Baker's Dictionary of Opera

Baker's Dictionary of Opera

LAURA KUHN

SCHIRMER BOOKS
An Imprint of The Gale Group
NEW YORK

Schirmer Books
An Imprint of The Gale Group
1633 Broadway
New York, New York 10019

Library of Congress Catalog Card Number: 99-16852

Printed in the United States of America

Printing number
1 2 3 4 5 6 7 8 9 10

Library of Congress Cataloging-in-Publication Data

Baker's dictionary of opera / Laura Kuhn.
p. cm.
ISBN 0-02-865349-1
1. Opera Dictionaries. I. Kuhn, Laura Diane.
ML 102.06B26 2000
782.1'03—dc21 99-16852
CIP

This paper meets the requirements of ANSI/NISO Z39.49-1992 (Permanence of Paper).

Contents

Foreword

Editor's note: It seems fitting and perfect to allow the late Nicolas Slonimsky, the de facto father of the present edition, as well as of the many and various *Baker's* reference volumes that have preceded and will follow it, to have the first word. The following materials on the subject of opera, its plots, and its libretti have been drawn from his *Lectionary of Music: An Entertaining Reference and Reader's Companion* (New York: McGraw-Hill Publishing, 1989), compiled by him in his ninety-fifth year.

—Laura Kuhn

In history, in literature, in art, in music, there comes a time when technical elaboration of available means reaches its limit, and a new turn in aesthetics becomes imperative. Such a point was reached in Italy, the historic progenitor of the art of music, toward the end of the sixteenth century, when a group of enlightened aristocratic men of science, poetry, and music assembled in Florence to discuss further advance in the arts. They assumed the modest name of Camerata, that is, a small chamber, and held regular gatherings in the villa of Count Giovanni Bardi. The participants, besides Bardi himself, included the poet Ottavio Rinuncini and the musicians Giulio Caccini, Jacopo Peri, and Vincenzo Galilei, father of the famous astronomer. Their project was to return music to the ideal of simplicity that was the essence of ancient Greek music. Accordingly, they published a collection, significantly entitled *Nuove musiche* (new musics), containing madrigals and airs by Caccini. The innovation of these pieces consisted in reducing music to a clearly outlined single voice with an accompaniment of static chords, expressly avoiding the polyphonic construction of the Renaissance masters. It was a state of musical entropy, in which the underlying matter remains stable in its solidity. Drawing a parallel from Greek philosophy, so beloved by the Florentine founders of the Camerata, the maxim of Heraclites "all is flux," immanent in flexible counterpoint, is controverted by the opposing principal of Parmenides, "all is immovable," basic to uniformity of harmonic progressions. The idiom adopted by the "new" musicians was monody, as opposed to counterpoint. Their theatrical productions, marked by monodic harmony, were to be called *dramma per musica,* or "drama by means of music." In the course of time this new type of composition received the name *opera,* which in Italian means simply "work." The greatest contribution to the art of early opera was in the sublime productions of Monteverdi, who introduced such refinements as discords of the dominant seventh and boldly depicted natural events, such as a tempest, in his instrumental accompaniment.

Structurally and historically, opera is a continuation of a suite of madrigals connected by a definite story. An introductory ensemble for instruments established the mood of the work. There were obligatory arias, most of them built on a symmetric plan, with the cadence recapitulating the opening. There were brief duets and climactic choral ensembles. The dramatic development included, almost necessarily, an amorous encounter, an opposition of inimical forces, and a concluding resolution of conflicts. A proverbial "happy ending" was not a necessity in the *dramma per musica,* and the finale of a typical opera may have been tragic, with the main actors meeting death. The principal forms of opera were *opera seria,* with dramatic or tragic content, and *opera buffa,* devoted to entertainment. *Opera seria* included an abundant application of arias; *opera buffa* exercised the spirit of the dance.

From the very inception of opera there was the debate of which was more important: the story represented in the action or the music accompanying that action. The German musician Christoph Willibald von Gluck, who was active mainly in Vienna and Paris in the eighteenth century, militated against the undue prominence given to singers in operatic productions and maintained that the poetry of the text must be paramount; music was to be the servant of the drama unfolded on the stage. Gluck remained faithful to the origin of opera as a revival of Greek tragedy. The opponent of this view was the Italian Niccolò Piccinni, who, like Gluck, was prominent in Paris. His style of composition was the very antithesis of Gluck's Grecian ideals, but he finally had to yield. Another operatic conflict arose in Paris in the middle of the eighteenth century, this time along national lines, as the Italian opera composers, who enjoyed the support of the French aristocracy, combated the popular adherents of French nationalism. The famous philosopher Jean-Jacques Rousseau, himself a composer, went so far as to maintain that the French language, with its weak vowels and uncertain consonants, was unfit for singing. In an extraordinary reversal of his views, Rousseau himself wrote a popular opera with a French libretto.

Italy remained for nearly four centuries the grand mistress of opera. Composers around the world, even such an incomparable genius as Mozart, selected Italian texts for their operas. Italian singers captivated audiences of all nations; opera companies were administered by Italians. French opera was largely the creation of the Florentine music master Lully, who became also the chief composer of French ballet. England tended to import Continental musicians to write theatrical music for the London Opera. Henry Purcell, the greatest English composer of the second half of the seventeenth century, bemoaned his compatriots' inability to write melodious music and proclaimed his determination to emulate the luscious melodies of sunny Italy in his own vocal works. In the eighteenth century, England was fortunate enough to engage Handel of Saxony as a royal musician to write operas for the London theaters. In opposition, another powerful British faction engaged Bononcini from Italy to provide operatic music. Their rivalry was immortalized in a celebrated stanza:

Some say, compar'd to Bononcini
That Mynheer Handel's but a Ninny;

Others aver, that he to Handel
Is scarcely fit to hold a Candle:
Strange all this Difference should be
Twixt Tweedledum and Tweedledee!

Patronized by the king of England (who was himself a German, the founder of the Hanover dynasty), Handel wrote a number of operas to Italian libretti for the London stage, but they were unsuccessful. To the supreme good of all music, Handel turned to oratorio with English texts.

It has been said that England produced no opera composers of significance between Purcell and Britten. This ignores the novel type of ballad opera that flourished on the English stage early in the eighteenth century and its comic sequel, *The Beggar's Opera,* designed to entertain the masses rather than the aristocracy. The glorious musical comedies of the nineteenth century by Gilbert and Sullivan were direct descendants of ballad opera. Other composers of the twentieth century, in addition to Britten, who wrote fine operas were Ralph Vaughan Williams, William Walton, and Michael Tippett.

Opera in the nineteenth century followed the spirit of the times in embracing Romantic and national ideals. Romantic nationalism was imbued with fantasy, which made it attractive to people of all categories. The first opera that successfully combined such diverse traits was *Der Freischütz* by Carl Maria von Weber. Its contents were colored by magic, its libretto was German, and its musical idiom was nationalistic. This romantically nationalistic trend was crowned in Germany by the development of a totally different type of opera. The formal elements of arias, vocal ensembles, and independently conceived instrumental parts gave way to the revolutionary creations of Richard Wagner, who wrote his own German libretti on the subject of German history and legend. Wagner's influence on the subsequent development of opera was universal; hardly an operatic composer in any country escaped the influence of his power and his imagination.

Italy continued to provide operas that were formal in structure and songful in treatment. Early in the nineteenth century this melodious and harmonious Italian operatic style became known as *bel canto* (beautiful song), with Donizetti, Bellini, and Rossini as its most proficient purveyors. Dramatic Italian opera was glorified by Giuseppe Verdi, born in the same year, 1813, as Wagner, and who lived a life so long that it projected into the twentieth century. Verdi kept the basic elements of Classical opera intact: there was a stately orchestral overture that included melodic allusions to the most important motifs in the entire opera; there were inspired arias and beautifully fashioned vocal ensembles; there was also dramatic tension in the manner of contemporary Romantic literature. Verdi's theatrical art led to the development of the Italian *verismo,* the music drama of verity, whose most brilliant representatives were Puccini, Mascagni, and Leoncavallo. Paradoxically, the only practitioner of verismo on the modern American scene is an Italian, Gian Carlo Menotti, who has never become an American citizen although he has resided most of his life in the United States and has written his own libretti in English.

Opera in the nineteenth century greatly increased the number of acting parts and augmented their participation in ensembles, in duos, trios, quartets, quintets, sextets, septets, octets, and even nonets. The role of the orchestra was also expanded, with newly chromatic brass instruments enhancing the harmony. To govern this exudation of sound, a conductor was assigned to give necessary cues to singers and orchestral players. The opera plots, enriched by exotic flights of fancy, further complicated the scene. The result was a much inflated spectacle that became known as *grand opera*; its principal dispenser was the newly established opera theater in Paris. Its greatest contributor was Meyerbeer, a German-Jewish composer who established himself in Paris and produced one opera after another, each a veritable archipelago of insular episodes in which arias and choral ensembles were artfully landscaped. Other composers who devoted most of their time and energy to grand opera in France were Auber, Halévy, Gounod, Delibes, Saint-Saëns, and Massenet. Verdi, who never sought popular success abroad, agreed to write a grand opera, *Aida,* to celebrate the opening of the Suez Canal under French auspices. In all such grand opera it was required, for commercial purposes, to include a ballet. Even Wagner had to submit to the fashion by inserting a ballet scene in *Tannhäuser,* but his attempt to meet the Parisian requirements failed dismally when *Tannhäuser* was taken out of the repertory after a few performances. Grand opera presentations included by necessity large, and loud, choruses. Mark Twain, no admirer of European cultures, attended one such spectacle during his trip abroad and commented that the screaming on the stage was louder than during the big fire that burned down the orphanage in his own town.

Russian operatic nationalism arose powerfully with the production of Glinka's *A Life for the Czar.* The so-called Russian national opera movement followed in the second half of the nineteenth century with a production of historical Russian operas by Rimsky-Korsakov, Borodin, and Mussorgsky. Tchaikovsky, who was their contemporary, did not join the national trend; instead, he wrote operas to meet the Romantic spirit of the Russian people.

A curious type of political nationalism followed the Russian national school during the revolutionary period, a style described as *socialist realism,* which was declared by the Soviet government to be the only proper musical development. Accordingly, when Shostakovich produced his dramatic opera *Lady Macbeth of the District of Mtzensk,* in which he exposed the moral decay of old Russia, it was condemned by the Soviet critics and taken off the boards. It was not until years later that it was allowed to be performed again, but the offensive interlude representing, in a passage for sliding trombones, a sexual act was removed from the score. Prokofiev, too, was harshly criticized for his last opera, *The Story of a Real Man,* even though it depicted a heroic deed of a Soviet pilot during World War II. This time, the official objection was the alleged excessive use of dissonances. It was eventually allowed to return to the stage, but by then Prokofiev had died.

Meanwhile, Wagner's influence remained incalculable among European composers, particularly in Germany. The greatest and most original opera composer in the Wagnerian mold was Richard Strauss, whose *Salome* and *Elektra* reach the height of modern harmony and vocal complexity. National German opera, on the other hand, free of Wagnerian domination, is represented by Hindemith's *Mathis der Maler.* In France, operatic development took a different course, that of impressionism, in which dramatic elements were understated rather than thrust forcefully upon the ear. The unquestionable masterpiece in this style was Debussy's *Pelléas et Mélisande*; in its score, the powerful dramatic events were conveyed in music by careful distillation of emotional expression.

Romantic nationalism was the natural style of operatic production among ethnic minorities within the sprawling Austro-Hungarian empire. Smetana and Dvořák expressed their Czech sentiment mainly through their instrumental music, but they also wrote operas to libretti in the Czech language. A modern representative of Czech opera was Janáček, who excelled both in dramatic and fairy-tale spectacles. In Hungary, Kodály wrote a national comic opera, *Háry János;* his close contemporary Béla Bartók limited his operatic activities to one short opera, *Bluebeard's Castle*.

Variegated as were opera productions at the threshold of the twentieth century, a veritable upheaval took place when opera composers adopted the ultramodern technique of composition elaborated by Arnold Schoenberg and his disciples. Of these creations, *Wozzeck* by Alban Berg was clad in atonality (but not yet dodecaphony), dissonant counterpoint, and neo-Baroque terms. Schoenberg preferred limited operatic forms of expressionism, applying allusion without direct depiction and premonitions without realization, so that an atmosphere of penetrating mystery and mystical presentiment was established, exemplified by *Die glückliche Hand* and particularly his unfinished opera, *Moses und Aron*.

The United States has never been an operatic nation. Attempts to produce genuine native operas by nineteenth-century American composers resulted in poor imitations of contemporary Italian models. Although the Italian management of the Metropolitan Opera House in New York expressed its eagerness to present an American opera, it did not succeed in doing so until 1906, when it staged a short-lived opera by Frederick Converse, *The Pipe of Desire*. Its subsequent productions of American operas by Howard Hanson, Deems Taylor, Samuel Barber, and others inevitably failed. Opera was simply not in the American arteries and veins; American hearts did not respond to the old tinsled glory of European operatic grandeur. Instead, they created a new tradition of gorgeously crafted musical comedies that were half operas, half revues. Gershwin's *Porgy and Bess,* announced as a "folk opera," became an American classic without adhering to the tradition of European opera. Finally, in the second half of the twentieth century, American composers inaugurated a modernistic operatic genre, a surrealistic collocation of contemporary events and dreamlike inconsistencies. The first work of this heterogeneous genre was the opera by Virgil Thomson, *Four Saints in Three Acts,* to a libretto by Gertrude Stein. Actually, there were in it many more saints than four and one act more than three, but this sort of oneiric inequity challenged and fascinated the listener. Systematic mixture of phantasmagorical reality in American opera was bewilderingly but somehow convincingly demonstrated in the hypnopompic opera *Einstein on the Beach* by Philip Glass. John Adams artfully combined a historic libretto with neo-Romantic minimalistic music in his would-be political opera *Nixon in China*. An utterly novel operatic event, cleverly named *Europeras 1 & 2,* created by John Cage, consisted of an astonishing array of excerpted selections from European nineteenth-century operas chosen by means of chance operations. Its immediate impact on the audience was that of a *fata morgana,* a mirage of familiar motifs arranged in arbitrary sequences.

It has long been customary to distribute opera librettos (or libretti, to use the correct Italian plural) to the audience to acquaint them with the subject of the opera. Italians were greatly adept as librettists. A paragon of the art was Metastasio, whose libretti were set to music by some fifty composers, including Gluck, Handel, Haydn, and Mozart, accounting for more than a thousand Italian operas. Da Ponte, who contributed the libretto to Mozart's *Don Giovanni,* led an adventurous life; he was exiled from Europe for adultery, and went to America to teach Italian grammar at Columbia College in New York, where he died at the age of nearly ninety. Italian libretti usually carried an *argomento* (a summary) listing the acts and scenes, the cast of characters, and sometimes a *protesta* (a protestation by the author of the libretto that his use of names of pagan deities should not be understood as a lack of Christian faith). Some libretti have independent literary value, such as Hofmannsthal's thoughtful texts for Richard Strauss. Then there are Gilbert and Sullivan, in whose comic operas the merit is distributed equally for literature and music. In a class by itself is the composer/librettist, of whom Wagner was the supreme example.

The plots of most early operas are based on standard formulas. Mistaken identities abound. Rigoletto hires assassins to kill the seducer of his daughter, but in the darkness of the night they mortally wound the daughter instead and deliver her body to her father in a sack. A most unlikely story, but plausibility is not a virtue among most librettists. A very common theme is seduction followed by desertion, which is the basis of *Faust, La Bohème,* and *La Traviata*. Suicides are also common, with female self-destruction exceeding that of the male by a large margin. Examples are the seduced granddaughter in *The Queen of Spades,* the murderess in *Lady Macbeth of the District of Mtzensk,* and Lakmé. Mascagni's Lodoletta does not commit suicide but dies in the snow outside her lover's Paris house. Infanticide is the central element in *Jenůfa*. Impersonation is also a common device in opera plots. The faithful Leonore dresses as a boy, assumes the symbolic name Fidelio, and penetrates the prison in which her beloved is unjustly held. The motif of rescue is so ubiquitous that *rescue opera* has entered the dictionaries of musical terms. Religious fanaticism, particularly in the Inquisition, is a convenient dramatic feature in most operas. Thus, in *La Juive* the fanatical cardinal has a girl boiled in a cauldron moments before he finds out that she is his natural daughter. Superstition plays a helpful role in libretti of all kinds. Operatic murders, particularly by stabbing, are too numerous to tabulate. Insanity should also not be overlooked; mad scenes in opera are most effective. Fortunately, most of the victims, practically all of them female, recover their sanity as soon as the dramatic situation improves.

It is easy to ridicule opera, but the difficulty is to suggest a rational and sensible substitute for operatic libretti. Of course, it is ludicrous for Verdi to have the king of Ethiopia overhear Radames as he relates military secrets to the king's daughter, Aida. The hidden king even offers comments in recitative from behind a potted palm. Here Coleridge's injunction regarding the poetic approach as being a "willing suspension of disbelief" is particularly helpful. An operagoer must leave his skepticism with his hat in the cloakroom. When he attended a rehearsal of the opera *Feramors* by Anton Rubinstein, Tolstoy, great writer that he was, felt insulted by the nonsense on the stage. His humorless account of the occasion in his extraordinary tract *What Is Art* (in which he also demolishes music, ballet, painting, and Shakespeare) is worth quoting:

> The procession began with a recitative of a person dressed up in Turkish costume who with a mouth open at an unnatural angle sings: "I accompany the bri-i-i-i-de." After singing this he waves his arm, naked of course, under his mantle. The procession opens, but here the French horn accompanying the recitative does something wrong, and the conductor, suddenly startled as if a disaster had struck, taps on the music stand with his stick, and the whole things starts all over again. The libretto of the opera is one of the greatest absurdities imaginable. An Indian king wants to marry; a bride is presented to him, and he changes his attire to that of a minstrel. The bride falls in love with the supposed minstrel, and becomes desperate at this development. Fortunately, she soon finds out that the minstrel is the king, and everyone is well content. That such Indians never existed, that the personages in the opera do not resemble any Indians or indeed any people, except those in other operas, can be in no doubt whatsoever; that nobody talks in recitative, that no group of four people place themselves at measured distances from one another to perform a quartet, constantly waving their arms to express their emotions; that nobody, except on the stage, walks in pairs carrying halberds made of foil and wearing slippers instead of shoes; that no one ever becomes angry or tender as in the theater, no one laughs or cries like that, and that no one can possibly be moved

> by such a spectacle, is obvious. And all this repellant nonsense is being put together not in the spirit of social entertainment and fun, but with malice and bestial brutality.

A historical footnote: the rehearsal in question was conducted by the famous Russian musician Wasily Safonov, and the participants were students of the Moscow Conservatory of which he was director. It was Tolstoy himself who asked Safonov's permission to be present at the rehearsal; his account of it did not endear him to Safonov, who never treated the orchestra or the singers with the "bestial brutality" of which Tolstoy accused him.

Sometimes the stories of operas are changed for political or social reasons. Glinka's *A Life for the Czar* could not very well be staged in Russia after the Revolution. The Soviet authorities actually changed the title to *Ivan Susanin,* and the self-sacrificial peasant hero, instead of saving the czar, is made to save a patriotic Russian commander. Attempts were made in Soviet Russia to rewrite other libretti to make them revolutionary. Thus *Tosca* became *The Commune,* and *The Huguenots* was changed to *The Decembrists* (the revolutionary Russian group of December 1825 who rebelled against Czar Nicholas I). Some operas cannot be performed in certain countries. *The Mikado* is forbidden in Japan because the Japanese emperor is portrayed in an undignified manner. Gounod's *Faust* was renamed *Gretchen* in Germany because the sentimental treatment of Goethe's great poem in the libretto was an affront to German literature. The libretto of Verdi's *Un ballo in maschera* was based on a historical event, the assassination of the king of Sweden. The opera was forbidden for performance in Italy for fear of inspiring a regicide in Europe at the time. Accordingly, the libretto was changed, and the mythical "Governor of Boston" substituted for the Swedish king. Sometimes religious restrictions make it impossible to have an opera performed under any circumstances. *Samson and Delilah* by Saint-Saëns could not be performed for nearly a century on the British stage because of a regulation that prohibited the representation of biblical personages in the theater. The restriction, however, did not apply to oratorios or cantatas. In czarist Russia there was a rule against the portrayal of a member of the reigning dynasty on the stage. So, when Catherine the Great was to make her entrance in Tchaikovsky's *The Queen of Spades,* the "Imperial March" announcing her presence was played, but the empress herself did not appear. No restrictions were applied to the depiction of Russian czars before the Romanov dynasty. In Mussorgsky's opera *Boris Godunov,* Czar Boris is a child murderer. Ivan the Terrible is treated by Rimsky-Korsakov in his opera *The Maid of Pskov* as the brute that he was. Ironically, Stalin decreed rehabilitation of the historic Ivan, perhaps because he felt an affinity with his remote precursor. Prokofiev had trouble in his scenic oratorio *Ivan the Terrible,* trying to conform to the new official attitude. And some minor changes had to be made in Pushkin's verses used as the libretto by Rimsky-Korsakov in his opera *Le Coq d'or* to avoid embarrassing similarities between the bumbling czar of the opera and the last czar, Nicholas II, who was not very bright.

In the nineteenth century it was common to supply a translation of the libretto into the language of the country in which the opera was being performed. Some of these translations are intentionally funny, as in the English translation of the exhortation of an operatic bandit to his gang upon recognizing his stepsister in the lady of the manor on which he is leading an assault: "Desist! On the same milk we were nurtured!" A unique hazard requires the adjustment of actual texts. The name of Pinkerton in Puccini's *Madama Butterfly* had to be changed in German productions to Linkerton because in colloquial German *pinkeln* means to urinate. When *Boris Godunov* was performed in Lisbon in 1921, the dying czar's injunction to his son containing the imperative *karai* had to be changed to another Russian word because *karai* means the male sexual organ in Portuguese. And the declaration of the young man in *Iolanthe* of Gilbert and Sullivan that he is "a fairy only down to the waist" continues to make sophisticated audiences of the twentieth century giggle.

Nicolas Slonimsky

Abbreviations

A.B.	Bachelor of Arts
ABC	American Broadcasting Company
A.M.	Master of Arts
ASCAP	American Society of Composers, Authors, and Publishers
assn./Assn.	association/Association
assoc.	associate
aug.	augmented
B.A.	Bachelor of Arts
BBC	British Broadcasting Corporation
B.M.	Bachelor of Music
CBC	Canadian Broadcasting Corporation
CBS	Columbia Broadcasting System
cons./Cons.	conservatory/Conservatory
dept./Dept.	department/Department
diss.	dissertation
D.M.A.	Doctor of Musical Arts
ed(s).	edit(ed), editor(s), edition(s)
enl.	enlarged
IRCAM	Institut de Recherche et de Coordination Acoustique/Musique
ISCM	International Society for Contemporary Music
inst./Inst.	institute/Institute
M.A.	Master of Arts
M.M.	Master of Music
MS(S)	manuscript(s)
Mus.B.	Bachelor of Music
Mus.D.	Doctor of Music
Mus.M.	Master of Music
NAACP	National Association for the Advancement of Colored People
NBC	National Broadcasting Company
n.d.	no date

NEA	National Endowment for the Arts
NHK	Japan Broadcasting Company
no(s).	number(s)
N.Y.	New York
op(p).	opus
orch./Orch.	orchestra/Orchestra
p(p).	page(s)
PBS	Public Broadcasting Service
perf.	performance
Ph.D.	Doctor of Philosophy
phil./Phil.	philharmonic/Philharmonic
posth.	posthumously
prof.	professor
publ.	publish(ed)
RAI	Radiotelevisione Italiana
rev.	revised
RIAS	Radio in the American Sector
S.	San, Santo, Santa
Ss.	Santi, Sante
St(e).	Saint(e)
sym(s).	symphony(-ies)
tr.	translate(d), translation
univ./Univ.	university/University
vol(s).	volume(s)
WDR	Westdeutscher Rundfunk (West German Radio)

Acknowledgments

Charles Amirkhanian, Artistic Director, "Other Minds," San Francisco, California
David Cummings, Editor, *International Who's Who in Music and Musicians' Directory*
Agnes Eisenberger, President, Colbert Artists Management, Inc., N.Y.
M. L. Falcone Public Relations, N.Y.
John Fennino, Assistant Archivist, Metropolitan Opera, N.Y.
R. Michael Fling, Collection Development and Acquisitions Librarian, William and Gayle Cook Music Library, Indiana University, Bloomington
Anni Heino, Information Manager, Finnish Music Information Centre, Helsinki
Indianapolis-Marion County Public Library, Central Library, Arts Division and Newspapers and Periodicals Division
Leipzig Opera
Tomas Löndahl, Head, Music Production, Swedish Broadcasting Corporation, Stockholm
Lars Mahinske, Editorial Division, *Encyclopaedia Brittanica*
Barbara Neumann, Archives Office, Hamburg State Opera
Alain Pâris, Editor, *Dictionnaire des Interprètes*
Joanne Rile Artists Management, Inc., N.Y.
Royal Opera, Stockholm
Dr. Stanley Sadie, C.B.E., Editor Emeritus, *The New Grove Dictionary of Music and Musicians*
Matthias Vogt Artists' Management, San Francisco
Laurence Wasserman, President and Director of the Vocal Division, Thea Dispeker, Inc., N.Y.

All photos: CORBIS

A

Aav, Evald, Estonian composer; b. Reval, Feb. 22, 1900; d. there (Tallinn), March 21, 1939. He studied composition in Reval with Arthur Kapp. He wrote mostly vocal music to words in the Estonian language. Among his works is *The Vikings* (Tallinn, Sept. 8, 1928), the first national Estonian opera.

Aavik, Juhan, Estonian conductor, pedagogue, and composer; b. Holstre, near Reval, Jan. 29, 1884; d. Stockholm, Nov. 26, 1982. He studied at the St. Petersburg Cons. After conducting in Tartu (1911–23), he was a prof. and director of the Reval (Tallinn) Cons. (1925–44) before settling in Sweden. He publ. a history of Estonian music (4 vols., Stockholm, 1965–69). He composed the opera *Autumn Dream* (1939).

Abbá-Cornaglia, Pietro, Italian pianist, organist, teacher, and composer; b. Alessandria, March 20, 1851; d. there, May 2, 1894. He studied with Antonio Angeleri (piano) and Lauro Rossi and Mazzucato (composition) at the Milan Cons. He was organist at Alessandri Cathedral (1880–94) and director of his own music school. His works included the operas *Isabella Spinola* (Milan, 1877), *Maria di Warden* (Venice, 1884), and *Una partita a scacchi* (Pavia, 1892).

Abbadia, Natale, Italian composer; b. Genoa, March 11, 1792; d. Milan, Dec. 25, 1861. He composed the opera *Giannina di Pontieu* (1812) and the musical farce *L'Imbroglione ed il castigamatti*.

Abbado, Claudio, outstanding Italian conductor, uncle of **Roberto Abbado**; b. Milan, June 26, 1933. His brother is the accomplished pianist and composer Marcello Abbado (b. Milan, Oct. 7, 1926). He received his early training in music from his father, a professional violinist; he then enrolled in the Milan Cons., graduating in 1955 in piano. He also received instruction in conducting from Votto and took piano lessons in Salzburg with Friedrich Gulda (1955). From 1956 to 1958 he attended the conducting classes of Swarowsky at the Vienna Academy of Music, spending the summers working with C. Zecchi and Galliera at the Accademia Musicale Chigiana in Siena. In 1958 he made his conducting debut in Trieste; he also won the Koussevitzky conducting prize at the Berkshire Music Center in Tanglewood, and in 1963 he was one of three winners of the Mitropoulos Competition in New York. He made his American conducting debut with the N.Y. Phil. on April 7, 1963. In 1965 he appeared as a sym. conductor at La Scala in Milan; he also began conducting the Vienna Phil., leading it in Salzburg, in Vienna, and on tour. He joined the opera at La Scala in 1967, and in 1972 he became principal guest conductor of the London Sym. Orch. In 1972–73 he took the Vienna Phil. to Japan and China; in 1974 he conducted concerts in Russia with the La Scala company; in 1976 he led appearances in the United States with both the Vienna Phil. and the La Scala company, which had its American debut during the celebrations of the Bicentennial. In 1978 he founded the European Community Youth Orch.; from 1981 he was principal conductor of the Chamber Orch. of Europe, which was composed of the former's members. In 1979 he was appointed principal conductor of the London Sym. Orch., and in 1982 he was named principal guest conductor of the Chicago Sym. Orch., which post he held until 1986. He founded La Filarmonica della Scala in Milan in 1982. From 1983 to 1988 he was music director of the London Sym. Orch. From 1986 to 1991 he was chief conductor of the Vienna State Opera. In 1989 he was elected Karajan's successor with the Berlin Phil. However, unlike the aristocratic and domineering Karajan, who had held the title of chief conductor-for-life of the Berlin Phil., the more democratically inclined Abbado asked for a regular contract as artistic director. He retained this position until 2002. In 1994 he also became artistic director of the Salzburg Easter Festival. Abbado's conducting engagements have taken him all over the globe. A fine technician, he is capable of producing distinguished performances of works ranging from the Classical era to the cosmopolitan avant-garde. Among his honors are the Mozart Medal of the Mozart-Gemeinde of Vienna (1973), the Golden Nicolai Medal of the Vienna Phil. (1980), the Gran Croce of his homeland (1984), and the Mahler Medal of Vienna (1985); in 1986 he was made a member of the Légion d'honneur of France.

BIBL.: H. Grünewald, H.-J. von Jena, and U. Meyer-Schoellkopf, *Das Berliner Philharmonische Orchester mit C. A.* (Berlin, 1994).

Abbado, Roberto, Italian conductor, nephew of **Claudio Abbado**; b. Milan, Dec. 30, 1954. Another uncle is the accomplished pianist and composer Marcello Abbado (b. Milan, Oct. 7, 1926). He was a student of Ferrara in Venice and at the Accademia Nazionale di Santa Cecilia in Rome (1976–77). While still a student, he appeared as a guest conductor with the Orch. di Santa Cecilia in 1977. In 1978 he made his debut as an opera conductor with *Simon Boccanegra* at the Macerata Festival. After conducting in Verona (1979) and Venice and Palermo (1980), he made his debut at the Vienna State Opera conducting *Il Barbiere di Siviglia* at the Zürich Opera and *Don Carlo* at the Deutsche Oper in Berlin. He made his debut at Milan's La Scala with *Il Barbiere di Siviglia* in 1983, and at the Teatro Comunale in Florence with *L'Italiana in Algeri* in 1986. In 1990 he conducted *Adriana Lecouvreur* at his first appearance at the Bavarian State Opera in Munich. In 1991 he made his North American debut as a guest conductor with the Orch. of St. Luke's in New York. From 1991 to 1998 he was chief conductor of the Munich Radio Orch. In 1992 he conducted *La forza del destino* at his first appearance at the San Francisco Opera. He made his Metropolitan Opera debut in New York on March 3, 1994, conducting *Adriana Lecouvreur*, and that year made his first appearance at the Hamburg State Opera with *Aida*. In 1995 he conducted *Lucia di Lammermoor* at the Opéra de la Bastille in Paris, and in 1996 *Norma* at the Houston Grand Opera. He also appeared as a guest conductor with many orchs. on both sides of the Atlantic.

Abbatini, Antonio Maria, distinguished Italian composer and teacher; b. Tiferno, 1609 or 1610; d. there, c. 1677. He received his musical training from the Nanino brothers in Rome, where he spent the greater portion of his life. From 1626 to 1628 he was maestro di cappella at St. John Lateran. After serving in that capacity at Orvieto Cathedral (1633), he returned to Rome to hold that position at S. Maria Maggiore (c.1640–46), S. Lorenzo a Damaso (1646–49), S. Maria Maggiore (1649–57), S. Luigi dei Francesi (1657–67), Santa Casa in Loreto (1667), and once more at S. Maria Maggiore (1672–77). With M. Marazzoli, he composed the opera *Dal male il bene* (Rome, Feb. 12, 1653), historically significant as one of the earliest examples of the inclusion of the ensemble finale. He also wrote the operas *Ione* (Vienna, 1664 or Rome, 1665) and *La comica del ciclo, overo La Baltasara* (Rome, 1668), and the dramatic cantata *Il pianto di Rodomonte* (publ. in Orvieto, 1633).

BIBL.: K. Andrae, *Ein römischer Kapellmeister im 17. Jahrhundert: A.M. A. (ca. 1600–1679). Studien zu Leben und Werk* (diss., Univ. of Hamburg, 1985).

Abbott, Emma, American soprano; b. Chicago, Dec. 9, 1850; d. Salt Lake City, Jan. 5, 1891. She was a pupil of her father, a singer and music teacher. After vocal training from Achille Errani in New York, she sang with Chapin's choir there (1870–72). She then pursued vocal studies in Milan with Sangiovanni and in Paris with Marchesi, Wartel, and Delle Sedie. On May 2, 1876, she made her professional debut as Maria in *La Fille du régiment* at London's Covent Garden. On Feb. 8, 1877, she made her U.S. debut in the same role in New York. From 1878 she toured with her own company in the United States giving performances of operas and operettas in English. She made a habit of interpolating hymns into her performances of operas by Bellini and Donizetti as a specialty.

BIBL.: S. Martin, *The Life and Professional Career of E. A.* (Minneapolis, 1891).

Abeille, (Johann Christian) Ludwig, German pianist, organist, and composer; b. Bayreuth, Feb. 20, 1761; d. Stuttgart, March 2, 1838. He studied in Stuttgart, where he settled. In 1782 he joined the private band of the Duke of Württemberg, and in 1802 he became Konzertmeister. By 1815 he was court organist and director of music. He retired in 1832. He wrote the Singspiels *Amor und Psyche* (Stuttgart, 1800) and *Peter und Ännchen* (Stuttgart, 1809).

Abell, John, Scottish countertenor, lutenist, and composer; b. Aberdeenshire, 1652; d. probably in Cambridge, after 1716. He was a chorister in the Chapel Royal in London, and about 1679 he also became a musician in the King's Private Music. In 1684 he took his Mus.B. at Cambridge. A Catholic sympathizer, he left England after the 1688 revolution and traveled throughout Europe. In 1699 he returned to England, where he was successful mainly as a singer until 1716. He publ. the uninspired vols. *A Collection of Songs, in Several Languages* (1701), *A Collection of Songs, in English* (1701), and *A Choice Collection of Italian Ayres* (1703).

Abert, Anna Amalie, distinguished German musicologist, daughter of **Hermann Abert**; b. Halle, Sept. 19, 1906; d. Kiel, Jan. 4, 1996. She studied musicology with her father, with Blume, and with Sachs at the Univ. of Berlin (Ph.D., 1934, with the diss. *Die stilistischen Voraussetzungen der "Cantiones sacrae" von Heinrich Schütz*); she then joined the staff of the Univ. of Kiel, where she completed her Habilitation in 1943 with *Claudio Monteverdi und das musikalische Drama* (publ. in Lippstadt, 1954); in 1950 she became a prof. there, and also a research fellow in 1962; she retired in 1971. From 1949 to 1958 she was an ed. of *Die Musik in Geschichte und Gegenwart*. She contributed important articles to the *Mozart-Jahrbuch*; her writings also include *Christoph Willibald Gluck* (Munich, 1959); *Die Opern Mozarts* (Wolfenbüttel, 1970; Eng. tr. in *The New Oxford History of Music*, vol. 7, London, 1973); *Richard Strauss: Die Opern* (Velber, 1972); *Geschichte der Oper* (Kassel, 1994).

BIBL.: K. Hortschansky, ed., *Opernstudien: A. A. A. zum 65. Geburtstag* (Tutzing, 1975).

Abert, Hermann, eminent German musicologist, father of **Anna Amalie Abert**; b. Stuttgart, March 25, 1871; d. there, Aug. 13, 1927. He studied with his father, Johann Joseph Abert (b. Kochowitz, Sept. 20, 1832; d. Stuttgart, April 1, 1915), then with Bellermann, Fleischer, and Friedlaender in Berlin; he received his Ph.D. from the Univ. of Berlin in 1897 with the diss. *Die Lehre vom Ethos in der griechischen Musik* (publ. in Leipzig, 1899); completed his Habilitation in 1902 at the Univ. of Halle with *Die ästhetischen Grundsätze der mittelalterlichen Melodiebildung* (publ. in Halle, 1902); and was named honorary prof. there in 1909 and lecturer in 1911. In 1920 he became prof. at the Univ. of Leipzig and in 1923 at the Univ. of Berlin. He was one of the outstanding scholars of his time, noted for his wide-ranging musicological interests. Among his important writings, his exhaustively rewritten and revised ed. of Jahn's biography of Mozart is still valuable; it was publ. as *Wolfgang Amadeus Mozart: Neu bearbeitete und erweitert Ausgabe von Otto Jahns "Mozart"* (2 vols., Leipzig, 1919–21; further rev. by his daughter and publ. in 1955–56). Other books include *Robert Schumann* (Berlin, 1903; 4th ed., 1920); *Die Musikanschauung des Mittelalters und ihre Grundlagen* (Halle, 1905); *Niccolo Jommelli als Opernkomponist* (Halle, 1908); *Goethe und die Musik* (Engelhorn, 1922); he also wrote a biography of his father (Leipzig, 1916). His collected writings were posthumously ed. by F. Blume as *Gesammelte Schriften und Vorträge* (Halle, 1929).

BIBL.: K. Funk, *H. A.: Musiker, Musikwissenschaftler, Musikpädagoge* (Stuttgart, 1994).

Abert, Johann Joseph, German composer, father of **Hermann Abert**; b. Kochowitz, Sept. 20, 1832; d. Stuttgart, April 1, 1915. He studied double bass and composition at the Prague Cons. (1846–53), then played the double bass in the Court Orch. at Stuttgart; in 1867 he became its conductor, and held this post until 1888. Abert's style, greatly influenced by Mendelssohn and Schumann, represents the German Romantic tradition at its most typical among worthy epigones. His composing technique was flawless, however. His son wrote a detailed biography, *J. J. A., 1832–1915: Sein Leben und seine Werke* (Leipzig, 1916). His opera *Astorga*, based on the life of the composer Emanuele d'Astorga (Stuttgart, May 27, 1866) was quite successful at the time. His other operas were *Anna von Landskron* (1858), *König Enzio* (1862), and *Ekkehard* (Berlin, Oct. 11, 1878).

Abos, Girolamo (baptismal name, **Geronimo**), Maltese composer; b. La Valetta, Nov. 16, 1715; d. Naples, Oct. 1760. He was a student of Francesco Durante and Gerolimo Ferraro in Naples. He served as secondo maestro at the Cons. Poveri di Gesù Cristo (1742–43), and was also secondo maestro at the Cons. della Pietà dei Turchini (1754–59). Among his pupils was Paisiello. Abos wrote 14 operas, which were produced in Naples and Rome; of these, *Tito Manlio* (May 30, 1751) was successful.

Abraham, Paul (originally, **Pál Ábrahám**), Hungarian composer; b. Apatin, Nov. 2, 1892; d. Hamburg, May 6, 1960. He studied in Budapest, and began his career as a composer of serious scores. Turning his attention to lighter music, he became conductor and composer at the Fäváriosi Operettszinház in 1927. He scored his greatest success with the operetta *Viktória* (Budapest, Feb. 21, 1930), which subsequently was performed widely abroad. Other works of merit included the operettas *Die Blume von Hawaii* (Leipzig, July 24, 1931) and *Ball im Savoy* (Berlin, Dec. 23, 1932), and his film score for *Die Privatsekretärin* (1931). With the rise of the Nazi regime, Abraham left Europe and settled in the U.S. in 1938, where he made ends meet as a pianist. He eventually settled in Hamburg, ill and largely forgotten. All the same, several of his works continued to be revived long after his death.

WORKS: MUSIC THEATER: *Zenebona* (Budapest, March 2, 1928); *Az utolsó Verebély lány* (Budapest, Oct. 13, 1928); *Szeretem a feleségem* (Budapest, June 15, 1929); *Viktória* (Budapest, Feb. 21, 1930; also known as *Viktoria und ihr Husar*); *Die Blume von Hawaii* (Leipzig, July 24, 1931); *Ball im Savoy* (Berlin, Dec. 23, 1932); *Märchen im Grand-Hotel* (Vienna, March 29, 1934); *Viki* (Budapest, Jan. 26, 1935); *Történnek még csodák* (Budapest, April 20, 1935); *Dschainah, das Mädchen aus dem Tanzhaus* (Vienna, Dec. 20, 1935); *3:1 a szerelem javára* (Budapest, Dec. 18, 1936); *Roxy und ihr Wunderteam* (Vienna, March 25, 1937); *Júlia* (Budapest, Dec. 23, 1937); *Fehér hattyú* (Budapest, Dec. 23, 1938).

BIBL.: G. Sebestyén, *P. A.: Aus dem Leben eines Operettenkomponisten* (Vienna, 1987).

Ábrányi, Emil, Hungarian conductor and composer; b. Budapest, Sept. 22, 1882; d. there, Feb. 11, 1970. His grandfather was the pianist, composer, and writer on music Kornél Ábrányi (b. Szentgyörgy-Ábrányi, Oct. 15, 1822; d. Budapest, Dec. 20, 1903). He studied composition with Koessler at the Royal Academy of Music in Budapest and conducting with Nikisch in Leipzig. After conducting in Cologne (1904–07) and Hannover (1907–11), he returned to Budapest as conductor at the Royal Opera; also was director of the municipal theater (1921–26).

WORKS: OPERAS: *A ködkirály* (The King of the Mist; Budapest, 1902), *Monna Vanna* (Budapest, March 2, 1907), *Paolo e Francesca* (Budapest, Jan. 13, 1912), *Don Quijote* (Budapest, Nov. 30, 1917), *Ave Maria* (Budapest, 1922), *Az éneklő dervis* (Singing Dervishes; 1935), *Liliomos herceg* (The Prince with the Lillies; 1938), *Bizánc* (Byzantium; 1942), *Éva boszorkány* (Sorceress Eve; 1944), *Balatoni rege* (The Tale of Balaton; 1945), and *A Tamás templom karnagya* (The Cantor of St. Thomas Church; 1947).

Abravanel, Maurice, distinguished Greek-born American conductor of Spanish-Portuguese Sephardic descent; b. Saloniki, Jan. 6, 1903; d. Salt Lake City, Sept. 22, 1993. He attended the univs. of Lausanne (1919–21) and Zürich (1921–22) before studying composition in Berlin with Kurt Weill. In 1924 he made his conducting debut in Berlin, and then conducted widely in Germany until he was compelled to go to Paris by the advent of the Nazis in 1933. After touring Australia (1934–36), he made his Metropolitan Opera debut in New York conducting *Samson et Dalila* on Dec. 26, 1936, remaining on its roster until 1938; then conducted on Broadway. In 1940–41 he was a conductor at the Chicago Opera. In 1947 he became music director of the Utah Sym. Orch. in Salt Lake City, which, by the time of his retirement in 1979, he had molded into one of the finest U.S. orchs. He also served as artistic director of the Music Academy of the West in Santa Barbara from 1954 to 1980. From 1982 he was active at the Tanglewood Music Center. On his 90th birthday on Jan. 6, 1993, the Utah Sym. Orch.'s concert hall was renamed in his honor.

BIBL.: L. Durham, *A.!* (Salt Lake City, 1989).

Absil, Jean, eminent Belgian composer and pedagogue; b. Bonsecours, Oct. 23, 1893; d. Brussels, Feb. 2, 1974. He studied organ and composition at the Brussels Cons., and later took lessons in advanced composition with Paul Gilson. He won the Prix Agniez for his First Sym. (1921); in 1922 he won a 2d Prix de Rome for the cantata *La Guerre*; he also received the Prix Rubens in 1934. His First Piano Concerto was commissioned by the 1938 Concours Ysaÿe in Brussels as the compulsory work for the 12 finalists in the contest eventually won by Emil Gilels. He was music director of the Academy of Etterbeek in Brussels (1922–64), taught at the Brussels Cons. (1930–59), and was one of the founders of the Revue Internationale de Musique. Absil evolved an individual style, characterized by rhythmic variety, free tonality, and compact counterpoint.

WORKS: DRAMATIC: *Peau d'âne*, lyrical poem (1937); *Ulysse et les sirènes*, radio play (1939); *Fansou ou Le Chapeau chinois*, musical comedy (1944); *Le Miracle de Pan*, ballet (1949); *Pierre Breughel l'Ancien*, radio play (1950); *Épouvantail*, ballet (1950); *Les Voix de la mer*, opera (1951; Brussels, March 26, 1954); *Les Météores*, ballet (1951).

BIBL.: R. de Guide, *J. A.: Vie et oeuvre* (Tournai, 1965).

Accardo, Salvatore, outstanding Italian violinist and conductor; b. Turin, Sept. 26, 1941. He studied with Luigi d'Ambrosio at the Cons. S. Pietro a Majella in Naples and with Yvonne Astruc at the Accademia Musicale Chigiana in Siena. He won the Vercelli (1955), Geneva (1956), and Paganini (Genoa, 1958) competitions, then pursued a remarkable career, appearing both as soloist with major orchs. of the world and as recitalist. He was also active in later years as a conductor. In 1993 he was appointed music director of the Teatro San Carlo in Naples. He publ. *L'arte del violino* (ed. by M. Delogu; Milan, 1987). As a violin virtuoso, Accardo excelled in a vast repertoire; in addition to the standard literature, he performed many rarely heard works, including those by Paganini. His playing was marked by a fidelity to the classical school of violin playing, in which virtuosity was subordinated to stylistic propriety.

Accorimboni, Agostino, Italian composer; b. Rome, Aug. 29, 1739; d. there, Aug. 13, 1818. He was a pupil of Rinaldo di Capua. He composed 13 stage works (1768–85), the most notable being his comic opera *Il regno delle Amazzoni* (Parma, Dec. 27, 1783). Among his other works is an oratorio.

Ackermann, Otto, admired Romanian-born Swiss conductor; b. Bucharest, Oct. 18, 1909; d. Wabern, near Bern, March 9, 1960. After attending the Bucharest Cons. (1920–25), he studied with Prüwer, Szell, and Valeska Burgstaller at the Berlin Hochschule für Musik (1926–28). He was active at the Royal Opera in Bucharest (1925–26) and at the Düsseldorf Opera (1928–32) before becoming chief conductor of the Brno Opera in 1932, and then of the Bern Opera in 1935. After conducting at the Theater an der Wien in Vienna (1947–53), he served as Generalmusikdirektor of the Cologne Opera (1953–58); subsequently conducted at the Zürich Opera. Ackermann distinguished himself as an interpreter of the standard operatic and symphonic repertory. He also had a special affinity for the operettas of the Viennese Strauss family and of Lehár.

Ackté (real name, **Achté**), **Aino,** Finnish soprano; b. Helsinki, April 23, 1876; d. Nummela, Aug. 8, 1944. She studied first with her mother, the soprano Emmy Strömer-Achté (1850–1924), and then with Duvernoy, Girodet, and P. Vidal at the Paris Cons. On Oct. 8, 1897, she made her operatic debut as Marguerite at the Paris Opéra, which role she also chose for her Metropolitan Opera debut in New York on Feb. 20, 1904; she sang there until 1905. On Jan. 16, 1907, she made her first appearance at London's Covent Garden as Elsa; on Dec. 8, 1910, she sang Salome in the first British perf. of Strauss's opera there, which led the satisfied composer to invite her to repeat her success in Dresden and Paris. In later years, Ackté pursued her career in Finland. In 1938–39 she was director of the Finnish National Opera in Helsinki. Her other notable roles included Elisabeth, Senta, Juliette, Ophélie, Gilda, and Nedda. She publ. *Minnen och fantasier* (Stockholm, 1916), *Muistojeni kirja* (The Book of My Recollections; Helsinki, 1925), and *Taiteeni taipaleelta* (My Life as an Artist; Helsinki, 1935).

Adam, Adolphe (-Charles), noted French composer, son of **Jean (Louis) Adam**; b. Paris, July 24, 1803; d. there, May 3, 1856. He was encouraged by his friend Hérold to pursue a career as a composer. After studying piano with Lemoine, he entered the Paris Cons. at 17 and received training from Benoist (organ), Reicha (counterpoint), and Boieldieu (composition). In 1825 he won a 2d prize in the Prix de Rome with his cantata *Ariane a Naxos*. His first successful stage score was the opéra comique *Pierre et Catherine* (Paris Opéra Comique, Feb. 9, 1829). Adam achieved his first great success with his opéra comique *Le chalet* (Opéra Comique, Sept. 25, 1834). It was followed by the even more successful opéra comique *Le postillon de Lonjumeau* (Opéra Comique, Oct. 13, 1836). His most celebrated score, the ballet *Giselle, ou Les Wilis* (Paris Opéra, June 28, 1841), has remained a repertory staple for over 150 years. In 1844 he was made a member of the Institut de France. He founded the Opéra-National in Paris in 1847, which was forced to close as a result of the revolutionary events of 1848. Adam was left bankrupt and was forced to take up music journalism to eke out a living. In 1849 he obtained the post of prof. of composition at the Paris Cons., which he held until his death. The opéra comique *Si j'étais roi* (Paris Théâtre-Lyrique, Sept. 4, 1852) proved one of his finest late works. His operetta *Les pantins de Violette* was premiered at the Paris Bouffes-Parisiens on April 29, 1856, just 4 days before his death. In addition to his *Giselle*, Adam is still fondly remembered for his "Cantique de Noël", known in Eng. as *O Holy Night*.

WORKS (all 1st perf. in Paris unless otherwise given): DRAMATIC: OPÉRAS COMIQUES: *Pierre et Catherine* (Feb. 9, 1829); *Danilowa* (April 23, 1830); *Trois jours en une heure* (Aug. 21, 1830; in collaboration with Romagnesi); *Joséphine, ou Le retour de Wagram* (Dec. 2, 1830); *Le morceau d'ensemble* (March 7, 1831); *Le grand prix, ou Le voyage à frais communs* (July 9, 1831); *Le proscrit, ou Le tribunal invisible* (Sept. 18, 1833); *Une bonne fortune* (Jan. 28, 1834); *Le chalet* (Sept. 25, 1834); *La marquise* (Feb. 28, 1835); *Micheline, ou L'heure d'esprit* (June 29, 1835); *Le postillon de Lonjumeau* (Oct. 13, 1836); *Le fidèle berger* (Jan. 6, 1838); *Le brasseur de Preston* (Oct. 31, 1838); *Régine, ou Les deux nuits* (Jan. 17, 1839); *Le reine d'un jour* (Sept. 19, 1839); *La rose de Péronne* (Dec. 12, 1840); *La main de fer, ou Le mariage secret* (Oct. 26, 1841); *Le roi d'Yvetot* (Oct. 13, 1842); *Lambert Simnel* (Sept. 14, 1843; completion of a work by H. Monpou); *Cagliostro* (Feb. 10, 1844); *Le toréador, ou l'accord parfait* (May 18, 1849); *Giralda, ou La nouvelle Psyché* (July 20, 1850); *La poupée de Nuremberg* (Feb. 21, 1852); *Le farfadet* (March 19, 1852); *Si j'étais roi* (Sept. 4, 1852); *Le sourd, ou L'auberge pleine* (Feb. 2, 1853); *Le roi des halles* (April 11, 1853); *Le bijou perdu* (Oct. 6, 1853); *Le muletier de Tolède* (Dec. 16, 1854); *A Clichy* (Dec. 24, 1854); *Le houzard de Berchini* (Oct. 17, 1855); *Falstaff* (Jan. 18, 1856); *Mam'zelle Geneviève* (March 24, 1856). OPERETTA: *Les pantins de Violette* (April 29, 1856). OPERAS: *Richard en Palestine* (Oct. 7, 1844); *La bouquetiâre* (May 31, 1847); *Le Fanal* (Dec. 24, 1849). Also various vaudevilles and other stage pieces. BALLETS: *La chatte blanche* (July 26, 1830; in collaboration with C. Gide); *Faust* (London, Feb. 16, 1833); *La fille du Danube* (Sept. 21, 1836); *Les mohicans* (July 5, 1837); *L'écumeur de mer* (Feb. 21, 1840); *Die Hamadryaden* (Berlin, April 28, 1840); *Giselle, ou Les Wilis* (June 28, 1841); *La jolie fille de Gand* (June 22, 1842); *Le diable à quatre* (Aug. 11, 1843); *The Marble Maiden* (London, Sept. 27, 1845); *Griselidis, ou Les cinq sens* (Feb. 16, 1848); *La filleule des fées* (Oct. 8, 1840; in collaboration with C. de Saint-Julien); *Orfa* (Dec. 29, 1852); *Le corsaire* (Jan. 23, 1856).

WRITINGS: *Souvenirs d'un musicien . . . précédés de notes biographiques* (Paris, 1857); *Derniers souvenirs d'un musicien* (Paris, 1859).

BIBL.: W. Studwell, ed., *A. A. and Léo Delibes: A Guide to Research* (Westport, Conn., 1987).

Ádám, Jeno, Hungarian conductor, pedagogue, and composer; b. Szigetszentmiklós, Dec. 12, 1896; d. Budapest, May 15, 1982. He studied organ and theory at the Budapest Teacher Training College (1911–15), composition with Kodály at the Budapest Academy of Music (1920–25), and conducting with Weingartner in Basel (1933–35). He was conductor of the orch. (1929–39) and the choir (1929–54) at the Budapest Academy of Music, where he also was a teacher (1939–59). In 1955 he was made a Merited Artist by the Hungarian government and in 1957 was awarded the Kossuth Prize. Among his writings were textbooks on singing (with Kodály) and *A muzsikáról* (On Music; Budapest, 1954). His compositions, written in a Romantic style, are notable for their utilization of Hungarian folk tunes, particularly in his operas, i.e. his *Magyar karácsony* (Hungarian Christmas; 1930; Budapest, Dec. 22, 1931) and *Mária Veronika* (1934–35; Budapest, Oct. 27, 1938).

Adam, Theo, distinguished German bass-baritone; b. Dresden, Aug. 1, 1926. As a boy, he sang in the Dresdner Kreuzchor and studied voice in his native city with Rudolf Dittrich (1946–49). On Dec. 25, 1949, he made his operatic debut as the Hermit in *Der Freischütz* at the Dresden State Opera, and in 1952 made his first appearance at the Bayreuth Festival, quickly rising to prominence as one of the leading Wagnerian heroic bass–baritones of his time. He was a principal member of the Berlin State Opera from 1953, and made guest appearances at London's Covent Garden, the Vienna State Opera, the Paris Opéra, the Salzburg Festivals, the San Francisco Opera, and the Chicago Lyric Opera. On Feb. 7, 1969, he made his debut at the Metropolitan Opera in New York as Hans Sachs. In addition to his Wagnerian roles, he also sang in operas by Mozart, Verdi, and R. Strauss with notable success; he appeared in various contemporary works as well, creating the leading roles in Cerha's *Baal* (1981) and Berio's *Un Re in ascolto* (1984). In 1979 he was made an Austrian Kammersänger. He publ. *Seht, hier ist Tinte, Feder, Papier . . .* (1980) and *Die hundertste Rolle, oder, Ich mache einen neuen Adam* (1987).

Adamberger, (Josef) Valentin, noted German tenor; b. Munich, July 6, 1743; d. Vienna, Aug. 24, 1804. He studied in Italy with Valesi, and made appearances there using the name **Adamonti**. He went to Munich in 1772, sang in London in 1777, and settled in Vienna in 1780. He created the role of Belmonte in *Die Entführung aus dem Serail* (July 16, 1782), and also sang the part of Herr Vogelsang in *Der Schauspieldirektor* (Feb. 7, 1786). In 1789 he became a member of the Italian Opera in Vienna, and remained there until his retirement in 1793. He then devoted himself to teaching voice.

Adams, Charles, American tenor and pedagogue; b. Charlestown, Mass., Feb. 9, 1834; d. West Harwich, Mass., July 4, 1900. He studied in Boston, where he appeared as a soloist in the Handel and Haydn Society's performance of *The Creation* in 1856. He appeared in opera and concert in the West Indies and Holland in 1861. After further training with Barbieri in Vienna, he sang with the Berlin Royal Opera (1864–67) and the Vienna Court Opera (1867–76). He also appeared at Milan's La Scala, at London's Covent Garden, and in the United States. In 1879 he settled in Boston as a voice teacher. Among his students were Melba and Eames. Adams was best known for his Wagnerian roles, especially Lohengrin and Tannhäuser.

Adams, John (Coolidge), prominent American composer; b. Worcester, Mass., Feb. 15, 1947. He spent the tender years of his life in the healthy atmosphere of Vermont and New Hampshire; his father taught him clarinet, and he later took clarinet lessons with Felix Viscuglia, a member of the Boston Sym. Orch. He subsequently entered Harvard University, receiving his B.A. (magna cum laude) in 1969 and his M.A. in music composition in 1971. At Harvard, his principal teacher was Leon Kirchner; he also studied composition with David Del Tredici and had some sessions with Sessions. While still in college, he conducted the Bach Soc.

Orch. and was a substitute clarinetist with the Boston Sym. Orch. and the Boston Opera Co. In 1969 he played the solo part in Piston's Clarinet Concerto at Carnegie Hall in New York. In 1971 he moved to San Francisco, where he found a congenial environment for his activities as a conductor and composer. He was head of the composition dept. at the San Francisco Cons. (1971–81). In 1978 he became adviser on new music to the San Francisco Sym. and subsequently was its composer-in-residence (1982–85). In 1982 he was awarded a Guggenheim fellowship. From 1988 to 1990 he held the title of creative adviser to the St. Paul (Minn.) Chamber Orch. In his compositions Adams reveals himself as an apostle of the idea that a maximum effect can be achieved with a minimum of means, a notion usually described by the somewhat inaccurate term "minimalism," wherein a composer postulates harmonic and melodic austerity with audacious repetitiveness, withal electing to use the simplest time-honored units of the musical structure, to wit, major triads in the fundamental positions, with the tonic in the bass. Adams is a modernist among minimalists, for he allows for a constant flow of divergent tonalities in his works while also exploiting such elementary harmonic progressions as the serenely cadential alternations of the tonic and the dominant, achieving a desired effect. Typical of such works are his *Harmonium* for Chorus and Orch. (1980) and the grandiose popular score *Grand Pianola Music* (1981–82). Many of his works have been performed by leading U.S. orchs. His topical opera *Nixon in China* (Houston, Oct. 22, 1987) brought him international attention. He also composed the opera *The Death of Klinghoffer* (Brussels, March 19, 1991), and a song play, *I Was Looking at the Ceiling and Then I Saw the Sky* (Berkeley, Calif., May 11, 1995). In 1995 he received the Grawemeyer Award of the Univ. of Louisville for his Violin Concerto (1993). In 1997 he was elected a member of the American Academy of Arts and Letters.

Adams, Suzanne, American soprano; b. Cambridge, Mass., Nov. 28, 1872; d. London, Feb. 5, 1953. She studied with Bouhy and Mathilde Marchesi in Paris, where she made her operatic debut as Gounod's Juliette at the Opéra on Jan. 9, 1895; she remained on its roster until 1898. On May 10, 1898, she made her first appearance at London's Covent Garden as Juliette and sang there until 1904; on Nov. 8, 1898, she sang Juliette again in her Metropolitan Opera debut during the company's visit to Chicago, and then again for her formal debut with the company in New York on Jan. 4, 1899. She remained on its roster until 1903, but also was active as an oratorio singer in the United States and Europe. After the death of her husband, the cellist Leo Stein, in 1904, she retired from the operatic stage but appeared in vaudeville in London before settling there as a voice teacher. Her best roles, in addition to the ubiquitous Juliette, were Donna Elvira, Marguerite de Valois, and Micaëla.

Adaskin, Murray, Canadian composer and teacher; b. Toronto, March 28, 1906. He studied violin in Toronto with his brother Harry Adaskin and with Luigi von Kunits, in New York with Kathleen Parlow, and in Paris with Marcel Chailley. Returning to Toronto, he was a violinist in the Sym. Orch. there (1923–36). He then pursued training in composition with Weinzweig (1944–48), with Milhaud at the Aspen (Colo.) Music School (summers, 1949–50; 1953), and with Charles Jones in California (1949–51). In 1952 he became head of the music dept. at the Univ. of Saskatchewan, where he also was composer-in-residence from 1966 until his retirement in 1972. From 1957 to 1960 he was conductor of the Saskatoon Sym. Orch. In 1973 he settled in Victoria, where he continued to be active as a teacher and composer. In 1931 he married **Frances James**. In 1981 he was made a member of the Order of Canada. Adaskin's output followed along neoclassical lines with occasional infusions of folk elements; in some of his works, he utilized serial techniques. He composed the operas *Grant, Warden of the Plains* (1966; Winnipeg, July 18, 1967) and *The Travelling Musicians* (1983).

BIBL.: G. Lazarevich, *The Musical World of Frances James and M. A.* (Toronto, 1987).

Addison, Adele, black American soprano; b. N.Y., July 24, 1925. She studied at Westminster Choir College, Princeton, and the Berkshire Music Center at Tanglewood, and also took lessons with Povla Frijsh. She made her New York debut at Town Hall in 1952, then sang with the New England Opera and the N.Y. City Opera; she made numerous appearances with major American orchs. Her extensive repertoire included works extending from the Baroque era to the 20th century.

Adelburg, August, Ritter von, Austrian violinist and composer; b. Pera, Turkey, Nov. 1, 1830; d. Vienna, Oct. 20, 1873. He studied with Mayseder (violin) in Vienna (1850–54) and with Hoffmann (composition), then toured Europe as a violinist. He wrote the operas *Zrinyi* (Pest, June 23, 1868) and *Martinuzzi* (Buda, 1870).

Adès, Thomas (Joseph Edmund), remarkable English composer and pianist; b. London, March 1, 1971. He studied piano with Paul Berkowitz and composition with Robert Saxton at the Guildhall School of Music and Drama in London, and then pursued his training with Hugh Wood, Alexander Goehr, and Robin Holloway at King's College, Cambridge (M.A., 1992) before taking his M.Phil. at St. John's College, Cambridge. He also took courses in Dartington (1991) and Aldeburgh (1992). In 1993 he attracted notice as a pianist and composer when he gave a London recital featuring the premiere of his *Still Sorrowing*. His *Living Toys* for Chamber Ensemble (1993) secured his reputation as a composer of promise. In 1993–94 he was a lecturer at the Univ. of Manchester, and also served as composer-in-association with the Hallé Orch. in Manchester from 1993 to 1995. His chamber opera *Powder Her Face* (Cheltenham Festival, July 1, 1995) established him as a dramatic composer of marked talent. From 1995 to 1997 he was fellow commoner in creative arts at Trinity College, Cambridge. He was the Benjamin Britten Prof. of Music at the Royal Academy of Music in London (from 1997), musical director of the Birmingham Contemporary Music Group (from 1998), and artistic director of the Aldeburgh Festival (from 1999). In 1998 he was awarded the Elise L. Stroeger Prize of the Chamber Music Society of Lincoln Center in New York. He is currently composing a commissioned 2d opera for Covent Garden, to a libretto by James Fenton, to premiere in 2001.

Adler, F. Charles, American conductor; b. London, July 2, 1889; d. Vienna, Feb. 16, 1959. He studied piano with August Halm, theory with Beer-Walbrunn, and conducting with Mahler. He was assistant to Felix Mottl at the Royal Opera in Munich (1908–11); in 1913 he became 1st conductor of the Municipal Opera in Düsseldorf; conducted sym. concerts in Europe (1919–33). He was owner of Edition Adler in Berlin until 1933, when he went to America. In 1937 he founded the Saratoga Springs Music Festivals in New York.

Adler, Guido, eminent Austrian musicologist; b. Eibenschütz, Moravia, Nov. 1, 1855; d. Vienna, Feb. 15, 1941. He studied at the Vienna Cons. under Bruckner and Dessoff; entered the Univ. of Vienna in 1874 and founded, in cooperation with Felix Mottl and K. Wolf, the academical Wagner Soc.; took the degree of Dr.Jur. in 1878, and, in 1880, that of Ph.D. (diss., *Die historischen Grundklassen der christlich-abendlandischen Musik bis 1600*); in 1882 he completed his Habilitation with *Studie zur Geschichte der Harmonie* (publ. in Vienna, 1881). With Chrysander and Spitta he founded, in 1884, the *Vierteljahrsschrift für Musikwissenschaft*. In 1885 he was appointed prof. of music history at the German Univ. at Prague. In 1892 he was elected president of the Central Committee of the Internationale Ausstellung für Musik und Theater. In 1895 he succeeded Hanslick as prof. of music history at the Univ. of Vienna, retiring in 1927. He was also ed. of the monumental collection *Denkmäler der Tonkunst in Österreich* from its inception (the 1st vol. appeared in 1894) until 1938 (83 vols. in all). He contributed many articles to music periodicals.

WRITINGS: *Richard Wagner: Vorlesungen* (Leipzig, 1904); *Joseph Haydn* (Vienna and Leipzig, 1909); *Der Stil in der Musik* (Leipzig, 1911; 2d ed., 1929); *Gustav Mahler* (Vienna, 1916); *Methode der Musikgeschichte* (Leipzig, 1919); ed. *Handbuch der*

Musikgeschichte (Frankfurt am Main, 1924; 2d ed., rev., 1930); *Wollen und Wirken: Aus dem Leben eines Musikhistorikers* (Vienna, 1935).

BIBL.: *Studien zur Musikgeschichte: Festschrift für G. A.* (Vienna, 1930); E. Reilly, *Gustav Mahler und G. A.* (Vienna, 1978).

Adler, Kurt, Czech-American conductor; b. Neuhaus, Bohemia, March 1, 1907; d. Butler, N.J., Sept. 21, 1977. He studied musicology with Guido Adler and Robert Lach at the Univ. of Vienna. After serving as assistant conductor of the Berlin State Opera (1927–29) and the German Theater in Prague (1929–32), he was conductor of the Kiev Opera (1933–35) and the Stalingrad Phil. (1935–37). In 1938 he settled in the United States. He was assistant conductor (1943–45), chorus master (1945–73), and a conductor (1951–68) at the Metropolitan Opera in New York. He publ. *The Art of Accompanying and Coaching* (Minneapolis, 1965) and *Phonetics and Diction in Singing* (Minneapolis, 1967).

Adler, Kurt Herbert, notable Austrian-American conductor and operatic administrator; b. Vienna, April 2, 1905; d. Ross, Calif., Feb. 9, 1988. He studied at the Vienna Academy of Music and the Univ. of Vienna. He made his debut as a conductor at the Max Reinhardt Theater in Vienna in 1925, and subsequently conducted at the Volksoper there, as well as in Germany, Italy, and Czechoslovakia. He served as assistant to Toscanini at the Salzburg Festival in 1936. As the dark cloud of Nazidom descended upon central Europe, Adler moved to the United States, and from 1938 to 1943 was on the staff of the Chicago Opera; he subsequently was appointed choirmaster (1943), artistic director (1953), and general director (1956) of the San Francisco Opera. After his retirement in 1981, he was made general director emeritus. Under his direction the San Francisco Opera prospered greatly, advancing to the foremost ranks of American opera theaters. In 1980 he was awarded an honorary knighthood by Queen Elizabeth II of England.

BIBL.: K. Lockhart, ed., *The A. Years* (San Francisco, 1981)

Adler, Peter Herman, Czech-American conductor; b. Gablonz, Bohemia, Dec. 2, 1899; d. Ridgefield, Conn., Oct. 2, 1990. He studied with Fidelio Finke, Vítěslav Novák, and Alexander von Zemlinsky at the Prague Cons. After conducting opera in Bremen (1929–32) and sym. concerts in Kiev (1933–36), he settled in the United States and appeared as a guest conductor. From 1949 to 1959 he was music director of the NBC-TV Opera in New York, and then of the Baltimore Sym. Orch. (1959–68). In 1969 he helped found the NET (National Educational Television) Opera in New York, with which he appeared as a conductor. On Sept. 22, 1972, he made his Metropolitan Opera debut in New York conducting *Un ballo in maschera*. He was director of the American Opera Center at the Juilliard School in New York (1973–81).

Adler, Samuel (Hans), German-born American composer, conductor, and pedagogue; b. Mannheim, March 4, 1928. His father was a cantor and composer, and his mother an amateur pianist. Adler began violin study as a child with Albert Levy; in 1939 the family emigrated to the United States. After composition lessons with Herbert Fromm in Boston (1941–46), he studied with Hugo Norden (composition) and Karl Geiringer (musicology) at Boston Univ. (B.M., 1948) before pursuing composition training with Piston, Randall Thompson, and Irving Fine at Harvard Univ. (M.A., 1950); also attended the classes of Copland (composition) and Koussevitzky (conducting) at the Berkshire Music Center in Tanglewood (summers, 1949–50). In 1950 he joined the U.S. Army, and was founder-conductor of the 7th Army Sym. Orch., for which he received the Army Medal of Honor. Upon his discharge, he went to Dallas as music director of Temple Emanu-El (1953–56) and of the Lyric Theater (1954–58). From 1957 to 1966 he was prof. of composition at North Texas State Univ. in Denton. He was prof. of composition (1966–94) and chairman of the music dept. (1973–94) at the Eastman School of Music in Rochester, N.Y. Adler received many honors and awards, including the ASCAP-Deems Taylor Award (1983) for his book *The Study of Orchestration*. In 1984–85 he held a Guggenheim fellowship. In 1990 he received an award from the American Academy and Inst. of Arts and Letters. In his compositions, he has followed a path of midstream modernism, in which densely interwoven contrapuntal lines support the basically tonal harmonic complex, with a frequent incidence of tangential atonal episodes. Much of his music is inspired by the liturgical cantilena of traditional Jewish music; oriental inflections also occur.

WORKS: DRAMATIC: *The Outcasts of Poker Flat*, opera (1959; Denton, Texas, June 8, 1962); *The Wrestler*, sacred opera (1971; Dallas, May 1972); *The Lodge of Shadows*, music drama for Baritone, Dancers, and Orch. (1973; Fort Worth, Texas, May 3, 1988); *The Disappointment*, reconstruction of an early American ballad opera of 1767 (1974; Washington, D.C., Nov. 1976); *The Waking*, celebration for Dancers, Chorus, and Orch. (1978; Louisville, April 1979).

WRITINGS: *Anthology for the Teaching of Choral Conducting* (N.Y., 1971; 2d ed., 1985, as *Choral Conducting: An Anthology*); *Singing and Hearing* (N.Y., 1979); *The Study of Orchestration* (N.Y., 1982; 2d ed., 1989).

Adlgasser, Anton Cajetan, German organist and composer; b. Inzell, Bavaria, Oct. 1, 1729; d. Salzburg, Dec. 22, 1777. He studied with Johann Eberlin in Salzburg. On Dec. 11, 1750, he was appointed organist at Salzburg Cathedral and held this post until his death (he died of a stroke while playing the organ). Adlgasser enjoyed a great reputation as a musical scholar and was admired by the young Mozart. He wrote an opera, *La Nitteti* (Salzburg, 1766), and several school dramas.

Adolfati, Andrea, Italian composer; b. Venice, c.1721; d. Genoa, Oct. 28, 1760. He was a student of Galuppi. After serving as maestro di cappella at S. Maria della Salute in Venice, he was in the service of the Modena court (1745–48). Subsequently he was director of music at the Annunziata church in Genoa (1748–60) and maestro di cappella in Padua (1760). He wrote 10 operas (1746–55).

Adomián, Lan, Russian-born Mexican composer; b. near Mogilev, April 29, 1905; d. Mexico City, May 9, 1979. He emigrated to the United States in 1923, and studied at the Peabody Cons. of Music in Baltimore (1924–26) and at the Curtis Inst. of Music in Philadelphia (1926–28), where his teachers were Bailly (viola) and R. O. Morris (composition). He moved to New York in 1928, where he conducted working-class choruses and bands. In 1936 he joined the Abraham Lincoln Brigade and went to Spain to fight on the Republican side during the Spanish Civil War. Upon his return to America, he wrote music for documentary films. In 1952 his radical politics made it prudent for him to leave the United States. He moved to Mexico and became a naturalized citizen. Adomián was uncommonly prolific as a composer. Among his voluminous works are an opera, *La Macherata* (1969–72), and a dramatic scene, *Auschwitz*, for Baritone and Instruments (1970).

BIBL.: *La voluntad de crear* (2 vols., Mexico City, 1980–81).

Afanasiev, Nikolai, Russian composer; b. Tobolsk, Jan. 12, 1821; d. St. Petersburg, June 3, 1898. He studied violin with his father, an amateur musician, and joined the orch. of the Moscow Opera at the age of 17. Later he conducted Italian opera in Moscow and St. Petersburg. He traveled in Europe in 1857. Afanasiev was regarded as the first Russian composer to write a string quartet (1860), but this is refuted by the discovery of 3 string quartets by Aliabiev. He further wrote 4 operas: *Ammalat-Bek* (Imperial Opera, St. Petersburg, Dec. 5, 1870), and *Stenka Razin, Vakula the Smith*, and *Taras Bulba*, which were never performed.

Affré, Agustarello, French tenor; b. St. Chinian, Oct. 23, 1858; d. Cagnes-sur-Mer, Dec. 27, 1931. He studied at the Toulouse Cons. and with Duvernoy at the Paris Cons. In 1890 he made his operatic debut as Edgardo at the Paris Opéra, singing there until 1911. On May 18, 1909, he made his first appearance at London's Covent Garden as Samson. He later sang in San Francisco (1911) and New Orleans (1912). He was esteemed for his lyric-heroic roles, being equally successful in operas by his countrymen, as well as those by Mozart and Wagner.

Aggházy, Károly, Hungarian pianist, composer, and teacher; b. Pest, Oct. 30, 1855; d. Budapest, Oct. 8, 1918. He studied at the National Cons. in Pest (1867–70) and at the Vienna Cons. (1870–73), then had piano lessons with Liszt and took a course in composition with Volkmann at the Budapest Academy of Music (1875–78). From 1878 to 1881 he toured in duo recitals with the violinist Jenő Hubay. From 1881 to 1883 he was a prof. of piano at the National Cons. in Budapest, and from 1883 to 1889 taught at the Stern and Kullak conservatories in Berlin. In 1889 he returned to Budapest and resumed his post at the National Cons. He composed 2 operas.

Agnelli, Salvatore, Italian composer; b. Palermo, 1817; d. Marseilles, 1874. He was a student of Furno, Zingarelli, and Donizetti at the Palermo Cons. After composing 10 comic operas for Naples and Palermo (1837–42), he settled in Marseilles and brought out serious operas, ballets, and sacred works.

Agnesi, Luigi (real name, **Louis Ferdinand Léopold Agniez**), Belgian bass; b. Erpent, Namur, July 17, 1833; d. London, Feb. 2, 1875. He studied at the Brussels Cons. and with Duprez in Paris. After touring Germany and the Netherlands with Eugenio Merelli's opera company, he sang at the Théâtre-Italien in Paris (1864) and at Her Majesty's Theatre in London (1865). He later appeared in concerts in England (1871–74). He was admired for his portrayals of roles in Rossini's operas.

Agnesi, Maria Teresa, Italian harpsichordist, singer, and composer; b. Milan, Oct. 17, 1720; d. there, Jan. 19, 1795. She made appearances in Milan as a harpsichordist and singer. She composed a successful pastorale, *Il ristoro d'Arcadia*, which was produced in Milan at the Teatro Ducale in 1747, and an opera, *Ciro in Armenia*, to her own libretto (Milan, Dec. 26, 1753). Her other stage works were *Sofonisba* (Naples, 1765), *Insubria consolata* (Milan, 1766), and *Nitocri* (Venice, 1771).

Agostini, Mezio, Italian composer, pianist, conductor, and pedagogue; b. Fano, Aug. 12, 1875; d. there, April 22, 1944. He studied with Carlo Pedrotti at the Liceo Rossini in Pesaro (1885–92), where he subsequently was a prof. of harmony (1900–09); he was then director of the Liceo Benedetto Marcello in Venice (1909–40). He was active as an opera conductor in Venice and other Italian cities, and gave chamber music concerts as a pianist. His *Trio* won 1st prize at the international competition in Paris in 1904. He wrote the operas *Iovo e Maria* (1896), *Il Cavaliere del Sogno* (Fano, Feb. 24, 1897), *La penna d'Airone* (1896), *Alcibiade* (1902), *America* (also entitled *Hail Columbia*, 1904), *L'ombra* (1907), *L'agnello del sogno* (1928), and *La Figlio del navarca* (Fano, Sept. 3, 1938).

Agostini, Pietro Simone, Italian composer; b. Forlí, c.1635; d. (murdered) Parma, Oct. 1, 1680. He led an adventurous life. After being expelled from Forlì due to his complicity in a murder, he studied music with Mazzaferrata in Ferrara. He saw military service in Crete and was made a Knight of the Golden Spur. In 1658 he commenced his career as a composer in Venice. In 1664 he went to Genoa and composed for the theater until his intimate association with a nun led to his banishment. He then went to Rome, where he became director of music at S. Agnese. Although Agostini excelled as a composer of secular cantatas, his opera *Gl'inganni innocenti, ovvero L'Adalina* was a notable success at its premiere in Ariccia, near Rome, in 1673. In 1679 he was called to the ducal court in Parma as maestro di cappella, but was murdered the next year.

Agricola, Benedetta Emilia (née **Molteni**), Italian soprano; b. Modena, 1722; d. Berlin, 1780. She studied with Porpora, Hasse, and Salimbeni, making her operatic debut at the Berlin Royal Opera in 1743 in C. H. Graun's *Cesare e Cleopatra*. She was married to **Johann Friedrich Agricola**; her connection with the court ceased upon his death in 1774, and she disappeared from the music scene.

Agricola, Johann Friedrich, German organist and composer; b. Dobitzschen, near Altenburg, Jan. 4, 1720; d. Berlin, Dec. 2, 1774. He entered the Univ. of Leipzig as a law student in 1738, studying music meanwhile with J. S. Bach, and later (1741) with Johann Quantz in Berlin. In 1751 Agricola was appointed court composer to Frederick the Great; in 1759 he succeeded C. H. Graun as director of the Royal Chapel. Agricola wrote 11 operas (produced between 1750 and 1772 at Berlin and Potsdam) and church music; he also made arrangements of the King's compositions. He taught singing and in 1757 tr. Pier Tosi's *Opinioni de' cantori* as *Anleitung zur Singkunst* (Eng. tr. and commentary by J. Baird, 1995). Under the pseudonym **Flavio Amicio Olibrio** Agricola printed some polemical pamphlets directed against the theorist Friedrich Marpurg; he was also a collaborator with Jakob Adlung in the latter's *Musica mechanica organoedi* (1768). His wife was **Benedetta Emilia** (née **Molteni**) **Agricola**.

BIBL.: H. Wucherpfennig, *J. F. A.* (diss., Univ. of Berlin, 1922).

Aguiari or **Agujari, Lucrezia,** brilliant Italian soprano, known as **La Bastardina** and **La Bastardella** on account of her being the illegitimate daughter of a nobleman; b. Ferrara, 1743; d. Parma, May 18, 1783. She received vocal training from the Abbot Lambertini. In 1764 she made her debut with notable success in Florence. In 1768 she was made a court singer in Parma, where Mozart heard her in 1770 and was greatly impressed by the beauty of her voice and its phenomenal compass, which embraced 3 octaves (C^1-C^4). In 1775–76 she sang at the Pantheon in London. She created leading roles in several operas by the Italian composer **Giuseppe Colla**, whom she married in 1780.

BIBL.: G. Vetro, *L. A., la "Bastardella"* (Parma, 1993).

Ahlersmeyer, Mathieu, German baritone; b. Cologne, June 29, 1896; d. Garmisch-Partenkirchen, July 23, 1979. He studied in Cologne. In 1929 he made his operatic debut as Wolfram in Mönchengladbach, and then sang at the Berlin Kroll Opera (1930–31) and the Hamburg Opera (1931–33). From 1934 to 1945 he was a member of the Dresden State Opera, where he created the Barber in Strauss's *Die schweigsame Frau* (June 14, 1935). In 1938 he created the role of Egk's Peer Gynt at the Berlin State Opera. From 1946 to 1961 he sang at the Hamburg State Opera, and again from 1962 to 1973. His prominent roles included Don Giovanni, Hans Sachs, Rigoletto, Scarpia, and Hindemith's Matthias Grünewald.

Ahlin, Čvetka, Yugoslav mezzo-soprano; b. Ljubljana, Sept. 28, 1928; d. Hamburg, June 30, 1985. She studied at the Ljubljana Academy of Music. In 1952 she made her operatic debut at the Ljubljana Opera; after winning 1st prize at the Munich Competition (1954) she was a member of the Hamburg State Opera (1955–74); she was also a guest artist in various European opera centers. From 1974 she taught at the Lübeck Hochschule für Musik. Among her best roles were Orpheus, Amneris, Azucena, and Marina.

Ahlstrom, David, American composer; b. Lancaster, N.Y., Feb. 22, 1927; d. San Francisco, Aug. 23, 1992. He studied composition with Henry Cowell and Bernard Rogers and became interested in Asian philosophy and had instruction from Haridas Chaudhuri. He obtained a Ph.D. in composition from the Eastman School of Music in Rochester, N.Y., in 1961, then taught theory at Northwestern Univ. (1961–62), Southern Methodist Univ. in Dallas (1962–67), and Eastern Illinois Univ. in Charleston (1967–76). In 1976 he moved to San Francisco, and became active in the production of new American stage music. Among his own works, the most significant is his opera *America, I Love You*, to a libretto by e.e. cummings (San Francisco, June 25, 1983, composer conducting); other operas were *Doctor Faustus Lights the Lights*, after Gertrude Stein (San Francisco, Oct. 29, 1982), and *3 Sisters Who Are Not Sisters*, also after Stein (San Francisco, Sept. 17, 1982).

Ahna, Pauline de, German soprano; b. Ingolstadt, Feb. 4, 1863; d. Garmisch-Partenkirchen, May 13, 1950. She received her musical training in Munich. In 1890 she made her operatic debut as Pamina in Weimar, where she subsequently appeared as Eva, Elsa, and Donna Elvira, and also created the role of Freihild in Strauss's *Guntram* (May 10, 1894). She likewise sang Agathe, Leonore, and Donna Anna in Karlsruhe (1890–91) and Elisabeth at the Bayreuth Festival (1891). On Sept. 10, 1894, she married Strauss, who dedicated several sets of lieder to her. He also depicted her in his *Ein Heldenleben*, *Symphonia domestica*, and *Intermezzo*.

Ahnsjö, Claes-H(åkan), noted Swedish tenor; b. Stockholm Aug. 1, 1942. He studied with Erik Saeden, Askel Schiøtz, and Max Lorenz in Stockholm. In 1969 he made his operatic debut as Tamino at the Royal Theater in Stockholm; from 1969 he also sang at the Drottningholm Court Theater. In 1973 he became a member of the Bavarian State Opera in Munich, where he was made a Kammersänger in 1977. His guest engagements took him to the major operatic and concert centers of Europe, the United States, and Japan. His operatic repertoire includes roles by Haydn, Mozart, Rossini, Verdi, and Wagner; also appeared as a soloist with orchs. and as a recitalist.

Aho, Kalevi, prominent Finnish composer, pedagogue, and writer on music; b. Forssa, March 9, 1949. He was a student of Rautavaara at the Sibelius Academy in Helsinki (composition diploma, 1971) and of Boris Blacher at the Staatliche Hochschule für Musik and Darstellende Kunst in Berlin (1971–72). From 1974 to 1988 he lectured on musicology at the Univ. of Helsinki, and then was acting prof. of composition at the Sibelius Academy (1988–93). He has written numerous articles on music for various publications. Among his honors are the Leonie Sonning Prize of Denmark (1974) and the Henrik Steffens Prize of Germany (1990). After composing in a neoclassical vein, he embraced a more modern idiom. In his later works, his style became refreshingly varied, ranging from the traditional to the postmodern. His stage works include *Avain* (The Key), dramatic monologue for Singer and Chamber Orch. (1978–79; Helsinki, Sept. 4, 1979), and *Hyönteiselämää* (Insect Life), opera (1985–87; Helsinki, Sept. 27, 1996).

Aiblinger, Johann Kaspar, German conductor and composer; b. Wasserburg, Bavaria, Feb. 23, 1779; d. Munich, May 6, 1867. He studied music in Munich, then at Bergamo under Simon Mayr (1802). From 1803 to 1811 he lived at Vicenza, then became 2d maestro di cappella to the viceroy at Milan. He founded the Odeon (a society for the cultivation of Classical vocal music) at Venice, in collaboration with Abbe Trentino. In 1819 he was engaged for the Italian opera in Munich as maestro al cembalo. He returned in 1833 to Bergamo, and amassed a fine collection of early Classical music, now in the Staatsbibliothek at Munich. He wrote 2 operas, including the popular *Rodrigo e Ximene* (Munich, 1821), and 3 ballets.

Ainsley, John Mark, English tenor; b. Crewe, July 9, 1963. He studied at Magdalen College, Oxford, and with Anthony Rolfe Johnson. After making his professional debut as a soloist in Stravinsky's Mass at London's Royal Festival Hall in 1984, he appeared frequently as a soloist with many early music groups from 1985. He made his first appearance with the English National Opera in London as Eurillo in Scarlatti's *Gli equivoci nel sembiante* in 1989. In 1990 he made his U.S. debut as a soloist in Bach's Mass in B Minor in New York under Hogwood's direction. In 1991 he appeared as Mozart's Ferrando with the Glyndebourne Touring Opera, and also sang that composer's Idamante with the Welsh National Opera in Cardiff. His first appearance at the Glyndebourne Festival followed in 1992 as Ferrando, the same year in which he made his debut as a soloist with the Berlin Phil. In 1993 he sang Mozart's Don Ottavio at the Aix-en-Provence Festival, a role he sang again at the San Francisco Opera in 1995. In 1997 he sang in concert at London's Royal Festival Hall.

Aitken, Hugh, American composer and teacher; b. N.Y., Sept. 7, 1924. He received his primary training at home; his father was an accomplished violinist, and his paternal grandmother was a pianist. He took clarinet lessons and also enrolled in a chemistry class at N.Y. Univ. From 1943 to 1945 he served as a navigator in the U.S. Army Air Corps. Returning from World War II, he entered the Juilliard School of Music in New York as a student in composition of Bernard Wagenaar, Vincent Persichetti, and Robert Ward (M.S., 1950); in 1960 he joined the faculty there, and in 1970 became a prof. of music at William Paterson College of N.J. in Wayne. In his music he professes moral dedication to Classical ideals, regarding deviation from the natural melodic flow and harmonic euphony as unjustifiable tonicide. He composed the chamber opera *Fables* (1975) and the opera *Felipe* (1981).

Akimenko (real name, **Yakimenko**), **Fyodor (Stepanovich),** Russian composer; b. Kharkov, Feb. 20, 1876; d. Paris, Jan. 3, 1945. He studied with Balakirev at the Court Chapel in St. Petersburg (1886–90), then with Liadov and Rimsky-Korsakov at the St. Petersburg Cons. (1895–1900). He was the first composition teacher of Stravinsky, whom he taught privately. After the Russian Revolution, he emigrated to Paris. He wrote mostly for piano in the manner of the Russian lyric school, but his compositions also include an opera, *The Fairy of the Snows* (1914).

Akses, Necil Kâzim, Turkish composer and pedagogue; b. Constantinople, May 6, 1908. He studied at the Constantinople Cons.; in 1926 he went to Vienna, where he had instruction with Joseph Marx; subsequently moved to Prague and took lessons with Alois Hába and Josef Suk (1931–34). Returning to Turkey in 1935, he was appointed to the Teachers College in Ankara; he also attended classes of Paul Hindemith, who was teaching in Ankara at the time. In 1936 Akses became a composition teacher at the Ankara State Cons.; in 1958 he was made a prof. there. His music incorporates elements of Turkish folk songs, but the contrapuntal and harmonic formulation is entirely modern. He composed the operas *Mete* (1933) and *Bayönder* (Ankara, Dec. 27, 1934).

Akutagawa, Yasushi, noted Japanese composer and conductor; b. Tokyo, July 12, 1925; d. there, Jan. 31, 1989. He received training in piano, conducting, and composition (from Hashimoto and Ifukube) at the Tokyo Academy of Music (1943–49). In subsequent years, he devoted himself mainly to composition while making occasional appearances as a conductor. He was president of the Japanese Federation of Composers (1980–89) and the Japanese Performing Rights Soc. (1981–89). His orch. music was widely disseminated outside his homeland. His father was the famous Japanese author of *Rashomon*.

WORKS: DRAMATIC: OPERA: *Kurai Kagami* (Dark Mirror; Tokyo, March 27, 1960; rev. ver. as *Orpheus in Hiroshima*, NHK-TV, Aug. 27, 1967). BALLETS: *The Dream of the Lake* (Tokyo, Nov. 6, 1950); *Paradise Lost* (Tokyo, March 17, 1951); *Kappa* (July 21, 1957); *Spider's Web* (Tokyo, March 17, 1969).

Alagna, Roberto, prominent Italian tenor; b. Clichy-sur-Bois, France, June 7, 1963. He received vocal training from Raphael Ruiz. In 1988 he won the Pavarotti Competition in Philadelphia and then made his operatic debut with the Glyndebourne Touring Opera in Plymouth as Alfredo. His first appearance at London's Covent Garden followed in 1990 as Rodolfo. In 1991 he made his debut at Milan's La Scala as Alfredo. Following an engagement as Roberto Devereux in Monte Carlo in 1992, he returned to Covent Garden as Gounod's Roméo in 1994. He sang the Duke of Mantua at his debut at the Vienna State Opera in 1995; the same year he sang Edgardo at the Opéra de la Bastille in Paris. He returned to Paris in 1996 as Don Carlos at the Théâtre du Châtelet. On April 10, 1996, he made his debut at the Metropolitan Opera in New York as Rodolfo. Shortly afterward he married **Angela Gheorghiu**, and then returned to the Metropolitan Opera that year as Nemorino and the Duke of Mantua and to Covent Garden as Don Carlos and Alfredo. In 1997 he was engaged as Macduff at La Scala. He sang Roméo to Gheorghiu's Juliette at the Metropolitan Opera in 1998 to notable acclaim, roles they reprised at the Lyric Opera in Chicago in 1999.

Alaleona, Domenico, Italian music theorist and composer; b. Montegiorgio, Nov. 16, 1881; d. there, Dec. 28, 1928. He studied organ and clarinet in his native town; in 1901, went to Rome, where he studied piano with Sgambati, organ with Renzi, and theory with De Sanctis at the Accademia di Santa Cecilia; he was then active as a choral conductor in Leghorn and Rome; in 1911, obtained the post of prof. of musical aesthetics at the Accademia di Santa Cecilia. He wrote an opera, *Mirra* (1912; Rome, March

31, 1920), but his importance lies more in his theoretical writings. His valuable book *Studi sulla storia dell'oratorio musicale in Italia* (Turin, 1908), once a standard, was reprinted in Milan (1945) as *Storia dell'oratorio musicale in Italia*. A believer in musical progress, Alaleona contributed several original ideas to the theory of modern music, notably in his article "L'armonia modernissima," *Rivista Musicale Italiana* 28 (1911); he also originated the term "dodecafonia."

BIBL.: G. Cardi, *D. A.: Musicista e musicologo* (Ascoli Piceno, 1957).

Alarie, Pierrette (Marguerite), Canadian soprano and teacher; b. Montreal, Nov. 9, 1921. She studied voice and acting with Jeanne Maubourg and Albert Roberval. After appearing on radio as an actress and singer of popular music, she continued vocal training with Salvator Issaurel (1938–43) and as a scholarship student with Elisabeth Schumann at the Curtis Inst. of Music in Philadelphia (1943–46). In 1943 she made her debut as Mozart's Barbarina in Montreal. She won the Metropolitan Opera Auditions of the Air in 1945, and on Dec. 8 of that year made her debut with the company in New York as Verdi's Oscar; she remained on its roster until 1947. In subsequent years, she appeared frequently in opera and in concert with her husband, **Léopold Simoneau**, whom she married in 1946. In addition to her festival appearances in Aix-en-Provence, Edinburgh, Glyndebourne, Vienna, and Munich, she sang opera in Montreal, Toronto, Vancouver, San Francisco, Philadelphia, New York, and New Orleans, becoming particularly well known for her performances of works by Mozart and of works from the French repertoire. In 1966 she retired from the operatic stage and in 1970 made her farewell appearance as a concert singer. After teaching and staging opera in California (1972–82), she went to Victoria, British Columbia, where she was founder-director with her husband of the Canada Opera Piccola. In 1967 she was made an Officer of the Order of Canada. In 1990 the French government made her a Chevalière of the Ordre des arts et des lettres de France.

BIBL.: R. Maheu, *P. A., Léopold Simoneau: Deux voix, un art* (Montreal, 1988).

Alary, Jules (Giulio) Eugène Abraham, Italian-French composer; b. Mantua, March 16, 1814; d. Paris, April 17, 1891. He studied at the Milan Cons., then played the flute at La Scala. In 1838 he settled in Paris as a successful voice teacher and composer. He wrote numerous operas, among them *Rosamunda* (Florence, June 10, 1840), *Le tre nozze* (Paris, March 29, 1851; a polka duet from it, sung by Henrietta Sontag and Lablache, was highly popular), and *Sardanapalo* (St. Petersburg, Feb. 16, 1852). His opera *La Voix humaine* had the curious distinction of being staged at the Paris Opéra (Dec. 30, 1861) with the sole purpose of making use of the scenery left over after the fiasco of *Tannhäuser* (the action of Alary's opera takes place in Wartburg, as does that of *Tannhäuser*). It held the stage for 13 performances (*Tannhäuser* had 3). Alary also wrote a mystery play, *Redemption* (Paris, April 14, 1850).

Albanese, Licia, noted Italian-born American soprano; b. Bari, July 22, 1909. She studied with Emanuel de Rosa in Bari and Giuseppina Baldassare-Tedeschi in Milan. In 1934 she made an unexpected operatic debut at Milan's Teatro Lirico when she was called in to substitute as Cio-Cio-San for the 2d act of *Madama Butterfly*. In 1935 she made her first appearance at Milan's La Scala as Puccini's Lauretta, and subsequently sang there with distinction in such roles as Mimi and Micaëla. In 1937 she made her debut at London's Covent Garden as Liù. On Feb. 9, 1940, she made her first appearance at the Metropolitan Opera in New York as Cio-Cio-San, and remained on its roster as one of its most admired artists until 1963. In 1964 she rejoined its roster and sang with it until her farewell appearance as Mimi in a concert performance at the Newport (R.I.) Opera Festival on July 12, 1966. During her years at the Metropolitan Opera, she was greatly admired for her portrayals in operas by Puccini. She also excelled as Mozart's Countess, Susanna, Adriana Lecouvreur, Desdemona, Massenet's Manon, and Violetta. In 1945 she became a naturalized American citizen. In 1995 she was awarded the Medal of Arts by President Clinton.

Albani (real name, **Lajeunesse**), **Dame (Marie Louise Cécile) Emma,** famous Canadian soprano; b. Chambly, near Montreal, Nov. 1, 1847; d. London, April 3, 1930. In childhood she studied piano with her mother, and then piano, harp, and singing with her father. In 1856 she made her first public appearance in Montreal as a pianist and singer. In 1860 she sang for the visiting Prince of Wales there. In 1865 her family went to Albany, N.Y., where she sang at St. Joseph's Catholic Church until 1868. She then went to Paris to study voice with Duprez and organ and harmony with Benoist, completing her vocal training with Lamperti in Milan. In 1870 she made her operatic debut as Amina in Messina, taking the professional name of Albani. On April 2, 1872, she made a notable debut at London's Covent Garden as Amina. In succeeding years her career was closely associated with Covent Garden, where she was greatly admired. On Oct. 21, 1874, she made her U.S. operatic debut as Amina with the Max Strakosch company at N.Y.'s Academy of Music. On Dec. 23, 1891, she made her Metropolitan Opera debut in New York as Gilda, but sang there for only one season. Her last great triumph at Covent Garden came on July 24, 1896, when she appeared as Valentine. Thereafter she devoted herself to a concert career, giving her farewell recital at London's Royal Albert Hall on Oct. 14, 1911. After retirement, she fell upon hard times and gave voice lessons and even appeared in English music halls. In 1920 the British government granted her a pension. She was awarded the Gold Medal of the Phil. Society of London in 1897. In 1925 she was made a Dame Commander of the Order of the British Empire. Her memoirs were publ. as *Forty Years of Song* (London, 1911). Albani was a remarkable artist, excelling in coloratura, spinto, and dramatic roles. She was also a distinguished concert artist.

BIBL.: C. Macdonald, *E. A.: Victorian Diva* (Toronto, 1984).

Albéniz, Isaac (Manuel Francisco), eminent Spanish composer and pianist; b. Camprodón, May 29, 1860; d. Cambo-les-Bains, May 18, 1909. He began piano lessons at a very early age with Narciso Oliveros in Barcelona. He was only 4 when he made his first public appearance as a pianist there with his sister Clementina. In 1867 the family went to Paris, where he had some instruction from A.-F. Marmontel. The family returned to Spain in 1868, and in 1869 Albéniz enrolled in the Madrid Cons. to study with Ajero and Mendizábal. He quit the Cons. by the time he was 10 and set out to roam his homeland, supporting himself by playing in various venues. After an adventuresome sojourn in South America in 1872–73, he returned to Spain to give concerts. In 1875 he played in Puerto Rico, and then visited Cuba and the United States before pursuing his studies at the Leipzig Cons. with Jadassohn and Reinecke. In 1877 Count Guillermo Morphy provided Albéniz with a scholarship to study at the Brussels Cons. with Brassin (piano) and Gevaert and Dupont (composition), where he graduated with a 1st prize in 1879. In 1880 he met Liszt who gave him valuable advice. Albéniz subsequently pursued a concert career in Spain and abroad. After settling in Paris in 1894, he devoted himself principally to composing but also taught at the Schola Cantorum (1897–98). In 1900 he returned to Spain but was again in Paris in 1902 before settling in Nice in 1903. Albéniz helped to forge the Spanish national idiom of composition, one reflecting indigenous rhythms and melodic patterns. A gifted pianist, he composed a remarkable body of music for his instrument. His suite *Iberia* (1905–09) is an outstanding example.

WORKS: DRAMATIC: *The Magic Opal*, operetta (London, Jan. 19, 1893); *San Antonio de la Florida*, zarzuela (Madrid, Oct. 26, 1894); *Henry Clifford*, opera (Barcelona, May 8, 1895); *Merlín*, opera (c.1895; unfinished); *Pepita Jiménez*, comic opera (Barcelona, Jan. 5, 1896).

BIBL.: H. Collet, *A. et Granados* (Paris, 1926; 2d ed., 1948); V. Ruiz Albéniz, *I. A.* (Madrid, 1948); A Sagardia, *I. A.* (Madrid, 1951); W. Clark, *I. A.: A Guide to Research* (Levittown, Pa., 1998).

Albergati Capacelli, Pirro, Conte d', Italian composer; b. Bologna, Sept. 20, 1663; d. there, June 22, 1735. He wrote 2 operas,

Gli amici (Bologna, Aug. 16, 1699) and *Il Principe selvaggio* (Bologna, 1712), and numerous oratorios, which were regularly performed at various churches in Bologna (1686–1732).

Albert, Eugen (Eugène Francis Charles), D', prominent Scottish-born German pianist, conductor, pedagogue, and composer of English-French descent; b. Glasgow, April 10, 1864; d. Riga, March 3, 1932. He began his training with his father, the composer Charles Louis Napoléon d'Albert (b. Nienstetten, near Hamburg, Feb. 25, 1809; d. London, May 26, 1886). At 10 he entered London's National Training School and studied piano with Pauer and theory with Stainer, Prout, and Sullivan. After appearances at London's Popular Concerts, he made his debut as soloist in the Schumann Concerto in London on Feb. 5, 1881. On Oct. 24, 1881, he was soloist in his own Piano Concerto under Richter in London, winning extraordinary acclaim. After further training in Vienna and with Liszt, who hailed him as the young Tausig, he pursued a highly successful career as a pianist. In addition to his brilliant performances of Liszt, he was greatly admired for his Bach, Beethoven, and Brahms. In 1895 he became conductor of the Weimar Opera. From 1907 he served as director of the Berlin Hochschule für Musik. During World War I, he repudiated his English heritage, became a naturalized German citizen, and changed his first name to Eugen. His first wife (1892–95) was **Teresa Carreño**. Subsequently, he married 5 more times. As a composer, d'Albert's output reflects German and Italian influences. Of his major works, he found some success with the operas *Die Abreise* (1898), *Tiefland* (1903), and *Flauto solo* (1905).

WORKS: OPERAS: *Der Rubin* (Karlsruhe, Oct. 12, 1893); *Ghismonda* (Dresden, Nov. 28, 1895); *Gernot* (Mannheim, April 11, 1897); *Die Abreise* (Frankfurt am Main, Oct. 20, 1898); *Kain* (Berlin, Feb. 17, 1900); *Der Improvisator* (Berlin, Feb. 20, 1902); *Tiefland* (Prague, Nov. 15, 1903); *Flauto solo* (Prague, Nov. 12, 1905); *Tragaldabas* or *Der geborgte Ehemann* (Hamburg, Dec. 3, 1907); *Izeÿl* (Hamburg, Nov. 6, 1909); *Die verschenkte Frau* (Vienna, Feb. 6, 1912); *Liebesketten* (Vienna, Nov. 12, 1912); *Die toten Augen* (Dresden, March 5, 1916); *Der Stier von Olivera* (Leipzig, March 10, 1918); *Revolutionshochzeit* (Leipzig, Oct. 26, 1919); *Scirocco* (Darmstadt, May 18, 1921); *Mareike von Nymwegen* (Hamburg, Oct. 31, 1923); *Der Goldem* (Frankfurt am Main, Nov. 14, 1926); *Die schwarze Orchidee* (Leipzig, Dec. 1, 1928); *Mister Wu* (unfinished; completed by L. Blech; Dresden, Sept. 29, 1932).

BIBL.: W. Raupp, *E. d'A.: Ein Künstler- und Menschenschicksal* (Leipzig, 1930); H. Heisig, *D'A.s Opernschaffen* (diss., Univ. of Leipzig, 1942).

Albert, Karel, Belgian composer; b. Antwerp, April 16, 1901; d. Liedekerke, May 23, 1987. He was a student of Jong at the Royal Flemish Cons. in Antwerp. From 1933 to 1961 he was active with the Belgian Radio. He publ. *De evolutie van de muziek van de Oudheid tot aan Beethoven aan de hand van fonoplaten* (Brussels, 1947). Among his stage works were the opera buffa *Europa ontvoerd* (1950) and the ballets *De toverlantaarn* (1942) and *Tornooi* (1953).

Alberti, Domenico, Italian singer, harpsichordist, and composer; b. Venice, 1710; d. Formio or Rome, c.1740. He studied with Lotti, and won considerable renown as a singer and harpsichord player. He composed 3 operas, *Endimione, Galatea, and Olimpiade*. In 1737 he was a member of the Venetian Embassy in Rome, and made several appearances there as a singer and player. His fame in music history rests on his reputed invention of the arpeggio style of keyboard accompaniment, which became known as the "Alberti Bass."

Albertini, Joachim (Gioacchino), Italian-born Polish composer; b. Pesaro, 1749; d. Warsaw, March 27, 1812. He was a conductor to Prince Karol Radziwill in Neiswiez, later serving as maitre de chapelle to King Stanislaw August Poniatowski in Warsaw (from 1782). In 1795 he received Poland's life pension.

WORKS: DRAMATIC: *La Cacciatrice brillante*, intermezzo (Rome, Feb. 1772); *Don Juan albo Ukarany libertyn* (Don Juan or The Rake Punished), opera (Warsaw, Feb. 23, 1783); *Virginia*, opera seria (Rome, Jan. 7, 1786); *Circe und Ulisses*, opera seria (Hamburg, Jan. 30, 1786); *Scipione Africano*, opera seria (Rome, 1789); *La Virgine vestale*, opera seria (Rome, Carnival, 1803); *Kapelmajster polski* (Polish Kapellmeister), intermezzo (Warsaw, Oct. 28, 1808).

Albertsen, Per Hjort, Norwegian organist and composer; b. Trondheim, July 27, 1919. He studied organ at the Oslo Cons., graduating in 1946; took lessons in composition with Sven Erik Tarp in Copenhagen, Ralph Downes in London, and Hanns Jelinek in Vienna. He was an organist in Trondheim (1947–68), then lectured in the music dept. of the univ. there (1968–72). Much of his music has been written for student performance, including the school opera *Russicola* (1956).

Albinoni, Tomaso Giovanni, esteemed Italian composer; b. Venice, June 8, 1671; d. there, Jan. 17, 1751. He was the son of a wealthy paper merchant. Although apprenticed to his father, he also received training in violin, singing, and composition. The lure of music led him to pursue the career of a dilettante (in the best sense of the word) composer. He first attracted attention with the premiere of his first opera, *Zenobia, Regina de' Palmireni*, in Venice in 1694. It was also in that year that his 12 trio sonatas, op.1, were publ. in Venice. In succeeding years, he produced an extensive output of secular vocal works and instrumental music. In 1705 he married the soprano Margherita Raimondi, known as "La Salarina," who pursued an intermittent operatic career until her death in 1721. In 1722 Albinoni was called to Munich to oversee the premiere of his opera *I veri amici*, composed for the marriage of the Prince-elector Karl Albert to Maria Amalia, the daughter of the late emperor Joseph I. Thereafter his operas were performed widely abroad, complementing the extensive dissemination of his instrumental music. Although a lesser master than such contemporaries as Bach, Handel, and Vivaldi, Albinoni developed an individual style marked by fine craftsmanship in which his melodic talent served him exceedingly well. Bach admired his music and composed 4 keyboard fugues on the Italian's op.1.

WORKS: DRAMATIC: OPERAS: Albinoni claimed to have written 80 operas, but his count may have included rev. versions and pasticcios. Of the 50 operas generally attributed to him, only 3 are extant in full: *Zenobia, Regina de' Palmireni* (Venice, 1694), *Engelberta* (Venice, 1709; in collaboration with Gasparini), and *La Statira* (Rome, 1726); arias from some of his other operas are also extant. He also wrote 3 comic intermezzos, of which *Vespetta e Pimpinone* (Venice, 1708) is extant, and 3 serenatas, of which *Il nascimento dell'aurora* (c.1710) and *Il nome glorioso in terra, santificato in cielo* (Venice, Nov. 4, 1724) are extant. ORATORIOS: *Trionfi di Giosuè* (pasticcio; Florence, 1703); *Maria annunziata* (Florence, 1712).

BIBL.: R. Giazotto, *T. A.* (Brescia, 1953); M. Talbot, *A.: Leben und Werk* (Adliswil, 1980); M. Talbot, *T. A.: The Venetian Composer and His World* (Oxford, 1990).

Alboni, Marietta (Maria Anna Marzia), famous Italian contralto; b. Città de Castello, March 6, 1823; d. Ville d'Avray, France, June 23, 1894. She studied with Mombelli, Bertinotti, and Rossini. On Oct. 3, 1842, she made her operatic debut as Climene in Pacini's *Saffo* in Bologna. On Dec. 30, 1842, she made her first appearance at Milan's La Scala in Rossini's *Assedio de Corinto*. In 1843 she sang to acclaim in Vienna, and in 1844–45 with great success in St. Petersburg. After highly successful engagements in other cities on the Continent, she went to London to open the first season of the Royal Italian Opera at Covent Garden as Arsace in *Semiramide* on April 6, 1847. In Oct. 1847 she gave 4 "concerts-spectacles" in Paris, returning there on Dec. 2 to make her debut as Arsace at the Théâtre-Italien. In 1848 she returned to London, where she became a rival to Jenny Lind. She continued to make appearances in London until 1858. From June 1852 to May 1853 she toured the United States in concert and opera. Due to obesity, she gradually withdrew from operatic appearances after 1863. In 1872 she sang for the last time in opera at the Théâtre-Italien. She subsequently gave occasional concerts seated in a large chair. Her exceptional vocal range extended from contralto G to high soprano C.

BIBL.: A Pougin, *M. A.* (Paris, 1912).

Albrecht, Evgeni, Russian violinist, son of **Karl Albrecht**; b. St. Petersburg, July 16, 1842; d. there, Feb. 9, 1894. He studied violin with Ferdinand David at the Leipzig Cons. (1857–60). Upon his return to Russia, he conducted the Italian opera in St. Petersburg (1860–77); he was also music director of military schools there (1872–77). In 1877 he became inspector of the Imperial Orchs., and in 1892 he was music librarian of the Imperial Theaters. His brother, Konstantin Albrecht (b. Elberfeld, Oct. 4, 1835; d. Moscow, June 26, 1893), was a cellist.

Albrecht, Gerd, German conductor; b. Essen, July 19, 1935. His father was the German musicologist Hans Albrecht (b. Magdeburg, March 31, 1902; d. Kiel, Jan. 20, 1961). He studied conducting with Brückner-Rüggeberg at the Hamburg Hochschule für Musik and musicology at the univs. of Kiel and Hamburg. After winning the Besançon (1957) and Hilversum (1958) conducting competitions, he conducted at the Württemberg State Theater in Stuttgart (1958–61). He was 1st conductor in Mainz (1961–63), and then Generalmusikdirektor in Lübeck (1963–66) and Kassel (1966–72). From 1972 to 1979 he was chief conductor of the Deutsche Oper in West Berlin and of the Tonhalle Orch. in Zürich from 1975 to 1980. From 1976 he was a guest conductor at the Vienna State Opera. In 1981 he made his U.S. debut conducting the U.S. premiere of Reimann's *Lear* at the San Francisco Opera. In 1986 he made his first appearance as a sym. conductor in the United States when he led a guest engagement with the Houston Sym. Orch. He served as chief conductor of the Hamburg State Opera and the Phil. State Orch. from 1988 to 1997. From 1994 to 1996 he was chief conductor of the Czech Phil. in Prague. In 1998 he became chief conductor of the Yomiuri Nippon Sym. Orch. in Tokyo and in 2000 of the Danish National Radio Sym. Orch. in Copenhagen. He publ. the book *Wie eine Opernaufführung zustande kommt* (Zürich, 1988).

Albrecht, Karl, German-Russian conductor, father of **Evgeni Albrecht**; b. Posen, Aug. 27, 1807; d. Gatchina, near St. Petersburg, March 8, 1863. Another son, Konstantin (b. Elberfeld, Oct. 4, 1835; d. Moscow, June 26, 1893), was a cellist. He studied harmony and counterpoint with Josef Schnabel in Breslau, and also learned to play on string and wind instruments. In 1825 he joined the Breslau Theater Orch. as 1st violinist; in 1835 he went to Düsseldorf, where he was engaged as répétiteur in the opera theater. In 1838 he went to St. Petersburg, where he conducted a German opera troupe. From 1840 to 1850 he conducted the Russian Opera there. In 1842 he conducted the first performance of Glinka's *Ruslan and Ludmila*.

Albright, William (Hugh), American composer, pianist, organist, and teacher; b. Gary, Ind., Oct. 20, 1944; d. Ann Arbor, Mich., Sept. 17, 1998. He studied piano with Rosetta Goodkind and theory with Hugh Aitken at the Juilliard Preparatory Dept. in New York (1959–62), then took courses in composition with Finney and Bassett at the Univ. of Mich. in Ann Arbor; he also studied organ with Marilyn Mason there (1963–70). He also received training from Rochberg, and at the Paris Cons. from Olivier Messiaen (1968); also took private lessons with Max Deutsch. In 1970 he joined the faculty of the Univ. of Mich., where he was a prof. of music from 1982; also served as assoc. director of its Electronic Music Studio. He received Guggenheim fellowships in 1976 and 1987; was composer-in-residence at the American Academy in Rome in 1979. In his compositions Albright pursued quaquaversal methods of experimental music, using varied techniques according to need. His stage works include *Cross of Gold*, music theater for Actors, Chorus, Saxophone, Trombone, Double Bass, Percussion, and Electric Organ (1975), and *Full Moon in March*, 5 songs and incidental music to a play by Yeats (1978; Ann Arbor, Jan. 13, 1979). He also made a concert career as a pianist and organist in ragtime, jazz, and contemporary music.

Alcaide, Tomâz (de Aquino Carmelo), Portuguese tenor; b. Estremoz, Feb. 16, 1901; d. Lisbon, Nov. 9, 1967. He studied at the Univ. of Coimbra; took voice lessons in Lisbon, and later in Milan. In 1925 he made his operatic debut at the Teatro Carcano in Milan as Wilhelm Meister in *Mignon*. He subsequently sang principal roles in Italian and French operas at La Scala in Milan, the Paris Opéra, the Vienna State Opera, the Salzburg Festival, and the Rome Opera; also made concert tours of Europe and the United States After his retirement from the stage in 1948, he settled in Lisbon. He wrote an autobiography, *Um cantor no palco e na vida* (Lisbon, 1961).

Alcantara, Theo, Spanish conductor; b. Cuenca, April 16, 1941. He studied at the Madrid Cons.; then took courses in conducting at the Mozarteum in Salzburg. He began his career as a conductor with the Frankfurt am Main Opera Orch. (1964–66), then went to the United States, where he served as director of orchs. at the Univ. of Mich. in Ann Arbor (1968–73), and then as music director of the Grand Rapids Sym. Orch. (1973–78). From 1978 to 1989 he was music director of the Phoenix Sym. Orch.; he was also artistic director of the Music Academy of the West in Santa Barbara from 1981 to 1984. In 1987 he became principal conductor of the Pittsburgh Opera.

Alda (real name, **Davies**), **Frances (Jeanne),** admired New Zealand-born American soprano; b. Christchurch, May 31, 1883; d. Venice, Sept. 18, 1952. She studied with Marchesi in Paris, where she made her operatic debut as Manon at the Opéra Comique (April 15, 1904). She then appeared at the Théâtre Royal de la Monnaie in Brussels (1905–08), London's Covent Garden (debut as Louise, 1906), Milan's La Scala (1908), and Buenos Aires's Teatro Colón (from 1908). On Dec. 7, 1908, she made her Metropolitan Opera debut in New York as Gilda, continuing on its roster until her farewell appearance as Manon Lescaut on Dec. 28, 1929. She also made appearances in Boston (1909–13) and Chicago (1914–15). From 1910 to 1928 she was married to **Giulio Gatti-Casazza**. Her autobiography was publ. as *Men, Women and Tenors* (Boston, 1937). In 1939 she became a naturalized American citizen. Among her other notable roles were Gounod's and Boito's Marguerite, Mimi, Nannetta, Desdemona, Violetta, and Aida.

Aldenhoff, Bernd, German tenor; b. Duisburg, June 14, 1908; d. Munich, Oct. 8, 1959. He studied in Cologne, where he began his operatic career; then sang at the Düsseldorf Opera (1938–44), the Dresden State Opera (1944–52), the Bayreuth Festivals (1951–52; 1957), and the Bavarian State Opera in Munich (1952–59). On Feb. 25, 1955, he made his Metropolitan Opera debut in New York as Tannhäuser. He was best known as a Wagnerian.

Aldrovandini, Giuseppe (Antonio Vincenzo), Italian composer; b. Bologna, June 8, 1671; d. there (drowned), Feb. 9, 1707. He most likely was a pupil of Giacomo Perti. In 1695 he became a member of Bologna's Accademia Filarmonica, serving as its principe from 1702. While inebriated, he fell into a canal and drowned. He wrote 15 operas. For Bologna, he composed *Gl'inganni amorosi scoperti in villa* (Jan. 28, 1696), *Dafne* (Aug. 10, 1696), and *Amor torna in s'al so'* . . . (Carnival 1698), all significant works in the history of the opera buffa in that city. He also wrote 6 oratorios.

Aler, John, American tenor; b. Baltimore, Oct. 4, 1949. He studied with Rilla Mervine and Raymond McGuire at the Catholic Univ. of America in Washington, D.C. (M.M., 1972), with Oren Brown at the American Opera Center at the Juilliard School in N.Y. (1972–76), with Marlene Malas, and at the Berkshire Music Center at Tanglewood. In 1977 he made his operatic debut as Ernesto at the American Opera Center, the same year he won 1st prize for men and for the interpretation of French art song at the Concours International de Chant in Paris. In 1979 he made his European operatic debut as Belmonte at the Théâtre Royal de la Monnaie in Brussels. He made his first appearance at London's Covent Garden as Ferrando in 1986. In 1988 he made his debut at the Salzburg Festival as Don Ottavio. In 1993 he sang at the

London Promenade Concerts. He also sang in many other operatic centers and pursued a career as a concert and oratorio singer.

Alessandrescu, Alfred, eminent Romanian composer and conductor; b. Bucharest, Aug. 14, 1893; d. there, Feb. 18, 1959. He studied piano and theory at the Bucharest Cons. with Kiriac and Castaldi (1903–11); then went to Paris, where he took composition courses with d'Indy at the Schola Cantorum and with Paul Vidal at the Cons. (1913–14). Returning to Bucharest, he was active as a pianist. In 1921 he was appointed conductor of the Romanian Opera in Bucharest, retaining this post until his death; he also conducted the Bucharest Phil. (1926–40) and was artistic director of the Bucharest Radio (1933–59). He was piano accompanist to Georges Enesco, Jacques Thibaud and others.

BIBL.: V. Tomescu, *A. A.* (Bucharest, 1962).

Alessandri, Felice, Italian composer; b. Rome, Nov. 24, 1747; d. Casinalbo, Aug. 15, 1798. He studied music in Naples; then lived in Paris (1765–68) and in London (1768). From 1784 to 1789 he was in Russia, then from 1789 to 1792 he was in Berlin as 2d conductor at the Royal Opera. He finally returned to Italy. Alessandri wrote about 30 operas in all. Two were produced in London, *La Moglie fedele* (1768) and *Il Re alla caccia* (1769), and 2 in Milan, *Ezio* (first given in Verona, Carnival, 1767; staged at La Scala, Feb. 1, 1782) and *Calliroe* (Dec. 26, 1778). In Potsdam he produced *Il ritorno di Ulisse a Penelope* (Jan. 25, 1790), *Dario* (1791), and the comic opera *La compagnia d'opera a Nanchino* (1790), which exhibited the colorful effects of pseudo-Chinese music. His opera *Virginia* was given in Venice (Dec. 26, 1793). He also wrote an oratorio, *Betulia liberata* (1781).

BIBL.: L. Valdrighi, *F. A.: Maestro di cappella di Federico Guglielmo II re di Prussia* (1790–92) (Modena, 1896).

Alexander, John, prominent American tenor; b. Meridian, Miss., Oct. 21, 1923; d. there, Dec. 8, 1990. He studied at the Cincinnati Cons. of Music and with Robert Weede. In 1952 he made his operatic debut as Faust with the Cincinnati Opera. On Oct. 11, 1957, he appeared for the first time at the N.Y. City Opera as Alfredo, where he sang regularly until 1977. On Dec. 19, 1961, he made his Metropolitan Opera debut in New York as Ferrando, remaining on its roster for more than 25 years. In 1968 he sang Rodolfo at his Vienna State Opera debut and in 1970 Pollione at his Covent Garden debut in London. In 1973 he appeared as Don Carlos in the U.S. premiere of the French version of Verdi's opera in Boston. He also toured widely as a concert artist. He taught at the Univ. of Cincinnati–College Cons. of Music from 1974. Alexander maintained an extensive repertory which embraced works from the bel canto era to the 20th century.

Alexander, Roberta, admired black American soprano; b. Lynchburg, Va., March 3, 1949. She was reared in a musical family; studied at the Univ. of Mich. in Ann Arbor (1969–71; M.Mus., 1971) and with Herman Woltman at the Royal Cons. of Music at The Hague. She appeared as Pamina at the Houston Grand Opera in 1980, as Daphne in Santa Fe (1981), and as Elettra in *Idomeneo* in Zürich (1982). Following a tour of Europe, she made a successful debut at the Metropolitan Opera in New York as Zerlina on Nov. 3, 1983; later sang Bess in *Porgy and Bess* and the title role in Janáček's *Jenůfa*, a role she repeated at her Glyndebourne Festival debut in 1989. In 1984 she made her first appearance at the Aix-en-Provence Festival in Mozart's *La finta giardiniera*. She made her debut in Vienna as Cleopatra in Handel's *Giulio Cesare* at the Theater an der Wien in 1985. In 1986 she was a soloist with the Vienna Phil. at the Salzburg Festival and in 1988 she appeared with the English Chamber Orch. at the London Promenade Concerts. In 1995 she appeared as Vitellia at the Glyndebourne Festival. Among her other operatic roles are Mozart's Fiordiligi, Donna Elvira, Ilia, and the Countess, Offenbach's Antonia, Verdi's Luisa Miller, and Massenet's Manon and Thaïs.

Alexandra, Liana, Romanian composer; b. Bucharest, May 27, 1947. She studied at the Porumbescu Academy of Music in Bucharest (1965–71) and in Darmstadt; subsequently lectured in orchestration and analysis at the Bucharest Academy of Music. She won many honors for her compositions, including the Weber Prize (Dresden, 1979), 1st prize from the Gaudeamus Foundation (Netherlands, 1980), and the Romanian State Prize (1980). She composed the children's opera *The Snow Queen* (1979) and the opera *Labyrinth* (1987).

Alexandrov, Anatoli, eminent Russian pianist, teacher, and composer; b. Moscow, May 25, 1888; d. there, April 16, 1982. He studied with Taneyev at the Moscow Cons. (1907–10); he also studied composition there with Vasilenko and piano with Igumnov, graduating in 1916; subsequently he was a prof. there (from 1923). He composed mainly for piano, including 14 sonatas (1914–71), but he also composed 2 operas, *Bela* (Moscow, Dec. 10, 1946) and *Wild Bara* (Moscow, March 2, 1957), as well as incidental music for plays. In his style of composition, he followed the main lines of Rachmaninoff and Scriabin.

Alfano, Franco, eminent Italian composer and teacher; b. Posilippo, March 8, 1875; d. San Remo, Oct. 27, 1954. He studied composition with Serrao in Naples, and with Jadassohn and Sitt in Leipzig. From the beginning of his musical career, Alfano was interested in opera. His first stage work, *Miranda*, was written when he was barely 20; another opera, *La fonte di Enchir*, followed (Breslau, Nov. 8, 1898). In 1899 he went to Paris and became fascinated by light theater music. While in Paris he wrote *Napoli*, a ballet in the folk manner, which was staged at the Folies-Bérgères (Jan. 28, 1901), proving so successful that it ran for 160 successive performances. Returning to Italy, he began work on an opera based on Tolstoy's novel *Resurrection*. It was premiered as *Risurrezione* in Turin (Nov. 4, 1904) with sensational acclaim; the American premiere (Chicago, Dec. 31, 1925) was equally successful; there were also numerous performances in Germany and France. The opera was widely praised for its dramatic power and melodic richness in the best tradition of realistic Italian opera. Alfano continued to compose industriously for another half-century, but his later operas failed to equal his earlier successes. Among these later works are *Il Principe Zilah* (Genoa, Feb. 3, 1909), *L'ombra di Don Giovanni* (Milan, April 3, 1914), *La leggenda di Sakuntala* (Bologna, Dec. 10, 1921; score destroyed during World War II; recomposed as *Sakuntala*, 1952), *Madonna Imperia*, lyric comedy (Turin, May 5, 1927), *L'Ultimo Lord* (Naples, April 19, 1930), *Cyrano de Bergerac* (Rome, Jan. 22, 1936), and *Il Dottor Antonio* (Rome, April 30, 1949). He completed Puccini's last opera, *Turandot*, adding the last scene. His *Hymn to Bolivar* for Chorus and Orch., written for the centennial of Bolivar's death, was performed in Caracas, Venezuela, on Dec. 22, 1930. He was director of the Liceo Musicale in Bologna (1918–23) and of the Turin Cons. (1923–39), superintendent of the Teatro Massimo in Palermo (1940–42), and acting director of the Rossini Cons. in Pesaro (1947–50).

BIBL.: A. della Corte, *Ritratto di F. A.* (Turin, 1935).

Alfvén, Hugo (Emil), eminent Swedish composer and choral conductor; b. Stockholm, May 1, 1872; d. Falun, May 8, 1960. He was a student of Johan Lindberg (violin) and Aron Bergenson (harmony) at the Stockholm Cons. (1887–90); during this period, he also pursued training in painting with Otto Hesselbom and Oscar Törnå. From 1890 to 1897 he was a violinist in the Royal Opera Orch. in Stockholm. He also studied violin with Lars Zetterquist and composition with Johan Lindegren (1891–97). In 1896, 1897, and 1899 he held the composer's scholarship of the Royal Academy of Music, which allowed him to travel abroad, including a sojourn in Brussels to study violin with César Thomson (1897–98). From 1900 to 1903 he was a Jenny Lind scholar, which enabled him to study in various European cities, including Dresden with Hermann Kutzschbach, where he also received training in conducting (1901–02). From 1910 to 1939 he served as Director Musices of the Univ. of Uppsala. He also was conductor of the Orphei Drängar (1910–47), the Uppsala studentkars allmänna sangförening (1919–31; 1934–38), and the Svenska sangarförbundet (1921–43). In 1908 he was made a member of the Royal Academy of Music. He was awarded an honorary doctorate by the Univ. of Uppsala in 1917. His vivid autobiography was publ. in 4 vols. in Stockholm as *Första satsen: Ungdomsminnen* (1946), *Tempo furioso: Vandringsår* (1948), *I dur och moll: Från Uppsalaåren* (1949), and *Final* (1952). Alfvén's early training in painting is reflected in his adoption as a composer of a carefully crafted but colorful late Romantic idiom. He won distinction as a composer of orch. music and choral works. His folk-song settings for chorus were particularly successful in Sweden. Outside his homeland, he remains best known for his popular first Swedish rhapsody for orch., *Midsommarvaka* (Midsummer Vigil; 1903).

WORKS: DRAMATIC: *Bergakungen* (The Mountain King), pantomime drama (1916–23; Stockholm, Feb. 7, 1923); *Gustav II Adolf*, incidental music (Stockholm, Nov. 6, 1932); *Den förlorade sonen* (The Prodigal Son), ballet (Stockholm, April 27, 1957).

BIBL.: J. Rudén, *H. A.: Kompositioner/Musical Works: Käll-och Verkförteckning/Thematic Index* (Stockholm, 1972); L. Hedwall, *H. A.: Ein bildbiografi* (Tierp, 1990).

Aliabiev, Alexander (Nikolaievich), Russian composer; b. Tobolsk, Siberia, Aug. 15, 1787; d. Moscow, March 6, 1851. His father was the governor of Tobolsk, and Aliabiev spent his childhood there. The family went to St. Petersburg in 1796, and in 1804 settled in Moscow. He studied music in Moscow and had his first songs publ. in 1810. During the War of 1812 he served in the Russian army, and participated in the entry of the Russian army into Dresden and Paris. Returning to Russia, he lived in St. Petersburg, in Voronezh, and in Moscow. In 1825 he was arrested on suspicion of murder after a card game, was sentenced to prison, and in 1828 he was deported to his birthplace in Siberia. There he organized concerts of popular music and also composed. In 1831 he was allowed to return to European Russia and lived in the Caucasus and in Orenburg. In 1843 he returned to Moscow, but was still under police surveillance. He wrote more than 100 songs, of which "The Nightingale" became extremely popular; it is often used in the music lesson scene in Russian productions of Rossini's opera *Il Barbiere di Siviglia*. Among his works for the theater are scores of incidental music to *The Prisoner of the Caucasus* and to Shakespeare's plays, as well as the stage ballads *The Village Philosopher, The Moon Night*, and *Theatrical Combat* (with Verstovsky and Mauer).

BIBL.: B. Steinpress, *A. in Exile* (Moscow, 1959); B. Dobrohotov, *A. A.* (Moscow, 1966).

Aliprandi, Bernardo, Italian cellist and composer; b. Milan, c.1710; d. Frankfurt am Main, c.1792. On Oct. 1, 1731, he became a member of the Court Orch. in Munich, retiring in 1778. He wrote 3 theatrical works with music: *Apollo tra le Muse in Parnasso* (Munich, Aug. 6, 1737), *Mitridate* (Munich, 1738), and *Semiramide riconosciuta* (Munich, 1740).

Allanbrook, Douglas, American composer and teacher; b. Melrose, Mass., April 1, 1921. He studied with Boulanger at the Longy School of Music in Cambridge, with Piston at Harvard University (B.A., magna cum laude, 1948), and again with Boulanger in Paris. During World War II, he served in the infantry in Italy, receiving a Bronze Star Medal. In 1950 he received a Fulbright fellowship to study harpsichord and early keyboard music with Ruggero Gerlin in Naples; returning to the United States in 1952, he taught at St. John's College in Annapolis. He composed the operas *Ethan Frome* (1952) and *Nightmare Abbey* (1960).

Allegranti, (Teresa) Maddalena, Italian soprano; b. Venice, 1754; d. probably in Ireland, c.1802. She made her debut in Venice in 1770. After going to Mannheim to study with Holzbauer, she sang at the court opera there (from 1772). She appeared in Venice and Florence (from 1778). On Dec. 11, 1781, she made her London debut in Anfossi's *I viaggiatori felici*. After serving as prima donna buffa at the Dresden court opera (1783–98), she again sang in London (1799–1801).

Allen, Betty, black American mezzo-soprano, teacher, and administrator; b. Campbell, Ohio, March 17, 1930. She attended Wilberforce Univ. (1944–46), the Hartford School of Music (1950–53), and the Berkshire Music Center in Tanglewood; among her mentors were Sarah Peck More, Zinka Milanov, and Paul Ulanowsky. She made her N.Y. City Opera debut as Queenie in *Showboat* (1954). She made her N.Y. recital debut in 1958. After making her U.S. operatic debut in San Francisco in 1966, she sang with other U.S. opera companies, including the Metropolitan Opera in New York (debut as Commère in *Four Saints in Three Acts* during the company's visit to the Manhattan Forum, Feb. 20, 1973) and the N.Y. City Opera (1973–75); she also toured as a concert singer. She taught at the North Carolina School of the Arts in Winston-Salem (1978–87), was executive director (1979–92) and president (1992) of the Harlem School of the Arts, and gave master classes at the Curtis Inst. of Music in Philadelphia (from 1987).

Allen, Thomas (Boaz), notable English baritone; b. Seaham, Sept. 10, 1944. He studied organ and voice at the Royal College of Music in London (1964–68). After singing in the Glyndebourne Festival Chorus (1968–69), he made his operatic debut as Rossini's Figaro at the Welsh National Opera in Cardiff in 1969, where he sang until 1972. In 1971 he made his first appearance at London's Covent Garden as Donald in *Billy Budd*, and quickly established himself there as a leading member of the company. He also sang at the Glyndebourne (from 1973) and Aldeburgh (from 1974) festivals. On Nov. 5, 1981, he made his Metropolitan Opera debut in New York as Papageno. In 1986 he sang the title role in Busoni's *Doktor Faust* in its first stage mounting in England with the English National Opera in London. He made his debut at Milan's La Scala as Don Giovanni in 1987. In 1990 he sang for the first time at the Chicago Lyric Opera as Rossini's Figaro. In 1993 he sang Count Almaviva at the Salzburg Festival. From 1994 he was the Prince Consort Prof. at the Royal College of Music. In 1997 he sang in Beckmesser at Covent Garden, and in 1999 he sang in Sondheim's *A Little Night Music* in Houston. He publ. *Foreign Parts: A Singer's Journal* (North Pomfret, 1994). In 1989 Allen was made a Commander of the Order of the British Empire.

Allers, Franz, Czech-born American conductor; b. Karlsbad, Aug. 6, 1905; d. Las Vegas, Jan. 26, 1995. He studied violin at the Prague Cons., violin, piano, conducting, and composition at the Berlin Hochschule für Musik (diploma, 1926), and musicology at the Univ. of Berlin (1926). After playing in the Berlin Phil. (1924–26), he conducted at the Wuppertal Theater (1926–33), in Ůstí nad Labem (1933–38), and with the Ballet Russe de Monte Carlo. He then settled in the United States and became a naturalized American citizen. He was active as a guest conductor with various orchs. and on Broadway. On Oct. 13, 1957, he made his N.Y. City Opera debut conducting *Die Fledermaus*, which score he also chose for his Metropolitan Opera debut in New York on Nov. 30, 1963. He conducted at the Metropolitan until 1969; he returned for the 1970–72 seasons and again in 1975–76. He was chief conductor of the Gärtnerplatz State Theater in Munich (1973–76).

Allin, Norman, English bass and teacher; b. Ashton-under-Lyne, Nov. 19, 1884; d. Hereford, Oct. 27, 1973. He studied at the Royal Manchester College of Music (1906–10). He made his operatic debut with the Beecham Opera Co. in London in 1916. In 1922 he became a director and leading bass of the British National Opera Co. in London, remaining with it until 1929; from 1942 to 1949 he was a member of the Carl Rosa Opera Co. He led vocal classes at the Royal Academy of Music in London (1935–60) and the Royal Manchester College of Music (1938–42). In 1958 he was made a Commander of the Order of the British Empire.

Almeida, Antonio (Jacques) de, French conductor of Portuguese-American descent; b. Paris, Jan. 20, 1928; d. Pittsburgh, Feb. 18, 1997. He studied with Alberto Ginastera in Buenos Aires, attended the Mass. Inst. of Technology, received training in theory from Paul Hindemith at Yale Univ. (B.Mus., 1949), and took courses in conducting with Koussevitzky and Bernstein at the Berkshire Music Center in Tanglewood. After serving as a conductor with the Portuguese Radio in Lisbon (1957–60), he was principal conductor of the Stuttgart Phil. (1960–64). He was the principal guest conductor of the Houston Sym. Orch. (1969–71), and then music director of the Nice Phil. (1976–78). In 1993 he became music director of the Moscow Sym. Orch. As a guest conductor, Almeida appeared with many of the world's major orchs. and opera houses; he also was active in researching and ed. the works of Offenbach.

Alpaerts, Flor, Belgian composer, conductor, and music educator; b. Antwerp, Sept. 12, 1876; d. there, Oct. 5, 1954. His son was the Belgian conductor and teacher Jef Alpaerts (b. Antwerp, July 17, 1904; d. there, Jan. 15, 1973). He studied composition with Benoit and Blockx and violin at the Flemish Cons. in Antwerp; in 1903 he joined its staff, serving as its director from 1934 to 1941. He conducted the local orch. at the Zoological Gardens (1919–51). His music is marked by an intense feeling for the modalities of Flemish folk songs. His catalog of works includes the opera *Shylock* (Antwerp, Nov. 22, 1913), and incidental music. His 5-vol. treatise *Muzieklezen en Zingen* was for many years the official textbook in all Flemish music institutions.

Alsina, Carlos Roqué, Argentine composer; b. Buenos Aires, Feb. 19, 1941. He studied theory with various local teachers; was active with the modern society Agrupación de Nueva Música in Buenos Aires (1959–64); from 1964 to 1966 he worked in Berlin on a Ford Foundation grant; there he took instruction with Luciano Berio, who inculcated him in the arcana of ultramodern compositional techniques. From 1966 to 1968 he lived in Buffalo, where he taught at the State Univ. of N.Y.; in 1969 he founded, along with Vinko Globokar, Jean-Pierre Drouet, and Michel Portal, the improvisatory group New Phonic Art, which toured Europe. His music is of a functional nature, peculiar to the cosmopolitan avant-garde; it presents a colorful synthesis of quaquaversal idioms, ranging from stark, cloistered dissonance to overt, triadic formalism. Aleatory techniques are in evidence in his improvisatory performances.

WORKS: DRAMATIC: *Texts 1967*, theater piece for Soprano, Flute, Trombone, Violin, Cello, Double Bass, Percussion, and Piano (1967); *Fusion*, choreographic music for Dancer, 2 Pianos, and 2 Percussionists (1974); *Encore*, musical spectacle (1976); *La Muraille*, opera (Avignon, July 28, 1981); *Del Tango*, azione scenica (1982).

Altani, Ippolit (Karlovich), Russian conductor; b. Ukraine, May 27, 1846; d. Moscow, Feb. 17, 1919. He was a pupil of Zaremba and A. Rubinstein in St. Petersburg. After conducting in Kiev (1867–82), he was chief conductor of Moscow's Bolshoi Theater (1882–1906), where he conducted the premieres of Tchaikovsky's *Mazeppa* (1884) and Rachmaninoff's *Aleko* (1893). He also conducted the Moscow premieres of many other notable works, including Mussorgsky's *Boris Godunov* (1888) and Tchaikovsky's *The Queen of Spades* (1891).

Althouse, Paul (Shearer), American tenor; b. Reading, Pa., Dec. 2, 1889; d. N.Y., Feb. 6, 1954. He studied at Bucknell Univ. and with Perley Aldrich in Philadelphia and Percy Stevens and Oscar Saenger in New York. In 1911 he made his operatic debut as Faust with the Chicago-Philadelphia Grand Opera Co. in New York. On March 19, 1913, he made his Metropolitan Opera debut in New York as Dimitri in the U.S. premiere of *Boris Godunov*, remaining on its roster until 1920. After further vocal studies in Europe, he returned to the Metropolitan Opera in 1934 as a Heldentenor, singing there until 1940. He also appeared in opera in San Francisco, Chicago, Berlin, Bayreuth, and Salzburg and sang with many U.S. orchs. He spent his last years in New York as a teacher, numbering among his students Eleanor Steber and Richard Tucker.

Altmann, Wilhelm, German music scholar; b. Adelnau, near Posen, April 4, 1862; d. Hildesheim, March 25, 1951. He studied philology and government in Marburg and Berlin (Ph.D., 1885). He served as librarian in Greifswald (1889–1900). In 1900 he was appointed a librarian of the Prussian Library in Berlin; in 1915 he became director of the music dept., retiring in 1927. In 1906 he founded, in cooperation with Breitkopf & Härtel, the Deutsche Musiksammlung at the Berlin Library. Altmann compiled a number of valuable bibliographical works, among them *Richard Wagners Briefe* (1905; a list of 3,143 letters with brief synopses) and *Wagners Briefwechsel mit seinen Verlegern* (2 vols., 1911).

Altmeyer, Jeannine (Theresa), American soprano; b. La Habra, Calif., May 2, 1948. She received instruction from Martial Singher and Lotte Lehmann in Santa Barbara, California; later took courses at the Salzburg Mozarteum. She made her operatic debut as the Heavenly Voice in *Don Carlos* at the Metropolitan Opera (N.Y., Sept. 25, 1971); then sang Freia in *Das Rheingold* at the Chicago Lyric Opera (1972), in Salzburg (1973), and at London's Covent Garden (1975). From 1975 to 1979 she was a member of the Württemberg State Theater in Stuttgart; subsequently appeared in Bayreuth (1979), Paris (1987), Zürich (1989), and Milan (1990). After appearing as Wagner's Venus at the Metropolitan Opera in 1997, she was engaged as Brünnhilde in the *Ring* cycle in Amsterdam in 1998–99. She is notably successful in Wagnerian roles, including Elisabeth, Gutrune, Eva, Brünnhilde, Elsa, and Sieglinde.

Altmeyer, Theo(dor David), German tenor; b. Eschweiler, March 16, 1931. He was educated in Cologne. In 1956 he joined the Berlin Städtische Oper, remaining on its roster until 1960; then became a member of the Hannover Opera; he later appeared at the Stuttgart Opera and the Vienna State Opera and also toured North America. In 1974 he joined the faculty of the Hochschule für Musik in Hannover; continued to appear in opera and concerts.

Alva, Luigi (real name, **Luis Ernesto Alva Talledo**), noted Peruvian tenor; b. Lima, April 10, 1927. He was a pupil of Rosa Morales in Lima, where he made his operatic debut as Beppe in 1950. He then completed his training at the La Scala opera school in Milan. In 1954 he made his European operatic debut as Alfredo at Milan's Teatro Nuovo, and then sang Paolino in *Il matrimonio segreto* at the opening of Milan's La Piccola Scala in 1955; his La Scala debut followed as Count Almaviva in 1956. In 1957 he sang at the Salzburg Festival, in 1960 at London's Covent Garden (debut as Count Almaviva), and in 1961 at the Chicago Lyric Opera. On March 6, 1964, he made his Metropolitan Opera debut in New York as Fenton; he remained on its roster until 1966, and again for the 1967–69, 1971–72, and 1973–75 seasons. In subsequent years, he continued to make appearances in Europe until his retirement in 1989. He served as artistic director of the Fundación Pro Arte Lírica in Lima from 1982. Alva was particularly esteemed for his roles in Mozart's operas, but he also won success for his Italian roles from the early 19th century repertory.

Alvarez (real name, **Gourron**), **Albert (Raymond),** French tenor; b. Cenon, near Bordeaux, May 16, 1861; d. Nice, Feb. 1, 1933. After studying with Martini in Paris, he made his operatic debut as Faust in Ghent in 1887. He then sang in Lyons and Marseilles before returning to Paris to make his debut at the Opéra as Faust in 1892. In 1894 he created the role of Nicias in *Thaïs* there. He made his first appearance at London's Covent Garden in 1893 as Leicester in de Lara's *Amy Robsart*. In 1894 he created the role of Aragui in *La Navarraise* there. On Dec. 12, 1899, he made his debut with the Metropolitan Opera as Roméo during the company's visit to Boston, and then made his formal debut with it in New York in the same role on Dec. 18, 1899. He remained on its roster until 1903, finding success as Radames, Otello, and Canio. Thereafter he taught voice in Paris.

Alvarez (de Rocafuerte), Marguerite d', English contralto of Peruvian descent; b. Liverpool, c.1886; d. Alassio, Oct. 18, 1953. She made her first public appearance at a London diplomatic reception when she was 16. After training in Brussels, she made her operatic debut in 1904 as Dalila in Rouen; in 1909 she made her U.S. debut with Hammerstein's company in New York as Fidès; in 1911 she appeared at the London Opera House as the Queen in *Hérodiade* and later sang at London's Covent Garden and in Chicago and Boston. In her later years she devoted herself mainly to a concert career, retiring in 1939. Her autobiography was publ. as *Forsaken Altars* (London, 1954; U.S. ed. as *All the Bright Dreams*, N.Y., 1956).

Alvary, Lorenzo, Hungarian-born American bass; b. Debrecen, Feb. 20, 1909; d. N.Y., Dec. 13, 1996. He studied law at the univs. of Geneva (B.L., 1930) and Budapest (LL.M., 1932) and voice in Milan and Berlin. In 1934 he made his operatic debut at the Budapest Royal Opera, and then sang at the Vienna State Opera in 1937. In 1938 he emigrated to the United States, becoming a naturalized American citizen in 1944. In 1939 he made his U.S. debut as the Police Commissioner in *Der Rosenkavalier* at the San Francisco Opera, where he returned regularly until 1977. On Nov. 26, 1942, he made his Metropolitan Opera debut in New York as Zuñiga, remaining on its roster until 1961; appeared there again (1962–72, 1977–78).

Alvary (real name, **Achenbach**), **Max(imilian),** German tenor; b. Düsseldorf, May 3, 1856; d. near Gross-Tabarz, Thuringia, Nov. 7, 1898. He studied with Stockhausen in Frankfurt am Main and Lamperti in Milan. In 1879 he made his operatic debut as Max Anders in *Alessandro Stradella* in Weimar. On Nov. 25, 1885, he made his Metropolitan Opera debut in New York as Don José, remaining on its roster until 1889. In 1891 he sang Tristan and Tannhäuser at the Bayreuth Festival, and in 1892 he made his debut at London's Covent Garden as the young Siegfried. He was compelled to retire from the operatic stage due to poor health in 1897. Alvary was especially successful as a Wagnerian.

Alwin, Karl (real name, **Alwin Oskar Pinkus**), German conductor; b. Königsberg, April 15, 1891; d. Mexico City, Oct. 15, 1945. He studied composition in Berlin with Humperdinck and Hugo Kaun; then conducted in Halle (1913), Posen (1914), Düsseldorf (1915–17), and Hamburg (1917–20). From 1920 to 1938 he was a conductor at the Vienna State Opera. He left Austria in 1938, after the Anschluss, and went to Mexico, where he conducted opera from 1941 until his death. From 1920 to 1936 he was married to **Elisabeth Schumann**.

Alwyn, William, English composer; b. Northampton, Nov. 7, 1905; d. Southwold, Sept. 11, 1985. He studied with McEwen at the Royal Academy of Music in London (1920–23), where he subsequently taught (1926–56), although he had failed to graduate. He was also active as a poet, translator, and painter. In 1978 he was made a Commander of the Order of the British Empire. Although Alwyn wrote a significant number of concert and stage works, including the operas *Juan, or The Libertine* (1965–71) and *Miss Julie* (1970–73; BBC, July 16, 1977), he was particularly facile when writing for films.

Amadei, Filippo, Italian opera composer; b. Reggio, c.1670; d. probably in Rome, c.1729. His claim to attention is that under the name of **Signor Pippo** (diminutive of Filippo) he wrote the first act of the opera *Muzio Scevola*, for which Bononcini wrote the 2d act and Handel the 3d, and which was produced at the Royal Academy of Music in London on April 15, 1721. His other works are the opera *Teodosio il Giovane* (Rome, 1711), the oratorio *Il trionfo di Tito* (Rome, 1709), and the cantata *Il pensiero* (Rome, 1709). Amadei's name was erroneously converted into **Filippo Mattei** by Mattheson in his *Critica musica*, and the mistake was carried into reference works and Handel's biographies.

Amaducci, Bruno, Swiss conductor; b. Lugano, Jan. 5, 1925. He studied at the École Normale de Musique in Paris and at the Milan Cons., then toured widely as an opera and sym. conductor in Europe, and also appeared in North America. On Oct. 5, 1967, he made his Metropolitan Opera debut in New York conducting *Falstaff*. He became closely associated with the Orch. della Radiotelevisione della Svizzera Italiana in Lugano, where he was active as a conductor and later as chief of music programming. He publ. *Music of the Five Composers of the Puccini Dynasty* (1973).

Amalia Friederike, Princess of Saxony who wrote comedies under the name of **Amalie Heiter**; b. Dresden, Aug. 10, 1794; d. there, Sept. 18, 1870. She composed several light operas (*Una Donna, Le tre cinture, Die Siegesfahne, Der Kanonenschuss*, etc.).

Amara (real name, **Armaganian**), **Lucine,** American soprano of Armenian descent; b. Hartford, Conn., March 1, 1927. She studied violin; began her vocal training in San Francisco after her parents moved west. She made her operatic debut at the Metropolitan Opera in New York on Nov. 6, 1950, as the Heavenly Voice in Verdi's *Don Carlos*. Although criticized for a lack of celestial quality in that part, she made progress in her career. In 1954 she sang at the Glyndebourne Festival, and at the Vienna State Opera in 1960. She made a world tour in 1968, which included several appearances in Russia. She also made a cameo film appearance, as the female interest in *The Great Caruso* (1951) opposite Mario Lanza.

Amato, Pasquale, remarkable Italian baritone; b. Naples, March 21, 1878; d. N.Y., Aug. 12, 1942. He studied at the Naples Cons. (1896–99). In 1900 he made his operatic debut as Germont at the Teatro Bellini in Naples, and then sang in other Italian music centers. In 1904 he sang Amonasro at his debut at London's Covent Garden. In 1907–08 he appeared at Milan's La Scala. On Nov. 20, 1908, he made his Metropolitan Opera debut in New York as Germont, and quickly established himself as one of its principal members, remaining on its roster until 1918 and returning there from 1919 to 1921, excelling in all the major Italian roles as well as several French and German. On Dec. 10, 1910, he created the role of Jack Rance in *La Fanciulla del West* there. After his retirement, he taught voice in New York. In 1933 he came out of retirement to celebrate the 25th anniversary of his Metropolitan Opera debut with a gala appearance at N.Y.'s Hippodrome. Amato's extraordinary vocal prowess was equaled by his dramatic versatility, which ran the gamut from serious to comic roles.

Ambros, August Wilhelm, eminent Austrian music historiographer; b. Mauth, near Prague, Nov. 17, 1816; d. Vienna, June 28, 1876. He studied law and music, and rapidly rose in the legal profession. He was appointed public prosecutor in Prague (1850), but continued to devote much time to music. He publ. his *Die Grenzen der Musik und Poesie* (Leipzig, 1856; Eng. tr., N.Y., 1893) as a reply to Hanslick's views on aesthetics, followed by a brilliant collection of essays under the title *Culturhistorische Bilder aus dem Musikleben der Gegenwart* (Leipzig, 1860); also 2 collections of articles, *Bunte Blätter* (1872–74; 2d ed. by E. Vogel, 1896). In 1869 Ambros was appointed prof. of music at the Univ. of Prague and the Prague Cons., and in 1872 received a post in the Ministry of Justice in Vienna; he also taught at the Vienna Cons. His major work was the monumental *Geschichte der Musik* commissioned by the publisher Leuckart in 1860. Ambros spent many years of research in the libraries of Munich, Vienna, and several Italian cities for this work, but died before completing the 4th vol., which was ed. from his notes by C. F. Becker and G. Nottebohm; a 5th vol. was publ. in 1882 by O. Kade from newly collected materials. W. Langhans wrote a sequel in a more popular style under the title *Die Geschichte der Musik des 17., 18. und 19. Jahrhunderts*, bringing the work up to date (2 vols., 1882–86). A list of names and a general index were issued by W. Bäumker (1882). A 2d ed. of the original 4 vols. (Leipzig, 1880) contains the following: vol. 1, *The Beginnings of Music*; vol. 2, *From the Christian Era to the First Flemish School*; vol. 3, *From the Netherlands Masters to Palestrina*; vol. 4, *Palestrina, His Contemporaries and Immediate Successors*. Vol. 1 has been rewritten, not always for the better, by B. Sokolovsky; vol. 2 was reprinted in a new revision by Riemann (1892), vol. 4 by Leichtentritt (1909); vol. 5 was revised and enl. by O. Kade (1911). Ambros was also an excellent practical musician, a proficient pianist, and a composer. He wrote an opera in Czech, *Bretislaw a Jitka*, and overtures to *Othello* and *Magico prodigioso*.

Ambros, Vladimír, Czech composer; b. Prostjov, Moravia, Sept. 18, 1890; d. there, May 12, 1956. He studied at the Brünn Organ School (1908–10) and at the Frankfurt am Main Cons., later becoming active as a conductor with the Carl Rosa Opera Co. in England. After World War I, he returned to Prostjov. His works

include the operas *Ukradené štěstí* (Stolen Happiness; 1924) and *Maryla* (1951).
BIBL.: V. Gregor, *V. A.* (Prostjov, 1969).

d'Ambrosio, Alfredo, Italian violinist and composer; b. Naples, June 13, 1871; d. Nice, Dec. 29, 1914. He studied composition with Enrico Bossi at the Naples Cons, then went to Madrid, where he took violin lessons with Sarasate; later he continued his violin study with Willhelmj in London. He then went to Nice, where he was active mainly as a violin teacher. He wrote an opera, *Pia de Tolomei*, and a ballet, *Ersilia*.

Ameling, Elly (Elisabeth Sara), outstanding Dutch soprano; b. Rotterdam, Feb. 8, 1934. After studies in Rotterdam and The Hague, she completed her training with Bernac in Paris; she won the 's-Hertogenbosch (1956) and Geneva (1958) competitions, then made her formal recital debut in Amsterdam (1961). Subsequent appearances with the Concertgebouw Orch. in Amsterdam and the Rotterdam Phil. secured her reputation. In 1966 she made her London debut and in 1968 her N.Y. debut; her first appearance in opera was as Ilia in *Idomeneo* with the Netherlands Opera in Amsterdam in 1973, but she chose to concentrate upon a career as a concert artist. She gained renown for her appearances with major European orchs. and for her lieder recitals. In 1971 she was made a Knight of the Order of Oranje Nassau by the Dutch government. She established the Elly Ameling Lied Prize to be awarded at the 's-Hertogenbosch competition. Her remarkable career came to a close with a series of farewell recitals in 1995.

Ameller, André (Charles Gabriel), French composer; b. Arnaville, Jan. 2, 1912; d. Garenne-Colombes, near Paris, May 14, 1990. He studied composition with Roger-Ducasse and Gaubert at the Paris Cons.; also violin and double bass. From 1953 to 1981 he was director of the Dijon Cons. He wrote the operas *La Lance de Fingal* (1947), *Sampiero Corso, Monsieur Personne* (1957), and *Cyrnos* (Nancy, April 6, 1962) and the ballets *La Coupe de sang* (1950) and *Oiseaux du vieux Paris* (1967).

Amicis, Anna Lucia de, Italian soprano; b. Naples, 1733; d. there, 1816. She went to London in 1763, where she appeared in concert with Johann Christian Bach. Returning to Naples, she married the physician Francesco Buonsollazzi (1768) and thenceforth appeared under the name De Amicis Buonsollazzi; she continued her active career as an opera singer until 1786. Her talent was appreciated by Mozart, who often mentioned her name in his correspondence.

Amirov, Fikret Dzhamil, Azerbaijani composer; b. Gyandzha, Nov. 22, 1922; d. Baku, Feb. 20, 1984. He received early music instruction from his father, a singer and guitarist; he then studied composition at the Azerbaijan Cons., graduating in 1948. His compositions reflect the melorhythmic patterns of popular Azerbaijani music, marked by characteristic oriental inflections, while retaining a classical format and development, particularly in variation form. Among his works are the operas *Ulduz* (1948) and *Sevil* (Baku, Dec. 25, 1953).
BIBL.: D. Danilov, *F. A.* (Baku, 1958).

Amorevoli, Angelo (Maria), Italian tenor; b. Venice, Sept. 16, 1716; d. Dresden, Nov. 15, 1798. He began his career in Rome in 1730. He sang in Venice (1730), Milan (1731–35), Naples (1736–40), and Florence (1741), then went to London, where he was on the staff of the King's Theatre (1741–43). In 1745 he settled in Dresden, where he served as a chamber and church singer at the court.

Amram, David (Werner, III), American horn player, conductor, and and composer; b. Philadelphia, Nov. 17, 1930. He studied horn at the Oberlin (Ohio) College-Cons. of Music (1948) and pursued his education at George Washington Univ. (B.A. in history, 1952); after playing horn in the National Sym. Orch. in Washington, D.C. (1951–52) and the 7th Army Sym. Orch. in Europe, he completed his training with Mitropoulos, Giannini, and Schuller at the Manhattan School of Music (1955) and privately with Charles Mills. He first gained recognition as a composer for theater, films, and television; he composed the operas *The Final Ingredient* (ABC-TV, April 11, 1965) and *Twelfth Night* (1965–68; Lake George, N.Y., Aug. 1, 1968), as well as incidental music and film scores. In 1966–67 he was the first composer-in-residence of the N.Y. Phil. He also was active in jazz settings and as a conductor. His autobiography was publ. as *Vibrations: The Adventures and Musical Times of David Amram* (N.Y., 1968).

Ancona, Mario, notable Italian baritone; b. Livorno, Feb. 28, 1860; d. Florence, Feb. 22, 1931. He studied with Giuseppe Cima in Milan. After making his operatic debut as Scindia in *Le Roi de Lahore* in Trieste in 1889, he made his first appearances at Milan's La Scala as the King in *Le Cid* in 1890. On May 22, 1892, he created the role of Silvio in *Pagliacci* at Milan's Teatro dal Verme. He made his London debut in 1892 as Alphonse in *La Favorita* at the New Olympic Theater, returning to London in 1893 to sing Tonio in the first mounting there of *Pagliacci* at Covent Garden. On Dec. 11, 1893, he made his Metropolitan Opera debut in New York as Tonio, remaining on its roster until 1897. He sang with the Manhattan Opera (1906–08), in Boston (1913–14), and in Chicago (1915–16) before retiring to Florence as a voice teacher. Ancona was one of the leading baritones of his day. Among his many outstanding roles were Mozart's Figaro and Don Giovanni, Germont, Hans Sachs, Escamillo, Telramund, Amonasro, and Iago.

Anday, Rosette, Hungarian mezzo-soprano; b. Budapest, Dec. 22, 1903; d. Vienna, Sept. 28, 1977. She studied violin with Jenő Hubay and voice with Mme. Cahier, Georg Anthes, and Gino Tessari. In 1920 she made her operatic debut at the Budapest Opera, then was a member of the Vienna State Opera (1921–61). She also made guest appearances throughout Europe and North and South America. Among her finest roles were Carmen, Clytemnestra, Dorabella, and Orfeo.

Anderberg, Carl-Olof, Swedish pianist, conductor, and composer; b. Stockholm, March 13, 1914; d. Malmö, Jan. 4, 1972. He studied piano with Olof Wibergh in Stockholm, and took courses in composition there and in Copenhagen, Paris, and London (1936–38), as well as in Vienna and Salzburg; he also studied conducting in Salzburg at the Mozarteum with Paumgartner, Walter, and Weingartner. In 1934 he made his debut as a pianist in Malmö as soloist in his own, youthful Concertino for Piano and Chamber Orch. He was active as a theater conductor, and also served as founder-conductor of the Malmö Chamber Orch. (1946–50). From 1956 he was active in his own music studio in Malmö. He publ. the vol. *Hän mot en ljudkonst* (Towards a New Sound Art; Malmö, 1961). Anderberg was a leading figure in Swedish avant-garde music circles. He developed an individual serial style that incorporated both aleatory techniques and improvisation. He composed the chamber opera *Episode* (1952).

Anders, Peter, distinguished German tenor; b. Essen, July 1, 1908; d. in an automobile accident in Hamburg, Sept. 10, 1954. He was a pupil of Grenzebach and Mysz-Gemeiner in Berlin, making his debut there in *La belle Hélène* (1931). After singing in Heidelberg (1932), Darmstadt (1933–35), Cologne (1935–36), Hannover (1937–38), and Munich (1938–40), he was a principal member of the Berlin State Opera (1940–48) and the Hamburg State Opera (1948–54). In 1950 he made his British debut as Bacchus at the Edinburgh Festival; in 1951, appeared as Walther von Stolzing at London's Covent Garden. Anders was one of the finest German tenors of his generation. He excelled in operas by Mozart, Wagner, and Verdi; he also was a noted lieder artist.
BIBL.: F. Pauli, *P. A.* (Berlin, 1963); F. Kösters, *P. A.: Biographie eines Tenors* (Stuttgart, 1995).

Anderson, Beth (Barbara Elizabeth), inventive American composer and performance artist; b. Lexington, Ky., Jan. 3, 1950. After piano studies at the Univ. of Kentucky (1966–68), she continued piano training at the Univ. of Calif. at Davis, where she also took courses in composition with Larry Austin, John Cage, and Richard Swift (B.A., 1971). Following further training in piano (M.F.A., 1973) and in composition (M.A., 1974) with Robert Ashley and

Terry Riley at Mills College in Oakland, California, she attended N.Y. Univ. (1977–78). She was coeditor and publ. of *Ear* magazine (1973–79); she also taught at the College of New Rochelle in N.Y. (1978–86). As a composer, she has pursued a diagonal tangent upon her own highly original path. Her resources are manifold, passing through a wide spectrum of sound, sight, and motion in specially designed multimedia productions. She espouses text-sound composition, and also applies collage techniques. Anderson is also a professional astrologer who's made an earnest attempt to connect ideas of harmony with cosmic consciousness, extrasensory perception, and numerology.

WORKS: DRAMATIC: *Queen Christina*, opera (Oakland, Calif., Dec. 1, 1973); *Soap Tuning*, theater piece (1976); *Zen Piece*, theater piece (1976); *Nirvana Manor*, musical (1981); *Elizabeth Rex*, musical (1983); *Riot Rot*, text-sound opera (1984); *The Fat Opera*, musical comedy (N.Y., April 22, 1991).

Anderson, Emily, Irish musicologist; b. Galway, March 17, 1891; d. London, Oct. 26, 1962. She went to Germany for her education, and attended the univs. of Berlin and Marburg. Returning to England, she was employed in the British Foreign Office while pursuing her interest in music history and biography as an avocation. Of value are her translations of the correspondence of Mozart and Beethoven as publ. in *Letters of Mozart and His Family* (3 vols., London, 1938; 2d ed., rev., 1966 by A. Hyatt King and M. Carolan; 3d ed., rev., 1985 by S. Sadie and F. Smart) and *The Letters of Beethoven* (3 vols., London, 1961).

Anderson, June, admired American soprano; b. Boston, Dec. 30, 1952. She received singing lessons as a child and at age 14 made her first appearance in opera in a production of Toch's *Die Prinzessin auf der Erbse*. In 1970 she was the youngest finalist in the Metropolitan Opera National Auditions. After taking her B.A. in French literature at Yale Univ. in 1974, she pursued vocal training in New York with Robert Leonard. In 1976 she attracted favorable notice as soloist in Mozart's Mass in C minor, K.427, with the N.Y. Choral Soc., and then sang at the Chicago Lyric Opera in 1977. On Oct. 26, 1978, she made her debut at the N.Y. City Opera as the Queen of the Night, and continued to appear there until 1982 when she made her European debut as Semiramide in Rome. In 1983 she scored a major success in New York when she sang Semiramide in a concert performance at Carnegie Hall. In 1984 she was tapped to sing the sound track for the Queen of the Night for the film version of *Amadeus*. She made her first appearance at the Paris Opéra as Isabelle in *Robert le diable* in 1985; in 1986 she won accolades at her debut at Milan's La Scala as Amina, and later that year sang for the first time at London's Covent Garden as Lucia. In 1988 she appeared with the Opera Orch. of N.Y. as Beatrice di Tenda with fine success. On Nov. 30, 1989, she made her Metropolitan Opera debut in New York as Gilda to critical acclaim. Her debut at N.Y.'s Carnegie Hall followed on Dec. 12, 1991. In 1992 she sang Lucia at the Metropolitan Opera. In 1993 she was heard as Bellini's Elvira at the San Francisco Opera. In 1996 she appeared as Giovanna d'Arco at Covent Garden, and in 1997 as Norma in Chicago. She also was active as a concert singer.

Anderson, Marian, celebrated black American contralto; b. Philadelphia, Feb. 27, 1897; d. Portland, Oreg., April 8, 1993. She was the aunt of the greatly talented black American conductor James (Anderson) DePreist (b. Philadelphia, Nov. 21, 1936). She gained experience as a member of the Union Baptist Church choir in Philadelphia. After studies with Giuseppe Boghetti, she pursued vocal training with Frank La Forge in New York. In 1925 she won 1st prize in the N.Y. Phil. competition, which led to her appearance as soloist with it at the Lewisohn Stadium on Aug. 27 of that same year. In 1929 she sang at N.Y.'s Carnegie Hall, and then made her European debut at London's Wigmore Hall in 1930. She subsequently toured Europe, with increasing success. Her first appearance at N.Y.'s Town Hall on Nov. 30, 1935, proved a notable turning point in her U.S. career, and she thereafter toured throughout the country. In spite of her success, she became the center of national attention in 1939 when the Daughters of the American Revolution denied her the right to give a concert at Constitution Hall in Washington, D.C. The ensuing controversy led to widespread support for Anderson, who subsequently appeared in concert at the Lincoln Memorial in Washington, D.C. (April 9, 1939). Her success was enormous and secured her reputation as one of America's outstanding musicians. In later years, she toured not only in the United States and Europe, but worldwide. On Jan. 7, 1955, she became the first black singer to appear at the Metropolitan Opera in New York when she made her debut as Ulrica. She then continued her concert career until retiring in 1965. Her autobiography appeared as *My Lord, What a Morning* (N.Y., 1956). Anderson received numerous honors from governments and institutions of higher learning, among them the U.S. Medal of Freedom (1963), a gold medal from the U.S. Congress (1977), and the National Medal of Arts (1986).

BIBL.: K. Vehanen, *M. A.* (N.Y., 1941); J. Sims, *M. A.: An Annotated Bibliography and Discography* (Westport, Conn., 1981); C. Patterson, *M. A.* (N.Y., 1988); A. Tedards, *M. A.* (N.Y., 1988).

Anderson, T(homas) J(efferson, Jr.), black American composer and teacher; b. Coatesville, Pa., Aug. 17, 1928. He studied at West Virginia State College (B.Mus., 1950) and at Pa. State Univ. (M.Ed., 1951) before pursuing training in composition with Scott Huston at the Univ. of Cincinnati College-Cons. of Music (1954), Philip Bezanson and Richard Hervig at the Univ. of Iowa (Ph.D., 1958), and Darius Milhaud at the Aspen (Colo.) School of Music (summer, 1964). He was prof. of music and chairman of the dept. at Langston (Okla.) Univ. (1958–63), and prof. of music at Tenn. State Univ. (1963–69). From 1969 to 1971 he was composer-in-residence of the Atlanta Sym. Orch. From 1972 to 1990 he was prof. of music at Tufts Univ., and also chairman of the dept. (1972–80). In 1988–89 he held a Guggenheim fellowship. Anderson played a major role in the revival of Scott Joplin's music. He arranged Joplin's opera *Treemonisha* for its first complete performance (Atlanta, Jan. 28, 1972). Anderson's own works are audaciously modern, while preserving a deeply felt lyricism. His harmonies are taut and intense without abandoning the basic tonal frame. His contrapuntal usages suggest folklike ensembles, but he freely varies his techniques according to the character of each particular piece.

WORKS: DRAMATIC: *The Shell Fairy*, operetta (1976–77); *Re-Creation* for 3 Readers, Dancer, and Instrumentalists (1978); *Soldier Boy, Soldier*, opera (Bloomington, Ind., Oct. 23, 1982); *Thomas Jefferson's Orbiting Minstrels and Contraband*, a "21st Century celebration of 19th Century form" for Dancer, Soprano, String Quartet, Woodwind Quintet, Jazz Sextet, Computer, Visuals, and Keyboard Synthesizer (1984; DeKalb, Ill., Feb. 12, 1986); *Walker*, chamber opera (1992; Boston, Dec. 9, 1993).

d'Andrade, Francesco, Portuguese baritone; b. Lisbon, Jan. 11, 1859; d. Berlin, Feb. 8, 1921. He studied with Miraglia and Ronconi. In 1882 he made his operatic debut as Amonasro in San Remo, then sang throughout Italy, Portugal, and Spain. In 1886 he made his debut at London's Covent Garden as Rigoletto, singing there until 1890. He then was a member of the Berlin Royal Opera (1906–19). He gained fame for his portrayal of Don Giovanni. His brother, Antonio d'Andrade, was a tenor.

Andrašovan, Tibor, Slovak composer and conductor; b. Slovenská Lupča, April 3, 1917. He studied with Suchoň, A. Moyzes, A. Kafendová, and others at the Bratislava Cons., later serving as artistic director of the Slovak Folk Artistic Ensemble (1955–58; 1969–74). He received many awards, including Merited Artist (1971). He was active in unifying folk elements with concert music and in promoting Slovak stage works. His opera *Gelo the Joker* (1957) was the first Slovak comic opera.

WORKS: DRAMATIC: *Orpheus and Euridice*, ballet (1948); *The Song of Peace*, ballet (1949); *Gelo the Joker*, opera (1957); *The Quadrille*, operetta (1960); *The White Disease*, music drama (1967); *The Gamekeeper's Wife*, opera (1973–74); *The King of Fools*, musical (1982); *The Festival of Solstice*, ballet (1985); also incidental music.

André, (Johann) Anton, German music publisher, 3d son of **Johann André**; b. Offenbach, Oct. 6, 1775; d. there, April 6, 1842. A precocious talent, he studied with Karl Vollweiler in Mannheim (1792–93). He was a fine pianist, violinist, and composer before entering the Univ. of Jena. After completing his studies, he made extensive travels; on his father's death, took charge of the business, adding particular luster to its good name by the purchase, in 1799, of Mozart's entire musical remains. He publ. Mozart's autograph thematic catalog, and supplemented it by a list of the works so acquired. By accepting the application of the lithographic process to music engraving (1799), he took another long stride toward placing his firm in the front rank. He was also a composer (2 operas), a successful teacher, and a noteworthy theorist. He wrote 2 vols. on harmony, counterpoint, canon, and fugue (1832–42; new rev. ed., abr., 1874–78), and *Anleitung zum Violinspiele*. His sons were (1) Carl August (b. Offenbach, June 15, 1806; d. Frankfurt am Main, Feb. 15, 1887), head (from 1835) of the Frankfurt am Main branch opened in 1828, and founder of a piano factory ("Mozartflügel") and author of *Der Klavierbau und seine Geschichte* (1855); (2) Julius (b. Offenbach, June 4, 1808; d. there, April 17, 1880), a fine organist and pianist, pupil of Aloys Schmitt (his grandfather's pupil), author of a *Praktische Orgelschule*, composer of several interesting organ compositions, and arranger of Mozart's works for piano, 4-hands; (3) Johann August (b. Offenbach, March 2, 1817; d. there, Oct. 29, 1887), his father's successor (1839) in the publishing establishment; and (4) Jean Baptiste (de St.-Gilles; b. Offenbach, March 7, 1823; d. Frankfurt am Main, Dec. 9, 1882), pianist and composer of various pieces for piano and voice, a pupil of A. Schmitt, Taubert (piano), and Kessler and Dehn (harmony). He lived for years in Berlin and had the honorary title of "Herzoglich Bernbergischer Hofkapellmeister." Johann's 2 sons, Karl (b. Aug. 24, 1853; d. June 29, 1914) and Adolf (b. April 10, 1855; d. Sept. 10, 1910), succeeded to their father's business.

André, Johann, German composer, publisher, and father of a musical family, including **(Johann) Anton André**; b. Offenbach, March 28, 1741; d. there, June 18, 1799. He founded (Sept. 1, 1774) at Offenbach a music publishing house under his name and had publ. 1,200 compositions by the time of his death. For 7 years (1777–84) he was Kapellmeister of Döbbelin's Theater in Berlin. He was a prolific composer, author of 19 Singspiels and 14 miscellaneous scores for the stage, among them *Der Töpfer* (Hanau, Jan. 22, 1773) and *Der Liebhaber als Automat* (Berlin, Sept. 11, 1782). Bretzner wrote the libretto of *Die Entführung aus dem Serail, or Belmont und Constanze*, for him; the opera was produced in Berlin, May 25, 1781. The same text was used the following year by Mozart for his celebrated work, which elicited Bretzner's haughty protest against "a certain man named Mozart" for the unauthorized use of his libretto. Among Andre's songs, the "Rheinweinlied" ("Bekranzt mit Laub") was widely performed. André is credited with being the composer of the first "durchkomponierte Ballade," "Die Weiber von Weinsberg" (1783).

Andreae, Volkmar, distinguished Swiss conductor, pedagogue, and composer; b. Bern, July 5, 1879; d. Zürich, June 18, 1962. He was the grandfather of the Swiss conductor Marc (Edouard) Andreae (b. Zürich, Nov. 8, 1939). He studied with Karl Munzinger in Bern and with Wüllner at the Cologne Cons. (1897–1900). After serving as répétiteur at the Munich Court Opera (1900–1902), he settled in Zürich and was conductor of its mixed chorus (1902–49) and men's chorus (1904–19); he was chief conductor of the Tonhalle Orch. (1906–49) and director of the Zürich Cons. (1914–41). He championed the works of Bruckner, Strauss, Reger, Mahler, and Debussy. In his own compositions, he reflected post-Romantic tendencies. Among his own compositions were the operas *Ratcliff* (Duisburg, May 25, 1914) and *Abenteuer des Casanova* (Dresden, June 17, 1924).

BIBL.: F. Seiler, *Dr. V. A. . . . zum Jubiläum seiner 25-jährigen Tätigkeit* (Zürich, 1931); M. Engeler and E. Lichtenhahn, eds., *Briefe an V. A.: Ein halbes Jahrhundert Züricher Musikleben, 1902–1959* (Zürich, 1986).

Andreozzi, Gaetano, Italian composer; b. Aversa, May 22, 1755; d. Paris, Dec. 21?, 1826. He was a pupil of Fenaroli and P. A. Gallo at the Cons. di S. Maria di Loreto in Naples. He also studied with Jomelli, and hence was nicknamed Jommelino. He pursued a successful career as a theater composer, producing some 45 operas.

Andrésen, Ivar, Norwegian bass; b. Christiania, July 27, 1896; d. Stockholm, Nov. 25, 1940. He studied at the Royal Opera School in Stockholm. He made his operatic debut in Stockholm in 1919 as the King in *Aida*. From 1925 to 1934 he was a member of the Dresden State Opera, and also appered at the Bayreuth Festivals (1927–36) and at London's Covent Garden (1928–31). On Nov. 1, 1930, he made his Metropolitan Opera debut in New York as Daland, continuing on its roster until 1932. From 1934 to 1936 he sang at the Berlin State Opera, and in 1935 appeared at the Glyndebourne Festival. His success in Germany led to his being made a Kammersänger. Although principally known as a Wagnerian, he also sang such roles as Sarastro and Osmin to great effect.

Andriessen, Hendrik (Franciscus), eminent Dutch organist, pedagogue, and composer, father of **Jurriaan** and **Louis (Joseph) Andriessen**; b. Haarlem, Sept. 17, 1892; d. Heemstede, April 12, 1981. His brother was the Dutch pianist, teacher, and composer Willem (Christiaan Nicolaas) Andriessen (b. Haarlem, Oct. 25, 1887; d. Amsterdam, March 29, 1964). He studied music with his brother; then took piano and organ lessons with Louis Robert and J. B. de Pauw; studied composition with Bernard Zweers at the Amsterdam Cons. (1914–16); he subsequently taught harmony there (1926–34). He succeeded his father as organist at St. Joseph's Church in Haarlem (1913–34) and then became organist at Utrecht Cathedral (1934–49). He was director of the Royal Cons. of Music in The Hague (1949–57) and special prof. at the Catholic Univ. in Nijmegen (1952–63). His music is romantically inspired; some of his instrumental works make use of modern devices, including melodic atonality and triadic polytonality. He was particularly esteemed for his revival of the authentic modalities of Gregorian chant; his choral works present a remarkable confluence of old usages with modern technical procedures. He composed the operas *Philomela* (Holland Festival, June 23, 1950) and *De Spiegel uit Venetië* (The Mirror from Venice; 1964; Dutch TV, Oct. 5, 1967).

BIBL.: A. de Jager, P. Op de Coul, and L. Samama, eds., *Duizend kleuren van muziek: Leven en werk van H. A.* (Zutphen, 1992).

Andriessen, Jurriaan, Dutch composer, son of **Hendrik (Franciscus)** and brother of **Louis (Joseph) Andriessen**; b. Haarlem, Nov. 15, 1925; d. Aug. 23, 1996. His uncle was the Dutch pianist, teacher, and composer Willem (Christiaan Nicolaas) Andriessen (b. Haarlem, Oct. 25, 1887; d. Amsterdam, March 29, 1964). After training in theory from his father, he studied conducting with Willem van Otterloo at the Utrecht Cons. (graduated, 1947); following studies in Paris, he was a composition student of Copland at the Berkshire Music Center in Tanglewood (summers, 1949–50). His television opera *Kalchas* (Dutch TV, June 28, 1959) was the first such score to be produced in the Netherlands. He also composed the opera buffa *Het Zwarte Blondje* (The Black Blonde; 1964) and incidental music to many plays.

Andriessen, Louis (Joseph), Dutch composer and teacher, son of **Hendrik (Franciscus)** and brother of **Jurriaan Andriessen**; b. Utrecht, June 6, 1939. His uncle was the Dutch pianist, teacher, and composer Willem (Christiaan Nicolaas) Adriessen (b. Haarlem, Oct. 25, 1887; d. Amsterdam, March 29, 1964). He first studied with his father and with Kees van Baaren at the Royal Cons. of Music in The Hague (1957–62), then took lessons with Berio in Milan (1962–64). In 1978 he became a prof. of composition at the Royal Cons. of Music at The Hague. His works from the start were conceived in an advanced idiom. In later years he embarked on ambitious collaborative stage pieces with Robert Wilson and Peter Greenaway.

WORKS: DRAMATIC: OPERAS: *Reconstructie*, anti-imperialist collective opera (1968–69; Holland Festival, June 29, 1969; in collaboration with Reinbert de Leeuw, Misha Mengelberg, Peter

Schat, and Jan van Vlijmen); *De Materie* (Amsterdam, June 1, 1989; in collaboration with Robert Wilson); *Rosa*, "a horse opera," libretto by Peter Greenaway (Amsterdam, Nov. 2, 1994); *Writing to Vemeer*, libretto by Peter Greenaway (1997–99; Amsterdam, Dec. 1, 1999). THEATER PIECES: *Mattheus passle* (Matthew Passion; 1976); *George Sand* (1980); *Orpheus* (1977). DANCE: *Dances* for Soprano and Chamber Orch. (Amsterdam, April 24, 1991); *Odysseus' Women* (Rotterdam, May 6, 1995).

Anfossi, Pasquale, Italian composer; b. Taggia, near Naples, April 5, 1727; d. Rome, Feb. 1797. He studied composition with Piccinni, and began writing operas in the prevalent Italian manner. His 3d opera, *L'Incognita perseguitata*, produced in Rome in 1773, won popular approval; its subject was the same as Piccinni's previously staged opera, but if contemporary reports are to be trusted, Anfossi's opera was more successful than that of his erstwhile master. Encouraged by his success, Anfossi proceeded to write one opera after another; according to some accounts, he wrote 76 operas; a more plausible computation credits him with no fewer than 60, but no more than 70 operas. In 1779 he was in Paris; from Dec. 1782 to 1786 he was at the King's Theater in London as director of the Italian opera there. He then traveled in Germany; returning to Italy, he was appointed maestro di cappella at the Lateran church in 1791, and turned his attention to sacred compositions. Mozart wrote 2 arias for use in Anfossi's opera *Il Curioso indiscreto* (Vienna, 1783) and *Le Gelosie fortunate* (Vienna, 1788).

Angel, Marie, Australian soprano; b. Pinnaroo, June 3, 1953. Following training in Australia, she joined the Opera Factory Zürich and made her London debut with the company as Handel's Galatea in 1980. From 1982 to 1992 she was a member of the Opera Factory London, with which she appeared in such roles as Monteverdi's Poppea and Euridice, both of Gluck's Iphigenias, Mozart's Countess, Donna Anna, and Fiordiligi, Denise in Tippett's *The Knot Garden*, and Pretty Polly in Birtwistle's *Punch and Judy*. In 1986 she created the role of the Oracle of the Dead in Birtwistle's *The Mask of Orpheus* at the English National Opera in London and in 1991 Morgana Le Fay in his *Gawain* at London's Covent Garden. In 1994 she created the role of Esmerelda in *Rosa* by Louis Andriessen in Amsterdam. She married **David Freeman** in 1985.

d'Angeli, Andrea, Italian composer and writer on music; b. Padua, Nov. 9, 1868; d. S. Michele, near Verona, Oct. 28, 1940. He studied at the Univ. of Padua; he then became an instructor at the Liceo Rossini in Pesaro. He wrote the operas *L'Innocente; Il Negromante; Al Ridotto di Venezia; Fiori e Colombi; Maurizio e Lazzaro*; also a number of libretti. He publ. monographs on Verdi (Milan, 1924) and Benedetto Marcello (Milan, 1930), and numerous essays on music for *La Cronaca Musicale*, of which he was ed. (1907–14).

d'Angelo, Louis, Italian-born American baritone; b. Naples, May 6, 1888; d. Jersey City, N.J., Aug. 9, 1958. He was taken to the United States as a child, and was first apprenticed as a glove cutter in Gloversville, N.Y., then sang in a local church choir. He went to New York City at the age of 18, studied at the College of Music, and appeared in vaudeville; he made his Metropolitan Opera debut as Wagner in *Faust* (Nov. 17, 1917), and remained on its roster until 1946. He had some 130 operatic roles in his repertoire.

Angeloni, Carlo, Italian composer; b. Lucca, July 16, 1834; d. there, Jan. 13, 1901. He wrote a number of operas, several of which were performed in Lucca: *Carlo di Viana* (1855), *Asraele degli Abenceragi* (1871), and *Dramma in montagna* (posth., 1902).

BIBL.: L. Landucci, *C. A.* (Lucca, 1905).

Angerer, Paul, Austrian conductor, teacher, and composer; b. Vienna, May 16, 1927. He received violin and piano lessons as a child; later he studied violin, piano, and composition at the Vienna Academy of Music. He was made a violist in the Vienna Sym. Orch. (1947), Zürich's Tonhalle Orch. (1948), and Geneva's l'Orchestre de la Suisse Romande (1949), then became 1st violist of the Vienna Sym. Orch. (1953–57). After serving as director and chief conductor of the Vienna Chamber Orch. (1956–63), he was 1st conductor at the Bonn Stadttheater (1964–66); he then became music director of the Ulm Theater (1966–68), chief conductor of the Salzburg Landestheater (1967–72), and director of the South West German Chamber Orch. in Pforzheim (1971–82). In 1982 he founded the Concilium Musicum of Vienna for the performance of 17th and 18th century music on original instruments. From 1982 to 1992 he taught at the Vienna Hochschule für Musik. In 1977 he was made an Austrian prof. Among his other honors were the Austrian State Prize (1956), the Theodor Körner Prize (1958), and the culture prizes of the city of Vienna (1983) and the State of Niederösterreich (1987). His stage works include *Das verräterische Herz*, pantomime and ballet (1956), *Die Passkontrolle*, television opera (1958), and *Hotel Comedie*, musical (1970).

Angermüller, Rudolph (Kurt), German musicologist, editor, and music librarian; b. Bielefeld, Sept. 2, 1940. He studied at the Försterling Cons. in Bielefeld and pursued training in musicology in Mainz, Münster, and at the Univ. of Salzburg (Ph.D., 1970, with the diss. *Antonio Salieri: Sein Leben und seine weltlichen Werke unter besonderer Berücksichtigung seiner "grossen" Opern*; publ. in 3 vols., Munich, 1971–74), where he joined its musicological inst. in 1968. He served as chief ed. of the Neue Mozart-Ausgabe (from 1972), and was librarian (from 1972), chief of the research dept. (from 1981), and general secretary (from 1988) of the International Mozarteum Foundation in Salzburg.

WRITINGS: *Untersuchungen zur Geschichte des Carmen-Stoffes* (1967); *W. A. Mozarts Musikalische Umwelt in Paris (1777–78): Eine Dokumentation* (1982); *"Auf Ehre und Credit": Die Finanzen des W. A. Mozart* (1983); with O. Schneider, *Mozart-Bibliographie, 1981–1985: Mit Nachträgen zur Mozart-Bibliographie bis 1980* (1987); *Vom Kaiser zum Sklaven: Personen in Mozarts Opern: Mit bibliographischen Notizen über die Mozart-Sänger der Uraufführungen und Mozarts Librettisten* (1989); with J. Senigl, *Mozart-Bibliographie, 1986–1991: Mit Nachträgen zur Mozart-Bibliographie bis 1985* (1992); *Der Salzburger Mozart-Denkmal: Eine Dokumentation (bis 1845) zut 150-Jahre-Enthüllungsgeier* (1992); *Delitiae Italiae: Mozarts Reisen in Italien* (1994); *Mozart auf der Reise nach Prag, Dresden, Leipzig und Berlin* (1995).

Anhalt, István, Hungarian-born Canadian composer and teacher; b. Budapest, April 12, 1919. He studied composition with Kodály at the Budapest Academy of Music (1937–41); then received training in composition from Boulanger, in conducting from Fourestier, and in piano from S. Stravinsky in Paris (1946–49). In 1949 he went to Montreal and joined the faculty of McGill Univ., where he was founder-director of its electronic music studio (1964–71); in 1969 he also was Slee Prof. at the State Univ. of N.Y. in Buffalo. From 1971 to 1981 he was head of the music dept. at Queen's Univ. in Kingston, Ontario, where he was made prof. emeritus in 1984. In 1982 he was awarded an honorary D.Mus. from McGill Univ. He publ. *Alternative Voices: Essays on Contemporary Vocal and Choral Composition* (Toronto, 1984). In a number of his works, he utilizes synthetic sounds. His dramatic works include *Arc en ciel*, ballet "in 3 nights" for 2 Pianos (1951), *Thisness*, duodrama for Mezzo-soprano and Piano (1985; Vancouver, Jan. 19, 1986), and *Traces (Tikkun)*, drama for Baritone and Orch. (1994).

Anitúa, Fanny, Mexican mezzo-soprano; b. Durango, Jan. 22, 1887; d. Mexico City, April 4, 1968. She studied in Rome, where she made her operatic debut as Gluck's Orfeo (1909). She then sang at Milan's La Scala (from 1910), and also throughout South (1911–27) and North (1913) America. Her other roles included Rosina, Cenerentola, Azucena, and Mistress Quickly.

Annibale, Domenico, Italian castrato soprano; b. Macerata, c.1705; d. probably in Rome, 1779. He sang in Rome in 1725. After appearances in Venice (1727, 1729), he was called to Dresden in the service of the Saxon court, where he won distinction in the operas of Hasse. He was retained there until being pensioned in 1764 and named Kammermusikus. He also sang in Rome (1730, 1732, 1739), Vienna (1731), and London (1736–37). While in London he sang in the premieres of Handel's *Arminio, Giustino*, and *Berenice*.

Anosov, Nikolai, Russian conductor and pedagogue, father of **Gennadi Rozhdestvensky**; b. Borisoglebsk, Feb. 18, 1900; d. Moscow, Dec. 2, 1962. He conducted orchs. in Rostov-na-Donu (1937–38) and Baku (1938–39); he studied piano and composition at the Moscow Cons. (graduated 1943), where he later joined the faculty. He appeared as a guest conductor in Germany, Hungary, Poland, and China. He was noted for reviving operas by Bortniansky and Fomin. He wrote a textbook on reading orch. scores, and also composed a few works, including a Concertino for Piano and Orch. He was married to the soprano Natalia Rozhdestvenskaya; their son, Gennadi, assumed his mother's name.

Ansani, Giovanni, Italian tenor and teacher; b. Rome, Feb. 11, 1744; d. Florence, July 15, 1826. He sang widely in Italy, as well as in Copenhagen and London with notable success, creating roles in operas by Paisiello, Cimarosa, and Anfosi. In 1795 he retired and settled in Naples as a singing teacher, his most celebrated pupils being Manuel García and Lablache.

Anselmi, Giuseppe, noted Italian tenor; b. Catania, Nov. 16, 1876; d. Zoagli, May 27, 1929. He studied voice with Luigi Mancinelli, making his operatic debut in Athens in 1896. He then sang in Naples, London, Buenos Aires, St. Petersburg, Warsaw, and Madrid, retiring in 1917. He was a remarkable bel canto stylist, winning acclaim for his Verdi and Puccini roles. His love for Madrid, where he was particularly successful, prompted him to bequeath his heart to that city; the rest of his body was deposed in Catania Cathedral.

Ansermet, Ernest (Alexandre), celebrated Swiss conductor; b. Vevey, Nov. 11, 1883; d. Geneva, Feb. 20, 1969. He studied mathematics at the Univ. of Lausanne and at the Paris Sorbonne, and received music training from Gédalge in Paris and from Denéréaz, Barblan, and Ernest Bloch in Geneva. In 1910 he made his conducting debut in Montreux, where he subsequently conducted sym. concerts. In 1915 he settled in Geneva as a conductor. From 1915 to 1923 he also conducted Diaghilev's Ballets Russes, which he took on tours on Europe and North and South America. During this period, Ansermet attracted favorable notice as the conductor of the premieres of several works by Stravinsky, Ravel, Falla, and Prokofiev. In 1918 he founded l'Orchestre de la Suisse Romande in Geneva, which he led as chief conductor for nearly 50 years. He added luster to his reputation through appearances as a guest conductor with the world's leading orchs. In 1946 he made his debut at the Glyndebourne Festival conducting the premiere of Britten's *The Rape of Lucretia*; subsequently appeared with various major U.S. orchs., and made his belated Metropolitan Opera debut in New York conducting *Pelléas et Mélisande* on Nov. 30, 1952. Ansermet acquired a distinguished reputation as an interpreter of Debussy, Stravinsky, Ravel, Prokofiev, and Bartók. While he conducted the works of various other 20th-century composers, his sympathies did not extend to Schoenberg or his disciples; indeed, Ansermet disdained the 12-tone system and other avant-garde techniques. Among his writings were *Le Geste du chef d'orchestre* (1943), *Les Fondements de la musique dans la conscience humaine* (2 vols., 1961), *Entretiens sur la musique* (with J.-C. Piguet; 1963), and *Les compositeurs et leurs oeuvres* (ed. by J.-C. Piguet; 1989).

BIBL.: F. Hundry, *E. A.: Pionnier de la Musique* (1983).

Ansseau, Fernand, Belgian tenor; b. Boussu-Bois, March 6, 1890; d. Brussels, May 1, 1972. He was a pupil of Demest in Brussels. In 1913 he made his operatic debut as Jean in *Hérodiade* in Dijon; in 1918 he sang in Brussels. In 1919 he made his first appearance at London's Covent Garden; after singing at the Paris Opéra-Comique (1920–21), he was a member of the Chicago Civic Opera (1923–28). In later years, he sang in France and Belgium, retiring in 1939; then taught voice in Brussels.

Antheil, George (Georg Carl Johann), remarkable American composer; b. Trenton, N.J., July 8, 1900; d. N.Y., Feb. 12, 1959. He began piano lessons at age 6; after studying theory and composition with Constantin Sternberg in Philadelphia (1916–19), he pursued composition lessons with Ernest Bloch in New York (1919–21). Defying the dictates of flickering musical conservatism, Antheil wrote piano pieces under such provocative titles as *Airplane Sonata, Sonata Sauvage, Jazz Sonata*, and *Mechanisms*. In 1922 he went to Europe and toured successfully as a pianist, giving a number of concerts featuring his own compositions. While living in Berlin (1922–23), he met Stravinsky, who greatly influenced him. In 1923 he went to Paris and entered the circle of Joyce, Pound, Yeats, Satie, and the violinist Olga Rudge, with whom he performed his 3 violin sonatas. Hailed as a genius, he soon became the self-styled *enfant terrible* of modern music. He became naively infatuated with the world of the modern machine, winning extraordinary success with his *Ballet mécanique* for Percussion Ensemble, including electric bells, propellers, and siren (Paris, June 19, 1926). His Piano Concerto (Paris, March 12, 1927) paled in comparison, so Antheil returned to New York to introduce his *Ballet mécanique* to U.S. audiences at Carnegie Hall (April 10, 1927), which precipitated an uproar both in the audience and in the press. Abandoning attempts to shock the public by extravaganza, he turned to opera. However, his *Transatlantic* (Frankfurt am Main, May 25, 1930) and *Helen Retires* (N.Y., Feb. 28, 1934) met with little success. In 1936 he went to Hollywood as a film composer. He also pursued various sidelines, including penning a syndicated lonely hearts column and patenting a radio-guided torpedo with the actress Hedy Lamarr (patent No. 2,292,387, June 10, 1941, for an invention relating to a "secret communication system involving the use of carrier waves of different frequencies, especially useful in the remote control of dirigible craft, such as torpedoes"; it is not known whether the Antheil-Lamarr device was ever used in naval warfare). While continuing to write film music, Antheil pursued serious composition. Among his most important later scores were the 4th (1942) and 5th (1947–48) syms., the opera *Volpone* (1949–52), and the ballet *Capital of the World* (1952). His colorful autobiography was publ. as *Bad Boy of Music* (N.Y., 1945). He was married to Elizabeth ("Boski") Markus, a niece of the Austrian dramatist and novelist Arthur Schnitzler, who died in 1978. Antheil was the subject of a monograph by Ezra Pound entitled *Antheil and the Treatise on Harmony with Supplementary Notes* (Paris, 1924; 2d ed., Chicago, 1927), which, however, had little bearing on Antheil and even less on harmony.

WORKS: DRAMATIC: OPERAS: *Transatlantic* (1927–28; Frankfurt am Main, May 25, 1930); *Helen Retires* (1930–31; N.Y., Feb. 28, 1934); *Volpone* (1949–52; Los Angeles, Jan. 9, 1953); *The Brothers* (Denver, July 28, 1954); *Venus in Africa* (1954; Denver, May 24, 1957); *The Wish* (1954; Louisville, April 2, 1955). OPERA BALLET: *Flight (Ivan the Terrible)* (1927–30; arr. as *Crucifixion Juan Miro* for String Orch., 1927; not extant). BALLETS: *Dance in Four Parts* (c.1933–34; N.Y., Nov. 11, 1934; not extant; based on *La femme 100 têtes*); *Eyes of Gutne* (c.1934; not extant); *The Seasons* (c.1934; not extant); *Dreams* (1934–35; N.Y., March 5, 1935); *Serenade* (N.Y., June 9, 1934; not extant; orchestrated from Tchaikovsky); *Transcendance* (Bryn Mawr, Pa., Feb. 7, 1935; not extant; orchestrated from Liszt); *Course* (1935; not extant); *The Cave Within* (c.1948; not extant); *Capital of the World* (1952; telecast, Dec. 6, 1953). Also music for plays, radio, film, and television.

BIBL.: E. Pound, *A. and the Treatise on Harmony with Supplementary Notes* (Paris, 1924; 2d ed., 1927); L. Whitesitt, *The Life and Music of G. A., 1900–1959* (Ann Arbor, 1983).

Anthony, James R(aymond), American musicologist; b. Providence, R.I., Feb. 18, 1922. He studied at Columbia Univ. (B.S., 1946; M.A., 1948), the Univ. of Paris (diploma, 1951), and the Univ. of Southern Calif. in Los Angeles (Ph.D., 1964, with the diss. *The Opera-ballets of André Campra: A Study of the First Period*

French Opera-ballet); he taught at the Univ. of Montana (1948–50) and the Univ. of Arizona (from 1952). He publ. the study *French Baroque Music from Beaujoyeulx to Rameau* (London, 1973; rev. and expanded ed., 1997); he also contributed articles to *The New Grove Dictionary of Music and Musicians* (1980).

BIBL.: J. Heyer, ed., *Jean-Baptist Lully and the Music of the French Baroque: Essays in Honour of J. A.* (Cambridge, 1988).

Antill, John (Henry), Australian composer; b. Sydney, April 8, 1904; d. there, Dec. 29, 1986. He studied with Alfred Hill at the New South Wales State Conservatorium of Music in Sydney; from 1934 to 1971 he worked for the Australian Broadcasting Commission (later Corp.). In 1971 he received the Order of the British Empire, and in 1981 was made a Companion of the Order of St. Michael and St. George.

WORKS: DRAMATIC: OPERAS: *Endymion* (1922; Sydney, July 22, 1953); *The Music Critic* (1953); *The First Christmas* (ABC, Dec. 25, 1969). BALLETS: *Corroboree* (c.1935–46; Sydney, July 3, 1950; rev. 1960); *Wakooka* (1957); *Black Opal* (1961); *Snowy* (1961); *Paean to the Spirit of Man* (1968).

Antonacci, Anna Caterina, Italian soprano; b. Ferrara, April 5, 1961. She received her vocal training in Bologna. Following her operatic debut in Arezzo as Rossini's Rosina in 1986, she was engaged to sing in such operatic centers as Bari, Rome, Venice, and Bergamo. In 1991 she appeared as Rossini's Anais in Bologna. In 1992 she sang the title role in Rossini's *Ermione* in the first British performance of that opera in concert in London. That same year she appeared as that composer's Elisabetta in Naples. In 1994 she made her debut at London's Covent Garden as Rossini's Elcia. After singing Ermione at the Glyndebourne Festival in 1995, she appeared as Gluck's Armide at Milan's La Scala in 1996. In 1998 she returned to Glyndebourne to sing Rodelinda. Among her other roles of distinction are Fiordiligi, Semiramide, Dorliska, and Adalgisa.

Antoni, Antonio d', Italian conductor and composer; b. Palermo, June 25, 1801; d. (suicide) Trieste, Aug. 18, 1859. He studied with his grandfather and with his father, both of whom were musicians, and appeared as conductor of his own Mass for St. Cecilia's Day when he was 12. He also conducted the premiere of his first opera, *Un duello*, in Palermo at the age of 16, and, after touring as a conductor in Italy, France, and England, scored notable success with his opera *Amina ossia L'Orfanella di Ginevra* (Trieste, Carnival 1825). He settled in Trieste and became conductor of the Società Filarmonico-Dramatica (1829).

Antonicelli, Giuseppe, Italian conductor; b. Castrovillari, Dec. 29, 1897; d. Trieste, March 10, 1980. He studied in Turin, where he began his career as a répétiteur at the Teatro Regio. After conducting at Milan's La Scala (1934–37), he served as artistic director of the Teatro Giuseppe Verdi in Trieste (1937–45). On Nov. 10, 1947, he made his Metropolitan Opera debut in New York conducting *Un ballo in maschera*, remaining on its roster until 1950; then served once more as artistic director of the Teatro Giuseppe Verdi in Trieste (1951–68). His wife was **Franca Somigli**.

Antoniou, Theodore, Greek-American composer, conductor, and teacher; b. Athens, Feb. 10, 1935. He studied in Athens at the National Cons. (violin and voice, 1947–58), with Manolis Kalomiris (composition), and at the Hellenic Cons. (composition and orchestration with Yannis Papaioannou, 1958–61); he continued his training in Munich with Günter Bialas and Mennerich (composition and conducting) at the Hochschule für Musik (1961–65), and with Riedl at the Siemens Studio for Electronic Music; he also attended courses on new music in Darmstadt (summers, 1963–66). Returning to Athens, he became director and chief conductor of the sym. orch. in 1967 and founder-director of the Group for New Music. In 1968 he was in Berlin under the auspices of the Deutscher Akademischer Austauschdienst. He was composer-in-residence at the Berkshire Music Center at Tanglewood (summer, 1969), Stanford Univ. (1969–70), and the Univ. of Utah in Salt Lake City (1970–72). From 1970 to 1979 he was prof. of composition and director of the New Music Group of the Philadelphia College of the Performing Arts; concurrently he was conductor of the Philadelphia Musical Academy Sym. Orch. (1971–75). From 1979 he was prof. of composition at Boston Univ. Antoniou's early music is remarkably compendious in its integration of quaquaversal layers of sound; folk elements in Greek modalities are also in evidence, and many titles have Greek philosophic or literary connotations. His later style developed to embrace a modified serialism.

WORKS: DRAMATIC: *Noh-Musik*, music theater (1964); *Klytemnestra*, sound-action for Actresses, Ballet, Orch., and Tape (1967; Kassel, June 4, 1968); *Kassandra*, sound-action for Dancers, Actors, Chorus, Orch., Tape, Lights, and Projections (1969; Barcelona, Nov. 14, 1970); *Protest I* for Actors and Tape (1970) and *II* for Medium Voice, Actors, Tape, and Synthesizer (Athens, Sept. 26, 1971); *Chorochronos I* for Baritone, Narrator, Instruments, Film, Slides, and Lighting (Philadelphia, May 11, 1973); *Circle of Accusation*, ballet (1975); *Periander*, mixed-media opera (1977–79); *Bacchae*, ballet (1980); *The Magic World*, ballet (1984); incidental music to many plays.

Antunes, Jorge, Brazilian composer and teacher; b. Rio de Janeiro, April 23, 1942. He enrolled at the National School of Music at the Univ. of Brazil in Rio de Janeiro in 1960 to study violin, then pursued training in composition and conducting there (from 1964) with Henrique Morelembaum, José Siqueira, and Eleazar de Carvalho; he also took courses in physics at the Univ. and studied composition with Guerra Peixe at Rio de Janeiro's Pró-Arte. In 1969–70 he held a postgraduate scholarship at the Torcuato Di Tella Inst. in Buenos Aires and studied with Ginastera, Luis de Pablo, Eric Salzman, Francisco Kröpfl, and Gerardo Gandini. Following research under Koenig and Greta Vermeulen at the Inst. of Sonology at the Univ. of Utrecht (1970), he went to Paris to work with the Groupe de Recherches Musicales de l'ORTF (1971–73) and to study with Daniel Charles at the Sorbonne (Ph.D. in music aesthetics, 1977, with the diss. *Son Nouveau, Nouvelle Notation*). Antunes's avant-garde convictions prompted him to pursue experimental byways while he was still a student at the Univ. of Brazil when he founded the Chromo-Music Research Studio. In 1967 he organized the music research center and became a prof. of electro acoustic music at the Villa-Lobos Inst. in Rio de Janeiro. In 1973 he became a teacher of composition at the Univ. of Brasilia, where he later served as prof. of composition and acoustics. He also oversaw its electronic music studio and founded the experimental music group GeMUnB. In 1972 he won Rio de Janeiro's National Composition Competition, and in 1983 its Funarte Prize. In 1991 he was awarded the Vitae Prize of São Paulo. His stage works include *Vivaldia MCMLXXV*, chamber opera buffa (1975), *Qorpo Santo*, opera (1983), *Olga*, opera (1987–93), and *The Single-tone King*, children's mini chamber opera (1991).

Aperghis, Georges, innovative Greek composer; b. Athens, Dec. 23, 1945. After studies with Yannis Papaioannou in Athens, he settled in Paris in 1963 and completed his training with Xenakis, who initiated him into the mysteries of ultramodern techniques involving such arcana as musical indeterminacy and audiovisual coordinates in spatial projection. He was founder-director of the Atelier Théâter et Musique (1976–91), an experimental workshop for theater, music, and language. From 1992 he pursued his career in Nanterre. Aperghis has followed an avant-garde path as a composer, and has produced numerous stage works, including the operas *Pandaemonium* (1973), *Jacques le Fataliste* (1974), *Histoires de loup* (1976), *Je vous dis que je suis mort* (1978), *Liebestod* (1981), *L'écharpe rouge* (1984), and *Tristes Tropiques* (Strasbourg, Oct. 5, 1996).

ApIvor, Denis, Irish-born English composer of Welsh descent; b. Collinstown, April 14, 1916. He studied at the Univ. of Wales (1933–34) and Univ. College, London (1934–39), and received training in composition from Patrick Hadley and Rawsthorne in London (1937–39). He contributed articles to several books and music journals; ed. works by and wrote articles on Bernard van Dieren; he also was active as a translator. In his compositions,

ApIvor adopted a fairly advanced technique of composition while adhering to tradition in formal design.

WORKS: DRAMATIC: OPERAS: *She Stoops to Conquer*, after Goldsmith (1943–47; rev. 1976–77); *Yerma*, after García Lorca (1955–58); *Ubu roi*, after Jarry (1965–66); *Bouvard and Pecuchet*, after Flaubert (1970). BALLETS: *The Goodman of Paris* (1951); *A Mirror for Witches* (1951); *Blood Wedding* (1953); *Saudades* (1954); *Corporal Jan* (1967); *Glide the Dark Door Wide* (1977).

Applebaum, Edward, American composer; b. Los Angeles, Sept. 28, 1937. He had piano lessons in his youth; later studied composition with Henri Lazarof and Lukas Foss at the Univ. of Calif. at Los Angeles (Ph.D., 1966). In 1969 he was composer-in-residence of the Oakland Sym. Orch.; in 1971 he became a prof. of theory and composition at the Univ. of Calif. at Santa Barbara. From 1985 to 1987 he was composer-in-residence of the Santa Barbara Sym. Orch., and then of the Music Academy of the West in Santa Barbara (1988). In 1989 he became prof. of composition and director of the new-music ensemble at Florida State Univ. in Tallahassee. He served as dean (1991–92) and as prof. of music (1991–94) at Edith Cowan Univ. in Perth, Australia. He composed the chamber opera *The Frieze of Life* (1974).

Aprile, Giuseppe, Italian castrato soprano, known as Sciroletto and Scirolino after his teacher; b. Martina Franca, Apulia, Oct. 28, 1731; d. there, Jan. 11, 1813. He studied voice with his father, who had him castrated at the age of 11. He then studied in Naples with Girolamo Abos and Gregorio Sciroli. After singing at the Naples royal chapel in 1752, he made his operatic debut at Naples's Teatro San Carlo in 1753. He then sang regularly at the Württemberg court in Stuttgart from 1765 to 1769, and also toured widely. He subsequently sang in Italy, being named 1st soprano at the Naples royal chapel in 1783. After making his final public appearance in 1785, he devoted himself to teaching voice, numbering among his students Cimarosa. He publ. *The Modern Italian Method of Singing, with a Variety of Progressive Examples and Thirty-six Solfeggi* (London, 1791).

Aragall (y Garriga), Giacomo (actually, **Jaime**), Spanish tenor; b. Barcelona, June 6, 1939. He was a pupil of Francesco Puig in Barcelona and of Vladimiro Badiali in Milan. In 1963 he won the Verdi Competition in Busseto, sang Gastone in *Jérusalem* in Venice, and appeared as Mascagni's Fritz at Milan's La Scala. In 1966 he made his London debut at Covent Garden as the Duke of Mantua and his Vienna State Opera debut as Rodolfo. On Sept. 19, 1968, he made his Metropolitan Opera debut in New York as the Duke of Mantua. He also sang in Rome, Berlin, Hamburg, Chicago, San Francisco, and other opera centers. In 1992 he sang in the gala ceremonies for the Olympic Games in Barcelona. He appeared as Cavaradossi at the Opéra de la Bastille in Paris in 1994. Among his other roles were Edgardo and Alfredo.

Araia or **Araja, Francesco**, Italian composer; b. Naples, June 25, 1709; d. c.1770. He devoted himself mainly to writing serious operas. In 1735 he was called to the Russian court in St. Petersburg as maestro di cappella, where he produced his most celebrated opera, *Cephalus and Procris* (March 9, 1755), the first such score sung in the Russian language. After an Italian sojourn (1740–42), he resumed his duties in St. Petersburg. In 1750 he retired to Italy, but visited Russia again in 1762 before settling in Bologna.

WORKS: DRAMATIC: OPERAS: *Berenice* (Florence, 1730); *Ciro riconosciuto* (Rome, Carnival 1731); *Il Cleomene* (Rome, 1731); *La forza dell'amore e dell'odio* (Milan, Jan. 1734); *Lucio Vero* (Venice, Carnival 1735); *Il finto Nino, overo La Semiramide riconosciuta* (St. Petersburg, Feb. 9, 1737); *Artaserse* (St. Petersburg, Feb. 9, 1738); *Seleuco* (Moscow, May 7, 1744); *Scipione* (St. Petersburg, Sept. 4 or 5, 1745); *Mitridate* (St. Petersburgs, May 7, 1747); *L'asilo della pace* (St. Petersburg, May 7, 1748); *Bellerofonte* (St. Petersburg, Dec. 9, 1750); *Eudossa incoronata, o sia Teodosio II* (St. Petersburg, May 9, 1751); *Cephalus and Procris* (St. Petersburg, March 9, 1755); *Amor prigioniero* (Oranienbaum, 1755); *Alessandro nell'Indie* (St. Petersburg, Dec. 29, 1755). OTHER: Various other stage pieces; *S. Andrea Corsini,* oratorio (Rome, 1731).

Araiza, (José) Francisco, Mexican tenor; b. Mexico City, Oct. 4, 1950. He was a student of Irma Gonzales at the Univ. of Mexico City, where he sang in its choir. He made his concert debut in Mexico City in 1969, where he subsequently appeared for the first time in opera in 1970 as Jaquino. Following additional training with Richard Holm and Erik Werba in Munich, he was a member of the Karlsruhe (1974–77) and Zürich (from 1977) operas. He appeared as a guest artist in Munich, Paris, Vienna, Salzburg, Bayreuth, San Francisco, Chicago, and other opera centers. On March 12, 1984, he made his Metropolitan Opera debut in New York as Belmonte. He scored remarkable success as Lohengrin in Venice in 1990 and as Walther von Stolzing at the Metropolitan Opera in 1993. In 1997 he portrayed Faust at the Zürich Opera. He also had fine success as a concert and lieder artist. Among his other distinguished operatic roles were Tamino, Ferrando, Gounod's Faust, Massenet's Des Grieux, Alfredo, and Rodolfo.

Arakishvili, Dmitri, Russian conductor, teacher, and composer; b. Vladikavkaz, Feb. 23, 1873; d. Tbilisi, Aug. 13, 1953. He studied composition at the Moscow Phil. Inst. with Ilyinsky and also took private lessons with Gretchaninov. At the same time, he studied archaeology and ethnic sciences. In 1901 he became a member of the Musical Ethnographic Commission at the Univ. of Moscow. In 1906 he took part in the organization of the Moscow People's Cons., which offered free music lessons to impecunious students. He was ed. of the Moscow publication *Music and Life* (1908–12). In 1918 he moved to Tiflis, where he was active as a teacher and conductor. He composed one of the earliest national Georgian operas, *The Legend of Shota Rustaveli* (Tiflis, Feb. 5, 1919), as well as a comic opera, *Dinara* (1926). However, his best compositions are some 80 art songs composed in a lyrico-dramatic manner reflecting Georgian modalities.

Arangi-Lombardi, Giannina, Italian soprano; b. Marigliano, near Naples, June 20, 1891; d. Milan, July 9, 1951. She studied with Beniamino Carelli at the Cons. di S. Pietro a Majella in Naples. She made her operatic debut as a mezzo-soprano in 1920 at the Teatro Costanzi in Rome as Lola in *Cavalleria rusticana*. After further training from Adelina Sthele in Milan, she sang soprano roles from 1923; appeared at La Scala in Milan (1924–30). In 1928 she accompanied Melba on an Australian tour; also sang in South America. After retiring from the stage, she taught voice at the Milan Cons. (1937–47) and, later, in Ankara. She was at her best in the lyrico-dramatic roles of the Italian repertoire.

Arapov, Boris (Alexandrovich), eminent Russian composer and pedagogue; b. St. Petersburg, Sept. 12, 1905; d. there, Jan. 27, 1992. He was a scion of an intellectual family; his grandfather was a lawyer; his father was a naturalist. He spent his childhood in Poltava, where he received his early musical training; in 1921 the family returned to St. Petersburg (at the time renamed Petrograd); he studied composition with Shcherbachev at the Cons. there, graduating in 1930; was then appointed to its faculty as an instructor (1930) and later prof. (1940). Among his pupils were many Soviet composers of stature, including Dmitri Tolstoy, Falik, Uspensky, Banshchikov, Knaifel, and Sergei Slonimsky. Arapov spent the years 1941–44 in Tashkent, in Uzbekistan, where the entire faculty of the Leningrad Cons. was evacuated during the siege of Leningrad. There he studied indigenous folklore, and wrote an Uzbeki opera, *Khodja Nasreddin*. After the siege was lifted, Arapov returned to Leningrad, resumed his pedagogical duties, and continued to compose. In 1955–56 he was in China, where he wrote several works on Chinese themes. In 1959 he visited Korea, and composed a sym. using the pentatonic Korean modes. During the years 1950–73, he also traveled in Europe. Arapov's compositions represent to perfection the evolutionary character of Soviet music, taking their source in the Russian traditions of the previous centuries, making ample use of ethnic materials of the constituent regions of the immense territory of the USSR, and integrating the native homophonic melorhythms in an increasingly complex tapestry of colorful fabrics, richly ornamented with occasional application of such modern devices as dodecaphonic melodic structures. However, Arapov was also able to produce a virtuoso display of instrumental techniques for piano and other instruments.

WORKS: DRAMATIC: OPERAS: *Khodja Nasreddin*, on Uzbeki motifs (Tashkent, April 1944); *Frigate Victory*, after Pushkin's novella *The Moor of Peter the Great* (radio premiere, Leningrad, Oct. 12, 1959); *Rain*, after Somerset Maugham (concert perf., Leningrad, April 25, 1968). BALLET: *The Picture of Dorian Gray* (1971; concert perf., Leningrad, April 20, 1973).

BIBL.: A. Kenigsberg, *B.A. A.* (Moscow and Leningrad, 1965); L. Danke, *B. A.* (Leningrad, 1980).

Arbós, Enrique Fernández, notable Spanish violinist, conductor, pedagogue, and composer; b. Madrid, Dec. 24, 1863; d. San Sebastián, June 2, 1939. He received training in violin from Monasterio in Madrid, Vieuxtemps in Brussels, and Joachim in Berlin. In 1886–87 he was concertmaster of the Berlin Phil. He also made successful concert tours of Europe. Returning to Madrid in 1888, he taught at the Cons. In 1889 he was concertmaster of the Glasgow Sym. Orch. From 1894 to 1916 he was a prof. at the Royal College of Music in London. In 1903–04 he was concertmaster of the Boston Sym. Orch. From 1904 to 1936 he was conductor of the Madrid Sym. Orch.; also appeared as a guest conductor in the United States (1928–31), and then in Europe. He composed the comic opera *El centro de la tierra* (Madrid, Dec. 22, 1895).

BIBL.: V. Espinós Moltó, *El Maestro A.* (Madrid, 1942).

Archer (originally **Balestreri**), **Violet,** Canadian composer and teacher; b. Montreal, April 24, 1913. She studied with Shearwood-Stubington (piano; Teacher's Licentiate, 1934) and Weatherseed (organ) at the McGill Cons., and composition with Champagne and Douglas Clarke at McGill Univ. (B.Mus., 1936). After receiving her assoc. diploma from the Royal Canadian College of Organists (1938), she studied composition with Bartók in New York (1942) and with Donovan and Hindemith at Yale Univ. (B.Mus., 1948; M.Mus., 1949). Later she pursued studies in electronic music at the Royal Cons. of Music of Toronto (1968) and at Goldsmith's College, Univ. of London (1973). From 1940 to 1947 she was percussionist in the Montreal Women's Sym. Orch.; from 1943 to 1947 she taught at the McGill Cons. After serving as percussionist of the New Haven (Conn.) Sym. Orch. (1947–49), she was composer-in-residence at North Texas State College in Denton (1950–53). From 1953 to 1961 she taught at the Univ. of Okla. She was assoc. prof. (1962–70) and then prof. (1970–78) at the Univ. of Alberta, where she also served as head of the theory and composition dept. (1962–78). In 1983 she was made a Member of the Order of Canada. In 1993 her 80th birthday was celebrated with a festival of her music under the auspices of the Univ. of Alberta and the CBC. Hindemith's influence is paramount in many of her works; also prevalent is the use of folk elements. Overall, her music is structurally strong, polyphonically disciplined, and generally kept within organized tonality, with occasional dodecaphonic episodes. Among her works are the operas *Sganarelle* (1973; Edmonton, Feb. 5, 1974) and *The Meal* (1983; Edmonton, Oct. 19, 1985).

BIBL.: L. Hartig, *V. A.: A Bio-Bibliography* (N.Y., 1991).

Arditi, Luigi, Italian composer and conductor; b. Crescentino, Piedmont, July 16, 1822; d. Hove, near Brighton, England, May 1, 1903. He studied violin, piano, and composition at the Milan Cons., where he also produced his first opera, *I Briganti* (1841). He then embarked on a career as an operatic conductor. From 1846 he traveled in Cuba, where he produced his opera *Il Corsaro* (Havana, 1846); also visited New York and Philadelphia. In New York he produced his opera *La Spia* (March 24, 1856). He finally settled in London (1858) as a conductor and vocal teacher, while making annual tours with the Italian Opera in Germany and Austria. He conducted in St. Petersburg in 1871 and 1873. His operas and other works were never revived, but he created a perennial success with his vocal waltz *Il bacio*. He wrote his autobiography, *My Reminiscences* (N.Y., 1896).

Arensky, Anton (Stepanovich), Russian composer; b. Novgorod, July 12, 1861; d. Terijoki, Finland, Feb. 25, 1906. He studied at the St. Petersburg Cons. with Johanssen and Rimsky-Korsakov (1879–82), then taught harmony at the Moscow Cons. (1882–94). Returning to St. Petersburg, he conducted the choir of the Imperial Chapel (1895–1901). A victim of tuberculosis, Arensky spent his last years in a sanatorium in Finland. In his music he followed Tchaikovsky's lyric style. He composed the operas *A Dream on the Volga* (Moscow, Jan. 2, 1891), *Raphael* (Moscow, May 18, 1894), and *Nal and Damayanti* (Moscow, Jan. 22, 1904). Other works are music to Pushkin's poem *The Fountain of Bakhtchissaray* and the ballet *Egyptian Nights* (St. Petersburg, 1900). He publ. *Manual of Harmony* (tr. into German) and *Handbook of Musical Forms*.

BIBL.: G. Tzypin, *A.S. A.* (Moscow, 1966).

Argenta (real name, **Herbison**), **Nancy,** Canadian soprano; b. Nelson, British Columbia, Jan. 17, 1957. She spent her early years in the settlement of Argenta, from which she later took her professional name. She was a student of Jacob Hamm in Vancouver and of Martin Chambers at the Univ. of Western Ontario. In 1980 she won 1st prize in the S.C. Eckhardt-Gramatté Competition. After further training with Jacqueline Richard in Düsseldorf (1980–81), she settled in London and completed her studies with Vera Rosza. In 1983 she attracted critical attention as La Chasseuresse in Rameau's *Hippolyte et Aricie* at the Aix-en-Provence Festival. As a gifted exponent of the early music repertoire, she was engaged by many of the leading early music groups and by the principal music festivals; in 1989 she appeared as soloist with the English Concert in New York and also made her Wigmore Hall recital debut in London. In 1990 she sang Rossane in the North American premiere of Handel's *Floridante* in Toronto. She made her debut at the Salzburg Festival as Gluck's Euridice in 1996. Among her other esteemed roles are Monteverdi's Poppea and Orfeo, Purcell's Dido and King Arthur, Handel's Astreia, and Mozart's Barbarina and Susanna. Her concert repertoire is expansive, ranging from the Baroque era to contemporary scores.

Argento, Dominick, greatly talented American composer; b. York, Pa., Oct. 27, 1927. He taught himself piano, theory, and harmony before pursuing formal training. In 1947 he enrolled at the Peabody Cons. of Music in Baltimore, where he took courses with Nicolas Nabokov and Hugo Weisgall, graduating in 1951 with a B.A. degree. He then went to Italy on a Fulbright fellowship and studied piano with Pietro Scarpini and composition with Luigi Dallapiccola at the Florence Cons. Upon returning to the United States, he attended classes of Cowell in composition at the Peabody Cons. of Music, taking his M.M. degree in 1954. Eager to pursue his studies further, he entered the Eastman School of Music in Rochester, N.Y., where his teachers were Howard Hanson, Bernard Rogers, and Hovhaness. In 1957 he received his doctorate in music there. In 1957 he was awarded a Guggenheim fellowship, which enabled him to go once more to Florence and work on his opera *Colonel Jonathan the Saint*; in 1964 he obtained his 2nd Guggenheim fellowship. In 1958 he was appointed to the music faculty of the Univ. of Minnesota in Minneapolis; in 1964 he became a founder of the Center Opera in Minnesota, later renamed the Minnesota Opera. The connection gave Argento an opportunity to present his operas under his own supervision. In 1975 he received the Pulitzer Prize in Music for his song cycle *From the Diary of Virginia Woolf.* In 1980 he was elected a member of the American Academy and Inst. of Arts and Letters. In 1997 he became composer laureate of the Minnesota Orch.

In the pantheon of American composers, Argento occupies a distinct individual category, outside any certifiable modernistic trend or technical idiom. He writes melodious music in a harmonious treatment, so deliberate in intent that even his apologists profess embarrassment at its unimpeded flow; there is also a perceptible ancestral strain in the bel canto style of his Italianate opera scores; most important, audiences, and an increasing number of sophisticated critics, profess their admiration for his unusual songfulness. All the same, an analysis of Argento's productions reveals the presence of acerbic harmonies and artfully acidulated melismas.

WORKS: DRAMATIC: OPERAS: *The Boor* (Rochester, N.Y., May 6, 1957); *Colonel Jonathan the Saint* (1958–61; Denver, Dec. 31, 1971); *Christopher Sly* (1962–63; Minneapolis, May 31, 1963); *The Masque of Angels* (1963; Minneapolis, Jan. 9, 1964); *The Shoemaker's Holiday* (Minneapolis, June 1, 1967); *Postcard from Morocco* (Minneapolis, Oct. 14, 1971); *The Voyage of Edgar Allan Poe* (1975–76; St. Paul, April 24, 1976); *Miss Havisham's Fire* (1977–78; N.Y., March 22, 1979); *Casanova's Homecoming* (1980–84; St. Paul, April 12, 1985); *The Aspern Papers* (Dallas, Nov. 19, 1988); *The Dream of Valentino* (1993; Washington, D.C., Jan. 15, 1994). MONODRAMAS: *A Water Bird Talk* (1974; N.Y., May 19, 1977); *Miss Havisham's Wedding Night* (1980; Minneapolis, May 1, 1981). BALLETS: *The Resurrection of Don Juan* (1955; Rochester, N.Y., May 5, 1956); *Royal Invitation, or Homage to the Queen of Tonga* (St. Paul, March 22, 1964). INCIDENTAL MUSIC: To Shaw's *St. Joan* (1964); Molière's *Volpone* (1964); O'Neill's *S.S Glencairn* (1966); Aeschylus's *Oresteia* (1967).

Argiris, Spiros, Greek conductor; b. Athens, Aug. 24, 1948; d. Nice, May 19, 1996. He studied piano with Alfons Kontarsky and received training in conducting in Vienna from Swarowsky and in Fontainebleau from Boulanger. Thereafter he appeared widely as a guest conductor in major opera houses in such locales as Berlin, Hamburg, Munich, Rome, Monte Carlo, Paris, Miami, Baltimore, and Montreal. He also was engaged as a conductor with leading orchs. in Europe and North America. In 1986 he became music director of the Festival of Two Worlds in Charleston, S.C., and Spoleto, Italy. He resigned his post in 1992 in the wake of the dispute between the festival's founder, Gian Carlo Menotti, and its board. In 1987 he was made music director of the Trieste Opera and in 1988 of the Nice Opera. From 1991 to 1994 he also served as music director of the Teatro Bellini in Catania. In 1993 he resumed his association with the Festival of Two Worlds in Charleston.

d'Arienzo, Nicola, Italian composer; b. Naples, Dec. 22, 1842; d. there, April 25, 1915. After composing an opera in the Neapolitan dialect at the age of 18, a series of Italian operas followed: *I due mariti* (Naples, Feb. 1, 1866), *Il Cacciatore delle Alpi* (Naples, June 23, 1870), *Il Cuoco* (Naples, June 11, 1873), *I Viaggi* (Milan, June 28, 1875), *La Figlia del diavolo* (Naples, Nov. 16, 1879; his most successful opera, which aroused considerable controversy for its realistic tendencies), was *I tre coscritti* (Naples, Feb. 10, 1880) . He publ. a treatise, *Introduzione del sistema tetracordale nella moderna musica*, favoring pure intonation, a historical essay, *Dell' opera comica dalle origini a Pergolesi* (1887; German tr., 1902), several monographs on Italian composers, and numerous articles.

Ariosti, Attilio (Malachia), Italian composer, singer, and instrumentalist; b. Bologna, Nov. 5, 1666; d. England, c.1729. He joined the order of S. Maria de' Servi at the Bologna monastery in 1688, took minor orders in 1689, and received his diaconate in 1692. Abandoning the order, he was in the service of the duke of Mantua in 1696. With Lotti and Caldara, he collaborated on the opera *Tirsi* (Venice, 1696). In 1697 he went to Berlin as a court composer and staged the first Italian operas there. From 1703 to 1711 he was in the service of the Vienna court. In 1716 he went to London, where he was a composer with the Royal Academy of Music. Among the operas he brought out there were *Coriolano* (Feb. 19, 1723), *Artaserse* (Dec. 1, 1724), *Dario* (April 5, 1725), and *Lucio Vero, imperator di Roma* (Jan. 7, 1727). In all, he composed at least 22 operas and 5 oratorios.

Arizaga, Rodolfo (Bernardo), Argentine composer; b. Buenos Aires, July 11, 1926; d. there, May 12, 1985. He studied philosophy at the Univ. of Buenos Aires and composition with Luis Gianneo; then went to Paris, where he took lessons with Boulanger and Messiaen. Beginning with folkloric composition of the traditional Latin American type, he traversed the entire gamut of modern techniques, including 12-tone structures and aleatory composition, and applied these diverse methods liberally according to need and intention. Arizaga also publ. the monographs *Manuel de Falla* (Buenos Aires, 1961) and *Juan José Castro* (Buenos Aires, 1963), and edited the *Enciclopedia de la música argentina* (Buenos Aires, 1971). With P. Camps, he wrote *Historia de la música en la Argentina* (Buenos Aires, 1990). His compositions include the opera *Prometeo 45* (1958).

Arkas, Nikolai, Ukrainian composer and writer on music; b. Nikolayev, Jan. 7, 1853; d. there, March 26, 1909. He collected and compiled many Ukrainian folk songs. He composed one of the earliest Ukrainian operas, *Katerina*, based on a poem by Shevchenko, a modern version of which was prepared from the publ. piano score by G. Taranov. He publ. a history of the Ukraine and Russia (St. Petersburg, 1904).

BIBL.: L. Kaufman, *N. A.* (Kiev, 1958).

Arkhipova, Irina (Konstantinovna), outstanding Russian mezzo-soprano; b. Moscow, Dec. 2, 1925. She attended vocal classes at the Moscow Architectural Inst., graduating in 1948; then continued vocal training with Leonid Savransky at the Moscow Cons., graduating in 1953. She sang with the Sverdlovsk Opera (1954–56), then made her debut as Carmen at Moscow's Bolshoi Theater (1956), where she quickly rose to prominence; she traveled with it outside Russia, garnering praise for her appearances at Milan's La Scala (1965) and at the Montreal EXPO (1967). She appeared as Amneris at the San Francisco Opera in 1972 and as Azucena at London's Covent Garden in 1975. In 1992 she sang the Countess in *The Queen of Spades* with the Kirov Opera of St. Petersburg during its visit to the Metropolitan Opera in New York She made her belated Metropolitan Opera debut in New York in a minor role in *Eugene Onegin* in 1997. In 1966 she was made a People's Artist of the USSR. She excelled particularly in the Russian repertoire, but also distinguished herself in French and Italian music.

Arkor, André d', Belgian tenor; b. Tilleur, near Liège, Feb. 23, 1901; d. Brussels, Dec. 19, 1971. He studied with Malherbe and Seguin at the Liège Cons. He made his operatic debut in 1925 as Gérard in *Lakmé* at the Liège Théâtre Royal; then sang in Ghent and Lyons; in 1930 he joined the Théâtre de la Monnaie in Brussels, where he remained as a leading tenor until 1945; from 1945 to 1965 he was director of the Liège Théâtre Royal. He was particularly esteemed as a Mozartean.

Armbruster, Karl, German conductor; b. Andernach-am-Rhein, July 13, 1846; d. London, June 10, 1917. He studied piano in Cologne, and at the age of 17 settled in London, where he made propaganda for Wagner by means of numerous lectures. He was Hans Richter's assistant at the Wagner concerts in London in 1884, and later conducted operas at London theaters. He was also one of the conductors of the Wagner *Ring* cycles at Bayreuth (1884–94).

Armin, Georg (Herrmann), German singer and pedagogue; b. Braunschweig, Nov. 10, 1871; d. Karlslunde Strand, Denmark, Feb. 16, 1963. He studied architecture; then turned to singing. He settled in Berlin as a voice teacher; from 1925 to 1942 he ed. the periodical *Der Stimmwart*. His home in Berlin was destroyed in an air raid during World War II; in 1949 he settled in Denmark. He publ. several papers on vocal production, among them *Das Stauprinzip* (1905) and *Von der Urkraft der Stimme* (1921).

BIBL.: J. Berntsen, *Ein Meister der Stimmbildungskunst* (Leipzig, 1936).

Armstrong, Karan, American soprano; b. Horne, Mont., Dec. 14, 1941. She was educated at Concordia College in Moorhead, Minn. (B.A., 1963) and received private vocal instruction from various teachers, including Lotte Lehmann in Santa Barbara. In 1966 she made her operatic debut as Elvira in *L'italiana in Algeri* at the San Francisco Opera. After singing minor roles at the Metropolitan Opera in New York (1966–69), she sang with several other U.S. opera companies, including the N.Y. City Opera (1975–78). In 1976 she made her European debut as Salome at the Strasbourg Opera. She made her Bayreuth Festival debut as Elsa in 1979 and her Covent Garden debut in London as Lulu in 1981.

She also sang in Vienna, Munich, Paris, Hamburg, and other European music centers. Among her finest roles are Violetta, Tosca, Mimi, Alice Ford, Countess Almaviva, Eva, Mélisande, and the Marschallin. She also sang contemporary roles, creating the role of Death in Gottfried von Einem's *Jesu Hochzeit* (1980) and the title role in Giuseppe Sinopoli's *Lou Salome* (1981). She married **Götz Friedrich**.

Armstrong, Richard, English conductor; b. Leicester, Jan. 7, 1943. He studied at Corpus Christi College, Cambridge. In 1966 he joined the staff of the Royal Opera House, Covent Garden, London; in 1968 he became assistant conductor of the Welsh National Opera, Cardiff; from 1973 to 1986 he was its music director; also appeared as a guest conductor. In 1993 he became music director of Glasgow's Scottish Opera and chief conductor of the new National Orch. of Scotland. That same year he was made a Commander of the Order of the British Empire.

Armstrong, Sheila (Ann), English soprano; b. Ashington, Northumberland, Aug. 13, 1942. She studied at the Royal Academy of Music in London, winning the Kathleen Ferrier Memorial Scholarship in 1965. Following her operatic debut as Despina at the Sadler's Wells Theatre in London in 1965, she made her debut at the Glyndebourne Festival as Belinda in *Dido and Aeneas* in 1966. In 1971 she made her first appearance in New York as a soloist with the N.Y. Phil. In 1973 she made her debut at London's Covent Garden as Marzelline in *Fidelio*. She toured extensively in England, Europe, North America, and the Far East as a concert singer. In her operatic appearances, she has had particular success in works by Mozart, Rossini, and Donizetti.

Arndt-Ober, Margarethe, German mezzo-soprano; b. Berlin, April 15, 1885; d. Bad Sachsa, March 24, 1971. She studied in Berlin with Benno Stolzenberg and later with Arthur Arndt, who became her husband. In 1906 she made her operatic debut as Azucena in Frankfurt an der Oder; in 1907 she joined the Berlin Royal Opera. On Nov. 21, 1913, she made her Metropolitan Opera debut in New York as Ortrud, remaining on its roster until 1917, then was interned until the end of World War I. In 1919 she became a member of the Berlin State Opera, where she sang until the end of World War II.

Arne, Michael, English composer, illegitimate son of **Thomas Augustine Arne**; b. London, c.1740; d. there, Jan. 14, 1786. He was trained as an actor and a singer, and made his debut in a concert in London on Feb. 20, 1750. He also acquired considerable skill as a harpsichord player. In 1771–72 he traveled in Germany as a conductor of stage music; from 1776 he was in Dublin; at some time prior to 1784 he returned to London. He was known for his eccentricities, among which was an earnest preoccupation with alchemy in search of the philosopher's stone to convert base metals into gold, a quest which proved a disappointment. He composed 9 operas (all perf. in London), including *Hymen* (Jan. 20, 1764), *Cymon* (Jan. 2, 1767), *The Artifice* (April 14, 1780), *The Choice of Harlequin* (Dec. 26, 1781), and *Vertumnus and Pomona* (Feb. 21, 1782); also collaborations with other composers in about 14 productions.

BIBL.: J. Parkinson, *An Index to the Vocal Works of Thomas Augustine Arne and M. A.* (Detroit, 1972).

Arne, Thomas Augustine, famous English composer, natural father of **Michael Arne**; b. London, March 12, 1710; d. there, March 5, 1778. His father, an upholsterer, sent him to Eton; he then spent 3 years in a solicitor's office. He studied music on the side, much against his father's wishes, and acquired considerable skill on the violin. He soon began to write musical settings, "after the Italian manner," to various plays. His first production was Addison's *Rosamond* (March 7, 1733). He renamed Fielding's *Tragedy of Tragedies* as *Opera of Operas*, and produced it at the Haymarket Theatre (Oct. 29, 1733); a masque, *Dido and Aeneas*, followed (Jan. 12, 1734). His most important work was the score of *Comus* (Drury Lane, March 4, 1738). On Aug. 1, 1740, he produced at Clivedon, Buckinghamshire, the masque *Alfred*, the finale of which contains the celebrated song "Rule Britannia," which became a national patriotic song of Great Britain. In the meantime, on March 15, 1737, Arne married Cecilia Young, daughter of the organist Charles Young, and herself a fine singer. In 1742 he went with her to Dublin, where he also stayed in 1755 and 1758. Of his many dramatic productions the following were performed at Drury Lane in London: *The Temple of Dullness* (Jan. 17, 1745), *Harlequin Incendiary* (March 3, 1746), *The Triumph of Peace* (Feb. 21, 1748), *Britannia* (May 9, 1755), *Beauty and Virtue* (Feb. 26, 1762), and *The Rose* (Dec. 2, 1772). The following were staged at Covent Garden: *Harlequin Sorcerer* (Feb. 11, 1752), *The Prophetess* (Feb. 1, 1758), *Thomas and Sally* (Nov. 28, 1760), *Love in a Village* (Dec. 8, 1762), and *The Fairy Prince* (Nov. 12, 1771). He further contributed separate numbers to 28 theatrical productions, among them songs to Shakespeare's *As You Like It*; "Where the Bee Sucks" in *The Tempest*; etc. He wrote 2 oratorios: *The Death of Abel* (Dublin, Feb. 18, 1744) and *Judith* (Drury Lane, Feb. 27, 1761), the latter remarkable for the introduction of female voices into the choral parts. He received the honorary degree of D.Mus. from the Univ. of Oxford (July 6, 1759), which accounts for his familiar appellation of "Dr. Arne."

BIBL.: J. Parkinson, *An Index to the Vocal Works of T. A. A. and Michael Arne* (Detroit, 1972).

d'Arneiro, (José Augusto) Ferreira Veiga, Viscount, distinguished Portuguese composer; b. Macao, China, Nov. 22, 1838; d. San Remo, July 7, 1903. He studied with Botelho, Schira, and Soares in Lisbon. The production of his ballet *Gina* (Lisbon, 1866) attracted attention; he then produced an opera, *L'Elisire di Giovinezza* (Lisbon, March 31, 1876), followed by *La Derelitta* (Lisbon, 1885).

Arnell, Richard (Anthony Sayer), English composer and teacher; b. London, Sept. 15, 1917. He studied with John Ireland at the Royal College of Music in London (1935–39). In 1939 he went to America; when Winston Churchill had a reception at Columbia Univ. in 1946, Arnell wrote *Prelude and Flourish* for Brass Instruments, performed at the occasion. In 1948 Arnell returned to London and taught at Trinity College of Music until 1964. From 1975 to 1988 he was music director of the International Film School. His music is festive without pomposity, and very English.

WORKS: DRAMATIC: OPERAS: *Love in Transit* (London, Feb. 27, 1958); *The Petrified Princess* (London, May 5, 1959); *Moonflowers* (Kent, July 23, 1959); *Combat Zone* (Hempstead, N.Y., April 27, 1969). BALLETS: *Harlequin in April* (London, May 8, 1951); *The Great Detective* (1953).

Arnold, Denis (Midgley), distinguished English musicologist; b. Sheffield, Dec. 15, 1926; d. Budapest, April 28, 1986. He was educated at the Univ. of Sheffield (B.A., 1947; B.Mus., 1948; M.A., 1950). From 1951 to 1960 he was a lecturer and from 1960 to 1964 a reader in music at Queen's Univ., Belfast; in 1964 he was made senior lecturer at the Univ. of Hull; in 1969 he became prof. of music at the Univ. of Nottingham; from 1975 he was Heather Prof. of Music at the Univ. of Oxford. From 1976 to 1980 he was joint ed. of *Music & Letters*. From 1979 to 1983 he was president of the Royal Musical Assn. In 1983 he was made a Commander of the Order of the British Empire. He was regarded as one of the foremost authorities on Italian music of the Renaissance and the early Baroque period.

WRITINGS: *Monteverdi* (London, 1963; 3rd ed., rev., 1990 by T. Carter); *Marenzio* (London, 1965); *Monteverdi Madrigals* (London, 1967); ed. with N. Fortune, *The Monteverdi Companion* (London, 1968; 2d ed., rev., 1985, as *The New Monteverdi Companion*); ed. with N. Fortune, *The Beethoven Companion* (London, 1971); *Giovanni Gabrieli* (London, 1974); *Giovanni Gabrieli and the Music of the Venetian High Renaissance* (Oxford, 1979); *Monteverdi Church Music* (London, 1982); ed. *The New Oxford Companion to Music* (2 vols., Oxford, 1983); *Bach* (Oxford, 1984); with E. Arnold, *The Oratorio in Venice* (London, 1986).

Arnold, Sir Malcolm (Henry), prolific and versatile English composer; b. Northampton, Oct. 21, 1921. He studied trumpet with Ernest Hall and composition with Gordon Jacob at the Royal

College of Music in London (1938–41). He played trumpet in the London Phil. (1941–42), serving as its first trumpeter (1946–48); also played trumpet in the BBC Sym. Orch. in London (1945). He then devoted himself chiefly to composition, developing a melodious and harmonious style of writing that possessed the quality of immediate appeal to the general public while avoiding obvious banality; many of his works reveal modalities common to English folk songs, often invested in acridly pleasing harmonies. His experience as a trumpeter and conductor of popular concerts provided a secure feeling for propulsive rhythms and brilliant sonorities. He had a particular knack for composing effective film music. In his sound track for *The Bridge on the River Kwai*, he popularized the rollicking march "Colonel Bogey," originally composed by Kenneth Alford in 1914. In 1970 Arnold was made a Commander of the Order of the British Empire, and in 1993 he was knighted.

WORKS: DRAMATIC: OPERAS: *The Dancing Master* (1951); *The Open Window* (London, Dec. 14, 1956). BALLETS: *Homage to the Queen* (London, June 2, 1953); *Rinaldo and Armida* (1954); *Sweeney Todd* (1958); *Electra* (1963). OTHER STAGE WORKS: *Song of Simeon*, nativity play (1958); *The Turtle Drum*, children's spectacle (1967).

BIBL.: A. Poulton, *M. A.: A Catalogue of His Music* (London, 1986); P. Burton-Page, *Philharmonic Concerto: The Life and Music of M. A.* (London, 1994).

Arnold, Maurice (real name **Maurice Arnold Strothotte**), American conductor, teacher, and composer; b. St. Louis, Jan. 19, 1865; d. N.Y., Oct. 23, 1937. He studied in Cincinnati, then in Germany with several teachers, including Bruch. The performance of his orch. work *American Plantation Dances* (N.Y., 1894) aroused the interest of Dvořák, because of the Negro melodies used in it, and he engaged Arnold to teach at the National Cons. of Music of America in New York, of which Dvořák was then head. Arnold subsequently was active as a conductor of light opera, and as a violin teacher. He wrote the comic opera *The Merry Benedicts* (Brooklyn, 1896), and the grand opera *Cleopatra*.

Arnold, Samuel, celebrated English composer, organist, and music scholar; b. London, Aug. 10, 1740; d. there, Oct. 22, 1802. He received his musical training from Gates and Nares as a chorister of the Chapel Royal. He showed a gift for composition early on, and was commissioned to arrange the music for the play *The Maid of the Mill*; for this he selected songs by some 20 composers, including Bach, and added several numbers of his own; the resulting pasticcio was produced with success at Covent Garden (Jan. 31, 1765). This was the first of his annual productions for Covent Garden and other theaters in London, of which the following were composed mainly by Arnold: *Harlequin Dr. Faustus* (Nov. 18, 1766); *The Royal Garland* (Oct. 10, 1768); *The Magnet* (June 27, 1771); *A Beggar on Horseback* (June 16, 1785); *The Gnome* (Aug. 5, 1788); *New Spain, or Love in Mexico* (July 16, 1790); *The Surrender of Calais* (July 30, 1791); *The Enchanted Wood* (July 25, 1792); *The 63rd Letter* (July 18, 1802). He also wrote several oratorios, among them *The Cure of Saul* (1767); *Abimelech; The Resurrection; The Prodigal Son*; and *Elisha* (1795; his last). On the occasion of a performance of *The Prodigal Son* at the Univ. of Oxford in 1773, Arnold was given the degree of D.Mus. In 1783, he became the successor of Nares as composer to the Chapel Royal, for which he wrote several odes and anthems. In 1789 Arnold was engaged as conductor of the Academy of Ancient Music; in 1793 he became organist of Westminster Abbey. He was buried in Westminster Abbey, near Purcell and Blow. Arnold's ed. of Handel's works, begun in 1786, was carried out by him in 36 vols., embracing about 180 numbers; it is, however, incomplete and inaccurate in many respects. His principal work is Cathedral Music (4 vols., 1790); its subtitle describes its contents: "A collection in score of the most valuable and useful compositions for that Service by the several English Masters of the last 200 years." It forms a sequel to Boyce's work of the same name. A new ed. of Arnold's Cathedral Music was issued by Rimbault (1847).

Arnold, Yuri, Russian composer and music theorist; b. St. Petersburg, Nov. 13, 1811; d. Karakash, Crimea, July 20, 1898. He was of German extraction. He studied at the German Univ. of Dorpat, Estonia, then from 1863 to 1871 he lived in Leipzig. He then returned to Russia, living in Moscow until 1894, when he moved to St. Petersburg. He wrote a comic opera, *Treasure Trove* (St. Petersburg, Feb. 1, 1853), the MS of which was lost in a fire at the St. Petersburg Opera Theater in 1859, together with the MS of his other opera, *St. John's Eve*. He further composed an overture, *Boris Godunov*. Arnold was the author of the first book in the Russian language dealing with the theory of composition (1841); also publ. *Theory of Old Russian Religious Dance* (Moscow, 1880) and many articles on Russian music for German periodicals. Among his publications in German was *Der Einflüss des Zeitgeistes auf die Entwicklung der Tonkunst* (Leipzig, 1867). He tr. into German the librettos of operas by Tchaikovsky and Glinka, and publ. historically valuable memoirs (3 vols., Moscow, 1893).

Arnoldson, Sigrid, Swedish soprano; b. Stockholm, March 20, 1861; d. there, Feb. 7, 1943. She began her training with her father, the tenor Oscar Arnoldson (1830–81). After further training from Maurice Strakosch and Désirée Artôt, she made her operatic debut as Rosina in Prague in 1885. In 1886 she sang in Moscow, and in 1887 at London's Drury Lane Theatre. In 1888 she returned to London to make her Covent Garden debut, where she sang again from 1892 to 1894. On Nov. 29, 1893, she made her Metropolitan Opera debut in New York as Baucis, where she sang for a season. She then pursued her career in Europe, retiring in 1916. From 1922 to 1938 she taught in Vienna, and then in Stockholm. She was noted for her command of coloratura and lyric roles, but she also was a fine Carmen.

Arnould, (Madeleine) Sophie, notable French soprano; b. Paris, Feb. 13, 1740; d. there, Oct. 22, 1802. She studied with Marie Fel and Hippolyte Clairon. In 1757 she joined the Paris Opéra, where she was one of its principal members until her retirement on a state pension of 2,000 livres in 1788. She created the title role in Gluck's *Iphigénie en Aulide* there on April 19, 1774, and also had fine success in operas by Rameau, Monsigny, and Francoeur. She also became a favorite in Parisian society. Pierné chose her as the subject of his opera *Sophie Arnould* (1927).

BIBL.: A. Deville, *A.iana* (Paris, 1813); E. and J. de Goncourt, *S. A. d'après sa correspondance et ses mémoires* (Paris, 1857); R. Douglas, *S. A., Actress and Wit* (Paris, 1898); B. Dussanc, *S. A.: La plus spirituelle des bacchantes* (Paris, 1938).

Arriaga (y Balzola), Juan Crisóstomo (Jacobo Antonio de), precocious Spanish composer; b. Rigoitia, near Bilbao, Jan. 27, 1806; d. Paris, Jan. 17, 1826. At the age of 11, he wrote an Octet for Horn, Strings, Guitar, and Piano, subtitled *Nada y mucho*, and at 13, a 2-act opera, *Los esclavos felices*. On the strength of these works he was accepted at the Paris Cons., where he studied with Baillot and Fétis. In Paris he wrote a biblical scene, *Agar*, among other works. On Aug. 13, 1933, a memorial to him was unveiled in Bilbao and a Comision Permanente Arriaga was formed to publ. his works. Under its auspices, the vocal score of the opera was printed. A bibliographical pamphlet, *Resurgimiento de las obras de Arriaga*, by Juan de Eresalde was also publ. (Bilbao, 1953).

Arrieta y Corera, Pascual Juan Emilio, Spanish composer; b. Puente la Reina, Oct. 21, 1823; d. Madrid, Feb. 11, 1894. He studied at the Milan Cons. (1839–45) with Vaccai. He returned to Spain in 1846, and was a prof. at the Madrid Cons. in 1857; became its director in 1868. He wrote more than 50 zarzuelas and several grand operas in Italian. Of these the most important is *La conquista de Granada*, produced in Madrid (Oct. 10, 1850), Arrieta conducting, and revived 5 years later under the title *Isabel la Católica* (Madrid, Dec. 18, 1855). Other successful zarzuelas and operas are *Ildegonda* (Milan, Feb. 28, 1845), *El Domino Azul* (Madrid, Feb. 19, 1853), *El Grumete* (Madrid, June 17, 1853; its sequel, *La Vuelta del Corsario*, perf. in Madrid, Feb. 18, 1863), *Marina* (Madrid, Sept. 21, 1855; rev. and produced as a grand opera, Madrid, Oct. 4, 1871), and *S. Francesco da Siena* (Madrid, Oct. 27, 1883).

Arrieu, Claude, French composer; b. Paris, Nov. 30, 1903; d. there, March 7, 1990. She studied piano with Marguerite Long and took courses in composition at the Paris Cons. with Dukas, G. Caussade, Roger-Ducasse, and N. Galloń, graduating with a premier prix in 1932. In 1949 she received the Prix Italia. She was notably successful as a composer for the theater.

WORKS: DRAMATIC: *Noël*, musical (1934; Strasbourg, Jan. 29, 1950); *Cadet Roussel*, comic opera (1938–39; Marseilles, Oct. 2, 1953); *Les Amours de Don Perlimplin et Belisa dans son jardin*, opera (1947; Tours, March 1, 1980); *Fête galante*, ballet (1947); *Les Deux Rendez-vouz*, comic opera (1948; Radio France, June 22, 1951); *La Princesse de Babylone*, comic opera (1953–55; Rheims, March 4, 1960); *La Cabine téléphonique*, radiophonic sketch (1958; Paris, March 15, 1959); *Cymbeline*, opera (1958–63); *La Statue*, ballet (1968); *Un clavier pour un autre*, comic opera (1969–70; Avignon, April 3, 1971).

Arrigo, Girolamo, Italian composer; b. Palermo, April 2, 1930. He studied at the Palermo Cons., and later in Rome and Paris. His works are mostly in small forms, and virtually all with programmatic connotations. He also wrote a "collage opera," *Orden* (1969), consisting of several not necessarily related numbers, to texts in French, Italian, and Spanish, and an "epopée musicale," *Addio Garibaldi* (Paris, Oct. 10, 1972).

Arrigoni, Carlo, Italian composer; b. Florence, Dec. 5, 1697; d. there, Aug. 19, 1744. He left Italy as a young man; in 1728 he was in Brussels. In 1732 he was invited to London by a group favorable to Italian composers in opposition to Handel; there he produced an opera, *Fernando* (Feb. 5, 1734). Arrigoni then went back to Italy through Vienna, where he produced an oratorio, *Esther* (1738); returning to Florence, he staged his new operas *Sirbace* and *Scipione nelle Spagne* (1739). Several airs from his opera *Fernando* are preserved in the British Museum; Burney mistakenly attributed the music of this opera to Porpora.

Arroyo, João Marcellino, eminent Portuguese composer, writer, and statesman; b. Oporto, Oct. 4, 1861; d. Colares, near Lisbon, May 18, 1930. A member of a musical family, he first took lessons with his father while at the same time studying law. From 1884 to 1904 he was a member of the Portuguese parliament; in 1900–1901 he held the posts of minister of foreign affairs and minister of public education. A royalist, he abandoned politics after the revolution of 1910, and received a professorship of law at the Univ. of Coimbra. Among his compositions are *Amor de Perdição* (Lisbon, March 2, 1907; Hamburg, Jan. 25, 1910), regarded as the first modern Portuguese opera, and *Leonor Teles*.

BIBL.: C.A. Dos Santos, *J. A.* (Lisbon, 1941).

Arroyo, Martina, esteemed American soprano of Hispanic and black descent; b. N.Y., Feb. 2, 1936. Her principal teacher was Marinka Gurewich, but she also studied with Turnau at Hunter College of the City Univ. of N.Y. (B.A., 1956). In 1958 she won the Metropolitan Opera Auditions of the Air and made her professional operatic debut in New York in the U.S. premiere of Pizzetti's *Assassinio nella cattedrale*. On March 14, 1959, she made her debut with the Metropolitan Opera as the Celestial Voice in *Don Carlos*; she subsequently sang minor roles there until 1963 when she went to Europe, where she appeared in major roles in Vienna, Düsseldorf, Berlin, and Frankfurt am Main. From 1963 to 1968 she sang in Zürich. On Feb. 6, 1965, she scored a remarkable success at the Metropolitan Opera when she substituted for Birgit Nilsson as Aida. In subsequent years, she sang major roles there, and also appeared at London's Covent Garden (from 1968) and the Paris Opéra (from 1973). In 1989 she retired from the operatic stage. She taught at the Indiana Univ. School of Music in Bloomington from 1993. Arroyo was especially admired in Verdi spinto roles, but she also acquitted herself well as Donna Anna, Liù, Santuzza, and Cio-Cio-San. She also proved herself technically equal to the complex soprano parts in the works of such avant-garde composers as Varèse, Dallapiccola, and Stockhausen.

Artôt, Désirée (baptismal name, **Marguerite-Joséphine Désiré Montagney**), Belgian mezzo-soprano; b. Paris, July 21, 1835; d. Berlin, April 3, 1907. She was the daughter of the Belgian horn player and composer Jean-Désiré Artôt (1803–1887). She studied with Mme. Viardot-García, then sang in Belgium, the Netherlands, and England (1857). Meyerbeer engaged her to sing in *Le Prophète* at the Paris Opéra (Feb. 5, 1858); she was greatly praised by Berlioz and other Paris musicians and critics. In 1858 she went to Italy, then made appearances in London. In 1868 she was in Russia, where she was briefly engaged to Tchaikovsky; however, this engagement was quickly disrupted by her marriage (on Sept. 15, 1869) to the Spanish baritone **Mariano Padilla y Ramos**. Their daughter was **Lola Artôt de Padilla**.

Arundell, Dennis (Drew), English actor, singer, opera producer, writer on music, and composer; b. London, July 22, 1898; d. there, Dec. 10, 1988. He studied at Tonbridge and with Rootham, Henry Moule, and Stanford at St. John's College, Cambridge. Although he made appearances as an actor and singer, he was particularly noted as an opera producer in Cambridge (from 1922) and at the Sadler's Wells Theatre in London (from 1946). In 1974 he became a teacher at the Royal Northern College of Music in Manchester. In 1978 he was made a Member of the Order of the British Empire. Among his compositions were the operas *Ghost of Abel* and *A Midsummer Night's Dream* (1927). He publ. the vols. *Henry Purcell* (London, 1927), *The Critic at the Opera* (London, 1957), and *The Story of Sadler's Wells* (London, 1965; 2d ed., 1977).

Asafiev, Boris (Vladimirovich), prominent Russian musicologist and composer; b. St. Petersburg, July 29, 1884; d. Moscow, Jan. 27, 1949. He took courses in history and philology at the Univ. of St. Petersburg (graduated, 1908), and in orchestration with Rimsky-Korsakov and in composition with Liadov at the St. Petersburg Cons. (graduated, 1910). In 1914 he began writing music criticism under the pseudonym Igor Glebov. In 1917 he helped to found the music dept. of the Petrograd Inst. of the History of the Arts, becoming director of its music history dept. in 1920. From 1924 to 1928 he was ed. of the journal *Novaya Muzyka*. From 1925 to 1943 he was prof. of history, theory, and composition at the Leningrad Cons. In 1943 he went to Moscow as a prof. and director of the research section of the Cons., and as a senior research fellow at the Inst. for the History of the Arts. In 1948 he was made chairman of the Union of Soviet Composers. Asafiev was an influential writer on music. Among his works are *Russkaya poeziya v russkoy muzïke* (Russian Poetry in Russian Music; Petrograd, 1921; 2d ed., rev., 1922); *Instrumental'noye tvorchestvo Chaykovskovo* (Tchaikovsky's Instrumental Works; Petrograd, 1922); *Pyotr Il'ich Chaykovsky: Evo zhizn' i tvorchestvo* (Piotr Ilyich Tchaikovsky: Life and Works; Petrograd, 1922); *Simfonicheskiye etyudï* (Symphonic Studies; Petrograd, 1922; 2d ed., 1968); *Kniga o Stravinskom* (A Book About Stravinsky; Leningrad, 1929); *Muzïkal'naya forma kak protsess* (Music Form as a Process; 2 vols., Moscow, 1930, 1947; 3d ed., 1971); *Russkaya muzïka ot nachala XIX stoletiya* (Russian Music from the Beginning of the XIX Century; Moscow, 1930; 2d ed., 1968, by E. Orlova as *Russkaya muzïka: XIX i nachala XX veka* [Russian Music: The XIX and Early XX Centuries]); *Kompozitorï pervoy polovinï XIX veka: Russkaya klassicheskaya muzïka* (Composers of the First Half of the XIX Century: Russian Classical Music; Moscow, 1945); *Glinka* (Moscow, 1947; 2d ed., 1950); *Kriticheskiye stat'i, ocherki i retsenzii* (Critical Articles, Essays and Reviews; Moscow, 1967); *Ob opere: Izbranniye stat'i* (Collected Opera Criticism; Leningrad, 1976). As a composer, Asafiev was much less significant, although numbering among his compositions were 11 operas and 28 ballets.

BIBL.: A. Ossovsky, *B. V. A..: Sovetskaya muzïka* (Moscow, 1945); D. Kabalevsky, *B. V. A.—Igor Glebov* (Moscow, 1954); E. Orlova, *B. V. A.: Put' issledovatel'ya i publitsista* (B. V. A.'s Development as a Researcher and Writer; Leningrad, 1964); J. Jiránek, *Asafajevova teorie intonance: Jeji geneze a vyznam* (A.'s Intonation Theory: Its Origins and Significance; Prague, 1967).

Aschaffenburg, Walter, German-born American composer and teacher; b. Essen, May 20, 1927. He went to the United States at the age of 11 and in 1944 became a naturalized American citizen. He studied composition with Robert Doellner at the Hartt School of Music in Hartford, Conn. (1945), Elwell at the Oberlin (Ohio) College-Cons. of Music (B.A., 1951), Rogers at the Eastman School of Music in Rochester, N.Y. (M.A., 1952), and Dallapiccola in Florence (1956). In 1952 he joined the faculty of the Oberlin College-Cons. of Music, serving as chairman of its theory dept. (1968–73). In 1971 he was made a prof. of composition and theory, and in 1983 chairman of the composition dept., positions he held until his retirement in 1987. In 1955–56 and 1973–74 he held Guggenheim fellowships. While Aschaffenburg has employed the 12-tone system in some of his works, his scores are often embued with a meticulous expressivity. He composed *The Flies*, incidental music to Sartre's play (1953), and *Bartleby*, an opera (1956–62; Oberlin, Nov. 12, 1964).

Ascher, Leo, Austrian composer; b. Vienna, Aug. 17, 1880; d. N.Y., Feb. 25, 1942. His received training in law and music. The success of his first operetta, *Vergeltsgott* or *Der Bettlerklub* (Vienna, Oct. 14, 1905), encouraged him to devote himself to composing for the theater. His first major work, *Die arme Lori* (Vienna, March 12, 1909), was followed by his first notable success, *Hoheit tanzt Walzer* (Vienna, Feb. 24, 1912); then followed the highly successful scores *Was tut man nicht alles aus Liebe* (Vienna, Dec. 17, 1914), *Botschafterin Leni* (Vienna, Feb. 19, 1915), *Der Soldat der Marie* (Berlin, Sept. 2, 1916), *Egon und seine Frauen* (Berlin, Aug. 25, 1917), and *Bruder Leichtsinn* (Vienna, Dec. 28, 1917). Among his later works were *Der Künstlerpreis* (Vienna, Oct. 1, 1919), *Was Mädchen träumen* (Vienna, Dec. 6, 1919), *Princessin Friedl* (Berlin, May 14, 1920), *Zwölf Uhr Nachts!* (Vienna, Nov. 12, 1920), *Baronesschen Sarah* (Berlin, Dec. 25, 1920), *Ein Jahr ohne Liebe* (Berlin, Jan. 12, 1923), *Sonja* (Vienna, March 6, 1925), *Das Amorettenhaus* (Hamburg, Jan. 1926), *Ich hab' dich Lieb . . .* (Vienna, April 16, 1926), *Ninon am Scheideweg* (Berlin, Dec. 27, 1926), *Frühling in Wienerwald* (Vienna, April 17, 1930), and *Bravo Peggy!* (Leipzig, March 27, 1932). He also composed film scores for *Purpur und Waschblau* (1931) and *Mein Leopold* (1932). His last stage work was *Um ein bisschen Liebe* (Vienna, June 5, 1936). With the Anschluss in 1938, Ascher emigrated to the United States.

Ascone, Vicente, Uruguayan composer of Italian descent; b. Siderno, Aug. 16, 1897; d. Montevideo, March 5, 1979. He was taken to Uruguay as a child, where he studied trumpet and composition. Most of his music is rooted in Uruguayan folk songs, while stylistically he followed traditional Italian formulas. He wrote 5 operas, including *Paraná Gauzú* (Montevideo on July 25, 1931), based on an Indian subject.

Ashley, Robert (Reynolds), pioneering American composer, performer, director, and writer; b. Ann Arbor, Mich., March 28, 1930. He studied theory at the Univ. of Mich. (B.Mus., 1952) and piano and composition with Wallingford Riegger at the Manhattan School of Music in New York (M.Mus., 1954); then returned to the Univ. of Mich. for further composition study with Ross Lee Finney, Leslie Bassett, and Roberto Gerhard (1957–60), where he also took courses in psychoacoustics and cultural speech patterns at its Speech Research Laboratories and was employed as a research assistant (1960–61) in acoustics at its Architectural Research Laboratory. He was active with Milton Cohen's Space Theater (1957–64), the ONCE Festival and ONCE Group (1958–69), and the Sonic Arts Union (1966–76), touring widely with them in the United States and Europe; also served as director of the Center for Contemporary Music at Mills College in Oakland, California (1970–81). As the first opera composer of the post-proscenium age, Ashley is one of the most influential and highly acclaimed artists in the 20th-century avant-garde music and experimental performance tradition. He has produced several hundred music and music-theater compositions for live performance as well as audio and video recordings and broadcast television series, which have been performed the throughout the world. In his compositions from the mid-1970s, often experimental, technologically driven, and collaborative, he has developed a complex, episodic treatment of his materials, marked by striking imagery, textual multiplicity, and a graceful and highly individualized integration of speech and song. Ashley has also provided music for the dance companies of Douglas Dunn (*Idea from the Church*, 1978), Steve Paxton (*The Park* and *The Backyard*, 1978), Trisha Brown (*Son of Gone Fishin'*, 1983), and Merce Cunningham (*Problems in the Flying Saucer*, 1988). In 1995 he was commissioned by the Florida Grand Opera, Miami-Dade Community College, and the South Florida Composers Alliance to do a new opera, *Balseros*, to be premiered in Miami in 1997. Its libretto, subtitled "Manual for a Desperate Crossing" and written by Maria Irene Fornes, is based on interviews with actual "rafters" (*balseros*), Cuban refugees who rowed and paddled their way to America. He was married first to the artist Mary Ashley, with whom he collaborated; then to Mimi Johnson, director of Performing Artservices in New York. Ashley is one of four featured composers (with Cage, Glass, and Laurie Anderson) in Peter Greenaway's video series *Four American Composers*. His *Perfect Lives* was published, in book form, in 1991.

WORKS: OPERAS: *The Wolfman* for Amplified Voice and *The Wolfman Tape* (1964); *That Morning Thing* for 5 Principal Voices, 8 Dancers, Women's Chorus, and Tape, in 4 parts: *Four Ways, Frogs, Purposeful Lady Slow Afternoon*, and *She Was a Visitor* (1967; Ann Arbor, Feb. 8, 1968); *Music with Roots in the Aether*, television opera for Voices and Electronics (Paris, 1976); *Title Withdrawn*, television opera for Voices and Electronics (Paris, 1976; from *Music with Roots in the Aether*); *What She Thinks*, television opera for Voices and Electronics (1976; from *Music with Roots in the Aether*); *Perfect Lives (Private Parts)*, television opera for Voices, Piano, and Electronic Orch. (1978–80), in 7 parts: *The Backyard, The Bank, The Bar, The Church, The Living Room, The Park*, and *The Supermarket*); *Music Word Fire And I Would Do It Again Coo Coo: The Lessons*, television opera for Voices, Piano, and Electronic Orch. (1981); *Atalanta (Acts of God)*, television opera for Voice, Chorus, and Instruments (Paris, 1982; concert version as *Atalanta (Acts of God), aka Songs from Atalanta* for Voice, Chorus, and Instruments, 1982); *Tap Dancing in the Sand* for Voice (1982); *Atalanta Strategy*, television opera (N.Y., 1984); *Now Eleanor's Idea*, tetralogy: *I: Improvement (Don Leaves Linda)* (1984–85), *II: Foreign Experiences* (1994), *III: eL/Aficionado* (1987), and *Now Eleanor's Idea* (1993); *Yellow Man with Heart with Wings* for Voice and Tape (1990); *Love Is a Good Example* for Voice (1994); *When Famous Last Words Fail You* for Voice (1994); *Yes, But Is It Edible?* for Voice (1994); *Balseros* (1997); *Dust*, multimedia television opera (N.Y., April 14, 1999; in collaboration with Y. Yoshihara). ELECTRONIC MUSIC THEATER: *# + Heat* (1961); *Public Opinion Descends Upon the Demonstrators* (1961; Ann Arbor, Feb. 18, 1962); *Boxing* (1963; Detroit, April 9, 1964); *Combination Wedding and Funeral* (1964; N.Y., May 9, 1965); *Interludes for the Space Theater* (1964; Cleveland, May 4, 1965); *Kitty Hawk (An Antigravity Piece)* (1964; St. Louis, March 21, 1965); *The Lecture Series* (1964; N.Y., May 9, 1965; in collaboration with M. Ashley); *The Wolfman Motorcity Revue* (1964; Newport Beach, Calif., Jan. 11, 1969); *Morton Feldman Says* (1965); *Orange Dessert* (1965; Ann Arbor, April 9, 1966); *Night Train* (1966; Waltham, Mass., Jan. 7, 1967; in collaboration with M. Ashley); *Unmarked Interchange* (Ann Arbor, Sept. 17, 1965); *The Trial of Anne Opie Wehrer and Unknown Accomplices for Crimes Against Humanity* (Sheboygan, Wisc., April 30, 1968); *Fancy Free or It's There* (1970; Ann Arbor, April 1971); *Illusion Models* (1970); *It's There* (Brussels, April 1970); *Night Sport* (L'Aquila, Italy, April 1973); *Over the Telephone* (N.Y., March 1975).

BIBL.: T. DeLio, *Circumscribing the Open Universe: Essays on Cage, Feldman, Wolff, A. and Lucier* (Washington, D.C., 1984).

Ashrafi, Mukhtar, Russian composer; b. Bukhara, June 11, 1912; d. Tashkent, Dec. 15, 1975. He studied at the Moscow Cons. (1934–37) and later at the Leningrad Cons. (1941–43). As the war situation led to a siege of Leningrad, he was evacuated to Tashkent. Since he never acquired comprehensive technique of composition, his operas were orchestrated by his teacher at the Moscow Cons., Vasilenkov; 2 were premiered in Tashkent: *Buran* (June 12, 1939) and *The Grand Canal* (Jan. 12, 1941). He further wrote several ballets.

Asioli, Bonifazio or **Bonifacio,** Italian composer; b. Correggio, Aug. 30, 1769; d. there, May 18, 1832. He began writing music at a very early age. He studied with Angelo Morigi in Parma (1780–82), then lived in Bologna and Venice as a harpsichord player. His first opera, *La Volubile*, was produced in Correggio (1785) with marked success; it was followed by *Le nozze in villa* (Correggio, 1786), *Cinna* (Milan, 1793), and *Gustavo al Malabar* (Turin, 1802). From 1787 he was private maestro to the Marquis Gherardini in Turin, then in Venice (1796–99); subsequently he went to Milan and taught at the Cons. (1808–14). Asioli wrote a total of 7 operas, as well as an oratorio, *Giuseppe in Galaad*. He was the author of the textbooks *Principi elementari di musica* (Milan, 1809; also in Eng., Ger., and Fr.) and *Trattato d'armonia e d'accompagnamento* (1813), as well as manuals for harpsichord, voice, and double bass. His theoretical book *Il Maestro di composizione* was publ. posth. (1836).

BIBL.: A. Coli, *Vita di B. A.* (Milan, 1834).

Aspa, Mario, Italian composer; b. Messina, 1799; d. there, Dec. 14, 1868. He studied with Zingarelli in Naples. He produced 42 operas, of which the most successful were *Paolo e Virginia* (Rome, April 29, 1843) and *Il Muratore di Napoli* (Naples, Oct. 16, 1850). His last opera, *Piero di Calais*, was produced posth. (Messina, March 6, 1872).

Aspestrand, Sigwart, Norwegian opera composer; b. Fredrikshald, Nov. 13, 1856; d. Oslo, Dec. 31, 1941. He studied at Leipzig and Berlin and spent 30 years of his life (1885–1915) in Germany. Of his 7 operas, *Die Seemansbraut* (Gotha, March 29, 1894), was the most successful. His other operas, all in German, are *Der Recke von Lyrskovsheid, Freyas Alter, Die Wette, Der Kuss auf Sicht, Robin Hood*, and *Pervonte*.

Asplmayr, Franz, Austrian composer; b. Linz (baptized), April 2, 1728; d. Vienna, July 29, 1786. He studied violin with his father; wrote ballets for the Austrian court. Historically, Asplmayr was important as one of the earliest Austrian composers to adopt the instrumental style, rich in dynamics, as established by the Mannheim school. He composed the Singspiel *Die Kinder der Natur*, music for Shakespeare's *Macbeth* (1777), and the ballets *Agamemnon vengé* (1771), *Ifigenie* (1772), and *Acis et Galathée*.

Aston, Peter (George), English conductor, teacher, and composer; b. Birmingham, Oct. 5, 1938. He studied composition and conducting at the Birmingham School of Music before completing his education at the Univ. of York (Ph.D., 1970, with the diss. *George Jeffreys and the English Baroque*). From 1958 to 1965 he was director of the Tudor Consort, and then of the English Baroque Ensemble (1968–70); subsequently was conductor of the Aldeburgh Festival Singers (1975–88). He lectured at the Univ. of York (1964–72), where he then was senior lecturer in music (1972–74); subsequently he served as prof. and head of music at the Univ. of East Anglia (from 1974), where he also was dean of the School of Fine Arts and Music (1981–84). He ed. the complete works of George Jeffreys, and publ. the vols. *Sound and Silence* (1970), *The Music of York Minster* (1972), and *Music Theory in Practice* (3 vols., 1992–93). He composed mainly sacred and secular vocal music, but included in his catalog is the children's opera *Sacrapant, the Sorcerer* (1967).

d'Astorga, Baron Emanuele (Gioacchino Cesare Rincón), Italian composer of Spanish descent; b. Augusta, Sicily, March 20, 1680; d. probably in Madrid, c.1757. He was of noble Spanish descent and was a baron in his own right. During the revolution of 1708, he was an officer in the Palermo municipal guard. After a sojourn in Vienna (1712–14), he served as a senator in Palermo. In 1744 he settled in Spain in the service of the king. Among his works were the operas *La moglie menica* (Palermo, 1698), *Dafni* (Genoa, April 21, 1709), and *Amor tirannico* (Venice, 1710). His *Stabat Mater* (Oxford, 1752) was his best-known work. Johann Joseph Abert wrote an opera on his life, *Astorga* (1866).

BIBL.: H. Volkmann, *E. d'A.* (2 vols., Leipzig, 1911, 1919).

Atanasov, Georgi, Bulgarian composer and bandmaster; b. Plovdiv, May 18, 1881; d. Fasano, Italy, Nov. 17, 1931. He went to Italy in 1901, and took lessons in composition with Mascagni at the Pesaro Cons. Returning to Bulgaria, he became active as a military bandmaster, as well as a composer. He wrote 2 of the earliest operas on national Bulgarian subjects, *Borislav* (Sofia, March 4, 1911) and *Gergana* (Sofia, June 19, 1917); other operas were *Zapustialata vodenitza* (The Abandoned Mill; Sofia, March 31, 1923), *Altzek*, and *Tzveta*; he also wrote 2 children's operas, *The Sick Teacher* and *About Birds*.

BIBL.: I. Sagaev, *Maestro G. A.* (Sofia, 1961).

Atlantov, Vladimir (Andreievich), distinguished Russian tenor and baritone; b. Leningrad, Feb. 19, 1939. He studied with Bolotina at the Leningrad Cons., taking the Glinka Prize in 1962 and graduating in 1963. After making his formal operatic debut at Leningrad's Kirov Theater in 1963, he was a student artist at Milan's La Scala (1963–65). He was a medalist at the Tchaikovsky Competition in Moscow in 1966, and in competitions in Montreal and Sofia in 1967. In 1967 he became a member of the Bolshoi Theater in Moscow, with which he later toured with notable success to Milan, New York, Paris, and Vienna. From 1977 he also sang baritone roles. In 1987 he made his debut at London's Covent Garden as Otello, one of his most famous roles. In 1990 he sang for the first time with an American opera company when he appeared as Canio with the San Francisco Opera. He returned to the San Francisco Opera as Tchaikovsky's Hermann in 1993. In 1997 he appeared as Otello with Opera Pacific in Costa Mesa, Calif. He also toured extensively as a concert artist. In addition to the Russian repertoire, Atlantov is esteemed for his portrayals of Don José, Cavardossi, Alfredo, Radames, Posa, and Siegmund.

Atterberg, Kurt (Magnus), eminent Swedish composer; b. Göteborg, Dec. 12, 1887; d. Stockholm, Feb. 15, 1974. He studied engineering and was employed in the wireless service; then took courses in composition at the Stockholm Cons. with Hallén, and in Berlin with Schillings (1910–12). In 1913 he was appointed conductor at the Drama Theater in Stockholm, holding this post until 1922; in 1919 he began writing music criticism and continued to contribute to Stockholm newspapers until 1957; concurrently he was also employed at the Swedish patent office (1912–68) and served as secretary of the Royal Swedish Academy of Music in Stockholm (1940–53). He was one of the founders of the Soc. of Swedish Composers in 1924, and was on its board until 1947. During all this time, he continued to compose with inexhaustible energy, producing works in all genres: operas, ballets, syms., concertos, choruses, and chamber music, all with preordained precision of form and technique. It is ironic that his music remained hermetically sealed within the confines of Sweden, rarely if ever performed beyond its borders. Atterberg's name attracted unexpected attention when he was declared winner of the ill-conceived Schubert Centennial Contest organized in 1928 by the Columbia Phonograph Co., with the declared intention to finish Schubert's *Unfinished Symphony*. The entire venture was severely criticized in musical circles as an attempt to derive commercial advantage under the guise of an homage to a great composer. Rumors spread that Atterberg had deliberately imitated the style of composition of some members of the jury (Glazunov, Alfano, Nielsen) in order to ingratiate himself with them so as to secure the prize, but Atterberg denied any such suggestion, pointing out that he knew the names only of those in the jury from the Nordic zone, whereas the international membership comprised 10 national zones. Furthermore, the sym. he had submitted was written in a far more advanced style than Atterberg's previous symphonic works and was certainly much more modern than any music by the jury members, using as it did such procedures as polytonality. There can be no doubt, however, that Atterberg was a master technician of his craft, and that his music had a powerful appeal. That it never gained a wider audience can be ascribed only to an unfathomable accident of world culture.

WORKS: DRAMATIC: OPERAS : (all first perf. in Stockholm): *Härvard Harpolekare* (Härvard the Potter; 1915–17; Sept. 29, 1919; rev. as *Harvard der Harfner* and perf. in German at Chemnitz, 1936; a later ver. with new 3rd act perf. in Linz, June 14, 1952); *Bäckahästen* (1923–24; Jan. 23, 1925); *Fanal* (1929–32; Jan. 27, 1934); *Aladdin* (1936–41; March 18, 1941); *Stormen*, after Shakespeare's *Tempest* (1946–47; Sept. 19, 1948). BALLETS: *Per Svinaherde* (Peter the Swineherd; 1914–15); *De fåvitska jungfrurna*, ballet-pantomime (The Wise and Foolish Virgins; Paris, Nov. 18, 1920).

Attwood, Thomas, English organist and composer; b. London, Nov. 23, 1765; d. there, March 24, 1838. He was a chorister at the Chapel Royal under Nares and Ayrton from the age of 9. Following a performance before the Prince of Wales (afterward George IV), he was sent to Italy for further study; there he received instruction in Naples from Filippo Cinque and Gaetano Latilla. He then went to Vienna, where Mozart accepted him as a pupil; his notes from these theory and composition lessons are printed in the *Neue Mozart Ausgabe*, X/30/1. In 1787 he returned to London and held various posts as an organist. He was also music tutor to the Duchess of York (1791) and to the Princess of Wales (1795). A founder of the London Phil. Soc. (1813), he conducted some of its concerts. He occupied an important position in the English music world; when Mendelssohn came to London as a young man, Attwood lent him enthusiastic support. Attwood was a prolific composer of operas, of which many were produced in London, including *The Prisoner* (Oct. 18, 1792), *The Mariners* (May 10, 1793), *The Packet Boat* (May 13, 1794), *The Smugglers* (April 13, 1796), *The Fairy Festival* (May 13, 1797), *The Irish Tar* (Aug. 24, 1797), *The Devil of a Lover* (March 17, 1798), *The Magic Oak* (Jan. 29, 1799), *True Friends* (Feb. 19, 1800), and *The Sea-Side Story* (May 12, 1801). In all, Attwood wrote 28 operas, in some of which he used material from other composers (e.g., Mozart in *The Prisoner* and *The Mariners*).

Atzmon (real name, **Groszberger**), **Moshe,** Hungarian-born Israeli conductor; b. Budapest, July 30, 1931. He was taken to Palestine in 1944, where he attended the Tel Aviv Academy of Music (1958–62), then pursued conducting studies at the Guildhall School of Music in London. In 1964 he won 1st prize in the Liverpool conducting competition, and then appeared as a guest conductor with various British orchs. He was chief conductor of the Sydney (Australia) Sym. Orch. (1969–71), the North German Radio Sym. Orch. in Hamburg (1972–76), the Basel Sym. Orch. (1972–77), and the Tokyo Metropolitan Sym. Orch. (1978–82). With Giuseppe Patane, he served as coprincipal conductor of the American Sym. Orch. in New York (1982–84); he was then chief conductor of the Nagoya Phil. in Japan (1986–92). From 1991 to 1995 he was Generalmusikdirektor of the Dortmund Opera.

Auber, Daniel-François-Esprit, notable French composer; b. Caen, Jan. 29, 1782; d. Paris, May 12, 1871. He was a pupil of Ignaz Anton Ladurner. His first work for the stage, *L'erreur d'un moment* (1805; rev. as *Julie*, 1811), attracted the notice of Cherubini, who became his mentor. Auber first gained success as a composer with his opéra comique, *La bergère châtelaine* (Paris, Jan. 27, 1820). Shortly after, he met the librettist Scribe, with whom he collaborated on many works for the stage until Scribe's death in 1861. Following the success of Auber's *Le maçon* (Paris, May 3, 1825), a significant work in the development of the opéra-comique genre, he scored an enormous success with his *La muette de Portici* (Paris, Feb. 29, 1828), a work that launched a new era in French grand opera. The latter's vivid portrayal of popular fury stirred French and Belgian audiences, leading to revolutionary disturbances following its premiere in Brussels (Aug. 25, 1830). Another fine success followed with his opéra comique *Fra Diavolo* (Paris, Jan. 28, 1830), the only score by Auber that remains in the standard repertory. Among his later stage works, the opéras comiques *La part du diable* (Paris, Jan. 16, 1843), *Haydée* (Paris, Dec. 28, 1847), and *Manon Lescaut* (Paris, Feb. 23, 1856) were influential in the development of the opéra-lyrique genre. From 1842 to 1870 he served as director of the Paris Cons. In 1825 he was named a member of the Légion d'honneur. He was elected to the Inst. of the Académie in 1829. In 1852 Napoleon III appointed him music director of the imperial chapel.

WORKS: DRAMATIC: (all 1st perf. in Paris): *L'erreur d'un moment* (amateur perf., 1805; rev. as *Julie*, 1811); *Jean de Couvin* (Sept. 1812); *Le séjour militaire* (Feb. 27, 1813); *Le testament et les billets-doux* (Sept. 18, 1819); *Le bergère châtelaine* (Jan. 27, 1820); *Emma, ou La promesse imprudente* (July 7, 1821); *Leicester, ou Le château de Kenilworth* (Jan. 25, 1823); *La neige, ou Le nouvel Éginard* (Oct. 8, 1823); *Vendôme en Espagne* (Dec. 5, 1823; in collaboration with Hérold); *Les trois genres* (April 27, 1824; in collaboration with Boieldieu); *Le concert à la cour, ou La débutante* (June 3, 1824); *Léocadie* (Nov. 4, 1824); *Le maçon* (May 3, 1825); *Le timide, ou Le nouveau séducteur* (May 30, 1826); *Fiorella* (Nov. 28, 1826); *La muette de Portici* (Feb. 29, 1828); *La fiancée* (Jan. 10, 1829); *Fra Diavolo, ou L'hôtellerie de Terracine* (Jan. 28, 1830); *Le dieu et la bayadère, ou La courtisane amourese* (Oct. 13, 1830); *Le philtre* (June 20, 1831); *La Marquise de Brinvilliers* (Oct. 31, 1831; in collaboration with Batton, Berton, Blangini, Boieldieu, Carafa, Cherubini, Hérold, and Paër); *Le serment, ou Les faux-monnayeurs* (Oct. 1, 1832); *Gustave III, ou Le bal masqué* (Feb. 27, 1833); *Lestocq, ou L'intrigue et l'amour* (May 24, 1834); *Le cheval de bronze* (March 23, 1835; rev. version, Sept. 21, 1857); *Actéon* (Jan. 23, 1836); *Les chaperons blancs* (April 9, 1836); *L'ambassadrice* (Dec. 21, 1836); *Le domino noir* (Dec. 2, 1837); *Le lac des fées* (April 1, 1839); *Zanetta, ou Jouer avec le feu* (May 18, 1840); *Les diamants de la couronne* (March 6, 1841); *Le Duc d'Olonne* (Feb. 4, 1842); *La part du diable* (Jan. 16, 1843); *La sirène* (March 26, 1844); *La barcarolle, ou L'amour et la musique* (April 22, 1845); *Les premiers pas* (Nov. 15, 1847; in collaboration with Adam, Carafa, and Halévy); *Haydée, ou Le secret* (Dec. 28, 1847); *L'enfant prodigue* (Dec. 6, 1850); *Zerline, ou La corbeille d'oranges* (May 16, 1851); *Marco Spada* (Dec. 21, 1852); *Jenny Bell* (June 2, 1855); *Manon Lescaut* (Feb. 23, 1856); *La circassienne* (Feb. 2, 1861); *La fiancée du Roi de Garbe* (Jan. 11, 1864); *Le premier jour de bonheur* (Feb. 15, 1868); *Rêve d'amour* (Dec. 20, 1869).

BIBL.: E. de Mirécourt, *A.* (Paris, 1857); B. Jouvin, *A.* (Paris, 1868); A. Pougin, *A.: Ses commencements, les origines de sa carrière* (Paris, 1873); J. Carlez, *A.* (Caen, 1875); A. Kohut, *A.* (Leipzig, 1895); C. Malherbe, *A.* (Paris, 1911); R. Longyear, *D. F. E. A.: A Chapter in French Opéra Comique 1800–1870* (diss., Cornell Univ., 1957); W. Börner, *Die Opern von D. F. E. A.* (diss., Univ. of Leipzig, 1962); H. Schneider, *Chronologische-thematisches Verzeichnis sämtlicher Werke von D. F. E. A. (AWV), Band 1.1–2* (Frankfurt am Main, 1994).

Aubert, Louis-François-Marie, French composer; b. Paramé, Ille-et-Vilaine, Feb. 19, 1877; d. Paris, Jan. 9, 1968. Of precocious talent, he entered the Paris Cons. as a child, and studied piano with Diémer, theory with Lavignac, and advanced composition with Fauré; he also sang in church choirs. His song *Rimes tendres* was publ. when he was 19. His *Fantaisie* for Piano and Orch. was performed in Paris by the Colonne Orch. with Diémer as soloist (Nov. 17, 1901). His *Suite brève* for 2 Pianos was presented at the Paris Exposition in 1900; an orch. version of it was performed for the first time in Paris on April 27, 1916. Aubert's major work was an operatic fairy tale, *La Forêt bleue* (Geneva, Jan. 7, 1913); a Russian production was given in Boston on March 8, 1913, attracting considerable attention. The Paris production of *La Forêt bleue*, delayed by World War I, took place on June 10, 1924, at the Opéra Comique. Aubert's style was largely determined by the impressionistic currents of the early 20th century; like Debussy and Ravel, he was attracted by the music of Spain and wrote several pieces in the Spanish idiom, of which the symphonic poem *Habanera* (Paris, March 22, 1919) was particularly successful. The list of Aubert's works further includes 4 ballets: *La Momie* (1903), *Chrysothémis* (1904), *La Nuit ensorcélée* (1922), and *Cinéma* (1953).

BIBL.: L. Vuillemin, *L. A. et son oeuvre* (Paris, 1921); M. Landowski and G. Morançon, *L. A.* (Paris, 1967).

Aubin, Tony (Louis Alexandre), French composer, conductor, and pedagogue; b. Paris, Dec. 8, 1907; d. there, Sept. 21, 1981. He studied at the Paris Cons. with Samuel-Rousseau, Noël Gallon, and Dukas; in 1930 he won the 1st Grand Prix de Rome. Upon his return to Paris from Rome, he studied conducting with Gaubert, and later was in charge of the music division at the Paris Radio until the collapse of France in 1940; from 1945 to 1960 he served as conductor with the French Radio; concurrently he taught at the Paris Cons. In 1968 he was elected a member of the Académie des Beaux-Arts. A pragmatic composer, Aubin cultivated an eclectic idiom calculated to impress professionals and please common music lovers. He composed the opera *Goya* (1970).

Audran, (Achille) Edmond, notable French composer, son of **Marius-Pierre Audran**; b. Lyons, April 12, 1840; d. Tierceville, Aug. 17, 1901. He was a student of Jules Duprato at the École Niedermeyer in Paris, graduating in 1859. In 1861 he became maître de chapelle of the church of St. Joseph in Marseilles, where he composed sacred music and attracted notice with his operetta *Le Grand Mogol* (Feb. 24, 1877). Settling in Paris, he scored a major success with his comic opera *Les Noces d'Olivette* (Nov. 13, 1879). Even more successful was his next score, *La Moscotte* (Dec. 29, 1880), one of the finest operettas of the day. No less successful was his next score, *Gillette de Narbonne* (Nov. 11, 1882). The revised version of *Le Grand Mogol* (Sept. 19, 1884) made it a repertoire staple. Among his later successful works were *La Cigale et la fourmi* (Oct. 30, 1886), *Miss Helyett* (Nov. 12, 1890), *L'Oncle Célestin* (March 24, 1891), *L'Enlèvement de la Toledad* (Nov. 17, 1894), and *La Poupée* (Oct. 21, 1896).

WORKS: MUSICAL THEATER (all 1st perf. in Paris unless otherwise given): *L'Ours et le pacha* (Marseilles, 1862); *La Chercheuse d'esprit* (Marseilles, 1864); *La Nivernaise* (Marseilles, Dec. 1862); *Le Petit Poucet* (Marseilles, April 1868); *Le Grand Gogol* (Marseilles, Feb. 24, 1877; rev. version, Paris, Sept. 19, 1884); *Les Noces d'Olivette* (Nov. 13, 1879); *La Mascotte* (Dec. 29, 1880); *Gillette de Narbonne* (Nov. 11, 1882); *Les Pommes d'or* (Feb. 12, 1883); *La Dormeuse éveillée* (Dec. 27, 1883); *Pervenche* (March 31, 1885); *Serment d'amour* (Feb. 19, 1886); *Indiana* (London, Oct. 11, 1886); *La Cigale et la fourmi* (Oct. 30, 1886); *La Fiancée des verts-poteaux* (Nov. 8, 1887); *Le Puits qui parle* (March 15, 1888); *Miette* (Sept. 24, 1888); *La Petite Fronde* (Nov. 16, 1888); *La Fille à Cacolet* (July 10, 1889); *L'Oeuf rouge* (March 14, 1890); *Miss Helyett* (Nov. 12, 1890); *L'Oncle Célestin* (March 24, 1891); *Article de Paris* (March 17, 1892); *Sainte-Freya* (Nov. 4, 1892); *Madame Suzette* (March 29,1893); *Mon Prince!* (Nov. 18, 1893); *L'Enlèvement de la Toledad* (Nov. 17, 1894); *La Duchesse de Ferrare* (Jan. 25, 1895); *La Reine des reines* (Oct. 14, 1896); *La Poupée* (Oct. 21, 1896); *Monsieur Lohengrin* (Nov. 30, 1896); *Les Petites* (Oct. 11, 1897); *Les Soeurs Graudichard* (April 21, 1899); *Le Curé Vincent* (Oct. 25, 1901).

Audran, Marius-Pierre, French tenor, pedagogue, and composer, father of **(Achille) Edmond Audran**; b. Aix, Provence, Sept. 26, 1816; Marseilles, Jan. 9, 1887. After singing in Marseilles, Bordeaux, and Lyons, he was first tenor at the Paris Opéra Comique. In 1863 he became a prof. of voice and director of the Marseilles Cons.

Auger, Arleen (Joyce), esteemed American soprano; b. Los Angeles, Sept. 13, 1939; d. Amsterdam, June 10, 1993. She majored in education at Calif. State Univ. in Long Beach (B.A., 1963); then studied voice with Ralph Errolle in Chicago. She made her European operatic debut as the Queen of the Night in *Die Zauberflöte* at the Vienna State Opera (1967), remaining on its roster until 1974; also chose that role for her N.Y. City Opera debut (March 16, 1969). She appeared with the conductor Helmuth Rilling on a tour of Japan in 1974, and subsequently gained prominence through a major series of recordings of the music of Bach under his direction; also devoted increasing attention to a concert career. On Oct. 2, 1978, she made her Metropolitan Opera debut in New York as Marzelline in *Fidelio*, and, in 1984, made a notably successful New York recital debut. Her appearance in the title role of Handel's *Alcina* in London (1985) and Los Angeles (1986) elicited further critical accolades. In 1986 she was chosen to sing at the royal wedding of Prince Andrew and Sarah Ferguson in London. During the 1986–87 season she made an extensive concert tour of the United States and Europe. In 1992 her career was tragically ended when she was stricken with a fatal brain tumor.

Auletta, Pietro, Italian composer; b. S. Angelo, Avellino, c.1698; d. Naples, Sept. 1771. He studied at the Cons. of S. Onofrio in Naples; gained renown with his comic opera *Orazio* (Naples, Carnival 1737). Only a few of his stage works are extant, but *La Locandiera* (Naples, July 10, 1738) survives as a testimony to his abilities as a dramatic composer.

Auric, Georges, notable French composer; b. Lodève, Hérault, Feb. 15, 1899; d. Paris, July 23, 1983. He first studied music at the Montpellier Cons.; then went to Paris, where he was a student of Caussade at the Cons. and of d'Indy and Roussel at the Schola Cantorum. While still in his early youth (1911–15), he wrote something like 300 songs and piano pieces; at 18, he composed a ballet, *Les Noces de Gamache*. At 20, he completed a comic opera, *La Reine de coeur*; however, he was dissatisfied with this early effort and destroyed the MS. In the aftermath of continental disillusion following World War I, he became a proponent of the anti-Romantic movement in France, with the apostles of this age of disenchantment, Erik Satie and Jean Cocteau, preaching the new values of urban culture, with modern America as a model. Satie urged young composers to produce "auditory pleasure without demanding disproportionate attention from the listener," while Cocteau elevated artistic ugliness to an aesthetic ideal. Under Satie's aegis, Auric joined several French composers of his generation in a group described as *Les Nouveaux Jeunes*, which later became known as *Les Six* (the other 5 were Milhaud, Honegger, Poulenc, Durey, and Tailleferre). Auric soon established an important connection with the impresario Serge Diaghilev, who commissioned him to write a number of ballets for his Paris company; Auric's facile yet felicitous manner of composing, with mock-Romantic connotations, fit perfectly into Diaghilev's scheme; particularly successful were Auric's early ballets *Les Fâcheux* (Monte Carlo, Jan. 19, 1924) and *Les Matelots* (Paris, June 17, 1925). He also wrote music for films, of which *A nous la liberté* (1932) achieved popular success as a symphonic suite. Auric's familiarity with the theater earned him important administrative posts; from 1962 to 1968 he acted as general administrator of both the Grand Opéra and the Opéra Comique in Paris. From 1954 to 1977 he served as president of the French Union of Composers and Authors. In 1962 he was elected to the membership of the Académie des Beaux-Arts. He publ. his memoirs as *Quand j'etais là* (Paris, 1979).

BIBL.: A. Goléa, *G. A.* (Paris, 1958); J. Roy, *Le groupe des six: Poulenc, Milhaud, Honegger, A., Tailleferre, Durey* (Paris, 1994).

Austin, Frederic, English baritone and composer; b. London, March 30, 1872; d. there, April 10, 1952. His brother was the English composer Ernest Austin (b. London, Dec. 31, 1874; d. Wallington, Surrey, July 24, 1947). He studied with Charles Lunn. After working as an organist and music teacher in Liverpool, he appeared as a singer in London in 1902. In 1908 he made his debut at London's Covent Garden as Gunther in the English-language mounting of the *Ring* cycle. He subsequently was principal baritone of the Beecham Opera Co. In 1920 he prepared a new version of *The Beggar's Opera* for London, in which he scored notable success in the role of Peachum. He then brought out a new edition of its sequel, *Polly* (London, Dec. 30, 1922). After serving as artistic director of the British National Opera Co. in London (1924–29), he devoted himself to teaching voice.

Austin, Larry (Don), American composer and teacher; b. Duncan, Okla., Sept. 12, 1930. He was a student of Violet Archer at the Univ. of North Texas in Denton (B.M.E., 1951; M.M., 1952). After studies with Milhaud at Mills College in Oakland, California (summer, 1955), he pursued graduate training with Imbrie at the Univ. of Calif. at Berkeley (1955–58). He later studied electronic music at the San Francisco Tape Music Center (1965–66), and computer music at Stanford Univ. (summer, 1969) and the Mass. Inst. of Technology (summer, 1978). In 1958 he joined the faculty of the Univ. of Calif. at Davis, where he was director of its bands (1958–72), founder and codirector of its New Music Ensemble (1963–68), and a prof. (1970–72). In 1966 he also helped to found the unique and invaluable avant-garde music journal *Source*, which he ed. until it suspended publ. with its 13th issue in 1971. From 1972 to 1978 Austin was a prof. at the Univ. of South Florida in Tampa, where he was chairman of the music dept. (1972–73) and founder-director of the Systems Complex for the Studio and Performing Arts (1972–78). In 1978 he became a prof. at the Univ. of North Texas, where he was director of the electronic music center (1981–82) and founder-director of the Center for Experimental Music and Intermedia (1982–91). He was cofounder and president of the Consortium to Distribute Computer Music (from 1986) and president of the International Computer Music Assn. (1990–94). With T. Clark, he publ. the textbook *Learning to Compose: Modes, Materials, and Models of Musical Invention* (Dubuque, 1989). Most of Austin's compositions are for mixed media, in which theatrical, acoustical, and dynamic elements are wholly integrated. Among them are *Catalogo Voce*, mini-opera for Bass-Baritone, Tape, and Slides (1979), *Euphonia: A Tale of the Future*, opera for Soloists, Chorus, Chamber Orch., Digital Synthesizer, and Tape (1981–82), and *Euphonia 2344*, intermezzo for Voices and Computer Music on Tape (1988).

Austin, William W(eaver), American musicologist; b. Lawton, Okla., Jan. 18, 1920. He studied at Harvard Univ., obtaining his Ph.D. in 1951 with the diss. *Harmonic Rhythm in Twentieth-Century Music*. In 1947 he was appointed to the faculty of Cornell Univ., retiring in 1990. In 1961–62 he held a Guggenheim fellowship. Among his books is *Music in the 20th Century from Debussy through Stravinsky* (N.Y., 1966); he also ed. *New Looks at Italian Opera: Essays in Honor of Donald J. Grout* (Ithaca, N.Y., 1968).

Austral, Florence (real name, **Mary Wilson**), Australian soprano; b. Richmond, near Melbourne, April 26, 1892; d. Newcastle, New South Wales, May 15, 1968. She studied on a scholarship at the Melbourne Cons. (1914–18), and then completed her training with Sibella in New York. In 1921 she made her London concert debut, followed by her operatic debut there as Brünnhilde with the British National Opera Co. on May 16, 1922. She subsequently appeared as Aida and Isolde with the company. In 1924, 1929, and 1933 she again sang Brünnhilde in London, and returned there to sing at Sadler's Wells (1937–39). She also sang in Australia and the United States. For a time, she was married to the flutist John Amadio. Austral was admired as a Wagnerian.

Auteri Manzocchi, Salvatore, Italian composer; b. Palermo, Dec. 26, 1845; d. Parma, Feb. 21, 1924. He studied in Palermo with Platania, and with Mabellini in Florence. His first opera, *Marcellina*, was never performed; his 2d, *Dolores* (Florence, Feb. 23, 1875), enjoyed considerable success, as did *Stella* (Piacenza, May 22, 1880). His other operas are *Il Negriero* (Milan, 1878), *Il Conte di Gleichen* (Milan, 1887), *Graziella* (Milan, Oct. 23, 1894), and *Severo Torelli* (Bologna, April 25, 1903).

Avdeyeva, Larissa (Ivanovna), prominent Russian mezzo-soprano; b. Moscow, June 21, 1925. She studied at the Stanislavsky Opera Studio in Moscow. In 1947 she joined the Stanislavsky Music Theater there; in 1952 she became a member of Moscow's Bolshoi Theater, where she distinguished herself as an outstanding interpreter in operas by Tchaikovsky, Borodin, Mussorgsky, and Rimsky-Korsakov; she also made tours of Europe, the United States, and Japan. She was made a People's Artist of the R.S.F.S.R. in 1964. She married **Evgeny Svetlanov**.

Averkamp, Anton, Dutch choral conductor and composer; b. Willige Langerak, Feb. 18, 1861; d. Bussum, June 1, 1934. He studied with Daniel de Lange in Amsterdam, with Friedrich Kiel in Berlin, and with Rheinberger in Munich. In 1890 he founded the famous chorus Amsterdam A Cappella Coor, with which he traveled in Europe, presenting programs of early polyphonic music. He wrote an opera, *De Heidebloem*, which was not produced. He contributed numerous historical articles to music periodicals, and also publ. a manual for singers, *Uit mijn practijk* (Groningen, 1916), and the book *De Koordirigent* (1933).

Avidom (real name, **Kalkstein**), **Menahem,** prominent Polish-born Israeli composer and administrator; b. Stanislawow, Jan. 6, 1908; d. Herzliya, Aug. 5, 1995. He emigrated to Palestine in 1925. After taking courses in art and science at the American Univ. in Beirut (B.A., 1928), he went to Paris to study with Rabaud at the Cons. (1928–31). Following a sojourn in Alexandria, Egypt (1931–35), he settled in Tel Aviv as a teacher. From 1945 to 1952 he was secretary-general of the Israel Phil. He was director-general of ACUM (Soc. of Authors, Composers, and Music Publishers) of Israel from 1955 to 1980. From 1958 to 1972 he also was chairman of the Israel Composers League, of which he was elected honorary chairman for life in 1982. In 1961 he received the Israel State Prize for his opera *Alexandra*. In 1982 ACUM awarded him its prize for his life's work. In his extensive output, Avidom ranged widely stylistically. While he utilized folk modalities of the Middle East, he also embraced dodecaphony.

WORKS: DRAMATIC: *Alexandra*, opera (1952; Tel Aviv, Aug. 15, 1959); *In Every Generation*, opera (1955); *The Crook*, comic opera (1966–67; Tel Aviv, April 22, 1967); *The Farewell*, radiophonic opera (1969; broadcast Nov. 1971); *The Pearl and the Coral*, ballet (1972); *The Emperor's New Clothes*, comic opera (1976); *Yodfat's Cave*, musical drama (1977); *The Cave of Jotapata*, dramatic scene (1977); *The End of King Og*, children's opera (1979); *The First Sin*, satirical opera (1980).

d'Avossa, Giuseppe, Italian composer; b. Paola, Calabria, 1708; d. Naples, Jan. 9, 1796. He studied with Gaetano Greco and Francesco Durante in Naples, and later held the position of maestro di cappella at S. Maria Verticelli, Naples, and at Pesaro, where he also conducted the orch. of the municipal theater. He wrote 4 operas, the most popular being *La Pupilla* (Naples, Carnival 1763).

Avshalomov, Aaron, Russian-born American composer; b. Nikolayevsk, Siberia, Nov. 11, 1894; d. N.Y., April 26, 1965. He was the father of the Russian-born American conductor, teacher, and composer Jacob (David) Avshalomov (b. Tsingtao, China, March 28, 1919). He studied at the Zürich Cons. In 1914 he went to China, where he wrote a number of works on Chinese subjects, making use of authentic Chinese themes. On April 24, 1925, he conducted the first performance in Beijing of his first opera, on a Chinese subject, *Kuan Yin*; his 2d opera, also on a Chinese subject, *The Great Wall*, was staged in Shanghai on Nov. 26, 1945, as were *The Soul of the Ch'in*, ballet (May 21, 1933), *Incense Shadows*, pantomime (March 13, 1935), and *Buddha and the 5 Planetary Deities*, choreographic tableau (April 18, 1942). In 1947 Avshalomov went to America, where he continued to compose works in large forms.

Azkué (Aberasturi), Resurrección María de, Spanish composer and musicologist; b. Lequeitio, Aug. 5, 1864; d. Bilbao, Nov. 9, 1951. He studied theology in Spain, then went to Paris and studied music at the Schola Cantorum. He wrote 2 operas to Basque texts: *Ortzuri* (Bilbao, 1911) and *Urlo* (Bilbao, 1913), and several zarzuelas. He publ. a valuable collection, *Cancionero popular Vasco* (11 vols.), and *Literatura popular del País Vasco* (4 vols., the last containing musical examples).

Aznavour, Charles (real name, **Varenagh Aznavurian**), French chansonnier; b. Paris, May 22, 1924. A son of an Armenian baritone from Tiflis, he received early music training at home, acted in Paris variety shows at the age of 5, and learned to play the guitar. He made several American tours as a nightclub entertainer with a valuable French accent; he also acted in films. He composed a great number of songs, of the genre of "tristesse chansons" and frustration ballads, among them the popular *On ne sait jamais, Comme des étrangers*, and *Ce jour tant attendu*. His operetta *Monsieur Carnaval* was performed in Paris on Dec. 17, 1965. He wrote an autobiography, *Aznavour par Aznavour* (Paris, 1970; Eng. tr., 1972).

B

Babayev, Andrei, Russian composer; b. Azerbaijan, Dec. 27, 1923; d. Moscow, Oct. 21, 1964. He studied in Baku where he played native instruments; he then entered the Baku Cons., where he was a student in composition of Gadzhibekov and Karayev, graduating in 1950; he later took advanced courses with Shaporin at the Moscow Cons. His music is inspired mainly by Armenian folk melodies; he also arranged songs of Central Asia and India. Among his works is the opera *Eagles' Bastion* (1957).

Babbi, (Pietro Giovanni) Cristoforo (Bartolomeo Gasparre), Italian violinist and composer, son of **Gregorio (Lorenzo) Babbi**; b. Cesena, May 6, 1745; d. Dresden, Nov. 19, 1814. He studied violin, counterpoint, and composition with Paolo Alberghi in Faenza; subsequently was primo violino at the festas there (1766, 1769, 1770, 1772) and also played in the orch. of the Rimini Opera (1773). In 1774 he was elected a member of the Accademia Filarmonica of Bologna, then was maestro di cappella at the Teatro Comunale there (1775–78). In 1779 he became primo violino and direttore d'orchestra in Forli. He was called to Dresden in 1781 as provisional Konzertmeister, receiving a permanent appointment in 1782, and proceeded to reorganize the Kapelle. He held an equal place with J. G. Naumann, the Dresden Kapellmeister. He composed operas.

Babbi, Gregorio (Lorenzo), famous Italian tenor, father of **(Pietro Giovanni) Cristoforo (Bartolomeo Gasparre) Babbi**; b. Cesena, Nov. 16, 1708; d. there, Jan. 2, 1768. He made his operatic debut in Florence in 1730. In 1741 he entered the service of Charles III, king of Naples, and in 1748 he was engaged by the Teatro San Carlo of Naples, where his wife, Giovanna Guaetta, was also a singer. He was pensioned in 1759.

Babini, Matteo, famous Italian tenor; b. Bologna, Feb. 19, 1754; d. there, Sept. 22, 1816. He studied with Cortoni, making his debut in 1780. He then toured England, Russia, Germany, and Austria with great acclaim. He settled in Paris as a court favorite until the Revolution forced him to leave France; he was in Berlin in 1792 and in Trieste in 1796. Brighenti publ. an "Elogio" in his memory (Bologna, 1821).

Bacarisse, Salvador, Spanish composer; b. Madrid, Sept. 12, 1898; d. Paris, Aug. 5, 1963. He studied at the Madrid Cons. with Conrado del Campo; he received the Premio Nacional de Música in 1923, 1930, and 1934. During the Spanish Civil War, he was active in the music section of the loyalist army; after its defeat in 1939, he settled in Paris. He wrote the operas *Charlot* (1933), *El Tesoro de Boabdil* (1958), and *Fuenteovejuna* (1962).

BIBL.: C. Heine, *S. B. (1898–1963): Die Kriterien seines Stils während der Schaffenszeit in Spanien (bis 1939)* (Frankfurt am Main, 1993).

Baccaloni, Salvatore, noted Italian bass; b. Rome, April 14, 1900; d. N.Y., Dec. 31, 1969. He began his training at the Sistine Chapel choir school at the Vatican, and then studied with Giuseppe Kaschmann. In 1922 he made his operatic debut as Rossini's Bartolo at the Teatro Adriano in Rome; from 1926 to 1940 he sang at Milan's La Scala, where he was esteemed in buffo roles. In 1928 he made his debut at London's Covent Garden as Puccini's Timur, and in 1930 his U.S. debut at the Chicago Civic Opera as Verdi's Melitone. From 1931 to 1941 he appeared at the Teatro Colón in Buenos Aires, and from 1936 to 1939 at the Glyndebourne Festival. On Dec. 3, 1940, he made his first appearance with the Metropolitan Opera as Mozart's Bartolo during the company's visit to Philadelphia; then sang for the first time on the Metropolitan stage in New York in the same role on Dec. 7, 1940, and subsequently was its leading buffo artist until 1962; his farewell appearance with the company was as Rossini's Bartolo in Brookville, N.Y., on Aug. 8, 1965. Baccaloni was the foremost comic bass of his generation. Among his memorable roles were Don Pasquale, Osmin, Leporello, Dulcamara, Varlaam, and Gianni Schicchi.

Bacewicz, Grażyna, notable Polish composer and violinist; b. Łódź, Feb. 5, 1909; d. Warsaw, Jan. 17, 1969. She learned to play the violin in her youth in Łódź, and began to compose at age 13.

She then was a student of Józef Jarzębski (violin), Józef Turczýnski (piano), and Sikorski (composition) at the Warsaw Cons., graduating in 1932. She also studied philosophy at the Univ. of Warsaw. A scholarship from Paderewski enabled her to study violin with André Touret and composition with Boulanger at the École Normale de Musique in Paris (1932–33). After teaching at the Łódź Cons. (1933–34), she returned to Paris to study violin with Flesch. In 1935 she received honorable mention at the 1st Wieniawski violin competition in Warsaw, and then played in the Polish Radio Sym. Orch. there (1936–38). From 1945 to 1955 she was active as a concert violinist. From 1966 until her death, she taught at the Warsaw State College of Music. In 1949 she won the Warsaw Prize, and in 1950 and 1952 the National Prize for composition. Bacewicz's large catalog of works generally adhered to neo-Classical principles. After the rise of the new Polish school of composition, she pursued more adventuresome paths.

WORKS: DRAMATIC: *Z chopa król* (The Peasant King), ballet (1953); *Przygody króla Artura* (The Adventures of King Arthur), radio comic opera (1959); *Esik w Ostendzie* (Esik in Ostend), ballet (1964); *Pożądanie* (Desire), ballet (1968); incidental music.

BIBL.: J. Rosen, *G. B.: Her Life and Works* (Los Angeles, 1984); S. Shafer, *The Contribution of G. B. (1909–1969) to Polish Music* (Lewiston, N.Y., 1992).

Bach (real name, **Bak**), **Albert,** Hungarian singer; b. Gyula, March 24, 1844; d. Edinburgh, Nov. 19, 1912. He studied at the Vienna Cons., giving his first concert there in 1871; continued his studies in Italy. He sang opera in Italy, Russia, Germany, and England. In his recitals he always performed Loewe's songs. He was a member of the Loewe-Verein in Berlin and ed. 3 vols. of Loewe's ballades with Eng. trs.; he also publ. several papers on music.

Bach, Jan (Morris), American composer and teacher; b. Forrest, Ill., Dec. 11, 1937. He pursued composition studies with Gaburo and Kelly at the Univ. of Illinois (B.M., 1959; D.M.A., 1971); also took courses with Copland (becoming cowinner of the Koussevitzky prize at the Berkshire Music Center in Tanglewood, 1961), Gerhard, and Musgrave. From 1966 he taught theory and composition at Northern Illinois Univ. in De Kalb. In his compositions, Bach effectively combines traditional and contemporary elements in an accessible style. He composed the operas *The System* (1973; N.Y., March 5, 1974) and *The Student from Salamanca*, opera (1979; N.Y., Oct. 9, 1980) and *Romeo and Juliet*, incidental music (1984).

Bach, Johann (John) Christian (the "London" Bach), esteemed German composer; b. Leipzig, Sept. 5, 1735; d. London, Jan. 1, 1782. He was the 11th and youngest surviving son of Johann Sebastian Bach (b. Eisenach, March 21 [baptized, March 23], 1685; d. Leipzig, July 28, 1750). He received early instruction in music from his father, after whose death in 1750 he went to Berlin to study with his brother Carl Philipp Emanuel. In 1754 he went to Italy, where he continued his studies with Padre Martini; he also found a patron in Count Agostino Litta of Milan. He converted to the Roman Catholic faith in order to be able to obtain work, and became one of the organists at the Cathedral in Milan (1760–62); he also traveled throughout the country and composed several successful operas during his stay in Italy. In 1762 he went to England; his highly acclaimed opera *Orione* was given its premiere in London on Feb. 19, 1763; in 1764 he was appointed music master to the Queen. From 1764 to 1781 he gave, together with C. F. Abel, a series of London concerts. When child Mozart was taken to London in 1764, J. C. Bach took great interest in him and improvised with him at the keyboard; Mozart retained a lifelong affection for him; he used 3 of J. C. Bach's piano sonatas as thematic material for his piano concertos. J. C. Bach was a highly prolific composer; he adopted the style galant of the 2d half of the 18th century, with an emphasis on expressive "affects" and brilliance of instrumental display. He thus totally departed from the ideals of his father, and became historically a precursor of the Classical era as exemplified by the works of Mozart. Although he was known mainly as an instrumental composer, J. C. Bach's operas, most of them to Italian librettos, were quite successful; among them were *Artaserse* (Turin, Dec. 26, 1760), *Catone in Utica* (Naples, Nov. 4, 1761), *Alessandro nell' Indie* (Naples, Jan. 20, 1762), *Orione, ossia Diana vendicata* (London, Feb. 19, 1763), *Zanaida* (London, May 7, 1763), *Adriano in Siria* (London, Jan. 26, 1765), *Carattaco* (London, Feb. 14, 1767), *Temistocle* (Mannheim, Nov. 4, 1772), *Lucio Silla* (Mannheim, Nov. 4, 1774), *La clemenza di Scipione* (London, April 4, 1778), and *Amadis de Gaule* (Paris, Dec. 14, 1779). See E. Warburton, general ed., *J. C. B., 1735–1782: The Collected Works* (48 vols., N.Y., 1988–90).

BIBL.: M. Schwarz, *J. C. B.: Sein Leben und seine Werke* (Leipzig, 1901); C. Terry, *John C. B.* (London, 1929; 2d ed. by H. C. Robbins Landon, 1967); A. Wenk, *Beiträge zur Kenntnis des Opernschaffens von J. C. B.* (diss., Univ. of Frankfurt am Main, 1932); K. Geiringer, *The Bach Family: Seven Generations of Creative Genius* (N.Y., 1954); R. Seebandt, *Arientypen J. C. B.s* (diss., Humboldt Univ., Berlin, 1956); E. Downes, *The Operas of J. C. B. as a Reflection of the Dominant Trends in Opera Seria 1750–1780* (diss., Harvard Univ., 1958); E. Warburton, *A Study of J. C. B.'s Operas* (diss., Univ. of Oxford, 1969); H. Gärtner, *J. C. B.: Mozart's Friend and Mentor* (Portland, Oreg., 1994).

Bach, Leonhard Emil, German pianist and composer; b. Posen, March 11, 1849; d. London, Feb. 15, 1902. He studied with T. Kullak (piano) and with Kiel (theory); in 1869 he became a teacher at Kullak's Academy in Berlin. He settled in London, and from 1882 taught at the Guildhall School of Music. He wrote several short operas, which were fairly successful at their premieres: *Irmengard* (London, 1892), *The Lady of Longford* (London, 1894), and *Des Königs Garde* (Cologne, 1895).

Bachelet, Alfred, French composer; b. Paris, Feb. 26, 1864; d. Nancy, Feb. 10, 1944. He studied at the Paris Cons.; received the Grand Prix de Rome for his cantata, *Cléopâtre* (1890). From his earliest works, Bachelet devoted himself mainly to opera. In his youth, he was influenced by Wagnerian ideas, but later adopted a more national French style. During World War I, he conducted at the Paris Opéra; in 1919 he became director of the Nancy Cons.; in 1939 he was elected a member of the Académie des Beaux Arts. He composed the lyric dramas *Scémo* (Paris, May 6, 1914) and *Un Jardin sur l'Oronte* (Paris, Nov. 3, 1932), the music drama *Quand la cloche sonnera* (Paris, Nov. 6, 1922), and the ballets *La Fête chez la Pouplinière* and *Castor et Pollux* by Rameau (adapted and rewritten).

Bachrich, Sigmund (real name, **Sigismund**), Hungarian violist and composer; b. Zsambokreth, Jan. 23, 1841; d. Vienna, July 16, 1913. He studied violin in Vienna. He spent several years in Paris, where he was viola player with the Hellmesberger and Rosé quartets. From 1869 to 1899 he was a member of the viola section in the Vienna Phil. He wrote several operas, among them *Muzzedin* (1883), *Heini von Steier* (1884), and *Der Fuchs-Major* (1889), as well as a ballet, *Sakuntala*. His memoirs were publ. posthumously under the title *Aus verklungenen Zeiten* (Vienna, 1914). In his professional activities he adopted Sigmund as his first name.

Bacilly, Bénigne de, French composer and teacher; b. c.1625; d. Paris, Sept. 27, 1690. He composed a number of sacred and secular vocal works, but became best known for an important vocal treatise, *Remarques curieuses sur l'art de bien chanter* (Paris, 1668; Eng. ed., 1968).

Bäck, Sven-Erik, significant Swedish composer; b. Stockholm, Sept. 16, 1919; d. there, Jan. 10, 1994. He studied violin at the Stockholm Musikhögskolan (1938–43) and also had training in composition from Rosenberg in Stockholm (1940–45) before pursuing studies in early music with Ina Lohr and Wenzinger at the Basel Schola Cantorum (1948–50). He later had advanced composition studies with Petrassi in Rome (1951–52). He played violin in the Kyndel (1940–44) and Barkel (1944–53) string quartets, as well as in the Lilla Chamber Orch. (1943–48). After conducting the "Chamber Orch. '53" (1953–57), he was director of the Swedish Radio music school at Edsberg Castle outside

Stockholm (from 1959). In 1961 he was elected to membership in the Royal Academy of Music in Stockholm. In his compositions, Bäck experimented with serialism and, later, electronic sound. His liturgical works are particularly notable.

WORKS: DRAMATIC: OPERAS: *Tranfjädrarna* (The Twilight Crane), a symbolist subject from Japanese Noh drama (1956; Swedish Radio, Feb. 28, 1957; 1st stage perf., Stockholm, Feb. 19, 1958); *Ett spel om Maria, Jesu Moder* (A Play about Mary, Mother of Jesus; Swedish Radio, April 4, 1958); *Gästabudet* (The Feast; Stockholm, Nov. 12, 1958); *Fågeln* (The Birds; 1960; Swedish Radio, Feb. 14, 1961). BALLETS: *Ikaros* (Stockholm, May 1963); *Movements* (Swedish TV, Feb. 27, 1966); *Kattresan* (Cat's Journey; 1969); *Mur och Port* (Wall and Gate; 1970; Stockholm, Jan. 17, 1971); *Genom Jorden, Genom Havet* (Through the Earth, Through the Sea; 1971–72; Stockholm, June 17, 1972).

Bacon, Ernst, remarkable American composer; b. Chicago, May 26, 1898; d. Orinda, Calif., March 16, 1990. He studied theory at Northwestern Univ. with P. C. Lutkin (1915–18), and later at the Univ. of Chicago with Arne Oldberg and T. Otterstroem (1919–20); also took private piano lessons in Chicago with Alexander Raab (1916–21). In 1924 he went to Vienna, where he took private composition lessons with Karl Weigl and Franz Schmidt. Returning to America, he studied composition with Ernest Bloch in San Francisco, and conducting with Eugene Goossens in Rochester, N.Y.; he completed his education at the Univ. of Calif. (M.A., 1935). From 1934 to 1937 he was supervisor of the Federal Music Project in San Francisco; he simultaneously deployed numerous related activities, as a conductor and a music critic. He was on the faculty of Converse College in South Carolina (1938–45) and Syracuse Univ. (1945–63). In 1939 and 1942 he held Guggenheim fellowships. He also engaged in literary pursuits—wrote poetry and publ. a book of aphorisms—and espoused radical politics. A musician of exceptional inventive powers, he publ. a brochure, *Our Musical Idiom* (Chicago, 1917), when he was 19; in it he outlines the new resources of musical composition. He later publ. *Words on Music* (1960) and *Notes on the Piano* (1963). In some of his piano works, he evolved a beguiling technique of mirror reflection between right and left hands, exact as to the intervals, with white and black keys in 1 hand reflected respectively by white and black keys in the other. However, Bacon is generally regarded as primarily a composer of lyric songs.

WORKS: DRAMATIC: *Take Your Choice* (San Francisco, 1936; in collaboration with P. Mathias and R. Stoll); *A Tree on the Plains*, musical play (Spartanburg, S.C., May 2, 1942); *A Drumlin Legend*, folk opera (N.Y., May 4, 1949); *Dr. Franklin*, musical play (1976). BALLETS: *Jehovah and the Ark* (1968–70); *The Parliament of Fowls* (1975).

Bacquier, Gabriel (-Augustin-Raymond-Théodore-Louis), noted French baritone; b. Béziers, May 17, 1924. He studied at the Paris Cons., winning 3 premiers prix. In 1950 he made his debut in Landowski's *Le Fou* in Nice with José Beckman's Compagnie Lyrique, and remained with the company until 1952; he then sang at the Théâtre Royal de la Monnaie in Brussels (1953–56). He was a member of the Opéra Comique (1956–58) and the Opéra (from 1958) in Paris. In 1962 he made his U.S. debut as the high priest in *Samson et Dalila* in Chicago; in 1964 he first appeared at London's Covent Garden; on Oct. 17, 1964, he made his Metropolitan Opera debut in New York as the aforementioned High Priest, and continued to sing there until 1982. In 1987 he became a teacher at the Paris Cons. He was made a Chevalier of the Légion d'honneur in 1975. He was equally at home in both dramatic and comic roles, numbering among his most esteemed portrayals Leporello, Dr. Bartolo, Dulcamara, Boccanegra, Falstaff, Golaud, and Scarpia.

Badescu, Dinu (Constantin), Romanian tenor; b. Craiova, Oct. 17, 1904. He studied in Bucharest. He made his operatic debut as a baritone in 1931 in Cluj as Germont, returning later that year to make his tenor debut as Lionel in *Martha*. He was a leading member of the Bucharest Opera (1936–61); he also sang at the Vienna Volksoper (1941–44) and at the Vienna State Opera (from 1948); he was highly successful as a guest artist with the Bolshoi Theater in Moscow, in Leningrad, Budapest, Prague, et al., making a specialty of lyrico-dramatic roles in Verdi's operas.

Badia, Carlo Agostino, Italian composer; b. probably in Venice, 1672; d. Vienna, Sept. 23, 1738. His first known work was his oratorio *La sete di Cristo in croce* (Innsbruck, 1691); soon thereafter he was made a court composer at Innsbruck. In 1694 he was called to Vienna, where he became Musik-Compositeur of the Imperial Court, a post he held for the rest of his life. His first wife was Anna Maria Elisabetta Nonetti, a prominent singer at the Viennese court (d. 1726). Badia was an important composer in his day, producing some 25 works for the stage and about 40 oratorios.

WORKS: DRAMATIC: *La Ninfa Apollo* (1692); *Amor che vince lo sdegno, ovvero Olimpia placata* (Rome, Carnival 1692); *La Rosaura ovvero Amore figlio della gratitudine* (Innsbruck, 1692); *L'Amazone corsara, ovvero L'Alvilda, regina de' Goti* (Innsbruck, 1692); *Bacco, vincitore dell'India* (Vienna, Carnival 1697); *La pace tra i numi discordi nella rovina di Troia* (Vienna, May 21, 1697); *L'idea del felice governo* (Vienna, June 9, 1698); *Lo squittinio dell'eroe* (Vienna, July 26, 1698); *Imeneo trionfante* (Vienna, Feb. 28, 1699); *Il Narciso* (Vienna, June 9, 1699); *Il commun giubilo del mondo* (Vienna, July 26, 1699); *Cupido fuggitivo da Venere e ritrovato a' piedi della Sacra Reale Maestà d'Amalia* (Vienna, Carnival 1700); *Le gare dei beni* (Vienna, Feb. 21, 1700); *Diana rappacificata con Venere e con Amore* (Vienna, April 21, 1700); *La costanza d'Ulisse* (Vienna, June 9, 1700); *L'amore vuol somiglianza* (Vienna, Jan. 7, 1702); *L'Arianna* (Vienna, Feb. 21, 1702); *Il Telemacco, ovvero Il valore coronato* (Vienna, March 19, 1702); *La concordia della Virtù e della Fortuna* (Vienna, April 21, 1702); *Enea negli Elisi* (Vienna, July 26, 1702); *La Psiche* (Vienna, Feb. 21, 1703); Napoli ritornata ai Romani (Vienna, Oct. 1, 1707); *Ercole, vincitore di Gerione* (Vienna, Nov. 4, 1708); *Gli amori di Circe con Ulisse* (Dresden, June 20, 1709); *Il bel genio dell'Austria ed il Fato* (Vienna, Nov. 1723).

Badia, Conchita (Conxita), noted Spanish soprano; b. Barcelona, Nov. 14, 1897; d. there, May 2, 1975. She studied piano and voice with Granados; she also had lessons with Casals and Manuel de Falla. She made her debut in Barcelona as a concert singer in 1913 in the first performance of *Canciónes amatorias* by Granados, with the composer as piano accompanist. She subsequently devoted herself to concert appearances, excelling as an interpreter of Spanish and Latin American music; often appeared in performances with Casals and his orch. in Barcelona. In later years she taught voice in Barcelona, where her most famous pupil was Montserrat Caballé.

BIBL.: J. Alavedra, *Conxita B.: Una vida d'artista* (Barcelona, 1975).

Badings, Henk (Hendrik Herman), eminent Dutch composer and pedagogue; b. Bandung, Dutch East Indies, Jan. 17, 1907; d. Maarheeze, June 26, 1987. He was orphaned at an early age and taken to the Netherlands; studied mining engineering at the Delft Polytechnic Univ. before taking up composition without formal training; an early sym. was premiered by Mengelberg and the Concertgebouw Orch. in Amsterdam (July 6, 1930). After composition lessons with Willem Pijper (1930–31), he taught at the Rotterdam Cons. (1934–37), the Amsterdam Lyceum (1937–41), and the Royal Cons. of Music at The Hague (1941–45). In 1945 he was barred from professional activities as a cultural collaborator during the Nazi occupation of his homeland, but in 1947 he was permitted to resume his career. From 1961 to 1977 he taught at the Univ. of Utrecht musicological inst.; he was also a prof. of composition at the Stuttgart Hochschule für Musik (1966–72). Badings began his career as a composer in the Romantic vein. In his melodic foundation, he often employed the scale of alternating major and minor seconds. From 1950 he experimented with electronic sound and also adapted some of his works to the scale of 31 melodic divisions devised by the Dutch physicist Adriaan Fokker.

WORKS: OPERAS: *De Nachtwacht* (The Night Watch; 1942; Antwerp, May 13, 1950); *Liebesränke* (Love's Ruses; 1944–45; Hilversum, Jan. 6, 1948); *Orestes*, radio opera (Florence, Sept. 24, 1954); *Asterion*, radio opera (Johannesburg, April 11, 1958); *Salto mortale*, television chamber opera (Dutch TV, Eindhoven, June 19, 1959; first opera to be accompanied solely by electronic sound); *Martin Korda, D.P.* (Amsterdam, June 15, 1960). BALLETS FOR INSTRUMENTS: *Balletto Grottesco* for 2 Pianos (1939); *Orpheus und Eurydike* for Soloists, Chorus, and Orch. (Amsterdam, April 17, 1941); *Balletto Serioso* for Orch. or 2 Pianos (1955); *Balletto Notturno* for 2 Pianos (1975). BALLETS FOR ELECTRONIC SOUND: *Kain und Abel* (The Hague, June 21, 1958; first all-electronic sound ballet); *Evolutions* (Hannover, Sept. 28, 1958); *Der sechste Tag* (Innsbruck, Nov. 7, 1959); *Jungle* (Amsterdam, 1959); *The Woman of Andras* (Hannover, April 14, 1960); *Marionetten* (Salzburg, 1961).

BIBL.: P. Klemme, *Catalog of the Works of H. B., 1907–87* (Warren, Mich., 1993).

Badini, Ernesto, Italian baritone; b. San Colombano al Lambro, Sept. 14, 1876; d. Milan, July 6, 1937. He studied at the Milan Cons. and with Cesari. In 1895 he made his operatic debut as Rossini's Figaro in San Colombano al Lambro; he sang in many regional opera houses of Italy. In 1913 Toscanini chose him for the Verdi centennial celebrations in Parma, then invited him to Milan's La Scala, where he created Puccini's Gianni Schicchi (1922); he remained on its roster until 1931. He also appeared at Rome's Teatro Costanzi (1921) and London's Covent Garden (debut as Gianni Schicchi, 1924). In addition to buffo roles, Badini also sang a number of contemporary roles.

Baeyens, August, Belgian composer; b. Antwerp, June 5, 1895; d. there, July 17, 1966. He studied at the Royal Flemish Cons. in Antwerp. From 1911 he was a violist in Belgian orchs., and later served as director of the Royal Flemish Opera in Antwerp (1944–48; 1953–58). Despite his intimate association with the Flemish currents in the music of Belgium, he turned away from the dominant national direction and wrote music in a distinctly expressionistic style, rooted in a quasi-atonal chromaticism. He composed *De Dode Dichter*, ballet (1920), *De Liefde en de Kakatoes*, a "grotesque" (1928), *Coriolanus*, radio opera (1941), *De Ring van Gyges*, opera (1943), and *De Triomferende Min*, opera (1948).

Baggiani, Guido, Italian composer; b. Naples, March 4, 1932. He studied composition at the Accademia di Santa Cecilia in Rome; then attended courses given by Stockhausen in Cologne, which were crucial for his further development. In Rome he organized a group for propagandizing contemporary music with the meaningful name of Nuova Consonanza. In 1970 he was appointed prof. of composition at the Pesaro Cons. In 1972 he formed a group with the curious Italian-American name Gruppo Team Roma for performances of electronic music. His works include the opera *Perso per Perso* (Naples, Dec. 7, 1996).

Bahner, Gert, German conductor; b. Neuwiese, March 26, 1930. He was educated at the Leipzig Hochschule für Musik. In 1957 he made his debut at the Berlin Komische Oper; from 1958 to 1962 he was music director in Potsdam; then Generalmusikdirektor of Karl-Marx-Stadt (1962–65). In 1965 he became first conductor of the Berlin Komische Oper; in 1969 its music director. In 1973 he became music director of the Leipzig Opera. In 1983 he settled in (East) Berlin as an opera conductor; also taught at the Hochschule für Musik.

Bahr-Mildenburg, (Bellschau-Mildenburg), Anna (von), famous Austrian soprano; b. Vienna, Nov. 29, 1872; d. there, Jan. 27, 1947. She was a pupil of Rosa Papier in Vienna and Bernhard Pollini, director of the Hamburg Opera, who engaged her to make her operatic debut there as Brünnhilde in *Die Walküre* on Sept. 12, 1895. In 1897 she appeared as Kundry at the Bayreuth Festival, and subsequently sang there with distinction until 1914. From 1898 to 1917 she was a leading member of the Vienna Court Opera, where she continued to make guest appearances until 1921. In 1906, 1910, and 1913 she sang at London's Covent Garden. She was a prof. at the Munich Academy of Music (from 1921) and stage director at the Bavarian State Opera in Munich (1921–26). In 1930 she made her farewell operatic apperance as Klytemnestra in Augsburg. In 1909 she married the playwright Hermann Bahr, with whom she wrote *Bayreuth und das Wagner Theater* (Leipzig, 1910; Eng. tr., 1912); she also publ. her memoirs (Vienna and Berlin, 1921) and *Darstellung der Werke Richard Wagner aus dem Geiste der Dichtung und Musik* (Leipzig, 1936). She was one of the foremost Wagnerians of her day.

BIBL.: P. Stefan, *A. B.-M.* (Vienna, 1922).

Bailey, Norman (Stanley), English baritone; b. Birmingham, March 23, 1933. He received a B.Mus. degree from Rhodes Univ. in South Africa; then studied at the Vienna Academy of Music; his principal teachers there were Julius Patzak, Adolf Vogel, and Josef Witt. He made his operatic debut with the Vienna Chamber Opera in 1959 in *Cambiale di matrimonio*; was then a member of the Linz Landestheater (1960–63), the Wuppertal Opera (1963–64), the Deutsche Oper am Rhein in Düsseldorf (1964–67), and the Sadler's Wells Opera in London (1967–71). In 1969 he made his first appearance at London's Covent Garden, and that same year his debut at Bayreuth at Hans Sachs. On Oct. 23, 1976, he made his Metropolitan Opera debut in New York as Hans Sachs. In 1985 he sang in the premiere of Goehr's *Behold the Sun* in Duisburg. He appeared as Stromminger in *La Wally* at the Bregenz Festival in 1990. In 1996 he made his Glyndebourne Festival debut as Schigolch in *Lulu*. In 1977 he was made a Commander of the Order of the British Empire. He was particularly noted for his performances in Wagner's operas. In 1985 he married **Kristine Ciesinski**.

Baillie, Dame Isobel (Isabella), esteemed Scottish soprano; b. Hawick, Roxburghshire, March 9, 1895; d. Manchester, Sept. 24, 1983. She was a pupil of Sadler Fogg in Manchester and of Guglielmo Somma in Milan. In 1921 she made her concert debut in Manchester, and thereafter made numerous appearances as an oratorio and lieder artist in England. In 1933 she sang for the first time in the United States She taught at the Royal College of Music in London (1955–57), Cornell Univ. in Ithaca, N.Y. (1960–61), and the Manchester School of Music (from 1970). In 1951 she was made a Commander of the Order of the British Empire; in 1978 she was made a Dame Commander of the Order of the British Empire. She sang in hundreds of performances of *Messiah*, and was also noted for her championship of works by Elgar, Vaughan Williams, and Howells. Her autobiography was aptly titled *Never Sing Louder Than Lovely* (London, 1982).

Bainton, Edgar Leslie, English composer and pedagogue; b. London, Feb. 14, 1880; d. Sydney, Australia, Dec. 8, 1956. He studied piano and composition at the Royal College of Music in London with Davies and Stanford. He taught piano and composition at the Cons. of Newcastle upon Tyne from 1901 until 1914, and also was its director (1912–14). The outbreak of World War I found him in Berlin, and he was interned as an enemy alien. After the end of the War, he resumed his pedagogical activities as director of the Newcastle Cons. In 1934 he went to Australia and was director of the State Cons. at Sydney until 1947. As a composer, he followed the tenets of the English national school, writing in broad diatonic expanses with a Romantic élan. His works include the operas *Oithona* (Glastonbury, Aug. 11, 1915) and *The Pearl Tree* (Sydney, May 20, 1944).

BIBL.: H. Bainton, *Remembered on Waking: E. L. B.* (Sydney, 1960).

Baird, Julianne, American soprano and teacher; b. Statesville, N.C., Dec. 10, 1952. She studied at the Eastman School of Music in Rochester, N.Y. (B.A. in music history, 1973, M.A. in musicology, 1976), with Harnoncourt at the Salzburg Mozarteum (diploma in performance practice, 1977), and with George Houle at Stanford Univ. (Ph.D., 1991, with the diss. *Johann Friedrich Agricola's Anleitung zur Singkunst (1757): A Translation and Commentary*; publ. 1995). She commenced her vocal career as a member of the Waverly Consort and Concert Royal in New York, where she made her operatic debut in Gluck's *Orfeo*. Following her solo debut with the N.Y. Phil. under Mehta's direction in 1983, she sang with many orchs. in the United States After singing in *The Fairy Queen* in Toronto in 1989, she appeared in the U.S. premiere of Handel's *Siroe* in New York in 1991. She also was a soloist in Bach's St. John Passion in London and sang in Handel's *Acis and Galatea* in Ottawa in the latter year. After singing in *Dido and Aeneas* in London in 1992, she toured France, Switzerland, and Poland in 1993 and Mexico in 1994. In 1995 she sang in recital at N.Y.'s Merkin Hall. She portrayed Handel's Galatea at N.Y.'s Lincoln Center in 1996. In 1998 she was engaged to sing in that composer's *Apollo and Dafne* in Portland, Oregon. As a teacher, Baird gave master classes in various locales and served on the faculty of Rutgers Univ. in Camden. Her fine vocal gifts are complemented by her expert knowledge of the early music repertoire in which she has excelled. She is especially admired for her performances of works by Monteverdi, Charpentier, Bach, Handel, Purcell, and Telemann.

Baird, Martha, American pianist and music patroness; b. Madera, Calif., March 15, 1895; d. N.Y., Jan. 24, 1971. She studied at the New England Cons. of Music in Boston and with Artur Schnabel in Berlin; appeared as soloist with Beecham in London and Koussevitzky in Boston. In 1957 she married John D. Rockefeller Jr. and became a benefactress of opera and concert music.

Baird, Tadeusz, prominent Polish composer; b. Grodzisk Mazowiecki, July 26, 1928; d. Warsaw, Sept. 2, 1981. He studied music privately in Łódź with Sikorski and Woytowicz (1943–44), then at the Warsaw Cons. with Rytel and Perkowski (1947–51); had piano lessons with Wituski (1948–51); he also studied musicology with Lissa at the Univ. of Warsaw (1948–52). In 1949, together with Krenz and Serocki, he founded a progressive society of composers under the name Group 49. In 1956 he became active in initiating the 1st International Festival of Contemporary Music, during the "Warsaw Autumn." In 1977 he was appointed prof. of composition at the Chopin Academy of Music in Warsaw. As a composer, Baird won numerous awards, among them the Fitelberg Competition of 1958, 3 prizes of the Tribune Internationale des Compositeurs in Paris (1959, 1963, 1966), and the Polish State Awards for his 3 syms. (1951, 1964, 1969). He also was awarded the Commander's Cross of the Order of Poland's Revival (1964) and the Order of the Banner of Labor, 2d and 1st Class (1974, 1981). His early music followed the neo-Romantic modalities characteristic of Polish music; further evolution was marked by complex structures in the manner of dynamic expressionism, with occasional applications of serialism. His catalog of works includes the opera *Jutro* (Tomorrow; 1964–66).

BIBL.: T. Zielinski, *T. B.* (Kraków, 1966).

Bakala, Břetislav, Czech conductor and composer; b. Fryšták, Feb. 12, 1897; d. Brno, April 1, 1958. He studied with Kurz (piano), Neumann (conducting), and Janáček (composition) at the Brno Cons. He was chief conductor of the Opera (1929–31), the Radio Sym. Orch. (1937–56), and the State Phil. (1956–58) in Brno, where he also taught conducting at the Janáček Academy of Music (1951–58). Bakala championed the music of Janáček.

Baker, Dame Janet (Abbott), celebrated English mezzo-soprano; b. Hatfield, Yorkshire, Aug. 21, 1933. Her parents were music-lovers and she grew up in an artistic atmosphere. She was a student of Hélène Isepp and Meriel St. Clair in London. She began her career singing in the Leeds Phil. Choir, with which she made her debut as a soloist in Haydn's *Lord Nelson Mass* in 1953. In 1955 she became a member of the Ambrosian Singers. In 1956 she won 2d prize in the Kathleen Ferrier Competition, making her operatic debut as Roza in Smetana's *The Secret* with the Univ. of Oxford Opera Club. In 1959 she was awarded the Queen's Prize and began to sing major roles with the Handel Opera Soc. From 1962 she also appeared at the Aldeburgh Festival. In 1964 she toured Russia as Lucretia with the English Opera Group. In 1966 she made her debut at London's Covet Garden as Hermia in Britten's *A Midsummer Night's Dream*, her U.S. debut as soloist in Mahler's *Das Lied von der Erde* with the San Francisco Sym., and her N.Y. recital debut. In 1967 she appeared as Dorabella with Glasgow's Scottish Opera, returning there as Berlioz's Dido in 1969, Strauss's Octavian in 1971 and Composer in 1975, and Gluck's Orfeo in 1979. In 1970 she sang Diana in *La Calisto* at Glyndebourne, returning there as Penelope in *Il ritorno d'Ulisse in patria* in 1972. On May 16, 1971, she created the role of Kate in Britten's *Owen Wingrave* on BBC-TV, a role she sang again at the work's premiere staging at Covent Garden in 1973. In 1971 she appeared as Monteverdi's Poppea with the Sadler's Wells Opera in London, returning there as Donizetti's Mary Stuart in 1973 and with its successor, the English National Opera, as Massenet's Charlotte in 1977. She sang in concert with Abbado and the London Sym. Orch. at the Salzburg Festival in 1973. In 1982 she retired from the operatic stage singing Gluck's Orfeo at Glyndebourne, although as late as 1989 she appeared in a concert performance of the role in New York From 1983 to 1991 she was president of the Scottish Academy of Music and Drama in Glasgow. She was chancellor of the Univ. of York from 1991. She publ. the autobiographical vol. *Full Circle* (London, 1982). In 1970 she was made a Commander of the Order of the British Empire. She was made a Dame Commander of the Order of the British Empire in 1976. In 1990 she was awarded the Gold Medal of the Royal Phil. Soc. of London, and in 1994 she was made a Companion of Honour. Baker was one of the outstanding singers of her era. In addition to her expansive operatic repertoire, she won great renown as a concert artist in a repertoire of Lieder, English and French songs, and oratorio. She was especially distinguished in her performances of Schubert, Schumann, and Mahler.

BIBL.: A. Blyth, *J. B.* (London, 1973).

Baklanov (real name, **Bakkis**), **Georgy (Andreievich),** esteemed Latvian baritone; b. Riga, Jan. 17, 1881; d. Basel, Dec. 6, 1938. He studied at the Kiev Cons. and with Vanya in Milan. In 1903 he made his operatic debut in Kiev as A. Rubinstein's Demon; after singing at Moscow's Bolshoi Theater and in St. Petersburg (1905–09), he appeared throughout Europe. On Nov. 8, 1909, he made his U.S. debut as Barnaba in *La Gioconda* in the first performance at the Boston Opera House, where he sang with notable success until 1911 and again from 1915 to 1917. On Feb. 16, 1910, he made his only appearance with the Metropolitan Opera as Rigoletto during the company's visit to Baltimore. From 1917 to 1926 he was a member of the Chicago Opera. He later was a principal artist of the Russian Opera Co. of N.Y. In addition to Rigoletto, Baklanov was also highly praised for his portrayals of Prince Igor, Boris Godunov, Méphistophélès, and Scarpia.

Balada, Leonardo, Spanish composer and teacher; b. Barcelona, Sept. 22, 1933. He was early on apprenticed to his father's tailoring shop in Barcelona, but after piano training at the Cons. there, he went to New York and pursued studies at the N.Y. College of Music (1956–57), the Juilliard School of Music (1958–60), and the Mannes College of Music (1961–62). His principal mentors in composition were Copland, Tansman, and Persichetti. He also studied conducting in Paris with Markevitch. He eked out a living by working at odd jobs in the garment district in New York; subsequently he obtained a teaching position at the United Nations International School (1963–70), and then joined the faculty of Carnegie-Mellon Univ. in Pittsburgh in 1970, where he served as a prof. from 1975. In his works, Balada has utilized both constructionist and expressionist elements. He composed the operas *Hangman, Hangman!* (Barcelona, Oct. 10, 1982), *Zapata!* (1982), *Cristóbal Colón* (1987; Barcelona, Sept. 24, 1989), and *Death of Columbus* (1994).

Balanchivadze, Meliton (Antonovich), noted Russian composer; b. Banodzha, Dec. 24, 1862; d. Kutaisi, Nov. 21, 1937. He was the father of the celebrated Russian-American choreographer George Balanchine (b. St. Petersburg, Jan. 22, 1904; d. N.Y., April 30, 1983) and the Russian composer Andrei Balanchivadze (b. St. Petersburg, June 1, 1906). He was educated in the ecclesiastical seminary in Tiflis, where he sang in a chorus. In 1880 he became a member of the local opera theater; in 1882 he organized a chorus and arranged Georgian folk songs. In 1889 he went to St. Petersburg, where he took voice lessons, and in 1891 entered Rimsky-Korsakov's class in composition. In 1895 he organized a series of choral concerts of Georgian music. After the Revolution he returned to Georgia, where he continued his work of ethnic research. He composed a national Georgian opera, *Tamara the Treacherous* (1897).

BIBL.: P. Khuchua, *M. B.* (Tbilisi, 1964).

Balart, Gabriel, Spanish composer; b. Barcelona, June 8, 1824; d. there, July 5, 1893. He studied at the Paris Cons. He composed various pieces of salon music, which enjoyed some success. In 1849 he went to Milan as a theater conductor, and in 1853 he was appointed music director of the Teatro del Liceo in Barcelona. For a time his light opera *Amor y Arte* enjoyed considerable success.

Balasanian, Sergei, Tadzhik composer; b. Ashkhabad, Aug. 26, 1902; d. Moscow, June 3, 1982. He studied at the Moscow Cons., graduating with a degree in music history in 1935. From 1936 to 1943 he was mainly active in Tadzhikistan; then was in charge of radio programming there. In 1948 he joined the faculty of the Moscow Cons.; was chairman of the composition dept. (1962–71). He was one of the founders of the national school of composition in Tadzhikistan; in his works, he made use of native folk motifs, in ingenious harmonic coloration. His works include the opera *The Revolt of Vose* (1939; rev. 1959), *The Blacksmith Kova* (1941), and *Bakhtyor and Nisso* (1954), and the ballets *Leyly and Medzhnun* (1947) and *Shakuntala* (1963).

Balassa, Sándor, Hungarian composer; b. Budapest, Jan. 20, 1935. He studied choral conducting at the Béla Bartók Music Secondary School (1952–56) and composition with Szervánszky at the Budapest Academy of Music (graduated, 1965). From 1964 to 1980 he was a music producer for the Hungarian Radio; then taught at the Budapest Academy of Music until 1996. In 1972 he was awarded the Erkel Prize, in 1983 the Kossuth Prize, and in 1988 the Bartók-Pásztory Award. In 1983 he was made a Merited Artist by the Hungarian government and was named an Outstanding Artist in 1989. He composed the operas *Az ajtón kívül* (The Man Outside; 1973–76) and *A harmadik bolygó* (The Third Planet; 1986–87).

Balbi, Melchiore, Italian theorist and composer; b. Venice, June 4, 1796; d. Padua, June 21, 1879. He was a pupil of Nini, Valeri, and Calegari in Padua. From 1818 to 1853 he was theater conductor in Padua, and from 1854 maestro di cappella at the Basilica San Antonio. He wrote 3 operas, all produced in Padua: *La notte perigliosa* (1820), *L'abitator del bosco* (1821), and *L'alloggio militare* (1825).

Baldwin, Dalton, American pianist; b. Summit, N.J., Dec. 19, 1931. He studied at the Juilliard School of Music in New York and at the Oberlin (Ohio) College-Cons. of Music; later pursued training with Boulanger and Madeleine Lipatti in Paris, and also received invaluable coaching from Sibelius, Poulenc, and others. He acquired a fine reputation as a discerning accompanist to such eminent singers as Gérard Souzay, Elly Ameling, Marilyn Horne, and Jessye Norman; he also gave master classes in the art of accompaniment in the United States and abroad.

Balfe, Michael William, notable Irish composer; b. Dublin, May 15, 1808; d. Rowney Abbey, Hertfordshire, Oct. 20, 1870. He was the son of a dancing master, and as a small child played the violin for his father's dancing classes. He subsequently took violin lessons with O'Rourke. After his father's death on Jan. 6, 1823, Balfe went to London, where he studied violin with Charles Edward Horn and composition with Carl Friedrich Horn. In 1824 he was engaged as a violinist at the Drury Lane Theatre; also sang in London and in the provinces. His patron, Count Mazzara, took him to Italy in 1825, where he took composition lessons with Federici in Milan and voice lessons with Filippo Galli and also produced his first ballet, *La Perouse* (1826). He met Rossini, who advised him to continue singing lessons with Bordogni; in 1828 he was engaged as principal baritone at the Italian Opera in Paris. In Italy he married the Hungarian vocalist Lina Rosa (b. 1808; d. London, June 8, 1888). Returning to England in 1833, he devoted himself to the management of opera houses and to composition. He was manager of the Lyceum Theatre during the 1841–42 season. He made London his principal residence, with occasional visits to Vienna (1846), Berlin (1848), St. Petersburg, and Trieste (1852–56). Apart from his administrative duties, he displayed great energy in composing operas, most of them to English librettos; of these, *The Bohemian Girl*, produced at the Drury Lane Theatre in London on Nov. 27, 1843, obtained an extraordinary success and became a perennial favorite on the English stage; it was also tr. into French, German, and Italian. In 1864 he retired to his country seat at Rowney Abbey. His daughter, Victoire, made her debut as a singer at the Lyceum Theatre in London in 1857.

WORKS: OPERAS: 3 early operas in Italian, *I rivali di se stessi* (Palermo, 1829), *Un avertimento ai gelosi* (Pavia, 1830), and *Enrico IV al Passo della Marna* (Milan, Feb. 19, 1833); in French, *L'étoile de Séville* (Paris Opéra, Dec. 17, 1845). The following operas were produced in English at Drury Lane and Covent Garden in London and other theaters: *The Siege of Rochelle* (Drury Lane, London, Oct. 29, 1835); *The Maid of Artois* (May 27, 1836); *Catherine Grey* (May 27, 1837); *Joan of Arc* (Nov. 30, 1837); *Diadeste, or The Veiled Lady* (May 17, 1838); *Falstaff* (in Italian, July 19, 1838); *Këolanthe, or The Unearthly Bride* (March 9, 1841); *Le Puits d'amour* (Opéra Comique, Paris, April 20, 1843; in Eng. as *Geraldine*, Princess's Theatre, London, Aug. 14, 1843); *The Bohemian Girl* (Drury Lane Theatre, London, Nov. 27, 1843); *Les Quatre Fils Aymon* (Opéra Comique, Paris, July 9, 1844; in Eng. as *The Castle of Aymon*, Princess's Theatre, London, Nov. 20, 1844); *The Daughter of St. Mark* (Nov. 27, 1844); *The Enchantress* (May 14, 1845); *The Bondman* (Dec. 11, 1846); *The Maid of Honour* (Dec. 20, 1847); *The Sicilian Bride* (March 6, 1852); *The Devil's in It* (July 26, 1852); *Moro, the Painter of Antwerp* (Jan. 28, 1882; orig. produced as *Pittore e duca*, Trieste, Nov. 21, 1854); *The Rose of Castille* (Oct. 29, 1857); *Satanella, or The Power of Love* (Dec. 20, 1858); *Bianca, or The Bravo's Bride* (Dec. 6, 1860); *The Puritan's Daughter* (Nov. 30, 1861); *Blanche de Nevers* (Nov. 21, 1863); *The Armourer of Nantes* (Feb. 12, 1863); *The Sleeping Queen*, operetta (Aug. 31, 1864); *The Knight of the Leopard* (Liverpool, Jan. 15, 1891; orig. produced in London as *Il talismano*, June 11, 1874).

BIBL.: W.A. Barrett, *B.: His Life and Work* (London, 1882); G. Biddlecombe, *English Opera From 1834 to 1864 With Particular Reference to the Works of M. B.* (N.Y., 1994).

Balkwill, Bryan (Havell), English conductor; b. London, July 2, 1922. He was educated at the Royal Academy of Music in London. He was an assistant conductor of the New London Opera Co. (1947–48) and assoc. conductor of the International Ballet Co. (1948–49); he then became music director of the London Festival Ballet (1950–52) and of Opera for All (1953–63); also conducted at the Glyndebourne Festival (1950–58), and in London at Covent Garden (from 1953) and at the Sadler's Wells Opera (from 1957). From 1959 to 1965 he was resident conductor at the Royal Opera, Covent Garden; then was music director of the Welsh National Opera in Cardiff (1963–67) and of the Sadler's Wells Opera (1966–69). He served as a prof. of music at the Indiana Univ. School of Music in Bloomington from 1978 to 1992.

Ball, Michael, English composer; b. Manchester, Nov. 10, 1946. He began composing at an early age, writing a children's opera when he was 11; in 1964 he entered the Royal College of Music in London, where he studied with Herbert Howells, Humphrey Searle, and John Lambert, and was awarded all of its major composition prizes; then completed his training with Donatoni in Siena (summers 1972–73), where he also attended the master classes of Luciano Berio and György Ligeti. He composed the chamber opera *The Belly Bag* (1992).

Ballard, Louis W(ayne), preeminent Native American composer and music educator; b. Devil's Promenade, Quapaw Indian Reservation, Okla., July 8, 1931. He is of distinguished Quapaw-Cherokee descent and was given the name Honganózhe (Grand

Eagle). In his youth, he was immersed in native American music but also received piano lessons at the local Baptist mission school. He later pursued an intensive study of the music of various native American tribes. He studied at the Univ. of Okla., and then at the Univ. of Tulsa, where he took B.M., B.M.E., and M.M. degrees. He also studied with Milhaud and Castelnuovo-Tedesco. From 1962 to 1969 he was an administrator with the Inst. of American Indian Arts in Santa Fe. From 1969 to 1979 he was in charge of the music curriculum of the U.S. Bureau of Indian Affairs school system. He also was chairman of minority concerns in music education for the state of New Mexico from 1976 to 1982. He publ. *My Music Reaches to the Sky* (1973) and *Music of North American Indians* (1975). In some of his compositions, he has used the name Joe Miami. In his music, Ballard combines native American elements with advanced Western compositional techniques.

WORKS: DRAMATIC: *Jijogweh, the Witch-water Gull*, ballet (1962); *Koshare*, ballet (1965; Barcelona, May 17, 1966); *The 4 Moons*, ballet commemorating the 60th anniversary of the statehood of Oklahoma (Tulsa, Oct. 28, 1967); *The Maid of the Mist and the Thunderbeings*, dance piece (Buffalo, Oct. 18, 1991; symphonic suite, Aptos, Calif., Aug. 8, 1993); *Moontide*, opera (1994).

Ballif, Claude (André François), French composer and pedagogue; b. Paris, May 22, 1924. After training at the Bordeaux Cons. (1942–48), he took courses with Tony Aubin, Noël Gallon, and Messiaen at the Paris Cons. (1948–51); he then studied with Blacher and Rufer at the Berlin Hochschule für Musik (1953–55), and also attended Scherchen's classes in Darmstadt. He was associated with the French Radio and Television in Paris (1959–63), and then was a prof. there at the École Normal de Musique (1963–65); after serving as a prof. at the Rheims Cons. (1964–71), he was prof. of analysis (1971–90) and assoc. prof. of composition (1982–90) at the Paris Cons.; he subsequently was prof. of composition at the Sevran Cons. (from 1990). In 1984 he was made a Commandeur des Arts et des Lettres. As a composer, Baliff has followed an independent course, developing a system he describes as metatonality, notable for its avoidance of the extremes of diatonicism and chromaticism.

WRITINGS: (all publ. in Paris): *Introduction à la métatonalité* (1956); *Berlioz* (1968); *Voyage de mon oreille* (1979); *économie musicale—Souhaits entre symboles* (1988).

WORKS: OPERAS: *Dracoula* (1982; rev. 1983; Paris, Sept. 19, 1984); *Il suffit d'un pue d'air* (1990; Montreal, Dec. 11, 1991).

BIBL.: M. Tosi, *C. B.* (Bezières, 1991).

Balmer, Luc, Swiss conductor and composer; b. Munich, July 13, 1898. He was the son of the painter Wilhelm Balmer. Following training with Hans Huber, Ernst Lévy, and Egon Petri at the Basel Cons. (1915–19), he attended Busoni's master class in composition at the Prussian Academy of Arts in Berlin (1921–22). He conducted the Kursaal in Lucerne (1928–32) and at the Zürich Opera (1932–35). Settling in Bern, he conducted at the Opera (1932–35), and then was conductor of the Orch. Assn. (1935–41) and the Music Soc. (1941–64); he also was on the staff of the Bern Radio (1938–68). In 1969 he was awarded the music prize of the City of Bern, and in 1986 the music prize of the Canton of Bern. His compositions, notable for their ludic craftsmanship, were in an accessible style. They include the opera *Die drei gefoppten Ehemänner* (1967–68).

Balsys, Eduardas, Lithuanian composer and teacher; b. Nikolayev, Dec. 20, 1919; d. Druskininkai, Nov. 3, 1984. He studied composition with Račiunas at the Lithuanian Cons. in Vilnius, graduating in 1950; then took music courses at the Leningrad Cons. (1953). In 1953 he joined the faculty of the Lithuanian Cons.; in 1960 he was appointed chairman of the composition dept. In his music, he adhered to classical forms but made experimental use of certain modern techniques, including dodecaphonic progressions. He composed the opera *The Journey to Tilže* (1980) and the ballet *Eglė žalči ų karalienė* (Egle, Queen of Grass Snakes; Vilnius, 1960; orch. suite, 1961; 4 fragments for Violin and Piano, 1963).

Baltsa, Agnes, prominent Greek mezzo-soprano; b. Lefkas, Nov. 19, 1944. She studied at the Athen Cons. and won the first Callas scholarship, then pursued her training in Munich and Frankfurt am Main. In 1968 she made her operatic debut as Cherubino at the Frankfurt am Main Opera, where she was a member until 1972. In 1970 she sang at the Deutsche Oper in Berlin, appeared as Octavian in Vienna, and made her debut at the Salzburg Festival as Bastien. Her U.S. debut followed in 1971 when she appeared as Carmen in Houston. In 1976 she sang for the first time at Milan's La Scala and London's Covent Garden as Dorabella, returning to Covent Garden in 1984 to portray Romeo in *I Capuleti e i Montecchi*. On Dec. 13, 1979, she made her Metropolitan Opera debut in New York as Octavian, returning to New York in 1987 as Carmen. In 1989 she sang Santuzza in Vienna, and returned there in 1993 as Azucena. Following an engagement as Elisabeth in *Maria Stuarda* in Barcelona in 1993, she sang Delilah in Zürich in 1996. She also pursued a fine concert career. Among her other roles of note were Rosina, Orpheus, Berlioz's Dido, and Strauss's Composer.

BIBL.: C. Baumann, *A. B.: Eine Bildmonographie* (Zürich, 1986).

Bamboschek, Giuseppe, Italian-American conductor; b. Trieste, June 12, 1890; d. N.Y., June 24, 1969. He studied at the Trieste Cons., graduating in 1907. In 1913 he went to the United States as accompanist for Pasquale Amato; in 1918 he joined the staff at the Metropolitan Opera in New York, specializing in the Italian repertoire. After 1929 he was active mainly as a conductor for radio and films.

Bampton, Rose (Elizabeth), American soprano; b. Cleveland, Nov. 28, 1909. She studied with Queena Mario at the Curtis Inst. of Music in Philadelphia; also took academic courses at Drake Univ. in Des Moines, Iowa, where she obtained a doctorate of fine arts. She sang as a contralto with the Philadelphia Opera (1929–32), then changed to mezzo-soprano and finally to soprano, so that she could sing the roles of both Amneris and Aida. She made her debut at the Metropolitan Opera in New York on Nov. 28, 1932, as Laura in *La Gioconda*, and continued on its staff until 1945 and again from 1947 to 1950. She made annual appearances at the Teatro Colón in Buenos Aires from 1942 to 1948; then returned to New York, where she taught voice at the Manhattan School of Music (1962–82) and at the Juilliard School (from 1974). She was married to **Wilfrid Pelletier**.

Banchieri, Adriano (Tomaso), eminent Italian organist and composer; b. Bologna, Sept. 3, 1568; d. there, 1634. He studied with Lucio Barbieri and Giuseppe Guami. On Sept. 8, 1589, he took Holy Orders and entered the monastery of Monte Oliveto. In 1592 he was at the monastery of S. Bartolomeo in Lucca and in 1593, in Siena; he was organist at S. Maria in Regola di Imola in 1600. In 1608 he returned to Bologna, remaining there until his death. Despite his clerical rank (he became abbot in 1620), Banchieri never abandoned music, and was active at the Accademia Filarmonica in Bologna (where he was known as "Il dissonante"). He wrote numerous stage works, historically important in the evolution of early opera. Among these dramatic works were *La pazzia senile* (1598), *Il zabaione musicale* (1604), *La barca da Venezia per Padova* (1605), *La prudenza giovanile* (1607), and *Tirsi, Filli e Clori* (1614). As a theorist, he advocated the extension of the hexachord and proposed to name the 7th degree of the scale by the syllables ba and bi (corresponding to B♭ and B). Banchieri's theoretical work *L'organo suonarino* (Venice, 1605) gives instructions for accompaniment with figured bass; his *Moderna prattica musicale* (Venice, 1613) contains further elaborations of the subject. Banchieri was the first to use the signs *f* and *p* for loudness and softness (in his *Libro III di nuovi pensieri ecclesiastici*, 1613). He also wrote dramatic plays under the name of Camillo Scaliggeri della Fratta. Banchieri further publ. the treatises *Cartella musicale del canto figurato, fermo e contrappunto* (Venice, 1614), *Direttorio monastico di canto fermo* (Bologna, 1615), and *Lettere armoniche* (Bologna, 1628).

BIBL.: O. Mischiati, *A. B.* (Bologna, 1972).

Bandrowska-Turska, Eva, Polish soprano; b. Kraków, May 20, 1897; d. Warsaw, June 25, 1979. She studied with her uncle, **Alexander Bandrowski-Sas**, then took further instruction with Helena Zboinska-Ruszkowska. She made her debut as a concert singer in 1919, and subsequently appeared in opera; in later years she gained distinction as a solo singer, excelling particularly as a congenial interpreter of the songs of Debussy, Ravel, Roussel, and Szymanowski.

BIBL.: Z. Bieske, *E. B.-T.: Wspomnienia artystki* (Warsaw, 1989).

Bandrowski-Sas, Alexander, noted Polish tenor; b. Lubaczów, April 22, 1860; d. Kraków, May 28, 1913. He made his stage debut as a baritone in an operetta production in Lemberg in 1881, using the name Barski. He then studied voice with Sangiovanni in Milan and Salvi in Vienna, and subsequently pursued a successful career as a tenor, using the name Brandt. He sang in Vienna (1890), Berlin (1896, 1898), and Dresden and Munich, and at La Scala in Milan (1896, 1899). From 1889 to 1901 he was a member of the Frankfurt am Main Opera, and also filled engagements in New York, Philadelphia, Chicago, and Boston. He retired from the stage in 1904, and then taught voice in Kraków. His niece was **Eva Bandrowska-Turska**.

Bank, Jacques, Dutch composer; b. Borne, April 18, 1943. He studied with Jos Kunst and Ton de Leeuw at the Amsterdam Cons., graduating in 1974. Apart from his musical activities, he taught English in Amsterdam schools. He composed the opera *Een Tanthologie* (1986–87).

Banister, John, English violinist and composer, father of **John Banister Jr.**; b. London, c.1625; d. there, Oct. 3, 1679. After he had received some musical instruction from his father, his skill earned him the patronage of King Charles II, who sent him to France for further study. He was later a member of Charles's band, until an outspoken preference for the English over the French musicians playing in it caused his expulsion. Banister was director of a music school, and established the first public concerts not associated with taverns or other gathering places in which music was of only incidental importance, in London (1672–78). He was a prominent figure in the English musical life of his day. He wrote music for Davenant's *Circe* and Shakespeare's *The Tempest* (both 1676) and also contributed to Playford's *Courtly Masquing Ayres* (1662) and to Lock's *Melothesia* (1673); also wrote music for plays by Dryden, Shadwell, and Wycherley.

Banister, John, Jr., English violinist and composer, son of **John Banister**; b. London, c.1663; d. there, c.1725. He studied violin with his father. He served as concertmaster at the Italian Opera in London. He composed mostly for the theater, and contributed to Playford's *Division Violin* (1685), the first violin manual publ. in England.

Banshchikov, Gennadi, Russian composer; b. Kazan, Nov. 9, 1943. He studied composition with Balasanian at the Moscow Cons. (1961–64) and with Arapov at the Leningrad Cons. (1965–66); in 1973 he was appointed to the faculty of the Leningrad Cons. In his works he adopts a fairly progressive, even aggressive, modern idiom, making occasional use of serial techniques.

WORKS: DRAMATIC: *The Legend Remained*, radio opera for children (1967); *Lyubov and Silin*, chamber opera (1968); *The Stolen Sun*, television opera (1969); *Vestris*, ballet (1969); *Opera about How Ivan Ivanovich Quarreled with Ivan Nikiforovich*, comic opera (1971); *The Death of Cornet Klauzov*, opera (1976).

Banti, Brigida (née **Giorgi**), famous Italian soprano; b. Monticelli d'Ongina, 1759; d. Bologna, Feb. 18, 1806. She sang in Paris cafés, where she attracted the attention of de Vismes, director of the Paris Opéra, who engaged her to sing there. She made her debut on Nov. 1, 1776, singing a song during the intermission. She then studied with Sacchini. In 1779 she went to London for a season, then sang in Vienna (1780), Venice (1782–83), Warsaw (1789), and Madrid (1793–94). Paisiello wrote for her his opera *Giuochi di Agrigento*, and she sang at its premiere (Venice, May 16, 1792). From 1794 to 1802 she sang at King's Theatre in London; then retired. She married the dancer Zaccaria Banti. Her son wrote her biography.

BIBL.: G. Banti, *Vita di B. B.-G.* (Bologna, 1869).

Bantock, Sir Granville, eminent English composer; b. London, Aug. 7, 1868; d. there, Oct. 16, 1946. He studied at the Royal Academy of Music in London, graduating in 1892; was the first holder of the Macfarren Scholarship. His earliest works were presented at the Academy concerts: an Egyptian ballet suite, *Rameses II*; an overture, *The Fire Worshippers*; and a short opera, *Caedmar*, later presented at London's Crystal Palace (Oct. 18, 1893). He then engaged in varied activities; he was founder and ed. of the *New Quarterly Musical Review* (1893–96); toured as a musical comedy conductor (1894–95); organized and conducted concerts devoted to works by young British composers; conducted a military band and later a full orch. at New Brighton (1897–1901). At the same time, he was engaged in teaching; in 1907 he succeeded Elgar as prof. of music at the Univ. of Birmingham, a post he retained until 1934, when he became chairman of the board of Trinity College of Music. He was knighted in 1930. As a composer, Bantock was attracted to exotic subjects with mystical overtones; his interests were cosmopolitan and embraced all civilizations, with a particular predilection for the Celtic and oriental cultures; however, his music was set in Western terms. Among his works are 3 Celtic operas: *Caedmar* (1892), *The Pearl of Iran* (1894), and *The Seal-Woman* (Birmingham, Sept. 27, 1924), and 3 ballets: *Egypt* (1892), *Lalla Rookh* (1902), and *The Great God Pan* (1902). He was a strong believer in the programmatic significance of musical images, and most of his works bear titles relating to literature, mythology, or legend. Yet he was a typically British composer in the treatment of his materials. His works are brilliantly scored and effective in performance, but few of them have been retained in the repertoire.

BIBL.: H. Anderton, *G. B.* (London, 1915); M. Bantock, *G. B.: A Personal Portrait* (London, 1972).

Bär, Olaf, prominent German baritone; b. Dresden, Dec 19, 1957. He sang in the Kreuzchor (1966–75) and studied at the Hochschule für Musik in Dresden. In 1982 he won 1st prize in the Dvořák vocal competition in Karlovy Vary, and, in 1983, 1st prize in the vocal competition sponsored by the East German opera houses and the Walter Grüner lieder competition in London. In 1981 he made his operatic debut in Dresden, and from 1985 to 1991 he was a principal member of the State Opera there. He made his British debut in a recital at London's Wigmore Hall in 1983, returning to London in 1985 to make his British operatic debut as Strauss's Harlekin at Covent Garden. In 1986 he appeared as Ariadne at the Aix-en-Provence Festival, and as Papageno at the Vienna State Opera and at La Scala in Milan. On March 19, 1987, he made his U.S. debut as Christ in Bach's St. Matthew Passion with Solti and the Chicago Sym. Orch., and that same year sang the role of the Count in *Capriccio* at the Glyndebourne Festival. On April 18, 1991, he made his N.Y. recital debut at Alice Tully Hall. He portrayed Mozart's Count at the Netherlands Opera in Amsterdam in 1993. He made his U.S. operatic debut as that composer's Papageno in Chicago in 1996. In addition to his roles in operas by Mozart and Strauss, he has won distinction as a concert and lieder artist.

Barab, Seymour, American cellist and composer; b. Chicago, Jan. 9, 1921. He studied with Persichetti, Wolpe, Varese, and Harrison. He played in the Indianapolis Sym. Orch., the Cleveland Orch., the CBS Sym. Orch., the Portland (Oreg.) Sym. Orch., the San Francisco Sym., the ABC Sym. Orch., and the Brooklyn Philharmonia; also played in the Galimir String Quartet, the N.Y. Pro Musica, the N.Y. Trio, the New Music Quartet, and the Composers Quartet. He served on the faculties of Black Mountain College, Rutgers, the State Univ. of N.J., and the New England Cons. of Music in Boston. As a cellist, Barab commissioned and premiered scores by several American composers. His own large output includes 3 full-length operas: *Phillips Marshall, Mortals*, and *A Piece of String*, as well as 25 one-act operas.

Baranović, Krešimir, Croatian conductor, pedagogue, and composer; b. Šibenik, July 25, 1894; d. Belgrade, Sept. 17, 1975. He studied piano, theory, and composition in Zagreb and in Vienna. He was subsequently a theater conductor in Zagreb (1915–27), then traveled with Anna Pavlova's ballet group (1927–28). Returning to Yugoslavia, he was director of the Zagreb Opera (1929–40), then served as a prof. at the Belgrade Academy of Music (1946–61); was also conductor of the Belgrade Phil. (1952–61). A prolific composer, he was successful mostly in music for the theater, including two comic operas, *Striženo-Košeno* (Clipped and Mowed; Zagreb, May 4, 1932) and *Nevjesta od Cetingrada* (The Bride from Cetingrad; Belgrade, May 12, 1951) and two ballets *Licitarsko srce* (The Gingerbread Heart; 1924) and *Kineska priča* (Chinese Tale; Belgrade, April 30, 1955).

Barati, George (real name, **György Baráti**), Hungarian-born American cellist, conductor, and composer; b. Györ, April 3, 1913; d. San Jose, Calif., June 22, 1996. After initial training at the Györ Music School (graduated, 1932), he studied at the Franz Liszt Academy of Music in Budapest (graduated, 1935; teacher's diploma, 1937; artist diploma, 1938); he also was a member of the Budapest Concert Orch. (1933–36) and 1st cellist of the Budapest Sym. Orch. and Municipal Opera orch. (1936–38). In 1939 he emigrated to the United States, becoming a naturalized American citizen in 1944; he studied composition with Georges Couvreur and Henri Switten at Westminster Choir College in Princeton, N.J. (1938–39), and with Sessions at Princeton Univ. (1939–43). He played cello in the Pro Ideale (later Westminster) String Quartet (1936–39), then taught at Princeton Univ. (1939–43). He also conducted the Princeton Ensemble and Choral Union (1941–43) and the Alexandria (La.) Military Sym. Orch. (1944–46). He was a cellist in the San Francisco Sym. Orch. and the California String Quartet (1946–50); he also was music director of the Barati Chamber Orch. of San Francisco (1948–52). From 1950 to 1968 he was music director of the Honolulu Sym. Orch. and Opera, leaving to become executive director of the Montalvo Center for the Arts and conductor of the Montalvo Chamber Orch. in Saratoga, California (1968–78). From 1971 to 1980 he was music director of the Santa Cruz County Sym. Orch. in Aptos, California; he then was music director of the Barati Ensemble (1989–92). In 1991 the George Barati Archive was opened at the Univ. of Calif. at Santa Cruz Library. In 1959 he received the Naumburg Award, in 1962 the Alice M. Ditson Award, and in 1965–66 a Guggenheim fellowship. As a composer, Barati wrote fine music in a modern European tradition. During his stay in Hawaii, he studied native melodic and rhythmic patterns of exotic South Sea islands, and these found reflection in some of his works of the period. He composed the opera *Noelani* (1968), the ballet *The Love of Don Perlimplin* (1947), and incidental music *Thirty Pieces of Silver* for Narrator and Chamber Orch. (1951).

Barbaia or Barbaja, Domenico, celebrated Italian impresario; b. Milan, 1778?; d. Posillipo, near Naples, Oct. 19, 1841. He worked as a scullion in local cafes and bars, and is reputed to have been the inventor of barbaiate or granita di caffe, a concoction of coffee or chocolate with whipped cream. In 1808 he obtained the lease of the gambling tables in the foyer of Milan's La Scala, and in 1809 also secured the position of manager of all the royal opera houses in Naples. He became so influential that he was dubbed the "Viceroy of Naples." From 1821 to 1828 he was manager of Vienna's Kärnthnertortheater and Theater an der Wien, and from 1826 to 1832 of Milan's La Scala. In 1811 he engaged Isabella Colbran as a singer in Naples, and she became his mistress only to leave him to marry Rossini in 1822. All the same, he remained a champion of Rossini. Among the other composers he championed were Mercadente, Pacini, Bellini, and Donizetti. Barbaia appears as a character in Auber's opera *La sirène* (1844) and was the inspiration for Emil Lucka's novel *Der Impresario* (Vienna, 1937).

Barber, Samuel, outstanding American composer of superlative gifts; b. West Chester, Pa., March 9, 1910; d. N.Y., Jan. 23, 1981. He was the nephew of **Louise Homer** and her husband, Sidney Homer, a composer whose output included some 100 songs (many of which won great favor), who encouraged him in his musical inclination. At the age of 6, he began piano lessons, and later had some cello lessons. He was only 10 when he tried his hand at composing a short opera, *The Rose Tree*. During his high school years, he gained practical experience as organist at Westminster Presbyterian Church. Even before graduating from high school at age 16, he entered the first class at the newly organized Curtis Inst. of Music in Philadelphia when he was 14, where he was a pupil of George Boyle and Isabelle Vengerova (piano), Rosario Scalero (composition), and Fritz Reiner (conducting). He also took voice lessons with Emilio de Gogorza and gave recitals as a baritone at the Curtis Inst., where he graduated in 1932. He then went to Vienna to pursue vocal training with John Braun, and also appeared in public as a singer there. In the meantime, his interest in composing grew apace. In 1928 his Violin Sonata won the Bearns Prize of Columbia Univ. It was followed by such enduring scores as his *Dover Beach* for Voice and String Quartet (1931), the *Serenade* for String Quartet (1932), and the Cello Sonata (1932). In 1933 he won the Bearns Prize again for his overture to *The School for Scandal*, which was favorably received at its premiere by the Philadelphia Orch. on Aug. 30 of that year. Then followed the successful premiere of his *Music for a Scene from Shelley* by the N.Y. Phil. on March 24, 1935, under Werner Janssen's direction. Thanks to a Pultizer Traveling Scholarship and a Rome Prize, Barber pursued composition at the American Academy in Rome in 1935 and 1936. During his sojourn there, he wrote his First Symphony, which was premiered under Molinari's direction on Dec. 13, 1936. He also wrote his String Quartet in 1936. Rodzinski conducted Barber's 1st Sym. at the Salzburg Festival on July 25, 1937, the first score by an American composer to be played there. Toscanini conducted the premiere of Barber's (1st) *Essay for Orchestra* with the NBC Sym. Orch. in New York on Nov. 5, 1938. On the same program, he also conducted the *Adagio* for Strings, a transcription of the 2d movement of the String Quartet, which was destined to become Barber's most celebrated work, an epitome of his lyrical and Romantic bent. From 1939 to 1942 he taught composition at the Curtis Inst. His most notable work of this period was his Violin Concerto, which was first performed by Albert Spalding with Ormandy and the Philadelphia Orch. on Feb. 7, 1941. With his friend Gian Carlo Menotti, he purchased a house ("Capricorn") in Mount Kisco, N.Y., which was to remain the center of his activities until 1974. In 1943 he was conscripted into the U.S. Army and was assigned to the Army Air Force. During his military service, he composed his Second Symphony, which included an electronic instrument producing sound in imitation of radio signals. Koussevitzky conducted its premiere with the Boston Sym. Orch. on March 3, 1944. After his discharge from military service in 1945, Barber revised the score; it was first performed by the Philadelphia Orch. on Jan. 21, 1948. Still dissatisfied with the work, he destroyed the MS except for the 2d movement, which he revised as *Night Flight*, which was first performed by Szell and the Cleveland Orch. on Oct. 8, 1964. Barber had better luck with his Cello Concerto (1945), which was introduced by Raya Garbousova with Koussevitzy conducting the Boston Sym. Orch. on April 5, 1946. In 1947 it won the N.Y. Music Critics' Circle Award. For Martha Graham, he composed the ballet *Medea* (N.Y., May 10, 1946), which was revised as *The Cave of the Heart* (N.Y., Feb. 27, 1947). He made an orch. suite from the ballet (Philadelphia, Dec. 5, 1947) and the orch. piece, *Medea's Meditation and Dance of Vengeance* (N.Y., Feb. 2, 1956). One of Barber's most distinguished scores, *Knoxville: Summer of 1915* for High Voice and Orch., after James Agee, was first performed by Eleanor Steber with Koussevitzky conducting the Boston Sym. Orch. on April 9, 1948. His remarkable Piano Sonata, premiered by Horowitz in Havana on Dec. 9, 1949, amply utilized contemporary resources, including 12-tone writing. In 1953 he composed the 1-act opera *A Hand of Bridge*, scored for 4 Soloists and chamber orch. The work was not performed until June 17, 1959, when it was mounted in Spoleto, Italy, without much impact. In the meantime, Barber composed his finest opera, *Vanessa* (1956–57), to a libretto by Menotti. It was successfuly premiered at the Metropolitan Opera in New York on Jan. 15, 1958, and was awarded the Pulitzer Prize in Music. It was followed by his strikingly brilliant Piano Concerto, which was first performed by John Browning with Leinsdorf conducting the Boston Sym. Orch. at N.Y.'s Lincoln Center for the Performing Arts on Sept. 24, 1962. Barber was awarded his 2d Pulitzer Prize in music for this work. A commission from the Metropolitan Opera spurred Barber on to compose his most ambitious work for the stage, the 3-act opera *Antony and Cleopatra*. With Zeffirelli as librettist, producer, director, and designer, it was premiered at the opening of the new Metropolitan Opera House in New York on Sept. 16, 1966. Unfortunately, the work found few admirers. Barber revised the score with a revamped libretto by Menotti, and the new version was given a more favorable reception at its first performance by N.Y.'s Opera Theater of the Juilliard School on Feb. 6, 1975.

During the final years of his life, Barber wrote only a handful of works. In 1945, 1947, and 1949 he held Guggenheim fellowships. He was elected to the National Inst. of Arts and Letters in 1941 and to the American Academy of Arts and Letters in 1958. Barber was one of the most distinguished American composers of the 20th century. He excelled primarily as a melodist, being remarkably sensitive in his handling of vocally shaped patterns. Although the harmonic structures of his music remained fundamentally tonal, he made free use of chromatic techniques, verging on atonality and polytonality, while his mastery of modern counterpoint enabled him to write canons and fugues in effective neo-Baroque sequences. His orchestration was opulent without being turgid, and his treatment of solo instruments was unfailingly congenial to their nature even though requiring a virtuoso technique.

WORKS: DRAMATIC: OPERAS: *A Hand of Bridge* (1953; Spoleto, June 17, 1959); *Vanessa* (1956–57; N.Y., Jan. 15, 1958, Mitropoulos conducting; rev. 1964); *Antony and Cleopatra* (N.Y., Sept. 16, 1966, Schippers conducting; rev. 1974; N.Y., Feb. 6, 1975, Conlon conducting). BALLETS: *Medea* or *Serpent Heart* (N.Y., May 10, 1946; rev. as *The Cave of the Heart*, N.Y., Feb. 27, 1947; as a ballet suite, Philadelphia, Dec. 5, 1947, Ormandy conducting; as *Medea's Meditation and Dance of Vengeance* for Orch., 1953; N.Y., Feb. 2, 1956, Mitropoulos conducting); *Souvenirs* (1952; N.Y., Nov. 15, 1955; as a ballet suite, 1952; Chicago, Nov. 12, 1953, Reiner conducting; also for Solo Piano or Piano, 4-hands).

BIBL.: N. Broder, *S. B.* (N.Y., 1954); R. Friedewald, *A Formal and Stylistic Analysis of the Published Music of S. B.* (diss., Univ. of Iowa, 1957); D. Hennessee, *S. B.: A Bio-Bibliography* (Westport, Conn., 1985); J. Kreiling, *The Songs of S. B.: A Study in Literary Taste and Text-Setting* (Ann Arbor, Mich., 1987); P. Wittke, *S. B.: An Improvsatory Portrait* (N.Y., 1994; includes works list by N. Ryan).

Barbier, René (Auguste-Ernest), Belgian composer and teacher; b. Namur, July 12, 1890; d. Brussels, Dec. 24, 1981. He studied with Gilson at the Brussels Cons. and with Dupuis at the Liège Cons. He taught at the Liège Cons. (1920–49) and at the Brussels Cons. (1949–55); concurrently was director of the Namur Cons. (1923–63). In 1923 he received the Belgian Royal Academy Prize for his symphonic poem *Les Génies du sommeil*, and in 1968 he was elected to membership in the Academy. He composed the operas *Yvette* (1910) and *La Fête du vieux Tilleul* (1912) and the ballet *Les Pierres magiques* (1957).

Barbieri, Carlo Emanuele, Italian conductor and composer; b. Genoa, Oct. 22, 1822; d. Pest, Sept. 28, 1867. He was educated at the Naples Cons., where he studied voice with Crescenti and composition with Mercadante. In 1845 he embarked on a career as an opera conductor; eventually settled in Buda, where he conducted at the National Theater from 1862 until his death. He wrote 5 operas: *Cristoforo Colombo* (Berlin, 1848), *Nisida, la perla di Procida* (1851), *Carlo und Carlin* (1859), *Arabella* (Buda, 1862), and *Perdita, ein Wintermärchen* (Leipzig, 1865).

Barbieri, Fedora, Italian mezzo-soprano; b. Trieste, June 4, 1920. She studied in Trieste with Luigi Toffolo and in Milan with Giulia Tess. She made her professional debut as Fidalma in Cimarosa's *Il matrimonio segreto* at Florence's Teatro Comunale in 1940; in 1942 she made her first appearance at Milan's La Scala as Meg Page; in 1950 she first sang at London's Covent Garden as a member of the visiting La Scala company, and returned to Covent Garden as a guest artist in 1957–58 and 1964. From 1947 she sang at the Teatro Colón in Buenos Aires. On Nov. 6, 1950, she made her Metropolitan Opera debut in New York as Eboli, remaining on its roster until 1954, and again for the 1956–57, 1967–68, 1971–72, and 1974–77 seasons. Her large repertory included over 80 roles, both standard and modern, among them Adalgisa, Carmen, Amneris, Santuzza, and Azucena.

Barbieri, Francisco Asenjo, Spanish composer; b. Madrid, Aug. 3, 1823; d. there, Feb. 19, 1894. He studied clarinet, voice, and composition at the Madrid Cons., then engaged in multifarious activities as a café pianist, music copyist, and choral conductor. He found his true vocation in writing zarzuelas, and composed 78 of them. The following, all produced in Madrid, were particularly successful: *Gloria y peluca* (March 9, 1850), *Jugar con fuego* (Oct. 6, 1851), *Los diamantes de la corona* (Sept. 15, 1854), *Pan y Toros* (Dec. 22, 1864), and *El Barberillo de Lavapiés* (Dec. 18, 1874). He also ed. a valuable collection, *Cancionero musical de los siglos XV y XVI*, and publ. a number of essays on Spanish music.

BIBL.: A. Martínez Olmedilla, *El maestro B. y su tiempo* (Madrid, 1941).

Barbieri-Nini, Marianna, Italian soprano; b. Florence, Feb. 18, 1818; d. there, Nov. 27, 1887. She studied with Luigi Barbieri, Pasta, and Vaccai, making her operatic debut in 1840 at La Scala in Milan in Donizetti's *Belisario*. Unfortunately, her peculiarly asymmetrical facial features and an ill-constructed bodily frame produced such a vociferous outburst of revulsion on the part of the notoriously unrestrained Italian opera audiences that she was advised to wear a mask and a bodice to conceal her repellent physique. However, she astutely selected the part of Lucrezia Borgia, a historically celebrated poisoner, in Donizetti's eponymous opera at her next appearance in Florence, and there her ugly countenance fitted the role to a high C. She was also very successful in other bloody roles, among them that of Lady Macbeth in Verdi's opera and of the sympathetic but murderous Gulnara in Verdi's *Il Corsaro*.

Barbirolli, Sir John (actually, **Giovanni Battista**), eminent English conductor of Italian-French descent; b. London, Dec. 2, 1899; d. there, July 29, 1970. He studied cello; received a scholarship to London's Trinity College of Music in 1910 and another to London's Royal Academy of Music, graduating in 1916; he made his first appearance as a cellist at the age of 12, on Dec. 16, 1911, at the Queen's Hall in London. In 1916 he became a member of the Queen's Hall Orch. In 1923 he joined the International String Quartet and toured with it. In 1924 he organized a chamber orch. in Chelsea, which he conducted for several years; was a conductor with the British National Opera Co. (1926–29). He gained recognition on Dec. 12, 1927, when he successfully substituted for Beecham at a concert of the London Sym. Orch. In 1928 he was a guest conductor at London's Covent Garden, and a regular conductor there from 1929 to 1933; in 1933 he was named conductor of the Scottish Orch., Glasgow, and the Leeds Sym. Orch. He made his American debut with the N.Y. Phil. on Nov. 5, 1936, and was engaged as its permanent conductor in 1937. However, he failed to impress the N.Y. critics, and in 1943 he returned to England, where he was named conductor of the Hallé Orch. of Manchester. In 1958 he was appointed its conductor-in-chief. Renewing his American career, he served as conductor of the Houston Sym. Orch. (1961–67), while continuing his tenancy of the Hallé Orch., from which he finally retired in 1968 with the title of Conductor Laureate for Life. He was knighted in 1949 and made a Companion of Honour in 1969. A commemorative postage stamp with his portrait was issued by the Post Office of Great Britain on Sept. 1, 1980. Barbirolli was distinguished primarily in the Romantic repertoire; his interpretations were marked by nobility, expressive power, and brilliance. He had a fine pragmatic sense of shaping the music according to its inward style, without projecting his own personality upon it. However, this very objectivity tempered his success with American audiences, accustomed to charismatic flamboyance. He had a special affinity for English music, and performed many works of Elgar, Delius, and Britten. He conducted the first performances of the 7th and 8th syms. by Vaughan Williams; he also made transcriptions for string orch. and horns of 5 pieces from the Fitzwilliam Virginal Book (perf. by him under the title *Elizabethan Suite* in Los Angeles, Dec. 4, 1941). For his 2d wife, the English oboist Lady Evelyn Barbirolli (née Rothwell; b. Wallingford, Jan. 24, 1911), he composed an Oboe Concerto on themes by Pergolesi.

BIBL.: C. Rigby, *J. B.* (Altrincham, 1948); M. Kennedy, *B., Conductor Laureate* (London, 1971); C. Reid, *J. B.* (London, 1971); H. Atkins and P. Cotes, *The B.s: A Musical Marriage* (London, 1983).

Barblan, Guglielmo, eminent Italian musicologist; b. Siena, May 27, 1906; d. Milan, March 24, 1978. He first studied jurisprudence, then entered the Rome Cons. as a cello student of Forino and Becker; also took courses in theory at the Bolzano Cons. and attended lectures on musicology by Liuzzi in Rome and Sandberger in Munich. He served as a music critic for *La Provincia di Bolzano* (1932–50), and concurrently lectured on music history at the Bolzano Cons. (1932–49). In 1949 he became head librarian of the Milan Cons.; in 1965 he was appointed prof. of music history there; he also taught at the Univ. of Milan from 1961. Barblan's principal contribution as a music scholar was in the field of Italian music history. In addition to his books, he ed. works by Bonporti and Cambini.

WRITINGS: *Un musicista trentino: F. A. Bonporti* (Florence, 1940); *Musiche e strumenti musicali dell'Africa orientale italiana* (Naples, 1941); *L'opera di Donizetti nell'età romantica* (Bergamo, 1948); ed. with A. Della Corte, *Mozart in Italia: I viaggi e le lettere* (Milan, 1956); *Guida al "Clavicembalo ben temperato" di J. S. Bach* (Milan, 1961); with C. Gallico and G. Pannain, *Claudio Monteverdi nel quarto centenario della nascita* (Turin, 1967); ed. *Conservatorio di musica G. Verdi, Milano; Catalogo della biblioteca* (Florence, 1972); with B. Zanolini, *Gaetano Donizetti: Vita e opera di un musicista romantico* (Bergamo, 1983).

Barbot, Joseph-Théodore-Désiré, French tenor; b. Toulouse, April 12, 1824; d. Paris, Jan. 1, 1897. He studied with García at the Paris Cons. He was engaged to sing at the Paris Opéra in 1848; sang Faust at the premiere of Gounod's opera (March 19, 1859). In 1875 he became a prof. at the Paris Cons., succeeding Viardot-García.

Bardi, Giovanni de', Count of Vernio, Italian nobleman, patron of music and art, and composer; b. Florence, Feb. 5, 1534; d. Rome, Sept. 1612. He was the founder of the Florentine Camerata, a group of musicians who met at his home (1576-c.1582) to discuss the music of Greek antiquity; this led to the beginnings of opera. Count Bardi was descended from an old Guelph banking family; he was a philologist, mathematician, neo-Platonic philosopher, and lover of Dante. He was a member of the Crusca Academy, a literary group founded in 1583 whose ideas had great influence on the Camerata. Bardi is known to have been in Rome in 1567; he lent support to Vincenzo Galilei, a member of the Camerata. In 1580 Bardi married Lucrezia Salvati. The masques of 1589, commemorating the marriage of Grand Duke Ferdinand, were conceived largely by Bardi. In 1592 he left for Rome to become chamberlain at the court of Pope Clement VIII. Caccini was his secretary in 1592. Bardi's writings are: *Discorso sopra il giuoco del calzio fiorentino* (Florence, 1580), *Ristretto delle grandezze di Roma* (Rome, 1600), and *Discorso mandato a Caccini sopra la musica antica in Doni's Lyra Barberina* (Florence, 1763). Among contemporary documents which refer to him is Vincenzo Galilei's *Dialogo della musica antica e della moderna* (tr. in part in O. Strunk's *Source Readings in Music History*, N.Y., 1951; also included is a letter from Bardi's son to G. B. Doni commenting on Bardi's ideas).

Barenboim, Daniel, greatly talented Israeli pianist and conductor; b. Buenos Aires, Nov. 15, 1942. He began music training with his parents, making his public debut as a pianist in Buenos Aires when he was only 7. During the summers of 1954 and 1955, he studied piano with Edwin Fischer, conducting with Igor Markevitch, and chamber music with Enrico Mainardi at the Salzburg Mozarteum. He also pursued training in theory with Boulanger in Paris (1954–56), was one of the youngest students to receive a diploma from the Accademia di Santa Cecilia in Rome (1956), and took a conducting course with Carlo Zecchi at the Accademia Musicale Chigiana in Siena. In 1955 he made his debut as a soloist with orch. in Paris, and then made his British debut in Bournemouth. In Jan. 1956 he made his first appearance in London as soloist with Krips and the Royal Phil. He made his U.S. debut as soloist in Prokofiev's 1st Piano Concerto with Stokowski and the Sym. of the Air at N.Y.'s Carnegie Hall on Jan. 20, 1957. Later that year he made his first appearance as a conductor in Haifa. On Jan. 17, 1958, he made his U.S. recital debut in New York. In 1960 he played cycles of all the Beethoven piano sonatas in Israel and South America, and later in London (1967, 1970) and New York (1970). From 1965 he was active as a soloist and conductor with the English Chamber Orch. in London. In 1967 he married the renowned English cellist Jacqueline DuPré (b. Oxford, Jan. 26, 1945; d. London, Oct. 19, 1987), with whom he subsequently appeared in numerous concerts until she was tragically stricken with multiple sclerosis in 1973 and was compelled to abandon her career. In 1967 he conducted the Israel Phil. on a tour of the United States, returning thereafter to appear as a guest conductor with various orchs. He also appeared as a guest conductor throughout Europe. He made his operatic debut in 1973 conducting *Don Giovanni* at the Edinburgh Festival. In 1975 he became music director of the Orchestre de Paris, a position he held until 1989. In 1981 he made his first appearance at the Bayreuth Festival conducting *Tristan und Isolde*. In 1988 he was named artistic director of the new Opéra de la Bastille in Paris by the French minister of culture. However, following the French presidential election, a new minister of culture was appointed and disagreements over artistic policy and remuneration led to Barenboim's abrupt dismissal in Jan. 1989. That same month he was appointed music director of the Chicago Sym. Orch., succeeding Solti. During the 1989–91 seasons, he served as its music director-designate before fully assuming his duties as music director for the orch.'s 100th anniversary season in 1991–92. In 1993 he also became Generalmusikdirektor of the Berlin State Opera. His autobiography appeared as *A Life in Music* (1991). From the earliest years of his professional career as a pianist, Barenboim has been held in the highest esteem. Particularly notable have been his performances of Bach, Mozart, Beethoven, Chopin, and Brahms. In addition to his distinguished appearances as a recitalist and chamber music artist, he has won great admiration as an accompanist. Barenboim's career as a conductor has been less remarkable. While he has maintained an extensive repertoire, he has been most successful with scores from the Romantic and late Romantic eras. He has also championed contemporary works, conducting premieres by such composers as Boulez and Corigliano.

Barilli, Bruno, Italian writer on music and composer; b. Fano, Dec. 14, 1880; d. Rome, April 15, 1952. He studied in Parma and later in Munich. His collections of essays were publ. under the titles *Il sorcio nel violino* (Milan, 1926) and *Il paese del melodramma* (Lanciano, 1929). He wrote the operas *Medusa* (1910; Bergamo, Sept. 11, 1938) and *Emiral* (Rome, March 11, 1924).

BIBL.: E. Falqui, ed., *Opere di B. B.* (Florence, 1963).

Barkauskas, Vytautas (Pranas Marius), outstanding Lithuanian composer; b. Kaunas, March 25, 1931. He studied piano at the Vilnius College of Music while also studying mathematics at the Pedagogical Inst. there (1949–53); then took composition classes with Račiunas and orchestration classes with Balsys at the Lithuanian State Cons. (1953–59); in 1961 he joined its faculty. He wrote several cantatas following the compositional tenets of socialist realism; in his instrumental compositions, he makes use of more advanced cosmopolitan techniques, including serialism and aleatory improvisation. His stage works include *Conflict*, "choreographic scene" for 3 Performers (1965) and *Legend about Love*, opera (Vilnius, March 29, 1975).

Barkin, Elaine R(adoff), American composer and writer on music; b. N.Y., Dec. 15, 1932. She studied with Karol Rathaus at Queens College of the City Univ. of N.Y. (B.A., 1954), with Irving Fine at Brandeis Univ. (M.F.A., 1956), and Boris Blacher at the Berlin Hochschule für Musik (1957); she completed her studies with Berger and Shapero at Brandeis Univ. (Ph.D., 1974). She taught at various colleges, finally joining the faculty of the Univ. of Calif. at Los Angeles in 1974. She was an ed. of the journal *Perspectives of New Music* (1963–85). In her early works, she utilized serial techniques, later delving into "group interactive autonomous alternative music-making culture." Among her dramatic works is *De amore*, chamber miniopera (1980).

Barlow, David (Frederick), English composer; b. Rothwell, May 20, 1927; d. Newcastle upon Tyne, June 9, 1975. He studied at Emmanuel College, Cambridge, with Jacob at the Royal College of Music in London, and with Boulanger in Fontainebleau; he was on the faculty of King's College, Newcastle upon Tyne (from 1951). After writing in a late Romantic style, he developed a lyrical serial mode of expression (from 1963). He composed *David and Bathsheba*, a church opera (1969), *The Selfish Giant*, a children's opera (1974–75), and *Judas Iscariot*, a church opera (1974–75).

Barlow, Fred, French composer of English and Alsatian descent; b. Mulhouse, Oct. 2, 1881; d. Boulogne, Jan. 3, 1951. He studied in Paris with Jean Huré and his cousin, Charles Koechlin.

WORKS: DRAMATIC: MUSICAL COMEDY: *Sylvie* (1919–21; Paris, March 2, 1923). OPERETTA: *Mam'zelle Prudhomme* (Monte Carlo, Dec. 22, 1932). BALLETS: *Gladys, ou La légère incartade* (1915–16; Mulhouse, Jan. 7, 1956); *Polichinelle et Colombine* (1926–27); *La grande Jatte* (1936–38; Paris, July 12, 1950).

Barlow, Samuel L(atham) M(itchell), American composer; b. N.Y., June 1, 1892; d. Wyndmoor, Pa., Sept. 19, 1982. He studied at Harvard Univ. (B.A., 1914), with Goetschius and Franklin Robinson in New York, with Philipp (piano) in Paris, and with Respighi (orchestration) in Rome (1923). He was active in various N.Y. music, civic, and liberal organizations, and also taught. Among his works are the operas *Mon ami Pierrot* (1934; Paris, Jan. 11, 1935) and *Amanda* (1936) and the ballet *Ballo sardo* (1928). His autobiography appeared as *The Astonished Muse* (N.Y., 1961).

Barlow, Stephen, English conductor; b. Seven Kings, Essex, June 30, 1954. He was educated at Trinity College, Cambridge, and the Guildhall School of Music and Drama in London. From 1979 to 1985 he was a conductor with the Glyndebourne Festival and the Glyndebourne Touring Opera. He was a conductor with Opera 80 from 1980, and was made its music director in 1987. From 1983 he was also a conductor at the Scottish Opera in Glasgow. In 1989 he made his debut at London's Covent Garden with *Turandot*, and in 1990 made his first appearance at the San Francisco Opera with *Capriccio*. His Australian debut followed in 1991 when he conducted *Die Zauberflöte* in Melbourne. In 1992 he conducted *Faust* at Opera Northern Ireland in Belfast. He conducted *Madama Butterfly* in Auckland in 1994. From 1997 he served as music director of Opera Northern Ireland. He also appeared as a guest conductor with various European and North American orchs.

Barnett, John (Manley), American conductor; b. N.Y., Sept. 3, 1917. He studied piano, violin, and trumpet; took courses at Teachers College of Columbia Univ., the Manhattan School of Music, and the Salzburg Mozarteum (1936); received training in conducting from Bruno Walter, Weingartner, Enesco, and Malko. He was assistant conductor of the National Orchestral Assn. in N.Y. (1937–41), and also a conductor with the WPA Federal Music Project there (1939–42), serving concurrently as conductor of the Stamford (Conn.) Sym. Orch. From 1946 to 1956 he was assoc. conductor of the Los Angeles Phil., and from 1956 to 1958 its assoc. music director. In 1947 he organized the Phoenix (Ariz.) Sym. Orch., conducting it until 1949. He later served as music director of the Hollywood Bowl (1953–57) and of the Los Angeles Guild Opera Co. (1954–79). From 1958 to 1972 he was music director of the National Orchestral Assn. in N.Y.; from 1961 to 1971 he held the post of music director of the Phil. Sym. Orch. of Westchester, N.Y. From 1972 to 1978 he served as artistic consultant to the NEA. From 1979 to 1985 he was music director of the Puerto Rico Sym. Orch. in Santurce.

Barolsky, Michael, Lithuanian-born German-Israeli composer; b. Vilnius, July 19, 1947. He studied piano, theory, and ethnology; in 1965 he took lessons in composition with Lutoslawski in Warsaw; in 1968 he went to Moscow and studied privately with Denisov and Schnittke. From 1969 to 1971 he was music adviser at the Lithuanian Radio. In 1971 he emigrated to Germany. In 1972 he attended seminars with Ligeti, Kagel, and Stockhausen in Darmstadt; in 1974 he went to Israel, and taught at the Pedagogic Inst. in Tel Aviv. In 1977 he settled in Cologne on a stipend of the Deutsche Akademie; he also worked on electronic music with Humpert. In his compositions, he devotes himself totally to contemporary means of expression, astutely applying the full resources of electronic music. He composed the opera *Blue Eye, Brown Eye* (Tel Aviv, July 29, 1976).

Baroni, Leonora, greatly esteemed Italian singer, lutenist, and viola da gambist, known as "L'Andrianella" and "L'Adrianetta," daughter of **Andreana Basile**; b. Mantua, Dec. 1611; d. Rome, April 6, 1670. She studied music with her mother at the Gonzaga court in Mantua, where she first attracted attention for her vocal gifts. At age 16, she garnered accolades for her performances in salons throughout Naples. In 1630 she appeared in Genoa, and then in Florence. In 1633 she went to Rome, where she secured her reputation as a brilliant vocal artist in aristocratic circles. Following a sojourn at the French court in Paris (1644–45), she returned to Rome and pursued her career. Her sister, Catarina Baroni (b. Mantua, after 1620; place and date of death unknown), was a singer, harpist, and poet.

Barraud, Henry, French composer; b. Bordeaux, April 23, 1900. He received training in harmony and counterpoint in Bordeaux, and then was a pupil of Dukas (composition), Caussade (fugue), and Aubert (composition and orchestration) at the Paris Cons. (1926–27). In 1937 he was director of music for the Paris International Exposition. He served as head of music (1944–48) and director of the national program (1948–65) of Radiodiffusion Française. He publ. *Berlioz* (Paris, 1955; 3d ed., 1979), *La France et la musique occidentale* (Paris, 1956), *Pour comprendre les musiques d'aujord'hui* (Paris, 1968), and *Les cinq grands opéras* (Paris, 1972).

WORKS: DRAMATIC: OPERAS: *La Farce du maître Pathelin* (1938; Paris, June 24, 1948); *Numance* (1950–52; Paris, April 15, 1955; rev. 1970; arranged as the *Symphonie de Numance*, Baden-Baden, Dec. 3, 1950); *Lavinia*, comic opera (1959; Aix-en-Provence, July 20, 1961); *Le roi Gordogne* (1979); *Tête d'or* (1980). BALLETS: *Le diable à la kermesse* (1943); *L'astrologue dans le puits* (1948).

Barrientos, Maria, celebrated Spanish soprano; b. Barcelona, March 10, 1884; d. Ciboure, France, Aug. 8, 1946. She entered the Barcelona Cons. at age 6, where she received training in piano, violin, and composition before graduating at 12, then studied voice with Francesco Bonet. In 1898 she made her operatic debut as Inèz in *L'Africaine*; while still a youth, she appeared in Rome, Berlin, Leipzig, Milan, and other European music centers. On Jan. 31, 1916, she made her Metropolitan Opera debut in New York as Lucia, continuing to sing there until 1920. She then devoted most of her time to concert engagements; she also taught in Buenos Aires (1939–45). In her heyday, Barrientos was acclaimed as one of the finest coloratura sopranos. Among her notable roles were Rosina, Gilda, Amina, Lakmé, Norina, and the Queen of Shemakha.

Barrios Fernandez, Angel, Spanish composer; b. Granada, Jan. 4, 1882; d. Madrid, Nov. 27, 1964. Of a musical family (his father was a guitarist), he studied violin and played in bands as a child. He later studied theory with Conrado del Campo in Madrid and with Gédalge in Paris. At the same time, he perfected his guitar playing; formed a trio, Iberia, and traveled in Europe playing Spanish popular music. In collaboration with Conrado del Campo, he wrote a successful operetta, *El Avapiés* (Madrid, 1919), and several zarzuelas: *La Suerte, La Romeria, Seguidilla gitana, Castigo de Dios, En Nombre del Rey*, and *Lola se va a los.*

Barry, Gerald (Anthony), Irish composer; b. County Clare, April 28, 1952. He studied at Univ. College, Dublin (B.Mus., 1973; M.A., 1975); he also studied composition with Peter Schat and organ with Piet Kee in Amsterdam, and with Stockhausen and Kagel at the Cologne Hochschule für Musik (1975–80), and received some guidance from Cerha in Vienna (1977). After a brief stint as a lecturer at Univ. College, Cork (1982–86), he concentrated on composing. Among his works are the ballet *Unkrautgarten* (1980), the opera *The Intelligence Park* (1981–87), and the television opera *The Triumph of Beauty and Deceit* (1992–93).

Barry, Jerome, American baritone; b. Boston, Nov. 16, 1939. He studied voice and linguistics; in 1963, received his master's degree in languages from Tufts Univ., and acquired fluency in 8 European languages and in Hebrew. He studied voice privately with Pierre Bernac, Jennie Tourel, and Luigi Ricci. He began his professional career in Italy; he gave a great many concerts in Israel; returning to the United States, he developed activities in many fields, as a lecturer and a singer; settled in Washington, D.C., where he organized the Washington Music Ensemble.

Barsova (real name, **Vladimirova**), **Valeria,** Russian soprano; b. Astrakhan, June 13, 1892; d. Sochi, Dec. 13, 1967. She studied voice with Umberto Mazetti at the Moscow Cons., graduating in 1919; from 1920 to 1948 she was on the staff of the Bolshoi Theater in Moscow. She distinguished herself mainly in the Russian repertoire, but also sang Violetta and Gilda. Her silvery coloratura enabled her to sing such demanding roles as Lakmé. From 1950 to 1953 she taught at the Moscow Cons. She gave solo recitals in Russia and abroad, including England and Germany.

BIBL.: G. Polyanovsky, *V. V. B.* (Moscow and Leningrad, 1941).

Barstow, Dame Josephine (Clare), noted English soprano; b. Sheffield, Sept. 27, 1940. She studied at the Univ. of Birmingham (B.A. in English), the London Opera Centre, and with Eva Turner and Andrew Field. In 1964 she made her operatic debut as Mimi with Opera for All. In 1967 she made her first appearance at the Sadler's Wells Opera in London as Cherubino, and sang with its successor, the English National Opera, from 1974; she also sang with the Welsh National Opera from 1968. In 1969 she joined London's Covent Garden, where she created the roles of Denise in *The Knot Garden* (1970), the Young Woman in *We Come to the River* (1976), and Gayle in *The Ice Break* (1977). On March 28, 1977, she made her Metropolitan Opera debut in New York as Musetta. In 1983 she appeared as Gutrune in the *Ring* cycle at Bayreuth. In 1986 she made her first appearance at the Salzburg Festival creating the role of Benigna in Penderecki's *Die schwarze Maske*. Her appearances in the title role of *Gloriana* with Opera North in Leeds in 1993 and at Covent Garden in 1994 won her critical accolades. She returned to Opera North to reprise her portrayal of Gloriana in 1997. In 1985 she was made a Commander of the Order of the British Empire and in 1995 a Dame Commander of the Order of the British Empire. Barstow is a versatile singer whose repertoire ranges from traditional to contemporary roles.

Bartay, Andreas, Hungarian composer; b. Széplak, April 7, 1799; d. Mainz, Oct. 4, 1854. He began his career as a civil servant. At the same time he was engaged in collecting Hungarian folk songs and became interested in music in general. In 1829 he became a director of the first Pest singing academy. In 1834 he publ. one of the earliest collections of Hungarian folk songs and also a Hungarian book on music theory, *Magyar Apollo* (1834). A militant patriot, he participated in the Hungarian struggle for independence of 1848; after its defeat he emigrated to France and eventually to Germany. He wrote 3 operas: *Aurelia, oder Das Weib am Konradstein* (Pest, Dec. 16, 1837), *Csel* (The Ruse; Pest, April 29, 1839), and *A magyarok Nápolyban* (The Hungarians in Naples; unperf.). His son was the Hungarian folk-song collector Ede Bartay (b. Pest, Oct. 6, 1825; d. Budapest, Aug. 31, 1901).

Bartels, Wolfgang von, German composer; b. Hamburg, July 21, 1883; d. Munich, April 19, 1938. He studied with Beer-Walbrunn in Munich and with Gédalge in Paris, then became a music critic in Munich. His early works show impressionist influences; later he adopted an eclectic style. Among his compositions were 2 melodramas: *The Little Dream*, after Galsworthy (Manchester, 1911) and *Li-I-Lan* (Kassel, 1918).

Barth, Hans, German-born American pianist, pedagogue, and composer; b. Leipzig, June 25, 1897; d. Jacksonville, Fla., Dec. 8, 1956. When still a child, he studied on scholarship at the Leipzig Cons. with Carl Reinecke. In 1907 he was taken to the United States and in 1908 he made his New York recital debut. In 1912 he became a naturalized American citizen. His meeting with Busoni inspired him to experiment with new scales; with George Weitz, he perfected a portable quarter tone piano (1928). He toured the United States and Europe playing piano, quarter tone piano, and harpsichord. He served as director of the Inst. of Musical Art in Yonkers and of the National School for Musical Culture in New York; also taught at the Mannes School in New York and at the Jacksonville (Fla.) College of Music (from 1948). He composed the operetta *Miragia* (1938).

Barthélemon, François-Hippolyte, French violinist and composer; b. Bordeaux, July 27, 1741; d. London, July 20, 1808. His father was French and his mother Irish. He held posts as violinist in various theater orchs. in London. He became acquainted with Haydn during Haydn's London visit in 1792. He was greatly praised as a violinist; Burney speaks of his tone as being "truly vocal." Barthélemon wrote mostly for the stage. Among his most notable operas are *Pelopida* (London, May 24, 1766), *The Judgement of Paris* (London, Aug. 24, 1768), *Le Fleuve Scamandre* (Paris, Dec. 22, 1768), *The Maid of the Oaks* (The Oaks, near Epsom, June 1774), and *Belphegor* (London, March 16, 1778). He was married to Mary Young, a noted singer descended from Anthony Young; his daughter contributed a biographical ed. (London, 1827) of selections from Barthélemon's oratorio *Jefte in Masfa*.

Bartlett, Homer Newton, American pianist, organist, and composer; b. Olive, N.Y., Dec. 28, 1845; d. Hoboken, N.J., April 3, 1920. He studied with Max Braun and Jacobsen. He was organist at the Madison Avenue Baptist Church, N.Y., for 31 years. He was one of the founders of the American Guild of Organists. Among his works left in MS are the opera, *La Vallière*, and the unfinished Japanese opera, *Hinotito*.

Bartók, Béla (Viktor János), great Hungarian composer; b. Nagyszentmiklós, March 25, 1881; d. N.Y., Sept. 26, 1945. His father was a school headmaster; his mother was a proficient pianist, from whom he received his first piano lessons. He began playing the piano in public at the age of 11. In 1894 the family moved to Pressburg, where he took piano lessons with László Erkel, son of the famous Hungarian opera composer; he also studied harmony with Anton Hyrtl. In 1899 he enrolled at the Royal Academy of Music in Budapest, where he studied piano with István Thomán and composition with Hans Koessler; he graduated in 1903. His earliest compositions reveal the combined influence of Liszt, Brahms, and Richard Strauss; however, he soon became interested in exploring the resources of national folk music, which included not only Hungarian melorhythms but also elements of other ethnic strains in his native Transylvania, including Romanian and Slovak. He formed a cultural friendship with Zoltan Kodály, and together they traveled through the land collecting folk songs, which they publ. in 1906. In 1907 Bartók succeeded Thomán as prof. of piano at the Royal Academy of Music. His interest in folk-song research led him to tour North Africa in 1913. In 1919 he served as a member of the musical directorate of the short-lived Hungarian Democratic Republic with Dohnányi and Kodály; was also deputy director of the Academy of Music. Bartók was a brilliant pianist whose repertoire extended from Scarlatti to Szymanowski, as well as his own works; he also gave concerts playing works for 2 pianos with his 2d wife, the Hungarian pianist Ditta Pásztory (b. Rimaszombat, Oct. 31, 1903; d. Budapest, Nov. 21, 1982). In his own compositions, he soon began to feel the fascination of tonal colors and impressionistic harmonies as cultivated by Debussy and other modern French composers. The basic texture of his music remained true to tonality, which he expanded to chromatic polymodal structures and unremittingly dissonant chordal combinations; in his piano works, he exploited the extreme registers of the keyboard, often in the form of tone clusters to simulate pitchless drumbeats. He made use of strong asymmetrical rhythmic figures suggesting the modalities of Slavic folk music, a usage that imparted a somewhat acrid coloring to his music. The melodic line of his works sometimes veered toward atonality in its chromatic involutions; in some instances, he employed melodic figures comprising the 12 different notes of the chromatic scale; however, he never adopted the integral techniques of the 12-tone method.

Bartók toured the United States as a pianist from Dec. 1927 to Feb. 1928; also gave concerts in the Soviet Union in 1929. He resigned his position at the Budapest Academy of Music in 1934, but continued his ethnomusicological research as a member of the Hungarian Academy of Sciences, where he was engaged in the preparation of the monumental Corpus Musicae Popularis Hungaricae. With the outbreak of World War II, Bartók decided to leave Europe; in the fall of 1940 he went to the United States, where he remained until his death from polycythemia. In 1940 he received an honorary Ph.D. from Columbia Univ.; he also undertook folk-song research there as a visiting assistant in music (1941–42). His last completed score, the *Concerto for Orchestra*, commissioned by Koussevitzky, proved to be his most popular work. His 3d Piano Concerto was virtually completed at the time of his death, except for the last 17 bars, which were arranged and orchestrated by his pupil Tibor Serly.

Throughout his life, and particularly during his last years in the United States, Bartók experienced constant financial difficulties, and complained bitterly of his inability to support himself and his family. Actually, he was apt to exaggerate his pecuniary troubles, which were largely due to his uncompromising character. He arrived in America in favorable circumstances; his traveling expenses were paid by the American patroness Elizabeth Sprague Coolidge, who also engaged him to play at her festival at the Library of Congress in Washington, D.C., for a generous fee. Bartók was offered the opportunity to give a summer course in composition at a midwestern college on advantageous terms, when he was still well enough to undertake such a task, but he proposed to teach piano instead, and the deal collapsed. Ironically, performances and recordings of his music increased enormously after his death, and the value of his estate reached a great sum of money. Posthumous honors were not lacking: Hungary issued a series of stamps with Bartók's image; a street in Budapest was named for him; the centenary of his birth was celebrated throughout the world by concerts and festivals devoted to his works. Forty-three years after his death, his remains were removed from the Ferncliff Cemetery in Hartsdale, N.Y., and taken to Budapest for a state funeral on July 7, 1988.

Far from being a cerebral purveyor of abstract musical designs, Bartók was an ardent student of folkways, seeking the roots of meters, rhythms, and modalities in the spontaneous songs and dances of the people. Indeed, he regarded his analytical studies of popular melodies as his most important contribution. Even during the last years of his life, already weakened by illness, he applied himself assiduously to the arrangement of Serbo-Croatian folk melodies of Yugoslavia from recordings placed in his possession. He was similarly interested in the natural musical expression of children; he firmly believed that children are capable of absorbing modalities and asymmetrical rhythmic structures with greater ease than adults trained in the rigid disciplines of established music schools. His remarkable collection of piano pieces entitled, significantly, *Mikrokosmos*, was intended as a method to initiate beginners into the world of unfamiliar tonal and rhythmic combinations; in this he provided a parallel means of instruction to the Kodály method of schooling.

WORKS: DRAMATIC: *A kékszákallú herceg vará* (Duke Bluebeard's Castle), opera in 1 act, op. 11 (1911; rev. 1912, 1918; Budapest, May 24, 1918, Egisto Tango conducting; U.S. premiere, N.Y., Oct. 2, 1952); *A fából faragott királyfi* (The Wooden Prince), ballet in 1 act, op. 13 (1914–16; Budapest, May 12, 1917, Egisto Tango conducting; orch. suite, 1924; Budapest, Nov. 23, 1931; rev. 1932); *A czodálatos mandarin* (The Miraculous Mandarin), pantomime in 1 act, op. 19 (1918–19; Cologne, Nov. 27, 1926; orch. suite, 1924; rev. 1927; Budapest, Oct. 15, 1928, Ernst von Dohnányi conducting).

WRITINGS: *Cântece poporale româneşti din comitatul Bihor (Ungaria)/Chansons populaires roumaines du département Bihar (Hongrie)* (Bucharest, 1913; rev. ed. in Eng. as incorporated in B. Suchoff, ed., *Rumanian Folk Music*, The Hague, vols. 1–3, 1967); with Z. Kodály, *Erdélyi magyarság népdalok* (Transylvanian Folk Songs; Budapest, 1923); *A magyar népdal* (Budapest, 1924; Ger. tr. as *Das ungarische Volkslied*, Berlin, 1925; Eng. tr. as *Hungarian Folk Music*, London, 1931; enl. ed., with valuable addenda, as *The Hungarian Folk Song*, ed. by B. Suchoff, Albany, N.Y., 1981); *Népzenenk és a szomszéd ńepek népzenéje* (Our Folk Music and the Folk Music of Neighboring Peoples; Budapest, 1934; Ger. tr. as *Die Volksmusik der Magyaren und der benachbarten Völker*, Berlin, 1935; French tr. as "La Musique populaire des Hongrois et des peuples voisins," *Archivum Europae Centro Orientalis*, II; Budapest, 1936); *Die Melodien der rumänischen Colinde (Weihnachtslieder)* (Vienna, 1935; Eng. tr. in B. Suchoff, ed., *Rumanian Folk Music*, The Hague, vol. IV, 1975); *Miért és hogyan gyűjtsünk népzenét* (Why and How Do We Collect Folk Music?, Budapest, 1936; French tr. as *Pourquoi et comment recueille-t-on la musique populaire?*, Geneva, 1948); with A. Lord, *Serbo-Croatian Folk Songs* (N.Y., 1951; reprinted in B. Suchoff, ed., *Yugoslav Folk Music*, vol. I, Albany, N.Y., 1978).

The N.Y. Bartók Archive publ. an ed. of Bartók's writings in English trs. in its Studies in Musicology series. The following vols., under the editorship of Benjamin Suchoff, were publ.: *Rumanian Folk Music* (The Hague, vols. I-III, 1967; vols. IV–V, 1975); *Turkish Folk Music from Asia Minor* (Princeton, 1976); *Béla Bartók's Essays* (selected essays; London and N.Y., 1976); *Yugoslav Folk Music* (4 vols., Albany, N.Y., 1978); *The Hungarian Folk Song* (Albany, N.Y., 1981).

BIBL.: An extensive literature in many languages exists concerning various aspects of Bartók's life and music; in addition to the selected list of writings listed below, see the journal *Documenta Bartókiana* (Budapest, 1964–70; 1977–). *Musikblätter des Anbruch*, III/5 (Vienna, 1921); *Zénei Szemle*, VIII (Budapest, 1928); D. Dille, *B. B.* (Antwerp, 1939); J. Demény, *B.* (Budapest, 1946); D. Dille, *B. B.* (Brussels, 1947); G. Láng, *B. élete és müvei* (Budapest, 1947); J. Deményi, ed., *Bartók Béla levelek* (Budapest, 3 vols., 1948, 1951, and 1955; 2d ed., 1976; Ger. tr., 1960; 2d ed., 1973; Eng. tr., 1971); S. Moreux, *B. B.: Sa vie, ses oeuvres, son langage* (Paris, 1949; Ger. tr., Zürich, 1950; Eng. tr., London, 1953); B. Rondi, *B.* (Rome, 1950); H. Stevens, *The Life and Music of B. B.* (N.Y., 1953; 2d ed., rev., 1964; 3d ed., rev. 1993, by M. Gillies); P. Csobádi, *B.* (Budapest, 1955); B. Szabolcsi, ed., *B.: Sa vie et son oeuvre* (Budapest, 1956; 2d ed., 1968; Ger. tr., 1957; enl. ed., 1972); A. Fassett, *The Naked Face of Genius; B. B.'s American Years* (Boston, 1958; reprint as *B. B.; The American Years*, N.Y., 1970); J. Uhde, *B. B.* (Berlin, 1959); J. Demény, ed., *Ausgewählte Briefe* (Budapest, 1960; Eng. tr., London, 1971); L. Lesznai, *B. B.: Sein Leben, seine Werke* (Leipzig, 1961; Eng. tr., 1973, as *B.*); B. Szabolcsi, *B. B.: Leben und Werk* (Leipzig, 1961; 2d ed., 1968); V. Bator, *The B. B. Archives: History and Catalogue* (N.Y., 1963); P. Citron, *B.* (Paris, 1963); J. Ujfalussy, *Bartók Béla* (Budapest, 1965; 3d ed., 1976; Eng. tr., Boston, 1972; in Russian, 1971; Ger. tr., 1973); I. Martynov, *B. B.* (Moscow, 1968); I. Nestyev, *B. B.*

(Moscow, 1969); *B. B.: A Complete Catalogue of His Published Works* (London, 1970); E. Lendvai, *B. B.: An Analysis of His Music* (London, 1971); D. Dille, *Thematisches Verzeichnis der Jugendwerke B. B.s 1890–1904* (Budapest, 1974); T. Crow, ed., *B. Studies* (Detroit, 1976); E. Lendvai, *B. and Kodály* (4 vols., Budapest, 1978–80); P. Autexier, ed., *B. B.: Musique de la vie* (Paris, 1981); B. Bartók, Jr., *Apám életének krónikája* (Budapest, 1981); idem, *Bartók Béla családi levelei* (Budapest, 1981); Y. Queffélec, *B. B.* (Paris, 1981); B. Bartók, Jr., *Bartók Béla műhelyében* (Budapest, 1982); H. Milne, *B.: His Life and Times* (Tunbridge Wells, 1982); E. Antokoletz, *The Music of B. B.* (Berkeley, Los Angeles, and London, 1984); P. Griffiths, *B.* (London, 1984); G. Ránki, ed., *B. and Kodály Revisited* (Budapest, 1987); E. Antokoletz, *B. B.: A Guide to Research* (N.Y., 1988; 2d ed., 1997); J. Platthy, *B.: A Critical Biography* (Santa Claus, Ind., 1988); M. Gillies, *B. in Britain: A Guided Tour* (Oxford, 1989); D. Dille, *B. B.: Regard sur le passé* (Louvain-la-Neuve, 1990); N. John, ed., *The Stage Works of B. B.* (London and Riverrun, N.Y., 1991); P. Wilson, *The Music of B. B.* (New Haven, 1992); J. de Waard, *B.* (Haarlem, 1993); C. Pesavento, *Musik von B. B. als pädagogisches Programm* (Frankfurt am Main and N.Y., 1994); K. Chalmers, *B. B.* (London, 1995); P. Laki, ed., *B. and His World* (Princeton, 1995); L. Somfai, *B. B.: Composition, Concepts, and Autograph Sources* (Berkeley, 1996).

Bartoletti, Bruno, noted Italian conductor; b. Sesto Fiorentino, June 10, 1926. He studied flute at the Florence Cons., and then received training in piano and composition while serving as a flutist in the orch. of the Florence Teatro Comunale. In 1949 he became an assistant conductor there, making his formal debut conducting *Rigoletto* in 1953. In 1954 he made his debut as a sym. conductor at the Maggio Musicale Fiorentino, where he later was director (1957–64). On Oct. 23, 1956, he made his U.S. debut at the Chicago Lyric Opera conducting *Il Trovatore*, and then served as its resident conductor until 1963. With Pino Donati, he was its co-artistic director from 1964 to 1975, and then its sole artistic director from 1975 to 2000 and then served as its music director emeritus. He also was artistic director of the Rome Opera (1965–69), and later artistic advisor (1986–87) and artistic director (1987–92) of the Florence Teatro Comunale. As a guest conductor, he appeared throughout Europe, the United States, and South America, becoming especially admired for his idiomatic readings of the Italian operatic repertoire; he also conducted various French and Russian operas with success.

Bartoli, Cecilia, outstanding Italian mezzo-soprano; b. Rome, June 4, 1966. She began vocal training at a very early age with her mother; at the age of 9, sang the off-stage role of the shepherd in *Tosca*. After studying trombone at the Accademia di Santa Cecilia in Rome, she pursued a vocal career, attracting favorable attention when she was 19 on an Italian television special with Ricciarelli and Nucci. Her formal stage debut followed in Verona in 1987. She then received valuable coaching from Karajan and Barenboim. On July 17, 1990, she made her U.S. debut as soloist at the Mostly Mozart Festival in New York. During the 1990–91 season, she made successful debuts with the Opéra de la Bastille in Paris as Cherubino, at La Scala in Milan as Isolier in *Le Comte Ory*, at the Maggio Musicale Fiorentino as Dorabella, and at the Teatro Liceo in Barcelona as Rosina. In 1992 she performed admirably as Cherubino and Dorabella in concert performances with Barenboim and the Chicago Sym. Orch.; also appeared as Despina at the Salzburg Festival. On April 23, 1993, she made a sensational U.S. operatic stage debut with the Houston Grand Opera as Rosina. She made her first appearance at the John F. Kennedy Center for the Performing Arts in Washington, D.C., on March 25, 1994. On Sept. 29, 1994, she regaled audiences at the opening of the 1994–95 season of N.Y.'s Carnegie Hall when she appeared as soloist with Marriner and the Academy of St. Martin-in-the-Fields. The event was later telecast to the nation over PBS. She made her debut at the Metropolitan Opera in New York as Despina on Feb. 9, 1996. Her recital debut followed at Carnegie Hall on March 28, 1996. In 1998 she appeared as Susanna at the Metropolitan Opera and as Paisiello's Nina in Zürich. The matchless combination of her vocal perfection and extraordinary dramatic gifts have made Bartoli one of the most heralded singers of her day. Among her other acclaimed operatic roles are Concepción, Bellini's Romeo, Massenet's Charlotte, and Offenbach's Hélène. In addition to opera, she pursues a remarkably successful concert career.

BIBL.: K. Chesnin and R. Stendahl, *C. B.: The Passion of Song* (N.Y., 1997); M. Hoelterhoff, *Cinderella & Company: Backstage at the Opera with C. B.* (N.Y., 1999).

Bartoš, Jan Zdeněk, Czech composer; b. Dvůr Králové nad Labem, June 4, 1908; d. Prague, June 1, 1981. He played the violin as a youth; then took composition lessons with Šín and Křička at the Prague Cons., graduating in 1943. He earned his living playing in dance orchs.; from 1945 to 1956 he was a member of the Music Section of the Ministry of Education and Culture; in 1958 he was appointed teacher of composition at the Prague Cons. In his music, he followed the national traditions of the Czech school.

WORKS: DRAMATIC: OPERAS: *Rýparka* (Ripar's Wife; 1949); *Prokletý zámek* (The Accursed Castle; 1949); *útok na nebe* (The Attack of Heaven; 1953–54). OPERETTA: *Je libo ananas?* (Do You Like Pineapples?; 1956. BALLETS: *Hanuman* (1941); *Mirella* (1956); *Král manéže* (King of the Manege; 1963).

Bartoš, Josef, Czech writer on music; b. Vysoké Myto, March 4, 1887; d. Prague, Oct. 27, 1952. He studied with Stecker at the Prague Cons., and with Hostinský and Nejedlý at the Univ. of Prague (1905–09); he also attended the Sorbonne in Paris. He was active as a teacher and music critic. He publ. an important work on the National Opera of Prague (1938).

Bary, Alfred (Erwin) von, German tenor; b. La Valetta, Malta, Jan. 18, 1873; d. Munich, Sept. 13, 1926. He studied medicine at the Univ. of Munich (M.D., 1898) and voice with Richard Müller in Leipzig. In 1903 he made his operatic debut as Lohengrin at the Dresden Court Opera, where he sang until 1915; he also appeared at the Bayreuth Festivals (1904–14); was a member of the Munich Court Opera (1915–18). Among his best roles were Parsifal, Siegmund, Tristan, and Siegfried.

Baselt, Fritz (Friedrich Gustav Otto), composer; b. Öls, Silesia, May 26, 1863; d. Frankfurt am Main, Nov. 11, 1931. He studied with Emil Kohler in Breslau and with Ludwig Bussler in Berlin, then was a musician, music dealer, composer, teacher, and conductor in Breslau, Essen, and Nuremberg. After 1894 he settled in Frankfurt am Main, where he conducted the Philharmonischer Verein and the Sängervereinigung. He wrote many light operas: *Der Fürst von Sevilla* (Nuremberg, 1888), *Don Alvaro* (Ansbach, 1892), *Der Sohn des Peliden* (Kassel, 1893), *Die Annaliese* (Kassel, 1896), *Die Musketiere im Damenstift* (Kassel, 1896), and *Die Circusfee* (Berlin, 1897); also 2 ballets: *Die Altweibermühle* (Frankfurt am Main, 1906) and *Rokoko* (Frankfurt am Main, 1907).

Basevi, Abramo, Italian composer and writer on music; b. Livorno, Nov. 29, 1818; d. Florence, Nov. 25, 1885. He studied music with Pietro Romani, and also took courses in medicine at the Univ. of Pisa. He founded and ed. the periodical *Harmonia* (1856–59) and the journal *Boccherini* (1862–82). He publ. *Studio sulle opere di G. Verdi* (1859), *Studi sull'armonia* (1865), and *Compendio della storia della musica* (1866). His 2 operas, *Romilda ed Ezzelino* (Florence, Aug. 11, 1840) and *Enrico Odoardo* (Florence, 1847), were not successful.

Basile, Andreana, famous Italian contralto and instrumentalist; b. Posilipo, c.1580; d. Rome, c.1640. She attracted the public by her extraordinary beauty and became known as "la bella Adriana." She often accompanied herself on the harp and guitar. In Naples she married Muzio Baroni, a Calabrian nobleman. In 1610 she was engaged by the court of Vincenzo Gonzaga, the Duke of Mantua, remaining a principal singer at his court until 1624. She was praised by Monteverdi for her musicianship. In 1633 she settled in Rome. Her daughter was Leonora Baroni, who became a famous singer in her own right.

Basili, Francesco, Italian composer and conductor; b. Loreto, Jan. 31, 1767; d. Rome, March 25, 1850. He studied with his father, Andrea Basili, and later with Giovanni Battista Borghi, then entered the Accademia di Santa Cecilia in Rome, where he took courses with Jannaconi. He served as conductor in various provincial Italian theaters; from 1827 to 1837 he was director of the Milan Cons. He wrote 13 operas. In 1837 he became conductor at St. Peter's Cathedral in Rome.

Basilides, Mária, Hungarian contralto; b. Jolsva, Nov. 11, 1886; d. Budapest, Sept. 26, 1946. She was educated at the Royal Academy of Music in Budapest; in 1915 she became a member of the Budapest Opera, remaining on its roster until her death; she also made appearances with the Berlin State Opera, the Dresden State Opera, and the Bavarian State Opera of Munich. She championed the music of Bartók and Kodály as a soloist in recitals and with sym. orchs.

BIBL.: J. Molnár, *Basilides Mária* (Budapest, 1967).

Basiola, Mario, Italian baritone; b. Annico, July 12, 1892; d. there, Jan. 3, 1965. He was a pupil of Cotogni in Rome. In 1918 he made his operatic debut, and then sang in Barcelona (1920) and Florence (1921) before appearing with the San Carlo Opera Co. in the United States (1923–25). On Nov. 11, 1925, he made his Metropolitan Opera debut in New York as Amonasro, remaining on its roster until 1932; he then sang at Milan's La Scala and in Rome (1933–38), and at London's Covent Garden (1939). In 1946 he toured Australia, where he taught until 1951; then settled in Milan as a voice teacher. Among his prominent roles were Rossini's Figaro, Valentin, Iago, Rigoletto, and Scarpia.

Bassani, (also **Bassano, Bassiani), Giovanni Battista**, Italian composer, organist, and violinist; b. Padua, c.1647; d. Bergamo, Oct. 1, 1716. He studied with Legrenzi and Castrovillari in Venice, and in 1667 became a member of the funereally named Accademia della Morte in Ferrara, serving as organist and composer. On July 3, 1677, he became a member of the more cheerful Accademia Filarmonica in Bologna; also served as maestro di cappella and organist of the apocalyptic Confraternità del Finale in Modena (1677–80). In 1680 he became maestro di cappella to the Duke of Mirandola; in 1682 he was appointed principe of the Accademia Filarmonica; in 1683 and 1684 he was maestro di cappella of the Accademia della Morte. In 1687 he was named maestro di cappella of the Ferrara Cathedral, and in 1712 at S. Maria Maggiore in Bergamo; he also taught at the music school of the Congregazione di Carita there. He is known to have written at least 9 operas, but these are lost; only a few arias from his opera *Gli amori alla moda* (Ferrara, 1688) have survived. Some 15 oratorios have been attributed to him, but these are also lost; however, the texts to 3 have survived.

BIBL.: R. Haselbach, *G. B. Bassani* (Kassel and Basel, 1955).

Bassi, Amedeo (Vittorio), Italian tenor; b. Montespertoli, near Florence, July 20, 1874; d. Florence, Jan. 14, 1949. He was a pupil of Pavesi in Florence, where he made his operatic debut in 1897 in Marchetti's *Ruy Blas*, then sang in various Italian opera houses. In 1902 he made his first tour of South America, and in 1908 sang Radames at the opening of the new Teatro Colón in Buenos Aires. On Dec. 19, 1906, he made his U.S. debut in that same role at N.Y.'s Manhattan Opera House, remaining on its roster until 1908. In 1907 he made his first appearance at London's Covent Garden; he also made appearances with the Chicago Grand Opera Co. (1910–16). He made his Metropolitan Opera debut in New York on March 2, 1911, as Ramerrez in *La Fanciulla del West*. After singing at Milan's La Scala (1921–26), he retired from the operatic stage and sang widely in concerts. He also taught in Florence. His most famous student was Ferruccio Tagliavini. Bassi was particularly known for his roles in Italian operas, but he also sang such Wagnerian roles as Loge, Siegfried, and Parsifal. He created the roles of Lionello in Mascagni's *Amica* (1905) and Angel Clare in d'Erlanger's *Tess* (1906).

Bassi, Carolina Manna, greatly esteemed Italian contralto; b. Naples, Jan. 10, 1781; d. Cremona, Dec. 12, 1862. She was the daughter of the comic bass Giovanni Bassi. With her brother, the comic bass Nicola Bassi (1767–1825), she began her career in her father's company of Raggazi Napoletani at the Teatro San Carlo in Naples in 1789. She subsequently pursued a distinguished career, creating major roles in Meyerbeer's *Semiramide riconosciuta* (Turin, March 1819), *Margherita d'Angiù* (Milan, Nov. 14, 1820), and *L'Esule di Granata* (Milan, March 12, 1821), in Rossini's *Bianca e Falliero, ossia Il consiglio dei tre* (Milan, Dec. 26, 1819), and in operas by Pacini and Mercadante. After retiring from the operatic stage in 1828, she appeared in concerts.

Bassi, Luigi, Italian baritone; b. Pesaro, Sept. 4, 1766; d. Dresden, Sept. 13, 1825. He studied with Pietro Morandi in Senigallia, making his debut in Pesaro at the age of 13. He then sang in Florence, and in 1784 went to Prague, where he soon became greatly appreciated. Mozart wrote the part of Don Giovanni for him and heeded his advice in matters of detail. Bassi was in Vienna from 1806 to 1814, then briefly in Prague. In 1815 he joined an Italian opera company in Dresden.

Bastianini, Ettore, Italian baritone; b. Siena, Sept. 24, 1922; d. Sirmione, Jan. 25, 1967. He studied in Florence with Flaminio Contini. In 1945 he made his debut as a bass singing Colline in Ravenna; in 1948 he made his first appearance at Milan's La Scala as Tiresias in *Oedipus Rex*. Following additional training with Rucciana Bertarini, he turned to baritone roles in 1952. He sang Andrei in the rev. version of *War and Peace* in Florence in 1953. On Dec. 5, 1953, he made his Metropolitan Opera debut in New York as Germont, and was on its roster until 1957 and again 1959–60 and 1964–66. From 1954 he also sang again at La Scala. In 1956 he made his first appearance in Chicago as Riccardo in *I Puritani*. In 1962 he made his debut at London's Covent Garden as Renato. Among his other roles were Rigoletto, Amonasro, Don Carlos, Escamillo, and Scarpia.

BIBL.: M. Boagno and G. Starone, *E. B.: Una voce di bronzo e di velluto* (Parma, 1991).

Bastin, Jules, Belgian bass; b. Pont, Aug. 18, 1933; d. Brussels, Dec. 2, 1996. He studied at the Brussels Cons. In 1960 he became a member of the Théâtre de la Monnaie in Brussels; he also appeared in London, Chicago, N.Y., and Toronto. He was best known for his appearances in such French operas as *Le Prophète, Benvenuto Cellini, Pelléas et Mélisande*, and Massenet's *Cendrillon*. In 1979 he took part in the Paris premiere of the 3-act version of Berg's *Lulu*. He also pursued an active concert career.

Bates, Sarah (née **Harrop**), English singer; b. c.1755; d. London, 1811. She was born into a poor family. She worked in a Halifax factory to support herself; finally making her way to London, where she studied with the English organist Joah Bates (b. Halifax [baptized], March 8, 1741; d. London, June 8, 1799), whom she married in 1780; she also took lessons with Antonio Sacchini. She made her formal debut at Covent Garden in *Judas Maccabaeus* on Feb. 14, 1777. She made regular appearances at her husband's Concerts of Antient Music series.

Bates, William, English composer who flourished in the 2d half of the 18th century. He wrote popular English operas in the ballad-opera style. His most popular work was *Flora or Hob in the Well*, which he wrote and arranged in 1760 (Covent Garden, April 25, 1770), using 7 of John Hippisley's songs from the 1729 *Flora or Hob's Opera*, together with 8 new songs of his own and a new overture. Neither of his works is to be confused with Thomas Doggett's 1711 farce with songs, a forerunner of the true ballad opera, variously titled *The Country Wake or Hob* or *The Country Wake*. His other stage works are *The Jovial Crew* (1760; altered to *The Ladies Frolick* in 1770), *The Theatrical Candidates* (1775), *The Device, or The Marriage Officer* (1777), and *Second Thought Is Best* (1778); also a grand opera, *Pharnaces* (London, Feb. 15, 1765).

Bath, Hubert, English composer and conductor; b. Barnstaple, Nov. 6, 1883; d. Harefield, Middlesex, April 24, 1945. He was a pupil of Beringer (piano) and Corder (composition) at the Royal

Academy of Music in London; he was active as a conductor of popular orch. and choral concerts. He composed the operas *Spanish Student* (1904), *Bubbles* (Belfast, Nov. 26, 1923), *The Sire de Maletroit's Door* (n.d.), *The 3 Strangers* (n.d.), *Trilby* (n.d.), and the comic opera *Young England* (Birmingham, 1915).

Bathori, Jane (real name, **Jeanne-Marie Berthier**), French mezzo-soprano; b. Paris, June 14, 1877; d. there, Jan. 21, 1970. She studied voice with Émile Engel at the Paris Cons., whom she married in 1908; she also received training in violin and piano there. In 1898 she made her concert debut in Paris and in 1900 her operatic debut in Nantes. She subsequently devoted herself to a concert career, often accompanying herself at the piano in her recitals. She gave first performances of works by Debussy, Ravel, Satie, Milhaud, and others. During World War II, she lived in Buenos Aires. After the War, she returned to Paris, where she taught. She publ. *Conseils sur le chant* (Paris, 1929) and *Sur l'interprétation des mélodies de Claude Debussy* (Paris, 1953).

BIBL.: L. Cuneo-Laurent, *The Performer as Catalyst: The Role of the Singer J. B. (1877–1970) in the Careers of Debussy, Ravel, Les Six, and their Contemporaries in Paris 1904–1926* (diss., N.Y. Univ., 1982).

Báthy, Anna, Hungarian soprano; b. Beregszász, June 13, 1901; d. Budapest, May 20, 1962. She studied voice at the Academy of Music in Budapest. She made her operatic debut at the Municipal Theater in Budapest in 1928 as Elisabeth in *Tannhäuser*; in 1929 she joined the Budapest Opera, where she sang mostly Verdi and Wagner.

BIBL.: V. Somogyi and I. Molnár, *Báthy Anna* (Budapest, 1969).

Battaille, Charles-Amable, French bass; b. Nantes, Sept. 30, 1822; d. Paris, May 2, 1872. He was originally a medical student, then turned to music and studied voice at the Paris Cons. He made his debut at the Opéra Comique in *La Fille du régiment* (June 22, 1848), and also created several roles in operas by Thomas, Adam, Halévy, and Meyerbeer. A throat disorder ended his stage career, and he retired in 1863. He was on the staff of the Paris Cons. from 1851. He publ. an extensive method of singing in 2 vols.: 1. *Nouvelles recherches sur la phonation* (1861) and 2. *De la physiologie appliquée au mécanisme du chant* (1863).

Battishill, Jonathan, English organist and composer; b. London, May 1738; d. Islington, Dec. 10, 1801. He was a chorister at St. Paul's (1747), and then later apprenticed to William Savage. He was deputy organist under Boyce at the Chapel Royal, then harpsichordist at Covent Garden and organist in several London parishes. He wrote an opera with Michael Arne, *Almena* (Drury Lane Theatre, Nov. 2, 1764), and a pantomime, *The Rites of Hecate* (Drury Lane Theatre, Dec. 26, 1763).

Battistini, Mattia, celebrated Italian baritone; b. Rome, Feb. 27, 1856; d. Colle Baccaro, near Rieti, Nov. 7, 1928. He studied with V. Persichini and E. Terziani. On Dec. 11, 1878, he made his operatic debut as Alfonso XI in *La Favorite* at the Teatro Argentino in Rome. In 1883 he made his first appearance at London's Covent Garden as Riccardo in *I Puritani*, and he returned to London regularly until 1906. In 1888 he made his debut at Milan's La Scala as Nélusko. He first sang in St. Petersburg in 1893 as Hamlet, and returned there every season until 1914. He also sang in various other European music centers and in South America to great acclaim. Although he never sang in the United States, he was acknowledged as the foremost Italian baritone of his time. In 1924 he retired from the operatic stage and then appeared in concerts until his farewell in Graz on Oct. 17, 1927. Battistini was a master of bel canto, with a remarkably expressive high register. His operatic repertoire included over 80 roles, among the most celebrated being those in operas by Bellini and Donizetti. He also was renowned for his portrayals of Rossini's Figaro, Rigoletto, Don Giovanni, Amonasro, Ruslan, Iago, Onegin, Rubinstein's Demon, Scarpia, and the tenor role of Werther.

BIBL.: F. Palmegiani, *M. B. (Il re dei baritone)* (Milan, 1948).

Battle, Kathleen (Deanna), outstanding black American soprano; b. Portsmouth, Ohio, Aug. 13, 1948. She studied with Franklin Bens at the Univ. of Cincinnati College-Cons. of Music (B.Mus., 1970; M.Mus., 1971). After making her professional debut as a soloist in the Brahms *Requiem* at the Spoleto Festival in 1972, she pursued further training with Italo Tajo in Cincinnati. In 1974 she captured 1st prize in the WGN-Illinois Opera Guild Auditions of the Air and in 1975 1st prize in the Young Artists Awards in Washington, D.C. In 1975 she made her formal operatic debut as Rosina with the Michigan Opera Theatre in Detroit, and later that year her first appearance at the N.Y. City Opera as Mozart's Susanna. On Dec. 22, 1977, she made her Metropolitan Opera debut in New York as the Shepherd in *Tannhäuser*, and quickly established herself as one of its most esteemed artists via such roles as Massenet's and Strauss's Sophie, Despina, Blondchen, Zerlina, and Pamina. She also appeared with other major opera houses in the United States and Europe, and toured extensively as a soloist with leading orchs. and as a recitalist. On June 17, 1985, she made her Covent Garden debut in London as Zerbinetta. In 1987 she appeared as soloist at the New Year's Day Concert of the Vienna Phil. conducted by Karajan, which was telecast throughout the world. Although Battle's vocal gifts were undeniable, she acquired a reputation as an extremely temperamental artist. In Jan. 1993 she quit the Metropolitan Opera's production of *Der Rosenkavalier* during rehearsal. During rehearsal for her starring role in its revival of *La Fille du Régiment* on Feb. 7, 1994, general manager Joseph Volpe found her behavior so objectionable that he summarily dismissed her from the Metropolitan Opera roster. She subsequently pursued an active concert career.

Batton, Désiré-Alexandre, French composer; b. Paris, Jan. 2, 1798; d. Versailles, Oct. 15, 1855. He was a pupil of Cherubini at the Paris Cons., winning the Prix de Rome in 1817 for his cantata *La Mort d'Adonis*. In 1851 he was appointed inspector of the branch schools of the cons. where he also taught singing. His most successful opera was *La Marquise de Brinvilliers*, written in collaboration with Auber, Hérold, and others, and produced in Paris on Oct. 31, 1831. His other operas were *La Fenêtre secrète* (Paris, Nov. 17, 1818), *Velleda* (1820), *Ethelvina* (1827), *Le Prisonnier d'etat* (1828), *Le Camp du drap d'or* (1828), and *Le Remplaçant* (1837).

Baudo, Serge (Paul), French conductor, nephew of **Paul Tortelier**; b. Marseilles, July 16, 1927. His father was a prof. of oboe at the Paris Cons. He studied conducting with Fourestier and theory with Jean and Noël Gallon at the Paris Cons., winning premiers prix in harmony, percussion, chamber music, and conducting. After serving as conductor of the orch. of Radio Nice (1959–62), he conducted at the Paris Opéra (1962–65). He held the post of 1st conductor of the Orchestre de Paris from 1967 to 1970. On Sept. 16, 1970, he made his Metropolitan Opera debut in New York conducting *Les Contes d'Hoffmann*. He was music director of the Lyons Opéra (1969–71), and then of the Orchestre Philharmonique Rhône-Alpes (later known as the Orchestre National de Lyons) from 1971 to 1987. He was also the founder-artistic director of the Berlioz Festival in Lyons (1979–89).

Bauermeister, Mathilde, German-English soprano; b. Hamburg, 1849; d. Herne Bay, Kent, Oct. 15, 1926. She was a pupil of Schira at the Royal Academy of Music in London. After recital appearances in Dublin (1866), she made her first appearance at London's Covent Garden in 1868 as Siebel, where she sang occasionally until 1885. She then was on its roster from 1887 to 1905. In 1879 she made the first of 16 visits to North America. On Nov. 11, 1891, she made her debut with the Metropolitan Opera as Amore in *Orfeo ed Euridice* during the company's visit to Chicago. She first appeared on the stage of the Metropolitan in New York on Dec. 14, 1891, as Gertrude in *Roméo et Juliette*. She then was again on its roster from 1893 to 1897 and from 1898 to 1906. Her repertoire included over 100 roles.

Bauer-Theussl, Franz (Ferdinand), Austrian conductor; b. Zillingdorf, Sept. 25, 1928. He was a pupil of Seidlhofer (piano) and Clemens Krauss (conducting) at the Vienna Academy of Music. After making his conducting debut with *Les Contes d'Hoffmann* at the Salzburg Landestheater in 1953, he was assistant conductor at the Salzburg Festivals (1953–57), then was resident conductor of the Vienna Volksoper (from 1957) and conductor of the Netherlands Opera in Amsterdam (1960–64).

Baum, Kurt, Czech-born American tenor; b. Prague, March 15, 1908; d. N.Y., Dec. 27, 1989. He studied with Garbin in Milan and Scolari in Rome; in 1933, won the Vienna International Competition, then made his operatic debut in the premiere of Zemlinsky's *Der Kreidekreis* in Zürich (Oct. 14, 1933). After singing with the German Theater in Prague (1934–39), he made his U.S. debut as Radames in Chicago in 1939, where he sang until 1941. On Nov. 27, 1941 he made his Metropolitan Opera debut in New York as the Singer in *Der Rosenkavalier*, remaining on its roster until 1962, and again from 1964 to 1966; also made guest appearances at Milan's La Scala (1947–48), the Florence Maggio Musicale (1952), London's Covent Garden (1953), the San Francisco Opera, and in South America.

Bausznern, Waldemar von, German composer; b. Berlin, Nov. 29, 1866; d. Potsdam, Aug. 20, 1931. He studied music with Kiel and Bargiel in Berlin, then was active mainly as a choral conductor. He also taught at the Cons. of Cologne (1903–08), at the Hochschule für Musik in Weimar (1908–16), where he also served as director, and at the Hoch Cons. in Frankfurt am Main, where he was a teacher and director (1916–23). He also taught at the Academy of Arts and the Academy for Church and School Music in Berlin. He was a prolific composer, numbering among his works the operas *Dichter und Welt* (Weimar, 1897), *Dürer in Venedig* (Weimar, 1901), *Herbort und Hilde* (Mannheim, 1902), and *Der Bundschuh* (Frankfurt am Main, 1904). He ed. the score of the opera *Der Barbier von Bagdad* by Peter Cornelius, and completed his unfinished opera *Gunlöd*, which was produced in this version in Cologne in 1906.

Bayer, Josef, Austrian composer and conductor; b. Vienna, March 6, 1852; d. there, March 12, 1913. He studied at the Vienna Cons. (1859–70) with Georg and Joseph Hellmesberger (violin), Dachs (piano), and Bruckner (theory). He wrote a great number of operettas and ballets that were quite popular, owing to his facility for melodic writing and piquant rhythms. He traveled a great deal through Europe as a conductor. He visited New York in 1881, and conducted there the first performance of his operetta *Chevalier von San Marco* on Feb. 4, 1881. Other operettas successfully produced in Vienna were *Menelaus* (1892), *Fräulein Hexe* (1898), and *Der Polizeichef* (1904). He also wrote 2 exotic comic operas: *Alien Fata*, on a Bosnian subject, and *Der Goldasoka*, on a Hindu theme. The list of his ballets produced in Vienna include *Wiener Walzer* (1886), *Die Puppenfee* (1888), *Sonne und Erde* (1889), *Ein Tanzmärchen* (1890), *Rouge et Noir* (1892), *Die Donaunixe* (1892), *Eine Hochzeit in Bosnien* (1893; with Bosnian folk melodies), *Burschenliebe* (1894), *Rund um Wien* (1894), *Die Braut von Korea* (1896), and *Die kleine Welt* (1904); ballets produced at Berlin include *Deutsche Märsche* (1887), *Die Welt in Bild und Tanz* (1892), *Die Engelsjäger* (1896), and *Columbia* (1893).

Bazin, François-Emmanuel-Joseph, French composer; b. Marseilles, Sept. 4, 1816; d. Paris, July 2, 1878. He studied with Berton and Halévy at the Paris Cons., winning the Prix de Rome in 1840. In 1844 he was appointed to the faculty of the Paris Cons. He wrote 8 comic operas, none of which was retained in the repertoire, although *Le Voyage en Chine*, produced in 1865, was temporarily acclaimed. He also publ. a manual, *Cours d'harmonie théorique et pratique*, which was adopted at the Paris Cons.

Bázlik, Miroslav, Slovak composer; b. Partizánská Lupča, April 12, 1931. He studied piano at the Bratislava Cons.; then took a course in composition with Cikker at the Bratislava Academy of Musical Arts, graduating in 1961. His musical idiom evolved along modern Romantic lines; in his later compositions, he resorted to serial techniques. He composed the opera *Petr a Lucie* (1962–66; Bratislava, 1967).

Bazzini, Antonio, Italian violinist and composer; b. Brescia, March 11, 1818; d. Milan, Feb. 10, 1897. Encouraged by Paganini, before whom he played in 1836, Bazzini embarked upon a series of successful tours through Italy, France, Spain, Belgium, Poland, England, and Germany (1837–63). He taught at the Milan Cons. from 1873, and in 1882 became its director. Among his compositions are *Turanda*, opera after Gozzi's *Turandot* (La Scala, Milan, Jan. 13, 1867), and symphonic overtures to Alfieri's *Saul* (1866) and to Shakespeare's *King Lear* (1868).

Beach, Mrs. H. H. A. (née **Amy Marcy Cheney**), important American composer; b. Henniker, N.H., Sept. 5, 1867; d. N.Y., Dec. 27, 1944. She was descended of early New England colonists, and was a scion of a cultural family. She entered a private school in Boston; studied piano with Ernest Perabo and Carl Baermann; received instruction in harmony and counterpoint from Junius W. Hill. She made her debut as a pianist in Boston on Oct. 24, 1883, playing Chopin's *Rondo* in E-flat major and Moscheles's G minor concerto under Neuendorff. On March 28, 1885, she made her first appearance with the Boston Sym. Orch. in Chopin's F minor concerto under Gericke. On Dec. 3, 1885, at the age of 18, she married Dr. H. H. A. Beach, a Boston surgeon, a quarter of a century older than she. The marriage was a happy one, and as a token of her loyalty to her husband, she used as her professional name Mrs. H. H. A. Beach. She began to compose modestly, mostly for piano, but soon embarked on an ambitious Mass, which was performed by the Handel and Haydn Soc. in Boston on Feb. 18, 1892, becoming the first woman to have a composition performed by that organization. On Oct. 30, 1896, her *Gaelic Symphony*, based on Irish folk tunes, was performed by the Boston Sym. Orch. with exceptional success. On April 6, 1900, she appeared as soloist with the Boston Sym. Orch. in the first performance of her Piano Concerto. She also wrote a great many songs in an endearing Romantic manner. When her husband died in 1910, she went to Europe; she played her works in Berlin, Leipzig, and Hamburg, attracting considerable attention as the first of her gender and national origin to be able to compose music of a European quality of excellence. She returned to the United States in 1914 and lived in New York. Her music, unpretentious in its idiom and epigonic in its historical aspect, retained its importance as the work of a pioneer woman composer in America. Among her works is the opera *Cabildo* (1932; Athens, Ga., Feb. 27, 1947).

BIBL.: P. Goetschius, *Mrs. H. H. A. B.* (Boston, 1906); E. Merrill, *Mrs. H. H. A. B.: Her Life and Music* (diss., Univ. of Rochester, 1963); M. Eden, *Energy and Individuality in the Art of Anna Huntington, Sculptor, and A. B., Composer* (Metuchen, N.J., 1987); W. Jenkins, *The Remarkable Mrs. B., American Composer: A Biographical Account Based on Her Diaries, Letters, Newspaper Clippings, and Personal Reminiscences* (Warren, Mich., 1994).

Beach, John Parsons, American composer; b. Gloversville, N.Y., Oct. 11, 1877; d. Pasadena, Calif., Nov. 6, 1953. He studied piano at the New England Cons. of Music in Boston, then took lessons with Gédalge in Paris and Malipiero in Venice. Returning to Boston, he took additional lessons with Loeffler. He held various teaching jobs; finally settled in Pasadena. His opera *Pippa's Holiday* was premiered in Paris in 1915. He also composed the ballets *Phantom Satyr* (Asolo, Italy, July 6, 1925) and *Mardi Gras* (New Orleans, Feb. 15, 1926).

Beard, John, renowned English tenor; b. c.1717; d. Hampton, Feb. 5, 1791. He studied with Bernard Gates at the Chapel Royalm and while still a youth sang in Handel's *Esther* in London (1732). He left the Chapel Royal in 1734, and on Nov. 9 of that year made his debut as Silvio in Handel's *Il Pastor fido* at Covent Garden. He subsequently appeared in about 10 operas, many oratorios, masques, and odes by Handel. In 1761 he became manager of Covent Garden, but continued to make appearances as a singer. He retired in 1767 owing to increasing deafness.

Beardslee, Bethany, American soprano; b. Lansing, Mich., Dec. 25, 1927. She studied at Michigan State Univ.; then received a scholarship to the Juilliard School of Music in New York, making her N.Y. debut in 1949. She soon became known as a specialist in modern music, evolving an extraordinary technique with a flutelike ability to sound impeccably precise intonation; she also mastered the art of *Sprechstimme*, which enabled her to give fine renditions of such works as Schoenberg's *Pierrot Lunaire*; she also was a brilliant performer of vocal parts in scores by Berg, Webern, and Stravinsky. In 1976 she joined the faculty of Westminster Choir College in Princeton, N.J.; in 1981–82 she was a prof. of music at the Univ. of Texas in Austin; after serving as performer-in-residence at the Univ. of Calif. at Davis (1982–83), she taught at Brooklyn College of the City Univ. of N.Y. (from 1983). She was married to the French pianist, conductor, editor, and composer Jacques-Louis Monod (b. Asnières, near Paris, Feb. 25, 1927) and, later, to the English-American composer and computer specialist Godfrey Winham (b. London, Dec. 11, 1934; d. Princeton, N.J., April 26, 1975).

Beattie, Herbert (Wilson), American bass and teacher; b. Chicago, Aug. 23, 1926. He studied voice with John Wilcox at the American Cons. of Music in Chicago and with Dick Marzzolo in N.Y.; he also studied at Colorado College (B.A., 1948), Westminster Choir College (M.M., 1950), and the Salzburg Mozarteum (1955). On Oct. 11, 1957, he made his debut at the N.Y. City Opera as Baron Bouphol in *La Traviata*, where he sang regularly until 1972 and again from 1980 to 1984; he also sang opera in other cities in the United States and Europe, and toured as a concert artist. He taught at Syracuse Univ. (1950–52), Pennsylvania State Univ. (1952–53), the Univ. of Buffalo (1953–58), and at Hofstra Univ. (1959–82). Among his best roles were Mozart's Osmin, Sarastro, Leporello, and Don Alfonso, and Rossini's Dr. Bartolo and Mustafà. He also sang in many contemporary operas.

Beaulieu (real name, **Martin-Beaulieu**), **Marie-Désiré,** French composer and author; b. Paris, April 11, 1791; d. Niort, Dec. 21, 1863. He studied violin with Kreutzer and composition with Bencincori and Abbé Roze, then with Méhul at the Paris Cons., winning the Prix de Rome in 1810. He wrote the operas *Anacréon* and *Philadelphie* and the oratorios *L'Hymne du matin*, *L'Hymne de la nuit*, etc. He publ. the essays *Du rythme, des effets qu'il produit et de leurs causes* (1852), *Mémoire sur ce qui reste de la musique de l'ancienne Grèce dans les premiers chants de l'église* (1852), *Mémoire sur le caractère que doit avoir la musique de l'Eglise* (1858), and *Mémoire sur l'origine de la musique* (1859). His main contribution to French musical culture was his organizing of annual music festivals in provincial towns. He founded the Association Musicale de l'Ouest in 1835, and in 1860 the Société des Concerts de Chant Classique, to which he bequeathed 100,000 francs.

Becerra (-Schmidt), Gustavo, Chilean composer; b. Temuco, Aug. 26, 1925. He studied at the Santiago Cons. with Pedro Allende, and then with Domingo Santa Cruz. In 1949 he graduated from the Univ. of Chile, where he became a prof. in 1952; he was its director of the Instituto de Extensión Musical (1959–63) and secretary-general of its music faculty (1969–71). From 1968 to 1970 he served as cultural attaché to the Chilean embassy in Bonn. In 1971 he received the Premio Nacional de Arte in music. His early works are set in the traditional neoclassical manner, but soon he adopted an extremely radical modern idiom, incorporating dodecaphonic and aleatory procedures and outlining a graphic system of notation, following the pictorial representation of musical sounds of the European avant-garde, but introducing some new elements, such as indication of relative loudness by increasing the size of the notes on a music staff with lines far apart. His works include the opera *La muerte de Don Rodrigo* (1958).

Bechgaard, Julius, Danish composer; b. Copenhagen, Dec. 19, 1843; d. there, March 4, 1917. He studied at the Leipzig Cons. and with Gade in Copenhagen. He lived in Germany, Italy, and Paris, then settled in Copenhagen. He wrote 2 operas: *Frode* (Copenhagen, May 11, 1893) and *Frau Inge* (Prague, 1894).

Bechi, Gino, notable Italian baritone; b. Florence, Oct. 16, 1913; d. there, Feb. 2, 1993. He studied in Florence with Frazzi and Di Giorgi and in Alessandria. In 1936 he made his operatic debut as Germont in Empoli, and then sang in Rome (1938–52) and at Milan's La Scala (1939–44; 1946–53), where he acquired an admirable reputation. In 1950 he sang with the La Scala company during its visit to London's Covent Garden, and he returned to London in 1958 to sing at Drury Lane. In 1952 he appeared in Chicago and San Francisco. He also made appearances in musical films. In later years, he was active as a teacher and opera producer. Bechi was best known for his Verdi roles, among them Falstaff, Amonasro, Hamlet, Iago, and Nabucco.

Beck, Franz, German violinist and composer; b. Mannheim, Feb. 20, 1734; d. Bordeaux, Dec. 31, 1809. He studied violin with his father and also had some instruction from Johann Stamitz. About 1750 he went to Italy; in 1761 he settled in Bordeaux, where he conducted at the Grand Théâtre. In 1783 he visited Paris to hear the first performance of his *Stabat Mater*. His works include the operas *La Belle Jardinière* (Bordeaux, Aug. 24, 1767), *Pandora*, melodrame (Paris, July 2, 1789), and *L'Île déserte* (not produced).

Beck, Karl, Austrian tenor; b. 1814; d. Vienna, March 3, 1879. He was the first to sing the role of Lohengrin (Weimar, Aug. 28, 1850).

Becker, Albert (Ernst Anton), German composer; b. Quedlinburg, June 13, 1834; d. Berlin, Jan. 10, 1899. He was a pupil of Dehn in Berlin (1853–56). He was appointed teacher of composition at the Scharwenka Cons. (1881), and became the conductor of the Berlin Cathedral Choir (1891). He wrote an opera, *Loreley* (1898).

Becker, Constantin Julius, German composer and author; b. Freiberg, Saxony, Feb. 3, 1811; d. Oberlössnitz, Feb. 26, 1859. He studied singing with Anacker and composition with Carl Becker. From 1837 to 1846 he ed. the *Neue Zeitschrift für Musik*, in association with Schumann. In 1843 he settled in Dresden, where he taught singing, composed, and wrote novels on musical subjects. In 1846 he went to Oberlössnitz, where he spent the remainder of his life. He wrote an opera, *Die Erstürmung von Belgrad* (Leipzig, May 21, 1848) and other works, but he is best known for his manuals: *Männergesangschule* (1845), *Harmonielehre für Dilettanten* (1842), and *Kleine Harmonielehre* (1844).

Becker, Heinz, prominent German musicologist; b. Berlin, June 26, 1922. He studied at the Berlin Hochschule für Musik, taking courses in clarinet, piano, conducting, and composition; he then enrolled at Humboldt Univ. in Berlin; received his Ph.D. in 1951 with the diss. *Zur Problematik und Technik der musikalischen Schlussgestaltung*; in 1956 he joined the musicological inst. of the Univ. of Hamburg as an assistant lecturer; he completed his Habilitation there with his *Studien zur Entwicklungsgeschichte der antiken und mittelalterlichen Rohrblattinstrumente* (1961; publ. in Hamburg, 1966). In 1966 he became a prof. of musicology at the Ruhr Univ. in Bochum, where he remained until his retirement in 1987. Among his numerous writings are *Der Fall Heine-Meyerbeer* (Berlin, 1958), *Beiträge zur Geschichte der Oper* (Regensburg, 1969), *Das Lokalkolorit in der Oper des 19. Jahrhunderts* (Regensburg, 1976), *Giacomo Meyerbeer in Selbstzeugnissen und Bilddokumenten* (Reinbek, 1980), and, with G. Becker, *Giacomo Meyerbeer: Ein Leben in Briefen* (Wilhelmshaven, 1983). He also ed. *Giacomo Meyerbeer: Briefwechsel und Tagebucher* (4 vols., Berlin, 1960–85).

BIBL.: J. Schläder and R. Quandt, eds., *H. B.: Festschrift zum 60. Geburtstag* (Laaber, 1982).

Becker, John J(oseph), remarkable American composer; b. Henderson, Ky., Jan. 22, 1886; d. Wilmette, Ill., Jan. 21, 1961. He studied at the Cincinnati Cons. (graduated, 1905), then at the Wisconsin Cons. in Milwaukee, where he was a pupil of Alexander von Fielitz, Carl Busch, and Wilhelm Middleschulte (Ph.D., 1923). From 1917 to 1927 he served as director of music at Notre Dame

Univ.; was chairman of the fine arts dept. at the College of St. Thomas in St. Paul, Minn. (1929–35). He was subsequently Minnesota State Director for the Federal Music Project (1935–41) and prof. of music at Barat College of the Sacred Heart at Lake Forest, Ill. (1943–57); he also taught sporadically at the Chicago Musical College. His early works are characterized by romantic moods in a somewhat Germanic manner. About 1930 he was drawn into the circle of modern American music; he was on the editorial board of the *New Music Quarterly*, founded by Cowell, and became associated with Charles Ives. He conducted modern American works with various groups in St. Paul. Striving to form a style that would be both modern and recognizably American, he wrote a number of pieces for various instrumental groups under the title *Soundpiece*. He also developed a type of dramatic work connecting theatrical action with music. Becker's music is marked by sparse sonorities of an incisive rhythmic character contrasted with dissonant conglomerates of massive harmonies.

WORKS: DRAMATIC: *The Season of Pan*, ballet suite for Small Ensemble (c.1910); *The City of Shagpat*, opera (c.1926–27; unfinished); *Salome*, film opera (c.1931; unfinished); *Dance Figure: Stagework No. 1*, ballet for Soprano and Orch. (1932; includes music from *Salome*); *The Life of Man: Stagework No. 4*, ballet for Speaking Chorus and Orch. (1932–43; unfinished); *Abongo, a Primitive Dance: Stagework No. 2*, ballet for Wordless Voices and 29 Percussion Instruments (1933; N.Y., May 16, 1963); *A Marriage with Space: Stagework No. 3*, ballet for Speaking Chorus and Orch. (1935; arr. as Sym. No. 4, *Dramatic Episodes*, 1940); *Nostalgic Songs of Earth*, ballet for Piano (Northfield, Minn., Dec. 12, 1938); *Vigilante 1938*, ballet for Piano and Percussion (Northfield, Minn., Dec. 12, 1938); *Privilege and Privation: Stagework No. 5c*, opera (1939; Amsterdam, June 22, 1982); *Rain Down Death: Stagework No. 5a*, incidental music to the play by A. Kreymborg for Chamber Orch. (1939; also as *A Prelude to Shakespeare* for Orch., 1937, rev. as Suite No. 1 for Orch., 1939); *Dance for Shakespeare's Tempest*, incidental music for Piano and Chamber Orch. (1940; unfinished; arr. by M. Benaroyo as *The Tempest* for 2 Pianos, 1954); *When the Willow Nods: Stagework No. 5b*, incidental music to the play by A. Kreymborg for Speaker and Chamber Orch. (1940; includes music from *4 Dances* for Piano and from *Nostalgic Songs of Earth*; rev. as Suite No. 2 for Orch., 1940); *Antigone*, incidental music to the play by Sophocles for Orch. (1940–44); *Trap Doors*, incidental music to the play by A. Kreymborg for Speaking Chorus and Piano (n.d.; unfinished); *Deirdre: Stagework No. 6*, opera (1945; unfished); *Faust: A Television Opera*, monodrama after Goethe for Tenor and Piano (1951; Los Angeles, April 8, 1985); *The Queen of Cornwall*, opera (1956; unfinished); *Madeleine et Judas*, incidental music to the play by R. Bruckberger for Orch. (1958; radio perf., Paris, March 25, 1959).

BIBL.: E. Becker, *J. J. B.: American Composer* (MS, 1958).

Beckmann, Johann Friedrich Gottlieb, German composer and organist; b. Celle, Sept. 6, 1737; d. there, April 25, 1792. He was one of the finest players and improvisers on the organ of his time. He was for many years active in Celle. He wrote an opera, *Lukas und Hännchen* (Braunschweig, 1768).

Beckwith, John, prominent Canadian composer, teacher, writer on music, and pianist; b. Victoria, British Columbia, March 9, 1927. He began piano lessons as a child with Ogreta McNeill and Gwendoline Harper; after attending Victoria College (1944–45), he settled in Toronto, studying piano privately with Alberto Guerrero (1945–50) and at the Univ. of Toronto (Mus.B., 1947). He also received private composition lessons from Boulanger in Paris (1950–52). He completed his education at the Univ. of Toronto (Mus.M., 1961). In 1950 he made his debut as a pianist in a lecture-recital in Toronto. He was assoc. ed. of the *Canadian Music Journal* (1957–62), music reviewer for the *Toronto Star* (1959–62; 1963–65), and program annotator for the Toronto Sym. (1966–70). From 1952 to 1966 he taught theory at the Royal Cons. of Music of Toronto, and in 1952 joined the faculty at the Univ. of Toronto; in 1984 he was named Jean A. Chalmers Prof. of Canadian Music there, the first position of its kind created by a Canadian univ., and also founded and directed its Inst. for Canadian Music. In 1990 he retired as prof. emeritus. He was area ed. for Canada for *The New Grove Dictionary of Music and Musicians* (1972–80) and general ed. of the Canadian Composers/Compositeurs Canadiens study series (from 1975); he was also coeditor of *The Modern Composer and His World* (with U. Kasemets; Toronto, 1961), *Contemporary Canadian Composers* (with K. MacMillan; Toronto, 1975), *Hello Out There!: Canada's New Music in the World, 1950–85* (with D. Cooper; Toronto, 1988), *Musical Canada: Words and Music Honouring Helmut Kallmann* (with F. Hall; Toronto, 1988), and *The Fifth Stream* (with P. Hatch; Toronto, 1991). In 1987 he was made a Member of the Order of Canada. His music is marked by pragmatic modernism, with ingenious applications of urban folklore and structural collage.

WORKS: DRAMATIC: *Night Blooming Cereus*, chamber opera (1953–58; radio premiere, Toronto, March 4, 1959; stage premiere, Toronto, April 5, 1960); *The Killdeer*, incidental music (1960); *The Shivaree*, opera (1965–66; 1978; Toronto, April 3, 1982); *Crazy to Kill*, opera (1987–88); *Taptoo!*, opera (1993–94).

Bedford, David (Vickerman), English composer, brother of **Steuart (John Rudolf) Bedford**; b. London, Aug. 4, 1937. He was the grandson of **Liza Lehmann**. After training in London at Trinity College of Music and with Berkeley at the Royal Academy of Music (1958–61), he completed his studies with Luigi Nono in Venice and worked in the RAI electronic music studio in Milan. Returning to England, he was active as a keyboardist and arranger with Kevin Ayers's rock band The Whole World. He was a teacher (1968–80) and composer-in-residence (1969–81) at Queen's College in London. From 1983 he was assoc. visiting composer at the Gordonstoun School in Scotland. In 1986 he became youth music director of the English Sinfonia in London, serving as its composer-in-assoc. from 1994. Bedford is a remarkably facile composer whose interests range from rock to art music, and from film scores to music for the young. Included in the latter category are the school operas *The Rime of the Ancient Mariner* (1978), *The Death of Baldur* (1979), *Fridiof's Saga* (1980), *The Ragnarok* (1982), *The Camlann Game* (1987), *The Return of Odysseus* (1988), and *Anna* (1992–93).

Bedford, Steuart (John Rudolf), English conductor, brother of **David (Vickerman) Bedford**; b. London, July 31, 1939. He was the grandson of **Liza Lehmann**. He received his training at the Royal Academy of Music in London and at Lancing College, Oxford. In 1967 he became conductor of the English Opera Group. After it was renamed the English Music Theatre Co. in 1975, he continued to conduct it until 1980. On June 16, 1973, he conducted the premiere of Britten's *Death in Venice* at the Aldeburgh Festival, where he subsequently conducted regularly. On Oct. 18, 1974, he made his Metropolitan Opera debut in New York conducting the same opera, and remained on its roster until 1977. He was music director of the English Sinfonia from 1981 to 1992. With Oliver Knussen, he served as co-artistic director of the Aldeburgh Festival from 1989. From 1969 to 1980 he was married to **Norma Burrowes**.

Beecham, Sir Thomas, celebrated English conductor; b. St. Helens, near Liverpool, April 29, 1879; d. London, March 8, 1961. His father, Sir Joseph Beecham, was a man of great wealth, derived from the manufacture of the once-famous Beecham pills; thanks to them, young Beecham could engage in life's pleasures without troublesome regard for economic limitations. He had his first music lessons from a rural organist; from 1892 to 1897 he attended the Rossall School at Lancashire, and later went to Wadham College, Oxford. In 1899 he organized, mainly for his own delectation, an amateur ensemble, the St. Helen's Orchestral Soc.; also in 1899 he conducted a performance with the prestigious Halle Orch. in Manchester. In 1902 he became conductor of K. Trueman's traveling opera company, which gave him valuable practical experience with theater music. In 1905 he gave his first professional sym. concert in London, with members of the Queen's Hall Orch.; in 1906 he became conductor of the New Sym. Orch., which he led until 1908; then formed a group in his own name, the Beecham Sym. Orch., which presented its first concert in London on Feb. 22, 1909. In 1910 he presented his first season of opera at London's Covent Garden, and in subsequent seasons conducted there and at other London theaters. In 1915 he organized the Beecham Opera Co., by which time his reputation as a forceful and charismatic conductor was securely established in England. His audiences grew; the critics, impressed by his imperious ways and his unquestioned ability to bring out spectacular operatic productions, sang his praise; however, some commentators found much to criticize in his somewhat cavalier treatment of the classics. In appreciation of his services to British music, Beecham was knighted in 1916; with the death of his father, he succeeded to the title of baronet. But all of his inherited money was not enough to pay for Beecham's exorbitant financial disbursements in his ambitious enterprises, and in 1920 his operatic enterprise went bankrupt. He rebounded a few years later and continued his extraordinary career. On Jan. 12, 1928, he made his U.S. debut as a guest conductor of the N.Y. Phil., at which concert Vladimir Horowitz also made his U.S. debut as soloist. In 1929 he organized and conducted the Delius Festival in London, to which Delius himself, racked by tertiary syphilitic affliction, paralyzed and blind, was brought from his residence in France to attend Beecham's musical homage to him. From 1932 to 1939 he conducted at Covent Garden. In 1932 Beecham organized the London Phil.; contemptuous of general distaste for the Nazi regime in Germany, he took the London Phil. to Berlin in 1936 for a concert which was attended by the Führer in person. As the war situation deteriorated on the Continent, Beecham went to the United States in May 1940, and also toured Australia. In 1941 he was engaged as conductor of the Seattle Sym. Orch., retaining this post until 1944; he also filled guest engagements at the Metropolitan Opera in New York from 1942 to 1944. In America he was not exempt from sharp criticism, which he haughtily dismissed as philistine complaints. On his part, he was outspoken in his snobbish disdain for the cultural inferiority of England's wartime allies, often spicing his comments with mild obscenities, usually of a scatological nature. Returning to England, he founded, in 1946, still another orch., the Royal Phil. In 1950 he made an extraordinarily successful North American tour with the Royal Phil. Beecham continued to conduct the orch. until ill health led him to nominate Rudolf Kempe as his successor in 1960. In 1957 Queen Elizabeth II made him a Companion of Honour. Beecham was married 3 times: to Utica Celestia Wells, in 1903 (divorced in 1942); to Betty Hamby (in 1943), who died in 1957; and to his young secretary, Shirley Hudson, in 1959. He publ. an autobiography, *A Mingled Chime* (London, 1943), and also an extensive biography of Delius (London, 1959; 2d ed., rev., 1975). To mark his centennial, a commemorative postage stamp with Beecham's portrait was issued by the Post Office of Great Britain on Sept. 1, 1980. In 1964 the Sir Thomas Beecham Soc., dedicated to preserving his memory, was organized, with chapters in America and England. The Soc. publishes an official journal, *Le Grand Baton*, devoted to Beecham and the art of conducting. In spite of the occasional criticism directed at him, Beecham revealed a remarkable genius as an orchestra builder. In addition to his outstanding interpretations of Haydn, Mozart, Schubert, Richard Strauss, Delius, and Sibelius, he had a particular affinity for the works of French and Russian composers of the 19th century.

BIBL.: C. Reid, *T. B.: An Independent Biography* (London, 1961); H. Procter-Gregg, ed., *Sir T. B., Conductor and Impresario: As Remembered by His Friends and Colleagues* (Kendal, 1972; 2d ed., 1976); A. Jefferson, *Sir T. B.: A Centenary Tribute* (London, 1979); J. Gilmour, *Sir T. B.—50 years in the "New York Times"* (London, 1988).

Beecke, (Notger) Ignaz (Franz) von, German clavierist and composer; b. Wimpfen, Oct. 28, 1733; d. Wallerstein, Jan. 2, 1803. He studied with Gluck. He was a captain of dragoons, and later became Musikintendant to the prince of Öttingen-Wallerstein. A highly accomplished pianist, he was a friend of Jommelli, Gluck, and Mozart. Among his compositions are 8 operas, and the oratorio *Die Auferstehung Jesu*.

Beecroft, Norma (Marian), Canadian composer; b. Oshawa, Ontario, April 11, 1934. She studied piano with Gordon Hallett and Weldon Kilburn at the Royal Cons. of Music of Toronto (1952–58), during which period she also studied composition with John Weinzweig; following composition training from Copland and Foss at the Berkshire Music Center in Tanglewood (summer, 1958), she went to Rome to continue studies with Petrassi at the Accademia di Santa Cecilia (1959–62); she also attended Maderna's classes in Darmstadt (summers, 1960–61), and then Schaeffer's electronic music classes at the Univ. of Toronto (1962–63) before working with Davidovsky at the Columbia-Princeton Electronic Music Center (1964). She was active as a producer, host, and commentator for the CBC. With Robert Aitken, she founded the New Music Concerts in Toronto in 1971, which she oversaw until 1989. In her music Beecroft has followed along modernistic paths. In a number of her works she has effectively utilized 12-tone techniques and electronics. Her dramatic works include *Undersea Fantasy*, puppet show (1967), *Hedda*, ballet (1982), and *The Dissipation of Purely Sound*, radiophonic opera (1988).

Beer-Walbrunn, Anton, German composer; b. Kohlberg, Bavaria, June 29, 1864; d. Munich, March 22, 1929. He was a pupil of Rheinberger, Bussmeyer, and Abel at the Akademie der Tonkunst in Munich where, from 1901, he was an instructor and, from 1908, a prof. He wrote the operas *Die Sühne* (Lübeck, Feb. 16, 1894), *Don Quijote* (Munich, Jan. 1, 1908), *Das Ungeheuer* (Karlsruhe, April 25, 1914), and *Der Sturm* (1914; after Shakespeare); also incidental music to *Hamlet* (1909). He also supervised new eds. of works of Wilhelm Friedemann Bach.

Beeson, Jack (Hamilton), American composer and teacher; b. Muncie, Ind., July 15, 1921. He studied with Burrill Phillips, Bernard Rogers, and Howard Hanson at the Eastman School of Music in Rochester, N.Y. (B.M., 1942; M.M., 1943), and with Bartók in New York (1944–45). He pursued graduate work at Columbia Univ. (1945–48), where he was active as a teacher from 1945. From 1967 to 1988 he was the MacDowell Prof. of Music there, and he also served as chairman of its music dept. (1968–72). He held the American Prix de Rome (1948–50), a Fulbright fellowship (1949–50), and a Guggenheim fellowship (1958–59). In 1976 he was elected a member of the American Academy and Inst. of Arts and Letters. Beeson was particularly adept at writing operas.

WORKS: OPERAS: *Jonah* (1950); *Hello, Out There* (N.Y., May 27, 1954); *The Sweet Bye and Bye* (1956; N.Y., Nov. 21, 1957); *Lizzie Borden* (N.Y., March 25, 1965); *My Heart's in the Highlands*, chamber opera (1969; NET, March 17, 1970); *Captain Jinks of the Horse Marines*, romantic comedy (Kansas City, Mo., Sept. 20, 1975); *Dr. Heidegger's Fountain of Youth*, after Hawthorne (N.Y., Nov. 17, 1978); *Cyrano* (1990).

Beeth, Lola, German soprano; b. Kraków, Nov. 23, 1860; d. Berlin, March 18, 1940. She studied in Lemberg and then was a pupil of Louise Dustmann in Vienna, Pauline Viardot-García in Paris, Francesco Lamperti in Milan, and Rosa Deruda in Berlin. In 1882 she made her operatic debut as Elsa in *Lohengrin* at the Berlin Royal Opera, where she sang until 1888, then was a member of the Vienna Court Opera (1888–95). On Dec. 2, 1895, she made her Metropolitan Opera debut in New York as Elsa, remaining on its roster for a season. After singing in London, St. Petersburg, Moscow, Monte Carlo, and Warsaw, she was again a member of the Vienna Court Opera (1898–1901). She then sang mainly in concerts and taught voice in Berlin.

Beethoven, Ludwig van, the great German composer whose unsurpassed genius marked a historic turn in the art of composition; b. Bonn, Dec. 15 or 16 (baptized, Dec. 17), 1770; d. Vienna, March 26, 1827. (Beethoven himself maintained, against all evidence, that he was born in 1772, and that the 1770 date referred to his older brother, deceased in infancy, whose forename was also Ludwig.) The family was of Dutch extraction. Beethoven's grandfather, Ludwig van Beethoven (b. Malines, Belgium, Jan. 5, 1712; d. Bonn, Dec. 24, 1773), served as choir director of the church of St. Pierre in Louvain in 1731. In 1732 he went to Liège, where he sang bass in the cathedral choir of St. Lambert, and in 1733 he became a member of the choir in Bonn, where he married Maria Poll. Prevalent infant mortality took its statistically predictable tribute; the couple's only surviving child was Johann van Beethoven, who married a young widow, Maria Magdalena Leym (née Keverich), daughter of the chief overseer of the kitchen at the palace in Ehrenbreitstein; they were the composer's parents.

Beethoven's father gave him rudimentary instruction in music. Tobias Friedrich Pfeiffer, a local musician, gave him formal piano lessons, the court organist in Bonn, Gilles van Eeden, instructed him in keyboard playing and in music theory, and Franz Rovantini gave him violin lessons; another violinist who taught Beethoven was Franz Ries. Beethoven also learned to play the French horn, under the guidance of the professional musician Nikolaus Simrock. He was also briefly enrolled at the Univ. of Bonn in 1789. His first important teacher of composition was Christian Gottlob Neefe, a thorough musician who seemed to understand his pupil's great potential. He guided Beethoven in the study of Bach and encouraged him in keyboard improvisation. At the age of 12, in 1782, Beethoven composed *9 Variations for Piano on a March of Dressler*, his first work to be publ. In 1783 he played the cembalo in the Court Orch. in Bonn, and in 1784 the Elector Maximilian Franz officially appointed him to the post of deputy court organist, a position he retained until 1792. From 1788 to 1792 Beethoven also served as a violist in theater orchs. In 1787 the Elector sent him to Vienna, where he stayed for a short time. After a few weeks in Vienna Beethoven went to Bonn when he received news that his mother was gravely ill; she died on July 17, 1787, and he was obliged to provide sustenance for his 2 younger brothers. Beethoven earned some money by giving piano lessons to the children of Helene von Breuning, the widow of a court councillor. He also met important wealthy admirers, among them Count Ferdinand von Waldstein, who was to be immortalized by Beethoven's dedication to him of a piano sonata bearing his name. Beethoven continued to compose; some of his works of the period were written in homage to royalty, as a cantata on the death of the Emperor Joseph II and another on the accession of Emperor Leopold II, while others were designed for performance at aristocratic gatherings.

In 1790 Haydn was honored in Bonn by the Elector on his way to London and it is likely that Beethoven was introduced to him, and that Haydn encouraged him to come to Vienna to study with him. Beethoven went to Vienna in Nov. 1792, and began his studies with Haydn. Not very prudently, Beethoven approached the notable teacher Johann Schenk to help him write the mandatory exercises prior to delivering them to Haydn for final appraisal. In the meantime, Haydn had to go to London again, and Beethoven's lessons with him were discontinued. Instead, Beethoven began a formal study of counterpoint with Johann Georg Albrechtsberger, which continued for about a year. Furthermore, he took lessons in vocal composition with Salieri, then Imperial Kapellmeister at the Austrian court. Beethoven found a generous benefactor in Prince Karl Lichnowsky, who awarded him, beginning about 1800, an annual stipend of 600 florins; Beethoven dedicated his *Sonate pathétique* to him, as well as his first opus number, a set of 3 piano trios. Among other dedicatees was Prince Franz Joseph Lobkowitz, whose name adorns the title pages of the 6 String Quartets, op. 18, the *Eroica* Symphony (after Beethoven unsuccessfully tried to dedicate it to Napoleon), the Triple Concerto, op. 56, and (in conjunction with Prince Razumovsky) the 5th and 6th syms. Prince Razumovsky, the Russian ambassador to Vienna, played an important role in Beethoven's life. From 1808 to 1816 he maintained in his residence a string quartet in which he himself played the 2d violin. It was to Razumovsky that Beethoven dedicated his 3 string quartets that became known as the Razumovsky. Razumovsky also shared with Lobkowitz the dedications of Beethoven's 5th and 6th syms. Another Russian patron was Prince Golitzyn, for whom Beethoven wrote his great string quartets opp. 127, 130, and 132.

Beethoven made his first public appearance in Vienna on March 29, 1795, as soloist in one of his piano concertos (probably the B-flat major Concerto, op. 19). In 1796 he played in Prague, Dresden, Leipzig, and Berlin. He also participated in "competitions," fashionable at the time, with other pianists, usually held in aristocratic salons. In 1799 he competed with Joseph Wölffl and in 1800 with Daniel Steibelt. On April 2, 1800, he presented a concert of his works in the Burgtheater in Vienna, at which his 1st Sym., in C major, and the Septet in E-flat major were performed for the first time. Other compositions at the threshold of the century were the Piano Sonata in C minor, op. 13, the *Pathétique*, the C-major Piano Concerto, op. 15, the "sonata quasi una fantasia" for Piano in C-sharp minor, op. 27, celebrated under the nickname "Moonlight Sonata," and the D-major Piano Sonata known as *Pastoral*.

Fétis was the first to suggest the division of Beethoven's compositions into 3 stylistic periods. It was left to Wilhelm von Lenz to fully elucidate this view in his *Beethoven et ses trois styles* (2 vols., St. Petersburg, 1852). Despite this arbitrary chronological division, the work became firmly established in Beethoven literature. According to Lenz, the first period embraced Beethoven's works from his early years to the end of the 18th century, marked by a style closely related to the formal methods of Haydn. The second period, covering the years 1801–14, was signaled by a more personal, quasi-Romantic mood, beginning with the "Moonlight Sonata." The third and last period, extending from 1814 to Beethoven's death in 1827, comprised the most individual, the most unconventional, the most innovative works, such as his last string quartets and the 9th Sym., with its extraordinary choral finale.

Beethoven's early career in Vienna was marked by fine success. He was popular not only as a virtuoso pianist and a composer, but also as a social figure who was welcome in the aristocratic circles of Vienna. His students included society ladies and even royal personages, such as Archduke Rudolf of Austria, to whom Beethoven dedicated the so-called Archduke Trio, op. 97. But his progress was fatefully affected by a mysteriously growing deafness, which reached a crisis in 1802. On Oct. 8 and 10, 1802, he wrote a poignant document known as the "Heiligenstadt Testament," drawn in the village of Heiligenstadt, where he resided at the time. The document, not discovered until after Beethoven's death, voiced his despair at the realization that his sense of hearing was inexorably failing. The impairment of his hearing may have been caused by an otosclerosis, resulting in the shriveling of the auditory nerves and concomitant dilation of the accompanying arteries. Externally, there were signs of tinnitus, a constant buzzing in the ears, about which Beethoven complained. However, his reverential biographer A. W. Thayer states plainly in a letter dated Oct. 29, 1880, that it was known to several friends of Beethoven that the cause of his combined ailments was syphilis.

Beethoven nonetheless continued his creative work with his usual energy. On April 5, 1803, he presented a concert of his compositions in Vienna at which he was soloist in his 3d Piano Concerto; the program also contained performances of his 2d Sym. and of the oratorio *Christus am Oelberge*. On May 24, 1803, he played in Vienna the piano part of his Violin Sonata, op. 47, known as the "Kreutzer" Sonata, although Kreutzer himself did not introduce it; in his place the violin part was taken over by the mulatto artist George Bridgetower. During the years 1803 and 1804 Beethoven composed his great Sym. No. 3, in E-flat major, op. 55, the *Eroica*.

In 1803 Emanuel Schikaneder, manager of the Theater an der Wien, asked Beethoven to compose an opera to a libretto he had prepared under the title *Vestas Feuer* (The Vestal Flame), but he soon lost interest in the project and instead began work on another opera, based on J. N. Bouilly's *Leonore, ou L'Amour conjugal*. The completed opera was named *Fidelio*, and it was given at the Theater an der Wien on Nov. 20, 1805, under difficult circumstances, a few days after the French army entered Vienna. There were only 3 performances before it was rescheduled for March 29 and April 10, 1806; after another long hiatus a greatly revised version was produced on May 23, 1814. Beethoven wrote 3 versions of the Overture for *Léonore*; for another performance, on May 26, 1814, he revised the Overture once more, and this time it was performed under the title *Fidelio Overture*.

An extraordinary profusion of creative masterpieces marked the years 1802–08: the 3 String Quartets, op. 59, dedicated to Count Razumovsky, the 4th, 5th, and 6th syms., the Violin Concerto, the 4th Piano Concerto, the Triple Concerto, the *Coriolan Overture,* and a number of piano sonatas. On Dec. 22, 1808, his 5th and 6th syms. were heard for the first time at a concert in Vienna, lasting some 4 hours. Still, financial difficulties beset Beethoven. The various annuities from patrons were uncertain, and the devaluation of the Austrian currency played havoc with his budget. In Oct. 1808, King Jerome Bonaparte of Westphalia offered the composer the post of Kapellmeister of Kassel at a substantial salary, but Beethoven decided to remain in Vienna. Between 1809 and 1812, Beethoven wrote his 5th Piano Concerto, the String Quartet in E-flat major, op. 74, the incidental music to Goethe's drama *Egmont,* the 7th and 8th syms., and his Piano Sonata in E-flat major, op. 81a, whimsically subtitled "Das Lebewohl, Abwesenheit und Wiedersehn," also known by its French subtitle, "Les Adieux, l'absence, et le retour." He also added a specific description to the work, "Sonate caractéristique."

Beethoven had many devoted friends and admirers in Vienna, but he spent most of his life in solitude. Carl Czerny reports in his diary that Beethoven once asked him to let him lodge in his house, but Czerny declined, explaining that his aged parents lived with him and he had no room. Deprived of the pleasures and comforts of family life, Beethoven sought to find a surrogate in his nephew, Karl, son of Caspar Carl Beethoven, who died in 1815. Beethoven regarded his sister-in-law as an unfit mother and went to court to gain sole guardianship over the boy; in his private letters, and even in his legal depositions, he poured torrents of vilification upon the woman, implying even that she was engaged in prostitution. In his letters to Karl he often signed himself as the true father of the boy. In 1826 Karl attempted suicide. However, it would be unfair to ascribe this act to Beethoven's stifling avuncular affection; Karl later went into the army and enjoyed a normal life.

Gallons of ink have been unnecessarily expended on the crucial question of Beethoven's relationship with women. That Beethoven dreamed of an ideal life companion is clear from his numerous utterances and candid letters to friends, in some of which he asked them to find a suitable bride for him. But there is no inkling that he kept company with any particular woman in Vienna. Beethoven lacked social graces, he could not dance, he was unable to carry on a light conversation about trivia, and behind it all there was the dreadful reality of his deafness. There were several objects of his secret passions, among his pupils or the society ladies to whom he dedicated his works. But somehow he never actually proposed marriage, and they usually married less hesitant suitors. It was inevitable that Beethoven should seek escape in fantasies. The greatest of these fantasies was the famous letter addressed to an "unsterbliche Geliebte," the "Immortal Beloved," couched in exuberant emotional tones characteristic of the sentimental romances of the time, and strangely reminiscent of Goethe's novel *The Sorrows of Young Werther*. The letter was never mailed, and was discovered in the secret compartment of Beethoven's writing desk after his death. Clues to the identity of the object of his passion were maddeningly few and who she might have been remains speculative to the present day.

The so-called 3d style of Beethoven included the composition of his monumental 9th Sym., completed in 1824 and first performed in Vienna on May 7, 1824; the program also included excerpts from the *Missa Solemnis* and *Die Weihe des Hauses*. With the 9th Sym., Beethoven completed the evolution of the symphonic form as he envisioned it. Its choral finale was his manifesto addressed to the world at large, to the text from Schiller's ode *An die Freude* (To Joy). In it, Beethoven, through Schiller, appealed to all humanity to unite in universal love. Here a musical work, for the first time, served a political ideal. Beethoven's last string quartets, opp. 127, 130, 131, and 132, served as counterparts in their striking innovations, dramatic pauses, and novel instrumental tone colors.

In Dec. 1826, on his way back to Vienna from a visit in Gneixendorf, Beethoven was stricken with a fever that developed into a mortal pleurisy. Dropsy and jaundice supervened to this condition, and surgery to relieve the accumulated fluid in his organism was unsuccessful. He died on the afternoon of March 26, 1827. It was widely reported that an electric storm struck Vienna as Beethoven lay dying. Its occurrence was indeed confirmed by the contemporary records in the Vienna weather bureau, but the story that he raised his clenched fist aloft as a gesture of defiance to an overbearing Heaven must be relegated to fantasy. His funeral was held in all solemnity.

Beethoven was memorialized in festive observations of the centennial and bicentennial of his birth, and of the centennial and sesquicentennial of his death. The house where he was born in Bonn was declared a museum. Monuments were erected to him in many cities, and commemorative postage stamps bearing his image were issued not only in Germany and Austria, but in Russia and other countries.

WORKS: DRAMATIC: OPERAS: *Fidelio*, op. 72 (1st version, 1804–05; Theater an der Wien, Vienna, Nov. 20, 1805; 2d version, 1805–06; Theater an der Wien, March 29, 1806; final version, Kärnthnertortheater, Vienna, May 23, 1814); also a fragment from the unfinished opera *Vestas Feuer*, Hess 115 (1803). SINGSPIELS: "Germania," finale of the pasticcio *Die gute Nachricht* (Kärnthnertortheater, April 11, 1814); "Es ist vollbracht," finale of the pasticcio *Die Ehrenpforten* (Kärnthnertortheater, July 15, 1815). INCIDENTAL MUSIC: Overture to Collin's *Coriolan*, in C minor, op. 62 (Vienna, March 1807); *Egmont*, op. 84, to Goethe's drama (with overture; 1809–10; Vienna, June 15, 1810); *Die Ruinen von Athen,* op. 113, to Kotzebue's drama (with overture; 1811; Pest, Feb. 10, 1812); *König Stephan,* op. 117, to Kotzebue's drama (with overture; 1811; Pest, Feb. 10, 1812); Triumphal March in C major for Kuffner's *Tarpeja* (March 26, 1813); music to Duncker's drama *Leonore Prohaska* (1815); Overture in C major, op. 124, to Meisl's drama *Die Weihe des Hauses* (Vienna, Oct. 3, 1822). Also the oratorio *Christus am Oelberge*, op.85 (1803; Vienna, April 5, 1805; rev. 1804 and 1811).

BIBL.: The standard thematic and bibliographic index of all of Beethoven's completed publ. works is to be found in G. Kinsky and H. Halm, *Das Werk B.s. Thematisch-Bibliographisches Verzeichnis seiner sämtlichen vollendeten Kompositionen* (Munich and Duisburg, 1955). An important supplement to this source is K. Dorfmüller, ed., *Beiträge zur B.-Bibliographie: Studien und Materialien zum Werkverzeichnis von Kinsky-Halm* (Munich, 1978). See also W. Hess, ed., *Verzeichnis der nicht in der Gesamtausgabe veröffentlichten Werke L. v.B.s* (Wiesbaden, 1957), which lists missing works in the old Leipzig edition. BIOGRAPHICAL: While countless biographic works have been written in the years since Beethoven's death, A. Thayer's *L. v.B.s Leben* is still the standard and most extensive biography. It was publ. in a German tr. from the Eng. MS by H. Deiters, 3 vols., Berlin, 1866, 1872, and 1877. After the author's death, Deiters completed vols. 4 and 5 from Thayer's material, but also died before their publication. He had also rev. and enl. vol. 1, Leipzig, 1901. Deiters's MS was rev. and ed. by H. Riemann, vol. 4, Leipzig, 1907; vol. 5, Leipzig, 1908. Vols. 2 and 3 were then rev. and enl. by Riemann and publ. in Leipzig, 1910–11. He completed his task by reediting vol. 1, Leipzig, 1917. Thayer's original Eng. MS was completed by H. Krehbiel and publ. as *The Life of L. v. B.*, 3 vols., N.Y., 1921. It was in turn rev. by E. Forbes and publ. as *Thayer's Life of B.*, 2 vols., Princeton, N.J., 1964; rev. ed., 1967). It may be supplemented by consulting H. C. Robbins Landon, *B.: A Documentary Study* (N.Y. and London, 1970), M. Solomon, *B.* (N.Y., 1977), L. Finscher, *L. v.B.* (Darmstadt, 1983), and D. Jones, *The Life of B.* (Cambridge, 1998). CRITICAL, ANALYTICAL: GENERAL: W. von Lenz, *B. et ses trois styles* (2 vols. in 1, St. Petersburg, 1852; new ed. by M.D. Calvocoressi, Paris, 1909); R. Wagner, *B.* (Leipzig, 1870; Eng. tr. by A. Parsons, N.Y., 1872; 3d ed., 1883); L. Nohl, *B., Liszt, Wagner* (Vienna, 1874); T. de Wyzewa, *B. et Wagner* (Paris, 1898; 4th ed., 1914); H. Mersmann, *B., Die Synthese der Stile* (Berlin, n.d. [1922]); J. W. N. Sullivan, *B.: His Spiritual Development* (London, 1927; 2d ed., 1936); D. Tovey, *Essays in Musical Analysis* (7 vols.,

London, 1935–44); A Schering, *B. und die Dichtung* (Berlin, 1936); D. Tovey, *B.* (London, 1944); P. Nettl, *B. und seine Zeit* (Hamburg, 1958); D. Arnold and N. Fortune, eds., *The B. Reader* (N.Y., 1971); T. Scherman and L. Biancolli, eds., *The B. Companion* (Garden City, N.Y., 1972); I. Kolodin, *The Interior B.: A Biography of the Music* (N.Y., 1975); W. Mellers, *B. and the Voice of God* (London, 1983); G. Pestelli, *The Age of Mozart and B.* (Cambridge, 1984); R. Wallace, *B.'s Critics: Aesthetic Dilemmas and Resolutions during the Composer's Lifetime* (Cambridge, 1986); M. Broyles, *B.: The Emergence and Evolution of B.'s Heroic Style* (N.Y., 1987); A. Comini, *The Changing Image of B.: A Study in Mythmaking* (N.Y., 1987). ON *FIDELIO*: M. Kufferath, *Fidelio de L. v. B.* (Paris, 1913); W. Hess, *B.s Oper Fidelio und ihre drei Fassungen* (Zürich, 1953); W. Hess, *Das Fidelio-Buch: B.s Oper Fidelio, ihre Geschichte und ihre drei Fassungen* (Winterthur, 1986); P. Robinson, ed., *L. v. B.: Fidelio* (Cambridge, 1996).

Begnis, Giuseppe de, admired Italian bass; b. Lugo, 1793; d. N.Y., Aug. 1849. After serving as a choirboy in Lugo, he made his operatic debut in Modena in 1813 in Pavesi's *Ser Marc'Antonio*. He then sang in various Italian music centers, establishing himself as one of the finest buffo artists of the day. In 1816 he married **Giuseppina Ronzi de Begnis**, with whom he often appeared in opera. Rossini chose him to create the role of Dandini in *La Cenerentola* (Rome, Jan. 25, 1817), and he subsequently excelled in roles by that composer as well as those by Mayr and Pacini. He and his wife went to Paris in 1819, where he appeared as Don Basilio opposite his wife's Rosina in Rossini's *Il Barbiere di Siviglia* at its first Paris production at the Théâtre-Italien on Oct. 26, 1819. They continued to sing in Paris until 1821, when they went to London. Begnis made his debut there as Don Geronio opposite his wife's Fiorilla in Rossini's *Il Turco in Italia* at the King's Theatre on May 19, 1821. They continued to appear in opera together until their separation in 1825. Begnis remained at the King's Theatre until 1827, but also served as an opera manager in Bath (1823–24) and later in Dublin (1834–37) before settling in New York.

Behm, Eduard, German composer and teacher; b. Stettin, April 8, 1862; d. Bad Harzburg, Feb. 6, 1946. He studied at the Leipzig Cons. He taught at the Erfurt Academy of Music; he was director of the Scharwenka Cons. in Berlin (until 1901), and later a prof. there from 1917. He was awarded the Mendelssohn prize for a Sym. and the Bösendorfer prize for a Piano Concerto. He wrote the operas *Der Schelm von Bergen* (Dresden, 1899), *Marienkind* (1902), and *Das Gelobnis* (1914).

Behrend, (Gustav) Fritz, German composer and teacher; b. Berlin, March 3, 1889; d. there, Dec. 29, 1972. He studied composition with H. van Eycken, P. Rufer, and Humperdinck, and piano with Breithaupt (1907–11). After serving as a coach at the Braunschweig Hoftheater (1911–12), he taught at the Ochs-Eichelberg Cons. (1918–42) and the Klindworth-Scharwenka Cons. in Berlin (1942–49). His compositions did not meet with favor during the Third Reich, but later they achieved a modicum of recognition.

WORKS: DRAMATIC: *König Renés Tochter* (1919); *Der schwangere Bauer* (1927); *Die lächerlichen Preziösen* (1928; Berlin, May 22, 1949); *Almansor* (1931); *Dornröschen* (1934); *Der Wunderdoktor* (1947); *Der fahrende Schüler im Paradies* (1949); *Der Spiegel* (1950); *Romantische Komödie* (1953).

Behrens, Hildegard, noted German soprano; b. Varel, Oldenburg, Feb. 9, 1937. After obtaining a law degree from the Univ. of Freiburg im Breisgau, she studied voice with Ines Leuwen at the Freiburg im Breisgau Staatliche Hochschule für Musik. In 1971 she made her operatic debut as Mozart's Countess at the Freiburg im Breisgau City Theater; that same year she became a member of the opera studio of the Deutsche Oper am Rhein in Düsseldorf, becoming a full-fledged member of the company in 1972; she also sang in Frankfurt am Main. In 1976 she made her debut at London's Covent Garden as Giorgetta in *Il Tabarro*. On Oct. 1, 1976, she made her first appearance at the Metropolitan Opera in New York singing *Dich teure Halle* from *Tannhäuser* in a marathon concert, returning to make her formal debut there as Giorgetta on Oct. 15, 1976; in subsequent seasons, she returned to sing such roles as Fidelio, Elettra, Sieglinde, Isolde, Donna Anna, Brünnhilde, Berg's Marie, and Tosca. In 1983 she sang Brünnhilde at the Bayreuth Festival. She made her N.Y. recital debut in 1985. In 1990 she portrayed Salome at Covent Garden. Her characterization of Elektra at the Metropolitan Opera in 1992 was a stunning tour de force. After singing Isolde in Munich in 1996, she appeared as Elektra at Covent Garden in 1997.

Behrens, Jack, American composer and teacher; b. Lancaster, Pa., March 25, 1935. He was a student of Bergsma, Persichetti, and Mennin at the Juilliard School of Music in New York (B.S., 1958; M.S., 1959), and then of Leon Kirchner and Sessions at Harvard Univ. (Ph.D., 1973); he also studied with Milhaud at the Aspen (Colo.) Music School (summer 1962) and with Wolpe and Cage in Saskatchewan (summers 1964–65). From 1962 to 1966 he taught at the Univ. of Saskatchewan, where he was head of the theory dept. at its cons. He taught at Simon Fraser Univ. (1966–70) and at Calif. State College in Bakersfield (1970–76). In 1976 he became a member of the faculty of music at the Univ. of Western Ontario, where he was chairman of the theory and composition dept. until 1980; he then served as dean of the faculty (1980–86). Behrens's music is in a sophisticated modern idiom, with judicious use of both serial and aleatoric procedures. Among his works is the opera *The Lay of Thrym* (Regina, Saskatchewan, April 13, 1968).

Beilschmidt, Curt, German composer; b. Magdeburg, March 20, 1886; d. Leipzig, March 7, 1962. He studied in Magdeburg with Fritz Kauffmann; then in Leipzig (1905–09) with Stephan Krehl (theory), Adolf Ruthardt (piano), and Hans Sitt (violin). He served in the German army in World War I; returned to Leipzig in 1923 and founded a choral-symphonic group, which he continued to lead until 1954; he also taught at the Leipzig Hochschule für Musik (1946–56). Among his works were the dance opera *Das Abenteuer im Walde* (Leipzig, March 13, 1918), the opera buffa *Meister Innocenz, Der schlaue Amor* (Leipzig, July 6, 1921), the pastoral play *Der schlaue Amor* (Leipzig, 1921), and the musical divertimento *Der Tugendwächter* (Halle, Oct. 14, 1927).

Bekker, (Max) Paul (Eugen), eminent German writer on music; b. Berlin, Sept. 11, 1882; d. N.Y., March 7, 1937. He studied violin with Rehfeld, piano with Sormann, and theory with Horwitz; began his career as a violinist with the Berlin Phil. He was music critic of the *Berliner Neueste Nachrichten* (1906–09) and of the *Berliner Allgemeine Zeitung* (1909–11); he also served as chief music critic of the *Frankfurter Zeitung* from 1911. Later he became Intendant of the Kassel Stadttheater (1925), then in Wiesbaden (1927). In 1933 he left Germany, being unable to cope with the inequities of the Nazi regime. He publ. *Das Musikdrama der Gegenwart* (1909), *Richard Wagner* (1924; Eng. tr., 1931), *Das Operntheater* (1930), and *Wandlungen der Oper* (1934; Eng. tr., 1935, as *The Changing Opera*).

Bekku, Sadao, Japanese composer; b. Tokyo, May 24, 1922. He studied theoretical physics at the Univ. of Tokyo (1943–50); then studied composition with Milhaud, Rivier, and Messiaen at the Paris Cons. (1951–54). Returning to Japan, he became engaged in pedagogy; was also a member of the Japanese section of the ISCM from 1955 (president, 1968–73). His works are set in neo-Classical forms, with occasional use of authentic Japanese modalities. He composed the operas *Prince Arima* (1963–67; Tokyo, March 13, 1967) and *Aoi-no-ue* (1979) and the opera buffa *Le Dit les trois femmes* (Rome, 1964). He publ. a book on the occult in music (Tokyo, 1971).

Bell, Donald (Munro), Canadian bass-baritone; b. South Burnaby, British Columbia, June 19, 1934. He began his studies with Nancy Paisley Benn in Vancouver; after attending the Royal College of Music in London on scholarship (1953–55), he pursued training with Hermann Weissenborn in Berlin (1955–57); later he studied with Judith Boroschek in Düsseldorf (1967–76) and Richard Miller in Oberlin, Ohio (from 1985). He was only 14 when he was engaged to sing with the Vancouver Sym. Orch. In 1955 he appeared at the Glyndebourne Opera and the Berlin State Opera. In 1958 he made his recital debut at London's Wigmore Hall, and then appeared at the Bayreuth Festivals (1958–61). He made his Carnegie Hall debut in New York in 1959. From 1964 to 1967 he was a member of the Deutsche Oper am Rhein in Düsseldorf, where he sang such roles as Don Giovanni, Count Almaviva, Wolfram, Amfortas, Kurwenal, and Gounod's Méphistophélès. He also sang at other European opera houses, but eventually became best known as a concert artist. In addition to the standard repertoire, he devoted much time to furthering the cause of contemporary music. After teaching at Carleton Univ. and the Univ. of Ottawa in 1977, he taught at the Univ. of Calgary from 1982.

Bell, W(illiam) H(enry), English composer; b. St. Albans, Aug. 20, 1873; d. Gordon's Bay, Cape Province, South Africa, April 13, 1946. He studied in his hometown; won the Goss Scholarship for the Royal College of Music in London (1889); he studied organ with Stegall, violin with Burnett, piano with Izard, and composition with Corder and Stanford. He taught harmony at his alma mater (1903–12); in 1912, was appointed director of the South African College of Music in Cape Town and then dean of the music faculty at the Univ. of South Africa (1919), retiring in 1936. He was extremely critical of himself as a composer, and destroyed many of his MSS. Among his surviving works are the operas *Hippolytus* (1914) and *Isabeau* (1924).

BIBL.: H. du Plessis, ed., *Letters from W.H. B.* (Cape Town and Johannesburg, 1973).

Bella, Johann Leopold (actually, **Ján Levoslav**), Slovak composer; b. Lipto-Szentmiklós, Upper Hungary, Sept. 4, 1843; d. Bratislava, May 25, 1936. He studied theology in Banska Bystrica, then went to Vienna, where he studied composition with Sechter (1863–65). He was ordained a priest in 1866 and served as church music director at Kremnica (1869). In 1873 he received a scholarship to study in Germany and in Prague. In 1881 he relinquished his priesthood, and subsequently was organist at the Protestant church in Hermannstadt, Transylvania, and music director of the municipality there. He went to Vienna in 1921, and in 1928 returned to Bratislava. In addition to a great quantity of church music in the strict style, he composed an opera, *Wieland der Schmied* (Bratislava, April 28, 1926).

BIBL.: D. Orel, *J. L. B.* (Bratislava, 1924); Ķ. Hudek, *J. L. B.* (Prague, 1937); E. Zavárský, *Ján Levoslav B.: Život a dielo* (Bratislava, 1955).

Belletti, Giovanni Battista, famous Italian baritone; b. Sarzana, Feb. 17, 1813; d. there, Dec. 27, 1890. He made his operatic debut in 1837 in Stockholm as Figaro in Rossini's *Il Barbiere di Siviglia*. He made many appearances there with Jenny Lind, and later toured with her in the United States. He had his greatest successes in dramatic roles in Romantic operas.

Bellezza, Vincenzo, Italian conductor; b. Bitonto, Bari, Feb. 17, 1888; d. Rome, Feb. 8, 1964. He studied piano with Alessandro Longo, composition with Nicola d'Arienzo, and conducting with Giuseppe Martucci at the Naples Cons. He made his conducting debut at the Teatro San Carlo in Naples in 1908, then conducted throughout Italy; also had guest engagements at Covent Garden, London (1926–30; 1935–36); served as guest conductor at the Metropolitan Opera in New York (1926–35). After his return to Italy, he was on the staff of the Rome Opera.

Belli, Domenico, Italian composer; b. c.1590; d. (buried) May 5, 1627. He lived most of his life in Florence. On Sept. 19, 1619, he and his wife entered the service of the Medici court. As a composer, he was one of the earliest representatives of the new monodic style; Caccini praised his music. However, the claim that his short opera, *Il pianto d'Orfeo, or Orfeo Dolente* (Florence, 1616), was the earliest opera ever written is questionable.

Bellincioni, Gemma (Cesira Matilda), noted Italian soprano; b. Monza, Aug. 18, 1864; d. Naples, April 23, 1950. She studied with her father, the comic bass Cesare Bellincioni, and her mother, the contralto Carlotta Soroldoni. At age 15, she made her operatic debut in dell'Orefice's *Il segreto della duchessa* at the Teatro della Società Felarmonica in Naples. After further studies with Luigia Ponti and Giovanni Corsi, she sang in Spain and Portugal (1882), and then in Rome (1885). In 1886 she made her first appearance at Milan's La Scala as Violetta, and that same year toured South America, where she became intimate with the tenor Roberto Stagno. In subsequent years, they toured together in opera and concert, although she never appeared in the United States. On May 17, 1890, she created the role of Santuzza opposite Stagno's Turiddu at the Teatro Costanzi in Rome. On Nov. 17, 1898, she created the role of Fedora at Milan's Teatro Lirico. With Strauss conducting, she was the first to sing Salome in Italy in Turin in 1900, a role she subsequently sang more than 100 times. In 1911 she made her farewell operatic appearance as Salome in Paris, although she came out of retirement to sing opera in the Netherlands in 1924. She taught in Berlin (1911–15), Vienna (1931–32), and at the Naples Cons. (from 1932). Her autobiography was publ. as *Io ed il palcoscenico* (Milan, 1920).

BIBL.: B. Stagno-Bellincioni, *Roberto Stagno e G. B., intimi* (Florence, 1943).

Bellini, Vincenzo, famous Italian opera composer and a master of operatic bel canto; b. Catania, Sicily, Nov. 3, 1801; d. Puteaux, near Paris, Sept. 23, 1835. He was a scion of a musical family; his grandfather was maestro di cappella to the Benedictines in Catania, and organist of the Sacro Collegio di Maria in Misterbianco; his father also served as maestro di cappella. Bellini received his first musical instruction from his father and grandfather, and soon revealed a fine gift of melody. The duke and duchess of San Martino e Montalbo took interest in him and in 1819 arranged to have him enter the Real Collegio di Musica di San Sebastiano in Naples, where he studied harmony and accompaniment with Giovanni Furno and counterpoint with Giacomo Tritto; Carlo Conti supervised him as a maestrino and tutor. He further studied the vocal arts with Girolamo Crescentini and composition with Nicola Zingarelli. Under their guidance he made a detailed study of the works of Pergolesi, Jommelli, Paisiello, and Cimarosa, as well as those of the German classics. His first opera, *Adelson e Salvini*, was given at the Collegio in 1825; it was followed by an important production on the stage of the Teatro San Carlo in Naples of his 2d opera, *Bianca e Gernando* (1826), a score later revised as *Bianca e Fernando* (1828). In 1827 Bellini went to Milan, where he was commissioned by the impresario Barbaja to write an "opera seria" for the famous Teatro alla Scala; it was *Il Pirata*, which obtained fine success at its production in 1827; it was also given in Vienna in 1828. It was followed by another opera, *La Straniera*, produced at La Scala in 1829; also in 1829 Bellini had the opera *Zaira* produced in Parma. He was then commissioned to write a new opera for the Teatro La Fenice in Venice, on a Shakespearean libretto; it was *I Capuleti ed i Montecchi*; produced in 1830, it had a decisive success. Even more successful was his next opera, *La Sonnambula*, produced in Milan in 1831 with the celebrated prima donna Giuditta Pasta as Amina. Pasta also appeared in the title role of Bellini's most famous opera, *Norma*, produced at La Scala in Milan in 1831, which at its repeated productions established Bellini's reputation as a young master of the Italian operatic bel canto. His following opera, *Beatrice di Tenda*, produced in Venice in 1833, failed to sustain his series of successes. He then had an opportunity to go to London and Paris, and it was in Paris that he produced in 1835 his last opera, *I Puritani*, which fully justified the expectations of his admirers. Next to *Norma*, it proved to be one of the greatest masterpieces of Italian operatic art; its Paris production featured a superb cast, which included Grisi, Rubini, Tamburini, and Lablache. Bellini was on his way to fame and universal artistic recognition when he was stricken with a fatal affliction of amebiasis, and died 6 weeks before his 34th birthday. His remains were reverently removed to his native Catania in 1876.

Bellini's music represents the Italian operatic school at its most glorious melodiousness, truly reflected by the term "bel canto."

In his writing, the words, the rhythm, the melody, the harmony, and the instrumental accompaniment unite in mutual perfection. The lyric flow and dramatic expressiveness of his music provide a natural medium for singers in the Italian language, with the result that his greatest masterpieces, *La Sonnambula* and *Norma*, remain in the active repertoire of opera houses of the entire world, repeatedly performed by touring Italian opera companies and by native forces everywhere.

WORKS: DRAMATIC: *Adelson e Salvini*, dramma semiserio (1824–25; Real Collegio di Musica di San Sebastiano, Naples, between Feb. 10 and 15, 1825; 2d version, 1826; not perf.); *Bianca e Gernando*, melodramma, (1825–26; Teatro San Carlo, Naples, May 30, 1826; rev. version as *Bianca e Fernando*, 1828; Teatro Carlo Felice, Genoa, April 7, 1828); *Il Pirata*, opera seria (1827; Teatro alla Scala, Milan, Oct. 27, 1827); *La Straniera*, opera seria (1828–29; Teatro alla Scala, Milan, Feb. 14, 1829); *Zaira*, opera seria (1829; Teatro Ducale, Parma, May 16, 1829); *I Capuleti ed i Montecchi*, tragedia lirica (1830; Teatro La Fenice, Venice, March 11, 1830); *La Sonnambula*, melodramma (1831; Teatro Carcano, Milan, March 6, 1831); *Norma*, opera seria (1831; Teatro alla Scala, Milan, Dec. 26, 1831); *Beatrice di Tenda*, opera seria (1833; Teatro La Fenice, Venice, March 16, 1833); *I Puritani*, melodramma serio (1834–35; 1st perf. as *I Puritani e i cavalieri* at the Théâtre-Italien, Paris, Jan. 24, 1835).

BIBL.: F. Gerardi, *Biografia di V. B.* (Rome, 1835); L. Scuderi, *Biografia di V. B.* (Catania, 1840); F. Cicconetti, *Vita di V. B.* (Prato, 1859); A. Pougin, *B.: Sa vie, ses oeuvres* (Paris, 1868); A. Amore, *V. B.: Arte—Studi e ricerche* (Catania, 1892); idem, *V. B.: Vita—Studi e ricerche* (Catania, 1894); A. Cametti, *B. a Roma* (Rome, 1900); P. Voss, *V. B.* (Leipzig, 1901); A. Amore, *Belliniana (Errori e smentite)* (Catania, 1902); C. Reina, *V. B. (1801–35)* (Catania, 1902; 2d ed. as *Il cigno catanese: B.—La vita e le opere*, Catania, 1935); I. Pizzetti, *La musica di V. B.* (Milan, 1916); L. Cambi, *B.* (Milan, 1934); N. Scaglione, *V. B. a Messina* (Messina, 1934); B. Condorelli, *Il Museo Belliniano: Catalogo storico-iconografico* (Catania, 1935); G. de Angelis, *V. B.: La vita, l'uomo, l'artista* (Brescia, 1935); A. Della Corte and G. Pannain, *V. B.: Il Carattere morale, i caratteri artistici* (Turin, 1935); G. Mezzatesta, *V. B. nella vita e nelle opere* (Palermo, 1935); F. Pastura, ed., *Le lettere di B. (1819–35)* (Catania, 1935); G. Policastro, *V. B. (1801–19)* (Catania, 1935); O. Tiby, *V. B.* (Rome, 1935); I. Pizzetti, ed., *V. B.: L'Uomo, le sue opere, la sua fama* (Milan, 1936); O. Tiby, *V. B.* (Turin, 1938); L. Cambi, ed., *V. B.: Epistolario* (Milan, 1943); F. Pastura, *B. secondo la storia* (Parma, 1959); F. Pastura, *V. B.* (Catania, 1959); L. Orrey, *B.* (London and N.Y., 1969); H. Weinstock, *V. B.: His Life and His Operas* (N.Y., 1971); M. Adamo, *V. B.* (Turin, 1981); G. Tintori, *B.* (Milan, 1983); D. Danzuso, F. Gallo, and R. Monti, *Omaggio a B.* (Milan, 1986).

Belloc-Giorgi, Teresa (née **Maria Teresa Ottavia Faustina Trombetta**), Italian mezzo-soprano of French descent; b. San Benigno Cavanese, near Turin, July 2, 1784; d. San Giorgio Cavanese, May 13, 1855. She made her debut in Turin in 1801, then sang in Paris in 1803, and at La Scala, Milan, from 1804 to 1824. She then toured through Italy, and also appeared in Paris and London. She retired in 1828. Her repertoire comprised roles in 80 operas, Rossini's being her favorites.

BIBL.: C. Boggio, *La cantante T. B.* (Milan, 1895).

Bemberg, Herman, French composer; b. Paris, March 29, 1859; d. Bern, Switzerland, July 21, 1931. He studied at the Paris Cons. with Dubois, Franck, and Massenet, winning the Rossini prize in 1885. Among his works are a short opera, *Le Baiser de Suzon* (Paris, 1888) and a grand opera, *Elaine* (Covent Garden, London, July 5, 1892; N.Y., Dec. 17, 1894).

Bembo, Antonia, Italian-born French composer; b. presumably in Venice, c.1670; place and date of death unknown. Between 1690 and 1695 she went to Paris. She sang for Louis XIV, and received a pension from him, enabling her to devote herself to composition. Extant works (in the Paris Bibliothèque Nationale) include an opera, *L'Ercole Amante* (1707).

Beňačková, Gabriela, prominent Czech soprano; b. Bratislava, March 25, 1947. After studies with Ondrej Francisi, she was a pupil of Tatiana Kresáková and Magda Móryová at the Cons. and of Janko Blaho at the Academy of Arts and Music in Bratislava. In 1969 she won the Dvořák vocal competition in Karlovy Vary, which led to her operatic debut as Prokofiev's Natasha at the Prague National Theater in 1970, where she sang regularly until 1981. She appeared as Tatiana in Moscow in 1977 and as Jenůfa at the Vienna State Opera in 1978, returning there as Marguerite in 1985 and as Rusalka in 1987. In 1979 she made her first appearance at London's Covent Garden as Tatiana. After singing Maddalena at the Cologne Opera in 1983, she appeared as Jenůfa at the San Francisco Opera in 1986, and as Desdemona in Stuttgart and as Leonore at the Salzburg Festival in 1990. On Feb. 25, 1991, she made her Metropolitan Opera debut in New York as Kát'a Kabanová. Following an engagement as Maddalena in Zürich in 1994, she appeared as Senta at the Hamburg State Opera in 1996. She also pursued an active career as a concert artist. In 1976 she was awarded the National Prize, and then received the titles of Artist of Merit in 1979 and National Artist in 1985 from her homeland. In 1988 she was honored as a Kammersängerin of the Vienna State Opera.

Benatzky, Ralph (Rudolf Josef František), Czech composer; b. Mährisch-Budwitz, June 5, 1884; d. Zürich, Oct. 16, 1957. He studied in Vienna, in Prague with Veit and Klinger, and in Munich with Mottl; he also took a Ph.D. in philology. After conducting at the Kleines Theater in Munich (1910–11), he went to Vienna as music director at the Kabarett Rideamus. He first gained notice as a composer for the theater with his operetta *Der lachende Dreibund* (Berlin, Oct. 31, 1913). His first notable success came with the operetta *Liebe im Schnee* (Vienna, Dec. 2, 1916), which was followed by the successful premieres of *Yuschi tanzt* (Vienna, April 3, 1920), *Apachen* (Vienna, Dec. 20, 1920), *Pipsi* (Vienna, Dec. 30, 1921), *Ein Märchen aus Florenz* (Vienna, Sept. 14, 1923), and *Adieu Mimi* (Vienna, June 9, 1926). From 1924 he also was active at the Grosses Schauspielhaus in Berlin, where he provided music for various productions, including the Johann Strauss pasticcio *Casanova* (Sept. 1, 1928) and *Die drei Musketiere* (Sept. 28, 1929). It was at that theater that he brought out his celebrated operetta *Im weissen Rössl* (Nov. 8, 1930), which was also made into a film in 1935. Among his other theater scores were *Cocktail* (Berlin, Dec. 15, 1930), *Zirkus Aimée* (Basel, March 5, 1932), *Bezauberndes Fräulein* (Vienna, May 24, 1933), *Deux sous de fleurs* (Paris, Oct. 6, 1933), *Das kleine Café* (Vienna, April 20, 1934), *Axel an der Himmelstur* (Vienna, Sept. 1, 1936), *Pairserinnin* (Vienna, May 7, 1937; rev. ver., Lucerne, Dec. 11, 1964), *Majestät-privat* (Vienna, Dec. 18, 1937), and *Der Silberhof* (Mainz, Nov. 4, 1941). During World War II, Benatzky lived in the United States. After the war, he returned to Europe and finally settled in Switzerland.

Benda, Friedrich (Wilhelm Heinrich), German violinist, nephew of **Georg Anton (Jiří Antonín) Benda**; b. Potsdam, July 15, 1745; d. there, June 19, 1814. His father was the famous Bohemian violinist and composer Franz (František) Benda (b. Alt-Benatek, Bohemia [baptized], Nov. 22, 1709; d. Neuendorf, near Potsdam, March 7, 1786). He studied violin with his father, and music theory with J. P. Kirnberger. From 1765 to 1810 he served as a royal chamber musician at Potsdam. He composed the operas *Orpheus* (Berlin, Jan. 16, 1785; concert perf.) and *Alceste* (Berlin, Jan. 15, 1786).

Benda, Friedrich Ludwig, German violinist and composer, son of **Georg Anton (Jiří Antonín) Benda**; b. Gotha, Sept. 4, 1752; d. Königsburg, March 20, 1792. In 1775 he joined the orch. of the Seyler troupe in Gotha. After 1779 he was employed as a violinist in theaters in Berlin and Hamburg. In 1782 he was engaged as violinist and Cammer-Compositeur to the Duke of Mecklenburg-Schwerin. In 1788 he settled in Königsburg. He composed the music for G. F. Grossmann's *Der Barbier von Sevilla* (Leipzig, May 7, 1776).

Benda, Georg Anton (Jiří Antonín), important Bohemian composer, father of **Friedrich Ludwig** and uncle of **Friedrich (Wilhelm Heinrich) Benda**; b. Alt-Benatek (baptized), June 30, 1722; d. Köstritz, Nov. 6, 1795. His brother was the famous Bohemian violinist and composer Franz (František) Benda (b. Alt-Benatek, Bohemia [baptized], Nov. 22, 1709; d. Neuendorf, near Potsdam, March 7, 1786). He studied at the Jesuit college in Jicin (1739–42), then went to Prussia. In May 1750 he was appointed Kapellmeister to Duke Friedrich III of Saxe-Gotha. In 1765 he received a ducal stipend to go to Italy for half a year. In 1778 he went to Hamburg. He also traveled to Vienna, finally settling in Köstritz. His works were distinguished for their dramatic use of rapidly alternating moods ("Affekte"), which became a characteristic trait of the North German school of composition and exercised considerable influence on the development of opera and ballad forms in Germany; his effective use of melodrama (spoken recitative accompanied by orch.) was an important innovation.

WORKS: DRAMATIC: OPERAS: *Ariadne auf Naxos* (Gotha, Jan. 27, 1775); *Medea* (Leipzig, May 1, 1775); *Philon und Theone*, also known as *Almansor und Nadine* (Gotha, Sept. 20, 1779). SINGSPIELS: *Der Dorfjahrmarkt* (1775); *Romeo und Julia* (1776); *Der Holzhauer* (1778).

BIBL.: R. Hodermann, *G. A. B.* (Coburg, 1895); F. Brückner, *G. A. B.* (Rostock, 1904); V. Helfert, G. *B. und J. J. Rousseau* (Munich, 1908); Z. Pilková, *Dramatická tvorba Jiřího Bendy* (Prague, 1960); F. Lorenz, *Die Musikerfamilie B. II. G. A. B.* (Berlin, 1971).

Bender, Paul, esteemed German bass-baritone and bass; b. Driedorf, July 28, 1875; d. Munich, Nov. 25, 1947. He was a student of Luise Reuss-Belce and Baptist Hoffmann in Berlin. In 1900 he made his operatic debut as the Hermit in *Der Freischütz* in Breslau; then was a principal member of the Munich Court Opera (1903–18), and its successor, the Bavarian State Opera (1918–33). In 1914 and 1924 he sang at London's Covent Garden. On Nov. 17, 1922, he made his Metropolitan Opera debut in New York as Baron Ochs, remaining on its roster until 1927. In later years, he was a prof. of voice at the Munich Academy of Music. A greatly admired artist, Bender was made a Bavarian Kammersänger. He was equally successful in serious and buffo roles, being particularly noted for his Mozart and Wagner. In 1917 he created the role of Pope Pius V in Pfitzner's *Palestrina*. He was also a fine lieder artist and did much to promote the songs of Carl Loewe.

Bendl, Karl (Karel), Czech composer and conductor; b. Prague, April 16, 1838; d. there, Sept. 20, 1897. He studied at the Prague Organ School with Blažek, Pietsch, and Zvonar. In 1864–65 he was active as a conductor in Brussels, Amsterdam, and Paris. Returning to Prague in 1865, he conducted the male choral society Hlahol for 12 years; also was briefly deputy conductor at the Provisional Theater in Prague. He subsequently served as an organist at the church of St. Nicholas in Prague. He was an ardent supporter of Dvořák and Smetana in the cause of creating a national school of Czech music.

WORKS: DRAMATIC: OPERAS: *Lejla* (1867; Prague, Jan. 4, 1868); *Břetislav* (1869; Prague, Sept. 18, 1870); *Starý ženich* (1871–74); *Die Wunderblume* (1876; Czech Radio, Prague, Aug. 30, 1940, in Czech); *Indická princezna*, operetta (1876–77; Prague, Aug. 26, 1877); *Černohorci* (1881; Prague, Oct. 11, 1881); *Karel Škréta* (1883; Prague, Dec. 11, 1883); *Gina* (1884; not perf.); *Dítě Tábora* (1886–88; Prague, March 13, 1892); *Máti Míla* (1893–95; Prague, June 25, 1895); *Švanda dudák* (1895–96; Prague, April 29, 1907). BALLET: *Česká svatba* (1894; Prague, Feb. 13, 1895).

BIBL.: E. Krasnohorska, *Z mládí Karla Bendla* (Prague, 1897; 2d ed. as *Z mého mládí*, 1920); J. Polák, *Karel B.* (Prague, 1938).

Benedetti, Michele, Italian bass; b. Loreto, Oct. 17, 1778; place and date of death unknown. He settled in Naples, where he appeared in the first Italian mounting of *La vestale* in 1811. He won the esteem of Rossini, who chose him to create there the roles of Elmiro Barberigo in *Otello, ossia Il Moro di Venezia* (1816), Idraste in *Armida* (1817), Mosè in *Mosè in Egitto* (1818), Ircano in *Ricciardo e Zoraide* (1818), Douglas d'Angus in *La donna del lago* (1819), and Leucippo in *Zelmira* (1822). He also created roles in operas by Pacini, Mayr, Mercadante, and Bellini.

Benedict, Sir Julius, German-English conductor and composer; b. Stuttgart, Nov. 27, 1804; d. London, June 5, 1885. He was the son of a Jewish banker. From his earliest childhood he showed a decisive musical talent. He took lessons with J. C. L. Abeille in Stuttgart, then had further instruction with Hummel at Weimar. Hummel introduced him to Weber, and he became Weber's private pupil. In 1823, Benedict was appointed conductor of the Kärnthnertortheater in Vienna; in 1825 he obtained a similar post at the Teatro San Carlo in Naples and also at the Fondo Theater there. He produced his first opera, *Giacinta ed Ernesto*, in Naples in 1827. His 2d opera was *I Portoghesi* in Goa, produced in Naples on June 28, 1830. In 1834 Benedict went to Paris, and in 1835 he proceeded to London, where he remained for the rest of his life. In 1836 he became music director at the Opera Buffa at the Lyceum Theatre. He conducted opera at the Drury Lane Theatre from 1838 to 1848. His first opera in English, *The Gypsy's Warning*, was produced at Drury Lane under his direction on April 19, 1838. He also conducted at Covent Garden; led the Monday Popular Concerts; served as music director of the Norwich Festivals (1845–78); and conducted the Liverpool Phil. Soc. (1876–80). In recognition of his services, he was knighted in 1871. From 1850 to 1852 he accompanied Jenny Lind on her American tours. His reputation as a conductor and composer was considerable, in both Europe and America. Among his operas the most successful was *The Lily of Killarney*, which was produced at Covent Garden on Feb. 8, 1862; it was also staged in America and Australia. His other operas are *The Brides of Venice* (Drury Lane, April 22, 1844), *The Crusaders* (Drury Lane, Feb. 26, 1846), *The Lake of Glenaston* (1862), and *The Bride of Song* (Covent Garden, Dec. 3, 1864); also an oratorio, *St. Peter* (1870). He publ. biographies of Mendelssohn (London, 1850) and Weber (London, 1881; 2d ed., 1913), both containing information gleaned from his personal acquaintances.

Benelli, Antonio Peregrino (Pellegrino), Italian tenor and composer; b. Forli, Romagna, Sept. 5, 1771; d. Börnichau, Saxony, Aug. 16, 1830. In 1790 he was first tenor at the Teatro San Carlo in Naples. He held the same position in London in 1798, and in Dresden from 1801 to 1822, when his voice failed. He then taught singing at the Royal Theater School in Berlin until 1829. His most valuable work is a vocal method, *Gesangslehre* (Dresden, 1819; orig. publ. in Italian as *Regole per il canto figurato*, 1814); he also wrote *Bemerkungen über die Stimme in the Allgemeine Musikalische Zeitung* (Leipzig, 1824).

Benincori, Angelo Maria, Italian composer; b. Brescia, March 28, 1779; d. Belleville, near Paris, Dec. 30, 1821. He studied in Parma with Rolla (violin) and counterpoint with Ghiretti. After several years in Spain, he settled in Paris in 1803, where he was active mostly as a violin teacher. He brought out 3 unsuccessful operas, but performed his most meritorious service in completing Isouard's opera *Aladin*.

Benjamin, Arthur, admired Australian pianist, teacher, and composer; b. Sydney, Sept. 18, 1893; d. London, April 9, 1960. After studies in Brisbane, he completed his training at the Royal College of Music in London with Frederick Cliffe (piano) and Sir Charles Stanford (composition). He taught at the Sydney Cons. (1919–21) and the Royal College of Music (from 1926). After pursuing his career in Vancouver, British Columbia (1939–46), he returned to England. Benjamin was an adept composer who produced works in a readily accessible style.

WORKS: DRAMATIC: OPERAS: *The Devil Take Her* (London, Dec. 1, 1931); *Prima Donna* (1933; London, Feb. 23, 1949); *A Tale of 2 Cities* (1949–50; BBC, London, April 17, 1953); *Mañana*, television opera (1956); *Tartuffe* (1960; completed by A. Boustead; London, Nov. 30, 1964). BALLET: *Orlando's Silver Wedding* (London, May 1951).

Bennett, Sir Richard Rodney, prominent English composer; b. Broadstairs, Kent, March 29, 1936. He studied with Lennox Berkeley and Howard Ferguson at the Royal Academy of Music in London (1953–57) and with Boulez in Paris (1957–59). After serving as a prof. of composition at the Royal Academy of Music (1963–65), he devoted himself mainly to composition; also served as vice-president of the Royal College of Music in London (from 1983). In 1995 he held the International Chair of Composition at the Royal Academy of Music in London. In 1977 he was made a Commander of the Order of the British Empire. In 1998 he was knighted. A prolific and facile composer, Bennett's output includes stage and concert works as well as film scores, including *Murder on the Orient Express* (1974) and *Equus* (1977). In some of his compositions, he utilizes serial techniques.

WORKS: DRAMATIC: OPERAS: *The Ledge* (London, Sept. 11, 1961); *The Mines of Sulphur* (London, Feb. 24, 1965); *Penny for a Song* (London, Oct. 31, 1967); *All the King's Men*, children's opera (Coventry, March 28, 1969); *Victory* (London, April 13, 1970). BALLETS: *Jazz Calendar* (1963–64); *Isadora* (1980; London, April 30, 1981); *Noctuary* (1981; Armidale, New South Wales, June 3, 1985).

BIBL.: S. Craggs, *R. R. B.: A Bio-Bibliography* (Westport, Conn., 1990).

Bennett, Robert Russell, American orchestrator, arranger, and composer; b. Kansas City, Mo., June 15, 1894; d. N.Y., Aug. 18, 1981. He was a member of a musical family: his father played in the Kansas City Phil. and his mother was a piano teacher. He studied in Kansas City with Carl Busch (1912–15), in Paris with Boulanger (1926–31), and in Berlin and London. In 1919 he orchestrated his first theatrical songs, and during the next 40 years reigned as the leading orchestrator of Broadway musicals. In all, he orchestrated about 300 such works, including ones by Kern, Gershwin, Porter, Rodgers, Berlin, and Loewe. His own music reveals not only a mastery of orchestration but a facile flow of melodies and rhythms in luscious harmonies. He publ. a book on orchestration, *Instrumentally Speaking* (N.Y., 1975).

WORKS: DRAMATIC: *Columbine*, pantomime ballet (1916); *Endimion*, operetta-ballet (1926; Rochester, N.Y., April 5, 1935); *An Hour of Delusion*, opera (1928); *Hold Your Horses*, musical play (N.Y., Sept. 25, 1933); *Maria Malibran*, opera (1934; N.Y., April 8, 1935); *The Enchanted Kiss*, opera (1944; WOR Radio, N.Y., Dec. 30, 1945); *Crystal*, opera (1972); incidental music and radio scores.

BIBL.: G. Ferencz, *R. R. B.: A Bio-Bibliography* (Westport, Conn., 1990).

Benoist, François, French composer and organist; b. Nantes, Sept. 10, 1794; d. Paris, May 6, 1878. He studied at the Paris Cons. (1811–15) with Adam and Catel, winning the Prix de Rome in 1815 with the cantata *Oenone*. Returning from Italy in 1819, he was appointed to the staff of the Paris Cons., where he taught for 53 years; he was pensioned in 1872. He wrote mostly for the theater, numbering among his operas *Léonore et Félix* (Paris Opéra Comique, Nov. 27, 1821, and *L'Apparition* (Paris Opéra, June 16, 1848). He also wrote the ballets *La Gipsy* (1839), *Le Diable amoureux* (1840), *Nisida, ou Les Amazones des Acores* (1848), and *Pâquerette* (1851).

Benoit, Peter (Léopold Léonard), eminent Flemish composer; b. Harlebeke, Belgium, Aug. 17, 1834; d. Antwerp, March 8, 1901. He studied at the Brussels Cons. with Fétis (1851–55); while there he earned his living by conducting theater orchs. and wrote music for Flemish plays. At the age of 22 he produced his first opera in Flemish, *Het dorp in't gebergte* (A Mountain Village), staged in Brussels on Dec. 14, 1856. With his cantata *Le Meurtre d'Abel* Benoit obtained the Belgian Prix de Rome (1857); however, he did not go to Italy, but traveled instead in Germany. As part of his duties he submitted a short *Cantate de Noël* to Fétis, who praised Benoit's music; he also wrote the essay *L'école de musique flamande et son avenir*, proclaiming his fervent faith in the future of a national Flemish school of composition, of which he was the most ardent supporter. His 1-act opera *Roi des Aulnes* was presented in Brussels (Dec. 2, 1859). The Théâtre-Lyrique of Paris tentatively accepted it, and Benoit spent many months in Paris awaiting its production, which never took place; in the meantime he acted as 2d conductor at the Bouffes-Parisiens. In 1863 he returned to Belgium, where he produced his 2d Flemish opera, *Isa* (Brussels, Feb. 24, 1867). In 1867 he founded the Flemish Music School in Antwerp; he militated for many years to obtain official status for it. In 1898 it was finally granted, and the school became the Royal Flemish Cons. Benoit remained its director to the end of his life. In Belgium Benoit is regarded as the originator of the Flemish musical tradition in both composition and education; but although he cultivated the Flemish idiom in most of his works, his musical style owes much to French and German influences. Apart from his successful early operas, he wrote the opera *Pompeja* (1895), which was not produced. He also composed the Flemish oratorios *Lucifer* (Brussels, Sept. 30, 1866; highly successful; considered his masterpiece), *De Schelde* (1868), *De Oorlog* (War; 1873), a dramatic musical score, *Charlotte Corday* (1876), a historical music drama, *De Pacificatie van Ghent* (1876), a children's oratorio *De Waereld in* (In the World; 1878), and the oratorio, *De Rhijn* (1889). He also composed many songs in French and in Flemish. In his propaganda for national Flemish music, Benoit contributed numerous papers and articles, among them *Considérations à propos d'un projet pour l'institution de festivals en Belgique* (1874), *Verhandeling over de nationale Toonkunde* (2 vols., Antwerp, 1877–79), *De Vlaamsche Muziekschool van Antwerpen* (1889; a history of the Flemish Music School), and *De Oorsprong van het Cosmopolitisme in de Muziek* (1876). In 1880 he was elected a corresponding member of the Belgian Royal Academy, and in 1882, a full member.

BIBL.: L. Mortelmans, *P. B.* (Antwerp, 1911); H. Baggaert, *P. B.: Een kampion der nationale gedachte* (Antwerp, 1919); J. Horemans, *P. B.* (Antwerp, 1934); A. Pols, *Het leven van P. B.* (Antwerp, 1934); C. van den Borren, *P. B.* (Brussels, 1942); R. Boschvogel, *P. B.* (Tiel, 1944); A. Corbet, *P. B.: Leven, werk en beteekenis* (Antwerp, 1944); G.-M. Matthijs, *P. B.* (Brussels, 1944); F. van der Mueren, *P. B. in het huidig perspectief* (Antwerp, 1968); H. Willaert, *P. B., de levenswekker* (Brussels, 1984).

Bentoiu, Pascal, Romanian composer and writer on music; b. Bucharest, April 22, 1927. He was a pupil of M. Jora in Bucharest (1943–48). After working at the Inst. for Folklore there (1953–56), he pursued research in ethnomusicology and aesthetics. He publ. 3 books on aesthetics: *Imagine şi sens* (Bucharest, 1971), *Deschideri spre lumea muzicii* (Bucharest, 1973), and *Gîndirea muzicală* (Bucharest, 1975), and a study of Enesco's works, *Capodopere enesciene* (Bucharest, 1984). As a composer, he won the State Prize in 1964, the Prix Italia of the RAI in 1968, and the Enesco Prize of the Romanian Academy in 1974. His catalog of works includes the operas *Amorul doctor* (The Love Doctor; 1964; Bucharest, Dec. 23, 1966), *Jertifirea Iphigeniei* (The Immolation of Iphigenia; Bucharest, Sept. 1968), and *Hamlet* (1969; Bucharest, Nov. 19, 1971). He was president of the Romanian Composers Union from 1990.

Benton, Joseph. See **Bentonelli, Joseph (Horace).**

Bentonelli (real name, **Benton**), **Joseph (Horace),** American tenor; b. Sayre, Okla., Sept. 10, 1898; d. Oklahoma City, April 4, 1975. Following the frequent practice among American singers, he adopted an Italian-sounding name when he embarked on a singing career. He was a student of Jean de Reszke in Paris. In 1925 he made his public debut with the de Reszke Ensemble in Nice. In 1934 he appeared at the Chicago Opera. On Jan. 10, 1936, he made his Metropolitan Opera debut in New York as Massenet's Des Grieux, singing there until 1937. His repertoire included many leading Italian roles.

Bentzon, Jørgen, Danish composer, cousin of **Niels Viggo Bentzon**; b. Copenhagen, Feb. 14, 1897; d. Horsholm, July 9, 1951. He studied composition with Carl Nielsen (1915–18). At the same time, he took courses in jurisprudence; subsequently he was attached to the Ministry of Justice in Denmark, and served as clerk of records of the Danish Supreme Court. He also taught piano and theory at a People's School of Music in Copenhagen. As a composer, he followed the Romantic trends current in Scandinavia; an influence of Nielsen pervades his music. His works include the opera *Saturnalia* (Copenhagen, Dec. 15, 1944).

Bentzon, Niels Viggo, prominent Danish pianist, pedagogue, and composer, cousin of **Jørgen Bentzon**; b. Copenhagen, Aug. 24, 1919. He began his piano training with his mother, and then took lessons with the jazz pianist Leo Mathisen; he subsequently studied piano with Christiansen, organ with Bangert, and theory with Jeppesen at the Copenhagen Cons. (1938–42). In 1943 he made his debut as a pianist, and later toured Europe and the United States. He taught at the Århus Cons. (1945–49) and the Royal Danish Cons. of Music in Copenhagen (from 1949). Although a prolific composer, Bentzon also found time to write music criticism, publ. poetry, and paint. He publ. *Tolvtoneteknik* (Copenhagen, 1953) and *Beethoven: En skitse af et geni* (Copenhagen, 1970). His compositions follow along avant-garde lines for the most part, encompassing happenings, audiovisual scores, and graphic notation.

WORKS: DRAMATIC: OPERAS: *Faust III* (1961–62; Kiel, June 21, 1964); *Automaten* (1973; Kiel, May 3, 1974). BALLETS: *Metafor* (Copenhagen, March 31, 1950); *Kurtisanen* (The Courtesan; Copenhagen, Dec. 19, 1953); *Døren* (The Door; Copenhagen, Nov. 14, 1962); *Jenny von Westphalen* (Århus, Sept. 9, 1965); *Jubilacumsballet 800* (1968); *Duell* (Stockholm, Nov. 12, 1977).

Benucci, Francesco, famous Italian bass; b. c.1745; d. Florence, April 5, 1824. He began his career in 1769. In 1783 he went to Vienna, where he created the roles of Figaro in *Le nozze di Figaro* (Vienna, May 1, 1786) and Guglielmo in *Così fan tutte* (Vienna, Jan. 26, 1790). He visited London in 1788–89, then lived again in Vienna. In 1795 he returned to Italy.

Benvenuti, Tommaso, Italian opera composer; b. Cavarzere (Venice), Feb. 4, 1838; d. Rome, Feb. 26, 1906. When he was 18 years old, his opera *Valenzia Candiano* was announced for performance in Mantua, but was taken off after a rehearsal. The following year, he succeeded in having his 2d opera, *Adriana Lecouvreur*, produced in Milan (Nov. 26, 1857). Other productions followed: *Guglielmo Shakespeare* (Parma, Feb. 14, 1861); *La Stella di Toledo* (Milan, April 23, 1864); *Il Falconiere* (Venice, Feb. 16, 1878); *Beatrice di Suevia* (Venice, Feb. 20, 1890); *Le baruffe Chiozzotte*, opera buffa (Florence, Jan. 30, 1895). Although Benvenuti's operas are workmanlike and effective, they failed to hold the stage after initial successes.

Benzell, Mimi, American soprano; b. Bridgeport, Conn., April 6, 1922; d. Manhasset, Long Island, N.Y., Dec. 23, 1970. Her grandfather was a singer of Jewish folk songs in Russia before his emigration to America. She studied at Hunter College of the City Univ. of N.Y. and with Olga Eisner at the Mannes College of Music in N.Y. In 1944 she made her operatic debut in Mexico City. On Dec. 3, 1944, she made her first appearance at the Metropolitan Opera in New York in a concert, and then returned there to make her formal operatic debut as the Queen of the Night on Jan. 5, 1945; she remained on its roster until 1949. In subsequent years she pursued a career as a singer of popular music, winning her greatest success in the Broadway musical *Milk and Honey* (1961–63).

Benzi, Roberto, French conductor; b. Marseilles, Dec. 12, 1937. He began music training as a small child and in 1948 appeared as a youthful conductor in Bayonne and of the Colonne Orch. in Paris. He pursued academic studies at the Sorbonne in Paris and was a conducting pupil of Cluytens (1947–50). In 1954 he made his debut as an opera conductor, and in 1959 he made his first appearance at the Paris Opéra conducting *Carmen*. He subsequently made guest appearances in Europe, Japan, and North and South America. On Dec. 11, 1972, he made his Metropolitan Opera debut in New York conducting *Faust*. From 1973 to 1987 he was music director in Bordeaux, and then was principal conductor and artistic advisor of Arnhem's Het Gelders Orch. from 1989. In 1966 he married **Jane Rhodes**.

Berberian, Cathy (Catherine), versatile American mezzo-soprano; b. Attleboro, Mass., July 4, 1925; d. Rome, March 6, 1983. She studied singing, dancing, and the art of pantomime; took courses at Columbia Univ. and N.Y. Univ.; then studied voice in Milan with Giorgina del Vigo. In 1957 she made her debut in a concert in Naples; attracted wide attention in 1958, when she performed John Cage's *Aria* (with *Fontana Mix*), which demanded a fantastic variety of sound effects. Her vocal range extended to 3 octaves, causing one bewildered music critic to remark that she could sing both *Tristan* and *Isolde*. Thanks to her uncanny abilities, she became the darling of inventive composers of the avant-garde, who eagerly dedicated to her their otherwise unperformable works. She married one of them, **Luciano Berio**, in 1950, but their marriage was dissolved in 1964. She could also intone classical music. Shortly before her death, she sang her own version of the *Internationale* for an Italian television program commemorating the centennial of the death of Karl Marx (1983). She was an avant-garde composer in her own right; she wrote multimedia works, such as *Stripsody*, an arresting soliloquy of labial and laryngeal sounds, and an eponymously titled piano piece, *Morsicat(h)y*.

Berbié, Jane (real name, **Jeanne Marie-Louise Bergougne**), French mezzo-soprano; b. Villefranche-de-Lauragais, May 6, 1931. She received training at the Toulouse Cons. After making her operatic debut in 1958, she appeared at Milan's La Scala for the first time in Ravel's *L'Enfant et les sortilèges* in 1960. She appeared at the Glyndebourne Festivals (1969–71; 1983–84), the Aix-en-Provence Festivals (1969–70), London's Covent Garden (1971), and the Salzburg Festival (1974). From 1975 she sang at the Paris Opéra, and later at the Théâtre des Champs Elysées in Paris. She also appeared in other operatic centers in Europe and was a prof. at the Paris Cons. (from 1982). She was especially admired for her coloratura roles in operas by Mozart and Rossini.

Berens, (Johann) Hermann, German pianist and pedagogue; b. Hamburg, April 7, 1826; d. Stockholm, May 9, 1880. He studied with his father, Karl Berens of Hamburg, then had instruction with Reissiger in Dresden, and later with Czerny in Vienna. In 1847 he emigrated to Sweden. He served as music director to the Hussar regiment in Orebro (1849–60), then was music director at Mindre Teatern, in Stockholm (from 1860). In 1861 he was appointed to the staff of the Stockholm Cons. where, in 1868, he was named prof. He wrote an operetta, *En sommarnattsdröm* (1856), and the operas *Violetta* (1855), *Lully och Quinault* (1859), *En utflykt i det gröne* (1862), and *Riccardo* (1869), which sank without a trace.

Berenstadt, Gaetano, German castrato alto who flourished in the first half of the 18th century. In 1711 he sang in Novara and Bologna, and then entered the service of the Grand Duchess of Tuscany. After appearances in Düsseldorf (1712–14), he made his London debut in Handel's *Rinaldo* on Jan. 5, 1716. He also gave concerts there. In 1717 he sang in Dresden and served as virtuoso to the King of Poland and Elector of Saxony. After singing in Rome (1719–20) and Venice (1721), he returned to London and appeared with the Royal Academy of Music (1722–24), creating roles in Handel's *Ottone* (Jan. 23, 1723), *Flavio* (May 25, 1723), and *Giulio Cesare* (Feb. 20, 1724). In 1726 he sang in Rome and in 1726–27 in Naples. He then served as a member of the royal chapel in the latter city from 1727 to 1734. He also sang in Florence (1727–28; 1729–30; 1733–34) and Rome (1728–29; 1732).

Berezovsky, Maximus (Sozontovich), Russian tenor and composer; b. Glukhov, Oct. 27, 1740; d. (suicide?) St. Petersburg, April 2, 1777. He studied at the Kiev Ecclesiastic Academy, then was chorister at the Court Chapel in St. Petersburg. He attracted attention by his lyric voice, and in 1765 was sent by the Russian government to Bologna for further study. He became a pupil of Padre Martini, and wrote an opera, *Demofoonte* (1773), which was produced in Bologna. Upon his return to Russia, he was unable to compete with Italian musicians who had acquired all the lucrative positions in the field of vocal teaching and opera. He became despondent and apparently cut his own throat.

Berezowsky, Nicolai (Nikolai Tikhonovich), talented Russian-born American violinist, conductor, and composer; b. St. Petersburg, May 17, 1900; d. (suicide) N.Y., Aug. 27, 1953. He studied at the court chapel in St. Petersburg (1908–16). After playing violin in the orchs. of the Saratov opera (1917–19) and Moscow's Bolshoi Theater (1919–20), he pursued violin training with Robert Pollack in Vienna. In 1922 he settled in the United States and in 1928 became a naturalized American citizen. He was a violinist in the orch. of the Capitol Theatre in New York (1922–23) and the N.Y. Phil. (1923–29). In 1927 he studied with Paul Kochanski (violin) and Rubin Goldmark (composition) at N.Y.'s Juilliard School of Music. He was assistant conductor with CBS (1932–36; 1941–46) and a member of the Coolidge String Quartet (1935–40). In 1948 he received a Guggenheim fellowship. His works followed along Romantic lines, with a later infusion of impressionistic harmonies. Among his compositions is the children's opera *Babar the Elephant* (N.Y., Feb. 21, 1953).

BIBL.: A. Berezowsky, *Duet with Nicky* (N.Y., 1943).

Berg, Alban (Maria Johannes), greatly significant Austrian composer whose music combined classical clarity of design and highly original melodic and harmonic techniques that became historically associated with the New Viennese School; b. Vienna, Feb. 9, 1885; d. there, Dec. 24, 1935. He played piano as a boy and composed songs without formal training. He worked as a clerk in a government office in Lower Austria; in 1904 he met Arnold Schoenberg, who became his teacher, mentor, and close friend; he remained Schoenberg's pupil for 6 years. A fellow classmate was Anton von Webern; together they initiated the radical movement known to history as the New or Second Viennese School of composition. In Nov. 1918 Schoenberg organized in Vienna the Soc. for Private Musical Performances (Verein für Musikalische Privataufführungen) with the purpose of performing works unacceptable to established musical society. So as to emphasize the independence of the new organization, music critics were excluded from attendance. The society was disbanded in 1922, having accomplished its purpose. In 1925 Berg joined the membership of the newly created ISCM, which continued in an open arena the promotion of fresh musical ideas.

Berg's early works reflected the Romantic style of Wagner, Wolf, and Mahler; typical of this period were his *3 Pieces for Orchestra* (1913–15). As early as 1917 Berg began work on his opera *Wozzeck* (after the romantic play by Büchner), which was to become his masterpiece. The score represents an ingenious synthesis of Classical forms and modern techniques; it is organized as a series of purely symphonic sections in traditional Baroque forms, among them a passacaglia with 21 variations, a dance suite, and a rhapsody, all cast in a setting marked by dissonant counterpoint. Its first production at the Berlin State Opera on Dec. 14, 1925, precipitated a storm of protests and press reviews of extreme violence; a similarly critical reception was accorded to *Wozzeck* in Prague on Nov. 11, 1926. Undismayed, Berg and his friends responded by publishing a brochure incorporating the most vehement of these reviews so as to shame and denounce the critics. Leopold Stokowski, ever eager to defy convention, gave the first American performance of *Wozzeck* in Philadelphia on March 19, 1931; it aroused a great deal of interest and was received with cultured equanimity. Thereafter, performances of *Wozzeck* multiplied in Europe, and in due time the opera became recognized as a modern masterpiece. Shortly after the completion of *Wozzeck*, Berg wrote a *Lyric Suite* for String Quartet in 6 movements; it was first played in Vienna by the Kolisch Quartet on Jan. 8, 1927; in 1928 Berg arranged the 2d, 3d, and 4th movements for String Orch., which were performed in Berlin on Jan. 31, 1929. Rumors of a suppressed vocal part for the 6th movement of the suite, bespeaking Berg's secret affection for a married woman, Hanna Fuchs-Robettin, impelled Douglas M. Greene to institute a search for the original score; he discovered it in 1976 and, with the help of George Perle, decoded the vocal line in an annotated copy of the score that Berg's widow, understandably reluctant to perpetuate her husband's emotional aberrations, turned over to a Vienna library. The text proved to be Stefan Georg's rendition of Baudelaire's *De Profundis clamavi* from *Les Fleurs du mal*. Indeed, Berg inserted in the score all kinds of semiotical and numerological clues to his affection in a sort of symbolical synthesis. The Lyric Suite with its vocal finale was performed for the first time at Abraham Goodman House, N.Y., by the Columbia String Quartet and Katherine Ciesinski, mezzo-soprano, on Nov. 1, 1979.

Berg's 2d opera, *Lulu* (1928–35), to a libretto derived from 2 plays by Wedekind, was left unfinished at the time of his death; 2 acts and music from the *Symphonische Stücke aus der Oper Lulu* of 1934 were performed posthumously in Zürich on June 2, 1937. Again, Berg's widow intervened to forestall any attempt to have the work reconstituted by another musician. However, Berg's publishers, asserting their legal rights, commissioned Friedrich Cerha to re-create the 3d act from materials available in other authentic sources, or used by Berg elsewhere; the task required 12 years (1962–74) for its completion. After Berg's widow died in 1976, several opera houses openly competed for the Cerha version of the work; the premiere of the complete opera, incorporating this version, was first presented at the Paris Opéra on Feb. 24, 1979; the first American performance followed in Santa Fe, N. Mex., on July 28, 1979. As in *Wozzeck*, so in *Lulu*, Berg organized the score in a series of classical forms; but while *Wozzeck* was written before Schoenberg's formulation of the method of composition in 12 tones related solely to one another, *Lulu* was set in full-fledged dodecaphonic techniques; even so, Berg allowed himself frequent divagations, contrary to the dodecaphonic code, into triadic tonal harmonies.

Berg's last completed work was a Violin Concerto commissioned by Louis Krasner, who gave its first performance at the Festival of the ISCM in Barcelona on April 19, 1936. The score bears the inscription "Dem Andenken eines Engels," the angel being the daughter of Alma Mahler and Walter Gropius who died at an early age. The work is couched in the 12-tone technique, with free and frequent interludes of passing tonality.

WORKS: OPERAS: *Wozzeck*, after a play of Büchner, op. 7 (1917–22; Berlin, Dec. 14, 1925, E. Kleiber conducting; 1st U.S. perf., Philadelphia, March 19, 1931, Stokowski conducting; 1st British perf., London, Jan. 22, 1952, Kleiber conducting); *Lulu*, after Wedekind's plays *Erdgeist* and *Die Büchse der Pandora* (1928–35; Acts 1 and 2 complete, with Act 3 in short score; Acts 1 and 2, with music from the *Symphonische Stücke aus der Oper Lulu* [1934] to accompany the Act 3 death of Lulu, Zürich, June 2, 1937; 1st British perf., London, Oct. 1, 1962, L. Ludwig conducting; 1st U.S. perf., Santa Fe, N. Mex., Aug. 7, 1963, R. Craft conducting; 2d version, with Act 3 realized by Friedrich Cerha, Paris, Feb. 24, 1979, Boulez conducting; 1st U.S. perf., Santa Fe, N.Mex., July 28, 1979, M. Tilson Thomas conducting; 1st British perf., London, Feb. 16, 1981, Sir Colin Davis conducting).

WRITINGS: Berg contributed articles to many contemporary music journals; also wrote analyses for Schoenberg's *Gurrelieder, Kammersymphonie*, and *Pelleas und Melisande*.

BIBL.: The International A. B. Soc. of the Graduate Center of the City Univ. of N.Y. issues a newsletter. See also: W. Reich, *A. B.: Mit B.s eigenen Schriftem und Beiträgen von Theodor Wiesengrund-Adorno und Ernst Křenek* (Vienna, 1937); R. Leibowitz, *Schoenberg et son école* (Paris, 1947; Eng. tr., 1949, as *Schoenberg and His School*); H. Redlich, *A. B.: Versuch einer Würdigung* (Vienna, 1957; abr. Eng. tr., 1957, as *A. B.: The Man and His Music*); W. Reich, ed., *A. B.: Bildnis im Wort. Selbstzeugnisse und Aussagen der Freunde* (Zürich, 1959); K. Vogelsang, *A. B.: Leben und Werk* (Berlin, 1959); W. Reich, *A. B.: Leben und Werk* (Zürich, 1963; Eng. tr., 1965, as *The Life and Work of A. B.*); H. Berg, ed., *A. B.: Briefe an seine Frau* (Vienna, 1965; Eng. tr., 1971, as *A. B.: Letters to His Wife*); T. Adorno, *A. B., der Meister des Kleinsten übergangs* (Vienna, 1968; rev. ed., 1978); M. Carner, *A. B.: The Man and the Work* (London, 1975; 2nd ed., rev., 1983); E. Hilmar, *Wozzeck von A. B.* (Vienna, 1975); V. Scherleiss, *A. B.* (Hamburg, 1975); D. Jarman, *The Music of A. B.* (Berkeley, 1979); K. Monson, *A. B.* (Boston, 1979); F. Grasberger and R. Stephan, eds., *Die Werke von A. B.: Handschriftenkatalog* (Vienna, 1981); G. Perle, *The Operas of A. B.* (2 vols., Berkeley, 1981, 1985); J. Schmalfeldt, *B.'s Wozzeck: Harmonic Language and Dramatic Design* (London, 1983); J. Brand, C. Hailey, and D. Harris, eds., *The B.-Schönberg Correspondence* (N.Y., 1986); S. Rode, *A. B. und Karl Kraus: Zur geistigen Biographie des Komponisten der "Lulu"* (Frankfurt am Main, 1988); D. Jarman, *A. B.: "Wozzeck"* (Cambridge, 1989); idem ed., *The B. Companion* (Boston, 1990); H.-U. Fuss, *Musikalisch-dramatische Prozesse in den Opern A. B.s* (Hamburg, 1991); D. Gable and R. Morgan, eds., *A. B.: Historical and Analytical Perspectives* (Oxford, 1991); D. Jarman, ed., *A. B.: Lulu* (Cambridge, 1991); A. von Massow, *Halbwelt, Kultur und Natur in A. B.s "Lulu"* (Stuttgart, 1992); T. Ertelt, *A. B.'s 'Lulu': Quellenstudien und Beiträge zur Analyse* (Vienna, 1993); P. Hall, *A View of B.'s Lulu Through the Autograph Sources* (Berkeley, 1995); B. Simms, *A. B.: A Guide to Research* (N.Y., 1996); A. Pople, ed., *The Cambridge Companion to B.* (Cambridge, 1998).

Berg, Josef, Czech composer; b. Brno, March 8, 1927; d. there, Feb. 26, 1971. He studied with Petrželka at the Brno Cons. (1946–50); was music ed. of Brno Radio (1950–53); wrote simple music for the Folk Art ensemble. Later he began using 12-tone techniques. His most original works are the operas *Odysse ů návrat* (Odysseus's Return; 1962), *Evropská turistika* (European Tourism; 1963–64), *Eufrides před branami Thymen* (Euphrides in Front of the Gates of Tymenas; 1964), and *Johannes Doktor Faust* (1966).

BIBL.: M. Štědroň, *J. B.* (Brno, 1992)

Berg, (Carl) Natanael, Swedish composer; b. Stockholm, Feb. 9, 1879; d. there, Oct. 14, 1957. He was a pupil of Julius Günther (voice) and J. Lindegren (counterpoint) at the Stockholm Cons. (1897–1900), but was essentially an autodidact in composition; he held state composer's fellowships for further studies in Berlin and Paris (1908–09), and in Vienna (1911–12); also took a degree in veterinary medicine (1902) and served as a veterinary surgeon in the Swedish Army until 1939. In 1918 he helped to found the Soc. of Swedish Composers, serving as its chairman until 1924. In 1932 he was elected a member of the Royal Swedish Academy of Music in Stockholm. His music is indulgent, reminiscent in its tumescent harmonies of Richard Strauss.

WORKS: OPERAS: (all 1st perf. in Stockholm): *Leila* (1910; Feb. 29, 1912); *Engelbrekt* (1928; Sept. 21, 1929); *Judith* (1935; Feb. 22, 1936); *Brigitta* (1941; Jan. 10, 1942); *Genoveva* (1944–46; Oct. 25, 1947). PANTOMIME BALLETS: *Alvorna* (1914); *Sensitiva* (1919); *Hertiginnans friare* (The Duchesse's Suitors; 1920).

Berganza, (Vargas), Teresa, admired Spanish mezzo-soprano; b. Madrid, March 16, 1935. She was a pupil of Lola Rodriguez Aragón in Madrid; after winning the singing prize at the Madrid Cons. in 1954, she made her debut in a Madrid concert in 1955; in 1957 she made her opertic debut as Dorabella at the Aix-en-Provence Festival. In 1958 she made her British debut as Cherubino at the Glyndebourne Festival, and that same year she sang at the Dallas Civic Opera. In 1960 she made her first appearance at London's Covent Garden as Rosina, and in 1962 her debut at the Chicago Lyric Opera as Cherubino, a role she repeated for her Metropolitan Opera debut in New York on Oct. 11, 1967; she remained on its roster until 1969. She toured widely as a concert artist, winning particular distinction for her Spanish song recitals. In 1992 she participated in the gala ceremonies at the Olympic Games in Barcelona. She appeared in recital at London's Wigmore Hall in 1997. In addition to her roles in operas by Mozart and Rossini, she was esteemed for her portrayals of Monteverdi's Octavia, Purcell's Dido, and Bizet's Carmen. Her career is the subject of her book *Meditaciones de na Cantante* (Madrid, 1985).

Berge, Sigurd, Norwegian composer; b. Vinstra, July 1, 1929. He studied composition with Thorleif Eken at the Oslo Cons. and with Finn Mortensen (1956–59); he later took courses in electronic music in Stockholm, Copenhagen, and Utrecht. From 1959 he taught at the Sagene College of Education. He served as chairman of the Norwegian Composers Union (1985–88). His output ranges from traditional works to electronic pieces. Among his works is the music drama *Gudbrandskalsspelet* (1980).

Berger, Erna, distinguished German soprano; b. Cossebaude, near Dresden, Oct. 19, 1900; d. Essen, June 14, 1990. She was a student of Böckel and Melita Hirzel in Dresden. In 1925 she made her operatic debut as the first boy in *Die Zauberflöte* at the Dresden State Opera, where she sang until 1930. In Berlin she sang at the City Opera (1929) and the State Opera (from 1934); also appeared at the Bayreuth (1930–33) and Salzburg (1932–54) festivals. In 1934 she made her debut at London's Covent Garden as Marzelline, and sang there until 1938 and again in 1947. On Nov. 21, 1949, she made her Metropolitan Opera debut in New York as Sophie, remaining on its roster until 1951. In 1955 she retired from the operatic stage but pursued a career as a lieder artist until 1968. From 1959 she was a prof. of voice at the Hamburg Hochschule für Musik. In 1985 the Berlin State Opera made her an honorary member. Her autobiography was publ. as *Auf Flügeln des Gesanges* (Zürich, 1988). Berger was an outstanding coloratura soprano. Among her other roles were the Queen of the Night, Rosina, Martha, Gilda, and Zerbinetta.

BIBL.: K. Höcker, *E. B.: Die singende Botschafterin* (Berlin, 1961).

Berger, Jean, German-born French, later American, conductor, teacher, and composer; b. Hamm, Sept. 27, 1909. He studied musicicology with Egon Wellesz at the Univ. of Vienna and with Heinrich Besseler at the Univ. of Heidelberg (Ph.D., 1931), and then composition with Louis Aubert and Capdevielle in Paris, where he conducted the choir Les Compagnons de la Marjolaine and in 1935 became a naturalized American citizen. After teaching at the Conservatorio Brasileiro de Música in Rio de Janeiro (1939–41), he settled in the United States, becoming a naturalized citizen in 1943. He taught at Middlebury (Vt.) College (1948–59), the Univ. of Ill. in Urbana (1959–61), and the Univ. of Colo. (1961–68). In 1964 he founded the John Sheppard Music Press in Boulder. He wrote mainly choral music in an accessible style, although within his catalog are the stage works *Pied Piper*, musical play for Dancers, Solo Voices, Choruses, and Small Orch. (1968), *Birds of a Feather: An Entertainment* (1971), *Yiphth and his Daughter*, opera (1972), and *The Cherry Tree Carol*, liturgical drama (1975). His best known work is the *Brazilian Psalm* for Chorus (1941).

Berger, Rudolf, Czech baritone and tenor; b. Brünn, April 17, 1874; d. N.Y., Feb. 27, 1915. He was a pupil of Adolf Robinson in Brünn. In 1896 he made his debut as a baritone in Brünn, and then sang at the Berlin Royal Opera (from 1898) and at the Bayreuth Festival (1901–08). He also made guest appearances in Vienna, London (Covent Garden), Paris, and Prague. After further studies with Oscar Saenger in New York, he concentrated on Heldentenor roles from 1909. On Feb. 5, 1914, he made his Metropolitan Opera debut in New York as Siegmund, and remained on its roster until his death. In 1913 he married **Marie Rappold**.

Berggreen, Andreas Peter, Danish composer; b. Copenhagen, March 2, 1801; d. there, Nov. 8, 1880. He studied law and turned to music late in life, and occupied various teaching posts in Copenhagen. His opera *Billedet og Busten* (The Portrait and the Bust) was produced in Copenhagen on April 9, 1832; he also wrote incidental music to plays. His most important contribution to music literature is the compilation of 11 vols. of folk songs, *Folke-sang og melodier, faedre landske og fremmede* (Copenhagen, 1842–55; 2d ed., enl., 1861–71); he further publ. 14 vols. of songs for use in schools (1834–76) and ed. church anthems. Among his students was Niels Gade.

BIBL.: C. Skou, *A. P. B.* (Copenhagen, 1895).

Bergh, Arthur, American violinist, conductor, and composer; b. St. Paul, Minn., March 24, 1882; d. aboard the S.S. *President Cleveland* en route to Honolulu, Feb. 11, 1962. He studied violin; played in the Metropolitan Opera orch. (1903–08) and conducted concerts in New York (1911–14); later worked for recording companies. Among his works are the opera *Niorada*, the melodramas

The Raven and *The Pied Piper of Hamelin,* and the operettas *In Arcady* and *The Goblin Fair.*

Berghaus, Ruth, German opera director; b. Dresden, July 2, 1927; d. Zeuthen, Jan. 25, 1996. She received training in dance at the Palucca School in Dresden (1947–50). In 1964 she became a choreographer with the Berliner Ensemble, serving as its Intendant (1971–77). She garnered notoriety as an opera director at the Berlin State Opera with her staging of *Il barbiere di Siviglia.* From 1980 to 1987 she was an opera director at the Frankfurt am Main Opera, where she oversaw outstanding productions of *Parsifal* (1982) and the *Ring* cycle (1985–87); she also was active as a guest director in other European opera centers, including Brussels, Hamburg, Munich, and Vienna. In her productions, Berghaus has pursued a radical course laden with symbolism and satire. She was married to **Paul Dessau**.

BIBL.: S. Neef, *Das Theater der R. B.* (Berlin, 1989); K. Bertisch, *R. B.* (Frankfurt am Main, 1990).

Bergiron de Briou, Nicolas-Antoine, Seigneur du Fort Michon, French composer; b. Lyons, Dec. 12, 1690; d. there, before April 27, 1768. He studied classical literature and law at the Univ. of Paris. With J. P. Christin, he established in 1713 the Académie des Beaux-Arts in Lyons, and remained associated with it in various capacities until 1764. He composed divertissements and several operas.

Berglund, Joel (Ingemar), Swedish bass-baritone; b. Torsåker, June 4, 1903; d. Stockholm, Jan. 21, 1985. He was a pupil of John Forsell at the Stockholm Cons. (1922–28). In 1928 he made his operatic debut as Lothario in *Mignon* at the Royal Opera in Stockholm, where he was a member until 1949; he then made guest appearances there until 1964. He also sang in Venice, Chicago, Bayreuth (as the Dutchman, 1949), and other operatic centers. On Jan. 9, 1946, he made his Metropolitan Opera debut in New York as Hans Sachs, remaining on its roster until 1949. He served as director of the Royal Opera in Stockholm (1949–52), and continued to make appearances in opera until his retirement in 1970.

Bergman, Erik (Valdemar), eminent Finnish composer, conductor, music critic, and pedagogue; b. Nykarleby, Nov. 24, 1911. He received training in musicology at the Univ. of Helsinki (1931–33) and in composition from Furuhjelm at the Helsinki Cons. (diploma, 1938). Following further studies with Tiessen at the Berlin Hochschule für Musik (1937–39), he studied with Vogel in Switzerland. Returning to Helsinki, he was conductor of the Catholic Church Choir (1943–50), the Akademiska Sangföreningen at the Univ. (1950–69), and the Sällskapet Muntra Musikanter (1951–78). As a music critic, he wrote for the *Nya Pressen* (1945–47) and *Hufvudstadsbladet* (1947–76). From 1963 to 1976 he was prof. of composition at the Sibelius Academy. In 1961 he received the International Sibelius Prize of the Wihuri Foundation. In 1982 he was made a Finnish Academician. In 1994 he was awarded the Nordic Council Music Prize for his opera *Det sjungande trädet* (The Singing Tree), which received its premiere in Helsinki on Sept. 3, 1995. Bergman ranks among the foremost Finnish composers of his era. He cultivates varied techniques, ranging from medieval modality to serialism. His major works, including the opera *Det sjungande tradet* (The Singing Tree; 1986–88; Helsinki, Sept. 3, 1995), have evolved along expressionistic lines.

BIBL.: J. Parsons, *E. B.: A Seventieth Birthday Tribute* (London, 1981).

Bergonzi, Carlo, eminent Italian tenor; b. Polisene, near Parma, July 13, 1924. He studied with Grandini in Parma, where he also took courses at the Boito Cons. During World War II, he was imprisoned for his fervent antifascist stance. After his liberation, he made his operatic debut in the baritone role of Rossini's Figaro in Lecce in 1948. In 1951 he made his debut as a tenor singing Andrea Chénier in Bari. He made his first appearance at Milan's La Scala in 1953, creating the title role in Napoli's *Masaniello*, and that same year he made his London debut as Alvaro at the Stoll Theatre. In 1962 he returned to London to make his Covent Garden debut in the same role. In 1955 he made his U.S. debut as Luigi in *Il Tabarro* at the Chicago Lyric Opera. On Nov. 13, 1956, he made his Metropolitan Opera debut in New York as Radames, remaining on its roster until 1972, and again for the 1974–75, 1976–77, and 1978–83 seasons. He gave his farewell N.Y. concert at Carnegie Hall on April 17, 1994; he then bade farewell to Europe that same year in a series of concerts. He was blessed with a voice of remarkable beauty and expressivity. Among his many outstanding roles were Pollione, Rodolfo, Alfredo, Canio, Manrico, Nemorino, and Cavaradossi.

Bergsma, William (Laurence), notable American composer and pedagogue; b. Oakland, Calif., April 1, 1921; d. Seattle, March 18, 1994. His mother, a former opera singer, gave him piano lessons; he also practiced the violin. After the family moved to Redwood City, Bergsma entered Burlingame High School, where he had theory lessons. In 1937 he began to take lessons in composition with Hanson at the Univ. of Southern Calif. in Los Angeles. He composed a ballet, *Paul Bunyan*, and Hanson conducted a suite from it with the Rochester Civic Orch. in Rochester, N.Y., on April 29, 1939. Bergsma also took courses at Stanford Univ. (1938–40); from 1940 to 1944 he attended the Eastman School of Music in Rochester, studying general composition with Hanson and orchestration with Bernard Rogers. He graduated in 1942, receiving his M.M. degree in 1943. In 1944 Bergsma became an instructor in music at Drake Univ. in Des Moines. In 1946 and in 1951 he held Guggenheim fellowships. In 1946 he was appointed to the faculty of the Juilliard School of Music in New York, where he taught until 1963. From 1963 to 1971 Bergsma served as director of the School of Music of the Univ. of Wash. in Seattle, remaining as a prof. there until 1986. In 1967 he was elected to membership in the National Inst. of Arts and Letters. During his teaching activities he continued to compose, receiving constant encouragement from an increasing number of performances. His style of composition is that of classical Romanticism, having a strong formal structure without lapsing into modernistic formalism. The Romantic side of his music is reflected in his melodious lyricism. He never subscribed to fashionable theories of doctrinaire modernity. His dramatic works include the operas *The Wife of Martin Guerre* (N.Y., Feb. 15, 1956) and *The Murder of Comrade Sharik* (1973; rev. 1978) and the ballets *Paul Bunyan* (San Francisco, June 22, 1939) and *Gold and the Senor Commandante* (Rochester, N.Y., May 1, 1942).

Berio, Luciano, eminent Italian composer, conductor, and pedagogue; b. Oneglia, Oct. 24, 1925. Following initial training from his father, Ernesto Berio, he entered the Milan Cons. in 1945 to study composition with Paribeni and Ghedini, obtaining his diploma in 1950. He married **Cathy Berberian** in 1950 (marriage dissolved in 1964), who became a champion of his most daunting vocal works. In 1952 he attended Luigi Dallapiccola's course at the Berkshire Music Center in Tanglewood. After attending the summer course in new music in Darmstadt in 1954, he returned to Milan and helped to organize the Studio di Fonologia Musicale of the RAI with Maderna, remaining active with it until 1961. In 1956 he founded the journal *Incontri Musicali*, and also served as director of the concerts it sponsored until 1960. He taught composition at the Berkshire Music Center (1960, 1982), the Dartington Summer School (1961–62), Mills College in Oakland, California (1962–64), and Harvard Univ. (1966–67). From 1965 to 1972 he taught composition at the Juilliard School of Music in New York, where he also conducted the Juilliard Ensemble. From 1974 to 1979 he worked at IRCAM in Paris. He also gave increasing attention to conducting, eventually appearing as a guest conductor with leading European and North American orchs. In 1987 he became founder-director of Tempo Reale in Florence, a research, educational, and composition center. During the 1993–94 academic year, he was the Charles Eliot Norton Prof. of Poetry at Harvard Univ., and then served as its Distinguished Composer-in-Residence from 1994. In 1980 he was awarded an honorary doctorate from the City Univ. of London. He received the Premio Italia in 1982 for his *Duo*. In 1989 he was awarded the Ernst von

Siemens-Musikpreis of Munich. In 1996 he won Japan's Premium Imperiale.

From the very beginning of his career as a composer, Berio embraced the ideals of the avant-garde. His early use of 12-tone writing was followed by imaginative explorations of aleatory, electronics, objets trouvés, and other contemporary means of expression. As one of the principal composers of his era, Berio has demonstrated a remarkable capacity for infusing new life into established forms. The theatrical nature of much of his music has rendered his vocal scores among the most challenging and significant works of their time. These works, like most of his output, have set daunting hurdles of virtuosity for the performer while demanding a level of tolerance from both critics and audiences alike.

WORKS: DRAMATIC: *Allez Hop*, racconto mimico for Mezzo-soprano, 8 Mimes, Ballet, and Orch. (1952–59; Venice, Sept. 23, 1959; rev. 1968); *Passaggio*, messa in scena for Soprano, 2 Choruses, and Orch. (1961–62; Milan, May 6, 1963); *Laborintus II* for Voices, Instruments, and Tape (1965); *Il combattimento di Tancredi e Clordina*, after Monteverdi (1966); *Opera* for 10 Actors, 2 Sopranos, Tenor, Baritone, Vocal Ensemble, Orch., and Tape (1969–70; Santa Fe, N.M., Aug. 12, 1970; rev. version, Florence, May 28, 1977); *Per la dolce memoria de quel giorno*, ballet (1974); *La vera storia*, opera (1977–78; Milan, March 9, 1982); *Un re in ascolto*, azione musicale (1979–83; Salzburg, Aug. 7, 1984); *Duo*, imaginary theater for radio for Baritone, 2 Violins, Chorus, and Orch. (1982); *Naturale*, theater piece (1985–86); *Wir Bauen eine Stadt*, children's opera, after Hindemith (1987); *Outis*, opera (Milan, Oct. 2, 1996).

BIBL.: R. Dalmonte and B. Varga, *L. B.: Two Interviews* (London, 1985); D. Osmond-Smith, *B.* (Oxford, 1991); F. Menezes Filho, *L. B. et la phonologie: Une approche jakobsonienne de son oeuvre* (Frankfurt am Main, 1993).

Berkeley, Sir Lennox (Randall Francis), eminent English composer and teacher, father of **Michael (Fitzhardinge) Berkeley**; b. Boars Hill, May 12, 1903; d. London, Dec. 26, 1989. He was educated at Merton College, Oxford (1922–26), and then studied composition with Boulanger in Paris (1927–32). Returning to London, he worked for the BBC (1942–45) before serving as a prof. of composition at the Royal Academy of Music (1946–68). In 1957 he was made a Commander of the Order of the British Empire, in 1970 he received an honorary D.Mus. from the Univ. of Oxford, and in 1974 he was knighted. In his early works, Berkeley was influenced by the Parisian neo-Classicists and the music of Britten. He later developed a complex individual style that was broadly melodious, richly harmonious, and translucidly polyphonic.

WORKS: DRAMATIC: OPERAS: *Nelson* (1949–54; London, Sept. 22, 1954; orch. suite, 1955); *A Dinner Engagement* (Aldeburgh Festival, June 17, 1954); *Ruth* (London, Oct. 2, 1956); *Castaway* (Aldeburgh Festival, June 3, 1967). BALLET: *The Judgement of Paris* (1938). Also incidental music for plays.

BIBL.: P. Dickinson, *The Music of L. B.* (London, 1988).

Berkeley, Michael (Fitzhardinge), English composer, son of **Sir Lennox (Randall Francis) Berkeley;** b. London, May 29, 1948. He was a chorister at Westminster Cathedral under the tutelage of George Malcolm; he also studied with his father at the Royal Academy of Music and then privately with Richard Rodney Bennett. He received the Guinness Prize for his *Meditations* for Chamber Orch. (1977); he was assoc. composer to the Scottish Chamber Orch. (1979) and composer-in-residence at the London College of Music (1987–88). In 1995 he became artistic director of the Cheltenham Festival and co-artistic director of the Spitalfields Festival. His anti-nuclear oratorio *Or Shall We Die?* (1982) brought him to international attention. His music is austere while still projecting a firm relationship to the English New Romantic movement. His catalog of works includes *The Mayfly*, a children's ballet (London, Sept. 30, 1984), and *Baa-Baa Black Sheep*, opera (Cheltenham, July 7, 1993).

Berlijn, Anton (real name, **Aron Wolf**), Dutch composer; b. Amsterdam, May 2, 1817; d. there, Jan. 18, 1870. He studied with Friedrich Schneider in Berlin and with Spohr in Kassel, then went to Leipzig, where he took lessons with G. W. Fink. Returning to Amsterdam in 1846, he became a conductor at the Royal Theater, but devoted himself mainly to composition. He wrote several operas, 2 of which were popular (*Die Bergknappen* and *Proserpina*); also 7 ballets and an oratorio (*Moses auf Nebo*). He enjoyed a certain prestige in the Netherlands. A memorial vol., *Nachruf an den verstorbenden Komponist A.W. Berlijn*, compiled by P. Böhm, was publ. in Amsterdam shortly after Berlijn's death.

Berlioz, (Louis-) Hector, great French composer who exercised profound influence on the course of modern music in the direction of sonorous grandiosity, and propagated the Romantic ideal of program music, unifying it with literature; b. La Côte-Saint-André, Isère, Dec. 11, 1803; d. Paris, March 8, 1869. His father was a medical doctor who possessed musical inclinations, and it was under his guidance that Berlioz learned to play the flute, and later took up the guitar; however, he never became an experienced performer on any instrument. Following his father's desire that he study medicine, he went to Paris, where he entered the École de Médecine. At the same time he began taking private lessons in composition from Jean François Le Sueur. In 1824, he abandoned his medical studies to dedicate himself entirely to composition. His first important work was a *Messe solennelle*, which was performed at a Paris church on July 10, 1825. He then wrote an instrumental work entitled *La Révolution grecque*, inspired by the revolutionary uprising in Greece against the Ottoman domination. He was 22 years old when he entered the Paris Cons. as a pupil of his first music teacher, Le Sueur, in composition, and of Anton Reicha in counterpoint and fugue. In 1826, Berlioz wrote an opera, *Les Francs-juges*, which never came to a complete performance. In 1827 he submitted his cantata *La Mort d'Orphée* for the Prix de Rome, but it was rejected. On May 26, 1828, he presented a concert of his works at the Paris Cons., including the *Resurrexit* from the *Messe solennelle*, *La Révolution grecque*, and the overtures *Les Francs-juges* and *Waverley*. Also in 1828 he won the 2d prize of the Prix de Rome with his cantata *Herminie*. In 1828–29 he wrote *Huit scènes de Faust*, after Goethe. This was the score that was eventually revised and produced as *La Damnation de Faust*. In 1829, he applied for the Prix de Rome once more with the score of *La Mort de Cléopâtre*, but no awards were given that year. He finally succeeded in winning the 1st Prix de Rome with *La Mort de Sardanapale*, which was performed in Paris on Oct. 30, 1830.

In the meantime, Berlioz became passionately infatuated with the Irish actress Harriet Smithson after he attended her performance as Ophelia in Shakespeare's *Hamlet*, given by a British drama troupe in Paris on Sept. 11, 1827. Romantically absorbed in the ideal of love through music, Berlioz began to write his most ambitious and, as time and history proved, his most enduring work, *Symphonie fantastique,* which was to be an offering of adoration and devotion to Miss Smithson. Rather than follow the formal subdivisions of a sym., Berlioz decided to integrate the music through a recurring unifying theme, which he called an idée fixe, appearing in various guises through the movements of the *Symphonie fantastique*. To point out the autobiographical nature of the work he subtitled it "Épisode de la vie d'un artiste." The 5 divisions of the score are: *I. Reveries, Passions, II. A Ball, III. Scene in the Fields, IV. March to the Scaffold*, and *V. Dream of a Witches' Sabbath*. Berlioz supplied a literary program to the music: a "young musician of morbid sensibilities" takes opium to find surcease from amorous madness. In the *Symphonie fantastique* the object of the hero's passion haunts him through the device of the idée fixe; she appears first as an entrancing, but unattainable, vision, then as an enticing dancer at a ball, and then as a deceptive pastoral image. He penetrates her disguise and kills her, a crime for which he is led to the gallows. At the end she reveals herself as a wicked witch at a Sabbath orgy. The fantastic program design does not interfere, however, with an orderly organization of the score, and the wild fervor of the music is astutely subordinated to the symphonic form. The idée fixe itself serves merely as a recurring motif, not unlike similar musical reminiscences in Classical syms. Interestingly, in the *March to the Scaffold* Berlioz makes use of a section from his earlier score *Les Francs-juges*, and merely inserts into it a few bars of the idée fixe to justify the incorporation of unrelated musical material. No matter; *Symphonie fantastique* with or without Miss Smithson, with or without the idée fixe, emerges as a magnificent tapestry of sound. The work was first performed at the Paris Cons. on Dec. 5, 1830, with considerable success, although the Cons.'s director, the strict perfectionist Cherubini, who failed to attend the performance, spoke disdainfully of it from a cursory examination of the score. Nor did Miss Smithson herself grace the occasion by her physical presence. Incongruously, the publ. score of the *Symphonie fantastique* is dedicated to the stern Russian czar Nicholas I. That this apotheosis of passionate love should have been inscribed to one of Russia's most unpleasant czars is explained by the fact that Berlioz had been well received in Russia in 1847. Berlioz followed the *Symphonie fantastique* with a sequel entitled *Lélio, ou Le Retour à la vie*, purported to signalize the hero's renunciation of his morbid obsessions. Both works were performed at a single concert in Paris on Dec. 9, 1832, and this time La Smithson made her appearance. A most remarkable encounter followed between them; as if to prove the romantic notion of the potency of music as an aid to courtship, Berlioz and Smithson soon became emotionally involved, and they were married on Oct. 3, 1833. Alas, their marriage proved less enduring than the music. Smithson broke a leg (on March 16, 1833) even before the marriage ceremony, and throughout their life together was beset by debilitating illnesses. They had a son, who died young. Berlioz found for himself a more convenient woman companion, one Maria Recio, whom he married shortly after Smithson's death in 1854. Berlioz survived his 2d wife, too, who died in 1862.

Whatever the peripeteias of his personal life, Berlioz never lost the lust for music. During his stay in Italy, following his reception of the Prix de Rome, he produced the overtures *Le Roi Lear* (1831) and *Rob Roy* (1831). His next important work was *Harold en Italie*, for the very unusual setting of a solo viola with orch., commissioned by Paganini (although never performed by him) and inspired by Lord Byron's poem *Childe Harold*. It was first performed in Paris on Nov. 23, 1834. Berlioz followed it with an opera, *Benvenuto Cellini* (1834–37), which had its first performance at the Paris Opéra on Sept. 10, 1838. It was not successful, and Berlioz revised the score; the new version had its first performance in Weimar in 1852, conducted by Liszt. About the same time, Berlioz became engaged in writing musical essays; from 1833 to 1863 he served as music critic for the *Journal des Débats*; in 1834 he began to write for the *Gazette Musicale*. In 1835 he entered a career as conductor. In 1837 he received a government commission to compose the *Grande messe des morts* (Requiem), for which he demanded a huge chorus. The work was first performed at a dress rehearsal in Paris on Dec. 4, 1837, with the public performance following the next day. On Dec. 16, 1838, Berlioz conducted a successful concert of his works in Paris; legend has it that Paganini came forth after the concert and knelt in homage to Berlioz; if sources (including Berlioz himself) are to be trusted, Paganini subsequently gave Berlioz the sum of 20,000 francs. In 1839, Berlioz was named assistant librarian of the Paris Cons. and was awarded the Order of the Légion d'Honneur. On Nov. 24, 1839, he conducted, in Paris, the first performance of his dramatic sym. *Roméo et Juliette*, after Shakespeare. The work is regarded as one of the most moving lyrical invocations of Shakespeare's tragedy, rich in melodic invention and instrumental interplay. In 1840 Berlioz received another government commission to write a *Grande symphonie funèbre et triomphale*. This work gave Berlioz a clear imperative to build a sonorous edifice of what he imagined to be an architecture of sounds. The work was to commemorate the soldiers fallen in the fight for Algeria, and if contemporary reports can be taken literally, he conducted it with a drawn sword through the streets of Paris, accompanying the ashes of the military heroes to their interment in the Bastille column.

The spirit of grandiosity took possession of Berlioz. At a concert after the Exhibition of Industrial Products in 1844 in Paris he conducted Beethoven's 5th Sym. with 36 double basses, Weber's *Freischütz Overture* with 24 horns, and the *Prayer of Moses* from Rossini's opera with 25 harps. He boasted that his 1,022 performers achieved an ensemble worthy of the finest string quartet. For his grandiose *L'Impériale*, written to celebrate the distribution of prizes by Napoleon III at the Paris Exhibition of Industrial Products in 1855, Berlioz had 1,200 performers, augmented by huge choruses and a military band. As if anticipating the modus operandi of a century thence, Berlioz installed 5 subconductors and, to keep them in line, activated an "electric metronome" with his left hand while holding the conducting baton in his right. Such indulgences generated a chorus of derision on the part of classical musicians and skeptical music critics; caricatures represented Berlioz as a madman commanding a heterogeneous mass of instrumentalists and singers driven to distraction by the music. Berlioz deeply resented these attacks and bitterly complained to friends about the lack of a congenial artistic environment in Paris.

But whatever obloquy he suffered, he also found satisfaction in the pervading influence he had on his contemporaries, among them Wagner, Liszt, and the Russian school of composers. Indeed, his grandiosity had gradually attained true grandeur; he no longer needed huge ensembles to exercise the magic of his music. In 1844 he wrote the overture *Le Carnaval romain*, partially based on music from his unsuccessful opera *Benvenuto Cellini*. There followed the overture *La Tour de Nice* (later rev. as *Le Corsaire*). In 1845 he undertook the revision of his early score after Goethe, which now assumed the form of a dramatic legend entitled *La Damnation de Faust*. The score included the *Marche hongroise*, in which Berlioz took the liberty of conveying *Faust* to Hungary. The march became extremely popular as a separate concert number.

In 1847 Berlioz undertook a highly successful tour to Russia, and in the following year he traveled to England. In 1849 he composed his grand *Te Deum*, conducting its first performance in Paris on April 28, 1855, at a dress rehearsal; it was given a public performance 2 days later, with excellent success. In 1852 he traveled to Weimar at the invitation of Liszt, who organized a festival of Berlioz's music. Between 1850 and 1854 he wrote the oratorio *L'Enfance du Christ*, which he conducted in Paris on Dec. 10, 1854. Although Berlioz was never able to achieve popular success with his operatic productions, he turned to composing stage music once more between 1856 and 1860. For the subject he selected the great epic of Vergil relating to the Trojan War; the title was to be *Les Troyens*. He encountered difficulties in producing this opera in its entirety, and in 1863 divided the score into 2 sections: *La Prise de Troie* and *Les Troyens à Carthage*. Only the 2d part was produced in his lifetime; it received its premiere at the Théâtre-Lyrique in Paris on Nov. 4, 1863; the opera had 22 performances, and the financial returns made it possible for Berlioz to abandon his occupation as a newspaper music critic. His next operatic project was *Béatrice et Bénédict*, after Shakespeare's play *Much Ado about Nothing*. He conducted its first performance in Baden-Baden on Aug. 9, 1862. Despite frail health and a state of depression generated by his imaginary failure as composer and conductor in France, he achieved a series of successes abroad. He conducted *La Damnation de Faust* in Vienna in 1866, and he went to Russia during the 1867–68 season. There he had a most enthusiastic reception among Russian musicians, who welcomed him as a true prophet of the new era in music.

Posthumous recognition came slowly to Berlioz, and long after his death some conservative critics still referred to his music as bizarre and willfully dissonant. No cult comparable to the ones around the names of Wagner and Liszt was formed to glorify Berlioz's legacy. Of his works only the overtures and the *Symphonie fantastique* became regular items on sym. programs. Performances of his operas were still rare events. Since Berlioz never wrote solo works for piano or any other instrument, concert recitals had no opportunity to include his name in the program. However, a whole literature was publ. about Berlioz in all European languages, securing his rightful place in music history.

WRITINGS: *Grand traité d'instrumentation et d'orchestration modernes* (Paris, 1843; numerous subsequent eds.; in Eng., 1948; eds. covering modern usages were publ. in German by Felix Weingartner, Leipzig, 1904, and Richard Strauss, Leipzig, 1905); *Le Chef d'orchestre, Théorie de son art* (Paris, 1855; in Eng. as *The Orchestral Conductor, Theory of His Art*, N.Y., 1902); *Voyage musical en Allemagne et en Italie, Études sur Beethoven, Gluck, et Weber. Mélanges et nouvelles* (2 vols., Paris, 1844); *Les Soirées de l'orchestre* (Paris, 1852; in Eng. as *Evenings in the Orchestra*, tr. by C. Roche, with introduction by Ernest Newman, N.Y., 1929; new Eng. tr. as *Evenings with the Orchestra* by J. Barzun, N.Y., 1956; 2d ed., 1973); *Les Grotesques de la musique* (Paris, 1859); *A travers chants: études musicales, adorations, boutades, et critiques* (Paris, 1862); *Les Musiciens et la musique* (a series of articles collected from the *Journal des Débats*; with introduction by A. Hallays, Paris, 1903); *Mémoires de Hector Berlioz* (Paris, 1870; 2d ed. in 2 vols., Paris, 1878; in Eng., London, 1884; new tr. by R. and E. Holmes, with annotation by Ernest Newman, N.Y., 1932; another Eng. tr. by D. Cairns, N.Y., 1969; corrected ed., 1975). An incomplete ed. of literary works of Berlioz was publ. in German by Breitkopf & Härtel: *Literarische Werke* (10 vols. in 5, Leipzig, 1903–04) and *Gesammelte Schriften* (4 vols., Leipzig, 1864).

WORKS: DRAMATIC: OPERAS: *Estelle et Némorin* (1823; not perf.; score destroyed); *Les Francs-juges* (1826; not perf.; rev. 1829 and 1833; overture and 5 movements extant); *Benvenuto Cellini* (1834–37; Paris Opéra, Sept. 10, 1838; rev. 1852; Weimar, Nov. 17, 1852); *La Nonne sanglante* (1841–47; score unfinished); *Les Troyens* (1856–58; rev. 1859–60; divided into 2 parts, 1863: I, *La Prise de Troie* [1st perf. in German under Mottl, Karlsruhe, Dec. 6, 1890]; II, *Les Troyens à Carthage* [1st perf. under Deloffre, Théâtre-Lyrique, Paris, Nov. 4, 1863]; 1st perf. of both parts in French, with major cuts, Brussels, Dec. 26–27, 1906; 1st complete perf., *sans* cuts, alterations, etc., in Eng. under Alexander Gibson, Glasgow, May 3, 1969; in French, under Colin Davis, Royal Opera House, Covent Garden, London, Sept. 17, 1969); *Béatrice et Bénédict* (1860–62; Baden-Baden, Aug. 9, 1862). OTHER: *La Révolution grecque*, scène héroïque (1825–26; Paris, May 26, 1828); *La Mort d'Orphée*, monologue et bacchanale (1827; 1st perf. under Cortot, Paris, Oct. 16, 1932); *Herminie*, scène lyrique (1828); *La Mort de Cléopâtre*, scène lyrique (1829); *Le Retour à la vie*, op. 14b, monodrame lyrique (1831–32; Paris, Dec. 9, 1832; rev. 1854 as *Lélio, ou Le Retour à la vie*); *La Damnation de Faust*, légende dramatique, op. 24 (1845–46; Paris, Dec. 6, 1846); *L'Enfance du Christ*, trilogie sacrée, op. 25 (1850–54; Paris, Dec. 10, 1854).

BIBL.: COLLECTED EDITIONS, SOURCE MATERIAL: The first major ed. of Berlioz's works (*Benvenuto Cellini, Les Troyens*, and several other scores excepted) was edited by C. Malherbe and F. Weingartner (20 vols., Leipzig, 1900–07); see Supplement 5 in J. Barzun's *B. and the Romantic Century* (2 vols., Boston, 1950; 3d ed., rev., 1969) for an extensive enumeration of its musical and other errors. A new critical ed. of all of the extant works, the *New B. Edition*, under the general editorship of Hugh Macdonald, began publication in Kassel in 1967. The definitive catalog is D. Holoman, *Catalogue of the Works of H. B.* (Kassel, 1987). The standard bibliography is C. Hopkinson, *A Bibliography of the Musical and Literary Works of H. B. 1803–1869* (Edinburgh, 1951; 2d ed. with additions and corrections by R. Macnutt, Tunbridge Wells, 1980). Another valuable source is M. Wright, *A Bibliography of Critical Writings on H. B.* (1967). BIOGRAPHICAL: W. Neumann, *B., Eine Biographie* (Kassel, 1855); E. de Mirecourt, *B.* (Paris, 1856); A. Jullien, *H. B.: La Vie et le combat, Les OEuvres* (Paris, 1882); J. Bennett, *B.* (London, 1883); A. Jullien, *H. B.: Sa vie et ses oeuvres* (Paris, 1888); E. Hippeau, *B. et son temps* (Paris, 1890); L. Pohl, *H. B.: Leben und Werke* (Leipzig, 1900); A. Hahn et al., *H. B.: Sein Leben und seine Werke* (Leipzig, 1901); R. Louis, *H. B.* (Leipzig, 1904); J.-G. Prod'homme, *H. B. (1803–1869): Sa vie et ses oeuvres* (Paris, 1904; 3rd ed., 1927); A. Boschot, *La Jeunesse d'un romantique; H. B., 1803–31* (Paris, 1906; rev. ed., 1946), *Un Romantique sous Louis-Philippe; H. B., 1831–42* (Paris, 1908; rev. ed., 1948), and *Le Crépuscule d'un romantique; H. B., 1842–69* (Paris, 1913; rev. ed., 1950); B. Schrader, *B.* (Leipzig, 1907); P.-L. Robert, *étude sur H. B.* (Rouen, 1914); J. Kapp, *B.: Eine Biographie* (Berlin and Leipzig, 1917; 7th ed., 1922); A. Boschot, *Une Vie romantique: H. B.* (Paris, 1919; numerous subsequent printings); P.-M. Masson, *B.* (Paris, 1923); E. Rey, *La Vie amoureuse de B.* (Paris, 1929); L. Constantin, *B.* (Paris, 1934); W. Turner, *B.: The Man and His Work* (London, 1934); T. Wotton, *H. B.* (London, 1935); J. Elliot, *B.* (London, 1938; 4th ed., rev., 1967); E. Lockspeiser, *B.* (London, 1939); G. de Pourtalès, *B. et l'Europe romantique* (Paris, 1939; rev. ed., 1949); P. Mouthier, *H. B.* (Dilbeck, 1944); J. Daniskas, *H. B.* (Stockholm, 1947; Eng. tr., 1949); F. Knuttel, *H. B.* (The Hague, 1948); J. Barzun, *B. and the Romantic Century* (2 vols., Boston, 1950; 3d ed., rev., 1969); A. Ganz, *B. in London* (London, 1950); T. Tienot, *H. B.: Esquisse biographique* (Paris, 1951); H. Kühner, *H. B.: Charakter und Schöpfertum* (Olten, 1952); H. Barraud, *H. B.* (Paris, 1955; 2d ed., 1966); C. Ballif, *B.* (Paris, 1968); S. Demarquez, *H. B.: L'Homme et son oeuvre* (Paris, 1969); J. Crabbe, *H. B.: Rational Romantic* (London, 1980); H. Macdonald, *B.* (London, 1982); R. Clarson-Leach, *B.: His Life and Times* (Tunbridge Wells, 1983); W. Dömling, *H. B. und seine Zeit* (Laaber, 1986); D. Cairns, *B., Volume One: The Making of an Artist* (London, 1989); D. Holoman, *B.* (Cambridge, Mass., 1989); P. Bloom, *The Life of B.* (Cambridge, 1998). CRITICAL, ANALYTICAL: Important articles may be found in the *Berlioz Society Bulletin* and the *Bulletin de Liaison*; the latter is publ. by the Association Nationale Hector Berlioz in Paris (1964-). See also: A. Ernst, *L'OEuvre dramatique de H. B.* (Paris, 1884); R. Pohl, *H. B.: Studien und Erinnerungen* (Leipzig, 1884); J.-G. Prod'homme, *La Damnation de Faust* (Paris, 1896); E. Destranges, *Les Troyens de B.: Étude analytique* (Paris, 1897); E. Bernoulli, *H. B. als Ästhetiker der Klangfarben* (Zürich, 1909); A. Boschot, *Le Faust de B.* (Paris, 1910; rev. ed., 1946); P.-L. Robert, *H. B.: Les Troyens* (Rouen, 1920); T. Mantovani, *La dannazione di Faust di Ettore B.* (Milan, 1923); J. Tiersot, *La Damnation de Faust de B.* (Paris, 1924); A. Court, *H. B.: The Role of Literature in His Life and Work* (diss., Univ. of London, 1961); G. Sandford, *The Overtures of H. B.: A Study in Musical Style* (diss., Univ. of Southern Calif., Los Angeles, 1964); E. Grabner, *B. and French Operatic Tradition* (diss., Univ. of York, 1967); A. Dickinson, *The Music of B.* (London, 1972); H. Cohen, *B. and the Opera (1829–1849)* (diss., N.Y. Univ., 1973); B. Primmer, *The B. Style* (London, 1973); F. Piatier, *Benvenuto Cellini de B. ou Le Mythe de l'artiste* (Paris, 1979); M. Clavaud, *H. B., Visages d'un masque* (Lyons, 1980); J. Rushton, *The Musical Language of B.* (Cambridge, 1983); idem., *B., Roméo et Juliette* (Cambridge, 1994).

Bernabei, Ercole, Italian composer, father of **Giuseppe Antonio Bernabei**; b. Caprarola, Papal States, 1622; d. Munich (buried), Dec. 6, 1687. He was a pupil of Orazio Benevoli, whom he succeeded in 1672 as chapel master at the Vatican. In 1674 he became court conductor in Munich. He wrote 5 operas, which were produced in Munich.

BIBL.: R. Casimiri, *E. B., Maestro di cappella musicale lateranse* (Rome, 1920); R. de Rensis, *E. B.* (Rome, 1920).

Bernabei, Giuseppe Antonio, Italian composer, son of **Ercole Bernabei**; b. Rome, 1649; d. Munich, March 9, 1732. He studied with his father, and served with him as a vice Kapellmeister in Munich beginning in 1677. After his father's death in 1687, he assumed his post as principal Kapellmeister. He wrote 15 operas and much sacred music.

BIBL.: K. Forster, *G. A. B. als Kirchenkomponist* (Munich, 1933).

Bernac (real name, **Bertin**), **Pierre,** eminent French baritone and teacher; b. Paris, Jan. 12, 1899; d. Villeneuve-les-Avignon, Oct. 17, 1979. He received private voice lessons in Paris. He began his career as a singer rather late in life, being first engaged in finance as a member of his father's brokerage house in Paris. His musical tastes were decidedly in the domain of modern French songs; on May 2, 1926, he made his debut recital in Paris with a program of songs by Francis Poulenc and Georges Auric; at other concerts he sang works by Debussy, Ravel, Honegger, and Milhaud. Eager to learn the art of German lieder, he went to Salzburg to study with Reinhold von Warlich. Returning to Paris, he devoted himself to concerts and to teaching. He became a lifelong friend to Poulenc, who wrote many songs for him and acted as his piano accompanist in many tours through Europe and America. He also conducted master classes in the United States and was on the faculty of the American Cons. at Fontainebleau. He publ. a valuable manual, *The Interpretation of French Song* (N.Y., 1970; 2d ed., 1976), and a monograph, *Francis Poulenc: The Man and His Songs* (N.Y., 1977).

Bernacchi, Antonio Maria, celebrated Italian castrato alto; b. Bologna (baptized), June 23, 1685; d. there, March 13, 1756. He studied voice with Pistocchi and G. A. Ricieri. In 1700 he was sopranist at the church of S. Petronio in Bologna. He made his operatic debut in Genoa in 1703, and between 1709 and 1735 had a number of engagements in Venice. Between 1712 and 1731 he made several appearances in Bologna. He also sang in Munich (1720–27). In 1716–17 he sang in London, and in 1729 he was engaged by Handel as a substitute for Senesino for the London seasons of the Italian Opera; however, he failed to please British operagoers and returned to his native town of Bologna, where he opened a singing school. In his singing he cultivated the style of vocal embellishments in the manner of the French roulades.

Bernard, Robert, Swiss-born French composer, editor, and writer on music; b. Geneva, Oct. 10, 1900; d. Paris, May 2, 1971. He studied in Geneva with G. T. Strong, Barblan, and Lauber. In 1926 he settled in Paris; in 1937 he became a lecturer at the Schola Cantorum and a music critic; from 1939 to 1951 he was ed. of *La Revue Musicale*. He publ. monographs on Franck, Aubert, Roussel, and other French composers, and a *Histoire de la musique* (Paris, 1961–64). Among his compositions are 3 operas: *Flen* (1918), *Le Chevalier au Barizel* (1919), and *Polyphème* (1929).

Bernardi, Bartolomeo, Italian violinist and composer; b. Bologna, c.1660; d. Copenhagen, May 23, 1732. He received an invitation from the Danish Court to serve as a violinist and composer, and began his work there on Jan. 1, 1703. After an absence of several years (1705–10), he returned to Copenhagen and was appointed director of court music. In Copenhagen he produced 2 operas, *Il Gige fortunato* (Aug. 26, 1703) and *Diana e la Fortuna* (Oct. 10, 1703); he also wrote an opera, *La Libussa*, for a production in Prague in 1703. The music for all three works is lost.

Bernardi, Mario (Egidio), Canadian conductor; b. Kirkland Lake, Ontario, Aug. 20, 1930. He was sent to Italy when he was 6, where he studied piano, organ, and composition with Bruno Pasut at the Manzato Cons. in Treviso (1938–45), taking his examination in the latter year at the Venice Cons. He then took courses with Lubka Kolessa (piano) and Ettore Mazzoleni (conducting) at the Royal Cons. of Music of Toronto (1948–51), later studying conducting with Erich Leinsdorf at the Salzburg Mozarteum (1959). He began his career as a church organist and concert pianist; he also worked as a coach and conductor with the Royal Cons. Opera School in Toronto (from 1953). In 1957 he made his first appearance as a conductor with the Canadian Opera Co., and in 1963 he became assistant conductor at Sadler's Wells in London. In 1967 he made his U.S. debut conducting *La Bohème* at the San Francisco Opera. From 1969 to 1982 he served as the first music director of the new National Arts Centre Orch. in Ottawa; then was principal conductor of the CBC Vancouver Orch. (from 1983) and music director of the Calgary Phil. (1984–93). In 1997 he was made conductor laureate of the National Arts Centre Orch. On Jan. 19, 1984, he made his Metropolitan Opera debut in New York conducting Handel's *Rinaldo*. In 1972 he was made a Companion of the Order of Canada.

Bernasconi, Andrea, Italian composer, stepfather of **Antonia Bernasconi**; b. probably in Marseilles, c.1706; d. Munich, Jan. 27?, 1784. In 1746–47 he was maestro di cappella at the Ospedale della Rieta in Venice. In 1753 he settled in Munich as assistant court Kappellmeister of vocal music and as electoral councillor. In 1755 he was made court Kappellmeister, where he brought out several successful operas. He taught music to Princess Maria Anna Josepha (1754–55), Princess Josepha Maria (1754–65), and to the Elector, Maximilian III Joseph.

WORKS: OPERE SERIE: *Flavio Anicio Olibrio* (Venice, 1737); *Didone abbandonata* (Milan, Dec. 26, 1738); *Alessandro Severo* (Venice, Dec. 27, 1738; rev. as *Sallustia*, Venice, May 31, 1753); *Temistocle* (Padua, June 6, 1740); *Demofoonte* (Rome, Carnival 1741); *Il Bajazet* (Venice, 1742); *Germanico* (Turin, Carnival 1744); *Antigono* (Venice, Carnival 1745); *Artaserse* (Vienna, Oct. 8, 1746); *Ezio* (Schönbrunn, Oct. 4, 1749); *Adriano in Siria* (Munich, Jan. 5, 1755); *Agelmondo* (Munich, Carnival 1760); *Olimpiade* (Munich, Jan. 1764); *Semiramide* (Munich, Jan. 7, 1765); *La clemenza di Tito* (Munich, Jan. 1768); *Demetrio* (Munich, Jan. 1772); various other dramatic works.

BIBL.: E. Weiss, *A. B. als Opernkomponist* (diss., Univ. of Munich, 1923).

Bernasconi, Antonio, German soprano, stepdaughter of **Andrea Bernasconi**; b. Stuttgart, c.1741; d. probably in Vienna, c.1803. She was the daughter of a valet in the service of the Duke of Württemberg. After her father's death, her mother married Andrea Bernasconi. Antonia received her vocal training from him and made her debut as Aspasia in his *Temistocle* in Munich on Jan. 21, 1762. About 1765 she went to Vienna, where she won accolades at the first performance of Gluck's *Alcestis* (Dec. 16, 1767). Mozart wrote the role of Aspasia for her in his *Mitridate* (Dec. 1770). After appearances in Venice (1771–72), Naples (1772–73; 1774–75), and at the King's Theatre in London (1778–80), she returned to Vienna to sing in 1781.

Berners, Lord (Sir Gerald Hugh Tyrwhitt-Wilson, Baronet), eccentric English composer, writer, and painter; b. Arley Park, Bridgnorth, Sept. 18, 1883; d. Farringdon House, Berkshire, April 19, 1950. He was mainly self-taught, although he received some music training in Dresden and England, and advice and encouragement from Stravinsky. He served as honorary attaché to the British diplomatic service in Constantinople (1909–11) and Rome (1911–19). Returning to England, he joined the literary smart set; he was on close terms with George Bernard Shaw, H. G. Wells, and Osbert Sitwell. He publ. half a dozen novels, including *The Girls of Radcliff Hall* (1937), *The Romance of a Nose* (1942), and *Far from the Madding War*, in which he portrays himself as Lord Fitzcricket. Berners affected bizarre social behavior; his humor and originality are reflected in his compositions, many of which reveal a subtle gift for parody. He wrote 2 autobiographical vols., *First Childhood* (London, 1934) and *A Distant Prospect* (London, 1945); he also had successful exhibitions of his oil paintings in London (1931, 1936).

WORKS: OPERA: *Le Carrosse du Saint-Sacrement* (Paris, April 24, 1924). BALLETS: *The Triumph of Neptune* (London, Dec. 3, 1926); *Luna Park* (London, March 1930); *A Wedding Bouquet* (London, April 27, 1937); *Cupid and Psyche* (London, April 27, 1939); *Les Sirènes* (London, Nov. 12, 1946).

BIBL.: J. Holbrooke, *B.* (London, 1925); H. Bridgeman and E. Drury, *The British Eccentric* (N.Y., 1975).

Bernet, Dietfried, Austrian conductor; b. Vienna, May 14, 1940. He studied at the Vienna Academy of Music and received training in conducting from Swarowsky and Mitropoulos. In 1962 he won 1st prize in the Liverpool conducting competition, and then was a conductor in Vienna at the State Opera and at the Volksoper from 1964. In 1973 he made his U.S. debut as a guest conductor with the Chicago Sym. Orch. He also was a guest conductor with various other orchs. on both sides of the Atlantic, and appeared with opera companies in Munich, Hamburg, Cologne, Stuttgart, London, Barcelona, Venice, Glyndebourne, and Geneva. In 1995 he was made chief guest conductor of the Royal Opera in Copenhagen.

Bernet Kempers, Karel Philippus, Dutch musicologist; b. Nijkerk, Sept. 20, 1897; d. Amsterdam, Sept. 30, 1974. He studied with Sandberger at the Univ. of Munich (Ph.D., 1926, with the diss. *Jacobus Clemens non Papa und seine Motetten*; publ. in Augsburg, 1928) and completed his Habilitation at the Univ. of Amsterdam in 1929 with his *Herinnerignsmotieven, leidmotieven, grondthema's*. He taught music history at the Royal Cons. in The Hague (1929–49) and at the Amsterdam Cons. (1934–53); he was also privatdozent (1929–38), lecturer (1938–46), reader (1946–53), and prof. (1953–63) in musicology at the Univ. of Amsterdam. He was the ed. of the complete works of Clemens non Papa. Among his writings is *De italiaanse opera van Peri tot Puccini* (Amsterdam, 1929; Eng. tr., 1947).

Bernstein, Leonard (Louis), prodigiously gifted American conductor, composer, pianist, and teacher; b. Lawrence, Mass., Aug. 25, 1918; d. N.Y., Oct. 14, 1990. He was born into a family of Russian-Jewish immigrants. When he was 16, he legally changed his given name to Leonard to avoid confusion with another Louis in the family. At age 13, he began piano training with Susan Williams at the New England Cons. of Music in Boston. When he was 14, he commenced piano studies with Heinrich Gebhard and his assistant, Helen Coates. In 1935 he entered Harvard Univ., where he took courses with Edward Burlingame Hill (orchestration), A. Tillman Merritt (harmony and counterpoint), and Piston (counterpoint and fugue). He graduated cum laude in 1939. On April 21, 1939, he made his first appearance as a conductor when he led the premiere of his incidental music to Aristophanes' *The Birds* at Harvard Univ. He then enrolled at the Curtis Inst. of Music in Philadelphia, where he studied with Reiner (conducting), Vengerova (piano), Thompson (orchestration), and Renée Longy (score reading), receiving his diploma in 1941. During the summers of 1940 and 1941, he was a pupil in conducting of Serge Koussevitzky at the Berkshire Music Center at Tanglewood, returning in the summer of 1942 as Koussevitzky's assistant. In 1942–43 he worked for the N.Y. publishing firm of Harms, Inc., using the pseudonym Lenny Amber.

In Aug. 1943 Artur Rodzinski, then music director of the N.Y. Phil., appointed Bernstein as his assistant conductor. On Nov. 14, 1943, Bernstein substituted at short notice for ailing guest conductor Bruno Walter in a N.Y. Phil. concert which was broadcast to the nation by radio. He acquitted himself magnificently and was duly hailed by the press as a musician of enormous potential. Thus the most brilliant conducting career in the history of American music was launched, and Bernstein was engaged to appear as a guest conductor with several major U.S. orchs. On Jan. 28, 1944, he conducted the premiere of his first sym., *Jeremiah*, with the Pittsburgh Sym. Orch. The score was well received and won the N.Y. Music Critics' Circle Award for 1944. That same year he brought out his ballet *Fancy Free*, followed by the musical *On the Town*, which scored popular and critical accolades. In 1945 he became music director of the N.Y. City Sym. Orch., a post he held until 1948. On May 15, 1946, he made his European debut as a guest conductor of the Czech Phil. in Prague. In 1947 he appeared as a guest conductor of the Palestine Sym. Orch. in Tel Aviv. During Israel's War of Independence in 1948, he conducted a series of concerts with it as the renamed Israel Phil. He then completed his 2d Sym. for Piano and Orch., *The Age of Anxiety*, a score that reflected the troubled times. It was given its first performance by Koussevitzky and the Boston Sym. Orch. on April 8, 1949, with the composer at the piano. In 1951 Bernstein composed his first opera, *Trouble in Tahiti*. During the Israel Phil.'s first tour of the U.S. in 1951, he shared the conducting duties with Koussevitzky. Upon the latter's death that year, he was named his mentor's successor as head of the orch. and conducting depts. at the Berkshire Music Center, where he was active until 1953 and again in 1955. He also taught intermittently at Brandeis Univ. from 1951 to 1954. In 1953 he produced his successful Broadway musical *Wonderful Town*.

Bernstein was the first American conductor ever to appear as a guest conductor at Milan's La Scala when he led Cherubini's *Medea* in Dec. 1953. In 1954 he wrote the score for the Academy Award winning film *On the Waterfront*. That same year he made an indelible impact as an expositor/performer on the *Omnibus* television program. Returning to the theater, he composed his comic operetta *Candide*, after Voltaire, in 1956. Bernstein was appointed coconductor (with Mitropoulos) of the N.Y. Phil. in 1956, and in 1958 he became its music director, the first American-born and trained conductor to attain that prestigious position. In 1957 he brought out his musical *West Side Story*, a significant social drama abounding in memorable tunes, which proved enduringly popular; in its film incarnation (1961), it won no less than 11 Academy Awards, including best film of the year. In the meantime, Bernstein consolidated his protean activities as music director of the N.Y. Phil. through his concerts at home and abroad, as well as his numerous recordings, radio broadcasts, and television programs. Indeed, he acquired a celebrity status rarely achieved by a classical musician. His televised N.Y. Phil. Young People's Concerts (1958–72) were extremely successful with viewers of all ages. In 1959 he took the N.Y. Phil. on a triumphant tour of 17 European and Near East nations, including the Soviet Union. On Jan. 19, 1961, he conducted the premiere of his *Fanfare* at the Inaugural Gala for President John F. Kennedy in Washington, D.C. Bernstein led the gala opening concert of the N.Y. Phil. in its new home at Phil. Hall at N.Y.'s Lincoln Center for the Performing Arts on Sept. 23, 1962. He then took the orch. on a transcontinental tour of the United States in 1963. On Dec. 10, 1963, he conducted the first performance of his 3d Sym., *Kaddish*, with the Israel Phil. in Tel Aviv. The score reflects Bernstein's Jewish heritage, but is also noteworthy for its admixture of both 12-tone and tonal writing. On March 6, 1964, he made his Metropolitan Opera debut in New York conducting *Falstaff*, which work he also chose for his Vienna State Opera debut on March 14, 1966. In 1967 he appeared for the first time as a guest conductor of the Vienna Phil. In subsequent years he became closely associated with it, appearing not only in Vienna but also on extensive tours, recordings, and films.

In 1969 Bernstein retired as music director of the N.Y. Phil. and was accorded the title of laureate conductor. From 1970 to 1974 he served as advisor at Tanglewood. For the opening of the John F. Kennedy Center for the Performing Arts in Washington, D.C., he composed his theater piece *Mass* (Sept. 8, 1971), a challenging and controversial liturgical score. During the 1973–74 academic year, he was the Charles Eliot Norton Prof. of Poetry at Harvard Univ., where he gave a series of lectures later publ. as *The Unanswered Question* (1976). He returned to the genre of the musical in 1976 with his *1600 Pennsylvania Avenue*, but the work was not successful. (A concert version was given as *The White House Cantata* in London, July 1997.) On Jan. 19, 1977, he conducted at the Inaugural Concert for President Jimmy Carter in Washington, D.C. In 1983 Bernstein completed work on his opera *A Quiet Place*, which he considered his most important creative achievement. However, its premiere in Houston on June 17, 1983, was not a success. He then revised the work and incorporated it into his earlier opera *Trouble in Tahiti*. The revised version was premiered at Milan's La Scala on June 19, 1984, the first opera by an American composer ever accorded such a distinction. All the same, the opera remained problematic. In July–Aug. 1985 he toured as conductor with the European Community Youth Orch. in a "Journey for Peace" program to Athens, Hiroshima, Budapest, and Vienna. Bernstein also conducted celebratory performances of Beethoven's 9th Sym. to mark the opening of the Berlin Wall, first at the Kaiser Wilhelm Memorial Church in West Berlin (Dec. 23, 1989), and then at the Schauspielhaus Theater in East Berlin (telecast to the world, Dec. 25, 1989).

Increasingly plagued by ill health, Bernstein was compelled to announce his retirement from the podium on Oct. 9, 1990. His death just 5 days later (of progressive emphysema, complicated by a chronic pleurisy, eventuating in a fatal heart attack) shocked the music world and effectively brought to a close a unique era in the history of American music. Bernstein was afforded innumerable honors at home and abroad. Among his foreign decorations were the Order of the Lion, Commander, of Finland (1965); Chevalier (1968), Officier (1978), and Commandeur (1985), of the Légion d'honneur, of France; Cavaliere, Order of Merit, of Italy (1969); Grand Honor Cross for Science and Art of Austria (1976); and the Grand Order of Merit of the Italian Republic (1988). In 1977 he was made a member of the Swedish Royal Academy of Music in Stockholm, in 1981 of the American

Academy and Inst. of Arts and Letters in New York, in 1983 of the Vienna Phil., and in 1984 of the N.Y. Phil. In 1987 he was awarded the Gold Medal of the Royal Phil. Soc. of London. He was made president of the London Sym. Orch. in 1987 and laureate conductor of the Israel Phil. in 1988. His 70th birthday was the occasion for an outpouring of tributes from around the world, highlighted by a major celebration at Tanglewood from Aug. 25 to 28, 1988.

Bernstein's extraordinary musical gifts were ably matched by an abundance of spiritual and sheer animal energy, a remarkable intellect, and an unswerving commitment to liberal, and even radical, political and humanitarian ideals. As a composer, he revealed a protean capacity in producing complex serious scores on the one hand, and strikingly original and effective works for the Broadway musical theater on the other. All the same, it was as a nonpareil conductor and musical expositor that Bernstein so profoundly enlightened more than one generation of auditors. Ebullient and prone to podium histrionics of a choreographic expressivity, he was a compelling interpreter of the Romantic repertory. Bernstein had a special affinity for the music of Mahler, whose works drew from him unsurpassed readings of great beauty and searing intensity. He was also a convincing exponent of Haydn, Mozart, and Beethoven.

WORKS: DRAMATIC: *The Birds*, incidental music to Aristophanes' play (1938; Cambridge, Mass., April 21, 1939, composer conducting); *The Peace*, incidental music to Aristophanes' play (1940; Cambridge, Mass., May 23, 1941); *Fancy Free*, ballet (N.Y., April 18, 1944, composer conducting); *On the Town*, musical comedy (Boston, Dec. 13, 1944, Goberman conducting); *Facsimile*, ballet (N.Y., Oct. 24, 1946, composer conducting; 2d version as *Parallel Lives*, Milwaukee, Oct. 19, 1986; 3d version as *Dancing On*, Zagreb, March 31, 1988); *Peter Pan*, incidental music to Barrie's play (N.Y., April 24, 1950); *Trouble in Tahiti*, opera (1951; Waltham, Mass., June 12, 1952, composer conducting); *Wonderful Town*, musical comedy (New Haven, Conn., Jan. 19, 1953); *The Lark*, incidental music to Anouilh's play, adapted by Lillian Hellman (Boston, Oct. 28, 1955); *Salomé*, incidental music to Wilde's play (CBS-TV, N.Y., Dec. 11, 1955; withdrawn); *Candide*, comic operetta (Boston, Oct. 29, 1956; rev. version, N.Y., Dec. 20, 1973, Mauceri conducting; operatic version, N.Y., Oct. 13, 1982, Mauceri conducting; rev., Glasgow, May 17, 1988, Mauceri conducting); *West Side Story*, musical (Washington, D.C., Aug. 19, 1957); *The Firstborn*, incidental music to Christopher Fry's play (N.Y., April 29, 1958; withdrawn); *Mass*, theater piece for Singers, Players, and Dancers (Washington, D.C., Sept. 8, 1971, Peress conducting; chamber version, Los Angeles, Dec. 26, 1972); *Dybbuk*, ballet (N.Y., May 16, 1974, composer conducting; retitled *Dybbuk Variations* for Orch.); *By Bernstein*, musical cabaret (N.Y., Nov. 23, 1975; withdrawn); *1600 Pennsylvania Avenue*, musical (Philadelphia, Feb. 24, 1976; concert version as *The White House Cantata*, London, July 1997); *A Quiet Place*, opera (Houston, June 17, 1983, DeMain conducting; withdrawn; rev. version, incorporating *Trouble in Tahiti*, Milan, June 19, 1984, Mauceri conducting).

WRITINGS: *The Joy of Music* (N.Y., 1959); *Leonard Bernstein's Young People's Concerts for Reading and Listening* (N.Y., 1961; rev. ed., 1970, as *Leonard Bernstein's Young People's Concerts*); *The Infinite Variety of Music* (N.Y., 1966); *The Unanswered Question: Six Talks at Harvard* (Cambridge, Mass., and London, 1976); *Findings* (N.Y., 1982).

BIBL.: J. Briggs, *L. B., The Man, His Work and His World* (Cleveland and N.Y., 1961); A. Holde, *L. B.* (Berlin, 1961); P. Robinson, *B.* (N.Y., 1982); P. Gradenwitz, *L. B.: Eine Biographie* (Zürich, 1984; 2d ed., 1990; Eng. tr., 1986); M. Freedland, *L. B.* (London, 1987); J. Peyser, *L. B.: A Biography* (N.Y., 1987); J. Gottlieb, ed., *L. B.: A Complete Catalog of His Works: Celebrating His 70th Birthday, August 25, 1988* (N.Y., 1988); M. Secrest, *L. B.: A Life* (N.Y., 1995).

Berry, Wallace (Taft), American composer and music theorist; b. La Crosse, Wis., Jan. 10, 1928; d. Vancouver, British Columbia, Nov. 16, 1991. He studied with Stevens at the Univ. of Southern Calif. in Los Angeles (B.Mus., 1949; Ph.D., 1956) and with Boulanger at the Paris Cons. (1953–54); then taught at the Univ. of Southern Calif. (1956–57), the Univ. of Mich. (1957–77), and (from 1978) the Univ. of British Columbia, where he was also head of the music dept. (1978–84). He served as president of the Soc. for Music Theory (1982–85). He publ. *Form in Music* (Englewood Cliffs, N.J., 1966; 2d ed., rev., 1985), *Eighteenth-Century Imitative Counterpoint: Music for Analysis* (with E. Chudacoff; N.Y., 1969), *Structural Functions in Music* (Englewood Cliffs, N.J., 1975; 2d ed., 1987), and *Musical Structure and Performance* (New Haven, Conn., 1989). He composed the chamber opera *The Admirable Bashville* (1954).

Berry, Walter, admired Austrian bass-baritone; b. Vienna, April 8, 1929. He studied engineering at the Vienna School of Engineering before pursuing vocal training with Hermann Gallos at the Vienna Academy of Music. In 1950 he made his debut at the Vienna State Opera in Honegger's *Jeanne d'Arc*, and subseuently sang there regularly; he also appeared at the Salzburg Festivals (from 1952). In 1957 he made his U.S. debut as Mozart's Figaro in Chicago. He made his Metropolitan Opera debut in New York as Barak on Oct. 2, 1966, remaining on its roster until 1974 and returning for its 1975–76 and 1977–78 seasons. In 1976 he made his first appearance at London's Covent Garden as Barak. He also sang in Berlin, Munich, Paris, Tokyo, Buenos Aires, and elsewhere. In 1957 he married **Christa Ludwig**, with whom he appeared in opera and concert; they were divorced in 1970. In 1963 he was made an Austrian Kammersänger. Among his other roles were Leporello, Papageno, Telramund, Wotan, Escamillo, Baron Ochs, Wozzeck, and Dr. Schön.

BIBL.: P. Lorenz, *Christa Ludwig-W. B.: Eine Künstler Biographie* (Vienna, 1968).

Bersa, Blagoje, Croatian composer and teacher; b. Ragusa, Dec. 21, 1873; d. Zagreb, Jan. 1, 1934. He studied music in Vienna, where he remained until 1919. He wrote 2 operas, *Fire* and *The Cobbler of Delft*. Bersa was for many years a prof. of composition at the Zagreb Cons., influencing the development of a new generation of Croatian composers.

Bertali, Antonio, Italian violinist and composer; b. Verona, March 11, 1605; d. Vienna, April 17, 1669. He studied with Steffano Bernardi in Verona, and in 1624 he went to Vienna, where he served as a court violinist. In 1649 he succeeded Giovanni Valentini as Imperial court Kapellmeister. He wrote about 11 operas and a number of secular oratorios.

Berté, Heinrich, Hungarian composer; b. Galgócz, May 8, 1857; d. Perchtoldsdorf, near Vienna, Aug. 23, 1924. He studied with Hellmesberger, Fuchs, and Bruckner in Vienna. He produced the ballets *Das Märchenbuch* (Prague, 1890), *Amor auf Reisen* (Vienna, 1895), *Der Karneval in Venedig* (Vienna, 1900), and *Automatenzauber* (Vienna, 1901), and the operettas *Die Schneeflocke* (Prague, 1896), *Der neue Bürgermeister* (Vienna, 1904), *Die Millionenbraut* (Munich, 1905), *Der kleine Chevalier* (Dresden, 1907), *Der schöne Gardist* (Breslau, 1907), *Der Glücksnarr* (Vienna, 1909), *Kreolenblut* (Hamburg, 1911), *Der Märchenprinz* (Hannover, 1914), and *Das Dreimäderlhaus* (Vienna, Jan. 15, 1916). The last, based on Schubert melodies, was produced in English under the title *Blossom Time*, arranged by Romberg (N.Y., Sept. 21, 1921; very popular); also as *Lilac Time*, arranged by Clutsam (London, Dec. 22, 1922).

Bertin, Louise (-Angélique), French composer; b. Les Roches, near Paris, Feb. 15, 1805; d. Paris, April 26, 1877. She was a pupil of Fétis. She composed the operas *Guy Mannering* (Les Roches, Aug. 25, 1825), *Le Loup-garou* (Paris, March 10, 1827), *Fausto* (Paris, March 7, 1831), and *La Esmeralda,* to a libretto adapted by Victor Hugo from his novel *Notre-Dame de Paris* (Paris, Nov. 14, 1836).

Bertin de la Doué, Thomas, French composer; b. Paris, c.1680; d. there, 1745. He was maître de musique to the Princess of Orléans, then held the post of organist at the Théatins church in Paris; also served as violinist and keyboard musician with the

28). In 1819 he toured Finland with his brother, Christian August Berwald, and Russia. In 1829 he went to Berlin and in 1835 opened an orthopedic establishment, which soon flourished. In 1841 he went to Vienna, where he obtained short-lived success as a composer with his symphonic poems. He then returned to Stockholm and secured a foothold as a composer with his operettas and cantatas. On Dec. 2, 1843, his cousin conducted the premiere of his *Sinfonie sérieuse* (his only acknowledged sym. performed in his lifetime), but poor execution of the score did little to further his cause. In 1846 he returned to Vienna, where Jenny Lind sang in his stage cantata *Ein ländliches Verlobungfest in Schweden* at the Theater an der Wien. In 1847 he was elected an honorary member of the Salzburg Mozarteum. In 1849 he returned to his homeland in hopes of securing the position of either conductor of the Royal Opera in Stockholm or director of music in Uppsala. Hopes dashed, he became manager of a glassworks in Sandö, Ångermanland (1850–58) and part owner of a sawmill (1853), and briefly operated a brick factory. Berwald was shunned by the Swedish musical establishment (which he disdained), and his extraordinary gifts as a composer went almost totally unrecognized in his lifetime. Finally, in 1864, he was made a member of the Swedish Royal Academy of Music in Stockholm. In the last year of his life he was named to its composition chair, only to be unseated, however briefly, on a 2d vote demanded by his enemies. Berwald's masterpiece is his *Sinfonie singulière* (1845), a singular work of notable distinction, which was not performed until 70 years after its composition. He composed the operas *Estrella di Soria* (1841; Stockholm, April 9, 1862) and *Drottningen av Golconda* (1864; Stockholm, April 3, 1968, for the 100th anniversary of Berwald's death), as well as operettas. His output reveals the influence of the German Romantic school in general, but with an unmistakably individual voice.

BIBL.: I. Bengtsson, N. Castegren, and E. Lomans, eds., *F. B.: Die Dokumente seines Lebens* (Kassel, 1979).

Berwald, Johan Fredrik (Johann Friedrich), Swedish violinist and composer, cousin of **Franz (Adolf) Berwald**; b. Stockholm, Dec. 4, 1787; d. there, Aug. 26, 1861. He was a member of a musical family of German nationality that settled in Sweden. A precocious musician, he played the violin in public at the age of 5; took lessons in composition with Abbé Vogler during the latter's stay in Sweden. At 16 he went to St. Petersburg and served as concertmaster in the Russian Imperial Court Orch. (1803–12). Returning to Sweden, he was appointed chamber musician to the King of Sweden, a post he held from 1815 until 1849. He also conducted (from 1819) the Royal Orch. in Stockholm. He wrote his sym. when he was 9 years old, but in his mature years he devoted himself mainly to theatrical productions. One of his light operas, *L'Héroïne de l'amour*, to a French libretto, was produced in St. Petersburg in 1811. In Stockholm he was also active as a teacher, numbering his cousin among his pupils.

Besanzoni, Gabriella, Italian mezzo-soprano; b. Rome, Sept. 20, 1888; d. there, June 6, 1962. She studied with Hilde Brizzi and Alessandro Maggi. In 1911 she made her operatic debut as a soprano in the role of Adalgisa in Viterbo; in 1913 she sang in Rome as Ulrica; appeared at the Teatro Colón in Buenos Aires from 1918. On Nov. 19, 1919, she made her Metropolitan Opera debut in New York as Amneris, singing there for only 1 season. From 1923 to 1932 she appeared at Milan's La Scala, making her farewell appearance in Rome in 1939 in her finest role, Carmen. Among her other roles were Isabella, Cenerentola, Dalila, and Mignon.

Best, Matthew, English conductor and bass; b. Farnborough, Feb. 6, 1957. He was a choral scholar at King's College, Cambridge (M.A.), and studied with Otakar Kraus, at the National Opera Studio (1978–80), and with Robert Lloyd and Patrick Maguigan. In 1973 he founded the Corydon Singers, which he subsequently conducted in an expansive repertoire. In 1978 he made his operatic debut as Seneca in Monteverdi's *L'incoronazione di Poppea* with the Cambridge Univ. Opera Soc. From 1980 to 1986 he was a member of the Royal Opera at London's Covent Garden. In 1982 he won the Kathleen Ferrier Prize. From 1998 he served as principal conductor of the Hanover Band in Hove, Sussex. His appearances as a bass took him to London, Glyndebourne, Leeds, Cardiff, Frankfurt am Main, Salzburg, and other music centers. As a conductor, he led various choral performances and appeared as a guest conductor with many orchs.

Bettinelli, Bruno, respected Italian composer and teacher; b. Milan, June 4, 1913. He studied harmony and counterpoint with Paribeni and orchestration with Bossi at the Milan Cons., taking diplomas in piano in 1931 and in composition and conducting in 1937, then pursued advanced training in composition with Frazzi at the Accademia Musicale Chigiana in Siena (1940). In 1941 he joined the faculty of the Milan Cons., where he was a prof. of composition from 1957 until his retirement in 1979. In 1961 he was made a member of the Accademia di Santa Cecilia in Rome and of the Accademia di Luigi Cherubini in Florence. In his extensive output, he reveals particular skill in instrumental writing which reflects the best in the central European tradition with infusions of contemporary techniques, including the 12-tone method. He composed the operas *Il pozzo e il pendolo* (1957; Bergamo, Oct. 24, 1967), *La Smorfia* (Como, Sept. 30, 1959), and *Count Down* (1969; Milan, March 26, 1970).

Bettoni, Vincenzo, Italian bass; b. Melegnano, July 1, 1881; d. there, Nov. 4, 1954. He made his operatic debut as Silva in 1902 in Pinerolo. In 1905 he made his first appearance at Milan's La Scala, where he was regularly engaged from 1926 to 1940. He also sang at the Teatro Colón in Buenos Aires from 1910. In 1923 he appeared as Gurnemanz in the first Spanish mounting of *Parsifal* in Barcelona. In 1934 he sang Don Alfonso in the first season of the Glyndebourne Festival. He first appeared at London's Covent Garden in 1935. Bettoni was especially admired for his portrayals of roles in Rossini's operas.

Betts, Lorne, Canadian composer, music critic, and teacher; b. Winnipeg, Aug. 2, 1918; d. Hamilton, Ontario, Aug. 5, 1985. He studied piano, organ, and theory in Winnipeg, and was a pupil of Weinzweig in Toronto (1947–53) before settling in Hamilton, Ontario. His catalog of works includes the operas *Riders to the Sea* (1955) and *The Woodcarver's Wife* (1960).

Betz, Franz, noted German baritone; b. Mainz, March 19, 1835; d. Berlin, Aug. 11, 1900. He studied in Karlsruhe. In 1856 he made his operatic debut as the Herald in *Lohengrin* in Hannover, and then sang in Altenburg, Gera, Cöthen, and Rostock. On May 16, 1859, he made his first appearance at the Berlin Royal Opera as Don Carlos in *Ernani*, and remained one of its principal members until 1897. He was particularly esteemed for his Wagnerian roles, and was chosen to create the roles of Hans Sachs in Munich (1868) and the Wanderer in *Siegfried* at Bayreuth (1876). Among his other prominent roles were Don Giovanni, Pizzaro, Amonasro, and Falstaff. His wife was the soprano Johanne Betz (1837–1906).

Beversdorf, (Samuel) Thomas, American composer and teacher; b. Yoakum, Texas, Aug. 8, 1924; d. Bloomington, Ind., Feb. 15, 1981. He studied trombone and baritone horn with his father, a band director; later studied composition with Kent Kennan, Eric DeLamarter, and Anthony Donato at the Univ. of Texas (B.M., 1945), Rogers and Hanson at the Eastman School of Music in Rochester, N.Y. (M.M., 1946; D.M.A., 1957), Honegger and Copland at the Berkshire Music Center in Tanglewood (summer, 1947), and privately with Anis Fuleihan. He was a trombonist in the Rochester (N.Y.) Phil. (1945–46), the Houston Sym. Orch. (1946–48), and the Pittsburgh Sym. Orch. (1948–49). After teaching at the Univ. of Houston (1946–48), he was a prof. of music at the Indiana Univ. School of Music in Bloomington (1951–77).

WORKS: DRAMATIC: *Threnody: The Funeral of Youth*, ballet (Bloomington, Ind., March 6, 1963; also as *Variations* for Orch.); *The Hooligan*, opera (1964–69); *Metamorphosis*, opera (1968); *Vision of Christ*, mystery play (Lewisburg, Pa., May 1, 1971).

Bevignani, Enrico, Italian conductor and composer; b. Naples, Sept. 29, 1841; d. there, Aug. 29, 1903. He was a pupil of Albanese and Lillo. In 1863 he went to London as a répétiteur at Her Majesty's Theatre. He then conducted at Covent Garden (1869–87; 1890–96), where he conducted the first London performances of *Aida* (1876), *La Gioconda* (1883), and *Pagliacci* (1893). On Nov. 29, 1893, he made his Metropolitan Opera debut in New York conducting the first performance there of *Philémon et Baucis*, and remained on its roster until 1897 and then again from 1898 to 1900.

Bial, Rudolf, German violinist, composer, and conductor; b. Habelschwerdt, Silesia, Aug. 26, 1834; d. N.Y., Nov. 26, 1881. He was a member of the Breslau Orch., then toured Africa and Australia with his brother Karl. He settled in Berlin as conductor of the Kroll Orch. and of the Wallner Theater, where his numerous farces, operettas, etc. were performed. He later conducted at the Italian opera in Berlin, and in 1879 settled in New York.

Bialas, Günter, German composer and pedagogue; b. Bielschowitz, Silesia, July 19, 1907; d. Glonn, July 8, 1995. His father was the business manager of a local theater, and Bialas absorbed much music through personal connections with professional organizations. He studied in Breslau (1925–27) and with Trapp in Berlin (1927–33). After teaching composition at the Weimar Hochschule für Musik (1947), he was a teacher (1947–50) and a prof. (1950–59) of composition at the North-West German Academy of Music in Detmold; then was prof. of composition at the Munich Hochschule für Musik (1959–72). In 1967 he received the music prize of the Bavarian Academy of Fine Arts, and in 1971 the Culture Prize of Upper Silesia. He developed a style using serial procedures, with diversions into medieval and African modes.

WORKS: DRAMATIC: OPERAS: *Hero und Leander* (Mannheim, Sept. 8, 1966); *Die Geschichte von Aucassin und Nicolette* (1967–69; Munich, Dec. 12, 1969); *Der gestiefelte Kater* (1973–74; Schwetzingen, May 15, 1975; rev. version, Munich, July 18, 1987). BALLET: *Meyerbeer-Paraphrasen* (1971; Hamburg, May 12, 1974).

BIBL.: M. Holl and H. Schaefer, *Wort und Musik: Ausstellung zum 85. Geburtstag von G. B.: Bayerische Staatsbibliothek München, Musikabteilung, 15. July bis 4. September 1992* (Munich, 1992).

Bianchi, Bianca (real name, **Bertha Schwarz**), German soprano; b. near Heidelberg, June 27, 1855; d. Salzburg, Feb. 1947. She studied in Heidelberg and Paris, making her debut as Barberina in *La nozze di Figaro* at Karlsruhe (1873). After singing in Vienna and London, she settled in 1905 in Salzburg as a vocal teacher. She married her manager, Pollini, in 1897.

Bianchi, Francesco, Italian composer; b. Cremona, c.1752; d. (suicide) London, Nov. 27, 1810. He studied in Naples with Jommelli and Cafaro. He wrote nearly 80 operas, some quite pleasing, but ephemeral. His first was *Giulio Sabino* (Cremona, 1772); it was followed by *Il Grand Cidde* (Florence, 1773). From 1775 to 1778 he was in Paris serving as maestro al cembalo at the Comédie-Italienne, where he produced his opera *La Réduction de Paris* (Sept. 30, 1775). In 1778 he went to Florence, and in 1783 he became 2d maestro at the Cathedral of Milan, a post he held until 1793. He concurrently worked in Venice from 1785 to 1791, and again from 1793 to 1797, when he served as 2d organist at S. Marco. He subsequently was in Naples, where he produced his most significant opera, *La Vendetta de Nino* (Nov. 12, 1790). In 1794 he went to London, where he officiated as conductor at the King's Theatre (1795–1801); several of his operas were produced there under his supervision. He publ. a theoretical treatise, *Dell'attrazione armonica*, which was publ. in excerpts, in Eng., in the *Quarterly Musical Magazine and Review* (1820–21). Bianchi was also a successful teacher, numbering among his English pupils Henry Bishop.

Bibalo, Antonio (Gino), Italian-born Norwegian composer of Slovak descent; b. Trieste, Jan. 18, 1922. After training with Luciano Gante (piano) and Giulio Viozzi (composition) at the Trieste Cons. (graduated, 1946), he went to London in 1953 to complete his composition studies with Elisabeth Luytens. In 1956 he settled in Norway and in 1967 became a naturalized Norwegian citizen. In 1991 he was awarded Norway's Prize for Culture for his opera *Macbeth* and was decorated with the St. Olaf Knight Cross of the King of Norway. In his music, Bibalo demonstrates a capacity for inventive tonal, melodic, and rhythmic writing with occasional excursions into serialism.

WORKS: DRAMATIC: OPERAS: *The Smile at the Foot of the Ladder* (1958–62; 1st complete perf. as *Das Lächeln am Fusse der Leiter*, Hamburg, April 6, 1965); *Frøken Julie* (Miss Julie; Århus, Sept. 8, 1975); *Askeladden* (Numskull Jack; 1976; Norwegian Radio, Dec. 26, 1977); *Gespenster* (Ghosts; Kiel, June 21, 1981); *Macbeth* (1989; Oslo, Sept. 29, 1990); *Die Glasmenagerie* (Trier, Nov. 3, 1996). BALLETS: *Pinocchio* (1967; Hamburg, Jan. 17, 1969); *Nocturne for Apollo* (1969); *Flammen* (1974).

Biber, Heinrich (Ignaz Franz von), famous Bohemian violinist and composer; b. Wartenberg, Bohemia, Aug. 12, 1644; d. Salzburg, May 3, 1704. He was in the service of the emperor Leopold I, who ennobled him on Dec. 5, 1690; he also served at other courts. In 1670 he was a member of the Kapelle at Salzburg, and in 1679 was appointed vice Kapellmeister there, becoming Kapellmeister in 1684. He was one of the founders of the German school of violin playing and was among the first to employ the "scordatura," a system of artificial mistuning to facilitate performance. He publ. a number of violin sonatas, several of which were reprinted in David's *Hohe Schule* and in Denkmäler der Tonkunst in Österreich. He composed 2 operas, *Chi la dura la vince* (Salzburg, 1687) and *L'ossequio de Salisburgo* (Salzburg, 1699), but his only extant stage work is the opera *Chi la dura la vince*.

Bible, Frances, American mezzo-soprano; b. Sackets Harbor, N.Y., Jan. 26, 1927. She studied with Belle Julie Soudant and Queena Mario at the Juilliard School of Music in New York (1939–47). She made her operatic debut as the Shepherd in *Tosca* at the N.Y. City Opera on Oct. 7, 1948, subsequently attaining a prominent place on its roster, singing principal roles there regularly until 1977. She was later a teacher (1979–82) and artist-in-residence (1982–83) at Rice Univ. in Houston. She was best known for her trouser and contemporary roles.

Bie, Oskar, German music critic; b. Breslau, Feb. 9, 1864; d. Berlin, April 21, 1938. He studied music with Philipp Scharwenka in Berlin; devoted himself principally to musical journalism, and publ. a number of informative monographs. In the spring of 1914, he accompanied Koussevitzky on his concert tour of the Volga and reported his impressions in a privately publ. illustrated ed. in 1920. Among his publications are *Die moderne Musik und Richard Strauss* (Berlin, 1906; Leipzig, 1916, 1925), *Die Oper* (Berlin, 1913), and *Richard Wagner und Bayreuth* (Zürich, 1931).

Bierdiajew, Walerian, Polish conductor; b. Grodno, March 7, 1885; d. Warsaw, Nov. 28, 1956. He studied composition with Max Reger and conducting with Arthur Nikisch at the Leipzig Cons. He began his conducting career in Dresden in 1906; in 1908 he became regular conductor at the Maryinsky Opera Theater in St. Petersburg; then conducted in various Russian opera houses; from 1921 to 1925 he lived in Poland; from 1925 to 1930 he was again engaged as a conductor in Russia. In 1930 he was appointed prof. of conducting at the Warsaw Cons.; from 1947 to 1949 he was conductor of the Kraków Phil.; then taught at the Poznán Cons. (1949–54) and at the Warsaw Cons. (1954–56); he also was director of the Warsaw Opera (1954–56).

Bierey, Gottlob Benedikt, German conductor and composer; b. Dresden, July 25, 1772; d. Breslau, May 5, 1840. He was a pupil of Christian E. Weinlig at Dresden, then director of a traveling opera troupe. He was appointed Kapellmeister at Breslau in 1808, succeeding Weber. He retired in 1828. In his sizeable catalog of works are 26 operas and operettas.

Bigot, Eugène, French conductor; b. Rennes, Feb. 28, 1888; d. Paris, July 17, 1965. He studied violin and piano at the Rennes Cons. and later at the Paris Cons. In 1913 he was named chorus master at the Théâtre des Champs-Élysées in Paris; subsequently he toured Europe with the Ballets Suédois and also conducted the Paris Cons. Orch. (1923–25), then served as music director at the Théâtres des Champs-Élysées (1925–27). In 1935 he became president and director of the Concerts Lamoureux in Paris, a post he held until 1950; he also was principal conductor of the Paris Opéra Comique (1936–47). From 1947 until his death he was chief conductor of the Paris Radio Orch.

Billington, Elizabeth (née **Weichsel**), famous English soprano; b. London, Dec. 27, 1765; d. near Venice, Aug. 25, 1818. Her mother, a singer, was a pupil of Johann Christian Bach, and Elizabeth, too, had some lessons with him. She received her early musical training from her father, a German oboist. She also studied with James Billington, a double-bass player by profession, whom she married on Oct. 13, 1783. Her operatic debut took place in Dublin (1784), as Eurydice in Gluck's opera. She went to London, where she appeared as Rosetta in *Love in a Village* at Covent Garden on Feb. 13, 1786. Her success was immediate: she was reengaged at Covent Garden and also sang at the Concerts of Antient Music in London. Her career was briefly disrupted by the publication, in 1792, of anonymous memoirs attacking her private life. This was immediately followed by an equally anonymous rebuttal, "written by a gentleman," defending her reputation. In 1794 she went to Italy, where she sang for the king of Naples. He made arrangements for her appearances at the San Carlo, where she performed in operas by Bianchi, Paisiello, Paer, and Himmel, all written specially for her. After her husband died in 1794, she remained in Italy for 2 more years, then lived in France, where she married M. Felissent. Returning to London in 1801, she sang alternately at Drury Lane and Covent Garden, with great acclaim, at 4,000 guineas a season. This period was the peak of her success. She retired in 1809, except for occasional performances. After a temporary separation from Felissent, she returned to him in 1817. They settled at their estate at St. Artien, near Venice.

Bilt, Peter van der, Dutch bass-baritone; b. Jakarta, Dutch East Indies, Aug. 30, 1936; d. Amsterdam, Sept. 25, 1983. He studied in Amsterdam, where he made his operatic debut as Dulcamara in 1960. After appearing as Rossini's Don Basilio at the San Francisco Opera in 1963, he joined the Deutsche Oper am Rhein in Düsseldorf in 1964; made guest appearances in Vienna, Munich, Edinburgh, Los Angeles, and other music centers. Among his prominent roles were Don Giovanni, Figaro, Don Pasquale, Beckmesser, and Gianni Schicchi. He also sang widely in concerts.

Bimboni, Alberto, Italian-American pianist and composer; b. Florence, Aug. 24, 1882; d. N.Y., June 18, 1960. He studied in Florence; went to the United States in 1912 as an opera conductor. In 1930 he was appointed to the faculty of the Curtis Inst. of Music in Philadelphia; he taught opera classes at the Juilliard School of Music in New York from 1933; he appeared as a pianist in concerts with Ysaÿe, John McCormack, and other celebrated artists. Among his compositions are the operas *Winona* (Portland, Oreg., Nov. 11, 1926), *Karin* (Minneapolis, 1928), *Il cancelleto d'oro* (N.Y., March 11, 1936), and *In the Name of Culture* (Rochester, N.Y., May 9, 1949).

Binder, Abraham Wolfe, American composer and teacher; b. N.Y., Jan. 13, 1895; d. there, Oct. 10, 1966. He studied at Columbia Univ.; subsequently taught liturgical music at the Jewish Inst. of Religion in New York He composed an opera, *A Goat in Chelm* (N.Y., March 20, 1960) and a choral ballet, *Hora Vehodayah* (Praise and Dance).

Binder, Karl, Austrian composer; b. Vienna, Nov. 29, 1816; d. there, Nov. 5, 1860. He was a theater conductor by profession. He composed mostly for the stage: a melodrama, *Der Wiener Schusterhut* (1840); an opera, *Die Drei Wittfrauen* (1841); a vaudeville comedy, *Purzel* (1843); overture and choruses to the drama *Elmar*; and a parody on *Tannhäuser* (1857).

Bindernagel, Gertrud, German soprano; b. Magdeburg, Jan. 11, 1894; d. Berlin, Nov. 3, 1932. She studied at the Magdeburg Cons., and then at the Berlin Hochschule für Musik (1913–17). At age 17, she began her career in Magdeburg, and then sang in Breslau (1917–19) and Regensburg (1919–20); she subsequently appeared in Berlin at the State Opera (1920–27) and the Städtische Oper (from 1927); also made guest appearances in Barcelona, Munich, Hamburg, and Mannheim, becoming particularly admired as a Wagnerian. Following her performance of Brünnhilde in *Siegfried* at the Berlin Städtische Oper, she was fatally wounded by a gunshot delivered by her jealous husband, the banker Wilhelm Hintze.

Bing, Sir Rudolf (Franz Joseph), prominent Austrian-born English opera manager; b. Vienna, Jan. 9, 1902; d. N.Y., Sept. 2, 1997. He studied at the Univ. of Vienna and took singing lessons. After working at the Darmstadt Landestheater (1928–30) and the Berlin Städtische Oper (1930–33), he went to England and joined the Glyndebourne Festival in 1934, where he then was its general manager (1936–49). In 1947 he also helped to found the Edinburgh Festival, which he led as artistic director until 1949. In 1946 he became a naturalized British subject. From 1950 to 1972 he was general manager of the Metropolitan Opera in New York His tenure there was a distinguished, if at times controversial, one. His self assurance and acerbic wit added color to his clashes with the board of directors, celebrated artists, and the press. In 1971 he was knighted. He publ. the books *5,000 Nights at the Opera* (N.Y., 1972) and *A Knight at the Opera* (N.Y., 1981). His last years were blighted by Alzheimer's disease.

Bingham, Seth (Daniels), American organist, pedagogue, and composer; b. Bloomfield, N.J., April 16, 1882; d. N.Y., June 21, 1972. He studied with Horatio Parker at Yale Univ. (B.A., 1904; B.Mus., 1908) and with d'Indy, Widor, Guilmant, and Harry Jepson in Paris (1906–07). He taught at Yale Univ. (1908–19), Columbia Univ. (1919–54), and the Union Theological Seminary School of Sacred Music (1953–65); also was organist at N.Y.'s Madison Ave. Presbyterian Church (1913–53). His music was contrapuntal, occasionally chromatic, and, later, highly modal. He composed the opera *La Charelzenn* (1917).

Binički, Stanislav, Serbian composer and conductor; b. Jasika, near Kruševca, July 27, 1872; d. Belgrade, Feb. 15, 1942. He studied at the Univ. of Belgrade; he later took courses in composition with Rheinberger in Munich. Returning to Belgrade, he helped organize the Serbian School of Music; he was also active as an opera conductor. He composed a number of incidental pieces for the theater as well as the opera *Na uranku* (Dawn; Belgrade, Jan. 2, 1904).

Biriukov, Yuri, Russian composer; b. Moscow, April 1, 1908; d. there, Nov. 1, 1976. He studied piano with Feinberg and composition with Miaskovsky at the Moscow Cons., graduating in 1936. Among his works are the operas *Peasant Gentlewoman* (1947) and *Knight of the Golden Star* (1956), the ballet *The Cosmonauts* (1962), and the musical *The Blue Express* (1971). He also composed much music for theater and films.

Birnbach, Karl Joseph, German composer; b. Köpernick, Silesia, 1751; d. Warsaw, May 29, 1805. During the last years of his life he was conductor at the German Theater in Warsaw. In his substantial catalog of works are 2 operas. His son was the pianist, music pedagogue, and composer Heinrich Birnbach (1793–1879).

Birtwistle, Sir Harrison (Paul), eminent English composer; b. Accrington, Lancashire, July 15, 1934. He was a student of Frederick Thurston (clarinet) and Richard Hall (composition) at the Royal Manchester College of Music (1952–60), and then of Reginald Kell (clarinet) at the Royal Academy of Music in London (1960–61). After serving as director of music at the Cranbourne Chase School in Dorset (1962–65), he was a visiting prof. at Princeton Univ. (1966). Returning to England, he cofounded with Peter Maxwell Davies the Pierrot Players in 1967, a contemporary music ensemble, with which he remained active until 1970. He was a visiting prof. of music at Swarthmore College (1973–74) and the State Univ. of N.Y. at Buffalo (1975). Returning once more to England, he was active as music director at the National Theater in London from 1975. In 1987 he received the Grawemeyer Award of the Univ. of Louisville for his opera *The Mask of Orpheus*. He was knighted in 1988. In his compositions, Birtwistle departed completely from the folkloric trends popular in modern English music and adopted an abstract idiom, one marked by an expert handling of various elements in a thoroughly contemporary idiom. His operas constitute a significant contribution to the British stage.

WORKS: DRAMATIC: *Punch and Judy*, tragical comedy or comical tragedy (1966–67; Aldeburgh, June 8, 1968; rev. version, London, March 3, 1970); *Down by the Greenwood Side*, dramatic pastorale (1968–69; Brighton, May 8, 1969); *The Mask of Orpheus*, opera (1973–75; 1981–84; London, May 21, 1986); *Pulse Field: Frames, Pulses, and Interruptions*, ballet (Snape, June 25, 1977); *Bow Down*, music theater (London, July 4, 1977); *Yan, Tan, Tethera*, opera (1983–84; London, Aug. 7, 1986); *Gawain*, opera (1990–91; London, May 30, 1991); *The Second Mrs. Kong*, opera (1993–94; Glyndebourne, Oct. 21, 1994); incidental music.

BIBL.: M. Hall, *H. B.* (London, 1984).

Bischof, Rainer, Austrian composer; b. Vienna, June 20, 1947. He studied law, philosophy, art history, and pedagogy at the Univ. of Vienna (Ph.D., 1973); also composition at the Vienna Academy of Music (1965) and privately with Apostel (1967–72). After serving as president of the Austrian Composers Union (1984–86), he was a lecturer on aesthetics at the Vienna Hochschule für Musik (from 1987) and general secretary of the Vienna Sym. Orch. (from 1988). His music follows the tenets of the Second Viennese School. Among his compositions is the chamber opera *Das Donauergeschenk* (1990; Vienna, June 22, 1991).

Bishop, Anna (née **Ann Riviere**), famous English soprano; b. London, Jan. 9, 1810; d. N.Y., March 18, 1884. She studied piano with Moscheles and voice with **Henry Bishop** in London, marrying the latter in 1831. On April 20, 1831, she made her debut in a London concert. In 1839 she toured with the harpist Bochsa, and then returned to London to appear at Her Majesty's Theatre. After she and Bochsa became intimate, they headed for the Continent and toured widely in concerts. In 1843 she was made prima donna assoluta at the Teatro San Carlo and the Teatro Fondo in Naples. In 1846 she returned to London to sing at the Drury Lane Theatre. In 1847 she made her U.S. debut in New York as Linda di Chamounix. She created the title role of *Martha* in the first U.S. performance of that opera in New York in 1850. After Bochsa's death in 1856, she married the N.Y. diamond merchant Martin Schulz. In subsequent years she toured as a concert artist all over the world, making her farewell appearance in New York in 1883. She was greatly praised for her superb vocal technique.

Bishop, Sir Henry Rowley, noted English composer; b. London, Nov. 18, 1786; d. there, April 30, 1855. He was a pupil of Francesco Bianchi. He attracted attention with his first opera, *The Circassian Bride* (Drury Lane, Feb. 23, 1809). From 1810 to 1824 he was conductor at Covent Garden, and, in 1813, alternate conductor of the Phil. In 1819 he was oratorio conductor at Covent Garden, and in 1825 conductor at the Drury Lane Theatre, then, in 1830, music director at Vauxhall. He took the degree of B.Mus. at Oxford Univ. (1839). From 1840 he was music director at Covent Garden, then prof. of music at Edinburgh (1841–43). He was knighted in 1842. He conducted the Concerts of Ancient Music from 1840 to 1848, then was appointed prof. of music at Oxford, where he received the degree of D.Mus. in 1853. In 1831 he married **Anna Bishop**, but they were divorced in 1848. He was a remarkably prolific dramatic composer, having produced about 130 operas, farces, ballets, adaptations, etc. His best operas, generally in the style of English ballad opera, include *Cortez, or The Conquest of Mexico* (1823), *The Fall of Algiers* (1825), *The Knight of Snowdoun* (after Walter Scott; 1811), and *Native Land* (1824). His *Clari, or The Maid of Milan* (Covent Garden, May 3, 1823) contains the famous song "Home Sweet Home," with text by the American John Howard Payne, which appears repeatedly throughout the opera. The tune, previously publ. by Bishop to other words, was thought to have been of Sicilian origin, but after much litigation was accepted as Bishop's original composition (the MS is owned by the Univ. of Rochester in N.Y.). A version of the melody was used by Donizetti in his opera *Anna Bolena*, giving rise to the erroneous belief that Donizetti was its composer. Bishop also wrote an oratorio, *The Fallen Angel* (1839), as well as many additions to revivals of older operas, etc. His glees and other lyric vocal compositions are deservedly esteemed. Bishop also publ. vol. I of *Melodies of Various Nations,* and 3 vols. of *National Melodies*, to which Moore wrote the poems.

BIBL.: R. Northcott, *The Life of Sir H. R. B.* (London, 1920).

Bispham, David (Scull), American baritone; b. Philadelphia, Jan. 5, 1857; d. N.Y., Oct. 2, 1921. He first sang as an amateur in church choruses in Philadelphia. In 1886 he went to Italy, where he studied with Vannuccini in Florence and Francesco Lamperti in Milan; later studied in London with Shakespeare and Randegger. He made his operatic debut as Longueville in Messager's *La Basoche* (English Opera House, London, Nov. 3, 1891), in which his comic acting ability, as well as his singing, won praise. He made his first appearance in serious opera as Kurwenal in *Tristan und Isolde* (Drury Lane, June 25, 1892). He was particularly effective in the Wagnerian baritone roles; he made his American debut with the Metropolitan Opera in New York as Beckmesser (Nov. 18, 1896), and was on the Metropolitan roster 1896–97, 1898–99, and 1900–03. He was a strong advocate of opera in English. A Soc. of American Singers was organized under his guidance, presenting light operas in the English language. He publ. an autobiography, *A Quaker Singer's Recollections* (N.Y., 1920). A Bispham Memorial Medal Award was established by the Opera Soc. of America in 1921 for an opera in English by an American composer.

Bissell, Keith (Warren), Canadian composer, music educator, and conductor; b. Meaford, near Owen Sound, Ontario, Feb. 12, 1912; d. Newmarket, near Toronto, May 9, 1992. He was a composition student of Leo Smith at the Univ. of Toronto (B.Mus., 1942), and later studied with Gunild Keetman and Orff in Munich (1960). After teaching in Toronto schools (1934–48), he was assistant supervisor (1948) and then supervisor (1949–55) of school music in Edmonton. From 1955 to 1976 he served as supervisor of school music in Scarborough (part of Metropolitan Toronto), where he introduced the Orff Schulwerk method. He also was conductor of the Scarborough Orff Ensemble (1960–73). In addition to his works for professional performance, he wrote much music for the young, including *The Miraculous Turnip*, children's opera (1980). Other stage works include *His Majesty's Pie*, operetta (1964), *The Centennial Play*, incidental music (1967), and *A Musical Play*, operetta (1977);

BIBL.: M. Irving, *K. B.: His Life, Career, and Contribution to Music Education from 1912–76* (thesis, Univ. of Western Ontario, 1982).

Bittner, Julius, Austrian composer and music critic; b. Vienna, April 9, 1874; d. there, Jan. 9, 1939. He studied law and received music lessons from Josef Labor. After serving as a lawyer and judge in Wolkersdorf (1905–08) and Vienna (from 1908), he was employed in the Ministry of Justice (1920–22); later he was active as a music critic. As a composer, Bittner was most successful in writing operas on fairy tale or folklore subjects, often to his own libretti. He wrote many of his operatic roles and songs for his wife, the contralto Emilie Werner (1885–1963).

WORKS: DRAMATIC: OPERAS: *Die rote Gret* (Frankfurt am Main, Oct. 26, 1907); *Der Musikant* (1909; Vienna, April 12, 1910); *Der Bergsee* (1910; Vienna, Nov. 9, 1911; rev. 1938); *Die Kohlhaymerin* (1920; Vienna, April 9, 1921); *Mondnacht* (Berlin, Nov. 13, 1928); *Das Veilchen* (Vienna, Dec. 8, 1934). OPERETTAS: *Die silberne Tänzerin* (1926); *Général d'amour* (1926). Also Singspiels, a mimodrama, incidental music, and a ballet.

BIBL.: U. Bittner, *J. B.* (Vienna, 1968).

Bizet, Georges (baptismal names, **Alexandre-César-Léopold**), great French opera composer; b. Paris, Oct. 25, 1838; d. Bougival, June 3, 1875. His parents were both professional musicians: his father, a singing teacher and composer; his mother, an excellent pianist. Bizet's talent developed early in childhood. At the age of 9 he entered the Paris Cons.; his teachers were Marmontel (piano), Benoist (organ), Zimmerman (harmony), and (for composition) Halévy, whose daughter, Geneviève, married Bizet in 1869. In 1852 he won a 1st prize for piano, in 1855 for organ and for fugue, and in 1857 the Grand Prix de Rome. Also in 1857 he shared (with Lecocq) a prize offered by Offenbach for a setting of a 1-act opera, *Le Docteur Miracle*; Bizet's setting was produced at the Bouffes-Parisiens on April 9, 1857. Instead of the prescribed Mass, he sent from Rome during his first year a 2-act Italian opera buffa, *Don Procopio* (not produced until March 10, 1906, when it was given in Monte Carlo in an incongruously ed. version); later he sent 2 movements of a sym., an overture (*La Chasse d'Ossian*), and a 1-act opera (*La Guzla de l'Émir*; accepted by the Paris Opéra Comique, but withdrawn by Bizet prior to production). Returning to Paris, he produced a grand opera, *Les Pêcheurs de perles* (Théâtre-Lyrique, Sept. 30, 1863), but this work, like *La Jolie Fille de Perth* (Dec. 26, 1867), failed to win popular approval. A 1-act opera, *Djamileh* (Opéra Comique, May 22, 1872), fared no better. Bizet's incidental music for Daudet's play *L'Arlésienne* (Oct. 1, 1872) was ignored by the audiences and literary critics; it was not fully appreciated until its revival in 1885, but an orch. suite from it brought out by Pasdeloup (Nov. 10, 1872) was acclaimed; a 2d suite was made by Guiraud after Bizet's death. Bizet's next major work was his masterpiece, *Carmen* (based on a tale by Mérimée, text by Halévy and Meilhac), produced, after many difficulties with the management and the cast, at the Opéra Comique (March 3, 1875). The reception of the public was not enthusiastic; several critics attacked the opera for its lurid subject, and the music for its supposed adoption of Wagner's methods. Bizet received a generous sum (25,000 francs) for the score from the publisher Choudens and won other honors (he was named a Chevalier of the Légion d'honneur on the eve of the premiere of *Carmen*); although the attendance was not high, the opera was maintained in the repertoire. There were 37 performances before the end of the season; the original cast included Galli-Marie as Carmen, Lherie as Don José, and Bouhy as Escamillo. Bizet was chagrined by the controversial reception of the opera, but it is a melodramatic invention to state (as some biographers have done) that the alleged failure of *Carmen* precipitated the composer's death (he died on the night of the 31st perf. of the opera). Soon *Carmen* became a triumphant success all over the world; it was staged in London (in Italian at Her Majesty's Theatre, June 22, 1878), St. Petersburg, Vienna, Brussels, Naples, Florence, Mainz, N.Y. (Academy of Music, Oct. 23, 1878), etc. The Metropolitan Opera produced *Carmen* first in Italian (Jan. 9, 1884), then in French, with Calvé as Carmen (Dec. 20, 1893). It should be pointed out that the famous Habanera is not Bizet's own, but a melody by the Spanish composer Yradier; Bizet inserted it in *Carmen* (with slight alterations), mistaking it for a folk song. Bizet also wrote an operetta, *La Prêtresse* (1854), and the operas *Numa* (1871) and *Ivan le Terrible*, in 4 acts (Bordeaux, Oct. 12, 1951; the score was believed to have been destroyed by Bizet, but was discovered among the MSS bequeathed to the Paris Cons. by the 2d husband of Bizet's widow). Bizet also completed Halévy's biblical opera, *Noë* (1869).

BIBL.: E. Galabert, *G. B.* (Paris, 1877); C. Pigot, *B. et son oeuvre* (1886; new ed., 1911); C. Bellaigue, *B.* (1891); P. Voss, *B.* (Leipzig, 1899); A. Weissmann, *B.* (Berlin, 1907); R. Brancour, *La Vie et l'oeuvre de B.* (Paris, 1913); J. Rabe, *B.* (Stockholm, 1925); D. Parker, *B., His Life and Works* (London, 1926); E. Istel, *B. und Carmen* (Stuttgart, 1927); R. Laparra, *B. et l'Espagne* (Paris, 1934); M. Cooper, *B.* (London, 1938); W. Dean, *G. B.: His Life and Work* (London, 1948; 3rd ed., 1975); J. Roy, *B.* (Paris, 1983); G. Corapi, *Invito all'ascolto di G. B.* (Milan, 1992).

Bjelinski, Bruno, Croatian composer and teacher; b. Trieste, Nov. 1, 1909. He studied in Zagreb at the Univ. (law) and at the Academy of Music, serving on the faculty of the latter (from 1945). His music was Romantically inclined. Among his compositions was the opera *Pčelica Maja* (Maya the Bee; 1952).

Bjoner, Ingrid, Norwegian soprano; b. Kraakstad, Nov. 8, 1927. She studied pharmacy at the Univ. of Oslo (graduated, 1951) and pursued vocal training at the Oslo Cons. with Gudrun Boellemose, at the Frankfurt am Main Hochschule für Musik with Paul Lohmann, and in New York with Ellen Repp. After making her operatic debut as the 3d Norn and Gutrune with the Norwegian Radio in Oslo in 1956, she made her stage debut as Mozart's Donna Anna with the Norwegian National Opera in Oslo in 1957. She sang at the Stockholm Drottningholm Court Theater (1957), the Wuppertal Theater (1957–59), the Deutsche Oper am Rhein in Düsseldorf (1959–61), the Bayreuth Festival (1960), and the Bavarian State Opera in Munich (from 1961). On Oct. 28, 1961, she made her Metropolitan Opera debut in New York as Elsa in *Lohengrin*, remaining on its roster until 1968 and returning again in 1971–72 and 1974–75. In 1967 she sang at London's Covent Garden and in 1974 she returned to New York to sing the Duchess of Parma in the U.S. premiere of Busoni's *Doktor Faust* at Carnegie Hall. In subsequent years, she concentrated her career on European engagements. She also toured throughout the world as a concert singer. Later she served as a prof. at the Royal Danish Cons. of Music in Copenhagen (from 1991) and at the Norwegian Academy of Music in Oslo (from 1992). Bjoner was especially admired for her roles in operas by Wagner, Verdi, and Richard Strauss. She also won praise as Beethoven's Leonore, Iphigenia, and Turandot.

Björlin, (Mats) Ulf (Stefan), Swedish conductor and composer; b. Stockholm, May 21, 1933; d. West Palm Beach, Fla., Oct. 23, 1993. He studied with Markevitch (conducting) in Salzburg and with Boulanger (composition) in Paris. Returning to Stockholm, he pursued an active career as a conductor and composer. After serving as director of music at the Royal Dramatic Theater there (1963–68), he conducted widely in Europe and North America. As a composer, he wrote some effective pieces for the theater.

WORKS: DRAMATIC: *Pinocchio*, children's musical (1966); *Om fem år*, opera (Stockholm, Oct. 27, 1967); *Den stora teatern* (Göteborg, Feb. 25, 1972); *Balladen om Kasper Rosenröd*, opera (Valberg-Karlstad, Nov. 15, 1972); *Kärlekin till Belisa*, radio opera (1981); *Tillfälle gör Tiufven*, opera buffa (1983); *Den främmande kvinnan*, opera (1983–84); *The Snow Queen*, dramatic music (1991); incidental music.

Björling, Jussi (Johan Jonatan), eminent Swedish tenor; b. Stora Tuna, Feb. 5, 1911; d. Siarö, near Stockholm, Sept. 9, 1960. He studied voice with his father, a professional singer, making his first public appearance in 1916 as a member of the Björling Male Quartet, which included his father, David Björling (1873–1926), and 2 other brothers, Johan Olof "Olle" (1909–65) and Karl Gustaf "Gösta" (1912–57), both of whom pursued careers as singers; another brother, Karl David "Kalle" (1917–75), was also a singer. The Björling Male Quartet gave concerts throughout Sweden (1916–19); made an extensive tour of the United States (1919–21); then continued to sing in Sweden until 1926. Jussi Björling had an excellent professional training with John Forsell at the Royal Academy of Music in Stockholm. He made his operatic debut as the Lamplighter in *Manon Lescaut* at the Royal Theater in Stockholm on July 21, 1930, and remained there until 1939; he also sang as a guest artist with the Vienna State Opera and the Dresden State Opera, and at the Salzburg Festival. He made his professional U.S. debut in a concert broadcast from Carnegie Hall in New York on Nov. 28, 1937, and his first appearance with the Metropolitan Opera as Rodolfo in *La Bohème* on Nov. 24, 1938; he continued to sing there until 1941, when his career was interrupted by World War II. He resumed his appearances at the Metropolitan Opera in 1945 and sang there until 1954, and then again in 1956–57 and 1959. On March 15, 1960, he suffered a heart attack as he was preparing to sing the role of Rodolfo at the Royal Opera House, Covent Garden, London, but in spite of his great discomfort, went through with the performance. He appeared for the last time at a concert in Stockholm on Aug. 20, 1960. Björling was highly regarded for his fine vocal technique and his sense of style. He excelled in Italian and French roles, and also essayed some Russian operas. He wrote an autobiography, *Med bagaget i strupen* (Stockholm, 1945). The Jussi Björling Memorial Archive was founded in 1968.

BIBL.: J. Porter and H. Henrysson, *A J. B. Discography* (comprehensive, with biographical profile; Indianapolis, 1982; 2d ed., rev., 1993); A.-L. Björling and A. Farkas, *J.* (Portland, Oregon, 1996).

Björling, Sigurd, Swedish baritone; b. Stockholm, Nov. 2, 1907; d. Helsingborg, April 8, 1983. He was a student of Louis Condé (1928–30); then of Torsten Lennartson at the Cons. (1933–34) and the Royal Opera School (1934–36) in Stockholm. In 1934 he made his operatic debut as Billy Jackrabbit in *La Fanciulla del West* in Stockholm, where he continued to sing regularly until 1973. He also made guest appearances in various European opera centers. In 1950 he made his U.S. debut as Kurwenal with the San Francisco Opera. In 1951 he appeared at London's Covent Garden as Amfortas. On Nov. 15, 1952, he made his Metropolitan Opera debut in New York as Telramund, singing there until 1953.

Blacher, Boris, remarkable German composer; b. Newchwang, China (of half-German, quarter-Russian, and quarter-Jewish ancestry), Jan. 19, 1903; d. Berlin, Jan. 30, 1975. His family moved to Irkutsk, Siberia, in 1914, remaining there until 1920. In 1922 Blacher went to Berlin, where he studied architecture and then took a course in composition with F. E. Koch. From 1948 until 1970 he was prof. at the Hochschule für Musik in West Berlin, and from 1953 to 1970 served as its director. A prolific composer, Blacher was equally adept in classical and experimental forms and procedures. He initiated a system of "variable meters," with time signatures following the arithmetical progression, alternatively increasing and decreasing, with permutations contributing to metrical variety. For the theater he developed a sui generis "abstract opera," incorporating an element of organized improvisation. In 1960 he was appointed director of the Seminar of Electronic Composition at the Technological Univ. in Berlin, and subsequently made ample use of electronic resources in his own compositions.

WORKS: DRAMATIC: OPERAS: *Habemeajaja* (1929; not extant); *Fürstin Tarakanowa* (1940; Wuppertal, Feb. 5, 1941); *Romeo und Julia* (1943; Berlin Radio, 1947); *Die Flut* (1946; Berlin Radio, Dec. 20, 1946; stage premiere, Dresden, March 4, 1947); *Die Nachtschwalbe*, "dramatic nocturne" (Leipzig, Feb. 22, 1948; aroused considerable commotion because of its subject, dealing with prostitutes and pimps); *Preussisches Märchen*, ballet-opera (1949; Berlin, Sept. 23, 1952); *Abstrakte Oper No. 1* (Frankfurt Radio, June 28, 1953; stage premiere, Mannheim, Oct. 17, 1953; rev. version, Berlin, Sept. 30, 1957); *Rosamunde Floris* (Berlin, Sept. 21, 1960); *Zwischenfälle bei einer Notlandung*, "reportage in 2 phases and 14 situations" for Singers, Instruments, and Electronic Devices (1965; Hamburg, Feb. 4, 1966); *200,000 Taler* (Berlin, Sept. 25, 1969); *Yvonne, Prinzessin von Burgund* (1972; Wuppertal, Sept. 15, 1973); *Das Geheimnis des entwendeten Briefes* (1974; Berlin, Feb. 14, 1975). BALLETS: *Fest im Süden* (Kassel, Feb. 4, 1935); *Harlekinade* (1939; Krefeld, Feb. 14, 1940); *Das Zauberbuch von Erzerum* (1941; Stuttgart, Oct. 17, 1942; rev. version as *Der erste Ball*, Berlin, June 11, 1950); *Chiarina* (1946; Berlin, Jan. 22, 1950); *Hamlet* (1949; Munich, Nov. 19, 1950); *Lysistrata* (1950; Berlin, Sept. 30, 1951); *Der Mohr von Venedig* (Vienna, Nov. 29, 1955); *Demeter* (1963; Schwetzingen, June 4, 1964); *Tristan* (Berlin, Oct. 10, 1965). INCIDENTAL MUSIC: *Romeo and Juliet* (1951); *Lulu* (1952); *Georges Dandin* (1955); *War and Peace* (1955); *Robespierre* (1963); *Henry IV* (1970).

BIBL.: H. Stuckenschmidt, *B. B.* (Berlin, 1973); H. Henrich, *B. B., 1903–1975: Dokumente zu Leben und Werk* (Berlin, 1993); J. Hunkemöller, *B. B., der Jazz-Komponist* (Frankfurt am Main, 1994).

Blachut, Beno, Czech tenor; b. Wittkowitz, June 14, 1913; d. Prague, Jan. 10, 1985. He was a pupil of Luis Kadeřábek at the Prague Cons. (1935–39); in 1938 he made his operatic debut as Jeník in *The Bartered Bride* in Olomouc, where he sang until 1941, then was a leading member of the Prague National Theater; also sang in concerts. He was particularly esteemed for his portrayals of roles in operas by Smetana, Dvořák, and Janáček.

Blaes, Elisa (née **Meerti**), Belgian soprano; b. Antwerp, Nov. 2, 1817; d. Brussels, Nov. 6, 1878. She first gained distinction in Leipzig as a soloist with Mendelssohn and the Gewandhaus Orch. (1839; 1841–42); she sang with the Phil. Soc. of London in 1839. In 1843 she appeared in Russia, where she married the Belgian clarinetist Arnold Joseph Blaes (1814–1892); she often appeared in concerts with him. In her later years she taught voice in Belgium.

Blahetka, Marie Léopoldine, Austrian pianist and composer; b. Guntramsdorf, near Vienna, Nov. 15, 1811; d. Boulogne, France, Jan. 12, 1887. She was a piano pupil of Kalkbrenner and Moscheles; also studied composition with Sechter. In 1840 she settled in Boulogne. She wrote a romantic opera, *Die Rauber und die Sänger*, which was produced in Vienna in 1830.

Blake, David (Leonard), English composer and teacher; b. London, Sept. 2, 1936. He studied music at Gonville and Caius College, Cambridge (1957–60). After receiving a Mendelssohn scholarship, he studied with Eisler in East Berlin at the Deutsche Akademie der Künste (1960–61). In 1963–64 he was a Granada Arts Fellow at the Univ. of York, where he then was a lecturer (1964–71), senior lecturer (1971–76), and prof. (from 1976); from 1980 to 1983 he was also head of its music dept. He ed. *Hanns Eisler: A Miscellany* (1995). After composing in a tonal idiom and then in the 12-tone system, he experimented with a variety of styles, becoming drawn toward the use of oriental scales and aleatory methods. He composed the operas *Toussaint* (1976; London, Sept. 28, 1977; rev. 1982; London, Sept. 6, 1983) and *The Plumber's Gift* (London, May 25, 1989).

Blake, Rockwell (Robert), gifted American tenor; b. Plattsburgh, N.Y., Jan. 10, 1951. He studied voice with Renata Booth as part of his high school education. Following attendance at the State Univ. of N.Y. at Fredonia, he receivd a scholarship to pursue vocal training at the Catholic Univ. of America in Washington, D.C.; completed his vocal studies in New York. He began his career singing with various small opera companies, first attracting notice when he appeared as Lindoro with the Washington, D.C., Opera in 1976; then sang with the Hamburg State Opera (1977–79) and the Vienna State Opera (1978). In 1978 he became the first recipient of the Richard Tucker Award. On Sept. 23, 1979, he made his N.Y. City Opera debut as Count Ory, and on Feb. 2, 1981, his Metropolitan Opera debut in New York as Lindoro. He sang at the Chicago Lyric Opera and at the Rossini Opera Festival in Pesaro in 1983, at the San Francisco Opera in 1984, at the Paris Opéra in 1985, at the Paris Opéra Comique and the Bavarian State Opera in Munich in 1987, and in Montreal and at the Salzburg Festival in 1989. In 1990 he appeared in the leading tenor role in Pergolesi's *Annibal* in Turin. In 1992 he sang James V in *La Donna del Lago* at Milan's La Scala. He sang in *Semiramide* at the Rossini Festival in Pesaro in 1994. In 1996 he was engaged as Jupiter in the French premiere of Handel's *Semele* in Aix-en-Provence. He also sang widely in concerts. Blessed with a remarkable coloratura, Blake won notable distinction as a true tenore di grazia, excelling in Mozart and Rossini.

Blangini, (Giuseppe Marco Maria) Felice, Italian composer; b. Turin, Nov. 18, 1781; d. Paris, Dec. 18, 1841. He was a choirboy at Turin Cathedral. In 1799 his family moved to Paris, where he gave concerts, wrote fashionable romances, and came into vogue as an opera composer when he completed Della-Maria's *La Fausse Duègne* (1802). He was also popular as a singing teacher. After producing an opera in Munich, he was appointed court Kapellmeister (1805); later he was Generalmusikdirektor at Kassel (1809). Upon his return to Paris in 1814, was made superintendent of the King's music, court composer, and prof. of singing at the Cons., positions he held until 1830. See his autobiography, *Sou-*

venirs de F. B., ed. by M. de Villemarest (Paris, 1834). He composed some 30 operas.

Blank, Allan, American composer; b. N.Y., Dec. 27, 1925. He studied at the High School of Music and Art in N.Y.; subsequently at the Juilliard School of Music (1945–47), Washington Square College (B.A., 1948), the Univ. of Minnesota (M.A., 1950), and the Univ. of Iowa. He was a violinist in the Pittsburgh Sym. Orch. (1950–52); after teaching instrumental music in N.Y. high schools (1956–65), he taught at Western Illinois Univ. in Macomb (1966–68), Paterson (N.J.) State College (1968–70), Lehman College of the City Univ. of N.Y. (1970–77), and Virginia Commonwealth Univ. in Richmond (from 1978). He was also conductor (1984) and music director (1986–89) of the Richmond Community Orch. In his works, Blank strives for lyrical and dramatic expressivity complemented by clarity of line and richness of content. His dramatic works include *Aria da capo*, chamber opera (1958–60), *The Magic Bonbons*, opera (1980–83), and *The Noise*, opera (1985–86), as well as incidental music to *Othello* (1983) and *Measure for Measure* (1984).

Blanter, Matvei (Isaakovich), Russian composer; b. Pochep, Feb. 10, 1903. He studied in Moscow with G. Conus, then devoted himself exclusively to the composition of light music. He wrote an operetta, *On the Banks of the Amur* (1939), and some incidental music, but he was best known for his songs, including the popular *Katyusha* (famous during World War II), which combined the melodic inflection of the typical urban ballad with the basic traits of a Russian folk song. Blanter was regarded in Russia as a creator of the new Soviet song style.

BIBL.: V. Zak, *M. B.* (Moscow, 1971).

Blaramberg, Pavel (Ivanovich), Russian composer; b. Orenburg, Sept. 26, 1841; d. Nice, March 28, 1907. His father was a geographer of French origin; his mother was Greek. At the age of 14 he went to St. Petersburg, where he later became a functionary of the Central Statistical Committee. He was largely self-taught in music, apart from occasional advice from Balakirev and Rimsky-Korsakov. In 1878 he settled in Moscow as an instructor at the newly founded Phil. Inst. In 1898 he went to the Crimea, then to France.

WORKS: OPERAS: *The Mummers* (1881); *Russalka* (Moscow, April 15, 1888); *Maria Tudor*, after Hugo (produced as *Mary of Burgundy* on account of the censor's objection to the original libretto; Moscow, Oct. 29, 1888); *Tushintsy* (Moscow, Feb. 5, 1895); *The Waves* (1902).

Blass, Robert, American bass of German parents; b. N.Y., Oct. 7, 1867; d. Berlin, Dec. 3, 1930. He went to Leipzig in 1887 to study violin, but then pursued vocal instruction from Stockhausen in Frankfurt am Main. In 1892 he made his operatic debut as King Heinrich in Weimar, and then sang in various German opera centers. In 1899 he appeared at London's Covent Garden. On Nov. 13, 1900, he made his Metropolitan Opera debut as Hermann in *Tannhäuser* during the company's visit to San Francisco. He first sang on the stage of the Metropolitan Opera in New York as Rocco on Dec. 28, 1900, and remaining on its roster until 1910 and again from 1920 to 1922. In 1901 he appeared as Gurnemanz and Hagen at Bayreuth and sang at the Berlin Deutsches Opernhaus from 1913 to 1919.

Blatný, Pavel, Czech pianist, conductor, teacher, and composer; b. Brno, Sept. 14, 1931. He was the son of the Czech organist, pedagogue, and composer Josef Blatný (b. Brünn, March 19, 1891; d. there [Brno], July 18, 1980). He began music studies with his father; then had instruction in piano and theory at the Brno Cons. (1950–55) and in musicology at the Univ. of Brno (1954–58); also took composition lessons with Bořkovec at the Prague Academy of Music (1955–59) and attended summer courses of new music at Darmstadt (1965–69); in 1968 he traveled to the United States and took lessons in jazz piano and composition at the Berklee College of Music in Boston. He became an exceedingly active musician in Czechoslovakia; wrote a vast number of works, some of them paralleling the development of "3d-stream music" initiated in the United States by Schuller. He also gave countless piano recitals in programs of modern music, conducted a great many concerts, and participated in programs of the Czech Radio. In 1971 he was appointed chief of the music division of the television station in Brno; he also taught at the Janáček Academy of Music and Dramatic Arts in Brno (from 1979). He retired from these posts in 1991. In his later compositions, he turned to "serious" music, albeit with tonal manifestations. Among his many scores are *Prohádky lesa (Studánka a Domeček)* (Forest Tales [The Well and Little House]), 2 television operas for children (1975).

Blauvelt, Lillian Evans, American soprano; b. Brooklyn, March 16, 1874; d. Chicago, Aug. 29, 1947. She received violin lessons and made her debut at a recital in N.Y.'s Steinway Hall when she was 8, then entered the National Cons. of Music of America there at age 15 to pursue vocal training with Bouhy and Fürsch-Madi; she continued studies in Paris with Bouhy before making her operatic debut in Gounod's *Mireille* in Brussels on Sept. 6, 1891. In 1899 she sang before Queen Victoria and in 1902 sang the coronation ode for Edward VII, who presented her with the Coronation Medal. In 1903 she made her first appearance at London's Covent Garden as Gounod's Marguerite. In later years, she appeared mainly in concerts. Following further training with **Alexander Savine**, whom she married in 1914, she created the title role in his opera *Xenia* (Zürich, May 29, 1919). She spent her last years as a voice teacher in New York and Chicago.

Blavet, Michel, renowned French flutist and composer; b. Besançon (baptized), March 13, 1700; d. Paris, Oct. 28, 1768. He was self-taught as a musician, mastering both bassoon and flute, He went to Paris in 1723 with Duke Charles-Eugène Lévis, and made his debut at the Concert Spirituel in 1726, remaining as its most celebrated artist for some 25 years. He was acknowledged as the foremost flute virtuoso of his time. Among his stage works were *Floriane, ou La Grotte des spectacles*, comédie-ballet (Château de Berny, Aug. 25, 1752), *Les Jeux olympiques*, ballet héroïque (Château de Berny, Aug. 25, 1753), and *La Fête de Cythère*, opera (Château de Berny, Nov. 19, 1753).

Blaze (called **Castil-Blaze**), **François-Henri-Joseph,** French writer on music; b. Cavaillon, Vaucluse, Dec. 1, 1784; d. Paris, Dec. 11, 1857. His son was the French music critic Henri Blaze, Baron de Bury (b. Avignon, May 17, 1813; d. Paris, March 15, 1888). He studied with his father, a lawyer and amateur musician, then went to Paris in 1799 as a law student; he held various administrative posts in provincial towns in France. At the same time he studied music and compiled information on the opera in France. The fruit of this work was the publication in 2 vols. of his book *De l'opéra en France* (Paris, 1820, 1826). He became music critic of the influential Paris *Journal des Débats* in 1822, signing his articles "XXX." He resigned from this post in 1832 but continued to publish books on music, including valuable compilations of musical lexicography: *Dictionnaire de musique moderne* (2 vols., 1821; 2d ed., 1825; 3d ed., ed. by J. H. Mees, 1828); *Chapelle-musique des Rois de France* (1832); *La Danse et les ballets depuis Bacchus jusqu'à Mlle. Taglioni* (1832); *Mémorial du Grand Opéra* (1847); *Molière musicien* (1852); *Théâtres lyriques de Paris* (2 vols., 1855–56); *Sur l'opéra français: Vérités dures mais utiles* (1856); *L'Art des jeux lyriques* (1858); tr. into French many librettos of German and Italian operas. He himself wrote 3 operas.

Blažek, Zdeněk, Czech composer and teacher; b. Žarošice, May 24, 1905; d. Prague, June 19, 1988. He was a pupil of Petrželka at the Brno Cons. (1924–29) and of Suk at the Prague Cons. (1933–35). Returning to Brno, he was a teacher (1941–61) and director (1947–57) at the Cons., and then a teacher at the Purkyně Univ. (1961–70). His music evolved from Moravian folk songs. His catalog includes two operas: *Verchovina* (The Highlands; 1950–51; Brno, 1956) and *R.U.R.* (1975).

Blech, Leo, eminent German conductor and composer; b. Aachen, April 21, 1871; d. Berlin, Aug. 25, 1958. As a young man, he was engaged in a mercantile career; then studied briefly at the Hochschule für Musik in Berlin; he returned to Aachen to conduct at the Municipal Theater (1893–99) and also took summer courses in composition with Humperdinck (1893–96). He was subsequently engaged as opera conductor in Prague (1899–1906); he then became conductor at the Berlin Royal Opera in 1906; he was named Generalmusikdirektor in 1913. In 1923 he became a conductor of the Deutsches Opernhaus in Berlin; in 1924 he was with the Berlin Volksoper, and in 1925 with the Vienna Volksoper. In 1926 he returned to Berlin as a conductor with the Staatsoper, remaining there until 1937; he was conductor of the Riga Opera (1937–41). From 1941 to 1949 he conducted in Stockholm. In 1949 he returned to Berlin and served as Generalmusikdirektor of the Stadtische Oper, retiring with the title of Generalmusikdirektor in 1953. Blech was considered a fine interpreter of the standard German and Italian repertoire, particularly in the works of Wagner and Verdi. His own music was composed in the Wagnerian tradition; his knowledge and understanding of instrumental and vocal resources enabled him to produce competent operas; however, after initial successes, they suffered almost total oblivion.

WORKS: DRAMATIC: OPERAS: *Aglaja* (1893); *Cherubina* (1894); *Das war ich*, an "opera-idyl" (Dresden, Oct. 6, 1902); *Alpenkönig und Menschenfeind* (Dresden, Oct. 1, 1903; rev. as *Rappelkopf*, Berlin, Oct. 2, 1917); *Aschenbrodel* (Prague, 1905); *Versiegelt* (Hamburg, Nov. 4, 1908). OPERETTA: *Die Strohwitwe* (Hamburg, 1920).

BIBL.: E. Rychnowsky, *L. B.* (Leipzig, 1909); W. Jacob, *L. B.* (Hamburg, 1931).

Bledsoe, Jules, black American baritone and composer; b. Waco, Texas, Dec. 29, 1898; d. Los Angeles, July 14, 1943. He studied at the Chicago Musical College (B.A., 1919), then in Paris and Rome. Returning to America, he distinguished himself as a fine performer in musical comedies and opera. He sang the central role in the premiere of Jerome Kern's *Show Boat* (1927), appeared in grand opera as Rigoletto and Boris Godunov, and sang the title role in Gruenberg's *Emperor Jones*. As a composer, he wrote an *African Suite* for Orch. and several songs in the manner of Negro spirituals.

Blegen, Judith, American soprano; b. Lexington, Ky., April 27, 1940. She studied violin and voice at the Curtis Inst. of Music in Philadelphia (1959–64). In 1963 she went to Italy, where she studied with Luigi Ricci, then sang at the Nuremberg Opera (1963–66). She made a successful appearance at the Santa Fe Opera on Aug. 1, 1969, in the role of Emily in Menotti's satirical opera *Help! Help! the Globolinks!*, which was written especially for her. She made her Metropolitan Opera debut on Jan. 19, 1970, in New York as Papagena, returning there regularly in subsequent seasons to sing such roles as Zerlina, Marzelline, Gilda, Sophie, Blondchen, Adele, Oscar, and Juliette. In 1975 she made her first appearance at London's Covent Garden, and in 1977 at the Paris Opéra.

Bleichmann, Yuli, Russian composer; b. St. Petersburg, Dec. 6, 1868; d. there, Jan. 8, 1910. He studied with Rimsky-Korsakov at the St. Petersburg Cons., and later with Jadassohn and Reinecke in Leipzig. Returning to St. Petersburg, he founded the Popular Sym. Concerts in 1893; he also conducted the Phil. Sym. Concerts. He composed 2 operas, greatly influenced by Wagner: *St. Sebastian* and *The Dream-Princess* (Moscow, Oct. 23, 1900).

Bleyle, Karl, German composer; b. Feldkirch, Vorarlberg, May 7, 1880; d. Stuttgart, June 5, 1969. He studied with Wehrle (violin) and S. de Lange (composition) in Stuttgart and with Thuille (composition) in Munich. He was active as a teacher and a theater conductor in Graz, Weimar, and Munich; in 1923 he returned to Stuttgart. Among his works are the operas *Hannele und Sannele* (Stuttgart, 1923) and *Der Teufelssteg* (Rostock, 1924).

Bliss, Sir Arthur (Drummond), eminent English composer; b. London, Aug. 2, 1891; d. there, March 27, 1975. He studied counterpoint with Charles Wood at the Univ. of Cambridge (Mus.B., 1913), and then pursued training with Stanford, Vaughan Williams, and Holst at the Royal College of Music in London (1913–14). While serving in the British Army during World War I, he was wounded in 1916 and gassed in 1918. After the Armistice, he gained recognition as something of an *enfant terrible* with his *Madame Noy* for Soprano and 7 Instruments (1918) and *Rout* for Soprano and 10 Instruments (1920). With such fine scores as *A Colour Symphony* (1921–22), the *Introduction and Allegro* for Orch. (1926), the Oboe Quintet (1927), and the Clarinet Quintet (1932), he rose to prominence as a composer of great distinction. His music for H. G. Wells's film *Things to Come* (1934–35) and the *Music* for Strings (1935) added luster to his reputation, which was further enhanced by his outstanding ballets *Checkmate* (1937), *Miracle in the Gorbals* (1944), and *Adam Zero* (1946). After a sojourn as a teacher in Berkeley, California (1939–41), Bliss served as director of music for the BBC in London (1942–44). In 1950 he was knighted and in 1953 he was made the Master of the Queen's Music. In 1969 he was made a Knight Commander of the Royal Victorian Order and in 1971 a Companion of Honour. G. Roscow ed. *Bliss on Music: Selected Writings of Arthur Bliss (1920–1975)* (Oxford, 1991).

WORKS: DRAMATIC: OPERAS: *The Olympians* (1944–49; London, Sept. 29, 1949); *Tobias and the Angel* (1958–59; BBC-TV, London, May 19, 1960). BALLETS: *Checkmate* (Paris, June 15, 1937); *Miracle in the Gorbals* (London, Oct. 26, 1944); *Adam Zero* (London, April 10, 1946); *The Lady of Shalott* (1957–58; Berkeley, Calif., May 2, 1958). INCIDENTAL MUSIC: *As You Like It* (1919); *The Tempest* (1921); *King Solomon* (1924).

BIBL.: S. Craggs, *A. B.: A Bio-Bibliography* (N.Y., 1988).

Bliss, P. Paul, American organist and composer; b. Chicago, Nov. 25, 1872; d. Oswego, N.Y., Feb. 2, 1933. He studied in Philadelphia; then went to Paris, where he was a pupil of Guilmant (organ) and Massenet (composition). Returning to America, he was active as an organist in Oswego; he served as music director with the John Church Co. (1904–10) and the Willis Music Co. (from 1911). He composed 3 operettas: *Feast of Little Lanterns, Feast of Red Corn*, and *In India*.

Blitzstein, Marc, significant American composer; b. Philadelphia, March 2, 1905; d. Fort de France, Martinique, Jan. 22, 1964. He studied piano and organ with Sternberg in Philadelphia. In 1921 he entered the Univ. of Pa. on a scholarship, but left the following year when he failed to meet the physical education requirements. He then studied piano with Siloti in New York. From 1924 to 1926 he was a composition student of Scalero at the Curtis Inst. of Music in Philadelphia. After further training with Boulanger in Paris and Schoenberg in Berlin (1926–28), he returned to the United States and wrote a few generic instrumental works in either a late Romantic or a more modern, Copland-influenced jazz style. However, he soon turned to creating works for the theater à la Brecht and Weill, in which "art for society's sake" and "social consciousness" of a fervent left-wing persuasion became the norm. Particularly notable was his play in music *The Cradle Will Rock* (N.Y., June 16, 1937). In 1940–41 and 1941–42 he held Guggenheim fellowships. From 1942 to 1945 he served in the U.S. Army Air Force in England, where he was music director of the American Broadcasting Station for Europe. Upon his return to the United States, he resumed composing for the theater. However, in the 1950s he was unable to sustain his musical standing as his unique blending of musical theater and opera went out of fashion, as did his penchant for social protest. During the last decade of his life his works became more conventional. In 1959 he was elected to membership in the National Inst. of Arts and Letters. In 1960 he received a Ford Foundation grant to compose an opera on the subject of Sacco and Vanzetti for the Metropolitan Opera in New York, but the work was never finished. Two other operas were also left incomplete. Blitzstein died from injuries sustained after a savage beating by 3 sailors in an alley. Three arias, 1 each from his 3 unfinished operas, were premiered at a memorial concert conducted by Bernstein in N.Y., April 19, 1964. Blitzstein remains best known for his adaptation of Weill's *Die Dreigroschenoper* as *The Threepenny Opera* (Waltham, Mass.,

June 14, 1952). It opened off Broadway on March 10, 1954, and had a remarkable 6-year N.Y. run, becoming a classic of the American theater.

WORKS: DRAMATIC: *Svarga*, ballet (1924–25); *Jig-Saw*, ballet (1927–28); *Triple Sec*, opera-farce (1928; Philadelphia, May 6, 1929); *Parabola and Circula*, opera ballet (1929); *Cain*, ballet (1930); *The Harpies*, satirical chamber opera (1931; N.Y., May 25, 1953); *The Condemned*, choral opera (1932); *The Cradle Will Rock*, "play in music" in 10 scenes with "social significance" (1936–37; N.Y., June 16, 1937, composer at the piano); *I've Got the Tune*, "radio song-play" (CBS, N.Y., Oct. 24, 1937); *No for an Answer*, short opera (1938–40; N.Y., Jan. 5, 1941); *The Guests*, ballet (1946–48; N.Y., Jan. 20, 1949; incorporates the unperformed ballet *Show*, 1946); *Regina*, musical theater to Hellman's play *The Little Foxes* (1946–49; tryout, New Haven, Oct. 6, 1949; N.Y. premiere, Oct. 31, 1949; rev. 1953 and 1958 for N.Y. opera house perfs.); *Reuben Reuben*, musical play (1949–55; Boston, Oct. 10, 1955); *Juno*, musical play (1957–59; N.Y., March 9, 1959); *Sacco and Vanzetti*, opera (1959–64; unfinished); *The Magic Barrel*, opera (1962–64; unfinished); *Idiots First*, opera (1962–64; unfinished but completed by L. Lehrman, 1973; piano score, Ithaca, N.Y., Aug. 1974). INCIDENTAL MUSIC TO: Shakespeare's *Julius Caesar* (1937), Büchner's *Danton's Death* (1938), Shaw's *Androcles and the Lion* (1946), Hellman's *Another Part of the Forest* (1946), Shakespeare's *King Lear* (2 versions, 1950, 1955), Jonson's *Volpone* (1956), Shakespeare's *A Midsummer Night's Dream* (1958) and *A Winter's Tale* (1958), and Hellman's *Toys in the Attic* (1960). OTHER: Tr. and adaptation of Weill's *Dreigroschenoper* as *The Threepenny Opera* (1950–52; Waltham, Mass., June 14, 1952).

BIBL.: R. Dietz, *The Operatic M. B.* (diss., Univ. of Iowa, 1970); E. Gordon, *Mark the Music: The Life and Work of M. B.* (N.Y., 1989).

Bloch, André, French composer; b. Wissembourg, Alsace, Jan. 18, 1873; d. Viry-Chatillon, Essome, Aug. 7, 1960. He studied at the Paris Cons. with Guiraud and Massenet; he received the Premier Grand Prix de Rome in 1893. He was conductor of the orch. of the American Cons. at Fontainebleau. His works include the operas *Maida* (Aix-les-Baines, April 12, 1909), *Une Nuit de Noël* (1922), *Broceliande* (Paris, Nov. 23, 1925), and *Guignol* (Lyons, March 1, 1936), and a ballet, *Feminaland* (1904).

Bloch, Augustyn (Hipolit), Polish composer; b. Grudziadz, Aug. 13, 1929. After attending the Gdansk School of Music (1946–50), he studied with Rączkowski (organ; 1950–55) and Szeligowski (composition; 1952–59) at the Warsaw Cons. He was a church organist in Gdansk and Warsaw (1946–56), and a composer for the theater of the Polish Radio in Warsaw (1954–77). He served as vice president of the Polish Composers Union (1977–79; 1983–87) and as chairman of the program committee of the Warsaw Autumn festivals (1979–87). His compositions, written in an accessible style, have won several competitions. In 1971 and 1985 he received awards from the Polish Ministry of Culture. In 1981 he was honored with the Polish Composers Union Award.

WORKS: DRAMATIC: *Voci*, ballet (1962; Polish TV, Sept. 20, 1967); *Awaiting*, ballet (1963; Warsaw, Sept. 9, 1964); *The Bullet*, ballet (1965); *Ayelet, Jephta's Daughter*, mystery-opera (1967; Warsaw, Sept. 22, 1968); *Gilgamesh*, ballet (1969); *Pan Żagtoba*, musical (1971); *Very Sleeping Beauty*, opera-ballet-pantomime (1973; Warsaw, Sept. 29, 1974); *The Mirror*, ballet-pantomime (1975).

Bloch, Ernest, remarkable Swiss-born American composer of Jewish descent; b. Geneva, July 24, 1880; d. Portland, Oreg., July 15, 1959. He studied solfeggio with Jaques-Dalcroze and violin with Louis Rey in Geneva (1894–97), then went to Brussels, where he took violin lessons with Ysaije and studied composition with Rasse (1897–99); while a student, he wrote a string quartet and a "symphonie orientale," indicative of his natural attraction to non-European cultures and coloristic melos. In 1900 he went to Germany, where he studied theory with Knorr at the Hoch Cons. in Frankfurt am Main and took private lessons with Thuille in Munich; there he began the composition of his first full-fledged sym., in C-sharp. He then spent a year in Paris, where he met Debussy; Bloch's first publ. work, *Historiettes au crépuscule* (1903), shows Debussy's influence. In 1904 he returned to Geneva, where he began the composition of his only complete opera, *Macbeth*, after Shakespeare (1904–09; Paris, Nov. 30, 1910); another opera, *Jézabel*, on a biblical subject, never materialized beyond a few initial sketches. As a tribute to his homeland, he outlined the orch. work *Helvetia*, based on Swiss motifs, as early as 1900, but the full score was not completed until 1928. During the season 1909–10, Bloch conducted symphonic concerts in Lausanne and Neuchâtel. In 1916 he was offered an engagement as conductor on an American tour accompanying the dancer Maud Allan; he gladly accepted the opportunity to leave war-torn Europe, and expressed an almost childlike delight upon docking in the port of N.Y. at the sight of the Statue of Liberty. Allan's tour was not successful, however, and Bloch returned to Geneva; in 1917 he received an offer to teach at the David Mannes School of Music in New York, and once more he went to America; he became a naturalized American citizen in 1924. This was also the period when Bloch began to express himself in music as an inheritor of Jewish culture, explicitly articulating his racial consciousness in several verbal statements. His *Israel Symphony*, *Trois poèmes juifs*, and *Schelomo*, a "Hebrew rhapsody" for Cello and Orch., mark the height of Bloch's greatness as a Jewish composer. In America, he found sincere admirers and formed a group of greatly talented students, among them Sessions, Bacon, Antheil, Moore, Rogers, Thompson, Porter, Stevens, and Kirchner. From 1920 to 1925 he was director of the Inst. of Music in Cleveland, and from 1925 to 1930, director of the San Francisco Cons. When the magazine *Musical America* announced in 1927 a contest for a symphonic work, Bloch won 1st prize for his "epic rhapsody" entitled simply *America*. It was performed with a great outpouring of publicity in 5 cities, but as happens often with prizewinning works, it failed to strike the critics and the audiences as truly great, and in the end remained a mere by-product of Bloch's genius. From 1930 to 1939 Bloch lived mostly in Switzerland; he then returned to the United States and taught classes at the Univ. of Calif. at Berkeley (1940–52); he finally retired and lived at his newly purchased house at Agate Beach, Oreg. In 1937 he was elected a member of the National Inst. of Arts and Letters, and in 1943 of the American Academy of Arts and Letters. In 1947 he was awarded the 1st Gold Medal of the American Academy of Arts and Sciences. In 1952 he received 2 N.Y. Music Critic's Circle awards for his String Quartet No. 3 and Concerto Grosso No. 2.

Bloch contributed a number of informative annotations for the program books of the Boston Sym., N.Y. Phil., and other orchs.; he also contributed articles to music journals, among them "Man and Music" in *Musical Quarterly* (Oct. 1933). An Ernest Bloch Soc. was formed in London in 1937 to promote performances of his music, with Albert Einstein as honorary president and with vice presidents that included Sir Thomas Beecham, Havelock Ellis, and Romain Rolland. His daughter, Suzanne Bloch (b. Geneva, Aug. 7, 1907), is a noted lutenist and harpsichordist.

BIBL.: R. Stackpole, *E. B.* (Turin, 1933); D. Kushner, *E. B. and His Music* (Glasgow, 1973); S. Bloch and I. Heskes, *E. B., Creative Spirit: A Program Source Book* (N.Y., 1976); R. Strassburg, *E. B., Voice in the Wilderness: A Biographical Study* (Los Angeles, 1977); D. Kushner, *E. B.: A Guide to Research* (N.Y., 1988).

Blochwitz, Hans Peter, German tenor; b. Garmisch-Partenkirchen, Sept. 28, 1949. He received an engineering degree in computer science; after singing in amateur choruses and occasional concerts, he pursued a vocal career. In 1984 he made his operatic debut as Lensky at the Frankfurt am Main Opera; he then sang in Brussels, Geneva, Hamburg, Milan, and Vienna. In 1987 he made his U.S. debut as the Evangelist in Bach's *St. Matthew Passion* with Solti and the Chicago Sym. Orch. In 1989 he made his first appearance at London's Covent Garden as Mozart's Ferrando, and that same year made his U.S. operatic debut in San Francisco as Mozart's Idamanto. On Sept. 27, 1990, he appeared as Don Ottavio at his debut at the Metropolitan Opera in New

York, and the following month made his U.S. recital debut in La Jolla, California; subsequently he sang in opera and concert on both sides of the Atlantic. In 1993 he was a soloist in Beethoven's 9th Sym. at the London Promenade Concerts. He was engaged to sing the title role in Henze's *Der Junge Lord* in Munich in 1995. His impressive oratorio and concert repertoire ranges from Bach and Handel to Zemlinsky and Britten, with a noteworthy regard for the lieder of Schubert and Schumann. Among his operatic roles are Mozart's Tito, Tamino, and Belmonte, as well as Rossini's Count Almaviva and Donizetti's Nemorino.

Blockx, Jan, significant Flemish composer; b. Antwerp, Jan. 25, 1851; d. Kapellenbos, near Antwerp, May 26, 1912. He studied organ with Callaerts and composition with Benoit. In 1885 he became a lecturer at the Flemish Music School; also was music director of the Cercle Artistique and other societies in Belgium. With Benoit, he is regarded as the strongest representative of the national Flemish school of composition. While the melodic and rhythmic materials in his music strongly reflect Flemish folk elements, the treatment, contrapuntal and harmonic, is opulent, approaching Wagnerian sonorities.

WORKS: DRAMATIC: OPERAS: *Jets vergeten* (Antwerp, Feb. 19, 1877); *Maître Martin* (Brussels, Nov. 30, 1892); *Herbergprinses* (Antwerp, Oct. 10, 1896; produced in French as *Princesse d'auberge*, N.Y., March 10, 1909); *Thyl Uylenspiegel* (Brussels, Jan. 12, 1900); *De bruid der zee* (Antwerp, Nov. 30, 1901); *De kapel* (Antwerp, Nov. 7, 1903); *Baldie* (Antwerp, Jan. 25, 1908; rev. and perf. under the title *Liefdelied*; Antwerp, Jan. 6, 1912). BALLET: *Milenka* (1887).

BIBL.: L. Solvay, *Notice sur J. B.* (Brussels, 1920); F. Blockx, *J. B.* (Brussels, 1943).

Blodek, Wilhelm (Vilém), Czech composer; b. Prague, Oct. 3, 1834; d. there, May 1, 1874. He studied with J. F. Kittl and A. Dreyschock. He taught for 3 years in Poland, then returned to Prague, and became a prof. of flute at the Prague Cons. (1860–70). In 1870 he became insane and spent the rest of his life in an asylum. His opera in the Czech language, *V studni* (In the Well), was produced with excellent success in Prague (Nov. 17, 1867); it was also given in German under the title *Im Brunnen* (Leipzig, 1893). His 2d opera, *Zitek*, remained unfinished at his death; it was completed by F. X. Vana, and produced in Prague at the centennial of Blodek's birth (Oct. 3, 1934).

BIBL.: R. Budiš, *V. B.* (Prague, 1964).

Blomdahl, Karl-Birger, significant Swedish composer; b. Växjö, Oct. 19, 1916; d. Kungsängen, near Stockholm, June 14, 1968. He studied composition with Hilding Rosenberg and conducting with Tor Mann in Stockholm; in 1946 he traveled in France and Italy on a state stipend; in 1954–55 he attended a seminar at Tanglewood on a grant of the American-Scandinavian Foundation. Returning to Sweden, he taught composition at the Stockholm Musikhögskolan (1960–64); in 1964 he was appointed music director at the Swedish Radio. He was an organizer (with Bäck, Carlid, Johanson, and Lidholm) of a "Monday Group" in Stockholm, dedicated to the propagation of an objective and abstract idiom as distinct from the prevalent type of Scandinavian romanticism. Blomdahl's early works are cast in a neoclassical idiom, but he then turned to more advanced techniques, including the application of electronic resources. His 3d Sym., *Facetter* (Facets), utilizes dodecaphonic techniques. In 1959 he brought out his opera *Aniara*, which made him internationally famous; it pictures a pessimistic future when the remnants of the inhabitants of the planet earth, devastated by atomic wars and polluted by radiation, are forced to emigrate to saner worlds in the galaxy; the score employs electronic sounds, and its thematic foundation is derived from a series of 12 different notes and 11 different intervals. At the time of his death, Blomdahl was working on an opera entitled *The Saga of the Great Computer*, incorporating electronic and concrete sounds, and synthetic speech.

WORKS: DRAMATIC: *Vaknatten* (The Wakeful Night), theater music (1945); *Aniara*, opera (1957–59; Stockholm, May 31, 1959); *Minotaurus*, ballet (Stockholm, April 5, 1958); *Spel för åtta* (Game for 8), ballet (Stockholm, June 8, 1962; also as a choreographic suite for Orch., 1964); *Herr von Hancken*, comic opera (Stockholm, Sept. 2, 1965).

BIBL.: G. Bucht, ed., *"Facetter" av och om K.-B. B.* (Stockholm, 1970).

Blondeau, Pierre-Auguste-Louis, French violist and composer; b. Paris, Aug. 15, 1784; d. there, 1865. He studied at the Paris Cons. with Baillot, Gossec, and Méhul, winning the Prix de Rome in 1808 with his cantata *Maria Stuart*. He was violist in the Grand Opéra Orch. until 1842. He wrote an opera, *Alla fontana*.

Bloomfield, Theodore (Robert), American conductor; b. Cleveland, June 14, 1923. He studied conducting with Maurice Kessler and piano at the Oberlin (Ohio) College-Cons. of Music (Mus.B., 1944), then took courses in conducting at the Juilliard Graduate School in New York with Edgar Schenkman; he also studied piano with Arrau and conducting with Monteux. In 1946–47 he was apprentice conductor to Szell at the Cleveland Orch., then conducted the Cleveland Little Sym. and the Civic Opera Workshop (1947–52). He was subsequently music director of the Portland (Oreg.) Sym. (1955–59) and of the Rochester (N.Y.) Phil. (1959–63). He then was first conductor of the Hamburg State Opera (1964–66) and Generalmusikdirektor of Frankfurt am Main (1966–68). From 1975 to 1982 he was chief conductor of the (West) Berlin Sym. Orch.

Blum, Robert (Karl Moritz), Swiss composer and teacher; b. Zürich, Nov. 27, 1900; d. there, Dec. 10, 1994. He was a student of Andreae, Baldegger, Jarnach, Laquai, and Vogler at the Zürich Cons. (1912–22). After attending Busoni's master class in composition at the Prussian Academy of Arts in Berlin (1923), he returned to Switzerland and conducted various amateur orchs. and choirs. From 1943 to 1976 he taught counterpoint and composition at the Zürich Cons. In his extensive output, Blum utilized various contemporary means of expression, from polytonal to 12-tone writing. He composed the opera *Amarapura* (1924).

BIBL.: G. Fierz, *R. B.: Leben und Werk* (Zürich, 1967); G. Lehmann, *Zur Musik von R. B.* (Baden, 1973).

Blumenfeld, Harold, American composer; b. Seattle, Oct. 15, 1923. He studied composition with Rogers at the Eastman School of Music in Rochester, N.Y. (1941–43) and with Hindemith at Yale Univ. (B.M., 1949; M.M., 1950). He also studied conducting with Shaw and Bernstein, and operatic stage direction with Goldovsky at the Berkshire Music Center at Tanglewood, and in 1948–49 he attended the Salzburg Mozarteum and the Univ. and Cons. in Zürich. In 1951 he joined the faculty of Washington Univ. in St. Louis, where he was director of its opera studio until 1971. In 1971–72 he was a visiting prof. at Queens College of the City Univ. of N.Y., and then was again on the faculty of Washington Univ. from 1972 to 1989. Blumenfeld has concentrated on composing various vocal scores, including the operas *Amphitryon 4* (1962), *Fritzi* (1979), *Fourscore: An Opera of Opposites* (1980–86), *Breakfast Waltzes* (1991; St. Louis, March 25, 1994), and *Seasons in Hell: A Life of Rimbaud* (1992–94; Cincinnati, Feb. 14, 1996). His style is thoroughly contemporary in nature.

Blumer, Theodor, German conductor and composer; b. Dresden, March 24, 1881; d. Berlin, Sept. 21, 1964. He studied at the Dresden Cons. He was active as a pianist, and from 1925 to 1931 as a conductor on Dresden Radio. From 1931 to 1942 he conducted radio broadcasts in Leipzig. He wrote several light operas, among them *Der Funf-Uhr-Tee* (Dresden, 1911) and *Trau schau wem!*

Boatwright, Helen (née **Strassburger**), American soprano and teacher; b. Sheboygan, Wis., Nov. 17, 1916. She began her training with Anna Shram Irving, and later studied with Marion Sims at Oberlin (Ohio) College. After making her operatic debut as Anna in an English language production of Nicolai's *Die lustigen Weiber von Windsor* at the Berkshire Music Center in 1942, she appeared in opera in Austin and San Antonio (1943–45). In 1943 she married the American violinist, conductor, and composer Howard

Boatwright (b. Newport News, Va., March 16, 1918; d. Syracuse, N.Y., Feb. 20, 1999), with whom she often appeared in concert. She taught in New Haven (1945–64), and in 1965 became adjunct prof. of voice at Syracuse Univ. In 1967 she made her N.Y. recital debut at Town Hall. She was prof. of voice at the Eastman School of Music in Rochester, N.Y. (1972–79) and at the Peabody Cons. of Music in Baltimore (1987–89); also gave master classes.

Boatwright, McHenry, black American bass-baritone; b. Tennile, Ga., Feb. 29, 1928; d. N.Y., Nov. 5, 1994. He studied piano (B.Mus., 1950) and voice (B.Mus., 1954) at the New England Cons. of Music in Boston. In 1953 and 1954 he received Marian Anderson awards. In 1956 he made his formal concert debut in Boston, and in 1958 his first N.Y. concert appearance. After making his operatic debut as Arkel in *Pelléas et Mélisande* at the New England Opera Theater in 1958, he appeared with various opera companies and as a soloist with orchs. He created the central role in Schuller's opera *The Visitation* (Hamburg, Oct. 12, 1966).

Bocelli, Andrea, handsome Italian pop star tenor, b. Lajatico, September 22, 1958. Bocelli was raised in a rural community 20 miles from Pisa. Suffering from glaucoma since birth, he lost the remainder of his sight from a head injury in a soccer game at age 12. He began studying piano at age 6, later playing both flute and saxophone, but his true passion was for singing along with opera recordings. He studied law at the University of Pisa, earning extra money by working at a piano bar as a lounge singer, and eventually earned a law degree. In 1987 he auditioned for Italian rock star Zicchero Fornaciari, who was looking for a tenor to perform on a demo recording of the song "Miserere," which Fornaciari wanted to record with superstar Luciano Pavarotti. Pavarotti made the record and was impressed with the singing on the demo, offering Bocelli private lessons. In 1993 Bocelli made his first solo recording and was a sensation at the San Remo opera festival; the following year he won the competition and his first album soared to the top of the Italian charts. Pavarotti then introduced the young star at his own festival in 1995, where Bocelli again took top honors. He broke through big time on the European pop charts in 1996 with his recording of the pop song "Con te Partiro (Time to Say Goodbye)," a duet with British stage star Sarah Brightman. The song was commissioned by the German world light-heavyweight boxing champion Henry Maske for his farewell fight; Maske made it a habit to enter the ring accompanied by a soaring, romantic song. (Maske lost the fight but the song was a major international hit.) A year later Bocelli was launched in the United States via a hightoned special on public television and the release of his album *Romanza*, which eventually sold over 12 million copies. Bocelli has occasionally performed on the opera stage but is primarily known as a solo performer who packs them in around the world. He has also recorded pop duets with big-lunged singers like Celine Dion, and has gained a following thanks to his matinee-idol looks and romantic voice. His 1999 album, *Sogno*, sold an amazing 6 million copies just 4 months after its release.

Bockelmann, Rudolf (August Louis Wilhelm), German bass-baritone; b. Bodenteich, April 2, 1892; d. Dresden, Oct. 9, 1958. He studied in Celle and with Lassner, Soomer, and Scheidemantel in Leipzig. In 1920 he made his operatic debut in Celle. In 1921 he sang the Herald in *Lohengrin* at the Leipzig Opera, where he appeared until 1926. From 1926 to 1932 he sang at the Hamburg City Theater. He also appeared at the Bayreuth Festivals (1928–42), London's Covent Garden (1929–30; 1934–38), and the Chicago Opera (1930–32). From 1932 to 1945 he was a member of the Berlin State Opera. Guest engagements also took him to Milan, Paris, Rome, Vienna, and Munich. His Nazi inclinations precluded engagements outside Germany after World War II. After teaching voice in Hamburg, he went to Dresden in 1955 as a prof. at the Hochschule für Musik. He was particularly esteemed as a Wagnerian, winning praise for his portrayals of Hans Sachs, Wotan, Kurwenal, Gunther, and the Dutchman.

Bodanzky, Artur, famous Austrian conductor; b. Vienna, Dec. 16, 1877; d. N.Y., Nov. 23, 1939. He studied at the Vienna Cons., and later with Zemlinsky. He began his career as a violinist in the Vienna Court Opera Orch. In 1900 he received his first appointment as a conductor, leading an operetta season in Budweis; in 1902 he became assistant to Mahler at the Vienna Court Opera; conducted in Berlin (1905) and in Prague (1906–09). In 1909 he was engaged as music director at Mannheim. In 1912 he arranged a memorial Mahler Festival, conducting a huge ensemble of 1,500 vocalists and instrumentalists. He conducted *Parsifal* at Covent Garden in London in 1914; his success there led to an invitation to conduct the German repertoire at the Metropolitan Opera in New York; he opened his series with *Götterdämmerung* (Nov. 18, 1915). From 1916 to 1931 he was director of the Soc. of Friends of Music in N.Y.; from 1919 to 1922 he also conducted the New Sym. Orch. He made several practical arrangements of celebrated operas (*Oberon, Don Giovanni, Fidelio*, etc.), which he used for his productions with the Metropolitan Opera. His style of conducting was in the Mahler tradition, with emphasis on climactic effects and contrasts of light and shade.

Boehm, Karl. See **Böhm, Karl.**

Boelza, Igor (Feodorovich), Russian musicologist and composer; b. Kielce, Feb. 8, 1904; d. Moscow, Jan. 5, 1994. He received training in composition from Liatoshinsky at the Kiev Cons. (1922–25), and studied philology at the Univ. of Kiev. He was a teacher (1925–36) and a prof. (1936–41) at the Kiev Cons., and then settled in Moscow, where he was a prof. at the Cons. (1942–49). After taking his Ph.D. in 1951 with a diss. on Czech classical music at the Univ. of Moscow, he was on the staff of the Inst. for the History of the Arts (1954–61). Thereafter he was active with the Inst. of Slavonic Studies at the Academy of Sciences of the USSR. He wrote biographies of Mozart (Kiev, 1941), Borodin (Moscow, 1944; 2d ed., 1946), Dvořák (Moscow, 1949), Karlowicz (Moscow, 1951), Glière (Moscow, 1955; 2d ed., 1962), Vítězslav Novák (Moscow, 1957), Chopin (Moscow, 1960; 2d ed., 1968), and Oginsky (Moscow, 1965). His most important work, however, was done on the history of Czech and Polish music, and included books on Czech classical opera (Moscow, 1951), the history of Polish music culture (Moscow, 1954–73), the history of Czech music culture (Moscow, 1959–73), and a study of Slav music (Moscow, 1965).

Boero, Felipe, Argentine composer and teacher; b. Buenos Aires, May 1, 1884; d. there, Aug. 9, 1958. He studied with Pablo Berutti; received a government prize for further study in Europe, and attended the classes of Vidal and Fauré at the Paris Cons. (1912–14). Returning to Buenos Aires, he became active as a teacher. Among his operas, the following were first perf. at the Teatro Colón: *Tucumán* (June 29, 1918), *Ariana y Dionisios* (Aug. 5, 1920), *Raquela* (June 25, 1923), *Las Bacantes* (Sept. 19, 1925), *El Matrero* (July 12, 1929), and *Siripo* (June 8, 1937).

Boesch, Christian, Austrian baritone; b. Vienna, July 27, 1941. He pursued his training at the Vienna Hochschule für Musik, and in 1966 made his operatic debut at the Bern Stadttheater. He became a member of the Vienna Volksoper in 1975, later scoring notable success at the Salzburg Festival in 1978 for his portrayal of Papageno, a role he also chose for his Metropolitan Opera debut in New York on Feb. 17, 1979. He later sang Wozzeck and Masetto at the Metropolitan.

Boesmans, Philippe, Belgian composer; b. Tongeren, May 17, 1936. He studied composition with Froidebise and Pousseur, and piano at the Liège Cons. (1954–62). His music adheres to the abstract trends of cosmopolitan modernism, with structural formulas determining the contents. He composed the opera *Reigen* (1992).

Boettcher, Wilfried, German cellist and conductor; b. Bremen, Aug. 11, 1929; d. Uzes-Saint Siffret, France, Aug. 22, 1994. He studied cello with Arthur Troester at the Hamburg Hochschule für Musik (diploma, 1955) and with Fournier in Paris (1955–56). He was first cellist in the Bremen Radio Orch. (1948–50) and in the Hannover Opera orch. (1956–58). From 1958 to 1965 he was a prof. of cello at the Vienna Academy of Music. In 1959 he founded Die Wiener Solisten, which he conducted until 1966. From 1965 to 1974 he was a prof. at the Hamburg Hochschule für Musik. He also was chief conductor of the Hamburg Sym. Orch. (1967–71), and a conductor at the Hamburg State Opera (1970–73). From 1974 to 1978 he was principal guest conductor of the RAI Orch. in Turin. He also was a conductor at the Berlin Deutsche Oper (1975–82) and the Vienna State Opera (1977–82). In later years, he became closely associated as a conductor with several British orchs.

Bogatyrev, Anatoly (Vasilievich), Russian composer and teacher; b. Vitebsk, Aug. 13, 1913. He studied composition with Zolotarev at the Belorussian Cons. in Minsk, graduating in 1937; he was an instructor there from 1948. He wrote 2 patriotic operas: *In the Forests of Polesye* (Minsk, Aug. 28, 1939) and *Nadezhda Durova* (Minsk, Dec. 22, 1956).

Bogdanov-Berezovsky, Valerian (Mikhailovich), Russian musicologist and composer; b. Starozhilovka, near St. Petersburg, July 17, 1903; d. Moscow, May 13, 1971. He studied with Maximilian Steinberg and Liapunov at the Leningrad Cons., graduating in 1927. He taught there from 1945 to 1948, and was in charge of the artistic direction of the Leningrad Theater of Opera and Ballet from 1951 to 1962. He wrote the operas *The Frontier* (1941), *The Leningraders* (1943), and *Nastasia Filippovna*, after Dostoevsky's novel *The Idiot* (1964), and several ballets, including *The Seagull*, after Chekhov (1959). However, he was known chiefly as a critic and historian of Russian music.

BIBL.: I. Gusin, *V. B.-B.* (Leningrad, 1966).

Bogianckino, Massimo, Italian pianist, musicologist, and administrator; b. Rome, Nov. 10, 1922. He studied piano with Casella at the Accademia di Santa Cecilia in Rome and with Cortot at the École Normale de Musique in Paris; he also took courses in musicology with Ronga at the Univ. of Rome and with P. M. Masson at the Sorbonne in Paris. He taught at the Carnegie Inst. in Pittsburgh (1948–51), the Pesaro Cons. (1951–57), and the Rome Cons. (1957–67). In 1967 he joined the faculty of the Univ. of Perugia. He served as artistic director of the Rome Opera (1963–68), the Spoleto Festival of Two Worlds (1968–71), La Scala in Milan (1972–74), and the Teatro Comunale in Florence (from 1975). From 1983 to 1985 he was director of the Paris Opéra, then was mayor of Florence. He wrote the vols. *L'arte clavicembalistica di Domenico Scarlatti* (Rome, 1956; Eng. tr., 1968, as *The Harpsichord Sonatas of Domenico Scarlatti*) and *Aspetti del teatro musicale in Italia e in Francia nell'età barocca* (Rome, 1968).

Boguslawski, Edward, Polish composer; b. Chorzów, Sept. 22, 1940. He studied composition with Szabelski in Katowice and with Haubenstock-Ramati in Vienna. In 1963 he joined the faculty of the State College of Music in Katowice. His music makes use of impressionistic techniques. He composed *Beelzebub's Sonata*, chamber opera (Wroclaw, Nov. 19, 1977), and *The Game of Dreams*, musical drama (1985).

Boháč, Josef, Czech composer; b. Vienna, March 25, 1929. After training in Vienna, he was a student of Petrželka at the Janáček Academy of Music and Dramatic Art in Brno (1955–59). He later was active with Czech TV and the music publishing concern Panton. As a composer, he followed the median line of Central European modernism, with occasional resort to serial methods.

WORKS: DRAMATIC: *Námluvy* (The Courtship), comic opera (1967; Prague, March 18, 1971); *Goya*, opera (1972–77; Ostrava, Sept. 30, 1978); *Oči* (Eyes), television opera (1973; Czech TV, Prague, Oct. 5, 1974); *Zvířatka a Petrovští* (The Little Animals and Petrovští), opera (1980); *Zlatá svatba* (The Golden Wedding), comic opera (1981); *Rumcajs*, opera (1985).

Böhm, Karl, renowned Austrian conductor; b. Graz, Aug. 28, 1894; d. Salzburg, Aug. 14, 1981. He studied law before enrolling at the Graz Cons., where he took lessons in piano and theory; subsequently he studied musicology with Mandyczewski at the the Univ. of Vienna. After service in the Austrian Army during World War I, he made his debut as a conductor at the Graz Opera in 1917. He then completed his training in law at the Univ. of Graz (Dr.Jur., 1919). In 1920 he was appointed first conductor at the Graz Opera. Although he never took formal lessons in conducting, he soon acquired sufficient technique to be engaged at the Bavarian State Opera in Munich (1921). In 1927 he was appointed Generalmusikdirektor in Darmstadt; having already mastered a number of works by Mozart, Wagner, and Richard Strauss, he included in his repertoire modern operas by Krenek and Hindemith. In 1931 he conducted *Wozzeck* by Berg, a performance which Berg himself warmly praised. From 1931 to 1933 Böhm held the post of Generalmusikdirektor of the Hamburg Opera; from 1934 to 1943 he was music director of the Dresden State Opera, where he gave the first performances of *Die Schweigsame Frau* (June 24, 1935) and *Daphne* (Oct. 15, 1938), which Strauss dedicated to him. In 1943 he became director of the Vienna State Opera, but his tenure was a brief one due to its closure by the Nazis in 1944 and by its destruction by Allied bombing during the closing weeks of World War II in 1945. The rumors were rife of his at least passive adherence to the Nazis, although he categorically denied that he was ever a member of the party. After the war, he was not allowed by the Allied authorities to give performances pending an investigation of his political past; he was cleared and resumed his career in 1947. From 1950 to 1953 he conducted the German repertoire at the Teatro Colón in Buenos Aires. He then served again as director of the Vienna State Opera from 1954 to 1956. On Nov. 5, 1955, he conducted Beethoven's *Fidelio* at the opening of the reconstructed Vienna State Opera House. He made his first appearance in the United States with the Chicago Sym. Orch. on Feb. 9, 1956; on Oct. 31, 1957, he made his first appearance at the Metropolitan Opera in New York with Mozart's *Don Giovanni*. He continued to conduct occasional performances at the Metropolitan until 1978. In 1961 he took the Berlin Phil. to the United States, and in 1963–64 he made a tour in Japan with it. In 1975 he conducted an American tour with the Deutsche Oper of Berlin. In 1979 he took the Vienna State Opera on its first U.S. tour. He also conducted radio and television performances. Böhm received numerous honors and tokens of distinction, among them the Golden Mozart Memorial Medal from the International Mozarteum Foundation in Salzburg, the Brahms Medal from Hamburg, and the Brückner Ring from the Vienna Sym. Orch. On his 70th birthday, a Böhm Day was celebrated in Vienna, and he was granted the rare honorary title of Generalmusikdirektor of Austria; both his 80th and 85th birthdays were observed in Salzburg and Vienna. In 1977 he was elected president of the London Sym. Orch. Böhm was admired for his impeccable rendition of classical opera scores, particularly those of Mozart, in which he scrupulously avoided any suggestion of improper romanticization; he was equally extolled for his productions of the operas of Wagner and Richard Strauss, and he earned additional respect for his authoritative performances of the Austro-German orch. repertoire. He publ. *Begegnung mit Richard Strauss* (Munich, 1964) and a personal memoir, *Ich erinnere mich ganz genau* (Zürich, 1968; Eng. tr., 1992, as *A Life Remembered: Memoirs*).

BIBL.: F. Endler, *K. B.: Ein Dirigentenleben* (Hamburg, 1981); H. Hoyer, *K. B. an der Wiener Staatsoper: Eine Dokumentation* (Vienna, 1981).

Böhme, Kurt (Gerhard), distinguished German bass; b. Dresden, May 5, 1908; d. Munich, Dec. 20, 1989. He was a student of Adolf Kluge at the Dresden Cons. In 1930 he made his operatic debut as Caspar in *Der Freischütz* at the Dresden State Opera, where he remained as one of its principal artists until 1950; then was a member of the Bavarian State Opera in Munich. In 1936 he made his first appearance at London's Covent Garden with the visiting Dresden State Opera; later made regular appearances there from 1956 to 1970; he also was a guest artist in Vienna, Bayreuth, and Milan. On Nov. 11, 1954, he made his Metropolitan Opera debut in New York as Pogner, and was again on its roster in 1956–57. Böhme was especially admired for his Wagnerian roles, but he also won great acclaim as Baron Ochs.

Bohnen, (Franz) Michael, noted German bass-baritone; b. Cologne, May 2, 1887; d. Berlin, April 26, 1965. He received training from Fritz Steinbach and Schulz-Dornburg at the Cologne Cons. In 1910 he made his operatic debut as Caspar in *Der Freischütz* in Düsseldorf. After singing in Wiesbaden (1912–13), he was a highly respected member of the Berlin Royal (later State) Opera from 1913 to 1921. He also made debuts in 1914 at London's Covent Garden and the Bayreuth Festival. On March 1, 1923, he made his Metropolitan Opera debut in New York as the Tourist/Francesco in Schillings's *Mona Lisa*, remaining on its roster until 1932. On Jan. 19, 1929, he sang the leading role there in the U.S. premiere of Krenek's *Jonny spielt auf.* From 1933 to 1945 he sang at the Berlin Deutsches Opernhaus, and subsequently served as Intendant at the renamed Städtische Oper from 1945 to 1947. He was equally well versed in baritone and bass roles, numbering among his finest Sarastro, Wotan, King Marke, Hagen, Gurnemanz, Méphistophélès, Baron Ochs, and Scarpia.

Boieldieu, François-Adrien, celebrated French opera composer; b. Rouen, Dec. 16, 1775; d. Jarcy, near Grosbois, Oct. 8, 1834. His father was a clerical functionary who at one time served as secretary to Archbishop Larochefoucauld; his mother owned a millinery shop; the parents were divorced in 1794. Boieldieu received his musical instruction from Charles Broche, then was apprenticed to Broche as an assistant organist at the church of St. André in Rouen. When he was 17 his first opera, *La Fille coupable* (to his father's libretto), achieved a production in Rouen (Nov. 2, 1793). He composed patriotic pieces which were in demand during the revolutionary period. His *Chant populaire pour la Fête de la Raison* for Chorus and Orch. was presented at the Temple of Reason (former cathedral) in Rouen on Nov. 30, 1793. His 2d opera, *Rosalie et Myrza*, was also staged in Rouen (Oct. 28, 1795). He was befriended by the composer Louis Jadin and the piano manufacturer Erard; he met Cherubini and Méhul, and made a tour in Normandy with the tenor Garat. A facile composer, Boieldieu produced one opera after another and had no difficulties in having them staged in Paris. Particularly successful was *Le Calife de Bagdad* (Paris, Sept. 16, 1800), which appealed to the public because of its exotic subject and pseudo-oriental arias. On March 19, 1802, Boieldieu married the dancer Clotilde Mafleurai, but separated from her the following year. Opportunely, he received an invitation to go to Russia. His contract called for an attractive salary of 4,000 rubles annually, in return for writing operas for the Imperial theaters in St. Petersburg. He attended to his duties conscientiously, and produced operas every year. His salary was raised, but Boieldieu decided to leave Russia in 1811 and return to Paris. His estranged wife died in 1826, and Boieldieu married the singer Jenny Phillis. True to his custom, he resumed composing operas for the Paris theaters. In 1817 he was appointed prof. of composition at the Paris Cons.; he resigned in 1826. In 1821 he was named a Chevalier of the Légion d'honneur. After a number of insignificant productions, he achieved his greatest success with his Romantic opera *La Dame blanche*, fashioned after Walter Scott's novels *The Monastery* and *Guy Mannering*; the dramatic subject and the effective musical setting corresponded precisely to the tastes of the public of the time. It was produced at the Opéra Comique in Paris on Dec. 10, 1825, and became a perennial success in Paris and elsewhere; it was produced in London on Oct. 9, 1826, and in N.Y. on Aug. 24, 1827. In 1833 he received a grant of 6,000 francs from the French government and retired to his country house at Jarcy, where he died. During the last years of his life he became interested in painting; his pictures show a modest talent in landscape. He was also successful as a teacher, numbering among his pupils Fétis, Adam, and P. J. G. Zimmerman. Boieldieu composed about 40 operas, of which several were written in collaboration with Méhul, Berton, Hérold, Cherubini, Catel, Isouard, Kreutzer, and Auber; 9 of these operas are lost. Boieldieu's significance in the history of French opera is great, even though the nationalistic hopes of the French music critics and others that he would rival Rossini did not materialize; Boieldieu simply lacked the tremendous power of invention, both in dramatic and comic aspects, that made Rossini a magician of 19th-century opera. Boieldieu's natural son, Adrien-Louis-Victor Boieldieu (b. Paris, Nov. 3, 1815; d. Quincy, July 9, 1883), was also a composer; his mother was Thérèse Regnault, a singer. He wrote 10 operas, including *Marguerite*, which was sketched by his father but left incomplete, and *L'Aïeule*.

WORKS: OPERAS: *La Fille coupable* (Rouen, Nov. 2, 1793); *Rosalie et Myrza* (Rouen, Oct. 28, 1795); *La Famille suisse* (Paris, Feb. 11, 1797); *Zoraine et Zulnare* (Paris, May 10, 1798); *La Dôt de Suzette* (Paris, Sept. 5, 1798); *Beniowski* (Paris, June 8, 1800); *Le Calife de Bagdad* (Paris, Sept. 16, 1800); *Ma tante Aurore* (Paris, Jan. 13, 1803); *Aline, reine de Golconda* (St. Petersburg, March 17, 1804); *Abderkhan* (St. Petersburg, Aug. 7, 1804); *La Jeune Femme colère* (St. Petersburg, April 30, 1805); *Un Tour de soubrette* (St. Petersburg, April 28, 1806); *Télémaque dans l'isle de Calypso* (St. Petersburg, Dec. 28, 1806); *Les Voitures versées* (St. Petersburg, April 16, 1808); *Rien de trop ou Les Deux Paravents* (St. Petersburg, Jan. 6, 1811); *Jean de Paris* (Paris, April 4, 1812); *Le Nouveau Seigneur de village* (Paris, June 29, 1813); *La Fête du village voisin* (Paris, March 5, 1816); *Le Petit Chaperon rouge* (Paris, June 30, 1818); *La Dame blanche* (Paris, Dec. 10, 1825). The following operas were products of collaboration: *La Prisonnière*, with Cherubini (1799); *Le Baiser et la quittance*, with Méhul, Kreutzer, and others (1803); *Bayard à Mézières*, with Cherubini, Catel, and Isouard (1803); *Les Béarnais, ou Henry IV en voyage*, with Kreutzer (1814); *Angéla, ou L'Atelier de Jean Cousin*, with Mme. Gail, a pupil of Fétis (1814); *Charles de France, ou Amour et gloire*, with Hérold (1816); *Blanche de Provence, ou La Cour des fées*, with Cherubini, Berton, and others (1821); *Les Trois Genres*, with Auber (1824); *La Marquise de Brinvilliers*, with Berton and others (1831).

BIBL.: G. Favre, *B.: Sa vie, son oeuvre* (2 parts, 1944–45).

Boismortier, Joseph Bodin de, French composer; b. Thionville, Moselle, Dec. 23, 1689; d. Roissy-en-Brie, Oct. 28, 1755. He lived in Metz and Perpignan before settling in Paris in 1724. A prolific composer of instrumental music, he wrote more than 100 opus numbers. He also wrote 3 ballet operas: *Les Voyages de l'Amour* (1736), *Don Quichotte* (1743), and *Daphnis et Chloé* (1747).

Boito, Arrigo (baptismal name, **Enrico**), important Italian poet and opera composer; b. Padua, Feb. 24, 1842; d. Milan, June 10, 1918. He studied at the Milan Cons. with Alberto Mazzucato and Ronchetti-Monteviti. His 2 cantatas, *Il 4 Giugno* (1860) and *Le Sorelle d'Italia* (1861), written in collaboration with Faccio, were performed at the Cons., and attracted a great deal of favorable attention; as a result, the Italian government granted the composers a gold medal and a stipend for foreign travel for 2 years. Boito spent most of his time in Paris, and also went to Poland to meet the family of his mother (who was Polish); he also visited Germany, Belgium, and England. He was strongly influenced by new French and German music. Upon his return to Milan, he undertook the composition of his first and most significant large opera, *Mefistofele*, which contains elements of conventional Italian opera but also dramatic ideas stemming from Beethoven and Wagner. It was performed for the first time at La Scala (March 5, 1868). A controversy followed when a part of the audience objected to the unusual treatment of the subject and the music, and there were actual disorders at the conclusion of the performance. After the 2d production, the opera was taken off the boards, and Boito undertook a revision to effect a compromise. In this new version, the opera had a successful run in Italian cities; it was also produced in Hamburg (1880), in London (in Italian, July 6, 1880), and in Boston (in Eng., Nov. 16, 1880). It was retained in the repertoire of the leading opera houses, but its success never matched that of Gounod's *Faust*. Boito never completed his 2d opera, *Nerone*, on which he worked for more than half a century (from 1862 to 1916). The orch. score was revised by Toscanini and performed by him at La Scala on May 1, 1924. There are sketches for an earlier opera, *Ero e Leandro*, but not enough material to attempt a completion. Boito's gift as a poet is fully equal to that as a composer. He publ. a book of verses (Turin, 1877) under the anagrammatic pen name of Tobia Gorrio; he wrote his own librettos for his operas and made admirable trs. of Wagner's operas (*Tristan und Isolde; Rienzi*). He wrote the librettos of *Otello* and *Falstaff* for Verdi, which are regarded as his masterpieces; also for *Gioconda* by Ponchielli, *Amleto* by Faccio, etc. Boito also publ. novels. He held various honorary titles from the king of Italy; in 1892 he was appointed inspector-general of Italian conservatories; was made honorary D.Mus. by the Univ. of Cambridge and the Univ. of Oxford; in 1912 he was made a senator by the king of Italy. Boito's letters were ed. by R. de Rensis (Rome, 1932), who also ed. Boito's articles on music (Milan, 1931).

BIBL.: A. Boccardi, *A. B.* (Trieste, 1877); R. Giani, *Il Nerone di A. B.* (Turin, 1901); M. Risolo, *Il primo Mefistofele di A. B.* (Naples, 1916); A. Pompeati, *A. B.* (Florence, 1919); C. Ricci, *A. B.* (Milan, 1919); V. Gui, *Il Nerone di A. B.* (Milan, 1924); A. Bonaventura, *A. B.; Mefistofele* (Milan, 1924); F. Ballo, *A. B.* (Turin, 1938); R. de Rensis, *A. B.; Aneddoti e bizzarrie poetiche e musicali* (Rome, 1942); P. Nardi, *Vita di A. B.* (Verona, 1942; 2d ed., Milan, 1944); M. Vajro, *A. B.* (Brescia, 1955); G. Mariani, *A. B.* (Parma, 1973); G. Scarsi, *Rapporto poesia-musica in A. B.* (Rome, 1973); D. Del Nero, *A. B.: Un artista europeo* (Florence, 1995).

Bok, Mary Louise Curtis, munificent American music patroness; b. Boston, Aug. 6, 1876; d. Philadelphia, Jan. 4, 1970. She inherited her fortune from Cyrus H. K. Curtis, founder of the Curtis Publishing Co. In 1917 she founded the Settlement School of Music in Philadelphia. In 1924 she established in Philadelphia the Curtis Inst. of Music and endowed it initially with a gift of $12.5 million in memory of her mother. The school had a faculty of the most distinguished American and European musicians, and it provided tuition exclusively on a scholarship basis; many talented composers and performers were among its students, including Bernstein, Barber, and Foss. She was first married to Edward W. Bok, in 1896, who died in 1930; in 1943 she married the eminent Russian-born American violinist and pedagogue Efrem Zimbalist (b. Rostov-na-Donu, April 21, 1889; d. Reno, Nev., Feb. 22, 1985), who was director of the Curtis Inst. from 1941 until 1968. In 1932 she received an honorary doctorate from the Univ. of Pa., and, in 1934, an honorary doctorate from Williams College.

BIBL.: E. Viles, *M.L.C.B. Zimbalist: Founder of the Curtis Institute of Music and Patron of American Arts* (diss., Bryn Mawr College, 1983).

Bokor, Margit, Hungarian soprano; b. Losoncz, near Budapest, 1905; d. N.Y., Nov. 9, 1949. She received her training in Budapest and Vienna. After making her operatic debut in Budapest (1928), she sang in Berlin (1930) and then with the Dresden State Opera (1931–35), where she created the role of Zdenka in Strauss's *Arabella* in 1933. Following appearances at the Salzburg Festival (from 1934) and the Vienna State Opera (1935–38), she settled in the United States. After appearances in Chicago and Philadelphia, on April 6, 1947, she made her N.Y. City Opera debut as the Composer in *Ariadne*.

Bolcom, William (Elden), American pianist and composer; b. Seattle, May 26, 1938. He studied at the Univ. of Wash. in Seattle with John Verrall (B.A., 1958); he took a course in composition with Milhaud at Mills College in Oakland, California (M.A., 1961); he attended classes in advanced composition with Leland Smith at Stanford Univ. (D.M.A., 1964), and studied at the Paris Cons. (2d prize in composition, 1965). He received Guggenheim fellowships in 1964–65 and 1968–69. He taught at the Univ. of Wash. in Seattle (1965–66), Queens College of the City Univ. of N.Y. (1966–68), and the N.Y. Univ. School of the Arts (1969–70). He joined the faculty of the school of music at the Univ. of Mich. in 1973; he was made a full prof. in 1983. He was composer-in-residence of the Detroit Sym. Orch. (from 1987). In 1988 he won the Pulitzer Prize in music for his *12 New Études* for Piano. In 1993 he was elected a member of the American Academy and Inst. of Arts and Letters. After absorbing a variety of techniques sine ira et studio, he began to experiment widely and wildly in serial thematics, musical collage, sophisticated intentional plagiarism, and microtonal electronics. He composed various works for the stage, including *Dynamite Tonite*, actors' opera (N.Y., Dec. 21, 1963), *Greatshot*, actors' opera (1969), *Theatre of the Absurd* for Actor and Chamber Group (1970), *The Beggar's Opera*, an adaptation of John Gay's work, for Actors and Chamber Orch. (1978), *Casino Paradise*, musical theater opera (Philadelphia, April 1990), and *McTeague*, opera (Chicago, Oct. 31, 1992). He was also active as a pianist, recording and giving recitals of ragtime piano; in 1975 he married **Joan Morris**, with whom he appeared in concerts. He publ., with Robert Kimball, a book on the black American songwriting and musical comedy team of Noble Sissle and Eubie Blake, *Reminiscing with Sissle and Blake* (N.Y., 1973); also ed. the collected essays of George Rochberg, under the title *The Aesthetics of Survival: A Composer's View of Twentieth-Century Music* (Ann Arbor, Mich., 1984).

Boldemann, Laci, Finnish-born Swedish composer; b. Helsinki, April 24, 1921; d. Munich, Aug. 18, 1969. He studied piano and conducting at the Royal Academy of Music in London. At the outbreak of World War II in 1939, he went to Sweden and pursued piano training with Gunnar de Frumerie. After being compelled to return to Germany for army service, he saw action in the campaigns in the Soviet Union, Poland, and Italy before being captured by the Allies. He was a prisoner-of-war in the United States for 2 years; upon his release at the end of the war, he returned to Sweden to pursue his career as a composer. He was also active as a teacher and from 1963 to 1969 was secretary and treasurer of the Swedish Composers' Soc. Boldemann's output was the work of a solid craftsman who placed great store in lyrical invention. His works for the stage include *Svart är vitt, sa kejsaren* (Black Is White, Said the Emperor), fairy tale opera (1964; Stockholm, Jan. 1, 1965), *Dårskapens timme* (Hour of Madness), opera-musical (Malmö, March 22, 1968), and *Och så drommer han om Per Jonathan* (And He Dreams of Per Jonathan), operatic scene (Stockholm, Nov. 29, 1969).

Bolshakov, Nikolai, Russian tenor; b. Kharkov, Nov. 23, 1874; d. Leningrad, Jan. 20, 1958. He studied in St. Petersburg; made his debut there with the Kharkov Opera Co. in 1899; in 1902 he went to Milan, where he studied voice with A. Brogi; he then sang with the Maryinsky Theater in St. Petersburg (1906–29); he participated in the spectacles of Diaghilev's "Russian Seasons" in Paris and London (1911–13); he also gave recitals. From 1923 to 1953 he taught voice at the Leningrad Cons. He was noted for his interpretations of Faust and Don José.

Bolton, Ivor, English conductor; b. Lancashire, May 17, 1958. He was educated at Clare College, Cambridge (Mus.B.; M.A.), at the Royal College of Music in London, and at the National Opera Studio. In 1981–82 he was conductor of the Schola Cantorum at Oxford. From 1982 to 1990 he was music director at St. James's, Piccadilly. He was founder-director of the St. James's Baroque Players in London from 1984, and also founder-music director of the Lufthansa Festival of Baroque Music from 1985. After serving as chorus master at the Glyndebourne Festival (1985–88), he returned there to conduct Gluck's *Orfeo* in 1989. From 1990 to 1993 he was music director of the English Touring Opera. He made his first appearance at the English National Opera in London conducting *Xerxes* in 1992, the same year he became music director of the Glyndebourne Touring Opera. From 1993 to 1996 he also was chief conductor of the Scottish Chamber Orch. in Glasgow. In 1995 he made his debut at London's Covent Garden conducting the premiere of Goehr's *Arianna*. He was a conductor at the Munich Festival in 1997. In addition to various guest conducting engagements with opera companies, he also appeared as a guest conductor with many British orchs.

Bolzoni, Giovanni, Italian composer and conductor; b. Parma, May 14, 1841; d. Turin, Feb. 21, 1919. He studied at the Parma Cons. He was active as a conductor in Perugia; served as director and prof. of composition at the Liceo Musicale in Turin (1887–1916); also conducted at the Teatro Regio there (1884–89). His most successful operas were *Il matrimonio civile* (Parma, 1870), *La stella delle Alpi* (Savona, 1876), and *Jella* (Piacenza, 1881).

Bon, Willem Frederik, Dutch composer and conductor; b. Amersfoort, June 15, 1940; d. Nijeholtpade, April 14, 1983. He studied clarinet, conducting, and composition at the Amsterdam Cons. and the Royal Cons. of Music at The Hague, receiving a conducting diploma in 1971. In 1972 he became conductor of the Eindhoven Baroque Ensemble, and in 1973 was named an assistant conductor of the Concertgebouw Orch. in Amsterdam. At the time of his death, he taught composition at the Groningen Cons. His works include *Erik's wonderbaarlijke reis* (Erik's Miraculous Journey), instrumental opera for Children, Narrator, and Orch. (1979).

Bonaventura, Arnaldo, Italian musicologist; b. Livorno, July 28, 1862; d. Florence, Oct. 7, 1952. He studied law, violin, and theory, but made musicology his career. He was a prof. of music history and librarian at the Florence Istituto Musicale until 1932, then became director and prof. of music history and aesthetics at the Florence Cons. His many writings include *Giacomo Puccini: L'uomo-l'artista* (Livorno, 1925), *L'opera italiana* (Florence, 1928), and *Rossini* (Florence, 1934).

Bonci, Alessandro, Italian tenor; b. Cesena, Feb. 10, 1870; d. Viserba, Aug. 8, 1940. He studied with Pedrotti and Coen in Pesaro, and with Delle Sedie in Paris. On Jan. 20, 1896, he made his operatic debut as Fenton in Parma; after appearances at Milan's La Scala (1897) and London's Covent Garden (debut as Rodolfo, 1900), he toured throughout Europe. On Dec. 3, 1906, he sang Lord Arthur Talbot in *I Puritani* at the opening of the new Manhattan Opera House in New York. On Nov. 22, 1907, he made his Metropolitan Opera debut in New York as the Duke of Mantua, and remained on its roster until 1910. He later sang in Chicago (1919–21) and at the Teatro Costanzi in Rome (1922–23) before settling in Milan as a voice teacher. Among his best roles were Count Almaviva, Ottavio, Wilhelm Meister, and Rodolfo. He also appeared in German lieder recitals.

Bond, Victoria, American conductor and composer; b. Los Angeles, May 6, 1945. Her father was a physician and an opera singer and her mother was a pianist. Following initial music instruction from her mother, she attended the Mannes School of Music in New York and pursued piano training with Nadia Reisenberg. Returning to Los Angeles, she studied composition with Dahl at the Univ. of Southern Calif. (B.M.A., 1968), and also worked with Paul Glass. Upon returning to New York, she pursued studies in composition with Sessions and in conducting with Morel, Ehrling, Karajan, Slatkin, and Blomstedt at the Juilliard School (M.M.A., 1975; D.M.A., 1977), where she also was an assistant to Boulez and the first woman to take a doctorate in orchestral conducting. She was an Exxon-Arts Endowment conductor with the Pittsburgh Sym. Orch. (1978–80), and concurrently music director of the Pittsburgh Youth Orch. From 1982 to 1986 she was music director of the Empire State Youth Orch. in Albany, and from 1982 to 1988 music director of the Bel Canto Opera in New York. She was music director of the Roanoke Sym. Orch. (1986–95) and artistic director of Opera Roanoke (1989–95). As a guest conductor, she appeared widely in the United States, Europe, and Asia. She has made special effort to champion out-of-the-ordinary repertoire, including scores by women composers. Among her own compositions is the opera *Gulliver* (1988; rev. 1995 as *Travels*) and the ballets *Equinox* (1978), *Other Selves* (1979), *Sandburg Suite* (1980), and *Great Gallopin' Gottschalk* (1981).

Bondeville, Emmanuel (Pièrre Georges) de, French composer; b. Rouen, Oct. 29, 1898; d. Paris, Nov. 26, 1987. He studied organ in Rouen and composition at the Paris Cons. He served as music director of the Eiffel Tower radio station (1935–49), artistic director of the Monte Carlo Opera (1945–49), and director of the Paris Opéra (1952–70). In 1959 he was elected a member of the Académie des Beaux-Arts of the Institut de France. His works include 3 operas: *L'École des maris* (Paris, June 19, 1935), *Madame Bovary* (Paris, June 1, 1951), and *Antoine et Cléopâtre* (Rouen, March 10, 1974).

Bondon, Jacques (Lauret Jules Désiré), French composer; b. Boulbon, Bouches-du-Rhône, Dec. 6, 1927. He studied violin and painting. In 1945 he settled in Paris, where he was a student of Dandelot, Koechlin, Milhaud, and Rivier. In 1963 he became a member of the music committee of the ORTF. In 1981 he became director of the Georges Bizet Cons. In 1979 he won the composition prize of the Institut de France. After early experimentation with ultramodern techniques, he tergiversated to prudential modernism. He composed *Mélusine au rocher*, radio opera (1968; Luxembourg, Oct. 30, 1969), *Ana et l'albatros*, opera (Metz, Nov. 21, 1970), and *i. 330*, opera-ballet (Nantes, May 20, 1975).

Bonelli, (Bunn), Richard, American baritone; b. Port Byron, N.Y., Feb. 6, 1887; d. Los Angeles, June 7, 1980. He studied at Syracuse Univ. and with Arthur Alexander and Jean de Reszke in Paris. On April 21, 1915, he made his operatic debut as Valentine at the Brooklyn Academy of Music. After appearances at the Monte Carlo Opera, Milan's La Scala, and in Paris, he sang with the Chicago Opera (1925–31). On Dec. 1, 1932, he made his Metropolitan Opera debut in New York as Germont, remaining on its roster until 1945. Thereafter he taught at the Curtis Inst. of Music in Philadelphia and in New York He was best known for his Verdi roles, but also was praised for his portrayals of Wolfram, Tonio, and Sharpless.

Bongartz, Heinz, German conductor; b. Krefeld, July 31, 1894; d. Dresden, May 2, 1978. He studied in Krefeld, and then at the Cologne Cons. with Fritz Steinbach (conducting), Otto Neitzel (composition), and Elly Ney (piano). In 1923 he became director of the Mönchen-Gladbach Opera. With Oskar Fried, he was conductor of the Blüthner-Orch. in Berlin (1924–26). After conducting in Meiningen (1926–31), he was music director in Gotha (1931–33), 1st conductor in Kassel (1933–37), Generalmusikdirektor in Saarbrücken (1937–44), and chief conductor of the Pfalz Orch. in Ludwigshafen (1944–46). In 1946–47 he was a prof. at the Leipzig Hochschule für Musik. From 1947 to 1964 he was chief conductor of the Dresden Phil.

Boninsegna, Celestina, Italian soprano; b. Reggio Emilia, Feb. 26, 1877; d. Milan, Feb. 14, 1947. Without the benefit of vocal training, she made her debut at the age of 15 at Reggio Emilia as Norina; then enrolled at the Pesaro Cons.; her official debut took place in Fano in 1896, when she appeared as Gilda, then sang in Milan, Rome, Genoa, and South America; also at London's Covent Garden (1904, 1905). On Dec. 21, 1906, she made her Metropolitan Opera debut in New York as Aida, but remained on the roster for only that 1 season. In 1909–10 she sang with the Boston Opera. Following her retirement she taught voice and spent her last years in the Casa di Riposo in Milan.

Bonner, Eugene (MacDonald), American composer and music critic; b. Jacksonville, N.C., 1889; d. Taormina, Sicily, Dec. 8, 1983. He studied at the Peabody Cons. of Music in Baltimore and received training in piano with Bachner and Hutcheson, in organ with Philips, and in composition with Bois and Brockway; during a European sojourn (1911–17), he pursued studies in composition and instrumentation with Scott, Lehmann, and Bedford; during a 2d European sojourn, he took courses in instrumentation and conducting with Wolff in Paris (1921–27). Returning to the United States, he became music ed. of *Outlook Magazine* (1927–29); subsequently he was a music critic for the *Brooklyn Eagle*, the *Daily Mirror, Cue Magazine*, and the *N.Y. Herald Tribune*, and managing ed. of the *Musical Record*. In 1955 he settled in Taormina. His compositions include the operas *Barbara Frietchie* (1921), *Celui qui Épousa une Femme Muette* (1923), *The Venetian Glass Nephew* (1927), *The Gods of the Mountain* (1936), and *Frankie and Johnnie* (1945); also incidental music to *The Young Alexander* (1929).

Bonney, Barbara, American soprano; b. Montclair, N.J., April 14, 1956. She received training in Canada and with Walter Raninger at the Salzburg Mozarteum. In 1979 she became a member of the Darmstadt Opera, where she made her first appearance as Anna in *Die lustigen Weiber von Windsor*; among her subsequent roles were Blondchen, Adina, Cherubino, Gilda, Massenet's Manon, and Natalie in Henze's *Der Prinz von Homburg*. In 1983–84 she appeared with the Frankfurt am Main Opera, the Hamburg State Opera, and the Bavarian State Opera in Munich. In 1984 she made her first appearance at London's Covent Garden as Sophie. In 1985 she made her debut at Milan's La Scala as Pamina. She made her Metropolitan Opera debut in New York on March 3, 1988, as Najade in *Ariadne auf Naxos*, where she returned to sing Adele and Sophie. In 1989 she made her first appearance at the Chicago Lyric Opera as Adele. In 1991 she sang in the Mozart Bicentenary Gala at Covent Garden. After singing Sophie at the Metropolitan Opera that year, she returned there as Adina in 1996 and as Susanna in 1997. She was engaged in 1997 as a soloist in the centenary performance of the Brahms *Requiem* in Vienna. On Aug. 7, 1997 she made her N.Y. recital debut at Alice Tully Hall, followed by her Carnegie Hall recital debut on Jan. 31, 1998. Her husband is **Håkan Hagegård**.

Bonno, Giuseppe, noted Austrian composer of Italian descent; b. Vienna, Jan. 29, 1711; d. there, April 15, 1788. His father, Lucrezio Bonno, was the imperial footman. Giuseppe Bonno began his musical studies with Johann Georg Reinhardt, the court organist. Charles VI sent Bonno to Naples in 1726 for further musical education; there he studied composition with Durante and Leo. His first opera, *Nigella e Nise*, was performed in Naples in 1732. In 1736 he returned to Vienna, where he brought out his 2d opera, *L'amore insuperabile*. In 1737 he was made a court scholar in composition, and in 1739 was named court composer. In 1739 he brought out his oratorio *Eleazaro*, which proved highly successful. He subsequently joined Gluck and Dittersdorf as a Kapellmeister to Field Marshall Joseph Friedrich, prince of Sachsen-Hildburghausen, in Schlosshof and Mannersdorf. In 1774 he succeeded Gassmann as Imperial Court Kapellmeister. Bonno was greatly esteemed as a teacher; Dittersdorf and Marianne di Martinez were among his pupils. He was a friend of the Mozart family, and recognized the budding genius of Mozart at an early date.

WORKS: DRAMATIC (all 1st perf. at the Burgtheater in Vienna unless otherwise given): *Nigella e Nise*, pastorale (Naples, 1732); *L'amore insuperabile*, festa di camera (July 26, 1736); *Trajano*, festa di camera (Oct. 1, 1736); *La gara del genio con Giunone*, serenata (Laxenburg, May 13, 1737); *Alessandro Severo*, festa di camera (Oct. 1, 1737); *La generosità di Artaserse*, serenata (Nov. 4, 1737); a pastorale (Nov. 19, 1737); *La pace richiamata*, festa di camera (July 26, 1738); *La pietà di Numa*, festa di camera (Oct. 1, 1738); *La vera nobilità*, festa di camera (July 26, 1739); *Il natale di Numa Pompilio*, festa di camera (Oct. 1, 1739); *Il nume d'Atene*, festa di camera (Nov. 19, 1739); *La generosa Spartana*, serenata (Laxenburg, May 13, 1740); *Il natale di Giove*, azione teatrale (Favorita, Vienna, Oct. 1, 1740); *Il vero omaggio*, componimento drammatico (Schloss Schönbrunn, Vienna, March 13, 1743); *La danza*, cantata (April 1744); *Danae*, opera (1744; not extant); *Ezio*, opera (1749; not extant); *Il Re pastore*, dramma per musica (Schloss Schönbrunn, Vienna, Oct. 27, 1751); *L'Ero cinese*, opera (Schloss Schönbrunn, Vienna, May 13, 1752); *L'isola disabitata*, azione teatrale (Sept. 23, 1754); *Didone abbandonata*, opera (1752; not extant); *Colloquio amoroso fra Piramo e Tisbe* (1757); *Complimento*, for the Prince of Sachsen-Hildburghausen (1761; not extant); *L'Atenaide ovvero Gli affetti più generosi*, azione teatrale (1762); *Il sogno di Scipione* (1763); also, in collaboration with others, *Catone in Utica* (1742) and *L'Armida placata* (Oct. 8, 1750). ORATORIOS: (all perf. in Vienna): *Eleazaro* (1739); *San Paolo in Athene* (March 31, 1740); *Isacco figura del redentore* (March 18, 1759); *Il Giuseppe riconosciuto* (March 20, 1774).

BIBL.: K. Breitner, *G. B. und sein Oratorienwerk* (diss., Univ. of Vienna, 1961).

Bononcini, Antonio Maria, Italian composer, brother of **Giovanni Bononcini**; b. Modena, June 18, 1677; d. there, July 8, 1726. His father was the composer Giovanni Maria Bononcini (b. Montecorone, Sept. 23, 1642; d. Modena, Nov. 18, 1678). He studied with his father, his first success coming with the production of his opera *Il trionfo di Camilla, regina dei Volsci* (Naples, Dec. 26, 1696). This opera was produced in many other theaters in Italy, sometimes under different titles, as *Amore per amore, La fede in cimento*, etc. It was presented in London (March 31, 1706) with great acclaim. In 1702 Bononcini was in Berlin; from 1704 to 1711 he was in Vienna, where he produced the operas *Teraspo* (Nov. 15, 1704), *Arminio* (July 26, 1706), *La conquista delle Spagne di Scipione Africano* (Oct. 1, 1707), *La presa di Tebe* (Oct. 1, 1708), and *Tigrane, re d'Armenia* (July 26, 1710). Returning to Italy, he produced the following operas in Milan: *Il Tiranno eroe* (Dec. 26, 1715), *Sesostri, re di Egitto* (Feb. 2, 1716), and *Griselda* (Dec. 26, 1718). In his native town of Modena, he directed his operas *L'enigma disciolto* (Oct. 15, 1716) and *Lucio Vero* (Nov. 5, 1716). His last opera, *Rosiclea in Dania*, was staged in Naples (Oct. 1, 1721). He wrote 19 operas in all, and 3 oratorios. His most famous opera, *Il trionfo di Camilla*, has often been erroneously attributed to his brother; several songs from it were publ. in London by Walsh.

BIBL.: L. F. Valdrighi, *I B. da Modena* (Modena, 1882).

Bononcini, Giovanni (not Giovanni Battista, despite the fact that this name appears on some of his compositions), Italian composer, brother of **Antonio Maria Bononcini**; b. Modena, July 18, 1670; d. Vienna, July 9, 1747. His father was the composer Giovanni Maria Bononcini (b. Montecorone, Sept. 23, 1642; d. Modena, Nov. 18, 1678). His first teacher was his father; he also studied with G. P. Colonna in Bologna, and took cello lessons from Giorgio. In 1687 he was a cellist in the chapel of S. Petronio in Bologna; in the same year he became maestro di cappella at S. Giovanni in Monte. He publ. his first work, *Trattenimenti da camera* for String Trio, in Bologna at the age of 15. In 1691 he went to Rome, where he produced his first opera, *Serse* (Jan. 25, 1694), and shortly afterward, another opera, *Tullo Ostilio* (Feb. 1694). In 1698 he went to Vienna as court composer; there he brought out his operas *La fede pubblica* (Jan. 6, 1699) and *Gli affetti piu grandi vinti dal piu giusto* (July 26, 1701). He spent 2 years (1702–4) at the court of Queen Sophie Charlotte in Berlin; at her palace in Charlottenburg he produced, in the summer of 1702, the opera *Polifemo*, and a new opera, *Gli amori di Cefalo e Procri* (Oct. 16, 1704). After the Queen's death (Feb. 1, 1705) the opera company was disbanded; Bononcini returned to Vienna and staged the following operas: *Endimione* (July 10, 1706), *Turno Aricino* (July 26, 1707), *Mario fuggitivo* (1708), *Abdolonimo* (Feb. 3, 1709), and *Muzio Scevola* (July 10, 1710). In 1711 Bononcini returned to Italy with his brother (who had also been in Vienna). In 1719 he was in Rome, where he produced the opera *Erminia*. In 1720 he received an invitation to join the Royal Academy of Music in London, of which Handel was director, and the Italian Opera Co. connected with it. A famous rivalry developed between the supporters of Handel, which included the king, and the group of noblemen (Marlborough, Queensberry, Rutland, and Sunderland) who favored Bononcini and other Italian composers. Indicative of the spirit of the time was the production at the King's Theatre of the opera *Muzio Scevola*, with the 1st act written by Amadei, the 2d by Bononcini (he may have used material from his earlier setting of the same subject), and the 3d by Handel (April 15, 1721). By general agreement Handel won the verdict of popular approval; this episode may have inspired the well-known poem publ. at the time ("Some say, compar'd to Bononcini, That Mynheer Handel's but a ninny," etc.). Other operas brought out by Bononcini in London were *Astarto* (Nov. 19, 1720), *Crispo* (Jan. 10, 1722), *Farnace* (Nov. 27, 1723), *Calpurnia* (April 18, 1724), and *Astianatte* (May 6, 1727). He then suffered a series of setbacks: first the death of his chief supporter, Marlborough (1722), and then the revelation that a madrigal he had submitted to the Academy of Music was an arrangement of a work by Lotti, which put Bononcini's professional integrity in doubt.

To this was added his strange association with one Count Ughi, a self-styled alchemist who claimed the invention of a philosopher's stone, and who induced Bononcini to invest his earnings in his scheme for making gold. After his London debacle Bononcini went (in 1732) to Paris, where he was engaged as a cellist at the court of Louis XV. He was referred to in *Le Mercure de France* (Feb. 7, 1735) as the composer of 78 operas. In 1735 he was in Lisbon; in 1737, in Vienna, where he produced the oratorio *Ezechia* (April 4, 1737) and a Te Deum (1740). Reduced to poverty, he petitioned the young Empress Maria Theresa for a pension, which was granted in Oct. 1742, giving him a monthly stipend of 50 florins, received regularly until his death on July 9, 1747, at the age of 77. This date and the circumstances of his last years in Vienna were first made known in the valuable paper by Kurt Hueber, *Gli ultimi anni di Giovanni Bononcini, Notizie e documenti inediti*, publ. by the Academy of Sciences, Letters and Arts of Modena (Dec. 1954). Among Bononcini's works are 7 oratorios (including *Ezechia*; all on various biblical subjects).

BIBL.: K. Hueber, *Die Wiener Opern G. B.s von 1697 bis 1710* (diss., Univ. of Vienna, 1955); L. Lindgren, *A Bibliographic Scrutiny of Dramatic Works Set by G. and His Brother Antonio Maria Bononcini* (diss., Harvard Univ., 1972).

Bontempi (real name, **Angelini**), **Giovanni Andrea,** Italian singer and composer; b. Perugia, c.1624; d. Torgiano, July 1, 1705. He was a castrato, and sang in the choir of S. Marco in Venice (1643–50). After studies with Mazzocchi, he was appointed joint Kapellmeister in Dresden, with Schütz and Vincenzo Albrici, in 1656. He assumed the name Bontempi after his patron, Cesare Bontempi. In 1680 he returned to Italy, sang at the Collegiata di S. Maria at Sapello, near Foligno, in 1682, and was maestro di cappella there during the first half of 1686. He was one of the earliest composers of Italian operas and oratorios. His first opera, *Il Paride in musica*, to his own libretto, was produced in Dresden, on Nov. 3, 1662; it was the first Italian opera ever produced there. Two later operas, both produced in Dresden, were *Apollo e Dafne*, written in collaboration with Peranda and produced in Dresden on Sept. 3, 1671, and *Giove e Io* (also with Peranda), produced in Dresden on Jan. 16, 1673. He also composed an oratorio, *Martirio di San Emiliano*. and publ. the treatises *Nova quatuor vocibus componendi methodus* (Dresden, 1660), *Tractus in quo demonstrantur occultae convenientiae sonorum systematis participati* (Bologna, 1690), and *Historia musica, nella quale si ha piena cognitione della teorica e della pratica antica della musica harmonica secondo la dottrina de' Greci* (Perugia, 1695).

BIBL.: G. B. Rossi Scotti, *Di G. A. B. di Perugia* (1878); F. Briganti, *G. A. Angelini-B. (1624–1705), Musicista, letterato, architto: Perugia-Dresda* (Florence, 1956).

Bonynge, Richard (Alan), noted Australian conductor; b. Sydney, Sept. 29, 1930. He studied piano at the New South Wales Conservatorium of Music in Sydney and at the Royal College of Music in London, beginning his career as a pianist. After marrying **Joan Sutherland** in 1954, he devoted himself to helping her master the bel canto operatic repertoire. In 1962 he made his conducting debut in a concert with his wife in Rome; he then made his debut as an opera conductor with a performance of *Faust* in Vancouver (1963). He made his first appearance at London's Covent Garden in 1964, leading a performance of *I Puritani*. On Dec. 12, 1966, he made his Metropolitan Opera debut in New York, conducting *Lucia di Lammermoor*, with his wife in the title role. In subsequent years he conducted concerts and operas throughout the world. He was music director of the Australian Opera in Sydney from 1976 to 1986. In 1977 he was made a Commander of the Order of the British Empire.

BIBL.: Q. Eaton, *Sutherland & B.: An Intimate Biography* (N.Y., 1987).

Bordogni, Giulio Marco, Italian tenor and singing teacher; b. Gazzaniga, near Bergamo, Jan. 23, 1789; d. Paris, July 31, 1856. He was a pupil of Simon Mayr. He made his operatic debut in 1808, at La Scala, Milan. From 1819 to 1833 he was engaged at the Théâtre-Italien in Paris; later devoted himself primarily to teaching. He joined the staff of the Paris Cons. in 1820. He publ. a collection of 36 vocalises, in 2 vols., which became a standard book of vocal exercises throughout Europe.

Borg, Kim, Finnish bass, teacher, and composer; b. Helsinki, Aug. 7, 1919. He studied voice with Heikki Teittinen in Helsinki (1936–41; 1945–47), where he also received training in theory and composition with Leo Funtek and Aarre Merikanto, and then pursued vocal studies with Andrejewa de Skilondz in Stockholm (1950–59). He also studied biochemistry at the Helsinki Inst. of Technology (diploma, 1946). In 1947 he made his formal concert debut in Helsinki, and in 1951 his formal operatic debut in Århus as Colline in *La Bohème*. In addition to his concert appearances, he sang regularly in opera in Helsinki and Copenhagen (1952–70), Stockholm (1963–75), and Hamburg (1964–70). On Oct. 30, 1959, he made his Metropolitan Opera debut in New York as Count Almaviva, remaining on its roster until 1962. In 1961 he appeared as Boris Godunov in Moscow. He retired from the stage in 1980. From 1972 to 1989 he was a prof. at the Royal Danish Cons. of Music in Copenhagen. He publ. the books *Suomalainen laulajanaapinen* (ABC for a Finnish Singer; Helsinki, 1972) and *Muistelmia* (Memoirs; Helsinki, 1992). Among his compositions were 2 syms., Sinfonietta for Strings, a Trombone Concerto, a Concerto for Double Bass and Strings, chamber music, a *Stabat Mater*, and songs. He also prepared orchestrations of Mussorgsky's *Songs and Dances of Death* and *Without Sun*, and of Wolf's *Michelangelo Lieder*. In addition to Boris Godnunov, he also had success in such roles as Osmin, Don Giovanni, King Marke, Hans Sachs, Don Carlos, Pimen, Gremin, Rossini's Don Basilio, and Debussy's Arkel.

Borgatti, Giuseppe, Italian tenor; b. Cento, March 17, 1871; d. Reno, Lago Maggiore, Oct. 18, 1950. He studied with Alessandro Busi in Bologna; he made his operatic debut as Faust in Castelfranco Veneto in 1892; in 1896 he sang the title role in *Andrea Chenier* at Milan's La Scala; also sang in Wagner's operas. He retired from the stage in 1914 owing to glaucoma, becoming totally blind in 1923. He publ. an autobiography, *La mia vita d'artista* (Bologna, 1927). His daughter, Renata Borgatti (b. Bologna, March 2, 1894; d. Rome, March 10, 1964), was a pianist.

Borghi, Adelaide, Italian mezzo-soprano; b. Bologna, Aug. 9, 1829; d. there, Sept. 28, 1901. Acting on the advice of Pasta, she trained herself for the stage, making her debut at Urbino (1846) in Mercadante's *Il Giuramento*. She toured through Italy and in Vienna and Paris (1854–56), sang with the Grand Opéra in Paris (1856–59), and appeared in London with great success (1860) before returning to Italy.

Borghi, Giovanni Battista, Italian composer; b. Camerino, Macerata, Aug. 25, 1738; d. Loreto, Feb. 25, 1796. He studied at the Cons. della Pietà dei Turchini in Naples (1757–59). From 1759 to 1778 he was maestro di cappella at the Macerata Cathedral; from 1778, at S. Casa of Loreto. He composed some 25 operas, including *La morte di Semiramide* (Milan, Feb. 9, 1791), which was moderately successful. He also wrote a number of oratorios and other sacred works.

Borgioli, Armando, Italian baritone; b. Florence, March 19, 1898; d. in an air raid on the Milan-Modena train near Codogno, Jan. 20, 1945. He made his debut as Amonasro at the Teatro Carcano in Milan in 1925, then sang at Milan's La Scala and London's Covent Garden. On Jan. 22, 1932, he made his Metropolitan Opera debut in New York, as Carlo in *La forza del destino*, remaining on the company's roster until 1935. He was best known for his dramatic roles in Verdi's operas.

Borgioli, Dino, Italian tenor; b. Florence, Feb. 15, 1891; d. there, Sept. 12, 1960. He studied in Florence with Eugenio Giachetti. In 1914 he made his operatic debut as Arturo in *I Puritani* at Milan's Teatro Corso and appeared in various Italian opera houses, including Milan's La Scala (debut as Ernesto in *Don Pasquale*, 1918). After singing with Melba on her farewell tour of Australia

(1924), he made his first appearance at London's Covent Garden as Edgardo in 1925, continuing to sing there until 1939. In 1932 he sang Cavaradossi in San Francisco, a role he again sang in Chicago in 1933. On Dec. 31, 1934, he made his Metropolitan Opera debut in New York as Rodolfo, but sang with the company for only that 1 season. In 1937 he sang Ottavio at the Glyndebourne Festival. From 1939 he taught voice in London, eventually retiring to Florence. His roles in operas by Mozart and Rossini were particularly esteemed.

Bori, Lucrezia (real name, **Lucrecia Borja y Gonzalez de Riancho**), distinguished Spanish soprano; b. Valencia, Dec. 24, 1887; d. N.Y., May 14, 1960. She studied at the Valencia Cons. and with Melchior Vidal in Milan. She made her operatic debut in Rome at the Teatro Adriano on Oct. 31, 1908, as Micaëla; she then sang in Milan, in Naples, and, in 1910, in Paris as Manon Lescaut with the Metropolitan Opera Co.; then made a European tour. In 1911 she sang at La Scala in Milan; made her debut at the Metropolitan Opera in New York as Manon Lescaut on Nov. 11, 1912, and sang there until the end of the 1914–15 season. After a period of retirement occasioned by a vocal affliction, she reappeared in 1919 at Monte Carlo as Mimi, returning to the Metropolitan in 1921 in the same role. Thereafter she appeared in New York with increasing success and popularity until the end of the 1935–36 season, when she retired from opera. Among her finest roles were Juliette, Despina, Massenet's Manon, Mélisande, Violetta, Norina, and Mimi.

Borkh, Inge (real name, **Ingeborg Simon**), famous German soprano; b. Mannheim, May 26, 1917. She first appeared as a stage actress, then decided upon a singing career. She studied at the Milan Cons. and at the Mozarteum in Salzburg. She made her debut as Czipra in Johann Strauss's *Zigeunerbaron* at the Lucerne Opera in 1940, remaining a member there until 1944; then sang at the Bern Opera until 1951. She made her American debut at the San Francisco Opera in 1953; on Jan. 24, 1958, she appeared at the Metropolitan Opera in New York as Salome, returning to its roster for the 1960–61 and 1970–71 seasons. In 1959 she made her first appearance at London's Covent Garden, also as Salome. She made her farewell operatic appearance at the Munich Festival in 1988. Her other notable roles included Leonore, Eglantine, Lady Macbeth, and Elektra. She wrote *Ich komm' vom Theater nicht los: Erinnerungen und Einsichten* (Berlin, 1996).

Bořkovec, Pavel, Czech composer; b. Prague, June 10, 1894; d. there, July 22, 1972. He originally studied philosophy, and turned to composition rather late in life; he took lessons with Křička and Foerster in 1919; from 1925 to 1927 he attended master classes with Suk at the Prague Cons. From 1946 to 1964 he was on the faculty of the Academy of Musical Arts in Prague. His early works were in the manner of Dvořák and Suk; later he experienced the influence of neoclassicism and adopted dissonant counterpoint. He composed the operas *The Satyr* (1937–38; Prague, Oct. 8, 1942) and *Paleček* (Tom Thumb; 1945–47; Prague, Dec. 17, 1958) and the ballet *Krysař* (The Pied Piper; 1939; concert perf., Prague, Jan. 15, 1941; 1st stage perf., Oct. 8, 1942).

Bornschein, Franz (Carl), American composer, conductor, and teacher; b. Baltimore, Feb. 10, 1879; d. there, June 8, 1948. He spent his entire career in his native city, where he first studied violin with Lawrence Rosenberger and Julius Zech; subsequently he studied violin with Joan Van Hulsteyn and harmony with Phillip Kahmer and Otis Boise at the Peabody Cons. of Music (diploma, 1902). In 1905 he joined its preparatory dept. and also was made the local correspondent of *Musical America*. From 1910 to 1913 he was music critic of the Baltimore *Sun*. In 1919 he became a teacher of violin, conducting, and composition at Peabody, remaining on its faculty until his death. He also conducted various local orch. and choral groups. Bornschein had modest success as a composer of choral works, some of which appeared under the pseudonym Frank Fairfield. His tone poems on American subjects were favorably received. For the stage, he composed *Mother Goose's Goslings*, children's operetta (1918), *Willow Plate*, operetta (1932), and *Song of Songs*, opera (1934).

Borodin, Alexander (Porfirievich), celebrated Russian composer; b. St. Petersburg, Nov. 12, 1833; d. there, Feb. 27, 1887. He was the illegitimate son of a Georgian prince, Gedianov; his mother was the wife of an army doctor. In accordance with customary procedure in such cases, the child was registered as the lawful son of one of Gedianov's serfs, Porfiry Borodin, hence, the patronymic Alexander Porfirievich. He was given an excellent education; learned several foreign languages, and was taught to play the flute. He played 4-hand arrangements of Haydn's and Beethoven's syms. with his musical friend M. Shchiglev. At the age of 14 he tried his hand at composition; wrote a piece for flute and piano and a String Trio on themes from *Robert le Diable*. In 1850 he became a student of the Academy of Medicine in St. Petersburg, and developed a great interest in chemistry; he graduated in 1856 with honors, and joined the staff as assistant prof. In 1858 he received his doctorate in chemistry; he contributed several important scientific papers to the bulletin of the Russian Academy of Sciences; and traveled in Europe on a scientific mission (1859–62). Although mainly preoccupied with his scientific pursuits, Borodin continued to compose. In 1863 he married Catherine Protopopova, who was an accomplished pianist; she remained his faithful companion and musical partner; together they attended concerts and operas in Russia and abroad; his letters to her from Germany (1877), describing his visit to Liszt in Weimar, are of great interest. Of a decisive influence on Borodin's progress as a composer was his meeting with Balakirev in 1862; later he formed friendships with the critic Stasov, who named Borodin as one of the "mighty 5" (actually, Stasov used the expression "mighty heap"), with Mussorgsky and other musicians of the Russian national school. He adopted a style of composition in conformity with their new ideas; he particularly excelled in a type of Russian orientalism which had a great attraction for Russian musicians at the time. He never became a consummate craftsman, like Rimsky-Korsakov; although quite proficient in counterpoint, he avoided purely contrapuntal writing; his feeling for rhythm and orch. color was extraordinary, and his evocation of exotic scenes in his orch. works and in his opera *Prince Igor* is superb. Composition was a very slow process for Borodin; several of his works remained incomplete, and were ed. after his death by Rimsky-Korsakov and Glazunov.

WORKS: OPERAS: *Prince Igor* (begun in 1869, on the subject of the famous Russian medieval chronicle Tale of Igor's Campaign; completed posth. by Rimsky-Korsakov and Glazunov; 1st perf., St. Petersburg, Nov. 4, 1890; London, June 8, 1914, in Russian; N.Y., Dec. 30, 1915, in Italian); an opera-farce, *Bogatyry* (The Valiant Knights; anonymously produced in Moscow on Oct. 29, 1867; rediscovered in 1932, and produced in Moscow, Nov. 12, 1936, with a new libretto by Demian Biedny, to serve propaganda purposes in an anti-religious campaign, but 2 days later banned by the Soviet government for its mockery of Russian nationalism); sketches for the 4th act of an opera, *Mlada* (never produced), each act of which was to have been written by a different composer.

BIBL.: V. Stasov, *A. B.* (St. Petersburg, 1882; French tr. by A. Habets, Paris, 1893); R. Newmarch, *B. and Liszt* (London, 1895); E. Braudo, *B.* (Moscow, 1922); G. Abraham, *B., the Composer and His Music* (London, 1927); G. Khubov, *B.* (Moscow, 1933); Y. Kremlev, *B.* (Leningrad, 1934); M. Ilyin and E. Segal, *B.* (Moscow, 1953); S. Dianin, *B.* (Moscow, 1955; Eng. tr., 1963); L. Velluz, *Du laboratoire au Prince Igor, Pages sur Borodine* (Paris, 1971); A. Gaub and M. Unseld, *Ein Fürst, zwei Prinzessinnen und vier Spieler: Anmerkungen zum Werk A. B.s* (Berlin, 1994).

Borodina, Olga (Vladimirovna), notable Russian mezzo-soprano; b. Minsk, July 29, 1963. She studied at the Leningrad Cons. and in San Francisco. In 1987 she won the All-Union Glinka Competition in her homeland and the Rosa Ponselle Competition in the United States, and in 1989 the Francisco Vignas Competition in Barcelona. In 1987 she joined the Kirov Opera, where she made her formal operatic debut as Siebel in *Faust*. Her appearances with the company on tour were warmly received, including visits to Hamburg in 1990, Edinburgh in 1991, and New York, Paris, and Palermo in 1992. In 1992 she made her debut at London's Covent Garden as Delilah, and in 1993 she appeared as Marina in Berlin. In 1995 she sang for the first time at the San Francisco Opera as Cenerentola, and returned there as Carmen in 1996. In 1997 she sang Marina in Salzburg, a role she chose for her Metropolitan Opera debut in New York on Dec. 19 of that year. Her subsequent engagements took her to most of the principal operatic centers of the world. In addition to her admired Russian roles, particularly Marina, Olga, and Marfa, she has won acclaim for her characterizations of Rosina, Marguerite in *La Damnation de Faust*, and Angelina.

Boronat, Olimpia, highly esteemed Italian soprano; b. Genoa, 1867; d. Warsaw, 1934. She was a pupil of Leoni at the Milan Cons. After appearing throughout Italy (from 1885), she toured in Spain, Portugal, and South America. In 1890 she became a member of the St. Petersburg Imperial Opera, where she was notably successful. In 1893 she married the Polish nobleman Rzewuski and retired from the stage. In 1901 she resumed her career and sang with renewed success in Russia. She also sang in Poland and then in Italy (from 1909). In 1922 she retired for good and settled in Warsaw as a voice teacher. Among her outstanding roles were Rosina, Elvira in *I Puritani*, Ophélie in *Hamlet*, and Violetta.

Boroni, Antonio, Italian composer; b. Rome, 1738; d. there, Dec. 21, 1792. He studied with Martini in Bologna and with Abos and Lorenzo Fago at the Cons. Pietà dei Turchini in Naples (1757–58). He then devoted himself to writing operas. After composing works for Turin, Treviso, and Venice, he accompanied the Bustelli opera troupe to Prague (1767–68) and Dresden (1768–70). He served as Kapellmeister in Stuttgart (1770–77), then returned to Rome as maestro di cappella at St. Peter's (from 1778); he also held similar posts at S. Luigi de' Francesi and at S. Apollinare, the church of the Collegio Germanica (from c.1790).

WORKS: DRAMATIC: *La Moda*, dramma giocoso (Turin, 1761; rev. Venice, 1769); *Demofoonte*, opera seria (Treviso, Carnival 1762); *L'amore in musica*, dramma giocoso (Venice, Oct. 15, 1763); *La Pupilla rapita*, dramma giocoso (Venice, 1763; in collaboration with S. Laurenti); *Sofonisba*, dramma per musica (Venice, Ascension 1764); *Siroe*, dramma per musica (Venice, 1764); *Le Villeggiatrici ridicole*, dramma comico (Venice, 1765); *La notte critica*, dramma giocoso (Venice, Carnival 1766); *Artaserse*, dramma per musica (Prague, Jan. 1767); *Didone*, dramma per musica (Prague, Carnival 1768); *Il carnevale*, dramma giocoso (Dresden, 1769); *Le Orfane svizzere*, dramma giocoso (Venice, 1770); *Le Contadine furlane*, dramma giocoso (Venice, Carnival 1771); *Le Déserteur*, opéra-comique (Stuttgart, 1774–75); *L'Amour fraternel*, opéra comique (Stuttgart, 1774–75); *Zémire et Azor*, opéra comique (Stuttgart, 1774–75); *L'isola disabitata*, intermezzo (Stuttgart, Dec. 31, 1775); *Enea nel Lazio*, dramma per musica (Rome, Carnival 1778).

Borosini, Francesco, Italian tenor; b. Modena, c.1690; d. c.1750. From 1712 to 1731 he sang at the imperial court in Vienna. He also made appearances in Italy and in 1724–25 in London, where he appeared in operas by Handel and Ariosti. In 1725 he created the role of Grimoaldo in Handel's *Rodelinda*. He was married to the Italian soprano Rosa (née d'Ambreville) Borosini (b. Modena, June 27, 1698; d. after 1740). She launched her career in 1713, and later sang in Vienna (1721–40).

Borowski, Felix, English-American composer, music critic, and teacher; b. Burton, March 10, 1872; d. Chicago, Sept. 6, 1956. He studied violin with his father, a Polish émigré; he took lessons with various teachers in London, and at the Cologne Cons.; he then taught in Aberdeen, Scotland. His early *Russian Sonata* was praised by Grieg, which provided impetus to his progress as a composer. In 1897 he accepted a teaching engagement at the Chicago Musical College; was its president from 1916 to 1925. Subsequently he became active in musical journalism; in 1942 he was appointed music ed. of the *Chicago Sun*; also served as program annotator for the Chicago Sym. Orch. (from 1908). He also taught musicology at Northwestern Univ. (1937–42). Among his many musical works, the violin piece *Adoration* became widely popular. For the stage, he composed *Boudour*, ballet-pantomime (Chicago, Nov. 25, 1919), and *Fernando del Nonsensico*, satiric opera (1935). Borowski revised G. P. Upton's *The Standard Operas* in 1928, and *The Standard Concert Guide* in 1930.

Børresen, (Aksel Ejnar) Hakon, Danish composer; b. Copenhagen, June 2, 1876; d. there, Oct. 6, 1954. He studied with Svendsen and was awarded the Ancker scholarship for composition in 1901. He was president of the Danish Composers Soc. from 1924 to 1949. His compositions include the operas *Den Kongelige Gaest* (Copenhagen, Nov. 15, 1919) and *Kaddara* (Copenhagen, March 16, 1921) and the ballet *Tycho Brahes Dröm* (Tycho Brahe's Dream; Copenhagen, March 1, 1924).

Borris, Siegfried, respected German music scholar, pedagogue, and composer; b. Berlin, Nov. 4, 1906; d. there, Aug. 23, 1987. He studied economics at the Univ. of Berlin (1925–27), where he then pursued training in musicology with Schering (Ph.D., 1933, with the diss. *Kirnbergers Leben und Werk*). He also studied composition with Hindemith at the Berlin Hochschule für Musik (1927–29), where he subsequently taught (1929–33). After teaching privately, he rejoined its faculty as a lecturer in music history in 1945; he also was director of Berlin's Julius Stern Inst. from 1967. He composed in an accessible style, highlighted by an effective use of folk music. His dramatic works include 2 radio operas: *Hans im Glück* (1947) and *Hirotas und Gerline* (1948), *Die Rübe*, Märchenoper (1953), *Frühlingsgesellen*, Liederspiel (1951), *Ruf des Lebens*, scenic cantata (1954), and *Das letzte Spiel*, ballet (1955).

Bortkiewicz, Sergei (Eduardovich), Russian pianist and composer; b. Kharkov, Feb. 28, 1877; d. Vienna, Oct. 25, 1952. He was a pupil of Liadov at the St. Petersburg Cons. (1896–99); later he studied with Jadassohn in Leipzig (1900–02). He made his debut as a pianist in Munich in 1902, and subsequently made concert tours of Germany, Australia, Hungary, France, and Russia. From 1904 to 1914 he lived in Berlin, and taught at the Klindworth-Scharwenka Cons.; he then returned to Russia; he was in Vienna from 1920 to 1929, in Berlin from 1929 to 1934, and again in Vienna from 1934. His compositions include an opera, *Acrobats*. He was the author of the book *Die seltsame Liebe Peter Tschaikowskys und der Nadezhda von Meck* (1938).

Bortniansky, Dimitri (Stepanovich), Russian composer; b. Glukhov, Ukraine, 1751; d. St. Petersburg, Oct. 10, 1825. He was a choirboy in the court chapel, where he attracted the attention of Galuppi, who was at the time conductor there. He was sent to Italy, where he studied with Galuppi and with other Italian masters in Venice, Bologna, Rome, and Naples (1769–79). In Italy he produced his operas *Creonte* (Venice, Nov. 26, 1776; lost) and *Quinto Fabio* (Modena, Dec. 26, 1778). In 1779 he returned to St. Petersburg and became director of vocal music at the court chapel (1796). As a conductor of the chapel choir he introduced radical reforms for improvement of singing standards; composed for his choir a number of sacred works of high quality, among them a Mass according to the Greek Orthodox. He also continued to compose for the stage; produced the comic operas, in French, *Le Faucon* (Gatchina, Oct. 22, 1786) and *Le Fils rival* (Pavlovsk, Oct. 22, 1787).

BIBL.: B. Dobrohotov, *D. B.* (Moscow, 1950).

Börtz, Daniel, Swedish composer; b. Osby, Hässleholm, Aug. 8, 1943. He studied composition privately with Fernström and Rosenberg, and then at the Stockholm Musikhögskolan with Blomdahl (1962–65) and Lidholm (1965–68); he also received training in violin from Barkel and Grünfarb, and later in electronic music from Koenig at the Univ. of Utrecht. From 1972 to 1979 he was secretary of the Swedish Composer's Soc. He taught at the Stockholm Musikhögskolan from 1987. Börtz's works, which reflect the state of contemporary usages, nevertheless display an individualistic approach to melodic and harmonic writing. He composed

Muren—Vägen—Ordet, liturgical opera (1971–72), *Landskab med flod*, chamber opera (1972), *Den heliga Birgittas död och Mottagande i himmelen*, liturgical opera (Lund, Oct. 7, 1973), *Bacchanterna*, opera (1988–90; Stockholm, Nov. 2, 1991), and *Marie Antoinette*, opera (1996–97; Stockholm, Jan. 24, 1998).

Boschi, Giuseppe Maria, Italian bass who flourished in the late 17th century and the first half of the 18th century. He married the contralto Francesca Vanini in 1698. After singing in Venice (1707; 1708–09), he went to London with his wife and made his first appearance there in Mancini's *Idaspe fedele* on Nov. 19, 1710. On Feb. 24, 1711, he created the role of Argante in Handel's *Rinaldo*. After singing again in Venice (1713–14), he appeared in Dresden (1717–20), after which he was called to London by Handel to serve as one of the principal members of his Royal Academy of Music opera productions (1720–28). He subsequently returned once more to Venice, where he sang in opera (1728–29) and later in the choir at San Marco.

Boschot, Adolphe, French music critic; b. Fontenay-sous-Bois, near Paris, May 4, 1871; d. Paris, June 1, 1955. He was music critic of *Echo de Paris* from 1910, and of *Revue Bleue* from 1919. He founded, with Théodore de Wyzewa, the Paris Mozart Soc. and was elected to the Institut de France in 1926, succeeding Widor as permanent secretary of the Académie des Beaux-Arts. His greatest work is an exhaustive biography of Berlioz in 3 vols.: *La Jeunesse d'un romantique, Hector Berlioz, 1803–31* (Paris, 1906; rev. ed., 1946), *Un Romantique sous Louis-Philippe, Hector Berlioz, 1831–42* (Paris, 1908; rev. ed., 1948), and *Le Crépuscule d'un romantique, Hector Berlioz, 1842–69* (Paris, 1913; rev. ed., 1950); also *Le Faust de Berlioz* (1910; new ed., 1945). He also publ. *La Lumière de Mozart* (1928) and *Mozart* (1935). Boschot tr. into French the librettos of several of Mozart's operas. He was also prominent as a poet; he publ. the collections *Poèmes dialogués* (1901) and *Chez nos poètes* (1925).

Boscovich, Alexander Uriah, significant Israeli composer; b. Klausenburg, Transylvania, Aug. 16, 1907; d. Tel Aviv, Nov. 13, 1964. He studied in Budapest; later he enrolled at the Vienna Academy of Music, where he studied piano with Victor Ebenstein and composition with Richard Stöhr; he then went to Paris, where he took courses with Dukas and Boulanger and also had a few lessons in piano with Cortot. From 1930 to 1938 he was engaged as conductor at the State Opera in Cluj; in 1938 he emigrated to Palestine; taught at the Tel Aviv Cons. (1945–64); wrote music criticism for the Israeli newspaper *Haaretz*.

Bose, Hans-Jürgen von, German composer; b. Munich, Dec. 24, 1953. He went to Frankfurt am Main and studied at the Hoch Cons. (1969–72) and with Hans Engelmann (composition) and Klaus Billing (piano) at the Hochschule für Musik (1972–75). In 1980 and 1985 he held scholarships at the Villa Massimo in Rome. In 1986 he was elected a member of the Akademie der Künste in Berlin.

WORKS: DRAMATIC: *Blütbund*, chamber opera (1974; Hamburg, June 8, 1977); *Das Diplom*, chamber opera (1975; Ulm, Nov. 26, 1976); *Die Nacht aus Blei*, ballet (1980–81; Berlin, Nov. 1, 1981); *Die Leiden des jungen Werthers*, lyrical scenes (1983–84; Schwetzingen, April 30, 1986); *Chimäre*, opera (Aachen, June 11, 1986); *Werther-Szenen*, ballet (1988; Schweinfurt, April 26, 1989); *63: Dream Palace*, opera (1989; Munich, May 6, 1990); *Medea*, ballet (Zürich, Feb. 20, 1994); *Schlachthof 5*, after Vonnegut's *Slaughterhouse 5* (Munich, July 1, 1996).

Bossi, (Marco) Enrico, Italian organist, pianist, pedagogue, and composer, father of **(Rinaldo) Renzo Bossi**; b. Salò, Brescia, April 25, 1861; d. at sea (en route from America to Europe), Feb. 20, 1925. Son and pupil of the organist Pietro Bossi of Morbegno (1834–96), he studied at the Liceo Rossini in Bologna (1871–73), and at Milan (1873–81) under Sangali (piano), Fumagalli (organ), Campanari (violin), Boniforti (counterpoint), and Ponchielli (composition). He was maestro di cappella and organist at Como Cathedral (1881–89), prof. of organ and harmony in the Royal Cons. San Pietro at Naples (until 1896), prof. of advanced composition and organ at the Liceo Benedetto Marcello in Venice (1896–1902), director of the Liceo Musicale at Bologna (1902–12), and director of the Music School of the Accademia di Santa Cecilia in Rome (1916–23); he toured Europe, England, and the United States as a pianist and organist. He wrote *Metodo di studio per l'organo moderno* (Milan, 1893). Among his compositions are the operas *Paquita* (Milan, 1881), *Il Veggente* (Milan, 1890; rev. version as *Il Viandante*, Mannheim, 1896), and *L'Angelo della notte*, and *Giovanna d'Arco*, mystery place (1913).

BIBL.: G. Paribeni, L. Orsini, and E. Bontempelli, *M. E. B.: Il Compositore, l'organista, l'uomo* (Milan, 1934); F. Mompellio, *M. E. B.* (Milan, 1952).

Bossi, (Rinaldo) Renzo, Italian conductor, teacher, and composer, son of **(Marco) Enrico Bossi**; b. Como, April 9, 1883; d. Milan, April 2, 1965. He studied in Venice and in Leipzig; he took a course in conducting with Nikisch; conducted at various cities in Italy; and in 1916 he was appointed instructor at the Verdi Cons. in Milan. His works include the operas *Passa la ronda* (Milan, March 3, 1919), *Volpino il calderaio* (Milan, Nov. 13, 1925), and *La rosa rossa* (Parma, Jan. 9, 1940) and the ballet *Il trillo del diavolo* (1948).

BIBL.: F. Mompellio, *M. E. B.* (Milan, 1952); S. Pintacuda, *R. B.* (Milan, 1955).

Bottenberg, Wolfgang (Heinz Otto), German-born Canadian composer and teacher; b. Frankfurt am Main, May 9, 1930. He entered the Jesuit order in 1952 and taught himself theory and organ. After graduating from the Theologische Hochschule Vallender (1957), he emigrated to Canada in 1958 and became a naturalized Canadian citizen in 1964. He studied theory with R. A. Stangeland at the Univ. of Alberta (B.Mus., 1961), and then completed his training with Huston, Takács, and Cooper at the Univ. of Cincinnati (M.Mus., 1962; D.M.A., 1970). He taught at the Acadia Univ. in Wolfville, Nova Scotia (1965–73) and at Concordia Univ. in Montreal (from 1973). His interest in early music prompted him to organize the Acadia Medieval Ensemble in Montreal in 1974. In addition to early music, Bottenberg's works have been notably influenced by Hindemith. He makes eclectic use of tonal, atonal, and serial resources. He composed the opera *Inook* (1986).

Bottesini, Giovanni, Italian double-bass player, conductor, and composer; b. Crema, Dec. 22, 1821; d. Parma, July 7, 1889. He took lessons in double-bass playing with Rossi at the Milan Cons. (1835–39). He played in various orchs. In 1847 he visited the United States, and in 1848 he went to England, where he appeared as a cello soloist. He made his independent concert debut in London on June 26, 1849. In 1853 he was once more in America; he was also active as a conductor in Paris, in Russia, and in Scandinavian countries. In 1871 he was invited by Verdi to conduct the world premiere of *Aida* in Cairo. He eventually retired to Parma as director of the cons. there. Bottesini was the first great virtuoso on the double bass, regarded as an unwieldy instrument, and thus became a legendary paragon for the few artists who essayed that instrument after him. He publ. a valuable *Metodo complete per contrabasso*, in 2 parts, treating the double bass as an orch. and as a solo instrument (in Eng., adapted by F. Clayton, London, 1870). Bottesini was the composer of a number of passable operas which had several performances in his lifetime.

WORKS: DRAMATIC: OPERAS: *Cristoforo Colombo* (Havana, 1847); *L'Assedio di Firenze* (Paris, Feb. 21, 1856); *Il Diavolo della notte* (Milan, Dec. 18, 1858); *Marion Delorme* (Palermo, Jan. 10, 1862); *Vinciguerra il bandito* (Monte Carlo, Feb. 22, 1870); *Alí Babà* (London, Jan. 18, 1871); *Ero e Leandro* (Turin, Jan. 11, 1879); *La Regina di Nepal* (Turin, Dec. 26, 1880). ORATORIO: *The Garden of Olivet* (Norwich Festival, Oct. 12, 1887).

BIBL.: C. Lesei, *G. B.* (Milan, 1886); A. Carniti, *In memoria di G. B.* (Crema, 1922).

Bottje, Will Gay, American flutist, teacher, and composer; b. Grand Rapids, June 30, 1925. He studied flute (B.S., 1947) and received instruction in composition (M.S., 1948) from Giannini at the Juilliard School of Music in New York, then pursued training with Badings in Holland and Boulanger in Paris (1952–53); subsequently he was a pupil of Rogers and Hanson (composition), Joseph Mariano (flute), and Paul White (conducting) at the Eastman School of Music in Rochester, N.Y. (D.M.A., 1955); he later worked at the Univ. of Utrecht electronic music studios (1962–63) and at the Stockholm Stiftlesen (1973). He taught at the Univ. of Mississippi (1955–57) before serving as prof. of theory and composition at Southern Illinois Univ. in Carbondale (1957–81), where he founded an electronic music studio (1965). His music is of a highly experimental nature, awash with corrosive dissonances in a manner influenced primarily by developments cultivated in the northern avant-garde music laboratories. He composed the operas *Altgeld* (Carbondale, Ill., March 6, 1968) and *Root!* (1971).

Boué, Geori (Georgette), French soprano; b. Toulouse, Oct. 16, 1918. After studying at the Toulouse Cons., she settled in Paris, where she sang with success in opera and operetta; in 1942 she made her first appearance at the Opéra as Marguerite, and subsequently appeared there regularly; also toured in Europe. She was married to **Roger Bourdin**. Although she was particularly esteemed for her French roles, she also sang Violetta, Leonore, Salome, Tosca, Desdemona and Cio-Cio-San.

Boughton, Rutland, English composer; b. Aylesbury, Jan. 23, 1878; d. London, Jan. 24, 1960. He studied at the Royal College of Music in London with Stanford and Davies; without obtaining his diploma, he engaged in professional activity; he was for a time a member of the orch. at the Haymarket Theatre in London; he taught at the Midland Inst. in Birmingham (1905–11); also conducted a choral society there. He became a firm believer in the universality of arts along Wagnerian lines; formed a partnership with the poet Reginald Buckley; their book of essays, *The Music Drama of the Future*, expounding the neo-Wagnerian idea, was publ. in 1911. To carry out these plans, Boughton organized stage festivals at Glastonbury, helped by his common-law wife, Christina Walshe. Boughton's opera, *The Immortal Hour*, was performed there on Aug. 26, 1914; his choral music drama, *The Birth of Arthur*, had a performance there in 1920; these productions were staged with piano instead of an orch. After an interruption during World War I, Boughton continued the Glastonbury festivals until 1926. In 1927 he settled in the country, in Gloucestershire. He continued to compose, however, and produced a number of stage works, as well as instrumental pieces. His ideas of universal art had in the meantime been transformed into concepts of socialist realism, with an emphasis on the paramount importance of folk music as against formal constructions. He publ. *The Death and Resurrection of the Music Festival* (1913); *The Glastonbury Festival Movement* (1922); *Bach, the Master* (1930); *Parsifal: A Study* (1920); *The Nature of Music* (1930); *The Reality of Music* (1934).

WORKS: DRAMATIC: *The Birth of Arthur* (1909; Glastonbury, Aug. 16, 1920); *The Immortal Hour* (1913; Glastonbury, Aug. 26, 1914); *The Round Table* (Glastonbury, Aug. 14, 1916); *The Moon Maiden*, choral ballet for girls (Glastonbury, April 23, 1919); *Alkestis*, music drama (Glastonbury, Aug. 26, 1922); *The Queen of Cornwall*, music drama (Glastonbury, Aug. 21, 1924); *May Day*, ballet (1926); *The Ever Young*, music drama (1928; Bath, Sept. 9, 1935); *The Lily Maid*, opera (Gloucester, Sept. 10, 1934); *Galahad*, music drama (1944); *Avalon*, music drama (1946).

BIBL.: *The Self-Advertisement of R. B.* (c.1909); M. Hurd, *Immortal Hour: The Life and Period of R. B.* (London, 1962; 2d ed., rev. and enl., 1993, as *R. B. and the Glastonbury Festivals*).

Bouhy, Jacques (-Joseph André), Belgian-born French baritone; b. Pepinster, June 18, 1848; d. Paris, Jan. 29, 1929. He studied at the Liège Cons., then entered the Paris Cons., where he studied piano, organ, and theory of composition, as well as singing. He made his debut as Méphistophélès in Gounod's *Faust* at the Paris Opéra on Aug. 2, 1871, and on March 3, 1875, he sang Escamillo in the first performance of *Carmen* at the Opéra Comique in Paris. He appeared at Covent Garden, London, on April 22, 1882, then sang at various opera houses in Europe, including that in St. Petersburg. In 1885 he went to New York and served as director of the N.Y. Cons. (until 1889); he was again in New York from 1904 to 1907; then returned to Paris and settled there as a singing teacher.

Boulanger, Lili (Juliette Marie Olga), talented French composer, sister of **Nadia (Juliette) Boulanger**; b. Paris, Aug. 21, 1893; d. Mézy, Seine-et-Oise, March 15, 1918. She studied composition with Vidal at the Paris Cons. (1909–13), attracting considerable attention when she became the first woman to win the Grand Prix de Rome at graduation with her cantata *Faust et Hélène*. Her early death at the age of 24 was lamented by French musicians. Her talent, delicate and poetic, continued the tradition of French Romanticism on the borderline of Impressionism. Besides her prize-winning cantata, she composed an opera to Maeterlinck's play *La Princesse Maleine*, which remained incomplete.

BIBL.: E. Lebeau, *L. B.* (Paris, 1968); L. Rosenstiel, *The Life and Works of L. B.* (Rutherford, 1978).

Boulanger, Nadia (Juliette), illustrious French teacher, sister of **Lili (Juliette Marie Olga) Boulanger**; b. Paris, Sept. 16, 1887; d. there, Oct. 22, 1979. Both her father and grandfather were teachers at the Paris Cons.; her mother, the Russian Countess Myshetskaya, was a professional singer, and it was from her that Boulanger received her first music lessons. She entered the Paris Cons., where she studied organ with Guilmant and Vierne, and composition with Fauré; she graduated with prizes in organ and theory; in 1908 she received the 2d Prix de Rome for her cantata *La Sirène*; she completed the composition of the opera by Raoul Pugno, *La Ville Morte*, left unfinished at his death. Realizing that she could not compare with her sister Lili in talent as a composer, she devoted herself to teaching, and it was in that capacity that she found her vocation. She was assistant in a harmony class at the Paris Cons. (1909–24); she was engaged as a teacher at the École Normale de Musique in Paris (1920–39); when the American Cons. was founded in 1921 at Fontainebleau, she joined its faculty as a teacher of composition and orchestration, becoming its director in 1950. She also had a large class of private pupils from all parts of the world, many of whom achieved fame; among Americans who went to Paris to study with her were Copland, Harris, Piston, Thomson, Carter, Diamond, Siegmeister, Irving Fine, Easley Blackwood, Berger, Vincent, and Shapero; others were Markevitch, Françaix, Lennox Berkeley, and Dinu Lipatti. She was a great admirer of Stravinsky, Debussy, and Ravel, but had little appreciation of Schoenberg and the modern Vienna School. She visited the United States several times; she played the organ part in Copland's Organ Sym. (which she advised him to compose) with the N.Y. Sym. Orch., under the direction of Walter Damrosch (Jan. 11, 1925), and was the first woman to conduct regular subscription concerts of the Boston Sym. Orch. (1938) and of the N.Y. Phil. (Feb. 11, 1939). During World War II, she stayed in America; she taught classes at Radcliffe College, Wellesley College, and the Juilliard School of Music in New York. Returning to Paris in 1946, she took over a class in piano accompaniment at the Cons.; continued her private teaching as long as her frail health permitted; her 90th birthday was celebrated in Sept. 1977, with sincere tributes from her many students in Europe and America.

BIBL.: A. Kendall, *The Tender Tyrant. N. B.: A Life Devoted to Music* (London, 1977); B. Mosaingeon, *Mademoiselle: Entretiens avec N. B.* (Luynes, 1980; Eng. tr., 1985); L. Rosenstiel, *N. B.: A Life in Music* (N.Y., 1982); J. Spycket, *N. B.* (Lausanne, 1987; Eng. tr., 1992).

Boulez, Pierre, celebrated French composer and conductor; b. Montbrison, March 26, 1925. He studied composition with Messiaen at the Paris Cons., graduating in 1945; later took lessons with Leibowitz, who initiated him into the procedures of serial music. In 1948 he became a theater conductor in Paris; made a tour of the United States with a French ballet troupe in 1952. In 1954 he organized in Paris a series of concerts, "Domaine Musical," devoted mainly to avant-garde music. From 1962 he pursued a career as a guest conductor. In 1966 he conducted *Parsifal* at the Bayreuth Festival, returning there until 1969. In 1969 he became principal guest conductor of the Cleveland Orch. In 1971 he was engaged as music director of the N.Y. Phil., a choice that surprised many and delighted many more. From the outset he asserted complete independence from public and managerial tastes, and proceeded to feature on his programs works by Schoenberg, Berg, Webern, Varèse, and other modernists, giving a relatively small place to Romantic composers. This policy provoked the expected opposition on the part of many subscribers, but the management decided not to oppose Boulez in his position as music director of the orch. The musicians themselves voiced their full appreciation of his remarkable qualities as a professional of high caliber, but they also described him derisively as a "French correction," with reference to his extraordinary sense of rhythm, perfect pitch, and memory, but a signal lack of emotional participation in the music. In America Boulez showed little interest in social amenities and made no effort to ingratiate himself with men and women of power. His departure in 1977 and the accession of the worldly Zubin Mehta as his successor were greeted with a sigh of relief, as an antidote to the stern regimen imposed by Boulez. While attending to his duties at the helm of the N.Y. Phil., Boulez accepted outside obligations; from 1971 to 1975 he served as chief conductor of the London BBC Sym. Orch.; he then conducted the *Ring* cycle for the centenary celebrations at the Bayreuth Festivals (1976–80). He established residence in Paris, where he had founded, in 1974, the Inst. de Recherche & Coordination Acoustique/Musique, a futuristic establishment generously subsidized by the French government; in this post he could freely carry out his experimental programs of electronic techniques with the aid of digital synthesizers and a complex set of computers capable of acoustical feedback. He served as its director until 1992. In 1989 he was awarded the Praemium Imperiale prize of Japan for his various contributions to contemporary music. On Dec. 7, 1992, he conducted Debussy's *La Mer* as part of the 150th anniversary concert of the N.Y. Phil., which was televised live to the nation by PBS. In 1995 he was named principal guest conductor of the Chicago Sym. Orch.

Boulez's music is an embodiment of futuristic techniques; it is fiendishly difficult to perform and even more difficult to describe in the familiar terms of dissonant counterpoint, free serialism, or indeterminism. He specifically disassociated himself from any particular modern school of music. He even publ. a pamphlet with the shocking title *Schoenberg est mort*, shortly after Schoenberg's actual physical death; he similarly distanced himself from other current trends. He is the author of *Stocktakings from an Apprenticeship* (Oxford, 1991).

WORKS: DRAMATIC: *Le Soleil des Eaux*, music for a radio play for Voice and Orch. (1948; rev. as a cantata for Soprano, Tenor, Bass, and Chamber Orch., 1948; withdrawn; rev. for Soprano, Tenor, Bass, Chorus, and Orch., 1958; rev. for Soprano, Chorus, and Orch., 1965); *L'Orestie*, incidental music (1948); *Symphonie Mécanique*, film music for Tape (1955); *Le Crépuscule de Yang Koui-Feï*, incidental music for radio (1967); *Ainsi parla Zarathoustra*, incidental music (1974).

BIBL.: A. Goléa, *Rencontres avec P. B.* (Paris, 1958); J. Peyser, *B., Composer, Conductor, Enigma* (N.Y., 1976); R. Miller, *Pli selon pli: P. B. and the "New Lyricism"* (diss., Case Western Reserve Univ., 1978); P. Griffiths, *B.* (N.Y., 1979); D. Jameux, *P. B.* (Paris, 1984; Eng. tr., 1990); J. Hausler, ed., *Festschrift P. B.* (Vienna, 1985); T. Hirsbrunner, *P. B. und sein Werk* (Laaber, 1985); W. Glock, ed., *P. B.: A Symposium* (London, 1986); P. Stacey, *B. and the Modern Concept* (Lincoln, Nebr., 1987); L. Koblyakov, *P. B.: A World of Harmony* (Chur and N.Y., 1990); J.-J. Nattiez and F. Davoine, eds., *P. B./John Cage: Correspondance et documents* (Winterthur, 1990; Eng. tr., 1993); G. Born, *Rational Music: IRCAM, B., and the Institutionalisation of the Avant-Garde* (Berkeley, 1995); M. Breatnach, *B. and Mallarmé: A Study in Poetic Influence* (Aldershot, 1996).

Boulnois, Joseph, French composer; b. Paris, Jan. 28, 1884; killed in battle at Chalaines, Oct. 20, 1918. He studied piano and composition at the Paris Cons., and later became a church organist and from 1909 choir leader at the Opéra Comique. He wrote an opera, *L'Anneau d'Isis*, and other works, which remain mostly in MS.

Bourdin, Roger, French baritone; b. Lavallois, June 14, 1900; d. Paris, Sept. 14, 1973. He studied at the Paris Cons.; he made his operatic debut as Lescaut in *Manon* in 1922 at the Paris Opéra Comique; he also sang at the Paris Opéra. He made his Covent Garden debut in London in 1930 as Debussy's Pélleas. He was married to **Geori Boué**.

Bourgault-Ducoudray, Louis-Albert, French composer; b. Nantes, Feb. 2, 1840; d. Paris, July 4, 1910. At the age of 18 he composed his first opera, *L'Atelier de Prague* (Nantes, 1858). He was a pupil of Ambroise Thomas at the Paris Cons., taking the Grand Prix de Rome in 1862 with a cantata, *Louise de Mézières*. He founded an amateur choral society in Paris (1868). He spent some time in research in Greece, after which he publ. *Souvenirs d'une mission musicale en Grèce, 30 mélodies populaires de Grèce et de l'Orient*, and *Études sur la musique ecclésiastique grecque* (1877). He was appointed prof. of music history at the Paris Cons. in 1878. He composed 5 operas: *Thamara* (Paris Opéra, Dec. 28, 1891), *Michel Colomb* (Brussels, May 7, 1887), *Anne de Bretagne* (Nantes, Dec. 1892), *Myrdhin* (Nantes, March 28, 1912), and *L'Atelier de Prague* (Nantes, 1858).

BIBL.: M. Emmanuel, *Éloge funèbre de L.-A. B.-D.* (Paris, 1911).

Bourguignon, Francis de, Belgian composer; b. Brussels, May 29, 1890; d. there, April 11, 1961. He was a student of Dubois and Tinel (composition) and de Greef (piano) at the Brussels Cons.; after touring extensively as a pianist, he pursued composition studies with Gilson in Brussels (1925). With 7 other students of Gilson, he formed the Groupe des Synthétistes to promote contemporary music. From 1939 to 1955 he taught at the Brussels Cons. Among his compositions are *La Mort d'Orphé*, ballet (1928), *Congo*, radio play (1936), and *Le Mauvais Pari*, chamber opera (1937).

BIBL.: A. Vandernoot, *F. d.B.* (Brussels, 1949).

Bovicelli, Giovanni Battista, Italian singer, music theorist, and composer who flourished in the late 16th century. He wrote the important treatise *Regole, passaggi di musica, madrigali et motetti passeggiati* (Venice, 1594; ed. by N. Bridgman, Kassel, 1957), notable for its treatment of singing and improvised vocal ornamentation.

Bovy, Vina (real name, **Malvina Johanna Pauline Félicité Bovi van Overberghe**), Belgian soprano; b. Ghent, May 22, 1900; d. there, May 16, 1983. She studied piano and voice at the Ghent Cons. (1915–17). In 1917 she made her debut in *Hänsel und Gretel* in Ghent; she sang at the Théâtre Royal de la Monnaie in Brussels (1920–23) and at the Teatro Colón in Buenos Aires (1927), and had guest engagements in Barcelona, Madrid, Monte Carlo, Venice, Milan, Rome, and Paris. On Dec. 24, 1936, she made her Metropolitan Opera debut in New York as Violetta, remaining on its roster until 1938. From 1947 to 1955 she was director of the Ghent Opera. Among her best roles were Gilda, Manon, Lakmé, Juliette, Pamina, Desdemona, and Elsa.

BIBL.: J. Deleersnyder, *V. B.* (Ghent, 1965).

Bovy-Lysberg, Charles-Samuel, Swiss pianist and composer; b. Lysberg, near Geneva, Feb. 1, 1821; d. Geneva, Feb. 15, 1873. He went to Paris and was one of the few young pianists to study with Chopin (1835). Returning to Switzerland, he settled at Dardagny, near Geneva, in 1848; taught piano at the Geneva Cons., and gave recitals in the French cantons. His opera, *La Fille du carillonneur*, was produced in Geneva in 1854, but he became known chiefly by his effective salon pieces for piano (numbering about 130). His real name was Bovy, but he hyphenated it with Lysberg, the name of his birthplace.

Bowles, Paul (Frederic), American man of letters and composer; b. N.Y., Dec. 30, 1910. He became fascinated with pictorial arts, belles lettres, and the vocal projection of poetry as a child, and when he was 8 he also began to study music. At 17 he had his first poem publ. in the literary review *transition*. In 1929 he made his way to Paris, where he was dazzled by its intellectual resplendence and the insouciant millieu of the Left Bank. Returning to New York, his hypnopomping musical talent manifested itself and in 1930 he became a student of Copland. In 1931 he returned to Paris, where he continued his studies with Copland and had a few lessons with Boulanger. He became a habitué of the circle surrounding Gertrude Stein and Alice B. Toklas, but his wanderlust led him to visit Berlin and North Africa. The latter sojourn proved the turning point in his artistic career, both as a composer and as a man of letters. After composing several orch., chamber, and vocal scores, Bowles attracted attention with his ballet *Yankee Clipper* (1936). During the following 2 decades he proved adept at composing film scores and incidental music for plays. In 1941 he received a Guggenheim fellowship, which resulted in his opera *The Wind Remains* (1941–43), after García Lorca. His psychological attraction to exotic lands prompted him to return to North Africa in 1947, which remained the center of his activities for the rest of his life with occasional sojourns to various lands abroad. Among his later compositions was the opera *Yerma* (1948–55), also after García Lorca. As a composer, he found his métier in works reflecting American, Mexican, and North African elements. Among his dramatic works are the operas *Denmark Vesey* (1938), *The Wind Remains* (1941–43), and *Yerma* (1948–55) and the ballets *Yankee Clipper* (1936), *The Ballroom Guide* (1937), *Pastorela* (1941), and *Colloque sentimental* (1944). He also composed incidental music to plays and various film scores. Bowles soon became best known, however, as a writer, when in 1949 he publ. the first of his many bone-chilling novels, *The Sheltering Sky*. He also wrote short stories and made trs. of native works about North Africa. His autobiography was publ. as *Without Stopping* (1972). The vol. *Paul Bowles: Music* (1995) is a collection of essays, interviews, and reviews. Bowles was married to the extraordinary novelist and playwright Jane Auer, who died in 1973.

BIBL.: C. Sawyer-Lauçanno, *An Invisible Spectator: A Biography of P. B.* (N.Y., 1989).

Bowman, James (Thomas), notable English countertenor; b. Oxford, Nov. 6, 1941. He was educated at New College, Oxford (Dip.Ed., 1964; M.A. in history, 1967) and received vocal instruction in London from De Rentz and Manen. In 1967 he made his operatic debut as Britten's Oberon at Aldeburgh with the English Opera Group. From 1967 he sang with the group regularly in London, and also was a member of the Early Music Consort (1967–76). In 1970 he appeared in *Semele* at the Sadler's Wells Opera there, and continued to sing there after it became the English National Opera in 1974. He sang Endymion in *La Calisto* at the Glyndebourne Festival in 1970, and sang there regularly until 1974. On July 12, 1972, he created the role of the Priest in Maxwell Davies's *Taverner* at London's Covent Garden. Britten then wrote the role of Apollo for him in *Death in Venice* (Aldeburgh, June 16, 1973). On July 7, 1977, he created the role of Astron in Tippett's *The Ice Break* at Covent Garden. In 1979 he appeared at the Opéra Comique in Paris and in 1983 he sang in Geneva. He was engaged as Jommelli's Fetonte at Milan's La Scala in 1988. In 1992 he portrayed Britten's Oberon at the Aix-en-Provence Festival. In 1996 he sang Daniel in Handel's *Belshazzar* at the Göttingen Festival. He was made a Commander of the Order of the British Empire in 1997.

Boxberg, Christian Ludwig, German composer; b. Sondershausen, April 24, 1670; d. Görlitz, Dec. 1, 1729. He studied at the Thomasschule in Leipzig, and from 1692 to 1702 was organist in Grossenhain; he also was active as a librettist, composer, and singer at the Leipzig Opera. In 1702 he became organist at Ss. Peter and Paul in Görlitz. He wrote librettos for the operas of N. A. Strungk. His own operas include *Orion* (Ansbach, 1697), *Die verschwiegene Treue* (Ansbach, 1698), *Sardanapolus* (Ansbach, 1698), and *Amyntas und Phyllis* (Leipzig, 1700).

BIBL.: H. Mersmann, *C. L. B. und seine Oper "Sardanapolus," Ansbach, 1698* (diss., Univ. of Berlin, 1916).

Boyd, Anne (Elizabeth), Australian composer; b. Sydney, April 10, 1946. She studied flute at the New South Wales Cons. (1960–63) and composition at the Univ. of Sydney (1963–66); she concluded her studies at York Univ. in England (Ph.D., 1972). She was a lecturer at the Univ. of Sussex (1975–77) and served as head of the music dept. at the Univ. of Hong Kong (1980–88). She composed two children's operas, *The Little Mermaid* (1978) and *The Beginning of the Day* (1980), and *The Rose Garden*, theater piece (1972).

Bozay, Attila, Hungarian composer and teacher; b. Balatonfüzfö, Aug. 11, 1939. He studied in Budapest at the Bartók Cons. (1954–57) and then with Farkas at the Academy of Music, graduating in 1962. After serving as a music producer for the Hungarian Radio (1963–66), he went to Paris on a UNESCO scholarship in 1967. Returning to Budapest, he devoted himself fully to composition and later taught at the Academy of Music. In 1968 and 1979 he received the Erkel Prize. In 1984 he was made a Merited Artist by the Hungarian government. In 1988 he received the Bartók-Pásztory Award. He composed the operas *Küngisz királynö* (Queen Kungisz; 1968–69) and *Csongor és Tünde* (1979–84; Budapest, Jan. 20, 1985).

Božič, Darijan, Slovenian composer; b. Slavonski Brod, April 29, 1933. He studied composition with Škerjanc and conducting with Švara at the Ljubljana Academy of Music (1958–61); upon graduation he served as an opera conductor and artistic director of the Slovenian Phil. (1970–74) and later was a prof. at the Univ. of Maribor (from 1988). His music was at first influenced by jazz; later he adopted radical serial techniques. He composed *Baletska jednočinka*, ballet (1957), *Humoreske*, opera (1958), *Spoštovanja vredna vlačuga*, opera (1960), *Polineikes*, collage (1966), *Gluha okna*, ballet (1967), *Ares Eros*, opera (1970), *Lizistrata*, opera (1975), and *King Lear*, opera (1985).

Bozza, Eugène, French composer and conductor; b. Nice, April 4, 1905; d. Valenciennes, Sept. 28, 1991. He studied at the Paris Cons.; received the Grand Prix de Rome in 1934. From 1939 to 1948 he was conductor of the Opéra Comique in Paris; then moved to Valenciennes, where he was appointed director of the local cons. His stage works include *Fête romaine*, ballet (1942), *Jeux de plage*, ballet (1946), *Léonidas*, opera (1947), *Beppo ou le Mort dont personne ne voulait*, comic opera (1963), and *La Duchesse de Langeais*, lyric drama (Lille, 1967).

Bradley, Gwendolyn, black American soprano; b. N.Y., Dec. 12, 1952. She received training at the North Carolina School of the Arts in Winston-Salem, N.C., the Curtis Inst. of Music in Philadelphia, and the Philadelphia Academy of Vocal Arts. In 1976 she made her operatic debut as Verdi's Nannetta at the Lake George (N.Y.) Opera, and on Feb. 20, 1981, she made her first appearance at the Metropolitan Opera in New York as the Nightingale in *L'Enfant et les sortilèges*, returning there to sing such roles as Blondchen, Gilda, and Offenbach's Olympia in subsequent years. She made her European debut at the Corfu (Greece) Festival in 1981, and later was guest artist with opera companies in Cleveland, Philadelphia, Amsterdam, Glyndebourne, Hamburg, Berlin, Monte Carlo, and Nice. She also appeared as a soloist with many distinguished orchs. and as a recitalist.

Braein, Edvard Fliflet, Norwegian composer and conductor; b. Kristiansund, Aug. 23, 1924; d. Oslo, April 30, 1976. He was of a musical family; his grandfather was an organist and choirmaster, and his father, Edvard Braein (1887–1957), was a composer, organist, and conductor. He studied at the Oslo Cons., graduating in 1943; then studied conducting with Grüner-Hegge and composition with Brustad; later he took private lessons with Rivier in Paris (1950–51). Upon returning to Oslo, he was active mainly as a choral conductor. He composed *Anne Pedersdotter*, opera (Oslo, 1971), *Den stundeslose* (The Wastrel), opera buffa (Oslo, 1975), and *The Little Matchstick Girl*, ballet (1976; unfinished).

Braga, Gaetano, Italian cellist and composer; b. Giulianova, Abruzzi, June 9, 1829; d. Milan, Nov. 21, 1907. He studied at the

Naples Cons. with C. Gaetano (1841–52). He made tours as a cellist in Europe and America but lived mostly in Paris and London. Braga wrote several operas: *Alina, or La spregiata* (1853), *Estella di San Germano* (Vienna, 1857), *Il ritratto* (Naples, 1858), *Margherita la mendicante* (Paris, 1859), *Mormile* (La Scala, Milan, 1862), *Ruy Blas* (1865), *Reginella* (Lecco, 1871), and *Caligola* (Lisbon, 1873).

BIBL.: V. Bindi, *G. B.: Da ricordi della sua vita* (Naples, 1927).

Braham (real name, **Abraham**), **John,** renowned English tenor; b. London, March 20, 1774; d. there, Feb. 17, 1856. He studied with Leoni in London, with Rauzzini in Bath, and with Isola in Genoa. He made his debut at Covent Garden (April 21, 1787); he then appeared at Drury Lane in 1796, in the opera *Mahmoud* by Storace. He was subsequently engaged to sing at the Italian Opera House in London. In 1798 he undertook an extensive tour in Italy, and also appeared in Hamburg. Returning to England in 1801, he was increasingly successful. Endowed with a powerful voice of 3 octaves in compass, he knew no difficulties in operatic roles. He was the original Huon in Weber's *Oberon* (1826). As a ballad writer, he was very popular; he wrote much of the music for the operatic roles that he sang; often he added portions to operas by other composers, as in *The Americans* (1811), with its famous song "The Death of Nelson"; he contributed incidental music to 12 productions. In 1831 he entered upon a theatrical business venture; he acquired the Colosseum in Regent's Park; in 1836 he had the St. James's Theatre built, but failed to recoup his investment and lost much of his considerable fortune. He made an American tour from 1840 to 1842 despite the weakening of his voice with age; however, his dramatic appeal remained undiminished and he was able to impress the American public in concert appearances. He then returned to London, making made his final appearance in 1852.

BIBL.: J. Mewburn Levien, *The Singing of J. B.* (London, 1945).

Braithwaite, Nicholas (Paul Dallon), English conductor, son of **(Henry) Warwick Braithwaite**; b. London, Aug. 26, 1939. He studied at the Royal Academy of Music in London, at the Bayreuth Festival master classes, and with Swarowsky in Vienna. He was assoc. conductor of the Bournemouth Sym. Orch. (1967–70), assoc. principal conductor of the Sadler's Wells Opera in London (1970–74), and music director of the Glyndebourne Touring Opera (1976–80). After serving as principal guest conductor of the Manchester Camerata (1977–84), he was its principal conductor (1984–91). He also was music director of the Stora Theater Opera and Ballet in Göteborg (1981–84), chief conductor of the Adelaide Sym. Orch. (1987–91), and dean of the Victorian College of the Arts in Melbourne (1988–91). He then was chief conductor of the Tasmanian Sym. Orch. (from 1991).

Braithwaite, (Henry) Warwick, New Zealand conductor, father of **Nicholas (Paul Dallon) Braithwaite**; b. Dunedin, Jan. 9, 1896; d. London, Jan. 18, 1971. He studied at the Royal Academy of Music in London; he won the Challen Gold Medal and the Battison Hayes Prize. He began his career as a conductor with the O'Mara Opera Co., then conducted with the British National Opera Co. He was assistant music director of the BBC, then went to its Cardiff studio in Wales as music director; he also conducted the Cardiff Musical Soc. (1924–31). He was a founder of the Welsh National Orch. From 1932 to 1940 he was a conductor at the Sadler's Wells Opera in London, then he led the Scottish Orch. in Glasgow (1940–46). Later he was a ballet conductor at the Royal Opera, Covent Garden, in London (1950–53), then conducted the National Orch. of New Zealand and served as artistic director of the National Opera of Australia (1954–55). From 1956 to 1960 he was music director of the Welsh National Opera, then was again a conductor at Sadler's Wells until 1968. He publ. *The Conductor's Art* (London, 1952).

Brambach, Caspar Joseph, German composer; b. Oberdollendorf, near Königswinter, July 14, 1833; d. there, June 19, 1902. He studied composition at the Cologne Cons., then taught there (1858–61) and later was active as a teacher and composer in Bonn (1861–69). He wrote many secular cantatas and also an opera, *Ariadne*. His brother was the musicologist Wilhelm Brambach (1841–1932).

Brambilla, Marietta, Italian contralto, sister of **Teresa Brambilla**; b. Cassano d'Adda, June 6, 1807; d. Milan, Nov. 6, 1875. She was a member of a musical family; her 4 sisters were singers. She studied at the Milan Cons., making her debut in London in 1827, then sang in Italy, Vienna, and Paris. She eventually settled in Milan as a teacher. She publ. collections of vocalises.

Brambilla, Teresa, Italian soprano, sister of **Marietta Brambilla**; b. Cassano d'Adda, Oct. 23, 1813; d. Milan, July 15, 1895. She studied singing at the Milan Cons., making her debut in 1831 in Milan and traveling through Europe, including Russia. Her appearances at La Scala were highly successful. After several seasons in Paris, she was engaged at the Teatro La Fenice in Venice, where she created the role of Gilda in *Rigoletto* (March 11, 1851).

Branchu, Alexandrine Caroline (née **Chevalier de Lavit**), famous French soprano; b. Cap Français, Santo Domingo, Nov. 2, 1780; d. Passy, Oct. 14, 1850. She was a pupil of Garat at the Paris Cons. In 1799 she married the ballet dancer Branchu, and that same year made her debut at the Théâtre Feydeau in Paris. From 1801 to 1826 she was one of the leading members of the Paris Opéra. She sang principal roles in the premieres of Cherubini's *Anacréon* (1803) and *Les Abencérages* (1813), winning the composer's approbation. She was also highly regarded for her portrayals of Gluck's Alcestis, Iphigenia, and Armida, and of Piccinni's Dido.

Brancour, René, French music critic; b. Paris, May 17, 1862; d. there, Nov. 16, 1948. Educated at the Paris Cons., he became curator of its collection of musical instruments; in 1906 he began a course of lectures on aesthetics at the Sorbonne; he also wrote newspaper criticism. A brilliant writer, he poured invective on the works of composers of the advanced school; his tastes were conservative, but he accepted French music of the Impressionist period. He wrote biographies of Felicien David (1911), Méhul (1912), Massenet (1923), and Offenbach (1929).

Brand, Max(imilian), Austrian-born American composer; b. Lemberg, April 26, 1896; d. Langenzersdorf, near Vienna, April 5, 1980. He became a student of Schreker in Vienna in 1919, and continued as his student in Berlin in 1920. He also received instruction from Alois Hàba and Erwin Stein. Brand's early use of 12-tone methods is revealed in his *Fünf Balladen nach Gedichten von Else Lasker-Schüler* (1927). He scored a sensation when he brought out his first opera, *Maschinist Hopkins* (Duisburg, April 13, 1929), which subsequently was performed throughout Europe. This expressionistic score of the "machine era" served as a remarkable precursor to Berg's *Lulu*. Brand pursued his interest in avant-garde expression by founding Vienna's Mimoplastisches Theater für Ballett and by serving as codirector of the Raimund Theater, where he oversaw the Wiener Opernproduktion company. He also was associated with Eisler in producing experimental films. As a Jew, Brand's works were banned by the Nazis in Germany in 1933. After the Anschluss in Austria in 1938, he was compelled to flee to Brazil. In 1940 he went to the United States and in 1944 became a naturalized American citizen. He was active in New York as director of the Music and Theatre Wing, Caravan of East and West. Around 1958 he began to experiment with electronics. In 1975 he returned to Austria and was active in his own electronic music studio.

WORKS: DRAMATIC: *Maschinist Hopkins*, opera (1928; Duisburg, April 13, 1929); *Kleopatra*, opera (1932–38); *Requiem*, opera (1933); *Die Chronik*, scenic cantata (1938); *The Gate*, scenic oratorio (N.Y., May 23, 1944); *Stormy Interlude*, opera (1955); ballets; incidental music.

Brandl, Johann Evangelist, German composer; b. Kloster Rohr, near Regensburg, Nov. 14, 1760; d. Karlsruhe, May 25, 1837. He studied in various religious schools and monasteries as a youth, then decided to devote himself to music, and became proficient as an organist and violinist. He was attached to the court of the Archduke of Baden as music director. He composed the operas *Germania* (1800), *Triumph des Vaterherzens* (Karlsruhe, Jan. 15, 1811), *Omar der Gute* (Karlsruhe, Aug. 24, 1811), and *Nanthild, das Mädchen von Valbella* (Karlsruhe, May 19, 1813); also oratorios.

BIBL.: O. Danzer, *J. E. B.s Leben und Werke* (Leipzig, 1936).

Brandt, Marianne (real name, **Marie Bischoff**), Austrian contralto; b. Vienna, Sept. 12, 1842; d. there, July 9, 1921. She studied voice in Vienna, and later with Pauline Viardot-García in Baden-Baden (1869–70). She made her debut as Rachel in *La Juive* in Olmütz on Jan. 4, 1867, then sang in Hamburg and at the Berlin Royal Opera (1868–82). In 1872 she appeared in London. She made her American debut as Leonore at the Metropolitan Opera in New York on Nov. 19, 1884, and remained on its staff until 1888; also sang Italian roles in operas by Verdi and Meyerbeer. In 1890 she settled in Vienna as a singing teacher.

Brandts-Buys, Jan (Willem Frans), Dutch composer; b. Zutphen, Sept. 12, 1868; d. Salzburg, Dec. 7, 1933. He was a pupil of M. Schwarz and A. Urspruch at the Raff Cons. in Frankfurt am Main; he lived for a time in Vienna; later he settled in Salzburg. His first opera, *Das Veilchenfest* (Berlin, Dec. 3, 1909), met with opposition; a second opera, *Das Glockenspiel* (Dresden, Dec. 4, 1913), was received more kindly, while a third, *Die drei Schneider von Schönau* (Dresden, April 1, 1916), was quite successful. Subsequent operas were *Der Eroberer* (Dresden, Jan. 14, 1918), *Micarême* (Vienna, Nov. 14, 1919), *Der Mann im Mond* (Dresden, June 18, 1922), *Traumland* (Dresden, Nov. 24, 1927), and *Ulysses* (German radio, March 12, 1937). He also wrote a ballet, *Machinalität* (Amsterdam, 1928).

Brannigan, Owen, English bass; b. Annitsford, March 10, 1908; d. Newcastle upon Tyne, May 9, 1973. He studied at the Guildhall School of Music in London (1934–42), where he won its gold medal in 1942. In 1943 he made his operatic debut as Sarastro with the Sadler's Wells Opera in London, where he sang until 1948 and again from 1952 to 1958; he also appeared at the Glyndebourne Festivals (1947–49), at London's Covent Garden, and with the English Opera Group. He became closely associated with the music of Britten, in whose operas he created Swallow in *Peter Grimes* (1945), Collatinus in *The Rape of Lucretia* (1946), Superintendent Budd in *Billy Budd* (1947), Noye in *Noye's Fludde* (1958), and Bottom in *A Midsummer Night's Dream* (1960). He also sang in oratorio, concerts, and lighter fare. In 1964 he was made a member of the Order of the British Empire.

Branzell, Karin Maria, noted Swedish contralto; b. Stockholm, Sept. 24, 1891; d. Altadena, Calif., Dec. 14, 1974. She was a pupil of Thekla Hofer in Stockholm, Louis Bachner in Berlin, and Enrico Rosati in N.Y. In 1912 she made her operatic debut as Prince Sarvilaka in d'Albert's *Izeijl* in Stockholm, where she sang at the Royal Opera until 1918; she was then a member of the Berlin State Opera until 1923. On Feb. 6, 1924, she made her Metropolitan Opera debut in New York as Fricka in *Die Walküre*, and remained on the roster until 1944; she sang there again in 1951. She also appeared at the Bayreuth Festivals (1930–31), London's Covent Garden (1935; 1937–38), and the San Francisco Opera (1941). In later years she taught at the Juilliard School of Music in New York. The exceptional range of her voice allowed her to sing both contralto and soprano roles. Although especially known for such Wagnerian roles as Ortrud, Venus, Erda, Brangäne, and the *Walküre* Brünnhilde, she also was admired as Amneris, Dalila, Herodias, and Clytemnestra.

Braslau, Sophie, American contralto; b. N.Y., Aug. 16, 1892; d. there, Dec. 22, 1935. She studied with Arturo Buzzi-Peccia. On Nov. 27, 1913, she made her Metropolitan Opera debut in New York as the voice in *Parsifal*, followed by her formal debut there the next day as Fyodor in *Boris Godunov*; she remained on its roster until 1920, creating Cadman's Shanewis on March 23, 1918. She gave concerts throughout the United States, and in 1931 made a tour of Europe. In 1934 she sang for the last time in New York

Braun, Carl, German bass; b. Meisenheim, Prussia, June 2, 1885; d. Hamburg, April 19, 1960. He studied with Hermann Gausche in Kreuznach and later with Eugen Robert Weiss. He sang at the Wiesbaden Opera (1906–11) and at the Vienna Court Opera (1911–12), then was engaged at the Berlin City Opera (1912–14). He also appeared at the Bayreuth Festivals (1906–31). On Feb. 8, 1913, he made his American debut at the Metropolitan Opera in New York as King Marke, but was dismissed as an enemy alien in the spring of 1917 when the United States entered the war against Germany. In 1922–23 he made a South American tour; he also sang in the United States in 1928 and 1931. In 1933 he was engaged as a stage director at the German Opera in Berlin, and in 1935–36 held similar posts at the Berlin Volksoper and at the Danzig Municipal Theater. In 1937 he retired from the stage and was thereafter active mainly as a concert agent in Hamburg. He was particularly esteemed for his Wagnerian roles.

Braunfels, Walter, German composer and pedagogue; b. Frankfurt am Main, Dec. 19, 1882; d. Cologne, March 19, 1954. He studied piano in Vienna with Leschetizky and composition in Munich with Thuille. In 1925 he became a codirector of the Hochschule für Musik in Cologne. With the advent of the Nazi regime in 1933, he was compelled to abandon teaching; after the collapse of the Third Reich in 1945, he reorganized the Hochschule für Musik in Cologne and served as its director until 1950. He excelled mainly as an opera composer; the following operas are notable: *Falada* (Essen, May 24, 1906); *Prinzessin Brambilla* (Stuttgart, March 25, 1909; rev. 1931); *Ulenspiegel* (Stuttgart, Nov. 9, 1913); *Die Vögel*, after Aristophanes (Munich, Dec. 4, 1920; his most successful opera); *Don Gil von den grünen Hosen* (Munich, Nov. 15, 1924); *Der glaserne Berg* (Krefeld, Dec. 4, 1928); *Galatea* (Cologne, Jan. 26, 1930); *Der Traum, Ein Leben* (1937); *Die heilige Johanna* (1942); also a mystery play, *Verkündigung*, after Paul Claudel (1936). He believed in the artistic and practical value of Wagnerian leading motifs; in his harmonies he was close to Richard Strauss, but he also applied impressionistic devices related to Debussy.

Bravničar, Matija, Slovenian composer and teacher; b. Tolmin, Feb. 24, 1897; d. Ljubljana, Nov. 25, 1977. After service in the Austrian army (1915–18) he was a violinist at the opera theater in Ljubljana; meanwhile he studied composition at the Cons. there, graduating in 1932. He was director of the Ljubljana Academy of Music (1945–49) where he later taught composition (1952–68); was president of the Soc. of Slovenian Composers (1949–52) and of the Union of Yugoslavian Composers (1953–57). In his works, he cultivated a neoclassical style, with thematic material strongly influenced by the melorhythmic inflections of Slovenian folk music.

WORKS: DRAMATIC: *Pohujšanje v dolini Sentflorijanski* (Scandal in St. Florian's Valley), opera buffa (Ljubljana, May 11, 1930); *Stoji, stoji Ljubljanca*, satirical revue (Ljubljana, Dec. 2, 1933); *Hlapec Jernij in njegova pravica* (Knight Jernej and His Justice), opera (Ljubljana, Jan. 25, 1941).

Brecher, Gustav, German conductor and editor; b. Eichwald, near Teplitz, Bohemia, Feb. 5, 1879; d. (suicide) Ostend, May 1940. His family moved to Leipzig in 1889, where he studied with Jadassohn. His first major work, the symphonic poem *Rosmersholm*, was introduced by R. Strauss at a Liszt-Verein concert in Leipzig (1896), where Brecher subsequently made his debut as a conductor (1897). He was a vocal coach and occasional conductor of operas in Leipzig (1898); he also conducted in Vienna (1901), and served as first conductor in Olmütz (1902), Hamburg (1903), and Cologne (1911–16); then was in Frankfurt am Main (1916–24) and Leipzig (1924–33). He committed suicide with his wife aboard a boat off the Belgian coast while attempting to flee from the advancing Nazi troops. He was the author of *Über die veristische Oper, Analysen zu Werken von Berlioz und Strauss*, and *Über Operntexte und Opernubersetzungen* (1911).

Brecknock, John, English tenor; b. Long Eaton, Nov. 29, 1937. He studied with Frederic Sharp and Dennis Dowling at the Birmingham School of Music. In 1967 he made his debut as Alfred in *Die Fledermaus* at the Sadler's Wells Opera in London, and continued to sing with fine success; he also appeared at the Glyndebourne Festival (1971) and at London's Covent Garden (debut as Fenton, 1974). On March 23, 1977, he made his Metropolitan Opera debut in New York as Tamino. He also appeared in various European operatic centers. Although best known for such roles as Mozart's Belmonte and Ottavio, Rossini's Count Almaviva and Comte Ory, and Verdi's Duke of Mantua, he also sang in contemporary roles.

Bredemeyer, Reiner, German composer; b. Velez, Colombia, Feb. 2, 1929; d. Berlin, Dec. 5, 1995. He studied composition with Karl Höller at the Akademie der Tonkunst in Munich (1949–53); he then took courses with Wagner-Regény at the Akademie der Künste in East Berlin (1955–57). In 1961 he was appointed conductor of the German Theater in East Berlin; in 1978 he joined the faculty of the Akademie der Künste there. In his music he was an astute experimenter, but he adhered to the tenets of classical forms and avoided the extremes of modernism. His dramatic works include *Leben der Andrea*, opera after Brecht's *Galileo* (1971), *Die Galoschenoper*, after *The Beggar's Opera* (1978), and *Candide*, after Voltaire (1981–82; Halle, Jan. 12, 1986).

Brediceanu, Tiberiu, Romanian composer, administrator, and music editor; b. Lugoj, Transylvania, April 2, 1877; d. Bucharest, Dec. 19, 1968. He studied music mainly in Romania; he was director of the Astra Cons. in Brasov (1934–40) and director-general of the Romanian Opera in Bucharest (1941–44). He publ. valuable collections of Romanian songs and dances, including 170 Romanian folk melodies, 810 tunes of the Banat regions, and 1,000 songs of Transylvania. Among his own compositions are the operas *Poemul muzical etnografic* (1905; rev. and retitled *Romania in port, joc si cintec*, 1929) and *La şezătoare* (1908). He also composed *Seara mare*, lyric scene (1924) and *Învierea*, pantomime (1932).

Brehm, Alvin, American double bass player, conductor, and composer; b. N.Y., Feb. 8, 1925. He studied with Fred Zimmerman (double bass) and Giannini (orchestration) at the Juilliard School of Music in New York (1942–43), then with Riegger (composition) at Columbia Univ. (M.A., 1951). After making his debut as a double-bass player (1942), he performed with the Pittsburgh Sym. Orch. (1950–51), the Contemporary Chamber Ensemble (1969–73), the Group for Contemporary Music (1971–73), the Philomusica Chamber Music Soc. (1973–83), and the Chamber Music Soc. of Lincoln Center (1984–89). After making his debut as a conductor (1947), he was active in promoting contemporary music. He was founder-conductor of the Composer's Theatre Orch. (1967), and also taught at the State Univ. of N.Y. at Stony Brook (1968–75), the Manhattan School of Music (1969–75), and the State Univ. of N.Y. at Purchase (from 1981), where he also was head of its music division (1981–90). He composed the chamber opera *The Final Theory* (1994).

Brehme, Hans (Ludwig Wilhelm), German composer; b. Potsdam, March 10, 1904; d. Stuttgart, Nov. 10, 1957. He studied piano in Berlin with Wilhelm Kempff; he taught at Stuttgart and elsewhere. A highly diligent composer, he wrote music in many genres; the idiom of his compositions is fundamentally Classical, with a generous admixture of moderately modern harmonies. He wrote the opera *Der Uhrmacher von Strassburg* (1941) and the operetta, *Versiegelten Bürgermeister* (1944).

Brema, Marie (real name, **Minny Fehrmann**), English mezzo-soprano; b. Liverpool (of a German father and an American mother), Feb. 28, 1856; d. Manchester, March 22, 1925. She was a pupil of Henschel (1890). Under the name Bremer (in honor of her father's native city of Bremen), she made her concert debut in London singing Schubert's *Ganymed* on Feb. 21, 1891. Her operatic debut followed on Oct. 19, 1891, when she sang Lola in the first English performance of *Cavalleria rusticana* at London's Shaftesbury Theatre. She was the first English-born singer to appear at the Bayreuth Festival when she sang Ortrud in 1894, and returned there to sing Fricka in the *Ring* cycle in 1896 and Kundry in 1897. During the 1894–95 season, she toured in the United States with the Damrosch Opera Co. On Nov. 27, 1895, she made her Metropolitan Opera debut in New York as Brangäne, remaining on its roster until 1896 and appearing there again from 1898 to 1900. In 1900 she was soloist in the premiere of Elgar's *The Dream of Gerontius*. She created the role of Beatrice in Stanford's *Much Ado About Nothing* at London's Covent Garden in 1901, and in 1902 she sang Brünnhilde in the first French mounting of *Götterdämmerung* in Paris. She oversaw opera productions in English at London's Savoy Theatre in 1910, where she also sang Orfeo. From 1913 until her death she was prof. of voice and director of the opera class at the Royal Manchester College of Music.

Brendel, Wolfgang, German baritone; b. Munich, Oct. 20, 1947. After vocal studies, he began his career in Kaiserslautern. He joined the Bavarian State Opera in Munich in 1971, and became Kammersänger there in 1977. On Nov. 20, 1975, he made his Metropolitan Opera debut in New York as Count Almaviva in *Le nozze di Figaro*; he then appeared at the San Francisco Opera as Rodrigo in *Don Carlos* (1979), at Milan's La Scala as Count Almaviva (1981), at the Chicago Lyric Opera as Miller in *Luisa Miller* (1982), and at the Bayreuth Festival as Wolfram in *Tannhäuser* (1985). He made his debut at London's Covent Garden as Conte Di Luna in *Il Trovatore* on Oct. 12, 1985. In 1990 he sang Eugene Onegin in Chicago. He portrayed Amfortas at La Scala in 1992. In 1997 he appeared as the Dutchman at the Deutsche Oper in Berlin. He appeared in opera centers throughout Europe and the United States; his most noted roles include Rossini's Figaro, Papageno, Eugene Onegin, Amfortas, Silvio, and Pelléas.

Brent, Charlotte, English soprano; b. c.1735; d. London, April 10, 1802. She studied with Arne, making her operatic debut in his Eliza at the Smock Alley Theatre in Dublin on Nov. 29, 1755; she then sang at London's Drury Lane Theatre and at Covent Garden. She was noted for her performances of Polly in *The Beggar's Opera* and for corresponding roles in Handel's operas.

Brenta, Gaston, Belgian composer; b. Brussels, June 10, 1902; d. there, May 30, 1969. He studied theory with Gilson; in 1925 he and 7 other pupils of Gilson formed the Belgian Groupe des Synthétistes, advocating a more modern approach to composition. From 1931 he was associated with the Belgian Radio; from 1953 to 1967 he was music director of the French Services there. His music follows the traditions of cosmopolitan Romanticism, with exotic undertones.

WORKS: DRAMATIC: *Le Khâdi dupé*, opera (Brussels, Dec. 16, 1929); 2 radio dramas: *Aucassin et Nicolette* (1934) and *Heracles* (1955); 3 ballets: *Zo'har* (1928); *Florilège de Valses* (1940); *Candide* (1955); *Le Bal chez la Lorette* (1954), which forms a part of *Les Bals de Paris*, a large ballet consisting of passages contributed by several Belgian composers.

Bresgen, Cesar, Austrian composer and teacher of German descent; b. Florence, Oct. 16, 1913; d. Salzburg, April 7, 1988. He studied organ, piano, conducting, and composition at the Munich Academy of Music (1930–36), his mentors being Emmanuel Gatscher, Gottfried Rüdinger, and Joseph Haas. In 1936 he won the Felix Mottl Prize for composition. After working in the music division of the Bavarian Eadio in Munich, he settled in Salzburg in 1939 and organized his own music school; he also taught composition at the Mozarteum. He served in the army during World War II, and then was a church organist and choir director in Mittersill. In 1947 he returned to the Salzburg Mozarteum as prof. of composition. In 1974 he was awarded the Austrian State Prize for music. He publ. the books *Musikalische Dokumentation* (Vienna, 1982) and *Die Improvisation in der Musik* (Wilhelmshaven, 1983), as well as folk-song collections. As a composer, Bresgen acquired a notable facility for writing effective *Gebrauchsmusik*.

WORKS: DRAMATIC: *Der Goggolore*, Singspiel (1937–39; unfinished); *Dornröschenm*, Singspiel (Strasbourg, April 15, 1942); *Paracelsus*, opera (1942–43); *Das Urteil des Paris*, komisches Singspiel (Göttingen, Jan. 31, 1943); *Der Igel als Brautigam*, children's opera (Esslingen, Nov. 3, 1948; rev. version, Nuremburg, Nov. 13, 1951); *Visiones amantis* or *Der Wolkensteiner*, Ludus tragicus (1951; Bremen Radio, Feb. 17, 1964; 1st stage perf., Innsbruck, Dec. 20, 1971); *Niño fliegt mit Niña*, "insect comedy" for Children (Munich, May 14, 1953); *Brüderlein Hund*, children's opera (Nuremberg, Nov. 12, 1953); *Der ewige Arzt*, Mysterein-spiel (Schwyz, Feb. 10, 1956); *Ercole*, opera (Hamburg Radio, 1956); *Der Mann im Mond*, musical fairy tale (Nuremberg, May 22, 1960); *Die alte Lokomotive*, scenic cantata (Munich, Oct. 7, 1960); *Die Schattendiebe* or *Ali und der Bilderdiebel*, children's Singspiel (Vienna, April 13, 1962); *Bastian der Faulpelz*, musical pantomime (Hamburg, 1966); *Trubloff*, Singspiel (1970); *Der Engel von Pra*, opera (Salzburg, Dec. 25, 1978; rev. 1985); *Pilatus*, opera (Villach, Aug. 2, 1980); *Krabat*, Singspiel (1982); *Albolina, oder der Kampf der Geister um die Morgenrote*, musical fairy tale (Villach, July 12, 1987).

BIBL.: D. Larese, *C. B.* (Amriswil, 1968); R. Lück, *C. B.* (Vienna, 1974).

Bressler, Charles, American tenor; b. Kingston, Pa., April 1, 1926; d. N.Y., Nov. 28, 1996. After studies with Lucia Dunham, Sergius Kagen, and Marjorie Schloss at the Juilliard School of Music in New York (graduated, 1950; postgraduate diploma, 1951), he became a founding member of the N.Y. Pro Musica, with which he toured widely (1953–63). He also was a founding member of the N.Y. Chamber Soloists (from 1957); likewise he appeared with the Santa Fe Opera and the Washington (D.C.) Opera Soc., and toured Europe as a concert artist. He taught at various schools, including N.Y.'s Mannes College of Music (from 1966) and Manhattan School of Music (from 1978). He was best known for his performances of early music, but also had success in contemporary roles.

Bressler-Gianoli, Clotilde, Italian contralto; b. Geneva (of Italian parents), June 3, 1875; d. there, May 12, 1912. She received her primary training at the Geneva Cons., then enrolled at the Milan Cons., where she studied singing with Sangiovanni, Giocosa, and Ronconi. She made her operatic debut at the age of 19 in Geneva in *Samson et Dalila*; later sang at La Scala in Milan, at the Opéra Comique in Paris, and with the San Carlo Co. at New Orleans. Her best roles were Carmen and Mignon.

Bretan, Nicolae, remarkable Romanian composer; b. Năsăud, April 6, 1887; d. Cluj, Dec. 1, 1968. He studied at the Klausenburg Cons., composition and voice with Farkas, and violin with Gyémánt (1906–08); then at the Vienna Academy of Music (1908–09) and at the Magyar Királyi Zeneakademia in Budapest (1909–12) with Siklos (theory) and Szerémi (violin). His primary career was that of an opera singer, performing baritone parts at the opera houses in Bratislava, Oradea, and Cluj between 1913 and 1944, also acting as a stage director. At the same time, he surprisingly asserted himself as a composer of operas and lieder in an effective veristic manner, marked by a high degree of professional expertise and considerable originality.

WORKS: DRAMATIC: OPERAS: *Luceafărul* (The Evening Star; in Romanian; tr. by the composer into Hungarian and German; Cluj, Feb. 2, 1921); *Golem* (in Hungarian; tr. by the composer into Romanian and German; Cluj, Dec. 23, 1924); *Eroii de la Rovine* (in Romanian; Cluj, Jan. 24, 1935); *Horia* (in Romanian; also tr. into German by the composer; Cluj, Jan. 24, 1937); *Arald* (in Romanian; 1939). OTHER: *Requiem*; mystery play, *An Extraordinary Seder Evening* (in Hungarian; also tr. into Eng.).

Bretón y Hernández, Tomás, Spanish composer; b. Salamanca, Dec. 29, 1850; d. Madrid, Dec. 2, 1923. As a youth he played in restaurants and theaters. He graduated from the Madrid Cons. (1872), then conducted at the Madrid Opera. In 1901 he joined the faculty of the Madrid Cons. A fertile composer, he contributed greatly to the revival of the zarzuela. He was at his best in the 1-act comic type (*género chico*). Among his operas and zarzuelas (all produced in Madrid) are *Los amantes de Teruel* (1889), *Juan Garín* (1892), *La Dolores* (1895), *El Domingo de Ramos* (1896), *La Verbena de la Paloma* (1894), *Raquel* (to his own libretto; Jan. 20, 1900), *El caballo del señorito* (1901); *Farinelli* (1903); and *Tabaré* (1913). He also wrote an oratorio, *Apocalipsia* (Madrid, 1882).

BIBL.: A. Salcedo, *T. B.: Su vida y sus obras* (Madrid, 1924).

Brett, Charles (Michael), English countertenor; b. Maidenhead, Oct. 27, 1941. He studied with Julian Smith (1957–60) and John Whitworth (1958–60), and at King's College, Cambridge (B.A., 1963; M.A., 1967), where his mentors were Willcocks, Dart, and Leppard. In 1964 he made his debut as a soloist with the Monteverdi Choir and Orch. under Gardiner's direction in Cambridge, and subsequently was engaged to sing around the globe with many of the leading conductors and orchs. He made his recital debut in 1968 at the Winter Gardens in Malvern. Following his operatic debut as Angelica in Fux's *Vinitrice di Alcina* at the Graz Opera in 1984, he sang in Handel's *Semele* in Ludwigsburg (1985), Gluck's *La clemenza di Tito* in Tourcoing and on tour in France (1986), and Britten's *A Midsummer Night's Dream* in Aachen (1987–88). In 1995 he directed a production of *Dido and Aeneas* at the Cervantino Festival in Mexico.

Breuer, Hans (real name, **Johann Peter Joseph**), German tenor; b. Cologne, April 27, 1868; d. Vienna, Oct. 11, 1929. He studied voice at the Cologne Cons. (1890–92), making his operatic debut in 1896 as Mime at Bayreuth, and appearing there regularly until 1914. He also sang at the Vienna Court Opera from 1900 until his death. He made his Metropolitan Opera debut in New York in *Die fliegender Holländer* on Jan. 6, 1900.

Breval, Jean-Baptiste Sébastien, outstanding French cellist and composer; b. Paris, Nov. 6, 1753; d. Colligis, Aisne, March 18, 1823. He studied cello with Jean-Baptiste Cupis, making his debut in 1778 at a Concert Spirituel performing one of his own sonatas; subsequently he was a member of its orch. (1781–91), then played in the orch. of the Théâtre Feydeau (1791–1800). He composed the opéra comique, *Ines et Leonore, ou La Soeur jalouse* (Versailles, Nov. 14, 1788).

Bréval, Lucienne (real name, **Berthe Agnes Lisette Schilling**), Swiss-born French soprano; b. Männedorf, Nov. 4, 1869; d. Paris, Aug. 15, 1935. She studied piano at the Lausanne Cons. and the Geneva Cons. and voice with Wartot at the Paris Cons., making her operatic debut at the Paris Opéra as Selika in *L'Africaine* on Jan. 20, 1892; subsequently she was a principal singer there for 25 years. In 1899 she sang at London's Covent Garden, and on Jan. 16, 1901, made her Metropolitan Opera debut in New York as Chimène in *Le Cid*, remaining on the company's roster until 1902. She excelled in the French repertoire.

Brevik, Tor, Norwegian composer, conductor, and music critic; b. Oslo, Jan. 22, 1932. He studied violin, viola, and theory at the Oslo Cons. before completing his training in Sweden. In 1958 he founded the Oslo Youth Chamber Orch. He was also active as a music critic. He composed the ballet *Contrasts* (1964) and the opera *Da kongen kom til Spilliputt* (1973).

Bréville, Pierre (-Onfroy de), French composer, teacher, and music critic; b. Bar-le-Duc, Feb. 21, 1861; d. Paris, Sept. 24, 1949. He studied at the Paris Cons. with Dubois (1880–82) and later with Franck. He was a prof. of counterpoint at the Paris Schola Cantorum from 1898 to 1902; he was active also as a music critic. He completed (with d'Indy and others) Franck's unfinished opera *Ghiselle*; in his own music, he followed the traditions of French Romanticism. He composed the opera *Eros Vainqueur* (Brussels, March 7, 1910); also overtures to Maeterlinck's plays *La Princesse Maleine* and *Les Sept Princesses*.

Brian, (William) Havergal, English composer of extreme fecundity and longevity; b. Dresden, Staffordshire, Jan. 29, 1876; d. Shoreham-by-the-Sea, Sussex, Nov. 28, 1972. He studied violin, cello, and organ with local teachers; left school at age 12 to earn his living and help his father, who was a potter's turner. At the same time he taught himself elementary theory and also learned French and German without an instructor. From 1904 to 1949 he engaged in musical journalism. He attained a reputation in England as a harmless eccentric possessed by inordinate ambitions to become a composer; he attracted supporters among English musicians, who in turn were derided as gullible admirers of a patent amateur. But Brian continued to write music in large symphonic forms; some of his works were performed, mostly by nonprofessional organizations; amazingly enough, he increased his productivity with age; he wrote 22 syms. after reaching the age of 80, and 7 more after the age of 90. The total number of syms. at the time of his death was 32. Finally, English musicians, critics, conductors, and concert organizations became aware of the Brian phenomenon, and performances, mostly posthumous, followed. A Havergal Brian Soc. was formed in London, and there were a few timorous attempts to further the Brian cause outside of England. The slow acceptance of Brian's music was not due to his overindulgence in dissonance. Quite the contrary is true; Brian was not an innovator; he followed the Germanic traditions of Richard Strauss and Mahler in the spirit of unbridled grandiosity, architectural formidability, and rhapsodically quaquaversal thematicism. Brian's modernism tended to be programmatic, as in the ominous whole-tone progressions in his opera *The Tigers*, illustrating the aerial attacks on London by zeppelins during World War I. Brian's readiness to lend his MSS to anyone showing interest in his music resulted in the loss of several of his works; a few of them were retrieved after years of search.

WORKS: OPERAS: *The Tigers*, to his own libretto (1916–19; lost until 1977; BBC, May 3, 1983); *Turandot*, to a German libretto after Schiller (1950–51); *The Cenci*, after Shelley (1952); *Faust*, after Goethe (1955–56); *Agamemnon*, to an English libretto after Aeschylus (1957; London, Jan. 28, 1972).

BIBL.: M. MacDonald, *H. B.: Perspective on the Music* (London, 1972); K. Eastaugh, *H. B.: The Making of a Composer* (London, 1976); R. Nettel, *H. B. and His Music* (London, 1976).

Briccetti, Thomas (Bernard), American conductor and composer; b. Mt. Kisco, N.Y., Jan, 14, 1936. He studied piano with Jean Dansereau and composition with Barber, Mennin, and Hovhaness; attended the Eastman School of Music in Rochester, N.Y. (1955). In 1959–60 he held the Prix de Rome, and then Ford Foundation Composer's fellowships (1961–63). He was music director of the St. Petersburg (Fla.) Sym. Orch. (1963–68) and the Florida Sun Coast Opera (1964–68). He was assoc. conductor of the Indianapolis Sym. Orch. (1968–72). From 1971 to 1978 he was music director of the Ft. Wayne (Ind.) Phil.; also of the Cleveland Inst. of Music Univ. Circle Orch. (1972–75). He was music director of the Omaha Sym. Orch. and Nebraska Sinfonia (1975–83). After serving as principal guest conductor of the Stavanger Sym. Orch. and Radio Ensemble (1986–87), he was artistic director of the Orch. Stabile in Bergamo (from 1988) and principal conductor of the Orch. Sinfonica in Umbria (from 1988). His compositions include the opera *Eurydice*.

Brice, Carol (Lovette Hawkins), black American contralto; b. Sedalia, N.C., April 16, 1918; d. Norman, Okla., Feb. 15, 1985. She received training at Palmer Memorial Inst. in Sedalia, at Talladega (Ala.) College (B.Mus., 1939), and from Francis Rogers at the Juilliard School of Music in New York (1939–43). She first attracted attention when she sang in *The Hot Mikado* at the N.Y. World's Fair (1939); she was also chosen to sing at a concert for President Roosevelt's 3d inauguration in 1941 and was the first black American to win the Naumburg Award (1943). Among her many stage roles were Addie in *Regina*, Maude in *Finian's Rainbow*, Maria in *Porgy and Bess*, Queenie in *Show Boat*, and Harriet Tubman in *Gentlemen, Be Seated*. She was a member of the Vienna Volksoper (1967–71), then taught at the Univ. of Okla. (from 1974). With her husband, the baritone Thomas Carey, she founded the Cimarron Circuit Opera Co.

Bridge, Frank, distinguished English composer; b. Brighton, Feb. 26, 1879; d. Eastbourne, Jan. 10, 1941. He studied composition with Stanford at the Royal College of Music in London (1899–1903). He was active as a violinist and violist in several string quartets, among them the Joachim, Grimson, and English string quartets. In 1910–11 he was conductor of the New Sym. Orch. in London, and in 1913 he conducted at Covent Garden there. In 1923 he toured the United States conducting his own works. As a composer, Bridge received recognition only in the last years of his life. After his death, greater appreciation arose, particularly in his homeland. In his early works, he followed the paths of Delius, Ireland, and Bax. After World War I, he pursued a more adventuresome route, influenced by the Second Viennese School, although never embracing serialism. Among his most remarkable advanced works are the 3d and 4th string quartets. Britten, his ardent student and admirer, composed his *Variations on a Theme of Frank Bridge* after the latter's *Idyll* No. 2 for String Quartet.

WORKS: DRAMATIC: *The 2 Hunchbacks*, incidental music (London, Nov. 15, 1910, composer conducting); *The Pageant of London* (1911); *Threads*, incidental music (London, Aug. 23, 1921); *In the Shop*, children's ballet (1921); *The Christmas Rose*, opera (1919–29; London, Dec. 8, 1931, composer conducting).

BIBL.: P. Pirie, *F. B.* (London, 1971); A. Payne and L. Foreman, *F. B.* (London, 1976); P. Hindmarsh, *F. B.: A Thematic Catalogue* (London, 1983); A. Payne, *F. B.: Radical and Conservative* (London, 1984); K. Little, *F. B.: A Bio-Bibliography* (N.Y., 1991).

Brilioth, Helge, Swedish tenor; b. Vaxjo, May 7, 1931. He studied at the Stockholm Musikhögskolan, the Accademia di Santa Cecilia in Rome, and the Salzburg Mozarteum. In 1958 he made his operatic debut in the baritone role of Bartolo in Paisiello's *Il Barbiere di Siviglia* in Stockholm; then sang in Bielefeld (1962–64). After further training in Stockholm, he made his debut as a tenor there in 1965 in the role of Don José. In 1969 he made his first appearance at the Bayreuth Festival as Siegmund. He sang Siegfried in *Götterdämmerung* at the Salzburg Easter Festival in 1970. On Nov. 14, 1970, he made his Metropolitan Opera debut in New York as Parsifal, where he remained on the roster until 1974. He subsequently concentrated his career in Europe.

Brînduş, Nicolae, Romanian composer, writer on music, and teacher; b. Bucharest, April 16, 1935. He studied piano (1952–57) and composition (1960–64) at the Bucharest Cons., and then attended intermittent summer courses in new music in Darmstadt (1969–80); later he worked at IRCAM in Paris (1985). After serving as pianist of the Ploieşti Phil. (1960–69), he taught chamber music at the Bucharest Cons. (1969–81). In 1981 he became an ed. of the journal *Musica*. He also was a prof. of chamber music at the Bucharest Cons. from 1992. In 1993 he lectured on contemporary music in New York, Washington, D.C., Los Angeles, and other U.S. cities. After serving on the executive committee of the ISCM (1991–93), he was president of its Romanian section (from 1994). He publ. the theoretical vol. *Interferenţe* (Interrelations; Bucharest, 1984). Among his honors are the prizes of the Romanian Composers and Musicologists Union (1974), the Romanian Radio and TV (1975, 1977), and the Romanian Academy (1977). In his compositions, Brînduş has explored the utilization of modal and serial elements, improvisation, and electronics. He is also a leading advocate of the syncretic form known as instrumental theater. He also composed *Logodna* (The Betrothal), opera pantomime (1964–66; Bucharest, Feb. 9, 1975), and *La Tigănci* (With the Gypsy Girls), opera (1978–85; Bucharest, June 19, 1987).

Bristow, George Frederick, patriotic American composer; b. Brooklyn, N.Y., Dec. 19, 1825; d. N.Y., Dec. 13, 1898. His father, William Richard Bristow, a professional English musician, went to America in 1824; he gave his son primary instruction in violin playing; Bristow's other teacher was the cellist W. Musgriff; he is also said to have taken violin lessons with Ole Bull. He began his career at the age of 13 by playing in the orch. of the Olympic Theater in New York; in 1843 he joined the violin section of the newly formed N.Y. Phil., and remained with the orch. for 36 years; he also conducted the Harmonic Soc. from 1851 to 1863 and the Mendelssohn Soc. from 1867 to 1871. He began to compose with a determination to prove the possibility and the necessity of forming a national American school of composition; he orated at various public occasions defending his cause. He even withdrew from the N.Y. Phil. for several months in 1854 in protest against the neglect of American music in favor of foreigners. Actually, the N.Y. Phil. frequently placed his works on its programs. He was the concertmaster of the circus orch. when P. T. Barnum took Jenny Lind to America as a special attraction. He also played in the orch. at the N.Y. concerts led by the sensational French conductor Louis Antoine Jullien, and elicited from him a statement praising Bristow's String Quartet as a "truly classical work." Unfortunately, Bristow's own ostensibly American music sounded like a feeble imitation of German models. He merits his place in the annals of American music not for the originality of his own works but for his pioneering efforts to write music on American subjects. Among his works is *Rip Van Winkle*, opera (N.Y., Sept. 27, 1855), the unfinished opera, *Columbus* (overture perf. by the N.Y. Phil., Nov. 17, 1866), and the oratorios *Praise to God* (N.Y. Harmonic Soc., March 2, 1861) and *Daniel* (N.Y., Dec. 30, 1867). He publ. *New and Improved Method for Reed or Cabinet Organ* (N.Y., 1888).

BIBL.: D. Rogers, *Nineteenth-Century Music in New York City as Reflected in the Career of G. F. B.* (diss., Univ. of Michigan, 1967).

Britain, Radie, American composer and teacher; b. Silverton, Texas, March 17, 1899; d. Palm Springs, Calif., May 23, 1994. After studying piano at the American Cons. in Chicago (B.M., 1924), she studied theory and composition with Noelte in Munich and organ with Dupré in Paris (1924–26); then continued her studies with Noelte in Chicago, and also had instruction in piano from Godowsky and organ from Yon. She taught harmony and composition at Chicago's Girvin Inst. of Music (1930–34); after teaching at the Chicago Cons. (1934–39), she taught piano and composition in Hollywood (1940–60). She publ. the book *Composer's Corner* (1978). Her autobiography appeared posthumously as *From Ridin' Herd to Writing Symphonies* (1995). Most of her compositions followed along traditional lines, inspired by various American subjects.

WORKS: DRAMATIC: *Ubiquity*, musical drama (1937); *Happyland*, children's operetta (1946); *Carillon*, opera (1952); *The Spider and the Butterfly*, children's operetta (1953); *Kuthara*, chamber opera (1960; Santa Barbara, June 24, 1961); *The Dark Lady Within*, drama with music (1962); *Western Temperament*, drama with music (telecast, Omaha, June 2, 1963); 4 ballets.

BIBL.: W. and N. Bailey, *R. B.: A Bio-Bibliography* (N.Y., 1990).

Britten, (Edward) Benjamin, Lord Britten of Aldeburgh, renowned English composer; b. Lowestoft, Suffolk, Nov. 22, 1913; d. Aldeburgh, Dec. 4, 1976. He grew up in moderately prosperous circumstances; his father was an orthodontist, his mother an amateur singer. He played the piano and improvised facile tunes; many years later he used these youthful inspirations in a symphonic work which he named *Simple Symphony*. In addition to piano, he began taking viola lessons with Audrey Alston. At the age of 13, he was accepted as a pupil in composition by Frank Bridge, whose influence was decisive on Britten's development as a composer. In 1930 he entered the Royal College of Music in London, where he studied piano with Arthur Benjamin and Harold Samuel, and composition with John Ireland until 1933. He progressed rapidly; even his earliest works showed a mature mastery of technique and a fine talent for lyrical expression. His *Fantasy Quartet* for Oboe and Strings was performed at the Festival of the ISCM in Florence on April 5, 1934. He became associated with the theater and the cinema and began composing background music for films. In 1936 he met Peter Pears. From 1937 they appeared in joint recitals, remaining intimate as well as professional companions until Britten's death. With the outbreak of World War II in 1939, Britten went to the United States; he returned to England in the spring of 1942; he was exempted from military service as a conscientious objector. After the war, he organized the English Opera Group (1947), and in 1948 the Aldeburgh Festival, in collaboration with Eric Crozier and Pears; this festival became an important cultural institution in England, serving as the venue for the first performances of many of Britten's own works, often under his direction; he also had productions at the Glyndebourne Festival. In his operas, he observed the economic necessity of reducing the orch. contingent to 12 performers, with the piano part serving as a modern version of the Baroque ripieno. This economy of means made it possible for small opera groups and univ. workshops to perform Britten's works, yet he succeeded in creating a rich spectrum of instrumental colors, in an idiom ranging from simple triadic progressions, often in parallel motion, to ultrachromatic dissonant harmonies; on occasion he applied dodecaphonic procedures, with thematic materials based on 12 different notes; however, he never employed the formal design of the 12-tone method of composition. A sui generis dodecaphonic device is illustrated by the modulatory scheme in Britten's opera *The Turn of the Screw*, in which each successive scene begins in a different key, with the totality of tonics aggregating to a series of 12 different notes. A characteristic feature in his operas is the inclusion of orch. interludes, which become independent symphonic poems in an impressionistic vein related to the dramatic action of the work. The cries of seagulls in Britten's most popular and musically most striking opera, *Peter Grimes*, create a fantastic quasi-surrealistic imagery. Britten was equally successful in treating tragic subjects, as in *Peter Grimes* and *Billy Budd*, comic subjects, exemplified by his *Albert Herring*, and mystical evocation, as in his *The Turn of the Screw*. He was also successful in depicting patriotic subjects, as in *Gloriana*, composed for the coronation of Queen Elizabeth II. He possessed a flair for writing music for children, in which he managed to present a degree of sophistication and artistic simplicity without condescension. In short, Britten was an adaptable composer who could perform a given task according to the specific requirements of the occasion. He composed a "realization" of Gay's *Beggar's Opera*. He also wrote modern "parables" for church performance, and produced a contemporary counterpart of the medieval English miracle play *Noye's Fludde*. Among his other works is the remarkable *War Requiem*, a profound tribute to the dead of many wars. In 1952 Britten was made a Companion of Honour, in 1965 he received the Order of Merit, and in 1976 he became the first English composer to be created a life peer, becoming Lord Britten of Aldeburgh. In collaboration with Imogen Holst, Britten wrote *The Story of Music* (London, 1958) and *The Wonderful World of Music* (Garden City, N.Y., 1968; rev. ed., 1970).

WORKS: OPERAS: *Paul Bunyan* (N.Y., May 5, 1941; rev. 1974; BBC, Feb. 1, 1976; Aldeburgh, June 14, 1976); *Peter Grimes* (London, June 7, 1945; Tanglewood, Aug. 6, 1946, Bernstein conducting); *The Rape of Lucretia* (Glyndebourne, July 12, 1946); *Albert Herring* (Glyndebourne, June 20, 1947, composer conducting); *The Beggar's Opera*, a new realization of the ballad opera by John Gay (Cambridge, May 24, 1948, composer conducting); *The Little Sweep*, or *Let's Make an Opera*, "an entertainment for young people" with optional audience participation (Aldeburgh, June 14, 1949); *Billy Budd* (1st version in 4 acts; London, Dec. 1, 1951, composer conducting; rev. version in 2 acts, 1960; BBC, Nov. 13, 1960); *Gloriana* (London, June 8, 1953, Pritchard conducting); *The Turn of the Screw*, chamber opera (Venice, Sept. 14, 1954, composer conducting); *Noye's Fludde*, 1-act children's opera (Aldeburgh, June 18, 1958); *A Midsummer Night's Dream* (Aldeburgh, June 11, 1960, composer conducting); *Curlew River*, church parable (Aldeburgh, June 12, 1964, composer conducting); *The Burning Fiery Furnace*, church parable (Aldeburgh, June 9, 1966, composer conducting); *The Prodigal Son*, church parable (Aldeburgh, June 10, 1968, composer conducting); *Owen Wingrave* (BBC-TV, May 16, 1971, composer conducting; stage premiere, London, May 10, 1973); *Death in Venice* (Aldeburgh, June 16, 1973); 2 realizations of operas by Purcell: *Dido and Aeneas* (London, May 1, 1951, composer conducting) and *The Fairy Queen*, a shortened version for concert perf. (Aldeburgh, June 25, 1967); a ballet, *The Prince of the Pagodas* (London, Jan. 1, 1957, composer conducting).

BIBL.: E. White, *B. B.* (London, 1948; 3d ed., rev., 1983); I. Holst, *B.* (London, 1966; rev. ed., 1970); M. Hurd, *B. B.* (London, 1966); P. Young, *B.* (London, 1966); P. Howard, *The Operas of B. B.* (N.Y., 1969); A. Kendall, *B. B.* (London, 1973); P. Evans, *The*

Music of B. B. (London, 1979); D. Herbert, ed., *The Operas of B. B.* (London, 1979); C. Headington, *B.* (London, 1981); M. Kennedy, *B.* (London, 1981; rev. ed., 1993); A. Whittall, *The Music of B. and Tippett: Studies in Themes and Techniques* (Cambridge, 1982; 2d ed., 1990); P. Brett, *Peter Grimes* (Cambridge, 1983); C. Palmer, ed., *The B. Companion* (London, 1984); S. Corse, *Opera and the Uses of Language: Mozart, Verdi, and B.* (London and Toronto, 1987); J. Evans, P. Reed, and P. Wilson, eds., *A B. Source Book* (Aldeburgh, 1987); D. Mitchell, *B. B.: Death in Venice* (Cambridge, 1987); P. Reed, *The Incidental Music of B. B.: A Study and Catalogue of His Music for Film, Theatre and Radio* (diss., Univ. of East Anglia, 1988); H. Carpenter, *B. B.: A Biography* (London, 1992); P. Banks, ed., *B.'s 'Gloriana': Essays and Sources* (Woodbridge, Suffolk, 1993); M. Cook and P. Reed, eds., *B. B.: Billy Budd* (Cambridge, 1993); P. Banks, ed., *The Making of Peter Grimes: The Facsimile of B.'s Composition Draft: Studies* (2 vols., Woodbridge, Suffolk, 1995); P. Hodgson, *B. B.: A Guide to Research* (N.Y., 1996).

Brkanović, Ivan, Croation composer; b. Skaljari, Dec. 27, 1906; d. Zagreb, Feb. 20, 1987. He studied with Bersa at the Zagreb Academy of Music (graduated, 1935) and Léfebre at the Paris Schola Cantorum; then taught in Zagreb secondary schools (1935–51) and was a visiting prof. at the Sarajevo Academy of Music (1957–62). His works utilized thematic materials derived from national folk music, but his harmonic idiom followed along modern lines. He composed the operas *Ekvinocij* (Equinox; 1945; Zagreb, Oct. 4, 1950) and *Zlato Zadra* (The Gold of Zadar; Zagreb, April 15, 1954) and the ballet *Heloti* (1959; Zagreb, March 17, 1963).

Broadstock, Brenton (Thomas), Australian composer and teacher; b. Melbourne, Dec. 12, 1952. He studied at Monash Univ. (B.A., 1976), Memphis (Tenn.) State Univ. (M.M., 1980), the Univ. of Sydney (with Sculthorpe; postgraduate composition diploma, 1981), Trinity College in London (A.Mus., 1981), and the Univ. of Melbourne (D.Mus., 1989). In 1988 he served as the first composer-in-residence of the Melbourne Sym. Orch. and in 1989 joined the faculty of the Univ. of Melbourne. He publ. the vol. *Sound Ideas: Australian Composers born since 1950* (Sydney, 1995). In his music Broadstock follows a stylistically diverse course frequently marked by adventuresome harmonies, dense and complex textures, and aleatoric structures. In his opera *Fahrenheit 451* (1992), he explores the potentials of electronic sound.

Broekman, David, Dutch-born American conductor and composer; b. Leiden, May 13, 1899; d. N.Y., April 1, 1958. He studied with Anrooy in The Hague and conducted at the Royal Opera there. After playing violin in the N.Y. Phil (1924–26), he went to Hollywood and contributed soundtracks for several films, including *All Quiet on the Western Front* and *The Phantom of the Opera*; he also conducted pageants and was music director of Universal Pictures (1929–31), Columbia Pictures (1931–34), and CBS radio station KHJ (1934–41). After World War II he conducted sym. orchs. and was music director of various television shows; he conducted the contemporary concert series "Music in the Making" at N.Y.'s Cooper Union (1952–57), introducing John Becker's Horn Concerto, among other works. He wrote a satirical autobiographical novel, *The Shoestring Symphony* (N.Y., 1948), exhibiting a mandatory jaundiced view of Hollywood. He composed three short operas: *Barbara Allen* (1953), *The Stranger* (1953), and *The Toledo War* (1954).

Brogi, Renato, Italian composer; b. Sesto Fiorentino, Feb. 25, 1873; d. San Domenico di Fiesole, Florence, Aug. 25, 1924. He studied music in Florence, then at the Milan Cons., winning the Steiner Prize in Vienna with his opera *La prima notte* (Florence, Nov. 25, 1898). He also composed the operas *L'Oblio* (Florence, Feb. 4, 1890) and *Isabella Orsini* (Florence, April 24, 1920) and the operettas *Bacco in Toscana* and *Follie Veneziane* (both produced in Florence, 1923).

Bronsgeest, Cornelis, Dutch baritone; b. Leiden, July 24, 1978; d. Berlin, Sept. 22, 1957. He studied with Schulz-Dornburg in Berlin and Stockhausen in Frankfurt am Main. In 1900 he made his operatic debut in Magdeburg, singing there until 1903; he then sang with the Hamburg Opera (1903–06). In 1906 he made his first appearance in Berlin at the Royal Opera as Amonasro; continued to sing in Berlin until 1935. In 1914 he made his London debut as Papageno at the Drury Lane Theatre; in 1919–20 he made a tour of North America. From 1924 to 1933 he served as director of opera broadcasts of the Berlin Radio. After World War II, he returned to Berlin to assist in restoring the operatic life of the city.

Bronskaya, Evgenya (Adolfovna), outstanding Russian soprano; b. St. Petersburg, Feb. 1, 1882; d. there (Leningrad), Oct. 12, 1953. She first studied with her mother, E. de Hacke, then in Milan with Teresa Arkel; she made her operatic debut in Tiflis in 1901; she subsequently sang in Kiev (1902–03) and in Moscow (1904–05). From 1907 to 1910 she sang with a traveling Italian opera troupe, performing in Italy, France, and the United States (Boston, Chicago, and Philadelphia). Returning to Russia, she was a member of the Maryinsky Theater in St. Petersburg (1910–23); from 1923 to 1950 she taught voice at the Leningrad Cons. She was a brilliant coloratura soprano, particularly impressive in the roles of Lucia, Gilda, and Violetta.

Brook, Peter (Stephen Paul), noted English theater and opera producer; b. London, March 21, 1925. He was educated at Magdalen College, Oxford. His career in the theater commenced at the age of 17 when he staged a performance of Marlowe's *The Tragedie of Dr. Faustus*. After producing plays in Birmingham, Stratford, and London, he served as director of productions at the Royal Opera in London from 1947 to 1950. His productions there included *Boris Godunov* and *La Bohème* in 1948, and *Le nozze di Figaro* and *Salome* in 1949. In 1953 he staged *Faust* at the Metropolitan Opera in New York, returning there in 1957 to produce *Eugene Onegin*. In 1962 he became codirector of the Royal Shakespeare Theatre. From 1971 he was also active in Paris with his Centre International de Créations Théâtrales, with which he attempted to synthesize theatrical elements in a total media art. His compressed version of *Carmen* as *La tragédie de Carmen* was produced in Paris in 1981 and in New York in 1983, and won him an Emmy Award and the Prix Italia in 1984. His similar treatment of *Pelléas et Mélisande* as *Impressions de Pelléas* was first mounted in Paris in 1992. Brook's autobiography, *The Shifting Point*, appeared in 1988. Among his other writings are *The Empty Space* (N.Y., 1978), *The Open Door: Thoughts on Acting and Theater* (N.Y., 1993), and *Threads of Time* (Washington, D.C., 1998). In 1965 he was made a Commander of the Order of the British Empire. He was made an Officier of the Légion d'honneur of France in 1995, and in 1998 Queen Elizabeth II made him a Companion of Honour.

BIBL.: A. Hunt and G. Reeves, *P. B.* (Cambridge, 1995).

Brooks, Patricia, American soprano; b. N.Y., Nov. 7, 1937; d. Mount Kisco, N.Y., Jan. 22, 1992. She studied at the Manhattan School of Music in New York; she also took dance lessons with Martha Graham. She made her operatic debut as Marianne in *Der Rosenkavalier* at the N.Y. City Opera on Oct. 12, 1960; she also sang with opera companies in San Francisco, Chicago, New Orleans, Philadelphia, Houston, and Santa Fe. She made her Covent Garden debut in London in 1969 as Shemakha in *The Golden Cockerel*. In 1978 she retired from the operatic stage and taught at the State Univ. of N.Y. in Purchase until 1981. Among her best roles were Gilda, Lucia, Violetta, Massenet's Manon, Sophie, and Mélisande.

Broqua, Alfonso, Uruguayan composer; b. Montevideo, Sept. 11, 1876; d. Paris, Nov. 24, 1946. He studied with d'Indy at the Schola Cantorum in Paris, where he settled. His works are characterized by a fine feeling for exotic material, which he presented in the brilliant manner of French modern music. He composed the opera *Cruz del Sur* (1918), as well as *Thelen at Nagouëy*, Inca ballet (1934), and *Isabelle*, romantic ballet (1936).

Brouwenstijn, Gré (actually, **Gerarda Demphina Van Swol**), Dutch soprano; b. Den Helder, Aug. 26, 1915. She studied at the Amsterdam Music Lyceum, then made her operatic debut as 1 of the 3 ladies in *Die Zauberflöte* in Amsterdam (1940); she joined the Netherlands Opera there in 1946. She made her debut at London's Covent Garden as Aida in 1951, and continued to make regular appearances there until 1964; she also sang at the Bayreuth Festivals (1954–56), Buenos Aires's Teatro Colón (1958), and the Chicago Lyric Opera (1959); she made her farewell appearance in *Fidelio* in Amsterdam in 1971. She was best known for her Verdi and Wagner roles.

Brown, David (Clifford), English musicologist; b. Gravesend, July 8, 1929. He studied at the Univ. of Sheffield (B.A., 1951; B.Mus., 1952); then was music librarian at the Univ. of London Library, Senate House (1959–62). In 1962 he was appointed a lecturer at the Univ. of Southampton; was prof. of musicology there from 1983 to 1989. He was awarded a Ph.D. in 1971 by the Univ. of Southampton for his book *Thomas Weelkes: A Biographical and Critical Study* (London, 1969). He also wrote *John Wilbye* (London, 1974) and then specialized in Russian music; publ. *Mikhail Glinka* (London, 1974) and an extended 4-vol. biography of Tchaikovsky (1978–91). Later he publ. *Tchaikovsky Remembered* (London and Boston, 1993).

Browne, John Lewis, English-American organist and composer; b. London, May 18, 1864; d. Chicago, Oct. 23, 1933. He was a pupil of his father, William Browne, a noted organist; later studied with S. P. Warren (1884) and F. Archer (1887). Settling in America, he was active as an organist in San Francisco, Atlanta, Philadelphia, and Chicago; during his career he gave more than 500 organ recitals. He designed an organ for Medinah Temple in Chicago, and inaugurated it with the first performance of Felix Borowski's Allegro de Concert, commissioned for the occasion. Among his compositions is the opera *La Corsicana* (Chicago, Jan. 4, 1923), which received an honorable mention in the 1902 Sonzogno Competition.

Brownlee, John (Donald Mackensie), Australian baritone; b. Geelong, Jan. 7, 1900; d. N.Y., Jan. 10, 1969. He was a pupil of Gilly in Paris, where he made his operatic debut as Nilakantha in *Lakmé* at the Théâtre-Lyrique in 1926. On June 8, 1926, he first appeared at London's Covent Garden as Marcello during Melba's farewell concert. From 1927 to 1936 he was a member of the Paris Opéra; he also sang at the Teatro Colón in Buenos Aires (1931) and the Glyndebourne Festivals (1935–39). On Feb. 17, 1937, he made his Metropolitan Opera debut in New York as Rigoletto, and continued to sing there until 1957. He also sang in Chicago (1937–38; 1945), San Francisco (1940–50), and again at Covent Garden (1949–50). From 1953 to 1967 he was president of the American Guild of Musical Artists. He founded the Empire State Music Festival near Ellenville, N.Y., in 1955. In 1956 he became president of the Manhattan School of Music, and then was its president from 1966 until his death. Among his most prominent roles were Don Giovanni, Count Almaviva, Papageno, Alfonso, Iago, and Scarpia.

Bruce, (Frank) Neely, American pianist, conductor, music scholar, and composer; b. Memphis, Tenn., Jan. 21, 1944. He studied piano with Roy McAllister at the Univ. of Alabama (B.M., 1965); he then was a pupil in piano (M.M., 1966) of Soulima Stravinsky and in composition (D.M.A., 1971) of Ben Johnston at the Univ. of Ill., where he also taught (1968–74). In 1974 he joined the faculty at Wesleyan Univ., where he also conducted the Wesleyan Singers. In 1977 he founded the American Music/Theatre Group, an ensemble devoted to the performance of American music from all eras. He composed *Pyramus and Thisbe*, chamber opera (1964–65), *The Trials of Psyche*, opera (1970–71), and *Americana, or, A New Tale of the Genii*, opera (1978–83); also incidental music to plays and dance scores.

Bruch, Max, celebrated German composer; b. Cologne, Jan. 6, 1838; d. Friedenau, near Berlin, Oct. 2, 1920. His mother, a professional singer, was his first teacher. He afterward studied theory with Breidenstein in Bonn; in 1852 he won a scholarship of the Mozart Foundation in Frankfurt for 4 years, and became a pupil of Ferdinand Hiller, Reinecke, and Breuning. At the age of 14, he brought out a Sym. at Cologne, and at 20 produced his first stage work, *Scherz, List und Rache*, adapted from Goethe's Singspiel (Cologne, Jan. 14, 1858). Between 1858 and 1861 he taught music in Cologne; he also made prolonged visits to Berlin, Leipzig, Dresden, and Munich. In 1863 he was in Mannheim, where he produced his first full-fledged opera, *Die Loreley* (April 14, 1863), to the libretto by Geibel, orig. intended for Mendelssohn. About the same time, he wrote an effective choral work, *Frithjof*, which was presented with great success in various German towns, and in Vienna. From 1865 to 1867 Bruch was music director of a concert organization in Koblenz, where he wrote his 1st Violin Concerto (in G minor), which became a great favorite among violinists; he then was court Kapellmeister in Sonderhausen. In 1870 he went to Berlin, where his last opera, *Hermione*, based on Shakespeare's *The Winter's Tale*, was produced at the Berlin Opera on March 21, 1872. In 1880 he accepted the post of conductor of the Liverpool Phil., and remained in England for 3 years; in 1883 he visited the United States and conducted his choral work *Arminius* in Boston. From 1883 to 1890 he was music director of an orch. society in Breslau; in 1891 he became a prof. of composition at the Hochschule für Musik in Berlin, retiring in 1910. Bruch was married to the singer Clara Tuczek (d. 1919). Cambridge Univ. conferred upon him the honorary degree of D.Mus. (1893), the French Academy elected him corresponding member, and in 1918 the Univ. of Berlin gave him the honorary degree of Dr.Phil.

Bruch's music, although imitative in its essence and even in its melodic and harmonic procedures, has a great eclectic charm; he was a master of harmony, counterpoint, and instrumentation; he was equally adept at handling vocal masses. He contributed a great deal to the development of the secular oratorio, using soloists, chorus, and orch.

BIBL.: F. Gysi, *M. B.* (Zürich, 1922); K. Fellerer, *M. B.* (Cologne, 1974).

Brückner-Rüggeberg, Wilhelm, German conductor and pedagogue; b. Stuttgart, April 15, 1906; d. Hamburg, April 1, 1985. He studied with August Schmid-Lindner and Siegmund von Hausegger in Munich, where he began his career as chorus master at the Bavarian State Opera in 1928. After conducting in various German music centers, he was a guest conductor with the Hamburg State Opera in 1936–37; subsequently he was on its roster from 1938 to 1971. He taught at the Hamburg Hochschule für Musik, becoming a prof. in 1955.

Brüll, Ignaz, Austrian pianist and composer; b. Prossnitz, Moravia, Nov. 7, 1846; d. Vienna, Sept. 17, 1907. He studied in Vienna with Epstein (piano) and Dessoff (composition). He subsequently made extended recital tours, eventually settling in Vienna, where he was a prof. of piano at the Horak Inst. (1872–78). He was a close friend of Brahms, who greatly valued his advice. Of his numerous stage works, *Das goldene Kreuz* (1875) and *Der Husar* (1898) were the most successful.

WORKS: DRAMATIC: OPERAS: *Die Bettler von Samarkand* (1864); *Das goldene Kreuz* (Berlin, Dec. 22, 1875); *Der Landfriede* (Vienna, Oct. 4, 1877); *Bianca* (Dresden, Nov. 25, 1879); *Königin Marietta* (Munich, 1883); *Gloria* (Hamburg, 1886); *Das steinerne Herz* (Vienna, 1888); *Gringoire* (Munich, March 19, 1892); *Schach dem Könige* (Munich, 1893); *Der Husar* (Vienna, 1898); *Rübezahl* (unfinished). BALLET: *Ein Märchen aus der Champagne* (1896).

BIBL.: H. Wecker, *Der Epigone, I. B.: Ein jüdischer Komponist im Wiener Brahms-Kreis* (Pfaffenweiler, 1994).

Brumby, Colin (James), Australian composer, conductor, and teacher; b. Melbourne, June 18, 1933. He was educated at the Melbourne Univ. Conservatorium of Music (B.Mus., 1957; D.Mus., 1971); he also received training in composition in Santiago de Compostela (1962), London (1962–64), and Rome (1972–73), and studied computer music at Stanford Univ. (1974). He was music director of the Victorian Chamber Players (1956), the South Melbourne Sym. Orch. (1957), and the Queensland Opera (1969–

71). In 1964 he joined the faculty of the Univ. of Queensland, where he was an assoc. prof. from 1977; he also was music director of its Musical Soc. (1966–68; 1977–86). After composing in an approved atonal style, Brumby forsook that path in 1974 to embrace an adventuresome tonal style. In both atonal and tonal scores, melodic writing is a salient feature.

WORKS: DRAMATIC: OPERAS: *The 7 Deadly Sins* (Brisbane, Sept. 12, 1970); *The Marriage Machine* (1971; Sydney, Jan. 28, 1972); *La Donna* (1986); *Lorenzaccio* (1986–87); *Fire on the Wind* (1990); *Summer Carol* (1990). BALLETS: *Bunyip*, television ballet (1966); *Cinderella*, after Rossini (Brisbane, Dec. 10, 1975); *Masques* (Brisbane, Aug. 18, 1980); *Alice, Memories of Childhood* (1987). Also operettas for children and incidental music.

Bruneau, (Louis-Charles-Bonaventure-) Alfred, French opera composer; b. Paris, March 3, 1857; d. there, June 15, 1934. In 1873 he entered the Paris Cons., where he was a pupil of Franchomme. He won the 1st cello prize in 1876, and later studied harmony with Savard and composition with Massenet; in 1881 he won the Prix de Rome with his cantata *Sainte-Geneviève*. He was a music critic for *Gil Blas* (1892–95), then for *Le Figaro* and *Le Matin*. In 1903–04 he was 1st conductor at the Opéra Comique. In 1900 he was made a member of the "Conseil Superieur" at the Paris Cons., and in 1909 succeeded Reyer as inspector of music instruction. He made extensive tours of Russia, England, Spain, and the Netherlands, conducting his own works. He was made a Knight of the Légion d'honneur in 1895, received the title "Commandeur de St.-Charles" in 1907, and became a member of the Académie des Beaux Arts in 1925. His role in the evolution of French opera is of great importance; he introduced realistic drama on the French musical stage, working along lines parallel with Zola in literature. He used Zola's subjects for his most spectacular opera, *L'Ouragan*, and also for the operas *Messidor* and *L'Enfant-Roi*. In accordance with this naturalistic trend, Bruneau made free use of harsh dissonance when it was justified by the dramatic action of the plot. He publ. *Musiques d'hier et de demain* (1900), *La Musique française* (1901), *Musiques de Russie et musiciens de France* (1903; German tr. by M. Graf in *Die Musik*, Berlin, 1904), *La Vie et les oeuvres de Gabriel Fauré* (1925), and *Massenet* (1934).

WORKS: DRAMATIC: OPERAS: (all 1st perf. in Paris unless otherwise given): *Kérim* (June 9, 1887); *Le Rêve* (June 18, 1891); *L'Attaque du Moulin* (Nov. 23, 1893); *Messidor* (Feb. 19, 1897); *L'Ouragan* (April 29, 1901); *Lazare* (1902); *L'Enfant-Roi* (March 3, 1905); *Naïs Micoulin* (Monte Carlo, Feb. 2, 1907); *La Faute de l'Abbé Mouret* (March 1, 1907); *Les Quatre Journees* (Dec. 25, 1916); *Le Roi Candaule* (Dec. 1, 1920); *Angelo, tyran de Padoue* (Jan. 16, 1928); *Virginie* (Jan. 7, 1931). BALLETS: *L'Amoureuse Leçon* (Feb. 6, 1913); *Les Bacchantes* (after Euripides; Oct. 30, 1912).

BIBL.: A. Boschot, *La Vie et les oeuvres d'A. B.* (Paris, 1937).

Brunetti, family of Italian musicians:

(1) Giovan Gualberto Brunetti, composer; b. Pistoia, April 24, 1706; d. Pisa, May 20, 1787. He studied with Atto Gherardeschi, in Pisa with Clari (1723–28), and in Naples at the Turchini Cons. (1728–33). After serving as maestro di cappella to the Duke of Monte Nero, he was secondo maestro at the Turchini Cons. (1745–54). He then was maestro di cappella in Pisa (from 1754). In 1756 he was made a member of Bologna's Accademia Filarmonica. He was ordained a priest in 1764.

WORKS: OPERAS: *Amore imbratta il senno* (Naples, 1733); *Don Pasquino* (Naples, 1735); *Il corrivo* (Naples, 1736); *Ortensio* (Naples, Carnival 1739); *Alessandro nell'Indie* (Pisa, Carnival 1763); *Arminio* (Luca, 1763); *Temistocle* (Lucca, 1776). Also *Ester*, oratorio (Florence, 1758).

(2) Antonio Brunetti, violinist, son of the preceding; b. Naples, c.1740; d. Salzburg, Dec. 25, 1786. He was Hofmusikdirektor and Hofkonzertmeister in Salzburg from 1776, succeeding Mozart as Konzertmeister in 1777. His intimacy with Maria Judith Lipps, the sister-in-law of Michael Haydn, resulted in the illegitimate birth of a child in 1778. Later that year they were finally married. Mozart wrote his works K.261, 269, 373, and 379 for Brunetti but personally loathed him.

(3) Giuseppe Brunetti, composer, brother of the preceding; b. Naples, c.1741; d. after 1780. He was active mainly in Pisa (1754–75), Siena (1779), and Florence (1780). He wrote the operas *Didone* (Siena, 1759) and *Galatea* (Braunschweig, 1762).

(4) Antonio Brunetti, composer, probably son of the preceding; b. c.1767; d. after 1845. He was maestro di cappella at Chieti Cathedral (1790–1800), at Urbino Cathedral (1810–16), and in Macerata (1816–26). In 1826 he was recalled to his former position at Urbino Cathedral, but in 1827 he resigned without having assumed his duties.

WORKS: OPERAS: *Lo sposo di tre e marito di nessuno* (Bologna, 1786); *La stravaganza in campagna* (Venice, 1787); *Il Bertoldo* (Florence, Carnival 1788); *Vologeso re de' Parti* (Florence, 1789); *Le nozze per invito, ossia Gli amanti capricciosi* (Rome, 1791); *Fatima* (Brescia, 1791); *Li contrasti per amore* (Rome, 1792); *Il pazzo glorioso* (Rome, Carnival 1797); *Il libretto alla moda* (Naples, Carnival 1808); *La colomba contrastata, ossia La bella carbonara* (Rimini, Carnival 1813); *Amore e fedeltà alla prova* (Bologna, May 1814); *La fedeltà coniugale* (Parma, Jan. 30, 1815).

Brunetti, Gaetano, Italian violinist and composer; b. probably in Fano, 1744; d. Culminal de Oreja, near Madrid, Dec. 16, 1798. He studied with Nardini, and in about 1762 went to Madrid; in 1767 he was appointed violinist in the Royal Chapel in Madrid, and in 1788 became director of the Royal Chamber Orch., remaining in this post until his death. He composed many works for the Spanish court, and also for the Duke of Alba; Boccherini, who was in Madrid during the same years as Brunetti, was also favored by the court and the aristocracy, but there was apparently no rivalry between them, as commissions were plentiful. While Brunetti's productivity was astounding, he composed but one opera, *Jason*, which produced in Madrid on Oct. 4, 1768. A large collection of his MSS are held at The Library of Congress in Washington.

BIBL.: A. Belgray, *G. B., An Exploratory Bio-bibliographical Study* (diss., Univ. of Michigan, 1970).

Bruni, Antonio Bartolomeo, Italian violinist and composer; b. Cuneo, Jan. 28, 1757; d. there, Aug. 5, 1821. He studied with Pugnani in Turin. In 1780 he went to Paris, and on May 15, 1780, appeared as a violinist at the Concert Spirituel; he then served as a member of the orch. of the Comédie-Italienne (1781–89). He was subsequently director of the orch. of the Opéra Comique (1799–1801), then at the Théâtre-Italienne (1801–06). He wrote 22 operas, of which the most successful were *Célestine* (Paris, Oct. 15, 1787), *Claudine* (Paris, March 6, 1794), and *La Rencontre en voyage* (Paris, April 28, 1798). He also publ. a violin method and a viola method (the latter reprinted in 1928).

BIBL.: G. Cesari, *H. Closson, L. de La Laurencie, A. Della Corte, and C. Zino, A. B. B., musicista cuneese* (Turin, 1931).

Brunswick, Mark, American composer and teacher; b. N.Y., Jan. 6, 1902; d. London, May 25, 1971. He studied with Goldmark and Bloch; then lived in Europe (1925–38), during which time he studied with Boulanger in Paris and was active in Vienna. Returning to the United States, he served as chairman of the National Committee for Refugee Musicians (1938–43); he was president of the American section of the ISCM (1941–50) and of the College Music Assn. (1953). After teaching at Black Mountain College (1944) and Kenyon College (1945), he was chairman of the music dept. at the City College of N.Y. (1946–67). He composed an opera, *The Master Builder*, after Ibsen. (1959–67), which was left unfinished.

Bruscantini, Sesto, Italian baritone; b. Porto Civitanova, Dec. 10, 1919. He studied law; then went to Rome to study music with Luigi Ricci. He made his debut at La Scala in Milan in 1949, singing the bass role of Don Geronimo in Cimarosa's *Il matrimonio segreto*. He then sang at several festivals in Glyndebourne (1951–

54); in 1952 he appeared at the Salzburg Festival. In 1961 he made his U.S. debut with the Chicago Lyric Opera. On Feb. 2, 1981, he made his Metropolitan Opera debut in New York as Taddeo in *L'Italiana in Algeri*, and sang there until 1983. He was particularly renowned for his buffo roles. In 1953 he married **Sena Jurinac**.

Brusilovsky, Evgeni (Grigorievich), Russian composer and pedagogue; b. Rostov-na-Donu, Nov. 12, 1905; d. Moscow, May 9, 1981. He studied composition with Maximilian Steinberg at the Leningrad Cons., graduating in 1931. In 1933 he was commissioned by the Leningrad Union of Composers to go to Kazakhstan to promote music education there and to help native composers write music based on their own ethnic sources. Brusilovsky taught at the Alma-Ata Cons. of Music. He wrote a number of works making use of native motifs; particularly notable are his operas on folk subjects. He composed the operas (all 1st perf. in Alma-Ata) *Kyz-Zhybek* (1934), *Zhalbyr* (1935; 2d version, 1938; 3d version, 1946), *Er-Targyn* (1937; 2d version, 1954), *Ayman-Sholpan* (1938), *Altyn Styk* (1940), *Guard, Alga!* (1942), *Amangeldy* (1945), *Dudaray* (1953), and *The Inheritors* (1963), and the ballet *Bayan-Slu* (1971).

Bruson, Renato, distinguished Italian baritone; b. Este, near Padua, Jan. 13, 1936. He received training at the Padua Cons. In 1961 he made his operatic debut as Count Di Luna in Spoleto, and then sang in various Italian music centers. On Feb. 1, 1969, he made his Metropolitan Opera debut in New York as Enrico in *Lucia di Lammermoor*. In 1972 he made his first appearance at Milan's La Scala as Antonio in *Linda di Chamounix*. He made his debut at London's Covent Garden as Renato in *Un ballo in maschera* in 1976. In 1982 he sang Falstaff in Los Angeles. He appeared as Don Giovanni at the Berlin Deutsche Oper in 1988. In 1990 he sang Montfort in *Les Vêpres siciliennes* at N.Y.'s Carnegie Hall. He appeared as Germont at Covent Garden in 1995. In 1997 he was engaged as Macbeth in Monte Carlo. His guest engagements also took him to Vienna, Munich, Chicago, Hamburg, Paris, San Francisco, and other cities.

Brustad, Bjarne, Norwegian violinist, violist, conductor, and composer; b. Christiania, March 4, 1895; d. there (Oslo), May 22, 1978. He studied at the Christiania Cons.; then took violin lessons with Flesch in Berlin (1915–16). From 1919 to 1922 he was a violinist in the Oslo Phil., and from 1929 to 1943 he played first viola there. He also conducted orchs. in Oslo; in 1951 he received a government life pension. His music is Romantic in its essence, and traditional in form. He composed the opera *Atlantis* (1945).

Bruzdowicz, Joanna, Polish-French composer; b. Warsaw, May 17, 1943. She studied piano with Irena Protasewicz and Wanda Losakiewicz, and composition with Sikorski at the Warsaw Cons. (M.A., 1966). She then pursued training in composition in Paris with Boulanger, Messiaen, and Schaeffer (1968–70), where she was active with the Groupe de Recherches Musicales of the ORTF. She later made her home in Belgium while pursuing activities as a composer, music critic, and teacher. Her output ranges the spectrum from traditional scores to electronic pieces.

WORKS: DRAMATIC: OPERAS: *In der Strafkolonie* or *La Colonie Pénitentiaire* (Tours, 1972; rev. version, Liège, Oct. 9, 1986); *Les Troyennes* (Paris, 1973; Polish version, Warsaw, July 20, 1979); *Bramy Raju* (The Gates of Paradise; Warsaw, Nov. 1987); *Tides and Waves* (1991–92; Barcelona, June 1992). BALLET: *Le Petit Prince* (Brussels, Dec. 10, 1976). CHILDREN'S MUSICAL: *En attendant Anaïs* (Brussels, Dec. 6, 1987). Many theater scores.

Bryars, (Richard) Gavin, significant English composer and teacher; b. Goole, Yorkshire, Jan. 16, 1943. He studied composition privately with Cyril Ramsey (1959–61) and George Linstead (1963–65) in England, and with Ben Johnston (1968) in the United States; also at the Univ. of Sheffield (B.A. in philosophy, 1964) and at the Northern School of Music (1964–66). After teaching at the Northampton College of Technology (1966–67), the Portsmouth College of Art (1969–70), and the Leicester Polytechnic (1970–85), he was prof. of music at De Montford Univ. (1985–96). In 1981 he founded his own Gavin Bryars Ensemble, with which he toured widely. Bryar's output is generally experimental in nature. His works are indeterminate, replete with repetition, and often utilize electronics. His warmth and humor is evidenced in his *The Sinking of the Titanic* (1969), a multimedia, meditative collage work composed of excerpts from pieces the drowning orch. might have been playing. His poignant *Jesus' Blood Never Failed Me Yet*, originally composed for Ensemble and Tape (1971), became an international success in its later version for Orch. and Tape (1994), incorporating the raspy voice of Tom Waits. Bryars has also collaborated with a number of well-known musicians, including Eno, Reich, and Cardew, as well as with the preeminent American theater director Robert Wilson. His stage compositions include *Irma*, opera (1977; realization of a work by Tom Phillips), *Medea*, opera (1982; rev. version, Lyons, Oct. 23, 1984), and *Doctor Ox's Experiment*, opera (1988–95; London, June 15, 1998); other theater music, dance scores, and incidental music.

Bryn-Julson, Phyllis (Mae), esteemed American soprano; b. Bowdon, N. Dak., Feb. 5, 1945. She studied piano, organ, violin, and voice at Concordia College, Moorehead, Minn.; she then spent several summers at the Berkshire Music Center at Tanglewood and completed her studies at Syracuse Univ. On Oct. 28, 1966, she made her formal debut as soloist in Berg's *Lulu Suite* with the Boston Sym. Orch., and in 1976 made her operatic debut as Malinche in the U.S. premiere of Sessions's *Montezuma* in Boston. She often appears in recital with her husband, the organist Donald Sutherland. In addition to teaching at Kirkland-Hamilton College in Clinton, N.Y., and at the Univ. of Maryland, she conducted master classes on both sides of the Atlantic. She is particularly renowned as a concert singer, at ease with all periods and styles of music.

Bucchi, Valentino, Italian composer and pedagogue; b. Florence, Nov. 29, 1916; d. Rome, May 9, 1976. He studied composition with Frazzi and Dallapiccola, and music history with Torrefranca at the Univ. of Florence, graduating in 1944; he subsequently held teaching posts at the Florence Cons. (1945–52; 1954–57), the Venice Cons. (1952–54), and the Perugia Cons. (1957–58). He was music director of the Accademia Filarmonica Romana (1958–60) and artistic director of the Teatro Comunale in Bologna (1963–65) and was director of the Florence Cons. (1974–76). In his works, he continued the national Italian tradition of the musical theater, while attempting to modernize the polyphony of the Renaissance along the lines established by Malipiero. He composed the operas *Il giuoco del barone* (Florence, Dec. 20, 1944), *Il Contrabasso* (Florence, May 20, 1954), *Una notte in Paradiso* (Florence, May 11, 1960), and *Il coccodrillo* (Florence, May 9, 1970), and the ballets *Racconto siciliano* (Rome, Jan. 17, 1956) and *Mirandolina* (Rome, March 12, 1957).

Bucci, Mark, American composer; b. N.Y., Feb. 26, 1924. He attended St. John's Univ. in New York (1941–42); after private training in composition from Serly (1942–45), he continued his studies with Jacobi and Giannini at the Juilliard School of Music in New York (B.S., 1951) and with Copland at the Berkshire Music Center in Tanglewood. In 1953–54 and 1957–58 he held Guggenheim fellowships. His modern, lyrical style is particularly effective in his stage works.

WORKS: DRAMATIC: OPERAS: *The Boor* (N.Y., Dec. 29, 1949); *The Dress* (N.Y., Dec. 8, 1953); *Sweet Betsy from Pike* (N.Y., Dec. 8, 1953); *Tale for a Deaf Ear* (Tanglewood, Aug. 5, 1957); *The Hero* (N.Y., Sept. 24, 1965); Midas (1981). MUSICALS: *Caucasian Chalk Circle* (1948); *The Thirteen Clocks* (1953); *The Adamses* (1956); *Time and Again* (1958); *The Girl from Outside* (1959); *Chain of Jade* (1960); *Pink Party Dress* (1960); *The Old Lady Shows Her Medals* (1960); *Cheaper by the Dozen* (1961); *Johnny Mishuga* (1961); *Our Miss Brooks* (1961); *The Best of Broadway* (1961); *Ask Any Girl* (1967); *Second Coming* (1976). INCIDENTAL MUSIC TO: *Cadenza* (1947); *Elmer and Lily* (1952); *Summer Afternoon* (1952); *The Western* (1954); *The Sorcerer's Apprentice* (1969).

Buchanan, Isobel, Scottish soprano; b. Glasgow, March 15, 1954. She studied at the Royal Scottish Academy of Music and Drama in Glasgow, graduating in 1974. In 1976 she made her operatic debut as Pamina with the Australian Opera in Sydney, where she sang until 1978 when she made her Glyndebourne Festival debut in the same role and as Micaëla at the Vienna State Opera. In 1979 she appeared at London's Covent Garden and at the Santa Fe (N. Mex.) Opera. In 1981 she sang at the Aix-en-Provence Festival. In subsequent years she appeared with various opera companies and toured widely as a concert artist. Among her most admired roles are Adina, Zerlina, Donna Elvira, Susanna, and Fiordiligi.

Bucharoff, (Buchhalter), Simon, Russian-American pianist and composer; b. Berdichev, April 20, 1881; d. Chicago, Nov. 24, 1955. He settled in America as a youth; he studied piano with Paolo Gallico in New York, and later with Julius Epstein and Emil Sauer in Vienna. He occupied various teaching posts; lived principally in Chicago and Hollywood. He publ. *The Modern Pianist's Textbook* (N.Y., 1931). Among his works were the operas *A Lover's Knot* (Chicago, Jan. 15, 1916) and *Sakahra* (Frankfurt am Main, Nov. 8, 1924; rev. 1953).

Bucht, Gunnar, Swedish composer, musicologist, and pedagogue; b. Stocksund, Aug. 5, 1927. He studied composition with Blomdahl (1947–51) and also took courses in musicology at the Univ. of Uppsala (Ph.D., 1953); he later pursued training in composition with Orff in Germany (1954), Petrassi in Italy (1954–55), and Deutsch in Paris (1961–62). He taught at the Univ. of Stockholm (1965–69), and then was in the diplomatic service as cultural attaché at the Swedish Embassy in Bonn (1970–73). From 1975 to 1985 he was a prof. of composition at the Stockholm Musikhögskolan, serving as its director from 1987 to 1993. From 1963 to 1969 he was chairman of the Soc. of Swedish Composers. In 1964 he was elected to membership in the Royal Swedish Academy of Music in Stockholm. His music retains traditional forms while adopting diverse modern techniques. He composed *Tronkrävarna* (The Pretenders), opera (1961–64; Stockholm, Sept. 10, 1966) and *Jerikos murar* (The Walls of Jericho), opera oratorio (1966–67; reworked as an electronic piece).

Büchtger, Fritz, German composer; b. Munich, Feb. 14, 1903; d. in an automobile accident in Starnberg, Dec. 26, 1978. He was a student of Beer-Walbrunn and Waltershausen at the Munich Akadamie der Tonkunst (1923–26). He was active as a choral conductor and teacher, and also in the promotion of contemporary music until the advent of the Nazi regime, when he was compelled to change course. After the collapse of the Third Reich, he again embraced the cause of contemporary music, helping to found the Studio for New Music in Munich in 1948. In 1953 he became president of the Musikalischen Jugend Deutschlands, and was a prominent figure in music education. In 1953 he received the music prize of the City of Munich and in 1977 the Schwabinger Kunstpreis. In his music, Büchtger developed a dodecaphonic technique which he adroitly utilized even in his sacred music. His stage works include *O Mensch, gib acht!*, Kalenderspiel (1939), and *Der Spielhansl*, musical play (1946).

BIBL.: L. Wismeyer, *F. B.* (Regensburg, 1963); A. Ott, ed., *F. B. 1973* (Munich, 1974; new ed., 1988, as *F. B. 1903–1978*); K. Hübler, *F. B. und die neue Musik in München* (Munich, 1983); K.-R. Danler et al., *F. B.* (Tutzing, 1989).

Bücken, Ernst, eminent German musicologist; b. Aachen, May 2, 1884; d. Overath, near Cologne, July 28, 1949. He studied musicology at the Univ. of Munich with Sandberger and Kroyer; he also took courses in composition with Courvoisier and received his Ph.D. there in 1912 with the diss. *Anton Reicha; Sein Leben und seine Kompositionen* (publ. in Munich, 1912); he completed his Habilitation at the Univ. of Cologne in 1920 with his *Der heroische Stil in der Oper* (publ. in Leipzig, 1924) and was a prof. there from 1925 to 1945, then retired to Overath. His elucidation of musical styles remains an important achievement in his work as a musicologist; as such, he ed. the monumental *Handbuch der Musikwissenschaft* in 10 vols., which began publication in 1927; he was also editor of the series Die Grossen Meister der Musik from 1932. His further writings include *Tagebuch der Gattin Mozarts* (Munich, 1915), *Ludwig van Beethoven* (Potsdam, 1934), *Richard Wagner* (Potsdam, 1934; 2d ed., 1943), *Wolfgang Amadeus Mozart: Schöpferische Wandlungen* (Hamburg, 1942), and *Richard Strauss* (Kevelaar, 1949). He also ed. *Richard Wagner: Die Hauptschriften* (Leipzig, 1937).

Buckley, Emerson, American conductor; b. N.Y., April 14, 1916; d. Miami, Nov. 17, 1989. He studied at Columbia Univ. (B.A., 1936), where he began his career as conductor of its Grand Opera (1936–38). He subsequently was conductor of the Palm Beach (Fla.) Sym. Orch. (1938–41), the N.Y. City Sym. Orch. (1941–42), the San Carlo Opera in N.Y. (1943–45), and WOR Radio in New York (1945–54). In 1950 he became music director of the Miami Opera, and from 1973 to 1985 he was its artistic director and resident conductor; he also served as music director of the Fort Lauderdale Sym. Orch. (later the Phil. Orch. of Florida) from 1963 to 1986. In 1963 he received the Alice M. Ditson Award for conducting. He was principally known as a favorite conductor on tour with Pavarotti. With his silver hair and goatee he cut a striking figure when he appeared in Pavarotti's film *Yes, Giorgio!* (1982); the film was unsuccessful, but Buckley's appearance produced an impression. He was also the conductor in a film documentary about Pavarotti, entitled *A Distant Harmony*.

Buckner, Thomas, leading American baritone, composer, and producer; b. N.Y., Aug. 13, 1941. After brief studies at Yale Univ., he took both B.A. (1964) and M.A. (1965) degrees in English literature at the Univ. of Santa Clara in California; he also took courses in linguistics at Stanford Univ. He then devoted himself to vocal training, numbering among his mentors W. A. Mathieu, Martial Singher, Alden Gilchrist, Marion Cooper, and Raymond Beegle; he also studied Indian music with Ali Akbar Kahn at the American Soc. for Eastern Arts in Berkeley, California (1967–67). Buckner was active in Berkeley from 1967 to 1983, where he founded and directed the 1750 Arch Concerts (1972–80) and 1750 Arch Records (1973–83); he also was cofounder/director (with Robert Hughes) of the 23-piece Arch Ensemble, which specialized in 20th-century music. From 1989 he curated the World Music Institute's "Interpretations" series in New York. While Buckner's repertoire spans the ages, he has become a stalwart proponent of the avant-garde, appearing in first performances of works by David First, Annea Lockwood, Henry Threadgill, Somei Satoh, Jin Hi Kim, and David Behrman, among many others; he is known particularly for his lengthy association with Robert Ashley, in whose *Perfect Lives* trilogy (*Atalanta [Acts of God]* [1982], and *El Aficionado* [1987] and *Improvement [Don Leaves Linda]* [1984–85] from *Now Eleanor's Idea*) he created critically acclaimed leading roles. Through these and other performances, including a number of noteworthy recitals in New York and frequent appearances with the improvisational group "Act of Finding," the experimental group "Roscoe Mitchell New Chamber Ensemble," and the pianist Joseph Kubera, Buckner has earned the critical sobriquet "*the* voice of the Downtown (N.Y.) new music scene." Among his many recordings are 2 solo compilations, *Full Voice Spectrum* (1992) and *Sign of Our Times* (1995), both featuring works written especially for him, as well as *Pilgrimage* (1995; with the Roscoe Mitchell New Chamber Ensemble) and *Act of Finding* (1995; with Ratzo B. Harris, Bruce Arnold, and Tom Hamilton). As a composer, Buckner creates primarily structured improvisations, in both solo (*Resonances*, 1995) and ensemble (*In Moments of Great Passion* for Improvising Baritone and String Orch., after John Ralston Saul's *Voltaire's Bastards*; N.Y., Dec. 19, 1995) settings.

Buczynski, Walter (Joseph), Canadian composer, pianist, and teacher; b. Toronto, Dec. 17, 1933. After studies with Earle Moss (piano) and Ridout (theory) at the Royal Cons. of Music of Toronto, he had lessons in composition with Milhaud and Charles Jones at the Aspen (Colo.) Music School (summer 1956); he then studied piano with Lhévinne in New York (1958–59) and Drzewiecki in Warsaw (1959, 1961), and composition with Boulanger in Paris (1960, 1962). He taught piano and theory at the Royal Cons. of Music of Toronto (from 1962), and piano, theory, and composition at the Univ. of Toronto (from 1969); until 1977 he also pursued an active career as a pianist. His early penchant for satirical and humorous expression eventually mellowed as he pursued a more lyrical but still adventuresome path. His stage works include *Mr. Rhinoceros and His Musicians*, children's opera (1965), *Do Re Mi*, children's opera (1967), *From the Buczynski Book of the Living*, chamber opera (1972), and *Naked at the Opera*, chamber opera (1978).

Budden, Julian (Midforth), English musicologist; b. Holylake, Cheshire, April 9, 1924. He was educated at Queen's College, Oxford (B.A., 1948; M.A., 1951) and the Royal College of Music, London (B.Mus., 1955); from 1951 he worked for the BBC, serving as a producer for music programs (1955–70), chief producer for opera (1970–76), and music organizer for external services (1976–83). His studies of 19th-century Italian opera are important; especially valuable is *The Operas of Verdi* (3 vols., London, 1973–81; rev. ed., 1992). He also publ. the biography *Verdi* (London, 1985; rev. ed., 1993). In 1991 he was made a member of the Order of the British Empire.

Buketoff, Igor, American conductor; b. Hartford, Conn., May 29, 1915. He studied at the Univ. of Kansas (1931–32), the Juilliard School of Music in New York (B.S., 1935; M.S., 1941), and the Los Angeles Cons. In 1942 he won the first Alice M. Ditson Award for Young Conductors. He was music director of the Chautauqua Opera (1941–47), the N.Y. Phil. Young People's Concerts (1948–53), the Fort Wayne (Ind.) Phil. (1948–66), the Iceland Sym. Orch. in Reykjavík (1964–65), the St. Paul (Minn.) Opera (1968–74), and the Texas Chamber Orch. (1980–81). He also taught at the Juilliard School of Music (1935–45), the Chautauqua School of Music (1941–47), Columbia Univ. (1943–47), Butler Univ. (1953–63), and the Univ. of Houston (1977–79). He prepared a new ed. of *Boris Godunov* which was first perf. at the Metropolitan Opera on Dec. 19, 1997, Gergiev conducting. Buketoff was notably active in the promotion of contemporary music.

Buller, John, English composer; b. London, Feb. 7, 1927. He studied music as a child, beginning formal composition lessons in 1959 with Anthony Milner in London. He served as composer-in-residence at the Univ. of Edinburgh (1975–76) and at Queens Univ. in Belfast (1985–86). In his catalog of works is the opera *Bakxai* (1991–92).

Bülow, Hans (Guido) von, celebrated German pianist and conductor of high attainment; b. Dresden, Jan. 8, 1830; d. Cairo, Feb. 12, 1894. At the age of 9 he began to study piano with Friedrich Wieck and theory with Max Eberwein; he then went to Leipzig, where he studied law at the univ. and took a music course with Moritz Hauptmann; he also studied piano with Plaidy. From 1846 to 1848 he lived in Stuttgart, where he made his debut as a pianist. In 1849 he attended the Univ. of Berlin; there he joined radical social groups; shortly afterward he went to Zürich and met Wagner, who was there in exile. After a year in Switzerland, where he conducted theater music, Bülow proceeded to Weimar, where he began to study with Liszt. In 1853 he made a tour through Germany and Austria as a pianist. In 1855 he was appointed head of the piano dept. at the Stern Cons. in Berlin, retaining this post until 1864. He married Liszt's natural daughter, Cosima, in 1857. In 1864 he was called by Ludwig II to Munich as court pianist and conductor; the king, who was a great admirer of Wagner, summoned Wagner to Munich from exile. Bülow himself became Wagner's ardent champion; on June 10, 1865, he conducted at the Court Opera in Munich the first performance of *Tristan und Isolde*, and on June 21, 1868, he led the premiere of *Die Meistersinger von Nürnberg*. It was about this time that Wagner became intimate with Cosima; after her divorce she married Wagner, in 1870. Despite this betrayal, Bülow continued to conduct Wagner's music; his growing admiration for Brahms cannot be construed as his pique against Wagner. It was Bülow who dubbed Brahms "the 3d B of music," the 1st being Bach, and the 2d Beethoven. In fact, the context of this nomination was more complex than a mere alphabetical adumbration; according to reports, Bülow was asked to name his favorite key; he replied that it was E-flat major, the key signature of the *Eroica*, with the 3 Bs (German colloquialism for flats) signifying Bach, Beethoven, and Brahms. Then he was asked why he did not instead nominate Bruckner for the 3d B, and he is supposed to have replied that Bruckner was too much of a Wagnerian for him. Bülow was indeed renowned for his wit and his aptitude for alliterative punning; his writings are of elevated literary quality. In 1872 Bülow lived in Florence; then resumed his career as a pianist, winning triumphant successes in England and Russia; during his American tour in 1875–76 he gave 139 concerts; he revisited America in 1889 and 1890. An important chapter in his career was his conductorship in Meiningen (1880–85). In 1882 he married a Meiningen actress, Marie Schanzer. He was conductor of the Berlin Phil. from 1887 to 1893, when a lung ailment forced him to seek a cure in Egypt. He died shortly after his arrival in Cairo.

As a conductor, Bülow was an uncompromising disciplinarian; he insisted on perfection of detail, and he was also able to project considerable emotional power on the music. He was one of the first conductors to dispense with the use of the score. His memory was fabulous; it was said that he could memorize a piano concerto by just reading the score, sometimes while riding in a train. The mainstay of his repertoire was Classical and Romantic music, but he was also receptive toward composers of the new school. When Tchaikovsky, unable to secure a performance of his 1st Piano Concerto in Russia, offered the score to Bülow, he accepted it, and gave its world premiere as soloist with a pickup orch. in Boston, on Oct. 25, 1875; however, the music was too new and too strange to American ears of the time, and the critical reactions were ambiguous. Bülow encouraged the young Richard Strauss, and gave him his first position as conductor. Bülow was a composer himself, but his works belong to the category of "Kapellmeister Musik," competent, well structured, but devoid of originality. Among his compositions was incidental music to Shakespeare's *Julius Caesar*. He made masterly transcriptions of the prelude to Wagner's *Meistersinger* and the entire opera *Tristan und Isolde*; he also arranged for piano the overtures to *Le Corsaire* and *Benvenuto Cellini* by Berlioz. He annotated and edited Beethoven's piano sonatas; these eds. were widely used by piano teachers, even though criticism was voiced against his cavalier treatment of some passages and his occasional alterations of Beethoven's original to enhance the resonance. His writings were publ. by his widow, Marie von Bülow, under the title *Briefe und Schriften H. v. B.s* (8 vols., Leipzig, 1895–1908; vol. 3, republ. separately in 1936, contains selected essays, while the other vols. contain letters); selected letters in Eng. tr. were publ. by C. Bache, *The Early Correspondence of H. v. B.* (London, 1896).

BIBL.: E. Zabel, *H. v. B.* (Hamburg, 1894); R. Sternfeld, *H. v. B.* (Leipzig, 1894); T. Pfeiffer, *Studien bei H. v. B.* (Berlin, 1894; 6th ed., 1909); H. Heimann, *H. v. B.: Sein Leben und sein Wirken* (Berlin, 1909); R. Du Moulin-Eckart, H. v. B. (1921); M. von Bülow, *H. v. B. in Leben und Wort* (1925); L. Schemann, *H. v. B. im Lichte der Wahrheit* (Regensburg, 1935); W. Stresemann, *The Berlin Philharmonic from B. to Karajan* (in Ger. and Eng.; Berlin, 1979).

Bumbry, Grace (Melzia Ann), greatly talented black American mezzo-soprano and soprano; b. St. Louis, Jan. 4, 1937. She attended Boston Univ. and Northwestern Univ., and pursued vocal training with Lehmann at the Music Academy of the West in Santa Barbara (1955–58) and with Bernac in Paris. With Martina Arroyo, she was cowinner of the Metropolitan Opera auditions in 1958. In 1960 she made a notably successful operatic debut as Amneris at the Paris Opéra. In 1961 she became the first black American singer to appear at the Bayreuth Festival when she sang Venus in *Tannhäuser*. In 1963 she made her Covent Garden debut in London as Eboli, and her Chicago Lyric Opera debut as Ulrica. In 1964 she sang Lady Macbeth at her first appearance at the Salzburg Festival. She made her Metropolitan Opera debut in New

York as Eboli on Oct. 7, 1965, and subsequently sang there regularly. From 1970 she concentrated on the soprano repertoire. Among her distinguished roles at the Metropolitan were Carmen (1967), Santuzza (1970), Tosca (1971), Salome (1973), Venus (1977), Leonora in *Il Trovatore* (1982), and Gershwin's Bess (1985). In 1990 she sang Berlioz's Cassandre at the opening of the new Opéra de la Bastille in Paris. She also appeared as a soloist with major orchs. and as a recitalist.

Bungert, (Friedrich) August, German composer; b. Mulheim, Ruhr, March 14, 1845; d. Leutesdorf, Oct. 26, 1915. He studied piano and composition at Cologne and Paris, then lived mostly in Berlin. An ardent admirer of Wagner, Bungert devoted his life to the composition of a parallel work to Wagner's *Ring*, taking Homer's epics as the source of his librettos. The result of this effort was the creation of 2 operatic cycles: *The Iliad*, comprising *Achilleus* and *Klytemnestra*, and *The Odyssey*, a tetralogy. The Iliad was never completed for performance, but all 4 parts of *The Odyssey* were performed in Dresden: *Kirke* (Jan. 29, 1898), *Nausikaa* (March 20, 1901), *Odysseus' Heimkehr* (Dec. 12, 1896, prior to premieres of parts I and II), and *Odysseus' Tod* (Oct. 30, 1903). There were also subsequent productions in other German cities, but everywhere Bungert's operas were received without enthusiasm, and the evident ambition to emulate Wagner without comparable talent proved his undoing. His most successful work was a comic opera, *Die Studenten von Salamanka* (Leipzig, 1884); he also wrote a mystery play, *Warum? woher? wohin?* (1908), and incidental music to Goethe's *Faust*.

BIBL.: M. Chop, *A. B., Ein deutscher Dichterkomponist* (Leipzig, 1916).

Bunin, Revol, Russian composer; b. Moscow, April 6, 1924; d. there, July 4, 1976. He was a student at the Moscow Cons., graduating in 1945 in the class of Shostakovich; in 1947 he became an assistant to Shostakovich at the Leningrad Cons. A prolific composer, he wrote an opera, *Masquerade*.

Burbure de Wesembeek, Léon-Philippe-Marie, Belgian music scholar; b. Dendermonde, Aug. 16, 1812; d. Antwerp, Dec. 8, 1889. A scion of an aristocratic family, he studied law at the Univ. of Ghent; he also received an excellent musical education at home with private teachers. In 1846 he settled at Antwerp, and became the keeper of Archives at the Cathedral. He made a profound study of materials on early music accessible to him, and publ. a number of valuable monographs dealing with the Renaissance music guilds of Antwerp, on lute makers, etc. He also composed some 200 works, including an opera.

BIBL.: F. A. Gevaert, *Notice sur le Chevalier Léon de Burbure* (Brussels, 1893).

Burchuladze, Paata, Russian bass; b. Tbilisi, Feb. 12, 1951. He studied at the Tbilisi Cons. In 1975 he made his operatic debut as Gounod's Méphistophélès in Tbilisi, and then sang throughout Russia and in Italy, where he pursued further training. In 1983 he made his British debut as a soloist in Elgar's *The Dream of Gerontius* at the Lichfield Festival, and in 1984 he made his first appearance at London's Covent Garden as Verdi's Ramfis. In 1987 he sang Mozart's Commendatore at the Salzburg Festival. He made his Metropolitan Opera debut in New York as Rossini's Don Basilio on Oct. 21, 1989. In 1994 he appeared as Boris Godunov at the New Israeli Opera in Tel Aviv. He sang Verdi's Zaccaria at the Verona Arena in 1996. In 1997 he appeared as Banquo in Hamburg.

Burg (real name, **Bartl**), **Robert,** German baritone; b. Prague, March 29, 1890; d. Dresden, Feb. 9, 1946. He studied with Hans Pokorny in Prague, where he made his operatic debut at the German Theatre (1915). After appearing in Augsburg (1915–16), he was a member of the Dresden Court (later State) Opera from 1916 to 1944; in addition to his Verdi roles there, he created the roles of Busoni's Doktor Faust (1925) and Hindemith's Cardillac (1926). He also sang at the Bayreuth Festivals (1933–42), where he was heard as Alberich, Klingsor, and Kothner, and made guest appearances in Munich, Berlin, Vienna, and other European cities.

Burgess, Anthony (real name, **John Anthony Burgess Wilson**), celebrated English novelist, critic, and composer; b. Manchester, Feb. 25, 1917; d. London, Nov. 22, 1993. He studied language and literature at the Univ. of Manchester (B.A., 1940); he also played piano in jazz combos and taught himself to compose by a close study of the Classical masters. He was active as a teacher in England and the Far East; later was writer-in-residence at the Univ. of North Carolina at Chapel Hill (1969–70), visiting prof. at Princeton Univ. and Columbia Univ. (1970), and distinguished prof. at City College of the City Univ. of N.Y. (1972–73). As a novelist, Burgess made a notable impression with his disturbing *A Clockwork Orange* (1962), which was followed by such novels as the *Napoleon Symphony* (1974) and his major literary achievement, *Earthly Powers* (1980). Among his other writings were *This Man and Music* (1982) and the autobiography *Little Wilson and Big God* (1987). As a composer, he produced a respectable body of works notable for being refreshingly rhythmical and tonal, but not without quirky quartal harmonies and atonal diversions. Among his compositions is the opera *Blooms of Dublin* (1981).

Burgess, Sally, South African–born English mezzo-soprano; b. Durban, Oct. 9, 1953. She was a student of Alan at the Royal College of Music in London; she later pursued private training with Studholme, Salaman, and Veasey. In 1976 she began her career as a soprano with her formal debut as a soloist in the Brahms *Requiem* in London. In 1977 she made her first appearance at the English National Opera there as Bertha in *Euryanthe*, returning there in subsequent years to sing such roles as Zerlina, Cherubino, Micaëla, Massenet's Charlotte, Mimi, and Strauss's Composer. In 1978 she made her Wigmore Hall Recital debut in London, and thereafter became well known via her many concert engagements. In 1983 she made her debut as a mezzo-soprano at London's Covent Garden as Siebel; she also appeared that year at Glyndebourne as Smeraldina in Prokofiev's *The Love for 3 Oranges*. In 1986 she sang Carmen at the English National Opera, and also appeared with Opera North. She sang Fricka in *Die Walküre* at Glasgow's Scottish Opera in 1991, returning there in 1992 as Annius in *La Clemenza di Tito*. In 1991 she also sang in the premiere of Paul McCartney's *Liverpool Oratorio*. She portrayed Delilah in Nantes in 1994. In 1996 she sang Strauss's Herodias at the English National Opera and Isabella in *The Voyage* at the Metropolitan Opera. In 1997 she appeared in the premiere of *Twice Through the Heart* at the Aldeburgh Festival.

Burghauser, Jarmil (real name, **Jarmil Michael Mokrý**), distinguished Czech composer, conductor, and musicologist; b. Písek, Oct. 21, 1921; d. Prague, Feb. 19, 1997. He took his mother's maiden name as his own surname in 1950. After training in composition with Kělčka (1933–37) and Jeremiáš (1937–40), he pursued studies in conducting at the Prague Cons. with Doležil and Dědeček (graduated, 1944), and then at its master school with Talich (graduated, 1946); subsequently he took courses in musicology and psychology at the Charles Univ. in Prague, but quit his studies in protest against the communist coup in 1948; it was not until 1991 that he presented his diss. and was awarded his Ph.D. He served as chorus master and conductor at the National Theater in Prague from 1946 to 1950, and thereafter devoted himself principally to composition and scholarship. Following the Soviet-bloc invasion of his homeland in 1968 and the restoration of hard-line communist rule, he became suspect. Although he had done valuable work on the critical edition of Dvořák's works, his name was not acknowledged in the new vols. In order to get his music before the public, he took the pseudonym Michal Hájků. From 1978 to 1989 he was choirmaster at St. Margaret's church in Prague. Following the overthrow of the communist regime by the "Velvet Revolution" in 1989, Burghauser became a leading figure in the restoration of the musical life of his country by serving as chairman of the Guild of Composers and as a member of the rehabilitation committee of the Ministry of Culture. In addition to his valuable work on the critical edition of Dvořák's compositions, he also ed. works for the critical editions of the music of Janáček,

Smetana, and Fibich. In his own compositions, he developed a style which he described as harmonic serialism. Under his pseudonym he composed an interesting series of works in the style of earlier periods which he called "Storica apocrifa della musica Boema."

WORKS: DRAMATIC: *Lakomec* (The Miser), opera (1949; Liberec, May 20, 1950); *Karolinka a lhář* (Caroline and the Liar), opera (1950–53; Olomouc, March 13, 1955); *Honza a čert* (Honza and the Devil), ballet (Ostrava, Nov. 23, 1954; rev. 1960); *Sluha dvou pánů* (Servant of 2 Masters), ballet (1957; Prague, May 9, 1958); *Most* (The Bridge), antiopera (1963–64; Prague, March 31, 1967); *Tristam a Izalda*, ballet (1969).

WRITINGS: (all publ. in Prague): *Orchestrace Dvořákových Slonvanských tanců* (Orchestration of Dvořák's Slavonic Dances; 1959); *Antonín Dvořák: Tematický katalog, bibliografie, přehled života a díla* (Antonín Dvořák: Thematic Catalog, Bibliography, Survey of Life and Work; 1960; 2d ed., 1997); *Nejen pomníky* (Not Monuments Only; 1966); *Antonín Dvořák* (1966); with A. Špelda, *Akustické základy orchestrace* (Acoustic Basis of Orchestration; 1967; Ger. tr., 1971); completion of J. Rychlik's *Moderni instrumentace* (Modern Instrumentation; 1968); *Česká interpretační tradice* (Czech Tradition of Interpretation; 1982).

Burgon, Geoffrey (Alan), English composer; b. Hambledon, July 15, 1941. He was a student of Peter Wishart (composition) and Bernard Brown (trumpet) at the Guildhall School of Music in London. After playing trumpet in various orchs., jazz ensembles, and theater orchs. (1964–71), he devoted himself to composing and to conducting for films and television. His scores for the television series *Tinker, Tailor, Soldier, Spy* (1979) and *Brideshead Revisited* (1981) established his reputation. He has demonstrated special talent in composing works for vocal forces.

WORKS: DRAMATIC: OPERA: *Hard Times* (1991). MUSIC THEATER: *Epitaph to Sir Walter Raleigh* (1968; London, Feb. 8, 1969); *Joan of Arc* (1970); *The Fall of Lucifer* (1977); *Mirandola* (1980–81); *Orpheus* (Wells, July 17, 1982). BALLETS: *The Golden Fish* (1964); *Ophelia* (1964); *The Calm* (1974); *Running Figures/Goldberg's Dream* (Leeds, March 25, 1975); *Step at a Time* (London, Nov. 4, 1976); *Persephone* (1979); *Lamentations and Praises* (Jerusalem, Aug. 7, 1979); *Mass* (1984; London, Sept. 16, 1985); *The Trial of Prometheus* (1988).

Burgstaller, Alois, German tenor; b. Holzkirchen, Sept. 21, 1871; d. Gmund, April 19, 1945. He was trained as a watchmaker, and also sang; encouraged by Cosima Wagner, he made a serious study of singing, and performed the roles of Siegfried, Siegmund, Erik, and Parsifal at the Bayreuth Festivals (1896–1902). He made his American debut at the Metropolitan Opera in New York as Siegmund in *Die Walküre* on Feb. 12, 1903; remained on its roster until his final appearance, again as Siegmund, on Jan. 14, 1909. He also sang the title role in the first staged American performance of *Parsifal*, in New York, on Dec. 24, 1903, in violation of the German copyright; as a result, he was permanently banned from Bayreuth. In 1910 he returned to Germany.

Burian, Emil František, Czech composer and stage director, nephew of **Karl Burian**; b. Pilsen, June 11, 1904; d. Prague, Aug. 9, 1959. His father was a baritone and his mother a singing teacher. He received his training at the Prague Cons. where he attended Foerster's master class in composition (graduated, 1927). Even before graduating, he was active in avant-garde quarters in Prague as a stage director, dramatist, actor, and musician. With his mother, he presented concerts of new music from 1920. In 1924 he organized Přítomnost, a soc. for contemporary music. In 1927 he organized the Voice Band, which sang according to prescribed rhythm but without definite pitch; it attracted considerable attention at the Sienna ISCM Festival on Sept. 12, 1928. Between 1929 and 1932 he was active in Brno and Oloumoc. In 1933 he founded his own D 34 theater in Prague. During the Nazi occupation, Burian's theater was shut down and he was placed in a concentration camp. After his liberation, he was a director in Brno (1945–46). In 1946 he returned to Prague and served that year as director of the Karlín musical theater. His long-standing commitment to the political Left led to his being made a deputy in the post–World War II National Assembly. As a composer, he followed an eclectic path, finding inspiration in Czech folk art, jazz, the music of Les Six, and Dada. Between the 2 world wars, he was one of the leading figures in the Czech avant-garde. After World War II and the installation of the communist regime, he embraced the tenets of socialist realism. His writings, all publ. in Prague, include *O moderní ruské hudbě* (1926); *Polydynamika* (1926); *Jazz* (1928); *Památnik bratří Burianů* (Almanac of the Burian Brothers; 1929); *Pražská dramaturgie* (1938); *Emil Burian* (1947); *Karel Burian* (1948); *Divadlo za našich dnů* (The Theater of Our Days; 1962).

WORKS: DRAMATIC: OPERAS: *Alladine a Palomid* (1923; rev. version, Prague, Oct. 14, 1959); *Před slunce východem* (Before Sunrise; Prague, Nov. 24, 1925); *Bubu z Montparnassu* (Bubu from Montparnasse; (1927); *Mastičkář* (The Quack; Prague, May 23, 1928; rev. by R. Krátký, 1955); *Milenci z kiosku* (The Lovers from the Market Stall; Prague, Nov. 13, 1935); *Maryša* (Brno, April 16, 1940); *Opera z pouti* (Country Fair Scenes; Prague, Jan. 28, 1956); *Račte odpusdit* (Please Forgive Me; Prague, Oct. 13, 1956). Also ballets.

BIBL.: B. Srba, *Poetické divadlo E. F. B.a* (The Poetic Theater of E. F. B.; Prague, 1971); I. Kladiva, *E. F. B.* (Prague, 1982).

Burian, Karl (Karel), noted Czech tenor, uncle of **Emil František Burian**; b. Rusínov, near Rakovník, Jan. 12, 1870; d. Senomaty, Sept. 25, 1924. He studied with Franz Piwoda in Prague and Felix von Kraus in Munich. On March 28, 1891, he made his operatic debut as Jeník in *The Bartered Bride* in Brünn, then sang in Reval (1892–94), Aachen (1894–95), Cologne (1895–96), Hannover (1897–98), and Hamburg (1898–1902). From 1902 to 1911 he was a principal member of the Dresden Court Opera, where he created the role of Herod in Strauss's *Salome* (Dec. 9, 1905). On Nov. 30, 1906, he made his Metropolitan Opera debut in New York as Tannhäuser, remaining on its roster until 1913; during this period he used the name Carl Burrian. He also sang at the Bayreuth Festivals, where he was greatly admired. In later years he appeared at the Vienna Court Opera, in Budapest, and in Prague. He was famous for his portrayal of Tristan; among his other distinguished roles were Parsifal, Siegmund, and both Siegfrieds.

Burkhard, Paul, Swiss conductor and composer; b. Zürich, Dec. 21, 1911; d. Zell, Sept. 6, 1977. He was trained at the Zürich Cons. After working at the Bern City Theater (1932–34), he was resident composer at the Zürich Theater (1939–44). From 1944 to 1957 he conducted the Zürich Radio Orch. As a composer, he was successful mainly with light theater pieces. His *Der schwarze Hecht* (Zürich, April 1, 1939) was partially reworked by Erik Charell as *Feuerwerk* (Munich, May 16, 1950), and became internationally known via its song, *O, mein Papa*. Among his other theater pieces were *Hopsa* (Zürich, Nov. 30, 1935; rev. version, Wiesbaden, Oct. 12, 1957), *Dreimal Georges* (Zürich, Oct. 3, 1936), *Die Frauen von Coraya* or *Der Paradies der Frauen* (Stettin, Feb. 19, 1938), *Casanova in der Schweiz* (Zürich, 1942), *Tic-Tac* (1942), *Die Pariserin* (1946; Zürich, Dec. 31, 1957), *Die kleine Niederdorfoper* (Zürich, Dec. 31, 1951), *Bunbury* (1963; Basel, Oct. 7, 1965), *Die Schneekönigin* (Zürich, 1964) and *Regenbogen* (Basel, Nov. 30, 1977). He also wrote various works for young people, including the Christmas opera *Ein Stern geht auf aus Jakob* (Hamburg, Dec. 6, 1970) and religious plays.

BIBL.: P. Flury and P. Kaufmann, *O mein Papa . . . P. B.: Leben und Werk* (Zürich, 1979).

Burkhard, Willy, significant Swiss composer and pedagogue; b. Leubringen bei Biel, April 17, 1900; d. Zürich, June 18, 1955. After graduating from the Muristalden teachers' training college, he took up music studies with E. Graf in Bern; he then pursued training with Karg-Elert and Teichmüller in Leipzig (1921), Courvoisier in Munich (1922–23), and d'Ollone in Paris (1923–24). He taught theory at the Bern Cons. (1928–33), and later theory and composition at the Zürich Cons. (1942–55). His music was neoclassical in form and strongly polyphonic; his astringent linear idiom was tempered by a strong sense of modal counterpoint. He composed the opera *Die Schwarze Spinne* (1947–48; Zürich, May 28, 1949; rev. 1954), although his most important contribution was to church music.

BIBL.: H. Zurlinden, *W. B.* (Erlenbach, 1956); E. Mohr, *W. B.: Leben und Werk* (Zürich, 1957); S. Burkhard and F. Indermühle, *W. B. (17. April 1900–18. Juni 1955) Werkverzeichnis* (Liebefeld, 1968).

Burrowes, Norma (Elizabeth), Welsh soprano; b. Bangor, April 24, 1944. She studied at the Queen's Univ. in Belfast and with Flora Nielsen and Rupert Bruce-Lockhart at the Royal Academy of Music in London. In 1970 she made her professional operatic debut as Zerlina with the Glyndebourne Touring Opera Co., and that same year she made her first appearance at London's Covent Garden as Fiakermilli in *Arabella*. From 1971 she sang at the Sadler's Wells (later the English National) Opera in London, and also appeared at the Salzburg, Glyndebourne, Aix-en-Provence, and other festivals. On Oct. 12, 1979, she made her Metropolitan Opera debut in New York as Blondchen. She also toured widely as a concert singer. In 1982 she retired from the operatic stage. From 1969 to 1980 she was married to **Steuart Bedford**.

Burrows, (James) Stuart, Welsh tenor; b. Pontypridd, Feb. 7, 1933. He was educated at Trinity College, Carmarthen. After winning a prize at the National Eisteddfod of Wales in 1959, he appeared as a concert singer. In 1963 he made his operatic debut as Ismaele in *Nabucco* at the Welsh National Opera in Cardiff. In 1967 he made his first appearance at London's Covent Garden as Beppe, and subsequently sang there regularly. He made his U.S. debut as Tamino at the San Francisco Opera that same year. In 1970 he sang for the first time at the Vienna State Opera and the Salzburg Festival. On April 13, 1971, he made his Metropolitan Opera debut in New York as Ottavio, and continued to make occasional appearances there until 1982. He also toured extensively as a concert artist. Among his other esteemed roles were Faust, Alfredo, Belmonte, Lensky, Ernesto, and Rodolfo.

Burt, Francis, English composer and teacher; b. London, April 28, 1926. He studied with Ferguson and Berkeley at the Royal Academy of Music in London (1948–51), and then with Blacher in Berlin (1951–54). After winning the Mendelssohn Scholarship in 1954, he completed his studies in Rome (1954–55). In 1956 he settled in Vienna, where he was a prof. of composition at the Hochschule für Musik and Darstellende Kunst from 1973 to 1993. In 1973 he received the Körner Prize. He was awarded the Würdigungspreis for music in 1978 and in 1981 he received the music prize of the City of Vienna. He was awarded the Great Silver Medal of Honor in 1992 for services to the Republic of Austria. He composed the operas *Volpone oder Der Fuchs* (1952–58; Stuttgart, June 2, 1960; rev. 1960–61) and *Barnstable oder Jemand auf dem Dachboden* (1967–69; Kassel, Nov. 30, 1969) and the ballet *Der Golem* (1959–63; Hannover, Jan. 31, 1965).

BIBL.: H. Krones, *Musikalisches Dokumentation F. B.* (Vienna, 1980).

Burton, Stephen Douglas, American composer and teacher; b. Whittier, Calif., Feb. 24, 1943. He studied at the Oberlin (Ohio) College-Cons. of Music (1960–62), with Henze at the Salzburg Mozarteum, and at the Peabody Cons. of Music in Baltimore (M.M., 1974). In 1969 he was awarded a Guggenheim fellowship. After teaching at the Catholic Univ. of America in Washington, D.C. (1970–74), he joined the faculty of George Mason Univ. in Fairfax, Va., in 1974, serving as a prof. there from 1983. He publ. *Orchestrtion* (1982). While his music draws upon the totality of modern resources, it remains faithful to the directness, energy, and spirit of the American experience.

WORKS: DRAMATIC: *The Nightingale and the Rose*, chamber ballet (1968; also as *Eurydice* for Violin, Clarinet, Trombone, Piano or Celesta, and Percussion, 1977); *No Trifling with Love*, opera (1970); *An American Triptych*, 3 1-act operas: *Maggie*, after Crane, *Dr. Heidegger's Experiment*, after Hawthorne, and *Benito Cereno*, after Melville (1974–75; Alexandria, Va., July 29, 1988); *The Starchild*, children's opera (1975); *The Duchess of Malfi*, opera (1975–78; Vienna, Va., Aug. 18, 1978); *Finisterre*, dance piece (Newport, R.I., Aug. 21, 1977); *The Merchant of Venice*, incidental music to Shakespeare's play (1988); *Brotherhood*, music theater (1991–92).

Burzio, Eugenia, Italian soprano; b. Milan, June 20, 1872; d. there, May 18, 1922. She studied in Milan with Aversa and Benvenuti. In 1903 she made her operatic debut in Turin, and then sang in Parma and Palermo (from 1904). In 1906 she made her first appearance at Milan's La Scala as Katusha in Alfano's *Risurrezione*, and in 1907 scored a fine success there as Catalani's Loreley. She also sang at the Teatro Colón in Buenos Aires (from 1909). In 1919 she made her final stage appearance as Ponchielli's Marion Delorme at Milan's Teatro Lirico. Although most successful in verismo roles, Burzio was also praised for her portrayals of Gluck's Armide, Pacini's Saffo, and Bellini's Norma.

Busch, Fritz, eminent German conductor; b. Siegen, Westphalia, March 13, 1890; d. London, Sept. 14, 1951. His brothers were the noted German violinist Adolf (Georg Wilhelm) Busch (b. Siegen, Westphalia, Aug. 8, 1891; d. Guilford, Vt., June 9, 1952) and the noted German cellist Hermann Busch (b. Siegen, Westphalia, June 24, 1897; d. Bryn Mawr, Pa., June 3, 1975). He studied at the Cologne Cons. with Steinbach, Boettcher, Uzielli, and Klauwell; he was then conductor of the Deutsches Theater in Riga (1909–10); in 1912 he became music director of the city of Aachen, and then of the Stuttgart Opera in 1918. In 1922 he was named Generalmusikdirektor of the Dresden State Opera; during his tenure he conducted many notable productions, including the premieres of Strauss's *Intermezzo* and *Die Aegyptische Helena*. On Nov. 27, 1927, he made his U.S. debut as a guest conductor with the N.Y. Sym. Orch. In 1933 he was dismissed from his Dresden post by the Nazi government; leaving Germany, he made many appearances as a conductor with the Danish Radio Sym. Orch. and the Stockholm Phil.; from 1934 to 1939 he served as music director of the Glyndebourne Festivals; from 1940 to 1945 he was active mainly in South America. On Nov. 26, 1945, he made his first appearance with the Metropolitan Opera in New York, conducting *Lohengrin*; he continued on its roster until 1949. He was equally distinguished as an operatic and symphonic conductor, becoming particularly renowned for his performances of Mozart. He wrote an autobiography, *Aus dem Leben eines Musikers* (Zürich, 1949; Eng. tr., 1953, as *Pages from a Musician's Life*).

BIBL.: G. Busch, *F. B., Dirigent* (Frankfurt am Main, 1970); B. Dopheide, *F. B.* (Tutzing, 1970).

Bush, Alan (Dudley), English composer and teacher; b. London, Dec. 22, 1900; d. Watford, Oct. 31, 1995. He was a student of Corder (composition) and Matthay (piano) at the Royal Academy of Music in London (1918–22); he also received private training in piano from Moiseiwitsch (1924–29) and Schnabel (1928), and in composition from Ireland (1927–32); he also studied musicology with Wolf and Blume at the Univ. of Berlin (1929–31). From 1925 to 1978 he was prof. of composition at the Royal Academy of Music. He also was active as a pianist and conductor. In 1935 he joined the Communist Party, to which he remained deeply committed. In 1936 he founded the Workers' Music Assn., which he served as president from 1941 to 1976. In 1947–48 he was chairman of the Composers Guild of Great Britain. He publ. *Strict Counterpoint in the Palestrina Style* (London, 1948), *In My Seventh Decade* (London, 1970), and *In My Eighth Decade* (London, 1980). His early works were highly modern, utilizing a thematic style in which every note retains thematic importance. After World War II, tonal elements were added.

WORKS: DRAMATIC: OPERAS: *Wat Tyler* (1948–51; [East] Berlin Radio, April 3, 1952); *Men of Blackmoor* (1954–55; Weimar, Nov. 18, 1956); *The Sugar Reapers* (1961–63; Leipzig, Dec. 11, 1966); *Joe Hill: The Man Who Never Died* (1966–68; East Berlin, Sept. 29, 1970); also operas for young people. BALLETS: *His Wars or Yours* (1935); *Mining* (1935).

BIBL.: R. Stevenson, ed., *Time Remembered—A. B.: An 80th Birthday Symposium* (Kidderminster, 1981).

Bush, Geoffrey, English composer and teacher; b. London, March 23, 1920. He received training in composition from Ireland and then pursued his education at Balliol College, Oxford (B.Mus., 1940; D.Mus., 1946). After lecturing in the extramural dept. at the Univ. of Oxford (1947–52), he tutored in the extramural dept. at the Univ. of London (1952–80), where he subsequently served as music consultant (1984–87). He also was a visiting prof. at King's College, Univ. of London (1969–89). In 1957 he was chairman of the Composers Guild of Great Britain. He ed. works for Musica Britannica and for the collected edition of Elgar's works. He publ. *Musical Creation and the Listener* (London, 1954; rev. 1967), *Left, Right and Centre: Reflections on Composers and Composing* (London, 1983), and *An Unsentimental Education* (London, 1990). His works are written in an engaging neo-Classical style.

WORKS: DRAMATIC: *The Blind Beggar's Daughter*, opera (1952; rev. 1964); *If the Cap Fits*, opera (Cheltenham, July 12, 1956); *The Equation*, opera (1967; BBC Radio, Feb. 7, 1976); *Lord Arthur Savile's Crime*, theater piece (1972; BBC Radio, July 27, 1986); *The Cat who went to Heaven*, music theater (1974); *Love's Labours Lost*, opera (1988).

Busoni, Ferruccio (Dante Michelangiolo Benvenuto), greatly admired Italian-German pianist, pedagogue, and composer; b. Empoli, near Florence, April 1, 1866; d. Berlin, July 27, 1924. Busoni grew up in an artistic atmosphere. He learned to play the piano as a child; at the age of 8, he played in public in Trieste. He gave a piano recital in Vienna when he was 10, and included in his program some of his own compositions. In 1877 the family moved to Graz, where Busoni took piano lessons with W. Mayer. He conducted his *Stabat Mater* in Graz at the age of 12. At 15 he was accepted as a member of the Accademia Filarmonica in Bologna; he performed there his oratorio *Il sabato del villaggio* in 1883. In 1886 he went to Leipzig and undertook a profound study of Bach's music. In 1889 he was appointed a prof. of piano at the Helsinki Cons., where among his students was Sibelius. At that time, Busoni married Gerda Sjostrand, daughter of a celebrated Swedish sculptor; their 2 sons became well-known artists. In 1890 Busoni participated in the Rubinstein Competition in St. Petersburg, winning 1st prize with his *Konzertstück* for Piano and Orch. He was engaged to teach piano at the Moscow Cons. (1890–91), then accepted the post of prof. at the New England Cons. of Music in Boston (1891–94); however, he also made several tours, maintaining his principal residence in Berlin. During the season of 1912–13, he made a triumphant tour of Russia. In 1913 he was appointed director of the Liceo Musicale in Bologna. The outbreak of the World War I in 1914 forced him to flee to the United States; after a tour of the country, he moved to neutral Switzerland. In 1923 he went to Paris, and then returned to Berlin, remaining there until his death. In various cities, at various times, he taught piano in music schools; among his students were Brailowsky, Ganz, Petri, Mitropoulos, and Grainger. He also taught composition, numbering Weill, Jarnach, and Vogel among his pupils. He exercised great influence on Varèse, who was living in Berlin when Busoni was there; Varèse greatly prized Busoni's advanced theories of composition.

Busoni was a philosopher of music who tried to formulate a universe of related arts; he issued grandiloquent manifestos urging a return to classical ideals in modern forms, and he sought to establish a unifying link between architecture and composition. In his eds. of Bach's works, he included drawings illustrating the architectonic plan of Bach's fugues. He incorporated his innovations in his grandiose piano work *Fantasia contrappuntistica*, which opens with a prelude based on a Bach chorale and closes with a set of variations on Bach's acronym, B-A-C-H. In his theoretical writings, he proposed a system of 113 different heptatonic modes, and also suggested the possibility of writing music in exotic scales and subchromatic intervals; he expounded those ideas in his influential essay *Entwurf einer neuen Aesthetik der Tonkunst* (Trieste, 1907; Eng. tr. by T. Baker, N.Y., 1911). Busoni's other publications of significance were *Von der Einheit der Musik* (1923; in Italian, Florence, 1941; in Eng., London, 1957) and *Über die Möglichkeiten der Oper* (Leipzig, 1926).

Despite Busoni's great innovations in his own compositions and his theoretical writing, the Busoni legend is kept alive mainly through his sovereign virtuosity as a pianist. In his performances, he introduced a concept of piano sonority as an orch. medium; indeed, some listeners reported having heard simulations of trumpets and French horns sounded at Busoni's hands. The few extant recordings of his playing transmit a measure of the grandeur of his style, but they also betray a tendency, common to Busoni's era, toward a free treatment of the musical text, surprisingly so, since Busoni preached an absolute fidelity to the written notes. On concert programs Busoni's name appears most often as the author of magisterial and eloquent transcriptions of Bach's works. His gothic transfiguration for piano of Bach's *Chaconne* for Unaccompanied Violin became a perennial favorite of pianists all over the world.

Busoni was honored by many nations. In 1913 he received the order of Chevalier de la Légion d'honneur from the French government, a title bestowed on only 2 Italians before him: Rossini and Verdi. In 1949 a Concorso Busoni was established. Another international award honoring the name of Busoni was announced by the Accademia di Santa Cecilia of Rome, with prizes given for the best contemporary compositions; at its opening session in 1950 the recipient was Stravinsky.

WORKS: OPERAS: *Sigune* (1885–88); *Die Brautwahl* (1906–11; Hamburg, April 12, 1912); *Arlecchino* (1914–16; Zürich, May 11, 1917, composer conducting); *Turandot* (1916–17; Zürich, May 11, 1917, composer conducting); *Doktor Faust* (1916–23; unfinished; completed by Jarnach, 1924–25; Dresden, May 21, 1925).

BIBL.: H. Leichtentritt, *F. B.* (Leipzig, 1916); G. Selden-Goth, *F. B.* (Vienna, 1922); S. Nadel, *F. B.* (Leipzig, 1931); E. Dent, *F. B., A Biography* (London, 1933); A. Santelli, *B.* (Rome, 1939); G. Guerrini, *F. B., La vita, la figura, l'opera* (Florence, 1944); H. Stuckenschmidt, *F. B., Zeittafel eines Europaers* (Zürich, 1967; Eng. tr., *F. B.: Chronicle of a European*, London, 1970); J. Kindermann, *Thematisch-chronologisches Verzeichnis der musikalischen Werke von F. B.* (Regensburg, 1980); S. Sablich, *B.* (Turin, 1982); A. Beaumont, *B. the Composer* (London, 1985); A. Beaumont, ed. and tr., *F. B.: Selected Letters* (London, 1987); A. Riethmüller, *F. B.s Poetik* (Mainz and London, 1988); M.-A. Roberge, *F. B.: A Bio-Bibliography* (N.Y., 1991); N. Weindel, *F. B.s Ästhetik in seinen Briefen und Schriften* (Wilhelmshaven, 1996).

Bussani, Dorothea, Austrian soprano; b. Vienna, 1763; d. after 1810. In 1786 she married the Italian bass **Francesco Bussani**. She created the roles of Cherubino in Mozart's *Le nozze di Figaro* (Vienna, May 1, 1786) and Despina in his *Così fan tutte* (Vienna, Jan. 26, 1790), opposite her husband's roles as Bartolo and Antonio. She made appearances in Italy with her husband between 1795 and 1805; she subsequently appeared in Lisbon and London until she disappeared from the scene in 1810.

Bussani, Francesco, Italian bass; b. Rome, 1743; d. after 1807. He sang tenor roles; he then turned to bass. He was active from 1783 to 1794 in Vienna, where he married **Dorothea Bussani** in 1786. He created the roles of Bartolo and Antonio in Mozart's *Le nozze di Figaro* (Vienna, May 1, 1786) and Don Alfonso in *Così fan tutte* (Vienna, Jan. 26, 1790), opposite his wife as Cherubino and Despina. He returned to Italy with her in 1795 and continued to make appearances there until they went to Lisbon in 1807.

Büsser, (Paul-) Henri, esteemed French conductor, pedagogue, and composer; b. Toulouse, Jan. 16, 1872; d. Paris, Dec. 30, 1973. He received initial music instruction as a choirboy at the Toulouse Cathedral under Aloys Kunc; at age 13 he was taken to Paris, where he studied with A. Georges at the School of Religious Music; he then pursued training at the Cons. (1889–92) as a pupil of Franck and Widor (organ) and Guiraud (composition); he also received advice from Gounod. In 1892 he became organist at St. Cloud, near Paris. In 1893 he won the Prix de Rome with his cantata *Antigone*. Returning to Paris, he became conductor at the Théâtre du Château d'Eau in 1900, and at the Opéra Comique in

1902; he was conductor at the Opéra (1905–39; 1946–51). In 1904 he became head of the vocal ensemble class at the Cons., and subsequently was prof. of composition there from 1931 to 1948. In 1938 he was elected to membership in the Académie. He married **Yvonne Gall** in 1958. Büsser was an accomplished composer for the theater. He also orchestrated Debussy's *Petite Suite* (1907), *Printemps* (1912), *La cathédrale engloutie* (1917), and other pieces. His writings comprise *Traité d'instrumentation* (with Guiraud; Paris, 1933), *De "Pelléas" aux "Indes galantes"* (Paris, 1955), and *Gounod* (Lyons, 1961).

WORKS: DRAMATIC: *Les accordailles*, opéra comique (1890); *Les Marivaudages*, pantomime (1891); *Daphnis et Chloé*, scenic pastorale (c.1896; Paris, Dec. 14, 1897); *Le miracle des perles*, drame lyrique (1898); *Blanc et noir*, pantomime (Paris, 1900); *Colomba*, drame lyrique (c.1910; Nice, Feb. 4, 1921); *Les noces corinthiennes*, tragédie lyrique (1916–18; Paris, May 10, 1922); *La pie borgne*, comédie lyrique (Aix-les-Bains, Aug. 5, 1927); *La carosse du Saint-Sacrement*, comédie lyrique (Paris, June 2, 1948); *Roxelane*, comédie lyrique (Mulhouse, Jan. 31, 1948); *Diafoirus 60*, farce musicale (Lille, April 4, 1963); *La Vénus d'Ille*, drame lyrique (Lille, April 15, 1964).

Bussotti, Sylvano, important Italian composer, opera director, and stage designer; b. Florence, Oct. 1, 1931. He began violin lessons at a very early age and also took up painting while still a youth. At the age of 9 he entered the Florence Cons., where he was a student in harmony and counterpoint of Roberto Lupi and in piano of Dallapiccola. His training there was soon interrupted by World War II. After the war he pursued composition study on his own (1949–56) before continuing his training in Paris with Max Deutsch (1956–58). He also attended courses in new music at Darmstadt (summers, 1958–61). In 1964–65 he was active in the United States on a Rockefeller Foundation grant. In 1972 he studied in Berlin under the auspices of the Deutscher Akademischer Austauschdienst. He taught at the Academy of Fine Arts in L'Aquila (1971–74), and then served as artistic director of the Teatro La Fenice in Venice (1975). He was artistic consultant to the Puccini Festival in Torre del Lago (1979–81), and later its artistic director. From 1980 he taught at the Fiesole School of Music. He publ. *I miei teatri: Diario segreto, diario pubblico, alcuni saggi* (Palermo, 1981). Bussotti's early interest in painting continued later in life; his visual works have been exhibited around the globe. As a composer, he found his exploration of serialism, indeterminacy, and other modern means of expression too restrictive. He thus charted a revolutionary course which led him to embrace an anarchistic aestheticism. In 1976 he established his own production company, "Bussottioperaballet," which, from 1984 to 1992, operated as a festival in Genazzano. From his *Lorenzaccio* (1972), much of Bussotti's energies have gone into operas, both his own (which often draw heavily upon earlier compositions) and the standard repertory, which he has explored as a director and stage designer in most luxurious terms. He has also continued to create films and to write poetry, and has elevated himself to Italian celebrity status through his flamboyant direction of the musical section of the Venice Biennale, of which his last, highly controversial term was 1991.

WORKS: DRAMATIC: *Juvenilia*, ballet (1951–53; Segromigno, Aug. 5, 1983); *La Passion selon Sade*, chamber mystery (Palermo, Sept. 5, 1965); *Lorenzaccio*, romantic melodrama (1968–72; Venice, Sept. 7, 1972); *Raramente*, choreographic mystery (Florence, Feb. 4, 1971); *Bergkristall*, ballet (1972–74; concert premiere, North German Radio, Hamburg, May 15, 1973; stage premiere, Rome, June 8, 1974); *Syro-Sadun-Settimino*, monodance (Royan, March 1974); *Oggetto amato*, dance piece (1975; Milan, April 7, 1976); *Phaidra/Heliogabalus*, ballet (1975–80; Turin, Feb. 15, 1981); *Nottetempo*, lyric drama (Milan, April 7, 1976); *Le rarita', potente*, lyric representation (1976–78; Treviso, Oct. 12, 1979); *Autotono*, divertimento (1977; Treviso, Oct. 12, 1979); *Le Racine*, theater piece (Milan, Dec. 9, 1980); *Miró, L'uccello luce*, ballet-pantomime (Venice, Sept. 25, 1981); *Cristallo di Rocca*, ballet (Milan, June 10, 1983); *Phèdre*, lyric tragedy (Rome, April 19, 1988); *L'Ispirazione*, melodrama (Florence, May 25, 1988).

BIBL.: F. Degrada, *S. B. e il suo teatrale* (Milan, 1976); M. Bucci, *L'opera di S. B.* (Florence, 1988).

Bustini, Alessandro, Italian composer and teacher; b. Rome, Dec. 24, 1876; d. there, June 23, 1970. He studied at the Accademia di Santa Cecilia in Rome with Sgambati (piano), Renzi (organ), and Falchi (composition), graduating in 1897. He was subsequently appointed to its faculty, and was its president from 1952 to 1964. His works, all written in the traditional Italian manner, include the opera *Maria Dulcis* (Rome, April 15, 1902).

Butt, Dame Clara (Ellen), notable English contralto; b. Southwick, Sussex, Feb. 1, 1872; d. North Stoke, Oxfordshire, July 13, 1936. She studied with J. H. Blower at the Royal College of Music in London; later took lessons with Bouhy in Paris and Gerster in Berlin. She made her operatic debut as Ursula in Sullivan's *Golden Legend* (London, Dec. 7, 1892); then sang at the music festivals at Hanley and Bristol. She visited the United States in 1899 and 1913; in 1913–14 she made a world tour with her husband, R. Kennerley Rumford, a baritone. Several composers wrote works for her, among them Elgar (*Sea-Pictures*) and H. Bedford (*Romeo and Juliet*). In 1920 she was made a Dame Commander of the Order of the British Empire.

BIBL.: W. Ponder, *C. B.* (London, 1928).

Butterley, Nigel (Henry), Australian composer, pianist, and teacher; b. Sydney, May 13, 1935. He attended the New South Wales State Conservatorium of Music in Sydney (1952–55), his principal mentors being Frank Warbick (piano) and Raymond Hanson (composition); later he pursued training in composition with Priaulx Rainier in London (1962). In 1966 he won the Prix Italia for his choral work *In the Head the Fire*. He was active as a pianist, especially as a proponent of contemporary music. He also was on the music staff of the Australian Broadcasting Commission. From 1973 to 1991 he was a lecturer at the Newcastle Conservatorium. In 1991 he received the Australian Creative Artists' Fellowship and was made a Member of the Order of Australia. As a composer, Butterley pursues a thoroughly individualistic style, notable for its assured technical command and penchant for lyricism. He composed the opera *Lawrence Hargrave Flying Alone* (Sydney, Sept. 24, 1988) and two radio pieces, *In the Head the Fire* (1966) and *Watershore* (1978).

Butting, Max, German composer; b. Berlin, Oct. 6, 1888; d. there, July 13, 1976. He studied organ in Berlin and composition in Munich. Returning to Berlin, he was a successful teacher, but in 1933 was deprived of his various positions for political reasons, being the former ed. of a socialist publication. He was able to return to his professional activities after the end of World War II. In 1948 he was appointed a lecturer in the music division of the East Berlin Radio; in 1968 he received an honorary doctor's degree from Humboldt Univ. in East Berlin. His music is animated by polyphonic purposefulness and is marked by rhythmic vitality and lyric meditation. Since many of his works were destined for amateur performances, Butting shunned modernistic involvements; however, in his 9th and 10th syms. he applied dodecaphonic structures. He composed the opera *Plautus im Nonnenkloster* (Leipzig, Oct. 3, 1959).

BIBL.: D. Brennecke, *Das Lebenswerk M. B.s* (Leipzig, 1973).

Buttykay (real name, **Gálszécsy és Butykai**), **Ákos,** Hungarian pianist, teacher, and composer; b. Halmi, July 22, 1871; d. Debrecen, Oct. 26, 1935. He studied in Budapest, where he took courses in law and also attended the Academy of Music; he pursued training in piano and composition in Weimar. After touring as a pianist, he taught piano at the Budapest Academy of Music (1907–22). He won success as a theater composer with his operetta *A bolygó görög* (The Wandering Greek; Budapest, Oct. 19, 1905). After composing the theater scores *A harang* (Budapest, Feb. 1, 1907), *Csibészkirály* (Budapest, Feb. 21, 1907), and *Hamupipőke* (Budapest, Oct. 26, 1912), he composed his most successful operetta, *Az ezüst sirály* (The Silver Seagull; Budapest, Feb. 6, 1920). His *Olivia hercegnő* was chosen to open the new Fővárosi Operettszinház in Budapest on Dec. 23, 1922.

Buzzolla, Antonio, Italian composer and conductor; b. Adria, March 2, 1815; d. Venice, March 20, 1871. He received his early education from his father, a professional theater conductor, then enrolled at the Naples Cons. as a student of Donizetti and Mercadante (1837–39). He was then active as a theater conductor in Italy, Germany, and France, returning to Venice in 1847. He wrote the operas *Ferramondo* (Venice, Dec. 3, 1836), *Mastino I della Scala* (Venice, May 31, 1841), *Gli Avventurieri* (Venice, May 14, 1842), *Amleto* (Venice, Feb. 24, 1848), and *Elisabetta di Valois* (Venice, Feb. 16, 1850). He also wrote an opera in Venetian dialect, *La Puta onorata*, which remained incomplete. In 1855 he was appointed maestro di cappella at S. Marco, for which he wrote much sacred music.

BIBL.: F. Passadore and L. Sirch, eds., *A. B.: Una vita musicale nella Venezia romantica* (Rovigo, 1994).

Bychkov, Semyon, Russian-born American conductor; b. Leningrad, Nov. 30, 1952. He was the brother of **Yakov Kreizberg**. He attended the Glinka Choir School in Leningrad as a youth; subsequently studied with Ilya Musin at the Leningrad Cons., graduating in 1974. In 1975 he emigrated to the United States, where he received an Artist Diploma from the Mannes College of Music in New York in 1976. From 1980 to 1985 he was music director of the Grand Rapids Sym. Orch. In 1983 he became a naturalized American citizen. After serving as assoc. conductor (1980–81) and principal guest conductor (1981–85) of the Buffalo Phil., he was its music director (1985–89). He subsequently was music director of the Orchestre de Paris (1989–98), and also was principal guest conductor of the orch. of the Maggio Musicale Fiorentino (from 1992) and of the St. Petersburg Phil. (from 1992). In 1998 he became chief conductor of the Cologne Radio Sym. Orch. and in 1999 of the Saxon State Opera in Dresden.

Byström, Oscar Fredrik Bernadotte, Swedish organist and composer; b. Stockholm, Oct. 13, 1821; d. there, July 22, 1909. After serving in the military, he became inspector of the cons. of the Royal Academy of Music in 1866; was named prof. there in 1872. In addition to the music he wrote for the church, he also composed an operetta, *Herman Vimpel*.

Paris Opéra orch. (1714–34). As a composer, he was best known for his opera ballet *Ajax* (Paris, April 30, 1716).

Bertini, Gary, Russian-born Israeli conductor and composer; b. Brichevo, May 1, 1927. He was taken to Palestine as a child and began violin lessons at age 16. After studies at the Milan Cons. (diploma, 1948), he continued his training with Seter and Singer at the Tel Aviv College of Music (diploma, 1951). He then went to Paris, where he studied at the Cons. and the École Normale de Musique, his principal mentors in composition being Honegger, Messiaen, and Boulanger; he also studied musicology at the Sorbonne with Chailley. Returning to Israel in 1954, he was music director of the Rinat (later Israel Chamber) Choir (1955–72), the Israel Chamber Ensemble Orch. (1965–75), and the Jerusalem Sym. Orch. (1977–86). He also served as principal guest conductor of the Scottish National Orch. in Glasgow (1971–81) and as artistic advisor of the Israel Festival (1976–83) and of the Detroit Sym. Orch. (1981–83). From 1983 to 1991 he was chief conductor of the Cologne Radio Sym. Orch. He also was Intendant and Generalmusikdirektor of the Frankfurt am Main Opera from 1987 to 1991, concurrently serving as chief conductor of its Museumgesellschaft concerts. In 1994 he became artistic director of the New Israeli Opera in Tel Aviv. In 1997 he became music director of the Rome Opera. Bertini has become well known for conducting 20th-century scores, including many first performances. As a composer, he has written stage music, incidental scores, orch. works, chamber music, and songs. In 1978 he was awarded the Israel State Prize for composition.

Bertinotti, (-Radicati), Teresa, Italian soprano; b. Savigliano, 1776; d. Bologna, Feb. 12, 1854. She studied with La Barbiera in Naples. She married the singer Felice Radicati in 1801, and toured with him in a vocal duo, visiting Austria and Germany. She sang at the King's Theatre in London from 1810 to 1812, then was in Lisbon from 1812 to 1814. Upon her husband's death in 1820, she retired from the stage and devoted herself to teaching voice.

Bertolli, Francesca, Italian contralto; d. Bologna, Jan. 9, 1767. She sang in Bologna in 1728, then was engaged by Handel in 1729 for his Royal Academy of Music operatic performances in London at the King's Theatre. In 1733 she left Handel's company to join his rival's establishment, the Opera of the Nobility. In 1736–37 she was again a member of Handel's company, after which she returned to Italy and soon retired. She was noted for her performances of male roles in lieu of castrati.

Berton, Henri-Montan, French conductor and composer, son of **Pierre-Montan Berton**; b. Paris, Sept. 17, 1767; d. there, April 22, 1844. He was a pupil of Rey and Sacchini. In 1782 he joined the orch. of the Paris Opéra as a violinist, and in 1795 he was appointed to the staff of the Paris Cons., where, in 1818, he succeeded Méhul as prof. of composition. From 1807 to 1809 he conducted at the Opéra-Bouffe, and in 1809 became chorus master at the Paris Opéra. In 1815 he was elected a member of the French Academy. He wrote 47 operas, of which the most successful were *Montano et Stéphanie* (1799), *Le Délire* (1799), and *Aline, reine de Colconde* (1803); also several oratorios.

BIBL.: D. Raoul-Rochette, *Notice historique sur la vie et les ouvrages de M. B.* (Paris, 1846); H. Blanchard, *H.-M. B.* (Paris, 1839).

Berton, Pierre-Montan, French tenor, conductor, and composer, father of **Henri-Montan Berton**; b. Maubert-Fontaines, Ardennes, Jan. 7, 1727; d. Paris, May 14, 1780. He studied organ, harpsichord, and composition at the Senlis Cathedral choir school, and then completed his training in Paris. After singing at the Paris Opéra and in Marseilles, he became director of the Bordeaux Grand Théatre. In 1755 he returned to Paris as conductor of the Opéra, serving as its general director (1775–78). Under his leadership, the Paris Opéra orch. attained notable distinction. Berton was an adept arranger of the operas of Lully, Rameau, and Gluck, in which he interpolated his own music.

WORKS: OPERA BALLET: *Deucalion et Pyrrha* (Paris, Sept. 30, 1755). OPERAS: *Silvie* (Fontainebleau, Oct. 17, 1765); *Érosine* (Paris, Aug. 29, 1766); *Théonis, ou Le toucher* (Paris, Oct. 11, 1767; in collaboration with Trial); *Adèle de Ponthieu* (Paris, Dec. 1, 1772; in collaboration with Laborde); *Linus* (unfinished).

Bertoni, Ferdinando (Gioseffo), esteemed Italian composer, organist, and pedagogue; b. Salò, near Venice, Aug. 15, 1725; d. Desenzano, Dec. 1, 1813. He was a student of Padre Martini in Bologna. He settled in Venice, where he successfully brought out his first opera in 1745, and soon established an enviable reputation as a composer for the theater. In 1752 he was appointed to the post of 1st organist at San Marco, where he succeeded Galuppi as maestro di cappella in 1785. He also was maestro di cappella at the Mendicanti (1757–97). As a teacher, he numbered among his pupils Calegari, Mayr, and Pacchierotti. In 1773 he was elected a member of the Accademia Filarmonica in Bologna, and in 1804 of the Accademia degli Unanimi in Salò. Bertoni was one of the leading Venetian opera composers of his day. Many of his operas were performed abroad, including several during his two visits to London (1778–81; 1781–83). He also was admired for his sacred music.

WORKS: DRAMATIC: (all 1st perf. in Venice unless otherwise given): COMIC OPERAS: *La vedova accorta* (Carnival 1745); *La pescatrici* (Dec. 26, 1751); *I bagni d'Abano* (Feb. 1753; in collaboration with Galuppi); *La moda* (Carnival 1754); *La vicende amorose* (1760); *La bella Girometta* (1761); *L'ingannatore ingannato* (Carnival 1764); *L'anello incantato* (1771); *L'orfane svizzere* (Livorno, Carnival 1774); *La governante* (London, May 15, 1779); *Il duca di Atene* (London, May 9, 1780); *Il convito, or The Banquet* (London, Nov. 2, 1782). OPERE SERIE: *Il Cajetto* (Carnival 1746); *Orazio e Curiazio* (1746); *Armida* (Dec. 26, 1746); *Ipermestra* (Genoa, Carnival 1748); *Antigono* (1752); *Ginevra* (1753); *Sesostri* (Turin, Dec. 26, 1754); *Antigona* (Genoa, Carnival 1756); *Lucio Vero* (Turin, Carnival 1757); *Il Vologeso* (Padua, 1759); *Ifigenia in Aulide* (Turin, 1762); *Achille in Sciro* (Carnival 1764); *Il Bajazetto* (Parma, May 3, 1765); *Olimpiade* (Carnival 1765); *Tancredi* (Turin, Dec. 26, 1766); *Ezio* (Carnival 1767); *Semiramide riconosciuta* (Naples, May 30, 1767); *Scipione nelle Spagne* (Milan, Jan. 30, 1768); *Alessandro nell'Indie* (Genoa, 1769); *Il trionfo di Clelia* (Padua, June 10, 1769); *Eurione* (Udine, Aug. 1770); *Decebalo* (Treviso, Oct. 1770); *Andromaca* (Dec. 26, 1771); *Narale* (May 25, 1774); *Aristo e Temira* (Jan. 3, 1776); *Orfeo ed Euridice* (Jan. 3, 1776); *Creonte* (Modena, Jan. 27, 1776); *Artaserse* (Forlì, 1776); *Telemaco ed Eurice nell'isola di Calipso* (Dec. 26, 1776); *Medonte* (Turin, Dec. 26, 1777); *Quinto Fabio* (Milan, Jan. 31, 1778); *Demofoonte* (London, Nov. 28, 1778); *Armida abbandonata* (Dec. 26, 1780); *Cago Mario* (1781); *Cimene* (London, Jan. 7, 1783); *Eumene* (Dec. 26, 1783); *Nitteti* (Feb. 6, 1789); *Angelica e Medoro* (Carnival 1791). He also wrote 18 occasional dramatic pieces and some 50 oratorios.

BIBL.: G. Bustico, *Per la storia del melodramma: F. B. e Rubinelli* (Salò, 1913); I. Haas, *F. B.: Leben und Instrumentalwerk* (Vienna, 1958).

Berutti (originally, **Beruti**), **Arturo,** Argentine composer of Italian descent; b. San Juan, March 27, 1862; d. Buenos Aires, Jan. 3, 1938. He received his early training in music with his father, then went to Leipzig, where he became a student of Jadassohn. He subsequently lived in Italy, where he composed 3 operas: *La Vendetta* (Vercelli, May 21, 1892), *Evangelina* (Milan, Sept. 19, 1893), and *Taras Bulba* (Turin, March 9, 1895). Returning to Argentina in 1896, he premiered the following operas in Buenos Aires: *Pampa* (July 27, 1897), *Yupanki* (July 25, 1899), *Khrise* (June 21, 1902), *Horrida Nox* (the opera by a native Argentine composer, written to a Spanish libretto, to be produced in Argentina; July 7, 1908), and *Los Heroes* (Aug. 23, 1919).

Berwald, Franz (Adolf), outstanding Swedish composer, cousin of **Johan Fredrik Berwald**; b. Stockholm, July 23, 1796; d. there, April 3, 1868. His father, Christian Friedrich Berwald (1740–1825), was a German musician who studied with Franz Benda and settled in Stockholm in the 1770s as a member of the orch. of the Royal Chapel. Franz received training in violin from his father and cousin, and in composition from J. B. E. du Puy. He was a violinist and violist in the orch. of the Royal Chapel in Stockholm (1812–

C

Caballé, Montserrat, celebrated Spanish soprano; b. Barcelona, April 12, 1933. She was a pupil of Eugenia Kemeny, Conchita Badia, and Napoleone Annovazzi at the Barcelona Conservatorio del Liceo; after her graduation in 1953, she made her operatic debut in Reus, near Barcelona, in *La Serva padrona*. She then sang in Basel (1956–59) and Bremen (1959–62), and also made guest appearances in Vienna as Salome and Donna Elvira (1958), Milan's La Scala as a Flowermaiden in *Parsifal* (1960), where she sang major roles from 1969, and Mexico City as Massenet's Manon (1962). She made a brilliant U.S. debut on April 20, 1965, when she substituted for Marilyn Horne in a concert performance of *Lucrezia Borgia* at N.Y.'s Carnegie Hall. After appearing as the Marschallin and the Countess at the Glyndebourne Festival (summer 1965), she made her Metropolitan Opera debut in New York on Dec. 22, 1965, as Gounod's Marguerite. In subsequent years, she returned to the Metropolitan Opera regularly, eliciting extraordinary praise for such roles as Desdemona, Norma, Violetta, Liù, Mimi, Aida, Adriana Lecouvreur, and Tosca, among others. She also sang with various other opera companies, including debut appearances as Violetta at the Chicago Lyric Opera (1970) and London's Covent Garden (1972). In addition, she toured extensively as a concert artist. Her performances of operas in concert allowed her to survey not only Wagner but roles seldom heard. On Sept. 24, 1989, she created the role of Queen Isabella in Balada's *Cristóbal Colón* in Barcelona, where in 1992 she also appeared at the opening gala ceremonies at the Olympic Games. The great beauty of Caballé's voice was ably complemented by an extraordinary vocal technique, one equally suited for the opera house and concert hall. Few singers of her day could match her command of such a large repertory, which ranged from standard to contemporary opera, and from art songs to zarzuela. In 1964 she married the Spanish tenor Bernabé Martí (b. 1934).

BIBL.: R. Pullen and S. Taylor, *M.C.: Casta diva* (London, 1994).

Cabel, Marie (-Josèphe), Belgian soprano; b. Liège, Jan. 31, 1827; d. Maisons-Laffitte, May 23, 1885. She was a pupil of Bouillon in Liège, then studied with F. Cabel and L. J. Cabel, becoming the latter's wife in 1847. She subsequently completed her training at the Paris Cons. In 1849 she made her operatic debut at the Paris Opéra Comique in Halévy's *Val d'Andorre*. After appearances in Brussels, Lyons, Strasbourg, and London, she returned to Paris as a member of the Opéra Comique in 1856, where she created Meyerbeer's Dinorah (April 4, 1859). She retired in 1877. Cabel's roles in French opera were particularly admired.

Caccini, Francesca (nicknamed **"La Cecchina"**), Italian composer, daughter of **Giulio Caccini**; b. Florence, Sept. 18, 1587; d. c.1640. She was probably the first woman composer of operas. Her opera-ballet *La liberazione di Ruggiero dall'isola d'Alcina* was produced at a palace near Florence on Feb. 2, 1625, and a book of songs from it was publ. in the same year. A modern reprint, ed. by D. Silbert, was publ. in Northampton, Mass. (1945). Caccini wrote further a *Ballo delle zingare* (Florence, Feb. 24, 1615) in which she acted as one of the gypsies. Her sacred opera *Il martirio di Sant'Agata* was produced in Florence, Feb. 10, 1622.

Caccini, Giulio, Italian composer (called **Romano**, because he lived mostly in Rome), father of **Francesca Caccini**; b. probably in Tivoli, Oct. 8, 1551; d. Florence (buried), Dec. 10, 1618. He was a pupil of Scipione delle Palla in singing and lute playing. His first compositions were madrigals in the traditional polyphonic style, but the new ideas generated in the discussions of the artists and literati of the "Camerata," in the houses of Bardi and Corsi at Florence, inspired him to write vocal soli in recitative form (then termed "musica in stile rappresentativo"), which he sang with consummate skill to his own accompaniment on the theorbo. These first compositions in a dramatic idiom were followed by his settings of separate scenes written by Bardi, and finally by the opera *Il combattimento d'Apolline col serpente* (poem by Bardi); next was *Euridice* (1600; poem by Rinuccini) and *Il rapimento di Cefalo* (in collaboration with others; 1st perf., Oct. 9, 1600, at the Palazzo Vecchio in Florence). Then followed *Le nuove musiche*, a series of madrigals for solo voice, with bass (Florence, 1602; new eds., Venice, 1607 and 1615; a modern ed.

of the 1602 publication, prepared by H. Wiley Hitchcock [Madison, Wis., 1970], includes an annotated Eng. tr. of Caccini's preface, realizations of the solo madrigals, airs, and the final section of *Il rapimento di Cefalo*, an introductory essay on Caccini, the music, the poetry, MSS, other eds., and a bibliography. A tr. of the preface is also available in O. Strunk, *Source Readings in Music History* [N.Y., 1950]). The song "Amarilli mia bella" from the first series became very popular. Caccini also publ. *Fuggilotio musicale* (Venice, 2d ed., 1613; including madrigals, sonnets, arias, etc.). From 1565 Caccini lived in Florence as a singer at the Tuscan court. He was called, by abbate Angelo Grillo, "the father of a new style of music"; Bardi said of him that he had "attained the goal of perfect music." But his claim to priority in writing vocal music in the "stile rappresentativo" is not supported by known chronology. Caccini's opera *Il rapimento di Cefalo* was performed 3 days after Peri's path-breaking *Euridice*; the closeness in time of operatic productions by both Caccini and Peri is further emphasized by the fact that when Peri produced *Euridice* in Florence (1600), he used some of Caccini's songs in the score. Caccini later made his own setting of *Euridice* (1600), but it was not produced until Dec. 5, 1602. On the other hand, Caccini was undoubtedly the first to publish an operatic work, for his score of *Euridice* was printed early in 1601, before the publication of Peri's work of the same title.

BIBL.: A. Ehrichs, *G. C.* (Leipzig, 1908).

Cadman, Charles Wakefield, important American composer; b. Johnstown, Pa., Dec. 24, 1881; d. Los Angeles, Dec. 30, 1946. His great-grandfather was the hymn composer Samuel Wakefield (1799–1895). After studies with William Steiner (organ), Edwin L. Walker (piano), and Leo Oehmler (theory), he received training in theory and conducting from Luigi von Kunits and Emil Paur. From 1908 to 1910 he was music ed. and critic of the *Pittsburgh Dispatch*. His interest in American Indian music resulted in various lecture-performance tours in the United States and Europe with the Cherokee-Creek Indian princess Tsianina Redfeather. In 1916 he settled in Los Angeles as a composer and teacher. Cadman wrote an opera based on the life of Redfeather, *Shanewis or The Robin Woman*, which was premiered at the Metropolitan Opera in New York on March 23, 1918.

WORKS: DRAMATIC: *The Land of the Misty Water*, opera (1909–12; rev. as *Ramala*); *Shanewis or The Robin Woman*, opera (N.Y., March 23, 1918); *The Sunset Trail*, operatic cantata (Denver, Dec. 5, 1922); *The Garden of Mystery*, opera (N.Y., March 20, 1925); *The Ghost of Lollypop Bay*, operetta (1926); *Lelawala*, operetta (1926); *A Witch of Salem*, opera (Chicago, Dec. 8, 1926); *The Belle of Havana*, operetta (1928); *South in Sonora*, operetta (1932); *The Willow Tree*, radio score (NBC, Oct. 3, 1932).

BIBL.: N. Fielder, *Complete Musical Works of C. W. C.* (Los Angeles, 1951; catalog); H. Perison, *C.W. C.: His Life and Works* (diss., Eastman School of Music, 1978).

Cafaro (also **Caffaro**), **Pasquale,** Italian composer; b. San Pietro, in Galatina, Lecce, Feb. 8, 1716; d. Naples, Oct. 23, 1787. He studied at the Naples Cons. He became 2d master at the Naples Cons. della Pietà in 1759, and 1st master in 1771. He composed the operas *Ipermestra* (Naples, Dec. 18, 1751), *La disfatta di Dario* (Naples, Jan. 20, 1756), *L'incendio di Troia* (Naples, Jan. 20, 1757), *L'Olimpiade* (Naples, Jan. 12, 1769), and *Antigono* (Naples, Aug. 13, 1770); also oratorios.

Caffarelli (real name, **Gaetano Majorano**), Italian castrato soprano; b. Bitonto, April 12, 1710; d. Naples, Jan. 31, 1783. A poor peasant boy endowed with a beautiful voice, he was discovered by a musician, Domenico Caffarelli, who taught him, and later sent him to Porpora at Naples. In gratitude to his patron, he assumed the name of Caffarelli. He studied for 5 years with Porpora, who predicted a brilliant career for him. Caffarelli became a master of pathetic song, and excelled in coloratura as well; read the most difficult music at sight, and was an accomplished harpsichord player. His debut at the Teatro Valle (Rome, 1724) in a female role was a triumph. From 1737 to 1745 he sang in London, then in Paris and Vienna. His last public appearance took place on May 30, 1754, in Naples. He was in Lisbon during the earthquake of 1755; he retired from the opera in 1756. Upon his return to Naples, he bought the dukedom of Santo-Durato with the fortune he had amassed during his career, and assumed the title of duke.

Cage, John (Milton, Jr.), singularly inventive and much beloved American composer, writer, philosopher, and visual artist of ultramodern tendencies; b. Los Angeles, Sept. 5, 1912; d. N.Y., Aug. 12, 1992. His father, John Milton Cage, Sr., was an inventor, and his mother, Lucretia Harvey, was active as a clubwoman and columnist in Southern Calif. He studied piano, and had early aspirations to be either a minister or a writer. After brief studies at Pomona College in Claremont, Calif (1928–30), he traveled to Europe, where he studied architecture with Ernö Goldfinger and piano with Lazare Lévy in Paris; he also traveled throughout Biskra, Majorca, Madrid, and Berlin (1930–31), painting, writing poetry, and producing his first musical compositions, which he abandoned prior to his return to Calif. Upon his return, he studied composition with Richard Buhlig, developing a method of composition employing two twenty-five tone ranges. At the suggestion of Henry Cowell, he pursued studies in harmony with Adolph Weiss; he also studied modern harmony, contemporary music, and Oriental and folk music with Cowell at the New School for Social Research in New York. Cage's studies culminated with counterpoint lessons from Schoenberg (1934), both privately and at the Univ. of Southern Calif.; he also attended Schoenberg's classes in counterpoint and analysis at the Univ. of Calif., Los Angeles. On June 7, 1935, Cage married Xenia Andreyevna Kashevaroff. Through his brief association with the filmmaker Oskar Fischinger, Cage became interested in noise, subsequently developing methods of writing complex rhythmic structures for percussion music; he then joined a modern dance group at the Univ. of Calif., Los Angeles, as an accompanist and percussion composer.

During the summer of 1937, Cage was on the faculty of Mills College in Oakland, Calif., where he worked as a composer for Marian Van Tuyl. He then moved to Seattle as composer-accompanist for Bonnie Bird's modern dance classes at the Cornish School, where he met Merce Cunningham, then a dance student there. He organized a percussion orchestra, collected musical instruments, and made tours throughout the Northwest; he also met Morris Graves, and arranged for an exhibition of his work as well as exhibitions of the work of Alexej Jawlensky, Kandinsky, Klee, and Mark Tobey. In 1939 he gave concerts of percussion music with Lou Harrison in San Francisco; also worked as a recreational leader for the Works Progress Administration there, and composed his *First Construction (in Metal)* for 6 Percussionists (Seattle, Dec. 9, 1939). He began developing Cowell's piano technique of making use of tone clusters and playing directly on the body of the instrument or on the strings, which culminated in his invention of the "prepared piano." His first prepared piano piece was music to accompany a dance by Syvilla Fort, *Bacchanale* (1938; rev. version, Seattle, April 28, 1940). The instrument rapidly gained acceptance among avant-garde composers, and in 1949, after the N.Y. premiere by Maro Ajemian of his *Sonatas and Interludes* for Prepared Piano (1946–48), he received a grant from the Guggenheim Foundation and a $1,000 award from the National Academy of Arts and Letters for having "extended the boundaries of music."

In 1941 Cage went to Chicago, where, at the invitation of László Moholy-Nagy, he taught a class in experimental music at the School of Design. He also accompanied dance classes there, and gave a concert of percussion music at the Arts Club. Commissioned by CBS ("Columbia Workshop") to create a radio program, he composed *The City Wears a Slouch Hat* for 4 Percussion and Sound Effects, to a text by Kenneth Patchen (Chicago, May 31, 1942). He then moved to New York (1942), where he began a lengthy association with Cunningham; they would collaborate for nearly 50 years on works that introduced radical innovations in musical and choreographic composition. When the Merce Cunningham Dance Co. was formed in 1953, Cage served as its first music director, a position he maintained for more than 30 years.

During this period Cage also gave a concert at the Museum of Modern Art, the first in a series of New York recitals that established his reputation. After his divorce from Xenia in 1945, he moved to N.Y.'s Lower East Side; he began a lifelong study of Eastern philosophies, first (Indian philosophy and music) with the visiting Indian musician and teacher Gira Sarabhai, and then (Zen Buddhism) with Daisetz Teitaro Suzuki, whose classes he attended at Columbia Univ. He also made numerous tours with Cunningham, and received an important commission from Lincoln Kirstein and the Ballet Soc., resulting in *The Seasons* (N.Y., May 18, 1947). In 1948 Cage taught at Black Mountain College in North Carolina, and in 1949 he spent 3 months in Europe, where he met Pierre Boulez. Returning to New York, Cage participated in the formation, with Robert Motherwell and others, of the Artists Club.

In 1950 Cage began developing means for composition with chance operations. He came under the influence of the *I Ching*, or "Book of Changes," one of the most influential books in the Chinese canon, which became his sole director as a composer, poet, and visual artist. An extremely significant collaboration stemming from this period, was with the pianist David Tudor, who was able to reify Cage's exotic inspirations, works in which the performer shares the composer's creative role. In 1950 Cage completed a score for Herbert Matter's film, *Works of Calder* for Prepared Piano and Tape (1949–50), which received 1st prize from the Woodstock Art Film Festival. He also composed his *Concerto for Prepared Piano and Chamber Orchestra* (1950–51; N.Y., Jan. 1952) as well as his *Imaginary Landscape No. 4* for 24 Performers on 12 Radios, commissioned by the New Music Soc. and presented at Columbia Univ.'s McMillin Theater on May 10, 1951. It was during this period as well that he began a lifelong friendship with Robert Rauschenberg. In 1952, at Black Mountain College, Cage presented a theatrical event historically marked as the earliest Happening; participants in this protypical adventure included Cunningham, Charles Olson, Rauschenberg, M. C. Richards, and Tudor. Cage's seminal *Music of Changes* was given its premiere performance by Tudor at the Cherry Lane Theater on Jan. 1, 1952. In this year, he also composed his first piece for tape as a score for a dance by Jean Erdman, *Imaginary Landscape No. 5* (N.Y., Jan. 18, 1952). Influenced at the Black Mountain Happening by Rauschenberg's all-black and all-white paintings, Cage composed his notoriously tacet *4′33″* (1952), which is heard in 3 movements (indicated by the pianist's closing and reopening of the piano key cover), during which no sounds are intentionally produced. It was first performed by Tudor in Woodstock, N.Y., on Aug. 29, 1952.

In 1954 Cage moved with Tudor, Richards, and Karen Weinrib to a cooperative community established by Paul and Vera Williams in Rockland County, N.Y. He also made a concert tour of Europe with Tudor, and, upon his return, met Jasper Johns, who would remain a lifelong friend and associate. He also began work on his *Music for Piano* series (ranging from *Music for Piano 1*, 1952, to *Music for Piano 85* for Piano and Electronics, 1962), using the imperfections in manuscript paper to guide his composition. From 1956 to 1960 he taught occasional classes at the New School for Social Research, where his students included George Brecht, Al Hansen, Dick Higgins, Toshi Ichiyanagi, Allan Kaprow, and Jackson Mac Low. In 1958 an historically-significant 25-year retrospective concert of his music was given at N.Y.'s Town Hall. He then spent a summer in Europe teaching a class in experimental music at Darmstadt and giving concerts and lectures elsewhere; he also appeared on an Italian quiz show, "Lascia o Raddoppia," as a mushroom expert, winning $6,000.

Returning to New York in 1959, Cage again taught at the New School for Social Research. In 1960–61 he was a fellow at the Center for Advanced Studies at Wesleyan Univ. in Middletown, Conn., where he completed his first book, *Silence* (1961), a classic study in 20th-century musical aesthetics. In 1961 he was commissioned by the Montreal Festivals Soc. to write the orch. piece *Atlas Eclipticalis* for 1 to 86 Specified Instruments (1961–62; Montreal, Aug. 3, 1961). In 1962 he founded, with Esther Dam, Ralph Ferrara, Lois Long, and Guy G. Nearing, the N.Y. Mycological Soc. He also made an extensive concert tour of Japan with Tudor. He also made a world tour with the Merce Cunningham Dance Co. Other activities in the late 1960s included the formation, with Johns, of the philanthropic Foundation for Contemporary Performance Arts in New York; he also was composer-in-residence at the Univ. of Cincinnati. In 1967 he publ. *A Year from Monday*. It was during this period also that he met the controversial Canadian media philosopher Marshall McLuhan, whose ideas resonated strongly in Cage, as well as Wendell Berry, who introduced him to the *Journals* of Henry David Thoreau, which subsequently appeared, in various guises, in many of Cage's works. He also was an assoc. at the Center for Advanced Study at the Univ. of Ill., where he created *HPSCHD* for 1 to 7 Amplified Harpsichords and 1 to 51 Tapes (1967–69; Champaign-Urbana, Ill., May 16, 1969; in collaboration with L. Hiller). In 1969 he was an artist-in-residence at the Univ. of Calif., Davis; he also publ. *Notations* (with A. Knowles), and executed his first visual work (with Calvin Sumsion), *Not Wanting to Say Anything About Marcel*, at Hollander's Workshop in New York. In 1970 he again, this time as an advanced fellow, at the Center for Advanced Studies at Wesleyan Univ.

Throughout the 1970s Cage traveled extensively and produced works in a variety of media. With Lois Long he publ. *Mushroom Book*, and also made a European tour with Tudor. In 1973 he publ. *M: Writings '67-'72*. In 1974–75 he composed his *Etudes Australes* (Witten, April 23 and 25, 1982), using star charts as his guide; in 1978 he created color etchings entitled *Score Without Parts (40 Drawings by Thoreau): Twelve Haiku*, incorporating drawings by Thoreau. Also from the 1970s his *Lecture on the Weather* for 12 Amplified Voices, optionally with Instruments, Tape, and Film (1975; Toronto, Feb. 26, 1976), a lavish audiovisual work commissioned by the Canadian Broadcasting Corp. on the occasion of American's Bicentennial, combining collages of spoken texts by Thoreau, a film, and weather recordings. He also composed *Renga* for 78 Instruments or Voices or combinations thereof (1975–76; Boston, Sept. 29, 1976) and *Apartment House 1776* for 4 Voices, optionally on Tape, and any number of Instruments (Boston, Sept. 29, 1976). He then began reading the works of James Joyce, being particularly influenced by *Finnegans Wake*. On the advice of Yoko Ono, he also began following the macrobiotic diet, which significantly improved his health. In 1977 he began work on his mammoth *Freeman Etudes* for Violin, which were completed only shortly before their premiere in Zürich on June 29, 1991. In 1978, Cage began making prints at Crown Point Press in Oakland (later San Francisco), Calif., returning annually and producing such works as *Seven Day Diary* (1978), *Dereau* (1982), *Where There Is Where There—Urban Landscape* (1987), *Dramatic Fire* (1989), and *Smoke Weather Stone Weather* (1991); Cage also produced a series of unique pencil rock tracings on handmade Indian paper, entitled *Where R = Ryoanji* (1983–92).

In 1979 Cage worked at Paris's IRCAM (with David Fullemann) to complete his *Roaratorio, an Irish Circus on Finnegans Wake*, a quintessential realization of his ________, ___ ________ *Circus On* ________ for Voice, Tape, and any number of Musicians, optionally on tape, a means of translating any book into music; the work was commissioned by the Westdeutscher Rundfunk, Cologne, and premiered in Donaueschingen on Oct. 20 of that same year. In 1981–82 he composed his fanciful hörspiel, *James Joyce, Marcel Duchamp, Erik Satie: Ein Alphabet* (Westdeutscher Rundfunk, Cologne, July 6, 1982). In 1981 he wrote *Composition in Retrospect* (Cambridge, Mass., 1993), and also composed *Thirty Pieces for Five Orchestras* (Pont-à-Mousson, Nov. 22, 1981) and *Dance/4 Orchestras* (Mission San Juan Bautista, Calif., Aug. 22, 1982). He also gave a nightlong reading of his *Empty Words: Writings '73–'78* (Middletown, Conn., 1979) over National Public Radio. In 1982 his scores and prints were exhibited for the first time at the Whitney Museum of American Art in New York and at the Philadelphia Museum of Art. In 1984 he began extensive work with the computer, employing programs made especially for him and producing his first computer-assisted mesostic poem, after Allen Ginsburg's *Howl*.

In 1987 several large-scale works were completed and premiered, including Cage's only installation, *Voiceless Essay*, based on texts from Thoreau's *Essay on Civil Disobedience* and ambient sounds. He also completed *Europeras 1 & 2* for any number of Voices, Chamber Orch., Tape, and Organ ad libitum (1984–87; Frankfurt am Main, Dec. 12, 1987), a chance-determined, musico-dramatic staged collage self-referentially comprised of excerpts from extant operas across historical time. Also from this year was his *Two* for Flute and Piano, the first in a series of "number pieces," each utilizing a flexible notation system of his devising called "time-bracket notation." In 1988 he extended his activities as a visual artist further with a series of watercolors with Ray Kass at the Mountain Lake Workship in Roanoke, Virginia. In 1988–89 he held the prestigious Charles Eliot Norton Chair at Harvard Univ., for which he wrote and delivered 6 large-scale, quasi-autobiographical mesostic poems incorporating the writings of Fuller, Thoreau, McLuhan et al.; these lectures, with texts from interspersed seminars with students, were later publ. as *I-VI* (Boston, 1990). In 1989 a joint exhibition, "Dancers on a Plane: John Cage, Merce Cunningham, Jasper Johns," was presented in London and Liverpool. In 1990 Cage's watercolors were exhibited as "New River Watercolors" at the Phillips Collection in Washington, D.C. Cage also saw the premiere of his his *Europeras 3 & 4* for at least 6 Voices, 2 Pianos, at least 6 Performers with 12 Gramophones and 1 Phonograph, and Tape and Light Operators at London's Almeida Music Festival (June 17, 1990). His *Europera 5* followed in 1991, a somewhat diminutive version in the *Europeras* series for 2 Voices, Piano, Phonograph, and Sound and Light Operators (Buffalo, N.Y., April 18, 1991). Cage also began designing his continually changing work for museum, *Rolywholyover A Circus*, which was seen successively, after his death, in Los Angeles, Houston, New York, Mito (Japan), and Philadelphia. In 1991 Cage attended the John Cage-James Joyce Zürich June Festival, where his *Europeras 1 & 2* was performed at the Zürich Opera; also premiered there was *Beach Birds*, his final collaboration with Cunningham. During this period, Cage also made suites of handmade paper and edible drawings at Rugg Toad Papers in Boston, Mass.

In 1992, the last year of his life, Cage attended innumerable 80th birthday celebrations around the world. He also composed a remarkable number of scores, including orch. works for the Hessischer Rundfunk (Frankfurt am Main), the Westdeutscher Rundfunk (Cologne), and the American Composers Orch. (N.Y.), as well as some 20 compositions, most of them "number pieces," for various smaller ensembles. He also completed his first and only film, the strikingly minimalist *One* [11], with Henning Lohner.

Cage's influence, while unquestionably profound, has likely yet to be fully felt. With the passing years, he departed from the pragmatism of precise musical notation and circumscribed ways of performance, electing instead to mark his creative intentions in graphic symbols, pictorial representations, generalized and often poetic instructions, and flexible time relationships. His principal contribution to the history of music was his establishment of the principle of indeterminacy in composition; by adapting Zen Buddhist meditative practices to composition, Cage succeeded in bringing both authentic spiritual ideas and a liberating attitude of play to the enterprise of Western art. His aesthetic of chance also, uniquely, produced a body of what might be called "once-only" works, any 2 performances of which can never be the same. In an effort to reduce the subjective element in composition, Cage developed methods of selecting the components of his pieces by chance, early on through the throwing of coins or dice and later through the use of various random number generators on the computer. Thus, Cage's works did not originate in psychology, motive, drama, or literary purpose, but, rather, were just sounds, free of judgments about whether they are musical or not, free of fixed relations, and free of memory and taste.

Cage was also a brilliant writer, much influenced by the manner, grammar, syntax, and glorious illogic of Gertrude Stein. While his books did not appear until the early 1960s (with the exception of the coauthored *Virgil Thomson: His Life in Music*; with K. Hoover, N.Y., 1959), he was early on a frequent reviewer and contributor on music and dance to such periodicals as *Perspectives of New Music* and *Modern Music*, the latter under the guiding editorship of his close friend Minna Daniel (née Lederman); he also was an assoc. ed. of the short-lived magazine *Possibilities*. Of singular importance to the field, however, was his development of a style of poetry he called "mesostic" (the name suggested by Norman O. Brown, to differentiate from the clearly-related "acrostic"), which uses an anchoring, generating string of letters down the center of the page that spell a name, a word, or line of text relating (or not) to the subject matter of the poem. Cage's mesostic poems, analogously indeterminate with respect to their composition to his musical works of the period, were eventually also composed via computer, the "source material" pulverized and later enhanced by Cage into semi-coherent, highly evocative poetic texts; the most extensive example is found in the 6 lectures comprising the afore-mentioned *I–VI*, composed for Harvard Univ.

Cage was elected to the American Academy and Inst. of Arts and Letters in 1968 and to the American Academy of Arts and Sciences in 1978; he was inducted into the more exclusive branch of the Academy, the American Academy of Arts and Letters, in 1989. In 1981 he received the Mayor's Award of Honor in N.Y. City. He was named Commander of the Order of Arts and Letters by the French Minister of Culture in 1982, and received an Honorary Doctorate of Performing Arts from the Calif. Inst. of the Arts in 1986. In the summer of 1989 he was guest artist at International Festivals in Leningrad and Moscow, at which he presented works entitled *Music for* ______ (1984; rev. 1987), incorporating flexible time-bracket notation, which he conducted chironomically. In late 1989 he traveled to Japan to receive, in traditional and quite formal Japanese dress, the highly prestigious and lucrative Kyoto Prize.

WORKS: DRAMATIC: *Music for Marriage at the Eiffel Tower* for Piano and Toy Instruments (Seattle, March 24, 1939; in collaboration with H. Cowell and G. McKay); *The City Wears a Slouch Hat*, music for a radio play for 4 Percussion and Sound Effects, to a text by K. Patchen (Chicago, May 31, 1942); *Works of Calder*, music for a film for Prepared Piano and Tape (1949–50); *Black Mountain Piece* for 3 Voices, Piano, Dancer, Gramophone, Radios, Films, Slides, and Painter (Black Mountain, N.C., Summer, 1952); *Water Music* for Piano and Various Stage Properties (N.Y., May 2, 1952); *Sounds of Venice* for Various Stage Properties and Tape (Milan, Jan. 1959); *Water Walk* for Piano and Various Stage Properties (Milan, Jan. 1959); *Theatre Piece* for 1 to 8 Performers (N.Y., March 7, 1960); *Mewanemooseicday*, musical exhibition around the music of Erik Satie (Davis, Calif., Nov. 21, 1969); *Dialogue* for 2 Performers (c.1970); *Song Books* for Any Number of Performers (Paris, Oct. 26, 1970); *Demonstration of the Sounds of the Environment* for 300 people silently following a chance-determined path (Milwaukee, Fall 1971); *Alla Ricerca del Silenzio Perduto* for Prepared Train (1977; Bologna and vicinity, June 26–28, 1978); *Silent Environment* for an indeterminate closed space (1979; Berlin, Jan. 20, 1980); *Evéne/EnvironneMetzment* for an audience possibly producing sounds (Metz, Nov. 21, 1981); *Europeras 1 & 2* for any number of Voices, Chamber Orch., Tape, and Organ ad libitum (1985–87; Frankfurt am Main, Dec. 12, 1987); *Europeras 3 & 4* for at least 6 Voices, 2 Pianos, at least 6 Performers with 12 Gramophones and 1 Phonograph, and Tape and Light Operators (London, June 17, 1990); *Europera 5* for 2 Voices, Piano, Phonograph, and Sound and Light Operators (Buffalo, N.Y., April 18, 1991). RADIO PLAYS: *James Joyce, Marcel Duchamp, Erik Satie: Ein Alphabet* (1981–82; Westdeutscher Rundfunk, Cologne, July 6, 1982); *Klassik nach Wunsch* (Westdeutscher Rundfunk, Cologne, April 23, 1982); *Fifteen Domestic Minutes* (National Public Radio, Nov. 5, 1982); *HMCIEX* (1983–84; Westdeutscher Rundfunk, July 10, 1984); *Empty Mind* (Westdeutscher Rundfunk, Cologne, Feb. 15, 1987).

WRITINGS: With K. Hoover, *Virgil Thomson: His Life and Music* (N.Y., 1959); *Silence: Lectures and Writings* (Middletown, Conn., 1961); *A Year from Monday: New Lectures and Writings* (Middletown, Conn., 1967); *To Describe the Process of Composition Used in Not Wanting to Say Anything about Marcel* (Cincinnati, 1969); with A. Knowles, *Notations* (N.Y., 1969); *M: Writings*

'67–'72 (Middletown, Conn., 1973); *Writings through Finnegans Wake* (N.Y., 1978; includes *Writing for the Second Time through Finnegans Wake*); *Empty Words: Writings '73–'78* (Middletown, Conn. 1979); with D. Charles, *For the Birds* (Boston, 1981); with S. Barron, *Another Song* (N.Y., 1981); W. Diamond and C. Hicks, eds., *John Cage: Etchings 1978–1982* (Oakland, Calif., 1982); with L. Long, *Mud Book* (N.Y., 1982; 2nd ed., 1988); *Themes and Variations* (N.Y., 1982); *X: Writings '79–'82* (Middletown, Conn., 1983); *I–VI* (Cambridge, Mass., 1990); *Composition in Retrospect* (Cambridge, Mass., 1993); R. Kostelanetz, ed., *John Cage, Writer: Previously Uncollected Pieces* (N.Y., 1993).

BIBL.: R. Kostelanetz, ed., *J. C.* (N.Y., 1970; new ed., 1991); E. Snyder, *J. C. and Music since World War II: A Study in Applied Aesthetics* (diss., Univ. of Wisc., 1970); W. Duckworth, *Expanding Notational Parameters in the Music of J. C.* (diss., Univ. of Ill., 1972); M. Nyman, *Experimental Music: C. and Beyond* (N.Y., 1974); F. Bayer, *De Schönberg à Cage: Essai sur la notion d'espace sonore dans la musique contemporaine* (Paris, 1981); P. Griffiths, *C.* (N.Y., 1981); P. Gena and J. Brent, eds., *A J. C. Reader: In Celebration of His 70th Birthday* (N.Y., 1982); H. Kepler, *J. C. und der Zen-Buddhismus* (diss., Univ. of Marburg, 1982); K. Schöning, *Roaratorio: Eine irischer Circus über Finnegans Wake* (Königstein, 1982); D. Campana, *Form and Structure in the Music of J. C.* (diss., Northwestern Univ., 1985); J. Petkus, *The Songs of J. C. (1932–1970)* (diss., Univ. of Conn., 1986); R. Kostelanetz, ed., *Conversing with C.* (N.Y., 1987); P. van Emmerik, *A C. Documentary* (thesis, Univ. of Amsterdam, 1988); E. Pedrini, *J. C. Happening and Fluxus* (Florence, 1988); H.-K. Metzger and R. Riehn, eds., special issue of *Musik-Konzept* (2 vols., Frankfurt am Main, 1990; includes list of works, discography, and extensive bibliography); W. Fetterman, *J. C.'s Theatre Pieces: Notations and Performances* (diss., N.Y. Univ., 1992); L. Kuhn, *J. C.'s "Europeras 1 & 2": The Musical Means of Revolution* (diss., Univ. of Calif., Los Angeles, 1992); D. Revill, *The Roaring Silence: J. C.: A Life* (N.Y., 1992); J. Pritchett, *The Music of J. C.* (Cambridge, 1993); G. Leonard, *Into the Light of Things: The Art of the Commonplace from Wordsworth to J. C.* (Chicago, 1994); M. Perloff and C. Junkerman, *J. C: Composed in America* (Chicago, 1994); J. Retallack, *MUSICAGE: C. Muses on Art, Music, Poetry* (Middletown, Conn., 1995); D. Patterson, *J. C., 1942–1954: A Language of Changes* (diss., Columbia Univ., 1996).

Cagnoni, Antonio, Italian composer; b. Godiasco, near Voghera, Feb. 8, 1828; d. Bergamo, April 30, 1896. He studied at the Milan Cons. (1842–47), where 3 of his operas were produced: *Rosalia di San Miniato* (1845), *I due Savojardi* (1846), and his most successful work, *Don Bucefalo* (1847). From 1852 to 1873 he was maestro di cappella in the Cathedral of Vigevano; from 1873, in the Cathedral of Novarra; from 1887, in S. Maria Maggiore in Bergamo. From 1848 to 1874 he brought out 15 operas in various Italian theaters.

Cahier, Sarah (Jane Layton-Walker), American contralto; b. Nashville, Jan. 8, 1870; d. Manhattan Beach, Calif., April 15, 1951. She studied in Indianapolis. After singing in concert and church settings under the name Mrs. Morris Black, she pursued training with Jean de Reszke in Paris, Gustav Walter in Vienna, and Amalie Joachim in Berlin. In 1904 she made her operatic debut in Nice, and then was a member of the Vienna Court Opera (1906–11). On Nov. 20, 1911, she was a soloist in the premiere of Mahler's *Das Lied von der Erde* in Munich. She then made her Metropolitan Opera debut in New York under the name Sarah Charles-Cahier, having married Charles Cahier in 1905, singing Azucena on April 3, 1912; she remained on its roster until 1913. She subsequently devoted herself to concert engagements, and later taught in Sweden, Salzburg, and N.Y. Among her best known roles were Carmen, Amneris, and Fricka.

Cahill, Teresa (Mary), English soprano; b. Maidenhead, July 30, 1944. She trained at the Guildhall School of Music and the Royal Academy of Music in London. In 1967 she made her operatic debut as Rosina with the Phoenix Opera Co. in London; from 1970 she appeared at the Glyndebourne Festivals and at Covent Garden in London; she also sang with the Welsh National Opera in Cardiff and Scottish National Opera in Glasgow. In 1972 she appeared for the first time at the Santa Fe Opera, in 1976 at Milan's La Scala, and in 1981 with the Philadelphia Opera. She also pursued an active career as a concert singer. Her operatic repertoire includes roles in operas by Mozart, Verdi, and R. Strauss.

Caldara, Antonio, Italian cellist and composer; b. Venice, 1670; d. Vienna, Dec. 26, 1736. He likely was a pupil of Legrenzi. He was maestro di cappella da chiesa e dal teatro to Ferdinando Carlo in Mantua (1699–1707); from 1709 to 1716 he served as maestro di cappella to Prince Ruspoli in Rome. Caldara was an extraordinarily prolific composer, numbering among his works 90 operas and sacred dramas and 43 oratorios.

BIBL.: U. Kirkendele, *A. C.: Sein Leben und seine venezianische-römischen Oratorien* (Graz, 1966); B. Pritchard, ed., *A. C.: Essays on His Life and Times* (London, 1987).

Caldwell, Sarah, remarkable American conductor and operatic impresario; b. Maryville, Mo., March 6, 1924. She studied at the Univ. of Ark. and at Hendrix College, and then was a violin pupil of Richard Burgin at the New England Cons. of Music in Boston; she also studied viola with Georges Fourel at the Berkshire Music Center in Tanglewood (summer, 1946), where she returned in 1947 to stage Vaughan Williams's *Riders to the Sea*. After studying with and serving as assistant to Boris Goldovsky, she was head of the Boston Univ. opera workshop (1952–60). In 1958 she founded the Boston Opera Group, which became the Opera Co. of Boston in 1965, which played a prominent role in the musical life of the city for some 25 years, disbanding in 1991. In addition to standard operatic fare, Caldwell conducted the U.S. stage premieres of such modern operas as Schoenberg's *Moses und Aron* (Nov. 30, 1966), Prokofiev's *War and Peace* (May 8, 1974), Sessions's *Montezuma* (March 31, 1976), and Tippett's *The Ice Break* (May 18, 1979). She also was the first woman to conduct at the Metropolitan Opera in New York (*La Traviata*, Jan. 13, 1976). She returned to the Metropolitan Opera in 1978 to conduct *L'Elisir d'Amore*. She also appeared as a guest conductor with various U.S. orchs.

Calegari, Antonio, Italian composer and music theorist; b. Padua, Feb. 17, 1757; d. there, July 22, 1828. He studied with Scalabrin and Betoni in Venice, then was active as a composer there and in Padua. He was a conductor at the Teatro Nuovo in Padua (c.1790–96). He spent the last years of his life, from 1801, as organist at the Church of San Antonio in Padua. He brought out 3 operas in Venice: *Le Sorelle rivali* (1784), *L'amor soldato* (1786), and *Il matrimonio scoperto* (1789), although the authorship of all 3 is dubious. The last may be attributable to Luigi Caligari. Antonio Calegari publ. a curious treatise on composition, *Gioco pittagorico musicale* (Venice, 1801), which was republ. in Paris, during his residence there, as *L'Art de composer la musique sans en connaître les éléments* (1802). A harmonic system, *Sistema armonico* (1829), and a vocal method, *Modi generali del canto* (1836), were publ. posth.

Callaerts, Joseph, Belgian organist and composer; b. Antwerp, Aug. 22, 1838; d. there, March 3, 1901. He studied with Lemmens at the Brussels Cons.. He was organist of the Jesuit College and later of the Antwerp Cathedral, and from 1876 he taught organ at the Music School in Antwerp. He composed a comic opera, *Le Retour imprévu* (Antwerp, 1889).

Callas, Maria (real name, **Maria Anna Sofia Cecilia Kalogeropoulos**), celebrated American soprano; b. N.Y., Dec. 3, 1923; d. Paris, Sept. 16, 1977. Her father was a Greek immigrant. The family returned to Greece when she was 13; she studied voice at the Royal Academy of Music in Athens with Elvira de Hidalgo, and made her debut as Santuzza in the school production of *Cavalleria rusticana* in Nov. 1938. Her first professional appearance was in a minor role in Suppe's *Boccaccio* at the Royal Opera in Athens when she was 16; her first major role, as Tosca, was there in July 1942. She returned to New York in 1945; she auditioned for the Metropolitan Opera and was offered a contract, but decided instead to go to Italy, where she made her operatic debut in the title role of *La Gioconda* (Verona, Aug. 3, 1947). She was encouraged in her career by Tullio Serafin, who engaged her to sing Isolde and Aida in various Italian productions. In 1951 she became a member of La Scala in Milan. She was greatly handicapped by her absurdly excessive weight (210 lbs.); by a supreme effort of will, she slimmed down to 135 pounds; with her classical Greek profile and penetrating eyes, she made a striking impression on the stage; in the tragic role of Medea in Cherubini's opera she mesmerized the audience by her dramatic representation of pity and terror. Some critics opined that she lacked a true bel canto quality in her voice and that her technique was defective in coloratura, but her power of interpretation was such that she was soon acknowledged to be one of the greatest dramatic singers of the century. Her personal life was as tempestuous as that of any prima donna of the bygone era. In 1949 she married the Italian industrialist Giovanni Battista Meneghini, who became her manager, but they separated 10 years later. Her romance with the Greek shipping magnate Aristotle Onassis was a recurrent topic of sensational gossip. Given to outbursts of temper, she made newspaper headlines when she walked off the stage following some altercation, or failed to appear altogether at scheduled performances, but her eventual return to the stage was all the more eagerly welcomed by her legion of admirers. After leaving La Scala in 1958, she returned there from 1960 to 1962. She also sang at London's Covent Garden (1952–53; 1957–59; 1964), in Chicago (1954–56), and Dallas (1958–59). Perhaps the peak of her success was her brilliant debut at the Metropolitan Opera in New York as Norma on Oct. 29, 1956. Following a well-publicized disagreement with its management, she quit the company only to reach an uneasy accommodation with it to return as Violetta on Feb. 6, 1958; that same year she left the company again, returning in 1965 to sing Tosca before abandoning the operatic stage altogether. In 1971–72 she gave a seminar on opera at the Juilliard School in New York, which was enthusiastically received. In 1974 she gave her last public performances in a series of concerts with Giuseppe di Stefano; she then returned to Europe. She died suddenly of a heart attack in her Paris apartment. Her body was cremated and her ashes scattered on the Aegean Sea. Callas was nothing short of a phenomenon, one whose popularity has only increased with time. One radio commentator's characterization of Callas was that "If an orgasm could sing, it would sound like Maria Callas." She excelled particularly in roles by Rossini, Bellini, Donizetti, and Verdi.

BIBL.: E. Gara and R. Hauert, *M. C.* (Geneva, 1957; Eng. tr., 1958); E. Callas, *My Daughter M. C.* (N.Y., 1960); G. Jellinek, *C.* (N.Y., 1960); S. Galatopoulos, *C.—La Divina: Art That Conceals Art* (London, 1963; 3d ed., rev. and aug., 1976, as *C.: Prima donna assoluta*); J. Ardoin and G. Fitzgerald, *C* (N.Y., 1974); H. Wisneski, *M. C.: The Art Behind the Music* (N.Y., 1975); J. Ardoin, *The C. Legacy: The Complete Guide to Her Recordings* (N.Y., 1977; 2nd ed., rev., 1982; new ed., 1991); P.-J. Rémy, *M. C.: A Tribute* (N.Y., 1978); S. Linakis, *Diva: The Life and Death of M. C.* (Englewood Cliffs, N.J., 1980); C. Verga, *M. C.: Mito e malinconia* (Rome, 1980); C. Chiarelli, *M. C.: Vita, immagini, parole, musica* (Venice, 1981); G. Menghini, *M. C. mia moglie* (Milan, 1981; Eng. tr., 1982); A. Stassinopoulos, *M. C.: The Woman Behind the Legend* (N.Y., 1981); D. Lowe, ed., *C., as They Saw Her* (N.Y., 1986); R. La Rochelle, *C.: La diva et le vinyle* (Montreal, 1987); N. Stancioff, *M. C. Remembered* (N.Y., 1987); J. Callas, *Sisters: A Revealing Portrait of the World's Most Famous Diva* (London and N.Y., 1989); J. Kesting, *M. D.* (Düsseldorf, 1990; Eng. tr., 1993); R. Allegri, *La vera storia di M. C.: Con documenti inediti* (Milan, 1991); A. Petrolli, *La divina C.: Vita ed arte* (Trento, 1991); M. Di Stefano, *C. nemica mia* (Milan, 1992); M. Scott, *M. M. C.* (Boston, 1992); E. Kanthou, *M. C.* (Wilhelmshaven, 1993); F. Rohmer, *C.: Gesichter eines Mediums* (Munich, 1993); B. Tosi, *Casta diva: L'incomparable C.* (Parma, 1993); D. Lelait, *M. C.: J'ai vécu d'art, j'ai vécu d'amour* (Paris, 1997).

Callaway, Paul (Smith), American organist and conductor; b. Atlanta, Ill., Aug. 16, 1909. After attending Westminster College in Fulton, Mo. (1927–29), he studied organ with Tercius Noble in New York (1930–35), with Leo Sowerby in Chicago (1936), and with Marcel Dupré in Paris. He was organist and choirmaster at St. Thomas's Chapel in New York (1930–35) and at St. Mark's Chapel in Grand Rapids (1935–39); then he was organist and music director of the Cathedral Church of St. Peter and St. Paul in Washington, D.C. (1939–42; 1946–77); also was music director of the Opera Soc. of Washington, D.C. (1956–57) and of the Lake George Opera Festival in Glens Falls, N.Y. (1967–77).

Calvé (real name, **Calvet de Roquer**), **(Rosa-Noémie) Emma,** famous French soprano; b. Décazeville, Aveyron, Aug. 15, 1858; d. Millau, Jan. 6, 1942. She studied voice with Puget in Paris and with Marchesi and Laborde. She made her operatic debut as Marguerite in Gounod's *Faust* at the Théâtre Royal de la Monnaie in Brussels on Sept. 23, 1881; she then sang at the Opéra Comique in Paris 3 years later. She sang at La Scala in Milan and at other Italian opera houses from 1886; she appeared at Covent Garden in London from 1892 to 1904. She made her American debut at the Metropolitan Opera in New York as Santuzza on Nov. 29, 1893, and remained on its staff until 1904; her greatest role was that of Carmen. Subsequently she sang at the Manhattan Opera (1907–09), in Boston (1912), and in Nice (1914) before retiring from the operatic stage; she continued to give concerts until 1927. Her life was made the subject of a novel by Gustav Kobbé, *Signora, A Child of the Opera House* (N.Y., 1903). She publ. an autobiography, in Eng., *My Life* (N.Y., 1922); she later publ. an additional vol. of memoirs, *Sous tous les ciels j'ai chanté* (Paris, 1940).

BIBL.: A. Gallus, *E. C., Her Artistic Life* (N.Y., 1902).

Calvocoressi, Michel Dimitri, eminent Greek writer on music; b. Marseilles, Oct. 2, 1877; d. London, Feb. 1, 1944. He studied music in Paris, but was mostly autodidact; also pursued study in the social sciences. In 1914 he settled in London. He wrote music criticism and correspondences for French and other journals. He mastered the Russian language and became an ardent propagandist of Russian music; made excellent trs. into English and French of Russian and German songs. Among his books are monographs on Liszt (Paris, 1906), Mussorgsky (Paris, 1908), Glinka (Paris, 1911), Schumann (Paris, 1912), and Debussy (London, 1941); a new extensive biography of Mussorgsky was posth. publ. (London, 1946). With G. Abraham, he publ. the valuable *Masters of Russian Music* (London, 1936).

Calzabigi, Ranieri (Simone Francesco Maria) di, Italian poet and music theorist; b. Livorno, Dec. 23, 1714; d. Naples, July 1795. In 1750 he went to Paris, then proceeded to Brussels in 1760. From 1761 until 1772 he remained in Vienna, and was in Pisa by 1775. He engaged in polemics regarding the relative merits of French and Italian operas, lending energetic support to Gluck in his ideas of operatic reform. He wrote for Gluck the libretti of *Orfeo, Alceste*, and *Paride ed Elena*. He publ. *Dissertazione su le poesie drammatiche del Sig. Abate Pietro Metastasio* (1755), a controversial work concerning Metastasio and Hasse.

BIBL.: G. Lazzeri, *La vita e l'opera letteraria di R. C.* (Città di Castello, 1907).

Cambefort, Jean de, French singer and composer; b. c.1605; d. Paris, May 4, 1661. He was a singer in Richelieu's private chapel. After Richelieu's death in 1642, Cambefort entered the service of Cardinal Mazarin. In 1644 he was named maître des enfants de la chambre du roi. In 1650 he become compositeur de la musique de la chambre to Louis XIV, and later served as surintendant de la musique de roi. He was highly regarded at the court as both a singer and as a composer of ballets de cour, airs de cour, and sacred works.

Cambert, Robert, French opera composer; b. Paris, c.1628; d. London, 1677. He was a pupil of Chambonnières. His first venture on the lyric stage was *La Pastorale*, written with the librettist Perrin and successfully produced at the Château d'Issy in 1659. It was followed by *Ariane, ou Le Mariage de Bacchus* (rehearsed in 1661) and *Adonis* (1662; not perf.; MS lost). In 1669 Perrin received letters patent for establishing the Académie Royale de Musique. He brought out, in collaboration with Cambert, the opera *Pomone* (1671); another opera, *Les Peines et les plaisirs de l'amour*, was written, and produced in Paris in March 1671, before Lully secured the patent. In 1673, after Lully secured the patent in violation of the agreement with Molière, Cambert went to London.

BIBL.: A. Pougin, *Les Vrais Créateurs de l'opéra français, Perrin et C.* (Paris, 1881).

Cambini, Giuseppe Maria (Gioacchino), Italian composer; b. Livorno, Feb. 13, 1746; d. Bicêtre, Dec. 29, 1825. He was a prolific composer of instrumental works, numbering among his works ballets, operas, and oratorios. He died in an almshouse.

Cambreling, Sylvain, French conductor; b. Amiens, July 2, 1948. He received training in music at the Paris Cons. In 1975 he became assistant conductor of the Orchestre de Lyon; he also conducted opera in Lyon; beginning with the 1979–80 season, he appeared regularly as a conductor at the Paris Opéra. In 1981 he became joint music director (with John Pritchard) of the Théâtre Royal de la Monnaie in Brussels. He also conducted at the Glyndebourne Festival, the Frankfurt am Main Opera, La Scala in Milan, in the United States, and in Canada. On Jan. 9, 1986, he made his Metropolitan Opera debut in New York conducting *Roméo et Juliette*. From 1993 to 1997 he was chief conductor of the Frankfurt am Main Opera.

Campana, Fabio, Italian singing teacher and composer; b. Livorno, Jan. 14, 1819; d. London, Feb. 2, 1882. He studied in Bologna. He produced the operas *Caterina di Guisa* (Livorno, 1838), *Giulio d'Este* (Livorno, 1841), *Vannina d'Ornano* (Florence, 1842), and *Luisa di Francia* (Rome, 1844), then went to London, where he settled as a singing teacher. His opera *Almina* was staged in London at Her Majesty's Theatre (April 26, 1860); another opera, *Esmeralda*, was produced in St. Petersburg (Dec. 20, 1869); Patti sang the title role in its productions in western Europe. Campana also wrote hundreds of songs.

Campanari, Giuseppe, Italian baritone, brother of **Leandro Campanari**; b. Venice, Nov. 17, 1855; d. Milan, May 31, 1927. He was a cellist in the orch. of Milan's La Scala, but also studied voice. After playing cello in the Boston Sym. Orch. (1884–93), he made his operatic debut as Tonio with Hinrich's Opera Co. in New York on June 15, 1893. On Nov. 30, 1894, he made his Metropolitan Opera debut in New York as Di Luna, and continued on its roster until 1912. In addition to Italian roles, he also appeared there as Papageno, Valentin, Nélusko, Escamillo, Kothner, and Nevers.

Campanini, Cleofonte, eminent Italian-American conductor, brother of **Italo Campanini**; b. Parma, Sept. 1, 1860; d. Chicago, Dec. 19, 1919. He studied violin at the Parma Cons. and later at the Milan Cons., making his conducting debut with *Carmen* at Parma (1882). He conducted the first American performance of *Otello* at the N.Y. Academy of Music (April 16, 1888) while his brother, Italo, was impresario. Between 1888 and 1906, he conducted in Italy, in England, and in South America. A larger field opened to him in 1906, when Hammerstein engaged him for the new Manhattan Opera House in New York. Differences with Hammerstein led him to resign in 1909. In the following year he was engaged as principal conductor of the newly formed Chicago Opera Co.; in 1913 he was appointed general director, which post he held until his death. Among opera conductors he occupied a place in the first rank; he seemed to be equally at home in all styles of music. He introduced many new operas in the United States, among them Massenet's *Hérodiade*, Debussy's *Pelléas et Mélisande*, Charpentier's *Louise*, Wolf-Ferrari's *Il segreto di Susanna*, et al. On May 15, 1887, he married, in Florence, Eva Tetrazzini (sister of **Luisa Tetrazzini**).

Campanini, Italo, famous Italian tenor, brother of **Cleofonte Campanini**; b. Parma, June 30, 1845; d. Corcagno, near Parma, Nov. 22, 1896. In his early years he was an apprentice in his father's blacksmith shop. He joined Garibaldi's army and was wounded in the Italian struggle for unification. Subsequently, he studied with Griffini and Lamperti, then appeared at Bologna in *Lohengrin* (Nov. 1, 1871), which started him on the road to fame. He made his London debut as Gennaro in *Lucrezia Borgia* (May 4, 1872), and his American debut, also as Gennaro, at the N.Y. Academy of Music (Oct. 1, 1873). He appeared in *Faust* at the opening of the Metropolitan Opera (Oct. 22, 1883); he was on its roster until 1894. He was briefly active as an impresario; brought over his brother Cleofonte Campanini to conduct the American premiere of Verdi's *Otello* at the N.Y. Academy of Music (April 16, 1888).

Campenhout, François van, Belgian tenor and composer, author of the Belgian national anthem; b. Brussels, Feb. 5, 1779; d. there, April 24, 1848. Beginning as violinist in the Théâtre de la Monnaie, he studied singing under Plantade, and became a fine tenor, appearing in Belgium, the Netherlands, and France. He wrote 6 operas, 9 cantatas, etc. He is, however, chiefly remembered as the composer of *La Brabançonne*, which was written during the revolution of 1830, and eventually became the national anthem of Belgium.

Campo (y Zabaleta), Conrado del, distinguished Spanish composer and teacher; b. Madrid, Oct. 28, 1878; d. there, March 17, 1953. He was a student of Hierro, Monasterio, Fontanilla, and Serrano at the Madrid Cons.; he also studied with Chapí. Having become proficient as a violinist and violist, he played in the sym. orch. at the Teatro Real in Madrid, and was a member of the Quarteto Francés and the Quinteto de Madrid. He helped to organize the orch. of the National Radio, which he conducted from 1947 to 1951. He served as prof. of harmony (1915–23) and of composition (1923–53) at the Madrid Cons., where his outstanding students included Cristóbal Halffter and Domingo Santa Cruz. While Spanish national traits are prominent in his works, he also adapted German Romantic sonorities.

WORKS: DRAMATIC: OPERAS: *El final de Don Alvaro* (Madrid, March 4, 1911); *La dama desconocida* (1911); *La tragedia del beso* (Madrid, May 18, 1915); *Los amantes de Verona* (1916); *Dies irae* (1917); *El Avapiés* (Madrid, March 8, 1919; in collaboration with A. Barrios); *Fantochines* (Madrid, 1924); *Leonor Telles* (1927); *El árbol de los ojos* (1931); *Lola la piconera* (Barcelona, Nov. 14, 1950); *El pájaro de dos colores* (1951); some 25 zarzuelas.

BIBL.: T. Borrás, *C. d.C.* (Madrid, 1954).

Campora, Giuseppe, Italian tenor; b. Tortona, Sept. 30, 1923. He studied voice in Genoa and Milan. In 1949 he made his operatic debut in Bari as Rodolfo; in 1951 he joined Milan's La Scala and also sang with other Italian opera houses. He made his Metropolitan Opera debut in New York as Rodolfo on Jan. 20, 1955, and remained on the roster until 1959; he was again on its roster from 1963 to 1965. Among his best known roles were Enzo, Massenet's Des Grieux, Gounod's Faust, Cavaradossi, Edgardo, and Alfredo.

Camporese, Violante, Italian soprano; b. Rome, 1785; d. there, 1839. She studied in Paris with Crescentini, and sang before Napoleon. On Jan. 11, 1817, she made her London debut at the King's Theatre as Cimarosa's Penelope, and continued to sing there until 1823 in such roles as Donna Anna, Dorabella, and Susanna. From 1817 to 1829 she appeared at Milan's La Scala, where she created the role of Bianca in Rossini's *Bianca e Faliero* (Dec. 26, 1819). She was held in high esteem as a Mozartian.

Campra, André, important French composer; b. Aix, Provence, Dec. 4, 1660; d. Versailles, June 29, 1744. He studied with Guillaume Poitevin, then embraced an ecclesiastical vocation. He was made chaplain at Aix on May 27, 1681; he served as maître de musique at St. Étienne in Toulouse from 1683 to 1694, and at Notre Dame from 1694 to 1700; he then was active at the Paris Opéra. In 1723 he received a court appointment as sous-maitre with Bernier and Gervais. His operas had numerous performances in Paris.

WORKS (all 1st perf. in Paris unless otherwise given): DRA-

MATIC: *L'Europe galante*, opéra ballet (Oct. 24, 1697); *Le Carnaval de Venise*, ballet (Jan. 20, 1699; Act 3 includes the Italian opera *Orfeo nell'inferni*); *Hésione*, tragédie lyrique (Dec. 20, 1700); *Aréthuse, ou La Vengeance de l'Amour*, tragédie lyrique (July 14, 1701); *Tancrède*, tragédie lyrique (Nov. 7, 1702); *Les Muses*, opéra ballet (Oct. 28, 1703); *Iphigénie en Tauride*, tragédie lyrique based on the unfinished work of Desmarets (May 6, 1704); *Télémaque*, extracts from operas by Campra et al. (Nov. 11, 1704); *Alcine*, tragédie lyrique (Jan 15, 1705); *Hippodamie*, tragédie lyrique (March 6, 1708); *Les Fêtes vénitiennes*, opéra ballet (June 17, 1710); *Idomenée*, tragédie lyrique (Jan. 12, 1712); *Les Amours de Vénus et de Mars*, ballet (Sept. 6, 1712); *Téléphe*, tragédie lyrique (Nov. 28, 1713); *Camille, reine des volsques*, tragédie lyrique (Nov. 9, 1717); *Ballet représenté à Lion devant M. le marquis d'Harlincourt*, ballet (Lyons, May 17, 1718; not extant); *Les Âges*, opéra ballet (Oct. 9, 1718); *Achille et Deidamie*, tragédie lyrique (Feb. 24, 1735).

BIBL.: J. Anthony, *The Opera-Ballet of A. C.: A Study of the First Period French Opera-Ballet* (diss., Univ. of Southern Calif., 1964); M. Bathélemy, *A. C., 1660–1744: Étude biographique et musicologique* (Arles, 1995).

Camps, Pompeyo, Argentine composer; b. Paraná, Oct. 27, 1924. After playing piano in bands in his native town, he settled in Buenos Aires in 1947, where he studied with Jaime Pahissa and adopted his "intertonal system" of convertible counterpoint. In 1964 Camps modified this technique by incorporating serial procedures. He composed the operas *La pendiente* (1959) and *La oscuridad de la razón* (Buenos Aires, Nov. 7, 1995). He was also active as a music critic.

Camussi, Ezio, Italian composer; b. Florence, Jan. 16, 1877; d. Milan, Aug. 11, 1956. He studied in Rome with Falchi and Sgambati; later with Massenet in Paris and at the Liceo Musicale in Bologna. He composed the operas *La Dubarry* (Milan, Nov. 7, 1912), *I fuochi di San Giovanni* (Milan, March 27, 1920), *Il donzello, Scampolo* (Trieste, Feb. 22, 1925), and *Il volto della Virgine* (Bari, Jan. 23, 1937), as well as *La principessa lontana*, *I Romanzeschi*, and *Intermezzi giocosi* for Puppet Theater.

Candeille, (Amélie) Julie, French pianist, harpist, singer, actress, composer, and writer, daughter of **Pierre Joseph Candeille**; b. Paris, July 31, 1767; d. there, Feb. 4, 1834. She received most of her musical training from her father, but also studied piano with Holaind and singing with Legros. At age 14 she joined the Paris Opéra, and at 15 appeared as Gluck's Iphigénie there. In 1783 she appeared as an instrumentalist at the Concert Spirituel. By 1785 she was a member of the Comédie Française, where she was active as both a performer and a composer. In 1816 she was granted a pension by Louis XVIII. Her most successful work was the comédie *Catherine, ou La belle fermière* (Paris, Nov. 27, 1792). In addition to other stage pieces, she also composed orch. works, chamber music, piano pieces, and songs. Among her writings were novels, dramas, and her memoirs, the last included in L. Aillaud, "J. C.," *Chronique mondaine, littéraire et artistique* (Nîmes, Oct. 27, 1923–Jan. 12, 1924).

Candeille, Pierre Joseph, French singer and composer, father of **(Amélie) Julie Candeille**; b. Estaires, Dec. 8, 1744; d. Chantilly, April 24, 1827. He received his training at the song school of the collegiate church of St. Pierre in Lille. After settling in Paris, he was a basse taille in the chorus of the Opéra (1767–71; 1773–81) and of the Concert Spirituel (1769–71; 1773–81), and later was chorus master of the Opéra (1800–02; 1804–05). He wrote about 20 stage works, of which the most successful was the opera *Castor et Pollux* (Paris, June 14, 1791).

Caniglia, Maria, Italian soprano; b. Naples, May 5, 1905; d. Rome, April 16, 1979. She was a pupil of Roche at the Naples Cons. In 1930 she made her operatic debut in Turin as Chrysothemis, and later that year made her first appearance at Milan's La Scala as Maria in Pizzetti's *Lo Straniero*. She continued to sing at La Scala until 1943, and again from 1948 to 1951; she also appeared with the company on its visits to London's Covent Garden (1937, 1939, 1950). On Nov. 21, 1938, she made her Metropolitan Opera debut in New York as Desdemona, but returned to Europe in 1939. In 1939 she married **Pino Donati**. Among her best known roles were Tosca, Aida, Alice Ford, the 3 Leonoras, Maria Boccanegra, and Adriana Lecouvreur. She also created the title role in Respighi's *Lucrezia* (Milan, Feb. 24, 1937).

Cannabich, (Johann) Christian (Innocenz Bonaventura), German composer, violinist, and conductor; b. Mannheim (baptized), Dec. 28, 1731; d. Frankfurt am Main, Jan. 20, 1798. He studied with Johann Stamitz in Mannheim, then became a violinist in the Mannheim Orch. (1746). He was sent by the elector to Rome, where he studied with Jommelli (1750–53); he returned to Mannheim and, after Stamitz's death (1757), became 1st violinist of the orch. In 1774 he was director of the instrumental music, and in 1778 he moved to Munich. Cannabich is usually credited with bringing the Mannheim Orch. to a degree of perfection theretofore never attained, particularly in the carefully graduated crescendo and diminuendo. He was also a prolific composer, numbering among his works a Singspiel, *Azakia* (Mannheim, 1778), a melodrama, *Elektra* (Mannheim, 1781), and 40 ballets.

BIBL.: H. Hofer, *C. C.: Biographie und vergleichende Analyse seiner Sinfonien* (diss., Univ. of Munich, 1921); R. Kloiber, *Die dramatischen Ballette von C. C.* (diss., Univ. of Munich, 1928).

Cannon, (Jack) Philip, English composer and teacher; b. Paris (of English-French parents), Dec. 21, 1929. He was educated in England; studied composition with Imogen Holst; then at the Royal College of Music in London with Gordon Jacob and Vaughan Williams. He subsequently took lessons with Paul Hindemith. From 1957 to 1959 he lectured at the Univ. of Sydney; in 1960 he joined the staff of the Royal College of Music in London. He composed the opera *Morvoren* (London, July 15, 1964).

Cantelli, Guido, brilliant Italian conductor; b. Novara, April 27, 1920; d. in an airplane crash in Orly, near Paris, Nov. 24, 1956. A gifted child, he was given a place in his father's military band when he was a small boy; he appeared as organist at the local church from age 10, and made his debut as a pianist at age 14. He pursued formal studies with Pedrollo and Ghedini at the Milan Cons. He then was conductor of Novara's Teatro Coccia in 1941, but was compelled to give up his post and join the Italian army in 1943. When he refused to support the Fascist cause, he was sent to the Nazi-run Stettin labor camp (1943–44); after being transferred to Bolzano, he escaped to Milan, but was captured and sentenced to death. He was saved by the liberation of his homeland in 1944. After World War II, he conducted at Milan's La Scala; Toscanini heard his performances and was sufficiently impressed to invite him as guest conductor with the NBC Sym. Orch. in New York. He made his American debut on Jan. 15, 1949, and subsequently conducted there regularly. From 1951 he also made appearances as a conductor with the Philharmonia Orch. in London. Cantelli was one of the most gifted conductors of his generation. A perfectionist, he conducted both rehearsals and concert and operatic performances from memory. He was able to draw the most virtuosic playing from his musicians. A few days before his death, he was appointed artistic director of La Scala.

BIBL.: L. Lewis, *G. C.: Portrait of a Maestro* (London, 1981).

Cantelo, April (Rosemary), English soprano; b. Purbrook, April 2, 1928. She studied piano and voice at the Royal College of Music in London; she was subsequently a member of the New English Singers and the Deller Consort; she also appeared in opera with the Glyndebourne Opera and the English Opera Group; she also gave solo recitals. From 1949 to 1964 she was married to **Colin Davis**.

Canteloube, (de Malaret), (Marie-) Joseph, French pianist, composer, and writer on music; b. Annonay, near Tournon, Oct. 21, 1879; d. Grigny, Seine-et-Oise, Nov. 4, 1957. His name was simply Canteloube, but he added "de Malaret" after the name of his ancestral estate. He studied piano in Paris with Amélie Doetzer and composition with d'Indy at the Schola Cantorum. He became an ardent collector of French folk songs and arranged and publ.

many of them for voice with instrumental accompaniment. His *Chants d'Auvergne* (4 sets for Voice, with Piano or Orch., 1923–30) are frequently performed. Among his other albums, *Anthologie des chants populaires français* (4 sets, 1939–44) is a comprehensive collection of regional folk songs. He also publ. a biography of d'Indy (Paris, 1949). He composed two operas: *Le Mas* (1910–13; Paris, April 3, 1929) and *Vercingetorix* (1930–32; Paris, June 26, 1933).

BIBL.: L. Boursiac, *C.* (Toulouse, 1941); F. Gougniaud-Taginel, *J. C.: Chantre dela terre* (Béziers, 1988).

Capdevielle, Pierre, French composer and pianist; b. Paris, Feb. 1, 1906; d. Bordeaux, July 9, 1969. He studied at the Paris Cons. with Gédalge and Paul Vidal, and privately with d'Indy. He composed an opera, *Les Amants captifs* (1947–50), and a lyric tragedy, *Fille de l'homme* (Paris Radio, Nov. 9, 1967).

Capecchi, Renato, Italian baritone; b. Cairo (of Italian parents), Nov. 6, 1923; d. Milan, June 30, 1998. He was a student in Milan of Ubaldo Carrozzi. After making his debut on the Italian Radio (1948), he made his stage debut as Amonasro in 1949 in Reggio Emilia. From 1950 he sang at Milan's La Scala. On Nov. 24, 1951, he made his Metropolitan Opera debut in New York as Germont *père*, remaining on its roster until 1954. In 1975 he returned there, and then made occasional visits until 1994. Between 1953 and 1983 he was a regular guest at the Verona Arena. In 1962 he made his debut at London's Covent Garden as Melitone, and sang there again in 1973. In 1977 and 1980 he appeared as Falstaff at Glyndebourne. His guest appearances took him not only all over Italy but to Berlin, Paris, Munich, Moscow, Stuttgart, Stockholm, and other European music centers. His vast repertoire included hundreds of roles, ranging from the traditional to the contemporary. He was particularly successful as a buffo artist, winning special praise for his portrayals of Rossini's Figaro, Dr. Bartolo, Dulcamara, Don Pasquale, and Gianni Schicchi.

Capell, Richard, English writer on music; b. Northampton, March 23, 1885; d. London, June 21, 1954. He studied cello in London and at the Lille Cons. He was music critic for the *London Daily Mail* (1911–33); then joined the *Daily Telegraph*; during World War II, he was its war correspondent in the French, Greek, and Italian campaigns. From 1928 to 1933 he was an ed. of the *Monthly Musical Record*; from 1950 to 1954 he edited *Music & Letters*. In 1946 he was made an Officer of the Order of the British Empire. His publications include a biography of Gustav Holst (London, 1928), and *Opera* (London, 1930; 2d ed., aug., 1948).

Caplet, André, French composer and conductor; b. Le Havre, Nov. 23, 1878; d. Paris, April 22, 1925. He studied violin in Le Havre, and played in theater orchs. there and in Paris; he entered the Paris Cons. (1896), where he studied with Leroux and Lenepveu; in 1901 he received the Grand Prix de Rome for his cantata *Myrrha* (1901). His *Marche solennelle* for the centennial of the Villa Medicis was performed in Rome (April 18, 1903). He was active in France as a choral and operatic conductor; he conducted the first performance of Debussy's *Le Martyre de St. Sébastien* (Paris, May 22, 1911); he also conducted the Boston Opera Co. (1910–14) and in London at Covent Garden (1912). Caplet was wounded in action while serving in the French Army during World War I, which seriously impaired his life and greatly curtailed his subsequent musical activities. His own music is unequivocally impressionistic, with a lavish use of whole-tone scales and parallel chord formations; he combined this impressionism with neo-archaic usages and mystic programmatic ideas. He was a close friend of Debussy, with whom he collaborated on several of his orch. works and even completed sections left unfinished by Debussy. Their correspondence was publ. in Monaco in 1957.

Capobianco, Tito, Argentine-born American opera director and administrator; b. La Plata, Aug. 28, 1931. He received training in law and philosophy in La Plata and in music at the Univ. of Buenos Aires. In 1953 he launched his career as an opera director with a production of *Pagliacci* in La Plata. Moving to Buenos Aires, he was technical director at the Teatro Colón (1958–62) and general director of the Teatro Argentino (1959–61); subsequently he was artistic director of the Cincinnati Opera Festival (1961–65) and the Cincinnati Opera (1962–65). In 1966 he began staging operas at the N.Y. City Opera, where he was resident stage director from 1967. In 1975 he organized the Las Palmas Festival in the Canary Islands. He also became artistic director of the San Diego Opera in 1975, serving as its general director from 1977. In 1983 he became general director of the Pittsburgh Opera, and in 1997 he was made its artistic director. He was prof. of acting and interpretation at the Academy of Vocal Arts in Philadelphia (1962–68); in 1967 he founded the American Opera Center at the Juilliard School of Music in New York, serving as its director until 1969. He was director of opera studies and festival stage director at the Music Academy of the West in Santa Barbara (from 1983), and prof. of acting, staging, and interpretation at the Graduate School of Music at Yale Univ. (from 1983). In many of his operatic stagings, he collaborated with his wife, the choreographer Elena Denda.

Capoul, (Joseph-Amédée-) Victor, French tenor; b. Toulouse, Feb. 27, 1839; d. Pujaudran-du-Gers, Feb. 18, 1924. He was a student of Revial and Mocker at the Paris Cons. On Aug. 26, 1861, he made his operatic debut as Daniel in Adam's *Le Châlet* at the Paris Opéra Comique. After a decade there, he sang at the Academy of Music in New York (1871–74) and at London's Drury Lane (1871–75). On April 5, 1877, he made his first appearance at London's Covent Garden as Fra Diavolo, where he sang until 1879. He made his Metropolitan Opera debut in New York as Faust on Oct. 27, 1883, remaining on its roster until 1884 and again in 1891–92 and 1895–96. From 1897 to 1905 he was stage manager at the Paris Opéra. His other prominent roles included Count Almaviva, Wilhelm Meister, Edgardo, and Roméo.

Cappuccilli, Piero, admired Italian baritone; b. Trieste, Nov. 9, 1929. He studied with Luciano Doaggio in Trieste. In 1957 he made his operatic debut at Milan's Teatro Nuovo as Tonio. On March 26, 1960, he made his Metropolitan Opera debut in New York as Germont *père*, but then pursued his career in Europe. In 1964 he made his first appearance at Milan's La Scala as Donizetti's Ashton, and subsequently sang there regularly with notable success. He made his debut at London's Covent Garden as Germont *père* in 1967, and returned there in 1976 as a member of the La Scala company. In 1969 he made his first appearance at the Chicago Lyric Opera as Francesco in *I Due Foscari*. He made his debut at the Salzburg Festival as Posa in 1975. In 1978 he sang Simon Boccanegra in Paris. While continuing to sing in various Italian operatic centers, he also appeared as a guest artist throughout Europe. Among his other fine roles were Iago, Renato, Rigoletto, Nabucco, Escamillo, and Macbeth.

Capuana, Franco, Italian conductor, brother of **Maria Capuana**; b. Fano, Sept. 29, 1894; d. while conducting Rossini's *Mosè in Egitto* at the Teatro San Carlo, Naples, Dec. 10, 1969. He studied composition at the Naples Cons. He began his career as an opera conductor in 1915; from 1930 to 1937 he was music director of the Teatro San Carlo in Naples; from 1937 to 1940, and again from 1946 to 1949, he was a conductor at La Scala in Milan, then its music director (1949–52). He specialized in Italian verismo operas, but also excelled in the operas of Wagner, Strauss, and several modern composers.

BIBL.: B. Cagnoli, *L'arte musicale di F. C.* (Milan, 1983).

Capuana, Maria, Italian contralto, sister of **Franco Capuana**; b. Fano, 1891; d. Cagliari, Feb. 22, 1955. She studied voice and piano at the Cons. San Pietro a Majella in Naples. In 1918 she made her operatic debut in Naples as Urbain in *Les Huguenots*; in 1920 she sang Brangäne in Turin, and in 1922 made her first appearance at Milan's La Scala as Ortrud, where she successfully sang various Wagnerian roles. She also appeared in other major Italian music centers, as well as in Barcelona, Lisbon, Cairo, and the Teatro Colón in Buenos Aires. Among her finest non-Wagnerian roles were Amneris and Herodias.

Caradori-Allan, Maria (Caterina Rosalbina née **de Munck)**, Alsatian soprano; b. Milan (of Alsatian parents), 1800; d. Surbiton, Surrey, Oct. 15, 1865. She received her musical training from her mother, whose name she chose as her own for professional purposes. After appearances in France and Germany, she made her London debut as Cherubino at the King's Theatre on Jan. 12, 1822. She continued to sing in London until 1827, and then again from 1834, becoming particularly known as a concert and oratorio artist. She created the role of Giulietta in Bellini's *I Capuleti e i Montecchi* (Venice, March 11, 1830) and sang in the premiere of Mendelssohn's *Elijah* (Birmingham Festival, Aug. 26, 1846). Among her finest operatic roles were Zerlina, Amina, and Rosina.

Carafa (de Colobrano), Michele (Enrico-Francesco-Vincenzo-Aloisio-Paolo), Italian composer; b. Naples, Nov. 17, 1787; d. Paris, July 26, 1872. He was a son of Prince Colobrano, Duke of Alvito, and began to study music at an early age. Though he became an officer in the army of Naples, and fought in Napoleon's Russian campaign, he devoted his leisure time to music, and after Waterloo adopted it as a profession. In 1827 he settled in Paris, succeeding Le Sueur as a member of the Academy (1837). In 1840 was appointed a prof. of composition at the Paris Cons.

WORKS: DRAMATIC: OPERAS: *Gabriella di Vergy* (Naples, July 3, 1816); *Ifigenia in Tauride* (Naples, June 19, 1817); *Berenice in Siria* (Naples, July 29, 1818); *Elisabetta in Derbyshire* (Venice, Dec. 26, 1818); the following operas were produced at the Opéra Comique in Paris: *Jeanne d'Arc* (March 10, 1821); *Le Solitaire* (Aug. 17, 1822); *Le Valet de chambre* (Sept. 16, 1823); *L'Auberge supposée* (April 26, 1824); *Sangarido* (May 19, 1827); *Masaniello* (Dec. 27, 1827; on the same subject as Auber's *La Muette de Portici*, staged at the Paris Opéra 2 months later; yet Carafa's *Masaniello* held the stage in competition with Auber's famous opera for 136 nights); *La Violette* (Oct. 7, 1828); *Jenny* (Sept. 26, 1829); *Le Livre de l'ermite* (Aug. 11, 1831); *La Prison d'Edimbourg* (July 20, 1833); *Une Journée de la Fronde* (Nov. 7, 1833); *La Grande Duchesse* (Nov. 16, 1835); *Thérèse* (Sept. 26, 1838). Also ballets.

Carelli, Emma, esteemed Italian soprano; b. Naples, May 12, 1877; d. in an automobile accident in Montefiascone, near Rome, Aug. 17, 1928. She was a pupil of her father, the composer B. Carelli, at the Cons. San Pietro a Majella in Naples. In 1895 she made her operatic debut in Altamura in Mercadante's *La Vestale*. After singing in various Italian opera houses, she made her debut at Milan's La Scala in 1899 as Desdemona; in 1901 she was the first to sing the role of Tatiana in Italy. She then sang throughout Europe, and also appeared at the Teatro Colón in Buenos Aires and in Rio de Janeiro. In 1910 she married Walter Mocchi, the director of Rome's Teatro Costanzi, where she was the first to sing Elektra in Italy in 1912. She succeeded her husband as its director (1912–26). Among her most acclaimed roles were Iris and Zazá.

Carena, Maria, Italian soprano; b. Turin, 1891; d. there, Oct. 9, 1966. She studied in Turin with Virginia Ferni-Germano, and made her operatic debut there in 1917 as Leonora in *Il Trovatore*. Following appearances in Rome, Naples, and Milan, she sang in Buenos Aires (1919), Lisbon (1920), and Madrid (1920–21). In 1922 she made her first appearance at Milan's La Scala as Suor Angelica, and continued to sing there until 1932. In 1924 she sang in the premiere of Boito's *Nerone* at La Scala. In 1932 she scored a fine success as Giulia in *La Vestale* in Rome.

Carestini, Giovanni, greatly renowned Italian castrato alto; b. Filottrano, near Ancona, c.1705; d. probably there, c.1760. He studied in Milan, then made his operatic debut in a female role in A. Scarlatti's *Griselda* in Rome (1721), where he continued to sing until 1723. He is known to have appeared in Venice (until 1726), Parma and Genoa (1726), Rome (1727–30), Milan (1727–32), Naples (1728–29), where he found a rival in Bernacchi, and again in Venice (1729, 1731); he also served as chamber virtuoso to the Duke of Parma. From 1731 to 1741 he was in the service of the Elector of Bavaria in Munich, but he remained active in other music centers. He made his London debut in the pasticcio *Semiramide riconosciuta* (Oct. 30, 1733); there Handel chose him to create the leading male roles in his *Arianna in Creta* (Jan. 26, 1734), *Il Parnasso in festa* (March 13, 1734), *Ariodante* (Jan. 8, 1735), and *Alcina* (April 16, 1735), as well as the completely revised role of Mirtillo in *Il Pastor fido* (May 18, 1734). After appearances in Venice (1735) and Naples and Bologna (1736), he sang once again in London (1739–40). On Dec. 26, 1740, he sang in the inaugural performance at Turin's Teatro Regio of Feo's *Arsace*; he also sang in Reggio (1741), Milan (1742–44), where he created the principal roles in Gluck's *Demofoonte* (Jan. 6, 1743) and *Sofonisba* (Jan. 13, 1744), Padua (1743), and Venice (1743–45). He entered the service of the Elector of Saxony in Dresden in 1747. After serving Frederick the Great in Berlin (1750–54), he went to St. Petersburg, where he won the approbation of the empress Elizabeth.

Carlos, Wendy (née **Walter**), American organist, composer, and electronics virtuoso; b. Pawtucket, R.I., Nov. 14, 1939. He played piano as a child; he later studied with Ron Nelson at Brown Univ. (A.B., 1962) and with Luening, Ussachevsky, and Beeson at Columbia Univ. (M.A., 1965). In 1964 he began working with Robert Moog in perfecting the Moog Synthesizer. The result of their experiments with versified tone colors was a record album under the title *Switched-on Bach* (1968), which became unexpectedly successful, selling some million copies. This was followed in 1969 by *The Well-Tempered Synthesizer*, engineered entirely by Carlos, and, in 1992, by his *Switched-on Bach 2000*. At the age of 32, Carlos became aware of his sexual duality, and underwent a transsexual operation. On St. Valentine's Day, 1979, he officially changed his first name from Walter to Wendy. She/he described his sexual tergiversation in a candid interview in *Playboy* (May 1979). He composed the opera *Noah* (1964–65).

Carlson, Claudine, French-American mezzo-soprano; b. Mulhouse, Feb. 26, 1937. She studied in California and at the Manhattan School of Music in New York with Jennie Tourel and Esther Andreas; then embarked on a successful career as a concert singer. On April 18, 1968, she made her first appearance at the N.Y. City opera as Cornelia in *Giulio Cesare*. She made her Metropolitan Opera debut in New York as Geneviève in *Pelléas et Mélisande* on Oct. 11, 1977, and sang there again in 1981. Gifted with a voice of fine quality, she gained particular renown in the French repertoire.

Carlyle, Joan (Hildred), English soprano; b. Wirral, April 6, 1931. She studied in London, making her operatic debut as Frasquita at London's Covent Garden in 1955. She continued to sing there regularly until 1969 in such roles as Mimi, Nedda, Sophie, Arabella, Pamina, Desdemona, Britten's Titania, and Tippett's Jenifer; she also appeared at the Edinburgh Festival, the Glyndebourne Festival, the Vienna State Opera, the Bavarian State Opera in Munich, and the Teatro Colón in Buenos Aires.

Carner, Mosco, Austrian-born English writer on music and conductor; b. Vienna, Nov. 15, 1904; d. Cornwall, Aug. 3, 1985. He studied at the New Vienna Cons., and then musicology with Adler at the Univ. of Vienna (Ph.D., 1928, with the diss. *Studien zur Sonatenform bei Robert Schumann*). After conducting opera in Opava (1929–30) and Gdansk (1930–33), he emigrated to England and became a naturalized British subject. He devoted himself mainly to writing music criticism in London, and later was music critic of *Time and Tide* (1949–62) and the *Evening News* (1957–61). Among his publications are *Dvořák* (London, 1941), *Puccini: A Critical Biography* (London, 1958; 3d ed., rev., 1992), *Alban Berg: The Man and the Work* (London, 1975; 2d ed., rev., 1983), *Madama Butterfly* (London, 1979), and *Tosca* (Cambridge, 1985).

Carnicer (y Batlle), Ramón, Spanish conductor, teacher, and composer; b. Tárrega, near Lérida, Oct. 24, 1789; d. Madrid, March 17, 1855. He studied in Barcelona with Francisco Queralt and Carlos Baguer. From 1818 to 1820 conducted the Coliseo Theater orch. in Barcelona, and from 1828 to 1830 he was conductor of the Royal Opera in Madrid. From 1830 to 1854 was a prof. of composition at the Madrid Cons. One of the creators of Spanish national opera (the zarzuela), he composed 10 operas. He also composed *Dulce Patria*, the national hymn of Chile.

Caron, Rose (Lucille née **Meuniez)**, French soprano; b. Monerville, Nov. 17, 1857; d. Paris, April 9, 1930. She entered the Paris Cons. in 1880, leaving in 1882 to study with Marie Sasse in Brussels, where her debut was made as Alice in *Robert le Diable* (1883). She sang for 2 years at the Paris Opéra, and again in Brussels, creating Lorance (in *Jocelyn*), Richilde, and Salammbô (1890); in 1890 she returned to the Paris Opéra, where she sang Sieglinde (1893) and Desdemona (1894) in the first performances of *Die Walküre* and *Otello* in France; in 1898 she sang Fidelio at the Opéra Comique. From 1900 she appeared almost exclusively on the concert stage. In 1902 she was appointed a prof. of singing at the Paris Cons.

Carpenter, John Alden, important American composer; b. Park Ridge, Ill., Feb. 28, 1876; d. Chicago, April 26, 1951. He studied in Chicago with Amy Fay and W.C.E. Seeboeck, and then with J. K. Paine at Harvard Univ. (B.A., 1897). During a trip to Rome (1906), he had some lessons with Elgar, and then completed his training in Chicago with B. Ziehn (1908–12). He was employed in his father's shipping supply business, later serving as its vice-president (1909–36). In subsequent years, he devoted himself entirely to composition. In 1918 he was elected a member of the National Inst. of Arts and Letters, and received its Gold Medal in 1947. In 1942 he was elected a member of the American Academy of Arts and Leters. Carpenter gained success as a composer with his first orch. score, the humorous suite *Adventures in a Perambulator* (1914). Adopting mildly modernistic technques, he was notably successful in his works on American subjects with a tinge of ragtime and jazz elements. His "jazz pantomime" *Krazy Kat* (Chicago, Dec. 23, 1921; rev. 1940), after the well-known comic strip by George Herriman, proved an immediate success. It was followed by his *Skyscrapers* (1923–24; N.Y., Feb. 19, 1926), "a ballet of American life," which retains its historial interest as a period piece. His other stage works include *The Birthday of the Infanta*, ballet (1917; rev. version, Chicago, Dec. 23, 1919; suite, 1930, rev. 1940; concert suite, 1949) and incidental music.

BIBL.: T. Pierson, *The Life and Music of J. A. C.* (diss., Univ. of Rochester, 1952); J. O'Connor, *J. A. C.: Bio-Bibliography* (Westport, Conn., 1994).

Carr, Benjamin, English-American composer and publisher; b. London, Sept. 12, 1768; d. Philadelphia, May 24, 1831. He studied music with Samuel Arnold, Samuel Wesley, and Charles Wesley; established himself as a composer in London. He went to America in 1793; he settled in Philadelphia and established Carr's Musical Repository, one of the most important early American music stores and music publishing houses; the following year (1794) he opened branches in New York and Baltimore. He was cofounder in 1820 of the Musical Fund Soc. in Philadelphia. A versatile musician, he was proficient as a singer, pianist, and organist, and was an influential figure in early American musical life. His works include *Philander and Silvia*, pastoral piece (London, Oct. 16, 1792), and *The Archers, or Mountaineers of Switzerland*, ballad opera (N.Y., April 18, 1796). The N.Y. Public Library owns the only known copy of Carr's *Federal Overture* (Philadelphia, 1794), a medley of popular airs, including the first printing of *Yankee Doodle*.

BIBL.: C. Sprenkle, *The Life and Works of B. C.* (diss., Peabody Cons. of Music, 1970).

Carré, Albert, French opera impresario; b. Strasbourg, June 22, 1852; d. Paris, Dec. 12, 1938. He assumed the directorship of the theater at Nancy in 1884, and from 1885 to 1890 headed the Cercle at Aix-les-Bains. From 1898 to 1912 he was director of the Opéra Comique, succeeding Carvalho. His uncle was the librettist Michael Carre.

Carré, Marguerite (née **Marthe Giraud)**, French soprano; b. Cabourg, Aug. 16, 1880; d. Paris, Dec. 26, 1947. She studied at the Bordeaux Cons. and the Paris Cons. In 1899 she made her operatic debut as Mimi in Nantes; in 1901 she joined the Paris Opéra Comique, where she appeared in such roles as Manon, Mélisande, Louise, Madama Butterfly, and Pamina, and where she created roles in operas by Charpentier, Leroux, and Rabaud. In 1914 she married Albert Carré, director of the Opéra Comique; they divorced in 1924 but remarried upon her retirement in 1929.

Carreño, (Maria) Teresa, famous Venezuelan pianist; b. Caracas, Dec. 22, 1853; d. N.Y., June 12, 1917. As a child, she studied with her father, an excellent pianist; driven from home by a revolution, the family settled in New York in 1862, where she studied with Gottschalk. At the age of 8, she gave a public recital in New York (Nov. 25, 1862). She began her career in 1866, after studying with G. Mathias in Paris and A. Rubinstein. She lived mainly in Paris from 1866 to 1870; then in England. She developed a singing voice and made an unexpected appearance in opera in Edinburgh as the Queen in *Les Huguenots* (May 24, 1872) in a cast that included Tietjens, Brignoli, and Mario; was again in the U.S. in 1876, when she studied voice in Boston. For the Bolivar centenary celebration in Caracas (Oct. 29, 1885), she appeared as singer, pianist, and composer of the festival hymn, written at the request of the Venezuelan government; hence the frequent but erroneous attribution to Carreño of the national hymn of Venezuela, *Gloria al bravo pueblo* (the music of which was actually composed in 1811 by J. Landaeta, and officially adopted as the Venezuelan national anthem on May 25, 1881). In Caracas she once again demonstrated her versatility, when for the last 3 weeks of the season she conducted the opera company managed by her husband, **Giovanni Tagliapietra**. After these musical experiments, she resumed her career as a pianist; she made her German debut in Berlin, Nov. 18, 1889; in 1907 toured Australia. Her last appearance with an orch. was with the N.Y. Phil. (Dec. 8, 1916); her last recital appearance was in Havana (March 21, 1917). She was married 4 times: to **Émile Sauret** (June 1873), **Tagliapietra** (1876), **Eugène D'Albert** (1892–95), and Arturo Tagliapietra, a younger brother of Giovanni (June 30, 1902). She was greatly venerated in Venezuela; her mortal remains were solemnly transferred from New York, where she died, and reburied in Caracas, on Feb. 15, 1938.

BIBL.: M. Milinowski, *T. C.* (New Haven, 1940); A. Marquez Rodriguez, *Esbozo biográfico de T. C.* (Caracas, 1953); R. Marciano, *T. C.* (Kassel, 1990).

Carreras, José (Maria), celebrated Spanish tenor; b. Barcelona, Dec. 5, 1946. He studied with Jaime Puig at the Barcelona Cons. before completing his training with Juan Ruax. In 1970 he made his operatic debut as Flavio in *Norma* in Barcelona, and later that year appeared as Gennaro opposite Caballé's Lucrezia Borgia. In 1971 he won the Verdi Competition in Parma, where he made his Italian debut as Rodolfo. He also made his first appearance in London that year singing Leicester in a concert performance of *Maria Stuarda*. On March 15, 1972, he made his U.S. debut as Pinkerton at the N.Y. City Opera, where he remained on the roster until 1975. In 1973 he sang for the first time at the San Francisco Opera as Rodolfo. He made his Metropolitan Opera debut in New York on Nov. 18, 1974, as Cavaradossi, and subsequently returned there regularly. In 1975 he sang for the first time at Milan's La Scala as Riccardo. In 1976 he made his first appearances at the Salzburg Festival (as Don Carlos) and at the Chicago Lyric Opera (as Riccardo). In addition to his engagements with principal opera houses of the world, Carreras pursued a notably successful career as a concert artist. However, in 1987 he was stricken with acute lymphocytic leukemia. Following exhaustive medical treatment, he was able to resume his career in 1988 when he appeared at a special Barcelona outdoor concert before an audience of 150,000 admirers. That same year he founded the José Carreras Leukemia Foundation in Barcelona. In 1989 he appeared in recitals in Seattle and New York, and also returned to the operatic stage as Jason in Cherubini's *Medea* in Mérida, Spain. On Sept. 24, 1989, he created the title role in Balada's *Cristóbal Colón* in Barcelona. On July 7, 1990, he appeared in a spectacular concert with fellow tenors Plácido Domingo and Luciano Pavarotti in Rome, with Zubin Mehta conducting. The event was telecast live to the world and subsequently became a best-selling video and compact disc. The "three tenors" subsequently staged such extravaganzas throughout the world. In 1998 he sang Wolf-Ferrari's Sly in Zürich, a role he reprised at the Washington (D.C.) Opera in 1999 in his first U.S. stage appearance in 12 years. His autobiography was publ. as *Singen mit der Seele* (Munich, 1989; Eng. tr., 1991, as *Singing from the Soul*). The title aptly describes his approach not only to singing but to living the life of one of the world's favorite tenors.

BIBL.: J. Pérez Senz, *J. C. El placer de cantar: Un retrato autobiográfico* (Barcelona, 1988).

Carrillo (-Trujillo), Julián (Antonio), Mexican composer; b. Ahualulco, San Luis Potosí, Jan. 28, 1875; d. Mexico City, Sept. 9, 1965. He was of Indian extraction; lived mostly in Mexico City, where he studied violin with Pedro Manzano and composition with Melesio Morales. He graduated from the National Cons. in 1899 and received a government stipend for study abroad as a winner of the President Diaz Prize. He took courses at the Leipzig Cons. with Hans Becker (violin), Jadassohn (theory), and Hans Sitt (orchestration); he also played violin in the Gewandhaus Orch. under Nikisch. From 1902 to 1904 he studied at the Ghent Cons., winning 1st prize as violinist. He returned to Mexico in 1905 and made numerous appearances as a violinist; also conducted concerts; he was appointed general inspector of music and director of the National Cons. (1913–14; 1920–24). He visited the United States many times, and conducted his works in New York and elsewhere. During his years in Leipzig, he wrote a sym., which he conducted there in 1902; at the same time, he began experimenting with fractional tones and developed a theory which he named *Sonido 13*, symbolically indicating divisions beyond the 12 notes of the chromatic scale. He further devised a special number notation for quarter tones, eighth tones, and sixteenth tones, and constructed special instruments for their realization, such as a harpzither with 97 strings to the octave; he also publ. several books dealing with music of fractional tones, and ed. a monthly magazine, *El Sonido 13*, in 1924–25. He composed the operas *Ossian* (1903), *Matilda* (1909), and *Zultil* (1922). He authored *Julián Carrillo, Su vida y su obra* (Mexico City, 1945) and *Leyes de metamorfósis musicales* (Mexico City, 1949).

Carroli, Silvano, Italian baritone; b. Venice, Feb. 22, 1939. He trained at the opera school of the Teatro La Fenice in Venice and with Marcello and Mario del Monaco. After making his operatic debut as Schanuard in Venice in 1963, he sang in various Italian music centers. In 1972 he made his U.S. debut as Tonio in Dallas. As a member of Milan's La Scala company, he toured the United States in 1976 and Japan in 1981. In 1977 he made his debut at London's Covent Garden as Jack Rance, and returned there in later seasons. In 1978 he made his first appearance at the Chicago Lyric Opera. On Oct. 28, 1983, he made his Metropolitan Opera debut in New York as Don Carlo in *La forza del destino*. In 1984 he sang at the Paris Opéra. His guest engagements also took him to Vienna, Barcelona, Brussels, Munich, and Berlin. Carroli is especially associated with roles in Italian opera, but he also sings roles to fine effect in operas by Mozart and Wagner.

Carron (real name, **Cox**), **Arthur,** English tenor; b. Swindon, Dec. 12, 1900; d. there, May 10, 1967. He joined London's Old Vic Theatre in 1929; also sang in London at the Sadler's Wells Opera until 1935 and at Covent Garden (1931, 1939). In 1936 he went to the United States, where he won the Metropolitan Opera Auditions of the Air, and made his debut with the Metropolitan on May 29, 1936, as Canio in *Pagliacci*; he was chosen to sing the role of Nolan in the world premiere of Walter Damrosch's *The Man without a Country* on May 12, 1937; remained on the roster of the Metropolitan until 1946; he then returned to England, where he sang at Covent Garden until 1951. Among his other roles were Tristan, Tannhäuser, Siegmund, Otello, and Manrico.

Carte, Richard D'Oyly, English impresario; b. London, May 3, 1844; d. there, April 3, 1901. He studied at Univ. College in London. He wrote an opera, *Dr. Ambrosias*, and later turned to music management, representing, among others, Gounod, Adelina Patti, and the tenor Mario. He then became interested in light opera and introduced in England Lecocq's *Giroflé-Girofla*, Offenbach's *La Périchole*, and other popular French operettas. His greatest achievement was the launching of comic operas by Gilbert and Sullivan; he commissioned and produced at the Royalty Theatre their *Trial by Jury* (1875) and then formed a syndicate to stage other productions of their works at the London Opéra Comique Theatre. Dissension within the syndicate induced him to build the Savoy Theatre (1881), which subsequently became celebrated as the home of Gilbert and Sullivan productions, with Carte himself as the leading "Savoyard." He successfully operated the Savoy Theatre until his death; the enterprise was continued by his wife (Helen Lenoir) until her death in 1913; thereafter by his sons, and finally by his granddaughter; it was disbanded in 1982, but was revived in 1998. In 1887 Carte attempted to establish serious English opera through the building of a special theater (now known as the Palace Theatre), and the production in 1891 of Sullivan's grand opera *Ivanhoe*, followed by commissions to other English composers to write operas. D'Oyly Carte introduced many improvements in theatrical management, including the replacement of gaslight by electric illumination.

BIBL.: F. Cellier and C. Bridgeman, *Gilbert, Sullivan and d'O. C.* (London, 1914).

Carter, Elliott (Cook, Jr.), outstanding American composer and teacher; b. N.Y., Dec. 11, 1908. Carter entered Harvard Univ., majoring in literature and languages; at the same time, he studied piano at the Longy School of Music in Cambridge, Mass. In 1930 he devoted himself exclusively to music at Harvard, taking up harmony and counterpoint with Piston, and orchestration with Hill; he also attended in 1932 a course given there by Holst. He obtained his M.A. in 1932, and then went to Paris, where he studied with Boulanger and at the École Normale de Musique, receiving a *licence de contrepoint*; in the interim, he learned mathematics, Latin, and Greek. In 1935 he returned to America; he was music director of the Ballet Caravan (1937–39); he gave courses in music and also in mathematics, physics, and classical Greek at St. John's College in Annapolis, Md. (1940–44); he then taught at the Peabody Cons. of Music in Baltimore (1946–48). He was on the faculty of Columbia Univ. (1948–50), Queens College of the City Univ. of N.Y. (1955–56), and Yale Univ. (1960–62). In 1963 he was composer-in-residence at the American Academy in Rome, and in 1964 held a similar post in West Berlin. In 1967–68 he was a prof.-at-large at Cornell Univ. He held Guggenheim fellowships in 1945–46 and 1950–51, and the American Prix de Rome in 1953. In 1965 he received the Creative Arts Award from Brandeis Univ. In 1953 he received 1st prize in the Concours International de Composition pour Quatuor a Cordes in Liège for his 1st String Quartet; in 1960 he received the Pulitzer Prize in Music for his 2d String Quartet, which also received the N.Y. Music Critics Circle Award and was further elected as the most important work of the year by the International Rostrum of Composers. He again won the Pulitzer Prize in music, for his 3d String Quartet, in 1973. In 1985 he was awarded the National Medal of Arts by President Ronald Reagan. In 1987 he was made a Commandeur dans l'Ordre des Arts des Lettres of France. In 1991 he was named a Commendatore of the Order of Merit in Italy. In 1998 he won the Prince Pierre Foundation Music Award of Monaco.

The evolution of Carter's compositional style is marked by his constant preoccupation with taxonomic considerations. His early works are set in a neoclassical style. He later absorbed the Schoenbergian method of composition with 12 equal tones. Finally he developed a system of serial organization in which all parameters, including intervals, metric divisions, rhythm, counterpoint, harmony, and instrumental timbres, become parts of the total conception of each individual work. In this connection, he introduced the term "metric modulation," in which secondary rhythms in a polyrhythmic section assume dominance expressed in constantly changing meters, often in such unusual time signatures as $\frac{10}{16}$, $\frac{21}{8}$, etc. Furthermore, he assigns to each participating instrument in a polyphonic work a special interval, a distinctive rhythmic figure, and a selective register, so that the individuality of each part is clearly outlined, a distribution which is often reinforced by placing the players at a specified distance from one another.

While not well known for his dramatic works, Carter composed the opera *Tom and Lily* (1934; withdrawn), the ballets *Pocahontas* (Keene, N.H., Aug. 17, 1936; withdrawn; orch. version, 1938–39; N.Y., May 24, 1939) and *The Minotaur* (N.Y., March 26, 1947), and incidental music to Sophocles's *Philoctetes* (1931; Cambridge, Mass., March 15, 1933), Plautus's *Mostellaria* (Cambridge, Mass., April 15, 1936), and Shakespeare's *Much Ado About Nothing* (1937; withdrawn).

BIBL.: E. and K. Stone, eds., *The Writings of E. C.: An American Composer Looks at Modern Music* (N.Y., 1977); D. Schiff, *The Music of E. C.* (N.Y., 1983); C. Rosen, *The Musical Languages of E. C.* (Washington, D.C., 1984); D. Harvey, *The Later Music of E. C.: A Study in Music Theory and Analysis* (N.Y., 1989); A. Edwards, C. Rosen, and H. Holliger, *Entretiens avec E. C.* (Geneva, 1992).

Caruso, Enrico (Errico), great Italian tenor; b. Naples, Feb. 25, 1873; d. there, Aug. 2, 1921. While attending the Scuola sociale e serale in Naples, he received some training in oratorio and choral singing. By the age of 11 he was serving as principal soloist in its choir. He also received lessons from Amelia Tibaldi Nicola. In 1891 he began vocal training with Guglielmo Vergine, who remained a mentor until 1895. In 1894 he was engaged to sing in *Mignon* at the Teatro Mercadante in Naples, but at the piano rehearsal he proved a dismal failure at sight-reading and was dismissed. Caruso finally made his operatic debut at the Teatro Nuovo in Naples in Mario Morelli's *L'Amico Francesco* on March 15, 1895. He then sang Turiddu and Faust in Caserta, and subsequently Faust, the Duke of Mantua, and Alfredo at the Teatro Bellini in Naples. After successful appearances in Cairo as Edgardo, Enzo Grimaldo, and Puccini's Des Grieux, he returned to Naples to sing Bellini's Tebaldo at the Teatro Mercadente. While engaged in Salerno (1896–97), he received vocal coaching from the conductor Vincenzo Lombardi. On May 29, 1897, he scored a fine success as Enzo Grimaldo at the opening of the Teatro Massimo in Palermo. He then won accolades as Rodolfo at the Teatro Goldoni in Livorno on Aug. 14, 1897. During the 1897–98 season, he sang at the Teatro Lirico in Naples with increasing success. The decisive turning point in his career came at that theater on Nov. 17, 1898, when he created the role of Loris in Giordano's *Fedora*. On Jan. 27, 1899, he made his first appearance in St. Petersburg as Alfredo, where he sang until 1900. He sang Loris at his debut in Buenos Aires on May 14, 1899, and continued to appear there until 1901, returning again in 1915 and 1917. On March 6, 1900, he made his first appearance in Moscow at a concert at the Bolshoi Theater, and then made his stage debut there as Radames on March 11. Caruso first sang at La Scala in Milan on Dec. 26, 1900, as Rodolfo. After appearing in the premiere of Mascagni's *Le Maschere* there on Jan. 17, 1901, he scored an enormous success there as Nemorino on Feb. 17. On March 11, 1902, he sang in the premiere of Franchetti's *Germania* there. His La Scala success prompted the Gramophone & Typewriter Co. of England to make a series of recordings of him in Milan in 1902–03. Caruso's fame was greatly enhanced through these and other recordings, especially those made with the Victor Talking Machine Co. of the United States between 1904 and 1920. On May 14, 1902, he made a notable British debut as the Duke of Mantua at Covent Garden in London. He appeared there again from 1904 to 1907, and in 1913–14. On Nov. 6, 1902, he sang in the premiere of Cilea's *Adriana Lecouvreur* at the Teatro Lirico in Milan. Caruso made an auspicious U.S. debut as the Duke of Mantua at the Metropolitan Opera in New York on Nov. 23, 1903. For the rest of his career, he remained a stellar artist on its roster, appearing not only with the company in New York but widely on tour. In his 18 seasons with the company, he sang 39 roles in 862 performances.

In addition to the Italian repertoire, Caruso won great success in such French roles as Massenet's Des Grieux, Saint-Saëns's Samson, Bizet's Don José, and Meyerbeer's Raoul. He also created the role of Ramerrez in Puccini's *La Fanciulla del West* on Dec. 10, 1910. Caruso chose his famous portrayal of the Duke of Mantua for his debut appearances at the Dresden Court Opera (May 8, 1904), the Vienna Court Opera (Oct. 6, 1906), and the Berlin Royal Opera (Oct. 23, 1907). His success in Vienna led Emperor Franz Joseph I to make him an Austrian Kammersänger in 1906, and he returned there to sing in 1907 and again from 1911 to 1913. He also continued to appear at the Berlin Royal Opera until 1909. In 1910 Kaiser Wilhelm II made him a German Kammersänger. From 1911 to 1913 he again sang at the Berlin Royal Opera. With the outbreak of World War I in 1914, Caruso concentrated his career mainly on the Metropolitan Opera, where he had become an idolized figure. He also made various appearances as a concert artist. On Dec. 11, 1920, while singing Nemorino at the Brooklyn Academy of Music, he was stricken with a throat hemorrhage. He managed to sing through the 1st act, but the remainder of the performance had to be canceled. Although in great physical distress, he insisted on meeting his contractual obligation to sing Eléazar at the Metropolitan on Christmas Eve, 1920. This was his last public appearance. A severe pleurisy necessitated several debilitating surgeries. On May 28, 1921, he set sail to his beloved Italy, where he died 8 weeks later.

Caruso was richly blessed with a voice of extraordinary beauty and refinement, with unsurpassed breath control and impeccable intonation. Following surgery to remove a node from his vocal cords in 1909, his voice took on the darker characteristics of the baritone range. Caruso's earnings were astounding in his day. During his highest paid season at the Metropolitan (1907–08), he received $140,000. His concert fees were most lucrative, and eventually reached $15,000 per appearance. His recordings likewise became a gold mine. For his last contract with the Victor Talking Machine Co. in 1919, he was guaranteed an annual payment of $100,000 per year, in addition to royalties. In spite of his great wealth, however, he never lost his common touch and gave generously to various causes. And as much as he loved to sing, he loved life even more. Unfortunately, his private life was wracked by numerous ill-fated love affairs, several of which led to unsavory court proceedings and widespread press coverage and gossip. In 1897 he became intimate with the soprano (Vittoria Matilde) Ada Giachetti (b. Florence, Dec. 1, 1874; d. Rio de Janeiro, Oct. 16, 1946), the wife of the wealthy manufacturer Gino Botti. Their liaison produced 2 sons, the younger of whom, Enrico (Roberto Giovanni) Caruso Jr. (b. Castello, near Florence, Sept. 7, 1904; d. Jacksonville, Fla., April 9, 1987), had a brief career as a tenor and actor. Caruso was also attracted to Ada's younger sister, the soprano Rina Giachetti, with whom he became intimate in 1906. It was also in 1906 that he was accused of making improper advances to a woman at N.Y.'s Central Park Zoo, which became known as the "monkey-house incident." Although Caruso pleaded not guilty and had a corroborating eyewitness, he was found guilty as charged and fined $10. He lost on appeal and paid the fine in 1907. In 1908 Ada deserted him for the family chauffeur. The bitter conflict that ensued between them culminated in a rancorous court battle in Milan in 1912. Caruso found solace in Rina, then in Dorothy Park Benjamin, whom he married in New York on Aug. 20, 1918. Caruso's colorful life was the subject of the fictionalized film biography *The Great Caruso* (1951), starring Mario Lanza. On Feb. 27, 1987, the U.S. Postal Service issued a commemorative stamp in his honor, with appropriate ceremonies at the Metropolitan Opera in New York, attended by his son Enrico Caruso Jr.

BIBL.: S. Fucito and B. Beyer, *C. and the Art of Singing* (N.Y., 1922); P. Key, *E. C.: A Biography* (Boston, 1922); D. Caruso and T. Goddard, *Wings of Song: The Story of C.* (N.Y., 1928; British ed., 1928, as *Wings of Song: An Authentic Life Story of E. C.*); N. Daspuro, *E. C.* (Milan, 1938); P. Suardon, *E. C.* (Milan, 1938); D. Caruso, *E. C.: His Life and Death* (N.Y., 1945); H. Steen, *C.: Eine Stimme erobert die Welt* (Essen-Steele, 1946); E. Gara, *C.: Storia di un emigrante* (Milan, 1947); T. Ybarra, *C.: The Man of Naples and the Voice of Gold* (N.Y., 1953); J.-P. Mouchon, *E. C., 1873–1921, sa vie et sa voix: Étude psycho-physiologique, physique, phonétique et esthétique* (Langres, 1966; Eng. tr., 1974); S. Jackson, *C.* (N.Y., 1972); H. Greenfield, *C.* (N.Y., 1983); M. Scott, *The Great C.* (N.Y., 1988); E. Caruso, Jr. and A. Farkas, *E. C.: My Father and My Family* (Portland, Oreg., 1990); S. Fucito, *C. and the Art of Singing* (Mineola, N.Y., 1995).

Caruso, Luigi, Italian composer; b. Naples, Sept. 25, 1754; d. Perugia, 1822. He was a student of his father, a church musician, and of Sala. He was maestro di cappella in Cingoli (1790–96?), Fabriano (1796?–98), Perugia (1798–1808), Urbino (1808–10), and again in Perugia (from 1810), where he also was director of the music school. His large output included over 60 operas, as well as oratorios.

Carvalho, Caroline (née **Caroline-Marie Félix-Miolan**), French soprano; b. Puys, Seine-Inférieure, Dec. 31, 1827; d. near Dieppe, July 10, 1895. She entered the Paris Cons. at 12; studied under Duprez. She made her operatic debut on Dec. 14, 1849, in *Lucia di Lammermoor* at the Opéra Comique, where she was engaged from 1849 to 1855; from 1856 to 1867 she sang at the Théâtre-Lyrique, where she created the soprano parts in Gounod's *Faust*, *Roméo et Juliette*, and *Mireille*, and in Clapisson's *La Fanchonette*. From 1868 to 1885 she sang at the Paris Opéra and at the Opéra Comique; she also appeared in London, Berlin, Brussels, St. Petersburg, etc. She retired in 1885. In 1853 she married **Léon Carvalho**.

BIBL.: E. Accoyer-Spoll, *Mme. C.* (Paris, 1885).

Carvalho, Eleazar de, Brazilian conductor and composer; b. Iguatú, July 28, 1912; d. São Paulo, Sept. 15, 1996. His father was of Dutch extraction and his mother was part Indian. He studied in Fortaleza at the Apprentice Seaman's School; later joined the National Naval Corps in Rio de Janeiro and played tuba in the band. In 1941 he became assistant conductor of the Brazilian Sym. Orch. in Rio de Janeiro. In 1946 he went to the United States to study conducting with Koussevitzky at the Berkshire Music Center in Tanglewood, and Koussevitzky invited him to conduct a pair of concerts with the Boston Sym. Orch. Carvalho demonstrated extraordinary ability and musicianship by leading all rehearsals and the concerts without score in a difficult program; his sense of perfect pitch was exceptional. He subsequently conducted a number of guest engagements with orchs. in America and in Europe. From 1963 to 1968 he was music director of the St. Louis Sym. Orch.; during his tenure, he introduced many modern works into his programs, much to the discomfiture of the financial backers of the orch. From 1969 to 1973 he was conductor of the Hofstra Univ. Orch. in Hempstead, N.Y., which offered him a more liberal aesthetic climate; then returned to Brazil, where he became artistic director of the São Paulo State Sym. Orch. He married the Brazilian composer and pianist of French and Portuguese descent Jocy de Oliveira (b. Curitiba-Parana, April 11, 1936). He composed the operas *Descuberta do Brasil* (Rio de Janeiro, June 19, 1939) and *Tiradentes* (Rio de Janeiro, Sept. 7, 1941).

Carvalho, João de Sousa, eminent Portuguese pedagogue and composer; b. Estremoz, Feb. 22, 1745; d. Alentejo, 1798. He studied at the Colégio dos Santos Reis in Vila Viçosa and with Cotumacci at the Cons. di S. Onofrio in Naples, then settled in Lisbon, where he became a member of the Brotherhood of St. Cecilia and prof. of counterpoint (1767), mestre (1769–73), and mestre de capela (1773–98) at the Seminario Patriarcal. He was the most gifted Portuguese composer of his day, excelling in both sacred and secular vocal music. In 1778 he became music teacher to the royal family.

WORKS: OPERAS: (all 1st perf. in Lisbon unless otherwise given): *La Nitteti* (Rome, Carnival 1766; not extant); *L'amore industrioso* (1769); *L'Eumene* (June 6, 1773); *L'Angelica* (July 25, 1778); *Perseo* (July 5, 1779); *Testoride argonauta* (July 5, 1780); *Seleuco rè di Siria* (July 5, 1781); *Everardo II rè di Lituania* (July 5, 1782); *Penelope nella partenza da Sparta* (Dec. 17, 1782); *Tomiri amazzone guerriéra* (Dec. 17, 1783); *L'Endimione* (July 25, 1783); *Adrasto rè degli Argivi* (July 5, 1784); *Nettuno ed Eglé* (April 25?, 1785); *Alcione* (July 25, 1787); *Numa Pompilio II rè dei romani* (June 24, 1789).

Carvalho (real name, **Carvaille**), **Léon,** distinguished French baritone and opera manager; b. Port-Louis, near Paris, Jan. 18, 1825; d. Paris, Dec. 29, 1897. He studied at the Paris Cons. He began his career as a singer; in 1853 he married the French soprano **Caroline Carvalho**. From 1856 to 1868 he was director of the Théâtre-Lyrique, and from 1869 to 1875 chief producer at the Paris Opéra; concurrently was manager of the Théâtre du Vaudeville (1872–74). He then acted as stage manager at the Opéra, and from 1876 to 1887 was director of the Opéra Comique, succeeding du Locle. After the fire at the Opéra Comique in 1887, in which 131 persons perished, he was arrested and sentenced to 6 months' imprisonment, but was acquitted on appeal, and reinstated in 1891. He had the reputation of an enlightened administrator, encouraging young artists and young composers.

Cary, Annie Louise, notable American contralto; b. Wayne, Maine, Oct. 22, 1841; d. Norwalk, Conn., April 3, 1921. She was a pupil of J. Q. Wetherbee and Lyman Wheeler in Boston, and of Giovanni Corsi in Milan. In 1867 she made her operatic debut as Azucena in Copenhagen. After additional training from Viardot-García in Baden-Baden, she sang in Hamburg, Stockholm, Brussels, and London. On Sept. 19, 1870, she made her U.S. debut in a N.Y. recital. She sang Amneris in the U.S. premiere of *Aida* at the N.Y. Academy of Music on Nov. 28, 1873. Following a tour of Europe (1875–77), she returned to the United States and became the first American woman to sing a Wagnerian role when she appeared as Ortrud in 1877. After singing with Clara Louise Kellog's opera company, she was a member of J. H. Mapleson's company (1880–82). She also made various appearances as a concert and oratorio singer in the United States.

Casabona, Francisco, Brazilian composer and pedagogue; b. São Paulo, Oct. 16, 1894; d. there, May 24, 1979. He studied in Brazil; he then attended classes of Alessandro Longo (piano), Camillo de Nardis (theory), and Giovanni Barbieri (composition) at the Naples Cons. Returning to Brazil, he became a prof. at the São Paulo Cons. In his music, Casabona followed an Italianate expressive style, excelling equally in vocal and instrumental works. His catalog of works includes 2 comic operas: *Godiamo la Vita* (Rome, 1917) and *Principessa dell'Atelier* (Naples, 1918).

Casadesus, François Louis, French conductor and composer; b. Paris, Dec. 2, 1870; d. there, June 27, 1954. His brothers were the French violinist Henri Casadesus (b. Paris, Sept. 30, 1879; d. there, May 31, 1947) and the French violinist and composer Marius Casadesus (b. Paris, Oct. 24, 1892; d. there, Oct. 13, 1981). He studied at the Paris Cons. He conducted the Opéra and the Opéra Comique of Paris on tour in France (1890–92); in 1895 he conducted the Opéra on a European tour; he was the founder and director (1918–22) of the American Cons. at Fontainebleau; later he was active as a radio conductor and wrote music criticism. A collection of valedictory articles was publ. in honor of his 80th birthday (Paris, 1950). He composed 4 operas: *Cachaprès* (Brussels, 1914), *La Chanson de Paris* (1924), *Bertran de Born* (Monte Carlo, 1925), and *Messie d'Amour* (Monte Carlo, 1928).

Casadesus, Jean-Claude, French conductor; b. Paris, Dec. 7, 1935. He was the nephew of the eminent French pianist and composer Robert (Marcel) Casadesus (b. Paris, April 7, 1899; d. there, Sept. 19, 1972) and the French pianist and teacher Gaby Casadesus (née Gabrielle L'Hôte; b. Marseilles, Aug. 9, 1901). He studied at the Paris Cons.; in 1959 he received the premier prix as a percussion player there; he was then engaged as timpanist of the Concerts Colonne (until 1968) and of the Domaine Musical in Paris; also studied conducting with Dervaux at the École Normale de Musique in Paris (premier prix, 1965) and with Boulez in Basel. In 1969 he became resident conductor of the Opéra and of the Opéra Comique in Paris. In 1971 he became assistant conductor to Dervaux with the Orchestre Philharmonique des Pays de la Loire in Angers. In 1976 he founded the Lille Phil.; also appeared as a guest conductor with various orchs. and opera houses in

Europe. He was made an officer of the National Order of Merit for his services to French culture.

Casanova, André, French composer; b. Paris, Oct. 12, 1919. He studied with Paul Baumgartner (piano) and Leibowitz (composition) in Paris. In 1960 he was the winner of the Queen Marie-José composition competition. In 1977 he received the Prix de la Fondation des Éditions Durand. His music generally followed along neo-Classical lines, with some atonal deviations. His dramatic works include *Le Livre de la Foi jurée*, lyric piece (1964), *La Clé d'argent*, lyric drama (1965), *Le Bonheur dans le crime*, lyric drama (1969), and *La Coupe d'or*, opera (1970).

Casavola, Franco, Italian composer; b. Modugno, July 13, 1891; d. Bari, July 7, 1955. He studied in Rome with Respighi; abandoning his academic pursuits, he joined the Futurist movement, and composed music glorifying the mechanical age; he also wrote futurist poetry. At a later period, he veered toward musical realism with Romantic overtones. He wrote the operas *Il gobbo del califfo* (Rome, May 4, 1929), *Astuzie d'amore* (Bari, Jan. 28, 1936), and *Salammbô* (1948), and the ballets *L'alba di Don Giovanni* (1932) and *Il castello nel bosco* (1931).

Casazza, Elvira, Italian mezzo-soprano; b. Ferrara, Nov. 15, 1887; d. Milan, Jan. 24, 1965. She studied in Ferrara and Milan; made her debut in Varese in 1909; then sang at La Scala in Milan (1915–42); she also sang at Covent Garden, London (1926, 1931). After her retirement in 1948, she taught voice in Rome and then in Pesaro. Her most noted role was Mistress Quickly.

Casella, Alfredo, outstanding Italian composer and teacher; b. Turin, July 25, 1883; d. Rome, March 5, 1947. He began to play the piano at the age of 4 and received his early instruction from his mother; in 1896 he went to Paris, and studied with Diémer and Fauré at the Cons.; he won the premier prix in piano in 1899. He made concert tours as a pianist in Europe; appeared as a guest conductor with European orchs.; he taught piano classes at the Paris Cons. from 1912 to 1915; returned to Rome and was appointed a prof. of piano at the Accademia di Santa Cecilia. In 1917 he founded the Società Nazionale di Musica (later the Società Italiana di Musica Moderna; from 1923 the Corporazione delle Musiche Nuove, Italian section of the ISCM). On Oct. 28, 1921, Casella made his American debut with the Philadelphia Orch. in the triple capacity of composer, conductor, and piano soloist; he also appeared as a guest conductor in Chicago, Detroit, Cincinnati, Cleveland, and Los Angeles; was conductor of the Boston Pops from 1927 to 1929, introducing a number of modern works, but failing to please the public. In 1928 he was awarded the 1st prize of $3,000 from the Musical Fund Soc. in Philadelphia; in 1934 he won the Coolidge Prize. In 1938 he returned to Italy. Apart from his activities as pianist, conductor, teacher, and composer, Casella was a prolific writer on music, and contributed numerous articles to various publications in Italy, France, Russia, Germany, and America; he possessed an enlightened cosmopolitan mind, which enabled him to penetrate the musical cultures of various nations; at the same time, he steadfastly proclaimed his adherence to the ideals of Italian art. In his music he applied modernistic techniques to earlier forms; his style may be termed neo-Classical, but in his early years he cultivated extreme modernism.

WORKS: DRAMATIC: OPERAS: *La donna serpente* (Rome, March 17, 1932); *La favola d'Orfeo* (Venice, Sept. 6, 1932); *Il deserto tentato* (Florence, May 6, 1937). BALLETS: *Il convento veneziano* (1912; Milan, Feb. 7, 1925); *La Giara*, "choreographic comedy" (Paris, Nov. 19, 1924); *La camera dei disegni*, for children (Rome, 1940); La rosa del sogno (Rome, 1943).

WRITINGS: *L'evoluzione della musica* (publ. in Italian, French, and Eng. in parallel columns; 1919); *Igor Stravinsky* (1926; new ed., 1951); *"21 & 26"* (1931); *Il pianoforte* (1938); *I segreti della Giara* (1941; Eng. tr., 1955, as *Music in My Time: The Memoirs of Alfredo Casella*); *La tecnica dell'orchestra contemporanea* (completed by V. Mortari; 1950).

BIBL.: L. Cortese, *A. C.* (Genoa, 1935); F. d'Amico & G. Gatti, eds., *A. C.* (Milan, 1958).

Casken, John (Arthur), English composer and teacher; b. Barnsley, Yorkshire, July 15, 1949. He was a student of Joubert and Dickinson at the Univ. of Birmingham (1967–71), and then pursued training in Warsaw with Dobrowolski and Lutoslawski (1971–73). He subsequently lectured at the Univ. of Birmingham (1973–79), the Huddersfield Polytechnic (1979–81), and Univ. of Durham (1981–92); he then was prof. of music at the Univ. of Manchester (from 1992). His early works were influenced by Lutoslawski but he later tended toward eclecticism. He composed a chamber opera, *Golem* (1986–88; London, June 28, 1989).

Cassel, (John) Walter, American baritone and teacher; b. Council Bluffs, Iowa, May 15, 1910. He studied voice with Harry Cooper in Council Bluffs, where he also received training in trumpet and piano; after attending Creighton Univ. in Omaha, he pursued vocal studies with Frank La Forge in New York. In 1938 he began singing on radio shows, and on Dec. 12, 1942, made his Metropolitan Opera debut in New York as Brétigny in *Manon*, remaining on its roster until 1945, and then again from 1954 to 1970 and in 1973–74. On March 21, 1948, he made his first appearance at the N.Y. City Opera as Escamillo, singing there regularly until 1954, and then intermittently until 1969. He taught at Indiana Univ. in Bloomington (from 1974). While he proved equally at home in both serious and light roles, he was best known for his roles in operas by Wagner and R. Strauss. He sang the role of Horace Tabor in the first performance of Douglas Moore's *The Ballad of Baby Doe* (1956).

Cassilly, Richard, American tenor; b. Washington, D.C., Dec. 14, 1927; d. Boston, Jan. 30, 1998. He studied at the Peabody Cons. of Music in Baltimore. After singing Michele in Menotti's *The Saint of Bleecker Street* in New York (1955), he made his N.Y. City Opera debut as Vakula in Tchaikovsky's *The Golden Slippers* (Oct. 13, 1955); was on its roster until 1959, and again from 1960 to 1963 and from 1964 to 1966. He made his European debut in Sutermeister's *Raskolnikoff* in Geneva (1965) and that same year sang at the Hamburg State Opera, where he appeared regularly (1966–77). He was concurrently a member of London's Covent Garden (1968–78) and also sang in major European opera centers. He made his Metropolitan Opera debut in New York as Radames on Jan. 20, 1973. He resumed his association with the Metropolitan Opera in 1978, and subsequently appeared there in such roles as Tannhäuser, Don José, Tristan, Samson, Otello, Jimmy Mahoney in *Mahagonny*, and Captain Vere in *Billy Budd*. From 1986 he was prof. of voice at Boston Univ.

Castagna, Bruna, Italian mezzo-soprano; b. Bari, Oct. 15, 1905; d. Pinamar, Argentina, July 10, 1983. She was a student of Scognamiglio in Milan. In 1925 she made her operatic debut as the Nurse in *Boris Godunov* in Mantua; that same year she made her first appearance at Milan's La Scala as Suzuki, and then sang there until 1928 and again from 1932 to 1934; she also appeared at the Teatro Colón in Buenos Aires (1927–30). On March 2, 1936, she made her Metropolitan Opera debut in New York as Amneris, remaining there until 1940, and then returning in 1943 and 1945. She eventually settled in Argentina. In addition to her roles in Verdi's operas, she became well known for her portrayals of Carmen, Adalgisa, Santuzza, and Dalila.

Castelmary, Armand (real name, **Comte Armand de Castan**), French bass; b. Toulouse, Aug. 16, 1834; d. on the stage of the Metropolitan Opera just after Act 1 of *Martha* in New York, Feb. 10, 1897. He was a member of the Paris Opéra (1863–70), where he created the roles of Don Diego in *L'Africaine* (April 28, 1865), the Grand Inquisitor in *Don Carlos* (March 11, 1867), and Hamlet in Thomas's opera (March 9, 1868). In 1870 he made his U.S. debut in New Orleans. From 1889 to 1896 he sang at London's Covent Garden. On Nov. 29, 1893, he made his Metropolitan Opera debut in New York as Vulcan in *Philémon et Baucis*, remaining on its roster until his death. He was particularly esteemed for his portrayal of Méphistophélès in the operas by Gounod and Boito. From 1864 to 1867 he was married to **Marie Sass**.

Castelnuovo-Tedesco, Mario, greatly significant Italian-born American composer; b. Florence, April 3, 1895; d. Los Angeles, March 16, 1968. He studied piano with Edoardo del Valle, and then continued his training at the Florence Cons., where he took diplomas in piano (1910) and in composition in Pizzetti's class (1913). He attained considerable eminence in Italy between the 2 world wars, and his music was often heard at European festivals. Political events forced him to leave Italy; in 1939 he settled in the United States and in 1946 he became a naturalized American citizen. He became active as a composer for films in Hollywood, but continued to write large amounts of orch. and chamber music. His style is remarkably fluent and adaptable, often reaching rhapsodic eloquence.

WORKS: DRAMATIC: *La mandragola*, opera (Venice, May 4, 1926); *The Princess and the Pea*, overture with Narrator (1943); *Bacco in Toscana*, dithyramb for Voices and Orch. (Milan, May 8, 1931); *Aucassin et Nicolette*, puppet show with Voices and Instruments (1938; Florence, June 2, 1952); *All's Well That Ends Well*, opera (1959); *Saul*, biblical opera (1960); *Il Mercante di Venezia*, opera (Florence, May 25, 1961); *The Importance of Being Earnest*, chamber opera (1962); *The Song of Songs*, scenic oratorio (Hollywood, Aug. 7, 1963); *Tobias and the Angel*, scenic oratorio (1965).

BIBL.: N. Rossi, *Complete Catalogue of Works by M. C.-T.* (N.Y., 1977); B. Scalin, *Operas by M. C.-T.* (diss., Northwestern Univ., 1980).

Castiglioni, Niccolò, Italian composer and teacher; b. Milan, July 17, 1932; d. there, Sept. 6, 1996. He took courses in piano and composition at the Milan Cons., and also was a student at the Salzburg Mozarteum; from 1958 to 1965 he was active at the summer courses in new music in Darmstadt. In 1966–67 he was composer-in-residence at the Center for the Creative and Performing Arts at the State Univ. of N.Y. in Buffalo, and then taught composition at the univs. of Michigan (1967), Washington in Seattle (1968–69), and California at San Diego (1970). In 1970 he returned to Italy. After teaching in Trento (1976–78), he joined the faculty of the Milan Cons. (1978). His music was pragmatically modernistic, making use of a vast panorama of styles, ranging from neoclassical to post-Webern and beyond.

WORKS: DRAMATIC: OPERAS: *Uomini e no* (1955); *Attraverso lo specchio* (RAI, Oct. 1, 1961) *Jabberwocky*, chamber opera (1962); *Sweet* (1968); *3 Mystery Plays*, opera triptych (Rome, Oct. 2, 1968); *Oberon, the Fairy Prince* (1980; Venice, Oct. 10, 1981); *The Lord's Masque* (1980; Venice, Oct. 10, 1981). BALLETS: *Inverno in-ver* (1973; rev. version, Palermo, Feb. 3, 1978); *Beth-Daleth* (Florence, May 21, 1980).

BIBL.: R. Cresti, *Linguaggio musicale di N. C.* (Milan, 1991).

Castro, José María, Argentine cellist, conductor, and composer, brother of **Juan José Castro**; b. Avellaneda, near Buenos Aires, Dec. 15, 1892; d. Buenos Aires, Aug. 2, 1964. He studied cello and composition in Buenos Aires. From 1913 he played in orchs. and chamber music ensembles, and later was solo cellist in the Orquesta Filharmónica of the Asociación del Profesorado Orquestal (1922–27). He was titular conductor of the Orquesta Filarmónica in Buenos Aires (1930–42), and also conducted the municipal band there (1933–53). He composed the monodrama *La otra voz* (1953; Buenos Aires, Sept. 24, 1954) and the ballets *Georgia* (1937; Buenos Aires, June 2, 1939), *El sueño de la botella* (1948), and *Falarka* (La Plata, Oct. 27, 1951). Another brother, Washington Castro (b. Buenos Aires, July 13, 1909), is also a conductor, teacher, and composer.

Castro, Juan José, eminent Argentine composer and conductor, brother of **José Maria Castro**; b. Avellaneda, near Buenos Aires, March 7, 1895; d. Buenos Aires, Sept. 3, 1968. After study in Buenos Aires, he went to Paris, where he took a course in composition with d'Indy. Returning to Argentina in 1929, he organized in Buenos Aires the Orquesta de Nacimiento, which he conducted; in 1930 he conducted the ballet season at the Teatro Colón; he conducted opera there from 1933; also became music director of the Asociación del Profesorado Orquestal and Asociación Sinfónica, with which he gave first local performances of a number of modern works. In 1934 he received a Guggenheim Foundation grant. From 1947 to 1951 he conducted in Cuba and Uruguay; from 1952 to 1953 he was principal conductor of the Victorian Sym. Orch. in Melbourne, Australia; from 1956 to 1960 he was conductor of the Orquesta Sinfónica Nacional in Buenos Aires; from 1959 to 1964 he was director of the Puerto Rico Cons. in San Juan. Castro was proficient in all genres of composition, but his works were rarely performed outside South America, and he himself conducted most of his symphonic compositions. His most notable success outside his homeland came when he won the prize for the best opera in a La Scala competition in Milan with his *Prosperpino e lo straniero* (in Spanish as *Prosperpina y el extranjero*) in 1952. He composed the operas *La Zapatera prodigiosa* (Montevideo, Dec. 23, 1949), *Prosperpina e lo straniero* (Milan, March 17, 1952), *Bodas de sangre* (Buenos Aires, Aug. 9, 1956), and *Cosecha negra* (1961) and the ballets *Mekhano* (Buenos Aires, July 17, 1937) and *Offenbachiana* (Buenos Aires, May 25, 1940). Another brother, Washington Castro (b. Buenos Aires, July 13, 1909), is also a conductor, teacher, and composer.

BIBL.: R. Arizaga, *J. J. C.* (Buenos Aires, 1963).

Catalani, Alfredo, greatly talented Italian composer; b. Lucca, June 19, 1854; d. Milan, Aug. 7, 1893. He studied music with his father, a church organist, and in 1872 with Fortunato Magi and Bazzini at the Istituto Musicale Pacini in Lucca. He then went to Paris, where he attended classes of Bazin (composition) and Marmontel (piano). He returned to Italy in 1873. In 1886 he became the successor of Ponchielli as prof. of composition at the Milan Cons. It was in Milan that he became acquainted with Boito, who encouraged him in his composition. He also met young Toscanini, who became a champion of his music. Catalani was determined to create a Wagnerian counterpart in the field of Italian opera, and he selected for his libretti fantastic subjects suitable for dramatic action. After several unsuccessful productions he finally achieved his ideal in his last opera, *La Wally* (Milan, Jan. 20, 1892). He died of tuberculosis the year after its production. His other operas include *La Falce* (Milan, July 19, 1875), *Elda* (Turin, Jan. 31, 1880; rev. as *Loreley*, Turin, Feb. 16, 1890), *Dejanice* (Milan, March 17, 1883), and *Edmea* (Milan, Feb. 27, 1886).

BIBL.: D. Pardini, *A. C.* (Lucca, 1935); A. Bonaccorsi, *A. C.* (Turin, 1942); C. Gatti, *A. C.* (Milan, 1953).

Catalani, Angelica, famous Italian soprano; b. Sinigaglia, May 10, 1780; d. Paris, June 12, 1849. She was educated in the convent of S. Lucia di Gubbio in Rome, and received vocal training from her father and from Morandi. After making her operatic debut as Mayr's Lodoïska at the Teatro La Fenice in Venice in 1795, she sang at La Pergola in Florence (1799), La Scala in Milan (1801), and in Lisbon (from 1801). In 1806 she made her London debut at the King's Theatre in Portugal's *Semiramide*, and soon became one of the most highly acclaimed and paid prima donnas of the era. She became well known for her roles in operas by Paër, Paisiello, and Piccinni. In 1812 she sang Susanna in the first London staging of *Le nozze di Figaro*. After serving as manager of the Théâtre-Italien in Paris (1814–17), she toured extensively in Europe. In 1821 she retired from the operatic stage but continued to appear in concerts until 1828. Catalani captivated her audiences by the sheer beauty and range of her coloratura.

BIBL.: H. Satter, *A. C.* (Frankfurt am Main, 1958); M. Zurletti, *C.* (Turin, 1982).

Catel, Charles-Simon, French composer and pedagogue; b. l'Aigle, Orne, June 10, 1773; d. Paris, Nov. 29, 1830. He studied in Paris with Gossec and Gobert at the École Royale de Chant, where he served as accompanist and teacher (1787). He was accompanist at the Opéra and assistant conductor (to Gossec) of the band of the Garde Nationale (1790). In 1795, on the establishment of the Cons., he was appointed prof. of harmony, and was commissioned to write a *Traité d'harmonie* (publ. 1802; a standard work at the Cons. for 20 years thereafter). In 1810, with Gossec, Méhul, and Cherubini, he was made an inspector of the Cons., resigning in 1816; he was named a member of the Académie des Beaux-Arts in 1817. As a composer, Catel was at his best in his operas, written in a conventional but attractive style of French stage music of the time.

WORKS: OPERAS (all 1st perf. in Paris): *Sémiramis* (May 4, 1802); *L'Auberge de Bagnères* (April 23, 1807); *Les Artistes par occasion* (Jan. 22, 1807); *Les Bayadères* (Aug. 8, 1810; his most successful work); *Les Aubergistes de qualité* (June 11, 1812); *Bayard a Mézières* (Feb. 12, 1814); *Le Premier en date* (Nov. 3, 1814); *Wallace, ou Le Ménestrel écossais* (March 24, 1817); *Zirphile et Fleur de Myrte, ou Cent ans en jour* (June 29, 1818); *L'Officier enlevé* (May 4, 1819).

BIBL.: J. Carlez, *C.: Étude biographique et critique* (Caen, 1895); S. Suskin, *The Music of C.-S. C. for the Paris Opéra* (diss., Yale Univ., 1972).

Cavalieri, Catarina (real name, **Franziska Cavalier**), Austrian soprano of Italian descent; b. Wahring, near Vienna, Feb. 19, 1760; d. Vienna, June 30, 1801. She studied with Salieri, making her operatic debut as Sandrina in Anfossi's *La finta giardiniera* at the Italian Opera in Vienna on April 29, 1775; she subsequently sang with notable success at the German Opera there. Salieri, with whom she maintained a liaison, composed several operas for her. Mozart, too, composed the roles of Constanze in *Die Entführung aus dem Serail* (July 16, 1782) and Mme. Silberklang in *Der Schauspieldirektor* (Feb. 7, 1786) for her, as well as the extra aria "Mi tradi" (K. 540c) in *Don Giovanni*, for the first Vienna performance in 1788. In a letter of May 21, 1785, Mozart described her as "a singer of whom Germany might well be proud." She retired from the stage in 1793.

Cavalieri, Emilio del, Italian composer; b. c.1550; d. Rome, March 11, 1602. He was a nobleman who served as Inspector-General of Art and Artists at the Tuscan court in Florence (1588). He was one of the "inventors" and most ardent champions of the monodic style, or "stile recitativo," which combines melody with accompanying harmonies. His chief work, *La rappresentazione di anima e di corpo* (publ. by A. Guidotti, Rome, 1600, with explanatory preface; reprints: L. Guidiccioni-Nicastro, Livorno, 1911; Munich, 1921), once regarded as the first oratorio, is really a morality play set to music; other dramatic works (*Il satiro*, 1590; *Disperazione di Filene*, 1590; *Giuoco della cieca*, 1595) exemplify in similar manner the beginnings of modern opera form. In all of Cavalieri's music there is a basso continuato with thoroughbass figuring; the melodies are also crudely figured. A facsimile ed. of the libretto for *La rappresentazione* was publ. by D. Alaleona (Rome, 1912); a facsimile ed. of the orch. score is to be found in Mantica's *Collezione di prime fioriture del melodramma italiano* (Rome, 1912).

Cavalieri, Lina (Natalina), famous Italian soprano; b. Viterbo, Dec. 25, 1874; d. in an air raid on Florence, Feb. 8, 1944. As a young woman of striking beauty, she became the cynosure of the Paris boulevardiers via her appearances in cafés (1893) and at the Folies-Bergère (1894). During a trip to Russia in 1900, she married Prince Alexander Bariatinsky, who persuaded her to take up an operatic career. After studying in Paris, she made a premature debut as Nedda at the Teatro São Carlo in Lisbon (1900); at her 2d appearance, the audience's disapproval brought the performance to a halt. She and the prince then parted company, but she continued vocal studies with Maddalena Mariani-Masi in Milan, returning successfully to the stage as Mimi at the Teatro San Carlo in Naples (1900); she then sang in St. Petersburg and Warsaw (1901). In 1905 she was chosen to create the role of L'Ensoleillad in Massenet's *Chérubin* in Monte Carlo, and on Dec. 5, 1906, she made her Metropolitan Opera debut in New York as Fedora, winning subsequent praise for her dramatic portrayals there of Tosca and Mimi. In 1907, after divorcing her husband, she contracted a lucrative marriage with the American millionaire Winthrop Chandler, but left him in a week, precipitating a sensational scandal that caused the Metropolitan to break her contract; she made her farewell appearance there in a concert on March 8, 1908. She sang at London's Covent Garden (1908), N.Y.'s Manhattan Opera House (1908), the London Opera House (1911), and the Chicago Grand Opera (1913–14; 1921–22). She married **Lucien Muratore** in 1913, but abandoned him in 1919; she then married Paolo D'Arvanni, making her home at her Villa Cappucina near Florence. Among her other fine roles were Adriana Lecouvreur, Manon Lescaut, and Salomé in *Hérodiade*. She publ. an autobiography, *La mie verità* (1936). She was the subject of an Italian film under the telling title *La Donna più bella dello mondo* (1957), starring Gina Lollobrigida.

Cavalli (real name, **Caletti**), **Pier Francesco,** historically significant Italian opera composer; b. Crema, Feb. 14, 1602; d. Venice, Jan. 14, 1676. His father, Giovanni Battista Caletti (known also as Bruni), was maestro di cappella at the Cathedral in Crema; he gave him his first instruction in music; as a youth he sang under his father's direction in the choir of the Cathedral. The Venetian nobleman Federico Cavalli, who was also mayor of Crema, took him to Venice for further musical training; and as it was a custom, he adopted his sponsor's surname. In December 1616 he entered the choir of S. Marco in Venice, beginning an association there that continued for the rest of his life; he sang there under Monteverdi; he also served as an organist at Ss. Giovanni e Paolo (1620–30). In 1638, he turned his attention to the new art form of opera, and helped to organize an opera company at the Teatro San Cassiano. His first opera, *Le nozze di Teti e di Peleo*, was performed there on Jan. 24, 1639; 9 more were to follow within the next decade. In 1639 he successfully competed against 3 others for the post of 2d organist at S. Marco. In 1660 Cardinal Mazarin invited him to Paris, where he presented a restructured version of his opera *Serse* for the marriage festivities of Louis XIV and Maria Theresa. He also composed the opera *Ercole amante* while there, which was given at the Tuileries on Feb. 7, 1662. He returned to Venice in 1662; on Jan. 11, 1665, he was officially appointed 1st organist at S. Marco; on Nov. 20, 1668, he became maestro di cappella there. After Monteverdi, Cavalli stands as one of the most important Venetian composers of opera in the mid–17th century. In recent years several of his operas have been revived; Raymond Leppard ed. *L'Ormindo* (London, 1969) and *Calisto* (London, 1975); Jane Glover ed. *L'Eritrea* (London, 1977).

WORKS: OPERAS: *Le nozze di Teti e di Peleo* (Venice, Jan. 24, 1639); *Gli amori d'Apollo e di Dafne* (Venice, 1640); *Didone* (Venice, 1641); *Amore innamorato* (Venice, Jan. 1, 1642; music not extant); *La virtù de' strali d'Amore* (Venice, 1642); *Egisto* (Venice, 1643); *L'Ormindo* (Venice, 1644); *Doriclea* (Venice, 1645); *Titone* (Venice, 1645; music not extant); *Giasone* (Venice, Jan. 5, 1649); *Euripo* (Venice, 1649; music not extant); *Orimonte* (Venice, Feb. 20, 1650); *Oristeo* (Venice, 1651); *Rosinda* (Venice, 1651); *Calisto* (Venice, 1652); *L'Eritrea* (Venice, 1652); *Veremonda l'amazzone di Aragona* (Naples, Dec. 21, 1652); *L'Orione* (Milan, June 1653); *Ciro* (composed by Francesco Provenzale; prologue and arias added by Cavalli for Venice, Jan. 30, 1654); *Serse* (Venice, Jan. 12, 1655); *Statira principessa di Persia* (Venice, Jan. 18, 1656); *Erismena* (Venice, 1656); *Artemisia* (Venice, Jan. 10, 1657); *Hipermestra* (Florence, June 12, 1658); *Antioco* (Venice, Jan. 21, 1659; music not extant); *Elena* (Venice, Dec. 26, 1659); *Ercole amante* (Paris, Feb. 7, 1662); *Scipione Affricano* (Venice, Feb. 9, 1664); *Mutio Scevola* (Venice, Jan. 26, 1665); *Pompeo Magno* (Venice, Feb. 20, 1666); *Eliogabalo* (composed in 1668; not perf.); *Coriolano* (Piacenza, May 27, 1669; music not extant); *Massenzio* (composed in 1673; not perf.; music not extant). The following operas have been ascribed to Cavalli but are now considered doubtful: *Narciso et Ecco immortalati; Deidamia; Il Romolo e 'l Remo; La prosperita infelice di Giulio Cesare dittatore; Torilda; Bradamante; Armidoro; Helena rapita da Theseo*; also *La pazzia in trono, overo Caligola delirante*, which is a spoken drama with some music. None of the music is extant for any of these works.

BIBL.: H. Prunières, *C. et l'opéra venetien au dix-septième siècle* (Paris, 1931); E. Rosand, *Aria in the Early Operas of F. C.* (diss., N.Y. Univ., 1971); L. Bianconi, *F. C. und die Verbreitung der ve-*

nezianischen Oper in Italien (diss., Univ. of Heidelberg, 1974); J. Glover, *C.* (N.Y., 1978).

Cavos, Catterino, Italian-Russian composer; b. Venice, Oct. 30, 1775; d. St. Petersburg, May 10, 1840. He studied with Francesco Bianchi. His first work was a patriotic hymn for the Republican Guard, performed at the Teatro La Fenice (Sept. 13, 1797); he then produced a cantata, *L'Eroe* (1798). That same year he received an invitation to go to Russia as conductor at the Imperial Opera in St. Petersburg. He was already on his way to Russia when his ballet *Il sotterraneo* was presented in Venice (Nov. 16, 1799). He remained in St. Petersburg for the rest of his life. His Russian debut as a composer was in a collaborative opera, *Rusalka* (adapted from *Das Donauweibchen* by F. Kauer; Nov. 7, 1803). This was followed by the operas *The Invisible Prince* (May 17, 1805), *The Post of Love* (1806), *Ilya the Bogatyr* (Jan. 12, 1807), *3 Hunchback Brothers* (1808), *The Cossack Poet* (May 27, 1812), and several ballets. His most significant work was *Ivan Susanin*, which he conducted at the Imperial Theater on Oct. 30, 1815. The subject of this opera was used 20 years later by Glinka in his opera *A Life for the Czar*; the boldness of Cavos in selecting a libretto from Russian history provided the necessary stimulus for Glinka and other Russian composers. (Cavos conducted the premiere of Glinka's opera.) His subsequent operas were also based on Russian themes: *Dobrynia Nikitich* (1818) and *The Firebird* (1822). Cavos was a notable voice teacher, numbering among his pupils several Russian singers who later became famous.

Cebotari (real name, **Cebutaru**), **Maria,** outstanding Moldavian soprano; b. Kishinev, Bessarabia, Feb. 23, 1910; d. Vienna, June 9, 1949. She sang in a church choir; from 1924 to 1929 she studied at the Kishinev Cons.; she then went to Berlin, where she took voice lessons with Oskar Daniel at the Hochschule für Musik. In 1929 she sang with a Russian émigré opera troupe in Bucharest and in Paris. In 1931 she made an auspicious debut as Mimi at the Dresden State Opera, where she was a principal member until 1943; she also appeared at the Salzburg Festival. In 1936 she joined the Berlin State Opera, singing with it until 1944; from 1946 she was a member of the Vienna State Opera. She also filled guest engagements in other European opera houses. She had a large repertoire which included the standard soprano roles, among them Violetta, Madama Butterfly, Pamina, and Manon; she also gave brilliant performances in modern operas; Richard Strauss greatly prized her abilities, entrusting to her the role of Aminta in the premiere of his *Die schweigsame Frau* (Dresden, June 24, 1935). Thanks to her cosmopolitan background, she sang the part of Tatiana in Russian in Tchaikovsky's opera *Eugene Onegin* and the part of Antonida in Glinka's *A Life for the Czar*. She also appeared in films. She was married to the Russian nobleman Count Alexander Virubov; after their divorce in 1938, she married the film actor Gustav Diessl.

BIBL.: A. Mingotti, *M. C., Das Leben einer Sängerin* (Salzburg, 1950).

Ceccato, Aldo, Italian conductor; b. Milan, Feb. 18, 1934. He studied at the Verdi Cons. in Milan (1948–55), with Albert Wolff and Willem van Otterloo in the Netherlands (1958), and at the Berlin Hochschule für Musik (1959–62). In 1960 he served as assistant to Celibidache at the Accademia Musicale Chigiana in Siena. In 1964 he won 1st prize in the RAI conducting competition, and in 1969 he made his U.S. debut at the Chicago Lyric Opera and his first appearance at London's Covent Garden. He was music director of the Detroit Sym. Orch. (1973–77) and Generalmusikdirektor of the Hamburg State Phil. (1975–83); he then was music director of the Bergen Sym. Orch. (1985–89) and chief conductor of the Hannover Radio Orch. (1985–89). He subsequently was chief conductor of the Slovak Phil. in Bratislava (1990–91), the RAI Orch. in Turin (from 1990), and the Orquesta Nacional de España in Madrid (1991). His father-in-law was **Victor de Sabata**.

Cehanovsky, George, Russian baritone, b. St. Petersburg, April 14, 1892; d. Yorktown Heights, N.Y., March 25, 1986. He was a member of the Russian navy in World War I; after the war he studied voice with his mother, a professional singer. He made his professional debut as Valentin in *Faust* in Petrograd in 1921. In 1923 he emigrated to the United States, and in 1926 he joined the roster of the Metropolitan Opera in New York, with which he remained until 1966. He filled 96 different roles during his long career; however, most were secondary roles, and thus he never reached the rank of celebrity. In 1956 he married **Elisabeth Rethberg**.

Čelanský, Ludvík Vítězslav, Czech conductor and composer; b. Vienna, July 17, 1870; d. Prague, Oct. 27, 1931. He studied at the Prague Cons.; he then conducted theater orchs. in Pilsen and Zagreb. Returning to Prague, he made the Czech Phil. into an independent organization (1901), and conducted its first season and again in 1918–19; he also conducted opera and concerts abroad. He composed the opera *Camille* (Prague, Oct. 23, 1897).

Celis, Frits, Belgian conductor and composer; b. Antwerp, April 11, 1929. He studied composition at the Royal Flemish Cons. in Antwerp and harp at the Brussels Cons.; he also attended the summer conducting course at the Mozarteum in Salzburg (1949–51) and similar courses at the Hochschule für Musik in Cologne (1953–54). He then conducted at the Théâtre Royal de la Monnaie in Brussels (1954–59). In 1960 he was appointed to the faculty of the Royal Flemish Cons. of Antwerp.

Cellier, Alfred, English conductor and composer; b. London (of French parents), Dec. 1, 1844; d. there, Dec. 28, 1891. He was a chorister at St. James' Chapel Royal. He studied music with Thomas Helmore. In 1866 he was conductor, at Belfast, of the Ulster Hall concerts and the Phil.; from 1871 to 1875 he conducted at the Prince's Theatre in Manchester; from 1877 to 1879 at the London Opéra Comique, and (with Sullivan) at the Promenade Concerts in Covent Garden. He then spent some years in America and Australia, returning to London in 1887.

WORKS: LIGHT OPERAS: *Charity Begins at Home* (London, 1870); *The Foster Brothers* (London, June 17, 1873); *The Sultan of Mocha* (Manchester, Nov. 16, 1874); *The Tower of London* (Manchester, Oct. 4, 1875); *Nell Gwynne* (Manchester, Oct. 16, 1876); *Dora's Dream* (London, Nov. 17, 1877); *The Spectre Knight* (London, Feb. 9, 1878); *Bella Donna, or The Little Beauty and the Great Beast* (Manchester, April 27, 1878); *After All* (London, Dec. 16, 1878); *In the Sulks* (London, Feb. 21, 1880); *The Masque of Pandora*, after Longfellow (Boston, Jan. 10, 1881); *The Carp* (London, Feb. 11, 1886); *Dorothy* (London, Sept. 25, 1886); *Mrs. Jarramie's Genie* (London, Feb. 14, 1888); *Doris* (London, April 20, 1889); *The Mountebanks* (London, Jan. 4, 1892); also a setting of Gray's *Elegy*, written for the Leeds Festival (Oct. 10, 1883).

Ceremuga, Josef, Czech composer; b. Ostrava, June 14, 1930. He studied composition with Rídký and Dobíaš and quarter-tone music with A. Hába at the Prague Academy of Music (1950–53); after completing his postgraduate studies there (1953–56), he joined its faculty in 1960, serving in a variety of capacities. His works reflect modern Czech and Russian styles, with broad neo-Romantic melos sharpened by euphonious dissonances. He composed the opera *Juraj Čup* (1958–60; Prague, April 27, 1963) and the ballet *Princezna se zlatou hvězdou na čele* (The Princess with a Golden Star on Her Forehead; 1980–82).

Cerha, Friedrich, notable Austrian composer and pedagogue; b. Vienna, Feb. 17, 1926. He was a student of Prihoda (violin) and Uhl (composition) at the Vienna Academy of Music (1946–51), and also took courses in philosophy and musicology at the Univ. of Vienna (Ph.D., 1950). With Kurt Schwertsik, he founded the new music ensemble Die Reihe. In 1960 he became a lecturer at the Vienna Academy of Music, where he also was director of its electronic music studio until 1969; he subsequently was assoc. prof. (1969–70) and prof. (from 1970) of music there. In 1986 he was awarded the Austrian State Prize. Cerha completed the 3d act of Berg's unfinished opera *Lulu* (1962–78), which was first given in its finished version in Paris on Feb. 24, 1979. He has also produced a considerable output of avant-garde scores notable for their innovative blending of contemporary techniques and traditional idioms. He composed the operas *Baal*, after Brecht (1974–81; Salzburg, Aug. 7, 1981; suite of songs, North German Radio, Hamburg, Jan. 22, 1982) and *Der Rattenfänger* (1984–86).

Cerquetti, Anita, Italian soprano; b. Montecosaro, near Macerata, April 13, 1931. After training in Perugia, she made her operatic debut in 1951 as Aida in Spoleto; then sang in various Italian opera houses. In 1955 she made her U.S. debut at the Chicago Lyric Theatre. In 1958 she scored a major success when she substituted for Callas in the role of Norma at the Rome Opera, and that same year she made her first appearance at Milan's La Scala as Abigaille. Her promising career was cut short by a debilitating illness that compelled her to retire in 1961.

Cesti, Antonio (baptismal name, **Pietro**), renowned Italian composer; b. Arezzo (baptized), Aug. 5, 1623; d. Florence, Oct. 14, 1669. Although earlier reference works give his name as Marc' Antonio Cesti, this rendering is incorrect; he adopted the name Antonio when he joined the Franciscan order. He was a choirboy in Arezzo before joining the Franciscan order in Volterra in 1637; he served his novitiate at S. Croce in Florence and then was assigned to the Arezzo monastery. He is reported to have received his musical training from Abbatini in Rome and Città di Castello (1637–40) and from Carissimi in Rome (1640–45). While in Volterra, he was accorded the patronage of the Medici family. His first opera, *Orontea* (Venice, Jan. 20, 1649), was highly successful. He was active at the court of Archduke Ferdinand Karl in Innsbruck from 1652 to 1657, then was a tenor in the Papal Choir in Rome (1659–60). After being released from his vows, he quit the Papal Choir with the intention of returning to his court duties in Innsbruck. In spite of a threat of excommunication, he went to Innsbruck until the death of the Archduke in 1665 led to the removal of its musical entourage to Vienna in 1666. He was made "Capelan d'honore und intendenta delle musiche theatrali" at the Vienna court in 1666, and in 1668 returned to Italy and served as maestro di cappella at the Tuscan court in Florence during the last years of his life. Cesti was one of the most important composers of secular vocal music of his time.

WORKS: OPERAS: *Orontea* (Venice, Jan. 20, 1649); *Alessandro vincitor di se stesso* (Venice, 1651); *Il Cesare amante* (Venice, 1651); *La Cleopatra* (Innsbruck, 1654); *L'Argia* (Innsbruck, 1655); *La Dori* (Innsbruck, 1657); *La magnanimità d'Alessandro* (Innsbruck, 1662); *Il Tito* (Venice, Feb. 13, 1666); *Nettunno e Flora festeggianti* (Vienna, July 12, 1666); *Le disgrazie d'Amore* (Vienna, Feb. 19, 1667); *La Semirami* (Vienna, July 9, 1667); *Il pomo d'oro* (Vienna, July 13–14, 1668); also several doubtful works. See D. Burrows, ed., *A. C.: The Italian Cantata*, I, Wellesley Edition, V (1963).

BIBL.: C. Schmidt, *The Operas of A. C.* (diss., Harvard Univ., 1973).

Cezar, Corneliu, Romanian composer; b. Bucharest, Dec. 22, 1937; d. there, Feb. 13, 1997. He studied composition at the Bucharest Cons. with Ciortea, Jora, Mendelsohn, and Vieru. He composed the opera *Galileo Galilei* (1962; Bucharest, Dec. 16, 1964) and the theater piece *Pinocchio* (1983).

Chabrier, (Alexis-) Emmanuel, famous French composer; b. Ambert, Puy de Dôme, Jan. 18, 1841; d. Paris, Sept. 13, 1894. He studied law in Paris (1858–61), and also studied composition with Semet and Hignard, piano with Edouard Wolff, and violin with Hammer. He served in the government from 1861, at the same time cultivating his musical tastes; with Duparc, d'Indy, and others he formed a private group of music lovers, and was an enthusiastic admirer of Wagner. He began to compose in earnest, and produced 2 light operas: *L'Étoile* (Paris, Nov. 28, 1877) and *Une Éducation manquée* (Paris, May 1, 1879). In 1879 he went to Germany with Duparc to hear Wagner's operas. Returning to Paris, he publ. some piano pieces; he then traveled to Spain; the fruit of this journey was his most famous work, the rhapsody *España* (Paris, Nov. 4, 1883), which produced a sensation when performed by Lamoureux in 1884. Another work of Spanish inspiration was the *Habanera* for Piano (1885). In the meantime he served as chorus master for Lamoureux; this experience developed his knowledge of vocal writing; he wrote a brief cantata for mezzo-soprano and women's chorus, *La Sulamite* (March 15, 1885), and his operas *Gwendoline* (Brussels, April 10, 1886), *Le Roi malgré lui* (Opéra Comique, Paris, May 18, 1887), and *Briseis* (concert perf., Paris, Jan. 31, 1897; stage perf., Royal Opera, Berlin, Jan. 14, 1899). In his operas Chabrier attempted a grand style; his idiom oscillated between passionate Wagnerianism and a more conventional type of French stage music; although these operas enjoyed a succès d'estime, they never became popular, and Chabrier's place in music history is secured exclusively by his *España*, and other piano pieces such as *Bourrée fantasque* (1891; orchestrated by Felix Mottl).

BIBL.: R. Martineau, *E. C.* (Paris, 1911); G. Servières, *E. C.* (Paris, 1912); J. Desaymard, *C. d'aprés ses lettres* (Paris, 1934); F. Poulenc, *E. C.* (Paris, 1961); R. Myers, *E. C. and His Circle* (London, 1969); F. Robert, *E. C.: L'Homme et son oeuvre* (Paris, 1970); R. Delage, *C.* (Geneva, 1982).

Chadwick, George Whitefield, eminent American composer and teacher; b. Lowell, Mass. Nov. 13, 1854; d. Boston, April 4, 1931. He began musical training with his brother. From the time he was 15, he was active as an organist, and in 1872 he became a Congregational church organist. He also pursued organ training with Dudley Buck and Eugene Thayer at the New England Cons. of Music in Boston. After serving as a prof. of music at Olivet College in Michigan (1876–77), he went to Leipzig to study privately with Jadassohn, and then entered the Cons. there in 1878. His *Rip Van Winkle* overture and his 2d String Quartet were selected as the finest works at the annual Cons. concerts in 1879. He then pursued training with Rheinberger at the Munich Hochschule für Musik (1879–80). Upon his return to Boston in 1880, he devoted himself mainly to composing and teaching. He also was active as an organist, as a pianist (prinicipally in programs of his own works), and as a symphonic and choral conductor. He served as director and conductor of the Springfield (1890–99) and Worcester (1897–1901) festivals. In 1882 he became a teacher at the New England Cons. of Music. In 1897 he became its director, and proceeded to make it one of the most distinguished conservatories in the United States. Many noted American composers were Chadwick's pupils. In 1898 he was elected a member of the National Inst. of Arts and Letters, and in 1909 of the American Academy of Arts and Letters, which awarded him its gold medal in 1928. Chadwick was one of the leading American composers of his day. While he is usually regarded as a pillar of the "Boston Classicists," his most important works actually reveal attempts to find a new American style, albeit one reflecting the tenets of late Romanticism. Among his most important works were the verismo opera *The Padrone* (1912–13), the 2d Sym. (1883–85), the *Symphonic Sketches* (1895–1904), the symphonic ballad *Tom O'Shanter* (1914–15), the 4th String Quartet (1896), and various songs.

WORKS: DRAMATIC: *The Peer and the Pauper*, comic operetta (1884); *A Quiet Lodging*, operetta (Boston, April 1, 1892); *Tabasco*, burlesque opera (1893–94; Boston, Jan. 29, 1894); *Judith*, lyric drama (1899–1900; Worcester Festival, Sept. 23, 1901); *Everywoman: Her Pilgrimage in Quest of Love*, incidental music (1910; Hartford, Conn., Feb. 9, 1911); *The Padrone*, opera (1912–13; concert perf., Thomaston, Conn., Sept. 29, 1995; stage perf., Boston, April 10, 1997); *Love's Sacrifice*, pastoral opera (1916–17; Chicago, Feb. 1, 1923).

WRITINGS: *Harmony: A Course of Study* (Boston, 1897; many subsequent eds.); *Key to the Textbook on Harmony* (Boston, 1902).

BIBL.: V. Yellin, *The Life and Operatic Works of G. W. C.* (diss., Harvard Univ., 1957); idem, *C.: Yankee Composer* (Washington, D.C., and London, 1990).

Chailley, Jacques, eminent French musicologist; b. Paris, March 24, 1910. He studied composition with Boulanger, Delvincourt, and Büsser, musicology with Pirro, Rokseth, and Smijers, and conducting with Mengelberg and Monteux; he also took courses in medieval French literature at the Sorbonne in Paris (1932–36; Ph.D., 1952, with 2 dissertations: *L'École musicale de Saint-Martial de Limoges jusqu'à la fin du XIe siècle* [publ. in Paris, 1960] and *Chansons de Gautier du Coinci* [publ. as *Les Chansons à la Vierge de Gautier de Coinci* in *Monuments de la musique ancienne*, XV, 1959]). He was general secretary (1937–47), vice principal (1947–51), and prof. of the choral class (1951–53) at the Paris Cons.; from 1952 to 1979 he was director of the Inst. of Musicology at the Univ. of Paris; also taught at the Paris Lycée La Fontaine (1951–69); from 1962 to 1981 he was director of the Schola Cantorum. He wrote authoritatively on many subjects, including medieval music, the music of ancient Greece, music history, and the music of Bach, Mozart, Wagner, and others. He also composed, numbering among his works 2 operas. Among his numerous books (all publ. in Paris unless otherwise given) are: *Tristan et Isolde de Wagner* (1963; 2d ed., 1972), *"La Flûte enchantée," opéra maçonnique: Essai d'explication du livret et de la musique* (1968; 2d ed., aug., 1983; Eng. tr., 1971, as *The Magic Flute, Masonic Opera*), and *Parsifal de R. Wagner, opéra initiatique* (1979).

Chailly, Luciano, prominent Italian music administrator, teacher, and composer, father of **Riccardo Chailly**; b. Ferrara, Jan. 19, 1920. He studied violin in Ferrara (diploma, 1941) and pursued academic training at the Univ. of Bologna (B.A., 1943); after composition studies with R. Bossi at the Milan Cons. (diploma, 1945), he studied with Hindemith in Salzburg (1948). He was director of music programming for the RAI (1950–67), and artistic director of Milan's La Scala (1968–71), Turin's Teatro Regio (1972), Milan's Angelicum (1973–75), and Verona's Arena (1975–76). He was again associated with La Scala (from 1977) and was artistic director of the Genoa Opera (1983–85); he also taught at the Milan Cons. (1968–83). In 1989–90 he was artistic director of the RAI orch. and choir in Turin. His music is composed in a communicative neoclassical idiom, with some dodecaphonic incrustations and electronic effects.

WORKS: DRAMATIC: OPERAS: *Ferrovia soprelevata* (Bergamo, Oct. 1, 1955); *Una domanda di matrimonio* (Milan, May 22, 1957); *Il canto del cigno* (Bologna, Nov. 16, 1957); *La riva delle Sirti* (Monte Carlo, March 1, 1959); *Procedura penale* (Como, Sept. 30, 1959); *Il mantello* (Florence, May 11, 1960); *Era proibito* (Milan, March 5, 1963); *L'Idiota* (1966–67; Rome, Feb. 14, 1970); *Vassiliev* (Genoa, March 16, 1967); *Markheim* (Spoleto, July 14, 1967); *Sogno (ma forse no)* (Trieste, Jan. 28, 1975); *Il libro dei reclami* (Vienna, May 29, 1975); *La Cantatrice calva* (Vienna, Nov. 5, 1985). BALLETS: *Fantasmi al Grand-Hotel* (Milan, 1960); *Il cappio* (Naples, 1962); *L'urlo* (Palermo, 1967); *Shee* (Melbourne, 1967); *Anna Frank* (Verona, 1981); *Es-Ballet* (1983).

BIBL.: R. Cresti, *Linguaggio musicale di L. C.* (Milan, 1993).

Chailly, Riccardo, noted Italian conductor, son of **Luciano Chailly**; b. Milan, Feb. 20, 1953. He studied composition with his father, and then with Bruno Bettinelli at the Milan Cons.; he also studied conducting with Piero Guarino in Perugia, Franco Caracciolo in Milan, and Franco Ferrara in Siena. He was assistant conductor of the sym. concerts at Milan's La Scala (1972–74); his international career began with his U.S. debut at the Chicago Lyric Opera conducting *Madama Butterfly* (1974); he subsequently was a guest conductor at the San Francisco Opera, Milan's La Scala, London's Covent Garden, and the Vienna State Opera. He made his Metropolitan Opera debut in New York with *Les Contes d'Hoffmann* on March 8, 1982. From 1982 to 1989 he was chief conductor of the (West) Berlin Radio Sym. Orch., which he led on its first tour of North America in 1985; he also was principal guest conductor of the London Phil. (1982–85) and artistic director of the Teatro Comunale in Bologna (1986–89). In 1988 he became chief conductor of the Concertgebouw Orch. of Amsterdam, which was renamed the Royal Concertgebouw Orch. that same year by Queen Beatrix in honor of its 100th anniversary. Chailly is one of the leading conductors of his generation, and has won praise for his performances in both the opera pit and the concert hall.

Chalabala, Zdenek, noted Czech conductor; b. Uherské Hradiště, April 18, 1899; d. Prague, March 4, 1962. He studied composition with Novák in Prague, then took courses in violin, conducting, and composition at the Brno Cons., where his principal teachers were Janáček and Neumann. He was conductor of the Slovak Phil. in Brno (1924–25), the National Theater in Brno (1925–29), where he served as music director (1929–36), and the Prague National Theater (1936–45), and chief conductor of the Ostrava Opera (1945–49), the Brno National Theater (1949–52), and the Slovak National Theater in Bratislava (1952–53). In 1953 he returned to the Prague National Theater as chief conductor, a post he held with distinction until his death.

Chaliapin, Feodor (Ivanovich), celebrated Russian bass; b. near Kazan, Feb. 13, 1873; d. Paris, April 12, 1938. He was born into a poverty-ridden peasant family, and thus was compelled to work in menial jobs from an early age and had little opportunity for formal schooling. While still a youth, he began to travel with various opera and operetta companies as a chorister and eventually appeared in stage roles. In 1890 he made his formal operatic debut as the Stolnik in *Halka* with the Semyonov-Smarsky company in Ufa. During his travels, he was accompanied by the writer Maxim Gorky, who also sang in a chorus; together they made their way through the Russian provinces, often walking the railroad tracks when they could not afford the fare. Chaliapin's wanderings took him to Tiflis, where his extraordinary vocal gifts deeply impressed the tenor and vocal pedagogue Dimitri Usatov (1847–1913), who taught him free of charge in 1892–93. After appearances in Tiflis in 1893–94, Chaliapin went to St. Petersburg and sang with Panayev's company in 1894. He then was a member of the St. Petersburg Imperial Opera from 1894 to 1896. He subsequently went to Moscow, where he sang with Mamontov's company (1896–99), producing a great impression with his portrayals of Boris Godunov, Ivan Susanin, Varlaam, Dosifey, Ivan the Terrible, Holofernes in Serov's *Judith*, the Viking Guest in *Sadko*, and the Miller in Dargomyzhsky's *Rusalka*. On Dec. 7, 1898, he created the role of Salieri in Rimsky-Korsakov's *Mozart and Salieri* with Mamontov's company. During this time, Chaliapin also acquired fame as a concert singer. In 1899 he joined Moscow's Bolshoi Theater, where he served as its principal bass until 1914. His first appearance outside his homeland was at Milan's La Scala in 1901 when he sang Boito's Mefistofele. He returned to La Scala in 1904, 1908, 1912, 1929–30, and 1933. From 1905 to 1937 he made frequent appearances in Monte Carlo, where he created the title role in Massenet's *Don Quichotte* on Feb. 19, 1910. On July 25, 1905, he made his London debut at a private concert, and returned there to sing in the Russian seasons at Drury Lane in 1913 and 1914. He made his Metropolitan Opera debut in New York as Mefistofele on Nov. 20, 1907. However, his dramatic characterizations failed to evoke sympathetic response from N.Y. audiences and critics, so he went to Paris to sing in Diaghilev's Russian seasons in 1908, 1910, and 1913. After the Russian Revolution, he became soloist and artistic director of the Petrograd Opera in 1918. He also was made a People's Artist by the Soviet government, but he soon became estranged by the course of events in his homeland and in 1921 settled in Paris. On Dec. 9, 1921, he made a triumphant return to the Metropolitan Opera with his compelling portrayal of Boris Godunov, and thereafter sang there with notable acclaim until 1929. From 1922 to 1924 he also sang with the Chicago Opera. In 1926 and in 1928–29 he appeared at London's Covent Garden, and in 1931 he returned to London to sing at the Lyceum Theatre. On March 3, 1935, he gave his farewell concert performance in New York; his operatic farewell followed in Monte Carlo in 1937 when he once again sang Boris Godunov. Chaliapin made many recordings and appeared in film versions of *Tsar Ivan the Terrible* (1915) and *Don Quixote* (1933). He wrote *Stranitsiiz moyey zhizni: Avtobiografiya* (Leningrad, 1926; Eng. tr., 1927, as *Pages from My Life*) and *Maska i dusha: Moi sorok let na teatrakh* (Paris, 1932; Eng.

tr., 1932, as *Man and Mask*). Chaliapin was one of the foremost singing actors ever to grace the operatic stage. He dominated every scene in which he appeared as much by his remarkable dramatic gifts as by his superlative vocal prowess. Even in his last years, when this prowess declined, he never failed to move audiences by the sheer intensity of his performances.

BIBL.: M. Yankovsky, *C.* (Leningrad, 1972); V. Borovsky, *C.: A Critical Biography* (N.Y., 1988).

Challender, Stuart, Australian conductor; b. Hobart, Tasmania, Feb. 19, 1947; d. Sydney, Dec. 13, 1991. After training at the Univ. of Melbourne, he served as music director of the Victorian Opera Co. in Melbourne, and of the Melbourne Youth Orch. He then pursued studies in Hamburg, with Ferrera in Siena, and with Kelterborn and Celibidache in Zürich. He served as assistant conductor of the operas in Nuremberg and Zürich (1970–74), as a conductor at the Lucerne Opera (1974–76), and as resident conductor of the Basel Opera (1976–80). From 1980 to 1986 he was resident conductor of the Australian Opera in Sydney, and also artistic director of the contemporary music ensemble, the Seymour Group (1981–83). In 1985 he made his U.S. debut conducting *Eugene Onegin* at the San Diego Opera. In 1986 he became principal guest conductor of the Sydney Sym. Orch., and in 1987 its chief conductor. In 1987 he made his English debut with the Royal Phil. of London. In 1988 he made a successful tour of the United States with the Sydney Sym. Orch. After contracting AIDS, he continued to pursue his career and returned to London in 1991 to conduct *Rusalka* at the English National Opera. Shortly before his death, he was named an Officer of the Order of Australia.

Chamlee, Mario (real name, **Archer Cholmondeley**), American tenor; b. Los Angeles, May 29, 1892; d. there, Nov. 13, 1966. He studied with Achille Alberti in Los Angeles, where he made his operatic debut as Edgardo in 1916. After singing with Scotti's company, he made his Metropolitan Opera debut in New York as Cavaradossi on Nov. 22, 1920, remaining on its roster until 1928. Following engagements in Europe, he was again on the Metropolitan's roster (1932–34; 1935–39). Among his prominent roles were Pinkerton, Count Almaviva, Boito's Faust, Turiddu, Alfredo, and Hageman's Caponsacchi, which he created on Feb. 4, 1937. In later years he was primarily active as a voice teacher.

Champein, Stanislas, French composer; b. Marseilles, Nov. 19, 1753; d. Paris, Sept. 19, 1830. He studied under Peccico and Chavet in Paris, and at 13 he became maître de musique at the Collegiate Church at Pignon. In 1776 he went to Paris, where some sacred works and 2 operettas made his name known. Up to 1792 he produced 30 works for the stage, the best of which were the operas *La Mélomanie* (1781), *Les Dettes* (1787), and *Le Nouveau Don Quichotte* (1789). From 1793 to 1804 he filled a government position. He continued to compose for the stage, but without success, and spent the last years of his life in poverty. A pension, arranged for him through the efforts of Boieldieu and Scribe, came only 18 months before his death. Though Champein was one of the best-known stage composers of his time, his works are wholly forgotten.

Chance, Michael, noted English countertenor; b. Penn, Buckinghamshire, March 7, 1955. He was a choral scholar at King's College, Cambridge (1974–77). He first made a name for himself as a concert artist via appearances with British ensembles, mainly as an exponent of early music. In 1983 he made his formal operatic debut at the Buxton Festival as Apollo in Cavalli's *Giasone*. His European operatic debut followed in 1985 in Lyons as Handel's Andronico. In 1987 he created the role of the military governor in Weir's *A Night at the Chinese Opera* in Cheltenham. He made his first appearance at the Paris Opéra in 1988 as Tolomeo in *Giulio Cesare*. In 1989 he sang Britten's Oberon at the Glyndebourne Festival, and in 1993 at the Australian Opera. He was engaged as the Voice of Apollo in *Death in Venice* for his debut at London's Covent Garden in 1992, and also appeared that year as Monteverdi's Anfinomo at the English National Opera in London and as Handel's Giulio Cesare at the Scottish Opera in Glasgow. In 1994 he appeared in the premiere of Birtwistle's *The Second Mrs. Kong* at the Glyndebourne Festival. After singing Dick in *The Fairy Queen* at the English National Opera in 1995, he returned there as Gluck's Orfeo in 1997. His engagements as a concert artist took him all over Europe and North America, and were greeted with critical accolades for his naturally cultivated vocal gifts.

Chanler, Theodore Ward, American composer; b. Newport, R.I., April 29, 1902; d. Boston, July 27, 1961. He studied in Boston with Hans Ebell (piano) and with Arthur Shepherd (composition) then at the Cleveland Inst. of Music with Ernest Bloch; later he took courses at the Univ. of Oxford (1923–25); he also studied with Boulanger in Paris. He returned to America in 1933 and wrote music criticism; he taught at the Peabody Cons. of Music in Baltimore (1945–47) and then at the Longy School in Cambridge, Mass. In 1944 he held a Guggenheim fellowship. His music, mostly in smaller forms, is distinguished by a lyrical quality; his songs are particularly expressive; he employed the modern idiom of polytonal texture without overloading the harmonic possibilities; the melody is free, but usually within tonal bounds. He composed *The Pot of Fat*, chamber opera (Cambridge, Mass., May 8, 1955), and *Pas de Trois*, ballet (1942).

BIBL.: E. Nordgren, *An Analytical Study of the Songs of T. C. (1902–1961)* (diss., N.Y. Univ., 1980).

Chapí (y Lorente), Ruperto, Spanish composer; b. Villena, near Alicante, March 27, 1851; d. Madrid, March 25, 1909. He studied at the Cons. of Madrid, then received a stipend from the Spanish Academy for further study in Rome (1874). He wrote some operas (*La hija de Jefte, La hija de Garcilaso*, et al.), but discovered that his talent found more suitable expression in the lighter zarzuela, in which form his first success was won with *La Tempestad* (Tivoli, March 11, 1882). His work is noted for elegance, grace, and exquisite orchestration; of one of his zarzuelas (*La revoltosa*, Apolo, Nov. 25, 1897), Saint-Saëns remarked that Bizet would have been proud to sign his name to the score. His last zarzuela, *Margarita la Tornera* (Madrid, Feb. 24, 1909), was produced shortly before his death. Chapi wrote 155 zarzuelas and 6 operas. In 1893 he founded the Sociedad de Autores, Compositores y Editores de Musica.

BIBL.: A. Salcedo, *R. C., Su vida y sus obras* (Madrid, 1929); J. Aguilar Gómez, *R. C. y su obra lirica* (Alicante, 1973).

Chapin, Schuyler G(arrison), American music administrator; b. N.Y., Feb. 13, 1923. He received training from Boulanger at the Longy School of Music in Cambridge, Mass. (1940–41). After working for NBC (1941–51), Tex and Jinx McCary Enterprises (1951–53), and Columbia Artists Management (1953–59), he was head of the Masterworks Division of Columbia Records (1959–63); he later was associated with N.Y.'s Lincoln Center for the Performing Arts, and, from 1969 to 1971, was executive producer for Amberson Enterprises. He then was general manager of N.Y.'s Metropolitan Opera (1972–75). From 1976 to 1987 he served as dean of Columbia Univ.'s School of the Arts. He was vice president of worldwide concert and artist activities for Steinway and Sons (1990–92). In 1994 he became chairman of cultural affairs for the city of N.Y. He publ. his memoirs as *Musical Chairs: A Life in the Arts* (1977). He also publ. *Leonard Bernstein: Notes From a Friend* (1992) and *Sopranos, Mezzos, Tenors, Basso and Other Friends* (1995).

Chapuis, Auguste (Paul Jean-Baptiste), French composer; b. Dampierre-sur-Salon, Haute-Saône, April 20, 1858; d. Paris, Dec. 6, 1933. He studied at the Paris Cons. with Dubois, Massenet, and Franck, winning 1st prize for organ playing. He was active as a church organist in Paris, and in 1894 was appointed prof. of harmony at the Paris Cons. He retired from there in 1923. He wrote several operas that were produced without much success: *Enguerrande* (1892), *Tancrède* (1898), and *Les Demoiselles de Saint-Cyr* (1921); also several oratorios and dramatic cantatas. He publ. a harmony manual, *Traité d'harmonie théorique et pratique*.

Charpentier, Gustave, famous French composer; b. Dieuze, Lorraine, June 25, 1860; d. Paris, Feb. 18, 1956. He studied at the Paris Cons. (1881–87), where he was a pupil of Massart (violin), Pessard (harmony), and Massenet (composition). He received the Grand Prix de Rome in 1887 with his cantata *Didon*. He evinced great interest in the social problems of the working classes, and in 1900 formed the society L'Oeuvre de Mimi Pinson, devoted to the welfare of the poor, which he reorganized during World War I as an auxiliary Red Cross society. His fame is owed to one amazingly successful opera, *Louise*, a "roman musical" to his own libretto (his mistress at the time was also named Louise, and like the heroine of his opera, was employed in a dressmaking shop), which was premiered at the Opéra Comique in Paris on Feb. 2, 1900. The score is written in the spirit of naturalism and includes such realistic touches as the street cries of Paris vendors. Its success was immediate, and it entered the repertoire of opera houses all over the world. Encouraged, Charpentier wrote a sequel under the title *Julien* (Paris, June 4, 1913), but it failed to arouse comparable interest.

BIBL.: A. Homonet, *Louise* (Paris, 1922); M. Delmas, *G. C. et le lyrisme français* (Paris, 1931).

Charpentier, Jacques, French composer and organist; b. Paris, Oct. 18, 1933. He studied piano with Maria Cerati-Boutillier; then lived in Calcutta (1953–54), where he made a study of Indian music; prepared a valuable thesis, *Introduction à l'étude de la musique de l'Inde*. Upon his return to Paris, he studied composition with Aubin and analysis with Messiaen at the Cons. In 1954 he was appointed organist at the church of St.-Benoit-d'Issy; in 1966 he was named chief inspector of music of the French Ministry of Cultural Affairs, and in 1975 Inspector General of the Secretariat of State for Culture. In 1974 he was named official organist of the Church of St. Nicolas du Chardonnet in Paris. From 1979 to 1981 he was director of music, lyric art, and dance in the French Ministry of Culture. Several of his works are based on Hindu melorhythms. He composed *La Femme et son ombre*, ballet (1967), and *Béatrice de Planisoles*, opera (Aix en Provence, July 23, 1971).

Charpentier, Marc-Antoine, significant French composer; b. Paris, c.1647; d. there, Feb. 24, 1704. He studied with Carissimi in Italy. After returning to Paris, he became active as a composer to Molière's acting troupe; he was also in the service of Marie de Lorraine, the duchess of Guise, later serving as her haute-contre, and finally as her maître de musique until her death (1688); likewise he was in the service of the grand dauphin. Louis XIV granted him a pension (1683), and he subsequently served as music teacher to Philippe, duke of Chartres, was maître de musique to the Jesuit church of St. Louis, and finally held that post at Sainte-Chapelle (1698–1704). Charpentier was one of the leading French composers of his era, distinguishing himself in both sacred and secular works. He wrote some 30 works for the stage, including the tragédies lyriques *David et Jonathas* (1688) and *Médée* (1693), cantatas, overtures, ballet airs, pastorals, incidental pieces, airs sérieux, airs a boire, and so on. H. Hitchcock has prepared *Les OEuvres de Marc-Antoine Charpentier: Catalogue raisonné* (Paris, 1982).

BIBL.: D. Loskant, *Untersuchungen über die Oratorien M.-A. C.s* (diss., Univ. of Mainz, 1957); A. Parmley, *The Secular Stage Works of M.-A. C.* (diss., Univ. of London, 1985); H. Hitchcock, *M.-A. C.* (Oxford, 1990); P. Ranum, ed., *Vers une chronologie des oeuvres de M.-A. C.* (Baltimore, 1994); C. Cessac, *M.-A. C.* (Portland, Oreg., 1995).

Charpentier, Raymond (Louis Marie), French composer and music critic; b. Chartres, Aug. 14, 1880; d. Paris, Dec. 27, 1960. He studied composition with Gédalge. From 1921 to 1943 he was music director of the Comedie Française in Paris; then was active on the French radio (1944–50). He wrote some 20 scores of incidental music for plays produced at the Comedie Française as well as a comic opera, *Gerard et Isabelle* (Paris, 1912).

Charton-Demeur, Anne, prominent French mezzo-soprano; b. Saujon, Charente Maritime, March 5, 1824; d. Paris, Nov. 30, 1892. She studied in Bordeaux with Bizot, making her operatic debut there as Lucia di Lammermoor in 1842. After appearances in Toulouse and Brussels, she made her first appearance in London as Madeleine in *Le Postillon de Longjumeau* on July 18, 1846. In 1847 she married the Belgian flutist Jules-Antoine Demeur in London and took the professional name of Charton-Demeur. In 1849–50 she was the leading female member of Mitchell's French troupe in London, and in 1852 she sang at Her Majesty's Theatre; she also appeared in concert with the Phil. Soc. in 1850. After singing at the Paris Opéra Comique, she appeared with notable success in St. Petersburg, Vienna, and America; she also became a great favorite at the Paris Théâtre-Italien. She was befriended by Berlioz and did much to promote his music. She created the roles of Béatrice in his *Béatrice et Bénédict* (Baden-Baden, Aug. 9, 1862) and Dido in his *Les Troyens à Carthage* (Paris, Nov. 4, 1863). From 1869 she pursued a concert career.

Chausson, (Amédée-) Ernest, distinguished French composer; b. Paris, Jan. 20, 1855; d. Limay, near Mantes, June 10, 1899 (in a bicycle accident). He studied with Massenet at the Paris Cons.; then took private lessons with Franck, and began to compose. The influence of Wagner as well as that of Franck determined the harmonic and melodic elements in Chausson's music; but despite these derivations, he succeeded in establishing an individual style, tense in its chromaticism and somewhat flamboyant in its melodic expansion. The French character of his music is unmistakable in the elegance and clarity of its structural plan. He was active in musical society in Paris and was secretary of the Société Nationale de Musique. He composed relatively little music; possessing private means, he was not compelled to seek employment as a professional musician. Among his compositions are the operas *Les Caprices de Marianne* (1882–84), *Hélène* (1883–84), and *Le Roi Arthus* (Brussels, Nov. 30, 1903); also incidental music to *The Tempest* (1888) and *La Légende de Sainte Cécile* (Paris, Jan. 25, 1892).

BIBL.: J. Barricelli and L. Weinstein, *E. C.* (Norman, Okla., 1955); J. Gallois, *E. C.: L'Homme et son oeuvre* (Paris, 1967); R.S. Grover, *E. C.: The Man and His Music* (London, 1980).

Chávez (y Ramírez), Carlos (Antonio de Padua), distinguished Mexican composer and conductor; b. Calzada de Tacube, near Mexico City, June 13, 1899; d. Mexico City, Aug. 2, 1978. He studied piano as a child with Pedro Luis Ogazón; then studied harmony with Juan B. Fuentes and Manuel Ponce. He began to compose very early in life; he wrote a sym. at the age of 16; made effective piano arrangements of popular Mexican songs and also wrote many piano pieces of his own. His first important work was a ballet on an Aztec subject, *El fuego nuevo* (1921), commissioned by the Secretariat of Public Education of Mexico. Historical and national Mexican subject matter remained the primary source of inspiration in many of his works, but he rarely resorted to literal quotations from authentic folk melodies; rather, he sublimated and distilled the melorhythmic Mexican elements, resulting in a sui generis style of composition. In 1922–23 he traveled in France, Austria, and Germany, and became acquainted with the modern developments in composition. The influence of this period on his evolution as a composer is reflected in the abstract titles of his piano works, such as *Aspectos*, *Energía*, and *Unidad*. Returning to Mexico, he organized and conducted a series of concerts of new music, giving first Mexican performances of works by Stravinsky, Schoenberg, Satie, Milhaud, and Varèse. From 1926 to 1928 he lived in New York. In 1928 he organized the Orquesta Sinfónica de Mexico, of which he remained the principal conductor until 1949. Works of modern music occupied an important part in the program of this orch., including 82 performances of works by Mexican composers, many of them commissioned by Chávez; Silvestre Revueltas was among those encouraged by Chávez to compose. During his tenure as conductor, Chávez engaged a number of famous foreign musicians as guest conductors, as well as numerous soloists. In 1948 the orch. was renamed the

Orquesta Sinfónica Nacional; it remains a permanent institution. Chávez served as director of the Conservatorio Nacional de Música from 1928 to 1933 and again in 1934; he was general director of the Instituto Nacional de Bellas Artes from 1946 to 1952. Beginning in 1936 Chávez conducted a great number of concerts with major American orchs., and also conducted concerts in Europe and South America. Culturally, he maintained a close connection with progressive artists and authors of Mexico, particularly the painter Diego Rivera; his *Sinfonía proletaria* for Chorus and Orch. reflects his political commitment. In 1958–59 he was the Charles Eliot Norton Prof. of Poetry at Harvard Univ.; these lectures were publ. as *Musical Thought* (Cambridge, Mass., 1960); Chávez also publ. a book of essays, *Toward a New Music* (N.Y., 1937).

WORKS: DRAMATIC: OPERA: *Panfilo and Lauretta* (1953; in Eng., N.Y., May 9, 1957; rev. Spanish version as *El Amor propiciado*, Mexico City, Oct. 28, 1959; later retitled *The Visitors*). BALLETS: *El fuego nuevo* (1921; Mexico City, Nov. 4, 1928); *Los cuatro soles* (1925; Mexico City, July 22, 1930); *Caballos de Vapor* (1926; 1st perf. in Eng. as *HP*, i.e., *Horsepower*, Philadelphia, March 31, 1932); *Antígona* (Mexico City, Sept. 20, 1940; 1st perf. as incidental music for Sophocles' *Antigone*, 1932); *La hija de Cólquide* (1943; 1st perf. as accompaniment to the Martha Graham Dance Company as *Dark Meadow*, N.Y., Jan. 23, 1946); *Pirámide* (1968).

BIBL.: R. Morillo, *C. C., vida y obra* (Buenos Aires, 1960); R. Halffter, compiler, *C. C.: Catalogo completo de sus obras* (Mexico City, 1971); R. Parker, *C. C.: Mexico's Modern-Orpheus* (Boston, 1983); G. Carmona, ed., *Epistolario selecto de C. C.* (Mexico City, 1989).

Chaynes, Charles, French composer and broadcasting administrator; b. Toulouse, July 11, 1925. He first studied violin at the Toulouse Cons., and then entered the Paris Cons., where he took courses in violin with Gabriel Bouillon, in chamber music with Joseph Calvet, in composition with Milhaud and Rivier, and in harmony and fugue with N. and J. Gallon (Grand Prix de Rome, 1951, with the cantata *Et l'homme vit se rouvrir les portes*). After composing at the French Academy in Rome (1952–55), he returned to Paris and joined the ORTF as a radio producer in 1956; he then was director of its France-Musique (1965–75) before serving as its chief of the music service (1975–90). As a composer, Chaynes has pursued an independent course in which free atonality is enlivened by infusions of East Asian and African modes of expression. He composed the operas *Erzsebet* (Paris, March 28, 1983), *Noces de sang* (1986), and *Jocaste* (1993).

Cheek, John (Taylor), American bass-baritone; b. Greenville, S.C., Aug. 17, 1948. He received a B.Mus. degree from the North Carolina School of the Arts; then studied in Siena with Gino Bechi at the Accademia Musicale Chigiana, where he received the Diploma of Merit; he subsequently served in the U.S. Army. He made his professional debut in 1975. On June 6, 1977, he made his first appearance with the Metropolitan Opera as Ferrando during the company's visit to the Wolf Trap Farm Park; he then made his formal debut with the company in New York as the physician in *Pelléas et Mélisande* on Oct. 11, 1977; he later sang Pimen in *Boris Godunov*, Ferrando in *Il Trovatore*, Wurm in *Luisa Miller*, Klingsor in *Parsifal*, and also Panthée in *Les Troyens* at the opening night celebration of the Metropolitan's centenary season in 1983–84. In 1987 he won the North Carolina Arts Prize. In 1990 he sang Ramfis in Cincinnati, and in 1996 he returned there as Don Pasquale.

Chélard, Hippolyte-André(-Jean)-Baptiste, French composer; b. Paris, Feb. 1, 1789; d. Weimar, Feb. 12, 1861. He studied with Fétis and Gossec at the Paris Cons., winning the Grand Prix de Rome in 1811. In Rome he studied with Baini, then took lessons in Naples with Paisiello. Returning to Paris, he produced the opera *Macbeth* (libretto by Rouget de Lisle) on June 29, 1827, with meager success. He was much more fortunate in Germany as an opera composer; in Munich he produced a German version of *Macbeth*, a new opera, *Mitternacht* (June 19, 1831), and a German version of his French opera *La Table et le logement*, under the title *Der Student* (Feb. 19, 1832). These were followed by the opera *Die Hermannsschlacht* (Munich, Sept. 12, 1835). From 1840 to 1852 he was court conductor at Weimar, where he brought out 2 comic operas, *Der Scheibentoni* (1842) and *Die Seekadetten* (1844).

Chelleri (real name, **Keller**), **Fortunato,** Italian composer; b. Parma, May 1690; d. Kassel, Dec. 11, 1757. He studied music with his uncle, F. M. Bassani, who was maestro di cappella at Piacenza Cathedral. His first opera, *Griselda* (Piacenza, 1707), was followed by 18 more, written for various Italian stages. He settled in Kassel in 1725 as court music director, and remained there until his death, except for brief journeys to London (1726) and Stockholm (1731).

Chemin-Petit, Hans (Helmuth), German composer and teacher; b. Potsdam, June 24, 1902; d. Berlin, April 12, 1981. His family was of remote French origin; both his father and grandfather were professional musicians. He studied cello in Berlin with Hugo Becker and composition with Paul Juon; subsequently he was mostly active as a cello teacher; was on the staff of the Berlin Hochschule für Musik and later at the Akademie der Künste; in 1968 he was appointed director of its music dept. As a composer, he followed the median line of neo-Classicism. He composed the chamber operas *Der gefangene Vogel* (1927), *Lady Monika* (1930), *König Nicolo* (1962), *Die Komödiantin* (1968), and *Die Rivalinnen* (1970).

BIBL.: A Witte, *H. C.-P.* (Berlin, 1987); V. Grützner, ed., *H. C.-P., 1902–1981: Dokumente zu Leben und Werk* (Berlin, 1994).

Cherbuliez, Antoine-Élisée, Swiss musicologist; b. Mulhouse, Alsace, Aug. 22, 1888; d. Zürich, Oct. 15, 1964. He studied science at the Univ. of Strasbourg and took private organ lessons with Albert Schweitzer. He studied music with his grandfather Adolphe Koekkert in Geneva, and took courses at the Zürich Cons. From 1913 until 1916 he studied privately with Max Reger in Jena. He served for a time as an organist; in 1923 he was appointed instructor in musicology at the Univ. of Zürich. He wrote some chamber music and choruses, but devoted his energies mainly to writing. He publ. biographies of Peter Cornelius, Handel, Verdi, and Tchaikovsky, and monographs on Mozart and Beethoven; also numerous other books and many articles for musical journals.

Chéreau, Patrice, prominent French theater, film, and opera producer; b. Lézigne, Maine-et-Loire, Nov. 2, 1944. He was a leading theater producer from 1964, serving as codirector of the Théâtre National Populaire (1979–81) and director of the Théâtre des Amandiers in Nanterre (from 1982). As an opera producer, he caused a major stir with his deconstructionist version of the centennial mounting of Wagner's *Ring* cycle at the Bayreuth Festival (1976–80); he also produced the premiere staging of the 3-act version of Berg's *Lulu* in Paris (1979) and brought out *Wozzeck* there (1992). In 1994 he staged *Don Giovanni* at the Salzburg Festival. He publ. the book *Si tant que l'opéra soit du théâtre: Notes sur le mise en scène de la création mondiale de l'oeuvre integrale d'Alban Berg "Lulu"* (Toulouse, 1992).

Cherepnin. See **Tcherepnin.**

Chernov, Vladimir, Russian baritone; b. Moscow, Sept. 22, 1953. He received training at the Moscow Cons. (graduated, 1981) and at the opera school at Milan's La Scala. He won prizes in the Tchaikovsky (Moscow, 1982), Bussetto (1983), and Helsinki (Tito Gobbi prize, 1984) competitions. In 1983 he became a member of the Kirov Theater in Leningrad, where he excelled in the baritone repertoire. In 1985 he made his first tour of England and Ireland as a soloist with the Moscow Radio Sym. Orch. His U.S. debut followed in 1988 when he sang Marcello with the Opera Co. of Boston. In 1990 he appeared as Figaro at London's Covent Garden. He sang Posa at the Metropolitan Opera in New York in 1992. In 1995 he made his debut at Milan's La Scala as Stankar in *Stiffelio*. In 1996 he appeared as Don Carlos at the Metropolitan Opera, and returned there in 1997 as Eugene Onegin. His guest engagements also took him to many other leading opera houses in Europe and North America. In addition to the Russian repertoire, Chernov has won special praise for his roles in the Italian and French repertoire.

Cherubini, (Maria) Luigi (Carlo Zenobio Salvatore), famous Italian composer and teacher; b. Florence, Sept. 14, 1760; d. Paris, March 15, 1842. He first studied music with his father, the maestro al cembalo at the Teatro della Pergola in Florence, and then composition with Bartolomeo Felici and his son Alessandro and with Bizarri and Castrucci. In 1778 he received a grant from the Grand Duke Leopold of Tuscany, which enabled him to continue his studies with Sarti in Milan. By this time he had composed a number of works for the church and also several stage intermezzi. While studying with Sarti, he wrote arias for his teacher's operas as well as exercises in the early contrapuntal style. His first operatic success came with *Armida abbandonata* (Florence, Jan. 25, 1782). In the autumn of 1784 he set out for London, where he was commissioned to write an opera for the King's Theatre. *La finta principessa* was given there on April 2, 1785, followed by *Il Giulio Sabino* (March 30, 1786), which brought him public acceptance and the admiration of the prince of Wales. He made his first visit to Paris in the summer of 1785, where he was introduced to Marie Antoinette by the court musician Giovanni Battista Viotti; in the spring of 1786 he made Paris his home. He made 1 last visit to Italy to oversee the production of his opera *Ifigenia in Aulide* (Turin, Jan. 12, 1788). His first opera for Paris, *Démophon* (Paris Opera, Dec. 2, 1788), was a failure, due largely to J. F. Marmontel's inept libretto and Cherubini's less than total command of French prosody. In 1789, Leonard, a member of the Queen's household, assisted by Viotti, obtained a license to establish an Italian opera company at the Tuileries (Théâtre de Monsieur); Cherubini became its music director and conductor. After the company moved to a new theater in the rue Feydeau, he produced his opera *Lodoïska* (July 18, 1791), with notable success; with this score, he effectively developed a new dramatic style, destined to have profound impact on the course of French opera. The increased breadth and force of its ensemble numbers, its novel and rich orchestral combinations, and its generally heightened dramatic effect inspired other composers to follow his lead, particularly Méhul and Le Sueur. With the French Revolution in full swing, the Italian Opera was disbanded (1792). Cherubini then went to Normandy, but returned to Paris in 1793 to become an inspector at the new Inst. National de Musique (later the Cons.). His opera *Médée* (March 13, 1797), noteworthy for its startling characterization of Medea and for the mastery of its orchestration, proved a major step in his development as a dramatic composer. With *Les Deux Journées, ou Le Porteur d'eau* (Jan. 16, 1800), he scored his greatest triumph with the public as a composer for the theater; the opera was soon performed throughout Europe to much acclaim.

In 1805 Cherubini received an invitation to visit Vienna, where he was honored at the court. He also met the foremost musicians of the day, including Haydn and Beethoven. He composed the opera *Faniska*, which was successfully premiered at the Kärnthnertortheater on Feb. 25, 1806. After Napoleon captured Vienna, Cherubini was extended royal favor by the French emperor, who expressed his desire that Cherubini return to Paris. When Cherubini's opera *Pimmalione* (Nov. 30, 1809) failed to please the Parisians, Cherubini retired to the château of the Prince of Chimay, occupying himself with botanizing and painting. At the request to compose a Mass for the church of Chimay, he produced the celebrated 3-part Mass in F major. He subsequently devoted much time to composing sacred music. In 1815 he was commissioned by the Phil. Soc. of London to compose a sym., a cantata, and an overture; he visited London that summer for their performances. In 1816 he was appointed co-superintendent (with Le Sueur) of the Royal Chapel, and in 1822 became director of the Paris Cons., a position he held until a month before his death. In 1814 he was made a member of the Inst. and a Chevalier of the Légion d'honneur, and in 1841 he was made a Commander of the Légion d'honneur, the first musician to be so honored. He was accorded a state funeral, during which ceremony his Requiem in D minor (1836) was performed.

Cherubini was an important figure in the transitional period from the Classical to the Romantic eras in music. His influence on the development of French opera was of great historical significance. Although his operas have not found a permanent place in the repertoire, several have been revived in modern times. He also played a predominant role in music education in France during his long directorship of the Paris Cons. His influence extended beyond the borders of his adoptive homeland through his valuable treatise *Cours de contrepoint et de fugue* (with Halévy; Paris, 1835; Eng. tr., 1837). As the all-powerful director of the Paris Cons., he established an authoritarian regimen; in most of his instruction of the faculty he pursued the Italian type of composition. He rejected any novel deviations from strict form, harmony, counterpoint, or orchestration, regarding Beethoven's 9th Sym. as an aberration of a great composer's mind. He rejected descriptive music and demonstratively refused to attend rehearsals or performances of the *Symphonie fantastique* by Berlioz, who was then a student at the Paris Cons.

WORKS: A. Bottée de Toulmon prepared a *Notice des manuscrits autographes de la musique composée par feu M.-L.-C.-Z.-S. C.* (Paris, 1843); it contains the composer's own catalog of works. A modern catalog is included in A. Damerini, ed., *L. C. nel II centenario della nascita* (Florence, 1962). DRAMATIC: (only wholly extant works listed): *Il giuocatore*, intermezzo (1775); untitled intermezzo (dei Serviti, Florence, Feb. 16, 1778); *Armida abbandonata*, opera (Teatro alla Pergola, Florence, Jan. 25, 1782); *Mesenzio re d'Eturia*, opera (Teatro alla Pergola, Florence, Sept. 6, 1782); *Il Quinto Fabio*, opera (Torre Argentina, Rome, Jan. 1783); *Lo sposo di tre e marito di nessuna*, opera (San Samuele, Venice, Nov. 1783); *Olimpiade*, opera (c.1783); Il *Giulio Sabino*, opera (King's Theatre, London, March 30, 1786); *Ifigenia in Aulide*, opera (Teatro Regio, Turin, Jan. 12, 1788); *Démophon*, opera (Opéra, Paris, Dec. 2, 1788); *La Molinarella*, parody (Tuileries, Paris, Oct. 31, 1789); *Lodoïska*, heroic comedy (Feydeau, Paris, July 18, 1791); *Eliza, ou Le Voyage aux glaciers du Mont St.-Bernard*, opera (Feydeau, Paris, Feb. 23, 1794); *Médée*, opera (Feydeau, Paris, March 13, 1797); *L'Hôtellerie portugaise*, comic opera (Feydeau, Paris, July 25, 1798); *La Punition*, opera (Feydeau, Paris, Feb. 23, 1799); *La Prisonnière*, pasticcio (with Boieldieu; Montansier, Paris, Sept. 12, 1799); *Les Deux Journées, ou Le Porteur d'eau*, opera (Feydeau, Paris, Jan. 16, 1800; in Eng. as *The Water Carrier* and in German as *Der Wasserträger*); *Epicure*, opera (with Méhul; Favart, Paris, March 14, 1800); *Anacréon, ou L'Amour fugitif*, opéra ballet (Opéra, Paris, Oct. 4, 1803); *Achille à Scyros*, ballet-pantomime (pasticcio, but most of the music by Cherubini; Opéra, Paris, Dec. 18, 1804); *Faniska*, opera (Kärnthnertortheater, Vienna, Feb. 25, 1806); *Pimmalione*, opera (Tuileries, Paris, Nov. 30, 1809); *Le Crescendo*, opera (Opéra Comique, Paris, Sept. 30, 1810); *Les Abencérages, ou L'Étendard de Grenade*, opera (Opéra, Paris, April 6, 1813); *Bayard à Mézières*, comic pasticcio (with Boieldieu, Catel, and Nicolo; Opéra-Comique, Paris, Feb. 12, 1814); *Blanche de Provence, ou La Cour de fées*, pasticcio (with Berton, Boieldieu, Kreutzer, and Paër; Tuileries, Paris, May 1, 1821); *La Marquise de Brinvilliers*, pasticcio (with 8 other composers; overture by Cherubini; Opéra Comique, Paris, Oct. 31, 1831); *Ali-Baba, ou Les Quarante Voleurs*, opera (Opéra, Paris, July 22, 1833).

BIBL.: C. Place, *Essai sur la composition musicale: Biographie et analyse phrénologique de C.* (Paris, 1842); L. Picchianti, *Notizie sulla vita e sulle opere di L. C.* (Milan, 1843); B. Gamucci, *Intorno alla vita ed alle opere di L. C.* (Florence, 1869); E. Bellasis, *C.: Memorials Illustrative of His Life* (London, 1874; 3d ed., rev., 1912); F. Crowest, *C.* (London, 1890); M. Wittmann, *C.* (Leipzig, 1895); R. Hohenemser, *L. C.: Sein Leben und seine Werke* (Leipzig, 1913); M. Quatrelles-L'Épine, *C. (1760–1842): Notes et documents inédits* (Lille, 1913); L. Schemann, *C.* (Stuttgart, 1925); P. Espil, *Les Voyages de C. ou l'enfance de Mozart* (Bayonne, 1946); G. Confalonieri, *Prigionia di un artista: Il romanzo di L. C.* (2 vols., Milan, 1948); M. Selden, *The French Operas of L. C.* (diss., Yale Univ., 1951); F. Schlitzer, *Ricerche su C.* (Siena, 1954); A.

Damerini, ed., *L. C. nel II centenario della nascità* (Florence, 1962); C. Reynolds, *C.* (Ilfracombe, 1963); B. Deane, *C.* (London, 1965); G. Confalonieri, *C.* (Turin, 1978).

Cheslock, Louis, English-born American composer, violinist, and teacher; b. London, Sept. 9, 1898; d. Baltimore, July 19, 1981. He was taken to the United States as a child and became a citizen through the naturalization of his father. He studied at the Peabody Cons. of Music in Baltimore, taking diplomas in violin (1917), harmony (1919), and composition (1921). After teaching violin there (1916–22), he remained on its faculty as a teacher of theory and composition (1922–76). He also was a violinist in the Baltimore Sym. Orch. (1916–37). His music was basically neo-Romantic, although in later years he experimented with modern elements ranging from jazz to dodecaphony. He composed *The Jewel Merchants*, opera (1930; Baltimore, Feb. 26, 1940), and *Cinderella*, ballet (Baltimore, May 11, 1946; rev. 1958). He publ. an *Introductory Study on Violin Vibrato* (Baltimore, 1931) and ed. *H. L. Mencken on Music* (N.Y., 1961).

BIBL.: E. Sprenkle, *The Life and Works of L. C.* (diss., Peabody Cons. of Music, 1979).

Chevreuille, Raymond, Belgian composer; b. Brussels, Nov. 17, 1901; d. Montignies-le-Tilleul, May 9, 1976. He took a course in harmony at the Brussels Cons., but was largely self-taught in composition. From 1936 to 1959 he was employed as a sound engineer at the Belgian Radio. His style of composition embodies distinct elements of French impressionism; his searing melodies and rich harmonies are often housed within a framework of emancipated tonality, often verging on polytonal syncretism. He composed the chamber opera *Atta Troll* (1952) and the ballets *Jean et les Argayons* (1934), *Cendrillon* (1946), *La Bal chez la portière* (1954), and *Spéléomagie*, miniature ballet for TV (1959); also 2 symphonic radio plays: *D'un diable de briquet* (1950) and *L'Élixir du révérend père Gaucher* (1951).

Chiara, Maria(-Rita), Italian soprano; b. Oderzo, near Venice, Nov. 24, 1939. She studied with Antonio Cassinelli, who later became her husband, and with Maria Carbone. In 1965 she made her operatic debut in Venice as Desdemona. She subsequently appeared with the Bavarian State Opera in Munich and with the Vienna State Opera (1970); her debut at London's Covent Garden came in 1973 as Liù. In 1977 she made her U.S. debut as Manon Lescaut at the Chicago Lyric Opera; her Metropolitan Opera debut in New York followed on Dec. 16, 1977, as Violetta. In 1985 she appeared as Aida at Milan's La Scala. She sang Amelia in *Un ballo in maschera* in Naples in 1989. In 1991 she appeared as Leonora in *Il Trovatore* in Turin. Among her most noted roles are Anna Bolena, Maria Stuarda, Amelia Boccanegra, Aida, and Elisabeth de Valois.

Chisholm, Erik, Scottish composer and conductor; b. Glasgow, Jan. 4, 1904; d. Rondebosch, South Africa, June 7, 1965. He first studied music in Glasgow; then in London and in Edinburgh with Donald Tovey (composition) and Puishnov (piano); he received his Mus.Bac. in 1931, and his Mus.Doc. in 1934 from the Univ. of Edinburgh. He was conductor of the Glasgow Grand Opera Soc. from 1930 to 1939; in 1940 he joined the Carl Rosa Opera Co. as conductor; in 1945 he founded the Singapore Sym. Orch.; in 1946 he was appointed prof. of music and director of the South African College of Music at Cape Town Univ.; he also conducted operas in South Africa. His book, *The Operas of Leos Janáček*, was publ. posth. (N.Y., 1971). Chisholm's style of composition was marked by considerable complexity; elements of oriental scale formations are notable.

WORKS: DRAMATIC: OPERAS: *The Feast of Samhain* (1941); *The Inland Woman* (Cape Town, Oct. 21, 1953); *Dark Sonnet*, after O'Neill (Cape Town, Oct. 20, 1952); *Simoon*, after Strindberg (1953); *Dark Sonnet* and *Simoon* were later combined with a 3d short opera, *Black Roses*, with a libretto by the composer, to form a trilogy entitled *Murder in 3 Keys* (N.Y., July 6, 1954). BALLETS: *The Pied Piper of Hamelin* (1937); *The Forsaken Mermaid* (1940); *The Earth Shapers* (1941); *The Hoodie* (1947).

Chlubna, Osvald, Czech composer; b. Brünn, June 22, 1893; d. there (Brno), Oct. 30, 1971. Following attendance at the Czech Technical College (1911–13) and the Commercial Academy (1913–14), he studied composition with Janáček at the Brno Organ School (1914–15); he later attended Janáček's master class in Brno (1923–24). Although Chlubna made his living as a bank clerk until 1953, he devoted much time to composing. He also taught at the Cons. (1919–35; 1953–59) and at the Janáček Academy of Music (1956–58) in Brno. His works followed along Romantic lines, being notable for their lyrical and rhapsodic elements. Chlubna orchestrated Act 3 of Janáček's 1st opera, *Šárka*. With B. Bakala, he rev. and reorchestrated Janáček's last opera, *Z mrtvého domu* (From the House of the Dead), for its posthumous premiere. He also completed Janáček's unfinished symphonic poem *Dunaj* (The Danube). His multivol. study of Janáček's compositional style remains in MS.

WORKS: OPERAS: *Pomsta Catullova* (Catullus's Revenge; 1917; Brno, Nov. 30, 1921; rev. 1959); *Alladina a Palomid čili Síla touhy* (Alladina and Palomid, or The Power of Desire; 1921–22; Brno, Jan. 31, 1925); *Nura* (1928–30; Brno, May 20, 1932); *V den počátku* (In the Day of the Beginning; Brno, Jan. 24, 1936); *Freje pana z Heslova* (The Affairs of the Lord of Heslov; 1939; Brno, Jan. 28, 1949); *Jiří z Kunštátu a Poděbrad* (Jiří of Kunštát and Poděbrady; 1941); *Kolébka* (The Cradle; 1952); *Eupyros* (n.d.).

BIBL.: M. Černohorská, *O. C.* (Brno, 1963).

Chollet, Jean Baptiste (Marie), French baritone, later tenor; b. Paris, May 20, 1798; d. Nemours, Jan. 10, 1892. He received his training at the Paris Cons. He appeared as a baritone in Switzerland, in Le Havre (1823–25), at the Paris Opéra Comique (1825), and in Brussels (1826). Returning to the Opéra Comique, he turned to tenor roles and sang in the premiere of Hérold's *Marie* (Aug. 12, 1826). He then created the title roles in Auber's *Fra Diavolo* (Jan. 28, 1830) and Hérold's *Zampa* (May 3, 1831) there. After engagements in Brussels (1832–34) and The Hague (1834–35), he returned once more to the Opéra Comique and created the role of Chapelou in Adam's *Le Postillon de Longjumeau* (Oct. 13, 1836). In 1844 his health declined and in 1847 he was compelled to leave the Opéra Comique. After serving as director of theaters in Bordeaux (1847–48) and The Hague (1851), he resumed his career as a singer with appearances in Toulouse (1848), London (1850), and Paris (1852–54) before retiring from the operatic stage.

BIBL.: A. Laget, *C.* (Toulouse, 1880).

Chookasian, Lili, American contralto; b. Chicago, Aug. 1, 1921. She studied with Phillip Manuel, then made her concert debut as soloist in Mahler's 3d Sym. with Bruno Walter and the Chicago Sym. Orch. (1957). Her operatic debut followed as Adalgisa at the Arkansas Opera Theater in Little Rock (1959), and, after additional training with Rosa Ponselle, she made her Metropolitan Opera debut in New York as La Cieca in *La Gioconda* (March 9, 1962). She remained on the Metropolitan roster until 1978, where she again was a member from 1979. She made her first European appearance at the Bayreuth Festival in 1963 and in subsequent years sang widely in both opera and concert performances, appearing often in contemporary works.

Christie, William (Lincoln), outstanding American-born French conductor and harpsichordist; b. Buffalo, Dec. 19, 1944. He began his musical training with his mother. After studying harpsichord with Igor Kipnis at the Berkshire Music Center in Tanglewood, he took courses in music and art history at Harvard Univ. (B.A., 1966), and in harpsichord with Ralph Kirkpatrick, organ with Charles Krigbaum, and musicology with Claude Palisca and Nicholas Temperley at Yale Univ. (M.Mus., 1970). In 1971 he proceeded to Europe to complete his harpsichord studies with Kenneth Gilbert and David Fuller. In 1979 he founded Les Arts Florissants, a vocal and instrumental ensemble he developed into one of the foremost performing groups of French, Italian, and English music of the 17th and 18th centuries. From 1982 to 1995 he was a prof. of early music at the Paris Cons., the first American ever to serve on its faculty. In 1983 he conducted Monteverdi's

In ballo delle ingrate at the Opéra du Rhin in Strasbourg, and returned there in 1985 with Rameau's *Anacréon* and Charpentier's *Actéon*. After conducting Rameau's *Hippolyte et Aricie* at the Opéra Comique in Paris in 1985, he returned there in 1987 to great critical acclaim with Lully's *Atys*. In 1989 he conducted the latter work at the Brooklyn Academy of Music, and also conducted Purcell's *The Fairy Queen* at the Aix-en-Provence Festival. His subsequent engagements in Aix-en-Provence included Rameau's *Les Indes galantes* in 1990 and *Castor et Pollux* in 1991, and Mozart's *Die Zauberflöte* in 1994. In 1990 he led performances of *Actéon* and Purcell's *Dido and Aeneas* in London. After conducting the latter composer's *King Arthur* at London's Covent Garden in 1995, he was engaged as a conductor at the Glyndebourne Festival in 1996 for Handel's *Rodelinda*. He led Les Arts Florissants on tours to many leading music centers of the world, and also appeared as a guest conductor in Europe and abroad. In 1993 he was awarded the Légion d'honneur of France. In addition to his performances of the celebrated masters of the Baroque era, Christie has also championed the works of such lesser-known composers as Bouzignac, Lambert, Montéclair, Moulinié, and Rossi.

Christoff, Boris (Kirilov), celebrated Bulgarian bass; b. Plovdiv, May 18, 1914; d. Rome, June 28, 1993. He sang in the Gusla Choir in Sofia, where he was heard by King Boris, who made it possible for him to go to Rome to study with Stracciari; he later studied in Salzburg with Muratti. He made his debut in a concert in Rome in 1946; that same year he made his operatic debut there at the Teatro Argentina as Colline in *La Bohème*. He made his first appearance at La Scala in Milan in 1947, at Covent Garden in London in 1949, and his U.S. debut as Boris Godunov with the San Francisco Opera on Sept. 25, 1956. During his distinguished career, he appeared with many leading opera houses, singing most of the principal bass roles in the operas of Verdi, as well as such roles as Gurnemanz, Ivan Susanin, Hagen, Rocco, Konchak, and King Marke. He was most renowned for his dramatic portrayal of Boris Godunov, which recalled the interpretation of Chaliapin. His brother-in-law was **Tito Gobbi**.

BIBL.: F. Barker, *Voice of the Opera: B. C.* (London, 1951); G. Lauri-Volpi, *Voci parallele: B. C.* (Milan, 1955); O. Dejkova, *B. D.* (Sofia, 1965); A. Bozhkov, *B. Khristov* (Sofia, 1985); V. Pravchanska-Ivanova and N. Pravchanski, *Sreshti s B. Khristov* (Sofia, 1990); C. Curami and M. Modugno, *B. C.: La vita, la voce, l'arte* (Parma, 1996).

Christoff, Dimiter, Bulgarian composer; b. Sofia, Oct. 2, 1933. He studied composition with M. Goleminov at the Bulgarian State Cons. in Sofia (1951–56), where he later taught (from 1970). He was also vice-president of the Bulgarian Composers Union (1972–85) and general secretary of the International Music Council of UNESCO (1975–79). He composed the opera *Game* (1978) and the chamber opera *The Golden Fish Line* (1984).

Christophers, Harry, English conductor; b. Goudhurst, Kent, Dec. 26, 1953. He received his initial training at the Canterbury Cathedral Choir School, and later pursued his education at Magdalen College, Oxford. In 1977 he organized the esteemed choral aggregation The Sixteen, which he led in a vast repertory from Palestrina to contemporary composers. In 1989 he toured Great Britain, Europe, Japan, and Brazil with his group, and in 1992 he toured the globe with it. From 1997 he likewise conducted the Symphony of Harmony and Invention. He also made appearances as a guest conductor throughout Great Britain and Europe.

Christou, Jani, remarkable Greek composer; b. Heliopolis, Egypt (of Greek parents), Jan. 8, 1926; d. in an automobile accident near Athens, Jan. 8, 1970. He studied at Victoria College in Alexandria; then took courses in philosophy under Wittgenstein at King's College, Cambridge (M.A., 1948); concurrently he studied composition with Hans Redlich in Letchworth (1945–48); then enrolled in the summer courses of the Accademia Musicale Chigiana in Siena (1949–50); during the same period, he attended Karl Jung's lectures on psychology in Zürich. Christou returned to Alexandria in 1951; then lived on his family estate on the island of Chios. He evolved a system of composition embracing the totality of human and metaphysical expression, forming a "philosophical structure" for which he designed a surrealistic graphic notation involving a "psychoid factor," symbolized by the Greek letter psi; aleatory practices are indicated by the drawing of a pair of dice; a sudden stop, by a dagger, and so on. His score *Enantiodromia* (Opposed Pathways) for Orch. (1965; rev. 1968; Oakland, Calif., Feb. 18, 1969), in such a graphic notation, is reproduced in the avant-garde publication *Source*, 6 (1969). His notation also includes poetry, choreographic acting, special lighting, film, and projection meant to envelop the listener on all sides. At his death, he left sketches for a set of 130 multimedia compositions of a category he called *Anaparastasis* ("proto-performances, meant to revive primeval rituals as adapted to modern culture"). He composed a "super opera," *Oresteia*, after Aeschylus (1967–70), which was left unfinished.

BIBL.: J. Papaioannou, *J. C. and the Metaphysics of Music* (London, 1970).

Christov, Dobri. See **Khristov, Dobri.**

Chueca, Federico, Spanish composer; b. Madrid, May 5, 1846; d. there, June 20, 1908. He was a medical student. He organized a band at the Univ. of Madrid, also conducted theater orchs. He began to compose for the stage in collaboration with Valverde, who helped him to harmonize and orchestrate his melodies. Thanks to his prodigious facility, he wrote a great number of zarzuelas, of which *La gran via*, produced in Madrid (July 2, 1886), became his greatest success, obtaining nearly 1,000 performances in Madrid alone; it has also been performed many times in Latin America and the United States. The march from his zarzuela *Cadiz* served for a time as the Spanish national anthem; dances from his *El año pasado por agua* and *Locuras madrileñas* also enjoyed great popularity. Chueca is regarded as one of the creators of the "género chico" (light genre) of Spanish stage music.

Chung, Myung-Whun, talented Korean-born American conductor and pianist; b. Seoul, Jan. 22, 1953. He is the brother of two brilliant siblings: the Korean violinist Kyung-Wha Chung (b. Seoul, March 26, 1948) and the Korean-born American cellist Myung-Wha Chung (b. Seoul, March 19, 1944). He played piano as a child, making his debut as soloist with the Seoul Phil. when he was 7; he then went to the United States, where he studied with Nadia Reisenberg (piano) and Carl Bamberger (conducting) at the Mannes College of Music in New York, and at the Juilliard School (diplomas in piano and conducting, 1974); he received additional tutelage in conducting there from Sixten Ehrling (1975–78). He made his conducting debut in Seoul (1971), subsequently winning 2d prize in piano at the Tchaikovsky Competition in Moscow (1974). He became a naturalized American citizen in 1973. He pursued a dual career as a pianist and conductor; he gave trio concerts with his sisters, and was assistant conductor of the Los Angeles Phil. (1978–81), and chief conductor of the Saarland Radio Sym. Orch. in Saarbrücken (1984–90). On Feb. 21, 1986, he made his Metropolitan Opera debut in New York conducting *Simon Boccanegra*. In 1989 he became music director-designate and in 1990 was confirmed in the position of music director of the new Opéra de la Bastille in Paris. While his tenure was initially successful, the election of a new French government led to a change in the administration of the Opéra. Although Chung's tenure as music director was to extend to the year 2000, the new administration in 1994 sought to end his tenure by 1997, freeze his salary, and deny him artistic control of the Opéra. His refusal to accept these altered terms led to an abrupt dismissal, although he conducted the opening performances of the season in Oct. 1994 with *Simon Boccanegra* before taking leave of the embattled company. In 1997 he was appointed music director of both the Orchestre Sinfonica dell'Accademia Nazionale di Santa Cecilia in Rome and the Asia Phil. in Tokyo.

Chusid, Martin, American musicologist; b. N.Y., Aug. 19, 1925. He studied at the Univ. of Calif. at Berkeley (B.A., 1950; M.A., 1955; Ph.D., 1961, with the diss. *The Chamber Music of Schubert*). Chusid taught at the Univ. of Southern Calif. in Los Angeles (1959–63) and at N.Y. Univ. (from 1963), where he also served as chairman of the music dept. (1967–70), assoc. dean of the graduate school of arts and sciences (1970–72), and director of the American Inst. for Verdi Studies (from 1976). He edited the Norton Critical Score ed. of Schubert's *Unfinished Symphony* (N.Y., 1968; 2d ed., 1971), and was a contributor to the new critical ed. of Verdi's complete works; he also edited *A Catalog of Verdi's Operas* (Hackensack, N.J., 1974) and, with W. Weaver, *The Verdi Companion* (N.Y., 1979).

Cibber, Susanne Maria, celebrated English actress and mezzo-soprano, sister of **Thomas Augustine Arne**; b. London, Feb. 17, 1714; d. there, Jan. 31, 1766. After vocal training from her brother, she made her debut at the Little Theatre in the Haymarket in 1732 in J. F. Lampe's *Amelia*. In 1734 she became a member of the Drury Lane Theatre. That same year she married Theophilus Cibber, the disreputable son of the actor and dramatist Colley Cibber who admired her talent and served as her mentor. Her first great success was as Polly in *The Beggar's Opera*, which made her one of the leading lights on the London stage. Her notoriety was further enhanced when her husband allowed one of her admirers, John Sloper, to become her intimate upon payment of a fee. The ensuing scandal prompted Susanna and her new mate to elope. All the same, Handel engaged her for his oratorio productions in Dublin in 1741. On April 13, 1742, she sang in the premiere of his *Messiah* there. Returning to London, she sang in other oratorios by Handel while pursuing her career as an actress. Handel chose her to create the roles of Micah in *Samson* (1743) and Lichas in *Hercules* (1745). From 1744 she was the leading lady at Drury Lane, where she was acclaimed as an actress in tragic roles.

BIBL.: *An Account of the Life of S. M. C.* (London, 1887); M. Nash, *The Provoked Wife: The Life and Times of S. C.* (London, 1977).

Ciccimarra, Giuseppe, admired Italian tenor and teacher; b. Altamura, May 22, 1790; d. Venice, Dec. 5, 1836. He became a principal member of the Teatro San Carlo in Naples, where he gained notable distinction for his roles in Rossini's operas. He created Rossini's Iago (1816), Goffredo in *Arminda* (1817), Aronne in *Mosè* (1818), Ernesto in *Ricciardo e Zoraide* (1818), Pilade in *Erminione* (1819), and Condulmiero in *Maometto II* (1820). After his retirement in 1826, he went to Vienna as a teacher of voice and piano. Among his pupils were Clara Heinefetter, Sophie Loewe, Joseph Staudigl, and Joseph Tichatschek.

Ciesinski, Katherine, American mezzo-soprano, sister of **Kristine Ciesinski**; b. Newark, Del., Oct. 13, 1950. She studied at Temple Univ. (B.M., 1972; M.M., 1973) and at the Curtis Inst. of Music in Philadelphia (opera diploma, 1976); she won 1st prize in the Geneva International Competition (1976) and Grand Prize in the Paris International Competition (1977). She made her concert debut with the Philadelphia Orch. (1974) and her operatic debut as Leonora in *La Favorite* with the Opera Co. of Philadelphia (1975). She sang Erika in Barber's *Vanessa* at the Spoleto Festival U.S.A. (1978), then gained wide recognition as Countess Geschwitz in the first U.S. production of the 3-act version of Berg's *Lulu* at the Santa Fe Opera (1979). In 1988 she sang in the premiere performance of Argento's *The Aspern Papers* in Dallas. She made her Metropolitan Opera debut in New York as Nicklausse in *Les Contes d'Hoffmann* in 1988. In 1993 she was engaged as Handel's Xerxes at the Santa Fe Opera. As a concert artist, she appeared with leading orchs. in both North America and Europe; she also gave duo recitals with her sister. Among her prominent roles are Ottavia in *L'incoronazione di Poppea*, Laura in *La Gioconda*, Eboli in *Don Carlos*, Dalila in *Samson et Dalila*, Charlotte in *Werther*, Octavian in *Der Rosenkavalier*, and the Composer in *Ariadne auf Naxos*.

Ciesinski, Kristine, American soprano, sister of **Katherine Ciesinski**; b. Wilmington, Del., July 5, 1952. She studied at Temple Univ. (1970–71), the Univ. of Delaware (1971–72), and Boston Univ. (1973–74; B.A., 1974); in 1977 she won the Gold Medal in the Geneva International Competition and 1st prize in the Salzburg International Competition. She made her N.Y. concert debut as a soloist in Handel's Messiah (1977) and her European operatic debut as Baroness Freimann in Lortzing's *Der Wildschütz* at the Salzburg Landestheater (1979), remaining on its roster until 1981; she was subsequently a member of the Bremen State Opera (1985–88). She made guest appearances with the Cleveland Opera (1985), Glasgow's Scottish National Opera (1985), Toronto's Canadian Opera Co. (1986), Leeds Opera North (1986), the Augsburg Opera (1986), Cardiff's Welsh National Opera (1986), Munich's Bavarian State Opera (1989), London's English National Opera (1989–93), and Milan's La Scala (1992). In 1996 she appeared as Salome at the English National Opera. She also sang extensively in concerts, often appearing with her sister. Her finest roles include Iphigénie, Medea, Beethoven's Leonora, Cassandra, La Wally, Eva, Elisabeth in *Tannhäuser*, Chrysothemis, Ariadne, Salome, and Tosca. She married **Norman Bailey** in 1985.

Cigna, Gina (real name, **Ginetta Sens**), French soprano of Italian descent; b. Paris, March 6, 1900. She was a pupil of Calvé, Darclée, and Storchio. After making her operatic debut as Freia at Milan's La Scala in 1927, she was on its roster (1929–43); also appeared at London's Covent Garden (1933; 1936–37; 1939). On Feb. 6, 1937, she made her Metropolitan Opera debut in New York as Aida, and sang there until 1938 in such roles as Leonora in *Il Trovatore*, Gioconda, Norma, Donna Elvira, and Santuzza. After World War II, she taught voice in Milan; she also was on the faculty of the Royal Cons. of Music of Toronto (1953–57).

Cikker, Ján, eminent Slovak composer and pedagogue; b. Banská Bystrica, July 29, 1911; d. Bratislava, Dec. 21, 1989. He was a student of Křička (composition), Dědeček (conducting), and Wiedermann (organ) at the Prague Cons. (1930–35), where he then attended Novák's master class in composition (1935–36); he concurrently studied musicology at the Univ. of Prague, and then pursued conducting studies with Weingartner in Vienna (1936–37). After settling in Bratislava, he was prof. of theory at the Cons. (1938–51) and prof. of composition at the Academy of Music and Dramatic Arts (1951–81). In 1955, 1963, and 1975 he was awarded state prizes. In 1966 he was named a National Artist by his homeland, and that same year was awarded the Herder Prize of the Univ. of Vienna. In 1979 he received the UNESCO Prize. In a number of his works, Cikker utilized Slovak melodies. In others, he moved toward expressionism and eventually embraced serial procedures. His works for the stage were particularly notable.

WORKS: OPERAS: *Juro Jánošík* (1953; Bratislava, Nov. 10, 1954; rev. version, Bratislava, May 7, 1956); *Beg Bajazid* (Bajazet Bey; 1956; Bratislava, Feb. 16, 1957); *Mr. Scrooge*, after Dickens (1957–59; 1st perf. as *Evening, Night, and Morning*, Kassel, Oct. 5, 1963); *Vzkriesenie* (Resurrection), after Tolstoy (1961; Prague, May 18, 1962); *Hra o láske a smrti* (A Play of Love and Death), after Romain Rolland (1968; Munich, Aug. 1, 1969); *Coriolanus* (1971; Prague, April 4, 1974); *Rozsudok: Zemetrasenie v Chile* (The Sentence: Earthquake in Chile; 1978; Bratislava, Oct. 8, 1979); *Obliehanie Bystrice* (The Siege of Bystrica; 1981; Bratislava, Oct. 8, 1983); *Zo života hmyzu* (From the Life of Insects; 1986; Bratislava, Feb. 21, 1987).

BIBL.: J. Samko, *J. C.* (Bratislava, 1955).

Cilèa, Francesco, Italian composer and pedagogue; b. Palmi, Calabria, July 23, 1866; d. Varazze, Nov. 20, 1950. He studied at the Naples Cons. (1881–89) with Cesi (piano) and Serrao (composition); taught piano there (1894–96); then harmony at the Istituto Musicale in Florence (1896–1904); was head of the Palermo Cons. (1913–16) and of the Cons. di San Pietro a Majella in Naples (1916–35). He was a member of the Reale Accademia Musicale in Florence (1898) and a knight of the Order of the Crown of Italy (1893).

WORKS: OPERAS: *Gina* (Naples, Feb. 9, 1889); *La Tilda* (Florence, April 7, 1892); *L'Arlesiana* (Milan, Nov. 27, 1897; rev. version, Milan, Oct. 22, 1898); *Adriana Lecouvreur* (Milan, Nov. 6, 1902); *Gloria* (Milan, April 15, 1907); *Il matrimonio selvaggio* (1909).

BIBL.: E. Moschino, *Sulle opere di F. C.* (Milan, 1932); C. Gaianus, *F. C. e la sua nuova ora* (Bologna, 1939); T. d'Amico, *F. C.* (Milan, 1960).

Cillario, Carlo Felice, Italian conductor; b. San Rafael, Argentina, Feb. 7, 1915. He began music training in Buenos Aires, then studied violin and composition at the Bologna Cons. After making appearances as a violinist, he received instruction in conducting from Enesco; he then went to Russia, where he continued his studies at the Odessa Cons. He made his conducting debut at the Odessa Opera (1942), and after World War II embarked on a far-flung career as an operatic and sym. conductor, making guest appearances in the leading music centers of Europe and North and South America. He was music director of the Australian Opera in Sydney (1969–71), serving as its principal guest conductor and music consultant from 1987.

Cimara, Pietro, Italian conductor and composer; b. Rome, Nov. 10, 1887; d. Milan, Oct. 1, 1967. He was a student of Respighi at the Accademia di Santa Cecilia in Rome. In 1916 he made his conducting debut in Rome, where he conducted until 1927. On March 11, 1932, he made his Metropolitan Opera debut in New York conducting *Lucia di Lammermoor*, remaining on its roster until 1937; was again on its roster (1938–50; 1952–57). He composed many songs.

Cimarosa, Domenico, famous Italian composer; b. Aversa, near Naples, Dec. 17, 1749; d. Venice, Jan. 11, 1801. He was the son of a stonemason. After his father's death, his mother placed him in the monastery school of the church of S. Severo dei Padri Conventuali in Naples, where he began his musical training with Father Polcano, the monastery organist. He then enrolled at the Cons. di S. Maria di Loreto (1761), where he studied voice, violin, and keyboard playing with Fenaroli, P.A. Gallo, and Carcais. Following his graduation in 1771, he studied voice with Giuseppe Aprile. His first opera, *Le stravaganze del conte*, was staged in Naples in 1772. From 1776 he composed operas at a prolific rate, producing about 65 works for the major Italian opera centers as well as those abroad. In 1779 he was named supernumerary organist of the Royal Chapel in Naples; in 1785 he became its 2d organist. He also served for a time as maestro of the Ospedaletto, a cons. for girls in Venice. In 1787 he was given the post of maestro di cappella to the court of Catherine the Great in St. Petersburg. During his Russian sojourn, he wrote 3 operas and various other works for the court and the nobility. However, the court cut back on its funding of music and Cimarosa's contract was allowed to lapse in 1791. He proceeded to Vienna, where Emperor Leopold II appointed him Kapellmeister. He then composed his masterpiece, *Il matrimonio segreto*, which was premiered with great acclaim at the Burgtheater on Feb. 7, 1792. The emperor was so taken by the opera that he ordered that it be repeated that evening, undoubtedly the most elaborate encore in operatic annals. The opera's fame spread throughout Europe, and Cimarosa returned to Italy in 1793 as one of the most celebrated musicians of the age. In 1796 he was appointed 1st organist of the Royal Chapel in Naples. In 1799 he welcomed the republican movement in Naples by composing a patriotic hymn for the burning of the royal flag; however, the monarchy was restored later that year and Cimarosa's efforts miscarried. In consequence of this, he was arrested in Dec. 1799 and sent to prison for 4 months. He was released only after the intervention of several prominent individuals. He then went to Venice, where he died while working on his opera Artemisia. It was rumored abroad that he had been poisoned by order of Queen Caroline of Naples; the rumor was so persistent, and popular feelings so pronounced, that the Pope's personal physician, Piccioli, was sent to Venice to make an examination; according to his sworn statement (April 5, 1801), Cimarosa died of a gangrenous abdominal tumor.

Cimarosa was an outstanding composer of Italian opera buffa in his day. His melodic inventiveness, command of form, superb vocal writing, and masterly orchestration were unexcelled until Rossini arrived upon the scene.

WORKS: DRAMATIC: OPERAS: *Le stravaganze del conte* (Naples, Carnival 1772); *La finta parigina* (Naples, Carnival 1773); *I sdegni per amore* (Naples, Jan. 1776); *I matrimoni in ballo* (Naples, Carnival 1776); *La Frascatana nobile* or *La finta frascatana* (Naples, 1776); *I tre amanti* (Rome, Carnival 1777); *Il Fanatico per gli antiche romani* (Naples, 1777); *L'armida immaginaria* (Naples, 1777); *Gli amanti comici, o sia La famiglia in scompiglio* (Naples, 1778?); *Il ritorno di Don Calandrino* (Rome, Carnival 1778); *Le stravaganze d'amore* (Naples, 1778); *Il matrimonio per raggiro* or *La Donna bizzarra* (Rome, 1778–79?); *L'Italiana in Londra* (Rome, Carnival 1779); *L'infedeltà fedele* (Naples, 1779); *Le Donne rivali* (Rome, Carnival 1780); *Cajo Mario* (Rome, Carnival 1780); *I finti nobili* (Naples, Carnival 1780); *Il Falegname* (Naples, 1780); *Il capriccio drammatico* (Turin, 1781?); *Il Pittor parigino* (Rome, Carnival 1781); *Alessandro nell'Indie* (Rome, Carnival 1781); *L'Amante combattuto dalle donne di Punto* (Naples, 1781); *Giunio Bruto* (Verona, 1781); *Giannina e Bernardone* (Venice, 1781); *Il convito* (Venice, Carnival 1782); *L'amor costante* (Rome, Carnival 1782); *L'Eroe cinese* (Naples, 1782); *La Ballerina amante* (Naples, 1782); *La Circe* (Milan, Carnival 1783); *I due baroni di Rocca Azzurra* (Rome, Carnival 1783); *La Villana riconosciuta* (Naples, 1783); *Oreste* (Naples, 1783); *Chi dell'altrui si veste presto si spoglia* (Naples, 1783); *I matrimoni impensati* or *La bella greca* (Rome, Carnival 1784); *L'apparenza inganna, o sia La villeggiatura* (Naples, 1784); *La vanità delusa* or *Il mercato di Malmantile* (Florence, 1784); *L'Olimpiade* (Vicenza, 1784); *I due supposti conti, ossia Lo sposo senza moglie* (Milan, 1784); *Artaserse* (Turin, 1784); *Il Marito disperato* or *Il Marito geloso* (Naples, 1785); *La Donna sempre al suo peggior s'appiglia* (Naples, 1785); *Il Credulo* (Naples, Carnival 1786); *Le trame deluse* (Naples, 1786); *L'Impresario in angustie* (Naples, 1786); *Volodimiro* (Turin, Carnival 1787); *Il Fanatico burlato* (Naples, 1787); *La felicità inaspettata* (St. Petersburg, March 1788); *La Vergine del sole* (St. Petersburg, 1788?); *La Cleopatra* (St. Petersburg, Oct. 8, 1789); *Il matrimonio segreto* (Vienna, Feb. 7, 1792); *Amor rende sagace* (Vienna, April 1, 1793); *I traci amanti* (Naples, June 19, 1793); *Le astuzie femminili* (Naples, Aug. 26, 1794); *Penelope* (Naples, Carnival 1795); *Le nozze in garbuglio* (Messina, 1795); *L'impegno superato* (Naples, 1795); *La finta ammalata* (Lisbon, 1796); *I Nemici generosi* (Rome, Carnival 1796); *Gli Orazi ed i Curiazi* (Venice, Carnival 1797); *Achille all'assedio di Troja* (Rome, Carnival 1797); *L'imprudente fortunato* (Rome, Carnival 1797); *Artemisia regina di Caria* (Naples, 1797); *L'apprensivo raggirato* (Naples, 1798); *Il secreto* (Turin, 1798); *Artemisia* (Venice, Carnival 1801; left unfinished); some 30 other stage works have been at tributed to Cimarosa, but many are doubtful. ORATORIOS: *Giuditta* (Venice, 1782?); *Absalom* (Venice, 1782); *Il sacrificio d'Abramo* (Naples, 1786); *Il trionfo delle fede* (Naples, May 1794); *Il martirio* (Naples, 1795); *S. Filippo Neri che risuscita Paolo Massimi* (Rome, 1797).

BIBL.: M. Trevisan, *Nel primo centenario di D. C.* (Venice, 1900); R. Vitale, *D. C., La vita e le opere* (Aversa, 1929); G. Biamonti, *Il matrimonio segreto di D. C.* (Rome, 1930); F. Schlitzer, *Goethe e C.* (Siena, 1950); J. Johnson, *D. C. (1749–1801)* (diss., Univ. College, Cardiff, 1976).

Cinti-Damoreau, Laure (née **Laure Cinthie Montalant**), noted French soprano; b. Paris, Feb. 6, 1801; d. Chantilly, Feb. 25, 1863. She studied with Plantade, Bordogni, and Catalani at the Paris Cons.. After Italianizing her middle name to Cinti, she made her operatic debut in *Una cosa rara* at the Théâtre-Italien on Jan. 8, 1816; she sang there until 1818, and then at the Théâtre-Louvois (1819–22). After appearing at the King's Theatre in London (1822–23), she became a prominent member of the Paris Opéra (1825–35), where she created leading roles in Rossini's *Le Siège de Corinthe* (1826), *Moïse et Pharaon* (1827), *Le Comte Ory* (1828), and *Guillaume Tell* (1829); she also created the role of Isabelle in Meyerbeer's *Robert le diable* (1831) and subsequently sang at the Opéra Comique (1836–41), creating leading roles in works by Auber, including *Le Domino noir* (1837). She also made concert tours of Europe and toured the United States with the violinist Artot in 1843–44, making her last concert appearance in 1848. She taught at the Paris Cons. (1833–56) and also publ. *Méthode de chant* (1849). In 1827 she married the tenor V.C. Damoreau (1793–1863).

Cirino, Giulio, Italian bass; b. Rome, Feb. 15, 1880; d. there, Feb. 26, 1970. He made his operatic debut in Rome in 1903; subsequently he sang at La Scala in Milan; was on the roster of the Teatro Colón in Buenos Aires from 1909 to 1923; he retired from the stage in 1935. He was particularly successful in buffo roles of the Italian repertoire, but he also sang in Wagner's operas.

Cisneros, Eleanora de (née **Broadfoot**), American mezzo-soprano; b. Brooklyn, Nov. 1, 1878; d. there (N.Y.), Feb. 3, 1934. She received training from Francesco Fanciulli and Adeline Murio-Celli in N.Y. Under the name Eleanor Francis, she made her operatic debut as Siebel at N.Y.'s American Theater in 1898. Her talent was recognized by Jean de Reszke, who arranged for her Metropolitan Opera debut as Rossweise in *Die Walküre* during the company's visit to Chicago on Nov. 24, 1899, under the name Eleanor Broadfoot. Her formal debut with the company followed in N.Y. in the same role on Jan. 5, 1900; she remained on its roster for the season. In 1901 she married Cuban Count Francesco de Cisneros and took his name professionally. After further training with Angelo Tabadello in Paris, she made her European debut in Turin in 1902. She then appeared at London's Covent Garden (1904–08) and at Milan's La Scala, where she created the role of Candia in Franchetti's *La figlia di Iorio* (1906); she also appeared in the first mountings there of Tchaikovsky's *The Queen of Spades* (1906) and Strauss's *Salome* (1906) and *Elektra* (1909). She was the principal artist with the Manhattan Opera House (1906–08), and also appeared at the Bayreuth Festival (1908). She sang in Chicago (1910–13; 1915–16), and also with Melba's opera company in London and Australia in 1911. In subsequent years, she concentrated her career in Europe. In 1932 she gave her farewell performance in Cleveland. In addition to her Wagnerian roles, she had success as Gioconda, Azucena, Santuzza, and Carmen.

Claflin, (Alan) Avery, American composer; b. Keene, N.H., June 21, 1898; d. Greenwich, Conn., Jan. 9, 1979. He studied law and banking, and also received instruction in music at Harvard Univ. from Davison. In 1919 he joined the employ of the French-American Banking Corp. in New York, later serving as its president (1947–54). His best known work was an amusing choral piece on a text of the Internal Revenue Service, *Lament for April 15* (Tanglewood, Aug. 11, 1955). He wrote the operas *The Fall of Usher* (1920–21), *Hester Prynne* (1929–33), *La grande bretèche*, after Balzac (1946–48; NBC Radio, Feb. 3, 1957), and *Uncle Tom's Cabin* (1961–64).

Clapp, Philip Greeley, American composer and pedagogue; b. Boston, Aug. 4, 1888; d. Iowa City, April 9, 1954. He studied piano with his aunt Mary Greeley James (1895–99) and violin with Jacques Hoffman in Boston (1895–1905); also took lessons in theory with John Marshall (1905). He then entered Harvard Univ., studying theory and composition with Spalding, Converse, and Edward Burlingame Hill (B.A., 1908; M.A., 1909; Ph.D., 1911). He also studied composition and conducting in Stuttgart with Max von Schillings (1909–10). He was a teaching fellow at Harvard (1911–12); he was music director at Dartmouth College (1915–18); in 1919 he was appointed director of the music dept. at the Univ. of Iowa, and remained at that post for the rest of his life. Clapp was a prolific composer and a competent teacher; he was also a brilliant pianist, but did not develop a concert career; he also appeared as a conductor of his own works and was in charge of the univ. orch. at Iowa City. His music was conceived in an expansive Romantic idiom much influenced by the modern German style of composition, and yet introducing some advanced melodic and harmonic patterns, such as harmonies built on fourths. He composed the operas *The Taming of the Shrew* (1945–48) and *The Flaming Brand* (1949–53).

BIBL.: D. Holcomb, *P.G. C.* (Iowa City, 1972); C. Calmer, *P.G. C.: The Later Years (1909–54)* (diss., Univ. of Iowa, 1992).

Clarey, Cynthia, black American mezzo-soprano; b. Smithfield, Va., April 25, 1949. She studied at Howard Univ. in Washington, D.C. (B.Mus.) and at the Juilliard School of Music in New York (postgraduate diploma). She began her career with the Tri-Cities Opera Co. in Binghamton, N.Y. In 1977 she appeared in Musgrave's *The Voice of Ariadne* at the N.Y. City Opera, and then in the U.S. premiere of Tippett's *The Ice Break* in Boston in 1979. She made her British debut as Monteverdi's Octavia at the Glyndebourne Festival in 1984, returning there in 1986 as Gershwin's Serena. In 1984 she sang in the premiere of Tippett's *The Mask of Time* in Boston. After singing Polinesso in *Ariodante* at the Wexford Festival in 1985, she returned there in 1986 as Thomas's Mignon. In 1992 she appeared as Serena in the Covent Garden premiere of *Porgy and Bess* in London, and then sang Bess in Cape Town in 1996. She appeared with major orchs. in the United States and abroad. Among her other roles were Handel's Rinaldo, Zerlina, Carmen, Dalila, Preziosilla, Octavian, and Cio-Cio-San.

Clari, Giovanni Carlo Maria, Italian composer; b. Pisa, Sept. 27, 1677; d. there, May 16, 1754. He studied with his father and with Francesco Alessi in Pisa, then under Colonna at Bologna, where his opera *Il Savio delirante* was produced in 1695. From 1703 to 1724 he was in Pistoia as maestro di cappella of the Cathedral, then went to Pisa. His best-known work is a collection of madrigals for 2 and 3 voices (1720).

Clark, Graham, English tenor; b. Littleborough, Nov. 10, 1941. He studied with Richard Bonynge, in London with Bruce Boyce, and in Bologna. In 1975 he became a member of the Scottish Opera in Glasgow. From 1976 to 1985 he also made regular appearances at the English National Opera in London. He made his Bayreuth Festival debut as David in *Die Meistersinger von Nürnberg* in 1981, and continued to sing there until 1992. On Oct. 17, 1985, he made his Metropolitan Opera debut in New York as Števa in *Jenůfa*, where he remained on the roster until 1993. In 1991 he sang in the premiere of Corigliano's *The Ghosts of Versailles* there. In 1997 he appeared at the Salzburg Festival in Ligeti's *Le Grand Macabre*. As a guest artist, he sang in Berlin, Vienna, Munich, Rome, Chicago, San Francisco, and elsewhere. He also appeared as a soloist with many orchs.

Clarke, Henry Leland, American composer and teacher; b. Dover, N.H., March 9, 1907. He received training in piano, organ, and violin before pursuing his education at Harvard Univ. (M.A., 1929), where he studied composition with Holst (1931–32; Ph.D., 1947, with a diss. on John Blow). He also studied with Boulanger at the École Normale de Musique in Paris (1929–31) and with Weisse and Luening in Bennington, Vt., and N.Y. (1932–38). Clarke taught at Bennington (Vt.) College (1936–38), Westminster Choir College in Princeton, N.J. (1938–42), the Univ. of Calif. at Los Angeles (1947–58), and the Univ. of Wash. in Seattle (1958–77). He publ. the book *Sound and Unsound: Ideas on Music* (Seattle, 1973). In his compositions, he developed such innovations as "Intervalescent Counterpoint" (with interval values constanting changing one voice to another), "Lipophony" (with certain notes systematically omitted), "Word Tones" (whenever a word recurs, it is assigned to the same pitch), and "Rotating Triskaidecaphony" (a 12-tone series returning to note 1 for the 13th note, with the next row starting and ending on note 2, etc.). He composed the operas *The Loafer and the Loaf* (1951; Los Angeles, May 1, 1956) and *Lysistrata* (1968–72; Marlboro, Vt., Nov. 9, 1984).

BIBL.: O. Daniel, *H.L. C.* (N.Y., 1970).

Clarke, Jeremiah, English composer and organist; b. London, c.1673; d. there (suicide), Dec. 1, 1707. He was a chorister in the Chapel Royal; in 1700 was made Gentleman Extraordinary of the Chapel Royal; in 1704 was appointed joint organist (with Croft) there. A hopeless love affair caused Clarke to take his own life.

He composed (with others) the stage works *The World in the Moon* (1697) and *The Island Princess* (1699); also incidental music to several plays. Clarke was the first composer to set Dryden's *Alexander's Feast* to music (for St. Cecilia's Day, Nov. 22, 1697). He was the real author of the famous *Trumpet Voluntary*, erroneously ascribed to Purcell, and popularized by Sir Henry Wood's orch. arrangement.

BIBL.: T. Taylor, *Thematic Catalog of the Works of J. C.* (Detroit, 1977).

Clarus, Max, German conductor and composer; b. Mühlberg, March 31, 1852; d. Braunschweig, Dec. 6, 1916. He studied with his father, who was a municipal music director, and with Loschhorn in Berlin. He became a theatrical conductor, traveling in Germany, Austria, and Hungary. He composed mostly for the stage, numbering among his works (all 1st perf. in Braunschweig) the operas *Des Königs-Rekrut* (1889) and *Ilse* (1895), the fairy operas *Der Wunschpeter* (1910) and *Der Zwerg Nase* (1912), and several ballets.

Claussen, Julia (née **Ohlson**), Swedish mezzo-soprano; b. Stockholm, June 11, 1879; d. there, May 1, 1941. She studied at the Royal Academy of Music in Stockholm (1897–1902), then in Berlin with Friedrich (1903–05). She made her operatic debut as Leonora in *La Favorite* at the Stockholm Opera (Jan. 19, 1903); was engaged there from 1903 until 1932; made her debut at Covent Garden in London in 1914; was a member of the Chicago Opera Co. (1912–14; 1915–17). She made her first appearance at the Metropolitan Opera in New York as Delilah on Nov. 23, 1917, and remained on its roster until 1929; in 1934 she returned to Stockholm as a teacher at the Cons.

Clay, Frédéric (Emes), English composer; b. Paris, Aug. 3, 1838; d. Great Marlow, near London, Nov. 24, 1889. He studied with Molique at Paris and with Hauptmann in Leipzig. His early operettas, *The Pirate's Isle* (1859) and *Out of Sight* (1860), were performed privately in London; his first operetta to be produced at Covent Garden was *Court and Cottage* (1862); other light dramatic works subsequently performed there included *Constance* (1865), *Ages Ago* (1869), *The Gentleman in Black* (1870), *Happy Arcadia* (1872), *Cattarina* (1874), *Princess Toto* (1876), and *Don Quixote* (1876).

Clemens, Hans, German tenor; b. Bicken-Gelsenkirchen, July 27, 1890; d. Montrose, Colo., Aug. 25, 1958. After successful appearances in Germany and at Covent Garden in London, he went to the United States. He made his Metropolitan Opera debut in New York as the Steersman in *Der fliegende Holländer* (Nov. 1, 1930); appeared also in other Wagnerian roles, being particularly effective as David in *Die Meistersinger von Nürnberg*. In 1938 he settled in Los Angeles as a vocal teacher.

Clément, Edmond (Frédéric-Jean), esteemed French tenor; b. Paris, March 28, 1867; d. Nice, Feb. 24, 1928. He was a pupil of Warot at the Paris Cons. in 1887, taking 1st prize in 1889. His debut was at the Opéra Comique, Nov. 29, 1889, as Vincent in Gounod's *Mireille*. His success was instantaneous, and he remained there until 1910 with frequent leave for extended tours; he sang in the principal theaters of France, Belgium, Spain, Portugal, England, and Denmark. On Dec. 6, 1909, he made his debut at the Metropolitan Opera in New York in one of his finest roles, Massenet's Des Grieux; from 1911 to 1913, sang with the Boston Opera Co. His voice was a light tenor of very agreeable quality, with a range of 2 octaves. He created the chief tenor parts in the following operas (all at the Opéra Comique): Bruneau's *L'Attaque du Moulin* (1893), Saint-Saëns's *Phryné* (1893), Cui's *Le Flibustier* (1894), Godard's *La Vivandière* (1895), Dubois's *Xavière* (1895), Hahn's *L'Île du rêve* (1898), Erlanger's *Le Juif polonais* (1900), Saint-Saëns's *Hélène* (1904), Dupont's *La Cabrera* (1905), and Vidal's *La Reine Fiammette* (1908).

Clementi, Aldo, prominent Italian composer and pedagogue; b. Catania, May 25, 1925. He began training in piano at age 13 and in composition at age 16 in Catania. He pursued piano studies with Giovanna Ferro at the Cons. di Santa Cecilia in Rome (diploma, 1946), and then attended Scarpini's master class at the Accademia Musicale Chigiana in Siena (1947). From 1945 to 1952 he also studied composition with Alfred Sangiorgi in Catania and Bolzano, who introduced him to 12-tone writing. Following further composition studies with Petrassi at the Cons. di Santa Cecilia (1952–54; diploma, 1954), he attended the summer courses in new music at Darmstadt (1955–62) and was active at the Studio di Fonologia in Milan (1956–62). From 1971 to 1992 he taught theory at the Univ. of Bologna. Among his honors were 1st prize in the ISCM competition in 1963 for his *Sette scene* for Chamber Orch. and the Abbiati Prize in 1992 for his opera *Interludi: Musica per il Mitro di Eco e Narciso*. Clementi is one of the leading avant-garde composers of Europe. As such, he sees his main task as that of creating works which fulfill his vision of contemporary music as a vehicle for the dissolution of music as we know it.

WORKS: DRAMATIC: *College*, azione musicale (Rome, May 14, 1962); *Blitz*, azione musicale (Royan, April 18, 1973); *Collage 4*, azione mimo-visiva (1979; Florence, May 30, 1981); *Finale*, azione lirica (Rome, Oct. 13, 1984); *Interludi: Musica per il Mito di Eco e Narciso*, opera (Gibellina, July 23, 1992); *Carillon*, opera (1994).

BIBL.: R. Cresti, *A. C.: Studio monografico e intervista* (Milan, 1990).

Clérambault, Louis Nicolas, French composer and organist; b. Paris, Dec. 19, 1676; d. there, Oct. 26, 1749. He studied with André Raison. He was organist at various Paris churches. He was a successful composer of theatrical pieces for the court, including *Le Soleil vainqueur* (Paris, Oct. 21, 1721) and *Le Départ du roi* (1745). His son, César François Nicolas Clérambault (1700–1760), was also an organist and composer.

Cleva, Fausto (Angelo), Italian-born American conductor; b. Trieste, May 17, 1902; d. while conducting at the odeum of Herodes Atticus in Athens, Aug. 6, 1971. He studied at the Trieste Cons. and the Milan Cons. After making his conducting debut with *La Traviata* at the Teatro Carcano in Milan in 1920, he emigrated to the United States and became a naturalized citizen in 1931. In 1921 he joined the staff of the Metropolitan Opera in New York, where he later was chorus master (1935–42). On Dec. 4, 1938, he made his first appearance there as a conductor in a Sunday evening concert. His formal debut with the company followed on Feb. 14, 1942, when he conducted *Il Barbiere di Siviglia*. He then conducted at the San Francisco Opera (1942–44; 1949–55) and was music director of the Cincinnati Summer Opera (1943–63). He also rejoined the roster of the Metropolitan Opera in 1950, where he conducted every season until his death.

Clive, Kitty (**Catherine** née **Raftor**), famous English actress and soprano; b. London, 1711; d. Twickenham, Dec. 6, 1785. She studied with Henry Carey. As a protégé of Colley Cibber, she was engaged at the Drury Lane Theatre in 1728 and gained renown in ballad opera in his *Love in a Riddle or Damon and Phillida* (Jan. 1729). She continued to sing there with extraordinary success until 1743. After appearing at Covent Garden (1743–45), she returned to Drury Lane and remained a leading figure there until her retirement in 1769. Although she was most celebrated as a comic actress, she acquitted herself well as a singer of ballad farces and comic songs. She also sang Irish ballads, and even works by Handel, Purcell, and Arne. Handel wrote the role of Delilah in *Samson* for her, as well as the arioso *But lo, the Angel of the Lord* in *Messiah*. Clive herself wrote a comedy, *The Rehearsal or Bays in Petticoats* (London, March 15, 1750), for which Boyce composed the music.

BIBL.: P. Fitzgerald, *The Life of Mrs. C. C. . . . together with her Correspondence* (London, 1888).

Cluytens, André, noted Belgian-born French conductor; b. Antwerp, March 26, 1905; d. Neuilly, near Paris, June 3, 1967. He studied piano at the Antwerp Cons. His father, conductor at the Théâtre Royal in Antwerp, engaged him as his assistant (1921); later he conducted opera there (1927–32). He then settled in

France, and became a naturalized French citizen in 1932. He served as music director at the Toulouse Opera (1932–35); in 1935 he was appointed opera conductor in Lyons. In 1944 he conducted at the Paris Opéra; in 1947 he was appointed music director of the Opéra Comique in Paris. In 1949 he was named conductor of the Société des Concerts du Conservatoire de Paris. In 1955 he became the first French conductor to appear at the Bayreuth Festival. On Nov. 4, 1956, he made his U.S. debut in Washington, D.C., as guest conductor of the Vienna Phil. during its first American tour. In 1960 he became chief conductor of the Orchestre National de Belgique in Brussels, a post he held until his death. Cluytens was highly regarded as an interpreter of French music.

BIBL.: B. Gavoty, *A. C.* (Geneva, 1955).

Coates, Albert, eminent English conductor; b. St. Petersburg, Russia (of an English father and a mother of Russian descent), April 23, 1882; d. Milnerton, near Cape Town, South Africa, Dec. 11, 1953. He went to England for his general education; enrolled in science classes at the Univ. of Liverpool, and studied organ with an elder brother who was living there at the time. In 1902 he entered the Leipzig Cons., studying cello with Julius Klengel, piano with Teichmüller, and conducting with Nikisch; served his apprenticeship there and made his debut as conductor in Offenbach's *Les Contes d'Hoffmann* at the Leipzig Opera in 1904. In 1905 he was appointed (on Nikisch's recommendation) chief conductor of the opera house at Elberfeld; from 1907 to 1909 he was a joint conductor at the Dresden Court Opera (with Schuch); then at Mannheim (1909–10, with Bodanzky). In 1911 he received the appointment at the Imperial Opera of St. Petersburg, and conducted many Russian operas. From 1919 he conducted in England, specializing in Wagner and the Russian repertoire; was a proponent of Scriabin's music. Having made his first appearance at London's Covent Garden in 1914 with *Tristan und Isolde*, he conducted there regularly from 1919. From 1919 to 1921 he was principal conductor of the London Sym. Orch. In 1920 he made his American debut as guest conductor of the N.Y. Sym. Orch.; during 1923–25, he led conducting classes at the Eastman School of Music in Rochester, N.Y., conducted the Rochester Phil., and appeared as guest conductor with other American orchs. Subsequent engagements included a season at the Berlin State Opera (1931) and concerts with the Vienna Phil. (1935). In 1938 he conducted for the last time at Covent Garden. In 1946 he settled in South Africa, where he conducted the Johannesburg Sym. Orch. and taught at the Univ. of South Africa at Cape Town. Coates was a prolific composer, but his works had few performances. He was, however, one of the most outstanding, if unheralded, conductors of his generation; he excelled in the Romantic operatic and symphonic repertoire, conducting particularly memorable performances of Russian music and Wagner's music dramas.

Coates, Edith (Mary), English mezzo-soprano; b. Lincoln, May 31, 1908; d. Worthing, Jan. 7, 1983. She studied at Trinity College of Music in London and with Carey and Borgioli. In 1924 she joined the Old Vic Theatre in London, where she sang major roles from 1931 to 1946. In 1937 she appeared at London's Covent Garden, where she was on the roster until 1939 and again from 1947 to 1963. She sang in the premieres of Britten's *Peter Grimes* (1945) and *Gloriana* (1953), and of Bliss's *The Olympians* (1949). Among her other roles were the Countess in *The Queen of Spades*, Carmen, Delilah, Amneris, Ortrud, and Azucena. In 1977 she was made an Officer of the Order of the British Empire.

Coates, John, English tenor; b. Girlington, Yorkshire, June 29, 1865; d. Northwood, Middlesex, Aug. 16, 1941. He studied with his uncle, J. G. Walton, at Bradford, sang as a small boy at a Bradford church, began serious study in 1893, and took lessons with William Shakespeare in London. He sang baritone parts in Gilbert and Sullivan operettas, making his debut at the Savoy Theatre in London in *Utopia Limited* (1894); he toured in the United States with a Gilbert and Sullivan company. He made his debut in grand opera as Faust at London's Covent Garden (1901); also sang Lohengrin in Cologne and other German cities with considerable success; later sang nearly all the Wagner roles in English with the Moody-Manners Co., the Carl Rosa Co., and with Beecham (1910); from 1911 to 1913 he toured with Quinlan's opera company in Australia and South Africa. He served in the British army during World War I; in 1919, he returned to London, devoting himself chiefly to teaching; he also gave recitals of songs by English composers. In 1926–27 he made a concert tour of the United States.

Cobelli, Giuseppina, Italian soprano; b. Maderno, Lake Garda, Aug. 1, 1898; d. Barbarano di Salò, Aug. 10, 1948. She studied in Bologna, Cologne, and Hamburg. In 1924 she made her operatic debut as Gioconda in Piacenza; after singing with the Italian Opera in the Netherlands, she joined Milan's La Scala in 1925, where she was one of its principal artists until deafness compelled her to leave the company in 1942. She was notably successful in such Wagnerian roles as Isolde, Sieglinde, and Kundry, as well as in the standard and modern Italian repertory.

Cocchi, Gioacchino, Italian composer; b. probably in Naples, c.1720; d. probably in Venice, after 1788. He may have studied with Giovanni Veneziano at the Cons. di S. Maria di Loreto in Naples. He began his career as a composer for the theater with the opera *Adelaide* (Rome, Carnival 1743), subsequently bringing out many operas for Rome and Naples, winning his most popular success with *La Maestra* (Naples, 1747). He was in Venice by 1750, where he served as choir director at the Ospedale degli Incurabili until 1757; he then went to London as composer and music director of the Haymarket Theatre until 1762; he returned to Venice c.1772. He excelled in opera buffa; among such works, in addition to those given above, were *L'Elisa* (Naples, 1744), *L'Irene* (Naples, 1745), *I due fratelli beffati* (Naples, 1746), *La Serva bacchettona* (Naples, 1749), *La mascherata* (Venice, Dec. 27, 1750), *Il Tutore* (Rome, 1752), and *Il Pazzo glorioso* (Venice, 1753). He also composed a significant number of other stage works and oratorios.

Coccia, Carlo, Italian composer; b. Naples, April 14, 1782; d. Novara, April 13, 1873. He was 9 when he began musical training with Pietro Casella. He then studied singing with Saverio Valente and counterpoint with Fedele Fenaroli at the Cons. S. Maria di Loreto in Naples, and with Paisiello. He served as maestro accompagnatore al pianoforte in the private musical establishment of Joseph Bonaparte, king of Naples (1806–8); he also began his career as a composer, becoming best known for his operas semiseria and scoring his greatest success with *Clotilde* (Venice, June 8, 1815). In 1820 he went to Lisbon as maestro concertatore at the Teatro San Carlos, and in 1824 went to London as conductor at the King's Theatre; he also taught at the Royal Academy of Music. He returned to Italy in 1827 and scored a fine success with his opera *Caterina di Guise* (Milan, Feb. 14, 1833); he was made inspector of music and director of singing at the Accademia Filarmonica in Turin in 1836, and then settled in Novara as maestro di cappella at S. Gaudenzio (1840). He wrote 38 operas, which, in addition to those listed above, included *La verita nella bugia* (Venice, 1809), *Maria Stuart, regina di Scozia* (London, June 7, 1827, excerpts only), *Enrico di Monfort* (Milan, Nov. 12, 1831), and *Giovanna II regina di Napoli* (Milan, March 12, 1840).

BIBL.: G. Carotti, *Biografia di C. C.* (Turin, 1873).

Cochran, William, American tenor; b. Columbus, Ohio, June 23, 1943. He studied at Wesleyan Univ., with Singher at the Curtis Inst. of Music in Philadelphia, and with Melchior and Lehmann in Calif. In 1968 he sang Froh in *Das Rheingold* in San Francisco, and on Dec. 21 of that year he made his Metropolitan Opera debut in New York as Vogelsang in *Die Meistersinger von Nürnberg*. After winning the Lauritz Melchior Heldentenor Foundation Award in 1969, he joined the Frankfurt am Main Opera in 1970. In 1974 he made his first appearance at London's Covent Garden as Laca in *Jenůfa*. He returned to San Francisco in 1977 to sing Tichon in *Kát'a Kabanová*. In 1985 he was engaged as Bacchus at the Metropolitan Opera. After appearing as Otello with the Welsh National Opera in Cardiff in 1990, he sang Siegfried in Paris in 1991. He sang Aegisthus in *Elektra* at the London Promenade Concerts in 1993. In 1997 he returned to San Francisco to portray Herod in *Salome*.

Cockshott, Gerald Wilfred, English composer; b. Bristol, Nov. 14, 1915; d. London, Feb. 3, 1979. He specialized in English literature; was head of the English dept. at Whittingehame College, Brighton (1948–64), and at Ifield Grammar School, Crawley, Sussex (1965–78). He studied composition privately with Vaughan Williams; became active primarily as a writer on musical subjects. His music is transparently tonal and impressed with melorhythms of English folk songs. He composed the operas *Apollo and Persephone* (N.Y., Feb. 22, 1956) and *A Faun in the Forest* (Westport, Conn., Aug. 9, 1959).

Coelho, Rui, Portuguese composer; b. Alcaçer do Sal, March 3, 1891; d. Lisbon, May 5, 1986. He was a student of Colaço (piano) and of Ferreira and Borba (composition) at the Lisbon Cons., and then of Humperdinck, Bruch, and Schoenberg in Berlin (1910–13) and of Vidal at the Paris Cons. Upon his return to Lisbon, he devoted himself mainly to composition and music criticism; he also made appearances as a pianist and conductor. His compositions were predicated upon nationalist principles.

WORKS: DRAMATIC: OPERAS: *O serão da infanta* (1913); *Crisfal* (1919); *Auto do berço* (1920); *Rosas de todo o ano* (1921; Lisbon, May 30, 1940); *Belkiss* (1923; Lisbon, June 9, 1928); *Inês de Castro* (1925; Lisbon, Jan. 15, 1927), *Cavaleiro das mãos irresistíveis* (1926); *Freira de beja* (1927); *Entre giestas* (Lisbon, 1929); *Tâmar* (Lisbon, 1936); *Dom João IV* (Lisbon, Dec. 1, 1940); *A feira* (1942); *A rosa de papel* (Lisbon, Dec. 18, 1947); *Auto da barca do inferno* (1949; Lisbon, Jan. 15, 1950); *Inês Pereira* (Lisbon, April 5, 1952); *O vestido de noiva* (1958; Lisbon, Jan. 4, 1959); *Auto da alma* (1960); *Orfeu em Lisboa* (1964–66); *Auto da barca da glória* (1970). BALLETS: *Princesa dos sapatos de ferro* (1912); *O sonho da princesa na rosa* (1916); *A história de carochinha* (1916); *Bailado do encantemento* (1917); *O sonho da pobrezinha* (1921); *A feira* (1921); *Bailado africano* (1930); *Inêz de Castro* (1939); *Passatempo* (1940); *Dom Sebastião* (1943); *Festa na aldeia* (1966).

BIBL.: *R. C.: Sua acção e sua obras de 1910 a 1967* (Lisbon, 1967).

Coerne, Louis (Adolphe), American composer; b. Newark, N.J., Feb. 27, 1870; d. Boston, Sept. 11, 1922. He studied violin with Kneisel in Boston and composition at Harvard Univ. with J. K. Paine (1888–90), then went to Germany, where he took courses with Rheinberger in Munich. Returning to America, he became the first recipient of the degree of Ph.D. in music given by an American univ., with the dissertation *The Evolution of Modern Orchestration* (1905; publ. in N.Y., 1908) at Harvard. He composed the opera *Zenobia* (1902; Bremen, Dec. 1, 1905).

Coertse, Mimi, South African soprano; b. Durban, June 12, 1932. She studied in Johannesburg and Vienna. She made her debut with the Vienna State Opera on tour in Naples in 1955; then sang in Basel and at the Teatro San Carlo in Naples. In 1957 she became a member of the Vienna State Opera; she also appeared in London, Cologne, Rome, Brussels, and other major European music centers.

Coeuroy, André (real name, **Jean Bélime**), distinguished French writer on music; b. Dijon, Feb. 24, 1891; d. Chaumont, Haute-Marne, Nov. 8, 1976. After training at the Dijon Cons., he went to Paris to study at the Lycée Louis le Grand and at the École Normale Supérieure (1911–14), where he took a degree in German; he also studied harmony and counterpoint with Reger in Leipzig (1910) and took a course in philology at the Univ. of Munich (1912–13). With Henry Prunières, he founded *La Revue Musicale* in 1920, with which he remained active until 1937. He also wrote music criticism for various newspapers and journals. His expertise in philology was reflected in his writings on music. Among his many writings are *La Walkyrie* (1922) and *Wagner et l'esprit romantique* (1965).

Cogan, Philip, Irish organist, teacher, and composer; b. Cork, 1748; d. Dublin, Feb. 3, 1833. He was a chorister at Cork. In 1772 he went to Dublin, where he occupied various posts as a church organist. He acquired great renown as a teacher and performer, numbering Michael Kelly and Thomas Moore among his pupils. Cogan wrote 2 comic operas: *The Ruling Passion* (Dublin, Feb. 24, 1778) and *The Contract* (Dublin, May 14, 1782; revived under the title *The Double Stratagem*, 1784).

Cohn, James (Myron), American musicologist, inventor, and composer; b. Newark, N.J., Feb. 12, 1928. He studied with Barlow at the Eastman School of Music in Rochester, N.Y. (1940–41), Harris at Cornell Univ. (1941–43), and Wagenaar at the Juilliard School of Music in New York (B.S., 1949; M.S., 1950); he later pursued postgraduate studies with Ruth Anderson at Hunter College of the City Univ. of N.Y. (1973). He was a musicologist for ASCAP from 1954 to 1984. Cohn invented devices that can be applied to keyboards or fingerboards to control pitch, intonation, loudness, vibrato, and tremolo. He composed the opera *The Fall of the City* (1952; Athens, Ohio, July 8, 1955).

Colasse, Pascal, French composer; b. Rheims, Jan. 22, 1649; d. Versailles, July 17, 1709. He was a pupil of Lully, who entrusted him with writing out the parts of his operas from the figured bass and melody. Later Colasse was accused of appropriating scores thrown aside by his master as incomplete. In 1683 he was appointed Master of the Music; in 1696, royal chamber musician. He was a favorite of Louis XIV, and obtained the privilege of producing operas at Lille, but the theater burned down. His opera *Polyxène et Pyrrhus* (1706) failed, and his mind became disordered. Of 10 operas, *Les Noces de Thétys et Pélée* (1689) was his best.

Colbran, Isabella (Isabel Angela), famous Spanish soprano; b. Madrid, Feb. 2, 1785; d. Bologna, Oct. 7, 1845. She studied with Pareja in Madrid, then with Marinelli and Crescentini in Naples. She made her debut in a concert in Paris in 1801. After her successful appearances in Bologna (1807) and La Scala in Milan (1808), the impresario Barbaja engaged her for Naples in 1811; she became his mistress, only to desert him for Rossini, whom she married on March 16, 1822 (they were legally separated in 1837). She created the leading soprano roles in several of Rossini's operas, beginning with *Elisabetta, Regina d'Inghilterra* (1815) and concluding with *Semiramide* (1823). With her voice in decline, she retired from the stage in 1824. During the early years of the 19th century she was acclaimed as the leading dramatic coloratura soprano.

Cole, Rossetter Gleason, American composer, organist, and teacher; b. near Clyde, Mich., Feb. 5, 1866; d. Lake Bluff, Ill., May 18, 1952. After training in harmony from Francis York in Ann Arbor, he studied engineering and the liberal arts, including music with Calvin Cady, at the Univ. of Mich. (graduated, 1888). He won a scholarship to pursue training at the Berlin Königliche Meisterschule in 1890, where he studied organ with Middelschulte, violin with Bruch, conducting with Gustav Kogel, and composition and counterpoint with Heinrich van Eyken. Upon his return to the United States in 1892, he became a prof. and head of the music dept. at Riper College in Wisconsin; then was a prof. at Grinnel College in Iowa (1894–1901). After teaching privately in Chicago (1901–07), he was a prof. at the Univ. of Wisc. (1907–09). He then taught again privately in Chicago (from 1909). During these years, he also was active as a church organist. In 1915 he became head of the theory dept. at the Cosmopolitan School in Chicago, where he was dean from 1935. From 1939 to 1941 he was president of the Soc. of American Musicians. He prepared the vol. *Choral and Church Music* (1916) in the Art of Music series. Among his compositions are *Hiawatha's Wooing*, melodrama (1904), *King Robert of Sicily*, melodrama (1906), *Pierrot Wounded* (1917), and *The Maypole Lovers*, opera (1919–31; 2 orch. suites, 1934, 1942).

Cole, Vinson, black American tenor; b. Kansas City, Mo., Nov. 20, 1950. He studied at the Curtis Inst. of Music in Philadelphia, where he sang Werther while still a student in 1975; then was an apprentice at the Santa Fe Opera, and was chosen to create the role of Innis Brown in Ulysses Kay's *Jubilee* in Jackson, Miss., in 1976; that same year he made his European debut as Belmonte with the Welsh National Opera in Cardiff. From 1976 to 1980 he appeared at the Opera Theatre of St. Louis. He sang Nicolai's Fenton at the N.Y. City Opera in 1981. In 1992 he was engaged as Donizetti's Edgardo in Detroit. After singing Nadir in *Les Pêcheurs de perles* in Seattle in 1994, he portrayed Jason in Cherubini's *Medea* in Athens in 1995. In 1996 he sang Renaud in Gluck's *Armide* at Milan's La Scala. He returned to Seattle as Werther in 1997, and then sang Idomeneo at the Lyric Opera in 1998. As a concert artist, he toured widely in the United States and abroad, appearing with major orchs. Among his admired operatic portrayals are Gluck's Orfeo, Percy in *Anna Bolena*, Des Grieux in *Manon*, Lensky, Gounod's Faust, and Bizet's Nadir.

Coleridge-Taylor, Samuel, important English composer, conductor, and teacher; b. London, Aug. 15, 1875; d. Croydon, Sept. 1, 1912. His father was a black Sierra Leone physician and his mother was English. After violin lessons with Joseph Beckwith in Croydon, he entered the Royal College of Music in London in 1890 to continue his violin training; in 1892 he became a composition student of Stanford there, and in 1893 he won a composition scholarship; before completing his studies in 1897, he had several of his works premiered there. His first public success came with his Ballade in A minor for Orch., which was premiered at the Three Choirs Festival in Gloucester on Sept. 14, 1898. It was soon followed by what proved to be his most successful score, the cantata *Hiawatha's Wedding Feast*, which was first performed under Stanford's direction at the Royal College of Music on Nov. 11, 1898. It was subsequently performed widely in Europe and the United States. Although he continued to compose in earnest, he never duplicated this popular success. He also was active as a conductor, leading various orchestral and choral aggregations. He likewise was engaged in teaching, serving as prof. of composition at Trinity College of Music (from 1903) and at the Guildhall School of Music (from 1910) in London. In 1904, 1906, and 1910 he visited the United States. While greatly influenced by Dvořák, Coleridge-Taylor's works also reveal a fascination with black subjects and melodies.

WORKS: DRAMATIC: *Dream Lovers*, operatic romance (1898); *The Gitanos*, cantata-operetta (1898); *Thelma*, opera (1907–09). Incidental music to Stephen Phillips's *Herod* (1900), *Ulysses* (1901–02), *Nero* (1906), and *Faust* (1908); also to Noyes's *The Forest of Wild Thyme* (1910) and Shakespeare's *Othello* (1910–11).

BIBL.: W. Berwick Sayers, *S. C.-T., Musician: His Life and Letters* (London, 1915; 2d ed., rev., 1927); J. Coleridge-Taylor, *C.-T.: Genius and Musician* (London, 1943); W. Tortolano, *S. C.-T.: Anglo-Black Composer, 1875–1912* (Metuchen, N.J., 1977); A. Coleridge-Taylor, *The Heritage of S. C.-T.* (London, 1979); J. Thompson, *S. C.-T.: The Development of His Compositional Style* (Metuchen, N.J., 1994); G. Self, *The Hiawatha Man: The Life and Work of S. C.-T.* (Brookfield, Vt., 1995).

Coletti, Filippo, noted Italian baritone; b. Anagni, May 11, 1811; d. there, June 13, 1894. He studied with Alessandro Busti in Naples, making his debut there at the Teatro del Fondo in Rossini's *Il Turco in Italia* in 1834. He subsequently established himself as a distinguished interpreter of roles in operas by Bellini, Donizetti, and Verdi.

Colgrass, Michael (Charles), American composer; b. Chicago, April 22, 1932. He received training in percussion and composition at the Univ. of Ill. (Mus.B., 1956), and also studied composition with Foss at the Berkshire Music Center in Tanglewood (summers, 1952, 1954) and Milhaud at the Aspen (Colo.) Music School (summer, 1953); he then took private composition lessons with Riegger (1958–59) and Ben Weber (1959–62) in New York. After working as a freelance solo percussionist in New York (1956–67), he settled in Toronto, where he devoted himself fully to composition. In 1964 and 1968 he held Guggenheim fellowships, and in 1978 he was awarded the Pulitzer Prize in Music for his *Déjà vu*, a concerto for 4 Percussionists and Orch. In his output, he has utilized various styles and techniques, with percussion often playing a significant melorhythmic role. He composed *Virgil's Dream*, music theater (1967), *Nightingale, Inc.*, comic opera (1971), and *Something's Gonna Happen*, children's musical (1978).

Collier, Marie, Australian soprano; b. Ballarat, April 16, 1926; d. in a fall from a window in London, Dec. 7, 1971. She studied with Wielaert and Gertrude Johnson in Melbourne, where she made her operatic debut as Santuzza; she then completed her training in Milan with Ugo Benvenuti Giusti (1955–56). In 1956 she made her first appearance at London's Covent Garden as Musetta, where she sang regularly until her death; she also appeared at the Sadler's Wells Opera in London. From 1965 to 1968 she sang at the San Francisco Opera. On March 17, 1967, she created the role of Christine Mannon in Levy's *Mourning Becomes Electra* at her Metropolitan Opera debut in New York; she remained on its roster until 1968, and then returned for the 1969–70 season. Collier was highly regarded for her performances of contemporary operas, excelling in such roles as Kát'a Kabanová, Emilia Marty in *The Makropulos Affair*, Jenůfa, Marie in *Wozzeck*, Katerina Izmailova, Walton's Cressida, and Hecuba in Tippett's *King Priam*, which she created.

Collin (Colin) de Blamont, François, prominent French composer; b. Versailles, Nov. 22, 1690; d. there, Feb. 14, 1760. He commenced his musical training with his father, Nicolas Colin, who served as ordinaire de la musique du roi, then entered the service of the Duchess of Maine when he was 17, becoming a pupil of Lalande. In 1719 he was made surintendant de la musique de la chambre, and, upon Lalande's death, was named his successor as a maître de musique de la chambre (1726); he received Letters of Nobility (1750) and was made Chevalier of the Order of St. Michel (1751). With Fuzelier, he created the ballet héroïque with their *Festes grecques et romaines* (1723). He publ. the polemical book *Essaie sur les goûts anciens et modernes de la musique françoise relativement aux paroles d'opéra* (Paris, 1754), which was aimed primarily at Rousseau.

WORKS: DRAMATIC: *Les Festes grecques et romaines*, ballet héroïque (Paris, July 13, 1723; in collaboration with Fuzelier); *Le Retour des dieux sur la terre*, divertissement (for the marriage of Louis XV, 1725); *La Caprice d'Erato ou Les Caractères de la Musique*, divertissement (1730); *Endymion*, pastorale héroïque (Paris, May 17, 1731); *Les Caractères de l'amour*, ballet héroïque (1736); *Les Fêtes de Thétis*, ballet héroïque (Versailles, Jan. 14, 1750).

BIBL.: C. Massip, *F. C.d.B.: Musicien du roi* (diss., Paris Cons., 1971).

Collingwood, Lawrance (Arthur), English conductor and composer; b. London, March 14, 1887; d. Killin, Perthshire, Dec. 19, 1982. He studied at the Guildhall School of Music in London and later at Exeter College, Oxford (1907–11). In 1912 he went to Russia and took courses at the St. Petersburg Cons. with Glazunov, Wihtol, Steinberg, and Tcherepnin; in 1918 he returned to England and became active as a conductor; was principal conductor (1931–41) and music director (1941–47) at Sadler's Wells in London. In 1948 he was made a Commander of the Order of the British Empire. His compositions include the operas *Macbeth* (London, April 12, 1934) and *The Death of Tintagiles* (concert perf., London, April 16, 1950).

Collins, Anthony (Vincent Benedictus), English conductor and composer; b. Hastings, Sept. 3, 1893; d. Los Angeles, Dec. 11, 1963. He studied violin at the Royal College of Music in London, and composition there with Holst; was then a violist in the London Sym. Orch. and in the orch. of the Royal Opera House, Covent Garden; from 1936 he pursued a career as conductor, appearing with the Carl Rosa Opera Co., the Sadler's Wells Opera, and the London Sym. Orch. From 1939 to 1945 he conducted and composed for films in the United States. After pursuing his career again in England (1945–53), he settled in the United States. He wrote 4 operas.

Comissiona, Sergiu, prominent Romanian-born American conductor; b. Bucharest, June 16, 1928. He studied conducting with Silvestri and Lindenberg, making his conducting debut at the age of 17 in Sibiu in a performance of Gounod's *Faust.* He became a violinist in the Bucharest Radio Quartet (1946), and then in the Romanian State Ensemble (1947), where he was subsequently assistant conductor (1948–50) and music director (1950–55). From 1955 to 1959 he was principal conductor of the Romanian State Opera in Bucharest. Being Jewish, he was moved to emigrate to Israel, where he was music director of the Haifa Sym. Orch. (1960–66) and founder-director of the Ramat Gan Chamber Orch. (1960–67). In 1963 he appeared in North America as conductor of the Israel Chamber Orch., and, in 1965, as guest conductor of the Philadelphia Orch. He then was music director of the Göteborg Sym. Orch. (1966–77), music adviser of the Northern Ireland Orch. in Belfast (1967–68), and music director of the Baltimore Sym. Orch. (1969–84). On July 4, 1976, he became a naturalized American citizen. He was music director of the Chautauqua (N.Y.) Festival Orch. (1976–80), music advisor of the Temple Univ. Festival in Ambler (1977–80), and music advisor of the American Sym. Orch. in New York (1977–82). He served as artistic director (1980–83), music director-designate (1983–84), and music director (1984–88) of the Houston Sym. Orch. From 1982 he was chief conductor of the Radio Phil. Orch. in Hilversum. In 1987–88 he was also music director of the N.Y. City Opera, and then was chief conductor of the Helsinki Phil. from 1990. He likewise served as music director-designate (1990–91) and music director (1991–94) of the Vancouver (B.C.) Sym. Orch.

Concone, (Paolo) Giuseppe (Gioacchino), Italian singing teacher and composer; b. Turin, Sept. 12, 1801; d. there, June 1, 1861. From 1837 until 1848 he lived in Paris, where he became a popular singing teacher. His collection of solfeggi in 5 vols. (50 Lezioni, 30 Esercizi, 25 Lezioni, 15 Vocalizzi, and 40 Lezioni per Basso) became a standard work for singing teachers, showing no signs of obsolescence and continuing much in use all over the world. He also wrote an opera, *Un episodio del San Michele* (Turin, June 8, 1836).

Confalonieri, Giulio, Italian music critic, pedagogue, and composer; b. Milan, May 23, 1896; d. there, June 29, 1972. He studied at the Univ. of Milan (graduated, 1920) and received training in composition from Alfano at the Bologna Cons. (diploma, 1921). After further studies with Dukas in Paris (1922), he lived in London (1923–26) before returning to Milan to pursue his career. He wrote the opera *Rosaspina* (Bergamo, Sept. 9, 1939) and other stage. He publ. *Prigionia di un artista: Il romanzo di Luigi Cherubini* (2 vols., Milan, 1948), *Guida alla musica* (Milan, 1950; 2nd ed., 1958, as *Storia della musica*), and *Come la musica* (Turin, 1966).

Conley, Eugene, American tenor; b. Lynn, Mass., March 12, 1908; d. Denton, Texas, Dec. 18, 1981. He studied with Harriet Barrows and Ettore Verna. After making his operatic debut as the Duke of Mantua at the Brooklyn Academy of Music (1940), he sang with the San Carlo Opera Co.; later appeared in Chicago (1942) and at Milan's La Scala (1949). On Jan. 25, 1950, he made his Metropolitan Opera debut in New York as Faust, remaining on its roster until 1956. He made guest appearances in San Francisco, Stockholm, at Paris's Opéra Comique, and at London's Covent Garden. From 1960 to 1978 he was artist-in-residence at North Texas State Univ. in Denton. Among his best known roles were Edgardo, Rodolfo, Pinkerton, and Tom Rakewell.

Conlon, James (Joseph), American conductor; b. N.Y., March 18, 1950. He studied at the High School of Music and Art in New York, and then was a pupil in conducting of Morel at the Juilliard School of Music in New York (B.M., 1972). After making his formal conducting debut with *Boris Godunov* at the Spoleto Festival in 1971, he conducted at the Juilliard School (1972–75). On April 12, 1974, he became the youngest conductor ever to lead a subscription concert of the N.Y. Phil. On Dec. 11, 1976, he made his Metropolitan Opera debut in New York conducting *Die Zauberflöte,* and remained on its roster until 1980; he was again on its roster from 1981 to 1983. He served as music director of the Cincinnati May Festival (from 1979) and chief conductor of the Rotterdam Phil. (1983–91). In 1989 he became chief conductor of the Cologne Opera; in 1991 he also was made Generalmusikdirektor of the city of Cologne and chief conductor of the Gürzenich Orch. there. He likewise was music advisor (1995–96) and principal conductor (from 1996) of the Opéra de la Bastille in Paris.

Connell, Elizabeth, Irish mezzo-soprano, later soprano; b. Port Elizabeth, South Africa, Oct. 22, 1946. She was a student of Otakar Kraus at the London Opera Centre. In 1972 she won the Maggie Teyte Prize and made her operatic debut at the Wexford Festival as Varvara in *Kát'a Kabanová.* In 1975 she sang with the Australian Opera in Sydney, and from 1975 to 1980 she was a member of the English National Opera in London, where she won notice as Eboli and Herodias. In 1976 she made her debut at London's Covent Garden as Verdi's Viclinda, and in 1980 at the Bayreuth Festival as Ortrud. In 1983 she turned to soprano roles, and in 1984 appeared as Electra at the Salzburg Festival and as Norma in Geneva. On Jan. 7, 1985, she made her Metropolitan Opera debut in New York as Vitellia, and then returned to Covent Garden to sing Leonora in *Il Trovatore* and Leonore in *Fidelio.* In 1990 she portrayed Lady Macbeth in Bonn, a role she reprised in Cologne in 1992. She appeared as Isolde at the Royal Festival Hall in London in 1993. In 1997 she was engaged as Elektra at the San Francisco Opera.

Conried (real name, **Cohn**), **Heinrich**, Austrian-American operatic impresario; b. Bielitz, Sept. 13, 1848; d. Meran, Tirol, April 27, 1909. He started as an actor in Vienna. In 1877 he managed the Bremen Municipal Theater, and then went to the United States in 1878 and took over the management of the Germania Theater in New York, then was in charge of various theatrical enterprises. From 1892 he was director of the Irving Place Theater in New York, which he brought to a high degree of efficiency. From 1903 till 1908 he was the manager of the Metropolitan Opera and was instrumental in engaging numerous celebrated artists, including Caruso. During his first season he gave the first American production of *Parsifal,* despite the heated controversy regarding the rights of Wagner's heirs. His decision to produce the opera *Salome* by Richard Strauss in 1907 also aroused a storm of protests. Conried resigned in 1908 because of dissension within the management of the Metropolitan, and retired in Europe. He was decorated by several European governments, and also received an honorary M.A. from Harvard Univ.

BIBL.: M. Moses, *H. C.* (N.Y., 1916).

Constant, Marius, Romanian-born French conductor, composer, and teacher; b. Bucharest, Feb. 7, 1925. He first studied at the Bucharest Cons., where he took prizes in piano, harmony, counterpoint, and composition. In 1946 he settled in Paris and eventually became a naturalized French citizen. He was a student of Honegger, and also at the Cons. of Messiaen, Aubin, and Boulanger (premiers prix in composition and analysis, 1949), and at the École Normale de Musique of Fournet (conducting degree, 1949). He was active with the Groupe de Recherches Musicales du Club d'Essai de la Radio (1952–54), and was cofounder and director of the program France-Musique (1954–66); he also was chief conductor of the Ballets de Roland Petit (1957–63). In 1963 he founded Ars Nova, a contemporary music ensemble, which he served as music director until 1971. From 1973 to 1978 he was director of dance at the Paris Opéra. He was prof. of orchestration at the Paris Cons. (1979–88), and also taught composition and analysis at Stanford Univ. in California. Constant has won a number of honors for his compositions, including the Italia Prize (1952, 1987), the Koussevitzky Prize (1962), the Grand Prix National de la Musique (1969), and the "Victoires" de la Musique (1991). In 1993 he was elected a member of the Académie des Beaux-Arts, succeeding to the chair of Messiaen. In his compositions, Constant at first wrote along impressionistic lines; he later adopted a more advanced style in which he often made use of both serial and aleatory procedures. Among his scores for films and television is the signature theme for *Twilight Zone* (1959).

WORKS: DRAMATIC: OPERAS: *Le Souper* (Besançon, Sept. 9, 1969); *Le jeu de Sainte Agnès* (Besançon, Sept. 6, 1974); *La Tragédie de Carmen* (Paris, Nov. 5, 1981); *Impressions de Pélléas* (Paris, Nov. 13, 1992); *Teresa* (1996). BALLETS: *Cyrano de Bergerac* (Paris, April 17, 1959); *Eloge de la folie* (Paris, March 11, 1966); *Paradis perdu* (London, Feb. 27, 1967); *Candide* (1970; Hamburg, Jan. 20, 1971); *Septentrion* (Marseilles, May 15, 1975); *Nana* (Paris, May 6, 1976); *L'Ange bleu* (Berlin, June 8, 1985).

Constantinescu, Paul, eminent Romanian composer and pedagogue; b. Ploiesti, July 13, 1909; d. Bucharest, Dec. 20, 1963. He studied with Castaldi, Jora, Cuclin, and Brăiloiu at the Bucharest Cons. (1928–33) and with Schmidt and Marx in Vienna (1934–35). Returning to Bucharest, he taught at the academy for religious music (1937–41) and then was a prof. of composition at the Cons. from 1941 until his death. In 1932 he received the Enesco prize and in 1956 the Romanian Academy prize. Constantiescu made use of folk and liturgical elements in his works, developing a style marked by an assured command of form and modal harmony. He did much to chart the course for the post-Enesco generation of Romanian nationalist composers. His stage works include *O noapte furtunoasă*, comic opera (1934; rev. 1950; Bucharest, May 19, 1951), *Nunta în Carpaţi*, choreographic poem (Bucharest, May 5, 1938), and *Pană Lesnea Rusalim*, opera (1954–55; Cluj-Napoca, June 26, 1956).

BIBL.: V. Tomescu, *P. C.* (Bucharest, 1967).

Conti, Carlo, Italian composer and pedagogue; b. Arpino, Oct. 14, 1796; d. Naples, July 10, 1868. He studied at the Naples Cons. with Zingarelli and J. S. Mayr, then taught there from 1819 to 1821 and again from 1846 to 1858, becoming its assistant director in 1862. An industrious composer, he wrote 11 operas and much church music. Rossini called him "the best Italian contrapuntist of the day." His distinction lies principally in his excellence as a teacher; among his famous pupils was Bellini.

Conti, Francesco Bartolomeo, Italian composer; b. Florence, Jan. 20, 1681; d. Vienna, July 20, 1732. He was assistant court theorbist (1701–08), principal theorbist (1708–26), and court composer (from 1713). He wrote about 30 stage works to Italian and German texts, including *Clotilda* (1706) and *Don Chisciotte in Sierra Morena* (1719); also 11 oratorios.

BIBL.: H. Williams, *F. B. C.: His Life and Operas* (diss., Columbia Univ., 1964).

Conti, Gioacchino, celebrated Italian castrato soprano, known as "Gizziello" and "Egizziello," after his teacher; b. Arpino, Feb. 28, 1714; d. Rome, Oct. 25, 1761. He began study at the age of 8 with Domenico Gizzi in Naples, making his debut in Vinci's *Artaserse* in Rome (Feb. 4, 1730), where he scored a triumph. He subsequently sang in various Italian music centers, and also appeared in Vienna. Handel then called him to London, where he made his debut in *Ariodante* at Covent Garden (May 5, 1736; he had no time to learn the title role, however, and was compelled to sing Italian arias); he then created the roles of Meleager in *Atalanta* (May 12, 1736), Sigismondo in *Arminio* (Jan. 12, 1737), Anastasio in *Giustino* (Feb. 16, 1737), and Alessandro in *Berenice* (May 18, 1737), all of which were composed for him by Handel. Returning to Italy, he sang in Rome (1738, 1741), Padua (1739), and Florence (1742); after a sojourn in Lisbon (from 1743), he returned to Italy and sang in Naples (1747–50), Lucca (1749), and Padua (1751). He appeared at the court theater of Lisbon (1752–55) before retiring in Italy. Conti possessed a brilliant voice with a compass of 2 octaves.

Contilli, Gino, Italian composer and teacher; b. Rome, April 19, 1907; d. Genoa, April 4, 1978. He studied at the Accademia di Santa Cecilia in Rome with Respighi. He taught at the Messina Liceo Musicale (1942–66) and was director of the Genoa Cons. (from 1966). He composed the opera *Saul* (1941).

BIBL.: G. Zaccaro, *G. C.* (Milan, 1980).

Converse, Frederick Shepherd, distinguished American composer and teacher; b. Newton, Mass., Jan. 5, 1871; d. Westwood, Mass., June 8, 1940. After graduating from Harvard Univ. (1893), he studied music in Boston with Carl Baermann and Chadwick (1894–96), then in Munich at the Royal Academy of Music with Rheinberger (graduated, 1898). Returning to Boston, he taught harmony at the New England Cons. of Music (1900–02; 1920–36; dean, 1931–37) and was a composition instructor at Harvard Univ. (1901–07). He received a Mus.Doc. from Boston Univ. (1933); became a member of the American Academy of Arts and Letters (1937). His early works reflect the influence of academic German training; later he began to apply more advanced harmonies; in his *Flivver 10 Million*, written to glorify the 10 millionth Ford car, he adopted a frankly modern idiom, modeled after Honegger's *Pacific 231*. He composed 4 syms., and sketched some material for a 5th in 1937, which was never completed. He also composed the operas *The Pipe of Desire* (1905; Boston, Jan. 31, 1906), *The Sacrifice* (1910; Boston, March 3, 1911), *Sinbad the Sailor* (1913), and *The Immigrants* (1914).

BIBL.: R. Garofalo, *The Life and Works of F. S. C. (1871–1940)* (diss., Catholic Univ. of America, Washington, D.C., 1969).

Conyngham, Barry (Ernest), Australian composer and teacher; b. Sydney, Aug. 27, 1944. He studied jurisprudence before taking private composition lessons with Meale; in 1966 he entered the New South Wales State Conservatorium in Sydney, and then took his M.A. under Sculthorpe at the Univ. of Sydney, and subsequently his D.Mus. at the Univ. of Melbourne. In 1970 he pursued private lessons with Takemitsu in Japan and in 1972–73 postdoctoral studies at the Univ. of Calif. in San Diego. After teaching at the Univ. of New South Wales and the National Inst. of Dramatic Art (1968–70), and at the Univ. of Western Australia (1971), he was a visiting fellow at Princeton Univ. (1973–74) and composer and researcher in residence at the Univ. of Aix-Marseilles (1974–75). From 1975 to 1990 he taught at the Univ. of Melbourne. He served as prof. and head of the School of Creative Arts at the Univ. of Wollongong in New South Wales from 1990. Both jazz and Japanese influences are evident in his work; he has also written much electronic music. His stage works include *Ned*, opera (1975–78), *The Apology of Bony Anderson*, opera (1978), *Fly*, opera (1981–84), *The Oath of Bad Brown Bill*, children's opera (1985), *Vast*, ballet (1987; Melbourne, March 4, 1988), *Diamentina Ghosts*, music theater (1988), and *Bennelong*, music theater (1988).

Cook, Thomas (Aynsley), English bass; b. London, July 1831 or 1836; d. Liverpool, Feb. 16, 1894. He was a pupil of Hopkins at the City Temple in London, and of Staudigl in Munich. After singing in Germany, he made his British debut as a member of Lucy Escott's National English Opera Co. in Manchester in 1856. Following a tour of the United States with Escott, he joined the Pyne-Harrison Co. in London in 1862. After singing with the English Opera Co., he appeared at the Gaiety Theatre from 1870 to 1872. From 1875 he was a member of the Carl Rosa Opera Co. Cook was the maternal grandfather of **Sir Eugene, Marie, Leon**, and **Sidonie Goossens**.

Cooke, Arnold (Atkinson), English composer and pedagogue; b. Gomersal, Yorkshire, Nov. 4, 1906. He studied with Dent at Caius College, Cambridge (B.A., 1928; B.Mus., 1929), returning there to take his D.Mus. in 1948; he also studied with Hindemith at the Berlin Hochschule für Musik (1929–32). He served as prof. of harmony, counterpoint, and composition at the Royal Manchester College of Music (1933–38), and later at Trinity College of Music in London (1947–77); in 1953 he also was chairman of the Composers Guild of Great Britain. His works are composed in an agreeable tonal idiom. He composed the operas *Mary Barton* (1949–52) and *The Invisible Duke* (1975) and the ballet *Jabez and the Devil* (1962).

Cooke, Deryck (Victor), English writer on music; b. Leicester, Sept. 14, 1919; d. Thornton Heath, Oct. 26, 1976. He studied composition with Hadley and Orr at the Univ. of Cambridge (B.A.,

1940; M.A., 1943; Mus.B., 1947) and then worked in the BBC music dept. (1947–59; 1965–76). He prepared a performing version of the odd-numbered movements of Mahler's 10th Sym. for a BBC broadcast on Dec. 19, 1960. The composer's widow, Alma, forbade any further broadcasts or performances, but was eventually convinced of the merits of the score and supplied Cooke with 24 unpubl. pages of fragments with which he completed the sym. (new version, London, Aug. 13, 1964). Further revisions were made with the assistance of Colin and David Matthews before the work was publ. in 1976. Since then the Mahler–Cooke version has been performed throughout the world. Among his publications are *Mahler 1860–1911* (London, 1960; rev. and enl. ed., 1980, as *Gustav Mahler: An Introduction to His Music*) and *I Saw the World End: A Study of Wagner's Ring* (London, 1979).

Cooke, Tom (Thomas Simpson), Irish tenor, instrumentalist, and composer; b. Dublin, 1782; d. London, Feb. 26, 1848. He studied with his father, the oboist Bartlett Cooke, and appeared in public playing a violin concerto when he was 7. He then studied with Giordani. At age 15, he became concertmaster of Dublin's Crow Street Theatre orch. He also ran a music shop (1806–12). In 1813 he settled in London, where he became a dominant figure at the Drury Lane Theatre as a singer, concertmaster, versatile instrumentalist (on some 9 instruments), manager, and composer. He also taught voice. Cooke composed many stage pieces. He also wrote the treatises *Singing Exemplified in a Series of Solfeggi* and *Singing in Parts* (London, 1842).

Cooper, Emil (Albertovich), respected Russian conductor of English descent; b. Kherson, Dec. 20, 1877; d. N.Y., Nov. 16, 1960. He studied at the Odessa Cons., with Hellmesberger Jr. and Nikisch in Vienna, and with Taneyev in Moscow. In 1896 he made his conducting debut in Odessa. He then conducted in Kiev (1899–1906), and at Moscow's Bolshoi and Zimin theaters (1904). On Oct. 7, 1909, he conducted the premiere of Rimsky-Korsakov's *The Golden Cockerel* in Moscow. From 1909 to 1911 he conducted Diaghilev's Russian seasons in Paris, and also appeared at London's Covent Garden. He continued to conduct in Russia until 1923, and then in Riga (1925–28). From 1929 to 1932 he conducted at the Chicago Opera, and then in Europe. In 1939 he returned to the Chicago Opera, remaining with it until his Metropolitan Opera debut in New York on Jan. 26, 1944, conducting *Pelléas et Mélisande*. He remained on the roster there until 1950, and then conducted the Montréal Opera Guild. In addition to the Russian repertory, he was esteemed for his interpretations of Wagner.

Cooper, Martin (Du Pré), English music writer on music; b. Winchester, Jan. 17, 1910; d. Richmond, Surrey, March 15, 1986. He studied at Hertford College, Oxford (B.A., 1931) and with Wellesz in Vienna (1932–34). He then was music critic for the London *Mercury* (1935–38), *Daily Herald* (1946–50), and the *Daily Telegraph* (1950–54; chief music critic, 1954–76); he also was ed. of the *Musical Times* (1953–56). His writings (all publ. in London unless otherwise given) include *Gluck* (1935), *Bizet* (1938), *Opéra comique* (1949), and *Russian Opera* (1951).

Cope, David (Howell), eclectic American writer, composer, and teacher; b. San Francisco, May 17, 1941. He was educated at Arizona State Univ. and the Univ. of Southern Calif. in Los Angeles; then served on the faculties of Miami Univ. of Ohio and the Univ. of Calif. at Santa Cruz. He is well known for his didactic books on contemporary composition, which include *New Directions in Music* (Dubuque, 1971; 6th ed., rev., 1993), *New Music Composition* (N.Y., 1977), and *Computer Analysis of Musical Style* (N.Y., 1990). Among his compositions is an opera, *Cradle Falling*, for Soprano and Orch. (1989).

Copland, Aaron, greatly distinguished and exceptionally gifted American composer; b. N.Y., Nov. 14, 1900; d. North Tarrytown, N.Y., Dec. 2, 1990. He was educated at the Boys' High School in Brooklyn, and began piano study with Leopold Wolfsohn, Victor Wittgenstein, and Clarence Adler as a young child. In 1917 he commenced lessons in harmony and counterpoint with Rubin Goldmark in New York, and soon began to compose. His first publ. piece, *The Cat and the Mouse* for Piano (1920), subtitled *Scherzo humoristique*, shows the influence of Debussy. In 1920 he entered the American Cons. in Fontainebleau, where he studied composition and orchestration with Boulanger. Returning to America in 1924, he lived mostly in New York; he became active in many musical activities, not only as a composer but also as a lecturer, pianist, and organizer in various musical societies. He attracted the attention of Serge Koussevitzky, who gave the first performance of his early score *Music for the Theater* with the Boston Sym. Orch. in 1925; Koussevitzky then engaged Copland as soloist in his Piano Concerto in 1927; the work produced a considerable sensation because of its jazz elements, and there was some subterranean grumbling among the staid subscribers to the Boston Sym. concerts. Koussevitzky remained Copland's steadfast supporter throughout his tenure as conductor of the Boston Sym., and later as the founder of the Koussevitzky Music Foundation. In the meantime, Walter Damrosch conducted in New York Copland's Sym. for Organ and Orch., with Boulanger as soloist. Other orchs. and their conductors also performed his music, which gained increasing recognition. Particularly popular were Copland's works based on folk motifs; of these the most remarkable are *El Salón México* (1933–36) and the American ballets *Billy the Kid* (1938), *Rodeo* (1942), and *Appalachian Spring* (1944). A place apart is occupied by Copland's *Lincoln Portrait* for Narrator and Orch. (1942), with texts arranged by the composer from speeches and letters of Abraham Lincoln; this work has had a great many performances, with the role of the narrator performed by such notables as Adlai Stevenson and Eleanor Roosevelt. His patriotic *Fanfare for the Common Man* (1942) achieved tremendous popularity and continued to be played on various occasions for decades; Copland incorporated it in toto into the score of his 3d Sym. He was for many years a member of the board of directors of the League of Composers in New York; with Sessions, he organized the Copland–Sessions Concerts (1928–31), and was also a founder of the Yaddo Festivals (1932) and of the American Composers' Alliance (1937); was also a participant in such organizations as the Koussevitzky Music Foundation, the Composers Forum, the Cos Cob Press, etc. He was head of the composition dept. at the Berkshire Music Center at Tanglewood from 1940 to 1965, and from 1957 to 1965 was chairman of the faculty. He lectured extensively and gave courses at The New School for Social Research in New York and at Harvard Univ. (1935 and 1944); he was the Charles Eliot Norton Lecturer at Harvard in 1951–52. He was the recipient of many awards: Guggenheim fellowship (1925–27); RCA Victor award of $5,000 for his *Dance Symphony*; Pulitzer Prize in Music and N.Y. Music Critics' Circle Award for *Appalachian Spring* (1945); N.Y. Music Critics' Circle Award for the 3d Sym. (1947); Oscar award for the film score *The Heiress* from the Academy of Motion Picture Arts and Sciences (1950); Gold Medal for Music from the American Academy of Arts and Letters (1956); Presidential Medal of Freedom (1964); Howland Memorial Prize of Yale Univ. (1970); he was also decorated with a Commander's Cross of the Order of Merit in West Germany and was elected to honorary membership of the Accademia di Santa Cecilia in Rome. He held numerous honorary doctor's degrees: Princeton Univ. (1956); Brandeis Univ. (1957); Wesleyan Univ. (1958); Temple Univ. (1959); Harvard Univ. (1961); Rutgers Univ. (1967); Ohio State Univ. (1970); N.Y. Univ. (1970); Columbia Univ. (1971). About 1955 Copland developed a successful career as a conductor, and led major sym. orchs. in Europe, the United States, South America, and Mexico; he also traveled to Russia under the auspices of the State Dept. In 1982 the Aaron Copland School of Music was created at Queens College of the City Univ. of N.Y. In 1983 he made his last appearance as a conductor in New York. His 85th birthday was widely celebrated; Copland attended a special concert given in his honor by Zubin Mehta and the N.Y. Phil., which was televised live by PBS. He was awarded the National Medal of Arts (1986). As a composer, Copland made use of a broad variety of idioms and techniques, tempering dissonant textures by a strong sense of tonality. He enlivened his musical textures by ingenious applications of syncopation and polyrhythmic combinations; but in such works as Piano Variations, he adopted an austere method of musical constructivism. He used a modified 12-tone technique in his Piano Quartet (1950) and an integral dodecaphonic idiom in the score of *Connotations* (1962).

WORKS: DRAMATIC: *Grohg*, ballet (1922–25; not perf.; material incorporated into *Dance Symphony*); *Hear Ye! Hear Ye!*, ballet (Chicago, Nov. 30, 1934); *The 2nd Hurricane*, play-opera for high school (1936; N.Y., April 21, 1937); *Billy the Kid*, ballet (Chicago, Oct. 16, 1938); *From Sorcery to Science*, music for a puppet show (N.Y., May 12, 1939); *Rodeo*, ballet (N.Y., Oct. 16, 1942); *Appalachian Spring*, ballet (Washington, D.C., Oct. 30, 1944); *The Tender Land*, opera (N.Y., April 1, 1954); *Dance Panels*, ballet (1959; rev. 1962; Munich, Dec. 3, 1963; arranged for Piano, 1965). INCIDENTAL MUSIC TO PLAYS: *Miracle at Verdun* (1931); *The 5 Kings* (1939); *Quiet City* (1939).

WRITINGS: *What to Listen for in Music* (N.Y., 1939; 2d ed., 1957); *Our New Music* (N.Y., 1941; 2d ed., rev. and enl. as *The New Music, 1900–1960*, N.Y., 1968); *Music and Imagination* (Cambridge, Mass., 1952); *Copland on Music* (N.Y., 1960); an autobiography, *Copland* (with V. Perlis; 2 vols., N.Y., 1984, 1989).

BIBL.: A. Berger, *A. C.* (N.Y., 1953); J. Smith, *A. C.: His Work and Contribution to American Music* (N.Y., 1955); C. Peare, *A. C.: His Life* (N.Y., 1969); N. Butterworth, *The Music of A. C.* (N.Y., 1985); J. Skowronski, *A. C.: A Bio-Bibliography* (Westport, Conn., 1985); V. Perlis, *C: 1900–1942* (N.Y., 1987); idem., *C.: Since 1943* (N.Y., 1990); H. Pollack, *A. C.: The Life and Work of an Uncommon Man* (N.Y., 1999).

Copley, John (Michael), English opera director; b. Birmingham, June 12, 1933. He studied with Joan Cross at the National School of Opera in London. He was active in London as a stage manager at the Sadler's Wells Opera, where he first turned to directing with his staging of *Il Tabarro* in 1957; he then worked at Covent Garden, where he garnered success with his production of *Così fan tutte* in 1968; from 1971 to 1988 he was resident opera director there, and also was active at the English National Opera. As a guest opera director, he staged works at the San Francisco Opera, the Australian Opera in Sydney, the Santa Fe Opera, and the Metropolitan Opera in New York. His respect for the score at hand and the singers engaged, combined with imaginative direction, have made Copley's productions notably successful.

Coppola, Piero, admired Italian conductor; b. Milan, Oct. 11, 1888; d. Lausanne, March 13, 1971. He studied at the Milan Cons. (graduated, 1909). After conducting in various Italian operatic centers, he conducted in London in 1914. During World War I, he pursued his career in Scandinavia. In 1921 he went to Paris, where he won distinction as music director of the recording firm La Voix de son Maître (1923–34), with whom he made a number of pioneering recordings. In 1930 he was awarded the Chevalier of the French Légion d'honneur for his services to French music. He conducted throughout Europe until World War II; after the war, he conducted in Switzerland and Italy. He also composed, producing 2 operas, *Sirmione* and *Nikita* (1914).

Coppola, Pietro Antonio, Italian composer; b. Castrogiovanni, Sicily, Dec. 11, 1793; d. Catania, Nov. 13, 1877. For a short time he studied at the Naples Cons., then began to compose operas, which obtained sufficient success to enable his friends and admirers to present him as a rival to Rossini. From the time he was 19, he produced one opera after another, but without much success until he composed *La Pazza per amore* (Rome, Feb. 14, 1835). This was his 4th opera and it became popular all over Europe (presented in Paris under the title *Eva*). From 1839 to 1843, and again from 1850 till 1871, he was conductor of the Lisbon Royal Opera. His other operas were *Gli Illinesi* (Turin, Dec. 26, 1835), *Enrichietta di Baienfeld* (Vienna, June 29, 1836), *La bella Celeste degli Spadari* (Milan, June 14, 1837), *Giovanna prima di Napoli* (Lisbon, Oct. 11, 1840), and *Il Folletto* (Rome, June 18, 1843).

BIBL.: U. Coppola, *P. A. C.* (Catania, 1898).

Coquard, Arthur (-Joseph), French composer and music critic; b. Paris, May 26, 1846; d. Noirmoutier, Vendée, Aug. 20, 1910. He took private lessons with Franck (1862–66). He was music critic for *Le Monde* and *Écho de Paris*. He publ. *De la musique en France depuis Rameau* (Paris, 1892), which received a prize from the Académie des Beaux-Arts. He composed the operas *L'Épée du roi* (Angers, 1884), *Le Mari d'un jour* (Paris, 1886), *L'Oiseau bleu* (Paris, 1894), *La Jacquerie* (Paris, 1895), *Jahel* (Lyons, 1900), and *La Troupe Jolicoeur* (Paris, May 30, 1902), and an oratorio, *Jeanne d'Arc*.

BIBL.: N. Dufourcq, *Autour de C., Franck et d'Indy* (Paris, 1952).

Corder, Frederick, English composer, teacher, and writer on music; b. London, Jan. 26, 1852; d. there, Aug. 21, 1932. He studied at the Royal Academy of Music in London (1873–75); after winning the Mendelssohn Scholarship in 1875, he pursued training with Hiller in Cologne (1878–79). He conducted the Brighton Aquarium concerts (1880–82); he then was prof. of composition (from 1888) and curator (from 1889) of the Royal Academy of Music. Among his outstanding students were Bantock, Bax, and Holbrooke. With his wife, Henrietta Luisa (née Walford) Corder, he made the 1st Eng. trs. of Wagner's *Parsifal* (1879), *Die Meistersinger von Nürnberg* (1882), *Der Ring des Nibelungen* (1882), *Tristan und Isolde* (1882), and *Lohengrin* (1894). His own compositions followed along late Romantic lines. His son, Paul Corder (b. London, Dec. 14, 1879; d. there, Aug. 6, 1942), was a composer and teacher. He studied with his father at the Royal Academy of Music, and taught there from 1907. Among his works were the stage pieces *La morte d'Arthur*, opera (1877–78), *A Storm in a Teacup*, operetta (1880; Brighton, Feb. 18, 1882), *Nordisa*, opera (1886; Liverpool, Jan. 26, 1887), and *Ossian*, opera (1905); also incidental music.

WRITINGS (all publ. in London): *Exercises in Harmony and Counterpoint* (1891); *A Plain and Easy Guide to Music: or The New "Morely"* (1893; 3d ed., 1920); *The Orchestra and How to Write for it* (1896); *Recitation with Music* (1897); *Modern Musical Composition* (1909); *Beethoven and his Music* (1912); *Wagner and his Music* (1912); *A History of the Royal Academy of Music from 1822 to 1922* (1922); *Beethoven* (1922); *Wagner* (1922; 2nd ed., 1948); *Ferencz Liszt* (1925).

Cordon, Norman, American baritone; b. Washington, N.C., Jan. 20, 1904; d. Chapel Hill, N.C., March 1, 1964. He attended the Fishburne Military School; later studied at the Univ. of North Carolina and at the Nashville Cons. of Music; was a voice student of Gaetano de Lucas and Hadley Outland. He sang with the San Carlo Opera Co.; in 1933 he made his debut as Scarpia at the Civic Opera in Chicago, of which he was a member until 1936; on May 13, 1936, he made his Metropolitan Opera debut in New York as Monterone, remaining on its roster until 1946; he also appeared with the San Francisco Opera, the Cincinnati Summer Opera, and on Broadway.

Corelli, Franco, outstanding Italian tenor; b. Ancona, April 8, 1921. He studied naval engineering at the Univ. of Bologna; in 1947 he entered the Pesaro Cons. to study voice; dissatisfied with the academic training, he left the Cons. and proceeded to learn the repertoire by listening to recordings of great singers. He made his operatic debut at the Spoleto Festival in 1952 as Don José, then sang at the Rome Opera in 1953 and at Milan's La Scala in 1954; he appeared at London's Covent Garden in 1957. On Jan. 27, 1961, he made his Metropolitan Opera debut in New York as Manrico in *Il Trovatore*; while continuing on its roster until 1975, he also appeared with major opera houses worldwide. Among his finest roles were Radames, Ernani, Don Alvaro, Raoul, and Calaf.

BIBL.: M. Boagno, *F. C.: Un uomo, una voce* (Parma, 1990; Eng. tr., 1996, as *F. C.: A Man, a Voice*).

Corena, Fernando, Swiss bass; b. Geneva, Dec. 22, 1916; d. Lugano, Nov. 26, 1984. He studied in Geneva and with Enrico Romani in Milan; after making his operatic debut in 1937, he sang with the radio and municipal theater in Zürich. He first gained wide notice as Varlaam in Trieste in 1947, and subsequently was invited to sing with major opera houses in Europe and the United States; he made his Metropolitan Opera debut in New York as Leporello (Feb. 6, 1954), and remained on its roster until 1979. He first appeared at London's Covent Garden on May 16, 1960, as Dr. Bartolo in *Il Barbiere di Siviglia*. He was particularly known for his buffo roles. Among his other roles were Don Pasquale, Dulcamare, Alfonso, Osmin, and Gianni Schicchi.

Corigliano, John (Paul), notable American composer and teacher; b. N.Y., Feb. 16, 1938. His father was the American violinist John Corigliano (b. N.Y., Aug. 28, 1901; d. Norfolk, Conn., Sept. 1, 1975). While still a child, he began to play the piano and to try his hand at composing. During his high school years, he studied orchestration on his own by listening to recordings with scores in hand. He then was a student of Luening at Columbia Univ. (B.A., 1959) and of Giannini at the Manhattan School of Music. He worked as a music programmer in New York for WQXR-FM and WBAI-FM (1959–64), as an assoc. producer of music programs for CBS-TV (1961–72), and as music director of the Morris Theater in New Jersey (1962–64). After teaching at the College of Church Musicians in Washington, D.C. (1968–71), he was on the faculties of the Manhattan School of Music (from 1971) and of Lehman College of the City Univ. of N.Y. (from 1973), where he later held the title of Distinguished Prof. (from 1986). He also taught at the Juilliard School in New York (from 1991). Corigliano established his considerable reputation as a composer with his Clarinet Concerto (N.Y., Dec. 6, 1977). From 1987 to 1990 he served as the first composer-in-residence of the Chicago Sym. Orch. His deeply-felt Sym. No. 1, dedicated to the victims of AIDS, was premiered by that orch. under Barenboim's direction on March 15, 1990. The highly successful premiere and subsequent recording of the score brought Corigliano international acclaim. His opera, *The Ghosts of Versailles*, added further lustre to his reputation at its critically acclaimed premiere by the Metropolitan Opera in New York under Levine's direction on Dec. 19, 1991. Corigliano has won many honors and awards and received major commissions. In 1968–69 he held a Guggenheim fellowship. In 1989 the American Academy and Inst. of Arts and Letters gave him its award for music, and in 1991 he was elected to its membership. He also won the Grawemeyer Award in 1991 from the Univ. of Louisville for his Sym. No. 1. In his diverse output, Corigliano has produced a body of music notable for its remarkable originality and craftsmanship. His stage works include *The Naked Carmen*, electric rock opera (1970; transcription of Bizet's *Carmen*) and *The Ghosts of Versailles*, grand opera buffa (N.Y., Dec. 19, 1991); also incidental music for plays.

BIBL.: M. Humphrey, *J. C.* (N.Y., 1989; rev. ed., 1994).

Cornelius, Peter, important German composer and writer; b. Mainz, Dec. 24, 1824; d. there, Oct. 26, 1874. A nephew of the painter Peter von Cornelius, he at first became an actor, but after an unsuccessful debut, changed his mind. He studied theory with Dehn at Berlin (1845–52) and then joined Liszt's following in Weimar as a champion of Wagner, contributing frequent articles to the *Neue Zeitschrift für Musik*. His masterpiece, the opera *Der Barbier von Bagdad*, was produced at Weimar (Dec. 15, 1858) under the direction of Liszt, who resigned his position there because of hostile demonstrations while he was conducting the opera. In 1861 Cornelius went to Wagner at Vienna, and followed him to Munich (1865), where he was appointed reader to King Ludwig II, and prof. of harmony and rhetoric at the Royal Music School. A 2d opera, *Der Cid*, was produced at Weimar on May 21, 1865, while a 3d, *Gunlöd* (from the Edda), remained unfinished (completed by Lassen and produced at Weimar, May 6, 1891). *Der Barbier von Bagdad* was revived at Karlsruhe on Feb. 1, 1884, in a drastically altered version by F. Mottl. A complete ed. of Cornelius's works was issued by Breitkopf & Härtel (1905–06).

BIBL.: A Sandberger, *Leben und Werke des Dichtermusikers P. C.* (Leipzig, 1887); E. Istel, *P. C.* (Leipzig, 1904); E. Sulger-Gebing, *P. C. als Mensch und Dichter* (Munich, 1908); M. Hasse, *Der Dichtermusiker P. C.* (2 vols., Leipzig, 1923); C. Cornelius, *P. C., der Wort-und Tondichter* (2 vols., Regensburg, 1925); P. Egert, *P. C.* (Berlin, 1940).

Cornelius, Peter (real name, **Lauritz Peter Corneliys Petersen**), esteemed Danish tenor; b. Labjerggaard, Jan. 4, 1865; d. Snekkersten, near Copenhagen, Dec. 30, 1934. He studied with Nyrop in Copenhagen, making his operatic debut there in the baritone role of Escamillo (1892). After further appearances as a baritone, he then studied with Lieban, Revilliers, and Spiro in Berlin and made his tenor debut as the Steersman in *Der fliegende Holländer* in Copenhagen (1899), where he was subsequently a principal member of the Royal Danish Theater until 1922. He also sang at the Bayreuth Festival in 1906 and at London's Covent Garden (1907–14), and made guest appearances in Paris, Stockholm, and Oslo. Although he returned briefly to the stage in 1927, his later years were devoted mainly to teaching. He was particularly known for his Wagnerian roles, which included Tannhäuser, Siegfried, Lohengrin, Siegmund, and Tristan.

BIBL.: C. Cornelius, *P. C.* (1925).

Cornelys, T(h)eresa (née **Imer**), colorful Italian singer; b. Venice, 1723; d. London, Aug. 19, 1797. After making her debut in Venice (c.1741), she pursued her career in Vienna, Hamburg, Copenhagen, and the Low Countries; while in the latter, she married the dancer Pompeati but generally used the professional name of Cornelys. In 1746 she made her London debut in Gluck's *Caduta de' giganti*. In 1759 she settled in London, where she received the support of Casanova, with whom she was intimate. In 1760 she began giving concerts at Carlisle House in Soho Square, but these came to an inglorious end when she was indicted in 1771 for running an establishment of ill repute. She was convicted and spent her remaining years in the Fleet Street prison, being survived by a daughter born out of wedlock to Casanova. Although her contemporaries considered her a gifted singer, her reputation suffered as a result of the vagaries of her private life.

Coronaro, Gellio (Benvenuto), Italian pianist and composer; b. Vicenza, Nov. 30, 1863; d. Milan, July 26, 1916. He was 8 years old when he made his debut as a pianist; at 13, was theater conductor at Marosteca, and chorus master at 15; in 1882 he entered the Liceo Rossini at Bologna, where his teachers were Busi, Parisini, and Mancinelli; he graduated in 1883, winning the 1st prize with a 1-act opera, *Jolanda*, which was produced at the Milan Cons. (1883). Other works include the 1-act dramatic sketch, *Festa a Marina* (took 1st Sonzogno Prize in 1892), the operetta, *Minestrone napoletano* (Messina, 1893), and the operas *Claudia* (Milan, 1895), *Turiddu* (Vicenza, Nov. 30, 1905), and *Bertoldo* (Milan, 1910).

Corri, Domenico, Italian composer; b. Rome, Oct. 4, 1744; d. London, May 22, 1825. He was a pupil of Porpora in Naples, and in 1771 went to Edinburgh as an opera conductor. His attempt to organize his own opera company and a publishing firm there was a failure, and he sought better fortune in London (1790). There he engaged in various enterprises as a publisher, composer, and impresario. His opera, *The Travelers, or Music's Fascination*, was given at Drury Lane on Jan. 22, 1806, with little success. He publ. 4 music manuals in Eng.: *A Complete Musical Grammar* (1787), *A Musical Dictionary* (1798), *The Art of Fingering* (1799), and *The Singer's Preceptor* (1810). His daughter, Sophia Giustina Corri Dussek (b. Edinburgh, May 1, 1775; d. after 1828), a talented pianist and singer, married Dussek; his sons, Montague Corri (1784–1849) and Haydn Corri (1785–1860), were also musicians.

Corsaro, Frank (Anthony), American theater, musical, and opera producer and administrator; b. N.Y., Dec. 22, 1924. He studied at City College in N.Y., the Yale Univ. School of Drama (graduated, 1947), and the Actors' Studio in New York. In 1952 he made his debut as a theater director, and from 1955 he was active on Broadway. In 1958 he made his debut as an opera producer with his staging of Floyd's *Susannah* at the N.Y. City Opera, where his subsequent productions included *Don Giovanni, Rigoletto, Faust, Pelléas et Mélisande, A Village Romeo and Juliet, The Cunning*

Little Vixen, and *The Makropulos Affair*. He staged the premieres of Floyd's *Of Mice and Men* in Seattle (1970), Hoiby's *Summer and Smoke* in St. Paul (1971), and Pasatieri's *The Seagull* in Houston (1974). In 1977 he was named artistic director of the Actors' Studio in New York. His production of Handel's *Rinaldo* was seen at the Metropolitan Opera in New York in 1984. In 1992 he oversaw the U.S. stage premiere of Busoni's *Doktor Faust* at the N.Y. City Opera. He staged *Faust* at the Lyric Opera in Chicago in 1996. Corsaro's dramatically compelling opera productions have also been seen in Europe and Australia.

Corselli (real name, **Courcelle**), **Francesco,** Italian composer; b. Piacenza, c.1702; d. Madrid, April 3, 1778. He became an accomplished tenor, violinist, and harpsichordist, then went to Parma, where he was made maestro di cappella at the Steccata Church (1727), a position that extended to include the period of rule by the duke of Parma (1727–33). He was then called to Madrid (1734), where he was appointed suffragan royal maestro de capilla and music teacher to the royal children. In 1737 he was named coadjutor of the royal chapel, serving as its titular maestro from 1738; he also was rector of the choir school.

WORKS: OPERAS (all 1st perf. in Madrid unless otherwise given): *Venere placata* (Venice, 1731); *Nino* (Venice, Carnival 1732); *La Cautela en la amistad y el robo de las Sabinas* (1735); *Alessandro nelle Indie* (May 9, 1738); *Farnace* (Nov. 4, 1739); *Achille in Sciro* (Dec. 8, 1744); *La clemencia de Tito* (Carnival 1747; Act 1 by Corselli, Act 2 by F. Corradini, and Act 3 by G. B. Mele); *El Polifemo* (Carnival 1748; Act 1 by Corselli, Act 2 by Corradini, and Act 3 by Mele).

Corsi, Jacopo, Italian nobleman and patron of art; b. Florence, July 17, 1560; d. there, Dec. 29, 1602. In his palace, as in Bardi's, were held the memorable meetings of the "Camerata" in which Peri, Caccini, Emilio del Cavaliere, Galilei, the poet Rinuccini, and others took part, leading to the creation of the earliest operas. Corsi was a good musician, a skillful player on the harpsichord, and a composer. He wrote the concluding 2 numbers of the first opera by Peri, *Dafne*, which was performed at his home in 1598. These settings are preserved in the library of the Brussels Cons., and were publ. in Solerti's *Albori del Melodramma* (Milan, 1905).

Corteccia, Francesco Bernardo (baptized **Pier Francesco**), Italian composer and organist; b. Florence, July 27, 1502; d. there, June 27, 1571. He studied music with Bernardo Pisano, and was a choirboy at S. Giovanni Battista in Florence. He later prepared for the priesthood, and was chaplain at S. Giovanni from 1527 to 1531; in 1531–32 was organist at S. Lorenzo, then at S. Giovanni (1535–39); he was maestro di cappella there and at the Florence Cathedral from 1540 until his death. He wrote musical intermezzi for various stage works, including *Il furto* by Francesco d'Ambra (1544). Modern eds. of his works include *Francesco Corteccia: Hinnario secondo l'uso della chiesa romana e fiorentina*, ed. by G. Haydon (Cincinnati, 1958 and 1960), A. C. Minor and B. Mitchell, eds., *A Renaissance Entertainment: Festivities for the Marriage of Cosimo I, Duke of Florence, in 1539* (Columbia, Mo., 1968), and *Francesco Corteccia: Eleven Works to Latin Texts*, ed. by A. McKinley in *Recent Researches in the Music of the Renaissance*, XXVI (1969).

Cortés, Ramiro, Jr., American composer and teacher; b. Dallas, Nov. 25, 1933; d. Salt Lake City, July 2, 1984. He was a student of Henry Cowell in New York (1952), of Donovan at Yale Univ. (1953–54), and of Halsey Stevens and Ingolf Dahl at the Univ. of Southern Calif. in Los Angeles (B.M., 1955); after training with Petrassi in Rome on a Fulbright fellowship (1956–58), he completed his studies with Sessions at Princeton Univ. (1958) and with Giannini at the Juilliard School of Music in New York (M.M., 1962). He taught in Los Angeles at the Univ. of Calif. (1966–67), and at the Univ. of Southern Calif. (1967–72); in 1972–73 he was composer-in-residence at the Univ. of Utah, where he subsequently served as a teacher and chairman of its theory and composition dept. (1973–84). In his works to the late 1960s, he followed strict serial procedures; later he became less dogmatic in approach. He composed the operas *The Christmas Garden* (children's opera; 1955), *Prometheus* (1960), and *The Eternal Return* (1981) and the musical *The Patriots* (1975–76; rev. 1978); also incidental music and dance scores.

Cortese, Luigi, Italian composer; b. Genoa, Nov. 19, 1899; d. there, June 10, 1976. He studied with Mario Ferrari in Genoa, Casella in Rome, and Gédalge in Paris. From 1951 to 1964 he served as director of the Istituto Musicale in Genoa. He was active as a music critic. He publ. the monographs *Alfredo Casella* (1935), *Il Bolero di Ravel* (1944), and *Chopin* (1949). He composed the operas *Prometeo* (1941–47; Bergamo, Sept. 22, 1951), *La notte veneziana* (1953–55; Turin Radio, 1955), and *Le notte bianche* (1970).

Cortis, Antonio, Spanish tenor; b. on a ship between Oran and Altea, Aug. 12, 1891; d. Valencia, April 2, 1952. He went to Madrid, where he sang in the children's (1901–05) and adult (from 1911) choruses at the Teatro Real; he was soon singing operatic roles in Barcelona and Valencia. He made appearances in South America (from 1917) and in Italy (1919), and was a member of the Chicago Opera (1924–32) and the San Francisco Opera (1925–26). In 1931 he sang at London's Covent Garden, and from 1935 pursued his career in Spain; he made his farewell appearance as Cavaradossi in Saragossa (1951). Held in high esteem in his homeland, Cortis became known as the Spanish Caruso. Among his most prominent roles were Radames, Canio, Don José, Edgardo, and Andrea Chénier.

Cortot, Alfred (Denis), famous French pianist, conductor, and teacher; b. Nyon, Switzerland (of a French father and a Swiss mother), Sept. 26, 1877; d. Lausanne, June 15, 1962. He was a pupil at the Paris Cons., and studied with Decambes, Rouquou, and Diémer; he won the 1st prize for piano in 1896; the same year he made his debut in Paris, playing Beethoven's C-minor Concerto at one of the Colonne concerts, and won signal success; he went to Bayreuth (1898) and studied Wagner's works with J. Kniese, and acted as répétiteur at the festivals from 1898 to 1901. Returning to Paris, he began a most active propaganda for the works of Wagner; on May 17, 1902, he conducted the French premiere of *Götterdämmerung* at the Théâtre du Château d'Eau, and in the same year established the Association des Concerts A. Cortot, which he directed for 2 years, educating the public to an appreciation of Wagner; in 1904 he became conductor of the orch. concerts of the Societe Nationale and of the Concerts Populaires at Lille (until 1908). In 1905, together with Jacques Thibaud (violin) and Pablo Casals (cello), he formed a trio, which soon gained a great European reputation, and which continued to perform until 1937. From 1907 to 1918 he was a prof. of piano at the Paris Cons. With A. Mangeot, he founded the École Normale de Musique in Paris in 1919, and subsequently served as its director. Cortot toured widely as a soloist and recitalist in Europe and the United States until the outbreak of World War II. During the German occupation of France, he was a highly visible artist and was associated with the cultural policies of the Vichy regime. After the liberation, he was compelled to make an accounting of his activities, but was soon allowed to resume his concert career. He subsequently gave numerous concerts until his farewell appearance at the Prades Festival in 1958. He was awarded the Gold Medal of the Royal Phil. Soc. of London in 1923 and was made a Commandeur de la Légion d'honneur of France in 1934. Among his outstanding pupils were Haskil, Solomon, Bachauer, and Lipatti. Although Cortot was technically a highly wayward pianist, he succeeded in infusing his readings of the Romantic repertory with a rare insight and poetic patina. He wrote several books on piano technique and style.

BIBL.: B. Gavoty, *A. C.* (Paris, 1977).

Cossa, Dominic, American baritone and teacher; b. Jessup, Pa., May 13, 1935. He studied at the Univ. of Scranton (B.S. in psychology, 1959), the Univ. of Detroit (M.A., 1961), the Detroit Inst. of Musical Arts, and the Philadelphia Academy of Vocal Arts, his principal vocal mentors being Anthony Marlowe, Robert Weede, and Armen Boyajin. On Oct. 13, 1961, he made his first appearance at the N.Y. City Opera as Morales in *Carmen*, and subsequently sang leading baritone roles there. On Jan. 30, 1970, he made his Metropolitan Opera debut in New York as Silvio, and remained on its roster until 1975; he returned for the 1978–79 season. He also appeared as a guest artist with other U.S. opera companies and in Europe. He taught at the Manhattan School of Music in New York and at the Univ. of Maryland. Among his best roles were Rossini's Figaro, Lescaut, Germont, Marcello, Rigoletto, and Dr. Malatesta.

Cossira (real name, **Coussival**), **Emil,** French tenor; b. Orthez, 1854; d. Quebec, Feb. 1923. After training in Bordeaux, he made his operatic debut as Grétry's Richard Coeur de Leon at the Paris Opéra Comique in 1883, where he was chosen to create the title role in Saint-Saëns's *Ascanio* (March 21, 1890). In 1891, 1894, and 1900 he appeared at London's Covent Garden, where he sang Faust, Roméo, Raoul, and Don José. In addition to the French repertoire, he appeared as a Wagnerian. He was the first to sing Tristan in Brussels (1894) and Walther von Stolzing in Lyons (1896).

Cossotto, Fiorenza, distinguished Italian mezzo-soprano; b. Crescentino, April 22, 1935. After training at the Turin Cons., she studied in Milan at the La Scala opera school with Ettore Campogalliani. While still a student, she sang at La Scala before making her formal operatic debut there as Sister Mathilde in *Les Dialogues des Carmélites* on Jan. 26, 1957; continued to sing there regularly until 1973, winning special praise for her Verdi roles and as Donizetti's Leonora. In 1958 she commenced an international career with her appearance in Wexford as Donizetti's Giovanna Seymour; she then made debuts at the Vienna State Opera (as Maddalena, 1958), London's Covent Garden (as Néris in *Médée*, 1959), and the Chicago Lyric Opera (as Donizetti's Leonora, 1964). On Feb. 6, 1968, she made her Metropolitan Opera debut in New York as Amneris, and continued to sing there with distinction in succeeding years in such roles as Adalgisa, Eboli, Mistress Quickly, Laura, and Carmen. In 1958 she married **Ivo Vinco**.

Cossutta, Carlo, Italian tenor; b. Trieste, May 8, 1932. He was a student of Manfredo Miselli, Mario Melani, and Arturo Wolken in Buenos Aires, where he made his operatic debut as Alfredo in 1956. In 1958 he made his first appearance at the Teatro Colón in Buenos Aires as Cassio, and created the title role in Ginastera's *Don Rodrigo* there in 1968. In 1963 he appered as Cassio at his Chicago Lyric Opera debut, and, in 1964, as the Duke of Mantua at his debut at London's Covent Garden. On Feb. 17, 1973, he made his first appearance at the Metropolitan Opera in New York as Pollione, where he sang for one season and then returned for the 1978–79 season. He also sang in Milan, Paris, Berlin, Munich, Hamburg, Philadelphia, Boston, and San Francisco. Among his other roles were Otello, Don Carlos, Turiddu, Cavaradossi, and Manrico.

Costa, Mary, American soprano; b. Knoxville, Tenn., April 5, 1932. She was trained at the Los Angeles Cons. of Music. She pursued work in films (was the voice of Walt Disney's Sleeping Beauty) and television commercials before taking up a serious vocal career. In 1958 she made her operatic debut with the Los Angeles Opera, and in 1959 she made her first appearance with the San Francisco Opera. On Jan. 6, 1964, she made her Metropolitan Opera debut in New York as Violetta, and returned there for occasional appearances until 1978. She also sang at the Glyndebourne Festival, London's Covent Garden, the Leningrad Opera, the Bolshoi Theater in Moscow, the Cincinnati Opera, the Philadelphia Opera, et al. She also appeared as a soloist with orchs. and as a recitalist around the world. In 1972 she starred in the film *The Great Waltz*. She founded the Knoxville (Tenn.) Opera Co. in 1978. In 1979 the Mary Costa Scholarship was established at the Univ. of Tenn. Among her best known roles were Manon, Rosalinde, Musetta, and Alice Ford.

Costa, Sir Michael (Andrew Agnus) (Michele Andrea Agniello), Italian-born English conductor of Spanish descent; b. Naples, Feb. 4, 1806; d. Hove, England, April 29, 1884. He studied with his maternal grandfather, Giacomo Tritto, with his father, Pasquale Costa (a composer of church music), and with Giovanni Furno. He then studied at the Naples Cons. with Crescentini (singing) and Zingarelli (composition). His operas *Il sospetto funesto* (Naples, 1826), *Il delitto punito* (1827), *Il carcere d'Ildegonda* (Naples, 1828), and *Malvina* (Naples, 1829) were well received. When Zingarelli was commissioned to write a Psalm (Super Flumina Babilonis) for the Music Festival at Birmingham, England, he sent Costa to conduct it. When Costa arrived in Birmingham, the directors of the Festival refused to accept him as a conductor owing to his extreme youth, but offered to pay him a similar fee for performance as tenor in Zingarelli's Psalm and in other works. He was compelled to accept, but his debut as a singer was disastrous. Despite this setback, he decided to remain in England, a decision in which he was encouraged by Clementi, who was impressed by Costa's scoring of a Bellini aria. In 1830 Costa was engaged as maestro al cembalo at the King's Theatre in London; in 1832 he became music director; and in 1833, director and conductor. During this time he produced 3 of his ballets, *Kenilworth* (1831), *Une Heure à Naples* (1832), and *Sir Huon* (1833, for Taglioni). In 1846 he became conductor of the Phil. and of the Royal Italian Opera, and from 1848 to 1882 he conducted the Sacred Harmonic Soc. From 1849 he was the regular conductor of the Birmingham Festivals; from 1847 to 1880, of the Handel Festivals. He was knighted in 1869, and, in 1871, was appointed "director of the music, composer, and conductor" at Her Majesty's Opera, Haymarket, serving until 1881. He produced 2 operas in London: *Malek Adel* (May 18, 1837; a revision of *Malvina*) and *Don Carlos* (June 20, 1844).

Cotapos (Baeza), Acario, Chilean composer; b. Valdivia, April 30, 1889; d. Santiago, Nov. 22, 1969. He studied music in Santiago; in 1916 he went to New York, where he took lessons with various teachers, including Bloch. He lived in France until 1934; then went to Spain to work in defense of the Loyalists during the Spanish Civil War; in 1939 he returned to Chile. An experimenter by nature, Cotapos adopted an advanced quasi-serial technique of monothematic mottoes of 8 or more notes. He wrote a music drama, *Voces de gesta* (1933).

Cotogni, Antonio, notable Italian baritone and pedagogue; b. Rome, Aug. 1, 1831; d. there, Oct. 15, 1918. He was a pupil of Fontemaggi and Faldi. After making his operatic debut in Rome in 1852 as Belcore, he sang in various Italian opera centers until joining Milan's La Scala in 1860. In 1867 he made his debut at London's Covent Garden as Valentine, and continued to appear there regularly until 1889. He also sang in Paris, Madrid, Lisbon, and Barcelona. From 1893 to 1898 he sang in St. Petersburg, where he also was active as a teacher. Upon returning to Rome, he became a prof. of voice at the Accademia di Santa Cecilia. His repertoire included over 125 roles. Among his students were Jean de Reszke, Battistini, Lauri-Volpi, Gigli, and Stabile.

Cotrubas, Ileana, outstanding Romanian soprano; b. Galaţi, June 9, 1939. After studies at the Scolă Specială de Muzică (1952–57) and with Eugenia Elinescu and Constantin Stroescu at the Bucharest Cons. (1957–63), she made her operatic debut as Yniod in *Pelléas et Mélisande* in Bucharest (1964). She took 1st prize in both the 's-Hertogenbosch (1965) and Munich Radio (1966) competitions, and then completed her studies at the Vienna Academy of Music (1967). She appeared at the Salzburg Festival in 1967, then was a member of the Frankfurt am Main Opera (1968–71). In 1969 she appeared as Mélisande at the Glyndebourne Festival and as Pamina at the Vienna State Opera, where she subsequently appeared regularly; she was made an Austrian Kammersängerin in 1981. In 1973 she made her U.S. debut as Mimi at the Chicago Lyric Opera; she then sang in Paris (1974) and at Milan's La Scala (1975). On March 23, 1977, she made her Metropolitan Opera debut in New York in the role of Mimi. In addition to her appearances at the world's leading opera houses and festivals, she also toured extensively as a concert artist until her retirement in 1989. Among her other notable roles were Amina, Susanna, Norina, Adina, Violetta, Gilda, Marguerite, Elisabetta, Antonia, and Micaëla.

Coulthard, Jean, Canadian composer and teacher; b. Vancouver, Feb. 10, 1908. She began her studies with her mother, Jean (Blake; née Robinson) Coulthard (b. Moncton, New Brunswick, Aug. 13, 1882; d. Vancouver, July 16, 1933), a pianist and teacher. Following lessons with Jan Cherniavsky (piano) and Frederick Chubb (theory) in Vancouver (1924–28), she continued her training on scholarship at the Royal College of Music in London (1928–30), where she was a composition student of R. O. Morris and Vaughan Williams; still later she worked with Arthur Benjamin (1939), Bernard Wagenaar (1945, 1949), and Gordon Jacob (1965–66). After serving as head of the music dept at St. Anthony's College (1934–36) and Queen's Hall School (1936–37) in Vancouver, she was a lecturer (1947–57) and senior instructor (1957–73) in composition at the Univ. of British Columbia. In 1978 she was named an Officer of the Order of Canada. Coulthard's well-crafted works follow along traditional lines. She composed the opera *The Return of the Native* (1956–79) and the ballets *Excursion* (1940) and *The Devil's Fanfare* (1958).

Cowell, Henry (Dixon), remarkable and innovative American composer; b. Menlo Park, Calif., March 11, 1897; d. Shady, N.Y., Dec. 10, 1965. His father, of Irish birth, was a member of a clergyman's family in Kildare; his mother was an American of progressive persuasion. Cowell studied violin with Henry Holmes in San Francisco; after the earthquake of 1906, his mother took him to New York, where they were compelled to seek support from the Soc. for the Improvement of the Condition of the Poor; they returned to Menlo Park, California, where Cowell was able to save enough money, earned from menial jobs, to buy a piano. He began to experiment with the keyboard by striking the keys with his fists and forearms; he named such chords "tone clusters" and at the age of 13 composed a piece called *Adventures in Harmony*, in which they appear. Later he began experimenting in altering the sound of the piano by placing various objects on the strings, and also by playing directly under the lid of the piano *pizzicato* and *glissando*, thus the later development of the "prepared piano." He first exhibited these startling innovations on March 5, 1914, at the San Francisco Musical Soc. at the St. Francis Hotel, much to the consternation of its members. The tone clusters per se were not new; they were used for special sound effects by composers in the 18th century to imitate thunder or cannon fire. Vladimir Rebikov applied them, for example, in his piano piece *Hymn to Inca*, and Charles Ives used them in his *Concord Sonata* to be sounded by covering a set of white or black keys with a wooden board. However, Cowell had a priority by systematizing tone clusters as harmonic amplifications of tonal chords, and he devised a logical notation for them. These tone clusters eventually acquired legitimacy in the works of many European and American composers. Cowell also extended the sonorities of tone clusters to instrumental combinations and applied them in several of his symphonic works. In the meantime, Cowell began taking lessons in composition with E. G. Strickland and Wallace Sabin at the Univ. of Calif. at Berkeley, and later with Frank Damrosch at the Inst. of Musical Art in New York, and, privately, with Charles Seeger (1914–16). After brief service in the U.S. Army in 1918, where he was employed first as a cook and later as arranger for its Band, he became engaged professionally to give a series of lectures on new music, illustrated by his playing his own works on the piano. In 1928 he became the first American composer to visit Russia, where he attracted considerable attention; some of his pieces were publ. in a Russian ed., the first such publications by an American. Upon his return to the United States, he was appointed lecturer on music at the New School for Social Research in New York.

In 1931 Cowell received a Guggenheim fellowship, and went to Berlin to study ethnomusicology with Hornbostel. This was the beginning of his serious study of ethnic musical materials. He had already experimented with Indian and Chinese devices in some of his works; in his *Ensemble for Strings* (1924), he included Indian thundersticks. In 1931 he formed a collaboration with Leon Theremin, then visiting the United States; with his aid he constructed an ingenious instrument, the Rhythmicon, which made possible the simultaneous production of 16 different rhythms on 16 different pitch levels of the harmonic series. He demonstrated the Rhythmicon at a lecture-concert in San Francisco on May 15, 1932. He also composed an extensive work entitled *Rhythmicana* for it, but it did not receive a performance until Dec. 3, 1971, at Stanford Univ., using advanced electronic techniques. In 1927 Cowell founded the *New Music Quarterly* for publication of ultramodern music, mainly by American composers.

Cowell's career was brutally interrupted in 1936, when he was arrested in California on charges of homosexuality (then a heinous offense) involving the impairment of the morals of a minor. Lulled by the deceptive promises of a wily district attorney of a brief confinement in a sanatorium, Cowell pleaded guilty to a limited offense; he was vengefully given a maximum sentence of imprisonment, up to 15 years. Incarcerated at San Quentin, he was assigned to work in a jute mill, but indomitably continued to write music. Thanks to interventions on his behalf by a number of eminent musicians, he was paroled in 1940 to Percy Grainger as a guarantor of his good conduct; he obtained a full pardon on Dec. 9, 1942, from the governor of California, Earl Warren, after it was discovered that the evidence against him was largely contrived. On Sept. 27, 1941, he married Sidney Robertson, a noted ethnomusicologist. He then resumed his full activities as an ed. and instructor; he held teaching positions at the New School for Social Research in New York (1940–62), the Univ. of Southern Calif. in Los Angeles, Mills College in Oakland, California, and the Peabody Cons. of Music in Baltimore (1951–56); he was also appointed adjunct prof. at summer classes at Columbia Univ. (1951–65). In 1951 Cowell was elected a member of the National Academy of Arts and Letters; he received an honorary Mus.D. from Wilmington College (1953) and from Monmouth (Ill.) College (1963). In 1956–57 he undertook a world tour with his wife through the Near East, India, and Japan, collecting rich prime materials for his compositions, which by now had acquired a decisive turn toward the use of ethnomusicological melodic and rhythmic materials, without abandoning, however, the experimental devices which were the signposts of most of his works. In addition to his symphonic and chamber music, Cowell composed several stage works, including *The Building of Bamba*, pageant (Halcyon, near Pismo Beach, Calif., Aug. 18, 1917), *O'Higgins of Chile*, opera (1949; unifnished), and *The Commission*, "operatic episode" (1954; Woodstock, N.Y., Sept. 26, 1992).

WRITINGS: *New Musical Resources* (N.Y., 1930); ed., *American Composers on American Music: A Symposium* (Stanford, Calif., 1933); with S. Cowell, *Charles Ives and His Music* (N.Y., 1955).

BIBL.: R. Mead, *H. C.'s New Music, 1925–1936* (N.Y., 1981); M. Manion, *Writings about H. C.: An Annotated Bibliography* (N.Y., 1982); W. Lichtenwanger, *The Music of H. C.: A Descriptive Catalog* (Brooklyn, 1986).

Cowie, Edward, English-born Australian composer, conductor, teacher, and painter; b. Birmingham, Aug. 17, 1943. He studied with Fricker and took his B.Ed. at the Univ. of London (1964); after training from A. Goehr (1964–68), he worked with Lutoslawski in Poland (1971); he also studied at the Trinity College of Music in London (L.T.C.L., 1968), and at the univs. of Southampton (B.Mus., 1970; D.Mus., 1979) and Lancaster (Ph.D., 1983). From 1974 to 1983 he was senior lecturer at the Univ. of Lancaster; in 1979 he also was a visiting prof. at the Univ. of Kassel. From 1983 to 1986 he was composer-in-residence at the Royal Liverpool Phil., and from 1983 to 1989 prof. of creative arts at the Univ. of Wollongong in New South Wales. In 1988 he became a naturalized Australian citizen. In 1989–90 he was prof. of creative arts at James Cook Univ. in Queensland. He then served as artistic director and prof. of arts fusion of the Australian Arts Fusion Centre in Brisbane (from 1991). In 1995 he became prof. and director of research at the Dartington College of Arts in Devon. He also was active as a conductor. His talent as a painter has been highlighted in various exhibitions. As a composer, his technique ranges from static triadic tonality to serialistic atonality; reflections of nature, including birdsong, and a preoccupation with form, are pervasive aspects of his works. He composed *Commedia*, opera (1976–78) and *Kate Kelly's Roadshow*, music theater (1982).

Cox, Jean, American tenor; b. Gadsen, Ala., Jan. 16, 1922. After attending the Univ. of Alabama and the New England Cons. of Music in Boston, he studied with Kitsamer in Frankfurt am Main, Ricci and Bertelli in Rome, and Lorenz in Munich. In 1951 he made his operatic debut as Lensky with the New England Opera Theater in Boston. In 1954 he made his European operatic debut as Rodolfo in Spoleto, and then sang in Kiel (1954–55) and Braunschweig (1955–59). He appeared at the Bayreuth Festivals (1956–75), at the Hamburg State Opera (1958–73), and at the Mannheim National Theater (from 1959). As a guest artist, he sang with various European opera houses, including the Paris Opéra (as Siegmund, 1971) and at London's Covent Garden (as Siegfried, 1975). In the United States he appeared at the Chicago Lyric Opera (1964, 1970, 1973) and made his Metropolitan Opera debut in New York as Walther von Stolzing on April 2, 1976, where he sang for the season before concentrating his career in Europe. He sang various Wagnerian roles, as well as Fra Diavolo, Don Carlos, Othello, Strauss's Herod and Bacchus, and the Cardinal in *Mathis der Maler*.

Cox, John, English opera and theater director and administrator; b. Bristol, March 12, 1935. He was educated at St. Edmund Hall, Oxford (M.A.), where he produced the first British staging of *L'Enfant et les sortilèges* in 1958. From 1967 to 1970 he was director of the Music Theatre Ensemble, and then was active at the Glyndebourne Festival from 1970 to 1983, where he served as director of productions from 1971 to 1981. He was general administrator of the Scottish Opera in Glasgow from 1981 to 1986, where he also was its artistic director in 1985–86. In 1982 he oversaw his first production at the Metropolitan Opera in New York with *Il Barbiere di Siviglia*. From 1988 to 1994 he was director of productions at London's Covent Garden. In 1995 he was a visiting fellow of the European Humanities Centre in Oxford. His inventive productions have been seen on the Continent, in the U.S., and Australia, as well as in England. He has won particular notice for his stagings of Mozart and Richard Strauss.

Crabbé, Armand (Charles), Belgian baritone; b. Brussels, April 23, 1883; d. there, July 24, 1947. He studied with Demest and Gilles at the Brussels Cons. (1902–04), and then with Cottone in Milan. In 1904 he made his operatic debut as the Nightwatchman in *Die Meistersinger von Nürnberg* at the Théâtre Royal de la Monnaie in Brussels. From 1906 to 1914 he sang at London's Covent Garden, and returned there in 1937. On Nov. 5, 1907, he made his U.S. debut as Escamillo at N.Y.'s Manhattan Opera; after appearances with the Chicago Grand Opera (1910–14), he sang at Milan's La Scala (1915–16; 1928–31), in Buenos Aires (1916–26), and in Belgium. In his last years, he taught voice in Brussels. With Auguste Maurage, he composed the opera *Les Noces d'or*. He publ. the books *Conseils sur l'art du chant* (Brussels, 1931) and *L'art d'Orphée* (Brussels, 1933). Among his many roles were Rossini's Figaro, Silvio, Beckmesser, Rabaud's Mârouf, Ford, and Valentin.

Cras, Jean Émile Paul, French composer; b. Brest, May 22, 1879; d. there, Sept. 14, 1932. He grew up in a musical atmosphere and when still a child began to compose; he took lessons with Henri Duparc, under whose influence he composed a number of miniatures in an impressionistic vein; he was at his best in lyrical songs and instrumental pieces. He pursued a career in the French navy, attaining the rank of vice admiral. He composed the opera *Polyphème* (Paris, Dec. 28, 1922).

Crass, Franz, German bass-baritone; b. Wipperfurth, Feb. 9, 1928. He was a student of Glettenberg at the Cologne Hochschule für Musik. In 1954 he made his operatic debut as Amonasro in Krefeld, and then sang in Hannover (1956–62), Bayreuth (1959–73), and Cologne (1962–64). He was a member of the Hamburg State Opera (from 1964), and also appeared at the Vienna State Opera, the Bavarian State Opera in Munich, at La Scala in Milan, and at Covent Garden in London. He was particularly known for his roles in operas by Mozart and Wagner, as well as for his appearances as a concert artist.

Creatore, Giuseppe, Italian-American conductor; b. Naples, June 21, 1871; d. N.Y., Aug. 15, 1952. He was a pupil of d'Arienzo and De Nardis at the Naples Cons. After conducting the Naples municipal band (1888–96), he went to the United States in 1900. In 1902 he founded his own band in New York, with which he toured North America; he also was head of his own opera company (1918–23). He was conductor of the N.Y. City Symphonic Orch. (1936–40) and the N.Y. State Symphonic Band (1937–40), remaining active as a conductor until 1946.

Crescentini, Girolamo, notable Italian castrato mezzo-soprano; b. Urbania, near Urbino, Feb. 2, 1762; d. Naples, April 24, 1846. He studied singing with Gibelli at Bologna. He began his career in Padua in 1782 and then sang in Rome in 1783; subsequent successes in other European capitals earned him the surname of "Orfeo Italiano." He sang at Livorno, Padua, Venice, Turin, London (1786), Milan, and Naples (1788–89). Napoleon, having heard him in 1805, decorated him with the Iron Crown, and engaged him to teach singing to his family from 1806 to 1812; Crescentini then retired from the stage and left Paris, on account of vocal disorders induced by the climate. In 1816 he became a prof. of singing in the Royal Cons. in Naples. Cimarosa wrote his *Orazi e Curiazi* for him. Crescentini publ. several collections of Ariette (Vienna, 1797) and a *Treatise on Vocalization in France and Italy*, with vocal exercises (Paris, 1811).

Crespin, Régine, outstanding French soprano, later mezzo-soprano; b. Marseilles, Feb. 23, 1927. She studied pharmacology; then began taking voice lessons with Suzanne Cesbron-Viseur and Georges Jouatte in Paris. She made her debut in Mulhouse as Elsa in 1950 and then sang at the Paris Opéra from 1951, where she quickly rose to prominence. She acquired a reputation as one of the best Wagnerian singers; she sang Kundry at the Bayreuth Festivals (1958–60); she appeared also at La Scala in Milan, at Covent Garden in London, and on Nov. 19, 1962, made her debut with the Metropolitan Opera in New York in the role of the Marschallin; she remained with the Metropolitan until her farewell appearance as Mme. De Croissy in *Les Dialogues des Carmélites* on April 16, 1987. From 1977 until her retirement in 1991 she sang mezzo-soprano roles. Her memoires were publ. as *La vie et l'amour d'une femme* (Paris, 1980; rev. Eng. tr., 1997, as *On Stage, Off Stage: A Memoir*). She sang the parts of Elsa in *Lohengrin*, Sieglinde in *Die Walküre*, and Amelia in *Un ballo in maschera*; she also appeared as a concert singer. Her sonorous, somewhat somber voice suited dramatic parts excellently.

Crews, Lucile, American composer; b. Pueblo, Colo., Aug. 23, 1888; d. San Diego, Calif., Nov. 3, 1972. She studied at the New England Cons. of Music in Boston, then with Boulanger in Paris and Hugo Kaun in Berlin. She wrote a "miniature opera," *Ariadne and Dionysus* (1935) and a "grand opera," *800 Rubles* (1926).

Crimi, Giulio, Italian tenor; b. Paterno, May 10, 1885; d. Rome, Oct. 29, 1939. He made his debut in Palermo in 1910 as Manrico; then sang at Covent Garden in London (1914). On Nov. 13, 1918, he made his Metropolitan Opera debut in New York as Radames; on Dec. 14, 1918, he sang there in the premieres of Puccini's *Gianni Schicchi* (as Rinuccio) and *Il Tabarro* (as Luigi); he continued to sing there until 1921; he also made appearances in Chicago (1916–18; 1922–24); then sang in Milan and Rome. After his retirement in 1928, he taught voice; one of his most famous pupils was Tito Gobbi.

Crist, Bainbridge, American composer and teacher; b. Lawrenceburg, Ind., Feb. 13, 1883; d. Barnstable, Mass., Feb. 7, 1969. He studied piano and flute; later law at George Washington Univ. (LL.B.). He went to Europe to complete his musical training (theory with P. Juon in Berlin and C. Landi in London, and singing with William Shakespeare. He taught singing in Boston (1915–

21) and Washington, D.C. (1922–23); he returned to Europe (1923) and spent 4 years in Florence, Paris, Lucerne, and Berlin; then settled in Washington, D.C. Crist devoted much time to teaching. Among his compositions are *Le Pied de la momie*, choreographic drama (1915), *Pregiwa's Marriage*, Javanese ballet (1920), and *The Sorceress*, choreographic drama (1926). He authored *The Art of Setting Words to Music* (N.Y., 1944).

BIBL.: J. Howard, *B. C.* (N.Y., 1929).

Cristoforeanu, Florica, Romanian soprano; b. Rimnicu-Sarat, Aug. 16, 1887; d. Rio de Janeiro, March 1, 1960. She studied at the Milan Cons. with Filippi and Bodrilla; she made her debut in Capodistria in 1908 as Lucia, then sang operetta in Bucharest and Milan (1909–19). From 1927 to 1932 she appeared at Milan's La Scala; also sang in Rome (1928–34) and in South America. She retired in 1940. In addition to her classical roles, she was known for her performances of works by contemporary Italian composers.

Crivelli, Gaetano, Italian tenor; b. Brescia, Oct. 20, 1768; d. there, July 10, 1836. He made his debut in Brescia in 1794, and then sang in Verona, Palermo, Venice, and Naples. After studies in Naples with Nozzari and Aprile, he made his first appearance at Milan's La Scala in 1805. On Jan. 19, 1811, he made his Paris debut in Paisiello's *Pirro*. He made his London debut at the King's Theatre as Ulysses in Cimarosa's *Penelope* on Jan. 11, 1817. On March 7, 1824, he created the role of Adriano in Meyerbeer's *Il Crociato in Egitto* in Venice, which role he made his own and which he chose for his farewell performance in 1831. He also sang in operas by Mozart and Paër. His son, Domenico Crivelli (b. Brescia, June 7, 1793; d. London, Nov. 11, 1851), was a singing teacher and composer who pursued his career in London. He publ. *The Art of Singing and New Solfeggios for the Cultivation of the Bass Voice* (London, 2d ed., 1844).

Croiza, Claire, French mezzo-soprano and teacher; b. Paris, Sept. 14, 1882; d. there, May 27, 1946. After training at the Paris Cons., she made her operatic debut in Nancy in 1905 in de Lara's *Messalina*. In 1906 she joined the Théâtre Royal de la Monnaie in Brussels. From 1908 she was a member of the Paris Opéra, where she was especially admired for her roles in operas by Gluck, Berlioz, Bizet, and Strauss. In 1922 she joined the faculty of the École Normale de Musique in Paris, and from 1934 she taught at the Paris Cons. Her performances of the French song repertory were highly regarded, particularly her interpretations of Fauré, Duparc, and Debussy. B. Bannerman ed. and tr. *The Singer as Interpreter: Claire Croiza's Master Classes* (London, 1989).

BIBL.: J.-M. Nectoux, ed., *C. C. 1882–1946* (Paris, 1984).

Crooks, Richard (Alexander), American tenor; b. Trenton, N.J., June 26, 1900; d. Portola Valley, Calif., Sept. 29, 1972. He studied voice with Sydney H. Bourne and also took lessons with Frank La Forge; he was a boy soprano (later tenor) soloist in N.Y. churches. He made his debut with the N.Y. Sym. Orch. under Damrosch in 1922, then gave concerts in London, Vienna, Munich, Berlin, and the United States (1925–27). On Sept. 20, 1927, he made his stage debut as Cavaradossi at the Hamburg Opera; he made his American debut in the same role with the Philadelphia Grand Opera Co. (Nov. 27, 1930); he made his debut at the Metropolitan Opera in New York as Des Grieux (Feb. 25, 1933), where he continued to sing until 1942. He toured Australia (1936–39); gave concerts from coast to coast in the United States and Canada; appeared in recitals, as an orch. soloist, and in festivals.

Crosby, John (O'Hea), American conductor, opera impresario, and music educator; b. N.Y., July 12, 1926. He received instruction in violin and piano from his mother, and later studied composition with Hindemith at Yale Univ. (B.A., 1950) and conducting with Rudolph Thomas at Columbia Univ. and Monteux in Hancock, Maine. From 1951 to 1956 he was on the staff of the N.Y. City Opera. In 1956 he founded the Opera Assn. of New Mexico, later renamed the Santa Fe Opera. During his long tenure as its general director and resident conductor, he gave premiere performances of numerous operas by American and foreign composers. Crosby was also president of the Manhattan School of Music in New York (1976–85) and of Opera America (from 1976).

Cross, Joan, English soprano, opera producer, and teacher; b. London, Sept. 7, 1900; d. Aldeburgh, Dec. 12, 1993. She received training from Holst at St. Paul's Girls School and from Dawson Freer at Trinity College of Music in London. In 1924 she became a member of the chorus at the Old Vic Theatre in London; in 1931 she joined the Sadler's Wells Opera in London, where she was principal soprano until 1946. In 1946 she helped to found the English Opera Group, with which she was active as both a soprano and producer. In 1948 she cofounded the Opera School, which became the National School of Opera in 1955. In 1951 she was made a Commander of the Order of the British Empire. Cross became particularly known for her roles in Britten's operas, in which she created Ellen Orford in *Peter Grimes* (1945), the Female Chorus in *The Rape of Lucretia* (1946), Lady Billows in *Albert Herring* (1947), Elizabeth I in *Gloriana* (1953), and Mrs. Grose in *The Turn of the Screw* (1954).

Crosse, Gordon, English composer; b. Bury, Lancashire, Dec. 1, 1937. He studied music history with Wellesz at the Univ. of Oxford (graduated, 1961), where he continued his research under Frank Harrison in 1961–62; he then studied with Petrassi at the Accademia di Santa Cecilia in Rome (1962). After working as senior music tutor in the extramural dept. at the Univ. of Birmingham (1964–66), he served as its Haywood fellow in music (1966–69). From 1969 to 1976 he was a fellow in music at the Univ. of Essex, and in 1973 composer-in-residence at King's College, Cambridge. In 1976 he was awarded the Cobbett Medal. In subsequent years, Crosse devoted himself to composition. His research into early music, combined with his love of literature, resulted in dramatic, vocal, and instrumental works notable for their rich expressivity in a strongly defined personal style.

WORKS: DRAMATIC: OPERAS: *Purgatory* (Cheltenham, July 7, 1966); *The Grace of Todd* (1967–68; Aldeburgh, June 7, 1969); *The Story of Vasco* (1968–73; London, March 13, 1974); *Potter Thompson* (1972–73; London, Jan. 9, 1975). BALLETS: *Wildboy* (Washington, D.C., Dec. 12, 1980); *Young Apollo* (London, Nov. 17, 1984).

Crossley, Ada (Jessica), Australian mezzo-soprano; b. Tarraville, Gippsland, March 3, 1874; d. London, Oct. 17, 1929. She was a pupil of Fanny Simonson (voice) in Melbourne. Having sung in several churches, she made her concert debut with the Melbourne Phil. Soc. in 1892. She went to London in 1894, studied with Santley, and later with Mme. Marchesi in Paris. She made her London debut at the Queen's Hall on May 18, 1895. Her success was so emphatic that she sang by command 5 times before Queen Victoria within the next 2 years; she appeared as a soloist at all important English festivals. Her tour of Australia in 1904 was a succession of triumphs, and she also made successful tours of the United States and South Africa.

Crouch, Frederick Nicholls, English conductor and composer; b. London, July 31, 1808; d. Portland, Maine, Aug. 18, 1896. He studied with Bochsa (cello), and entered the Royal Academy of Music in London in 1822 (teachers: Crotch, Attwood, Howes, Lindley, and Crivelli). At the age of 9 he was a cellist in the Royal Coburg Theater. He played in Queen Adelaide's private band till 1832, and then was a teacher and singer in Plymouth, and cellist in various theaters. He went to New York in 1849; he was in Philadelphia in 1856 as conductor of Mrs. Rush's Saturday Concerts. He served in the Union Army, and settled in Baltimore as a singing teacher. Cora Pearl, the famous Parisian courtesan of the 2d Empire, was his daughter. He composed 2 operas.

Cruft, Adrian (Francis), English double-bass player, teacher, and composer; b. Mitcham, Surrey, Feb. 10, 1921; d. Hill Head, Hampshire, Feb. 20, 1987. He first studied double bass with his father, Eugene (John) Cruft (b. London, 1887; d. there, June 4, 1976). In 1938 he was awarded the Boult conducting scholarship at the Royal College of Music in London, where he studied conducting with W. H. Reed and Reginald Goodall, clarinet with Frederick Thurston, piano with Arthur Benjamin, and composition with Jacob and Rubbra. From 1947 to 1969 he played double bass in various London orchs. In 1966 he was chairman of the Composer's Guild of Great Britain. In 1972 he became a prof. of theory and composition at the Royal College of Music, and also taught at the Guildhall School of Music in London (1972–75). His output followed along traditional lines. He composed many pieces for young performers, including the melodrama *The Horse Trough* (1974), the vaudeville opera *The Eatanswill Election* (1981), and the "operina" *Dr. Syn* (1983).

Cruvelli, Sofia (real name, **Johanne Sophie Charlotte Crüwell**), esteemed German soprano; b. Bielefeld, Aug. 29, 1824; d. Nice, Nov. 6, 1907. She studied in Paris with Piermarini, and completed her training with Bordogni and Lamperti. In 1847 she made her operatic debut in Venice as Odabella in Verdi's *Attila*, and then appeared as Elvira and Abigaille at Her Majesty's Theatre in London in 1848. After singing in Milan (1850), she sang at the Théâtre-Italien in Paris (1851–53), where she appeared as Elvira, Norma, Semiramide, and Leonore. In 1854 she sang Donna Anna, Leonore, and Rossini's Desdemona at London's Covent Garden, and that same year she joined the Paris Opéra, where she was notably successful as Valentine, Rachel, Giulia, and Hélène in Verdi's *Les Vêspres siciliennes*, which role she created on June 13, 1855. Upon her marriage to Comte Vigier in 1856, she retired from the operatic stage. Her sister was Friederike Marie Crüwell (1824–68), a mezzo-soprano who studied with Roger and then pursued her career in France and Italy.

Cruz-Romo, Gilda, Mexican soprano; b. Guadalajara, Feb. 12, 1940. She studied at the Cons. of Mexico, making her debut there in 1962. On May 8, 1970, she appeared at the Metropolitan Opera in New York as Maddalena in *Andrea Chénier* ; continued to sing there in subsequent seasons; also sang in Chicago, Houston, and Dallas. In Europe, she appeared in London, Milan, Moscow, Paris, and Vienna. Her large repertory included both Verdi Leonoras, Violetta, Amelia, Aida, Elisabeth de Valois, Cherubini's Medea, Donna Anna, Cio-Cio-San, Manon, Suor Angelica, and Tosca.

Cuberli, Lella (Alice), American soprano; b. Austin, Texas, Sept. 29, 1945. She was educated at Southern Methodist Univ. (B.Mus., 1974). In 1975 she made her operatic debut as Violetta in Budapest. Following her first appearance at Milan's La Scala as Mozart's Constanze in 1978, she sang there frequently in later years. She also toured with the company to the Edinburgh Festival in 1982 in Handel's *Ariodante*. In 1985 she made her debut as a soloist at the Berlin Festival. She sang Mozart's Countess at her first appearance at the Salzburg Festival in 1986. After an engagement as Violetta in Brussels in 1987, she made her debut at the Vienna State Opera in 1988 in *Il viaggio a Reims*. On Nov. 30, 1990, she made her Metropolitan Opera debut in New York as Rossini's Semiramis. She sang Antonia in *Les Contes d'Hoffmann* at the Opéra de la Bastille in Paris in 1992, and that same year appeared as Mozart's Countess with the Royal Opera, Covent Garden, London, on the company's visit to Japan. In 1996 she was engaged as Donna Anna at the Salzburg Festival. As a concert artist, she sang with many major orchs.

Cuclin, Dimitrie, Romanian composer and pedagogue; b. Galaţi, April 5, 1885; d. Bucharest, Feb. 7, 1978. He studied with Kiriac, Castaldi, and Dinicu at the Bucharest Cons. (1904–07), and then in Paris at the Cons. and at the Schola Cantorum with Widor and d'Indy (1908–14). After teaching at the Brooklyn College of Music (1922–30), he returned to his homeland to serve as a prof. at the Bucharest Cons. (1930–48). His prolific output reflected the influence of the French and German Romantic tradition. He composed the operas *Soria* (1910–11), *Traiansi Dochia* (1921), *Agamemnon* (1922), *Bellérophon* (1925), and *Meleagridele* (1958) and the ballet *Tragedie în pădure* (1962).

Cuénod, Hugues (-Adhémar), notable Swiss tenor; b. Corseaux-sur-Vevey, June 26, 1902. He received training at the Ribaupierre Institut in Lausanne, at the conservatories in Geneva and Basel, and in Vienna. He commenced his career as a concert singer. In 1928 he made his stage debut in *Jonny spielt auf* in Paris, and in 1929 he sang for the first time in the United States in *Bitter Sweet*. From 1930 to 1933 he was active in Geneva, and then in Paris from 1934 to 1937. During the 1937–39 seasons, he made an extensive concert tour of North America. From 1940 to 1946 he taught at the Geneva Cons. In 1943 he resumed his operatic career singing in *Die Fledermaus* in Geneva. He subsequently sang at Milan's La Scala (1951), the Glyndebourne Festival (from 1954), and London's Covent Garden (1954, 1956, 1958). Cuénod pursued his career into old age, making his belated debut at the Metropolitan Opera in New York as the Emperor in *Turandot* just 3 months before his 85th birthday. In his 87th year, he appeared as Monsieur Taupe in *Capricuio* at the Geneva Opera in 1989. Among his finest roles were Mozart's Basilio, the Astrologer in *The Golden Cockerel*, and Sellem in *The Rake's Progress*. He was particularly known for his championship of early music and of the French song repertory.

Cui, César (Antonovich), Russian composer; b. Vilnius, Jan. 18, 1835; d. Petrograd, March 26, 1918. He was the son of a soldier in Napoleon's army who remained in Russia, married a Lithuanian noblewoman, and settled as a teacher of French in Vilnius. Cui learned musical notation by copying Chopin's mazurkas and various Italian operas; then tried his hand at composition on his own. In 1849 he took lessons with Moniuszko in Vilnius. In 1850 he went to St. Petersburg, where he entered the Engineering School in 1851 and later the Academy of Military Engineering (1855). After graduation in 1857 he became a topographer and later an expert in fortification. He participated in the Russo-Turkish War of 1877; in 1878 he became a prof. at the Engineering School and was tutor in military fortification to Czar Nicholas II. In 1856 Cui met Balakirev, who helped him master the technique of composition. In 1858 he married Malvina Bamberg; for her he wrote a scherzo on the theme BABEG (for the letters in her name) and CC (his own initials). In 1864 he began writing music criticism in the St. Petersburg *Vedomosti* and later in other newspapers, continuing as music critic until 1900. Cui's musical tastes were conditioned by his early admiration for Schumann; he opposed Wagner, against whom he wrote vitriolic articles; he attacked Strauss and Reger with even greater violence. He was an ardent propagandist of Glinka and the Russian national school, but was somewhat critical toward Tchaikovsky. He publ. the first comprehensive book on Russian music, *Musique en Russie* (Paris, 1880). Cui was grouped with Rimsky-Korsakov, Mussorgsky, Borodin, and Balakirev as one of the "Moguchaya Kuchka" (Mighty 5). The adjective in his case is not very appropriate, however, for Cui was at his best in delicate miniatures, e.g., *Orientale*, from the suite *Kaleidoscope*, op. 50. A vol. of his *Selected Articles* (1864–1917) was publ. in Leningrad in 1953. In addition to his own compositions, from 1914 to 1916 he completed Mussorgsky's opera *The Fair at Sorotchinsk*.

WORKS: DRAMATIC: OPERAS: *The Mandarin's Son* (1859; St. Petersburg, Dec. 19, 1878); *The Prisoner of the Caucasus* (1857–59; rev. 1881; St. Petersburg, Feb. 16, 1883); *William Ratcliff* (St. Petersburg, Feb. 26, 1869); *Angelo* (St. Petersburg, Feb. 13, 1876); *Le Flibustier* (Opéra Comique, Paris, Jan. 22, 1894); *The Saracen* (St. Petersburg, Nov. 14, 1899); *Mam'zelle Fifi* (Moscow, Nov. 17, 1903); *The Snow Giant*, children's opera (Yalta, May 28, 1906); *Matteo Falcone* (Moscow, Dec. 27, 1907); *The Captain's Daughter* (1907–09; St. Petersburg, Feb. 27, 1911); *Puss in Boots*, children's opera (Tiflis, Jan. 12, 1916). Cui's *A Feast in Time of Plague*, orig. written as a dramatic cantata, was produced as a 1-act opera (Moscow, Nov. 24, 1901).

BIBL.: L. Mercy-Argenteau, *C. C.: Esquisse critique* (Paris, 1888); P. Weimarn, *C. C. as a Songwriter* (St. Petersburg, 1896).

Culp, Julia, Dutch contralto; b. Groningen, Oct. 6, 1880; d. Amsterdam, Oct. 13, 1970. She first studied violin as a child; then became a voice pupil of Cornelia van Zanten at the Amsterdam Cons. (1897), and later of Etelka Gerster in Berlin. She made her formal debut in Magdeburg in 1901; her tours of Germany, Austria, the Netherlands, France, Spain, and Russia were highly successful, establishing her as one of the finest singers of German lieder. Her American debut took place in New York on Jan. 10, 1913; for many years, she visited the United States every season.

Culshaw, John (Royds), English recording producer; b. London, May 28, 1924; d. there, April 27, 1980. He studied music while serving in the British army. From 1954 to 1967 he was manager and chief producer with the Decca Record Co.; from 1967 to 1975 he held the same post with the BBC. He was awarded the rank of Officer of the Order of the British Empire in 1966. He made a mark in the recording industry by introducing the stereo-reproduction process, which created a 3-dimensional effect. His principal achievement was the stereophonic recording of *Der Ring des Nibelungen*, issued by Decca under the direction of Solti. Culshaw related the background of this undertaking in his books *Ring Resounding* (London, 1967) and *Reflections on Wagner's Ring* (London, 1976). His other publications are *Sergei Rachmaninov* (London, 1949) and *A Century of Music* (London, 1952). He also publ. an autobiography, *Odyssey of a Recording Pioneer: Putting the Record Straight* (N.Y., 1981).

Cummings, Conrad, American composer and teacher; b. San Francisco, Feb. 10, 1948. He studied with Bulent Arel at Yale Univ., took courses at the State Univ. of N.Y. at Stony Brook, was a student of Davidovsky and Ussachevsky at Columbia Univ., attended the Berkshire Music Center at Tanglewood, and pursued training at Stanford Univ. After teaching at the Columbia-Princeton Electronic Music Center (1974–76), he was electronic music coordinator at Brooklyn College of the City Univ. of N.Y. (1976–79). From 1980 he taught at the Oberlin College-Cons. of Music. His dramatic works include *Eros and Psyche* (Oberlin, Nov. 16, 1983), *Cassandra* (1984–85; rev. 1986), *Positions 1956* (N.Y., March 11, 1988), *Insertions* (N.Y., March 18, 1988), *Photo-Op* (N.Y., May 19, 1989), and *Tonkin* (Wilmington, Nov. 27, 1993).

Cunningham, Arthur, black American composer; b. Piermont, N.Y., Nov. 11, 1928; d. Nyack, N.Y., March 31, 1997. He commenced piano studies at the age of 6 and was composing for his own jazz group when he was 12; he later received formal training at Fisk Univ. (B.A., 1951), Columbia Univ. Teachers College (M.A., 1957), and the Juilliard School of Music. In addition to composing, he was active as a teacher and conductor. His output runs the gamut of styles and techniques, ranging from serious to rock. His works include the rock opera *His Natural Grace* (1969), two musicals, *The Beauty Part* and *Violetta* (both 1963), and a ballet, *Harlem Suite* (1971).

Cupido, Alberto, Italian tenor; b. Portofino, March 19, 1948. He studied at the Milan Cons. and at the Accademia Musicale Chigiana in Siena. In 1977 he made his operatic debut in Genoa as Pinkerton, and then his German debut as Rodolfo in Frankfurt am Main. He made his British debut in 1978 as Rodolfo at the Glyndebourne Festival. Following an engagement as Faust at the Bavarian State Opera in Munich in 1982, he made his U.S. debut in San Francisco in 1983. He portrayed Edgardo at his first appearance at Milan's La Scala in 1983, a role he reprised in Monte Carlo in 1987. He sang Faust in Geneva in 1988 and in Rome in 1990. Following an appearance as Faust at the Lyric Opera in Chicago in 1991, he portrayed Cavaradossi at London's Covent Garden in 1993. In 1995 he sang Reyer's Sigurd in Marseilles, and then appeared as Rodolfo in Genoa in 1996.

Cura, José, Argentine tenor; b. Rosario, 1962. He received training in composition and conducting at the Univ. of Rosario, and in voice at the School of the Arts at the Teatro Colón in Buenos Aires and later in Italy. In 1993 he appeared as Albert Gregor in *The Makropulos Affair* in Turin, and returned there as Ruggero in *La rondine* in 1994. He also sang in *Fedora* at the Lyric Opera in Chicago in 1994. In 1995 he was engaged as Paolo in Zandonai's *Francesca da Rimini* in Palermo, as Stiffelio at London's Covent Garden, and as Ismaele in *Nabucco* in Paris. He returned to Covent Garden in 1996 as Samson and Cavaradossi, and also sang Osaka in *Iris* in Rome, the title role in *Il corsaro* in Turin, and Pollione in Los Angeles. In 1997 he portrayed Enzo Grimaldi at Milan's La Scala, Turiddu in Bologna, and Otello and Samson in Turin. He returned to La Scala as Des Grieux and to Palermo as Radames in 1998.

Curci, Giuseppe, Italian composer; b. Barletta, June 15, 1808; d. there, Aug. 5, 1877. He studied in Naples with Zingarelli and Crescentini. He became a singing teacher, and also composed several operas, including *Il Proscritto* (Turin, 1837) and *Don Desiderio* (Venice, 1837). He traveled in Germany and Austria. He taught voice in Paris (1848–56), where his opera *Il Baccelliere* was produced; then returned to his native town. He publ. a manual, *Il bel canto*.

Curschmann, Karl Friedrich, German singer and composer; b. Berlin, June 21, 1805; d. Langfuhr, near Danzig, Aug. 24, 1841. Originally a law student, he devoted himself to music, studying with Hauptmann and Spohr at Kassel, where his 1-act opera *Abdul und Erinnieh* was produced (Oct. 29, 1828). He was also a noted singer and gave concerts in Germany and Italy.

BIBL.: G. Meissner, *K. F. C.* (Bautzen, 1899); D. Curschman-Undenheim, *Das Geschlecht C.* (Oppenheim am Rhein, 1937).

Curti, Franz, German composer; b. Kassel, Nov. 16, 1854; d. Dresden, Feb. 6, 1898. He became a dentist by profession, at the same time taking music courses in Dresden with Kretschmer and Schulz-Beuthen. Among his dramatic works are the operas *Hertha* (Altenburg, 1887), *Reinhardt von Ufenau* (Altenburg, 1889), *Erlöst* (Mannheim, 1894), and *Das Rösli vom Säntis* (Zürich, 1898), the melodrama, *Schneefried* (Mannheim, 1895), and the 1-act Japanese fairy opera, *Lili-Tsee* (Mannheim, 1896).

Curtin, Phyllis (née **Smith**), esteemed American soprano and teacher; b. Clarksburg, W.Va., Dec. 3, 1921. She studied at Wellesley College (B.A., 1943) and received vocal instruction from Olga Avierino, Joseph Regnaeas, and Goldovsky. In 1946 she made her operatic debut as Lisa in *The Queen of Spades* with the New England Opera Theatre in Boston. Her recital debut followed in 1950 at N.Y.'s Town Hall. On Oct. 22, 1953, she made her first appearance with the N.Y. City Opera as Fräulein Burstner in Gottfried von Einem's *The Trial*, where she remained on the roster until 1960; then returned in 1962, 1964, and 1975–76. She also made appearances at the Teatro Colón in Buenos Aires (1959), the Glyndebourne Festival (1959), the Vienna State Opera (1960–61), and at La Scala in Milan (1962). On Nov. 4, 1961, she made her Metropolitan Opera debut in New York as Fiordiligi, remaining on its roster for the season; she returned for the 1966–70 and 1972–73 seasons. Her tours as a soloist with orchs. and as a recitalist took her all over the globe until her retirement in 1984. She taught at the Aspen (Colo) School of Music and the Berkshire Music Center in Tanglewood. After serving as prof. of voice at the Yale Univ. School of Music (1974–83), she was prof. of voice and dean of the school of the arts at Boston Univ. (from 1983); in 1992 she retired as its dean but continued to teach there. Curtin became well known for such roles as Mozart's Countess, Donna Anna, Rosalinde, Eva, Violetta, Alice Ford, Salome, and Ellen Orford. She also created Floyd's Susannah (1955) and Cathy in *Wuthering Heights* (1958).

Curzon, (Emmanuel-) Henri (-Parent) de, French music critic and writer; b. Le Havre, July 6, 1861; d. Paris, Feb. 25, 1942. He was keeper of the government archives at Paris from 1892 until 1926; then became librarian of the Opéra Comique; he also was music critic of the *Gazette de France* (1889–1918). His numerous writings include *Les Dernières Années de Piccini à Paris* (1890), *La Légende de Sigurd dans l'Edda; L'Opéra d'Ernest Reyer* (1890), *Grétry, biographie critique* (1907), *L'Evolution lyrique au théâtre* (1908), *Meyerbeer, Biographie critique* (1910), with A. Soubies, *Documents inédits sur le "Faust" de Gounod* (1912), *Mozart, Biographie critique* (1914), *Rossini* (1920), *L'Oeuvre de Richard Wagner à Paris et ses interprètes* (1920), *Ambroise Thomas* (1921), *Ernest Reyer* (1924), *Cosima Wagner et Bayreuth* (1930), and *Berlioz, L'Homme et le musicien* (1932).

Cuvillier, Charles (Louis Paul), French composer; b. Paris, April 24, 1877; d. there, Feb. 14, 1955. He studied privately with Fauré and Messager, and with Massenet at the Paris Cons. He then devoted himself to the musical theater, bringing out his first light stage work, *Avant-hier matin* (Paris, Oct. 20, 1905; rev. version as *Les Adam*, Paris, Feb. 20, 1913). Its success led to the Parisian premieres of his *Son p'tit frère* (April 10, 1907; rev. version as *Laïs, ou la courtisane amoureuse*, 1930), *Afgar, ou Les Loisirs andalous* (April 10, 1909), and *Les Muscadines* (April 28, 1910; rev. version as *La Fausse Ingénue*, Paris, March 17, 1918). Following premieres of *L'Astronome et l'étoile* (Buenos Aires, July 1911) and *Les Trois Sultanes* (Monca, Jan. 1912), he brought out one of his most ambitious works, *Der lila Domino* (Leipzig, Feb. 3, 1912). His *Sappho* (Paris, Feb. 27, 1912; rev. version as *La République des vierges*, Paris, Sept. 6, 1917) was followed by his *La Reine s'amuse* (Marseilles, Dec. 31, 1912; rev. version as *La Reine joyeuse*, Paris, Nov. 1, 1918), a notably successful score which featured the famous waltz "Ah! la troublante volupté." *La Reine s'amuse* was a great success in London in its adapted version as *The Naughty Princess*. Among Cuvillier's other stage works were *Flora Bella* (Munich, Sept. 5, 1913), *The Sunshine of the World* (London, Feb. 18, 1920), *Bob et moi* (Paris, April 6, 1924), *Qui êtes vous?* (Monte Carlo, Nov. 13, 1926), and *Boulard et ses filles* (Paris, Nov. 8, 1929).

Cuzzoni, Francesca, celebrated Italian soprano; b. Parma, c.1700; d. Bologna, 1770. She studied with Lanzi. She sang in Parma, Bologna, Genoa, and Venice (1716–18), then was engaged at the Italian opera in London, making her debut as Teofane in Handel's opera *Ottone* (Jan. 12, 1723). She made a profound impression on London opera lovers, and was particularly distinguished in lyric roles, but later her notorious rivalry with Faustina Bordoni nearly ruined her career. Following some appearances in Venice, she returned to London (1734); after several seasons she went to the Netherlands, where she became impoverished and was imprisoned for debt. Eventually, she returned to Bologna, where she subsisted by making buttons.

Czerwenka, Oskar, Austrian bass; b. Vöcklabruck bei Linz, July 5, 1924. He was a student of O. Iro in Vienna. In 1947 he made his operatic debut as the Hermit in *Der Freischütz* in Graz. He joined the Vienna State Opera in 1951, where he became successful in such roles as Baron Ochs, Osmin, and Kecal in *The Bartered Bride*, and in operas by Lortzing; in 1961 he was made an Austrian Kammersänger. From 1953 he also appeared at the Salzburg Festival. In 1959 he sang Baron Ochs at the Glyndebourne Festival and, on Dec. 26 of that year, made his Metropolitan Opera debut in New York in the same role. He also appeared in Hamburg, Berlin, Munich, Frankfurt am Main, Cologne, and Stuttgart. He also appeared widely as a concert artist. He publ. the book *Lebenszeiten-Ungebetene Briefe* (Vienna, 1987).

Czibulka, Alphons, Hungarian bandmaster and composer; b. Szepes-Varallya, May 14, 1842; d. Vienna, Oct. 27, 1894. Originally a pianist, he became Kapellmeister at the Karltheater in Vienna in 1865. He was bandmaster of the 17th Regiment, and later of the 25th Regiment at Prague. He finally settled in Vienna, where he brought out the operetta *Pfingsten* in Florenz (Dec. 20, 1884). Other stage works are *Der Glücksritter* (1887), *Gil Blas* (Hamburg, 1889), *Der Bajazzo* (Vienna, 1892), and *Signor Annibale* (1893).

D

Dabadie, Henri-Bernard, French baritone; b. Pau, Jan. 19, 1797; d. Paris, May 1853. He received his training at the Paris Cons. In 1819 he made his operatic debut as Cinna in *La Vestale* at the Paris Opéra, where he sang until 1835. He became especially well known there for his roles in Rossini's operas, creating Pharaon in *Moïse et Pharaon* (March 26, 1827), Raimbaud in *Le Comte Ory* (Aug. 20, 1828), and the title role in *Guillaume Tell* (Aug. 3, 1829). He also created the role of Belcore in Donizetti's *L'elisir d'amore* in Milan (May 12, 1832). His wife was the soprano Louise Zulme Léroux (b. Boulogne, Oct. 4, 1796; d. Paris, Nov. 1877), who sang at the Paris Opéra (1824–35), where she created the roles of Sinaïde in *Moïse et Pharaon* and Jemmy in *Guillaume Tell*.

D'Accone, Frank A(nthony), American musicologist; b. Somerville, Mass., June 13, 1931. He studied with Geiringer and Read at Boston Univ. (B.Mus., 1952; M.Mus., 1953), then with Pirrotta, Merritt, and Piston at Harvard Univ. (M.A., 1955; Ph.D., 1960). He taught first at the State Univ. of N.Y. at Buffalo (1960–68); he also was a visiting prof. at the Univ. of Calif. at Los Angeles (1965–66), to which he returned as a prof. of music in 1968. He is ed. of the Music of the Florentine Renaissance in the Corpus Mensurabilis Musicae series, XXXII (1966 et seq.); he also publ. *Alessandro Scarlatti's "Gli equivoci nel sambiante": The History of a Baroque Opera* (N.Y., 1985).

BIBL.: I. Alm, A. McLamore, and C. Reardon, eds., *Musica franca: Essays in Honor of F. A. D.* (Stuyvesant, N.Y., 1996).

Daffner, Hugo, German composer and musicologist; b. Munich, June 2, 1882; d. in the concentration camp in Dachau, Oct. 9, 1936. He studied composition with Thuille and musicology with Sandberger and Kroyer at the Royal Academy in Munich (Ph.D., 1904, with the diss. *Die Entwicklung des Klavierkonzerts bis Mozarts*; publ. in Leipzig, 1908); subsequently took private lessons with Reger. He conducted opera in Munich from 1904 to 1906; was active as a music critic in Königsberg and Dresden; he decided to study medicine, and obtained the degree of M.D. in 1920; in 1924 he went to live in Berlin as a practicing physician. He became a victim of the Nazi program of extermination of Jews. Among his works were the operas *Macbeth*, *Truffaldino*, and *Der eingebildete*.

Dahlhaus, Carl, eminent German musicologist and editor; b. Hannover, June 10, 1928; d. Berlin, March 13, 1989. He studied musicology at the Univ. of Göttingen with Gerber and also at the Univ. of Freiburg with Gurlitt. He received his Ph.D. from the Univ. of Göttingen in 1953 with the diss. *Studien zu den Messen Josquins des Prés*. He was a dramatic adviser for the Deutsches Theater in Göttingen from 1950 to 1958; from 1960 to 1962, and an ed. of the *Stuttgarter Zeitung*; he then joined the Inst. für Musikalische Landesforschung of the Univ. of Kiel; he completed his Habilitation there in 1966 with his *Untersuchungen uber die Entstehung der harmonischen Tonalität* (publ. in Kassel, 1968; Eng. tr., 1991, as *Studies on the Origin of Harmonic Tonality*). In 1966–67 he was a research fellow at the Univ. of Saarbrücken; in 1967 he became prof. of music history at the Technical Univ. of Berlin. In 1984 he was made a corresponding member of the American Musicological Soc. He was the ed.-in-chief of the complete edition of Wagner's works, which began publication in 1970; he was also an ed. of the Supplement to the 12th edition of the *Riemann Musik-Lexikon* (2 vols., Mainz, 1972, 1975); with Hans Eggebrecht, of the *Brockhaus-Riemann Musik-Lexikon* (2 vols., Wiesbaden and Mainz, 1978–79); and of *Pipers Enzyklopadie des Musiktheaters* (from 1986); in addition, he was coed. of the *Neue Zeitschrift für Musik* (1972–74), *Melos/NZ für Musik* (1975–78), *Musik und Bildung* (1978–80), and *Musica* (from 1981). He was one of the foremost musicologists of the 2d half of the 20th century. A scholar of great erudition, he wrote authoritatively and prolifically on a vast range of subjects, extending from the era of Josquin to the present day.

WRITINGS: *Musikästhetik* (Cologne, 1967; 4th ed., 1986; Eng. tr., 1982, as *Aesthetics of Music*); *Studien zur Trivialmusik des 19. Jahrhunderts* (Regensburg, 1967); *Analyse und Werturteil* (Mainz, 1970; Eng. tr., 1983, as *Analysis and Value Judgment*); *Das Drama Richard Wagners als musikalisches Kunstwerk* (Regensburg, 1970); *Richard Wagner: Werk und Wirkung* (Regensburg, 1971); *Wagners Konzeption des musikalischen Dramas* (Regensburg, 1971); *Richard Wagners Musikdramen* (Velber, 1971; 2d ed., 1985; Eng. tr., 1979, as *Richard Wagner's Music Dramas*); *Wagner's ästhetik* (Bayreuth, 1971); *Zwischen Romantik und Moderne: Vier Studien zur Musikgeschichte des späteren 19. Jahrhunderts* (Munich, 1974; Eng. tr., 1980, as *Between Romanticism and Modernism: Four Studies in the Music of the Later Nineteenth Century*); *Grundlagen der Musikgeschichte* (Cologne, 1977; Eng. tr., 1983, as *Foundations of Music History*); *Die Idee der absoluten Musik* (Kassel, 1978; Eng. tr., 1989, as *The Idea of Absolute Music*); *Schönberg und andere: Gesammelte Aufsätze zur Neuen Musik* (Mainz, 1978; Eng. tr., 1988, as *Schoenberg and the New Music*); *Die Musik des 19. Jahrhunderts* (Wiesbaden, 1980; 2d ed., 1988; Eng. tr., 1989, as *Nineteenth Century Music*); *Musikalischer Realismus: Zur Musikgeschichte des 19. Jahrhunderts* (Munich and Zürich, 1982; Eng. tr., 1985, as *Realism in Nineteenth Century Music*); with H. de la Motte-Haber, *Systematische Musikwissenschaft* (Laaber, 1982); *Vom Musikdrama zur Literaturoper: Aufsätze zur neueren Operngeschichte* (Munich and Salzburg, 1983); with J. Deathridge, *Wagner* (London, 1984); *Die Musiktheorie im 18. und 19. Jahrhundert: Erster Teil: Grundzüge einer Systematik* (Darmstadt, 1984); *Die Musik des 18. Jahrhunderts* (Laaber, 1985); with R. Katz, *Contemplating Music: Source Readings in the Aesthetics of Music* (N.Y., 1987); *Ludwig van Beethoven und seine Zeit* (Laaber, 1987; 2d ed., 1988; Eng. tr., 1991, as *Ludwig van Beethoven: Approaches to His Music*); *Klassische und romantische Musikästhetik* (Laaber, 1988).

BIBL.: H. Danuser et al., eds., *Das musikalische Kunstwerk: Geschichte, Ästhetik, Theorie: Festschrift C. D. zum 60. Geburtstag* (Laaber, 1988); M. Zimmermann, ed., *Oper nach Wagner: In memoriam C. D.* (Laaber, 1993).

Dalayrac, Nicolas (-Marie), French composer; b. Muret, Haute-Garonne, June 8, 1753; d. Paris, Nov. 26, 1809. (He signed his name d'Alayrac, but dropped the nobiliary particle after the Revolution.) His early schooling was in Toulouse. Returning to Muret in 1767, he studied law and played violin in a local band. He then entered the service of the Count d'Artois in his Guard of Honor, and at the same time took lessons in harmony with François Langlé at Versailles; he also received some help from Grétry. His first theater work was a 1-act comedy, *L'Eclipse totale* (Paris, March 7, 1782). From then on, he devoted most of his energies to the theater. He wrote over 56 operas; during the Revolution he composed patriotic songs for special occasions. He also enjoyed Napoleon's favors later on. During his lifetime, and for some 3 decades after his death, many of his operas were popular not only in France but also in Germany, Italy, and Russia; then they gradually disappeared from the active repertoire, but there were several revivals even in the 20th century. Dalayrac's natural facility enabled him to write successfully in all operatic genres.

WORKS: OPERAS (most 1st perf. in Paris, most at the Opéra Comique): *Le Petit Souper, ou L'Abbé qui veut parvenir* (1781); *Le Chevalier à la mode* (1781); *Nina* (May 15, 1786); *Sargines* (May 14, 1788); *Les Deux Petits Savoyards* (Jan. 14, 1789); *Raoul, Sire de Créqui* (Oct. 31, 1789); *La Soirée orageuse* (May 29, 1790); *Camille* (March 19, 1791); *Philippe et Georgette* (Dec. 28, 1791); *Ambroise* (Jan. 12, 1793); *Adèle et Dorsan* (April 27, 1795); *Marianne* (July 7, 1796); *La Maison isolée* (May 11, 1797); *Gulnare* (Dec. 30, 1797); *Alexis* (Jan. 24, 1798); *Adolphe et Clara* (Feb. 10, 1799); *Maison à vendre* (Oct. 23, 1800); *Léhéman* (Dec. 12, 1801); *L'Antichambre* (Feb. 26, 1802); *La Jeune Prude* (Jan. 14, 1804); *Une Heure de mariage* (March 20, 1804); *Gulistan* (Sept. 30, 1805); *Deux mots* (June 9, 1806); *Koulouf* (Dec. 18, 1806); *Le Poète et le musicien* (Paris, May 30, 1811).

BIBL.: R. de Pixérécourt, *Vie de D.* (Paris, 1810).

Dal Barba, Daniel, Italian singer, violinist, teacher, and composer; b. Verona, May 5, 1715; d. there, July 16, 1801. He made his debut as a singer in Chiarini's *I fratelli riconosciuti* in Venora in 1743. After singing in his own opera *Il Tigrane* (1744) and others, he devoted himself to a career as a violinist, teacher, and composer in his native city. He became maestro di cappella of the Filarmonica and Filotima academies, posts he retained for the next 30 years. He also was temporary maestro di cappella (1762–70) and maestro di cappella (1770–79) at the Cathedral. Among his works were 7 operas.

BIBL.: M. Dubiaga, Jr., *The Life and Works of D. P. D. B. (1715–1801)* (diss., Univ. of Colorado, 1977).

D'Albert, Eugène. See **Albert, Eugen d'.**

Dalcroze, Emile Jaques. See **Jaques-Dalcroze, Emile.**

Dale, Clamma, black American soprano; b. Chester, Pa., July 4, 1948. She studied at the Philadelphia Settlement Music School, and later with Hans Heinz, Alice Howland, and Cornelius Reed at the Juilliard School of Music in New York (B.Mus., 1970; M.S., 1975). On Feb. 20, 1973, she appeared as St. Teresa I in *4 Saints in 3 Acts* in the Mini-Met staging at N.Y.'s Manhattan Forum. On Sept. 30, 1975, she made her N.Y. City Opera debut as Antonia in *Les Contes d'Hoffmann*, and subsequently appeared with opera companies throughout North America and abroad; she also toured extensively as a concert artist. In 1988 she sang Gershwin's Bess at the Theater des Westens in Berlin, and in 1989 she sang Puccini's Liù at the Deutsche Oper there. Among her other principal roles were Pamina, Countess Almaviva, Nedda, and Musetta.

Dalis, Irene, American mezzo-soprano, teacher, and operatic administrator; b. San Jose, Calif., Oct. 8, 1925. She studied at San Jose State Univ. (A.B., 1946; M.S., 1957) and at Columbia Univ. Teachers College (M.A., 1947); received vocal training from Edyth Walker (1947–50) and Paul Althouse (1950–51) in New York, and from Otto Müller (1952) in Milan. In 1953 she made her operatic debut as Eboli in *Don Carlos* at the Oldenburg Landestheater; sang with the Städtische Oper in Berlin (1955–60). On March 16, 1957, she made her Metropolitan Opera debut in New York as Eboli, and continued to sing there regularly until 1977. She also made guest appearances at Covent Garden in London, the Chicago Lyric Opera, and the Bayreuth Festivals. In 1976 she became a prof. of music at San Jose State Univ.; she also directed its opera workshop, which served as the nucleus for the fully professional Opera San Jose, with Dalis as executive director (1984–88) and artistic director (from 1988).

Dallapiccola, Luigi, eminent Italian composer and pedagogue; b. Pisino, Istria, Feb. 3, 1904; d. Florence, Feb. 19, 1975. He took piano lessons at an early age in Pisino. After training in piano and harmony in Trieste (1919–21), he studied with Ernesto Consolo (piano diploma, 1924) and Vito Frazzi (composition diploma, 1931) at the Florence Cons., where he subsequently was a distinguished member of the faculty (1934–67). A collection of his essays appeared as *Appunti incontri meditazioni* (Milan, 1970). As a composer, Dallapiccola adopted dodecaphonic procedures but added considerable innovations, such as the use of mutually exclusive triads and thematic structure and harmonic progressions. He particularly excelled in his handling of vocal lines in a complex modern idiom.

WORKS: DRAMATIC: OPERAS: *Volo di notte* (1937–39; Florence, May 18, 1940); *Il Prigioniero* (1944–48; rev. version, Turin Radio, Dec. 4, 1949; stage premiere, Florence, May 20, 1950); *Ulisse* (1959–68; in Ger. as *Odysseus*, Berlin, Sept. 29, 1968). BALLET: *Marsia* (1942–43; Venice, Sept. 9, 1948).

BIBL.: B. Zanolini, *L. D.: La conquista di un linguaggio* (Padua, 1974); D. Kamper, *Gefangenschaft und Freiheit: Leben und Werk des Komponisten L. D.* (Cologne, 1984); J. Hees, *L. D.s Bühnewerk Ulisse: Untersuchungen zu Werk und Werkgenese* (Kassel, 1994).

Dallapozza, Adolf, Italian-born Austrian tenor; b. Bolzano, March 14, 1940. His parents settled in Austria when he was 5 months old. He received his musical education at the Vienna Cons.; he then joined the Chorus of the Volksoper; in 1962 he made his debut as soloist in the role of Ernesto in Donizetti's *Don Pasquale*. In 1967 he became a member of the Vienna State Opera; also sang with the Bavarian State Opera in Munich and made appearances in Milan, Basel, Hamburg, Zürich, and Buenos Aires. In 1976 the president of Austria made him a Kammersänger.

He is highly regarded for his versatility, being equally competent in opera, oratorio, and operetta.

Dalla Rizza, Gilda, Italian soprano; b. Verona, Oct. 2, 1892; d. Milan, July 4, 1975. She received her musical training in Bologna where she made her operatic debut as Charlotte in *Werther* in 1912; in 1915 she sang at La Scala in Milan; Puccini so admired her singing that he created the role of Magda in *La Rondine* for her (Monte Carlo, March 27, 1917). She sang in Rome (1919), at London's Covent Garden (1920), and again at La Scala (1923–39); she then taught voice at the Venice Cons. (1939–55). Her students included Anna Moffo and Gianna d'Angelo. She was married to the tenor Agostino Capuzzo (1889–1963). Her most famous role was Violetta.

BIBL.: P. Badoer, *G.d. R.: La cantante prediletta di Giacomo Puccini* (Abano Terme, 1991).

Dal Monte, Toti (real name, **Antonietta Meneghelli**), outstanding Italian soprano; b. Mogliano, near Treviso, June 27, 1893; d. Pieve di Soligo, Treviso, Jan. 26, 1975. She studied piano at the Venice Cons., then voice with Barbara Marchisio. She made her operatic debut at La Scala in Milan as Biancafiore in Zandonai's *Francesca da Rimini* in 1916, and then sang throughout Italy. After a brilliant appearance as Gilda at La Scala in 1922, she pursued a notably acclaimed career in Europe, singing in Paris, Vienna, London, and Berlin with extraordinary success. On Dec. 5, 1924, she made her Metropolitan Opera debut in New York as Lucia, remaining on its roster for 1 season; she also sang at the Chicago Civic Opera (1924–28) and at London's Covent Garden (1926). She continued to sing in opera until World War II, after which she made her farewell performance at the Verona Arena in 1949; thereafter she taught voice. She publ. an autobiography, *Una voce nel mondo* (Milan, 1962). Her other remarkable roles included Cio-Cio-San, Mimi, and Stravinsky's Nightingale.

Dalmorès, Charles (real name, **Henry Alphonse Boin**), French tenor; b. Nancy, Jan. 1, 1871; d. Los Angeles, Dec. 6, 1939. After taking 1st prizes at the local Cons. for solfeggio and horn at 17, he received from the city of Nancy a stipend for study at the Paris Cons., where he took 1st prize for horn at 19; he played in the Colonne Orch. and the Lamoureux Orch.; at 23, he became a prof. of horn at the Lyons Cons. His vocal teacher was Dauphin. His stage debut as a tenor took place on Oct. 6, 1899, at Rouen as Siegfried; later he sang at the Théâtre Royal de la Monnaie in Brussels (1900–06) and at London's Covent Garden (1904–05; 1909–11). On Dec. 7, 1906, he made his debut as Faust at the Manhattan Opera House in New York, then was with the Chicago Opera Co. (1910–18). His repertoire was large, and included Wagnerian as well as French operas; in Chicago he sang Tristan and the title role in the first performance of *Parsifal* to be presented there.

Dal Pane, Domenico, noted Italian castrato soprano and composer; b. probably in Rome, c.1630; d. there, Dec. 10, 1694. He became a treble at S. Maria Maggiore in Rome in his youth. After studies with Abbatini, he went to Vienna as a singer at the imperial court about 1650. Upon his return to Rome in 1654, he became active at the Sistine Chapel, where he later was its maestro di cappella (1669–79). He also was in the service of the Pamphili family. Among his finest works are 2 vols. of madrigals for 5 Voices and Basso Continuo (Rome, 1652, 1678) and the vol. *Sagri concerti ad honore del Ss. Sagramento* for 2 to 5 Voices and Basso Continuo (Rome, 1675).

Damase, Jean-Michel, French composer and pianist; b. Bordeaux, Jan. 27, 1928. He was a student of Delvincourt at the Paris Cons. and winner of the Grand Prix de Rome in 1947. He made appearances as a pianist while devoting time to composition. In 1954 he made his first appearance in the United States as a pianist-composer in New York. His stage works include *Colombe*, lyric comedy (Bordeaux, May 5, 1961), *Le Tendre Eleonore*, opera-bouffe (1962), *Eurydice*, lyric comedy (Bordeaux, May 26, 1972), and *L'heritiere*, opera (1974); also the ballets *Le Saut du Tremplin* (1944), *La Croqueuse de diamants* (1950), *Piège de lumière* (1952), *Lady in the Ice* (1953), *Le prince du désert* (1955), *Balance à trois* (1955), *La boucle* (1957), *Othello* (1957); *La noce forcaine* (1961), and *Suite monégasgue* (1964).

Damrosch, Leopold, eminent German-American conductor and violinist, father of **Frank (Heino)** and **Walter (Johannes) Damrosch**; b. Posen, Oct. 22, 1832; d. N.Y., Feb. 15, 1885. He took the degree of M.D. at the Univ. of Berlin in 1854, but then, against his parents' wishes, embraced the career of a musician, studying with Ries, Dehn, and Böhmer. He appeared at first as a solo violinist in several German cities, later as a conductor at minor theaters, and in 1857 procured, through Liszt, the position of solo violinist in the Weimar Court Orch. While there, he was intimate with Liszt and many of his most distinguished pupils, and won Wagner's lifelong friendship; in Weimar, too, he married the singer Helene von Heimburg (b. Oldenburg, 1835; d. N.Y., Nov. 21, 1904). From 1858 to 1860 Damrosch was conductor of the Breslau Phil. Concerts; he gave up the post to make tours with Bülow and Tausig; organized the Breslau Orch. Soc. in 1862. Besides this, he founded quartet soirées, and a choral society; he conducted the Soc. for Classical Music, and a theater orch. (for 2 years) and frequently appeared as a solo violinist. In 1871 he was called to New York to conduct the Arion Soc., and made his debut, in April 1871, as conductor, composer, and violinist. In New York his remarkable capacity as an organizer found free scope; besides bringing the Arion to the highest pitch of efficiency and prosperity, he was conductor of the N.Y. Phil. (1876–77); he founded the Sym. Soc. in 1878, the latter's concerts succeeding those of the Thomas Orch. at Steinway Hall. In 1880 Columbia College conferred on him the honorary degree of D.Mus.; in 1881 he conducted the first major music festival held in New York, with an orch. of 250 and a chorus of 1,200; in 1883 he made a highly successful Western tour with his orch.; in 1884–85 he organized the German Opera Co., and, together with Anton Seidl, conducted a season of German opera at the Metropolitan Opera, presenting Wagner's *Der Ring des Nibelungen*, *Tristan und Isolde*, and *Die Meistersinger von Nürnberg* for the first time in the United States He also tried his hand at composing, producing a large output of music of little lasting value.

BIBL.: G. Martin, *The D. Dynasty: America's First Family of Music* (N.Y., 1983).

Damrosch, Walter (Johannes), distinguished German-American conductor, music educator, son of **Leopold Damrosch**; b. Breslau, Jan. 30, 1862; d. N.Y., Dec. 22, 1950. His brother was the German-American conductor and teacher Frank (Heino) Damrosch (b. Breslau, June 22, 1859; d. N.Y., Oct. 22, 1937). He received lessons in piano and composition before going to N.Y. with his family in 1871, where he continued his music studies. During the 1884–85 season of the Metropolitan Opera, he served as his father's assistant. When his father fell ill, he received some deathbed coaching from him and made his Metropolitan Opera debut conducting *Tannhäuser* on Feb. 11, 1885, just 4 days before his father succumbed. He remained on the roster of the Metropolitan Opera until 1891, and also served as his father's successor as conductor of the Oratorio Soc. of N.Y. (1885–98) and the Sym. Soc. of N.Y. (from 1885). In 1887 he pursued training in conducting with Bülow in Frankfurt am Main. In 1894 he founded the Damrosch Opera Co. in New York, which he conducted in performances of German operas until 1899, both there and in other major U.S. cities. From 1900 to 1902 he was again on the roster of the Metropolitan Opera. He was conductor of the N.Y. Phil. in 1902–03. After the reorganization of the Sym. Soc. of N.Y. in 1903, he was its conductor until it merged with the N.Y. Phil. in 1928. In 1920 he conducted the Sym. Soc. of N.Y. on a major tour of Europe. In 1912 he took over the sym. concerts for young people originally organized by his brother, and he also conducted young people's concerts with the Sym. Soc. of N.Y. His interest in music education prompted him to utilize the medium of radio to further the cause of music appreciation; on Oct. 19, 1923, he conducted the Sym. Soc. of N.Y. in its first radio broadcast from Carnegie Hall. In 1926 he inaugurated a regular series of radio broadcasts, which were later aired as the "NBC Music Appreciation Hour" throughout the United States and Canada from 1928 to 1942. He also served as musical counsel to NBC from 1927 to 1947. Damrosch conducted the U.S. premieres of Tchaikovsky's 4th and 6th syms. as well as scores by Wagner, Mahler, and Elgar. He also conducted premieres of works by American composers, including Gershwin's *An American in Paris*. He received honorary doctorates from Columbia Univ. (1914), Princeton Univ. (1929), N.Y. Univ. (1935) et al. In 1929 he was awarded the David Bispham medal. In 1932 he was elected to membership in the American Academy of Arts and Letters, and in 1938 he received the gold medal. His autobiography was publ. as *My Musical Life* (N.Y., 1923; 2d ed., 1930).

WORKS: DRAMATIC: OPERAS: *The Scarlet Letter* (Boston, Feb. 10, 1896); *The Dove of Peace*, comic opera (Philadelphia, Oct. 15, 1912); *Cyrano de Bergerac* (N.Y., Feb. 27, 1913; rev. 1939); *The Man without a Country* (May 12, 1937); *The Opera Cloak* (N.Y., Nov. 3, 1942). INCIDENTAL MUSIC TO: Euripides' *Iphigenia in Aulis* (Berkeley, 1915) and *Medea* (Berkeley, 1915); Sophocles' *Electra* (N.Y., 1917).

BIBL.: F. Himmelein, *W. D.: A Cultural Biography* (diss., Univ. of Virginia, 1972); G. Martin, *The D. Dynasty: America's First Family of Music* (N.Y., 1983).

Dan, Ikuma, Japanese composer; b. Tokyo, April 7, 1924. He studied at the Tokyo Music Academy with K. Shimofusa and S. Moroi. After teaching at the Tokyo Music School (1947–50), he was active as a film music director and composer.

WORKS: DRAMATIC: OPERAS: *Yûzuru* (The Twilight Crane; 1950–51; Tokyo, Jan. 30, 1952; rev. 1956); *Kikimimi-zukin* (The Listening Cap; 1954–55; Tokyo, March 18, 1955); *Yang Kwei-fei* (1957–58; Tokyo, Dec. 11, 1958); *Chanchiki* (Cling-Clang; 1961–63); *Hikarigoke* (1972; Osaka, April 27, 1972). DANCE DRAMA: *Futari Shizuka* (1961).

Danbé, Jules, French violinist, conductor, and composer; b. Caen, Nov. 16, 1840; d. Vichy, Nov. 10, 1905. He was a pupil at the Paris Cons. He was 2d conductor of the Cons. concerts until 1892, then conductor at the Opéra Comique (1877–98). From 1899 until his death, he was conductor at the Théâtre-Lyrique.

Danco, Suzanne, admired Belgian soprano; b. Brussels, Jan. 22, 1911. She began her training at the Brussels Cons.; after winning the Vienna vocal competition (1936), she studied with Fernando Carpi in Prague. She then went to Italy, where she made her debut as a concert artist in 1940. In 1941 she made her operatic debut as Fiordiligi in Genoa, and later sang in various Italian operatic centers. She had much success at Milan's La Scala, where she sang in the local premieres of *Peter Grimes* (as Ellen Orford, 1947) and *Oedipus Rex* (as Jocasta, 1948). From 1948 to 1951 she appeared at the Glyndebourne Festivals. She sang in the United States for the first time in 1950. In 1951 she appeared as Mimi at London's Covent Garden. In later years, she concentrated on concert engagements and also was active as a teacher at the Accademia Musicale Chigiana in Siena. Among her other notables roles were Donna Anna, Mélisande, and Berg's Marie. She was especially praised as a concert artist, excelling in the French repertory, particularly in works by Berlioz, Debussy, and Ravel.

Dandelot, Georges (Edouard), French composer and teacher; b. Paris, Dec. 2, 1895; d. St.-Georges de Didonne, Charente-Maritime, Aug. 17, 1975. He studied with Widor at the Paris Cons.; later he took lessons with Dukas and Roussel. He was in the French army during World War I, and received the Croix de Guerre for valor. In 1919 he became an instructor at the École Normale de Musique in Paris; in 1942, was appointed a prof. at the Paris Cons. Dandelot composed the operas *Midas* (1947) and *L'Ennemi* (1948) and the ballets *Le Souper de famine* (1943), *Le Jardin merveilleux* (1944), and *Pierrot et la rose* (1948).

Daneau, Nicolas, Belgian composer and teacher; b. Binche, June 17, 1866; d. Brussels, July 12, 1944. He studied at the Ghent Cons. with Adolphe Samuel, graduating in 1892; won the 2d Prix de Rome in 1895. He was director of the Tournai Cons. (1896–1919), and of the Mons Cons. (1919–31). His daughter, Suzanne Daneau (b. Tournai, Aug. 17, 1901; d. there, Nov. 29, 1971), was his pupil. Among her scant compositions are *Linario*, lyric drama (Tournai, 1906), *Myrtis*, opera-idyll (Tournai, 1910), *Le Sphynx*, opera, and *La Brute*, lyric drama.

BIBL.: L. Beatrice, *D.: Histoire d'une famille d'artistes* (Brussels, 1944).

D'Angeri, Anna (real name, **Anna von Angermayer de Redernburg**), Austrian soprano; b. Vienna, Nov. 14, 1853; d. Trieste, Dec. 14, 1907. She studied with Marchesi in Vienna. In 1872 she made her operatic debut as Selika in Mantua, and then appeared at London's Covent Garden (1874–77). She was admired as a Wagnerian, and was the first to sing Ortrud and Venus in London (1875–76). After singing at the Vienna Court Opera (1878–79), she appeared at Milan's La Scala (1879–81), where she sang Amelia in the rev. version of *Simon Boccanegra* in 1881. She then married Vittorio Dalem, director of the Teatro Rossetti in Trieste, and retired from the stage.

Daniel, Paul (Wilson), English conductor; b. Birmingham, July 1, 1958. He was a chorister at Coventry Cathedral, and pursued his musical training at King's College, Cambridge (1976–79) and at the Guildhall School of Music and Drama in London (1979–80). His mentors in conducting were Boult and Downes in England, and Ferrara in Italy. He was on the staff of the English National Opera in London from 1980 to 1985. In 1982 he made his debut as an operatic conductor with *The Beggar's Opera* with the Opera Factory in London. In 1985 he joined its staff, subsequently serving as its music director from 1987 to 1990. In 1988 he made his U.S. debut in New York with the London Sinfonietta. From 1990 to 1997 he was artistic director of Opera North in Leeds, where he concurrently served as principal conductor of the English Northern Philharmonia. He made his first appearance at London's Covent Garden in 1993 conducting *Mitridate*. In 1997 he became music director of the English National Opera. As a guest conductor, his engagements took him all over England and Europe in appearances with major opera houses and orchs. In 1988 he married **Joan Rodgers**. Daniel's operatic repertoire is an expansive one, ranging from Cavalli, Mozart, and Verdi to Birtwistle, Maxwell Davies, and Böse.

Daniel-Lesur, Jean Yves (real name, **Daniel Jean Yves Lesur**), prominent French composer and pedagogue; b. Paris, Nov. 19, 1908. He spent his entire life in Paris, where he studied at the Cons. (1919–29) with J. Gallon and Caussade (harmony and fugue), Armand Ferté (piano), and Tournemiere (organ and composition). He was assistant organist at St. Clotilde (1927–37) and organist at the Benedictine Abbey (1935–39; 1942–44). With Messiaen, Baudrier, and Jolivet, he founded the Groupe Jeune France in 1936. He taught counterpoint (1935–64) and was director (1957–62) of the Schola Cantorum. He was responsible for music information for the French Radio (from 1939) and was music councilor for the French TV (from 1968). From 1969 to 1971 he was inspector general of music for the Ministry of Culture. He was administrator of the Réunion des Théâtres Lyriques Nationaux from 1971 to 1973. With B. Gavoty, he publ. *Pour ou contre la musique moderne* (Paris, 1957). He was made a Commandeur de la Légion d'honneur and a Commander de l'Ordre National du Merité et Commandeur des Arts et Lettres. In 1982 he was made a member of the Académie des Beaux-Arts. In his compositions, Daniel-Lesur perfected an ascetic modal style. He composed the operas *Andrea del Sarto* (1968; Marseilles, Jan. 24, 1969), *Ondine* (Paris, April 26, 1982), and *La Reine morte* (1987) and the ballets *L'Infante et le monstre* (1938; in collaboration with A. Jolivet) and *Le Bal du destin* (1956).

Daniels, Barbara, American soprano; b. Newark, Ohio, May 7, 1946. She studied at Ohio State Univ. (B.Mus., 1969) and the Univ. of Cincinnati College-Cons. of Music (M.A., 1971). In 1973 she made her operatic debut as Susanna in *Le nozze di Figaro* at the West Palm Beach (Fla.) Opera; she then was a member of the Innsbruck Landestheater (1974–76), Kassel Staatstheater (1976–

78), and Cologne Opera (1978–82). In 1978 she appeared as Rosalinde at London's Covent Garden, and on Sept. 30, 1983, she made her Metropolitan Opera debut in New York as Musetta, also making guest appearances at the Vienna State Opera, the Chicago Lyric Opera, the Paris Opéra, and the Bavarian State Opera in Munich. Among her other roles are Violetta, Alice Ford, Massenet's Manon, and Micaëla.

Daniels, David, extraordinary American countertenor; b. Spartanburg, S.C., March 12, 1966. He was reared in a musical family. Following studies at the Univ. of Cincinnati College-Cons. of Music, he pursued graduate training with George Shirley at the Univ. of Mich. (M.A., 1992). He sang minor roles with the Los Angeles Opera and appeared in oratorios before attracting notice as Nerone in *L'incoronazione di Poppea* at the Glimmerglass Opera in Cooperstown, N.Y., in 1994. In 1995 he returned there to great critical acclaim as Handel's Tamerlano. He sang Arsamene in Handel's *Xerxes* with the Boston Lyric Opera, Didymus in Handel's *Theodora* at the Glyndebourne Festival, and Oberon in his London debut in 1996. On Dec. 2, 1996, he made his N.Y. recital debut at Lincoln Center. In 1997 he won the Richard Tucker Music Foundation Award, and sang Sesto in Handel's *Giulio Cesare* at London's Covent Garden, Nerone in Munich, and Arsamene at the N.Y. City Opera. He was engaged to make his Metropolitan Opera debut in New York as Arsamene on April 10, 1999. Daniels's remarkable artistry combines a mastery of vocal splendor and dramatic power.

Daniels, Mabel Wheeler, American composer; b. Swampscott, Mass., Nov. 27, 1878; d. Boston, March 10, 1971. She studied at Radcliffe College (B.A., 1900), with Chadwick in Boston, and with Thuille in Munich (1904–05). She was director of the Radcliffe Glee Club (1911–13) and head of music at Simmons College in Boston (1913–18). In 1931 she held a MacDowell fellowship, and was awarded honorary doctorates from Boston Univ. (1939), Wheaton College (1957), and the New England Cons. of Music (1958). Although she composed numerous stage pieces, including the operettas *A Copper Complication* (1900), *The Court of Hearts* (1900; Cambridge, Mass., Jan. 2, 1901), and *The Show Girl* (1902; in collaboration with D. Stevens) and the opera sketch *Alice in Wonderland Continued* (Brookline, Mass., May 20, 1904), Daniels became best known as a composer of choral music. Her experiences abroad were captured in her *An American Girl in Munich: Impressions of a Music Student* (Boston, 1905).

Dankevich, Konstantin, eminent Ukrainian composer and teacher; b. Odessa, Dec. 24, 1905; d. Kiev, Feb. 26, 1984. He studied with Zolotarev at the Odessa Cons., graduating in 1929. In 1942 he was made artistic director of the Red Army Ensemble of Songs and Dance in Tbilisi. From 1944 to 1953 he was a prof. of composition at the Odessa Cons.; in 1953 he was appointed to the faculty of the Kiev Cons. In his works Dankevich utilized motifs of Ukrainian and Russian folk songs. He first attracted attention with his opera *Bogdan Khmelnitsky* (Kiev, Jan. 29, 1951), on a subject from Ukrainian history, which was attacked for its libretto and its unsuitable music; Dankevich revised the score, after which it gained favorable notices in Russia. He also wrote the opera *Nazar Stodolya* (Kharkov, May 28, 1960). His most popular score was *Lileya*, a ballet (1939). A monograph on him was publ. in Ukrainian in Kiev (1959).

Danon, Oskar, Serbian conductor; b. Sarajevo, Feb. 7, 1913. He was educated at the Prague Cons. and the Univ. of Prague (Ph.D., 1938). In 1940 he became a conductor at the Belgrade Opera; was its director (1945–60). He also conducted throughout Europe, both opera and sym. concerts.

Danzi, Franz (Ignaz), German composer and teacher; b. Schwetzingen, June 15, 1763; d. Karlsruhe, April 13, 1826. He received primary instruction in music from his father, Innocenz Danzi, a cellist, and later took theory lessons with Abbé Vogler. In 1783 he joined the Court Orch. in Munich, then from 1807 to 1812 he served as Kapellmeister at Stuttgart, where he was the teacher of Carl Maria von Weber. He was an excellent singing teacher, and wrote vocal exercises of practical value.

WORKS: DRAMATIC: *Cleopatra*, duodrama (Mannheim, Jan. 30, 1780); *Azakia*, comedy (Mannheim, June 6, 1780); *Die Mitternachtsstunde*, Singspiel (Munich, April 1788); *Der Sylphe*, Singspiel (Munich, 1788); *Der Triumph der Treue*, melodrama (Munich, Feb. 1789; not extant); *Der Quasi-Mann*, comedy (Munich, Aug. 1789; not extant); *Deucalion et Pirrha*, opera (c.1795); *Der Kuss*, comedy (Munich, June 27, 1799); *El Bondocani*, Singspiel (Munich, 1802; not extant); *Iphigenie in Aulis*, grand opera (Munich, Jan. 27, 1807); *Dido*, melodrama (Stuttgart, 1811; not extant); *Camilla und Eugen oder Der Gartenschlüssel*, comedy (Stuttgart, March 15, 1812); *Rübezahl*, Singspiel (Karlsruhe, April 19, 1813); *Malvina*, Singspiel (Karlsruhe, Dec. 20, 1814); *Turandot*, Singspiel (Karlsruhe, Feb. 9, 1817); *Die Probe*, opera (Karlsruhe, Oct. 1817); *L'Abbe de Attaignant oder Die Theaterprobe*, opera (Karlsruhe, Sept. 14, 1820). Also oratorios.

BIBL.: E. Reipschläger, *Schubaur, D. und Poissl als Opernkomponisten* (diss., Univ. of Rostock, 1911); M. Herre, *F. D.* (diss., Univ. of Munich, 1924).

Da Ponte, Lorenzo (real name, **Emanuele Conegliano**), famous Italian librettist; b. Ceneda, near Venice, March 10, 1749; d. N.Y., Aug. 17, 1838. He was of a Jewish family, but was converted to Christianity at the age of 14, and assumed the name of his patron, Lorenzo da Ponte, Bishop of Ceneda. He then studied at the Ceneda Seminary and at the Portogruaro Seminary, where he taught from 1770 to 1773; in 1774 he obtained a post as prof. of rhetoric at Treviso, but was dismissed in 1776 for his beliefs concerning natural laws. He then went to Venice, where he led an adventurous life, and was banished in 1779 for adultery; subsequently he lived in Austria and in Dresden, and in 1782 he settled in Vienna and became official poet to the Imperial Theater. He met Mozart and became his friend and librettist of his most famous operas, *Le nozze di Figaro, Don Giovanni*, and *Così fan tutte*. From 1792 to 1798 he was in London, then traveled in Europe, and went to New York in 1805. After disastrous business ventures, with intervals of teaching, he became interested in various operatic enterprises. In his last years he was a teacher of Italian at Columbia College. He publ. *Memorie* (4 vols., N.Y., 1823–27; Eng. tr., London, 1929, and Philadelphia, 1929).

BIBL.: A. Marchesan, *Della vita e delle opere di L. d.P.* (Treviso, 1900); J. Russo, *L. d.P., Poet and Adventurer* (N.Y., 1922); A. Fitzlyon, *The Libertine Librettist* (London, 1955); S. Hodges, *L. d.P.: The Life and Times of Mozart's Librettist* (London, 1985); A. Steptoe, *The Mozart-D.P. Operas: The Cultural and Musical Background to Le nozze di Figaro, Don Giovanni, and Così fan tutte* (Oxford, 1988).

Darclée, Hariclea (real name, **Haricly Hartulary**), Romanian soprano; b. Braila, June 10, 1860; d. Bucharest, Jan. 10, 1939. She studied in Bucharest and Paris; made her debut as Marguerite at the Paris Opéra in 1888, then sang at La Scala in Milan, creating La Wally on Jan. 20, 1892; she also sang in Rome, New York, St. Petersburg, Moscow, and in South America before retiring in 1918. She was particularly distinguished for her Italian repertoire; she created the role of Tosca (Rome, Jan. 14, 1900); she also was known for her performances of roles in Wagner's operas.

Dargomyzhsky, Alexander (Sergeievich), outstanding Russian composer; b. Tula province, Feb. 14, 1813; d. St. Petersburg, Jan. 17, 1869. From 1817 he lived in St. Petersburg, where he studied piano with Schoberlechner and Danilevsky, and violin with Vorontsov. At 20 he was a brilliant pianist. From 1827 to 1843 he held a government position, but then devoted himself exclusively to music, studying assiduously for 8 years; he visited Germany, Brussels, and Paris in 1845. In Moscow (Dec. 17, 1847) he produced an opera, *Esmeralda* (after Victor Hugo's *Notre-Dame de Paris*), with great success (excerpts publ. in piano score, Moscow, 1948). From 1845 to 1855 he publ. over 100 minor works. On May 16, 1856, he brought out his best opera, *Rusalka*, at St. Petersburg (vocal score, with indications of instruments, publ. at Moscow, 1937); in 1867, an opera ballet, *The Triumph of Bacchus* (written in 1845; perf. in Moscow, Jan. 23, 1867); a posthumous opera, *Kamennyi gost* (The Stone Guest, after Pushkin's poem of the same title), was scored by Rimsky-Korsakov and produced at St. Petersburg on Feb. 28, 1872; of *Rogdana*, a fantasy opera, only a few scenes were sketched. At first a follower of Rossini and Auber, Dargomyzhsky gradually became convinced that dramatic realism with nationalistic connotations was the destiny of Russian music; he applied this realistic method in treating the recitative in his opera *The Stone Guest* and in his songs (several of these to satirical words). In 1867 he was elected president of the Russian Music Soc.

BIBL.: N. Findeisen, *A. S. D.: His Life and Work* (Moscow, 1902); S. Fried, *A. S. D.* (St. Petersburg, 1913); A. Drozdov, *A. S. D.* (Moscow, 1929); M. Pekelis, *A. D. and His Circle* (2 vols., Moscow, 1966, 1973).

Darnton, (Philip) Christian, English composer; b. near Leeds, Oct. 30, 1905; d. Hove, April 14, 1981. He began piano lessons at the age of 4 and began composing at 9; after studies with F. Corder, Sr., at the Brighton School of Music, he went to London for studies with Craxton (piano) at the Matthay School and Dale (composition) at the Royal Academy of Music; later he was a student of Wood (composition) and Rootham (theory) at Caius College, Cambridge (1923–26), Jacob at the Royal College of Music, London (1927), and Butting in Berlin (1928–29). He publ. *You and Music* (Harmondsworth, 1939; 2d ed., 1946). He composed the opera *Fantasy Fair*.

Dashow, James (Hilyer), American composer; b. Chicago, Nov. 7, 1944. After studies with Babbitt, Cone, Kim, and Randall at Princeton Univ. (B.A., 1966), with Berger, Boykan, and Shifrin at Brandeis Univ. (M.F.A., 1969), and with Petrassi at the Accademia di Santa Cecilia in Rome (diploma, 1971), he founded the Forum Players (1971–75), a contemporary chamber music group. He served as director of the Studio di Musica Elettronica Sciadoni in Rome (from 1975). From 1982 to 1989 he taught computer music at the Centro di Sonologia Computazionale at the Univ. of Padua; he also was guest lecturer in various European and U.S. cities. He was a producer of contemporary music programs for the RAI from 1985 to 1992. In 1969 he held a Fulbright fellowship; later accolades included grants from the NEA (1976, 1981) and the Rockefeller Foundation (1982), an award from the American Academy and Inst. of Arts and Letters (1984), and a Guggenheim fellowship (1989). He composed the opera *Il piccolo principe* (1981–82) and the theater piece *Archimede* (1988);

Daugherty, Michael, American composer; b. Cedar Rapids, Iowa, April 28, 1954. He studied with Wuorinen at the Manhattan School of Music (M.A., 1976) and with Druckman, Brown, Reynolds, Rands, and Evans at Yale Univ. (M.M.A., 1982; D.M.A., 1986); he then traveled to Hamburg, where he studied with Ligeti at the Hochschule für Musik (1982–84). He also studied at IRCAM on a Fulbright fellowship (1978–80). He received an NEA Composition Fellowship in 1980; he subsequently joined the faculty at the Oberlin (Ohio) College Cons. of Music (1986), becoming director of its Summer Electronic Music Workshop. In 1991 he became associate prof. of composition at the Univ. of Michigan. He composed the opera *Jackie O* (Houston, March 14, 1997).

Daussoigne-Méhul, Louis-Joseph, French composer; b. Givet, Ardennes, June 10, 1790; d. Liège, March 10, 1875. He was the nephew and foster son of **Etienne-Nicolas Méhul**, under whom he studied; he also studied with Catel at the Cons., taking the Grand Prix de Rome in 1809. After writing 4 operas, which were rejected, he at length produced his 1-act *Aspasie* at the Grand Opéra (1820) with moderate success. He did still better with *Valentine de Milan*, a 3-act opera left unfinished by his foster father, which he completed. In 1827 he accepted the directorship of the Liège Cons., which he retained, with great benefit to the school, until 1862. He was an associate of the Royal Academy, Brussels.

Dauvergne, Antoine, French composer, violinist, and conductor; b. Moulins, Oct. 3, 1713; d. Lyons, Feb. 11, 1797. He received his first instruction from his father, then went for further study to Paris, where he was appointed a violinist in the chambre du roi (1739) and in the orch. of the Opera (1744). In 1755 he was appointed composer to the court and in 1762 became conductor and one of the directors of the Concerts Spirituels; he was one of the directors of the Opéra (1769–76; 1780–82; 1785–90) before retiring to Lyons. He introduced into France the forms of the Italian intermezzo, substituting spoken dialogue for the recitative, and thus was the originator of a style that soon became typical of French dramatic composition. He composed 18 stage works, the first being *Les Troqueurs* (Paris, July 30, 1753), which is regarded as the first opéra comique.

d'Avalos, Francesco, Italian composer, conductor, and teacher; b. Naples, April 11, 1930. He received lessons in piano from age 12 from Vincenzo Vitale, and then studied orchestration with Renato Parodi. He pursued training in philosophy at the Univ. of Naples, and also studied composition at the Cons. of San Pietro a Majella in Naples (diploma with high honors, 1955) and conducting with Kempen, Celibidache, and Ferrara at the Accademia Musicale Chigiana in Siena. After making his conducting debut with the RAI Orch. in Rome in 1964, he appeared as a guest conductor in Italy and Europe. He taught at the Bari Cons. before joining the faculty of the Cons. of San Pietro a Majella in 1979. As a composer, d'Avalos followed an avant-, later post-avant-, garde path. Among his works is the music drama *Maria di Venosa* (1992). As a conductor, he strives to preserve the composer's intentions even in the face of received tradition. He has won particular distinction for his performances of the Italian symphonic repertoire of the 19th and early 20th centuries.

Davaux, Jean-Baptiste, prominent French composer; b. La Côte-St. André, July 19, 1742; d. Paris, Feb. 2, 1822. He studied music with his parents, then settled in Paris, where he made a name for himself as a violinist and composer. Although he continued to be active as a composer in subsequent years, he found employment in the Ministry of War; upon retiring, he was made a member of the Légion d'honneur (1814). Davaux was highly regarded as a composer of orch. and chamber music; in his *Trois simphonies à grand orchestre*, op. 11 (1784), he included his chronometre, thus anticipating Maelzel's invention. He also composed the operas *Théodore, ou Le Bonheur inattendu*, comic opera (Fontainebleau, March 4, 1785; not extant) and *Cécilia, ou Les Trois Tuteurs*, comic opera (Paris, Dec. 14, 1786).

Davico, Vincenzo, Italian composer; b. Monaco, Jan. 14, 1889; d. Rome, Dec. 8, 1969. He was a student of Cravero in Turin and of Reger in Leipzig. After living in Paris (1918–40), he settled in Rome. He composed the operas *La dogaressa* (1919; Monte Carlo, Feb. 26, 1920), *Berlingaccio* (1931), and *La principessa prigioniera* (Bergamo, Sept. 29, 1940), and the ballets *L'agonia della rosa* (Paris, May 2, 1927) and *Narciso* (San Remo, Feb. 19, 1935).

BIBL.: C. Valabrega, *La lirica da camera di V. D.* (Rome, 1953).

David, Félicien (-César), French composer; b. Cadenet, Vaucluse, April 13, 1810; d. St.-Germain-en-Laye, Aug. 29, 1876. After the death of his parents, he was sent to be a chorister at the cathedral of St. Sauveur in Aix-en-Provence. He entered the Paris Cons. in 1830, where he studied with F.-J. Fétis (fugue) and Benoist (organ); he also studied privately with H. Reber. In 1831 he joined the St. Simonians, a messianic socialistic cult patterned after the ideas of Claude-Henri de Rouvroy, Count of St.-Simon (1760–1825). After its forced disbanding in 1832, he made a pilgrimage to Egypt and the Near East, where he absorbed the flavor of the Orient. Returning to Paris in 1836, he produced a number of works based upon his travels, many with titles reflecting oriental exoticism. His first success came in 1844 with the symphonic ode *Le Désert* for Soloists, Men's Chorus, and Orch. After visiting Mendelssohn and Meyerbeer in Germany in 1845, he turned his attention to opera; he achieved little success, with the exception of his *Lalla-Roukh* (Paris, May 12, 1862), which retained its popularity for many years. Although he received many awards, including the rank of Officier de la Légion d'honneur (1862) and membership into the Académie des Beaux Arts (succeeding Berlioz, 1869), his music virtually disappeared; occasional revivals are fostered by those with an interest in the exoticism of the period. Among other stage works are the operas *La Perle du Brésil* (Paris, Nov. 22, 1851), *Le Fermier de Franconville* (1857), *Herculanum* (Paris, March 4, 1859), *La Captive* (1860–64), and *Le Saphir* (based on Shakespeare's *All's Well That Ends Well*; Paris, March 8, 1865); also *Le Jugement dernier, ou La Fin du monde*, incidental music (Paris, 1849), and the oratorios *Moïse au Sinai* (Paris, March 24, 1846) and *L'Eden* (Paris, Aug. 25, 1848; full score lost).

BIBL.: S. St.-Etienne, *Biographie de F. D.* (Marseilles, 1845); A. Azevedo, *F. D.* (Paris, 1863); R. Brancour, *F. D.* (Paris, 1911); M. Achter, *F. D., Ambroise Thomas and French Opéra Lyrique* (diss., Univ. of Michigan, 1972); R. Locke, *Music and the St. Simonians: The Involvement of F. D. and Other Musicians in a Utopian Socialist Movement* (diss., Univ. of Chicago, 1980); D. Hagan, *F. D. 1810–1876: A Composer and a Cause* (Syracuse, N.Y., 1985).

David, Ferdinand, noted German violinist, pedagogue, and composer; b. Hamburg, Jan. 19, 1810; d. near Klosters, Switzerland, July 18, 1873. In 1823–24 he studied with Spohr and Hauptmann at Kassel. He played in the Gewandhaus Orch. in Leipzig in 1825, and from 1826 to 1829 was a member of the Königstadt Theater in Berlin. In 1829 he became the 1st violinist in the private string quartet of the wealthy amateur Baron von Liphardt of Russia, whose daughter he married. He remained in Russia until 1835, giving concerts in Riga, Moscow, and St. Petersburg with great acclaim. In 1836 he was appointed 1st violinist of the Gewandhaus Orch., of which Mendelssohn was the conductor. They became warm friends; Mendelssohn had a great regard for him, and consulted him while writing his Violin Concerto; it was David who gave its first performance (Leipzig, March 13, 1845). When the Leipzig Cons. was established in 1843, David became one of its most important teachers; his class was regarded as the finishing school of the most talented violinists in Europe; among his pupils were Joachim and Wilhelmj. He publ. many valuable eds. of violin works by classical composers, notably *Die hohe Schule des Violinspiels*, containing French and Italian masterpieces of the 17th and 18th centuries. His pedagogical activities did not interfere with his concert career; he played in England in 1839 and 1841 with excellent success and was compared with Spohr as a virtuoso; also made occasional appearances on the Continent. He composed an opera, *Hans Wacht* (Leipzig, 1852).

BIBL.: J. Eckardt, *F. D. und die Familie Mendelssohn-Bartholdy* (Leipzig, 1888).

David, Giacomo, Italian tenor, father of **Giovanni David**; b. Presezzo, near Bergamo, 1750; d. Bergamo, Dec. 31, 1830. He studied in Naples, making his debut in 1773 in Milan. He then made many appearances at La Scala in Milan (1782–83; 1799–1800; 1802–03; 1806–08), and also sang in concert in London (1791); he was a featured singer at the first performances given at the Teatro Nuovo in Trieste (1801) and at the Teatro Carcano in Milan (1803).

David, Giovanni, Italian tenor, son of **Giacomo David**; b. Naples, Sept. 15, 1790; d. St. Petersburg, 1864. He studied with his father, making his debut in 1808 in Siena. He created the role of Narciso in Rossini's *Il Turco in Italia* at La Scala in Milan on Aug. 14, 1814; he also created other roles in Rossini operas. He sang in London in 1818 and 1831. He quit the stage in 1839 and later became manager of the St. Petersburg Opera.

David, Karl Heinrich, Swiss composer; b. St. Gallen, Dec. 30, 1884; d. Nervi, Italy, May 17, 1951. He studied in Cologne and Munich; taught at the Basel Cons. (1910–14), then at Cologne and Berlin (1914–17); in 1918 he returned to Switzerland. He was the ed. of the *Schweizer Musikzeitung* in Zürich (1928–41). He composed the operas *Aschenputtel* (Basel, Oct. 21, 1921), *Der Sizilianer* (Zürich, Oct. 22, 1924), *Jugendfestspiel* (Zürich, June 8, 1924), *Traumwandel* (Zürich, Jan. 29, 1928), and *Weekend*, comic opera (1933).

David, Léon, French tenor; b. Sables-d'Olonne, Dec. 18, 1867; d. there, Oct. 27, 1962. He studied at the Nantes Cons. and later at the Paris Cons. He made his debut at the Opéra Comique in Paris in 1892; appeared subsequently in Brussels, Monte Carlo, Marseilles, Bordeaux, Cairo, Lisbon, Bucharest, and other cities. From 1924 to 1938 he was a prof. of singing at the Paris Cons. His son was the singer José David (b. Sables-d'Olonne, Jan. 6, 1913).

David, Thomas Christian, noted Austrian composer and teacher; b. Wels, Dec. 22, 1925. His father was the outstanding Austrian composer and teacher Johann Nepomuk David (b. Eferding, Nov. 30, 1895; d. Stuttgart, Dec. 22, 1977). He was a choirboy at Leipzig's Thomaskirche and studied with his father at the Leipzig Hochschule für Musik before studying musicology at the Univ. of Tübingen (1948). He taught flute at the Salzburg Mozarteum (1945–48) and was founder-director of the South German Madrigal Choir (1952–57); he then went to Vienna, where he taught harmony and composition at the Academy of Music (from 1957), later serving as prof. of harmony at the Hochschule für Musik (from 1973) and director of the Austrian Composers Soc. (from 1986). He also taught at the Univ. of Teheran and was director of the Iranian Television Orch. (1967–73). He made various appearances as a flutist, harpsichordist, pianist, choral director, and conductor. David received several awards for his compositions, which are noted for their innovative, modernistic uses of contrapuntal devices. His substantial catalog includes the operas *Atossa* (1968), *Der Weg nach Emmaus* (Alpbach, Aug. 28, 1982), and *Als Oedipus kam* (1986).

Davidenko, Alexander, Russian composer; b. Odessa, April 13, 1899; d. Moscow, May 1, 1934. He organized, with Bely, the Procoll (Production Collective of Composers) in Russia in 1925. His most important work is the opera *1905* (1929–33; with B. Shekhter); another opera, *Down the Cliff*, was left incomplete.

BIBL.: N. Martynov, ed., *A. D.* (Leningrad, 1968).

Davidov, Stepan Ivanovich, Russian composer; b. 1777; d. St. Petersburg, May 22, 1825. He studied with Giuseppe Sarti in St. Petersburg and was subsequently active as a singing teacher, répétiteur, and composer at the Drama School there. After serving as music director to Count Sheremetev, he was a singing teacher at the Moscow Drama School. He was one of the leading Russian composers of music for the stage in his day.

WORKS: DRAMATIC: OPERAS: *Lesta, the Dnepr Water Nymph* (St. Petersburg, Nov. 6, 1805); *Rusalka* (St. Petersburg, 1807); also numbers for Kauer's *Das Donauweibchen*, given in Russian as *Rusalka* (St. Petersburg, Nov. 7, 1803). BALLETS: *Virtue Crowned* (St. Petersburg, Oct. 7, 1801); *Thank Offering* (St. Petersburg, 1802); *The Victory Celebration* (1814). Also several comical divertissements; incidental music; sacred works.

Davidson, Tina, American composer; b. Stockholm (of American parents), Dec. 30, 1952. She studied piano at the State Univ. of N.Y. at Oneonta (1962–70) and at the School of Music in Tel Aviv (1971), and composition with Brant, Fine, and Nowak at Bennington (Vt.) College (1972–76). From 1978 to 1989 she was assoc. director of RELACHE, a Philadelphia-based ensemble for the performance of contemporary music. From 1981 to 1985 she taught piano at Drexel Univ. She was composer-in-residence of the Orch. Soc. of Philadelphia (1992–94) and of Opera Delaware in Wilmington (1994–97). From 1997 to 1999 she was the Fleischer Art Memorial Composer-in-Residence in Philadelphia. Her music is replete with colorful sonoric effects and extramusical influences. She composed the opera *Billy and Zelda* (Wilmington, Del., Dec. 11, 1998).

Davies, Arthur, Welsh tenor; b. Wrexham, April 11, 1941. He was a student at the Royal Northern College of Music in Manchester. After appearing with Opera for All and singing in the Welsh National Opera chorus in Cardiff, he made his formal operatic debut as Squeak in *Billy Buddy* with the Welsh National Opera. In subsequent seasons, he sang such roles as Nero, Nadir, Nemorino, Lensky, Rodolfo, Don José, Pinkerton, and Števa. In 1976 he made his first appearance at London's Covent Garden in the premiere of Henze's *We Come to the River*, and returned in later seasons to sing such roles as Alfredo, the Italian Singer in *Der Rosenkavalier*, Pinkerton, Števa, and Walton's Troilus. He also made guest appearances with the Scottish Opera in Glasgow, the Edinburgh Festival, the English National Opera in London, and in Leipzig, Chicago, Moscow, and Buenos Aires. As a concert artist, he was known for his performances in works by Elgar.

Davies, Ben(jamin) Grey, Welsh tenor; b. Pontardawe, near Swansea, South Wales, Jan. 6, 1858; d. Bath, England, March 28, 1943. After winning 1st prize for solo singing at the Swansea Eisteddfod in 1877, he studied at the Royal Academy of Music in London (1878–80) under Randegger, Sr., and Fiori, winning the bronze, silver, and gold medals for best declamatory English singing. His debut was in Birmingham, Oct. 11, 1881, in *The Bohemian Girl*. He created the title role in Sullivan's *Ivanhoe* (London, Jan. 31, 1891). In 1892 he made his debut at London's Covent Garden as Faust. He made his first appearance in the United States at the Chicago World's Fair in 1893, then was mainly active as a concert and oratorio singer. He sang regularly at the Handel Festivals until 1926.

Davies, Cecilia, English soprano; b. c.1755; d. London, July 3, 1836. A precocious child, she toured with her parents and her sister, Marianne Davies (b. 1743 or 1744; d. c.1818), who played the harpsichord and flute, and then the glass harmonica from 1762. Cecilia appeared in Ireland in 1763, and then with her sister in London in 1767 before touring throughout Europe. During their stay in Vienna, Cecilia studied with Hasse, in whose *Ruggiero* she appeared in Naples in 1772. Following appearances in other Italian cities, she sang in London (1773–74; 1776–77) before pursuing her career on the Continent. She gave concerts in London and other British cities in 1787 and 1791, but her career then waned and she ended her days in poverty.

Davies, Dennis Russell, significant American conductor; b. Toledo, Ohio, April 16, 1944. He studied piano with Lonny Epstein and Sascha Gorodnitzki and conducting with Morel and Mester at the Juilliard School of Music in New York (B.Mus., 1966; M.S., 1968; D.M.A., 1972), where he also taught (1968–71) and was cofounder (with Berio) of the Juilliard Ensemble (1968–74). He was music director of the Norwalk (Conn.) Sym. Orch. (1968–73), the St. Paul (Minn.) Chamber Orch. (1972–80), the Cabrillo (Calif.) Music Festival (1974–91), and the American Composers Orch. in New York (from 1977). In 1978 he made his first appearance at the Bayreuth Festival, conducting *Der fliegende Holländer*. He was Generalmusikdirektor of the Württemberg State Theater in Stuttgart (1980–87), principal conductor and director of Classical music programming at the Saratoga (N.Y.) Performing Arts Center (1985–88), and Generalmusikdirektor of Bonn (1987–95), where he was chief conductor of the Orchester der Beethovenhalle and of the Opera. In 1994 he led the orch. on a tour of North America. From 1991 to 1996 he was music director of the Brooklyn Academy of Music and principal conductor of the Brooklyn Phil. He likewise was chief conductor of the Stuttgart Chamber Orch. (from 1995) and the Austrian Radio Sym. Orch. in Vienna (from 1996). In 1987 he received the Alice M. Ditson conductor's award. Davies has acquired a notable reputation as a champion of contemporary music. He has conducted numerous premieres in the United States and Europe.

Davies, Sir Peter Maxwell, distinguished English composer and conductor; b. Manchester, Sept. 8, 1934. He studied at the Royal Manchester College of Music (graduated, 1952) and at the Univ. of Manchester (Mus.B., 1956). In 1957 he won an Italian government scholarship to study in Rome with Petrassi. After serving as director of music at Cirencester Grammar School (1959–62), he received a Harkness fellowship to pursue studies with Sessions and Babbitt at Princeton Univ. (1962–64). In 1966 he was composer-in-residence at the Univ. of Adelaide. In 1967 he became co-founder (with Harrison Birtwistle) of the Pierrot Players in London, a contemporary music ensemble. In 1970 it was renamed the Fires of London, and Davies remained its artistic director until 1987. In 1970 he made his residence on the island of Hoy, Orkney, where in 1977 he founded the St. Magnus Festival of Orkney, serving as its artistic director, and, from 1986, its president. From 1979 to 1983 he also was director of Music of the Dartington Hall Summer School. In 1985 he became composer-in-residence and assoc. conductor of the Scottish Chamber Orch. in Glasgow, with which he toured widely. In 1992 he assumed similar positions with the BBC Phil. in Manchester and the Royal Phil. in London. In 1995 he became president of the Society for the Promotion of New Music. Davies received honorary doctorates from various institutions of higher learning, among them the univs. of Edinburgh (1979), Aberdeen (1981), Manchester (1983), and Bristol (1984). In 1981 he was made a Commander of the Order of the British Empire and in 1987 he was knighted.

In his works, Davies combines seemingly incongruous elements, which include reverential evocations of medieval hymnody, surrealistic depictions of historical personages, and hedonistic musical theatrics. Among his most arresting works in this synthetic manner is his *8 Songs for a Mad King* (1969), a fantastic suite of heterogeneously arranged pieces representing the etiology of the madness of King George III; at the other end of the spectrum is his *Vesalii Icones* (1969), inspired by the anatomical drawings of Christ's Passion and Resurrection by the Renaissance artist Vesalius. In his later scores, he often found inspiration in the Orkney landscape and literary heritage.

WORKS: DRAMATIC: OPERAS: *Taverner* (1962–70; London, July 12, 1972); *The Martyrdom of St. Magnus* (1976; Orkney, June 18, 1977); *The Lighthouse* (1979; Edinburgh, Sept. 2, 1980); *Resurrection* (1987; Darmstadt, Sept. 18, 1988); *Redemption* (1988); *The Doctors of Myddfai* (1993–96; Cardiff, July 5, 1996). MUSIC THEATER: *8 Songs for a Mad King* for Baritone, Flute, Clarinet, Keyboards, Percussion, Violin, and Cello (London, April 22, 1969); *Vesalii Icones* for Dancer, Cello, Flute, Clarinet, Piano, Percussion, and Viola (London, Dec. 9, 1969); *Blind Man's Bluff* for Mime, Soprano, Mezzo-soprano, and Small Orch. (London, May 29, 1972); *Miss Donnithorne's Maggot* for Female Singer, Flute, Clarinet, Violin, Cello, Piano, Percussion, and 4 Mechanical Metronomes (Adelaide, March 9, 1974); *Salome*, ballet (Copenhagen, Nov. 10, 1978; concert suite, London, March 16, 1979); *Le Jongleur de Notre Dame* for Mime, Baritone, Flute, Clarinet, Violin, Cello, Piano, Percussion, and Children's Band (Orkney, June 18, 1978); *The Yellow-Cake Revue*, anti-nuclear cabaret for Singer and Piano (Orkney, June 21, 1980); *The Medium*, monodrama for Mezzo-soprano (Orkney, July 21, 1981); *The No. 11 Bus* for Mime, 2 Dancers, Mezzo-soprano, Tenor, Baritone, Flute, Clarinet, Violin, Cello, Piano, and Percussion (London, March 20, 1984); *Caroline Mathilde*, ballet (1990).

BIBL.: P. Griffiths, *P. M. D.* (London, 1982); M. Seabrook, *Max: The Life and Music of P. M. D.* (London, 1994).

Davies, Ryland, Welsh tenor; b. Cwm, Ebbw Vale, Feb. 9, 1943. He studied at the Royal Manchester College of Music. He made his operatic debut as Almaviva in 1964 with the Welsh National Opera; then sang in Glasgow, Glyndebourne, and London (1969). He sang in San Francisco in 1970; made his Metropolitan Opera debut in New York on Oct. 15, 1975, as Ferrando in *Così fan tutte*. He appeared in major European operatic centers, and also toured widely as a concert singer. Among his best known roles were Tamino, Don Ottavio, Belmonte, Lensky, Nemorino, and Pelléas. From 1966 to 1981 he was married to **Anne Howells**.

Davies, Tudor, Welsh tenor; b. Cymmer, Nov. 12, 1892; d. London, April 2, 1958. He studied in Cardiff and at the Royal Academy of Music in London. He appeared at the Old Vic; joined the British National Opera Co. in 1922; created the title role in *Hugh the Drover* by Vaughan Williams (London, July 14, 1924); in 1928 he sang in the United States with the Civic Opera in Philadelphia. He then was a principal singer with the Old Vic and the Sadler's Wells Opera (1931–41); he was a member of the Carl Rosa Opera Co. (1941–46) and also appeared in concerts.

Davis, Andrew (Frank), esteemed English conductor; b. Ashridge, Hertfordshire, Feb. 2, 1944. He studied piano at the Royal

Academy of Music in London, and after taking organ lessons with Peter Hurford and Piet Kee, was an organ scholar at King's College, Cambridge (1963–67). He then received instruction in conducting from Franco Ferrara at the Accademia di Santa Cecilia in Rome. Following a successful guest conducting engagement with the BBC Sym. Orch. in London in 1970, he served as assistant conductor of the BBC Scottish Sym. Orch. in Glasgow until 1973, making his debut as an opera conductor that same year at the Glyndebourne Festival. He was assoc. conductor of the New Philharmonia Orch. in London (1973–75) and principal guest conductor of the Royal Liverpool Phil. (1974–76). In 1974 he made his North American debut as a guest conductor with the Detroit Sym. Orch. He then was music director of the Toronto Sym. (1975–88), which, under his guidance, acquired a fine international reputation via major tours of North America, Europe, the People's Republic of China, and Japan. In 1982 he inaugurated the orch.'s new home, the Roy Thomson Hall in Toronto, in a gala concert. After completing his tenure, he served as the orch.'s conductor laureate from 1988 to 1990. In 1988 he was named chief conductor of the BBC Sym. Orch. in London and music director of the Glyndebourne Festival. In 1994 he conducted the 100th anniversary season of the Henry Wood Promenade Concerts in London with the BBC Sym. Orch. In 1999–2000 he became the music director designate of the Lyric Opera of Chicago, and from 2000 its music director and principal conductor. His 3d marriage was to **Gianna Rolandi**. In 1992 he was made a Commander of the Order of the British Empire. His vast repertoire encompasses works from virtually every era, all of which display his wide sympathies, command of technique, and musical integrity.

Davis, Anthony, black American composer and pianist; b. Paterson, N.J., Feb. 20, 1951. He studied at Yale Univ. (B.A., 1975), proving himself to be an extremely facile jazz pianist; was co-founder of Advent (1973), a free jazz ensemble that included trombonist George Lewis, and then played in trumpeter Leo Smith's New Delta Ahkri band (1974–77). He also played in New York with violinist Leroy Jenkins (1977–79) and with flutist James Newton, both active proponents of the Assn. for the Advancement of Creative Musicians. His compositions, while strictly notated, are improvisational in tone. His opera *X*, based on the life of Malcolm X, was premiered in Philadelphia in 1985; a performance followed in 1989 at N.Y.'s Lincoln Center. On June 14, 1992, his opera *Tania*, inspired by the Patty Hearst-Symbionese Liberation Army exploits, was performed for the first time in Philadelphia. His opera *Amistad* was premiered in Chicago on Nov. 29, 1997.

Davis, Carl, American conductor and composer; b. N.Y., Oct. 28, 1936. He was educated at the New England Cons. of Music in Boston and at Bard college (B.A.), his mentors in composition in the U.S. being Paul Nordoff and Hugo Kauder; also studied with Per Nørgård in Copenhagen. He became active in England as a conductor and composer. From 1984 to 1987 he was principal conductor of the Bournemouth Pops. In 1987–88 he was assoc. conductor of the London Phil. He composed much stage, film, and television music. He also collaborated with Paul McCartney on the *Liverpool Oratorio* (1991).

WORKS: DRAMATIC: OPERA: *Peace* (1978). TELEVISION OPERAS: *The Arrangement* (1967); *Orpheus in the Underground* (1976). MUSICALS: *The Projector* (1971); *Pilgrim* (1975); *Cranford* (1976); *Alice in Wonderland* (1977); *The Wind in the Willows* (1986); *Kip's War* (1987). BALLETS: *Dances of Love and Death* (1981); *Fire and Ice* (1986); *The Portrait of Dorian Gray* (1987); *A Simple Man* (1987); *Liaisons Amoureuses* (1989); *Lipizzaner* (1989); *A Christmas Carol* (1992); *Savoy Suite* (1993).

Davis, Sir Colin (Rex), eminent English conductor; b. Weybridge, Sept. 25, 1927. He studied clarinet at the Royal College of Music in London, and played in the band of the Household Cavalry while serving in the army. He began his conducting career with the Kalmar Chamber Orch. and the Chelsea Opera Group; in 1958 he conducted a performance of *Die Entführung aus dem Serail* in London; from 1961 to 1965 he served as music director of Sadler's Wells. He made his U.S. debut as a guest conductor with the Minneapolis Sym. Orch. on Dec. 30, 1960; subsequently he had engagements with the N.Y. Phil., the Philadelphia Orch., and the Los Angeles Phil. From 1972 to 1983 he served as principal guest conductor of the Boston Sym. Orch. On Jan. 20, 1967, he made his Metropolitan Opera debut in New York conducting *Peter Grimes*. From 1967 to 1971 he was chief conductor of the BBC Sym. Orch. in London. In 1965 he conducted at the Royal Opera at Covent Garden; he succeeded Solti as its music director in 1971. Among his notable achievements was a production at Covent Garden of the *Ring* cycle between 1974 and 1976; in 1977 he became the first British conductor to appear at the Bayreuth Festival, conducting *Tannhäuser*. He conducted the Royal Opera during its tours in South Korea and Japan in 1979, and in the United States in 1984. In 1983 he was appointed chief conductor of the Bavarian Radio Sym. Orch. in Munich, which he led on a tour of North America in 1986. In 1986 he stepped down as music director at Covent Garden to devote himself fully to his duties in Munich and to pursue far-flung engagements as a guest conductor with major orchs. and opera houses of the world. In 1988 he was named to an international chair at the Royal Academy of Music. In 1993 he stepped down from his Munich position. In 1995 he became principal conductor of the London Sym. Orch. and in 1998 he became principal guest conductor of the N.Y. Phil. Davis is an authoritative interpreter of such masters as Mozart, Berlioz, Sibelius, and Stravinsky. He has also championed the cause of his British contemporaries, most notably Sir Michael Tippett. He was made a Commander of the Order of the British Empire in 1965, and was knighted in 1980. From 1949 to 1964 he was married to **April Cantelo**.

BIBL.: A. Blyth, *C. D.* (London, 1972).

Davis, John David, English composer and teacher; b. Birmingham, Oct. 22, 1867; d. Estoril, Portugal, Nov. 20, 1942. He studied in Frankfurt am Main and in Brussels. After returning to England in 1889, he taught in various schools in Birmingham; in 1905, was appointed prof. of composition at the Guildhall School of Music in London. He wrote an opera on a Russian subject, *The Zaporoges* (Birmingham, May 7, 1895).

Davison, A(rchibald) T(hompson), eminent American music educator; b. Boston, Oct. 11, 1883; d. Brant Rock, Mass., Feb. 6, 1961. He studied at Harvard Univ. (B.A., 1906; M.A., 1907; Ph.D., 1908, with the diss. *The Harmonic Contributions of Claude Debussy*); he then took lessons in organ with Widor in Paris (1908–9). Returning to America, he was organist and choirmaster at Harvard Univ. (1910–40); he conducted the Harvard Glee Club (1912–33) and the Radcliffe Choral Soc. (1913–28); he began teaching at Harvard in 1917 as assistant prof.; subsequently he was assoc. prof. (1920–29), prof. of choral music (1929–40), and the James Edward Ditson Prof. of Music (1940–54). He held numerous honorary degrees, including those of D.Mus. at Williams College and the Univ. of Oxford; Fellow of the Royal College of Music, London; Litt.D. from Washington Univ. (1953); and L.H.D. from Temple Univ. (1955). He wrote 2 comic operas, and the musical comedy *The Girl and the Chauffeur* (Boston, April 16, 1906), but his greatest achievement was as an educator and popularizer of musical subjects.

Davy, Gloria, black American soprano; b. N.Y., March 29, 1931. She was a student of Belle Julie Soudent at the Juilliard School of Music in New York (1948–53) and of Victor de Sabata in Milan. In 1953 she sang in the touring production of *Porgy and Bess*. On April 2, 1954, she appeared as the Countess in the U.S. premiere of *Capriccio* in New York. She made her European operatic debut in Nice as Aida in 1957, a role she repeated for her Metropolitan Opera debut in New York on Feb. 12, 1958. She remained on the Metropolitan roster until 1961, appearing as Pamina, Nedda, and Leonora in *Il Trovatore*. Aida was her debut role at the Vienna State Opera in 1959 and at London's Covent Garden in 1960. From 1961 she appeared at the Berlin Deutsche Oper, singing such roles as Aida, Fiordiligi, Donna Anna, Cio-Cio-San, Donna Elvira, and Salome. She also pursued guest engagements in other European operatic centers (1963–69). From 1975 to 1985 she made regular concert tours in Europe. In 1983 she made her London recital debut at Wigmore Hall. She served as a prof. at the Indiana Univ. School of Music in Bloomington from 1985 to 1993.

Dawson, Lynne, English soprano; b. York, June 3, 1953. She received vocal training at the Guildhall School of Music and Drama in London. In 1975 she began to make regular appearances in the Baroque repertoire, with which she became closely identified. In 1986 she made her formal operatic debut with the Kent Opera as Mozart's Countess. After appearing in Florence as Monteverdi's Orfeo in 1987, she sang Pamina with the Scottish Opera in Glasgow and Zdenka in *Arabella* at the Théâtre du Châtelet in Paris in 1988. In 1990 she sang in Monteverdi's *Orfeo* at the Salzburg Festival and as Mozart's Countess in Brussels. She appeared as Cornelia in Graun's *Cesare e Cleopatra* at the Berlin State Opera in 1992. In 1996 she was a soloist in Handel's *Belshazzar* in Göttingen. Her performances of Monteverdi, Purcell, Handel, Gluck, Mozart, and Rossini have won her well-deserved accolades.

Deák, Csaba, Hungarian-born Swedish composer; b. Budapest, April 16, 1932. He studied clarinet and composition at the Béla Bartók Cons. in Budapest (1949–55) and composition with Ferenc Farkas at the Budapest Academy of Music (1955–56); he subsequently went to Sweden, where he took composition lessons with Hilding Rosenberg. He also studied composition, clarinet, and conducting at the Ingesund School of Music in Arvika; he received his music teacher's certification from the Stockholm Musikhögskolan (1969). He taught at the Swedish State School of the Dance in Stockholm (from 1969) and at the Univ. of Göteborg (1971–74). His compositions include *Fäderna* (The Fathers), chamber opera (Stockholm, Oct. 16, 1968), *Etude on Spring*, electronic ballet (1970), *Lucie's Ascent into Heaven*, an "astrophonic minimelodrama" (1973), and *Bye-bye, Earth, A Play about Death* (1976–77); also theater music.

De Amicis, Anna Lucia, famous Italian soprano; b. Naples, c.1733; d. there, 1816. She studied with her father and began her career singing with her family in comic opera productions in Pisa and Florence (1754), Bologna (1755), Paris (1758), Brussels (1759), and Dublin (1762). In 1762 she appeared for the first time in London at the King's Theatre, where she made her debut in serious opera in J. C. Bach's *Orione* (Feb. 19, 1763); she subsequently sang in Milan (1764–65), Venice (1764), Innsbruck (1765), and Naples (1766), then again in Venice (1768–69; 1770–71) and Naples (1769–70; 1771–72). Mozart attended her performances in the latter cities and chose her to sing in the premiere of his *Lucio Silla* (Milan, Dec. 26, 1772). After further engagements in Naples (1773–76), Turin (1776–79), and Bologna (1778), she settled in Naples, where she continued to sing in private performances during the next decade, before retiring. She was generally considered one of the greatest singers of her time, winning acclaim for her astounding vocal as well as dramatic gifts.

Dean, Stafford (Roderick), English bass; b. Kingswood, Surrey, June 20, 1937. He studied at Epsom College and at the Royal College of Music in London; also received private lessons from Howell Glynne and Otakar Kraus. He first sang with Opera for All (1962–64); in 1964 he made his debut at the Glyndebourne Festival as Lictor in *L'incoronazione de Poppea*, and at Sadler's Wells in London as Zuniga, where he appeared regularly until 1970; in 1969 he made his debut at London's Covent Garden as Masetto, and remained on its roster. On Feb. 6, 1976, he made his Metropolitan Opera debut in New York as Figaro. He also sang opera in Chicago, San Francisco, Toronto, Hamburg, Berlin, Vienna, Paris, and other cities, and likewise toured widely as a concert artist. His extensive repertoire includes such roles as Sarastro, Leporello, Osmind, Sparafucile, and King Philip. He married **Anne Howells**.

Dean, Winton (Basil), English writer on music; b. Birkenhead, March 18, 1916. He pursued studies in the liberal arts at King's College, Cambridge (B.A., 1938; M.A., 1941); he took private music lessons with Philip Radcliffe, then devoted himself to musicological research. He publ. several valuable biographical essays on Handel, Bizet, and others. In 1989 he was made a corresponding member of the American Musicological Soc.

WRITINGS: *Bizet* (London, 1948; 2d ed., rev., 1965, as *Georges Bizet: His Life and Work*; 3d ed., 1976); *Carmen* (London, 1949); *Franck* (London, 1950); *Introduction to the Music of Bizet* (London, 1950); *Handel's Dramatic Oratorios and Masques* (London, 1959; rev. ed., 1900); *Handel and the Opera Seria* (Berkeley, 1969); with J. Knapp, *Handel's Operas 1704–1726* (Oxford, 1987); *Essays on Opera* (Oxford, 1990).

BIBL.: N. Fortune, ed., *Music and Theatre: Essays in Honour of W. D.* (Cambridge, 1987).

De Angelis, Nazzareno, noted Italian bass; b. Aquila, Nov. 17, 1881; d. Rome, Dec. 14, 1962. As a boy, he sang in the Sistine and Justine chapel choirs in Rome. He made his operatic debut in Aquila in 1903; then appeared with major Italian opera houses. In 1909–10 he was on the roster of the Manhattan Opera House in New York, then of the Chicago Opera (1910–11; 1915–20); he later made appearances with the Rome Opera (until 1938) and also gave song recitals. He was regarded as one of the most cultured bass singers of the Italian school of opera, and he was equally appreciated in Wagnerian roles.

De Bassini (real name, **Bassi**), **Achille,** Italian baritone; b. Milan, May 5, 1819; d. Cavadei Tirreni, July 3, 1881. He studied with Perelli, and then made his operatic debut in Voghera (c.1837). He won the admiration of Verdi, who chose him to create the roles of Francisco in *I due Foscari* (Rome, Nov. 3, 1844), Corsaro (Trieste, Oct. 25, 1848), Miller in *Luisa Miller* (Naples, Dec. 8, 1849), and Melitone in *La forza del destino* (St. Petersburg, Nov. 10, 1862). In 1859 he sang at London's Covent Garden. In addition to his Verdi roles, he won distinction in operas by Bellini and Donizetti. His wife, Rita (Gabriella) Gabussi (b. Bologna, c.1815; d. Naples, Jan. 26, 1891), was also a singer. After making her operatic debut as Rosina in Milan in 1830, she sang widely in Italy. In 1851 she created the title role in Mercadante's *Medea* in Naples and then retired. Their son, Alberto De Bassini (b. Florence, July 14, 1847; place and date of death unknown), was also a singer. In 1869 he made his operatic debut in *Belisario* in Venice. After singing mainly French roles, he appeared with the Royal Italian Grand Opera Co. on tour in the United States in 1898. He later taught voice.

De Boeck, August, Belgian organist, pedagogue, and composer; b. Merchtem, May 9, 1865; d. there, Oct. 9, 1937. He went to Brussels to study organ at the Cons., and also had lessons in orchestration from Gilson. He was active as a church organist in Brussels, where he also was a teacher of organ (1893–1902) and of harmony (1920–30) at the Cons. He also taught organ at the Royal Flemish Cons. in Antwerp (1909–21) and was director of the Mechelen Cons. (1920–30). De Boeck's compositions generally followed along the lines of the French impressionists.

WORKS: DRAMATIC: OPERAS: *Théroigne de Mérincourt* (Antwerp, Jan. 1901); *Winternachtsdroom* (Antwerp, Dec. 1902); *De Rijndwergen* (Antwerp, Oct. 1906); *Reinaert de Vos* (Antwerp, Jan. 1, 1909); *La Route d'Emeraude* (Ghent, Feb. 1921). OPERETTAS: *Papa Poliet* (1914–18); *Totole* (1929). BALLETS: *Cendrillon* (1895); *La Phalène* (1896). INCIDENTAL MUSIC TO: G. Eekhoud's *La Chevalière d'Eon* (1894); R. Verhulst's *Jesus de Nazarener* (1909).

BIBL.: F. Rasse, *A. D. B.* (Brussels, 1943).

Debussy, (Achille-) Claude, great French composer whose music created new poetry of mutating tonalities and became a perfect counterpart of new painting in France; b. St.-Germain-en-Laye, Aug. 22, 1862; d. Paris, March 25, 1918. Mme. Mauté de Fleurville, the mother-in-law of the poet Verlaine, prepared him for the Paris Cons.; he was admitted at the age of 10 and studied piano with Marmontel (2d prize, 1877) and solfège with Lavignac (3d medal, 1874; 2d, 1875; 1st, 1876). He further took courses in harmony with Emile Durand (1877–80) and practiced score reading under

Bazille. In 1880 Marmontel recommended him to Mme. Nadezhda von Meck, Tchaikovsky's patroness. She summoned him to Interlaken, and they subsequently visited Rome, Naples, and Fiesole. During the summers of 1881 and 1882, Debussy stayed with Mme. von Meck's family in Moscow, where he became acquainted with the syms. of Tchaikovsky; however, he failed to appreciate Tchaikovsky's music and became more interested in the idiosyncratic compositions of Mussorgsky. Back in France, he became friendly with Mme. Vasnier, wife of a Paris architect and an amateur singer.

Debussy made his earliest professional appearance as a composer in Paris on May 12, 1882, at a concert given by the violinist Maurice Thieberg. In Dec. 1880 he enrolled in the composition class of Guiraud at the Paris Cons. with the ambition of winning the Grand Prix de Rome; after completing his courses, he won the 2d Prix de Rome in 1883. Finally, on June 27, 1884, he succeeded in obtaining the Grand Prix de Rome with his cantata *L'Enfant prodigue*, written in a poetic but conservative manner reflecting the trends of French romanticism. During his stay in Rome, he wrote a choral work, *Zuleima* (1885–86), after Heine's *Almanzor*, and began work on another cantata, *Diane au bois*. Neither was preserved. His choral suite with orch., *Printemps* (1887), failed to win formal recognition. He then set to work on another cantata, *La Damoiselle Élue* (1887–89), which gained immediate favor among French musicians.

In 1888 Debussy visited Bayreuth, where he heard *Parsifal* and *Die Meistersinger von Nürnberg* for the first time, but Wagner's grandiloquence never gained his full devotion. What thoroughly engaged his interest was the oriental music that he heard at the Paris World Exposition in 1889. He was fascinated by the asymmetric rhythms of the thematic content and the new instrumental colors achieved by native players; he also found an inner valence between these oriental modalities and the verses of certain French impressionist poets, including Mallarmé, Verlaine, Baudelaire, and Pierre Louÿs. The combined impressions of exotic music and symbolist French verses were rendered in Debussy's vocal works, such as *Cinq poèmes de Baudelaire* (1887–89), *Ariettes oubliées* (1888), *Trois mélodies* (1891), and *Fêtes galantes* (1892). He also wrote *Proses lyriques* (1892–93) to his own texts. For the piano, he composed *Suite bergamasque* (1890–1905), which includes the famous *Clair de lune*. In 1892 he began work on his instrumental *Prélude à l'après-midi d'un faune*, after Mallarmé, which comprises the quintessence of tonal painting with its free modal sequences under a subtle umbrage of oscillating instrumentation. The work was first heard in Paris on Dec. 22, 1894. It was about that time that Debussy attended a performance of Maeterlinck's drama *Pelléas et Mélisande*, which inspired him to begin work on an opera on that subject. In 1893 there followed *Trois chansons de Bilitis*, after prose poems by Louÿs, marked by exceptional sensuality of the text in a musical context of free modality; a later work, *Les Chansons de Bilitis* for 2 harps, 2 flutes, and celesta, was heard in Paris in 1901 as incidental music to accompany recited and mimed neo-Grecian poetry of Louÿs. Between 1892 and 1899 Debussy worked on *3 Nocturnes* for orch.: *Nuages*, *Fêtes*, and *Sirènes*.

As the 20th century dawned, Debussy found himself in a tangle of domestic relationships. A tempestuous liaison with Gabrielle Dupont (known as Gaby Lhéry) led to a break, which so distressed Gaby that she took poison. She survived, but Debussy sought more stable attachments; on Oct. 19, 1899, he married Rosalie Texier, with whom he made his first attempt to form a legitimate union. But he soon discovered that like Gaby before her, Rosalie failed to satisfy his expectations, and he began to look elsewhere for a true union of souls. This he found in the person of Emma Bardac, the wife of a banker. He bluntly informed Rosalie of his dissatisfaction with their marriage. Like Gaby 7 years before, Rosalie, plunged into despair by Debussy's selfish decision, attempted suicide; she shot herself in the chest but missed her suffering heart. Debussy, now 42 years old, divorced Rosalie on Aug. 2, 1905. Bardac and her husband were divorced on May 4, 1905; Debussy married her on Jan. 20, 1908. They had a daughter, Claude-Emma (known as "Chouchou"), born Oct. 15, 1905; she was the inspiration for Debussy's charming piano suite, *Children's Corner* (the title was in English, for Chouchou had an English governess). She survived her father by barely a year, dying of diphtheria on July 14, 1919.

With his opera *Pelléas et Mélisande*, Debussy assumed a leading place among French composers. It was premiered at the Opéra Comique in Paris on April 30, 1902, after many difficulties, including the open opposition of Maeterlinck, who objected to having the role of Mélisande sung by the American soprano Mary Garden, whose accent jarred Maeterlinck's sensibilities; he wanted his mistress, Georgette Leblanc, to be the first Mélisande. The production of the opera aroused a violent controversy among French musicians and littérateurs. The press was vicious in the extreme: "Rhythm, melody, tonality, these are 3 things unknown to Monsieur Debussy," wrote the doyen of the Paris music critics, Arthur Pougin. "What a pretty series of false relations! What adorable progressions of triads in parallel motion and fifths and octaves which result from it! What a collection of dissonances, sevenths and ninths, ascending with energy! . . . No, decidedly I will never agree with these anarchists of music!" Camille Bellaigue, who was Debussy's classmate at the Paris Cons., conceded that *Pelléas et Mélisande* "makes little noise," but, he remarked, "it is a nasty little noise." The English and American reports were no less vituperative, pejorative, and deprecatory. "Debussy disowns melody and despises harmony with all its resources," opined the critic of the *Monthly Musical Record* of London. Echoing such judgments, the *Musical Courier* of New York compared Debussy's "disharmony" with the sensation of "an involuntary start when the dentist touches the nerve of a sensitive tooth." And the American writer James Gibbons Huneker exceeded all limits of permissible literary mores by attacking Debussy's physical appearance. "I met Debussy at the Café Riche the other night," he wrote in the N.Y. *Sun*, "and was struck by the unique ugliness of the man. . . . [H]e looks more like a Bohemian, a Croat, a Hun, than a Gaul." These utterances were followed by a suggestion that Debussy's music was fit for a procession of headhunters of Borneo, carrying home "their ghastly spoils of war."

Debussy's next important work was *La Mer*, which he completed during a sojourn in England in 1905. It was first performed in Paris on Oct. 15, 1905. Like his String Quartet, it was conceived monothematically; a single musical idea permeated the entire work despite a great variety of instrumentation. It consists of 3 symphonic sketches: *De l'aube à midi sur la mer*, *Jeux de vagues*, and *Dialogue du vent et de la mer*. *La Mer* was attacked by critics with even greater displeasure than *Pelléas et Mélisande*. The American critic Louis Elson went so far as to suggest that the original title was actually "Le Mal de mer," and that the last movement represented a violent seizure of vomiting. To summarize the judgment on Debussy, a vol. entitled *Le Cas Debussy* was publ. in Paris in 1910. It contained a final assessment of Debussy as a "déformateur musical," suffering from a modern nervous disease that affects one's power of discernment.

Meanwhile, Debussy continued to work. To be mentioned is the remarkable orch. triptych *Images* (1906–12), comprising *Gigues*, *Ibéria*, and *Rondes de printemps*. In 1908 he conducted a concert of his works in London; he also accepted engagements as conductor in Vienna (1910), Turin (1911), Moscow and St. Petersburg (1913), and Rome, Amsterdam, and The Hague (1914). Among other works of the period are the piano pieces, *Douze préludes* (2 books, 1909–10; 1910–13) and *Douze Études* (2 books, 1915). *En blanc et noir*, for 2 pianos, dates from 1915. On May 15, 1913, Diaghilev produced Debussy's ballet *Jeux* in Paris. On May 5, 1917, Debussy played the piano part of his Violin Sonata at its premiere in Paris with violinist Gaston Poulet. But his projected tour of the United States with the violinist Arthur Hartmann had to be abandoned when it was discovered that Debussy had irreversible colon cancer. Surgery was performed in Dec. 1915, but there was little hope of recovery. The protracted 1st World War depressed him; his hatred of the Germans became intense as the military threat to Paris increased. He wrote the lyrics and the accompaniment to a song, *Noël des enfants*, in which he begged Santa Claus not to bring presents to German children whose parents were destroying the French children's Christmas. To underline his national sentiments, he emphatically signed his last works "musicien français." Debussy died on the evening of March 25, 1918, as the great German gun "Big Bertha" made the last attempt to subdue the city of Paris by long distance (76 miles) bombardment.

Debussy emphatically rejected the term "impressionism" as applied to his music. But it cannot alter the essential truth that like Mallarmé in poetry, he created a style peculiarly sensitive to musical mezzotint, a palette of half-lit delicate colors. He systematically applied the oriental pentatonic scale for exotic evocations, as well as the whole-tone scale (which he did not invent, however; earlier samples of its use are found in works by Glinka and Liszt). His piece for piano solo *Voiles* is written in a whole-tone scale, while its middle section is set entirely in the pentatonic scale. In his music Debussy emancipated discords; he also revived the archaic practice of consecutive perfect intervals (particularly fifths and fourths). In his formal constructions, the themes are shortened and rhythmically sharpened, while in the instrumental treatment the role of individual solo passages is enhanced and the dynamic range made more subtle.

WORKS: DRAMATIC AND LITERARY: *Axel*, music for a scene to Villiers de l'Isle Adam's drama (1889); *Rodrigue et Chimène*, opera (1890–92; piano score only, partially lost; reconstructed by Richard Smith and orchestrated by Edison Denisov; Lyons, May 14, 1993); *Pelléas et Mélisande*, opera (1893–95; 1901–02; Paris, April 30, 1902, Messager conducting); *F.E.A. (Frères en art)*, play written with René Peter (1896–1900; unfinished); *Esther et la maison des fous*, text for a dramatic work (1900); *Le Diable dans le beffroi*, opera after Poe's *The Devil in the Belfry* (1902–03; unfinished; only notes for the libretto and sketch for Scene I extant); *Masques et Bergamasques*, scenario for a ballet (1910); *La Chute de la maison Usher*, opera after Poe's *The Fall of the House of Usher* (1908–18; unfinished; only sketches and final version of the libretto and incomplete vocal score extant); *Le Martyre de Saint-Sébastien*, incidental music to the mystery play by d'Annunzio for Soprano, 2 Contraltos, Chorus, and Orch. (Paris, May 22, 1911); *Jeux*, ballet (1912; Paris, May 15, 1913, Monteux conducting); *Khamma*, ballet (1912; Paris, Nov. 15, 1924, Pierné conducting).

WRITINGS: Debussy contributed numerous critical articles to *La Revue Blanche, Gil Blas, Musica, La Revue S.I.M.* et al. A selection of these, some abridged, appeared as *Monsieur Croche, antidilettante* (Paris, 1921; 2d ed., 1926; Eng. tr., 1927, as *Monsieur Croche the Dilettante-Hater*; 2d ed., 1962; new ed. by F. Lesure as *Monsieur Croche et autres Écrits*, Paris, 1971; Eng. tr., 1977, as *D. on Music: The Critical Writings of the Great French Composer C. D.*).

BIBL.: SOURCE MATERIAL: A periodical, *Cahiers D.*, began publication in 1974 (issued by the Centre de Documentation C. D. in St.-Germain-en-Laye, France). F. Lesure has prepared a *Catalogue de l'oeuvre de C. D.* (Geneva, 1977). The *Oeuvres complètes* began publication in 1986. Other sources include the following: A. Martin, *C. D.: Chronologie de sa vie et de ses oeuvres* (Paris, 1942); A. Gauthier, *D.: Documents iconographiques* (Geneva, 1952); *Catalogue de la collection Walter Straram: Manuscrits de C. D.* (Rambouillet, 1961); F. Lesure, *C. D., Catalogue de l'Exposition* (Paris, 1962); C. Abravanel, *C. D.: A Bibliography* (Detroit, 1974); F. Lesure, *Iconographie musicale: D.* (Geneva, 1974); J. Briscoe, *C. D.: A Guide to Research* (N.Y., 1990). BIOGRAPHICAL: L. Liebich, *C.-A. D.* (London, 1908); L. Laloy, *C. D.* (Paris, 1909; 2d ed., aug., 1944); E. Vuillermoz, *C. D.* (Paris, 1920); R. Jardillier, *C. D.* (Dijon, 1922); A. Suarés, *D.* (Paris, 1922; 2d ed., aug., 1936); R. Paoli, *D.* (Florence, 1924; 2d ed., 1947); F. Shera, *D. and Ravel* (London, 1925); F. Gysi, *C. D.* (Zürich, 1926); R. van Santen, *D.* (The Hague, 1926; 2d ed., 1947); C. Koechlin, *D.* (Paris, 1930); R. Peter, *C. D.* (Paris, 1931; 2d ed., aug., 1944); L. Vallas, *C. D. et son temps* (Paris, 1932; 2d ed., 1958; Eng. tr., 1973); E. Decsey, *C. D.* (Graz, 1936); E. Lockspeiser, *D.* (London, 1936; 5th ed., rev., 1980); O. Thompson, *D., Man and Artist* (N.Y., 1937); H. Strobel, *C. D.* (Zürich, 1940; 3d ed., rev., 1948); L. Vallas, *A.-C. D.* (Paris, 1944); R. Paoli, *D.* (Florence, 1947; 2d ed., 1951); G. Ferchault, *C. D., musicien français* (Paris, 1948); H. Harvey, *C. of France: The Story of D.* (N.Y., 1948); R. Malipiero, *D.* (Brescia, 1948); J. van Ackere, *C. D.* (Antwerp, 1949); R. Myers, *D.* (London, 1949); W. Danckert, *C. D.* (Berlin, 1950); G. and D.-E. Inghelbrecht, *C. D.* (Paris, 1953); V. Seroff, *D., Musician of France* (N.Y., 1956); E. Vuillermoz, *C. D.* (Geneva, 1957); J. Barraqué, *D.* (Paris, 1962; Eng. tr., 1972); E. Lockspeiser, *D.: His Life and Mind* (2 vols., London, 1962 and 1965; rev. ed., Cambridge, 1978); Y. Tiénot and O. d'Estrade-Guerra, *D.: L'Homme, son oeuvre, son milieu* (Paris, 1962); A. Goléa, *D.* (Paris, 1965); P. Young, *D.* (London, 1966); G. Gourdet, *D.* (Paris, 1970); R. Nichols, *D.* (London, 1973); C. Goubault, *C. D.* (Paris, 1986); L. Knödler, *D.* (Haarlem, 1989); F. Lesure, *C. D.: Biographie critique* (Paris, 1994); R. Langham Smith, ed., *D. Studies* (Cambridge, 1997); R. Nichols, *The Life of D.* (Cambridge, 1998). CRITICAL, ANALYTICAL: L. Gilman, *D.'s "Pelléas et Mélisande"* (N.Y., 1907); F. Santoliquido, *Il Dopo-Wagner, C. D. e Richard Strauss* (Rome, 1909); C. Caillard and J. de Bérys, *Le Cas D.* (Paris, 1910); G. Setaccioli, *D. é un innovatore?* (Rome, 1910); D. Chennevière, *C. D. et son oeuvre* (Paris, 1913); C. Paglia, *Strauss, D., e compagnia bella* (Bologna, 1913); L. Vallas, *Les Idées de C. D., musicien français* (Paris, 1927; Eng. tr., 1929, as *The Theories of C. D.*); H. Kolsch, *Der Impressionismus bei D.* (Düsseldorf, 1937); G. Schaeffner, *C. D. und das Poetische* (Bern, 1943); A. Gauthier, *Sous l'influence de Neptune: Dialogues avec D.* (Paris, 1945); J. d'Almendra, *Les Modes grégoriens dans l'oeuvre de C. D.* (Paris, 1948); E. Decsey, *D.s Werke* (Graz, 1949); V. Jankélévitch, *D. et le mystère* (Neuchâtel, 1949; 2d ed., 1962); J. van Ackere, *Pelléas et Mélisande* (Brussels, 1952); A. Goléa, *Pelléas et Mélisande, analyse poetique et musicale* (Paris, 1952); H. Büsser, *De Pelléas aux Index galantes* (Paris, 1955); E. Lockspeiser, *D. et Edgar Poe* (Monaco, 1962); S. Jarocinski, *D., a impresionizm i synmbolizm* (Kraków, 1966; French tr., 1971; Eng. tr., 1976, as *D.: Impressionism and Symbolism*); R. Park, *The Later Style of C. D.* (diss., Univ. of Mich., 1967); V. Jankélévitch, *La Vie et la mort dans la musique de D.* (Neuchâtel, 1968); C. Zenck, *Versuch über die wahre Art D. zu analysieren* (Munich, 1974); V. Jankélévitch, *D. et le mystère de l'instant* (Paris, 1976); A. Wenk, *D. and the Poets* (Berkeley and Los Angeles, 1976); R. Holloway, *D. and Wagner* (London, 1979); R. Orledge, *D. and the Theatre* (Cambridge, 1982); A. Wenk, *C. D. and Twentieth-Century Music* (Boston, 1983); G.-P. Biasih, *Montale, D., and Modernism* (Princeton, N.J., 1989); R. Nichols and R. Smith, *C. D.: Pelléas et Mélisande* (Cambridge, 1989); R. Parks, *The Music of C. D.* (New Haven and London, 1989); F. Lesure, *C. D. avant "Pelléas" ou Les Années symbolistes* (Paris, 1992); J. Arndt, *Der Einfluss der javanischen Gamelan-Musik auf Kompositionen von C. D.* (Frankfurt am Main and N.Y., 1993); idem, *Einheitlichkeit versus Widerstreit: Zwei gründsätzlich verschiedene Gestaltungsarten in der Musik C. Ds* (Frankfurt am Main and N.Y., 1993).

Decsényi, János, Hungarian composer; b. Budapest, March 24, 1927. He studied in Budapest with Sugár at the Cons. (1948–52) and with Szervánszky at the Academy of Music (1952–56). From 1951 he was active with the Hungarian Radio, becoming head of its dept. of serious music and director of its electronic music studio. In 1986 he was made a Merited Artist by the Hungarian government. He composed the ballet *Képtelen történet* (An Absurd Story; 1962) and the pantomime *Az orr* (The Nose; 1979).

Decsey, Ernst (Heinrich Franz), German-born Austrian writer on music; b. Hamburg, April 13, 1870; d. Vienna, March 12, 1941. He studied law in Vienna (doctorate, 1894), then composition with Bruckner and Robert Fuchs at the Vienna Cons. He was active as a music critic in Graz and in Vienna. He was the author of a major biography of Hugo Wolf (4 vols., Berlin, 1903–06; abridged 1-vol. ed., 1921). He also wrote *Anton Bruckner* (Berlin, 1920); *Johann Strauss* (Berlin, 1922; 2d ed., 1947); *Franz Lehár* (Vienna, 1924); *Franz Schubert* (Vienna, 1924); *Maria Jeritza* (Vienna, 1931); *Claude Debussy* (2 vols., Graz, 1936); and *Debussys Werke* (Graz and Vienna, 1948).

DeFabritiis, Oliviero (Carlo), Italian conductor; b. Rome, June 13, 1902; d. there, Aug. 12, 1982. He studied with Setaccioli and Refice. He made his conducting debut at the Teatro Adriano in

Rome in 1920; subsequently he was a conductor at the Rome Opera (1934–61). He made numerous guest appearances with major European opera houses; also conducted in the United States.

Defossez, René, Belgian conductor, pedagogue, and composer; b. Spa, Oct. 4, 1905; d. Brussels, May 20, 1988. He studied with Rasse at the Liège Cons., winning the Belgian Prix de Rome in 1935 with his opera cantata *Le Vieux Soudard*. He was conductor at the Théâtre Royal de la Monnaie in Brussels (1936–59) and prof. of conducting at the Brussels Cons. (1946–71). In 1969 he was elected a member of the Royal Belgian Academy.

WORKS: DRAMATIC: OPERA: *Le Subterfuge improvisé* (1938). OPERA CANTATAS: *La Conversion de St. Hubert* (1933); *Le Vieux Soudard* (1935). BALLETS: *Floriante* (1942); *Le Sens du divin* (1947); *Le Rêve de l'astronome* (1950); *Les Jeux de France* (1959); *Le Regard* (1970). BALLET CANTATA: *Le Pêcheur et son âme* (1965). HISTORIC FRESCO: *Lièges libertes* (1981).

DeGaetani, Jan(ice), remarkable American mezzo-soprano; b. Massillon, Ohio, July 10, 1933; d. Rochester, N.Y., Sept. 15, 1989. She studied at the Juilliard School of Music in New York with Sergius Kagan. Upon graduation, she joined the Contemporary Chamber Ensemble, with which she developed a peculiar technique essential for performance of ultramodern vocal works. She devoted herself to a detailed study of Schoenberg's *Pierrot lunaire*, which became one of her finest interpretations. She mastered the most challenging techniques of new vocal music, including fractional intervals. She also mastered foreign languages so as to be able to perform a wide European repertoire. She became a faithful interpreter of the most demanding works by modern composers, among them Boulez, Crumb, Druckman, Maxwell Davies, Ligeti, Carter, and Davidovsky. She also developed a fine repertoire of Renaissance songs, and soon became a unique phenomenon as a lieder artist, excelling in an analytical capacity to express the most minute vocal modulations of the melodic line while parsing the words with exquisite intellectual penetration of their meaning, so that even experienced critics found themselves at a loss of superlatives to describe her artistry. From 1973 she taught at the Eastman School of Music. With N. and R. Lloyd, she publ. the useful vol. *The Complete Sightsinger* (1980).

Degrada, Francesco, esteemed Italian musicologist; b. Milan, May 23, 1940. He studied piano, composition, and conducting at the Milan Cons., obtaining a simultaneous arts degree from the Univ. of Milan (1964), where he was a prof. (from 1976). He joined the music history faculty of the Univ. of Milan in 1964, where he was prof. (from 1976) and director of the arts dept. (from 1983); also taught at the Milan Cons. (1966–73) and gave lectures at various European and U.S. univs., including N.Y. Univ. (1986). His interest in Baroque music led him to organize the chamber group Complesso Barocco di Milan in 1967, with which he was associated as director and harpsichordist until 1976. His research ranges from the Renaissance period to the contemporary era. In addition to numerous scholarly articles in various publications, he has also ed. works by Pergolesi, Vivaldi, Durante, D. Scarlatti, and Sarti.

WRITINGS: *Al gran sole carico d'amore. Per un nuovo teatro musicale* (Milan, 1974; 2d ed., 1977); *Sylvano Bussotti e il suo teatro* (Milan, 1976); *Antonio Vivaldi da Venezia all'Europa* (Milan, 1977); *Il palazzo incantato. Studi sulla tradizione del melodramma dal Barocco al Romanticismo* (2 vols., Florence, 1979); *Vivaldi veneziano europeo* (Florence, 1980); ed. *Studi Pergolesiani/Pergolesi Studies* (2 vols., N.Y., 1986, 1988); *Andrea Gabrieli e il suo tempo* (Florence, 1988).

De Koven, (Henry Louis) Reginald, American composer; b. Middletown, Conn., April 3, 1859; d. Chicago, Jan. 16, 1920. He was educated in Europe from 1870, taking his degree at St. John's College, Oxford, in 1879. Before this he studied piano under W. Speidel at Stuttgart, and after graduation studied there another year under Lebert (piano) and Pruckner (harmony). After a 6-month course in Frankfurt am Main under Hauff (composition), he studied singing with Vannuccini at Florence, and operatic composition under Genée in Vienna and Delibes in Paris. In 1902 he organized the Phil. Orch. at Washington, D.C., which he conducted for 3 seasons. He was music critic for the *Chicago Evening Post* (1889–90), *Harper's Weekly* (1895–97), *N.Y. World* (1898–1900; 1907–12), and later for the *N.Y. Herald*.

WORKS: OPERETTAS: *The Begum* (Philadelphia, Nov. 7, 1887); *Don Quixote* (Boston, Nov. 18, 1889); *Robin Hood* (Chicago, June 9, 1890; as *Maid Marian*, London, Jan. 5, 1891; the celebrated song "O Promise Me" was introduced into the score shortly after its first perf.; it was originally publ. as a separate song in 1889); *The Fencing Master* (Boston, 1892); *The Knickerbockers* (Boston, 1893); *The Algerian* (Philadelphia, 1893); *Rob Roy* (Detroit, 1894); *The Tzigane* (N.Y., 1895); *The Mandarin* (Cleveland, 1896); *The Paris Doll* (Hartford, Conn., 1897); *The Highwayman* (New Haven, 1897); and the following, all of which had their premieres in New York: *The 3 Dragoons* (1899); *Red Feather* (1903); *Happyland* (1905); *Student King* (1906); *The Golden Butterfly* (1907); *The Beauty Spot* (1909); *The Wedding Trip* (1911); *Her Little Highness* (1913). A grand opera, *The Canterbury Pilgrims*, was produced at the Metropolitan Opera, New York, March 8, 1917; another grand opera, *Rip van Winkle*, was performed by the Chicago Grand Opera (Jan. 2, 1920).

BIBL.: A. de Koven, *A Musician and His Wife* (N.Y., 1926).

Delalande (also **de La Lande, Lalande**, etc.), **Michel-Richard,** noted French organist, harpsichordist, and composer; b. Paris, Dec. 15, 1657; d. Versailles, June 18, 1726. He was the 15th child of a Paris tailor. He joined the choir of the royal church of St.-Germain-l'Auxerrois about 1666 and sang there until his voice broke at age 15. He became a distinguished organist and harpsichordist, giving instruction on the latter to 2 of the daughters of Louis XIV by his mistress Mme. de Montespan. He was also active as a church organist in Paris. In 1683 he became 1 of the 4 sous-maîtres of the Royal Chapel; he was in sole charge from 1714 until 1723, when Louis XV restored the other 3 positions; he then was joined by Campra, Bernier, and Gervais. In 1685 he was named compositeur de la musique de la chambre, a title he solely held from 1709 to 1718. He also was surintendant de la musique de la chambre from 1689 to 1719. He was made a Chevalier of the Order of St. Michel by Louis XV in 1722. Delalande's grand motets are outstanding, being notable for their mastery of the Versailles style. He is also distinguished by his music for the stage. He deftly used music from his ballets and divertissements in his Sinfonies pour les soupers du Roi, which were played at the dinners of Louis XIV and Louis XV.

WORKS: DRAMATIC: OPERA BALLET: *Les Éléments* (Tuileries Palace, Paris, Dec. 31, 1721; major portion by Destouches; ed. by d'Indy, 1883). BALLETS, PASTORALES, AND DIVERTISSEMENTS: *La Sérénade* (Fontainebleau, 1682); *L'Amour berger* (Paris, 1683); *Les Fontaines de Versailles* (Versailles, April 5, 1683); *Epithalame* (Versailles, June 25, 1685; music not extant); *Le Ballet de la jeunesse* (Versailles, Jan. 28, 1686); *Le Palais de Flore* (Versailles, Jan. 5, 1689); *Ballet de M. de La Lande* (Versailles, Aug. 25, 1691); *Adonis* (1696); *L'Amour, fléchy par la constance* (Fontainebleau, 1697); *La Noce de village* (Sceaux, Feb. 21, 1700); *L'Hymen champestre* (Marly, 1700); *Ode à la louange du Roy* (Sceaux, Oct. 24, 1704; music not extant); *Ballet de la paix* (Marly, July 1713); *L'Inconnu* (Paris, Feb. 1720); *Les Folies de Cardenio* (Paris, Dec. 30, 1720); etc.

BIBL.: J. Richards, *The "Grand Motet" of the Late Baroque in France as Exemplified by M.-R. d.L.* (diss., Univ. of Southern Calif., 1950).

De Lamarter, Eric, American organist, conductor, music critic, teacher, and composer; b. Lansing, Mich., Feb. 18, 1880; d. Orlando, Fla., May 17, 1953. He studied organ with Fairclough in St. Paul, Middleschulte in Chicago, and Guilmant and Widor in Paris (1901–2), then held several organ positions in Chicago, notably with the 4th Presbyterian Church (1914–36). He was music critic for the *Chicago Inter-Ocean* (1901–14), the *Chicago Record-Herald* (1905–08), and the *Chicago Tribune* (1909–10); he also taught at Olivet College (1904–5), Chicago Musical College (1909–10), Univ. of Missouri, Ohio State Univ., and the Univ. of Texas. He was assistant conductor of the Chicago Sym. Orch. and conductor of the Chicago Civic Orch. (1918–36). His compositions include *The Betrothal*, incidental music (N.Y., Nov. 19, 1918), and *The Black Orchid*, suite taken from *The Dance of Life*, ballet (Chicago, Feb. 27, 1931).

Delannoy, Marcel, French composer; b. La Ferté-Alais, July 9, 1898; d. Nantes, Sept. 14, 1962. He took lessons with Gédalge and Honegger. He wrote an effective stage work, *Poirier de Misère* (Paris, Feb. 21, 1927), which obtained excellent success. Other stage works are the ballet cantata *Le Fou de la dame* (concert perf., Paris, Nov. 9, 1928; stage perf., Geneva, April 6, 1929), *Cinderella*, ballet (Chicago, Aug. 30, 1931; rev. as *La Pantoufle de vair*, Paris, May 14, 1935), *Ginevra*, comic opera (Paris, July 25, 1942), *Arlequin radiophile*, chamber opera (Paris, April 1, 1946), *Puck*, fairy opera after Shakespeare (Strasbourg, Jan. 29, 1949), *Travesti*, ballet (Enghien-les-Bains, June 4, 1952), and *Les Noces fantastiques*, ballet (Paris, Feb. 9, 1955).

Delcroix, Léon Charles, Belgian composer; b. Brussels, Sept. 15, 1880; d. there, Nov. 14, 1938. He studied piano with J. Wieniawski, organ with A. Mailly, and composition with Ysaÿe in Brussels and d'Indy in Paris. He conducted theater orchs. in Belgium (1909–27); then devoted himself to composition, numbering among his compositions the opera *Le Petit Poucet* (Brussels, Oct. 9, 1913) and the ballet *La Bacchante*, ballet (Ghent, 1912). He wrote a biography of J. Wieniawski (Brussels, 1908).

Deldevez, Edouard (-Marie-Ernest), French conductor and composer; b. Paris, May 31, 1817; d. there, Nov. 6, 1897. He studied violin with Habeneck and music theory with Halevy and Berton at the Paris Cons. He was assistant conductor (1859–73) and then principal conductor (1873–77) at the Paris Opéra; he also was assistant conductor (1860–72) and then principal conductor (1872–85) of the Société des Concerts du Conservatoire. He taught orch. playing at the Paris Cons. (1874–85). He composed the operas *Samson* and *Le Violon enchanté*, and the ballets *Eucharis* (1844), *Paquita* (1846), and *Vert-Vert* (1851, with Tolbecque).

WRITINGS: *Curiosités musicales* (1873); *L'Art du chef d'orchestre* (1878); *La Société des Concerts de 1860 à 1885* (1887); *De l'exécution d'ensemble* (1888); Mes mémoires (1890); *Le Passé à propos du présent* (1892).

de Leone, Francesco (Bartolomeo), American conductor, pedagogue, and composer; b. Ravenna, Ohio (of Italian parents), July 28, 1887; d. Akron, Ohio, Dec. 10, 1948. He studied at Dana's Musical Inst., Warren, Ohio (1901–03), and at the Royal Cons. of Naples (1903–10); returning to the United States, he settled in Akron, Ohio, where he founded the de Leone School of Music and organized and directed the music dept. of the Univ. of Akron; he also conducted the Akron Sym. Orch. He wrote the operas *Alglala* (Akron, May 23, 1924) and *A Millionaire Caprice* (in Italian; Naples, July 26, 1910), the operettas *Cave Man Stuff* and *Princess Ting-Ah-Ling*, and the sacred musical dramas *Ruth*, *The Prodigal Son*, *The Golden Calf*, and *David*.

Delibes, (Clément-Philibert-) Léo, famous French composer; b. St.-Germain-du-Val, Sarthe, Feb. 21, 1836; d. Paris, Jan. 16, 1891. He received his early musical training with his mother and an uncle, then enrolled in the Paris Cons. in 1847 as a student of Tariot. He won a premier prix in solfège in 1850, and also studied organ with Benoist and composition with Adam. In 1853 he became organist of St. Pierre de Chaillot and accompanist at the Théâtre-Lyrique. In 1856 his first work for the stage, *Deux sous de charbon*, a 1-act operetta, humorously designated an "asphyxie lyrique," was produced at the Folies-Nouvelles. His 2d work, the opérette bouffe *Deux vieilles gardes*, won considerable acclaim at its premiere at the Bouffes-Parisiens on Aug. 8, 1856. Several more operettas were to follow, as well as his first substantial work for the stage, *Le Jardinier et son seigneur*, given at the Théâtre-Lyrique on May 1, 1863. In 1864 he became chorus master of the Paris Opéra. With Louis Minkus, he collaborated on the ballet score *La Source*, which was heard for the first time at the Paris Opéra, on Nov. 12, 1866. It was with his next ballet, *Coppélia, ou La Fille aux yeux d'émail*, that Delibes achieved lasting fame after its premiere at the Paris Opéra on May 25, 1870. Another ballet, *Sylvia, ou La Nymphe de Diane* (Paris Opéra, June 14, 1876), was equally successful. He then wrote a grand opera, *Jean de Nivelle* (Opéra Comique, March 8, 1880), which was moderately successful; it was followed by his triumphant masterpiece, the opera *Lakmé* (Opéra Comique, April 14, 1883), in which he created a most effective lyric evocation of India; the "Bell Song" from *Lakmé* became a perennial favorite in recitals. In 1881 he was appointed prof. of composition at the Paris Cons.; in 1884, was elected a member of the Inst. His last opera, *Kassya*, was completed but not orchestrated at the time of his death; Massenet orchestrated the score, and it was premiered at the Opéra Comique on March 24, 1893. Delibes was a master of melodious elegance and harmonious charm; his music possessed an autonomous flow in colorful timbres, and a finality of excellence that seemed effortless while subtly revealing a mastery of the Romantic technique of composition.

WORKS: DRAMATIC (all 1st perf. at the Bouffes-Parisiens in Paris unless otherwise given): *Deux sous de charbon, ou Le Suicide de Bigorneau*, asphyxie lyrique (Folies-Nouvelles, Feb. 9, 1856); *Deux vieilles gardes,* opérette bouffe (Aug. 8, 1856); *Six demoiselles à marier,* opérette bouffe (Nov. 12, 1856); *Maître Griffard,* opéra comique (Théâtre-Lyrique, Oct. 3, 1857); *La Fille du golfe,* opéra comique (publ. 1859); *L'Omelette à la Follembuche,* opérette bouffe (June 8, 1859); *Monsieur de Bonne-Etoile,* opéra comique (Feb. 4, 1860); *Les Musiciens de l'orchestre,* opérette bouffe (Jan. 25, 1861; in collaboration with Offenbach, Hignard, and Erlanger); *Les Eaux d'Ems,* comédie (1861); *Mon ami Pierrot,* operette (1862); *Le Jardinier et son seigneur,* opéra comique (Théâtre-Lyrique, May 1, 1863); *La Tradition,* prologue en vers (Jan. 5, 1864); *Grande nouvelle,* operette (publ. 1864); *Le Serpent à plumes,* farce (Dec. 16, 1864); *Le Boeuf Apis,* opéra bouffe (April 25, 1865); *La Source, ou Naila,* ballet (Opéra, Nov. 12, 1866; in collaboration with Louis Minkus); *Valse, ou Pas de fleurs,* divertissement (Opéra, Nov. 12, 1867; for Adam's *Le Corsaire*); *Malbrough s'en va-t-en guerre*, Act 4, opérette bouffe (Athénée, Dec. 13, 1867; Act 1 by Bizet, 2 by E. Jonas, and 3 by Legouix); *L'écossais de Chatou,* operette (Jan. 16, 1869); *La Cour du roi Petaud,* opéra bouffe (Variétés, April 24, 1869); *Coppélia, ou La Fille aux yeux d'email,* ballet (Opéra, May 25, 1870); *Le Roi l'a dit,* opéra comique (Opéra Comique, May 24, 1873); *Sylvia, ou La Nymphe de Diane,* ballet (Opéra, June 14, 1876); *Jean de Nivelle,* opera (Opéra Comique, March 8, 1880); *Le Roi s'amuse, six airs de danse dans le style ancien,* incidental music to Hugo's play (Comédie-Française, Nov. 22, 1882); *Lakmé,* opera (Opéra Comique, April 14, 1883); *Kassya,* drame lyrique (Opéra Comique, March 24, 1893; orchestrated by Massenet); also sketches for *Le Roi des montagnes,* opéra comique; 2 works not extant: *Le Don Juan suisse,* opéra bouffe, and *La Princesse Ravigote,* opéra bouffe.

BIBL.: E. Guiraud, *Notice sur la vie et les oeuvres de L. D.* (Paris, 1892); H. de Curzon, *L. D.* (Paris, 1926); A. Coquis, *L. D.: Sa vie et son oeuvre (1836–1891)* (Paris, 1957); W. Studwell, ed., *Adolphe Adam and L. D.: A Guide to Research* (N.Y., 1987).

Delius, Frederick (Fritz Theodor Albert), significant English composer of German parentage; b. Bradford, Jan. 29, 1862; d. Grez-sur-Loing, France, June 10, 1934. His father was a successful merchant, owner of a wool company; he naturally hoped to have his son follow a career in industry, but did not object to his study of art and music. Delius learned to play the piano and violin. At the age of 22 he went to Solano, Fla., to work on an orange plantation owned by his father; a musical souvenir of his sojourn there was his symphonic suite *Florida*. There he met an American organist, Thomas F. Ward, who gave him a thorough instruction in theory; this study, which lasted 6 months, gave Delius a foundation for his further progress in music. In 1885 he went to Danville, Va., as a teacher. In 1886 he enrolled at the Leipzig Cons., where he took courses in harmony and counterpoint with Reinecke, Sitt, and Jadassohn. It was there that he met Grieg, becoming his friend and admirer. Indeed, Grieg's music found a deep resonance in his own compositions. An even more powerful influence was Wagner, whose principles of continuous melodic line and thematic development Delius adopted in his own works. Euphonious serenity reigns on the symphonic surface of his music, diversified by occasional resolvable dissonances. In some works, he made congenial use of English folk motifs, often in elaborate variation forms. Particularly successful are his evocative symphonic sketches *On Hearing the First Cuckoo in Spring*, *North Country Sketches*, *Brigg Fair*, and *A Song of the High Hills*. His orch. nocturne *Paris: The Song of a Great City* is a tribute to a city in which he spent many years of his life. Much more ambitious in scope is his choral work *A Mass of Life*, in which he draws on passages from Nietzsche's *Also sprach Zarathustra*.

Delius settled in Paris in 1888; in 1897 he moved to Grez-sur-Loing, near Paris, where he remained for the rest of his life, except for a few short trips abroad. In 1903 he married the painter Jelka Rosen. His music began to win recognition in England and Germany; he became a favorite composer of Sir Thomas Beecham, who gave numerous performances of his music in London. But these successes came too late for Delius; a syphilitic infection that he had contracted early in life eventually grew into an incurable illness accompanied by paralysis and blindness; as Beecham phrased it, "Delius had suffered a heavy blow in the defection of his favorite goddess, Aphrodite Pandemos, who had returned his devotions with an affliction which was to break out many years later." Still eager to compose, he engaged as his amanuensis the English musician Eric Fenby, who wrote down music at the dictation of Delius, including complete orch. scores. In 1929 Beecham organized a Delius Festival in London (6 concerts; Oct. 12 to Nov. 1, 1929) and the composer was brought from France to hear it. In the same year Delius was made a Companion of Honour by King George V and an Hon.Mus.D. by Oxford. A film was made by the British filmmaker Ken Russell on the life and works of Delius. However, he remains a solitary figure in modern music. Affectionately appreciated in England, in America, and to some extent in Germany, his works are rarely performed elsewhere.

WORKS: DRAMATIC: *Zanoni*, incidental music after Bulwer Lytton (1888; unfinished); *Irmelin*, opera (1890–92; Oxford, May 4, 1953); *The Magic Foundation*, lyric drama (1893–95; BBC, London, Nov. 20, 1977); *Koanga*, lyric drama (1895–97; Elberfeld, March 30, 1904); *Folkeraadet*, incidental music to G. Heiberg's drama (Christiania, Oct. 18, 1897); *A Village Romeo and Juliet*, lyric drama (1899–1901; Berlin, Feb. 21, 1907); *Margot la Rouge*, lyric drama (1902; concert perf. BBC, London, Feb. 21, 1982; stage perf., St. Louis, June 8, 1983); *Fennimore and Gerda*, opera (1908–10; Frankfurt am Main, Oct. 21, 1919); *Hassan, or The Golden Journey to Samarkand*, incidental music to J. Flecker's drama (1920–23; Darmstadt, June 1, 1923; full version, London, Sept. 20, 1923).

BIBL.: P. Heseltine, *F. D.* (London, 1923; 2d ed., rev., 1952); R. Hull, *F. D.* (London, 1928); E. Fenby, *D. as I Knew Him* (London, 1936; 3d ed., 1966); A. Hutchings, *D., A Critical Biography* (London, 1948); T. Beecham, *F. D.* (London, 1959; 2d ed., rev., 1975); G. Jahoda, *The Road to Samarkand: F. D. and His Music* (N.Y., 1969); E. Fenby, *D.* (London, 1971); L. Carley and R. Threlfall, *D. and America* (London, 1972); A. Jefferson, *D.* (London, 1972); R. Lowe, *F. D., 1862–1934; A Catalogue of the Music Archives of the D. Trust, London* (London, 1974); L. Carley, *D.: The Paris Years* (London, 1975); C. Palmer, *D.: Portrait of a Cosmopolitan* (London, 1976); C. Redwood, ed., *A D. Companion* (London, 1976; 2d ed., 1980); L. Carley and R. Threlfall, *D.: A Life in Pictures* (London, 1977; 2d ed., 1984); R. Threlfall, *F. D. (1862–1934): A Catalogue of the Compositions* (London, 1977); C. Redwood, *Flecker and D.: The Making of "Hassan"* (London, 1978); L. Carley, *D.: A Life in Letters*: vol. 1, *1862–1908* (London, 1983; Cambridge, Mass., 1984) and vol. 2, *1909–1934* (Aldershot, 1988); R. Threlfall, *F. D.: A Supplementary Catalogue* (London, 1986); P. Jones, *The American Source of D.' Style* (N.Y., 1989); L. Carley, ed., *Grieg and D.: A Chronicle of their Friendship in Letters* (N.Y., 1993); idem, ed., *F. D.: Music, Art and Literature* (Aldershot, 1998).

Della Casa, Lisa, noted Swiss soprano; b. Burgdorf, Feb. 2, 1919. She commenced vocal studies with Margarete Haeser in Zürich when she was 15. She made her operatic debut as Cio-Cio-San in Solothurn-Biel (1941), then was a member of the Zürich Stadttheater (1943–50). She made her first appearance at the Salzburg Festival as Zdenka in 1947, then appeared as the Countess in *Le nozze di Figaro* at the Glyndebourne Festival in 1951. That same year she sang Sophie and Arabella, her most celebrated portrayal, in Munich. She subsequently was a leading member of the Vienna State Opera (1952–74). She made her Metropolitan Opera debut in New York as Mozart's Countess on Nov. 20, 1953, and continued to sing there with distinction until 1968. Della Casa was chosen to sing the role of the Marschallin at the opening of the new Salzburg Festspielhaus (1960). She was held in great esteem for her remarkable portrayals of roles in operas by Mozart and Richard Strauss.

BIBL.: D. Debeljevirć, *Ein Leben mit L. d. C.* (Zürich, 1975).

Della Corte, Andrea, eminent Italian musicologist; b. Naples, April 5, 1883; d. Turin, March 12, 1968. He was self-taught in music; he devoted himself mainly to musical biography and analysis. He taught music history at the Turin Cons. (1926–53) and at the Univ. of Turin (1939–53). From 1919 till 1967 he was music critic of *La Stampa*. Among his many writings are *Paisiello* (Turin, 1922), *L'opera comica italiana del 1700* (2 vols., Bari, 1923), *Niccolò Piccinni* (Bari, 1928), with G. Pannain, *Vincenzo Bellini* (Turin, 1936), *Pergolesi* (Turin, 1936), *Un Italiano all'estero: Antonio Salieri* (Turin, 1937), *Tre secoli di opera italiana* (Turin, 1938), *Verdi* (Turin, 1939), *Toscanini* (Vicenza, 1946), *Le sei più belle opere di Verdi: Rigoletto, Il Trovatore, La Traviata, Aida, Otello, Falstaff* (Milan, 1947), and *Gluck* (Florence, 1948).

Della Maria, (Pierre-Antoine-) Dominique, French opera composer; b. Marseilles, June 14, 1769; d. Paris, March 9, 1800. Son of an Italian mandolinist, he was remarkably precocious. He played the mandolin and cello at an early age, and at 18 produced a grand opera at Marseilles. He then studied composition in Italy (for a time with Paisiello) and produced in Naples a successful opera, *Il maestro di cappella* (1792). He went to Paris in 1796; obtaining a libretto *(Le Prisonnier)* from Duval, he set it to music in 8 days, brought it out at the Opéra Comique (Jan. 29, 1798), and was at once famous. Before his death he finished 6 more operas, 4 of which were produced during his lifetime; a posthumous opera, *La Fausse Duegne* (completed by Blangini), was produced at Paris in 1802.

Delle Sedie, Enrico, Italian baritone and singing teacher; b. Livorno, June 17, 1822; d. La Garennes-Colombes, near Paris, Nov. 28, 1907. His teachers were Galeffi, Persanola, and Domeniconi. After imprisonment as a revolutionist (1848), he resumed the study of singing and made his debut in San Casciano (1851) in Verdi's *Nabucco*. Until 1861 he sang in the principal Italian cities; appeared in London in 1861, and then was engaged at the Théâtre-Italien, Paris, and was prof. of singing in the Cons. (1867–71); he was regarded as one of the best singing teachers in Paris. His basic manuals, *Arte e fisiologia del canto* (Milan, 1876; in French as *L'Art lyrique*, Paris, 1876) and *L'estetica del canto e dell'arte melodrammatica* (Milan, 1886), were publ. in New York in Eng. as *Vocal Art* (3 parts) and *Esthetics of the Art of Singing, and of the Melodrama* (4 vols.). A condensation (by the author) of both manuals was publ. in 1 vol. as *A Complete Method of Singing* (N.Y., 1894).

Deller, Alfred (George), English countertenor; b. Margate, May 31, 1912; d. Bologna, July 16, 1979. He studied voice with his father; began singing as a boy soprano, later developing the alto range. He sang in the choirs of the Canterbury Cathedral (1940–47) and at St. Paul's in London. In 1950 he formed his own vocal and instrumental ensemble, the Deller Consort, acting as conductor and soloist in a repertoire of early English music. This unique enterprise led to a modest revival of English madrigals of the

Renaissance. In 1963 he founded the Stour Music Festival in Kent. Britten wrote the part of Oberon in his *A Midsummer Night's Dream* for him. In 1970 Deller was named a Commander of the Order of the British Empire.

BIBL.: M. and M. Hardwick, *A. D.: A Singularity of Voice* (London, 1968; 2d ed., rev., 1982).

Dellinger, Rudolf, German composer and conductor; b. Graslitz, Bohemia, July 8, 1857; d. Dresden, Sept. 24, 1910. He was a pupil at the Prague Cons. He played clarinet in the city orch. at Brünn, becoming 2d conductor there in 1880; in 1883, occupied the same post at the Carl Schulze Theater in Hamburg, and from 1893 until his death he was conductor at the Residenz-Theater in Dresden. He produced the operettas *Don Caesar* (Hamburg, March 28, 1885; highly popular), *Lorraine* (Hamburg, 1886), *Capitän Fracassa* (Hamburg, 1889), *Saint-Cyr* (Hamburg, 1891), *Die Chansonnette* (Dresden, 1894; Prague, 1895, as Die *Sängerin*), *Jadwiga* (Dresden, 1901), and *Der letzte Jonas* (1910).

Dello Joio, Norman, able American composer and teacher; b. N.Y., Jan. 24, 1913. His family's original name was Ioio. His father, grandfather, and great-grandfather were church organists. Dello Joio acquired skill as an organist and pianist at home; at the age of 12, he occasionally substituted for his father on his job at the Church of Our Lady of Mount Carmel in New York He took additional organ lessons from his godfather, the well-known Italian-born American organist, composer and teacher Pietro Yon (b. Settimo Vittone, Aug. 8, 1886; d. Huntington, N.Y., Nov. 22, 1943), and studied piano with Gaston Déthier at the Inst. of Musical Art in New York (1933–38); in the meantime, he played jazz piano in various groups in New York. From 1939 to 1941 he studied composition with Wagenaar at the Juilliard School of Music in New York; in 1941 he enrolled in the summer class of composition led by Hindemith at the Berkshire Music Center in Tanglewood; he continued to attend Hindemith's courses at Yale Univ. from 1941 to 1943. During this period he wrote several works of considerable validity, among them a piano trio, a ballet entitled *The Duke of Sacramento*, a Magnificat, a Piano Sonata, and other pieces. He taught composition at Sarah Lawrence College (1945–50); he held 2 consecutive Guggenheim fellowships (1944, 1945), and composed music with utmost facility and ingratiating felicity. His *Concert Music* was premiered by the Pittsburgh Sym. Orch., conducted by Fritz Reiner, on Jan. 4, 1946, and his *Ricercari* for Piano and Orch. was introduced by the N.Y. Phil. on Dec. 19, 1946, with George Szell conducting, with the piano part played by Dello Joio himself. There followed a number of major works in a distinctive Joioan manner, some of them deeply rooted in medieval ecclesiasticism, profoundly liturgical, and yet overtly modern in their neomodal moderately dissonant counterpoint. He also exhibited a flair for writing on topical American themes, ranging from impressions of the Cloisters in New York to rhythmic modalities of Manhattan's Little Italy. On May 9, 1950, at Sarah Lawrence College, he produced his first opera, *The Triumph of Joan*; he later used its thematic material in a sym. in 3 movements, *The Triumph of St. Joan*, originally titled *Seraphic Dialogue*. He then wrote another opera on the subject of St. Joan, to his own libretto, *The Trial of Rouen*, first performed on television, by the NBC Opera Theater, April 8, 1956; still another version of the St. Joan theme was an opera in which Dello Joio used the original title, *The Triumph of St. Joan*, but composed the music anew; it had its premiere at the N.Y. City Opera on April 16, 1959. In 1957 Dello Joio received the Pulitzer Prize in Music for his *Meditations on Ecclesiastes*, scored for string orch.; it was first performed in Washington, D.C., on Dec. 17, 1957, but the material was used previously for a ballet, *There Is a Time*. In 1961 he produced an opera, *Blood Moon*, brought out by the San Francisco Opera, to a scenario dealing with the life and times of an adventurous actress, Adah Menken, who exercised her charms in New Orleans at the time of the Civil War. Returning to liturgical themes, Dello Joio composed three masses (1968, 1975, 1976). He continued his activities as a teacher; from 1956 to 1972 he was on the faculty of the Mannes College of Music in New York; from 1972 to 1979 he taught at Boston Univ. He held honorary doctorates in music from Lawrence College in Wisconsin (1959), Colby College in Maine (1963), and the Univ. of Cincinnati (1969). He received the N.Y. Music Critics' Circle Award in 1947 and 1959.

WORKS: DRAMATIC: *Prairie*, ballet (1942; arranged from the Sinfonietta, 1941); *The Duke of Sacramento*, ballet (1942); *On Stage*, ballet (1945); *Diversion of Angels*, ballet (New London, Conn., Aug. 13, 1948; for Martha Graham); *The Triumph of Joan*, opera (1949; Bronxville, N.Y., May 9, 1950; withdrawn); *The Triumph of St. Joan Symphony*, ballet (Louisville, Dec. 5, 1951; based on the opera *The Triumph of St. Joan*; rechoreographed as *Seraphic Dialogue* [by Martha Graham], 1955); *The Ruby*, opera (1953; Bloomington, Ind., May 13, 1955); *The Tall Kentuckian*, incidental music to B. Anderson's play (Louisville, June 15, 1953); *The Trial at Rouen*, opera (1955; NBC-TV, April 8, 1956; rev. as *The Triumph of St. Joan*, N.Y., April 16, 1959); *There Is a Time*, ballet (1956; arranged from *Meditations on Ecclesiastes* for Strings, 1956); *Air Power*, television music (1956–57; arranged as a symphonic suite, 1957); *Profile of a Composer*, television music (CBS-TV, Feb. 16, 1958; includes *Ballad of the 7 Lively Arts*); *Here Is New York*, television music (1959; includes excerpts from *New York Profiles*; arranged as an orch. suite); *The Saintmaker's Christmas Eve*, television music (1959); *Vanity Fair*, television music (1959); *Women's Song*, ballet (1960; arranged from the Harp Concerto, 1945); *Anthony and Cleopatra*, incidental music to Shakespeare's play (1960); *Time of Decision*, television music (1962); *The Louvre*, television music (1965; arranged for Band, 1965); *A Time of Snow*, ballet (1968; arranged for Band as *Songs of Abelard*, 1969); *The Glass Heart*, ballet (1968; arranged from *Meditations on Ecclesiastes* for Strings, 1956); *Satiric Dances for a Comedy by Aristophanes* for Band (1974; Concord, Mass., July 17, 1975); *As of a Dream*, masque (1978).

BIBL.: T. Bumgardner, *N. D. J.* (Boston, 1986).

Dell'Orefice, Giuseppe, Italian composer; b. Fara, Abruzzio Chietino, Aug. 22, 1848; d. Naples, Jan. 3, 1889. He was a pupil of Fenaroli and Miceli at the Naples Cons. From 1878 he was conductor at the San Carlo Theater in Naples. He wrote the ballet *I fantasmi notturni* (Naples, 1872) and the operas *Romilda de' Bardi* (Naples, 1874), *Egmont* (Naples, 1878), *Il segreto della Duchesa* (Naples, 1879), and *L'oasi* (Vicenza, 1886).

Del Mar, Norman (René), respected English conductor, teacher, and writer on music; b. London, July 31, 1919; d. Bushey, Feb. 6, 1994. He studied composition with Morris and Vaughan Williams at the Royal College of Music in London, and also had lessons in conducting with Lambert. In 1944 he founded the Chelsea Sym. Orch., with which he championed rarely performed works in England. He also played horn in and was assistant conductor of the Royal Phil. In London (1947–48). From 1949 to 1955 he was principal conductor of the English Opera Group, and from 1953 to 1960 conductor and prof. at the Guildhall School of Music in London. In 1954–55 he was conductor with the Yorkshire Sym. Orch. After serving as principal conductor of the BBC Scottish Sym. in Glasgow (1960–65), he was principal guest conductor of the Göteborg Sym. Orch. (1969–73). In 1972 he joined the faculty of the Royal College of Music, where he taught conducting and conducted its First Orch. He also conducted the chamber orch. of the Royal Academy of Music in London (1973–77) and was principal conductor of the Academy of the BBC (1974–77), a training ensemble. After serving as principal guest conductor of the Bournemouth Sinfonietta (1982–85), he was artistic director of the Århus Sym. Orch. (1985–88). In 1990 he retired from the faculty of the Royal College of Music. In 1975 he was made a Commander of the Order of the British Empire. Among his many writings were *Paul Hindemith* (London, 1957) and *Richard Strauss: A Critical Commentary of His Life and Works* (3 vols., London, 1962, 1968, 1972).

Delmas, Jean-François, famous French bass-baritone; b. Lyons, April 14, 1861; d. St. Alban de Monthel, Sept. 29, 1933. He was a pupil of Bussine and Obin at the Paris Cons., where he won the premier prix for singing in 1886. He made his operatic debut at the Paris Opéra in 1886 as St.-Bris in *Les Huguenots*; he then was a regular member there until his retirement in 1927, idolized by the public, and unexcelled as an interpreter of Wagner, in whose works he created the principal bass parts in several French premieres; he created also the chief roles in Massenet's *Le Mage* (1891) and *Thaïs* (1894), Leroux's *Astarté* (1901), Saint-Saëns's *Les Barbares* (1901), and Erlanger's *Le Fils de l'étoile* (1904). In addition to his enormous French repertoire, Delmas also sang in the operas of Gluck, Mozart, and Weber.

Delmas, Marc-Jean-Baptiste, talented French composer; b. St. Quentin, March 28, 1885; d. Paris, Nov. 30, 1931. He was a pupil of Vidal and Leroux; won the Prix de Rossini (1911), the Grand Prix de Rome (1919), the Chartier Prix for chamber music, the Prix Cressent, and other awards for various compositions. He composed the operas *Jean de Calais* (1907), *Laïs* (1909), *Stéfano* (1910), *Cyrca* (1920), *Iriam* (1921), *Anne-Marie* (1922), and *Le Giaour* (1925). He wrote the books *Georges Bizet* (Paris, 1930), *Gustave Charpentier et le lyrisme française* (Coulommiers, 1931), and *Massenet: Sa vie, ses oeuvres* (Paris, 1932).

Del Monaco, Giancarlo, Italian opera producer and administrator, son of **Mario Del Monaco**; b. Venice, Dec. 27, 1943. He received training in languages and music in Lausanne. In 1964 he staged his first opera, *Samson et Dalila*, in Siracusa, and then was an assistant to Günter Rennert, Wieland Wagner, and Walter Felsenstein (1965–68). After serving as personal assistant to the general director of the Vienna State Opera (1968–70), he was principal stage director in Ulm (1970–73). From 1980 to 1982 he was Intendant of the Kassel State Theater, and then was director of the Macerata Festival from 1986 to 1988. In 1989 he staged *La forza del destino* at the Vienna State Opera, *La Fille du régiment* in Zürich, and *Samson et Dalila* in Barcelona. His production of *Les Huguenots* opened the new opera house in Montpellier in 1990. In 1991 he staged *La fanciulla del West* at the Metropolitan Opera in New York. From 1992 to 1997 he was Intendant of the Bonn Opera, where his productions included *Cavalleria rusticana* and *Pagliacci* (1993), *Les Contes d'Hoffmann* (1994), and *Manon Lescaut* (1995). In 1997 he staged *Aida* in Cologne. He became general director of the Nice Opera in 1997.

Del Monaco, Mario, renowned Italian tenor, father of **Giancarlo Del Monaco**; b. Florence, July 27, 1915; d. Mestre, near Venice, Oct. 16, 1982. His father was a government functionary, but his mother loved music and sang. Del Monaco haunted provincial opera theaters, determined to be a singer; indeed, he sang a minor part in a theater in Mondolfo, near Pesaro, when he was only 13. Rather than take formal voice lessons, he listened to operatic recordings; at 19 he entered the Rossini Cons. in Pesaro, but left it after an unhappy semester of academic vocal training with unimaginative teachers. In 1935 he won a prize in a singing contest in Rome. In 1939 he made his operatic debut as Turriddu in Pesaro. On Jan. 1, 1941, he made his Milan debut as Pinkerton, but had to serve time out in the Italian army during World War II. After the war's end, he developed a busy career singing opera in a number of Italian theaters, including La Scala of Milan. In 1946 he sang at the Teatro Colón in Buenos Aires, and also in Rio de Janeiro, Mexico City, and at London's Covent Garden. On Sept. 26, 1950, he sang the role of Radames at the San Francisco Opera in his first appearance in the United States; on Nov. 27, 1950, he made his Metropolitan Opera debut in New York as Des Grieux in *Manon Lescaut*; he continued to sing at the Metropolitan until 1958 in virtually every famous tenor part, including Don José, Manrico, Cavaradossi, Canio, Andrea Chénier, Otello, etc. In 1973 he deemed it prudent to retire, and he spent the rest of his life in a villa near Venice, devoting his leisure to his favorite avocations, sculpture and painting. Del Monaco was buried in his Otello costume, while the funeral hymns were intoned in his own voice on a phonograph record.

Delna (real name, **Ledan**), **Marie,** French contralto; b. Meudon, near Paris, April 3, 1875; d. Paris, July 23, 1932. She was a pupil of Laborde and Savary in Paris, where she made her debut at the Opéra Comique on June 9, 1892, as Dido in Berlioz's *Les Troyens*; sang there for 6 years with great success; she also appeared at London's Covent Garden in 1894. She sang at the Paris Opéra (1898–1901) and at Milan's Teatro Lirico (1898–1901); then again at the Opéra Comique. In 1903 she married a Belgian, A. H. de Saone, and retired temporarily from the stage; her reappearance at the Opéra Comique in 1908 was greatly acclaimed and after that she was a prime favorite. On March 5, 1910, she sang Gluck's Orfeo at her Metropolitan Opera debut in New York and later Marcelline in Bruneau's *L'Attaque du moulin* at the New Theater, making a deep impression; then returned to Paris, where she continued to sing at the Opéra Comique until her retirement in 1922.

De Los Angeles, Victoria. See **Los Angeles** (real name **Gómez Cima**), **Victoria de.**

De Luca, Giuseppe, notable Italian baritone; b. Rome, Dec. 25, 1876; d. N.Y., Aug. 26, 1950. He studied with Vinceslao Persichini at the Accademia di Santa Cecilia in Rome. He made his first professional appearance in Piacenza (Nov. 6, 1897) as Valentine in *Faust*; then sang in various cities of Italy; from 1902, was chiefly in Milan at the Teatro Lirico, and from 1903 at La Scala; he created the principal baritone role in the premieres of *Adriana Lecouvreur* at the Teatro Lirico (Nov. 6, 1902) and *Madama Butterfly* at La Scala (Feb. 17, 1904). He made his Metropolitan Opera debut in New York as Figaro in *Il Barbiere di Siviglia* on Nov. 25, 1915, with excellent success, immediately establishing himself as a favorite; on Jan. 28, 1916, he sang the part of Paquiro in the premiere of *Goyescas* by Granados, at the Metropolitan, of which he was a member until 1935. After a sojourn in Italy, he returned to the United States in 1940, and made a few more appearances at the Metropolitan, his vocal powers undiminished by age; he made his farewell appearance in a concert in New York in 1947. He sang almost exclusively the Italian repertoire; his interpretations were distinguished by fidelity to the dramatic import of his roles and he was praised by critics for his finely graduated dynamic range and his mastery of *bel canto*.

De Lucia, Fernando, famous Italian tenor; b. Naples, Oct. 11, 1860; d. there, Feb. 21, 1925. He made his debut in Naples on March 9, 1885, as Faust, then appeared in London at Drury Lane (1887). On Oct. 31, 1891, he created in Rome the role of Fritz in Mascagni's *L'Amico Fritz*; on Jan. 10, 1894, he made his American debut at the Metropolitan Opera in New York, again as Fritz in Mascagni's opera; he then returned to Europe. He retired from the stage in 1917, singing for the last time in public at Caruso's funeral (1921). De Lucia was one of the finest representatives of the bel canto era, being especially praised for his authentic interpretations of Italian operatic roles, excelling in operas by Rossini, Bellini, and Verdi.

Delune, Louis, Belgian composer; b. Charleroi, March 15, 1876; d. Paris, Jan. 5, 1940. He studied with Tinel at the Brussels Cons.; won the Belgian Prix de Rome with his cantata *La Mort du roi Reynaud* (1905); he then traveled as accompanist for César Thomson. He lived for many years in Paris, and wrote most of his works there, including the opera *Tania* and the ballet *Le Fruit défendu*.

Delvincourt, Claude, outstanding French composer and music educator; b. Paris, Jan. 12, 1888; d. in an automobile accident in Orbetello, Italy, April 5, 1954. He studied with Boellmann, Büsser, Caussade, and Widor at the Paris Cons.; in 1913 he received the Prix de Rome for his cantata *Faust et Hélène* (sharing the prize with Lili Boulanger). He was in the French army during World War I, and on Dec. 31, 1915, he suffered a crippling wound. He recovered in a few years, and devoted himself energetically to musical education and composition. In 1931 he became director of the Versailles Cons.; in 1941 he was appointed director of the Paris Cons. His music was distinguished by strong dramatic and lyric qualities; he was most successful in his stage works, including *Offrande à Siva*, choreographic poem (Frankfurt am Main,

July 3, 1927), *La Femme à barbe*, musical farce (Versailles, June 2, 1938), and *Lucifer*, mystery play (Paris, Dec. 8, 1948).

BIBL.: W. Landowski, *L'Oeuvre de C. D.* (Paris, 1947).

De Main, John (Lee), American conductor; b. Youngstown, Ohio, Jan. 11, 1944. He studied with Adele Marcus (piano; B.A., 1966) and Jorge Mester (conducting; M.S., 1968) at the Juilliard School of Music in New York. He was an assistant conductor at the WNET opera project in New York and in 1972 at the N.Y. City Opera. After serving as assoc. conductor of the St. Paul (Minn.) Chamber Orch. (1972–74), he became music director of the Texas Opera Theater in 1975, the touring company of the Houston Grand Opera. In 1978 he was appointed principal conductor of the Houston Grand Opera, serving as its music director from 1980 to 1994; he also was principal conductor of the Chatauqua (N.Y.) Opera (1982–87) and music director of Opera Omaha (1983–91). He was music director of the Madison (Wis.) Sym. Orch. and artistic director of the Madison (Wis.) Opera from 1994. From 1997 he also was music director of Opera Pacific in Costa Mesa, Calif. In addition to conducting rarely heard works, De Main gave many premiere performances of contemporary operas.

Demian, Wilhelm, Romanian composer and conductor; b. Braşov, June 22, 1910. He studied in his hometown (1925–28) and in Vienna (1929–33); from 1935 to 1940 he conducted the Phil. in Cluj; after 1949 he was conductor of the Hungarian State Opera there. His music is marked by a distinct neoclassical idiom in the manner of the modern German school. Among his works are *Capcana*, opera (1964) and *Attention! On tourne!*, musical (1972).

Demougeot, (Jeanne Marguerite) Marcelle (Decorne), remarkable French soprano; b. Dijon, June 18, 1871; d. Paris, Nov. 24, 1931. She studied in Dijon and Paris. She made her operatic debut at the Paris Opéra in 1902 as Donna Elvira; she continued to sing there until 1925. She was one of the foremost French Wagnerian sopranos of her time, noted for her fine renditions as Brünnhilde, Elisabeth, Kundry, and Venus.

Demuth (real name, **Pokorný**), **Leopold,** esteemed Austrian baritone; b. Brunn, Nov. 2, 1861; d. while giving a concert in Czernowitz, March 4, 1910. He studied with Joseph Gänsbacher in Vienna, making his debut in 1889 in Halle as Hans Heiling. He sang in Leipzig (1891–95) and Hamburg (1895–97), then joined the Vienna Court Opera, remaining on its roster until his death. He also sang at Bayreuth (1899), where he gained recognition as a fine Wagnerian.

Demuth, Norman, English composer, writer on music, and teacher; b. South Croydon, July 15, 1898; d. Chichester, April 21, 1968. He was a student of Parratt and Dunhill at the Royal College of Music in London, and then continued private studies with Dunhill. After military service during World War I (1915–17), he was active as a church organist and later conducted in provincial music centers. He became prof. of composition at the Royal Academy of Music in London in 1930; with the exception of his military service in World War II, he retained this post throughout his life. Demuth's high regard for French music led to his being made a corresponding member of the Institut. In 1951 he became an officer of the French Académie and in 1954 a chevalier of the Légion d'honneur. In his compositions, he followed a course set by d'Indy and Roussel. His works include the operas *Conte venitien* (1947), *Le Flambeau* (1948), *Volpone* (1949), *The Oresteia* (1950), and *Rogue Scapin* (1954), and the ballets *The Temptation of St. Anthony* (1937), *Planetomania* (1940), *Complainte* (1946), *Bal des fantômes* (1949), and *La débutante* (1949). Also incidental music and film scores. Among his many writings (all publ. in London unless otherwise given) were *Gounod* (1951) and *French Opera: Its Development to the Revolution* (Horsham, 1963).

Denis, Didier, French composer; b. Paris, Nov. 5, 1947. He studied at the Paris Cons. with Challan (harmony), Bitsch (counterpoint and fugue), Messiaen (analysis), and Rivier (composition), where he won several premiers prix (1958–71). He then was active at the Villa Medici in Rome under the auspices of the French Academy (1971–73). From 1982 to 1991 he was an inspector of music for the French Ministry of Culture. In 1992 he became a prof. of composition at the Toulouse Cons. He is currently composing an opera, *Urbicande*.

Denisov, Edison, remarkable, innovative Russian composer; b. Tomsk, April 6, 1929; d. Paris, Nov. 23, 1996. He was named after Thomas Alva Edison by his father, an electrical engineer. He studied mathematics at the Univ. of Moscow, graduating in 1951, and composition at the Moscow Cons. with Shebalin (1951–56). In 1959 he was appointed to the faculty of the Cons. An astute explorer of tonal possibilities, Denisov wrote instrumental works of an empirical genre. The titles of his pieces reveal a lyric character of subtle nuances, often marked by impressionistic colors. He composed *Soldier Ivan*, opera (1959), *L'Ecume des jours*, lyric drama (1981), and *Confession*, ballet (1984).

BIBL.: J.-P. Armengaud, *Entretiens avec E. D.: Un compositeur sous le regime communist* (Paris, 1993); I. Kholopov, *E. D.* (Moscow, 1993).

Dent, Edward J(oseph), eminent English musicologist, teacher, and music critic; b. Ribston, Yorkshire, July 16, 1876; d. London, Aug. 22, 1957. He studied with C. H. Lloyd at Eton College; then went to Cambridge to continue his studies with Charles Wood and Stanford (Mus.B., 1899; M.A., 1905); he was elected a Fellow of King's College there in 1902, and subsequently taught music history, harmony, counterpoint, and composition until 1918. He was also active in promoting operatic productions in England by preparing translations of libretti for performances at Cambridge, particularly of the operas of Mozart. From 1918 he wrote music criticism in London. In 1919 he became one of the founders of the British Music Soc., which remained active until 1933. The ISCM came into being in 1922 largely through his efforts, and he served as its president until 1938 and again in 1945; he also was president of the Société Internationale de Musicologie from 1931 until 1949. In 1926 he was appointed prof. of music at Cambridge, a position he held until 1941. He was made an honorary Mus.D. at the Univ. of Oxford (1932), Harvard Univ. (1936), and the Univ. of Cambridge (1947). In 1937 he was made a corresponding member of the American Musicological Soc. After his death, the Royal Musical Assn. created, in 1961, the Dent Medal, which is given annually to those selected for their important contributions to musicology. A scholar of the widest interests, Dent contributed numerous articles to music journals, encyclopedias, dictionaries, and symposia.

WRITINGS: *Alessandro Scarlatti* (London, 1905; 2d ed., rev. by F. Walker, 1960); *Mozart's Operas: A Critical Study* (London, 1913; 3d ed., rev., 1955); *Terpander, or Music and the Future* (London, 1926); *Foundations of English Opera: A Study of Musical Drama in England during the Seventeenth Century* (Cambridge, 1928); *Ferruccio Busoni* (London, 1933; 2d ed., 1966); *Handel* (London, 1934); *Opera* (Harmondsworth, 1940; 5th ed., rev., 1949); *Notes on Fugue for Beginners* (Cambridge, 1941); *A Theatre for Everybody: The Story of the Old Vic and Sadler's Wells* (London, 1945; 2d ed., rev., 1946); *The Rise of Romantic Opera* (ed. by W. Dean; Cambridge, 1976); *Selected Essays* (ed. by H. Taylor; Cambridge, 1979).

BIBL.: P. Radcliffe, *E. J. D.: A Centenary Memoir* (Rickmansworth, 1976).

Denzler, Robert, Swiss conductor and composer; b. Zürich, March 19, 1892; d. there, Aug. 25, 1972. He studied with Andreae at the Zürich Cons.; after further training in Cologne, he was an assistant at Bayreuth. He was music director of the Lucerne (1912–15) and then of the Zürich Opera (1915–27); after serving as 1st conductor of the Berlin Städtische Oper (1927–32), he was again music director of the Zürich Opera (1934–47).

De Rensis, Raffaello, Italian music critic; b. Casacalenda, Campobasso, Feb. 17, 1879; d. Rome, Nov. 3, 1970. He founded the weekly magazine *Musica* in 1908; wrote music criticism in daily newspapers. He publ. *Il cantore del popolo, Beniamino Gigli*

(Rome, 1934), *Franco Faccio e Verdi* (Milan, 1934), *Ottorino Respighi* (Turin, 1935), *Ermanno Wolf-Ferrari* (Milan, 1937), *Arrigo Boito* (Florence, 1942), *Umberto Giordano e Ruggiero Leoncavallo* (Siena, 1949), *Francesco Cilea* (Palmi, 1950), and *Musica vista* (Milan, 1960).

De Reszke, Edouard, famous Polish bass, brother of **Jean (Jan Mieczislaw)** and **Josephine de Reszke**; b. Warsaw, Dec. 22, 1853; d. Garnek, May 25, 1917. He studied with Ciaffei in Warsaw; also was trained by his brother, Jean, and by Steller and Coletti. He then went to Italy, where he continued his study with various teachers. His professional debut was at the Théâtre-Italien in Paris, when he sang Amonasro in *Aida* under Verdi's direction (April 22, 1876). He continued to make appearances in Paris for 2 seasons, and later sang at La Scala in Milan. From 1880 to 1884 he sang in London with extraordinary success. He made his American debut in Chicago as the King in *Lohengrin* (Nov. 9, 1891), then as Frère Laurent in *Roméo et Juliette* at the Metropolitan Opera in New York (Dec. 14, 1891); his brother, Jean, made his N.Y. debut as Roméo at the same performance. Edouard's greatest role was that of Méphistophélès in *Faust*; he sang this part at its 500th performance at the Paris Opéra (his brother, Jean, sang the title role), on Nov. 4, 1887; he made a special final appearance at a Metropolitan gala on April 27, 1903, in the last act of *Faust*. He then retired, and died in extreme poverty as a result of the depredations brought on by World War I.

De Reszke, Jean (Jan Mieczislaw), celebrated Polish tenor, brother of **Edouard** and **Josephine de Reszke**; b. Warsaw, Jan. 14, 1850; d. Nice, April 3, 1925. His mother gave him his first singing lessons; he then studied with Ciaffei and Cotogni. He sang at the Warsaw Cathedral as a boy; then went to Paris, where he studied with Sbriglia. He was first trained as a baritone, and made his debut in Venice (1874) as Alfonso in *La Favorite* under the name of Giovanni di Reschi. He continued singing in Italy and France in baritone parts; his first appearance as a tenor took place in Madrid on Nov. 9, 1879, in *Robert le Diable*. He created the title role in Massenet's *Le Cid* at the Paris Opéra (Nov. 30, 1885) and became a favorite tenor there. He appeared at Drury Lane in London as Radames on June 13, 1887 (having previously sung there as a baritone in 1874). He then sang at Covent Garden (until 1900). On Nov. 9, 1891, he made his American debut in Chicago as Lohengrin; he made his Metropolitan Opera debut in New York on Dec. 14, 1891, as Romeo; he remained with the Metropolitan for 11 seasons. In order to sing Wagnerian roles, he learned German, and made a sensationally successful appearance as Tristan (N.Y., Nov. 27, 1895). His last appearance at the Metropolitan was as Tristan on April 29, 1901, in Act 2 during a postseason gala performance. The secret of his success rested not so much on the power of his voice (some baritone quality remained in his singing to the end) as on his controlled interpretation, musical culture, and fine dynamic balance. When he retired from the stage in 1902, settling in Paris as a voice teacher, he was able to transmit his method to many of his students, several of whom later became famous on the opera stage.

BIBL.: C. Leiser, *J. d. R. and the Great Days of Opera* (London, 1933).

De Reszke, Josephine, Polish soprano, sister of **Jean (Jan Mieczislaw)** and **Edouard de Reszke**; b. Warsaw, June 4, 1855; d. there, Feb. 22, 1891. She studied at the St. Petersburg Cons., first appearing in public under the name of Giuseppina di Reschi at Venice in 1874. She sang Marguerite in Gounod's *Faust* (Aug. 1, 1874), with her brother Jean as Valentin; then was engaged at the Paris Opéra, where she made her debut as Ophelia in *Hamlet* by Ambroise Thomas (Paris, June 21, 1875); later sang in Madrid and Lisbon, and appeared as Aida at Covent Garden in London on April 18, 1881. She retired from the stage upon her marriage in 1885 and settled in Poland.

Dérivis, Henri Etienne, French bass, father of **Prosper Dérivis**; b. Albi, Aug. 2, 1780; d. Livry, Feb. 1, 1856. He made his debut at the Paris Opéra as Sarastro in the French version of *Die Zauberflöte* under the title of *Les Mystères d'Isis* in 1803. During the next 25 years he was a principal singer there, creating roles in works by Spontini (*La Vestale, Fernand Cortez*, and *Olympie*), Cherubini (*Les Abencérages*), Rossini (*Le Siège de Corinthe*), and others.

Dérivis, Prosper, distinguished French bass, son of **Henri Etienne Dérivis**; b. Paris, Oct. 28, 1808; d. there, Feb. 11, 1880. He studied with Pellegrini and Nourrit in Paris, making his debut at the Paris Opéra in 1831. He subsequently created roles there in operas by Berlioz (*Benvenuto Cellini*), Meyerbeer (*Les Huguenots*), Donizetti (*Les Martyrs*), and others. He appeared at La Scala in Milan (1842–43), singing in the premieres of Verdi's *Nabucco* and *I Lombardi*; he also sang in the first performance of Donizetti's *Linda di Chamounix* in Vienna in 1842. After his retirement from the stage in 1857, he taught voice in Paris.

Dermota, Anton, Austrian tenor of Slovenian descent; b. Kropa, June 4, 1910; d. Vienna, June 22, 1989. After training at the Ljubljana Cons., he was a student in Vienna of Elisabeth Rado. In 1934 he made his operatic debut in Cluj; in 1936 he joined the Vienna State Opera, where he sang regularly during the next 40 years; in 1946 he was made a Kammersänger and in 1955 he sang Florestan at the reopening celebration of the restored Vienna State Opera house. He also sang at the Salzburg Festival, Milan's La Scala, the Paris Opéra, and London's Covent Garden, and appeared as a concert artist. In 1966 he became a prof. at the Vienna Academy of Music. He was best known for his roles in Mozart's operas, but he also was admired as Des Grieux, Lensky, Rodolfo, and Palestrina.

Dernesch, Helga, Austrian soprano; b. Vienna, Feb. 3, 1939. She was educated at the Vienna Cons. She made her operatic debut at the Bern Stadttheater in 1961; she then sang in Wiesbaden and Cologne; subsequently appeared at the Bayreuth Festivals. In 1969 Herbert von Karajan chose her for his Salzburg Easter Festival; in 1970 she made her debut at Covent Garden, London; she also sang with the Hamburg State Opera, the Berlin Städtische Oper, and the Vienna State Opera. She sang many Wagnerian dramatic roles and those of Richard Strauss; from 1979 she turned her attention to mezzo-soprano parts. From 1982 she sang at the San Francisco Opera. On Oct. 14, 1985, she made her Metropolitan Opera debut in New York as Mussorgsky's Marfa. In 1990 she appeared as Verdi's Mistress Quickly in Los Angeles. She sang Strauss's Clytemnestra at the Opéra de la Bastille in Paris in 1992. In 1996 she appeared as Frau von Luber in Weill's *Silbersee* at the London Promenade Concerts. She married **Werner Krenn**.

De Rogatis, Pascual, Argentine composer and teacher; b. Teora, Italy, May 17, 1880; d. Buenos Aires, April 2, 1980. He studied piano and composition with Alberto Williams and violin with Pietro Melani and Rafael Albertini in Buenos Aires, where he then devoted himself to teaching and composing. His stage works included *Huemac*, lyric drama (1913–14; Buenos Aires, July 22, 1916), and *La novia del hereje* or *La Inquisición en Lima*, opera (c.1924; Buenos Aires, June 13, 1935); also incidental music and dance scores.

Dervaux, Pierre, noted French conductor and teacher; b. Juvisy-sur-Orge, Jan. 3, 1917; d. Marseilles, Feb. 20, 1992. He studied at the Paris Cons. with Philipp, Armand Ferté, Nat, J. and N. Gallon, and Samuel-Roussel. After conducting at the Paris Opéra Comique (1945–53), he was permanent conductor at the Paris Opéra (1956–70); from 1958 he was also president and chief conductor of the Concerts Colonne in Paris. He was music director of the Orchestre Symphonique de Québec (1968–71), the Orchestre Philharmonique des Pays de la Loire (1971–78), and in Nice (1979–82). He taught at the École Normale de Musique in Paris (1964–86), the Montreal Cons. (1965–72), and the Nice Academy (1971–82). Dervaux was especially admired for his brilliant and colorful interpretations of the French repertoire.

Derzhinskaya, Xenia (Georgievna), notable Russian soprano; b. Kiev, Feb. 6, 1889; d. Moscow, June 9, 1951. She was a pupil of F. Pash and M. Marchesi in Kiev. After appearing in concerts there, she settled in Moscow and sang at the Narodniy Dom Opera (1913–15), and subsequently was a leading member of the Bolshoi Theater (1915–48); also pursued a concert career, and taught voice at the Moscow Cons. (1947–51). In 1937 she was named a People's Artist of the USSR. She won high praise in her homeland for her compelling portrayals of roles in Russian operas.

BIBL.: E. Grosheva, *X. G. D.* (Moscow, 1952).

De Sabata, Victor (Vittorio), outstanding Italian conductor and composer; b. Trieste, April 10, 1892; d. Santa Margherita Ligure, Dec. 11, 1967. He studied with Michele Saladino and Giacomo Orefice at the Milan Cons. (1901–11). An extremely versatile musician, he could play piano with considerable Élan, and also took lessons on cello, clarinet, oboe, and bassoon. He was encouraged in his career as a conductor by Toscanini; at the same time, he began to compose operas; his first production was *Il Macigno*, which was first performed at La Scala in Milan on March 30, 1917. His symphonic poem *Juventus* (1919) was conducted at La Scala by Toscanini. De Sabata's style of composition involved Romantic Italian formulas, with lyric and dramatic episodes receiving an equal share of attention. In the meantime, he filled engagements as an opera and sym. conductor in Italy. In 1927 he conducted concerts in New York and Cincinnati, in 1936 he conducted at the Vienna State Opera, in 1939 he was a guest conductor with the Berlin Phil., and in 1946 he conducted in Switzerland. On April 21, 1946, he was invited to conduct a sym. concert in London, the first conductor from an "enemy country" to conduct in England after World War II. He then was a guest conductor with the Chicago Sym. Orch. in 1949, and with the N.Y. Phil. and the Boston Sym. Orch. in 1950. He became popular with American audiences, and in 1952 was engaged to conduct in New York, Philadelphia, Washington, D.C., Baltimore, St. Louis, and Detroit. In 1953 he conducted in Philadelphia, Los Angeles, San Francisco, and Santa Barbara, California. On Feb. 18, 1957, he conducted at the funeral of Toscanini; this was his last appearance on the podium. He was the father-in-law of the Italian conductor Aldo Ceccato (b. Milan, Feb. 18, 1934). As a conductor, De Sabata acquired a brilliant reputation in both operatic and symphonic repertoire. He was an impassioned and dynamic conductor who excelled particularly in the works of Verdi and Wagner. Among his own dramatic compositions are *Il Macigno*, opera (Milan, March 30, 1917; 2d version, Driada, Turin, Nov. 12, 1935), *Lisistrata*, opera (1920), *Le mille e una notte*, ballet (Milan, Jan. 20, 1931), and theater music for Max Reinhardt's production of *The Merchant of Venice* (Venice, July 18, 1934).

BIBL.: R. Mucci, *V. d.S.* (Lanciano, 1937); T. Celli, *L'arte di V. d.S.* (Turin, 1978).

Deschamps-Jehin, (Marie-) Blanche, outstanding French contralto; b. Lyons, Sept. 18, 1857; d. Paris, June 1923. She studied at the Cons. in Lyons and later at the Paris Cons., making her debut in Brussels in *Giroflé-Girofla* in 1874. She then sang at the Théâtre Royal de la Monnaie in Brussels (1879–85), during which tenure she created the role of Hérodiade in Massenet's opera (1881); then sang in Paris at the Opéra Comique (1885–91) and the Opéra (1891–1902), and at Covent Garden in London (1891). In later years she appeared at the Monte Carlo Opera and then mainly in concerts. She was married to **Léon Jehin**.

De Segurola, Andrés (Perello), Spanish bass; b. Valencia, March 27, 1874; d. Barcelona, Jan. 22, 1953. He studied with Pietro Farvaro in Barcelona, where he made his operatic debut in 1898 at the Teatro Liceo. On Oct. 10, 1901, he made his first appearance with the Metropolitan Opera in a concert during the company's visit to Toronto, and 2 days later sang Laurent in *Roméo et Juliet* there; his debut with the company in New York came on March 3, 1902, as the King in *Aida*, and he remained on its roster until the end of the season; then was again on its roster from 1909 to 1920. He later appeared in films and taught in Hollywood (1931–51) before settling in Barcelona. Among his most prominent roles were Basilio, Alvise, Varlaam, Colline, Sparafucile, and Geronte in *Manon Lescaut*. G. Creegan ed., *Through My Monocle: Memoirs of the Great Basso Andreas de Segurola* (Steubenville, Ohio, 1991).

Deshevov, Vladimir, Russian composer; b. St. Petersburg, Feb. 11, 1889; d. there (Leningrad), Oct. 27, 1955. He studied with Steinberg and Liadov at the St. Petersburg Cons. Many of his themes were drawn from folk sources. Among his works were the revolutionary operas *The Red Hurricane* (Leningrad, Oct. 29, 1924), *Ice and Steel*, based on the Kronstadt rebellion of 1921 (Leningrad, May 17, 1930), and *The Hungry Steppe*, about socialist distribution of land in Uzbekistan.

Des Marais, Paul (Emile), American composer; b. Menominee, Mich., June 23, 1920. He studied with Sowerby in Chicago (1937–41), Boulanger in Cambridge, Mass. (1941–42) and Paris (1949), and Piston at Harvard Univ. (B.A., 1949; M.A., 1953). He received the Lili Boulanger prize (1947–48), the Boott prize in composition from Harvard (1949), and a John Knowles Paine Traveling Fellowship (1949–51). After teaching at Harvard (1953–56), he was on the faculty of the Univ. of Calif. at Los Angeles (from 1956), where he received the Inst. of Creative Arts Award (1964–65); he later received the Phoebe Ketchum Thorne award (1970–73). He publ. the study *Harmony* (1962) and contributed articles to *Perspectives of New Music*. His early music was oriented toward neoclassicism, with pandiatonic excrescences in harmonic structures. He later moved to a free combination of serial and nonserial elements, functioning on broad tonal planes.

WORKS: DRAMATIC: *Epiphanies*, chamber opera (1968); *Orpheus*, theater piece for Narrator and Instruments (1987); incidental music to Dryden's *A Secular Masque* (1976), Shakespeare's *A Midsummer Night's Dream* (1976), Sophocles' *Oedipus* (1978), G. B. Shaw's *St. Joan* (1980), Dryden's *Marriage à la Mode* (1981), Shakespeare's *As You Like It* (1983), and G. Etherege's *The Man of Mode* (1984).

Desmarets, Henri, important French composer; b. Paris, Feb. 1661; d. Lunéville, Sept. 7, 1741. He was a boy soprano in the Paris royal chapel, subsequently becoming one of the most highly regarded musicians of his day. Many of his works were performed at the court of Louis XIV. He served as maître de chapelle at the Jesuit College of Louis-le-Grand. His personal life was stormy; after the death of his wife, he became involved with one of his students; when the girl's father objected, the lovers fled to Brussels in 1699. In 1701 he was made maître de musique de la chambre to Philip V in Madrid, and in 1707 became surintendant de la musique to Leopold I, duke of Lorraine, in Lunéville. Having been sentenced to death in absentia for personal indiscretions, he was unable to return to France until he was pardoned by the regent in 1720. For the most part, he spent his remaining years in Lunéville.

WORKS: DRAMATIC: OPERAS (all 1st perf. in Paris): *Didon* (Sept. 11, 1693); *Circé* (Oct. 1, 1694); *Venus et Adonis* (March 7, 1697); *Théagène et Cariclée* (Feb. 3, 1695); *Iphigénie en Tauride* (May 6, 1704); *Renaud, ou La Suite d'Armide* (March 5, 1722). BALLETS: *Les Amours de Momus* (May 25, 1695); *Les Fêtes galantes* (May 10, 1698).

BIBL.: M. Antoine, *Henry D.* (Paris, 1965).

Desmond, Astra, English mezzo-soprano and teacher; b. Torquay, April 10, 1893; d. Faversham, Aug. 16, 1973. She studied in London at Westfield College and with Blanche Marchesi at the Royal Academy of Music. Following additional training in Berlin, she returned to London and made her recital debut in 1915. While she made some appearances with the Carl Rosa Opera Co., she devoted herself principally to the concert and oratorio repertory; was a prof. of voice at the Royal Academy of Music (from 1947). In 1949 she was made a Commander of the Order of the British Empire. Her interpretations of English music, particularly works by Elgar and Vaughan Williams, were outstanding. Having mastered 12 languages, she also excelled as an interpreter of the Scandinavian song literature.

Désormière, Roger, brilliant French conductor; b. Vichy, Sept. 13, 1898; d. Paris, Oct. 25, 1963. He studied with Koechlin in Paris. After serving as music director of the Paris Ballets Suédois (1924–25) and the Ballets Russes (1925–29), he was conductor (from 1936) and director (1944–46) of the Opéra Comique; in 1945–46 he also was assoc. director of the Paris Opéra. In 1946–47 he was a guest conductor with the BBC Sym. Orch. in London, and in 1949 he returned to that city with the Opéra Comique to conduct *Pelléas et Mélisande* at Covent Garden. He also appeared as a guest conductor of opera and sym. throughout Europe. Désormière was an outstanding interpreter of the French repertory. He also championed 20th-century French music, conducting premieres of works by Satie, Koechlin, Roussel, Milhaud, Poulenc, Messiaen, Boulez et al. After being stricken with aphasia and other disorders, he abandoned his career in 1952.

BIBL.: D. Mayer and P. Souvchinsky, *R. D. et son temps* (Monaco, 1966).

Dessau, Paul, prominent German composer; b. Hamburg, Dec. 19, 1894; d. Königs Wusterhausen, near Berlin, June 27, 1979. He studied violin with Florian Zajic at the Klindworth-Scharwenka Cons. in Berlin (1910–12), and then returned to Hamburg to study piano and score reading with Eduard Behm and composition with Max Loewengard. In 1912 he became corépétiteur at the Hamburg City Theater, and then went to Bremen in 1913 as an operetta conductor at the Tivoli Theater. After military service during World War I, he returned to Hamburg in 1918 as conductor and composer at the Kammerspiele. He was corépétiteur and conductor at the Cologne Opera (1919–23) and at the Mainz City Theater (1923–25), and then was 1st conductor at the Berlin Städtische Oper from 1925. When the Nazis came to power in 1933, Dessau lost his post and made his way to Paris, where he came into contact with René Leibowitz and 12-tone music. In 1939 he went to the United States. While in New York, he commenced a long collaboration with Bertolt Brecht. In 1944 he went to Hollywood, where he composed for films. He also composed the music for his most successful collaboration with Brecht, *Mutter Courage und ihre Kinder* (1946). In 1948 he settled in East Germany, where he continued to work with Brecht until the latter's death in 1956. In 1952 Dessau was made a member of the German Academy of Arts, becoming vice president and prof. there in 1959. He taught at the Zeuthen school, near Berlin, from 1960. In 1953, 1956, 1965, and 1974 he was awarded state prizes by the German Democratic Republic, and in 1964 he received its National Order of Merit. His wife was **Ruth Berghaus**. In his earliest scores, Dessau pursued expressionist and neoclassical precepts. He then developed an interest in Jewish folk music while exploring 12-tone music. His association with Brecht led him into more popular modes of expression. His works after settling in East Germany are imbued with the progressive ideals of socialist realism, but with increasing serial applications.

WORKS: DRAMATIC: OPERAS: *Giuditta* (1910–12; unfinished); *Orpheus 1930/31*, radio operetta (Berlin, 1931; rev. as *Orpheus und der Bürgmeister*); *Die Reisen des Glücksgotts* (1945; unfinished); *Das Verhöor des Lukullus* (1949; Berlin, March 17, 1951; rev. version as *Die Verurteilung des Lukullus*, Berlin, Oct. 12, 1951); *Puntila* (1956–59; Berlin, Nov. 15, 1966); *Lanzelot* (1967–69; Berlin, Dec. 19, 1969); *Einstein* (1971–73; Berlin, Feb. 16, 1974); *Leonce und Lena* (1977–78; Berlin, Nov. 24, 1979). INCIDENTAL MUSIC TO: Brecht's *99%*, later retitled *Furcht und Elend des Dritten Reiches* (1938), *Mutter Courage und ihre Kinder* (1946), *Der gute Mensch von Sezuan* (1947), *Herr Puntila und sein Knecht* (1949), *Mann ist Mann* (1951), and *Der kaukasische Kreidekreis* (1953–54); also Goethe's *Faust*, part I (1949) and *Urfaust* (1952), F. Wolf's *Der arme Konrad* (1951), J. Becher's *Der Weg nach Fussen* (1956), Shakespeare's *Coriolanus* (1964), Weiss's *Vietnam-Diskurs* (1968), and Müller's *Zement* (1973). Also film scores, tanzscenen, lehrstücke, and schulstücke.

WRITINGS: *Musikarbeit in der Schule* (Berlin, 1968); *Aus Gesprächen* (Leipzig, 1975); *Notizen und Noten* (Leipzig, 1974); F. Hennenberg, ed., *Opern* (Berlin, 1976).

BIBL.: F. Hennenberg, *D.-Brecht: Musikalische Arbeiten* (Berlin, 1963); idem, *P. D.: Eine Biographie* (Leipzig, 1965); idem, *Für Sie porträtiert: P. D.* (Leipzig, 1974; 2d ed., 1981).

Dessauer, Josef, composer; b. Prague, May 28, 1798; d. Mödling, near Vienna, July 8, 1876. He studied piano with Tomaschek and composition with Dionys Weber in Prague. He wrote several operas: *Lidwina* (Prague, 1836), *Ein Besuch in Saint-Cyr* (Dresden, May 6, 1838; his best work), *Paquita* (Vienna, 1851), *Domingo* (1860), and *Oberon* (not perf.).

BIBL.: O. Sestl, *J. D. (1798–1876): Ein Liedermeister des Wiener Biedermeier* (diss., Univ. of Innsbruck, 1951).

Dessay, Natalie, remarkable French soprano; b. Lyons, April 19, 1965. Following training at the Bordeaux Cons., she completed her studies in Paris. In 1990 she won the Mozart Competition in Vienna. After singing Bizet's Don Procopio at the Opéra Comique in Paris in 1990, she appeared as Adele in Geneva in 1991. She sang at the Lyons Opera from 1991, where she won notable success for her Mozart roles. In 1992 she was engaged as Olympia in *Les Contes d'Hoffmann* at the Opéra de la Bastille in Paris and as Blondchen in Lausanne. In 1993 she portrayed Olympia at the Vienna State Opera. On Oct. 13, 1994, she made her debut at the Metropolitan Opera in New York as Fiakermilli in *Arabella*. In 1995 she appeared as Lakmé at the Opéra Comique. Her portrayal of Ophélie in Thomas's *Hamlet* was acclaimed in Geneva in 1996, the same year she sang Aminta at the Vienna State Opera. In 1997 she appeared as Stravinsky's Nightingale at the Théâtre du Châtelet in Paris. She was also highly successful as a concert artist.

Destinn, Emmy (real name, **Emilie Pavlína Kittlová**), famous Czech soprano; b. Prague, Feb. 26, 1878; d. České Budějovice, Jan. 28, 1930. She first studied the violin; her vocal abilities were revealed later by Marie Loewe-Destinn, whose 2d name she adopted as a token of appreciation. She made her debut as Santuzza at the Kroll Opera in Berlin (July 19, 1898) and was engaged at the Berlin Royal Opera as a regular member until 1908. She specialized in Wagnerian operas, and became a protégée of Cosima Wagner in Bayreuth, where she sang for the first time in 1901 as Senta; because of her ability to cope with difficult singing parts, Richard Strauss selected her for the title role in the Berlin and Paris premieres of his *Salome*. She made her London debut at Covent Garden on May 2, 1904, as Donna Anna; her success in England was spontaneous and unmistakable, and she continued to sing opera in England until the outbreak of World War I. She made her American debut in *Aida* with the Metropolitan Opera in New York on Nov. 16, 1908, and remained with the company until 1916, and then was on its roster again from 1919 to 1921. She retired from the opera stage in 1926 but continued to make concert appearances until shortly before her death. For a few years following World War I, she used her Czech name, Ema Destinnová, but later dropped it. She was a versatile singer with a pure soprano voice of great power; her repertoire included some 80 parts. A film biography of her life, *The Divine Emma*, was produced in Czechoslovakia in 1982.

BIBL.: A. Rektorys, *Ema D.ová* (Prague, 1936); M. Martínková, *Život Emy D.ová* (Pilzen, 1946); V. Holzknecht and B. Trita, *E. D.ová ve slovech a obrazech* (E. D. in Words and Pictures; Prague, 1972); M. Pospíšil, *Veliké srdce: Život a umění Emy Destinové* (A Great Heart: The Life and Art of E. D.; Prague, 1974).

Destouches, André-Cardinal, French composer; b. Paris (baptized), April 6, 1672; d. there, Feb. 7, 1749. After attending a Jesuit school in Paris, he went as a boy to Siam with his teacher, the missionary Gui Tachard (1686). He returned to France in 1688; served in the Royal Musketeers (1692–94), and later took lessons from André Campra, contributing 3 airs to Campra's opéra ballet *L'Europe galante* (1697). After this initiation, Destouches produced his first independent work, *Issé*, a "heroic pastorale" in 3 acts (Fontainebleau, Oct. 7, 1697); its popularity was parodied in several productions of a similar pastoral nature (*Les Amours de Vincennes* by P. F. Dominique, 1719; *Les Oracles* by J.A. Romagnesi, 1741). Among his other operas, the following were produced in Paris: *Amadis de Grèce* (March 22, 1699), *Omphale*

(Nov. 10, 1701), and *Callirhoé* (Dec. 27, 1712). With Delalande, he wrote the ballet *Les Eléments*, which was produced at the Tuileries Palace in Paris on Dec. 22, 1721. In 1713 Louis XIV appointed him inspector general of the Académie Royale de Musique; in 1728 he became its director, retiring in 1730. A revival of *Omphale* in 1752 evoked Baron Grimm's famous *Lettre sur Omphale*, inaugurating the so-called Guerre des Bouffons between the proponents of the French school, as exemplified by Destouches, and Italian opera buffa.

BIBL.: K. Dulle, *A. C. D.* (Leipzig, 1908).

Destouches, Franz (Seraph) von, German conductor and composer; b. Munich, Jan. 21, 1772; d. there, Dec. 10, 1844. He was a pupil of Haydn in Vienna in 1787. He was appointed music director at Erlangen (1797), then was 2d concertmaster at the Weimar theater (1799), later becoming first concertmaster and director of music (1804–08). In 1810 he was a prof. of theory at Landshut Univ.; then a conductor at Homburg (1826–42). He retired to Munich in 1842.

WORKS: DRAMATIC: OPERAS: *Die Thomasnacht* (Munich, Aug. 31, 1792); *Das Missverständniss*, operetta (Weimar, April 27, 1805); *Der Teufel und der Schneider*, comic opera (1843; not perf.). INCIDENTAL MUSIC TO: Schiller's version of Gozzi's *Turandot* (1802); Schiller's *Die Braut von Messina* (1803), *Die Jungfrau von Orleans* (1803), and *Wilhelm Tell* (1804); Kotzebue's *Die Hussiten vor Naumburg* (1804); Zacharias Werner's play *Wanda, Königin der Sarmaten* (1808). ORATORIO: *Die Anbetung am Grabe Christi*.

BIBL.: E. von Destouches, *F. v.D.* (Munich, 1904).

Deutekom, Cristina (real name, **Stientje Engel**), notable Dutch soprano; b. Amsterdam, Aug. 28, 1931. She was a student of Johan Thomas and Coby Riemersma at the Amsterdam Cons. In 1962 she made her operatic debut as the Queen of the Night in Amsterdam, a role she subsequently sang with great distinction at her Metropolitan Opera debut in New York on Sept. 28, 1967; was again on its roster (1973–75). She subsequently sang in principal opera houses of the world, becoming equally adept in both coloratura and dramatic roles. Deutekom excelled particularly in the operas of Mozart, Rossini, Bellini, Donizetti, and Verdi.

Deutsch, Otto Erich, eminent Austrian musicologist; b. Vienna, Sept. 5, 1883; d. there, Nov. 23, 1967. He studied literature and art history at the univs. of Vienna and Graz; was art critic of Vienna's *Die Zeit* (1908–09); he then served as an assistant at the Kunsthistorisches Institut of the Univ. of Vienna (1909–12); he later was a bookseller, and then music librarian of the important collection of Anthony van Hoboken in Vienna (1926–35). In 1939 he emigrated to England and settled in Cambridge; in 1947 he became a naturalized British subject, but returned to Vienna in 1951. A scholar of impeccable credentials, Deutsch was an acknowledged authority on Handel, Mozart, and Schubert; his documentary biographies of these composers constitute primary sources; he was also responsible for initiating the critical edition of Mozart's letters, which he ed. with W. Bauer and J. Eibl as *Mozart: Briefe und Aufzeichnungen* (7 vols., Kassel, 1962–75).

WRITINGS: *Schubert-Brevier* (Berlin, 1905); *Beethovens Beziehungen zu Graz* (Graz, 1907); *Franz Schubert: Die Dokumente seines Lebens und Schaffens* (in collaboration, 1st with L. Scheibler, then with W. Kahl and G. Kinsky), which was planned as a comprehensive work in 3 vols. containing all known documents, pictures, and other materials pertaining to Schubert, arranged in chronological order, with a thematic catalog, but of which only 2 vols. were publ.: vol. 3, *Sein Leben in Bildern* (Munich, 1913), and vol. 2, part 1, *Die Dokumente seines Lebens* (Munich, 1914; Eng. tr. 1946, by E. Blom, as *Schubert: A Documentary Biography*; American ed., 1947, as *The Schubert Reader: A Life of Franz Schubert in Letters and Documents*; 2d German ed., 1964, enl., in the *Neue Ausgabe sämtlicher Werke of Schubert*); *Franz Schuberts Briefe und Schriften* (Munich, 1919; Eng. tr., 1928; 4th German ed., Vienna, 1954); *Die historischen Bildnisse Franz Schuberts in getreuen Nachbildungen* (Vienna, 1922); *Die Originalausgaben von Schuberts Goethe-Liedern* (Vienna, 1926); *Franz Schubert: Tagebuch: Faksimile der Originalhandschrift* (Vienna, 1928); *Mozart und die Wiener Logen* (Vienna, 1932); with B. Paumgartner, *Leopold Mozarts Briefe an seine Tochter* (Salzburg, 1936); *Das Freihaustheater auf der Wieden 1787–1801* (Vienna, 1937); *Wolfgang Amadé Mozart: Verzeichnis aller meiner Werke. Faksimile der Handschrift mit dem Beiheft "Mozarts Werkverzeichnis 1784–1791"* (Vienna, 1938; Eng. tr., 1956); *Schubert: Thematic Catalogue of All His Works in Chronological Order* (with D. Wakeling; London, 1951; Ger tr. as *Franz Schubert: Thematisches Verzeichnis seiner Werke*, in the *Neue Ausgabe samtlicher Werke of Schubert* in a rev. ed., 1978); *Handel: A Documentary Biography* (N.Y., 1954; London, 1955); *Franz Schubert: Die Erinnerungen seiner Freunde* (Leipzig, 1957; Eng. tr., 1958); *Mozart: Die Dokumente seines Lebens* (Kassel, 1961; Eng. tr., 1965, as *Mozart: A Documentary Biography*; 2d ed., 1966; supplement, 1978); *Mozart und seine Welt in zeitgenössischen Bildern* (completed by M. Zenger, Kassel, 1961).

BIBL.: *O. E. D. zum 75. Geburtstag* (Vienna, 1958); W. Gerstenberg, J. LaRue, and W. Rehm, eds., *Festschrift O. E. D.* (Kassel, 1963).

Devčič, Natko, Croatian composer; b. Glina, June 30, 1914. He studied piano and composition at the Zagreb Academy of Music, graduating in 1939; he later studied with Marx in Vienna (1949–50) and Rivier in Paris (1953), and attended courses led by Boulez at Darmstadt (summer 1965); he also researched the potentials of electronic sound with Davidovsky at the Columbia-Princeton Electronic Music Studio in New York (1966–67). His early works are based on folk resources; later he experimented with advanced techniques. He composed *Labinska vještica* (The Witch of Labin), opera (Zagreb, Dec. 25, 1957), and *Dia . . .*, ballet (Zagreb, May 20, 1971).

Devienne, François, versatile French musician; b. Joinville, Haute-Marne, Jan. 31, 1759; d. in the insane asylum at Charenton, Sept. 5, 1803. A flutist and bassoonist, member of the band of the Gardes Suisses, bassoonist at the Théâtre de Monsieur (1789–1801), and a prof. at the Paris Cons. (from 1795), he was an extraordinarily prolific composer of peculiar importance from the impulse which he gave to perfecting the technique of wind instruments. Among his works were 12 operas. His valuable *Méthode de flûte* (Paris, 1795) went through several eds.

BIBL.: W. Montgomery, *The Life and Works of F. D., 1759–1803* (diss., Catholic Univ. of America, 1975).

Devlin, Michael (Coles), American bass-baritone; b. Chicago, Nov. 27, 1942. He studied at Louisiana State Univ. (Mus.B., 1965) and received vocal training from Norman Treigle and Daniel Ferro in New York. In 1963 he made his operatic debut as Spalanzani in *Les Contes d'Hoffmann* in New Orleans, and in 1966 he made his first appearance at the N.Y. City Opera as the Hermit in the U.S. premiere of Ginastera's *Don Rodrigo*, continuing on its roster until 1978. In 1974 he made his British debut at the Glyndebourne Festival as Mozart's Almaviva; he first sang at London's Covent Garden in 1975, then appeared at the Holland Festival, the Frankfurt am Main Opera, and the Bavarian State Opera in Munich in 1977. On Nov. 23, 1978, he made his Metropolitan Opera debut in New York as Escamillo, and subsequently returned there regularly. In later years, he sang with opera companies in San Francisco, Hamburg, Paris, Monte Carlo, Dallas, Chicago, Los Angeles, and other cities. He also appeared as a soloist with the world's major orchs.

Devol, Luana, American soprano; b. San Francisco, Nov. 30, 1942. She studied at the Univ. of San Diego, in London with Vera Rozsa, and with Jess Thomas. In 1983 she made her operatic debut as Strauss's Ariadne in San Francisco, and that same year made her European operatic debut in Stuttgart as Beethoven's Leonore. In 1986 she appeared for the first time in Berlin at both the State Opera and the Deutsche Oper. From 1987 to 1991 she was a member of the Mannheim National Theater. In 1989 she appeared as Irene in *Rienzi* at the Hamburg State Opera and as Eva in Schreker's *Irrelohe* in Vienna. Her debut at the Bayreuth Festival followed in 1990 as Brünnhilde, the same year she sang Leonore in a concert perf. in London. In 1991 she sang Wagner's Gutrune in a concert perf. In Rome. She appeared as Andromache in Reimann's *Troades* in Frankfurt am Main in 1992. After singing Strauss's Empress in Munich in 1993, she reprised that role in Paris in 1994. Among her other admired roles were Donna Anna, Agathe, Euryanthe, Amelia, Isolde, Elisabeth in *Tannhäuser*, and Elisabeth de Valois.

Devreese, Frédéric, Belgian conductor and composer, son of **Godefroid Devreese**; b. Amsterdam, June 2, 1929. He studied first at the Mechelen Cons., then took courses in composition from Poot and conducting from Defossez at the Brussels Cons.; subsequently he studied with Pizzetti at the Accademia di Santa Cecilia in Rome (1952–55). Returning to Belgium, he became associated with the Flemish TV as program director. His compositions include the operas *Willem van Saeftinghe* (Brussels TV, Sept. 28, 1964; 1st stage perf., Antwerp, Nov. 21, 1964) and *De vreemde ruiter* (1966) and the ballet *Mascarade* (1955; Aix-les-Bains, France, 1956) and *L'Amour de Don Juan* (1973).

Devreese, Godefroid, Belgian conductor, teacher, and composer, father of **Frédéric Devreese**; b. Kortrijk, Jan. 22, 1893; d. Brussels, June 4, 1972. He studied at the Brussels Cons. with Ysaÿe and César Thomson (violin) and Rasse and Gilson (composition). He was a conductor of the Antwerp Opera (1919–20), a violinist with the Concertgebouw Orch. in Amsterdam (1925–30), and director of the Mechelin Cons. (1930–58), concurrently giving courses at the Brussels Cons. (1944–59). He composed the ballet *Tombelène* (1927).

Devrient, Eduard (Philipp), German baritone, librettist, and writer on music; b. Berlin, Aug. 11, 1801; d. Karlsruhe, Oct. 4, 1877. He studied singing and thorough-bass with Zelter in Berlin, giving his first public performance there in 1819. He then joined the Royal Opera, but after the loss of his voice (1834) he went over to the spoken drama, without losing his interest in music. He sang the role of Christ in the famous performance of Bach's St. Matthew Passion under Mendelssohn on March 11, 1829. He was chief producer and actor at the Dresden Court Theater (1844–46) and director at the Karlsruhe Court Theater (1852–70); also the author of the text to Marschner's *Hans Heiling*, and created the title role (1833). His chief work is *Geschichte der deutschen Schauspielkunst* (5 vols., 1848–74); his works concerning music are *Briefe aus Paris* (1840; about Cherubini) and *Meine Erinnerungen an Felix Mendelssohn-Bartholdy und seine Briefe an mich* (Leipzig, 1869). Within weeks after publication of the latter, Wagner issued a polemical pamphlet entitled *Herr Eduard Devrient und sein Styl* (Munich, 1869) under the pseudonym Wilhelm Drach, violently attacking Devrient for his literary style. Devrient's book was publ. in Eng. (London, 1869; 3d ed., 1891).

BIBL.: J. Bab, *Die D.s* (Berlin, 1932).

De Waart, Edo (Eduard). See **Waart, Edo (Eduard) de.**

Dew, John, English opera producer and administrator; b. Santiago di Cuba, June 1, 1944. He received training in opera production in Germany from Walter Felsenstein and Wieland Wagner. In 1971 he began his career with a staging of *The Rake's Progress* in Ulm, and then attracted notice with his Mozart and Wagner productions in Krefeld. He was named head of production with the Bielefeld Theater in 1981, where he staged Schreker's *Irrelohe*, Brand's *Maschinist Hopkins*, Hindemith's *Neues von Tage*, and Krenek's *Der Sprung über den Schatten*. As a guest producer, he staged Neikrug's *Las Alamos* at the Berlin Deutsche Oper (1988), *Les Huguenots* at London's Covent Garden (1991), *Aida* at the Hamburg State Opera (1993), and *I Puritani* at the Vienna State Opera (1994). In 1995 he returned to Hamburg to stage the premiere of Schnittke's *Historia von D. Johann Fausten*. From 1995 he was Generalintendant of the Dortmund Theater.

Dexter, John, English opera director; b. Derby, Aug. 2, 1925; d. London, March 23, 1990. He worked in London in the theater and in films; from 1957 to 1972 he was associated with the English Stage Company, and also was assoc. director of the National Theatre from 1963. In 1966 he staged his first opera, *Benvenuto Cellini*, at London's Covent Garden. After staging operas in Hamburg (1969–72) and Paris (1973), he was director of production at the Metropolitan Opera in New York (1974–81), where his memorable achievements included *Les Dialogues des Carmélites* and *Lulu* (1977), *Billy Budd* (1978), *Aufstieg und Fall der Stadt Mahagonny* (1979), and the triple bill of Satie's *Parade*, Poulenc's *Les Mamelles de Tirésias*, and Ravel's *L'Enfant et les sortilèges* (1981). From 1981 to 1984 he served as production advisor at the Metropolitan.

Deyo, Ruth Lynda, American pianist and composer; b. Poughkeepsie, N.Y., April 20, 1884; d. Cairo, March 4, 1960. She studied piano with William Mason and Teresa Carreño and composition with MacDowell. She made her debut at the age of 9 at the World's Columbian Exposition in Chicago (1893); she made her concert debut in Berlin (March 23, 1904); subsequently played with major orchs. in the United States and in Europe; appeared in recitals with Kreisler and Casals. In 1925 she settled in Egypt and devoted herself mainly to composition. In 1930 she completed the full score of an opera on Egyptian themes, *The Diadem of Stars*, to a libretto by her husband, Charles Dalton; its *Prelude* was perf. by Stokowski and the Philadelphia Orch. (April 4, 1931). She was the 2d cousin of the American composer and pianist Felix Deyo (Poughkeepsie, N.Y., April 21, 1888; d. Baldwin, N.Y., June 21, 1959).

Dezède, Nicolas, composer; b. c.1742; d. Paris, Sept. 11, 1792. He is believed to have been of noble birth. After initial training in the fundamentals of music and the harp, he settled in Paris and studied composition. He subsequently launched a successful career as a composer for the theater, scoring a major triumph with his opéra comique *Blaise et Babet, ou La Suite des trois fermiers* (Versailles, April 4, 1783) and finding a patron in Duke Maximilian of Zweibrücken in 1785. Dezède's liaison with Mme. Belcour of the Comédie-Française resulted in a daughter, Florine (b. c.1766; d. c.1792), who wrote the comedy *Lucette et Lucas, ou La Paysanne curieuse* (Paris, 1781). Mozart used the air "Lison dormait dans un bocage" from Dezède's opéra comique *Julie* as the theme for his 9 variations for piano, K. 264. Dezède is believed to have composed the air "Ah, vous dirais-je, Maman?," celebrated in English as "Twinkle, Twinkle, Little Star."

WORKS: DRAMATIC (all 1st perf. in Paris unless otherwise given): *Julie,* opéra comique (Sept. 28, 1772); *L'erreur d'un moment, ou La Suite de Julie,* opéra comique (June 14, 1773); *Le Stratageme découvert,* comédie (Oct. 4, 1773); *Les Trois Fermiers*, comédie (May 24, 1777); *Fatmé, ou Le Langage des fleurs,* comédie ballet (Fontainebleau, Oct. 30, 1777); *Zulima ou L'Art et la nature, ou La Nature et l'art*, opéra comique (May 9, 1778); *Le Porteur de chaise*, opéra comique (Dec. 10, 1778; rev. as *Jerôme et Champagne*, Jan. 11, 1781); *Cécile,* opéra comique (Versailles, Feb. 24, 1780); *A trompeur, trompeur et demi, ou Les Torts du sentiment*, opéra comique (May 3, 1780; also known as *Fin contre fin*); *Blaise et Babet, ou La Suite des trois fermiers,* opéra comique (Versailles, April 4, 1783); *Péronne sauvée,* opera (May 27, 1783); *Alexis et Justine,* opéra comique (Versailles, Jan. 14, 1785); *Alcindor,* opéra féerie (April 17, 1787); *Auguste et Théodore, ou Les Deux Pages,* opéra comique (March 6, 1789); *Les Trois Noces,* pièce champêtre (Feb. 23, 1790); *Ferdinand, ou La Suite des Deux Pages,* comédie (June 19, 1790); *Adèle et Didier,* opéra comique (Nov. 5, 1790); *Paulin et Clairette, ou Les Deux Espiègles*, prose comédie (Jan. 5, 1792); *Mélite*, opéra comique (March 19, 1792); *La Fête de la cinquantaine,* opera (Jan. 9, 1796).

D'Hoedt, Henri-Georges, Belgian composer; b. Ghent, June 28, 1885; d. Brussels, May 14, 1936. He was a student of Emile Mathieu and Leo Moeremans. He became director of the Louvain Cons. in 1924, serving until his death. He was one of the first Belgian composers to depart from late-19th-century Romanticism and come under the influence of French Impressionism. Among his few compositions is the opera *Klaas au Pays de Cocagne* (Antwerp, 1926).

Diaghilev, Sergei (Pavlovich), famous Russian impresario; b. Gruzino, Novgorod district, March 31, 1872; d. Venice, Aug. 19, 1929. He was associated with progressive artistic organizations in St. Petersburg, but his main field of activity was in western Europe. He established the Ballets Russes in Paris in 1909; he commissioned Stravinsky to write the ballets *The Firebird*, *Petrouchka*, and *Le Sacre du printemps*; he also commissioned Prokofiev, Milhaud, Poulenc, Auric, and other composers of the younger generation. Ravel and Falla also wrote works for him. The great importance of Diaghilev's choreographic ideas lies in the complete abandonment of the classical tradition; in this respect he was the true originator of the modern dance.

BIBL.: A. Haskell, *D.: His Artistic and Private Life* (London, 1935); V. Kamenev, *Russian Ballet through Russian Eyes* (London, 1936); S. Lifar, *S. D.: His Life, His Work, His Legend* (London, 1940); S. Grigoriev, *The D. Ballet* (London, 1953); B. Kochno, *D. and the Ballets Russes* (N.Y., 1970); R. Buckle, *D.* (N.Y., 1979).

Diamond, David (Leo), eminent American composer; b. Rochester, N.Y., July 9, 1915. After attending the Cleveland Inst. of Music (1927–29), he was a student of Rogers at the Eastman School of Music in Rochester, N.Y. (1930–34); he then studied at the New Music School and the Dalcroze Inst. in New York (1934–36) with Boepple and Sessions. In 1936 he went to Paris to pursue studies with Boulanger, and during the summers of 1937 and 1938 he attended the American Cons. in Fontainebleau; he also studied with Ribaupierre and Scherchen. While in Paris, he became associated with the most important musicians and writers of his time, including Stravinsky, Ravel, Roussel, and Milhaud. His *Psalm* for Orch. (1936) won the Juilliard Publication Award in 1937 and brought him wide recognition. In 1941 he received the Prix du Rome and in 1942 the American Academy in Rome Award. With his *Rounds* for Strings (1944), he established himself as one of America's most important composers. This highly successful score won the N.Y. Music Critics' Circle Award in 1944. In subsequent years Diamond received various commissions and had his works performed by major conductors. After serving as the Fulbright Prof. at the Univ. of Rome (1951–52), he settled in Florence. In 1961 and 1963 he was the Slee Prof. at the State Univ. of N.Y. at Buffalo. In 1965 he moved to the United States and taught at the Manhattan School of Music in New York until 1968, serving as chairman of its music dept. in 1967–68. In 1970 he was a visiting prof. at the Univ. of Colo. in Boulder. In 1971–72 he was composer-in-residence at the American Academy in Rome. He then was prof. of composition and lecturer in graduate studies at the Juilliard School in New York from 1973. In 1983 he also was a visting prof. at the Univ. of Denver. From 1991 to 1994 he was composer-in-residence at the Tisch Center for the Arts in New York. In 1938, 1941, and 1958 he held Guggenheim fellowships. In 1966 he was elected to membership in the National Inst. of Arts and Letters. In 1985 he received the William Schuman Lifetime Achievement Award and in 1991 the Edward MacDowell Gold Medal. In 1995 he received the Medal of Arts from President William Clinton. As a composer, Diamond developed an original and recognizable style of harmonic and contrapuntal writing with the clearest sense of tonality. The element of pitch, often inspired by natural folklike patterns, is strong in all of his music. He later adopted a modified dodecaphonic method, while keeping free of doctrinaire serialism. His orch., chamber, and vocal output constitutes a significant contribution to 20th-century American music.

WORKS: DRAMATIC: OPERA: *The Noblest Game* (1971–75). MUSICAL COMEDY: *Mirandolina* (1958). MUSICAL FOLK PLAY: *The Golden Slippers* (N.Y., Dec. 5, 1965). DANCE DRAMA: *Icaro* (1937). BALLETS: *A Myriologue* (1935); *Formal Dance* (N.Y., Nov. 10, 1935); *Dance of Liberation* (1936; N.Y., Jan. 23, 1938); *Tom* (1936); *Duet* (1937); *Prelude* (1937); *The Dream of Audubon* (1941); *Labyrinth* (N.Y., April 5, 1946). INCIDENTAL MUSIC TO: Shakespeare's *The Tempest* (1944; N.Y., Jan. 25, 1945; rev. 1946 and 1968) and *Romeo and Juliet* (1947; rev. 1950; N.Y., March 10, 1951); Williams's *The Rose Tattoo* (1950–51; N.Y., Feb. 3, 1951).

BIBL.: V. Kimberling, *D. D.: A Bio-bibliography* (Metuchen, N.J., 1987); C. Shore, ed., *D. D.: A Musical Celebration* (Stuyvesant, N.Y., 1995).

Dianin, Sergei, Russian writer on music; b. St. Petersburg, Dec. 26, 1888; d. Davidovo, Oct. 26, 1968. A son of Borodin's assistant in chemistry, he became a mathematician by profession; having access to Borodin's archives, he publ. 4 vols. of Borodin's letters (Moscow, 1928, 1936, 1949, 1950) and a vol. devoted to Borodin's life, materials, and documents (Moscow, 1955; 2d ed., 1960; Eng. tr., 1963).

Díaz, Justino, noted Puerto Rican bass; b. San Juan, Jan. 29, 1940. He studied at the Univ. of Puerto Rico (1958–59) and at the New England Cons. of Music in Boston (1959–62); he also received training from Frederick Jagel. In 1957 he made his operatic debut as Ben in Menotti's *The Telephone* in San German, Puerto Rico, and in 1961 he appeared with the New England Opera Theater in Boston. After winning the Metropolitan Opera Auditions of the Air, he made his debut with the company in New York as Monterone on Oct. 23, 1963; was chosen to create the role of Antony in Barber's *Antony and Cleopatra* at the opening of the new Metropolitan Opera house at Lincoln Center on Sept. 16, 1966. He made guest appearances in Salzburg, Hamburg, Vienna, Munich, Milan, and other European music centers. On Sept. 10, 1971, he appeared in the premiere of Ginastera's *Beatrix Cenci*, which inaugurated the opera house at the Kennedy Center in Washington, D.C. On March 4, 1973, he made his N.Y. City Opera debut as Francesco in the same opera. In 1976 he made his first appearance at London's Covent Garden as Escamillo. In 1987 he sang Iago in Zeffirelli's film version of *Otello*. In 1990 he made his debut with the Cincinnati Opera as Amonasro.

Dibdin, Charles, English composer; b. Dibdin, near Southampton (baptized), March 15, 1745; d. London, July 25, 1814. From 1756 to 1759 he was a chorister at Winchester Cathedral. He took lessons there from Kent and Fussell, but was chiefly self-taught in composition. At 15 he went to London, where he was engaged at Covent Garden as a singing actor, and soon began to write for the stage. His first piece, *The Shepherd's Artifice*, was produced at his benefit performance, at Covent Garden, on May 21, 1764. He was engaged at Birmingham from 1763 to 1765, and at Covent Garden again until 1768, when he went over to Drury Lane. Falling out with Garrick, he went to France in 1776 to avoid imprisonment for debt, remaining there until 1778, when he was appointed composer to Covent Garden, having up to that time brought out 8 operas. From 1782 to 1784, he was manager of the newly erected Royal Circus (later the Surrey Theatre). After the failure of certain theatrical enterprises, and a projected journey to India, he commenced a series of monodramatic "table-entertainments," of which song was a principal feature, and which were extremely popular from 1789 to 1805; in these Dibdin appeared as author, composer, narrator, singer, and accompanist. He then built and managed a small theater of his own, which opened in 1796; he retired in 1805 on a pension, which was withdrawn for a time, but subsequently restored. Dibdin also composed numerous sea songs which were very popular at the time. He publ. *The Musical Tour of Mr. Dibdin* (1788), *History of the Stage* (5 vols., 1795), *The Professional Life of Mr. Dibdin* (4 vols., 1803), and various novels. His grandson, Henry Edward Dibdin (b. London, Sept. 8, 1813; d. Edinburgh, May 6, 1866), was an organist, harpist, and teacher who compiled the collection *The Standard Psalm Tune Book* (1851).

BIBL.: E. Dibdin, *A C. D. Bibliography* (Liverpool, 1937); E. Holmes, *C. D.* (diss., Univ. of Southampton, 1974).

Dickie, Murray, Scottish tenor; b. Bishopton, April 3, 1924. After studies in Glasgow, he pursued training with Dino Borgioli in London, Stefan Pollmann in Vienna, and Guido Farinelli in Milan. In 1947 he made his operatic debut as Count Almaviva in London, where he appeared at the Cambridge Theatre (1947–49) and at Covent Garden (1949–52). He sang at the Glyndebourne Festivals (1950–54), the Vienna State Opera (from 1951), and the Salzburg Festivals (from 1955). On Oct. 18, 1962, he made his Metropolitan

Opera debut in New York as David in *Die Meistersinger von Nürnberg*, remaining on the roster until 1965; he was again on its roster (1966–67; 1970–72). He became well known for his buffo roles.

Dickinson, Meriel, English mezzo-soprano; b. Lytham St. Annes, Lancashire, April 8, 1940. She studied piano and voice in England, and also attended the Vienna Academy of Music. After making her London debut in 1964, she devoted herself mainly to the performance of modern music; her brother toured with her as accompanist, and also composed a number of works for her. In 1986 she made her N.Y. debut in Berio's *Laborintus*. Her brother is the English composer, pianist, and teacher Peter Dickinson (b. Lytham St. Annes, Lancashire, Nov. 15, 1934).

Di Domenica, Robert (Anthony), American composer, flutist, and teacher; b. N.Y., March 4, 1927. He studied music education at N.Y. Univ. (B.S., 1951), composition with Riegger and Josef Schmid, and flute with Harold Bennett (1949–55). He was a flutist with various orchs. and ensembles, and also taught flute. In 1969 he joined the faculty of the New England Cons. of Music in Boston, where he was an assoc. dean (1973–76) and dean (1976–78), and then a teacher of theory and composition (from 1978). In 1972 he held a Guggenheim fellowship. In 1994 the Robert Di Domenica Collection was completed at the Library of Congress in Washington, D.C. In his works, he follows a serial course while utilizing such diverse elements as jazz and American popular music. He composed the operas *The Balcony* (1972; Boston, June 16, 1990), *The Scarlet Letter* (1986), *Beatrice Cenci* (1993), *The Cenci* (1995), and *Francesco Cenci* (1996).

Didur, Adamo, famous Polish bass; b. Wola Sekowa, near Sanok, Galicia, Dec. 24, 1874; d. Katowice, Jan. 7, 1946. He studied with Wysocki in Lemberg and Emmerich in Milan, where he made his concert debut in 1894; later that year he made his operatic debut as Méphistophélès in Rio de Janeiro. He sang at the Warsaw Opera (1899–1903), Milan's La Scala (1903–06), London's Covent Garden (1905), and Buenos Aires's Teatro Colón (1905–08). On Nov. 4, 1907, he made an auspicious N.Y. debut as Alvise at the Manhattan Opera; his Metropolitan Opera debut followed as Ramfis on Nov. 16, 1908, and he remained on its roster as one of its leading artists until 1932. He then returned to Poland; his appointment as director of the Warsaw Opera in 1939 was aborted by the outbreak of World War II. He later settled in Katowice as a voice teacher, founding an opera company (1945) and becoming director of the Cons. His portrayals of Leporello and Boris Godunov were particularly memorable.

Diepenbrock, Alphons (Johannes Maria), eminent Dutch composer; b. Amsterdam, Sept. 2, 1862; d. there, April 5, 1921. He received training in piano, violin, and voice. As a composer, he was autodidact, having made a thorough study of 16th-century Netherlands polyphony, Beethoven's late string quartets, and Wagner's music. He pursued his education at the Univ. of Amsterdam, where he studied classical literature (graduated 1888, with a thesis on Seneca). After teaching classics at the 's-Hertogenbosch grammar school, he returned to Amsterdam in 1894 as a private teacher of Latin and Greek. He also pursued his career as a composer, eventually developing a personal style in which Wagnerian elements were entertwined with impressionistic modalities à la Debussy (from 1910). Diepenbrock was a notable composer of sacred music, creating such outstanding works as the *Missa in die festo* (1891) and the *Te Deum* (1897). Among his other distinguished vocal works were the 2 *Hymnen an die Nacht* (1899) and *Die Nacht* (1911). His incidental scores were also noteworthy. He left a number of incomplete MSS at his death. E. Reeser ed. his letters and documents as *Alphons Dieprenbrock: Brieven en documenten* (4 vols., Amsterdam, 1962–74). His compositional output includes incidental music to Verhagen's *Marsyas* (1910), J. van der Vondel's *Gijsbrecht van Aemstel* (1912), Aristophanes's *The Birds* (1917), Goethe's *Faust* (1918), and Sophocles' *Electra* (1920).

Dieren, Bernard van, Dutch-English composer and writer; b. Rotterdam, Dec. 27, 1887; d. London, April 24, 1936. He began playing the violin at an early age but later pursued his enthusiasm for literature and science. As a composer, he was self-taught. In 1909 he settled in 1909 in England, where he devoted much time to writing criticism for continental newspapers and magazines. Among his writings were a study of the sculptor Jacob Epstein (London, 1920) and an interesting collection of essays, *Down Among the Dead Men* (London, 1935). As a composer, he developed a highly personal style of harmonic and contrapuntal complexity. He composed the opera *The Tailor* (1917).

BIBL.: A. Chisolm, *B. v.D.: An Introduction* (London, 1984).

Dietrich, Albert (Hermann), German conductor and composer; b. Forsthaus Golk, near Meissen, Aug. 28, 1829; d. Berlin, Nov. 19, 1908. He was a pupil of J. Otto in Dresden (1842–47) and of Moscheles and Rietz at Leipzig (1847–51); also studied with Schumann (one of his best pupils) at Düsseldorf (1851–54). From 1855 to 1861 he was a concert conductor, and from 1859 municipal music director, at Bonn; from 1861, at Oldenburg. He retired in 1890 and lived in Berlin, being made Royal Prof. in 1899. He wrote *Erinnerungen an Johannes Brahms in Briefen, besonders aus seiner Jugendzeit* (Leipzig, 1898; in Eng., 1899). He composed the operas *Robin Hood* (Frankfurt am Main, 1879) and *Das Sonntagskind* (Bremen, 1886); also incidental music.

Dietsch, (Pierre-) Louis (-Philippe), French conductor and composer; b. Dijon, March 17, 1808; d. Paris, Feb. 20, 1865. He studied at Choron's Institution Royale de Musique Classique et Religieuse in Paris, then with A. Reicha (counterpoint) and M.-P. Chenie (double bass) at the Paris Cons., winning a premier prix for the latter (1830). He played double bass in the orchs. of the Théâtre-Italien and the Paris Opéra; was also maître de chapelle at St. Eustache (1830–39) and at the Madeleine (from 1849), as well as chorus master at the Opéra (from 1840). With Paul Foucher and Henri Revoil as librettists, he wrote the opera *Le Vaisseau fantôme* (Opéra, Nov. 9, 1842), a subject also treated by Wagner in his opera *Der fliegende Holländer*. Dietsch's opera received only 11 hearings and then was totally forgotten. He became conductor of the Paris Opéra in 1860, where he led the 3 notorious performances of the Paris version of Wagner's *Tannhäuser* in 1861; after an argument with Verdi, he resigned his post in 1863.

Di Giuseppe, Enrico, American tenor; b. Philadelphia, Oct. 14, 1932. He was a pupil of Richard Bonelli at the Curtis Inst. of Music in Philadelphia and of Hans Heinz at the Juilliard School of Music in New York. In 1959 he made his operatic debut as Massenet's Des Grieux in New Orleans; then toured with the Metropolitan Opera National Co. On March 18, 1965, he made his first appearance at the N.Y. City Opera as Michele in Menotti's *The Saint of Bleecker Street*; he then sang there regularly from 1967 to 1981. He made his Metropolitan Opera debut in New York as Turiddu on June 20, 1970, where he later sang many Italian and French roles. He also sang opera in other major U.S. operatic centers and toured as a concert artist. Among his finest portrayals were Mozart's Ferrando and Almaviva, Bellini's Pollione, Verdi's Alfredo, Massenet's Werther, and Puccini's Pinkerton.

Dijk, Jan van, Dutch pianist, teacher, and composer; b. Oostzaan, June 4, 1918. He studied composition with Pijper in Rotterdam (1936–46); gave piano recitals; he taught at the Brabant Cons. in Tilburg from its founding in 1955, and at the Royal Cons. of Music in The Hague from 1961. A prolific composer, he wrote hundreds of works. He also produced music in the 31-tone system devised by the Dutch physicist Adriaan Fokker. Within his substantial catalog of works are the operas *Flying Dutchman* (1953) and *Protesilaus and Laodamia* (1968).

Dimitrova, Ghena, Bulgarian soprano; b. Beglj, May 6, 1941. She studied with Christo Brumbarov at the Bulgarian State Cons. in Sofia; she then sang with the Sofia Opera. After winning 1st prize in the Sofia Competition in 1970, she scored a major success as Amelia in *Un ballo in maschera* in Parma (1972); she subsequently held engagements in France, Spain, South America, Moscow, Vienna, and Rome. In 1983 she made her London debut in a concert performance of *La Gioconda*; later that year she appeared as Turandot at Milan's La Scala. In 1984 she sang at N.Y.'s Carnegie Hall and at the Salzburg Festival; later operatic roles included Turandot at London's Covent Garden (1985) and Leonora in *Il Trovatore* at the San Francisco Opera (1986). On Dec. 14, 1987, she made her Metropolitan Opera debut in New York as Turandot. In 1992 she appeared as Leonora in *La forza del destino* in Naples. She sang Lady Macbeth in Athens in 1997. Among her other roles were Aida, Norma, Santuzza, and Tosca.

Dimov, Ivan, Bulgarian composer; b. Kazanlak, Dec. 13, 1927. He studied composition with Goleminov at the Bulgarian State Cons. in Sofia, graduating in 1953; then took courses in advanced composition at the Moscow Cons. He composed the operas *They Have Stolen the Council* (1966) and *The Emigrant* (1973) and the ballet *Laughter of Africa* (1966).

D'Indy, Vincent. See **Indy, Vincent d'.**

Dineşcu, Violeta, Romanian-born German composer, teacher, and writer on music; b. Bucharest, July 13, 1953. She studied at the Bucharest Cons. (B.A. in composition, piano, and pedagogy, 1977; M.A. in composition, 1978). After teaching at the George Enescu Music School in Bucharest (1978–82), she settled in West Germany and in 1989 became a naturalized German citizen. From 1987 to 1990 she taught at the Heidelberg Cons. for Church Music, and from 1989 to 1991 at the Frankfurt am Main Cons. From 1990 to 1994 she was on the faculty of the Bayreuth Academy of Music. In 1996 she became prof. of composition at the Univ. of Oldenburg. She contributed articles on music to publs. in Europe and the United States. In her compositions, melodic and rhythmic elements are complemented by a concern for mathematical exactitude, the exploration of sound potentials, and the utilization of electronic instruments. Among her works is the film score *Tabu*, for the 1931 F. Murnau film (Frankfurt am Main, April 5, 1988).

WORKS: DRAMATIC: OPERAS: *Hunger and Thirst*, chamber opera (1985; Freiburg im Breisgau, Feb. 1, 1986); *Der 35. Mai*, children's opera (Mannheim, Nov. 30, 1986); *Eréndira*, chamber opera (1992); *Schachnovelle*, opera (1994). BALLET: *Der Kreisel* (Ulm, May 26, 1985).

Dippel, (Johann) Andreas, German-American tenor and operatic impresario; b. Kassel, Nov. 30, 1866; d. Los Angeles, May 12, 1932. He studied with Nina Zottmayr in Kassel, Julius Hey in Berlin, Alberto Leoni in Milan, and Johannes Ress in Vienna. In 1887 he made his operatic debut as Lionel in *Martha* in Bremen, where he sang until 1892; he also appeared at the Bayreuth Festival in 1889. On Nov. 26, 1890, he made his Metropolitan Opera debut in New York as Asrael, returning on its roster from 1898 to 1902 and from 1903 to 1910; he also sang in Breslau (1892–93), at the Vienna Court Opera (1893), and at London's Covent Garden (1897–1900). With Gatti-Casazza, he shared administrative duties at the Metropolitan Opera (1908–10), then was manager of the Chicago Grand Opera (1910–13). After managing his own light opera company, he settled in Los Angeles as a vocal coach. His repertoire included almost 150 roles; he was particularly successful in operas by Wagner.

Di Stefano, Giuseppe, noted Italian tenor; b. Motta Santa Anastasia, near Catania, July 24, 1921. He was a pupil of Adriano Torchi and Luigi Montesanto in Milan. During World War II, he was conscripted into the Italian Army but in 1943 he went AWOL to Switzerland, where he was interned as a refugee. After making appearances on the Swiss radio and in concert in 1944, he returned to Italy and made his operatic debut in 1946 as Massenet's Des Grieux in Reggio Emilia, a role he also chose for his first appearance at Milan's La Scala the following year. He made his Metropolitan Opera debut in New York on Feb. 25, 1948, as the Duke of Mantua; he remained on its roster until 1952, appearing as Rossini's Almaviva, Faust, Nemorino, Rinuccio in *Gianni Schicchi*, Alfredo, Rodolfo, and Pinkerton; he returned for the 1955–56 and 1964–65 seasons. From 1948 to 1952 he appeared in Mexico City. In 1950 he made his San Francisco Opera debut as Rodolfo. From 1952 to 1961 he was a principal member at La Scala, where he appeared as Radames, Canio, and Turiddu, and where he created the role of Giuliano in Pizzetti's *Calzare d'Argento* in 1961. In 1954 he made his first appearance at the Lyric Theatre of Chicago as Edgardo. His British debut followed in 1957 as Nemorino at the Edinburgh Festival. In 1961 he made his debut at London's Covent Garden as Cavaradossi. He also sang at the Vienna State Opera, the Berlin State Opera, the Paris Opéra, and the Teatro Colón in Buenos Aires. In 1973–74 he made a concert tour of the world with Maria Callas.

Dittersdorf, Karl Ditters von (original name, **Karl Ditters**), eminent Austrian composer and violinist; b. Vienna, Nov. 2, 1739; d. Schloss Rothlhotta, Neuhof, Bohemia, Oct. 24, 1799. He played violin as a child, then studied with König and Ziegler. The prince of Sachsen-Hildburghausen made it possible for him to take private violin lessons with Trani and to study composition with Bonno; he played in the prince's orch. from 1751 to 1761. In 1761 he went to Vienna, where he was engaged as a member of the Court Theater Orch. (until 1764). He was befriended by Gluck, who took him along on his Italian journey, where he had an occasion to appear in public as a violinist. In 1765 he assumed the post of Kapellmeister to the Bishop of Grosswardein in Hungary, where he remained until 1769. His career as a composer began in earnest at this time; he wrote an oratorio, *Isacco, figura del redentore,* several cantatas, and many pieces of orch. and chamber music. In 1770 he became Kapellmeister to the prince-bishop of Breslau, Count von Schaffgotsch, at Johannisberg in Silesia. There he wrote mostly for the stage, bringing out 12 works between 1771 and 1776. However, he wrote his most important dramatic works in Vienna and for the ducal theater in Oels. He gained fame with his first Singspiel, *Doctor und Apotheker*, produced in Vienna on July 11, 1786; it was followed by other successful stage works, *Betrug durch Aberglauben, Die Liebe im Narrenhause, Das rote Käppchen*, and *Hieronymus Knicker*. He received several honors during his lifetime: in 1770 the Pope bestowed upon him the Order of the Golden Spur; in 1773 he was ennobled by the emperor as von Dittersdorf. Upon the death of the prince-bishop in 1795, he was granted a small pension, and found himself in straitened circumstances until a friend, Baron von Stillfried, took him into his castle, Rothlhotta, where he remained until his death. Dittersdorf was an important figure in the Viennese Classical school of composition, although he lacked the genius of Haydn and Mozart. He was able to fuse the common folk-song elements of the period with brilliant ensembles characteristic of opera buffa. His Singspiels reveal a jovial humor, melodic charm, and rhythmic vitality. His syms. and concertos are also of interest as characteristic specimens of the period.

WORKS: DRAMATIC: *Il viaggiatore americano in Joannesberg*, farce (Johannisberg, May 1, 1771; not extant); *L'amore disprezzato (Pancratio; Amore in musica)*, operetta buffa (Johannisberg, 1771); *Il finto pazzo per amore*, operetta giocosa (Johannisberg, June 3, 1772); *Il tutore e la pupilla*, dramma giocoso (Johannisberg, May 1, 1773); *Lo sposo burlato*, operetta giocosa (Johannisberg, 1773 or 1775; another version as *Der gefoppte Bräutigam*); *Il tribunale di Giove*, serenade with prologue (Johannisberg, 1774); *Il maniscalco*, operetta giocosa (Johannisberg, May 1, 1775); *La contadina fedele*, opera giocosa (Johannisberg, 1776); *La moda ossia Gli scompigli domestici*, dramma giocoso (Johannisberg, June 3, 1776); *L'Arcifanfano, re de' matti*, opera giocosa (Johannisberg, 1776); *Il barone di Rocca Antica*, operetta giocosa (Johannisberg, 1776); *I visionari* (Johannisberg, 1776; not extant); *Doctor und Apotheker (Der Apotheker und der Doctor)*, Singspiel (Vienna, July 11, 1786); *Betrug durch Aberglauben oder Die Schatzgräber (Der glückliche Betrug; Die dienstbaren Geister)*, Singspiel (Vienna, Oct. 3, 1786); *Democrito corretto*, opera giocosa (Vienna, Jan. 24, 1787; performed under various titles); *Die Liebe im Narrenhause*, Singspiel (Vienna, April 12, 1787); *Das rote Käppchen oder Hilft's nicht so schadt's nicht (Die rote Kappe; Das Rotkäppchen)*, comic operetta (Vienna, 1788); *Im Dunkeln ist nicht gut munkeln oder Irrung über Irrung (25,000 Gulden)*, comic opera (Vienna, Feb. 1789); *Hieronymus Knicker (Lucius Knicker; Chrisostomus Knicker; Hokus Pokus oder Die Lebensessenz)*, Singspiel (Vienna, July 7, 1789); *Die Hochzeit des Figaro*, Singspiel (Brunn, 1789?; music not extant); *Der Schiffspatron oder Der neue Gutsherr*, Singspiel (Vienna, 1789); *Hokus-Pokus oder Der Gaukelspiel*, comic opera (Vienna, 1790); *Der Teufel ein Hydraulikus*, comedy (Gratz, 1790); *Der Fürst und sein Volk*, pasticcio (Leipzig, March 5?, 1791; music not extant; in collaboration with F. Piterlin and F. Bertoni); *Das Gespenst mit der Trommel (Geisterbanner)*, Singspiel (Oels, Aug. 16, 1794); *Don Quixote der Zweyte (Don Chisciotto)*, Singspiel (Oels, Feb. 4, 1795); *Gott Mars und der Hauptmann von Bärenzahn (Gott Mars oder Der eiserne Mann)*, Singspiel (Oels, May 30, 1795); *Der Durchmarsch*, an arrangement of J. Paneck's *Die christliche Judenbraut* (Oels, Aug. 29, 1795); *Der Schach von Schiras*, Singspiel (Oels, Sept. 15, 1795); *Die befreyten Gwelfen (Die Guelfen)*, prologue (Oels, Oct. 29, 1795); *Ugolino*, serious Singspiel (Oels, June 11, 1796); *Die lustigen Weiber von Windsor*, Singspiel (Oels, June 25, 1796); *Der schöne Herbsttag*, dialogue (Oels, Oct. 29, 1796); *Der Ternengewinnst oder Der gedemütigte Stolz (Terno secco)*, Singspiel (Oels, Feb. 11, 1797); *Der Mädchenmark*, Singspiel (Oels, April 18, 1797); *Die Opera buffa*, comic opera (Vienna, 1798); *Don Coribaldi ossia L'usurpata prepotenza*, drama (Dresden, 1798?); *Ein Stück mit kleinen Liedern*, opera based on *Frau Sybilla trinkt keinen Wein* and *Das Reich der Toten*; comic opera version based on *Amore in musica* (Grosswardein, 1767?; not extant); etc. OTHER: *Isacco, figura del redentore*, oratorio (Grosswardein, 1766); *Il Davide nella Valle di Terebintho (Davidde penitente)*, oratorio (Johannisberg, 1771); *L'Esther ossia La Liberatrice del popolo giudaico nella Persia*, oratorio (Vienna, Dec. 19, 1773); *Giobbe (Hiob)*, oratorio (Vienna, April 8–9, 1786); etc.

WRITINGS: "Briefe über Behandlung italienischer Texte bei der Composition," *Allgemeine musikalische Zeitung* (Leipzig, 1799); an autobiography publ. as *K. v. D.s Lebensbeschreibung, Seinem Sohne in die Feder diktiert* (Leipzig, 1801; Eng. tr., London, 1896; new ed. by N. Miller, Munich, 1967).

BIBL.: C. Krebs, *D.iana* (Berlin, 1900); K. Holl, *Carl D. v. D.s Opern für das wiederhergestellte Johannisberger Theater* (diss., Univ. of Bonn, 1913); H. Unverricht, *Carl D. v.D. 1739–1799: Der Schlesische Opernkomponist* (Würzburg, 1991).

Dittrich, Paul-Heinz, German composer and teacher; b. Gornsdorf, Dec. 4, 1930. He studied composition at the Leipzig Hochschule für Musik (1951–56; diploma, 1958), and then attended Wagner-Régeny's master classes at the Academy of Arts in East Berlin (1958–60). From 1960 to 1976 he taught at the Hanns Eisler Hochschule für Musik in East Berlin, returning there as a prof. of composition in 1990. In 1991 he founded the Bandenburgische Colloquium für Neue Musik in Zeuthen. He received the Artist's Prize in 1981 and the National Prize in 1988 of the German Democratic Republic. In 1983 he became a member of the Academy of Arts in Berlin, serving as secretary of its music section from 1990. His works astutely utilize modern forms and technical idioms, while observing and preserving the pragmatic elements of instrumental and vocal writing. He composed the opera *Poesien*, opera (1987–91).

Dlugoszewski, Lucia, innovative American composer, performer, teacher, and inventor; b. Detroit, June 16, 1931. She studied piano with Agelageth Morrison at the Detroit Cons. (1940–46); after courses in physics at Wayne State Univ. in Detroit (1946–49), she went to New York and studied analysis with Salzer at the Mannes College of Music (1950–53); she also had lessons in piano with Grete Sultan and in composition with Varèse. The latter greatly influenced her, as did the N.Y. School of painters and poets. In an effort to expand her compositional parameters, she invented several instruments. Her most noteworthy creation was the so-called timbre piano (c.1951), a revamped conventional piano activated by striking the strings with mallets, or having the strings bowed and picked. She became especially successful as a composer for the dance, and was closely associated with the Erick Hawkins Dance Co. From 1960 she was also with the Foundation for Modern Dance. In 1966 she received the National Inst. of Arts and Letters Award and in 1977 she became the first woman to receive the Koussevitzky International Recording Award for her *Fire Fragile Flight*.

WORKS: DRAMATIC: OPERAS: *Tiny Opera* (1953); *The Heidi Songs* (1970). DANCE: *Openings of the Eye* (1952); *Here and Now with Watchers* (1954–57); *8 Clear Places* (1958–60); *Cantilever* (1964); *To Everyone Out There* (1964); *Geography of Noon* (1964); *Lords of Persia* No. 1 (1965), No. 2 (1968), and No. 3 (1971); *Dazzle on a Knife's Edge* (1966); *Tight Rope* (1968); *Agathlon Algebra* (1968); *Black Lake* (1969); *Of Love . . . Or He Is a Cry, She Is His Ear* (1971); *Angels of the Inmost Heaven* (1972); *Avanti* (1983); *The Woman Deunde Amor* (1984–85). Also incidental music.

Döbber, Johannes, German composer; b. Berlin, March 28, 1866; d. there, Jan. 26, 1921. He was a pupil, in the Stern Cons. in Berlin, of R. Radecke, L. Bussler (composition), and C. Agghazy (piano). He taught the first piano class in the Kullak Cons. in Berlin; he became Kapellmeister at Darmstadt, then was at Coburg-Gotha as tutor in music to Princess Beatrice. He was a teacher and music critic of the Volkszeitung in Berlin (1908).

WORKS: DRAMATIC: OPERAS: *Die Strassensängerin* (Gotha, 1890); *Der Schmied von Gretna-Green* (Berlin, 1893); *Dolcetta* (Brandenburg, 1894); *Die Rose von Genzano* (Gotha, 1895); *Die Grille* (Leipzig, 1897); *Die drei Rosen* (Coburg, 1902); *Der Zauberlehrling* (Braunschweig, 1907); *Die Franzosenzeit* (Berlin, 1913); *Fahrende Musikanten,* song play (Magdeburg, 1917). OPERETTAS: *Die Millionenbraut* (Magdeburg, 1913); *Des Kaisers Rock* (Berlin, 1915).

Dobbs, Mattiwilda, black American soprano and teacher; b. Atlanta, July 11, 1925. She was educated at Spelman College in Atlanta (B.A., 1946) and at Columbia Univ. (M.A., 1948); pursued vocal training with Lotte Leonard in New York (1946–50) and Bernac in Paris (1950–52). In 1948 she won the Marian Anderson scholarship contest and made her debut as a concert artist; in 1951 she won 1st prize in singing in the Geneva Competition. After appearing in opera and recitals in Holland (1952), she sang at Milan's La Scala, the Glyndebourne Festival, and London's Covent Garden (1953). In 1955 she appeared at the San Francisco Opera; on Nov. 9, 1956, she made her Metropolitan Opera debut in New York as Gilda. In 1957 she made her first appearance at the Royal Swedish Opera in Stockholm; also sang at the Hamburg State Opera (1961–63; 1967). In addition to her operatic and concert engagements in the United States and Europe, she also toured in Australia, New Zealand, and Israel. She was a visiting prof. at the Univ. of Texas in Austin (1973–74); then was a prof. at the Univ. of Ill. (1975–76), the Univ. of Georgia (1976–77), and Howard Univ. in Washington, D.C. (from 1977).

Döbricht, Johanna Elisabeth, German soprano; b. Weissenfels, Sept. 16, 1692; d. Darmstadt, Feb. 23, 1786. Her parents were the singers Daniel Döbricht (1650–94) and Katharina Elisabeth Grosse. She studied in Weimar with Christoph Alt. After singing at the Leipzig Opera, she became a court and church singer in Darmstadt. She also made tours as a concert artist. In 1740 she was granted a pension by the Darmstadt court, but she continued to appear in public for many years thereafter. In 1713 she married **Ernst Christian Hesse**.

Dobronič, Antun, Croatian composer and teacher; b. Jelsa, island of Hvar, April 2, 1878; d. Zagreb, Dec. 12, 1955. He studied music with Novák in Prague; he then returned to Yugoslavia, and in 1921 was appointed a prof. at the Zagreb Cons. He wrote many stage works, among them the operas *Ragusean Diptych*, *The Man of God, Mara, Dubrovnički triptihon* (1925), *Udovica Rozlinka* (1934), *Rkac* (1938), and *Goran* (1944), and a ballet, *The Giant Horse*.

Dobrowen, Issay (Alexandrovich) (real name, **Ishok Israelevich Barabeichik**), distinguished Russian conductor; b. Nizhny-Novgorod, Feb. 27, 1891; d. Oslo, Dec. 9, 1953. His orphaned mother was adopted by Israil Dobrovel; Issay Dobrowen changed his legal name, Dobrovel, to Dobrowein, and later to Dobrowen. He studied at the Nizhny-Novgorod Cons. as a small child (1896–1900); then entered the Moscow Cons. and studied with Igumnov (piano) and Taneyev (composition); he went to Vienna for additional training with Godowsky (piano). Returning to Moscow, he made his conducting debut at the Kommisarzhevsky Theater in 1919; he then conducted at the Bolshoi Theater (1921–22); in 1922 he led the Dresden State Opera in the German premiere of Mussorgsky's opera *Boris Godunov*; he subsequently conducted at the Berlin Volksoper (1924–25) and the Sofia Opera (1927–28). In 1931 he made his American debut conducting the San Francisco Sym. Orch.; was guest conductor with the Minneapolis Sym. Orch., the Philadelphia Orch., and the N.Y. Phil. He was a regular conductor of the Budapest Opera from 1936 to 1939; at the outbreak of World War II he went to Sweden, where he won his greatest successes as conductor and producer at the Stockholm Royal Theater (1941–45). From 1948 he conducted at La Scala in Milan. In 1952 he conducted at London's Covent Garden. He was a prolific composer; wrote several piano concertos and pieces for piano solo, in a Romantic vein; also an orch. fairy tale, *1,001 Nights* (Moscow, May 27, 1922).

Dobrzynski, Ignacy Felix, Polish pianist and composer; b. Romanov, Volhynia, Feb. 15, 1807; d. Warsaw, Oct. 10, 1867. The son of composer Ignacy Dobrzynski (b. Warsaw, Feb. 2, 1779; d. there, Aug. 16, 1841), he was taught by his father; then, being a fellow pupil and close friend of Chopin, by Chopin's teacher Elsner. On subsequent pianistic tours to Leipzig, Dresden, and Berlin (1845–47), he had great success. For a time he directed opera in Warsaw, where he finally settled. He wrote an opera, *Monbar or The Filibuster* (1838; Warsaw, Jan. 10, 1863). His son Bronislaw Dobrzynski publ. a monograph on him (Warsaw, 1893).

Doche, Joseph-Denis, French organist, conductor, and composer; b. Paris, Aug. 22, 1766; d. Soissons, July 20, 1825. He was a chorister at the Cathedral of Meaux, then organist at Coutances in Normandy. He played string instruments in a theater orch. in Paris from 1794 until 1810, then became a conductor, retiring in 1823. He wrote numerous successful vaudevilles, as well as the operas *Point de bruit, ou Le Contrat simulé* (Paris, Oct. 25, 1802) and *Les Deux Sentinelles* (Paris, Sept. 27, 1803).

Dodgson, Stephen (Cuthbert Vivian), English composer; b. London, March 17, 1924. He studied with R.O. Morris at the Royal College of Music in London, where he subsequently taught (1965–82). He was also active as a broadcaster. Among his numerous compositions is the opera *Margaret Catchpole* (1979).

Doese, Helena, Swedish soprano; b. Göteborg, Aug. 13, 1946. She received training in Göteborg and from Luigi Ricci in Rome and Erik Werba and Gerald Moore in Vienna. Following her operatic debut in 1971 as Aida in Göteborg, she sang with the Bern Opera. In 1974 she made her first appearance at the Glyndebourne Festival as Mozart's Countess and made her debut at London's Covent Garden as Mimi. From 1975 she made regular appearances at the Royal Opera in Stockholm, where her roles included Eva, Liù, Mimi, and Kát'a Kabanová. She made her U.S. debut in 1982 at the San Francisco Opera as Countess Almaviva. In 1987 she portrayed Agathe at the Berlin Deutsche Oper. In 1992 she was engaged as Ariadne in Stuttgart. She appeared as Chrysothemis in Frankfurt am Main in 1994. Among her other roles were Fiordiligi, Amelia Boccanegra, Sieglinde, the Marschallin, and Jenůfa.

Döhl, Friedhelm, German composer and teacher; b. Göttingen, July 7, 1936. He was a pupil of Fortner at the Freiburg im Breisgau Hochschule für Musik (1956–64) and pursued his academic studies at the Univ. of Göttingen (Ph.D., 1966, with the diss. *Weberns Beitrag zur Stilwende der neuen Musik*; publ. in Munich, 1976). After lecturing at the Düsseldorf Hochschule für Musik (1965–68), he was principal lecturer (1969–72) and prof. (1972–74) at the Musicological Inst. of the Free Univ. in Berlin; then was founder-director of the studio for electronic music, for music and theater, and for non-European music at the Basel Academy of Music (1974–82). He served as a prof. of composition at the Lübeck Hochschule für Musik from 1983, and as its director from 1991. Döhl's earliest creative efforts were heavily influenced by Webern and Schoenberg; he later developed an innovative style notable for both exploration of color and experimental instrumentation. He composed the opera *Medea* (1987–90) and the ballets *Ikaros* (1977–78) and *Fiesta* (1982).

Döhler, Theodor (von), Austrian pianist and composer; b. Naples, April 20, 1814; d. Florence, Feb. 21, 1856. He was a pupil of Julius Benedict at Naples and of Czerny (piano) and Sechter (composition) at Vienna. In 1831 he became pianist to the duke of Lucca; lived for a time in Naples; made brilliant pianistic tours from 1836 to 1846 in Germany, Italy, France, the Netherlands, and England. In 1843 went to Copenhagen, thence to Russia, and in 1846 to Paris; settled in Florence in 1848. In 1846 the duke, his patron, ennobled him, and he married a Russian countess. He wrote an opera, *Tancreda*, which was performed posthumously in Florence in 1880.

Dohnányi, Christoph von, eminent German conductor of Hungarian descent, grandson of **Ernst (Ernö) von Dohnányi**; b. Berlin, Sept. 8, 1929. He began to study the piano as a child; his musical training was interrupted by World War II. His father, Hans von Dohnányi, a jurist, and his uncle, Dietrich Bonhoeffer, the Protestant theologian and author, were executed by the Nazis for their involvement in the July 20, 1944, attempt on Hitler's life. After the war, he studied jurisprudence at the Univ. of Munich; in 1948 he enrolled at the Hochschule für Musik in Munich, and won the Richard Strauss Prize for composition and conducting. Making his way to the United States, he continued his studies with his grandfather at Florida State Univ. at Tallahassee; also attended sessions at the Berkshire Music Center at Tanglewood. Returning to Germany, he received a job as a coach and conductor at the Frankfurt am Main Opera (1952–57). Progressing rapidly, he served as Generalmusikdirektor in Lübeck (1957–63) and Kassel (1963–66), chief conductor of the Cologne Radio Sym. Orch. (1964–70), and director of the Frankfurt am Main Opera (1968–77). From 1977 to 1984 he was Staatsopernintendant of the Hamburg State Opera. In 1984 he assumed the position of music director of the Cleveland Orch., having been appointed music director designate in 1982, succeeding Lorin Maazel. In the meantime, he had engagements as a guest conductor of the Vienna State Opera, Covent Garden in London, La Scala in Milan, the Metropolitan Opera in New York, the Berlin Phil., the Vienna Phil., and the Concertgebouw Orch. in Amsterdam. In 1992 the Cleveland Orch., under Dohnányi's direction, became the resident orch. of the Salzburg Festival, the first time this honor was bestowed upon an American orch. On Dec. 12, 1993, he conducted Beethoven's 9th Sym. in a gala concert at Cleveland's Public Auditorium marking the 75th anniversary of the founding of the Cleveland Orch. He also was principal guest conductor (1994–97) and principal conductor (from 1997) of the Philharmonia Orch. in London. From 1998 to 2000 he also was principal guest conductor and artistic director of the Orchestre de Paris. As both a sym. and opera conductor, Dohnányi has proved himself a master technician and a versatile musician capable of notably distinguished interpretations of all types of music, from Baroque to the avant-garde. He married **Anja Silja**.

Dohnányi, Ernst (Ernö) von, eminent Hungarian pianist, composer, conductor, and pedagogue, grandfather of **Christoph von Dohnányi**; b. Pressburg, July 27, 1877; d. N.Y., Feb. 9, 1960. He began his musical studies with his father, an amateur cellist; then studied piano and theory with Károly Forstner. In 1894 he entered the Royal Academy of Music in Budapest, where he took courses in piano with Thomán and in composition with Koessler. In 1896 he received the Hungarian Millennium Prize, established to commemorate the thousand years of existence of Hungary, for his sym. He graduated from the Academy of Music in 1897, and then went to Berlin for additional piano studies with d'Albert. He made his debut in a recital in Berlin on Oct. 1, 1897; on Oct. 24, 1898, he played Beethoven's 4th Piano Concerto in London; then followed a series of successful concerts in the United States. Returning to Europe, he served as prof. of piano at the Hochschule für Musik in Berlin (1908–15). He then returned to Budapest, where he taught piano at the Royal Academy of Music; served briefly as its director in 1919, when he was appointed chief conductor of the Budapest Phil. In 1928 he became head of the piano classes at the Academy of Music; in 1934 he became its director. In 1931 he assumed the post of music director of the Hungarian Radio. As Hungary became embroiled in the events of World War II and partisan politics that invaded even the arts, Dohnányi resigned his directorship in 1941, and in 1944 he also resigned his post as chief conductor of the Budapest Phil. Personal tragedy also made it impossible for him to continue his work as a musician and teacher: both of his sons lost their lives. One of them, the German jurist Hans von Dohnányi, was executed for his role in the abortive attempt on Hitler's life; the other son was killed in combat. Late in 1944 he moved to Austria. At the war's end rumors were rife that Dohnányi used his influence with the Nazi overlords in Budapest to undermine the position of Bartók and other liberals, and that he acquiesced in anti-Semitic measures. But in 1945 the Allied occupation authorities exonerated him of all blame; even some prominent Jewish-Hungarian musicians testified in his favor. In 1947–48 he made a tour of England as a pianist; determined to emigrate to America, he accepted the position of piano teacher at Tucuman, Argentina; in 1949 he became composer-in-residence at Florida State Univ. in Tallahassee.

Dohnányi was a true virtuoso of the keyboard, and was greatly esteemed as a teacher; among his pupils were Solti, Anda, and Vázsonyi. His music represented the terminal flowering of European Romanticism, marked by passionate eloquence of expression while keeping within the framework of Classical forms. Brahms praised his early efforts. In retrospect, Dohnányi appears as a noble epigone of the past era, but pianists, particularly Hungarian pianists, often put his brilliant compositions on their programs. His most popular work with orch. is *Variations on a Nursery Song*; also frequently played is his Orch. Suite in F-sharp minor. Dohnányi himself presented his philosophy of life in a poignant pamphlet under the title *Message to Posterity* (Jacksonville, Fla., 1960).

WORKS: DRAMATIC: *Der Schleier der Pierrette*, pantomime (1908–09; Dresden, Jan. 22, 1910); *Tante Simona*, comic opera (1911–12; Dresden, Jan. 10, 1913); *A vajda tornya* (The Tower of the Voivod), opera (1915–22; Budapest, March 19, 1922); *Der Tenor*, comic opera (1920–27; Budapest, Feb. 9, 1929).

BIBL.: V. Papp, *D. E.* (Budapest, 1927); M. Reuth, *The Tallahassee Years of E. v.D.* (diss., Florida State Univ., 1962); B. Vázsonyi, *D. E.* (Budapest, 1971).

Dohnányi, Oliver von, Czech conductor; b. Trencin, March 2, 1955. He received training in violin, conducting, and composition at the Bratislava Cons., and in conducting at the Prague Academy of Music and the Vienna Hochschule für Musik. From 1979 to 1986 he conducted the Slovak Radio Sym. Orch. in Bratislava, where he also served as principal conductor of the Slovak National Opera. He was music director of the National Theater in Prague from 1993 to 1996. He appeared as a guest conductor with many of the major European opera companies and orchs.

Doire, René, French composer; b. Evreux, June 13, 1879; d. Paris, July 9, 1959. He studied in Rouen and later in Paris with Widor and d'Indy; he then was engaged as a bandleader in the casinos of various French spas. He composed an opera, *Morituri* (1903).

Dolega-Kamiénski. See **Kamiénski, Lucian.**

Dolin, Samuel (Joseph), Canadian composer and teacher; b. Montreal, Aug. 22, 1917. He received training in piano and theory in Montreal, and then pursued his education at the Univ. of Toronto (B.Mus., 1942). In 1945 he joined the staff of the Toronto Cons. of Music, where he studied composition with Weinzweig. He also studied piano and had lessons in composition with Krenek before completing his education at the Univ. of Toronto (D.Mus., 1958). Dolin continued to serve on the staff at the Cons. as a teacher for 50 years, founding its electronic music studio in 1966. He served as vice president (1967–68) and president (1969–73) of the Canadian League of Composers, and also as chairman (1970–74) of the Canadian section of the ISCM. In 1984 he was founding artistic director of the Canadian Contemporary Music Workshop. Dolin's music ranges widely in scope, from the traditional in manner to multimedia scores.

WORKS: DRAMATIC: *Casino (Greed)*, opera (1966–67); *Drakkar*, entertainment for Narrator, Mezzo-soprano, 2 Baritones, 2 Dancers, Chamber Ensemble, 2 Synthesizers, and Amplifiers (1972; Toronto, Feb. 17, 1973); *Golden Section: The Biography of a Woman* for Soprano, Dancer, Slides, Narrator, Lighting, and Orch. (1981); *Hero of Our Time* for Baritone, Men's Chorus, Dancers, and Orch. (1985).

Dolukhanova, Zara, Russian mezzo-soprano of Armenian descent; b. Moscow, March 5, 1918. She studied with private teachers. She joined the Moscow Radio staff in 1944. A lyric singer, she excelled in the Romantic Russian repertoire. In 1959 she made her first American tour, enjoying great acclaim; she toured America again in 1970. In 1966 she was awarded the Lenin Prize.

Domanínská (real name, **Klobásková**), **Libuše,** Czech soprano; b. Brno, July 4, 1924. She was a student at the Brno Cons. of Hana Pírková and Bohuslav Sobeský. In 1945 she made her operatic debut as Blaženka in Smetana's *Tajemství*, and continued to sing there until 1955. In 1955 she became a member of the Prague National Theater, where she was a principal artist until 1985. She also was a member of the Vienna State Opera (1958–68) and a guest artist with other European opera companies. She likewise pursued an active concert career. In 1966 she was made an Artist of Merit and in 1974 a National Artist by the Czech government. In addition to her roles in operas by Mozart, Verdi, and Puccini, she won particular praise for her portrayals in operas by Czech and Russian masters.

Domgraf-Fassbänder, Willi, German baritone, father of **Brigitte Fassbänder**; b. Aachen, Feb. 9, 1897; d. Nuremberg, Feb. 13, 1978. He first studied in Aachen, where he made his operatic debut (1922), then with Jacques Stückgold and Paul Bruns in Berlin and with Giuseppe Borgatti in Milan. He sang in Berlin, Düsseldorf, and Stuttgart, and was a leading member of the Berlin State Opera from 1928 until the end of World War II; he also appeared at the Glyndebourne Festivals (1934–35; 1937). After the war he sang in Hannover, Vienna, Munich, and Nuremberg, serving as chief producer at the latter opera house (1953–62). He also taught at the Nuremberg Cons. (from 1954). Among his finest roles were Figaro, Papageno, and Guglielmo.

Domingo, Plácido, famous Spanish tenor and able conductor; b. Madrid, Jan. 21, 1941. His parents were zarzuela singers; after a tour of Mexico, they settled there and gave performances with their own company. Domingo joined his parents in Mexico at the age of 7 and began appearing with them in various productions while still a child; he also studied piano with Manuel Barajas in Mexico City and voice with Carlo Morelli at the National Cons. there (1955–57). He made his operatic debut in the tenor role of Borsa in *Rigoletto* with the National Opera in Mexico City in 1959. His first major role was as Alfredo in *La Traviata* in Monterrey in 1961; that same year he made his U.S. debut as Arturo in *Lucia di Lammermoor* with the Dallas Civic Opera, then was a member of the Hebrew National Opera in Tel Aviv (1962–64). He made his first appearance with the N.Y. City Opera as Pinkerton in *Madama Butterfly* on Oct. 17, 1965. On Aug. 9, 1966, he made his Metropolitan Opera debut as Turiddu in a concert performance of *Cavalleria rusticana* at N.Y.'s Lewisohn Stadium; his formal debut on the stage of the Metropolitan followed on Sept. 28, 1968, when he essayed the role of Maurice de Saxe in *Adriana Lecouvreur*, establishing himself as one of its principal members. He also sang regularly at the Vienna State Opera (from 1967), Milan's La Scala (from 1969), and London's Covent Garden (from 1971). His travels took him to all the major operatic centers of the world, and he also sang for recordings, films, and television. He also pursued conducting. He made his formal debut as an opera conductor with *La Traviata* at the N.Y. City Opera on Oct. 7, 1973, and on Oct. 25, 1984, he appeared at the Metropolitan Opera, conducting *La Bohème*. He commissioned Menotti's opera *Goya* and sang the title role at its premiere in Washington, D.C., on Nov. 15, 1986. In 1987 he sang Otello at the 100th anniversary performances at La Scala. On New Year's Eve 1988 he appeared as a soloist with Zubin Mehta and the N.Y. Phil in a gala concert televised live to millions, during which he also conducted the orch. in the overture to *Die Fledermaus*. On July 7, 1990, he participated in a celebrated concert with fellow tenors José Carreras and Luciano Pavarotti in Rome, with Mehta conducting. The concert was telecast live to the world and subsequently became a best-selling video and compact disc. Thereafter the "three tenors" toured the globe. In 1993 he sang Parsifal at the Bayreuth Festival with extraordinary success. Domingo celebrated his 25th anniversary with the Metropolitan Opera singing Siegmund in Act 1 of *Die Walküre* in a performance broadcast live on radio throughout the world on Sept. 27, 1993. In 1994 Domingo was named principal guest conductor of the Los Angeles Opera, where he sang the title role in Verdi's *Stiffelio* (1995). In 1996 he assumed the position of artistic director of the Washington (D.C.) Opera. In 1996 he also appeared as Siegfried at the Metropolitan Opera, where he returned in a remarkable portrayal of Siegmund in 1997. He sang Samson there in 1998. From 2000 he was artistic director of the Los Angeles Opera while retaining his position in Washington, D.C. One of the best-known lyric tenors of his era, Domingo has gained international renown for his portrayals of such roles as Cavaradossi, Des Grieux, Radames, Don Carlos, Otello, Don José, Hoffmann, Canio, and Samson. He publ. an autobiography, *Plácido Domingo: My First Forty Years* (N.Y., 1983).

BIBL.: D. Snowman, *The World of P. D.* (London, 1985); L. Fayer, *Von Don Carlos bis Parsifal: P. D., 25 Jahre an der Wiener Staatsoper* (Vienna, 1992); R. Stefoff, *P. D.* (N.Y., 1992).

Dominguez, Oralia, Mexican contralto; b. San Luis Potosí, Oct. 15, 1927. She studied at the National Cons. in Mexico City, during which time she made her first appearance as a singer in Debussy's *La Damoiselle élue*. After making her stage debut at the Mexico City Opera in 1950, she made her European debut at a concert at London's Wigmore Hall in 1953, and then toured in France, Spain, Germany, and the Netherlands; that same year she appeared as Princess de Bouillon in *Adrienne Lecouvreur* at Milan's La Scala. She then sang opera in Naples, Brussels, Vienna, and Paris. In 1955 she created the role of Sosostris in Tippett's *A Midsummer Marriage* at London's Covent Garden, and then appeared regularly at the Glyndebourne Festival from 1955 to 1964. She was a member of the Deutsche Oper am Rhein in Düsseldorf from 1960. She also appeared as soloist with major orchs. and as a recitalist.

Dominiceti, Cesare, Italian composer; b. Desenzano, July 12, 1821; d. Sesto di Monza, June 20, 1888. He studied in Milan, where all his operas were brought out. He lived for a long time in Bolivia, where he made a fortune. In 1881 he was appointed prof. of composition at the Milan Cons. He wrote the operas *Due mogli in una* (June 30, 1853), *La maschera* (March 2, 1854), *Morovico* (Dec. 4, 1873), *Il lago delle fate* (May 18, 1878), and *L'Ereditiera* (Feb. 14, 1881).

Donalda (real name, **Lightstone**), **Pauline,** Canadian soprano; b. Montreal, March 5, 1882; d. there, Oct. 22, 1970. The original family name was Lichtenstein, which her father changed to Lightstone when he became a British subject. She received her first musical training at Royal Victoria College in Montreal, and then was a private pupil of Duvernoy in Paris. She made her operatic debut as Massenet's Manon in Nice, Dec. 30, 1904; the next year she appeared at the Théâtre Royal de la Monnaie in Brussels and at Covent Garden in London; in 1906–07 she appeared at the Manhattan Opera House in New York, and in London and Paris, mainly in oratorios and concerts. From the time of her retirement in 1922 until 1937 she had a singing school in Paris; in 1937 she returned to Montreal. In 1938 she presented her valuable music library (MSS, autographs, and music) to McGill Univ. In 1942 she founded the Opera Guild in Montreal, serving as its president until it ceased operations in 1969. In 1967 she was made an Officer of the Order of Canada. Her stage name was taken in honor of Sir Donald Smith (later Lord Strathcona), who endowed the Royal Victoria College and was her patron.

BIBL.: C. Brotman, *P. D.* (Montreal, 1975).

Donath, Helen (née **Erwin**), American soprano; b. Corpus Christi, Texas, July 10, 1940. After attending Del Mar College in Corpus Christi, she studied voice with Paola Novikova and Maria Berini. She then joined the Cologne Opera studio, where she made her formal operatic debut as Inez in *Il Trovatore* in 1960. From 1963 to 1967 she sang at the Hannover Opera, and then joined the Bavarian State Opera in Munich in 1967, where she quickly rose to prominence. In 1971 she made her U.S. operatic debut as Sophie at the San Francisco Opera. In 1979 she made her first appearance at London's Covent Garden as Anne Trulove. She also appeared as a guest artist in Salzburg, Vienna, Hamburg, Berlin, Bayreuth, Milan, and Zürich. In 1990 she was made a Bavarian Kammersängerin. Among her many roles were Susanna, Zerlina, Ilia in *Idomeneo*, Marcelline in *Fidelio*, Ännchen in *Der Freischütz*, Micaëla, Mélisande, and Mimi.

Donati, Pino, Italian opera director, administrator, and composer; b. Verona, May 9, 1907; d. Rome, Feb. 24, 1975. After studying violin, he received instruction in composition from Paribeni. He was an opera director at the Verona Arena (1936–43), in Lisbon (1946–50), and in Bologna (1950–56). In 1958 he became artistic director of the Chicago Lyric Opera; from 1964 until his death he served as its co-artistic director with Bruno Bartoletti; from 1968 he also was director of the Florence Opera. In 1939 he married **Maria Caniglia**. Among his works were the operas *Corradino lo Svevo* (Verona, April 4, 1931) and *Lancillotto del lago* (Bergamo, Oct. 2, 1938), and chamber music.

Donato, Anthony, American violinist, conductor, teacher, and composer; b. Prague, Nebr., March 8, 1909. He studied violin with Gustave Tinlot, conducting with Goossens, and composition with Hanson, Royce, and Rogers at the Eastman School of Music in Rochester, N.Y. (B.M., 1931; M.M., 1937; Ph.D., 1947). After playing violin in the Rochester Phil. (1927–31) and the Hochstein Quartet (1929–31), he served as head of the violin depts. at Drake Univ. (1931–37), Iowa State Teachers College (1937–39), and the Univ. of Texas (1939–46); he then was prof. of theory and composition at Northwestern Univ. (1947–76), where he also conducted its chamber orch. (1947–58). He publ. a valuable textbook on notational techniques, *Preparing Music Manuscripts* (Englewood Cliffs, N.J., 1963). As a composer, Donato was particularly successful writing choral works and piano pieces. He composed the opera *The Walker Through Walls* (1964; Evanston, Ill., Feb. 26, 1965).

Donatoni, Franco, noted Italian composer and pedagogue; b. Verona, June 9, 1927. He commenced his musical training with Piero Bottagisio at the Verona Liceo Musicale. After further studies in composition with Desderi at the Milan Cons. (1946–48), he was a student of Liviabella at the Bologna Cons., where he took diplomas in composition and band orchestration (1949), choral music (1950), and composition (1951). He pursued advanced composition studies with Pizzetti at the Accademia di Santa Cecilia in Rome (graduated, 1953), and then attended the summer courses in new music in Darmstadt (1954, 1956, 1958, 1961). He taught at the Bologna Cons. (1953–55), the Turin Cons. (1956–69), and the Milan Cons. (1969–78) before holding the chair in advanced composition at the Accademia di Santa Cecilia. He also taught advanced composition at the Accademia Musicale Chigiana in Siena (from 1970), and was concurrently on the faculty of the Univ. of Bologna (1971–85). In addition, he taught at the Civica Scuola in Milan, the Perosi Academy in Biella, and the Forlanini Academy in Brescia; also gave master classes. He publ. the vols. *Questo* (1970), *Antecedente X* (1980), *Il sigaro di Armando* (1982), and *In-oltre* (1988). In addition to his memberships in the Accademia

Nazionale di Santa Cecilia and the Accademia Filarmonica of Rome, the French government honored him as a Commandeur of l'Order des Arts et des Lettres in 1985. As a composer, Donatoni was deeply influenced by Schoenberg, Boulez, and Stockhausen, particularly in his mature aleatoric style. His gifts as a master of his craft are most fully revealed in his orch. works and chamber music, which are notable for their imaginative manipulation of sonorities and colors. Within his sizeable catalog of works is the opera *Atem* (1983–84; Milan, Feb. 16, 1985) and the ballet *La lampara* (1957).

BIBL.: G. Mazzola Nangeroni, *F. D.* (Milan, 1989).

Dönch, Karl, German bass-baritone; b. Hagen, Jan. 8, 1915; d. Vienna, Sept. 16, 1994. He studied at the Dresden Cons., then made his operatic debut in Görlitz (1936). He sang in Reichenberg, Bonn, and Salzburg, later becoming a member of the Vienna State Opera (1947) and making regular appearances at the Salzburg Festivals (from 1951). He was a guest artist at the Berlin Städtische Oper, the Deutsche Oper am Rhein in Düsseldorf, Milan's La Scala, and the Teatro Colón in Buenos Aires. On Jan. 22, 1959, he made his Metropolitan Opera debut in New York as Beckmesser; he was on its roster from 1962 to 1965 and again from 1966 to 1969. From 1973 to 1986 he was director of the Vienna Volksoper. In addition to the standard Austro-German repertoire, Dönch sang in several contemporary works, including Liebermann's *Penelope* (1954) and Frank Martin's *Tempest* (1956).

Donizetti (real name, **Ciummei**), **Alfredo,** composer; b. Smyrna, Sept. 2, 1867; d. Rosario, Argentina, Feb. 4, 1921. He studied (1883–89) at the Milan Cons. under Ponchielli and Dominiceti, then settled in Argentina. He wrote the operas *Nama* (Milan, 1890) and *Dopo l'Ave Maria* (Milan, 1896).

Donizetti, (Domenico) Gaetano (Maria), famous Italian composer, brother of Giuseppe Donizetti; b. Bergamo, Nov. 29, 1797; d. there, April 1, 1848. His father was from a poor family of artisans who obtained the position of caretaker in the local pawnshop. At the age of 9 Gaetano entered the Lezioni Caritatevoli di Musica, a charity institution which served as the training school for the choristers of S. Maria Maggiore; he studied singing and harpsichord there; later studied harmony and counterpoint with J. S. Mayr. With the encouragement and assistance of Mayr, he enrolled in the Liceo Filarmonico Comunale in Bologna in 1815, where he studied counterpoint with Pilotti; later studied counterpoint and fugue with Padre Mattei. His first opera, *Il Pigmalione* (1816), appears never to have been performed in his lifetime. He composed 2 more operas in quick succession, but they were not performed. Leaving the Liceo in 1817, he was determined to have an opera produced. His next work, *Enrico di Borgogna*, was performed in Venice in 1818, but it evoked little interest. He finally achieved popular success with his opera buffa *Il Falegname di Livonia, o Pietro il grande, czar delle Russie* (Venice, Dec. 26, 1819). In Dec. 1820 he was exempted from military service when a woman of means paid the sum necessary to secure his uninterrupted work at composition. His opera seria *Zoraide de Granata* (Rome, Jan. 28, 1822) proved a major success. During the next 9 years, Donizetti composed 25 operas, none of which remain in the active repertoire today; however, the great success of his *L'Ajo nell'imbarazzo* (Rome, Feb. 4, 1824) brought him renown at the time. In 1825–26 he served as musical director of the Teatro Carolino in Palermo. From 1829 to 1838 he was musical director of the royal theaters in Naples. With *Anna Bolena* (Milan, Dec. 26, 1830), Donizetti established himself as a master of the Italian operatic theater. Composed for Pasta and Rubini, the opera was an overwhelming success. Within a few years it was produced in several major Italian theaters, and was also heard in London, Paris, Dresden, and other cities. His next enduring work was the charming comic opera *L'elisir d'amore* (Milan, May 12, 1832). The tragic *Lucrezia Borgia* (Milan, Dec. 26, 1833), although not entirely successful at its premiere, soon found acceptance and made the rounds of the major opera houses. In 1834 Donizetti was appointed prof. of counterpoint and composition at the Conservatorio di San Pietro a Majella in Naples. His *Maria Stuarda* (Oct. 18, 1834) was given its first performance as Buondelmonte in Naples after the queen objected to details in the libretto. He then went to Paris, where his Marino Faliero had a successful premiere at the Théâtre-Italien on March 12, 1835. Returning to Italy, he produced his tragic masterpiece *Lucia di Lammermoor* (Naples, Sept. 26, 1835). Upon the death of Zingarelli in 1837, Donizetti was named director pro tempore of the Conservatorio in Naples. On July 30, 1837, he suffered a grievous loss when his wife died following the 3d stillbirth of a child, after 9 years of marriage. On Oct. 29, 1837, *Roberto Devereux* garnered acclaim at its first performance in Naples. In 1838 Donizetti resigned his positions at the Conservatorio when his post as director was not made a permanent appointment. When the censor's veto prevented the production of *Poliuto* due to its sacred subject (it was written for Nourrit after Corneille's *Polyeucte*), he decided to return to Paris. He produced the highly successful *La Fille du régiment* there on Feb. 11, 1840. It was followed by *Les Martyrs* (April 10, 1840), a revision of the censored *Poliuto*, which proved successful. His *La Favorite* (Dec. 2, 1840) made little impression at its first performance, but it soon became one of his most popular operas. He spent 1841–42 in Italy, and then went to Vienna. His *Linda di Chamounix* received an enthusiastic reception at its premiere there on May 19, 1842. The emperor appointed Donizetti Maestro di Cappella e di Camera e Compositore di Corte. In 1843 he once more went to Paris, where he brought out his great comic masterpiece *Don Pasquale*. With such famous singers as Grisi, Mario, Tamburini, and Lablache in the cast, its premiere on Jan. 3, 1843, was a triumph. He then returned to Vienna, where he conducted the successful premiere of *Maria di Rohan* on June 5, 1843. Back again in Paris, he produced *Dom Sébastien* (Nov. 11, 1843). The audience approved the work enthusiastically, but the critics were not pleased. Considering the opera to be his masterpiece, Donizetti had to wait until the Vienna premiere (in German) of 1845 before the work was universally acclaimed. The last opera produced in his lifetime was *Caterina Cornaro* (Naples, Jan. 12, 1844). By this time Donizetti began to age quickly; in 1845 his mental and physical condition progressively deteriorated as the ravages of syphilis reduced him to the state of an insane invalid; in 1846 he was placed in a mental clinic at Ivry, just outside Paris; in 1847 he was released into the care of his nephew, and was taken to his birthplace to await his end. Donizetti was a prolific composer of operas whose fecundity of production was not always equaled by his inspiration or craftsmanship. Many of his operas are hampered by the poor librettos he was forced to use on so many occasions. Nevertheless, his genius is reflected in many of his operas. Indeed, his finest works serve as the major link in the development of Italian opera between the period of Rossini and that of Verdi. Such operas as *Anna Bolena, L'elisir d'amore, Lucia di Lammermoor, Roberto Devereux, La Favorite, La Fille du régiment*, and *Don Pasquale* continue to hold a place in the repertoire.

WORKS: OPERAS: Il *Pigmalione,* scena drammatica (1816; Teatro Donizetti, Bergamo, Oct. 13, 1960); *L'ira d'Achille* (1817; not perf.); *L'Olimpiade* (1817; not perf.); *Enrico di Borgogna*, opera semiseria (1818; Teatro San Luca, Venice, Nov. 14, 1818); *Una follia (di Carnevale)*, farsa (1818; Teatro San Luca, Venice, Dec. 15, 1818); *Piccioli Virtuosi ambulanti* (also known as *Piccoli Virtuosi di musica ambulanti*), opera buffa (1819; Bergamo, 1819); *Il Falegname di Livonia, o Pietro il grande, czar delle Russie*, opera buffa (1819; Teatro San Samuele, Venice, Dec. 26, 1819); *Le nozze in villa*, opera buffa (1820; Teatro Vecchio, Mantua, 1820 or 1821); *Zoraide di Granata*, opera seria (1822; Teatro Argentina, Rome, Jan. 28, 1822); *La Zingara*, opera seria (1822; Teatro Nuovo, Naples, May 12, 1822); *La lettera anonima*, farsa (1822; Teatro del Fondo, Naples, June 29, 1822); *Chiara e Serafina, o I Pirati*, opera semiseria (1822; Teatro alla Scala, Milan, Oct. 26, 1822); *Alfredo il grande*, opera seria (1823; Teatro San Carlo, Naples, July 2, 1823); *Il Fortunato inganno*, opera buffa (1823; Teatro Nuovo, Naples, Sept. 3, 1823); *L'Ajo nell'imbarazzo, o Don Gregorio*, opera buffa (1823–24; Teatro Valle, Rome, Feb. 4, 1824); *Emilia di Liverpool* (also known as *Emilia* or *L'eremitaggio di Liverpool*), opera semiseria (1824; Teatro Nuovo, Naples, July

28, 1824); *Alahor di Granata*, opera seria (1825; Teatro Carolino, Palermo, Jan. 7, 1826); *Il castello degli invalidi*, farsa (1825–26?; 1st perf. may have taken place at the Teatro Carolino, Palermo, 1826); *Elvida*, opera seria (1826; Teatro San Carlo, Naples, July 6, 1826); *Gabriella di Vergy*, opera seria (1826; Teatro San Carlo, Naples, Nov. 22, 1869; 2d version, 1838?; Whitla Hall, Belfast, Nov. 7, 1978); *La bella prigioniera*, farsa (1826; not perf.); *Olivo e Pasquale*, opera buffa (1826; Teatro Valle, Rome, Jan. 7, 1827); *Otto Mesi in due ore, ossia Gli Esiliati in Siberia*, opera romantica (1827; Teatro Nuovo, Naples, May 13, 1827); *Il Borgomastro di Saardam*, opera buffa (1827; Teatro Nuovo, Naples, Aug. 19, 1827); *Le convenienze ed inconvenienze teatrali*, farsa (1827; Teatro Nuovo, Naples, Nov. 21, 1827); *L'Esule di Roma, ossia Il Proscritto* (also known as *Settimio il proscritto*), opera seria (1827; Teatro San Carlo, Naples, Jan. 1, 1828); *Alina, regina di Golconda* (also known as *La Regina di Golconda*), opera buffa (1828; Teatro Carlo Felice, Genoa, May 12, 1828); *Gianni di Calais*, opera semiseria (1828; Teatro del Fondo, Naples, Aug. 2, 1828); *Il Giovedì grasso, o Il nuovo Pourceaugnac*, farsa (1828; Teatro del Fondo, Naples, 1828); *Il Paria*, opera seria (1828; Teatro San Carlo, Naples, Jan. 12, 1829); *Elisabetta al castello di Kenilworth* (also known as *Il castello di Kenilworth*), opera seria (1829; Teatro San Carlo, Naples, July 6, 1829); *I Pazzi per progetto*, farsa (1830; Teatro del Fondo, Naples, Feb. 7, 1830); *Il diluvio universale*, azione tragico-sacra (1830; Teatro San Carlo, Naples, Feb. 28, 1830); *Imelda de' Lambertazzi*, opera seria (1830; Teatro San Carlo, Naples, Aug. 23, 1830); *Anna Bolena*, opera seria (1830; Teatro Carcano, Milan, Dec. 26, 1830); *Francesca di Foix*, opera semiseria (1831; Teatro San Carlo, Naples, May 30, 1831); *La Romanziera e l'uomo nero*, opera buffa (1831; Teatro del Fondo, Naples, June 18, 1831); *Gianni di Parigi*, opera comica (1831; Teatro alla Scala, Milan, Sept. 10, 1839); *Fausta*, opera seria (1831; Teatro San Carlo, Naples, Jan. 12, 1832); *Ugo, conte di Parigi*, opera seria (1832; Teatro alla Scala, Milan, March 13, 1832); *L'elisir d'amore*, opera comica (1832; Teatro della Canobbiana, Milan, May 12, 1832); *Sancia di Castiglia*, opera seria (1832; Teatro San Carlo, Naples, Nov. 4, 1832); *Il Furioso all'isola di San Domingo*, opera semiseria (1832; Teatro Valle, Rome, Jan. 2, 1833); *Parisina*, opera seria (1833; Teatro della Pergola, Florence, March 17, 1833), *Torquato Tasso* (also known as *Sordello il trovatore* or *Sordello*), opera seria (1833; Teatro Valle, Rome, Sept. 9, 1833); *Lucrezia Borgia*, opera seria (1833; Teatro alla Scala, Milan, Dec. 26, 1833); *Rosmonda d'Inghilterra*, opera seria (1834; Teatro della Pergola, Florence, Feb. 27, 1834); *Maria Stuarda*, opera seria (1834; 1st perf. as *Buondelmonte* at the Teatro San Carlo, Naples, Oct. 18, 1834; 1st perf. as *Maria Stuarda* at the Teatro alla Scala, Milan, Dec. 30, 1835); *Gemma di Vergy*, opera seria (1834; Teatro alla Scala, Milan, Dec. 26, 1834); *Adelaide*, opera comica (1834?; not completed); *Marino* (or *Marin*) *Faliero*, opera seria (1835; Théâtre-Italien, Paris, March 12, 1835); *Lucia di Lammermoor*, opera seria (1835; Teatro San Carlo, Naples, Sept. 26, 1835); *Belisario*, opera seria (1835–36; Teatro La Fenice, Venice, Feb. 4, 1836); *Il campanello (di notte or dello speziale)*, farsa (1836; Teatro Nuovo, Naples, June 1, 1836); *Betly* (or *Bettly*), *ossia La Capanna svizzera*, opera giocosa (1836; Teatro San Carlo, Naples, Aug. 24, 1836); *L'assedio di Calais*, opera seria (1836; Teatro San Carlo, Naples, Nov. 19, 1836); *Pia de' Tolomei*, opera seria (1836–37; Teatro Apollo, Venice, Feb. 18, 1837); *Roberto Devereux, ossia Il Conte di Essex*, opera seria (1837; Teatro San Carlo, Naples, Oct. 29, 1837); *Maria di Rudenz*, opera seria (1837; Teatro La Fenice, Venice, Jan. 30, 1838); *Poliuto*, opera seria (1839; 1st perf. as *Les Martyrs* at the Opéra, Paris, April 10, 1840; 1st perf. as *Poliuto* at the Teatro San Carlo, Naples, Nov. 30, 1848); *L'Ange de Nisida* (incomplete opera; transformed into *La Favorite* [1840]); *Le Duc d'Albe* (1839 and later; not completed; finished by Matteo Salvi and tr. into Italian by Angelo Zanardini as *Il Duca d'Alba*, Teatro Apollo, Rome, March 22, 1882); *La Fille du régiment*, opéra comique (1839–40; Opéra Comique, Paris, Feb. 11, 1840); *Les Martyrs*, grand opera (1840; rev. version of *Poliuto* [1839]; Opéra, Paris, April 10, 1840); *La Favorite*, grand opera (1840; rev. version of *L'Ange de Nisida* [1839]; Opéra, Paris, Dec. 2, 1840); *Adelia, o La Figlia dell'arciere*, opera seria (1840–41; Teatro Apollo, Rome, Feb. 11, 1841); *Rita, ou Le Mari battu* (also known as *Deux hommes et une femme*), opéra comique (1841; Opéra Comique, Paris, May 7, 1860); *Maria Padilla*, opera seria (1841; Teatro alla Scala, Milan, Dec. 26, 1841); *Linda di Chamounix*, opera semiseria (1842; Kärnthnertortheater, Vienna, May 19, 1842); *Don Pasquale*, opera buffa (1842; Théâtre-Italien, Paris, Jan. 3, 1843); *Maria di Rohan*, opera seria (1843; Kärnthnertortheater, Vienna, June 5, 1843); *Dom Sébastien, roi de Portugal*, grand opera (1843; Opéra, Paris, Nov. 11, 1843); *Caterina Cornaro*, opera seria (1842–43; Teatro San Carlo, Naples, Jan. 12, 1844).

BIBL.: F. Regli, *G. D. e le sue opere* (Turin, 1850); F. Cicconetti, *Vita di G. D.* (Rome, 1864); A. Bellotti, *D. e i suoi contemporanei* (Bergamo, 1866); F. Marchetti and A. Parisotti, eds., *Lettere inedite di G. D.* (Rome, 1892); I. Valetta, *D.* (Rome, 1897); A. Gabrielli, *G. D.* (Rome and Turin, 1904); C. Caversazzi, *G. D.: La casa dove nacque, La famiglia, L'inizio della malattia* (Bergamo, 1924); G. Donati-Petténi, *D.* (Milan, 1930; 3d ed., 1940); G. Gavazzeni, *D.: Vita e musiche* (Milan, 1937); A. Geddo, *D.* (Bergamo, 1938); G. Monaldi, *G. D.* (Turin, 1938); G. Zavadini, *G. D.: Vicende della sua vita artistica* (Bergamo, 1941); G. Barblan, *L'opera di D. nell'età romantica* (Bergamo, 1948); G. Zavadini, *D.: Vita—Musiche—Epistolario* (Bergamo, 1948); L. Bossi, *D.* (Brescia, 1956); A. Geddo, *D. (L'uomo—le musiche)* (Bergamo, 1956); H. Weinstock, *D. and the World of Opera in Italy, Paris, and Vienna in the First Half of the Nineteenth Century* (N.Y., 1963); W. Ashbrook, *D.* (London, 1965); F. Speranze, ed., *Studi D.ani, II* (1972); W. Ashbrook, *D. and His Operas* (Cambridge, 1982); G. Barblan and B. Zanolini, *G. D.: Vita e opera di un musicista romantico* (Bergamo, 1983); P. Gossett, *Anna Bolena and the Artistic Maturity of G. D.* (Oxford, 1985); S. Fayad, *Vita di D.* (Milan, 1995).

Donzelli, Domenico, Italian tenor; b. Bergamo, Feb. 2, 1790; d. Bologna, March 31, 1873. He was a student of Branchi in Bergamo, where he made his operatic debut in Mayr's *Elisa* in 1808. He then continued his training in Naples with Viganoni and Crivelli. After appearing throughout his homeland, he made his Paris debut as Rossini's Otello in 1825. In 1829 he sang at the King's Theatre in London. On Dec. 26, 1831, he created the role of Pollione in Bellini's *Norma* at Milan's La Scala. He continued to sing widely until his retirement in 1844.

Dooley, William (Edward), American baritone; b. Modesto, Calif., Sept. 9, 1932. He was a pupil of Lucy Lee Call at the Eastman School of Music in Rochester, N.Y., and of Viktoria Prestel and Hedwig Fichtmüller in Munich. In 1957 he made his operatic debut as Rodrigo in *Don Carlos* in Heidelberg; after singing at the Bielefeld Stadttheater (1959–62), he was a member of the Berlin Deutsche Oper (from 1962), where he sang in the premieres of Sessions's *Montezuma* (1964), Reimann's *Gespenstersonate* (1984), and Rihm's *Oedipus* (1987). In 1964 he appeared at the Salzburg Festival, returning there in 1966 to sing in the premiere of Henze's *The Bassarids*. On Feb. 15, 1964, he made his Metropolitan Opera debut in New York as Eugene Onegin, remaining on its roster until 1977. His engagements as a concert artist took him to many of the principal North American and European music centers. Among his prominent roles were Pizarro, Kothner, Escamillo, Macbeth, Amonasro, Telramund, Mandryka, Nick Shadow, and Wozzeck.

Dopper, Cornelis, Dutch conductor and composer; b. Stadskanaal, near Groningen, Feb. 7, 1870; d. Amsterdam, Sept. 18, 1939. He was a student of Jadassohn and Reinecke at the Leipzig Cons. (1887–90). After serving as a coach and conductor with the Netherlands Opera in Amsterdam (1896–1903), he was conductor of the Savage Opera Co., with which he toured North America. From 1908 to 1931 he held the post of 2d conductor under Mengelberg with the Concertgebouw Orch. in Amsterdam. He introduced youth concerts to the Netherlands. His well-crafted scores were composed in a late Romantic vein. He composed the operas *Het blinde meisje von Castel Cuillé* (1892; The Hague, Dec. 17, 1894), *Frithof* (1895), *William Ratcliff* (1896–1901; Weimar, Oct. 19, 1909), *Het eerekruis* (1902; Amsterdam, Jan. 9, 1903), and *Don Quichotte* (unfinished), and the ballet *Meidevorn*.

Doppler, Árpád, Austrian pianist and composer; b. Pest, June 5, 1857; d. Stuttgart, Aug. 13, 1927. His father was the Austrian flutist, composer, and conductor Karl (Károly) Doppler (b. Lemberg, Sept. 12, 1825; d. Stuttgart, March 10, 1900). He went to Stuttgart as a young man and studied there, after which he was engaged to teach in New York and spent 3 years there (1880–83). He later returned to Stuttgart and taught at the Cons. He wrote 2 operas, *Halixula* (Caligula; Stuttgart, 1891) and *Much Ado about Nothing*.

Doppler, (Albert) Franz (Ferenc), Austrian flutist, composer, and conductor, uncle of **Árpád Doppler**; b. Lemberg, Oct. 16, 1821; d. Baden, near Vienna, July 27, 1883. His brother was the Austrian flutist, composer, and conductor Karl (Károly) Doppler (b. Lemberg, Sept. 12, 1825; d. Stuttgart, March 10, 1900). He studied music with his father, then played 1st flute in the Pest Opera Orch. In 1858 settled in Vienna as ballet conductor at the court opera. He taught flute at the Vienna Cons. from 1865. His first opera, *Benjowsky*, was well received in Pest (Sept. 29, 1847) and had several revivals under the title *Afanasia*; the following operas were also produced in Pest: *Ilka* (Dec. 29, 1849); *Wanda* (Dec. 20, 1850); *A két huszár* (March 12, 1853); his last opera, *Judith*, was produced in Vienna (Dec. 30, 1870). He also wrote 15 ballets.

Doran, Matt (Higgins), American composer and teacher; b. Covington, Ky., Sept. 1, 1921. He was a student at Los Angeles City College and of Toch, Kubik, and Eisler at the Univ. of Southern Calif. in Los Angeles (B.M., 1947; D.M.A., 1953); he also received training in flute and played in several orchs. He taught at Del Mar College in Corpus Christi (1953–55) and at Ball State Univ. in Muncie (1956–57); he then was an instructor (1957–66) and a prof. (from 1966) at Mount St. Mary College in Los Angeles. He composed 10 operas, including *The Committee* (1953; Corpus Christi, May 25, 1955) and *The Marriage Counselor* (Los Angeles, March 12, 1977).

Doráti, Antal, distinguished Hungarian-born American conductor and composer; b. Budapest, April 9, 1906; d. Gerzensee, near Bern, Nov. 13, 1988. He studied with Leo Weiner, both privately and at the Franz Liszt Academy of Music in Budapest, where he also received instruction in composition from Kodály (1920–24). He was on the staff of the Budapest Opera (1924–28); after conducting at the Dresden State Opera (1928–29) he was Generalmusikdirektor in Münster (1929–32). In 1933 he went to France, where he conducted the Ballets Russes de Monte Carlo, which he took on a tour of Australia (1938). He made his U.S. debut as guest conductor with the National Sym. Orch. in Washington, D.C., in 1937. In 1940 he settled in the United States, becoming a naturalized citizen in 1947. He began his American career as music director of the American Ballet Theatre in New York (1941–44); after serving as conductor of the Dallas Sym. Orch. (1945–49), he was music director of the Minneapolis Sym. Orch. (1949–60). From 1963 to 1966 he was chief conductor of the BBC Sym. Orch. in London; then of the Stockholm Phil. (1966–70). He was music director of the National Sym. Orch. in Washington, D.C. (1970–77), and of the Detroit Sym. Orch. (1977–81); he was also principal conductor of the Royal Phil. in London (1975–79). He made numerous guest conducting appearances in Europe and North America, earning a well-deserved reputation as an orch. builder. His prolific recording output made him one of the best-known conductors of his time. His recordings of the Haydn syms. and operas were particularly commendable. In 1984 he was made an honorary Knight Commander of the Order of the British Empire. In 1969 he married the Austrian pianist Ilse von Alpenheim (b. Innsbruck, Feb. 11, 1927), who often appeared as a soloist under his direction. His autobiography was publ. as *Notes of Seven Decades* (London, 1979). Among his compositions are the ballet *Graduation Ball*, arranged from the waltzes of Johann Strauss, and the dramatic cantata *The Way of the Cross* (Minneapolis, April 19, 1957);

Doret, Gustave, Swiss composer and conductor; b. Aigle, Sept. 20, 1866; d. Lausanne, April 19, 1943. He received his first instruction at Lausanne; studied violin with Joachim in Berlin (1885–87); then entered the Paris Cons. as a pupil of Marsick (violin) and Dubois and Massenet (composition). He was conductor of the Concerts d'Harcourt and of the Société Nationale de Musique in Paris (1893–95), and at the Opéra Comique (1907–09); he also appeared as a visiting conductor in Rome, London, and Amsterdam. In his music, Doret cultivated the spirit of Swiss folk songs; his vocal writing is distinguished by its natural flow of melody. He publ. *Musique et musiciens* (1915), *Lettres à ma nièce sur la musique en Suisse* (1919), *Pour notre indépendance musicale* (1920), and *Temps et contretemps* (1942).

WORKS: DRAMATIC: OPERAS: *Maedeli* (1901); *Les Armaillis* (Paris, Oct. 23, 1906; rev. version, Paris, May 5, 1930); *Le Nain du Hasli* (Geneva, Feb. 6, 1908); *Loÿs*, dramatic legend (Vevey, 1912); *La Tisseuse d'Orties* (Paris, 1926); incidental music.

BIBL.: J. Dupérier, *G. D.* (Paris, 1932).

Dorn, Alexander (Julius Paul), German pianist, conductor, and composer, son of **Heinrich (Ludwig Egmont) Dorn**; b. Riga, June 8, 1833; d. Berlin, Nov. 27, 1901. He studied with his father, then traveled as a pianist and choral conductor. He was in Egypt (1855–65), then settled in Berlin, where he taught piano at the Hochschule für Musik. He wrote more than 400 compositions, including operettas.

Dorn, Heinrich (Ludwig Egmont), noted German conductor, pedagogue, and composer, father of **Alexander (Julius Paul) Dorn**; b. Königsberg, Nov. 14, 1800; d. Berlin, Jan. 10, 1892. He was a law student at Königsberg in 1823, but studied music diligently, continuing in Berlin under L. Berger (piano), Zelter, and B. Klein. After teaching in Frankfurt am Main, he became Kapellmeister of the Königsberg Theater in 1828; in 1829 he became music director of the Leipzig Theater; in 1830 Schumann became his pupil. In 1832 he went to the Hamburg Theater; he was concurrently music director at St. Peter's Cathedral in Riga. Wagner conducted the premiere of his opera *Der Schöffe von Paris* in Riga in 1838; after Wagner lost his post at the Riga Theater in 1839, Dorn was named his successor, and the 2 subsequently became bitter enemies. Dorn next went to Cologne, where he served as Kapellmeister at the theater and of the concerts of the Singverein and Musikalischen Gesellschaft (1843–44), then was conductor of the Lower Rhenish Music Festivals (1844–47). In 1845 he founded the Rheinische Musikschule, which became the Cologne Cons. under Hiller's directorship in 1850. For his services to music in Cologne, he was accorded the title of Royal Musikdirektor in 1847. In 1849 he succeeded Nicolai as court Kapellmeister of the Royal Opera in Berlin. In 1854 he anticipated Wagner by bringing out his opera *Die Nibelungen*; although initially successful, it was eventually supplanted by Wagner's masterful Ring cycle. Dorn was pensioned with the title of Royal Prof. in 1869. He subsequently busied himself with teaching and writing music criticism. He publ. an autobiography, *Aus meinem Leben* (7 vols., Berlin, 1870–86; includes various essays).

WORKS: DRAMATIC: OPERAS: *Die Rolandsknappen* (Berlin, 1826); *Der Zauberer und das Ungethüm* (Berlin, 1827); *Die Bettlerin* (Königsberg, 1827); *Abu Kara* (Leipzig, 1831); *Das Schwärmermädchen* (Leipzig, 1832); *Der Schöffe von Paris* (Riga, Sept. 27, 1838); *Das Banner von England* (Riga, 1841); *Die Musiker von Aix-la-Chapelle* (1848); *Artaxerxes* (Berlin, 1850); *Die Nibelungen* (Berlin, March 27, 1854); *Ein Tag in Russland* (Berlin, 1856); *Der Botenläufer von Pirna* (Mannheim, March 15, 1865); *Gewitter bei Sonnenschein* (Dresden, 1865). BALLET: *Amors Macht* (Leipzig, 1830).

BIBL.: A. Rauh, *H. D. als Opernkomponist* (diss., Univ. of Munich, 1939).

Dorus-Gras, Julie (**-Aimée-Josephe** née **Van Steenkiste**), South Netherlands soprano; b. Valenciennes, Sept. 7, 1805; d. Paris, Feb. 6, 1896. After training at the Paris Cons., she made her operatic debut at the Théâtre Royal de la Monnaie in Brussels in 1825. On Feb. 12, 1829, she sang in the first Brussels staging of Auber's *La muette de Portici*. She later sang in the famous staging of the score there on Aug. 25, 1830, which set the spark of the Belgian revolution. In 1831 she joined the Paris Opéra, where she created roles in many operas, among them Alice in *Robert le diable* (Nov. 21, 1831), Eudoxie in *La juive* (Feb. 23, 1835), Marguerite de Valois in *Les Huguenots* (Feb. 29, 1836), and Teresa in *Benvenuto Cellini* (Sept. 3, 1838). She continued to sing there until 1846. In 1839 she appeared as a concert artist in London, returning there to sing Lucia at Drury Lane in 1847 and Elvira in *La muette de Portici* at Covent Garden in 1849.

Dostal, Nico(laus Josef Michäel), Austrian composer; b. Korneuburg, Nov. 25, 1895; d. Vienna, Oct. 27, 1981. He was the nephew of Hermann Dostal (1874–1930), a composer of operettas and military marches. After studies in Linz and Vienna, he was active at the Innsbruck City Theater; then conducted in St. Pölten, Romania, and Salzburg. In 1924 he went to Berlin and was active as an arranger and orchestrator of operettas, and as a composer of songs for the theater and films. In 1927 he became a conductor at the Theater am Nollendorfplatz, where he scored a fine success with his first operetta *Clivia* (Dec. 23, 1933). It was followed by the successful operettas *Die Vielgeliebt* (March 5, 1935), *Monika* (Stuttgart, Oct. 3, 1937), *Die ungarische Hochzeit* (Stuttgart, Feb. 4, 1939), and *Manina* (Berlin, Nov. 28, 1942). Among his well-received postwar scores was *Doktor Eisenbart* (Nuremberg, March 29, 1952). His autobiography was publ. as *Ans Ende deiner Träume kommst du nie: Berichte, Bekenntniss, Betrachtungen* (Innsbruck, 1982).

WORKS: MUSIC THEATER: *Clivia* (Berlin, Dec. 23, 1933); *Die Vielgeliebte* (Berlin, March 5, 1935); *Prinzessin Nofretete* (Cologne, Sept. 12, 1936); *Extrablätter* (Bremen, Feb. 17, 1937); *Monika* (Stuttgart, Oct. 3, 1937); *Die ungarische Hochzeit* (Stuttgart, Feb. 4, 1939); *Die Flucht ins Glück* (Stuttgart, Dec. 23, 1940); *Die grosse Tänzerin* (Chemnitz, Feb. 15, 1942); *Eva im Abendkleid* (Chemnitz, Nov. 21, 1942); *Manina* (Berlin, Nov. 28, 1942); *Süsse kleine Freundin* (Wuppertal, Dec. 31, 1949); *Zirkusblut* (Leipzig, March 3, 1950); *Der Kurier der Königin* (Hamburg, March 2, 1950); *Doktor Eisenbart* (Nuremberg, March 29, 1952); *Der dritte Wunsch* (Nuremberg, Feb. 20, 1954); *Liebesbriefe* (Vienna, Nov. 25, 1955); *So macht man Karriere* (Nuremberg, April 29, 1961); *Rhapsodie der Liebe* (Nuremberg, Nov. 9, 1963).

Doubrava, Jaroslav, Czech composer; b. Chrudim, April 25, 1909; d. Prague, Oct. 2, 1960. He was a student of Otakar Jeremiáš (1931–37). During the German occupation of his homeland, he was active in the partisan movement. After the liberation in 1945, he joined the staff of the Czech Radio in Prague, where he served as head of music (1950–55). Among his compositions are particularly well-crafted works for the theater.

WORKS: DRAMATIC: OPERAS: *Sen noci svatojanské* (A Midsummer Night's Dream; 1942–49; Opava, Dec. 21, 1969); *Křest svatého Vladimíra* (The Conversion of St. Vladimir; 1949–50; unfinsihed); *Líný Honza* (Lazy Honza; 1952; unfinished); *Balada o lásce* (Ballad of Love) or *Láska čarovana* (Love Bewitched), opera ballad (1960; orchestrated by J. Hanuš; Prague, June 21, 1962). BALLETS: *Král Lávra* (King Lavra; 1951); *Don Quijote* (1955).

Dougherty, Celius (Hudson), American pianist and composer; b. Glenwood, Minn., May 27, 1902; d. Effort, Pa., Dec. 22, 1986. After training in piano and composition with Ferguson at the Univ. of Minnesota, he was a piano scholarship student of J. Lhévinne and Goldmark at the Juilliard School of Music in New York. He toured as an accompanist to noted singers of the day, several of whom championed his songs; he also toured in duo-piano recitals with Vincent Ruzicka, giving first performances of works by Stravinsky, Schoenberg, Berg, Hindemith et al. Among his compositions is *Many Moons*, opera (Poughkeepsie, N.Y., Dec. 6, 1962).

BIBL.: J. Bender, *The Songs of C. D.* (thesis, Univ. of Minnesota, 1981).

Douglas, Clive (Martin), Australian conductor and composer; b. Rushworth, Victoria, July 27, 1903; d. Melbourne, April 29, 1977. He received lessons in violin, piano, orchestration, and conducting before pursuing training with Nickson and Heinze at the Univ. of Melbourne Conservatorium of Music (Mus.B., 1934). In 1936 he joined the conducting staff of the Australian Broadcasting Commission, appearing as a conductor with its orchs. in Hobart (1936–41) and Brisbane (1941–47), and then as assoc. conductor in Sydney (1947–53) and assoc. and resident conductor in Melbourne (1953–66). In 1953 he received the Coronation Medal, in 1958 he was awarded a Doctor of Music degree from the Univ. of Melbourne, and in 1963 he was made a Life Fellow of the International Inst. of Arts and Letters. In many of his scores, Douglas made use of aboriginal melorhythmic patterns.

WORKS: DRAMATIC: *The Scarlet Letter*, opera (1925–29; unfinished); *Ashmadai*, operetta (1929; 1934–35; 1st public perf. in a radio broadcast, Melbourne, Aug. 17, 1936); *Kaditcha* or *A Bush Legend*, operetta (1937–38; ABC, Tasmania, June 22, 1938; rev. 1956); *Corroboree*, ballet from the operetta *Kaditcha* (1939); *Eleanor*, *Maid Rosamond*, and *Henry of Anjou*, opera trilogy (1941–43); documentary film scores; music for radio and television.

Dourlen, Victor (-Charles-Paul), French pedagogue and composer; b. Dunkerque, Nov. 3, 1780; d. Batignolles, near Paris, Jan. 8, 1864. He studied with Gossec and Boieldieu at the Paris Cons. (1799–1805), sharing the Prix de Rome in 1805 for his cantata *Cupidon pleurant Psyché*. He subsequently taught there (1812–42). Of his 9 operas, 8 were produced at the Opéra Comique: *Philoclès* (Oct. 4, 1806); *Linnée, ou La Mine de Suéde* (Sept. 10, 1808); *La Dupe de son art* (Sept. 9, 1809); *Cagliostro, ou Les Illuminés* (with A. Reicha; Nov. 27, 1810); *Plus heureux que sage* (May 25, 1816); *Le Frère Philippe* (Jan. 20, 1818); *Marini, ou Le Muet de Venise* (June 12, 1819); *La Vente après décès* (Théâtre du Gymnase-Dramatique; Aug. 1, 1821); *Le Petit Souper* (Feb. 22, 1822). He publ. 3 harmony textbooks based upon the methods of C. S. Catel.

Downes, Sir Edward (Thomas), respected English conductor; b. Birmingham, June 17, 1924. After studies at the Univ. of Birmingham (M.A., 1944), he took courses in horn and composition at the Royal College of Music in London (1944–46); in 1948 he received the Carnegie Scholarship and pursued training in conducting with Scherchen. He was an assistant conductor with the Carl Rosa Opera (1950–52); he then was on the conducting staff at London's Covent Garden (1952–69), where he led an extensive repertoire of standard and modern scores, including his own translation of Shostakovich's *Katerina Ismailova* (1963); he also conducted Wagner's *Ring* cycle there (1967). In 1972 he became musical director of the Australian Opera in Sydney, inaugurating the new Sydney Opera House in 1973 with his own translation of Prokofiev's *War and Peace*. In 1976 he left this post, and in 1980 became principal conductor of the BBC Northern Sym. Orch. in Manchester, a post he retained in 1983 when it was renamed the BBC Phil. In 1992 he left this post, having been appointed assoc. music director and principal conductor at Covent Garden in 1991. In 1986 he was made a Commander of the Order of the British Empire, and in 1991 he was knighted.

Downes, Edward O(lin) D(avenport), American music critic and lecturer, son of **(Edwin) Olin Downes**; b. Boston, Aug. 12, 1911. He studied at Columbia Univ. (1929–30), the Univ. of Paris (1932–33), the Univ. of Munich (1934–36, 1938), and Harvard Univ. (Ph.D., 1958, with the diss. *The Operas of Johann Christian Bach as a Reflection of the Dominant Trends in "opera seria," 1750–1780*). Under the tutelage of his father, he embarked upon a career as a music critic; he wrote for the *N.Y. Post* (1935–38), the *Boston Transcript* (1939–41), and the *N.Y. Times* (1955–58) and was program annotator for the N.Y. Phil. (from 1960); from 1958 he acted as quizmaster for the Metropolitan Opera broadcasts. He was a lecturer at Wellesley College (1948–49), Harvard Univ. (1949–50), and the Univ. of Minnesota (1950–55). After serving as musicologist-in-residence at the Bayreuth master classes (1959–65), he was prof. of music history at Queens College of the City Univ. of N.Y. (1966–81) and at N.Y. Univ. (1981–86). From 1986 he was a prof. of music at the Juilliard School. Most of his publ. books focus on the symphonic repertory, but he also produced *Verdi, The Man in His Letters* (tr. of Werfel and Stefan's *Giuseppe Verdis Briefe*, Berlin, 1926; N.Y., 1942).

Downes, (Edwin) Olin, eminent American music critic, father of **Edward O(lin) D(avenport) Downes**; b. Evanston, Ill., Jan. 27, 1886; d. N.Y., Aug. 22, 1955. He studied piano at the National Cons. of Music of N.Y. and was a pupil in Boston of Louis Kelterborn (history and analysis), Carl Baermann (piano), Homer Norris and Clifford Heilman (theory), and John Marshall (music criticism). After establishing himself as a music critic of the *Boston Post* (1906–24), he was the influential music critic of the *N.Y. Times* from 1924 until his death. He was also active as a lecturer and served as quizmaster of the Metropolitan Opera broadcasts. His valuable collection of letters (about 50,000) to and from the most celebrated names in 20th-century music history is housed at the Univ. of Georgia. Downes did much to advance the cause of Strauss, Stravinsky, Sibelius, Prokofiev, and Shostakovich in the United States. In 1937 he received the Order of Commander of the White Rose of Finland and in 1939 an honorary Mus.Doc. from the Cincinnati Cons. of Music. He authored numerous books and also ed. *Ten Operatic Masterpieces, From Mozart to Prokofiev* (N.Y., 1952).

BIBL.: G. Goss, *Jean Sibelius and O. D.: Music, Friendship, Criticism* (Boston, 1995).

Draeseke, Felix (August Bernhard), significant German composer; b. Coburg, Oct. 7, 1835; d. Dresden, Feb. 26, 1913. He entered the Leipzig Cons. at the age of 17, where he studied composition with Julius Rietz; his advanced proclivities met with opposition there, so he continued his studies privately with Rietz. In 1857 he met Liszt and in 1861 Wagner, and thereafter was an ardent champion of the New German School of composition. In 1862 he went to Switzerland and was active as a piano teacher; in 1876 he returned to Germany and in 1884 joined the faculty of the Dresden Cons. Although regarded as a radical composer by many, he did not accept the modern tendencies in music of the early years of the 20th century, which he attacked in his pamphlet *Die Konfusion in der Musik* (1906), directed chiefly against Richard Strauss. He was a prolific composer, but his works are virtually unknown outside Germany. A Draeseke Soc., formed in Germany in 1931, issued sporadic bulletins.

WRITINGS: *Answeisung zum kunstgerechten Modulieren* (Freienwalde, 1876); *Die Beseitigung des Tritonus* (Leipzig, 1880); *Die Lehre von der Harmonia in lustige Reimlein gebracht* (Leipzig, 1883; 2d ed., aug., 1887); *Der gebundene Stil: Lehrbuch für Kontrapunkt und Fuge* (Hannover, 1902).

WORKS: OPERAS: *König Sigurd* (1853–57; fragment perf., Meiningen, 1867); *Herrat (Dietrich von Bern)* (1877–79; Dresden, March 10, 1892); *Gudrun* (Hannover, Jan. 11, 1884); *Bertrand de Born* (1892–94); *Fischer und Kalif* (1894–95; Prague, April 15, 1905); *Merlin* (1903–05; Gotha, May 10, 1913).

BIBL.: H. Platzbecker, *F. D.* (Leipzig, 1909); O. zur Nedden, *F. D.s Opern und Oratorien* (diss., Univ. of Marburg, 1925); E. Röder, *F. D.* (2 vols., Dresden, 1930, Berlin, 1935).

Draghi, Antonio, noted Italian-born Austrian composer; b. Rimini, c.1634; d. Vienna, Jan. 16, 1700. He received musical training in his homeland and was active as a bass singer in Venice by 1657. He settled in Vienna in 1658, where he was assistant Kapellmeister (1668–69) and then Kapellmeister (1669–82) to the dowager empress Eleonora. He was appointed director of dramatic music at the Imperial court in 1673 and then its Kapellmeister in 1682. Draghi was a leading representative of the Venetian school of composition at Vienna's Imperial court, being a prolific composer of operas, oratorios, and other dramatic works. From 1666 to 1700 he composed over 100 operas, prologues, and intermezzi, much of which is not extant.

BIBL.: R. Schnitzler, *The Sacred-Dramatic Music of A. D.* (diss., Univ. of North Carolina, 1971); N. Hiltl, *Die Oper am Hofe Kaiser Leopolds I. mit besonderer Berücksichtigung der Tätigkeit von Minato und D.* (diss., Univ. of Vienna, 1974); H. Seifert, *Neues zu A. D.s weltlichen Werken* (Vienna, 1978).

Drăgoi, Sabin V(asile), eminent Romanian composer, folklorist, and pedagogue; b. Selişte, June 18, 1894; d. Bucharest, Dec. 31, 1968. He studied harmony with Zirra in Iaşi (1918–19), theory with Bena and counterpoint with Klee in Cluj (1919–20), and composition with Novák, conducting with Ostrčil, and music history with Krupka in Prague (1920–22). After teaching music in Deva (1922–24), he was director of the Timişoara Cons. (1925–43) and then a teacher at the Cluj Cons. (1943–45). He served as prof. of folklore at the Cons. (1950–52) and as director of the Folklore Inst. (1950–64) in Bucharest. He received the Enesco prize 3 times (1922, 1923, 1928) and the Romanian Academy prize (1933). His extensive folklore research in the Banat and in Transylvania is often reflected in his compositions.

WORKS: DRAMATIC: *Năpasta* (Disaster), opera (1927; Bucharest, May 30, 1928; rev. 1958; Bucharest, Dec. 23, 1961); *Constantin Brîncoveanu*, scenic oratorio (1929; Bucharest, Oct. 25, 1935); *Kir Ianulea*, comic-fantastic opera (1930–38; Cluj-Napoca, Dec. 22, 1939); *Horia*, historical opera (1945; rev. 1959); *Păcală*, comic opera (1954–56; Brasov, May 6, 1962).

BIBL.: N. Rădulescu, *S. V. D.* (Bucharest, 1971).

Dranishnikov, Vladimir, Russian conductor and composer; b. St. Petersburg, June 10, 1893; d. Kiev, Feb. 6, 1939. He studied at the St. Petersburg Cons. with Essipova (piano), Steinberg, Liadov, and Wihtol (composition), and N. Tcherepnin (conducting). He was employed as a rehearsal pianist at the St. Petersburg Imperial Opera (1914–18); in 1918 he became conductor there, earning great esteem for his skill in both the classical and the modern repertoire; he conducted the first Soviet performance of Berg's *Wozzeck*, and of numerous Soviet operas. In 1930 he was appointed conductor of the Kiev Opera.

Drdla, Franz (František Alois), Bohemian violinist and composer; b. Saar, Moravia, Nov. 28, 1868; d. Badgastein, Sept. 3, 1944. After training with Bennewitz (violin) and Foerster (composition) at the Prague Cons. (1880–82), he studied at the Vienna Cons. (1882–88) with J. Hellmesberger Jr. (violin) and Krenn and Bruckner (composition), winning 1st prize for violin and the medal of the Gesellschaft der Musikfreunde. He was a violinist in the orch. of the Vienna Court Opera (1890–93); after serving as concertmaster of the orch. of the Theater an der Wien (1894–99), he made successful tours as a violinist in Europe (1899–1905) and the United States (1923–25). His lighter pieces for violin and piano won enormous popularity in their day, especially his *Serenade No. 1* (1901), *Souvenir* (1904), and *Vision*. He also wrote the operettas *Zlatá sít* (1st perf. as *Das goldene Netz*, Leipzig, 1916; rev. as *Bohyně lásky* [The Goddess of Love], Brno, 1941) and *Komtesa z prodejny* (1st perf. as *Die Ladenkomtesse*, Brünn, 1917).

BIBL.: J. Květ, *F. D.* (Ždár nad Sázavou, 1968).

Drechsler, Joseph, Bohemian-born Austrian composer; b. Wällisch-Birken, May 26, 1782; d. Vienna, Feb. 27, 1852. He was a pupil of the organist Grotius at Florenbach. He was assistant Kapellmeister (1812) at the Vienna Court Opera, then conductor in the theaters at Baden (near Vienna) and Pressburg. Returning to Vienna, he became organist of the Servite church. In 1816 he was precentor at St. Ann's, and in 1823 Kapellmeister at the Univ. church and the Hofpfarrkirche. From 1824 to 1830 he was also Kapellmeister at the Leopoldstadt Theater. He composed 6 operas, including *Die Feldmühle,* Singspiel (Vienna, Sept. 29, 1812) and *Pauline*, opera (Vienna, Feb. 23, 1821), and about 30 operettas, vaudevilles, and pantomimes. He publ. a method for organ and a treatise on harmony.

BIBL.: C. Preiss, *J. D.* (Graz, 1910).

Dreier, Per, Norwegian conductor; b. Trondheim, Dec. 25, 1929. He studied conducting with Paul van Kempen and Willem van Otterloo at the Royal Cons. of Music in The Hague. He made his debut with the Trondheim Sym. Orch. in 1953. He then was a conductor at the Württemberg State Theater at Stuttgart (1953–57) and chief conductor and artistic director of the Århus Sym. Orch. (1957–73); he also served as chief conductor of the Jutland

Opera (1957–71). Dreier has done much to promote contemporary Norwegian music.

Dresden, Sem, notable Dutch composer and pedagogue; b. Amsterdam, April 20, 1881; d. The Hague, July 30, 1957. He studied composition with Zweers at the Amsterdam Cons., and then composition and conducting with Pfitzner at the Stern Cons. in Berlin (1903–05). Returning to Amsterdam, he was conductor of the Motet and Madrigal Soc. (1914–26); he also taught composition at (1919–24) and was director (1924–37) of the Cons. In 1937 he became director of the Royal Cons. of Music in The Hague, but was removed from his position by the Nazi occupation authorities in 1940; upon the liberation in 1945, he was restored to his position, which he held until 1949. He publ. *Het Muziekleven in Nederlands sinds 1880* (Amsterdam, 1923) and *Stromingen en Tegenstromingen in de Muziek* (Haarlem, 1953); he also rev. Worp's *Algemeene Muziekleer* (Groningen, 1931; 9th ed., 1956). His compositions reveal both German and French influences with a distinctive Dutch strain. Among his diverse works is the opera *François Villon* (1956–57; orchestrated by J. Mul; Amsterdam, June 15, 1958) and the operetta *Toto* (1945).

Dresher, Paul (Joseph), American composer and performer; b. Los Angeles, Jan. 8, 1951. He studied music at the Univ. of Calif. at Berkeley (B.A., 1977) and composition with Erickson, Reynolds, and Oliveros at the Univ. of Calif. at San Diego (M.A., 1979); he also received training in Ghanaian drumming, Javanese and Balinese gamelan, and North Indian classical music. In 1984 he founded the Paul Dresher Ensemble. His awards include an NEA grant (1979), the Goddard Lieberson fellowship of the American Academy and Inst. of Arts and Letters (1982), and a Fulbright fellowship (1984). In addition to orch. and chamber works, he has written experimental operatic and theater pieces (many in collaboration with theater director George Coates), as well as various electroacoustic taped scores for use in theater, dance, video, radio, and film. As a composer, his intent has been to integrate the more traditional formal aspects of music with what he terms a "pre-maximalist" vocabulary.

WORKS: DRAMATIC: *The Way of How*, music theater (1981); *Are Are*, music theater (1983); *Seehear*, music theater (1984); *re:act:ion* for Orch. (1984); *Was Are/Will Be*, staged concert piece (1985); *Freesound* (1985–88); *Slow Fire*, music theater/opera (1985–88); *Figaro Gets a Divorce*, theater score (1986); *The Tempest*, theater score (1987); *Shelflife*, live perf. dance piece (1987); *Loose the Thread*, dance piece for Violin, Piano, and Percussion (1988); *Power Failure*, music theater/opera (1988–89); *Pioneers*, music theater/opera (1989–90; Spoleto Festival, May 26, 1990); *Awed Behavior*, music theater (1992–93; Los Angeles, May 1, 1993).

Dressel, Erwin, German pianist, conductor, and composer; b. Berlin, June 10, 1909; d. there, Dec. 17, 1972. He studied in Berlin with Klatte at the Stern Cons. and with Juon at the Hochschule für Musik. He was active in Berlin as a pianist, theater conductor, arranger, and composer. He composed the operas *Der arme Columbus* (Kassel, Feb. 19, 1928), *Der Kuchentanz* (Kassel, May 18, 1929), *Der Rosenbusch der Maria* (Leipzig, June 23, 1930), *Die Zwillingsesel* (Dresden, April 29, 1932), *Jery und Bätely* (Berlin, 1932), *Die Laune der Verliebten* (Hamburg and Leipzig, 1949), and *Der Bar* (Bern, 1963).

Drew, James, multifaceted American composer, playwright, pianist, and teacher; b. St. Paul, Minn., Feb. 9, 1929. He studied at the N.Y. School of Music (1954–56), with Varèse (1956), and with Riegger (1956–59). Following further training at Tulane Univ. (M.A., 1964), he pursued postgraduate studies at Washington Univ. in St. Louis (1964–65). In 1972–73 he held a Guggenheim fellowship. He taught at Northwestern Univ. (1965–67), Yale Univ. (1967–73), the Berkshire Music Center at Tanglewood (summer, 1973), Louisiana State Univ. (1973–76), Calif. State Univ. at Fullerton (1976–77), and the Univ. of Calif. at Los Angeles (1977–78). As a composer and playwright, Drew has pursued an active career outside of academia. Except for master classes and lectures, he has worked since 1980 on independent projects for the theater, concert stage, and film. His Grey Wolf Atelier International, which is devoted to the arts education of children, parents, and teachers, was founded in 1993. With his colleague, the educator Mary Gae George, the Atelier operates in Florida, Utah, Indiana, and the Netherlands.

WORKS: DRAMATIC: *Toward Yellow*, ballet (1970); *Mysterium*, television opera (1974–75); *Crucifixus Domini Christi* (1975); *Suspense Opera* (1975); *Dr. Cincinnati* (1977); *5 O'Clock Ladies* (1981); *Himself, the Devil* (1982); *Whisper*, video piece (1982); *Becket: The Final Moments*, automated drama (1984); *One Last Dance*, theater and/or video piece (1985); *Blue in Atlantis*, audiotheater piece (1986); *"Live" from the Black Eagle* (1987–88); *Rat's Teeth* (1989); *Surprise Operas* (1989); *Theater of Phantom Sounds* (1993); *The Voice* (1995); *Club Berlin is Closed: Hello?*, theater piece (1995); *Survivors in Pale Light* (1995); *Powder Songs of the Lady Magicians* (1999); *The Voice* (1999).

Dreyfus, George (Georg), German-born Australian bassoonist, conductor, and composer; b. Wuppertal, July 22, 1928. He emigrated to Australia in 1939. He studied clarinet and bassoon at the Melbourne Conservatorium, then completed his training at the Vienna Academy of Music (1955–56). He played in various Australian orchs., including the Melbourne Sym. Orch. (1953–64); in 1958 he founded the New Music Ensemble in Melbourne, which became the George Dreyfus Chamber Orch. in 1970. In 1976 he held the Prix de Rome of the German Academy in Rome, and in 1983 was artist-in-residence at the Tianjin Cons. of Music in China. He publ. an autobiography, *The Last Frivolous Book* (Sydney, 1984).

WORKS: DRAMATIC: OPERAS: *Garni Sands* (1965–66; Sydney, July 12, 1972); *The Takeover*, school opera (1969); *The Gilt-Edged Kid* (1970; Melbourne, April 11, 1976); *The Lamentable Reign of Charles the Last*, "pantopera" (1975; Adelaide, March 23, 1976); *Rathenau* (1993); *Die Marx Sisters* (1995). MUSICALS: *Smash Hit!* (1980); *The Sentimental Bloke* (Melbourne, Dec. 17, 1985). MIMEDRAMA: *The Illusionist* (1972).

Dreyschock, Alexander, brilliant Bohemian pianist, teacher, and composer; b. Zack, Oct. 15, 1818; d. Venice, April 1, 1869. His brother was the Bohemian violinist Raimund Dreyschock (b. Zack, Aug. 20, 1824; d. Leipzig, Feb. 6, 1869). A student of Tomaschek, he acquired a virtuoso technique and was regarded as a worthy rival of Liszt in technical dexterity. At 8 he was able to play in public; he toured North Germany (1838), spent 2 years in Russia (1840–42), and visited Brussels, Paris, and London, then the Netherlands and Austria. In 1862 he was called to St. Petersburg as a prof. at the newly founded Cons. In 1868 he went to Italy. His astounding facility in playing octaves, double sixths, and thirds, and performing solos with the left hand alone cast a glamour about his performance. Among his compositions is the opera *Florette, oder Die erste Liebe Heinrichs des IV.*

Drieberg, Friedrich von, German music historian and composer; b. Charlottenburg, Dec. 10, 1780; d. there, May 21, 1856. He served in the Prussian army until 1804, when he went to Paris to study composition with Spontini; also traveled to Vienna. He produced 2 operas, *Don Cocagno* (Berlin, 1812) and *Der Sänger und der Schneider* (Berlin, Nov. 23, 1814), but became known mainly through his speculative publications concerning Greek music, promulgating theories and conclusions that were utterly unfounded. However, they were publ. and seriously discussed, if only in refutation. These are *Die mathematische Intervallenlehre der Griechen* (1818), *Aufschlüsse über die Musik der Griechen* (1819), *Die praktische Musik der Griechen* (1821), *Die pneumatischen Erfindungen der Griechen* (1822), *Wörterbuch der griech. Musik* (1835), *Die griechische Musik, auf ihre Grundgesetze zurückgeführt* (1841), and *Die Kunst der musikalischen Composition . . . nach griechischen Grundsätzen bearbeitet* (1858).

Driessler, Johannes, German composer and pedagogue; b. Friedrichsthal, Jan. 26, 1921. He received training in organ, choral conducting, and theory from Karl Rahner at the Saarbrücken

Cons. and in composition from William Maler at the Cologne Cons. In 1946 he became a teacher of church music at the North West German Music Academy in Detmold, where he was a prof. of composition (from 1958) and deputy director (1960–83). He was especially adept at composing choral works in an acceptable tonal idiom. His stage works include the operas *Claudia amata* (1952), *Prinzessin Hochmut* (1952), *Der Umfried* (youth opera; 1957), and *Doktor Luzifer Trux* (1958).

Dring, Madeleine, English violinist, pianist, singer, and composer; b. Hornsey, Sept. 7, 1923; d. London, March 26, 1977. She studied violin at the Junior Dept. of the Royal College of Music in London, and also acquired professional skill as a pianist, singer, and actress. She took courses in composition at the Royal College of Music with Howells and Vaughan Williams. She developed a knack for writing attractively brief pieces. She also wrote a short opera, *Cupboard Love*.

Drummond, Dean, American composer, conductor, instrumentalist, and inventor of musical instruments; b. Los Angeles, Jan. 22, 1949. He was educated at the Univ. of Southern Calif. in Los Angeles (B.M. in composition, 1971) and the Calif. Inst. of the Arts in Valencia (M.F.A. in composition, 1973), where he studied composition with Leonard Stein; while a student, he also worked closely with Harry Partch, whose instruments and works he later championed. In 1977 he cofounded Newband with the flutist Stefanie Starin, whom he subsequently married; in 1990 he became director of the Harry Partch Music Instrument Collection which in 1993 moved to the State Univ. of N.Y. at Purchase, where Drummond was also composer-in-residence. Drummond's compositions frequently feature newly invented instruments (including his own zoomoozophone and juststrokerods), synthesizers, microtones, new techniques for winds and strings, and large ensembles of specialized percussion. He also made 3 arrangements of works by Partch (1978), Thelonius Monk (1990; rev. 1993), and John Coltrane (1994). Among his awards are a Guggenheim fellowship (1995–96), awards from the Koussevitzky Foundation (1992), Fromm Foundation (1993), and the Cary Trust Commission (1993), NEA fellowships (1988–89; 1995–96), a N.Y. Foundation for the Arts fellowship (1989), and 2d prize in the John F. Kennedy Center Friedheim Award for Chamber Music for his *Dance of the Seven Veils* (1993); in 1995–96 he also received a Meet the Composer/Reader's Digest commission for his live film score, *Der Lezte Mann*. Among his other works is the chamber opera *Cafe Buffe*, for 5 Singers, 9 Instrumentalists, and 4 Dancers, after the poet Charles Bernstein (1997).

Dubensky, Arcady, Russian-American violinist and composer; b. Viatka, Oct. 15, 1890; d. Tenafly, N.J., Oct. 14, 1966. He learned to play the violin in his youth, and then was a student of Hřímalý (violin), Ilyinsky (composition), and Arends (conducting) at the Moscow Cons. (1904–09; diploma, 1909). After playing 1st violin in the Moscow Imperial Opera orch. (1910–19), he settled in New York in 1921 and was a violinist in the N.Y. Sym. Orch. (1922–28) and the N.Y. Phil. (1928–53). While he composed in a conservative idiom, he made adroit use of unusual instrumental combinations. His dramatic works include the operas *Romance with Double Bass* (1916; N.Y., Oct. 31, 1936), *Downtown* (1930), *On the Highway* (1936), and *2 Yankees in Italy* (1944), and incidental music to Tarkington's *Mowgli* (1940).

Dubois, Pierre-Max, French composer; b. Graulhet, Tarn, March 1, 1930; d. Rocquencourt, Aug. 29, 1995. He studied at the Tours Cons., obtaining a prize in piano at the age of 15; he later studied composition with Milhaud at the Paris Cons. In 1955 he won the Grand Prix de Rome and the music prize of the City of Paris. His dramatic works include *Impressions foraines*, ballet (1951), *Le Docteur OX*, ballet-bouffe, after Jules Verne (Lyons, Feb. 23, 1964), *Cover Girls*, choreographic spectacle (1965), *Comment causer*, opéra pouf (1970), *Les Suisses*, opera (1972), and *Hommage à Hoffnung*, ballet (1980).

Dubois, (François-Clément) Théodore, eminent French organist and composer; b. Rosnay, Marne, Aug. 24, 1837; d. Paris, June 11, 1924. He entered the Paris Cons. in 1853, working under Marmontel (piano), Benoist (organ), and Bazin and Ambroise Thomas (composition); he graduated in 1861, the recipient of the Grand Prix de Rome with the cantata *Atala*, after having taken 1st prizes in all depts. Returning to Paris, he was maître de chapelle at Sainte-Clotilde until 1869 and at the Madeleine until 1877, and then succeeded Saint-Saëns there as organist. In 1871 he was made prof. of harmony at the Paris Cons., succeeding Elwart; in 1891 he became prof. of composition, and in 1894 he was elected to the chair in the Academy left vacant by Gounod's death. In 1896 he succeeded Ambroise Thomas as director of the Paris Cons.; he retired in 1905. Dubois publ. a practical manual, *Traité de contrepoint et de fugue* (1901), which was a standard work at the Paris Cons.

WORKS: DRAMATIC (all 1st perf. in Paris): COMIC OPERAS: *La Guzla de l'émir* (April 30, 1873); *Le Pain bis, ou La Lilloise* (Feb. 26, 1879); *Aben Hamet* (produced in Italian, Dec. 16, 1884). IDYLLE DRAMATIQUE: *Xavière* (Nov. 26, 1895). BALLET: *La Farandole* (Dec. 14, 1883). Also 2 oratorios: *Les Sept Paroles du Christ* (1867) and *Le Paradis perdu* (1878; won the City of Paris prize).

BIBL.: M. Widor, *Notice sur la vie et les travaux de T. D.* (Paris, 1924).

Dubrovay, László, Hungarian composer; b. Budapest, March 23, 1943. He studied at the Bartók Cons. and the Academy of Music in Budapest (graduated, 1966), his principal mentors being István Szelényi, Ferenc Szabó, and Imre Vincze; then continued his training in West Germany on a scholarship from the Deutscher Akademischer Austauschdienst, receiving instruction in composition from Stockhausen and in electronic music from Hans-Ulrich Rumpert (1972–74). Returning to Budapest, he taught theory at the Academy of Music (from 1976); he was awarded the Erkel Prize (1985). In some of his works, he utilizes electronic and computer resources. He composed the opera *Il ricatto* (1991) and the dance-play *The Sculptor* (1993).

Ducloux, Walter (Ernest), Swiss-born American conductor and teacher; b. Kriens, April 17, 1913; d. Austin, Texas, Jan. 27, 1997. He was educated at the Univ. of Munich (Ph.D., 1935) and studied conducting at the Vienna Academy of Music (diploma, 1937). After conducting in Lucerne (1937–39), he emigrated to the United States and became a naturalized citizen in 1943. He appeared as a conductor in the United States and Europe, and also served on the faculties of the Univ. of Southern Calif. in Los Angeles (1953–68) and the Univ. of Texas in Austin (from 1968). He was music director of the Austin (Texas) Sym. Orch. (1973–75) and the Austin (Texas) Lyric Opera (from 1986).

Duesing, Dale, American baritone; b. Milwaukee, Sept. 26, 1947. He studied voice at Lawrence Univ. in Appleton, Wis. Following appearances in Bremen (1972) and Düsseldorf (1974–75), he sang in the premiere of Imbrie's *Angle of Repose* in San Francisco in 1976; that same year, made his first appearance at the Glyndebourne Festival as Strauss's Olivier. On Feb. 22, 1979, he made his Metropolitan Opera debut in New York as Strauss's Harlekin, returning there in later seasons as Rossini's Figaro, as Pelléas, and as Billy Budd; he also sang opera in Seattle, Santa Fe, Chicago, Houston, Brussels, Barcelona, Salzburg, and Milan. Duesing won critical acclaim when he created the tasking role of I in the premiere of Schnittke's *Zhizn s Idiotom* (Life with an Idiot) in Amsterdam in 1992. Among his other operatic roles are Guglielmo, Eugene Onegin, Belcore, Wolfram, and Janáček's Goryanshikov.

Dufallo, Richard (John), American conductor; b. East Chicago, Ind., Jan. 30, 1933. He played clarinet as a youngster; then enrolled at the American Cons. of Music in Chicago. He subsequently studied composition with Foss at the Univ. of Calif., Los Angeles; in 1957 he joined the Improvisation Chamber Ensemble organized by Foss, and showed an exceptional talent for controlled improvisation in the ultramodern manner. He then joined Foss as his assoc. conductor with the Buffalo Phil. (1962–67); he also served on the faculty of the State Univ. of N.Y. at Buffalo (1963–67), where he directed its Center of Creative and Performing Arts. He attended a conducting seminar with William Steinberg in New York (1965); Boulez gave him additional instruction in Basel (1969). In 1967 he went to Japan and other Asian countries as assistant tour conductor with the N.Y. Phil. In 1971 he made his European conducting debut in Paris. He served as conductor of the "Mini-Met," an adjunct to the Metropolitan Opera in New York (1972–74), and was director of the series of new music sponsored by the Juilliard School in New York (1972–79). From 1970 to 1985 he was artistic director of the Aspen Music Festival's Conference on Contemporary Music. From 1980 to 1982 he also served as artistic adviser of Het Gelders Orkest in Arnhem, the Netherlands. In 1984–85 he was acting director of the Aspen Inst. Italia in Rome. He secured a reputation as an advocate of contemporary music. He publ. the useful book *Trackings: Composers Speak with Richard Dufallo* (N.Y. and Oxford, 1989).

Dufranne, Hector (Robert), Belgian bass-baritone; b. Mons, Oct. 25, 1870; d. Paris, May 3, 1951. He studied in Brussels, making his operatic debut there at the Théâtre Royal de la Monnaie as Valentine in *Faust* (Sept. 9, 1896), then went to Paris as a member of the Opéra Comique (1899–1909) and the Opéra (from 1909). He also sang at the Manhattan Opera in New York (1908–10), the Chicago Grand Opera (1910–22), and London's Covent Garden (1914); he retired from the stage in 1939. He created roles in several French operas, including Golaud in Debussy's *Pelléas et Mélisande* (1902).

Dugazon, Louise (Rosalie), famous French mezzo-soprano; b. Berlin, June 18, 1755; d. Paris, Sept. 22, 1821. She was brought up in the atmosphere of the theater. Her father, F. J. Lefèbvre, was a French dancer at the Berlin Royal Opera and the Paris Opéra, and she herself began her career as a ballet dancer; encouraged mainly by Grétry, who thought highly of her talent, she studied with Favart. She made her debut in Paris in Grétry's opera *Sylvain* (June 19, 1774). In 1776 she married an actor who used the professional name Dugazon; although they were soon separated, she adopted this name for her professional appearances. She sang mostly at the Opéra Comique, where she created some 60 new roles. Her last public appearance was at the Paris Opéra on Feb. 29, 1804. She was greatly admired by her contemporaries, and her name became a designation of certain types of operatic parts ("jeune Dugazon"; i.e., an ingenue). Her son Gustave (1782–1826) was a composer.

BIBL.: H. and A. Leroux, *La D.* (Paris, 1926).

Duhamel, Antoine, French composer; b. Valmondois, near Paris, July 30, 1925. He was the son of the writer Georges Duhamel and of the actress Blanche Albane. He studied at the Paris Cons. with Messiaen, Dufourcq, and de la Presle, but pursued his major training privately with Leibowitz who provided him with a thorough grounding in modern techniques. Although he composed some concert works, he devoted much time to the theater. In addition to film and television scores, he wrote much stage music. Among the latter were *L'ivrogne* (1952; Tours, 1984); *Gala de cirque* (Strasbourg, 1965); *Lundi, Monsieur, vous serez riche* (Paris, Jan. 23, 1969); *L'opéra des oiseaux* (Lyons, May 19, 1971); *Ubu à l'opéra* (Avignon, July 16, 1974); *Gambara* (Lyons, June 2, 1978); *Le cirque impérial* (Avignon, July 30, 1979); *Les travaux d'Hercule* (Vaise, June 15, 1981); *Le transsibérien* (1983); *Le scieur de long* (Tours, March 9, 1984); *Quatrevingt-treize* (Fourvières, July 10, 1989); *Les Adventures de Sinbad le marin* (Colmar, Feb. 12, 1991).

Dukas, Paul, famous French composer and teacher; b. Paris, Oct. 1, 1865; d. there, May 17, 1935. From 1882 to 1888 he was a student at the Paris Cons., studying under Mathias (piano), Dubois (harmony), and Guiraud (composition); he won 1st prize for counterpoint and fugue in 1886, and the 2d Prix de Rome with a cantata, *Velléda* (1888). He began writing music reviews in 1892; he was music critic of the *Revue Hebdomadaire* and *Gazette des Beaux-Arts*. In 1906 he was made a Chevalier of the Légion d'honneur. From 1910 to 1913, and again from 1928 to 1935, he was prof. of the orch. class at the Cons.; in 1918 he was elected Debussy's successor as a member of the *Conseil de l'enseignement supérieur* there; also taught at the École Normale de Musique. Although he was not a prolific composer, Dukas wrote a masterpiece in his orch. scherzo *L'Apprenti Sorcier*; his opera *Ariane et Barbe-Bleue* (1899–1906; Paris, May 10, 1907) is one of the finest French operas in the impressionist style. Among his other notable works is the ballet *La Péri* (1911–12; Paris, April 22, 1912). Shortly before his death he destroyed several MSS of his unfinished compositions.

BIBL.: G. Samazeuilh, *P. D.* (Paris, 1913; 2d ed., 1936); V. d'Indy, *Emmanuel Chabrier et P. D.* (Paris, 1920); G. Samazeuilh, *P. D.: Musicien français* (Paris, 1936); G. Favre, *P. D.: Sa vie, son oeuvre* (Paris, 1948); N. Demuth, *P. D.* (London, 1949); G. Favre, *L'Oeuvre de P. D.* (Paris, 1969); idem, ed., *Correspondance de P. D.* (Paris, 1971); W. Moore, *The Significance of Late Nineteenth-Century French Wagnérisme in the Relationship of P. D. and Edouard Dujardin: A Study of Their Correspondence, Essays on Wagner, and D.'s Opera Ariane et Barbe-Bleue* (diss., Univ. of Texas, 1986).

Duke, John (Woods), American pianist, pedagogue, and composer; b. Cumberland, Md., July 30, 1899; d. Northampton, Mass., Oct. 26, 1984. He studied piano with Harold Randolph and composition with Gustav Strube at the Peabody Cons. of Music in Baltimore (1915–18), then studied piano with Franklin Cannon and composition with Howard Brockway and Bernard Wagenaar in New York; later he received instruction in piano from Schnabel in Berlin and in composition from Boulanger in Paris (1929). He was assistant prof. (1923–38) and prof. (1938–67) of music at Smith College in Northampton, Mass., becoming prof. emeritus at his retirement. He composed *Captain Lovelock*, opera (Hudson Falls, N.Y., Aug. 18, 1953), *The Sire de Maledroit*, opera (Schroon Lake, N.Y., Aug. 15, 1958), and *The Yankee Pedlar*, operetta (Schroon Lake, N.Y., Aug. 17, 1962). He also wrote over 200 songs, some of which are outstanding contributions to the genre.

Duke, Vernon. See **Dukelsky, Vladimir (Alexandrovich).**

Dukelsky, Vladimir (Alexandrovich), versatile Russian-born American composer who used the name **Vernon Duke**; b. Parfianovka, Oct. 10, 1903; d. Santa Monica, Calif., Jan. 16, 1969. He was a student of Glière (1916–19) and Dombrovsky (1917–19) at the Kiev Cons. After living in Constantinople (1920–21), he went to New York in 1922 and to Paris in 1924, where Diaghilev commissioned him to write the ballet *Zéphyr et Flore* (Monte Carlo, April 28, 1925); he also found a champion in Koussevitzky, who conducted his works in Paris and later in Boston. After composing for the London stage (1926–29), he returned to New York and studied orchestration with Schillinger (1934–35). In 1936 he became a naturalized American citizen. Upon settling in the United States, Dukelsky pursued a dual career as a composer of both serious and popular music. At George Gershwin's suggestion, he adopted the name Vernon Duke for his popular scores, and in 1955 he dropped his real name entirely. He scored his greatest success with the Broadway musical *Cabin in the Sky* (Oct. 25, 1940), which was also made into a film (1943). His amusing autobiography was publ. as *Passport to Paris* (Boston, 1955); he also wrote the polemical book *Listen Here! A Critical Essay on Music Depreciation* (N.Y., 1963).

WORKS: DRAMATIC (all 1st perf. in N.Y. unless otherwise given): REVUES: *Walk a Little Faster* (Dec. 7, 1932); *Ziegfeld Follies of 1934* (Jan. 4, 1934); *Ziegfeld Follies of 1936* (Jan. 30, 1936); *The Show is On* (Dec. 25, 1936); *Dancing in the Streets* (Boston, 1943); *Sweet Bye and Bye* (New Haven, Conn., Oct. 10, 1946); *Two's Company* (Dec. 15, 1952). OPERETTA: *Yvonne* (London, May 22, 1926; in collaboration with J. Gilbert). MUSICAL COMEDY: *The Yellow Mask* (London, Feb. 8, 1928). MUSICALS: *Cabin in the Sky* (Oct. 25, 1940; film version in collaboration with H. Arlen, 1943); *Banjo Eyes* (Dec. 25, 1941); *The Lady Comes Across* (Jan. 9, 1942); *Jackpot* (Jan. 13, 1944); *Sadie Thompson* (Nov. 16, 1944). OPERAS: *Mistress into Maid* (Santa Barbara, Calif., 1958); *Zenda* (San Francisco, Aug. 1963). INCIDENTAL MUSIC: *Time Remembered* (1957). BALLETS: *Zéphyr et Flore* (Monte Carlo, April 28, 1925); *Public*

Gardens (Chicago, March 8, 1935); *Le bal des blanchisseuses* (Paris, Dec. 19, 1946); *Emperor Norton* (San Francisco, 1957); *Lady Blue* (1961). He also completed G. Gershwin's *The Goldwyn Follies* (1938).

Dumesnil, René (Alphonse Adolphe), French writer; b. Rouen, June 19, 1879; d. Paris, Dec. 24, 1967. He studied literature at the Sorbonne in Paris; was active as a literary critic. Besides his publications dealing with literature, he wrote a number of books on music, including *Le Don Juan de Mozart* (1927; 2d ed., 1955), *Richard Wagner* (1929), *Histoire illustrée du théâtre lyrique* (1954), *Richard Wagner* (1954; a much larger work than his 1929 edition), *L'Opéra* (1964), and *Mozart présent dans ses oeuvres lyriques* (1965).

BIBL.: G. van der Kemp, *Notice sur la vie et les travaux de R. D.* (Paris, 1970).

Dumitrescu, Gheorghe, Romanian composer and teacher; b. Oteşani, Dec. 28, 1914. His brother was the Romanian composer and teacher Ion Dumitrescu (b. Oteşani, June 2, 1913; d. Bucharest, Sept. 6, 1996). He studied with Cuclin, Perlea, and Jora at the Bucharest Cons. (1935–41). He was active as a violinist, conductor, and composer at the National Theater in Bucharest (1935–46), and was composer-counselor for the Armatei artistic ensemble (1947–57). In 1951 he was appointed a prof. at the Bucharest Cons. He won the Enesco prize 3 times (1942, 1943, 1946) and was awarded the Great Prize of the Romanian Composers Union (1985). He was especially adept at writing music for the stage.

WORKS: DRAMATIC: *Tarsiţaşi Rosiorul*, operetta (1949; Bucharest, Dec. 12, 1950); *Ion Vodă cel Cumplit*, opera (1955; Bucharest, April 12, 1956); *Decebal*, musical tragedy (1957); *Răscoala*, popular music drama (Bucharest, Nov. 20, 1959); *Fata cu garoafe*, opera (Bucharest, May 6, 1961); *Meşterul Manole*, opera legend (1970; Bucharest, Oct. 4, 1971); *Geniu pustiu*, opera (1973); *Vlad Tepeş*, musical drama (1974); *Orfeu*, lyric tragedy (1976–77); *Luceafărul*, ballet opera (concert perf., Bucharest, Dec. 29, 1981); *Marea iubire*, opera (concert perf., Dec. 13, 1982); *Ivan Turbincă*, opera (1983); *Prometheu*, lyric tragedy (1985); *Mihai Viteazul*, music drama (1986).

Duncan, (Robert) Todd, black American baritone; b. Danville, Ky., Feb. 12, 1903; d. Washington, D.C., Feb. 28, 1998. He was educated at Butler Univ. in Indianapolis (B.A., 1925) and at Columbia Univ. Teachers College (M.A., 1930); then taught voice at Howard Univ. in Washington, D.C. (until 1945). In 1934 he made his operatic debut with the Aeolian Opera in New York as Alfio in *Cavalleria rusticana*. On Oct. 10, 1935, he created the role of Porgy in Gershwin's *Porgy and Bess* in New York, and subsequently sang in revivals of the score. He was the first black American to become a member of a major opera company when he made his first appearance at the N.Y. City Opera on Sept. 28, 1945, as Tonio. He appeared as Stephen Kumalo in Weill's *Lost in the Stars* (1949–50), winning both the Donaldson and N.Y. Drama Critics' Circle awards in 1950.

Dunhill, Thomas (Frederick), English composer, teacher, and writer on music; b. London, Feb. 1, 1877; d. Scunthorpe, Lincolnshire, March 13, 1946. He entered the Royal College of Music in London in 1893, and studied with Franklin Taylor (piano) and Stanford (theory); in 1905 he was appointed a prof. there. In 1907 he founded the Concerts of British Chamber-Music, which he oversaw until 1916. He publ. *Chamber Music* (1912), *Mozart's String Quartets* (2 vols., 1927), *Sullivan's Comic Operas* (1928), and *Sir Edward Elgar* (1938). He composed the operas *The Enchanted Garden* (London, March 1928), *Tantivy Towers* (London, Jan. 16, 1931), and *Happy Families* (Guildford, Nov. 1, 1933) and the ballet *Gallimaufry* (Hamburg, Dec. 11, 1937).

Duni, Egidio (Romualdo), noted Italian composer; b. Matera, Feb. 9, 1709; d. Paris, June 11, 1775. Nothing definitive is known about his musical training. He may have studied at the Loreto Cons. in Naples. His first opera, *Nerone*, was successfully premiered in Rome on May 21, 1735. He visited London in 1737; produced his opera *Demofoonte* at the King's Theatre there on May 24, 1737. Making his way to Holland, he studied at the Univ. of Leiden (1738). He returned to Italy in 1739; he was appointed maestro di cappella of S. Nicola di Bari in Naples in 1743, and took up the same post at the court of the duke of Parma about 1748, where he also served as music teacher to the duke's daughter. His opéra comique *Le Peintre amoureux de son modèle* was premiered in his presence in Paris on July 26, 1757. Following its success, he settled in Paris. From 1761 to 1768 he was music director of the Comédie-Italienne, where he brought out such successful works as *Mazet* (1761), *Les Deux Chasseurs et la laitière* (1763), *L'école de la jeunesse* (1765), *La Clochette* (1766), and *Les Moissonneurs* (1768). Duni was a significant contributor to the opéra comique genre. By fusing Italian and French strains in his work, he was instrumental in developing the comédie melée d'ariettes.

Dunn, James Philip, American organist, teacher, and composer; b. N.Y., Jan. 10, 1884; d. Jersey City, N.J., July 24, 1936. He studied at the College of the City of N.Y. (B.A., 1903) and with MacDowell, Leonard McWhood, and Rybner at Columbia Univ. (M.A., 1905). He was active as an organist in Catholic churches in New York and Jersey City, and also devoted time to teaching and writing on music. He composed two stages works, *The Galleon* (1918) and *Lyric Scenes* (n.d.).

BIBL.: J. Howard, *Studies of Contemporary American Composers: J. P. D.* (N.Y., 1925).

Dunn, Mignon, American mezzo-soprano; b. Memphis, Tenn., June 17, 1931. She attended Southwestern Univ. in Memphis and the Univ. of Lausanne; at 17 she was awarded a Metropolitan Opera scholarship and pursued vocal training in New York with Karin Branzell and Beverley Johnson. In 1955 she made her operatic debut as Carmen in New Orleans, and then appeared as Maddalena in Chicago later that year; on March 28, 1956, she made her N.Y. City Opera debut as the 4th Lady in Walton's *Troilus and Cressida*, remaining on its roster until 1957; sang there again in 1972 and 1975. On Oct. 29, 1958, she made her Metropolitan Opera debut in New York as the Nurse in *Boris Godunov*; in subsequent seasons she appeared in more than 50 roles there, including Amneris, Azucena, Fricka, Herodias, Marina, and Ortrud. She also made guest appearances in San Francisco, London, Paris, Berlin, Hamburg, Milan, and Vienna. In 1972 she married the conductor Kurt Klippstatter.

Dunn, Susan, American soprano; b. Malvern, Ark., July 23, 1954. She was educated at Hendrix College in Arkansas and at Indiana Univ. in Bloomington. In 1982 she made her operatic debut as Aida in Peoria. After winning the Richard Tucker Award in 1983, she attracted favorable notice as Sieglinde in a concert performance of Act I of *Die Walküre* at N.Y.'s Carnegie Hall in 1985. She subsequently appeared with the Chicago Lyric Opera, the Washington (D.C.) Opera, the Houston Grand Opera, and the San Francisco Opera. In 1986 she made her European operatic debut in Bologna as Hélène in *Les Vêpres siciliennes*; also sang Aida at Milan's La Scala and appeared at the Vienna State Opera. On Feb. 5, 1990, she made her debut at the Metropolitan Opera in New York as Leonora in *Il Trovatore*.

Dupin, Paul, French composer; b. Roubaix, Aug. 14, 1865; d. Paris, March 6, 1949. He worked in a factory; then was a menial clerk, but turned to music against all odds; took some lessons with Emile Durand, and then proceeded to compose with fanatic compulsion, seeing some 200 of his works published. Among his compositions was an opera, *Marcelle*, which he later renamed *Lyszelle*. He was much admired in Paris for his determination, but his works were rarely performed.

BIBL.: P. Ladmirault, *Les Choeurs en canon de P. D.: Notice biographique et analytique* (Paris, 1925).

Duprez, Gilbert(-Louis), French tenor and pedagogue; b. Paris, Dec. 6, 1806; d. there, Sept. 23, 1896. He began his training in Paris at Choron's Inst. de Musique Classique et Religieuse, then continued his studies with Rogat at the Cons. He made his operatic debut as Count Almaviva at Paris's Odéon (1825); dissatisfied with his performance, he pursued further vocal training in Italy, where he became notably successful in Italian roles (1829–35); Donizetti chose him to create the role of Edgardo in *Lucia di Lammermoor* (Naples, 1835). Returning to France, he was a principal member of the Paris Opéra (1837–49), where he created a number of roles, including Berlioz's Benvenuto Cellini (1838), Donizetti's Polyeucte in *Les Martyrs* (1840), and Fernando in *La Favorite* (1840); he retired from the stage in 1855. He taught at the Paris Cons. (1842–50) and founded his own vocal school (1853). His most famous pupil was Emma Albani. He wrote several operas and other works. He also publ. the methods *L'Art du chant* (Paris, 1845) and *La Mélodie, Études complémentaires vocales et dramatiques de l'Art du chant* (Paris, 1846); he also publ. *Souvenirs d'un chanteur* (Paris, 1880) and *Récréations de mon grand âge* (Paris, 1888). His wife, Alexandrine (née Duperron) (b. Nantes, 1808; d. Brussels, Feb. 27, 1872), and daughter, Caroline (b. Florence, April 10, 1832; d. Pau, April 17, 1875), were also singers.

BIBL.: A. Elwart, *D.: Sa vie artistique* (Paris, 1838).

Dupuis, Albert, eminent Belgian composer; b. Verviers, March 1, 1877; d. Brussels, Sept. 19, 1967. He studied piano, violin, and flute at the Verviers Cons. before pursuing training with d'Indy and others at the Paris Schola Cantorum (1897–99). Returning to his homeland, he won the Belgian Prix de Rome in 1903 with his cantata *La chanson d'Halewyn*, which was premiered in Brussels on Nov. 25 of that year; it later was rev. as the opera of the same title and premiered in Antwerp on Feb. 14, 1914. In 1907 he became director of the Verviers Cons., which post he held until 1947. He distinguished himself as a composer for the theater, in a style reflecting his French training.

WORKS: OPERAS: *Idylle* (Verviers, March 5, 1895); *Bilitis* (Verviers, Dec. 21, 1899); *Jean-Michel* (1901–02; Brussels, March 5, 1903); *Martille* (1904; Brussels, March 3, 1905); *Fidélaine* (Liège, March 30, 1910); *Le château de la Bretêche* (Nice, March 28, 1913); *La chanson d'Halewyn* (Antwerp, Feb. 14, 1914; based on the cantata of the same title, 1903); *La passion* (Monte Carlo, April 2, 1916); *La délivrance* (Verviers, Dec. 19, 1918); *La barrière* (Verviers, Feb. 26, 1920); *La victoire* (Brussels, March 28, 1923); *Un drame sous Philippe II* (Liège, Dec. 29, 1926); *Hassan* (Antwerp, Nov. 5, 1931); *Ce n'était qu'un rêve* (Antwerp, Jan. 26, 1932).

BIBL.: J. Dor, *A. D.* (Liège, 1935); R. Michel, *Un grand musicien belge méconnu: A. D.* (Verviers, 1967).

Durante, Francesco, celebrated Italian composer and pedagogue; b. Frattamaggiore, March 31, 1684; d. Naples, Sept. 30, 1755. His uncle, Don Angelo Durante, was a priest and composer. Francesco most likely received his early training at home from his uncle, then continued his studies with him at the Cons. S. Onofrio a Capuana in Naples (1702–05) and with the violinist Gaetano Francone there; he may have subsequently studied with Pasquini and Pitoni in Rome. He taught at the Cons. S. Onofrio a Capuana (1710–11) and was maestro of the Congregatione and Accademia di Santa Cecilia in Rome (1718). Little else is known about him until he was appointed primo maestro of the Cons. Poveri di Gesù Cristo in Naples in 1728, which position he held until 1739. In 1742 he became primo maestro there of the Cons. S. Maria di Loreto, and also of the Cons. S. Onofrio a Capuana in 1745; he retained both positions until his death. With his fellow Neapolitans Porpora, Leo, Feo, and Vinci, Durante ranks among the most important composers of his era. Although the former were renowned as composers of opera, Durante was a particularly significant composer of sacred music, his output being notable for its resourcefulness of styles and practices as well as for originality. He was greatly renowned as a teacher; among his pupils were Pergolesi, Abos, Anfossi, Traetta, Sacchini, Piccini, and Paisiello.

WORKS: SACRED DRAMAS: *Prodigii della divina misericordia verso i devoti del gloriosa S. Antonio di Padova*, scherzo drammatico (Naples, June 13, 1705; music not extant); *La cerva assetata ovvero L'anima nelle fiamme della gloria* (Naples, Feb. 18, 1719; not extant); *Abigaile* (Rome, Nov. 22, 1736; music not extant); *S. Antonio di Padova* (Venice, 1754). Also 5 choruses for *Flavio Valente*, a tragedy by Duke Annibale Marchese (publ. in *Tragedie cristiane*, Naples, 1729).

Durey, Louis (Edmond), French composer; b. Paris, May 27, 1888; d. St. Tropez, July 3, 1979. He received training in solfège, harmony, counterpoint, and fugue from Léon Saint-Requier at the Paris Schola Cantorum (1910–14); he was self-taught in orchestration. In 1936 he joined the French Communist Party. During the German occupation (1940–44), he was a member of the Résistance. He was secretary-general of the Fédération Musicale Populaire (1937–56) and of the Assn. Française des Musiciens Progressistes (from 1948); he also wrote music criticism for the Paris Communist newspaper *L'Humanité* (from 1950). In 1961 he received the Grand Prix de la Musique Française. Although Durey was one of Les Six, he early on adopted a distinct path as a composer. His works owe much to the examples of Satie and Stravinsky. He was at his best writing chamber and vocal works.

WORKS: DRAMATIC: *Judith*, monodrama for Voice and Piano (1918); *L'occasion*, comic opera (1923–25; Strasbourg Radio, May 22–25, 1974); *L'intruse*, puppet play (1936); *Feu la mère de madame*, radio score (1945); *Chant des partisans coréens*, incidental music (1952).

BIBL.: F. Robert, *L. D.: L'aîné des Six* (Paris, 1968); J. Roy, *Le groupe des six: Poulenc: Poulenc, Milhaud, Honegger, Auric, Tailleferre, D.* (Paris, 1994).

Durkó, Zsolt, prominent Hungarian composer; b. Szeged, April 10, 1934; d. Budapest, April 2, 1997. He was a student of Farkas at the Budapest Academy of Music (1955–60) and of Petrassi at the Accademia di Santa Cecilia in Rome (1961–63). After teaching at the Budapest Academy of Music (1971–77), he was active with the Hungarian Radio (from 1982). In 1978 he won the Kossuth Prize, and in 1983 the Bartók-Pasztory Award. He was made a Merited Artist in 1983 and an Outstanding Artist in 1987 by the Hungarian government. His varied output reveals an assured craftsmanship and imaginative use of traditional forms in a contemporary style. He composed the opera *Mózes* (1972–77; Budapest, May 15, 1977).

Dussek, Johann Ladislaus (real name, **Jan Ladislav Dusík**), outstanding Bohemian pianist and composer; b. Tschaslau, Feb. 12, 1760; d. St.-Germain-en-Laye, March 20, 1812. He studied piano at age 5 and organ at age 9, then became a chorister at the Iglau Minorite church and a pupil at the Jesuit Gymnasium. After further studies at the Kuttenberg Jesuit Gymnasium, he continued his studies at Prague's New City Gymnasium (1776–77) and at the Univ. of Prague (1778). He found a patron in Count Männer, with whose assistance he was able to go to Malines in 1779, where he became active as a piano teacher; he made his public debut there as a pianist on Dec. 16, 1779, and then set out on a highly successful tour, visiting Bergen op Zoom, Amsterdam, and The Hague. He then went to Hamburg, where he gave a concert on July 12, 1782; he also met C. P. E. Bach, with whom he may have studied. In 1783 he played at the St. Petersburg court; after spending about a year in the service of Prince Karl Radziwill as Kapellmeister in Lithuania, he made a major tour of Germany in 1784, winning notable acclaim in Berlin, Mainz, Kassel, and Frankfurt am Main as a piano and glass harmonica virtuoso. In 1786 he went to Paris, where he performed at the court for Marie Antoinette; except for a brief trip to Milan and Bohemia, he remained in Paris until the outbreak of the French Revolution in 1789 compelled him to flee to London. On June 1, 1789, he made his London debut at the Hanover Square Rooms. He soon became successful as a pianist and teacher in the British capital, appearing regularly at Salomon's concerts and actively participating in these concerts during Haydn's 2 visits. In 1792 Dussek married the singer, pianist, and harpist Sophia Corri. With his father-in-law, Domenico Corri, he became active as a music publisher. Both men were ill suited for such a venture, however, and Dussek's love for the good life further contributed to the failure of the business. Dussek fled to Hamburg in 1799, leaving his father-in-law to serve a jail sentence for debt. Dussek apparently never saw his wife or daughter again. He seems to have spent about 2 years in Hamburg, where he was active as a performer and teacher. In 1802 he played in his birthplace, and then in Prague; from 1804 to 1806 he served as Kapellmeister to Prince Louis Ferdinand of Prussia. After the latter's death at the battle of Saalfeld (Oct. 10, 1806), Dussek composed a piano sonata in his memory, the *Élégie harmonique sur la mort du Prince Louis Ferdinand de Prusse*, op. 61. He then was briefly in the service of Prince Isenburg. In 1807 he settled in Paris, where he served Prince Talleyrand, gave concerts, and taught. His health began to fail due to excessive drinking, and he was compelled to abandon his career. Dussek was a remarkable composer for the piano, proving himself a master craftsman capable of producing the most brilliant works for the instrument. In his later works he presaged the development of the Romantic school, anticipating such composers as Chopin, Mendelssohn, Schumann, and even Brahms. As a celebrated virtuoso of the keyboard, he shares with Clementi the honor of having introduced the "singing touch." He publ. *Instructions on the Art of Playing the Piano Forte or Harpsichord* (London, 1796; numerous later eds.; in French as *Methode pour le piano forte*, Paris, 1799; in German as *Pianoforte-Schule*, Leipzig, 1802). Among his compositions are *The Captive of Spilberg*, musical drama (London, Nov. 14, 1798), and incidental music to Sheridan's melodrama *Pizarro* (London, Jan. 19, 1799). A complete ed. of his works was publ. by Breitkopf & Härtel (12 vols., Leipzig, 1813–17; reprint, 6 vols., N.Y., 1976). A number of his works have appeared in modern eds. in the Musiqua Antiqua Bohemica series.

BIBL.: H. Craw, *A Biography and Thematic Catalog of the Works of J. L. D. (1760–1812)* (diss., Univ. of Southern Calif., 1964).

Dutilleux, Henri, distinguished French composer and teacher; b. Angers, Jan. 22, 1916. He was a student at the Paris Cons. (1933–38) of J. and N. Gallon (harmony and counterpoint), Büsser (composition), and Emmanuel (music history), winning the Grand Prix de Rome in 1938. He pursued his career in Paris, where he worked for the French Radio (1944–63) and was a prof. of composition at the École Normale de Musique (1961–70). In 1970–71 he was a guest prof. at the Paris Cons. In 1967 he was awarded the Grand Prix National de la Musique. In 1987 he received the Prix Maurice Ravel for his complete works. He was awarded the Praemium Imperial of Japan in 1994. In 1995 he was composer-in-residence at the Tanglewood Festival of Contemporary Music. Dutilleux developed a thoroughly individualistic contemporary style of composition, marked by a meticulous craftsmanship.

WORKS: DRAMATIC: *L'anneau du roi*, lyric scene (1938); *Petite Lumière et L'Ourse*, music for a radio play (1944); *Les Hauts de Hurle-vent*, incidental music (1945; orch. suite, 1945); *La Princesse d'élide*, incidental music (1946); *Monsieur de Pourceaugnac*, incidental music (1948); *Hernani*, incidental music (1952); *Le Loup*, ballet (Paris, March 18, 1953).

Dutoit, Charles (Edouard), outstanding Swiss conductor; b. Lausanne, Oct. 7, 1936. He took courses in violin, piano, and conducting at the Lausanne Cons., graduating at age 17; he then pursued training in conducting with Baud-Bovy at the Geneva Cons. (1st prize, 1958), with Galliera at the Accademia Musicale Chigiana in Siena (diploma, 1958), and with Munch at the Berkshire Music Center in Tanglewood (summer, 1959). He was a choral conductor at the Univ. of Lausanne (1959–63), and then conducted the Lausanne Bach Choir. After appearing as a guest conductor with the Bern Sym. Orch. in 1963, he served as its 2d conductor (1964–66) and music director (1966–78); he also was chief conductor of the Zürich Radio Orch. (1964–66), assoc. conductor of the Zürich Tonhalle Orch. (1966–71), and conductor of the National Sym. Orch. in Mexico City (1973–75) and the Göteborg Sym. Orch. (1976–79). On Aug. 31, 1972, he made his U.S. debut conducting at the Hollywood Bowl. In subsequent years, he made extensive guest conducting tours of Europe, North and South America, Australia, Japan, and Israel. In 1977 he became music director of the Orchestre Symphonique de Montréal, which gained international recognition under his guidance. He also was principal guest conductor of the Minnesota Orch. in Minneapolis (from 1983). On Dec. 21, 1987, he made his Metropolitan Opera debut in New York conducting *Les Contes d'Hoffmann*. While retaining his position in Montreal, he also served as chief conductor of the Orchestre National de France in Paris (from 1990). He likewise was chief conductor of the NHK (Japan Broadcasting Corp.) Sym. Orch. in Tokyo (from 1996). Dutoit's extensive repertoire embraces works from the Baroque era to modern scores, but he has won a particularly notable reputation as a consummate interpreter of French music. He was married 3 times, his 2d wife being **Martha Argerich**.

BIBL.: G. Nicholson, *C.D.: Le Maître de l'orchestre* (Lausanne, 1986).

Duval, Denise, French soprano; b. Paris, Oct. 23, 1921. She studied at the Bordeaux Cons. In 1941 she made her operatic debut as Lola at the Bordeaux Grand Théâtre. In 1944 she joined the Folies Bergères in Paris, where she won notice; in 1947 she was chosen to create Thérese in Poulenc's *Les Mamelles de Tirésias* at the Paris Opéra Comique, where she also created Elle in his *La Voix Humaine* in 1959; she also appeared regularly at the Paris Opéra. In 1953 she sang in New York, in 1960 at the Edinburgh Festival (as Elle), and in 1962 at the Glyndebourne Festival (as Mélisande); she also made guest appearances in Milan, Cologne, Brussels, Amsterdam, Geneva, and Buenos Aires. After retiring in 1965, she taught voice in Paris. Among her other roles were Massenet's Salomé, Ravel's Concepción, and Poulenc's Blanche.

Duvernoy, Victor-Alphonse, French pianist and composer; b. Paris, Aug. 30, 1842; d. there, March 7, 1907. He was a pupil of Bazin and Marmontel at the Paris Cons., taking the 1st prize for piano (1855). In 1869 he founded, together with Leonard, Stiehle, Trombetta, and Jacquard, a series of chamber music concerts. He devoted his time otherwise to composing and teaching, and held a professorship at the Cons. For some 11 years, he was music critic of the *République Française*; he was made a Chevalier of the Légion of Honor, and was an officer of public instruction. As a dramatic composer, he produced the opera *Sardanapale* (concert perf., Paris, 1882), the "scene lyrique" *Cléopâtre*, the opera *Hellé* (Paris, 1896), and the ballet, *Bacchus* (1902).

Dux, Claire, German-American soprano; b. Witkowicz, Aug. 2, 1885; d. Chicago, Oct. 8, 1967. She was a student of Maria Schwadtke, Adolf Deppe, and Teresa Arkel in Berlin before completing her training in Milan. In 1906 she made her operatic debut as Pamina in Cologne, singing there until 1911. From 1911 to 1918 she was a member of the Berlin Royal Opera; she also sang in London, where she was the first British Sophie at Covent Garden (1913) and appeared as Pamina at Drury Lane (1914). After singing at Stockholm's Royal Theater (1918–21), she was a member of the Chicago Grand (later Civic) Opera (1921–22; 1923–24); she also toured the United States with the German Opera Co. In 1926 she married her 3d husband, the wealthy Chicagoan Charles H. Swift, and retired from the operatic stage. She then sang in concerts until making her farewell in Berlin in 1932.

Dvarionas, Balis, Lithuanian composer, conductor, and teacher; b. Leipaia, June 19, 1904; d. Vilnius, Aug. 23, 1972. He studied at the Leipzig Cons. with Teichmüller (piano) and Karg-Elert (composition); he also received training in piano from Petri at the Berlin Hochschule für Musik and in conducting from Abendroth. In 1926 he went to Kaunas and taught piano there until 1940; in 1947 he became a prof. at the Lithuanian Cons. in Vilnius; also conducted the Lithuanian Phil. there (1940–41; 1958–61). Among his works is the opera, *Dalia* (1959). He wrote the music for the national anthem of the Lithuanian Soviet Socialist Republic (1950).

BIBL.: Y. Gaudrimas, *B. D.* (Moscow, 1960).

Dvŏráček, Jiří, prominent Czech composer and pedagogue; b. Vamberk, June 8, 1928. He studied organ at the Prague Cons. (1943–47) and composition with Řídký and Dobiáš at the Prague Academy of Music (1949–53), where he subsequently taught (from 1953), later serving as a prof. of composition and chairman of the composition dept. (1979–90). In 1983 he was made an Artist of Merit by the Czech government. From 1987 to 1989 he was president of the Union of Czech Composers and Concert Artists. His works represent a median course of Central European modernism. He composed the opera *Ostrov Afrodity* (Aphrodite's Island; 1967; Dresden, Feb. 13, 1971).

Dvořák, Antonín (Leopold), famous Czech composer; b. Mühlhausen, Sept. 8, 1841; d. Prague, May 1, 1904. His father ran a village inn and butcher shop and intended Antonín to learn his trade. However, when he showed his musical inclinations, his father let him study piano and violin with a local musician. He also received financial help from an uncle. Later, Dvořák went to Prague, where he studied with the director of a church music school, Karel Pitsch, and his successor, Josef Krejcí. He also began to compose assiduously, including 2 operas. His first public appearance as a composer took place in Prague on March 9, 1873, with a perf. of his cantata *The Heirs of the White Mountain (Hymnus)*. An important event in his career occurred in Prague on March 29, 1874, when Smetana conducted his Sym. in E-flat major, op. 10. Dvořák then entered several of his works in a competition for the Austrian State Prize, adjudicated by a distinguished committee that included Herbeck, Hanslick, and Brahms. He won the prize in 1875 and twice in 1877. Brahms, in particular, appreciated Dvořák's talent and recommended him to Simrock for publication of his *Moravian Duets* and the highly popular *Slavonic Dances*. His *Stabat Mater* (Prague, Dec. 23, 1880) and Sym. in D major, op. 60 (Prague, March 25, 1881), followed in close succession, securing for him a leading position among Czech composers.

At the invitation of the Phil. Soc. of London, Dvořák visited England in 1884 and conducted several of his works. He then was commissioned to compose a new sym. for the Phil. Soc.; this was his Sym. in D minor, op. 70, which he conducted in London on April 22, 1885. His cantata *The Spectre's Bride*, composed for the Birmingham Festival, was accorded an excellent reception when he conducted the English performance there on Aug. 27, 1885. On his 3d visit to England, he conducted the premiere of his oratorio *St. Ludmila*, at the Leeds Festival on Oct. 15, 1886. In 1890 he appeared as a conductor of his own works in Russia. On Feb. 2, 1890, he conducted in Prague the first performance of his Sym. in G major, op. 88, which became one of his most popular works. In 1891 Dvořák was appointed prof. of composition at the Prague Cons.; he then received honorary degrees from the Charles Univ. in Prague (Ph.D.) and the Univ. of Cambridge (D.Mus.). There followed his brilliant Carnival Overture of 1891.

In 1892 Dvořák accepted the position of director of the National Cons. of Music of America in New York. He composed his *Te Deum* for his first U.S. appearance as a conductor (N.Y., Oct. 21, 1892); he also conducted a concert of his music at the 1892 World Columbian Exposition in Chicago. It was in the United States that he composed his most celebrated work, the Sym. in E minor, op. 95, *From the New World*, which received its premiere performance on Dec. 15, 1893, with Anton Seidl conducting the N.Y. Phil. The sym. is essentially a Czech work from the old world; nevertheless, by appearing as a proponent of the use of Negro-influenced themes in symphonic music, Dvořák had a significant impact on American musical nationalism. He discussed the idea in an article, "Music in America" (*Harper's New Monthly Magazine*, Feb. 1895). Dvořák also composed his great Cello Concerto during his American sojourn, and conducted its first performance in London on March 19, 1896. Resigning his N.Y. position in 1895, he returned home to resume his duties at the Prague Cons.; he became its director in 1901. During the last years of his life, Dvořák devoted much of his creative efforts to opera; *Rusalka* (1900) remains best known outside Czechoslovakia. He made his last appearance as a conductor on April 4, 1900, leading a concert of the Czech Phil. in Prague. He was made a member of the Austrian House of Lords in 1901, the first Czech musician to be so honored. Czechs celebrated his 60th birthday with special performances of his music in Prague.

Dvořák's musical style was eclectic. His earliest works reflect the influence of Beethoven and Schubert, then Wagner, culminating in the Classicism of Brahms. After mastering his art, he proved himself to be a composer of great versatility and fecundity. A diligent and meticulous craftsman, he brought to his finest works a seemingly inexhaustible and spontaneous melodic invention, rhythmic variety, judicious employment of national folk tunes, and contrapuntal and harmonic skill. Many of his last works have become staples of the repertoire.

WORKS (the B. numbers are those established by J. Burghauser in *A. D.: Thematic Catalogue, Bibliography, and Survey of Life and Work* [Prague, 1960; 2d ed., 1997]): OPERAS: *Alfred*, B.16 (1870; Czech Theater, Olomouc, Dec. 10, 1938); *Kraál a uhlíř* (King and Charcoal Burner), B.21 (1st version, 1871; National Theater, Prague, May 28, 1929; 2d version, 1874, with music recomposed, op. 14, B.42; Provisional Theater, Prague, Nov. 24, 1874; rev. 1887 and listed as B.151; National Theater, Prague, June 15, 1887); *Tvrdé palice* (The Stubborn Lovers), op. 17, B.46 (1874; New Czech Theater, Prague, Oct. 2, 1881); *Vanda*, op. 25, B.55 (1875; Provisional Theater, Prague, April 17, 1876; rev. 1879 and 1883); *Šelma sedlák* (The Cunning Peasant), op. 37, B.67 (1877; Provisional Theater, Prague, Jan. 27, 1878); *Dmitrij*, op. 64, B.127 (1881–82; New Czech Theater, Prague, Oct. 8, 1882; rev. 1883, 1885, and 1894–95; the latter is listed as B.186; National Theater, Prague, Nov. 7, 1894); *Jakobín* (The Jacobin), op. 84, B.159 (1887–88; National Theater, Prague, Feb. 12, 1889; rev. 1897 and listed as B.200; National Theater, Prague, June 19, 1898): *Čert a Káča* (The Devil and Kate), op. 112, B.201 (1898–99; National Theater, Prague, Nov. 23, 1899); *Rusalka*, op. 114, B.203 (1900; National Theater, Prague, March 31, 1901); *Armida*, op. 115, B.206 (1902–03; National Theater, Prague, March 25, 1904). Also the overture *Domov můj* (My Home), B.125a, and the incidental music to F. Samberk's drama *Josef Kajetán Tyl*, op. 62, B.125 (1881–82; Provisional Theater, Prague, Feb. 3, 1882).

BIBL.: O. Šourek inaugurated a complete ed. of D.'s works, which commenced publ. in Prague in 1955. The standard thematic catalog was compiled by J. Burghauser as *A. D.: Thematic Catalogue, Bibliography, and Survey of Life and Work* (in Czech, Ger., and Eng.; Prague, 1960; 2d ed., 1997). See also the following: J. Bartoš, *A. D.* (Prague, 1913); O. Šourek, *Zivot a dílo A.a D.a* (The Life and Work of A. D.; 4 vols., Prague, 1916–33; Vols. 1-2, 3d ed., 1955–56; Vols. 3–4, 2d ed., 1957–58; in Ger. as *D.: Leben und Werk*, 1 vol., abr. by P. Stefan, Vienna, 1935; in Eng. tr. by Y. Vance as *A. D.*, N.Y., 1941); K. Hoffmeister, *A. D.* (Prague, 1924; Eng. tr. by R. Newmarch, London, 1928); O. Šourek, *A. D.* (Prague, 1929; 4th ed., 1947; Eng. tr. as *A. D.: His Life and Work*, Prague, 1952); H. Sirp, *A. D.* (Potsdam, 1939); A. Robertson, *D.* (London, 1945; 2d ed., 1964); R. Smetana, *A. D.: O místo a význam skladatelského díla v českém hudebním vyvoji* (A. D.: The Place and Meaning of D.'s Compositions in the Development of Czech Music; Prague, 1956); A. Hetschko, *A. D.* (Leipzig, 1965); M. Aborn, *The Influence on American Musical Culture of D.'s Sojourn in America* (Ann Arbor, 1966); J. Burghauser, *A. D.* (Prague, 1966; in Ger. and Eng., 1967); J. Clapham, *A. D.: Musician and Craftsman* (London and N.Y., 1966); G. Hughes, *D.: His Life and Music* (N.Y., 1967); J. Berkovec, *A. D.* (Prague, 1969); J. Clapham, *D.* (London and N.Y., 1979); N. Butterworth, *D.: His Life and Times* (Tunbridge Wells, 1980); H.-H. Schönzeler, *D.* (London, 1984); K. Döge and P. Jost, eds., *D.-Studien* (Mainz and N.Y., 1994); D. Beveridge, ed., *Rethinking D.: Views from Five Countries* (Oxford, 1996).

Dvořáková, Ludmila, Czech soprano; b. Kolin, July 11, 1923. She was a pupil of Jarmila Vavrdova at the Prague Cons. (1942–49). In 1949 she made her operatic debut as Kát'a Kabanová in Ostrava, and then appeared in Bratislava and at the Smetana Theater in Prague from 1952; she was a member of the Prague National Theater (1954–57). In 1956 she made her first appearance at the Vienna State Opera, and from 1960 she sang at the Berlin State Opera; she also sang at the Bayreuth Festivals (1965–71) and at London's Covent Garden (1966–71). On Jan. 12, 1966, she made her Metropolitan Opera debut in New York as Beethoven's Leonore, remaining on its roster until 1968. In addition to her roles in Czech operas, she was admired for her Wagner, Verdi, and Strauss.

Dvorský, Peter (Petr), esteemed Czech tenor; b. Partizánske, Sept. 25, 1951. He studied at the Bratislava Cons. and with Gina Cigna in Palermo. In 1972 he made his operatic debut as Lensky at the Slovak National Theater in Bratislava. In 1974 he took 5th prize in the Tchaikovsky Competition in Moscow, and then 1st prize in the Geneva Competition in 1975. From 1975 he sang at the Vienna State Opera, where he was made a Kammersänger in 1986. On Nov. 15, 1977, he made his Metropolitan Opera debut in New York as Alfredo, where he sang Rodolfo in 1987. He made his first appearance at London's Covent Garden as the Duke of Mantua in 1978, returning there as Alfredo in 1986 and as Lensky in 1988. In 1981 he sang Rodolfo at Milan's La Scala. In 1986 he toured Japan with the Vienna State Opera. After portraying Cavaradossi at the Salzburg Festival in 1989, he appeared as Massenet's Des Grieux in Barcelona in 1990. He sang Don Alvaro at the Maggio Musicale di Fiorentino in 1992. In 1997 he appeared again in Japan. While Dvorský has won particular praise for his roles in operas by Smetana, Dvořák, and Janáček, he has also been admired for his various Verdi and Puccini portrayals.

BIBL.: D. Štilichová, *P. D.* (Bratislava, 1991).

Dzegelenok, Alexander (Mikhailovich), Russian composer; b. Moscow, Aug. 24, 1891; d. there, Jan. 31, 1969. He studied piano (diploma, 1914) and composition (with Koreshchenko, 1918) at the Music and Drama School of the Moscow Phil. Soc. In 1919 he organized the Moscow People's Cons., serving as its director (1920–21); then taught piano at the Moscow Technical School of Music (1926–34). He composed the opera *Niyazgyul* (1941).

Dzerzhinsky, Ivan (Ivanovich), Russian composer; b. Tambov, April 9, 1909; d. Leningrad, Jan. 18, 1978. He went to Moscow and studied piano with Yavorsky at the First Music School (1925–29) and composition with Gnessin at the Gnessin Music School (1929–30); he then went to Leningrad to pursue training in composition with Popov and Riazanov at the Central Music School (1930–32) and with Asafiev at the Cons. (1932–34). While still a student, he composed his first opera, *Tikhiy Don* (Quiet Flows the Don). After its failure in an opera competition, he sought the assistance of Shostakovich who helped him to revamp the score. It received its premiere in Leningrad on Oct. 22, 1935. After Stalin attended a performance of the work in Moscow on Jan. 17, 1936, the Soviet propaganda machine was set in motion to proclaim it a model for the development of the so-called song opera in the socialist realist manner. Dzerzhinsky's limited compositional gifts frustrated him in repeating this signal success, although he continued to compose a large catalog of music. He held various administrative positions with the Union of Soviet Composers from 1936, serving on its central committee from 1948.

WORKS: DRAMATIC: OPERAS: *Tikhiy Don* (Quiet Flows the Don; 1932–34; Leningrad, Oct. 22, 1935; rev. version, Leningrad, Nov. 7, 1947); *Podnyataya tselina* (Virgin Soil Upturned; Moscow, Oct. 23, 1937; rev. version, Perm, May 30, 1964); *Volochayevskiye dni* (Volochayev Days; 1939); *Groza* (The Storm; 1940–55; concert perf., Moscow, April 17, 1956); *Krov naroda* (The Blood of the People; 1941; Orenburg, Jan. 21, 1942); *Nadezhda Svetlova* (1942; Orenburg, Sept. 8, 1943); *Metel (v zimnyuyu noch)* (The Blizzard [on a Winter's Night]), comic opera (Leningrad, Nov. 24, 1946); *Knyaz-ozero* (The Prince Lake), folk opera (Leningrad, Oct. 26, 1947); *Daleko ot Moskvï* (Far from Moscow; Leningrad, July 19, 1954; rev. version, Leningrad, Nov. 8, 1954); *Sudba cheloveka* (The Fate of a Man; 1959; Moscow and Leningrad, Oct. 17, 1961); *Grigori Melekhov* (Leningrad, Nov. 4, 1967); incidental music.

Samuel Barber

Mrs. H. H. A. Beach (née Amy Marcy)

Ludwig van Beethoven

Hector (Louis-) Berlioz

Leonard Bernstein addressing muscicians

Georges Bizet

Arthur Bliss

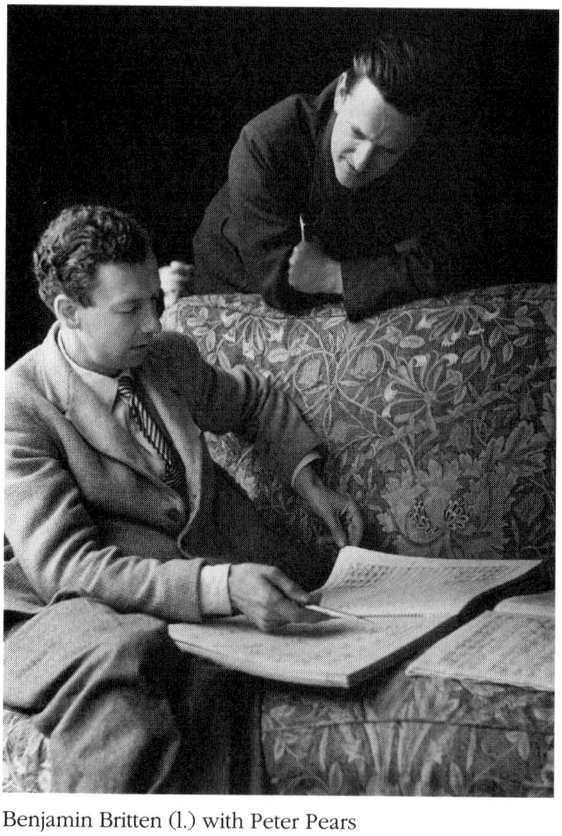
Benjamin Britten (l.) with Peter Pears

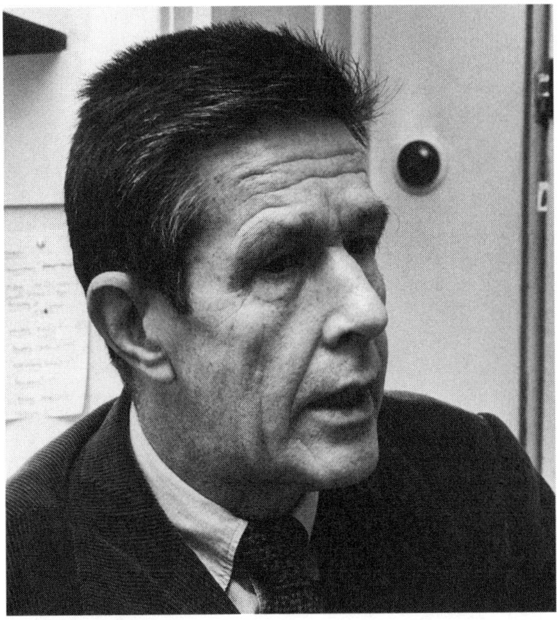

John Cage

Gustave Charpentier

Birthday gala for Aaron Copland (second from right)

Walter (Johannes) Damrosch

Vincent d'Indy

Antonín Dvořák

Sir Edward Elgar

George Gershwin

Philip Glass

Oscar Hammerstein II

Paul Hindemith

Ernst Theodor Amadeus Hoffman

Arthur Honegger (standing)

Oliver Knussen

Zoltán Kodály

Franz Lehár

Franz Liszt

Charles Martin Loeffler

Frank Martin

Pietro Mascagni

Gian Carlo Menotti

Olivier Messiaen

Wolfgang Amadeus Mozart

Modest (Petrovich) Mussorgsky

Luigi Nono

Jacques Offenbach

Nigel Osborne

Ignacy (Jan) Paderewski

Horatio William Parker

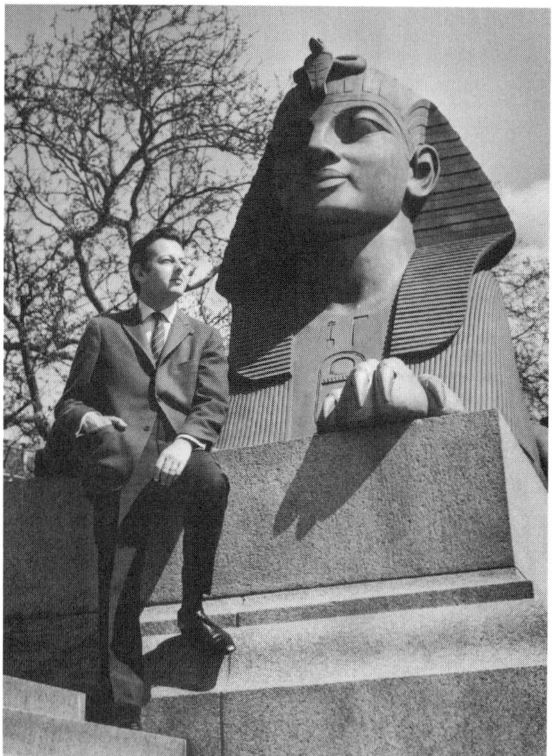

André Previn on the Thames embankment

Giacomo Puccini

Sergei Rachmaninoff

Jean-Philippe Rameau

Maurice Ravel (seated at piano)

Aribert Reimann joining music rehearsals

Tim Rice (l.) and Andrew Lloyd Webber

Mikel Rouse/Photo: Susan San Giovanni

Max von Schillings

Arnold Schoenberg

Clara and Robert Schumann

Peter Sellars

John Philip Sousa

Igor Stravinsky

Michael Tippett with Adrian Boult (seated)

Joaquín Turina (center) with singers

Antonio Vivaldi by François Morellon La Cave

Richard Wagner

Charles Marie Widor

Ralph Vaughn Williams

Malcolm Williamson at rehearsal

Hugo Wolf

Franco Zeffirelli

E

Eaglen, Jane, remarkable English soprano; b. Lincoln, April 4, 1960. She was a student of Joseph Ward at the Royal Northern College of Music in Manchester (1978–83). In 1984 she made her debut at the English National Opera in London as Lady Ella in *Patience*, where she served as principal soprano until 1991. She made her first appearance at London's Covent Garden as Berta in *La Barbiere di Siviglia* in 1986. After singing Mimi at the Scottish Opera in Glasgow in 1988, she returned there to sing Brünnhilde in *Die Walküre* in 1991. She first appeared at the London Promenade Concerts as Sieglinde in Act III of *Die Walküre* in 1989. Following her debut at the Vienna State Opera in 1993 as Donna Anna, she made first appearances at Milan's La Scala as Brünnhilde in *Die Walküre*, the Seattle Opera as Norma, and the Opéra de la Bastille in Paris as Amelia in 1994. In 1995 she sang Brünnhilde in *Die Walküre* at the San Francisco Opera. She made her Metropolitan Opera debut in New York as Donna Anna on Jan. 18, 1996, and appeared that same season at the Lyric Opera in Chicago as Brünnhilde in its mounting of the *Ring* cycle and at the Seattle Opera as Turandot. She made her first appearance with the N.Y. Phil. on May 22, 1997, singing the Liebestod from *Tristan und Isolde* under Masur's direction. That same year she returned to the Metropolitan Opera as Turandot. Her return to the Seattle Opera to sing Isolde on Aug. 1, 1998, proved a triumph. Eaglen's outstanding vocal gifts have rendered her one of the leading Wagnerian interpreters of her era.

Eames, Emma (Hayden), famous American soprano; b. Shanghai, China, Aug. 13, 1865; d. N.Y., June 13, 1952. Her mother, who was her first teacher, took her to America as a child; she then studied with Clara Munger in Boston and with Marchesi in Paris. She made her operatic debut at the Paris Opéra on March 13, 1889, as Juliette in Gounod's *Roméo et Juliette*, singing there until 1891. On April 7, 1891, she made her first appearance at London's Covent Garden as Marguerite, and continued to sing there until 1901. On Nov. 9, 1891, she made her first appearance with the Metropolitan Opera as Elsa in *Lohengrin* during its visit to Chicago. On Dec. 14, 1891, she made her formal debut with the company as Juliette in New York. She remained with the Metropolitan until 1909, appearing as Marguerite in *Faust*, Desdemona in *Otello*, Elisabeth in *Tannhäuser*, Aida, Tosca, and Donna Anna in *Don Giovanni*. In 1911–12 she was a member of the Boston Opera, and then retired from the operatic stage. She received the Jubilee Medal from Queen Victoria, and was decorated by the French Academy with the order of Les Palmes Académiques. Her emotional life was turbulent; she married the painter Julian Story in 1891, but they were separated in the midst of a widely publicized scandal; in 1911 she married **Emilio de Gogorza**, but left him too. She publ. an autobiography, *Some Memories and Reflections* (N.Y., 1927).

Easdale, Brian, English composer; b. Manchester, Aug. 10, 1909; d. Oct. 30, 1995. He studied at the Royal College of Music in London (1925–33). He became interested in theatrical music; wrote 3 operas, *Rapunzel* (1927), *The Corn King* (1935), and *The Sleeping Children* (1951); also incidental music to Shakespeare's plays and several film scores, of which the most successful was *The Red Shoes* (1948).

Easton, Florence (Gertrude), English soprano; b. South Bank, Yorkshire, Oct. 25, 1882; d. N.Y., Aug. 13, 1955. She studied with Agnes Larkcom at the Royal Academy of Music in London and with Elliott Haslam in Paris; in 1903 she made her operatic debut as the Shepherd in *Tannhäuser* with the Moody-Manners Co. in Newcastle upon Tyne; toured the United States with Savage's opera company in 1904–05 and 1906–07. She was a member of the Berlin Royal Opera (1907–13) and the Hamburg Opera (1912–16); after singing with the Chicago Grand Opera (1915–17), she made her Metropolitan Opera debut in New York as Santuzza on Dec. 7, 1917, remaining on its roster until 1929; she created the role of Lauretta in *Gianni Schicchi* there in 1918. In 1927 and 1932 she sang at London's Covent Garden and in 1934 appeared at Sadler's Wells Opera in London. She then returned to the Metropolitan Opera in 1936 as Brünnhilde in *Die Walküre* before retiring from the stage.

Eaton, John (Charles), American composer and teacher; b. Bryn Mawr, Pa., March 30, 1935. He studied composition with Babbitt, Cone, and Sessions at Princeton Univ. (1953–59; B.A., M.F.A.). He also received training in piano from Steuermann, Erich Kahn, and Frank Sheridan. In 1959, 1960, and 1962 he held American Prix de Rome prizes. In 1962 and 1965 he held Guggenheim fellowships. In 1970 he became composer-in-residence at the Indiana Univ. School of Music in Bloomington, where he was assoc. prof. (1971–73) and prof. (1973–91). In 1976–77 he was composer-in-residence at the American Academy in Rome. In 1990 he received the MacArthur Award. He was a prof. at the Univ. of Chicago from 1991. He publ. the book *Involvement with Music: New Music since 1950* (1976). Eaton has made use of various modern resources in his compositions, including electronics. In some pieces, he has employed the Syn-Ket, a synthesizer invented by Paolo Ketoff.

WORKS: DRAMATIC: *Ma Barker*, opera (1957); *Heracles*, opera (1964; Turin, Oct. 10, 1968); *Myshkin*, television opera (1971; Bloomington, Ind., April 23, 1973); *The 3 Graces*, theater piece (1972); *The Lion and Androcles*, children's opera (1973; Indianapolis, May 1, 1974); *Danton and Robespierre*, opera (Bloomington, Ind., April 21, 1978); *The Cry of Clytaemnestra*, opera (1979; Bloomington, Ind., March 1, 1980); *The Tempest*, opera (1983–85; Santa Fe, July 27, 1985); *The Reverend Jim Jones*, opera (1988); *Peer Gynt*, theater piece (1990; Chicago, May 29, 1992); *Let's Get This Show on the Road: An Alternative View of Genesis*, opera (Chicago, Dec. 8, 1993); *Don Quixote*, theater piece (1994).

Eben, Petr, Czech composer, pianist, and teacher; b. Žamberk, Jan. 22, 1929. He studied with František Rauch (piano) and Pavel Bořkovec (composition) at the Prague Academy of Music (1948–52). From 1955 to 1990 he taught music history at the Charles Univ. in Prague, and also served as prof. of composition at the Royal Northern College of Music in Manchester (1978–79); he then taught at the Prague Academy of Music (from 1990). Eben was imprisoned during the Nazi occupation of his homeland, and then endured the suffocating communist regime until its undoing by the "velvet revolution" in 1989. As a composer, he found solace in plainchant and folk music, thus his liturgical works and organ music represent significant aspects of his oeuvre. However, he also composed numerous stage works, including *Faust*, incidental music to Goethe's play (1976), *Hamlet*, incidental music to Shakespeare's play (1977), *Curses and Blessings*, ballet (1983), and *Jeremias*, church opera (1997).

BIBL.: K. Vondrovicová, *P. E.* (Prague, 1993).

Eberl, Anton (Franz Josef), Austrian pianist and composer; b. Vienna, June 13, 1765; d. there, March 11, 1807. On Feb. 27, 1787, he produced in Vienna the Singspiel *La Marchande des modes*. There followed several other stage works, including *Die Zigeuner* (Vienna, 1793). His syms. and piano music were praised by Mozart and Gluck. He made a concert tour with Mozart's widow in 1795, then lived in St. Petersburg from 1796 to 1799, revisiting Russia in 1801. He gave concerts there on Dec. 8, 15, and 28, 1801, presenting the first performances in Russia of Haydn's *The Creation*. He returned to Vienna early in 1802, traveling once more through Germany in 1806.

Eberlin (also **Eberle), Johann Ernst**, German composer; b. Jettingen, Bavaria, March 27, 1702; d. Salzburg, June 19, 1762. He settled in Salzburg, where he studied at the Benedictine Univ. (1721–23). He was 4th organist (1726–29) and principal organist and choirmaster (1727–49) at the cathedral, then was court and cathedral Kapellmeister (1749–62). Anton Adlgasser was his pupil and son-in-law. Among his compositions are a pastoral play, *Daphne* (1758), 61 school plays, intermezzos, and much sacred music, including 21 oratorios.

Ebert, (Anton) Carl, noted German opera producer and administrator; b. Berlin, Feb. 20, 1887; d. Santa Monica, Calif., May 14, 1980. He studied acting with Max Reinhardt; then appeared in theaters in Berlin and Frankfurt am Main. In 1927 he became general administrator of the State Theater in Darmstadt and began to produce operas there. He then held a similar post at the Berlin City Opera (1931–33); he left Germany when the Nazis came to power. Ebert was one of the founders of the Glyndebourne Festival (1934), serving as its artistic director until 1939; in 1936 he organized the Turkish National School for Opera and Drama in Ankara, serving as its director until 1947, then was again artistic director at Glyndebourne (1947–59). He was also a prof. and head of the opera dept. at the Univ. of Southern Calif., Los Angeles (1948–54). He subsequently was administrator of the Berlin Städtische Oper (1956–61). As a producer, he gave much importance to the fusion of the music with the dramatic action on stage.

Eberwein, (Franz) Carl (Adalbert), German violinist and composer, brother of **Traugott (Maximilian) Eberwein**; b. Weimar, Nov. 10, 1786; d. there, March 2, 1868. He was a member of a musical family. After a study of general subjects at the Weimar Hochschule für Musik, he received an appointment as a court musician at the age of 16. He then studied with Zelter in Berlin. Returning to Weimar, he held the posts of chamber musician (1810–18), music director of the Weimar cathedral church (1818–26), and conductor of the Weimar Opera (1826–49). He was a friend of Goethe, who often mentions him, and for whom he composed some songs. His works include 3 Singspiels: *Die Heerschau*, *Der Graf zu Gleichen*, and *Der Teppichhändler*.

Eberwein, Traugott (Maximilian), German violinist and composer, brother of **(Franz) Carl (Adalbert) Eberwein**; b. Weimar, Oct. 27, 1775; d. Rudolstadt, Dec. 2, 1831. He played the violin in the Weimar Court Orch. as a very young man. Like his brother, he was a protégé of Goethe. He wrote 2 singspiels, *Claudine von Villa Bella* (1815) and *Der Jahrmarkt von Plundersweilen* (1818), to texts by Goethe.

Eckerberg, (Axel) Sixten (Lennart), Swedish conductor, pianist, and composer; b. Hjältevad, Sept. 5, 1909; d. Göteborg, April 9, 1991. After training at the Stockholm Cons. (1927–32), he studied conducting with Weingartner in Basel (1932–34) and piano with Sauer in Vienna and Philipp in Paris. From 1937 to 1969 he was chief conductor of the Göteborg Radio Orch. His autobiography was publ. as *Musiken och mitt lif* (Stockholm, 1970). In his compositions his contrapuntal writing tended toward the austere with occasional impressionist elements. He composed the operas *Det stora bankränet* (1975) and *Uppståndelse* (1975–76) and the musical *Ånger* (1972; Swedish Radio, July 22, 1975).

Eckert, Karl (Anton Florian), German composer and conductor; b. Potsdam, Dec. 7, 1820; d. Berlin, Oct. 14, 1879. At the age of 6 he was considered a prodigy; the poet F. Förster became interested in him and sent him to the best teachers; he studied piano with Rechenberg and Greulich, violin with Botticher and Ries, and composition with Rungenhagen in Berlin. At the age of 10 he wrote an opera, *Das Fischermädchen,* and at 13, an oratorio, *Ruth*. After completing his training with Mendelssohn in Leipzig, he began his career as a conductor at the Berlin Royal Opera, where his opera *Das Käthchen von Nürnberg* was premiered in 1837. With the outbreak of revolution in 1848, he went to the Netherlands and Belgium. He then conducted at the Théâtre-Italien in Paris (1851–53), and also toured the United States as an accompanist to Henriette Sontag (1852). He was conductor of the Vienna Court Opera (1853–60) and of the Vienna Phil. (1854–60). After serving as conductor of the Stuttgart Court Opera (1860–67), he was called to Berlin in 1869 to succeed Heinrich Dorn as conductor of the Royal Opera. Unlike Dorn, Eckert was a friend and champion of Wagner. Although he composed several ambitious works, his music met with little success. Among his other compositions are the operas *Der Laborant im Riesengebirge* (1838), *Scharlatan* (Königsberg and Berlin, 1840), and *Wilhelm von Oranien* (Berlin, 1846), as well as oratorios.

Eckert, Rinde, American avant-garde vocalist, librettist, and composer; b. Mankato, Minn., Sept. 20, 1951. He studied at the Univ. of Iowa (B.M., 1973) and Yale Univ. (M.M., 1975), then was on the faculty of the Cornish Inst. (1980–82) and resident stage director of the Cornish Opera Theater. Since 1980 he has worked primarily with the composer Paul Dresher, and is principal performer and collaborator on their American opera trilogy (*Slow Fire* [1985–88], *Power Failure* [1989], and *Pioneers*). He was also principal performer and collaborator on the *How Trilogy* with George Coates Performance Works (*The Way of How* [1981], *are are* [1983], and *Seehear* [1984]; music by Dresher). Other works with Dresher include *Was Are/Will Be* (1983–85), *Shelf Life* (1987, with choreographer Margaret Jenkins), and *Secret House* (1990, with the Oberlin Dance Collective). His intense vocal style indicates both classical and rock training; his libretti are complex explorations, drenched with verbal paradox, of the pressure and instability of contemporary life. Among his own musical compositions is the radio opera, *Shoot the Moving Things* (1987).

Eckstein, Pavel, Czech musicologist; b. Opava, April 27, 1911. He studied jurisprudence at Charles Univ. in Prague, graduating in 1935; received his musical education there. During the German occupation (1941–45), he was in a concentration camp in Łódz, but survived and returned to Prague, where he became active as an organizer of music festivals, an ed., and a writer on music. From 1969 to 1992 he was artistic advisor of the Prague National Theater, and subsequently was chief dramaturg there from 1992 to 1995. Among his books are *Czechoslovak Opera* (Prague, 1964) and *The Czechoslovak Contemporary Opera—Die tschechoslowakische zeitgenössische Oper* (Prague, 1967).

Eda-Pierre, Christiane, esteemed French soprano; b. Fort-de-France, Martinique, March 24, 1932. She studied at the Paris Cons., graduating with 3 premiers prix in 1957. In 1958 she made her operatic debut in Nice as Leila in *Les Pêcheurs de perles*; after singing Pamina at the Aix-en-Provence Festival (1959), she went to Paris and made debuts at the Opéra Comique (as Lakmé, 1961) and the Opéra (as Lucia di Lammermoor, 1962). In 1966 she made her first appearance at London's Covent Garden as Teresa in *Benvenuto Cellini*. She appeared as Mozart's Countess with the Paris Opéra during its visit to New York in 1976. On April 3, 1980, she made her Metropolitan Opera debut in New York as Mozart's Constanze, and returned there for the 1981–82 season. In 1983 she created the role of the Angel in Messiaen's *St. François d'Assise* in Paris. She also served as a prof. of voice at the Paris Cons. (from 1977). Among her other admired roles were Rameau's Dardanus, the Queen of the Night, Berlioz's Hero, Zerbinetta, Gilda, and Milhaud's Médée.

Edelmann, Jean-Frédéric (also **Johann Friedrich**), famous Alsatian harpsichordist, pianist, composer, and teacher; b. Strasbourg, May 5, 1749; d. (executed by guillotine) Paris, July 17, 1794. He studied law at the Univ. of Strasbourg (matriculated, 1770). He went to Paris about 1774, where he gained distinction as a performer, teacher, and composer. His students included Jean-Louis Adam and Méhul. His life took a tempestuous and ultimately tragic turn after he joined the Jacobin cause. Returning to Strasbourg in 1789, he was appointed administrator of the Lower Rhine. However, he soon fell out with his former friend Philippe-Frédéric Dietrich, the mayor of Strasbourg. Edelmann assisted in bringing about his arrest, trial, and execution in 1793. After further Jacobin intrigues, Edelmann himself became a victim of the Reign of Terror and was executed by guillotine. Through his teaching and compositions, Edelmann helped to make the piano a fashionable instrument in Paris. Many of his keyboard works were publ. in his lifetime. Ironically, his lyric drama *Arianne dans l'isle de Naxos* (1782) was dedicated to Joseph Ignace Guillotin.

WORKS: DRAMATIC: OPERAS: *La Bergère des Alpes*, scene lyrique (Paris, July 20, 1781); *Ariane dans l'isle de Naxos*, drame lyrique (Opéra, Paris, Sept. 24, 1782); *Diane et l'amour*, opéra ballet (Paris, 1802). BALLET: *Feu* (Opéra, Paris, Sept. 24, 1782). Also the oratorio *Esther* (Concert Spirituel, Paris, April 8, 1781; not extant).

Edelmann, Otto (Karl), noted Austrian bass-baritone; b. Brünn am Gebirge, near Vienna, Feb. 5, 1917. He studied with Lierhammer and Graarud at the Vienna Academy of Music, making his operatic debut as Mozart's Figaro in Gera in 1937; he then sang in Nuremberg (1938–40). After military service during World War II, he resumed his career as a leading member of the Vienna State Opera from 1947. He also sang at the Bayreuth Festival, the Salzburg Festival, La Scala in Milan, the Hamburg State Opera, the Edinburgh Festival, and other major operatic centers. On Nov. 11, 1954, he made his Metropolitan Opera debut in New York as Hans Sachs, a role in which he particularly excelled; he continued to sing there regularly until 1976. His most famous role was that of Baron Ochs in *Der Rosenkavalier*.

BIBL.: S.-M. Schlinke, *O. E.: Ein Meistersinger aus Wien* (Vienna, 1987).

Eder, Helmut, Austrian composer and pedagogue; b. Linz, Dec. 26, 1916. He studied at the Linz teacher training inst. (diploma, 1937). In 1938 he entered the Austrian Army. During his service in World War II, he was taken prisoner of war. After his release, he studied with Hindemith in Salzburg (1947, 1950), Orff in Munich (1953–54), and J. N. David in Stuttgart (1954). From 1950 to 1967 he was prof. of theory at the Linz Cons. He subsequently was prof. of composition at the Salzburg Mozarteum from 1967. In 1962 he was awarded the Austrian State Prize. In 1963 he received the Theodor Körner Prize for music. He was awarded the Würdigungspreis in 1972. In 1986 he was made an honorary member of the Austrian Composers Guild.

WORKS: DRAMATIC: OPERAS: *Ödipus* (1958); *Der Kardinal* (1962); *Die weisse Frau* (1968); *Konjugationen 3*, television opera (1969); *Der Aufstand* (1975); *Georges Dandin oder Der betrogene Ehemann* (1978–79); *Mozart in New York* (1989–90; Salzburg, Aug. 15, 1991). BALLETS: *Moderner Traum* (Linz, Sept. 29, 1957); *Anamorphose* (1963; Linz, June 22, 1966); *Die Irrfahrten des Odysseus* (1964–65).

BIBL.: G. Gruber and G. Kraus, *H. E.* (Vienna, 1988).

Edlund, Lars, Swedish organist, conductor, teacher, and composer; b. Karlstad, Nov. 6, 1922. He studied in Arvika and at the Stockholm Musikhögskolan (1942–47). After serving as an organist in Tranås and Södertälje (1948–60), he taught aural training at the Stockholm Musikhögskolan until 1971; he then devoted himself to performing and composing. He publ. 2 influential books, *Modus novus: Lärobok i fritonal melodiläsning* (New method: Textbook in atonal melody reading: 1963) and *Modus vetus: Gehörstudier i dur/moll-tonalitet* (Old method: Ear training in major/minor tonalities; 1967), which have guided his path as a composer. He won particular distinction for his choral music. Among his works is a chamber opera, *Flickan i ögat* (1979). His son, Mikael Edlund (b. Tranås, Jan. 19, 1950), is also a composer.

Edwards, Ross, Australian composer; b. Sydney, Dec. 23, 1943. He studied at the New South Wales State Conservatorium of Music in Sydney (1959–62), the Univ. of Sydney (1963), and the Univ. of Adelaide (B.Mus., 1968; M.Mus., 1971), his principal mentors being Meale and Sculthorpe. A Commonwealth postgraduate scholarship enabled him to pursue studies in London with Maxwell Davies. He also studied with Veress. After serving as senior tutor (1973–76) and lecturer (1976–80) in composition at the New South Wales State Conservatorium of Music, he was composer-in-residence at the Univ. of Wollongong (1983). In 1989 he was made the Australia Council's Don Banks fellow. In 1990 he received the D.Mus. degree from the Univ. of Sydney. He held 2 Australian Creative Artists fellowships. Edwards has developed a highly imaginative style of composition. In his works, designated as his "sacred series," an austere meditative aura prevails. In other scores he has been much influenced by the sounds of the natural world, including those of insects and birds. He composed a chamber opera, *Christina's World* (1983; rev. 1989), and a television dance score, *Sensing* (1993).

Edwards, Sian, English conductor; b. Sussex, May 27, 1959. She studied horn before entering the Royal Northern College of Music in Manchester, where she turned to conducting; following studies with Sir Charles Groves and Norman Del Mar, and in the Netherlands with Neeme Järvi, she pursued diligent training with Ilya Musin at the Leningrad Cons. (1983–85). In 1984 she won the

Leeds Competition and subsequently appeared as a guest conductor with principal British orchs. In 1986 she made her first appearance as an operatic conductor at Glasgow's Scottish Opera with Weill's *Mahogonny*. In 1987 she conducted *La Traviata* at the Glyndebourne Festival. She became the first woman ever to conduct at London's Covent Garden when she led a performance of Tippett's *The Knot Garden* in 1988; that same year she conducted the premiere of Turnage's *Greek* at the Munich Biennale. In 1989 she made her U.S. debut as a guest conductor with the St. Paul (Minn.) Chamber Orch.; she continued to conduct at Covent Garden, leading performances of *Rigoletto* (1989), *Il Trovatore* (1990), and *Carmen* (1991). From 1993 to 1995 she was music director of the English National Opera in London.

Effinger, Cecil, American composer; b. Colorado Springs, July 22, 1914; d. Boulder, Colo., Dec. 22, 1990. He took courses in mathematics at Colorado College (B.A., 1935); then studied harmony and counterpoint with Frederick Boothroyd in Colorado Springs (1934–36). He then studied composition with Wagenaar in New York (1938) and Boulanger in Fontainebleau (1939), where he was awarded the Stoval composition prize. He was oboist in the Colorado Springs Sym. Orch. (1932–41) and the Denver Sym. Orch. (1937–41); he taught at Colorado College (1936–41) and the Colorado School for the Blind (1939–41). During World War II, he conducted the 506th Army Band (1942–45), then taught at the American Univ. in Biarritz, France (1945–46). After teaching at Colorado College (1946–48), he was music ed. of the *Denver Post* (1947–48), then was head of the composition dept. (1948–81) and composer-in-residence (1981–84) at the Univ. of Colo. in Boulder. In 1954 he patented a practical music typewriter as the "Musicwriter." In his music he maintained a median modern style, making use of polytonal and atonal procedures, without abandoning the basic sense of tonality. He composed *Pandora's Box*, children's opera (1961), *Cyrano de Bergerac*, opera (Boulder, July 21, 1965), and *The Gentleman Desperado*, music theater (1976); also incidental music.

Eggen, Arne, Norwegian organist and composer; b. Trondheim, Aug. 28, 1881; d. Baerum, near Oslo, Oct. 26, 1955. He studied at the Christiania Cons. (1903–05) and then with Straube (organ) and Krehl (composition) at the Leipzig Cons. (1906–07). He toured Norway and Sweden giving organ recitals; from 1927 to 1945 he was president of the Soc. of Norwegian Composers. In 1934 he received a government life pension. He composed 2 operas: *Olav Liljekrans* (1931–40; Oslo, 1940) and *Cymbeline* (1943–48; Oslo, Dec. 7, 1951). His brother was the Norwegian music scholar and composer Erik Eggin (1877–1957).

Eggerth, Martha (real name, **Márta Eggert**), Hungarian soprano; b. Budapest, April 17, 1912. She was only 12 when she began appearing in juvenile roles in light theater performances in Budapest. In 1930 she attracted favorable notice in the title role of *Das Veilchen vom Montmartre* in Vienna, and in subsequent years had a notably successful career both on stage and in films. Her theater engagements took her all over Europe and to New York, where she was notably successful in *The Merry Widow* with her husband, **Jan Kiepura**. She pursued her career to an advanced age, appearing in her 80th year in Stolz's *Servus Du* in Vienna.

Egk (real name, **Mayer**), **Werner,** significant German composer; b. Auchsesheim, near Donauwörth, May 17, 1901; d. Inning, near Munich, July 10, 1983. Rumor had it that he took the name Egk as a self-complimentary acronym for "ein grosser (or even ein genialer) Komponist." Egk himself rejected this frivolous suspicion, offering instead an even more fantastic explanation that Egk was a partial acronym of the name of his wife, Elisabeth Karl, with the middle guttural added "for euphony." He studied piano with Anna Hirzel-Langenhan and composition with Carl Orff in Munich, where he made his permanent home. Primarily interested in theater music, he wrote several scores for a Munich puppet theater; he was also active on the radio; then wrote ballet music to his own scenarios and a number of successful operas. He was also active as an opera conductor and music pedagogue. He conducted at the Berlin State Opera from 1938 to 1941, and was head of the German Union of Composers from 1941 to 1945. He was commissioned to write music for the Berlin Olympiad in 1936, for which he received a Gold Medal. He also received a special commission of 10,000 marks from the Nazi Ministry of Propaganda. The apparent favor that Egk enjoyed during the Nazi reign made it necessary for him to stand trial before the Allied Committee for the de-Nazification proceedings in 1947; it absolved him of political taint. From 1950 to 1953 he was director of the Berlin Hochschule für Musik. As a composer, Egk continued the tradition of Wagner and Richard Strauss, without excluding, however, the use of acidulous harmonies, based on the atonal extension of tonality. The rhythmic investiture of his works is often inventive and bold. He publ. a vol. of essays under the title *Musik, Wort, Bild* (Munich, 1960).

WORKS: DRAMATIC: *Columbus*, radio opera (1932; Bavarian Radio, Munich, July 13, 1933; 1st stage perf., Frankfurt am Main, Jan. 13, 1942); *Die Zaubergeige*, opera (Frankfurt am Main, May 19, 1935; rev. version, Stuttgart, May 2, 1954); *Peer Gynt*, opera (Berlin, Nov. 24, 1938); *Joan von Zarissa*, ballet (1939; Berlin, Jan. 20, 1940); *Circe*, opera (1945; Berlin, Dec. 18, 1948; rev. version as *17 Tage und 4 Minuten*, Stuttgart, June 2, 1966); *Abraxas*, ballet (South West Radio, Baden-Baden, Dec. 7, 1947; 1st stage perf., Munich, June 6, 1948); *Ein Sommertag*, ballet (Berlin, June 11, 1950); *Die chinesische Nachtigall*, ballet (Munich, May 6, 1953); *Irische Legende*, opera (Salzburg, Aug. 17, 1955; rev. 1970); *Der Revisor*, opera (Schwetzingen, May 9, 1957); *Die Verlobung in San Domingo*, opera (Munich, Nov. 27, 1963); *Casanova in London*, ballet (Munich, Nov. 23, 1969).

BIBL.: B. Kohl and E. Nölle, eds., *W. E.: Das Bühnenwerk* (Munich, 1971); E. Krause, *W. E.: Oper und Ballet* (Wilhelmshaven, 1971).

Egmond, Max (Rudolf) van, admired Dutch bass-baritone; b. Semarang, Java, Feb. 1, 1936. He studied with Tine van Willingen-de Lorme and took prizes in the 's-Hertogenbosch (1959), Brussels (1962), and Munich (1964) competitions. He then pursued a distinguished career as a concert and oratorio artist, touring extensively in Europe and North America. From 1973 he also taught singing at the Amsterdam Musieklyceum. He was particularly associated with Baroque music, excelling in the works of Bach.

BIBL.: J. Müller, *M. v. E., toonaangevend kunstenaar* (Zutphen, 1984).

Ehrenberg, Carl (Emil Theodor), German conductor, teacher, and composer; b. Dresden, April 6, 1878; d. Munich, Feb. 26, 1962. He studied with Draeseke at the Dresden Cons. (1894–98); from 1898 on was engaged as a conductor in Germany; from 1909 to 1914 he conducted concerts in Lausanne; from 1915 to 1918 he was 1st conductor at the Augsburg Opera, then conducted at the Berlin State Opera (1922–24). Subsequently he was a prof. at the Cologne Hochschule für Musik (1924–35) and at the Akademie der Tonkunst in Munich (1935–45). He composed 2 operas: *Und selig sind* (1904) and *Anneliese* (1922).

Ehrlich, Abel, German-born Israeli composer and teacher; b. Cranz, Sept. 3, 1915. He began violin lessons at the age of 6, and later was a student at the Zagreb Academy of Music (1934–38). After emigrating to Palestine, he studied composition with Rosowsky at the Jerusalem Academy of Music (1939–44); later he attended the Darmstadt summer courses in new music under Stockhausen, Nono et al. (1959, 1961, 1963, 1967). He taught composition in various Israeli academies, conservatories, and teacher training colleges; from 1966 to 1982 he was on the faculty of the Univ. of Tel Aviv. He received many awards and prizes for his works. In 1989 he was awarded the Israeli government prize. In his early works, he adhered to a Romantic line with infusions of Middle Eastern themes. Later he adopted an advanced idiom marked by a personal amalgam of traditional Jewish cantillation and serialism. He composed *Immanuel Haromi*, musical spectacle (1971), and *Dead Souls*, opéra bouffe (1978).

Ehrling, (Evert) Sixten, noted Swedish conductor; b. Malmö, April 3, 1918. He studied piano, organ, composition, and conducting at the Royal Academy of Music's Cons. in Stockholm. After a brief career as a concert pianist, he joined the staff of the Royal Opera in Stockholm as a rehearsal pianist, and made his conducting debut there in 1940. He then took conducting lessons with Karl Böhm in Dresden (1941) and, after the end of World War II, with Albert Wolff in Paris. In 1942 he was appointed conductor in Göteborg; in 1944 he became a conductor at the Royal Opera in Stockholm, where he served as chief conductor from 1953 to 1960. From 1963 to 1973 he was music director of the Detroit Sym. Orch., then headed the orch. conducting class at the Juilliard School in New York. In 1978 he became music adviser and principal guest conductor of the Denver Sym. Orch., and from 1979 to 1985, he was its principal guest conductor; he was also artistic adviser to the San Antonio Sym. Orch. (1985–88). He was chief conductor and musical advisor of the orchs. at the Manhattan School of Music in New York from 1993.

Eichheim, Henry, American composer and violinist; b. Chicago, Jan. 3, 1870; d. Montecito, near Santa Barbara, Calif., Aug. 22, 1942. He received elementary musical training from his father, Meinhard Eichheim, a cellist in the Theodore Thomas Orch., then studied with Becker, L. Lichtenberg, and S. Jacobson at the Chicago Musical College. After a season as a violinist in the Thomas Orch. in Chicago, he was a member of the Boston Sym. Orch. (1890–1912), then he devoted himself to concert work and composition. He made 5 trips to the Orient (1915, 1919, 1922, 1928, mid–1930s) and collected indigenous instruments, which he subsequently used in his orch. music. All of his works are based on oriental subjects, with their harmonic idiom derived from Debussy and Scriabin. He composed *The Rivals*, ballet (1924; Chicago, Jan. 1, 1925; rev. as *Chinese Legend* for Orch., Boston, April 3, 1925) and *A Burmese pwé*, incidental music (N.Y., March 16, 1926).

Eichhorn, Kurt (Peter), German conductor; b. Munich, Aug. 4, 1908; d. Murnau am Staffelsee, June 29, 1994. He studied with Hermann Zilcher and made his professional debut at the Bielefeld Opera in 1932. In 1941 he conducted at the Dresden State Opera. After World War II he returned to Munich as a conductor at the Gärtnerplatz State Theater; he also conducted at the Bavarian State Opera. From 1967 to 1975 he served as chief conductor of the Munich Radio Orch.

Eilers, Albert, German bass; b. Cothen, Dec. 21, 1830; d. Darmstadt, Sept. 4, 1896. He studied at the Milan Cons., making his opera debut in Dresden (1854). He sang at the German Theater in Prague (1858–65). In 1876 Wagner selected him to sing the part of the giant Fasolt at Bayreuth. In 1882 he became a member of the Darmstadt Opera. He wrote a fairly successful comic opera, *Die Johannisnacht* (Koblenz, 1889).

Einem, Gottfried von, outstanding Austrian composer; b. Bern, Switzerland, Jan. 24, 1918; d. Obern Durenbach, Austria, July 12, 1996. He was taken to Germany as a child and pursued academic studies in Plön and Ratzeburg. In 1938 he was arrested and briefly imprisoned by the Gestapo, but that same year he became a coach at the Bayreuth Festival and at the Berlin State Opera. After studying composition with Blacher in Berlin (1941–42), he went to the Dresden State Opera in 1944 as resident composer and musical advisor. Later that year he settled in Austria, where he studied counterpoint with J. N. David. From 1963 to 1972 he taught at the Vienna Hochschule für Musik. He also served as president of the Austrian Soc. of Authors, Composers, and Music Publishers (1965–70). Einem publ. the books *Das musikalische Selbstporträt von Komponisten, Dirigenten, Sängerinnen und Sänger unserer Zeit* (Hamburg, 1963) and *Komponist und Gesellschaft* (Karlsruhe, 1967). Einem achieved an original mode of expression within tonal parameters which allowed him to explore a remarkable range of dynamic, rhythmic, and harmonic effects. He especially excelled as a composer of dramatic scores, but he also revealed himself as a distinguished composer of instrumental music.

WORKS: DRAMATIC: OPERAS: *Dantons Tod* (1944–46; Salzburg, Aug. 6, 1947); *Der Prozess* (1950–52; Salzburg, Aug. 17, 1953); *Der Zerrissene* (1961–64; Hamburg, Sept. 17, 1964); *Der Besuch der alten Dame* (1970; Vienna, May 23, 1971); *Kabale und Liebe* (1975; Vienna, Dec. 17, 1976); *Jesu Hochzeit* (Vienna, May 18, 1980); *Tulifant* (1989–90; Vienna, Oct. 30, 1990); *Luzifers Lacheln* (Vienna, Feb. 4, 1998). BALLETS: *Prinzessin Turandot* (1942–43; Dresden, Feb. 5, 1944); *Rondo von goldenen Kalb* (1950; Hamburg, Feb. 1, 1952); *Pas de coeur* (Munich, July 22, 1952); *Glück, Tod und Traum* (1953; Alpbach, Aug. 23, 1954); *Medusa* (Vienna, Jan. 16, 1957; rev. 1971).

BIBL.: D. Hartmann, *G. v. E.* (Vienna, 1967); H. Hopf and B. Sonntag, eds., *G. v. E.: Ein Komponist unseres Jahrhunderts* (Münster, 1989); K. Lezak, *Das Opernschaffen G.v. E.s.* (Vienna, 1990).

Eiríksdóttir, Karólína, Icelandic composer; b. Reykjavík, Jan. 10, 1951. She studied composition with Thorkell Sigurbjornsson at the Reykjavík College of Music and with George Wilson and William Albright at the Univ. of Mich. (M.M., 1978); she taught at the Kopavogur School of Music and the Reykjavík College of Music. In 1985 she received an Icelandic Artists' Grant. Her music is stark and austere, laden with northern Romanticism. She composed the chamber opera *Someone I Have Seen* (1988).

Eisler, Hanns (Johannes), remarkable German composer; b. Leipzig, July 6, 1898; d. Berlin, Sept. 6, 1962. He began to study music on his own while still a youth, then studied with Weigl at the New Vienna Cons. and later privately with Schoenberg (1919–23); he also worked with Webern. In 1924 he won the Vienna Arts Prize. He went to Berlin in 1925 and taught at the Klindworth-Scharwenka Cons. In 1926 he joined the German Communist party; after the Nazis came to power in 1933, he left Germany; made visits to the United States and was active in Austria, France, England, and other European countries. He taught at the New School for Social Research in New York (1935–36; 1937–42) and at the Univ. of Calif. in Los Angeles (1942–48); then left the United States under the terms of "voluntary deportation" on account of his communist sympathies. In 1949 he settled in East Berlin and became a prof. at the Hochschule für Musik and a member of the German Academy of the Arts. Under Schoenberg's influence, Eisler adopted the 12-tone method of composition for most of his symphonic works. However, he demonstrated a notable capacity for writing music in an accessible style. His long association with Bertolt Brecht resulted in several fine scores for the theater; he also worked with Charlie Chaplin in Hollywood (1942–47). His songs and choral works became popular in East Germany. He composed the music for the East German national anthem, *Auferstanden aus Ruinen*, which was adopted in 1949. His writings include *Composing for the Films* (with T. Adorno; N.Y., 1947), *Reden und Aufsätze* (Berlin, 1959), and *Materialen zu einer Dialektik der Musik* (Berlin, 1973). G. Mayer ed. his *Musik und Politik* (2 vols., Berlin, 1973 and Leipzig, 1982).

WORKS: DRAMATIC: *Johannes Faustus*, opera (Berlin, March 11, 1953); some 38 scores of incidental music, to works by Brecht (*Rote Revue*, 1932; *Die Rundköpfe und die Spitzköpfe*, 1934–36; *Furcht und Elend des dritten Reiches*, 1945; *Galileo Galilei*, 1947; *Tage der Kommune*, 1950; *Die Gesichte der Simone Machard*, 1957; *Schweyk im zweiten Weltkrieg*, 1943–59), by Feuchtwanger (*Kalkutta, 4.Mai*, 1928), by Ernst Toller (*Feuer aus den Kesseln*, 1934; *Peace on Earth*, 1934), by Ben Jonson (*Volpone*, 1953), by Aristophanes (*Lysistrata*, 1954), by Shakespeare (*Hamlet*, 1954), by Schiller (*Wilhelm Tell*, 1961), etc.

BIBL.: H. Brockhaus, *H. E.* (Leipzig, 1961); N. Notowicz, *H. E.: Quellennachweise* (Leipzig, 1966); H. Bunge, *Fragen Sie mehr über Brecht: H. E. im Gespräch* (Munich, 1970); E. Klemm, *H. E.: Für Sie porträtiert* (Leipzig, 1973); A. Betz, *H. E.: Musik einer Zeit* (Munich, 1976; Eng. tr., 1982, as *H. E.: Political Musician*); M. Grabs, *H. E.: Kompositionen, Schriften, Literatur: Ein Handbuch* (Leipzig, 1984); D. Blake, *H. E.: A Miscellany* (London, 1995).

Eisler, Paul, Austrian pianist, conductor, and composer; b. Vienna, Sept. 9, 1875; d. N.Y., Oct. 16, 1951. He was a pupil of Bruckner at the Vienna Cons. He conducted in Riga, Vienna, and at the Metropolitan Opera in New York (1916–17; 1920–29); he also made numerous tours as an accompanist to Caruso, Ysaÿe, and others. He composed several operettas, including *Spring Brides*, *The Sentinel*, *The Little Missus*, and *In the Year 1814*.

Eklund, Hans, prominent Swedish composer and teacher; b. Sandviken, July 1, 1927. He studied at the Stockholm Musikhogskolan with Åke Uddén and Lars-Erik Larsson (1947–52) and with Ernst Pepping in Berlin (1954) before completing his training in Rome (1957). He was prof. of harmony and counterpoint at the Stockholm Musikhögskolan (from 1964). In 1975 he was elected a member of the Royal Swedish Academy of Music; in 1985 he was awarded the degree of Litteris et Artibus from the King of Sweden. Edlund's large output is notable for its imaginative handling of traditional forms. He composed the radio opera *Moder Svea* (Mother Svea; Swedish Radio, Oct. 7, 1972).

El-Dabh, Halim (Abdul Messieh), Egyptian-born American composer; b. Cairo, March 4, 1921. He studied piano and Western music at the Sulcz Cons. in Cairo (1941–44), then went to the United States in 1950 on a Fulbright fellowship, studying with Copland and Irving Fine at the Berkshire Music Center at Tanglewood and taking graduate degrees from the New England Cons. of Music and Brandeis Univ. In 1961 he became a naturalized American citizen. He taught at Haile Selassie Univ. in Ethiopia (1962–64), Howard Univ. (1966–69), and Kent State Univ. (from 1969), where he later also was codirector of its Center for the Study of World Musics (from 1979). His compositions reveal Afro-Arab influences, especially in their rhythmic structures and their incorporation of unusual percussive devices. He publ. *The Derabucca: Hand Techniques in the Art of Drumming* (1965).

WORKS: DRAMATIC: *Clytemnestra*, epic dance drama (for Martha Graham; 1958); *The Egyptian Series: Lament of the Pharaohs, Pyramid Rock to the Sky, Gloria Aton*, and *Prayer to the Sphinx* for Solo Voices, Chorus, and Orch. (1960); *The Islamic Series: Allahu Akbar, Al-khaheera, Ya Leiyly, Saladin and the Citadel*, and *The Nile* for Voices ad libitum and Orch. (1960); *Theodora in Byzantium* (1965); *Black Epic*, opera pageant (1968); *Opera Flies* (1971); *Ptahmose and the Magic Spell*, opera trilogy: *The Osiris Ritual, Aton, the Ankh, and the World*, and *The 12 Hours Trip* (1972–73); *Drink of Eternity*, opera pageant (1981).

Elder, Mark (Philip), prominent English conductor; b. Hexham, June 2, 1947. He studied in Bryanston and played bassoon in the National Youth Orch. before pursuing his education at the Univ. of Cambridge (B.A., M.A.). In 1969–70 he was on the music staff of the Wexford Festival. In 1970 he became an assistant conductor at the Glyndebourne Festival, serving as chorus master until 1972. From 1972 to 1974 he was a staff conductor at the Australian Opera in Sydney. In 1974 he became a conductor at the English National Opera in London. He made his debut at London's Covent Garden in 1976 conducting *Rigoletto*. In 1977 he became assoc. conductor at the English National Opera, and subsequently served as its music director from 1979 to 1993. During his tenure there Elder conducted the British premieres of several operas by masters of the past as well as the world premieres of operas by contemporary composers. From 1980 to 1983 he was principal guest conductor of the London Mozart Players, and, from 1982 to 1985, of the BBC Sym. Orch. in London. In 1981 he made his first appearance at the Bayreuth Festival conducting *Die Meistersinger von Nürnberg*. He made his U.S. debut as a guest conductor of the Chicago Sym. Orch. in 1983. In 1988 he conducted *Le Nozze di Figaro* at the Metropolitan Opera in New York. From 1989 to 1994 he was music director of the Rochester (N.Y.) Phil. From 1992 to 1995 he was principal guest conductor of the City of Birmingham Sym. Orch. In 1989 he was made a Commander of the Order of the British Empire.

Elgar, Sir Edward (William), great English composer; b. Broadheath, near Worcester, June 2, 1857; d. Worcester, Feb. 23, 1934. He received his earliest music education from his father, who owned a music shop and was organist for the St. George's Roman Catholic Church in Worcester; he also took violin lessons from a local musician. He rapidly acquired the fundamentals of theory and served as arranger with the Worcester Glee Club, becoming its conductor at the age of 22; simultaneously he accepted a position with the County of Worcester Lunatic Asylum at Powick, where he was for several years in charge of the institution's concert band.. In 1885 he succeeded his father as organist at St. George's. He married in 1889 and moved to Malvern, where he stayed from 1891 to 1904. During these years, he conducted the Worcestershire Phil. (1898–1904); in 1905 he accepted the position of Peyton Prof. of Music at the Univ. of Birmingham, and in 1911–12 served as conductor of the London Sym. Orch. He then settled in Hampstead. His wife died in 1920, at which time he returned to Worcester.

Elgar's first signal success was with the concert overture *Froissart* (Worcester, Sept. 9, 1890). His cantata *The Black Knight* was produced at the Worcester Festival (April 18, 1893) and was also heard in London at the Crystal Palace (Oct. 23, 1897); the production of his cantata *Scenes from the Saga of King Olaf* at the North Staffordshire Music Festival (Oct. 30, 1896) attracted considerable attention; he gained further recognition with his *Imperial March* (1897), composed for the Diamond Jubilee of Queen Victoria. From then on, Elgar's name became familiar to the musical public. There followed the cantata *Caractacus* (Leeds Festival, Oct. 5, 1898) and Elgar's great masterpiece, the oratorio *The Dream of Gerontius* (Birmingham Festival, Oct. 14, 1900). He began to give more and more attention to orch. music. On June 19, 1899, Hans Richter presented the first performance of Elgar's *Variations on an Original Theme* (generally known as the *Enigma Variations*) in London. This work consists of 14 sections, each marked by initials of fancied names of Elgar's friends; in later years, Elgar issued cryptic hints as to the identities of these persons, which were finally revealed. Its success was followed (1901–30) by the production of Elgar's *Pomp and Circumstance* marches, the first of which became his most famous piece through a setting to words by Arthur Christopher Benson, used by Elgar in the *Coronation Ode* (1902) as *Land of Hope and Glory*; another successful orch. work was the *Cockaigne Overture* (London, June 20, 1901). Elgar's 2 syms., written between 1903 and 1910, became staples in the English orch. repertoire. His Violin Concerto, first performed by Fritz Kreisler (London, Nov. 10, 1910), won notable success; there was also a remarkable Cello Concerto (London, Oct. 26, 1919, Felix Salmond soloist, composer conducting).

The emergence of Elgar as a major composer about 1900 was all the more remarkable since he had no formal academic training. Yet he developed a masterly technique of instrumental and vocal writing. His style of composition may be described as functional Romanticism; his harmonic procedures remain firmly within the 19th-century tradition; the formal element is always strong, and the thematic development logical and precise. Elgar had a melodic gift, which asserted itself in his earliest works, such as the popular *Salut d'amour*; his oratorios, particularly *The Apostles*, were the product of his fervent religious faith (he was a Roman Catholic). He avoided archaic usages of Gregorian chant; rather, he presented the sacred subjects in a communicative style of secular drama.

Elgar was the recipient of many honors. He was knighted in 1904. He received honorary degrees of Mus.Doc. from Cambridge (1900), Oxford (1905), and Aberdeen (1906); also an LL.D. from Leeds (1904). During his first visit to the United States, in 1905, he received a D.Mus. degree from Yale Univ.; in 1907 he was granted the same degree from the Univ. of Western Pa. (now the Univ. of Pittsburgh). He received the Order of Merit in 1911; was made a Knight Commander of the Royal Victorian Order in 1928 and a baronet in 1931; was appointed Master of the King's Musick in 1924. He was not a proficient conductor, but appeared on various occasions with orchs. in his own works; during the 3d of his 4 visits to the United States (1905, 1906, 1907, 1911), he conducted his oratorio *The Apostles* (N.Y., 1907); he also led the mass chorus at the opening of the British Empire Exhibition in 1924. His link with America was secured when the hymnlike section from his first *Pomp and Circumstance* march became a popular recession march for American high school graduation exercises.

WORKS: DRAMATIC: OPERA: *The Spanish Lady*, op. 89 (unfinished; sketches date from 1878; 15 excerpts orchestrated by Percy M. Young; BBC, London, Dec. 4, 1969). INCIDENTAL MUSIC TO: *Grania and Diarmid*, op. 42 (Yeats and Moore; Dublin, Oct. 1901); *The Starlight Express*, op. 78 (Blackwood and Pearn; London, Dec. 29, 1915); *King Arthur* (Binyon; London, March 12, 1923); *Beau Brummel* (Matthews; Birmingham, Nov. 5, 1928, composer conducting). MASQUE: *The Crown of India*, op. 66 (1902–12; London, March 11, 1912; as a suite for Orch., Hereford Festival, Sept. 11, 1912, composer conducting). BALLET: *The Sanguine Fan*, op. 81 (London, March 20, 1917).

BIBL.: The Elgar Soc. of England began issuing the *Elgar Society Newsletter* in 1973; it became the *Elgar Society Journal* in 1979. Other writings include: R. Buckley, *Sir E. E.* (London, 1904; new ed., 1925); E. Newman, *E.* (London, 1906); J. Porte, *Sir E. E.* (London, 1921); B. Maine, *E., His Life and Works* (2 vols., London, 1933); J. Porte, *E. and His Music* (London, 1933); A. Sheldon, *E. E.* (London, 1933); W. Reed, *E.* (London, 1939); W. Anderson, *Introduction to the Music of E.* (London, 1949); D. McVeagh, *E. E., His Life and Music* (London, 1955); P. Young, *E., O.M.* (London, 1955; new ed., 1973); M. Kennedy, *Portrait of E.* (London, 1968; 2d ed., rev., 1982); M. Hurd, *E.* (London, 1969); I. Parrott, *E.* (London, 1971); S. Mundy, *E.: His Life and Times* (Tunbridge Wells, 1980); G. Hodgkins, *Providence and Art: A Study of E.'s Religious Beliefs* (London, 1982); M. De-la-Noy, *E. the Man* (London, 1983); C. Redwood, ed., *An E. Companion* (Ashbourne, 1983); D. Bury, *E. and the Two Mezzos* (London, 1984); J. Northrop Moore, *Spirit of England: E. E. and His World* (London, 1984); R. Monk, ed., *E. Studies* (Aldershot, 1990); J. Northrop Moore, *E. E.: Letters of a Lifetime* (Oxford, 1990); C. Kent, *E. E.: A Guide to Research* (N.Y., 1993); R. Monk, ed., *E. E.: Music and Literature* (Aldershot, 1993); S. Craggs, *E. E.: A Source Book* (Aldershot, 1995); P. Young, *E., Newman and the Dream of Gerontius: In the Tradition of English Catholicism* (Brookfield, Vt., 1995).

Elias, Rosalind, American mezzo-soprano; b. Lowell, Mass., March 13, 1930. She began her training at the New England Cons. of Music in Boston; during her student days there, she sang Poppaea in *L'incoronazione di Poppea*, and also appeared with the Boston Sym. Orch.; she then studied at the Berkshire Music Center in Tanglewood. After singing with the New England Opera Co. (1948–52), she completed her training in Italy with Luigi Ricci and Nazareno de Angelis. Following engagements at Milan's La Scala and Naples's Teatro San Carlos, she made her Metropolitan Opera debut in New York as Grimgerde in *Die Walküre* on Feb. 23, 1954; she created roles there in Barber's *Vanessa* (Erika, 1958) and *Antony and Cleopatra* (Charmian, 1966), remaining on its roster for over 30 years. She also made guest appearances in Europe and toured as a concert artist. Among her other roles were Dorabella, Rosina, Cherubino, Giordano's Bersi, Carmen, and Octavian.

Eliasson, Anders, Swedish composer; b. Borlänge, April 3, 1947. He was a pupil of Ingvar Lidholm (composition) and Valdemar Söderholm (harmony and counterpoint) at the Stockholm Musikhögskolan (1966–72); he also studied with Ligeti. In 1983 he was awarded the Royal Swedish Academy of Music prize in Stockholm. His music reveals a searching exploration of new forms while retaining conventional compositional techniques. He composed *En av oss*, church opera (1974), and *Backanterna*, incidental music to Euripides (Swedish Radio, April 4, 1982).

Elizalde, Federico, Spanish conductor and composer; b. Manila, Philippines (of Spanish parents), Dec. 12, 1908; d. there, Jan. 16, 1979. He studied piano at the Madrid Cons. (1st prize, 1923), law at Stanford Univ., and composition with Ernest Bloch. In 1930 he became conductor of the Manila Sym. Orch. and in 1948 president of the Manila Radio. His works include *Paul Gauguin*, opera (1948).

Elizza, Elise (real name, **Elisabeth Letztergroschen**), Austrian soprano; b. Vienna, Jan. 6, 1870; d. there, June 3, 1926. She studied in Vienna with Adolf Limley, making her debut there at the Carl Theater in 1892 in Weinberger's operetta *Lachenden Erben*. She then made her operatic debut in 1894 in Olmütz. After further studies with Materna, she joined the Vienna Court Opera in 1895, where she sang until 1919. She retired in 1923. She was admired for her coloratura roles but she also had success as a Wagnerian.

Elkus, Jonathan (Britton), American conductor, pedagogue, and composer; b. San Francisco, Aug. 8, 1931. His father was the American composer and teacher Albert (Israel) Elkus (b. Sacramento, April 30, 1884; d. Oakland, Feb. 19, 1942). He studied composition with Cushing and Denny at the Univ. of Calif. in Berkeley (B.A., 1953), Ernst Bacon and L. Ratner at Stanford Univ. (M.A., 1957), and Milhaud at Mills College in Oakland, California (1957). He taught at Lehigh Univ. in Bethlehem, Pa. (1957–73), and also conducted its bands. After serving as director of music (1979–85) and chairman of the humanities dept. (1985–89) at Cape Cod Academy in Osterville, he was chairman of the history dept. at Stuart Hall School in Stauton (1989–92). In 1992 he became director of bands at the Univ. of Calif. at Davis. He publ. *Charles Ives and the American Band Tradition: A Centennial Tribute* (Exeter, England, 1974). He composed the operas *The Outcasts of Poker Flat* (1959; Bethlehem, Pa., April 16, 1960), *Medea* (1963; Milwaukee, Nov. 13, 1970), *The Mandarin* (N.Y., Oct. 26, 1967), and *Helen in Egypt* (Milwaukee, Nov. 13, 1970), and the musicals *Tom Sawyer* (San Francisco, May 22, 1953), *Treasure Island* (1961), and *A Little Princess* (1980); also incidental music.

Ellberg, Ernst (Henrik), Swedish composer and pedagogue; b. Söderhamm, Dec. 11, 1868; d. Stockholm, June 14, 1948. He studied with J. Lindberg (violin) and J. Dente (composition) at the Stockholm Cons. (1886–92), and then held a state composer's fellowship (1894–96). From 1887 to 1905 he was a violist in the Royal Orch. in Stockholm; he taught composition, counterpoint, and orchestration at the Stockholm Cons. (1904–33), and then taught military musicians there until 1943. In 1912 he was made a member of the Swedish Royal Academy of Music, and in 1916 he was granted the title of prof. Ellberg was an influential teacher. His music is steeped in the Romantic tradition. Among his compositions are the operas *Den röda liljan* (The Red Lily) and *Rassa*, and ballets.

Elleviou, (Pierre-) Jean (-Baptiste-François), notable French tenor; b. Rennes, June 14, 1769; d. Paris, May 5, 1842. He made his operatic debut as a baritone in Monsigny's *Le Déserteur* at the Comédie-Italienne in Paris in 1790. Turning to tenor roles, he made his first appearance there in Dalayrac's *Philippe et Georgette* in 1791. During the French Revolution, he was compelled to leave its roster but was able to return in 1797. In 1801 he became a leading member of the Paris Opéra Comique, where he won distinction in roles created especially for him by Grétry. He also created roles in operas by various other composers, including Méhul's Joseph (1807) and Boieldieu's Jean de Paris (1812). In 1813 he retired from the operatic stage. He wrote the libretto for Berton's *Délia et Verdikan* (1805).

BIBL.: E.-H.-P. de Curzon, *J. E.* (Paris, 1930).

Elling, Catharinus, Norwegian organist, composer, and writer on music; b. Christiania, Sept. 13, 1858; d. there (Oslo), Jan. 8, 1942. He studied in Christiania, Leipzig (1877–78), and with Herzogenberg at the Berlin Hochschule für Musik (1886–87). Returning to Christiania in 1896, he taught counterpoint and composition at the Cons. until 1908; he was also active as a choral conductor (1897–1901) and as a church organist (1909–26). In 1898 he received a government subvention to study Norwegian folk songs, which resulted in essays and books; he also wrote biographies of Bull, Grieg, Svendsen, and Kjerulf. He composed the opera *Kosakkerne* (The Cossacks; 1890–94) and also incidental music to plays.

BIBL.: Ø. Gaukstad, *Melodi- og tekstregister til C. E.s opptegnelser av folkemusikk* (Oslo, 1963).

Elliott, Paul, English tenor; b. Macclesfield, Cheshire, March 19, 1950. He was a choral scholar at Magdalen College, Oxford (1969–72), later pursuing his education at the Univ. of Oxford (B.A., 1973; M.A., 1977). His principal vocal teachers were David Johnston and Peter Pears. He served as vicar choral at St. Paul's Cathedral (1972–75) and sang with various choral and early music groups, including the John Alldis Choir (1972–76), the Deller Consort (1973–82), the Monteverdi Choir (1973–78), and the Academy of Ancient Music (from 1973); also was a founding member of the Hilliard Ensemble (1974–84) and the London Early Music Group (1976–79). From 1984 to 1989 he sang with the Newberry Consort in Chicago. He toured widely as a solo concert artist, and also sang in opera, scoring success as Handel's Acis in St. Gallen (1984) and as Mozart's Belmonte in Chicago (1988). In 1987 he joined the faculty of the Indiana Univ. School of Music in Bloomington, but continued to make appearances as a singer.

Ellis, Brent, American baritone; b. Kansas City, Mo., June 20, 1946. He studied with Edna Forsythe (1962–65), Marian Freschl (1965–71), and Daniel Ferro in New York (from 1971), where he also attended classes at the Juilliard School of Music (1965–67; 1970–72). In 1965 he made his first appearance at the Santa Fe Opera, where he later sang regularly (1972–82); he also appeared at the Houston Grand Opera (1972–81). In 1973 he won both the WGN Radio Auditions of the Air and the Montreal International Competition, and on April 28, 1974, made his N.Y. City Opera debut as Ottone in *L'incoronazione di Poppea*; then sang with the Chicago Lyric Opera (1974), the San Francisco Opera (1974–78), the Boston Opera (1975–83), the Glyndebourne Festival (1977–78), the Hamburg State Opera (1977–79), and the Vienna State Opera (1977–79). On Oct. 25, 1979, he made his Metropolitan Opera debut in New York as Silvio in *Pagliacci*. From 1984 he sang at the Cologne Opera. In 1989 he made his first appearance at London's Covent Garden as Rigoletto. He sang Amonasro in Seattle in 1992. In 1996 he portrayed Dandini in *La Cenerentola* in Toronto.

Elmendorff, Karl (Eduard Maria), eminent German conductor; b. Düsseldorf, Oct. 25, 1891; d. Hofheim am Taunus, Oct. 21, 1962. He was a student of Steinbach and Abendroth at the Cologne Hochschule für Musik. After conducting opera in Düsseldorf, Mainz, Hagen, and Aachen, he held the post of 1st conductor at the Berlin State Opera and the Bavarian State Opera in Munich (from 1925). He won distinction as a conductor at the Bayreuth Festivals (1927–42); he also was Generalmusikdirektor in Kassel and Wiesbaden (1932–35), and then conducted in Mannheim (1935–42), at the Berlin State Opera (1937–45), and at the Dresden State Opera (1942–45); he subsequently was Generalmusikdirektor in Kassel (1948–51) and Wiesbaden (1951–56). Elmendorff was greatly esteemed as a Wagnerian.

Elming, Poul, Danish tenor; b. Ålborg, July 21, 1949. He studied at the Alborg Cons. and the Århus Cons., and was a student in Wiesbaden of Paul Lohmann. In 1979 he joined the Jutland Opera in Århus, where he began his career singing baritone roles. He became a member of the Royal Opera in Copenhagen in 1984. Following further training with Susanna Eken in Copenhagen and Oren Brown in New York, he returned to the Royal Opera in 1989 to make his tenor debut as Parsifal. In 1990 he made his first appearance at the Bayreuth Festival as Siegmund, which role he then sang at London's Covent Garden in 1991. He sang Parsifal at the Berlin State Opera in 1992, and returned there in 1993 as Lohengrin and in 1995 as Parsifal. As a guest artist, he sang with many European opera houses. He also was active as a recitalist and concert artist. Among his other roles were Erik in *Der fliegende Holländer* and Max in *Der Freischütz*.

Elmo, Cloe, Italian mezzo-soprano; b. Lecce, April 9, 1910; d. Ankara, May 24, 1962. She was a pupil of Chibaudo at the Accademia di Santa Cecilia in Rome; after winning the Vienna singing competition (1932), she pursued training with Rinolfi and Pedrini. In 1934 she made her operatic debut as Santuzza in Cagliara, and then was a valued member of Milan's La Scala (1936–43). On Nov. 14, 1947, she made her Metropolitan Opera debut in New York as Azucena, remaining on its roster until 1949. From 1951 to 1954 she again sang at La Scala, and then taught voice at the Ankara Cons. Her repertoire included both standard and contemporary roles in Italian operas.

Elmore, Robert Hall, American organist, teacher, and composer; b. Ramapatnam, India (of American parents), Jan. 2, 1913; d. Ardmore, Pa., Sept. 22, 1985. He studied with Pietro Yon (organ) and Harl McDonald (composition), at the Royal Academy of Music in London (licentiate, 1933), and at the Univ. of Pa. (B.Mus., 1937). He taught organ at Philadelphia's Clarke Cons. of Music (1936–53) and Musical Academy (from 1939), and composition at the Univ. of Pa. (from 1940); he also was organist at various churches. His *It Began at Breakfast* (Philadelphia, Feb. 8, 1941) was the first televised opera by an American composer.

Elsner, Joseph (Anton Franciskus) (also **Józef Antoni Franciszek**), noted Polish pedagogue and composer of German descent; b. Grottkau, Silesia, June 1, 1769; d. Warsaw, April 18, 1854. After singing in the local church choir, he studied at the Breslau Jesuit Gymnasium (1781–88), concurrently singing in the opera chorus, playing violin in chamber music concerts, and beginning to compose. After studying theology and medicine at the Univ. of Breslau and the Univ. of Vienna (1789), he turned decisively to music. He was concertmaster of the Brünn Opera orch. (1791–92) and Kapellmeister in Lemberg (1792–99), then settled in Warsaw, where he served as director of the Opera for 25 years; he was also active as a teacher (Chopin was his most famous student) and founded several music schools, one of which later became the Warsaw Cons. In 1823 he was awarded the Order of St. Stanislaw. His compositions presage the development of the Polish national school.

WRITINGS: *Poczstki muzyki a szczególniej śpiewania* (The Beginnings of Music, Especially of Singing; Warsaw, 1818–21); *Szkola śpiewu* (School of Singing; Warsaw, 1834; 2d ed., Leipzig, 1855); *Sumarius moich utworów z objaśnieniami o czynnościach i dzialaniach moich jako artysty muzycznego* (Summary of My Works with Explanations of My Functions and Activities as a Musician; 1840–49; Kraków, 1957).

WORKS (all 1st perf. in Warsaw unless otherwise given): OPERAS: *Amazonki czyli Herminia* (The Amazons, or Herminia; Lemberg, July 26, 1797); *Sultan Wampum czyli Nieroztropne zyczenie* (Sultan Vampum, or The Rash Wish; 1800); *Siedem razy jeden* (7 Times 1; Dec. 14, 1804); *Stary trzpiot i mlody mdrzec* (The Old Dolt and the Young Sage; Feb. 15, 1805); *Wiezczka Urzella czyli To co sie damom podoba* (The Soothsayer Urzella, or What Pleases the Ladies; March 7, 1806); *Andromeda* (Jan. 14, 1807); *Chimère et réalité or Urojenie i rzeczywistość* (April 22, 1808); *Leszek Bialy czyli Czarownica z-Lysej Góry* (Leszek the White or The Witch of the Bald Mountain; Dec. 2, 1809); *Wawozy Sierra Modena* (The Ravines of the Sierra Modena; Jan. 31, 1812); *Kabalista* (The Cabalist; Jan. 29, 1813); *Król Lokietek czyli Wiśliczanki* (King Lokietek, or The Women of Wislica; April 3, 1818); *Jagiello w Tenczynie* (Jagiello in Tenczyn; Jan. 1, 1820). Also melodramas, duodramas, 4 oratorios, and ballets.

BIBL.: J. Reiss, *Ślaszak Józef E.: Nauczyciel Chopina* (Silesian J. E.: Chopin's Teacher; Katowice, 1936); A. Nowak-Romanowicz, *Józef E.* (Kraków, 1957).

Elson, Arthur, American writer on music; b. Boston, Nov. 18, 1873; d. N.Y., Feb. 24, 1940. He was the son of the American music historian Louis Elson (b. Boston, April 17, 1848; d. there, Feb. 14, 1920). After training from his father, he studied at the New England Cons. of Music in Boston, Harvard Univ. (graduated, 1895), and the Mass. Inst. of Technology (graduated, 1897). He served as music critic of the *Boston Advertiser* (from 1920). Among his numerous books was *A Critical History of the Opera* (1901; new ed., 1926, as *A History of Opera*).

Elston, Arnold, American composer; b. N.Y., Sept. 30, 1907; d. Vienna, June 6, 1971. He studied harmony and counterpoint with Goldmark in New York and took courses at City College (B.A.,

1930) and Columbia Univ. (M.A., 1932); after composition studies with Webern in Vienna (1932–35), he continued his training at Harvard Univ. (Ph.D., 1939), while concurrently studying conducting with Fiedler in Boston (1939). He taught at the Longy School of Music in Cambridge, Mass. (1939–40), the Univ. of Oregon (1941–58), and the Univ. of Calif. at Berkeley (1958–71). He wrote the books *Music and Medicine* (1948) and *A Modern Guide to Symphonic Music* (1966). Among his compositions is the chamber opera *Sweeney Agonistes* (1948–50) and the opera *The Love of Don Perlimplin* (1957–58).

Elvira, Pablo, Puerto Rican baritone; b. Santurce, Sept. 24, 1937. He studied voice at the Puerto Rico Cons., becoming a finalist in the Metropolitan Opera auditions in 1966. He taught at the Indiana Univ. School of Music in Bloomington (1966–74), where he made his formal debut as Rigoletto (1968). On Feb. 23, 1974, he made his first appearance at the N.Y. City Opera as Germont, where he sang regularly in subsequent seasons. He made his Metropolitan Opera debut in New York as Rigoletto on March 22, 1978. In 1985 he sang Germont at the Lyric Opera in Chicago, and in 1989 he was engaged as Sharpless at the Pittsburgh Opera. He appeared in the gala opening performance of the restored Detroit Opera House in 1996. In addition to his operatic engagements, he also sang frequently in concert. Among his finest roles were Rossini's Figaro, Don Carlos, Renato, Leoncavallo's Tonio, and Puccini's Lescaut.

Elwart, Antoine (-Aimable-Élie), French writer on music and composer; b. Paris, Nov. 18, 1808; d. there, Oct. 14, 1877. A chorister at St.-Eustache when 10 years old, he was apprenticed at 13 to a mechanic, but ran away, and joined a small theater orch. as a violinist. From 1825 to 1834 he studied at the Paris Cons., taking the Grand Prix de Rome in 1834. He taught at the Paris Cons. from 1836 to 1871, numbering among his pupils Gouvy, Grisar, and Weckerlin. His compositions include *Les Catalans*, opera (Rouen, 1840), *Noé, ou Le Déluge universel*, "oratorio symphonie" (Paris, 1845), *La Naissance d'Eve*, oratorio (Paris, 1846), and *Les Noces de Cana*, mystery (1853). He publ. various theoretical and vocal studies.

Elwes, Gervase (Cary), noted English tenor; b. Billing Hall, near Northampton, Nov. 15, 1866; d. Boston, Jan. 12, 1921. He began his career as a diplomat, and, while stationed in Vienna (1891–95), he studied singing. During his sojourn in Paris he took voice lessons with Bouhy, and soon achieved competence as a concert singer. He made a tour of Germany in 1907 and 2 tours in the United States (1909 and 1921; he died on his 2d tour, killed by a train in the railroad station in Boston). He excelled in oratorio, singing Elgar's *Dream of Gerontius* about 150 times. Winifred and Richard Elwes publ. an impassioned family monograph, *Gervase Elwes: The Story of His Life* (London, 1935).

Emmanuel, (Marie François) Maurice, eminent French music scholar, pedagogue, and composer; b. Bar-sur-Aube, May 2, 1862; d. Paris, Dec. 14, 1938. He received his primary education in Dijon; then studied at the Paris Cons. (1880–87) with Savard, Dubois, Delibes, and Bourgault-Ducoudray, then specialized in the musical history of antiquity under Gevaert in Brussels; he also studied ancient languages at the Sorbonne in Paris, becoming a licencié ès lettres (1887) and a docteur ès lettres (1895) with the theses *De saltationis disciplina apud Graecos* (publ. in Latin, Paris, 1895) and *La Danse grecque antique d'après les monuments figurés* (Paris, 1896; Eng. tr., 1916, as *The Antique Greek Dance after Sculptured and Painted Figures*), completing his study of composition with Guiraud. He was a prof. of art history at the Lycée Racine and Lycée Lamartine (1898–1905) and maître de chapelle at Ste.-Clotilde (1904–07); in 1909 he succeeded Bourgault-Ducoudray as prof. of music history at the Paris Cons., and held this post until 1936. Among his numerous writings was *Pelléas et Mélisande de Claude Debussy* (Paris, 1926; 2d ed., 1950). He composed several works for the stage, including *Pierrot Peintre*, pantomime (1886), *Prométhée enchaîné,* opera (1916–18), *Salamine*, opera (1921–23; 1927–28; Paris, June 28, 1929), and *Amphitryon*, opéra bouffe (1936; Paris, Feb. 20, 1937).

Encina, Juan del, Spanish poet, dramatist, and composer; b. Salamanca, July 12, 1468; d. León, late 1529 or 1530. He was the son of a shoemaker of Salamanca named Juan de Fermoselle. He became a chorister at Salamanca Cathedral, and studied music under his elder brother, Diego de Fermoselle, and under Fernando de Torrijos. He took his law degree at Salamanca Univ., where he enjoyed the favor of the chancellor, Don Gutiérrez de Toledo. In 1492 he entered the household of the 2d duke of Alba, for whom he wrote a series of pastoral eclogues that form the foundation of the Spanish secular drama. These eclogues included "villancicos," or rustic songs, for which Encina composed the music. He went to Rome in 1500; on May 12, 1500, he was appointed canon at the Cathedral of Salamanca; from Feb. 2, 1510, until 1512, he was archdeacon and canon of Málaga; on May 2, 1512, he again went to Rome, where his *Farsa de Plácida e Vittoriano* was performed in the presence of Pope Julius II on Jan. 11, 1513. In 1517, he was "subcollector of revenues to the Apostolic Chamber." In 1519 he was appointed prior of León, and that same year made a pilgrimage to Jerusalem, where he was ordained a priest. He described his sacred pilgrimage in *Tribagia o Via Sacra de Hierusalem* (Rome, 1521). After the death of Pope Leo X in 1521, Encina returned to Spain and spent his last years as prior at León. Besides being a leading figure in the development of the Spanish drama, Encina was the most important Spanish composer of the reign of Ferdinand and Isabella; he cultivated with notable artistry a type of part-song akin to the Italian "frottola," setting his own poems to music. Some 62 works are found in H. Anglès, ed., *La música en la corte de los Reyes Catolicos: Cancionero de Palacio*, in Monumentos de la Música Española, V, X, and XIV (1947–65). Another modern ed. was publ. by C. Terni, *Juan del Encina: L'opera musicale* (Florence, 1974-).

Enesco, Georges (real name, **George Enescu**), famous Romanian violinist, conductor, teacher, and composer; b. Liveni-Virnav, Aug. 19, 1881; d. Paris, May 4, 1955. He began to play the piano when he was 4, taking lessons with a Gypsy violinist, Nicolas Chioru, and began composing when he was 5; he then studied with Caudella in Iaşi. On Aug. 5, 1889, he made his formal debut as a violinist in Slânic, Moldavia. In the meantime, he had enrolled in the Cons. of the Gesellschaft der Musikfreunde in Vienna (1888), where he studied violin with S. Bachrich, J. Grün, and J. Hellmesberger Jr.; piano with L. Ernst; harmony, counterpoint, and composition with R. Fuchs; chamber music with J. Hellmesberger Sr.; and music history with A. Prosnitz, winning 1st prizes in violin and harmony (1892). After his graduation (1894), he entered the Paris Cons., where he studied violin with Marsick and J. White, harmony with Dubois and Thomas, counterpoint with Gédalge, composition with Fauré and Massenet, and early music with Diémer, winning 2d accessit for counterpoint and fugue (1897) and graduating with the premier prix for violin (1899). At the same time, he also studied cello, organ, and piano, attaining more than ordinary proficiency on each. On June 11, 1897, he presented in Paris a concert of his works, which attracted the attention of Colonne, who brought out the youthful composer's op. 1, *Poème roumain*, the next year. Enesco also launched his conducting career in Bucharest in 1898. In 1902 he first appeared as a violinist in Berlin and also organized a piano trio; in 1904 he formed a quartet. On March 8, 1903, he conducted the premiere of his 2 *Romanian Rhapsodies* in Bucharest, the first of which was to become his most celebrated work. He soon was appointed court violinist to the queen of Romania. In 1912 he established an annual prize for Romanian composers, which was subsequently won by Jora, Enacovici, Golestan, Otescu, and others. In 1917 he founded the George Enescu sym. concerts in Iaşi. After the end of World War I, he made major tours as a violinist and conductor; he also taught violin in Paris, where his pupils included Menuhin, Grumiaux, Gitlis, and Ferras. He made his U.S. debut in the triple role of conductor, violinist, and composer with the Philadelphia Orch. in New York on Jan. 2, 1923; he returned to conduct the N.Y. Phil. on Jan. 28, 1937. He led several subsequent concerts with it with remarkable success; led it in 14 concerts in 1938, and also appeared twice as a violinist; he conducted 2 concerts at the N.Y. World's Fair in 1939. The outbreak of World War II found him in Romania, where he lived on his farm in Sinaia, near Bucharest. He visited New York again in 1946 as a teacher. On Jan. 21, 1950, during the 60th anniversary season of his debut as a violinist, he gave a farewell concert with the N.Y. Phil. in the multiple capacity of violinist, pianist, conductor, and composer, in a program comprising Bach's Double Concerto (with Menuhin), a violin sonata (playing the piano part with Menuhin), and his 1st *Romanian Rhapsody* (conducting the orch.). He then returned to Paris, where his last years were marked by near poverty and poor health. In July 1954 he suffered a stroke and remained an invalid for his remaining days.

Although Enesco severed relations with his communist homeland, the Romanian government paid homage to him for his varied accomplishments. His native village, a street in Bucharest, and the State Phil. of Bucharest were named in his honor. Periodical Enesco festivals and international performing competitions were established in Bucharest in 1958. Enesco had an extraordinary range of musical interests. His compositions include artistic stylizations of Romanian folk strains; while his style was neo-Romantic, he made occasional use of experimental devices, such as quarter tones in his only opera, *Oedipe,* op. 23 (1921–31; Paris, March 10, 1936). He also composed about 25 songs, many to words by the queen of Romania, who wrote poetry in German under the pen name Carmen Sylva. He possessed a fabulous memory and was able to perform innumerable works without scores. He not only distinguished himself as a violinist and conductor, but he was also a fine pianist and a gifted teacher.

BIBL. (all publ. in Bucharest unless otherwise given): M. Costin, *G. E.* (1938); V. Cheorghiu, *Un muzician genial: G. E.* (1944); F. Brulez, *G. E.* (1947); B. Gavoty, *Yehudi Menuhin—G. E.* (Geneva, 1955); A. Tudor, *E.* (1956); L. Voiculescu, *G. E. i opera şa Oedip* (1956); A. Tudor, *G. E.: Viaţâ in imagini* (1959; French tr., 1961); *G. E. on the 80th Anniversary of His Birth* (1961); G. Bălan, *G. E.: Mesajul—estetica* (1962); idem, *E.* (1963; German tr., 1964); F. Foni, *N. Missir, M. Voicana, and E. Zottoviceanu, G. E.* (1964); B. Kotlyarov, *G. E.* (Moscow, 1965); E. Ciomac, *E.* (1968); M. Voicana et al., eds., *G. E.: Monografie* (2 vols., 1971); R. Draghici, *G. E.* (Bacau, 1973); M. Voicana, ed., *Enesciana*, 1 (1976; in French, German, and Eng.); A Cosmovici, *G. E. în lumea muzicii şi în familie* (1990); N. Malcolm, *G. E.: His Life and Music* (London, 1990); V. Cosma, *G.E.: Cronica unei vieţi zbuciumstei* (1991).

Engel, Lehman, American conductor, composer, and writer on music; b. Jackson, Miss., Sept. 14, 1910; d. N.Y., Aug. 29, 1982. He attended the Univ. of Cincinnati and studied composition at the Cincinnati Cons. of Music (1927–29) before completing his training in New York with Goldmark at the Juilliard Graduate School (1930–34) and with Sessions (1931–37). After conducting his own Lehman Engel Singers and the Madrigal Singers (1935–39), he concentrated on conducting and composing for the serious and popular N.Y. theater.

WORKS: DRAMATIC: OPERAS: *The Pierrot of the Minuet* (1927; Cincinnati, April 3, 1928); *Malady of Love* (N.Y., May 27, 1954); *The Soldier* (1955; concert perf., N.Y., Nov. 25, 1956). MUSICAL COMEDIES: *Golden Ladder* (Cleveland, May 28, 1953); *Serena* (1956). BALLETS: *Ceremonials* (1932; N.Y., May 13, 1933); *Phobias* (N.Y., Nov. 18, 1932); *Ekstasis* (1933); *Transitions* (N.Y., Feb. 19, 1934); *Imperial Gesture* (1935); *Marching Song* (1935); *Traditions* (1938); *The Shoe Bird* (1967; Jackson, Miss., April 20, 1968). Also incidental music to over 50 plays.

Engelmann, Hans Ulrich, German composer and pedagogue; b. Darmstadt, Sept. 8, 1921. He had piano lessons while in high school; he then took courses in composition with Fortner in Heidelberg (1945–49); from 1948 to 1950 he attended the classes of Leibowitz and Krenek in Darmstadt; also enrolled at the Univ. of Frankfurt am Main (1946–52), taking classes in musicology (with Gennrich and Osthoff) and philosophy (with Adorno). In 1952 he received his Ph.D. there with a diss. on Bartók's *Mikrokosmos* (publ. in Würzburg, 1953). In 1949 he held a Harvard Univ. stipend at the Salzburg Seminar in American Studies; was active in radio programming and in composition for films and for the theater in Iceland (1953–54), and then was theater composer in Darmstadt (1954–61). In 1969 he was appointed an instructor at the Frankfurt am Main Hochschule für Musik. His early works are impregnated by chromaticism with an impressionistic tinge. He adopted the 12-tone method of composition, expanding it into a sui generis "field technique" of total serialism, in which rhythms and instrumental timbres are organized systematically. In his theater music, he utilizes aleatory devices, *musique concrète*, and electronic sonorities.

WORKS: DRAMATIC: *Ballet colore* (1948); *Doktor Fausts Hollenfahrt*, chamber opera (1949–50; North German Radio, Hamburg, Jan. 11, 1951); *Noche de luna*, ballet (1958); *Operette*, music theater (1959); *Verlorener Schatten*, opera (1960); *Serpentina*, ballet (1962–63); *Der Fall Van Damm*, opera (1966–67; Westdeutscher Rundfunk, Cologne, June 7, 1968); *Ophelia*, multimedia theater piece (Hannover, Feb. 1, 1969); *Revue*, music theater piece (1972–73); much incidental music.

BIBL.: K. Carius et al., *Commedia humana: H. U. E. und sein Werk* (Wiesbaden, 1985).

English, Granville, American composer; b. Louisville, Jan. 27, 1895; d. N.Y., Sept. 1, 1968. He studied with Borowski, Reuter, and Gunn at the Chicago Musical College (B.M., 1915), and with Boulanger, Haubiel, Riegger, and Serly. He taught in Chicago and N.Y., and in 1961 was composer-in-residence at Baylor Univ. He composed the folk opera *Wide, Wide River* and the ballet *Sea Drift*.

Enna, August (Emil), eminent Danish composer; b. Nakskov, May 13, 1859; d. Copenhagen, Aug. 3, 1939. He was taken to Copenhagen as a child, and learned to play piano and violin; he had sporadic instruction in theory; he later became a member of a traveling orch. and played with it in Finland (1880). Upon his return to Copenhagen, he taught piano and played for dancers; in 1883 he became music director of Werner's Theatrical Soc. and wrote his first stage work, *A Village Tale*, which he produced the same year. After these practical experiences, he began to study seriously; he took lessons with Schjorring (violin), Matthesson (organ), and Rasmussen (composition) and soon publ. a number of piano pieces, which attracted the attention of Gade, who used his influence to obtain a traveling fellowship for Enna; this made it possible for Enna to study in Germany (1888–89) and acquire a complete mastery of instrumental and vocal writing. He followed the German Romantic school, being influenced mainly by Weber's type of opera, and by Grieg and Gade in the use of local color; the first product of this period was his most successful work, the opera *Heksen* (The Witch), premiered in Copenhagen (Jan. 24, 1892), then in Germany.

WORKS (all 1st perf. in Copenhagen unless otherwise given): DRAMATIC: OPERAS: *Agleia* (1884); *Heksen* (The Witch; Jan. 24, 1892); *Kleopatra* (Feb. 7, 1894); *Aucassin og Nicolette* (Feb. 2, 1896); *Den lille pige med svovlstikkerne* (The Match Girl; Nov. 13, 1897); *Lamia* (Antwerp, Oct. 3, 1899); *Ung Elskov* (as *Heisse Liebe*, Weimar, Dec. 6, 1904); *Prinsessen paa aerten* (Princess and the Pea; Århus, Sept. 15, 1900); *Nattergallen* (The Nightingale; Nov. 10, 1912); *Gloria Arsena* (April 15, 1917); *Brnene fra Santa Fé* (The Children from Santa Fé; March 16, 1918); *Komedianter* (Comedians; April 8, 1920); *Don Juan Mañara* (April 17, 1925); *Afrodites praestinde* (Aphrodite's Priestess; 1925); *Ghettoens dronning* (The Queen of the Ghetto; 1932). BALLETS: *The Shepherdess and the Chimney Sweep* (Oct. 6, 1901); *St. Cecilia's Golden Shoe* (Dec. 26, 1904); *The Kiss* (Oct. 19, 1927).

Eötvös, Peter, Hungarian conductor and composer; b. Székelyudvarhely, Jan. 2, 1944. He studied composition with Pál Kardos at the Budapest Academy of Music (1958–65) and conducting at the Cologne Hochschule für Musik (1966–68). From 1966 he worked closely with Stockhausen, and was also associated with the electronic music studio of Cologne's West German Radio (1971–79). From 1974 he appeared as a guest conductor in contemporary programs with major European orchs. He became music director of the Ensemble InterContemporain in Paris in 1979, a position he held until 1992. He also was principal guest conductor of the BBC Sym. Orch. in London (1985–88). In 1992 he was named a prof. and director of the new music ensembles at the Karlsruhe Hochschule für Musik. In 1994 he became co-principal conductor (with Ton Koopman) of the Netherlands Radio Chamber Orch. in Hilversum. Among his compositions are the comedy madrigals *Moro Lasso*, for 5 Soloists (1963; rev. version, 1972; Witten, April 28, 1974), and *Hochzeitsmadrigal*, for 6 Soloists (1963; rev. version, 1976; Metz, Nov. 20, 1976), and the opera *Trois Soeurs* (Lyons, March 13, 1998).

Eppert, Carl, American composer and conductor; b. Carbon, Ind., Nov. 5, 1882; d. Milwaukee, Oct. 1, 1961. He studied with Harris and Wells at the American Cons. in Chicago, and then with Kaun, Nikisch, and Kunwald in Berlin (1907–14). After conducting the Seattle Grand Opera, he led the Milwaukee Civic Orch. (1921–26) and was head of the theory and composition dept. at the Wisconsin Cons. in Milwaukee (1921–23). Among his compositions is the opera *Kaintuckee* (1915).

Equiluz, Kurt, esteemed Austrian tenor and teacher; b. Vienna, June 13, 1929. He received instruction in piano and violin as a child, and was a member of the Vienna Boys Choir (from 1939). In 1944 he entered the Vienna Academy of Music, where he studied with Hubert Jelinek (harp), Adolf Vogel (voice), and Ferdinand Grossmann (choral conducting). He then was a member of the Vienna Academy Chamber Choir (1946–51), and in 1949 won the Vienna Mozart Competition. In 1950 he joined the Vienna State Opera chorus, making his debut as a solo artist in 1957 and subsequently singing roles in operas by Mozart, Beethoven, and Strauss. However, it was as an oratorio and lieder artist that he acquired an international reputation, excelling particularly in the works of Bach. In 1980 he was made an Austrian Kammersänger. In 1964 he joined the faculty of the Graz Hochschule für Musik, and in 1981 the faculty of the Vienna Hochschule für Musik.

Erb, Karl, noted German tenor; b. Ravensburg, July 13, 1877; d. there, July 13, 1958. He was self-taught. He made his debut in Stuttgart in 1907, then sang in Lübeck (1908–10), Stuttgart (1910–13), and Munich (1913–25); he later embarked on a series of appearances as a concert and oratorio singer. He was best known for his portrayal of roles in the works of Mozart; he created the title role in Pfitzner's *Palestrina* (1917). From 1921 to 1932 he was married to **Maria Ivogün**.

Erbse, Heimo, German composer; b. Rudolstadt, Thuringia, Feb. 27, 1924. He studied in Weimar, and in Berlin with Boris Blacher; in 1957 he moved to Salzburg. In his catalog of works is *Julietta*, opera semi-seria (Salzburg, Aug. 17, 1959) and *Der Herr in Grau*, comic opera (1966).

Erede, Alberto, Italian conductor; b. Genoa, Nov. 8, 1908. After training in Genoa and at the Milan Cons., he studied conducting with Weingartner in Basel (1929–31) and Busch in Dresden (1930). In 1930 he made his debut at the Accademia di Santa Cecilia in Rome, then was on the staff of the Glyndebourne Festival (1934–39); he also conducted the Salzburg Opera Guild (1935–38). In 1937 he made his U.S. debut with the NBC Sym. Orch. in New York. After serving as chief conductor of the RAI Orch. in Turin (1945–46), he was music director of the New London Opera Co. (1946–48). On Nov. 11, 1950, he made his Metropolitan Opera debut in New York conducting *La Traviata*, remaining on its roster until 1955; he conducted there again in 1974. He was Generalmusikdirektor of the Deutsche Oper am Rhein in Düsseldorf (1958–62). In 1968 he conducted *Lohengrin* at the Bayreuth Festival. He subsequently was active as a guest conductor in Europe, and in 1975 became artistic director of the Paganini Competition in Genoa.

Erkel, Franz (Ferenc), distinguished Hungarian pianist, conductor, composer, and pedagogue; b. Gyula, Nov. 7, 1810; d. Budapest, June 15, 1893. He studied in Bratislava at the Benedictine Gymnasium (1822–25) and with Heinrich Klein, then went to Klausenburg, where he began his career as a pianist and became conductor of the Kaschau opera troupe (1834), with which he traveled to Buda (1835). He became conductor of the German Municipal Theater in Pest in 1836; in 1838 he was made music director of the newly founded National Theater, an influential post he held until 1874. He was conductor at the Opera House from 1884, and also founded the Phil. concerts (1853), which he conducted until 1871. He was the first prof. of piano and instrumentation at the Academy of Music, serving as its director from 1875 to 1888. He gave his farewell performance as a pianist in 1890 and as a conductor in 1892. Erkel was one of the most significant Hungarian musicians of his era. After successfully producing his opera *Báthory Mária* (1840), he gained lasting fame in his homeland with the opera *Hunyady László* (1844), which is recognized as the first truly national Hungarian work for the theater. He composed the Hungarian national anthem in 1844. He later achieved extraordinary success with the opera *Bánk-Bán* (1861), written in collaboration with his sons Gyula (b. Pest, July 4, 1842; d. Ujpest, March 22, 1909) and Sandor (b. Pest, Jan. 2, 1846; d. Bekescsaba, Oct. 14, 1900). He also collaborated with his other sons, Elek (b. Pest, Nov. 2, 1843; d. Budapest, June 10, 1893) and László (b. Pest, April 9, 1844; d. Bratislava, Dec. 3, 1896), who were successful musicians. A catalog of his works was publ. by E. Major (Budapest, 1947; 2d ed., rev., 1967).

WORKS: OPERAS: *Báthory Mária* (Pest, Aug. 8, 1840); *Hunyady László* (Pest, Jan. 27, 1844); *Erzsébet* (Pest, May 6, 1857; in collaboration with Franz and Karl Doppler); *Bánk-Bán* (Pest, March 9, 1861; orchestrated with Gyula and Sandor Erkel); *Sarolta*, comic opera (Pest, June 26, 1862; mainly orchestrated by Gyula Erkel); *Dózsa György* (Pest, April 6, 1867; in collaboration with Gyula and Sandor Erkel); *Brankovics György* (Budapest, May 20, 1874; in collaboration with Gyula and Sandor Erkel); *Névtelen hösök* (Budapest, Nov. 30, 1880; in collaboration with Gyula, Sandor, Elek, and László Erkel); *István király* (Budapest, March 14, 1885; generally believed to be principally the work of Gyula Erkel); *Sakk-játék*, ballet (Pest, Feb. 2, 1853; not extant). Also incidental music.

BIBL.: K. Abrányi, *Erkel Franz* (Budapest, 1895); F. Scherer, *Erkel Franz* (Gyula, 1944); A. Németh, *Erkel Ferenc* (Budapest, 1967); D. Legány, *Erkel Ferenc müvei* (Works of Ferenc E.; Budapest, 1974).

d'Erlanger, Baron Frédéric, French-born English composer; b. Paris, May 29, 1868; d. London, April 23, 1943. He was born into the family of French bankers. He studied music with Ehmant in Paris, then settled in London, where he was active as a banker and a composer. In 1897 he assumed the pseudonym Regnal, formed by reading backward the last 6 letters of his name. He composed the operas *Jehan de Saintre* (Aix-les-Bains, Aug. 1, 1893), *Inez Mendo* (London, July 10, 1897), *Tess* (Naples, April 10, 1906), and *Noël* (Paris, Dec. 28, 1910), and the ballet *Les cent baisers* (London, 1935).

Erlanger, Camille, French composer; b. Paris, May 25, 1863; d. there, April 24, 1919. He was a pupil of the Paris Cons. under Delibes, Durand, and Matthias. In 1888 he took the Grand Prix de Rome for his cantata *Velléda*. He earned fame with his opera *Le Juif polonais* (Paris, April 11, 1900). His other operas are *Kermaria* (Paris, Feb. 8, 1897), *Le Fils de l'étoile* (Paris, April 20, 1904), *Aphrodite* (Paris, March 27, 1906), *Bacchus triomphant* (Bordeaux, Sept. 11, 1909), *L'Aube rouge* (Rouen, Dec. 29, 1911), *La Sorcière* (Paris, Dec. 18, 1912), *Le Barbier de Deauville* (1917), and *Forfaiture* (Paris, 1921).

Ermler, Mark, Russian conductor; b. Leningrad, May 5, 1932. He studied with Khaiken and Rabinovich at the Leningrad Cons., graduating in 1956. In 1952 he made his debut with the Leningrad Phil., and in 1953 his debut as an opera conductor with *Die Entführung aus dem Serail* in Leningrad. From 1956 he was on the conducting staff of the Bolshoi Theater in Moscow, where he led a vast operatic and ballet repertoire; he also appeared with the company on its tours to Montreal (1967), Paris and Tokyo (1970), Milan (1974), New York and Washington, D.C. (1975), Berlin (1980), and other major music centers. As a guest conductor, he appeared throughout Europe, North America, and Japan.

Ernster, Deszö, Hungarian bass; b. Pécs, Nov. 23, 1898; d. Zürich, Feb. 15, 1981. He studied in Budapest and Vienna; then sang in Plauen, Gera, and Düsseldorf; in 1929 he appeared at the Berlin State Opera, in 1931 at the Bayreuth Festival, and in 1933 at the Vienna State Opera; he then was a member of the Graz City Theater (1935–36). He made his first visit to the United States during the 1938–39 season, when he sang in New York with the Salzburg Opera Guild. During World War II, he was interned in a concentration camp. On Nov. 20, 1946, he made his Metropolitan Opera debut in New York as Marke in *Tristan und Isolde*; remained on its roster until 1964; was also a member of the Deutsche Oper am Rhein in Düsseldorf (1950–67).

BIBL.: J. Fábián, *E.* (Budapest, 1969).

Errani, Achille, Italian tenor and vocal pedagogue; b. Faenza, Aug. 1823; d. N.Y., Jan. 6, 1897. He was trained by Vaccai at the Milan Cons. After appearances throughout Italy, Spain, and Greece, he joined Maretzek's Italian Opera Co. in Havana in 1858. In 1860 he made his U.S. debut as Verdi's Alfredo in Philadelphia, and toured widely with Maretzek's company until the end of the Civil War, when he settled in New York as a teacher. Among his many students were Emma Abbott, Minnie Hauk, Clara Louise Kellogg, and Emma Thursby. His death from a heart attack followed a suicide-murder attempt involving a domestic in his household and her lover.

Ershov, Ivan (Vasilievich), celebrated Russian tenor; b. Maly Nesvetai, near Novocherkassk, Nov. 20, 1867; d. Tashkent, Nov. 21, 1943. He studied voice in Moscow with Alexandrova-Kochetova and in St. Petersburg with Gabel and Paleček. In 1893 he made his operatic debut at the Maryinsky Theater in St. Petersburg as Faust, which became one of his most popular roles; he then went to Italy and took voice lessons with Rossi in Milan; he appeared in Turin as Don José in *Carmen*. He returned to Russia in 1894 and joined the Kharkov Opera; in 1895 he became a member of the Maryinsky Opera Theater in St. Petersburg, and served with it until 1929. He achieved fabulous success as the greatest performer of the tenor roles in the Russian repertoire, and he also was regarded by music critics and audiences as the finest interpreter of the Wagnerian operas; he sang Siegfried, Tannhäuser, Lohengrin, and Tristan with extraordinary lyric and dramatic penetration; as an opera tenor in his time, he had no rivals on the Russian stage. In 1929, at the age of 62, he sang Verdi's Otello; he also appeared in oratorio and solo recitals. From 1916 to 1941 he taught voice at the Petrograd (Leningrad) Cons. At the beginning of the siege of Leningrad in 1941, Ershov was evacuated with the entire personnel of the Cons. to Tashkent in Central Asia, where he died shortly afterward.

BIBL.: V. Bogdanov-Berezovsky, *I. E.* (Leningrad, 1951).

Eschenbach (real name, **Ringmann**), **Christoph,** remarkably talented German pianist and conductor; b. Breslau, Feb. 20, 1940. His mother died in childbirth; his father, the musicologist Heribert Ringmann, lost his life in battle soon thereafter; his grandmother died while attempting to remove him from the advancing Allied armies; placed in a refugee camp, he was rescued by his mother's cousin, who adopted him in 1946. He began studying piano at age 8 with his foster mother; his formal piano training commenced at the same age with Eliza Hansen in Hamburg, and continued with her at the Hochschule für Musik there; he also studied piano with Hans-Otto Schmidt in Cologne, and received instruction in conducting from Brückner-Ruggeberg at the Hamburg Hochschule für Musik. In 1952 he won 1st prize in the Steinway Piano Competition; after winning 2d prize in the Munich International Competition in 1962, he gained wide recognition by capturing 1st prize in the 1st Clara Haskil Competition in Montreux (1965). In 1966 he made his London debut; following studies with Szell (1967–69), the latter invited him to make his debut as soloist in Mozart's Piano Concerto in F major, K. 459, with the Cleveland Orch. on Jan. 16, 1969. In subsequent years, he made numerous tours as a pianist, appearing in all of the major music centers of the world. He also gave duo concerts with the pianist Justus Frantz. In 1972 he began to make appearances as a conductor; made his debut as an opera conductor in Darmstadt with *La Traviata* in 1978. He pursued a successful career as both a pianist and a conductor, sometimes conducting from the keyboard. After serving as Generalmusikdirektor of the Rheinland-Pfalz State Phil. (1979–81), he was first permanent guest conductor of the Zürich Tonhalle Orch. (1981–82), then was its chief conductor (1982–85). From 1988 to 1999 he was music director of the Houston Sym. Orch. He also served as music director of the Ravinia Festival in Chicago from 1995. In 1998 he became chief conductor of the North German Radio Sym. Orch. in Hamburg. He also served as music director of the Orchestre de Paris from 2000. Eschenbach maintains a varied repertoire, as both a pianist and a conductor; his sympathies range from the standard literature to the cosmopolitan avant-garde.

BIBL.: W. Erk, ed., *Für C. E. zum 20. Februar 1990: Eine Festgabe* (Stuttgart, 1990).

Esham, Faith, American soprano; b. Vanceburg, Ky., Aug. 6, 1948. Following training with Vasile Venettozzi in Ky., she pursued vocal studies at the Juilliard School of Music in New York with Adele Addison, Beverly Johnson, and Jennie Tourel. She made her formal operatic debut in 1977 as Cherubino at the N.Y. City Opera, and then her European operatic debut in 1980 as Nedda in Nancy. In 1981 she won the Concours International de Chant in Paris, and sang Cherubino at the Glyndebourne Festival. After appearing in the same role at Milan's La Scala in 1982, she sang Micaëla at the Vienna State Opera and Mélisande at the Geneva Opera in 1984. On Dec. 27, 1986, she made her Metropolitan Opera debut in New York as Marzelline. She appeared as Desdemona at the Welsh National Opera in Cardiff in 1990, and then as Musetta at the Cologne Opera and as Pamina at the Washington (D.C.) Opera. In 1992 she sang Micaëla at the Cincinnati Opera, Cio-Cio-San at the Opera Theatre of St. Louis, and Cherubino at the Dallas Opera. She also pursued an active concert career and sang with major American orchs.

Eshpai, Andrei (Yakovlevich), Russian composer and pianist; b. Kozmodemiansk, May 15, 1925. He studied piano with Safranitsky and composition with Miaskovsky and Golubev (1948–53) at the Moscow Cons., where he completed his training in composition with Khatchaturian (1953–56). From 1965 to 1970 he was on its faculty. He made tours as a pianist throughout Russia and abroad. In 1986 he received the Lenin Prize. His output, which includes both serious and light scores, is written in an accessible style. He has made use of folk motifs of the Mari nation. He composed operettas, musicals, ballets, including *The Circle* (1980; Kuibishev, Feb. 23, 1981), and incidental music to plays. His father was the Russian composer of Mari descent Yakov (Andreievich) Eshpai (1890–1963).

Eslava (y Elizondo), (Miguel) Hilarión, Spanish composer and scholar; b. Burlada, Navarra, Oct. 21, 1807; d. Madrid, July 23, 1878. He was a choirboy at the Cathedral of Pamplona, studying organ and violin; in 1827 he went to Calahorra, where he studied with Francisco Secanilla. At the age of 20 he was appointed music director at the Cathedral of Burgo de Osma, where he was ordained a priest. In 1832 he became music director at Seville. In 1844 he obtained the appointment as chapel master to Queen Isabella in Madrid, and in 1854 he became a prof. at the Madrid Cons. and in 1866 its director. He also ed. a periodical, *Gaceta Musical de Madrid* (1855–56). He wrote 3 operas with Italian texts: *Il solitario del Monte Selvaggio* (Cádiz, 1841), *La tregua di Ptolemaide* (Cádiz, May 24, 1842), and *Pietro il crudele* (Seville, 1843). His fame rests, however, on his great collection in 10 vols., *Lira sacro-hispana* (Madrid, 1869), an anthology of Spanish sacred music from the 16th to the 19th century, including some of

Eslava's own works. He also publ. *Método de solfeo* (1846) and *Escuela de armonía y composición* (1861).

Esplá (y Triay), Oscar, Spanish music educator and composer; b. Alicante, Aug. 5, 1886; d. Madrid, Jan. 6, 1976. He began his musical studies in Alicante, and then pursued training in engineering and philosophy at the Univ. of Barcelona (1903–11); subsequently he studied with Reger in Meiningen and Munich (1912) and Saint-Saëns in Paris (1913). In 1930 he became a prof. at the Madrid Cons., serving as its director (1936–39); was also president of the Junta Nacional de Música y Teatros Líricos (1931–34). He became director of the Laboratoire Musical Scientifique in Brussels in 1946; returning to Spain, he became director of his own cons. in Alicante (1958). He publ. *El arte y la musicalidad* (Alicante, 1912), *Fundamento estético de las actividades del espíritu* (Munich, 1915), and *Función musical y música contemporánea* (Madrid, 1955). A. Iglesias ed. *Escritos de Oscar Esplá* (3 vols., 1977–86). His compositions show the influence of Spanish folk music; he utilized his own Levantine scale in his works.

WORKS: DRAMATIC: OPERAS: *La bella durmiente* (Vienna, 1909); *La balteira* (N.Y., 1935); *Plumes au vent* (1941); *El pirata cautivo* (Madrid, 1974); *Calixto y Melibea* (1974–76). SCENIC CANTATA: *Nochebuena del diablo* for Soprano, Chorus, and Orch. (1923). BALLETS: *Ciclopes de Ifach* (1920?); *El contrabandista* (Paris, 1928); *Fiesta* (1931; unfinished).

BIBL.: E. García Alcázar, *O. E.y.T.: (Alicante, 5–8–1886-Madrid, 6–1–1976): Estudio monográfico documental* (Alicante, 1993).

Esposito, Michele, Italian composer, pianist, and conductor; b. Castellammare di Stabia, near Naples, Sept. 29, 1855; d. Florence, Nov. 23, 1929. He studied at the Cons. San Pietro e Majella at Naples with Cesi (piano) and Serrao (theory); then gave piano concerts in Italy; in 1882 he was engaged as a piano teacher at the Royal Irish Academy of Music in Dublin; he organized the Dublin Orch. Soc. in 1899 and conducted it until 1914, and again in 1927. He composed several works on Irish subjects, including the Irish operetta, *The Post Bag* (London, Jan. 27, 1902), and incidental music for *The Tinker and the Fairy* (Dublin, 1910). He received 1st prizes for his cantata *Deirdre* (Irish Festival, Dublin, 1897); and *Irish Symphony* (Irish Festival, Dublin, 1902).

Esswood, Paul (Lawrence Vincent), English countertenor; b. West Bridgford, June 2, 1942. He studied with Gordon Clinton at the Royal College of Music in London (1961–64), and then was a lay vicar at Westminster Abbey until 1971. In 1965 he made his formal debut as a countertenor in a BBC performance of Handel's *Messiah*; his operatic debut followed in Cavalli's *Erismena* in Berkeley, California, in 1968. In 1967 he cofounded the Pro Cantione Antiqua, an a cappella male vocal group, but he also continued to pursue his solo career, appearing at many major European festivals. He also was a prof. at the Royal College of Music (1977–80) and at the Royal Academy of Music (from 1985). While he was best known for his performances of such early masters as Monteverdi, Cavalli, Purcell, Bach, and Handel, he also appeared in modern works, including the premieres of Penderecki's *Paradise Lost* (Chicago, Nov. 29, 1978) and Glass's *Akhnaten* (Stuttgart, March 24, 1984).

Estes, Simon (Lamont), noted black American bass-baritone; b. Centerville, Iowa, Feb. 2, 1938. He sang in a local Baptist church choir as a child, then studied voice with Charles Kellis at the Univ. of Iowa and on scholarship at N.Y.'s Juilliard School of Music. He made his operatic debut as Ramfis at the Berlin Deutsche Oper (1965); after winning a silver medal at the Tchaikovsky Competition in Moscow (1966), he appeared with the San Francisco Opera and the Chicago Lyric Opera, but was mainly active as a concert artist. On June 10, 1976, he made his first appearance with the Metropolitan Opera as Oroveso in *Norma* during the company's visit to the Wolf Trap Farm Park in Vienna, Va. However, it was not until he sang the Dutchman at the Bayreuth Festival in 1978 that his remarkable vocal gifts began to be widely appreciated. He subsequently appeared as the Dutchman throughout Europe to notable acclaim. In 1980 he made his U.S. recital debut at N.Y.'s Carnegie Hall, and in 1981 returned to the Metropolitan Opera roster, singing Wotan opposite Birgit Nilsson's Brünnhilde in a concert performance of Act III of *Die Walküre* in New York. He finally made his formal stage debut with the company there as the Landgrave on Jan. 4, 1982. In 1985 he returned to sing Porgy in *Porgy and Bess*. He sang Wotan in the *Ring* cycle at the Metropolitan Opera from 1986 to 1988. He made his debut at the London Promenade Concerts in 1989. In 1990 he appeared in the title role of the musical *King* in London. In 1992 he appeared as Macbeth in Miami and as Wotan in Bonn. He portrayed Zaccaria at the Orange Festival in 1994. After singing Porgy in Cape Town in 1996, he appeared as Jochanaan in Toronto in 1998. His comprehensive operatic and concert repertoire ranges from Handel to spirituals.

Esteve (also **Estebe**) **y Grimau, Pablo**, Catalonian composer; b. probably in Barcelona, c.1730; d. Madrid, June 4, 1794. He went to Madrid about 1760. He was maestro di cappella to the Duke of Osuna, and in 1778 was appointed official composer for the municipal theaters of Madrid. He composed over 400 tonadillas, and some zarzuelas. His song *El jilguerito con pico de oro* was arranged for soprano and orch. by Joaquín Nin.

Estrada, Carlos, Uruguayan conductor, music educator, and composer; b. Montevideo, Sept. 15, 1909; d. there, May 7, 1970. He was a student in Montevideo of Adelina Pérez Montero (piano), Carlos Correa Luna (violin), and Manuel Fernández Espiro (harmony, counterpoint, and composition), and at the Paris Cons. of Roger-Ducasse and Büsser (composition), N. Gallon (counterpoint and fugue), and Paray, Wolff, and Gaubert (conducting). He was active in Montevideo as a conductor, and also was director of the National Cons. (1954–68). Among his works was the opera *L'Annonce faite à Marie* (1943).

Etcheverry, Henri-Bertrand, French bass-baritone; b. Bordeaux, March 29, 1900; d. Paris, Nov. 14, 1960. He studied in Paris, where he made his operatic debut as Ceprano in *Rigoletto* at the Opéra in 1932; from 1937 he was a member of the Paris Opéra Comique, and he also sang at London's Covent Garden (1937, 1949). He was greatly admired for his portrayal of Golaud; among his other notable roles were Don Giovanni, Wotan, Boris Godunov, and Gounod's Méphistophélès and Friar Lawrence.

Ettinger, Max (Markus Wolf), German conductor and composer; b. Lemberg, Dec. 27, 1874; d. Basel, July 19, 1951. He studied with Herzogenberg in Berlin and with Thuille and Rheinberger at the Munich Akademie der Tonkunst. After conducting in Munich (1900–20), Leipzig (1920–29), and Berlin (1929–33), he settled in Switzerland in 1938. He composed the operas *Judith* (Nuremberg, Nov. 24, 1921), *Der eifersüchtige Trinker* (Nuremberg, Feb. 7, 1925), *Juana* (Nuremberg, Feb. 7, 1925), *Clavigo* (Leipzig, Oct. 19, 1926), *Frühlings Erwachen* (Leipzig, April 14, 1928), and *Dolores* (1930–31).

Evangelisti, Franco, Italian composer; b. Rome, Jan 21, 1926; d. there, Jan. 28, 1980. He studied with Daniele Paris in Rome (1948–53) and Harald Genzmer at the Freiburg im Breisgau Hoschschule für Musik (1953–56); he also attended the Darmstadt summer courses in new music with Eimert and Stockhausen, and worked at the electronic music studios in Cologne and Warsaw. He was active in new music circles in Rome, where he became president of Nuova Consonanza in 1961; he taught there at the Accademia di Santa Cecilia (1968–72), the Cons. dell'Aquila (1969–75), and the Cons. Santa Cecilia (1974–80). He composed the opera *Die Schachtel* (1963), and also authored the book *Dal silenzio ad una nuova musica* (Palermo, 1967).

Evans, Anne, esteemed English soprano; b. London, Aug. 20, 1941. She was a student of Ruth Packer at the Royal College of Music in London and of Maria Carpi, Herbert Graf, and Lofti Mansouri at the Geneva Cons. After singing secondary roles at the Geneva Grand Théâtre, she returned to London in 1968 to join the Sadler's Wells Opera (later the English National Opera), where she was notably successful in such roles as Mimi, Tosca, Elsa, the Marschallin, and Sieglinde; she also appeared with the Welsh National Opera in Cardiff as Senta, Chrysothemis, the Empress, Donna Anna, and Brünnhilde (1985). Her Brünnhilde elicited critical acclaim when the company visited London's Covent Garden in 1986, which role she also sang at the Bayreuth Festival for the first time in 1989. On Feb. 6, 1992, she made her Metropolitan Opera debut in New York as Elisabeth in *Tannhäuser*. In 1993 she appeared as Isolde with the Welsh National Opera in Cardiff, and then with the company at London's Covent Garden. She appeared as the Marschallin at the English National Opera in 1994. In 1996 she sang Brünnhilde at Covent Garden. She portrayed Isolde at the Semper Opera in Dresden in 1997.

Evans, Sir Geraint (Llewellyn), distinguished Welsh baritone; b. Pontypridd, South Wales, Feb. 16, 1922; d. Aberystwyth, Sept. 19, 1992. He began to study voice in Cardiff when he was 17, and, after serving in the RAF during World War II, resumed his vocal studies in Hamburg with Theo Hermann; he then studied with Fernando Carpi in Geneva and Walter Hyde at the Guildhall School of Music in London. He made his operatic debut as the Nightwatchman in *Die Meistersinger von Nürnberg* at London's Covent Garden (1948); thereafter was a leading member of the company. He also sang at the Glyndebourne Festivals (1949–61). In 1959 he made his U.S. debut with the San Francisco Opera; first appearances followed at Milan's La Scala (1960), the Vienna State Opera (1961), the Salzburg Festival (1962), N.Y.'s Metropolitan Opera (debut as Falstaff, March 25, 1964), and the Paris Opéra (1975). In 1984 he made his farewell operatic appearance as Dulcamara at Covent Garden. He was also active as an opera producer. In 1959 he was made a Commander of the Order of the British Empire and was knighted in 1969. With N. Goodwin, he publ. an entertaining autobiography, *Sir Geraint Evans: A Knight at the Opera* (London, 1984). His finest roles included Figaro, Leporello, Papageno, Beckmesser, Falstaff, Don Pasquale, and Wozzeck.

Everding, August, German opera director and administrator; b. Bottrop, Oct. 31, 1928; d. Munich, Jan. 27, 1999. He received training in piano and also took courses in Germanic studies, philosophy, theology, and dramaturgy at the univs. of Bonn and Munich. From 1959 he worked regularly at the Munich Kammerspiele, later serving as its Intendant (1963–73). From 1973 to 1977 he was Intendant at the Hamburg State Opera, and from 1977 to 1982 at the Bavarian State Opera in Munich, where he subsequently was Generalintendant of the Bavarian State Theater (1982–93). In 1993 he became founder-president of the Bavarian Theater Academy. In addition to staging operas during his tenures in Hamburg and Munich, he worked as a guest opera director at the Bayreuth Festival, the Savonlinna Festival, London's Covent Garden, N.Y.'s Metropolitan Opera, and other music centers. He publ. *Mir ist die Ehre widerfahren: An-Reden, Mit-Reden, Aus-Reden, Zu-Reden* (Munich, 1985) and *Wenn für Romeo der letzte Vorhang fällt: Theater, Musik, Musiktheater: Zur aktuellen Kulturszene* (Munich, 1993).

BIBL.: K. Seidel, *Die ganze Welt ist Bühne: A. E.* (Munich, 1988).

Evstatieva, Stefka, Bulgarian soprano; b. Rousse, May 7, 1947. She was a pupil of Elena Kiselova at the Bulgarian State Cons. in Sofia. In 1971 she made her operatic debut as Amelia at the Rousse Opera, where she was a member until 1979; she was also a member of the Bulgarian State Opera in Sofia from 1978. In 1980 she made her first appearance with the Royal Opera, Covent Garden, London as Desdemona during its visit to Manchester; in 1981 she sang with the company in London as Donna Elvira. After engagements in Berlin and Vienna in 1982, and in Milan and Paris in 1983, she made her Metropolitan Opera debut in New York as Elisabeth in *Don Carlos* on April 9, 1984. In 1984 she appeared with the San Francisco Opera. In subsequent years, she sang with many of the principal opera houses of Europe and North America, and also toured as a concert artist. Among her other roles were Donna Elvira, Leonora, Aida, Mimi, Suor Angelica, Tosca, Madeleine de Coigny, and Lisa in *The Queen of Spades*.

Ewen, David, Polish-born American writer on music; b. Lemberg, Nov. 26, 1907; d. Miami Beach, Dec. 28, 1985. He was taken to the United States in 1912 and pursued his training in New York at City College and Columbia Univ.; he also studied theory with Max Persin. He was music ed. of *Reflex Magazine* (1928–29), *The American Hebrew* (1935), and *Cue* (1937–38), and then was active with the publ. firm of Allen, Towne, and Heath (1946–49); in 1965 he joined the faculty of the Univ. of Miami, which awarded him an honorary D.Mus. in 1974; in 1985 he received the ASCAP Award for Lifetime Achievement in Music. Ewen publ. more than 80 books during a career of some 50 years, including *The Book of Modern Composers* (1942; 3d ed., 1961, as *The New Book of Modern Composers*), *Encyclopedia of the Opera* (1955; 2d ed., rev., 1971 as *New Encyclopedia of the Opera*), *Complete Book of the American Musical Theater* (1958; 3d ed., rev., 1976 as *New Complete Book of the American Musical Theater*), and *The Story of America's Musical Theater* (1961; 2d ed., rev., 1968).

Ewing, Maria (Louise), noted American mezzo-soprano and soprano; b. Detroit, March 27, 1950. She commenced vocal training with Marjorie Gordon, continuing her studies with Steber at the Cleveland Inst. of Music (1968–70), and later with Tourel and O. Marzolla. In 1973 she made her professional debut at the Ravinia Festival with the Chicago Sym. Orch., and subsequently was engaged to appear with various U.S. opera houses and orchs.; she also appeared as a recitalist. On Oct. 14, 1976, she made her Metropolitan Opera debut in New York as Cherubino, and returned there to sing such roles as Rosina, Dorabella, Mélisande, Blanche in *Les Dialogues des Carmélites*, and Carmen. In 1976 she made her first appearance at Milan's La Scala as Mélisande; in 1978 she made her Glyndebourne Festival debut as Dorabella, and returned there as a periodic guest. In 1986 she sang Salome in Los Angeles and appeared in *The Merry Widow* in Chicago in 1987. In 1988 she sang Salome at London's Covent Garden, a role she sang to enormous critical acclaim in Chicago that same year; she returned there as Tosca in 1989 and Susanna in 1991. After a dispute over artistic matters at the Metropolitan Opera in 1987, she refused to sing there until 1993 when she returned as Dido. After singing Katerina Ismailova there in 1994, she was engaged as Tosca at Covent Garden in 1995. In 1997 she returned to the Metropolitan Opera as Berg's Marie. She was married for a time to **Sir Peter Hall**.

Eybler, Joseph Leopold, Edler von, Austrian composer; b. Schwechat, near Vienna, Feb. 8, 1765; d. Vienna, July 24, 1846. He began his musical training with his father. Settling in Vienna, he continued his studies at St. Stephen's choir school and also received instruction from Albrechtsberger (1776–79). Haydn became his friend and mentor, and he was also befriended by Mozart. From 1794 to 1824 he was choirmaster of the Schottenkloster; he also became music teacher at the court (1801) and was named deputy Hofkapellmeister under Salieri (1804), succeeding him as Hofkapellmeister (1824). In 1833 he suffered a stroke while conducting Mozart's Requiem and was compelled to retire. He was ennobled by the Emperor in 1835. His works include the opera *Das Zauberschwert*, and the oratorios *Die Hirten bei der Krippe* (1794) and *Die vier letzten Dirge* (1810).

BIBL.: R. Ricks, *The Published Works of J. E.* (diss., Catholic Univ. of America, 1967); H. Herrmann, *Thematische Verzeichnis der Werke von J. E.* (Munich and Salzburg, 1976).

Eyser, Eberhard, German violist and composer; b. Kwidzyn, Poland, Aug. 1, 1932. He studied composition at the Hannover Hochschule für Musik (1952–57); his principal mentor was Fritz von Bloh, but he also attended the Salzburg Mozarteum, the Accademia Musicale Chigiana in Siena, and seminars with Xenakis, Maderna, and Scherchen. He was a violist in the Hannover Opera orch. (1956–57), the Stuttgart Radio Sym. Orch. (1957–61), and the Royal Theater orch. in Stockholm (from 1961).

WORKS: DRAMATIC: OPERAS: *Molonne*, chamber opera (Stockholm, Oct. 27, 1970); *Abu Said, Kalifens son* (1970–76; Stockholm, March 10, 1976); *Sista resan*, chamber opera (1972–73; Vadstena, July 24, 1974); *Carmen 36*, chamber opera (1972–77); *Det djupa vattnet*, lyric scene (1979); *Sensommardag*, chamber opera (1979); *Sista dagen på jorden*, chamber opera (1979); *Altaret* (1980); *Bermuda-Triangeln* (1981); *Der letzte Tag auf Erden* (1979–82); *Rid i natt* (1982–91); *Destination Mars*, chamber opera (1983); *Das gläserne Wand*, chamber opera (1985); *Herr Karls likvaka*, madrigal-opera (1985–88); *The Picture of Dorian Gray* (1986); *Intimate Letters*, chamber opera (1989); *Charley McDeath*, chamber opera (1992). BALLET: *Golgata* (1983).

Eysler (Eisler), Edmund, noted Austrian composer; b. Vienna, March 12, 1874; d. there, Oct. 4, 1949. He was a student of Door (piano), R. Fuchs (harmony and counterpoint), and J. N. Fuchs (composition) at the Vienna Cons. He made Vienna the center of his activities, beginning with the premiere of his operetta *Bruder Straubinger* (Feb. 20, 1903). Its waltz song *Kussen ist keine Sund* became celebrated. Success continued with *Pufferl* (Feb. 10, 1905), *Die Schützenliesel* (Oct. 7, 1905), *Künstlerblut* (Oct. 20, 1906), and *Vera Violetta* (Nov. 30, 1907). Further success attended his *Der unsterbliche Lump* (Oct. 14, 1910), *Der Natursänger* (Dec. 22, 1911), *Der Frauenfresser* (Dec. 23, 1911), *Der lachende Ehemann* (March 19, 1913), and *Ein Tag im Paradies* (Dec. 23, 1913). Even during World War I, his works were produced unabated: *Die—oder keine* (Oct. 9, 1915), *Wenn zwei sich lieben* (Oct. 29, 1915), *Warum geht's denn jetzt?* (July 5, 1916), *Hanni geht's tanzen* (Nov. 7, 1916), and *Graf Toni* (March 2, 1917). After the War, Eysler brought out a steady stream of additional scores. His greatest postwar success came with *Die goldene Meisterin* (Sept. 13, 1927), which was acclaimed as one of his finest scores. His last major success came with *Ihr erster Ball* (Nov. 21, 1929). As a Jew, Eysler was compelled to go into hiding during World War II. After the War, his status was restored as one of Vienna's master melodists of the operetta genre.

WORKS: MUSICAL THEATER (all 1st perf. in Vienna unless otherwise given): *Das Gastmahl des Lucullus* (Nov. 23, 1901); *Bruder Straubinger* (Feb. 20, 1903); *Pufferl* (Feb. 10, 1905); *Die Schützenliesel* (Oct. 7, 1905); *Phryne* (Oct. 6, 1906); *Künstlerblut* (Oct. 20, 1906); *Vera Violetta* (Nov. 30, 1907); *Ein Tag auf dem Mars* (Jan. 17, 1908); *Das Glücksschweinchen* (June 26, 1908); *Johann der Zweite* (Oct. 3, 1908); *Der junge Papa* (Feb. 3, 1909); *Lumpus und Pumpus* (Jan. 21, 1910); *Der unsterbliche Lump* (Oct. 14, 1910); *Der Zirkuskind* (Feb. 18, 1911); *Der Natursänger* (Dec. 22, 1911); *Der Frauenfresser* (Dec. 23, 1911); *Der lachende Ehemann* (March 19, 1913); *Ein Tag im Paradies* (Dec. 23, 1913); *Komm, deutscher Brüder* (Oct. 4, 1914); *Der Kriegsberichterstatter* (Oct. 9, 1914; in collaboration with others); *Frühling am Rhein* (Oct. 10, 1914); *Der Durchgang der Venus* (Nov. 28, 1914); *Die—oder keine* (Oct. 9, 1915); *Wenn zwei sich lieben* (Oct. 29, 1915); *Das Zimmer der Pompadour* (Dec. 1, 1915); *Warum geht's denn jetzt?* (July 5, 1916); *Hanni geht's tanzen* (Nov. 7, 1916); *Der berühmte Gabriel* (Nov. 8, 1916); *Graf Toni* (March 2, 1917); *Der Aushilfsgatte* (Nov. 7, 1917); *Leute von heute* (June 22, 1918; in collaboration with R. Stolz and A. Werau); *Der dunkel Schatz* (Nov. 14, 1918); *Der fidele Geiger* (Jan. 17, 1919); *Rund um die Bühne* (March 1, 1920); *Der König heiratet* (April 1920); *Wer hat's gemacht* (Oct. 1, 1920); *La bella Mammina* (Rome, April 9, 1921; German version as *Die schöne Mama*, Vienna, Sept. 17, 1921); *Die fromme Helene* (Dec. 22, 1921); *Die Parliamentskathi* (April 15, 1922); *Fräulein Sopherl, die schöne vom Markt* (May 19, 1922); *Schummel macht alles* (July 1, 1922); *Drei auf einmal* (March 29, 1923); *Der ledige Schwiegersohn* (April 20, 1923); *Vierzehn Tage (im) Arrest* (June 16, 1923); *Lumpenlieschen* (May 21, 1923); *Das Land der Liebe* (Aug. 27, 1926); *Die goldene Meisterin* (Sept. 13, 1927); *Ihr erster Ball* (Nov. 21, 1929); *Das Strumpfband der Pompadour* (Augsburg, March 16, 1930); *Durchlaucht Mizzi* (Dec. 23, 1930); *Die schlimme Paulette* (Augsburg, March 1, 1931); *Zwei alte Wiener* (Feb. 12, 1932); *Die Rakete* (Innsbruck, Dec. 23, 1932); *Donauliebchen* (Dec. 25, 1932); *Das ist der erste Liebe(lei)* (Dec. 23, 1934); *Wiener Musik* (Dec. 22, 1947). OTHER: 2 operas: *Der Hexenspiegel* (1900) and *Hochzeitspräludium* (1946); ballet: *Schlaraffenland* (1899); dances; piano pieces; songs.

BIBL.: K. Ewald, *E. E.: Ein Musiker aus Wien* (Vienna, 1934); R. Prosl, *E. E.* (Vienna, 1947).

F

Fabbri, Inez (real name, **Agnes Schmidt**), Austrian-American soprano and operatic impresario; b. Vienna, Jan. 26, 1831; d. San Francisco, Aug. 30, 1909. She was trained in Vienna and made her operatic debut as Abigail in *Lucrezia Borgia* in Kaschau on Oct. 5, 1847. In 1857 she sang at the Hamburg Opera and then joined the traveling opera company of Richard Mulder (b. Amsterdam, Dec. 31, 1822; d. San Francisco, Dec. 22, 1874). She toured throughout North and South America with his company, eventually becoming his wife and adopting the professional name of Inez Fabbri. In 1860 she attracted much notice when she appeared at N.Y.'s Winter Garden as a rival to Adelina Patti. After singing at the Frankfurt am Main Stadttheater (1864–70), she and her husband teamed up with the Theodore Habelmann-Karl Formes troupe in New York in 1872, but that same year they went to San Francisco to produce operas until Mulder's death. In 1877 she married the German tenor Jacob Müller (1845–1901), and remained active as a singer until 1880. After teaching voice in Los Angeles (1892–99), she settled in San Francisco.

Fabri, Annibale Pio, famous Italian tenor, known as "Il Bolognese" and "Il Balino"; b. Bologna, 1697; d. Lisbon, Aug. 12, 1760. He studied with Pistocchi. While in the service of Prince Ruspoli in Rome, he sang female roles in operas by Caldara (1711), then made his public debut in Bologna in 1716. He quickly gained renown for his performances throughout Italy (1716–28); then was engaged by Handel for the King's Theatre in London, making his debut there in Handel's *Lotario* on Dec. 2, 1729, creating the role of Berengario. During his 2 seasons in London, he also created the roles of Handel's Emilio in *Partenope* (1730) and Alexander in *Poro* (1731). He subsequently appeared throughout Italy again, and then retired in Lisbon as a member of the royal chapel. He was also a composer; he was elected to membership in the Accademia Filarmonica in Bologna in 1719 and from 1725 to 1750 served intermittently as its president.

Fabrizi, Vincenzo, Italian composer; b. Naples, 1764; d. after 1812. After bringing out operas in Naples and Bologna, he went to Rome and was elected maestro di cappella at the Univ. in 1786. From then until 1788 he was musical director of Rome's Teatro Capranica, where he won particular success with his comic operas *La sposa invisibile* (Feb. 20, 1786) and *Il convitato di pietra*, also known as *Don Giovanni Tenorio ossia Il convitato di pietra* (Carnival 1787). The latter was performed throughout Europe with fine success.

Faccio, Franco (Francesco Antonio), prominent Italian conductor and composer; b. Verona, March 8, 1840; d. Monza, July 21, 1891. He was a pupil of Giuseppe Bernasconi and Gaetano Costalunga in Verona, and then at the Milan Cons. (1855–64), where his principal mentor was Stefano Ronchetti-Montevito. He toured Germany and Scandinavia (1866–68), and then went to Milan as a conductor at the Teatro Carcano in 1868. In 1869 he became deputy conductor at Milan's La Scala. From 1871 to 1890 he was its principal conductor, also serving in that capacity with the Società Orchestrale delle Scala (1879–90). During his notable tenure, he conducted the premieres of Ponchielli's *La Gioconda* (April 8, 1876) and his friend Verdi's *Otello* (Feb. 5, 1887), as well as the Italian premieres of many other operas, including those by Wagner. From 1868 to 1878 he was prof. of composition at the Milan Cons. He composed the operas *I profughi fiamminghi* (Milan, Nov. 11, 1863) and *Amleto* (Genoa, May 30, 1865; rev. 1871). Stricken with syphilis, he went insane in 1890 and was confined to an asylum in Monza. His sister, Chiarina Faccio (1846–1923), was a soprano.

BIBL.: R. de Rensis, *F. F. e Verdi: Carteggi e documenti inediti* (Milan, 1934).

Fago, (Francesco) Nicola, Italian composer, called "Il virtuosissimo Tarantino" after his place of birth; b. Taranto, Feb. 26, 1677; d. Naples, Feb. 18, 1745. He was a pupil of Provenzale at the Cons. della Pietà dei Turchini in Naples (1693–95), becoming his assistant in 1697 and his successor in 1705. From 1704 to 1708 he was maestro di cappella at the Conservatorio di S. Onofrio; from 1709 to 1731 he was maestro di cappella at the Tesoro di S. Gennaro, then at the S. Giacomo degli Spagnuoli Church (1736–45). He was the teacher of Leonardo Leo, Francesco Feo, Jommelli, and Sala. He composed 4 operas: *Radamisto* (1707), *Astarto* (1709), *La Cassandra indovina* (1711), and *Lo Masillo* (1712), and 3 oratorios, including *Faraone sommerso* and *Il monte fiorito*. His son Lorenzo Fago (b. Naples, Aug. 13, 1704; d. there, April 30, 1793), an organist and composer, was his successor at the Tesoro di S. Gennaro (1731–66 and 1771–80), and taught at the Cons. della Pietà dei Turchini for 56 years (1737–93) until his death.

Failoni, Sergio, Italian conductor; b. Verona, Dec. 18, 1890; d. Sopron, July 25, 1948. He received his musical education in Verona and Milan. He conducted opera throughout Italy; from 1932 he made appearances at La Scala in Milan. From 1928 to 1947 he was chief conductor of the State Opera in Budapest. In 1947 he was invited to make his debut at the Metropolitan Opera in New York; however, he suffered a stroke and died the following year. He was regarded as one of the leading interpreters of the Italian repertoire.

Fairlamb, James Remington, American organist and composer; b. Philadelphia, Jan. 23, 1838; d. Ingleside, N.Y., April 16, 1908. As a youth he played the organ in several Philadelphia churches; in 1858 went to Paris, where studied piano there with Marmontel. While in Europe he was appointed by President Lincoln as American consul at Zürich (1861) and stayed in Zürich until 1865, when he returned to the United States. He organized an amateur opera company with which he brought out his 4-act grand opera *Valérie, or Treasured Tokens* (Philadelphia, Dec. 15, 1869). From 1872 to 1898 he was church organist in Philadelphia, Jersey City, and New York. He wrote another grand opera, *Lionello*, and 2 light operas, *Love's Stratagem* and *The Interrupted Marriage*. He was one of the founders of the American Guild of Organists.

Faith, Percy, Canadian-born American conductor, arranger, and composer; b. Toronto, April 7, 1908; d. Los Angeles, Feb. 9, 1976. He took up violin at age 7 and piano at 10. After training at Toronto's Canadian Academy, he entered the Toronto Cons. of Music at 14 to study with Frank Welsman. At 18, he abandoned his hopes for a career as a concert pianist after his hands were severely burned in an accident, and pursued training in composition with Louis Waizman. From 1927 he was active as a conductor and arranger of popular music for Canadian radio programs. In 1940 he settled in the United States and in 1945 became a naturalized American citizen. He was music director of *The Carnation Contented Hour* on NBC Radio (1940–47), Coca-Cola's *The Pause That Refreshes* on CBS Radio (1946–49), and *The Woolworth Hour* on CBS Radio (1955–57). He also was an arranger-conductor for Columbia Records in New York (1950–59) and Los Angeles (1960–76). Although he wrote an operetta, *The Gandy Dancer* (1943), he was especially adept as a composer, arranger, and orchestrator of popular music. He also wrote numerous film scores.

Falabella, (Correa), Roberto, Chilean composer; b. Santiago, Feb. 13, 1926; d. there, Dec. 15, 1958. He was paralyzed by polio as a child. He pursued his studies with Lucila Césped (1945–46), Alfonso Letelier (1949–50), Gustavo Becerra (1952), and Miguel Aguilar and Esteban Eitler (1956–57). His music was Classical in form, Romantic in content, and modernistic in technique. He composed the chamber operas *Epitafios fúnebres* (1952) and *La tirana* (1957), a miniature opera, *Del diario morir* (1954), and the ballets *El peine de oro* (1954) and *Andacollo* (1957).

Falco, Michele, Italian composer; b. Naples, c.1688; d. after 1732. He was trained at the Cons. di S. Onofrio in Naples, where he became a member of the Reale Congregazione e Monte dei Musici in 1712. He served as maestro di cappella and organist at the church of S. Geronimo in Naples, and also as maestro di cappella in Pollena, near Naples. Falco was one of the most important exponents of opera buffa, composing the following scores for Naples: *Lo Lollo pisciaportelle* (1700), *Lo Masiello* (1712; Acts 1 and 3 by N. Fago), *Lo Imbruoglio d'ammore* (Dec. 27, 1717), *Armida abbandonata* (Oct. 1, 1719), *Lo castiello saccheiato* (Oct. 1720), and *Le pazzie d'ammore* (April 1723). He also wrote oratorios and cantatas.

Falcon, (Marie-) Cornélie, renowned French soprano; b. Paris, Jan. 28, 1814; d. there, Feb. 25, 1897. She studied with Henri, Pelegrini, Bordogni, and Nourrit at the Paris Cons. (1827–31), taking premiers prix in singing and lyric declamation. On July 20, 1832, she made her operatic debut as Alice in *Robert le diable* at the Paris Opéra, where she subsequently sang with such brilliant success that she was chosen to create the roles of Rachel in *La Juive* (Feb. 23, 1835) and Valentine in *Les Huguenots* (Feb. 29, 1836). In the spring of 1837 she suffered a vocal collapse, but soon managed to resume her career at the Opéra and sang there until her final performance in *Les Huguenots* on Jan. 15, 1838. She made many attempts to regain her vocal prowess, resorting to various quack remedies and bogus treatments, all to no avail. On March 14, 1840, she made an unsuccessful return to the Opéra in a special benefit performance, but her attempt proved disastrous and she retired to her villa near Paris. Despite the brevity of her remarkable career, her portrayals of Donna Anna, Giulia in *Vestale*, and the heroines in all 4 Rossini French operas, as well as those already noted, brought her great fame. Indeed, so much fame, that the description "Falcon type" subsequently was given to those singers who excelled in her chosen repertory.

BIBL.: C. Bouvet, *C. F.* (Paris, 1927).

Falcon, Ruth, American soprano; b. New Orleans, Nov. 2, 1946. She studied in New Orleans before pursuing training in New York and with Tito Gobbi and Luigi Ricci in Italy. In 1968 she sang Frasquita in New Orleans. In 1974 she made her first appearance at the N.Y. City Opera as Micaëla, and in 1975 her European debut in the title role of Mayr's *Medea in Corinto* in Bern. She made her first appearance at the Bavarian State Opera in Munich in 1976 as Leonora, and continued to appear there until 1980. Her debut at the Paris Opéra followed in 1981 as Donna Anna. In 1983 she was engaged as Leonora at the Vienna State Opera. After singing Anna Bolena in Nice in 1985, she portrayed Leonora at London's Covent Garden in 1987. On Nov. 13, 1989, she made her Metropolitan Opera debut in New York as Strauss's Empress. In 1990 she sang Norma in New Orleans. After appearing as Turandot at the Teatro Colón in Buenos Aires in 1993, she returned to New Orleans as Chrysothemis in 1994 and as Leonora in 1997.

Falik, Yuri, Russian cellist and composer; b. Odessa, July 30, 1936. He studied cello with A. Strimer at the Leningrad Cons.; in 1962 he won 1st cello prize at the International Competition in Helsinki. He composed music from adolescence; in 1955 he enrolled in the composition class of Boris Arapov at the Leningrad Cons., graduating in 1964. He subsequently joined the staff of the Leningrad Cons., teaching both cello and composition. In his music, Falik reveals a quasi-Romantic quality, making use of tantalizingly ambiguous melodic passages approaching the last ramparts of euphonious dissonance. His angular rhythms, with their frequently startling pauses, suggest a theatrical concept. He composed *Till Eulenspiegel*, "mystery ballet" (1967), *Oresteia*, choreographic tragedy (1968), and *Les Fourberies de Scapin*, opéra bouffe (Tartu, Dec. 22, 1984).

Falkner, Sir (Donald) Keith, English bass-baritone and pedagogue; b. Sawston, Cambridgeshire, March 1, 1900; d. Bungay, Suffolk, May 17, 1994. He studied at New College, Oxford, and with Plunkett Greene in London, Lierhammer in Vienna, Grenzebach in Berlin, and Dossert in Paris. From 1923 to 1946 he was active mainly as a concert singer, appearing principally in oratorios. After serving as visiting prof. (1950–51), assoc. prof. (1951–56), and prof. (1956–60) at Cornell Univ., he was director of the Royal College of Music in London (1960–74). He was joint artistic director of the Kings Lynn Festival (1981–83). In 1974 he was knighted.

Fall, Leo(pold), notable Austrian composer; b. Olmütz, Feb. 2, 1873; d. Vienna, Sept. 16, 1925. He began his musical training with his father, Moritz Fall (1840–1922), a military bandmaster and composer. At 14 he enrolled at the Vienna Cons. to study violin and piano, and also had courses in harmony and counterpoint with J. N. Fuchs and R. Fuchs. He was active as a theater conductor in Berlin (1894–96), and then was conductor of the Centralhallen-Theater in Hamburg (1896–98). Returning to Berlin, he conducted in theaters before becoming music director of the Intimes-Theater, a cabaret. There he brought out his comic opera *Paroli* (Oct. 4, 1902). After the failure of his grand opera *Irrlicht* (Mannheim, 1905), Fall concentrated his efforts on lighter stage works. Although his first operetta *Der Rebell* (Vienna, Nov. 28, 1905) was a failure at its premiere, its revised version as *Der liebe Augustin* (Berlin, Feb. 3, 1912) was a resounding success. In the meantime, Fall scored his first unqualified success with *Der fidele Bauer* (Mannheim, July 25, 1907). With *Die Dollarprinzessin* (Vienna, Nov. 2, 1907), Fall also was acclaimed in Great Britain and America, establishing him as one of the principal operetta composers of his time. His *Die geschiedene Frau* (Vienna, Dec. 23, 1908) was so successful that it was heard around the world. His success continued with *Das Puppenmädel* (Vienna, Nov. 4, 1910), *Die shöne Risette* (Vienna, Nov. 19, 1910), *Die Sirene* (Vienna, Jan. 5, 1911), and *The Eternal Waltz* (London, Dec. 22, 1911). During World War I, Fall continued to compose, producing the outstanding *Die Kaiserin* or *Fürstenliebe* (Berlin, Oct. 16, 1916) and the popular *Die Rose von Stambul* (Vienna, Dec. 2, 1916). With the war over, Fall turned out the notable scores *Der goldene Vogel* (Dresden, May 21, 1920), *Die spanische Nachtigall* (Berlin, Nov. 18, 1920), and *Die Strassensängerin* (Berlin, Sept. 24, 1921). His greatest postwar success came with his *Madame Pompadour* (Berlin, Sept. 9, 1922), which became an international favorite. His brother, Richard Fall (b. Gewitsch, April 3, 1882; d. in the concentration camp in Auschwitz about Nov. 20, 1943), was also a composer. He wrote operettas, revues, and film scores. Among his best known stage works were *Der Wiener Fratz* (Vienna, Jan. 1, 1912), *Der Weltenbummler* (Berlin, Nov. 18, 1915), *Die Puppenbaronessen* (Vienna, Sept. 1, 1917), and *Grossstadtmärchen* (Vienna, Jan. 10, 1920).

WORKS: MUSIC THEATER: *Lustige Blätter* (Hamburg, July 25, 1896); *1842* or *Der grosse Brand* (Hamburg, Aug. 1, 1897); *Der Brandstifter* (Berlin, Jan. 1, 1899); *Die Jagd nach dem Glück* (Berlin, Feb. 1, 1900); *'ne feine Nummer* (Berlin, Feb. 16, 1901; in collaboration with V. Hollander); *Paroli* or *Frau Denise* (Vienna, Oct. 4, 1902); *Der Rebell* (Vienna, Nov. 28, 1905; rev. version as *Der liebe Augustin*, Berlin, Feb. 3, 1912); *Der Fuss* (Chemnitz, Sept. 18, 1906); *Der fidele Bauer* (Mannheim, July 25, 1907); *Die Dollarprinzessin* (Vienna, Nov. 2, 1907); *Die geschiedene Frau* (Vienna, Dec. 23, 1908); *Brüderlein fein* (Berlin, Dec. 31, 1908); *Die Schrei nach der Ohrfeige* (1909); *Brüderlein fein* (Vienna, Dec. 1, 1909); *Das Puppenmädel* (Vienna, Nov. 4, 1910); *Die schöne Risette* (Vienna, Nov. 19, 1910); *Die Sirene* (Vienna, Jan. 5, 1911); *The Eternal Waltz* (London, Dec. 11, 1911); *Die Studentengräfin* (Berlin, Jan. 18, 1913); *Der Nachtschnellzug* (Vienna, Dec. 18, 1913); *Jung England* (Berlin, Feb. 14, 1914; rev. version as *Frau Ministerpräsident*, Dresden, Feb. 3, 1920); *Der künstliche Mensch* (Berlin, Oct. 2, 1915); *Die Kaiserin* or *Fürstenliebe* (Berlin, Oct. 16, 1915); *Tantalus im Dachstüberl* (Würzburg, March 26, 1916); *Seemansliebchen* (Berlin, Sept. 4, 1916; in collaboration with F. Warnke); *Die Rose von Stambul* (Vienna, Dec. 2, 1916); *Der goldene Vogel* (Dresden, May 21, 1920); *Die spanische Nachtigall* (Berlin, Nov. 18, 1920); *Die Strassensängerin* (Berlin, Sept. 24, 1921); *Der heilige Ambrosius* (Berlin, Nov. 3, 1921); *Madame Pompadour* (Berlin, Sept. 9, 1922); *Der süsse Kavalier* (Vienna, Dec. 11, 1923); *Jugen in Mai* (Dresden, Oct. 22, 1926); *Rosen aus Florida* (Vienna, Feb. 22, 1929; arranged by E. Korngold).

BIBL.: W. Zimmerli, *L.F.* (Zürich, 1957).

Falla (y Matheu), Manuel (Maria) de, great Spanish composer; b. Cadíz, Nov. 23, 1876; d. Alta Gracia, Córdoba province, Argentina, Nov. 14, 1946. He studied piano with his mother; after further instruction from Eloisa Galluzo, he studied harmony, counterpoint, and composition with Alejandro Odero and Enrique Broca; then went to Madrid, where he studied piano with José Tragó and composition with Felipe Pedrell at the Cons. He wrote several zarzuelas, but only *Los amores de la Inés* was performed (Madrid, April 12, 1902). His opera *La vida breve* won the prize of the Real Academia de Bellas Artes in Madrid in 1905, but it was not premiered until 8 years later. In 1905 he also won the Ortiz y Cussó Prize for pianists. In 1907 he went to Paris, where he became friendly with Debussy, Dukas, and Ravel, who aided and encouraged him as a composer. Under their influence, he adopted the principles of Impressionism without, however, giving up his personal and national style. He returned to Spain in 1914 and produced his tremendously effective ballet *El amor brujo* (Madrid, April 2, 1915). It was followed by the evocative *Noches en los jardines de Espaüa* for Piano and Orch. (Madrid, April 9, 1916). In 1919 he made his home in Granada, where he completed work on his celebrated ballet *El sombrero de tres picos* (London, July 22, 1919). Falla's art was rooted in both the folk songs of Spain and the purest historical traditions of Spanish music. Until 1919 his works were cast chiefly in the Andalusian idiom, and his instrumental technique was often conditioned by effects peculiar to Spain's national instrument, the guitar. In his puppet opera *El retablo de maese Pedro* (1919–22), he turned to the classical tradition of Spanish (especially Castilian) music. The keyboard style of his Harpsichord Concerto (1923–26), written at the suggestion of Wanda Landowska, reveals in the classical lucidity of its writing a certain kinship with Domenico Scarlatti, who lived in Spain for many years. Falla became president of the Instituto de Espana in 1938. When the Spanish Civil War broke out, and General Franco overcame the Loyalist government with the aid of Hitler and Mussolini, Falla left Spain and went to South America, never to return to his homeland. He went to Buenos Aires, where he conducted concerts of his music. He then withdrew to the small locality of Alta Gracia, where he lived the last years of his life in seclusion, working on his large scenic cantata *Atlántida*. It remained unfinished at his death and was later completed by his former pupil Ernesto Halffter.

WRITINGS: *Escritos sobre música y músicos* (ed. by F. Sopeüa; Madrid, 1950; 3d ed., 1972; Eng. tr., 1979, as *On Music and Musicians*); *Cartas a Segismondo Romero* (ed. by P. Recuero; Granada, 1976); *Correspondencia de Manuel de Falla* (ed. by E. Franco; Madrid, 1978).

WORKS: DRAMATIC: *La vida breve*, opera (1904–05; Nice, April 1, 1913); *El amor brujo*, ballet (1914–15; Madrid, April 2, 1915; concert version, 1916); *El corregidor y la molinera*, farsa mimica (1916–17; Madrid, April 7, 1917; rev. and expanded as *El sombrero de tres picos*); *El sombrero de tres picos*, ballet (rev. and expanded from *El corregidor y la molinera*; 1918–19; 2 orch. suites, 1919; London, July 22, 1919); *El retablo de maese Pedro*, puppet opera (1919–22; concert perf., Seville, March 23, 1923; private stage perf. in the salon of Princess de Poligna, Paris, June 25, 1923; public stage perf., Paris, Nov. 13, 1923); *Atlántida*, cantata escenica (1925–46; unfinished; completed by E. Halffter; Milan, June 18, 1962; rev. and perf. in concert form, Lucerne, Sept. 9, 1976); also several zarzuelas, including *Los amores de la Inés* (Madrid, April 12, 1902); incidental music, and a comic opera, *Fuego fatuo* (1918–19).

BIBL.: J. Trend, *M. d.F. and Spanish Music* (N.Y., 1929; new ed., 1934); Roland-Manuel, *M. d.F.* (Paris, 1930); A. Sagardia, *M. d.F.* (Madrid, 1946); J. Thomas, *M. d.F. en la Isla* (Palma, 1947); J. Jaenisch, *M. d.F. und die spanische Musik* (Zürich and Freiburg im Breisgau, 1952); L. Campodonico, *F.* (Paris, 1959); R. Arizaga, *M. d.F.* (Buenos Aires, 1961); E. Molina Fajardo, *M. d.F. y el "cante jondo"* (Granada, 1962); J. Viniegra, *M. d.F.: Su vida intima* (Cádiz, 1966); A. Saeardia, *Vida y Obra de M. d.F.* (Madrid, 1967); J. Grunfeld, *M. d.F.: Spanien und die neue Musik* (Zürich, 1968); A. Campoamor Gonzalez, *M. d.F., 1876–1946* (Madrid, 1976); R. Crichton, *M. d.F.: Descriptive Catalogue of His Works* (London, 1976); B. James, *M. d.F. and the Spanish Musical Renaissance* (London, 1979); R. Crichton, *F.* (London, 1982); G. Chase and A. Budwig, *M. d.F.: A Bibliography and Research Guide* (N.Y., 1986); J. de Persia, *Los últimos aüos de M. d.F.* (Madrid, 1989); T. Garms, *Der Flamenco und der spanische Folklore in M. d.F.s Werken* (Wiesbaden, 1990); K. Pahlen, *M. d.F. und der Musik in Spaniern* (Mainz, 1993).

Famintsyn, Alexander (Sergeievich), Russian music critic and composer; b. Kaluga, Nov. 5, 1841; d. Ligovo, near St. Petersburg, July 6, 1896. He studied with Jean Vogt in St. Petersburg, and then with Hauptmann and Richter in Leipzig. He taught music history at the St. Petersburg Cons. (1865–72); he tr. into Russian the textbooks *Allgemeine Musiklehre* by Marx and *Harmonielehre* by Richter. However, he soon abandoned his teaching activities and devoted himself chiefly to music criticism, taking a very conservative attitude. He indulged in frequent polemics against the Russian composers of the National School, and Mussorgsky caricatured him in his satirical song *The Classicist* and in a section of his burlesque *Rayok*. Famintsyn's publications on Russian instruments are valuable. He publ. essays on the gusli (1890) and the domra (1891). His opera *Sardanapal* was produced in St. Petersburg on Dec. 5, 1875, but without any success; his other opera, *Uriel Acosta* (1883), was not performed.

Fancelli, Giuseppe, admired Italian tenor; b. Florence, Nov. 24, 1833; d. there, Dec. 23, 1887. He had no formal musical instruction and never learned to read music. However, his natural vocal gifts were discovered and he made his operatic debut as the Fisherman in *Guglielmo Tell* at Milan's La Scala in 1860. After singing in Ancona, Rome, and Trieste, he appeared at London's Covent Garden (1866–68; 1870–72), where he excelled as Edgardo, Alfredo, Raoul, and Pollione. In 1872 he sang Radames in the first Italian staging of *Aida* at La Scala. Fancelli's marvelous high C endeared him to a generation of opera aficionados.

Fano, (Aronne) Guido Alberto, Italian composer, teacher, and writer on music; b. Padua, May 18, 1875; d. Tauriano di Spilimbergo, Friuli, Aug. 14, 1961. He was a pupil of Orefice and Pollini in Padua, then of Martucci at the Bologna Liceo Musicale (composition diploma, 1897); he received a law degree from the Univ. of Bologna (1901). He taught piano at the Bologna Liceo Musicale (1900–05), then was director of the conservatories in Parma (1905–12), Naples (1912–16), and Palermo (1916–22); he subsequently taught piano at the Milan Cons. (1922–38; 1945–47). He composed the poema drammatico *Astraea* and the dramma musicale *Juturna*.

Farberman, Harold, American conductor and composer; b. N.Y., Nov. 2, 1929. He was educated at the Juilliard School of Music in New York (diploma, 1951) and the New England Cons. of Music in Boston (B.S., 1956; M.S., 1957). He was a percussionist in the Boston Sym. Orch. (1951–63) and conductor of the New Arts Orch. in Boston (1955–63); he then was conductor of the Colorado Springs (Colo.) Phil. (1967–68) and the Oakland (Calif.) Sym. Orch. (1971–79); subsequently he was principal guest conductor of the Bournemouth Sinfonietta (from 1986). In 1975 he became founder-president of the Conductors' Guild. In 1980 he organized the Conductors' Inst. at the Univ. of West Virginia, which moved to the Univ. of South Carolina in 1987. His dramatic works include *Medea*, chamber opera (1960–61; Boston, March 26, 1961) and *The Losers*, opera (N.Y., March 26, 1971); also ballets and film scores.

Fariñas, Carlos, Cuban composer and teacher; b. Cienfuegos, Nov. 28, 1934. He was a student of Ardévol and Gramatges at the Havana Cons., of Copland at the Berkshire Music Center at Tanglewood (summer, 1956), and of Pirumov and Rogal-Levitski at the Moscow Cons. (1961–63); later he worked in Berlin on a grant from the Deutscher Akademischer Austauschdienst (1975–77). After serving as director of the Cons. Alejandro García Caturla in Havana (1963–67), he was head of the music dept. of the Biblioteca Nacional de Cuba there (1967–77). In 1978 he joined the faculty of music at the Instituto Superior de Arte de Cuba in Havana, where he was founder-director of the Estudio de Música Electroacustica y por Computadoras (from 1989). His works are generally cast along avant-garde lines, and include the opera *Escenas* (1990) and the ballets *Despertar* (1959–60) and *Yagruma* (1975).

Farinelli (real name, **Carlo Broschi**), celebrated Italian castrato soprano; b. Andria, Jan. 24, 1705; d. Bologna, July 15, 1782. His father, Salvatore Broschi, was a musician and most likely Carlo's earliest instructor in music. He later adopted the name Farinelli to honor his benefactor, Farina. He studied with Porpora in Naples, making his first public appearance there in his teacher's serenata *Angelica e Medoro* in 1720; subsequent appearances brought him great success, and he soon became famous as "il ragazzo" ("the boy"). He also sang in Rome, appearing in Porpora's opera *Eumene* at the age of 16. His repeated successes brought him renown throughout Italy and abroad, and led to his first appearance in Vienna (1724). He met the celebrated castrato alto Bernacchi in Bologna in 1727; in a singing contest with him, Farinelli acknowledged defeat and persuaded Bernacchi to give him lessons to achieve virtuosity in coloratura. After further visits to Vienna in 1728 and 1731, Porpora called him to London to sing with the Opera of the Nobility; he made his London debut in Hasse's *Artaserse* on Oct. 27, 1734, appearing with Senesino and Cuzzoni; he remained with the company until the summer of 1736, when he went to Paris, then returned to it for the 1736–37 season. Having amassed a fortune in London, Farinelli went to Madrid in 1737. He attained unparalleled success as court singer to King Philip V; his duty was to sing arias every night to cure the king's melancholy, and his influence on the ailing monarch, and on the queen, was such that he was able to command considerable funds to engage famous performers for the Madrid court. When his voice began to fail, he served as impresario, decorator, and stage director. He continued to enjoy the court's favor under Philip's successor, Ferdinand VI, who made him a knight of the order of Calatrava in 1750. However, when Carlos III became king in 1759, Farinelli was dismissed. He then returned to Italy in possession of great wealth. He built a palatial villa for himself near Bologna and spent the last years of his life in contentment.

BIBL.: G. Sacchi, *Vita del Cavaliere Don Carlo Broschi, detto F.* (Venice, 1784); C. Ricci, *Burney, Casanova, e F. in Bologna* (Milan, 1890); J. Desastre, *Carlo Broschi* (Zürich, 1903).

Farinelli (real name, **Finco**), **Giuseppe (Francesco),** prolific Italian composer; b. Este, May 7, 1769; d. Trieste, Dec. 12, 1836. In 1785 he entered the Cons. della Pietà dei Turchini at Naples, his teachers being La Barbiera, Fago, Sala, and Tritto. His first opera, *Il dottorato di Pulcinella*, produced in 1792, was followed by 50 or 60 others, not original, but in very happy imitation of Cimarosa's style and chiefly comic. During the years 1810–17 he lived at Turin, then went to Trieste as maestro di cappella and organist at the Cathedral of San Giusto. He also wrote several oratorios.

Farjeon, Harry, English composer; b. Hohokus, N.J. (of English parents), May 6, 1878; d. London, Dec. 29, 1948. He was a son of the English novelist B. L. Farjeon, and grandson of the famous actor Joseph Jefferson. He was educated in England, taking music lessons with Landon Ronald and John Storer; he then studied composition with Corder at the Royal Academy of Music in London; won the Lucas Medal and other prizes. In 1903 he became an instructor at the Royal Academy of Music. He composed the opera *Floretta* (1899) and the operettas *The Registry Office* (1900) and *A Gentleman of the Road* (1902).

Farkas, Ferenc, prominent Hungarian composer and teacher; b. Nagykanizsa, Dec. 15, 1905. He began to study piano as a child; took courses with Leo Weiner and Albert Siklós at the Academy of Music in Budapest (1922–27); a state scholarship enabled him to study with Respighi at the Accademia di Santa Cecilia in Rome (1929–31). Returning to Hungary, he was a music teacher at the municipal school in Budapest (1935–41). From 1941 to 1944 he taught at the Cluj Cons.; he was director of the music school in Székesfehérvár (1946–48); from 1949 to 1975 he was a prof. of composition at the Academy of Music in Budapest. In 1950 and 1991 he was awarded the Kossuth Prize and in 1960 the Erkel Prize and was made Merited Artist (1965) and Honored Artist (1970) of the Hungarian People's Republic. He also received the Herder Prize of Hamburg (1979) and was made a Cavaliere dell'Ordine della Repubblica Italiana (1985).

WORKS: DRAMATIC: *The Magic Cupboard*, comic opera (1938–

42; Budapest, April 22, 1942; also a separate overture, 1952); *The Sly Students*, ballet (1949); *Csinom Palkó*, musical play (1950; rev. 1960); *Vidróczki*, radio ballad (1959; rev. as an opera, 1964); *Piroschka*, musical comedy (1967); *Story of Noszty Junior with Mari Tóth*, musical comedy (1971); *Panegyricus*, ballet (1972); *A Gentleman from Venice*, opera (1980). Also incidental music and film scores.

BIBL.: J. Ujfalussy, *F. F.* (Budapest, 1969).

Farley, Carole Ann, talented American soprano; b. Le Mars, Iowa, Nov. 29, 1946. She studied at the Indiana Univ. School of Music (Mus.B., 1968), with Reid in New York, and on a Fulbright scholarship with Schech at the Munich Hochschule für Musik (1968–69). In 1969 she made her debut at the Linz Landestheater and also her U.S. debut at N.Y.'s Town Hall; subsequently appeared as a soloist with major orchs. of the United States and Europe, and sang with the Welsh National Opera (1971–72), the Cologne Opera (1972–75), the Strasbourg Opera (1975), the N.Y. City Opera (1976), and the Lyons Opera (1976–77). She made her formal Metropolitan Opera debut in New York as Lulu on March 18, 1977, and continued to sing there in later seasons; she also sang at the Zürich Opera (1979), the Deutsche Oper am Rhein in Düsseldorf (1980–81; 1984), the Chicago Lyric Opera (1981), the Florence Maggio Musicale (1985), and at the Teatro Colón in Buenos Aires (1989). In addition to her esteemed portrayal of Lulu, which she essayed over 80 times in various operatic centers, she also sang Poppea, Donna Anna, Violetta, Massenet's Manon, Mimi, and various roles in Richard Strauss's operas. She married **José Serebrier** in 1969.

Farncombe, Charles (Frederick), English conductor; b. London, July 29, 1919. He first studied engineering at the Univ. of London (B.Sc., 1940); after military service in World War II, he enrolled at the Royal School of Church Music, Canterbury, and the Royal Academy of Music, London. In 1955 he organized the Handel Opera Soc., serving as its music director and conductor. From 1970 to 1979 he was chief conductor of the Drottningholm Court Theater in Stockholm, then was music director of the London Chamber Opera (from 1983) and the Malcolm Sargent Festival Choir (from 1986). In 1977 he was made a Commander of the Order of the British Empire.

Farquhar, David (Andross), New Zealand composer and teacher; b. Cambridge, New Zealand, April 5, 1928. He studied with Douglas Lilburn, at Canterbury College, and at Victoria College (B.A., B.Mus., 1948); went to England and took his M.A. at Emmanuel College, Cambridge (1951), completing his training with Benjamin Frankel at the Guildhall School of Music in London (1951–52). Returning to New Zealand, he was a lecturer (1953–76) and prof. of music (1976–93) at Victoria Univ. of Wellington; in 1974 he was founding president of the Composers Assn. of New Zealand. His music is contrapuntal in structure and neo-Romantic in mood. He composed the operas *A Unicorn for Christmas* (1962) and *Shadow* (1970; Wellington, Sept. 19, 1988); also incidental music.

Farrar, Geraldine, celebrated American soprano; b. Melrose, Mass., Feb. 28, 1882; d. Ridgefield, Conn., March 11, 1967. She studied music with Mrs. J. H. Long of Boston; she took lessons with Emma Thursby in New York, Trabadello in Paris, and Graziani in Berlin; she made a successful debut at the Berlin Royal Opera on Oct. 15, 1901, as Marguerite, under the direction of Karl Muck; she then studied with Lilli Lehmann. She sang at the Monte Carlo Opera (1903–06). Her career in Europe was well established before her American debut as Juliette at the Metropolitan Opera in New York (Nov. 26, 1906); she remained on the roster for 16 years; she made her farewell appearance in *Zaza* on April 22, 1922, but continued to sing in concert; she gave her last public performance at Carnegie Hall in New York in 1931 and then retired to Ridgefield, Conn. Her greatest success was as Cio-Cio-San, which she sang opposite Caruso's Pinkerton in *Madama Butterfly* at its American premiere at the Metropolitan on Feb. 11, 1907; she subsequently sang this part in America more than 100 times. Her interpretation of Carmen was no less remarkable. She also appeared in silent films between 1915 and 1919; her film version of *Carmen* aroused considerable interest. On Feb. 8, 1916, she married the actor Lou Tellegen, from whom she was subsequently divorced. She made adaptations of pieces by Kreisler, Rachmaninoff, and others, for which she publ. the lyrics. She wrote an autobiography, *Such Sweet Compulsion* (N.Y., 1938), which had been preceded in 1916 by *Geraldine Farrar: The Story of an American Singer*.

BIBL.: E. Wagenknecht, *G. F.: An Authorized Record of Her Career* (Seattle, 1929); E. Nash, *Always First Class: The Career of G. F.* (Washington, D.C., 1982); A. Truxall, ed., *All Good Greetings, G. F.: Letters of G. F. to Ilka Marie Stolker, 1946–1958* (Pittsburgh, 1991).

Farrell, Eileen, brilliant American soprano; b. Willimantic, Conn., Feb. 13, 1920. Her parents were vaudeville singers; she received her early vocal training with Merle Alcock in New York, and later studied with Eleanor McLellan. In 1940 she sang on the radio; in 1947–48 she made a U.S. tour as a concert singer; toured South America in 1949. Her song recital in New York on Oct. 24, 1950, was enthusiastically acclaimed and secured for her immediate recognition. She was soloist in Beethoven's 9th Sym. with Toscanini and the NBC Sym. Orch.; she also appeared many times with the N.Y. Phil. She made her operatic debut as Santuzza with the San Carlo Opera in Tampa, Fla., in 1956. In 1958 she joined the San Francisco Opera and in 1957 became a member of the Lyric Opera of Chicago. On Dec. 6, 1960, she made a successful debut with the Metropolitan Opera in New York as Gluck's Alcestis; she remained on its roster until 1964, then returned in 1965–66. She was a Distinguished Prof. of Music at the Indiana Univ. School of Music in Bloomington from 1971 to 1980; then held that title at the Univ. of Maine in Orono from 1983 to 1985.

Fassbänder, Brigitte, noted German mezzo-soprano, opera producer, and Intendant, daughter of **Willi Domgraf-Fassbänder;** b. Berlin, July 3, 1939. She studied with her father and attended the Nuremberg Cons. (1952–61). In 1961 she made her operatic debut as Nicklausse in *Les Contes d'Hoffman* at the Bavarian State Opera in Munich, where she became one of its most esteemed members. In 1970 she was honored as a Bavarian Kammersängerin. She appeared as Carmen at the San Francisco Opera in 1970, as Octavian at London's Covent Garden in 1971, and as Brangäne at the Paris Opéra in 1972. From 1972 to 1978 she appeared regularly at the Salzburg Festivals. On Feb. 16, 1974, she made her Metropolitan Opera debut in New York as Octavian, returning there as Fricka in *Die Walküre* in 1986. In 1989 she sang Clytemnestra at the Salzburg Festival, returning in 1990 as Clairon in *Capriccio*. On Jan. 9, 1994, she made her N.Y. recital debut at Alice Tully Hall. In 1995 she retired from singing. From 1999 she was the Intendant of the Innsbruck Opera. While her operatic repertoire ranged from Gluck to contemporary scores, she won special distinction for her roles in operas by Mozart and Strauss. She also pursued a distinguished concert career.

Fassbender, Zdenka, Bohemian soprano; b. Děčín, Dec. 12, 1879; d. Munich, March 14, 1954. She studied voice in Prague with Sophie Löwe-Destinn; she made her operatic debut in Karlsruhe in 1899; from 1906 to 1919 she was one of the principal singers at the Munich Opera; she also sang at Covent Garden in London (1910, 1913). **Felix Mottl** married her on his deathbed to sanction their long-standing alliance.

Faull, Ellen, American soprano and teacher; b. Pittsburgh, Oct. 14, 1918. She studied at the Curtis Inst. of Music in Philadelphia and at Columbia Univ. She made her debut as Donna Anna in *Don Giovanni* with the N.Y. City Opera on Oct. 23, 1947, establishing herself as one of its principals, singing there regularly until 1979. She also appeared in San Francisco, Boston, and Chicago, and as a soloist with many U.S. orchs. Faull taught at N.Y.'s Manhattan School of Music (from 1971) and the Juilliard School (from 1981). She was particularly noted for her roles in Italian operas.

Fauré, Gabriel (-Urbain), great French composer and pedagogue; b. Pamiers, Ariège, May 12, 1845; d. Paris, Nov. 4, 1924. His father was a provincial inspector of primary schools; noticing the musical instinct of his son, he took him to Paris to study with Louis Niedermeyer; after Niedermeyer's death in 1861, Fauré studied with Saint-Saëns, from whom he received thorough training in composition. In 1866 he went to Rennes as organist at the church of St.-Sauveur; returned to Paris on the eve of the Franco-Prussian War in 1870, and volunteered in the light infantry. He was organist at Notre Dame de Clignancourt (1870), St.-Honoré d'Elyau (1871), and St.-Sulpice (1871–74). He then was named deputy organist (to Saint-Saëns, 1874), choirmaster (1877), and chief organist (1896) at the Madeleine. In 1896 he was appointed prof. of composition at the Paris Cons. He was an illustrious teacher; among his students were Ravel, Enesco, Koechlin, Roger-Ducasse, Florent Schmitt, and Nadia Boulanger. In 1905 he succeeded Théodore Dubois as director and served until 1920. Then, quite unexpectedly, he developed ear trouble, resulting in gradual loss of hearing. Distressed, he made an effort to conceal it but was eventually forced to abandon his teaching position. From 1903 to 1921 he wrote occasional music reviews in *Le Figaro* (a selection was publ. as *Opinions musicales*, Paris, 1930). He was elected a member of the Académie des Beaux Arts in 1909, and in 1910 was made a Commander of the Légion d'honneur. Fauré's stature as a composer is undiminished by the passage of time. He developed a musical idiom all his own; by subtle application of old modes, he evoked the aura of eternally fresh art; by using unresolved mild discords and special coloristic effects, he anticipated procedures of Impressionism; in his piano works, he shunned virtuosity in favor of the Classical lucidity of the French masters of the clavecin; the precisely articulated melodic line of his songs is in the finest tradition of French vocal music. His great *Requiem* and his *Élégie* for Cello and Piano have entered the general repertoire.

WORKS: DRAMATIC: *Barnabé*, opéra comique (1879; unfinished; not perf.); *Caligula*, op. 52, incidental music to a play by A. Dumas père (Paris, Nov. 8, 1888); *Shylock*, incidental music to a play by E. de Haraucourt, after Shakespeare, op. 57 (Paris, Dec. 17, 1889); *La Passion*, incidental music to a play by Haraucourt (Paris, April 21, 1890); *Le Bourgeois Gentilhomme*, incidental music to a play by Molière (1893); *Pelléas et Mélisande*, incidental music to a play by Maeterlinck, op. 80 (London, June 21, 1898); *Prométhée*, tragédie lyrique, op. 82 (Béziers, Aug. 27, 1900); *Le Voile du bonheur*, incidental music to a play by Clémenceau, op. 88 (Paris, Nov. 4, 1901); *Pénélope*, drame lyrique (Monte Carlo, March 4, 1913); *Masques et bergamasques*, comédie musicale, op. 112 (Monte Carlo, April 10, 1919).

BIBL.: L. Vuillemin, *G. F. et son oeuvre* (Paris, 1914); L. Aguettant, *La Génie de G. F.* (Lyons, 1924); A. Bruneau, *La Vie et les oeuvres de G. F.* (Paris, 1925); C. Koechlin, *G. F.* (Paris, 1927; Eng. tr., 1945; 2d ed., 1949); P. Fauré-Fremiet, *G. F.* (Paris, 1929; 2d ed., aug., 1957); G. Servières, *G. F.* (Paris, 1930); V. Jankélévitch, *G. F. et ses mélodies* (Paris, 1938; 3d ed., aug., 1974, as *G. F. et l'inexprimable*); G. Fauré, *G. F.* (Paris, 1945); C. Rostand, *L'Oeuvre de G. F.* (Paris, 1945); N. Suckling, *F.* (London, 1946); E. Vuillermoz, *G. F.* (Paris, 1960; Eng. tr., 1969); M. Long, *Au piano avec G. F.* (Paris, 1963); J.-M. Nectoux, *F.* (Paris, 1972; 3d ed., aug., 1995); idem, *Phonographie de G. F.* (Paris, 1979); R. Orledge, *G. F.* (London, 1979); J. Barrie Jones, tr. and ed., *G. F.: A Life in Letters* (London, 1989); R. Tait, *The Musical Language of G. F.* (N.Y. and London, 1989); J. Nectoux, *G. F.: Le voix du clair-obscur* (Paris, 1990; Eng. tr., 1991, as *G. F.: A Musical Life*); E. Phillips, *G. F.: A Guide to Research* (Levittown, Pa., 1998).

Faure, Jean-Baptiste, famous French baritone; b. Moulins, Jan. 15, 1830; d. Paris, Nov. 9, 1914. He was a choirboy in Paris, then entered the Paris Cons. in 1851. On Oct. 20, 1852, he made his operatic debut at the Opéra Comique as Pygmalion in Massé's *Galathée*. He subsequently created the roles of Malipieri in Auber's *Haydée* (July 5, 1853) and Hoël in Meyerbeer's *Dinorah, ou Le Pardon de Ploërmel* (April 4, 1859) there. It was as Hoël that he made his Covent Garden debut in London on April 10, 1860; he continued to sing there, as well as at Drury Lane and Her Majesty's Theatre, until 1877. He made his debut at the Paris Opéra as Julien in Poniatowsky's *Pierre de Médicis* on Oct. 14, 1861; he continued to sing there until 1869, and then again from 1872 to 1876 and in 1878. Among the roles he created at the Opéra were Nelusko in Meyerbeer's *L'Africaine* (April 28, 1865), Posa in Verdi's *Don Carlos* (March 11, 1867), and Hamlet in Thomas's opera (March 9, 1868). In later years he appeared in concerts, garnering notable acclaim in Vienna and London. He excelled in dramatic roles in French and Italian operas, and was particularly renowned for his portrayals of Don Giovanni, Méphistophélès, and Guillaume Tell. He publ. 2 books on singing, and also taught at the Paris Cons. (1857–60). He was married to the singer Constance Caroline Lefèbvre (1828–1905).

Favart, Charles-Simon, French librettist and impresario; b. Paris, Nov. 13, 1710; d. Belleville, near Paris, March 12, 1792. He publ. satirical plays as a youth. After a successful performance of one of his vaudevilles at the Opéra Comique, he was appointed stage manager there; in 1758 he became its director. In 1745 he married **Marie Favart**. He wrote about 150 librettos for operas by Duni, Philidor, and Gluck. He also was the author of *Les Amours de Bastien et Bastienne* (1753), used by Mozart in a German version for his early opera (1768).

Favart, Marie (née **-Justine-Benoîte Duronceray**), French soprano, actress, and dramatist; b. Avignon, June 15, 1727; d. Paris, April 21, 1772. Her father was André-Réné Duronceray, a musician in the Chapel Royal under Louis XV. In 1744 she began her career under the name Mlle. de Chantilly in **Charles-Simon Favart**'s *Les Fêtes publiques* at the Paris Opéra Comique, becoming his wife in 1745. They subsequently were active in Flanders until the unwanted advances of her patron, the Maréchal de Saxe, caused them to flee in 1747. In 1749 she appeared at the Paris Comédie-Italienne, and then was notably successful in soubrette roles at the Théâtre-Italien there from 1751 to 1771. Her most famous role was Serpina in *La Serva padrona*. She also collaborated with her husband on several works, and often appeared in many of the works he wrote. Her career was marked by various theatrical intrigues, leading Offenbach to compose the operetta *Mme. Favart* (1878).

BIBL.: A. Pougin, *Madame F.* (Paris, 1912).

Favero, Mafalda, Italian soprano; b. Portamaggiore, near Ferrara, Jan. 6, 1903; d. Milan, Sept. 3, 1981. She studied at the Bologna Cons. with Alessandro Vezzani. Under the stage name of Maria Bianchi, she made her operatic debut in 1926 in Cremona as Lola; in 1927 she made her formal operatic debut as Liù in Parma. In 1928 she made her first appearance at Milan's La Scala as Eva in *Die Meistersinger von Nürnberg*, and subsequently sang there regularly until 1943, then again from 1945 to 1950. In 1937 and 1939 she appeared at London's Covent Garden. On Nov. 24, 1938, she made her Metropolitan Opera debut in New York as Mimi, remaining on its roster for a season. Among her finest roles were Mimi, Adriana Lecouvreur, Manon, and Thaïs.

BIBL.: I. Buscaglia, *M.F. nella vita e nell'arte* (1946).

Fayer, Yuri, Russian conductor; b. Kiev, Jan. 17, 1890; d. Moscow, Aug. 3, 1971. After attending the Kiev Cons., he studied violin and composition at the Moscow Cons. He played in various orchs. before conducting opera in Riga (1909–10); in 1916 he joined the orch. of the Bolshoi Theater in Moscow, where he was assistant conductor (1919–23) and chief conductor (1923–63) of its ballet; he toured with it in Europe, the United States, and China. His memoirs were publ. in 1970.

Federici, Vincenzo, Italian composer; b. Pesaro, 1764; d. Milan, Sept. 26, 1826. He became an orphan at 16. He lived in Turin, where he produced his first opera, *L'Olimpiade* (Dec. 26, 1789). He then made his way to London, where he became cembalist at the Italian Opera. He returned to Italy in 1802, and in 1808 he became a teacher of harmony at the Milan Cons.

Fehr, Max, Swiss musicologist; b. Bulach, near Zürich, June 17, 1887; d. Winterthur, April 27, 1963. He studied at the Univ. of Zürich with Eduard Bernoulli (Ph.D., 1912). In 1917 he became librarian, and in 1923 president, of the Allgemeine Musikgesellschaft of Zürich; he retired as librarian in 1957. In addition to his scholarly works on music, he wrote a satirical novelette, *Die Meistersinger von Zürich* (Zürich, 1916).

WRITINGS: *Spielleute im alten Zürich* (Zürich, 1916); *Unter Wagners Taktstock* (Winterthur, 1922); *Geschichte des Musikkollegiums Winterthur, I. Teil: 1629–1830* (Winterthur, 1929); *Richard Wagners Schweizer Zeit* (2 vols., Aarau, 1934, 1953); *Die Familie Mozart in Zürich* (Zürich, 1942); *Die wandernden Theatertruppen in der Schweiz: Verzeichnis der Truppen, Aufführungen und Spieldaten für das 17. und 18. Jahrhundert* (Einsiedeln, 1949); with L. Caflisch, *Der junge Mozart in Zürich* (Zürich, 1952); *Musikalische Jagd* (Zürich, 1954).

BIBL.: E. Nievergelt, *M. F.* (Zürich, 1968).

Feinhals, Fritz, distinguished German baritone; b. Cologne, Dec. 4, 1869; d. Munich, Aug. 30, 1940. He studied in Milan and Padua. He made his operatic debut in Essen in 1895 as Silvio; in 1898 he joined the Munich Court (later State) Opera, where he remained until his retirement in 1927. On Nov. 18, 1908, he made his debut at the Metropolitan Opera in New York as Wotan in *Die Walküre*, but was on its roster for only the 1908–09 season. He also made appearances in London, Paris, and Vienna. He was a Wagnerian singer par excellence; his portrayal of Wotan was imperious in its power; he was also successful in the role of Hans Sachs. He also excelled in operas by Mozart and Verdi.

Fel, Marie, famous French soprano; b. Bordeaux, Oct. 24, 1713; d. Paris, Feb. 2, 1794. She studied with Christina VanLoo in Paris, making her debut as Venus in the prologue to La Coste's *Philomèle* at the Opéra on Oct. 29, 1734; she subsequently sang with notable success there, and also at court and at the Concert Spirituel. She retired from the operatic stage in 1758. She was renowned for her performances of roles in French operas. Sophie Arnould was one of her pupils. Her brother, Antoine Fel (b. Bordeaux, 1694; d. Bicêtre, June 27, 1771), was a singer at the Paris Opéra as well as a composer.

Felciano, Richard, American composer; b. Santa Rosa, Calif., Dec. 7, 1930. He studied with Milhaud at Mills College in Oakland, California (1952) and subsequently at the Paris Cons. (1953–55). As a student living in San Francisco, he supported himself by singing in a liturgical choir of men and boys, during which time he twice sang the complete liturgical year in Dominican chant and from neumatic notation. This experience had a profound effect on his style, even in orchestral and electronic music, and it was reinforced by several residencies at the Abbey of Solesmes while he was a student in Paris. After a period of service in the U.S. Army, he studied privately with Dallapiccola in Florence. While there, he met and married Rita Baumgartner, a native of Zürich, who later, as Rita Felciano, became a recognized American dance critic. In 1959 he took his Ph.D. at the Univ. of Iowa. In 1964 he received a Ford Foundation fellowship to serve as composer-in-residence to Cass Technical High School in Detroit, during which time he composed a number of works for student ensembles. Returning to San Francisco in 1965, he received a series of commissions for the Roman Catholic liturgy in the wake of the liberalizing directives of the 2d Vatican Council (1964). One of these commissions, *Pentecost Sunday*, introduced electronic sound into liturgical music and assumed a permanent place in its repertory. In 1967 he was appointed resident composer to the National Center for Experiments in Television in San Francisco, a pioneering effort by the Rockefeller Foundation to explore television as a nondocumentary, nonnarrative medium. As a participant in this project, he created *Linearity*, a television piece for harp and live electronics, the first musical work using the technical properties of a television system as an instrumental component. In the same year, he joined the music faculty of the Univ. of Calif. at Berkeley. In 1968 he received a Guggenheim fellowship and in 1971 a 2-year fellowship from the Ford Foundation as composer-in-residence to the City of Boston. During that residency, he created a 14-channel electronic environment with light sculptures of his own design for Boston City Hall and *Galactic Rounds* (1972), an orchestral work whose climax deploys rotating trumpets and trombones to create Doppler shifts, an early indication of his interest in acoustics which was to become pronounced in later decades. In 1974 he received an award from the American Academy of Arts and Letters and in 1975 was a resident fellow at the Rockefeller Foundation's International Study and Conference Center in Bellagio. From 1974 to 1978 he served as a panelist for the NEA and from 1976 to 1980 was an Art Commissioner for the City of San Francisco. In 1976 he was commissioned to compose a work joining an Eastern with a Western instrument for the 12th World Congress of the International Musicological Society at Berkeley, a pioneering forum in the growth of East-West studies in music. The result was *In Celebration of Golden Rain* (1977) for Indonesian gamelan and pipe organ, a work which addressed the conflicting scales, design, and intent of the instruments of these 2 cultures as a problem of symbiosis rather than one of fusion, making a philosophical as well as a musical statement. Many subsequent works show the influence of non-Western cultures. In 1982–83 he was active at IRCAM in Paris; he returned to Berkeley and in 1987 founded the Center for New Music and Audio Technologies (CNMAT), an interdisciplinary facility linking music, cognitive psychology, linguistics, computer science, and architecture. His music reflects an acute interest in acoustics and sonority, and an attempt to cast them in ritual, architectural, or dramatic forms. He composed the chamber opera *Sir Gawain and the Green Knight* (San Francisco, April 4, 1964).

Feld, Jindřich, Czech composer; b. Prague, Feb. 19, 1925. He studied violin and viola with his father, a prof. of violin at the Prague Cons.; he then took courses in composition there with Hlobil (1945–48) and with Řídký at the Prague Academy of Music (1948–52); he also studied musicology, aesthetics, and philosophy at the Charles Univ. in Prague (Ph.D., 1952). His 4th string quartet was awarded the State Prize in 1968. In 1968–69 he was a visiting prof. at the Univ. of Adelaide. During this time, he composed his *Dramatic Fantasy: The Days of August*, an orch. score in protest to the Soviet invasion of his homeland. From 1972 to 1986 he was a prof. of composition at the Prague Cons. He subsequently was head of the music dept. of the Czech Radio from 1990. After composing works reflective of the Czech tradition, he developed a distinctive voice utilizing a variety of modern compositional methods. Among his works is the children's opera *Pošťácká pohádka* (The Postman's Tale; 1956).

Feldbusch, Eric, Belgian cellist, music educator, and composer; b. Grivegnée, March 2, 1922. He studied cello at the Liège Cons. (1934–39); he later took courses in composition with Quinet and Legley (1947–48). He was director of the Mons Cons. (1963–72) and of the Brussels Cons. (1974–87). He composed the opera *Orestes* (1969) and the ballet *El Diablo Cojuelo* (1972).

Felderhof, Jan (Reindert Adriaan), Dutch composer and pedagogue; b. Bussum, near Amsterdam, Sept. 25, 1907. He studied violin with Felice Togni and Hendrik Rynbergen (diploma, 1931) and theory and composition with Sem Dresden (diploma, 1933) at the Amsterdam Cons.; he later studied with Chris Bos at the Utrecht Cons. (diploma, 1958). He taught at the Amsterdam Cons. (1934–54; 1958–68), where he was adjunct director (1968–73); he also taught at the Bussum music school (1944–54), served as director of the Rotterdam Cons. (1954–55), and taught at the Utrecht Cons. (1956–67). In 1970 he was made a Knight of the Order of Oranje Nassau by the Dutch government. His works have an agreeable veneer of simple musicality, and all are excellently written. He composed the opera *Vliegvuur* (Wildfire; 1959–64; Dutch Radio, Nov. 10, 1965).

Feldhoff, Gerd, German baritone; b. Radervormwald, near Cologne, Oct. 29, 1931. He studied at the North West Music Academy in Detmold. He made his operatic debut in Essen in 1959 as Figaro in *Le nozze di Figaro*, then sang at the Städtische Oper in Berlin, the Hamburg State Opera, and the Frankfurt am Main Opera. From 1968 to 1978 he appeared at the Bayreuth Festivals. He made his Metropolitan Opera debut in New York as Kaspar in *Der Freischütz* on Sept. 28, 1971. He was especially noted as a dramatic baritone; he also made tours as a concert artist.

Feldman, Jill, esteemed American soprano; b. Los Angeles, April 21, 1952. She studied with Michael Ingham at the Univ. of Calif. at Santa Barbara (B.A. in musicology, 1975), Lillian Loran in San Francisco (1975–95), Andrea von Ramm in Basel (1980–81), and Nicole Fallien (1987–91) and Anna Maria Bondi (1992–93) in Paris. In 1977 she made her recital debut in Berkeley, returning there in 1978 to make her first appearance as a soloist with the Univ. of Calif. Orch. In 1979 she made her operatic debut in the role of La Musica in *Orfeo* in Berkeley, and then made her European operatic debut in 1980 as Clerio in Cavalli's *Erismena* in Spoleto. In 1981 she became a leading member of William Christie's Les Arts Florissants in Paris, where she won acclaim in the title role of Charpentier's *Medée* at the Salle Pleyel in 1983. In 1986 she made her first appearance with the Philharmonia Baroque Orch. under Nicholas McGegan's direction. She appeared in recital at London's Wigmore Hall in 1987, and returned to England in 1988 to sing with the Taverner Players under Andrew Parrott's direction at the Bath Festival. In 1990 she was engaged as a soloist in Haydn's *Die Schöpfung* under Frans Bruggen's direction at the Flanders Festival and the Utrecht Festival. She gave solo recitals in Boston, Geneva, and Paris in 1995. Feldman's superb vocal gifts are complemented by her expert knowledge of early music performance practice. Her repertoire ranges from the medieval to Romantic periods, and includes works by Hildegard von Bingen, Monteverdi, Charpentier, Cavalli, Purcell, Cesti, Handel, Campra, Rameau, Mozart, and Meyerbeer.

Felix, Václav, prominent Czech composer and pedagogue; b. Prague, March 29, 1928. He studied composition with Bořkovec and Dobiáš at the Prague Academy of Music (graduated, 1953), then did postgraduate study in theory with Janeček (1953–56); he completed his education at the Charles Univ. in Prague (Ph.D. in philosophy, 1957; Candidatus scientiarum, 1961). He was ed. of *Hudebni Rozhledy* in Prague (1959–61). In 1960 he joined the faculty of the Prague Academy of Music, where he was head of the theory and music history dept. (1979–85), dean of the music faculty (1985–90), and a prof. (1985–92). From 1978 to 1989 he was vice president of the central committee of the Union of Czech Composers and Concert Artists. He received the prize of the Czech Minister of Culture (1976), was made an Artist of Merit (1978), and received the prize of the Union of Czech Composers and Concert Artists (1980) and the National Prize (1986). His music follows the golden mean of agreeable Central European modernism. He composed the following operas, all 1st perf. in Prague: *Nesmělý Kasanova aneb Čím zrají muži* (Shy Casanova or What Makes Men Ripe; 1966; Dec. 13, 1967), *Inzerát* (The Advertisement; Brno, April 25, 1975), and *Mariana* (1982; April 11, 1985).

Felsenstein, Walter, influential Austrian opera producer; b. Vienna, May 30, 1901; d. East Berlin, Oct. 8, 1975. He studied at a Graz technical college; then went to Vienna, where he enrolled in drama courses at the Burgtheater. In 1923 he appeared as an actor in Lübeck. In 1925 he became dramatic adviser and producer in Beuthen, Silesia; in 1927 he was called to Basel to become chief opera and drama producer at the Stadttheater; in 1929 he went to Freiburg im Breisgau as both actor and dramatic adviser and producer. He served as chief producer at the Cologne Opera in 1932 and at the Frankfurt am Main Opera in 1934. Despite his differences with the policies of the Nazi authorities, he was able to continue producing operas and dramas. From 1938 to 1940 he produced plays in Zürich; he then served as producer in Berlin (1940–44); he was drafted by the military despite his age, and served for a year. From 1947 until his death he was director of the Komische Oper in East Berlin. During his tenure, the Komische Oper established itself as one of the best opera houses of Europe; his productions of *Die Fledermaus, Carmen, Le nozze di Figaro, Otello, Les Contes d'Hoffmann*, and *Die Zauberflöte* were artistically of the first rank. He also made operatic films and gave courses on theater arts. Among his students were the opera producers Götz Friedrich and Joachim Herz. With S. Melchinger, he compiled *Musiktheater* (Bremen, 1961); with G. Friedrich and J. Herz, he publ. *Musiktheater: Beiträge zur Methodik und zu Inszenierungs-Konzeptionen* (Leipzig, 1970).

BIBL.: R. Münz, *Untersuchungen zum realistischen Musiktheater W. F.s* (diss., Humboldt Univ., Berlin, 1964); G. Friedrich, *W. F.: Weg und Werk* (Berlin, 1967); P. Fuchs, ed. and tr., *The Music Theater of W. F.: Collected Articles, Speeches and Interviews by F. and Others* (N.Y., 1975); I. Kobán, ed., *W. F.: Theater: Gespräche, Briefe, Dokumente* (Berlin, 1991).

Fenaroli, Fedele, Italian music theorist, pedagogue, and composer; b. Lanciano, April 25, 1730; d. Naples, Jan. 1, 1818. He studied with his father, a church organist, then went to Naples, where he became a pupil of Francesco Durante and P. A. Gallo at the Cons. of S. Maria di Loreto. In 1762 he became 2d maestro di cappella there, and in 1777 the 1st; also taught at the Cons. della Pietà. He trained many famous musicians (Cimarosa, Conti, Mercadante, Zingarelli, et al.), and his theoretical manuals were highly regarded. He publ. *Partimento ossia Basso numerato* (Rome, 1800), *Studio del contrappunto* (Rome, 1800), and *Regole musicali per i principianti di cembalo* (Naples, 1775). He was a prolific composer, including in his catalog 3 oratorios and 2 operas.

BIBL.: T. Consalvo, *La teoria musicale del F.* (Naples, 1826).

Fénelon, Philippe, French composer; b. Suèvres, Nov. 23, 1952. He studied at the Orléans Cons. and with Messiaen at the Paris Cons. (premier prix in composition, 1977). In 1984 he received the Prix Hervé Dugardin and in 1991 the Prix Villa Médicis. Among his works are the operas *Le Chevalier imaginaire*, after Cervantes and Kafka (1984–86), *Les Roi* (1988–89), and *Salammbô*, after Flaubert (1993; Paris, May 28, 1998).

Feo, Francesco, celebrated Italian composer and pedagogue; b. Naples, 1691; d. there, Jan. 18, 1761. He studied with Andrea Basso and Nicola Fago at the Cons. S. Maria della Pietà dei Turchini (1704–12), subsequently serving as maestro (with Ignazio Prota) at the Cons. S. Onofrio (1723–39) and as primo maestro at the Cons. dei Poveri di Gesù Cristo (1739–43). His most famous pupil was Nicolò Jommelli, who studied with him at the Cons. S. Onofrio.

WORKS: DRAMATIC: OPERAS: *L'amor tirannico, ossia Zenobia* (Naples, Jan. 18, 1713); *La forza della virtù* (Naples, Jan. 22, 1719); *Teuzzone* (Naples, Jan. 20, 1720); *Siface, re di Numidia* (Naples, Nov. 4, 1720); *Ipermestra* (Rome, Jan. 1728); *Arianna* (Turin, Carnival 1728); *Tamase* (Naples, 1729); *Andromaca* (Rome, Feb. 5, 1730); *L'Issipile* (Turin, 1733?); *Arsace* (Turin, Dec. 26, 1740). INTERMEZZOS: *Morano e Rosina* (Naples, 1723), *Don Chisciotte della Mancia* (Rome, Carnival 1726); *Coriando lo speciale* (Rome, Carnival 1726); *Il vedovo* (Naples, 1729).

Ferchault, Guy, French musicologist; b. Mer, Loire-et-Cher, Aug. 16, 1904; d. Paris, Nov. 14, 1980. He studied with C. Lalo, Pirro, and Masson at the Cons. and philosophy at the Sorbonne (graduated, 1942) in Paris. He held teaching positions in music education in Paris, Orléans (1941), Poitiers (1942–49), Tours (1948–51), and Roubaix (from 1952); from 1943 to 1967 he was also a prof. of music history at the Cons. Régional de Musique in Versailles, and then at St. Maur.

WRITINGS: *Henri Duparc, Une Amitié mystique, d'après ses lettres à Francis Jammes* (Paris, 1944); *Les Créatures du drame musical: De Monteverdi à Wagner* (Paris, 1944); *Introduction à l'esthétique de la mélodie* (Gap, 1946); *Claude Debussy, musicien français* (Paris, 1948); *Faust, J.-S. Bach et l'esthétique de son temps* (Zürich, 1950).

Fere, Vladimir, Russian composer and ethnomusicologist; b. Kamyshin, May 20, 1902; d. Moscow, Sept. 2, 1971. He studied piano with Goldenweiser and composition with Glière and Miaskovsky at the Moscow Cons. (1921–29). In 1936 he went to Frunze, Kirghizia, where he composed, in collaboration with Vlasov, a number of operas based on native folk motifs, all first premiered there: *Golden Girl* (May 1, 1937), *Not Death but Life* (March 26, 1938), *Moon Beauty* (April 15, 1939), *For People's Happiness* (May 1, 1941), *Patriots* (Nov. 6, 1941), *Son of the People* (Nov. 8, 1947), *On the Shores of Issyk-Kul* (Feb. 1, 1951), *Toktogul* (July 6, 1958), *The Witch* (1965), and *One Hour before Dawn* (1969).

Ferencsik, Jânos, noted Hungarian conductor; b. Budapest, Jan. 18, 1907; d. there, June 12, 1984. He studied organ and theory at the Budapest Cons.; he became répétiteur at the Hungarian State Opera (1927), and subsequently conductor there (from 1930); he was also an assistant at the Bayreuth Festivals (1930, 1931). He was chief conductor of the Hungarian Radio and Television Sym. Orch. (1945–52), the Hungarian State Sym. Orch. (1952–84), and the Budapest Phil. (1953–76); he also appeared as a guest conductor in Europe and North America. He was awarded the Kossuth Prize (1951, 1961); the Order of the Banner was bestowed upon him by the Hungarian government on his 70th birthday. He was a persuasive interpreter of the Hungarian repertoire.

Ferenczy, Oto, Slovak composer; b. Brezovica nad Torysou, March 30, 1921. He studied philosophy, aesthetics, and musicology at the Comenius Univ. in Bratislava (Ph.D., 1945); he was mainly self-taught in composition. In 1951 he joined the staff of the Bratislava Academy of Music and Dramatic Arts; from 1962 to 1966 was its rector; subsequently he was prof. of theory there until 1990. From 1982 to 1987 he served as president of the Union of Slovak Composers. His music, expertly crafted, is entrenched well within the inoffensive idiom of Central European neoclassicism. His works include the comic opera *Nevšedna humoreska* (An Uncommon Humoresque; 1966–67).

Fernândez, Oscar Lorenzo. See **Lorenzo Fernândez, Oscar.**

Fernandez, Wilhelmina, black American soprano; b. Philadelphia, Jan. 5, 1949. Following training in Philadelphia (1969–73), she completed her studies at the Juilliard School in New York. She made her debut as Gershwin's Bess at the Houston Grand Opera in 1977, and then toured the United States and Europe in that role. After appearing as Musetta at the Paris Opéra in 1979, she sang with the N.Y. City Opera, and in Boston, Toulouse, Strasbourg, and Liège. She sang Bess at the Theater des Westens in Berlin in 1988, and then Aida in Bonn in 1989. In 1991 she scored a great success as Carmen Jones in London. During the 1994–95 season, she sang Aida at the Deutsche Oper in Berlin. She also appeared widely as a concert artist and recitalist. Among her other roles were Purcell's Dido, Mozart's Countess, Donna Anna, Marguerite, and Luisa Miller.

Ferni-Giraldoni, Carolina, Italian soprano, mother of **Eugenio Giraldoni**; b. Como, Aug. 20, 1839; d. Milan, June 4, 1926. She studied violin in Paris and Brussels, and later took voice lessons with Pasta. She made her debut as Leonora in *La Favorite* in Turin in 1862, then sang at La Scala in Milan (1866–68). She retired in 1883 and taught voice, numbering Caruso as one of her pupils. She was married to **Leone Giraldoni**.

Fernström, John (Axel), Swedish violinist, conductor, teacher, and composer; b. Ichang, China (of Swedish parents), Dec. 6, 1897; d. Lund, Oct. 19, 1961. He was the son of a Swedish missionary in China. After settling in Sweden, he studied violin at the Malmö Cons. (1913–15); also with Max Schlüter in Copenhagen (1917–21; 1923–24), and with Issay Barmas in Berlin (1921–22); he also studied composition with Peder Gram in Copenhagen (1923–30) and pursued composition and conducting studies at the Sonderhausen Cons. (1930). After playing violin in the Hälsingborg Sym. Orch. (1916–39), he was director of the Malmö Radio (1939–41). He then settled in Lund, where he was director of the municipal music school (1948–61); he also was conductor of the Orch. Soc. and founder-conductor of the Nordic Youth Orch. In 1953 he was made a member of the Royal Academy of Music in Stockholm. In addition to his writings on music theory, he was the author of the interesting autobiography *Jubals son och blodsarvinge* (1967). Although he wrote three operas, *Achnaton* (1931), *Isissystarnas bröllop* (1942), and *Livet en dröm* (1946), Fernström was particularly adept with instrumental music. In his works, he pursued a median course between traditional idioms and avant-garde styles.

Ferrani (real name, **Zanaggio**), **Cesira,** admired Italian soprano; b. Turin, May 8, 1863; d. Pollone, May 4, 1943. She studied with Antonietta Fricci in Turin, where she made her operatic debut in 1887 at the Teatro Carignano as Gilda. She then sang at the Teatro Regio there, where she created the roles of Manon Lescaut (Feb. 1, 1893) and Mimi (Feb. 1, 1896). From 1894 to 1909 she was a principal singer at Milan's La Scala. Among her other notable roles were Elsa, Eva, and Mélisande.

Ferraresi del Bene, Adriana (née **Gabrieli**), Italian soprano, known as **La Ferrarese**; b. Ferrara, c.1755; d. Venice, after 1799. She was trained at Venice's Ospedaletto. After marrying Luigi del Bene in 1783, she was generally known as Ferraresi del Bene or La Ferrarese. In 1785 she appeared in Cherubini's *Demetrio* at His Majesty's Theatre in London, and then created the role of Epponina in his *Giulio Sabbino* at Milan's La Scala in 1787. In 1788 she made her debut in Vienna in Martín y Soler's *L'arbore di Diana*, and then sang there in operas by Salieri, Guglielmi, and Paisiello. As the mistress of Da Ponte, she became acquainted with Mozart, who wrote the role of Fiordiligi for her in his *Così fan tutte* (Jan. 26, 1790). All the same, Mozart thought little of her vocal abilities. Indeed, her quarrels with singers and her scandalous conduct in general led to her dismissal from the Viennese court in 1792.

Ferrari, Benedetto, Italian librettist and composer, called "Dalla Tiorba" for his proficiency on the theorbo; b. Reggio Emilia, c.1603; d. Modena, Oct. 22, 1681. He studied music in Rome, then served as a choirboy at the Collegio Germanico in Rome (1617–18). He subsequently was a musician at the Farnese court in Parma (1619–23). In 1637 he proceeded to Venice, where he wrote the libretto for Manelli's opera *L'Andromeda;* it was produced at the Teatro di San Cassiano in 1637, the first Venetian opera performed in a theater open to the public. He then wrote librettos for *La Maga fulminata* by Manelli (1638), *L'inganno d'Amore* by Bertali (Regensburg, 1653), *La Licasta* by Manelli (Parma, 1664), and 4 of his own operas, all produced in Venice: *L'Armida* (Feb. 1639), *Il Pastor regio* (Jan. 23, 1640), *La Ninfa avara* (1641), and *Il Principe giardiniero* (Dec. 30, 1643). From 1651 to 1653 he was in Vienna. From 1653 to 1662 he served as court choirmaster in Modena; after a hiatus of employment, he was reinstated in 1674, remaining in this post until his death. In Modena he produced the opera *L'Erosilda* (1658). Six of Ferrari's librettos were publ. in Milan in 1644 under the title *Poesie drammatiche*.

Ferrari, Carlotta, Italian composer; b. Lodi, Jan. 27, 1837; d. Bologna, Nov. 23, 1907. She studied with Strepponi and Mazzucato at the Milan Cons., then devoted herself to the composition of operas to her own librettos. The following operas were produced: *Ego* (Milan, 1857), *Sofia* (Lodi, 1866), and *Eleanora d'Armorea* (Cagliari, 1871).

Ferrari, Giacomo (Gotifredo), Italian composer; b. Rovereto, Tirol (baptized), April 2, 1763; d. London, Dec. 1842. He studied harpsichord at Verona with Marcola and theory with Marianus Stecher at the Monastery of Mariaberg in Switzerland. He then went to Naples, where he studied with Latilla. There he met Chevalier Campan, household master for Marie-Antoinette. He was then appointed as court musician at the Tuileries in Paris in 1787; after the Revolution he went to London (1792), where he settled as a singing teacher. He produced in London the operas *I due Svizzeri* (May 14, 1799), *Il Rinaldo d' Asti* (March 16, 1802), *L'Eroina di Raab* (April 8, 1813), and *Lo sbaglio fortunato* (May 8, 1817); he also wrote 2 ballets. He publ. *Studio di musica pratica, teorica* (1830) and a book of reminiscences, *Anedotti piacevoli e interresanti occorsi nella vita G. G. F. da Rovereto* (1830; contains some vivid recollections of Haydn and other celebrities).

Ferrari, Gustave, Swiss pianist, singer, conductor, and composer; b. Geneva, Sept. 28, 1872; d. there, July 29, 1948. He studied at the Geneva Cons. and in Paris. After a period as an operetta conductor, he toured as accompanist to Yvette Guilbert; he later toured on his own as a singer-pianist in the folk-song repertoire. He wrote some dramatic music.

Ferrari-Fontana, Edoardo, Italian tenor; b. Rome, July 8, 1878; d. Toronto, July 4, 1936. He studied voice and gained experience singing in operetta in Argentina and Milan before making an impressive operatic debut as Tristan in Turin on Dec. 23, 1909. He sang at Milan's La Scala (1912–14), where he created the role of Avito in *L'amore dei tre re* on April 10, 1913. It was as Avito that he made his Metropolitan Opera debut in New York on Jan. 2, 1914, remaining on its roster until 1915. He also sang with the Boston Opera Co. (1913–14) and the Chicago Grand Opera Co. (1915–16). In 1926 he settled in Toronto as a voice teacher. He was married for a time to **Margarete Matzenauer**. In addition to the Italian repertory, he was esteemed for his portrayals of Siegfried, Siegmund, and Tannhäuser.

Ferrari-Trecate, Luigi, Italian composer; b. Alessandria, Piedmont, Aug. 25, 1884; d. Rome, April 17, 1964. He studied with Antonio Cicognani at the Pesaro Cons., and also with Mascagni. Subsequently he was engaged as a church organist; he was prof. of organ at the Liceo Musicale in Bologna (1928–31); from 1929 to 1955 he was director of the Parma Cons. He wrote several operas which had considerable success: *Pierozzo* (Alessandria, Sept. 15, 1922), *La Bella e il mostro* (Milan, March 20, 1926), *Le astuzie di Bertoldo* (Genoa, Jan. 10, 1934), *Ghirlino* (Milan, Feb. 4, 1940), *Buricchio* (Bologna, Nov. 5, 1948), *L'Orso Re* (Milan, Feb. 8, 1950), *La capanna dello Zio Tom* (Parma, Jan. 17, 1953), and *Lo spaventapasseri* (1963); also music for a marionette play, *Ciottolino* (Rome, Feb. 8, 1922).

Ferrero, Lorenzo, Italian composer; b. Turin, Nov. 17, 1951. He was basically self-taught in music, but received some training from Bruni and Zaffiri. He also attended the Milan Cons. and studied aesthetics with Battimo at the Univ. of Turin (graduated, 1974, with a study of the writings of John Cage). In 1974 he began working with the group Musik-Dia-Licht-Film-Galerie in Munich. In 1980–81 he was assistant to Bussotti at the Puccini Festival in Torre del Lago, where he was artistic director in 1984. In 1981 he became a prof. at the Milan Cons. In 1982–83 he worked at IRCAM in Paris. He was artistic director of the Unione Musicale concert series in Turin from 1982 to 1988, and of the Verona Arena from 1991 to 1994. In his music, Ferrero bridges the gap between traditional opera and rock and popular music. Among his dramatic works are *Rimbaud ou Le fils de soleil*, melodrama (1978), *Marilyn*, theater piece (1980), *La figlia del mago*, children's opera (1981), *Mare nostro*, comic opera (1985); *Salvatore Giuliano*, opera (1986), and *Carlotta Corday*, opera (1988).

Ferri, Baldassare, celebrated Italian castrato soprano; b. Perugia, Dec. 9, 1610; d. there, Nov. 18, 1680. He was a choirboy in Orvieto, where he entered the service of Cardinal Crescenzio in 1622. He then studied in Naples and with Vincenzo Ugolini in Rome. He entered the service of Prince Wladyslaw of Poland in Warsaw in 1625 and continued in his employ when he became King Wladyslaw IV Vasa in 1632. In 1655 he went to Vienna, where he served the emperors Ferdinand III and Leopold I until about 1665; he then returned to Italy. He gained public renown with his appearances in major music centers, his travels taking him as far as London. According to contemporary accounts, he possessed a phenomenal voice and accumulated a great fortune.

Ferrier, Kathleen (Mary), remarkable English contralto; b. Higher Walton, Lancashire, April 22, 1912; d. London, Oct. 8, 1953. She grew up in Blackburn, where she studied piano and began voice lessons with Thomas Duerden. In 1937 she won 1st prizes for piano and singing at the Carlisle Competition; she then decided on a career as a singer, and subsequently studied voice with J. E. Hutchinson in Newcastle upon Tyne and with Roy Henderson in London. After an engagement as a soloist in *Messiah* at Westminster Abbey in 1943, she began her professional career in full earnest. Britten chose her to create the title role in his *Rape of Lucretia* (Glyndebourne, July 12, 1946); she also sang Orfeo in Gluck's *Orfeo ed Euridice* there in 1947 and at Covent Garden in 1953. She made her American debut with the N.Y. Phil. on Jan. 15, 1948, singing *Das Lied von der Erde*, with Bruno Walter conducting. She made her American recital debut in New York on March 29, 1949. Toward the end of her brief career, she acquired in England an almost legendary reputation for vocal excellence and impeccable taste, so that her untimely death (from cancer) was greatly mourned. In 1953 she was made a Commander of the Order of the British Empire and received the Gold Medal of the Royal Phil. Soc.

BIBL.: N. Cardus, ed., *K. F., A Memoir* (London, 1955; 2d ed., rev., 1969); W. Ferrier, *The Life of K. F.* (London, 1955); C. Rigby, *K. F.* (London, 1955); W. Ferrier, *K. F., Her Life* (London, 1959); P. Lethbridge, *K. F.* (London, 1959); M. Leonard, *K.: The Life of K. F.: 1912–1953* (London, 1988); J. Spycket, *K. F.* (Lausanne, 1990); P. Campion, *F.: A Career Recorded* (London, 1992); B. Mailliet Le Penven, *La voix de K. F.: Essai* (Paris, 1997).

Ferro, Gabriele, Italian conductor; b. Pescara, Nov. 15, 1937. He studied with Franco Ferrara at the Cons. di Santa Cecilia in Rome. In 1967 he founded the Bari Sym. Orch., and from 1974 he conducted sym. concerts with the La Scala Orch. in Milan. He made his U.S. debut as a guest conductor with the Cleveland Orch. in 1978. He was music director of the Orchestra Sinfonica Siciliana in Palermo, and, from 1988, served as chief conductor of the RAI Orch. in Rome. From 1992 to 1997 he was Generalmusikdirektor of the Stuttgart Opera.

Ferroud, Pierre-Octave, French composer and music critic; b. Chasselay, near Lyons, Jan. 6, 1900; d. in an automobile accident near Debrecen, Hungary, Aug. 17, 1936. He studied harmony with Commette in Lyons and attended the Univ. there, and then pursued his training with Ropartz in Strasbourg (1920–22) and Schmitt in Lyons. In 1923 he settled in Paris as a composer and music critic. His output was influenced by Schmitt and Bartók and includes an operatic sketch, *Chirurgie* (Monte Carlo, March 20, 1928). He publ. *Autour de Florent Schmitt* (Paris, 1927).

BIBL.: C. Rostand, *L'oeuvre de P.-O. F.* (Paris, 1958).

Fesca, Alexander (Ernst), German pianist and composer, son of **Friedrich (Ernst) Fesca**; b. Karlsruhe, May 22, 1820; d. Braunschweig, Feb. 22, 1849. He studied with his father, and later with Taubert in Berlin. He was extremely successful as a concert pianist from 1839; in 1841 he became chamber musician to Prince Fürstenberg, and in 1842 settled in Braunschweig, where he brought out his opera *Der Troubadour* (July 25, 1847). He also wrote 3 other operas. His early death at the age of 28 was regretted by many admirers who believed that he was a composer of uncommon talent.

Fesca, Friedrich (Ernst), German composer, father of **Alexander (Ernst) Fesca**; b. Magdeburg, Feb. 15, 1789; d. Karlsruhe, May 24, 1826. He studied violin, making his debut in his own Violin Concerto in Magdeburg at the age of 11. In 1806 he joined the orch. of the duke of Oldenburg, and in 1808 he obtained a similar position at the Westphalian court at Kassel. In 1813 he was in Vienna, and in 1814 he became a member of the grand duke of Baden's chapel orch. in Karlsruhe. He was a prolific composer of chamber music and also wrote 2 operas, *Cantemire* (Karlsruhe, April 27, 1820) and *Omar und Leila* (Karlsruhe, Feb. 26, 1824).

Fetler, Paul, American composer and teacher; b. Philadelphia, Feb. 17, 1920. His family moved to Europe when he was a child; he had early music studies in Latvia, the Netherlands, Sweden, and Switzerland; he composed 2 dozen small works and part of a sym. that were later discarded. In 1939 he returned to the United States and studied briefly at the Chicago Cons. of Music; he then studied composition with David Van Vactor at Northwestern Univ. (graduated, 1943). Drafted into military service, he was sent at the end of World War II to Berlin as a liaison officer and Russian interpreter assigned to the Allied Control Council. It was during this time that he became a student of Celibidache, who arranged the premiere of his *Prelude* for Orch. with members of the Berlin Phil. (July 13, 1946, composer conducting). In 1946 he returned to the United States to study with Porter and Hindemith at Yale Univ. (M.M., 1948). In 1948 he was appointed to the music faculty of the Univ. of Minnesota, which became his permanent position and where he earned his Ph.D. degree in 1956. He retired in 1990. He returned to Berlin in 1953 to study with Blacher on a Guggenheim fellowship. His 2d Guggenheim fellowship (1960) took him to Kreuth, Bavaria, where he composed his *Soundings* for Orch. (Minneapolis, Oct. 12, 1962). One of his most successful scores, *Contrasts* for Orch. (Minneapolis, Nov. 7, 1958), was widely performed. He received 3 NEA grants (1975, 1977, 1980). His other works include *Sturge Maclean*, opera for youth (St. Paul, Minn., Oct. 11, 1965), and incidental music to plays and film scores.

Février, Henri, French composer; b. Paris, Oct. 2, 1875; d. there, July 6, 1957. He studied at the Paris Cons. with Fauré, Leroux, Pugno, and Massenet; also privately with Messager. He publ. a monograph on the latter (Paris, 1948). He composed the operas *Le Roi aveugle* (Paris, May 8, 1906), *Monna Vanna* (Paris, Jan. 13, 1909), *Gismonda* (Chicago, Jan. 14, 1919; Paris, Oct. 15, 1919), *La Damnation de Blanche-Fleur* (Monte Carlo, March 13, 1920), and *La Femme nue* (Monte Carlo, March 23, 1929), and the operettas *Agnès, dame galante* (1912), *Carmosine* (1913), and *Ile désenchantée* (Paris, Nov. 21, 1925).

Fibich, Zdeněk (Antonín Václav), important Czech composer; b. Všebořiče, Dec. 21, 1850; d. Prague, Oct. 15, 1900. He studied piano with Moscheles and theory with E. F. Richter at the Leipzig Cons. (1865–66), then composition privately with Jadassohn (1866–67) and in Mannheim with V. Lachner (1869–70). Upon his return to Prague (1871), he was deputy conductor and chorus master at the Provisional Theater (1875–78) and director of the Russian Orthodox Church Choir (1878–81). He was a fine craftsman and facile melodist, and one of the leading representatives of the Czech Romantic movement in music. His extensive output reveals the pronounced influence of Weber, Schumann, and especially Wagner. His operas *Nevěsta mesinská* (The Bride of Messina) and *Pád Arkuna* (The Fall of Arkun) are recognized as significant achievements, although they have not gained a place in the standard repertoire. He remains best known for his effective music for piano. A critical ed. of his works was publ. in Prague (1950–67).

WORKS (all 1st perf. in Prague unless otherwise given): OPERAS: *Bukovín* (1870–71; April 16, 1874); *Blaník* (1874–77; Nov. 25, 1881); *Nevěsta mesinská* (The Bride of Messina, after Schiller; 1882–83; March 28, 1884); *Bouře* (The Tempest, after Shakespeare; 1893–94; March 1, 1895); *Hedy*, after Byron's Don Juan (1894–95; Feb. 12, 1896); *Šárka* (1896–97; Dec. 28, 1897); *Pád Arkuna* (The Fall of Arkun; 1898–99; Nov. 9, 1900). STAGE MELODRAMA TRILOGY: *Hippodamie (Hippodamia)*, after Sophocles and Euripides: *Námluvy Pelopovy* (The Courtship of Pelops; 1888–89; Feb. 21, 1890), *Smír Tantaluv* (The Atonement of Tantalus; 1890; June 2, 1891), and *Smrt Hippodamie* (Hippodamia's Death; Nov. 8, 1891). CONCERT MELODRAMAS (for reciter and piano): *Štědrý den* (Christmas Day; 1875; orchestrated 1899); *Pomsta květin* (The Revenge of the Flowers; 1877); *Věčnost* (Eternity; 1878); *Královna Ema* (Queen Emma; 1883); (for reciter and orch.): *Vodník* (The Water Goblin; 1883); *Hakon* (1888).

BIBL.: J. Bartoš, *Z. F.* (Prague, 1914); J. Plavec, *Z. F.: Mistr české balady* (Z. F.: Master of the Czech Ballad; Prague, 1940); K. Jirák, *Z. F.* (Prague, 1947).

Ficher, Jacobo, Russian-Argentine composer; b. Odessa, Jan. 15, 1896; d. Buenos Aires, Sept. 9, 1978. He studied violin with Stolarsky and Korguev in Odessa and composition with Kalafati and Steinberg at the St. Petersburg Cons., graduating in 1917. In 1923 he emigrated to Argentina. In 1956 he was appointed prof. of composition at the National Cons. of Music in Buenos Aires. His music is characterized by a rhapsodic fluency of development and a rich harmonic consistency. He composed the chamber operas *El oso* (1952) and *Pedido de mano* (1955) and the ballets *Colombina de Hoy* (1933), *Los Invitados* (1933), *Melchor* (1938–39), and *Golondrina* (1942), but he particularly excelled in chamber music.

BIBL.: B. Zipman, *J. F.* (Buenos Aires, 1966).

Field, Helen, Welsh soprano; b. Awyn, May 14, 1951. She was educated at the Royal Northern College of Music in Manchester and at the Royal College of Music in London. In 1976 she made her operatic debut as Offenbach's Eurydice at the Welsh National Opera in Cardiff, where she returned in subsequent years in such roles as Desdemona, Tatiana, Marzelline, Micaëla, the Vixen, and Jenůfa. Following her debut at London's Covent Garden as Emma in *Khovanshchina* in 1982, she sang at the English National Opera in London from 1983, where she was particularly admired for her portrayals of Pamina, Gilda, Marguerite, and Violetta. In 1987 she sang the title role in the British premiere of Strauss's *Daphne* with Opera North in Leeds. She created the role of JoAnn in Tippett's *New Year* in Houston in 1989, a role she reprised at her Glyndebourne Festival debut in 1990. In 1994 she returned to Glyndebourne to create the role of Pearl in Birtwistle's *The Second Mrs. Kong*. She created the title role in MacMillan's *Inés de Castro* at the Edinburgh Festival in 1996. In 1997 she sang Salome at Covent Garden, and then was engaged for that role in Los Angeles in 1998. As a concert artist, she appeared with leading British and European orchs.

Fielitz, Alexander von, German conductor and composer; b. Leipzig, Dec. 28, 1860; d. Bad Salzungen, July 29, 1930. He was of partly Slavic origin; his mother was Russian. He studied piano with Julius Schulhoff and composition with Kretschmer in Dresden; in conducting he profited by the advice of Nikisch. He conducted opera in various German towns. A nervous disorder caused him to take a prolonged rest in Italy (1887–97), after which he settled in Berlin as a teacher. From 1905 to 1908 he was in Chicago, where he organized an orch. and conducted it for a season; in 1908 he returned to Berlin as a teacher at, and later (1916) director of, the Stern Cons. He wrote 2 operas, *Vendetta* (Lubeck, 1891) and *Das stille Dorf* (Hamburg, March 13, 1900).

Fiévet, Paul, French composer; b. Valenciennes, Dec. 11, 1892; d. Paris, March 15, 1980. His father, Claude Fievet (1865–1938), was a composer. Paul Fievet studied piano and theory at the Paris Cons., where he was a student of Xavier Leroux, Caussade, and Widor, obtaining the premier prix in harmony in 1913, and the premier prix in composition in 1917, 1918, and 1919. He received the Grand Prix International in Ostende in 1931 and the Grand Prix of Paris in 1932. Among his works is the operetta *Le Joli Jeu* (Lyons, 1933).

Figner, Medea, famous Italian-Russian mezzo-soprano, later soprano; b. Florence, April 3, 1858; d. Paris, July 8, 1952. She studied voice with Bianchi, Carozzi-Zucchi, and Panofka in Florence. She made her debut as Azucena in Sinalunga, near Florence, in 1875; then sang in the opera theaters of Florence. From 1877 to 1887 she toured in Italy, Spain, and South America; she met **Nikolai (Nikolaievich) Figner** during her travels, and followed him to Russia; after their marriage in 1889, she appeared under the name Medea Mei-Figner; they were divorced in 1903. She became extremely successful on the Russian operatic stage, and was a member of the Maryinsky Imperial Opera Theater in St. Petersburg from 1887 until 1912. She then devoted herself mainly to voice teaching. Her voice was described by critics as engagingly soft, rich, "velvety," and "succulent." She could sing soprano roles as impressively as those in the mezzo-soprano range. She was fortunate in having been coached by Tchaikovsky in the role of Liza in his opera *The Queen of Spades*, which she sang at its premiere in St. Petersburg (Dec. 19, 1890); her husband sang the role of her lover in the same opera. Her other successful roles were Tosca, Mimi, Donna Anna, Elsa, Brünnhilde, Marguerite, Desdemona, Aida, Amneris, and Carmen. She publ. a book of memoirs (St. Petersburg, 1912).

Figner, Nikolai (Nikolaievich), celebrated Russian tenor; b. Nikiforovka, Feb. 21, 1857; d. Kiev, Dec. 13, 1918. He was a lieutenant in the Russian navy before deciding upon a career in music, then studied voice with Prianishnikov and Everardi in St. Petersburg (1881–82), and with De Roxas in Naples, where he made his operatic debut at the Teatro Sannazaro in Gounod's *Philémon et Baucis* in 1882. After singing in various Italian cities and in Latin America, he was a leading member of the Maryinsky Imperial Opera Theater in St. Petersburg (1887–1907). He made his debut at Covent Garden in London on May 26, 1887, as the Duke in *Rigoletto*. After singing in private Russian theaters (1907–10), he served as director of the Narodny Dom in St. Petersburg (1910–15). He was married to **Medea Mei** (1889–1903); she described their careers in her memoirs (St. Petersburg, 1912). He was the favorite tenor of Tchaikovsky and was selected to create the roles of Hermann in *The Queen of Spades* (Dec. 19, 1890) and Count Vaudemont in *Yolanta* (Dec. 18, 1892) at their St. Petersburg premieres. His other roles included Lensky, Otello, Don José, Faust, Radames, Werther, Lohengrin, and Roméo.

BIBL.: L. Kutateladse, *N. F.: Recollections, Letters, Materials* (Leningrad, 1968).

Figuš-Bystrý, Viliam, Slovak composer; b. Banská Bystrica, Feb. 28, 1875; d. there, May 11, 1937. He spent many years collecting Slovak folk melodies, which he publ. in 5 vols. (1906–15) for voice and piano; also publ. a collection of 1,000 arranged for piano only (1925–31). He further wrote an opera, *Detvan* (1924; Bratislava, Aug. 1, 1928).

Filiasi, Lorenzo, Italian composer; b. Naples, March 25, 1878; d. Rome, July 30, 1963. He studied at the Cons. di S. Pietro a Majella in Naples with Nicola d'Arienzo. His first success came with the opera *Manuel Menendez* (Milan, May 15, 1904), which won the Sonzogno Competition Prize in 1902. His other operas included *Fior di Neve* (Milan, April 1, 1911) and *Messidoro* (1912). He also wrote a pantomime, *Pierrot e Bluette* (1895).

Filleul, Henry, French composer; b. Laval, May 11, 1877; d. Saint-Omer, May 1, 1959. He studied at the Paris Cons. with Lavignac and Casadesus. In 1908 he became director of the École Nationale de Musique at St. Omer. He composed the comic opera *Le Jugement de Triboulet* (1923).

BIBL.: *Hommage à Henri F.* (St. Omer, 1952).

Finazzi, Filippo, Italian castrato soprano and composer; b. Bergamo, c.1706; d. Jersbeck, near Hamburg, April 21, 1776. After singing in Venice in 1726, he was a member of the Italian Opera in Breslau (1728–30). By 1732 he was again in Venice and by 1739 he was in the service of the Duke of Modena. In 1743 he joined Pietro Mingotti's opera company in Linz, and then was active with it in Hamburg in 1743–44. Thereafter he worked with the company mainly as a composer, giving his last public appearance as a singer in his own opera *Temistocle* (Hamburg, Feb. 16, 1746). After a decade of teaching, he retired to his country estate in Jersbeck. In 1762 a special decree of the Hamburg Senate allowed him to marry his housekeeper. Among his publ. works were 6 Sinfonien (Hamburg, 1754).

Finck, Henry T(heophilus), prominent American music critic; b. Bethel, Mo., Sept. 22, 1854; d. Rumford Falls, Maine, Oct. 1, 1926. He studied philosophy at Harvard Univ. (graduated, 1876), where he also received instruction in music from J. K. Paine. After writing for several U.S. periodicals in Europe, he was again at Harvard (1877–78), where he won the Harris fellowship, which enabled him to study philosophy and comparative psychology in Berlin, Heidelberg, and Vienna. Upon returning to the United States, he was made music critic of the *N.Y. Evening Post* and *The Nation* in 1881, retiring in 1924. He also taught music history at the National Cons. of Music of America from 1888. In addition to his perceptive writings on music, he publ. books on psychology, anthropology, and other nonmusical subjects. In 1890 he married the pianist Abbie Cushman. A fine literary stylist, she succeeded in copying his style so effectively that she wrote music reviews for him. His numerous writings include *Wagner and His Works: The Story of His Life, With Critical Comments* (N.Y., 1893), *Massenet and His Operas* (N.Y., 1910), and *Richard Strauss: The Man and His Works* (Boston, 1917).

Fine, Vivian, American composer, teacher, and pianist; b. Chicago, Sept. 28, 1913. She became a scholarship student in piano at the age of 5 at the Chicago Musical College; she studied piano with Djane Lavoie-Herz, harmony and composition with Ruth Crawford and Adolf Weidig, and composition with Cowell; in 1931 she went to New York, where she studied piano with Whiteside, composition with Sessions, and orchestration with Szell; she also appeared as a pianist. She held teaching positions at N.Y. Univ. (1945–48), the Juilliard School of Music in New York (1948), the State Univ. of N.Y. at Potsdam (1951), the Conn. College School of Dance (1963–64), and Bennington (Vt.) College (1964–87). In 1980 she received a Guggenheim fellowship and was elected to the American Academy and Inst. of Arts and Letters. She was particularly adept at writing vocal and instrumental works in a dissonant but acceptable style. In 1935 she married the sculptor Benjamin Karp. She composed the chamber opera *The Women in the Garden* (1977; San Francisco, Feb. 12, 1978) and numerous theater pieces.

Finger, Gottfried, Moravian composer; b. probably in Olomouc, c.1660; d. Mannheim (buried), Aug. 31, 1730. After traveling in Italy, he made his way to England, where he was an instrumentalist in the Roman Catholic chapel of King James II (1687–88). He subsequently was active as a composer of operas and of incidental music for the London stage.. He left England in 1704, in 1706 entering the service of Duke Karl Philipp of Neuburg in Breslau, where he remained until 1723.

WORKS: DRAMATIC: OPERAS: *The Rival Queens, or The Death of Alexander* (also known as *Alexander the Great;* London, 1696 or 1703; with D. Purcell); *The Virgin Prophetess, or The Fate of Troy* (London, May 15, 1701); *Der Sieg der Schönheit über die Helden* (Berlin, 1706; with Greber and Stricker; not extant). Also incidental music to plays by Congreve, Dryden, Shakespeare, Cibber, and others, as well as masques.

Fink, Myron S(amuel), American composer; b. Chicago, April 19, 1932. He received training from Borowski and Castelnuovo-Tedesco, and studied at the Juilliard School of Music in New York with Wagenaar and at the Univ. of Illinois with Burrill Phillips. He was awarded a Woodrow Wilson Memorial Fellowship and studied with Robert Palmer at Cornell Univ. (1954–55) before completing his training on a Fulbright Scholarship in Vienna (1955–56). Fink subsequently taught at Alma College, Hunter College, the Curtis Institute of Music in Philadelphia, the State Univ. of N.Y. at Purchase, and the City Univ. of N.Y. Graduate Center. He wrote the operas *The Boor* (St. Louis, Feb. 14, 1955), *Susanna and the Elders* (1955), *Jeremiah* (Binghamton, N.Y., May 25, 1962), *Judith and Holofernes* (concert perf., Purchase, N.Y., Feb. 4, 1978), *Chinchilla* (Binghamton, N.Y., Jan. 18, 1986), *The Island of Tomorrow* (N.Y., June 19, 1986), and *The Conquistador* (San Diego, March 1, 1997).

Finke, Fidelio F(ritz or **Friedrich),** German composer and pedagogue; b. Josefsthal, near Gablonz, Bohemia, Oct. 22, 1891; d. Dresden, June 12, 1968. He studied with his father and with his uncle, Romeo Finke, director of the German Academy of Music in Prague, and then attended Novák's master classes in composition at the Prague Cons. (1908–11). He joined its faculty as a teacher of theory and piano in 1915, becoming a prof. in 1926; he also was national inspector of the German music schools in Czechoslovakia (1920–38) and head of the master classes in composition at the German Academy of Music in Prague (1927–45). After serving as director and as a teacher of a master class in composition at the Dresden Akademie für Musik und Theater (1946–51), he was a prof. of composition at the Leipzig Hochschule für Musik (1951–59). His works evolved from German classicism to the exploration of the Second Viennese School and neoclassicism before embracing a readily accessible style.

WORKS: DRAMATIC: OPERAS: *Die versunkene Glocke* (1915–18);

Die Jakobsfahrt (Prague, Oct. 17, 1936); *Der schlagfertige Liebhaber* (1950–54); *Der Zauberfisch* (Dresden, June 3, 1960). DANCE PANTOMIME: *Lied der Zeit* (1946).

BIBL.: D. Härtwig, *F. F. F.: Leben und Werk* (Habilitationsschrift, Univ. of Leipzig, 1970).

Finko, David, Russian-born American composer and teacher; b. Leningrad, May 15, 1936. He received training in piano and violin at the Rimsky-Korsakov School of Performing Arts in Leningrad (1950–55; 1956–58), and then studied composition and theory (1960–65) and conducting (with Musin, 1970–79) at the Leningrad Cons. He then emigrated to the United States and became a naturalized American citizen in 1986. After lecturing at the Univ. of Pa. in Philadelphia (1980–84), he was an adjunct prof. of music there (1986–92); he also was composer-in-residence at the Univ. of Texas in El Paso (1981–84) and a faculty member of the Combs College of Music in Philadelphia (1984–90). In 1981 he founded Deko Publishers in Philadelphia. He frequently appeared as a pianist, violinist, and conductor of his own works. His music reflects his Jewish heritage and is set in a modern style but not without melodic overtones. He composed the operas *Polinka* (1965), *That Song* (1970; rev. 1991), *The Enchanted Tailor* (1983–93), *The Klezmers* (1989), *The Kabbalists* (1990), *Abraham and Hanna* (1993), and *The Woman is a Devil* (1993; Philadelphia, July 15, 1995).

Finney, Ross Lee, distinguished American composer and teacher; b. Wells, Minn., Dec. 23, 1906; d. Carmel, Calif., Feb. 4, 1997. He studied at the Univ. of Minnesota with Donald Ferguson and received a B.A. in 1927 from Carleton College. In 1927 he went to Paris, where he took lessons with Boulanger; returning to America, he enrolled at Harvard Univ., where he studied with Edward Burlingame Hill (1928–29); in 1935 he had instructive sessions with Sessions. From 1929 to 1949 he was on the faculty of Smith College; concurrently he taught at Mt. Holyoke College (1938–40). In 1931–32 he was in Vienna, where he took private lessons with Berg; in 1937 he studied with Malipiero in Asolo. He then taught composition at the Hartt School of Music in Hartford, Conn. (1941–42), and at Amherst College (1946–47). His professional career was facilitated by 2 Guggenheim fellowships (1937, 1947) and a Pulitzer traveling fellowship (1937). In 1948–49 he was a visiting lecturer at the Univ. of Mich. in Ann Arbor; from 1949 to 1973 he was a prof. there, and also served as chairman of the dept. of composition; furthermore, he established there an electronic music laboratory. He was the author of *Profile of a Lifetime: A Musical Autobiography* (N.Y., 1992). In 1962 he was elected a member of the National Inst. of Arts and Letters. F. Goossen ed. *Thinking About Music: The Collected Writings of Ross Lee Finney* (Tuscaloosa, 1990). Because of the wide diversification of his stylistic propensities, Finney's works represent a veritable encyclopedic inventory of styles and idioms, from innocently pure modalities to highly sophisticated serialistic formations. About 1950 he devised a sui generis dodecaphonic method of composition which he called "complementarity." In it a 12-tone row is formed by 2 mutually exclusive hexachords, often mirror images of each other; tonal oases make their welcome appearances; a curious air of euphony of theoretically dissonant combinations is created by the contrapuntal superposition of such heterophonic ingredients, and his harmonies begin to sound seductively acceptable despite their modernity. He composed the operas *Weep Torn Land* (1984) and *Computer Marriage* (1987) and the dance works *Heyoka* (N.Y., Sept. 14, 1981), *The Joshua Tree* (N.Y., Oct. 10, 1984), and *Ahab* (1985). His brother was the American music educator Theodore M(itchell) Finney (b. Fayette, Iowa, March 14, 1902; d. Pittsburgh, May 19, 1978).

Finnie, Linda, Scottish mezzo-soprano; b. Paisley, May 9, 1952. She was a student of Winifred Busfield at the Royal Scottish Academy of Music in Glasgow. In 1976 she made her operatic debut with Glasgow's Scottish Opera. In 1977 she won the Kathleen Ferrier Prize at the 's-Hertogenbosch Competition in the Netherlands, and then pursued successful engagements in both opera and concert. In 1979 she became a member of the Welsh National Opera in Cardiff; also appeared as a guest artist in London with the English National Opera and at Covent Garden. In 1986 she was a soloist in Mahler's 8th Sym. at the London Promenade Concerts and in Verdi's *Requiem* in Chicago; in 1988, she made her first appearance at the Bayreuth Festival. In 1995 she sang in the *Ring* cycle at the Vienna State Opera. Among her prominent operatic roles are Amneris, Eboli, Ortrud, Brangäne, Fricka, and Waltraute. Her concert repertoire extends from Handel to Prokofiev.

Finnilä, Birgit, Swedish contralto; b. Falkenberg, Jan. 20, 1931. She studied with I. Linden in Göteborg and with Roy Henderson at the Royal Academy of Music in London. In 1963 she made her formal concert debut in Göteborg, and then sang regularly in her homeland. After making her London debut in 1966, she sang in Germany. In 1967 she made her operatic debut as Gluck's Orfeo in Göteborg. In 1968 she toured North America, and then appeared in many of the major European music centers. She was active principally as a concert artist, appearing as a soloist with the major orchs. and as a recitalist.

Finnissy, Michael (Peter), English composer; b. London, March 17, 1946. He studied composition with Bernard Stevens and Humphrey Searle at the Royal College of Music in London (1964–66) and with Roman Vlad in Rome. In 1969 he organized the music dept. of the London School of Contemporary Dance, where he taught until 1974; later he taught at Winchester College (from 1987). He served as president of the ISCM from 1991.

WORKS: MUSIC THEATER: *Mysteries*, in 8 parts, for Vocal and Instrumental Forces, some with Dancers and Mimes: *1, The Parting of Darkness from Light; 2, The Earthly Paradise; 3, The Great Flood; 4, The Prophecy of Daniel; 5, The Parliament of Heaven; 6, The Annunciation; 7, The Betrayal and Crucifixion of Jesus of Nazareth; 8, The Deliverance of Souls* (1972–79); *Circle, Chorus, and Formal Act* for Baritone, Women's Chorus, Percussion, Chorus, 6 Sword Dancers, 4 Mimes, and Small Ensemble (1973); *Mr. Punch* for Speaker, 5 Instruments, and Percussion (1976–77); *Vaudeville* for Mezzo-soprano, Baritone, 2 Mimes, 6 Instruments, and Percussion (1983); *The Undivine Comedy*, opera for 5 Singers and 9 Instruments (1988; rev. version, 1992); *Thérèse Raquin*, opera (1992–93); *Shameful Vice* (1994).

Finzi, Gerald (Raphael), gifted English composer; b. London, July 14, 1901; d. Oxford, Sept. 27, 1956. After training with Ernest Farrar in Harrogate (1914–16) and Edward Bairstow in York (1917–22), he studied counterpoint with R. O. Morris in London (1925). From 1930 to 1933 he taught composition at the Royal Academy of Music in London. In 1940 he founded the Newbury String Players, which he conducted in varied programs, including music of 18th-century English composers. During World War II, he worked in the Ministry of War Transport (1941–45). He also made his home a haven for German and Czech refugees. In 1951 he was stricken with Hodgkin's disease, but he continued to pursue his activities until his death. While the influence of Parry, Elgar, and Vaughan Williams may be discerned in some of his works, he found a distinctive style that is reflected in a fine body of orch. and vocal scores. Among his most notable works are the Concerto for Clarinet and Strings, the Cello Concerto, the cantata *Dies Natalis*, the *Intimations of Immortality* for Tenor, Chorus, and Orch., and *For St. Cecilia* for Tenor, Chorus, and Orch. However, he also wrote *Love's Labours Lost*, incidental music to Shakespeare's play (BBC, Dec. 16, 1946; orch. suite, 1952, 1955; 1st complete perf., BBC, July 26, 1955).

Finzi, Graciane, French composer; b. Casablanca, Morocco, July 10, 1945. She entered the Paris Cons. in 1955 and studied with Joseph Benvenuti (piano) and Barraine and Aubin (theory), taking premiers prix in harmony (1962), counterpoint and fugue (1964), and composition (1969). After organizing music festivals in Casablanca, she became a prof. at the Paris Cons. in 1979. Her dramatic works include *Avis de recherche*, music theater (1981), *3 Opéras drôles* (1984), and *Pauvre Assassin*, opera (1987; Strasbourg, Jan. 1992).

Fiocco, Pietro Antonio, Italian-born Belgian composer; b. Venice, c.1650; d. Brussels, Sept. 3, 1714. He was the father of Jean-Joseph Fiocco (b. Brussels [baptized], Dec. 15, 1686; d. there, March 30, 1746), the Belgian organist and composer, and Joseph-Hector Fiocco (b. Brussels, Jan. 20, 1703; d. there, June 22, 1741), the Belgian organist, harpsichordist, and composer. He traveled to Germany, then settled in Brussels, marrying a Belgian lady in 1682; she died in 1691, and Fiocco remarried in 1692. He was music master of the ducal chapel in Brussels from 1687, and in 1694 he established an opera enterprise. In 1698 he was director, with Giovanni Paolo Bombarda, of the Opéra du Quai du Forn. Fiocco wrote special prologues for the operas of Lully, as well as music for the court; his pastoral play *Le Retour du printemps* was produced in 1699. A collection of his sacred concertos was publ. in Antwerp (1691).

Fioravanti, Valentino, Italian composer, father of **Vincenzo Fioravanti**; b. Rome, Sept. 11, 1764; d. Capua, June 16, 1837. He studied in Rome with Jannacconi and with Sala in Naples. Returning to Rome in 1782, he began his career as a prolific composer of operas. He visited Naples quite often; succeeded Zingarelli as maestro di cappella at St. Peter's in Rome in 1816. Between 1784 and 1824 he composed 77 operas. His earliest work, an intermezzo, was *Le avventure di Bertoldino* (Rome, 1784); he produced a comic opera, *Gl' inganni fortunati*, in Naples (1786); there followed *Il furbo contro al furbo* (Venice, Dec. 29, 1796). His greatest success was achieved by his comic opera *Le Cantatrici villane*, first produced in Naples (1799) and then in Venice in a new version under the title *Le Virtuose ridicole* (Dec. 28, 1801); there were performances all over Europe, including Russia; the opera was particularly in favor with German audiences (under the title *Die Dorfsängerinnen*). Other operas were *La capricciosa pentita* (Milan, Oct. 2, 1802) and *I Virtuosi ambulanti* (Paris, Sept. 26, 1807). His autobiographical sketch was reprinted by G. Roberti in *La Gazzetta Musicale* (1895).

Fioravanti, Vincenzo, Italian composer, son of **Valentino Fioravanti**; b. Rome, April 5, 1799; d. Naples, March 28, 1877. He studied with his father, and also with his father's teacher, Jannacconi; also took lessons with Donizetti. He wrote a number of operas in the Neapolitan dialect, only a few of which (tr. into conventional Italian) were produced outside Italy. He also composed sacred works, including 2 oratorios.

Fiorillo, Ignazio, Italian composer; b. Naples, May 11, 1715; d. Fritzlar, near Kassel, June 1787. He studied with Durante and Leo in Naples. He composed his first opera, *Mandane*, at the age of 20 (Venice, 1736). Other operas were *Artimene* (Milan, 1738), *Partenope nell' Adria* (Venice, 1738), and *Il Vincitor di se stesso* (Venice, 1741). He traveled as a theater conductor; he was appointed court conductor at Braunschweig (1754); in 1762 he received a similar post at Kassel, retiring in 1780. He wrote a number of German operas in Braunschweig and 3 Italian operas in Kassel. An oratorio, *Isacco*, is also noteworthy. His son Federigo Fiorillo (b. Braunschweig [baptized], June 1, 1755; d. after 1823) was a violinist and composer.

Firsova, Elena (Olegovna), Russian composer; b. Leningrad, March 21, 1950. She was a student of Pirumov (composition) and Kholopov (analysis) at the Moscow Cons. (1970–75); she also profited from further studies with Denisov. From 1979 her works were heard abroad. In 1993 she became a prof. and composer-in-residence at the Univ. of Keele in England. In 1972 she married **Dmitri Smirnov**. In her works, she has developed an intimate style notable for its poetic handling of both harmony and melody. She composed *Feast in Plague Time*, chamber opera (1972), and *The Nightingale and the Rose,* opera (1991; London, July 8, 1994).

BIBL.: B. Brand, ed., *E. F.* (Berlin, 1991).

Fischer, Ádám, Hungarian conductor, brother of **Iván Fischer**; b. Budapest, Sept. 9, 1949. He studied at the Béla Bartók Cons. in Budapest, and then took conducting courses with Swarowsky at the Vienna Academy of Music and with Ferrara in Venice and Siena (1970–71). In 1971–72 he was an assistant conductor in Graz. In 1972–73 he was chief conductor in St. Pölten. He won 1st prize in the Cantelli Competition in Milan in 1973. After serving as an assistant conductor at the Vienna State Opera (1973–74), he was a conductor at the Finnish National Opera in Helsinki from 1974 to 1977. From 1977 to 1979 he held the position of 1st conductor at the Karlsruhe Opera. In 1980 he made his first appearance at the Salzburg Festival, and in 1981 he made his U.S. debut at the San Francisco Opera conducting *Don Giovanni*. From 1981 to 1984 he was Generalmusikdirektor in Freiburg im Breisgau. In 1984 he conducted *Der Rosenkavalier* at his first appearance at the Paris Opéra, and in 1986 he made his debut at Milan's La Scala conducting *Die Zauberflöte*. From 1987 to 1992 he was Generalmusikdirektor in Kassel. He also founded the Austro-Hungarian Haydn Festival in Eisenstadt, and served as music director of the Austro-Hungarian Haydn Orch. In 1989 he made his debut at London's Covent Garden conducting *Die Fledermaus*. He returned to London in 1991 to make his first appearance at the English National Opera with *Bluebeard's Castle*. On April 14, 1994, he made his debut at the Metropolitan Opera in New York conducting *Otello*. He also appeared as a guest conductor with major orchs. on both sides of the Atlantic.

Fischer, Betty, Austrian operetta singer; b. Vienna, Oct. 27, 1887; d. there, Jan. 19, 1969. She centered her career in Vienna, where she sang in variety productions and operetta at a young age. After establishing herself as a valuable member of the Raimundtheater (1900–03), she was prima donna at the Theater an der Wien (1903–28). In 1928 she starred at the Johann Strauss Theater. She also made guest appearances at other theaters in Vienna and other music centers. In later years, she appeared in character roles at the Raimundtheater and taught at the Vienna Cons. Fischer was an outstanding operetta singer in her day, excelling in both traditional and contemporary roles.

Fischer, Emil (Friedrich August), distinguished German bass; b. Braunschweig, June 13, 1838; d. Hamburg, Aug. 11, 1914. He received his vocal training entirely from his parents, who were opera singers. He made his debut in Graz in 1857, then was with the Danzig Opera (1863–70), in Rotterdam (1875–80), and with the Dresden Opera (1880–85). He made his debut with the Metropolitan Opera in New York on Nov. 23, 1885, as King Heinrich, and remained on the staff for 5 years; he then sang with the Damrosch Opera Co. (1894–98). He lived mostly in New York as a vocal teacher, returning to Germany shortly before his death. On March 15, 1907, a testimonial performance was held in his honor at the Metropolitan Opera, at which he sang one of his greatest roles: that of Hans Sachs (Act 3, Scene 1). He was particularly famous for his Wagnerian roles.

Fischer, György, Hungarian-born Austrian conductor and pianist; b. Budapest, Aug. 12, 1935. He received training at the Franz Liszt Academy of Music in Budapest and at the Salzburg Mozarteum. After working as an assistant to Karajan at the Vienna State Opera, where he conducted works by Mozart, he was active as a conductor at the Cologne Opera (from 1973). In 1973 he made his British debut conducting *Die Zauberflöte* with the Welsh National Opera in Cardiff; he made his London debut conducting *Mitridate* in 1979. From 1980 he appeared as a conductor with the English Chamber Orch. in London; also conducted widely in other European music centers, as well as in North and South America, and in Australia. As a piano accompanist, he toured the world with many outstanding artists. For a time he was married to **Lucia Popp**.

Fischer, Iván, Hungarian conductor, brother of **Ádám Fischer**; b. Budapest, Jan. 20, 1951. He studied cello and composition at the Béla Bartók Cons. in Budapest (1965–70), then took lessons in conducting with Swarowsky at the Vienna Academy of Music and with Harnoncourt in Salzburg. During the 1975–76 season, he conducted concerts in Milan, Florence, Vienna, and Budapest; beginning in 1976, he filled engagements with the BBC Sym. Orch. in London and the BBC regional orchs. From 1979 to 1982 he was coconductor of the Northern Sinfonia Orch. in Newcastle upon Tyne. In 1983 he became music director of the Budapest Festival Orch. Also in 1983 he made his first appearance in the United States as a guest conductor with the Los Angeles Phil. He was music director of the Kent Opera (1984–88), and then its artistic director. From 1989 to 1995 he was principal guest conductor of the Cincinnati Sym. Orch.

Fischer, Jan (Frank), Czech composer; b. Louny, Sept. 15, 1921. He studied at the Prague Cons. (1940–45) and took lessons in composition from Řídký at the master class there (1945–48); also attended the Charles Univ. in Prague (1945–48), where he later received his Ph.D. (1990). He won prizes from the city of Prague (1966) and the Guild of Composers (1986). His music occupies the safe ground of Central European Romanticism, not without some audacious exploits in euphonious dissonance.

WORKS: DRAMATIC: OPERAS: *Ženichové* (Bridegrooms; 1956; Brno, Oct. 13, 1957); *Romeo, Julie a tma* (Romeo, Juliet, and Darkness; 1959–61; Brno, Sept. 14, 1962); *Oh, Mr. Fogg*, comic chamber opera after Jules Verne's *Around the World in 80 Days* (1967–70; Saarbrücken, June 27, 1971); *Miracle Theater*, radio opera (1970); *Decamerone*, chamber opera (1975–76); *Copernicus* (1981); *Rites* (1990); *"Tys mě tak rozčíli . . . !"* ("You've annoyed me so much . . .!"), mini-opera (1996); *Varta*, mini-opera (1996). BALLETS: *Eufrosyne* (1951); *Le Marionnettists* (1978).

Fischer, (Johann Ignaz) Ludwig, renowned German bass; b. Mainz, Aug. 18, 1745; d. Berlin, July 10, 1825. He studied voice with Anton Raaff in Mannheim, then obtained the post of virtuoso da camera at the Mannheim court (1772); he also taught voice at the Mannheim Seminario Musico from 1775, continuing in the court's service when it moved to Munich in 1778. He then proceeded to Vienna (1780), where he first gained recognition as a leading opera singer. He became a friend of Mozart, who wrote the role of Osmin in his *Die Entführung aus dem Serail* (July 16, 1782) for him. In 1783 he went to Paris, where he was notably successful at the Concert Spirituel; he subsequently toured Italy, and then sang in Vienna, Prague, and Dresden (1785). After serving the Prince of Thurn und Taxis in Regensburg (1785–89), he received an appointment for life in Berlin. He continued to make guest appearances in other cities, including London (1794, 1798), giving his last public performance in Berlin in 1812; he was pensioned in 1815. The MS of his autobiography, which covers his life to 1790, is in the Berlin Staatsbibliothek.

Fischer, Res (Maria Theresia), German contralto; b. Berlin, Nov. 8, 1896; d. Stuttgart, Oct. 4, 1974. She studied in Stuttgart and Prague; then took lessons in Berlin with Lilli Lehmann. She made her debut in 1927 in Basel, where she sang until 1935; she then appeared with the Frankfurt am Main Opera (1935–41); in 1941 she joined the Stuttgart Opera, remaining on its roster until 1961; she was made its honorary member in 1965. She also sang at the festivals of Salzburg and Bayreuth, and with the state operas in Vienna, Hamburg, and Munich. She created the title role in Orff's *Antigonae* (Salzburg, 1949) and sang in the first performance of Wagner-Régeny's *Bergwerk von Falun* (Salzburg, 1961).

Fischer-Dieskau, (Albert) Dietrich, celebrated German baritone; b. Berlin, May 28, 1925. The surname of the family was originally Fischer; his paternal grandmother's maiden surname of Dieskau was legally conjoined to it in 1937. His father, a philologist and headmaster, was self-taught in music; his mother was an amateur pianist. He began to study piano at 9, and voice at 16; he then studied voice with Hermann Weissenborn at the Berlin Hochschule für Musik (1942–43). In 1943 he was drafted into the German army. He was made a prisoner of war by the Americans while serving in Italy in 1945; upon his release in 1947, he returned to Germany and made his first professional appearance as a soloist in the Brahms *Requiem* in Mülheim. He continued his vocal training with Weissenborn in Berlin, where he soon was heard on radio broadcasts over the RIAS. On May 6, 1948, he made his operatic debut in the bass role of Colas in an RIAS broadcast of Mozart's *Bastien und Bastienne*. On Nov. 18, 1948, he made his stage debut as Rodrigo, Marquis of Posa, in *Don Carlos* at the Berlin Städtische Oper, where he remained an invaluable member for 35 years. He also pursued his operatic career with appearances at leading opera houses and festivals in Europe. It was as a lieder and concert artist, however, that Fischer-Dieskau became universally known. On April 5, 1955, he made his U.S. debut with the Cincinnati Sym. Orch.; his U.S. recital debut followed at N.Y.'s Town Hall on May 2, 1955. In subsequent years, he made tours all over the world to enormous critical acclaim. On Dec. 31, 1992, he gave his farewell stage performance in Munich. However, he made occasional appearances as a conductor. His finest operatic roles included Count Almaviva, Don Giovanni, Papageno, Macbeth, Falstaff, Hans Sachs, Mandryka, Mathis der Maler, and Wozzeck. He created the role of Mittenhofer in Henze's *Elegy for Young Lovers* (1961) and the title role in Reimann's *Lear* (1978). His honors include membership in the Berlin Akademie der Künste (1956), the Mozart Medal of Vienna (1962), Kammersänger of Berlin (1963), the Grand Cross of Merit of the Federal Republic of Germany (1978), honorary doctorates from the Univ. of Oxford (1978) and the Sorbonne in Paris (1980), and the Gold Medal of the Royal Phil. Soc. of London (1988). In 1978 he married his 4th wife, **Julia Varady**.

WRITINGS: *Texte deutscher Lieder: Ein Handbuch* (Munich, 1968; 7th ed., 1986; Eng. tr., 1976, as *The Fischer-Dieskau Book of Lieder*); *Auf den Spuren der Schubert-Lieder: Werden-Wesen-Wirkung* (Wiesbaden, 1971; Eng. tr., 1976, as *Schubert: A Biographical Study of His Songs*; U.S. ed., 1977, as *Schubert's Songs: A Biographical Study*); *Wagner und Nietzsche: Der Mystagoge und sein Abtrunniger* (Stuttgart, 1974; Eng. tr., 1976, as *Wagner and Nietzsche*); *Robert Schumann: Das Vokalwerk* (Munich, 1985); *Töne sprechen, Worte klingen: Zur Geschichte und Interpretation des Gesangs* (Stuttgart and Munich, 1985); *Nachklang: Ansichten und Erinnerungen* (Stuttgart, 1987; Eng. tr., 1989, as *Reverberations: The Memoirs of Dietrich Fisher-Dieskau*); *Wenn Musik der Liebe Nahrung ist: Künstlerschicksale im 19. Jahrhundert* (Stuttgart, 1990); *Weil nicht alle Blütenträume reiften: Johann Friedrich Reichardt, Hofkapellmeister dreier Preussenkönige: Porträt und Selbstporträt* (Stuttgart, 1992); *Fern die Klage des Fauns: Claude Debussy und seine Welt* (Stuttgart, 1993).

BIBL.: W.-E. von Lewinski, *D. F.-D.* (Munich and Mainz, 1988); H. Neunzig, *D. F.-D.: Eine Biographie* (Stuttgart, 1995; Eng. tr., 1997, as *D. F.-D.: A Biography*).

Fischietti, Domenico, Italian composer; b. Naples, c.1725; d. probably in Salzburg, c.1810. He was the son of the organist, teacher, and composer Giovanni Fischietti (1692–1743). He was a student at the S. Onofrio Cons. in Naples of Leo and Durante. After beginning his career as an opera composer in Naples, he went to Venice to collaborate with Goldoni on 4 highly successful comic operas: *Lo speziale* (Carnival 1754; Act 1 by V. Pallavicini), *La ritornata di Londra* (Feb. 1756), *Il mercato di Malmantile* (Dec. 26, 1757), and *Il Signor dottore* (1758). He then was active in Prague and Dresden, serving as court Kapellmeister in the latter city (1765–72). Upon settling in Salzburg, he was Kapellmeister to the Archbishop (1772–75) and a teacher at the Institut der Domsängerknaben (1779–83). In all, he wrote some 20 operas, as well as the oratorio *La morte d'Abele* (1767).

Fišer, Luboš, Czech composer; b. Prague, Sept. 30, 1935. He studied composition with Hlobil at the Prague Cons. (1952–56) and with Bořkovec at the Prague Academy of Music, graduating in 1960. His music is often associated with paintings, archeology, and human history; his style of composition employs effective technical devices without adhering to any particular doctrine. His *15 Prints after Dürer's Apocalypse* for Orch. (1964–65), his most successful work, received the UNESCO prize in Paris in 1967. He also composed *Lancelot*, chamber opera (1959–60; Prague, May 19, 1961), *Dobrý voják Švejk* (The Good Soldier Schweik), musical (Prague, 1962), *Changing Game*, ballet (1971), and *Faust Eternal*, television opera (1986).

Fisher, John Abraham, English violinist and composer; b. Dunstable or London, 1744; d. probably in London, 1806. After training with Thomas Pinto, he was a violinist in various theater orchs. in London. From about 1769 to 1778 he was concertmaster at Covent Garden, where he had success as a composer for the stage. In 1777 he received his B.Mus. and D.Mus. degrees from the Univ. of Oxford. During the next few years, he made successful tours of Europe as a violinist. While in Vienna in 1783, he took **Nancy Storace** as his 2d wife, but his poor treatment of her led the emperor to expel him the following year and his marriage collapsed. After a sojourn in Ireland (1786–88), he settled in London.

WORKS: DRAMATIC (all 1st perf. at Covent Garden, London): *The Court of Alexander,* burlesque opera (Jan. 5, 1770); *The Golden Pippin*, burletta (Feb. 5, 1773); *The Beggar's Opera*, ballad opera after John Gay (Sept. 27?, 1776); *The Tempest*, dramatic opera after Shakespeare (Dec. 27, 1776); *Love Find the Way*, comic opera (Nov. 18, 1777); also pantomimes, masques, and incidental music. Also *Providence*, oratorio (Oxford, July 2, 1777).

Fisher, Sylvia (Gwendoline Victoria), admired Australian soprano; b. Melbourne, April 18, 1910. She was a student of Adolf Spivakovsky at the Melbourne Cons. In 1932 she made her operatic debut as Hermione in Lully's *Cadmus et Hermione* in Melbourne. After settling in London, she made her first appearance at Covent Garden as Beethoven's Leonore in 1949; subsequently she was a leading dramatic soprano there until 1958, excelling particularly as Sieglinde, the Marschallin, and Kostelnička in *Jenůfa*. In 1958 she sang at the Chicago Lyric Opera. She was a member of the English Opera Group in London (1963–71), and also sang there with the Sadler's Wells (later the English National) Opera. She created the role of Miss Wingrave in Britten's *Owen Wingrave* (BBC-TV, London, May 16, 1971), and was notably successful as Elizabeth I in his *Gloriana*.

Fiske, Roger (Elwyn), English musicologist; b. Surbiton, Sept. 11, 1910; d. London, July 22, 1987. He attended Wadham College, Oxford (B.A. in English, 1932), then received instruction in composition from Herbert Howells at the Royal College of Music in London before completing his education at the Univ. of Oxford (D.Mus., 1937). He was active as a BBC broadcaster (1939–59), and served as general ed. of the Eulenburg miniature scores (1968–75). Among his writings is *Ballet Music* (London, 1958) and *English Theatre Music in the Eighteenth Century* (London, 1973; 2d ed., 1986).

Fistoulari, Anatole, Russian-born English conductor; b. Kiev, Aug. 20, 1907; d. London, Aug. 21, 1995. He studied with his father, Gregory Fistoulari, an opera conductor. He was only 7 when he conducted Tchaikovsky's 6th Sym. in Kiev, and he subsequently conducted throughout Russia. At 12, he made his first conducting tour of Europe. In 1931 he appeared as conductor with the Grand Opera Russe in Paris, and later conducted the Ballets Russes de Monte Carlo on tours of Europe and in 1937 on a tour of the United States. In 1939 he joined the French Army; after its defeat in 1940, he made his way to London. In 1942 he appeared as a guest conductor with the London Sym. Orch., and then served as principal conductor of the London Phil. (1943–44). He subsequently appeared as a conductor of sym. concerts and opera in England, becoming a naturalized British subject in 1948. In 1956 he toured the Soviet Union with the London Phil. In 1942 he married Mahler's daughter Anna, but their union was dissolved in 1956.

Fiume, Orazio, Italian composer and teacher; b. Monopoli, Jan. 16, 1908; d. Trieste, Dec. 21, 1976. He studied piano and theory in Palermo and Naples; he was later a student of Pizzetti (composition) and Molinari (conducting) in Rome. He taught harmony at the Parma Cons. (1941–51), in Milan (1951–59), and in Pesaro (1959–60); he was director of the Trieste Cons. (from 1961). His music, which included the opera *Il tamburo di panno* (Rome, April 12, 1962), followed the tradition of expansive Italian Romanticism.

Flagello, Ezio (Domenico), American bass, brother of **Nicolas (Oreste) Flagello;** b. N.Y., Jan. 28, 1931. He was a pupil of Schorr and Brownlee at the Manhattan School of Music in New York. In 1952 he made his debut in a concert performance of *Boris Godunov* at N.Y.'s Carnegie Hall, followed in 1955 by his stage debut as Dulcamara at the Empire State Festival in Ellenville, N.Y. He then pursued his training in Rome on a Fulbright scholarship with Luigi Rossi, appearing as Dulcamara with the Opera there in 1956. In 1957 he won the Metropolitan Opera Auditions of the Air, which led to his debut with the company in New York as the Jailer in *Tosca* on Nov. 9 of that year. He subsequently sang regularly there until 1987. In 1966 he created the role of Enobarbus in Barber's *Antony and Cleopatra* at the opening of the new Metropolitan Opera house. He also was a guest artist in Vienna, Berlin, and Milan. He was particularly known for his buffo roles, excelling in operas by Mozart and Rossini. He also was successful in operas by Verdi and Wagner.

Flagello, Nicolas (Oreste), American composer and conductor, brother of **Ezio (Domenico) Flagello**; b. N.Y., March 15, 1928; d. New Rochelle, N.Y., March 16, 1994. He began piano lessons at the incredible age of 3, and played in public at 5. At 6, he began taking violin lessons with Francesco di Giacomo. He also learned to play the oboe, and was a member of the school band, performing on these instruments according to demand. In 1945–46 he played the violin in Stokowski's All-American Youth Orch. in New York. In 1946 he entered the Manhattan School of Music (B.M., 1949; M.M., 1950), studying with a variety of teachers in multifarious subjects (Harold Bauer, Hugo Kortschak, Hugh Ross, and Vittorio Giannini). He also took conducting lessons with Mitropoulos. It was with Giannini that he had his most important training in composition (1935–50), and it was Giannini who influenced him most in his style of composition—melodious, harmonious, euphonious, singingly Italianate, but also dramatically modern. After obtaining his master's degree, Flagello took lessons with Pizzetti at the Accademia di Santa Cecilia in Rome (Mus.D., 1956). He taught composition and conducting at the Manhattan School of Music from 1950 to 1977. He also appeared as a guest conductor with the Chicago Lyric Opera and the N.Y. City Opera, and toured as accompanist to Tito Schipa, Richard Tucker, and other singers. His own works include the operas *Mirra* (1953), *The Wig* (1953), *Rip Van Winkle* (1957), *The Sisters* (1958; N.Y., Feb. 23, 1961), *The Judgment of St. Francis* (1959; N.Y., March 18, 1966), *The Piper of Hamelin* (1970), and *Beyond the Horizon* (1983).

Flagstad, Kirsten (Malfrid), famous Norwegian soprano; b. Hamar, July 12, 1895; d. Oslo, Dec. 7, 1962. She studied voice with her mother and with Ellen Schytte-Jacobsen in Christiania, then made her operatic debut there as Nuri in d'Albert's *Tiefland* (Dec. 12, 1913). During the next 2 decades, she sang throughout Scandinavia, appearing in operas and operettas, and in concert. In 1933 she sang a number of minor roles at Bayreuth, and then scored her first major success there in 1934 when she appeared as Sieglinde. She made an auspicious Metropolitan Opera debut in New York in that same role on Feb. 2, 1935, and was soon hailed as the foremost Wagnerian soprano of her time. On May 18, 1936, she made her first appearance at London's Covent Garden as Isolde. While continuing to sing at the Metropolitan Opera, she made guest appearances at the San Francisco Opera (1935–38) and the Chicago Opera (1937), and also gave concerts with major U.S. orchs. She returned to her Nazi-occupied homeland in 1941 to be with her husband, a decision that alienated many of her admirers. Nevertheless, after World War II, she resumed her career with notable success at Covent Garden. In 1951 she also returned to the Metropolitan Opera, where she sang Isolde and Leonore; she made her farewell appearance there in Gluck's *Alceste* on April 1, 1952. She retired from the operatic stage in 1954, but continued to make recordings. From 1958 to 1960 she was director of the Norwegian Opera in Oslo. Among her other celebrated roles were Brünnhilde, Elisabeth, Elsa, and Kundry. She narrated an autobiography to L. Biancolli, which was publ. as *The Flagstad Manuscript* (N.Y., 1952).

BIBL.: E. McArthur, *F.: A Personal Memoir* (N.Y., 1965); T. Gunnarson, *Sannheten om K. F.: En dokumentarbiografi* (Oslo, 1985); H. Vogt, *F.* (London, 1987).

Flament, Édouard, French bassoonist, conductor, and composer; b. Douai, Aug. 27, 1880; d. Bois-Colombes, Seine, Dec. 27, 1958. He studied at the Paris Cons. with Bourdeau (bassoon), Lavignac, Caussade, and Lenepveu (composition). After graduation (1898), he played the bassoon in the Lamoureux Orch. (1898–1907) and in the Société des Instruments à Vent (1898–1923) in Paris; he conducted opera and concerts in Paris (1907–12), Algiers (1912–14), and Marseilles (1919–20), and summer concerts at Fontainebleau (1920–22), then with the Diaghilev ballet in Monte Carlo, Berlin, London, and Spain (1923–29). In 1930 he became conductor at the Paris Radio. He composed the operas *La Fontaine de Castalie*, *Le Coeur de la rose*, and *Lydéric et Rosèle*.

Flanagan, William (Jr.), American composer and music critic; b. Detroit, Aug. 14, 1923; d. of an overdose of barbituates in New York, Aug. 31, 1969. He studied composition at the Eastman School of Music in Rochester, N.Y., with Phillips and Rogers, then at the Berkshire Music Center in Tanglewood with Honegger, Berger, and Copland; also, in New York, with Diamond. Concurrently, he became engaged in musical journalism; was a reviewer for the *N.Y. Herald Tribune* (1957–60) and later wrote for *Stereo Review*. His style of composition was characterized by an intense pursuit of an expressive melodic line, projected on polycentric but firmly tonal harmonies. He composed the operas *Bartleby* (1952–57; N.Y., Jan. 24, 1961) and *The Ice Age* (1967; unfinished); also incidental music to E. Albee's plays *The Sandbox* (1961), *The Death of Bessie Smith* (1961), *The Ballad of the Sad Café* (1963), and *Malcolm* (1966).

Fleming, Renée, gifted American soprano; b. Indiana, Pa., Feb. 14, 1959. She received vocal training in New York After winning a Metropolitan Opera Audition in 1988, she made her debut at London's Covent Garden as Dircé in Cherubini's *Médée* in 1989. In 1990 she received the Richard Tucker Award, and also took the Grand Prix in the Belgian singing competition. Following engagements as Dvořák's Rusalka at the Houston Grand Opera and the Seattle Opera, she made her Metropolitan Opera debut in New York as Mozart's Countess on March 16, 1991, which role she also sang at the Teatro Colón in Buenos Aires. On Dec. 19, 1991, she appeared as Rosina in the premiere of Corigliano's *The Ghosts of Versailles* at the Metropolitan Opera, returning in subsequent seasons to sing Mozart's Countess and Pamina, and Desdemona. In 1992 she returned to Covent Garden as Rossini's Mme. de Folleville, sang Mozart's Donna Elvira at Milan's La Scala and his Fiordiligi at the Geneva Opera and the Glyndebourne Festival, and appeared as Mimi at the opening of the new Bath and Wessex Opera. She made her N.Y. recital debut at Alice Tully Hall on March 29, 1993. In Aug. 1993 she was the soloist in Barber's *Knoxville: Summer of 1915* at the opening of the new concert hall in Aspen, Colo. In Oct. 1993 she sang the title role in the revival of Floyd's *Susannah* at the Chicago Lyric Opera. She appeared as Mozart's Countess at the opening of the new opera theater at the Glyndebourne Festival on May 28, 1994. On Sept. 10, 1994, she sang Mme. de Tourvel in the premiere of Susa's *The Dangerous Liaisons* at the San Francisco Opera. In 1995 she appeared as Rusalka at the San Diego Opera and at the San Francisco Opera, and sang Desdemona at the Metropolitan Opera. She returned to the Metropolitan Opera in 1997 as Gounod's Marguerite and as Manon, the latter role being one she also portrayed that year in Paris at the Opéra de la Bastille. After singing Arabella in Houston and Lucrezia Borgia at La Scala in 1998, she created Previn's Blanche in *A Streetcar Named Desire* in San Francisco (Sept. 19, 1998). She appeared in recital at N.Y.'s Carnegie Hall in 1999. As a concert and oratorio artist, Fleming had many engagements in North America and Europe. Among her other outstanding operatic roles are Rossini's Armida, Tatiana, the Marschallin, Salome, Jenůfa, and Ellen in *Peter Grimes*.

Fleta, Miguel, Spanish tenor, father of **Pierre Fleta**; b. Albalate, Dec. 28, 1893; d. La Coruña, May 30, 1938. He studied at the Barcelona and Madrid conservatories; also took vocal lessons in Italy with Louisa Pierrick, who became his wife. He made his debut in Trieste on Nov. 14, 1919, as Paolo in Zandonai's *Francesca da Rimini*. After several busy tours in Europe, Mexico, and South America, he made his debut at the Metropolitan Opera in New York on Nov. 8, 1923, as Cavaradossi; he remained on its roster until 1925; from 1923 to 1926 he sang at La Scala in Milan, where he created the role of Prince Calaf in *Turandot* (April 25, 1926). In 1926 he returned to Spain.

Fleta, Pierre, French tenor of Spanish descent, son of **Miguel Fleta;** b. Villefranche-sur-Mer, July 4, 1925. He studied with his mother, Luisa Pierrick. In 1949 he made his operatic debut in Barcelona, and then sang in Nice (1949–51) and at the Théâtre Royal de la Monnaie in Brussels (from 1952); he also toured as a concert artist.

Fletcher, (Horace) Grant, American composer and teacher; b. Hartsburg, Ill., Oct. 25, 1913. He studied composition with William Kritch, theory with Bessie Louise Smith, and conducting with Henry Lamont at Illinois Wesleyan Univ. (1932–35); he took a course in conducting with Thor Johnson; for 3 summers (1937–39) he attended composition classes with Krenek at the Univ. of Mich., then took classes with Willan in Toronto. He later studied at the Eastman School of Music in Rochester, N.Y., where his teachers were Rogers and Hanson (1947–49; Ph.D., 1951); he also had private lessons with Elwell in Cleveland. From 1945 to 1948 he was conductor of the Akron (Ohio) Sym. Orch., and from 1952 to 1956 of the Chicago Sinfonietta; from 1949 to 1951 he was on the faculty of the Chicago Musical College; he later taught at Arizona State Univ. at Tempe (1956–78). In his music, he follows the median line of modern techniques. Among his works are *The Carrion Crow*, buffa fantasy opera (1948), *Lomotawi*, ballet pantomime (1957), *The Sack of Calabasas*, opera (1964–66), and *Cinco de Mayo*, ballet (1973); also incidental music.

Floquet, Étienne-Joseph, French composer; b. Aix-en-Provence, Nov. 23, 1748; d. Paris, May 10, 1785. After studying in his native town, he went to Paris, where he wrote the opéra ballet *L'Union de l'amour et des arts*, produced with great success at the Académie Royale de Musique (Sept. 7, 1773). His 2d opera, *Azolan, ou Le Serment indiscret* (Nov. 22, 1774, also at the Académie), was a fiasco. Floquet then went to Italy, where he perfected his knowledge by studying with Sala in Naples and with Martini in Bologna. Returning to Paris, he had 2 operas performed at the Académie: *Hellé* (Jan. 5, 1779) and *Le Seigneur bien-faisant* (Dec. 14, 1780). He also wrote a comic opera, *La Nouvelle Omphale* (Comédie-Italienne, Nov. 22, 1782). In an attempt to challenge Gluck's superiority, Floquet wrote the opera *Alceste* on the same subject as Gluck's famous work, but it was never produced.

BIBL.: A. Pougin, *É.-J. F.* (Paris, 1863); F. Huot, *Étude biographique sur É.-J. F.* (Aix, 1903).

Floros, Constantin, distinguished Greek musicologist; b. Thessalonika, Jan. 4, 1930. He studied composition with Uhl and conducting with Swarowsky and Kassowitz at the Vienna Academy of Music, graduating in 1953; he concurrently studied musicology with Schenck at the Univ. of Vienna (Ph.D., 1955, with the diss. *C. A. Campioni als Instrumentalkomponist*) and then continued his training with Husmann at the Univ. of Hamburg, where he completed his Habilitation in 1961; in 1967 he became ausserplanmässiger prof. and in 1972 prof. of musicology there. P. Petersen ed. a Festschrift in honor of his 60th birthday (Wiesbaden, 1990). Among his writings are *Mozart-Studien I: Zu Mozarts Sinfonik, Opern- und Kirchenmusik* (Wiesbaden, 1979) and *Alban Berg: Musik als Autobiographie* (Wiesbaden, 1992).

Flotow, Friedrich (Adolf Ferdinand) von, famous German opera composer; b. Teutendorf, April 27, 1813; d. Darmstadt, Jan. 24, 1883. He was a scion of an old family of nobility. He received his first music lessons from his mother, then was a chorister in Güstrow. At the age of 16 he went to Paris, where he entered the

Cons. to study piano with J. P. Pixis and composition with Reicha. After the revolution of 1830, he returned home, where he completed his first opera, *Pierre et Cathérine*, set to a French libretto; it was premiered in a German tr. in Ludwigslust in 1835. Returning to Paris, he collaborated with the Belgian composer Albert Grisar on the operas *Lady Melvil* (1838) and *L'Eau merveilleuse* (1839). With the composer Auguste Pilati, he composed the opera *Le Naufrage de la Méduse* (Paris, May 31, 1839; perf. in a German tr. as *Die Matrosen*, Hamburg, Dec. 23, 1845). He scored a decisive acclaim with his romantic opera *Alessandro Stradella*, based on the legendary accounts of the life of the Italian composer; it was first performed in Hamburg on Dec. 30, 1844, and had numerous subsequent productions in Germany. He achieved an even greater success with his romantic opera *Martha, oder Der Markt zu Richmond* (Vienna, Nov. 25, 1847); in it he demonstrated his ability to combine the German sentimental spirit with Italian lyricism and Parisian elegance. The libretto was based on a ballet, *Lady Henriette, ou La Servante de Greenwich* (1844), for which Flotow had composed the music for Act I; the ballet in turn was based on a vaudeville, *La Comtesse d'Egmont*; the authentic Irish melody *The Last Rose of Summer* was incorporated into the opera by Flotow, lending a certain nostalgic charm to the whole work. Flotow's aristocratic predilections made it difficult for him to remain in Paris after the revolution of 1848. He accepted the post of Intendant at the grand ducal court theater in Schwerin (1855–63), then moved to Austria; he returned to Germany in 1873, settling in Darmstadt in 1880.

WORKS: DRAMATIC: OPERAS: *Pierre et Cathérine* (1st perf. in a German version, Ludwigslust, 1835); *Die Bergknappen*; *Alfred der Grosse*; *Rob-Roy* (Royaumont, Sept. 1836); *Sérafine* (Royaumont, Oct. 30, 1836); *Alice* (Paris, April 8, 1837); *La Lettre du préfet* (Paris, 1837; rev. 1868); *Le Comte de Saint-Mégrin* (Royaumont, June 10, 1838; rev. as *Le Duc de Guise*, Paris, April 3, 1840; in German, Schwerin, Feb. 24, 1841); *Lady Melvil* (with Albert Grisar; Paris, Nov. 15, 1838); *L'Eau merveilleuse* (with Grisar; Paris, Jan. 30, 1839); *Le Naufrage de la Méduse* (with Auguste Pilati; Paris, May 31, 1839; in German as *Die Matrosen*, Hamburg, Dec. 23, 1845); *L'Esclave de Camoëns* (Paris, Dec. 1, 1843; subsequent revisions under different titles); *Alessandro Stradella* (Hamburg, Dec. 30, 1844); *L'Âme en peine* (Der Förster; Paris, June 29, 1846); *Martha, oder Der Markt zu Richmond* (Vienna, Nov. 25, 1847); *Sophie Katharina, oder Die Grossfürstin* (Berlin, Nov. 19, 1850); *Rübezahl* (private perf., Retzien, Aug. 13, 1852; public perf., Frankfurt am Main, Nov. 26, 1853); *Albin, oder Der Pflegesohn* (Vienna, Feb. 12, 1856; rev. as *Der Müller von Meran*, Königsberg, 1859); *Herzog Johann Albrecht von Mecklenburg, oder Andreas Mylius* (Schwerin, May 27, 1857); *Pianella* (Schwerin, Dec. 27, 1857); *La Veuve Grapin* (Paris, Sept. 21, 1859; in German, Vienna, June 1, 1861); *La Châtelaine* (*Der Märchensucher*, 1865); *Naida* (St. Petersburg, Dec. 11, 1865); *Zilda, ou La Nuit des dupes* (Paris, May 28, 1866); *Am Runenstein* (Prague, April 13, 1868); *L'Ombre* (Paris, July 7, 1870; in German as *Sein Schatten*, Vienna, Nov. 10, 1871); *Die Musikanten, or La Jeunesse de Mozart* (Mannheim, June 19, 1887). BALLETS: *Lady Henriette, ou La Servante de Greenwich* (Act II by R. Burgmüller and Act III by E. Deldevez; Paris, Feb. 21, 1844); *Die Libelle, or La Demoiselle, ou Le Papillon ou Dolores* (Schwerin, Aug. 8, 1856); *Die Gruppe der Thetis* (Schwerin, Aug. 18, 1858); *Der Tannkönig* (Schwerin, Dec. 22, 1861); *Der Königsschuss* (Schwerin, May 22, 1864).

BIBL.: G. von Flotow, *Beiträge zur Geschichte der Familie von F.* (Dresden, 1844); A. Bussensius, *F. v.F.: Eine Biographie* (Kassel, 1855); B. Bardi-Poswiansky, *F. als Opernkomponist* (diss., Univ. of Königsberg, 1924); J. Weissmann, *F.* (London, 1950).

Flower, Sir (Walter) Newman, English publisher and writer on music; b. Fontmell Magna, Dorset, July 8, 1879; d. Blandford, Dorset, March 12, 1964. He joined the firm of Cassel & Co. in 1906 and purchased it in 1927. He became deeply interested in music; publ. an extensive biography, *George Frideric Handel: His Personality and His Times* (London, 1923; 2d ed., rev., 1947); also *Sir Arthur Sullivan: His Life, Letters and Diaries* (London, 1927; 2d ed., rev., 1950); *Franz Schubert: The Man and His Circle* (London, 1928; 2d ed., rev., 1949); also prepared a *Catalogue of a Handel Collection Formed by Newman Flower* (Sevenoaks, 1921); publ. a vol. of memoirs, *Just as It Happened* (London, 1950). He was knighted in 1938.

BIBL.: A. Walker, *George Frideric Handel: The N. F. Collection* (Manchester, 1972).

Floyd, Carlisle (Sessions, Jr.), American composer and teacher; b. Latta, S.C., June 11, 1926. He studied at Syracuse Univ. with Ernst Bacon (Mus.B., 1946; Mus.M., 1949); he also took private piano lessons with Rudolf Firkušný and Sidney Foster. In 1947 he joined the staff of the School of Music of Florida State Univ., Tallahassee; in 1976 he became a prof. of music at the Univ. of Houston. His musical drama *Susannah* was premiered in Tallahassee (Feb. 24, 1955); it was later staged at the City Center in New York (Sept. 27, 1956), winning the N.Y. Music Critics Circle Award. Floyd's other works include *Slow Dusk*, musical play (1949); *Fugitives*, musical drama (1951); operas: *Wuthering Heights* (Santa Fe, July 16, 1958); *The Passion of Jonathan Wade* (N.Y., Oct. 11, 1962); *The Sojourner and Mollie Sinclair* (Raleigh, N.C., Dec. 2, 1963); *Markheim* (New Orleans, March 31, 1966); *Of Mice and Men* (Seattle, Jan. 22, 1970); *Bilby's Doll* (Houston, Feb. 29, 1976); *Willie Stark* (Houston, April 24, 1981). He further wrote the ballet *Lost Eden* for 2 Pianos (1952).

Flury, Richard, Swiss composer, conductor and teacher; b. Biberist, March 26, 1896; d. there, Dec. 23, 1967. He studied musicology in Basel, Bern, and Geneva, then theory and composition with Kurth, Hubert, Lauber, and Marx. He conducted orchs. and choral societies in Switzerland; taught at the Solothurn Canton School. He wrote an autobiography, *Lebenserinnerungen* (1950). He composed the operas *Eine florentinische Tragödie* (1926), *Die helle Nacht* (1932), and *Casanova e l'Albertolli* (1937), and the ballet *Die alte Truhe* (1945).

Fodor-Mainvielle, Joséphine, famous French soprano; b. Paris, Oct. 13, 1789; d. Saint-Génis, near Lyons, Aug. 14, 1870. She made her debut in 1808 in St. Petersburg in Fioravanti's *Le Cantatrici villane*. She gained renown for her performances in the operas of Mozart and Rossini at the King's Theatre in London (1816–18); was likewise successful in her many engagements in Paris, Naples, and Vienna. During a performance of the title role of *Sémiramide* in Paris on Dec. 9, 1825, she suddenly lost her voice and was eventually compelled to quit the stage. She went to Naples in the hopes of recovery under the warm sun, but her attempts to renew her career in 1828 and 1831 failed, and she spent the rest of her long life in retirement.

Foerster, Josef Bohuslav, eminent Czech composer and teacher; b. Prague, Dec. 30, 1859; d. Nový Vestec, near Stará Boleslav, May 29, 1951. He was the son of the organist, teacher, and composer Josef Förster (b. Osojnitz, Feb. 22, 1833; d. Prague, Jan. 3, 1907). He studied at the Prague Organ School (1879–82), then was organist at St. Vojtěch (1882–88) and choirmaster of Panna Marie Sněžná (1889–94). He married the Czech soprano Berta Foerstrová-Lautererová (b. Prague, Jan. 11, 1869; d. there, April 9, 1936) in 1888; when she became a member of the Hamburg Opera in 1893, he settled there as a music critic and later became a prof. of piano at the Cons. in 1901. After his wife became a member of the Vienna Court Opera in 1903, he became a prof. of composition at the New Vienna Cons. He returned to Prague in 1918; then taught composition at the Cons. (1919–22), at its master school (1922–31), and at the Univ. of Prague (1920–36). He served as president of the Czech Academy of Sciences and Art (1931–39), and was awarded the honorary title of National Artist of the Czech government in 1945. He continued to teach privately and to compose during the last years of his long life. He taught many distinguished Czech composers of the 20th century. He publ. a detailed autobiography (Prague, 1929–47), as well as several vols. of essays and articles. Of his numerous compositions, the most important are his operas, instrumental music, and choral pieces written before World War I. His works from this period are suffused with lyric melos, and reveal characteristic national traits in Foerster's treatment of melodic and rhythmic material; his harmonic idiom represents the general style of Central European Romanticism.

WORKS: DRAMATIC: OPERAS (all 1st perf. in Prague): *Debora* (1890–91; Jan. 27, 1893); *Eva* (1895–97; Jan. 1, 1899); *Jessika* (1902–04; April 16, 1905); *Nepřemožení* (Invincibilities; 1917; Dec. 19, 1918); *Srdce* (Hearts; 1921–22; Nov. 15, 1923); *Bloud* (The Fool; 1935–36; Feb. 28, 1936); incidental music for various plays.

BIBL.: Z. Nejedlý, *J. B. F.* (Prague, 1910); J. Bartoš, *J. B. F.* (Prague, 1923); J. Bartoš, P. Pražák, and J. Plavec, eds., *J. B. F.: Jeho životní pout a tvorba: 1859–1949* (Prague, 1949); F. Pala, *J. B. F.* (Prague, 1962).

Foignet, Charles Gabriel, French singer and composer; b. Lyons, 1750; d. Paris, 1823. He settled in Paris in 1779, where he taught harpsichord, harp, and singing. After publishing keyboard pieces and songs, he devoted himself to composing for the stage from 1791. With his son, François Foignet (b. Paris, Feb. 17, 1782; d. Strasbourg, July 22, 1845), who was also a singer and composer, he was active with his own Théâtre des Jeunes-Artistes from 1798 to 1807. François scored his most celebrated success there when he sang in his own *La naissance d'Arlequin, ou Arlequin dans un oeuf* (July 15, 1803). After 1807, François pursued his singing career in Liège, Bruges, Nantes, Lille, Ghent, and Rouen. Charles had another son, Gabriel Foignet, who was a harpist and composer.

Foli (real name, **Foley**), **A(llan) J(ames),** Irish bass; b. Cahir, Tipperary, Aug. 7, 1835; d. Southport, Oct. 20, 1899. He was a pupil of Bisaccia in Naples. Following a widespread fashion among aspiring English opera singers, he changed his name to an Italian-sounding homonym, Foli, and made a career as "Signor Foli." He made his professional debut as Elmiro in Rossini's *Otello* in Catania in 1862, then sang throughout Italy. He appeared in London at Her Majesty's Theatre in 1865, and later at Covent Garden and Drury Lane. He toured the United States with Mapleson's opera company (1878–79), and also traveled in South Africa, Australia, and Russia.

Fomin, Evstignei, Russian composer; b. St. Petersburg, Aug. 16, 1761; d. there, April 27, 1800. He was sent to Bologna to study with Padre Martini, returning to St. Petersburg in 1785. He then became a singing teacher and operatic coach at the theatrical school there. He composed about 10 operas, including *Novgorod Hero Vassily Boyeslavich* (St. Petersburg, Dec. 8, 1786), *Yamshchiki* (Coachmen; St. Petersburg, Jan. 13, 1787), *Orpheus and Eurydice* (St. Petersburg, Jan. 13, 1792), and *The Americans* (St. Petersburg, Feb. 19, 1800; the title refers to the Russians in Alaska; vocal score publ. in 1893; the opera was revived in a perf. at Moscow, Jan. 17, 1947). A number of other operas were erroneously attributed to Fomin, among them the popular *Miller, Wizard, Cheat, and Marriage-Broker*, produced in Moscow on Jan. 31, 1779, the music of which was actually written by an obscure violinist named Sokolovsky.

BIBL.: B. Dobrokhotov, *E. F.* (Moscow, 1949; 2d ed., 1968).

Fongaard, Björn, Norwegian composer and guitarist; b. Christiania, March 2, 1919; d. there (Oslo), Oct. 26, 1980. He took up the guitar at an early age before pursuing his musical training at the Oslo Cons. with Per Steenberg, Bjarne Brustad, and Karl Andersen. He appeared as a guitarist and also taught guitar at the Oslo Cons. His interest in the potentialities of fractional intervals led him to devise special guitars for playing microtonal music with the aid of electronic techniques which he described as "orchestra microtonalis." He composed a prolific corpus of works in every conceivable genre, including *Skapelse II* (Creation II), church opera (1972), *Andromeda*, ballet music (1972), and *Dimensions*, ballet music (1974).

Ford, Bruce (Edwin), American tenor; b. Lubbock, Texas, Aug. 15, 1956. He studied at West Texas A. & M. Univ., Texas Tech Univ., and the Houston Opera Studio, where he appeared in student productions. In 1981 he sang in the premiere of Floyd's *Willie Stark* at the Houston Grand Opera. From 1983 to 1985 he was a member of the Wuppertal Opera. In 1985 he sang Count Almaviva in Bordeaux and Tamino at the Minnesota Opera. He was a member of the Mannheim National Theatre from 1985 to 1987. In 1986 he appeared as Rossini's Argirio at the Wexford Festival. After singing that composer's Agorante in Pesaro in 1990, he made his debut at London's Covent Garden as Count Almaviva in 1991. In 1992 he appeared as Rossini's Uberto at Milan's La Scala and as his Rodrigo at the San Francisco Opera in 1994. He sang Ernesto in *Don Pasquale* at the Lyric Opera in Chicago in 1995. His Metropolitan Opera debut in New York followed as Count Almaviva on Oct. 22, 1997. In 1998 he was engaged as Lindoro in Paris.

Formes, Karl Johann, German bass, brother of **Theodor Formes**; b. Mülheim, Aug. 7, 1815; d. San Francisco, Dec. 15, 1889. He was a pupil of Basodowa in Vienna. After making his operatic debut as Sarastro in Cologne (Jan. 6, 1842), he sang in Mannheim before appearing in Vienna (1843–49). In 1849 he made his London debut at Drury Lane. On March 16, 1850, he made his first appearance at London's Covent Garden as Caspar in *Der Freischütz*, returning there regularly until 1868. He also sang at London's Royal Italian Opera (1852–57). In 1857 he made his N.Y. debut as Bertram in *Robert le diable* at the Academy of Music, where he sang for some 20 years. After his retirement, he settled in San Francisco as a voice teacher. He publ. a *Method of Singing* (3 vols., 1865; 2d ed., 1885) and an autobiography, *Aus meinem Kunst- und Bühnenleben: Erinnerungen des Bassisten* (Cologne, 1888; Eng. tr., 1891, as *My Memoirs*). Among his best known roles were Leporello, Rocco, Nicolai's Falstaff, and Flotow's Plunkett.

Formes, Theodor, German tenor, brother of **Karl Johann Formes**; b. Mülheim, June 24, 1826; d. Endenich, near Bonn, Oct. 15, 1874. He made his debut at Ofen (1846), then sang in Vienna (1848) and Berlin (1851–66); he made a tour in America with his brother. He lost his voice temporarily. After returning to the stage for a few years, he suffered a setback, became insane, and died in an asylum.

Formichi, Cesare, Italian baritone; b. Rome, April 15, 1883; d. there, July 21, 1949. He studied in Rome. He made his debut at the Teatro Lirico in Milan in 1911; he then sang at the Teatro Colón in Buenos Aires, in Madrid, in Barcelona, and at the Paris Opéra; he appeared with the Chicago Opera Co. (1922–32); he sang at Covent Garden in London (1924). He was particularly effective in dramatic roles, such as Rigoletto, Iago, and Scarpia.

Fornerod, Aloÿs, Swiss violinist, music critic, educator, and composer; b. Montet-Cudrefin, Nov. 16, 1890; d. Fribourg, Jan. 8, 1965. He studied violin and theory at the Lausanne Cons. and at the Schola Cantorum in Paris. He was a member of the Lausanne Sym. Orch.; in 1954 he was appointed director of the Fribourg Cons. As a composer, he followed the French modern style, in the spirit of fin-de-siècle Impressionism. He publ. *Les Tendances de la musique moderne* (Lausanne, 1924); he was for 40 years a critic for *La Tribune de Lausanne*. Among his works was the comic opera *Geneviève* (Lausanne, May 20, 1954).

BIBL.: J. Viret, *A. F., ou, Le Musicien et le pays* (Lausanne, 1982).

Fornia-Labey, Rita (née **Regina Newman**), American soprano, later mezzo-soprano; b. San Francisco, July 17, 1878; d. Paris, Oct. 27, 1922. She adopted the name Fornia after California; following her marriage to J. P. Labey in 1910, she used the name Fornia-Labey. She studied with Emil Fischer and Sofia Scalchi in New York and Selma Nicklass-Kempner in Berlin. After making her operatic debut in Hamburg in 1901, she completed her training with Jean de Reszke in Paris. In 1903 she made her N.Y. debut as Siebel in *Faust* at the Brooklyn Academy of Music, and then toured with H. W. Savage's Opera Co. On Dec. 6, 1907, she made her Metropolitan Opera debut in New York as the Geisha in Mascagni's *Iris*, remaining on its roster for the rest of her life.

Forrest, Hamilton, American composer; b. Chicago, Jan. 8, 1901; d. London, Dec. 26, 1963. He was a student of Weidig at the American Cons. of Music in Chicago (M.M., 1926). His opera *Yzdra* (1925) received the Bispham Memorial Medal, and his opera *Camille*, with Mary Garden in the title role, was highly praised at its premiere (Chicago, Dec. 10, 1930). He prepared settings of 33 Kentucky mountain melodies and Negro folk songs, including "He's Got the Whole World in His Hands," which were championed by Marian Anderson. He composed the operas *Yzdra* (1925), *Camille* (Chicago, Dec. 10, 1930), *Marie Odile* (n.d.), *Don Fortunio* (Interlochen, Mich., July 22, 1952), *Daelia* (Interlochen, July 21, 1954), and *Galatea* (1957); also ballets and incidental music.

Forrester, Maureen (Kathleen Stewart), outstanding Canadian contralto; b. Montreal, July 25, 1930. She studied piano and sang in Montreal church choirs. At 16, she began vocal training with Sally Martin in Montreal; at 19, she became a student of Frank Rowe; at 20, she found a mentor in Bernard Diamant, with whom she continued to work for over a decade; she also had lessons with Michael Raucheisen in Berlin in 1955. On Dec. 8, 1951, she made her professional debut in Elgar's *The Music Makers* with the Montreal Elgar Choir. Her recital debut followed in Montreal on March 29, 1953. On Feb. 14, 1955, she made her European debut in a recital at the Salle Gaveau in Paris, and then toured throughout Europe. She made her N.Y. debut at Town Hall on Nov. 12, 1956. Her extraordinary success as a soloist in Mahler's 2d Sym. with Bruno Walter and the N.Y. Phil. on Feb. 17, 1957, set the course of a brilliant international career as a concert artist. In subsequent years, she appeared as a soloist with most of the principal conductors and orchs. of the world, and also gave numerous recitals. From 1965 to 1974 she was a member of the Bach Aria Group in New York, and also served as chairman of the voice dept. at the Philadelphia Musical Academy (1966–71). She also began to give increasing attention to opera. On May 28, 1962, she made her Toronto stage debut as Gluck's Orfeo. In 1963 she appeared as Brangäne at the Teatro Colón in Buenos Aires. She made her U.S. stage debut as Cornelia in Handel's *Julius Caesar* at the N.Y. City Opera on Sept. 27, 1966. On Feb. 10, 1975, she made her Metropolitan Opera debut in New York as Erda in *Das Rheingold*. In 1982 she appeared as Madame de la Haltière in Massenet's *Cendrillon* at the San Francisco Opera. In 1990 she made her debut at Milan's La Scala as the Countess in *The Queen of Spades*. From 1983 to 1988 she was chairperson of the Canada Council, and from 1986 to 1990 she was chancellor of Wilfrid Laurier Univ. She received over 30 honorary doctorates. In 1967 she was made a Companion of the Order of Canada and in 1990 received the Order of Ontario. With M. MacDonald, she wrote *Out of Character: A Memoir* (Toronto, 1986). In spite of her later success in opera, Forrester's reputation was first and foremost that of a remarkable interpreter of solo works with orch., oratorio, and lieder.

Forsell, John (Carl Johan Jacob), famous Swedish baritone and pedagogue; b. Stockholm, Nov. 6, 1868; d. there, May 30, 1941. He served as an officer in the Swedish Army before pursuing vocal training in Stockholm. On Feb. 26, 1896, he made his operatic debut as Figaro in *Il Barbiere di Siviglia* at the Royal Opera in Stockholm, where he was a member until 1901, and again from 1903 to 1909. On June 26, 1909, he made his debut at London's Covent Garden as Don Giovanni, his most celebrated role. He made his Metropolitan Opera debut in New York on Nov. 20, 1909, as Telramund, but remained on its roster for only that season before pursuing his career in Europe. He made guest appearances in Berlin, Vienna, Bayreuth, and other music centers. In 1938 he appeared as Don Giovanni for the last time in Copenhagen. From 1923 to 1939 he was director of the Royal Opera in Stockholm, and he also was prof. of voice at the Stockholm Cons. from 1924 to 1931. His notable students included Jussi Björling, Set Svanholm, and Aksel Schiøtz. The beauty of his voice was ably seconded by his assured vocal technique. Among his other roles were Hans Sachs, Beckmesser, Amfortas, Eugene Onegin, Germont, and Scarpia.

BIBL.: E. Ljungberger, *J. F.* (Stockholm, 1916); *Boken om J. F.* (Stockholm, 1938); K. Liliedahl, *J. F.: A Discography* (Trelleborg, 1972).

Fortner, Wolfgang, important German composer and pedagogue; b. Leipzig, Oct. 12, 1907; d. Heidelberg, Sept. 5, 1987. He studied composition with Grabner at the Leipzig Cons., and musicology with Kroyer at the Univ. there (1927–31). Upon graduation, he was engaged for 22 years as instructor in theory at the Inst. of Sacred Music in Heidelberg, then was a prof. of composition at the North West Music Academy in Detmold (1954–57) and held a similar position at the Hochschule für Musik in Freiburg im Breisgau (1957–73). Concurrently he led the concerts of Music Viva in Heidelberg, Freiburg, and Munich; after 1954 he was also a lecturer at the Academy of the Arts in West Berlin. His music is marked by exceptional contrapuntal skills, with the basic tonality clearly present even when harmonic density reaches its utmost; in some of his works from 1947, Fortner gave a dodecaphonic treatment to melodic procedures; in his textures, he often employed a "rhythmic cell" device. He was equally adept in his works for the musical theater and purely instrumental compositions; the German tradition is maintained throughout, both in the mechanics of strong polyphony and in rational innovations.

WORKS: DRAMATIC: OPERAS: *Bluthochzeit* (1956; Cologne, June 8, 1957; rev. 1963; a reworking of a dramatic scene, *Der Wald* for Voices, Speaker, and Orch., Frankfurt am Main, June 25, 1953); *Corinna*, opera buffa (Berlin, Oct. 3, 1958); *In seinem Garten liebt Don Perlimlín Belisa* (1961–62; Schwetzingen, May 10, 1962); *Elisabeth Tudor* (1968–71; Berlin, Oct. 23, 1972); *That Time* (Baden-Baden, April 24, 1977). BALLETS: *Die weisse Rose* (1949; concert premiere, Baden-Baden, March 5, 1950; stage premiere, Berlin, April 28, 1951); *Die Witwe von Ephesus* (Berlin, Sept. 17, 1952); *Carmen* (1970; Stuttgart, Feb. 28, 1971).

BIBL.: B. Weber, *W. F. und seine Opernkompositionen* (Mainz, 1995).

Fortunato, D'Anna, American mezzo-soprano; b. Pittsburgh, Feb. 21, 1945. She studied with Frederick Jagel, Gladys Miller, and John Moriarty at the New England Cons. of Music in Boston (1965–72) and with Phyllis Curtin at the Berkshire Music Center in Tanglewood (1971, 1972). She made her European opera debut with the Boston Camerata as Dido in Purcell's *Dido and Aeneas* in Paris in 1980, and her U.S. opera debut at the N.Y. City Opera as Ruggiero in Handel's *Alcina* in 1983. From 1974 to 1982 she taught at the Longy School of Music in Cambridge, Mass. Her operatic and concert repertoire is extensive, ranging from early music to contemporary works.

Forti, Anton, famous Austrian tenor and baritone; b. Vienna, June 8, 1790; d. there, June 16, 1859. He first sang in Esterháza (1807–11), then went to Vienna, where he appeared at the Theater an der Wien (1811–13). In 1813 he joined the Court Theater, singing both tenor and baritone roles; also sang in Prague, Hamburg, and Berlin, continuing to sing until late in his life. He was particularly esteemed for his performances in the roles of Figaro and Don Giovanni.

Fortune, Nigel (Cameron), English musicologist; b. Birmingham, Dec. 5, 1924. He studied at the Univ. of Birmingham (B.A., 1950); received his Ph.D. in 1954 from Gonville and Caius College, Cambridge, with the diss. *Italian Secular Song from 1600 to 1635: The Origins and Development of Accompanied Monody*. He was music librarian at the Univ. of London (1956–59); in 1959 he became a lecturer at the Univ. of Birmingham; from 1969 to 1986 was a reader in music there. He was a senior consulting ed. of *The New Grove Dictionary of Music and Musicians* (1980) and joint ed. of *Music & Letters* (from 1981). With D. Arnold, he ed. *The Monteverdi Companion* (London, 1968; 2d ed., rev., 1985, as *The New Monteverdi Companion*) and *The Beethoven Companion* (London, 1971). He also ed. *Music and Theatre: Essays in Honour of Winton Dean* (Cambridge, 1987).

Foss (real name, **Fuchs**), **Lukas,** brilliant German-born American pianist, conductor, and composer; b. Berlin, Aug. 15, 1922. He was a scion of a cultural family; his father was a prof. of philosophy; his mother, a talented painter. He studied piano and theory with Julius Goldstein-Herford in Berlin. When the dark shadow of the Nazi dominion descended upon Germany in 1933, the family prudently moved to Paris; there Foss studied piano with Lazare Lévy, composition with Noël Gallon, and orchestration with Felix Wolfes. He also took flute lessons with Louis Moÿse. In 1937 he went to the United States and enrolled at the Curtis Inst. of Music in Philadelphia, where he studied piano with Vengerova, composition with Scalero, and conducting with Reiner; in 1939–40 he took a course in advanced composition with Hindemith at Yale Univ., and also studied conducting with Koussevitzky at the Berkshire Music Center in Tanglewood (summers, 1939–43). He became a naturalized American citizen in 1942. He was awarded a Guggenheim fellowship in 1945; in 1960 he received his 2d Guggenheim fellowship. His first public career was that of a concert pianist, and he elicited high praise for his appearances as soloist with the N.Y. Phil. and other orchs. He made his conducting debut with the Pittsburgh Sym. Orch. in 1939. From 1944 to 1950 he was pianist of the Boston Sym. Orch.; then traveled to Rome on a Fulbright fellowship (1950–52). From 1953 to 1962 he taught composition at the Univ. of Calif. at Los Angeles, where he also established the Improvisation Chamber Ensemble to perform music of "controlled improvisation." In 1963 he was appointed music director of the Buffalo Phil.; during his tenure, he introduced ultramodern works, much to the annoyance of some regular subscribers; he resigned his position in 1970. In 1971 he became principal conductor of the Brooklyn Philharmonia; also established the series "Meet the Moderns" there. From 1972 to 1975 he conducted the Jerusalem Sym. Orch. He became music director of the Milwaukee Sym. Orch. in 1981; he relinquished his position in 1986 after a tour of Europe, and was made its conductor laureate; he continued to hold his Brooklyn post until 1990. In 1986 he was the Mellon Lecturer at the National Gallery of Art in Washington, D.C. In 1962 he was elected a member of the National Inst. of Arts and Letters. He was elected a member of the American Academy and Inst. of Arts and Letters in 1983. Throughout the years, he evolved an astounding activity as conductor, composer, and lately college instructor, offering novel ideas in education and performance. As a composer, he traversed a protean succession of changing styles, idioms, and techniques. His early compositions were marked by the spirit of Romantic lyricism, adumbrating the musical language of Mahler; some other works reflected the neoclassical formulas of Hindemith; still others suggested the hedonistic vivacity and sophisticated stylization typical of Stravinsky's productions. But the intrinsic impetus of his music was its "pulse," which evolves the essential thematic content into the substance of original projection. His earliest piano pieces were publ. when he was 15 years old; there followed an uninterrupted flow of compositions in various genres. Foss was fortunate in being a particular protégé of Koussevitzky, who conducted many of his works with the Boston Sym. Orch.; and he had no difficulty in finding other performers. As a virtuoso pianist, he often played the piano part in his chamber music, and he conducted a number of his symphonic and choral works.

WORKS: DRAMATIC: OPERAS: *The Jumping Frog of Calaveras County* (1949; Bloomington, Ind., May 18, 1950); *Griffelkin* (1953–55; NBC-TV, Nov. 6, 1955); *Introductions and Goodbyes* (1959; N.Y., May 7, 1960). BALLETS: *The Heart Remembers* (1944); *Within These Walls* (1944); *Gift of the Magi* (1944; Boston, Oct. 5, 1945). INCIDENTAL MUSIC TO: Shakespeare's *The Tempest* (1939–40; N.Y., March 31, 1940).

BIBL.: K. Perone, *L. F.: A Bio-Bibliography* (N.Y., 1991).

Foster, Lawrence (Thomas), noted American conductor; b. Los Angeles, Oct. 23, 1941. He studied conducting with F. Zweig in Los Angeles. He made his first conducting appearance with the Young Musicians Foundation Debut Orch. in Los Angeles in 1960. At the age of 24, he was appointed assistant conductor of the Los Angeles Phil., a post he held until 1968; in 1966, received the Koussevitzky Memorial Conducting Prize at the Berkshire Music Center at Tanglewood. From 1969 to 1974 he was chief guest conductor of the Royal Phil. in London. From 1971 to 1978 he was conductor-in-chief of the Houston Sym. Orch. From 1979 to 1990 he was chief conductor of the Opera and the Orchestre National de Monte Carlo (called Orchestre Philharmonique de Monte Carlo from 1980). He also became Generalmusikdirektor in the city of Duisburg in 1981, remaining in that position until 1988. From 1990 to 1998 he was music director of the Aspen (Colo.) Music Festival. In 1992 he resumed the position of chief conductor of the Orchestre Philharmonique in Monte Carlo. He was also music director of the Lausanne Chamber Orch. (1985–90) and the Jerusalem Sym. Orch. (1988–92). In 1996 he became music director of the Barcelona Sym. Orch. Foster is particularly notable for his dynamic interpretations of modern works, but has also been acclaimed for his precise and intelligent presentations of the Classical and Romantic repertoire.

Fotek, Jan, Polish composer; b. Czerwinsk, Nov. 28, 1928. He studied composition with Wiechowicz at the State College of Music in Kraków and with Szeligowski at the State College of Music in Warsaw. His works include *Galileo*, musical drama (1969), *A Forest King's Daughter*, opera ballet (1977), and *Anyone*, opera mystery (1983);

Foulds, John (Herbert), significant English composer and music theorist; b. Manchester, Nov. 2, 1880; d. Calcutta, April 24, 1939. He was precocious and began to compose at a single-digit age; he learned to play cello and earned a living by playing in theater orchs. In 1900 he joined the Hallé Orch. in Manchester; then moved to London in 1910, where he served as music director for the Central YMCA (1918–23); he also conducted the Univ. of London Music Soc. (1921–26). In 1935 he went to India; he undertook a thorough study of Indian folk music; he served as director of European music for the All-India Radio at Delhi and Calcutta (1937–39) and also formed an experimental "Indo-European" orch., which included both European and Asian instruments. He was the first English composer to experiment with quarter tones, and as early as 1898 wrote a string quartet with fractional intervals; he also composed semiclassical pieces using traditional Indian instruments. Unfortunately, many of his MSS are lost. He authored *Music To-Day: Its Heritage from the Past, and Legacy to the Future* (London, 1934).

WORKS: DRAMATIC: *The Vision of Dante*, concert opera (1905–08); *Cleopatra*, miniature opera (1909; not extant); *The Tell-Tale Heart*, melodrama (1910); *Avatara*, opera (1919–30; not extant); music for the ritual play *Veils* (1926; unfinished).

BIBL.: M. MacDonald, *J. F. and His Music* (N.Y. and London, 1990).

Fourdrain, Félix, French composer; b. Nice, Feb. 3, 1880; d. Paris, Oct. 22, 1923. He studied with Widor.

WORKS: DRAMATIC: OPERAS: *Echo* (Paris, 1906); *La Légende du point d'Argentan* (Paris, April 17, 1907); *La Glaneuse* (Lyons, 1909); *Vercingétorix* (Nice, 1912); *Madame Roland* (Rouen, 1913); *Les Contes de Perrault* (Paris, 1913); *Les Maris de Ginette; La Mare au diable; La Griffe*. OPERETTAS: *Dolly* (Paris, 1922); *L'Amour en cage; Le Million de Colette; La Hussarde* (Paris, 1925). Also incidental music to Cain's *Le Secret de Polichinelle* (Cannes, 1922).

Fourestier, Louis (Félix André), French conductor, pedagogue, and composer; b. Montpellier, May 31, 1892; d. Boulogne-Billancourt, Sept. 30, 1976. He was a student of Gédalge and Leroux at the Paris Cons., winning the Grand Prix de Rome with his cantata *La Mort d'Adonis* in 1925. After conducting in the French provinces, he returned to Paris and conducted at the Opéra Comique (1927–32) and the Opéra (1938–45). On Nov. 11, 1946, he made his Metropolitan Opera debut in New York conducting *Lakmé*, and remained on its roster until 1948. From 1945 to 1963 he was a prof. at the Paris Cons. He wrote mainly orch. works and chamber music.

Fournet, Jean, distinguished French conductor and pedagogue; b. Rouen, April 14, 1913. He received training in flute from M. Moyse (premier prix, 1932) and in conducting from Gaubert (1930–36) at the Paris Cons. In 1936 he made his conducting debut in Rouen, where he was active until 1940. After conducting in Marseilles (1940–44), he returned to Paris and served as music director of the Opéra Comique (1944–57) and as a teacher of conducting at the École Normale de Musique (1944–62). From 1961 to 1968 he was principal guest conductor of the Hilversum Radio Orch. in the Netherlands, where he was also engaged in teaching conducting. In 1965 he made his debut with the Chicago Lyric Opera. After serving as music director of the Rotterdam Phil. (1968–73) and l'Orchestre de l'Ile-de-France (1973–82), he was active as a guest conductor. He made his belated Metropolitan Opera debut in New York on March 28, 1987, conducting *Samson et Dalila*. Fournet was especially esteemed for his idiomatic interpretations of scores from the French symphonic and operatic repertory.

Fournier, Émile-Eugène-Alix, French composer; b. Paris, Oct. 11, 1864; d. Joinville-le-Pont, Sept. 12, 1897. He was a pupil of Delibes and Dubois at the Paris Cons., taking the 2d Grand Prix de Rome in 1891 and the Prix Cressent in 1892 for the 1-act opera *Stratonice* (Paris, 1892). He publ. a number of songs.

Frackenpohl, Arthur (Roland), American composer and teacher; b. Irvington, N.J., April 23, 1924. He studied with Rogers at the Eastman School of Music in Rochester, N.Y. (B.A., 1947; M.A., 1949); he took courses with Milhaud at the Berkshire Music Center in Tanglewood (summer, 1948) and with Boulanger in Fontainebleau (1950); he completed his studies at McGill Univ. in Montreal (D.M.A., 1957). He became a teacher at the Crane School of Music at the State Univ. of N.Y. at Potsdam (1949); he was a prof. there (1961–85). He publ. *Harmonization at the Piano* (1962; 6th ed., 1990). He composed the chamber opera *Domestic Relations ("To Beat or Not to Beat")*, after O. Henry (1964).

Fraenkel, Wolfgang, German composer; b. Berlin, Oct. 10, 1897; d. Los Angeles, March 8, 1983. He studied violin, piano, and theory at the Klindworth-Scharwenka Cons. in Berlin; at the same time, he took courses in jurisprudence and was a judge in Berlin until the advent of the Nazi regime in 1933; he was interned in the Sachsenhausen concentration camp, but as a 50 percent Jew (his mother was an Aryan, as was his wife), he was released in 1939, and went to China, where he enjoyed the protection of Chiang Kai-shek, who asked him to organize music education in Nanking and Shanghai. In 1947 he emigrated to the United States and settled in Los Angeles. He earned a living by composing background music for documentary films in Hollywood, supplementing his income by copying music (he had a calligraphic handwriting). Fraenkel's music was evolved from the standard German traditions, but at a later period he began to experiment with serial methods of composition. His 3d string quartet (1960) won the Queen Elisabeth of Belgium Prize and his *Symphonische Aphorismen* (1965) won 1st prize at the International Competition of the City of Milan. His works, both publ. and in MS, were deposited in the Moldenhauer Archive in Spokane, Wash. Among them is the opera *Der brennende Dornbusch* (1924–27).

Framery, Nicolas Étienne, French composer, writer on music, and poet; b. Rouen, March 25, 1745; d. Paris, Nov. 26, 1810. He composed the text and music for the comic opera *La Sorcière par hasard* (1768); its performance at Villeroy earned him the position of superintendent of music with the Count of Artois. The opera was performed at the Comédie-Italienne (Paris, Sept. 3, 1783), but suffered a fiasco because of the antagonism against Italian opera generated by the adherents of Gluck. He also wrote librettos for Sacchini, Salieri, Paisiello, Anfossi, and other Italian composers; ed. the *Journal de Musique* (1770–78) and *Calendrier Musical Universel* (1788–89) in Paris. He compiled, together with Ginguène and Feytou, the musical part of vol. 1 of *Encyclopédie méthodique* (1791; vol. 2 by Momigny, 1818); besides smaller studies, he wrote *De la nécessité du rythme et de la césure dans les hymnes ou odes destinées à la musique* (1796); tr. into French *Azopardi's Musico prattico, as Le Musicien pratique* (2 vols., 1786).

BIBL.: J. Carlez, *F.: Littérateur-musicien* (Caen, 1893).

Françaix, Jean, significant French composer; b. Le Mans, May 23, 1912; d. Paris, Sept. 25, 1997. He first studied at the Le Mans Cons., of which his father was director, and later took courses at the Paris Cons. with Philipp (piano) and Boulanger (composition). In his music, he associated himself with the new French school of composers, pursuing the twofold aim of practical application and national tradition; his instrumental works represent a stylization of Classical French music; in this respect, he came close to Ravel.

WORKS: DRAMATIC: OPERAS: *Le Diable boîteux*, comic chamber opera (1937; Paris, June 30, 1938); *L'Apostrophe*, musical comedy, after Balzac (1940; Amsterdam, July 1, 1951); *Paris à nous deux (ou Le Nouveau Rastignac)*, comic opera (Fontainebleau, Aug. 7, 1954); *La Princesse de Clèves* (1961–65; Rouen, Dec. 11, 1965). BALLETS: *Scuola de Ballo*, on themes of Boccherini (1933); *Les Malheurs de Sophie* (1935; Paris, Feb. 25, 1948); *Le Roi nu* (1935; Paris, June 15, 1936); *Le Jeu sentimental* (Brussels, July 8, 1936); *La Lutherie enchantée* (Antwerp, March 21, 1936); *Le Jugement d'un fou* (1938; London, Feb. 6, 1939); *Verreries de Venise* (1938; Paris, June 22, 1939); *Les Demoiselles de la nuit* (Paris, May 20, 1948); *Les Zigues de mars* (1950); *La Dame dans la lune* (Paris, Feb. 18, 1958); *Pierrot ou Les Secrets de la nuit* (1980).

BIBL.: M. Lanjean, *J. F.* (Paris, 1961).

Franchetti, Alberto, Italian composer; b. Turin, Sept. 18, 1860; d. Viareggio, Aug. 4, 1942. He studied in Turin with Niccolò Coccon and Fortunato Magi; then with Rheinberger in Munich and with Draeseke in Dresden. He devoted his entire life to composition, with the exception of a brief tenure as director of the Cherubini Cons. in Florence (1926–28).

WORKS: OPERAS: *Asrael* (Reggio Emilia, Feb. 11, 1888); *Cristoforo Colombo* (Genoa, Oct. 6, 1892); *Fior d'Alpe* (Milan, March 15, 1894); *Il Signor di Pourceaugnac* (Milan, April 10, 1897); *Germania* (Milan, March 11, 1902); *La Figlia di Jorio* (Milan, March 29, 1906); *Notte di leggenda* (Milan, Jan. 14, 1915); *Giove a Pompei* (Rome, June 5, 1921; in collaboration with U. Giordano); *Glauco* (Naples, April 8, 1922).

Franci, Benvenuto, Italian baritone, father of **Carlo Franci;** b. Pienza, near Siena, July 1, 1891; d. Rome, Feb. 27, 1985. He was a student of Cotogni and Rosati in Rome. In 1918 he made his operatic debut at Rome's Teatro Costanzi as Giannetto in Mascagni's *Lodoletta*, where he later sang in the premiere of that composer's *Il piccolo Marat* in 1921. In 1923 he sang Amonasro at Milan's La Scala, where he returned to sing in the premieres of Giordano's *Cena delle Beffe* in 1924 and Zandonai's *Cavalieri di Ekebù* in 1925. From 1928 to 1949 he was a principal member of the Rome Opera. He also made guest appearances at London's Covent Garden in 1925, 1931, and 1946. In 1955 he made his farewell appearance in Trieste. Among his other roles were Rigoletto, Macbeth, Gerard, Telramund, Barnaba, Barak, and Scarpia.

Franci, Carlo, Italian conductor and composer, son of **Benvenuto Franci;** b. Buenos Aires, July 18, 1927. He went to Rome and studied composition with Turchi and Petrassi at the Cons. and conducting with Previtali at the Accademia di Santa Cecilia. After conducting the Radio Eireann Sym. Orch. in Dublin (1955–57) and the RAI in Rome (1961–63), he appeared with the Rome Opera. In 1968 he conducted the Rome Opera production of Rossini's *Otello* during its visit to the Metropolitan Opera in New York. On Feb. 1, 1969, he made his debut at the Metropolitan Opera conducting *Lucia di Lammermoor*, and remained on its roster until 1972. As a guest conductor, he appeared with opera houses in Milan, Berlin, Budapest, Munich, Madrid, Paris, Hamburg, Zürich et al. In 1988 he appeared as a guest conductor with the PACT (Performing Arts Council, Transvaal) Opera in Pretoria, where he subsequently served as principal conductor of the

Transvaal Phil. Among his compositions are *4 Studies* for Orch. (1993) and the *African Oratorio* (1994).

Franck, César (-Auguste-Jean-Guillaume-Hubert), great Belgian composer and organist; b. Liège, Dec. 10, 1822; d. Paris, Nov. 8, 1890. His brother was the Belgian-French organist and composer Joseph Franck (1825–1891). He studied first at the Royal Cons. of Liège with Daussoigne and others. At the age of 9 he won 1st prize for singing, and at 12 1st prize for piano. As a child prodigy, he gave concerts in Belgium. In 1835 his family moved to Paris, where he studied privately with Anton Reicha; in 1837 he entered the Paris Cons., studying with Zimmerman (piano), Benoist (organ), and Leborne (theory). A few months after his entrance examinations he received a special award of "grand prix d'honneur" for playing a fugue a third lower at sight; in 1838 he received the 1st prize for piano; in 1839, a 2d prize for counterpoint; in 1840, 1st prize for fugue; and in 1841, 2d prize for organ. In 1842 he was back in Belgium. In 1843 he returned to Paris, and settled there for the rest of his life. On March 17, 1843, he presented there a concert of his chamber music; on Jan. 4, 1846, his first major work, the oratorio *Ruth*, was given at the Paris Cons. On Feb. 22, 1848, in the midst of the Paris revolution, he married. In 1851 he became organist of the church of St.-Jean-St.-François, in 1853 maître de chapelle, and, in 1858, organist at Ste.-Clotilde, which position he held until his death. In 1872 he succeeded Benoist as prof. of organ at the Paris Cons. Franck's organ classes became the training school for a whole generation of French composers; among his pupils were d'Indy, Chausson, Breville, Bordes, Duparc, Ropartz, Pierné, Vidal, Chapuis, Vierne, and a host of others, who eventually formed a school of modern French instrumental music. Until the appearance of Franck in Paris, operatic art dominated the entire musical life of the nation, and the course of instruction at the Paris Cons. was influenced by this tendency. By his emphasis on organ music, based on the contrapuntal art of Bach, Franck swayed the new generation of French musicians toward the ideal of absolute music. The foundation of the famous Schola Cantorum by d'Indy, Bordes, and others in 1894 realized Franck's teachings. After the death of d'Indy in 1931, several members withdrew from the Schola Cantorum and organized the École César Franck (1938).

Franck was not a prolific composer, but his creative powers rose rather than diminished with advancing age. Lucidity of contrapuntal design and fullness of harmony are the distinguishing traits of Franck's music, and in his melodic writing he balanced the diatonic and chromatic elements in fine equilibrium. Although he did not pursue innovation for its own sake, he was not averse to using unorthodox procedures. The novelty of introducing an English horn into the score of his Sym. aroused some criticism among academic musicians of the time. Franck was quite alien to the Wagner-Liszt school of composition, which attracted many of his own pupils; the chromatic procedures in Franck's music derive from Bach rather than from Wagner.

WORKS: DRAMATIC: OPERAS: *Le Valet de Ferme* (1851–53); *Hulda* (1882–85; Monte Carlo, March 8, 1894); *Ghisèle* (unfinished; orchestration completed by d'Indy, Chausson, Bréville, Rousseau, and Coquard; 1st perf., Monte Carlo, March 30, 1896). ORATORIOS: *Ruth* (1843–46; Paris, Jan. 4, 1846; rev. 1871); *La Tour de Babel* (1865); *Les Béatitudes* (1869–79; Dijon, June 15, 1891); *Rédemption* (1st version, Paris, April 10, 1873; final version, Paris, March 15, 1875); *Rébecca* (Paris, March 15, 1881; produced as a 1-act sacred opera at the Paris Opéra, May 25, 1918).

BIBL.: A. Coquard, *C. F.* (Paris, 1890; new ed., 1904); E. Destranges, *L'OEuvre lyrique de C. F.* (Paris, 1896); G. Derepas, *C. F.: Étude sur sa vie, son enseignement, son oeuvre* (Paris, 1897); A. Meyer, *Les Critiques de C. F.* (Orléans, 1898); P. Garnier, *L'Héroïsme de C. F.: Psychologie musicale* (Paris, 1900); F. Baldensperger, *C. F.: L'Artiste et son oeuvre* (Paris, 1901); C. Van den Borren, *L'OEuvre dramatique de C. F.* (Brussels, 1906); V. d'Indy, *C. F.* (Paris, 1906; Eng. tr., 1910); M. de Rudder, *C. F.* (Paris, 1920); E. Closson, *C. F.* (Charleroi, 1923); M. Emmanuel, *C. F.* (Paris, 1930); C. Tournemire, *C. F.* (Paris, 1931); T. Lynn, *C. F.: A Bio-bibliography* (N.Y., 1934); M. Kunel, *La Vie de C. F.* (Paris, 1947); J. Horton, *C. F.* (London, 1948); N. Demuth, *C. F.* (London, 1949); N. Dufourcq, *C. F.: Le Milieu, l'oeuvre, l'art* (Paris, 1949); L. Vallas, *La Véritable Histoire de C. F.* (Paris, 1950; Eng. tr., 1951); C. Taube, *C. F. und wir: Eine Biographie* (Berlin, 1951); E. Buenzod, *C. A. F.* (Paris, 1966); W. Mohr, *C. F.* (Tutzing, 1969); L. Davies, *C. F. and His Circle* (Boston, 1970).

Franck, Johann Wolfgang, German composer; b. Unterschwaningen (baptized), June 17, 1644; d. c.1710. He was brought up in Ansbach, and served there as court musician from 1665 until 1679. He produced 3 operas at the Ansbach court: *Die unvergleichliche Andromeda* (1675), *Der verliebte Fobus* (1678), and *Die drei Töchter Cecrops* (1679). On Jan. 17, 1679, in a fit of jealousy, he allegedly killed the court musician Ulbrecht, and was forced to flee. He found refuge in Hamburg with his wife, Anna Susanna Wilbel (whom he had married in 1666), and gained a prominent position at the Hamburg Opera. Between 1679 and 1686 he wrote and produced 17 operas, the most important of which was *Diokletian* (1682). His private life continued to be stormy; he deserted his wife and their 10 children, and went to London, where he remained from 1690 to about 1702. The exact place and date of his death are unknown. In London he organized (with Robert King) a series of Concerts of Vocal and Instrumental Music. He publ. *Geistliche Lieder* (Hamburg, 1681, 1685, 1687, 1700; republ. in 1856 by D. H. Engel, with new words by Osterwald; newly ed. by W. Krabbe and J. Kromolicki in vol. 45 of Denkmaler Deutscher Tonkunst) and *Remedium melancholiae* (25 secular solo songs with Basso Continuo; London, 1690).

BIBL.: F. Zelle, *J. W. F.: Ein Beitrag zur Geschichte der ältesten deutschen Oper* (Berlin, 1889); R. Klages, *J. W. F.: Untersuchungen zu seiner Lebensgeschichte und zu seinen geistlichen Kompositionen* (Hamburg, 1937).

Franckenstein, Clemens von, German composer; b. Wiesentheid, July 14, 1875; d. Hechendorf, Aug. 19, 1942. He spent his youth in Vienna, then went to Munich, where he studied with Thuille; he later took courses with Knorr at the Hoch Cons. in Frankfurt am Main. He traveled with an opera company in the United States in 1901; he then was a theater conductor in London (1902–07). From 1912 to 1918 and from 1924 to 1934 he was Intendant at the Munich Opera. He wrote several operas, the most successful of which was *Des Kaisers Dichter* (on the life of the Chinese poet Li-Tai Po), premiered in Hamburg (Nov. 2, 1920). Other operas were *Griselda* (Troppau, 1898), *Fortunatus* (Budapest, 1909), and *Rahab* (Hamburg, March 25, 1911). He also wrote several orch. works.

BIBL.: A. McCredie, *C. v. F.* (Tutzing, 1992).

Francoeur, Louis-Joseph, French violinist, conductor, and composer; b. Paris, Oct. 8, 1738; d. there, March 10, 1804. He entered the orch. of the Paris Opéra at the age of 14, becoming its conductor in 1767. During the Revolution he was imprisoned as a suspect, but was released after the Thermidor coup d'état (1794) and was administrator of the Paris Opéra until 1799. He wrote an act for the opera *Lindor et Ismène* (Paris, Aug. 29, 1766), and also publ. a treatise, *Diapason général de tous les instruments à vent* (1772). His uncle was the French violinist and composer François Francoeur (b. Paris, Sept. 8, 1698; d. there, Aug. 5, 1787).

Frandsen, John, respected Danish conductor; b. Copenhagen, July 10, 1918. He was educated at the Royal Danish Cons. of Music in Copenhagen; then was organist at the Domkirke there (1938–53); he also made appearances as a conductor. After serving as conductor with the Danish Radio Sym. Orch. in Copenhagen (1945–46), he became a conductor at the Royal Danish Theater there; also made appearances with the Royal Danish Orch. in Copenhagen. In 1958 he toured the United States with the Danish Radio Sym. Orch. He was also active as a teacher, at both the Royal Danish Cons. of Music and the Opera School of the Royal Danish Theater. In 1980 he was named orch. counselor of the Danish Radio. He was particularly noted for his outstanding performances of Danish music.

Frank, Ernst, German conductor and composer; b. Munich, Feb. 7, 1847; d. Oberdöbling, near Vienna, Aug. 17, 1889. He studied with M. de Fontaine (piano) and F. Lachner (composition). In 1868 he was conductor at Würzburg, and in 1869 chorus master at the Vienna Court Opera. From 1872 to 1877 he was conductor at Mannheim, from 1877 to 1879 at Frankfurt am Main, and from 1879 to 1887 at the Hannover Court Opera. He wrote the operas *Adam de la Halle* (Karlsruhe, April 9, 1880), *Hero* (Berlin, Nov. 26, 1884), and *Der Sturm* (after Shakespeare; Hannover, Oct. 14, 1887). He also completed H. Götz's opera *Francesca da Rimini* and produced it at Mannheim (1877). Frank was a friend of Brahms. Mental illness led to his being committed to an asylum in April 1887.

Frankel, Benjamin, English composer; b. London, Jan. 31, 1906; d. there, Feb. 12, 1973. He worked as an apprentice watchmaker in his youth; he then went to Germany to study music; returning to London, he earned his living by playing piano or violin in restaurants. It was only then that he began studying composition seriously. In the interim, he made arrangements, played in jazz bands, and wrote music for films; some of his film scores, such as that for *The Man in the White Suit*, are notable for their finesse in musical characterization. In 1946 he was appointed to the faculty of the Guildhall School of Music and Drama in London. Frankel also took great interest in political affairs; he was for many years a member of the British Communist party and followed the tenets of socialist realism in some of his compositions. He composed the opera *Marching Son* (1972–73).

Franko, Nahan, American violinist and conductor; b. New Orleans, July 23, 1861; d. Amityville, N.Y., June 7, 1930. As a child prodigy, he toured with Adelina Patti, then studied in Berlin with Joachim and Wilhelmj. Returning to America, he joined the orch. of the Metropolitan Opera in New York; he was its concertmaster from 1883 to 1905, making his debut there as a conductor on April 1, 1900, the first native-born American to be so engaged there (1904–07). His brother Sam Frank (b. New Orleans, Jan. 20, 1857; d. N.Y., May 6, 1937) was also a violinist.

Frantz, Ferdinand, German bass-baritone; b. Kassel, Feb. 8, 1906; d. Munich, May 26, 1959. He made his debut at the opera in Kassel in 1927 as Ortel in *Die Meistersinger von Nürnberg*; then sang in Halle (1930–32) and Chemnitz (1932–37). He was a leading member of the Hamburg State Opera (1937–43) and the Bavarian State Opera in Munich (1943–59). He made a fine impression at his Metropolitan Opera debut in New York on Dec. 12, 1949, as Wotan in *Die Walküre*; he sang there until 1951 and again in 1953–54; he also appeared at Covent Garden in London in 1953–54. He was primarily known as an effective Wagnerian bass and baritone.

Franz, Paul (real name, **François Gautier**), French tenor; b. Paris, Nov. 30, 1876; d. there, April 20, 1950. After private voice studies with Louis Delaquerrière, he made his debut at the Paris Opéra in 1909 as Lohengrin; he remained on its roster until 1938; he also appeared at London's Covent Garden (1910–14). From 1937 he taught voice at the Paris Cons.

Fränzl, Ferdinand (Ignaz Joseph), German violinist, conductor, and composer, son of **Ignaz (Franz Joseph) Fränzl**; b. Schwetzingen, May 25, 1767; d. Mannheim, Oct. 27, 1833. He studied with his father, and later was a pupil in composition of F. X. Richter and Pleyel at Strasbourg and of Mattei at Bologna. He entered the Mannheim Court Orch. at the age of 22, and in 1785 began to travel on concert tours with his father. He was appointed conductor of the Munich Opera in 1806, but continued his tours. He retired in 1826, finally settling in Mannheim. As a master violinist, he enjoyed great renown. A prolific composer, he composed a number of operas.

Fränzl, Ignaz (Franz Joseph), German violinist, conductor, and composer, father of **Ferdinand (Ignaz Joseph) Fränzl**; b. Mannheim, June 3, 1736; d. there, Sept. 3, 1811. He entered the Mannheim Court Orch. as a boy of 11, becoming co-concertmaster in 1774, and serving as conductor from 1790 to 1803. He made several concert tours with his son. Among his compositions were various works for the stage, including his Singspiel *Die Luftbälle*, which was produced in Mannheim with excellent success (April 15, 1787). He also wrote music for Shakespeare's plays.

BIBL.: R. Würtz, *I. F.* (Mainz, 1970).

Fraschini, Gaetano, noted Italian tenor; b. Pavia, Feb. 16, 1816; d. Naples, May 23, 1887. He studied with F. Moretti, making his debut in Pavia in 1837. He subsequently sang in Milan, Venice, Trieste, Rome, and other Italian cities, and also appeared in London at Her Majesty's Theatre (1847) and Drury Lane (1868). He created the role of Genaro in Donizetti's *Caterina Cornaro*. Much esteemed by Verdi, he sang in the premieres of *Attila, Il Corsaro, La battaglia di Legnano, Alzira, Stiffelio*, and *Un ballo in maschera*. The opera house in Pavia is named for him.

Frazzi, Vito, Italian composer and teacher; b. San Secondo Parmense, Aug. 1, 1888; d. Florence, July 8, 1975. He studied organ at the Parma Cons.; he also took courses in piano and theory. From 1912 to 1958 he taught at the Florence Cons.; he also taught at the Accademia Chigiana in Siena (1932–63). He wrote a music drama, *Re Lear*, after Shakespeare (Florence, 1939), and an opera, *Don Quixote* (Florence, April 27, 1952). He also orchestrated Monteverdi's stage works.

Freed, Isadore, Russian-born American composer and teacher; b. Brest-Litovsk, March 26, 1900; d. Rockville Centre, N.Y., Nov. 10, 1960. He went to the United States at an early age; graduated from the Univ. of Pa. in 1918 (Mus.Bac.), then studied with Bloch and with d'Indy in Paris. He returned to the United States in 1934; held various teaching positions; in 1944 he was appointed head of the music dept. at the Hartt College of Music in Hartford, Conn. He composed the operas *Homo Sum* (1930) and *The Princess and the Vagabond* (Hartford, May 13, 1948) and the ballet *Vibrations* (Philadelphia, 1928).

BIBL.: E. Steinhauer, *A Jewish Composer by Choice, I. F.: His Life and Work* (N.Y., 1961).

Freedman, Harry, Polish-born Canadian composer; b. Łódz, April 5, 1922. He was taken to Canada as a child and became a naturalized citizen in 1931. At 13, he became a student at the Winnipeg School of Art to study painting. At 18, he took up the clarinet; he then studied oboe with Perry Bauman and composition with John Weinzweig at the Royal Cons. of Music of Toronto (1945–51); he also attended Messiaen's class in composition at the Berkshire Music Center in Tanglewood (summer, 1949). He began his career performing with and composing for dance bands and jazz ensembles; he played English horn in the Toronto Sym. Orch. (1946–70), then served as its composer-in-residence (1970–71); he was a founder and president (1975–78) of the Canadian League of Composers. In 1985 he was made an Officer of the Order of Canada. In his works, he reveals a fine command of writing in various idioms, ranging from symphonic to jazz scores. He composed the opera *Abracadabra* (1979), the ballets *Rose Latulippe* (Stratford, Aug. 16, 1966), *5 over 13* (1969), *The Shining People of Leonard Cohen* (1970), *Star Cross'd* (1973; rev. 1975; retitled *Romeo and Juliet*), *Oiseaux exotiques* (1984–85), *Heroes of Our Time* (1986), and *Breaks* (1987), and incidental music and film and television scores.

Freeman, David, Australian opera producer; b. Sydney, May 1, 1952. He was educated at the Univ. of Sydney (1971–74). In 1973 he founded the Opera Factory in Sydney, in 1976 the Opera Factory Zürich, and in 1981 the Opera Factory London. In 1985 he oversaw the British premiere in London of Glass's *Akhnaten*. In 1986 he was producer of the premieres of Osborne's *Hell's Angels* and Birtwistle's *The Mask of Orpheus* and *Yan Tan Tethera* in London. He produced the British premieres of Ligeti's *Aventures & Nouvelles aventures* in 1988 and Reimann's *Die Gespenstersonate* in 1989. Freeman founded Opera Factory Films in 1991. In 1992 he produced Prokofiev's *The Fiery Angel* in St. Petersburg, at London's Covent Garden, and at the Metropolitan Opera in New York. His production of *Die Zauberflöte* was mounted in

London in 1996. He married **Marie Angel** in 1985, the same year he was made a Chevalier of l'Ordre des arts et lettres of France.

Freeman, Harry Lawrence, black American composer, conductor, and teacher; b. Cleveland, Oct. 9, 1869; d. N.Y., March 24, 1954. He studied theory with J. H. Beck and piano with E. Schonert and Carlos Sobrino. He taught at Wilberforce Univ. (1902–04) and the Salem School of Music (1910–13); he organized and directed the Freeman School of Music (1911–22) and the Freeman School of Grand Opera (from 1923); conducted various theater orchs. and opera companies; in 1920 he organized the Negro Opera Co.; he conducted a pageant, *O Sing a New Song*, at the Chicago World's Fair in 1934. He was the first black composer to conduct a sym. orch. in his own work (Minneapolis, 1907), and the first of his race to write large operatic compositions. All of his music is written in folk-song style, his settings in simple harmonies; his operas, all on Negro, oriental, and Indian themes, are constructed of songs and choruses in simple concatenation of separate numbers.

WORKS: DRAMATIC: OPERAS: *The Martyr* (Denver, 1893); *Zuluki* (1898); *African Kraal* (Chicago, June 30, 1903; rev. 1934); *The Octoroon* (1904); *Valdo* (Cleveland, May 1906); *The Tryst* (N.Y., May 1911); *The Prophecy* (N.Y., 1912); *The Plantation* (1914); *Athalia* (1916); *Vendetta* (N.Y., Nov. 12, 1923); *American Romance*, jazz opera (1927); *Voodoo* (N.Y., Sept. 10, 1928); *Leah Kleschna* (1930); *Uzziah* (1931); *Zululand*, tetralogy of music dramas: *Nada, The Lily* (1941–44), *Allah* (1947), and *The Zulu King* (1934). BALLET: *The Slave* for Choral Ensemble and Orch. (N.Y., Sept. 22, 1932).

Freeman, Robert (Schofield), American musicologist, pianist, and educator; b. Rochester, N.Y., Aug. 26, 1935. He received training in piano from Gregory Tucker, Artur Balsam, and Rudolf Serkin, and pursued his academic studies at Harvard College (A.B., *summa cum laude*, 1957) and at Princeton Univ. (M.F.A., 1960; Ph.D., 1967, with the diss. *Opera without Drama: Currents of Change in Italian Opera, 1675–1725*; publ. in Ann Arbor, 1981); he also studied at the Univ. of Vienna on a Fulbright fellowship (1960–62). He taught at Princeton Univ. (1963–68) and at the Mass. Inst. of Technology (1968–73), and also was a visiting assoc. prof. at Harvard Univ. (1972). In 1972 he became director and prof. of musicology at the Eastman School of Music in Rochester, N.Y., where he revitalized its administration and oversaw an extensive renovation of its facilities. In 1997 he became president of the New England Cons. of Music in Boston.

Freer, Eleanor (née **Everest**), American composer; b. Philadelphia, May 14, 1864; d. Chicago, Dec. 13, 1942. She studied singing in Paris (1883–86) with Mathilde Marchesi, then took a course in composition with Benjamin Godard. Upon her return to the United States, she taught singing at the National Cons. of Music of America in New York (1889–91); she settled in Chicago, where she studied theory with Bernhard Ziehn (1902–07). She publ. some light pieces under the name Everest while still a young girl, but most of her larger works were written after 1919. She also wrote an autobiography, *Recollections and Reflections of an American Composer* (Chicago, 1929). Among her works were 9 operas, of which the following were performed: *The Legend of the Piper* (South Bend, Ind., Feb. 28, 1924), *The Court Jester* (Lincoln, Nebr., 1926); *A Christmas Tale* (Houston, Dec. 27, 1929), *Frithiof* (concert perf., Chicago, Feb. 1, 1931), and *A Legend of Spain* (concert perf., Milwaukee, June 19, 1931).

BIBL.: A. Foster, *E. F. and Her Colleagues* (Chicago, 1927).

Freitas (Branco), Frederico (Guedes) de, Portuguese conductor and composer; b. Lisbon, Nov. 15, 1902; d. there, Jan. 12, 1980. He studied piano with Aroldo Silva, composition with A. E. da Costa Ferreira, musicology with Luis de Freitas Branco, and violin at the National Cons. in Lisbon (1919–24); he won the National Composition prize (1926). He conducted the Lisbon Emissora Nacional Orch. (from 1934), the Lisbon Choral Soc. (1940–47), the Oporto Sym. Orch. (1949–53), and the Orquesta de Concierto (from 1955). In his Violin Sonata (1923) he made the first known use of linear polyphony by a Portuguese composer. He composed the operas *O eremita* (1952), *A igreja do mar*, radio opera (1957; Lisbon, Feb. 5, 1960), and *Don João e a máscara*, radio opera (1960) and the ballet *Muro do derrete* (1940), *A dança da Menina Tonta* (1941), *Imagens da terra e do mar* (1943), and *Nazaré* (1948).

Fremstad, Olive, famous Swedish-born American soprano; b. Stockholm, March 14, 1871 (entered into the parish register as the daughter of an unmarried woman, Anna Peterson); d. Irvington-on-Hudson, N.Y., April 21, 1951. She was adopted by an American couple of Scandinavian origin, who took her to Minnesota; she studied piano in Minneapolis; she went to New York in 1890 and took singing lessons with E. F. Bristol. She then held several church positions; in 1892 she sang for the first time with an orch. (under C. Zerrahn) in Boston. In 1893 she went to Berlin to study with Lilli Lehmann; made her operatic debut in Cologne as Azucena (1895); she sang contralto parts. at the Bayreuth Festival in 1896; in 1897 she made her London debut; she also sang in Cologne, Vienna, Amsterdam, and Antwerp. From 1900 to 1903 she was at the Munich Court Opera. She made her American debut as Sieglinde at the Metropolitan Opera in New York on Nov. 25, 1903. Subsequently she sang soprano parts in Wagnerian operas; at first she was criticized in the press for her lack of true soprano tones; however, she soon triumphed over these difficulties, and became known as a soprano singer to the exclusion of contralto parts. She sang Carmen with great success at the Metropolitan (March 5, 1906) with Caruso; her performance of Isolde under Mahler (Jan. 1, 1908) produced a deep impression; until 1915 she was one of the brightest stars of the Metropolitan, specializing in Wagnerian roles, but she was also successful in *Tosca* and other Italian operas. She sang Salome at the first American performance of the Strauss opera (N.Y., Jan. 22, 1907) and in Paris (May 8, 1907). After her retirement from the Metropolitan, she appeared with the Manhattan Opera, the Boston Opera, and the Chicago Opera, and in concerts; she presented her last song recital in New York on Jan. 19, 1920. In 1906 she married Edson Sutphen of New York (divorced in 1911); in 1916 she married her accompanist, Harry Lewis Brainard (divorced in 1925). In Willa Cather's novel *The Song of the Lark*, the principal character was modeled after Fremstad.

Freni (real name, **Fregni**), **Mirella,** noted Italian soprano; b. Modena, Feb. 27, 1935. Curiously enough, her mother and the mother of the future celebrated tenor Luciano Pavarotti worked for a living in the same cigarette factory; curiouser still, the future opera stars shared the same wet nurse. Freni studied voice with her uncle, Dante Arcelli; she made her first public appearance at the age of 11; her accompanist was a child pianist named Leone Magiera, whom she married in 1955. She later studied voice with Ettore Campogalliani. Freni made her operatic debut in Modena on Feb. 3, 1955, as Micaëla; she then sang in provincial Italian opera houses. In 1957 she took 1st prize in the Viotti Competition in Vercelli. In 1959 she sang with the Amsterdam Opera at the Holland Festival, then at the Glyndebourne Festival (1960), Covent Garden in London (1961), and La Scala in Milan (1962). She gained acclaim as Mimi in the film version of *La Bohème*, produced at La Scala in 1963 under Karajan's direction. When La Scala toured Russia in 1964, Freni joined the company and sang Mimi at the Bolshoi Theater in Moscow. She also chose the role of Mimi for her American debut with the Metropolitan Opera in New York on Sept. 29, 1965. She subsequently sang with the Vienna State Opera, the Bavarian State Opera in Munich, the Teatro San Carlo in Naples, and the Rome Opera. In 1976 she traveled with the Paris Opéra during its first American tour. In addition to Mimi, she sang the roles of Susanna, Zerlina, Violetta, Amelia in *Simon Boccanegra*, and Manon. She won acclaim for her vivid portrayal of Tatiana, which she sang with many major opera companies, including the Metropolitan Opera in 1989. In 1990 she celebrated the 35th anniversary of her debut in Modena by returning there as Manon Lescaut. In 1992 she sang Alice Ford at the Metropolitan Opera, and that year also appeared as Mimi in Barcelona and

Rome. She was engaged in 1994 as Fedora at La Scala, at the Lyric Opera in Chicago, and at Covent Garden, and then sang that role at the Metropolitan Opera in 1997.

Freschi, (Giovanni) Domenico, Italian composer; b. Bassano del Grappa, c.1625; d. Vicenza, July 2, 1710. He was a singer and priest at the Cathedral of Vicenza. He publ. 2 masses and a number of Psalms (1660, 1673). In 1677 he went to Venice, remaining there for 8 years. Freschi wrote 15 operas, which were successfully produced there, and a series of short pieces for an opera house in Piazzola, near Padua. He also wrote at least 3 oratorios, including *Giuditta* and *Il Miracolo del mago*.

Frešo, Tibor, Slovak conductor and composer; b. Spišský, Nov. 20, 1918; d. Bratislava, July 7, 1987. He studied composition with A. Moyzes and conducting with J. Vincourek at the Bratislava Cons., graduating in 1938; he then studied with Pizzetti at the Accademia di Santa Cecilia in Rome (1939–42). Returning to Czechoslovakia, he served as conductor of the Slovak National Theater in Bratislava (1942–49) and the Košice Opera (1949–52); in 1953 he was appointed chief opera conductor of the Slovak National Opera. Among his compositions are the children's opera *Martin and the Sun* (Bratislava, Jan. 25, 1975) and the opera *Poor François* (1982–84).

Freudenberg, Wilhelm, German composer and conductor; b. Raubacher Hütte, near Neuwied, March 11, 1838; d. Schweidnitz, May 22, 1928. He studied at the Leipzig Cons. with Moscheles and others. In 1870 he went to Wiesbaden, where he was active as a choral conductor, and in 1886 he settled in Berlin, where he was a theater conductor and teacher. He wrote several light operas, including *Die Pfahlbauer* (Mainz, 1877), *Die Mühle im Wispertale* (Magdeburg, 1883), and *Das Jahrmarktsfest zu Plundersweilen* (Bremen, 1908).

Freund, Marya, German soprano; b. Breslau, Dec. 12, 1876; d. Paris, May 21, 1966. She was a student of Sarasate (violin) and Stockhausen (voice). After making her debut in 1909, she appeared as a soloist with orchs. and as a recitalist in Europe and the United States, gaining distinction as a champion of contemporary music. She settled in Paris and taught voice during the last 30 years of her life.

Frey, Paul, Canadian tenor; b. Heidelberg, Ontario, April 20, 1941. He received vocal instruction from Douglas Campbell and Victor Martens, and then studied at the Univ. of Toronto Opera School with Louis Quilico and at the Royal Cons. of Music in Toronto. In 1976 he made his debut as Werther with Opera in Concert. He joined the Basel Opera in 1978, where he made his debut in that same role. In 1985 he sang Lohengrin in Karlsruhe, and then portrayed that role with great success in Mannheim in 1986. In 1987 he appeared in that role at his Bayreuth Festival debut. On Sept. 23, 1987, he made his Metropolitan Opera debut in New York as Strauss's Bacchus. He sang Lohengrin at his first appearance at London's Covent Garden in 1988. After appearing as Huon in *Oberon* at Milan's La Scala in 1989, he was engaged as Siegmund at the Cologne Opera for the 1990–91 season. In 1994 he created the title role in Jost Meier's *Dreyfus—Die Affäre* at the Deutsche Oper in Berlin. He appeared as Schoeck's Venus in Geneva in 1997. Among his other roles were Mozart's Titus and Don Ottavio, Florestan, Max, Parsifal, and Strauss's Flamand and Emperor.

Frezzolini, Erminia, Italian soprano; b. Orvieto, March 27, 1818; d. Paris, Nov. 5, 1884. She studied with her father, the bass Giuseppe Frezzolini, and with Nencini, Ronconi, Manuel García, and Tacchinardi. In 1838 she made her operatic debut in *Beatrice di Tenda* in Florence, and then appeared in London in 1842. On Feb. 11, 1843, she created the role of Viclinda in *I Lombardi* in Milan, returning there to create the title role in *Giovanna d'Arco* on Feb. 15, 1845. In 1850 she again sang in London, and in 1855 she appeared in New York, where she was the first Gilda. She also sang in Vienna, St. Petersburg, Madrid, and Paris. In 1860 she retired from the stage, but resumed her career in 1863. In 1868 she retired for good.

Fribec, Krešimir, Croatian composer; b. Daruvar, May 24, 1908. He studied with Zlatko Grgošević in Zagreb; later he was active as music ed. of the Zagreb Radio (1943–64); he also served as director of the Croatian Music Soc. Most of his large output was composed in an accessible style.

WORKS: DRAMATIC: OPERAS: *Sluga Jernej* (1951); *Krvava svadba* (Blood Wedding; 1958); *Prometej* (1960); *Jerma* (1960); *Maljiva* (1962); *Čehovljev humoristicon* (1962); *Nova Eva* (1963); *Juduška Golovljiev* (1964); *Adagio melancolico* (1965); *Dolazi revisor* (The Government Inspector; 1965); *Dunja u kovčegu* (1966); *Veliki val* (The Large Wave; 1966); *Heretik* (1971); *Ujak Vanja* (Uncle Vanya; 1972). Also many ballets.

Fricci (real name, **Frietsche**), **Antonietta,** Austrian soprano; b. Vienna, Jan. 8, 1840; d. Turin, Sept. 7, 1912. She studied with Marchesi in Vienna, making her debut in 1858 in Pisa as Violetta. She was a principal singer at La Scala in Milan (1865–73). After her retirement in 1878, she taught voice in Florence and Turin.

Frick, Gottlob, German bass; b. Olbronn, Württemberg, July 28, 1906; d. Mühlacker, near Pforzheim, Aug. 18, 1994. He studied at the Stuttgart Cons. and also took vocal lessons with Neudörfer-Opitz. After singing in the Stuttgart Opera chorus, he made his operatic debut as Daland in *Der fliegende Holländer* in Coburg (1934), then sang in Freiburg im Breisgau and Königsberg, and subsequently he was a leading member of the Dresden State Opera (1941–52). He appeared at the Städtische Oper in West Berlin (from 1950), the Bavarian State Opera in Munich (from 1953), and the Vienna State Opera (from 1953); he made his debut at London's Covent Garden (1951), and later sang there regularly (1957–67). On Dec. 27, 1961, he made his Metropolitan Opera debut in New York as Fafner in *Das Rheingold*; he also sang at Bayreuth, Milan's La Scala, and Salzburg. He gave his farewell performance in 1970, but continued to make a few stage appearances in later years. A fine Wagnerian, he excelled as Gurnemanz and Hagen; was also admired for his portrayal of Rocco in *Fidelio*.

Fricke, Heinz, German conductor; b. Halberstadt, Feb. 11, 1927. He studied in Halberstadt and with Abendroth in Weimar (1948–50). From 1950 to 1960 he was conductor at the Leipzig City Theater. In 1960–61 he was Generalmusikdirektor in Schwerin, and then held that title with the Berlin State Opera from 1961 to 1992. He also appeared as a guest conductor with many opera houses in Europe and South America. In 1992 he conducted *Parsifal* at the reopening of the Chemnitz Opera House. In 1993 he became music director of the Washington (D.C.) Opera.

Fricker, Peter Racine, distinguished English composer and pedagogue; b. London, Sept. 5, 1920; d. Santa Barbara, Calif., Feb. 1, 1990. He studied theory and composition with R.O. Morris at the Royal College of Music in London; following service in the Royal Air Force (1941–46), he completed his training with Mátyás Seiber (1946–48). He was director of music at Morley College in London (from 1952) and a prof. of composition at the Royal College of Music (from 1955). In 1964 he was a visiting prof. at the Univ. of Calif. at Santa Barbara, where he then was a full prof. (from 1965); he also was chairman of its music dept. (1970–74). In his works, Fricker utilized various techniques. His output revealed a fascination for the development of small cells, either melodically, harmonically, or rhythmically. He composed the radio opera *The Death of Vivien* (1956) and the ballet *Canterbury Prologue* (1951).

Fricsay, Ferenc, distinguished Hungarian-born Austrian conductor; b. Budapest, Aug. 9, 1914; d. Basel, Feb. 20, 1963. He received his initial musical training from his father, a military bandmaster, and then was a pupil of Bartók (piano) and Kodály (composition) at the Budapest Academy of Music; he learned to play almost every orchestral instrument. He was conductor in Szeged (1933–44), and also held the post of 1st conductor at the Budapest Opera (1939–45). In 1945 he became music director of the Hungarian State Opera in Budapest. On Aug. 6, 1947, he made an impressive debut at the Salzburg Festival conducting the premiere of Gottfried von Einem's opera *Dantons Tod*, which led to engagements in Europe and South America. In 1948 he became a conductor at the Städtische Oper in West Berlin; in 1951–52 he was its artistic director but resigned after a conflict over artistic policies. In 1949 he became chief conductor of the RIAS (Radio in the American Sector) Sym. Orch. in Berlin, an esteemed position he retained until 1954. After it became the Radio Sym. Orch. of Berlin in 1955, he appeared with it regularly until 1961. On Nov. 13, 1953, he made his U.S. debut as a guest conductor of the Boston Sym. Orch. In 1954 he was engaged as conductor of the Houston Sym. Orch., but he resigned his position soon afterward following a disagreement with its management over musical policies. From 1956 to 1958 he was Generalmusikdirektor of the Bavarian State Opera in Munich. In 1959 he became a naturalized Austrian citizen. In 1961 he was invited to conduct *Don Giovanni* at the opening of the Deutsche Oper in West Berlin. Soon thereafter leukemia compelled him to abandon his career. Fricsay excelled as an interpreter of the Romantic repertory but he also displayed a special affinity for the masterworks of the 20th century. He was the author of the book *Über Mozart und Bartók* (Frankfurt am Main, 1962).

BIBL.: F. Herzfeld, *F. F.: Ein Gedenkbuch* (Berlin, 1964).

Frid, Géza, Hungarian-born Dutch composer; b. Máramarossziget, Jan. 25, 1904; d. Beverwijk, Sept. 13, 1989. He studied composition with Kodály and piano with Bartók at the Budapest Academy of Music (1912–24). He settled in Amsterdam in 1929, becoming a naturalized Dutch citizen in 1948; he later taught at the Utrecht Cons. (1964–69). He composed the opera *De zwarte bruid* (1959) and the ballets *Luctor et Emergo* (1953) and *Euridice* (1961).

Friebert, (Johann) Joseph, Austrian tenor and composer; b. Gnadendorf, Lower Austria (baptized), Dec. 5, 1724; d. Passau, Aug. 6, 1799. After vocal studies with Bonno, he entered the service of the Prince of Saxe-Hildburgshausen in Vienna. In 1755 he became a member of the Vienna Court Theater, and then was Kapellmeister to the prince-bishop of Passau from 1763 until his death. He was a composer of Singspiels, Italian operas, oratorios, and cantatas. His brother, Karl Friebert (b. Wullersdorf, Lower Austria, June 7, 1736; d. Vienna, Aug. 6, 1816), was also a tenor and composer. After singing in Eisenstadt (1759–76), he settled in Vienna as Kapellmeister to the two Jesuit churches and the Minorite Church.

Fried, Oskar, German-born Russian conductor and composer; b. Berlin, Aug. 10, 1871; d. Moscow, July 5, 1941. He studied with Humperdinck in Frankfurt am Main and P. Scharwenka in Berlin. He played the horn in various orchs. until the performance of his choral work with orch. *Das trunkene Lied*, given by Muck in Berlin (April 15, 1904), attracted much favorable attention; he continued to compose prolifically. At the same time, he began his career as a conductor, achieving considerable renown in Europe; he was conductor of the Stern Choral Soc. in Berlin (from 1904), of the Gesellschaft der Musikfreunde in Berlin (1907–10), and of the Berlin Sym. Orch. (1925–26). He left Berlin in 1934 and went to Russia; became a naturalized Russian citizen in 1940. For several years he was conductor of the Tbilisi Opera; he later was chief conductor of the All-Union Radio Orch. in Moscow.

BIBL.: P. Bekker, *O. F.* (Berlin, 1907); P. Stefan, *O. F.* (Berlin, 1911); D. Rabinovitz, *O. F.* (Moscow, 1971).

Friedrich, Götz, notable German opera producer and administrator; b. Naumburg, Aug. 4, 1930. He was educated at the Deutsches Theaterinstitut in Weimar (1949–53). In 1953 he became an assistant to Walter Felsenstein at the Komische Oper in Berlin, where he was a producer from 1959 to 1968, and then its chief producer from 1968 to 1972. In 1972 he gained wide notoriety with his highly controversial staging of *Tannhäuser* at the Bayreuth Festival, and then returned there to produce *Lohengrin* in 1978 and *Parsifal* in 1982. In 1973 he became Oberspielleiter at the Hamburg State Opera, and then was its Chefregisseur from 1977 to 1981. His first *Ring* cycle was staged at London's Covent Garden from 1974 to 1976, and from 1977 to 1981 he served as director of productions there. In 1981 he staged the 3-act version of *Lulu* there. In 1981 he became Generalintendant of the Deutsche Oper in Berlin, where he produced the *Ring* cycle in 1984–85, a staging later seen in many opera houses. In 1982 he staged *Wozzeck* at the Houston Grand Opera. He produced the premiere of Berio's *Un re in ascolto* in Salzburg in 1984. From 1984 to 1993 he was artistic director of the Theater des Westens in Berlin while retaining his position at the Deutsche Oper. After staging *Otello* in Los Angeles in 1986, he returned there to produce *Kát'a Kabanová* in 1988. In 1987 he oversaw the premiere of Rihm's *Oedipus* in Berlin. He produced the premiere of Matthus's *Desdemona und ihre Schwestern* at the Schwetzingen Festival in 1992. After staging *Faust* at the Zürich Opera in 1997, he produced *Samson et Dalila* at the New Israeli Opera in Tel Aviv in 1998.

Friedrich's productions reflect his humanistic ideals and commitment to the Left. His writings include *Die humanistische Idee der Zauberflöte* (Berlin, 1954), *Die Zauberflöte in der Inszenierung Walter Felsensteins an der Komischen Oper Berlin* (Berlin, 1958), *Walter Felsenstein: Weg und Werk* (Berlin, 1961), *Musiktheater: Beiträge zur Methodik und zu Inszenierungs-Konzeptionen* (Leipzig, 1970; 2d ed., 1978), *Wagner-Regie* (Zürich, 1983), and *Musiktheater: Ansichten, Einsichten, Konzepte, Versuche, Erfahrungen* (Frankfurt am Main, 1986). He married **Karan Armstrong**.

BIBL.: D. Kranz, *Der Regisseur G. F.* (Berlin, 1972); P. Barz, *G. F.: Abenteur Musiktheater* (Bonn, 1978); N. Ely, *Richard Wagner: Der Ring des Nibelungen in der Inszenierung von G. F.: Deutsche Oper Berlin* (Vienna, 1987); *Zeit für Oper: G. F.s Musiktheater, 1958–90* (Frankfurt am Main, 1991).

Friedrich, Karl, Austrian tenor; b. Vienna, Jan. 15, 1905; d. there, March 8, 1981. He received his musical education at the Vienna Academy of Music. He sang operatic engagements in Düsseldorf and Hamburg; in 1938, he joined the roster of the Vienna State Opera, retiring in 1969.

Friedrichs (real name, **Christofes**), **Fritz,** German baritone; b. Braunschweig, Jan. 13, 1849; d. Königslutter, May 15, 1918. He joined the chorus of the Braunschweig Opera in 1869, where he soon appeared in minor operatic roles. After singing in provincial opera centers, he was a member of the operas in Nuremberg (from 1883) and Bremen (from 1886), where he acquired distinction as a Wagnerian. From 1888 to 1902 he sang at the Bayreuth Festivals, most notably as Alberich, Beckmesser, and Klingsor. His guest engagements took him to Berlin, Vienna, London, Hamburg, and N.Y.'s Metropolitan Opera (debut as Beckmesser, Jan. 24, 1900).

Friemann, Witold, Polish composer and teacher; b. Konin, Aug. 20, 1889; d. Laski, near Warsaw, March 22, 1977. He was a student of Noskowski (composition) and Michalowski (piano) at the Warsaw Cons. (graduated, 1910), and of Reger in Leipzig. After teaching at the Lwów Cons. (1921–29) and the Katowice Military School of Music (1929–33), he was head of the music division of the Polish Radio (1934–39); he later taught at a school for the blind in Laski. Among his works are the operas *Giewont* (1934), *Polski misterium narodowe* (1946), *Kain* (1952), and *Bazyliszek* (1958).

Frijsh, Povla (real name, **Paula Frisch**), Danish-American soprano; b. Århus, Aug. 3, 1881; d. Blue Hill, Maine, July 10, 1960. She studied piano and theory in Copenhagen with O. Christensen, later, voice in Paris with Jean Périer. She made her debut in Paris at the age of 19; she appeared in concert and recital in Paris and briefly in opera in Copenhagen and made her American debut in 1915. She gave many first performances of modern vocal music and made a specialty of the modern international song literature.

Friml (Frimel), (Charles) Rudolf, notable Bohemian-born American composer and pianist; b. Prague, Dec. 2, 1879; d. Los Angeles, Nov. 12, 1972. He was a student of Dvořák (composition) and Jiránek (piano) at the Prague Cons. He toured Europe as accompanist to Kubelik, with whom he visited the United States in 1900 and 1906, settling there in the latter year. In 1907 he appeared as soloist in his 1st Piano Concerto with Damrosch and the N.Y. Sym. Orch., and subsequently gave recitals throughout the United States. While he continued to perform for most of his career, he also pursued his career as a composer of concert and lighter fare. His first great success in the latter came with his operetta *The Firefly* (N.Y., Dec. 2, 1912). With his musical farce *High Jinks* (N.Y., Dec. 10, 1913), he acquired global fame. His *Katinka* (N.Y., Dec. 23, 1915) proved another extraordinary success. Among a spate of succeeding N.Y. productions, the most successful were *You're in Love* (Feb. 6, 1917), *Sometime* (Oct. 4, 1918), *Glorianna* (Oct. 28, 1918), *The Little Whopper* (Oct. 13, 1919), and *The Blue Kitten* (Jan. 13, 1922). Then, in collaboration with Herbert Stothart, he brought out the enormously successful musical *Rose Marie*, which was first heard in United States on Sept. 2, 1924. Its title song and the song "Indian Love Call" became celebrated. Among his subsequent scores, acclaim was accorded *The Vagabond King* (N.Y., Sept. 21, 1925) and *The 3 Musketeers* (N.Y., March 13, 1928). In 1925 Friml settled in Los Angeles. His final success as a composer came with his reworking of "Chansonette," first heard in the *Ziegfeld Follies of 1923*, as "The Donkey Serenade" for the film version of *The Firefly* (1937). In a number of his works, Friml used the pseudonym of Roderick Freeman.

WORKS: MUSIC THEATER (all 1st perf. in N.Y. unless otherwise given): *The Firefly* (Dec. 2, 1912); *High Jinks* (Dec. 10, 1913); *The Ballet Girl* (Albany, N.Y., Nov. 12, 1914); *Katinka* (Dec. 23, 1915); *You're in Love* (Feb. 6, 1917); *Kitty Darlin'* (Nov. 7, 1917); *Sometime* (Oct. 4, 1918); *Glorianna* (Oct. 28, 1918); *Tumble In* (March 24, 1919); *The Little Whopper* (Oct. 13, 1919); *June Love* (April 25, 1921); *Ziegfeld Follies of 1921* (June 21, 1921; in collaboration with others); *The Blue Kitten* (Jan. 13, 1922); *Bibi of the Boulevards* (Providence, R.I., Feb. 12, 1922); *Cinders* (April 3, 1923); *Ziegfeld Follies of 1923* (Oct. 20, 1923; in collaboration with others); *Rose Marie* (Sept. 2, 1924; in collaboration with H. Stothart); *The Vagabond King* (Sept. 21, 1925); *No Foolin'* (June 24, 1926; in collaboration with J. Hanley); *The Wild Rose* (Oct. 20, 1926); *The White Eagle* (Dec. 26, 1927); *The 3 Musketeers* (March 13, 1928); *Luana* (Sept. 17, 1930); *Annina* or *Music Hatch Charm* (Dec. 29, 1934).

Frischenschlager, Friedrich, Austrian composer and teacher; b. Gross Sankt Florian, Styria, Sept. 7, 1885; d. Salzburg, July 15, 1970. He studied music in Graz. In 1909 he went to Berlin, where he studied musicology with J. Wolf and Kretzschmar, and also attended Humperdinck's master classes in composition. In 1918 he was engaged as a music teacher at the Mozarteum in Salzburg, and remained there until 1945; he also ed. its bulletin. An industrious composer, Fritschenschlager wrote the fairy tale operas *Der Schweinehirt*, after Hans Christian Andersen (Berlin, May 31, 1913), *Die Prinzessin und der Zwerg* (Salzburg, May 12, 1927), and *Der Kaiser und die Nachtigall*, also after Andersen (Salzburg, March 27, 1937).

Froidebise, Pierre (Jean Marie), eminent Belgian composer, musicologist, and organist; b. Ohey, May 15, 1914; d. Liège, Oct. 28, 1962. Following training in harmony and organ with Camille Jacquemin (1932–35), he studied with Barbier at the Namur Cons.; he then was a student of Moulaert (composition), J. Jongen (fugue), Malengreau (premier prix in organ, 1939), and Absil (composition) at the Brussels Cons. He also studied composition with Gilson, and then went to Paris to complete his training in organ with Tournemire. Returning to Belgium, he won the 2d Prix de Rome with his cantata *La navigation d'Ulysse* in 1943. In 1947 he became prof. of harmony at the Liège Cons. In 1949 he organized his so-called "Variation" group for young performers and composers, which sought to champion a broad expanse of music, ranging from the 13th to the 20th centuries. Froidebise was especially known for his championship of early organ music, and was ed. of the monumental *Anthologie de la musique d'orgue des primitifs à la renaissance* (Paris, 1958). In his own compositions, he favored an advanced idiom utilizing aleatoric and serial procedures. Among his works are the radio operas *La lune amère* (1956), *L'aube* (n.d.), and *La bergère et le ramoneur* (n.d.), the ballet *Le bal chez le voisin* (c.1953), and incidental music to Sophocles' *Antigone* (1936) and *Oedipe roi* (c.1946), A. Curvers' *Ce vieil Oedipe* (c.1946), M. Lambilliotte's *Jan van Nude* (1951), Aeschylus' *Les choéphores* (1954), Euripides' *Hippolyte* (n.d.), Calderón's *La maison a deux portes* (n.d.).

Frühbeck de Burgos (originally, **Frühbeck**), **Rafael,** eminent Spanish conductor; b. Burgos, Sept. 15, 1933. His father was German, his mother Spanish. He studied violin before pursuing musical training at the Bilbao Cons. and the Madrid Cons. (1950–53); he then received instruction in conducting from Eichhorn at the Munich Hochschule für Musik (1956–58). He was conductor of the Bilbao Municipal Orch. (1958–62), chief conductor of the Orquesta Nacional de Espaüa in Madrid (1962–77), Generalmusikdirektor of the Düsseldorf Sym. Orch. (1966–71), and music director of the Orchestre Symphonique de Montréal (1975–76). He appeared as a guest conductor with major European and North American orchs.; he served as principal guest conductor of the National Sym. Orch. in Washington, D.C. (1980–89) and of the Yomiuri Nippon Sym. Orch. in Tokyo (1980–93). He was chief conductor of the Vienna Sym. Orch. (1991–96), Generalmusikdirektor of the Deutsche Oper in Berlin (1992–97), and chief conductor of the Berlin Radio Orch. In Berlin (from 1993). His idiomatic performances of Spanish music have won him many accolades; he has also demonstrated expertise as an interpreter of the standard orch. repertoire.

Frumerie, (Per) Gunnar (Fredrik) de, esteemed Swedish composer, pianist, and teacher; b. Nacka, near Stockholm, July 20, 1908; d. Mörby, Sept. 9, 1987. He was a student of Lundberg (piano) and Ellberg (composition) at the Stockholm Cons. (1923–29); after pursuing his training with Sauer (piano) and Stein (composition) on a Jenny Lind Foundation stipend in Vienna (1929–31), he completed his studies with Cortot (piano) and Sabaneyev (composition) in Paris. He was active as a concert pianist in Sweden, and also taught piano at the Stockholm Musikhögskolan (1945–74). In 1943 he was made a member of the Royal Swedish Academy of Music. His music reflected the influence of Scandinavian Romanticism, crafted along traditional lines with a respect for folk elements. Among his compositions are *En Moder*, melodrama (1932), *Singoalla*, opera (1937–40; Stockholm, March 16, 1940), and *Johannesnatten*, ballet (1947).

Fry, William Henry, American composer and journalist; b. Philadelphia, Aug. 10, 1813; d. Santa Cruz, West Indies, Dec. 21, 1864. He was one of the most vociferous champions of American music, and particularly of opera on American subjects in the English language. Ironically, his own opera *Leonora* (Philadelphia, June 4, 1845), for which he claimed the distinction of being the first grand opera by a native American composer, was a feeble imitation of Italian vocal formulas in the manner of Bellini, with a libretto fashioned from a novel by Bulwer-Lytton, *The Lady of Lyons*. Leonora ran for 16 performances before closing. A revival of some numbers in concert form was attempted in New York on Feb. 27, 1929, but was met with puzzled derision. Fry continued his campaign in favor of American opera in English, and composed 3 more operas, 1 of which, *Notre Dame de Paris*, after Victor Hugo, was produced in Philadelphia on May 3, 1864; 2 other operas, *The Bridal of Dunure* and *Aurelia the Vestal*, were not performed. Fry's various proclamations, manifestos, and prefaces to publ. eds. of his works are interesting as illustrations of the patriotic bombast and humbug that agitated American musicians in the mid-19th century.

BIBL.: W. Upton, *The Musical Works of W. H. F.* (Philadelphia, 1946); idem, *W. H. F., American Journalist and Composer-Critic* (N.Y., 1954).

Fuchs, Lukas. See **Foss, Lukas.**

Fuchs, Marta, admired German soprano; b. Stuttgart, Jan. 1, 1898; d. there, Sept. 22, 1974. She was trained in Stuttgart, Munich, and Milan. In 1928 she made her operatic debut in Aachen as a mezzo-soprano, singing there until 1930. She then was a prominent member of the Dresden State Opera (1930–45); she also was a guest artist at the Berlin State Opera, the Bayreuth Festival, and the Vienna State Opera, and toured as a concert singer. Among her notable roles were Brünnhilde, Isolde, Kundry, Donna Anna, the Marschallin, and Ariadne.

Fuerstner, Carl, German-born American pianist, conductor, teacher, and composer; b. Strasbourg, June 16, 1912; d. Bloomington, Ind., Dec. 5, 1994. He studied composition and conducting at the Cologne Hochschule für Musik (1930–34), where his teachers were Abendroth, Braunfels, Jarnach, and Klussmann. While still a student, he composed incidental music for theatrical plays. In 1939 he went to the United States as assistant conductor of the San Francisco Opera; he became a naturalized American citizen in 1945. From 1945 to 1950 he was head of the opera dept. at the Eastman School of Music in Rochester, N.Y.; he then served on the faculty of Brigham Young Univ. in Provo, Utah (1951–61), where he was resident pianist, opera conductor, principal piano teacher, and head of the composition dept. (1955–61); he also toured widely as a piano accompanist to many celebrated artists of the day and conducted an impressive repertoire of standard and modern operas in the United States and Europe. From 1963 to 1982 he was principal opera coach at the Indiana Univ. School of Music in Bloomington, where he also conducted operas. He also was on the faculty of the Summer Academy of the Salzburg Mozarteum (1973–82); he then was active with the American Inst. of Musical Studies in Graz (1983–85); concurrently he was associated with the "Festa Musica Pro" in Assisi, Italy. From 1981 to 1989 he was music director of the Bloomington (Ind.) Sym. Orch.

Fuga, Sandro, Italian pianist, teacher, and composer; b. Mogliano Veneto, Nov. 26, 1906; d. Turin, March 1, 1994. He studied piano, organ, and composition at the Turin Cons. He was a concert pianist until 1940; he became a lecturer at the Turin Cons. in 1933, and in 1966 its director, which post he held until 1977. His works included the dramatic scores *La croce deserta* (Bergamo, 1950), *Otto Schnaffs* (Turin, 1950), and *Confessione* (RAI Radio, 1962).

Fugère, Lucien, remarkable French baritone; b. Paris, July 22, 1848; d. there, Jan. 15, 1935. He was a student at the Paris Cons. of Raguneau and Batiste. In 1870 he began his career singing at the Café-Concert, Ba-ta-can. In 1874 he joined the Bouffes-Parisiens. He made his debut at the Paris Opéra Comique in 1877 as Jean in Masse's *Les noces de Jeannette*, and remained on its roster until 1910. He appeared in over 100 roles there, including the premieres of Chabrier's *Le roi malgré lui* (1887), Messager's *La Basoche* (1890), Saint-Saëns' *Phryné* (1893), Massenet's *Cendrillon* (1899), and Charpentier's *Louise* (1900). In 1897 he sang at London's Covent Garden. After appearing at the Gaîté-Lyrique in Paris (1910–19), he returned to the Opéra Comique, where he celebrated his 50th anniversary as a singer on March 5, 1920. He continued to make appearances until he was 80, singing his farewell performance in *La Basoche* in Le Touquet in 1928, the year he was awarded the Légion d'honneur. He was particularly celebrated for his portrayals of Leporello, Papageno, Figaro, and Bartolo. Mary Garden was among his students.

BIBL.: R. Duhamel, *L. F.* (Paris, 1929).

Fuleihan, Anis, Cypriot-born American pianist, conductor, and composer; b. Kyrenia, April 2, 1900; d. Palo Alto, Calif., Oct. 11, 1970. He studied at the English School in Kyrenia; went to the United States in 1915 and continued his study of the piano in New York with Alberto Jonás; toured the United States, also the Near East, from 1919 to 1925; then lived in Cairo, returning to the United States in 1928. He was on the staff of G. Schirmer, Inc. in New York (1932–39); in 1947 he became a prof. at Indiana Univ. in Bloomington, in 1953, director of the Beirut Cons. in Lebanon. In 1962 he went to Tunis under the auspices of the State Dept.; in 1963, organized the Orch. Classique de Tunis; remained there until 1965. He composed the opera *Vasco* (1960).

Fulkerson, James (Orville), American composer and trombonist; b. Streator, Ill., July 2, 1945. He studied composition with Wilbur Ogdon and Abram Plum and trombone with John Silver at Illinois Wesleyan Univ. (B.A., 1966) and composition with Martirano, Gaburo, Hiller, and Brun at the Univ. of Ill. (M.M., 1969). He was a creative assoc. of the Center for the Creative and Performing Arts at the State Univ. of N.Y. in Buffalo (1969–72); then was composer-in-residence at the Deutscher Akademischer Austauschdienst in Berlin (1973), the Victorian College of the Arts in Melbourne (1977–79), and Dartington College in Devon, England (from 1981). He is a virtuoso on the trombone, and he makes a specialty of playing the most fantastically difficult modern pieces. His own compositions, which include the dramatic scores *Raucasity and the Cisco Kid . . . or, I Skate in the Sun* (1977–78), *Vicarious Thrills* (1978–79), *Cheap Imitations II: Madwomen* (1980), *Force Fields and Spaces* (1981), *Cheap Imitations IV* (1982), *Put Your Foot Charlie* (1982), *Rats Tale* (1983), and *Studs*, ballet music (1992), are no less advanced.

Fulton, Thomas, American conductor; b. Memphis, Sept. 18, 1949; d. Milan, Aug. 4, 1994. He studied at the Curtis Inst. of Music in Philadelphia, where his conducting mentors were Max Rudolf and Eugene Ormandy. He began his career as a staff conductor at the San Francisco Opera and the Hamburg State Opera. In 1978 he joined the conducting staff of the Metropolitan Opera in New York, where he made his house debut with *Manon Lescaut* on April 4, 1981. He also made guest appearances with various opera companies, including the Paris Opéra (1979), the Rome Opera (1986), the Berlin Deutsche Oper (1986), and the Greater Miami Opera (1989).

Fumi, Vinceslao, Italian conductor and composer; b. Montepulciano, Tuscany, Oct. 20, 1823; d. Florence, Nov. 20, 1880. He conducted opera in various Italian cities, in Constantinople, Montevideo, and Buenos Aires, and finally at Florence. His compositions include the opera *Atala* (Buenos Aires, 1862). A collection of folk songs of all times and nations which he undertook remained unfinished.

Furlanetto, Ferruccio, Italian bass; b. Pordenone, Sicily, May 16, 1949. He was a student of Campogaliahi and Casagrande. After making his operatic debut as Sparafucile in Vicenza in 1974, he held engagements in Turin, Trieste, Bologna, Venice, Parma, and Aix-en-Provence. In 1978 he made his U.S. debut as Zaccaria with the New Orleans Opera. He first appeared at the San Francisco Opera as Alvise in 1979. On Feb. 26, 1980, he made his Metropolitan Opera debut in New York as the Grand Inquisitor; he also appeared at the Glyndebourne Festival (1980), the San Diego Opera (1985), the Paris Opéra (1985), the Salzburg Festival (1986), and the Royal Opera, Covent Garden, London (1988). In addition to such Mozart roles as Figaro, Don Alfonso, Leporello, and Don Giovanni, he has sung in many operas by Rossini and Verdi.

Fürsch-Madi(er), Emma or **Emmy**, French soprano; b. Bayonne, 1847; d. Warrenville, N.J., Sept. 19, 1894. She studied at the Paris Cons., making her operatic debut as Marguerite in Paris (1868). She then sang with the French Opera Co. in New Orleans (1873–74), making her first appearance at London's Covent Garden as Valentine in *Les Huguenots* (May 9, 1881). After adopting the name Fürsch-Madi (1882), she sang there again (1883–88). She made her Metropolitan Opera debut in New York as Ortrud on Nov. 7, 1883, appearing again on its roster in 1893–94. She was particularly noted for her portrayals of Donna Anna, Lucrezia Borgia, and Aida.

Furtwängler, (Gustav Heinrich Ernst Martin) Wilhelm, great German conductor; b. Berlin, Jan. 25, 1886; d. Ebersteinburg, Nov. 30, 1954. His father, Adolf Furtwängler, was a distinguished archaeologist and director of the Berlin Museum of Antiquities, and his mother, Adelheid (née Wendt) Furtwängler, was a painter. A precocious child, he received instruction in piano at a very early age from his mother and his aunt; by the time he was 7, he had begun to compose. After his father was called to the Univ. of

Munich as prof. of archaeology in 1894, he was tutored at home by the archaeologist Ludwig Curtius, the art historian and musicologist Walter Riezler, and the sculptor Adolf Hildebrand. He commenced formal training in composition with Beer-Walbrunn, and then pursued the study of advanced counterpoint with Rheinberger (1900–01); he subsequently completed his studies with Schillings. After working as répétiteur at the Breslau Opera (1905–06), he became 3d conductor at the Zürich Opera in 1906; that same year he scored a notable success conducting Bruckner's 9th Sym. in Munich with the Kaim Orch. From 1907 to 1909 he was an assistant conductor under Mottl at the Munich Court Opera. He then was 3d conductor under Pfitzner at the Strasbourg Municipal Opera from 1909 to 1911. In 1911 he was appointed music director in Lübeck, a position he held until 1915 when he was called to Mannheim as Generalmusikdirektor. It was during this period that Furtwängler began to secure his reputation as a conductor of great promise. In 1915 he made his first appearance in Vienna conducting the Konzertvereinsorchester. He scored a notable success at his debut with the Berlin Phil. on Dec. 14, 1917. In 1920 he resigned his position in Mannheim to serve as Strauss's successor as music director of the Berlin State Opera orch. concerts, remaining there until 1922; concurrently he served as Mengelberg's successor as music director of the Frankfurt am Main Museumgesellschaft concerts. On Aug. 30, 1921, he made his debut with the Leipzig Gewandhaus Orch. to critical acclaim. Upon the death of Nikisch in 1922, Furtwängler was appointed his successor as music director of both the Berlin Phil. and the Leipzig Gewandhaus Orch., retaining the latter position until 1928. On March 27, 1922, he made his debut with the Vienna Phil. He made his first appearance in Milan in 1923 when he conducted the La Scala Orch. On Jan. 24, 1924, Furtwängler made his British debut with the Royal Phil. Soc. in London. His auspicious U.S. debut followed on Jan. 3, 1925, with the N.Y. Phil.; he returned to conduct there again in 1926 and 1927. Upon Weingartner's resignation as regular conductor of the Vienna Phil. in 1927, Furtwängler was elected his successor. He made his debut at the Vienna State Opera conducting *Das Rheingold* on Oct. 17, 1928. That same year he was awarded an honorary doctorate by the Univ. of Heidelberg. His debut as an opera conductor in Berlin took place on June 13, 1929, when he conducted *Le nozze di Figaro* at the Berlin Festival. In 1929 the German government awarded him the medal Pour le Mérite in recognition of his outstanding contributions to German musical culture. In 1930 he resigned his position with the Vienna Phil., having been named Generalmusikdirektor of Berlin. In 1930 he was made music director of the Bayreuth Festival. He made his first appearance there conducting *Tristan und Isolde* on July 23, 1931, but resigned his position at the close of the season. He then made his debut at the Berlin State Opera on Nov. 12, 1931, conducting the local premiere of Pfitzner's *Das Herz*, and in 1932 was appointed its music director.

After the Nazis came to power in 1933, they moved quickly to appropriate Furtwängler's stature as Germany's greatest conductor for their own propaganda purposes. He was made vice president of the newly organized Reichsmusikkammer and then was appointed one of the newly created Prussian State Councilors, an honorary lifetime title that Furtwängler refused to use. He also refused to join the Nazi party. Early on, he began to encounter difficulties with the authorities over personal and artistic matters. He opposed the regime's policies against the Jews and others, and did all he could to assist those who sought him out, both musicians and nonmusicians alike, often at great personal risk. For the 1933–34 season of the Berlin State Opera, Furtwängler scheduled the premiere of Hindemith's *Mathis der Maler*, even though the Nazis had branded the composer a "cultural Bolshevist" and a "spiritual non-Aryan" (his wife was half Jewish). The Nazis compelled Furtwängler to withdraw the work, but he attempted to defy them by conducting a symphonic version of the score with the Berlin Phil. on March 11, 1934. It elicited a prolonged ovation from the audience, but drew condemnation from the Nazi press as a contemptible example of "degenerate" music. The ensuing polemical campaign against Furtwängler led him to resign all of his positions on Dec. 4, 1934. (As a propaganda ploy, the Nazis would not accept his resignation as a Prussian State Councilor since this was a lifetime "honor" granted by the regime.) Furtwängler's devotion to what he considered to be the true (non-Nazi) Germany and his belief that it was his duty to preserve its great musical heritage compelled him to make an uneasy peace with the regime. On April 25, 1935, he returned as a conductor with the Berlin Phil. Although he appeared regularly with it in succeeding years, he refused an official position with it so as not to be beholden to the Nazis. In 1936 he was offered the position of conductor of the N.Y. Phil. in succession to Toscanini, but he declined the offer in the face of accusations in the American press that he was a Nazi collaborator. In 1937 he was invited to London to participate in the musical celebrations in honor of the coronation of King George VI, where he conducted the *Ring* cycle at Covent Garden and Beethoven's 9th Sym. On Aug. 27, 1937, he made his first appearance at the Salzburg Festival conducting Beethoven's 9th Sym. In 1939 he was honored by the French government as a Commandeur of the Légion d'honneur. After the outbreak of World War II on Sept. 1, 1939, Furtwängler confined his activities almost exclusively to Germany and Austria, principally with the Berlin Phil. and the Vienna Phil. In 1944, after learning that Himmler had placed him on the Nazi's liquidation list, Furtwängler sent his family to Switzerland for safety, while he remained behind to keep his conducting engagements for the 1944–45 season. However, after conducting the Vienna Phil. in Jan. 1945, he too fled to Switzerland. His decision to pursue his career in his homeland during the Third Reich left him open to charges by the Allies after the war of being a Nazi collaborator. Although the Vienna denazification commission cleared him on March 9, 1946, as a German citizen he was ordered to stand trial in Berlin before the Allied Denazification Tribunal for Artists. Following his trial on Dec. 11 and 17, 1946, he was acquitted of all charges; it was not until March 1947, however, that he was formally "normalized." On May 25, 1947, he conducted the Berlin Phil. for the first time since the close of World War II, leading an all-Beethoven concert to extraordinary approbation. On Aug. 10, 1947, he also resumed his association with the Vienna Phil. when he conducted it at the Salzburg Festival. He made his first postwar appearance at the Berlin State Opera on Oct. 3, 1947, conducting *Tristan und Isolde*. In Feb. 1948 he returned to England for the first time in more than a decade to conduct a series of concerts with the London Phil. He also became active as a conductor with the Philharmonia Orch. of London. When the management of the Chicago Sym. Orch. announced Furtwängler's engagement as a guest conductor for the 1949–50 season, a campaign against him as a Nazi collaborator compelled him to cancel his engagements. However, in Western Europe his appearances on tours with the Berlin Phil. and the Vienna Phil. were acclaimed. In 1950 he made his debut at Milan's La Scala conducting the *Ring* cycle. With Flagstad as soloist, he conducted the premiere of Strauss's *Vier letzte Lieder* in London on May 22, 1950. On July 29, 1951, he reopened the Bayreuth Festival conducting Beethoven's 9th Sym. In 1952 he resumed his position of music director of the Berlin Phil., but increasing ill health and growing deafness clouded his remaining days. He was scheduled to conduct the Berlin Phil. on its first tour of the United States in the spring of 1955, but his health further declined, leading to his death in the fall of 1954; Herbert von Karajan was elected his successor.

Furtwängler was the perfect embodiment of all that was revered in the Austro-German tradition of the art of conducting. As its foremost exponent, he devined and made manifest the spiritual essence of the great masterworks of the symphonic and operatic repertory. His often refulgent and always inspired interpretations of Mozart, Beethoven, Schubert, Schumann, Brahms, Wagner, and Bruckner, many of which have been preserved on recordings, attest to his greatness as a recreative artist of the highest order. Furtwängler was also a creative artist who composed in an expansive Romantic style. Sketches for an early sym. (1903) were utilized in a mature sym. (1937–41), premiered in Marl kreis Recklinghausen on April 27, 1991, Alfred Walter conducting. Another sym. (1943–47) had 3 of its movements premiered in Berlin on Jan. 26, 1956, Joseph Keilberth conducting. Among his other works were a *Te Deum* (1910); Piano Quintet (1935); Symphonie Concertante for Piano and Orch. (1937); 2 violin sonatas (1937, 1940).

WRITINGS: *Johannes Brahms und Anton Bruckner* (Leipzig, 1941; 2d ed., 1952); W. Abendroth, ed., *Gespräche über Musik* (Zürich, 1948; 7th ed., 1958; Eng. tr., 1953, as *Concerning Music*); *Ton und Wort* (Wiesbaden, 1954; 8th ed., 1958); M. Hürlimann, ed., *Der Musiker und sein Publikum* (Zürich, 1955); S. Brockhaus, ed., *Vermächtnis* (Wiesbaden, 1956; 4th ed., 1958); F. Thiess, ed., *Briefe* (Wiesbaden, 1964); E. Furtwängler and G. Birkner, *Wilhelm Furtwängler Aufzeichnungen 1924–54* (Mainz, 1980; Eng. tr., 1989); R. Taylor, tr. and ed., *Furtwängler on Music: Essays and Addresses* (Aldershot and Brookfield, Vt., 1991).

BIBL.: R. Specht, *W. F.* (Vienna, 1922); O. Schrenck, *W. F.* (Berlin, 1940); F. Herzfeld, *W. F.: Weg und Wesen* (Leipzig, 1941; 3d ed., rev., 1950); B. Geissmar, *Two Worlds of Music* (N.Y., 1946); W. Siebert, *F.: Mensch und Künstler* (Buenos Aires, 1950); C. Riess, *F.: Musik und Politik* (Bern, 1953; abridged Eng. tr., 1955); B. Gavoty and R. Hauert, *W. F.* (Geneva, 1954); M. Hürlimann, ed., *W. F.: Im Urteil seiner Zeit* (Zürich, 1955); D. Gillis, ed., *F. Recalled* (Tuckahoe, N.Y., 1966); idem, *F. and America* (Woodhaven, N.Y., 1970); E. Furtwängler, *Über W.F.* (Wiesbaden, 1979; Eng. tr., 1993); K. Hoecker, *Die nie vergessenen Klänge: Erinnerungen an W. F.* (Berlin, 1979); P. Pirie, *F. and the Art of Conducting* (London, 1980); J. Hunt, *The F. Sound* (London, 1985; 3d ed., 1989); J. Squire and J. Hunt, *F. and Great Britain* (London, 1985); B. Wessling, *W. F.: Eine kritische Biographie* (Stuttgart, 1985); G. Gefen, *F.: Une Biographie par le Disque* (Paris, 1986); J. Matzner, *F.: Analyse, Dokument, Protokoll* (Zürich, 1986); F. Prieberg, *Kraftprobe: W. F. im Dritten Reich* (Wiesbaden, 1986; Eng. tr., 1991); H.-H. Schönzeler, *F.* (London, 1990); S. Shirakawa, *The Devil's Music Master: The Controversial Life and Career of W. F.* (Oxford, 1992).

Fussell, Charles C(lement), American composer and conductor; b. Winston-Salem, N.C., Feb. 14, 1938. He received lessons in piano from Clemens Sandresky in Winston-Salem; in 1956 he enrolled in the Eastman School of Music in Rochester, N.Y., where he studied composition (B.M., 1960) with Thomas Canning, Wayne Barlow, and Bernard Rogers, piano with José Echaniz, and conducting with Herman Genhart; in 1962 he received a Fulbright grant and studied with Blacher at the Berlin Hochschule für Musik; attended Friedelind Wagner's Bayreuth Festival Master Class in opera production and conducting in 1963, then completed his training in composition at the Eastman School of Music (M.M., 1964). In 1966 he joined the faculty of the Univ. of Mass. in Amherst; also founded its Group for New Music in 1974 (later renamed Pro Musica Moderna). He taught composition at the North Carolina School of the Arts in Winston-Salem (1976–77) and at Boston Univ. (1981); in 1981–82 he conducted the Longy School Chamber Orch. in Cambridge, Mass. In his music, he adopts a prudent modernistic idiom and favors neo-Romantic but never overladen sonorities, without doctrinaire techniques. He composed the opera *Caligula* (1962).

Füssl, Karl Heinz, Austrian composer, musicologist, publisher, and music critic; b. Jablonec, Czechoslovakia, March 21, 1924; d. Eisenstadt, Sept. 4, 1992. He went to Berlin and began his formal training at 15 with Konrad Friedrich Noetel (composition), Gerd Otto (piano), and Hugo Distler (choral conducting). Following World War II, he settled in Vienna and completed his studies with Alfred Uhl (composition), Erwin Ratz (analysis), and Hans Swarowsky (conducting). He was active as a music critic and served as head of production for Universal Edition. In addition to overseeing its Urtext Editions, he was associated with the publication of the works of Haydn, Mozart, Johann Strauss, and Mahler. In 1974 he became a teacher of form analysis at the Vienna Academy of Music, where he served as a prof. from 1985. In his music, Füssl demonstrated an adept handling of dodecaphonic procedures. Within his catalog of works are *Die Maske*, ballet (1954), *Dybuk*, opera (1958–70; Karlsruhe, Sept. 26, 1970), *Celestina*, opera (1973–75), *Kain*, religious play (1984–85), and *Resurrexit*, musical play (1991–92); also incidental music.

Fux, Johann Joseph, renowned Austrian organist, music theorist, pedagogue, and composer; b. Hirtenfeld, near St. Marein, Styria, 1660; d. Vienna, Feb. 13, 1741. He was born into a peasant family. He enrolled in the Jesuit Univ. in Graz as a "grammatista" in 1680, then in 1681 entered the Ferdinandeum there, a Jesuit residential school made up mostly of musically gifted students. He also studied at the Jesuit Univ. of Ingolstadt, being listed as logica studiosus in 1683. He served as organist at St. Moritz there until 1688. By 1696 he was in Vienna, where he was organist at the Schottenkirche until 1702; he was made court composer by the emperor in 1698; about 1700 the latter is believed to have sent him to Rome, where he studied composition. He became vice Kapellmeister at St. Stephen's Cathedral in Vienna in 1705; he was then its principal Kapellmeister from 1712 to 1715; he became vice Kapellmeister to the court in 1713; he was named Ziani's successor as principal Kapellmeister to the court in 1715. Among his noted students were Gottlieb Muffat, G. C. Wagenseil, and J. D. Zelenka. Fux was the last representative of the Baroque tradition in composition and music theory in Austria. As a composer, he was an outstanding contrapuntist. He found inspiration in the a cappella polyphonic mastery of Palestrina, which led to his adoption of 2 contrasting styles in his sacred music: the *stylus a cappella* (without instruments) and the *stylus mixtus* (with instruments). In his solo motets, operas, and oratorios, he prepared the way for the Viennese Classicists. More than 200 works have been added to the original 405 cataloged by Köchel. As a music theorist, he produced the classic treatise on counterpoint, *Gradus ad Parnassum* (1725). It had a profound influence on his successors, and remains an invaluable textbook. A complete edition of his works, ed. by H. Federhofer and O. Wessely under the auspices of the J. J. Fux-Gesellschaft, began publication in 1959.

WRITINGS: *Gradus ad Parnassum* (Vienna, 1725; partial Eng. tr. as *Steps to Parnassus: The Study of Counterpoint*, N.Y., 1943; 2d ed., rev., 1965, as *The Study of Counterpoint*); *Singfundament* (Vienna, c.1832); *Exempla dissonantiarum ligatarum et non ligatarum* (publ. in H. Federhofer, "Drei handscriftliche Quellen zur Musiktheorie in Österreich um 1700," *Musa—mens—musici: Im Gedenken an Walther Vetter* (Leipzig, 1969).

WORKS: DRAMATIC: OPERAS (all 1st perf. at the Hoftheater, Vienna, unless otherwise given): *Il fato monarchico, festa teatrale* (Feb. 18, 1700; music not extant); *Neo-exoriens phosphorus, id est neo-electus et infulatus praesul Mellicensis*, Latin school opera (1701; music not extant); *L'offendere per amare ovvero La Telesilla*, dramma per musica (June 25, 1702; music not extant); *La clemenza d'Augusto*, poemetto drammatico (Nov. 15, 1702; music not extant); *Julo Ascanio, rè d'Alba*, poemetto drammatico (March 19, 1708); *Pulcheria*, poemetto drammatico (June 21, 1708); *Il messe di Marzo, consecrato a Marte*, componimento per musica (March 19, 1709); *Gli ossequi della notte*, componimento per musica (July 15, 1709); *La decima fatica d'Ercole, ovvero La Sconfitta di Gerione in Spagna*, componimento pastorale-eroico (Oct. 1, 1710); *Dafne in Lauro,* componimento per camera (Oct. 1, 1714); *Orfeo ed Euridice*, componimento da camera per musica (Oct. 1, 1715); *Angelica vincitrice di Alcina*, festa teatrale (Sept. 14, 1716); *Diana placata*, componimento da camera (Nov. 19, 1717); *Elisa*, festa teatrale per musica (Laxenburg, Aug. 28, 1719); *Psiche*, componimento da camera per musica (Nov. 19, 1720); *Le nozze di Aurora*, festa teatrale per musica (Oct. 6, 1722); *Costanza e Fortezza*, festa teatrale (Prague, Aug. 28, 1723); *Giunone placata*, festa teatrale per musica (Nov. 19, 1725); *La corona d'Arianna*, festa teatrale (Aug. 28, 1726); *Enea negli Elisi, ovvero Il tempio dell'Eternita*, festa teatrale (Aug. 28, 1731). ORATORIOS: *Die Heilige Dimpna, Infantin von Irland* (1702; only part 2 extant); *La fede sacrilega nella morte del Precursor S. Giovanni Battista* (1714); *La donna forte nelle madre de' sette Maccabei* (1715); *Il trionfo della fede* (1716); *Il disfacimento di Sisara* (1717); *Cristo nell'orto* (1718); *Gesù Cristo negato da Pietro* (1719); *Santa Geltrude* (1719); *La cena del Signore* (1720); *Ismaele* (1721); *Il testamento di nostro Signor Gesù Cristo sul cal-*

vario (1726); *Oratorium germanicum de passione Domini* (1731; music not extant).

BIBL.: L. von Köchel, *J. J. F.* (Vienna, 1872; includes thematic catalog and list of works); A. Liess, *F.iana* (Vienna, 1958); J. van der Meer, *J. J. F. als Opernkomponist* (3 vols., Bilthoven, 1961); E. Wellesz, *F.* (London, 1965); R. Flotzinger, *F. Studien* (Graz, 1985); B. Habla, ed., *J. J. F. und die barocke Bläsertradition* (Tutzing, 1987).

G

Gabichvadze, Revaz (Kondratevich), Georgian composer; b. Tiflis, June 11, 1913. He was a student of Bagrinovsky, Shcherbachev, and Tuskia at the Tiflis Cons. (graduated, 1935), where he took postgraduate courses with Aranov and Ryazanov. In 1938 he joined its faculty, but he also was active as a theater conductor. He was founder-director of the State Light Orch. (1941–43), and also music ed. of the Georgian Radio. In 1967 he was named a People's Artist of the Georgian SSR. In his earlier compositions, Gabichvadze wrote in a traditional style which often utilized folk elements. Around 1960 he adopted an advanced style which partook of dodecaphonic and aleatoric techniques, as well as electronics and collage.

WORKS: DRAMATIC: *Nana*, opera (1949; rev. 1960); *Strekoza* (The Dragonfly), operetta (Sverdlovsk, Dec. 31, 1952); *Mï, materi mira: Vosstaniye Niobey* (We, Mothers of the World: The Revolt of Niobe), opera (1966); *Hamlet*, ballet (1971); incidental music; film scores.

Gabold, Ingolf, German-born Danish composer; b. Heidelberg, March 31, 1942. He studied theory and music history at the Royal Danish Cons. of Music in Copenhagen, and composition with Nørgård at the Århus Cons. His stated goal is to "combine music with Jung's depth psychology." Among his works are *Syv scener til Orfeus* (7 Visions to Orpheus), opera for 4 Singers, Actor, Dancers, and Orch. (1969–70; Danish TV, Sept. 28, 1970), and *Mod Vandmandens tegn* (Toward Aquarius), television play for Soprano, Bass, Chorus, and Organ (1971–72; Copenhagen, Nov. 11, 1973).

Gabrielli, Caterina, famous Italian soprano; b. Rome, Nov. 12, 1730; d. there, Feb. 16, 1796. Her father served as a cook to Prince Gabrielli, and the prince made it possible for her to pursue vocal training. She thus took his name in appreciation; her nickname "La Coghetta" ("Little Cook") derives from her father's position. She most likely studied with Porpora in Venice (1744–47), then sang throughout Italy with notable success. She subsequently went to Vienna, where she made her concert debut at the Burgtheater on Feb. 16, 1755. She found a friend and mentor in Metastasio, and quickly established herself as one of the leading singers of the day. In 1758 she went to Milan, where she found another mentor in the castrato Gaetano Guadagni. That same year she was in Padua and Lucca, and later appeared in Parma (1759–60). She then returned to Vienna, where she created the title roles in Gluck's *Tetide* (Oct. 8, 1760) and Traetta's *Armide* (Jan. 3, 1761). Following further appearances in Italy, she sang in St. Petersburg (1772–75) and in London (1775–76); she then returned to Italy, singing in Naples, Venice, Lucca, and Milan until her 1780 retirement. Her reputed beauty and scandalous liaisons made her a legendary figure in operatic lore.

BIBL.: H. de Koch, *La G.* (Paris, 1878).

Gabrielli, Nicolò, Italian composer; b. Naples, Feb. 21, 1814; d. Paris, June 14, 1891. He was a pupil of Buonamici, Conti, Donizetti, and Zingarelli at the Naples Cons. From 1854 he lived in Paris. He wrote about 20 operas and 60 ballets, produced at Naples, Paris, and Vienna.

Gaburo, Kenneth (Louis), American composer and teacher; b. Somerville, N.J., July 5, 1926; d. Iowa City, Jan. 26, 1993. He studied composition, piano, and theory at the Eastman School of Music in Rochester, N.Y. (B.M., 1944; M.M., 1949), composition and conducting at the Conservatorio di Santa Cecilia in Rome (1954–55), and composition, theater, and linguistics at the Univ. of Ill., Urbana (D.M.A., 1962); he also studied composition at the Berkshire Music Center at Tanglewood (summer, 1956), and attended the Princeton Seminar in Advanced Musical Studies (summer, 1959). After teaching at Kent State Univ. (1950), he was assoc. prof. at McNeese State Univ. (1950–54); he then was a prof. at the Univ. of Ill. (1955–67) and at the Univ. of Calif. at San Diego (1967–75); he also was founder-director of the Studio for Cognitive Studies in San Diego (1975–83) and a prof. at the Univ. of Iowa (from 1983). He was the recipient of a Fulbright fellowship (1954), ASCAP awards (from 1960), a Guggenheim fellowship (1967), and an NEA award (1975); in 1985 he received the Milhaud Chair fellowship at Mills College in Oakland, California. Among his works are the operas *The Snow Queen* (Lake Charles,

La., May 5, 1952), *Blur* (Urbana, Ill., Nov. 7, 1956), and *The Widow* (Urbana, Ill., Feb. 26, 1961).

Gade, Niels (Wilhelm), greatly significant Danish composer, conductor, and pedagogue; b. Copenhagen, Feb. 22, 1817; d. there, Dec. 21, 1890. The son of a maker of instruments, he studied violin with F. T. Wexschall and theory and composition with A. P. Berggreen. After making his debut as a violinist in 1833, he joined the Royal Orch. in 1834. He first came to prominence as a composer with his concert overture *Efterklange af Ossian* (1840), which won the prize of the Copenhagen Musical Soc. This popular score was followed by his outstanding 1st Sym. (1841–42), which Mendelssohn conducted in its premiere performance in Leipzig at a Gewandhaus concert on March 2, 1843, with extraordinary success. Gade was appointed assistant conductor to Mendelssohn and the Gewandhaus Orch.; he also joined the faculty of the Leipzig Cons. Upon Mendelssohn's death in 1847, Gade was named Gewandhaus Kapellmeister. However, with the outbreak of the Schleswig–Holstein War in 1848, he returned to Copenhagen and quickly assumed a preeminent place in the musical life of his homeland. He reorganized the Copenhagen Musical Soc. and became its chief conductor in 1850, leading its orch. and choir in distinguished performances of his own music as well as that of other composers. In 1866 he helped to organize the Copenhagen Cons., and thereafter served as one of its directors; also taught composition and music history there. In 1876 the Danish government awarded him a life pension. Gade was an ardent admirer of Mendelssohn and Schumann and thus adopted the prevalent German Romantic style in his own works; his influence was nonetheless great in Denmark. His activities as a conductor and teacher were also extremely important. Among his works are *Mariotta*, Singspiel (1848–49), and the ballets *Faedrelandets muser* (The Muses of Our Fatherland; 1840), *Napoli* (1842; Act 2 only), and *Et folkesagn* (1853–54; Act 2 by J. P. E. Hartmann). He also composed incidental music. His son was the violinist Axel Willy Gade (1860–1921).

BIBL.: R. Henriques, *N. W. G.* (Copenhagen, 1891); D. Gade, *N. W. G.: Optengenelser og breve* (Copenhagen, 1892; Ger. tr., 1894); C. Kjerulf, *N. W. G.* (Copenhagen, 1917); W. Behrend, *Minder om N. W. G.* (Copenhagen, 1930); J. Gade, *Omkring N. W. G.: Breve fra fader og søn* (Copenhagen, 1967); *N. W. G.—Katalog* (Copenhagen, 1986).

Gadski, Johanna (Emilia Agnes), celebrated German soprano; b. Anklam, June 15, 1872; d. as a result of an automobile accident, Berlin, Feb. 22, 1932. She studied with Schroeder-Chaloupka in Stettin, making her operatic debut as Lortzing's Undine at Berlin's Kroll Opera (1889). She continued to appear there until 1893, and also sang in Mainz, Stettin, and Bremen. On March 1, 1895, she made her U.S. debut as Elsa in *Lohengrin* with the Damrosch Opera Co. in New York; she continued to sing with it until 1898, appearing in such roles as Elisabeth, Eva, and Sieglinde. She made her first appearance at London's Covent Garden as Elisabeth on May 15, 1899, and sang there until 1901; she also appeared as Eva in Bayreuth (1899). On Jan. 6, 1900, she made her Metropolitan Opera debut in New York as Senta, and quickly established herself there as an outstanding interpreter of such compelling roles as Brünnhilde and Isolde. She made 2 transcontinental concert tours of the United States (1904–06), then returned to the Metropolitan Opera (1907), making her farewell performance there as Isolde on April 13, 1917. Having married Lt. Hans Tauscher on Nov. 11, 1892, she returned to Germany in 1917 when her husband was deported as an enemy alien. She sang opera again in the United States with a touring German company from 1929 to 1931.

Gadzhibekov, Sultan, Azerbaijani conductor, pedagogue, and composer; b. Shusha, May 8, 1919; d. Baku, Sept. 19, 1974. He studied composition with B. Zeidman at the Baku Cons. (graduated, 1946), where he then taught instrumentation and composition, later becoming a prof. (1965) and rector (1966); he also conducted the Azerbaijan Phil. (1955–62). He received state prizes for his ballet *Gulshen* (1952) and for his *Concerto for Orchestra* (1970). He was named a People's Artist of the Azerbaijan SSR (1960). His other stage works include *The Red Rose*, musical comedy (1940) and *Iskender and the Shepherd*, children's opera (1947).

Gadzhibekov, Uzeir, Azerbaijani composer; b. Agdzhabedy, near Shusha, Sept. 17, 1885; d. Baku, Nov. 23, 1948. He studied in Shusha; then lived in Baku, where he produced his first opera on a native subject, *Leyly and Medzhnun* (Jan. 25, 1908). His comic opera *Arshin Mal Alan* (Baku, Nov. 27, 1913) had numerous performances; another opera, *Kyor-Oglu* (A Blind Man's Son), was premiered at the Azerbaijan Festival in Moscow (April 30, 1937).

Gadzhiev, (Akhmed) Jevdet, Azerbaijani composer; b. Nukha, June 18, 1917. He studied with M. Rudolf and U. Gadzhibekov at the Baku Cons. (1936–38), and with Anatoli Alexandrov, S. Vasilenko, and Shostakovich at the Moscow Cons. (1938–41; graduated, 1947). He then taught composition at the Baku Cons., where he later was a prof. (from 1963) and rector (until 1969). He received state prizes for his opera *Veten* (1945; in collaboration with K. Karayev) and for the symphonic poem *For Peace* (1952). He was made a People's Artist of the Azerbaijan S.S.R. (1960). His other operas are *Ghazal My Flower* (1956) and *The Maiden Gathering Apples* (1957).

BIBL.: E. Muradova, *J. G.* (Baku, 1962); K. Abezgauz, *J. G.* (Baku, 1965); E. Abasova, *J. G.* (Baku, 1967).

Gagliano, Marco da, significant Italian composer; b. Florence, May 1, 1582; d. there, Feb. 25, 1643. He studied with Luca Bati, and became his assistant at S. Lorenzo in 1602; concurrently he studied with the Compagnia dell'Arcangelo Raffaello, serving as maestro di cappella in 1607 and 1609; he also took Holy Orders. In 1607 he went to Mantua, where his opera *La Dafne* was given with great success in 1608. After returning to Florence, he succeeded Bati as maestro di cappella at the Cathedral in 1608; he was later in the service of the Medici court; he was made canon in 1610 and Apostolic Protonotary in 1615. He founded the Accademia degli Elevati in 1607. With Jacopo Peri, he wrote the opera *Lo sposalizio di Medoro e Angelica*, which was performed in honor of the election of Emperor Ferdinand III at the Palazzo Pitti on Sept. 25, 1619. He also composed the opera *La Flora,* for which Peri wrote the role of Clori; it was performed in honor of the wedding of Margherita de' Medici and Duke Odoardo Farnese of Parma at the Palazzo Pitti on Oct. 14, 1628. Gagliano was one of the earliest composers to write in the stile rappresentativo, which he developed further by ornamentation. In addition to his own listed operas, his *La liberazione di Tirreno e d'Arnea* (Florence, Feb. 6, 1617), may be by Gagliano; he may have collaborated with Peri on the score, or it may be entirely the work of Peri.

WORKS: OPERAS: *La Dafne* (Mantua, 1608); *Lo sposalizio di Medoro e Angelica* (Palazzo Pitti, Florence, Sept. 25, 1619; in collaboration with J. Peri); *La Flora, overo Il natal di Fiori* (Palazzo Pitti, Florence, Oct. 14, 1628; major portion by Gagliano, with the role of Clori by Peri).

BIBL.: D. Butchart, *I Madrigali di M. d.G.* (Florence, 1982).

Gailhard, Pierre, noted French bass and opera manager; b. Toulouse, Aug. 1, 1848; d. Paris, Oct. 12, 1918. He began his vocal studies in his native city, and entered the Paris Cons. in 1866. After a year of study under Revial, he graduated in 1867, winning 3 1st prizes. He made his debut at the Opéra Comique (Dec. 4, 1867) as Falstaff in Thomas's *Songe d'une nuit d'été*; on Nov. 3, 1871, he made his debut at the Opéra as Méphistophélès in Gounod's *Faust*. At the height of his powers and success he gave up the stage when, in 1884, he accepted, jointly with M. Ritt, the management of the famous institution; on the appointment of M. Bertrand as successor to Ritt, in 1892, he retired, but joined Bertrand the following year as codirector; after the latter's death, in 1899, he remained sole director until 1908. His administration was remarkably successful, considering both the novelties produced and the engagement of new singers (Melba, Eames, Bréval,

Caron, Ackté, Alvarez, Saléza, Renaud, the 2 de Reszkes, et al.). Against violent opposition he introduced, and maintained in the repertoire, *Lohengrin* (1895), *Die Walküre* (1893), *Tannhäuser* (1895; the 1st perf. after the notorious fiasco of 1861), *Meistersinger* (1897), and *Siegfried* (1902). His son, André Gailhard (b. Paris, June 29, 1885; d. Ermont, Val d'Oise, July 3, 1966), composed the operas *Amaryllis* (Toulouse, 1906), *Le Sortilège* (Paris, 1913), and *La Bataille* (Paris, 1931).

Gaito, Constantino, Argentine composer and teacher; b. Buenos Aires, Aug. 3, 1878; d. there, Dec. 14, 1945. He studied in Naples with Platania, then lived in Buenos Aires as a teacher. He wrote the operas (all premiered in Buenos Aires) *Shafras* (1907), *I Doria* (1915), *I paggi di Sua Maestà* (1918), *Caio Petronio* (Sept. 2, 1919), *Flor de nieve* (Aug. 3, 1922), *Ollantay* (July 23, 1926), *Lazaro* (1929), and *La sangre de las guitarras* (Aug. 17, 1932) and the ballet *La flor del Irupé* (July 17, 1929).

Gál, Hans, Austrian musicologist and composer; b. Brunn, near Vienna, Aug. 5, 1890; d. Edinburgh, Oct. 3, 1987. He studied with Mandyczewski and Adler at at the Univ. of Vienna, where he lectured (1919–29); he then was director of the Mainz Cons. (1929–33). He returned to Vienna in 1933; after the Anschluss, he was compelled to leave Vienna in 1938, and settled in Edinburgh, where he lectured on music at the Univ. (1945–65) while continuing to compose. Among his compositions are the operas *Der Arzt der Sobeide* (Breslau, 1919), *Die heilige Ente* (Düsseldorf, April 29, 1923), *Das Lied der Nacht* (Breslau, April 24, 1926), *Der Zauberspiegel* (Breslau, 1930; also as an orch. suite), and *Die beiden Klaas* (1933). His numerous writings include *Richard Wagner* (Frankfurt am Main, 1963) and *Giuseppe Verdi und die Oper* (Frankfurt am Main, 1982).

BIBL.: W. Waldstein, *H. G.* (Vienna, 1965); *H. G. zum 100. Geburtstag* (Mainz, 1990).

Galeffi, Carlo, esteemed Italian baritone; b. Malamocco, near Venice, June 4, 1882; d. Rome, Sept. 22, 1961. He was a student of Sbrigilia in Paris and of Cotogni in Rome. In 1903 he made his operatic debut in Rome as Enrico, and then won success in Naples as Amonasro and Rigoletto. On Nov. 29, 1910, he made his only appearancce at the Metropolitan Opera in New York as Germont. In 1911 he sang in the premiere of Mascagni's *Isabeau* in Buenos Aires. From 1912 to 1938 he was a leading member of Milan's La Scala, winning particular distinction in such roles as Tell, Rigoletto, Boccanegra, Nabucco, Luna, and Germont; he also created the roles of Manfredo in Montemezzi's *L'amore dei tre Re* (1913) and Fanuel in Boito's *Nerone* (1924). His operatic farewell performance took place in 1954.

BIBL.: A. Marchetti, *C. G.: Una vita per el canto* (Rome, 1973).

Gall, Jeffrey (Charles), American countertenor; b. Cleveland, Sept. 19, 1950. He was educated at Princeton Univ. (B.A., 1972) and Yale Univ. (M.Phil., 1976), and received vocal instruction from Blake Stern (1972–75) and Arthur Burrows (1976–80). After singing with the Waverly Consort (1974–78), he made his debut in Cavalli's *Erismena* at the Brooklyn Academy of Music in 1980. He sang at Milan's La Scala (1981), the Edinburgh Festival (1982), the Lyric Opera in Chicago (1986), and the Santa Fe Opera (1986). On Sept. 27, 1988, he made his Metropolitan Opera debut in New York as Tolomeo in *Giulio Cesare*. He appeared as Britten's Oberon in Los Angeles in 1992. Following an engagement as Monteverdi's Ottone in Cologne in 1993, he returned to the Metropolitan Opera in 1994 in Britten's *Death in Venice*. In 1996 he sang Ottone at the Dallas Opera. He also appeared in roles in operas by Cesti, Purcell, Lully, Jommelli, Pergolesi, Scarlatti, and Mozart.

Gall (real name, **Galle**), **Yvonne,** French soprano; b. Paris, March 6, 1885; d. there, Aug. 21, 1972. She studied at the Paris Cons. She made her operatic debut at the Paris Opéra in 1908 as Mathilde, and remained on its roster until 1935; she also sang at the Opéra Comique in Paris (1921–34). From 1918 to 1921 she was a member of the Chicago Grand Opera, then sang in San Francisco (1931). After her retirement, she taught voice at the Paris Cons. She was highly successful in the French and Italian operatic repertoire. In 1958 she married **Henri Büsser**, who, although much older, outlived her and reached the age of 101.

Galli, Amintore, Italian composer; b. Talamello, near Rimini, Oct. 12, 1845; d. Rimini, Dec. 8, 1919. He was a pupil of Mazzucato at the Milan Cons. (1862–67). He was music editor for the publisher Sonzogno, and critic of *Il Secolo*; he was later ed. *Il Teatro Illustrato* and *Musica Popolare*. He publ. *Musica e musicisti dal secolo X sino ai nostri giorni* (1871), *Estetica della musica* (1900), *Storia e teoria del sistema musicale* (1901), and *Piccolo lessico di musica* (1902).

WORKS: DRAMATIC: OPERAS: *Il corno d'oro* (Turin, Aug. 30, 1876); *David* (Milan, Nov. 12, 1904). ORATORIOS: *Espiazione* (after Moore's *Paradise and Peri*); *Cristo al Golgota*.

Galli, Caterina, Italian mezzo-soprano; b. c.1723; d. Chelsea, 1804. She went to London and sang for the first time at the King's Theatre in 1742. She then became a favorite of Handel, who engaged her to sing in his oratorios (1747–54) and for whom he wrote several parts. About 1754 she left England to pursue her career in Genoa, Naples, Venice, and Mantua. In 1773 she returned to England and sang in opera, oratorios, and concerts until 1797.

Galli, Filippo, celebrated Italian bass; b. Rome, 1783; d. Paris, June 3, 1853. He made his debut as a tenor in Naples in 1801. After an interruption caused by an illness, he returned to the stage as a bass in Padua in 1811, singing in the premiere of Rossini's *La cambiale di matrimonio*; his success was so great that Rossini wrote several other roles for him, including Fernando in *La gazza ladra* and the title role in *Maometto II*. Donizetti wrote the role of Henry VIII for him in *Anna Bolena*. He sang in London at the King's Theatre (1827–33). His voice began to decline about 1840, and he abandoned the stage. He was then active as a chorus master in Lisbon and Madrid, and taught voice at the Paris Cons. (1842–48).

Galli-Curci, Amelita, brilliant Italian soprano; b. Milan, Nov. 18, 1882; d. La Jolla, Calif., Nov. 26, 1963. She studied in Milan and intended to be a pianist; she graduated in 1903 from the Milan Cons., winning 1st prize. She then had a few voice lessons with Carignani and Dufes, and received advice from Mascagni and William Thorner. She made her operatic debut in Trani as Gilda (Dec. 26, 1906), then sang in various opera houses in Italy and in South America (1910). She continued her successful career as an opera singer in Europe until 1915; she then made a sensationally successful U.S. debut with the Chicago Opera Co. as Gilda (Nov. 18, 1916); she made her first appearance with the Metropolitan Opera in New York as Violetta (Nov. 14, 1921); she remained as a member of the Metropolitan until 1930, and then toured as a recitalist. She was married to the painter Luigi Curci (1910; divorced 1920) and to Homer Samuels, her accompanist.

BIBL.: C. LeMassena, *G.-C.'s Life of Song* (N.Y., 1945).

Galli-Marié, Cêlestine (Laurence née **Mariê de l'Isle)**, French mezzo-soprano; b. Paris, Nov. 1840; d. Vence, near Nice, Sept. 22, 1905. Her father, an opera singer, was her only teacher. She made her debut at Strasbourg (1859), then sang in Toulouse (1860) and in Lisbon (1861). She sang *La Bohème* at Rouen (1862) with such success that she was immediately engaged for the Paris Opéra Comique; made her debut there (1862) as Serpina in *La Serva padrona*. She created the roles of Mignon (1866) and Carmen (1875).

Galliard, Johann Ernst, German oboist, organist, and composer; b. Celle, c.1680; d. London, 1749. He was a pupil of A. Steffani in Hannover. A skillful oboist, he went to London (1706) as chamber musician to Prince George of Denmark; he succeeded Draghi as organist at Somerset House. In 1713 he played in the Queen's Theatre orch., and from 1717 to 1736 he was engaged in writing music for the stage productions at Covent Garden and Lincoln's Inn Fields. He last appeared as an oboist probably in 1722. Besides the music to numerous plays, masques, and pantomimes, he wrote several operas, including *Calypso* and *Telemachus* (London, Queen's Theatre, May 17, 1712), *Circe* (London, Lincoln's Inn Fields, April 11, 1719; 3 songs extant), and *The Happy Captive* (London, Little Theatre in the Haymarket, April 16, 1741; music not extant).

Gallico, Paolo, Italian-American pianist, teacher, and composer; b. Trieste, May 13, 1868; d. N.Y., July 6, 1955. At the age of 15, he gave a recital at Trieste, then studied at the Vienna Cons. under Julius Epstein, graduating at 18 with highest honors. After successful concerts throughout Europe, he settled in New York in 1892 as a pianist and teacher; he toured the United States frequently as pianist in recitals and as a soloist with the principal orchs. He wrote the opera *Harlekin* (1926). His son, Paul Gallico, was a well-known writer.

Galliera, Alceo, Italian conductor and composer; b. Milan, May 3, 1910; d. Brescia, April 20, 1996. He studied piano, organ, and composition at the Milan Cons., and then was on its faculty. After World War II, he appeared as a conductor throughout Europe and South America; he was music director of the Victorian Sym. Orch. in Melbourne (1950–51), at the Teatro Carlo Felice in Genoa (1957–60), and of the Strasbourg Phil. (1964–71).

Gallignani, Giuseppe, Italian composer and writer on music; b. Faenza, Jan. 9, 1851; d. (suicide) Milan, Dec. 14, 1923. He studied at the Milan Cons., then was choir leader at the Milan Cathedral. He ed. the periodical *Musica Sacra* (1886–94), then was director of the Parma Cons. (1891–97); from 1897 he was director of the Milan Cons. He produced the operas *Il Grillo del focolare* (Genoa, Jan. 27, 1873), *Atala* (Milan, March 30, 1876), and *Nestorio* (Milan, March 31, 1888), which were unsuccessful, but his church music was greatly appreciated.

Gallmeyer, Josefine (real name, **Josefina Tomaselli**), German soprano; b. Leipzig, Feb. 27, 1838; d. Vienna, Feb. 2, 1884. She began her stage career at 15. After appearing in Brünn, Budapest, Hermannstadt, and Temesvár, she became a star soubrette artist at Vienna's Theater an der Wien in 1865. She was bested in a rivalry there with Marie Geistinger, and in 1867 went to Berlin. Upon returning to Vienna, she became one of the principal singers at the Carltheater. She later was active at the Strampfertheater and the Theater an der Wien. After her final appearance at the Carltheater in 1882, she went to New York for engagements at the Thalia Theater. Her N.Y. appearances were bedeviled by illness, and she died shortly after returning to Vienna. Gallmeyer was affectionately known as Pepi. Her roles in the lighter scores of the Viennese musical theater were memorable. Her career was the subject of a Volksstuck (1905) and a Singspiel by Paul Knepler (1921).

BIBL.: M. Waldstein, *Erinnerungen an J. G.* (Berlin, 1885).

Gallo, Fortune, Italian-American impresario; b. Torremaggiore, May 9, 1878; d. N.Y., March 28, 1970. After piano studies, he emigrated to the United States in 1895. In 1909 he founded the San Carlo Opera Co., which toured throughout the United States until it disbanded in 1955. In 1926 he built the Gallo Theater in New York. He was a pioneering figure in the production of operatic sound films, *Pagliacci* being the first such effort in 1928.

Gallois-Montbrun, Raymond, French violinist, music educator, and composer; b. Saigon, Aug. 15, 1918; d. Paris, Aug. 13, 1994. He studied at the Paris Cons. (1929–39) with Firmin Touche (violin), Büsser (composition), and Jean and Noël Gallon (theory). In 1944 he won the Prix de Rome with his cantata *Louise de la miséricorde*. He made concert tours in Europe, and also played in Japan and Africa. He served as director of the Versailles Cons. (1957–62), and then of the Paris Cons. (1962–83). In 1980 he was made a member of the Académie des Beaux-Arts. He composed *Le Rossignol et l'Empereur*, chamber opera (1959) and *Stella ou le Piège de sable*, opera (1964).

Gallon, Jean, French composer and pedagogue, brother of **Noël Gallon**; b. Paris, June 25, 1878; d. there, June 23, 1959. He studied piano with Diémer and theory with Lavignac and Lenepveu at the Paris Cons. He was chorus master of the Paris Société des Concerts du Conservatoire (1906–14) and at the Paris Opéra (1909–14). From 1919 to 1949 he taught harmony at the Paris Cons. Among his pupils were Robert Casadesus, Marcel Delannoy, Henri Dutilleux, Olivier Messiaen, and Jean Rivier. He publ. harmony exercises for use at the Cons.; with his brother, the composer and pedagogue Noël Gallon (b. Paris, Sept. 11, 1891; d. there, Dec. 26, 1966), he composed several pieces of theater music, among them a ballet, *Hansli le Bossu* (1914).

Galuppi, Baldassare, celebrated Italian composer, called "Il Buranello" after his birthplace; b. on the island of Burano, near Venice, Oct. 18, 1706; d. Venice, Jan. 3, 1785. He began his musical training with his father, a barber and violinist, writing his first opera, *La fede nell'incostanza ossia Gli amici rivali*, when he was 16; it failed at its premiere in Vicenza in 1722, so he pursued a thorough course of instruction in composition and keyboard playing with Antonio Lotti. He garnered his first unqualified success as a composer with the opera *Dorinda* (Venice, June 9, 1729), written in collaboration with G. B. Pescetti, and subsequently wrote numerous operas for the leading Italian opera houses. From 1740 to 1751 he was maestro di musica of the Ospedale dei Mendicanti in Venice. He was active as a composer in London at the King's Theatre at the Haymarket (1741–43); he also visited Vienna in 1748. He was named vice maestro of the cappella ducale of S. Marco in Venice in 1748; he was made Venice's maestro di cappella in 1762. Turning to the new form of opera buffa, he established himself as a master of the genre with his *L'Arcadia in Brenta* (Venice, May 14, 1749), sealing his fame with his *Il Filosofo di campagna* (Venice, Oct. 26, 1754), which was performed with great acclaim all over Europe. He was called to Russia in 1765 to serve as music director of the court chapel of Catherine the Great in St. Petersburg; his opera seria *Ifigenia in Tauride* was given at the court on May 2, 1768. He returned to Venice in 1768, and resumed his post at S. Marco; that same year he also became maestro di coro of the Ospedale degli Incurabili. Galuppi was a pivotal figure in the development and refinement of opera buffa. His effective vocal and orch. writing, combined with Goldoni's innovative librettos, ensured popular success. He was also a distinguished composer for the keyboard; his sonatas confirm his contemporary renown as a harpsichord virtuoso.

WORKS: OPERAS (all 1st perf. in Venice unless otherwise given): SERIA: *Gl'odj delusi dal sangue* (1728; in collaboration with G. B. Pescetti); *L'odio placato* (1729); *Argenide* (1733); *L'ambizione depressa* (1733); *Tamiri* (1734); *Elisa regina di Tiro* (1736); *Ergilda* (1736); *L'Alvilda* (1737); *Issipile* (Turin, 1737); *Alessandronelle Indie* (Mantua, 1738); *Adriano in Siria* (Turin, 1740); *Gustavo primo re di Svezia* (1740); *Oronte re de' Sciti* (1740); *Didone abbandonata* (Modena, 1741); *Penelope* (London, 1741); *Scipione in Cartagine* (London, 1742); *Enrico* (London, 1743); *Sirbace* (London, 1743); *Ricimero* (Milan, 1745); *Antigono* (London, 1746); *Scipione nelle Spagne* (1746); *Evergete* (Rome, 1747); *L'Arminio* (1747); *Vologeso* (Rome, 1748); *Demetrio* (Vienna, 1748); *Clotilde* (1748); *Demofoonte* (Madrid, 1749); *Olimpia* (Naples, 1749); *Alcimena principessa dell'Isole Fortunate, ossia L'amore fortunato ne' suoi disprezzj* (1749); *Antigona* (Rome, 1751); *Dario* (Turin, 1751); *Lucio Papirio* (Reggio Emilia, 1751); *Artaserse* (Padua, 1751); *Le Virtuose ridicole* (1752); *La calamità de' cuori* (1752); *I bagni d'Abano* (1753; in collaboration with Bertoni); *Sofonisba* (Rome, 1753); *Siroe* (Rome, 1754); *Attalo* (Padua, 1755); *Idomeneo* (Rome, 1756); *Ezio* (Milan, 1757); *Sesostri* (1757); *Ipermestra* (Milan, 1758); *Adriano in Siria* (Livorno, 1758); *Meilite riconosciuto* (Rome, 1759); *La clemenza di Tito* (1760); *Solimano* (Padua, 1760); *Antigono* (1762); *Il Re pastore* (Parma, 1762); *Siface*, later known as *Viriate* (1762); *Il Muzio Scevola* (Padua, 1762); *Arianna e Teseo* (Padua, 1763); *Sonofisba* (Turin, 1764); *Cajo Mario* (1764); *Ifigenia in Tauride* (St. Petersburg, 1768); *Montezuma* (1772). DRAMMA GIOCOSO: *L'Arcadia in Brenta* (1749); *Il Conte Caramella* (Verona, 1749?); *Arcifanfano re dei matti* (1749); *Il paese della Cuccagna* (1750); *Il mondo alla roversa, ossia Le Donne che comandano* (1750); *La mascherata* (1750); *Il Filosofo di campagna* (1754); *Il Povero superbo* (1755);

Le nozze (Bologna, 1755); *La Diavolessa* (1755); *L'Amante di tutte* (1760); *Li tre amanti ridicoli* (1761); *Il caffe di campagna* (1761); *Il Marchese villano* (1762); *L'Uomo femmina* (1762); *Il puntiglio amoroso* (1762); *Il Re alla caccia* (1763); *La Donna di governo* (Rome, 1761; rev. version, Prague, 1763); *La partenza il ritorno de' marinari* (1764); *La Cameriera spiritosa* (Milan, 1764); *Il Villano geloso* (1769); *Amor lunatico* (1770); *L'inimico delle donne* (1771); *La Serva per amore* (1773; Act 1 unfinished); also several other dramatic works, including farsettas, pastorales, intermezzos, serenatas, and cantatas.

BIBL.: W. Bollert, *Die Buffoopern B. G.s* (diss., Univ. of Berlin, 1935); R. Wiesend, *Studien zur Opera Seria von B. G.* (2 vols., Tutzing, 1984).

Galvani, Giacomo, noted Italian tenor; b. Bologna, Nov. 1, 1825; d. Venice, May 7, 1889. He studied in Bologna with Gamberini and Zamboni, making his debut in *I Masnadieri* in Spoleto in 1849. He subsequently sang in Bologna, Milan, London, Barcelona, and other cities with great success. After his retirement, he taught voice in Venice and at the Moscow Cons. (1869–87). He was acclaimed for his performances in the operas of Rossini and Donizetti.

Gandini, Gerardo, Argentine composer, pianist, and teacher; b. Buenos Aires, Oct. 16, 1932. He studied with Pia Sebastini, Roberto Caamaño, and Ginastera in Buenos Aires (1956–59); he completed studies in Rome with Petrassi (1966–67). He taught in Buenos Aires and New York. As a pianist, he specialized in contemporary music. He composed the chamber opera *La Pasión de Buster Keaton* (1978) and the opera *La ciudad ausente* (Buenos Aires, Oct. 25, 1995).

Gandolfi, Riccardo (Cristoforo Daniele Diomede), Italian composer; b. Voghera, Piedmont, Feb. 16, 1839; d. Florence, Feb. 5, 1920. He was a pupil of Carlo Conti at the Naples Cons., then of Mabellini in Florence. He was appointed inspector of studies at the Real Istituto di Musica in Florence (1869), chief librarian in 1889; was pensioned in 1912. He began as a dramatic composer, then turned to the larger instrumental and vocal forms, and finally abandoned composition altogether, devoting himself to historical studies, which won him distinction.

WORKS: OPERAS: *Aldina* (Milan, 1863); *Il Paggio* (Turin, 1865); *Il Conte di Monreale* (Genoa, 1872); *Caterina di Guisa* (Catania, 1872).

WRITINGS: *Sulla relazione della poesia colla musica melodrammatica* (1868); *Una riparazione a proposito di Francesco Landino* (1888); *Commemorazioni di W. A. Mozart* (1891); *Illustrazioni di alcuni cimeli concernanti l'arte musicale in Firenze* (1892); *Appunti di storia musicale* (1893); *Onoranze Fiorentine a G. Rossini* (1902).

Ganelin, Viacheslav, Russian pianist and composer; b. Kraskovo, 1944. He graduated from the Lithuanian State Cons. in Vilnius and was music director of the Russian Dramatic Theater. He wrote much theater music, film scores, an opera, *The Red-Haired Liar and the Soldier*, and a rock musical, *The Devilish Bride*. When he met the percussionist Vladimir Tarasov (b. Archangelsk, 1947) in Vilnius, the 2 formed what was to be the basis of the Ganelin Trio; after playing at the Jazz Club in Sverdlovsk in the early 1960s, they were joined by Chaksin (b. Sverdlovsk, 1947), a graduate of the Sverdlovsk Cons. The Ganelin Trio has an eclectic and ironic style, synthesizing strong formal structural ideas with improvisation and stressing constant innovation and Ganelin's conviction that the 2 most important elements of jazz are "swing and improvisation."

Gange, Fraser, distinguished Scottish-American baritone and pedagogue; b. Dundee, June 17, 1886; d. Baltimore, July 1, 1962. He studied with his father in Dundee and with Amy Sherwin in London. After making his debut at 16, he toured in England, Scotland, Australia, and New Zealand. On Jan. 18, 1924, he made his U.S. debut in New York, and subsequently toured as an oratorio and lieder artist. He also taught at the Peabody Cons. of Music in Baltimore (1931–57) and at the Juilliard School of Music in New York (summers 1932–46).

Ganne, (Gustave) Louis, French conductor and composer; b. Buxières-les-Mines, Allier, April 5, 1862; d. Paris, July 13, 1923. He studied at the Paris Cons. with Dubois, Massenet, and Franck. He was a conductor for the Bals de l'Opéra in Paris and in various spa towns. In 1905 he organized his own Concerts Louis Ganne series in Monte Carlo. As a composer, Ganne wrote many light scores. His circus musical *Les Saltimbanques* (Paris, Dec. 30, 1899) was notably successful, but he scored his greatest success with the operetta *Hans, le joueur de flûte* (Monte Carlo, April 14, 1906). He also composed the popular *La Marche Lorraine* and the march *Le Père de la Victoire*.

WORKS: DRAMATIC: MUSIC THEATER (all 1st perf. in Paris unless otherwise given): *Tout Paris* (June 16, 1891); *Rabelais* (Oct. 25, 1892); *Les Colles des femmes* (Sept. 29, 1893); *Les Saltimbanques* (Dec. 30, 1899); *Hans, le joueur de flûte* (Monte Carlo, April 14, 1906); *Rhodope* (Monte Carlo, Dec. 13, 1910); *Cocorico* (Nov. 29, 1913); *L'Archiduc des Folies-Bergère* (Oct. 7, 1916); *La Belle de Paris* (Oct. 22, 1921); vaudevilles; ballet music; other dances.

Ganzarolli, Wladimiro, Italian bass-baritone; b. Venice, Jan. 9, 1936. He received his training at the Venice Cons. In 1958 he made his operatic debut as Méphistophélès in *Faust* at Milan's Teatro Nuovo, and from 1959 he was a member of Milan's La Scala; from 1964 he also sang at the Vienna State Opera. In 1965 he made his debut at London's Covent Garden as Figaro. His guest engagements in the United States took him to San Francisco, Chicago, Dallas, and New York. In addition to his roles in Italian operas, he was especially admired for his roles in Mozart's operas.

Garat, (Dominique) Pierre (Jean), famous French singer and teacher; b. Ustaritz, Bas-Pyrénées, April 25, 1762; d. Paris, March 1, 1823. His talent was discovered early, and he studied theory and singing with Franz Beck in Bordeaux. His father wished him to become a lawyer, and sent him to the Univ. of Paris in 1782. However, he neglected his legal studies, and, aided by the Count d'Artois, he was introduced to Marie Antoinette, whose special favor he enjoyed up to the Revolution. He earned his livelihood as a concert singer; accompanied Rode, in 1792, to Rouen, where he gave numerous concerts before being arrested as a suspect during the Terror; subsequently he went to Hamburg. He returned to Paris in 1794, and sang (1795) at the Feydeau Concerts, where his triumphs speedily procured him a professorship of singing in the newly established Cons. For 20 years longer, his fine tenor-baritone voice, trained to perfection, made him the foremost singer on the French concert stage. Nourrit, Levasseur, and Ponchard were his pupils.

BIBL.: P. Lafond, *G.* (Paris, 1899); B. Miall, *P. G., Singer and Exquisite: His Life and His World* (London, 1913); I. de Fagoaga, *P. G., le chanteur* (Bayonne, 1944).

Garbin, Edoardo, Italian tenor; b. Padua, March 12, 1865; d. Brescia, April 12, 1943. He studied with Alberto Selva and Vittorio Orefice in Milan. In 1891 he made his operatic debut in Vicenza as Alvaro in *La forza del destino*; he also sang in Milan (Teatro dal Verme), Naples, and Genoa. On Feb. 9, 1893, he created the role of Fenton in Verdi's *Falstaff* at La Scala in Milan. Garbin made guest appearances in Rome, Vienna, Berlin, London, Russia, and South America. He married **Adelina Stehle**. He was particularly distinguished in *verismo* roles.

García, Eugénie, French soprano and teacher; b. Paris, 1815; d. there, Aug. 12, 1880. She was a pupil of **Manuel (Patricio Rodríguez) García**, who became her husband. After singing in Italy, she appeared at the Paris Opéra Comique (1840) and in London (1842). Upon separating from her husband, she settled in Paris to teach voice.

García Mansilla, Eduardo, American-born French-Argentine composer; b. Washington, D.C., March 7, 1870; d. Paris, May 9, 1930. He studied composition with Massenet, Saint-Saëns, and Vincent d'Indy in Paris and with Rimsky-Korsakov in St. Petersburg. His opera *Ivan* was premiered in St. Petersburg in 1905, and another opera, *La angelica Manuelite*, in Buenos Aires in 1917.

García, Manuel (del Popolo Vicente Rodríguez), famous Spanish tenor, singing teacher, and composer, father of **Manuel Patricio Rodríguez García**; b. Seville, Jan. 21, 1775; d. Paris, June 9, 1832. A chorister in the Seville Cathedral at 6, he was taught by Ripa and Almarcha, and at 17 was already well known as a singer, composer, and conductor. After singing in Cadiz, Madrid, and Málaga, he proceeded (1807) to Paris, and sang to enthusiastic audiences at the Théâtre-Italien. In 1809, at his benefit, he sang his own monodrama *El poeta calculista* with extraordinary success. From 1811 to 1816 he was in Italy. On his return to Paris, his disgust at the machinations of Catalani, the manageress of the Théâtre-Italien, caused him to break his engagement and go to London (1817), where his triumphs were repeated. From 1819 to 1824 he was again the idol of the Parisians at the Théâtre-Italien; he sang as 1st tenor at the Royal Opera in London (1824) and in 1825 embarked for New York with his wife, his son, Manuel, and his daughter Maria (Malibran), and the distinguished artists Crivelli *fils*, Angrisani, Barbieri, and de Rosich; from Nov. 29, 1825, to Sept. 30, 1826, they gave 79 performances at the Park and Bowery theaters in New York; the troupe then spent 18 months in Mexico. García returned to Paris, and devoted himself to teaching and composition. His operas, all forgotten, comprise 17 in Spanish, 18 in Italian, and 8 in French, besides a number never performed, and numerous ballets. He was a preeminently successful teacher, numbering his 2 daughters, **Maria Malibran** and **Pauline Viardot-García**, and Nourrit, Rimbault, and Favelli among his best pupils.

BIBL.: G. Malvern, *The Great G.s* (N.Y., 1958).

García, Manuel Patricio Rodríguez, distinguished Spanish vocal teacher, son of **Manuel (del Popolo Vicente Rodríguez) García**; b. Madrid, March 17, 1805; d. London, July 1, 1906. He was intended to be a stage singer; in 1825 went to New York with his father, but in 1829 adopted the vocation of a singing teacher (in Paris), with conspicuous success. An exponent of his father's method, he carefully investigated the functions of the vocal organs; in 1855 he invented the laryngoscope, for which the Univ. of Königsberg made him a Dr.Phil. In 1840 he sent to the Academy a *Mémoire sur la voix humaine*, a statement of the conclusions arrived at by various investigators, with his own comments. He was appointed prof. at the Paris Cons. in 1847, but resigned in 1848 to accept a similar position at the London Royal Academy of Music, where he taught uninterruptedly until 1895. Among García's pupils were his first wife, **Eugênie García**, Jenny Lind, Henriette Nissen, and Stockhausen. His *Traité complet de l'art du chant* was publ. in 1847 (Eng. ed., 1870; rev. ed. by García's grandson Albert García as *García's Treatise on the Art of Singing*, London, 1924). He also publ. (in Eng.) *Hints on Singing* (London, 1894).

BIBL.: M. Sterling Mackinlay, *G.: The Centenarian, and His Time* (Edinburgh, 1908); J. Levien, *The G. Family* (London, 1932); G. Malvern, *The Great G.s* (N.Y., 1958).

García, Pauline Viardot- . See **Viardot-García, Pauline.**

García Fajer, Francisco Javier, Spanish composer; b. Nalda, 1730; d. Saragossa, Feb. 26, 1809. He lived for some years in Rome as a student and singing teacher; in 1756 he was appointed maestro at Saragossa Cathedral. His works show a marked contrast to the fugal style prevailing before, being more natural and simple. He wrote the componimento sacro *Il Tobia* (Rome, 1752), and the operas *La finta schiava* (Rome, 1754), *Pompeo Magno in Armenia* (Rome, 1755), *La Pupilla* (Rome, 1755), and *Lo Scultore deluso* (Rome, 1756).

BIBL.: J. Carreras López, *La musica en las catedrales durante el siglo XVIII: F. J. G. "El Españoleto" (1730–1809)* (Saragossa, 1983).

Gardelli, Lamberto, distinguished Italian conductor; b. Venice, Nov. 8, 1915; d. Munich, July 17, 1998. He studied piano and composition at the Liceo Musicale Rossini in Pesaro, and then completed his training in Rome with Zanella, Ariani, Petrassi, and Bustini. He was an assistant to Serafin in Rome, where he made his conducting debut at the Opera with *La Traviata* in 1944; then he conducted at the Royal Opera in Stockholm (1946–55). From 1955 to 1961 he was conductor of the Danish Radio Sym. Orch., and then conducted at the Hungarian State Opera in Budapest (1961–65) and at the Glyndebourne Festivals (1964–65; 1968). In 1964 he made his first appearance in the United States conducting *I Capuleti e i Montecchi* at N.Y.'s Carnegie Hall. On Jan. 30, 1966, he made his Metropolitan Opera debut in New York conducting *Andrea Chénier;* he remained on its roster until 1968. He made his first appearance at London's Covent Garden in 1969 conducting *Otello*, and returned for the 1970–71, 1975–76, and 1979–80 seasons. From 1970 to 1975 he was music director of the Bern City Theater. From 1973 he also conducted at the Royal Opera in Copenhagen. He later was chief conductor of the Munich Radio Orch. (1983–88) and of the Danish Radio Sym. Orch. in Copenhagen (1986–89). Gardelli acquired a notable reputation as an interpreter of the Italian operatic repertory. He himself composed 4 operas.

Garden, Mary, celebrated Scottish soprano; b. Aberdeen, Feb. 20, 1874; d. Inverurie, Jan. 3, 1967. She went to the United States as a child; studied violin and piano; in 1893 she began the study of singing with Mrs. Robinson Duff in Chicago; in 1895 she went to Paris, where she studied with Sbriglia, Bouhy, Trabadello, Mathilde Marchesi, and Lucien Fugere. Her funds, provided by a wealthy patron, were soon depleted, and Sybyl Sanderson introduced her to Albert Carré, director of the Opéra Comique. Her operatic debut was made under dramatic circumstances on April 10, 1900, when the singer who performed the title role of Charpentier's *Louise* at the Opéra Comique was taken ill during the performance, and Garden took her place. She revealed herself not only as a singer of exceptional ability, but also as a skillful actress. She subsequently sang in several operas of the general repertoire; she also created the role of Diane in Pierné's *La Fille de Tabarin* (Opéra Comique, Feb. 20, 1901). A historic turning point in her career was reached when she was selected to sing Mélisande in the premiere of Debussy's *Pelléas et Mélisande* (Opéra Comique, April 30, 1902); she became the center of a raging controversy when Maurice Maeterlinck, the author of the drama, voiced his violent objection to her assignment (his choice for the role was Georgette Leblanc, his common-law wife) and pointedly refused to have anything to do with the production. Garden won warm praise from the critics for her musicianship, despite the handicap of her American-accented French. She remained a member of the Opéra Comique; she also sang at the Grand Opéra, and at Monte Carlo. She made her U.S. debut as Thaïs at the Manhattan Opera House, N.Y. (Nov. 25, 1907), and sang Mélisande there, the first U.S. performance of *Pelléas et Mélisande* (Feb. 19, 1908). In 1910 she joined the Chicago Opera Co.; she was its general director for the 1921–22 season, during which the losses mounted to about $1,000,000. She continued to sing at the Chicago Opera until 1931, and then made sporadic operatic and concert appearances until giving her farewell performance at the Paris Opéra Comique in 1934. In 1939 she settled in Scotland. With L. Biancolli, she publ. *Mary Garden's Story* (N.Y., 1951).

BIBL.: M. Turnbull, *M. G.* (Portland, Oregon, 1997).

Gardiner, Sir John Eliot, outstanding English conductor; b. Fontmell Magna, Dorset, April 20, 1943. His great-uncle was the English composer H(enry) Balfour Gardiner (b. London, Nov. 7, 1877; d. Salisbury, June 28, 1950. As a child, he attended the Bryanston Summer School of Music and later played in the National Youth Orch. He studied history at King's College, Cambridge (M.A., 1965) and pursued advanced training in music with Dart at King's College, London (1966); a French government scholarship enabled him to study with Boulanger in Paris and Fontainebleau (1966–68). In 1964 he founded the Monteverdi Choir, followed by its complement, the Monteverdi Orch., in 1968. In the latter year, he conducted his own performing edition of Monteverdi's *Vespers* at the London Promenade Concerts. He made his first appearance at the Sadler's Wells Opera in London in 1969 conducting *Die Zauberflöte*. In 1971 he discovered in Paris the MS of Rameau's opera *Abaris, ou Les Boréades*, which he conducted in its concert premiere in London on April 19, 1975, and in its stage premiere at the Aix-en-Provence Festival on July 21, 1982. In 1973 he made his debut at London's Covent Garden conducting Gluck's *Iphigénie en Tauride*. He founded the English Baroque Soloists in 1977, which he conducted in performances utilizing original instruments of the Baroque era. From 1980 to 1983 he was principal conductor of the CBC Orch. in Vancouver. He served as artistic director of the Göttingen Handel Festivals from 1981 to 1990. From 1983 to 1988 he was music director of the Lyons Opera. In 1990 he organized the Orchestre Révolutionaire et romantique, an orch. devoted to performing scores on instruments of the period. He conducted it in Beethoven's 9th Sym. at its U.S. debut in New York in 1996. From 1991 to 1994 he was chief conductor of the North German Radio Sym. Orch. in Hamburg. As a guest conductor, Gardiner has appeared in many of the principal music centers of the world. In 1990 he was made a Commander of the Order of the British Empire. In 1998 he was knighted. His repertoire is immense, ranging from the pre-Baroque to modern eras. His interpretations reflect his penchant for meticulous scholarship while maintaining stimulating performance standards.

Gardner, John (Linton), English composer and teacher; b. Manchester, March 2, 1917. He studied organ with Sir Hugh Allen, Ernest Walker, and Thomas Armstrong, and composition with R. O. Morris at Exeter College, Oxford (Mus.B., 1939). He pursued his career in London, where he was a tutor (1952–76) and director of music (1965–69) at Morley College; he also taught at the Royal Academy of Music (1956–86) and was director of music at St. Paul's Girls' School (1962–75). In 1976 he was made a Commander of the Order of the British Empire. His extensive catalogue of works reveals a fine craftsmanship in an eclectic style.

WORKS: DRAMATIC: OPERAS: *A Nativity Opera* (1950); *The Moon and Sixpence* (1956; London, May 24, 1957); *The Visitors* (1971; Aldeburge, June 10, 1972); *Bel and the Dragon* (1973); *Tobermory* (1976). MUSICAL: *Vile Bodies* (1960). MASQUE: *The Entertainment of the Senses* (1973; London, Feb. 2, 1974). BALLETS: *Reflection* (1952); *Dress Rehearsal* (1958). Also incidental music.

Garrett, Lesley, English soprano; b. Thorne, Doncaster, April 10, 1955. She studied at the Royal Academy of Music in London and pursued postgraduate studies at the National Opera Studio. In 1979 she was cowinner of the Kathleen Ferrier Memorial Competition. After making her operatic debut with the English National Opera in London in 1980 as Alice in *Le comte Ory*, she sang Dorinda in Handel's *Orlando* that year at the Wexford Festival. In 1984 she made her first appearance at the Gyndebourne Festival as Damigella in *L'incoronazione de Poppea*. She returned to the English National Opera in 1984 as its principal soprano, winning praise for her appearances in such roles as Susanna in 1990, Zerlina in 1992, and Euridice in 1997. Her other roles of note included Despina, Adele, Oscar, Musetta, Janáček's Bystrouška, Weill's Jenny, and Tippett's Bella. As a guest artist, she appeared in Geneva, Florence, Moscow, St. Petersburg, and other European operatic centers. She also was engaged as a concert artist in her homeland and abroad.

Garrido, Pablo, Chilean composer and ethnomusicologist; b. Valparaiso, March 26, 1905; d. Santiago, Sept. 14, 1982. He studied in Santiago; conducted concerts of Chilean music and gave lectures; publ. a valuable monograph, *Biografía de la Cueca Chilena* (Santiago, 1942). He composed an opera, *La sugestión* (Santiago, Oct. 18, 1961) and a ballet, *El Guerrillero* (1963).

Garrison, Jon, American tenor; b. Higgensville, Mo., Dec. 11, 1944. He was educated at the Univ. of New Hampshire (B.A., 1966) and at N.Y. Univ. (M.A., 1968), and also pursued private vocal training with Arthur Hackett in Durham, N.H. (1965–66), and Raymond Buckingham (1969–75) and Bonnie Hamilton (1990–99) in New York. In 1974 he was engaged to sing a minor role at the Metropolitan Opera in New York, returning in 1975 to sing Rinuccio and in 1976 Tamino. In 1977 he appeared as Ferrando at the Santa Fe Opera, and in 1978 as Ramiro in *La Cenerentola* in Spoleto, Italy, and as Don Ottavio at the Metropolitan Opera. He made his debut as a soloist with the N.Y. Phil. under Kostelanetz's direction in 1979, and subsequently sang with the Cleveland Orch., the San Francisco Sym., the Boston Sym. Orch., the Philadelphia Orch., the Los Angeles Phil., the St. Louis Sym. Orch., and various other orchs. In 1982 he made his first appearance at the N.Y. City Opera as Admete in *Alceste*, and subsequently sang there frequently until 1990. He appeared as Nadir at the Théâtre du Châtelet in Paris in 1983, and in 1984 as Des Grieux in Cincinnati. His recital debut followed in 1985 at Oregon State Univ. in Corvalis, the same year he sang Ferrando at the Metropolitan Opera, where he returned as Roméo in 1986. He portrayed Alfredo at the Washington (D.C.) Opera in 1988. In 1993 he was engaged as Lensky at the Pittsburgh Opera. After singing Desportes in *Die Soldaten* at the English National Opera in London in 1996, he appeared as Eisenstein at the Metropolitan Opera in 1998. He sang Pedro in MacMillan's *Inés de Castro* at the Scottish Opera in Glasgow in 1999.

Garrison, Mabel, American soprano; b. Baltimore, April 24, 1886; d. N.Y., Aug. 20, 1963. She attended Western Maryland College and then pursued vocal training with Heinendahl and Minetti at the Peabody Cons. of Music in Baltimore (1909–11), and in New York with Saenger (1912–14) and Witherspoon (1916). In 1908 she married the composer George Siemonn. On April 18, 1912, she made her operatic debut under her married name as Philine in *Mignon* with the Aborn Opera Co. in Boston. On Feb. 15, 1914, she first sang at the Metropolitan Opera in a concert; her stage debut there followed as a Flower Maiden in *Parsifal* on Nov. 26, 1914, with her formal debut coming the next day as Frasquita. She continued to sing at the Metropolitan Opera until her farewell as Lucia on Jan. 22, 1921. In 1921 she made guest appearances at the Berlin State Opera, the Vienna State Opera, and the Cologne Opera, and then launched a concert tour of the globe. After singing with the Chicago Opera (1925–26), she taught at Smith College (1933–39). Among her finest roles were the Queen of the Night, Rosina, Gilda, Urbain, Martha, and the Queen of Shemakha. In her recitals, she often included songs by her husband, who frequently appeared as her accompanist.

Gasdia, Cecilia, Italian soprano; b. Verona, Aug. 14, 1960. She studied in Verona. After winning the Maria Callas competition of the RAI in 1981, she made her operatic debut as Bellini's Giulietta in Florence. In 1982 she made her first appearance at Milan's La Scala as Anna Bolena, and also sang in Perugia and Naples. She made her debut at the Paris Opéra in 1983 as Anais in Rossini's *Moïse*. In 1985 she made her U.S. debut as Gilda in a concert performance of *Rigoletto* in Philadelphia. In 1986 she sang for the first time at the Chicago Lyric Opera and at the Metropolitan Opera in New York. In subsequent years, she sang at leading opera houses and festivals on both sides of the Atlantic, winning particular notice for her Rossini, Verdi, and Puccini roles.

Gasparini, Francesco, eminent Italian composer and pedagogue; b. Camaiore, near Lucca, March 5, 1668; d. Rome, March 22, 1727. He became a member of the Accademia Filarmonica in Bologna in 1685, then studied with Legrenzi in Venice in 1686. He subsequently went to Rome (1689), where he became a member of the Accademia di Santa Cecilia; he may have received further instruction from Corelli and Pasquini. In 1701 he became maestro di coro of the Ospedale della Pieta in Venice. In 1713 he returned to Rome, where he became maestro di cappella of S. Lorenzo in Lucina in 1717; he was appointed to the same position at St. John Lateran in 1725, but ill health prevented him from assuming his duties. He distinguished himself as a composer of both secular and sacred music, writing about 50 operas in all. He was also an esteemed teacher, numbering Domenico Scarlatti, Quantz, and Benedetto Marcello among his students. He publ. the valuable treatise *L'armonico pratico al cimbalo* (Venice, 1708;

many subsequent eds.; Eng. tr. by F. Stillings as *The Practical Harmonist at the Keyboard*, New Haven, 1963).

WORKS: DRAMATIC: OPERAS (all 1st perf. in Venice unless otherwise given): *Il Roderico* (Rome, 1694); *L'Ajace* (Rome, 1697); *Mirena e Floro* (Naples, 1699); *Tiberio Imperatore d'Oriente* (Venice?, 1702); *Gli imenei stabiliti dal caso* (1702); *Il più fedel fra i vassalli* (1703); *Il miglior d'ogni amore per il peggiore d'ogni odio* (1703); *La fede tradita e vendicata* (1704); *La maschera levata al vitio* (1704); *La Fredegonda* (1704); *Ambleto* (1705); *Il principato custodito dalla frode* (1705); *Statira* (1705); *Antioco* (1705); *Flavio Anicio Olibrio* (1707); *Anfitrione* (1707); *L'amor generoso* (1707); *Taican Rè della Cina* (1707); *Engelberta* (1708); *Atenaide* (Vienna, 1709; Act 1 by A. S. Fiore, Act 2 by Caldara, and Act 3 by Gasparini); *Sesostri Rè d'Egitto* (1709); *La Ninfa Apollo* (1709); *Alciade, overo La violenza d'amore* (Bergamo, 1709; Act 1 by Gasparini, Act 2 by C. F. Pollarolo, and Act 3 by G. Ballarotti); *La Principessa fedele* (1709); *Tamerlano* (1710); *L'amor tirannico* (1710); *Merope* (1711); *Costantino* (1711); *Amor vince l'odio, overo Timocrate* (Florence, 1715); *Il Tartaro nella Cina* (Reggio Emilia, 1715); *Il comando non inteso ed ubbedito* (Florence, 1715); *Ciro* (Rome, 1716); *Teodosio ed Eudossa* (Braunschweig, 1716; in collaboration with J. Fux and A. Caldara); *Il trace in catena* (Rome, 1716–17); *Intermezzi in derisione della setta maomettana* (Rome, 1717?); *Pirro* (Rome, 1717); *Il gran Cid* (Naples, 1717); *Democrito* (Turin, 1718); *Lucio Vero* (Rome, 1719); *Astianatte* (Rome, 1719); *L'oracolo del fato* (Vienna, 1719); *La pace fra Seleuco e Tolomeo* (Milan, 1720); *Nino* (Reggio Emilia, 1720; Act 1 by G. M. Capelli, Act 2 by Gasparini, and Act 3 by A. M. Bononcini); *L'Avaro* (Florence, 1720?); *Il Faramondo* (Rome, 1720); *Dorinda* (Rome, 1723); *Gl'equivoci d'amore e d'innocenza* (1723); *Tigrane* (Rome, 1724). ORATORIOS: *Santa Maria egittiaca, piacere, pentimento, e Lucifero* (n.d.); *Moisé liberato dal Nilo* (Vienna, 1703?); *L'Atalia* (n.d.); *La nascita di Cristo* (1724); *Le nozze di Tobia* (1724).

Gassmann, Florian Leopold, important Bohemian composer; b. Brüx, May 3, 1729; d. Vienna, Jan. 20, 1774. He studied voice, violin, and harp with Johann Woborschil (Jan Voboril), the regens chori in Brüx; his father opposed his interest in music, so he ran away from home, eventually making his way to Italy, where he may have studied with Padre Martini in Bologna. His first opera, *Merope*, was given in Venice in 1757. After serving Count Leonardo Veneri there, he was invited to Vienna to become ballet composer at the court in 1763. He soon established himself as an opera composer, gaining fame with his comic operas *L'amore artigiano* (Vienna, April 26, 1767) and *La Contessina* (Mährisch-Neustadt, Sept. 3, 1770). In 1772 he was appointed court composer and also founded and served as first vice president of the Tonkünstler-Sozietät, a benevolent society for musicians. In addition to his operas, he distinguished himself as an accomplished symphonist. He was highly esteemed by Mozart, Gerber, Burney, and Salieri, the last having been his student in Vienna. His 2 daughters, Maria Anna Fux (b. Vienna, 1771; d. there, Aug. 27, 1852) and (Maria) Therese Rosenbaum (b. Vienna, April 1, 1774; d. there, Sept. 8, 1837), were pupils of Salieri, and both were active as singers.

WORKS: DRAMATIC: OPERAS: *Merope* (Venice, Carnival 1757; only the overture and Act 1 extant); *Issipile* (Venice, Carnival 1758); *Gli Uccellatori*, dramma giocoso (Venice, Carnival 1759); *Filosofia ed amore*, dramma giocoso (Venice, Carnival 1760); *Catone in Utica* (Venice, 1761; only 1 aria extant); *Un Pazzo ne fa cento*, dramma giocoso (Venice, 1762); *L'Olimpiade* (Vienna, 1764); *Il trionfo d'amore*, azione teatrale (Vienna, 1765); *Achille in Sciro* (Venice, 1766); *Il Viaggiatore ridicolo*, dramma giocoso (Vienna, 1766); *L'amore artigiano*, dramma giocoso (Vienna, 1767); *Amore e Psiche* (Vienna, 1767); *La notte critica*, dramma giocoso (Vienna, 1768); *L'opera seria*, commedia per musica (Vienna, 1769); *Ezio* (Rome, Carnival 1770); *La Contessina*, dramma giocoso (Mährisch-Neustadt, 1770); *Il Filosofo inamorato*, dramma giocoso (Vienna, 1771); *Le Pescatrici*, dramma giocoso (Vienna, 1771); *Don Quischott von Mancia*, comedy (Vienna, 1771; Acts 1 and 2 by Paisiello, Act 3 by Gassmann); *I rovinati*, comedy (Vienna, 1772); *La casa di campagna*, dramma giocoso (Vienna, 1773). ORATORIO: *La Betulia liberata* (Vienna, 1772). Also 27 opera overtures.

BIBL.: E. Girach, *F. L. G.* (Reichenberg, 1930).

Gastinel, Léon-Gustave-Cyprien, French composer; b. Villers, near Auxonne, Aug. 13, 1823; d. Fresnes-les-Rurgis, Oct. 20, 1906. He was a pupil of Halévy at the Paris Cons., taking 1st Grand Prix de Rome for his cantata *Vélasquez* in 1846. A successful composer of operas, he produced *Le Miroir* (1853), *L'Opéra aux fenêtres* (1857), *Titus et Bérénice* (1860), *Le Buisson vert* (1861), *Le Barde* (Nice, 1896), and the ballet *Le Rêve* (Paris Opéra, 1890), besides other stage works: *La Kermesse, Eutates, Ourania*, and *La Tulipe bleue*, and 4 oratorios.

BIBL.: F. Boisson, *L. G.* (Paris, 1893).

Gatti, Daniele, Italian conductor; b. Milan, Nov. 6, 1961. He received training in conducting and composition at the Milan Cons. After making his debut as an opera conductor in Milan with *Giovanni d'Arco* in 1982, he appeared with opera houses and orchs. throughout Italy, including the orchs. of the RAI. In 1986 he became founder-conductor of the Stradivari Chamber Orch. He made his first appearance at Milan's La Scala in 1988 conducting Rossini's *L'Occasion fa il Ladro*. In 1991 he made his U.S. debut conducting *Madama Butterfly* in Chicago. In 1992 he became music director of the Orch. Sinfonica dell'Accademia Nazionale di Santa Cecilia in Rome, and also made his debut at the Royal Opera in London conducting *I Puritani*. During the 1993–94 season, he appeared as a guest conductor with the Chicago Sym. Orch., the Cincinnati Sym. Orch., the London Phil., the London Sym. Orch., the Philadelphia Orch., and the San Francisco Sym.; also toured Germany and South America with his Rome orch. In 1994 he was appointed principal guest conductor of the Royal Opera in London, and also made his debut as guest conductor with the Royal Phil. in the British capital. On Dec. 1, 1994, he made his first appearance at the Metropolitan Opera in New York conducting *Madama Butterfly*. He made an auspicious U.S. debut with the N.Y. Phil. conducting Mahler's Sym. No. 6 (Feb. 22, 1996). In 1996 he became music director of the Royal Phil. in London.

Gatti, Guido M(aggiorino), eminent Italian writer on music, critic, and editor; b. Chieti, May 30, 1892; d. Grottaferrata, May 10, 1973. He took up violin training at 6 and piano studies at 12, and later studied engineering at the Univ. of Turin (1909–14). He was ed.-in-chief of *Riforma musicale* (1913–15; 1918). In 1920 he founded *Il pianoforte*, which was renamed the *Rassegna musicale* in 1928. He ed. it until it ceased publication in 1944, and then again from 1947 when it resumed publication in Rome. In 1962 it was renamed again as *Quaderni della Rassegna*. He also was director-general of the Teatro di Torino (1925–31), administrator of Lux films (1934–66), music critic of *Tempo* (1951–69), and ed. of *Studi musicali* (1972–73). In addition, he was ed. of several series, was music ed. of the *Dizionario Bompiani delle opere e dei personaggi* (1946–49) and the *Dizionario degli autori* (1956), and was a contributor of numerous articles to European and U.S. journals. Gatti was particularly influential in contemporary music circles.

WRITINGS: *I "Lieder" di Schumann* (Turin, 1914); *Figure di musicisti francesi* (Turin, 1915); *Giorgio Bizet* (Turin, 1915); *Musicisti moderni d'Italia e di fuori* (Bologna, 1920; 2d ed., enl., 1925); *Débora e Jaèle di I. Pizzetti* (Milan, 1922); ed. with A. della Corte, *Dizionario di musica* (Turin, 1925; 6th ed., 1959); *Le barbier de Séville de Rossini* (Paris, 1925); *Ildebrando Pizzetti* (Turin, 1934; 2d ed., 1955; Eng. tr., 1951); ed. with L. Dallapiccola, *F. B. Busoni: Scritti e pensieri sulla musica* (Florence, 1941; 2d ed., rev., 1954); ed. with others, *L'opera di Gian Francesco Malipiero* (Treviso, 1952); *Cinquanta anni di opera a balletto in Italia* (Rome, 1954); with F. D'Amico, *Alfredo Casella* (Milan, 1958); *V. de Sabata* (Milan, 1958); ed. with A. Basso, *La musica: enciclopedia storica* (Turin, 1966) and *La musica: Dizionario* (Turin, 1968–71); ed. with B. Marziano, *Riccardo Gualino e la cultura torinese: Le manifestazioni del Teatro di Torino* (Turin, 1971).

Gatti-Casazza, Giulio, distinguished Italian operatic administrator; b. Udine, Feb. 3, 1868; d. Ferrara, Sept. 2, 1940. He was educated at the univs. of Ferrara and Bologna, and graduated from the Naval Engineering School at Genoa; he abandoned his career as engineer and became director of the opera in Ferrara in 1893. His ability attracted the attention of the Viscount di Modrone and A. Boito, who, in 1898, offered him the directorship of La Scala at Milan. During the 10 years of his administration, the institution came to occupy first place among the opera houses of Italy. From 1908 to 1935 he was general director of the Metropolitan Opera in New York, a tenure of notable distinction. During his administration, he engaged many celebrated musicians, produced over 175 works, including premieres by American as well as foreign composers, and expanded audiences through major tours and regular nationwide broadcasts. On April 3, 1910, Gatti-Casazza married **Frances Alda**; they were divorced in 1929; in 1930 he married Rosina Galli, premiere danseuse and ballet mistress. Gatti-Casazza's *Memories of the Opera* was posth. publ. in Eng. in 1941.

Gaubert, Philippe, French conductor and composer; b. Cahors, July 3, 1879; d. Paris, July 8, 1941. He studied flute with Taffanel at the Paris Cons.; in 1905, he won the 2d Prix de Rome. From 1919 to 1938 he was conductor of the Paris Cons. concerts; from 1920 to 1941 he was also principal conductor at the Paris Opéra. He composed the operas *Sonia* (Nantes, 1913) and *Naila* (Paris, April 7, 1927) and a ballet *Philotis* (Paris, 1914). He publ. a *Méthode complète de flûte* (8 parts, 1923).

Gauthier, (Ida Joséphine Phoebe) Eva, notable Canadian mezzo-soprano and teacher; b. Ottawa, Sept. 20, 1885; d. N.Y., Dec. 26, 1958. She began her training in Ottawa, where she had lessons in piano and harmony with J. Edgar Birch, and then in voice with Frank Buels. She gained experience as soloist at St. Patrick Church in Ottawa, and then made her professional debut at the Ottawa Basilica at the commemoration service for Queen Victoria in 1902. After pursuing her studies in Paris with Auguste-Jean Dubulle, and then with Jacques Bouhy, Emma Albani invited her to tour the British Isles with her in 1905. In 1906 she accompanied Albani on her farewell tour of Canada. In 1907 she was soloist in C. Harriss's *Coronation Mass for Edward VII* at the Queen's Hall in London. During this time, she also had vocal lessons with William Shakespeare in London. Following further studies with Giuseppe Oxilia in Milan (1907–08), she made her only stage appearance as Micaëla in Pavia in 1909. From 1910 to 1914 she toured extensively as a recitalist in Southeast Asia. After making her N.Y. recital debut in 1915, she appeared regularly there in imaginative programs, which included works by Stravinsky, Schoenberg, Ravel, Bartók, Hindemith, Kern, Berlin, and Gershwin, not to mention works by lesser known composers of the past and even non-Western works. From 1936 she devoted herself principally to teaching.

BIBL.: N. Turbide, *Biographical Study of E. G. (1885–1958): First French-Canadian Singer of the Avant-garde* (diss., Univ. of Montreal, 1986).

Gavazzeni, Gianandrea, Italian conductor, writer on music, and composer; b. Bergamo, July 27, 1909; d. there, Feb. 5, 1996. He studied at the Accademia di Santa Cecilia in Rome (1921–25), and then took courses in piano with Renzo Lorenzoni and in composition with Ildebrando Pizzetti and Mario Pilati at the Milan Cons. (1925–31). While he devoted much time to musical journalism, he also pursued a conducting career from 1940. In 1948 he became a regular conductor at Milan's La Scala, where he served as artistic director from 1966 to 1968. He took La Scala companies on visits to the Edinburgh Festival (1957), to Moscow (1964), and to Montreal (1967). In 1957 he conducted *La Bohème* at the Lyric Opera of Chicago and in 1965 *Anna Bolena* at the Glyndebourne Festival. On Oct. 11, 1976, he made his Metropolitan Opera debut in New York conducting *Il Trovatore*. He then pursued his career in Europe, where he was especially admired for his interpretations of the Italian operatic repertory. Among his numerous writings were *Donizetti* (Milan, 1937); *Musorgskij e la musica russa dell'800* (Florence, 1943); *Le feste musicali* (Milan, 1944); *Il suono è stanco* (Bergamo, 1950); *Quaderno del musicista* (Bergamo, 1952); *Musicisti d'Europa* (Milan, 1954); *La musica e il teatro* (Pisa, 1954); *La morte dell'opera* (Milan, 1954); *La casa di Arlecchino* (Milan, 1957); *Trent'anni di musica* (Milan, 1958); *Diario di Edimburgo e d'America* (Milan, 1960); *La campane di Bergamo* (Milan, 1963); *I nemici della musica* (Milan, 1965); *Carta da musica* (Milan, 1968); *Non eseguire Beethoven e altri scritti* (Milan, 1974). He composed the opera *Paolo e Virginia* (1932; Bergamo, 1935) and the ballet *Il furioso all'isola di S. Domingo* (1940).

Gaveaux, Pierre, French singer and composer; b. Béziers, Oct. 9, 1760; d. Charenton, near Paris, Feb. 5, 1825. He was a choirboy at the Béziers Cathedral, where he later sang as a soloist. After composition lessons with Abbé Combés, the cathedral organist, he studied with Franz Beck. He settled in Paris, where he sang in opera from 1780. From 1793 he ran a music shop with his brother, and publ. his own works. In 1804 he became a singer at the imperial chapel, but was stricken with mental illness in 1812. In 1819 he entered an asylum. He composed more than 30 works for the stage, principally opéras comiques. His most notable stage works were *Sophie et Moncars, ou L'intrigue portugaise* (Paris, Sept. 30, 1797) and *Léonore, ou L'amour conjugal* (Paris, Feb. 19, 1798). The latter was composed to a libretto by Bouilly, which was also set by Beethoven as *Fidelio*. Among Gaveaux's other works were Revolutionary pieces, overtures, and songs.

Gaviniès, Pierre, noted French violinist and composer; b. Bordeaux, May 11, 1728; d. Paris, Sept. 8, 1800. He learned to play the violin as a child in the workshop of his father, a violin maker. In 1734 the family moved to Paris. Gaviniès made his first public appearance at a Concert Spirituel at the age of 13; he reappeared at these concerts as a youth of 20, his success with the public such that Viotti described him as "the French Tartini." From 1773 to 1777 he was director (with Gossec) of the Concert Spirituel. When the Paris Cons. was organized in 1795, he was appointed prof. of violin. His book of technical exercises, *Les 24 Matinées* (violin studies in all the 24 keys), demonstrates by its transcendental difficulty that Gaviniès must have been a virtuoso; he attracted numerous pupils, and is regarded as the founder of the French school of violin pedagogy. His compositions are of less importance, among them a comic opera, *Le Prétendu* (Paris, Nov. 6, 1760).

BIBL.: C. Pipelet, *Éloge historique de P. G.* (Paris, 1802).

Gay, John, English poet and dramatist, librettist of *The Beggar's Opera*; b. Barnstaple, Devon (baptized), Sept. 16, 1685; d. London, Dec. 4, 1732. *The Beggar's Opera* was premiered in London on Jan. 29, 1728, and was immensely popular for a century, chiefly because of its sharp satire and the English and Scots folk melodies it used. It has had a number of successful revivals. The government disliked it, and forbade the performance of its sequel, *Polly*, the score of which was printed in 1729. When *Polly* was finally performed in London on June 19, 1777, it was a fiasco, because the conditions satirized no longer prevailed.

BIBL.: C. Pearce, *Polly Peachum: The Story of "Polly" and "The Beggar's Opera"* (London, 1923); W. Schultz, *G.'s Beggar's Opera* (New Haven, Conn., 1923); O. Sherwin, *Mr. G.; Being a Picture of the Life and Times of the Author of The Beggar's Opera* (N.Y., 1929); C. Tolksdorf, *J. G.'s Beggar's Opera und Bert Brechts Dreigroschenoper* (Rheinberg, 1934).

Gay, Maria (née **Pitchot**), Spanish contralto; b. Barcelona, June 13, 1879; d. N.Y., July 29, 1943. She studied sculpture and the violin; became a singer almost by chance, when Pugno, traveling in Spain, heard her sing and was impressed by the natural beauty of her voice. She sang in some of his concerts and also with Ysaÿe in Brussels; she made her operatic debut there as Carmen (1902), a role that became her finest. She then studied in Paris with Ada Adiny, and when she returned to the operatic stage, made an international reputation. After tours in Europe, including appearances at London's Covent Garden (1906) and Milan's La Scala

(1906–07), she made her American debut at the Metropolitan Opera in New York as Carmen on Dec. 3, 1908, with Toscanini conducting. She sang with the Boston Opera Co. from 1910 to 1912 and with the Chicago Opera Co. from 1913 to 1927, when she retired from the stage. She and her husband, **Giovanni Zenatello**, whom she married in 1913, settled in New York as teachers (1927).

Gayarre, Julián (real name, **Gayarre Sebástian**), famous Spanish tenor; b. Valle de Roncal, Jan. 9, 1844; d. Madrid, Jan. 2, 1890. He received his training in Madrid and from Lamperti in Milan. In 1867 he made his operatic debut in Varese as Nemorino. After appearances in St. Petersburg (1873–75), he created the role of Enzo in *La Gioconda* at Milan's La Scala on April 8, 1876. Gayarre created a sensation at his debut at London's Covent Garden as Fernando in *La Favorite* on April 7, 1877, and was engaged to sing there until 1880, and again in 1886–87. On March 22, 1882, he created the title role in *Il Duca d'Alba* in Rome. In 1885 he appeared at the Théâtre-Italien in Paris, returning there in 1886 to sing at the Opéra. During a performance of *Les Pêcheurs de perles* in Madrid on Dec. 8, 1889, he suffered a vocal breakdown that compelled him to abandon his career. Gayarre was one of the foremost lyrico-dramatic tenors of his time. His roles in Italian and French operas were outstanding.

BIBL.: F. Hernandel Girbal, *J. G.: El tenor de la voz de ángel* (Madrid, 1955).

Gayer, (Ashkenasi), Catherine, American soprano; b. Los Angeles, Feb. 11, 1937. She studied at the Univ. of Calif. at Los Angeles and in Berlin. She made her operatic debut in Venice in the premiere of *Intolleranza* as the Companion on April 13, 1961; she then joined the Deutsche Oper in West Berlin, and was made a Kammersängerin in 1970; she also appeared at the East Berlin Komische Oper. She made guest appearances in Vienna, Salzburg, and Milan. She excelled in the modern operatic repertoire, but also was admired for her Queen of the Night, Constanze, Sophie, Gilda, Mélisande, and Zerbinetta.

Gaztambide (y Garbayo), Joaquín (Romualdo), Spanish conductor and composer; b. Tudela, Navarre, Feb. 7, 1822; d. Madrid, March 18, 1870. He studied at Pamplona and at the Madrid Cons. with Pedro Albéniz (piano) and Ramón Carnicer (composition). After a stay in Paris, he returned to Madrid as manager of several theaters and director of the Cons. concert society in 1862. He was best known, however, for his zarzuelas, the satiric musical productions which are identified with the Madrid stage. He wrote 44 zarzuelas, many of which became popular; one, *El juramento*, first produced in 1858, was revived in Madrid in 1933. His most popular work was *Catalina* (Madrid, Oct. 23, 1854). He took his own zarzuela company to Mexico and Havana in 1869–70.

Gazzaniga, Giuseppe, Italian composer; b. Verona, Oct. 5, 1743; d. Crema, Feb. 1, 1818. He studied with Porpora, first in Venice and then at the Cons. di S. Onofrio a Capuana in Naples (1760–66); subsequently studied with Piccinni. He composed 47 operas, his *Don Giovanni Tenorio osia Il Convitato di pietra* (Venice, Feb. 5, 1787; ed. by S. Kunze, Kassel and Basel, 1974) anticipating Mozart's great masterpiece *Don Giovanni*.

Geck, Martin, German musicologist; b. Witten, March 19, 1936. He was educated at the Univ. of Kiel (Ph.D., 1962, with the diss. *Die Vokalmusik Dietrich Buxtehude und der frühe Pietismus*; publ. in Kassel, 1965). In 1976 he became a prof. at the Dortmund Padagogischen Hochschule. He was prof. of musicology at the Univ. of Dortmund from 1980. Among his various writings were *Die Bildnisse Richard Wagners* (Munich, 1970), *Deutsche Oratorien 1800 bis 1840: Verzeichnis der Quellen und Aufführungen* (Wilhelmshaven, 1971), and, with J. Deathridge and E. Voss, *Wagner-Werk-Verzeichnis* (Mainz, 1986).

Gédalge, André, eminent French pedagogue and composer; b. Paris, Dec. 27, 1856; d. Chessy, Feb. 5, 1926. He began to study music rather late in life, and entered the Paris Cons. at the age of 28. However, he made rapid progress, and obtained the 2d Prix de Rome after a year of study (with Guiraud). He then elaborated a system of counterpoint, later publ. as *Traité de la fugue* (Paris, 1901; Eng. tr., 1964), which became a standard work. In 1905 he became a prof. of counterpoint and fugue at the Paris Cons.; among his students were Ravel, Enesco, Koechlin, Roger-Ducasse, Milhaud, and Honegger. He also publ. *Les Gloires musicales du monde* (1898) and other pedagogic works. As a composer, he was less significant. Among his works are a pantomime, *Le Petit Savoyard* (Paris, 1891), an opera, *Pris au piège* (Paris, 1895), and 3 operas that were not performed: *Sita, La Farce du Cadi*, and *Hélène*.

Gedda (real name, **Ustinov**), **Nicolai (Harry Gustav),** noted Swedish tenor; b. Stockholm, July 11, 1925. Gedda was his mother's name, which he assumed in his professional life. His father was a Russian who went to Sweden after the Civil War. He studied at the opera school at the Stockholm Cons. On April 8, 1952, he made his operatic debut as Chapelou in *Le Postillon de Longjumeau* at the Royal Opera in Stockholm. In 1953 he made his debut at La Scala in Milan; in 1954 he sang Faust at the Paris Opera and the Duke of Mantua at Covent Garden in London; in 1957 he sang Don José in *Carmen* at the Vienna State Opera. He made his U.S. debut as Faust with the Pittsburgh Opera on April 4, 1957; his Metropolitan Opera debut followed in New York on Nov. 1, 1957, in that same role; he created the role of Anatol in Barber's *Vanessa* at the Metropolitan on Jan. 15, 1958. Because of his natural fluency in Russian and his acquired knowledge of German, French, Italian, and English, he was able to sing with total freedom the entire standard operatic repertoire. In 1980 and 1981 he made highly successful appearances in Russia, both in opera and on the concert stage. In 1986 he made his London recital debut. In 1991 he appeared as Christian II in a revival of Naumann's *Gustaf Wasa* in Stockholm. He sang in *Palestrina* at Covent Garden in 1997. His memoirs were publ. as *Gåvan är inte gratis* (Stockholm, 1978).

Gedike, Alexander. See **Goedike, Alexander.**

Gedzhadze, Irakly, Russian composer; b. Mtskheta, Oct. 26, 1925. He studied with Matchavariani at the Tbilisi Cons., graduating in 1957. His works include the opera *Sunrise* (Tbilisi, Nov. 23, 1961).

Gefors, Hans, Swedish composer; b. Stockholm, Dec. 8, 1952. He studied composition with Per-Gunnar Alldahl and Maurice Karkoff, with Ingvar Lidholm at the Stockholm Musikhögskolan (1972), and with Nørgård at the Århus Cons.; also wrote music criticism and worked as an ed. In 1988 he joined the faculty at the Univ. of Lund.

WORKS: DRAMATIC: OPERAS: *Poeten och glasmästaren*, chamber opera (1979; Århus, April 26, 1980); *Christina* (1983–86; Stockholm, Oct. 18, 1986); *Der Park* (1986–91; Wiesbaden, April 25, 1992); *Vargen kommer* (1994–96; Malmö, Jan. 17, 1997); *Clara* (Paris, Dec. 7, 1998). OTHER: *Syndabocken*, theater music (1979).

Geissler, Fritz, German composer; b. Wurzen, near Leipzig, Sept. 16, 1921; d. Bad Saarow, Jan. 11, 1984. He studied at the Leipzig Hochschule für Musik with Max Dehnert and Wilhelm Weismann (1948–50); he later taught there (1962–70), then joined the faculty of the Dresden Cons.; he was named a prof. there in 1974. His music is dialectical and almost Hegelian in its syllogistic development and climactic synthesis; the ground themes are carefully adumbrated before their integration in a final catharsis; formal dissonances are emancipated by a freely modified application of 12-tone writing. He composed the operas *Der Schatten*, fantastic opera (1975), *Die Stadtpfeifer* (1977), and *Das Chagrinleder* (1978), and the ballets *Pigment* (1960), *Sommernachtstraum* (1965), and *Der Doppelganger* (1969). Also *Der verrückte Jourdain*, a "Rossiniada" (1971).

Geistinger, Marie (Maria Charlotte Cäcilia), noted Austrian soprano; b. Graz, July 26, 1836; d. Klagenfurt, Sept. 30, 1903. She appeared on the stage while still a child. At 16, she sang the title role in *Die falsche Pepita* in Vienna. After singing in Berlin, Hamburg, Riga, and again in Berlin in juvenile comedy roles, she returned to Vienna in 1865 to sing the title role in Offenbach's *La Belle Helene* at the Theater an der Wien. During the following decade, she sang there regularly and acquired the status of queen of the Vienna musical theater. She became particularly well known for her roles in Offenbach's works, but also was acclaimed as Fantasca in Johann Strauss's *Indigo und die vierzig Rauber* in 1871. In 1874 she created the role of Rosalinde in Strauss's *Die Fledermaus*. In 1877 she was seen in dramatic roles at the Vienna Stadttheater. After appearances in Leipzig (1877–79), she returned to Vienna's Theater an der Wien. In 1881 she made her U.S. debut as Offenbach's Grande-Duchess in New York, subsequently starring in various productions there and in other cities. In 1884 she returned to Vienna and appeared at the Carltheater. She also had guest engagements in other Austrian and German music centers. In 1891, 1896, and 1899 she made return visits to the United States. She retired from the stage in 1900.

BIBL.: E. Pirchan, *M. G.* (Vienna, 1947).

Gelbrun, Artur, Polish-born Israeli composer and teacher; b. Warsaw, July 11, 1913; d. Tel Aviv, Dec. 24, 1985. He studied at the Warsaw Cons., then took courses with Molinari and Casella at the Accademia di Santa Cecilia in Rome; he later studied composition with W. Burkhard and conducting with Scherchen in Zürich. He was an orch. and solo violinist in Warsaw, Lausanne, and Zürich (1936–47). In 1949 he emigrated to Israel and joined the staff of the Tel Aviv Academy of Music as prof. of conducting and composition.

WORKS: DRAMATIC: RADIOPHONIC ORATORIO: *Le Livre du Feu* (1964; Jerusalem, 1966). BALLETS: *Hedva* (concert premiere, Ein-Gev, May 27, 1951; stage premiere, St. Gallen, 1958); *Miadoux* (1966–67); *Prologue to the Decameron* (1968); *King Solomon and the Hoopoes* (1976).

Gelmetti, Gianluigi, Italian conductor; b. Rome, Sept. 11, 1945. He studied conducting at the Accademia di Santa Cecilia in Rome (diploma, 1965); his principal mentor was Ferrara (1962–67), but he also studied with Celibidache and in Vienna with Swarowsky. After serving as music director of the Orch. of the Pomeriggi Musicale in Milan (until 1980), he was chief conductor of the RAI Orch. in Rome (1980–84) and music director of the Rome Opera (1984–85). He was chief conductor of the Stuttgart Radio Sym. Orch. (1989–96) and music director of the Orchestre Philharmonique de Monte Carlo (1990–92).

Gencer, Leyla, Turkish soprano; b. Constantinople, Oct. 10, 1924. She studied at the Ankara Cons. with Elvira de Hidalgo; she also studied with Arangi-Lombardi in Istanbul. After making her operatic debut as Santuzza in Ankara in 1950, she completed her training in Italy with Apollo Granforte. In 1953 she sang in Naples, and then joined Milan's La Scala in 1956; she also appeared at the San Francisco Opera (1956–58). Her career was mainly concentrated in Europe, where she first sang at the Spoleto Festival (1959), the Salzburg Festival (1961), London's Covent Garden (1962), the Glyndebourne Festival (1962), and the Edinburgh Festival (1969). Among her admired roles were Donna Anna, Countess Almaviva, Anna Bolena, Norma, Elisabeth de Valois, and Maria Stuarda.

Genée, (Franz Friedrich) Richard, German conductor and composer; b. Danzig, Feb. 7, 1823; d. Baden, near Vienna, June 15, 1895. He studied under Stahlknecht in Berlin. He was a theater conductor (1847–67) at Riga, Cologne, Düsseldorf, Danzig, Amsterdam, and Prague; from 1868 to 1878 he was conductor at the Theater an der Wien in Vienna, then retired to his villa at Pressbaum, near Vienna. He wrote several of his own librettos (some with F. Zell); he also wrote librettos for Strauss, Suppé, and Millöcker.

WORKS: OPERETTAS: *Der Geiger aus Tirol* (1857); *Der Musikfeind* (1862); *Die Generalprobe* (1862); *Rosita* (1864); *Der schwarze Prinz* (1866); *Am Runenstein* (with Flotow; 1868); *Der Seekadett* (1876); *Nanon* (1877); *Im Wunderlande der Pyramiden* (1877); *Die letzten Mohikaner* (1878); *Nisida* (1880); *Rosina* (1881); *Die Zwillinge* (1885); *Die Piraten* (1886); *Die Dreizehn* (1887).

Gentele, Goeran, brilliant Swedish opera manager; b. Stockholm, Sept. 20, 1917; d. in an automobile accident near Olbia, Sardinia, July 18, 1972. He studied political science in Stockholm, and art at the Sorbonne in Paris. He was first engaged as an actor, then was stage director at the Royal Drama Theater (1941–52) and at the Royal Opera (1952–63) in Stockholm, where he was appointed director in 1963. In 1970 he was appointed general manager of the Metropolitan Opera in New York, effective June 1972; great expectations for his innovative directorship in America were thwarted by his untimely death during a vacation in Italy.

George, Earl, American composer, conductor, teacher, and music critic; b. Milwaukee, May 1, 1924. He studied composition with Hanson and Rogers and conducting with Paul White and Herman Genhart at the Eastman School of Music in Rochester, N.Y. (B.M., 1946; M.M., 1947; Ph.D., 1958); he also attended courses of Lopatnikoff and Martinů at the Berkshire Music Center in Tanglewood (summer, 1946), and continued his studies with the latter in New York (1947). In 1947 he received the Gershwin Prize and in 1957 held a Guggenheim followship. From 1948 to 1956 he taught theory and composition at the Univ. of Minnesota, and in 1955–56 was a Fulbright lecturer at the Univ. of Oslo. He then was prof. of theory and composition at Syracuse Univ. (1959–88), where he was founder-conductor of the Univ. Singers (1963–69) and conductor of the Univ. Sym. Orch. (1971–80). He also was music critic of the Syracuse *Herald-Journal* from 1961. His works follow an astute median course of prudent American modernism. He composed *Birthdays*, 2 operas individually titled *Pursuing Happiness* and *Another 4th of July* (Syracuse, April 23, 1976), and *Genevieve,* opera (Berea, Ohio, Feb. 10, 1984).

Georgescu, Dan Corneliu, Romanian composer; b. Craiova, Jan. 1, 1938. He studied at the Popular School for the Arts (1952–56) and with Ion Dumitrescu, Ciortea, Olah, and Mendelsohn at the Bucharest Cons. (1956–61). From 1962 to 1983 he was head of research at the Ethnography and Folklore Inst. of the Romanian Academy; he then pursued research at the Inst. for the History of Art (from 1984). In 1987 he went to Berlin, and then was active in ethnomusicological pursuits at the Free Univ. from 1991. His output extends from traditional to electronic scores. His works include the opera ballet *Model mioritic* (1973; Cluj, Oct. 1, 1975).

Georgescu, George, Romanian conductor; b. Sulina, Sept. 12, 1887; d. Bucharest, Sept. 1, 1964. After initial training in Bucharest, he went to Berlin and studied cello with H. Becker and conducting with Nikisch and Strauss. He began his conducting career in Berlin in 1918, and then returned to Bucharest as music director of the Phil. (1920–49) and the Opera (1922–26; 1932–34); from 1954 until his death he was music director of the George Enesco State Phil. He also made guest appearances throughout Europe.

BIBL.: T. Georgescu, *G. G.* (Bucharest, 1971).

Gerber, René, Swiss composer and teacher; b. Travers, June 29, 1908. He attended the Univ. of Zürich (1929) and studied with Andreae and Müller at the Zürich Cons. (1931–33) before completing his training in Paris (1934) with Dukas, Boulanger, Siohan, and Dupont. After serving as prof. of music at the Latin College in Neuchâtel (1940–47), he was director of the Neuchâtel Cons. (1947–51). His works, which include the operas *Roméo et Juliette* (1957–61) and *Le Songe d'une nuit d'été* (1978–81), were marked by tonal and modal writing.

Gerber, Rudolf, learned German musicologist; b. Flehingen, Baden, April 15, 1899; d. Göttingen, May 6, 1957. He studied at the Univ. of Halle, and then at the Univ. of Leipzig (Ph.D., 1922, with the diss. *Die Arie in den Opern Johann Adolf Hasses*; publ. as *Der Operntypus Johann Adolf Hasses und seine textlichen Grundlagen*, Leipzig, 1925). In 1923 he became Abert's assistant at the Univ. of Berlin. He completed his Habilitation in 1928 at the Univ. of Giessen with his *Das Passionsrezitativ bei Heinrich Schütz und seine stilgeschichtlichen Grundlagen* (publ. in Gütersloh,

1929). In 1928 he joined its faculty, where he later was a prof. and head of its Music-Historical Inst. (1937–43). In 1943 he became a prof. at the Univ. of Göttingen. Among his other writings is *Christoph Willibald Ritter von Gluck* (Potsdam, 1941; 2d. ed., rev., 1950). He also ed. works by Schütz, J. S. Bach, and Gluck.

Gerelli, Ennio, Italian conductor and composer; b. Cremona, Feb. 12, 1907; d. there, Oct. 5, 1970. He studied at the Bologna Cons. He conducted ballet and opera in Italy. From 1935 to 1940 he was on the staff of La Scala in Milan; in 1961 he founded the Camerata di Cremona.

Gergiev, Valery (Abissalovich), notable Russian conductor; b. Moscow, May 2, 1953. He received training in piano and conducting at the Ordzhoniskidze College of Music, then pursued conducting studies with Ilya Musin at the Leningrad Cons. (graduated, 1977). In 1975 he won 1st prize in the All-Union Conductors' Competition in Moscow. In 1977 he captured 2d prize in the Karajan competition in Berlin and was named assistant conductor at the Kirov Opera in Leningrad, where he made his debut conducting *War and Peace* in 1978; in 1979 he was made permanent conductor there. He also served as chief conductor of the Armenian State Sym. Orch. in Yerevan (1981–85). In 1988 he was appointed artistic director and principal conductor of the Kirov Opera. From 1989 to 1992 he also was principal guest conductor of the Rotterdam Phil. He conducted the Kirov Opera on many tours abroad, including its first visit to the United States in 1992 when it appeared at the Metropolitan Opera in New York. On March 21, 1994, he made his Metropolitan Opera debut conducting *Otello*. In the autumn of 1994 he made a concert tour of the United States conducting the Kirov Orch. In 1995 he became music director of the Rotterdam Phil. In 1997 he became principal guest conductor of the Metropolitan Opera, where on Dec. 19 he conducted the first perf. of Buketoff's ed. of *Boris Godunov*. Gergiev's interpretative insights, backed by an assured conducting technique, make him one of the most admired conductors of his generation. While his idiomatic performances of the Russian repertoire are particularly compelling, he has demonstrated skills in a broad operatic and symphonic repertoire well beyond the Russian tradition.

Gerhard, Roberto, eminent Catalonian-born English composer and teacher of Swiss-German and Alsatian descent; b. Valls, Sept. 25, 1896; d. Cambridge, Jan. 5, 1970. After training in piano from Granados (1915–16) and in composition from Pedrell (1916–20) in Barcelona, he pursued advanced studies in composition with Schoenberg in Vienna (1922–25) and Berlin (1925–28). Returning to Barcelona, he was made a prof. of music at the Ecola Normal de la Generalitat in 1931 and head of the music dept. of the Catalan Library in 1932, positions he held until the defeat of the Republic in the Spanish Civil War in 1939. He settled in Cambridge, where he held a research scholarship at King's College. In 1956 he taught at the Dartington Summer School of Music. In 1960 he was a visiting prof. of composition at the Univ. of Mich. in Ann Arbor. He taught at the Berkshire Music Center at Tanglewood in the summer of 1961. In 1960 he became a naturalized British subject. Gerhard was made a Commander of the Order of the British Empire in 1967 and was awarded an honorary doctor of music degree by the Univ. of Cambridge in 1968. In his early works, Gerhard followed traditional Spanish melodic and rhythmic patterns. The influence of Schoenberg is felt in his serial usage in the Wind Quintet (1928), but it was not until he settled in England that he began to reassess Schoenberg's 12-tone method with a detailed study of Hauer's and A. Hába's serial procedures. In 1952 he turned to the athematic procedures of Hába, which led to his composition of scores of great originality and merit. Among his finest works were the opera *The Duenna* and the ballet *Don Quixote*.

WORKS: DRAMATIC: OPERA: *The Duenna* (1945–47; BBC, 1947; rev. 1950; concert perf., Wiesbaden, June 27, 1951; stage perf., Madrid, Jan. 21, 1992; also *Interlude and Arias from The Duenna* for Mezzo-soprano and Orch., London, Sept. 18, 1961). BALLETS: *Ariel* (1934; concert perf., Barcelona, May 18, 1936); *Soirées de Barcelone* (1936–38; unfinished; orch. suite, 1936–38; also for Piano, c.1958; London, Jan. 12, 1985); *Don Quixote* (1940–41; 1947–49; London, Feb. 20, 1950; also *Dances from Don Quixote* for Piano, BBC, London, Nov. 26, 1947, and for Orch., 1958); *Alegrías* (1942; Birmingham, July 16, 1943; orch. suite, BBC, April 4, 1944); *Pandora* (1943–44; Cambridge, Jan. 26, 1944; orchestrated 1945; orch. suite, BBC, London, Feb. 1950). Also incidental music to plays, and film, radio, and television scores.

BIBL.: K. Potter, *The Life and Works of R. G.* (diss., Univ. of Birmingham, 1972); R. Paine, *Hispanic Traditions in Twentieth-Century Catalan Music with Particular Reference to G., Mompou, and Montsalvatge* (N.Y. and London, 1989); J. Homs, *R. G. i la seva obra* (Barcelona, 1991).

Gerhardt, Elena, celebrated German-born English mezzo-soprano; b. Leipzig, Nov. 11, 1883; d. London, Jan. 11, 1961. She studied at the Leipzig Cons. (1899–1903) with Marie Hedmont. She made her public debut on her 20th birthday in a recital, accompanied by Nikisch; after appearing at the Leipzig Opera (1903–04), she toured Europe as a lieder artist with great success; made her English debut in London in 1906, and her American debut in New York, Jan. 9, 1912. In 1933 she settled in London, making appearances as a singer, and teaching. She compiled *My Favorite German Songs* (1915), ed. a selection of Hugo Wolf's songs (1932), and wrote an autobiography, *Recital* (London, 1953).

Gerl, Franz Xaver, German bass and composer; b. Andorf, Nov. 30, 1764; d. Mannheim, March 9, 1827. He sang in the choir at Salzburg. In 1789 he became principal bass at the Theater auf der Wieden in Vienna, remaining on its roster until 1793. He created the role of Sarastro in Mozart's *Die Zauberflöte* in 1791. His wife, Barbara Reisinger (1770–1806), created the role of Papagena in that production. He composed several works for the stage, collaborating with Benedikt Schack.

German, Sir Edward (real name, **German Edward Jones**), admired English composer; b. Whitchurch, Salop, Feb. 17, 1862; d. London, Nov. 11, 1936. After studies with W. C. Hay in Shrewsbury (1880), he pursued his training at the Royal Academy of Music in London (1880–87) with Steggall (organ), Weist-Hill and Burnett (violin), Banister (theory), and Prout (composition and orchestration). He played violin in theater orchs., and soon began conducting them. From 1888 he was active with various London theaters, establishing his reputation as a composer with his incidental music. German scored his most notable stage success with the comic opera *Merrie England* (London, April 2, 1902). In 1928 he was knighted and in 1934 was awarded the Gold Medal of the Royal Phil. Soc. of London.

WORKS: DRAMATIC: OPERAS: *The Rival Poets* (1883–86); *The Emerald Isle* (London, April 27, 1901; completion of an unfinished work by Sullivan); *Merrie England* (London, April 2, 1902); *A Princess of Kensington* (London, Jan. 22, 1903); *Tom Jones* (1907; London, April 17, 1908); *Fallen Fairies* or *Moon Fairies* (London, Dec. 15, 1909). INCIDENTAL MUSIC TO: *Richard III* (1889); *Henry VIII* (1892); *The Tempter* (1893); *Romeo and Juliet* (1895); *As You Like It* (1896); *Much Ado About Nothing* (1898); *Nell Gwyn* (1900); *The Conqueror* (1905).

BIBL.: W. Scott, *Sir E. G.: An Intimate Biography* (London, 1932); B. Rees, *A Musical Peacemaker: The Life and Works of Sir E. G.* (Bourne End, Buckinghamshire, 1987).

Gershfeld, David, Moldavian composer; b. Bobrinets, Aug. 28, 1911. After studying horn and theory in Odessa, he moved to Kishinev, where he produced 2 operas on Moldavian subjects: *Grozovan* (June 9, 1956) and *Aurelia* (April 26, 1959). In 1966 he moved to Sochi in the Caucasus.

Gershwin, George (real name, **Jacob Gershvin**), immensely gifted American composer, brother of **Ira Gershwin**; b. N.Y., Sept. 26, 1898; d. Los Angeles, July 11, 1937. His father was an immigrant from Russia whose original name was Gershovitz. Gershwin's extraordinary career began when he was 16, playing the piano in music stores to demonstrate new popular songs. His studies were desultory; he took piano lessons with Ernest Hutcheson and Charles Hambitzer in New York; he studied harmony with Edward Kilenyi and Rubin Goldmark; later on, when he was already a famous composer of popular music, he continued to take private lessons; he studied counterpoint with Cowell and Riegger and, during the last years of his life, applied himself with great earnestness to his studies with Joseph Schillinger in an attempt to organize his technique in a scientific manner; some of Schillinger's methods he applied in *Porgy and Bess*. But it was his melodic talent and his genius for rhythmic invention, rather than any studies, that made Gershwin a genuinely important American composer. As far as worldly success was concerned, there was no period of struggle in Gershwin's life; one of his earliest songs, "Swanee," written at the age of 19, became enormously popular, selling more than a million copies of sheet music and some 2,250,000 recordings. He also took time to write a lyrical *Lullaby* for String Quartet (1920). Possessing phenomenal energy, he produced musical comedies in close succession, using fashionable jazz formulas in original and ingenious ways. A milestone in his career was *Rhapsody in Blue* for Piano and Jazz Orch., in which he applied the jazz idiom to an essentially classical form. He played the solo part at a special concert of the work conducted by Paul Whiteman at Aeolian Hall in New York on Feb. 12, 1924. The orchestration was by Ferde Grofé, a circumstance that generated rumors of Gershwin's inability to score for instruments; these rumors, however, were quickly refuted by his production of several orch. works, scored by himself in a brilliant fashion. He played the solo part of his Piano Concerto in F, with Walter Damrosch and the N.Y. Sym. Orch. (Dec. 3, 1925); this work had a certain vogue, but its popularity never equaled that of the *Rhapsody in Blue*. Reverting again to a more popular idiom, Gershwin wrote a symphonic work, *An American in Paris* (N.Y., Dec. 13, 1928, Damrosch conducting). His *Rhapsody No. 2* was performed by Koussevitzky and the Boston Sym. Orch. on Jan. 29, 1932, but was unsuccessful; there followed a *Cuban Overture* (N.Y., Aug. 16, 1932) and Variations for Piano and Orch. on his song "I Got Rhythm" (Boston, Jan. 14, 1934, composer soloist). In the meantime, Gershwin composed his *Of Thee I Sing* (Dec. 26, 1931), an engaging and political satire; he also became engaged in his most ambitious and, what would be in time, his most important, undertaking: the composition of *Porgy and Bess*, an American opera in a folk manner, for black singers, after the book by Dubose Heyward. It was first staged in Boston on Sept. 30, 1935, and in New York on Oct. 10, 1935. Its reception by the press was not uniformly favorable, but its songs, and especially "Summertime," "I Got Plenty o' Nuthin'," "It Ain't Neccessarily So," and "Bess, You Is My Woman Now," rapidly attained great popularity. Gershwin's death (of a gliomatous cyst in the right temporal lobe of the brain) at the age of 38 was mourned as a great loss to American music. The 50th anniversary of his death brought forth a number of special tributes in 1987, including a major joint broadcast of his music by the PBS and BBC television networks. His stage works (all musical comedies with 1st N.Y. perf. unless otherwise given) comprised: *Half Past 8*, revue (Dec. 9, 1918); *La La Lucille* (May 26, 1919); *George White's Scandals of 1920*, revue (June 7, 1920); *A Dangerous Maid* (Atlantic City, N.J., March 21, 1921); *George White's Scandals of 1921*, revue (July 11, 1921); *Blue Monday*, opera (Aug. 28, 1922; retitled *135th Street*); *George White's Scandals of 1922*, revue (Aug. 28, 1922); *Our Nell* (Dec. 4, 1922); *The Rainbow*, revue (London, April 3, 1923); *George White's Scandals of 1923*, revue (June 18, 1923); *Sweet Little Devil* (Jan. 21, 1924); *George White's Scandals of 1924*, revue (June 30, 1924); *Primrose* (London, Sept. 11, 1924); *Lady, Be Good!* (Dec. 1, 1924); *Tell Me More* (April 13, 1925); *Tip-toes* (Dec. 28, 1925); *Song of the Flame*, operetta (Dec. 30, 1925); *Oh, Kay!* (Nov. 8, 1926); *Strike Up the Band* (Philadelphia, Sept. 5, 1927; rev. version, N.Y., Jan. 14, 1930); *Funny Face* (Nov. 22, 1927); *Rosalie* (Jan. 10, 1928); *Treasure Girl* (Nov. 8, 1928); *Show Girl* (July 2, 1929); *Girl Crazy* (Oct. 14, 1930); *Of Thee I Sing* (Dec. 26, 1931); *Pardon My English* (Jan. 20, 1933); *Let 'em Eat Cake* (Oct. 21, 1933); *Porgy and Bess*, folk opera (Boston, Sept. 30, 1935). He also wrote the film scores for *Delicious* (1931), *Shall We Dance?* (1937), *A Damsel in Distress* (1937), and *The Goldwyn Follies* (1938; completed by V. Duke), as well as many songs.

BIBL.: I. Goldberg, *G. G., A Study in American Music* (N.Y., 1931; 2d ed., rev., 1958); M. Armitage, ed., *G. G.* (N.Y., 1938); O. Levant, *A Smattering of Ignorance* (N.Y., 1938); D. Ewen, *A Journey to Greatness; G. G.* (N.Y., 1956; 2d ed., rev., 1970, as *G. G., His Journey to Greatness*); E. Jablonski and L. Stewart, *The G. Years* (Garden City, N.Y., 1958; 2d ed., rev., 1973); C. Schwartz, *G.: His Life and Music* (Indianapolis, 1973); idem, *G. G.: A Selective Bibliography and Discography* (Detroit, 1974); E. Jablonski; *G.: A Biography* (Garden City, N.Y., 1987); A. Kendall, *G. G.: A Biography* (N.Y., 1987); P. Kresh, *An American Rhapsody: The Story of G. G.* (N.Y., 1988); H. Alpert, *The Life and Times of Porgy and Bess: The Story of an American Classic* (N.Y., 1990); E. Jablonski, *G.* (Boston, 1990); D. Rosenberg, *Fascinating Rhythm: The Collaboration of G. and Ira G.* (N.Y., 1991); J. Peyser, *The Memory of All That: The Life of G. G.* (N.Y., 1993).

Gershwin (real name, **Gershvin**), **Ira,** greatly talented American librettist and lyricist, brother of **George Gershwin**; b. N.Y., Dec. 6, 1896; d. Beverly Hills, Aug. 17, 1983. He attended night classes at the College of the City of N.Y., wrote verses and humorous pieces for the school paper, and served as cashier in a Turkish bath of which his father was part owner. He began writing lyrics for shows in 1918, using the pseudonym Arthur Francis. His first full-fledged libretto was for the musical comedy *Be Yourself*, for which he used his own name for the first time. He achieved fame when he wrote the lyrics for his brother's musical comedy *Lady, Be Good!* (1924). He remained his brother's collaborator until George Gershwin's death in 1937, and his lyrics became an inalienable part of the whole, so that the brothers became artistic twins, like Gilbert and Sullivan, indissolubly united in some of the greatest productions of the musical theater in America: *Strike Up the Band* (1927), *Of Thee I Sing* (1931), and the culminating product of their brotherly genius, the folk opera *Porgy and Bess* (1935). Ira Gerschwin also wrote lyrics for other composers, among them Vernon Duke (*The Ziegfeld Follies of 1936*), Kurt Weill (*Lady in the Dark*, and several films), and Jerome Kern (the enormously successful song "Long Ago and Far Away" for the film *Cover Girl*). R. Kimball ed. *The Complete Lyrics of Ira Gershwin* (N.Y., 1993).

BIBL.: D. Rosenberg, *Fascinating Rhythm: The Collaboration of George and I. G.* (N.Y., 1991); P. Furia, *I. G.: The Art of the Lyricist* (Oxford, 1995).

Gerster, Etelka, noted Hungarian soprano; b. Kaschau, June 25, 1855; d. Pontecchio, near Bologna, Aug. 20, 1920. She studied with Mathilde Marchesi in Vienna, then made her debut in Venice as Gilda in *Rigoletto*, Jan. 8, 1876. Her great success resulted in engagements in Berlin and Budapest in Italian opera under the direction of Carlo Gardini. She married Gardini on April 16, 1877. She then continued her successful career, making her London debut on June 23, 1877, as Amina in *La Sonnambula*, and her U.S. debut in the same role on Nov. 11, 1878, at the N.Y. Academy of Music. She returned to London for 2 more seasons (1878–80), then sang again in New York from 1880 to 1883 and in 1887. After retiring, she taught singing in Berlin (1896–1917). She wrote the treatise *Stimmführer* (1906; 2d ed., 1908).

Gerster, Ottmar, German violinist, composer, and pedagogue; b. Braunfels, June 29, 1897; d. Leipzig, Aug. 31, 1969. He studied theory with Sekles at the Frankfurt am Main Cons. (1913–16); then studied violin with Adolf Rebner (1919–21). He played viola in string quartets (1923–27), and concurrently was concertmaster of the Frankfurt am Main Museumgesellschaft Orch. From 1927 to 1939 he taught violin and theory at the Folkwang-Schule in Essen; he then was on the faculty of the Hochschule für Musik in Weimar (1947–52) and in Leipzig (1952–62). His music is marked by melodious polyphony in a neoclassical vein; in his operas, he used folklike thematic material. He composed the operas *Madame Liselotte* (Essen, 1933), *Enoch Arden* (Düsseldorf, 1936), *Die Hexe von Passau* (Düsseldorf, 1941), *Das Verzauberte Ich*

(Wuppertal, 1949), and *Der fröhliche Sünder* (Weimar, 1963), and the ballet *Der ewige Kreis* (Duisburg, 1939).

BIBL.: O. Goldhammer, *O. G.* (Berlin, 1953); R. Malth, *O. G.: Leben und Werk* (Leipzig, 1988).

Gerville-Réache, Jeanne, French contralto; b. Orthez, March 26, 1882; d. N.Y., Jan. 5, 1915. She was a student of Rosine Laborde and Pauline Viardot-García in Paris, where she made her operatic debut as Orféo at the Opéra Comique in 1899. She continued to sing there until 1903, during which time she was chosen to create the role of Geneviève in *Pélleas et Mélisande* on April 30, 1902. In 1903–04 she appeared at Brussels's Théâtre Royal de la Monnaie, and then sang Orféo at London's Covent Garden in 1905. In 1907 she made her first appearance at the Manhattan Opera in New York as Cieca, and sang there until 1910. She then appeared in Chicago, Boston, Philadelphia, and Montreal. Among her other roles were Delilah, Clytemnestra, and Hérodiade.

Geszty (real name, **Witkowsky**), **Sylvia,** Hungarian soprano; b. Budapest, Feb. 28, 1934. She studied at the Budapest Cons. In 1959 she made her operatic debut at the Hungarian State Opera in Budapest and was a member of the Berlin State Opera (1961–70), the Berlin Komische Oper (1963–70), the Hamburg State Opera (1966–72; 1973), and the Württemberg State Theater in Stuttgart (from 1970). She sang the Queen of the Night at London's Covent Garden in 1966, and repeated the role at the Salzburg Festival in 1967; at the Munich Opera Festival she also sang Zerbinetta, a favorite soubrette role, which she chose for her Glyndebourne Festival debut in 1971. She made her North American debut as Sophie in *Der Rosenkavalier* with the N.Y. City Opera during its visit to Los Angeles on Nov. 19, 1973; she also appeared with the Berlin Städtische Oper, the Paris Opéra, La Scala in Milan, and the Teatro Colón in Buenos Aires, and in concerts and recitals.

Getty, Gordon, American composer; b. Los Angeles, Dec. 20, 1933. He was the scion of the billionaire oil executive and art collector Jean Paul Getty. In 1945 he was taken to San Francisco, where he studied English literature at San Francisco State College (graduated, 1956) and took courses at the San Francisco Cons. of Music. From his earliest attempts at composition, he proclaimed faith in the primacy of consonance and a revival of Romantic ideals. His preference lay with vocal music, and he possessed a natural gift for writing a fetching melodic line. He produced an opera, *Plump Jack*, based on the character of Shakespeare's Falstaff (excerpts only; San Francisco, March 13, 1985).

Ghedini, Giorgio Federico, Italian composer and pedagogue; b. Cuneo, July 11, 1892; d. Nervi, March 25, 1965. He studied piano and organ with Evasio Lovazzano, cello with S. Grossi, and composition with G. Cravero at the Turin Cons., then composition at the Liceo Musicale in Bologna with M. E. Bossi, graduating in 1911. He was prof. of harmony and composition at the conservatories in Turin (1918–37), Parma (1938–41), and Milan (from 1941), serving as director of the latter (1951–62). His works evolved from neoclassicism to more advanced contemporary techniques.

WORKS: DRAMATIC: OPERAS: *Gringoire* (1915); *Maria d'Alessandria* (Bergamo, Sept. 9, 1937); *Re Hassan* (Venice, Jan. 26, 1939); *La pulce d'oro* (Genoa, Feb. 15, 1940); *Le Baccanti* (Milan, Feb. 21, 1948); *Billy Budd*, after Melville (Venice, Sept. 7, 1949); *Lord Inferno*, "harmonious comedy" for radio, after Beerbohm's *The Happy Hypocrite* (RAI, Oct. 22, 1952; rev. version as *L'Ipocrita felice*, Milan, March 10, 1956); *La Via della Croce* (Venice, April 9, 1961). BALLET: *Girotondo*, mime play for children (Venice, 1959).

BIBL.: N. Castiglioni, *G. F. G* (Milan, 1955).

Gheluwe, Leon van, Belgian composer; b. Wanneghem-Lede, Sept. 15, 1837; d. Ghent, July 14, 1914. He studied in Ghent with Gevaert and others. He became a prof. at the Ghent Cons. (1869–71), and later was director of the École de Musique in Bruges (1871–1900). He wrote a Flemish opera, *Philippine van Vlaanderen* (Brussels, 1876).

Gheorghiu, Angela, admired Romanian soprano; b. Adjud, Sept. 7, 1965. She was a student of Mia Burbu at the George Enescu Lyceum in Bucharest, and then pursued training at the Bucharest Cons. (graduated, 1988). Following engagements in Romania, she made her first appearance at London's Covent Garden in 1992 as Zerlina. On Dec. 4, 1993, she made her Metropolitan Opera debut in New York as Mimi. She returned to Covent Garden in 1994 as Violetta. In 1995 she was engaged as Gounod's Juliette at the Washington (D.C.) Opera and Verdi's Desdemona at the Salzburg Festival. In 1996 she returned to the Metropolitan Opera as Micaëla, and that same year married **Roberto Alagna**. She sang again at Covent Garden in 1997 as Adina. Her return to the Metropolitan Opera in 1998 to sing Juliette to Alagna's Roméo elicited critical accolades. They reprised those roles at the Lyric Opera in Chicago in 1999. Among her other esteemed roles are Liù, Nina in Massenet's *Chérubin*, Suzel in *L'Amico Fritz*, and Magda in *La Rondine*.

Ghiaurov, Nicolai, outstanding Bulgarian bass; b. Lydjene, near Velingrad, Sept. 13, 1929. He was a student of Brambarov at the Sofia Cons., and then pursued his training at the Moscow Cons. (1950–55). After making his operatic debut as Don Basilio at the Moscow Opera Studio in 1955, he reprised that role for his Sofia debut in 1956. In 1957 he sang for the first time at the Paris Opéra, the Vienna State Opera, and at the Bolshoi Theater in Moscow, where he quickly established his reputation. In 1959 he made an impressive debut as Varlaam at Milan's La Scala, and in 1962 sang for the first time at London's Covent Garden as the Padre Guardino. In 1964 he made his first appearance at the Lyric Opera of Chicago as Gounod's Méphistophélès, which role he also chose for his Metropolitan Opera debut in New York on Nov. 8, 1965. In subsequent years, he appeared with most of the principal opera houses of Europe and North America, as well as at many of the leading festivals. Ghiaurov's remarkable vocal and dramatic gifts placed him among the foremost bassos of his day. His other roles included Don Giovanni, Pimen, Ramfis, Boris Godunov, Philip II, Massenet's Don Quichotte, and Boito's Mefistofele. In 1981 he married **Mirella Freni.**

Ghisi, Federico, Italian musicologist and composer; b. Shanghai, Feb. 25, 1901; d. Luzerna San Giovanni, July 18, 1975. His father was in the diplomatic corps in China. After the family settled in Italy in 1908, he studied harmony and counterpoint at the Milan Cons., and also piano privately with Faggioni; later he pursued training in chemistry at the Univ. of Pavia (graduated, 1923). While employed as a chemist, he took courses in composition with Ghedini at the Turin Cons. and in music history with Torrefranca at the Univ. of Florence (libera docenza, 1936). He then taught at the latter (1937–40), at the Università per Stranieri in Perugia (1945–74), and at the Univ. of Pisa (1963–70). Ghisi wrote many articles on Florence during the Renaissance era. Among his compositions were the operas *Il dono dei Re Magi* (1959) and *Il Vagabondo e la guardia* (1960), and the oratorio *L'ultima visione* (1967–72).

WRITINGS: *I canti carnascialeschi nelle fonti musicali del XV e XVI secolo* (Florence, 1937); *Le feste musicali della Firenze Medicea* (Florence, 1939); *Alle Fonti della Monodia: Nuovi brani della "Dafne" di J. Peri e "Il fuggilotio musicale" di G. Caccini* (Milan, 1940).

Ghislanzoni, Antonio, Italian writer and dramatic poet; b. Barco, near Lecco, Nov. 25, 1824; d. Caprino-Bergamasco, July 16, 1893. He was intended for the church, but his fine baritone voice led him to adopt the career of a stage singer (Lodi, 1846), which he speedily abandoned, however, for literary work. He became the manager of Italia Musicale, and was for years the ed. of the *Milan Gazzetta Musicale*, to which he remained a faithful contributor until his death. He wrote over 80 opera librettos, that of *Aida* being the most famous. He publ. *Reminiscenze artistiche* (contains an episode entitled *La casa di Verdi a Sant' Agata*).

Giacomelli, Geminiano, Italian composer; b. Piacenza, c.1692; d. Loreto, Jan. 25, 1740. He studied with Capelli at Parma, and wrote his first opera, *Ipermestra*, in 1724. It was the first of 19 operas he wrote for Venice, Parma, Naples, and other Italian towns; the most popular was *Cesare in Egitto* (Milan, 1735). He was maestro di cappella at the court of Parma and the Chiesa della Steccata from 1719 to 1727; he returned to both posts from 1732 to 1737; was maestro di cappella for the church of S. Giovanni in Piacenza from 1727 to 1732; he held a similar post at the Santa Casa in Loreto from 1738. His many church compositions include an oratorio, *La conversione di Santa Margherita*.

BIBL.: C. Anguisola, *G. G. e Sebastiano Nasolini, musicisti piacentini* (Piacenza, 1935).

Gialdini, Gialdino, Italian conductor and composer; b. Pescia, Nov. 10, 1843; d. there, March 6, 1919. He was a pupil of T. Mabellini in Florence. His first opera, *Rosamunda* (prize opera in a competition instituted by the Pergola Theater, Florence), given in 1868, was unsuccessful; after producing 2 "opere buffe," *La Secchia rapita* (Florence, 1872) and *L'Idolo cinese* (1874), in collaboration with other musicians, he devoted himself to conducting. Later he again turned to dramatic composition, producing the operas *I due soci* (Bologna, Feb. 24, 1892), *La Pupilla* (Trieste, Oct. 23, 1896), and *La Bufera* (Pola, Nov. 26, 1910). He also publ. *Eco della Lombardia*, a collection of 50 folk songs.

Gianettini (or **Zanettini**), **Antonio**, Italian organist and composer; b. Fano, 1648; d. Munich, July 12, 1721. He was organist at S. Marco, Venice (1677–86). He produced 3 operas in Venice, winning a reputation that led to his appointment as maestro di cappella at the court of Modena; he was organist at Modena from 1686 to 1721, except during 1695, when he brought out 3 operas in Hamburg. He moved to Munich with his family in 1721. He composed several operas, as well as 9 oratorios.

BIBL.: E. Luin, *A. G. e la musica a Modena alla fine del secolo 17* (Modena, 1931).

Giannini, Dusolina, American soprano, daughter of **Ferruccio** and sister of **Vittorio Giannini**; b. Philadelphia, Dec. 19, 1900; d. Zürich, June 26, 1986. She received early musical training at home, then studied voice with Sembrich in New York, where she made her concert debut on March 14, 1920. She made her operatic debut as Aida with the Hamburg Opera on Sept. 12, 1925, then sang in Berlin, Vienna, and London. She made her Metropolitan Opera debut in New York as Aida on Feb. 12, 1936, and remained on its roster until 1941; she also appeared with other American opera houses. She sang again in Europe (1947–50), then taught voice. Giannini created the role of Hester in her brother's *The Scarlet Letter* (Hamburg, June 2, 1938).

Giannini, Ferruccio, Italian-American tenor, father of **Dusolina** and **Vittorio Giannini**; b. Ponte d'Arnia, Nov. 15, 1868; d. Philadelphia, Sept. 17, 1948. He emigrated to the United States in 1885, and studied with Eleodoro De Campi in Detroit. He made his debut in Boston in 1891, then toured the United States with the Mapleson Opera Co. (1892–94); he made the first operatic recordings, which were issued by Emile Berliner in 1896. He later settled in Philadelphia, where he presented operas, concerts, and plays in his own theater.

Giannini, Vittorio, American composer and teacher, son of **Ferruccio** and brother of **Dusolina Giannini**; b. Philadelphia, Oct. 19, 1903; d. N.Y., Nov. 28, 1966. Brought up in a musical family, he showed a precocious talent. He was sent to Italy at the age of 10, and studied at the Milan Cons. (1913–17). After returning to the United States, he took private lessons with Martini and Trucco in New York; in 1925 he entered the Juilliard graduate school, where he was a pupil of Rubin Goldmark in composition and Hans Letz in violin; in 1932 he won the American Prix de Rome; he was in Rome for a period of 4 years. Upon his return to New York, he was appointed to the faculty of the Juilliard School of Music in 1939 as a teacher of composition and orchestration; in 1941 he also became an instructor in theory; furthermore, he was appointed prof. of composition at the Curtis Inst. of Music in Philadelphia in 1956. In 1965 became the 1st director of the North Carolina School of the Arts in Winston-Salem. As a composer, Giannini was at his best in opera, writing music of fine emotional éclat, excelling in the art of bel canto and avoiding extreme modernistic usages; in his symphonic works, he also continued the rich Italian tradition; these qualities endeared him to opera singers, but at the same time left his music out of the mainstream of contemporary music making.

WORKS: OPERAS: *Lucedia* (Munich, Oct. 20, 1934); *Not all Prima Donnas are Ladies* (n.d.); *The Scarlet Letter* (1937; Hamburg, June 2, 1938); *Flora* (1937); *Beauty and the Beast* (CBS, Nov. 24, 1938; stage premiere, Hartford, Conn., Feb. 14, 1946); *Blennerhasset* (CBS, Nov. 22, 1939); *Casanova* (n.d.); *The Taming of the Shrew* (1952; concert premiere, Cincinnati, Jan. 31, 1953; television premiere, NBC, March 13, 1954); *Christus* (1956); *The Harvest* (Chicago, Nov. 25, 1961); *Rehearsal Call* (1961; N.Y., Feb. 15, 1962); *The Servant of 2 Masters* (1966; N.Y., March 9, 1967); *Edipus Rex* (unfinished).

BIBL.: M. Mark, *The Life and Works of V. G. (1903–1966)* (diss., Catholic Univ. of America, 1970).

Giardini, Felice de', Italian violinist and composer; b. Turin, April 12, 1716; d. Moscow, June 8, 1796. He was a chorister at the Cathedral of Milan; studied singing and harpsichord with Paladini and violin with Somis in Turin. As a young man he played in various theater orchs. in Rome and Naples, often improvising cadenzas at the end of operatic numbers. He acquired popularity in Italy and made a tour in Germany (1748); he then went to London (1750), where he made a series of successful appearances as a concert violinist. In 1752 he joined the Italian opera in London as concertmaster; he became its impresario in 1755, and was connected with the management, with interruptions, for some 40 years. He was concertmaster at the Pantheon Concerts (1774–80). From 1784 to 1789 he was in Italy; he returned to London in 1790 and led 3 seasons of Italian opera. In 1796 he was engaged as a violinist in Russia and gave his initial concert in Moscow, on March 24, 1796, but soon became ill, and died shortly afterward. As a violinist, he was eclipsed in London by Salomon and Cramer, but he left his mark on musical society there. Among operas entirely by him were *Rosmira* (April 30, 1757), *Siroe* (Dec. 13, 1763), *Enea e Lavinia* (May 5, 1764), and *Il Re pastore* (March 7, 1765); he also wrote music for various pasticcios.

BIBL.: S. McVeigh, *The Violinist in London's Concert Life, 1750–1784: F. G. and His Contemporaries* (diss., Univ. of Oxford, 1980).

Giazotto, Remo, Italian musicologist; b. Rome, Sept. 4, 1910. He studied piano and composition at the Milan Cons. (1931–33), his principal mentors being Torrefranca, Pizzetti, and Paribeni; he also took courses in literature and philosophy at the Univ. of Genoa. In 1932 he joined the staff of the *Rivista Musicale Italiana*, serving as its ed. (1945–49), and later as coed. of the *Nuova Rivista Musicale Italiana* (from 1967); he also was a prof. of music history at the Univ. of Florence (1957–69). The popular *Adagio* for Strings and Organ frequently attributed to Albinoni is almost totally the work of Giazotto.

WRITINGS: *Il melodramma a Genova nel XVII e XVIII secolo* (Genoa, 1942); *Tomaso Albinoni, musico di violino, dilettante veneto* (Milan, 1945); *Busoni: La vita nell'opera* (Milan, 1948); *Poesia melodrammatica e pensiero critico nel Settecento* (Milan, 1952); *La musica a Genova nella vita pubblica e privata dal XIII al XVIII secolo* (Genoa, 1952); *La musica italiana a Londra negli anni di Purcell* (Rome, 1955); *Giovanni Battista Viotti* (Milan, 1956); *Musurgia nova* (Milan, 1959); *Vita di A. Stradella: Un "Orfeo assassinato"* (2 vols., Milan, 1962); *Vivaldi* (Milan, 1965); *Quattro secoli di storia dell'Accademia di Santa Cecilia* (2 vols., Milan, 1970); *Le due patri di Giulio Caccini, musico mediceo (1551–1618)* (Florence, 1984); *Puccini in Casa Puccini* (Lucca, 1992).

Gibbs, Cecil Armstrong, English composer; b. Great Braddow, near Chelmsford, Aug. 10, 1889; d. Chelmsford, May 12, 1960. He studied at Trinity College, Cambridge (B.A., 1911; Mus.B., 1913); took courses in composition with Charles Wood and Vaughan Williams and in conducting with Boult at the Royal College of

Music in London, where he also taught (1921–39). In 1934 he received the Cobbett Gold Medal for his services to British chamber music. His style adhered to the Romantic school; he was best known for his songs, many to texts by Walter De la Mare.

WORKS: DRAMATIC: *The Blue Peter*, comic opera (London, 1923); *The Sting of Love*, comic opera (1926); *When One Isn't There*, operetta (1927); *Twelfth Night*, opera (1946–47); *The Great Bell of Burley*, children's opera (1952); also incidental music.

Gibson, Sir Alexander (Drummond), distinguished Scottish conductor; b. Motherwell, Feb. 11, 1926; d. London, Jan. 14, 1995. He studied piano at the Royal Scottish Academy of Music in Glasgow, and also was a student in music at the Univ. of Glasgow; he then held a piano scholarship at the Royal College of Music in London, where he first studied conducting; he later received additional training in conducting from Markevitch at the Salzburg Mozarteum and from Kempen at the Accademia Musicale Chigiana in Siena. In 1951 he became a répétiteur and in 1952 a conductor at the Sadler's Wells Opera in London. After serving as assoc. conductor of the BBC Scottish Sym. Orch. in Glasgow (1952–54), he again conducted at the Sadler's Wells Opera (from 1954), where he later was music director (1957–59). In 1959 he made his first appearance at London's Covent Garden. From 1959 to 1984 he was principal conductor and artistic director of the Scottish National Orch. in Glasgow. In 1962 he founded Glasgow's Scottish Opera and was its artistic director until 1987. He also was principal guest conductor of the Houston Sym. Orch. (1981–83). In 1991 he became president of the Scottish Academy of Music and Drama in Glasgow. In 1967 he was made a Commander of the Order of the British Empire. He was knighted in 1977. Gibson was equally admired as an interpreter of the orch. and operatic repertoire.

Gideon, Miriam, American composer and teacher; b. Greeley, Colo., Oct. 23, 1906; d. N.Y., June 18, 1996. She studied piano in New York with Hans Barth and in Boston with Felix Fox, and pursued her education at Boston Univ. (B.A., 1926); later she took courses in musicology at Columbia Univ. (M.A., 1946) and in composition at the Jewish Theological Seminary of America (D.S.M., 1970), and also studied with Saminsky and Sessions. She taught at Brooklyn College (1944–54) and the City College of the City Univ. of N.Y. (1947–55; 1971–76); she also was an assoc. prof. of music at the Jewish Theological Seminary (from 1955) and a teacher at the Manhattan School of Music (from 1967). In 1975 she was elected to the National Inst. of Arts and Letters. Her music was distinguished by its attractive modernism. She composed the opera *Fortunato* (1958).

Giebel, Agnes, Dutch soprano of German descent; b. Heerlen, Aug. 10, 1921. She studied with Hilde Weselmann at the Folkwangschule in Essen. She began a career as a concert singer in 1947. She gained wide recognition for her radio broadcasts of the Bach cantatas over the RIAS in Berlin in 1950. At a later period, she promoted modern music; her performances of works by Schoenberg, Berg, Hindemith, and Henze were praised. She made several tours as a concert artist in the United States.

Gielen, Michael (Andreas), noted German conductor; b. Dresden, July 20, 1927. His father, Josef Gielen, was an opera director who settled in Buenos Aires in 1939; his uncle was **Eduard Steuermann**. Gielen studied piano and composition with Erwin Leuchter in Buenos Aires (1942–49). He was on the staff of the Teatro Colón there (1947–50), then continued his training with Polnauer in Vienna (1950–53). In 1951 he became a répétiteur at the Vienna State Opera, and later was its resident conductor (1954–60). He was principal conductor of the Royal Opera in Stockholm (1960–65), a regular conductor with the Cologne Radio Sym. Orch. (1965–69), and chief conductor of the Orchestre National de Belgique in Brussels (1968–73) and the Netherlands Opera in Amsterdam (1973–75). From 1977 to 1987 he was artistic director of the Frankfurt am Main Opera and chief conductor of its Museumgesellschaft concerts; he also was chief guest conductor of the BBC Sym. Orch. in London (1979–82) and music director of the Cincinnati Sym. Orch. (1980–86). In 1986 he became chief conductor of the South-West Radio Sym. Orch. in Baden-Baden; he also was prof. of conducting at the Salzburg Mozarteum (from 1987). Gielen has acquired a fine reputation as an interpreter of contemporary music; he has also composed a number of works of his own.

Gifford, Helen (Margaret), Australian composer; b. Hawthorn, Victoria, Sept, 5, 1935. She studied with Roy Shepherd (piano) and Dorian Le Gallienne (harmony) at the Univ. of Melbourne Conservatorium of Music (Mus.Bac., 1958). From 1970 to 1982 she was active as a composer for the Melbourne Theatre Co.; in 1974 she was also composer-in-residence of the Australian Opera in Sydney. Among her compositions are the operas *Jo Being* (1974), *Regarding Faustus* (1983), and *Iphigenia in Exile* (1985); also incidental music to plays.

Gigli, Beniamino, celebrated Italian tenor; b. Recanati, March 20, 1890; d. Rome, Nov. 30, 1957. He was a chorister at Recanati Cathedral; commenced serious vocal studies with Agnese Bonucci in Rome, and continued his training with Cotogni and Rosati as a scholarship student at the Liceo Musicale there. After winning 1st prize in the Parma competition in 1914, he made his operatic debut as Enzo in *La Gioconda* in Rovigo on Oct. 14, 1914; subsequently he sang in various Italian theaters, including Milan's La Scala in 1918 as Boito's Faust, a role he repeated in his Metropolitan Opera debut in New York on Nov. 16, 1920. He remained on the Metropolitan roster as one of its leading singers until 1932, then returned for the 1938–39 season. He made his Covent Garden debut in London as Andrea Chénier on May 27, 1930; he sang there again in 1931, 1938, and 1946. He spent the years during World War II in Italy; he then resumed his operatic appearances, making his farewell to the stage in 1953; however, he continued to give concerts, making a final, impressive tour of the United States in 1955. Gigli's voice, with its great beauty and expressivity, made him one of the foremost tenors of his era; he was famous for such roles as the Duke of Mantua, Nemorino, Lionel, Des Grieux, Nadir, and Gounod's Faust, as well as for the leading roles in Puccini's operas. His memoirs were publ. in an Eng. tr. in London in 1957.

BIBL.: R. Rosner, *B. G.* (Vienna, 1929); D. Silvestrini, *B. G.* (Bologna, 1937); R. Gigli, *B. G. mio padre: A cura di Celso Minestroni* (Parma, 1986).

Gilardi, Gilardo, Argentine composer; b. San Fernando, May 25, 1889; d. Buenos Aires, Jan. 16, 1963. He studied with Pablo Berutti, then devoted himself to teaching and composing. Two of his operas were premiered at the Teatro Colón in Buenos Aires: *Ilse* (July 13, 1923) and *La leyenda de Urutau* (Oct. 25, 1934).

Gilbert, Anthony (John), English composer and teacher; b. London, July 26, 1934. He studied composition with Milner, Goehr, and Seiber in London both privately and at Morley College (1958–63); he studied conducting at Morley with Del Mar (1967–69) and received training in composition from Nono and Berio at the Dartington Summer School (1961, 1962) and from Schuller, Shifrin, Carter, and Sessions at the Berkshire Music Center in Tanglewood (summer, 1967); he studied piano with Denis Holloway at London's Trinity College of Music and completed his training at the Univ. of Leeds (M.A., 1984; Mus.D., 1990). He taught at Goldsmiths' College, Univ. of London (1968–73); he served as composer-in-residence (1970–71) and visiting lecturer (1971–72) at the Univ. of Lancaster; then taught at Morley College (1971–74). In 1973 he joined the faculty of the Royal Northern College of Music in Manchester; in 1978–79 he also was senior lecturer in composition at the New South Wales State Conservatorium of Music in Sydney, and in 1981 was composer-in-the-community of Bendigo, Australia. A modernist by nature, Gilbert nevertheless writes music in Classical forms and is not averse to representational music; on the purely structural side, he adopts various attenuated forms of serial music, and in thematic development uses disparate agglutinative blocks. Among his numerous compositions are *The Scene Machine,* opera (1970; Kassel, April 1, 1971) and *The Chakravaka-bird,* radio opera (1977; BBC, Jan. 1982).

Gilbert, Henry F(ranklin Belknap), remarkable American composer; b. Somerville, Mass., Sept. 26, 1868; d. Cambridge, Mass., May 19, 1928. He studied at the New England Cons. of Music in Boston and with E. Mollenhauer; from 1889 to 1892 he was a pupil of MacDowell (composition) in Boston. Rather than do routine music work to earn his livelihood (he had previously been a violinist in theaters, etc.), he took jobs of many descriptions, becoming, in turn, a real estate agent, a factory foreman, and a collector of butterflies in Florida, and composed when opportunity afforded. In 1893, at the Chicago World's Fair, he met a Russian prince who knew Rimsky-Korsakov and gave him many details of contemporary Russian composers whose work, as well as that of Bohemian and Scandinavian composers which was based on folk song, influenced Gilbert greatly in his later composition. In 1894 he made his first trip abroad and stayed in Paris, subsequently returning to the United States; when he heard of the premiere of Charpentier's Louise, he became intensely interested in the work because of its popular character, and, in order to hear it, earned his passage to Paris, in 1901, by working on a cattle boat; the opera impressed him so much that he decided to devote his entire time thereafter to composition. In 1902 he became associated with Arthur Farwell, whose Wa-Wan Press publ. Gilbert's early compositions. From 1903 he employed Negro tunes and rhythms extensively in his works. The compositions of his mature period (from 1915) reveal an original style, not founded on any particular native American material but infused with elements from many sources, and are an attempt at "un-European" music, expressing the spirit of America and its national characteristics.

WORKS: DRAMATIC: OPERAS: *Uncle Remus* (c.1906; unfinished); *Fantasy in Delft* (1915–20). INCIDENTAL MUSIC TO: *Cathleen ni Houlihan* (1903); *Pot of Broth* (1903); *Riders to the Sea* (1904; rev. 1913; symphonic prologue, Peterboro, N.H., Aug. 20, 1914); *The Twisting of the Rope* (1904); *The Redskin, or The Last of his Race* (1906; not extant). PAGEANT: *Pilgrim Tercentenary Pageant* for Band (1921; orch. suite, 1921; Boston, March 31, 1922).

BIBL.: K. Longyear, *H. F. G.: His Life and Works* (diss., Univ. of Rochester, 1968).

Gilbert, Jean (real name, **Max Winterfeld**), German composer; b. Hamburg, Feb. 11, 1879; d. Buenos Aires, Dec. 20, 1942. He was trained in Kiel, Sondershausen, Weimar, and Berlin. In 1897 he began his career as a conductor at the Bremerhaven City Theater. Soon after, he went to Hamburg as conductor at the Carl-Schultze Theater. In 1900 he became conductor at the Centralhallen-Theater, where he brought out his first stage work, *Das Jungfernstift* or *Comtesse* (Feb. 8, 1901). After conducting in provincial music centers, he devoted himself to composing for the theater. He attained his first notable success with the musical comedy *Polnische Wirtschaft* (Cottbus, Dec. 26, 1909). Then followed an even greater success with *Die keusche Susanne* (Magdeburg, Feb. 26, 1910), which was subsequently performed throughout Germany, France, England, and Spain. In 1910 he went to Berlin, where he brought out *Autoliebchen* (March 16, 1912), *Puppchen* (Dec. 19, 1912), *Die Kino-Königen* (March 8, 1913; rev. version of *Die elfte Muse*, Hamburg, Nov. 22, 1912), and *Die Tango-Prinzessin* (Oct. 4, 1913). He also had success with *Fräulein Tralala* (Königsberg, Nov. 15, 1913). During World War I, he continued to compose numerous stage works, including the Berlin favorites *Die Fräulein von Amt* (Sept. 2, 1915), *Blondinchen* (March 4, 1916), *Die Fahrt ins Glück* (Sept. 2, 1916), *Das Vagabundenmädel* (Dec. 2, 1916), and *Die Dose seiner Majestät* (Sept. 1, 1917). Also notable were *Arizonda* (Vienna, Feb. 1, 1916) and *Eheurlaub* (Breslau, Aug. 1, 1918). With the War over, Gilbert had a tremendous success with *Die Frau im Hermelin* (Berlin, Aug. 23, 1919) and *Katja, die Tänzerin* (Vienna, Jan. 5, 1922). Subsequent works included *Dorine und der Zufall* (Berlin, Sept. 15, 1922), *Die kleine Sünderin* (Berlin, Oct. 1, 1922), *Das Weib im Purpur* (Vienna, Dec. 21, 1923), *Geliebte seiner Hoheit* (Berlin, Sept. 24, 1924), *Uschi* (Hamburg, Jan. 24, 1925; later used in the pasticcio *Yvonne*, London, May 22, 1926), *Annemarie* (Berlin, July 2, 1915), and *Hotel Stadt Lemberg* (Hamburg, July 1, 1929). After the Nazis came to power in Germany in 1933, Gilbert lived in several European cities before emigrating to Buenos Aires in 1939. His son, Robert Gilbert (real name, David Robert Winterfeld; b. Berlin, Sept. 29, 1899; d. Minusio, March 20, 1978), was a librettist, lyricist, and composer. He collaborated with his father on several scores and also wrote many of his own. However, he became best known for his German-language adaptations of such American musicals as *Annie Get Your Gun* (1956), *My Fair Lady* (1961), *Hello, Dolly!* (1966), and *Man of La Mancha* (1968).

Gilbert, Pia, spirited German-born American composer and pedagogue; b. Kippenheim, June 1, 1921. She began her career as a dance accompanist in the N.Y. studios of Lotte Goslar, Doris Humphreys, and Martha Graham; then found her niche as a composer for dance and theater. She served in various capacities during her lengthy tenure as prof. in the dance dept. at the Univ. of Calif., Los Angeles (1947–85), including resident composer and music director of its dance company; in 1986 she joined the music faculty at the Juilliard School in New York. As a teacher, Gilbert is distinguished by her commitment to the musical literacy of dancers, as well as for her interdisciplinary approach. Her compositions, whether for dance, theater, or simply "music per se," are always subtly dramatic, and a certain sly humor invades several of her vocal works; *Vociano*, first performed by Jan DeGaetani at the 1978 Aspen (Colo.) Music Festival, is pleasing for its use of imaginary languages, and her later chamber opera, *Dialects* (1990–91; Bonn, May 21, 1991), is a modern-day recreation of the most playful of Futurist ideals. With A. Lockhart, she publ. *Music for the Modern Dance* (1961).

WORKS: DRAMATIC: CHAMBER OPERA: *Dialects* (1990–91; Bonn, May 21, 1991). DANCE: *In 2s It's Love* (1949); *Songs of Innocence and Experience* (1952); *Trio* for Piano, Dancer, and Lights (1956); *Valse* for Lotte Goslar (1959); *Bridge of the 7th Moon* (1960); *Freke-Phreec-Freake-Phreaque-Freak* (1969); *Irving, the Terrific* (1971); *Requiem for Jimmy Dean* (1972); *Legend* (1985). THEATER (all 1st perf. by the Mark Taper Forum Theatre Group, Los Angeles): *The Deputy*, after R. Hochhuth (1966); *Murderous Angels*, after C. C. O'Brien (1970); *Tales from Hollywood*, after C. Hampton (1982).

Gilibert, Charles, French baritone; b. Paris, Nov. 29, 1866; d. N.Y., Oct. 11, 1910. He studied at the Paris Cons. After making his operatic debut at the Paris Opéra Comique in 1888, he sang in Brussels at the Théâtre Royal de la Monnaie (from 1889) and at London's Covent Garden (1894–1909). On Nov. 9, 1900, he made his debut with the Metropolitan Opera as Schaunard during the company's visit to Los Angeles. His formal debut with the company in New York followed on Dec. 18, 1900, as the Duke of Verona, and he remained with the company until 1903. He then appeared at the Manhattan Opera House (1906–10). Among his other roles were Mozart's and Rossini's Bartolo, Masetto, Don Pasquale, and Monterone.

Gillis, Don, American composer; b. Cameron, Mo., June 17, 1912; d. Columbia, S.C., Jan. 10, 1978. He was educated at Texas Christian Univ. (graduated, 1936) and at North Texas State Univ. (M.M., 1943). In 1943 he joined NBC in Chicago, and then worked for the network in New York (1944–54), mainly as a producer. In 1967–68 he was chairman of the music dept. at Southern Methodist Univ.; after serving as chairman of fine arts and director of media instruction at Dallas Baptist College (1968–72), he was composer-in-residence and director of the inst. for media arts at the Univ. of South Carolina (from 1973). His compositions, clothed in a conservative garb, were often enlivened by a whimsical bent.

WORKS: DRAMATIC: OPERAS: *The Park Avenue Kids* (Elkhart, Ind., May 12, 1957); *Pep Rally* (Interlochen, Mich., Aug. 15, 1957); *The Libretto* (1958; Norman, Okla., Dec. 1, 1961); *The Legend of Star Valley Junction* (1961–62; N.Y., Jan. 7, 1969); *The Gift of the Magi* (Forth Worth, Texas, Dec. 7, 1965); *World Premiere* (1966–

67); *The Nazarene* (1967–68); *Behold the Man* (1973); also ballets.

Gilly, Dinh, French baritone; b. Algiers, July 19, 1877; d. London, May 19, 1940. He studied at the Toulouse Cons. and with Cotogni in Rome; after completing his studies at the Paris Cons., he made his debut as the Priest in *Sigurd* at the Paris Opéra in 1899; continued to sing there until 1908. On Nov. 16, 1909, he made his debut with the Metropolitan Opera in New York at the New Theatre as Albert in *Werther*; his formal debut at the Metropolitan Opera was as Alfio in *Cavalleria rusticana* on Nov. 24, 1909, and remained on its roster until 1914; he first appeared at London's Covent Garden as Amonasro in *Aida* on May 15, 1911; he sang there until 1914 and again from 1919 to 1924. He also made appearances with the Beecham, Carl Rosa, and British National Opera companies. He made London his home and was active in later years as a teacher; among his pupils was John Brownlee.

Gilman, Lawrence, American music critic; b. Flushing, N.Y., July 5, 1878; d. Franconia, N.H., Sept. 8, 1939. He was self-taught in music. From 1901 to 1913 he was music critic of *Harper's Weekly*; from 1915 to 1923, music, dramatic, and literary critic of the *North American Review*; from 1921 to 1939 he was author of the program notes of the N.Y. Phil. and Philadelphia Orch. concerts; from 1923 to 1939 he was music critic of the *N.Y. Herald Tribune*. He was a member of the National Inst. of Arts and Letters. Among his writings are *Aspects of Modern Opera* (1909) and *Wagner's Operas* (1937).

Gilse, Jan van, Dutch conductor and composer; b. Rotterdam, May 11, 1881; d. Oegstgeest, near Leiden, Sept. 8, 1944. He studied with Wüllner at the Cologne Cons. (1897–1902) and with Humperdinck in Berlin (1902–03). He was a conductor of the Bremen Opera (1905–08) and of the Dutch Opera at Amsterdam (1908–09); he was music director of the City of Utrecht (1917–22). He lived again in Berlin (1922–33); then was director of the Utrecht Cons. (1933–37). His music is heavily imbued with German Romanticism. Among his works are the operas *Frau Helga von Stavern* (1911) and Thijl (1938–40; 1st complete perf., Amsterdam, Sept. 21, 1976; also a symphonic extract, *Funeral Music*, 1940).

Gilson, Paul, notable Belgian composer, pedagogue, and writer on music; b. Brussels, June 15, 1865; d. there, April 3, 1942. He studied with Auguste Cantillon (theory) and Charles Duyck (harmony) before pursuing his training at the Brussels Cons. (1887–89) with Gevaert (composition), where he won the Belgian Prix de Rome with his cantata *Sinai* (1889). His orch. work *La mer* (1892) placed him in the forefront of Belgian musical life. During the following decade, he composed his finest scores before concentrating on teaching and writing. He was prof. of harmony at the Brussels Cons. (1899–1909) and the Antwerp Cons. (1904–09), and then was inspector of music education in the Belgian schools (1909–30). He was music critic of *Le Soir* (1906–14), *Le Diapason* (1910–14), and of *Midi*. In 1925 a group of his students formed the Synthetistes to carry on his ideals, which led to the founding of the journal *Revue Musicale Belge*. Gilson's compositions reflect the considerable gifts of a traditionalist.

WRITINGS (all publ. in Brussels unless otherwise given): *Le tutti orchestral* (1913); *Traité d'harmonie* (1919); *Quintes, octaves, secondes et polytonie* (1921); *Manuel de musique militaire* (Antwerp, 1926); *Notes de musique et souvenirs* (1942).

WORKS: DRAMATIC: OPERAS: *Le démon* (1890; Mons, April 9, 1893); *Prinses Zonneschijn* (Antwerp, Oct. 10, 1903; as *La princesse Rayon de Soleil*, Brussels, Sept. 9, 1905); *Gens de mer* (Antwerp, Oct. 15, 1904; in French, Brussels, Dec. 16, 1929); *Rooversliefde* (Antwerp, Jan. 30, 1910). BALLETS: *La captive* (1896–1900); *Les deux bossus* (1910–21).

BIBL.: G. Brenta, *P. G.* (Brussels, 1965).

Giménez (Jiménez) (y Bellido), Jerônimo, Spanish conductor and composer; b. Seville, Oct. 10, 1854; d. Madrid, Feb. 19, 1923. He studied with Alard, Savard, and A. Thomas at the Paris Cons. He was conductor of the Sociedad de Conciertos in Madrid. He wrote over 100 zarzuelas.

Gimenez, Raul, Argentine tenor; b. Santa Fe, Sept. 14, 1950. He received training in Buenos Aires. Following his operatic debut there in 1980 at the Teatro Colón as Ernesto, he appeared in concert and opera in various South American music centers. In 1984 he made his European debut at the Wexford Festival as Filandro in Cimarosa's *La astuzie femminili*, and subsequently sang in Paris, Venice, Pesaro, Amsterdam, Rome, Aix-en-Provence, Zürich, and Geneva. He made his U.S. debut as Ernesto in Dallas in 1989, choosing that role for his first appearance at London's Covent Garden in 1990. He sang Rossini's Count Almaviva at his debut at the Vienna State Opera in 1990. In 1993 he sang for the first time at Milan's La Scala in *Tancredi*. In 1994 he portrayed Rossini's Don Ramiro in Dallas. Gimenez is highly regarded for his roles in Rossini operas, among them Almaviva, Argiro, Rodrigo, Count Alberto, Giocondo, and Florville.

Ginastera, Alberto (Evaristo), greatly talented Argentine composer; b. Buenos Aires, April 11, 1916; d. Geneva, June 25, 1983. He was of Catalan-Italian descent. He took private lessons in music as a child; he then entered the National Cons. of Music in Buenos Aires, where he studied composition with José Gil, Athos Palma, and José André; he also took piano lessons with Argenziani. He began to compose in his early youth; in 1934 he won 1st prize of the musical society El Únisono for his *Piezas infantiles* for Piano. His next piece of importance was *Impresiones de la Puna* for Flute and String Quartet, in which he made use of native Argentine melodies and rhythms; he discarded it, however, as immature; he withdrew a number of his other works, some of them of certain value, for instance, his *Concierto argentino*, which he wrote in 1935, and *Sinfonia Porteña*, his 1st Sym. (which may be identical in its musical material with *Estancia*). Also withdrawn was his 2d Sym., the *Sinfonía elegíaca*, written in 1944, even though it was successfully performed. In 1946–47 Ginastera traveled to the United States on a Guggenheim fellowship. Returning to Argentina, he served as director of the Cons. of the province of Buenos Aires in La Plata (1948–52; 1956–58); he then taught at the Argentine Catholic Univ. and also was a prof. at the Univ. of La Plata. In 1968 he left Argentina and lived mostly in Geneva. From his earliest steps in composition, Ginastera had an almost amorous attachment for the melodic and rhythmic resources of Argentine folk music, and he evolved a fine harmonic and contrapuntal setting congenial with native patterns. His first significant work in the Argentine national idiom was *Panambí*, a ballet, composed in 1935 and performed at the Teatro Colón in Buenos Aires on July 12, 1940. There followed a group of *Danzas argentinas* for Piano, written in 1937; in 1938 he wrote 3 songs; the first one, *Canción al árbol del olvido*, is a fine evocation of youthful love; it became quite popular. In 1941 he was commissioned to write a ballet for the American Ballet Caravan, to be called *Estancia*; the music was inspired by the rustic scenes of the pampas; a suite from the score was performed at the Teatro Colón on May 12, 1943, and the complete work was brought out there on Aug. 19, 1952. A series of works inspired by native scenes and written for various instrumental combinations followed, all infused with Ginastera's poetic imagination and brought to realization with excellent technical skill. Soon, however, he began to search for new methods of musical expression, marked by modern and sometimes strikingly dissonant combinations of sound, fermented by asymmetrical rhythms. Of these works, one of the most remarkable is *Cantata para América Mágica*, scored for dramatic soprano and percussion instruments, to apocryphal pre-Columbian texts, freely arranged by Ginastera; it was first performed in Washington, D.C., on April 30, 1961, with excellent success. An entirely new development in Ginastera's evolution as composer came with his first opera, *Don Rodrigo* (1964), produced on July 24, 1964, at the Teatro Colón. In it he followed the general formula of Berg's *Wozzeck* in its use of classical instrumental forms, such as rondo, suite, scherzo, and canonic progressions; he also introduced *Sprechstimme*. In 1964 he wrote the *Cantata Bomarzo* on a commission from the Elizabeth Sprague Coolidge Foundation in Washington, D.C. He used the same libretto by Manuel Mujica Láinez in his opera *Bomarzo*, which created a sensation at its production in Washington, D. C., on May 19, 1967, by its unrestrained spectacle of sexual violence. It was announced for performance at the Teatro Colón on Aug. 9, 1967, but was canceled at the order of the Argentine government because of its alleged immoral nature. The score of *Bomarzo* reveals extraordinary innovations in serial techniques, with thematical employment not only of different chromatic sounds, but also of serial progressions of different intervals. His last opera, *Beatrix Cenci*, commissioned by the Opera Soc. of Washington, D.C., and produced there on Sept. 10, 1971, concluded his operatic trilogy. Among instrumental works of Ginastera's last period, the most remarkable was his 2d Piano Concerto (1972), based on a tone-row derived from the famous dissonant opening of the finale of Beethoven's 9th Sym.; the 2d movement of the concerto is written for the left hand alone. He was married to the pianist Mercedes de Toro in 1941. After their divorce in 1965, Ginastera married the Argentine cellist Aurora Natola, for whom he wrote the Cello Sonata, which she played in New York on Dec. 13, 1979, and his 2d Cello Concerto, which she performed in Buenos Aires on July 6, 1981.

WORKS: DRAMATIC: OPERAS: *Don Rodrigo* (1963–64; Buenos Aires, July 24, 1964); *Bomarzo* (1966–67; Washington, D.C., May 19, 1967); *Beatrix Cenci* (Washington, D.C., Sept. 10, 1971). BALLETS: *Panambí* (1935; suite, Buenos Aires, Nov. 27, 1937; 1st complete perf., Buenos Aires, July 12, 1940); *Estancia* (1941; Buenos Aires, Aug. 19, 1952). Also film music.

BIBL.: P. Suárez Urtubey, *A. G.* (Buenos Aires, 1967); *A. G.: A Catalogue of His Published Works* (London, 1976); F. Spangemacher, ed., *A. G.* (Bonn, 1984).

Giordani, Giuseppe, Italian composer, called **Giordanello**; b. Naples, Dec. 9, 1743; d. Fermo, Jan. 4, 1798. He studied with Fenaroli at the S. Loreto Cons., Naples, where Cimarosa and Zingarelli were fellow students. His 2d opera, *Epponina*, was given in Florence in 1779. He continued to write operas for various Italian towns, but they were not outstanding, and few of the 30-odd he wrote have survived. He also wrote several oratorios and church music. From 1791 until his death he was maestro di cappella at the Fermo Cathedral. He is sometimes credited with *Il bacio* and other operas and works produced in London by Tommaso Giordani; Giuseppe was not related to Tommaso, and never left Italy. The famous song "Caro mio ben," popularized in London by Pacchierotti, was probably written by Giuseppe.

Giordani, Tommaso, Italian composer; b. Naples, c.1730; d. Dublin, Feb. 23 or 24, 1806. His family formed a strolling opera company, with the father as impresario and singer and the rest of the family, except Tommaso, as singers. Tommaso was probably a member of the orch. and the arranger of music. They left Naples about 1745 and moved northward, appearing in Italian towns, then in Graz (1748), Frankfurt am Main (1750), Amsterdam (1752), and Covent Garden, London (Dec. 17, 1753); they returned in 1756, at which time Tommaso first appeared as a composer, with his comic opera *La Comediante fatta cantatrice* (Covent Garden, Jan. 12, 1756). The Giordani company next went to Dublin, appearing there in 1764; Tommaso continued to be active both in Dublin and in London. He was conductor and composer at the King's Theatre, London, in 1769 and many following seasons, and in Dublin, where he lived after 1783, was conductor and composer at the Smock Alley and Crow St. theaters; he also taught piano. In 1794 he was elected president of the Irish music fund. He played an important part in Irish music circles, and wrote altogether more than 50 English and Italian operas, including pasticcios and adaptations. The most notable were *L'Eroe cinese* (Dublin, 1766), *Il Padre e il figlio rivali* (London, 1770), *Artaserse* (London, 1772), *Il Re pastore* (London, 1778), and *Il bacio* (London, 1782). He also wrote several cantatas, including *Aci e Galatea* (London, 1777), and an oratorio, *Isaac* (Dublin, 1767).

Giordano, Umberto, noted Italian composer; b. Foggia, Aug. 28, 1867; d. Milan, Nov. 12, 1948. He studied with Gaetano Briganti at Foggia, and then with Paolo Serrao at the Naples Cons. (1881–90). His first composition performed in public was a symphonic poem, *Delizia* (1886); he then wrote some instrumental music. In 1888 he submitted a short opera, *Marina*, for the competition established by the publisher Sonzogno; Mascagni's *Cavalleria rusticana* received 1st prize, but *Marina* was cited for distinction. Giordano then wrote the opera *Mala vita*, which was performed in Rome, Feb. 21, 1892; it was only partly successful; it was then revised and presented under the title *Il voto in Milan* (Nov. 10, 1897). There followed the opera *Regina Diaz* (Rome, Feb. 21, 1894), which obtained a moderate success. Then he set to work on a grand opera, *Andrea Chénier*; its premiere at La Scala in Milan (March 28, 1896) was a spectacular success and established Giordano as one of the best composers of Italian opera of the day. The dramatic subject gave Giordano a fine opportunity to display his theatrical talent, but the score also revealed his gift for lyric expression. Almost as successful was his next opera, *Fedora* (Teatro Lirico, Milan, Nov. 17, 1898), but it failed to hold a place in the world repertoire after the initial acclaim; there followed *Siberia* (La Scala, Dec. 19, 1903; rev. 1921; La Scala, Dec. 5, 1927). Two short operas, *Marcella* (Milan, Nov. 9, 1907) and *Mese Mariano* (Palermo, March 17, 1910), were hardly noticed and seemed to mark a decline in Giordano's dramatic gift; however, he recaptured public attention with *Madame Sans-Gêne*, produced at a gala premiere at the Metropolitan Opera in New York on Jan. 25, 1915, conducted by Toscanini, with Geraldine Farrar singing the title role. With Franchetti, he wrote *Giove a Pompei* (Rome, July 5, 1921); he then produced *La cena delle beffe*, which was his last signal accomplishment; it was staged at La Scala, Dec. 20, 1924. He wrote 1 more opera, *Il Re* (La Scala, Jan. 10, 1929). During his lifetime, Giordano received many honors, and was elected a member of the Accademia Luigi Cherubini in Florence and of several other institutions. Although not measuring up to Puccini in musical qualities or to Mascagni in dramatic skill, Giordano was a distinguished figure in the Italian opera field for some 4 decades.

BIBL.: G. Paribeni, *Madame Sans-Gêne di U. G.* (Milan, 1923); D. Cellamare, *U. G.: La vita e le opere* (Milan, 1949); R. Giazotto, *U. G.* (Milan, 1949); G. Confalonieri, *U. G.* (Milan, 1958); D. Cellamare, *U. G.* (Rome, 1967); M. Morini, ed., *U. G.* (Milan, 1968).

Giorza, Paolo, Italian composer; b. Milan, Nov. 11, 1832; d. Seattle, May 5, 1914. He was especially known for his ballet music, his ballets numbering more than 70 ballets; also 2 operas. He lived in New York, London, and San Francisco. In 1906 he settled in Seattle.

Giraldoni, Eugenio, notable Italian baritone; b. Marseilles, May 20, 1871; d. Helsinki, June 23, 1924. He was the son of **Leone Giraldoni** and **Carolina Ferni-Geraldoni**. He received his training from his mother. In 1891 he made his operatic debut as Escamillo in Barcelona, and then sang in various Italian music centers, including Milan's La Scala and Rome's Teatro Costanzi; at the latter he created the role of Scarpia on Jan. 14, 1900. On Nov. 28, 1904, he made his Metropolitan Opera debut in New York as Barnaba, singing there for a season; he then pursued his career in Europe and South America. Among his other roles of distinction were Amonasro, Valentin, Boris Godunov, Rigoletto, and Gérard.

Giraldoni, Leone, Italian baritone and pedagogue, father of **Eugenio Giraldoni**; b. Paris, 1824; d. Moscow, Oct. 1, 1897. He was a student of Ronzi in Florence. After making his operatic debut in Lodi in 1847, he sang in various Italian opera houses until his retirement in 1885. He then taught voice in his homeland, and later at the Moscow Cons. (from 1891). He created Verdi's Simon Boccanegra (Venice, March 12, 1857) and Renato (Rome, Feb. 17, 1859), and Donizetti's Duca d'Alba (Rome, March 22, 1882). His wife was **Carolina Ferni-Giraldoni**. He publ. *Guida teorico-practico ad uso dell'artista cantante* (Bologna, 1864).

Girardi, Alexander, famous Austrian tenor and actor; b. Graz, Dec. 5, 1850; d. Vienna, April 20, 1918. He made his stage debut at the Kurtheater in Rohitsch-Sauerbrunn in 1869. After appearing in Krems, Karlsbad, Ischl, and Salzburg, he went to Vienna in 1870 and joined the Strampfertheater. In 1874 he became a member of the Theater an der Wien, acquiring renown in 1881 when he created the role of Marchese Sebastiani in Johann Strauss's *Der lustige Krieg*. In 1882 he had enormous success when he created the title role in Millöcker's *Der Bettelstudent*. After creating the role of Kálmán Zsupán in Strauss's *Der Zigeunerbaron* in 1885, he scored a resounding success in 1890 when he created the title role of Jonathan in Millöcker's *Der arme Jonathan*. Further acclaim came when he created the title role of Adam in Zeller's *Der Vogelhändler* in 1891. In 1894 he joined the Carltheater. In 1896 he became a member of the Deutsches Volkstheater, where he was active as an actor. From 1899 he was once more a favorite on the musical stages of Vienna. In 1902 he rejoined the Theater an der Wien, where he had triumphs creating the title roles in Eysler's *Bruder Straubinger* (1903) and *Pufferl* (1905). Returning to the Carltheater, his success continued as he created roles in Eysler's *Die Schützenliesel* (1905) and *Künstlerblut* (1906). In 1907 he went to Berlin as a member of the Thalia-Theater. In 1909 he returned to Vienna and joined the Raimundtheater. His last great success came at the Johann Strauss-Theater in 1912 when he created the role of Pali Rácz in Kálmán's *Der Zigeunerprimas*. Girardi continued to make appearances until the end of his life, being duly recognized as the foremost singer of the golden era of Vienna operetta. He is honored in Graz with a street named after him and in Vienna by the Girardigasse near the Theater an der Wien.

BIBL.: K. Nowak, *G.* (Berlin, 1908); A. Wutzky, *G.* (Vienna, 1943).

Giraud, Fiorello, Italian tenor; b. Parma, Oct. 22, 1870; d. there, March 29, 1928. He was the son of the tenor Lodovico Giraud (1846–82). He studied with Babacini in Parma. He made his debut as Lohengrin in 1891 in Vercelli; he then sang in Barcelona, Lisbon, and South America, and at La Scala in Milan. He created the role of Canio in Leoncavallo's *Pagliacci* (Milan, May 21, 1892). He was a fine interpreter of other verismo roles.

Giraudet, Alfred-Auguste, French bass and pedagogue; b. Etampes, March 29, 1845; d. N.Y., Oct. 17, 1911. He studied with Delsarte, making his operatic debut at the Théâtre-Lyrique in Paris as Méphistophélès (1868). He then sang at the Théâtre-Italien, the Opéra Comique, and the Opéra. In 1883 he retired from the stage and devoted himself to teaching. He eventually settled in New York.

Girdlestone, Cuthbert (Morton), English music scholar; b. Bovey-Tracey, Sept. 17, 1895; d. St. Cloud, France, Dec. 10, 1975. He was educated at the Sorbonne (licence ès lettres, 1915) and the Schola Cantorum in Paris; then entered Trinity College, Cambridge. He became a lecturer at Cambridge in 1922; from 1926 to 1960 he was prof. of French at the Univ. of Durham, Newcastle division (later the Univ. of Newcastle upon Tyne). He publ. a valuable analysis of Mozart's piano concertos, *Mozart et ses concertos pour piano* (Paris, 1939; Eng. tr., 1948; 2d ed., 1964); also the important monograph *Jean-Philippe Rameau: His Life and Work* (London, 1957; 2d ed., rev., 1969). He further wrote *La Tragédie en musique (1673–1750) considérée comme genre littéraire* (Paris, 1972).

BIBL.: N. Suckling, ed., *Essays Presented to C. M. G.* (Newcastle upon Tyne, 1960).

Giro, Manuel, Spanish composer; b. Lérida, Catalonia, Sept. 5, 1848; d. Barcelona, Dec. 20, 1916. He studied organ and composition at the cathedral school in Lérida and later in Barcelona and Paris. In 1884 he settled in Barcelona, where in 1885 he brought out his opera *Il rinegato Alonso García*, which proved a popular success. Another opera, *El sombrero de tres picos* (Madrid, 1893), was also well received. He further wrote ballets.

Giteck, Janice, American composer and pianist; b. N.Y., June 27, 1946. She studied with Milhaud and Subotnick at Mills College in Oakland, California (B.A., 1968; M.A., 1969), and with Messiaen at the Paris Cons. (1969–70). She also studied electronic music with Lowell Cross and Anthony Gnazzo, Javanese gamelan with Daniel Schmidt, and West African drumming with Obo Addy. From 1979 she taught at the Cornish Inst. in Seattle. Her compositions, variously scored, reflect interest in the language and lore of American Indians; her best-known work is the ceremonial opera *A'agita* (orig. and sacrilegiously entitled *Wi'igita*) for 3 Singing Actors, Dancing Actor, and 8 Instrumentalists/Actors (1976), based on the legends and mythologies of the Pima and Papago, a native American tribe living in southwestern Arizona and Mexico. She also composed *Messalina*, mini-opera for Man's Voice, Cello, and Piano (1973), *Thunder, Like a White Bear Dancing*, ritual performance for Soprano, Flute, Piano, Hand Percussion, and Slide Projections, after the *Mide Picture Songs of the Ojibwa Indians* (1977), and *Callin' Home Coyote*, burlesque for Tenor, Steel Drums, and String Bass (1977).

Giuglini, Antonio, Italian tenor; b. Fano, 1827; d. Pesaro, Oct. 12, 1865. He studied with Cellini, making his debut in Fermo. He was highly successful in London when he sang at Her Majesty's Theatre in 1857; he also sang at Drury Lane and the Lyceum there. In 1865 he was in St. Petersburg, where he displayed symptoms of mental aberrations. Upon his return to London, he was committed to an asylum; in the same year he was taken to Pesaro, where he died.

Giulini, Carlo Maria, eminent Italian conductor; b. Barletta, May 9, 1914. He began to study the violin as a boy; at 16 he entered the Cons. di Musica di Santa Cecilia in Rome, where he studied violin and viola with Remy Principe, composition with Alessandro Bustini, and conducting with Bernardino Molinari; he also received instruction in conducting from Casella at the Accademia Musicale Chigiana in Siena. He then joined the Augusteo Orch. in Rome in the viola section. He was drafted into the Italian army during World War II, but went into hiding as a convinced anti-Fascist; after the liberation of Rome by the Allied troops in 1944, he was engaged to conduct the Augusteo Orch. in a special concert celebrating the occasion. He then became assistant conductor of the RAI Orch. in Rome, and was made its chief conductor in 1946. In 1950 he helped to organize the RAI Orch. in Milan; in 1952 he conducted at Milan's La Scala as an assistant to Victor de Sabata; in 1954 he became principal conductor there; his performance of *La Traviata*, with Maria Callas in the title role, was particularly notable. In 1955 he conducted Verdi's *Falstaff* at the Edinburgh Festival, earning great praise. On Nov. 3, 1955, he was a guest conductor with the Chicago Sym. Orch. and later was its principal guest conductor (1969–72); during its European tour of 1971, he was joint conductor with Sir Georg Solti. From 1973 to 1976 he was principal conductor of the Vienna Sym. Orch., and in 1975 he took it on a world tour. On Oct. 24, 1975, he led it at a televised concert from the United Nations in New York. In 1978 he succeeded Zubin Mehta as music director of the Los Angeles Phil., and succeeded in maintaining it at a zenith of orchestral brilliance until 1984. His conducting style embodies the best traditions of the Italian school as exemplified by Toscanini, but is free from explosive displays of temper. He is above all a Romantic conductor who can identify his musical *Weltanschauung* with the musical essence of Mozart, Beethoven, Schubert, Schumann, Brahms, Bruckner, Verdi, and Mahler; he leads the classics with an almost abstract contemplation. In the music of the 20th century, he gives congenial interpretations of works by Debussy, Ravel, and Stravinsky; the expressionist school of composers lies outside of his deeply felt musicality, and he does not actively promote the experimental school of modern music. His behavior on the podium is free from self-assertive theatrics, and he treats the orch. as comrades-in-arms, associates in the cause of music, rather than subordinate performers of the task assigned to them. Yet his personal feeling for music is not disguised; often he closes his eyes in fervent self-absorption when conducting without score the great Classical and Romantic works.

BIBL.: A. Foletto, *C. M. G.* (Milan, 1997).

Glanville-Hicks, Peggy, Australian-born American composer; b. Melbourne, Dec. 29, 1912; d. Sydney, June 25, 1990. She entered the Melbourne Cons. in 1927 as a composition student of Hart; in 1931 she went to London and studied with Benjamin (piano), Morris and Kitson (theory), Vaughan Williams (composition), Jacob (orchestration), and Lambert and Sargent (conducting); she then pursued further training with Boulanger in Paris and with Wellesz (musicology and advanced composition) in Vienna (1936–38). In 1938 she married **Stanley Bate,** but they divorced in 1948. In 1939 she went to the United States and in 1948 became a naturalized American citizen. From 1948 to 1958 she wrote music criticism for the *N.Y. Herald Tribune*, and also was active in contemporary music circles. In 1956 and 1958 she held Gugggenheim fellowships. After living in Athens (1959–76), she returned to Australia. She utilized serial techniques in her music but not without explorations of early and non-Western modalities.

WORKS: DRAMATIC: OPERAS: *Caedmon* (1933); *The Transposed Heads* (1952–53; Louisville, April 3, 1954); *The Glittering Gate* (1957; N.Y., May 14, 1959); *Nausicaa* (1959–60; Athens, Aug. 19, 1961); *Carlos Among the Candles* (1962); *Sappho* (1963); *Beckett* (1989–90). BALLETS: *Hylas and the Nymphs* (1935); *Postman's Knock* (1938); *Killer-of-Enemies* (1946); *The Masque of the Wild Man* (Spoleto, June 10, 1958); *Triad* (Spoleto, June 10, 1958); *Saul and the Witch of Endor* (CBS-TV, June 7, 1959; also for Orch. as *Drama*); *A Season in Hell* (1965; N.Y., Nov. 15, 1967); *Tragic Celebration: Jephthah's Daughter* (CBS-TV, Nov. 6, 1966). Also film scores.

BIBL.: D. Hayes, *P. G.-H.: A Bio-Bibliography* (Westport, Conn., 1990).

Glaser, Franz (Joseph), Bohemian composer and conductor; b. Obergeorgenthal, April 19, 1798; d. Copenhagen, Aug. 29, 1861. He studied at the Prague Cons. He was active in Vienna as a composer for the theater from 1817. In 1830 he went to Berlin, where he produced the successful opera *Des Adlers Horst* (Dec. 29, 1832); in 1842 he settled in Copenhagen, where he became court conductor (1845). His Danish operas were *Bryllupet vet Como-soen* (The Wedding by Lake Como; Copenhagen, Jan. 29, 1849), *Nokken* (The Water Sprites; Copenhagen, Feb. 12, 1853), and *Den forgyldte svane* (The Golden Swan; Copenhagen, March 17, 1854). Hans Christian Andersen prepared the librettos for the first 2 for the Danish capital.

BIBL.: W. Neumann, *F. G.* (Leipzig, 1859); N. Pfeil, *F. G.* (Leipzig, 1870).

Glaser, Werner Wolf, German-born Swedish pianist, conductor, teacher, and composer; b. Cologne, April 14, 1910. He studied composition with Jarnach at the Cologne Hochschule für Musik, where he also received training in piano and conducting; he later studied composition with Hindemith at the Berlin Hochschule für Musik, art history at the Univ. of Bonn, and psychology at the Univ. of Berlin, receiving a Ph.D. After conducting the Chemnitz Opera orch. (1929–31) and serving as chorus master in Cologne (1931–33), he went to Copenhagen as a teacher at the Fredriksberg Cons. (1936–43); with I. Skovgaard, he founded the Lyngby School of Music in 1939. He settled in Sweden, becoming a naturalized citizen in 1951; was conductor of the Södra Västmanland Orch. Soc. (1944–59) and was active as a music critic. With I. Andrén and G. Axén, he founded the Västerås School of Music in 1945, and was its director of studies from 1954 until his retirement in 1975. A man of wide interests, he studied modern art and literature and wrote poetry; he also investigated the potentialities of music therapy. A prolific composer, he followed the neoclassical line.

WORKS: DRAMATIC: OPERAS: *Kagekiyo*, chamber opera (1961); *Encounters*, chamber opera (Västerås, Dec. 13, 1970); *A Naked King* (1971; Göteborg, April 6, 1973); *Cercatori*, chamber opera (1972); *The Boy and the Voice*, children's opera (1973); *Freedom Bells* (1980). BALLETS: *Persefone* (1960); *Les Cinq Pas de l'homme* (1973).

Glass, Philip, remarkable American composer; b. Baltimore, Jan. 31, 1937. He entered the Peabody Cons. of Music in Baltimore as a flute student when he was 8; he then took courses in piano, mathematics, and philosophy at the Univ. of Chicago (1952–56) and subsequently studied composition with Persichetti at the Juilliard School of Music in New York (M.S., 1962). He received a Fulbright fellowship in 1964 and went to Paris to study with Boulanger; much more important to his future development was his meeting with Ravi Shankar, who introduced him to Hindu ragas. During a visit to Morocco, Glass absorbed the modalities of North African melorhythms, which taught him the art of melodic repetition. When he returned to New York in 1967, his style of composition became an alternately concave and convex mirror image of Eastern modes, undergoing melodic phases of stationary harmonies in lieu of modulations. He formed associations with modern painters and sculptors who strove to obtain maximum effects with a minimum of means. He began to practice a similar method in music, which soon acquired the factitious sobriquet of minimalism. Other Americans and some Europeans followed this practice, which was basically Eastern in its catatonic homophony; Steve Reich was a close companion in minimalistic pursuits of maximalistic effects. Glass formed his own phonograph company, Chatham Square, which recorded most of his works. He also organized an ensemble of electrically amplified instruments, which became the chief medium of his compositions. On April 13, 1968, he presented the first concert of the Philip Glass Ensemble at Queens College in New York. He subsequently toured widely with it, making visits abroad as well as traveling throughout the United States. His productions, both in America and in Europe, became extremely successful among young audiences, who were mesmerized by his mixture of rock realism and alluring mysticism; undeterred by the indeterminability and interminability of his productions, some lasting several hours, these young people accepted him as a true representative of earthly and unearthly art. The mind-boggling titles of his works added to the tantalizing incomprehensibility of the subjects that he selected for his inspiration. The high point of his productions was the opera *Einstein on the Beach* (in collaboration with Robert Wilson), which involved a surrealistic comminution of thematic ingredients and hypnotic repetition of harmonic subjects. It was premiered at the Avignon Festival on July 25, 1976, and was subsequently performed throughout Europe. It was given on Nov. 21, 1976, at the Metropolitan Opera in New York, where it proved something of a sensation of the season; however, it was not produced as part of the regular subscription series. In Rotterdam on Sept. 5, 1980, he produced his opera *Satyagraha*, a work based on Gandhi's years in South Africa ("Satyagraha" was Gandhi's slogan, composed of 2 Hindu words: satya [truth] and āgraha [firmness]). Another significant production was the film scores *Koyaanisqatsi* (Hopi Indian word meaning "life out of balance," 1983) and *Powaqqatsi* (Hopi Indian word meaning "life in transformation," 1990). The music represented the ultimate condensation of the basic elements of Glass's compositional style; here the ritualistic repetition of chords arranged in symmetrical sequences becomes hypnotic, particularly since the screen action is devoid of narrative; the effect in the first film score is enhanced particularly by the opening deep bass notes of an Indian chant. His mixed media piece *The Photographer: Far from the Truth*, based on the life of the photographer Eadweard Muybridge, received its first U.S. performance in New York on Oct. 6, 1983. It was followed by the exotic opera *Akhnaton*, set in ancient Egypt, with a libretto in ancient Akkadian, Egyptian, and Hebrew, with an explanatory narration in English; it was produced in Stuttgart on March 24, 1984. In collaboration with Robert Moran, he produced the opera *Juniper Tree* (Cambridge, Mass., Dec. 11, 1985). After bringing out the dance-theater piece *A Descent into the Maelstrom* (1986) and the dance piece *In the Upper Room* (1986), he wrote a Violin Concerto (1987). His symphonic score *The Light* was first performed in Cleveland on Oct. 29, 1987. It was followed by his opera *The Making of the Representative for Planet 8* (to a text by Doris Lessing), which received its premiere in Houston on July 8, 1988. His next opera, *The Fall of the House of Usher*, was first performed in Cambridge, Mass., on May 18, 1988. The music theater piece *1000 Airplanes on the Roof* was produced in Vienna in 1988. On Nov. 2, 1989, his *Itaipu* for Chorus and Orch. was premiered in Atlanta. His opera *The Voyage*, celebrating the voyages of discovery of Christopher Columbus, was performed for the first time at the Metropolitan Opera in New York on Oct. 12, 1992. On Nov. 13, 1992, his *Low Symphony*, based on music of David Bowie and Brian Eno, was given its premiere in New York. His opera *Orphée*, after Jean Cocteau's film, was first presented in Cambridge, Mass., on May 14, 1993. Glass's 2d Sym. was performed for the first time in New York on Oct. 14, 1994. On Dec. 7, 1994, his opera *La Belle et la Bête* was premiered in New York. In June 1997 his opera *The Marriages Between Zones Three, Four, and Five* was mounted in Heidelberg. In 1998, in collaboration with R. Wilson, he produced the opera *Monsters of Grace,* based on the poems of the 13th-century Sufi mystic Mevlana Jalaluddin Rumi; slowly moving images are projected on a screen requiring audiences to wear special 3-D glasses. With R. Jones, he publ. *Music by Philip Glass* (N.Y., 1987; new ed., with supplement, 1988, as *Opera on the Beach: On His New World of Music Theatre*).

BIBL.: W. Mertens, *American Minimal Music: La Monte Young, Terry Riley, Steve Reich, P. G.* (London, 1991); R. Kostelanetz, ed., *Writings on G.* (N.Y., 1997).

Glaz, Herta, Austrian-American contralto; b. Vienna, Sept. 16, 1908. She was trained in Vienna and made her operatic debut at the Breslau Opera in 1931, presaging a successful career, but in 1933 was forced to leave Germany. She toured Austria and Scandinavia as a concert singer; she sang at the German Theater in Prague in 1935–36; in 1936 she took part in the American tour of the Salzburg Opera Guild; she subsequently sang at the Chicago Opera (1940–42); on Dec. 25, 1942, she made her debut with the Metropolitan Opera in New York as Amneris, and remained on its roster until 1956; she then taught voice at the Manhattan School of Music, retiring in 1977. Her husband was **Joseph Rosenstock**.

Glebov, Evgeny, Russian composer; b. Roslavl, near Smolensk, Sept. 10, 1929. He studied at the Belorussian Cons. in Minsk with Bogatyrev; later he was appointed to its faculty. Several of his compositions reflect the events of World War II, which devastated Belorussia in 1941. Among his scant compositions is the opera *Our Spring* (1963).

BIBL.: L. Mukharinskaya, *E. G.* (Moscow, 1959); E. Rakova, *E. G.* (Minsk, 1971).

Glière, Reinhold (Moritsovich), eminent Russian composer and pedagogue; b. Kiev, Jan. 11, 1875; d. Moscow, June 23, 1956. Following training in Kiev (1891–94), he studied violin with Hrimaly at the Moscow Cons., where he also took courses with Arensky, Taneyev, and Ippolitov-Ivanov (1894–1900), graduating with a gold medal. He completed his studies in Berlin (1905–07). Returning to Russia, he became active as a teacher; he was appointed prof. of composition at the Kiev Cons., and was its director from 1914 to 1920, then was appointed to the faculty of the Moscow Cons., a post he retained until 1941. He traveled extensively in European and Asiatic Russia, collecting folk melodies; he also conducted many concerts of his own works. He was a prolific composer, and was particularly distinguished in symphonic works, in which he revealed himself as a successor of the Russian national school. He never transgressed the natural borderline of traditional harmony, but he was able to achieve effective results. His most impressive work is his 3d Sym., subtitled *Ilya Muromets*, an epic description of the exploits of a legendary Russian hero. In his numerous songs, Glière showed a fine lyrical talent. He wrote relatively few works of chamber music, most of them early in his career. In his opera *Shah-Senem*, he made use of native Caucasian songs. Glière was the teacher of 2 generations of Russian composers; among his students were Prokofiev and Miaskovsky. He received Stalin prizes for the String Quartet No. 4 (1948) and the ballet *The Bronze Knight* (1950).

WORKS: DRAMATIC: OPERAS: *Zemlya i nebo* (Earth and Sky; 1900); *Shah-Senem* (1923; Baku, 1926; rev. 1934); *Gyulsara*, music drama (1936; Moscow, 1937; in collaboration with Sadikov; rev. version as an opera, Tashkent, Dec. 25, 1949); *Leyli i Mejnun* (Tashkent, July 18, 1940); *Rashel*, after Maupassant's *Mademoiselle Fifi* (1942; Moscow, April 19, 1947). BALLETS: *Khirzis* (Moscow, Nov. 30, 1912); *Ovechiy istochnik* (Sheep's Spring; 1922; rev. as *Komedianti* [The Comedians], 1930; Moscow, April 5, 1931); *Kleopatra* (1925; Moscow, Jan. 11, 1926); *Krasniy mak* (The Red Poppy; 1926–27; Moscow, June 14, 1927; rev. as *Krasniy tsvetok* [The Red Flower], 1949); *Medniy vsadnik* (The Bronze Horseman; 1948–49; Leningrad, March 14, 1949); *Taras Bulba* (1951–52); *Dog Kastilii* (1955). Also incidental music to plays.

BIBL.: I. Boelza, *R. M. G.* (Moscow, 1955; 2d ed., 1962); N. Petrova, *R. M. G.* (Leningrad, 1962).

Glinka, Mikhail (Ivanovich), great Russian composer, often called "the father of Russian music" for his pioneering cultivation of Russian folk modalities; b. Novospasskoye, Smolensk district, June 1, 1804; d. Berlin, Feb. 15, 1857. A scion of a fairly rich family of landowners, he was educated at an exclusive school in St. Petersburg (1817–22); he also took private lessons in music; his piano teacher was a resident German musician, Carl Meyer; he also studied violin; when the pianist John Field was in St. Petersburg, Glinka had an opportunity to study with him, but he had only 3 lessons before Field departed. He began to compose even before acquiring adequate training in theory. As a boy he traveled in the Caucasus, then stayed for a while at his father's estate. At 20 he entered the Ministry of Communications in St. Petersburg; he remained in government employ until 1828, at the same time constantly improving his general education by reading; he had friends among the best Russian writers of the time, including the poets Zhukovsky and Pushkin. He also took singing lessons with an Italian teacher, Belloli. In 1830 he went to Italy; he continued irregular studies in Milan (where he spent most of his Italian years), and also visited Naples, Rome, and Venice. He met Donizetti and Bellini. He became enamored of Italian music, and his early vocal and instrumental compositions are thoroughly Italian in melodic and harmonic structure. In 1833 he went to Berlin, where he took a course in counterpoint and general composition with Dehn; thus he was nearly 30 when he completed his theoretical education. In 1834 his father died, and Glinka went back to Russia to take care of the family affairs. In 1835 he was married; the marriage was unhappy, and he soon separated from his wife, finally divorcing her in 1846. The return to his native land led him to consider the composition of a truly national opera on a subject (suggested to him by Zhukovsky) depicting a historical episode in Russian history: the saving of the first czar of the Romanov dynasty by a simple peasant, Ivan Susanin. (The Italian composer Cavos wrote an opera on the same subject 20 years previously, and conducted it in St. Petersburg.) Glinka's opera was produced in St. Petersburg on Dec. 9, 1836, under the title *A Life for the Czar*. The event was hailed by the literary and artistic circles of Russia as a milestone of Russian culture, and indeed the entire development of Russian national music received its decisive creative impulse from Glinka's patriotic opera. It remained in the repertoire of Russian theaters until the Revolution made it unacceptable, but it was revived, under the original title, *Ivan Susanin*, on Feb. 27, 1939, in Moscow, without alterations in the music, but with the references to the czar eliminated from the libretto, the idea of saving the country being substituted for that of saving the czar. Glinka's next opera, *Ruslan and Ludmila*, after Pushkin's fairy tale, was produced in St. Petersburg on Dec. 9, 1842; this opera, too, became extremely popular in Russia. Glinka introduced into the score many elements of oriental music; one episode contains the earliest use of the whole-tone scale in an opera. Both operas retain the traditional Italian form, with arias, choruses, and orch. episodes clearly separated. In 1844 Glinka was in Paris, where he met Berlioz; he also traveled in Spain, where he collected folk songs; the fruits of his Spanish tour were

2 orch. works, *Jota Aragonesa* and *Night in Madrid*. On his way back to Russia, he stayed in Warsaw for 3 years. The remaining years of his life were spent in St. Petersburg, Paris, and Berlin.

WORKS: DRAMATIC: OPERAS: *A Life for the Czar* (1st perf. as *Ivan Susanin*, St. Petersburg, Dec. 9, 1836); *Ruslan and Ludmila* (St. Petersburg, Dec. 9, 1842); sketches for 3 unfinished operas. BALLET: *Chao-Kang* (1828–31). OTHER: Incidental music for Kukolnik's tragedy *Prince Kholmsky* (1840) and for the play *The Moldavian Gypsy* (1836).

BIBL.: Glinka's autobiographical sketch intended for inclusion in the *Biographie universelle des musiciens* by Fétis was publ. for the first time in *Muzikalnaya Letopis'* in 1926; his collected letters, ed. by N. Findeisen, were publ. in 1907. See also O. Fouque, *G.* (Paris, 1880); P. Weimarn, *M. I. G.* (Moscow, 1892); N. Findeisen, *M. I. G.* (St. Petersburg, 1896); M. D. Calvocoressi, *G.* (Paris, 1913); M. Montagu-Nathan, *G.* (London, 1916); I. Martinov, *M. I. G.* (Moscow, 1947); B. Asafiev, *G.* (Moscow, 1947); A. Orlova, *M. I. G., Chronicle of Life and Work* (Moscow, 1952; ed. by M. Brown and tr. by R. Hoops, Ann Arbor, 1988); P. Dippel, *Klingende Einkehr: G. und Berlin* (Berlin, 1953); D. Brown, *G.: A Biographical and Critical Study* (London, 1974).

Gliński, Mateusz, Polish conductor, musicologist, and composer; b. Warsaw, April 6, 1892; d. Welland, Ontario, Jan. 3, 1976. He studied at the Warsaw Cons. with Barcewicz (violin) and Statkowski (composition), then took courses in Leipzig with Reger (composition), Riemann and Schering (musicology), and Nikisch (conducting). He went to St. Petersburg in 1914 where he studied composition with Glazunov and Steinberg and conducting with Nikolai Tcherepnin. In 1918 he went to Warsaw; from 1924 to 1939 he was ed. of the periodical *Muzyka*. At the outbreak of World War II in 1939, he went to Rome, where he engaged in various activities as music critic and ed. In 1949 he established in Rome the Istituto Internazionale Federico Chopin. From 1959 to 1965 he taught at Assumption Univ. in Windsor, Ontario. In 1965 he established the Niagara Sym. Orch., which he conducted. His works include an opera, *Orlotko*, after Rostand's play *L'Aiglon* (1918–27). He publ. a monograph on *Scriabin* (Warsaw, 1933); *Chopin's Letters to Delfina Potocka* (Windsor, 1961), in which he subscribes to the generally refuted belief that these letters, which came to light in 1945, are indeed genuine; and *Chopin the Unknown* (Windsor, 1963).

Glodeanu, Liviu, Romanian composer; b. Dârja, Aug. 6, 1938; d. Bucharest, March 31, 1978. He studied at the Cluj Cons. and the Bucharest Cons., his principal teachers being Comes, Negrea, and Mendelsohn. In his music, he respected Romanian musical tradition while subtly employing modern means of expression. His works include the operas *Ulysse* (1967–72; Cluj, April 25, 1973) and *Zamolxe* (1968–69; Cluj, April 25, 1973).

Glossop, Peter, English baritone; b. Sheffield, July 6, 1928. He was a student of Mosley, Rich, and Hislop. In 1952 he joined the chorus of the Sadler's Wells Opera in London, where he then was a principal member of the company (1953–62). In 1961 he won the Sofia Competition and made his debut at London's Covent Garden as Demetrius in *A Midsummer Night's Dream*, appearing there regularly until 1966. On Aug. 18, 1967, he made his Metropolitan Opera debut as Rigoletto during the company's visit to Newport, R.I. His formal debut at the Metropolitan Opera in New York took place as Scarpia on June 5, 1971. He also sang with other opera houses in Europe and North America. Among his other roles were Nabucco, Iago, Simone Boccanegra, Falstaff, Wozzeck, and Billy Budd.

Glover, Jane (Alison), English conductor and musicologist; b. Helmsley, Yorkshire, May 13, 1949. She was educated at St. Hugh's College, Oxford (B.A., M.A.; Ph.D., 1978, with a diss. on Cavalli). She was a junior research fellow (1973–75), lecturer in music (1976–84), and senior research fellow (1982–91) at St. Hugh's College, Oxford. In 1975 she made her professional conducting debut at the Wexford Festival with her own performing ed. of Cavalli's *Eritrea*. She was a lecturer in music at St. Anne's College (1976–80) and at Pembroke College (1979–84) at Oxford, and from 1979 she served on the music faculty at the Univ. of Oxford. From 1982 to 1985 she was music director of the Glyndebourne Touring Opera. In 1983 she became principal conductor of the London Choral Soc. From 1984 to 1991 she was artistic director of the London Mozart Players. In 1988 she made her first appearance at London's Covent Garden conducting *Die Entführung aus dem Serail*, and then at the English National Opera in London in 1989 with *Don Giovanni*. From 1989 to 1996 she was principal conductor of the Huddersfield Choral Soc. In 1995 she conducted Britten's *War Requiem* at the London Promenade Concerts. She was engaged to conduct *Orfeo* at the English National Opera in 1997. As a guest conductor, she appeared with orchs. and opera companies around the world.

Glover, John William, Irish composer; b. Dublin, June 19, 1815; d. there, Dec. 18, 1899. He studied in Dublin. From 1848 he taught vocal music at the Normal Training School of the Irish National Education Board and was also director of music in the Roman Catholic procathedral. He was noted for his promotion of choral music in Ireland. He ed. *Moore's Irish Melodies* (1859). Among his works is the opera *The Deserted Village*, after Goldsmith (London, 1880), as well as 2 Italian operas to librettos by Metastasio.

Glover, William Howard, English conductor and composer; b. London, June 6, 1819; d. N.Y., Oct. 28, 1875. He played the violin in the Lyceum Theater orch. in London, and also conducted opera in Manchester, Liverpool, and London. In 1868 he went to New York, where he was conductor at Niblo's Garden until his death. Among his works are the opera *Ruy Blas* (London, Oct. 21, 1861), and the operettas *Aminta* (London, Jan. 26, 1852), *Once Too Often* (London, Jan. 20, 1862), and *Palomita, or The Veiled Songstress* (publ. in N.Y., 1875).

Gluck, Alma (née **Reba Fiersohn**), famous Romanian-born American soprano; b. Bucharest, Romania, May 11, 1884; d. N.Y., Oct. 27, 1938. She was taken to the United States as an infant and was educated in New York. In 1902 she married Bernard Gluck; although they were divorced in 1912, she used the name Alma Gluck throughout her professional career. After vocal training with Arturo Buzzi-Peccia in New York (1906–09), she made her first appearance with the Metropolitan Opera as Massenet's Sophie during the company's visit to the New Theatre on Nov. 16, 1909. Her formal debut at the Metropolitan Opera took place as the Spirit in Gluck's *Orfeo ed Euridice* on Dec. 23, 1909. She remained on its roster until 1912, winning acclaim in such roles as Mimi, Nedda, and Gilda. After additional training with Sembrich in Berlin, she devoted herself to a distinguished concert career. During the 1913–15 and 1916–18 seasons, she was engaged to sing at the Sunday Concerts at the Metropolitan Opera. She became one of the leading recording artists of her day, excelling in both serious and popular genres. She had a daughter with Bernard Gluck, (Abigail) Marcia Davenport, who became a noted novelist and writer on music. In 1914 she married **Efrem Zimbalist.** Their son, Efrem Zimbalist Jr., became a well-known actor. His daughter, Stefanie Zimbalist, also followed a thespian bent.

Gluck, Christoph Willibald, Ritter von, renowned German composer; b. Erasbach, near Weidenwang, in the Upper Palatinate, July 2, 1714; d. Vienna, Nov. 15, 1787. His father was a forester at Erasbach until his appointment as forester to Prince Lobkowitz of Eisenberg about 1729. Gluck received his elementary instruction in the village schools at Kamnitz and Albersdorf near Komotau, where he also was taught singing and instrumental playing. Some biographers refer to his study at the Jesuit college at Komotau, but there is no documentary evidence to support this contention. In 1732 he went to Prague to complete his education, but it is doubtful that he took any courses at the Univ. He earned his living by playing violin and cello at rural dances in the area; also sang at various churches. He met Bohuslav Černohorsky, and it is probable that Gluck learned the methods of church music from him. He went to Vienna in 1736, and was chamber musician to young Prince Lobkowitz, son of the patron of Gluck's father. In 1737 he was taken to Milan by Prince Melzi; this Italian sojourn was of the greatest importance to Gluck's musical development. There he became a student of G. B. Sammartini and acquired a solid technique of composition in the Italian style. After 4 years of study, he brought out his first opera, *Artaserse*, to the text of the celebrated Metastasio; it was produced in Milan (Dec. 26, 1741) with such success that he was immediately commissioned to write more operas. There followed *Demetrio, or Cleonice* (Venice, May 2, 1742), *Demofoonte* (Milan, Jan. 6, 1743), *Il Tigrane* (Crema, Sept. 9, 1743), *La Sofonisba, or Siface* (Milan, Jan. 13, 1744), *Ipermestra* (Venice, Nov. 21, 1744), *Poro* (Turin, Dec. 26, 1744), and *Ippolito, or Fedra* (Milan, Jan. 31, 1745). He also contributed separate numbers to several other operas produced in Italy. In 1745 he received an invitation to go to London; on his way, he visited Paris and met Rameau. He was commissioned by the Italian Opera of London to write 2 operas for the Haymarket Theatre, as a competitive endeavor to Handel's enterprise. The first of these works was *La Caduta dei giganti*, a tribute to the Duke of Cumberland on the defeat of the Pretender; it was produced on Jan. 28, 1746; the 2d was a pasticcio, *Artamene*, in which Gluck used material from his previous operas; it was produced March 15, 1746. Ten days later, he appeared with Handel at a public concert, despite the current report in London society that Handel had declared that Gluck knew no more counterpoint than his cook (it should be added that a professional musician, Gustavus Waltz, was Handel's cook and valet at the time). On April 23, 1746, Gluck gave a demonstration in London, playing on the "glass harmonica." He left London late in 1746 when he received an engagement as conductor with Pietro Mingotti's traveling Italian opera company. He conducted in Hamburg, Leipzig, and Dresden; on June 29, 1747, he produced a "serenata," *Le nozze d'Ercole e d'Ebe*, to celebrate a royal wedding; it was performed at the Saxon court, in Pillnitz. He then went to Vienna, where he staged his opera *Semiramide riconosciuta*, after a poem of Metastasio (May 14, 1748). He then traveled to Copenhagen, where he produced a festive opera, *La Contesa dei Numi* (March 9, 1749), on the occasion of the birth of Prince Christian; his next productions (all to Metastasio's texts) were *Ezio* (Prague, 1750), *Issipile* (Prague, 1752), *La clemenza di Tito* (Naples, Nov. 4, 1752), *Le Cinesi* (Vienna, Sept. 24, 1754), *La danza* (Vienna, May 5, 1755), *L'innocenza giustificata* (Vienna, Dec. 8, 1755), *Antigono* (Rome, Feb. 9, 1756), and *Il Re pastore* (Vienna, Dec. 8, 1756).

In 1750 Gluck married Marianna Pergin, daughter of a Viennese merchant, and for several years afterward conducted operatic performances in Vienna. As French influence increased there, he wrote several entertainments to French texts, containing spoken dialogue, in the style of opéra comique; of these, the most successful were *Le Cadi dupé* (Dec. 1761) and *La Rencontre imprévue* (Jan. 7, 1764; perf. also under the title *Les Pèlerins de la Mecque*, his most popular production in this genre). His greatest work of the Vienna period was *Orfeo ed Euridice*, to a libretto by Calzabigi (in a version for male contralto, Oct. 5, 1762, with the part of Orfeo sung by the famous castrato Gaetano Guadagni). Gluck revised it for a Paris performance, produced in French on Aug. 2, 1774, with Orfeo sung by a tenor. There followed another masterpiece, *Alceste* (Vienna, Dec. 16, 1767), also to Calzabigi's text. In the preface to *Alceste*, Gluck formulated his aesthetic credo, which elevated the dramatic meaning of musical stage plays above a mere striving for vocal effects: "I sought to reduce music to its true function, that of seconding poetry in order to strengthen the emotional expression and the impact of the dramatic situations without interrupting the action and without weakening it by superfluous ornaments." Among other productions of the Viennese period were *Il trionfo di Clelia* (Vienna, May 14, 1763), *Il Parnaso confuso* (Schönbrunn Palace, Jan. 24, 1765), *Il Telemacco* (Vienna, Jan. 30, 1765), and *Paride ed Elena* (Vienna, Nov. 30, 1770).

The success of his French operas in Vienna led Gluck to the decision to try his fortunes in Paris, yielding to the persuasion of Francois du Roullet, an attache at the French embassy in Vienna, who also supplied him with his first libretto for a serious French opera, an adaptation of Racine's *Iphigénie en Aulide* (Paris, April 19, 1774). He set out for Paris early in 1773, preceded by declarations in the Paris press by du Roullet and Gluck himself, explaining in detail his ideas of dramatic music. These statements set off an intellectual battle in the Paris press and among musicians in general between the adherents of traditional Italian opera and Gluck's novel French opera. It reached an unprecedented degree of acrimony when the Italian composer Nicola Piccinni was engaged by the French court to write operas to French texts, in open competition with Gluck; intrigues multiplied, even though Marie Antoinette never wavered in her admiration for Gluck, who taught her singing and harpsichord playing. However, Gluck and Piccinni themselves never participated in the bitter polemics unleashed by their literary and musical partisans. The sensational successes of the French version of Gluck's *Orfeo* and of *Alceste* were followed by the production of *Armide* (Sept. 23, 1777), which aroused great admiration. Then followed his masterpiece, *Iphigénie en Tauride* (May 17, 1779), which established Gluck's superiority to Piccinni, who was commissioned to write an opera on the same subject but failed to complete it in time. Gluck's last opera, *Echo et Narcisse* (Paris, Sept. 24, 1779), did not measure up to the excellence of his previous operas. By that time, his health had failed; he had several attacks of apoplexy, which resulted in partial paralysis. In the autumn of 1779 he returned to Vienna, where he lived as an invalid. His last work was a *De profundis* for Chorus and Orch., written 5 years before his death.

Besides his operas, Gluck wrote several ballets, of which *Don Juan* (Vienna, Oct. 17, 1761) was the most successful; he also wrote a cycle of 7 songs to words by Klopstock, 7 trio sonatas, several overtures, etc. Wagner made a complete revision of the score of *Iphigénie en Aulide*; this arrangement was so extensively used that a Wagnerized version of Gluck's music became the chief text for performances during the 19th century. A complete ed. of Gluck's works was begun by the Barenreiter Verlag in 1951. A thematic catalogue was publ. by A. Wotquenne (Leipzig, 1904; Ger. tr. with supplement by J. Liebeskind). See also C. Hopkinson, *A Bibliography of the Printed Works of C. W. von Gluck, 1714–1787* (2d ed., N.Y., 1967).

BIBL.: F. Riedel, *Über die Musik des R.s C. v.G.* (Vienna, 1775); C. Coqueau, *Entretiens sur l'etat actuel de l'opéra de Paris* (Paris, 1779; dialogue on the Gluck-Piccinni controversy); G. Leblond, *Mémoires pour servir à l'histoire de la révolution opérée dans la musique par M. le Chevalier G.* (Paris, 1781; Ger. tr., 1823; 2d ed., 1837); J. Siegmeyer, *Über den R. G. und seine Werke* (Berlin, 1837); E. Miel, *Notice sur G.* (Paris, 1840); A. Schmid, *C. W. R. v.G.* (Leipzig, 1854); W. Neumann, *C. W. G.* (Kassel, 1855); J. Baudoin, *L'Alceste de G.* (Paris, 1861); A. Marx, *G. und die Oper* (Berlin, 1863); L. Nohl, *G. und Wagner* (Munich, 1870); G. Desnoiresterres, *G. et Piccinni* (Paris, 1875); E. Thoinan, *Notes bibliographiques sur la guerre musicale des G.istes et Piccinnistes* (Paris, 1878); H. Barbedette, *G.* (Paris, 1882); A. Reissmann, *C. W. v.G.* (Berlin, 1882); K. Bitter, *Die Reform der Oper durch G. und Wagner* (Braunschweig, 1884); H. Welti, *G.* (Leipzig, 1888); E. Newman, *G. and the Opera* (London, 1895); J. d'Udine, *G.* (Paris, 1906); J. Tiersot, *G.* (Paris, 1910); G. Scuderi, *C. G.: Orfeo* (Milan, 1924); R. Haas, *G. und Durazzo im Burgtheater* (Vienna, 1925); L. de la Laurencie, *G., Orphee: Etude et analyse musicale* (Paris, 1934); M. Cooper, *G.* (London, 1935); A. Einstein, *G.* (London, 1936); P. Landormy, *G.* (Paris, 1941); A. Della Corte, *G.* (Turin, 1942); W. Brandl, *C. W. R. v.G.* (Wiesbaden, 1948); A. Della Corte, *G. e i suoi tempi* (Florence, 1948); J.-G. Prod'homme, *G.* (Paris, 1948; rev. ed., 1985, by J. Faquet); R. Gerber, *C. W. R. v.G.* (Potsdam, 1950); R. Tenschert, *C. W. G.: Der grosse Reformator der Oper* (Freiburg, 1951); A. Abert, *C. W. G.* (Munich, 1959); P. Howard, *G. and the Birth of Modern Opera* (N.Y., 1964); W. Vetter, *C. W. G.* (Leipzig, 1964); P. Howard, *C. W. G.: A Guide to Research* (N.Y., 1987); idem, *G.: An Eighteenth-Century Portrait in Letters and Documents* (Oxford, 1995).

Glynne, Howell, Welsh bass; b. Swansea, Jan. 24, 1906; d. in an automobile accident in Toronto, Nov. 24, 1969. He labored as a miner while pursuing vocal training with Davies and Warlich. He gained a place in the chorus of the Carl Rosa Opera Co., and in 1931 made his operatic debut with it as Sparafucile. He was a member of the Sadler's Wells Opera in London (1946–50; 1956–63); from 1947 he also appeared at London's Covent Garden, and was active as a concert artist. In 1964 he joined the faculty of the Univ. of Toronto. Among his best roles were Bartolo, Varlaam, and Baron Ochs.

Gnecchi, Vittorio, Italian composer; b. Milan, July 17, 1876; d. there, Feb. 1, 1954. He studied at the Milan Cons. His opera *Cassandra* was performed at Bologna on Dec. 5, 1905; some years later, after the premiere of Strauss's *Elektra*, there was considerable discussion when Giovanni Tebaldini pointed out the identity of some 50 themes in the two works ("Telepatia Musicale," *Rivista Musicale Italiana*, XVII, 1909). Gnecchi also wrote the operas *Virtu d'amore* (1896) and *La rosiera*, after a comedy by Alfred de Musset (in German, Gera, Feb. 12, 1927; in Italian, Trieste, Jan. 24, 1931).

Gnessin, Mikhail (Fabianovich), Russian composer and pedagogue; b. Rostov-na-Donu, Feb. 2, 1882; d. Moscow, May 5, 1957. After lessons with O. Fritch in Rostov, he studied with Rimsky-Korsakov and Liadov at the St. Petersburg Cons. (1901–05; 1906–09). He later went to Moscow, where he was a prof. of composition at the Gnessin Academy (from 1923) and at the Cons. (from 1925); after serving as a prof. at the Leningrad Cons. (1935–44), he returned to Moscow and was head of the Gnessin State Inst. for Musical Education (1944–51). Most of his works composed after 1914 reflect his interest in Jewish themes. Among his works is the opera *Yunost Avraama* (Abraham's Youth; 1921–23); also incidental music and film scores. He publ. his reflections and reminiscences of Rimsky-Korsakov in Moscow in 1956.

Gobbi, Tito, famous Italian baritone; b. Bassano del Grappa, near Venice, Oct. 24, 1913; d. Rome, March 5, 1984. He received vocal lessons from Barone Zanchetta in Bassano del Grappa before going to Rome to train with Giulio Crimi; he made his operatic debut as Count Rodolfo in *La Sonnambula* in Gubbio (1935). During the 1935–36 season, he was an understudy at Milan's La Scala, where he made a fleeting stage appearance as the Herald in Pizzetti's *Oreseolo* (1935). In 1936 he won 1st prize in the male vocal section of the Vienna International Competition; he then went to Rome, where he sang Germont *père* at the Teatro Adriano (1937); that same year he made his first appearance at the Teatro Reale, in the role of Lelio in Wolf-Ferrari's *Le Donne curiose*; after singing secondary roles there (1937–39), he became a principal member of the company; he appeared as Ford in *Falstaff* during its visit to Berlin in 1941. He also sang on the Italian radio and made guest appearances with other Italian opera houses; in Rieti in 1940 he first essayed the role of Scarpia, which was to become his most celebrated characterization. In 1942 he made his formal debut at La Scala as Belcore in *L'elisir d'amore*. In 1947 he appeared as Rigoletto in Stockholm, and in 1948 he sang in concerts in London and also made his U.S. debut as Figaro in *Il Barbiere di Siviglia* at the San Francisco Opera. In 1950 he made his Covent Garden debut in London as Renato in *Un ballo in maschera*. He made his first appearance at the Chicago Opera as Rossini's Figaro in 1954. On Jan. 13, 1956, he made his Metropolitan Opera debut in New York as Scarpia. In subsequent years, his engagements took him to most of the principal music centers of the world. He was also active as an opera producer from 1965. In 1979 he bade farewell to the operatic stage. He was the brother-in-law of **Boris Christoff**. Gobbi was acclaimed as an actor as well as a singer; his mastery extended to some 100 roles. He publ. *Tito Gobbi: My Life* (1979) and *Tito Gobbi and His World of Italian Opera* (1984).

Gockley, (Richard) David, American opera administrator; b. Philadelphia, July 13, 1943. He was educated at Brown Univ. (B.A., 1965), Columbia Univ. (M.B.A., 1970), and the New England Cons. of Music in Boston. Following engagements as an opera singer, he was on the staff of the Santa Fe Opera (1968–70) and of Lincoln Center for the Performing Arts in New York (1970). In 1970 he joined the Houston Grand Opera as its business manager. After serving as its associate director in 1971–72, he was its general director from 1972. Under his guidance, it became one of America's finest opera companies. Gockley's tenure has been especially noteworthy for his championship of contemporary works, among them Adams's *Nixon in China* (1987) and Wallace's *Harvey Milk* (1995). He also promoted educational programs, introduced the use of surtitles, and inaugurated the touring Texas Opera Theater.

Godard, Benjamin (Louis Paul), French composer; b. Paris, Aug. 18, 1849; d. Cannes, Jan. 10, 1895. He studied violin with Richard Hammer and Vieuxtemps and composition with Reber at the Paris Cons. He publ. his first work, a Violin Sonata, at the age of 16 and wrote several other chamber music pieces, obtaining the Prix Chartier. In 1878 he received a municipal prize for an orch. work; in the same year he produced his first opera, *Les Bijoux de Jeannette*. His 2d opera was *Pedro de Zalamea* (Antwerp, Jan. 31, 1884), but it left little impact; then came his masterpiece, *Jocelyn*, after Lamartine's poem (Brussels, Feb. 25, 1888). The famous *Berceuse* from this opera became a perennial favorite, exhibiting Godard's lyric talent at its best. There followed the opera *Dante et Béatrice*, produced at the Opéra Comique in Paris on May 13, 1890. His opera *La Vivandière* was left unfinished at his death, and the orchestration was completed by Paul Vidal; it was staged in Paris on April 1, 1895; another posthumous opera, *Les Guelphes*, was produced in Rouen (Jan. 17, 1902).

BIBL.: M. Clerjot, *B. G.* (Paris, 1902); M. Clavie, *B. G.* (Paris, 1906).

Godfrey, Isidore, English conductor; b. London, Sept. 27, 1900; d. Sussex, Sept. 12, 1977. He was educated at the Guildhall School of Music in London. In 1925 he joined the D'Oyly Carte Opera Co. as a conductor; from 1929 to 1968 he served as its music director. In 1965 he was named an Officer of the Order of the British Empire.

Goedike, Alexander, Russian pianist, pedagogue, and composer of German descent; b. Moscow, March 4, 1877; d. there, July 9, 1957. He studied with Safonov and G. Pabst (piano) and Arensky (composition) at the Moscow Cons. (graduated, 1898), where he was a prof. of piano from 1909. His compositions include the operas *Virineya* (1915), *At the Crossing* (1933), *Jacquerie* (1937), and *Macbeth* (1944).

BIBL.: V. Yakovlev, *A. G.* (Moscow, 1927); K. Adzhemov, *A. G.* (Moscow, 1960).

Goehr, (Peter) Alexander, prominent German-born English composer and teacher, son of **Walter Goehr;** b. Berlin, Aug. 10, 1932. He was a student of Richard Hall at the Royal Manchester College of Music (1952–55), and then of Messiaen and Loriod in Paris (1955–56). After lecturing at Morely College in London (1955–57), he was a music assistant at the BBC (1960–68). In 1968–69 he served as composer-in-residence at the New England Cons. of Music in Boston, and then was an assoc. prof. of music at Yale Univ. in 1969–70. From 1971 to 1976 he was the West Riding prof. of music at the Univ. of Leeds, and in 1975 he also was artistic director of the Leeds Festival. He subsequently was prof. of music at the Univ. of Cambridge from 1976. In 1980 he was a visiting prof. at the Beijing Cons. of Music. In 1989 he was made an honorary member of the American Academy and Inst. of Arts and Letters. Goehr's oeuvre has been notably influenced by Schoenberg, although he has succeeded in developing an individual mode of expression utilizing serial, tonal, and modal means.

WORKS: DRAMATIC: *La belle dame sans merci*, ballet (1958); *Arden muss sterben* or *Arden must die*, opera (1966; Hamburg, March 5, 1967); *Triptych*, theater piece consisting of *Naboth's Vineyard* (London, July 16, 1968), *Shadowplay* (London, July 8, 1970), and *Sonata about Jerusalem* (1970; Tel Aviv, Jan. 1971); *Behold the Sun* or *Die Wiedertäufer*, opera (1981–84; Duisburg,

April 19, 1985); *Arianna*, opera (1994–95; London, Sept. 15, 1995).

BIBL.: B. Northcott, ed., *The Music of A. G.: Interviews and Articles* (London, 1980).

Goehr, Walter, German-born English conductor and composer, father of **(Peter) Alexander Goehr**; b. Berlin, May 28, 1903; d. Sheffield, Dec. 4, 1960. He studied theory with Schoenberg in Berlin; he then was a conductor with the Berlin Radio (1925–31). In 1933 he went to England and was music director of the Columbia Graphophone Co. until 1939; from 1945 to 1948 he was conductor of the BBC Theatre Orch.; he also was conductor of the Morley College concerts from 1943 until his death. He composed theater, radio, and film scores.

Goerne, Matthias, admired German baritone; b. Weimar, March 31, 1967. He sang in the children's choir of the Chemnitz Civic Opera before pursuing vocal studies with Hans Joachim Beyer in Leipzig (1985–91), Fischer-Dieskau in Berlin (1988–93), and Schwarzkopf in Zürich (1989–91). In 1987 he began his career as a soloist with orchs. and as a recitalist in Germany. Following an engagement as Lazarus in the St. Matthew Passion with the Leipzig Gewandhaus Orch. under Masur's direction in 1990, he appeared with many major orchs. In 1992 he made his operatic debut in the title role of Henze's *Der Prinz von Homburg* in Cologne. From 1993 to 1995 he sang at the Dresden State Opera. In 1994 he made his London recital debut at Wigmore Hall. He made his U.S. debut as a soloist as Christus in the St. John Passion with the Philadelphia Orch. under Rilling's direction in 1996, the same year he made his N.Y. recital debut at the Frick Collection. In 1997 he made his first appearance at the Salzburg Festival as Papageno. In 1998 he sang in recitals at the Edinburgh Festival and at N.Y.'s Alice Tully Hall, and on Dec. 14th of that year he made his Metropolitan Opera debut in New York as Papageno. He sang *Die Winterreise* and *Schwanengesang* with Brendel as his accompanist at N.Y.'s Carnegie Hall in 1999, the same year he portrayed Wozzeck at the Zürich Opera. In addition to his esteemed interpretations of Schubert's lieder, Goerne has also won critical accolades for his Schumann, Wolf, and Mahler.

Goetz, Hermann (Gustav), German composer; b. Königsberg, Dec. 7, 1840; d. Hottingen, near Zürich, Dec. 3, 1876. He studied in Berlin (1860–62), with von Bülow in piano and H. Ulrich in composition. In 1863 he took the post of organist at Winterthur, Switzerland, then lived in Zürich, where he gave private lessons and conducted a singing society. His most famous work is the opera *Der Widerspenstigen Zähmung*, based on Shakespeare's play *The Taming of the Shrew*, which was given in Mannheim, Oct. 11, 1874. His other works include the opera *Francesca da Rimini* (Mannheim, Sept. 30, 1877; unfinished; 3d act completed by Ernst Frank) and incidental music for Widmann's play *Die heiligen drei Könige* (Winterthur, Jan. 6, 1866).

BIBL.: A. Steiner, *H. G.* (Zürich, 1907); E. Kreuzhage, *H. G.: Sein Leben und seine Werke* (Leipzig, 1916); G. Kruse, *H. G.* (Leipzig, 1920).

Goetze, Walter W(ilhelm), German composer; b. Berlin, April 17, 1883; d. there, March 24, 1961. He was trained in Berlin. After working as a bassoonist and theater conductor, he had his first success as a theater composer with his *Parkettsitz Nr. 10* (Hamburg, Sept. 24, 1911). After bringing out such scores as *Zwischen zwölf und eins* (Leipzig, Feb. 9, 1913), *Der liebe Pepi* or *Der Bundesbruder* (Berlin, Dec. 23, 1914), and *Am Brunnen vor dem Tore* (Hannover, May 26, 1918), he had his finest success with *Ihre Hoheit die Tänzerin* (Stettin, May 8, 1919). Among the best of his subsequent works were *Adrienne* (Hamburg, April 24, 1926), *Henriette Sontag* (Altenberg, Jan. 20, 1929; rev. version as *Die göttliche Jette*, Berlin, Dec. 31, 1931), *Der goldene Pierrot* (Berlin, March 31, 1934), *Schach dem König!* (Berlin, May 16, 1935), and *Liebe im Dreiklang* (Heidelberg, Nov. 15, 1950; in collaboration with E. Malkowsky).

Gogorza, Emilio (Edoardo) de, American baritone and teacher; b. Brooklyn, May 29, 1874; d. N.Y., May 10, 1949. After singing as a boy soprano in England, he returned to the United States and studied with C. Moderati and E. Agramonte in New York. He made his debut in 1897 with Marcella Sembrich in a concert; sang throughout the country in concerts and with leading orchs. Beginning in 1925, he was an instructor of voice at the Curtis Inst. of Music in Philadelphia. He married **Emma Eames** in 1911.

Goh, Taijiro, Japanese composer; b. Dairen, Manchuria, Feb. 15, 1907; d. Shizuoka, July 1, 1970. He studied in Tokyo. He organized the Soc. of Japanese Composers, and created the Japan Women's Sym. Orch. (1963). His music follows the European academic type of harmonic and contrapuntal structure.

WORKS: DRAMATIC: OPERAS: *Madame Rosaria* (1943); *Tsubaki saku koro* (When Camellias Blossom; 1949; unfinished); *Tais* (1959; unfinished). BALLET: *Oni-Daiko* (Devil Drummers; 1956). CHOREOGRAPHIC PLAYS: *Koku-sei-Ya* (1954); *Rashômon* (1954).

Göhler, (Karl) Georg, German conductor and composer; b. Zwickau, June 29, 1874; d. Lübeck, March 4, 1954. He was a pupil of Vollhardt in Zwickau, then studied at the Cons. and the Univ. of Leipzig (Ph.D., 1897, with a diss. on Cornelius Freundt). He then pursued a career as a conductor, becoming best known as a champion of Bruckner and Mahler. Among his own works is the opera *Prinz Nachtwächter* (1922).

Goldberg, Reiner, noted German tenor; b. Crostau, Oct. 17, 1939. He was a student of Arno Schellenberg at the Dresden Hochschule für Musik. In 1966 he began his career in Radebeul, and that same year made his Dresden debut as Luigi in *Il Tabarro*. In 1973 he became a member of the Dresden State Opera, and in 1977 of the (East) Berlin State Opera; he toured with both companies in Europe and abroad. In 1982 he made his debut at London's Covent Garden as Walther von Stolzing, in Paris as Midas in a concert perf. of *Die Liebe der Danae*, at the Salzburg Easter Festival as Erik, and at the Salzburg Summer Festival as Florestan. He also sang Parsifal on the soundtrack for the Syberberg film version of Wagner's opera. In 1983 he made his N.Y. debut as Guntram in a concert perf. of Strauss's opera. He sang for the first time at Milan's La Scala as Tannhäuser in 1984. In 1987 he first appeared at the Bayreuth Festival as Walther von Stolzing. He made his Metropolitan Opera debut in New York on Jan. 27, 1992, as Florestan. As one of the leading Heldentenors of his day, Goldberg won considerable distinction for his portrayals of Siegmund, Tannhäuser, Siegfried, Erik, and Parsifal. His versatile repertoire also included Bacchus, Max, Hermann in *The Queen of Spades*, Faust, the Drum Major in *Wozzeck*, and Sergei in *Lady Macbeth of the District of Mtzensk*.

Goldberg, Theo, German-born Canadian composer and teacher; b. Chemnitz, Sept. 29, 1921. He received training in composition from Blacher at the Berlin Hochschule für Musik (1945–50). In 1954 he emigrated to Canada and in 1973 became a naturalized Canadian citizen. He taught school in Vancouver but pursued his education at Washington State Univ. in Pullman (M.A., 1969) and the Univ. of Toronto (D.Mus., 1972). From 1970 to 1987 he taught music education at the Univ. of British Columbia in Vancouver. In his output from 1975, he placed special emphasis on mixed media, tape, and computers.

WORKS: DRAMATIC: *Nacht mit Kleopatra*, opera ballet (1950; Karlsruhe, Jan. 20, 1952); *Robinson und Freitag*, radio opera (1951); *Engel-Étude*, chamber opera (Berlin, Sept. 20, 1952); *Galatea Elettronica*, chamber opera (1969); *The Concrete Rose*, rock opera (1970); *Orphée aux enfers*, "opéra son et lumières" (1975); *Daedalus*, "opéra son et lumières" (1977); *Orion*, sound images (1978); incidental music for stage, radio, and television; various multimedia pieces, among them *Variations of a Mandala* (1973), *The Magic Carpet* (1982), and *The Hoard of the Nibelungen, as performed by a company of Baenkelsaengers* (1988).

Golde, Walter, American pianist, vocal teacher, and composer; b. Brooklyn, Jan. 4, 1887; d. Chapel Hill, N.C., Sept. 4, 1963. After piano training with Hugo Troetschel in Brooklyn, he studied at Dartmouth College, graduating in 1910; he then went to Vienna, where he took vocal lessons and studied counterpoint and composition with Robert Fuchs at the Cons. Returning to the United States, he was accompanist to many famous musicians of the day. From 1944 to 1948 he headed the voice dept. of Columbia Univ.; in 1953 he was appointed director of the Inst. of Opera at the Univ. of North Carolina. He composed a number of attractive songs and piano pieces.

Goldmann, Friedrich, German conductor, teacher, and composer; b. Siegmar-Schönau, April 27, 1941. After attending Stockhausen's seminar in Darmstadt (summer 1959), he studied composition with Thilman at the Dresden Hochschule für Musik (1959–62); he then attended the master classes of Wagner-Régeny at the Akademie der Künste in East Berlin (1962–64); subsequently he took courses in musicology with Knepler and Meyer at Humboldt Univ. in East Berlin (1964–68). In 1973 he received the Hanns Eisler Prize, and later the German Democratic Republic's Arts Prize (1977) and the National Prize (1987). In 1978 he became a member of the Akademie der Künste in East Berlin, and in 1990 was made president of the German section of the ISCM. In 1988 he became conductor at the Berlin Hochschule der Künste, where he was prof. of composition and conducting from 1991. His works include the opera fantasy *R. Hot bzw. die Hitze* (1976).

Goldmark, Karl (Károly), eminent Hungarian composer; b. Keszthely, May 18, 1830; d. Vienna, Jan. 2, 1915. His nephew was the American composer and teacher Rubin Goldmark (b. N.Y., Aug. 15, 1872; d. there, March 6, 1936). The son of a poor cantor, he studied at the school of the Musical Soc. of Sopron (1842–44). The talent he showed there as a violinist resulted in his being sent to Vienna, where he studied with L. Jansa (1844–45); he later studied at the Vienna Cons., as a pupil of Preyer (harmony) and Bohm (violin). He spent most of his life in Vienna, where the first concert of his compositions was given on March 20, 1857. Landmarks in his career were the first performance of his *Sakuntala* overture by the Vienna Phil. on Dec. 26, 1865, and the premiere of his first opera, *Die Königin von Saba*, at the Vienna Court Opera on March 10, 1875; both were very successful. He publ. an autobiography, *Erinnerungen aus meinem Leben* (Vienna, 1922; in Eng. as *Notes from the Life of a Viennese Composer*, N.Y., 1927).

WORKS: OPERAS: *Die Königin von Saba* (Vienna, March 10, 1875); *Merlin* (Vienna, Nov. 19, 1886); *Das Heimchen am Herd*, after Dickens's *The Cricket on the Hearth* (Vienna, March 21, 1896); *Die Kriegsgefangene* (Vienna, Jan. 17, 1899); *Götz von Berlichingen*, after Goethe's play (Budapest, Dec. 16, 1902); *Ein Wintermärchen*, after Shakespeare's *A Winter's Tale* (Vienna, Jan. 2, 1908).

BIBL.: O. Keller, *K. G.* (Leipzig, 1901); H. Schwarz, *Ignaz Brüll und sein Freundeskreis: Erinnerungen an Brüll, G. und Brahms* (Vienna, 1922); L. Koch, ed., *K. G.* (Budapest, 1930); P. Varnai, *Károly G.* (Budapest, 1957).

Goldovsky, Boris, Russian-American pianist, conductor, opera producer, lecturer, and broadcaster, son of **Lea** and nephew of **Pierre Luboshutz**; b. Moscow, June 7, 1908. He studied piano with his uncle and took courses at the Moscow Cons. (1918–21); in 1921 he made his debut as a pianist with the Berlin Phil., and continued his studies with Schnabel and Kreutzer at the Berlin Academy of Music (1921–23); after attending Dohnányi's master class at the Budapest Academy of Music (graduated, 1930), he received training in conducting from Reiner at the Curtis Inst. of Music in Philadelphia (1932). He served as head of the opera depts. at the New England Cons. of Music in Boston (1942–64), the Berkshire Music Center at Tanglewood (1946–61), and the Curtis Inst. of Music (from 1977). In 1946 he founded the New England Opera Theater in Boston, which became the Goldovsky Opera Inst. in 1963; he also toured with his own opera company until 1984. He was a frequent commentator for the Metropolitan Opera radio broadcasts (from 1946) and also lectured extensively; he prepared Eng. trans. of various operas.

WRITINGS: *Accents on Opera* (1953); *Bringing Opera to Life* (1968); with A. Schoep, *Bringing Soprano Arias to Life* (1973); with T. Wolf, *Manual of Operatic Touring* (1975); with C. Cate, *My Road to Opera* (1979); *Good Afternoon, Ladies and Gentlemen!: Intermission Scripts from the Met Broadcasts* (1984); *Adult Mozart: A Personal Perspective* (4 vols., 1991–93).

Goldschmidt, Adalbert von, Austrian composer; b. Vienna, May 5, 1848; d. Hacking, near Vienna, Dec. 21, 1906. He studied at the Vienna Cons. From his earliest efforts in composition, he became an ardent follower of Wagner. At the age of 22, he wrote a cantata, *Die sieben Todsünden* (Berlin, 1875); this was followed by a music drama, *Helianthus* (Leipzig, 1884), for which he wrote both words and music. A dramatic trilogy, *Gaea* (1889–92), was his most ambitious work along Wagnerian lines. He also brought out a comic opera, *Die fromme Helene* (Hamburg, 1897).

BIBL.: E. Friedegg, *Briefe an einen Komponisten: Musikalische Korrespondenz an A. v.G.* (Berlin, 1909).

Goldschmidt, Berthold, German-born English composer and conductor; b. Hamburg, Jan. 18, 1903; d. London, Oct. 17, 1996. He studied at the Univ. of Hamburg (1918–22) and took courses in composition (with Schreker) and in conducting at the Berlin State Academy of Music (1922–24). He participated as a répétiteur and celesta player in the premiere of Berg's opera *Wozzeck* in Berlin in 1925. After working as an assistant conductor at the Darmstadt Opera (1927–29), he was a conductor in Berlin with the Radio and the Städtische Oper (from 1931). With the Nazi takeover in 1933, he was dismissed. In 1935 he fled to England and in 1947 became a naturalized British subject. He made numerous appearances as a guest conductor in England. In 1959 he conducted the first complete British performance of Mahler's 3d Sym. That same year he was consulted by Deryck Cooke on the latter's performing version of Mahler's 10th Sym. Goldschmidt conducted Cooke's first though incomplete reconstruction of the sym. in a London recording studio on Dec. 19, 1960. He conducted the first complete performance of the sym. at a London Promenade Concert on Aug. 13, 1964. Goldschmidt's inability to secure a performance of his opera *Beatrice Cenci* led him to cease composing in 1958. It was nearly 25 years before he broke his silence with his Clarinet Quartet of 1983. By the end of the 1980s he had been "discovered," and was composing again with renewed vigor. Several of his works were either lost during World War II (*Passacalia* for Orch. and *Requiem* for Chorus and Orch.) or were withdrawn by the composer (Sym. and Harp Concerto). He wrote *Berthold Goldschmidt: Komponist und Dirigent: Ein Musiker-Leben zwischen Hamburg, Berlin und London* (ed. by P. Peterson, Hamburg, 1994).

WORKS: DRAMATIC: OPERAS: *Der gewaltige Hahnrei* (1929–30; Mannheim, Feb. 14, 1932); *Beatrice Cenci* (1949; concert version, London, April 16, 1988; stage version, Magdeburg, Sept. 10, 1994). BALLET: *Chronica* for 2 Pianos (1938; orch. suite, 1958).

BIBL.: S. Hilger and W. Jacobs, eds., *B. G.* (Bonn, 1993).

Goléa, Antoine, Austrian-born French writer on music of Romanian descent; b. Vienna, Aug. 30, 1906; d. Paris, Oct. 12, 1980. He studied at the Bucharest Cons. (1920–28). After further training at the Sorbonne in Paris (1928–31), he settled in that city as a journalist. His wife was the soprano Colette Herzog (1923–86).

WRITINGS (all publ. in Paris unless otherwise given): *Pelléas et Mélisande, analyse poétique et musicale* (1952); *Esthétique de la musique contemporaine* (1954); *L'Avénement de la musique classique, de Bach à Mozart* (1955); *Recontres avec Pierre Boulez* (1958); *Georges Auric* (1958); *Recontres avec Olivier Messiaen* (1959); *La Musique dans la société européenne depuis le moyen âge jusqu'a nos jours* (1960); *L'Aventure de la musique au XXe siècle* (1961); with A. Hodier and C. Samuel, *Panorama de l'art musical contemporaine* (1962); *Vingt ans de musique contemporaine* (1962); *J.-S. Bach* (1963); *Claude Debussy: L'homme et son oeuvre* (1965); *Richard Strauss* (1965); *Entretiens avec Wieland Wagner* (1967; German tr., 1968); *Histoire du ballet* (Lausanne, 1967); *Marcel Landowski: L'homme et son oeuvre* (1969); *Je suis un violoniste raté* (1973); *La Musique de la nuit des temps aux aurores nouvelles* (1977).

Goleminov, Marin, Bulgarian composer and pedagogue; b. Kjustendil, Sept. 28, 1908. He studied at the Bulgarian State Academy of Music in Sofia (graduated, 1931), in Paris with d'Indy (composition) and Labé (conducting) at the Schola Cantorum, with Dukas (composition) at the École Normale de Musique, and aesthetics and music history at the Sorbonne (1931–34), and with J. Haas (composition) and H. Knappe and E. Erenberg (conducting) at the Munich Akademie der Tonkunst (1938–39). From 1943 he taught at the Bulgarian State Academy of Music, where he was a prof. of orchestration, composition, and conducting, and its rector. From 1965 to 1967 he was director of the National Opera. He received various honors from the Bulgarian government. In 1976 he was awarded the Gottfried von Herder Prize of the Univ. of Vienna. In 1991 he became a member of the Bulgarian Academy of Sciences. He publ. books in Sofia on the sources of Bulgarian musical composition (1937), instrumentation (1947), orchestration (2 vols., 1953; 3d ed., 1966), and on the creative process (1971). In his music, he utilized folk elements, particularly the asymmetrical rhythms of Bulgarian folk motifs, in a fairly modern but still quite accessible idiom.

WORKS: DRAMATIC: OPERAS: *Ivailo* (1958; Sofia, Feb. 13, 1959); *Zlatnata ptica* (The Golden Bird; Sofia, Dec. 20, 1961); *Zahari the Icon Painter* (1971; Sofia, Oct. 17, 1972); *Thracian Idols* (1981). BALLETS: *Nestinarka* (1940; Sofia, Jan. 4, 1942); *The Daughter of Kaloyan* (Sofia, Dec. 23, 1973).

BIBL.: B. Arnaudova, *M. G.* (Sofia, 1968); S. Lazarov, *M. G.* (Sofia, 1971); R. Apostolova, *M. G.* (Sofia, 1988); L. Braschowanowa and M. Miladinova, *M. G.: Biobibliografski ocherk* (Sofia, 1990).

Golovanov, Nikolai (Semyonovich), Russian conductor, composer, and pedagogue; b. Moscow, Jan. 21, 1891; d. there, Aug. 28, 1953. He studied choral conducting with Kastalsky at the Synodal School in Moscow, graduating in 1909; he then entered the composition classes of Ippolitov-Ivanov and Vassilenko at the Moscow Cons. After graduation in 1914 he was engaged as assistant chorusmaster at the Bolshoi Theater in Moscow; he was its chief conductor (1919–28; 1948–53); he was also chief conductor of the Moscow Phil. (1926–29), the USSR All-Union Radio Sym. Orch. (1937–53), and the Stanislavsky Opera Theater (1938–53). He was awarded the Order of the Red Banner in 1935, and was 4 times recipient of the 1st Stalin Prize (1946, 1948, 1950, 1951). He wrote an opera, *Princess Yurata*. He was married to **Antonina Nezhdanova**.

Golschmann, Vladimir, notable French-born American conductor of Russian descent; b. Paris, Dec. 16, 1893; d. N.Y., March 1, 1972. He studied violin and piano, and received training at the Paris Schola Cantorum in harmony, counterpoint, and composition. He played violin in orchs. in Paris, where he founded the Concerts Golschmann in 1919, at which he conducted many premieres of contemporary works; he also conducted opera and from 1920 was a conductor of ballet for Diaghilev. In 1923 he conducted in the United States for the first time with Les Ballets Suédois, and returned in 1924 as a guest conductor of the N.Y. Sym. Orch. A successful engagement as a guest conductor of the St. Louis Sym. Orch. in 1931 led to his appointment that year as its music director, a position he held with distinction for 27 years. In 1947 he became a naturalized American citizen. He later was music director of the Tulsa Phil. (1958–61) and the Denver Sym. Orch. (1964–70). Throughout his long career, he appeared as a guest conductor in North America and Europe. In addition to the 20th-century repertory, Golschmann's brilliance as an interpreter was at its best in the colorful works of the Romantic era.

Goltz, Christel, German soprano; b. Dortmund, July 8, 1912. She studied in Munich with Ornelli-Leeb. In 1935 she joined the chorus of the Fürth Opera, where she soon made her operatic debut as Agathe; from 1936 to 1950 she was a member of the Dresden State Opera; she also sang with the Berlin State Opera and the Berlin City Opera. In 1951 she sang Salome at her debut at London's Covent Garden. From 1951 to 1970 she made many appearances with the Vienna State Opera; in 1952 she was named a Kammersängerin. On Dec. 15, 1954, she made her Metropolitan Opera debut in New York as Salome, remaining on its roster for the season. She sang in many productions of modern operas.

Gomes, (Antônio) Carlos, Brazilian composer; b. Campinas (of Portuguese parents), July 11, 1836; d. Belem, Sept. 16, 1896. He studied with his father, then at the Rio de Janeiro Cons., where he produced 2 operas, *A Noite do Castello* (Sept. 4, 1861) and *Joana de Flandres* (Sept. 15, 1863). The success of these works induced Emperor Don Pedro II to grant him a stipend for further study in Milan; there he soon made his mark with a humorous little piece entitled *Se sa minga* (a song from this work, *Del fucile ad ago*, became popular), produced in 1867. After another piece in the same vein (*Nella Luna*, 1868), he made a more serious bid for fame with the opera *Il Guarany*, produced at La Scala on March 19, 1870, with brilliant success; this work, in which Amazon Indian themes are used, quickly went the round of Italy, and was given in London (Covent Garden) on July 13, 1872. Returning to Rio de Janeiro, Gomes brought out a very popular operetta, *Telegrapho elettrico*. His other operas are *Fosca* (La Scala, Milan, Feb. 16, 1873), *Salvator Rosa* (Genoa, March 21, 1874), *Maria Tudor* (La Scala, Milan, March 27, 1879), *Lo Schiavo* (Rio de Janeiro, Sept. 27, 1889), and *Condor* (La Scala, Milan, Feb. 21, 1891). He wrote the hymn *Il saluto del Brasile* for the centenary of American independence (Philadelphia, July 19, 1876); also the cantata *Colombo*, for the Columbus Festival (Oct. 12, 1892). In 1895 he was appointed director of the newly founded Belém Cons., but he died soon after arriving there.

BIBL.: S. Boccanera Júnior, *Um artista brasileiro: In memoriam* (Bahia, 1904); H. Vieira, *C. G.: Sua arte e sua obra* (São Paulo, 1934); I. Gomes Vaz de Carvalho, *A vida de C. G.* (Rio de Janeiro, 1935; Italian tr., Milan, 1935); R. Seidl, *C. G.: Brasileiro e patriota* (Rio de Janeiro, 1935); J. Prito, *C. G.* (São Paulo, 1936); L. Vieira Souto, *A. C. G.* (Rio de Janeiro, 1936); R. Almeida, *C. G.* (Rio de Janeiro, 1937); M. de Andrade, *C. G.* (Rio de Janeiro, 1939); P. Cerquera, *C. G.* (São Paulo, 1944).

Gomes de Araújo, João, Brazilian composer; b. Pindamonhangaba, Aug. 5, 1846; d. São Paulo, Sept. 8, 1942. He studied at São Paulo and Milan. In 1905 he became a teacher at the São Paulo Cons., remaining there almost to the end of his long life. Among his works were 4 operas: *Edmea*, *Carminosa* (Milan, 1888), *Maria Petrowna* (1904; São Paulo, 1929), and *Helena* (São Paulo, 1910).

Gomez, Jill, British Guianan soprano; b. New Amsterdam, Sept. 21, 1942. She studied in London at the Royal Academy of Music and the Guildhall School of Music. After her operatic debut in a minor role in *Oberon* with the Cambridge Univ. Opera in 1967, she sang Adina with the Glyndebourne Touring Opera in 1968. In 1969 she made her first appearance at the Glyndebourne Festival as Mélisande. On Dec. 2, 1970, she created the role of Flora in Tippett's *The Knot Garden* at London's Covent Garden. She appeared as the Countess in Musgrave's *The Voice of Ariadne* with the English Opera Group in 1974. In 1977 she sang Tatiana at the Kent Opera. On March 25, 1979, she created the title role in the posthumous premiere of Prokofiev's *Maddalena* on the BBC. She appeared as the Governess in Britten's *The Turn of the Screw* at the English National Opera in London in 1984. She also sang opera in Glasgow, Cardiff, Zürich, Geneva, Frankfurt am Main, Lyons, and other cities. Among her other roles were Fiordiligi, Donna Anna, Handel's Cleopatra, Berlioz's Teresa, Bizet's Leïla, and Britten's Helena. As a concert artist, she was engaged for many appearances in Europe and North America.

Gomez Martínez, Miguel Angel, Spanish conductor; b. Granada, Sept. 17, 1949. After piano studies with his mother, he enrolled at the Granada Cons.; also studied composition, piano, and violin at the Madrid Cons.; he later attended the conducting classes of Boult and Leinsdorf at the Berkshire Music Center at Tanglewood; he then studied with Markevitch in Madrid and Swarowsky in Vienna. He was music director of the St. Pölten Stadttheater (1971–72) and principal conductor of the Lucerne Stadttheater (1972–74); in 1973 he conducted at the Deutsche Oper in Berlin; he was subsequently its resident conductor (1974–77). In 1976 he was made resident conductor at the Vienna State Opera; he also conducted in Berlin, Munich, Hamburg, London (at Covent Garden), Geneva, and Paris; in 1980 he made his U.S. debut, conducting at the Houston Grand Opera. From 1984 to 1987 he was principal conductor of the Orquestra Sinfónica de Radiotelevisión Española in Madrid. He was artistic director and chief conductor of the Teatro Lérico Nacional in Madrid from 1985 to 1991. In 1990 he became Generalmusikdirektor in Mannheim. He then served as chief conductor of the Finnish National Opera in Helsinki (1993–96), and of the Hamburg Sym. Orch. (1993–2000).

Gondek, Juliana (Kathleen), American soprano; b. Pasadena, Calif., May 20, 1953. She studied at the Univ. of Southern Calif. in Los Angeles (B.M., 1975; M.M., 1977), and also attended the Britten-Pears School of Advanced Musical Studies in Aldeburgh. After singing with the San Diego Opera (1979–81), she appeared in 1983 with the Baltimore Opera and sang Giovanna d'Arco with the N.Y. Grand Opera. She won the gold medals at the Geneva (1983) and Francisco Viñas (Barcelona, 1984) competitions; she then appeared as Mozart's Countess with the Netherlands Opera in Amsterdam (1986). In 1987 she sang Alcina with the Opera Theatre of St. Louis and Bianca with the Greater Miami Opera. She made her Metropolitan Opera debut in New York as Marianne in *Der Rosenkavalier* on Sept. 25, 1990. In 1991 she appeared as Vitellia with Glasgow's Scottish Opera and as Elvira with the Seattle Opera. She sang Ginevra in *Ariodante* in Göttingen and appeared in the premiere of *Harvey Milk* in Houston in 1995. In 1996 she created the role of Ela in David Carlson's *Dreamkeepers* in Salt Lake City. Gondek also pursued wide-ranging concert engagements with major orchs. in North America and Europe; also appeared at leading festivals and as a recitalist.

Gönnenwein, Wolfgang, German conductor, pedagogue, and operatic administrator; b. Schwäbisch-Hall, Jan. 29, 1933. He was educated at the Stuttgart Hochschule für Musik and at the univs. of Heidelberg and Tübingen. In 1959 he became conductor of the South German Madrigal Choir of Stuttgart, with which he toured Germany and Europe. In 1968 he was made prof. of choral conducting at the Stuttgart Hochschule für Musik, and in 1973 was named its director. He also was conductor of the Bach Choir of Cologne (1969–73) and later Intendant of the Württemberg State Theater in Stuttgart (1985–92).

Goodall, Sir Reginald, notable English conductor; b. Lincoln, July 13, 1901; d. Barham, May 5, 1990. He studied piano, violin, and conducting at the Royal College of Music in London, and later pursued his training in Munich and Vienna. In 1936 he made his debut conducting *Carmen* in London, and became a répétiteur at Covent Garden there. From 1936 to 1939 he was assistant conductor of the Royal Choral Soc. in London. His decision to join the British Union of Fascists just 5 days after Hitler invaded Poland in 1939 undoubtedly played a role in delaying his career opportunities. From 1944 to 1946 he was a conductor at the Sadler's Wells Opera in London, where he was chosen to conduct the premiere of Britten's *Peter Grimes* on June 7, 1945. From 1946 to 1961 he was on the conducting staff at Covent Garden, but then was relegated to the position of a répétiteur there from 1961 to 1971. Thereafter he again had the opportunity to conduct there. In 1968 he emerged as a major operatic conductor when he conducted a remarkable performance of *Die Meistersinger von Nürnberg* in English at the Sadler's Wells Opera. In 1973 he conducted an acclaimed traversal of the *Ring* cycle there in English. In subsequent years, he was ranked among the leading Wagnerian interpreters of the day. In 1975 he was made a Commander of the Order of the British Empire. He was knighted in 1985.

BIBL.: J. Lucas, *Reggie: The Life of R. G.* (London, 1993).

Goodman (real name, **Guttmann**), **Alfred,** German-American composer; b. Berlin, March 1, 1920. After training in Berlin, he went to England in 1939 and then to the United States in 1940, and subsequently served in the U.S. Army. Following studies with Cowell and Luening at Columbia Univ. (B.S., 1952; M.A., 1953), he returned to Germany in 1960 and was a composer and broadcaster with the Bavarian Radio in Munich; he later was its music adviser (1971–85). In 1973 he received his Ph.D. from the Free Univ. of Berlin, and then taught at the Munich Hochschule für Musik (from 1976). His compositions include the operas *The Audition* (1948–54; Athens, Ohio, July 27, 1954), *Der Läufer* (1969), and *The Lady and the Maid* (1984). He publ. *Musik von A-Z* (Munich, 1971) and *Sachwörterbuch der Musik* (Munich, 1982).

Goodman, Roy, English conductor, violinist, and keyboard player; b. Guilford, Surrey, Jan. 26, 1951. After serving as a chorister at King's College, Cambridge (1959–64), he studied at the Royal College of Music in London (1968–70) and the Berkshire College of Education (1970–71). He then was director of music at the Univ. of Kent and of early music at the Royal Academy of Music in London, and then founded the Brandenburg Consort in 1975. From 1979 to 1986 he was codirector of the Parley of Instruments. He was principal conductor of the Hanover Band from 1986 to 1994, an orch. specializing in period instrument performances of scores from the Baroque and Classical eras. He also conducted operas from that period, especially those by Handel and Mozart. In 1988 he became music director of the European Union Baroque Orch. He also was music director of the Umeå Sym. Orch. in Sweden from 1996.

Goossens, prominent family of English musicians of Belgian descent:

(1) Eugène Goossens, conductor; b. Bruges, Feb. 25, 1845; d. Liverpool, Dec. 30, 1906. He studied violin at the Bruges Cons. and violin and composition at the Brussels Cons.; in 1873 he went to London, where he appeared as an operetta conductor; he was 2d conductor (1883–89) and principal conductor (1889–93) of the Carl Rosa Opera Co., he then settled in Liverpool, where he was founder-conductor of the Goossens Male Voice Choir (from 1894).

(2) Eugène Goossens, violinist and conductor, son of the preceding; b. Bordeaux, Jan. 28, 1867; d. London, July 31, 1958. He studied in Bruges and at the Brussels Cons. (1883–86); then went to England, where he worked as a violinist, répétiteur, and assistant conductor under his father with the Carl Rosa Opera Co.; he also continued his studies at London's Royal Academy of Music (1891–92). After conducting various traveling opera companies, he served as principal conductor of the Carl Rosa Opera Co. (1899–1915); later he was a conductor with the British National Opera Co. He had the following 4 children, who became musicians:

(3) Sir (Aynsley) Eugene Goossens, distinguished conductor and composer; b. London, May 26, 1893; d. there, June 13, 1962. He first studied at the Bruges Cons. (1903–04), then at the Liverpool College of Music. After winning a scholarship to the Royal College of Music in London in 1907, he studied there with Rivarde (violin), Dykes (piano), and C. Wood and Stanford (composition). He was a violinist in the Queen's Hall Orch. (1912–15), then was assistant conductor to Beecham (1915–20). In 1921 he founded his own London orch.; he conducted opera and ballet at Covent Garden (1921–23). After serving as conductor of the Rochester (N.Y.) Phil. (1923–31), he greatly distinguished himself as conductor of the Cincinnati Sym. Orch. from 1931 to 1947. He then was conductor of the Sydney (Australia) Sym. Orch. and director of the New South Wales Conservatorium (1947–56). In 1955 he was knighted. He was a discriminating interpreter of the late 19th- and early 20th-century repertoire of the Romantic and Impressionist schools. As a composer, he wrote in all genres; his style became a blend of impressionistic harmonies and neoclassical polyphony; while retaining a clear tonal outline, he often resorted to expressive chromatic melos bordering on atonality. His dramatic works include *L'École en crinoline*, ballet (1921), *East of Suez*, incidental music to Maugham's play (1922), *Judith*, opera (1925; London, June 25, 1929), and *Don Juan de Mañana*, opera

(1934; London, June 24, 1937); also *Apocalypse*, oratorio (1951; Sydney, Nov. 22, 1954, composer conducting). He publ. *Overture and Beginners: A Musical Autobiography* (London, 1951).

(4) Marie (Henriette) Goossens, harpist; b. London, Aug. 11, 1894; d. Dorking, Surrey, Dec. 18, 1991. She studied at the Royal College of Music in London. She made her debut in Liverpool in 1910, then was principal harpist at Covent Garden, the Diaghilev Ballet, the Queen's Hall Orch. (1920–30), the London Phil. (1932–39), the London Sym. Orch. (1940–59), and the London Mozart Players (from 1972). She was also prof. of harp at the Royal College of Music (1954–67). In 1984 she was made an Officer of the Order of the British Empire. Her autobiography was publ. as *Life on a Harp String* (1987).

(5) Leon Goossens, eminent oboist; b. Liverpool, June 12, 1897; d. Tunbridge Wells, Feb. 13, 1988. He studied at the Royal College of Music in London (1911–14). He played in the Queen's Hall Orch. (1914–24), and later in the orchs. of Covent Garden and the Royal Phil. Soc.; subsequently he was principal oboe of the London Phil. (1932–39); he was also prof. of oboe at the Royal Academy of Music (1924–35) and the Royal College of Music (1924–39). In succeeding years, he appeared as a soloist with major orchs. and as a chamber music artist; in 1962 he suffered injuries to his lips and teeth as a result of an automobile accident, but after extensive therapy he was able to resume his virtuoso career. He commissioned works from several English composers, among them Elgar and Vaughan Williams. In 1950 he was made a Commander of the Order of the British Empire.

(6) Sidonie Goossens, harpist; b. Liscard, Cheshire, Oct. 19, 1899. She studied at the Royal College of Music in London. She made her orch. debut in 1921; she was principal harpist of the BBC Sym. Orch. in London (1930–80), and served as prof. of harp at the Guildhall School of Music there (from 1960). She was made a Member of the Order of the British Empire in 1974 and an Officer of the Order of the British Empire in 1981.

BIBL.: C. Rosen, *The G.: A Musical Century* (London, 1993).

Gorchakova, Galina, compelling Russian soprano; b. Novokuznetsk, March 1, 1962. She was born into a musical family, her father being a baritone and her mother a soprano. She studied at the Novokuznetsk Academy of Music and Cons. From 1988 to 1990 she sang with the Sverdlovsk Opera. During this time, she also appeared as a guest artist throughout Russia. In 1990 she made her debut at the Kirov Opera in St. Petersburg as Yaroslavna in *Prince Igor*. She secured her position as one of the company's leading artists shortly thereafter with her stunning portrayal of Renata in *The Fiery Angel*. In 1991 she sang Renata again in a concert performance in London, and again in 1992 with the visiting Kirov Opera at the Metropolitan Opera in New York. In 1994 she made her San Francisco Opera debut as Prokofiev's Renata. On Jan. 4, 1995, she made her debut with the Metropolitan Opera as Cio-Cio-San. Later that year she sang in Rome, Los Angeles, Edinburgh, and London, and appeared as Tosca at the Opéra de la Bastille in Paris. In 1996 she was engaged as Cio-Cio-San at Milan's La Scala and as Tosca at London's Covent Garden. In 1997 she appeared as Tchaikovsky's Tatiana at the Metropolitan Opera. She also pursued a highly successful career as a recitalist. In addition to her compelling interpretations of the Russian operatic repertoire, Gorchakova has won distinction in operas by Verdi and Puccini.

Goritz, Otto, German baritone; b. Berlin, June 8, 1873; d. Hamburg, April 11, 1929. He received his musical education from his mother, Olga Nielitz. He made his debut on Oct. 1, 1895, as Matteo (*Fra Diavolo*) at Neustrelitz; his success led to an immediate engagement for 3 years; from 1898 to 1900 he was in Breslau; from 1900 to 1903, in Hamburg. On Dec. 24, 1903, he made his American debut at the Metropolitan Opera in New York as Klingsor in the first production of *Parsifal* outside Bayreuth; he remained there until 1917. In 1924 he returned to Germany, where he sang in Berlin and Hamburg.

Gorr, Rita (real name, **Marguerite Geirnaert**), noted Belgian mezzo-soprano; b. Zelzaete, Feb. 18, 1926. She was a student in Ghent of Poelfiet and in Brussels of Pacquot-d'Assy. After winning 1st prize in the Verviers Competition in 1946, she made her formal operatic debut as Fricka in Antwerp in 1949, and then sang in Strasbourg (1949–52). In 1952 she won 1st prize in the Lausanne Competition, which led to engagements at the Opéra Comique and the Opéra in Paris that same year. In 1958 she appeared at the Bayreuth Festival for the first time. In 1959 she made her debut at London's Covent Garden as Amneris, where she sang regularly with notable success until 1971. In 1960 she sang at Milan's La Scala for the first time as Kundry. She made her Metropolitan Opera debut in New York as Amneris on Oct. 17, 1962, and remained on its roster until 1967. Gorr was a remarkably versatile artist, excelling in the works of Wagner and Verdi as well as in the French repertory. Among her memorable roles were Fricka, Kundry, Ortrud, Azucena, Eboli, Amneris, Ulrica, Charlotte, Delilah, and Berlioz's Dido.

Gossec, François-Joseph, significant South Netherlands composer; b. Vergnies, Jan. 17, 1734; d. Paris, Feb. 16, 1829. He showed musical inclinations at an early age; as a child he studied at the collegiate church in Walcourt and sang in the chapel of St. Aldegonde in Maubeuge; he then joined the chapel of St. Pierre there, where he studied violin, harpsichord, harmony, and composition with Jean Vanderbelen. In 1742 he was engaged as a chorister at the Cathedral of Notre Dame in Antwerp, where he received some instruction with André-Joseph Blavier in violin and organ. In 1751 he went to Paris, and in 1754 joined a private musical ensemble of the rich amateur La Pouplinière. There he wrote chamber music and little syms., in which he seems to have anticipated Haydn; several works for string quartet followed in 1759. After the death of La Poupliniere in 1762, Gossec became director of the private theater of Louis-Joseph de Bourbon, prince of Condé, in Chantilly. In 1760 he wrote a Requiem; he then turned his attention to stage music, producing a 3-act opéra comique, *Le Faux Lord* (Paris, June 27, 1765); he obtained a decisive success with another short opéra comique, *Les Pêcheurs* (Paris, April 23, 1766). In 1769 he organized a performing society, Concerts des Amateurs; he became a director of the Concert Spirituel (1773–77), and was also an associate director of the Paris Opéra (1780–85) and director of the École Royale de Chant (1784–89); when this school became the Cons. in 1795, Gossec became one of the inspectors, and also taught composition there. He publ. a manual, *Exposition des principes de la musique*, for use at the Cons. In 1795 he became a member of the newly founded Académie des Beaux-Arts of the Institut de France. Gossec welcomed the French Revolution with great enthusiasm, and wrote many festive works to celebrate Revolutionary events, among them *L'Offrande à la Liberté* (1792), *Le Triomphe de la République* (1793), and numerous marches and hymns. During his long life he saw many changes of regime, but retained his position in the musical world and in society throughout the political upheavals. He retired to Passy, then a suburb of Paris, at the age of 80.

Gossec's historic role consists in his creation of a French type of symphonic composition, in which he expanded the resources of instrumentation so as to provide for dynamic contrasts; he experimented with new sonorities in instrumental and choral writing; his string quartets attained a coherence of style and symmetry of form that laid the foundation of French chamber music. In his choral works, Gossec was a bold innovator, presaging in some respects the usages of Berlioz; his *Te Deum* (1790), written for a Revolutionary festival, is scored for 1,200 singers and 300 wind instruments; in his oratorio *La Nativité* (1774), he introduced an invisible chorus of angels placed behind the stage; in other works, he separated choral groups in order to produce special antiphonal effects.

WORKS: DRAMATIC: *Le Périgourdin*, intermezzo (private theater of the Prince of Conti, Paris, June 7, 1761); *Le Tonnelier*, opéra comique (Comédie-Italienne, Paris, March 16, 1765); *Le Faux Lord*, opéra comique (Comédie-Italienne, June 27, 1765); *Les Pêcheurs*, opéra comique (Comédie-Italienne, April 23, 1766); *To-*

inon et Toinette, opéra comique (Comédie-Italienne, June 20, 1767); *Le Double Déguisement*, opéra comique (Comédie-Italienne, Sept. 28, 1767); *Les Agréments d'Hylas et Sylvie*, pastorale (Comédie-Française, Dec. 10, 1768); *Sabinus*, tragédie lyrique (Versailles, Dec. 4, 1773); *Berthe*, opera (Théâtre Royal de la Monnaie, Brussels, Jan. 18, 1775; not extant); *Alexis et Daphné*, pastorale (Opéra, Paris, Sept. 26, 1775); *Philémon et Baucis*, pastorale (Opéra, Sept. 26, 1775); *Annette et Lubin*, ballet (Opéra, 1778); *La Fête de village*, intermezzo (Opéra, May 26, 1778); *Mirza*, ballet (Opéra, Nov. 18, 1779; rev. 1788); *La Fête de Mirza*, ballet pantomime (Opéra, Feb. 17, 1781); *Thésée*, tragédie lyrique (Opéra, March 1, 1782); *Electre*, incidental music (1782); *Nitocris*, opera (1783); *Le Premier Navigateur, ou Le Pouvoir de l'amour*, ballet (Opéra, July 26, 1785); *Athalie*, incidental music (Fontainebleau, Nov. 3?, 1785); *Rosine, ou L'Eposue abandonnée*, opera (Opéra, July 14, 1786); *Le Pied de boeuf*, divertissement (Opéra, June 17, 1787); *Les Sabots et le cerisier*, opera (Théâtre des Jeunes Eleves, Paris, 1803). Also the oratorios *La Nativité* (1774; ed. by D. Townsend, N.Y., 1966) and *L'Arche d'alliance* (1781; not extant).

BIBL.: P. Hédouin, *G.: Sa vie et ses ouvrages* (Valenciennes, 1852); É. Gregoir, *Notice biographique sur F.-J. Gossé dit G., compositeur de musique* (Mons, 1878); F. Hellouin, *G. et la musique française à la fin du XVIIIe siècle* (Paris, 1903); L. Dufrane, *G.: Sa vie, ses oeuvres* (Paris, 1927); F. Tonnard, *F.-J. G.: Musicien hennuyer de la Révolution française* (Brussels, 1938).

Gossett, Philip, esteemed American musicologist; b. N.Y., Sept. 27, 1941. He was educated at Amherst College (B.A., 1963), Columbia Univ. (1961–62), and Princeton Univ. (M.F.A., 1965; Ph.D., 1970, with the diss. *The Operas of Rossini: Problems of Textual Criticism in Nineteenth-Century Opera*); he held a Fulbright fellowship (1965–66) and a Guggenheim fellowship (1971–72). He joined the faculty at the Univ. of Chicago in 1968, where he was a prof. (from 1977) and chairman of the music dept. (1978–84). From 1995 to 1996 he was president of the American Musicological Soc. He ed. and tr. Rameau's *Traité de l'harmonie* as *Treatise on Harmony by Jean-Philippe Rameau* (N.Y., 1971); with C. Rosen, he ed. *Early Romantic Opera* (44 vols., N.Y., 1977–83); he also ed. *Italian Opera 1810–1840* (58 vols., N.Y., 1984-) and served as general ed. of *The Works of Giuseppe Verdi*. He publ. *The Tragic Finale of Tancredi* (Pesaro, 1977), *Le Sinfonie di Rossini* (Pesaro, 1981), and *Anna Bolena and the Artistic Maturity of Gaetano Donizetti* (Oxford, 1985), for which he received the ASCAP–Deems Taylor Award in 1986.

Gotovac, Jakov, Croatian conductor and composer; b. Split, Oct. 11, 1895; d. Zagreb, Oct. 16, 1982. He studied law at the Univ. of Zagreb, and music with Antun Dobronic in Zagreb and with Joseph Marx in Vienna. In 1923 he was appointed conductor of the Croatian National Opera in Zagreb, retaining this post until 1958. He composed mostly for the theater; his instrumental music is imbued with the folkways of Croatia, enhancing the simple native materials by carefully proportioned modernistic mutations while preserving the impulsive asymmetrical patterns of the original songs.

WORKS: OPERAS: *Dubravka* (1928); *Morana* (Brno, Nov. 29, 1930); *Ero s onoga svijeta* (A Rogue from the World Beyond; Zagreb, Nov. 2, 1935; in Ger. as *Ero der Schelm*, Karlsruhe, April 3, 1938); *Kamenik* (The Quarry; Zagreb, Dec. 17, 1946); *Mila Gojsalica* (Zagreb, May 18, 1952); *Stanac* (Zagreb, Dec. 6, 1959); *Dalmaro* (Zagreb, Dec. 20, 1964); *Petar Svačiç*, opera oratorio (1969).

Gottlieb, Jack, American composer; b. New Rochelle, N.Y., Oct. 12, 1930. He was a student of Rathaus at Queens College in New York (B.A., 1953), of Fine at Brandeis Univ. (M.F.A., 1955), of Copland and Blacher at the Berkshire Music Center in Tanglewood (summers, 1954–55), and of Phillips and Palmer at the Univ. of Ill. (D.M.A., 1964, with the diss. *The Music of Leonard Bernstein: A Study of Melodic Manipulations*). From 1958 to 1966 he was Bernstein's assistant at the N.Y. Phil. After serving as music director of Temple Israel in St. Louis (1970–73), he returned to New York and was composer-in-residence (1973–75) and assistant prof. (1975–77) at the School of Music at Hebrew Union College–Jewish Inst. of Religion. From 1977 he worked for Amberson Enterprises, the company responsible for Bernstein's musical activities. After Bernstein's death, he served as an archivist-consultant for the Bernstein Estate. He also was president of the American Soc. for Jewish Music from 1991. In both his secular and sacred music, Gottlieb has followed a generally contemporary course.

WORKS: DRAMATIC: *Tea Party*, opera (1955; Athens, Ohio, Aug. 4, 1957); *Public Dance*, opera (1964); *The Song of Songs, Which Is Solomon's*, operatorio (1968–76); *The Movie Opera* (1982; rev. 1994); *Death of a Ghost*, opera (N.Y., Dec. 13, 1988); *After the Flood*, musical fable (1990–91; rev. 1995); *Monkey Biz'nis*, musical diversion (1991–93); *Love, Divorce, and Other Considerations*, theater piece (1994–95).

Gottlieb, (Maria) Anna, Austrian singer and actress; b. Vienna, April 29, 1774; d. there, Feb. 4, 1856. She was reared in a theatrical family and made her first appearance in the theater as a child. At the age of 12 she created the role of Barbarina in Mozart's *Le nozze di Figaro* (Vienna, May 1, 1786). Mozart later chose her to create the role of Pamina in his *Die Zauberflöte* (Vienna, Sept. 30, 1791). She subsequently pursued a career mainly as a singer in Singspiels and musical parodies, and as an actress. She was a member of the Freihaustheater (1790–93) and of the Theater in der Leopoldstadt (1792–1809; 1813–28) in Vienna.

Gottwald, Clytus, German choral conductor, musicologist, and composer; b. Bad Salzbrunn, Silesia, Nov. 25, 1925. He received training in voice, choral conducting, and musicology at the Univ. of Tübingen, and also took courses in sociology, theology, and folklore. He completed his education at the Univ. of Frankfurt am Main (Ph.D., 1961, with the diss. *Johannes Ghiselen—Johannes Verbonnet: Stilkritische Untersuchung zum Problem ihrer Identität*; publ. in Wiesbaden, 1962). In 1960 he founded the Schola Cantorum Stuttgart, a polyphonic vocal ensemble he conducted in enterprising concerts until 1990. In addition to works of the 15th and 16th ceturies, he also conducted contemporary avant-garde scores. From 1969 to 1989 he was an ed. for new music for the South German Radio in Stuttgart. He contributed valuable articles to many journals and other publications on subjects ranging from early music to the avant-garde, from Josquin to John Cage. He ed. the complete works of Ghiselen in Corpus Mensurabilis Musicae, XXIII/1–4 (1961–68) and publ. *Codices musici* (series 1, *Die Handschriften der Württembergischen Landesbibliothek Stuttgart*, Wiesbaden, 1964; series 2, *Die Handschriften de ehemals Königlichen Hofbibliothek*, Wiesbaden, 1965) and *Katalog der Musikalien in der Schermar-Bibliothek Ulm* (Wiesbaden, 1993). As a composer, he tended toward the experimental, producing a number of advanced vocal works.

Götze, Johann Nikolaus Konrad, German violinist and composer; b. Weimar, Feb. 11, 1791; d. there, Feb. 5, 1861. He studied with Kreutzer in Paris. Returning to Weimar, he was music director to the Grand Duke (1826–48). He played concerts in Germany and Austria. He wrote operas, some of which he produced in Weimar.

Götze, Karl, German conductor and composer; b. Weimar, 1836; d. Magdeburg, Jan. 14, 1887. He was a pupil of Töpfer and Gebhardi, later of Liszt. He then was active as a theater conductor. Among his works were the operas *Die Korsen* (Weimar, 1866), *Gustav Wasa, Der Held des Nordens* (Weimar, 1868), and *Judith* (Magdeburg, 1887).

Gounod, Charles (François), famous French composer; b. St. Cloud, June 17, 1818; d. Paris, Oct. 18, 1893. His father, Jean François Gounod, was a painter, winner of the 2d Grand Prix de Rome, who died when Gounod was a small child. His mother, a most accomplished woman, supervised his literary, artistic, and musical education, and taught him piano. He completed his academic studies at the Lycée St. Louis, and in 1836 entered the Paris Cons., studying with Halévy, Le Sueur, and Paër. In 1837 he won the 2d

Prix de Rome with his cantata *Marie Stuart et Rizzio*, and in 1839 he won the Grand Prix with his cantata *Fernand*. In Rome, he studied church music, particularly the works of Palestrina; he composed a Mass for 3 Voices and Orch., which was performed at the church of San Luigi dei Francesi. In 1842, during a visit to Vienna, he conducted a Requiem of his own; upon his return to Paris, he became precentor and organist of the Missions Etrangeres. He studied theology for 2 years, but decided against taking Holy Orders, yet he was often referred to as l'Abbé Gounod; some religious choruses were publ. in 1846 as composed by Abbé Charles Gounod. Soon he tried his hand at stage music. On April 16, 1851, his first opera, *Sapho*, was produced at the Opéra, with only moderate success; he revised it much later, extending it to 4 acts from the original 3, and it was performed again on April 2, 1884; but it was unsuccessful. His 2nd opera, *La Nonne sanglante*, in 5 acts, was staged at the Opéra on Oct. 18, 1854; there followed a comic opera, *Le Médecin malgré lui*, after Molière (Jan. 15, 1858), which also failed to realize his expectations. In the meantime, he was active in other musical ways in Paris; he conducted the choral society Orphéon (1852–60) and composed for it several choruses. Gounod's great success came with the production of *Faust*, after Goethe (Théâtre-Lyrique, March 19, 1859; perf. with additional recitatives and ballet at the Opéra, March 3, 1869); *Faust* remained Gounod's greatest masterpiece, and indeed the most successful French opera of the 19th century, triumphant all over the world without any sign of diminishing effect through a century of changes in musical tastes. However, it was widely criticized for the melodramatic treatment of Goethe's poem by the librettists, Barbier and Carre, and for the somewhat sentimental style of Gounod's music. The succeeding operas *Philémon et Baucis* (Paris, Feb. 18, 1860), *La Colombe* (Baden-Baden, Aug. 3, 1860), *La Reine de Saba* (Paris, Feb. 29, 1862), and *Mireille* (Paris, March 19, 1864) were only partially successful, but with *Roméo et Juliette* (Paris, April 27, 1867), Gounod recaptured universal acclaim. In 1870, during the Franco-Prussian War, he went to London, where he organized Gounod's Choir, and presented concerts; when Paris fell, he wrote an elegiac cantata, *Gallia*, to words from the Lamentations of Jeremiah, which he conducted in London on May 1, 1871; it was later performed in Paris. He wrote some incidental music for productions in Paris: *Les Deux Reines*, to a drama by Legouvé (Nov. 27, 1872), and *Jeanne d'Arc*, to Barbier's poem (Nov. 8, 1873). In 1874 he returned to Paris, where he produced his operas *Cinq-Mars* (April 5, 1877), *Polyeucte* (Oct. 7, 1878), and *Le Tribut de Zamora* (April 1, 1881), without signal success. The last years of his life were devoted mainly to sacred works, of which the most important was *La Rédemption*, a trilogy, first performed at the Birmingham Festival in 1882. He continued to write religious works in close succession. One of his most popular settings to religious words is *Ave Maria*, adapted to the first prelude of Bach's *Well-tempered Clavier*, but its original version was *Méditation sur le premier Prélude de Piano de J. S. Bach* for Violin and Piano (1853); the words were added later (1859). Among his literary works were *Ascanio de Saint-Saëns* (1889), *Le Don Juan de Mozart* (1890; Eng. tr., 1895), and an autobiography, *Mémoires d'un artiste* (Paris, 1896; Eng. tr. by W. Hutchenson, N.Y., 1896).

BIBL.: M. de Bovet, *C. G.* (Paris, 1890; Eng. tr., 1891); L. Pagnerre, *C. G.: Sa vie et ses oeuvres* (Paris, 1890); C. Saint-Saëns, *C. G. et le Don Juan de Mozart* (Paris, 1893); T. Dubois, *Notice sur C. G.* (Paris, 1894); H. Tolhurst, *G.* (London, 1905); P. Hillemacher, *C. G.* (Paris, 1906); C. Bellaigue, *G.* (Paris, 1910); J.-G. Prod'homme and A. Dandelot, *G.: Sa vie et ses oeuvres* (2 vols., Paris, 1911); H. Soubiès and H. de Curzon, *Documents inédits sur le Faust de G.* (Paris, 1912); P. Landormy, *G.* (Paris, 1942); idem, *Faust de G.: Étude et analyse* (Paris, 1944); J. Harding, *G.* (London, 1973); M. Rustman, *Lyric Opera: A Study of the Contribution of C. G.* (diss., Univ. of Kansas, 1986); S. Huebner, *The Operas of G.* (Oxford, 1990).

Gouvy, Louis Théodore, French composer; b. Goffontaine, near Saarbrücken, July 5, 1819; d. Leipzig, April 21, 1898. The son of French parents, he graduated from the college at Metz. He went to Paris to study law, but turned to music, presenting a concert of his works in Paris in 1847; also made frequent trips to Germany, where his music was received with great favor. He composed about 200 works, including an opera, *Der Cid* (1863).

BIBL.: O. Klauwell, *L. T. G.: Sein Leben und seine Werke* (Berlin, 1902).

Graarud, Gunnar, Norwegian tenor; b. Holmestrand, near Christiania, June 1, 1886; d. Stuttgart, Dec. 6, 1960. He was a student in Berlin of Husler and Zawilowski. Following his operatic debut in Kaiserslautern in 1919, he sang at the Mannheim National Theater (1920–22), the Berlin Volksoper (1922–25), the Hamburg Opera (1926–28), the Bayreuth Festivals (from 1927), and the Vienna State Opera (1928–37). He also was a guest artist in London, Paris, Milan, and Salzburg. Among his best roles were Tristan, Siegmund, Parsifal, and Siegfried.

Grabner, Hermann, Austrian composer and music theorist; b. Graz, May 12, 1886; d. Bolzano, Italy, July 3, 1969. He took his degree in law at the Univ. of Graz. in 1909; then studied music with Reger and Sitt at the Leipzig Cons. He became a lecturer in theory at the Strasbourg Cons. in 1913; served in the German army in World War I; after the Armistice he taught at the Mannheim Cons.; from 1924 to 1938 he was prof. of composition at the Leipzig Cons.; he then taught at the Hochschule für Musik (1938–45) and Cons. (1950–51) in Berlin. He wrote an opera, *Die Richterin* (Barmen, May 7, 1930).

WRITINGS: *Die Funktionstheorie Hugo Riemanns und ihre Bedeutung für die praktische Analyse* (Munich, 1923); *Allgemeine Musiklehre* (Stuttgart, 1924; 5th ed., 1949); *Lehrbuch der musikalischen Analyse* (Leipzig, 1925); *Der lineare Satz; Ein Lehrbuch des Kontrapunktes* (Stuttgart, 1930; rev. ed., 1950); *Handbuch der Harmonielehre* (Berlin, 1944).

Grabovsky, Leonid, Ukrainian composer; b. Kiev, Jan. 28, 1935. He studied at the Univ. of Kiev (1951–56) and took courses in composition with Revutsky and Liatoshinsky at the Kiev Cons. (1954–62; diploma, 1962). After teaching at the latter (1961–63; 1966–68), he was active as a composer, editor, and translator. He was one of the earliest composers in the Soviet Union to espouse minimalism. His works also reveal Asian influences. Among his works are the chamber operas *The Bear* (1963) and *The Marriage Proposal* (1964).

Gracis, Ettore, Italian conductor; b. La Spezia, Sept. 24, 1915; d. Treviso, April 12, 1992. He studied violin at the Parma Cons. and piano and composition at the Venice Cons.; he also took courses in composition with Malipiero and Guarnieri at the Accademia Musicale Chigiana in Siena. He made his conducting debut in 1942; from that time, he appeared with many opera houses of Italy. He also conducted sym. concerts. He was active in bringing out contemporary scores; he conducted a number of works by Malipiero and other leading Italian composers.

Grad, Gabriel, Lithuanian composer; b. Retovo, near Kovno, July 9, 1890; d. Tel Aviv, Dec. 9, 1950. He studied in Ekaterinoslav and in Berlin. He was founder-director of a Jewish music school in Kovno (1920–22); he went to Palestine in 1924, then was founder-director of the Benhetov Cons. in Tel Aviv (from 1925). He wrote an opera, *Judith and Holofernes*, and about 250 other works.

Grädener, Carl (Georg Peter), German cellist, conductor, and composer, father of **Hermann (Theodor Otto) Grädener**; b. Rostock, Jan. 14, 1812; d. Hamburg, June 10, 1883. He studied cello with Mattstedt. From 1838 he was music director at the Univ. of Kiel for 10 years; in 1851 he established an academy for vocal music in Hamburg. After 3 years at the Vienna Cons. (1862–65), he returned to Hamburg, and was a teacher at the Cons. there until 1873. He was also cofounder and a president of the Hamburger Tonkünstlerverein. He wrote *System der Harmonielehre* (Hamburg, 1877); his articles for music periodicals were collected and publ. as *Gesammelte Aufsätze* (Hamburg, 1872). He composed the operas *König Harald* and *Der Mullerin Hochzeit*, and the oratorio *Johannes der Täufer*.

Grädener, Hermann (Theodor Otto), German violinist, conductor, and composer, son of **Carl (Georg Peter) Grädener**; b. Kiel, May 8, 1844; d. Vienna, Sept. 18, 1929. He studied at the Vienna Cons. He was violinist in the Court Orch. in Vienna, then taught theory at the Horaksche Klavierschule in 1873, and at the Cons. of the Gesellschaft der Musikfreunde in Vienna from 1877 to 1913; he was also a prof. at the Univ. of Vienna (from 1882), and in 1899 succeeded Bruckner there. He wrote 2 operas, *Der Richter von Zalamea* and *Die heilige Zita*.

Graener, Paul, significant German composer; b. Berlin, Jan. 11, 1872; d. Salzburg, Nov. 13, 1944. He studied composition with Albert Becker at the Veit Cons. in Berlin. He traveled in Germany as a theater conductor; in 1896 he went to London, where he taught at the Royal Academy of Music (1897–1902). He was then in Vienna as a teacher at the Neues Konservatorium; he subsequently directed the Mozarteum in Salzburg (1910–13); after serving as prof. of composition at the Leipzig Cons. (1920–25), he was director of the Stern Cons. in Berlin (1930–33); thereafter he was vice president of the Reichsmusikkamer (1933–41). His many songs reveal a penchant for folk-like melodies. His other works follow along traditional Romantic lines with some neo-Baroque aspects.

WORKS: OPERAS: *Don Juans letztes Abenteuer* (Leipzig, June 11, 1914); *Theophano* (Munich, June 5, 1918); *Schirin und Gertraude* (Dresden, April 28, 1920); *Hanneles Himmelfahrt* (Dresden, Feb. 17, 1927); *Friedemann Bach* (Schwerin, Nov. 13, 1931); *Der Prinz von Homburg* (Berlin, March 14, 1935); *Schwanhild* (Cologne, Jan. 4, 1941).

BIBL.: G. Graener, *P. G.* (Leipzig, 1922); P. Grümmer, *Verzeichnis der Werke P. G.s* (Berlin, 1937).

Graf, Hans, Austrian conductor; b. Linz, Feb. 15, 1949. He studied piano at the Bruckner Cons. in Linz (1957–59) and later took diplomas in piano and conducting at the Graz Hochschule für Musik (1971); he also pursued training in conducting with Ferrara in Siena (1970, 1971) and Hilversum (1972), Celibidache in Bologna (1972), and Yansons in Weimar (1972) and Leningrad (1972–73). In 1975–76 he was music director of the Iraqi National Sym. Orch. in Baghdad. In 1979 he won 1st prize in the Karl Böhm conducting competition in Salzburg. He subsequently made appearances as a guest conductor with the Vienna Sym. Orch. (from 1980), the Vienna State Opera (from 1981), and at the Salzburg Festival (from 1983). From 1984 to 1995 he was music director of the Mozarteum Orch. and the Landestheater in Salzburg. In 1985 he made his first tour of the United States and Japan with the Mozarteum Orch. In 1987 he made his British debut as a guest conductor with the Royal Liverpool Phil. In 1995 he became principal conductor of the Calgary (Alberta) Phil.

Graf, Herbert, Austrian-born American opera producer and director; b. Vienna, April 10, 1903; d. Geneva, April 5, 1973. His father was the Austrian music critic, teacher, and musicologist Max Graf (b. Vienna, Oct. 1, 1873; d. there, June 24, 1958). He studied at the Univ. of Vienna with Adler; received his Ph.D. in 1925. He then was a producer at the opera houses in Münster, Breslau, Frankfurt am Main, and Basel. In 1934 he went to the United States; he was associated with the Philadelphia Opera in 1934–35; in 1936 he was appointed producer of the Metropolitan Opera in New York; in 1949 he also became head of the opera dept. at the Curtis Inst. of Music in Philadelphia. He later returned to Europe, where he was director of the Zürich Opera (1960–62) and the Grand Theatre in Geneva (1965–73). He publ. *The Opera and Its Future in America* (N.Y., 1941), *Opera for the People* (Minneapolis, 1951), and *Producing Opera for America* (Zürich, 1961).

Graffigna, Achille, Italian composer; b. S. Martino dall' Argine, near Mantua, May 5, 1816; d. Padua, July 19, 1896. He studied with Alessandro Rolla in Milan. He wrote church music and theatrical cantatas, then devoted himself to opera; his *Ildegonda e Rizzardo* (La Scala, Milan, Nov. 3, 1841) was accepted with favor. In 1842 he went to Verona, where he produced *Eleonora di San Bonifacio* (March 11, 1843); there followed *Maria di Brabante* (Trieste, Oct. 16, 1852), *L'assedio di Malta* (Padua, July 30, 1853), *Gli Studenti* (Milan, Feb. 7, 1857), *Veronica Cibo* (Mantua, Feb. 13, 1858; rev. and produced at the Théâtre-Italien, Paris, March 22, 1865, as *La Duchessa di San Giuliano*), *Il Barbiere di Siviglia* (Padua, May 17, 1879; intended as an homage to Rossini), *Il matrimonio segreto* (Florence, Sept. 8, 1883), and *La buona figliuola* (Milan, May 6, 1886).

Graham, Colin, English opera director and librettist; b. Hove, Sussex, Sept. 22, 1931. He attended the Royal Academy of Dramatic Art in London (1951–52). After working as a stage manager, he directed his first opera, Britten's *Noye's Fludde*, at the Aldeburgh Festival in 1958. In subsequent years, he worked closely with Britten, becoming an artistic director at the Aldeburgh Festival in 1968. He worked with the English Opera Group, serving as its director of productions from 1963 to 1975; from 1961 he was active at the Sadler's Wells (later English National) Opera in London, where he was director of productions from 1977 to 1982. He was also associated with London's Covent Garden (1961–73). In 1975 he created the English Music Theatre Co., with which he was active until 1978. In 1978 he was named director of production at the Opera Theatre of St. Louis, serving as its artistic director from 1985. Graham also pursued theological studies at the New Covenant School of Ministry in St. Louis, and was ordained in 1988. He staged the first British productions of *The Cunning Little Vixen* (1961), *From the House of the Dead* (1965), and *War and Peace* (1972). Among the 50 world premieres he directed were Britten's *Curlew River* (1964), *The Burning Fiery Furnace* (1966), *The Golden Vanity* (1967), *The Prodigal Son* (1968), *Owen Wingrave* (1972), and *Death in Venice* (1973), Bennett's *Mines of Sulphur* (1963) and *A Penny for a Song* (1967; librettist), Paulus's *The Postman Always Rings Twice* (1982; librettist), and Minoru Miki's *Joruri* (1985; librettist), Minoru Miki's *Joruri* (1985; librettist), and Susa's *The Dangerous Liaisons* (1994). Graham's early training in the dramatic arts, combined with his extraordinary command of every aspect of the music theater, have placed him among the leading masters of his craft.

Graham, Susan, admired American mezzo-soprano; b. Roswell, N. Mex., July 23, 1960. She studied with Cynthia Hoffman at the Manhattan School of Music in New York (M.M., 1987). While still a student there, she attracted critical notice as Massenet's Chérubin, and then appeared with the operas in St. Louis and Seattle. During the 1989–90 season, she sang Annius in *La clemenza di Tito* at the Chicago Lyric Opera, Sonia in Argento's *The Aspern Papers* in Washington, D.C., Dorabella and Strauss's Composer in Santa Fe, and as soloist in *Das Knaben Wunderhorn* at N.Y.'s Carnegie Hall. In 1990–91 she appeared as Minerva in Monteverdi's *Il ritorno d'Ulisse in patria* at the San Francisco Opera and as Berlioz's Beatrice in Lyons. Her success in the Metropolitan Opera National Auditions led to her debut with the company in New York during the 1991–92 season as the 2d Lady in *Die Zauberflöte*, where she subsequently was engaged to sing Cherubino, Tebaldo in *Don Carlos*, Meg Page, Octavian, Ascanio, and Dorabella. From 1993 she sang at the Salzburg Festivals as well. During the 1993–94 season, she made her debut at London's Covent Garden as Chérubin. In 1995 she sang for the first time at Milan's La Scala as Berlioz's Marguerite and at the Vienna State Opera as Octavian, and on Sept. 15 of that year she created the title role in Goehr's *Arianna* at Covent Garden. She sang Beatrice in Santa Fe and Strauss's Composer at the Lyric Opera in Chicago in 1998. Her engagements as a concert artist have taken her to principal North American and European music centers, where she has appeared with many notable orchs.

Gramm (real name, **Grambasch**), **Donald (John),** American bass-baritone; b. Milwaukee, Feb. 26, 1927; d. N.Y., June 2, 1983. He studied piano and organ at the Wisconsin College–Cons. of Music (1935–44); also studied voice with George Graham. He made his professional debut in Chicago at the age of 17 when he sang the role of Raimondo in *Lucia di Lammermoor*; he continued his vocal studies at the Chicago Musical College and at the

Music Academy of the West in Santa Barbara, where he was a student of Martial Singher. On Sept. 26, 1952, he made his debut at the N.Y. City Opera as Colline in *La Bohème*, and continued to appear with the company for the rest of his life. On Jan. 10, 1964 he made his Metropolitan Opera debut in New York as Truffaldino in *Ariadne auf Naxos*, and then sang major roles there until his death. He was extremely versatile in his roles; he sang Méphistophélès, Leporello, Mozart's Figaro, Falstaff in Verdi's opera, Baron Ochs, and Scarpia. He also distinguished himself as an interpreter of such difficult parts as Dr. Schön in Berg's *Lulu* and as Moses in Schoenberg's *Moses und Aron*.

Grammann, Karl, German composer; b. Lubeck, June 3, 1844; d. Dresden, Jan. 30, 1897. He studied at the Leipzig Cons. He spent some years in Vienna, and in 1885 settled in Dresden. As a youth, he wrote 2 operas, *Die Schatzgräber* and *Die Eisjungfrau*, which were not produced; the following operas were staged with some success: *Melusine* (Wiesbaden, 1875), *Thusnelda und der Triumphzug des Germanicus* (Dresden, 1881), *Das Andreasfest* (Dresden, 1882), and 2 short operas, *Ingrid* and *Das Irrlicht* (Dresden, 1894). His last opera, *Auf neutralem Boden*, was produced posth. (Hamburg, 1901).

BIBL.: F. Pfohl, *K. G.: Ein Künstlerleben* (Berlin, 1910).

Granados (y Campiña), Eduardo, Spanish conductor and composer, son of **Enrique Granados (y Campiña)**; b. Barcelona, July 28, 1894; d. Madrid, Oct. 2, 1928. He studied in Barcelona with his father; then at the Madrid Cons. with Conrado del Campo. He taught at the Granados Academy in Barcelona; he was also active as a conductor; presented many works by his father. He wrote several zarzuelas, of which the first, *Bufon y Hostelero*, was performed with some success in Barcelona (Dec. 7, 1917); other stage works were *Los Fanfarrones*, comic opera; *La ciudad eterna*, mystery play; *Los Cigarrales*, operatic sketch; and musical comedies.

Granados (y Campiña), Enrique, distinguished Spanish composer, pianist, and teacher, father of **Eduardo Granados (y Campiña);** b. Lérida, July 27, 1867; d. in the aftermath of the torpedoing of the S.S. *Sussex* by a German submarine in the English Channel, March 24, 1916. He went to Barcelona and studied piano with Francisco Jurnet at the Escolania de la Marcé and privately with Joan Baptista Pujol, and from 1883 took private composition lessons with Pedrell. In 1887 he went to Paris to pursue his training in piano with Charles de Bériot. In 1889 he returned to Barcelona, and in 1890 made his recital debut there. He continued to make successful appearances as a pianist in subsequent years while pursuing his interest in composing. On Nov. 12, 1898, he scored a notable success as a composer with the premiere of his zarzuela *María del Carmen* in Madrid. In 1900 he organized the Sociedad de Conciertos Clasicos in Barcelona, and from 1901 taught there at his own Academia Granados. He secured his reputation as a composer with his imaginative and effective piano suite *Goyescas* (1911). He subsequently utilized music from the suite and from some of his vocal tonadillas to produce the opera *Goyescas*, which received its premiere at the Metropolitan Opera in New York on Jan. 28, 1916, with the composer in attendance. It was on his voyage home that Granados perished. Although he was picked up by a lifeboat after the attack on the S.S. *Sussex*, he dove into the sea to save his drowning wife and both were lost. Granados's output reflected the influence of the Spanish and Romantic traditions, and the Castilian tonadilla. His finest scores are notable for their distinctive use of melody, rhythm, harmony, and color.

WORKS: DRAMATIC: *María del Carmen*, zarzuela (Madrid, Nov. 12, 1898); *Blancaflor* (Barcelona, Jan. 30, 1899); *Petrarca*, lyric drama (n.d.); *Picarol*, lyric drama (Barcelona, Feb. 23, 1901); *Follet*, lyric drama (Barcelona, April 4, 1903); *Gaziel*, lyric drama (Barcelona, Oct. 27, 1906); *Liliana*, lyric drama (Barcelona, July 9, 1911); *La cieguecita de Belén* or *El portalico de Belén* (1914); *Goyescas*, opera (1915; N.Y., Jan. 28, 1916); also *Miel de la Alcarria*, incidental music (n.d.) and *Ovillejos o La gallina ciega*, Sainte lírico (n.d.; unfinished).

BIBL.: G. Boladeres Ibern, *E. G.: Recuerdos de su vid y estudio critico de su obra por su antiguo discipulo* (Barcelona, 1921); H. Collet, *Albéniz et G.* (Paris, 1925; 2d ed., 1948); J. Subirá, *E. G.: Su producción musical, su madrileñismo, su personalidad artística* (Madrid, 1926); A. Fernández-Cid, *G.* (Madrid, 1956); P. Vila San-Juan, *Papeles intimos de E. G.* (Barcelona, 1966); J. Riera, *E. G.: Estudio* (Lérida, 1967); A. Tarazona, *E. G.: El último romántico* (Madrid, 1975); A. Carreras i Granados, *G.* (Barcelona, 1988); M. Larrad, *The Goyescas of G.* (thesis, Univ. of Liverpool, 1988); C. Hess, *E. G.: A Bio-Bibliography* (N.Y., 1991); M. Larrad, *The Catalan Theater Works of E. G.* (diss., Univ. of Liverpool, 1991).

Grandert, Johnny, Swedish composer; b. Stockholm, July 11, 1939. He studied under Lidholm at the Stockholm Musikhögskolan (1959–64); he also took music courses in Germany, Italy, and America. He was mainly antodidact in music and was also active as a painter. In 1972 he became principal and in 1986 director of music at the Norrtalje School of Music. The titles of his compositions betray a desire to puzzle and tantalize, but the music itself is not forbidding, despite the application of startling effects (as in his *Mirror 25* for Chorus and Orch. [1966], in which a machine gun is included in the orchestra and in which the chorus is invited to belch at certain points). He composed the opera *Gyllene jord* (1984).

Grandi, Margherita (née **Margaret Garde**), Australian soprano; b. Hobart, Oct. 4, 1894; d. Milan, 1972. She studied at the Royal College of Music in London, with Calvé in Paris, and with Russ in Milan. In 1919 she made her operatic debut under the stage name of Djema Vécla (an anagram of Calvé) at the Paris Opéra Comique in *Werther*. In 1922 she created the title role in Massenet's *Amadis* in Monte Carlo. After marrying the scenic designer Giovanni Grandi, she sang under her married name. In 1932 she appeared as Aida at Milan's Teatro Carcano, and returned to that city to sing Elena in *Mefistofele* at La Scala in 1934. She sang at the Glyndebourne Festivals in 1939, 1947, and 1949. In 1946 she appeared at the Verona Arena. In 1947 she sang Tosca and Donna Anna at London's Cambridge Theatre. In 1949 she returned to London to create the role of Diana in Bliss's *The Olympians* at Covent Garden. She also made guest appearances in South America. In 1951 she retired from the operatic stage. Grandi's most acclaimed roles were Lady Macbeth and Tosca, which she projected in the grand manner.

Granichstaedten, Bruno, Austrian composer; b. Vienna, Sept. 1, 1879; d. N.Y., May 20, 1944. He was a student of Jadassohn at the Leipzig Cons. Returning to Vienna, he began his career as a songwriter and singer. He scored a notabale success as a composer for the theater with his first operetta, *Bub oder Mädel?* (Vienna, Nov. 13, 1908), which was later heard in New York as *The Rose Maid*. He then had success with such scores as *Majestät Mimi* (Vienna, Feb. 17, 1911), *Madame Serafin* (Hamburg, Sept. 1, 1911), *Casimirs Himmelfahrt* (Vienna, Dec. 25, 1911), *Die verbotene Stadt* (Berlin, Dec. 23, 1913; in collaboration with C. Lindau), *Auf Befehl der Kaiserin* or *Auf Befehl der Herzogin* (Vienna, March 20, 1915), *Walzerliebe* (Vienna, Feb. 16, 1918; in collaboration with R. Bodanzky), *Indische Nächte* (Vienna, Nov. 25, 1921), and *Die Bacchusnacht* (Vienna, May 18, 1923; in collaboration with E. Marischka). Following the remarkable success of *Der Orlow* (Vienna, April 3, 1925; in collaboration with Marischka), he went on to compose such popular scores as *Das Schwalbennest* (Vienna, Sept. 2, 1926; in collaboration with Marischka), *Die Königin* (Vienna, Feb. 4, 1927; in collaboration with O. Straus and Marischka), *Evelyne* or *Die Milliardärin* (Berlin, Dec. 23, 1927; in collaboration with P. Hertz and A. Schutz), and *Reklame* (Vienna, Feb. 28, 1930; in collaboration with Marischka). With the Nazi assumption of power in Germany in 1933, his career was derailed. After the Anschluss in Austria in 1938, he made his way to New York, where he was compelled to make ends meet playing piano in bars.

Grant, Clifford (Scantlebury), Australian bass; b. Randwick, Sept. 11, 1930. He studied at the New South Wales State Conservatorium of Music in Sydney and with Otakar Kraus in London. In 1951 he made his operatic debut with the New South Wales Opera as Raimondo in *Lucia di Lammermoor*. After further appearances in Australia, he made his debut at the Sadler's Wells Opera in London in 1966 as Silva in *Ernani*, where he later sang Pogner, Sarastro, Hunding, the Commendatore, and Hagen. He also made his U.S. debut in 1966 at the San Francisco Opera as Lord Walton in *I Puritani*, and returned there to sing such roles as the King in *Aida*, Monterone, and Oroveso. He first sang at the Glyndebourne Festival as Nettuno in *Il Ritorno d'Ulisse* in 1972. His Covent Garden debut followed in London in 1974 as Mozart's Bartolo. On Nov. 19, 1976, he made his debut at the Metropolitan Opera in New York as Phorcas in *Esclarmonde*. From 1976 to 1990 he pursued his operatic career in Australia. In 1993 he appeared as Alvise with England's Opera North.

Grantham, Donald, American composer; b. Duncan, Okla., Nov. 9, 1947. He studied composition at the Univ. of Okla. (B.Mus., 1970) and then entered the Univ. of So. Calif. in Los Angeles in the composition classes of Robert Linn and Halsey Stevens (M.M., 1974; D.M.A., 1980). In the summers of 1973 and 1974 he studied with Boulanger at the American Cons. in Fontainebleau. After lecturing at the Univ. of So. Calif. in Los Angeles (1974–75), he joined the faculty of the Univ. of Texas at Austin in 1975, where he became a prof. in 1991. With K. Kennan, he was coauthor of the 4th ed. of *The Technique of Orchestration* (Englewood Cliffs, N.J., 1990). His compositions include the opera *The Boor* (1989).

Grassini, Josephina (Giuseppina Maria Camilla), Italian contralto; b. Varese, April 8, 1773; d. Milan, Jan. 3, 1850. She studied in Varese with Domenico Zucchinetti and in Milan with Antonio Secchi. She made her operatic debut in Parma in 1789 in Guglielmi's *La Pastorella nobile*; she sang at La Scala in Milan in 1790, and soon attained popularity on all the leading Italian stages. In 1800 she sang in Milan before Napoleon, and became his mistress; he took her with him to Paris, where she sang at national celebrations. She was in London from 1804 to 1806, then returned to Paris and sang at the French court. She was noted for her beauty and her acting, as well as her voice.

BIBL.: A. Pougin, *Une Cantatrice "amie" de Napoleon: G. G.* (Paris, 1920); A. Gavoty, *La G.* (Paris, 1947).

Grau, Maurice, Moravian-born American operatic impresario; b. Brünn, 1849; d. Paris, March 14, 1907. He was taken to New York at 5. After studying at Columbia Univ. Law School, he turned to artist management and organized the American tours of many celebrated artists. He later became a partner in the successful theater management firm of Abbey, Schoeffel, and Grau. In 1890 they presented their own special season of Italian opera at the Metropolitan Opera in New York with such stellar artists as Albani, Nordica, Patti, and Tamagno. In 1891 their firm secured the lease of the Metropolitan Opera. Upon Abbey's death in 1896, Grau took over the lease. After a hiatus (1897–98), Grau returned to run the Metropolitan Opera under the aegis of the Maurice Grau Opera Co. until 1903. His astute understanding of public taste led him to engage the most famous singers of the day. He showcased their talents in the French and Italian, and later Wagner, repertory with notable artistic and financial success. From 1897 to 1900 he also managed London's Covent Garden. In 1883 he married the opera singer Marie Durand.

Graun, Carl Heinrich, noted German composer; b. Wahrenbruck, near Dresden, May 7, 1704; d. Berlin, Aug. 8, 1759. He was the brother of the German organist and composer August Friedrich Graun (1699–1765) and the distinguished German composer Johann Gottlieb Graun (c.1703–1771). He studied voice with Grundig and Benisch, keyboard playing with Pezold, and composition with Johann Christoph Schmidt at the Dresden Kreuzschule (1713–21); he also sang in the chorus of the Dresden Court Opera. He became a tenor at the Braunschweig court in 1725; he was made vice Kapellmeister about 1727, and wrote several operas for the Court Theater. He then joined the court establishment of Crown Prince Ferdinand (later Frederick II the Great) in Ruppin in 1735, becoming his Kapellmeister in Rheinsberg in 1736. After Frederick became king, Graun went to Berlin as Royal Kapellmeister (1740); the new opera house was inaugurated with his opera *Cesare e Cleopatra* on Dec. 7, 1742; many others followed, several with librettos by the king. Graun enjoyed royal favor and public esteem throughout his career in Berlin, his only serious challenger being Hasse. His operas were firmly rooted in the Italian tradition; although not without merit, they vanished from the repertoire after he passed from the scene. His gifts were more strikingly revealed in his sacred music, particularly in his *Te Deum* (written to commemorate Frederick's victory at the battle of Prague in 1756) and his Passion oratorio, *Der Tod Jesu*; the latter, his finest and most famous work, was performed in Germany regularly until the end of the 19th century.

WORKS: OPERAS (all 1st perf. in Berlin unless otherwise given): *Sancio und Sinilde* (Braunschweig, 1727); *Polydorus* (Braunschweig, 1726 or 1728); *Iphigenia in Aulis* (Braunschweig, 1731); *Scipio Africanus* (Wolfenbüttel, 1732); *Lo specchio della fedeltà* or *Timareta* (Braunschweig, 1733; music not extant); *Pharao Tubaetes* (Braunschweig, 1735); *Rodelinda, regina de' langobardi* (Potsdam, Dec. 13, 1741); *Venere e Cupido* (Potsdam, 1742); *Cesare e Cleopatra* (1742); *Artaserse* (1743); *Catone in Utica* (1744); *La festa del Imeneo* (1744); *Lucio Papirio* (1745); *Adriano in Siria* (1746); *Demofoonte, rè di Tracia* (1746; 3 arias by Frederick II); *Cajo Fabricio* (1746); *Le feste galanti* (1747); *Il Rè pastore* (Charlottenburg, 1747; recitative, duet, and 2 choruses by Graun; remainder by Frederick II, Nichelmann, and Quantz); *L'Europa galante* (Schloss Monbijou, 1748); *Galatea ed Acide* (Potsdam, 1748; overture, 1 recitative, and 1 aria by Quantz; arias by Frederick II); *Ifigenia in Aulide* (1748); *Angelica e Medoro* (1749); *Coriolano* (1749); *Fetonte* (1750); *Il Mitridate* (1750); *L'Armida* (1751); *Britannico* (1751); *L'Orfeo* (1752); *Il giudizio di Paride* (Charlottenburg, 1752); *Silla* (1753; libretto by Frederick II); *Il trionfo della fedeltà* (Charlottenburg, 1753; major portion of the work by G. Benda and Hasse); *Semiramide* (1754); *Montezuma* (1755; libretto by Frederick II); *Ezio* (1755); *I Fratelli nemici* (1756; libretto by Frederick II); *La Merope* (1756; libretto by Frederick II). Also the sacred Passion oratorio, *Der Tod Jesu* (Berlin, 1755).

Graupner, (Johann) Christoph, German composer; b. Kirchberg, Saxony, Jan. 13, 1683; d. Darmstadt, May 10, 1760. He studied music in Kirchberg with the cantor Michael Mylius and the organist Nikolaus Kuster, and later at the Thomasschule in Leipzig with Johann Kuhnau and Johann Schelle. He then went to Hamburg, where he became harpsichordist at the Oper-am-Gänsemarkt (1707–09); during this time he composed 5 operas. In 1709 he was called to Darmstadt as vice Kapellmeister to the Landgraf Ernst Ludwig; in 1712 he was appointed Kapellmeister, a post he held until his death. Graupner was a highly industrious composer, including in his substantial catalog 8 operas. Several of his compositions were publ. during his lifetime; he also brought out a *Neu vermehrtes Darmstädtisches Choralbuch* (Darmstadt, 1728). He was proficient as an engraver, and printed several keyboard pieces in his own workshop. His operas include *Dido, Königin von Carthago* (Hamburg, 1707); *Il fido amico, oder Der getreue Freund Hercules und Theseus* (Hamburg, 1708; not extant); *L'amore ammalato: Die Krankende Liebe, oder Antiochus und Stratonica* (Hamburg, 1708); *Bellerophon, oder Das in die preussisch Krone verwandelte Wagenstirn* (Hamburg, Nov. 28, 1708; not extant); *Der Fall des grossen Richters in Israel, Simson, oder Die abgekuhlte Liebesrache der Deborah* (Hamburg, 1709; not extant); *Berenice und Lucilla, oder Das tugendhafte Lieben* (Darmstadt, March 4, 1710; not extant); *Telemach* (Darmstadt, Feb. 16, 1711; not extant); *La costanza vince l'inganno* (Darmstadt, 1715). An incomplete edition of his works was ed. by F. Noack (4 vols., Kassel, 1955–57).

Graveure, Louis (real name, **Wilfred Douthitt**), English baritone; b. London, March 18, 1888; d. Los Angeles, April 27, 1965. He studied voice with Clara Novello-Davies. He sang in the operetta *The Lilac Domino* in New York on Oct. 28, 1914. In 1915 he reappeared in New York as Louis Graveure (after his mother's maiden name) and became a popular concert artist, singing all types of music. On Feb. 5, 1928, he gave a concert in New York as a tenor; from 1931 to 1938 he was in Germany; from 1938 to 1940, in France; from 1940 to 1947, in England. In 1947 he returned to the United States and taught in various music schools.

Gray, Linda Esther, Scottish soprano; b. Greenock, May 29, 1948. After training at the Royal Scottish Academy of Music in Glasgow, she went to London to pursue her studies at the Opera Centre and with Dame Eva Turner. During her student days, she made her first appearances in opera at the Sadler's Wells Theatre in London (1970). In 1972 she sang Mimi with the Glyndebourne Touring Opera Co., and then made her first appearance at the Glyndebourne Festival in 1973 as Mozart's 1st Lady. She then sang with the Scottish Opera in Glasgow. In 1978 she made her debut as Micaëla at the English National Opera in London, and in 1979 sang for the first time at the Welsh National Opera in Cardiff as Isolde. She made her debut at London's Covent Garden in 1980 as Gutrune, followed by her U.S. debut in Dallas in 1981 as Sieglinde. Although highly admired for her talent, she inexplicably ceased singing in 1983. Among her other roles were Donna Elvira, Countess Almaviva, Leonore, Kundry, Aida, Tosca, and Ariadne.

Graziani, Francesco, noted Italian baritone, brother of **Giuseppe** and **Lodovico Graziani**; b. Fermo, April 26, 1828; d. there, June 30, 1901. Following vocal training with Cellini, he made his operatic debut in *Gemma di vergy* in Ascoli Piceno in 1851. From 1853 to 1861 he sang at the Théâtre-Italien in Paris. On April 26, 1855, he made his first appearance at London's Covent Garden as Carlo in *Ernani*. He continued to sing there regularly during the next 25 years, making his farewell appearance in *La Traviata* on July 17, 1880. In 1854 he sang in the United States. In 1861 he appeared for the first time in St. Petersburg, where he was chosen to create the role of Don Carlos in *La forza del destino* on Nov. 10, 1862. He continued to sing there until 1871. Graziani's roles in Verdi's operas were particularly remarkable, especially Rigoletto, Germont, Di Luna, Renato, and Amonasro. He also was a convincing exponent of roles in operas by Mozart, Rossini, and Donizetti.

Graziani, Giuseppe, Italian bass, brother of **Francesco** and **Lodovico Graziani**; b. Fermo, Aug. 28, 1819; d. Porto S. Giorgio, March 6, 1905. After training in Naples with Mercadante, he devoted himself to a career as a concert artist.

Graziani, Lodovico, Italian tenor, brother of **Francesco** and **Giuseppe Graziani**; b. Fermo, Nov. 14, 1820; d. there, May 15, 1885. He was a pupil of Cellini. In 1845 he made his operatic debut in Cambiaggio's *Don Procopio* in Bologna. In 1851 he sang at the Théâtre-Italien in Paris, and then in Venice, where he later created the role of Alfredo in *La Traviata* (March 6, 1853). He subsequently appeared at Milan's La Scala (1855, 1862) and in Vienna (1860). Among his other Verdi roles were Manrico, the Duke of Mantua, and Riccardo.

Greef, Arthur de, Belgian pianist, teacher, and composer; b. Louvain, Oct. 10, 1862; d. Brussels, Aug. 29, 1940. He studied at the Brussels Cons. with L. Brassin (piano) and Gevaert (composition); then traveled as a pianist in Europe. In 1885 he became a prof. of piano at the Brussels Cons., retaining that post until 1930. He composed the opera *De Marketenster* (Louvain, 1879).

Greenawald, Sheri (Kay), American soprano; b. Iowa City, Nov. 12, 1947. She studied with Charles Matheson at the Univ. of Northern Iowa (B.A., 1968), with Maria DeVarady, Hans Heinz, and Daniel Ferro in New York, and with Audrey Langford in London. In 1974 she made her professional debut in Poulenc's *Les Mamelles de Tirésias* at N.Y.'s Manhattan Theater Club, and then sang with the San Francisco Opera, the Houston Grand Opera, the Santa Fe Opera, the Washington (D.C.) Opera, and elsewhere. In 1980 she made her European debut as Mozart's Susanna with the Netherlands Opera. In 1991 she sang Pauline in the U.S. stage premiere of Prokofiev's *The Gambler* at the Lyric Opera in Chicago. After portraying Mélisande in Seattle in 1993, she appeared as the Marschallin at the Welsh National Opera in Cardiff in 1994. On Nov. 25, 1995, she made her Metropolitan Opera debut in New York as Weill's Jenny. She sang in Susa's *Transformations* in St. Louis in 1997. She toured extensively as a concert artist. Among her many roles were Zerlina, Despina, Massenet's Sophie, Violetta, Mimi, and Britten's Ellen Orford. She also created roles in Pasatieri's *Signor Deluso* (1974) and *Washington Square* (1976), Floyd's *Bilby's Doll* (1976), and Bernstein's *A Quiet Place* (1983).

Greenaway, Peter, Welsh film director, writer, painter, and librettist; b. Newport, April 5, 1942. He went to England and studied at the Walthamstow College of Art. From 1965 to 1976 he worked as a film editor in the Central Office of Information. His first exhibition of paintings was mounted in 1964, and his first one-man show was held in Canterbury in 1989. As a film director and writer, he began producing short films in 1966 and feature-length films in 1978, all highly structured, visually complex, and elaborate; among the best known are *The Cook, The Thief, His Wife and Her Lover* (1990), *Prospero's Books* (1991), and *The Pillow Book* (1996). His book *The Falls* appeared in 1993. He collaborated with Louis Andriessen as librettist for the operas *Rosa* (Amsterdam, Nov. 2, 1994) and *Writing to Vermeer* (1997–99; Amsterdam, Dec. 1, 1999). Greenaway was made a Chevalier de l'Ordre des Arts et des Lettres of France in 1990.

Greenberg, Noah, American conductor; b. N.Y., April 9, 1919; d. there, Jan. 9, 1966. He studied music privately, and then organized choruses in New York. In 1952 he founded the N.Y. Pro Musica Antiqua, an organization specializing in Renaissance and medieval music, performed in authentic styles and on copies of early instruments; he revived the medieval liturgical music dramas *The Play of Daniel* (1958) and *The Play of Herod* (1963); traveled with his ensemble in Europe in 1960 and 1963. It was primarily through the efforts of this group (later known as the N.Y. Pro Musica) that early music, in the United States, became a viable idiom available to modern audiences. He held a Guggenheim fellowship in 1955 and Ford fellowships in 1960 and 1962.

Greene, (Harry) Plunket, Irish bass-baritone and teacher; b. Old Connaught House, County Wicklow, June 24, 1865; d. London, Aug. 19, 1936. He was a student of Hromada in Stuttgart, Vannuccini in Florence, and J. B. Welsh and A. Blume in London. On Jan. 21, 1888, he made his debut as a soloist in Handel's *Messiah* in Stepney. In 1890 he appeared at London's Covent Garden, but soon became a successful concert artist; from 1893 he appeared in recitals with Leonard Borwick, and that same year made his first tour of the United States. In 1899 he married Parry's daughter, Gwendolen. Greene devoted his later years to vocal pedagogy. He publ. the manual *Interpretation in Song* (London, 1912) and a book of reminiscences, *From the Blue Danube to Shannon* (London, 1934); also a biography of Stanford (London, 1935). He was a fine interpreter of Schumann and Brahms, and also sang in the premieres of works by Parry, Stanford, Elgar, and Vaughan Williams.

Gregh, Louis, French composer and music publisher; b. Philippeville, Algeria, March 16, 1843; d. St. Mesme, Seine-et-Oise, Jan. 21, 1915. He began his musical career with the production of a light opera, *Un Lycée de jeunes filles* (Paris, 1881), which won a decided success. It was followed by several other operettas, including *Le Présomtif* (1884) and *Le Capitaine Roland* (1895), and ballets. He then turned to publishing; the firm was continued by his son, Henri Gregh, who established it as Henri Gregh & Fils (1902); Henri Gregh's son, André, succeeded him as director in 1934.

Gregoir, Édouard (Georges Jacques), Belgian pianist, composer, and writer on music, brother of **Jacques (Mathieu Jo-**

seph) Gregoir; b. Turnhout, near Antwerp, Nov. 7, 1822; d. Wyneghem, June 28, 1890. He studied piano, and was a professional accompanist; in 1851 he settled in Antwerp. He was a prolific composer, his works numbering 150 in all. His Flemish opera, *Willem Beukels*, was produced in Brussels (July 21, 1856); he also wrote incidental music to various patriotic plays, including *De Belgen* (1848) and *La Dernière Nuite du Comte d'Egmont,* etc., and a symphonic oratorio, *Le Déluge* (1849).

WRITINGS: *Essai historique sur la musique et les musiciens dans les Pays-Bas* (1861); *Histoire de l'orgue* (1865); *Galerie biographique des artistes-musiciens belges du XVIIIe et du XIXe siècles* (1862; 2d ed., 1885); *Notice sur l'origine du célèbre compositeur Louis van Beethoven* (1863); *Les Artistes-Musiciens néerlandais* (1864); *Recherches historiques concernant les journaux de musique depuis les temps les plus reculés jusqu'à nos jours* (1872); *Réponse à un critique de Paris* (1874); *Documents historiques relatifs à l'art musical et aux artistes-musiciens* (4 vols., 1872–76); *Panthéon musical populaire* (6 vols., 1876–77); *Notice biographique sur F. J. Gossé dit Gossec* (1878); *L'Art musical en Belgique sous les règnes de Léopold I et Léopold II* (1879); *Les Gloires de l'Opéra et la musique à Paris* (4 vols., 1880–83); *A.-E.-M. Grétry* (1883); *Souvenirs artistiques* (3 vols., 1888–89).

Gregoir, Jacques (Mathieu Joseph), Belgian pianist and composer, brother of **Édouard (Georges Jacques) Gregoir**; b. Antwerp, Jan. 19, 1817; d. Brussels, Oct. 29, 1876. He studied with Henri Herz in Paris and with Rummel in Biebrich. He gave a number of successful piano recitals in Belgium, Germany, and Switzerland, and also wrote salon pieces for piano and several practical methods of piano playing. He publ. duets for violin and piano in collaboration with Vieuxtemps. He also wrote an opera, *Le Gondolier de Venise* (1848).

Gregor, Bohumil, Czech conductor; b. Prague, July 14, 1926. He studied at the Prague Cons. with Alois Klima. After conducting at the 5th of May Theater in Prague (1947–49) and in Brno (1949–51), he served as music director in Ostrava (1958–62). From 1962 he was a regular guest conductor at the National Theater in Prague; he also appeared as a guest conductor throughout Europe; in 1969 he made his U.S. debut with the San Francisco Opera conducting *Jenůfa*. He was closely associated with the music of Janáček and other Czech composers.

Gregor, Čestmír, Czech composer; b. Brno, May 14, 1926. He began his training with his father, Josef Gregor, who had been a student of Novák; later he studied with Kvapil (1950–54) and Kapr (1965–70) at the Janáček Academy of Music in Brno. From 1959 to 1972 he was director of music for Czech Radio in Ostrava. In his works, he pursued an atonal style of composition. Among his works is the opera *Profesionální žena* (A Professional Woman; 1983) and the ballets *Závrat* (Vertigo; 1963; ballet version of the *Choreographic Symphony)* and *Horko* (Heat; 1978).

Greindl, Josef, German bass; b. Munich, Dec. 23, 1912; d. Vienna, April 16, 1993. He was a student in Munich of Paul Bender and Anna Bahr-Mildenburg. In 1936 he made his formal operatic debut as Hunding in Krefeld. After singing in Düsseldorf (1938–42), he was a member of the Berlin State Opera (from 1942); in 1949 he became a member of the Berlin Städtische (later Deutsche) Oper. In 1943 he made his first appearance at the Bayreuth Festival as Pogner, and returned to sing there regularly from 1951 to 1969. On Nov. 15, 1952, he made his Metropolitan Opera debut in New York as Wagner's Heinrich, but remained on the roster for only a season. From 1956 to 1969 he sang at the Vienna State Opera. In 1963 he appeared at London's Covent Garden. In 1961 he was made a prof. at the Saarbrücken Hochschule für Musik, and in 1973 at the Vienna Hochschule für Musik. Greindl was equally convincing in dramatic and buffo roles. Among his other roles were Sarastro, Don Alfonso, Hans Sachs, and the Wanderer in *Siegfried*.

Grešák, Jozef, Slovak composer; b. Bardejov, Dec. 30, 1907; d. Piešt'any, April 17, 1987. He studied piano and organ, but was mainly autodidact as a composer.

WORKS: DRAMATIC: *Prichod Slovákov* (The Arrival of the Slovaks), opera (1925); *Radúz and Mahuliena*, ballet (1954–55); *With Rosary*, opera (1970–73); *Zuzanka Hrašovie*, monodrama (1973; Bratislava, Jan. 15, 1975).

Gresnick, Antoine-Frédéric, Belgian composer; b. Liège (baptized), March 2, 1755; d. Paris, Oct. 16, 1799. He was a chorister at the St. Lambert Church in Liège, and studied in Naples under Sala. He made several trips to London, where he produced his operas *Demetrio, Alessandro nell'Indie, Donna di Cattiva Umore*, and *Alceste* with considerable success. He was in Lyons from 1789 to 1793, where his opera *L'Amour exilé de Cythère* was produced in 1793. He returned to Paris in 1794, and had varying success. He died there in poverty.

BIBL.: P. Mercier, *A.-F. G.: Compositeur liégeois* (Louvain, 1977).

Gretchaninoff, Alexander (Tikhonovich), Russian-born American composer; b. Moscow, Oct. 25, 1864; d. N.Y., Jan. 3, 1956. He studied at the Moscow Cons. (1881–91) with Safonov (piano) and Arensky (composition); he then studied composition at the St. Petersburg Cons. as a pupil of Rimsky-Korsakov (1891–1903). He was a prof. of composition at the Moscow Inst. from 1891 to 1922; then lived in Paris. He visited the United States, where he appeared with considerable success as a guest conductor of his own works (1929–31); went to the United States again in 1939, settling in New York. He became a naturalized American citizen on July 25, 1946. He continued to compose until the end of his long life. A concert of his works was presented in his presence on the occasion of his 90th birthday at Town Hall in New York (Oct. 25, 1954). Gretchaninoff's music is rooted in the Russian national tradition; influences of both Tchaikovsky and Rimsky-Korsakov are in evidence in his early works; toward 1910 he attempted to inject some impressionistic elements into his vocal compositions, but without signal success. His masterly sacred works are of historical importance, for he introduced a reform into Russian church singing by using nationally colored melodic patterns; in several of his masses, he employed instrumental accompaniment contrary to the prescriptions of the Russian Orthodox faith, a circumstance that precluded the use of these works in Russian churches. His *Missa oecumenica* represents a further expansion toward ecclesiastical universality; in this work, he makes use of elements pertaining to other religious music, including non-Christian. His instrumental works are competently written, but show less originality. His early *Lullaby* (1887) and the song "Over the Steppes" long retained their popularity, and were publ. in numerous arrangements. After the Revolution, Gretchaninoff wrote a new Russian national anthem, "Hymn of Free Russia" (sung in New York at a concert for the benefit of Siberian exiles, May 22, 1917), but it was never adopted by any political Russian faction. He publ. a book of reminiscences as *My Life* (Paris, in Russian, 1934; Eng. tr., 1951, with a complete catalogue of works as well as additions and an introduction by N. Slonimsky).

WORKS: DRAMATIC: OPERAS: *Dobrinya Nikititch* (Moscow, Oct. 27, 1903); *Sister Beatrice* (Moscow, Oct. 25, 1912; suppressed after 3 perfs. as being irreverent); *The Dream of a Little Christmas Tree*, children's opera (1911); *The Cat, the Fox, and the Rooster*, children's opera (1919); *The Castle Mouse*, children's opera (1921); *Marriage*, comic opera after Gogol (1945–46; Tanglewood, Aug. 1, 1948). BALLET DIVERTISSEMENT: *Idylle forestière* (N.Y., 1925). INCIDENTAL MUSIC TO: Ostrovsky's *Snegoruchka* (Moscow, Nov. 6, 1900); Tolstoy's *Tsar Feodor* (Moscow, Oct. 26, 1898) and *Death of Ivan the Terrible* (1899).

Grétry, André-Ernest-Modeste, greatly significant French composer; b. Liège, Feb. 8, 1741; d. Montmorency, near Paris, Sept. 24, 1813. He was a choirboy and 2d violinist at the collegiate church of St. Denis in Liège (1750–60), where his father served as violinist; he subsequently studied voice with Francois Leclerc, thoroughbass with H. F. Renkin, and composition with Henri Moreau. About 1754 an Italian opera company gave a season in Liège, and young Grétry thus received his first impulse toward dramatic music. His early works were instrumental; his first syms.

were performed at the home of his patron, Canon Simon de Harlez; the latter helped him to obtain a scholarship to the Collège de Liège in Rome, where he studied harmony with G. B. Casali (1761–65). While in Rome he composed mainly sacred music; however, he did write 2 intermezzos entitled *La Vendemmiatrice* for Carnival 1765. He was in Geneva in 1766 as a music teacher; there he met Voltaire, who advised him to go to Paris; before his departure, he produced the opéra comique *Isabelle et Gertrude* (Dec. 1766), to a libretto by Favart, after Voltaire. He arrived in Paris in the autumn of 1767, where he sought the patronage of aristocrats and diplomats; the Swedish ambassador, the Count de Creutz, gave him the first encouragement by obtaining for him Marmontel's comedy *Le Huron*; it was performed with Grétry's music at the Comédie-Italienne (Aug. 20, 1768). From then on, he produced operas one after another, without interruption, even during the years of the French Revolution.

The merit of Grétry's operas lies in their melodies and dramatic expression. He was not deeply versed in the science of music; yet despite this lack of craftsmanship, he achieved fine effects of vocal and instrumental writing. His operas suffered temporary eclipse when Méhul and Cherubini entered the field, but public interest was revived by the magnificent tenor Elleviou in 1801. The changes in operatic music during the next 30 years caused the neglect of his works. Nevertheless, Gretry—the "Molière of music," as he was called—founded the school of French opéra comique, of which Boieldieu, Auber, and Adam were worthy successors. He was greatly honored; he was elected a member of many artistic and learned institutions in France and abroad; the Prince-Bishop of Liège made him a privy councillor in 1784; a street in Paris was named for him in 1785; he was admitted to the Institut de France in 1795, as one of the first 3 chosen to represent the dept. of musical composition; he was also appointed inspector of the Paris Cons. in 1795, but resigned after just a few months. Napoleon made him a Chevalier of the Légion d'honneur in 1802, and granted him a pension of 4,000 francs in compensation for losses during the Revolution. His daughter, Lucille (real name, Angélique-Dorothée-Lucie; b. Paris, July 15, 1772; d. there, Aug. 25, 1790), was a gifted musician; at the age of 13, with some assistance from her father, she composed an opera, *Le Mariage d'Antonio*, which was produced at the Opéra Comique on July 29, 1786; her 2d opera, *Toinette et Louis*, was produced on March 23, 1787. F. A. Gevaert, E. Fetis, A. Wotquenne, and others ed. a *Collection complète des oeuvres* (Leipzig, 1884–1936).

WORKS: DRAMATIC (all 1st perf. in Paris unless otherwise given): OPÉRAS COMIQUES: *Isabelle et Gertrude, ou Les Sylphes supposés* (Geneva, Dec. 1766); *Le Huron* (Comédie-Italienne, Aug. 20, 1768); *Lucile* (Comédie-Italienne, Jan. 5, 1769); *Le Tableau parlant* (Comédie-Italienne, Sept. 20, 1769); *Silvain* (Comédie-Italienne, Feb. 19, 1770); *Les Deux Avares* (Fontainebleau, Oct. 27, 1770); *L'Amitié à l'épreuve* (Fontainebleau, Nov. 13, 1770); *L'Ami de la maison* (Fontainebleau, Oct. 26, 1771); *Zémire et Azor* (Fontainebleau, Nov. 9, 1771); *Le Magnifique* (Comédie-Italienne, March 4, 1773); *La Rosière de Salency* (Fontainebleau, Oct. 23, 1773); *La Fausse Magie* (Comédie-Italienne, Feb. 1, 1775); *Matroco* (Nov. 3, 1777); *Le Jugement de Midas* (March 28, 1778); *Les Fausses Apparences, ou L'Amant jaloux* (Versailles, Nov. 20, 1778); *Les Evénements imprévus* (Versailles, Nov. 11, 1779); *Aucassin et Nicolette, ou Les Moeurs du bon vieux temps* (Versailles, Dec. 30, 1779); *Théodore et Paulin* (Versailles, March 5, 1784); *Richard Coeur-de-lion* (Comédie-Italienne, Oct. 21, 1784); *Les Méprises par ressemblance* (Fontainebleau, Nov. 7, 1786); *Le Comte d'Albert* (Fontainebleau, Nov. 13, 1786); *Le Prisonnier anglais* (Comédie-Italienne, Dec. 26, 1787); *Le Rival confident* (Comédie-Italienne, June 26, 1788); *Raoul Barbe-bleue* (Comédie-Italienne, March 2, 1789); *Pierre le Grand* (Comédie-Italienne, Jan. 13, 1790); *Guillaume Tell* (Comédie-Italienne, April 9, 1791); *Cécile et Ermance, ou Les Deux Couvents* (Comédie-Italienne, Jan. 16, 1792); *Basile, ou À trompeur, trompeur et demi* (Comédie-Italienne, Oct. 17, 1792); *Le Congrès des rois* (Opéra Comique; Feb. 26, 1794; in collaboration with others); *Joseph Barra* (Opéra Comique, June 5, 1794); *Callias, ou Nature et patrie* (Opéra Comique, Sept. 19, 1794); *Lisbeth* (Opéra Comique, Jan. 10, 1797); *Le Barbier du village, ou Le Revenant* (Théâtre Feydeau, May 6, 1797); *Elisca, ou L'Amour maternel* (Opéra Comique, Jan. 1, 1799). OTHER: *La Vendemmiatrice*, 2 intermezzos (Rome, Carnival 1765); *Les Mariages samnites*, opéra (Jan. 1768?; rev. version, Comédie-Italienne, June 12, 1776); *Céphale et Procris, ou L'Amour conjugal*, opéra ballet (Versailles, Dec. 30, 1773); *Amour pour amour*, 3 divertissements (Versailles, March 10, 1777); *Les Trois Âges de l'opéra*, prologue (Opéra, April 27, 1778); *Andromaque*, opera (Opéra, June 6, 1780); *Emilie, ou La Belle Esclave*, opéra ballet (Opéra, Feb. 22, 1781); *L'Embarras des richesses*, opera (Opéra, Nov. 26, 1782); *Thalie au nouveau théâtre*, prologue (Comédie-Italienne, April 28, 1783); *La Caravane du Caire*, opéra ballet (Fontainebleau, Oct. 30, 1783); *Panurge dans l'île des lanternes*, opera (Opéra, Jan. 25, 1785); *Amphitryon*, opera (Versailles, March 15, 1786); *Aspasie*, opera (Opéra, March 17, 1789); *Denys le tyran, maître d'école à Corinthe*, opera (Opéra, Aug. 23, 1794); *La Fête de la raison,* later called *La Rosière républicaine, ou La Fête de la vertu*, opera (Opéra, Sept. 2, 1794); *Anacréon chez Polycrate*, opera (Opéra, Jan. 17, 1797); *Le Casque et les colombes*, opéra ballet (Opéra, Nov. 7, 1801); *Le Ménage*, later called *Delphis et Mopsa*, opera (Opéra, Feb. 15, 1803). Several other stage works listed by Grétry were either never performed or were left unfinished.

BIBL.: Comte de Livry, *Recueil de lettres écrites à G., ou à son sujet* (Paris, 1809); A. J. Grétry, *G. en famille . . . précédées de son oraison funèbre par M. Bouilly* (Paris, 1814); F. Van Hulst, *G.* (Liège, 1842); L. de Saegher, *Notice biographique sur A. G.* (Brussels, 1869); E. Gregoir, *G.: Célèbre compositeur belge* (Brussels, 1883); J. Rongé and F. Delhasse, *G.* (Brussels, 1883); C. Gheude, *G.* (Liège, 1906); H. de Curzon, *G.* (Paris, 1907); E. Closson, *A.-M. G.* (Turnhout and Brussels, 1920); P. Long des Clavières, *La Jeunesse de G. et ses débuts à Paris* (Besançon, 1921); H. Wichmann, *G. und das musikalische Theater in Frankreich* (Halle, 1929); J. Bruyr, *G.* (Paris, 1931); J. Sauvenier, *A. G.* (Brussels, 1934); M. Degey, *A.-M. G.* (Brussels, 1939); S. Clercx, *G., 1741–1813* (Brussels, 1944); G. de Froidcourt, *G., Rouget de Lisle et la Marseillaise* (Liège, 1945); idem ed., *La Correspondance générale de G.* (Brussels, 1962); R. Jobe, *The Operas of A.-E.-M. G.* (diss., Univ. of Michigan, 1965); D. Charlton, *G. and the Growth of Opéra Comique* (Cambridge, 1986).

Grevillius, Nils, Swedish conductor; b. Stockholm, March 7, 1893; d. Mariefred, Aug. 15, 1970. He was a violin student of Book at the Stockholm Cons. (1905–11), where he received 1st prize and the Prix Marteau, and later was a conducting student in Sondershausen and London. He began his career as concertmaster of the Royal Theater Orch. in Stockholm (1911–14). After serving as assistant conductor of the Stockholm Concert Soc. (1914–20), he conducted the Ballet Suédois in Paris (1922–23) and the Vienna Tonkünstlerverein (1923). Upon his return to Stockholm, he was conductor of the Royal Orch. (1924–53) and the Radio Orch. (1927–39), and also was court music director (1931–53).

Grey, Madeleine (real name, **Madeleine Nathalie Grumberg**), French mezzo-soprano; b. Villaines-la-Juhel, Mayenne, June 11, 1896; d. Paris, March 13, 1979. She was a student of Cortot (piano) and Hettich (voice) at the Paris Cons., and then devoted herself to a concert career. Fauré wrote his *Mirages* for her, and served as her accompanist at the cycle's premiere in Paris in 1919. Grey became particularly associated with the music of Ravel, who accompanied her in recordings of his *Chansons hébraïques* and *Chansons madécasses* in 1932. Canteloube dedicated his *Chants d'Auvergne* to her. Grey made many tours abroad, winning success in Italy, the United States, and South America. She retired in 1952. While her command of diction and clarity of vocal timbre were especially suited to the French repertoire, she also championed works by Respighi, Malipiero, Villa Lobos, and other composers of her era.

Griebling, Karen (Jean), American violist, violinist, conductor, teacher, and composer; b. Akron, Ohio, Dec. 31, 1957. She was trained at the Eastman School of Music in Rochester, N.Y. (B.M., 1980), the Univ. of Houston (M.M., 1982), and the Univ. of Texas at Austin (D.M.A., 1986). She played in the Texas Chamber Orch. (1980–81), the Houston Ballet Orch. (1980–82), the Corpus Christi Sym. Orch. (1985–86), and the Albany (N.Y.) Sym. Orch. (1986–87). In 1987 she joined the faculty of Hendrix College in Conway, Ark., became a member of the Fort Smith Sym. Orch., and was made codirector of the Conway Civic Orch.; she also was a member of the Arkansas String Quartet (from 1988). In 1990 she founded and became conductor of the Conway Chamber Orch. Among her works is the opera *The House of Bernarda Alba* (1986).

Griesbach, John Henry, English composer; b. Windsor, June 20, 1798; d. London, Jan. 9, 1875. He studied cello with his father, and played in the court band. His major work was a sacred opera, *Belshazzar's Feast* (1835; rev. as the oratorio *Daniel*, London, June 30, 1854).

Griffes, Charles Tomlinson, outstanding American composer; b. Elmira, N.Y., Sept. 17, 1884; d. N.Y., April 8, 1920. He began piano lessons at an early age with his sister; about 1899 he became a piano student of Mary Selena Broughton, an instructor at Elmira College. Thanks to Broughton's financial assistance, Griffes was able to go to Berlin in 1903 to pursue his training at the Stern Cons. with Ernst Jedliczka and Gottfried Galston (piano), Philippe Rufer and Humperdinck (composition), and Max Lowengard and Klatte (counterpoint). After private composition lessons with Humperdinck (1905–06), he again studied piano with Galston (1906–07). Upon his return to the United States in 1907, he was made director of music at the Hackley School in Tarrytown, N.Y. Until about 1911 Griffes's works followed along the path of German Romanticism. He then pursued his fascination with impressionism in a number of piano pieces and songs. His subsequent interest in the potentialities of the oriental scale resulted in such scores as his Japanese pantomime *Sho-jo* (1917) and the orch. version of his remarkable piano piece *The Pleasure-Dome of Kubla Khan* (1917). In his last works, such as his Piano Sonata (1917–18), he revealed a strong individual style tending toward extreme dissonance.

WORKS: DRAMATIC: *The Kairn of Koridwen*, dance drama (1916; N.Y., Feb. 10, 1917); *Sho-jo*, Japanese pantomime (Atlantic City, N.J., Aug. 5, 1917); *The White Peacock*, ballet (N.Y., June 22, 1919; arrangement of the piano piece, 1915); *Salut au monde*, festival drama (1919; N.Y., April 22, 1922).

BIBL.: J. Howard, *C. T. G.* (N.Y., 1923); E. Maisel, *C. T. G.: The Life of an American Composer* (N.Y., 1943); G. Conrey, *The Published Songs of C. T. G.: A Stylistic Examination* (diss., Chicago Musical College, 1955); D. Boda, *The Music of C. G.* (diss., Florida State Univ., 1962); D. Anderson, *C. T. G.: An Annotated Bibliography-Discography* (Detroit, 1977); idem, *The Works of C. T. G.: A Descriptive Catalogue* (Ann Arbor, 1984); idem, *C. T. G.: A Life in Music* (Washington, D.C., 1993).

Griffes, Elliot, American pianist, teacher, and composer; b. Boston, Jan. 28, 1893; d. Los Angeles, June 8, 1967. He studied at Ithaca College (graduated, 1913), then with Horatio Parker at the Yale Univ. School of Music (1915–16), and with Chadwick, Stuart Mason, and Pattison at the New England Cons. of Music in Boston (1917–18); he won a Juilliard scholarship (1922) and a Pulitzer scholarship (1931). He was active as a recitalist; he also taught in various institutions, including Grinnell College in Iowa (1920–22), the Brooklyn Settlement School (1923–24), the St. Louis School of Music (head of theory dept., 1935–36), and the Westchester Cons. in White Plains, N.Y. (director, 1942–43); he settled in Los Angeles as a composer of film scores. He wrote works in ingratiatingly Romantic colors. Among his works are *The Blue Scarab*, operetta (1934), and *Port of Pleasure*, opera (Los Angeles, June 29, 1963).

Griffiths, Paul, English music critic and writer on music; b. Bridgend, Glamorgan, Wales, Nov. 24, 1947. He received his education at Lincoln College, Oxford. From 1971 he wrote music criticism for many publications. He was chief music critic of *The Times* of London from 1982 to 1992, and then of the *New Yorker* from 1992. He served as area ed. for 20th-century music for the *New Grove Dictionary of Music and Musicians* (1980) and the *New Oxford Companion to Music* (1983). Among his books are *The Rake's Progress* (1982) and *Stravinsky* (1992).

Grist, Reri, black American soprano; b. N.Y., Feb. 29, 1934. While still a child, she appeared as a dancer and singer in musicals. She was educated at N.Y.'s High School of Music and Art, and then at Queens College; her voice teacher was Claire Gelda. In 1957 she sang Consuelo in the Broadway staging of *West Side Story*. In 1959 she made her operatic debut as Blöndchen at the Sante Fe Opera, and then sang with the N.Y. City Opera. In 1960 she made her European debut in Cologne as the Queen of the Night, and then sang in Zürich as Zerbinetta. She appeared as Despina at the Glyndebourne Festival in 1962, the year she also made her debut at London's Covent Garden as the Queen of Shemakha. In 1965 she sang Blondchen at the Salzburg Festival. On Feb. 25, 1966, she made her Metropolitan Opera debut in New York as Rossini's Rosina, returning for the 1968–73 and 1977–78 seasons. She was a prof. at the Indiana Univ. School of Music in Bloomington (1981–83), the Munich Hochschule für Musik (1984–95), and the Stearns Inst. at Ravinia (from 1992). Her operatic engagements also took her to many other music centers in North America and Europe. She also sang widely as a soloist with orchs. and as a recitalist. Among her other roles were Susanna, Adina, Norina, Gilda, Oscar, and Sophie.

Grisar, Albert, Belgian composer; b. Antwerp (of German-Belgian parents), Dec. 26, 1808; d. Asnières, near Paris, June 15, 1869. He studied for a short time (1830) with Reicha in Paris. Returning to Antwerp, he brought out his opera *Le Mariage impossible* (Brussels, March 4, 1833), and obtained a government subsidy for further study in Paris. On April 26, 1836, he produced *Sarah* at the Opéra Comique; then *L'An mille* (June 23, 1837), *La Suisse à Trianon* (March 8, 1838), *Lady Melvil* (Nov. 15, 1838, with Flotow), *L'Eau merveilleuse* (Jan. 31, 1839, with Flotow), *Le Naufrage de la Méduse* (May 31, 1839, with Flotow and Pilati), *Les Travestissements* (Nov. 16, 1839), and *L'Opéra à la cour* (July 16, 1840, with Boieldieu, Jr.). In 1840 he went to Naples for further serious study under Mercadante; returning to Paris in 1848, he brought out *Gilles ravisseur* (Feb. 21, 1848), *Les Porcherons* (Jan. 12, 1850), *Bonsoir, M. Pantalon* (Feb. 19, 1851), *Le Carillonneur de Bruges* (Feb. 20, 1852), Les Amours du diable (March 11, 1853), *Le Chien du jardinier* (Jan. 16, 1855), *Voyage autour de ma chambre* (Aug. 12, 1859), *Le Joaillier de St. James* (9 songs from *Lady Melvil*; Feb. 17, 1862), *La Chatte merveilleuse* (March 18, 1862), *Les Bégaiements d'amour* (Dec. 8, 1864), and *Les Douze Innocentes* (Oct. 19, 1865). He left, besides, 12 finished and unfinished operas; also dramatic scenes, over 50 romances, etc. His statue (by Brackeleer) was placed in the vestibule of the Antwerp Theater in 1870.

BIBL.: A. Pougin, *A. G.* (Paris, 1870).

Grisi, Giuditta, Italian mezzo-soprano, sister of **Giulia Grisi**; b. Milan, July 28, 1805; d. Robecco d'Oglio, near Cremona, May 1, 1840. She studied at the Milan Cons., making her first appearance in Vienna in 1826. Afterward she sang with success in Italy and in Paris at the Théâtre-Italien under Rossini's management, retiring in 1838, after her marriage to Count Barni. Bellini wrote for her the part of Romeo in *I Capuleti ed i Montecchi* (Venice, March 11, 1830); her sister sang Juliet.

Grisi, Giulia, celebrated Italian soprano, sister of **Giuditta Grisi**; b. Milan, July 28, 1811; d. Berlin, Nov. 29, 1869. She received training from her sister and from her aunt, Grassini. She also studied with Celli and Guglielmi, with Marliani in Milan, and with Giacomelli in Bologna. In 1828 she made her operatic debut as Emma in Rossini's *Zelmira* in Bologna. She soon won the admiration of Bellini, who wrote the role of Juliet for her in his *I Capuleti ed i Montecchi*, which role she created in Venice on March 11, 1830. In 1831 she made her debut at Milan's La Scala in Strepponi's *L'ullà di Bassor*, where she then created Adalgisa in Bellini's *Norma* (Dec. 26, 1831) and Adelia in Donizetti's *Ugo, conte* *di Parigi* (March 13, 1832). Dissatisfied with her La Scala contract and unable to break it legally, she fled to Paris. On Oct. 16, 1832, she made her debut there with phenomenal success at the Théâtre-Italien as Rossini's Semiramide. She sang there regularly from 1834 to 1846, creating Elvira in Bellini's *I Puritani* (Jan. 24, 1835), Elena in Donizetti's *Marin Faliero* (March 12, 1835), and Norina in the latter's *Don Pasquale* (Jan. 3, 1843). On April 18, 1834, she made her London debut as Rossini's Ninetta at the King's Theatre, and subsequently sang regularly in the British capital with remarkable success. On April 6, 1847, she appeared as Semiramide in the first production of the newly organized Royal Italian Opera at London's Covent Garden. She continued to sing there until her farewell appearance on July 24, 1861. In 1836 she married, but later separated from her husband. In 1839 she met the tenor Mario in London, with whom she became intimate. Although she was never divorced from her husband, she continued to live with Mario as his wife. They made a tour of the United States in 1854–55. Her outstanding vocal gifts were matched by her compelling dramatic talent. Her other famous roles included Alice in *Robert le diable*, Valentine, Anna Bolena, Lucrezia Borgia, and Leonora in *Il Trovatore*.

BIBL.: E. Forbes, *Mario and G.* (London, 1985).

Griswold, Putnam, American bass-baritone; b. Minneapolis, Dec. 23, 1875; d. N.Y., Feb. 26, 1914. He went to London to study at the Royal College of Music and with A. Randegger. After making his operatic debut at Covent Garden as Leonato in Stanford's *Much Ado About Nothing* (1901), he pursued his training in Paris with Bouhy, in Frankfurt am Main with Stockhausen, and in Berlin with Emerich. In 1904 he sang at the Berlin Royal Opera; after touring the United States with Savage's opera company as Gurnemanz in an English language production of *Parsifal* (1904–05), he returned to Berlin to sing with fine success at the Royal Opera (1906–11). On Nov. 23, 1911, he made his Metropolitan Opera debut in New York as Hagen, and sang there until his death. He was highly admired as a Wagnerian, being notably successful as Wotan, King Marke, Pogner, and Daland.

Grob-Prandl, Gertrud, Austrian soprano; b. Vienna, Nov. 11, 1917; d. there, May 16, 1995. She was a student of Burian in Vienna. In 1938 she made her operatic debut as Santuzza at the Vienna Volksoper; after singing at the Zürich Opera (1946–47), she was a valued member of the Vienna State Opera (1947–64); she also appeared at London's Covent Garden (from 1951), in Milan, Berlin, and South America. She was known for her Wagnerian roles, most notably Ortrud, Brünnhilde, and Isolde.

Grobe, Donald (Roth), American tenor; b. Ottawa, Ill., Dec. 16, 1929; d. Berlin, April 1, 1986. He attended the Mannes College of Music in New York and also received vocal coaching from Robert Long, Martial Singher, Robert Weede, and Marguerite von Winterfeldt. In 1952 he made his operatic debut as Borsa in *Rigoletto* in Chicago, and then sang in musicals, on television, and in concerts in New York. After singing opera in Krefeld/Mönchengladbach (1956–57) and Hannover (1957–60), he was a member of the Berlin Deutsche Oper, where he created the roles of Wilhelm in Henze's *Der Junge Lord* (1965) and Arundel in Fortner's *Elisabeth Tudor* (1972); in 1970, he was made a Kammersänger. He also appeared at the Hamburg State Opera (1958–61; 1966–75) and the Bavarian State Opera in Munich (from 1967). On Nov. 22, 1968, he made his Metropolitan Opera debut in New York as Froh in *Das Rheingold*. His other roles included Ferrando, Eisenstein, Hoffmann, Alwa in *Lulu*, and Flamand in *Capriccio*.

Grosheim, Georg Christoph, German writer on music and composer; b. Kassel, July 1, 1764; d. there, Nov. 18, 1841. He played viola in the Court Orch. at Kassel. He ed. the magazine *Euterpe* in 1797–98, and also wrote biographical articles on composers, and corresponded with Beethoven. His autobiography was publ. by G. Heinrichs (1926). He composed 3 operas: *Titania, oder Liebe durch Zauberei* (1792), *Das heilige Kleeblatt* (1793; Oct. 1794), and *Les Esclaves d'Alger* (Kassel, Oct. 14, 1808; not extant).

Grossi, Giovanni Francesco, famous Italian castrato soprano, known as **Siface**; b. Chiesina Uzzanese, near Pescia, Feb. 12, 1653; d. (murdered) near Ferrara, May 29, 1697. He gained renown and his nickname when he appeared as Siface in Cavalli's *Scipione affricano* in Rome in 1671. After singing in the Papal Chapel (1675–79), he was in the service of Francesco II d'Este, Duke of Modena. He also appeared in opera throughout Italy, and in 1687 visited London and sang before King James II in his private chapel. He then pursued his career in Modena, Naples, Parma, Bologna, Milan, and Reggio Emilia. When he became intimate with a female member of the Marsili family, affronted members of the family took revenge by having assassins kill him.

Grosz, Wilhelm, Austrian composer; b. Vienna, Aug. 11, 1894; d. N.Y., Dec. 10, 1939. He studied in Vienna with Richard Robert (piano), at the Cons. with Heuberger, Fuchs, and Schreker (theory and composition), and at the Univ. with Adler (musicology; Ph.D., 1920, with the diss. *Die Fugenarbeit in W.A. Mozarts Vokal- und Instrumentalwerken*). He was active mainly in Vienna, where he was conductor of the Kammerspiele in 1933–34. As a Jew, he sought refuge in London before emigrating to the United States in 1938.

WORKS: DRAMATIC: *Sganarell*, opera (Dessau, Nov. 21, 1925); *Der arme Reinhold*, dance fable (Berlin, Dec. 22, 1928); *Achtung, Aufnahme!*, musical comedy (Frankfurt am Main, March 23, 1930); incidental music for plays, films, and radio.

Grout, Donald J(ay), eminent American musicologist; b. Rock Rapids, Iowa, Sept. 28, 1902; d. Skaneateles, N.Y., March 9, 1987. He studied philosophy at Syracuse Univ. (A.B., 1923) and musicology at Harvard Univ. (A.M., 1932; Ph.D., 1939); he also received piano instruction in Boston, and took a course in French music in Strasbourg and in the history of opera in Vienna. After serving as a visiting lecturer at Mills College in Oakland, California (1935–36), he was on the faculties of Harvard Univ. (1936–42) and the Univ. of Texas at Austin (1942–45); subsequently he was a prof. of musicology at Cornell Univ. (1945–70). He held a Guggenheim Foundation grant in 1951. He served as president of the American Musicological Soc. (1952–54; 1960–62); in 1966 he became curator of the Accademia Monteverdiana in New York.

WRITINGS: *A Short History of Opera* (2 vols., N.Y., 1948; 3d ed., 1988); *A History of Western Music* (N.Y., 1960; 4th ed., 1988); *Mozart in the History of Opera* (Washington, D.C., 1972); *Alessandro Scarlatti: An Introduction to His Operas* (Berkeley, 1979).

BIBL.: W. Austin, ed., *New Looks at Italian Opera: Essays in Honor of D. J. G.* (Ithaca, N.Y., 1968).

Grové, Stefans, South African composer and teacher; b. Bethlehem, Orange Free State, July 23, 1922. He studied with his mother and his uncle, David Roode, and learned to play the piano and organ. He continued his piano training in Cape Town at the South African College of Music (diploma, 1948) and was a student in composition of W. H. Bell (1945–46). In 1953 he went to the United States on a Fulbright scholarship and pursued his studies at Harvard Univ., taking the M.A. in musicology and the M.Mus. under Walter Piston in 1955; he also studied composition with Copland at the Berkshire Music Center in Tanglewood (summer, 1954). After teaching at Bard College in Annandale-on-Hudson, N.Y. (1956–57), he was on the faculty of the Peabody Cons. of Music in Baltimore (1957–71). In 1972 he was a lecturer at the South African College of Music, and then taught theory and composition at the Univ. of Pretoria from 1974. With the composition of his Violin Sonata on African motives (1984), he has pursued a style which is characterized by the incorporation of African elements in his music. These ethnic elements consist mainly of rhythmic and melodic procedures, resulting in complex rhythmic patterns with constant metric changes, as well as ostinato figures with constant changes. His works include the opera *Die bose Wind* (1983) and the ballets *Waratha* (1977) and *Pinocchio* (1983).

Groves, Sir Charles (Barnard), distinguished English conductor; b. London, March 10, 1915; d. there, June 20, 1992. He received training in piano and organ at the Royal College of Music in London. In 1938 he joined the BBC as a chorus master, and then was assoc. conductor of the BBC Theatre Orch. (1942–44) and subsequently conductor of the BBC Northern Orch. in Manchester (1944–51). In 1951 he became conductor of the Bournemouth Municipal Orch.; after it was renamed the Bournemouth Sym. Orch. in 1954, he continued as its conductor until 1961. After serving as music director of the Welsh National Opera in Cardiff (1961–63), he was principal conductor of the Royal Liverpool Phil. from 1963 to 1977. He launched the career of several conductors through his sponsorship of the Liverpool International Conductors' Competition. In 1978–79 he was music director of the English National Opera in London, and later was principal conductor of the Guildford Phil. (from 1986). In 1958 he was made an Officer and in 1968 a Commander of the Order of the British Empire, and in 1973 he was knighted. Groves acquitted himself admirably as a conductor of the orch., operatic, and choral repertory.

Grovlez, Gabriel (Marie), French conductor and composer; b. Lille, April 4, 1879; d. Paris, Oct. 20, 1944. He studied at the Paris Cons. with Descombes, Diémer, Fauré, Gédalge, and Lavignac, taking a premier prix in piano in 1899. He toured Europe as accompanist to Marteau. He concentrated his activities on Paris, where he was prof. of piano at the Schola Cantorum (1899–1909), and also choirmaster and conductor at the Opéra Comique (1905–08). After serving as music director of the Théâtre des Arts (1911–13), he was director of the Opéra (1914–34); he also conducted opera abroad. In 1939 he became prof. of chamber music at the Cons. His works reflect the finest qualities of the Gallic tradition.

WORKS: DRAMATIC: OPERAS: *Coeur de rubis* (1906; Nice, 1922); *Le marquis do Carabas* (1926). BALLETS: *La princesse au jardin* (1914; Paris, 1941); *Maïmouna* (1916; Paris, 1921); *Le vrai arbre de Robinson* (1921; N.Y., 1922).

Grozăvescu, Trajan, Romanian tenor; b. Lugoj, Nov. 21, 1895; d. (murdered) Vienna, Feb. 15, 1927. He studied in Bucharest and Cluj. After making his debut in Cluj as Pinkerton in 1920, he continued his vocal studies in Vienna with F. Steiner. He made appearances with the Vienna Volksoper, the Prague National Theater, and the Vienna State Opera. He was shot to death by his wife.

BIBL.: M. Demeter-Grozăvescu and I. Voledi, *T. G.* (Bucharest, 1965).

Grua, Carlo Luigi Pietro, Italian composer; b. Florence, c.1665; place and date of death unknown. He most likely was the father of **Carlo (Alisio) Pietro Grua**. He was in Dresden from 1691 to 1694, first as singer in the electoral chapel, then as assistant Kapellmeister; his opera *Camillo generoso* was produced in Dresden in 1693; he next went to the Palatine court at Düsseldorf as assistant Kapellmeister; his opera *Telegono* was given there during the 1697 Carnival; he then went to Venice, where he produced 2 operas: *Il Pastor fido* (1721) and *Romolo e Tazio* (1722).

Grua, Carlo (Alisio) Pietro, Italian composer, father of **Franz Paul (Francesco da Paula or Paolo) Grua**; b. probably in Milan, c.1700; d. Mannheim (buried), April 11, 1773. He may have been a son of **Carlo Luigi Pietro Grua**. He was Kapellmeister at Mannheim from about 1734 until his death. During this time, he wrote the operas *Meride* (1742) and *La clemenza di Tito* (1748); also 5 oratorios.

Grua, Franz Paul (Francesco da Paula or Paolo), German composer of Italian descent, son of **Carlo (Alisio) Pietro Grua**; b. Mannheim (baptized), Feb. 1, 1753; d. Munich, July 5, 1833. He studied with Holzbauer in Mannheim, then went to Bologna, where he was a pupil of Padre Martini, and to Parma, where he studied with Traetta. Returning to Mannheim, he became a member of the electoral orch.; in 1778 he accompanied the court to Munich; he became court conductor there in 1784. He wrote one opera, *Telemaco*, given at the Munich Carnival in 1780.

Gruber, H(einz) K(arl) "Nali," Austrian composer and double bass player; b. Vienna, Jan. 3, 1943. He was the great-great-grandson of Austrian composer Franz Xaver Gruber (b. Unterweizburg, near Hochburg, Nov. 25, 1787; d. Hallein, near Salzburg, June 7, 1863). After singing in the Vienna Boys' Choir (1953–57), he studied double bass with Planyavsky and Streicher, composition with Uhl and Ratz, and serial techniques with Jelinek at the Vienna Academy of Music (1957–63). In 1963–64 he attended a master class in composition there with Einem. He pursued his career in Vienna, where he joined the die reihe ensemble as a double bass player in 1961. From 1963 to 1969 he was principal double bass in the Niederösterreiches Tonkünstler Orch. In 1968 he cofounded with Schwertsik and Zykan the avant-garde group MOB art & tone ART, with which he was active until 1971. He played double bass in the Austrian Radio Sym. Orch. from 1969. In 1979 he was awarded the music prize of the Austrian Ministry of Culture and Education. While Gruber's works are basically tonal in nature, he has developed an unbuttoned personal style in which serious and lighter elements are given free reign as the mood strikes him. His self-described "pan-demonium" *Frankenstein!!* (1976–77) brought him international recognition.

WORKS: DRAMATIC: *Die Vertreibung aus dem Paradies*, melodrama (1966; ORF, Vienna, Feb. 11, 1969; rev. 1979); *Gomorra*, musical spectacle (1970–72; withdrawn; new version, 1984–91; Vienna, Jan. 18, 1993); *Reportage aus Gomorra* for 5 Singers and 8 Players (1975–76); *Frankenstein!!*, "pan-demonium" for Baritone Channsonier and Orch. (1976–77; Liverpool, Nov. 25, 1978; also for Baritone Channsonier and 12 Instruments, Berlin, Sept. 30, 1979); *Bring me the head of Amadeus*, music for the television series *Not Mozart* (BBC2-TV, London, Nov. 17, 1991); *Gloria von Jaxtberg*, music theater (1992–93).

Gruberová, Edita, Czech soprano; b. Bratislava, Dec. 23, 1946. She was a student in Prague of Maria Medvecká and in Vienna of Ruthilde Boesch. In 1968 she made her operatic debut as Rossini's Rosina at the Slovak National Theater in Bratislava. In 1970 she made her first appearance at the Vienna State Opera as the Queen of the Night, and subsequently sang there regularly. In 1973 she sang at the Glyndebourne Festival and in 1974 at the Salzburg Festival. On Jan. 5, 1977, she made her Metropolitan Opera debut in New York as the Queen of the Night. She appeared as Giulietta in *I Capuleti e i Montecchi* at London's Covent Garden in 1984. After singing Lucia at Milan's La Scala in 1984, she reprised that role in Chicago in 1986 and in Barcelona in 1987. In 1989 she portrayed Violetta at the Metropolitan Opera. She sang Donizetti's Elizabeth I in Vienna in 1990, and then appeared as Semiramide in Zürich in 1992. She returned to Vienna as Linda di Chamounix in 1997 and also sang Anna Bolena that year in Munich. She also toured widely as a concert singer. Among her other admired roles were Donna Anna, Gilda, and Ariadne.

Gruenberg, Louis, Russian-born American composer; b. near Brest Litovsk, Aug. 3, 1884; d. Los Angeles, June 9, 1964. He went with his family to the United States when he was 2; after piano lessons with Adele Margulies in New York, he went to Berlin in 1903 to study piano and composition with Busoni and Friedrich Koch. In 1912 he made his debut as a soloist with the Berlin Phil. under Busoni's direction, and then toured Europe and the United States; he also became an instructor at the Vienna Cons. that year. Upon winning the Flagler Prize in 1920 for his orch. piece *The Hill of Dreams*, he decided to settle in the United States and devote himself to composition. In 1923 he helped found the League of Composers and became a champion of contemporary music. The influence of jazz and spirituals resulted in one of his most successful scores, *The Daniel Jazz* for Tenor, Clarinet, Trumpet, and String Quartet (1924). In 1930 he was awarded the RCA Victor Prize for his 1st Sym. He then composed his most successful stage work, the opera *The Emperor Jones*, which was premiered at the Metropolitan Opera in New York on Jan. 7, 1933. It received the David Bispham Medal. After serving as head of the composition dept. at the Chicago Musical College (1933–36), Gruenberg settled in California. His film scores for *The Fight for Life* (1940), *So Ends our Night* (1941), and *Commandos Strike at Dawn* (1942) won him Academy Awards. He was elected a member of the National Inst. of Arts and Letters in 1947.

WORKS: DRAMATIC: *Signor Formica*, operetta (1910); *The Witch of Brocken*, operetta (1912); *Piccadillymädel*, operetta (1913); *The Bride of the Gods*, opera (1913); *Roly-boly Eyes*, musical (1919; in collaboration with E. Brown); *The Dumb Wife*, chamber opera (1923); *Hallo! Tommy!*, operetta (1920s); *Lady X*, operetta (c.1927); *Jack and the Beanstalk*, opera (N.Y., Nov. 19, 1931); *The Emperor Jones*, opera (1931; N.Y., Jan. 7, 1933); *Helena's Husband*, opera (1936); *Green Mansions*, radio opera (CBS, Oct. 17, 1937); *Volpone*, opera (1945); *One Night of Cleopatra*, opera (n.d.); *The Miracle of Flanders*, musical legend (1954); *The Delicate King*, opera (1955); *Antony and Cleopatra*, opera (1955; rev. 1958 and 1961); ballets; pantomimes; incidental music; film scores.

BIBL.: R. Nisbett, *L. G.: His Life and Work* (diss., Ohio State Univ., 1979).

Gruhn (originally, **Grunebaum**), **Nora,** English soprano of German descent; b. London, March 6, 1905. She studied at the Royal College of Music in London and with Hermine Bosetti in Munich. She made her operatic debut in Kaiserslautern in 1928; sang with the Cologne Opera (1929–30); she appeared at Covent Garden (1929–33; 1936–37) and Sadler's Wells (1946–48) in London. She sang the part of Gretel in an English production of Humperdinck's *Hansel und Gretel* reportedly more than 400 times.

Grümmer, Elisabeth, distinguished German soprano; b. Niederjeutz, near Diedenhofen, Alsace-Lorraine, March 31, 1911; d. Berlin, Nov. 6, 1986. She began her career as an actress; after being persuaded to study voice by Karajan, she had lessons with Schlender in Aachen. In 1940 she made her operatic debut in Aachen as the 1st Flowermaiden in *Parsifal*, and then sang her first major role there in 1941 as Octavian. After appearances in Duisburg (1942–44), she was a member of the Berlin Städtische Oper (from 1946). On June 29, 1951, she made her first appearance at London's Covent Garden as Eva in *Die Meistersinger von Nürnberg*. She then made debuts at the Vienna State Opera and the Salzburg Festival in 1953, at the Glyndebourne Festival in 1956, and at the Bayreuth Festival in 1957. On Feb. 17, 1967, she made her debut at the N.Y. City Opera as the Marschallin, followed by her Metropolitan Opera debut in New York as Elsa in *Lohengrin* on April 20, 1967. She then continued her career in Europe until retiring in 1972. In addition to opera, she toured extensively as a concert artist. From 1959 she was a prof. of voice at the (West) Berlin Hochschule für Musik. Grümmer's exquisite voice and admirable dramatic gifts made her an exemplary interpreter of the music of Mozart and Richard Strauss. Among her other outstanding roles were Pamina, Donna Anna, Ilia, and the Mozart and Strauss Countess.

Grünbaum (originally, **Müller**), **Therese,** famous Austrian soprano, daughter of **Wenzel Müller**; b. Vienna, Aug. 24, 1791; d. Berlin, Jan. 30, 1876. She studied with her father, and appeared on stage while still a child. In 1807 she went to Prague, and in 1816 she joined the Kärnthnertortheater in Vienna, remaining as a principal member there until 1826. While in Vienna, she gained fame for her Rossini roles; also created the role of Eglantine in Weber's *Euryanthe*. After appearances in Berlin (1828–30), she taught voice. She married the tenor Johann Christoff (b. Haslau, Oct. 28, 1785; d. Berlin, Oct. 10, 1870); a daughter, Caroline (b. Prague, March 18, 1814; d. Braunschweig, May 26, 1868), was also a soprano.

Grundheber, Franz, German baritone; b. Trier, Sept. 27, 1937. He studied in Trier, Hamburg, at Indiana Univ., and at the Music Academy of the West in Santa Barbara. In 1966 he became a member of the Hamburg State Opera. In 1983 he sang Strauss's Mandryka at the Vienna State Opera, and in 1985 Strauss's Olivier at the Salzburg Festival. After appearing as Amonasro at the Savonlinna Festival in 1989, he sang Strauss's Barak at the Holland Festival in 1990. In 1992 he was engaged as Germont in Barcelona, and as Wozzeck in Paris and at London's Covent Garden. He also sang Wozzeck at the Lyric Opera in Chicago in 1994, and then appeared as Wagner's Dutchman at the Los Angeles Opera in 1995. In 1997 he returned to Covent Garden as Rigoletto, which role he sang at his Metropolitan Opera debut in New York on March 8, 1999.

Grunenwald, Jean-Jacques, distinguished French organist and composer; b. Cran-Gevrier, near Annecy (of Swiss parents), Feb. 2, 1911; d. Paris, Dec. 19, 1982. He studied with Dupré (organ; premier prix, 1935) and Büsser (composition; premier prix, 1937) at the Paris Cons. From 1936 to 1945 he was Dupré's assistant at St.-Sulpice in Paris; from 1955 to 1970 he was organist at St.-Pierre-de-Montrouge. He was a prof. at the Schola Cantorum in Paris from 1958 to 1961, and from 1961 to 1966 was on the faculty of the Geneva Cons. Through the years, he played more than 1,500 concerts, presenting the complete organ works of Bach, Franck et al. He also became famous for the excellence of his masterly improvisations, which rivaled those of Dupré. Among his own compositions is the lyric drama *Sardanapale* (1945–50).

Grüner-Hegge, Odd, Norwegian conductor and composer; b. Christiania, Sept. 23, 1899; d. there (Oslo), May 11, 1973. He studied piano and composition at the Christiania Cons. and conducting with Weingartner. In 1927 he began his conducting career; from 1931 he was a conductor with the Oslo Phil., subsequently serving as its chief conductor from 1945 to 1961; he then was manager of the Norwegian Opera in Oslo from 1961 to 1969. He also appeared as a guest conductor with many of the leading European orchs. Among his works were orch. scores, chamber music, and piano pieces.

Grünfeld, Alfred, Austrian pianist and composer; b. Prague, July 4, 1852; d. Vienna, Jan. 4, 1924. He studied in Prague, and at Kullak's Academy in Berlin. He settled in Vienna in 1873, and established himself as a pianist and teacher; he also made tours in other European countries. He composed an operetta, *Der Lebemann* (Vienna, Jan. 16, 1903), and the comic opera *Die Schonen von Fogaras* (Dresden, 1907); he also made brilliant arrangements for piano of waltzes by Johann Strauss Jr. and publ. piano studies and various other pieces. His brother Heinrich Grünfeld (1855–1931) was also a pianist and composer.

Guadagno, Anton, Italian-born American conductor; b. Castellammare del Golfo, May 2, 1925. He studied at the Palermo Cons.; after obtaining degrees in conducting and composition at the Accademia di Santa Cecilia in Rome, he took 1st prize in conducting at the Salzburg Mozarteum; his principal conducting mentors were Ferrara, Molinari, C. Zecchi, and Karajan. Following engagements in Italy and South America, he emigrated to the United States and became a naturalized American citizen. In 1952 he made his U.S. debut conducting at a Carnegie Hall concert in New York. In 1958–59 he was an assistant conductor at the Metropolitan Opera in New York. From 1966 to 1972 he was music administrator of the Philadelphia Lyric Opera. In 1970 he made his London debut conducting *Andrea Chénier* at Drury Lane, and returned to London in 1971 to make his debut at Covent Garden conducting *Un ballo in maschera*. On Nov. 9, 1982, he made his formal debut at the Metropolitan Opera in New York conducting the latter opera. He was artistic director of the Palm Beach (Fla.) Opera from 1984.

Guadagni, Gaetano, celebrated Italian castrato contralto, later soprano; b. Lodi or Vicenza, c.1725; d. Padua, Nov. 1792. He was a contralto at the Basilica del Santo in Padua in 1746, and that same year he commenced his stage career at the Teatro San Moise in Venice. In 1748 he went to London and appeared at the Haymarket Theatre. Handel was so impressed with Guadagni's voice that he arranged contralto parts for him in *Messiah* and *Samson*, and also composed the role of Didimus in *Theodora* for him, which role Guadagni created at Covent Garden on March 16, 1750. Guadagni seems to have made his way to Lisbon in 1753 to study with Gioacchino "Gizziello" Conti. In 1754 he appeared at the Concert Spirituel in Paris, and also sang in Versailles. After another London sojourn in 1755, he sang throughout Europe.

While in Vienna, he created the title role in Gluck's *Orfeo* on Oct. 5, 1762, and also sang in concerts. He then accompanied Gluck to Frankfurt am Main for the coronation of the emperor in 1764. After singing in Innsbruck (1765), Venice (1767–69), and once again at London's Haymarket Theatre (1770), he returned to his homeland. In 1772 he was granted the title of Cavaliere di San Marco in Venice. Following appearances in Munich in 1773 and 1775, he sang before Frederick the Great in Potsdam in 1776. In 1777 he settled in Padua, where he sang mainly at the Basilica del Santo. Guadagni was renowned for both his vocal and dramatic gifts. He composed several arias, including *Pensa a serbarmi, o cara* for Metastasio's *Ezio*.

Guarducci, Tommaso, notable Italian castrato soprano; b. Montefiascone, c. 1720; d. after 1770. He was a pupil in Bologna of Bernacchi. From about 1745 he sang in many Italian music centers. In 1750 he became a prominent singer at the Spanish court; he also appeared at the Vienna court from 1752, while continuing his career in Italy. After singing at the King's Theatre in London (1766–68), he retired to his homeland in 1770.

Guarino, Carmine, Italian composer; b. Rovigo, Oct. 1, 1893; d. Genoa, June 5, 1965. He studied violin and composition at the Naples Cons. His first opera, *Madama di Challant*, set in the tradition of Verdi, was premiered there on March 9, 1927, attracting favorable comments. He was also the composer of the first Italian radio opera, *Cuore di Wanda* (Radio Italiano, Dec. 20, 1931). Other works for the stage were an operetta, *Gaby* (San Remo, March 20, 1924); *Tabarano alla Corte di Nonesiste*, musical fable (1931); 2 operas: *Balilla* (Rome, March 7, 1935) and *Sogno di un mattino d'autunno* (Cluj, March 30, 1936); and a ballet, *El Samet, il silenzioso* (1958).

Guarino, Piero, Italian pianist, conductor, pedagogue, and composer; b. Alexandria, Egypt, June 20, 1919; d. Rovereto, May 23, 1991. He studied piano and composition at the Athens Cons. (1936–39) before pursuing his training at the Accademia di Santa Cecilia in Rome; he completed advanced studies with Casella and Bonucci. From 1939 he was active as a pianist and conductor. After serving as director of the Alexandria Cons. (1950–60), he was director of the chamber orch. of the Accademia Musicale Napoletana (1962–73); he also taught at the Salzburg Mozarteum (1963–67) and the Perugia Cons. (1965–66). He then was director of the Sassari Cons. (1969–75) and the Parma Cons. (1975–89). He composed the chamber opera *Vettura-letto* (1969).

Guarnieri, Antonio, distinguished Italian conductor; b. Venice, Feb. 1, 1880; d. Milan, Nov. 25, 1952. He studied cello, piano, and composition in Venice. He began his career as a cellist in the Martucci Quartet. After making his conducting debut in Siena in 1904, he conducted in various Italian theaters. Following an engagement at the Vienna Court Opera (1912–13), he returned to Italy and founded the Società Sinfonica Italiana in Milan in 1915. In 1922 he made his first appearance at Milan's La Scala, where he subsequently was one of its principal conductors from 1929 until shortly before his death. Guarnieri was highly esteemed for his interpretations of the Italian operatic repertory.

Guarnieri, (Mozart) Camargo, esteemed Brazilian composer, conductor, and teacher; b. Tietê, Feb. 1, 1907; d. São Paulo, Jan. 13, 1993. His father was an Italian emigrant, his mother a Brazilian. After musical instruction from his parents, he went to São Paulo in 1922 and studied with Lamberto Baldi and Mário de Andrade; later he pursued his training with Koechlin (composition) and Rühlmann (conducting) in Paris (1938–39). Upon returning to São Paulo, he served as resident conductor of the Municipal Sym. Orch. and, from 1975, was conductor of the Univ.'s Sym. Orch.; he also was engaged in teaching. Between 1941 and 1981 he made a number of visits to the United States, occasionally appearing as a conductor of his own works. His extensive catalogue of music, skillfully crafted in a tonal style, is basically reflective of Brazilian national elements. His catalog of works includes *Pedro Malazarte*, comic opera (1931), and *O Homen Só*, opera (1960).

Guarrera, Frank, American baritone; b. Philadelphia, Dec. 3, 1923. He studied voice with Richard Bonelli in Philadelphia. On Dec. 14, 1948, he made his Metropolitan Opera debut in New York as Escamillo in *Carmen*, where he remained on its roster until 1976. He was invited by Toscanini to sing at La Scala in Milan; he also made guest appearances in San Francisco, Chicago, Paris, and London. He was best known for his performances of Italian roles.

Gubaidulina, Sofia (Asgatovna), remarkable Russian composer; b. Chistopol, Oct. 24, 1931. She received training in piano from Maria Piatnitskaya and in theory from Nazib Zhiganov at the Academy of Music (1946–49), and in piano from Leopold Lukomsky and Grigory Kogan, and in composition from Albert Leman at the Cons. (1949–54) in Kazan; she then studied composition with Nikolai Peiko and Vissarion Shebalin at the Moscow Cons. (1954–63), and later pursued research at the Moscow Electronic Music Studio (from 1968). In 1991 she settled in Germany. Gubaidulina's heritage—her grandfather was a mullah, her father was a Tatar, and her mother was of Russian, Polish, and Jewish descent—has played a significant role in her development as a composer. Claiming that "I am the place where East meets West," the spiritual quality of her works is reflected in the influence of the Muslim, Orthodox, Jewish, and Roman Catholic faiths. While she has pursued advanced compositional methods along avant-garde lines, she has done so in victorially divergent paths that have allowed her to retain a unique individuality. Her extensive catalog of works includes the opera-ballet-oratorio *Oration for the Age of Aquarius* (1991), and the ballets *Volshebnaya svirel* (1960), *Flute of Tania* (1961), and *Begushchaya po volnam* (1962).

Gubrud, Irene (Ann), American soprano; b. Canby, Minn., Jan. 4, 1947. She studied at St. Olaf College in Northfield, Minn. (B.M., 1969), and with Marion Freschel at the Juilliard School of Music in New York. She won the Naumburg International Voice Competition (1980), and made her operatic debut as Mimi in St. Paul, Minn., in 1981; she also toured widely as a recitalist. She was successful in a comprehensive repertoire, extending from early music to the avant-garde.

Gudehus, Heinrich, distinguished German tenor; b. Altenhagen, near Celle, March 30, 1845; d. Dresden, Oct. 9, 1909. He was a student of Malvina Schnorr von Carolsfeld in Braunschweig and of Gustav Engel in Berlin. After making his operatic debut in Berlin as Nadori in *Jessonda* (Jan. 7, 1871), he sang in Lübeck, Freiburg, and Bremen. From 1880 to 1890 he was a principal member of the Dresden Court Opera. On July 28, 1882, he made his Bayreuth debut as Parsifal in its second staging, and returned there as Tristan in 1886 and as Walther von Stolzing in 1888. On June 4, 1884, he made his first appearance at London's Covent Garden in the latter role. He made his Metropolitan Opera debut in New York on Nov. 28, 1890, as Tannhäuser, and remained on its roster for the season. After singing at the Berlin Royal Opera (1891–96), he settled in Dresden as a voice teacher. Among his other outstanding roles were Florestan, John of Leyden, Siegmund, Lohengrin, and Siegfried.

Gueden, Hilde, noted Austrian soprano; b. Vienna, Sept. 15, 1917; d. Klosterneuburg, Sept. 17, 1988. She studied with Wetzelsberger at the Vienna Cons., then made her debut in operetta at the age of 16. She made her operatic debut as Cherubino in 1939 in Zürich, where she sang until 1941. After appearing in Munich (1941–42) and Rome (1942–46), she sang at the Salzburg Festival (1946); subsequently she was a leading member of the Vienna State Opera until 1973. She first appeared at London's Covent Garden with the visiting Vienna State Opera in 1947; her Metropolitan Opera debut followed in New York on Nov. 15, 1951, when she appeared as Gilda; she continued to sing there until 1960. In 1951 she was made an Austrian Kammersängerin. She maintained a wide-ranging repertoire, singing roles from Mozart to contemporary composers such as Britten and Blacher; she also was a fine operetta singer. She particularly excelled as Despina, Sophie, Zerbinetta, and Daphne.

Guelfi, Giangiacomo, Italian baritone; b. Rome, Dec. 21, 1924. He studied law in Florence and received vocal training from Ruffo. In 1950 he made his operatic debut as Rigoletto in Spoleto, and then sang at Milan's La Scala (from 1952); he also made appearances in Chicago (from 1954) and in London (from 1958). On Feb. 5, 1970, he made his Metropolitan Opera debut in New York as Scarpia, remaining on its roster for only that season. In 1975 he sang Scarpia at London's Covent Garden.

Guerrini, Guido, Italian composer and pedagogue; b. Faenza, Sept. 12, 1890; d. Rome, June 13, 1965. He studied with Torchi and Busoni at the Bologna Liceo Musicale. After teaching on its faculty (1920–24), he taught at the Parma Cons. (1925–28); he then was director of the Florence Cons. (1928–47), the Bologna Cons. (1947–49), and the Cons. di Santa Cecilia in Rome (1950–60). In addition to books on harmony and orchestration, he publ. *Ferrucio Busoni: La vita, la figura e l'opera* (Florence, 1941) and *Antonio Vivaldi: La vita e l'opera* (Florence, 1951). He was especially effective in composing orch., sacred, and chamber pieces.

WORKS: OPERAS: *Zalebi* (1915); *Nemici* (Bologna, Jan. 19, 1921); *La vigna* (1923–25; Rome, March 7, 1935); *L'arcangelo* (1930; Bologna, Nov. 26, 1949); *Enea* (Rome, Feb. 11, 1953).

BIBL.: A. Damerini, *Profilo critico di G. G.: Biografia e bibliografia* (Milan, 1928); P. Fragapane, *G. G. e i suoi poemi sinfonici* (Florence, 1932); *Catalogo delle opere di G. G. al suo settantesimo anno di età e curriculum della sua vita e cura dell'interessato, come saluto e ricordo agli amici* (Rome, 1961).

Guéymard, Louis, French tenor; b. Chapponay, Aug. 17, 1822; d. Paris, July 1880. Following his operatic debut in Lyons in 1845, he joined the Paris Opéra in 1848, where he was one of its principal singers until 1868 and where he created the roles of Jonas in *Le Prophéte* (1849) , Arrigo in *Les Vêpres siciliennes* (1855), and Assad in *La Reine de Saba* (1862). He also sang at London's Covent Garden (1852) and in New Orleans (1873–74). His wife was the Belgian soprano Pauline Lauters-Guéymard (b. Brussels, Dec. 1, 1834; place and date of death unknown) who sang at the Paris Théâtre-Lyrique in 1854. She then was a member of the Paris Opéra (1857–76), where she created the roles of Balkis in *La Reine de Saba* (1862), Eboli in *Don Carlos* (1867), and Gertrude in Thomas's *Hamlet* (1868).

Guglielmi, Pietro Alessandro, noted Italian composer, father of **Pietro Carlo Guglielmi**; b. Massa di Carrara, Dec. 9, 1728; d. Rome, Nov. 18, 1804. He began his musical training with his father, Jacopo Guglielmi, then studied with Durante at the S. Maria di Loreto Cons. in Naples. His first opera, *Lo solachianello 'mbroglione*, was given in Naples in 1757. During the next decade, he wrote no fewer than 25 operas; these included such popular works as *Il ratto della sposa* (Venice, 1765) and *La Sposa fedele* (Venice, 1767), which, along with *L'impresa d'opera* (Venice, 1769), were performed throughout Europe with notable success. In 1767 he went to London, where he brought out several operas; his wife, known as Maria Leli or Lelia Acchiapati (or Acchiappati), sang in his Ezio at the King's Theatre (Jan. 13, 1770). He returned to Italy in 1772, and continued to compose stage works with abandon; among the most popular were *La Villanella ingentilita* (Naples, Nov. 8, 1779), *La Quakera spiritosa* (1782), *Le vicende d'amore* (Rome, 1784), *La Virtuosa di Mergellina* (Naples, 1785), *La Pastorella nobile* (Naples, April 15, 1788), *La bella pescatrice* (Naples, Oct. 1789), and *La Serva innamorata* (Naples, 1790). His oratorios were also highly successful, and were often performed in stage versions; *La morte di Oloferne* (Rome, April 22, 1791) was a great favorite. In 1793 he was appointed maestro di cappella at S. Pietro in the Vatican; in 1797 he also assumed the post of maestro di cappella at S. Lorenzo Lucina. Guglielmi was one of the major Italian composers of his day. His productivity and facility were remarkable, making it possible for him to write for the stage or the church with equal aplomb.

WORKS: OPERAS (all 1st perf. in Naples unless otherwise given): COMIC: *Lo solachianello 'mbroglione* (1757); *Il Filosofo burlato* (1758); *I capricci di una vedova* (1759); *La Moglie imperiosa* (1759); *I du soldati* (1760); *L'Ottavio* (1760); *Il finto cieco* (1761); *La Donna di tutti i caratteri* (1762); *La Francese brillante* (1763); *Li Rivali placati* (1764); *Il ratto della sposa* (Venice, 1765); *La Sposa fedele* (Venice, 1767); *I Viaggiatori ridicoli tornati in Italia* (London, 1768); *L'impresa d'opera* (Venice, 1769); *Il Disertore* (London, 1770); *L'Amante che spende* (Venice, 1770); *Le pazzie di Orlando* (London, 1771); *Il carnevale di Venezia, o sia La Virtuosa* (London, 1772); *L'assemblea* (London, 1772); *Mirandolina* (Venice, 1773); *Il matrimonio in contrasto* (1776); *I fuoriusciti* (1777); *Il raggiratore di poca fortuna* (1779); *La Villanella ingentilita* (1779); *La Dama avventuriera* (1780); *La Serva padrona* (1780); *Le nozze in commedia* (1781); *Mietitori* (1781); *La semplice ad arte* (1782); *La Quakera spiritosa* (1783); *La Donna amante di tutti, e fedele a nessuno* (1783); *I finti amori* (1784); *La Virtuosa di Mergellina* (1785); *L'inganno amoroso* (1786); *Le astuzie villane* (1786); *Lo scoprimento inaspettato* (1787); *La Pastorella nobile* (1788); *Gl'inganni delusi* (1789); *La bella pescatrice* (1789); *La Serva innamorata* (1790); *L'azzardo* (1790); *Le false apparenze* (1791); *La Sposa contrastata* (1791); *Il Poeta di campagna* (1792); *Amor tra le vendemmie* (1792); *La lanterna di Diogene* (Venice, 1793); *La Pupilla scaltra* (Venice, 1795); *L'amore in villa* (Rome, 1797). SERIOUS: *Tito Manlio* (Rome, 1763); *L'Olimpiade* (1763); *Siroe re di Persia* (Florence, 1764); *Farnace* (Rome, 1765); *Tamerlano* (Venice, 1765); *Adriano in Siria* (Venice, 1765); *Sesostri* (Venice, 1766); *Demofoonte* (Treviso, 1766); *Antigono* (Milan, 1767); *Il Re pastore* (Venice, 1767); *Ifigenia in Aulide* (London, 1768); *Alceste* (Milan, 1768); *Ruggiero* (Venice, 1769); *Ezio* (London, 1770); *Demetrio* (London, 1772); *Tamas Kouli-Kan nell'Indie* (Florence, 1774); *Merope* (Turin, 1775); *Vologeso* (Milan, 1775); *La Semiramide riconosciuta* (1776); *Artaserse* (Rome, 1777); *Ricimero* (1777); *Enea e Lavinia* (1785); *Laconte* (1787); *Arsace* (Venice, 1788); *Rinaldo* (Venice, 1789); *Ademira* (1789); *Alessandro nell'Indie* (1789); *Il trionfo di Camilla* (1795); *La morte di Cleopatra* (1796); *Ippolito* (1798); *Siface e Sofonisba* (1802). He also composed many other stage works and vocal works.

BIBL.: G. Bustico, *Pier A. G.: Appunti biografici* (Massa, 1898); idem, *Un musicista massese: Pier A. G.* (Barga, 1926).

Guglielmi, Pietro Carlo, Italian composer, son of **Pietro Alessandro Guglielmi**; b. Rome or Naples, c.1763; d. Naples, Feb. 21, 1817. After study at the S. Maria di Loreto Cons. in Naples, he went to Spain. His first opera was performed at Madrid in 1794; he then lived in Italy, producing operas in Naples, Florence, and Rome. He went to London in 1809, presenting several operas at the King's Theatre; returned to Italy in 1811, and was appointed maestro di cappella to the Duchess Beatrice at Massa di Carrara. A list of his works, including some 40 operas, oratorios, and cantatas, was publ. by Francesco Piovano in the *Rivista Musicale Italiana* (1909–10). Although several works were popular in their day, their lack of intrinsic worth doomed them to eventual oblivion.

Gui, Vittorio, eminent Italian conductor; b. Rome, Sept. 14, 1885; d. Florence, Oct. 16, 1975. He studied composition with Falchi at the Liceo Musicale di Santa Cecilia in Rome, and also attended the Univ. of Rome. On Dec. 7, 1907, he made his debut conducting *La Gioconda* at Rome's Teatro Adriano. After conducting in Naples, he appeared at Milan's La Scala (1923–25; 1932–34). In 1925 he was a founder and conductor of the Teatro di Torino. In 1928 he organized the Orch. Stabile in Florence, which served as the foundation of the famous Maggio Musicale Fiorentino, which he instituted in 1933; he also was a conductor at the Teatro Comunale there. In 1938–39 he conducted at London's Covent Garden, and returned there in 1952. He was chief conductor of the Glyndebourne Festivals from 1952 to 1960, and then was its artistic counsellor from 1960 to 1965. Gui continued to conduct in Italy until the close of his long life, making his final appearance only a few weeks before his death at the age of 90. He was one of the leading Italian conductors of his day, excelling not only in opera but also in symphonic music. He also composed the operas *David* (Rome, 1907) and *Fata Malerba* (Turin, May 15, 1927); the orch. works *Giulietta e Romeo* (1902), *Il tempo che fu* (1910), *Scherzo fantastico* (1913), *Fantasia bianca* (1919), and *Giornata di festa* (1921); chamber music; songs. Gui publ. the study *Nerone di Arrigo Boito* (Milan, 1924) and a vol. of critical essays *Battute d'aspetto* (Florence, 1944).

Guiraud, Ernest, French composer; b. New Orleans, June 23, 1837; d. Paris, May 6, 1892. He studied with his father, Jean Baptiste Guiraud, producing his first opera, *Le Roi David*, in New Orleans at the age of 15. He then went to Paris, which was his home for the rest of his life. He studied at the Cons. with Marmontel (piano) and Halévy (composition), winning the Grand Prix de Rome in 1859 with his cantata *Bajazet et le joueur de flûte*. He stayed in Rome for 4 years, then returned to Paris, where his one-act opera *Sylvie* was produced at the Opéra Comique (May 11, 1864). He was appointed a prof. at the Cons. in 1876; among his students were Debussy, Gédalge, and Loeffler. He wrote the recitatives to Bizet's *Carmen* and completed the orchestration of Offenbach's *Les Contes d'Hoffmann*. His operas (all 1st perf. in Paris) include *En prison* (March 5, 1869), *Le Kobold* (July 2, 1870), *Madame Turlupin* (Nov. 23, 1872), *Piccolino* (April 11, 1876; his most popular stage work), *Galante aventure* (March 23, 1882), and *Frédégonde* (completed by Saint-Saëns; Dec. 18, 1895). He also wrote a ballet, *Gretna Green* (Paris, May 5, 1873). He publ. a treatise on instrumentation (Paris, 1892).

Gulak-Artemovsky, Semyon Stepanovich, Russian baritone and composer; b. Gorodishche, Feb. 16, 1813; d. Moscow, April 17, 1873. He studied voice with Glinka in St. Petersburg. He sang at the Imperial Opera there (1842–64), then lived in Moscow. His opera *Zaporozhets za Dunayem* (A Cossack beyond the Danube) was produced in St. Petersburg on April 26, 1863, and subsequently acquired considerable popularity in Russia.

BIBL.: L. Kaufman, *S. S. G.-A.* (Kiev, 1962).

Gulbranson, Ellen (née **Norgren**), Swedish soprano; b. Stockholm, March 4, 1863; d. Oslo, Jan. 2, 1947. She studied at the Stockholm Cons. and with M. and B. Marchesi in Paris. In 1886 she made her concert debut in Stockholm, and in 1889 her operatic debut at that city's Royal Opera as Amneris. She gained distinction as a Wagnerian, singing Brünnhilde at every Bayreuth Festival from 1896 to 1914; she also appeared as Kundry. She sang in Berlin from 1895 and in Vienna from 1896; in 1900 she appeared as Brünnhilde at London's Covent Garden, returning there in 1907–08. She also sang in other major music centers until her retirement in 1915.

Guleghina, Maria, Russian soprano; b. Odessa, Aug. 9, 1959. She received vocal training at the Odessa Cons. In 1984 she won 1st prize in the All-Union Glinka Competition, and then sang at the Minsk Opera until 1990. She made her first appearance at Milan's La Scala as Amelia in 1986, and subsequently sang such roles there as Tosca, Lisa, and Elisabetta. In 1990 she sang Tosca at the Hamburg State Opera, a role she also portrayed at her Metropolitan Opera debut in New York on March 30, 1991, and at the San Francisco Opera in 1992. In 1994 she sang Verdi's Elvira at the Barbican Hall in London, and in 1995 appeared as that composer's Odabella in Houston. In 1997 she was engaged as Tosca at the Metropolitan Opera and at London's Covent Garden. Following an appearance as Lady Macbeth at La Scala that year, she returned to the Metropolitan Opera as Lina in *Stiffelio* in 1998.

Gundry, Inglis, English composer; b. London, May 8, 1905. He studied law at Balliol College, Oxford (M.A., 1927) and at the Middle Temple (1927–29) before pursuing his musical training with Vaughan Williams, Gordon Jacob, and R.O. Morris at the Royal College of Music in London (1935–38). In 1936 he won the Cobbett Prize. From 1946 he lectured on music, and later was founder-music director of the Sacred Music Drama Soc. (1960–86). He publ. *Opera in a Nutshell* (1945), *The Nature of Opera as a Composite Art* (1947), and *Composers by the Grace of God: A Study of Music and Religion* (1989).

WORKS: DRAMATIC: OPERAS: *Naaman: The Leprosy of War* (1936–37); *The Return of Odysseus* (1938); *The Partisans* (London, May 28, 1946); *Avon* (London, April 11, 1949); *The Tinners of Cornwall* (London, Sept. 30, 1953); *The Logan Rock* (Porthcurno, Aug. 15, 1956); *The Prince of Coxcombs* (London, Feb. 3, 1965); *The 3 Wise Men* (Kings Langley, Hertfordshire, Jan. 7, 1967); *The Prisoner Paul* (London, Oct. 16, 1970); *A Will of her Own* (1971–73; London, May 31, 1985); *The Rubicon* (1981–83); *Lindisfarne* (1984–86); *Claudia's Dream* (1986–89); *Galileo* (1992–93). OTHER: *The Daytime of Christ*, oratorio.

Günther, Mizzi, greatly talented Austrian soprano; b. Warnsdorf, Feb. 8, 1879; d. Vienna, March 18, 1961. After appearances in provincial theaters, she settled in Vienna and first gained attention as O Mimosa San in *Die Geisha* in 1901. Later that year she had her first starring role as Lotti in *Die drei Wünsche* at the Carltheater, then had her first great success as Lola Winter there in *Das süsse Mädel*. She joined the Theater an der Wien in 1905 singing Jessie in *Vergeltsgott*. On Dec. 30, 1905, she created the role of Hanna Glawari in Lehár's *Die lustige Witwe*, and thereafter was recognized as one of the leading operetta stars of her era. She went on to appear to great acclaim as Alice in *Die Dollarprinzessin* (1907) and as Lori in *Der Mann mit den drei Frauen* (1908). In 1909 she became a member of the Johann Strauss-Theater, where she created the role of Mary Ann in Lehár's *Das Fürstenkind*. In 1911 she rejoined the Theater an der Wien and created the title role in Lehár's *Eva*. After again appearing at the Johann Strauss-Theater (from 1915), she once more sang at the Theater an der Wien (from 1919), where she created the role of Katja in *Katja, die Tänzerin* (1923). In subsequent years, she concentrated on character roles. She later appeared at the Raimundtheater and the Volksoper. As late as 1948 she was seen on the Vienna stage, marking some 50 years in the musical theater.

Gura, Eugen, distinguished German bass-baritone, father of **Hermann Gura**; b. Pressern, near Saatz, Bohemia, Nov. 8, 1842; d. Aufkirchen, Bavaria, Aug. 26, 1906. He studied in Vienna and with Joseph Herger in Munich. In 1865 he made his operatic debut in Lortzing's *Der Waffenschmied* in Munich, where he sang until 1867. He then appeared in Breslau (1867–70) and Leipzig (1870–76). In 1876 he sang Donner and Gunther at the first Bayreuth Festival, and returned there regularly until 1892. In 1882 he sang the first British Hans Sachs and King Marke at London's Drury Lane. From 1882 to 1896 he sang at the Hamburg Opera. On Aug. 20, 1901, he made his farewell appearance in opera as Hans Sachs in Munich, the day before the official opening of the Prinzregententheater. Among his other notable roles were Wotan, Wolfram, Amfortas, Leporello, Iago, and Falstaff. He publ. *Erinnerungen aus meinem Leben* (Leipzig, 1905).

Gura, Hermann, German baritone, son of **Eugen Gura**; b. Breslau, April 5, 1870; d. Bad Wiessee, Bavaria, Sept. 13, 1944. He studied with Hasselbeck and Zenger in Munich, making his debut as the Dutchman in Weimar in 1890; he then sang throughout Europe (1890–96). He subsequently was a singer and producer at the Schwerin Hoftheater in Munich (1896–1908), then director of the Berlin Komische Opera (from 1911); he also worked at London's Covent Garden as a producer in 1913. After producing opera in Helsinki from 1920 to 1927, he taught voice in Berlin.

Guridi (Bidaola), Jésus, Spanish organist, teacher, and composer; b. Vitoria, Álava province, Sept. 25, 1886; d. Madrid, April 7, 1961. He studied harmony with Valentín Arín, and then with José Sainz Besabé in Bilbao; he took courses in piano with Grovlez, organ with Decaux, composition with Sérieyx, and counterpoint and fugue with d'Indy at the Paris Schola Cantorum; studied organ and composition with Jongen in Liège; he finally took a course in instrumentation with Neitzel in Cologne. He was an organist in Bilbao (1909–29); he also conducted the Bilbao Choral Soc. (1911–26). In 1939 he settled in Madrid, where he became prof. of organ at the Cons. in 1944. During his years in Bilbao, he promoted the cause of Basque folk music; he publ. an album of 22 Basque songs. His zarzuelas make frequent use of Basque folk music; of these, *El caserio* (Madrid, 1926) attained enormous success in Spain. Other stage works include *Mirentxu*, idyll (Madrid, 1915), *Amaya*, lyric drama (Bilbao, 1920), and *La Meiga* (Madrid, 1928).

BIBL.: J. de Arozamena, *J. G.* (Madrid, 1967).

Gurlitt, Cornelius, German organist and composer; b. Altona, Feb. 10, 1820; d. there, June 17, 1901. He studied piano with Johann Peter Reinecke in Altona, and with Weyse in Copenhagen. In 1845 he made a journey through Europe, meeting Schumann, Lortzing, Franz, and other eminent composers. In 1864 he was appointed organist of the Altona Cathedral, retaining this post until 1898; he also taught at the Hamburg Cons. (1879–87). He wrote an opera, *Die römische Mauer* (Altona, 1860); another opera, *Scheik Hassan*, was not performed. He also composed 3 violin sonatas, 3 cello sonatas, several cycles of songs, etc., but he is chiefly remembered for his numerous piano miniatures, in Schumann's style, a collection of which was publ. by W. Rehberg, under the title *Der neue Gurlitt* (2 vols., Mainz, 1931).

Gurlitt, Manfred, German conductor, teacher, and composer; b. Berlin, Sept. 6, 1890; d. Tokyo, April 29, 1972. He was a student in Berlin of Mayer-Mahr and Breithaupt (piano), Kaun (theory and composition), and Humperdinck (composition). In 1911 he became an assistant at the Bayreuth Festivals, and also conducted opera in Essen and Augsburg. After serving as 1st conductor and opera director at the Bremen City Theater (1914–24), he returned to Berlin and was granted the title of Generalmusikdirektor, appeared as a guest conductor at the State Opera and on the radio, and taught at the Hochschule für Musik. After the Nazis proscribed his activities, he settled in Tokyo in 1939 as a conductor and teacher. He conducted his own opera company there from 1953. His cousin was the eminent German musicologist and editor Willibald Gurlitt (b. Dresden, March 1, 1889; d. Freiburg im Breisgau, Dec. 15, 1963).

WORKS: OPERAS: *Die Heilige* (Bremen, Jan. 27, 1920); *Wozzeck* (Bremen, April 22, 1926); *Soldaten* (Düsseldorf, Nov. 1930); *Nana* (Dortmund, 1933); *Nächtlicher Spuk* (1937); *Warum?* (1940); *Nordische Ballade* (1944); *Wir schreiten aus* (1958).

Guschlbauer, Theodor, Austrian conductor; b. Vienna, April 14, 1939. He was educated at the Vienna Academy of Music and in Salzburg. He was conductor of the Vienna Baroque Ensemble (1961–69); subsequently he served as chief conductor of the Salzburg Landestheater (1966–68); he then went to Lyons as conductor of the Opera. In 1975 he was appointed chief conductor of the Landestheater in Linz; concurrently he assumed the post of chief conductor of the Linz-Bruckner Sym. Orch. and director of the annual Bruckner Festival. From 1983 to 1988 he was chief conductor of the Deutsche Oper am Rheim in Düsseldorf, and from 1983 to 1997 of the Strasbourg Phil. In 1997 he became chief conductor of the Rhineland-Palatinate Phil.

Gustafson, Nancy, American soprano; b. Evanston, Ill., June 27, 1956. She received vocal training in San Francisco. In 1983 she made her operatic debut as Woglinde at the San Francisco Opera, where she returned as Freia, Musetta, Antonia, and Elettra. She made her European operatic debut in Paris in 1985 as Rosalinde. Her first engagement with the Glyndebourne Opera was as Donna Elvira during the company's visit to Hong Kong in 1986. In 1988 she made her formal debut at the Glyndebourne Festival as Kát'a Kabanová, and also made her first appearance at London's Covent Garden as Freia. She sang Violetta with the Scottish Opera in Glasgow and Marguerite at the Lyric Opera in Chicago in 1989. On March 28, 1990, she made her debut at the Metropolitan Opera in New York as Musetta. That same year she also sang Freia in Munich, Eva at Milan's La Scala, and Amelia Boccanegra in Brussels. In 1993 she appeared at the London Promenade Concerts. After singing Floyd's Susannah in Houston in 1996, she returned to Covent Garden in 1997 as Eva.

Gutheil-Schoder, Marie, prominent German mezzo-soprano; b. Weimar, Feb. 16, 1874; d. Bad Ilmenau, Oct. 4, 1935. She was largely self-taught, although she received some coaching from Richard Strauss in Weimar, where she made her operatic debut as the 1st Lady in *Die Zauberflöte* in 1891. After singing in Berlin and Leipzig, she was engaged by Mahler for the Vienna Court Opera (debut as Nedda, Feb. 16, 1900). In her early performances, she was criticized for her small voice; Mahler made note of her "disagreeable middle register," but he also declared that she was a musical genius; her strong dramatic characterizations made her a favorite there until 1926. She was successful as Carmen, Elektra, Eva, and the 3 principal soprano roles in *Les Contes d'Hoffmann*; her Mozart roles included Pamina, Elvira, Susanna, and Cherubino. Her only London appearance was at Covent Garden as Octavian in 1913; 3 years later she sang the role of the Composer, under Strauss's direction, in a Zürich production of the revised version of *Ariadne auf Naxos*. She was closely associated with the music of Schoenberg; she took part in the premiere of his 2d String Quartet (Vienna, Feb. 5, 1907), and later frequently performed in his *Pierrot Lunaire*; Schoenberg conceived the part of the Woman in his monodrama *Erwartung* as a "Gutheil part"; she appeared in its first performance (Prague, June 6, 1924). After her retirement, she was active as a teacher and producer in Vienna and Salzburg. She was successively married to the violinist and composer Gustav Gutheil and the Viennese photographer Franz Setzer.

Guyonnet, Jacques, Swiss composer; b. Geneva, March 20, 1933. He studied at the Geneva Cons. (1950–58) and had courses in new music with Boulez at the summer sessions held in Darmstadt (1958–61). In 1959 he founded the Studio de Musique Contemporaine in Geneva; from 1976 to 1981 was president of the ISCM. Among his works are *Entremonde*, ballet for Flute, Piano, 4 Percussionists, and Tape (1967), and *Electric Sorcerers*, rock opera (1980–81).

Gyrowetz, Adalbert (Mathias) (original name, **Vojtěch Matyáš Jirovec**), noted Bohemian composer and conductor; b. Budweis, Feb. 19, 1763; d. Vienna, March 19, 1850. He studied piano, violin, and composition with his father, a local choirmaster, and began to compose while a student at the Piarist Gymnasium in his native town; he then studied philosophy and law in Prague. He subsequently became secretary to Count Franz von Fünfkirchen, and was also a member of his private orch. In 1784 he went to Vienna, where he was befriended by Mozart; the latter arranged for one of his syms. to be performed in 1785. He then became secretary and music master to Prince Ruspoli, who took him to Italy. While in Rome (1786–87), he composed a set of 6 string quartets, the first of his works to be publ. After leaving Ruspoli's service, he studied with Sala in Naples. He made a brief visit to Paris in 1789, and then proceeded to London, where he met and befriended Haydn, who was also visiting the British capital. During his London sojourn, Gyrowetz was commissioned by the Pantheon to write an opera, *Semiramis*; however, before the work could be mounted, both the theater and his MS were destroyed by fire (1792). He returned to the Continent in 1793; in 1804 he became composer and conductor of the Vienna Hoftheater, where he produced such popular operas as *Agnes Sorel* (Dec. 4, 1806) and *Der Augenarzt* (Oct. 1, 1811). He also wrote *Il finto Stanislao* (Milan, July 5, 1818), to a libretto by Romani, which Verdi subsequently used for his *Un giorno di regno*. He likewise anticipated Wagner by writing the first opera on the subject of Hans Sachs's life in his *Hans Sachs im vorgerückten Alter* (Dresden, 1834). He retired from the Hoftheater in 1831, and his fame soon dissipated; he spent his last years in straitened circumstances and relative neglect, having outlived the great masters of the age. He composed a variety of stage works, including operas, Singspiels, and melodramas.

Gysi, Fritz, Swiss music critic and musicologist; b. Zofingen, Feb. 18, 1888; d. Zürich, March 5, 1967. He studied at the Basel Cons., and then took courses in musicology and art history at the univs. of Zürich, Berlin, and Bern (Ph.D., 1913, with the diss. *Die En-*

H

Haas, Joseph, eminent German composer and pedagogue; b. Maihigen, March 19, 1879; d. Munich, March 30, 1960. He was a pupil of Reger (composition) in Munich and Leipzig, and also in the latter city of Straube (organ) and Ruthardt (piano). In 1911 he became a teacher and in 1916 a prof. of composition at the Stuttgart Cons. In 1921 he settled in Munich as a prof. in the Catholic church music dept. of the Akademie der Tonkunst, and later was president of the Hochschule für Musik (1945–50). In 1949 a Joseph Haas Soc. was formed to promote his music, which is written in a well-crafted and accessible style. Among his compositions are the operas *Die Bergkönigin* (1927), *Tobias Wunderlich* (Kassel, Nov. 24, 1937), and *Die Hochzeit des Jobs* (Dresden, July 2, 1944), and the oratorios *Die Heilige Elisabeth* (1931), *Das Lebensbuch Gottes* (1934), *Das Lied von Mutter* (1939), *Das Jahr im Lied* (1952), and *Die Seligen* (1956). He publ. a biography of Reger (Bonn, 1949), and a collection of his speeches and articles appeared as *Reden und Aufsätze* (Mainz, 1964).

BIBL.: K. Laux, *J. H.* (Mainz, 1931); K. Laux, *J. H.* (Berlin and Düsseldorf, 1954); S. Gmeinwieser, W. Haas, H.-M. Palm-Beulich, and F. Schieri, *J. H.* (Tutzing, 1994).

Haas, Pavel, Czech composer; b. Brünn, June 21, 1899; d. in the concentration camp in Auschwitz, Oct. 17, 1944. He studied piano and composition in Brünn and was a soldier in the Austrian army in World War I; after the Armistice he continued his study with Petřzelka at the Brno Cons. (1919–21) and at the master class there with Janáček (1920–22). He tried to leave Czechoslovakia after its occupation by the Nazi hordes, but the outbreak of World War II made this impossible; in 1941 he was deported to the Jewish ghetto camp in Theresienstadt, where he continued to compose until, in Oct. 1944, he was sent to Auschwitz and put to death. His extant MSS are preserved in the Moravian Museum in Brno. Among his works is the opera *Šarlatán* (The Charlatan), to his own libretto (1934–37; Brno, April 2, 1938).

BIBL.: L. Peduzi, *P. H.: Života dilo skladatele* (Brno, 1993).

Haas, Robert (Maria), distinguished Austrian musicologist; b. Prague, Aug. 15, 1886; d. Vienna, Oct. 4, 1960. He received his primary education in Prague; he then studied music history at the Univs. of Prague, Berlin, and Vienna and obtained his Ph.D. in 1908 from the Univ. of Prague with his diss. *Das Wiener Singspiel*. He then was an assistant to Guido Adler at the Inst. for Music History in Vienna (1908–09). During World War I he was in the Austrian army; he then joined the staff of the Nationalbibliothek in Vienna, becoming chief of the music division in 1920. He completed his Habilitation at the Univ. of Vienna in 1923 with his *Eberlins Schuldramen und Oratorien*; he then became a lecturer there; he also devoted much of his time to the music of the Baroque and Classical eras. After the founding of the International Bruckner Soc., he became ed. of the critical edition of Bruckner's works; he also edited works for the Denkmäler der Tonkunst in Österreich. He retired in 1945.

WRITINGS: *Gluck und Durazzo im Burgtheater* (Vienna, 1925); *Die estensischen Musikalien: Thematisches Verzeichnis mit Einleitung* (Regensburg, 1925); *Die Wiener Oper* (Vienna, 1926); *Wiener Musiker vor und um Beethoven* (Vienna, 1927); *Die Musik des Barocks* (Potsdam, 1928); *Aufführungspraxis der Musik* (Potsdam, 1931); *W. A. Mozart* (Potsdam, 1933; 2d ed., 1950); *Anton Bruckner* (Potsdam, 1934); *Bach und Mozart in Wien* (Vienna, 1951); *Ein unbekanntes Mozart-Bildnis* (Vienna, 1955).

Hába, Alois, notable Czech composer and pedagogue, brother of **Karel Hába**; b. Vizovice, Moravia, June 21, 1893; d. Prague, Nov. 18, 1973. He studied with Novák at the Prague Cons. (1914–15), then privately with Schreker in Berlin (1918–20), continuing as his student at the Hochschule für Musik (1920–22). He became interested in the folk music of the Orient, which led him to consider writing in smaller intervals than the semitone. His first work in the quarter-tone system was the 2d String Quartet (1920); in his 5th String Quartet (1923), he first applied sixth-tones; in his 16th String Quartet (1967), he introduced fifth-tones. He notated these fractional intervals by signs in modified or inverted sharps and flats. The piano manufacturing firm of A. Förster constructed for him 3 types of quarter-tone pianos (1924–31), a quarter-tone (1928) and a sixth-tone (1936) harmonium, and a quarter-tone guitar (1943); other firms manufactured at his request a quarter-tone clarinet (1924) and trumpet (1931). From 1924 to 1951 (World War II excepted) he led a class of composition in fractional tones at the Prague Cons., attracting a large number of students, among them his brother, Karel, the conductors Ančerl and Susskind, and the composers Dobiáš, Ježek, Kowalski, Kubín, Lucký, Ponc, Reiner (who, along with E. Schulhoff, specialized in quarter-tone piano playing and premiered 10 of Hába's works), Seidel and Srnka, as well as such foreigners as Iliev, Osterc, and Akses. Hába publ. an important manual of modern harmony, *Neue Harmonielehre des diatonischen, chromatischen, Viertel-, Drittel-, Sechstel-, und Zwölfteltonsystems* (New Principles of Harmony of the Diatonic, Chromatic, Fourth-, Third-, Sixth-, and Twelfth-Tone Systems; Leipzig, 1927), detailing new usages introduced by him in his classes; he further publ. *Harmonicke základy čtvrttónove soustavy* (Harmonic Foundation of the Quarter-Tone System; Prague, 1922), *Von der Psychologie der musikalischen Gestaltung, Gesetzmässigkeit der Tonbewegung und Grundlagen eines neuen Musikstils* (On the Psychology of Musical Composition; Rules of Tonal Structure and Foundation of New Musical Style; Vienna, 1925), and *Mein Weg zur Viertel- und Sechstonmusik* (Düsseldorf, 1971). As a composer, he cultivated a "nonthematic" method of writing, without repetition of patterns and devoid of development. In 1963 he was made an Artist of Merit and in 1968 he received the Order of the Republic in recognition of his contributions to Czech music.

WORKS: OPERAS: *Matka* (Mother; 1927–29; in quarter tones, 1st perf. in German as *Die Mutter*, Munich, May 17, 1931; 1st perf. in Czech, Prague, May 27, 1947); *Nová Země* (The New Land; 1934–36; only overture perf., Prague, April 8, 1936); *Přijd královstvi Tvé* (Thy Kingdom Come; 1937–40; in fractional tones).

BIBL.: J. Vysloužil, *A. H.: Život a dílo* (Prague, 1974).

Hába, Karel, Czech composer and music educator, brother of **Alois Hába;** b. Vizovice, Moravia, May 21, 1898; d. Prague, Nov. 21, 1972. He spent his entire life in Prague, where he studied violin with Karel Hoffmann and Jan Mařák, and theory with Novák, Křička, and Foerster at the Cons.; he also attended his brother's class in quarter-tone music there (1925–27). After playing violin in the Czech Radio Orch. (1929–36), he was head of the music education dept. of the Czech Radio (1936–50); he then lectured on music education at the Charles Univ. (1951–63); he also was active as a music critic. Hába faithfully followed the athematic method of composition espoused by his brother.

WORKS: OPERAS: *Jánošík* (1929–32; Prague, Feb. 23, 1934); *Stará historia* (The Old Story; 1934–37); *Smolíček*, children's opera (Prague, Sept. 28, 1950); *Kalibův zločin* (Kaliba's Crime; 1957–61; Košice, May 16, 1968).

Habich, Eduard, German baritone; b. Kassel, Sept. 3, 1880; d. Berlin, March 15, 1960. He studied in Frankfurt am Main with Max Fleisch. He made his operatic debut in Koblenz in 1904, then sang in Posen, Halle, and Düsseldorf, at the Berlin Royal (later State) Opera (1910–30), at the Bayreuth Festivals (1911–31), at London's Covent Garden (1924–36; 1938), and at the Chicago Civic Opera (1930–32). He made his Metropolitan Opera debut in New York on Dec. 20, 1935, as Peter in *Hänsel und Gretel*, and remained on its roster until 1937; he later taught voice in Berlin. Among his admired roles were Beckmesser, Faninal, Alberich, Telramund, and Klingsor.

Hackett, Charles, American tenor; b. Worcester, Mass., Nov. 4, 1889; d. N.Y., Jan. 1, 1942. He was a student of Arthur J. Hubbard at the New England Cons. of Music in Boston and of Vincenzo Lombardi in Florence. After making his operatic debut in Genoa as Thomas's Wilhelm Meister in 1914, he sang throughout Italy, including Milan (La Scala, 1916); he also sang at the Teatro Colón in Buenos Aires. On Jan. 31, 1919, he made his Metropolitan Opera debut in New York as Count Almaviva, remaining on the roster until 1921; after singing with the Chicago Civic Opera (1923–32), he was again on the roster of the Metropolitan Opera (1933–39). His other roles included the Duke of Mantua, Alfredo, Roméo, Rodolfo, Lindoro, and Pinkerton.

Hadley, Henry (Kimball), noted American conductor and composer; b. Somerville, Mass., Dec. 20, 1871; d. N.Y., Sept. 6, 1937. He received training in piano, violin, and conducting from his father, and then studied harmony with Emery and counterpoint and composition with Chadwick in Somerville and at the New England Cons. of Music in Boston; he then took lessons in counterpoint with Mandyczewski in Vienna (1894–95) and in composition with Thuille in Munich (1905–07). After teaching at St. Paul's School in Garden City, N.Y. (1895–1902), he devoted himself fully to conducting and composing. He was conductor of the Mainz Stadttheater (1907–09) and of the Seattle Sym. Orch. (1909–11). In 1911 he became conductor of the newly organized San Francisco Sym. Orch., which he conducted until 1915. After serving as assoc. conductor of the N.Y. Phil. (1920–27), he was founder-conductor of the Manhattan Sym. Orch. (1929–32). In 1934 he founded the Berkshire Music Festival in Stockbridge, Mass., which he conducted for 2 seasons. In 1924 he was elected a member of the American Academy of Arts and Letters. In 1933 he organized the National Assn. for American Composers and Conductors, which subsequently endowed the Henry Hadley Memorial Library at the N.Y. Public Library. In 1938 the Henry Hadley Foundation was organized in New York to further Hadley's championship of American music. In his own compositions, Hadley wrote well-crafted scores in a late Romantic vein. His 2d Sym. received the Paderewski Prize in 1901.

WORKS: DRAMATIC: *Happy Jack*, operetta (1897); *Nancy Brown*, operetta (1903); *Safie*, opera (Mainz, April 4, 1909); *The Atonement of Pan*, incidental music (1912; also an orch. suite, 1912); *The Pearl Girl*, operetta (n.d.); *Azora, Daughter of Montezuma*, opera (1914; Chicago, Dec. 26, 1917); *The Masque of Newark*, pageant (1916); *Bianca*, opera (1917; N.Y., Oct. 15, 1918); *The Fire Prince*, operetta (1917); *Cleopatra's Night*, opera (1918; N.Y., Jan. 31, 1920); *Semper virens*, music drama (1923); *A Night in Old Paris*, opera (1924); *The Legend of Hani*, incidental music (1933; also an orch. suite, 1933); *The Red Flame*, musical (n.d.). Also *Resurgam*, oratorio for Soloists, Chorus, and Orch. (1922).

BIBL.: H. Boardman, *H. H.: Ambassador of Harmony* (Atlanta, 1932); P. Berthoud, ed., *The Musical Works of Dr. H. H.* (N.Y., 1942); J. Canfield, *H. K. H. (1871–1937): His Life and Works* (diss., Florida State Univ., 1960).

Hadley, Jerry, American tenor; b. Princeton, Ill., June 12, 1952. He studied music education at Bradley Univ. (B.A., 1974) and voice at the Univ. of Ill. (M.A., 1977), where he found a mentor in David Lloyd; then studied with Thomas LoMonaco in New York In 1976 he made his professional operatic debut as Ferrando at the Lake George (N.Y.) Opera Festival. On Sept. 14, 1979, he made his first appearance at the N.Y. City Opera as Lord Arturo Bucklaw in *Lucia de Lammermoor*, remaining with the company until 1985; he also appeared regularly with the Washington (D.C.) Opera (from 1980). He made his debut at the Vienna State Opera in 1982 as Nemorino, and in 1983 he sang for the first time at the Bavarian State Opera in Munich, the Glyndebourne Festival, and the Netherlands Opera in Amsterdam. In 1984 he made his debut at London's Covent Garden as Fenton and his Carnegie Hall recital debut in New York; his Metropolitan Opera debut in New York followed on March 7, 1987, as Massenet's Des Grieux; he sang there regularly from 1990. In 1991 he sang in the premiere of McCartney's *Liverpool Oratorio*. In 1994 he was engaged as Tom Rakewell in London and at the Lyric Opera in Chicago, a role he reprised at the Metropolitan Opera in 1997. In 1997 he also created the title role in Myron Fink's *The Conquistador* in San Diego. He also toured extensively as a concert artist. In addition to his Mozart and *bel canto* roles, Hadley has found success as Berlioz's and Gounod's Faust, Offenbach's Hoffmann, Verdi's Alfredo, and Stravinsky's Tom Rakewell. His performances in works by Weill, Kern, Rodgers and Hammerstein, Bernstein, and Lerner and Lowe have added further luster to his success.

Haeffner, Johann Christian Friedrich, German organist, conductor, and composer; b. Oberschönau, near Suhl, March 2, 1759; d. Uppsala, May 28, 1833. He was a pupil of Vierling in Schmalkalden. He studied at the Univ. of Leipzig, and served as proofreader for Breitkopf; he then became conductor of a traveling opera troupe. In 1781 he arrived in Stockholm, where he was an organist at St. Gertrud until 1793. He composed several operas in the style of Gluck that had a favorable reception: *Electra* (July 22, 1787), *Alcides inträde i Världen* (Nov. 11, 1793), and *Renaud* (Jan. 29, 1801). In 1792 he was appointed director of the Swedish Royal Orch. In 1808 he went to Uppsala, where he remained for the rest of his life, acting as organist of the Cathedral and music director of the Univ. He took great interest in Swedish national music, publishing Swedish folk songs with accompaniment and revising the melodies of the Geijer-Afzelius collection. He also ed. a *Svenska Choralbok* (2 parts, 1819–21), in which he restored the choral melodies of the 17th century, and added preludes (1822); he also arranged a collection of old Swedish songs in 4 parts (1832–33; he finished only 2 books).

Haefliger, Ernst, noted Swiss tenor; b. Davos, July 6, 1919. He studied at the Zürich Cons., with Fernando Carpi in Geneva, and with Julius Patzak in Vienna. After making his debut as the Evangelist in Bach's St. John Passion in 1942, he sang at the Zürich Opera (1943–52). He gained wide recognition when he created the role of Tiresias in Orff's *Antigonae* at the Salzburg Festival on Aug. 9, 1949. From 1952 to 1974 he was a member of the Berlin Städtische (later Deutsche) Oper, but he also appeared as a guest artist with many of the principal European opera houses. His roles in Mozart's operas were particularly esteemed. He pursued a distinguished career as a concert singer and lieder artist. His appearances as the Evangelist in Bach's passions and his lieder recitals were notable. He was a prof. at the Munich Hochschule für Musik (from 1971). Haefliger publ. the book *Die Singstimme* (Bern, 1983).

Haenchen, Hartmut, German conductor; b. Dresden, March 21, 1943. He was a student of Matschke, Neuhaus, and Förster at the Dresden Hochschule für Musik (1960–66), and of Koch and Höft in Berlin; in 1971 he won 1st prize in the Carl Maria von Weber competition in Dresden. After serving as director of the Robert-Franz-Singakadamie and the Halle orch. (1966–72), he was chief conductor of the Zwickau Theater (1972–73). From 1973 to 1976 he was permanent conductor of the Dresden Phil., and from 1974 to 1976, of the Phil. Choir of Dresden; he then was chief conductor of the Mecklenburg State Theater (1976–79). He was a prof. of conducting at the Dresden Hochschule für Musik (1980–86), and also music director of the C. P. E. Bach Chamber Orch. in Berlin (from 1980). In 1986 he became music director of the Netherlands Opera in Amsterdam. Haenchen has appeared as a guest conductor with major opera houses throughout Europe, North America, and Japan.

Hafgren, Lily (Johana Maria), Swedish soprano; b. Stockholm, Oct. 7, 1884; d. Berlin, Feb. 27, 1965. She was educated in Frankfurt am Main; began her career as a pianist; Siegfried Wagner encouraged her to consider an operatic career, and she studied voice in Stuttgart with Max Fleisch. In 1908 she made her operatic debut as Freia at the Bayreuth Festival, where she sang again in 1911, 1912, and 1924; she also sang in Mannheim (1908–12) and at the Royal (later State) Opera in Berlin (1912–21) and also appeared in Paris, Rome, Milan, Dresden, Stockholm, Prague, and other operatic centers. She retired in 1934. In later years, she used her married names, Hafgren-Waag and Hafgren-Dinkela. Among her finest roles were Brünnhilde, Eva, and Isolde.

Hagegård, Håkan, outstanding Swedish baritone; b. Karlstad, Nov. 25, 1945. After initial training in Karlstad, he studied at the Stockholm Musikhögskolan and with Erik Werba and Gerald Moore in Salzburg. He made his operatic debut at the Royal Theater in Stockholm as Papageno (1968); after further study with Tito Gobbi, he made his first venture outside his homeland at the Glyndebourne Festival in 1973. He gained wide recognition through his notable portrayal of Papageno in Ingmar Bergman's film version of *Die Zauberflöte* (1975); subsequently appeared throughout Europe in opera and concert. On Dec. 7, 1978, he made his Metropolitan Opera debut in New York as Dr. Malatesta. He appeared as Wolfram at his debut at London's Covent Garden in 1987. On Dec. 19, 1991, he created the role of Beaumarchais in the premiere of Corigliano's *The Ghosts of Versailles* at the Metropolitan Opera in New York. In 1992 he portrayed Wolfram at the Deutsche Oper in Berlin. He sang at the Metropolitan Opera Gala in 1996. He is married to **Barbara Bonney**. He particularly distinguished himself in operas by Mozart, Rossini, Donizetti, and Verdi; he also became highly esteemed as a concert singer, excelling as an interpreter of lieder.

Hageman, Richard, distinguished Dutch-American pianist, conductor; b. Leeuwarden, July 9, 1882; d. Beverly Hills, March 6, 1966. He studied music with his father, the Dutch violinist, conductor, and composer Maurits (Leonard) Hageman (1829–1906), then took courses at the Brussels Cons. with Gevaert and Arthur de Greef. He held an auxiliary position as conductor at the Royal Opera in Amsterdam (1899–1903). After playing accompaniments for Mathilde Marchesi in Paris (1904–05), he went to the United States as accompanist for Yvette Guilbert in 1906; he was on the conducting roster of the Metropolitan Opera in New York (1908–10; 1911–21; 1935–37), the Chicago Civic Opera (1922–23), and the Los Angeles Grand Opera (1923). In 1938 he settled in Hollywood, where he was engaged as a composer of film music. He wrote 2 operas: *Caponsacchi* (1931; 1st perf. as *Tragödie in Arezzo*, Freiburg im Breisgau, Feb. 18, 1932; received the David Bispham Memorial Medal) and *The Crucible* (Los Angeles, Feb. 4, 1943). However, he achieved a lasting reputation mainly through his solo songs, of which "Do Not Go My Love" (to words by Rabindranath Tagore; 1917) and "At the Well" (1919) became extremely popular.

Hager, Leopold, Austrian conductor; b. Salzburg, Oct. 6, 1935. He took courses in piano, organ, harpsichord, conducting, and composition at the Salzburg Mozarteum (1949–57); his principal teachers were Paumgartner, Wimberger, Bresgen, J. N. David, and Kornauth. He was assistant conductor at the Mainz City Theater (1957–62); after conducting the Linz Landestheater (1962–64), he held the post of 1st conductor of the Cologne Opera (1964–65). After serving as Generalmusikdirektor in Freiburg im Breisgau (1965–69), he was chief conductor of the Mozarteum Orch. and of the Landestheater in Salzburg (1969–81). On Oct. 14, 1976, he made his Metropolitan Opera debut in New York conducting *Le Nozze di Figaro*, and remained on its roster until 1978. He also appeared as a guest conductor with other opera houses as well as orchs. in Europe and the United States. In 1981 he became chief conductor of the Orchestre Symphonique de Radio-Télé Luxembourg.

Hagerup Bull, Edvard, Norwegian composer; b. Bergen, June 10, 1922. He was an organ student of Sandvold at the Oslo Cons. (graduated, 1947); he also received training in piano from Erling Westher and Reimar Riefling, and in composition from Brustad and Irgens Jensen; after further studies at the Paris Cons. with Milhaud, Koechlin, and Rivier (Prix de composition, 1952), he completed his training with Blacher and Rufer at the Berlin Hochschule für Musik. Hie early neoclassical style tended later toward free tonality. Among his works are the operas *Fyrtøjet* (1973–74) and *Den Grimme Aelling* (1972–77) and the ballet *Munchhausen* (1961).

Hahn, Reynaldo, Venezuelan-born French conductor, music critic, and composer; b. Caracas, Aug. 9, 1874; d. Paris, Jan. 28, 1947. His father, a merchant from Hamburg, settled in Venezuela c.1850; the family moved to Paris when Reynaldo was 5 years old. He studied singing and apparently had an excellent voice; a professional recording he made in 1910 testifies to that. He studied theory with Dubois and Lavignac and composition with Massenet at the Paris Cons., who exercised the most important influence on Hahn's own music. He also studied conducting, achieving a high professional standard as an opera conductor. In 1934 he became music critic of *Le Figaro*. He remained in France during the Nazi occupation at a considerable risk to his life, since he was

Jewish on his father's side. In 1945 he was named a member of the Institut de France and in 1945–46 was music director of the Paris Opéra. Hahn's music is distinguished by a facile, melodious flow and a fine Romantic flair. Socially, he was known in Paris for his brilliant wit. He maintained a passionate youthful friendship with Marcel Proust, who portrayed him as a poetic genius in his novel *Jean Santeuil*; their intimate correspondence was publ. in 1946. He was a brilliant journalist; his articles were publ. as *Du Chant* (Paris, 1920; 2d ed., 1957), *Notes. Journal d'un musicien* (Paris, 1933), *L'Oreille au guet* (Paris, 1937), and *Thèmes variés* (Paris, 1946). A series of his letters dating from 1913–14 were publ. in an Eng. tr. by L. Simoneau as *On Singers and Singing* (Portland, Oreg., 1990).

WORKS: DRAMATIC: *Fin d'amour*, ballet-pantomime (1892); *L'île du reve*, opera (Paris, March 23, 1898); *La carmélite*, opéra comique (Paris, Dec. 16, 1902); *La pastorale de Noël*, Christmas mystery (1908); *Le bal de Béatrice d'Este*, ballet (1909); *La fête chez Thérèse*, ballet (1909); *Le bois sacré*, ballet-pantomime (1912); *Le dieu bleu*, ballet (Paris, May 14, 1912); *Fête triomphale*, opera (Paris, July 14, 1919); *Nausicaa*, opéra comique (Monte Carlo, April 10, 1919); *La colombe de Bouddah*, conte lyrique (Cannes, March 21, 1921); *Ciboulette*, operetta (Paris, April 7, 1923); *Mozart*, musical comedy (Paris, Dec. 2, 1925); *La reine de Sheba*, scène lyrique (1926); *Une revue* (1926); *Le temps d'aimer*, musical comedy (Paris, Nov. 6, 1926); *Brummel*, operetta (1930; Paris, Jan. 20, 1931); *O mon bel inconnu!*, musical comedy (Paris, Oct. 5, 1933); *Malvina*, operetta (Paris, March 23, 1935); *Le marchand de Venise*, opera (Paris, March 25, 1935); *Beaucoup de bruit pour rien*, musical comedy (1936); *Aux bosquets d'Idalie*, ballet (1937); *Le oui des jeunes filles*, opera (orchestrated by H. Büsser; Paris, June 21, 1949); also incidental music to Daudet's *L'obstacle* (1890), Croisset's *Les deux courtisanes* (1902), Hugo's *Angelo* (1905), Racine's *Esther* (1905), Mendès's *Scarron* (1905), Hugo's *Lucrèce Borgia* (1911), and Magre's *Méduse* (1911).

BIBL.: D. Bendahan, *R. H.: Su vida y su obra* (Caracas, 1973); B. Gavoty, *R. H.: Le Musicien de la belle époque* (Paris, 1976); M. Milanca Guzmán, *R. H., caraqueño: Contribución a la biografía caraqueña de R. H. Echenagucia* (Caracas, 1989).

Haibel, (Johann Petrus) Jakob, Austrian tenor and composer; b. Graz, July 20, 1762; d. Djakovar, March 24, 1826. He was engaged in Vienna as a tenor. In 1806 he settled in Djakovar, where he married Sophie Weber, sister of Mozart's widow. He produced several stage works in Vienna, among them the ballet *Le nozze disturbate* (May 18, 1795) and a Singspiel, *Der Tyroler Wastl* (May 14, 1796), which became very popular.

Hailstork, Adolphus (Cunningham), black American composer and teacher; b. Rochester, N.Y., April 17, 1941. He studied composition with Mark Fax at Howard Univ. in Washington, D.C. (B.Mus., 1963), Boulanger at the American Cons. in Fontainebleau (summer, 1963), Ludmila Ulehla, Flagello, Giannini, and Diamond at the Manhattan School of Music in New York (B.Mus., 1965; M.Mus., 1966), and H. Owen Reed at Michigan State Univ. in East Lansing (Ph.D., 1971). He also attended sessions on synthesizer and computer music given by John Appleton and Herbert Howe at the New Hampshire Electronic Music Inst. (summer 1972), and on contemporary music at the State Univ. of N.Y. at Buffalo (summer 1978). In 1987 he held a Fulbright fellowship for study in Guyana. He taught at Michigan State Univ. (1969–71), Youngstown (Ohio) State Univ. (1971–76), and Norfolk (Va.) State Univ. (from 1977). Several of his works reflect his Afro-American experience. He has received various commissions, and a number of his works have been performed by major U.S. orchs. He composed the opera *Paul Laurence Dunbar: Common Ground* (1994).

Haitink, Bernard (Johann Herman), eminent Dutch conductor; b. Amsterdam, March 4, 1929. He studied violin as a child, and later at the Amsterdam Cons., where he took a conducting course with Felix Hupka. He then played in the Radio Phil. in Hilversum. In 1954–55 he attended the conducting course of Ferdinand Leitner, sponsored by the Netherlands Radio; in 1955 he was appointed to the post of 2d conductor of the Radio Phil. in Hilversum, becoming its principal conductor in 1957. In 1956 he made his first appearance as a guest conductor with the Concertgebouw Orch. of Amsterdam. He made his U.S. debut with the Los Angeles Phil. in 1958. In 1959 he conducted the Concertgebouw Orch. in England. In 1961 he became co-principal conductor of the Concertgebouw Orch., sharing his duties with Eugen Jochum; that same year he led it on a tour of the United States, followed by one to Japan in 1962. In 1964 he became chief conductor of the Concertgebouw Orch., a position he held with great distinction until 1988. In 1982 he led it on an acclaimed transcontinental tour of the United States. In 1967 he also assumed the post of principal conductor and artistic adviser of the London Phil., becoming its artistic director in 1969; he resigned from this post in 1978. He made his first appearance at the Glyndebourne Festival in 1972, and from 1978 to 1988 was its music director. In 1977 he made his Covent Garden debut in London conducting *Don Giovanni*. On March 29, 1982, he made his debut at the Metropolitan Opera in New York conducting *Fidelio*. In 1987 he became music director of the Royal Opera House at London's Covent Garden. He also was guest conductor with the Berlin Phil., Vienna Phil., N.Y. Phil., Chicago Sym., Boston Sym., and Cleveland Orch. In his interpretations, Haitink avoids personal rhetoric, allowing the music to speak for itself. Yet he achieves eloquent and colorful effect; especially fine are his performances of the syms. of Bruckner and Mahler; equally congenial are his projections of the Classical repertoire. He has received numerous international honors, including the Netherlands' Royal Order of Orange-Nassau (1969), the Medal of Honor of the Bruckner Soc. of America (1970), and the Gustav Mahler Soc. Gold Medal (1971); he was named a Chevalier de l'Ordre des Arts et des Lettres of France (1972). He received the rare distinction of being made an Honorary Knight Commander of the Order of the British Empire by Queen Elizabeth II in 1977. In 1991 he was awarded the Erasmus Prize of the Netherlands.

BIBL.: S. Mundy, *B. H.: A Working Life* (London, 1987).

Haizinger, Anton, esteemed Austrian tenor; b. Wilfersdorf, March 14, 1796; d. Karlsruhe, Dec. 31, 1869. He studied harmony with Wölkert and voice with Mozzati in Vienna, and later was a student of Salieri. In 1821 he made his operatic debut as Gianetto in *La gazza ladra* at the Theater an der Wien. Weber chose him to create the role of Adolar in *Euryanthe* (Vienna, Oct. 25, 1823). After engagements in Prague, Pressburg, Frankfurt am Main, Mannheim, and Stuttgart, he was a member of the Théâtre-Italien in Paris (1829–30) and of Covent Garden in London (1832–33). Following appearances in St. Petersburg (1835) and Vienna (1838), he settled in Karlsruhe and ran his own singing school. He was the author of a manual on singing. Haizinger's most distinguished roles were Mozart's Tamino, Beethoven's Florestan, and Weber's Max.

Hajdu, André, Hungarian-born Israeli composer and teacher; b. Budapest, March 5, 1932. He studied with Kodály, Szabó, Szervánsky, and Kosá at the Budapest Academy of Music (1947–56) and with Milhaud and Messiaen at the Paris Cons. (1957–59). He taught at the Tunis Cons. (1959–61), emigrated to Israel in 1966, and in 1967 became a teacher at the Tel Aviv Academy of Music. His music is folkloristic in its sources of inspiration, while the harmonic idiom is fairly advanced. Among his works is the children's opera *Jonah* (1986); also *Jacob and His Comforters*, oratorio (1992).

Hajdu, Mihály, Hungarian composer and teacher; b. Orosháza, Jan. 30, 1909. He settled in Budapest and studied composition with Kodály and piano with Thomán and Székely at the Academy of Music (1929–33). After teaching in a private music school (1933–40), he taught at the Upper Music School (1941–49) and the Béla Bartók Music School (1949–60); subsequently he was prof. of theory at the Academy of Music (1960–77). In 1957 he received the Erkel Prize. His works include the opera *Kádár Kata* (1957).

Hale, Robert, American bass-baritone; b. Kerrville, Texas, Aug. 22, 1943. He studied with Gladys Miller at the New England Cons. of Music in Boston, with Ludwig Bergman at Boston Univ., in Oklahoma, and with Boris Goldovsky in New York. In 1965 he made his operatic debut as Mozart's Figaro in Denver, and then joined the N.Y. City Opera in 1967. He made guest appearances in Philadelphia, Pittsburgh, San Diego, San Francisco, and other U.S. opera centers. In 1978 he made his European debut in Stuttgart as the Dutchman. He sang Escamillo in Cologne in 1983. After appearing as Scarpia in Berlin in 1987, he sang for the first time at London's Covent Garden in 1988 as Jochanaan. On Jan. 17, 1990, he made his Metropolitan Opera debut in New York as the Dutchman, the same year that he appeared as Pizarro at the Salzburg Festival and as Wotan at the San Francisco Opera. In 1992 he sang Barak at the Salzburg Festival. During the 1992–93 season, he appeared as Wotan in the *Ring* cycle at the Vienna State Opera, and then sang that role at the Théâtre du Châtelet in Paris in 1994 and at the Metropolitan Opera in 1996. He married **Inga Nielsen**.

Halévy (real name, **Levy**), **(Jacques-François-) Fromental (-Elie),** celebrated French composer; b. Paris, May 27, 1799; d. Nice, March 17, 1862. The family changed its name to Halévy in 1807. He entered the Paris Cons. at age 9 as a student of Cazot, then studied with Lambert (piano), Berton (harmony), and Cherubini (counterpoint); he also studied with Méhul, winning the 2d Prix de Rome in 1816 and 1817 and the Grand Prix de Rome in 1819 with his cantata *Herminie*. He became chef du chant at the Théâtre-Italien in 1826. His first stage work to be performed was the opéra comique *L'Artisan* (Opéra Comique, Jan. 30, 1827), which had a modicum of success. He gained further notice with his *Clari*, introduced to Paris by Malibran (Théâtre-Italien, Dec. 9, 1828). His first major success came with *Le Dilettante d'Avignon* (Opéra Comique, Nov. 7, 1829). He then was chef du chant at the Paris Opéra (1829–45), where he scored his greatest triumph with *La Juive* (Feb. 23, 1835), which established his name and was performed throughout Europe and the United States. His next opera, *L'Éclair* (Opéra Comique, Dec. 16, 1835), also enjoyed a favorable reception. Among later operas of note were *La Reine de Chypre* (Dec. 22, 1841), *Charles VI* (March 15, 1843), and *La Magicienne* (March 17, 1858), all first performed at the Opéra. He was also active as a teacher at the Paris Cons., being made a prof. of harmony and accompaniment (1827), of counterpoint and fugue (1833), and of composition (1840). His students included Gounod, Bizet (who became his son-in-law), and Saint-Saëns. He was elected to membership in the Institut in 1836, and served as its secretary from 1854. Halévy was an extremely apt composer for the stage, winning the admiration of both Berlioz and Wagner. Yet he could never equal Meyerbeer in popular success; as time went by, only *La Juive* gained a permanent place in the world repertoire.

WRITINGS: *Leçons de lecture musicale . . . pour les écoles de la ville de Paris* (Paris, 1857); *Souvenirs et portraits* (Paris, 1861); *Derniers souvenirs et portraits* (Paris, 1863).

WORKS: DRAMATIC: OPERAS (all 1st perf. in Paris unless otherwise given): *L'Artisan*, opéra comique (Opéra Comique, Jan. 30, 1827); *Le Roi et le batelier*, opéra comique (Opéra Comique, Nov. 8, 1827; in collaboration with L. Rifaut); *Clari*, opera semi-seria (Théâtre-Italien, Dec. 9, 1828); *Le Dilettante d'Avignon*, opéra comique (Opéra Comique, Nov. 7, 1829); *Attendre et courir*, opéra comique (Opéra Comique, May 28, 1830; in collaboration with H. de Ruolz); *La Langue musicale*, opéra comique (Opéra Comique, Dec. 11, 1830); *La Tentation*, ballet opera (Opéra, June 20, 1832; in collaboration with C. Gide); *Les Souvenirs de Lafleur*, opéra comique (Opéra Comique, March 4, 1833); *Ludovic*, opéra comique (Opéra Comique, May 16, 1833; completion of an opera by Herold); *La Juive* (Opéra, Feb. 23, 1835); *L'Éclair*, opéra comique (Opéra Comique, Dec. 16, 1835); *Guido et Ginevra, ou La Peste de Florence* (Opéra, March 5, 1838); *Les Treize*, opéra comique (Opéra Comique, April 15, 1839); *Le Sherif*, opéra comique (Opéra Comique, Sept. 2, 1839); *Le Drapier* (Opéra, Jan. 6, 1840); *Le Guitarrero*, opéra comique (Opéra Comique, Jan. 21, 1841); *La Reine de Chypre* (Opéra, Dec. 22, 1841); *Charles VI* (Opéra, March 15, 1843); *Le Lazzarone, ou Le Bien vient en dormant* (Opéra, March 23, 1844); *Les Mousquetaires de la reine*, opéra comique (Opéra Comique, Feb. 3, 1846); *Les Premiers Pas*, prologue (Opéra-National, Nov. 15, 1847; in collaboration with Adam, Auber, and Carafa); *Le Val d'Andorre*, opéra comique (Opéra Comique, Nov. 11, 1848); *La Fée aux roses*, opéra comique (Opéra Comique, Oct. 1, 1849); *La Tempestà*, opera italien (Her Majesty's Theatre, London, June 8, 1850); *La Dame de pique*, opéra comique (Opéra Comique, Dec. 28, 1850); *Le Juif errant* (Opéra, April 23, 1852); *Le Nabab*, opéra comique (Opéra Comique, Sept. 1, 1853); *Jaguarita l'indienne*, opéra comique (Théâtre-Lyrique, May 14, 1855); *L'Inconsolable*, opéra comique (Théâtre-Lyrique, June 13, 1855; perf. under the nom de plume Alberti); *Valentine d'Aubigny*, opéra comique (Opéra Comique, April 26, 1856); *La Magicienne* (Opéra, March 17, 1858); *Noé* (unfinished; completed by Bizet and perf. as *Le Déluge*, Karlsruhe, April 5, 1885); *Vanina d'Ornano* (unfinished). BALLET: *Manon Lescaut* (Opéra, May 3, 1830).

BIBL.: C. de Lorbac, *Fromenthal H.: Sa vie, ses oeuvres* (Paris, 1862); L. Halévy, *F. H.: Sa vie et ses oeuvres* (Paris, 1862; 2d ed., 1863); A. Catelin, *F. H.: Notice biographique* (Paris, 1863); E. Monnais, *F. H.: Souvenirs d'un ami* (Paris, 1863); A. Pougin, *F. H.: Écrivain* (Paris, 1865); R. Jordan, *F. H.: His Life and Music, 1799–1862* (N.Y., 1996).

Halffter (Jiménez-Encina), Cristóbal, prominent Spanish composer and conductor, nephew of **Ernesto** and **Rodolfo Halffter (Escriche);** b. Madrid, March 24, 1930. He studied composition with Conrado del Campo at the Madrid Cons. (1947–51) and with Tansman in Paris (1959). From 1953 he was active as a conductor in Spain, and later conducted abroad. After serving as a teacher of composition (1961–66) and as director (1964–66) at the Madrid Cons., he lectured at the Univ. of Navarra (1970–78). He was president of the Spanish section of the ISCM (1976–78). In 1979 he was artistic director of the electronic music studio of the Heinrich Strobel-Stiftung in Freiburg im Breisgau. He was made a member of the Royal Academy of Fine Arts of San Fernando in 1983, of the Berlin Academy of Arts in 1985, and of the Swedish Royal Academy in Stockholm in 1988. As a composer, Halffter has perfected a highly personal style which makes use of the full range of contemporary means of expression, from dodecaphony to electronics.

WORKS: DRAMATIC: *Saeta*, ballet (Madrid, Oct. 28, 1955); *El pastor y la estrella*, children's television chamber opera (Madrid, Dec. 28, 1959); *Don Quichotte*, opera (1969).

BIBL.: T. Marco, *C. H.* (Madrid, 1972); E. Casares Rodicio, *C. H.* (Oviedo, 1980).

Halffter (Escriche), Ernesto, esteemed Spanish composer and conductor, brother of **Rodolfo Halffter (Escriche)** and uncle of **Cristóbal Halffter (Jiménez-Encina);** b. Madrid, Jan. 16, 1905; d. there, July 5, 1989. He was trained in composition by Manuel de Falla and Adolfo Salazar. At the outbreak of the Spanish Civil War in 1936, he went to Lisbon. In 1960 he returned to Madrid. In addition to Falla, his output reflects the influence of such French masters as Ravel and Poulenc. He completed and orchestrated Falla's scenic cantata *Atlántida* (Milan, June 18, 1962; he later rev. and perf. in concert form, Lucerne, Sept. 9, 1976). Among his works is the chamber opera *Entr'acte* (1964) and the ballets *Sonatina* (1928), *Dulcinea* (1940), *Cojo enamorado* (1954), and *Fantasía galaica* (1955).

Halffter (Escriche), Rodolfo, eminent Spanish-born Mexican composer and pedagogue, brother of **Ernesto Halffter (Escriche)** and uncle of **Cristóbal Halffter (Jiménez-Encina);** b. Madrid, Oct. 30, 1900; d. Mexico City, Oct. 14, 1987. He was mainly autodidact although he received some instruction from Falla in Granada (1929). Halffter became a prominent figure in the promotion of modern Spanish music, and was made chief of the music section of the Ministry of Propaganda (1936) and then a member of the Central Music Council (1937) of the Spanish Republic. Following the defeat of the regime in the Spanish Civil

War, Halffter fled in 1939 to France and then to Mexico, where he became a naturalized Mexican citizen. In 1940 he founded the contemporary ballet ensemble La Paloma Azul. From 1941 to 1970 he taught at the Cons. Nacional de México in Mexico City. In 1946 he founded the publishing firm Ediciones Mexicanas de Música and the journal *Nuestra Música*, which he ed. until 1952. In 1969 he was made a member of the Academia de Artes de Mexico and in 1984 he was made an honorary member of the Real Academia de Bellas Artes in Madrid. In his early works, Halffter followed in the path of Falla but he later explored contemporary techniques, including 12-tone writing. His *Tres Hojas de Album* (1953) was the earliest 12-tone music publ. in Mexico.

WORKS: DRAMATIC: *Clavileño*, opera buffa (1934–36; not extant); *Don Lindo de Almería*, ballet (1935; Mexico City, Jan. 9, 1940; orch. suite, 1936); *La madrugada del panadero*, ballet (Mexico City, Sept. 20, 1940; orch. suite, 1940); *Lluvia de toros*, ballet (1940); *Elena la traicionera*, ballet (Mexico City, Nov. 23, 1945); *Tonanzintla*, ballet (1951; also as *Tres Sonatas de Fray Antonio* for Orch.); much film music.

BIBL.: J. Alcaraz, *R. H.* (Madrid, 1987); X. Ruiz Ortiz, *R. H.: Antología, Introducción y Catalogos* (Mexico City, 1990); A. Iglesias, *R. H.: Tema, Nueve décadas y Final* (Madrid, 1991).

Hall, Sir Peter (Reginald Frederick), noted English theater and opera producer; b. Bury St. Edmunds, Nov. 22, 1930. He was educated at St. Catharine's College, Cambridge. In 1955–56 he was director of the Arts Theatre, London. He was managing director of the Royal Shakespeare Theatre from 1960 to 1968; from 1973 to 1988 he was director of the National Theatre; he also worked at the Royal Opera House, Covent Garden. In 1970 he began a long and fruitful association as an opera producer at Glyndebourne, serving as its artistic director from 1984 to 1990. He was head of his own Peter Hall Production Co. (from 1988). For several years he was married to **Maria Ewing**. He was made a Commander of the Order of the British Empire in 1963 and was knighted in 1977. He is known for his versatility, having produced operas by Cavalli, Mozart, Wagner, Tchaikovsky, Schoenberg, and Tippett. In 1983 he produced the new *Ring* cycle at Bayreuth for the 100th anniversary of Wagner's death, with Solti conducting.

Hallberg, Björn Wilho, Norwegian-born Swedish composer; b. Oslo, July 9, 1938. After training with Brustad and Mortensen at the Oslo Cons., he settled in Stockholm in 1962 and completed his studies at the Musikhögskolan with Blomdahl, Wallner, and Linholm. In 1968 he became a naturalized Swedish citizen.

WORKS: DRAMATIC: OPERAS: *Evakueringen* (Stockholm, Dec. 9, 1969); *Josef* (1976–79); *Förföraren* (Stockholm, Dec. 22, 1981); *Regina* (1985); *Majdagar* (Stockholm, Dec. 16, 1989); *Orfika* (1990–95). Ballet music.

Hallén, (Johannes) Andreas, Swedish conductor and composer; b. Göteborg, Dec. 22, 1846; d. Stockholm, March 11, 1925. He studied with Reinecke in Leipzig, Rheinberger in Munich, and Rietz in Dresden. Upon his return to Sweden, he conducted in Göteborg (1872–78; 1883–84), then was conductor of the Phil. Concerts in Stockholm (1885–95) and of the Royal Opera (1892–97). From 1908 to 1919 he was a prof. of composition at the Stockholm Cons. He composed in a Wagnerian style. His works include the operas *Harald der Wiking* (Leipzig, Oct. 16, 1881), *Häxfällan* (Stockholm, March 16, 1896; rev. version as *Walpurgis Night*, Stockholm, March 15, 1902), and *The Treasure of Waldemar* (Stockholm, April 8, 1899).

BIBL.: P. Vretblad, *A. H.* (Stockholm, 1918).

Hallström, Ivar (Christian), Swedish composer; b. Stockholm, June 5, 1826; d. there, April 11, 1901. He studied jurisprudence at the Univ. of Uppsala, where he became a friend of Prince Gustaf, who was himself a musical amateur. On April 9, 1847, jointly with Gustaf, he produced in Stockholm an opera, *Hvita frun på Drottningholm* (The White Lady of Drottningholm). In 1853 he became librarian to Prince Oscar, and from 1861 to 1872 he was director of Lindblad's music school in Stockholm. His opera *Hertig Magnus och sjöjungfrun* (Duke Magnus and the Mermaid) was produced at the Royal Opera in Stockholm on Jan. 28, 1867, but had only 6 performances in all, purportedly because it contained more arias in minor keys (10, to be exact) than those in major (only 8). He then produced another opera, *Den förtrollade Katten* (The Enchanted Cat; Stockholm, April 20, 1869), which was more successful. With his next opera, *Den Bergtagna* (The Bewitched One), produced in Stockholm on May 24, 1874, he achieved his greatest success; it had repeated performances not only in Sweden, but also in Germany and Denmark. In this work Hallstrom made use of Swedish folk motifs, a pioneering attempt in Scandinavian operatic art. His next opera, *Vikingarna* (Stockholm, June 6, 1877), was but moderately successful; there followed *Neaga* (Stockholm, Feb. 24, 1885), to a libretto by Carmen Sylva (Queen Elisabeth of Romania). He also wrote several ballets, cantatas, and arrangements of Swedish folk songs for piano.

Halmen, Pet(re), Romanian opera designer and producer; b. Talmaciu, Nov. 14, 1943. He received training in Berlin. After working in Kiel and Düsseldorf, he collaborated as a designer on productions with Jean-Pierre Ponnelle. Their staging of a Monteverdi cycle in Zürich in 1975 won critical accolades. From 1978 he was active at the Bavarian State Opera in Munich, where he prepared designs for the premieres of Reimann's *Lear* that year and for his *Troades* in 1986, as well as for Wagner's *Das Liebesverbot* in 1983 and Berg's *Lulu* in 1985. His designs for *Aida*, in collaboration with Ponnelle, were seen in Berlin in 1982, Chicago in 1983, and at London's Covent Garden in 1984, where controversy raged over his iconoclastic leanings. In 1987 he produced *Lohengrin* in Düsseldorf. With Ponnelle, he mounted a controversial production of *Parsifal* in San Francisco in 1988. After producing Paër's *Achille* in Bologna (1988) and *La straniera* at the Spoleto Festival in Charleston, S.C. (1989), he staged *Nabucco* in Munich in 1990 and *La clemenza di Tito* in Toulouse in 1992. He produced *Don Giovanni* in Hamburg in 1996, followed by *Orfeo* in Halle in 1997, and *Idomeneo* in Salzburg in 1998.

Halvorsen, Johan, notable Norwegian conductor and composer; b. Drammen, March 15, 1864; d. Oslo, Dec. 4, 1935. He began violin lessons at 7 and while still a youth, played several instruments in the local civil defense band. He pursued his musical training with Lindberg and Nordquist at the Stockholm Cons. In 1885 he made his debut as a soloist in the Beethoven Violin Concerto in Bergen, where he served as concertmaster of the Harmonien Music Soc. He then was a violinist in the Gewandhaus Orch. in Leipzig, where he studied violin with Brodsky. After serving as concertmaster of the Aberdeen Musical Soc., he taught at the Helsinki Cons. (1889–92). He also completed his studies in St. Petersburg, Berlin (composition with Becker), and Liège (violin with Thomson). Upon returning to Bergen in 1893, he became conductor of the orch. of the theater and of the Harmonien Music Soc. In 1899 he was called to Christiania (Oslo) as conductor of the orch. of the newly opened National Theater, where he led symphonic as well as theater scores until his retirement in 1929. He was married to a niece of Grieg. Halvorsen's compositions were influenced by Grieg, Svendsen, and the folk melodies of his native land. Outside of Norway he is best known for his celebrated orch. march *Entry of the Boyars* (1893), as well as the Passacaglia for Violin and Viola, after a Handel keyboard suite (1897), the *Andante religioso* for Violin and Orch. (1903), and *Bergensiana, Rococo Variations on an Old Melody from Bergen* for Orch. (1913). Among his other works were incidental music to more than 30 plays; also *Reisen til Julestjernen* (Journey to the Christmas Star), a popular children's Christmas play (1924).

Hamari, Julia, Hungarian mezzo-soprano; b. Budapest, Nov. 21, 1942. She studied with Fatime Martin; after further training at the Budapest Academy of Music, she won the Erkel competition in 1964, and then completed her studies at the Stuttgart Hochschule für Musik. In 1966 she made her debut as a soloist in the St. Matthew Passion in Vienna, and subsequently was notably successful as a concert and lieder artist in Europe. In 1967 she made her stage debut in Salzburg. In 1972 she made her U.S. debut as a soloist with the Chicago Sym. Orch. As an opera singer, she appeared with the opera houses in Düsseldorf and Stuttgart. On April 24, 1982, she made her Metropolitan Opera debut in New York as Rossini's Rosina. Her concert and lieder repertoire extends from Monteverdi to Verdi. Among her other operatic roles are Cherubino, Dorabella, Cenerentola, Carmen, and Octavian.

Hambraeus, Bengt, prominent Swedish composer, organist, musicologist, and pedagogue; b. Stockholm, Jan. 29, 1928. He studied organ with Alf Linder (1944–48), and also pursued training in musicology at the Univ. of Uppsala (1947–56; M.A., 1950; Fil.Lic., 1956) and attended the summer courses in new music in Darmstadt (1951–55). After service with the Inst. of Musicology at the Univ. of Uppsala (1948–56), he joined the music dept. of the Swedish Broadcasting Corp. in Stockholm in 1957, where he later was head of its chamber music section (1965–68) and production manager (1968–72). He subsequently was a prof. at McGill Univ. in Montreal from 1972. In 1967 he was made a member of the Swedish Royal Academy of Music in Stockholm. In addition to his numerous articles and essays, he publ. *Codex Carminum Gallicorum* (Uppsala, 1961), *Portrait av Bach* (with others; Stockholm, 1968), and *Om Notskrifter* (Stockholm, 1970). Hambraeus is one of the pioneering figures of the Swedish avant-garde. His *Doppelrohr* for Tape (1955) was one of the earliest electronic pieces by a Scandinavian composer. While he has found inspiration in both the Western and non-Western musical traditions, he has pursued an adventuresome course in his oeuvre.

WORKS: OPERAS: *Experiment X*, church opera (1968–69; Stockholm, March 9, 1971); *Se människen*, church opera (1970; Stockholm, May 15, 1972); *Sagan*, radio opera (1978–79; Swedish Radio, Aug. 31, 1980); *L'Oui-dire* (1984–86).

Hamerik (real name, **Hammerich**), **Asger,** Danish composer, father of **Ebbe Hamerik**; b. Frederiksberg, April 8, 1843; d. there, July 13, 1923. He studied with Gade in Copenhagen and with Bülow in Berlin. He met Berlioz in Paris in 1864, and accompanied him to Vienna in 1866, studying orchestration. Hamerik was probably the only pupil that Berlioz had. He received a gold medal for his work *Hymne de la paix* at the contest for the Paris Exposition. His opera *Tovelille* was performed in Paris in concert form (May 6, 1865); another opera, *Hjalmar and Ingeborg*, was not performed in its entirety. In 1870 he visited Italy and produced his Italian-language opera, *La vendetta* (Milan, Dec. 23, 1870). He then received an invitation to become director of the newly organized Peabody Cons. in Baltimore. He accepted, and remained in Baltimore until 1898, when he returned to Copenhagen. His other works include 8 syms. (1881–98), 5 Nordic Suites (1872–77), and the opera *Den rejsende* (1871). His brother was the Danish musicologist Angul Hammerich (b. Copenhagen, Nov. 25, 1848; d. Frederiksberg, April 26, 1931).

Hamerik (real name, **Hammerich**), **Ebbe,** Danish conductor and composer, son of **Asger Hamerik**; b. Copenhagen, Sept. 5, 1898; d. there (drowned in the Kattegat), Aug. 11, 1951. He studied with his father, then was active mainly as a conductor. He held the post of 2d conductor at the Royal Danish Theater in Copenhagen (1919–22) and conductor of the Copenhagen music society (1927–31) and the State Radio Sym. Orch. He composed the operas *Stepan* (Mainz, Nov. 30, 1924), *Leonardo da Vinci* (Antwerp, March 28, 1939), *Marie Grubbe* (Copenhagen, May 17, 1940), *Rejsekammeraten*, after Andersen (Copenhagen, Jan. 5, 1946), and *Drommerne* (posthumous; Århus, Sept. 9, 1974). His uncle was the Danish musicologist Angul Hammerich, (b. Copenhagen, Nov. 25, 1848; d. Frederiksberg, April 26, 1931).

Hamilton, David (Peter), American music critic; b. N.Y., Jan. 18, 1935. He was educated at Princeton Univ. (1952–56; A.B., 1956; M.F.A., music history, 1960). He was music and record librarian there (1961–65); in 1965 he became assistant music ed. of W. W. Norton & Co. in New York; he was music ed. from 1968 to 1974. In 1967 he became a contributing ed. of *High Fidelity*, and in 1968, music critic of the *Nation*; he also served as N.Y. music correspondent for the *Financial Times* of London (1969–74) and assoc. ed. of the *Musical Newsletter* (1971–77). He wrote *The Listener's Guide to Great Instrumentalists* (N.Y., 1981) and *The Metropolitan Opera Encyclopedia: A Comprehensive Guide to the World of Opera* (N.Y., 1987); he also publ. *The Music Game: An Autobiography* (London, 1986).

Hamilton, Iain (Ellis), remarkable Scottish composer; b. Glasgow, June 6, 1922. He was taken to London at the age of 7, and attended Mill Hill School; after graduation, he became an apprentice engineer, but studied music in his leisure time. He was 25 years old when he decidedly turned to music; he won a scholarship to the Royal Academy of Music, where he studied piano with Harold Craxton and composition with William Alwyn; concurrently he studied at the Univ. of London (B.Mus., 1950). He made astonishing progress as a composer, and upon graduation from the Royal Academy of Music received the prestigious Dove Prize (1950); other awards included the Royal Phil. Soc. Prize for his Clarinet Concerto (1951), the Koussevitzky Foundation Award for his 2d Sym. (1951), the Edwin Evans Prize (1951), the Arnold Bax Gold Medal (1957), and the Vaughan Williams Award (1974). From 1951 to 1960 he was a lecturer at Morley College in London; he also lectured at the Univ. of London (1952–60). He served as Mary Duke Biddle Prof. of Music at Duke Univ. in Durham, N.C. (1961–78), where he was chairman of its music dept. (1966–67); he also was composer-in-residence at the Berkshire Music Center at Tanglewood, Mass. (summer, 1962). In 1970 he received an honorary D.Mus. from the Univ. of Glasgow. His style of composition is marked by terse melodic lines animated by a vibrant rhythmic pulse, creating the impression of kinetic lyricism; his harmonies are built on a set of peculiarly euphonious dissonances, which repose on emphatic tonal centers. For several years he pursued a sui generis serial method, but soon abandoned it in favor of a free modern manner; in his operas, he makes use of thematic chords depicting specific dramatic situations.

WORKS: DRAMATIC: *Clerk Saunders*, ballet (1951); *The Royal Hunt of the Sun*, opera (1966–68; 1975; London, Feb. 2, 1977); *Agamemnon*, dramatic narrative (1967–69); *Pharsalia*, dramatic commentary (1968); *The Cataline Conspiracy*, opera (1972–73; Stirling, Scotland, March 16, 1974); *Tamburlaine*, lyric drama (1976; BBC, London, Feb. 14, 1977); *Anna Karenina*, opera (1977–78; London, May 7, 1981); *Dick Whittington*, lyric comedy (1980–81); *Lancelot*, opera (1982–83; Arundel, England, Aug. 24, 1985); *Raleigh's Dream*, opera (1983; Durham, N.C., June 3, 1984); *The Tragedy of Macbeth*, opera (1990); *London's Fair*, opera (1992).

Hamm, Charles (Edward), American musicologist; b. Charlottesville, Va., April 21, 1925. He studied at the Univ. of Virginia (B.A., 1947) and Princeton Univ. (M.F.A., 1950; Ph.D., 1960, with the diss. *A Chronology of the Works of Guillaume Dufay*; publ. in Princeton, 1964). He taught at Princeton Univ. (1948–50; 1958), at the Cincinnati Cons. of Music (1950–57), and at Tulane Univ. (1959–63). In 1963 he was appointed prof. of musicology at the Univ. of Ill.; in 1976 he joined the faculty of Dartmouth College. He served as president of the American Musicological Soc. from 1973 to 1974, and in 1993 he was made an honorary member. A versatile scholar, Hamm publ. books on a variety of subjects, including *Opera* (Boston, 1966).

Hammerstein, Oscar, celebrated German-American impresario, grandfather of **Oscar (Greeley Clendenning) Hammerstein, II**; b. Stettin, May 8, 1846; d. N.Y., Aug. 1, 1919. At the age of 16 he ran away from home. He spent some time in England, then went to America, where he worked in a N.Y. cigar factory. Possessing an inventive mind, he patented a machine for shaping tobacco leaves by suction; he later ed. a tobacco trade journal. At the same time, he practiced the violin, learned to write music, and dabbled in playwriting. In 1868 he produced in New York a comedy in German and also wrote the libretto and music of an operetta, *The Kohinoor* (N.Y., Oct. 24, 1893). His main activity, however, was in management. He built the Harlem Opera House (1888), the Olympia Music Hall (1895), and the Republic Theater (1900), and presented brief seasons of plays and operas in all 3. In 1906 he announced plans for the Manhattan Opera House in

New York, his crowning achievement. The enterprise was originally planned as a theater for opera in English, but it opened with an Italian company in Bellini's *I Puritani* (Dec. 3, 1906). Hammerstein entered into bold competition with the Metropolitan Opera, and engaged celebrated singers, among them Melba, Nordica, Tetrazzini, and Garden; among the spectacular events presented by him were the first U.S. performances of 5 operas by Massenet, Charpentier's *Louise*, and Debussy's *Pelléas et Mélisande*. The new venture held its own for 4 seasons, but in the end Hammerstein was compelled to yield; in April 1910 he sold the Manhattan Opera House to the management of the Metropolitan for $1.2 million, and agreed not to produce grand opera in New York for 10 years. He also sold to the Metropolitan (for $100,000) his interests in the Philadelphia Opera House, built by him in 1908. Defeated in his main ambition in the United States, he transferred his activities to England. There he built the London Opera House, which opened with a lavish production of *Quo Vadis* by Nougues (Nov. 17, 1911). However, he failed to establish himself in London, and after a season there, returned to New York In contravention of his agreement with the Metropolitan, he announced a season at the newly organized American Opera House in New York, but the Metropolitan secured an injunction against him, and he was forced to give up his operatic venture.

BIBL.: V. Sheean, *O. H., I: The Life and Exploits of an Impresario* (N.Y., 1956); J. Cone, *O. H.'s Manhattan Opera Company* (Norman, Okla., 1966).

Hammerstein, Oscar (Greeley Clendenning), II, outstanding American lyricist, grandson of **Oscar Hammerstein**; b. N.Y., July 12, 1895; d. Highland Farms, Doylestown, Pa., Aug. 23, 1960. He studied law at Columbia Univ., graduating in 1917; he then became interested in the theater. He collaborated on the librettos for Friml's *Rose Marie* (1924), Romberg's *The Desert Song* (1926), and Kern's *Show Boat* (1927; included the celebrated song "Ol' Man River"). In 1943 he joined forces with the composer Richard Rodgers, and together they produced some of the most brilliant and successful musical comedies in the history of the American theater: *Oklahoma!* (1943; Pulitzer Prize); *Carousel* (1945); *Allegro* (1947); *South Pacific* (1949; Pulitzer Prize); *The King and I* (1951); *Me and Juliet* (1953); *Pipe Dream* (1955); *Flower Drum Song* (1958); and *The Sound of Music* (1959). His lyrics are characterized by a combination of appealing sentiment and sophisticated nostalgia, making them particularly well suited to the modern theater.

BIBL.: D. Taylor, *Some Enchanted Evenings: The Story of Rodgers and H.* (N.Y., 1953); M. Wilk, *They're Playing Our Song* (N.Y., 1973); H. Fordin, *Getting to Know Him, A Biography of O. H. II* (N.Y., 1977); S. Citron, *The Wordsmiths: O. H. II and Alan Jay Lerner* (Oxford, 1995).

Hammond, Frederick (Fisher), American musicologist and harpsichordist; b. Binghamton, N.Y., Aug. 7, 1937. He received his B.A. and Ph.D. from Yale Univ., where he studied harpsichord with Kirkpatrick. He taught at the Univ. of Chicago (1962–65) and at Queens College (1966–68), then joined the faculty at the Univ. of Calif. at Los Angeles (1968). In 1989 he became Irma Brandeis Prof. of Romance Studies at Bard College. He made his N.Y. recital debut in 1969. He was assistant music director of the Castelfranco Veneto Festival (1975–80), assistant music director of the Clarion Music Soc. (from 1978), and director of the Nakamichi Festival of Baroque Music (from 1986). His research focuses on Italian harpsichord composers; his *Girolamo Frescobaldi* (Cambridge, Mass., 1983) is the definitive biography. He also publ. *Girolamo Frescobaldi: A Guide to Research* (N.Y., 1988). His honors include a Rome Prize fellowship (1965–66) and the Cavaliere al merito della Repubblica (1986).

Hammond, Dame Joan (Hood), prominent New Zealand soprano; b. Christchurch, May 24, 1912; d. Bowral, Australia, Nov. 26, 1996. She studied at the Sydney Cons., in Vienna, and with Borgioli in London. In 1929 she made her operatic debut in Sydney as Siebel. In 1938 she made her London debut in a recital, and then sang in Vienna. From 1942 to 1945 she appeared with the Carl Rosa Opera Co. in London. On Oct. 6, 1948, she made her debut at London's Covent Garden as Verdi's Leonora, and continued to sing there until 1951; she appeared there again in 1953. She made her N.Y. City Opera debut as Cio-Cio-San on Oct. 16, 1949, and remained on its roster for the season. She also pursued an active concert career. After her retirement in 1965, she taught voice in Wellington at Victoria Univ. Her autobiography was publ. as *A Voice, a Life* (London, 1970). She was made an Officer (1953), a Commander (1963), and a Dame Commander (1974) of the Order of the British Empire. Among her finest operatic roles were Beethoven's Leonore, Violetta, Marguerite, Tatiana, Rusalka, Salome, and Tosca.

Hammond-Stroud, Derek, English baritone; b. London, Jan. 10, 1929. He was a student of Elena Gerhardt in London and of Gerhard Hüsch in Vienna and Munich. In 1954 he made his London recital debut, followed by his operatic debut there in 1955 as Creon in Haydn's *L'anima del filosofo ossia Orfeo ed Euridice* at St. Pancras Town Hall. From 1961 to 1971 he was a principal member of the Sadler's Wells Opera in London, and then sang at London's Covent Garden from 1971. In 1973 he made his first appearance at the Glyndebourne Festival. He made his U.S. debut with the Houston Grand Opera in 1975. On Dec. 5, 1977, he made his first appearance at the Metropolitan Opera in New York as Faninal. In addition to his operatic appearances, he also pursued an active concert career. In 1987 he was made an Officer of the Order of the British Empire. His successful operatic roles included Papageno, Bartolo, Don Magnifico, Melitone, Alberich, and Beckmesser.

Hampe, Michael (Hermann), German opera and theater director and Intendant; b. Heidelberg, June 3, 1936. He studied cello at Syracuse Univ. in New York and pursued training in literature, musicology, and philosophy at the Univ. of Munich and the Univ. of Vienna (Ph.D.). After working as a theater producer in Bern (1961–64) and Zürich (1965–70), he was director of the Mannheim National Theater from 1972 to 1975. From 1975 to 1995 he served as Intendant of the Cologne Opera. In 1993 he became Intendant of the Dresden Music Festival. Hampe has worked in many principal opera houses and theaters, including those of Germany, Austria, England, France, the United States, and Australia.

Hampson, Thomas, admired American baritone; b. Elkhart, Ind., June 28, 1955. He studied at Eastern Washington Univ. (B.A., 1977), Fort Wright College (B.F.A., 1979), the Univ. of Southern Calif., and the Music Academy of the West at Santa Barbara, where he won the Lotte Lehmann award (1978). In 1980 he took 2d prize at the 's-Hertogenbosch International Vocal Competition, and in 1981 1st place in the Metropolitan Opera Auditions. In 1981 he appeared with the Deutsche Oper am Rhein in Düsseldorf, and in 1982 attracted wide notice as Guglielmo in *Così fan tutte* with the Opera Theatre of St. Louis. In subsequent seasons, he appeared with opera companies in Santa Fe, Cologne, Lyons, and Zürich. In 1985 he made his N.Y. recital debut. On Oct. 9, 1986, he made his Metropolitan Opera debut in New York as Mozart's Count Almaviva. During the 1986–87 season, he sang for the first time with the Bavarian State Opera in Munich and the Vienna State Opera. In 1988 he appeared at the Salzburg Festival as Mozart's Count Almaviva. In 1989 he made his debut at the Berlin Deutsche Oper as Don Giovanni. He appeared for the first time at the San Francisco Opera as Ulisse in *Il Ritorno d'Ulisse* in 1990. In 1992 he made his Carnegie Hall recital debut in New York. In 1993 he made his debut at London's Covent Garden as Rossini's Figaro. He created the role of Vicomte de Valmont in Susa's *Dangerous Liaisons* in San Francisco in 1994. In 1997 he was engaged as Riccardo in *I Puritani* at the Metropolitan Opera, portrayed Eugene Onegin at the Vienna State Opera, and sang in Schubert's *Alfonso und Estrella* at the Vienna Festival. After singing Guillaume Tell at the Vienna State Opera in 1998, he returned to the Metropolitan Opera as Werther in 1999. He has won particular success for roles in operas by Mozart, Rossini, Donizetti, Verdi, and Puccini. As a concert artist, Hampson has appeared as a soloist with orchs. and as a recitalist in principal music centers of the world. His concert repertoire embraces works from Bach to Cole Porter and beyond.

Hampton, Calvin, esteemed American organist, choirmaster, and composer; b. Kittanning, Pa., Dec. 31, 1938; d. Port Charlotte, Fla., Aug. 5, 1984. He studied organ and composition at the Oberlin (Ohio) College-Cons. of Music (B.M., 1960), and then at Syracuse Univ. (M.M., 1962). He was organist-choirmaster at N.Y.'s Calvary Episcopal Church (later combined with Holy Communion and St. George's; 1963–83). Hampton was a brilliant recitalist who played his own notable transcriptions of works by Chopin and Mussorgsky. On March 2, 1980, at St. George's, he conducted what is thought to be the first complete U.S. performance, in French, of Franck's oratorio *Les Béatitudes*. His compositions fuse popular and classical influences with striking effect, producing a lyrical and romantic underpinning that belies the modernity of their instrumentation. Some of his anthems are found in supplements to the Episcopal hymnal. Among his works is *It Happened in Jerusalem*, music drama for Soli, Speakers, Actors, Dancers, Chorus, Organ, Percussion, and Tape (1982).

Handel, George Frideric (the Anglicized form of the name, adopted by Handel in England; the original German spelling was **Georg Friedrich Händel**; other forms used in various branches of the family were Hendel, Hendeler, Händler, and Hendtler; the early spelling in England was Hendel; in France it is spelled Haendler; the Russian transliteration of the name from the Cyrillic alphabet, which lacks the aspirate, is Gendel), great German-born English composer; b. Halle, Feb. 23, 1685; d. London, April 14, 1759. His father was a barber-surgeon and valet to the prince of Saxe-Magdeburg; at the age of 61 he took a 2d wife, Dorothea Taust, daughter of the pastor of Giebichenstein, near Halle; Handel was their 2d son. As a child, he was taken by his father on a visit to Saxe-Weissenfels, where he had a chance to try out the organ of the court chapel. The duke, Johann Adolf, noticing his interest in music, advised that he be sent to Halle for organ lessons with Friedrich Wilhelm Zachau, the organist of the Liebfrauenkirche there. Zachau gave him instruction in harpsichord and organ playing and also introduced him to the rudiments of composition. Handel proved to be an apt student, and substituted for Zachau as organist whenever necessary; he also composed trio sonatas and motets for Sunday church services. After the death of his father in 1697, he entered the Univ. of Halle in 1702, and was named probationary organist at the Domkirche there. In 1703 he went to Hamburg, where he was engaged as "violino di ripieno" by Reinhard Keiser, the famous composer and director of the Hamburg Opera. There he met Johann Mattheson, and in 1703 the 2 undertook a journey to Lübeck together, with the intention of applying for the post of organist in succession to Buxtehude, who was chief organist there. There was apparently a quarrel between Mattheson and Handel at a performance of Mattheson's opera *Cleopatra*, in which he sang the leading male role of Antonio, while Handel conducted from the keyboard as maestro al cembalo. When Mattheson completed his stage role, he asked Handel to yield his place at the keyboard to him; Handel declined, and an altercation ensued, resulting in a duel with swords, which was called off when Mattheson broke his sword on a metal button of Handel's coat. There is no independent confirmation of this episode, however, and the 2 apparently reconciled.

Handel's first opera, *Almira*, was produced at the Hamburg Opera on Jan. 8, 1705; his next opera, *Nero*, was staged there on Feb. 25, 1705. He was then commissioned to write 2 other operas, *Florindo* and *Daphne*, originally planned as a single opera combining both subjects. In 1706 he undertook a long voyage to Italy, where he visited Florence, Rome, Naples, and Venice. The first opera he wrote in Italy was *Rodrigo*, presented in Florence in 1707. Then followed *Agrippina*, produced in Venice on Dec. 26, 1709; it obtained an excellent success, being given 27 performances. In Rome, he composed the serenata *Il trionfo del Tempo e del Disinganno*, performed there in the spring of 1707. Handel's oratorio *La Resurrezione* was given in Rome on April 8, 1708. On July 19, 1708, he brought out in Naples his serenata *Aci, Galatea, e Polifemo*; its score was remarkable for a bass solo that required a compass of 2 octaves and a fifth. During his Italian sojourn he met Alessandro and Domenico Scarlatti. In 1710 he returned to Germany and was named Kapellmeister to the elector of Hannover, as successor to Agostino Steffani. Later that year he visited England, where he produced his opera *Rinaldo* at the Queen's Theatre in London on Feb. 24, 1711; it received 15 performances. After a brief return to Hannover in June 1711, he made another visit to London, where he produced his operas *Il Pastor fido* (Nov. 22, 1712) and *Teseo* (Jan. 10, 1713). He also wrote an ode for Queen Anne's birthday, which was presented at Windsor Palace on Feb. 6, 1713; it was followed by 2 sacred works, performed on July 7, 1713, to celebrate the Peace of Utrecht; these performances won him royal favor and an annuity of 200 pounds sterling.

An extraordinary concurrence of events persuaded Handel to remain in London, when Queen Anne died in 1714 and Handel's protector, the elector of Hannover, became King George I of England. The king bestowed many favors upon the composer and augmented his annuity to 400 pounds sterling. Handel became a British subject in 1727, and Anglicized his name to George Frideric Handel, dropping the original German umlaut. He continued to produce operas, invariably to Italian librettos, for the London stage. His opera *Silla* was produced in London on June 2, 1713; it was followed by *Amadigi di Gaula* on May 25, 1715. In 1716 Handel wrote *Der für die Sünden der Welt gemarterte und sterbende Jesus*, to the text of the poet Heinrich Brockes. In 1717 he produced one of his most famous works, written expressly for King George I, his *Water Music*. On July 17, 1717, an aquatic fête on the Thames River was held by royal order; the king's boat was followed by a barge on which an orch. of 50 musicians played Handel's score, or at least a major portion of it. The final version of the *Water Music* combines 2 instrumental suites composed at different times: one was written for the barge party; the other is of an earlier provenance. In 1717 Handel became resident composer to the duke of Chandos, for whom he wrote the so-called *Chandos Anthems* (1717–18), the secular oratorio *Acis and Galatea* (1718), and the oratorio *Esther* (1718). He also served as music master to the daughters of the prince of Wales; for Princess Anne he composed his first collection of *Suites de pièces pour le clavecin* (1720), also known as *The Lessons*, which includes the famous air with variations nicknamed "The Harmonious Blacksmith." In 1719 he was made Master of Musick of a new business venture under the name of the Royal Academy of Music, established for the purpose of presenting opera at the King's Theatre. The first opera he composed for it was *Radamisto* (April 27, 1720). In the fall of 1720 the Italian composer Giovanni Bononcini joined the company. A rivalry soon developed between him and Handel that was made famous by a piece of doggerel by the poet John Byrom ("Some say, compar'd to Bononcini, that Mynheer Handel's but a ninny. Others aver that he to Handel is scarcely fit to hold a candle. Strange all this difference should be twixt tweedledum and tweedledee"). Handel won a Pyrrhic victory when Bononcini had the unfortunate idea of submitting to the London Academy of Music a madrigal which he had appropriated *in extenso* from a choral piece by the Italian composer Antonio Lotti; Lotti discovered it, and an embarrassing controversy ensued, resulting in Bononcini's disgrace and expulsion from London (he died in obscurity in Vienna, where he sought refuge). The irony of the whole episode is that Handel was no less guilty of plagiarism. An article on Handel in the 1880 ed. of the *Encyclopaedia Britannica* spares no words condemning Handel's conduct: "The system of wholesale plagiarism carried on by Handel is perhaps unprecedented in the history of music. He pilfered not only single melodies but frequently entire movements from the works of other masters, with few or no alterations, and without a word of acknowledgment." Between 1721 and 1728 he produced the following operas at the King's Theatre: *Florindante, Ottone, Flavio, Giulio Cesare, Tamerlano, Rodelinda Scipione, Alessandro, Admeto, Riccardo Primo, Siroe*, and *Tolomeo*; of these, *Giulio Cesare* and *Rodelinda* became firmly established in the operatic repertoire. In 1727 he composed 4 grand anthems for the coronation of King George II and Queen Caroline. In the spring of 1728 the

Royal Academy of Music ceased operations, and Handel became associated with the management of the King's Theatre. The following year, he went to Italy to recruit singers for a new Royal Academy of Music. Returning to London, he brought out the operas *Lotario, Partenope, Poro, Ezio, Sosarme*, and *Orlando*; only *Orlando* proved a lasting success. On May 2, 1732, Handel gave a special performance of a revised version of his oratorio *Esther* at the King's Theatre; it was followed by the revised version of *Acis and Galatea* (June 10, 1732) and the oratorio *Deborah* (March 17, 1733). On July 10, 1733, he produced his oratorio *Athalia* at Oxford, where he also appeared as an organist; he was offered, but declined, the degree of Mus.Doc. (*honoris causa*).

Discouraged by the poor reception of his operas at the King's Theatre, Handel decided to open a new season under a different management. But he quarreled with the principal singer, the famous castrato Senesino, who was popular with audiences, and thus lost the support of a substantial number of his subscribers, who then formed a rival opera company called Opera of the Nobility. It engaged the famous Italian composer Porpora as director, and opened its first season at Lincoln's Inn Fields on Dec. 29, 1733. Handel's opera *Arianna in Creta* had its premiere at the King's Theatre on Jan. 26, 1734, but in July of that year both Handel's company and the rival enterprise were forced to suspend operations. Handel set up his own opera company at Covent Garden, inaugurating his new season with a revised version of *Il Pastor fido* (Nov. 9, 1734); this was followed by *Ariodante, Alcina, Atalanta, Arminio, Giustino*, and *Berenice*, all staged between 1735 and 1737; only *Alcina* sustained a success; Handel's other operas met with indifferent reception. On Feb. 19, 1736, he presented his ode *Alexander's Feast* at Covent Garden, and on March 23, 1737, he brought out a revised version of his oratorio *Il trionfo del Tempo e della Verità*. His fortunes improved when he was confirmed by the queen as music master to princesses Amelia and Caroline. He continued to maintain connections with Germany, and traveled to Aachen in 1737. Upon his return to London, he suffered from attacks of gout, an endemic illness of British society at the time, but he managed to resume his work. On Jan. 3, 1738, he produced his opera *Faramondo*, and on April 15, 1738, presented his opera *Serse* (a famous aria from this opera, *Ombra mai fù*, became even more famous in an instrumental arrangement made by parties unknown, under the title "Handel's Celebrated Largo"). There followed a pasticcio, *Giove in Argo* (May 1, 1739), and *Imeneo* (Nov. 22, 1740). On Jan. 10, 1741, he produced his last opera, *Deidamia*, which marked the end of his operatic enterprise.

In historical perspective, Handel's failure as an operatic entrepreneur was a happy turn of events, for he then directed his energy toward the composition of oratorios, in which he achieved greatness. For inspiration, he turned to biblical themes, using English texts. On Jan. 16, 1739, he presented the oratorio *Saul*; on April 4, 1739, there followed *Israel in Egypt*. He also wrote an *Ode for St. Cecilia's Day*, after Dryden (Nov. 22, 1739), and his great set of 12 Concerti grossi, op. 6. Milton's *L'Allegro* and *Il Penseroso* inspired him to write *L'Allegro, il Penseroso, ed il Moderato* (Feb. 27, 1740). In 1741 he was invited to visit Ireland, where he produced his greatest masterpiece, *Messiah*; working with tremendous concentration of willpower and imagination, he completed Part I in 6 days, Part II in 9 days, and Part III in 6 days. The work on orchestration took him only a few more days; he signed the score on Sept. 14, 1741. The first performance of *Messiah* was given in Dublin on April 13, 1742, and its London premiere was presented on March 23, 1743. If contemporary reports can be trusted, King George II rose to his feet at the closing chords of the "Hallelujah" chorus, and the entire audience followed suit. This established a tradition, at least in England. Handel's oratorio *Samson*, produced in London on Feb. 18, 1743, was also successful, but his next oratorio, *Semele* (Feb. 10, 1744), failed to arouse public admiration. Continuing to work, and alternating between mythological subjects and religious themes, he produced *Joseph and His Brethren* (March 2, 1744), *Hercules* (Jan. 5, 1745), and *Belshazzar* (March 27, 1745). His subsequent works, composed between 1746 and 1752, were the *Occasional Oratorio, Judas Maccabaeus, Joshua, Alexander Balus, Susanna, Solomon, Theodora, The Choice of Hercules*, and *Jephtha*. Of these, *Judas Maccabaeus, Solomon*, and *Jephtha* became public favorites. Besides oratorios, mundane events also occupied his attention. To celebrate the Peace of Aachen, he composed the remarkable *Music for the Royal Fireworks*, heard for the first time in Green Park in London on April 27, 1749. In 1750 he revisited Germany. But soon he had to limit his activities on account of failing eyesight, which required the removal of cataracts; the operation proved unsuccessful, but he still continued to appear in performances of his music, with the assistance of his pupil John Christopher Smith. Handel's last appearance in public was at the London performance of *Messiah* on April 6, 1759; 8 days later, on April 14, the Saturday between Good Friday and Easter, he died. He was buried at Westminster Abbey; a monument by Roubiliac marks his grave. (It should be noted that the year of birth on Handel's gravestone is marked as 1684 rather than 1685; this discrepancy is explained by the fact that at that time the calendar year in England and other European countries began in March, not in Jan.)

A parallel between the 2 great German contemporaries, Bach and Handel, is often drawn. Born a few months apart, Bach in Eisenach, Handel in Halle, at a distance of about 130 kilometers, they never met. Bach visited Halle at least twice, but Handel was then away, in London. The difference between their life's destinies was profound. Bach was a master of the Baroque organ who produced religious works for church use, a schoolmaster who regarded his instrumental music as a textbook for study; he never composed for the stage, and traveled little. By contrast, Handel was a man of the world who dedicated himself mainly to public spectacles, and who became a British subject. Bach's life was that of a German burgher; his genius was inconspicuous; Handel shone in the light of public admiration. Bach was married twice; survivors among his 20 children became important musicians in their own right. Handel remained celibate, but he was not a recluse. Physically, he tended toward healthy corpulence; he enjoyed the company of friends, but had a choleric temperament, and could not brook adverse argument. Like Bach, he was deeply religious, and there was no ostentation in his service to his God. Handel's music possessed grandeur of design, majestic eloquence, and lusciousness of harmony. Music lovers did not have to study Handel's style to discover its beauty, while the sublime art of Bach could be fully understood only after knowledgeable penetration into the contrapuntal and fugal complexities of its structure.

Handel bequeathed the bulk of his MSS to his amanuensis, John Christopher Smith, whose son presented them in turn to King George III. They eventually became a part of the King's Music Library; they comprise 32 vols. of operas, 21 vols. of oratorios, 7 vols. of odes and serenatas, 12 vols. of sacred music, 11 vols. of cantatas, and 5 vols. of instrumental music. Seven vols. containing sketches for various works are in the Fitzwilliam Collection at Cambridge.

WORKS: OPERAS: *Almira* (Theater am Gänsemarkt, Hamburg, Jan. 8, 1705; part of music not extant); *Nero* (Theater am Gänsemarkt, Feb. 25, 1705; music not extant); *Rodrigo* (Accademia degli Infuocata, Florence, 1706 or 1707; part of music not extant); *Florindo* and *Daphne* (presented as 2 separate operas, Theater am Gänsemarkt, Jan. 1708; only a small part of music extant); *Agrippina* (Teatro San Giovanni Crisostomo, Venice, Dec. 26, 1709); *Rinaldo* (Queen's Theatre, London, Feb. 24, 1711; major rev., King's Theatre, London, April 6, 1731); *Il Pastor fido* (Queen's Theatre, Nov. 22, 1712; rev. versions, King's Theatre, May 18, 1734, and Nov. 9, 1734 [the latter with ballet *Terpsicore*]); *Teseo* (Queen's Theatre, Jan. 10, 1713); *Silla* (Queen's Theatre, or Burlington House, June 2, 1713); *Amadigi di Gaula* (King's Theatre, May 25, 1715); *Radamisto* (King's Theatre, April 27, 1720; rev. versions there, Dec. 28, 1720, and Jan.-Feb. 1728); *Floridante* (King's Theatre, Dec. 9, 1721; rev. version there, March 3, 1733); *Ottone, rè di Germania* (King's Theatre, Jan. 12, 1723; rev. versions there, Feb. 8, 1726, and Nov. 13, 1733); *Flavio, rè di Longobardi* (King's Theatre, May 14, 1723; major rev. there, April 18,

1732); *Giulio Cesare in Egitto* (King's Theatre, Feb. 20, 1724; rev. versions there, Jan. 2, 1725, and Jan. 17, 1730); *Tamerlano* (King's Theatre, Oct. 31, 1724); *Rodelinda, regina de' Longobardi* (King's Theatre, Feb. 13, 1725); *Scipione* (King's Theatre, March 12, 1726; rev. version there, Nov. 3, 1730); *Alessandro* (King's Theatre, May 5, 1726); *Admeto, rè di Tessaglia* (King's Theatre, Jan. 31, 1727; rev. version there, Dec. 7, 1731); *Riccardo Primo, rè d'Inghilterra* (King's Theatre, Nov. 11, 1727); *Siroe, rè di Persia* (King's Theatre, Feb. 17, 1728); *Tolomeo, rè di Egitto* (King's Theatre, April 30, 1728; major rev. there, May 19, 1730); *Lotario* (King's Theatre, Dec. 2, 1729); *Partenope* (King's Theatre, Feb. 24, 1730; rev. version there, Dec. 12, 1730; later rev. for Covent Garden, London, Jan. 29, 1737); *Poro, rè dell'Indie* (King's Theatre, Feb. 2, 1731; rev. versions there, Nov. 23, 1731, and Dec. 8, 1736); *Ezio* (King's Theatre, Jan. 15, 1732); *Sosarme, rè di Media* (King's Theatre, Feb. 15, 1732); *Orlando* (King's Theatre, Jan. 27, 1733); *Arianna in Creta* (King's Theatre, Jan. 26, 1734; rev. for Covent Garden, Nov. 27, 1734); *Oreste*, a pasticcio with music by Handel (Covent Garden, Dec. 18, 1734); *Ariodante* (Covent Garden, Jan. 8, 1735); *Alcina* (Covent Garden, April 16, 1735); *Atalanta* (Covent Garden, May 12, 1736); *Arminio* (Covent Garden, Jan. 12, 1737); *Giustino* (Covent Garden, Feb. 16, 1737); *Berenice* (Covent Garden, May 18, 1737); *Faramondo* (King's Theatre, Jan. 3, 1738); *Alessandro Severo*, pasticcio with music by Handel (King's Theatre, Feb. 25, 1738); *Serse* (King's Theatre, April 15, 1738); *Giove in Argo*, pasticcio (King's Theatre, May 1, 1739); *Imeneo* (Lincoln's Inn Fields, London, Nov. 22, 1740); *Deidamia* (Lincoln's Inn Fields, Jan. 10, 1741). Also *Muzio Scevola* (Act 3 by Handel; Act 1 by F. Amadei and Act 2 by G. Bononcini; King's Theatre, April 15, 1721); *Genserico* (only part of Act 1 drafted); *Tito* (only scenes 1–3 of Act 1 composed); *Alceste* (greater part of music used in the oratorio *The Choice of Hercules*; see below).

ORATORIOS: *Oratorio per la Resurrezione di Nostro Signor Gesu Cristo* (Palazzo Ruspoli, Rome, April 8, 1708); *Acis and Galatea* (Cannons, 1718; major rev., King's Theatre, June 10, 1732; also subsequent revs.); *Esther* (Cannons, 1718; major rev., King's Theatre, May 2, 1732; also subsequent additions); *Deborah* (King's Theatre, March 17, 1733; also subsequent revs.); *Athalia* (Sheldonian Theatre, Oxford, July 10, 1733; major rev., Covent Garden, April 1, 1735); *Il Parnasso in festa* (greater part of music from *Athalia*; King's Theatre, March 13, 1734); *Saul* (King's Theatre, Jan. 16, 1739; also subsequent revs.); *Israel in Egypt* (King's Theatre, April 4, 1739; also subsequent extensive changes); *Messiah* (New Music Hall, Dublin, April 13, 1742; also numerous revs. made for many subsequent perfs.); *Samson* (Covent Garden, Feb. 18, 1743; also subsequent revs.); *Semele* (Covent Garden, Feb. 10, 1744); *Joseph and His Brethren* (Covent Garden, March 2, 1744; also subsequent revs.); *Hercules* (King's Theatre, Jan. 5, 1745); *Belshazzar* (King's Theatre, March 27, 1745; rev. version, Covent Garden, Feb. 22, 1751); *Occasional Oratorio*, pasticcio (Covent Garden, Feb. 14, 1746); *Judas Maccabaeus* (Covent Garden, April 1, 1747; also many subsequent revs.); *Alexander Balus* (Covent Garden, March 23, 1748; rev. version, March 1, 1754); *Susanna* (Covent Garden, Feb. 10, 1749); *Solomon* (Covent Garden, March 17, 1749); *Theodora* (Covent Garden, March 16, 1750); *The Choice of Hercules* (greater part of music from *Alceste*; Covent Garden, March 1, 1751); *Jephtha* (Covent Garden, Feb. 26, 1752); *The Triumph of Time and Truth* (greater part of music from *Il trionfo del Tempo e della Verità*; Covent Garden, March 11, 1757).

BIBL.: COLLECTED EDITIONS, SOURCE MATERIAL: The first ed. of Handel's collected works was edited by S. Arnold in 180 installments in 54 vols. (1787–97). It was superseded by the monumental ed. prepared by F. Chrysander under the title *G. F. H.s Werke: Ausgabe der deutschen Händelgesellschaft* (100 vols., Leipzig and Bergedorf bei Hamburg, 1858–94; 6 supplementary vols., 1888–1902). In 1955 the Hallische H.-Ausgabe was begun as a supplement to the Chrysander ed.; however, it soon became a new critical ed. in its own right, being edited by M. Schneider and R. Steglich as the *Hallische H.-Ausgabe im Auftrage der Georg Friedrich H.-Gesellschaft*, and publ. in Kassel. A. Bell ed. a *Chronological Catalogue of H.'s Work* (Greenock, Scotland, 1969).

Other sources include the following: N. Flower, *Catalogue of a H. Collection Formed by Newman Flower* (Sevenoaks, 1920); W. Squire, *Catalogue of the King's Music Library, I: The H. Manuscripts* (London, 1927); H. Shaw, *A First List of Word-books of H.'s "Messiah," 1742–83* (Worcester, 1959); W. Smith and C. Humphries, *H.: A Descriptive Catalogue of the Early Editions* (London, 1960; 2d ed., rev., 1970); H. Federhofer, *Unbekannte Kopien von Werken G. F. H.s* (Kassel, 1963); K. Sasse, *H.-Bibliographie* (Leipzig, 1963; new ed., 1967; with supplement, 1969); W. Smith, *A H.ian's Notebook* (London, 1965); P. Krause, *Handschriften und altere Drucke der Werke G. F. H.s in der Musikbibliothek der Stadt Leipzig* (Leipzig, 1966); A. Hyatt King, *H. and His Autographs* (London, 1967); W. Meyerhoff, ed., *50 Jahre Göttinger H.-Festspiele. Festschrift* (Kassel, 1970); H. Clausen, *H.s Direktionspartituren ("Handexemplare")* (Hamburg, 1972); A. Walker, *G. F. H.: The Newman Flower Collection in the Henry Watson Music Library* (Manchester, 1972); H. Marx, *Göttinger H.-Beitrage I* (Kassel, 1984); B. Baselt, *Verzeichnis der Werke G. F. H.s (HWV)* (Leipzig, 1986); M. Parker-Hale, *G. F. H.: A Guide to Research* (N.Y., 1988).

BIOGRAPHICAL: J. Mainwaring, *Memoirs of the Late G. F. H.* (London, 1760; reprint, 1967); J. Mattheson, *G. F. H.s Lebensbeschreibung* (based almost entirely on Mainwaring's biography; Hamburg, 1761; reprint, 1976); C. Burney, *An Account of the Musical Performances in Westminster Abbey and the Pantheon May 26th, 27th, 29th; and June the 3d and 5th, 1784: In Commemoration of H.* (London, 1785; reprint, 1965); W. Coxe, *Anecdotes of G. F. H. and John Christopher Smith* (London, 1799; reprint, 1980); R. Clark, *Reminiscences of H.* (London, 1836); K. Förstemann, *G. F. H.s Stammbaum* (Leipzig, 1844); W. Callcott, *A Few Facts in the Life of H.* (London, 1850); H. Townsend, *An Account of H.'s Visit to Dublin: With Incidental Notices of His Life and Character* (Dublin, 1852); V. Schoelcher, *The Life of H.* (London, 1857); A. Stothard, *H.: His Life, Personal and Professional* (London, 1857); F. Chrysander, *G. F. H.* (3 vols., Leipzig, 1858–67; reprint, 1966); J. Marshall, *H.* (London, 1881; 3d ed., 1912); W. Rockstro, *The Life of G. F. H.* (London, 1883); J. Opel, *Mitteilungen zur Geschichte der Familie des Tonkünstlers H.* (Leipzig, 1885); A. Ademollo, *G. F. H. in Italia* (Milan, 1889); F. Volbach, *G. F. H.* (Berlin, 1897; 3d ed., 1914); W. Cummings, *H.* (London, 1904); F. Williams, *H.* (London, 1904); J. Hadden, *Life of H.* (London, 1905); R. Streatfeild, *H.* (London, 1909; reprint, 1964); R. Rolland, *H.* (Paris, 1910; 2d ed., 1974; Eng. tr., 1916; reprint, 1975); M. Brenet, *H.* (Paris, 1912); H. Davey, *H.* (London, 1912); G. Thormälius, *G. F. H.* (Stuttgart, 1912); R. Streatfeild, *H., Canons and the Duke of Chandos* (London, 1916); N. Flower, *G. F. H.: His Personality and His Times* (London, 1923; 3d ed., rev., 1959); H. Leichtentritt, *H.* (Stuttgart, 1924); H. Moser, *Der junge H. und seine Vorgänger in Halle* (Halle, 1929); J. Müller-Blattau, *G. F. H.* (Potsdam, 1933); E. Dent, *H.* (London, 1934); L. Liebeman, *G. F. H. und Halle* (Halle, 1935); E. Müller, ed., *The Letters and Writings of G. F. H.* (London, 1935); C. Williams, *H.* (London, 1935); H. Weinstock, *H.* (N.Y., 1946; 2d ed., rev., 1959); P. Young, *H.* (London, 1946; 3d ed., rev., 1975); W. Smith, *Concerning H., His Life and Works* (London, 1948); A.-E. Cherbuliez, *G. F. H.: Leben und Werk* (Olten, 1949); H. and E. H. Müller von Asow, *G. F. H.: Briefe und Schriften* (Lindau, 1949); O. Deutsch, *H.: A Documentary Biography* (N.Y., 1954, and London, 1955); W. Siegmund-Schultze, *G. F. H.: Leben und Werke* (Leipzig, 1954; 3d ed., rev., 1962); W. Serauky, *G. F. H.: Sein Leben, sein Werk* (only vols. III–V publ.; Kassel, 1956–58); P. Nettl, *G. F. H.* (Berlin, 1958); R. Friedenthal, *G. F. H. in Selbstzeugnissen und Bilddokumenten* (Hamburg, 1959; 3d ed., Reinbeck, 1967); J. Müller-Blattau, *G. F. H.: Der Wille zur Volldendung* (Mainz, 1959); W. Rackwitz and H. Steffens, *G. F. H.: Persönlichkeit, Umwelt, Vermächtnis* (Leipzig, 1962); S. Sadie, *H.* (London, 1962); P. Lang, *G. F. H.* (N.Y., 1966); K. Sasse, *Bildsammlung; Hogarth-Grafik; Darstellung zur Geschichte, H.-pfege und Musikkunde* (Halle, 1967); M. Szentkuthy, *H.* (Budapest, 1967); W. Siegmund-Schultze, ed., *G.F. H.: Beiträge zu seiner Biographie aus dem 18. Jahrhundert* (Leipzig, 1977); C. Hogwood, *H.* (London, 1984); H. C. Robbins Landon, *H. and His World* (Boston, 1984); J. Keates, *H.: The Man and His Music* (London, 1985); W. Rackwitz, *G. F. H.: Lebensbeschreibung in Bildern*

(Wiesbaden, 1986); C. Ludwig, *G. F. H.: Composer of Messiah* (Milford, Mich., 1987); D. Burrows, *H.* (N.Y., 1994); S. Pettitt, *H.* (N.Y., 1994).

CRITICAL, ANALYTICAL (in addition to the writings listed below, important articles may be found in the *H.-Jahrbuch* [1928–33; 1955-]): J. Weissebeck, *Der grosse Musikus H. im Universalruhme* (Nuremberg, 1809); H. Chorley, *H.-Studies* (2 vols., London, 1859); R. Franz, *Über Bearbeitungen älterer Tonwerke, namenlich Bachscher und Händelscher Vokalmusik* (Leipzig, 1871; reprinted by R. Bethge as *Gesammelte Schriften über die Wiederbelebung Bachscher und Händelscher Werke*, Leipzig, 1910); F. Chrysander, *H.s biblische Oratorien in geschichtlicher Betrachtung* (Hamburg, 1897); S. Taylor, *The Indebtedness of H. to Works by Other Composers* (Cambridge, 1906); P. Robinson, *H. and His Orbit* (London, 1908); H. Abert, *H. als Dramatiker* (Göttingen, 1921); E. Bairstow, *The Messiah* (London, 1928); E. Bredenfoerder, *Die Texte der H.-Oratorien* (Leipzig, 1934); E. Völsing, *G. F. H.s englische Kirchenmusik* (Leipzig, 1940); J. Eisenschmidt, *Die szenische Darstellung der Opern H.s auf der Londoner Bühne seiner Zeit* (Wölfenbuttel, 1940–41); J. Herbage, *Messiah* (London, 1948); R. Myers, *H.'s Messiah: A Touchstone of Taste* (N.Y., 1948); P. Young, *The Oratorios of H.* (London, 1949); G. Abraham, ed., *H.: A Symposium* (London, 1954); R. Myers, *H., Dryden and Milton* (London, 1956); J. Larsen, *H.'s Messiah: Origins, Composition, Sources* (London, 1957; 2d ed., rev., 1972); H. Wolff, *Die H.-Oper auf der modernen Bühne* (Leipzig, 1957); W. Dean, *H.'s Dramatic Oratorios and Masques* (London, 1959); H. Shaw, *The Story of H.'s Messiah* (London, 1963); J. Tobin, *H. at Work* (London, 1964); H. Shaw, *A Textual and Historical Companion to H.'s Messiah* (London, 1965); D. Kimbell, *A Critical Study of H.'s Early Operas* (diss., Univ. of Oxford, 1968); W. Dean, *H. and the Opera Seria* (Berkeley, Calif., 1969); J. Tobin, *H.'s Messiah* (London, 1969); H. Friedrichs, *Das Verhältnis von Text und Musik in den Brockespassionen Keisers, H.s, Telemanns und Matthesons* (Munich and Salzburg, 1975); E. Harris, *H. and the Pastoral Tradition* (London, 1980); H. Hoffmann, *G. F. H.: Vom Opernkomponisten zum Meister des Oratoriums* (Marburg an der Lahn, 1983); D. Burrows, *H. and the Chapel Royal* (London, 1984); R. Strohm, *Essays on H. and Italian Opera* (Cambridge, 1985); P. Williams, ed., *Bach, H. and Scarlatti: Tercentenary Essays* (Cambridge, 1985); H. Meynell, *The Art of H.'s Operas* (Lewiston, N.Y., 1986); W. Dean and J. Knapp, *H.'s Operas 1704–1726* (Oxford, 1987); N. Pirrotta and A. Zino, eds., *H. e gli Scarlatti a Roma: Atti del convegno internazionale di studi (Roma, 12–14 giugno 1985)* (Florence, 1987); J. Larsen, *Essays on H., Haydn, and the Viennese Classical Style* (tr. by U. Krämer; Ann Arbor, 1988); S. Sadie and A. Hicks, eds., *H. Tercentenary Collection* (Ann Arbor, 1988); C. Larue, *H. and His Singers: The Creation of the Royal Academy Operas, 1720–1728* (Oxford, 1995).

Handt, Herbert, American tenor and conductor; b. Philadelphia, May 26, 1926. He studied at the Juilliard School of Music in New York and the Vienna Academy of Music, making his operatic debut at the Vienna State Opera (1949). After making his conducting debut in Rome (1960), he prepared performing eds. of rarely heard Italian scores; he later settled in Lucca, where he was founder-director of the Associazione Musicale Lucchese, the Lucca Chamber Orch., and the Marlia International Festival.

Hanfstängel, Marie (née **Schröder**), German soprano; b. Breslau, April 30, 1846; d. Munich, Sept. 5, 1917. She studied at Baden-Baden with Viardot-García, making her debut as Agathe in *Der Freischütz* at the Théâtre-Lyrique in Paris (Feb. 27, 1867). On the declaration of the Franco-Prussian War, she returned to Germany, and was engaged at the Stuttgart Opera (1870). She publ. *Meine Lehrweise der Gesangskunst* (1902).

Hanke, Karl, German composer; b. Rosswald, Silesia, c.1750; d. Flensburg, June 10, 1803. As a young man he was sent to Vienna to pursue his music studies, where he briefly associated himself with Gluck, and profited by the master's advice. He then held the post of music director in Brünn (1778–81), Warsaw (1781–83), and Hamburg (1783–86); was in Schleswig from 1786 to 1792. In 1792 he settled in Flensburg, where he remained until the end of his life. He composed several pieces for the stage; his Singspiel *Der Wunsch mancher Mädchen* (1781), dedicated to Gluck, was performed on various occasions with some success.

Hann, Georg, Austrian bass-baritone; b. Vienna, Jan. 30, 1897; d. Munich, Dec. 9, 1950. He was a student of Lierhammer at the Vienna Academy of Music. From 1927 until his death he was a member of the Bavarian State Opera in Munich; he also made guest appearances in Vienna, Berlin, Salzburg, London, Milan, and Paris. He was noted for such buffo portrayals as Leporello, Nicolai's Falstaff, Kecal, Baron Ochs, and La Roche, which he created (Munich, Oct. 28, 1942); his admired dramatic roles included Sarastro, Pizarro, Amfortas, Gunther, and Rigoletto.

Hannay, Roger D(urham), talented American composer; b. Plattsburg, N.Y., Sept. 22, 1930. He studied composition with F. Morris and D. Newlin at Syracuse Univ. (1948–52), H. Norden at Boston Univ. (1952–53), Rogers and Hanson at the Eastman School of Music in Rochester, N.Y. (1954–56; Ph.D., 1956), and Foss and Copland at the Berkshire Music Center at Tanglewood (summer, 1959); he had sessions with Sessions and attended lectures by Carter at the Princeton Seminar for Advanced Studies (1960). He taught at various colleges; in 1966, joined the music faculty of the Univ. of North Carolina at Chapel Hill, was founder and director of the New Music Ensemble (1967–82), and also served as chairman of the Division of Fine Arts there (1979–82). An unprejudiced and liberal music maker, Hannay makes use of varied functional resources, from neoclassical pandiatonism to dodecaphony; resorts also to the device of "objets trouvés," borrowing thematic materials from other composers.

WORKS: DRAMATIC: *2 Tickets to Omaha, The Swindlers*, chamber opera (1960); *The Fortune of St. Macabre*, chamber opera (1964); *Marshall's Medium Message* for Mod Girl Announcer, Percussion Quartet, 2 Action Painters, Tape, Films, and Slides (1967); *Live and in Color!* for Mod Girl Announcer, Percussion Quartet, 2 Action Painters, Tape, Films, and Slides (1967); *The Inter-Planetary Aleatoric Serial Factory* for Soprano, String Quartet, Rock Band, Actors, Dancers, Tapes, Film, and Slides (1969); *The Journey of Edith Wharton*, opera (1982); *The Nightingale and the Rose*, theater piece (1986); *Dates and Names*, monodrama for Soprano and Piano, after original and adapted texts from *Baker's Biographical Dictionary of Musicians* (1991).

Hanslick, Eduard, greatly renowned Austrian music critic of Czech descent; b. Prague, Sept. 11, 1825; d. Baden, near Vienna, Aug. 6, 1904. He studied law in Prague and Vienna, taking the degree of Dr.Jur. in 1849 and qualifying himself for an official position. But having already studied music under Tomaschek at Prague, in 1848–49 he served as music critic for the *Wiener Zeitung*, and soon adopted a literary career. His first work, *Vom Musikalisch-Schön: Ein Beitrag zur Revision der Aesthetik der Tonkunst* (Leipzig, 1854; Fr. tr., 1877; Span., 1879; Ital., 1884; Eng., 1891; Russ., 1895), brought him worldwide fame. Its leading idea is that the beauty of a musical composition lies wholly and specifically in the music itself; i.e., it is immanent in the relations of the tones, without any reference whatever to extraneous (non-musical) ideas, and can express no others. Such being his point of view through life, it follows logically that he could not entertain sympathy for Wagner's art; his violent opposition to the music-drama was a matter of profound conviction, not personal spite; he in fact wrote a moving tribute after Wagner's death. On the other hand, he was one of the very first and most influential champions of Brahms. From 1855 to 1864 Hanslick was music ed. of the *Presse*; thereafter of the *Neue Freie Press*; he became a lecturer on music history and aesthetics at Vienna Univ., prof. extraordinary in 1861, and full prof. in 1870, retiring in 1895. What gives his writings permanent value is the sound musicianship underlying their brilliant, masterly style. Yet in music history he is chiefly known as a captious and intemperate reviler of genius; Wagner caricatured him in the part of Beckmesser (in any early version of *Die Meistersinger von Nürnberg* the name was to have been Veit Hanslich). A collection of Hanslick's articles in the *Neue*

Freie Presse was publ. in Eng. tr. as *Vienna's Golden Years of Music, 1850–1900* (N.Y., 1950).

WRITINGS: *Geschichte des Concertwesens in Wien* (1869); *Aus dem concertsaal* (1870); a series begun with *Die moderne Oper* (1875) and followed by 8 more vols.: 2, *Musikalische Stationen* (188), 3, *Aus dem Opernleben der Gegenwart* (1884), 4, *Musikalisches Skizzenbuch* (1888), 5, *Musikalisches und Litterarisches* (1889), 6, *Aus dem Tagebuch eines Jahrhunderts* (1899), and 9, *Aus neuer und neuester Zeit* (1900); *Suite, Aufsätze über Musik und Musiker* (1885); *Konzerte, Komponisten und Virtuosen der letzten fünfzehn Jahre* (1886); *Aus menem Leben* (2 vols., 1894).

BIBL.: R. Schafke, *E. H. und die Musikästhetik* (1922); S. Deas, *In Defence of H.* (London, 1940); A. Wilhemer, *Der junge H.* (Klagenfurt, 1959); D. Glatt, *Zur geschichtichlen Bedeutung der Musikästhetik E. H.s* (Munich, 1972); W. Abegg, *Musikästhetik und Musikkritik bei E. H.* (Regensburg, 1974).

Hanson, Howard (Harold), eminent American composer, music educator, and conductor; b. Wahoo, Nebr., Oct. 28, 1896; d. Rochester, N.Y., Feb. 26, 1981. After obtaining a diploma from Luther College in Wahoo (1911), he studied with Goetschius at the Inst. of Musical Art in New York (1914) and with Oldberg and Lutkin at Northwestern Univ. in Evanston, Ill. (B.A., 1916). In 1915–16 he was an assistant teacher at Northwestern Univ. In 1916 he became a teacher of theory and composition at the College of the Pacific in San Jose, California, where he was made dean of its Cons. of Fine Arts in 1919. In 1921 he received the Rome Prize for his *California Forest Play of 1920*. During his stay at the American Academy in Rome, he received training in orchestration from Respighi and composed his first major work, the Sym. No. 1, *Nordic*, which he conducted in its premiere on May 17, 1923. Returning to the United States, he conducted the premiere of his "symbolic" poem *North and West* with the N.Y. Sym. Orch. in Jan. 1924. In subsequent years, Hanson appeared often as a guest conductor throughout the United States and Europe championing not only his own music but numerous scores by other American composers. In 1924 he was appointed director of the Eastman School of Music in Rochester, N.Y., which he molded into one of the outstanding music schools of the United States. As both a music educator and conductor, he proved profoundly influential. He promoted the cause of music education through his energetic work with many national organizations, among them the Music Teachers National Assn., of which he was president (1930–31), the Music Educators National Conference, the National Assn. of Schools of Music, and the National Music Council, of which he was founder-president. From 1925 to 1935 he conducted a series of American Composers' Concerts, and from 1935 to 1971 he was director of the Festivals of American Music. For the 50th anniversary of the Boston Sym. Orch., Hanson was commissioned to compose his Sym. No. 2, *Romantic*. Koussevitzky conducted its premiere on Nov. 28, 1930, and the score remains Hanson's most famous orch. work. His opera *Merry Mount* was first heard in a concert performance under the composer's direction in Ann Arbor on May 20, 1933. It received its stage premiere at the Metropolitan Opera in New York on Feb. 10, 1934. While it failed to find a place in the operatic repertoire, an orch. suite (1936) won favor. Hanson's Sym. No. 4, *The Requiem*, was composed in memory of his father. The composer conducted its first performance with the Boston Sym. Orch. on Dec. 3, 1943. In 1944 it was awarded the Pulitzer Prize in music. Hanson remained as director of the Eastman School of Music until 1964, the year he founded the Inst. of American Music. In 1935 he was elected a member of the National Inst. of Arts and Letters. In 1979 he was elected a member of the American Academy and Inst. of Arts and Letters. He also received many other notable honors, including various awards and numerous honorary doctorates. As a composer, Hanson eschewed serialism and other modern techniques to pursue a neo-Romantic course. While much has been made of the influence of Grieg and especially of Sibelius on his works, his compositions remain basically true to the American spirit. At his most inspired, Hanson's oeuvre displays an array of sonorous harmonies, bold asymmetrical rhythms, and an overall mastery of orchestration one would expect of a remarkable compositional craftsman.

WORKS: DRAMATIC: *California Forest Play of 1920* (1919; Calif. State Redwood Park, July 1920, composer conducting); *Merry Mount*, opera (1933; concert perf., Ann Arbor, May 20, 1933, composer conducting; stage perf., N.Y., Feb. 10, 1934, Serafin conducting; suite, N.Y., March 23, 1936, Iturbi conducting); *Nymphs and Satyr*, ballet (Chautauqua, N.Y., Aug. 9, 1979).

WRITINGS: *Harmonic Materials of Modern Music: Resources of the Tempered Scale* (N.Y., 1960).

BIBL.: R. Watanabe, *Music of H. H.* (Rochester, N.Y., 1966); R. Monroe, *H. H.: American Music Educator* (diss., Florida State Univ., 1970); J. Perone, *H. H.: A Bio-Bibliography* (Westport, Conn., 1993).

Hanssens, Charles-Louis, Belgian cellist, conductor, and composer; b. Ghent, July 12, 1802; d. Brussels, April 8, 1871. As a child of 10 he played in the orch. of the National Theater in Amsterdam. He was 1st cellist of the orch. in the Brussels theater (1824–27), then taught harmony at the Brussels Cons. He subsequently conducted opera at The Hague and in Ghent. From 1848 to 1869 he was conductor at the Théâtre de la Monnaie in Brussels. Among his works are 8 operas and 15 ballets.

BIBL.: L. de Burbure, *Notice sur C.-L. H.* (Antwerp, 1872); L. Bäwolf, *C.-L. H.* (Brussels, 1895).

Hanuš, Jan, Czech composer; b. Prague, May 2, 1915. He became a composition student of Jeremiáš in 1934; he also studied conducting at the Prague Cons. with Dědeček (1935–37; 1939–41). He worked as an ed. in music publishing houses and was active in Czech music organizations. His music is marked by a lyrical Romanticism tinged by stringent dissonant textures. Hanuš completed the instrumentations of the unfinished operas *Tkalci* by Nejedlý and *Balada o lásce* by Doubrava.

WORKS: DRAMATIC: OPERAS: *Plameny* (Flames; 1942–44); *Sluha dvou pánů* (Servant of 2 Masters; 1958); *Pochodeň Prométheova* (Torch of Prometheus; 1961–63); *Pohádka jedné noci* (Story of 1 Night; 1961–68). BALLETS: *Sůl nad zlato* (Salt is Worth More than Gold; 1953); *Othello* (1955–56); *Labyrint* (1981). OTHER: *Ecce Homo*, oratorio (1980).

Harašta, Milan, Czech composer; b. Brno, Sept. 16, 1919; d. there, Aug. 29, 1946. He studied musicology at the Univ. of Brno before taking a course in composition with Kaprál at the Brno Cons. (1938–42). His music, written in a forward-looking, post-Janáček style, included the opera *Nikola Šuhaj* (1941–44).

BIBL.: M. Barík, *M. H.* (Prague, 1956).

Harbison, John (Harris), esteemed American composer, conductor, and teacher; b. Orange, N.J., Dec. 20, 1938. He studied violin, viola, piano, tuba, and voice while attending Princeton (N.J.) High School. During this time, he also profited from advice from Sessions and developed a facility as a jazz pianist. At 16, he won an award in a BMI composition contest. He pursued his education with Piston at Harvard Univ. (B.A., 1960), Blacher at the Berlin Hochschule für Musik (1961), and Sessions and Kim at Princeton Univ. (M.F.A., 1963). He also attended the conducting courses of Carvalho at the Berkshire Music Center in Tanglewood and of Dean Dixon in Salzburg. In 1968–69 he was composer-in-residence at Reed College in Portland, Oreg. In 1969 he joined the faculty of the Mass. Inst. of Technology. He also conducted the Cantata Singers and Ensemble (1969–73; 1980–82), and then the new music group Collage (from 1984). He was composer-in-residence of the Pittsburgh Sym. Orch. (1982–84) and of the Berkshire Music Center in Tanglewood (summer, 1984). After serving as new music advisor of the Los Angeles Phil. (1985–86), he was its composer-in-residence (1986–88). In 1992 he returned to Tanglewood as composer-in-residence, and also served as director of its contemporary music festival. In 1978 he received a Guggenheim fellowship. In 1980 he won the Kennedy Center Friedheim Award for his Piano Concerto. He was awarded the Pulitzer Prize in music in 1986 for his sacred ricercar *The Flight into Egypt*. In 1989 he received a MacArthur fellowship. In 1992 he was elected to membership in the American Academy and Inst. of Arts and Letters. In 1998 he won the Heinz Award in arts and humanities. Harbison's works are distinguished by their outstanding craftsmanship, rhythmic intensity, and lyricism. His experience as a conductor has made him a master of orchestral resources. He has also demonstrated a rare sensitivity in setting vocal texts.

WORKS: DRAMATIC: *The Merchant of Venice*, incidental music to Shakespeare's play (1971; Francestown, N.H., Aug. 12, 1973); *Winter's Tale*, opera (1974; San Francisco, Aug. 20, 1979; rev. 1991); *Full Moon in March*, opera (1977; Cambridge, Mass., April 30, 1979); *Ulysses*, ballet (1983).

Harewood, Sir George (Henry Hubert Lascelles), 7th Earl of, distinguished English arts administrator, music critic, and music editor; b. London, Feb. 7, 1923. He was educated at Eton and King's College, Cambridge. In 1950 he founded the journal *Opera*, of which he was ed. until 1953. He was on the board of directors of the Royal Opera at Covent Garden (1951–53; 1969–72), serving as its administrative executive (1953–60); he was general-director of the Leeds Festival (1958–74), later serving as its chairman (1988–90); he also was director of the Edinburgh Festivals (1961–65), and chancellor of the Univ. of York (1962–67). In 1972 he was appointed managing director of the Sadler's Wells Opera (known after 1974 as the English National Opera) in London; retained this position until 1985, and then was its chairman from 1986. In 1988 he was artistic director of the Adelaide Festival. He was knighted in 1987. He ed. *Kobbé's Complete Opera Book* in 1954, 1963, and 1972; it was publ. as *The New Kobbé's Complete Opera Book* in 1976, then as *The Definitive Kobbé's Opera Book* (1987). His autobiography was publ. as *The Tongs and the Bones* (1982).

Harling, William Franke, English-American composer; b. London, Jan. 18, 1887; d. Sierra Madre, Calif., Nov. 22, 1958. He was taken to the United States in his infancy. He filled various jobs as a church organist. Eventually he settled in Hollywood. He wrote an opera, *A Light from St. Agnes* (Chicago, Dec. 26, 1925), and *Deep River*, a "native opera with jazz" (Lancaster, Pa., Sept. 18, 1926); instrumental music; more than 100 songs. He was also the composer of the march "West Point Forever."

Harman, Carter, American music critic, recording-firm executive, and composer; b. N.Y., June 14, 1918. He studied with Sessions at Princeton Univ. (B.A., 1940) and continued his studies at Columbia Univ. (M.A., 1949). He was a music critic for the *N.Y. Times* (1947–52) and later music ed. of *Time* magazine (1952–57); from 1958 to 1967 he lived in Puerto Rico, where he became president of the West Indies Recording Corp. In 1967 Harman became producer and executive vice president of Composers Recordings, Inc., in New York, devoted mainly to recording contemporary American music; was its executive director from 1976 to 1984. He publ. *A Popular History of Music from Gregorian Chant to Jazz* (N.Y., 1956; rev. 1968). Among his compositions are the ballet *Blackface* (N.Y., May 18, 1947) and 2 children's operas: *Circus at the Opera* (1951) and *Castles in the Sand* (1952).

Harmati, Sândor, Hungarian-born American violinist, conductor, and composer; b. Budapest, July 9, 1892; d. Flemington, N.J., April 4, 1936. He studied at the Royal Academy of Music in Budapest. After serving as concertmaster of the Budapest Sym. Orch., he emigrated to the United States in 1914 and became a naturalized American citizen in 1920. He was a violinist in the Letz (1917–21) and Lenox (1922–25) string quartets, conductor of the Omaha Sym. Orch. (1925–30) and the Musicians' Sym. Orch. for the Unemployed in New York, and prof. of music at Bard College in Annandale-on-Hudson, N.Y. (1934–36). He wrote the opera *Prelude to a Melodrama* (1928) and incidental music to *The Jeweled Tree* (1926).

Harper, Edward (James), English composer, pianist, and teacher; b. Taunton, March 17, 1941. After studies at Christ Church, Oxford (1959–63), he received instruction in composition from Gordon Jacob at the Royal College of Music in London (1963–64) and with Donatoni in Milan (1968). From 1964 he lectured on music at the Univ. of Edinburgh. He also was director of the New Music Group of Scotland (1973–91). His works include the operas *Fanny Robin* (1974; Edinburgh, Feb. 5, 1975), *Hedda Gabler* (1984–85; Glasgow, June 5, 1985), and *The Mellstock Quire* (1987–88; Edinburgh, Feb. 10, 1988).

Harper, Heather (Mary), distinguished Irish soprano; b. Belfast, May 8, 1930. She studied at Trinity College of Music in London and also took voice lessons with Helene Isepp and Frederic Husler. She made her debut as Lady Macbeth with the Oxford Univ. Opera in 1954. She was a member of the English Opera Group (1956–75); she first sang at the Glyndebourne Festival in 1957, at Covent Garden as Helena in *A Midsummer Night's Dream* in 1962, and at the Bayreuth Festival as Elsa in 1967; she also sang in the United States and South America. Although she formally retired as a singer in 1990, she sang with Rattle and the City of Birmingham Sym. Orch. at the London Proms in 1994. From 1985 she was a prof. at the Royal College of Music in London; she also was director of singing studies at the Britten-Pears School in Snape (from 1986) and the first visiting lecturer-in-residence at the Royal Scottish Academy of Music in Glasgow (from 1987). Her notable roles included Arabella, Marguerite, Antonia, Gutrune, Hecuba, Anne Trulove in *The Rake's Progress*, The Woman in *Erwartung*, and Ellen Orford in *Peter Grimes*; she also created the role of Nadia in Tippett's *The Ice Break* (1977). An esteemed concert artist, she sang in the premieres of Britten's *War Requiem* (1962) and Tippett's 3d Sym. (1972). In 1965 she was made a Commander of the Order of the British Empire.

Harrell, Mack, distinguished American baritone; b. Celeste, Texas, Oct. 8,1909; d. Dallas, Jan. 29, 1960. He studied violin and voice at the Juilliard School of Music in New York. In 1938 he made his concert debut at N.Y.'s Town Hall. After winning the Metropolitan Opera Auditions in 1938, he made his debut with the company in New York on Dec. 16, 1939, as Biterolf; he remained on the roster until 1948, and returned there for the 1949–50, 1952–54, and 1957–58 seasons. On May 18, 1944, he made his first appearance at the N.Y. City Opera as Germont, and returned there in 1948, 1951–52, and 1959. He also pursued a notably successful concert career. From 1945 to 1956 he taught voice at the Juilliard School of Music. He publ. *The Sacred Hour of Song* (N.Y., 1938). Harrell's voice was one of remarkable lyrical beauty. Among his operatic roles were Papageno, Kothner, Amfortas, Jochanaan, Wozzeck, and Nick Shadow in *The Rake's Progress*, which role he created in its U.S. premiere at the Metropolitan Opera on Feb. 14, 1953. His son is the outstanding American cellist and teacher Lynn Harrell (b. N.Y., Jan. 30, 1944).

Harrhy, Eiddwen (Mair), Welsh soprano; b. Trowbridge, England, April 14, 1949. She studied at the Royal Manchester College of Music, where she sang Mozart's Despina in 1970. After further training in London and Paris, she made her formal operatic debut as Mozart's Ilia in Oxford in 1974. That same year she appeared at London's Covent Garden as Wellgunde. In 1977 she made her first appearance at the English National Opera in London as Adele in *Le Comte Ory*. She sang for the first time at the Glyndebourne Festival in 1979 as Diana in *La Fedeltà premiata*. In 1986 she sang Berg's Marie at the Welsh National Opera in Cardiff and made her U.S. debut in Los Angeles as Morgana in Handel's *Alcina*. She returned to the English National Opera in 1989 to create the role of Marian Singleton in Blake's *The Plumber's Gift*, and also appeared at the London Promenade Concerts. In 1991 she sang Hecuba in *King Priam* with Opera North in Leeds. She appeared in *Owen Wingrave* at the Glyndebourne Festival in 1997.

Harries, Kathryn, English soprano; b. Hampton Court, Feb. 15, 1951. She was a student of Constance Shacklock at the Royal Academy of Music in London. In 1977 she made her concert debut at London's Royal Festival Hall. Her operatic debut followed in 1982 as Leonore with the Welsh National Opera in Cardiff, where she returned as Sieglinde in 1984 and as Gutrune in 1985. In 1983 she made her first appearance at the English National Opera in London as Irene in *Rienzi*, and returned there in such roles as

Eva, Kát'a Kabanová and Donna Anna. She created the title role in Edward Harper's *Hedda Gabler* at the Scottish Opera in Glasgow in 1985. Her debut at the Metropolitan Opera in New York followed on April 10, 1986, as Kundry, where she returned as Gutrune in 1989. In 1987 she sang Berlioz's Dido in Lyons and Senta at the Paris Opéra. She made her first appearance at London's Covent Garden in 1989 in the British premiere of Berio's *Un re in ascolto*, and returned there in 1991 as Gutrune. Following engagements as Dido in Brussels and as Carmen in Orange in 1992, she appeared as Brangäne at the Scottish Opera in 1994. In 1997 she sang Kundry at the Opéra de la Bastille in Paris.

Harris, Sir Augustus (Henry Glossop), celebrated English operatic impresario; b. Paris, 1852; d. Folkestone, June 22, 1896. He was an assistant manager to Mapleson before becoming a prominent figure in London operatic circles. In 1879 he became lessee of the Drury Lane Theatre. In 1883 he brought the Carl Rosa Opera Co. to London and managed its seasons until 1887. In 1887–88 he oversaw his own Italian opera season before becoming manager of Covent Garden in 1888. He presented brilliant seasons of opera at Covent Garden, whose audiences were exposed to operas in the original language. Among the famous artists he engaged were Melba, the de Reszkes, Maurel, and Mahler. He did much to promote the cause of Wagner's music. In 1891 he was knighted.

Harris, Donald, American composer and music educator; b. St. Paul, Minn., April 7, 1931. He was a student of Paul Wilkinson in St. Paul, of Ross Lee Finney at the Univ. of Mich. at Ann Arbor (B.Mus., 1952; M.Mus., 1952), and of Max Deutsch in Paris. He also studied with Boulanger in Paris, Blacher and Foss at the Berkshire Music Center in Tanglewood (summers, 1954–55), and Jolivet at the Centre Français d'Humanisme Musical in Aix-en-Provence (1960). From 1968 to 1977 he held administrative posts at the New England Cons. of Music in Boston. In 1977 he became prof. of music at the Hartt School of Music at the Univ. of Hartford, where he was chairman of the composition and theory dept. (1977–80) and then dean of the school (1980–88). In 1988 he became dean of the College of the Arts at Ohio State Univ. in Columbus, where he also was a prof. (from 1988) and acting director (1989–91) of the School of Music. From 1994 to 1996 he also served as president of the International Council of Fine Arts Deans. With C. Hailey and J. Brand, he ed. *The Berg-Schoenberg Correspondence* (N.Y., 1987), which won the ASCAP/Deems Taylor Award in 1989. In 1956 he received a Fulbright scholarship. In 1962 he won the Prince Rainier III of Monaco Composition Award. He held a Gugggenheim fellowship in 1966. From 1973 he received annual ASCAP awards. In 1974 he received an NEA fellowship grant. He received an award from the American Academy and Inst. of Arts and Letters in 1991. As a composer, he follows the trends of the cosmopolitan avant-garde.

WORKS: DRAMATIC: *The Legend of John Henry*, ballet (1954; rev. 1979); *The Golden Deer*, ballet (1955); *Intervals*, dance piece (1959); *The Little Mermaid*, opera (1985–95); *Twelfth Night*, incidental music to Shakespeare's play (1989).

Harrison, Julius (Allan Greenway), English conductor, composer, and teacher; b. Stourport, Worcestershire, March 26, 1885; d. Harpenden, Hertfordshire, April 5, 1963. He studied with Bantock in Birmingham and at the Midland Inst. In 1913 he conducted for the first time at London's Covent Garden; after serving as conductor of the Scottish Orch. in Glasgow (1920–23), he was a conductor with the Beecham Opera Co. and the British National Opera Co. in London (1922–27); he subsequently was conductor of the Hastings Municipal Orch. (1930–40) and a prof. of composition at the Royal Academy of Music in London. His music was principally influenced by Elgar. Among his compositions is the opera *The Canterbury Pilgrims*.

BIBL.: G. Self, *J. H. and the Importunate Muse* (Brookfield, 1993).

Harrison, Lou (Silver), inventive American composer and performer; b. Portland, Oreg., May 14, 1917. He studied with Cowell in San Francisco (1934–35) and with Schoenberg at the Univ. of Calif. at Los Angeles (1941). From 1945 to 1948 he was a music critic for the *N.Y. Herald-Tribune*; he was also an active promoter of contemporary music, including the works of Ives, Ruggles, Varèse, and Cowell; he prepared for publication Ives's 3d Sym., and conducted its premiere (N.Y., April 5, 1946). He taught at Reed College in Portland, Oreg. (1949–50) and at Black Mountain College in North Carolina (1951–52). In 1952 and 1954 he held Guggenheim fellowships. In 1961 he visited the Far East. In 1963 he served as the senior scholar at the East-West Center of the Univ. of Hawaii. From 1967 to 1980 he taught at San Jose State Univ., and from 1980 to 1985 at Mills College in Oakland, California. In 1983 he was a senior Fulbright scholar in New Zealand. Harrison's extensive output reflects his belief that the entire sound world is open to the creative musician. He has made use of both Western and non-Western musical traditions. He has demonstrated a preoccupation with pitch relations, most notably just intonation. In some of his works, he has utilized non-Western instruments or folk instruments, and he has also constructed various instruments of his own invention. He has even been bold enough to explore the use of unconventional "instruments," such as flowerpots, washtubs, and packing cases. Whatever the resources used, Harrison molds them into his own eclectic style in which melody and rhythm predominate.

WORKS: DRAMATIC: OPERAS: *Rapunzel* (Rome, 1954); *Young Caesar*, puppet opera (Aptos, Calif., Aug. 21, 1971). THEATER PIECE: *Jeptha's Daughter* (1940–63; Aptos, Calif., March 9, 1963). DANCE SCORES: *Changing World* (1936); *Green Mansions* (1939); *Something to Please Everybody* (1939); *Johnny Appleseed* (1940); *Omnipotent Chair* (1940); *Orpheus* (1941–69); *Perilous Chapel* (1948); *Western Dance* (1948); *The Marriage at the Eiffel Tower* (1949); *The Only Jealousy of Emer* (1949); *Solstice* (1949); *Almanac of the Seasons* (1950); *Io and Prometheus* (1951); *Praises for Hummingbirds and Hawks* (1951). Also incidental music to plays and film scores.

WRITINGS: *About Carl Ruggles* (N.Y., 1946); *Music Primer: Various Items About Music to 1970* (N.Y., 1971); with others, *Soundings: Ives, Ruggles, Varèse* (Santa Fe, N.M., 1974); P. Garland, ed., *A Lou Harrison Reader* (Santa Fe, N.M., 1987).

BIBL.: V. Rathbun, *L. H. and his Music* (thesis, San Jose State Univ., 1976); L. Miller and F. Lieberman, *L. H.: Composing a World* (Oxford and N.Y., 1998).

Harrison, William, English tenor and operatic impresario; b. London, June 15, 1813; d. there, Nov. 9, 1868. He was trained at the Royal Academy of Music in London. On May 2, 1839, he made his operatic debut at London's Covent Garden in Rooke's *Henrique*. He then sang at London's Drury Lane, where he created roles in works by Balfe (*The Bohemian Girl*, 1844), Benedict (*The Brides of Venice*, 1844, and *The Crusaders*, 1846), and Wallace (*Maritana*, 1845). In 1854 he made a concert tour of the United States. With the soprano Louisa Pyne, he organized the Pyne-Harrison English Opera Co. in 1856. It presented performances at Covent Garden (1858–64), premiering works by Balfe, Benedict, Wallace, and other British composers.

Harsanyi, Janice (née **Morris**), American soprano and teacher; b. Arlington, Mass., July 15, 1929. She studied at Westminster Choir College in Princeton, N.J. (B.Mus., 1951) and at the Philadelphia Academy of Vocal Arts (1952–54). In 1954 she launched her career, concentrating on appearances as a soloist with orchs. and as a recitalist; she also sang in opera, becoming especially well known for her championship of contemporary music. She taught voice (1951–63) and was chairman of the voice dept. (1963–65) at Westminster Choir College; she also lectured on music at the Princeton Theological Seminary (1956–63). After serving as artist-in-residence at the Interlochen (Mich.) Arts Academy (1967–70), she taught voice at the North Carolina School of the Arts in Winston-Salem (1971–78) and at Salem College (1973–76). She was prof. of voice at Florida State Univ. in Tallahassee from 1979. In 1952 she married the Hungarian-born American conductor and teacher Nicholas Harsanyi (b. Budapest, Dec. 17, 1913; d. Tallahassee, July 19, 1987).

Harsányi, Tibor, Hungarian composer; b. Magyarkanizsa, June 27, 1898; d. Paris, Sept. 19, 1954. He studied at the Budapest Academy of Music with Kodály; in 1923 he settled in Paris, where he devoted himself to composition. The melodic material of his music stems from Hungarian folk melos; his harmonic idiom is largely polytonal; the rhythms are sharp, often with jazzlike syncopation; the form remains classical.

WORKS: DRAMATIC: OPERAS: *Les Invités*, chamber opera (Gera, Germany, 1930); *Illusion*, radio opera (Paris, June 28, 1949). BALLETS: *Le Dernier Songe* (Budapest, Jan. 27, 1920); *Pantins* (Paris, 1938); *Chota Roustaveli* (Monte Carlo, 1945; in collaboration with A. Honegger and A. Tcherepnin); *L'Amour et la vie* (1951). OTHER: *L'Histoire du petit tailleur*, puppet show for 7 Instruments and Percussion (1939).

Harshaw, Margaret, outstanding American mezzo-soprano, later soprano; b. Narberth, Pa., May 12, 1909; d. Libertyville, Ill., Nov. 7, 1997. She studied in Philadelphia and then was a scholarship student at the Juilliard Graduate School of Music in New York, where she studied voice with Anna Schoen-René, graduating in 1942. Shortly after graduation, she won the Metropolitan Opera Auditions of the Air and made her debut with the company in New York as a mezzo-soprano in the role of the 2d Norn in *Gotterdämmerung* on Nov. 25, 1942; she subsequently sang contralto and mezzo-soprano roles in German, Italian, and French operas; she also acquitted herself brilliantly as a dramatic soprano in her debut appearance in that capacity as Senta at the Metropolitan Opera on Nov. 22, 1950; was particularly successful in Wagnerian roles; she sang Isolde, Sieglinde, Kundry, Elisabeth, and all 3 parts of Brünnhilde. She also excelled as Donna Anna in *Don Giovanni* and Leonore in Beethoven's *Fidelio*. She was a guest soloist with the opera companies of Philadelphia, Cincinnati, San Francisco, and Covent Garden in London, and at the Glyndebourne Festivals. On March 10, 1964, she made her farewell appearance at the Metropolitan Opera as Ortrud. In 1962 she joined the faculty of the Indiana Univ. School of Music in Bloomington, where she taught voice until retiring in 1993.

Hart, Fritz (Bennicke), English conductor and composer; b. Brockley, Kent, Feb. 11, 1874; d. Honolulu, July 9, 1949. He studied at the Royal College of Music in London (1893–96). In 1908 he went to Australia and in 1915 became director of the Melbourne Cons.; in 1927 he was appointed joint artistic director of the Melbourne Sym. Orch.; he conducted the Honolulu Sym. Orch. (1932 until his death); he settled in Honolulu in 1936 when appointed prof. of music at the Univ. of Hawaii; retired in 1942. He wrote operas, operettas, orch. works, chamber music, choruses, and over 500 songs.

Hart, James, English bass and composer; b. York, 1647; d. London, May 8, 1718. He was a singer in York Minster until 1670. He was then appointed Gentleman of the Chapel Royal and lay-vicar of Westminster Abbey. He settled in London and composed songs, publ. in *Choice Ayres and Songs* (1673–84), *The Theater of Music* (1685–87), *Banquet of Musick* (1688–90), and *Comes amoris* (1687–94). He wrote *Adieu to the pleasures and follies of love* for Shadwell's operatic adaptation of *The Tempest* (1674), publ. as one of 6 "Ariel's Songs."

Hart, Lorenz (Milton), American lyricist; b. N.Y., May 2, 1895; d. there, Nov. 22, 1943. He began as a student of journalism at Columbia Univ. (1914–17); then turned to highly successful theatrical writing. During his 24-year collaboration with Richard Rodgers, he wrote the lyrics for *Connecticut Yankee* (1927); *On Your Toes* (1936); *Babes in Arms* (1937); *The Boys from Syracuse* (1938); *I Married an Angel* (1938); *Too Many Girls* (1939); *Pal Joey* (1940); *By Jupiter* (1942). Some of their best songs ("Manhattan," "Here in My Arms," "My Heart Stood Still," "Small Hotel," "Blue Moon," "Where or When," "I Married an Angel") are publ. in the album *Rodgers & Hart Songs* (N.Y., 1951).

BIBL.: S. Marx and J. Clayton, *Rodgers and H.* (N.Y., 1976); D. Hart, *Thou Swell, Thou Witty: The Life and Lyrics of L. H.* (N.Y., 1976); F. Nolan, *L. H.: A Poet on Broadway* (Oxford, 1994).

Hartig, Heinz (Friedrich), German composer; b. Kassel, Sept. 10, 1907; d. Berlin, Sept. 16, 1969. He studied piano at the Kassel Cons., and musicology at the Univ. of Vienna. Unable to hold a teaching post under the Nazi regime, he occupied himself with performances as a harpsichord player; in 1948 he joined the Hochschule für Musik in Berlin. In his compositions, he applied varied techniques of modern music, from neoclassicism to serialism, with formal unity achieved by the principle of free variations. He wrote a ballet, *Schwarze Sonne* (1958), and a chamber opera, *Escorial* (1961).

BIBL.: W. Burde, *H. H.* (Berlin, 1967).

Hartmann, family of eminent Danish musicians of German descent:

(1) Johann Ernst (Joseph) Hartmann, violinist and composer; b. Gross Clogau, Silesia, Dec. 24, 1726; d. Copenhagen, Oct. 21, 1793. He was a member of the orch. of the Prince-Bishop of Breslau (1754–57). In 1761 he was at the Rudolstadt court and at the ducal court in Plön Holstein, where he became Konzertmeister. He then was a member of Sarti's Italian opera orch. in Copenhagen (1762–64), where he settled as a member of the Royal Chapel (1766), becoming 1st violinist (1767) and music director (1768). He is recognized as the founder of the Danish national school of Romantic opera. His most notable Singspiels, among the many composed for the Royal Theater, are *Balders død* (The Death of Balder; Copenhagen, Jan. 30, 1779) and *Fiskene* (The Fishermen; Copenhagen, Jan. 31, 1780); the latter includes the final stanza of the Danish national anthem, *Kong Christian stod ved højen mast*; however, the present melody was not in the original score, so Hartmann may not have composed it. Most of his other MSS were destroyed in the Christiansborg Palace fire of 1794. He prepared a *Violin-Schule* (MS, 1777).

(2) August Wilhelm Hartmann, violinist, organist, and composer, son of the preceding; b. Copenhagen, Nov. 6, 1775; d. there, Nov. 15, 1850. He studied with his father. He was 1st violinist in the Royal Chapel (1796–1817) and then organist and choirmaster at Copenhagen's Garnisonskirke (1817–24).

(3) Johann Peter Emilius Hartmann, celebrated organist and composer, son of the preceding; b. Copenhagen, May 14, 1805; d. there, March 10, 1900. He studied piano, organ, violin, and theory with his father, and began to compose when still a child. He succeeded his father as organist at Copenhagen's Garnisonskirke (1824), and then studied law at the Univ. of Copenhagen (graduated, 1828). While retaining a government post (1828–70), he pursued an active career as a musician. He joined the faculty of Siboni's cons. in 1827 and helped to organize the Musikforening in 1836; he also was active with the Studentersanforening from 1839, serving as its president from 1868. He expanded his musical horizons with trips abroad; he visited Germany, Switzerland, Austria, and France in 1836, meeting such famous musicians as Marschner, Cherubini, Chopin, Rossini, Paër, Spohr, and Spontini; met Franz Berwald and Clara Wieck in Berlin and Mendelssohn and Schumann in Leipzig in 1839. He won the critical admiration of Schumann, who wrote about him in the pages of the *Neue Zeitschrift für Musik*; subsequently met Liszt in Hamburg in 1841. He was a guest conductor with the Leipzig Gewandhaus Orch. in 1844. He was appointed organist of Vor Frue Kirke, Copenhagen's cathedral, in 1843, and continued in that capacity until his death. He was also a founder of the Copenhagen Cons. (1866), serving as joint director with Gade (his son-in-law) and Paulli. As the leading representative of the Danish Romantic movement in music, he was held in the greatest esteem by his countrymen; he received an honorary Ph.D. from the Univ. of Copenhagen in 1874.

WORKS: DRAMATIC: OPERAS: *Ravnen, eller Broderprøven* (The Raven, or The Brother Test; Copenhagen, Oct. 29, 1832; rev. version, Copenhagen, April 23, 1865); *Korsarerne* (The Corsairs; Copenhagen, April 23, 1835); *Liden Kirsten* (Little Christina; Copenhagen, May 12, 1846; rev. version, Copenhagen, Oct. 29, 1858). BALLETS: *Et folkesagn* (A Folk Tale; Copenhagen, March 20, 1854; in collaboration with Gade); *Valkyrien* (Copenhagen, Sept. 13, 1861); *Thrymskviden* (The Legend of Thrym; Copenhagen, Feb. 21, 1868); *Arcona* (Copenhagen, May 7, 1875). Also a melodrama, *Guldhornene* (The Golden Horns; 1834), and incidental music to more than 15 plays.

BIBL.: W. Behrend, *J. P. E. H.* (Copenhagen, 1895); A. Hammerich, *J. P. E. H.: Biografiske essays* (Copenhagen, 1916); W. Behrend, *J. P. E. H.* (Copenhagen, 1918); R. Hove, *J. P. E. H.* (Copenhagen, 1934); V. Bitsch, *J. P. E. H.* (Hellerup, 1955).

(4) Emil (Wilhelm Emilius Zinn) Hartmann, organist and composer, son of the preceding; b. Copenhagen, Feb. 21, 1836; d. there, July 18, 1898. He studied organ and theory with his father and piano with Anton Ree; he later studied in Leipzig. He began composing songs as a child. His first mature work was the *Passionssalme* (1858), followed by the ballet *Fjeldstuen* (The Mountain Cottage; Copenhagen, May 13, 1859), written in collaboration with his brother-in-law August Winding. Although he continued to write for the stage, he became best known as a composer of instrumental music. He was organist of St. John's (1861–71) and of the Christiansborg Palace Church (1871–98).

WORKS (all 1st perf. in Copenhagen): DRAMATIC: OPERAS: *En nat mellem fjeldene* (A Night in the Mountains; April 11, 1863); *Elverpigen* (The Elf Girl; Nov. 5, 1867); *Korsikaneren* (The Corsican; April 7, 1873); *Ragnhild* (Runic Spell; 1896); *Det store lod* (The Big Prize; 1897; probably not perf.). BALLETS: *Fjeldstuen* (The Mountain Cottage; May 13, 1859; in collaboration with A. Winding); *En bryllupsfest i Hardanger* (A Wedding Feast in Hardanger; 1897; not perf.).

Hartmann, Carl, German tenor; b. Solingen, May 2, 1895; d. Munich, May 30, 1969. He was a student in Düsseldorf of Senff. In 1928 he made his operatic debut as Tannhäuser in Elberfeld, and then toured the United States as a member of Gadski's opera company in 1930. After appearing with the Cologne Opera (1933–35), he sang in Berlin and Vienna, and also made guest appearances in Italy, France, and Switzerland. On Dec. 3, 1937, he made his Metropolitan Opera debut in New York as Siegfried, and remained on its roster until 1940; in 1938 he sang Tristan at the Bayreuth Festival. He was principally known as a Wagnerian.

Hartmann, Karl Amadeus, outstanding German composer; b. Munich, Aug. 2, 1905; d. there, Dec. 5, 1963. He was a student of Haas at the Munich Academy of Music (1923–27) and later of Scherchen. His first major composition was his Trumpet Concerto of 1933. During the Third Reich, he withdrew from public life and forbade the performance of his music. His defiance of the Nazi regime was manifested in his *Concerto funebre* for Violin and String Orch. (1939), composed in tribute to Czechoslovakia in the wake of its dismemberment; the score is notable for its metamorphosis, in the minor, of the famous Hussite chorale *Ye Who are God's Warriors*. In 1941–42 Hartmann pursued advanced training in composition and analysis with Webern in Vienna. After the defeat of the Third Reich in 1945, he organized the Musica Viva concerts for new music in Munich. In 1948 he received a prize from the city of Munich and in 1952 was elected to membership in the German Academy of Fine Arts. Despite his acceptance of a highly chromatic, atonal idiom and his experimentation in the domain of rhythm (patterned after Blacher's "variable meters"), Hartmann retained the orthodox form and structural cohesion of basic Classicism. He was excessively critical of his early works, and discarded many of them, some of which were retrieved and performed after his death.

WORKS: DRAMATIC: 5 small operas under the collective title of *Wachsfigurenkabinett* (1929–30; 1, *Leben und Sterben des heiligen Teufels*; 2, *Der Mann, der vom Tode auferstand*, completed by G. Bialas and H.W. Henze; 3, *Chaplin-Ford-Trott*, completed by W. Hiller; 4, *Fürwahr . . . ?!*, completed by H. W. Henze; 5, *Die Witwe von Ephesus)*; chamber opera, *Des Simplicius Simplicissimus Jugend* (1934–35; Cologne, Oct. 20, 1949; rev. 1955 as *Simplicius Simplicissimus)*.

BIBL.: A. McCredie, *K. A. H.* (Wilhelmshaven, 1980); R. Wagner, ed., *K. A. H. und die Musica Viva* (Mainz, 1980); A. McCredie, ed., *K. A. H.: Thematic Catalogue of His Works* (Wilhelmshaven, 1982).

Hartmann, Rudolf, German opera director and administrator; b. Ingolstadt, Oct. 11, 1900; d. Munich, Aug. 26, 1988. He was trained in stage design in Munich and was a student of Berg-Ehlert in Bamberg. He was an opera director in Altenburg (1924–27), Nuremberg (1928–34; 1946–52), the Berlin State Opera (1934–37), and the Bavarian State Opera in Munich (1937–44); from 1952 to 1967 he was the Bavarian Staatsintendant. He was especially known for his staging of works by Richard Strauss, and was chosen to stage the premieres of Strauss's *Friedenstag* (Munich, 1938) and *Capriccio* (Munich, 1942); he also directed the official premiere of Strauss's *Der Liebe der Danae* (Salzburg, 1952). In his stagings he fused the best of traditional elements with contemporary stage practices. He publ. an autobiography as *Das geliebte Haus: Mein Leben mit der Oper* (Munich, 1975). His other writings included *Oper: Regie und Bühnenbild heute* (Stuttgart, 1977) and *Richard Strauss: Die Bühnenwerke von der Uraufführung bis heute* (Munich and Fribourg, 1980; Eng. tr., 1982, as *Richard Strauss: The Staging of His Operas and Ballets)*. His correspondence with Strauss was ed. by R. Schlötterer as *Richard Strauss—Rudolf Hartmann: Ein Briefwechsel* (Tutzing, 1984).

Hartmann, Thomas (Alexandrovich de), Russian composer; b. Khoruzhevka, Ukraine, Sept. 21, 1885; d. Princeton, N.J., March 26, 1956. He studied piano with Essipova and composition with Taneyev and Arensky at the St. Petersburg Cons. His first important work, the ballet *The Little Crimson Flower*, was premiered at the Imperial Theater in St. Petersburg on Dec. 16, 1907, with Pavlova, Karsavina, Nijinsky, and Fokine. After the Revolution, he went to the Caucasus; taught at the Tiflis Cons. (1919); then went to Paris, where he remained until 1951, when he settled in New York. His early music is in the Russian national style, influenced particularly by Mussorgsky; from about 1925, he made a radical change in his style of composition, adopting many devices of outspoken modernism. His other works include the opera *Esther* (not perf.). and the ballet *Babette* (Nice, March 10, 1935). He also composed music to Kandinsky's *The Yellow Sound* (arranged by G. Schuller; N.Y., Feb. 9, 1982).

Härtwig, Dieter, distinguished German musicologist; b. Dresden, July 18, 1934. He was a student of Besseler, Serauky, Wolff, and Eller at the Univ. of Leipzig (Ph.D., 1963, with the diss. *Der Opernkomponist Rudolf Wagner-Régeny: Leben und Werk*; publ. in Berlin, enl. ed., 1965 as *Rudolf Wagner-Régeny: Der Opernkomponist*; Habilitation, 1970, with his *Fidelio F. Finke: Leben und Werk)*. He was a dramaturg at the theaters in Schwerin (1959–60) and Dresden-Radebeul (1960–65), and then was chief dramaturg of the Dresden Phil. (from 1965). He also was a lecturer (1960–62; 1973–80), Dozent (1980–84), and prof. (1984–91) of music history at the Dresden Hochschule für Musik.

WRITINGS: *Die Dresdner Philharmonie: Eine Chronik des Orchesters 1870 bis 1970* (Leipzig, 1970); *Kurt Masur* (Leipzig, 1975); *Die Dresdner Philharmonie* (Leipzig, 1985; 2d ed., 1989; new ed., Berlin, 1992); *Carl Maria von Weber* (Leipzig, 1986; 2d ed., 1989).

Harvey, Jonathan (Dean), significant English composer; b. Sutton Coldfield, Warwickshire, May 3, 1939. He was a scholarship student at St. John's College, Cambridge, and also received private instruction from Erwin Stein and Hans Keller; after obtaining his Ph.D. from the Univ. of Glasgow (1964), he attended the Darmstadt summer courses in new music (1966) and studied with Babbitt at Princeton Univ. He taught at the Univ. of Southampton (1964–77) and at the Univ. of Sussex (from 1977). In 1985 he received the Koussevitzky Foundation Award. In his ultimate style of composition, he astutely synthesized a number of quaquaversal idioms and techniques ranging from medieval modalities to ultramodern procedures, occasionally making use of electronic resources. Among his works are *Passion and Resurrection*, church opera (Winchester Cathedral, March 21, 1981), and *Inquest of Love,* opera (1992).

Harwood, Elizabeth (Jean), English soprano; b. Barton Seagrave, May 27, 1938; d. Ingatestone, June 21, 1990. She studied at the Royal Manchester College of Music (1955–60). In 1960 she won the Kathleen Ferrier Memorial Prize and in 1963 the Verdi Prize of Busseto. She made her operatic debut in 1960 as the 2d boy in *Die Zauberflöte* at the Glyndebourne Festival, and returned there to sing Fiordiligi, Countess Almaviva, and the Marschallin. In 1961 she became a member of the Sadler's Wells Opera in London, where she appeared as Susanna, Zerbinetta, and Massenet's Manon. In 1967 she made her first appearance at London's Covent Garden as Fiakermilli, and returned there to sing such roles as Marzelline, Gilda, Norina, and Donna Elvira; she also sang at Glasgow's Scottish Opera (1967–74). In 1970 she sang for the first time at the Salzburg Festival and in 1972 at Milan's La Scala. On Oct. 15, 1975, she made her Metropolitan Opera debut in New York as Fiordiligi, remaining on the roster for that season; she returned for the 1977–78 season. In 1986 she made a tour of Australia. Among her other roles were Constanze, Lucia, Musetta, Sophie, and Hanna Glawari.

Häser, August Ferdinand, German composer, brother of **Charlotte (Henriette) Häser**; b. Leipzig, Oct. 15, 1779; d. Weimar, Nov. 1, 1844. He was educated at the Thomasschule in Leipzig, and studied theology at Leipzig Univ. In 1817 he was engaged in Weimar as music teacher to Princess Augusta (the future German empress); he also conducted the chorus at the Court Opera there and was a church organist and a teacher of Italian. He publ. *Versuch einer systematischen Übersicht der Gesanglehre* (Leipzig, 1822) and *Chorgesangschule für Schul- und Theaterchöre* (Mainz, 1831). He composed 3 operas and an oratorio, *Die Kraft des Glaubens.*

Häser, Charlotte (Henriette), German soprano, sister of **August Ferdinand Häser**; b. Leipzig, June 24, 1784; d. Rome, May 1, 1871. She studied with her father, the composer Johann Georg Häser (1729–1809), then sang in Dresden. In 1806 she went to Italy, where she enjoyed tremendous success; she was also one of the first women to sing male roles. After she left the stage, she settled in Rome.

Hass, Sabine, German soprano; b. Braunschweig, April 8, 1949. She received vocal training in Berlin and Munich. In 1970 she made her operatic debut in Stuttgart as Pamina, where she continued to sing regularly. In 1976 she appeared for the first time at the Bavarian State Opera in Munich and at the Vienna State Opera. Following an engagement as Reiza in *Oberon* at the Bregenz Festival in 1977, she sang in various European festivals and opera houses. In 1983 she made her debut at Milan's La Scala as Isabella in *Das Liebesverbot.* She made her Metropolitan Opera debut in New York on Jan. 4, 1986, as Elsa. In 1988 she appeared in the title role in *Die Liebe der Danae* at the Munich Festival, and also portrayed Sieglinde at the Berlin Deutsche Oper. Following engagements in Seattle and Paris as Leonore in 1989, she sang Senta at the Bayreuth Festival in 1991. In 1992 she portrayed Wagner's Elisabeth in Berlin and his Brünnhilde in *Götterdammerung* in Bologna. She appeared as Strauss's Empress in Florence in 1993, the same year she sang his Dyer's Wife at the Théâtre du Châtelet and Wagner's Senta at the Opéra de la Bastille in Paris. In 1997 she was engaged as Elektra in Rome.

Hasse, Faustina (née **Bordoni**), famous Italian mezzo-soprano; b. Venice, c.1700; d. there, Nov. 4, 1781. She found patrons in Alessandro and Benedetto Marcello, who entrusted her vocal training to M. Gasparini. She made her debut in Pollarolo's *Ariodante* in Venice in 1716, and then entered the service of the Elector Palatine. In addition to appearances in Venice until 1725, she also sang in Reggio (1719), Modena (1720), Bologna (1721–22), Naples (1721–23), and Rome (1722). She made her first appearance in Germany in P. Torri's Griselda in Munich in 1723 with notable success, returning in 1724, 1728, and 1729. She created a number of roles in operas by Handel, including Rossane in *Alessandro* (London debut, May 5, 1726), Alcestis in *Ameto* (Jan. 31, 1727), Pulcheria in *Riccardo Primo* (Nov. 11, 1727), Emira in *Siroe* (Feb. 17, 1728), and Elisa in *Tolomeo* (April 30, 1728). Her rivalry with Cuzzoni became a public scandal, culminating in a physical altercation during a performance of *Astianatte* on June 6, 1727. Her other performances were in Florence (1728–29), Parma (1729–30), Turin (1729, 1731), Venice (1729–32), Milan (1730), and Rome (1731). She sang in the premieres of **Johann Adolf Hasse**'s *Dalisa* and *Arminio* in Venice in 1730, and married the composer that same year. Her career thereafter was closely related to her husband's, and she frequently appeared in his operatic and concert works. In 1731 they were called to the Saxon court in Dresden, where she became prima donna assoluta and her husband Kapellmeister; she also made frequent visits to Italy to sing in the principal music centers. She made her farewell stage appearance in the premiere performance of her husband's *Ciro riconosciuto* in Dresden on Jan. 20, 1751. She continued to receive her salary of 3,000 thaler and retained her title of virtuosa da camera until 1763, when she and her husband were dismissed by the new elector. They lived in Vienna until 1773, and then retired to Venice. According to contemporary accounts, she possessed one of the finest voices of the day. She also possessed great physical beauty, which greatly enhanced her dramatic gifts.

BIBL.: A. Niggli, *F. B.-H.* (Leipzig, 1880); M. Hogg, *Die Gesangskunst der F. H. und das Sängerinnenwesen ihrer Zeit in Deutschland* (Berlin, 1931).

Hasse, Johann Adolf, celebrated German composer; b. Bergedorf, near Hamburg (baptized), March 25, 1699; d. Venice, Dec. 16, 1783. He studied in Hamburg (1714–17), and then was engaged as a tenor at the Opera there (1718); he was a member of the Braunschweig Opera (1719–21), where he sang in the premiere of his opera *Antioco* (Aug. 11, 1721). He then went to Naples, where he studied with A. Scarlatti. The success of his serenata *Antonio e Cleopatra* (Naples, Sept. 1725), sung by the famous castrato Farinelli and Vittoria Tesi, brought him a commission from the Teatro San Bartolomeo. There he produced his opera *Il Sesostrate* (Naples, May 13, 1726), which launched his career as a major dramatic composer. His *Artaserse* (Venice, Feb. 1730) was a particular favorite of Farinelli, who was later called upon to sing the arias *Per questo dolce amplesso* and *Pallido il sole* while in the service of the ailing King Philip V of Spain (1737–46). Hasse married **Faustina Hasse** (née **Bordoni**) in 1730, the same year in which she sang in the premieres of his *Dalisa* and *Arminio* in Venice. He went to the Saxon court in Dresden in 1731 as Kapellmeister; his wife joined him there as prima donna. His first opera for Dresden was *Cleofide* (Sept. 13, 1731). As his fame increased, the court allowed him frequent leaves of absence to produce his operas in other major music centers, often with his wife singing leading roles. He scored a major success with *Seroe, rè de Persia* (Bologna, May 2, 1733). His admiration for the renowned librettist Metastasio led to their remarkable personal and professional relationship from 1743. During this period, Hasse was acknowledged as the preeminent composer of opera seria in Germany, Austria, and Italy. Although Porpora served the Dresden court as Kapellmeister from 1748 to 1751, Hasse succeeded in maintaining his own position and was elevated to the post of Oberkapellmeister in 1750. His wife made her farewell appearance in opera in the premiere of his *Ciro riconosciuto* (Jan. 20, 1751). His *Solimano* (Feb. 5, 1753), with its huge cast of singers, actors, and even animals, proved a major court event. His last opera written for Dresden was *L'Olimpiade* (Feb. 16, 1756); he remained in the court's service until the advent of the new elector in 1763. In the meantime, he found an appreciative court in Vienna, where he produced the operas *Alcide al bivio* (Oct. 8, 1760), *Zenobia* (Carnival 1761), and *Il trionfo di Clelia* (April 27, 1762). Following the success of these works, he settled in Vienna; after bringing out his opera *Egeria* there (April 24, 1764), he wrote *Romolo ed Ersilia* for the Innsbruck court (Aug. 6, 1765). His success in Vienna continued with the productions of his *Partenope* (Sept. 9, 1767) and *Piramo e Tisbe* (Nov. 1768). But his *Il Ruggiero ovvero L'eroica gratitudine* (Milan, Oct. 16, 1771) failed to please the Italian public, and he decided to cease composing for the stage. In 1773 he retired to Venice. Hasse was a master of bel canto writing; his extraordinary craftsmanship is revealed in his command of harmony and orchestration; in addition to his dramatic works, he also distinguished himself as a composer of sacred music.

WORKS: DRAMATIC: OPERAS: *Antioco* (Braunschweig, Aug. 11, 1721); *Antonio e Cleopatra*, serenata (Naples, Sept. 1725); *Il Sesostrate* (Naples, May 13, 1726); *La Semele o sia La richiesta fatale*, serenata (Naples, 1726); *L'Astarto* (Naples, Dec. 1726); *Enea in Caonia*, serenata (Naples, 1727); *Gerone tiranno di Siracusa* (Naples, Nov. 19, 1727); *Attalo, rè di Bitinia* (Naples, May 1728); *L'Ulderica* (Naples, Jan. 29, 1729); *La Sorella amante*, commedia per musica (Naples, 1729); *Tigrane* (Naples, Nov. 4, 1729; rev. version, Naples, Nov. 4, 1745); *Artaserse* (Venice, Feb. 1730; rev. version, Dresden, Sept. 9, 1740); *Dalisa* (Venice, May 1730); *Arminio* (Milan, Aug. 28, 1730); *Ezio* (Naples, 1730; rev. version, Dresden, Jan. 20, 1755); *Cleofide* (Dresden, Sept. 13, 1731; rev. version, Venice, Carnival 1736; subsequent revs. 1738 and 1743); *Catone in Utica* (Turin, Dec. 26, 1731); *Cajo Fabricio* (Rome, Jan. 12, 1732; subsequent revs. for Naples, 1733; Dresden, July 8, 1734; Berlin, Sept. 1766); *Demetrio* (Venice, Jan. 1732; subsequent revs. for Vienna [as *Cleonice*], Feb. 1734; Venice, Carnival 1737; Dresden [as *Cleonice*], Feb. 8, 1740; Venice, Carnival 1747); *Euristeo* (Venice, May 1732); *Issipile* (Naples, Oct. 1, 1732; rev. version by Leo, Naples, Dec. 19, 1742; 2d rev. version by P. Cafaro, Naples, Dec. 26, 1763); *Siroe rè di Persia* (Bologna, May 2, 1733; subsequent revs. for Naples, Nov. 4, 1747; Warsaw, Carnival 1763); *Sei tu, Lidippe, ò il sole*, serenata (Dresden, Aug. 4, 1734); *Senz'attender che di maggio*, cantata (Dresden, 1734); *Tito Vespasiano* (Pesaro, Sept. 24, 1735; subsequent revs. for Dresden, Jan. 17, 1738; Naples, Jan. 20, 1759); *Senocrita* (Dresden, Feb. 27, 1737); *Atalanta* (Dresden, July 26, 1737); *Asteria*, favola pastorale (Dresden, Aug. 3, 1737); *Irene* (Dresden, Feb. 8, 1738); *Alfonso* (Dresden, May 11, 1738); *Viriate* (Venice, Carnival 1739); *Numa Pompilio* (Hubertusburg, Oct. 7, 1741); *Lucio Papirio* (Dresden, Jan. 18, 1742; rev. version by G. de Majo, Naples, Nov. 4, 1746; 2d rev. version by Hasse or Graun, Berlin, Jan. 24, 1766); *Asilio d'amore*, festa teatrale (Naples, July 1742); *Didone abbandonata* (Hubertusburg, Oct. 7, 1742; rev. version by N. Logroscino, Naples, Jan. 20, 1744; subsequent revs. for Berlin, Dec. 29, 1752; Versailles, Aug. 28, 1753); *Endimione*, festa teatrale (Naples, July 1743); *Antigono* (Hubertusburg, Oct. 10, 1743?; rev. version by A. Palella, Naples, Dec. 19, 1744); *Ipermestra* (Vienna, Jan. 8, 1744; rev. version by A. Palella, Naples, Jan. 20, 1746; 2d rev. version, Hubertusburg, Oct. 7, 1751); *Semiramide riconosciuta* (Naples, Nov. 4, 1744; subsequent revs. for Dresden, Jan. 11, 1747; Warsaw, Oct. 7, 1760); *Arminio* (Dresden, Oct. 7, 1745; rev. version, Dresden, Jan. 8, 1753); *La Spartana generosa, ovvero Archidamia* (Dresden, June 14, 1747); *Leucippo*, favola pastorale (Hubertusburg, Oct. 7, 1747; subsequent revs. for Venice, May 1749; Dresden, Jan. 7, 1751; Berlin, Jan. 7, 1765); *Demofoonte* (Dresden, Feb. 9, 1748; subsequent revs. for Venice, Carnival 1749; Naples, Nov. 4, 1758); *Il natal di Giove*, serenata (Hubertusburg, Oct. 7, 1749); *Attilio Regolo* (Dresden, Jan. 12, 1750); *Ciro riconosciuto* (Dresden, Jan. 20, 1751); *Adriano in Siria* (Dresden, Jan. 17, 1752); *Solimano* (Dresden, Feb. 5, 1753; rev. version, Dresden, Jan. 7, 1754); *L'Eroe cinese* (Hubertusburg, Oct. 7, 1753; rev. version, Potsdam, July 18, 1773); *Artemisia* (Dresden, Feb. 6, 1754); *Il Rè pastore* (Hubertusburg, Oct. 7, 1755); *L'Olimpiade* (Dresden, Feb. 16, 1756; subsequent revs. for Warsaw, Carnival 1761; Turin, Dec. 26, 1764); *Nitteti* (Venice, Jan. 1758; rev. version, Vienna, 1762); *Il sogno di Scipione*, azione teatrale (Warsaw, Oct. 7, 1758); *Achille in Sciro* (Naples, Nov. 4, 1759); *Alcide al bivio*, festa teatrale (Vienna, Oct. 8, 1760); *Zenobia* (Vienna, Carnival 1761); *Il trionfo di Clelia* (Vienna, April 27, 1762; rev. version by G. de Majo, Naples, Jan. 20, 1763); *Egeria*, festa teatrale (Vienna, April 24, 1764); *Romolo ed Ersilia* (Innsbruck, Aug. 6, 1765); *Partenope*, festa teatrale (Vienna, Sept. 9, 1767; rev. version, Berlin, July 18, 1775); *Piramo e Tisbe*, intermezzo tragico (Vienna, Nov. 1768; rev. version, Vienna, Sept. 1770); *Il Ruggiero ovvero L'eroica gratitudine* (Milan, Oct. 16, 1771).

INTERMEZZOS: *Miride e Damari* (Naples, May 13, 1726); *Larinda e Vanesio* (Naples, Dec. 1726; subsequent revs. for Dresden, July 8, 1734; Venice, Carnival 1739); *Grilletta e Porsugnacco* (Venice, May 1727; subsequent revs. for Naples, Nov. 19, 1727; Dresden, Aug. 4, 1747); *Carlotta e Pantaleone* (Naples, May 1728; subsequent revs. for Naples, Carnival 1734; Potsdam, 1749); *Scintilla e Don Tabarano* (Naples, 1728; subsequent revs. for Venice, 1731; Dresden, July 26, 1737); *Merlina e Galoppo* (Naples, Jan. 29, 1729; subsequent revs. for Venice, 1741; Dresden, 1749); *Dorilla e Balanzone* (Naples, Nov. 4, 1729; rev. version, Venice, 1732); *Lucilla e Pandolfo* (Naples, 1730; subsequent revs. for Dresden, 1738; Venice, 1739; Dresden, 1755); *Arrighetta e Cespuglio* (Naples, c.1730); *Pimpinella e Marcantonio* (Hubertusburg, Oct. 7, 1741; subsequent revs. for Dresden, Jan. 14, 1743; Versailles, Aug. 28, 1753); *Rimario e Grilantea* (Nov. 3, 1741).

ORATORIOS: *Daniello* (Vienna, Feb. 15, 1731); *Serpentes ignei in deserto* (Venice, c.1731); *S. Petrus et S. Maria Magdalena* (Venice, c.1731); *Il cantico de'tre fanciulli* (Dresden, April 23, 1734); *Le virtù appiè della croce* (Dresden, April 19, 1737); *Giuseppe riconosciuto* (Dresden, March 31, 1741); *I Pellegrini al sepolcro de Nostro Signore* (Dresden, March 23, 1742); *La caduta di Gerico* (Dresden, April 12, 1743); *La deposizione dalla croce di Gesu Cristo, salvatore nostro* (Dresden, April 4, 1744); *S. Elena al Calvario* (Dresden, April 9, 1746); *La conversione di S. Agostino* (Dresden, March 28, 1750).

BIBL.: F. Kandler, *Cenni storico-critici intorno alla vita ed alle opere del cel. Gio. Adolfo H. detto il Sassone* (Venice, 1820); B. Zeller, *Das Recitativo accompagnato in den Opern J. A. H.s* (Halle, 1911); W. Müller, *J. A. H. als Kirchenkomponist* (Leipzig, 1911; with a thematic catalog); L. Kamienski, *Die Oratorio von J. A. H.* (Leipzig, 1912); R. Gerber, *Der Operntypus J. A. H. und seine textlichen Grundlagen* (Leipzig, 1925); F. Millner, *The Operas of J. A. H.* (Ann Arbor, 1979).

Hasselmans, Louis, French cellist and conductor; b. Paris, July 15, 1878; d. San Juan, Puerto Rico, Dec. 27, 1957. His father was the Belgian-born French harpist and composer Alphonse (Jean) Hasselmans (b. Liège, March 5, 1845; d. Paris, May 19, 1912). He studied with Godard, Lavignac, and Massenet; he also studied cello with Jules Delsart at the Paris Cons., winning the premier prix in 1893. He was a member of the Capet Quartet (1904–09); he made his conducting debut with the Lamoureux Orch. (1905), then conducted at the Opéra Comique (1909–11; 1919–22), the Montreal Opera and Marseilles Concerts Classiques (1911–13), and the Chicago Civic Opera (1918–19); he later was a conductor at the Metropolitan Opera in New York (1922–36). From 1936 to 1948 he taught at the Louisiana State Univ. School of Music.

Hatrík, Juraj, Slovak composer and teacher; b. Orkučany, May 1, 1941. He was a student of A. Moyzes at the Bratislava Academy of Music (1958–63), where he pursued his postgraduate training (1965–68). After teaching at the Košice Cons. (1963–65) and the Bratislava Academy of Music (1968–71), he was a specialist with the Slovak Music Fund (1972–90); he then served as assoc. prof. of composition at the Bratislava Academy of Music (from 1990). His output is replete with traditional and modern elements.

WORKS: DRAMATIC: *Janko Polienko* (1976); *Šťastný princ* (The Happy Prince; 1977–78); *Mechúrik Koščúrik*, musical fairy tale (1980); *Turčan Poničan* (1985); *Adamove deti* (Adam's Children), tragifarce (1990).

Hatton, John Liptrot, English composer; b. Liverpool, Oct. 12, 1808; d. Margate, Sept. 20, 1886. He acquired facility as a pianist and singer, and appeared on the vaudeville stage as a musical comedian. He publ. a great number of songs, among which "Anthea" and "Good-bye, Sweetheart, Good-bye" became extremely popular. In 1832 he went to London, where he produced his operetta, *The Queen of the Thames, or The Anglers* (Feb. 25, 1842). He then went to Vienna, where he staged his opera *Pascal Bruno* (March 2, 1844). For some of his numbers he used the punning pseudonym Czapek (genitive plural of the Hungarian word for "hat"). From 1848 to 1850 he made an extensive American tour. Returning to England, he was music director at the Princess's Theatre (1853–59). He wrote music for several Shakespeare plays there; wrote a cantata, *Robin Hood* (Bradford Festival, Aug. 26, 1856), a grand opera, *Rose, or Love's Ransom* (London, Nov. 26, 1864), and a sacred drama, *Hezekiah* (Dec. 15, 1877). He also ed. collections of old English songs.

Haubenstock-Ramati, Roman, Polish composer; b. Kraków, Feb. 27, 1919; d. Vienna, March 3, 1994. He studied with J. Koffler at the Lwów Academy of Music (1939–41); he also took courses in philosophy at the univs. of Kraków and Lwów. From 1947 to 1950 he was music director of Radio Kraków, then was director of the State Music Library in Tel Aviv (1950–56). In 1957 he settled in Vienna, where he worked for Universal Edition until 1968, then was a prof. of composition at the Vienna Academy of Music (from 1973); in 1981 he was awarded the Austrian State Prize. In 1959 he organized in Donaueschingen the first exhibition of musical scores in graphic notation; he evolved an imaginative type of modern particella in which the right-hand page gives the outline of musical action for the conductor while the left-hand page is devoted to instrumental and vocal details. This type of notation combined the most advanced type of visual guidance with an aide-memoire of traditional theater arrangements. Several of his works bear the subtitle "Mobile" to indicate the flexibility of their architectonics. His dramatic works include *Amerika*, opera after Kafka's novel (1962–64; Berlin, Oct. 8, 1966), *Divertimento*, text collage for Actors, Dancer, and/or Mime, and 2 Percussionists (1968; after *Jeux 2*), and *La Comédie*, "anti-opera," after Beckett, for 1 Male and 2 Female Speech-singers and 3 Percussionists (St. Paul-de-Vence, Alpes-Maritimes, France, July 21, 1969; German version as *Spiel*, Munich, 1970; Eng. version as *Play*).

Haubiel (real name, **Pratt**), **Charles Trowbridge,** American composer; b. Delta, Ohio, Jan. 30, 1892; d. Los Angeles, Aug. 26, 1978. His father's last name was Pratt, but he adopted his mother's maiden name, Haubiel, as his own. He had piano lessons with his sister Florence Pratt, an accomplished pianist. In 1911 he went to Europe, where he studied piano with Rudolph Ganz in Berlin; also took composition lessons with Alexander von Fielitz in Leipzig. Returning to the United States in 1913, he taught music at various schools in Oklahoma. When the United States entered World War I in 1917, he enlisted in the field artillery and served in France. After the Armistice, he resumed serious study of composition with Rosario Scalero at the David Mannes Music School in New York (1919–24), while continuing piano lessons with Rosina and Josef Lhévinne (1920–26). In 1928 he won 1st prize in the Schubert Centennial Contest with his symphonic variations *Karma*. Intermittently he taught musical subjects at the Inst. of Musical Art in New York (1921–31) and at N.Y. Univ. (1923–47). In 1935 he organized the Composers Press, Inc., with the purpose of promoting the publication of American music, and served as its president until 1966. His compositions reveal an excellent theoretical and practical grasp of harmony, counterpoint, instrumentation, and formal design. In his idiom, he followed the models of the Romantic school of composition, but he embroidered the basic patterns of traditional music with winsome coloristic touches, approaching the usage of French Impressionism. He was extremely prolific; many of his works underwent multiple transformations from a modest original, usually for solo piano or a chamber group, to a piece for full orch.; in all these forms, his compositions remain eminently playable.

WORKS: DRAMATIC: *Brigands Preferred*, comic opera (1929–46); *Passionate Pilgrim*, incidental music (c.1937); *The Witch's Curse*, fairy tale opera (1940); *The Birthday Cake*, operetta (c.1942); *Sunday Costs 5 Pesos*, folk opera (1947; Charlotte, N.C., Nov. 6, 1950); *The Enchanted Princess* (c.1955); *Adventures on Sunbonnet Hill*, children's operetta (c.1971).

Hauer, Josef Matthias, significant Austrian composer and music theorist; b. Wiener-Neustadt, near Vienna, March 19, 1883; d. Vienna, Sept. 22, 1959. After attending a college for teachers, he became a public-school instructor; at the same time, he studied music. An experimenter by nature, with a penchant for mathematical constructions, he developed a system of composition based on "tropes," or patterns, which aggregated to thematic formations of 12 different notes. As early as 1912 he publ. a piano piece, entitled *Nomos* (Law), which contained the germinal principles of 12-tone music; in his theoretical publications, he elaborated his system in greater detail. These were *Über die Klangfarbe*, op. 13 (Vienna, 1918; aug. as *Vom Wesen des Musikalischen*, Leipzig and Vienna, 1920; 3d ed., rev. and aug., 1966); *Deutung des Melos: Eine Frage an die Künstler und Denker unserer Zeit* (Leipzig, Vienna, and Zürich, 1923); *Vom Melos zur Pauke: Eine Einführung in die Zwölftonmusik* (Vienna, 1925; 2d ed., 1967); *Zwölftontechnik: Die Lehre von den Tropen* (Vienna, 1926; 2d ed., 1953); *Zwölftonspiel-Neujahr 1947* (Vienna, 1962). Hauer vehemently asserted his priority in 12-tone composition; he even used a rubber stamp on his personal stationery proclaiming himself the true founder of the 12-tone method. This claim was countered, with equal vehemence but with more justification, by Schoenberg; indeed, the functional basis of 12-tone composition in which the contrapuntal and harmonic structures are derived from the unifying tone row did not appear until Schoenberg formulated it and put it into practice in 1924. Hauer lived his entire life in Vienna, working as a composer, conductor, and teacher. Despite its forbidding character, his music attracted much attention. Among his works are 2 operas: *Salambo* (1930; Austrian Radio, Vienna, March 19, 1983) and *Die schwarze Spinne* (1932; Vienna, May 23, 1966); also the oratorio *Wandlungen* for 6 Soloists, Chorus, and Chamber Orch. (1927; Baden-Baden, April 16, 1928).

BIBL.: W. Szmolyan, *J. M. H.* (Vienna, 1965); H. Götte, *Die Kompositionstechniken J. M. H.s: Unter besonderer Berücksichtigung deterministischer Verfahren* (Kassel, 1989).

Haufrecht, Herbert, American composer; b. N.Y., Nov. 3, 1909; d. Albany, N.Y., June 23, 1998. He studied piano with Severin Eisenberger at the Cleveland Music School Settlement and composition with Herbert Elwell and Quincy Porter at the Cleveland Inst. of Music; he then completed his training in composition with Rubin Goldmark at the Juilliard Graduate School in New York (1930–34). He was a composer and arranger for the WPA Federal Theater in New York (1937–39), national music director of Young Audiences, Inc. (1961–68), and an ed. and arranger for several N.Y. music publishers (1968–77). He also was active as a collector of folk music and publ. such vols. as *Folk Sing* (1960), *'Round the World Folk Sing* (1964), *Travelin' on with the Weavers* (1966), *The Judy Collins Songbook* (1969), *Folk Songs in Settings by Master Composers* (1970), and, with N. Cazden and N. Studer, *Folk Songs of the Catskills* (1982). Among his own works are the folk operas *Boney Quillen* (1951) and *A Pot of Broth* (1961–63).

Haug, Hans, Swiss conductor, teacher, and composer; b. Basel, July 27, 1900; d. Lausanne, Sept. 15, 1967. He studied with Petri and Levy at the Basel Cons., with Busoni, and with Courvoisier and J. Pembaur Jr. at the Munich Academy of Music. He served as music director in Grandson and Solothurn; after working as choirmaster and assistant conductor at the Basel City Theater (1928–34), he conducted at the Interlaken Kursaal and at the Swiss Radio in Lausanne (1935–38) and in Zürich (1938–43). He subsequently devoted himself mainly to teaching and composing. His works were in an eminently appealing style.

WORKS: DRAMATIC: OPERAS: *Don Juan in der Fremde* (1929; Basel, Jan. 15, 1930); *Madrisa* (1933; Basel, Jan. 15, 1934); *Tartuffe* (Basel, May 24, 1937); *Der unsterbliche* (1946; Zürich, Feb. 8, 1947); *La colombe égarée* (Basel Radio, 1951); *Le miroir d'Agrippine* (1953–54); *Les fous* (1957; Geneva Radio, Nov. 1959); *Le souper de Venise* (1966); *Le gardien vigilant* (1966). OPÉRA BALLET: *Orfée* (RTF, Paris, Sept. 24, 1954; 1st stage perf., Lausanne, June 12, 1955). OPERETTAS: *Liederlig Kleeblatt* (1938); *Gilberte de Courgenay* (1940); *Annely us der Linde* (1940); *Barbara* (1942); *Leute von der Strasse* (1944); *La mère Michel* (1945). Other stage pieces and incidental music. OTHER: *Michelangelo*, oratorio (1942; Solothurn, Feb. 28, 1943).

BIBL.: J.-L. Matthey, eds., *H. H. Werkverzeichnis* (Lausanne, 1971).

Haugland, Aage, Danish bass-baritone; b. Copenhagen, Feb. 1, 1944. He studied with Mogens Wöldike and Kristian Riis in Copenhagen, making his operatic debut as the Brewer in Martinů's *Veselohra na mostě* at the Norwegian Opera in Oslo in 1968; he then sang with the Royal Opera in Copenhagen (from 1973) and also made guest appearances with other major European opera houses, including London's Covent Garden as Hunding (1975), Milan's La Scala as the King in *Lohengrin* (1981), in Salzburg as Rocco (1982), and in Bayreuth as Hagen (1983). In 1979 he made his U.S. debut as Boris Godunov in St. Louis, as well as his Metropolitan Opera debut in New York (Dec. 13, 1979) as Baron Ochs. He continued to sing at the Metropolitan Opera with success in operas by Wagner, Mussorgsky, Tchaikovsky, Strauss, and Janáček. In 1990 he appeared as King Marke at the Edinburgh Festival. After singing Boris in *Lady Macbeth of the District of Mtsensk* at La Scala in 1992, he was engaged as Varlaam at the Salzburg Easter Festival in 1994. During the 1996–97 season, he appeared as Schoenberg's Moses at the Royal Festival Hall in London. His other roles include Leporello, Sarastro, Gounod's Méphistophélès, and the Grand Inquisitor.

Hauk, Minnie (real name, **Amalia Mignon Hauck**), celebrated American soprano; b. N.Y., Nov. 16, 1851; d. Triebschen, near Lucerne, Switzerland, Feb. 6, 1929. Her father was a German carpenter who became involved in the political events of 1848, emigrated to America, and married an American woman; he named his daughter Mignon after the character in Goethe's *Wilhelm Meister*. The family moved to Atchison, Kansas, when Minnie was very young; her mother maintained a boarding house at a steamboat landing on the Missouri. In 1860 they moved to New Orleans, where Minnie began to sing popular ballads for entertainment. She made her operatic debut at the age of 14 in Brooklyn, in *La Sonnambula* (Oct. 13, 1866), then took lessons with Achille Errani in New York. On Nov. 15, 1867, she sang Juliette at the American premiere of Gounod's opera in New York. She attracted the attention of the rich industrialist Leonard Jerome and the music publisher Gustave Schirmer, who financed her trip to Europe. She sang in opera in Paris during the summer of 1868; she made her London debut at Covent Garden on Oct. 26, 1868; in 1870 she sang in Vienna. She sang the title roles in the first American performances of *Carmen* (N.Y., Oct. 23, 1878) and Massenet's *Manon* (N.Y., Dec. 23, 1885); she made her debut at the Metropolitan Opera in New York as Selika in *L'Africaine* on Feb. 10, 1891. She continued to appear there for that season, but following a disagreement with the management, decided to organize her own opera group; with it, she gave the first Chicago performance of *Cavalleria rusticana* (Sept. 28, 1891). She then settled in Switzerland with her husband, Baron Ernst von Hesse-Wartegg, whom she had married in 1881; after his death she lived mostly in Berlin; she lost her fortune in the depreciation of her holdings in Germany. In 1919 Geraldine Farrar launched an appeal to raise funds for her in America. Hauk's autobiography, collated by E. Hitchcock, was publ. as *Memories of a Singer* (London, 1925).

Hauptmann, Cornelius, German bass; b. Stuttgart, 1951. He studied at the Stuttgart Hochschule für Musik (graduated, 1982), and with Jakob Stampfli at the Bern Cons., Fischer-Dieskau in Berlin, and Tappy and Schwarzkopf in Salzburg. In 1981 he joined the Stuttgart Opera, where he first attracted notice as Masetto. From 1985 to 1987 he sang with the Heidelberg Opera, where he portrayed King Philip and Osmin. In 1987 he joined the Karlsruhe State Theater and appeared in such roles as Monteverdi's Plutone, Mozart's Sarastro and Figaro, and Verdi's Sparafucile. His appearance as a soloist in the St. Matthew Passion under Gardiner's direction in Stuttgart in 1988 led to frequent appearances with leading conductors of the day. In 1991 he sang Osmin at the Royal Festival Hall in London and Sarastro at the Deutsche Oper in Berlin. He portrayed the Speaker in *Die Zauberflöte* at the Opéra de la Bastille in Paris in 1993. In 1995 he was engaged as Sarastro at the Lyons Opera, where he returned in 1996 as Rocco. He also pursued an active career as a lieder artist.

Hauschild, Wolf-Dieter, German conductor; b. Greiz, Sept. 6, 1937. He was a student of Gerster, Abendroth, and Pflüger at the Weimar Hochschule für Musik before completing his training with Scherchen and Celibidache. After conducting at the Weimar National Theater and at the Kleist Theater in Frankfurt an der Oder, he was conductor of the Radio Choir (1971–74) and the Radio Sym. Orch. (1974–78) in East Berlin. From 1978 to 1985 he was chief conductor of the Leipzig Radio Sym. Orch. and Choir, during which time, in 1981, he became a prof. of conducting at the Berlin Hochschule für Musik. He was music director of the Stuttgart Phil. from 1985 to 1991, and also chief guest conductor of the Berlin Sym. Orch. In 1988 he became a prof. of conducting at the Stuttgart Hochschule für Musik. From 1991 to 1997 he was Generalmusikdirektor in Essen, where his tenure culminated in a mounting of the *Ring* cycle. He also appeared as a guest conductor with various opera houses and orchs. in Germany and abroad.

Hausegger, Siegmund von, esteemed Austrian conductor and composer; b. Graz, Aug. 16, 1872; d. Munich, Oct. 10, 1948. He studied with his father, the Austrian musicologist Friedrich von Hausegger (b. St. Andrä, Carinthia, April 26, 1837; d. Graz, Feb. 23, 1899) and with Karl Pohlig. At the age of 16 he composed a grand Mass, which he himself conducted; at 18 he brought out in Graz an opera, *Helfrid* (1890). Richard Strauss thought well enough of Hausegger as a composer to accept for performance his comic opera *Zinnober*, which he conducted in Munich on June 19, 1898. In 1895–96 Hausegger conducted at the Graz City Theater; in 1897 he was an assistant conductor in Bayreuth. He was the conductor of the Volk-Symphonie-Konzerte in Munich (1899–1902), the Museum Concerts in Frankfurt am Main (1903–06), and the Phil. Concerts in Hamburg (1910–20). From 1918 to 1934 he was director of the Academy of Musical Art in Munich; in 1920 he was named Generalmusikdirektor of the Munich Konzertverein, which became the Munich Phil. in 1928; he remained there until his retirement in 1938. He acquired a fine reputation as a conductor in Germany, becoming a champion of Bruckner's syms. in their original versions. As a composer, he wrote in a late German Romantic style. He publ. a monograph, *Alexander Ritter: Ein Bild seines Charakters und Schaffens* (Berlin, 1907), and his father's correspondence with Peter Rosegger (Leipzig, 1924). His collected articles appeared under the title *Betrachtungen zur Kunst* (Leipzig, 1921).

Hausswald, Günter, distinguished German musicologist; b. Rochlitz an der Mülde, March 11, 1908; d. Stuttgart, April 23, 1974. He studied piano with Max Pauer and composition with Karg-Elert in Leipzig, theory with Grabner at the Leipzig Hochschule für Musik, and musicology with Kroyer and others at the Univ. of Leipzig, where he took his Ph.D. in 1937 with the diss. *Johann David Heinichens Instrumentalwerke* (publ. in Wolfenbüttel and Berlin, 1937); he completed his Habilitation in 1949 at the Dresden Technical College with his *Mozarts Serenaden* (publ. in Leipzig, 1951). From 1933 to 1945 he taught school in Dresden; he then was dramaturge at the Dresden State Opera (1947–53); he also lectured at the Dresden Hochschule für Musik and at the Univ. of Jena from 1950 to 1953. He then settled in West Germany, where he ed. the monthly *Musica* (1958–70); he was also program director for the South German Radio at Stuttgart (1960–68). His important monographs include *Heinrich Marschner* (Dresden, 1938); *Die deutsche Oper* (Cologne, 1941); *Die Bauten des Staatstheater Dresden* (Dresden, 1948); *Das neue Opernbuch* (Dresden, 1951; 5th ed., 1956); *Richard Strauss* (Dresden, 1953); *Dirigenten: Bild und Schrift* (Berlin, 1966). He also contributed exemplary eds. to the complete works of Telemann, Gluck, Bach, and Mozart.

Hawes, William, English composer and conductor; b. London, June 21, 1785; d. there, Feb. 18, 1846. As a boy he was a chorister at the Chapel Royal (1793–1801), then violinist at Covent Garden (1802–5). He became Gentleman of the Chapel Royal (1805), vicar-choral and master of choristers at St. Paul's Cathedral (1812), master of the children of the Chapel Royal (1817), and lay vicar of Westminster Abbey (1817–20). He was director of English opera at the Lyceum (1824–36); it was at his suggestion that Weber's *Der Freischütz* was given for the first time in England (July 22, 1824; he contributed some airs of his own composition to this production). Subsequently, he adapted and produced many Italian, French, and German operas for the English stage. He wrote and staged several light operas, among them *Broken Promises* (1825), *The Quartette, or Interrupted Harmony* (1828), and *The Sister of Charity* (1829).

Hayashi, Hikaru, Japanese composer; b. Tokyo, Oct. 22, 1931. He was a student of Otaka and Ikenouchi at the Tokyo Academy of Music.

WORKS: DRAMATIC: OPERAS: *The Naked King*, radio opera (1955); *Amanjaku and Urikohime*, television opera (1958); *The Wife in the Picture* (1961); *The Chalk Circle* (1978; orch. suite, 1982); *Legend of White Beasts* (1979); *Gorsh, the Cellist* (1986); *Joan of Arc Wearing a Skirt* (1987); *12th Night* (1989); *Hamlet's Hour* (1990); *12 Months and a Girl* (1992). Also ballet music and *Beggar's Song*, oratorio (1962).

Haydn, (Franz) Joseph, great Austrian composer who was a master of the Classical style, brother of **(Johann) Michael Haydn**; b. Rohrau, Lower Austria, probably March 31, 1732 (baptized, April 1, 1732); d. Vienna, May 31, 1809. He was the 2d of 12 children born to Mathias Haydn, a wheelwright, who served as village sexton, and Anna Maria Koller, daughter of the market inspector and a former cook in the household of Count Harrach, lord of the village. On Sundays and holidays music was performed at home, the father accompanying the voices on the harp, which he had learned to play by ear. When Haydn was a small child his paternal cousin Johann Mathias Franck, a choral director, took him to Hainburg, where he gave him instruction in reading, writing, arithmetic, and instrumental playing. When Haydn was 8 years old, Karl Georg Reutter, Kapellmeister at St. Stephen's Cathedral in Vienna, engaged him as a soprano singer in the chorus. After his voice began to break, he moved to the household of Johann Michael Spangler, a music teacher. He obtained a loan of 150 florins from Anton Buchholz, a friend of his father's, and was able to rent an attic room where he could use a harpsichord. In the same house lived the famous Italian poet and opera librettist Metastasio, who recommended Haydn to a resident Spanish family as a music tutor. He was also engaged as accompanist to students of Nicolo Porpora, for whom he performed various menial tasks in exchange for composition lessons. He made a diligent study of *Gradus ad Parnassum* by Fux and *Der vollkommen Capellmeister* by Mattheson. Soon he began to compose keyboard music. In 1751 he wrote the Singspiel *Der krumme Teufel*. A noblewoman, Countess Thun, engaged him as harpsichordist and singing teacher; he met Karl Joseph von Fürnburg, for whom he wrote his first string quartets. In 1759 Haydn was engaged by Count Ferdinand Maximilian von Morzin as Kapellmeister at his estate in Lukaveč. On Nov. 26, 1760, he married Maria Anna Keller, the eldest daughter of his early benefactor, a Viennese wigmaker.

A decided turn in Haydn's life was his meeting with Prince Paul Anton Esterházy. Esterházy had heard one of Haydn's syms. during a visit to Lukaveč, and engaged him to enter his service as 2d Kapellmeister at his estate in Eisenstadt; Haydn signed his contract with Esterházy on May 1, 1761. Prince Paul Anton died in 1762, and his brother, Prince Nikolaus Esterházy, known as the "Magnificent," succeeded him. He took Haydn to his new palace at Esterháza, where Haydn was to provide 2 weekly operatic performances and 2 formal concerts. Haydn's service at Esterháza was long-lasting, secure, and fruitful; there he composed music of all descriptions, including most of his known string quartets, about 80 of his 104 syms., a number of keyboard works, and nearly all his operas; in 1766 he was elevated to the rank of 1st Kapellmeister. Prince Nikolaus Esterházy was a cultural patron of the arts, but he was also a stern taskmaster in his relationship to his employees. His contract with Haydn stipulated that each commissioned work had to be performed without delay, and that such a work should not be copied for use by others. Haydn was to present himself in the "antichambre" of the palace each morning and afternoon to receive the Prince's orders, and he was obliged to wear formal clothes, with white hose and a powdered wig with a pigtail or a hairbag; he was to have his meals with the other musicians and house servants. In particular, Haydn was obligated to write pieces that could be performed on the baryton, an instrument which the prince could play; in consequence, Haydn wrote numerous pieces for the baryton. He also wrote 3 sets of 6 string quartets each (opp. 9, 17, and 20), which were brought out in 1771–72. His noteworthy syms. included No. 49, in F minor, *La passione*; No. 44, in E minor, known as the *Trauersinfonie*; No. 45, in F-sharp minor; and the famous *Abschiedsinfonie* (the Farewell Sym.), performed by Haydn at Esterháza in 1772. In 1780 Haydn was elected a member of the Modena Phil. Soc.; in 1784 Prince Henry of Prussia sent him a gold medal; in 1785 he was commissioned to write a "passione istrumentale," *The 7 Last Words*, for the Cathedral of Cádiz; in 1787 King Friedrich Wilhelm II gave him a diamond ring; many other distinctions were conferred upon him. During his visits to Vienna he formed a close friendship with Mozart, who was nearly a quarter of a century younger, and for whose genius Haydn had great admiration. If the words of Mozart's father can be taken literally, Haydn told him that Mozart was "the greatest composer known to me either in person or by name." Mozart reciprocated Haydn's regard for him by dedicating to him a set of 6 string quartets. Prince Nikolaus Esterházy died in 1790, and his son Paul Anton (named after his uncle) inherited the estate. After he disbanded the orch., Haydn was granted an annuity of 1,000 florins; nominally he remained in the service of the new prince as Kapellmeister, but he took up permanent residence in Vienna.

In 1790 Johann Peter Salomon, the enterprising London impresario, visited Haydn and persuaded him to travel to London for a series of concerts. Haydn accepted the offer, arriving in London on Jan. 1, 1791. On March 11 of that year he appeared in his first London concert in the Hanover Square Rooms, presiding at the keyboard. Haydn was greatly feted in London by the nobility; the king himself expressed his admiration for Haydn's art. In July 1791 he went to Oxford to receive the honorary degree of Mus.D. For this occasion, he submitted his Sym. No. 92, in G major, which became known as the Oxford Sym.; he composed a 3-part canon, *Thy Voice, O Harmony, Is Divine*, as his exercise piece. It was also in England that he wrote his Sym. No. 94, in G major, the *Surprise* Sym. On his journey back to Vienna in the summer of 1792 Haydn stopped in Bonn, where young Beethoven showed him some of his works, and Haydn agreed to accept him later as his student in Vienna. In 1794 Haydn went to London once more. His first concert, on Feb. 10, 1794, met with great success. His London syms., also known as the Salomon syms., because Haydn wrote them at Salomon's request, were 12 in number, and they included No. 99, in E-flat major; No. 100, in G major, known as the *Military Sym.*, No. 101, in D major, nicknamed *The Clock*, No. 102, in B-flat major; No. 103, in E-flat major, known as the *Drum Roll Sym.*, and No. 104, in D major. A philatelic note: Haydn sent the MS of his oratorio *The Creation* to Salomon in London for its first performance there. The package was delivered on March 23, 1800, by stagecoach and sailboat from Vienna, and the postage was £30 16s. 0d., a sum equal to £650 today, c.$1,000. In 1800, this sum was enough to buy a horse, or to pay the living expenses for a family of 4 for a year.

Returning to Vienna, Haydn resumed his contact with the Esterházy family. In 1794 Prince Paul Anton died and was succeeded by his son Nikolaus; the new prince revived the orch. at Eisenstadt, with Haydn again as Kapellmeister. Conforming to the new requirements of Prince Nikolaus, Haydn turned to works for the church, including 6 masses. Between 1796 and 1798 Haydn composed his great oratorio *Die Schöpfung*, which was first performed at a private concert for the nobility at the Schwarzenburg Palace in Vienna on April 29, 1798. In 1796 he wrote the Concerto in E-flat major for Trumpet, which became a standard piece for trumpet players. In 1797 Haydn was instructed by the court to compose a hymn-tune of a solemn nature that could be used as the national Austrian anthem. He succeeded triumphantly in this task; he made use of this tune as a theme of a set of variations in his String Quartet in C major, op. 76, no. 3, which itself became known as the Emperor Quartet. The original text for the hymn, written by Lorenz Leopold Haschka, began "Gott erhalte Franz den Kaiser." This hymn had a curious history: a new set of words was written by August Heinrich Hoffmann during a period of revolutionary disturbances in Germany preceding the general European revolution of 1848; its first line, "Deutschland, Deutschland über alles," later assumed the significance of German imperialism; in its original it meant merely "Germany above all (in our hearts)." Between 1799 and 1801 Haydn completed the oratorio *Die Jahreszeiten*; its text was tr. into German from James Thomson's poem *The Seasons*. It was first performed at the Schwarzenburg Palace in Vienna on April 24, 1801. In 1802, beset by illness, Haydn resigned as Kapellmeister to Prince Nikolaus.

Haydn made his last public appearance at a concert given in his honor in the Great Hall of the Univ. of Vienna on March 27, 1808, with Salieri conducting *Die Schöpfung*. When Vienna capitulated to Napoleon, he ordered a guard of honor to be placed at Haydn's residence. Haydn died on May 31, 1809, and was buried at the Hundsturm Cemetery. In consequence of some fantastic events, his skull became separated from his body before his reinterment at Eisenstadt in 1820; it was actually exhibited under glass in the hall of the Gesellschaft der Musikfreunde in Vienna for a number of years, before being reunited with his body in the Bergkirche in Eisenstadt on June 5, 1954, in a solemn official ceremony.

In schoolbooks Haydn is usually described as "father of the symphony," the creator of the classical form of the sym. and of the string quartet. Historically, this absolute formulation cannot be sustained, as the symphonic form was established by Stamitz and his associates at the Mannheim School, and the string quartet was of an even earlier provenance. But Haydn's music was not limited to formal novelty; its greatness was revealed in the variety of moods, the excellence of variations, and the contrast among the constituent movements of a sym. String quartets, as conceived by Haydn, were diminutions of the sym.; both were set in sonata form, consisting in 3 contrasting movements, *Allegro, Andante, Allegro*, with a *Minuet* interpolated between the last 2. It is the quality of invention that places Haydn above his contemporaries and makes his music a model of classical composition. Haydn played a historic role in the evolution of functional harmony by adopting 4-part writing as a fundamental principle of composition, particularly in his string quartets. This practice has also exercised a profound influence on the teaching of music theory.

WORKS: DRAMATIC: *Der krumme Teufel*, Singspiel (1751?; 1st confirmed perf., Vienna, May 29, 1753; not extant); *Der neue krumme Teufel (Asmodeus, der krumme Teufel)*, Singspiel (1758?; music not extant); *Acide*, festa teatrale (1762; Eisenstadt, Jan. 11, 1763; only fragment and libretto extant; rev. version, 1773; only fragment extant); *Marchese (La Marchesa Nespola)*, comedia (1762?; only fragment extant; dialogues not extant); *Il Dottore*, comedia (1765?; not extant); *La Vedova*, comedia (1765?; not extant); *Il scanarello*, comedia (1765?; not extant); *La Canterina*, intermezzo in musica (1766; Bratislava, Sept. 11?, 1766); *Lo speziale (Der Apotheker)*, dramma giocoso (1768; Esterháza, Autumn 1768); *Le Pescatrici (Die Fischerinnen)*, dramma giocoso (1769; Esterháza, Sept. 16?, 1770); *L'infedeltà delusa (Liebe macht erfinderisch; Untreue lohnt sich nicht; Deceit Outwitted)*, burletta per musica (1773; Esterháza, July 26, 1773); *Philemon und Baucis oder Jupiters Reise auf die Erde*, Singspiel/marionette opera (1773; Esterháza, Sept. 2, 1773); *Hexenschabbas*, marionette opera (1773?; not extant); *L'incontro improvviso (Die unverhoffte Zusammenkunft; Unverhofftes Begegnen)*, dramma giocoso (1775; Esterháza, Aug. 29, 1775); *Dido*, Singspiel/marionette opera (1776?; Esterháza, March ?, 1776; music not extant); *Opéra comique vom abgebrannten Haus* (not extant; may be identical with the following work); *Die Feuerbrunst*, Singspiel/marionette opera (1775?-78?; may be by Haydn; dialogues not extant); *Il mondo della luna (Die Welt auf dem Monde)*, dramma giocoso (1777; Esterháza, Aug. 3, 1777); *Die bestrafte Rachbegierde*, Singspiel/marionette opera (1779?; Esterháza, 1779; music not extant); *La vera costanza*, dramma giocoso (1778?; Esterháza, April 25, 1779; only music extant appears in the rev. version of 1785); *L'isola disabitata (Die wüste Insel)*, azione teatrale (1779; Esterháza, Dec. 6, 1779; rev. 1802); *La fedeltà premiata (Die belohnte Treue)*, dramma pastorale giocoso (1780; Esterháza, Feb. 25, 1781); *Orlando paladino (Der Ritter Roland)*, dramma eroicomico (1782; Esterháza, Dec. 6, 1782); *Armida*, dramma eroico (1783; Esterháza, Feb. 26, 1784); *L'anima del filosofo ossia Orfeo ed Euridice*, dramma per musica (1791; composed for London but not perf.; 1st confirmed perf., Florence, June 10, 1951); *Alfred, König der Angelsachsen, oder Der patriotische König* (1796; perf. as the incidental music to *Haldane, König der Danen*, Eisenstadt, Sept. 1796). ORATORIOS: *Stabat Mater* (1767); *Applausus (Jubilaeum virtutis Palatium)*, allegorical oratorio/cantata (1768; Zwettl, April 17, 1768); *Il ritorno di Tobia* (1774–75; Vienna, April 2 and 4, 1775, in 2 parts; rev. 1784); *Die sieben letzten Worte unseres Erlösers am Kreuze* (1795–96; Vienna, 1796); *Die Schöpfung* (1796–98; 1st private perf., Schwarzenburg Palace, Vienna, April 29, 1798; 1st public perf., Kärnthnertortheater, Vienna, March 19, 1799); *Die Jahreszeiten* (1799–1801; Schwarzenburg Palace, Vienna, April 24, 1801).

BIBL.: COLLECTED EDITIONS, SOURCE MATERIAL: The first attempt to publ. a complete edition was made by Breitkopf & Härtel; *J. H.s Werke*, ed. by G. Adler, H. Kretzschmar, E. Mandyczewski, M. Seiffert, and others, reached only 10 vols. in its coverage (Leipzig, 1907–33). An attempt to continue it after World War II as *J. H.: Kritische Gesamtausgabe*, under the editorship of Jens Peter Larsen and the sponsorship of the Haydn Soc. of Boston, also failed; only 4 vols. were issued (Boston, Leipzig, and Vienna, 1950–51). Finally, in 1955, through the efforts of Friedrich Blume and the publisher Gunter Henle, the Joseph Haydn-Institut of Cologne was founded to sponsor a monumental critical ed. The new ed., *J. H.: Werke*, also includes accompanying *Kritische Berichte*. Jens Peter Larsen ed. the first series of vols. (Munich, 1958–61); he was succeeded as editor by Georg Feder. Expected to be completed by the year 2000, this exhaustive ed. will contain more than 100 vols. H. C. Robbins Landon has ed. all of the syms. in a separate series, issued in miniature score as *J. H.: Kritische Ausgabe sämtlicher Symphonien* (1–12, Vienna, 1965–68). A. van Hoboken prepared a thematic catalog, *J. H.: Thematisch-bibliographisches Werkverzeichnis* (2 vols., Mainz, 1957 and 1971).

Invaluable articles may be found in the *H. Yearbook* (1962-) and *H. Studien* (Joseph Haydn-Institut, Cologne, 1965-). Other sources include: A. Csatkai, *J. H.: Katalog der Gedächtnisausstellung in Eisenstadt 1932* (Eisenstadt, 1932); A. Orel, *Katalog der H.-Gedächtnisausstellung Wien 1932* (Vienna, 1932); J. Larsen, *Die H.-Überlieferung* (Copenhagen, 1939); idem, ed., *Drei H. Kataloge in Faksimile: Mit Einleitung und ergänzenden Themenverzeichnissen* (Copenhagen, 1941; 2d ed., rev., 1979); R. Feuchtmüller, *F. Hadamowsky, and L. Nowak, J. H. und seine Zeit: Ausstellung Schloss Petronell (N. Ö.) Mai bis Oktober 1959* (Vienna, 1959); L. Nowak, ed., *J. H.: Ausstellung zum 150. Todestag: Vom 29. Mai bis 30. September 1959* (Vienna, 1959); E. Badura-Skoda, ed., *Congress Report: International F. J. H. Congress: Vienna 1982* (Munich, 1987); F. and M. Grave, *F. J. H.: A Guide to Research* (N.Y., 1990). BIOGRAPHICAL: S. Mayr, *Brevi notizie istoriche della vita e delle opere di H.* (Bergamo, 1809); A. Dies, *Biographische Nachrichten von J. H.: Nach mündlichen Erzählungen desselben entworfen und herausgegeben von Albert Christoph Dies, Landschaftmahler* (Vienna, 1810; modern ed. by H. Seeger, Berlin, 1959; 4th ed., 1976; Eng. tr. in V. Gotwals, ed., *J. H.: Eighteenth-century Gentleman and Genius*, Madison, 1963; 2d ed., 1968, as *H.: Two Contemporary Portraits*); G. Carpani, *Le Haydine, ovvero Lettere su la vita e le opere del celebre maestro Giuseppe H.* (Milan, 1812; 2d ed., 1823; Eng. tr. as *The Life of H. in Letters*, 1839); T. von Karajan, *J. H. in London, 1791 und 1792* (Vienna, 1861); C. von Wurzbach, *J. H. und sein Bruder Michael: Zwei bio-bibliographische Kunstler-Skizzen* (Vienna, 1861); C. Pohl, *Mozart und H. in London: vol. 2, H. in London* (Vienna, 1867); idem, *J. H.* (incomplete; 2 vols.; vol. 1, Berlin, 1875; 2d ed., 1878; vol. 2, Leipzig, 1882; vol. 3, completed by H. Botstiber, Leipzig, 1927); J. Hadden, *H.* (London and N.Y., 1902; 2d ed., rev., 1934); F. Artaria and H. Botstiber, *J. H. und das Verlagshaus Artaria: Nach den Briefen des Meisters an das Haus Artaria & Compagnie dargestellt* (Vienna, 1909); M. Brenet, *H.* (Paris, 1909; 2d ed., 1910; Eng. tr., 1926); H. von Hase, *J. H. und Breitkopf & Härtel* (Leipzig, 1909); A. Schnerich, *J. H. und seine Sendung* (Zürich, 1922; 2d ed., 1926, with supplement by W. Fischer); K. Geiringer, *J. H.* (Potsdam, 1932); E. Schmid, *J. H.: Ein Buch von Vorfahren und Heimat des Meisters* (Kassel, 1934); K. Geiringer, *H.: A Creative Life in Music* (N.Y., 1946; 3d ed., rev., 1983); R. Hughes, *H.* (London, 1950; 6th ed., rev., 1989); L. Nowak, *J. H.: Leben, Bedeutung und Werk* (Zürich, 1951; 3d ed., rev., 1966); D. Bartha and L. Somfai, *H. als Opernkapellmeister: Die H.-Dokumente der Esterházy-Opernsammlung* (Budapest, 1960; rev. ed. in *New Looks at Italian Opera: Essays in Honor of Donald J. Grout*, Ithaca, N.Y., 1968); H. Seeger, *J. H.* (Leipzig, 1961); A. van Hoboken, *Discrepancies in H. Biographies* (Washington, D.C., 1962); L. Somfai, *J. H.: Sein Leben in zeitgenossischen Bildern* (Budapest and Kassel, 1966; Eng. tr., 1969); H. C. Robbins Landon, *H.* (London, 1972); B. Redfern, *H.: A Biography, with a Survey of Books, Editions and Recordings* (London, 1972); H. C. Robbins Landon, *H.: Chronicle and Works* (5 vols., Bloomington, Ind., and London; vol. 1, *H.: The Early Years, 1732–1765* [1980]; vol. 2, *H. at Esterhaza, 1766–1790* [1978]; vol. 3, *H. in England, 1791–1795* [1976]; vol. 4, *H.: The Years of "The Creation," 1796–1800* [1977]; vol. 5, *H.: The Late Years, 1801–1809* [1977]); idem, *H.: A Documentary Study* (London, 1981); N. Butterworth, *H.* (Sydney, 1983); H. C. Robbins Landon and D. Jones, *H.: His Life and Music* (London, 1988); M. Vignal, *J. H.* (Paris, 1988); W. Marggraf, *J. H.: Versuch einer Annäherung* (Leipzig, 1990); E. Sisman, ed., *H. and His World* (Princeton, 1997). CRITICAL, ANALYTICAL: L. Wendschuh, *Über J. H.'s Opern* (Halle, 1896); H. Wirth, *J. H. als Dramatiker: Sein Bühnenschaffen als Beitrag zur Geschichte der deutschen Oper* (Wolfenbüttel and Berlin, 1940); H. Wirth, *J. H.: Orfeo ed Euridice; Analytical Notes* (Boston, 1951); D. Cushman, *J. H.'s Melodic Materials: An Exploratory Introduction to the Primary and Secondary Sources Together with an Analytical Catalogue and Tables of Proposed Melodic Correspondence and/or Variance* (diss., Boston Univ., 1972); W. Koller, *Aus der Werkstatt der Wiener Klassiker: Bearbeitung H.s* (Tutzing, 1975); M. Huss, *J. H.: Klassiker zwischen Barock und Biedermeier* (Eisenstadt, 1984); S. Fisher, *H.'s Overtures and Their Adaptations as Concert Orchestral Works* (diss., Univ. of Pa., 1985); A. Peter Brown, *Performing H.'s Creation* (Bloomington, Ind., 1986); J. Larsen, *Essays on Handel, H., and the Viennese Classical Style* (tr. by U. Krämer; Ann Arbor, 1988); G. Wheelock, *H.'s Ingenious Jesting with Art: Contexts of Musical Wit and Humor* (N.Y., 1992); R. Wochnik, *Die Musiksprache in den opere semiserie J. H.s* (Eisenach, 1993); W. Sutcliffe, *H. Studies* (Cambridge, 1998).

Haydn, (Johann) Michael, distinguished Austrian composer, brother of **(Franz) Joseph Haydn**; b. Rohrau, Lower Austria (baptized), Sept. 14, 1737; d. Salzburg, Aug. 10, 1806. He went to Vienna about 1745 and became a chorister at St. Stephen's Cathedral; his voice was remarkable for its wide range, extending 3 octaves. In addition to the academic and musical training he received as a chorister, he also studied composition on his own by absorbing the theories of Fux as propounded in his *Gradus ad Parnassum*. He then obtained the post of Kapellmeister to the Bishop of Grosswardein in 1757, and subsequently was named a court musician and Konzertmeister to Archbishop Sigismund Schrattenbach of Salzburg in 1762. In 1768 he married Maria Magdalen Lipp (1745–1827), the daughter of the court organist Franz Ignaz Lipp; she was a soprano in the archbishop's service. Haydn also became principal organist of the Dreifatigkeitskirche in 1777, and was Mozart's successor as cathedral organist in 1781. Part of his time he devoted to teaching; Weber and Diabelli were among his students. When Archbishop Hieronymus Colloredo abdicated in 1800 and the French took control of Salzburg, Haydn lost his positions. Although his last years were made difficult by this change in his fortunes, he turned down the post of vice Kapellmeister to Prince Nikolaus Esterházy, his famous brother's patron. He was a prolific composer of both sacred and secular music, and particularly esteemed for his mastery of church music. His outstanding Requiem in C minor, *Pro defuncto Archiepiscopo Sigismundo*, was composed in memory of his patron in 1771; it was also performed at Joseph Haydn's funeral. He also wrote a fine Mass, the *Sotto il titulo di S. Teresia*, for the empress Maria Theresia, who sang the soprano solos under his direction in Vienna in 1801. His secular output included dramatic works, syms., serenades, divertimentos, chamber music, etc. His Sym. in G major (1783) was long attributed to Mozart (who composed an introduction to its 1st movement) as K.444/425a.

WORKS: DRAMATIC: SINGSPIELS: *Rebekka als Braut* (Salzburg, April 10, 1766); *Die Hochzeit auf der Alm* (Salzburg, May 6, 1768); *Die Wahrheit der Natur* (Salzburg, July 7, 1769); *Der Bassgeiger zu Wörgl* (c.1773–75); *Abels Tod* (c.1778; only fragment extant); *Der englische Patriot* (c.1779); *Die Ährenleserin* (Salzburg, July 2, 1788). OPERA SERIA: *Andromeda e Perseo* (Salzburg, March 14, 1787). ORATORIOS: *Die Schuldigkeit des ersten Gebots* (1767; part 2 by Haydn; remainder in collaboration with Mozart and Adlgasser; not extant); *Der Kampf der Busse und Bekehrung* (Salzburg, Feb. 21, 1768); *Kaiser Constantin I. Feldzug und Sieg* (Salzburg, Feb. 20, 1769; part 3 by Haydn, part 1 by Adlgasser, and part 2 by Scheicher); *Der reumütige Petrus* (Salzburg, March 11, 1770); *Der büssende Sünder* (Salzburg, Feb. 15, 1771); *Oratorium de Passione Domini nostri Jesu Christi* (c.1775); *Figura: In emigratione nostra* (Salzburg, Aug. 24, 1782). Also incidental music to Voltaire's *Zaïre* (Salzburg, Sept. 29, 1777).

BIBL.: [J.]G. Schinn and [F.]J. Otter, *Biographische Skizze von M. H.* (Salzburg, 1808); C. von Wurzbach, *Joseph Haydn und sein Bruder M.* (Vienna, 1861); J. Engl, *Zum Gedenken J. M. H.s* (Salzburg, 1906); O. Schmid, *J. M. H. . . . Sein Leben und Wirken* (Langensalza, 1906); H. Jancik, *M. H.: Ein vergessener Meister* (Vienna, 1952); G. Croll and K. Vossing, *J. M. H.: Sein Leben—sein Schaffen—seine Zeit: Eine Bildbiographie* (Vienna, 1987).

Hayes, Catherine, Irish soprano; b. Limerick, Oct. 25, 1825; d. London, Aug. 11, 1861. She studied with Antonio Sapio in Dublin, where she began her career as a concert artist in 1840. She later pursued training with Manuel García in Paris and Domenico Ronconi in Milan. On May 10, 1845, she made her operatic debut as Bellini's Elvira in Marseilles, and then sang with fine success at Milan's La Scala and in Vienna. From 1849 she appeared in London. She also made tours of the United States, Australia, and India. She was especially admired for her roles in operas by Rossini, Mercadante, Donizetti, and Verdi.

Hayes, Roland, outstanding black American tenor; b. Curryville, Ga., June 3, 1887; d. Boston, Jan. 1, 1977. He was born to former slaves. After vocal studies with A. Calhoun in Chattanooga, he attended Fisk Univ. He then pursued his vocal training with Arthur J. Hubbard in Boston. On Nov. 15, 1917, he made his recital debut there, and then made a successful concert tour of the United States. In 1920 he went to Europe to complete his studies, finding mentors in Ira Aldridge, Victor Beigel, Sir George Henschel, and Theodor Lierhammer. After singing with leading orchs. in London, Paris, Berlin, Vienna, and Amsterdam, and giving recitals, he returned to the United States and made his first appearance at N.Y.'s Carnegie Hall in recital in 1923. In subsequent years, he made numerous appearances in the United States until retiring from the concert stage in 1973. Hayes was greatly esteemed for his compelling interpretations of German lieder and French songs, as well as for his unforgettable and poignant performances of black spirituals. He publ. expert arrangements of 30 black spirituals as *My Songs* (1948).

BIBL.: M. Helm, *Angel Mo' and her Son, R. H.* (Boston, 1942).

Haym (Haim), Nicola Francesco, Italian cellist, composer, and librettist of German descent; b. Rome, July 6, 1678; d. London, Aug. 11, 1729. He was a violone player in the private orch. of Cardinal Ottoboni in Rome under Corelli (1694–1700), then went to London, where he was composer and cellist to the 2d duke of Bedford (1701–11); later was a bass player in the employ of the duke of Chandos. He was a major figure in organizing performances of Italian opera in London. In 1722 he became the official librettist and Italian secretary of the Royal Academy of Music, the business venture responsible for presenting Italian opera in London. His works include 2 oratorios, *David sponsae restitutus* (1699) and *Santa Costanza* (1700), a serenata, *Il reciproco amore di Tirsi e Clori* (1699), a secular cantata, *Lontan del idol mio* (1704), and instrumental pieces. His historical importance, however, rests upon his adaptations for Handel's scores, including *Teseo* (1713), *Radamisto* (1720), *Ottone* (1723), *Flavio* (1723), *Giulio Cesare* (1724), *Tamerlano* (1724), *Rodelinda* (1725), *Siroe* (1728), and *Tolomeo* (1728).

Haymon, Cynthia, black American soprano; b. Jacksonville, Fla., Sept. 6, 1958. She was educated at Northwestern Univ. In 1984 she made her operatic debut at the Santa Fe Opera in the U.S. premiere of Henze's *We Come to the River*, returning there to sing Xanthe in the United States premiere of Strauss's *Die Liebe de Danae* in 1985. That same year, she created the title role in Musgrave's *Harriet, the Woman Called Moses* at the Norfolk (Va.) Opera. In 1986 she made her European debut as Gershwin's Bess at the Glyndebourne Festival. In subsequent years, she was engaged with opera companies on both sides of the Atlantic, including London's Covent Garden, the Hamburg State Opera, the Bavarian State Opera in Munich, the Deutsche Oper in Berlin, the Canadian Opera, the Baltimore Opera, the San Francisco Opera, and the Opéra de la Bastille in Paris. She also appeared as a soloist with notable orchs. Among her other roles are Gluck's Amor, Mozart's Pamina and Susanna, Bizet's Micaëla, and Puccini's Liù and Mimi.

Hays, Sorrel (Doris Ernestine), American composer, pianist, and mixed-media artist; b. Memphis, Tenn., Aug. 6, 1941. She was educated at the Univ. of Chattanooga (B.M., 1963), the Munich Hochschule für Musik (piano and harpsichord diploma, 1966), the Univ. of Wisc. (M.M., 1968), and the Univ. of Iowa (composition and electronic music, 1969). In 1971 she won 1st prize in the International Competition for Interpreters of New Music in Rotterdam, and subsequently toured as a performer of contemporary music; was prof. of theory at Queens College of the City Univ. of N.Y. (1974–75), and a guest lecturer and performer at various institutions. In 1984 she adopted Sorrel as her first name.

WORKS: DRAMATIC: *Love in Space*, radio opera/music theater (1986); *The Glass Woman*, opera (1989–95); *Touch of Touch*, video opera (1989); *Dream in Her Mind*, opera (1994–95; Westdeutscher Rundfunk, Cologne, April 14, 1995); film scores; various works for radio.

Head, Michael (Dewar), English singer, pianist, and composer; b. Eastbourne, Jan. 28, 1900; d. Cape Town, South Africa, Aug. 24, 1976. He studied composition with Frederick Corder at the Royal Academy of Music in London, and in 1927 joined its faculty as a piano instructor. In 1947 he made a grand tour through Asia, Canada, and Australia, performing both as singer and pianist. He publ. several collections of English songs; also wrote 2 children's operas, *The Bachelor Mouse* (1954) and *Key Money* (1966).

Headington, Christopher (John Magenis), English pianist, writer on music, and composer; b. London, April 28, 1930; d. Chamonix, France, March 19, 1996. He studied piano with Percy Waller and composition with Lennox Berkeley at the Royal Academy of Music in London; he also received private instruction in composition from Britten (1947–54) and studied piano with Lefébure and composition with Lutosławski at the Dartington International Summer School (1963). He then devoted much time to teaching; he was also active with the BBC in London (1964–65). He toured as a pianist in Europe, the Middle East, and the Far East and also was active as a broadcaster. Among his writings are *Britten* (1981), *Opera: A History* (1987), and *Peter Pears: A Biography* (1993). Among his compositions is the ballet *Chanson de l'eternelle tristesse* (1957).

Healey, Derek, English composer and pedagogue; b. Wargrave, May 2, 1936. He was a student of Darke (organ) and Howells (composition) at the Univ. of Durham (B.Mus., 1961), and received training in piano, organ, and flute at the Royal College of Music in London; he then continued his composition studies with Petrassi and Berio in Italy, principally with Porena in Rome (1962–66). He also studied conducting with Celibidache at the Accademia Musicale Chigiana in Siena (summers, 1961–63 and 1966). He taught at the Univ. of Victoria, British Columbia (1969–71) and at the Univ. of Toronto (1971–72); he concurrently taught at the Univ. of Waterloo. After teaching at the Univ. of Guelph (1972–78), he was prof. of theory and composition at the Univ. of Oregon in Eugene from 1979 to 1988. In 1980 he was awarded the International Composition Prize of the Univ. of Louisville.

WORKS: DRAMATIC: *Il Carcerato,* ballet (1965); *The 3 Thieves*, ballet (1967); *Mr. Punch*, children's opera (1969); *Seabird Island*, opera (Guelph, May 7, 1977).

Heartz, Daniel (Leonard), American musicologist; b. Exeter, N.H., Oct. 5, 1928. He studied at the Univ. of New Hampshire in Durham (A.B., 1950) and at Harvard Univ. (A.M., 1951; Ph.D., 1957, with the diss. *Sources and Forms of the French Instrumental Dance in the Sixteenth Century*). From 1957 to 1960 he was on the faculty of the Univ. of Chicago; in 1960 he was appointed to the music faculty of the Univ. of Calif., Berkeley. In 1967–68 and 1978–79 he held Guggenheim fellowships. He publ. *Pierre Attaingnant, Royal Printer of Music: A Historical Study and Bibliographical Catalogue* (Berkeley, 1969), *Mozart's Operas* (Berkeley, 1990), and *Haydn, Mozart, and the Viennese School, 1740–1780* (N.Y., 1995).

Hedges, Anthony (John), English composer and teacher; b. Bicester, March 5, 1931. He studied at Keble College, Oxford (M.A., B.Mus.) and at the Royal Academy of Music in London. After teaching at the Royal Scottish Academy of Music in Glasgow (1957–63), he was on the faculty of the Univ. of Hull from 1963, where he was made senior lecturer in 1968 and then reader in composition in 1978. Among his works are *The Birth of Freedom*, ballet (1961), *Shadows in the Sun*, opera (1976), and *Minotaur*, musical (1978); also music for films and television. He publ. the book *Basic Tonal Harmony* (1987).

Hedwall, Lennart, Swedish pianist, organist, conductor, teacher, writer on music, and composer; b. Göteborg, Sept. 16, 1932. He received training in organ and piano; he was a composition student of Bäck and Blomdahl at the Stockholm Musikhögskolan (1951–59), and also studied conducting with Mann and in Vienna with Swarowsky; he also pursued his composition studies abroad with Fortner, Krenek, and Jelinek. He conducted at the Riksteatern (1958–60), the Stora Teatern in Göteborg (1962–65), the Drottningsholmteatern (1966–70) and the Royal Theater (1967–68) in Stockholm, and with the Örebro Orchestral Foundation (1968–74). After teaching at the Göteborg College of Speech and Drama (1963–67), he taught at the school of the Royal Theater in Stockholm (1968–70; 1974–80; 1985–97); he also served as director of the Swedish National Music Museum in Stockholm (1981–83). As a performing musician, he was very active as an accompanist. His writings include 2 books on Alfvén (monograph, 1973; pictorial biography, 1990), a study of the Swedish symphony (1983), and a pictorial biography of Peterson-Berger (1983). The idiom of his music ranges from the traditional to the audaciously modern. His works include the operas *Herr Sleeman kommer* (1976–78; Örebro, March 16, 1979) and *Amerika, Amerika* (1980–81).

Heger, Robert, German conductor and composer; b. Strasbourg, Aug. 19, 1886; d. Munich, Jan. 14, 1978. He studied in Strasbourg, with Kempter in Zürich, and with Schillings in Berlin. After conducting opera in Strasbourg (1907–08), Ulm/Donau (1908–11), and Barmen (1911), he conducted at the Vienna Volksoper (1911–13). From 1913 to 1921 he was conductor of the Nuremberg Opera, and then conducted at the Bavarian State Opera in Munich. He conducted at the Vienna State Opera from 1925 to 1933; concurrently he conducted the concerts of Vienna's Gesellschaft der Musikfreunde and conducted opera at London's Covent Garden. From 1933 to 1945 he conducted at the Berlin State Opera; he also was music director of the Kassel State Theater (1935–41) and of the Zoppot Waldoper. After conducting at the Berlin Städtische Oper (1945–50), he settled in Munich as a regular conductor at the Bavarian State Opera. He also served as president of the Munich Hochschule für Musik (1950–54). Heger acquired a respectable position among opera conductors in Germany. While his compositions failed to maintain themselves in the repertoire, his orchestrations of several of Richard Strauss's songs have become well known.

WORKS: OPERAS: *Ein Fest auf Haderslev* (Nuremberg, Nov. 12, 1919; rev. 1943); *Der Bettler Namenlos* (1931; Munich, April 8, 1932); *Der verlorene Sohn* (1935; Dresden, March 11, 1936; rev. 1942); *Lady Hamilton* (1941; Nuremberg, Feb. 11, 1951); *Das ewige Reich* (n.d.; rev. 1972 as *Trägodie der Zweitracht*).

Heiden, Bernhard, German-born American composer and pedagogue; b. Frankfurt am Main, Aug. 24, 1910. He studied piano, clarinet, violin, theory, and harmony; from 1929 to 1933 he studied at the Hochschule für Musik in Berlin, where his principal teacher was Hindemith. In 1935 he emigrated to the United States and became a naturalized American citizen in 1941. He taught at the Art Center Music School in Detroit; he was also conductor of the Detroit Chamber Orch., as well as pianist, harpsichordist, and chamber music artist. He served in the U.S. Army (1943–45), then studied musicology with Grout at Cornell Univ. (A.M., 1946). In 1946 he joined the faculty of the Indiana Univ. School of Music in Bloomington; he retired in 1981. His music is neoclassical in its formal structure, and strongly polyphonic in texture; it is distinguished also by its impeccable sonorous balance and effective instrumentation.

WORKS: DRAMATIC: Incidental music to *Henry IV* (1940) and *The Tempest* (1942); *Dreamers on a Slack Wire*, dance drama for 2 Pianos and Percussion (1953); *The Darkened City*, opera (1962; Bloomington, Ind., Feb. 23, 1963).

Heidingsfeld, Ludwig, German composer; b. Jauer, March 24, 1854; d. Danzig, Sept. 14, 1920. He studied at the Stern Cons. in Berlin, and later taught there. He subsequently settled in Danzig, and founded a cons. (1899). He wrote 2 operettas, *Der neue Dirigent* (Danzig, 1907) and *Alle Burchenherrlichkeit* (Danzig, 1911).

Heinefetter, family of German opera singers:

(1) Sabine Heinefetter, soprano; b. Mainz, Aug. 19, 1809; d. Illemau, Nov. 18, 1872. She made her operatic debut in Ritter's *Der Mandarin* in Frankfurt am Main in 1822. Spohr then engaged her for Kassel, but she broke her contract to continue vocal study with Banderali and Tadolini in Paris. After appearances at the Théâtre-Italien there, she sang with brilliant success all over Europe. She created the role of Adina in *L'elisir d'amore* (Milan, 1832). She made her farewell appearances in Marseilles in 1846. She died insane.

(2) Clara Heinefetter, soprano, sister of the preceding; b. Mainz, Sept. 7, 1813; d. Vienna, Feb. 23, 1857. She studied with her sister Sabine and with Ciccimarra in Vienna, making her debut there in 1831. She subsequently sang under the name of Mme. Stöckl-Heinefetter; appeared in London (1840–42). She also died insane.

(3) Kathinka Heinefetter, soprano, sister of the preceding; b. Mainz, Sept. 12, 1819; d. Freiburg, Dec. 20, 1858. She studied with her sister Sabine and with Ponchard in Vienna, making her debut in Frankfurt am Main in 1836; she retired from the stage in 1853. Three other Heinefetter sisters, Fatima, Eva, and Nanetta, also appeared professionally on the operatic stage.

Heinichen, Johann David, notable German composer and music theorist; b. Krössuln, near Weissenfels, April 17, 1683; d. Dresden, July 16, 1729. He was educated at the Thomasschule in Leipzig, studying with Schell and Kuhnau; at the same time, he studied law, and practiced as a lawyer in Weissenfels. His first opera, *Der Karneval von Venedig, oder Der angenehme Betrug*, was performed in Leipzig in 1709. He then held a position as conductor at Zeitz. Councillor Buchta of Zeitz supplied the funds for Heinichen to accompany him to Italy (1710–16), where he produced several operas. In Venice he joined the elector of Saxony, Frederick Augustus, and followed him to Dresden as Kapellmeister of the Italian opera company there (1717). However, as a result of confusion brought about by a violent quarrel between Heinichen and the singer Berselli, the Dresden opera was dissolved. Heinichen remained in Dresden as director of church and chamber music. He was a prolific composer; a thematic catalog of his works is found in G. Seibel, *Das Leben des J. D. H.* (Leipzig, 1913). Most of his compositions were preserved in the Dresden Court (later State) Library, but unfortunately many perished in the firebombing of Dresden in 1945. Few of his works have been publ., although the championship of his music by Reinhard Goebel via recordings has proved noteworthy. Heinichen wrote the important theoretical work, *Neu erfundene und gründliche Anweisung zu vollkommener Erlernung des General-Basses* (Hamburg, 1711; 2d ed., rev. and greatly augmented, as *Der General-Bass in der Composition*, Dresden, 1728).

BIBL.: R. Tanner, *J. D. H. als dramatischer Komponist* (Leipzig, 1916).

Heininen, Paavo (Johannes), significant Finnish composer and teacher; b. Helsinki, Jan. 13, 1938. After studying privately with Merilainen, he took courses with Merikanto, Rautavaara, Englund, and Kokkonen at the Sibelius Academy in Helsinki (composition diploma, 1960); he later took courses with Zimmermann in Cologne (1960–61), and with Persichetti and Steuermann at the Juilliard School of Music in New York (1961–62); he also worked with Lutosławski in Poland, and attended theory classes at the Univ. of Helsinki. In 1962–63 he was on the faculty of the Sibelius Academy; taught in Turku (1963–66) before resuming his position at the Sibelius Academy, where he was mentor to a generation of Finnish composers. He was also active as a pianist, conductor, and program annotator. He developed a highly complex compositional style, employing styles and techniques ranging from neoclassicism to dodecaphonic and serial procedures culminating in a stream-of-consciousness modality.

WORKS: DRAMATIC: *Silkkirumpu* (The Silken Drum), concerto for Singers, Players, Words, Images, and Movements (1981–83; Helsinki, April 5, 1984); *Veitsi* (The Knife), opera (1985–88; Helsinki, July 3, 1989).

Heinsheimer, Hans (Walter), German-born American publishing executive and writer on music; b. Karlsruhe, Sept. 25, 1900; d. N.Y., Oct. 12, 1993. He studied law in Heidelberg, Munich, and Freiburg im Breisgau (Juris Dr., 1923); then joined Universal Edition in Vienna, where he was in charge of its opera dept. (1924–38), and supervised the publication of such important stage works as Berg's *Wozzeck*, Krenek's *Jonny spielt auf*, Weinberger's *Schwanda*, Weill's *Aufstieg und Fall der Stadt Mahagonny*, and Antheil's *Transatlantic*. He went to the United States in 1938 and was associated with the N.Y. branch of Boosey & Hawkes. In 1947 he was appointed director of the symphonic and operatic repertoire of G. Schirmer, Inc.; in 1957 he became director of publications and in 1972 vice president of the firm; in these capacities, he promoted the works of Barber, Menotti, Bernstein, and Carter. He retired in 1974 and devoted himself mainly to writing. A brilliant stylist in both German and English, he contributed numerous informative articles to *Melos*, *Musical Quarterly*, *Holiday*, *Reader's Digest*, etc. He publ. the entertaining books *Menagerie in F-sharp* (N.Y., 1947) and *Fanfare for Two Pigeons* (1952); the 2 works were publ. in German in a single vol. entitled *Menagerie in Fis-dur* (Zürich, 1953); he also wrote *Best Regards to Aida* (publ. in Ger. as *Schönste Grüsse an Aida*; Munich, 1968).

Heinze, Gustav Adolf, German conductor and composer; b. Leipzig, Oct. 1, 1820; d. Muiderberg, near Amsterdam, Feb. 20, 1904. He received his early musical education from his father, a clarinetist in the Gewandhaus Orch. in Leipzig, and joined that orch. as clarinetist at the age of 16. He then conducted at the Breslau City Theater (1844–49), where he successfully produced 2 operas: *Loreley* (1846) and *Die Ruinen von Tharandt* (1847). In 1850 he went to Amsterdam, where he founded a singing school (1862–69); he later founded a music school in Bussum

(1885). He composed, besides his operas, several oratorios and other choral works. He publ. an autobiography (Amsterdam, 1905).

Heise, Peter (Arnold), esteemed Danish composer; b. Copenhagen, Feb. 11, 1830; d. Stockkerup, Sept. 12, 1879. He studied music with Berggreen in Copenhagen and with Hauptmann at the Leipzig Cons. Returning to Denmark, he became a music teacher and organist at Sorö, where he remained until 1865. He then settled in Copenhagen, where he produced 2 successful operas, *Paschaens datter* (The Pasha's Daughter; Sept. 30, 1869) and *Drot og marsk* (King and Marshal; Sept. 25, 1878). However, it was in his many lieder to Danish texts that Heise achieved enduring fame.

BIBL.: G. Hetsch, *P. H.* (Copenhagen, 1926).

Hekster, Walter, Dutch clarinetist, teacher, and composer; b. Amsterdam, March 29, 1937. He studied clarinet and composition at the Amsterdam Cons. (graduated, 1961). After playing clarinet in the Connecticut Sym. Orch. (1962–65), he studied with Sessions at the Berkshire Music Center in Tanglewood (summer 1966). He taught clarinet and composition at Brandon Univ. in Canada (1965–71), and then at the conservatories in Utrecht and Arnhem. His compositions include the chamber opera *The Fog* (1987).

Heldy, Fanny (real name, **Marguerite Virginia Emma Clémentine Deceuninck**), Belgian-born French soprano; b. Ath, near Liège, Feb. 29, 1888; d. Paris, Dec. 13, 1973. She studied in Liège and Brussels. She made her operatic debut as Elena in Gunsbourg's *Ivan le Terrible* at the Théâtre Royal de la Monnaie in Brussels, where she sang regularly while accepting guest engagements in Monte Carlo, Warsaw, and St. Petersburg. In 1917 she made her Paris debut as Violetta at the Opéra Comique, and sang there until 1920; she then was a member of the Paris Opéra (1920–39). In 1926 and 1928 she sang at London's Covent Garden. Among her admired portrayals were Marguerite, Nedda, Mélisande, Louise, Manon, Concepción, and Thaïs.

Heller, Hans Ewald, German-American composer; b. Vienna, April 17, 1894; d. N.Y., Oct. 1, 1966. He studied with J. B. Foerster and Camillo Horn; was engaged in Vienna as a music critic and teacher. In 1938 he settled in the United States. Among his compositions were the light operas *Satan* (Vienna, 1927), *Messalina* (Prague, 1928), and *Der Liebling von London* (Vienna, 1930).

Hellermann, William (David), American composer and guitarist; b. Milwaukee, July 15, 1939. He studied mechanical engineering at the Univ. of Wisc. (B.S., 1962) and composition at Columbia Univ. (M.A., 1965; D.M.A., 1969), his principal mentors being Wolpe, Chou Wen-chung, Luening, and Ussachevsky. From 1966 to 1972 he was on the music faculty at Columbia Univ. He also held a composer's fellowship to the Berkshire Music Center at Tanglewood (summer 1967) and the Prix de Rome fellowship to the American Academy in Rome (1972). In 1977 he was composer-in-residence at the Center for the Creative and Performing Arts at the State Univ. of N.Y. at Buffalo. As a guitarist, he has been especially active as a proponent of contemporary music. His compositions are thoroughly modern in range and utilization of resources. He has become particularly well known for his creations in the realm of music sculpture. Among his dramatic works are *Parts Sequences 1 for an Open Space* for 4 Musicians, 4 Actors, 4 Dancers, and 4 Sets (N.Y., March 24, 1972), *Extraordinary Histories*, experimental opera (N.Y., April 28, 1982), *3 Sisters Who Art Not Sisters*, theater piece (1984; Barcelona, Oct. 23, 1985), and *Blood on the Dining Room Floor*, theater piece (N.Y., Nov. 21, 1991).

Hellmesberger, family of famous Austrian musicians:

(1) Georg Hellmesberger Sr., violinist, conductor, and composer; b. Vienna, April 24, 1800; d. Neuwaldegg, near Vienna, Aug. 16, 1873. His father, a country schoolmaster, gave him his first instruction in music; he succeeded Schubert as a chorister in the Hofkapelle. After making his concert debut on Dec. 9, 1819, he studied violin with Böhm and composition with E. Förster at the Vienna Cons.; he then was made assistant to Bohm in 1821; subsequently he was titular prof. (1826–33) and prof. (1833–67). He became concertmaster of the Court Opera in 1830, and also a member of the Hofkapelle; he served as conductor of the Vienna Phil. with Nicolai (1845–47), and then was its sole conductor (1847–48). He made appearances as a violinist in London in 1847; was also active as a teacher; in addition to his sons, he taught Ernst, Auer, and Joachim. He composed 2 violin concertos, some chamber music, and some pieces for solo violin. His 2 sons became musicians of distinction:

(2) Joseph Hellmesberger Sr., violinist and conductor; b. Vienna, Nov. 3, 1828; d. there, Oct. 24, 1893. He studied violin with his father at the Vienna Cons., and was named soloist in the orch. of the Court Opera when he was 17. He was artistic director and conductor of the Gesellschaft der Musikfreunde concerts (1851–59), concurrently teaching violin at the Vienna Cons. (1851–77), then was its director until 1893. He was also concertmaster of the Vienna Phil. (1855–77) and the Court Opera (1860–77); he was named Hofkapellmeister in 1877. In 1849 he founded the renowned Helmesberger Quartet, in which he played 1st violin, retiring in 1891.

BIBL.: A. Barthlmé, *Vom alten H.* (Vienna, 1908); R. Prosl, *Die H.: Hundert Jahre aus dem Leben einer Wiener Musikerfamilie* (Vienna, 1947).

(3) Georg Hellmesberger Jr., violinist and composer; b. Vienna, Jan. 27, 1830; d. Hannover, Nov. 12, 1852. He studied violin and music theory with his father and composition with Rotter; then toured Germany, and subsequently accompanied his father to London in 1847; he was named Hofkonzertmeister in Hannover in 1850. Among his 9 operas were *Die Bürgschaft* and *Die beiden Königinnen*. His promising career was tragically cut short by tuberculosis.

(4) Joseph Hellmesberger Jr., violinist, conductor, and composer, son of **Joseph Hellmesberger Sr.**; b. Vienna, April 9, 1855; d. there, April 26, 1907. He studied with his father, making his debut at a Vienna Cons. concert when he was 8 and becoming 2d violinist in his father's quartet when he was 15. He was concertmaster of the Vienna Phil. (1870–84); he was also made solo violinist of the Hofkapelle and the Court Opera in 1878, and prof. of violin at the Cons. He became conductor of the new Ringtheater in 1881, but his tenure was cut short by a disastrous fire (Dec. 8, 1881), which destroyed the building. He then became conductor of the Carltheater in 1882, and subsequently (1884) was made concertmaster and music director of the ballet at the Court Opera; he was named Vizehofkapellmeister in 1889, and then Hofkapellmeister in succession to Richter in 1890; he also succeeded his father as 1st violin in the Hellmesberger Quartet in 1891, and later served as conductor of the Vienna Phil. (1901–03) and of the Stuttgart Opera (1904–05). He wrote 10 operettas, the most celebrated being *Das Veilchenmädel* (Vienna, Feb. 27, 1904).

(5) Ferdinand Hellmesberger, cellist and conductor, son of **Joseph Hellmesberger Sr.**; b. Vienna, Jan. 24, 1863; d. there, March 15, 1940. He studied at the Vienna Cons.. He became a member of the Hofkapelle in 1879, and also played in his father's quartet (from 1883). He taught cello at the Vienna Cons. (1884–1902), and was solo cellist in the orch. of the Court Opera (1886–1902). He then was conductor of the Volksoper (1902–05), and subsequently ballet conductor at the Berlin Court Opera (1905–10); later conducted various spa orchs.

Hellwig, Karl (Friedrich) Ludwig, German organist and composer; b. Wriezen, July 23, 1773; d. Berlin, Nov. 24, 1838. He learned to play all the string instruments and piano, then studied theory with Zelter and others; at the same time, he was engaged in the manufacture of paint, which enabled him to pursue his musical studies as an avocation. He became a member of the Singakademie in 1793; he was a conductor with it from 1803, serving as joint deputy conductor (1815–33). In 1813 he became organist of the Berlin Cathedral; he was its director of music from

1815. He wrote 2 operas, *Die Bergknappen* (Dresden, April 27, 1820) and *Don Sylvio di Rosalbo* (unperf.) and a number of German lieder, which show a certain poetic sensitivity and a ballad-like quality in the manner of Zelter and other early German Romanticists.

Helm, Anny, Austrian soprano; b. Vienna, July 20, 1903. She was a student of Gutheil-Schoder and Gertrude Förstel in Vienna, and of Grenzebach in Berlin. In 1924 she made her operatic debut in Magdeburg, and then appeared at the Berlin State Opera (1926–33) and at the Bayreuth Festivals (1927–31). In 1933 she settled in Italy, where she sang under the name Anny Helm-Sbisa (her husband, Giuseppe Sbisa, was director of the Teatro Giuseppe Verdi in Trieste). In 1939 she appeared at London's Covent Garden. She devoted herself mainly to teaching from 1941. Her finest roles included Donna Anna, Brangäne, Isolde, Brünnhilde, Turandot, and Elektra.

Helm, Everett (Burton), American composer and musicologist; b. Minneapolis, July 17, 1913. He studied at Harvard Univ. (M.A., 1936; Ph.D., 1939) and also in Europe (1936–38) with Malipiero, Vaughan Williams, and Alfred Einstein. Returning to the United States, he taught at Western College in Oxford, Ohio (1943–44). From 1948 to 1950 he was a music officer under the U.S. military government in Germany. He was ed. of *Musical America* (1961–63). A linguist, he contributed articles to various music magazines in several languages; he made a specialty of the music of Yugoslavia and was a guest lecturer at the Univ. of Ljubljana (1966–68).

WRITINGS: *Béla Bartók in Selbstzeugnissen und Biddokumenten* (Reinbek-bei-Hamburg, 1965; reduction and Eng. tr., N.Y., 1972); *Composer, Performer, Public: A Study in Communication* (Florence, 1970); *Franz Liszt* (Hamburg, 1972); *Music and Tomorrow's Public* (Wilhelmshaven, 1981). His works include *Adam and Eve*, an adaptation of a medieval mystery play (Wiesbaden, Oct. 28, 1951), *The Siege of Tottenburg*, radio opera (1956), *Le Roy fait battre tambour*, ballet (1956), and *500 Dragon-Thalers*, Singspiel (1956).

Hemberg, (Bengt Sven) Eskil, Swedish composer, administrator, and conductor; b. Stockholm, Jan. 19, 1938. He studied organ and was a student of Blomstedt (conducting) at the Stockholm Musikhögskolan (1957–64). From 1959 to 1964 he conducted the Stockholm Academic Choir, and then was its artistic director from 1964 to 1984. He was executive producer for the Swedish Broadcasting Corp., serving as head of its choral section (1963–70); he then was head of planning of the Inst. for National Concerts (1970–83) and president of the Swedish Soc. of Composers (1971–83). After serving as artistic director of the Stora Teatern in Göteborg (1984–87), he held that title with the Royal Theater in Stockholm from 1987 to 1996. In 1974 he was elected a member of the Royal Academy of Music in Stockholm. He has written much vocal music, ranging from operas to sacred scores, in which traditional procedures are enhanced by ventures into contemporary harmony. Among his dramatic works are *Love, love, love,* opera (1973–80), *The Pirates in the Deep Green Sea,* opera (1975–77), *St. Erik's Crown*, church opera (1979), *Herr Apfelstädt wird Kunstler*, chamber opera (1989), and *Utopia,* opera (1997); also film music.

Hemel, Oscar van, Dutch composer; b. Antwerp, Aug. 3, 1892; d. Hilversum, July 9, 1981. He was a student of L. Mortelmans and de Boeck at the Royal Flemish Cons. in Antwerp; in 1914 he settled in the Netherlands, and later pursued his training with Pijper in Rotterdam (1931–33). The style of his works oscillated between Austro-German Romantic trends and the more complex technical structures of the Dutch modernists. He composed the radio opera *Viviane* (Hilversum Radio, 1950).

Heming, Percy, English baritone; b. Bristol, Sept. 6, 1883; d. London, Jan. 11, 1956. He studied in London at the Royal Academy of Music and with Henschel and Thomas Blackburn; also with Grose in Dresden. In 1915 he made his operatic debut as Paris in *Roméo et Juliette* with the Beecham Opera Co. in London, with which he appeared until 1919. In 1920 he made a tour of the United States in *The Beggar's Opera*. In 1922 he joined the British National Opera Co. in London, and also appeared there at Sadler's Wells (1933–35; 1940–42); he also served as artistic director of London's Covent Garden English Co. (1937–39) and as artistic advisor at Covent Garden (1946–48). He was greatly admired as one of England's finest baritones. His repertory was extensive, but he excelled particularly as Mozart's Dr. Bartolo, Ford, Amfortas, Macheath, and Scarpia.

Hempel, Frieda, brilliant German soprano; b. Leipzig, June 26, 1885; d. Berlin, Oct. 7, 1955. She studied piano at the Leipzig Cons. (1900–02) before pursuing vocal training with Selma Nicklass-Kempner at the Stern Cons. in Berlin (1902–05). After making her operatic debut in Breslau in 1905, she appeared with the Berlin Royal Opera for the first time on Aug. 22, 1905, as Frau Fluth in Nicolai's *Die lustigen Weiber von Windsor*. Following appearances with the Schwerin Court Opera (1905–07), she returned to Berlin and was a leading member of the Royal Opera until 1912. On May 2, 1907, she made her debut at London's Covent Garden as Bastienne in Mozart's opera and as Gretel in Humperdinck's opera in a double bill. She made her first appearance at the Metropolitan Opera in New York on Dec. 27, 1912, as the Queen in *Les Huguenots*. She remained on its roster until 1919, gaining renown for her portrayals of such roles as the Queen of the Night, Susanna, Rosina, Lucia, Offenbach's Olympia, Eva, and Violetta. In 1914 and again in 1920–21 she sang with the Chicago Grand Opera. Thereafter she devoted herself to concert appearances in which she impersonated Jenny Lind in period costume. Her memoirs were publ. as *Mein Leben dem Gesang* (Berlin, 1955). Hempel possessed a remarkable coloratura voice. Her repertoire extended from Mozart to Richard Strauss, including the latter's Marschallin.

Hemsley, Thomas (Jeffery), English baritone; b. Coalville, April 12, 1927. He studied at Brasenose College, Oxford, and received private vocal training from Lucie Manén. In 1951 he made his operatic debut as Purcell's Aeneas at London's Mermaid Theatre; he then sang regularly at the Glyndebourne Festival (1953–71). He also sang at the Aachen City Theater (1953–56), the Deutsche Oper am Rhein in Düsseldorf (1957–63), the Zürich Opera (1963–67), the Bayreuth Festivals (1968–70), and at London's Covent Garden (from 1970). He likewise pursued a career as a concert singer. In later years, he was active as an opera director and as a teacher. Prominent among his roles were such portrayals as Don Fernando, Count Almaviva, Dr. Malatesta, Beckmesser, and Massetto.

Henderson, Alva, American composer; b. San Luis Obispo, Calif., April 8, 1940. He studied voice and theory at San Francisco State College. He wrote mainly vocal works, including the operas *Medea* (San Diego, Nov. 29, 1972), *The Tempest* (n.d.), and *The Last of the Mohicans* (Wilmington, Del., June 12, 1976).

Henderson, Roy (Galbraith), Scottish baritone, conductor, and pedagogue; b. Edinburgh, July 4, 1899. He studied at the Royal Academy of Music in London (1920–25). He made his London debut as Zarathustra in *A Mass of Life* by Delius in 1925; his operatic debut followed in 1928 as Donner in Wagner's *Das Rheingold* at Covent Garden; he also sang at the Glyndebourne Festival (1934–39). He was founder and conductor of the Nottingham Oriana Choir (1936–52); he was a prof. of singing at the Royal Academy of Music (1940–74). He was made a Commander of the Order of the British Empire in 1970. Henderson was especially esteemed as a concert singer, becoming well known for his championship of music by English composers. As a teacher, he numbered Kathleen Ferrier among his gifted students.

Henderson, W(illiam) J(ames), noted American music critic; b. Newark, N.J., Dec. 4, 1855; d. (suicide) N.Y., June 5, 1937. He was a graduate of Princeton Univ. (B.A., 1876; M.A., 1886); he also studied piano with Carl Langlotz (1868–73) and voice with Torriani (1876–77); he was chiefly self-taught in theory. He was first a reporter (1883–87), then music critic of the *N.Y. Times*

(1887–1902) and the *N.Y. Sun* (1902–37); lectured on music history at the N.Y. College of Music (1889–95; 1899–1902); from 1904 he lectured on the development of vocal art at the Inst. of Musical Art in New York. A brilliant writer, Henderson was an irreconcilable and often venomous critic of modern music; he loved Wagner, but savagely attacked Debussy and Richard Strauss. Henderson, in turn, was the butt of some of Charles Ives's caustic wit. Among his many writings (all publ. in New York) are *Richard Wagner, His Life and His Dramas* (1901; 2d ed., 1923), *The Art of the Singer* (1906; 2d ed., aug., 1938, as *The Art of Singing*), *Some Forerunners of Italian Opera* (1911), and *Early History of Singing* (1921).

Hendricks, Barbara, greatly admired black American soprano; b. Stephens, Ark., Nov. 20, 1948. She sang in church and school choirs before majoring in chemistry and mathematics at the Univ. of Nebraska (graduated, 1969); during the summer of 1968 she began vocal training with Tourel at the Aspen (Colo.) Music School, continuing under her guidance at the Juilliard School in New York (1969–71); she also attended Callas's master class there. In 1971 she won the Geneva International Competition, and in 1972 both the International Concours de Paris and the Kosciuszko Foundation Vocal Competition. On Feb. 20, 1973, she made her debut in Thomson's *4 Saints in 3 Acts* in the Mini-Metropolitan Opera production presented at the Lincoln Center Forum Theatre in New York; later that year she made her first concert tour of Europe. In 1974 she appeared as Erisbe in Cavalli's *Ormindo* at the San Francisco Spring Opera, and in the title role of Cavalli's *La Calisto* at the Glyndebourne Festival. On Feb. 26, 1975, she made her formal N.Y. debut as Inez in a concert performance of *La Favorite* at Carnegie Hall. In 1976 she sang Amor in Gluck's *Orfeo ed Euridice* with the Netherlands Opera at the Holland Festival, and on Nov. 14 of that year made her N.Y. recital debut at Town Hall. At the Berlin Deutsche Oper in 1978 she appeared as Mozart's Susanna, a role she quickly made her own. In 1980 she sang Gilda and in 1981 Pamina at the Orange Festival in France; in 1982 she appeared as Gounod's Juliet at both the Paris Opéra and London's Covent Garden. On Oct. 30, 1986, she made her Metropolitan Opera debut in New York as Strauss's Sophie. In 1988 she sang at the 70th birthday celebration for Leonard Bernstein at the Tanglewood Festival, and also starred as Mimi in Luigi Comencini's film version of *La Bohème*. In 1989 she appeared at the Bolshoi Theater in Moscow. In addition to her operatic career, she has won notable distinction as a recitalist. In 1991 she sang Manon in Parma and in 1992 she sang Micaëla in Orange. Her interpretations of the German and French lieder repertoire, as well as of Negro spirituals, have won accolades. In 1986 she was made a Commandeur des Arts et des Lettres of France. Her unswerving commitment to social justice led the High Commissioner for Refugees at the United Nations to name her a goodwill ambassador of the world body in 1987.

Henkemans, Hans, Dutch pianist, composer, physician, and psychiatrist; b. The Hague, Dec. 23, 1913; d. Dec. 29, 1995. He studied piano and composition with Sigtenhorst-Meyer (1926–31), and then composition with Pijper (1933–38); he also took courses in medicine at the Univ. of Utrecht (from 1931) and later took his doctorate at the Univ. of Amsterdam (1981). After making his debut as a pianist in his own Piano Concerto at 19, he pursued a successful concert career until 1969 when he decided to practice medicine and psychiatry. In his compositions, which include the opera *Winter Cruise* (1977), he succeeded in developing an original voice while utilizing traditional forms.

Henneberg, (Carl) Albert (Theodor), Swedish composer; b. Stockholm, March 27, 1901; d. Sollentuna, April 14, 1991. His father was the German conductor and composer Richard Henneberg (b. Berlin, Aug. 5, 1853; d. Malmö, Oct. 19, 1925). He studied composition with Ellberg at the Stockholm Cons. (1920–24) and later in Vienna and Paris (1926–30). Returning to Stockholm in 1931, he became active as a conductor; later he served as secretary (1945–49) and treasurer (1947–63) of the Soc. of Swedish Composers. His compositions were conceived in a late Romantic style. Among his works are the operas *Inka* (1935–36), *Det jäser i Småland* (1937–38), *Den lyckliga staden* (1940–41), *Bolla och Badin* (1942–44), and *I madonnans skugga* (1946).

Henneberg, Johann Baptist, Austrian organist, conductor, and composer; b. Vienna, Dec. 6, 1768; d. there, Nov. 26, 1822. He conducted at Vienna theaters (1790–1803), then became a member of the orch. of Count Esterházy. In 1818 he returned to Vienna, where he became choirmaster at the Am Hof Church; was named court organist in 1818. He wrote a great number of Singspiels, of which the most successful were *Die Waldmänner* (Vienna, Oct. 14, 1793) and *Liebe macht kurzen Prozess* (Leipzig, 1799).

Henriques, Fini (Valdemar), Danish violinist, conductor, and composer; b. Copenhagen, Dec. 20, 1867; d. there, Oct. 27, 1940. He studied violin with Valdemar Tofte in Copenhagen, and with Joachim at the Hochschule für Musik in Berlin; he studied composition with Svendsen. Returning to Copenhagen, he was a violinist in the Court Orch. (1892–96); he also appeared as a soloist. He organized his own string quartet, and traveled with it in Europe; he also conducted orchs. As a composer, he followed the Romantic school; he possessed a facile gift of melody; his "Danish Lullaby" became a celebrated song in Denmark. He also wrote an opera, *Staerstikkeren* (Copenhagen, May 20, 1922), and several ballets (*The Little Mermaid*, after Hans Andersen; *Tata*; etc.).

BIBL.: S. Berg, *F. V. H.* (Copenhagen, 1943).

Henry, Pierre, influential French composer and acoustician; b. Paris, Dec. 9, 1927. He studied with Messiaen (composition) and Boulanger (piano) at the Paris Cons. (1938–48). In 1950 he was a founder of the Groupe de Recherche de Musique Concrète with Pierre Schaeffer, but in 1958 separated from the group to experiment on his own projects in the field of electro-acoustical music and electronic synthesis of musical sounds. In virtually all of his independent works, he applied electronic effects, often with the insertion of prerecorded patches of concrete music and sometimes "objets trouvés" borrowed partially or in their entirety from preexistent compositions. In collaboration with Schaeffer, he wrote *Symphonie pour un homme seul* (1950) and the experimental opera *Orphée 53* (1953); independently, he wrote 4 ballets: *Haut voltage* (1956), *Coexistence* (1959), *Investigations* (1959), and *Le Voyage* (1962); also *Futuristie 1*, "electro-acoustical musical spectacle," with the reconstruction of the "bruiteurs" introduced by the Italian futurist Luigi Russolo in 1909 (Paris, Oct. 16, 1975).

BIBL.: M. Chion, *P. H.* (Paris, 1980).

Henschel, Sir (Isidor) George (Georg), esteemed German-born English baritone, pianist, conductor, teacher, and composer; b. Breslau, Feb. 18, 1850; d. Aviemore, Scotland, Sept. 10, 1934. His parents were of Polish-Jewish descent but he converted to Christianity when young. He was a student of Julius Shäffer in Breslau, of Moscheles (piano), Götze (voice), Papperitz (organ), and Reinecke (theory) at the Leipzig Cons. (1867–70), and of Kiel (composition) and Adolf Schulze (voice) at the Berlin Cons. He gave concerts as a tenor before making his debut as a pianist in Berlin in 1862. In 1866 he first appeared as a bass in Hirschberg, and then as a baritone as Hans Sachs in a concert performance in Leipzig in 1868. He subsequently sang throughout Europe. In 1881 he was selected as the first conductor of the Boston Sym. Orch., which post he held until 1884; he also appeared as a concert singer in Boston and New York He then settled in England, where he was founder-conductor of the London Sym. Concerts (1886–97). He taught voice at the Royal College of Music in London (1886–88) and was conductor of the Scottish Orch. in Glasgow (1891–95); later he taught voice at the Inst. of Musical Art in New York (1905–08). In 1928, at the age of 78, he sang Schubert lieder in London in commemoration of the 100th anniversary of the composer's death. In 1931 he was invited to conduct the 50th anniversary concert of the Boston Sym. Orch. In 1881 he married **Lillian June** (née **Bailey**) **Henschel**. In 1890 he became a naturalized British subject and in 1914 he was knighted. He publ. *Personal Recollections of Johannes Brahms* (1907), *Musings and*

Memories of a Musician (1918), and *Articulation in Singing* (1926). His compositions were in the German Romantic tradition. They included the opera *Nubia* (Dresden, Dec. 9, 1899); *Stabat Mater* (Birmingham, Oct. 4, 1894); *Requiem* (Boston, Dec. 2, 1902); Mass (London, June 1, 1916); String Quartet; about 200 songs.

Henschel, Lillian June (née **Bailey**), American soprano; b. Columbus, Ohio, Jan. 17, 1860; d. London, Nov. 4, 1901. She made her professional debut in Boston at 16, then went to Paris to study with Viardot-García. On April 30, 1879, she appeared in London, at a Phil. concert, when she sang, besides her solo number, a duet with **George Henschel**. She then studied with him and on March 9, 1881, married him. When Henschel was appointed 1st conductor of the Boston Sym. Orch., she appeared as a soloist with him accompanying her at the piano, also in duets at Boston Sym. concerts. Until her untimely death, the Henschels were constantly associated in American artistic life. Her well-trained voice and fine musical feeling won her many admirers.

BIBL.: H. Henschel, *When Soft Voices Die: A Musical Biography* (London, 1944).

Hensel, Heinrich, German tenor; b. Neustadt, Oct. 29, 1874; d. Hamburg, Feb. 23, 1935. He studied with Gustav Walter in Vienna and with Eduard Bellwidt in Frankfurt am Main. He sang in Freiburg im Breisgau (1897–1900), Frankfurt am Main (1900–06), and then at Wiesbaden (1906–11), where Siegfried Wagner heard him and engaged him to create the chief tenor part in his opera *Banadietrich* (Karlsruhe, 1910) and also to sing Parsifal at the Bayreuth Festival. He obtained excellent success; subsequently he sang at Covent Garden, London (1911–14). He made his American debut at the Metropolitan Opera in New York as Lohengrin (Dec. 22, 1911) and was hailed by the press as one of the finest Wagnerian tenors; he also appeared with the Chicago Opera (1911–12); he then was a leading Heldentenor at the Hamburg Opera (1912–29). He was married to the soprano Elsa Hensel-Schweitzer (1878–1937), who sang in Dessau (1898–1901) and then in Frankfurt am Main (from 1901).

Hentschel, Franz, German conductor and composer; b. Berlin, Nov. 6, 1814; d. there, May 11, 1889. He studied with A. W. Bach. After conducting theater orchs. in provincial towns, he settled in Berlin as a music teacher. He wrote an opera, *Die Hexenreise*, and numerous marches for military band.

Hentschel, Theodor, German conductor and composer; b. Schirgiswalde, March 28, 1830; d. Hamburg, Dec. 19, 1892. He studied with Reissiger and Ciccarelli in Dresden. He was active as a theater conductor in Bremen (1860–90), and then at Hamburg. He wrote the operas *Matrose und Sänger* (Leipzig, 1857), *Der Königspage* (Bremen, 1874), *Die Braut von Lusignan, oder Die schöne Melusine* (Bremen, 1875), *Lancelot* (Bremen, 1878), and *Des Königs Schwerdt* (Hamburg, 1891).

Henze, Hans Werner, outstanding German composer; b. Gütersloh, Westphalia, July 1, 1926. His early studies at the Braunschweig School of Music (1942–44) were interrupted by military service during World War II, and for a year he was in the German Army on the Russian front. In 1946 he took music courses at the Kirchenmusikalisches Inst. in Heidelberg; he also studied privately with Fortner (1946–48). He became fascinated with the disciplinary aspects of Schoenberg's method of composition with 12 tones, and attended the seminars on the subject given by Leibowitz at Darmstadt. A musician of restless temperament, he joined a radical political group and proclaimed the necessity of writing music without stylistic restrictions in order to serve the masses. In 1953 he moved to Italy, and later joined the Italian Communist Party. From 1961 to 1967 he taught composition at the Salzburg Mozarteum, in 1969–70 in Havana, and in 1980 at the Cologne Hochschule für Musik. He successfully integrated musical idioms and mannerisms of seemingly incompatible techniques; in his vocal works, he freely adopted such humanoid effects as screaming, bellowing, and snorting; he even specified that long sustained tones were to be sung by inhaling as well as exhaling. Nonetheless, Henze managed to compose music that was feasible for human performance. But political considerations continued to play a decisive role in his career. In 1967 he withdrew from the membership of the Academy of the Arts of West Berlin, in a gesture of protest against its artistic policies. His political stance did not preclude his acceptance in "bourgeois" musical centers, for his works were performed widely in Europe. He held the International Chair of Composition Studies at the Royal Academy of Music in London from 1986. In 1989 he helped found the Munich Biennale. In 1990 he served as the first composer-in-residence of the Berlin Phil.

WORKS: DRAMATIC: *Das Wundertheater*, opera for Actors, after Cervantes (1948; Heidelberg, May 7, 1949; rev. for Singers, 1964; Frankfurt am Main, Nov. 30, 1965); *Ballet Variations* (concert premiere, Düsseldorf, Oct. 3, 1949; stage premiere, Wuppertal, Dec. 21, 1958); *Jack Pudding*, ballet (1949; Wiesbaden, Jan. 1, 1951); *Rosa Silber*, ballet (1950; concert premiere, Berlin, May 8, 1951; stage premiere, Cologne, Oct. 15, 1958); *Labyrinth*, choreographic fantasy (1951; concert premiere, Darmstadt, May 29, 1952); *Die schlafende Prinzessin*, ballet, after Tchaikovsky (1951; Essen, June 5, 1954); *Ein Landarzt*, radio opera, after Kafka (Hamburg, Nov. 19, 1951; broadcast, Nov. 29, 1951; rev. as a monodrama for Baritone and Orch., 1964; Berlin, Oct. 12, 1965; radio opera rev. for the stage, 1964; Frankfurt am Main, Nov. 30, 1965); *Boulevard Solitude*, opera (1951; Hannover, Feb. 17, 1952); *Der Idiot*, ballet pantomime, after Dostoyevsky (Berlin, Sept. 1, 1952); *Pas d'action*, ballet (Munich, 1952; withdrawn by the composer and rev. as *Tancredi*, 1964; Vienna, May 14, 1966); *König Hirsch*, opera (1952–55; Berlin, Sept. 23, 1956; rev. as *Il Re cervo*, 1962; Kassel, March 10, 1963); *Das Ende einer Welt*, radio opera (Hamburg, Dec. 4, 1953; rev. for the stage, 1964; Frankfurt am Main, Nov. 30, 1965); *Maratona*, ballet (1956; Berlin, Sept. 24, 1957); *Ondine*, ballet (1956–57; London, Oct. 27, 1958); *Der Prinz von Homburg*, opera (1958; Hamburg, May 22, 1960); *L'Usignolo dell'Imperatore*, pantomime, after Andersen (Venice, Sept. 16, 1959); *Elegy for Young Lovers*, chamber opera (1959–61; in German, Schwetzingen, May 20, 1961; 1st perf. to Auden's original Eng. libretto, Glyndebourne, July 13, 1961); *Der junge Lord*, comic opera (1964; Berlin, April 7, 1965); *The Bassarids*, opera seria (1965; in German, Salzburg, Aug. 6, 1966; 1st perf. to the original Eng. libretto by Auden and Kallman, Santa Fe, N. Mex., Aug. 7, 1968); *Moralities*, scenic cantatas, after Aesop, to texts by Auden (1967; Cincinnati, May 18, 1968); *Der langwierige Weg in die Wohnung der Natascha Ungeheuer*, show (RAI, Rome, May 17, 1971); *La cubana, oder Ein Leben für die Kunst*, vaudeville (1973; NET Opera Theater, N.Y., March 4, 1974; stage premiere, Munich, May 28, 1975); *We Come to the River*, actions for music (1974–76; London, July 12, 1976); *Don Chisciotte*, opera, arrangement of Paisiello (Montepulciano, Aug. 1, 1976); *Orpheus*, ballet (1978; Stuttgart, March 17, 1979); *Pollicino*, fairy-tale opera (1979–80; Montepulciano, Aug. 2, 1980); *The English Cat*, chamber opera (1980–83; Schwetzingen, June 2, 1983); *Il ritorno d'Ulisse in patria*, realization of Monteverdi's opera (1981; Salzburg, Aug. 18, 1985); *Ödipus der Tyrann oder Der Vater vertreibt seinem Sohn und Schickt die Tochter in die Küche* (Kindberg, Oct. 30, 1983); *Das verratene Meer*, opera (1989; Berlin, May 5, 1990); *Venus und Adonis* (1996; Munich, Jan. 11, 1997). CONCERT: *Der Vorwurf*, concert aria for Baritone, Trumpet, and Strings, after Werfel (Darmstadt, July 29, 1948); 5 Neapolitan songs for Baritone and Orch. (Frankfurt am Main, May 26, 1956); *Nocturnes and Arias* for Soprano and Orch. (Donaueschingen, Oct. 20, 1957); *Ariosi* for Soprano, Violin, and Orch., after Tasso (1963; Edinburgh Festival, Aug. 23, 1964); *Das Floss der Medusa*, oratorio to the memory of Ché Guevara (1968; concert premiere, Vienna, Jan. 29, 1971; stage premiere, Nuremberg, April 15, 1972); *Jephtha*, realization of Carissimi's oratorio (London, July 14, 1976, composer conducting).

WRITINGS: *Musik und Politik: Schriften und Gespräche, 1955–1975* (Munich, 1976; in Eng. as *Music and Politics: Collected Writings, 1953–81*, London and Ithaca, N.Y., 1982).

BIBL.: K. Geitel, *H. W. H.* (Berlin, 1968); E. Restagno, ed., *H.* (Turin, 1986); D. Rexroth, ed., *Der Komponist H. W. H.: Ein Buch der Alten Oper Frankfurt, Frankfurt Feste '86* (Mainz and N.Y., 1986); P. Petersen, *H. W. H., ein politischer Musiker: Zwölf Vorlesungen* (Hamburg, 1988); W. Schottler, *"Die Bassariden" von H. W. H.: Der Weg eines Mythos von der antiken Tragödie zur modernen Oper: Eine Analyse von Stoff, Libretto und Musik* (Trier, 1992); D. Hochgesang, *Die Opern von H. W. H. im Spiegel der deutschsprachigen, zeitgenössischen Musikkritik bis 1966* (Trier, 1995); P. Petersen, *H. W. H.: Werke der Jahre 1984–1993* (Mainz and N.Y., 1995).

Heppener, Robert, Dutch composer and teacher; b. Amsterdam, Aug. 9, 1925. He studied piano with Jan Öde and Johan van den Boogert at the Amsterdam Cons., and composition with Bertus van Lier. He then taught at the Cons. of the Music Lyceum Soc. in Amsterdam. His works include the opera *Een Ziel van Hout* (A Soul of Wood; Amsterdam, June 10, 1998).

Heppner, Ben, outstanding Canadian tenor; b. Murrayville, British Columbia, Jan. 14, 1956. He studied at the Univ. of British Columbia and the Univ. of Toronto. In 1979 he took 1st prize in the CBC Talent Festival, and then sang in concert and oratorio settings in Canada. In 1987 he appeared as Strauss's Bacchus at the Victoria State Opera in Sydney. He made his European operatic debut as Lohengrin at the Royal Opera in Stockholm in 1988. That same year, he won the Metropolitan Opera Auditions and the Birgit Nilsson Prize, which led to his U.S. debut at a state concert for the king and queen of Sweden at N.Y.'s Carnegie Hall. Following an engagement as Lohengrin at the San Francisco Opera in 1989, he sang Bacchus at the Vienna State Opera and Walther von Stolzing at Milan's La Scala and London's Covent Garden in 1990. He made his debut at the Metropolitan Opera in New York on Dec. 11, 1991, as Idomeneo. In 1992 he sang Dvořák's Dimitrij in Munich and Mozart's Tito in Salzburg, and also created the title role in Bolcom's *McTeague* in Chicago. In 1994 he was engaged as Lohengrin at the Seattle Opera. He appeared as Peter Grimes in Vancouver and as Tchaikovsky's Hermann at the Metropolitan Opera in 1995. After singing Andrea Chénier in Seattle in 1996, he appeared as Calaf in Chicago in 1997. In 1998 he returned to Seattle as Tristan and to the Metropolitan Opera as Lohengrin and Walther von Stolzing. He made his N.Y. recital debut at Carnegie Hall on Jan. 30, 1999. Heppner's engagements as a soloist with orchs. and as a recitalist have taken him to the world's leading music centers.

Herberigs, Robert, Belgian composer and novelist; b. Ghent, June 19, 1886; d. Oudenaarde, Sept. 20, 1974. He studied voice at the Ghent Cons. In 1908 he made his operatic debut as a baritone at the Flemish Opera in Antwerp, but then abandoned his operatic aspirations to study composition. In 1909 he won the Belgian Grand Prix with his cantata *La Legénde de St. Hubert*, and subsequently composed prolifically. He also publ. several novels. His compositions followed along Romantic lines.

WORKS: DRAMATIC: *Le Mariage de Rosine*, comic opera (1919; Ghent, Feb. 13, 1925); *L'Amour médecin*, comic opera (1920); *Lam Godsspel* or *Jeu de l'Agneau Mystique*, open-air play (1948); *Antoine et Cleopatra*, radio play (1949); *Le Château des comtes de Gand*, light and sound play (1960).

Herbert, Victor (August), famous Irish-born American composer, cellist, and conductor; b. Dublin, Feb. 1, 1859; d. N.Y., May 26, 1924. He was a grandson of Samuel Lover, the Irish novelist; his father died when he was an infant; his mother married a German physician and the family moved to Stuttgart in 1867. He entered the Stuttgart high school, but did not graduate; his musical ability was definitely pronounced by then, and he selected the cello as his instrument, taking lessons from Bernhard Cossmann in Baden-Baden (1874–76). He soon acquired a degree of technical proficiency that enabled him to take a position as cellist in various orchs. in Germany, France, Italy, and Switzerland; in 1880 he became a cellist of the Eduard Strauss waltz band in Vienna; in 1881, he returned to Stuttgart, where he joined the Court Orch., and studied composition with Max Seifritz at the Cons. His earliest works were for cello with orch.; he performed his Suite with the Stuttgart orch. on Oct. 23, 1883, and his 1st Cello Concerto on Dec. 8, 1885. On Aug. 14, 1886, he married the Viennese opera singer Therese Förster (1861–1927); in the same year, she received an offer to join the Metropolitan Opera in New York, and Herbert was engaged as an orch. cellist there, appearing in New York also as a soloist (played his own Cello Concerto with the N.Y. Phil., Dec. 10, 1887). In his early years in New York, Herbert was overshadowed by the celebrity of his wife, but soon he developed energetic activities on his own, forming an entertainment orch. which he conducted in a repertoire of light music; he also participated in chamber music concerts; was a soloist with the Theodore Thomas and Seidl orchs. He was the conductor of the Boston Festival Orch. in 1891; Tchaikovsky conducted this orch. in Philadelphia in a miscellaneous program, and Herbert played a solo. He was assoc. conductor of the Worcester Festival (1889–91), for which he wrote a dramatic cantata, *The Captive* (Sept. 24, 1891). In 1893 he became bandmaster of the 22d Regiment Band, succeeding P. S. Gilmore. On March 10, 1894, he was soloist with the N.Y. Phil. in his 2d Cello Concerto. In the same year, at the suggestion of William MacDonald, the manager of the Boston Ideal Opera Co., Herbert wrote his first operetta, *Prince Ananias*, which was premiered with encouraging success in New York (Nov. 20, 1894). He quickly established himself as a leading composer in the genre, winning enduring success with such scores as *The Serenade* (1897), *Babes in Toyland* (1903), *Mlle. Modiste* (1905), *Naughty Marietta* (1910), *Sweethearts* (1913), and *The Only Girl* (1914). In 1900 he directed at Madison Square Garden, New York, an orch. of 420 performers for the benefit of the sufferers in the Galveston flood. On April 29, 1906, he led a similar monster concert at the Hippodrome for the victims of the San Francisco earthquake. In 1904 he organized the Victor Herbert Orch. in New York. In 1908 he was elected to the National Inst. of Arts and Letters.

In his finest operettas, Herbert united spontaneous melody, sparkling rhythm, and simple but tasteful harmony; his experience as a symphonic composer and conductor imparted a solidity of texture to his writing that placed him far above the many gifted amateurs in this field. Furthermore, his music possessed a natural communicative power, which made his operettas spectacularly successful with the public. In the domain of grand opera, he was not so fortunate. When the premiere of his first grand opera, *Natoma*, took place in Philadelphia on Feb. 25, 1911, it aroused great expectations; but the opera failed to sustain lasting interest. Still less effective was his second opera, *Madeleine*, staged by the Metropolitan Opera in New York on Jan. 24, 1914. Herbert was one of the founders of ASCAP in 1914, and was vice president from that date until his death. In 1916 he wrote a special score for the film *The Fall of a Nation*, in synchronization with the screenplay. He also wrote a film score for *Indian Summer* (1919).

WORKS: DRAMATIC: OPERETTAS: *Prince Ananias* (N.Y., Nov. 20, 1894); *The Wizard of the Nile* (Wilkes Barre, Pa., Sept. 26, 1895); *The Gold Bug* (N.Y., Sept. 21, 1896); *The Serenade* (Cleveland, Feb. 17, 1897); *The Idol's Eye* (Troy, N.Y., Sept. 20, 1897); *The Fortune Teller* (Toronto, Sept. 14, 1898); *Cyrano de Bergerac* (Montreal, Sept. 11, 1899); *The Singing Girl* (Montreal, Oct. 2, 1899); *The Ameer* (Scranton, Pa., Oct. 9, 1899); *The Viceroy* (San Francisco, Feb. 12, 1900); *Babes in Toyland* (Chicago, June 17, 1903); *Babette* (Washington, D.C., Nov. 9, 1903); *It Happened in Nordland* (Harrisburg, Pa., Nov. 21, 1904); *Miss Dolly Dollars* (Rochester, N.Y., Aug. 30, 1905); *Wonderland* (Buffalo, Sept. 14, 1905); *Mlle. Modiste* (Trenton, Oct. 7, 1905); *The Red Mill* (Buffalo, Sept. 3, 1906); *Dream City* (N.Y., Dec. 25, 1906); *The Magic Knight* (N.Y., Dec. 25, 1906); *The Tattooed Man* (Baltimore, Feb. 11, 1907); *Algeria* (Atlantic City, Aug. 24, 1908; rev. as *The Rose of Algeria*, Wilkes Barre, Pa., Sept. 11, 1909); *Little Nemo* (Philadelphia, Sept. 28, 1908); *The Prima Donna* (Chicago, Oct. 5, 1908); *Old Dutch* (Wilkes Barre, Pa., Nov. 6, 1909); *Naughty Marietta* (Syracuse, Oct. 24, 1910); *When Sweet 16* (Springfield, Mass., Dec. 5, 1910); *Mlle. Rosita* (later called *The Duchess*; Boston, March 27, 1911); *The Enchantress* (Washington, D.C., Oct. 9, 1911); *The Lady of the Slipper* (Philadelphia, Oct. 8, 1912); *Sweethearts* (Baltimore, March 24, 1913); *The Madcap Duchess* (Rochester, N.Y., Oct. 13, 1913); *The Débutante* (Atlantic City, Sept. 21, 1914); *The Only Girl* (Atlantic City, Oct. 1, 1914); *The Princess Pat* (Atlantic City, Aug. 23, 1915); *Eileen* (Cleveland, Jan. 1, 1917, as *Hearts of Erin*); *Her Regiment* (Springfield, Mass., Oct. 22, 1917); *The Velvet Lady* (Philadelphia, Dec. 23, 1918); *Angel Face* (Chicago, June 8, 1919); *My Golden Girl* (Stamford, Conn., Dec. 19, 1919); *Oui Madame* (Philadelphia, March 22, 1920); *The Girl in the Spotlight* (Stamford, Conn., July 7, 1920); *Orange Blossoms* (Philadelphia, Sept. 4, 1922); *The Dream Girl* (New Haven, April 22, 1924). OPERAS: *Natoma* (Philadelphia, Feb. 25, 1911); *Madeleine* (1913; N.Y., Jan. 24, 1914). OTHER: *The Captive,* dramatic cantata (Worcester Festival, Sept. 24, 1891); *Miss Camille,* burlesque (1907); *The Song Birds,* musical skit (1907); *The Century Girl,* revue (N.Y., Nov. 6, 1916; in collaboration with I. Berlin); music for the films *The Fall of a Nation* (1916) and *Indian Summer* (1919), and for Ziegfeld's Follies.

BIBL.: J. Kaye, *V. H.* (N.Y., 1931); C. Purdy, *V. H.—American Music Master* (N.Y., 1944); E. Waters, *V. H.: A Life in Music* (N.Y., 1955).

Herincx, Raimund (Fridrik), English bass-baritone of Belgian descent; b. London, Aug. 23, 1927. He received his training from Van Dyck in Belgium and from Valli in Italy. In 1950 he made his operatic debut as Mozart's Figaro with the Welsh National Opera. In 1956 he joined the Sadler's Wells Opera in London, where his roles included Count Almaviva, Pizzaro, Germont, Rigoletto, and Stravinsky's Nick Shadow and Creon. In 1966 he was a soloist in Delius's *A Mass of Life* in New York, and in 1967 he sang in opera in Boston. From 1968 he appeared at London's Covent Garden, winning success as the King Fisher in the *Midsummer Marriage*, Macbeth, and Escamillo, and creating roles in the premieres of *The Knot Garden* (1970) and *Taverner* (1972). In 1973–74 he sang at the Salzburg East Festivals, and then in the *Ring* cycles at the English National Opera in London (1974–76). On Jan. 18, 1977, he made his debut as Mathiesen in *Le Prophète* at the Metropolitan Opera in New York, and then sang with the Seattle (1977–81) and San Francisco (1983) operas. In 1986 he returned to Boston to sing in the U.S. premiere of *Taverner.*

Héritte-Viardot, Louise-Pauline-Marie, French voice teacher and composer, daughter of **Pauline Viardot-García**; b. Paris, Dec. 14, 1841; d. Heidelberg, Jan. 17, 1918. She was for many years a singing teacher at the St. Petersburg Cons., then taught in Frankfurt am Main, Berlin, and Heidelberg. Her opera *Lindoro* was performed in Weimar (1879); she further wrote the cantatas *Das Bacchusfest* (Stockholm, 1880) and *Le Feu de ciel*; some chamber music; and vocal exercises. Her memoirs (tr. from the original Ger.) were publ. in Eng. as *Memories and Adventures* (London, 1913).

Hermann, Roland, German baritone; b. Bochum, Sept. 17, 1936. He attended the Univs. of Freiburg im Bresgau, Mainz, and Frankfurt am Main, and received his vocal training from Margarete von Winterfeldt, Paul Lohmann, and Flaminio Contini. In 1961 he took 1st prize in the competition of the German radio stations. In 1967 he made his operatic debut as Mozart's Figaro in Trier, then joined the Zürich Opera in 1968. He also sang opera in Munich, Cologne, Buenos Aires, Paris, Berlin, and other cities. His engagements as a soloist with orchs. and as a recitalist took him to many of the major music centers of Europe, the United States (debut with the N.Y. Phil., 1983), and the Far East. In addition to such operatic roles as Don Giovanni, Wolfram, Germont, and Amfortas, he sang in such rarely performed works as Schumann's *Genoveva*, Marschner's *Der Vampyr*, Busoni's *Doktor Faust*, and Schoenberg's *Moses und Aron*. He also sang in several premieres, among them Keltenborn's *Der Kirschgarten* (Zürich, 1984) and Höller's *Der Meister und Margarita* (Paris, 1989).

Hernández Sales, Pablo, Spanish composer; b. Saragossa, Jan. 25, 1834; d. Madrid, Dec. 10, 1910. He was first a church chorister, and at 14 played organ at the San Gil church in Saragossa. At 22 he went to Madrid to study with Eslava at the Madrid Cons.; he graduated with a gold medal (1861), and joined the faculty in 1863 as a singing teacher. He wrote 2 zarzuelas: *Gimnasio higienico* and *Un Sevillano en la Habana*.

Hernándo (y Palomar), Rafael (José María), Spanish composer; b. Madrid, May 31, 1822; d. there, July 10, 1888. He studied with Carnicer, Saldoni, and P. Albéniz at the Madrid Cons. (1837–43), then went to Paris, where he took lessons with Auber. His *Stabat Mater* was performed there, and a grand opera, *Romilda*, was accepted for performance at the Theatre des Italiens, but the revolutionary upheaval of 1848 prevented its production. Hernándo returned to Madrid, where he produced a number of zarzuelas, of which the most successful was *El duende* (June 6, 1849); others were *Palo de ciego* (Feb. 15, 1849), *Colegialas y soldados* (March 21, 1849), *Bertoldo y Comparsa* (May 23, 1850), *Cosas de Juan* (Sept. 9, 1854), *El tambor* (April 28, 1860), and *Aurora*. He also collaborated with Barbieri, Oudrid, and Gaztambide in *Escenas de Chamberi* (Nov. 19, 1850) and *Don Simplicio Bobadilla* (May 7, 1853). In 1852 he became secretary of the Madrid Cons., where he also taught harmony.

Hernried, Robert (Franz Richard), Austrian-American musicologist and composer; b. Vienna, Sept. 22, 1883; d. Detroit, Sept. 3, 1951. He was trained in Vienna at the Cons. and the Univ. He taught theory at the Mannheim Academy of Music (1919–22), the Heidelberg Cons. (1923), in Erfurt (1924–26), and in Berlin at the Stern Cons. (1926–28) and the Staatliche Akademie für Kirchen- und Schulmusik (1927–34). In 1939 he went to the United States and taught at St. Ambrose College in Davenport, Iowa (1940–42), the State Teachers College in Dickinson, N. Dak. (1942–43), and St. Francis College in Fort Wayne, Ind. (1943–46); he then was prof. of theory and composition at the Detroit Inst. of Musical Art (1946–51). He publ. studies on Jaques-Dalcroze (Geneva, 1929) and Brahms (Leipzig, 1934), as well as *Allgemeine Musiklehre* (Berlin, 1932) and *Systematische Modulationslehre* (Berlin, 1935; 2d ed., 1948). Among his compositions were the operas *Francesca da Rimini* and *Die Bäuerin*.

Hérold, (Louis-Joseph) Ferdinand, celebrated French composer; b. Paris, Jan. 28, 1791; d. Thernes, near Paris, Jan. 19, 1833. His father, François-Joseph Hérold (b. Seltz, Bas-Rhin, March 18, 1755; d. Paris, Oct. 1, 1802), a piano teacher and composer, did not desire his son to become a musician, and sent him to the Hix school, where his aptitude for music was noticed by Fétis, then assistant teacher there. After his father's death, Hérold began to study music seriously; in 1806 he entered the Paris Cons., taking piano lessons with Louis Adam, and winning 1st prize for piano playing in 1810. He studied harmony under Catel, and (from 1811) composition under Méhul; in 1812 his cantata *Mlle. de la Vallière* won the Prix de Rome. From Rome he went to Naples, where he became pianist to Queen Caroline; he produced his first opera, *La gioventù di Enrico Quinto* (Jan. 5, 1815), which was well received. From Naples he went to Vienna, and after a few months' stay returned to Paris, where he finished the score of Boieldieu's *Charles de France*, an "opéra d'occasion" (Opéra Comique, June 18, 1816), and where all the rest of his operas were produced. The flattering reception of *Charles de France* led to the successful production of *Les Rosières* (Jan. 27, 1817), *La Clochette* (Oct. 18, 1817), *Le Premier Venu* (Sept. 28, 1818), *Les Troqueurs* (Feb. 18, 1819), and *L'Auteur mort et vivant* (Dec. 18, 1820); the failure of the last-named opera caused him to distrust his natural talent, and to imitate, in several succeeding stage works, the style then in vogue—that of Rossini. With the comic opera *Marie* (Aug. 12, 1826) Hérold returned, however, to his true element, and won instant and brilliant success. Meantime he had obtained the post of chorus master at the Italian Opera (1824); during this period he brought out *Le Muletier* (May 12, 1823), *Lasthénie* (Sept. 8, 1823), *Vendôme en Espagne* (Dec. 5, 1823), *Le Roi René* (Aug. 24, 1824), and *Le Lapin blanc* (May 21, 1825). In 1826 he was appointed to the staff of the Grand Opéra, for which he wrote several melodious and elegant ballets: *Astolphe et Jaconde* (Jan. 29, 1827), *La Somnambule* (Sept. 19, 1827), *Lydie* (July 2, 1828), *La Fille mal gardée* (Nov. 17, 1828), *La Belle au bois dormant* (April 27, 1829), and *La Noce de village* (Feb.

11, 1830). *La Somnambule* furnished Bellini with the subject of his popular opera. On July 18, 1829, Hérold produced *L'Illusion*, a 1-act opera full of charming numbers. *Emmeline*, a grand opera (Nov. 28, 1829), was a failure, but his next opera, *Zampa* (May 3, 1831), was sensationally successful and placed him in the first rank of French composers. He then wrote *L'Auberge d'Aurey* (May 11, 1830) jointly with Carafa, and *La Marquise de Brinvilliers* (Oct. 31, 1831), in collaboration with Auber, Batton, Berton, Blangini, Boieldieu, Carafa, Cherubini, and Paër; he also produced *La Médecine sans médecin* (Oct. 15, 1832). His last completed work, *Le Pré aux clercs* (Dec. 15, 1832), had a remarkable vogue. He died of tuberculosis shortly before his 42d birthday. His unfinished opera *Ludovic* was completed by Halévy and produced posthumously at the Opéra Comique on May 16, 1833.

BIBL.: B. Jouvin, *H.: Sa vie et ses oeuvres* (Paris, 1868); A. Pougin, *H.* (Paris, 1906).

Herold, Vilhelm (Kristoffer), Danish tenor; b. Hasle, March 19, 1865; d. Copenhagen, Dec. 15, 1937. He studied in Copenhagen, and then with Devillier and Sbriglia in Paris. He made his debut at the Royal Danish Theater in Copenhagen in 1893 as Faust; he was a member of the Royal Theater in Stockholm (1901–03; 1907–09); he also made guest appearances in London, Berlin, Dresden, and Hamburg. In 1915 he retired from the operatic stage. He served as director of Copenhagen's Royal Theater (1922–24). Herold was best known for his Wagnerian roles.

Herreweghe, Philippe, esteemed Belgian conductor; b. Ghent, May 2, 1947. He studied piano with Marcel Gazelle at the Ghent Cons. He also pursued training in medicine and psychiatry at the Univ. of Ghent, graduating in 1975. His musical training continued at the Ghent Cons. with Gabriel Verschraegen (organ) and Johan Huys (harpsichord), where he took a prize in 1975. In 1969 he founded the Collegium Vocale in Ghent, which soon acquired distinction as one of Europe's finest early music groups. He organized the Ensemble Vocal La Chapelle Royale in Paris in 1977, which won acclaim for its performances of a vast repertoire ranging from the Renaissance to the contemporary era. From 1982 he also served as artistic director of the Saintes early music festival. In 1989 he founded the Ensemble Vocal Européen, which also won distinction. He organized the Orchestre des Champs-Elysées in Paris in 1991, which he conducted in performances of Classical and Romantic scores on original instruments. From 1998 he was chief conductor of the Royal Phil. in Flanders.

Herrmann, Bernard, American conductor and composer; b. N.Y., June 29, 1911; d. Los Angeles, Dec. 24, 1975. He studied violin and began to compose as a child. At 16 he commenced formal training in composition with Gustav Heine, and then attended N.Y. Univ. (1929–30) where he studied with James (composition) and Stoessel (conducting); he subsequently continued his studies with the latter as a fellowship student at the Juilliard School of Music in New York (1930–32), where he also studied with Wagenaar (composition and harmony). In 1932–33 he attended Grainger's lectures at N.Y. Univ. In 1933 he organized the New Chamber Orch. in New York and then in 1934 joined the staff of CBS in New York working as an arranger, composer, and rehearsal conductor. In 1935 he became a staff conductor at CBS. As a composer, he found success with the various scores he wrote for such CBS programs as the *Columbia Workshop* (1937) and the *Mercury Theatre on the Air* (1938–39), where he was closely associated with Orson Welles. It was Welles who chose Herrmann to compose the score for his film *Citizen Kane* (1941), and thereafter Herrmann devoted much of his creative efforts to writing for films, with outstanding success. His score for the film *All That Money Can Buy* (1941) won him an Academy Award. From 1943 to 1951 Herrmann was chief conductor of the CBS Sym. Orch., with which he pursued a bold approach to programming. In addition to conducting broadcasts of early and rarely heard works, he also led programs of much contemporary music, ranging from Ives and Schoenberg to Elgar and Vaughan Williams. After leaving CBS, he made occasional guest conducting appearances but devoted most of his time to composing film scores and for television. Particularly outstanding were his film scores for Hitchcock's *Vertigo* (1958) and *Psycho* (1960), and Truffaut's *Fahrenheit 451* (1966). Throughout his career, Herrmann also composed serious works, generally along neo-Romantic lines. These included ballet music for *Americana Revue* (1932), *The Skating Rink*, ballet (1934), ballet music for the play *The Body Beautiful* (1935), *Wuthering Heights*, opera (1943–51; recorded 1966; stage premiere in a drastically cut version, Portland, Oreg., Nov. 6, 1982), *The King of Schnorrers*, musical comedy (1968; East Haddam, Conn., April 17, 1970), and many radio scores and television music, including the operas *A Christmas Carol* (CBS-TV, Dec. 23, 1954) and *A Child Is Born* (CBS-TV, Dec. 23, 1955).

BIBL.: E. Johnson, *B. H.: Hollywood's Music Dramatist* (London, 1977); G. Bruce, *B. H.: Film Music and Narrative* (Ann Arbor, 1985); S. Smith, *A Heart at Fire's Center: The Life and Music of B. H.* (Berkeley, 1991).

Herrmann, Hugo, German composer, teacher, and organist; b. Ravensburg, April 19, 1896; d. Stuttgart, Sept. 7, 1967. He studied at the Stuttgart Cons., and then with Gmeindl and Schreker at the Berlin Hochschule für Musik. He was organist and choirmaster in Balingen and Ludwigsburg (1919–23), and then at the Church of the Holy Redeemer in Detroit (1923–25). After working in Reutlingen (1925–29; 1932–35) and Wiesbaden (1929–32), he served as director of the Trossingen Städtische Musikschule (1935–62), where he was a prof. (from 1950). Herrmann was an advocate of Gebrauchsmusik, of which he left many examples. He wrote significant pieces for the accordion and also composed for the harmonica. Among his operas are *Gazellenhorn* (1929), *Vasantasena* (1930), *Das Wunder* (1937), and *Paracelsus* (1943).

BIBL.: A. Fett, *H. H. sum 60. Geburtstag* (Trossingen, 1956).

Hertog, Johannes den, Dutch conductor and composer; b. Amsterdam, Jan. 20, 1904; d. there, Oct. 18, 1982. He studied with his father, Herman Johannes den Hertog; then with Cornelis Dopper. He was director and conductor of the Wagner Soc. in Amsterdam; from 1938 to 1941 he was assistant conductor of the Concertgebouw Orch. there; in 1948 he was appointed conductor of the Flemish Opera in Antwerp, and from 1960 to 1965 was artistic director of the Netherlands Opera in Amsterdam. He wrote an opera, *Pygmalion* (1957), and a musical play, *Pandora* (1968).

Hertz, Alfred, eminent German-born American conductor; b. Frankfurt am Main, July 15, 1872; d. San Francisco, April 17, 1942. After completing his academic studies, he entered the Hoch Cons. in Frankfurt am Main, where he studied with Anton Urspruch; he then held positions as an opera conductor in Halle (1891–92), Altenburg (1892–95), Barmen-Elberfeld (1895–99), and Breslau (1899–1902). On Nov. 28, 1902, he made his first appearance at the Metropolitan Opera in New York conducting *Lohengrin*; he conducted the first American performance of *Parsifal* there (Dec. 24, 1903), which took place against the wishes of the Wagner family; consequently, Hertz could no longer obtain permission to conduct Wagner in Germany. He made his Covent Garden debut in London in 1910. From 1915 to 1930 he led the San Francisco Sym. Orch.; he also founded the summer series of concerts at the Hollywood Bowl (1922), and conducted more than 100 concerts there; he was affectionately known as the "Father of the Hollywood Bowl." From 1930 he was director of the Federal Music Project for Northern California and conductor of the San Francisco Federal Sym. Orch. His autobiography was publ. in the *San Francisco Chronicle* (May 3–14, 1942).

Hervé (real name, **Florimond Ronger**), French organist, singer, and composer; b. Houdain, near Arras, June 30, 1825; d. Paris, Nov. 3, 1892. He was a chorister at St.-Roch, then studied with Elwart at the Paris Cons.; became organist at various churches in Paris. In 1848 he sang in *Don Quichotte et Sancho Pansa*, an interlude of his own composition, at the Opéra National. In 1851 he conducted at the Palais Royal; in 1854 he opened the Folies-Concertantes, a small theater for the production of pantomimes, *saynètes* (musical comediettas for 2 persons), etc., and with phenomenal activity, he developed the light French operetta from these diminutive and frivolous pieces, writing both librettos and music, conducting the orch., and often appearing as an actor. From 1856 to 1869 he led this feverish life in Paris, producing his works at various theaters, and responding to failures by doubling his efforts. In 1870–71, when the Franco-Prussian War and the Commune stopped theatrical activities in Paris, he went to London, where he produced several of his light operas; he revisited London many times afterward; he was music director of the Empire Theater there from 1886. He wrote about 50 operettas, of which only 1 became a universal success, *Mam'zelle Nitouche* (Paris, Jan. 26, 1883, followed by numerous productions in European cities); other fairly successful works were *L'Œil crevé* (Paris, Oct. 12, 1867) and *Le Petit Faust* (Paris, April 28, 1869). He also wrote a grand opera, *Les Chevaliers de la table ronde* (Paris, Nov. 17, 1866), and the ballets *Sport, La Rose d'Amour, Les Bagatelles*, etc.

BIBL.: L. Schneider, *Les Maîtres de l'operette française, H. et Charles Lecocq* (Paris, 1924).

Herz, Joachim, German opera director; b. Dresden, June 15, 1924. After training in piano, clarinet, and theory, he studied at the Dresden Hochschule für Musik (1945–49) and took courses in musicology at the Humboldt Univ. in Berlin (1949–51). In 1950 he began his career as an opera director at the Dresden State Opera, and worked with its touring company (1951–53). After serving as an assistant to Felsenstein at the Berlin Komische Oper (1953–56), he worked at the Cologne Opera (1956–57). In 1957 he became principal stage director of the Leipzig Opera, and later served as its opera director (1959–76). During his Leipzig years, he staged *Die Meistersinger von Nürnberg* for the inauguration of the new opera house in 1960, and later staged a *Ring* cycle replete with social significance (1973–76). From 1976 to 1980 he was Intendant of the Berlin Komische Oper. He was principal opera director at the Dresden State Opera from 1981 to 1991. In 1985 he staged *Der Freischütz* at the inauguration of the restored Semper Opera in Dresden. His productions have been staged in various European and North American opera centers. Herz has lectured widely at home and abroad.

WRITINGS: With W. Felsenstein, *Musiktheater: Beiträge zur Methodik und su Inszenierungskonzeptionen* (Leipzig, 1970; 2d ed., 1976); *Joachim Herz über Musiktheater* (Berlin, 1974); *Und Figaro lässt sich scheiden: Oper als Idee und Interpretation* (Munich, 1985); *Joachim Herz: Theater, Kunst des erfüllten Augenblicks: Briefe, Vorträge, Notate, Gespräche, Essays* (Berlin, 1989).

BIBL.: H.-J. Irmer and W. Stein, *J. H.: Regisseur im Musiktheater* (Berlin, 1977); U. and U. Müller, eds., *Opern und Opernfiguren: Festschrift für J. H.* (Anif, 1989); I. Kobán, ed., *J. H.: Interviews* (Berlin, 1990).

Herzog, Emilie, Swiss soprano; b. Ermatingen, Dec. 17, 1859; d. Aarburg, Sept. 16, 1923. She studied in Zürich and Munich. She made her debut in a minor role at the Munich Court Opera in 1880, and afterward sang in other German opera houses, including Bayreuth. In 1889 she was engaged at the Berlin Royal Opera, where she became one of the best interpreters of soubrette roles; also gave recitals in Germany as a lieder artist. She made guest appearances in the opera houses of London, Paris, Vienna, and Brussels, and in 1896 sang at the Bolshoi Theater in Moscow; she made her Metropolitan Opera debut in New York as a Flower Maiden in *Parsifal* on Nov. 24, 1904. Returning to Europe, she continued to sing at the Berlin Royal Opera (until 1910). She then taught at the Zürich Cons. (1910–22).

Hesch, Wilhelm (real name, **Vilêm Heš**), Bohemian bass; b. Týnec nad Labem, July 3, 1860; d. Vienna, Jan. 3, 1908. He studied with Jan Ludvík Lukes and František Pivoda. On Dec. 5, 1880, he made his operatic debut as Kečal in *The Bartered Bride* in Brünn. He then sang with the Pištěk Theater Co. before becoming a principal member of the Prague National Theater in 1882. After singing at the Hamburg Opera (1893–96), he was a leading member of the Vienna Court Opera (from 1896). He was especially notable in buffo roles, particularly in Smetana's operas and as Papageno, Leporello, Dr. Bartolo, and Beckmesser.

Hess, Ludwig, German tenor and composer; b. Marburg, March 23, 1877; d. Berlin, Feb. 5, 1944. He studied singing with Vidal in Milan. He gave concerts of German lieder throughout Europe, specializing in the modern repertoire; he made a successful tour of the United States and Canada in 1911; he conducted a choral society in Königsberg (1917–20); then settled in Berlin. He wrote the operas *Abu und Nu* (Danzig, 1919), *Vor Edens Pforte*, after Byron (n.d.), and *Kranion* (Erfurt, 1933); Sym.; *Himmelskonig mit musizierenden Engeln*, symphonic poem; *Ariadne*, cantata; many choral works; numerous songs. He publ. *Die Behandlung der Stimme vor, während und nach der Mutation* (Marburg, 1927).

Hess, Willy, noted Swiss musicologist; b. Winterthur, Oct. 12, 1906; d. there, May 9, 1997. He studied piano and theory at the Zürich Cons. and musicology at the Univ. of Zürich. He played bassoon in the Winterthur Stadtorchester (1942–71). As a musicologist, he devoted most of his effort to the compilation of a Beethoven catalog. He ed. a valuable *Verzeichnis der nicht in der Gesamtausgabe veröffentlichten Werke Ludwig van Beethovens* (Wiesbaden, 1957); he also ed. the extensive supplement *Ludwig van Beethoven: Sämtliche Werke: Supplement zur Gesamtausgabe* (14 vols., Wiesbaden, 1959–71). His other important writings include *Ludwig van Beethoven* (Geneva, 1946); *Beethovens Oper Fidelio und ihre drei Fassungen* (Zürich, 1953); *Beethoven* (Zürich, 1956; 2d ed., rev., 1976); *Die Harmonie der Künste* (Vienna, 1960); *Die Dynamik der musikalischen Formbildung* (2 vols., Vienna, 1960; 1964); *Vom Doppelantlitz des Bösen in der Künst, dargestellt am Beispiel der Musik* (Munich, 1963); *Vom Metaphysischen im Künstlerischen* (Winterthur, 1963); *Parteilose Künst, parteilose Wissenschaft* (Tutzing, 1967); *Beethoven-Studien* (Munich, 1972); also an autobiography, *Aus meinem Leben: Erlebnisse, Bekenntnisse, Betrachtungen* (Zürich, 1976). He was also a prolific composer, including in his works several fairytale operas.

Hesse, Ernst Christian, German viola da gambist and composer; b. Grossgottern, April 14, 1676; d. Darmstadt, May 16, 1762. He studied the viola da gamba, first at Darmstadt, then in Paris; he gave successful demonstrations of his virtuosity in various European towns. From 1707 to 1714 he was Kapelldirektor in Darmstadt. In 1713 he married **Johanna Döbricht**. Among his works is the Italian opera *La fedeltà coronata* (c.1712).

Hetsch, (Karl) Ludwig Friedrich, German conductor; b. Stuttgart, April 26, 1806; d. Mannheim, June 28, 1872. He studied with Abeille. He was attached to the court of the king of Wurttemberg, then conducted in Heidelberg (1846–56) and in Mannheim (from 1856 until his death). He wrote an opera, *Ryno* (Stuttgart, 1833).

Heuberger, Richard (Franz Joseph), Austrian choral conductor, music critic, and composer; b. Graz, June 18, 1850; d. Vienna, Oct. 27, 1914. By profession a civil engineer, in 1876 he turned his full attention to music. He became choral master of the Vienna Akademischer Gesangverein and conductor of the Singakademie (1878); he was conductor of the Männergesangverein (1902–09) and prof. at the Vienna Cons. (1902). From 1881 to 1896 he was music critic of the *Wiener Tageblatt*, from 1896 to 1901 of the *Neue Freie Presse*, and from 1904 to 1914 of the *Neue Musikalische Presse*. He also was ed. of the *Musikbuch aus Österreich* (1904–06).

WRITINGS: *Im Foyer: Gesammelte Essays über das Opernrepertoire der Gegenwart* (Lepizig, 1901); *Musikalische Skizzen* (Leipzig, 1901); *Franz Schubert* (Berlin, 1902; 3d ed., rev., 1920, by H. von der Pfordten); *Anleitung zum Modulieren* (Vienna, 1910).

WORKS: DRAMATIC: OPERAS: *Abenteuer einer Neujahrsnacht* (Leipzig, 1886); *Manuel Venegas* (Leipzig, March 27, 1889;, remodeled as the 3-act grand opera *Mirjam, oder Das Maifest*, Vienna, Jan. 20, 1894); *Barfüssele* (Dresden, 1905). OPERETTAS (all 1st perf. in Vienna): *Der Opernball* (Jan. 5, 1898); *Ihre Excellenz* (1899; new version as *Eine entzückende Frau*); *Der Sechsuhrzug*

(1900); *Das Baby* (1902); *Der Furst von Düsterstein* (1909); *Don Quixote* (1910). BALLET: *Struwwelpeter* (Dresden, 1897).

Heward, Leslie (Hays), esteemed English conductor; b. Littletown, Liversedge, Yorkshire, Dec. 8, 1897; d. Birmingham, May 3, 1943. He studied with his father, an organist; he then continued his training at the Manchester Cathedral Choir School, where he served as assistant cathedral organist; was made organist of St. Andrew's, Ancoats (1914); he then won a scholarship in composition to the Royal College of Music in London (1917), where he studied with Stanford and Vaughan Williams. After appearing as a conductor with the British National Opera Co., he was music director of the South African Broadcasting Corp. and conductor of the Cape Town Orch. (1924–27); he then was conductor of the City of Birmingham Orch. (from 1930). He was acknowledged as one of England's finest conductors. He was also a composer, but he destroyed many of his MSS; his works included 2 unfinished operas.

BIBL.: E. Blom, ed., *L. H.: A Memorial Volume* (London, 1944).

Hewitt, Harry Donald, unimaginably fecund American composer; b. Detroit, March 4, 1921. His paternal grandmother was a Winnebago Indian. He was completely autodidact in music, and achieved such mastery of composition in quaquaversal directions without stylistic prejudice, that in some 40 years of writing music he produced 3,300 works in every conceivable manner, using every speculative idiom, from jazz to pop, couched in every available tonal, atonal, polytonal, and incommensurate oriental scale. Entirely free from supercilious elitism, he was not ashamed to admit the authorship of a *Hymn to Mickey Mouse* or an *Homage to Bugs Bunny*. None of his 30 syms. was ever performed. The brute weight of his collected MSS is 1 1/2 tons. Included are the operas *The Shadowy Waters, Moby Dick, The Song of Kawas, The Happy Hymadrayad, Doctor Too-Big, Clara's Friend, Remember George*, and *Pierre*.

Hewitt, James, English-born American composer, publisher, organist, and violinist; b. Dartmoor, June 4, 1770; d. Boston, Aug. 1, 1827. He played in London as a youth. In 1792 he went to America and settled in was New York, where he was described as one of the "professors of music from the Opera House, Hanover Square, and Professional Concerts under the direction of Haydn, Pleyel, etc., London." On Sept. 21, 1792, he gave a benefit concert with the violinists J. Gehot and B. Bergmann, the flutist W. Young, and a cellist named Phillips, which included Hewitt's Overture in 9 Movements, expressive of a battle. Subsequently, Young and Gehot went to Philadelphia, and in 1793 Hewitt, Bergmann, and Phillips gave a series of 6 subscription concerts; at their 5th concert (March 25, 1793) they presented for the first time in America Haydn's *Passion of Our Saviour* (i.e., *The 7 Last Words*); in 1794 Henri Capron joined Hewitt in promoting his "City Concerts"; meanwhile, Hewitt became the leader of the Old American Co. Orch., and in 1795 gave up his activities in connection with the subscription concerts. In 1798 he bought out the N.Y. branch of Carr's "Musical Repository" and established a publishing business of his own. In 1811 he went to Boston, where he played organ at Trinity Church and was in charge of the music presented at the Federal St. Theatre. In 1816 he returned to New York; also traveled in the South. In New York he was director of the Park Theatre. Among his works are the ballad operas *Tammany* (N.Y., 1794, under the auspices of the Tammany Soc.; only 1 song, "The Death Song of the Cherokee Indians," survives), *The Patriot or Liberty Asserted* (1794), *The Mysterious Marriage* (1799), *Columbus* (1799), *Pizarro, or The Spaniards in Peru* (1800), *Robin Hood* (1800), *The Spanish Castle* (N.Y., Dec. 5, 1800), and *The Wild Goose Chase* (1800). His eldest son, John Hill Hewitt (b. N.Y., July 12, 1801; d. Baltimore, Oct. 7, 1890), studied at West Point Academy; he was a theatrical manager, newspaperman, and drillmaster of Confederate recruits in the Civil War. He wrote poems and plays, about 300 songs ("The Minstrel's Return from the War," "All Quiet along the Potomac," "Our Native Land," "The Mountain Bugle," etc.), cantatas (*Flora's Festival, The Fairy Bridal, The Revelers, and The Musical Enthusiast*), and ballad operas (*Rip Van Winkle, The Vivandiere, The Prisoner of Monterey*, and *The Artist's Wife*). His admirers dubbed him the "father of the American ballad," but the ballad form existed in America long before him. He wrote a book of memoirs, *Shadows on the Wall* (1877; reprinted 1971). Another son, James Lang Hewitt (b. N.Y., Sept. 28, 1803; d. there, March 24, 1853), was associated with the publishing firm of J. A. Dickson in Boston (1825); after his father's death he returned to New York and continued his father's publishing business.

BIBL.: C. Huggins, *John Hill H.: Bard of the Confederacy* (diss., Florida State Univ., 1964); J. Wagner, *James H.: His Life and Works* (diss., Indiana Univ., 1969); W. Winden, *The Life and Music Theater Works of John Hill H.* (diss., Univ. of Illinois, 1972); F. Hoogerwerf, *John Hill H.: Sources and Bibliography* (Atlanta, 1982).

Hey, Julius, German singing teacher; b. Irmelshausen, April 29, 1832; d. Munich, April 22, 1909. He first studied painting, but turned to music, taking courses in harmony and counterpoint with Franz Lachner and Friedrich Schmitt. He became an ardent Wagnerian after his introduction to the master by King Ludwig II, and worked under the direction of Hans von Bülow at the Munich School of Music (established by the king in accordance with Wagner's plans). After Bülow's departure (1869), Hey vainly tried to effect a reform from a German national standpoint in the cultivation of singing, but met with so many obstacles that he resigned when Wagner died (1883), and devoted himself to finishing his method of singing, *Deutscher Gesangsunterricht* (4 vols., Mainz, 1885; ed. by F. Volbach and H. Hey as *Der kleine Hey*, Mainz, 1912; 2d ed., rev., 1956, by F. Reusch). It contains a complete and logical exposition of Wagner's views on vocal training. His book *Richard Wagner als Vortragsmeister* (Leipzig, 1911) was publ. posthumously by his son Hans.

Hickox, Richard (Sidney), esteemed English conductor; b. Stokenchurch, Buckinghamshire, March 5, 1948. He studied organ, piano, and composition at the Royal Academy of Music in London (1966–67) and was an organ scholar at Queens' College, Cambridge (M.A., 1970). In 1971 he made his professional debut as a conductor at St. John's Smith Square in London. He founded the City of London Sinfonia in 1971, and subsequently served as its music director. That same year he also organized the Richard Hickox Singers, which later became the City of London Sinfonia Singers. From 1972 to 1982 he was organist and master of music at St. Margaret's, Westminster. He made his debut at the London Promenade Concerts in 1973. From 1976 he was music director of the London Sym. Chorus, and from 1978 of the Bradford Festival Choral Soc. In 1979 he made his debut as an opera conductor at the English National Opera in London. From 1980 to 1984 he was principal guest conductor of the Netherlands Radio Orch. in Hilversum. After serving as artistic director of the Northern Sinfonia in Newcastle upon Tyne from 1982 to 1990, he was its principal guest conductor from 1990. In 1983–84 he was associate conductor of the San Diego Sym. Orch., and from 1985 of the London Sym. Orch. In 1985 he conducted for the first time at London's Covent Garden, and in 1986 at the Los Angeles Opera. With Simon Standage, he founded the Collegium Musicum 90 of London in 1990. From 1998 he was principal conductor of the Spoleto Festival in Italy. As a guest conductor, he was engaged by leading orchs. in Europe and North America. Hickox's vast repertoire embraces works from the 14th century to the present era. He reveals a rare capacity for surmounting the various interpretative challenges posed by both standard and seldom performed scores of the orch., choral, and operatic repertoires.

Hidalgo, Elvira de, Spanish soprano and teacher; b. Aragón, Dec. 27, 1892; d. Milan, Jan. 21, 1980. She studied with Bordalba in Barcelona and Vidal in Milan. In 1908 she made her operatic debut as Rossini's Rosina in Naples. On March 7, 1910, she sang that role in her Metropolitan Opera debut in New York, returning there for the 1924–26 seasons. She also appeared at Milan's La Scala (1916), in Rome (1919), at Buenos Aires's Teatro Colón (1922), and at London's Covent Garden (1924). From 1932 she devoted herself to teaching, being the mentor of Maria Callas in Athens. She later taught in Ankara (1949–59) and then in Milan. In addition to Rosina, she was greatly admired for her portrayals of Gilda, Linda, Philine, Elvira, Musetta, and Lakmé.

Hidas, Frigyes, Hungarian composer; b. Budapest, May 25, 1928. He was a student of Viski at the Budapest Academy of Music. He served as music director of the National Theater in Budapest (1951–66), and then at the Municipal Operetta Theater in Budapest (1974–79). In subsequent years, he devoted himself solely to composition. In 1959 and 1980 he was awarded the Erkel Prize. In 1986 the Hungarian government made him a Merited Artist.

WORKS: DRAMATIC: *Színek* (Colors), ballet (1960); *Riviera*, operetta (1963); *Az Asszony és az igazság* (The Woman and the Truth), chamber opera (1965); *Tökéletes alattvaló* (The Perfect Subject), opera (1973); *Cédrus* (Cedar), ballet (1975); *Bösendorfer*, opera (1977); *Dunakanyar* (Danube Bend), opera (1984); *Almodj Bachot* (Dream Bach), musical play (1991; Budapest, May 25, 1993).

Hignard, (Jean-Louis) Aristide, French composer; b. Nantes, May 20, 1822; d. Vernon, March 20, 1898. He studied with Halevy at the Paris Cons., taking the 2d Grand Prix de Rome. He was an earnest composer of lofty aims, but brought out operas and other works of secondary importance; his best opera, *Hamlet*, composed in 1868, was to be performed in Paris; unluckily for him, *Hamlet* by Ambroise Thomas was produced that same year, with such spectacular success that Hignard could not compete with it; accordingly, he had to be content with a provincial production in his native city (Nantes, April 21, 1888). His other operas included *Le Visionnaire* (Nantes, 1851), *Le Colin-Maillard* (Paris, 1853), *Les Compagnons de la Marjolaine* (Paris, 1855), *M. de Chimpanzé* (Paris, 1858), *Le Nouveau Pourceaugnac* (Paris, 1860), *L'Auberge des Ardennes* (Paris, 1860), and *Les Musiciens de l'orchestre* (Paris, 1861).

Hildach, Eugen, German baritone, teacher, and composer; b. Wittenberge-an-der-Elbe, Nov. 20, 1849; d. Zehlendorf, near Berlin, July 29, 1924. He began to study voice at the age of 24; he married Anna Schubert, a singer, and went to Dresden, where they both taught at the Cons.; they also toured together in Germany. In 1904 they established their own singing school in Frankfurt am Main. He publ. a number of songs, several of which became well known, including the popular "Der Lenz."

Hill, Alfred (Francis), noted Australian composer; b. Melbourne, Nov. 16, 1870; d. Sydney, Oct. 30, 1960. He played violin in traveling theater orchs., then studied with Paul, Schreck, and Sitt at the Leipzig Cons. (1887–91); he subsequently was active in New Zealand and Australia as a conductor, and later as a prof. at the New South Wales State Conservatorium (1916–34). He was made an Officer of the Order of the British Empire in 1953 and a Companion of the Order of St. Michael and St. George in 1960. He wrote over 500 works, some of which employ Maori and Australian aboriginal materials. He publ. *Harmony and Melody* (London, 1927).

WORKS: OPERAS: *Whipping Boy* (1893); *Lady Dolly* (1898; Sydney, 1900); *Tapu* (1902–03); *A Moorish Maid or Queen of the Riffs* (Auckland, 1905); *Teora—The Weird Flute* (1913; Sydney, 1928); *Giovanni, the Sculptor* (1913–14; Melbourne, 1914); *Rajah of Shivapore* (Sydney, 1914); *Auster* (1919; Sydney, 1922); *The Ship of Heaven* (1923; 1st complete perf., Sydney, 1933).

BIBL.: J. Thomson, *A Distant Music: The Life and Times of A. H., 1870–1960* (Oxford, 1982).

Hillebrecht, Hildegard, German soprano; b. Hannover, Nov. 26, 1927. She made her operatic debut as Leonora in *Il Trovatore* in Freiburg im Breisgau (1951); then sang in Zürich (1952–54), Düsseldorf (1954–59), Cologne (1956–61), Munich (from 1961), and again in Zürich (from 1972). She also made guest appearances in Vienna, Hamburg, Berlin, Salzburg, Paris, and Rome. In 1967 she made her Covent Garden debut in London as the Empress in *Die Frau ohne Schatten*; on Nov. 8, 1968, she made her Metropolitan Opera debut in New York as Sieglinde in *Die Walküre*. She was best known for her roles in operas by Mozart, Wagner, Puccini, Strauss, and Verdi; she also sang in the premiere of Dallapiccola's *Ulisse* in Berlin (1968).

Hiller, Ferdinand (von), noted German conductor, composer, and writer on music; b. Frankfurt am Main, Oct. 24, 1811; d. Cologne, May 10, 1885. He studied piano with A. Schmitt, making his public debut at age 10, then went to Weimar to study with Hummel (1825), whom he accompanied to Vienna for a visit with Beethoven (1827). He subsequently was in Paris (1828–35), where he was befriended by Chopin, Liszt, Berlioz, and other famous musicians. He became conductor of Frankfurt am Main's Cäcilien-Verein (1836). After studies in Italy (1841), he devoted himself mainly to conducting, composing, and writing on music. He was a conductor with the Leipzig Gewandhaus Orch. (1843–44), then in Dresden, where he brought out 2 of his operas (1845–47); he subsequently conducted in Düsseldorf (1847–50). He settled in Cologne as a conductor (1850), gaining distinction in particular with the Lower Rhine Festival; he also reorganized the municipal music school, serving as its director until his death. He appeared as a guest conductor in Paris (1851–52), London (1852–72), and St. Petersburg (1870). A musical conservative, Hiller violently attacked Wagner. His own compositions met with indifferent success, although his career as a conductor and writer on music won him many admirers.

WORKS: DRAMATIC: OPERAS: *Romilda* (Milan, 1839); *Der Traum in der Christnacht* (Dresden, 1845); *Konradin* (Dresden, Oct. 13, 1847); *Der Advokat* (Cologne, 1854); *Die Katakomben* (Wiesbaden, Feb. 15, 1862); *Der Deserteur* (Cologne, Feb. 17, 1865). ORATORIOS: *Die Zerstörung Jerusalems* (Leipzig, April 2, 1840); *Saul*.

WRITINGS: *Die Musik und das Publikum* (Cologne, 1864); *Aus dem Tonleben unserer Zeit* (2 vols., Leipzig, 1868, 1871); *Ludwig van Beethoven; Gelegentliche: Aufsätze* (Leipzig, 1871); *Felix Mendelssohn Bartholdy: Briefe und Erinnerungen* (Cologne, 1874); *Musikalisches und Persönliches* (Leipzig, 1876); *Briefe an eine Ungenannte* (Cologne, 1877); *Kunstlerleben* (Cologne, 1880); *Wie hören wir Musik?* (Leipzig, 1881); *Goethes musikalisches Leben* (Cologne, 1883); *Erinnerungsblatter* (Cologne, 1884).

BIBL.: R. Sietz, ed., *Aus F. H.s Briefwechsel* (7 vols., Cologne, 1958–70); idem, *Der Nachlass F. H.s* (Cologne, 1970).

Hiller, Friedrich Adam, German singer, conductor, and composer, son of **Johann Adam Hiller**; b. Leipzig, c.1767; d. Königsberg, Nov. 23, 1812. He studied music with his father. He was a conductor at various provincial theaters in Germany, and wrote a number of light operas, including *Biondetta* (Schwerin, 1792), *Das Schmuckkästchen* (Königsberg, 1804), and *Die drei Sultaninen* (Königsberg, 1809).

Hiller, Johann Adam, important German conductor, composer, and writer on music, father of **Friedrich Adam Hiller**; b. Wendisch-Ossig, near Görlitz, Dec. 25, 1728; d. Leipzig, June 16, 1804. He began his musical training as a child. After attending the Görlitz Gymnasium (1740–45), he won a scholarship to the Dresden Kreuzschule, where he studied keyboard playing and thoroughbass with Homilius (1746–51); he then studied law at the Univ. of Leipzig (1751). He was active as a bass singer and flutist in Leipzig's Grosses Concert prior to serving as steward to Count Brühl in Dresden (1754–58), and also later in Leipzig (1758–60). Thereafter he assumed a major role in the musical life of Leipzig. He organized his own subscription concert series (1762), and was director of the revived Grosses Concert (1763–71); he also founded a singing school, which evolved into a music school. He was the erudite ed. of the *Wöchentliche Nachrichten* (1766–70), the first major specialized journal on music. During this same period, he helped to establish the German Singspiel in collaboration with the poet Christian Felix Weisse. He mastered the genre in his *Lottchen am Hofe* (Leipzig, April 24, 1767), in which he created effective characterizations by writing simple songs for the country people and arias in the opera seria tradition for the people of means. His finest Singspiels were *Die Liebe auf dem Lande* (Leipzig, May 18, 1768) and *Die Jagd* (Weimar, Jan. 29, 1770). He founded the Musikabende Gesellschaft (1775), with which he gave many concerts; then became conductor of the Gewandhaus concerts in 1781, leading them until 1785. This famous series of concerts has continued without interruption for more than 200 years. He also was music director of the Univ.'s Paulinerkirche (1778–85) and of the Neukirche (1783–85); then was Kapellmeister to the duke of Courland in Mitau (1785–86) and civic music director in Breslau (1787–89). He returned to Leipzig as Kantor of the Thomaskirche in 1789, remaining there until his retirement in 1800.

WORKS: SINGSPIELS (all 1st perf. in Leipzig unless otherwise given): *Die verwandelten Weiber oder Der Teufel ist los, erster Teil* (May 28, 1766; 12 pieces by J. Standfuss); *Der lustige Schuster oder Der Teufel ist los, zweiter Teil* (1766; 7 pieces by Hiller, remainder by Standfuss); *Lisuart und Dariolette oder Die Frage und die Antwort* (Nov. 25, 1766); *Lottchen am Hofe* (April 24, 1767); *Die Muse* (Oct. 3, 1767); *Die Liebe auf dem Lande* (May 18, 1768); *Die Jagd* (Weimar, Jan. 29, 1770); *Der Dorfbalbier* (1771; with pieces by C. Neefe); *Der Aerndtekranz* (1771); *Der Krieg* (1772); *Die Jubelhochzeit* (April 5, 1773); *Die kleine Aehrenleserin*, children's operetta (publ. in Leipzig, 1778); *Das Grab des Mufti oder Die beiden Geitzigen* (Jan. 17, 1779); *Poltis oder Das gerettete Troja* (1777?).

WRITINGS: *Anekdoten zur Lebensgeschichte grosser Regenten und berühmter Staatsmänner* (Leipzig, 1766–72); ed. *Wöchentliche Nachrichten und Anmerkungen die Musik betreffend* (Leipzig, 1766–70; supplement publ. as *Musikalische Nachrichten und Anmerkungen*, Leipzig, 1770); *Anweisung zur Singekunst in der deutschen und italienischen Sprache* (Frankfurt am Main and Leipzig, 1773); *Musikalisches Handbuch für die Liebhaber des Gesanges und Claviers* (Leipzig, 1773); *Anweisung zum musikalisch-richtigen Gesange* (Leipzig, 1774; 2d ed., aug., 1798); *Exempelbuch der Anweisung zum Singen* (Leipzig, 1774); *Anweisung zum musikalisch-zierlichen Gesange* (Leipzig, 1780); *Lebensbeschreibungen berühmter Musikgelehrten und Tonkünstler neuerer Zeit* (vol. 1, Leipzig, 1784); *Über Metastasio und seine Werke* (Leipzig, 1786); *Nachricht von der Aufführung des Händelschen Messias in . . . Berlin den 19. May 1786* (Berlin, 1786); *Fragmente aus Händels Messias, nebst Betrachtungen über die Aufführung Händelscher Singcompositionen* (Leipzig, 1787); *Über Alt und Neu in der Musik* (Leipzig, 1787); *Was ist wahre Kirchenmusik?* (Leipzig, 1789); *Beyträge zu wahrer Kirchenmusik von J.A. Hasse und J.A. Hiller* (Leipzig, 1791); *Kurze und erleichterte Anweisung zum Singen* (Leipzig, 1792); *Anweisung zum Violinspielen für Schulen und zum Selbstunterrichte* (Leipzig, 1792); *Erinnerungen gegen das Melodien-Register in Freyes kleiner Lieder-Konkordanz* (Leipzig, 1798).

BIBL.: C. Naumann, *J. A. H.: Eine bescheidene Würdigung seiner Verdienste als Mensch, Künstler und Schulmann* (Leipzig, 1804); K. Peiser, *J. A. H.* (Leipzig, 1894); G. Calmus, *Die ersten deutschen Singspiele von Standfuss und H.* (Leipzig, 1908); A. Schering, *Das Zeitalter J. S. Bachs und J. A. H.s* (Leipzig, 1940); G. Sander, *Das Deutschtum im Singspiel J. A. H.s* (diss., Univ. of Berlin, 1943); K. Kawada, *Studien zu den Singspiel von J. A. H. (1728–1804)* (Marburg, 1969).

Hillier, Paul (Douglas), distinguished English baritone, conductor, and teacher; b. Dorchester, Feb. 9, 1949. He trained at the Guildhall School of Music in London, and then served as vicar-choral at St. Paul's Cathedral (1973–74). In 1974 he made his formal concert debut at London's Purcell Room and also founded the Hilliard Ensemble, which he directed in performances of early music until 1990. In 1989 he founded the Theatre of Voices. He also was a prof. of music at the Univ. of Calif. at Davis from 1990. In 1996 he became a prof. and director of the Early Music Institute at the Indiana Univ. School of Music. He publ. *300 Years of English Partsongs* (1983), *Romantic English Partsongs* (1986), and *The Catch Book* (1987).

Hillis, Margaret (Eleanor), American conductor; b. Kokomo, Ind., Oct 1, 1921; d. Evanston, Ill., Feb. 5, 1998. She studied piano as a child and played the tuba and double bass in school bands. After taking her B.A. at Indiana Univ. (1947), she studied choral conducting at the Juilliard School of Music in New York (1947–49) and with Robert Shaw, who engaged her as his assistant (1952–53). In 1950 she became music director of the American Concert Choir and Orch. in New York. From 1952 to 1968 she was conductor of the chorus of the American Opera Soc. there, and also was choral director of the N.Y. City Opera (1955–56). From 1956 to 1960 she was music director of the N.Y. Chamber Soloists. In 1957 Fritz Reiner, music director of the Chicago Sym. Orch., asked Hillis to organize its chorus. She conducted it with great distinction until her retirement in 1994. She also was choral director of the Santa Fe (N.M.) Opera (1958–59), music director of the Kenosha (Wis.) Sym. Orch. (1961–68), resident conductor of the Chicago Civic Orch. (1967–90), conductor of the Cleveland Orch. Chorus (1969–71), music director of the Elgin (Ill.) Sym. Orch. (1971–85), and conductor of the San Francisco Sym. Chorus (1982–83). From 1950 to 1960 she taught at the Union Theological Seminary in New York, and also at the Juilliard School of Music (1951–53). After serving as director of choral activities at Northwestern Univ. (1970–77), she was a visiting prof. at the Indiana Univ. School of Music in Bloomington (from 1978). She also led various master classes in choral conducting. In 1954 she founded and became director of the American Choral Union. In 1994 she was honored with the Theodore Thomas Award in recognition of her long and distinguished career.

Himmel, Friedrich Heinrich, German composer; b. Treuenbrietzen, Brandenburg, Nov. 20, 1765; d. Berlin, June 8, 1814. He studied theology at the Univ. of Halle, and at the same time, cultivated music. He received a stipend from Friedrich Wilhelm II to study with Naumann in Dresden; subsequently he went to Italy, where he acquired skill in stage music. His cantata *Il primo navigatore* was performed in Venice (March 1, 1794), and his opera *La morte di Semiramide* in Naples (Jan. 12, 1795). He then returned to Berlin and was appointed court composer. In 1798 he went to St. Petersburg, where he produced his opera *Alessandro* (Jan. 1799). In 1800 he returned from Russia by way of Sweden and Denmark; in Berlin he produced his Italian opera *Vasco di Gama* (Jan. 12, 1801). His subsequent operas, staged in Berlin, were in the nature of Singspiels, to German words: *Frohsinn und Schwärmerei* (March 9, 1801), *Fanchon das Leiermädchen* (May 15, 1804; his most successful work), *Die Sylphen* (April 14, 1806), etc. His last opera, *Der Kobold*, was produced in Vienna (May 22, 1813). Many of his songs had great vogue. He also composed an oratorio, *Isacco figura del Redentore* (Berlin, March 14, 1792).

BIBL.: L. Odendahl, *F. H. H.: Bemerkungen zur Geschichte der Berliner Oper um die Wende des 18. und 19. Jahrhunderts* (diss., Univ. of Bonn, 1914).

Hindemith, Paul, eminent German-born American composer and teacher; b. Hanau, near Frankfurt am Main, Nov. 16, 1895; d. Frankfurt am Main, Dec. 28, 1963. He began studying violin at the age of 9; at 14, he entered the Hoch Cons. in Frankfurt am Main, where he studied violin with A. Rebner, and composition with Arnold Mendelssohn and Sekles. His father was killed in World War I, and Hindemith was compelled to rely on his own resources to make a living. He was concertmaster of the orch. of the Frankfurt am Main Opera (1915–23), and later played the viola in the string quartet of his teacher Rebner; from 1922 to 1929 he was violist in the Amar String Quartet; he also appeared as a soloist on the viola and viola d'amore and later was engaged as a conductor, mainly of his own works. As a composer, he joined the modern movement and was an active participant in the contemporary music concerts at Donaueschingen, and later in Baden-Baden. In 1927 he was appointed instructor in composition at the Berlin Hochschule für Musik. With the advent of the Hitler regime in 1933, Hindemith began to experience increasing difficulties, both artistically and politically. Although his own ethnic purity was never questioned, he was married to Gertrud Rottenberg, daughter of the Jewish conductor Ludwig Rottenberg, and he stubbornly refused to cease ensemble playing with undeniable Jews. Hitler's propaganda minister, Goebbels, accused Hindemith of cultural Bolshevism, and his music fell into an official desuetude. Unwilling to compromise with the barbarous regime, Hindemith accepted engagements abroad. Beginning in 1934, he made 3 visits to Ankara at the invitation of the Turkish government, and helped to organize the music curriculum at the Ankara Cons. He made his first American appearance at the Coolidge Festival at the Library of Congress in Washington, D.C., in a performance of his Unaccompanied Viola Sonata (April 10, 1937). Hindemith was an instructor at the Berkshire Music Center at Tanglewood in the summer of 1940; from 1940 to 1953 he was a prof. at Yale Univ.; during the academic year 1950–51, he was the Charles Eliot Norton Lecturer at Harvard Univ. He became a naturalized American citizen in 1946. In 1953 he went to Switzerland and gave courses at the Univ. of Zürich. He also was active as a guest conductor in Europe and the United States.

Hindemith's early music reflects rebellious opposition to all tradition; this is noted in such works as the opera *Mörder, Hoffnung der Frauen* (1919) and *Suite 1922* for Piano (1922); at the same time, he cultivated the techniques of constructivism, evident in his theatrical sketch *Hin und Zurück* (1927), in which *Krebsgang* (retrograde movement) is applied to the action on the stage, so that events are reversed; in a work of a much later period, *Ludus Tonalis* (1943), the postlude is the upside-down version of the prelude. Along constructive lines is Hindemith's cultivation of *Gebrauchsmusik*, that is, music for use; he was also an ardent champion of *Hausmusik*, to be played or sung by amateurs at home; the score of his *Frau Musica* (as revised in 1944) has an obbligato part for the audience to sing. A neoclassical trend is shown in a series of works, entitled *Kammermusik*, for various instrumental combinations, polyphonically conceived, and Baroque in style. Although he made free use of atonal melodies, he was never tempted to adopt an integral 12-tone method, which he opposed on aesthetic grounds. Having made a thorough study of early music, he artfully assimilated its polyphony in his works; his masterpiece of this genre was the opera *Mathis der Maler*. A prolific composer, Hindemith wrote music of all types for all instrumental combinations, including a series of sonatas for each orch. instrument with piano. His style may be described as a synthesis of modern, Romantic, Classical, Baroque, and other styles, a combination saved from the stigma of eclecticism only by Hindemith's superlative mastery of technical means. As a theorist and pedagogue, he developed a self-consistent method of presentation derived from the acoustical nature of harmonies.

WORKS: DRAMATIC: OPERAS: *Mörder, Hoffnung der Frauen*, op. 12 (1919; Stuttgart, June 4, 1921); *Das Nusch-Nuschi*, op. 20, marionette opera (1920; Stuttgart, June 4, 1921; rev. version, Königsberg, Jan. 22, 1931); *Sancta Susanna*, op. 21 (1921; Frankfurt am Main, March 26, 1922); *Cardillac*, op. 39 (Dresden, Nov. 9, 1926; rev. version, Zürich, June 20, 1952); *Hin und Zurück*, op. 45a, 1-act sketch (Baden-Baden, July 17, 1927); *Neues vom Tage* (1928–29; Berlin, June 8, 1929; rev. 1953; Naples, April 7, 1954, composer conducting); *Mathis der Maler* (1934–35; Zürich, May 28, 1938); *Orfeo*, realization of Monteverdi's opera (1943); *Die Harmonie der Welt* (1950–57; Munich, Aug. 11, 1957, composer conducting); *Das lange Weihnachtsmahl* (1960; Mannheim, Dec. 17, 1961). INCIDENTAL MUSIC: *Tuttifantchen* (Darmstadt, Dec. 13, 1922). BALLETS: *Der Dämon*, op. 28, pantomime (1922; Darmstadt, Dec. 1, 1923); *Nobilissima visione*, dance legend in 6 scenes (perf. as *St. Francis* by the Ballets Russes de Monte Carlo, London, July 21, 1938, composer conducting); *Theme and Variations: The 4 Temperaments* for String Orch. and Piano (1940; N.Y., Nov. 20, 1946); *Hérodiade*, after Mallarmé (perf. as *Mirror before Me* by the Martha Graham Dance Co., Washington, D.C., Oct. 30, 1944).

The Auftrag der Hindemith-Stiftung began issuing a collected ed. in 1975. Thematic indexes have been compiled by K. Stone (N.Y., 1954; verified by the composer) and H. Rösner, *Paul Hindemith—Katalog seiner Werke, Diskographie, Bibliographie, Einführung in das Schaffen* (Frankfurt am Main, 1970).

WRITINGS: *Unterweisung im Tonsatz* (2 vols., 1937, 1939; Eng. ed. as *The Craft of Musical Composition*, N.Y., 1941; rev., 1945); *A Concentrated Course in Traditional Harmony* (2 vols., N.Y., 1943, 1953); *Elementary Training for Musicians* (N.Y., 1946); *J. S. Bach: Heritage and Obligation* (New Haven, Conn., 1952; Ger. ed., *J. S. Bach: Ein verpflichtendes Erbe*, Wiesbaden, 1953); *A Composer's World: Horizons and Limitations* (Cambridge, Mass., 1952).

BIBL.: The *H.-Jahrbuch* began publication in 1971. See also H. Strobel, *P. H.* (Mainz, 1928; 3d ed., aug., 1948); H. Schilling, *P. H.'s Cardillac* (Würzburg, 1962); A. Briner, *P. H.* (Zürich, 1970; Eng. tr., 1987); I. Kemp, *H.* (London, 1970); E. Zwink, *P. H.s Unterweisung im Tonsatz* (Göppingen, 1974); G. Skelton, *P. H.: The Man behind the Music* (London, 1975); G. Metz, *Melodische Polyphonie in der Zwölftonordnung: Studien zum Kontrapunkt P. H.s* (Baden-Baden, 1976); D. Rexroth, *Erprobungen und Erfahrungen: Zu P. H.s Schaffen in den Zwanziger Jahren* (Frankfurt am Main, 1978); G. Schubert, *H.* (Hamburg, 1981); D. Rexroth, *P. H. Briefe* (Frankfurt am Main, 1982); E. Preussner, *P. H.: Ein Lebensbild* (Innsbruck, 1984); D. Neumeyer, *The Music of P. H.* (New Haven, 1986); S. Cook, *Opera During the Weimar Republic: The Zeitopern of Ernst Krenek, Kurt Weill, and P. H.* (Ann Arbor, 1987); A. Briner, D. Rexroth, and G. Schubert, *P. H.: Leben und Werk in Bild und Text* (Zürich, 1988); S. Hinton, *The Idea of Gebrauchsmusik: A Study of Musical Aesthetics in the Weimar Republic (1919–1933) with Particular Reference to the Works of P. H.* (N.Y. and London, 1989); L. Noss, *P. H. in the United States* (Urbana, 1989); J. Berger and K. Velten, eds., *Experiment und Erbe: Studien zum Frühwerk P. H.s* (Saarbrücken, 1993).

Hines (real name, **Heinz**), **Jerome (Albert Link),** distinguished American bass; b. Los Angeles, Nov. 8, 1921. He received training in mathematics, chemistry, and physics at the Univ. of Calif. at Los Angeles (B.A., 1943), and concurrently took vocal lessons with Gennaro Curci in Los Angeles; he later studied voice with Samuel Margolis in New York. In 1940 he made his stage debut as Bill Bobstay in *H.M.S. Pinafore* with the Los Angeles Civic Light Opera. On Oct. 19, 1941, he made his San Francisco Opera debut as Monterone. He then made appearances as a soloist with American orchs., and also sang with the New Orleans Opera (1944–46). After winning the Caruso Award in 1946, he made his debut at the Metropolitan Opera in New York as the Sergeant in *Boris Godunov* on Nov. 21, 1946; he first sang its title role there on Feb. 18, 1954, making a memorable impression. In the meantime, he sang in South America and Europe. He appeared at the Glyndebourne and Edinburgh Festivals in 1953, at the Bavarian State Opera in Munich in 1954, and at La Scala in Milan and the Bayreuth Festival in 1958. On Sept. 23, 1962, he made a dramatic debut at the Bolshoi Theater in Moscow when he sang Boris Godunov in Russian. He continued to sing regularly at the Metropolitan Opera, where he remained on the roster for over 45 years. In addition to his commanding portrayal of Boris Godunov, he also won distinction for such roles as Don Giovanni, Sarastro, Wotan, Philip II, Don Basilio, and King Marke. His deep religious faith was revealed in his choice of Christ as the subject of his opera *I Am the Way*, and in the title of his autobiography *This is My Story, This is My Song* (1968). He also publ. a book of interviews as *Great Singers on Great Singing* (1982) and the volume *The Four Voices of Man* (1997).

Hinrichs, Gustav, German-American conductor, teacher, and composer; b. Ludwigslust, Dec. 10, 1850; d. Mountain Lake, N.J., March 26, 1942. He studied violin and piano with his father, and received training in composition in Hamburg from Marxsen. He began conducting at 15, and at 20 went to San Francisco, where he conducted the Fabbri Opera. In 1885 he went to New York as assistant conductor to Theodore Thomas and the American Opera Co. In 1888 he founded his own opera company in Philadelphia, where he conducted the U.S. premieres of *Cavalleria rusticana* (Sept. 9, 1891) and *Manon Lescaut* (Aug. 29, 1894); he also conducted the U.S. premiere of *Pagliacci* in New York (June 15, 1893). On Oct. 14, 1899, he conducted *Il Barbiere di Siviglia* with the Metropolitan Opera Co. during its visit to Syracuse, N.Y.; on Oct. 19, 1899, he conducted *Faust* at the Metropolitan Opera in New York, remaining on its roster for the season; he returned there for the 1903–04 season. He taught at the National Cons. and at Columbia Univ. (1895–1906). Among his works was the opera *Onti-Ora* (Philadelphia, July 28, 1890, composer conducting).

Hinshaw, William Wade, American baritone, pedagogue, and operatic impresario; b. near Union, Iowa, Nov. 3, 1867; d. Washington, D.C., Nov. 27, 1947. He studied civil engineering (B.S., 1888), music (Mus.B., 1890), and law (LL.B., 1897) at Valparaiso (Ind.) Univ.; he also pursued vocal training with Arturo Marescalchi and Alfred Hertz. In 1893 he made his debut at a concert at the World's Columbian Exposition in Chicago. From 1895 to 1899 he was head of the music dept. at Valparaiso Univ. On Nov. 6, 1899, he made his operatic debut as Gounod's Méphistophélès with Henry Savage's opera company in St. Louis. Returning to Chicago, he became secretary of the Hinshaw School of Opera and Drama; when it merged with the Chicago Cons. in 1903, he became president of the new institution; subsequently he was director of the Hinshaw Cons. (1907–10). With the tenor James Sheehan, he organized the Metropolitan Grand Opera Co. to stage operas in English at the International Theatre; Hinshaw sang Telramund in the company's first production in 1908. On Nov. 16, 1910, he made his debut at the Metropolitan Opera in New York at Biterolf, and subsequently remained on its roster as a distinguished Wagnerian until 1913; he also appeared at the Wagner Festivals in Graz (1912) and Berlin (1914). In 1916 he offered a prize of $1,000 for the best 1-act opera by an American composer, which was won by Hadley with his opera *Bianca*. After serving as president of the Soc. of American Singers in New York (1918–20), he toured the United States, Canada, and Cuba with his own opera company (1920–26). He spent his remaining years compiling the *Encyclopedia of American Quaker Genealogy* (6 vols., 1936–47).

Hirai, Kozaburo, Japanese composer; b. Kochi, Sept. 10, 1910. He studied violin with Robert Pollak and composition and conducting with Klaus Pringsheim at the Tokyo Imperial Academy of Music (1929–34); he taught at the Academy (1937–47) and in 1966 he organized the Assn. of Composers and Authors (ACA). Among his compositions is the operetta *Taketori-Monogatari* (1949) and the ballet *Spirit of the Snow* (1942; rev. 1968).

Hirao, Kishio, Japanese composer; b. Tokyo, July 8, 1907; d. there, Dec. 15, 1953. He graduated from Keio Univ. in 1930, then studied composition with Guy de Lioncourt at the Schola Cantorum in Paris (1931–34). He became a prof. at the Tokyo Music Academy. Among his scant compositions is the choreographic drama *Histoire de Wanasa—Otome* (1943).

Hirst, Grayson, American tenor; b. Ojai, Calif., Dec. 27, 1939. He studied at the Music Academy of the West in Santa Barbara, California, with Singher at the Univ. of Calif. at Los Angeles, and with Tourel at the Juilliard School of Music in New York (1963–72), making his professional debut as Cavalli's Ormindo with the Opera Soc. of Washington, D.C. (1969). His first appearance in New York was as Tonio in a concert performance of *La Fille du régiment* at Carnegie Hall (1970); after singing Quint in *The Turn of the Screw* at the N.Y. City Opera (1972), he appeared in opera throughout the United States and Europe while also pursuing an extensive concert career. In 1986 he joined the faculty at the Univ. of Arizona. His operatic repertoire includes over 70 roles, ranging from Mozart to contemporary roles.

Hislop, Joseph, Scottish tenor; b. Edinburgh, April 5, 1884; d. Upper Largo, Fife, May 6, 1977. He studied in Stockholm with Gillis Bratt. On Sept. 12, 1914, he made his operatic debut at the Royal Opera in Stockholm as Faust, and subsequently was active in Scandinavia before singing at the Teatro San Carlo in Naples (1919–20). On May 14, 1920, he made his first appearance at London's Covent Garden as Rodolfo; that same year, he made his U.S. debut in Chicago, then appeared in New York in 1921 before touring the country with Scotti's company. In 1923 he sang in Venice and Turin, and was the first British tenor to sing a leading role at Milan's La Scala when he appeared as Edgardo. In 1925 he appeared at the Teatro Colón in Buenos Aires. After retiring in 1937, he taught voice in Stockholm, where his most gifted students were Jussi Björling and Birgit Nilsson. In 1947 he went to London, where he was artistic advisor at Covent Garden and subsequently at the Sadler's Wells Opera. In later years, he was active as a teacher at the Guildhall School of Music. He was admired for his roles in operas by Verdi and Puccini, the latter praising him as the ideal Rodolfo. His French roles were also noteworthy.

BIBL.: M. Turnbull, *J. H.: Gran Tenore* (Aldershot, 1992).

Hitchcock, H(ugh) Wiley, eminent American musicologist and editor; b. Detroit, Sept. 28, 1923. He was educated at Dartmouth College (A.B., 1943) and the Univ. of Mich. (M.Mus., 1948; Ph.D., 1954, with the diss. *The Latin Oratorios of Marc-Antoine Charpentier*). He taught music at the Univ. of Mich. (1947–61); then was prof. of music at Hunter College (1961–71); in 1971 he became prof. of music at Brooklyn College (named Distinguished Prof. of Music in 1980), where he also served as director of the Inst. for Studies in American Music. A recipient of numerous grants, including Fulbright senior research fellowships in 1954–55 (Italy) and 1968–69 (France), and a Guggenheim fellowship in 1968–69, Hitchcock also served on the boards of numerous organizations; in 1991–92 he was president of the American Musicological Soc., and in 1994 was made an honorary member. He was also ed. of the Prentice-Hall History of Music Series (Englewood Cliffs, N.J., 1965–), *Earlier American Music* (reprints of music; N.Y., 1972–), and *Recent Researches in American Music* (Madison, Wis., 1976–). He was coed. of *The New Grove Dictionary of American Music* (4 vols., N.Y., 1986). His research interests are wide and meritorious, covering French Baroque and American music; his editorial contributions include the works of Caccini, Leonardo Leo, Charpentier, and Lully.

WRITINGS: *Music in the United States: A Historical Introduction* (Englewood Cliffs, N.J., 1969; 2d ed., rev. and enl., 1974; 3d ed., 1988); *Charles Ives Centennial Festival-Conference 1974* (program book; N.Y., 1974); *Ives* (London, 1977; rev. 1983); coed. with V. Perlis, *An Ives Celebration: Papers and Panels of the Charles Ives Centennial Festival-Conference* (Urbana, Ill., 1977); *The Phonograph and Our Musical Life* (Brooklyn, 1980); with L. Inserra, *The Music of Ainsworth's Psalter (1612)* (Brooklyn, 1981); *The Works of Marc-Antoine Charpentier: A Catalogue Raisonné* (Paris, 1982); *Ives: A Survey of the Music* (N.Y., 1983); *Marc-Antoine Charpentier* (Oxford, 1990).

BIBL.: R. Crawford, R. Lott, and C. Oja, eds., *A Celebration of American Music: Words and Music in Honor of H. W. H.* (Ann Arbor, 1989).

Hlobil, Emil, Czech composer and teacher; b. Veselí nad Lužnici, Oct. 11, 1901; d. Prague, Jan. 25, 1987. He studied with Křička at the Prague Cons. (1920–23) and in the master classes of Suk there (1924–25; 1927–30). After teaching at the Prague Women Teachers' Inst. (1930–41) he taught at the Cons. (1941–58) and afterward at the Academy of Music and Dramatic Arts in Prague. He was made an Artist of Merit (1972) and a National Artist (1981) for his services to Czech music. He followed the national tradition of the modern Czech school, and also cautiously experimented with serial methods of composition. Among his compositions are the operas *Anna Karenina* (1962; České Budějovice, April 16, 1972), *Le Bourgeois gentilhomme* (1965), and *Král Václav IV* (1981).

BIBL.: J. Bajer, *E. Hlovil: Hudební putování stoletím* (Prague, 1984).

Hoch, Beverly, American soprano; b. Marion, Kansas, Aug. 26, 1951. She studied at Friends Univ. in Wichita (1969–73), Oklahoma City Univ. (B.M., 1975), and Wichita State Univ. (M.M., 1978), and in New York with Michael Trimble (1977–82) and Ellen Faull (1982–86). In 1980 she won the Young Concert Artists International Auditions, made her recital debut at the 92nd Street Y in New York, and sang for the first time in opera at the Opera Theatre in St. Louis. From 1980 to 1988 she was a soloist with the Chamber Music Soc. of Lincoln Center in New York. In 1981 she made her debut as a soloist with orch. when she appeared at N.Y.'s Carnegie Hall with the St. Paul Chamber Orch. under Zukerman's direction. After singing Filene in *Mignon* at the Wexford Festival in 1986, she was engaged to sing Offenbach's Olympia at the Théâtre des Champs Elysées in Paris in 1987. She portrayed the Queen of the Night with the London Classical Players under Norrington's direction in 1990, a role she reprised in 1991 at the Glyndebourne Festival, the San Antonio Opera, and the London Promenade Concerts. She appeared as Adele at the Opéra du Rhin in Strasbourg in 1993. From 1994 she was the soprano of the Bach Aria Group in New York. In 1997 she sang Vespina in Haydn's *L'infedeltà delusa* at the Bard Festival in New York. As a soloist, Hoch has appeared with major orchs. around the world.

Hochberg, Hans Heinrich, XIV, Bolko Graf von, German theater Intendant and composer; b. Fürstenstein Castle, Silesia, Jan. 23, 1843; d. near Salzbrunn, Dec. 1, 1926. He established and for several years maintained the Hochberg Quartet; he also founded the Silesian music festivals (1878) and was general Intendant of the Berlin Royal Theater (1886–1902). His works include the operas *Claudine von Villabella* (Schwerin, 1864) and *Die Falkensteiner* (Hannover, 1876; rewritten as *Der Wärwolf*, Dresden, 1881).

Hoddinott, Alun, prominent Welsh composer and teacher; b. Bargoed, Aug. 11, 1929. He studied at Univ. College in Cardiff (B.A., 1949; Ph.D., 1960), and also had private instruction from Arthur Benjamin. After teaching at the Cardiff College of Music and Drama (1951–59), he was a lecturer (1959–65), reader (1965–67), and prof. (1967–87) of music at Univ. College. From 1966 to 1989 he served as artistic director of the Cardiff Festival of Twentieth Century Music. In 1957 he was awarded the Arnold Bax Medal and in 1983 he was made a Commander of the Order of the British Empire. Hoddinott's extensive output displays a notable command of various styles, ranging from the traditional to serial and aleatoric techniques.

WORKS: OPERAS: *The Beach of Falesá* (1973; Cardiff, March 26, 1974); *Murder, the Magician* (1975; Welsh TV, Feb. 11, 1976; stage version as *The Magician*, Cardiff, April 1976); *What the Old Man Does Is Always Right* (1975; Fishguard, July 27, 1977); *The Rajah's Diamond* (television premiere, Nov. 24, 1979); *The Trumpet Major* (Manchester, April 1, 1981).

BIBL.: B. Deane, *A. H.* (Cardiff, 1977); S. Craggs, *A. H.: A Bio-Bibliography* (Westport, Conn., 1993).

Hodgson, Alfreda (Rose), English contralto; b. Morecombe, June 7, 1940; d. there, April 16, 1992. She received training at the Northern School of Music in Manchester. In 1961 she made her concert debut in Liverpool, followed by her first appearance in London (in 1963). In subsequent years, she appeared as a soloist with all of the principal British orchs.; her concert engagements abroad took her to Israel, the United States, and Canada. She also appeared in opera, singing for the first time in London at the English National Opera in 1974 and at Covent Garden in 1983. Her concert repertoire ranged from Bach to Britten.

Hodkinson, Sydney P(hillip), Canadian-born American conductor, teacher, and composer; b. Winnipeg, Jan. 17, 1934. He studied composition with Louis Mennini and Bernard Rogers, and conducting with Paul White and Frederick Fennell at the Eastman School of Music in Rochester, N.Y. (M.Mus., 1958); after attending the Seminar in Advanced Musical Studies given by Carter, Sessions, and Babbitt at Princeton Univ. (1960), he studied conducting with Max Rudolf; completed his training in composition with Bassett, Castiglioni, Finney, and George B. Wilson at the Univ. of Mich. (D.M.A., 1968). From 1970 to 1972 he was music director of the St. Paul (Minn.) Chamber Orch.; concurrently he served as artist-in-residence in Minneapolis-St. Paul. He taught at the Univ. of Virginia (1958–63), Ohio Univ. (1963–66), and the Univ. of Mich. (1968–73), where he conducted its Contemporary Directions Ensemble. In 1973 he joined the faculty of the Eastman School of Music, where he was also conductor of its Musica Nova Ensemble. From 1984 to 1986 he was a visiting prof. at Southern Methodist Univ. in Dallas. In 1971 he received an award from the American Academy and National Inst. of Arts and Letters; he was granted 4 awards from the NEA (1976, 1978, 1980, 1984); in 1978–79 he held a Guggenheim fellowship. In his compositions, he explores modern techniques with pragmatic coherence.

WORKS: DRAMATIC: OPERAS: *The Swinish Cult* (1969–75); *The Wall* (1980); *In the Gallery* (1981); *Catsman* (1985). OTHER: *Lament*, fable with music for Guitar and 2 Lovers (1962); *Taiwa*, myth for Actors, Dancers, and Musicians (1965); *Vox Populous*, active oratorio for 2 Actors, Electronics Technician, 4 Vocal Soloists, and Chorus (1971–72).

Hoesslin, Franz von, German conductor and composer; b. Munich, Dec. 31, 1885; d. in an airplane crash in southern France, Sept. 28, 1946. He studied at the Univ. of Munich and with Mottl (conducting) and Reger (composition). He conducted in St. Gallen (1908–11), Riga (1912–14), Lübeck (1919–20), Mannheim (1920–22), and at the Berlin Volksoper (1922–23). After serving as Generalmusikdirektor in Dessau (1923–26), he conducted in Barmen-Elberfeld (1926–27), Bayreuth (1927–28), and Breslau (1932–35). After his wife, the singer Erna Liebenthal, was forced out of Nazi Germany, they settled in Switzerland.

Høffding, (Niels) Finn, Danish composer and pedagogue; b. Copenhagen, March 10, 1899; d. Frederiksberg, March 29, 1997. He studied violin with K. Sandby (1911–21), composition and harmony with Jeppesen (1918–21), organ with R. Rung-Keller (1919–21), and music history with Laub (1920–23) in Copenhagen; he also studied with Marx in Vienna (1921–22). He taught at the Royal Danish Cons. of Music in Copenhagen (1931–69), where he was its director (1954–69). His large output followed along post-Nielsen lines.

WORKS: OPERAS: *Kejserens nye Klaeder* (The Emperor's New Clothes; 1926; Copenhagen, Dec. 29, 1928); *Kilderejsen* (The Healing Spring; 1931; Copenhagen, Jan. 13, 1942); *Pasteur*, school opera (1935; Copenhagen, March 9, 1938).

BIBL.: S. Bruhns and D. Fog, *F. H.s Kompositionen* (Copenhagen, 1969).

Höffer, Paul, German composer and teacher; b. Barmen, Dec. 21, 1895; d. Berlin, Aug. 31, 1949. He studied with Georgii, Bölsche, and Abendroth at the Cologne Cons., and with Schreker at the Berlin Hochschule für Musik, where he joined the faculty as a piano instructor in 1923. From 1930 he taught composition and theory, and was made a prof. in 1933; in 1948 he became its director. He made use of polytonality and atonality in his compositions, which included the operas *Borgia* (1931) and *Der falsche Waldemar* (1934) and the ballet *Tanz um Liebe und Tod* (1939).

Höffgen, Marga, German contralto; b. Mülheim an der Ruhr, April 26, 1921; d. Müllheim, Baden, July 7, 1995. She studied at the Berlin Hochschule für Musik and with Hermann Weissenborn. She made her concert debut in Berlin in 1952; in 1953 she made a highly successful appearance in Vienna as a soloist in the St. Matthew Passion conducted by Karajan; she then was active as a concert singer in Europe; she also appeared in opera at Covent Garden in London, at the Vienna State Opera, and at the Bayreuth Festival.

Hoffman, Grace (Goldie), American mezzo-soprano; b. Cleveland, Jan. 14, 1925. She was educated at Western Reserve Univ. in Cleveland; then studied voice with Schorr in New York and Basiola in Milan. After appearances in the United States, she sang in Florence and Zürich; in 1955 she became a member of the Württemberg State Theater in Stuttgart. On March 27, 1958, she made her Metropolitan Opera debut in New York as Brangäne in *Tristan und Isolde*. She made many appearances at La Scala in Milan, Covent Garden in London, Bayreuth, and the Vienna State Opera. In 1978 she became a prof. of voice at the Hochschüle für Musik in Stuttgart. She was noted for her performances of the music of Wagner and Verdi, particularly for her roles of Brangäne, Kundry, and Eboli; also sang widely in concerts.

Hoffmann, E(rnst) T(heodor) A(madeus) (his 3d Christian name was Wilhelm, but he replaced it with Amadeus, from love of Mozart), famous German writer, who was also a composer; b. Königsberg, Jan. 24, 1776; d. Berlin, June 25, 1822. He studied law at the Univ. of Königsberg; he also studied violin with Christian Gladau, piano with Carl Gottlieb Richter, and thoroughbass and counterpoint with Christian Podbielski; after further studies with Gladau, he completed his training by taking a course in composition with J. F. Reichardt in Berlin. He served as music director at the theater in Bamberg, then conducted opera performances in Leipzig and Dresden (1813–14). In 1814 he settled in Berlin. He used the pen name of Kapellmeister Johannes Kreisler (subsequently made famous in Schumann's *Kreisleriana*); his series of articles in the *Allgemeine Musikalische Zeitung* under that name were reprinted as *Phantasiestucke* in Callot's *Manier* (1814). As a writer of fantastic tales, he made a profound impression on his period, and influenced the entire Romantic school of literature; indirectly, he was also a formative factor in the evolution of the German school of composition. His own compositions are passable from the technical viewpoint, but strangely enough, for a man of his imaginative power, they lack the inventiveness that characterizes his literary productions. His writings on music were ed. by H. von Ende (Cologne, 1896); see also D. Charlton, ed., *E. T. A. Hoffmann's Musical Writings: Kreisleriana, The Poet and the Composer, Music Criticism* (Cambridge, 1989).

WORKS: DRAMATIC: OPERAS: *Die Maske* (1799); *Scherz, List und Rache* (Posen, 1801); *Der Renegat* (Plozk, 1803); *Faustine* (Plozk, 1804); *Die ungeladenen Gäste, oder Der Canonicus von Mailand* (Warsaw, 1805); *Lustige Musikanten* (Warsaw, 1805); *Liebe aus Eifersucht* (Warsaw, 1807); *Der Trank der Unsterblichkeit* (Bamberg, 1808); *Das Gespenst* (Warsaw, 1809); *Aurora* (1811; rev. version by L. Böttcher, Bamberg, Nov. 5, 1933); *Undine* (Berlin, Aug. 3, 1816; his best work; vocal score ed. by Pfitzner, 1907); *Julius Sabinus* (unfinished). BALLET: *Harlekin*.

BIBL.: H. von Wolzogen, *E. T. A. H. und R. Wagner* (Berlin, 1906); E. Kroll, *E. T. A. H.s musikalische Anschauungen* (Königsberg, 1909); H. Ehinger, *E. T. A. H. als Musiker und Musikschriftsteller* (Cologne, 1954); H. Dechant, *E. T. A. H.s Oper Aurora* (Regensburg, 1975); R. Murray Schafer, *E. T. A. H. and Music* (Toronto, 1975); W. Keil, *E. T. A. H. als Komponist: Studien zur Kompositionstechnik an ausgewählten Werken* (Wiesbaden, 1986).

Hoffmann, Hans, German conductor and musicologist; b. Neustadt, Silesia, Jan. 26, 1902; d. Bielefeld, Aug. 8, 1949. He studied musicology at the Univ. of Breslau, and later in Leipzig, Berlin, and Kiel. Concurrently he took instruction in singing and for several years sang in oratorio performances in Germany. In 1933 he became a choral conductor in Hamburg, and taught theory at the Univ. of Hamburg. He was also active as a sym. and opera conductor, and in 1940 was appointed music director of the Bielefeld Opera. Among his publications were *Heinrich Schütz und Johann Sebastian Bach: Zwei Tonsprachen und ihre Bedeutung für die Aufführungspraxis* (Kassel, 1940) and *Vom Wesen der zeitgenössischen Kirchenmusik* (Kassel, 1949).

Hofmann, Peter, outstanding German tenor; b. Marienbad, Aug. 12, 1944. He studied at the Hochschule für Musik in Karlsruhe. He made his operatic debut in 1972 in Lübeck as Tamino; in 1973 he joined the Württemberg State Theater in Stuttgart. He came to prominence in his performance of the role of Siegmund in the centennial Bayreuth productions of *Der Ring des Nibelungen* (1976); that same year, he made his first appearance at London's Covent Garden in the same role. He made his U.S. debut as Siegmund with the San Francisco Opera in 1977; he sang Lohengrin on Jan. 24, 1980, at his Metropolitan Opera debut in New York. In 1986 he sang Tristan at the Bayreuth Festival. His other roles included Max, Florestan, Alfred in *Die Fledermaus*, Loge, and Bacchus.

BIBL.: M. Müller, *P. H.: Singen ist wie Fliegen* (Bonn, 1983).

Hogwood, Christopher (Jarvis Haley), prominent English harpsichordist, conductor, and musicologist; b. Nottingham, Sept. 10, 1941. He studied classics as well as music at Pembroke College, Cambridge (B.A., 1964); he received instruction in harpsichord from Puyana and Leonhardt, and also took courses at the Charles Univ. and the Academy of Music in Prague. In 1967 he joined David Munrow in organizing the Early Music Consort, an ensemble devoted to the performance of medieval music. In 1973 he founded the Academy of Ancient Music with the aim of performing music of the Baroque and early Classical periods on original instruments; he toured widely with the ensemble and made many recordings with it, including a complete set of Mozart's syms. utilizing instruments of Mozart's time. He also served as artistic director of the Handel and Haydn Soc. of Boston (from 1986) and music director of the St. Paul (Minn.) Chamber Orch. (1988–92), subsequently serving as principal guest conductor of the latter (from 1992). He also was the International Prof. of Early Music Performance at the Royal Academy of Music in London (from 1992) and a visiting prof. at King's College, London (from 1992). His guest conducting engagements took him all over Europe and North America. In 1989 he was made a Commander of the Order of the British Empire. He ed. works by J. C. Bach, Purcell, and Croft; was a contributor to *The New Grove Dictionary of Music and Musicians* (1980). He publ., in London, *Music at Court* (1977), *The Trio Sonata* (1979), and *Handel* (1984).

Hoiby, Lee, talented American composer and pianist; b. Madison, Wis., Feb. 17, 1926. He began piano study at age 5, and while attending high school received instruction from Gunnar Johansen; then studied at the Univ. of Wisc. (B.A., 1947); attended Petri's master class in Ithaca, N.Y. (1944), and at Mills College in Oakland, California (M.A., 1952), where he also studied composition with Milhaud; he also received instruction in composition from Menotti at the Curtis Inst. of Music in Philadelphia. He received a Fulbright fellowship (1953), an award from the National Inst. of Arts and Letters (1957), and a Guggenheim fellowship (1958). In addition to his career as a composer, he appeared as a concert pianist; he made his N.Y. recital debut on Jan. 17, 1978. He has composed a number of highly successful vocal and instrumental works, being particularly adept in writing operas in a manner reminiscent of Menotti—concise, dramatic, and aurally pleasing, and sometimes stimulating.

WORKS: DRAMATIC: OPERAS: *The Scarf*, after Chekhov (Spoleto, June 20, 1958); *Beatrice*, after Maeterlinck (Louisville, Oct. 23, 1959; withdrawn); *Natalia Petrovna*, after Turgenev (N.Y., Oct. 8, 1964; rev. version as *A Month in the Country*, Boston, Jan. 1981); *Summer and Smoke*, after Tennessee Williams (1970; St. Paul, Minn., June 19, 1971); *Something New for the Zoo* (1979; Cheverly, Md., May 17, 1982); *The Tempest*, after Shakespeare (1982–86; Indianola, Iowa, June 21, 1986); *This Is the Rill Speaking* (1993); also *The Italian Lesson*, monodrama for Mezzo-soprano and Chamber Orch. (1980; Newport, R.I., 1982); incidental music to various plays. BALLETS: *Hearts, Meadows, and Flags* (1950); *After Eden* (1966); *Landscape* (1968). Also *Galileo Galilei*, oratorio for Soloists, Chorus, and Orch. (1975).

Hol, Richard (Rijk), Dutch composer, conductor, pianist, and organist; b. Amsterdam, July 23, 1825; d. Utrecht, May 14, 1904. He studied organ with Martens and theory with Bertelmann. After traveling in Germany, he taught music in Amsterdam; in 1862 he became city music director at Utrecht, succeeding Kufferath, then cathedral organist (1869–87) and director of the School of Music (1875–1904). He conducted concerts in The Hague and Amsterdam. From 1886 to 1900 he was ed. of *Het Orgel*; wrote a monograph on Sweelinck (1860). Among his compositions are the operas *Floris V* (Amsterdam, April 9, 1892), *Uit de branding* (Amsterdam, 1894), and *De schoone schaapster*, and the oratorio, *David* (1879).

BIBL.: H. Nolthenius, *R. H.: Levensschets* (Haarlem, 1904).

Holbrooke, Joseph (Josef Charles), English composer; b. Croydon, July 5, 1878; d. London, Aug. 5, 1958. He was a student of Corder (composition) and Westlake (piano) at the Royal Academy of Music in London. He then worked as a conductor and pianist. The success of his symphonic poem *The Raven* (1900) encouraged him to write a large body of music along Romantic lines. His most ambitious work was the operatic trilogy *The Caul-*

dron of Annwn (1909–29). Holbrooke's initial success as a composer was not sustained. Especially in his early years he was a trenchant critic of the musical establishment. He was the author of *Contemporary British Composers* (London, 1925).

WORKS: DRAMATIC: *Pierrot and Pierrette*, lyric drama (London, Nov. 11, 1909; rev. version as *The Stranger*, Liverpool, Oct. 1924); *The Cauldron of Annwn*, operatic trilogy: 1, *The Children of Don* (London, June 15, 1912); 2, *Dylan: Son of the Wave* (1909; London, July 4, 1914); and 3, *Bronwen* (Huddersfield, Feb. 1, 1929); *The Red Mask*, ballet; *The Moth and the Flame*, ballet; *The Enchanter*, opera ballet (Chicago, 1915); *Coromanthe*, ballet; *The Sailor's Arms*, comic opera; *The Snob*, comic opera; *Aucassin et Nicolette*, ballet.

BIBL.: G. Lowe, *J. H. and his Work* (London, 1920); *J. H.: Various Appreciations by Many Authors* (London, 1937).

Holewa, Hans, Austrian-born Swedish composer; b. Vienna, May 26, 1905; d. Bromma, April 24, 1991. He studied conducting at the New Cons. of Music in Vienna, and piano and theory with J. Heinz. In 1937 he settled in Stockholm as a pianist and pedagogue; there he introduced Schoenberg's 12-tone technique. From 1949 to 1970 he worked in the music library of the Swedish Broadcasting Corp. Among his works is the opera *Apollos förvandling* (1967–71).

Holguín, Guillermo. See **Uribe-Holguín, Guillermo.**

Holl, Robert, Dutch bass-baritone; b. Rotterdam, March 10, 1947. He studied with Jan Veth and David Hollestelle. After winning 1st prize in the 's-Hertogenbosch Competition in 1971, he pursued training with Hans Hotter in Munich. In 1972 he captured 1st prize in the Munich International Competition. After appearing with the Bavarian State Opera in Munich (1973–75), he pursued a concert career. From 1981 to 1983 he was engaged in opera at the Mozartwochen in Salzburg. In 1988 he sang in Schubert's *Fierabras* at the Theater an der Wien in Vienna. He appeared as Assur in *Semiramide* and as La Roche in *Capriccio* in Zürich in 1992. Following an engagement as Hans Sachs at the Bayreuth Festival and as Amfortas in Zürich in 1996, he sang in Schubert's *Des Teufels Lustschloss* at the Vienna Festival in 1997. In 1990 he was made an Austrian Kammersänger. Holl's engagements as a soloist with orchs., as an oratorio singer, and as a lieder artist have taken him all over the world.

Hollaender, Viktor, German conductor and composer; b. Leobschütz, Silesia, April 20, 1866; d. Los Angeles, Oct. 24, 1940. After training in Berlin with Kullak, he was a theater conductor in Hamburg, Milwaukee (1890), Berlin, Chicago, and London (1894–1901). Returning to Berlin, he was musical director at the Metropoltheater (1901–08) and the Thalia-Theater (1908–09), where he brought out various revues. His more ambitious light theater scores included *San Lin* (Breslau, Jan 28, 1898), *Der rote Kosak* (Berlin, Dec. 21, 1901), *Der Sonnenvogel* or *Der Phönix* (St. Petersburg, Aug. 22, 1903), *Die schöne vom Strand* (Berlin, Feb. 5, 1915), and *Die Prinzessin vom Nil* (Berlin, Sept. 18, 1915). He had his finest success with the incidental music he composed for the pantomime *Sumurun* (Berlin, 1910). In 1934 he emigrated to the United States. His son, Friedrich Hollaender (b. London, Oct. 18, 1896; d. Munich, Jan. 18, 1976), was a composer. He was a student at the Berlin Hochschule für Musik and of Humperdinck. After composing revues, operettas, and other light theater scores, he became best known as a composer of film scores. His autobiography appeared as *Von Kopf bis Fuss, mein Leben mit Text und Musik* (Munich, 1965). His brother was the German violinist, pedagogue, and composer Gustav Hollaender (1855–1915).

Holland, Charles, black American tenor; b. Norfolk, Va., Dec. 27, 1909; d. Amsterdam, Nov. 7, 1987. He studied with May Hamaker Henley, Georges Le Pyre in Los Angeles, and Clyde Burrows in New York. He sang with the bands of Benny Carter and Fletcher Henderson, appeared in the film *Hullabaloo* (1941), and had his own concert program on NBC radio. In 1949 he settled in France, where he appeared on radio and television; he made his European operatic debut in *Die Zauberflöte* at the Paris Opéra in 1954, and in 1955 he became the first black artist to sing at the Paris Opéra Comique. He later sang throughout Europe, Australia, New Zealand, and Canada, making his N.Y. debut in a recital at Carnegie Hall in 1982.

Holland, Theodore (Samuel), English composer and teacher; b. London, April 25, 1878; d. there, Oct. 29, 1947. He studied with F. Corder at the Royal Academy of Music in London and with Joachim at the Hochschule für Musik in Berlin. In 1927 he became prof. of composition at the Royal Academy of Music. He was an estimable composer, particularly proficient in writing for the theater. Among his works were a children's operetta, *King Goldemar*, and a musical play, *Santa Claus*; *Evening on a Lake* for Chamber Orch. (1924).

Hölle, Matthias, German bass; b. Rottweil am Nekkar, July 8, 1951. He was a student of Georg Jelden in Stuttgart and of Josef Metternich in Cologne. In 1976 he joined the Cologne Opera, where he made frequent appearances until 1987. From 1981 he sang at the Bayreuth Festival, where he became best known for such roles as Hunding, Fasolt, Titurel, and King Marke. He appeared in the premiere of Stockhausen's *Donnerstag aus Licht* in Milan in 1981, and returned there in 1984 to create the role of Lucifer in that composer's *Samstag aus Licht*. On Dec. 10, 1986, he made his debut at the Metropolitan Opera in New York as Rocco. He portrayed Don Fernando in Brussels in 1989, and Hunding in Bonn in 1992. Following his first appearance at London's Covent Garden in 1994 as Hunding, he returned there in 1996 as Fafner.

Höller, York (Georg), German composer; b. Leverkusen, Jan. 11, 1944. He studied composition with Zimmermann and Eimert, piano with Alfons Kontarsky, conducting, and music education (diploma, 1967) at the Cologne Hochschule für Musik. He also took courses in musicology and philosophy at the Univ. of Cologne, and attended Boulez's analysis sessions at the summer course in new music in Darmstadt (1965). In 1971–72 he was active at the WDR Electronic Music Studio in Cologne. In 1974–75 he was in residence at the Cite Internationale des Arts in Paris. From 1976 to 1989 he taught analysis and theory at the Cologne Hochschule für Musik. His *Antiphon* for String Quartet was commissioned for the opening of the Centre Pompidou in Paris in 1977. In 1978 he realized his *Arcus* at IRCAM in Paris, which was commissioned for the opening of its Espace de Projection. The score was subsequently performed on both sides of the Atlantic by the Ensemble Inter-Contemporain. In 1979 he received the Bernd Alois Zimmermann Prize of Cologne. In 1984–85 he was in residence at the Villa Massimo in Rome. He was named Chevalier dans l'Ordre des Arts et des Lettres of France in 1986. The International Composer's Forum of UNESCO awarded him its prize for his 2d Piano Concerto in 1987. In 1990 he became director of the WDR Electronic Music Studio. He wrote *Fortschritt oder Sackgasse?: Kritische Betrachtungen zum frühen Serialismus* (Saarbrücken, 1994). In his oeuvre, Höller has effectively utilized both traditional and electronic modes of expression. Within his catalog of works are the operas *Der Meister und Margarita* (1984–89; Paris, May 20, 1989) and *Caligula* (1992).

Holliger, Heinz, outstanding Swiss oboist, pedagogue, and composer; b. Langenthal, May 21, 1939. He commenced playing the recorder at 4 and the piano at 6; he later studied oboe with Cassagnaud and composition with Veress at the Bern Cons., then oboe with Pierlot and piano with Lefébure at the Paris Cons. In 1959 he won 1st prize in the Geneva competition, and then played in the Basel Sym. Orch.; he also attended Boulez's master classes in composition in Basel (1961–63). After winning 1st prize in the Munich competition in 1961, he embarked upon a brilliant international career; he toured in Europe and the United States as soloist with the Lucerne Festival Strings in 1962. He also gave concerts with his wife, the harpist Ursula Hanggi, and his own Holliger Ensemble. In addition to giving master classes, he was a prof. at the Freiburg im Breisgau Hochschule für Musik (from 1965). He is generally recognized as the foremost oboist of his era, his mastery extending from early music to the commissioned works of such modern composers as Penderecki, Henze, Stockhausen, Krenek, Berio, Jolivet, and Lutoslawski. In his own works, he is an uncompromising avant-gardist.

WORKS: DRAMATIC: *Der magische Tänzer* for 2 Singers, 2 Dancers, 2 Actors, Chorus, Orch., and Tape (1963–65; Basel, April 26, 1970); *Come and Go/Va et vient/Kommen und Gehen*, chamber opera, after Samuel Beckett (1976–77; Hamburg, Feb. 16, 1978); *Not I*, monodrama for Soprano and Tape, after Beckett (1978–80; Avignon, July 15, 1980); *What Where*, chamber opera, after Beckett (1988; Frankfurt am Main, May 19, 1989).

Hollingsworth, Stanley, American composer and teacher; b. Berkeley, Calif., Aug. 27, 1924. He studied at San Jose State College; then with Milhaud at Mills College and with Menotti at the Curtis Inst. of Music in Philadelphia; subsequently he was at the American Academy in Rome (1955–56). He received a Guggenheim fellowship in 1958; he also was awarded several NEA grants. From 1961 to 1963 he taught at San Jose State College; in 1963 he joined the faculty of Oakland Univ. in Rochester, Mich. His music follows the principles of practical modernism; in this respect, he emulates Menotti. He used the pseudonym Stanley Hollier in some of his works.

WORKS: OPERAS: *The Mother*, after Andersen (1949; Philadelphia, March 29, 1954); *La Grande Bretèche*, after Balzac (1954; NBC-TV, Feb. 10, 1957); *The Selfish Giant* (1981); *Harrison Loved His Umbrella* (1981).

Holloway, Robin (Greville), English composer, teacher, and writer on music; b. Leamington Spa, Oct. 19, 1943. He studied privately with Goehr (1959–63), and also attended King's College, Cambridge (1961–64); he completed his education at New College, Oxford (1965–67; Ph.D., 1971, with a diss. on Debussy and Wagner; publ. in London, 1979). He was a lecturer at the Univ. of Cambridge (from 1975); he also contributed various articles to periodicals and anthologies. His output is notable for its remarkable command of various styles and genres. While he has tended along tonal paths, he is not averse to nontonal and constructivist techniques. He has also made much use of "objets trouvés." His works include the opera *Clarissa* (1976; also *Clarissa Symphony* for Soprano, Tenor, and Orch., Birmingham, Dec. 9, 1982).

Hollreiser, Heinrich, German conductor; b. Munich, June 24, 1913. He studied at the Munich Academy of Music; took lessons in conducting with Elmendorff. He subsequently was engaged as an opera conductor in Wiesbaden (1932), Darmstadt (1935–38), Mannheim (1938–39), Duisburg (1939–42), and Munich (1942–45). From 1945 to 1952 he was Generalmusikdirektor in Düsseldorf. He then was a conductor at the Vienna State Opera (1952–61) and chief conductor of the Deutsche Oper in West Berlin (1961–64); he also served as a regular conductor at Bayreuth for several seasons. In 1978 he made his U.S. debut with the Cleveland Orch. In subsequent years, he appeared as a guest conductor with various European orchs. and opera houses. In 1993 he became permanent guest conductor of the Deutsche Oper in Berlin.

Hollweg, Ilse, German soprano; b. Solingen, Feb. 23, 1922; d. there, Feb. 9, 1990. She studied with Gertrude Förstel at the Cologne Hochschule für Musik. In 1942 she made her operatic debut as Blondchen in Saarbrücken. From 1946 to 1951 she sang in Düsseldorf, and also appeared as Constanze at the Glyndebourne Festival (1950) and then as Zerbinetta at the Edinburgh Festival. In 1951 she made her debut at London's Covent Garden as Gilda. Her guest engagements also took her to Berlin, Hamburg, Vienna, Salzburg, and Bayreuth. From 1955 to 1970 she was a member of the Deutsche Oper am Rhein in Düsseldorf. She also sang in works by Schoenberg, Krenek, Karl Amadeus Hartmann, Boulez, and Nono to great effect.

BIBL.: K. Ruhrberg, *I. H.* (Duisburg, 1971).

Hollweg, Werner (Friedrich), German tenor; b. Solingen, Sept. 13, 1936. He received his training in Detmold, Lugano, and Munich. After making his debut with the Vienna Chamber Opera in 1962, he sang in Bonn (1963–67) and Gelsenkirchen (1967–68). His success as Belmonte in Florence in 1969 and as a soloist in Beethoven's 9th Sym. under Karajan in Osaka in 1970 led to engagements with the Hamburg State Opera, the Bavarian State Opera in Munich, the Deutsche Oper in Berlin, the Deutsche Oper am Rhein in Düsseldorf, and the Vienna State Opera. He also appeared in Rome, Paris, New York, Los Angeles, and at London's Covent Garden (debut as Titus, 1976). He won particular distinction in such Mozart portrayals as Don Ottavio, Idomeneo, Tamino, Basilio, and Ferrando. He also sang in contemporary operas, creating the role of Matthew Levi in Höller's *Der Meister und Margarita* (Paris, 1989). His concert repertoire ranged from Haydn to Kodály. His interpretations of the songs of Schubert, Schumann, and Loewe were especially esteemed.

Holm, Mogens Winkel, Danish composer; b. Copenhagen, Oct. 1, 1936. He was a student of Jørgen Jersild (theory and composition) and Mogens Andreassen (oboe) at the Royal Danish Cons. of Music in Copenhagen (1955–61). He then was an oboist in several Copenhagen orchs.; he was a music critic for the Copenhagen newspapers *Ekstra Bladet* and *Politiken* (1965–71), and subsequently served as chairman of the Danish Composers' Soc. (1971–75; from 1982).

WORKS: DRAMATIC: OPERAS: *Aslak*, chamber opera (1962; Copenhagen, Jan. 27, 1963); *Sonata for 4 Opera Singers*, textless chamber opera (Copenhagen, April 19, 1968). BALLETS: *Tropismer II* (Copenhagen, May 24, 1964); *Kontradans* (Danish Radio, July 16, 1965); *Bikt* (Swedish Radio, May 5, 1969; rev. as *Krønike* [Chronicle]); *Galgarien* (Malmö, Nov. 27, 1970); *Rapport* (Report; Danish Radio, March 19, 1972); *Tarantel* (1975); *Eurydike tøver* (Eurydice Hesitates; 1977); *Gaerdesanger under kunstig stjernehimmel* (Whitethroat Under an Artificial Firmament; 1979–80); *Til Blåskaeg* (To Bluebeard; 1982).

Holm, Peder, Danish composer; b. Copenhagen, Sept. 30, 1926. He studied violin with Thorval Nielsen and counterpoint with Jeppesen at the Royal Danish Cons. of Music in Copenhagen (1945–47). He became a lecturer at the Esbjerg Cons. in 1949 and in 1964 was named its director. Among his works is the opera *Ingen mad i dag, men i morgen* (No Food Today but Tomorrow; 1962).

Holm, Renate, German soprano; b. Berlin, Aug. 10, 1931. After winning 1st prize in a vocal competition sponsored at the RIAS in Berlin in 1952, she embarked upon a career as a pop singer; she also pursued vocal training with Maria Ivogün in Vienna. In 1958 she made her debut in Oscar Straus's *Ein Walzertraum* at the Vienna Volksoper, where she subsequently sang with fine success. In 1961 she joined the Vienna State Opera. Her guest engagements took her to the Salzburg Festival, Covent Garden in London, the Bolshoi Theater in Moscow, and the Teatro Colón in Buenos Aires. She was notably successful as Blondchen, Papagena, Rosina in *Il Barbiere di Siviglia*, Marie in *Zar und Zimmermann*, and Musetta, as well as in Viennese operettas. She was the author of *Ein Leben nach Spielplan: Stationen einer ungewöhnlichen Karriere* (Berlin, 1991).

Holm, Richard, German tenor; b. Stuttgart, Aug. 3, 1912; d. Munich, July 20, 1988. He studied in Stuttgart with Rudolf Ritter. In 1937 he made his operatic debut in Kiel; he became a member of the Kiel Opera and also made guest appearances at other German opera houses; in 1948 he joined the Bavarian State Opera in Munich. On March 15, 1952, he made his Metropolitan Opera debut in New York as David in *Die Meistersinger von Nürnberg*; was on its roster until 1953. He also made successful appearances in London, Vienna, Salzburg, and Bayreuth. In 1967 he became a prof. of voice at the Hochschule für Musik in Munich. Among his roles were Xerxes, Titus, Belmonte, Tamino, Loge, Flamand, Novagerio in *Palestrina*, Robespierre in *Dantons Tod*, and Aschenbach in *Death in Venice*.

Holmboe, Vagn, eminent Danish composer and pedagogue; b. Horsens, Jutland, Dec. 20, 1909; d. Ramlse, Sept. 1, 1996. He was a student of Høffding and Jeppesen at the Copenhagen Cons. (1925–29), and then of Toch at the Berlin Hochschule für Musik

(1930). After pursuing ethnomusicological research in Romania (1933–34), he returned to Copenhagen as a private teacher. He taught at the Royal Danish Inst. for the Blind (1940–49), and also was a music critic for the newspaper *Politiken* (1947–55). In 1950 he became a teacher at the Royal Danish Cons. of Music in Copenhagen, where he subsequently was a prof. of theory and composition from 1955 to 1965. He held a lifetime government grant to pursue composition. He publ. *Mellemspil* (Interlude; Copenhagen, 1961) and *Det Uforklarlige* (Copenhagen, 1981; Eng. tr., 1991, as *Experiencing Music: A Composer's Notes*). As the leading Danish composer in the post–Nielsen era, Holmboe pursued a neoclassical style in which he displayed a thorough command of counterpoint and instrumentation. His symphonic compositions were notable for their development of "germ themes" that grow metamorphically. In addition to his important contribution to the symphony, he also composed an outstanding series of string quartets.

WORKS: DRAMATIC: *Fanden og borgemesteren* (The Devil and the Mayor), symphonic fairy play (1940); *Den galsindede tyrk*, ballet (1942–44); *Lave og Jon*, opera (1946–48); *Kniven* (The Knife), chamber opera (1959–60; Copenhagen, Dec. 2, 1963); music for plays, films, and radio.

BIBL.: P. Rapoport, *V. H.: A Catalogue of His Music, Discography, Bibliography, Essays* (London, 1974; 2d. ed., rev. and enl., Copenhagen, 1979); idem, *V. H.'s Symphonic Metamorphoses* (diss., Univ. of Ill., 1975).

Holmès (real name, **Holmes**), **Augusta (Mary Anne),** French composer; b. Paris (of Irish parents), Dec. 16, 1847; d. there, Jan. 28, 1903. She progressed very rapidly as a child pianist, and gave public concerts; also composed songs, under the pen name Hermann Zenta. She studied harmony with H. Lambert, an organist, and later became a pupil of Franck. She then began to compose works in large forms, arousing considerable attention, mixed with curiosity, for she was one of the very few professional women composers of the time. Her music lacks individuality or strength; at best, it represents a conventional by-product of French Romanticism, with an admixture of fashionable exotic elements. Her works include the operas *La Montagne noire* (Paris Opéra, Feb. 8, 1895), *Héro et Léandre, Astarte*, and *Lancelot du lac*.

BIBL.: P. Barillon-Bauché, *A. H. et la femme compositeur* (Paris, 1912); R. Pichard du Page, *A. H.: Une Musicienne versaillaise* (Paris, 1921).

Holoman, D(allas) Kern, American musicologist and conductor; b. Raleigh, N.C., Sept. 8, 1947. He pursued his academic training at Duke Univ. (B.A., 1969) and Princeton Univ. (M.F.A., 1971; Ph.D., 1974, with the diss. *Autograph Musical Documents of Hector Berlioz, c.1818–1840*; publ. in a rev. and corrected ed. as *The Creative Process in the Autograph Musical Documents of Hector Berlioz, c.1818–1840*, Ann Arbor, 1980), receiving a Fulbright fellowship (1972–73). In 1973 he joined the faculty of the Univ. of Calif. at Davis, where he was founder-director of its Early Music Ensemble (1973–77; 1979), conductor of its sym. orch. (from 1978), and chairman of the music dept. (1980–88). With J. Kerman and R. Winter, he was founding ed. of the distinguished journal *19th Century Music* (1977), subsequently serving as its managing ed. In 1989 he became general ed. of the series Recent Researches in the Music of the Nineteenth and Twentieth Centuries. His writings are notable for their accessible prose style and engaging, dry wit. An authority on Berlioz, he publ. the first thematic catalog of that composer's output, *Catalogue of the Works of Hector Berlioz* (Kassel, 1987), and ed. his *Roméo et Juliette* for the New Berlioz Edition.

Holoubek, Ladislav, Slovak conductor and composer; b. Prague, Aug. 13, 1913. He studied composition with Moyzes at the Bratislava Academy of Music (1926–33) and with Novák at the Prague Cons. (1934–36). He conducted at the Slovak National Theater in Bratislava (1933–52; 1959–66) and at the State Theater in Košice (1955–58; from 1966). His operas have contributed significantly to the advancement of modern Slovak opera.

WORKS: OPERAS (all 1st perf. in Bratislava unless otherwise given): *Stella* (March 18, 1939; rev. 1948–49 and 1954–55); *Svitanie* (Dawn; March 12, 1941); *Tužba* (Yearning; Feb. 12, 1944; rev. 1963 and 1969); *Rodina* (The Family; Nov. 12, 1960); *Professor Mamlock* (May 21, 1966); *Bačovské žarty* (Shepherds' Games; 1975; Košice, Jan. 16, 1981).

Holst, Gustav(us Theodore von), significant English composer, father of **Imogen (Clare) Holst**; b. Cheltenham, Sept. 21, 1874; d. London, May 25, 1934. He was of Swedish descent. He received his primary musical training from his parents. In 1892 he became organist and choirmaster in Wyck Rissington, Gloucestershire; in 1893 he entered the Royal College of Music in London, where he studied composition with Stanford and Rockstro, organ with Hoyte, and piano with Sharpe; he also learned to play the trombone. After graduating in 1898 he was a trombonist in the orch. of the Carl Rosa Opera Co. (until 1900) and the Scottish Orch. in Glasgow (1900–03). His interest in Hindu philosophy, religion, and music during this period led to the composition of his settings from the Sanskrit of *Hymns from the Rig Veda* (1907–08). He worked as a music teacher in a Dulwich girls' school (1903–20) and was director of music at St. Paul's Girls' School, Hammersmith (1905–34), and of London's Morley College (1907–24). He became a teacher of composition at the Royal College of Music (1919); he was also prof. of music at Univ. College, Reading (1919–23). Plagued by suspicions of his German sympathies at the outbreak of World War I in 1914, he removed the Germanic-looking (actually Swedish) nobiliary particle "von" from his surname; his early works had been publ. under the name Gustav von Holst. He was deemed unfit for military service, but served as YMCA musical organizer among the British troops in the Near East in 1918. After the war, he visited the United States as a lecturer and conductor in 1923 and 1932. However, his deteriorating health limited his activities; his daughter described his mind in the last years of his life as "closed in gray isolation." Holst's most celebrated work, the large-scale orch. suite *The Planets*, was inspired by the astrological significance of the planets. It consists of 7 movements, each bearing a mythological subtitle: *Mars, the Bringer of War; Venus, the Bringer of Peace; Mercury, the Winged Messenger; Jupiter, the Bringer of Jollity; Saturn, the Bringer of Old Age; Uranus, the Magician; Neptune, the Mystic*, with an epilogue of female voices singing wordless syllables. It was first performed privately in London (Sept. 29, 1918); 5 movements were played in public (Feb. 15, 1920); the first complete performance followed (Nov. 15, 1920). The melodic and harmonic style of the work epitomizes Holst's musical convictions, in which lyrical, dramatic, and triumphant motifs are alternately presented in coruscatingly effective orch. dress. His music in general reflects the influence of English folk songs and the madrigal. He was a master of choral writing; one of his notable works utilizing choral forces was *The Hymn of Jesus* (1917). His writings were ed. by S. Lloyd and E. Rubbra as *Gustav Holst: Collected Essays* (London, 1974).

WORKS: DRAMATIC: OPERAS: *The Revoke*, op. 1 (1895); *The Youth's Choice*, op. 11 (1902); *Sita*, op. 23 (1899–1906); *Savitri*, chamber opera, op. 25 (1908; London, Dec. 5, 1916); *The Perfect Fool*, op. 39 (1918–22; London, May 14, 1923); *At the Boar's Head*, op. 42 (1924; Manchester, April 3, 1925); *The Wandering Scholar*, chamber opera, op. 50 (1929–30; Liverpool, Jan. 31, 1934). OTHER: *Lansdown Castle*, operetta (Cheltenham, Feb. 7, 1893); *The Idea*, children's operetta (c.1898); *The Vision of Dame Christian*, masque, op. 27a (London, July 22, 1909). BALLETS: *The Lure* (1921); *The Golden Goose*, choral ballet, op. 45/1 (BBC, London, Sept. 21, 1926); *The Morning of the Year*, choral ballet, op. 45/2 (1926–27; London, March 17, 1927). INCIDENTAL MUSIC: *The Sneezing Charm* (1918); 7 choruses from *Alcestis* (1920); *The Coming of Christ* (1927; Canterbury, May 28, 1928).

See I. Holst and C. Matthews, eds., *Gustav Holst: Collected Facsimile Edition of Autograph Manuscripts of the Published Works* (4 vols., London, 1974–83).

BIBL.: L. Dyer, *G. H.* (London, 1931); I. Holst, *G. H.: A Biography* (London, 1938; 2d ed., 1969); E. Rubbra, *G. H.* (Monaco, 1947); I. Holst, *The Music of G. H.* (London, 1951; 3d ed., rev.,

1986, including *H.'s Music Reconsidered*); U. Vaughan Williams and I. Holst, eds., *Heirs and Rebels* (London, 1959); I. Holst, *H.* (London, 1974; 2d ed., 1981); idem, *A Thematic Catalogue of G. H.'s Music* (London, 1974); M. Short, ed., *G. H. (1874–1934): A Centenary Documentation* (London, 1974); M. Short, *G. H.: The Man and His Music* (Oxford, 1990).

Holst, Imogen (Clare), English conductor and writer on music, daughter of **Gustav(us Theodore von) Holst**; b. Richmond, Surrey, April 12, 1907; d. Aldeburgh, March 9, 1984. She studied at the St. Paul's Girls' School and the Royal College of Music in London. From 1943 to 1951 she was music director of the Dartington Hall arts center. From 1952 to 1964 she was musical assistant to Britten; she also conducted the Purcell Singers (1953–67) and served as artistic director of the Aldeburgh Festival (from 1956). In 1975 she was made a Commander of the Order of the British Empire. Her most important writings include *Gustav Holst: A Biography* (London, 1938; 2d ed., 1969), *The Music of Gustav Holst* (London, 1951; 3d ed., rev., 1986, including *Holst's Music Reconsidered*), and *A Thematic Catalogue of Gustav Holst's Music* (London, 1974). With C. Matthews, she ed. *Gustav Holst: Collected Facsimile Edition of Autograph Manuscripts of the Published Works* (London, 1974–83).

BIBL.: P. Cox and J. Dobbs, eds., *I. H. at Dartington* (Dartington, 1988).

Holstein, Franz (Friedrich) von, German composer; b. Braunschweig, Feb. 16, 1826; d. Leipzig, May 22, 1878. His father was an army officer, at whose behest Holstein entered the Cadet School; he concurrently studied music theory with Griepenkerl. While a lieutenant, he privately produced his operetta, *Zwei Nächte in Venedig* (1845). He fought in the Schleswig-Holstein campaign, then wrote a grand opera, *Waverley*, after Walter Scott. He sent the score to Hauptmann at the Leipzig Cons.; the latter expressed his willingness to accept Holstein as a student. Accordingly, he resigned from the army (1853) and studied with Hauptmann, H. Richter, and Moscheles at the Leipzig Cons. He then devoted himself to composition. He was also a poet, and wrote his own librettos. The style of his operas was close to the French type, popularized by Auber. He was a man of means, and left a valuable legacy for the benefit of indigent music students. Among his works were the operas *Der Haideschacht* (Dresden, Oct. 22, 1868), *Der Erbe von Morley* (Leipzig, Jan. 23, 1872), *Die Hochländer* (Mannheim, Jan. 16, 1876), and *Marino Faliero* (unfinished); also an overture, *Frau Aventiure* (sketches only; orchestrated by A. Dietrich; Leipzig, Nov. 13, 1879).

BIBL.: G. Glaser, *F. v.H.: Ein Dichterkomponist des 19. Jahrhunderts* (Leipzig, 1930).

Holt, Henry, Austrian-born American conductor and opera administrator; b. Vienna, April 11, 1934; Charlottesville, Va., Oct. 4, 1997. He studied with Strelitzer at Los Angeles City College and with Dahl at the Univ. of Southern Calif. in Los Angeles. In 1961 he made his conducting debut with *Rigoletto* with the American Opera Co. in Los Angeles. He was general director of the Portland (Oreg.) Opera from 1964 to 1966. From 1966 to 1984 he was general director of the Seattle Opera, where he conducted its acclaimed Wagner Festivals.

Holten, Bo, Danish conductor and composer; b. Copenhagen, Oct. 22, 1948. He studied at the Univ. of Copenhagen but was principally autodidact. He acquired a fine reputation as a conductor with his own vocal ensemble, Ars Nova, in Copenhagen; in 1990 he became a guest conductor of the BBC Singers in London. He has frequently led challenging concerts in which works from various eras and nations have appeared on the same program. As a composer, Holton has been particularly noted for his inventive counterpoint and melodic writing. Among his works is the opera *The Bond* (1978–79).

Holzbauer, Ignaz (Jakob), noted Austrian composer; b. Vienna, Sept. 17, 1711; d. Mannheim, April 7, 1783. He studied law and at the same time received instruction in music from members of the choir at St. Stephen's in Vienna; he also perused *Gradus ad Parnassum* by Fux, whom he met later and who advised him to go to Italy for further studies. He then proceeded to Venice, but soon returned home. For a brief period he served as Kapellmeister to Count Rottal of Holešov in Moravia; in 1737 he married Rosalie Andreides, a singer; shortly thereafter they moved to Vienna, where he became a conductor and she a singer at the Court Theater; they also spent several years in Italy. In 1751 he was named Oberkapellmeister in Stuttgart. In 1753 he became Kapellmeister at the court of the elector Karl Theodor in Mannheim, a post he held until the court moved to Munich in 1778. He visited Rome in 1756, Turin in 1758, and Milan in 1759; during these visits he produced several of his operas. Holzbauer was greatly respected as a composer, especially for his church music; Mozart heard one of his masses in Mannheim in 1777 and found it excellent. He was an important figure among symphonic composers of the Mannheim school; he wrote some 65 works for orch. Of his operas, *Günther von Schwarzburg* (Mannheim, Jan. 5, 1777) is historically significant for its departure from Italian convention; it is thoroughly German in subject and treatment, and is noteworthy for the inclusion of accompanied recitative in place of the dialogue of the Singspiel. It was publ. in Mannheim in 1776. His other operas include *Il Figlio delle selve* (Schwetzingen, 1753), *L'isola disabitata* (Schwetzingen, 1754), *L'issipile* (Mannheim, Nov. 4, 1754), *Don Chisciotte* (Schwetzingen, 1755), *I Cinesi* (Mannheim, 1756), *Le nozze d'Arianna* (Mannheim, 1756), *Il Filosofo di campagna* (Mannheim, 1756), *La clemenza di Tito* (Mannheim, Nov. 4, 1757), *La Nitteti* (Turin, 1758), *Alessandro nell'Indie* (Milan, 1759), *Ippolito ed Aricia* (Mannheim, Nov. 4, 1759), *Adriano in Siria* (Mannheim, Nov. 4, 1768), and *Tancredi* (Munich, Jan. 1783). He also wrote ballet music for operas by J. A. Hasse: *L'Ipermestra* (Vienna, Jan. 8, 1744) and *Arminio* (Vienna, May 13, 1747). In addition, he composed 4 oratorios.

Holzmair, Wolfgang (Friedrich), esteemed Austrian baritone; b. Vöcklabruck, April 24, 1952. He graduated from the Vienna Univ. of Economics but pursued training in voice with Rössl-Madjan and in lieder interpretation with Werba at the Vienna Academy of Music. After taking a prize at the 1982 International Song Competition of the Vienna Musikverein, he appeared in opera in Bern and Gelsenkirchen; also sang at the Bavarian State Opera in Munich, the Zürich Opera, and the Vienna State Opera. In 1989 he made his London debut in a recital at the Wigmore Hall. His U.S. debut followed in 1992 as soloist in Mahler's *Rückert-Lieder* with Dohnányi and the Cleveland Orch. He made his N.Y. debut in 1993 in a recital at the Frick Museum, and that same year made his debut at London's Covent Garden as Papageno; he also appeared at the Salzburg Festival. Holzmair's operatic repertoire includes Gluck's Orfeo, Don Giovanni, Rossini's Figaro, Eugene Onegin, Wolfram, Pélleas, and Wozzeck. His concert and oratorio repertoire is notably expansive, including works from all periods since the Baroque era, but he has become especially well known for his interpretations of Schubert and Mahler.

Homer, Louise (Dilworth née **Beatty**), esteemed American contralto; b. Shadyside, near Pittsburgh, April 30, 1871; d. Winter Park, Fla., May 6, 1947. She studied in Philadelphia and at the New England Cons. of Music in Boston, where she received instruction in harmony from the noted American song composer Sidney Homer (1864–1953), who later became her husband (1895). She then went to Paris to study voice with Fidèle Koenig and dramatic acting with Paul Lhérie, making her operatic debut as Leonora in *La Favorite* in Vichy (June 5, 1898). She made her first appearance at London's Covent Garden as Lola in *Cavalleria rusticana* on May 9, 1899, and appeared there again in 1900; she was also on the roster of the Théâtre Royal de la Monnaie in Brussels (1899–1900). On Nov. 14, 1900, she made her U.S. debut as Amneris with the touring Metropolitan Opera in San Francisco, which role she sang at her formal debut on Dec. 22, 1900, with the company in New York. She remained on its roster until 1919, the 1914–15 season excepted. She was acclaimed for her interpretation of Gluck's Orfeo in Paris in 1909, a role she repeated later that year at the Metropolitan Opera under Toscanini; she also created the roles of the Witch in Humperdinck's *Königskinder* (Dec. 28, 1910) and of Mona in Parker's opera (March 14, 1912) there. After singing with opera companies in Chicago (1920–25) and in San Francisco and Los Angeles (1926), she returned to the Metropolitan (1927), continuing on its roster until her farewell performance as Azucena on Nov. 28, 1929. She subsequently appeared in recitals with her daughter, the soprano Louise Homer Stires. In addition to Italian and French roles, she sang with great success such Wagernian roles as Brangäne, Erda, Fricka, Ortrud, and Waltraute. Her nephew was **Samuel Barber**.

BIBL.: S. Homer, *My Wife and I* (N.Y., 1939); A. Homer, *L. H. and the Golden Age of Opera* (N.Y., 1973).

Honegger, Arthur (Oscar), remarkable French composer; b. Le Havre (of Swiss parents), March 10, 1892; d. Paris, Nov. 27, 1955. He studied violin in Paris with Capet; then took courses with Kempter and Hegar at the Zürich Cons. (1909–11). Returning to France in 1912, he entered the Paris Cons., in the classes of Gédalge and Widor; he also took lessons with d'Indy. His name first attracted attention when he took part in a concert of Les Nouveaux Jeunes in Paris on Jan. 15, 1918. In 1920 Henri Collet publ. an article in *Comoedia* in which he drew a fortuitous parallel between the Russian Five and a group of young French composers whom he designated as Les Six. These Six were Honegger, Milhaud, Poulenc, Auric, Durey, and Tailleferre. The label persisted, even though the 6 composers went their separate ways and rarely gave concerts together. In the early years of his career, Honegger embraced the fashionable type of urban music, with an emphasis on machine-like rhythms and curt, pert melodies. In 1921 he wrote a sport ballet, *Skating Rink*, and a mock-militaristic ballet, *Sousmarine*. In 1923 he composed the most famous of such machine pieces, *Mouvement symphonique No. 1*, subtitled *Pacific 231*. The score was intended to be a realistic tonal portrayal of a powerful American locomotive, bearing the serial number 231. The music progressed in accelerating rhythmic pulses toward a powerful climax, then gradually slackened its pace until the final abrupt stop; there was a simulacrum of a lyrical song in the middle section of the piece. *Pacific 231* enjoyed great popularity and became in the minds of modern-minded listeners a perfect symbol of the machine age. Honegger's 2d *Mouvement symphonique*, composed in 1928, was a musical rendering of the popular British sport rugby. His *Mouvement symphonique No. 3*, however, bore no identifying subtitle. This abandonment of allusion to urban life coincided chronologically with a general trend away from literal representation and toward absolute music in classical forms, often of historical or religious character. Among his most important works in that genre were *Le Roi David*, to a biblical subject, and *Jeanne d'Arc au bûcher*, glorifying the French patriot saint on the semimillennium of her martyrdom. Honegger's syms. were equally free from contemporary allusions; the first 2 lacked descriptive titles; his 3d was entitled Liturgique, with a clear reference to an ecclesiastical ritual; the 4th was named Deliciae Basilienses, because it was written to honor the city of Basel; the somewhat mysterious title of the 5th, *Di tre re*, signified nothing more arcane than the fact that each of its movements ended on the thrice-repeated note D. Honegger spent almost all of his life in France, but he retained his dual Swiss citizenship, a fact that caused some biographers to refer to him as a Swiss composer. In 1926 he married the pianist-composer Andrée Vaurabourg (1894–1980), who often played piano parts in his works. In 1929 he paid a visit to the United States; he returned in 1947 to teach summer classes at the Berkshire Music Center at Tanglewood, but soon after his arrival was stricken with a heart ailment and was unable to complete his term; he returned to Paris and remained there until his death. He publ. a book, *Je suis compositeur* (Paris, 1951; Eng. tr., London, 1966).

WORKS: DRAMATIC: *Le Roi David*, dramatic Psalm for Narrator, Soloists, Chorus, and 15 Instruments (Mézières, June 11, 1921; rev. as an oratorio with Full Orch., 1923; Winterthur, Dec. 2, 1923); *Antigone*, opera (1924–27; Brussels, Dec. 28, 1927); *Judith*, biblical drama (Mézières, June 11, 1925; expanded as an opera, Monte Carlo, Feb. 13, 1926); *Amphion*, melodrama (1929; Paris, June 23, 1931); *Les Aventures du Roi Pausole*, operetta (1929–30; Paris, Dec. 12, 1930); *Cris du Monde*, stage oratorio for Soprano, Contralto, Baritone, Chorus, and Orch. (1930; Solothurn, May 3, 1931); *La Belle de Moudon*, operetta (Mézières, May 30, 1931); *Jeanne d'Arc au bûcher*, dramatic oratorio (1934–35; concert version, without Prologue, Basel, May 12, 1938; stage premiere, in German, Zürich, June 13, 1942); *L'Aiglon*, opera (1935; Monte Carlo, March 11, 1937; in collaboration with J. Ibert); *Les Mille et Une Nuits*, spectacle for Soprano, Tenor, Chorus, and Orch. (Paris Exhibition, 1937); *Les Petites Cardinal*, operetta (1937; Paris, Feb. 20, 1938; in collaboration with J. Ibert); *Nicolas de Flue*, dramatic legend for Narrator, Chorus, Children's Chorus, and Orch. (1939; concert premiere, Solothurn, Oct. 26, 1940; stage premiere, Neuchâtel, May 31, 1941). BALLETS: *Vérité-Mensonge*, marionette ballet (Paris, Nov. 1920); *Skating Rink* (1921; Paris, Jan. 20, 1922); *Sousmarine* (1924; Paris, June 27, 1925); *Roses de métal* (Paris, 1928); *Sémiramis*, ballet melodrama (1931; Paris, May 11, 1934); *Un Oiseau blanc s'est envolé* (Paris, June 1937); *Le Cantique des cantiques* (1937; Paris, Feb. 2, 1938); *La Naissance des couleurs* (1940; Paris, 1949); *Le Mangeur de rêves* (Paris, 1941); *L'Appel de la montagne* (1943; Paris, July 9, 1945); *Chota Roustaveli* or *L'Homme à la peau de léopard* (1945; Monte Carlo, May 5, 1946; scenes 2 and 3 by Harsányi and A. Tcherepnin); *De la musique* (1950). INCIDENTAL MUSIC: *Les Dit des jeux du monde* for Flute, Trumpet, Percussion, and Strings (1918; as a ballet, Paris, Dec. 2, 1918); *La Mort de Sainte Alméenne* (1918); *La Danse macabre* (1919); *Saül* (Paris, June 16, 1922); *Fantasio* (1922); *Antigone* (1922); *La Tempête* (1923); *Liluli* (1923); *Le Miracle de Notre-Dame* (1925); *L'Impératrice aux rochers* (1925; Paris, Feb. 17, 1927); *Phèdre* (1926); *800 mètres* (1941); *Le Soulier de satin* for Soprano, Baritone, and Orch. (Paris, Nov. 17, 1943); *Charles le Téméraire* for Chorus, 2 Trumpets, 2 Trombones, and Percussion (1943–44; Mézières, May 27, 1944); *Hamlet* for Narrator, Chorus, and Orch. (Paris, Oct. 17, 1946); *Prométhée* (1946); *L'État de siège* (Paris, Oct. 27, 1948); *Tête d'or* (1948); *Oedipe-Roi* (1948). RADIO MUSIC: *Les Douze Coups de minuit*, "radio-mystère" for Chorus and Chamber Orch. (Paris Radio, Dec. 27, 1933); *Radio panoramique* for Tenor, Soprano, Organ, String Quintet, Wind Instruments, and Percussion (Geneva Radio, March 4, 1935; concert premiere, Paris, Oct. 19, 1935); *Christophe Colomb*, radio oratorio for 2 Tenors, Chorus, and Orch. (Lausanne Radio, April 17, 1940); *Les Battements du monde* for Woman's Voice, Child's Voice, Chorus, and Orch. (Lausanne Radio, May 18, 1944); *Saint François d'Assise* for Narrator, Baritone, Chorus, and Orch. (Lausanne Radio, Dec. 3, 1949). FILM MUSIC: *Les Misérables* (1934); *Mayerling* (1935); *Regain* (1937); *Mlle. Doctor* (1937); *Pygmalion*, after G. B. Shaw's play (1938); *Mermoz* (1943); *Bourdelle* (1950); 36 others.

BIBL.: Roland-Manuel, *A. H.* (Paris, 1925); A. George, *A. H.* (Paris, 1926); W. Tappolet, *A. H.* (in German, Zürich, 1933; 2d Ger. ed., Zürich, 1954; French ed., Neuchâtel, 1938; 2d Fr. ed., Neuchâtel, 1957); C. Gérard, *A. H.: Catalogue succinct des oeuvres* (Brussels, 1945); J. Bruyr, *H. et son oeuvre* (Paris, 1947); J. Matter, *H. ou La Quête de joie* (Lausanne, 1956); A. Gauthier, *A. H.* (London, 1957); M. Landowski, *H.* (Paris, 1957); J. Feschotte, *A. H.: L'Homme et son oeuvre* (Paris, 1966); P. Meylan, *A. H., Humanitäre Botschaft der Musik* (Frauenfeld, 1970); G. Spratt, *The Music of A. H.* (Cork, 1987); H. Halbreich, *A. H.: Un musicien dans la cité des hommes* (Paris, 1992); J. Roy, *Le groupe des six: Poulenc, Milhaud, H., Auric, Tailleferre, Durey* (Paris, 1994).

Höngen, Elisabeth, esteemed German mezzo-soprano; b. Gevelsberg, Dec. 7, 1906; d. Vienna, Aug. 7, 1997. She studied voice with Hermann Weissenborn and Ludwig Horth in Berlin. In 1933 she made her operatic debut as Lady Macbeth at the Wuppertal Opera, where she was a member until 1935. She then sang with the Düsseldorf Opera (1935–40) and the Dresden State Opera (1940–43). In 1943 she joined the Vienna State Opera, where she remained one of its principal artists during the next 2 decades. In 1947 she was honored as an Austrian Kammersängerin. She first sang at London's Covent Garden in 1947 as a member of the visiting Vienna State Opera, returning there in 1959–60. From 1948 to 1950, and again in 1959, she appeared at the Salzburg

Festivals. In 1951 she was a soloist in Beethoven's 9th Sym. under Furtwängler at the reopening of the Bayreuth Festival. On Jan. 10, 1952, she made her Metropolitan Opera debut in New York as Hérodias, returning there that season as Waltraute and Klytemnestra. She also was a guest artist in Berlin, Munich, Paris, Milan, Buenos Aires, and other operatic centers. From 1957 to 1960 she was a prof. at the Vienna Academy of Music. Among her other notable portrayals were Dorabella, Marcellina, Ortrud, Eboli, and Fricka.

Hoof, Jef van, Belgian composer; b. Antwerp, May 8, 1886; d. there, April 24, 1959. He studied composition at the Antwerp Cons. with Gilson, Mortelmas, and Huybrechts. He composed 3 operas: *Tycho-Brahe* (1911), *Meivuur* (1916), and *Jonker Lichthart* (1928). His style of composition was neo-Romantic, with a penchant for expansive sonorities.

Hopf, Hans, German tenor; b. Nuremberg, Aug. 2, 1916; d. Munich, June 25, 1993. He studied in Munich with Paul Bender and in Oslo with Ragnvald Bjärne. In 1936 he made his operatic debut as Pinkerton at the Bavarian Landesbühnen in Munich, and then sang with the Augsburg Opera (1939–42), the Dresden State Opera (1942–43), the Oslo Opera (1943–44), and the Berlin State Opera (1946–49). In 1949 he joined the Bavarian State Opera in Munich, and sang there regularly until his retirement in 1988. In 1951 he was a soloist in Beethoven's 9th Sym. under Furtwängler at the reopening of the Bayreuth Festival, where he later sang from 1961 to 1966. From 1951 to 1953 he appeared at London's Covent Garden, returning there in 1963. On March 15, 1952, he made his Metropolitan Opera debut in New York as Walther von Stolzing, remaining on the roster until 1953; he was again on its roster for the 1954–55, 1960–62, and 1963–64 seasons. He also sang at the Salzburg Festivals from 1954, and was a guest artist in Milan, Moscow, Zürich, San Francisco, Chicago, and Buenos Aires. Among his prominent roles were Florestan, Max in *Der Freischütz*, Siegfried, Parsifal, Tristan, Tannhäuser, Otello, and the Kaiser in *Die Frau ohne Schatten*.

Hopkins, Charles Jerome, American writer on music and composer; b. Burlington, Vt., April 4, 1836; d. Athenia, N.J., Nov. 4, 1898. Self-taught in music (he took only 6 lessons in harmony), he learned to play piano sufficiently well to attain professional status. He studied chemistry at the N.Y. Medical College; he played organ in N.Y. churches, and was active in various educational enterprises. In 1856 he founded the American Music Assoc., which promoted concerts of music by Gottschalk, Bristow, and other American composers. In 1868 he founded the N.Y. Philharmonic Journal, and was its ed. until 1885. In 1886 he organized several "Free Singing and Opera Schools," for which he claimed nearly 1,000 pupils. In 1889 he went to England on a lecture tour, announcing himself as "the first American Operatic Oratorio composer and Pianist who has ever ventured to invade England with New World Musical theories and practices." Throughout his versatile career, he was a strong advocate of American music; his sensational methods and eccentric professional conduct brought him repeatedly into public controversy; in England he was sued for libel. Hopkins claimed a priority in writing the first "musicianly and scientific Kinder-Oper" (*Taffy and Old Munch*, a children's fairy tale, 1880). He further wrote an operatic oratorio, *Samuel*, and a great number of choruses and songs, few of which were publ. He compiled 2 collections of church music and an *Orpheon Class-Book*.

Horák, Antonín, Czech conductor and composer; b. Prague, July 2, 1875; d. Belgrade, March 12, 1910. He was an opera conductor in Prague and Belgrade. His opera, *Babička* (Grandmother), was fairly successful at its first production in Prague (March 3, 1900).

Horenstein, Jascha, distinguished Russian-born American conductor; b. Kiev, May 6, 1898; d. London, April 2, 1973. He began his musical training in Königsberg as a piano student of his mother, and he also studied with Max Brode. In 1911 he went to Vienna, where he studied philosophy at the Univ. and was a pupil of A. Busch (violin), Marx (theory), and Schreker (composition) at the Academy of Music; he then continued his training with Schreker at the Berlin Hochschule für Musik (1920). He served as an assistant to Furtwängler and began his career conducting the Schubert Choir in Berlin. In 1923 he was a guest conductor with the Vienna Sym. Orch. Returning to Berlin, he conducted the Blüthner Concerts (1924) and was conductor of the Berlin Sym. Orch. (1925–28); he also appeared as a guest conductor with the Berlin Phil. In 1929 he became music director of the Düsseldorf Opera, but was removed from that position in 1933 by the Nazi regime because he was a Jew. After conducting in Europe, Australia, New Zealand, and Palestine, he went to the United States in 1940 and became a naturalized American citizen. Following the end of World War II, he resumed his career in Europe. He became especially admired in England, where he appeared as a guest conductor with the London Sym. Orch. In 1961 he made his debut at London's Covent Garden conducting *Fidelio*. While Horenstein's repertoire ranged widely from the Baroque era to the 20th century, he acquired his greatest renown as an interpreter of Bruckner and Mahler.

Horký, Karel, Czech composer; b. Štěmechy, near Třebíč, Sept. 4, 1909; d. Brno, Nov. 27, 1988. He played in a military band as a boy; he studied bassoon, took lessons in composition with V. Polivka and Pavel Haas, and then entered the Prague Cons. as a student of Křička, graduating in 1944. He taught harmony (1945–52) and was director (1964–71) at the Brno Cons.

WORKS: DRAMATIC: OPERAS: *Jan Hus* (Brno, May 27, 1950); *Hejtman Šarovec* (Brno, 1953); *Jed z Elsinoru* (The Poison from Elsinor), freely after Shakespeare's *Hamlet* (Brno, Nov. 11, 1969); *Dawn* (Brno, July 4, 1975); *Atlantida* (1980). BALLETS: *Lastura* (The Shell; Brno, Oct. 23, 1945); *Král Ječmínek* (King Ječmínek; Brno, Sept. 21, 1951).

Horn, Charles Edward, English singer, conductor, and composer; b. London, June 21, 1786; d. Boston, Oct. 21, 1849. He studied with his father, the German organist and composer Karl Friedrich Horn (1762–1830), and received vocal guidance from Rauzzini. On June 26, 1809, he made his debut as a singer in M. P. King's *Up All Night* at London's Lyceum Theatre. After further vocal training with Thomas Welsh, he returned to the stage in 1814. He also was active as a conductor and composer for the theater. In 1827 he went to New York and staged several of his operas. After serving as music director of London's Olympic Theatre (1831–32), he was music director of N.Y.'s Park Theatre (1832–47) and conductor of Boston's Handel and Haydn Soc. (from 1847). In addition to his stage works, he wrote the oratorio *The Remission of Sin* (N.Y., May 7, 1835; perf. in London as *Satan*, March 18, 1845).

BIBL.: R. Montague, *C. E. H.: His Life and Works* (diss., Florida State Univ., 1959).

Horne, Marilyn (Bernice), outstanding American mezzo-soprano; b. Bradford, Pa., Jan. 16, 1934. She studied with William Vennard at the Univ. of Southern Calif. in Los Angeles; also attended Lotte Lehmann's master classes. She then went to Europe, where she made her professional operatic debut as Giulietta at the Gelsenkirchen Opera in 1957; she remained on its roster until 1960, appearing in such roles as Mimi, Tatiana, Minnie, Fulvia in *Ezio*, and Marie in *Wozzeck*, the role she repeated in her U.S. debut at the San Francisco Opera on Oct. 4, 1960. She married **Henry Lewis** in 1960, and subsequently made a number of appearances under his direction; they were separated in 1976. In 1965 she made her debut at London's Covent Garden, again as Marie. She appeared at Milan's La Scala in 1969, and on March 3, 1970, she made her Metropolitan Opera debut in New York as Adalgisa; subsequently she became one of the Metropolitan's principal singers. Her notable performances there included Rosina in *Il Barbiere di Siviglia* (Jan. 23, 1971), Carmen (Sept. 19, 1972), Fides in *Le Prophète* (Jan. 18, 1977), Rinaldo (the first Handel opera to be staged there, Jan. 19, 1984), Isabella in *L'Italiana in Algeri* (telecast live by PBS, Jan. 11, 1986), and Samira in the premiere of Corigliano's *The Ghosts of Versailles* (Dec. 19, 1991).

In 1992 President Bush awarded her the National Medal of Arts. On Jan. 20, 1993, she sang at the inauguration of President Clinton in Washington, D.C. That same year, she founded the Marilyn Horne Foundation with the goal of encouraging young singers as art song recitalists. In 1994 she began teaching at the Music Academy of the West in Santa Barbara, where she was artist-in-residence and director of the voice program from 1995. In 1995 she received a Kennedy Center Honor. Acclaimed for her brilliant portrayals in roles by Handel, Rossini, and Meyerbeer, she won equal praise as an outstanding concert artist. She publ. an autobiography (with J. Scovell; N.Y., 1983).

Horneman, Christian Frederik Emil, Danish choral conductor, teacher, and composer; b. Copenhagen, Dec. 17, 1840; d. there, June 8, 1906. His father was the Danish publisher and composer Johan Ole Emil Horneman (1809–70). He studied at the Leipzig Cons. (1858–60), where he became a friend of Grieg. He composed light music under various pseudonyms. Returning to Copenhagen, he organized a concert society there; then was founder-director of the Koncertforeningen (1874–79) and of his own Cons. (1880–1906). He wrote an opera, *Aladdin* (Copenhagen, Nov. 18, 1888).

Hornstein, Robert von, German composer; b. Donaueschingen, Dec. 6, 1833; d. Munich, July 19, 1890. He studied at the Leipzig Cons., then went to Munich, where he became a teacher at the municipal school of music. He was a close friend of Wagner; composed operas in a Romantic vein; one of these, *Adam und Eva*, was produced in Munich in 1870; other works are a ballet, *Der Blumen Rache*, and incidental music to Shakespeare's *As You Like It*.

Horovitz, Joseph, Austrian-born English composer, conductor, and teacher; b. Vienna, May 26, 1926. He went to England in 1938 and studied music (with Westrup) and literature at New College, Oxford (M.A. and B.Mus., 1948), with Jacob at the Royal College of Music in London, and with Boulanger in Paris. In 1950–51 he was music director of the Bristol Old Vic Co. From 1952 to 1963 he was assoc. director of the Intimate Opera Co. He was prof. of composition at the Royal College of Music from 1961. From 1981 to 1989 he served as president of the International Council of Composers and Lyricists. In 1959 he received the Commonwealth Medal for Composition and in 1961 the Leverhulme Music Research Award. His facility as a composer is evident in both his handling of serious and light scores.

WORKS: DRAMATIC: *Gentleman's Island*, opera (Cheltenham, July 9, 1959); *The Dumb Wife*, opera (Antwerp, Jan. 10, 1972); 16 ballets, including *Alice in Wonderland* (1953), *Les Femmes d'Alger*, *Miss Carter Wore Pink*, and *Concerto for Dancers*; theater, radio, and television scores.

Horst, Louis, American composer; b. Kansas City, Mo., Jan. 12, 1884; d. N.Y., Jan. 23, 1964. He studied violin and piano in San Francisco, and composition with Richard Stöhr in Vienna, as well as with Max Persin and Riegger in New York (1925). From 1915 to 1925 he was music director of the Denishawn Dance Co., and from 1926 to 1948, of Martha Graham's dance company, for which he wrote a number of works that played a crucial role in the development of modern dance. He wrote extensively on the subject of music and dance; he founded and ed. the journal *Dance Observer* (1934), and publ. the books *Pre-classic Dance Forms* (1940) and *Modern Dance Forms* (with C. Russell; 1961). He was also active as a teacher at Bennington (Vt.) College (1934–45), Columbia Univ. Teachers College (1938–41), and the Juilliard School of Music in New York (1958–63).

BIBL.: E. Pease, *L. H.: His Theories on Modern Dance Composition* (diss., Univ. of Mich., 1953); J. Soares, *L. H.: Musician in a Dancer's World* (Durham, N.C., 1992).

Horvat, Milan, Yugoslav conductor; b. Pakrac, July 28, 1919. He was educated in Zagreb, studying law at the Univ. and taking courses with Svetislav Stančič (piano), Fritz Zaun (conducting), and Zlatko Grgošević (composition) at the Academy of Music (1939–46). In 1945 he became conductor of the Zagreb Radio Chorus, and from 1946 he conducted the Zagreb Radio Orch. From 1953 to 1958 he conducted the Radio Telefís Eireann Sym. Orch. in Dublin. He was music director of the Phil. (1956–70) and Opera (1958–65) in Zagreb. After serving as chief conductor of the Austrian Radio Sym. Orch. in Vienna (1969–75), he held that title with the Zagreb Radio Orch. (from 1975). As a guest conductor, he appeared widely in Europe.

Horvat, Stanko, Croatian composer; b. Zagreb, March 12, 1930. He studied composition with Šulek at the Zagreb Academy of Music, graduating in 1956; he then took a course with Aubin at the Paris Cons. and private composition lessons with Leibowitz (1958–59); returning to Yugoslavia, he was appointed to the music faculty of the Zagreb Academy of Music in 1961. In his style of composition, he traversed successively a period of neoclassical mannerisms, serialism in its dodecaphonic aspect, aleatory expressionism, and sonorism; eventually he returned to a median technique of pragmatic modernism. Among his works are a ballet, *Izabranik* (The Chosen One; 1961) and a television opera, *3 Legends* (Salzburg, 1971).

Hoschna, (Hoschner), Karl, Czech-American composer; b. Kuschwarda, Aug. 16, 1876; d. N.Y., Dec. 23, 1911. He studied piano, harmony, and composition at the Vienna Cons., then played oboe in an Austrian army band before going to the United States (1896), where he was an oboist in Victor Herbert's orch. After working as a music copyist and arranger, he turned to composing, turning out a number of successful operettas, mostly in collaboration with the lyricist Otto Harbach.

WORKS: OPERETTAS: *The Belle of the West* (Chicago, Oct. 29, 1905); *The Girl from Broadway* (Philadelphia, Dec. 3, 1906); *3 Twins* (N.Y., June 15, 1908); *Prince Humbug* (Boston, Sept. 3, 1908); *The Photo Shop* (1910); *Bright Eyes* (N.Y., Feb. 28, 1910); *Madame Sherry* (N.Y., Aug. 30, 1910); *Katie Did* (Chicago, Feb. 18, 1911); *Jumping Jupiter* (N.Y., March 6, 1911); *Dr. Deluxe* (N.Y., April 17, 1911); *The Girl of My Dreams* (N.Y., Aug. 7, 1911); *The Fascinating Widow* (N.Y., Sept. 11, 1911); *The Wall Street Girl* (N.Y., April 15, 1912).

Hotter, Hans, greatly esteemed German bass-baritone; b. Offenbach am Main, Jan. 19, 1909. He studied voice with Matthäus Roemer, making his debut as the Speaker in *Die Zauberflöte* in Opava in 1929; was a member of the opera there from 1930, and also sang at the German Theater in Prague (1932–34). He then sang at the Hamburg State Opera (1934–45), Bavarian State Opera in Munich (1937–72), Berlin State Opera (1939–42), and Vienna State Opera (1939–72). He made his first appearance at London's Covent Garden with the visiting Vienna State Opera in 1947; he made appearances regularly at Covent Garden until 1967 and was a principal singer at the Bayreuth Festivals (1952–64), where he became renowned for his portrayal of Wotan; he also distinguished himself in such roles as Kurwenal, Hans Sachs, Amfortas, Gurnemanz, King Marke, and Pogner. He made his Metropolitan Opera debut in New York as the Dutchman in *Der fliegende Holländer* on Nov. 9, 1950, remaining on its roster until 1954; he also sang at La Scala in Milan, the Paris Opéra, the Salzburg Festival, the Chicago Opera, and the Teatro Colón in Buenos Aires. He became a member of the faculty of the Vienna Hochschule für Musik in 1977. In addition to his Wagnerian roles, Hotter also sang in several first performances of operas by Richard Strauss; he created the roles of the Kommandant in *Friedenstag* (Munich, July 24, 1938), of Olivier in *Capriccio* (Munich, Oct. 28, 1942), and of Jupiter in *Die Liebe der Danae* (public dress rehearsal, Salzburg, Aug. 16, 1944).

BIBL.: B. Wessling, *H. H.* (Bremen, 1966); P. Turing, *H. H.: Man and Artist* (London, 1983).

Hovhaness (real name, **Chakmakjian**), **Alan (Vaness Scott),** prolific American composer of Armenian-Scottish descent; b. Somerville, Mass., March 8, 1911. He took piano lessons with Adelaide Proctor and Heinrich Gebhard in Boston; his academic studies were at Tufts Univ.; in 1932 he enrolled in the New England Cons. of Music in Boston as a student of Frederick Converse, then was a scholarship student of Martinů at the Berkshire Music Center at Tanglewood in the summer of 1942. He served on the faculty of the New England Cons. of Music (1948–51), then moved to New York. He was awarded 2 Guggenheim fellowships (1954 and 1958). In 1959 he received a Fulbright fellowship and traveled to India and Japan, where he collected native folk songs for future use and presented his own works, as pianist and conductor, receiving acclaim. In 1962 he was engaged as composer-in-residence at the Univ. of Hawaii; then traveled to Korea. In 1967 he was composer-in-residence of the Seattle Sym. Orch. From his earliest attempts at composition, he took great interest in the musical roots of his paternal ancestry, studying the folk songs assembled by Komitas. He gradually came to believe that music must reflect the natural monody embodied in national songs and ancient church hymns. In his music, he adopted modal melodies and triadic harmonies. This *parti pris* had the dual effect of alienating him from the milieu of modern composers while exercising great attraction for the music consumer at large. By dint of ceaseless repetition of melodic patterns and relentless dynamic tension, he succeeded in creating a sui generis type of impressionistic monody, flowing on the shimmering surfaces of euphony, free from the upsetting intrusion of heterogeneous dissonance; an air of mysticism pervaded his music, aided by the programmatic titles which he often assigned to his compositions. A composer of relentless fecundity, he produced over 60 syms.; several operas, quasi-operas, and pseudo-operas, and an enormous amount of choral music. The totality of his output is in excess of 370 opus numbers. In a laudable spirit of self-criticism, he destroyed 7 of his early syms. and began numbering them anew so that his 1st numbered sym. (subtitled *Exile*) was chronologically his 8th. He performed a similar auto-da-fé on other dispensable pieces. Among his more original compositions is a symphonic score *And God Created Great Whales*, in which the voices of humpback whales recorded on tape were used as a solo with the orch.; the work was performed to great effect in the campaign to save the whale from destruction by human (and inhuman) predators.

WORKS: DRAMATIC: OPERAS: *Etchmiadzin* (1946); *The Blue Flame* (San Antonio, Dec. 13, 1959); *Spirit of the Avalanche* (Tokyo, Feb. 15, 1963); *Wind Drum* and *The Burning House* (both at Gatlinburg, Tenn., Aug. 23, 1964); *Pilate* (Los Angeles, June 26, 1966); *The Travelers* (Los Altos Hills, Calif., April 22, 1967); *Pericles* (1975); *Tale of the Sun Goddess Going into the Stone House* (1979). OPERETTA: *Afton Water*, after William Saroyan (1951). BALLETS: *Killer of Enemies* (1983); *God the Revenger* (1986). Also *The Way of Jesus*, folk oratorio (N.Y., Feb. 23, 1975).

Hovland, Egil, Norwegian organist, music critic, and composer; b. Mysen, Oct. 18, 1924. He studied organ and composition at the Oslo Cons. (1946–49), later studying privately with Brustad (1951–52, in Oslo), Holmboe (1954, in Copenhagen), Copland (1957, at Tanglewood), and Dallapiccola (1959, in Florence). He then was active as an organist, music critic, and composer. In 1983 he was made a Knight of the Royal Order of St. Olav for his services to Norwegian music. He cultivates a peculiarly Scandinavian type of neoclassical polyphony, but is apt to use serial techniques.

WORKS: DRAMATIC: OPERAS: *Brunnen*, church opera (1971–72; Oslo, March 17, 1982); *Fange og fri* (1990). BALLETS: *Dona Nobis Pacem* (1982); *Den Heliga Dansen* (1982); *Veni Creator Spiritus* (1984); *Danses de la Mort* (Bergen, June 8, 1983).

Howard, Ann (real name, **Pauline Swadling**), English mezzo-soprano; b. London, July 22, 1936. She was a student of Topliss Green and Rodolfa Lhombino; after singing in musical theater, she joined the chorus of the Royal Opera House, Covent Garden, London, and was awarded a grant to pursue her training with Modesti in Paris. In 1964 she made her operatic debut as Azucena with the Welsh National Opera in Cardiff; that same year, she made her first appearance at the Sadler's Wells Opera in London as Czipra in *Der Zigeunerbaron*, and subsequently appeared there regularly, and later with its successor, the English National Opera. In 1973 she made her Covent Garden debut as Amneris. As a guest artist, she sang in Europe, the United States (debut as Carmen in New Orleans, 1971), Canada, Mexico, and South Africa. Among her many roles were Fricka, Brangäne, Ortrud, Eboli, Clytemnestra, Dalila, Carmen, Offenbach's Hélène, Herodiade, and Jocasta. She also sang in operetta and in contemporary operas.

Howard, Kathleen, Canadian-American contralto; b. Niagara Falls, Ontario, July 17, 1884; d. Los Angeles, Aug. 15, 1956. She studied in New York with Bouhy and in Paris with Jean de Reszke. She appeared at the Metz Opera (1907–09), at Darmstadt (1909–12), at Covent Garden in London (1913), and with the Century Opera in New York (1914–15). After appearing as the nurse in *Boris Godunov* with the Metropolitan Opera in Brooklyn on Nov. 14, 1916, she made her formal debut with the company in New York as the 3d Lady in *Die Zauberflöte* on Nov. 20, 1916, remaining on its roster until 1928. After her retirement from the stage, she was engaged in magazine work and was fashion ed. of *Harper's Bazaar* (1928–33). She publ. an autobiography, *Confessions of an Opera Singer* (N.Y., 1918).

Howard, Leslie (John), Australian pianist, organist, conductor, musicologist, and composer; b. Melbourne, April 29, 1948. He was educated at Monash Univ., Victoria (B.A., 1969; M.A., 1972), the Univ. of Melbourne (1966–71), and the Accademia Musicale Chigiana in Siena (1972–75); also received private instruction from Guido Agosti (piano), Donald Britton (organ and harpsichord), Fritz Rieger (conducting), and Franco Donatoni (composition). After making his formal debut as a pianist in Melbourne in 1967, he appeared as a soloist with orchs., as a recitalist, and as a chamber music artist in Australia, Europe, North and South America, and Asia. He also taught at Monash Univ. (1970–72) and was a prof. of piano at the Guildhall School of Music and Drama in London (1987–92). While Howard's keyboard repertoire extends from classical masterpieces to contemporary scores, he has become particularly associated with the music of Liszt, both as a performer and a researcher. In 1988 he became president of the Liszt Soc. in England. Among his honors are the Liszt Medal of Honor of the Hungarian government (1986) and the Medal of Honor of the Liszt Soc. of America (1993). His writings have appeared in various publications. His compositions include *Fruits of the Earth*, ballet (1971), and *Hreidar the Fool*, opera (1973–74).

Howarth, Elgar, English conductor and composer; b. Cannock, Staffordshire, Nov. 4, 1935. He studied at the Univ. of Manchester (Mus.B.) and at the Royal Manchester College of Music. After playing trumpet in the orch. of the Royal Opera, Covent Garden, London (1958–63), he was principal trumpeter of the Royal Phil. of London (1963–69). He was a trumpeter with the Philip Jones Brass Ensemble (1965–76) and the London Sinfonietta (1968–71). From 1970 he pursued a career as a conductor. In 1978 he conducted the premiere of Ligeti's *Le Grand Macabre* in Stockholm, and in 1982 its first British performance at the English National Opera in London. In 1985 he made his debut at Covent Garden with Tippett's *King Priam*. From 1985 to 1988 he was principal guest conductor of Opera North in Leeds. He conducted the premieres of Birtwistle's *The Mask of Orpheus* at the English National Opera in 1986, *Gawain* at Covent Garden in 1991, and *The Second Mrs. Kong* at the Glyndebourne Festival in 1994. In 1997 he conducted the British premiere of Strauss's *Die ägyptische Helena* in Garsington. With Patrick Howarth, he publ. *What a Performance! The Brass Band Plays . . .* (London, 1988). He composed mainly for brass instruments.

Howarth, Judith, English soprano; b. Ipswich, Sept. 11, 1962. She was trained at the Royal Scottish Academy of Music and Drama in Glasgow and at the National Opera School, and received vocal instruction from Patricia Macmahon. In 1984 she made her debut as a soloist with the English Chamber Orch. In 1985 she was awarded the Kathleen Ferrier Prize and made her first appearance at London's Covent Garden as the First Maid in Zemlinsky's *Der Zwerg*. Her U.S. debut followed in 1989 when she appeared in concert in Seattle. In 1991 she was engaged at the London Promenade Concerts, in Salzburg, and in Aix-en-Provence. She portrayed Morgana in *Alcina* at Covent Garden in 1992, and returned there as Gilda in 1993 and as Walton's Cressida in 1995. In 1998 she sang Donizetti's Marie in Geneva.

Howell, Gwynne (Richard), Welsh bass; b. Gorseinon, June 13, 1938. He was educated at the Univ. of Wales in Swansea (B.Sc.) and pursued training in town planning at the Univ. of Manchester; he also studied voice with Redvers Llewellyn, at the Royal Manchester College of Music with Gwilym Jones, and in London with Otakar Kraus (1968–72). While in Manchester, he gained experience singing Hunding, Fasolt, and Pogner. In 1968 he made his first appearance at the Sadler's Wells Opera in London as Monterone, where he became a principal artist, and with its successor, the English National Opera. In 1970 he made his debut at Covent Garden in London as the 1st Nazarene in *Salome*, where he later created the title role in Maxwell Davies's *Taverner* (July 12, 1972) and sang various Italian, German, and French roles. On Jan. 21, 1985, he made his Metropolitan Opera debut in New York as Lodovico. Among his finest roles were the Commendatore, Sarastro, Pimen, Timur, Gurnemanz, the Landgrave, Philip II, and Hans Sachs. He also sang widely in concert. In 1998 he was made a Commander of the Order of the British Empire.

Howells, Anne (Elizabeth), English mezzo-soprano; b. Southport, Jan. 12, 1941. She was a student of Frederick Cox at the Royal Manchester College of Music, where she sang Eros in the first English production of Gluck's *Paride ed Elena* (1963). Following further training with Vera Rosza, she made her professional operatic debut as Flora in *La Traviata* with the Welsh National Opera in Cardiff in 1966. From 1966 she appeared regularly at the Glyndebourne Festivals. In 1967 she made her first appearance at London's Covent Garden as Flora, returning there in subsequent years as Rosina, Cherubino, Siébel, Ascanio, Mélisande, Meg Page, Despina, and Giulietta. In 1972 she made her U.S. debut as Dorabella with the Chicago Lyric Opera, a role she also sang at her debuts at the Metropolitan Opera in New York (Oct. 15, 1975), and the San Francisco Opera (1979). She also had guest engagements in Geneva, Salzburg, Berlin, and Paris. In 1966 she married **Ryland Davies.** After their divorce in 1981, she married **Stafford Dean.**

Howland, William Legrand, American composer; b. Asbury Park, N.J., 1873; d. Long Island, N.Y., July 26, 1915. He studied with Philip Scharwenka in Berlin, and lived most of his life in Europe. His 1-act opera *Sarrona*, to his own libretto, was produced in Italian in Bruges (Aug. 3, 1903), and subsequently had a number of performances in Italy; it was staged in New York (in Eng.) on Feb. 8, 1910, and in Philadelphia (in Ger.) on March 23, 1911. He wrote another opera, *Nita*, and 2 oratorios, *The Resurrection* and *Ecce Homo*.

Hoyland, Vic(tor), English composer; b. Wombwell, Yorkshire, Dec. 11, 1945. He studied at the Univ. of Hull and with Robert Sherlaw Johnson and Bernard Rands at the Univ. of York, where he served as a visiting lecturer in 1984, then was a lecturer at the Univ. of Birmingham (from 1985). Among his compositions are *Xingu*, music theater piece (1979) and *Le Madre*, opera (1990).

Hřimalý, Adalbert (Vojtěch), Czech violinist, conductor, and composer, father of **Otakar Hřimalý**; b. Pilsen, July 30, 1842; d. Vienna, June 15, 1908. A member of an exceptionally musical family, he received an early training at home; then studied with Mildner at the Prague Cons. (1855–61). He was subsequently active as a conductor, composer, and teacher in various towns in the Netherlands, Sweden, and Romania. He wrote a great number of works, including an opera, *Zaklety princ* (The Enchanted Prince; Prague, May 13, 1872). His brother was the celebrated Czech violinist and teacher Johann (Jan) Hrimaly (b. Pilsen, April 13, 1844; d. Moscow, Jan. 24, 1915).

Hřimalý, Otakar, Czech violinist, conductor, and composer, son of **Adalbert (Vojtěch) Hřimalý**; b. Czernowitz, Bukovina, Dec. 20, 1883; d. Prague, July 10, 1945. His uncle was the Czech violinist and teacher Johann Hřimalý (b. Pilsen, April 13, 1844; d. Moscow, Jan. 24, 1915). He was trained in Vienna at the Cons. and the Univ. He went to Moscow, where he was conductor of the Cons. opera dept. (1910–16) and at the Opera (1919–22); he then lived in Czernowitz until the Russian occupation forced him to flee to Prague, where he joined the Cons. in 1940. He wrote an opera.

Hristić, Stevan, Serbian conductor, teacher, and composer; b. Belgrade, June 19, 1885; d. there, Aug. 21, 1958. He studied with Nikisch (conducting) and Krehl and Hofmann at the Leipzig Cons., and then pursued studies in Moscow, Rome, and Paris. Returning to Belgrade, he was conductor of the National Opera Theater (1912–14); he then was chief conductor of the Belgrade Phil. (1923–34) and Opera (1924–34) and a prof. of composition at the Academy of Music (1937–50). He composed a music drama, *Suton* (Sunset, 1925; rev. 1954), and a ballet, *Legend of Okhrid* (1933; rev. 1958).

Hsu, Tsang-houei, Chinese composer, musicologist, and teacher; b. Changhau, Taiwan, Sept. 6, 1929. He studied violin in Tokyo from the age of 11, remaining in Japan until 1945, when he returned to Taiwan. He studied violin and composition at the National Univ. (1949–53); in 1954 he went to Paris to study violin at the École César Franck and music history and analysis at the Sorbonne (1956–58). He also studied with Jolivet and Messiaen at the Paris Cons. In 1959 he returned to Taiwan; his first concert (1960), which introduced avant-garde ideas to Taiwan audiences, met with both censure and enthusiasm. He taught advanced composition techniques and founded several organizations to promote contemporary music, including the Chinese Composers' Forum (1961) and the Chinese Soc. for Contemporary Music (1969); he was also active in the League of Asian Composers. Hsu made extensive study of Taiwanese folk music, elements of which are integrated into his compositions. He cofounded the Centre for Chinese Folk Music Research (1967), and was appointed examiner in charge of folk-music research by the Taiwanese provincial government (1976). He held professorships at the National Academy of Arts, Soochow Univ., and the College of Chinese Culture, and lectured throughout East Asia and the United States. His early compositions show a variety of influences, including aspects of impressionism, atonality, and serialism, along with traditional Chinese and Taiwanese elements; his later works are less aggressively modern, but have a distinctive identity and unified style. His writings reflect his interest in folk music research. Among his works is the opera *The Legend of White Horse* (1979–87) and the ballets *Chang-o Flies to the Moon* (1968), *The Peach Blossom* (1977), *Peach Blossom Girl* (1983), and *Chen San and the 5th Madame* (1985).

Hubay, Jenö, celebrated Hungarian violinist, pedagogue, and composer; b. Budapest, Sept. 15, 1858; d. Vienna, March 12, 1937. He received his initial training from his father, Karl Hubay, prof. of violin at the Budapest Cons.; he gave his first public concert at the age of 11; he then studied with Joachim in Berlin (1873–76). His appearance in Paris, at a Pasdeloup concert, attracted the attention of Vieuxtemps, of whom he became a favorite pupil; in 1882 he succeeded Vieuxtemps as prof. at the Brussels Cons. In 1886 he became a prof. at the Budapest Cons. (succeeding his father); from 1919 to 1934 he was its director. In Budapest he formed the celebrated Hubay String Quartet. In 1894 he married the Countess Rosa Cebrain. Among his pupils were Vecsey, Szigeti, Telmanyi, Eddy Brown, and other renowned violinists. He ed. the violin études of Kreutzer (1908), Rode, Mayseder, and Saint Lubin (1910).

WORKS: OPERAS (all 1st perf. in Budapest): *Alienor* (Dec. 5, 1891); *Le Luthier de Crémone* (Nov. 10, 1894); *A Falu Rossza* (The Village Vagabond; March 20, 1896); *Moosröschen* (Feb. 21, 1903); *Anna Karenina* (Nov. 10, 1923); *Az álarc* (The Mask; Feb. 26, 1931).

Huber, Hans, Swiss composer; b. Eppenberg, near Olten, June 28, 1852; d. Locarno, Dec. 25, 1921. He studied at the Leipzig Cons. with Richter, Reinecke, and Wenzel (1870–74), then taught music in Wesserling, Thann (Alsace), and Basel. He received an honorary degree of Dr.Phil. from Univ. of Basel (1892). In 1896 he became director of the Basel Cons., a post he held until 1917. Huber composed prolifically in all genres; his style combined the rhapsodic form typical of Lisztian technique with simple ballad-like writing. He often used Swiss songs for thematic material. In Switzerland his reputation is very great and his works are frequently performed, but they are virtually unknown elsewhere. Among his compositions are the operas *Weltfrühling* (Basel, March 28, 1894), *Kudrun* (Basel, Jan. 29, 1896), *Der Simplicius* (Basel, Feb. 22, 1912), *Die schöne Bellinda* (Bern, April 2, 1916), and *Frutta di mare* (Basel, Nov. 24, 1918).

BIBL.: E. Refardt, *H. H.* (Leipzig, 1906); idem, *H. H.: Beiträge zu einer Biographie* (Leipzig, 1922); C. Bundi, *H. H.: Die Persönlichkeit nach Briefen und Erinnerungen* (Basel, 1925); E. Refardt, *H. H.* (Zürich, 1944).

Huber, Klaus, Swiss composer and pedagogue; b. Bern, Nov. 30, 1924. He studied violin with Geyer (1947–49) and theory and composition with his godfather Burkhard (1947–55) at the Zürich Cons., and then completed his training with Blacher at the Berlin Hochschule für Musik (1955–56). He taught violin at the Zürich Cons. (1950–60) and music history at the Lucerne Cons. (1960–63). From 1961 to 1972 he taught at the Basel Academy of Music, where he was director of the composition and instrumentation classes (1964–68) and then of the master composition class (1968–72). In 1969 he founded the international composers' seminar in Boswil, with which he was active until 1980. In 1973 he held the Deutscher Akademischer Austauschienest scholarship in Berlin. From 1973 to 1990 he taught composition and was head of the inst. for contemporary music at the Freiburg im Breisgau Hochschule für Musik. He served as president of the Swiss Composers' Assn. from 1979 to 1982. In 1975 he won the Composers' Prize of the Swiss Composers' Assn. and in 1978 was awarded the art's prize of the City of Basel. He was a member of the Bayerische Akademie der Schönen Künste of Munich and the Akademie der Künste of Berlin. He publ. *Klaus Huber: Gesammelte Schriften* (Cologne, 1995). In his music, Huber has written a large body of works notable for their exquisite craftsmanship in a highly personal style evocative of contemporary means of expression. His works include the operas *Jot, oder wann kommt der Herr zurück* (1972–73; Berlin, Sept. 27, 1973) and *Im Paradies oder Der Alte vom Berge* (1973–75).

Hüe, Georges (Adolphe), French composer and teacher; b. Versailles, May 6, 1858; d. Paris, June 7, 1948. After piano lessons with his mother, he studied counterpoint and fugue with Paladilhe and organ and composition with Franck and Reber at the Paris Cons. In 1879 he won the Prix de Rome with his cantata *Médée* and in 1881 he received the Prix Crescent with his comic opera *Les pantins*. He devoted himself to composing and teaching in Paris. In 1922 he succeeded to Saint-Saëns's seat in the Académie des Beaux-Arts.

WORKS: DRAMATIC (all 1st perf. in Paris): *Les pantins*, opéra comique (Dec. 18, 1881); *Le roi de Paris*, opera (April 26, 1901); *Titania*, opera (1902; Jan. 20, 1903); *Le miracle*, opera (Dec. 14, 1910); *Dans l'ombre de la cathédrale*, opera (Dec. 7, 1921); *Siang-Sin*, ballet pantomime (March 12, 1924); *Riquet à la houppe*, comédie musicale (Dec. 17, 1928).

Huehn, Julius, American baritone; b. Revere, Mass., Jan. 12, 1904; d. Rochester, N.Y., June 8, 1971. He studied engineering at the Carnegie Inst. of Technology; he later took voice lessons with Anna Schoen-René at the Juilliard School of Music in New York. He made his operatic debut with the Metropolitan Opera in New York as the Herald in *Lohengrin* on Dec. 21, 1935, singing there until 1944; he then served in the U.S. Air Force and carried out missions in Europe as a bombardier. He sang again at the Metropolitan after the war (1945–46). He was particularly noted for his performances of heroic baritone parts in Wagner's operas.

Hughes, Arwel, Welsh conductor and composer, father of **Owain Arwel Hughes**; b. Rhosllanerchrugog, Aug. 25, 1909; d. Cardiff, Sept. 23, 1988. He studied with Kitson and Vaughan Williams at the Royal College of Music in London, then returned to Wales, where he became a member of the music dept. of the BBC in 1935; from 1965 to 1971 he was head of music there. He was made an Officer of the Order of the British Empire in 1969. He wrote the operas *Menna* (1950–51) and *Serch yw'r doctor* (Love's the Doctor), after Molière (1959).

Hughes, Owain Arwel, Welsh conductor, son of **Arwel Hughes**; b. Cardiff, March 21, 1942. He first studied at Univ. College in Cardiff; then (1964–66) at the Royal College of Music in London, where his teachers included Boult and Harvey Philips; subsequently he studied with Kempe in London and Haitink in Amsterdam. He made his London debut in 1968, then appeared as a guest conductor with leading English orchs.; he also conducted at the Welsh National Opera and the English National Opera. In 1977 he became music director of the Royal National Eisteddfod of Wales; also was assoc. conductor of the BBC Welsh Sym. Orch. (from 1980) and music director of the Huddersfield Choral Soc. (1980–86); he then was assoc. conductor of the Philharmonia Orch. of London (from 1987).

Hughes, Robert Watson, Scottish-born Australian composer; b. Leven, Fyfeshire, March 27, 1912. He emigrated to Australia in 1930 and studied with A. E. H. Nickson at the Univ. of Melbourne Conservatorium of Music (1938–40). He worked as a music librarian at the Australian Broadcasting Commission in Melbourne; was chairman of the Australian Performing Right Assn. (1977–85). In 1978 he was made a Member of the Order of the British Empire. He withdrew most of his early compositions. Among his works is the opera *The Intriguers* (1975) and the ballets *Xanadu* (1954) and *The Forbidden Rite* (1962).

Humble, (Leslie) Keith, Australian pianist, conductor, teacher, and composer; b. Geelong, Victoria, Sept. 6, 1927; d. there, May 23, 1995. After obtaining his diploma at the Melbourne Cons. (1949), he studied with Vivian Langrish (piano) and Howard Ferguson (composition) at the Royal Academy of Music in London (1950–51). He then went to Paris and studied with Cortot (piano) at the École Normale de Musique (1951–52), and then privately with Leibowitz (composition and conducting, 1952–54). In 1959 he founded Le Centre de Musique in Paris, which he led as musical director until 1968. In 1966 he became senior lecturer in composition at the Melbourne Cons., and also founded its electronic music studio. From 1971 to 1974 he was a prof. at the Univ. of Calif. at San Diego. In 1974 he became the Foundation Prof. in the music dept. of La Trobe Univ. in Victoria, Australia, which position he held until 1989 when he became prof. emeritus. From 1975 to 1978 he was music director of the Australia Contemporary Music Ensemble. He was a visiting prof. at the Univ. of Calif. at San Diego from 1982 to 1990, where he made appearances as a soloist and conductor with the Ensemble Sonor. In 1982 he was made a Member of the Order of Australia. A confirmed avant-gardist, Humble early on developed a personal 12-tone method. He later experimented with improvisation in a series of works he called *Nuniques*. Still later he explored the realm of temporal composition. Among his various works is the opera *Now V* (1971).

Humel, Gerald, American composer; b. Cleveland, Nov. 7, 1931. He studied at Hofstra Univ. in New York (B.A., 1954), the Royal College of Music in London (A.R.C.M., 1956), the Oberlin (Ohio) College-Cons. of Music (M.M., 1958), and the Univ. of Mich. in Ann Arbor (1958–60); in 1960 he went to Berlin, where he took private lessons with Blacher and Rufer. His music at first maintained a median line of cosmopolitan modernism, in a neoclassical direction, but gradually he became oriented toward dodecaphonic techniques. His compositions include the operas *The Proposal* (1949) and *The Triangle* (Oberlin, Nov. 14, 1958) and the ballets *Devil's Dice* (1957), *First Love* (1965), and *Herodias* (1967).

Hummel, Ferdinand, German harpist and composer; b. Berlin, Sept. 6, 1855; d. there, April 24, 1928. He gave concerts as a child harpist (1864–67), then studied music at Kullak's Academy in Berlin and later at the Hochschule für Musik there. He established himself as a teacher in Berlin, and also became a prolific composer. Much impressed by the realistic school of Italian opera (Mascagni), he wrote several short operas in the same genre: *Mara* (Berlin, 1893), *Angla* (Berlin, 1894), *Assarpai* (Gotha, 1898), *Sophie von Brabant* (Darmstadt, 1899), *Die Beichte* (Berlin, 1900), *Ein treuer Schelm* (Altenburg, 1894), and *Die Gefilde der Seligen* (Altenburg, 1917).

Hummel, Johann Nepomuk, celebrated Austrian pianist, composer, and pedagogue; b. Pressburg, Nov. 14, 1778; d. Weimar, Oct. 17, 1837. A child prodigy, he began to study the violin and the piano under his father's tutelage; when he was 8 the family moved to Vienna, where his father became music director of the Theater auf der Wieden. Mozart interested himself in the young musician, took him into his house, and for 2 years instructed him. Hummel made his Vienna debut in 1787, then toured under his father's guidance, visiting Bohemia, Germany, Denmark, Scotland, the Netherlands, and England, where he presented his String Quartet in Oxford. He returned to Vienna in 1793 and studied counterpoint with Albrechtsberger, composition with Salieri, and organ with Haydn. He served as Konzertmeister to Prince Nikolaus Esterházy (1804–11), carrying out the duties of Kapellmeister, although Haydn retained the title. His opera *Mathilde von Guise* was produced in Vienna on March 26, 1810. He returned there in 1811 as a teacher; he then resumed his appearances as a pianist in 1814, being particularly successful at the Congress of Vienna, and subsequently toured Germany in 1816. He served as court Kapellmeister in Stuttgart (1816–18); then in 1819 became Grand Ducal Kapellmeister in Weimar, a position he held until his death. His years in Weimar were marked by his friendship with Goethe. He traveled widely as a pianist; he visited St. Petersburg (1822); Paris (1825), where he was made a Chevalier of the Légion d'honneur; and Belgium and the Netherlands (1826). In 1827 he was in Vienna, where he visited Beethoven on the composer's deathbed; he traveled to Warsaw in 1828 and to Paris and London in 1830. He revisited London in 1831 and 1833; during the latter visit, he conducted German opera at the King's Theater. The last years of his life were marred by ill health and much suffering. At the peak of his career as a pianist, he was regarded as one of the greatest virtuosos of his time; both as a pianist and as a composer, he was often declared to be the equal of Beethoven. His compositions were marked by excellent craftsmanship; his writing for instruments, particularly for piano, was impeccable; his melodic invention was rich, and his harmonic and contrapuntal skill was of the highest caliber. Yet with his death, his music went into an immediate eclipse; performances of his works became increasingly rare, until the name of Hummel all but vanished from active musical programs. However, some of his compositions were revived by various musical societies in Europe and America, and as a result, at least his Trumpet Concerto (1803) and chamber music were saved from oblivion. He wrote works in all genres except the sym. He also publ. *Anweisung zum Pianofortespiel* (1828), an elaborate instruction book and one of the first to give a sensible method of fingering. His wife, Elisabeth Hummel-Rockl (1793–1883), was an opera singer; they had 2 sons, a pianist and a painter.

WORKS: DRAMATIC: *Il Viaggiator ridicolo*, opera (1797; unfinished); *Dankgefühl einer Geretteten*, monodrama (March 21, 1799); *Demagorgon*, comic opera (c.1800; only fragment extant; used in the following opera); *Don Anchise Campione*, opera buffa (c.1800; unfinished); *Le vicende d'amore*, opera buffa (1804; rev. as *Die vereitelten Ränke*, Eisenstadt, Sept. 1806); *Die beyden Genies*, Lustspiel (1805; not extant); *Die Messenier*, grosse heroische Oper (c.1805–10); *Pimmalione,* azione teatrale (c.1805–15); *Mathilde von Guise*, opera (Vienna, March 26, 1810; rev. version, Weimar, Feb. 17, 1821); *Stadt und Land*, Singspiel (c.1810; unfinished); *Dies Haus ist zu verkaufen*, Singspiel (Vienna, May 5, 1812, based on *Die vereitelten Ränke*); Aria in Castelli's pasticcio *Fünf sind Zwey* (Vienna, March 21, 1813); *Der Junker in der Mühle*, Singspiel (Nov. 1813); *Die Eselshaut, oder Die blaue Insel*, Feenspiel (Vienna, March 10, 1814); *Die Rückfahrt des Kaisers*, Singspiel (Vienna, June 15, 1814); *Attila*, opera (c.1825–27; not extant). Also music to operas by others, incidental music to plays, ballets, and pantomimes.

BIBL.: K. Benyovszky, *J. N. H.: Der Mensch und Künstler* (Bratislava, 1934); D. Zimmerschied, *Thematisches Verzeichnis der Werke von J. N. H.* (Hofheim am Taunus, 1971); J. Sachs, *Kapellmeister H. in England and France* (Detroit, 1977).

Humperdinck, Engelbert, famous German composer and pedagogue; b. Siegburg, near Bonn, Sept. 1, 1854; d. Neustrelitz, Sept. 27, 1921. He began to study piano at 7. He commenced composing at 14, then studied at the Cologne Cons. (1872–76), where his teachers were Hiller, Gernsheim, and Jensen (harmony and composition), Hompesch, Mertke, and Seiss (piano), F. Weber (organ), and Ehlert and Rensburg (cello). After winning the Mozart Prize (1876), he studied counterpoint and fugue with Rheinberger at Munich's Royal Music School (1877); he also studied composition privately there with F. Lachner. In 1879 he won the Mendelssohn Prize of Berlin for his choral work *Die Wallfahrt nach Kevelaar* (1878); he then went to Italy, where he met Wagner in Naples (1880); at Wagner's invitation, he worked in Bayreuth (1881–82). In 1881 he won the Meyerbeer Prize of Berlin, which enabled him to visit Paris in 1882. He taught at the Barcelona Cons. (1885–86) and the Cologne Cons. (1887–88); he subsequently worked for the Schott publishing firm in Mainz (1888–89). After serving as private teacher to Siegfried Wagner (1889–90), he joined the faculty of the Hoch Cons. in Frankfurt am Main in 1890; was made prof. there in 1896, but resigned in 1897. During this period he also was music critic of the *Frankfurter Zeitung*. His fame as a composer was assured with the extraordinary success of his opera *Hänsel und Gretel* (Weimar, Dec. 23, 1893), written to a libretto by his sister Adelheid Wette. This fairy-tale score, with its melodies of ingenuous felicity in a Wagnerian idiom, retains its place in the repertoire. Although he continued to write for the stage, his succeeding works left little impression. He was director of a master class in composition at Berlin's Akademische Meisterschule (1900–20); was also a member of the senate of the Berlin Academy of Arts.

WORKS: DRAMATIC: OPERAS: *Hänsel und Gretel* (Weimar, Dec. 23, 1893, R. Strauss conducting); *Dornröschen* (Frankfurt am Main, Nov. 12, 1902); *Die Heirat wider Willen* (Berlin, April 14, 1905); *Königskinder* (N.Y., Dec. 28, 1910; based on his incidental music to Rosmer's *Königskinder*); *Die Marketenderin* (Cologne, May 10, 1914); *Gaudeamus* (Darmstadt, March 18, 1919). Also *Die sieben Geislein*, children's fairy play for Voice and Piano (Berlin, Dec. 19, 1895). INCIDENTAL MUSIC: To Rosmer's *Königskinder* (Munich, Jan. 23, 1897; later expanded into an opera); for the Berlin productions of Shakespeare's *The Merchant of Venice* (Nov. 5, 1905), *The Winter's Tale* (Sept. 15, 1906), *The Tempest* (Oct. 26, 1906), *Romeo and Juliet* (Jan. 29, 1907), and *Twelfth Night* (Oct. 17, 1907); also to Aristophanes's *Lysistrata* (Berlin, Feb. 27, 1908) and Maeterlinck's *The Blue Bird* (Berlin, Dec. 23, 1912), as well as for Reinhardt's production of *The Miracle* (London, Dec. 23, 1911).

BIBL.: O. Besch, *E. H.* (Leipzig, 1914); H. Kuhlmann, *Stil und Form in der Musik von H.s Oper "Hänsel und Gretel"* (Borna and Leipzig, 1930); L. Kirsten, *Motivik und Form in der Musik zu E. H.s Oper "Königskinder"* (diss., Univ. of Jena, 1942); K. Pullen, *Die Schauspielmusiken H.s* (diss., Univ. of Cologne, 1951); E. Thamm, *Der Bestand der lyrischen Werke E. H.s* (diss., Univ. of Mainz, 1951); W. Humperdinck, *E. H.* (Frankfurt am Main, 1965); H. Irmen, *Die Odyssee des E. H.: Eine biographische Dokumentation* (Siegburg, 1975); idem, ed., *E. H.: Briefe und Tagebucher* (Cologne, 1976); E. Humperdinck and J. Nickel, *E. H. zum 70. Todestag* (Siegburg, 1992); W. Humperdinck, *E. H.: Das Leben meines Vaters* (Koblenz, 1993); E. Humperdinck, *E. H. Werkverzeichnis: Zum 140 Geburtstag: Seinem Andenken gewidmet* (Koblenz, 1994).

Hüni-Mihacsek, Felice, Hungarian soprano; b. Pécs, April 3, 1891; d. Munich, March 26, 1976. She studied in Vienna with Rosa Papier. She made her operatic debut as the 1st Lady in *Die Zauberflöte* with the Vienna State Opera in 1919, remaining there until 1926; she was then a member of the Bavarian State Opera in Munich (1926–44); she retired from the stage in 1953. She particularly excelled in Mozart's operas, winning distinction as the Queen of the Night, Constanze, Fiordiligi, and Donna Anna. Among her other admired roles were Elsa and Eva.

Hunter, Rita (Nellie), distinguished English soprano; b. Wallasey, Aug. 15, 1933. She studied with Edwin Francis in Liverpool and with Clive Carey and Redvers Llewellyn in London; she sang in the Sadler's Wells chorus (1954–56) before touring with the Carl Rosa Opera Co. (1956–58); after further studies with Dame Eva Turner, she joined the Sadler's Wells Opera (1959), singing leading roles there from 1965, including Brünnhilde in the English-language version of *Die Walküre* (June 29, 1970); she later sang Brünnhilde in the first complete English-language version of the *Ring* cycle (July–Aug. 1973). On Dec. 19, 1972, she made her Metropolitan Opera debut in New York as Brünnhilde; appeared as Norma at the San Francisco Opera in 1975. Her other notable roles included Donna Anna, Aida, Senta, and Santuzza. In 1980 she was made a Commander of the Order of the British Empire. She publ. an autobiography, *Wait Till the Sun Shines, Nellie* (London, 1986).

Hurd, Michael (John), English composer, conductor, broadcaster, and writer on music; b. Gloucester, Dec. 19, 1928. He was a pupil of Thomas Armstrong and Bernard Rose at Pembroke College, Oxford (1950–53), and of Lennox Berkeley (1954–56). He taught at the Royal Marines School of Music (1953–59), and from 1956 was a broadcaster with the BBC. His compositions are written in an accessible style; among his lighter scores, the "pop" cantatas have been particularly successful.

WORKS: DRAMATIC: *Little Billy*, children's opera (1964); *Mr. Punch*, operatic entertainment for young people (1970); *The Widow of Ephesus*, chamber opera (Stroud, Oct. 23, 1971); *The Aspern Papers*, opera (1993).

WRITINGS: *Immortal Hour: The Life and Period of Rutland Boughton* (1962; rev. and enl. ed, 1993, as *Rutland Boughton and the Glastonbury Festivals*); *The Composer* (1968); *An Outline History of European Music* (1968; 2d ed., rev., 1988); *Elgar* (1969); *Vaughan Williams* (1970); *Mendelssohn* (1970); *The Ordeal of Ivor Gurney* (1978); *The Oxford Junior Companion to Music* (1979); *Vincent Novello and Company* (1981); *The Orchestra* (1981).

Huré, Jean, French pianist, organist, composer, and writer on music; b. Gien, Loiret, Sept. 17, 1877; d. Paris, Jan. 27, 1930. He received his musical education at a monastery in Angers. He went to Paris in 1895, where he founded the École Normale de Musique (1910), the École Normale pour Pianistes (1912), and the monthly magazine *L'Orgue et les Organistes* (1923). In 1925 he became church organist at St. Augustin; in 1926 he won the Prix Chartier for composition. His ballet, *Le Bois sacré*, was produced at the Opéra Comique in Paris on June 28, 1921; he further wrote incidental music to Musset's *Fantasio*.

BIBL.: G. Migot, *J. H.* (Paris, 1926).

Hurley, Laurel, American soprano; b. Allentown, Pa., Feb. 14, 1927. Of a musical family, she studied with her mother, a church organist; at 16, she appeared on Broadway (Aug. 21, 1943) as Kathie in Romberg's operetta *The Student Prince*; then toured with the company that produced it. In 1952 she made her N.Y. City Opera debut as Zerlina. She was the winner of the Walter W. Naumburg Foundation Award, which enabled her to give a song recital in New York (Nov. 6, 1952). She made her debut at the Metropolitan Opera in New York on Feb. 8, 1955, as Oscar; she remained at the Metropolitan until 1967, singing such roles as Musetta, Susanna, Périchole, Adele, Mimi, and Despina.

Hurník, Ilja, Czech pianist and composer; b. Poruba, near Svinov, Nov. 25, 1922. He moved to Prague in 1938 and had piano lessons with Kurz (1939–45); he studied composition with Řídký and was the last pupil of Novák (1941–44); he later studied piano with Štepánová at the Cons. (1945–48) before completing his training at the Academy of Music (1948–52). He then made several concert tours in Czechoslovakia. He taught at the Prague Cons. (from 1970) and at the Bratislava Academy of Music. His works are marked with modernistic tendencies.

WORKS: DRAMATIC: OPERAS: *Dámá a lupiči* (The Lady and the Gangster), after the film *The Ladykillers* (1966); *Mudrci a bloudi* (The Wise and the Foolish; 1968); *Diogenes* (1974); *Oldřich a Boženka* (1985); *Stažená hrdla* (Tightened Throat), mini-opera (1997). BALLET: *Ondráš* (1950).

Hüsch, Gerhard (Heinrich Wilhelm Fritz), esteemed German baritone and pedagogue; b. Hannover, Feb. 2, 1901; d. Munich, Nov. 23, 1984. He received his training from Hans Emge in Hannover. In 1923 he made his operatic debut as Lieberau in Lortzing's *Der Waffenschmied* in Osnabrück. After singing in Bremen, he was a member of the Cologne Opera (1927–30). He then went to Berlin and sang with the City and State Operas (1930–42); he also appeared in Dresden, Hamburg, Munich, Vienna, Milan, Bayreuth (1930–31), and London (Covent Garden debut as Falke, 1930; returned there, 1931 and 1938). In later years, Hüsch became well known as an exponent of lieder. He also taught voice in Munich.

Huston, (Thomas) Scott (, Jr.), American composer and pedagogue; b. Tacoma, Wash., Oct. 10, 1916; d. Cincinnati, March 1, 1991. After attending the Univ. of Puget Sound (1934–35), he studied with Phillips, Rogers, and Hanson at the Eastman School of Music in Rochester, N.Y. (B.M., 1941; M.M., 1942; Ph.D., 1952). He taught at several schools of higher learning before joining the Cincinnati Cons. of Music in 1952; after it merged with the College of Music in 1955, he was dean until 1956; he then taught there until 1988. His output was marked by a fine command of tonal and atonal writing. Among his works is the opera *Blind Girl* (1981; concert perf., Lake George, N.Y., May 1984).

Huszka, Jenő, Hungarian composer; b. Szeged, April 24, 1875; d. Budapest, Feb. 2, 1960. He was a student of Hubay (violin) and Koessler (composition) at the Royal Academy of Music in Budapest. At age 24, he launched a career as a composer for the theater in Budapest. His first operetta, *Bob herceg* (Dec. 12, 1902), was followed by such successful scores as *Aranyvirág* (Nov. 6, 1903), *Gül Baba* (Dec. 9, 1905), *Rébusz báró* (Nov. 20, 1909), *Nemtudomka* (Jan. 14, 1914), *Lili bárónő* (March 7, 1919), *Mária főhadnagy* (Sept. 23, 1942), and *Szabadság, szerelem* (April 1, 1955).

Hüttenbrenner, Anselm, Austrian composer; b. Graz, Oct. 13, 1794; d. Ober-Andritz, near Graz, June 5, 1868. At the age of 7 he studied with the organist Gell, then studied law at the Univ. of Graz; in 1815 he went to Vienna to study with Salieri. Schubert was his fellow student, and they became close friends. Hüttenbrenner also knew Beethoven intimately, and was present at his death. He was an excellent pianist and a prolific composer; Schubert praised his works, which included 6 operas and an operetta. One of his songs, "Erlkönig," was included in the collection *12 Lieder der deutschen Romantik*, ed. by H. Rosenwald (1929). His reminiscences of Schubert (1854) were publ. by Otto Deutsch in 1906. It was Huttenbrenner who came into the possession of many Schubert MSS after Schubert's death, among them that of the "Unfinished Sym.," which he held until 1865. It has been suggested that Huttenbrenner lost the 3d and 4th movements of Schubert's work, but the extant sketches for the Scherzo make that unlikely.

BIBL.: K. Kurth, *A. H. als Liederkomponist* (diss., Univ. of Cologne, 1932).

Huttenlocher, Philippe, Swiss baritone; b. Neuchâtel, Nov. 29, 1942. He received vocal training in Fribourg, and then began his career with the Ensemble Vocal de Lausanne and the Choeurs de la Foundation Gulbenkian in Lisbon. In 1975 he made his first appearance at the Zürich Opera as Monteverdi's Orfeo, and thereafter sang various Baroque roles there. His guest engagements took him to such leading European music centers as London, Vienna, Berlin, Hamburg, Edinburgh, Montreux, Milan, and Strasbourg. He was especially admired for his interpretations of works by Gabrieli, Monteverdi, Charpentier, Carissimi, Bach, Handel, Rameau, Haydn, and Mozart.

Hvorostovsky, Dmitri, prominent Russian baritone; b. Krasnoyarsk, Oct. 16, 1962. He was a student of Ekaterina Yofel at the Krasnoyarsk School of the Arts (1982–86). In 1986 he joined the Krasnoyarsk Opera. In 1987 he won the Glinka Prize, and in 1989 the BBC Cardiff Singer of the World Competition, which resulted in an appearance on BBC-TV; that same year, he made his London recital debut at the Wigmore Hall, and sang Tchaikovsky's Yeletsky in Nice. On March 4, 1990, he made an acclaimed U.S. debut in recital at N.Y.'s Alice Tully Hall. In 1991 he appeared in *War and Peace* at the San Francisco Opera. In 1992 he was engaged to sing in *I Puritani* at London's Covent Garden and appeared as Posa at Milan's La Scala. In 1993 he made his U.S. operatic debut as Germont at the Lyric Opera of Chicago and his first appearance at the London Promenade Concerts. On Oct. 26, 1995, he made his Metropolitan Opera debut in New York as Yeletsky in *The Queen of Spades*. After singing in recital at the Barbican Hall in London in 1997, he was engaged as Francesco in *I masnadieri* in Baden-Baden in 1998. In addition to the Russian operatic and song repertoires, he has won distinction for his roles in Verdi's operas.

Hvoslef (real name, **Saeverud**), **Ketil,** Norwegian composer, son of **Harald Saeverud**; b. Fana, near Bergen, July 19, 1939. He took his mother's maiden name in 1980. He studied piano with Thomas Rayna in London (1961) and took an organ diploma at the Bergen Cons. (1962); he then studied composition with Blomdahl and Lidholm in Stockholm, Jersild in Copenhagen, and Lazaroff in London. From 1963 to 1979 he was on the faculty of the Bergen Cons. After a period of hesitant serialism, he evolved a "motivic assimilation technique," wherein a central motif influences all the other thematic material in the manner of a theme with variations. Among his works are the operas *The Ballad of Narcissus and Echo* (1981), *Dode Sardiner* (1986–87), and *Trio for Tretten; Acotral* (1987), as well as much incidental music.

Hyde, Walter, English tenor; b. Birmingham, Feb. 6, 1875; d. London, Nov. 11, 1951. He studied with Gustave Garcia at the Royal College of Music in London, where he sang in student performances. He then sang in light opera before he undertook Wagnerian roles, which became his specialty. He sang Siegmund in the English-language production of the *Ring* cycle at Covent Garden in London in 1908; his other roles included Walther von Stolzing and Parsifal. He made his Metropolitan Opera debut in New York on March 28, 1910, as Siegmund in *Die Walküre*; he then returned to England and made regular appearances at Covent Garden until 1924; he later sang with the Beecham Opera Co. and the British National Opera Co., serving as a director of the latter. He was a frequent participant at many musical festivals in England.

Hye-Knudsen, Johan, Danish conductor and composer; b. Nyborg, May 24, 1896; d. Copenhagen, Sept. 28, 1975. He studied cello at the Copenhagen Cons. with Rudinger; also in Paris with André Hekking; studied conducting in Dresden with Fritz Busch. In 1925 he was named a conductor of the Royal Danish Theater in Copenhagen, concurrently leading concerts of the Royal Danish Orch. He wrote 2 operas: *Orfeus i underverdenen* (Copenhagen, Jan. 1, 1934) and *Kirke og orgel* (Copenhagen, Nov. 8, 1947).

Hynninen, Jorma, distinguished Finnish baritone and opera administrator; b. Leppävirta, April 3, 1941. He studied at the Sibelius Academy in Helsinki (1966–70); he also took courses in Rome with Luigi Ricci and in Salzburg with Kurt Overhoff. He won 1st prize at the singing competition in Lappeenranta in 1969, and in the Finnish division of the Scandinavian singing competition in Helsinki in 1971. In 1970 he made his concert debut in Helsinki, as well as his operatic debut as Silvio in *Pagliacci* with the Finnish National Opera there, and subsequently sang leading roles with the company. He also made first appearances at La Scala in Milan (1977), the Vienna State Opera (1977), the Hamburg State Opera (1977), the Bavarian State Opera in Munich (1979), and the Paris Opéra (1980); he gave recitals throughout Europe and the United States. He made his N.Y. debut in a recital in 1980; his operatic debut followed in 1983, when he sang with the Finnish National Opera during its visit to America; made his Metropolitan Opera debut in New York as Rodrigo in *Don Carlos* on March 30, 1984. He was artistic director of the Finnish National Opera from 1984 to 1990, and then of the Savonlinna Festival from 1992. In addition to such traditional operatic roles as Pelléas, Wolfram, Orpheus, Valentin in *Faust*, and Macbeth, he has sung parts in contemporary Finnish operas; he created the King in Sallinen's *The King Goes Forth to France* (Savonlinna, July 7, 1984), Thomas in Rautavaara's opera (Joensuu, June 21, 1985), Kullervo in Sallinen's opera (Los Angeles, Feb. 25, 1992), and Aleksis Kivi in Rautavaara's opera (Savonlinna, July 10, 1997).

Hytner, Nicholas, English theater and opera producer; b. Manchester, May 7, 1956. He was educated at Trinity College, Cambridge (graduated, 1977), where he produced Weill's *The Threepenny Opera* while still a student. In 1979 he launched his professional career when he oversaw the production of *The Turn of the Screw* at the Kent Opera. In 1983 he brought out *Rienzi* at the English National Opera in London. He was the producer for the British premiere of Sallinen's *The King Goes Forth to War* at London's Covent Garden in 1987. Following productions of Handel's *Giulio Cesare* in Paris in 1987 and Mozart's *Le nozze di Figaro* in Geneva in 1989, he brought out the latter composer's *La clemenza di Tito* at the Glyndebourne Festival in 1991. In 1992 he staged *La forza del destino* at the English National Opera. In 1996 he oversaw the production of *The Cunning Little Vixen* in Paris. His film version of *The Crucible* appeared in 1997. In addition to his work in opera, he has also pursued an active career as a producer of stage plays. His work in the legitimate theater is reflected in his approach to opera, most notably in his ability to harmonize the dramatic and musical elements into a satisfying theater experience.

I

Ibert, Jacques (François Antoine), distinguished French composer; b. Paris, Aug. 15, 1890; d. there, Feb. 5, 1962. He studied at the Paris Cons. with Gédalge and Fauré (1911–14). During World War I, he served in the French navy, then returned to the Paris Cons. after the Armistice and studied with Vidal, and received the Prix de Rome in 1919 for his cantata *Le Poète et la fée*. While in Rome he wrote his most successful work, the symphonic suite *Escales*, inspired by a Mediterranean cruise while serving in the navy. In 1937 he was appointed director of the Académie de France of Rome, holding this post until 1960; he was also administrator of the Réunion des Théâtres Lyriques Nationaux in Paris (1955–56). He was elected a member of the Institut de France (1956). In his music Ibert combined the most felicitous moods and techniques of Impressionism and neoclassicism; his harmonies were opulent, and his instrumentation was coloristic. There was also an element of humor in lighter works, such as his popular orch. *Divertissement* (1930). His craftsmanship was excellent; an experimenter in tested values, he never failed to produce the intended effect.

WORKS: DRAMATIC: OPERAS: *Angélique* (Paris, Jan. 28, 1927); *Persée et Andromède, ou Le Plus Heureux des trois* (1921; Paris, May 15, 1929); *Le Roi d'Yvetot* (Paris, Jan. 15, 1930); *Gonzague* (Monte Carlo, Dec. 7, 1931); *L'Aiglon* (Monte Carlo, March 11, 1937; in collaboration with A. Honegger); *Les Petites Cardinal* (Paris, 1938; in collaboration with A. Honegger); *Barbebleue*, radio opera (Lausanne Radio, Oct. 10, 1943). BALLETS (all 1st perf. in Paris): *Les Rencontres* (Nov. 21, 1925); *Diane de Poitiers* (April 30, 1934); *Les Amours de Jupiter* (March 9, 1946); *Le Chevalier errant* (May 5, 1950); *Tropismes pour des Amours Imaginaires* (1957).

BIBL.: J. Feschotte, *J. I.* (Paris, 1959); G. Michel, *J. I.: L'Homme et son oeuvre* (Paris, 1968).

Ichiyanagi, Toshi, Japanese composer; b. Kobe, Feb. 4, 1933. He studied composition with Kishio Hirao and piano with Chieko Hara, and then pursued training in New York at the Juilliard School of Music and the New School for Social Research (1954–58), receiving instruction in composition from Cage and in piano from Beveridge Webster. He worked at the NHK electronic music studio in Tokyo, and also received a Rockefeller Foundation grant in 1967. In 1976 he was the Deutscher Akademischer Austauschdienst composer-in-residence in Berlin. In addition to various composition prizes, he was made a member of the Ordre des Arts et des Lettres of France in 1985. Ichiyanagi's output reflects his penchant for experimentation in the best avant-garde tradition, and includes the utilization of unusual performance techniques, chance, electronics, and graphic notation. Among his many works is the opera *Hino yuigon* (Testament of Fire; Tokyo, Nov. 16, 1995).

Ikebe, Shin-Ichiro, Japanese composer and teacher; b. Mito City, Sept. 15, 1943. He studied with Ikenouchi, Yashiro, and Miyoshi at the Tokyo Univ. of Fine Arts and Music (graduated, 1967), where he later was an assistant (1971–77). Subsequently he served as a prof. at the Tokyo College of Music. He won the Prix Italia in 1976, the music prize of the Japanese Academy in 1980, 1984, and 1992, and the Otaka Prize in 1991.

WORKS: DRAMATIC: *The Death Goddess*, opera (NHK-TV, July 25, 1971); *The Whistling of the Wind*, television musical fantasy (1976); *The Silence*, radiophonic music drama (1977); *The Adventures of Pinocchio*, musical comedy (1981); *Hoichi, the Earless*, opera (1982); *Cleopatra, Her Love and Death*, ballet (1983); *Mobile et Immobile*, ballet (1984); *The Window*, musical drama (1986); *Chichibu-Bansho*, opera (1988); *Taro's Tree*, choral opera (1991–92).

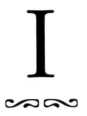

Ikenouchi, Tomojirô, Japanese composer and pedagogue; b. Tokyo, Oct. 21, 1906; d. there, March 9, 1991. He was the first Japanese student at the Paris Cons. (1926–36), where he studied with Fauchet (harmony), Caussade (fugue), and Büsser (composition), taking the premier prix in harmony. In 1936 he joined the faculty of Nihon Univ. in Tokyo, and then was prof. of composition at the Tokyo National Univ. of Fine Arts and Music from 1947. Ikenouchi was highly esteemed as a teacher. His small but well-crafted output reflects the influence of his Western training. Among his works is the opera *Yuya* (1942; Tokyo, Feb. 1, 1943).

Ikonomov, Boyan Georgiev, Bulgarian composer; b. Nikopol, Dec. 14, 1900; d. Sofia, March 27, 1973. He studied in Sofia (1920–26), then went to Paris, where he attended classes of **d'Indy** and Lioncourt at the Schola Cantorum (1928–32); he also studied with Boulanger and Roussel, and then took a course in conducting with Weingartner in Basel (1934). Returning to Bulgaria, he was music director of Sofia Radio (1937–48) and of the Bulgarian film center (1948–56); he then was head of the music dept. of Sofia Radio (1957–60). His music was rooted in Bulgarian folk songs, with an emphasis on modal melodic progressions and asymmetric rhythms. Among his compositions is the opera *Indje Voivoda* (1960) and the ballets *The 7 Mortal Sins* (1933), *The Tragedy of Othello* (1946), and *The Light Floods Everything* (1967); also 2 oratorios: *The Legend of Shipka* (1968) and *Vassil Levsky* (1972).

Iliev, Konstantin, Bulgarian conductor, teacher, and composer; b. Sofia, March 9, 1924; d. there, March 6, 1988. He studied composition with Khadzhiev and Vladigerov, and conducting with Goleminov, at the Bulgarian State Cons. in Sofia (1942–46); he later took courses in composition with Řídký and A. Hába, and in conducting with Talich, at the Prague Cons. (1946–47). He conducted at the Sofia Opera (1948–49); after serving as chief conductor of the Ruse Opera and Sym. Orch. (1949–52), and then of the Varna Sym. Orch. (1952–56), he was principal conductor of the Sofia Phil. (1956–85). From 1964 to 1985 he was on the faculty of the Bulgarian State Cons. in Sofia. As a composer, Iliev evolved a rather stimulating idiom, adroitly exploring the asymmetric Balkan rhythms and oriental melismas to create an aura of folkloric authenticity; in nonethnic pieces he often applied serial principles of melodic formations. His works include the operas *The Master of Boyana* (Sofia, Oct. 3, 1962) and *The Kingdom of the Deer* (1975); also the oratorio *Eulogy to Constantin the Philosopher* (1971).

Ilitsch, Daniza, Serbian soprano; b. Belgrade, Feb. 21, 1914; d. Vienna, Jan. 15, 1965. She studied at the Stankovic Cons. in Belgrade, then in Berlin. She made her operatic debut as Nedda in *Pagliacci* with the Berlin State Opera (Nov. 6, 1936); she was on its roster for 2 seasons, then was a member of the Vienna State Opera (1938–41). The German army of occupation put her in a concentration camp in 1944, and she spent 4 months there until the liberation of Vienna. She made her debut with the Metropolitan Opera in New York as Desdemona (March 12, 1947), remaining on its roster until 1948. Thereafter she pursued her career in Europe and South America. In 1959 she settled in Vienna. She was principally known for her roles in Italian opera, including Aida, Desdemona, Gioconda, Amelia, and Cio-Cio-San.

Imbrie, Andrew (Welsh), distinguished American composer and pedagogue; b. N.Y., April 6, 1921. He studied piano and composition with Ornstein (until 1942), and also received instruction in composition from Boulanger (1937) and in piano with R. Casadesus (1941). From 1937 he pursued composition studies with Sessions, graduating from Princeton Univ. with a B.A. in 1942. After serving in the U.S. Army during World War II, he completed his studies with Sessions at the Univ. of Calif. at Berkeley, where he took his M.A. in 1947. In the latter year he joined its faculty as an instructor in music, becoming an assistant prof. in 1951, assoc. prof. in 1957, and prof. in 1960, a position he held until 1991. He also taught at the San Francisco Cons. of Music, serving as chairman of its composition dept. from 1970. In 1991 he was the composer-in-residence at the Tanglewood Festival of Contemporary Music. In 1982 he was the Jacob Ziskind Visiting Professor at Brandeis Univ. He was a fellow at the American Academy in Rome (1947–49), returning there on a Guggenheim fellowship (1953–54) and as its composer-in-residence (1967–68). In 1959–60 he was in Tokyo on a 2d Guggenheim fellowship. In addition to various commissions, he won the N.Y. Music Critics's Circle Award for his 1st String Quartet (1944), the Alice M. Ditson Award (1947), and the Naumburg Award for his Violin Concerto (1954). In 1969 he was elected a member of the National Inst. of Arts and Letters, and in 1980 of the American Academy of Arts and Sciences. Imbrie's style of composition is marked by a sharp and expressive melodic line, while the polyphony is vigorously motile; harmonic confluence is dissonant but euphoniously tonal. His natural propensity is toward instrumental writing, although his mastery is displayed in other genres, including dramatic. In his extensive catalog are the operas *Three Against Christmas* or *Christmas in Peebles Town* (1960; Berkeley, Dec. 3, 1964) and *Angle of Repose* (San Francisco, Nov. 6, 1976).

Inbal, Eliahu, prominent Israeli-English conductor; b. Jerusalem, Feb. 16, 1936. He received training in violin and theory at the Jerusalem Academy of Music (diploma, 1956). In 1956 he made his debut conducting the Youth Sym. Orch. of Israel. During military service, he was active with a combined army and youth orch. A recommendation from Bernstein in 1958 resulted in his receiving a scholarship from the Israel-America Foundation to pursue conducting studies with Fourestier at the Paris Cons. (1960–62); he also studied with Ferrara and Celibidache. After winning 1st prize in the Cantelli Competition in 1963, he appeared as a guest conductor with leading orchs. in Europe and the United States; he also was active as an opera conductor from 1969. From 1974 to 1990 he was chief conductor of the Frankfurt am Main Radio Sym. Orch., which he led on its first tour of the United States in 1980. He also was artistic director of the Teatro La Fenice in Venice from 1983 to 1986. During his tenure in Frankfurt am Main, Inbal conducted many premieres. He also became particularly well known for his performances of cycles of works by Schumann, Bruckner, Mahler, and Scriabin. From 1996 he served as principal conductor of the Orch. Nazionale d'Italia in Turin.

d'Indy, (Paul-Marie-Théodore-) Vincent, eminent French composer and pedagogue; b. Paris, March 27, 1851; d. there, Dec. 2, 1931. Owing to the death of his mother at his birth, his education was directed entirely by his grandmother, Countess Rézia d'Indy, a woman of culture and refinement who had known Grétry and Monsigny, and who had shown a remarkable appreciation of the works of Beethoven when that master was still living. From 1862 to 1865 he studied piano with Diémer and Marmontel; in 1865 he studied harmony with Lavignac. In 1869 he made the acquaintance of Duparc, and with him spent much time studying the masterpieces of Bach, Beethoven, Berlioz, and Wagner; at that time, he wrote his opp. 1 and 2, and contemplated an opera on Hugo's *Les Burgraves* (1869–72; unfinished). During the Franco-Prussian War he served in the Garde Mobile, and wrote of his experiences in *Histoire du 105ᵉ bataillon de la Garde nationale de Paris en l'année 1870–71* (1872). He then began to study composition with Franck (1872); when the latter was appointed prof. of organ at the Paris Cons. (1873), d'Indy joined the class, winning a 2d *accessit* in 1874 and the 1st the following year. On his first visit to Germany in 1873, he met Liszt and Wagner, and was introduced to Brahms; in 1876 he heard the first performances of the *Ring* cycle at Bayreuth, and for several years thereafter made regular trips to Munich to hear all the works of Wagner; he also attended the premiere of *Parsifal* in 1882. From 1872 to 1876 he was organist at St. Leu-la-Forêt, and from 1873 to 1878, chorusmaster and timpanist with the Colonne Orch. For the Paris premiere of *Lohengrin* in 1887, he drilled the chorus and was Lamoureux's assistant. In 1871 he joined the Société Nationale de Musique as a junior member, serving as its secretary from 1876 to 1890, when, after Franck's death, he became president. In 1894 he founded, with Bordes and Guilmant, the famous Schola Cantorum (opened 1896), primarily as a school for plainchant and the Palestrina style. Gradually the scope of instruction was enlarged to include all musical disciplines, and the inst. became one of the world's foremost music schools. D'Indy's fame as a composer began with the performance of his *Le Chant de la cloche* at a Lamoureux concert in 1886; the work itself had won the City of Paris Prize in the competition of the preceding year. As early as 1874, Pasdeloup had played the overture *Les Piccolomini* (later embodied as the 2d part in the Wallenstein trilogy), and in 1882 the 1-act opera *Attendez-moi sous l'orme* had been produced at the Paris Opéra Comique; but the prize work attracted general attention, and d'Indy was recognized as one of the most important French composers of his day. Although he never held an official position as a conductor, he frequently, and with marked success, appeared in that capacity (chiefly upon invitation to direct his own works); thus he visited Spain in 1897, Russia in 1903 and 1907, and the United States in 1905, when he conducted the Boston Sym. Orch. In 1892 he was a member of the commission appointed to revise the curriculum of the Cons., and refused a proffered professorship of composition, but in 1912 he accepted an appointment as prof. of the ensemble class. Besides his other duties, he was, from 1899, inspector of musical instruction in Paris. He was made a Chevalier of the Légion d'honneur in 1892, and an Officer in 1912. Both as teacher and creative artist, d'Indy continued the traditions of Franck. Although he cultivated almost every form of composition, his special talent was in the field of the larger instrumental forms. Some French critics assign to him a position in French music analogous to that of Brahms in German music. His style rests on Bach and Beethoven; however, his deep study of Gregorian chant and the early contrapuntal style added an element of severity, and not rarely of complexity, that renders his approach somewhat difficult, and has prompted the charge that his music is lacking in emotional force. He wrote numerous articles for various journals, which are remarkable for their critical acumen and literary finish.

WRITINGS: *Cours de Composition musicale* (Book I, 1903; Book II: Part 1, 1909, Part 2, 1933); *César Franck* (1906; Eng. tr., 1910); *Beethoven: Biographie critique* (1911; Eng. tr., 1913); *La Schola Cantorum en 1925* (1927); *Wagner et son influence sur l'art musical français* (1930); *Introduction à l'étude de Parsifal* (1937).

WORKS: DRAMATIC: *Les Burgraves*, opera (1869–72; unfinished); *Attendez-moi sous l'orme*, comic opera (Paris, Feb. 11, 1882); *Karadec*, incidental music (Paris, May 2, 1891); *Le Chant de la cloche*, dramatic legend (Brussels, Nov. 21, 1912); *Fervaal*, lyric drama (Brussels, March 12, 1897); *Medée*, incidental music (1898); *L'Étranger*, lyric drama (Brussels, Jan. 7, 1903); *La Légende de Saint-Christophe*, lyric drama (Paris, June 9, 1920); *Le Rêve de Cynias*, lyric comedy (Paris, June 10, 1927).

BIBL.: E. Deniau, *V. d'I.* (Toulouse, 1903); F. Starczewski, *La Schola Cantorum de Paris, ou V. d'I. considéré comme professeur* (Warsaw, 1905); L. Borgex, *V. d'I.: Sa vie et son oeuvre* (Paris, 1913); A. Sérieyx, *V. d'I.* (Paris, 1913); M. de Fraguier, *V. d'I.* (Paris, 1933); L. Vallas, *V. d'I.: I. La Jeunesse, II. La Maturité, La Vieillesse* (Paris, I, 1946; II, 1950); J. Canteloube, *V. d'I.* (Paris, 1949); N. Demuth, *V. d'I.* (London, 1951); J. Guy-Ropartz, ed., *Le Centenaire de V. d'I., 1851–1951* (Paris, 1952); A. Thomson, *V. d.'I. and His World* (Oxford, 1996).

Ingarden, Roman (Witold), important Polish music theorist and aesthetician; b. Kraków, Feb. 5, 1893; d. there, June 14, 1970. He studied philosophy with Husserl and mathematics with Hilbert at the univs. of Göttingen and Freiburg im Breisgau (Ph.D., 1918). After completing his Habilitation (1921), he joined the faculty at the Univ. of Lwów. In 1945 he became chairman of the philosophy dept. at the Jagellonian Univ. in Kraków, only to be barred from teaching in 1950 by the Communist government because of his adherence to "idealism"; during his forced sabbatical, he tr. Kant's *Critique of Pure Reason*. He regained his academic post in 1956, retiring in 1963. Ingarden is regarded as the ablest of Husserl's students, preserving the cognitive core of Husserl's phenomenology that was lost in Heidegger's and Sartre's emotional reduction of it to existentialism. His *The Work of Music and the Problem of Its Identity* (Berkeley, 1986), an excerpt from his *Studia z estetyki* (Studies in Aesthetics; Warsaw, 1957–70), is an important consideration of ontology and epistemology in musical aesthetics. His other publications include *Spór o istnienie świata* (Controversy over the Existence of the World; Kraków, 1947–48); *Untersuchungen zur Ontologie der Kunst: Musikwerk, Bild, Architektur, Film* (Tübingen, 1962); *The Literary Work of Art: An Investigation on the Borderlines of Ontology, Logic, and Theory of Literature, with an Appendix on the Functions of Language in the Theater* (Evanston, Ill., 1973); *Selected Papers in Aesthetics* (Washington, D.C., 1985).

Inghelbrecht, D(ésiré)-É(mile), noted French conductor and composer; b. Paris, Sept. 17, 1880; d. there, Feb. 14, 1965. He began violin lessons as a child, and later studied solfège and harmony with Taudou at the Paris Cons. only to be expelled as musically unpromising. After working as an orch. player, he became conductor of the Théâtre des Arts in Paris in 1908. In 1912 he organized l'Association Chorale Professionnelle. After serving as music director at the Théâtre des Champs-Elysées in Paris, he founded the Concerts Ignace Pleyel in 1919 to promote the music of the 17th and 18th centuries. From 1920 to 1923 he toured Europe as conductor of the Ballets Suédois, and then returned to Paris as music director of the Opéra Comique in 1924–25; he then held the post of 2d conductor of the Concerts Pasdeloup (1928–32). After serving as director of the Algiers Opera (1929–30), he was again music director of the Opéra Comique (1932–33). In 1934 he founded l'Orchestre National de la Radio Française, serving as its director until 1944. From 1945 to 1950 he was chief conductor of the Paris Opéra, and subsequently appeared as a conductor with Radio Française. Inghelbrecht was greatly admired for his interpretations of French music, particularly the works of Debussy, Ravel, and Roussel. He was also an accomplished composer in his own right. He was the author of *Comment on ne doit pas interpréter Carmen, Faust et Pelléas* (1933), *Diabolus in musica* (1933), *Mouvement contraire: Souvenirs d'un musicien* (1947), *Le Chef d'orchestre et son équipe* (1948; Eng. tr., 1953, as *The Conductor's World*), *Claude Debussy* (1953), and *Le Chef d'orchestre parle au public* (1957).

WORKS: DRAMATIC: OPERA: *La nuit vénitienne* (1908). OPERETTA: *Virage sur l'aile* (1947). OPERA BALLET: *Le chêne et le tilleul* (1960). BALLETS: *El Greco* (Paris, Nov. 18, 1920); *Le diable dans le beffroi* (1921; Paris, June 1, 1927); *La métamorphose d'Eve* (1928); *Jeux de Couleurs* (Paris, Feb. 21, 1933).

Inghilleri, Giovanni, Italian baritone and composer; b. Porto Empedocle, March 9, 1894; d. Milan, Dec. 10, 1959. He made his operatic debut as Valentine at the Teatro Carcano in Milan in 1919, and then sang throughout Italy; he was a member of La Scala in Milan from 1945. He also sang at London's Covent Garden (1928–30; 1935) and at the Chicago Civic Opera (1929–30). After his retirement in 1953, he taught voice in Pesaro and Milan. Among his best known roles were Amonasro, Amfortas, Gérard, and Scarpia. He composed an opera, *La burla*, a ballet, and songs.

Inzenga (y Castellanos), José, Spanish composer; b. Madrid, June 3, 1828; d. there, June 28, 1891. He first studied with his father, then at the Madrid Cons. and the Paris Cons. He became a prof. at the Madrid Cons. (1860). He was commissioned by the Minister of Public Instruction to make a collection of Spanish folk songs, which he publ. as *Cantos y bailes populares de España* (3 vols., 1874–88); he also wrote a treatise on accompaniment (Madrid, 1876) and *La música en el templo católico* (Madrid, 1878). He was very successful as a composer of zarzuelas, which included *Para seguir una mujer* (Madrid, Dec. 24, 1851), *Don Simplicio Bobadilla* (1853), *Un día de reino* (1854), *El campamento* (Madrid, May 8, 1861), and *Si yo fuera rey* (1862).

Ipavec, Benjamin, Slovenian composer; b. St. Jurij, Dec. 24, 1829; d. Graz, Dec. 20, 1909. He studied medicine in Vienna and became a professional physician, with music as an avocation; he was the first to cultivate national Slovenian motifs systematically. He wrote a national Slovenian opera, *Teharski plemiči* (The Nobles of Teharje; Ljubljana, 1892), and an operetta, *Tičnik* (The Aviary; 1862).

Ippolitov-Ivanov (real name, **Ivanov**), **Mikhail (Mikhailovich),** important Russian composer and pedagogue; b. Gatchina, Nov. 19, 1859; d. Moscow, Jan. 28, 1935. He assumed his mother's name to distinguish himself from Michael Ivanov, the music critic. He studied composition with Rimsky-Korsakov at the St. Petersburg Cons., graduating in 1882. He then received the post of teacher and director of the Music School in Tiflis, where he remained until 1893. He became deeply interested in Caucasian folk music, and many of his works were colored by the semi-oriental melodic and rhythmic inflections of that region. Upon Tchaikovsky's recommendation, he was appointed prof. of composition at the Moscow Cons. in 1893; in 1906 he became its director, retiring in 1922; he then taught at the Tiflis Cons. (1924–25). Among his pupils were Glière and Vasilenko. He was also active as a conductor in Moscow, where he led the Russian Choral Soc. (1895–1901), the Mamontov Opera (1898–1906), and the Bolshoi Theater (from 1925). Outside Russia, he is known mainly for his effective symphonic suite *Caucasian Sketches* (1895). He publ. his memoirs (Moscow, 1934; Eng. tr. in the *Musical Mercury*, N.Y., 1937).

WORKS: OPERAS: *Ruf* (Ruth; 1883–86; Tiflis, Feb. 4, 1887); *Azra* (Tiflis, Dec. 4, 1890); *Asya* (Moscow, Oct. 11, 1900); *Izmena* (Treason; 1908–09; Moscow, Dec. 17, 1910); *Ole iz Nordlands* (Ole from the Northland; Moscow, Nov. 21, 1916); *Poslednyaya barrikada* (The Last Barricade; 1933); also completed Mussorgsky's unfinished opera *Zhenitba* (Marriage; Moscow, Oct. 18, 1931).

BIBL.: S. Chemodanov, *M. M. I.-I.* (Moscow, 1933); S. Boguslavsky, *I.-I.* (Moscow, 1936); L. Podzemskaya, *M. M. I.-I. i gruzinskaya muzikalnaya kultura* (Tbilisi, 1963); N. Sokolov, ed., *M. M. I.-I.: Pisma, stati, vospominaniya* (M. M. I.-I.: Letters, Articles, Reminiscences; Moscow, 1986).

Irino, Yoshirō, Japanese composer and pedagogue; b. Vladivostok, Nov. 13, 1921; d. Tokyo, June 28, 1980. Although of pure Japanese ancestry, he was baptized in the Greek Orthodox faith, which he retained throughout his life. His family took him to Tokyo when he was 6. He studied economics at the Univ. of Tokyo; at the same time, he took composition lessons with Saburo Moroi. He became a teacher at the Tōhō Gakuen School of Music in 1952, serving as its director (1960–70), then was prof. at the Tokyo Music College (from 1973). A prolific composer, he wrote music of all categories, adopting a style decidedly modern in character, marked by fine instrumental coloration, with a complete mastery of contemporary techniques. Most of his vocal and stage music is imbued with a pronounced Japanese sensibility, with touches that are almost calligraphic in their rhythmic precision.

WORKS: DRAMATIC: *Kamisama ni shikarareta otoko* (The Man in Fear of God), radio operetta (NHK, May 25, 1954); *Fuefuki to Ryuo no musumetachi* (The Piper and the Dragon King's Daughters), radio opera (1959); *Sarudon no mukoiri* (The Marriage of Mr. Monkey), radio opera (NHK, Nov. 26, 1961; 1st stage perf., Tokyo, March 15, 1962; in collaboration with Moroi and Shimizu); *Aya no tsuzumi* (The Damask Drum), television opera (NHK, Aug. 9, 1962; 1st stage perf., Tokyo, March 26, 1975); *Sonezaki shinju* (The Lover's Suicide at Sonezaki), chamber opera (Osaka, April 10, 1980).

Irving, Robert (Augustine), English conductor; b. Winchester, Aug. 28, 1913; d. there, Sept. 13, 1991. He studied at Winchester College (1926–32), at New College, Oxford (B.A., 1935), and with Sargent and Lambert at the Royal College of Music in London (1934–36). He was assoc. conductor of the BBC Scottish Orch. in Glasgow (1945–48). After serving as principal conductor of the Sadler's Wells (later Royal) Ballet in London (1948–58), he was music director of the N.Y. City Ballet (1958–89); he also conducted for the Martha Graham Dance Co. in New York (1960–65; 1974–77). Although he appeared as a guest conductor with various orchs. in England and the United States, it was as an exemplary conductor of ballet that he secured his reputation. He also wrote music for the theater and for films.

Isaac, Adèle, French soprano; b. Calais, Jan. 8, 1854; d. Paris, Oct. 22, 1915. She studied with Duprez in Paris, making her debut at the Théâtre Montmartre in Paris in 1870 in *Noces de Jeannette*. She then sang at the Paris Opéra Comique (1873; 1878–88) and the Paris Opéra (1883–85), retiring from the stage in 1894. She was noted for her performances of French operatic roles.

Isepp, Martin (Johannes Sebastian), Austrian pianist, harpsichordist, and conductor; b. Vienna, Sept. 30, 1930. He studied at Lincoln College, Oxford, and at the Royal Academy of Music in London. In 1957 he joined the music staff of the Glyndebourne Festival, serving as head of its music staff from 1978 to 1993. From 1973 to 1976 he was head of opera training at the Juilliard School in New York; he also was head of music studies at the National Opera Studio in London (1978–95) and head of the academy of singing at the Banff Centre School of Fine Arts in Canada (1981–93). He became best known as an accompanist to many of the foremost singers of the day.

Ishii, Kan, Japanese composer; b. Tokyo, March 30, 1921. He is one of two sons of Baku Ishii, a renowned scholar of modern dance. His brother, Maki Ishii (b. Tokyo, May 28, 1936) is also a composer and conductor. He studied in Tokyo at the Musashino Music School with Goh, Ikenouchi, and Odaka (1939–43); in 1952 he took lessons with Orff at the Hochschule für Musik in Munich. Returning to Japan, he taught at the Tōhō Gakuen School of Music in Tokyo (1954–66), the Aichi-Prefectural Arts Univ. in Nagoya (1966–86), and the Showa Music College (from 1986).

WORKS: DRAMATIC: OPERAS: *Mermaid and Red Candle* (1961); *Kaguyahime* (Prince Kaguya; 1963); *En-no-Gyojia* (Tokyo, 1964); *Lady Kesa and Morito* (Tokyo, Nov. 24, 1968); *Women are Wonderful* (1978); *Kantomi* (1981). OPERETTA: *Blue Lion* (1989). BALLETS: *God and the Bayadere* (Tokyo, Nov. 6, 1950); *Birth of a Human* (Tokyo, Nov. 27, 1954); *Frökln Julie* (1955); *Shakuntara* (1961); *Marimo* (Tokyo, 1963); *Biruma no tategoto* (Harp of Burma; 1963); *Haniwa* (1963); *Hakai* (1965); *Ichiyo Higuchi* (1966).

Isouard, Nicolò, important Maltese-born French composer; b. Malta, Dec 6, 1775; d. Paris, March 23, 1818. He was sent to Paris to study at the Pensionnat Berthaud, a preparatory school for engineers and artillerymen; he also studied piano there with Pin. With the outbreak of the French Revolution (1789), he returned to Malta, where he worked in a merchant's office and took courses in composition with Michel-Ange Vella and counterpoint with Azzopardi; his father then sent him to Italy to act as his assistant, but he found time to study harmony with Nicolas of Amendola in Palermo. He later studied composition with Sala in Naples, where he also received counsel from Guglielmi. His first opera, *L'avviso ai maritati* (Florence, 1794), proved so successful that he decided to devote himself fully to composition. In order not to embarrass his family, he used the name Nicolò de Malte, or simply Nicolò, professionally. The singer Senesino commissioned his 2d opera, *Artaserse* (Livorno, 1794), which also was a success. After serving as organist of the church of St. John of Jerusalem in Malta (1795–98), he went to Paris, gaining his first major success with the opera *Michel-Ange* (Opéra Comique, Dec. 11, 1802) and quickly establishing himself as the leading composer at the Opéra Comique. His *Cendrillon* (Feb. 22, 1810), *Joconde ou Les Coureurs d'aventures* (Feb. 28, 1814), and *Jeannot et Colin* (Oct. 17, 1814) were popular favorites. In spite of the competition from his friend and rival Boieldieu, he remained a protean figure in the musical life of Paris until his death.

WORKS (all 1st perf. in Paris unless otherwise given): DRAMATIC: OPERAS COMIQUES: *Le Petit Page ou La Prison d'état* (Feb. 14, 1800; in collaboration with R. Kreutzer); *Le Tonnelier* (May 17, 1801); *La Statue ou La Femme avare* (April 26, 1802); *Les Confidences* (March 31, 1803); *Le Baiser et la quittance ou Une Aventure de garnison* (June 18, 1803; in collaboration with Boieldieu, Kreutzer, and Méhul); *Le Médecin turc* (Nov. 19, 1803); *L'Intrigue aux fenêtres* (Feb. 25, 1805); *La Ruse inutile ou Les Rivaux par convention* (May 30, 1805); *Léonce ou Le Fils adoptif* (Nov. 18, 1805); *La Prise de Passaw* (Feb. 8, 1806); *Idala ou La Sultane* (July 30, 1806); *Les Rendez-vous bourgeois* (May 9, 1807); *Les Créanciers ou Le Remède à la goutte* (Dec. 10, 1807); *Un Jour à Paris ou La Leçon singulière* (May 24, 1808); *Cimarosa* (June 28, 1808); *La Victime des arts* (Feb. 27, 1811; in collaboration with Solie and Berton Fils); *La Fête au village* (March 31, 1811); *Le Billet de loterie* (Sept. 14, 1811); *Le Magicien sans magic* (Nov.

4, 1811); *Lully et Quinault* (Nov. 27, 1812); *Les Français à Venise* (June 14, 1813); *Bayard à Mézières ou Le Siège de Mézières* (Feb. 12, 1814; in collaboration with Boieldieu, Catel, and Cherubini); *Joconde ou Les Coureurs d'aventures* (Feb. 28, 1814); *Jeannot et Colin* (Oct. 17, 1814); *Les Deux Maris* (March 18, 1816); *L'Une pour l'autre ou L'Enlèvement* (May 11, 1816). OTHER: *L'avviso ai maritati*, opera (Florence, 1794); *Artaserse*, opera (Livorno, 1794); *Rinaldo d'Asti*, opera (Malta, c.1796); *Il Barbiere di Siviglia*, opera buffa (Malta, c.1796); *L'improvisata in campagna*, opera buffa (Malta, 1797; rev. as *L'impromptu de campagne*, June 30, 1801); *I due avari*, opera buffa (Malta, c.1797); *Ginevra di Scozia*, opera (Malta, c.1798); *Il Barone d'Alba chiara*, opera (Malta, c.1798); *Flaminius à Corinthe*, opera (Feb. 27, 1801; in collaboration with Kreutzer); *Michel-Ange*, opera (Dec. 11, 1802); *Cendrillon*, opéra-féerie (Feb. 22, 1810); *Le Prince de Catane*, opera (March 4, 1813); *Aladin ou La Lampe merveilleuse*, opera (Feb. 6, 1822; completed by A. Benincori).

BIBL.: E. Wahl, *N. I.: Sein Leben und sein Schaffen auf dem Gebiet der Opéra Comique* (Munich, 1906).

Israel, Brian M., American composer, pianist, and teacher; b. N.Y., Feb. 5, 1951; d. Syracuse, N.Y., May 8, 1986. He wrote an opera before he was 8, and received BMI student composer awards in 1966 and 1968. He pursued training in composition with Kay at Lehman College in New York (B.A., 1971) and with Palmer, Phillips, and Husa at Cornell Univ. (M.F.A., 1974; D.M.A., 1975), where he was on the faculty (1972–75). In 1975 he began teaching at Syracuse Univ., and in 1984 was made a prof. there. As a pianist, he performed much contemporary music. At the time of his death from leukemia, he was at the height of his compositional creativity. His works form an eclectic traversal from Baroque contrapuntal devices to serialism, juxtaposing humor and grotesqueries. He wrote extensively for concert band and frequently featured lesser used instruments in solos.

WORKS: OPERAS: *Ladies' Voices*, mini-opera (1970); *The Obtaining of Portia*, chamber opera (Bloomington, Ind., April 13, 1976); *Love and Other Important Nonsense* (1977); *Winnie the Pooh*, children's opera (Syracuse, June 1, 1979).

Istel, Edgar, eminent German musicologist; b. Mainz, Feb. 23, 1880; d. Miami, Fla., Dec. 17, 1948. He studied composition with Volbach in Mainz, and then took courses with Thuille at the Munich Hochschule für Musik and Sandberger at the Univ. of Munich (Ph.D., 1900, with the diss. *J. J. Rousseau als Komponist seiner lyrischen Scene "Pygmalion,"* publ. in *Publikationen der Internationalen Musikgesellschaft*, I/i, Leipzig, 1901). He was active as a lecturer, critic, and writer on music in Munich (1900–13), and then taught at Berlin's Humboldt Academy (1913–19) and Lessing Hochschule (1919–20). In 1920 he moved to Madrid, where he remained until the outbreak of the civil war in 1936; he then went to England, and eventually to the United States (1938). He was also a composer, numbering 5 operas, oratorios, and smaller pieces among his works.

WRITINGS: *Das deutsche Weihnachtsspiel und seine Wiedergeburt aus dem Geiste der Musik* (1901); *Richard Wagner im Lichte eines zeitgenössischen Briefwechsels* (1902); *Peter Cornelius* (1906); *Die Entstehung des deutschen Melodramas* (1906); *Die komische Oper* (1906); *Die Blütezeit der musikalischen Romantik in Deutschland* (1909); *Das Kunstwerk Richard Wagners* (1910); *Das Libretto* (1914; Eng. tr., 1922, as *The Art of Writing Opera Librettos*); *Die moderne Oper vom Tode Wagners bis zum Weltkrieg* (1915); *Niccolò Paganini* (1919); *Revolution und Oper* (1919); *Das Buch der Oper* (1919); *Die deutschen Meister von Gluck bis Wagner* (1919); *Bizet und Carmen* (1927).

Ito, Ryûta, Japanese composer; b. Kure, March 4, 1922. He graduated from the faculty of medicine of the Univ. of Tokyo in 1946 (Doctor of Medical Science, 1955), then studied composition with Takata, Moroi, Ikenouchi, and Fukai. Subsequently he divided his interests between music and medicine and became a prof. of pharmacy at the school of medicine of Toho Univ.; he also served as secretary and a member of the committee of the Japanese Soc. for Contemporary Music (1952–61). Among his works is the chamber opera *The Court of Judgment* (1954).

Ivanov, Nikolai (Kuzmich), Russian tenor; b. Voronezh, Oct. 22, 1810; d. Bologna, July 19, 1880. He sang as a child in the Imperial Court Chapel in St. Petersburg, where he attracted the attention of Glinka, who took him to Italy in 1830; he studied with Bianchi in Milan and with Josephine Fodor-Mainvielle and Nozzari in Naples. He made his debut at the Teatro San Carlo in Naples in 1832 as Percy in Donizetti's *Anna Bolena*; subsequently he sang in Paris at the Théâtre-Italien (1833–37) and concurrently appeared in London. Later he was a member of La Scala in Milan. He retired in 1852. He was reputed to be one of the best representatives of the Italian school of bel canto, and enjoyed the friendship of Rossini and other famous contemporaries.

Ivanov-Boretzky, Mikhail Vladimirovich, Russian musicologist and composer; b. Moscow, June 16, 1874; d. there, April 1, 1936. He studied jurisprudence at the Univ. of Moscow, graduating in 1896; at the same time, he took music lessons, and, in 1898, went to St. Petersburg and became a student of composition of Rimsky-Korsakov. From 1921 to 1936 he taught at the Moscow Cons. His music was mainly imitative of Rimsky-Korsakov's works. He wrote the operas *Adolfina* (Moscow, Dec. 10, 1908) and *The Witch* (Moscow, Aug. 14, 1918). His importance to Russian music, however, lies in his writings. He publ. monographs on Palestrina, Handel, Schumann, Mendelssohn, and Beethoven, as well as a useful anthology of music history, with a synoptic table of 18th-century music (Moscow, 1934). A collection of his articles was publ. in Moscow in 1972.

Ivogün, Maria (real name, **Ilse Kempner**), esteemed Hungarian soprano; b. Budapest, Nov. 18, 1891; d. Beatenberg, Switzerland, Oct. 2, 1987. Her mother was the singer Ida von Günther. She studied voice with Schlemmer-Ambros in Vienna, then with Schöner in Munich, where she made her debut as Mimi at the Bavarian Court Opera (1913). She became renowned there for her portrayal of Zerbinetta, and also created the role of Ighino in Pfitzner's *Palestrina* (1917). In 1925 she joined the Berlin Städtische Oper; she also made guest appearances with the touring German Opera Co. in the United States (1923), at the Chicago Opera (1923), at London's Covent Garden (1924, 1927), and at the Salzburg Festivals (1925, 1930). She gave her farewell performance as Zerbinetta at the Berlin Städtische Oper (1934). She was subsequently active as a teacher, later serving on the faculties of the Vienna Academy of Music (1948–50) and the Berlin Hochschule für Musik (1950–58); her most celebrated pupil was Elisabeth Schwarzkopf. She was married to **Karl Erb** (1921–32), then to her accompanist Michael Raucheisen (from 1933). Among her other notable roles were Constanze, the Queen of the Night, Norina, Gilda, and Oscar.

Ivry, Richard d', French composer; b. Beaune, Feb. 4, 1829; d. Hyères, Dec. 18, 1903. He studied music as an avocation. He wrote mostly for the stage, numbering among his works several grand operas, including *Les Amants de Vérone*, after *Romeo and Juliet* (Paris, Oct. 12, 1878), and *Fatma, Omphale et Pénélope*. He used the anagram Yrvid as a nom de plume.

Iwaki, Hiroyuki, Japanese conductor; b. Tokyo, Sept. 6, 1932. He received training in percussion at the Academy of Music and in conducting from Saito and Watanabe (1951–54) at the Univ. of Arts in Tokyo. In 1954 he became assistant conductor of the NHK (Japanese Broadcasting Corp.) Sym. Orch. in Tokyo, serving as its principal resident conductor from 1969. From 1965 to 1967 he was also music director of the Fujiwara Opera Co., and from 1974 chief conductor of the Melbourne Sym. Orch. In 1988 he was named music director of the new Orchestra-Ensemble Kanazawa, but continued to hold his post with the NHK Sym. Orch. As a guest conductor, he appeared throughout the Far East, Europe, and North America.

J

Jachimecki, Zdzislaw, eminent Polish musicologist; b. Lemberg, July 7, 1882; d. Kraków, Oct. 27, 1953. He studied music with Niewiadomski and Jarecki in Lemberg, then musicology with Adler at the Univ. of Vienna (Ph.D., 1906, with the diss. *Psalmy Mikolaja Gomólki*, publ. in an abr. ed., Kraków, 1907); he also studied composition with Grädener and Schoenberg in Vienna and completed his Habilitation at the Univ. of Kraków in 1911 with his *Wplywy wloskie w muzyce polskiej cześč I. 1540–1560* (The Influence of Italian Music on Polish Music, Part 1, 1540–1560; publ. in Kraków, 1911); he then was a lecturer in music history there, later being made a reader (1917) and a prof. (1921); he was also a guest lecturer at many European univs. He conducted sym. concerts in Kraków (1908–24), and composed a number of orch. pieces and songs. Among his writings is *Ryszard Wagner: Zycie i twórczošč* (Richard Wagner: Life and Works; Lemberg, 1911; 2d ed., aug., 1922; 4th ed., 1973).

Jachino, Carlo, Italian composer; b. San Remo, Feb. 3, 1887; d. Rome, Dec. 23, 1971. He studied with Luporini in Lucca and then with Riemann in Leipzig (1909–10). He taught in Parma (1928–33), Naples (1933–38), and Rome (1938–51). After serving as director of the conservatories in Naples (1951–53) and Bogotá, Colombia (1953–56), he was artistic director of the Teatro San Carlo in Naples (1961–69). He publ. *Tecnica dodecafonica* (Milan, 1948) and *Gli strumenti d'orchestra* (Milan, 1950). In his early compositions he followed the Romantic Italian style; after adopting a modified 12-tone method, he finally returned to tonality in his last years. Among his works is the opera *Giocondo e il suo re* (1915–21; Milan, June 24, 1924).

Jacobi, Frederick, American composer, conductor, and teacher; b. San Francisco, May 4, 1891; d. N.Y., Oct. 24, 1952. He was a student of Gallico, Joseffy, Goldmark, and Bloch in New York, and of Juon at the Berlin Hochschule für Musik. After studying the music of the Pueblo Indians in New Mexico and Arizona, he returned to New York and taught harmony at the Master School of the United Arts (1924–36) and composition at the Juilliard Graduate School (1936–50). He also served as director of the American section of the ISCM, and actively promoted the cause of contemporary American music. In 1945 he received the David Bispham Award for his opera *The Prodigal Son* (1943–44). In some of his works, he made use of native American Indian themes. However, his music as a whole was characterized by an assured usage of Classical and Romantic idioms.

Jacobi, Georg, German violinist, conductor, and composer; b. Berlin, Feb. 13, 1840; d. London, Sept. 13, 1906. He studied violin with Eduard and Leopold Ganz in Berlin, Beriot in Brussels (1849–52), and Massart at the Paris Cons. (1852) and also composition there with Reber, Gevaert, and Cheri. After graduating with a premier prix in violin (1861) he played in the orchs. of the Opéra Comique (1861–63) and the Opéra (1863–69); he then was conductor of the Bouffes-Parisiens (1869–71). He subsequently settled in London as conductor of the Alhambra Theatre (1871–98), then conducted at the Crystal Palace and also taught at the Royal College of Music (from 1896). He wrote a comic opera, *The Black Crook*, which attained temporary popularity, as well as 103 ballets and divertissements.

Jacobs, Arthur (David), English music critic, editor, writer on music, and translator; b. Manchester, June 14, 1922; d. Oxford, Dec. 13, 1996. He studied at Merton College, Oxford. He was music critic for the *Daily Express* (1947–52) and deputy ed. of the journal *Opera* (1960–71). He was a prof. at the Royal Academy of Music in London (1964–79) and head of the music dept. at Huddersfield Polytechnic (1979–84); he also ed. the British Music Yearbook (1971–80). An accomplished linguist, he prepared admirable trs. of some 20 operas into English; he also wrote the libretto for Maw's opera *One Man Show* (1964).

WRITINGS: *Gilbert and Sullivan* (London, 1951); *A New Dictionary of Music* (Harmondsworth, 1958; new ed., rev., 1978 as *The New Penguin Dictionary of Music*; 6th ed., rev., 1996); with S. Sadie, *The Pan Book of Opera* (London, 1964; rev. ed., 1972, as *Opera: A Modern Guide*; new ed., 1984); *A Short History of Western Music* (Harmondsworth, 1972); *Arthur Sullivan: A Victorian Musician* (Oxford, 1984; 2d ed., rev. and enl., 1992); *The*

Pan Book of Orchestral Music (London, 1988); *The Penguin Dictionary of Musical Performers* (Harmondsworth, 1990); *Henry J. Wood: Maker of the Proms* (London, 1994).

Jacobs, René, noted Belgian countertenor and conductor; b. Ghent, Oct. 30, 1946. He pursued training in philology at the Univ. of Ghent, then studied voice with Louis Devos in Brussels and Lucie Frateur in The Hague; subsequently he pursued an international career as a performer with various early-music groups, as an opera singer, and as a recitalist; he also taught at the Schola Cantorum Basiliensis in Basel. He has been particularly successful in works by Cavalli, Monteverdi, Charpentier, Gluck, and Handel. As a conductor, he was active with his own Collegium Vocale. He conducted his own eds. of Cavalli's *Giasone* at the Innsbruck Festival in 1988 and of Monteverdi's *L'Orfeo* at the Salzburg Festival in 1993. He is the author of *La Controverse sur le timbre de contre-ténor* (1985).

Jacquillat, Jean-Pierre, French conductor; b. Versailles, July 13, 1935; d. in an automobile accident in Chambo-sur-Lignon, Aug. 6, 1986. He was educated at the Paris Cons., winning premiers prix in harmony, percussion, and piano; he also studied conducting with Munch, Cluytens, and Dervaux. He was assistant conductor (1967) and assoc. conductor (1968) of the Orch. de Paris; he toured with it in the Soviet Union, North America, and Mexico. In 1970 he was named resident conductor and music director of the Angers Phil.; in 1971 he became permanent conductor of the Lyons Opera and the Rhône-Alpes Phil.; he then was resident conductor and music adviser to the Lamoureux Orch. in Paris (1975–78) and subsequently he was chief conductor of the Iceland Sym. Orch. in Reykjavík (1980–86).

Jadlowker, Hermann, distinguished Latvian tenor; b. Riga, July 17, 1877; d. Tel Aviv, May 13, 1953. He studied with J. Gänsbacher at the Vienna Cons. He made his operatic debut as Gomez in *Nachtlager von Granada* in Cologne (1897); after appearances in Königsberg, Stettin, Rostock, and Riga, he sang in Karlsruhe (1906–10) and at Berlin's Kroll Opera (from 1907). He made his Metropolitan Opera debut in New York as Gounod's Faust (Jan. 22, 1910), and sang there until 1912; he also sang in Boston (1910–12), and at the Berlin Royal Opera (1911–12). He created the role of Bacchus in Richard Strauss's *Ariadne auf Naxos* (Stuttgart, Oct. 25, 1912). After guest appearances in Europe and a period with the Berlin State Opera (1922–23), he served as chief cantor of the Riga synagogue (1929–38) and taught at the Riga Cons. (1936–38); he then settled in Tel Aviv as a teacher.

Jaffee, Michael, American early-music performer and instrument builder; b. N.Y., April 21, 1938. He studied music at N.Y. Univ. (B.A., 1959; M.A., 1963), and learned to play the guitar. While still a student, he married Kay Cross (b. Lansing, Mich., Dec. 31, 1937), a keyboard player, in 1961. Their interest in early music led Michael to master the lute and Kay the recorder; they subsequently organized the Waverly Consort, a group dedicated to performances of music from the medieval and Renaissance eras using period instruments and costumes; the group made its formal debut at N.Y.'s Carnegie Hall in 1966. The two founders became highly proficient on a variety of instruments or copies, many of which they built themselves. The Waverly Consort toured extensively, becoming one of the most successful early-music groups in the United States.

Jagel, Frederick, American tenor and teacher; b. Brooklyn, June 10, 1897; d. San Francisco, July 5, 1982. He sang in local choirs as a youth and later appeared as a tenor soloist. After training from William Brady in New York, he completed his studies in Milan. In 1924 he made his operatic debut under the name Federico Jeghelli in Livorno as Rodolfo, and then appeared throughout Italy and with an Italian opera company in the Netherlands. On Nov. 8, 1927, he made his Metropolitan Opera debut in New York as Radamès, and remained on its roster until 1950. Among his prominent roles there were Alfredo, the Duke of Mantua, Cavaradossi, Turiddu, Pinkerton, Pollione, and Peter Grimes. He also appeared in Buenos Aires (1928; 1939–41), San Francisco (debut as Jack Rance, 1930), Chicago (debut as Lohengrin, 1934), and at the N.Y. City Opera (debut as Herod, 1947). From 1949 to 1970 he taught voice at the New England Cons. of Music in Boston.

Jahn, Wilhelm, Austrian conductor and opera adminstrator; b. Hof, Moravia, Nov. 24, 1834; d. Vienna, April 21, 1900. At the age of 20 he became a theater conductor in Budapest, then occupied similar posts in Agram, Amsterdam, and Prague. He was in Wiesbaden (1864–80). He was music director of the Vienna Court Opera (1880) and conductor of the Vienna Phil. (1882–83). Jahn retired in 1897, and was succeeded by Mahler.

Jalas (real name, **Blomstedt**), **Jussi,** Finnish conductor; b. Jyväskylä, June 23, 1908. He studied at the Helsinki Cons. and with Ilmari Krohn at the Univ. of Helsinki; he later studied in Paris with Rhené-Baton and Monteux. He was active as a theater conductor in Helsinki (1930–45); subsequently he conducted at the Finnish National Opera there, serving as its music director until 1973; he also made guest conducting appearances throughout Europe, the United States, and Japan. He was highly regarded as an interpreter of the music of **Sibelius**, his father-in-law; he also excelled in performances of 20th-century works, ranging from Puccini to Shostakovich.

James, Dorothy, American composer and teacher; b. Chicago, Dec. 1, 1898; d. St. Petersburg, Fla., Dec. 1, 1982. She was a student of Gruenberg and Weidig at the Chicago Musical College and the American Cons. of Music in Chicago (M.M., 1927), of Hanson at the Eastman School of Music in Rochester, N.Y., of Willan in Toronto, and of Krenek at the Univ. of Mich. In 1927 she joined the faculty of Eastern Michigan Univ. in Ypsilanti, where she was later a prof. (1962–68); she also was music critic of the *Ypsilanti Press*. She was the author of *Music of Living Women Composers* (1976). Her compositions display fine craftsmanship, particularly her choral works. She also composed an opera, *Paola and Francesca* (partial concert perf., Rochester, N.Y., April 2, 1931).

James, (Mary) Frances, Canadian soprano and teacher; b. Saint John, New Brunswick, Feb. 3, 1903; d. Victoria, British Columbia, Aug. 22, 1988. She studied with Walter Clapperton at the McGill Cons. in Montreal, and with Emmy Hein at the Toronto Cons. of Music (1934), then was a student of Jeanne Dusseau (1936), had lessons with Enrico Rosati and Maria Kurenko in New York, and worked with Roland Hayes in Boston. She became well known to Canadian audiences via radio, and as a soloist and recitalist; in 1940 she made her first appearance in the United States. From 1952 to 1973 she taught at the Univ. of Saskatchewan, and then in Victoria at the Cons. of Music and at the Univ. In 1931 she married **Murray Adaskin**. She was especially admired for her championship of the 20th-century vocal repertoire.

BIBL.: G. Lazarevich, *The Musical World of F. J. and Murray Adaskin* (Toronto, 1987).

Janáček, Leoš, greatly significant Czech composer; b. Hukvaldy, Moravia, July 3, 1854; d. Moravská Ostrava, Aug. 12, 1928. At the age of 11, he was sent to Brno to serve as a chorister at the Augustinian Queen's Monastery, where he was schooled under its choirmaster, Křízkovský. After studies at the German College he was a scholarship student at the teacher's training college (1869–72). He then began his teaching career while serving as choirmaster at the monastery; he also served as choirmaster of the men's chorus, Svatopluk (1873–77), taking an opportunity to study organ with Skuherský at the Prague Organ School (1874–75). He conducted the Beseda Choral Soc. in Brno (1876–88), and also pursued studies at the Leipzig Cons., where he took music history courses with Oskar Paul and composition courses with Leo Grill (1879–80). He continued his composition studies with Franz Krenn at the Vienna Cons. (1880). Returning to Brno, he was appointed the first director of the new organ school (1881). His social position in Brno was enhanced by his marriage to Zdenka Schulzová, the daughter of the director of the teachers' training college. He also engaged in scholarly activities; from 1884 to 1886 he was ed. of the music journal *Hudební Listy* (Music Bulletins); he further became associated with František Bartoš in collecting Moravian folk songs. From 1886 to 1902 he taught music at the Brno Gymnasium. In 1919 he retired from his directorship of the Brno Organ School, and then taught master classes in Brno (1920–25). Throughout all these busy years, he worked diligently on his compositions, showing particular preference for operas.

Janáček's style of composition underwent numerous transformations, from Romantic techniques of established formulas to bold dissonant combinations. He was greatly influenced by the Russian musical nationalism exemplified by the "realistic" speech inflections in vocal writing. He visited St. Petersburg and Moscow in 1896 and 1902, and publ. his impressions of the tour in the Brno press. From 1894 to 1903 he worked assiduously on his most important opera, *Její pastorkyňa* (Her Foster Daughter), to a highly dramatic libretto set in Moravia in the mid-19th century, involving a jealous contest between 2 brothers for the hand of Jenůfa (the innocent heroine), and infanticide at the hands of a foster mother, with an amazing outcome absolving Jenůfa and her suitors. The opera encountered great difficulty in securing production in Prague because of its grisly subject, but was eventually produced on various European stages, mostly in the German text, and under the title *Jenůfa*. Another opera by Janáček that attracted attention was *Výlet pana Broučka do XV stoleti* (Mr. Brouček's Excursion to the 15th Century), depicting the imaginary travel of a Czech patriot to the time of the religious struggle mounted by the followers of the nationalist leader Hus against the established church. There followed an operatic fairy tale, *Příhody Lišky Bystroušky* (The Adventures of the Vixen Bystrouška, or The Cunning Little Vixen), and a mystery play, *Věc Makropulos* (The Makropulos Affair). Janáček's great interest in Russian literature was reflected in his opera *Kát'a Kabanová*, after the drama *The Storm* by the Russian playwright Ostrovsky, and one after Dostoyevsky, *Z mrtvého domu* (From the House of the Dead). He further composed a symphonic poem, *Taras Bulba* (the fictional name of a Ukrainian patriot, after a story by Gogol). In 1917 Janáček became enamored of Kamila Stösslová, the 26-year-old wife of an antique dealer. His unconsummated love for her proved an inspiration and led to the composition of several major works by an aging composer. Like most artists, writers, and composers of Slavic origin in the old Austro-Hungarian Empire, Janáček had a natural interest in the Pan-Slavic movement, with an emphasis on the common origins of Russian, Czech, Slovak, and other kindred cultures; his *Glagolitic Mass*, to a Latin text tr. into the Czech language, is an example. Janáček lived to witness the fall of the old Austrian regime and the national rise of the Slavic populations. He also showed great interest in the emerging Soviet school of composition, even though he refrained from any attempt to join that movement. Inevitably, he followed the striking innovations of the modern school of composition as set forth in the works of Stravinsky and Schoenberg, but he was never tempted to experiment along those revolutionary lines. He remained faithful to his own well-defined style, and it was as the foremost composer of modern Czech music that he secured for himself his unique place in history.

WORKS: DRAMATIC: OPERAS: *Šárka* (1887–88; rev. 1918–19, with Act 3 orchestrated by O. Chlubna; rev. 1924–25; Brno, Nov. 11, 1925); *Počátek romanu* (The Beginning of a Romance; 1891; Brno, Feb. 10, 1894); *Její pastorkyňa* (Her Foster Daughter; generally known by its German title, *Jenůfa*; 1894–1903; Brno, Jan. 21, 1904; several subsequent revisions, including final version by K. Kovařovic, 1916; Prague, May 26, 1916); *Osud* (Fate; 1903–05; rev. 1906–07; 1st complete perf., Brno Radio, Sept. 18, 1934; 1st stage perf., National Theater, Brno, Oct. 25, 1958); *Výlet pana Broučka do měsíce* (Mr. Brouček's Excursion to the Moon; 1908–17; National Theater, Prague, April 23, 1920); a sequel to the preceding, *Výlet pana Broučka do XV stoleti* (Mr. Brouček's Excursion to the 15th Century; 1917; National Theater, Prague, April 23, 1920); *Kát'a Kabanová* (1919–21; Brno, Nov. 23, 1921); *Příhody Lišky Bystroušky* (The Adventures of the Vixen Bystrouška; The Cunning Little Vixen; 1921–23; Brno, Nov. 6, 1924); *Věc Makropulos* (The Makropulos Affair; 1923–25; Brno, Dec. 18, 1926); *Z mrtvého domu* (From the House of the Dead; 1927–28; rev. and reorchestrated by O. Chlubna and B. Bakala, 1930; Brno, April 12, 1930). FOLK BALLET: *Rákos Rákoczy* (National Theater, Prague, July 24, 1891).

WRITINGS: J. Vysloužil, ed., *O lidové písni a lidové hudbě* (Folk Song and Folk Music; Prague, 1955); Z. Blaček, ed., *Hudebně teoretické dilo* (Music Theory Works; 2 vols., Prague, 1968, 1974); M. Boyars, ed., *J.'s Uncollected Essays on Music* (London and N.Y., 1989).

BIBL.: SOURCE MATERIAL: His correspondence was ed. by A. Rektorys and J. Rocek (9 vols., Prague, 1934–53); J. Rocek, ed., *L. J.: Obraz života a dila* (L. J.: A Picture of His Life and Works; Brno, 1948); B. Štědroň, *L. J. v obrazech* (L. J. in Pictures; Prague, 1958); idem, *Dilo Leoše Janáčka: Abecedni seznam Janáčkových skladeb a úprav* (L. J.'s Works: An Alphabetical Catalog of J.'s Compositions and Arrangements; Prague, 1959; Eng. tr., 1959, as *The Work of L. J.*); T. Strakova, ed., *Iconographia janáčkiana* (Brno, 1975); N. Simeone, *The First Editions of L. J.: A Bibliographical Catalogue, with Reproductions of Title Pages* (Tutzing, 1991); M. Beckerman and G. Bauer, eds., *Proceedings of the International Conference on J. and Czech Music* (Stuyvesant, N.Y., 1993); J. Tyrrell, ed. and tr., *Intimate Letters: L. J. to Kamila Stösslová* (Princeton, N.J., 1994). BIOGRAPHICAL: M. Brod, *L. J.: Život a dilo* (L. J.: Life and Works; Prague, 1924; Ger. ed., 1925; 2d ed., rev., 1956); D. Muller, *L. J.* (Paris, 1930); A. Vašek, *Po stopách dra Leoše Janáčka* (On the Track of Dr. L. J.; Brno, 1930); H. Kašlik, *L. J. dirigent* (Prague, 1936); O. Jeremiáš, *L. J.* (Prague, 1938); V. Helfert, *L. J.* (Brno, 1939); idem, *O Janáčkovi* (About J.; ed. by B. Štědroň, Prague, 1949); H. Richter, *L. J.* (Leipzig, 1958); J. Vogel, *L. J.: Leben und Werk* (Kassel, 1958; Eng. tr., 1962; 2d ed., rev., 1980); J. Šeda, *L. J.* (Prague, 1961); J. Racek, *L. J.: Mensch und Künstler* (Leipzig, 1962; 2d ed., 1971; Czech ed., 1963); H. Hollander, *L. J.* (London, 1963; Ger. ed., 1964); M. Černohorská, *L. J.* (in Eng.; Prague, 1966); B. Štědroň, *L. J.: K jeho lidskému a uměleckému profilu* (L. J.'s Image as Man and Artist; Brno, 1976); J. Vysloužil, *L. J.* (Brno, 1978); I. Horsbrugh, *L. J.* (Newton Abbot, 1981); K. Honolka, *L. J.: Sein Leben, sein Werk, seine Zeit* (Stuttgart, 1982); S. Přibáňová, *L. J.* (Prague, 1984); C. Susskind, *J. and Brod* (London, 1986); F. Pulcini, *J.: Vita, opere, scritti* (Florence, 1993). CRITICAL, ANALYTICAL: L. Firkušný, *Odkaz Leoše Janáčka české opeře* (L. J.'s Legacy to Czech Opera; Brno, 1939); B. Štědroň, *Zur Genesis von L. J.s Oper Jenůfa* (Brno, 1968; 2d ed., 1971); A. Tučapský, *Mužské sbory Leoše Janáčka a jejich interpretačni tradice* (L. J.'s Male Voice Choruses and Their Performance Tradition; Ostrava, 1968); E. Chisholm, *The Operas of L. J.* (Oxford, 1971); T. Kneif, *Die Bühnenwerke von L. J.* (Vienna, 1974); A. Geck, *Das Volksliedmaterial L. J.s: Analysen der Strukturen unter Einbeziehung von J.s Randbemerkungen und Volkstudien* (Regensburg, 1975); D. Ströbel, *Motiv und Figur in den Kompositionen der Jenufa-Werkgruppe* (Freiburg, 1975); M. Ewans, *J.'s Tragic Operas* (London, 1977); J. Tyrrell, ed., *J.'s Operas: A Documentary Account* (Princeton, N.J., 1992); M. Beckerman, *J. as Theorist* (Stuyvesant, N.Y., 1993).

Jander, Owen (Hughes), American musicologist; b. Mount Kisco, N.Y., June 4, 1930. He was educated at the Univ. of Virginia (B.A., 1951) and Harvard Univ. (M.A., 1952; Ph.D., 1962, with the diss. *The Works of Alessandro Stradella Related to the Cantata and the Opera*). In 1960 he joined the dept. of music at Wellesley College, where he later became the Catherine Mills Davis Prof. in Music History; he was founder of its Collegium Musicum for the performance of early music and also initiated the project to construct the outstanding Fisk Organ there for the performance of the pre-Bach repertoire; also served as ed. of the Wellesley Edition and the Wellesley Edition Cantata Index Series (1962–74). In 1966–67 he held a Guggenheim fellowship, and in 1985 he received an NEH Fellowship for Senior Scholars. He initially devoted himself to 17th-century Italian music, but later turned to Beethoven. He contributed numerous articles to *The New Grove Dictionary of Music and Musicians* (1980), and also served as coed. of *Charles Benton Fisk: Organ Builder* (2 vols., 1986).

Jankélévitch, Vladimir, French philosopher and writer on music; b. Bourges, Aug. 31, 1903; d. Paris, June 6, 1985. He was educated in Paris at the School of Oriental Languages and at the École Normale Supérieure; received a degree in philosophy in 1925 and the doctorat es lettres in 1933. He was a prof. of philosophy at the Institut de Prague (1927–33), then at the univs. of Lille (1933–39; 1945–52) and Toulouse (1939–45); he was a prof. of ethics and moral philosophy at the Sorbonne in Paris (1952–78). His writings on music reflect his philosophical bent; these include *Gabriel Fauré et ses mélodies* (Paris, 1938; 2d ed., aug., 1951, as *Gabriel Fauré: Ses mélodies, son esthétique*); *Maurice Ravel* (Paris, 1939; 2d ed., aug., 1956, as *Ravel*); *Debussy et le mystère* (Neuchâtel, 1949); *La Rhapsodie, verve et improvisation musicale* (Paris, 1955); *Le Nocturne: Fauré: Chopin et la nuit: Satie et le matin* (Paris, 1957); *La Musique et l'ineffable* (Paris, 1961; 2d ed., 1983); *La Vie et la mort dans la musique de Debussy* (Neuchâtel, 1968); *Fauré et l'inexprimable* (Paris, 1974); *Debussy et le mystère de l'instant* (Paris, 1976); with B. Berlowitz, *Quelque part dans l'inachevé, Moussorgsky, Liszt, Bartók, Chopin...* (Paris, 1978); *Liszt et la rhapsodie: Essai sur la virtuosité* (Paris, 1979); *La Présence lointaine, Albéniz, Severac, Mompou* (Paris, 1983).

BIBL.: L. Jerphagnon, *J.* (Paris, 1969).

Janků, Hana, Czech soprano; b. Brno, Oct. 25, 1940; d. Vienna, April 28, 1995. She studied with Jaroslav Kvapil in Brno, making her operatic debut there as the Countess in Novák's *Lucerna* in 1959; she later sang with the Prague National Theater Opera. She made her first appearance at Milan's La Scala in 1967 as Turandot; appeared regularly at the Deutsche Oper am Rhein in Düsseldorf and the Deutsche Oper in West Berlin (from 1970). In 1973 she sang Tosca at her Covent Garden debut in London. She also made guest appearances at the Vienna State Opera, the Bavarian State Opera in Munich, the Hamburg State Opera, the San Francisco Opera, and the Teatro Colón in Buenos Aires. In addition to the Czech repertory, she was also known for such roles as Gioconda, Elsa, Kundry, Desdemona, and Ariadne.

Janowitz, Gundula, esteemed German soprano; b. Berlin, Aug. 2, 1937. She studied with Herbert Thöny at the Graz Cons. She made her formal operatic debut as Barbarina at the Vienna State Opera (1959), and later became one of its leading members; she also sang at the Bayreuth Festival (1960–63) and the Salzburg Festival (from 1963); she was a member of the Frankfurt am Main Opera (1963–66), then joined the Deutsche Oper in West Berlin. She appeared at the Glyndebourne Festival (1964); she sang at Karajan's Salzburg Easter Festival (1967–68). She made her Metropolitan Opera debut in New York as Sieglinde on Nov. 21, 1967. She was chosen to sing the role of Mozart's Countess at the reopening of the Paris Opéra in 1973; she subsequently made her debut at London's Covent Garden as Donna Anna (1976). She was made an Austrian Kammersängerin in 1970. In 1990–91 she was director of the Graz-Steiermark Theater. Her other notable roles included Fiordiligi, Agathe, Eva, Aida, Elisabeth, Desdemona, and Ariadne. She was also well known as a concert and lieder artist.

Janowski, Marek, esteemed Polish-born German conductor; b. Warsaw, Feb. 18, 1939. He was taken to Germany while young; he studied mathematics and music at the Univ. of Cologne; he continued his musical studies in Vienna and at the Accademia Musicale Chigiana in Siena. He conducted sym. concerts in Italy, and then opera in Aachen and Cologne; he subsequently held the post of 1st conductor at the Deutsche Oper am Rhein in Düsseldorf (1964–69) and at the Hamburg State Opera (1969–74); he also made guest appearances in Stuttgart, Cologne, and Munich. In 1969 he made his English debut conducting the visiting Cologne Opera in the British premiere of Henze's *Der junge Lord*. From 1973 to 1975 he was chief conductor in Freiburg im Breisgau, and from 1975 to 1979 Generalmusikdirektor in Dortmund. He made his U.S. debut conducting *Lohengrin* at the Chicago Lyric Opera in 1980. He was principal guest conductor (1980–83) and artistic advisor (1983–86) of the Royal Liverpool Phil.; he was also chief conductor of the Nouvel Orch. Philharmonique de Radio France in Paris (from 1984) and of the Gürzenich Orch. in Cologne (1986–91).

Janson, Alfred, Norwegian composer and pianist; b. Oslo, March 10, 1937. His mother, a piano teacher, oversaw his early music instruction. He also learned to play the accordion and began appearing in Oslo restaurants when he was 12. He later received some instruction in composition from Finn Mortensen. In 1962 he made his debut as a pianist in Oslo, and subsequently was frequently engaged in jazz settings. After composing in a decidedly contemporary idiom, his works took on more tonal leanings. His interest in jazz and electronics also played a role in his path as a composer. Among his works are *Mot solen* (Towards the Sun), ballet (1969), *Et Fjelleventyret* (A Mountain Adventure), opera (1970–73; Oslo, April 9, 1973), and music for theater, films, and television.

Janssen, Herbert, noted German-born American baritone; b. Cologne, Sept. 22, 1892; d. N.Y., June 3, 1965. He studied in Cologne, and then with Oskar Daniel in Berlin, making his operatic debut in Schreker's *Der Schatzgräber* at the State Opera there (May 5, 1922), and remaining on its roster until 1938; he also made regular appearances at London's Covent Garden (1926–39) and at the Bayreuth Festivals (1930–37), where he excelled in such roles as Amfortas, the Dutchman, Gunther, Kurwenal, and Wolfram. He made his Metropolitan Opera debut as Wotan during the company's visit to Philadelphia (Jan. 24, 1939); his formal debut with the company followed in New York as Wolfram (Jan. 28, 1939); he continued as a prominent member on its roster until 1952. He became a naturalized American citizen in 1946. In later years he was active as a voice teacher. He was also well known for his portrayal of Kothner.

Janssens, Jean-François-Joseph, Belgian composer; b. Antwerp, Jan. 29, 1801; d. there, Feb. 3, 1835. He studied with his father and later with Le Sueur in Paris. Returning to Antwerp, he practiced law until the siege of 1832, composing in his leisure hours. Going to Cologne, he lost his MSS and other possessions in a fire on the night of his arrival; this misfortune so affected him that he became insane. Among his works were 4 operas.

BIBL.: E. van der Straeten, *J.-F.-J. J.: Compositeur de musique* (Brussels, 1866).

Jaques-Dalcroze, Emile, Swiss music educator and composer, creator of "Eurhythmics"; b. Vienna (of French parents), July 6, 1865; d. Geneva, July 1, 1950. In 1873 his parents moved to Geneva; having completed his courses at the Univ. and at the Cons. there, he went to Vienna for further study under Fuchs and Bruckner, then to Paris, where he studied with Delibes and Fauré; he returned to Geneva as instructor of theory at the Cons. (1892). Since he laid special stress on rhythm, he insisted that all his pupils beat time with their hands, and this led him, step by step, to devise a series of movements affecting the entire body. Together with the French psychologist Edouard Claparide, he worked out a special terminology and reduced his practice to a regular system, which he called "Eurhythmics." When his application to have his method introduced as a regular course at the Cons. was refused, he resigned, and in 1910 established his own school at Hellerau, near Dresden. As a result of World War I, the school was closed in 1914; he then returned to Geneva and founded the Institut Jaques-Dalcroze. Interest in his system led to the opening of similar schools in London, Berlin, Vienna, Paris, New York, Chicago, and other cities. Aside from his rhythmical innovations, he also commanded respect as a composer of marked originality and fecundity of invention; many of his works show how thoroughly he was imbued with the spirit of Swiss folk music.

WRITINGS: *Le coeur chante: Impressions d'un musicien* (Geneva, 1900); *Vorschläge zur Reform des musikalischen Schulunterrichts* (Zürich, 1905); *La respiration et l'innervation musculaire* (Paris, 1906); *Méthode Jaques-Dalcroze* (Paris, 1906–17); *La rythmique* (Lausanne, 1916–17); *La portée musicale* (Lausanne, n.d.); *Introduction à l'étude de l'harmonie* (Geneva, n.d.); *Le rhythme, la musique et l'education* (Paris, 1919; 2d ed., 1965;

Eng. tr., 1921; 2d ed., 1967); C. Cox, ed., *Eurhythmics, Art and Education* (London, 1930); *Rhythmics Movement* (London, 1931); *Métrique et rythmique* (Paris, 1937–38); *Souvenirs, notes et critiques* (Neuchâtel, 1942); *La musique et nous: Notes de notre double vie* (Geneva, 1945); *Notes bariolées* (Geneva, 1948).

WORKS: DRAMATIC: OPERETTA: *Riquet à la houppe* (1883). OPÉRAS COMIQUES: *Onkel Dazumal* (Cologne, 1905; as *Le Bonhomme Jadis*, Paris, 1906); *Les jumeaux de Bergame* (Brussels, 1908). COMÉDIE LYRIQUE: *Sancho Pança* (Geneva, 1897).

BIBL.: P. Boepple, *Der Rhythmus als Erziehungsmittle für das Leben und die Kunst: Sechs Vorträge von E. J.-D. zur Begründung seiner Methode der rhythmischen Gymnastik* (Basel, 1907); W. Dohrn, *Die Bildungsanstalt E. J.-D.* (Dresden, 1912); M. Sadler, *The Eurhythmics of J.-D.* (London, 1912; 3d ed., rev., 1920); K. Storck, *E. J.-D.: Seine Stellung und Aufgabe in unserer Zeit* (Stuttgart, 1912); H. Brunet-Lecomte, *J.-D.: Sa vie, son oeuvre* (Geneva, 1950); F. Martin et al., *E. J.-D.: L'Homme, le compositeur, le créateur de la rhythmique* (Neuchâtel, 1965); M.-L. Bachmann, *Le Rhythmique J.-D.: Une éducation par la musique et pour la musique* (Neuchâtel, 1984; Eng. tr., 1991, as *D. Today: An Education Through and Into Music*); I. Spector, *Rhythm and Life: The Work of E. J.-D.* (Stuyvesant, N.Y., 1990).

Jarecki, Henryk, Polish conductor and composer, father of **Tadeusz Jarecki**; b. Warsaw, Dec. 6, 1846; d. Lwów, Dec. 18, 1918. He studied composition with Moniuszko at the Warsaw Music Inst. After playing double bass in the orch. of the Wielki Theater there (1864–72), he served as conductor of the Polish Theater in Posen (1872–73); he then was deputy conductor (1873–74) and chief conductor and director (1874–1900) of the Lemberg Opera. Among his works were 9 operas.

Jarecki, Tadeusz, Polish conductor and composer, son of **Henryk Jarecki**; b. Lemberg, Dec. 31, 1888; d. N.Y., April 29, 1955. He studied with his father, then with Niewiadomski in Lemberg; subsequently went to Moscow, where he studied with Taneyev at the Cons., graduating in 1913; he also studied with Jaques-Dalcroze in Geneva (1912–13). In 1917–18 he lived in the United States; he then returned to Poland and conducted opera in Stanislawow (1932–37); after a sojourn in Paris and London, he returned to the United States in 1946. In 1921 he married the American soprano Louise Llewellyn (b. N.Y., Dec. 10, 1889; d. there, March 6, 1954). He publ. the book *The Most Polish of Polish Composers: Frédéric Chopin 1810–1849* (N.Y., 1949).

Järnefelt, (Edvard) Armas, distinguished Finnish-born Swedish conductor and composer; b. Vyborg, Aug. 14, 1869; d. Stockholm, June 23, 1958. He studied with Wegelius and Busoni at the Helsinki Cons. (1887–90), with Becker in Berlin (1890), and with Massenet in Paris (1893–94); he then was conductor of the Vyborg Municipal Orch. (1898–1903) and director of the Helsinki Music Inst. (1906–07). He became a conductor at the Royal Opera in Stockholm in 1907; he was named court conductor in 1910, the same year he became a naturalized Swedish citizen; later was chief conductor of the Royal Opera (1923–32). He subsequently was chief conductor of the Finnish National Opera in Helsinki (1932–36) and the Helsinki Phil. (1942–43). He married the soprano Maikki Pakarinen (b. Joensuu, Aug. 26, 1871; d. Turku, July 4, 1929) in 1893; they were divorced in 1908; in 1910 he married the soprano Liva Edström (b. Vänersborg, March 18, 1876; d. Stockholm, June 24, 1971). Jarnefelt was the brother-in-law of **Sibelius**. His compositions, which included the symphonic poem *Korsholma* (1894), a Symphonic Fantasy for Orch. (1895), and *Berceuse* for Small Orch. (1904), were written in the Finnish national style.

Jarno, Georg (real name, **György Kohner**), Hungarian conductor and composer; b. Budapest, June 3, 1868; d. Breslau, May 20, 1920. He worked as a theater conductor in Bremen, Halle, Metz, Chemnitz, Magdeburg, and other cities before concentrating on composing light theater scores. After bringing out such pieces as *Die schwarze Kaschka* (Breslau, May 27, 1895) and *Der Richter von Zalamea* (1899), he produced his first operetta, *Der zerbrochene Krug* (Hamburg, Jan. 15, 1903). The respectable staging of his *Der Goldfisch* (Breslau, Jan. 20, 1907) led to the notable Viennese premieres of his *Die Förster-Christl* (Dec. 17, 1907), *Das Musikantenmädel* (Feb. 18, 1910), and *Die Marinen-Gustl* (March 22, 1912). He went on to score further successes with *Das Farmermädchen* (Berlin, March 22, 1913), *Mein Annerl* (Vienna, Oct. 7, 1916), *Jungfer Sonnenschein* (Hamburg, Feb. 16, 1918), and *Die Csikós-Baroness* (Hamburg, Oct. 28, 1919).

Jarre, Maurice (Alexis), French composer; b. Lyons, Sept. 13, 1924. He studied electrical engineering before entering the Paris Cons. in 1943, where he was a student of La Presle (harmony) and Aubert (orchestration). He also profited from advice from Honegger. After working with Radiodiffusion Française (1946–50), he served as director of music at the Théâtre National Populaire in Paris (1951–63). In 1955 and 1962 he won the Prix Italia. He became especially successful as a film composer, winning Academy Awards for *Lawrence of Arabia* (1962), *Dr. Zhivago* (1965), and *A Passage to India* (1984). Among his other film scores were *The Longest Day* (1962), *Ryan's Daughter* (1970), *Shogun* (1980), and *Dead Poets Society* (1989). His other dramatic compositions include *Armida*, opéra ballet (1954), *Fâcheuse rencontre*, ballet (1958), *Loin de Rueil*, musical comedy (1961), and *Notre-Dame de Paris*, ballet (1966).

Järvi, Neeme, prominent Estonian conductor; b. Tallinn, June 7, 1937. He graduated with degrees in percussion and choral conducting from the Tallinn Music School, then studied conducting with Mravinsky and Rabinovich at the Leningrad Cons. (1955–60); he pursued postgraduate studies in 1968, and in 1971 captured 1st prize in the Accademia di Santa Cecilia conducting competition in Rome. He was active in Tallinn as music director of the Estonian State Sym. Orch. (1960–80) and of the Estonian Opera Theater (1964–77). He subsequently served as principal guest conductor of the City of Birmingham Sym. Orch. in England (1981–84). In 1982 he became music director of the Göteborg Sym. Orch. in Sweden; he also was principal conductor of the Scottish National Orch. in Glasgow (1984–88). In 1990 he became music director of the Detroit Sym. Orch. His guest conducting engagements have taken him to most of the principal music centers of the world. He has won particular notice in concert settings and on recordings for his efforts in championing such rarely performed composers as Berwald, Gade, Svendsen, Stenhammar, and Tubin.

Jedlička, Dalibor, Czech bass-baritone; b. Svojanov, May 23, 1929. He received his training from Rudolf Vašek in Ostrává. In 1953 he made his operatic debut as Mumalal in Smetana's *The 2 Widows* in Opava. In 1957 he became a member of the National Theater in Prague, where his extensive repertoire included not only standard German, Italian, and French roles but various Czech roles. He toured with the company abroad, including its visit to Edinburgh in 1970 when he sang in the first British performance of Janáček's *The Excursions of Mr. Brouček*; he also appeared as a guest artist in Amsterdam, Zürich, Warsaw, Venice, Bologna, and other cities. In 1993 he made his U.S. debut at the San Francisco Opera as Kolenaty in Janáček's *The Makropulos Affair*.

Jehin, Léon, Belgian conductor; b. Spa, July 17, 1853; d. Monte Carlo, Feb. 14, 1928. He was trained in Liège and Brussels. He conducted at the Théâtre de la Monnaie in Brussels (1882–93), the Paris Opéra (1889–93), at Covent Garden in London (1891–92), and in Monte Carlo. His wife was **(Marie-) Blanche Deschamps-Jehin**.

Jelinek, Hanns, Austrian composer; b. Vienna, Dec. 5, 1901; d. there, Jan. 27, 1969. He studied harmony and counterpoint with Schoenberg (1918–19) and piano, harmony, and counterpoint with F. Schmidt (1920–22) at the Vienna Academy of Music. Jelinek's output ranged from light music to works utilizing serial techniques. He made a living by playing piano in bars, leading his own band, and composing for films under the name Hanns Elin. He became a lecturer (1955) and a prof. (1965) at the Vienna Academy of Music. He publ. the manual *Anleitung zur Zwölfton-*

komposition (2 vols., Vienna, 1952 and 1958; 2d ed., 1967). Among his compositions is the operetta *Bubi Caligula* (1947).

Jellinek, George, Hungarian-born American writer on music and broadcaster; b. Budapest, Dec. 22, 1919. He studied violin in Hungary (1925–37). In 1941 he went to the United States and became a naturalized American citizen in 1943; he served in the U.S. Army. He was active in broadcasting; in 1968 he was named music director of radio station WQXR in New York, where he produced such popular programs as *The Vocal Scene* and *Music at First Hearing*. From 1958 he was a contributing ed. of *Stereo Review*; he also wrote articles for the *Saturday Review, Opera News*, and other publs. In 1976 he became an adjunct assistant prof. of music at N.Y. Univ. He received an honorary doctorate from Long Island Univ. in 1984. He wrote librettos for Eugene Zador's operas *The Magic Chair* and *The Scarlett Mill*. His study *Maria Callas, Portrait of a Prima Donna*, was publ. in 1960.

Jélyotte, Pierre de, French tenor and composer; b. Lasseube, April 13, 1713; d. Oloron, Oct. 12, 1797. He received training in harpsichord, cello, guitar, voice, and composition in Toulouse. In 1733 he made his operatic debut in Collin de Blamont's *Les fêtes grecques et romaines* at the Paris Opéra, where he was a leading singer from 1738 until his retirement in 1765. He was widely admired for his leading haute-contre roles in Rameau's operas, which displayed his brilliant vocal range (up to d''). He also appeared at the court, and in 1745 was named maître de guitare to the king. He likewise served as a cellist to Madame de Pompadour. Among his compositions was the comédie ballet *Zéliska* (1746), as well as several vocal pieces.

Jemnitz, Sándor (Alexander), Hungarian conductor, composer, and music critic; b. Budapest, Aug. 9, 1890; d. Balatonföldvár, Aug. 8, 1963. He studied with Koessler at the Budapest Royal Academy of Music (1906–08), then briefly with Nikisch (conducting), Reger (composition), Straube (organ), and Sitt (violin) at the Leipzig Cons. After conducting in various German opera houses (1911–13) he studied with Schoenberg in Berlin; he returned to Budapest (1916) and was music critic of *Népszava* (1924–50); he subsequently taught at the Budapest Cons. (from 1951). He publ. monographs on Mendelssohn (1958), Schumann (1958), Beethoven (1960), Chopin (1960), and Mozart (1961). As a composer, he followed the median line of Middle European modernism of the period between the 2 world wars, representing a curious compromise between the intricate contrapuntal idiom of Reger and the radical language of atonality modeled after Schoenberg's early works. He wrote mostly instrumental music, but also the ballet *Divertimento* (1921; Budapest, April 23, 1947).

Jenkins, Graeme (James Ewers), English conductor; b. London, Dec. 31, 1958. He was a chorister at Dulwich College, attended the Univ. of Cambridge, where he conducted the British premiere of *Stiffelio*, and studied conducting with Del Mar and Willcocks at the Royal College of Music in London, where he conducted student performances of *Albert Herring* and *The Turn of the Screw*. In 1982 he made his professional conducting debut with the Kent Opera with *The Beggar's Opera*. In 1986 he became music director of the Glyndebourne Touring Opera, a position he retained until 1991. He made his first appearance at the Glyndebourne Festival in 1987 conducting *Carmen*, the same year that he made his debut on the Continent in Geneva conducting *Hänsel und Gretel*. In 1988 he made his first appearance at the English National Opera in London conducting *Così fan tutte*. As a guest conductor, Jenkins has appeared with opera companies and orchs. at home and abroad. From 1992 he was music director of the Arundel Festival. In 1994 he became music director of the Dallas Opera. From 1997 he also was principal guest conductor of the Cologne Opera.

Jenkins, Speight, American opera administrator; b. Dallas, Jan. 31, 1937. He was educated at the Univ. of Texas at Austin (B.A., 1957) and at Columbia Univ. (LL.B., 1961). He was an ed. for *Opera News* (1967–73), music critic of the *N.Y. Post* (1973–81), and host for the *Live from the Met* telecasts on PBS (1981–83). In 1983 he became general director of the Seattle Opera. His tenure was highlighted with stagings of the *Ring* cycle (1986–87; 1991; 1995), Glass's *Satyagraha* (1988), Prokofiev's *War and Peace* (1990), *Pelléas et Mélisande* (1993), *Lohengrin* (1994), *Andrea Chénier* (1996), and *Tristan und Isolde* (1998).

Jensen, Adolf, German composer; b. Königsberg, Jan. 12, 1837; d. Baden-Baden, Jan. 23, 1879. He began his studies with E. Sobolewski, the Königsberg Kapellmeister. He publ. a vol. of songs as his op.1 (1849; withdrawn and publ. as 6 songs, op.1, in 1859), then continued his studies with Ehlert, Köhler, and F. Marpurg (1849–52). He went to Brest Litovsk as a music tutor (1856), then was a theater conductor in Posen, Bromberg, and Copenhagen (1857–58). He returned to Königsberg as assistant director of the Academy (1861), and then subsequently taught at Tausig's school in Berlin (1866–68). He ultimately settled in Baden-Baden, where he died of consumption. A great admirer of Schumann, he closely imitated him in his songs, of which about 160 were publ. He also wrote an opera, *Die Erbin von Montfort* (1864–65; rev. by Kienzl, to a new libretto by Jensen's daughter, as *Turandot*). P. Kuczynski ed. his letters (Berlin, 1879). His brother, Gustav Jensen (1843–1895), was a violinist and composer.

BIBL.: A. Niggli, *A. J.* (Zürich, 1895); idem, *A. J.* (Berlin, 1900); G. Schweizer, *Das Liedschaffen A. J.s* (Frankfurt am Main, 1933).

Jeppesen, Knud (Christian), eminent Danish musicologist and composer; b. Copenhagen, Aug. 15, 1892; d. Risskov, June 14, 1974. He began his career as an opera conductor, using the name Per Buch, in Elbing and Liegnitz (1912–14), then studied organ at the Royal Danish Cons. of Music (diploma, 1916) and musicology with Angul Hammerich at the Univ. of Copenhagen (M.A., 1918); he also received instruction from Carl Nielsen and Thomas Laub. He prepared his Ph.D. diss., *Die Dissonanzbehandlung bei Palestrina*, at the Univ. of Copenhagen; however, the retirement of Hammerich made it necessary for the diss. to be approved by and completed under Guido Adler at the Univ. of Vienna (1922; publ., in an aug. ed., in Copenhagen in 1923 as *Palestrinastil med saerligt henblik paa dissonansbehandlingen*; Eng. tr. by M. Hamerik as *The Style of Palestrina and the Dissonance*, Copenhagen, 1927; 2d ed., 1946). Jeppesen served as organist of Copenhagen's St. Stephen's (1917–32) and of the Holmens Church (1932–47); he also taught theory at the Royal Danish Cons. of Music (1920–46). He became the first prof. of musicology at the Univ. of Århus (1946), where he founded its musicological inst. in 1950, retiring in 1957. He was ed. in chief of *Acta Musicologica* (1931–54) and president of the International Musicological Soc. (1949–52). Jeppesen was an authority on Palestrina and the music of the Italian Renaissance. As a composer, he demonstrates his erudition in his music: precise in its counterpoint, unfailingly lucid in its harmonic structure, and set in impeccable classical forms. Among his works is the opera *Rosaura, eller Kaerlighed besejrer alt* (1946; Copenhagen, Sept. 20, 1950).

WRITINGS: *Kontrapunkt (vokalpolyfoni)* (Copenhagen, 1930; German tr., 1935; 5th ed., 1970; Eng. tr., 1939; new ed., 1992; 3d Danish ed., 1962); *La frottola* (Copenhagen, 1968–70).

EDITIONS: With V. Brøndal, *Der Kopenhagener Chansonnier* (Copenhagen and Leipzig, 1927; 2d ed., rev., 1965); *Vaerker af Mogens Pedersn* (Copenhagen, 1933); with V. Brøndal, *Die mehrstimmige italienische Laude um 1500* (Copenhagen and Leipzig, 1935); *Die italienische Orgelmusik am Anfang des Cinquecento* (Copenhagen, 1943; 2d ed., rev. and aug., 1960); *La flora, arie &c antiche italiane* (Copenhagen, 1949); *Antichi balli veneziani per cembalo* (Copenhagen, 1962); *Italia sacra musica: Musiche corali italiane sconosciute della prima metà del cinquecento* (Copenhagen, 1962).

BIBL.: B. Hjelmborg and S. Sørenson, eds., *Natalicia musicologica K. J. septuagenario collegis oblata* (Copenhagen, 1962).

Jepson, Helen, American soprano; b. Titusville, Pa., Nov. 28, 1904; d. Bradenton, Fla., Sept. 16, 1997. She studied in Philadelphia with Queena Mario at the Curtis Inst. of Music (B.Mus., 1934); in 1936, she went to Paris to study with Mary Garden. She sang with the Philadelphia Grand Opera (1928–30), then made her

Metropolitan Opera debut in New York as Helene in Seymour's *In the Pasha's Garden* on Jan. 24, 1935, remaining on its roster until 1943; also sang with the Chicago Opera (1935–42). Her roles of note included Eva in *Die Meistersinger von Nürnberg*, Marguerite in *Faust*, Desdemona in *Otello*, and Nedda in *Pagliacci*.

Jeremiáš, Jaroslav, Czech pianist and composer, brother of **Otakar Jeremiáš**; b. Pisek, Aug. 14, 1889; d. Ceské Budějovice, Jan. 16, 1919. His father was the well-known Czech conductor, composer, and teacher Bohuslav Jeremiáš (b. Řestorky, Chrudim district, May 1, 1859; d. Česke Budjěvicé, Jan. 18, 1918). He studied at his father's music school in Pisek; he then studied piano with A. Miks at the Prague Cons. and privately with Novák (1909–10). Although he died at the age of 29, he left several significant works, including the opera *Starý král* (The Old King; 1911–12; Prague, April 13, 1919) and the oratorio *Mistr Jan Hus* (1914–15; Prague, June 13, 1919).

BIBL.: B. Bělohlávek, *J. J.* (Prague, 1935).

Jeremiáš, Otakar, Czech conductor and composer, brother of **Jaroslav Jeremiáš**; b. Pisek, Oct. 17, 1892; d. Prague, March 5, 1962. His father was the well-known Czech conductor, composer, and teacher Bohuslav Jeremiáš (b. Řestorky, Chrudim district, May 1, 1859; d. Česke Budjěvicé, Jan. 18, 1918). He began his musical training with his parents, then studied composition at the Prague Cons. (1907) and privately with Novák (1909–10); he also took cello lessons with Jan Burian. He was a cellist in the Czech Phil. (1911–13); he took over his father's music school (1919). He then was conductor of the Prague Radio orch. (1929–45); subsequently he was director of the Prague National Theater (1945–47); he was also the first chairman of the Union of Czech Composers. He was made a National Artist (1950) and received the Order of the Republic (1960). His music continues the traditions of the Czech national school, with a pronounced affinity to the style of Smetana, Foerster, and Ostrčil. Among his works were *Romance o Karlu IV*, melodrama (1917), *Bratři Karamazovi* (The Brothers Karamazov), opera, after Dostoyevsky (1922–27; Prague, Oct. 8, 1928), and *Enšpígl* (Til Eulenspiegel), opera (1940–44; Prague, May 13, 1949).

BIBL.: J. Plavec, *O. J.* (Prague, 1943); idem, *Národni umělec: O. J.* (National Artist: O. J.; Prague, 1964).

Jerger, Alfred, noted Austrian bass-baritone; b. Brünn, June 9, 1889; d. Vienna, Nov. 18, 1976. He studied at the Vienna Academy of Music, where his teachers included Fuchs, Grädener, and Gutheil; he then became an operetta conductor at the Zürich Opera (1913). He began his vocal career in 1915, appearing as Lothario in *Mignon* at the Zürich Opera in 1917; he then sang at the Bavarian State Opera in Munich (1919–21). He was a leading member of the Vienna State Opera (1921–53); he also sang at the Salzburg Festivals, at London's Covent Garden, and other major music centers of Europe. In 1947 he joined the faculty of the Vienna Academy of Music; he was also a producer at the Vienna Volksoper. He created the role of the Man in Schoenberg's *Die Glückliche Hand* (Vienna, Oct. 14, 1924) and the role of Mandryka in Strauss's *Arabella* (Dresden, July 1, 1933). His other outstanding Strauss roles included Baron Ochs, Orestes, John the Baptist, and Barak. He also was a fine Leporello, Don Giovanni, Pizzaro, Hans Sachs, Beckmesser, Grand Inquisitor, and King Philip.

Jeritza (real name, **Jedlitzková**), **Maria,** celebrated Moravian-born American soprano; b. Brünn, Oct. 6, 1887; d. Orange, N.J., July 10, 1982. She studied in Brünn and sang in the Stadttheater chorus there; after completing her training in Prague, she made her formal operatic debut as Elsa in *Lohengrin* in Olomouc (1910); she then became a member of the Vienna Volksoper. In 1912 Emperor Franz Josef heard her sing in Bad Ischl, after which he decreed that she should be engaged at the Vienna Court Opera, where she made her first appearance as Oberleitner's Aphrodite. Strauss then chose her to create the title role in his opera *Ariadne auf Naxos* (Stuttgart, Oct. 25, 1912), and also in its revised version (Vienna, Oct. 4, 1916); she likewise created the role of the Empress in his *Die Frau ohne Schatten* (Vienna, Oct. 10, 1919). On Nov. 19, 1921, she made her U.S. debut at the Metropolitan Opera in New York in the first U.S. production of Korngold's opera *Die tote Stadt*. Her compelling portrayals of Tosca and Turandot quickly secured her place as the prima donna assoluta there, and she remained on its roster until 1932. She made her debut at London's Covent Garden as Tosca on June 16, 1926. Throughout the years she remained a leading singer in Vienna as well, continuing to appear there until 1935. In 1943 she became a naturalized American citizen. She again sang in Vienna (1949–52); she also appeared as Rosalinda in a Metropolitan Opera benefit performance of *Die Fledermaus* in New York (Feb. 22, 1951). At the zenith of her career in the years between the 2 world wars, she won extraordinary acclaim in such roles as Sieglinde, Elisabeth, Santuzza, Fedora, Thaïs, Carmen, Salome, Octavian, Tosca, and Turandot. She led a colorful life, both on and off the operatic stage: she married 3 times, had many romantic affairs, and her spats with fellow artists became legendary. She publ. an autobiography, *Sunlight and Song* (N.Y., 1924).

BIBL.: E. Decsey, *M. J.* (Vienna, 1931); R. Werba, *M. J.: Primadonna des Verismo* (Vienna, 1981).

Jerusalem, Siegfried, prominent German tenor; b. Oberhausen, April 17, 1940. He received training in violin and piano at the Essen Folkwangschule, where he played principal bassoon in its orch. He began his career as an orchestral bassoonist in 1961; he was a member of the Stuttgart Radio Sym. Orch. (1972–77). He began serious vocal study in Stuttgart with Hertha Kalcher in 1972, appearing in minor roles at the Württemberg State Theater from 1975. He sang Lohengrin in Darmstadt and Aachen in 1976, and then at the Hamburg State Opera in 1977; that same year he made his debut at the Bayreuth Festival as Froh, returning in later seasons as Lohengrin, Walther, Parsifal, and Loge in the Solti-Hall mounting of the *Ring* cycle in 1983. After making his first appearance at the Berlin Deutsche Oper as Tamino in 1978, he became a leading member of the company. He made his U.S. debut with the Metropolitan Opera in New York as Lohengrin on Jan. 10, 1980, his British debut at London's Coliseum as Parsifal on March 16, 1986, and his Covent Garden debut in London on March 18, 1986, singing Erik; he also appeared at the Vienna State Opera, Milan's La Scala, and the Paris Opéra. His later appearances at Bayreuth were highlighted by his portrayals of Siegfried (1990, 1992, 1995) and Tristan (1993). He also sang Siegfried at the Lyric Opera in Chicago in 1995 and in Berlin in 1996. His portrayal of Tristan at the Los Angeles Opera in 1997 was acclaimed, and he also won accolades for his Loge and Siegfried at the Metropolitan Opera that year.

Jessel, Leon, German composer; b. Stettin, Jan. 22, 1871; d. Berlin, Jan. 4, 1942. At age 20 he began working as a theater conductor, appearing in Gelsenkirchen, Mülheim, Celle, Freiburg im Breisgau, Stettin, Chemnitz, and Lübeck. As a composer, he first attracted notice with his piano and instrumental pieces. His *Die Parade der Zinnsoldaten* (1905) became internationally celebrated. In 1911 he settled in Berlin, where he first won success as an operetta composer with his *Die beiden Husaren* (Feb. 6, 1913). He scored a signal triumph with his *Das Schwarzwaldmädel* (Aug. 25, 1917). Of his subsequent scores, the most successful were *Die närrische Liebe* (Nov. 28, 1919), *Die Postmeisterin* (Feb. 3, 1921), *Das Detektivmädel* (Oct. 28, 1921), *Des Königs Nachbarin* (April 15, 1923), and the Viennese premiered *Meine Tochter Otto* (May 5, 1927). As a Jew, Jessel's works were banned after the Nazis came to power in 1933. His last operetta, *Die goldene Mühle*, received its premiere in Olten, Switzerland (Oct. 29, 1936). Jessel died as a result of manhandling by the Gestapo.

Ježek, Jaroslav, Czech composer; b. Prague, Sept. 25, 1906; d. N.Y., Jan. 1, 1942. He studied composition with Jirák and Suk; he also experimented with quarter-tone techniques under the direction of Alois Hába. In 1928 he became resident composer for the "Liberated Theater," a Prague satirical revue; he produced the scenic music for 20 of its plays. He also composed a ballet, *Nerves*

(1928). In 1939, shortly before the occupation of Czechoslovakia by the Nazis, he emigrated to the United States.

Jílek, František, Czech conductor; b. Brünn, May 22, 1913; d. there (Brno), Sept. 16, 1993. He took courses with Balatka, Chalabala, and Kvapil at the Brno Cons. and with Novák at the Prague Cons.; he then was répétiteur and conductor at the Brno Opera (1936–39). After serving as assistant conductor at the Ostrava Opera (1939–48), he returned to Brno as conductor (1948–52) and chief conductor (1952–78) at the Opera; he also taught at the Janáček Academy of Music there; he was chief conductor of the Brno State Phil. (1978–83). He acquired a fine reputation through his championship of the music of his homeland, most notably of works by Smetana and Janáček.

Jiménez-Mabarak, Carlos, Mexican composer and pedagogue; b. Tacuba, Jan. 31, 1916; d. Cuautla, Morelos, June 21, 1994. He studied piano with Jesús Castillo in Guatemala (1923–27); he continued his piano training at the Cons. in Santiago, Chile (1928–29), where he then attended the Liceo de Aplicación (1930–33); in 1933 he went to Brussels, where he received instruction in piano and harmony at the Inst. of Advanced Studies in Music and Drama, in harmony, counterpoint, and analysis with Wouters at the Cons., and in musicology with Van den Borren at the Univ.; returning to his homeland, he studied orchestration with Revueltas at the Cons. (1938); still later (1953–56) he studied composition with Turchi at the Accademia di Santa Cecilia in Rome and dodecaphonic techniques with Leibowitz in Paris. From 1942 to 1965 he was prof. of music education, harmony, and composition at the National Cons. of Music in Mexico City. After serving as a prof. at the Villahermosa School of the Arts in Tabasco (1965–68), he was the cultural attaché of the Mexican Embassy in Vienna (1972–74). He first composed in a neoclassical style but later became an accomplished dodecaphonist. He was one of the first Mexican composers to utilize electronics and to experiment with "musique concrète."

WORKS: DRAMATIC: OPERAS: *Misa de seis* (1960; Mexico City, June 21, 1962); *La guerra* (1980; Mexico City, Sept. 26, 1982). BALLETS: *Perifonema* (Mexico City, March 9, 1940); *El amor del agua* (1945); *Balada del pájaro y las doncellas* (1947); *Balada del venado y la luna* (1948); *Danza fúnebre* (1949); *Recuerdo a zapata*, ballet-cantata (1950); *Balada mágico o danza de las cuatro estaciones* (1951); *Retablo de la annunciación* (1951); *El nanual herido* (1952); *La maestra rural* (1952); *Balada de los quetzales* (1953); *El paraíso de los Ahogados* (1960); *La llorona* (1961); *La portentosa vida de la muerte* (1964); *Pitágoras dijo . . .* (1966); *Balada de los rios de Tabasco* (1990). OTHER: Incidental music to several plays, including Camus's *Caligula* (1947), and various film scores.

Jirák, K(arel) B(oleslav), distinguished Czech conductor and composer; b. Prague, Jan. 28, 1891; d. Chicago, Jan. 30, 1972. He received training in law and philosophy at the Univ. of Prague, and studied composition privately with Novák (1909–11) and J. B. Foerster (1911–12). He was a répétiteur and conductor at the Hamburg Opera (1916–19); he also conducted opera in Brno and Moravska Ostrava (1918–20). He then was conductor of Prague's Hlahol choir and 2d conductor of the Czech Phil. (1920–21); he was prof. of composition at the Prague Cons. (1920–30). From 1930 to 1945 he was music director of the Czech Radio. From 1935 to 1946 he was married to **Marta Krásová**. In 1947 he went to the United States; in 1948 he became chairman of the theory dept. at Roosevelt College (later Univ.) in Chicago; he held the same position also at Chicago Cons. College from 1967 to 1971. His music represents the finest traditions of Middle European 20th-century Romanticism. His 5th Sym. won the Edinburgh International Festival prize in 1951. Among his other works is the opera *Žena a bůh* (A Woman and God; 1911–14; Brno, March 10, 1928). He publ. a textbook on musical form (Prague, 1922; 5th ed., 1946); also biographies of Fibich (Ostrava, 1947), Mozart (Ostrava, 1948), and Dvořák (N.Y., 1961).

BIBL.: M. Očadlík, *K. B. J.* (Prague, 1941); A. Tischler, *K. B. J.: A Catalog of his Works* (Detroit, 1975).

Jirásek, Ivo, Czech composer; b. Prague, July 16, 1920. He studied composition with Šin in Prague and was a student at the Prague Cons. (1938–45) of Krejčí and A. Hába (composition) and Dědeček (conducting). After working as assistant to Kubelik and the Czech Phil. in Prague (1945–46), he conducted at the Zdeněk Nejedlý Theater in Opava (1946–53), where he then was director of its opera company (until 1956). From 1969 to 1978 he was active with the copyright union in Prague. In 1980 he was made a Merited Artist by the Czech government. His output was greatly influenced by French music, but it also owed much to Stravinsky and Berg.

WORKS: DRAMATIC: OPERAS: *Pan Johanes* (Mr. Johanes; 1951–52; Opava, March 24, 1956); *Svítání nad vodami* (Daybreak Over the Waters; 1960–61; Plzeň, Nov. 23, 1963); *Medvěd* (The Bear), after Chekhov (1962–64; Prague, Jan. 25, 1965); *Klíč* (The Key; 1967–68; Prague, March 15, 1971); *Danse macabre* (1970–71; Prague, Sept. 27, 1972); *Mistr Jeroným* (Master Jerome; 1979–80; Prague, March 26, 1992); *Zázrak* (Miracle; 1981). BALLET: *Faust* (1982–85).

Jirko, Ivan, Czech composer; b. Prague, Oct. 7, 1926; d. there, Aug. 20, 1978. He studied medicine at the Univ. of Prague (graduated, 1951), and also studied composition with K. Janeček (1944–49) and Bočkovec (1949–52) at the Prague Cons. He then pursued a dual career as a psychiatrist and a composer.

WORKS: DRAMATIC: OPERAS: *The Twelfth Night*, after Shakespeare (1963–64; Liberec, Feb. 25, 1967); *The Strange Story of Arthur Rowe*, after Graham Greene's novel *Ministry of Fear* (1967–68; Liberec, Oct. 25, 1969); *The Millionairess*, operatic divertimento (1969–71); *The Strumpet* (1970; Olomouc, June 23, 1974); *The Way Back* (1974). OTHER: *Štěsí* (Happiness), musical panorama for Narrator, Soprano, Baritone, and Orch. (1975–76).

Jo, Sumi, Korean soprano; b. Seoul, Nov. 22, 1962. She received her training in Seoul and at the Accademia di Santa Cecilia in Rome (1983–86). In 1986 she made her operatic debut as Gilda in Trieste. After engagements in Lyons, Nice, and Marseilles (1987–88), she won particular distinction as Barbarina at the Salzburg Festival in 1988, the year in which she also made her first appearance in Munich and her debut at Milan's La Scala as Thetis/Fortune in Jommelli's *Fetonte*. In 1989 she made her Metropolitan Opera debut in New York as Gilda, and also sang in Vienna. She appeared at the Chicago Lyric Opera in 1990 as the Queen of the Night. In 1991 she made her debut at London's Covent Garden as Olympia in *Les Contes d'Hoffmann*. In 1992 she sang Matilde in Rossini's *Elisabetta regina d'Inghilterra* in Naples. In 1996 she was engaged as Zerbinetta in Lisbon. She portrayed Lucio Silla in New York in 1997. Among her other roles are Fiorilla in *Il Turco in Italia*, Elvira in *I Puritani*, Adèle in *Le Comte Ory*, Zerlina in *Fra Diavolo*, and Oscar in *Un Ballo in Maschera*.

Joachim, Amalie (née **Schneeweiss**), German soprano, later mezzo-soprano; b. Marburg, May 10, 1839; d. Berlin, Feb. 3, 1899. She began her career as a soprano, appearing in Vienna under the name Weiss (1854); she later became a mezzo-soprano. She married Joseph Joachim in 1863, but after a bitter lawsuit, in which he accused her of infidelity with the publisher Fritz Simrock, they were divorced (1884). She was a fine lieder artist, excelling particularly in songs by Schumann.

BIBL.: O. Plaschke, *A. J.* (Berlin, 1899).

Jochum, Eugen, eminent German conductor, brother of **Georg Ludwig** and **Otto Jochum;** b. Babenhausen, Nov. 1, 1902; d. Munich, March 26, 1987. He began playing the piano at 4 and the organ at 7; after attending the Augsburg Cons. (1914–22), he studied composition with Waltershausen and conducting with Hausegger at the Munich Academy of Music (1922–25). He commenced his career as a répétiteur at the Bavarian State Opera in Munich and in Mönchengladbach; appeared as a guest conductor with the Munich Phil. in 1926; he then was a conductor at the Kiel Opera (1926–29) and conducted the Lübeck sym. concerts. After conducting at the Mannheim National Theater (1929–30), he served as Generalmusikdirektor in Duisburg (1930–32); then was music director of the Berlin Radio and a frequent guest conductor with the Berlin Phil. From 1934 to 1945 he was Generalmusikdirektor of the Hamburg State Opera. Although his tenure coincided with the Nazi era, Jochum successfully preserved his artistic independence; he avoided joining the Nazi party, assisted a number of his Jewish players, and programmed several works by officially unapproved composers. From 1934 to 1949 he also was Generalmusikdirektor of the Hamburg State Phil. In 1949 he was appointed chief conductor of the Bavarian Radio Sym. Orch. in Munich, a position he held with great distinction until 1960. He also appeared as a guest conductor throughout Europe. In 1953 he made his first appearance at the Bayreuth Festival, conducting *Tristan und Isolde*. He made his U.S. debut as a guest conductor with the Los Angeles Phil. in 1958. From 1961 to 1964 he was co-principal conductor of the Concertgebouw Orch. of Amsterdam, sharing his duties with Bernard Haitink. From 1969 to 1973 he was artistic director of the Bamberg Sym. Orch.; he also served as laureate conductor of the London Sym. Orch. (1977–79). His many honors included the Brahms Medal (1936), the Bruckner Medal (1954), the Bülow Medal of the Berlin Phil. (1978), and the Bruckner Ring of the Vienna Sym. Orch. (1980); he was also made an honorary prof. by the senate of the city of Hamburg (1949). Jochum became known as an outstanding interpreter of the music of Bruckner; he also gained renown for his performances of Bach, Haydn, Mozart, Beethoven, Schubert, Brahms, and Richard Strauss. His daughter was the gifted German pianist (Maria) Veronica Jochum (b. Berlin, Dec. 6, 1932).

Jochum, Georg Ludwig, German conductor, brother of **Eugen** and **Otto Jochum**; b. Babenhausen, Dec. 10, 1909; d. Mülheim an der Ruhr, Nov. 1, 1970. He studied at the Augsburg Cons. and then with Haas (composition) and Hausegger (conducting) at the Munich Academy of Music. He was music director in Münster (1932–34); he then was a conductor at the Frankfurt am Main Opera and Museumgesellschaft concerts (1934–37) and subsequently was Generalmusikdirektor in Linz (1940–45) and Duisburg (1946–58); he was also director of the Duisburg Cons. (1946–58). He appeared as a guest conductor in Europe, South America, and Japan.

Jochum, Otto, German composer, brother of **Eugen** and **Georg Ludwig Jochum**; b. Babenhausen, March 18, 1898; d. Bad Reichenhall, Oct. 24, 1969. He studied at the Augsburg Cons. and at the Munich Academy of Music with Heinrich Kasper Schmid, Gustav Geierhaas, and Joseph Haas (1922–31). From 1932 to 1951 he served as director of the Augsburg Municipal Singing School. Among his compositions were the oratorios *Der jungste Tag* and *Ein Weihnachtssingen*.

Johanos, Donald, American conductor; b. Cedar Rapids, Iowa, Feb. 10, 1928. He studied violin and conducting at the Eastman School of Music in Rochester, N.Y. (Mus.B., 1950; Mus.M., 1952); he received grants from the American Sym. Orch. League and the Rockefeller Foundation for conducting studies with Ormandy, Szell, Beecham, Beinum, Karajan, and Klemperer (1955–58). He won the Netherlands Radio Union conducting competition in 1957. From 1953 to 1956 he was music director of the Altoona (Pa.) Sym. Orch., and also of the Johnstown (Pa.) Sym. Orch. in 1955–56. In 1957 he became assoc. conductor of the Dallas Sym. Orch., and then its resident conductor in 1961, and subsequently its music director in 1962, achieving estimable results. He was assoc. conductor of the Pittsburgh Sym. Orch. and director of its chamber orch. (1970–80); he was music director of the Honolulu Sym. Orch. (1979–94) and artistic director of the Hawaii Opera Theatre (1979–83).

Johanson, Sven-Eric (Emanuel), Swedish composer, organist, and pedagogue; b. Västervik, Dec. 10, 1919; d. Göteborg, Sept. 29, 1997. He studied at the Ingesund School of Music (1938), then obtained diplomas as a music teacher (1943) and organist and choirmaster (1946) at the Stockholm Musikhögskolan; he also studied composition with Melchers, and later with Valen (1951) and finally with Dallapiccola in Florence (1957). After serving as organist and choirmaster at the Uppsala Missionary Church (1944–50), he settled in Göteborg in 1952 and was organist at the Alvsborg Church (until 1977); he was also active as a teacher. In 1971 he was made a member of the Royal Swedish Academy of Music in Stockholm. His output ranges from electro-acoustic compositions to popular scores.

WORKS: DRAMATIC: OPERAS: *Bortbytingarna* (1954–55); *Kunskapens vin* (Göteborg, May 21, 1959); *Sagan om ringen* (1972); *Reliken* (1974; Borås, Jan. 18, 1975); *Skandal, Ers Majestät* (Umeå, May 8, 1978); *Du människa* (1980); *Pojken med flöjten* (Göteborg, Dec. 3, 1980); *Tjuvens pekfinger*, opera buffa (1968–82; Göteborg, Jan. 14, 1983); *Denize* (1994–95). OTHER: Radio operas; incidental music; *Rivalerna*, microdrama (1967; Swedish Radio, March 16, 1969); *Kassandras omvändelse*, monodrama (1977); *Slottet*, ballet (1983).

BIBL.: P.-G. Bergfors, *Mitt hjärtas melodi: En Bok om S.-E. J.* (1994).

Johansson, Bengt (Viktor), Finnish composer; b. Helsinki, Oct. 2, 1914; d. Visuvesi, June 22, 1989. He studied composition with Sulho Ranta and Selim Palmgren and cello at the Sibelius Academy in Helsinki, graduating in 1947; he made study trips to Europe, Italy, and America. Returning to Finland, he served as director of music broadcasting for the Finnish Radio (1952–74); he was a teacher (from 1960) and a lecturer in music history (from 1965) at the Sibelius Academy. His music makes use of a wide variety of resources, including electronic sound. Among his works is the opera *Linna* (1975); also *It's Perfectly True*, "musical fairy tale" for Narrator, Solo Voices, Women's Chorus, and Orch. (1957).

Johns, Paul Emile, Polish-born American pianist, music publisher, and composer; b. Kraków, c.1798; d. Paris, Aug. 10, 1860. He settled in New Orleans by 1818, where he was active as a pianist until 1830; had his own music store in New Orleans (1830–46). During a visit to Paris in 1832, he was befriended by Chopin, who dedicated his 5 mazurkas, op. 7, to him. With Pleyel, he publ. his *Album louisianais*, a vol. of piano pieces and songs. His other works, including a comic opera, *The Military Stay*, are not extant. In later years he was active as a cotton magnate. From 1848 to 1860 he was Russian consul in New Orleans.

Johnsen, Hallvard Olav, Norwegian flutist and composer; b. Hamburg (of Norwegian parents), June 27, 1916. He went to Norway as a youth and studied flute with Stenseth and Wang, conducting with Fjeldstad, harmony and counterpoint with Steenberg, and composition with Brustad at the Oslo Cons. (1930–41); he then studied composition with Karl Andersen in Oslo (1942–45), and later with Holmboe in Copenhagen (1956). He was a flutist in the orch. of the National Theater in Oslo (1945–47) and played in military bands (1947–73). His style of composition evolved from late Romanticism to free tonal techniques. Among his works are the operas *The Legend of Svein and Maria* (1971; Oslo, Sept. 9, 1973), *Det Kjempende Menneske* (1982), and *Nattergalen* (1991); also *Logos*, oratorio for 8 Solo Voices, Chorus, Organ, and Orch. (1979), and *Bergammen*, melodrama for Man's Voice and Orch. (1980).

Johnson, Bengt-Emil, Swedish composer and poet; b. Ludvika, Dec. 12, 1936. He studied piano and composition with Knut Wiggen (1956–62), at the same time pursuing his abiding interest in modernistic poetry. In 1966 he joined the staff of the Swedish Radio in Stockholm, where he later was named director of the music dept. (1979) and program director (1984). He publ. 14 collections of poetry (1963–86). Many of his compositions take the form of text-sound scores. Among his works is *Döden sopran*, radio opera (Swedish Radio, Sept. 7, 1986).

Johnson, Edward, distinguished Canadian-born American tenor and operatic administrator; b. Guelph, Ontario, Aug. 22, 1878; d. there, April 20, 1959. He sang in concert and oratorio performances before going to New York in 1899 to study with Mme. von Feilitsch; after appearing in the U.S. premiere of Oscar Straus's *A Waltz Dream* in 1907, he continued his studies with

Richard Barthélemy in Paris (1908) and Vincenzo Lombardi in Florence (1909). He made his operatic debut as Andrea Chénier at the Teatro Verdi in Padua on Jan. 10, 1912, using the stage name of Edoardo Di Giovanni; he subsequently appeared in Milan at La Scala, where he sang the title role in *Parsifal* at its first complete stage production in Italy, on Jan. 4, 1914. He made his U.S. debut as Loris in *Fedora* at the Chicago Grand Opera on Nov. 20, 1919, remaining on its roster until 1922, then made his Metropolitan Opera debut in New York as Avito in *L'amore dei tre Re* on Nov. 16, 1922, continuing to sing there until 1935, when he became its general manager, guiding its fortunes through the difficult years of World War II and the postwar era; he retired in 1950. Although he became a naturalized American citizen in 1922, he maintained a close connection with Canada; he returned there after his retirement. He was particularly esteemed for such roles as Romeo, Tannhäuser, Don José, Siegfried, Canio, and Pelléas; he also created leading roles in Deems Taylor's *The King's Henchman* (1927) and *Peter Ibbetson* (1931) at the Metropolitan.

BIBL.: R. Mercer, *The Tenor of His Time: E. J. of the Met* (Toronto, 1976).

Johnson, (Francis) Hall, black American choral conductor, composer, and arranger; b. Athens, Ga., June 2, 1887; d. N.Y., April 30, 1970. He studied at the Univ. of Pa. (B.A., 1910), where he took a course in composition with Hugh A. Clark; he later studied with Goetschius at the Inst. of Musical Art in New York (1923–24). In 1925 he formed the Hall Johnson Choir, with which he gave numerous concerts; from 1938 to 1946 he conducted the Festival Choir of Los Angeles, and then settled in New York as conductor of the Festival Negro Chorus, with which he toured Germany and Austria under the auspices of the U.S. State Dept. (1951). He composed a folk opera, *Run Littl' Chillun* (1933).

Johnson, James Weldon, black American man of letters, brother of **J(ohn) Rosamond Johnson**; b. Jacksonville, Fla., June 17, 1871; d. in an automobile accident in Wiscasset, Maine, June 26, 1938. He studied literature at Atlanta Univ. (B.A., 1894; M.A., 1904) and also passed the Florida bar examination to practice law (1897). As a poet, he began writing texts to his brother's compositions; their song "Lift Ev'ry Voice and Sing" (1900) proved popular, becoming known as "the Negro National Anthem." The brothers settled in New York in 1902, where they joined Bob Cole in the enormously successful songwriting team of Cole and Johnson Bros.; among their hit songs, mostly in black dialect, were "Under the Bamboo Tree" (1902), which was parodied by T. S. Eliot in "Fragment of an Agon," and "Congo Love Song" (1903). Under the pseudonym Will Handy, they produced "Oh, Didn't He Ramble" (1902), which became a jazz standard; the team's success was such that they became known as "Those Ebony Offenbachs." Johnson was then active as a diplomat (1906–14), serving as consul to Venezuela and, later, to Nicaragua. His tr. of Granados's *Goyescas* was used for the Metropolitan Opera's first performance of this work. He publ. anonymously the novel *The Autobiography of an Ex-Colored Man* (Boston, 1912), which includes vivid descriptions of the ragtime era in New York. He collaborated with his brother in compiling 2 books of American Negro spirituals (N.Y., 1926 and 1927); wrote *Black Manhattan* (N.Y., 1930), a history of blacks in New York, which includes valuable information on black musical life; also publ. an autobiography, *Along This Way* (1931). His papers are on deposit at Yale Univ.

BIBL.: E. Levy, *J. W. J.* (Chicago, 1973).

Johnson, J(ohn) Rosamond, black American composer and bass, brother of **James Weldon Johnson**; b. Jacksonville, Fla., Aug. 11, 1873; d. N.Y., Nov. 11, 1954. He studied at Atlanta Univ. and at the New England Cons. of Music in Boston; took voice lessons with David Bispham. He set his brother's poem "Lift Ev'ry Voice and Sing" (1900) to music, which later became known as "the Negro National Anthem." The brothers collaborated on many other songs, selling them to various musical reviews in New York; in 1902 they formed, with Bob Cole, the songwriting team of Cole and Johnson Bros.; Johnson also wrote some songs that were accepted on the concert stage, among them "Li'l Gal" and "Since You Went Away." In 1911–12 he was music director of Hammerstein's Opera House in London; he also sang in opera, and later toured the United States and Europe in programs of Negro spirituals. With his brother, he compiled 2 vols. of Negro spirituals (1926, 1927), adding piano accompaniments; he wrote a ballet, *African Drum Dance*, and many vocal works; also *Rolling Along in Song* (a history of black music with 85 song arrangements). He sang the role of Lawyer Frazier in the early performances of Gershwin's *Porgy and Bess*.

Johnson, Lockrem, American pianist, music publisher, and composer; b. Davenport, Iowa, March 15, 1924; d. Seattle, March 5, 1977. He studied at the Cornish School of Music in Seattle (1931–38) and at the Univ. of Wash. (1938–42); he subsequently was a member of its faculty (1947–49) and concurrently served as music director of the Eleanor King Dance Co. (1947–50) and pianist in the Seattle Sym. Orch. (1948–51). In 1952 he held a Guggenheim fellowship; he lived in New York, where he served as education director for Mercury Music (1951–54), head of the orch. dept. of C. F. Peters (1954–58), and president of Dow Publishers (1957–62); he subsequently returned to Seattle as head of the music dept. at the Cornish School of Music (1962–69); he also founded Puget Music Publications (1970), which was devoted to publishing works by composers of the Northwest. His works reveal a fine lyrical gift of expression. Among his compositions are the ballet *She* (1948; rev. 1950) and the chamber opera *A Letter to Emily* (1951; N.Y., Jan. 25, 1955).

Johnson, Mary Jane, American soprano; b. Pampa, Texas, March 22, 1950. She studied at West Texas A. & M. Univ. In 1981 she made her operatic debut in New York singing Weber's Agathe. In 1982 she made her first appearance at the Santa Fe Opera as Rosalinde, and subsequently sang there with fine success in later seasons. In 1983 she appeared as Freia in *Das Rheingold* at the San Francisco Opera. She made regular appearances at the Washington (D.C.) Opera from 1984, and at the Cincinnati Opera from 1986. After singing Desdemona at the Pittsburgh Opera and Helen of Troy in *Mefistofele* at the Lyric Opera in Chicago in 1991, she was engaged as Shostakovich's Lady Macbeth at Milan's La Scala and at the Opéra de la Bastille in Paris in 1992. In 1996 she sang Janáček's Emilia Marty at the Vancouver Opera. Among her other roles of note were Mozart's Countess, Leonore, Senta, Alice in *Falstaff*, Salome, and Tosca.

Johnson, Robert Sherlaw, English pianist and composer; b. Sunderland, May 21, 1932. He was educated at King's College, Univ. of Durham (1950–53), and at the Royal Academy of Music in London (1953–57); he then studied piano with Fevrier and composition with Boulanger in Paris (1957–58), where he also attended Messiaen's classes at the Cons.; returning to England, he gave piano recitals in programs of 20th-century music. He lectured at the univs. of Leeds (1961–63) and York (1965–70). In 1970 he was appointed to the faculty of the Univ. of Oxford; he was a visiting prof. at the Eastman School of Music in Rochester, N.Y. (1985). He wrote a study on Messiaen (1974). In his music, he re-creates Renaissance forms and mannerisms in a modern modal idiom. Although he wrote the opera *The Lambton Worm* (1976), he composes mainly for chamber ensembles and vocal groups.

Johnson, Tom, American composer; b. Greeley, Colo., Nov. 18, 1939. He was educated at Yale Univ. (B.A., 1961; M.Mus., 1967) and studied with Morton Feldman in New York. After writing music criticism for N.Y.'s *Village Voice* newspaper (1972–82), he settled in Paris to pursue his career as a composer. An anthology of his articles from the *Village Voice* appeared as *The Voice of New Music* (Eindhoven, 1991). In his music Johnson has made use of minimalist resources while steering his own independent course made refreshing by his wit and penchant for ironical expression.

WORKS: DRAMATIC: OPERAS: *The 4-Note Opera* (1972); *The Masque of Clouds* (1975); *Window* (1978); *Dryer* (1978); *Drawers* (1978); *Door* (1978); *Sopranos Only* (1984); *Riemannoper* (1988); *Deux cents ans* (1989); *Una opera Italiana* (1991). RADIO SCORE:

Cling Clang (1993). OTHER: *Bonhoeffer Oratorio* for 4 Soloists, 2 Choruses, and Orch. (1990).

Johnston, Ben(jamin Burwell), American composer and pedagogue; b. Macon, Ga., March 15, 1926. He studied at the College of William and Mary in Williamsburg, Va. (A.B., 1949), the Cincinnati Cons. of Music (M.Mus., 1950), and Mills College in Oakland, California (M.A., 1953); he held a Guggenheim fellowship (1959–60). He taught at the Univ. of Ill. in Urbana (1951–83).

WORKS: DRAMATIC: OPERAS: *Gertrude, or Would She Be Pleased to Receive It?* (1965); *Carmilla* (1970). BALLETS: *St. Joan* (1955); *Gambit* for Dancers and Orch. (1959; also concert version entitled *Ludes* for 12 Instruments).

BIBL.: H. Von Gunden, *The Music of B. J.* (Metuchen, N.J., and London, 1986).

Jolas, Betsy (real name, **Elizabeth Illouz**), American composer and teacher; b. Paris (of American parents), Aug. 5, 1926. She went to the United States in 1940 and studied with Boepple (composition), Helen Schnabel (piano), and Weinrich (organ) at Bennington (Vt.) College (B.A., 1946). Returning to Paris, she completed her training with Milhaud (composition), Plé-Caussade (fugue), and Messiaen (analysis) at the Cons. From 1971 to 1974 she taught Messiaen's course at the Cons., and then served on its faculty from 1975 to 1991. She won the Grand Prix National de la Musique (1974), the Grand Prix de la Ville de Paris (1981), the Grand Prix de la SACEM (1982), the Maurice Ravel Prix International (1992), and the Prix SACEM (1994). In 1983 she was elected a member of the American Academy of Arts and Letters. In 1985 she was made a Commandeur des Arts et des Lettres. Her Franco-American training is reflected in her music, which is particularly notable for its imaginative handling of form and structure with judicious infusions of color and lyricism.

WORKS: OPERAS: *Le Pavillon au bord de la rivière*, chamber opera after a medieval Chinese play (Avignon, July 25, 1975); *Le Cyclope*, chamber opera (Avignon, July 27, 1986); *Schliemann* (1988; concert perf., Paris, April 4, 1990; stage perf., Lyons, May 1995).

Jolivet, André, prominent French composer; b. Paris, Aug. 8, 1905; d. there, Dec. 20, 1974. A son of artistically inclined parents, he took an interest in the fine arts, wrote poetry, and improvised at the piano; he studied cello with Louis Feuillard and theory with Aimé Théodas at Notre Dame de Clignancourt. At the age of 15 he wrote a ballet and designed a set for it, then undertook a prolonged study of musical techniques with Le Flem (1928–33). Of decisive importance to the maturation of his creative consciousness was his meeting in 1930 with Varèse, then living in Paris, who gave him a sense of direction in composition. In 1935 he organized in Paris the progressive group La Spirale. In 1936, in association with Baudrier, Messiaen, and Daniel-Lesur, he founded La Jeune France, dedicated to the promotion of new music in a national French style. He served as conductor and music director of the Comédie Française (1943–59) and was technical adviser of the Direction Générale des Arts et des Lettres (1959–62) and president of the Concerts Lamoureux (1963–68); he also was prof. of composition at the Paris Cons. (1965–70). He toured throughout the world as a conductor of his own music. Jolivet injected an empiric spirit into his music, making free use of modernistic technical resources, including the electronic sounds of the Ondes Martenot. Despite these esoteric preoccupations, and even a peripheral deployment of serialism, his music was designed mainly to provide aural stimulation and aesthetic satisfaction.

WORKS: DRAMATIC: OPERA BUFFA: *Dolorès, Le Miracle de la femme laide* (1942; Paris Radio, May 4, 1947). BALLETS: *Guignol et Pandore* (1943; Paris, April 29, 1944); *L'Inconnue* (Paris, April 19, 1950); *Ariadne* (1964; Paris, March 12, 1965). OTHER: Incidental music.

BIBL.: V. Fédorov and P. Guinard, compilers, *A. J.: Catalogue des oeuvres* (Paris, 1969); H. Jolivet, *Avec A. J.* (Paris, 1978).

Joll, Philip, Welsh baritone; b. Merthyr Tydfil, March 14, 1954. He was a student of Nicholas Powell and Frederick Cox at the Royal Northern College of Music in Manchester (1975–78) and of Hotter and Goodall at the National Opera Studio (1978–79). In 1978 he made his formal operatic debut as the Bonze in *Madama Butterfly* with the English National Opera in London, and then sang Donner and the Dutchman there. He made his first appearance at the Welsh National Opera in Cardiff as Strauss's Orestes in 1979, where he returned as Wotan in its *Ring* cycle (1983–85). In 1982 he made his debut at London's Covent Garden as the Second Nazarene in *Salome*, and was engaged as Wotan in its *Ring* cycle in 1986. In 1983 he sang Amfortas in Frankfurt am Main. He made his Metropolitan Opera debut in New York on Oct. 9, 1987, as Donner. His Australian debut followed in 1988 in Queensland as Jochanaan, the same year he appeared as the Dutchman at the Bregenz Festival. In 1990 he was engaged as Jochanaan for a tour to Japan with the Welsh National Opera. In 1992 he sang Orestes and in 1993 Macbeth with the company in Cardiff. In the latter year, he also sang Verdi's Francesco Foscari at the Edinburgh Festival and the Sacristan in *Tosca* at the Scottish Opera in Glasgow. He portrayed Sharpless in Auckland in 1994, and then sang Wozzeck in Brussels in 1995. In 1996 he was engaged as Simon Boccanegra and as Falstaff in Stuttgart, and as Scarpia at the English National Opera. He returned to the Welsh National Opera in 1997 as Rigoletto. He married **Penelope Walker**.

Jommelli, Niccolò, greatly significant Italian composer; b. Aversa, near Naples, Sept. 10, 1714; d. Naples, Aug. 25, 1774. He began his musical studies with Canon Muzzillo, the director of the Cathedral choir in Aversa. In 1725 he entered the Cons. S. Onofrio in Naples, where he studied with Prota and Feo; in 1728 he enrolled in the Cons. Pietà dei Turchini in Naples, where he continued his studies with Fago, Sarcuni, and Basso. In 1737 he composed a comic opera, *L'errore amoroso*, for Naples; this was followed by a 2d comic opera, *Odoardo* (Naples, 1738). On Jan. 16, 1740, his first serious opera, *Ricimero rê de' Goti*, was produced in Rome. After composing *Astianatte* (Rome, Feb. 4, 1741), he went to Bologna for the premiere of his *Ezio* (April 29, 1741). There he studied with Padre Martini, and was also elected to membership in the Accademia Filarmonica. He then proceeded to Venice, where his opera *Merope* was given on Dec. 26, 1741. In 1743 he became music director of the Ospedale degli Incurabili there; during this time he composed several notable sacred works, including the oratorios *Isacco figura del Redentore* and *La Betulia liberata*. In 1747 he left Venice for Rome, and in 1749 he went to Vienna, where his opera *Achille in Sciro* was successfully staged on Aug. 30, 1749. Several of his operas had been performed in Stuttgart, resulting in a commission for a new opera from Karl Eugen, the duke of Württemberg. *Fetonte* was premiered in Stuttgart on the duke's birthday on Feb. 11, 1753. On Jan. 1, 1754, Jommelli became Ober-Kapellmeister in Stuttgart. Among the operas he composed for Stuttgart were *Pelope* (Feb. 11, 1755), *La Nitteti* (Feb. 11, 1759), and *L'Olimpiade* (Feb. 11, 1761); he also composed sacred music, including a *Miserere* and a *Te Deum*, both of which were widely performed. In 1768 Jommelli accepted an offer from King José of Portugal to compose operas and sacred music for the court of Lisbon. He left Stuttgart in 1769 and returned to Italy; for Naples he composed the operas *Armida abbandonata* (May 30, 1770) and *Ifigenia in Tauride* (May 30, 1771). His opera *Il trionfo di Clelia* was produced in Lisbon with great success on June 6, 1774.

The historical significance of Jommelli lies in his being a mediator between the German and Italian styles of composition, especially in opera. He introduced into Italian opera the German solidity of harmonic texture and also the expressive dynamics associated with the "Mannheim" school of composition; he also abandoned the formal Neapolitan convention of the da capo aria, thus contributing to a more progressive and realistic operatic form. This earned him the sobriquet "the Italian Gluck." On the other hand, he influenced the development, during his long stay in Stuttgart, of German opera in the direction of simple melodiousness and natural rhythmic flow without dependence on contrapuntal techniques. Thus his influence was beneficial both for his native art and for the most austere German operatic traditions.

WORKS: DRAMATIC: OPERAS: *L'errore amoroso*, comic opera (Naples, 1737; not extant); *Odoardo*, comic opera (Naples, 1738; not extant); *Ricimero rè de' Goti* (Rome, Jan. 16, 1740); *Astianatte* (Rome, Feb. 4, 1741; also known as *Andromaca*); *Ezio* (Bologna, April 29, 1741; 2d ver., Naples, Nov. 4, 1748; 3d ver., Stuttgart, Feb. 11, 1758, not extant; 4th ver., 1771; rev. by da Silva, Lisbon, April 20, 1772); *Merope* (Venice, Dec. 26, 1741); *Semiramide riconosiuta* (Turin, Dec. 26, 1741; 2d ver., Piacenza, 1753; 3d ver., Stuttgart, Feb. 11, 1762); *Don Chichibio*, intermezzi (Rome, 1742); *Eumene* (Bologna, May 5, 1742; 2d ver., as *Artemisia*, Naples, May 30, 1747); *Semiramide* (Venice, Dec. 26, 1742); *Tito Manlio* (Turin, 1743; 2d ver., Venice, 1746, not extant; 3d ver., Stuttgart, Jan. 6, 1758, not extant); *Demofoonte* (Padua, June 13, 1743; 2d ver., Milan, 1753; 3d ver., Stuttgart, Feb. 11, 1764; rev., Ludwigsburg, Feb. 11, 1765; rev. by da Silva, Lisbon, June 6, 1775; 4th ver., Naples, Nov. 4, 1770); *Alessandro nell'Indie* (Ferrara, 1744, not extant; 2d ver., Stuttgart, Feb. 11, 1760, not extant; rev. by da Silva, Lisbon, June 6, 1776); *Ciro riconosciuto* (Bologna, May 4, 1744; 2d ver., 1747?; 3d ver., Venice, 1749; completely new ver., 1751 or 1758); *Sofonisba* (Venice, 1746; not extant); *Cajo Mario* (Rome, Feb. 6, 1746; 2d ver., Bologna, 1751); *Antigono* (Lucca, Aug. 24, 1746); *Didone abbandonata* (Rome, Jan. 28, 1747; 2d ver., Vienna, Dec. 8, 1749; 3d ver., Stuttgart, Feb. 11, 1763); *L'amore in maschera*, comic opera (Naples, 1748; not extant); *La cantata e disfida di Don Trastullo*, intermezzi (Rome, 1749; 2d ver., Lucca, 1762); *Artaserse* (Rome, Feb. 4, 1749; 2d ver., Stuttgart, Aug. 30, 1756); *Demetrio* (Parma, 1749); *Achille in Sciro* (Vienna, Aug. 30, 1749; 2d ver., Rome, Jan. 26, 1771); *Cesare in Egitto* (Rome, 1751; not extant); *La Villana nobile*, comic opera (Palermo, 1751; not extant); *Ifigenia in Aulide* (Rome, Feb. 9, 1751; rev. with arias by Traetta, Naples, Dec. 18, 1753); *L'Uccellatrice*, intermezzi (Venice, May 6, 1751; 2d ver. as *Il paratajo [ovvero] La Pipée*, Paris, Sept. 25, 1753); *Ipermestra* (Spoleto, Oct. 1751); *Talestri* (Rome, Dec. 28, 1751); *I Rivali delusi*, intermezzi (Rome, 1752); *Attilio Regolo* (Rome, Jan. 8, 1753); *Fetonte* (Stuttgart, Feb. 11, 1753, not extant; 2d ver., Ludwigsburg, Feb. 11, 1768); *La clemenza di Tito* (Stuttgart, Aug. 30, 1753, not extant; 2d ver., Ludwigsburg, Jan. 6, 1765, not extant; rev. by da Silva, Lisbon, June 6, 1771); *Bajazette* (Turin, Dec. 26, 1753); *Don Falcone*, intermezzi (Bologna, Jan. 22, 1754); *Lucio Vero* (Milan, 1754); *Catone in Utica* (Stuttgart, Aug. 30, 1754; not extant); *Pelope* (Stuttgart, Feb. 11, 1755; rev. by da Silva, Salvaterra, 1768); *Enea nel Lazio* (Stuttgart, Aug. 30, 1755, not extant; rev. by da Silva, Salvaterra, 1767); *Creso* (Rome, Feb. 5, 1757); *Temistocle* (Naples, Dec. 18, 1757; 2d ver., Ludwigsburg, Nov. 4, 1765); *La Nitteti* (Stuttgart, Feb. 11, 1759, not extant; rev. by da Silva, Lisbon, June 6, 1770); *Endimione ovvero Il trionfo d'amore*, pastorale (Stuttgart, 1759, not extant; 2d ver., Queluz, June 29, 1780); *Cajo Fabrizio* (Mannheim, Nov. 4, 1760; includes arias by G. Cola); *L'Olimpiade* (Stuttgart, Feb. 11, 1761; rev. by da Silva, Lisbon, March 31, 1774); *L'isola disabitata*, pastorale (Ludwigsburg, Nov. 4, 1761, not extant; 2d ver., Queluz, March 31, 1780); *Il trionfo d'amore*, pastorale (Ludwigsburg, Feb. 16, 1763; not extant); La pastorella illustre, pastorale (Stuttgart, Nov. 4, 1763, not extant; rev. by da Silva, Salvaterra, 1773); *Il Re pastore* (Ludwigsburg, Nov. 4, 1764, not extant; rev. by da Silva, Salvaterra, 1770); *Imeneo in Atene*, pastorale (Ludwigsburg, Nov. 4, 1765; rev. by da Silva, Lisbon, March 19, 1773); *La Critica*, comic opera (Ludwigsburg, 1766; rev. as *Il giuoco di picchetto*, Koblenz, 1772; rev. as *La conversazione [e] L'accademia di musica*, Salvaterra, 1775); *Vologeso* (Ludwigsburg, Feb. 11, 1766; rev. by da Silva, Salvaterra, 1769); *Il matrimonio per concorso*, comic opera (Ludwigsburg, Nov. 4, 1766, not extant; rev. by da Silva, Salvaterra, 1770); *Il Cacciatore deluso [ovvero] La Semiramide in bernesco*, serious-comic opera (Tübingen, Nov. 4, 1767; rev. by da Silva, Salvaterra, 1771); *La Schiava liberata*, serious-comic opera (Ludwigsburg, Dec. 18, 1768; rev. by da Silva, Lisbon, March 31, 1770); *Armida abbandonata* (Naples, May 30, 1770; rev. by da Silva, Lisbon, March 31, 1773); *L'amante cacciatore*, intermezzi (Rome, 1771; not extant); *Le avventure di Cleomede*, serious-comic opera (Naples, 1771?; rev. by da Silva, Lisbon, June 6, 1772); *Ifigenia in Tauride* (Naples, May 30, 1771; rev. by da Silva, Salvaterra, 1776); *Il trionfo di Clelia* (Naples, 1774?; rev. by da Silva, Lisbon, June 6, 1774); etc. OTHER STAGE WORKS: *Componimento drammatico* (Rome, Feb. 9, 1747; not extant); *Componimento drammatico* (Ronciglione, Feb. 28, 1751; not extant); *La reggia de' Fati* (with G. B. Sammartini; Milan, March 13, 1753); *La pastorale offerta* (with G. B. Sammartini; Milan, March 19, 1753); *Il giardino incanto* (Stuttgart, 1755; not extant); *L'asilo d'amore* (Stuttgart, Feb. 11, 1758; not extant); *Le Cinesi* (Ludwigsburg, 1765; not extant); *L'unione coronata* (Solitude, Sept. 22, 1768; not extant); *Cerere placata* (Naples, Sept. 14, 1772). Also contributions to a number of pasticcios.

BIBL.: S. Mattei, *Elogio del J.* (Colle, 1785); P. Alfieri, *Notizie biografiche di N. J.* (Rome, 1845); H. Abert, *N. J. als Opernkomponist* (Halle, 1908); L. Tolkoff, *The Stuttgart Operas of N. J.* (diss., Yale Univ., 1974); M. McClymonds, *N. J.: The Last Years, 1769–1774* (Ann Arbor, Mich., 1980).

Jonas, Émile, French composer; b. Paris, March 5, 1827; d. St.-Germain-en-Laye, May 21, 1905. He studied at the Paris Cons. (1841–49), graduating with the 2d Grand Prix de Rome for his cantata Antonio. He was an instructor there (1847–66), and also music director at the Portuguese Synagogue, for which he publ. *Receuil de chants hébraïques* (1854).

WORKS: LIGHT OPERAS (all 1st perf. in Paris): *Le Duel de Benjamin* (1855); *La Parade* (Aug. 2, 1856); *Le Roi boit* (April 1857); *Les Petits Prodiges* (Nov. 19, 1857); *Job et son chien* (Feb. 6, 1863); *Le Manoir de La Renardière* (Sept. 29, 1864); *Avant la noce* (March 24, 1865); *Les Deux Arlequins* (Dec. 29, 1865); *Le Canard à trois becs* (Feb. 6, 1869); *Désiré, sire de Champigny* (April 11, 1869). Also an operetta to an Eng. libretto, *Cinderella the Younger* (London, Sept. 25, 1871; in French as *Javotte*, Paris, Dec. 22, 1871).

Jonas, Peter, English opera administrator; b. London, Oct. 14, 1946. He was educated at the Univ. of Sussex (B.A., 1968), the Northern College of Music, the Royal College of Music in London, and the Eastman School of Music in Rochester, N.Y. From 1974 to 1976 he was assistant to the music director of the Chicago Sym. Orch., and then served as artistic administrator of that orch. from 1976 to 1985. He also was director of artistic administration of the Orchestral Assn. of Chicago from 1977 to 1985. He was managing director (later general director) of the English National Opera in London from 1985 to 1993. In 1993 he became Staatsintendant of the Bavarian State Opera in Munich and was made a Commander of the Order of the British Empire. Jonas's tenures in London and Munich were marked by his encouragement of contemporary opera performances.

Joncières, Victorin de (real name, **Felix Ludger Rossignol**), French composer; b. Paris, April 12, 1839; d. there, Oct. 26, 1903. He was first a student of painting; music was his avocation. At the age of 20 he produced a light opera for a student performance. Encouraged by its success with the critics, he began to study music seriously, first with Elwart, then with Leborne at the Paris Cons. He was a great admirer of Wagner, and when Leborne expressed his opposition to Wagner, Joncières impulsively left his class.

WORKS: OPERAS (all 1st perf. in Paris): *Sardanapale* (Feb. 8, 1867); *Le Dernier Jour de Pompei* (Sept. 21, 1869); *Dimitri* (May 5, 1876; his most successful work); *La Reine Berthe* (Dec. 27, 1878); *Le Chevalier Jean* (March 11, 1885; successful in Germany under the title *Johann von Lothringen*); *Lancelot du lac* (Feb. 7, 1900). Also music to *Hamlet* (Nantes, Sept. 21, 1867).

Jones, Daniel (Jenkyn), remarkable Welsh composer; b. Pembroke, Dec. 7, 1912; d. Swansea, April 23, 1993. Both his parents were musicians, and he absorbed the natural rudiments of music instinctively at home. He studied English literature at Univ. College of Wales, Swansea (B.A., 1934; M.A., 1939), and also attended the Royal Academy of Music in London (1935–38), where he studied composition with Farjeon, conducting with Wood, viola with

Lockyear, and horn with Aubrey Brain; he later completed his education at Univ. College of Wales (D.Mus., 1951). He retained interest in literature; was ed. of the collected poems of Dylan Thomas (1971) and the author of *My Friend Dylan Thomas* (1973). He was made an Officer of the Order of the British Empire (1968). In 1936 he promulgated a system of "complex metres," in which the numerator in the time signature indicates the succession of changing meters in a clear numerical progression, e.g., 32–322–3222–322–32, followed by 332–3332–332, etc.; his other innovation is a category of "continuous modes," with the final note of the mode (nonoctaval) serving as the initial note of a transposed mode. Among his compositions are the operas *The Knife* (1961; London, Dec. 2, 1963) and *Orestes* (1967). He authored numerous articles expounding his philosophy of music, some of which were incorporated in the book *Music and Esthetic* (1954).

Jones, Della, Welsh mezzo-soprano; b. Neath, April 13, 1946. She studied at the Royal College of Music in London (1964–68), in Geneva (1968–70), and with Denis Dowling. After winning the Kathleen Ferrier Memorial Scholarship in 1969, she made her operatic debut as Fyodor in *Boris Godunov* in Geneva in 1970. She made her first appearance at the Sadler's Wells Opera in London in 1973 as Ninon in the British premiere of Penderecki's *The Devils of Loudon*. In 1977 she made her debut at the Welsh National Opera in Cardiff as Rosina. From 1977 she also made frequent appearances at the English National Opera in London, where she sang Rossini's Isabella in 1987. She made her debut at London's Covent Garden in 1983 as the Female Cat in *L'Enfant et les sortilèges*. Her U.S. debut came in 1986 when she sang Ruggiero in *Alcina* in Los Angeles. In 1990 she was engaged as Preziosilla at the Scottish Opera in Glasgow. After returning to the Welsh National Opera as Brangäne in 1993, she portrayed Clytemnestra at Opera North in Leeds in 1996. She appeared as a soloist with orchs. and as a recitalist in Europe, North America, and the Far East.

Jones, Dame Gwyneth, prominent Welsh soprano; b. Pontnewynydd, Nov. 7, 1936. She studied at the Royal College of Music in London, and in Siena, Geneva, and Zürich, where she made her operatic debut as Gluck's Orfeo (1962). In 1963 she first appeared at the Welsh National Opera in Cardiff and at London's Covent Garden; she also sang at the Vienna State Opera and at the Bayreuth Festivals from 1966. In 1966 she made her U.S. debut in New York in a concert version of Cherubini's *Médée*; her Metropolitan Opera debut followed there as Sieglinde in *Die Walküre* on Nov. 24, 1972. She also sang at the San Francisco Opera, Milan's La Scala, Munich's Bavarian State Opera, and the Rome Opera; she appeared as Brünnhilde in the centenary performances of the *Ring* cycle at Bayreuth in 1976. In 1976 she was made a Commander of the Order of the British Empire and in 1986 a Dame Commander of the Order of the British Empire. On Sept. 12, 1988, she celebrated the 25th anniversary of her Covent Garden debut by opening its season as Turandot. In 1997 she celebrated the 35th anniversary of her operatic debut and was engaged to sing Ortrud at Covent Garden. In addition to Wagner and Verdi roles, she also won praise for her portrayals of Donna Anna, Medea, Leonore, the Marschallin, Tosca, and Salome.

BIBL.: T. Haberfeld, *G. J.: Pictures of Her Life and Career* (Zürich, 1991).

Jones, (Herbert) Kelsey, American-born Canadian composer, harpsichordist, and teacher; b. South Norwalk, Conn., June 17, 1922. He went to Canada in 1939; became a naturalized Canadian citizen in 1956. He studied with Harold Hamer at Mount Allison Univ. (B.Mus., 1945), then with Sir Ernest MacMillan, Healey Willan, and Leo Smith at the Univ. of Toronto (B.Mus., 1946; D.Mus., 1951), and with Boulanger in Paris (1949–50). He was founder-conductor of the St. John (New Brunswick) Sym. Orch. (1950–54). From 1954 to 1984 he taught at McGill Univ. in Montreal. His output is traditional in nature but not without effective utilization of dissonant writing. Among his works is the chamber opera *Sam Slick* (Halifax, Sept. 5, 1967).

Jones, Parry, Welsh tenor; b. Blaina, Monmouthshire, Feb. 14, 1891; d. London, Dec. 26, 1963. He studied at the Royal College of Music in London; also with Colli in Italy, Scheidemantel in Dresden, and John Coates in England. He made his debut in London in 1914; he then sang in the United States. He survived the German submarine attack on the S.S. *Lusitania* on his return trip to England in 1915, and then sang with the Beecham and D'Oyly Carte opera companies. He was a leading member of the Carl Rosa Opera Co. (1919–22) and the British National Opera Co. (1922–28); made his Covent Garden debut in London in 1921 as Turiddu; he sang there again (1925–26; 1930–32; 1935; 1937), serving as a principal tenor there from 1949 to 1955, the 1953–54 season excepted. He then taught voice at the Guildhall School of Music in London. In 1962 he was made an Officer of the Order of the British Empire. He sang in the first British performances of *Wozzeck*, *Mathis der Maler*, and *Doktor Faust* in concert broadcasts by the BBC; was also active as an oratorio singer.

Jones, Richard, English opera and theater producer; b. London, June 7, 1953. He was educated at the Univ. of Hull and the Univ. of London. In 1982 he commenced his career as an opera producer with Argento's *A Water Bird Talk* at the Scottish Opera in Glasgow, where he returned to stage *Das Rheingold* in 1989 and *Die Walküre* in 1991. In 1984–85 he produced operas by Mozart, Salieri, and Paisiello at the Battignano Festival. After staging *Don Pasquale* at Opera Northern Ireland in Belfast (1985) and *Mignon* at the Wexford Festival (1986), he produced *Manon* and *Carmen* at Opera North in Leeds (1987). His staging of Weir's *A Night at the Chinese Opera* was seen at the Kent Opera in 1988. In 1989 he produced the premiere of Blake's *The Plumber's Gift* at the English National Opera in London. After staging *Mazeppa* at the Bregenz Festival (1991), he oversaw the production of *Der fliegende Holländer* at the Netherlands Opera in Amsterdam (1993). In 1994 he staged *Giulio Cesare* at the Bavarian State Opera in Munich. Jones was responsible for the staging of the *Ring* cycle at London's Covent Garden in 1994–95. In 1998 he returned to Munich to produce *The Midsummer Marriage*.

Jones, (James) Sidney, English composer and conductor; b. London, June 17, 1861; d. there, Jan. 29, 1946. He was the son of Sidney James, the conductor of the Leeds Grand Theatre and municipal band. He learned to play the clarinet and served as a musician under his father before setting out on his own as a touring theater conductor. In 1891 he toured the United States and Australia as conductor of London's Gaiety Theater company. Returning to England, he composed his first operetta, *Our Family Legend* (Brighton, Oct. 8, 1892). He made London the center of his activities, where he conducted at several theaters and had his first major success as a composer with *A Gaiety Girl* (Oct. 14, 1893). After bringing out *An Artist's Model* (Feb. 2, 1895), Jones scored a triumphant success with *The Geisha* (April 25, 1896). It subsequently was given around the globe and remained a staple in the repertoire of light theater works for decades. Following the premiere of *A Greek Slave* (June 8, 1898), he scored another outstanding success with *San Toy* (Oct. 21, 1899). Success also attended *My Lady Molly* (Brighton, Aug. 11, 1902). His London efforts resumed with the unsuccessful *The Medal and the Maid* (April 25, 1903), but he had better luck with *See See* (June 20, 1906). While his *King of Caledonia* (Sept. 3, 1908) met with public favor, *A Persian Princess* (April 27, 1909) did not. After an unsuccessful collaboration with Paul Rubens on *The Girl from Utah* (Oct. 18, 1913) and *The Happy Day* (May 13, 1916), Jones abandoned the musical theater.

Jones, Sissieretta (born **Matilda Sissieretta Joyner**), noted black American soprano, known as the "Black Patti" (with reference to Adelina Patti); b. Portsmouth, Va., Jan. 5, 1868; d. Providence, R.I., June 24, 1933. She studied at the New England Cons. of Music in Boston, and with Louise Capianni and Mme. Scongia in London. She made her debut at a concert at N.Y.'s Steinway Hall on April 5, 1888, then began to tour from 1890, giving concerts in the West Indies, North America, and Europe. She gained prominence as a result of her appearances at the Grand Negro

Jubilee at N.Y.'s Madison Square Garden and at the White House in a command performance for President Harrison (1892); she then sang at the Pittsburgh Exposition and the Chicago World's Columbian Exposition (1893). N.Y.'s Metropolitan Opera considered her for African roles in *Aida* and *L'Africaine*, but racial attitudes and conservative management policies precluded such appearances. She was the principal soprano of the vaudeville troupe known as Black Patti's Troubadours (1896–1915), with which she toured throughout the world; she starred in its operatic "kaleidoscope," in which she sang a medley of arias from operas in staged scenes; she also sang art songs and popular ballads.

Jong, Marinus de, Dutch-born Belgian composer, pianist, and pedagogue; b. Osterhout, Aug. 14, 1891; d. Ekeren, June 13, 1984. He was a student of Bosquet (piano) and Mortelmans (composition) at the Antwerp Cons. After touring Europe and the United States as a pianist, he settled in Belgium in 1926; he was made a prof. of piano (1931) and of counterpoint and fugue (1948) at the Antwerp Cons. His works were in a neo-impressionistic style, with polytonal counterpoint as its mainstay.

WORKS: DRAMATIC: OPERAS: *Mitsanoboe* (1962); *Die häslichen Mädchen von Bagdad* (1966; Antwerp, Jan. 7, 1967); *Esmoreit* (Antwerp, Sept. 11, 1970). BALLETS: *De vrouwen van Zalongo* (1951); *De kleine haven* (1952); *De kringloop* (1955); *Carrefour* (1956); *De Reiskameraad* (1959). OTHER: 4 oratorios: *Hiawatha's Lied* (1947), *Imitatio Christi* (1956), *Kerkhofblommen* (1957), and *Proverbia Bruegeliana* (1961).

Jongen, Léon (Marie-Victor-Justin), respected Belgian composer and pedagogue; b. Liège, March 2, 1884; d. Brussels, Nov. 18, 1969. His brother was the eminent Belgian composer and teacher (Marie-Alphonse-Nicolas-) Joseph Jongen (b. Liège, Dec. 14, 1873; d. Sart-lez-Spa, July 12, 1953). He was trained at the Liège Cons. From 1898 to 1904 he was organist at St. Jacques in Liège. In 1913 he won the Belgian Grand Prix de Rome with his cantata *Les Fiancés de Noël* (1913). From 1927 to 1929 he was conductor of the Tonkin Opera in Hanoi. He was his brother's successor as director of the Brussels Cons. (1939–49). His Violin Concerto (1962) was the compulsory work for the 12 finalists of the 1963 Queen Elisabeth violin competition held in Brussels.

WORKS: DRAMATIC: *L'Ardennaise*, opera (1909); *Le Rêve d'une nuit de Noël*, musical fairy tale (1917; Paris, March 18, 1918); *Thomas l'Agnelet*, opera (1922–23; Brussels, Feb. 14, 1924); *Le Masque de la Mort rouge*, ballet, after Poe (1956).

Joplin, Scott, remarkable black American pianist and composer; b. probably near Marshall, Texas, Nov. 24, 1868; d. N.Y., April 1, 1917. He learned to play the piano at home in Texarkana, and later studied music with a local German musician. He left home at 17 and went to St. Louis, earning his living by playing piano in local emporia. In 1893 he moved to Chicago (drawn by the prospect of music making and other gaiety of the World's Fair), and in 1896 went to Sedalia, Mo., where he took music courses at George Smith College, a segregated school for blacks. His first music publications were in 1895, of genteel, maudlin songs and marches, typical of the period. His success as a ragtime composer came with the "Maple Leaf Rag" (1899; the most famous of all piano rags), which he named after a local dance hall, the Maple Leaf Club. The sheet-music ed. sold so well that Joplin was able to settle in St. Louis and devote himself exclusively to composition. He composed a ragtime ballet, *The Ragtime Dance* (1902), and a ragtime opera, *A Guest of Honor* (copyright 1903, but the music is lost; newspaper notices indicate it was probably perf. by the Scott Joplin Opera Co. in 1903). In 1907 he went to New York, where he continued his career as a composer and teacher. Still intent on ambitious plans, he wrote an opera, *Treemonisha*, to his own libretto; he completed the score in 1911 and produced it in concert form in 1915 without success. Interest in the opera was revived almost 60 years later; T. J. Anderson orchestrated it from the piano score, and it received its first complete performance in Atlanta on Jan. 28, 1972. Despite Joplin's ambitious attempts to make ragtime "respectable" by applying its principles to European forms, it was with the small, indigenous dance form of the piano rag that he achieved his greatest artistic success. Altogether, he wrote about 50 piano rags, in addition to the 2 operas, and a few songs, waltzes, and marches. The designations of some of these rags reflect his desire to transcend the trivial and create music on a more serious plane, i.e., "Sycamore, A Concert Rag" (1904), "Chrysanthemum, An Afro-American Intermezzo" (1904), "Sugar Cane, A Ragtime Classic 2 Step" (1908), "Fig Leaf Rag, A High Class Rag" (1908), and "Reflection Rag, Syncopated Musings" (1917). In his last years, he lamented at having failed to achieve the recognition he felt his music merited. Suffering from syphilis, he became insane and died shortly afterward in a state hospital. More than 50 years later, an extraordinary sequence of events—new recordings of his music and its use in an award-winning film, *The Sting* (1974)—brought Joplin unprecedented popularity and acclaim: among pop recordings, *The Entertainer* (1902) was one of the best-selling discs for 1974. Among classical recordings, Joplin albums represented 74 percent of the best-sellers of the year. In 1976 he was awarded exceptional posthumous recognition by the Pulitzer Prize Committee. See V. Lawrence, ed., *The Collected Works of Scott Joplin* (2 vols., N.Y., 1971; 2d ed., rev., 1981 as *The Complete Works of Scott Joplin*).

BIBL.: K. Preston and N. Huggins, *S. J.* (N.Y., 1988); E. Berlin, *S. J.* (Oxford, 1994); S. Curtis, *Dancing to a Black Man's Tune: A Life of S. J.* (Columbia, Mo., 1994); S. Otfinoski, *S. J.: A Life in Ragtime* (N.Y., 1995).

Jordan, Armin (Georg), Swiss conductor; b. Lucerne, April 9, 1932. He received his musical training in Lucerne and Geneva. After holding the post of 1st conductor at the Zürich Opera (1963–68), he was conductor in St. Gallen (1968–71) and at the Basel Opera (1968–89). From 1973 to 1985 he was music director of the Lausanne Chamber Orch., with which he toured the United States in 1983. From 1985 to 1997 he was chief conductor of l'Orchestre de la Suisse Romande in Geneva, while concurrently serving as principal guest conductor of the Ensemble Orchestral de Paris from 1986 to 1993. He conducted the sound track and also portrayed the role of Amfortas, with the vocal part dubbed in by Wolfgang Schöne, for the Syberberg film version of *Parsifal*. Jordan has appeared as a guest conductor with various opera houses and orchs., and has won particular distinction for his performances of the French repertoire.

Jordan, Irene, American soprano; b. Birmingham, Ala., April 25, 1919. She studied at Judson College in Marion, Ala. (A.B., 1939) and with Clytie Mundy in New York. On Nov. 11, 1946, she made her Metropolitan Opera debut in New York in the mezzo-soprano role of Mallika in *Lakmé*, and remained on its roster until 1948. After training as a soprano (1949–52), she sang opera in Chicago (1954), at the Metropolitan Opera (1957), and at the N.Y. City Opera (1957); she also appeared as a soloist with various American orchs. Among his admired roles were Donna Elvira, the Queen of the Night, Leonore, Lady Macbeth, and Aida.

Jørgensen, Erik, Danish composer and teacher; b. Copenhagen, May 10, 1912. He received lessons in theory from Jeppesen, in organ from Rung-Keller, and in piano from Anders Rachlew. Following training in composition with Høffding at the Copenhagen Cons. (from 1931), he took a course in conducting with Scherchen in Geneva (1936). From 1947 to 1982 he taught at the Copenhagen Inst. for the Blind. In his music, Jørgensen developed a personal style that utilized 12-tone procedures and aleatory. His works include the chamber opera *Skyggen af en drøm* (Shadow of a Dream; 1969) and the madrigal comedy *Eventyret* (Fairytale; 1973–74).

Jörn, Karl, Latvian tenor of German descent; b. Riga, Jan. 5, 1873; d. Denver, Dec. 19, 1947. He studied with Schütte-Harmsen, Jacobs, and Ress in Berlin. He made his operatic debut as Lyonel in Martha in Freiburg im Breisgau (1896), then sang in Zürich (1898–99) and Hamburg (1899–1902). He was a member of Berlin's Royal Opera (1902–08). On Jan. 22, 1909, he made his Metropolitan Opera debut in New York as Walther von Stolzing, remaining on its roster until 1914; after further appearances in Berlin

(1914), he returned to the United States; toured with Gadski's German opera company (1929–31) and then taught voice in New York and later in Denver, where he settled. He was best known for his Wagnerian roles.

Josephs, Wilfred, esteemed English composer; b. Newcastle upon Tyne, July 24, 1927; d. London, Nov. 18, 1997. He studied music with Arthur Milner (1947) and took a degree in dental surgery in 1951 from the Univ. of Durham Sutherland Dental School; then was an orthodontist in the British army. In 1954 he entered the Guildhall School of Music in London, where he studied with Alfred Nieman until 1956, then had private lessons with Max Deutsch in Paris (1958–59). In 1956 he won the Cobbett Prize, in 1957 the Harriett Cohen Medal, and in 1963 the first City of Milan and La Scala international composition competition for his *Requiem* set to the Hebrew Kaddish. He was a visiting prof. at the Univ. of Wisc. in Milwaukee (1970), Roosevelt Univ. in Chicago (1972), and Ohio State Univ. (1992). In 1988 he became a musical consultant to the London International Film School. He developed an individualistic style based on dodecaphony but not without exploiting his mastery of melodic invention.

WORKS: DRAMATIC: *The Magic Being*, ballet (1961; Newcastle upon Tyne, May 31, 1963); *The Nottingham Captain*, music theater (Wellingborough, Sept. 11, 1962); *The King of the Coast*, children's musical (1962–67); *Pathelin*, theater piece (1963); *La Répétition de Phèdre*, ballet (Newcastle upon Tyne, June 22, 1964); *The Appointment*, television opera (1968); *A Child of the Universe*, theater piece (1971); *Through the Looking Glass and What Alice Found There*, children's opera (1977–78; Harrogate, Aug. 3, 1978); *Equus*, ballet (Baltimore, March 21, 1980); *Rebecca*, opera (1981–83; Leeds, Oct. 15, 1983); *Alice in Wonderland*, children's opera (1985–88); *Cyrano de Bergerac*, ballet (1990–91); also numerous film and television scores.

Joteyko, Tadeusz, Polish conductor and composer; b. Poczujki, near Kiev, April 1, 1872; d. Cieszyn, Silesia, Aug. 19, 1932. He studied at the Brussels Cons. with Jacobs (cello) and Gevaert (composition) and with Noskowski (composition) and Cinke (cello) at the Warsaw Cons. He conducted the Warsaw Phil. (1914–18) and taught at the Warsaw Cons. He wrote the operas *Grajek* (The Player; Warsaw, Nov. 23, 1919), *Zygmunt August* (Warsaw, Aug. 29, 1925), and *Królowa Jadwiga* (Queen Jadwiga; Warsaw, Sept. 7, 1928), but is best remembered for his choral music. He publ. *Zasady muzyki* (Principles of Music; Warsaw, 1914) and *Historia muzyki polskiej i powszechnej w zarysie* (Warsaw, 1916).

Joubert, John (Pierre Herman), prominent South African-born English composer; b. Cape Town, March 20, 1927. After attending the Diocesan College in Rondebosch (1934–44), he studied composition with Bell at the South African College of Music in Cape Town (1944–46); subsequently he completed his training in London with Holland and Ferguson at the Royal Academy of Music (B.Mus., 1950). In 1949 he won the Royal Phil. Soc. Prize. He taught at the univs. of Hull (1950–62) and Birmingham (1962–86). In 1991 he was awarded an Hon. Doc. in Music from the Univ. of Durham. Joubert has succeeded in developing an effective means of expression within the tonal tradition.

WORKS: DRAMATIC: *Legend of Princess Vlei*, ballet (Cape Town, Feb. 21, 1952); *Antigone*, radio opera (BBC, London, July 21, 1954); *In the Drought*, chamber opera (1955; Johannesburg, Oct. 20, 1956); *Silas Marner*, opera, after George Eliot (Cape Town, May 20, 1961); *The Quarry*, opera for young players (1964; London, March 25, 1965); *Under Western Eyes*, opera, after Joseph Conrad (1968; London, May 20, 1969); *The Prisoner*, school opera (London, March 14, 1973); *The Wayfarers*, opera for young people (1983; Huntington, April 4, 1984).

Jouret, Léon, Belgian composer; b. Ath, Oct. 17, 1828; d. Brussels, June 6, 1905. He studied at the Brussels Cons. where, in 1874, he was appointed prof. of singing. His 2 operas, *Quentin Metsys* and *Le Tricorne enchanté*, were produced semiprivately in Brussels (1865 and 1868). Of more importance is his collection of folk melodies of his native region, *Chants populaires du pays d'Ath*.

Journet, Marcel, distinguished French bass; b. Grasse, Alpes Maritimes, July 25, 1867; d. Vittel, Sept. 5, 1933. He studied at the Paris Cons. with Obin and Seghettini. He made his operatic debut in *La Favorite* in Montpellier (1891), then sang at the Théâtre Royal de la Monnaie in Brussels (1894–1900). On July 10, 1897, he made his debut at London's Covent Garden as the Duke of Mendoza in d'Erlanger's *Inez Mendo*; he appeared there regularly until 1907, and returned in 1927–28. He made his Metropolitan Opera debut in New York on Dec. 22, 1900, as Ramfis, and remained on its roster until 1908; he then was a member of the Paris Opéra (1908–32); he also sang at the Chicago Grand Opera (1915–17; 1918–19) and at Milan's La Scala (1917; 1922–27), where he created the role of Simon Mago in Boito's *Nerone* (May 1, 1924). Among his finest roles were Hans Sachs, Gurnemanz, Wotan, Méphistophélès, Golaud, and Scarpia.

Jozzi, Giuseppe, Italian castrato soprano, harpsichordist, and composer; b. probably in Rome, c.1710; d. probably in Amsterdam, c.1770. He sang in various theaters in Rome (1729–40). After appearances in Venice, Milan, and Bologna (1740–45), he sang in London at the Haymarket Theater. While in London, he appeared as a harpsichordist playing sonatas by Domenico Alberti, which he publ. under his own name. Walsh later publ. them under Alberti's name (1748). Jozzi sang in Stuttgart from 1750 to 1756. The Alberti sonatas were republ. in Amsterdam under Jozzi's name (1761, 1765). Jozzi's own sonatas are closely patterned after those of Alberti.

Juch, Emma (Antonia Joanna), noted American soprano; b. Vienna (of Austrian-born American parents), July 4, 1863; d. N.Y., March 6, 1939. She was taken at the age of 4 to the United States, where she studied with her father and with Murio Celli in Detroit. She made her recital debut in N.Y.'s Chickering Hall (1881), then her stage debut as Philine in *Mignon* at London's Her Majesty's Theatre (1881); that same year she appeared at N.Y.'s Academy of Music. She was a leading member of the American (later National) Opera Co. (1884–89), subsequently touring the United States, Canada, and Mexico with her own Emma Juch Grand Opera Co. (1889–91); she retired from the operatic stage upon her marriage (1894). She was a great advocate of opera in English. Her voice was admired for its extensive range, which enabled her to sing a wide repertoire.

Judd, James, English conductor; b. Hertford, Oct. 30, 1949. He studied piano with Alfred Kitchin and conducting with Bernard Keefe at Trinity College of Music in London (1967–71), then was active with the London Opera Centre; he subsequently was assistant conductor of the Cleveland Orch. (1973–75). He was co-founder and conductor of the Chamber Orch. of Europe in 1981; toured with it in the United States (1984–85). He also appeared widely as a guest conductor in England, on the Continent, and in the United States. In 1987 he became music director of the Phil. Orch. of Florida in Fort Lauderdale. He also was artistic director of the Greater Miami Opera from 1993.

Jung, Manfred, German tenor; b. Oberhausen, July 9, 1945. He studied with Hilde Wesselmann at the Essen Folkwangschule. After singing in the Bayreuth Festival chorus (1970–73), he made his operatic debut in Dortmund in 1974, and then sang in Kaiserslautern, Saarbrücken, and Karlsruhe. In 1977 he became a member of the Deutsche Oper am Rhein in Düsseldorf; he made his debut at the Bayreuth Festival as Siegfried in *Götterdämmerung* (1977), and then appeared in the televised version of that role in the *Ring* cycle. He made his Metropolitan Opera debut in New York in the title role of *Siegfried* on Sept. 24, 1981, and subsequently sang other Wagnerian roles there. He returned to the Bayreuth Festival in 1983 to sing Siegfried in the Solti–Hall production, commemorating the 100th anniversary of Wagner's death; also appeared in concert throughout Europe, North America, and the Far East.

Jungwirth, Manfred, Austrian bass; b. St. Pölten, June 4, 1919. He studied voice in St. Pölten, Vienna, Bucharest, Munich, and Berlin; he entered the Univ. of Vienna to study medicine in 1937, but passed the examinations in voice, piano, and conducting instead (1940). He sang for German troops in Romania and Bulgaria (1941–45); he made his operatic debut as Gounod's Méphistophélès at the Bucharest Opera (1942), and then sang at the Innsbruck Landestheater (1945–47). In 1948 he was awarded his Ph.D. in musicology in Vienna and also won 1st prize in the Geneva voice competition; he then sang in Zürich, Berlin, Hamburg, Paris, and London; he made regular appearances at the Frankfurt am Main Opera (1960–67) and the Vienna State Opera (from 1967). On Feb. 16, 1974, he made his debut at the Metropolitan Opera in New York as Baron Ochs, which became his most famous role.

Juozapaitis, Jurgis, Lithuanian composer; b. near Šiauliai, June 29, 1942. He studied with Juzeliunas at the Lithuanian State Cons. in Vilnius, graduating in 1968. His music is rooted in native folk modes, which are enhanced by a modernistic harmonic investiture and a rich employment of polyrhythmic percussion. Among his works is the opera *Sea Bird* (1976).

Jurinac, Sena (Srebrenka), famous Yugoslav soprano; b. Travnik, Oct. 24, 1921. She studied at the Zagreb Academy of Music, and also with Milka Kostrenñiń, making her operatic debut as the 1st Flower Maiden at the Zagreb Opera (1942); her first major role there was Mimi that same year. In 1945 she made her Vienna State Opera debut as Cherubino, and soon established herself as one of its outstanding members; she accompanied it on its visit to London's Covent Garden in 1947, where she sang Dorabella; that same year, she made her debut at the Salzburg Festival. She also appeared at the Glyndebourne Festival (1949–56). She made her U.S. debut at the San Francisco Opera (1959); sang regularly at Covent Garden (1959–63; 1965; 1973). In 1953 she married **Sesto Bruscantini**. A distinguished interpreter of Mozart, she excelled as Fiordiligi, Cherubino, Pamina, and Donna Elvira, and later mastered the more demanding roles of Donna Anna and the Countess. She was also renowned for her portrayals of Octavian, the Composer, Elektra, and the Marschallin in the operas of Richard Strauss.

BIBL.: U. Tamussino, *S. J.* (Augsburg, 1971).

Jurovský, Šimon, Slovak composer; b. Ulmanka, Feb. 8, 1912; d. Prague, Nov. 8, 1963. He attended the Bratislava Academy of Music (1931–36); then took courses in composition with Joseph Marx at the Vienna Academy of Music (1943–44). He was manager of the Bratislava Opera and director of the Slovak Folk Art Ensemble. In his music, he followed the broad tenets of national Romanticism, with frequent references to folk themes. He composed the opera *Dcery Abelovy* (The Daughters of Abel, 1961) and the ballet *Rytierska balada* (The Song of Chivalry; Bratislava, 1960).

BIBL.: Z. Bokesová, *Š. J.* (Bratislava, 1955).

Juzeliunas, Julius, Lithuanian composer; b. Čepales, Feb. 20, 1916. He studied with Gruodis at the Kaunas Cons. (graduated, 1948), then entered the Leningrad Cons. in the class of Voloshinov (graduated, 1952). Returning to Lithuania, he taught at the State Cons. in Vilnius (from 1952). His compositions follow the spirit of socialist realism, treating heroic themes in stage productions and romantic subjects in instrumental music; on occasion, he uses modern techniques, including dodecaphony. Among his works are the operas *Sukilėliai* (The Rebels; 1957; Vilnius, 1960) and *Žaidimas* (The Game; 1968); also *Cantus magnificat*, sym.-oratorio for 2 Soloists, 2 Choruses, Organ, and Orch. (1979).

K

Kabaivanska, Raina (Yakimova), Bulgarian soprano; b. Burgas, Dec. 15, 1934. She studied at the Bulgarian State Cons. in Sofia. In 1957 she made her operatic debut at the National Opera as Tatiana. She then studied with Zita Fumagalli-Riva in Milan and with Giulia Tess in Vercelli; she then made her first appearance at La Scala as Agnese in *Beatrice di Tenda* (1961), and subsequently sang there regularly. In 1962 she made her debut at London's Covent Garden as Desdemona; made her American debut at the Metropolitan Opera in New York as Nedda on Oct. 27, 1962; she first sang at the Paris Opéra as Leonora in *La forza del destino* in 1975. She also made guest appearances in Chicago, San Francisco, Dallas, Vienna, and Buenos Aires. She was best known for her Verdi and Puccini roles.

Kabalevsky, Dmitri (Borisovich), noted Russian composer and pedagogue; b. St. Petersburg, Dec. 30, 1904; d. Moscow, Feb. 14, 1987. When he was 14 years old, his family moved to Moscow; he received his primary music education at the Scriabin Music School (1919–25); he also studied theory privately with Gregory Catoire; in 1925 he entered the Cons. as a student of Miaskovsky in composition and Goldenweiser in piano. In 1932 he was appointed instructor in composition there; in 1939 he became a full prof. As a pedagogue, he developed effective methods of musical education; in 1962 he was elected head of the Commission of Musical Esthetic Education of Children; in 1969 he became president of the Scientific Council of Educational Aesthetics in the Academy of Pedagogical Sciences of the USSR; in 1972 he received the honorary degree of president of the International Soc. of Musical Education. As a pianist, composer, and conductor, he made guest appearances in Europe and the United States. Kabalevsky's music represents a paradigm of the Russian school of composition in its Soviet period; his melodic writing is marked by broad diatonic lines invigorated by an energetic rhythmic pulse; while adhering to basic tonality, his harmony is apt to be rich in euphonious dissonances. In his operas, he successfully reflected both the lyrical and the dramatic aspects of the librettos, several of which are based on Soviet subjects faithful to the tenets of socialist realism. His instrumental writing was functional, taking into consideration the idiomatic capacities of the instruments.

WORKS: DRAMATIC: OPERAS: *Kola Bryunon: Master iz Klamsi* (Colas Breugnon: The Master of Klamsi), after Romain Rolland (1936–38; Leningrad, Feb. 22, 1938; rev. version, Leningrad, April 16, 1970); *V ogne: Pod Moskvoi* (Into the Fire: Near Moscow; 1942; Moscow, Sept. 19, 1943; rev. version, Moscow, Nov. 7, 1947); *Semya Tarasa* (The Family of Taras; Moscow, Nov. 2, 1947; rev. version, Leningrad, Nov. 7, 1950; 2d rev. version, Moscow, Nov. 17, 1967); *Nikita Vershinin* (1954–55; Moscow, Nov. 26, 1955). OPERETTAS: *Vesna poyot* (Spring Sings; Moscow, Nov. 4, 1957); *Syostrï* (The Sisters; 1967; Perm, May 31, 1969). Also incidental music for plays and film scores.

BIBL.: L. Danilevich, *D. K.* (Moscow, 1954); G. Abramovsky, *D. K.* (Moscow, 1960); R. Glezer, *K.* (Moscow, 1969); P. Nazarevsky, ed., *D. B. K.: Notograficheskiy i bibliografischeskiy spravochnik* (D. B. K.: Worklist and Bibliography; Moscow, 1969); Y. Korev, *K.* (Moscow, 1970).

Kadosa, Pál, esteemed Hungarian composer and pedagogue; b. Léva, Sept. 6, 1903; d. Budapest, March 30, 1983. He studied piano with Arnold Székely and Kodály at the Budapest Academy of Music (1921–27); he had a brief career as a concert pianist, then taught at Budapest's Fodor Music School (1927–43) and Goldmark Music School (1943–44), then at the Academy of Music (from 1945). He won the Kossuth Prize (1950) and the Erkel Prize (1955, 1962); he was made a Merited Artist (1953) and an Honored Artist (1963) of the Hungarian People's Republic. In his music, he combined the elements of the cosmopolitan modern idiom with strong Hungarian rhythms and folklike melodies; in his treatment of these materials, and particularly in the energetic asymmetrical passages, he was closer to the idiom of Bartók than to that of Kodály. The lyrical element in modal interludes adds to the Hungarian charm of his music. Among his works is the opera *A huszti kaland* (The Adventure of Huszt; 1949–50; Budapest, Dec. 22, 1951).

BIBL.: F. Bónis, *K. P.* (Budapest, 1965).

Kaffka (real name, **Engelmann**), **Johann Christoph,** German violinist, singer, and composer; b. Regensburg, 1754; d. Riga, Jan. 29, 1815. He studied violin with his father and theory with Riepel. He appeared on the stage as a singer and actor in various German cities (from 1777); he settled in Riga as a bookseller (1803). He wrote Singspiels, ballets, oratorios, masses, and songs, most of which are lost.

Kagel, Mauricio (Raúl), notable Argentine composer and pedagogue; b. Buenos Aires, Dec. 24, 1931. He studied in Buenos Aires, taking courses in theory with Juan Carlos Paz and in piano, cello, organ, conducting, and voice with Alfredo Schiuma et al.; he also studed philosophy and literary history at the Univ. there. In 1949 he became active with the Agrupación Nueva Música and joined the staff of the Teatro Colón in Buenos Aires. In 1957 he went to Cologne on a stipend from the Deutscher Akademischer Austauschdienst. He taught at the courses for new music in Darmstadt from 1960, and was founder-director of the Cologne Ensemble for New Music from 1961. After serving as the Slee Prof. of Composition at the State Univ. of N.Y. in Buffalo (1964–65), he was director of the Inst. for New Music at the Rheinische Musikschule in Cologne (from 1969). In 1974 he became a prof. at the Cologne Hochscule für Musik. In 1989 he was composer-in-residence at the Cologne Philharmonie. In 1977 he became a member of the Akademie der Künste in Berlin. He was awarded the Mozart Medal of Frankfurt am Main in 1983 and was made a Commandeur de L'Ordre des Arts et des Lettres of France in 1985. He is the author of *Worte über Musik: Gespräche, Aufsätze, Reden, Hörspiele* (Munich, 1991). Kagel has developed an extremely complex system of composition in which a fantastically intricate and yet wholly rational serial organization of notes, intervals, and durations is supplemented by aleatory techniques. Some of these techniques are derived from linguistic permutations, random patterns of light and shadows on exposed photographic film, and other processes.

WORKS: DRAMATIC: *Sur Scène*, chamber-music theater piece (1959–60); *Antithese* for 1 or 2 Performers and Electronics (1962); *Tremens*, scenic montage (1963–65); *Die Himmelsmechanik*, piece with theater scenery (1965); *Pas de cing*, variable scene for 5 Performers (1965); *Staatstheater*, scenic piece (1967–70); *Con voce* for 3 Mimes and Instruments ad libitum (1972); *Mare nostrum*, scenic piece (1973–75); *Présentation* for Speaker, Piano, and Tape (1976–77); *Variété*, concert spectacle for Artists and Musicians (1976–77); *Die Erschöpfung der Welt*, scenic illusion (1976–78); *Umzug* for Mime (1977); *Die Rhythmusmaschinen*, action for 10 Gymnasts and Instruments (1977–78); *Ex-Position*, action for Vocal Ensemble and Instruments (1977–78); *Aus Deutschland*, lieder opera (1977–80); *Der Tribun* for Political Orator, Marching Band, and Loudspeaker (1978–79); *Der mündliche Verrat* or *La Trahison orale*, musical epic on the Devil for 1 Female Performer, 2 Male Singers, Tuba, Viola or Violin, Double Bass, Piano or Electric Organ, 3 Percussion, and Tape (1981–83); *... nach einer Lektüre von Orwell*, theater picture or scenic environment (1982–83); *Tantz-Schul*, ballet d'action (1985–87); *Zwei Akte* for 2 Actors, Saxophone, and Harp (1988–89).

Kagen, Sergius, Russian-born American pianist, teacher, and composer; b. St. Petersburg, Aug. 22, 1909; d. N.Y., March 1, 1964. He went to Berlin in 1921 and studied with Leonid Kreutzer and Paul Juon at the Hochschule für Musik. He emigrated to the United States in 1925 and became a naturalized American citizen in 1930; he studied with Carl Friedberg, Rubin Goldmark, and Marcella Sembrich at the Juilliard School of Music in New York (diploma, 1930); he later joined its faculty (1940), and also taught at the Union Theological Seminary (1957–64). He wrote the books *Music for the Voice* (N.Y., 1949; 2d ed., rev., 1968) and *On Studying Singing* (N.Y., 1950). He also composed an opera, *Hamlet* (Baltimore, Nov. 9, 1962), and more than 70 songs.

BIBL.: B. Woods, *S. K.: His Life and Works* (diss., George Peabody College for Teachers, 1969).

Kahn, Otto Hermann, German-American music patron; b. Mannheim, Feb. 21, 1867; d. N.Y., March 29, 1934. He was engaged in the banking profession in London (1888–93); he settled in New York in 1893; he was a member of the firm Kahn, Loeb & Co. He became interested in the musical affairs of New York City, and from 1907 to his death was on the board of the Metropolitan Opera; he also was vice president of the N.Y. Phil. His brother, Robert Kahn (1865–1951), was a pianist and composer.

BIBL.: M. Matz, *The Many Lives of O. K.* (N.Y., 1963); J. Kobler, *O. the Magnificent: The Life of O. K.* (N.Y., 1989).

Kaipainen, Jouni (Ilari), Finnish composer; b. Helsinki, Nov. 24, 1956. He studied with Sallinen (1973–76) and Heininen (1976–82) at the Sibelius Academy in Helsinki. From 1991 to 1993 he was artistic director of the Helsinki Festival. His style of composition is typical of the modern school of Finnish music, drawing away from the nationalistic trends of Sibelius, creating a thoroughly individual style. He composed the television opera *Konstanzin Ihme* (The Miracle of Konstanz; 1987).

Kaiser, Alfred, Belgian-born English composer; b. Brussels, Feb. 29, 1872; d. Bournemouth, Oct. 1, 1917. He studied composition with Bruckner in Vienna and with Foerster in Prague, then went to London to live. During World War I, he changed his name to De Keyser to escape the odium attached to the Kaiser of Germany. Among his works are the operas *Le Billet de Joséphine* (Paris, 1902), *Die schwarze Nina* (Elberfeld, 1905), and *Stella Maris* (Düsseldorf, 1910).

Kakinuma, Toshie, significant Japanese musicologist and music critic; b. Shizuoka Prefecture, July 31, 1953. She was educated in Tokyo at the Kunitachi College of Music (B.M., 1977) and Ochanomizu Univ. (M.A., 1981); then took her Ph.D. at the Univ. of Calif., San Diego in 1989 with the diss. *The Musical Instruments of Harry Partch as an Apparatus of Production in Musical Theatre*. She taught at the Yoshiro Irino Music Inst. (from 1990), Nippon Electronics College (from 1992), and Takushoku Univ. (from 1995); she also was a guest lecturer at Nippon Univ. (1995). Kakinuma has been an important figure in the organization of new music festivals in Japan, including "Music History of Quotation" (1983) and "Sound Culture Festival" (1993). Her important writings, primarily on contemporary Japanese, American, and English composers, have appeared widely in publs. in both Japan and the United States; she is a regular writer/reviewer to *Ongakugeijutsu* (from 1980), *On-Stage* (from 1989), and *inTune* and the *Asahi Evening News* (from 1994); from 1981 to 1991 she was a regular contributor to *Philharmony*, the program guide for the NHK Sym. Orch. (1982–91). She also publ., with others, a number of music reference works (1982, 1983, 1993), and prepared a Japanese tr. of John Cage's *Silence* (Tokyo, 1995).

Kalafati, Vasili (Pavlovich), Russian composer and pedagogue of Greek descent; b. Eupatoria, Feb. 10, 1869; d. Leningrad, Jan. 30, 1942. He studied at the St. Petersburg Cons. with Rimsky-Korsakov, graduating in 1899; subsequently he was on its teaching staff (1907–29). A musician of thorough knowledge, he was held in great esteem by his colleagues and students; Rimsky-Korsakov sent Stravinsky to him for additional training in harmony. As a composer Kalafati faithfully continued the traditions of the Russian national school; his works include an opera, *Zygany* (The Gypsies; 1939–41), and a number of songs, all set in impeccably euphonious harmonies.

Kalaš, Julius, Czech composer; b. Prague, Aug. 18, 1902; d. there, May 12, 1967. He studied composition with Foerster and Křička at the Prague Cons. (1921–24), then attended Suk's master classes there (1924–28). He was pianist and artistic director of the satirical male sextet the Teachers of Gotham (1925–53), for which he wrote numerous witty ballads and songs. He was a prof. in the film dept. of the Prague Academy of Musical Arts from 1948; was its dean (1949–50) and vice dean (1955–57). He wrote 6 operas, the most notable being *Nepokoření* (The Proud Ones; 1960), 6 operettas, including the popular *Mlynárka z Granady* (The Miller's Wife of Granada; 1954), and 2 ballets.

Kalenberg, Josef, German tenor; b. Cologne, Jan. 7, 1886; d. Vienna, Nov. 8, 1962. He received his training at the Cologne Cons. In 1911 he made his operatic debut as Turiddu at the Cologne Opera. After singing in Krefeld (1912–16), Barmen (1919–21), Düsseldorf (1921–25), and Cologne (1925–27), he made his first appearance at the Vienna State Opera as Parsifal in 1927, remaining on its roster until 1942. He also sang at the Salzburg Festivals (1928–36) and made guest appearances in France, Italy, and England before retiring in 1949.

Kalhauge, Sophus Viggo Harald, Danish composer; b. Copenhagen, Aug. 12, 1840; d. there, Feb. 19, 1905. He studied with P. Heise, C. Rongsted, and J. C. Gebauer; he also studied in Germany, Switzerland, and Italy. He taught piano and singing in Copenhagen. Among his works are the operas *Zouavens Hjemkomst* (1868), *Paa Krigsfod* (1880), and *Mantillen* (1889).

Kálik, Václav, Czech pianist, conductor, and composer; b. Opava, Oct. 18, 1891; d. Prague, Nov. 18, 1951. He studied with Novák at the Univ. of Prague (1911–13); he later attended Suk's master classes at the Prague Cons. (1924–26). He was mainly active as a pianist and conductor. Among his compositions are the operas *Jarní jitro* (A Spring Morning; 1933; Olomouc, 1943), *Lásky div* (Love's Miracle; 1942–43; Liberec, Nov. 20, 1950), and *Posvěcení mládí* (Consecration of Youth; 1946–48).
BIBL.: J. Vratislavský, *V. K.* (Ostrava, 1961).

Kalisch, Paul, German tenor; b. Berlin, Nov. 6, 1855; d. St. Lorenz am Mondsee, Austria, Jan. 27, 1946. He studied architecture; then went to Milan, where he took voice lessons with Leoni and Lamperti. He made his operatic debut under the name Paolo Alberti in Rome as Edgardo (1879); subsequently he sang in Milan's La Scala (1882) and other Italian opera houses. After appearing in Munich (1883), he was a member of Berlin's Royal Opera (1884–87); made his first appearance in London at Her Majesty's Theatre (1887). In 1888 he married **Lilli Lehmann**, with whom he frequently appeared in operatic performances. On Jan. 30, 1889, he sang Tannhäuser in his Metropolitan Opera debut in New York; he sang there again in 1890 and 1891. He later separated from Lehmann, although they never legally divorced; after her death in 1929, he settled on her estate.

Kallenberg, Siegfried Garibaldi, German composer; b. Bad Schachen, near Lindau, Nov. 3, 1867; d. Munich, Feb. 9, 1944. He studied with Faisst at the Stuttgart Cons. and at the Munich Academy of Music. He became director of the Stettin Cons. (1892), and later taught in Königsberg, Hannover, and Munich (from 1910). He publ. *Musikalische Kompositionsformen* (Leipzig, 1913) and monographs on R. Strauss (Leipzig, 1926) and Reger (Leipzig, 1930). As a composer, he was inspired by neo-Romanticism; in some of his works there are touches of Impressionism; in others, his absorption in symbolic subjects brought him into a kinship with the Expressionist school in Germany. Apart from works on exotic subjects, he wrote music in a traditional style; he was particularly strong in choral polyphony. Among his compositions are 3 operas: *Sun Liao*, *Das goldene Tor*, and *Die lustigen Musikanten*; also some 300 songs.

Kalliwoda (Kalivoda), Johann Wenzel (Jan Křtitel Václav), Bohemian violinist, conductor, and composer; b. Prague, Feb. 21, 1801; d. Karlsruhe, Dec. 3, 1866. He studied at the Prague Cons. (1811–16) with Pixis (violin) and D. Weber (composition), then played in the orch. of the Stavovské Theater in Prague (1816–21). In 1822 he became conductor of Prince Fürstenberg's orch. in Donaueschingen, where he remained for some 30 years; his duties were minimal after the orch. was dissolved in the wake of the 1848 Revolution and the destruction of the theater by fire (1856). After giving a farewell concert as a violinist in Prague (1858), he retired to Karlsruhe. His early success as a composer was not sustained in the later years of his career; some of his music was praised by Schumann. Among his compositions were the operas *Blanda, die silberne Birke* (Prague, Nov. 29, 1827) and *Prinzessin Christine von Wolfenburg* (Donaueschingen, 1828). His son, Wilhelm Kalliwoda (1827–1893), was a pianist, composer, and conductor.
BIBL.: K. Strunz, *J. W. K.* (Vienna, 1910).

Kálmán, Emmerich (Imre), remarkable Hungarian composer; b. Siófolk, Oct. 24, 1882; d. Paris, Oct. 30, 1953. He went to Budapest, where he studied law at the Univ. and theory and composition with Koessler at the Royal Academy of Music. From 1904 to 1908 he was a répétiteur at the Vigszinhás, and also wrote music criticism. Although he attracted notice as a composer with his symphonic poem *Saturnalia* (1904) and a song cycle, which was awarded the Franz-Josef Prize (1907), he soon concentrated his activities on the musical theater. His first operetta, *Tatárjárás* (The Happy Hussars; Feb. 22, 1908), was so successful that it was subsequently performed throughout Europe and eventually made its way to New York. His next score, *Az obsitos* (March 16, 1910), assured his reputation when it was subsequently staged in Vienna as *Der gute Kamerad* (Oct. 10, 1911; rev. version as *Gold gab ich für Eisen*, Oct. 16, 1914). Its unqualified success led Kálmán to settle in Vienna, where he brought out the highly successful *Der Zigeunerprimás* (Oct. 11, 1912), which subsequently triumphed on various European stages and as *Sari* on Broadway. After producing *The Blue House* (London, Oct. 28, 1912), *Der kleine König* (Vienna, Nov. 27, 1912), and *Kivándorlók* (Budapest, Sept. 26, 1913), Kálmán had a notable success with *Zsuzsi kisasszony* (Budapest, Feb. 23, 1915), which later became a Broadway favorite as *Miss Springtime*. With Vienna again the center of his activities, he scored a triumph with his *Die Csárdásfürstin* (Nov. 17, 1915), which ran for almost 600 performances and became a beloved repertoire piece. The success of *Die Faschingsfee* (Sept. 21, 1917) was followed by the popular *Das Hollandweibchen* (Jan. 31, 1920). Kálmán then composed 2 outstanding scores, *Die Bajadere* (Dec. 23, 1921) and *Gräfin Mariza* (Feb. 28, 1924), which were heard throughout Europe to great acclaim. The latter was so successful that it also became a repertoire work. After further success with *Die Zirkusprinzessin* (March 26, 1926), Kálmán attempted to transfer his golden touch to Broadway with *Golden Dawn* (Nov. 30, 1927) but without success. Back in Vienna, success was his again with *Die Herzogin von Chicago* (April 5, 1928), although *Das Veilchen vom Montmartre* (March 21, 1930) and *Der Teufelsreiter* (March 10, 1932) elicited little interest. He also wrote the film score for *Ronny* (1931). After composing *Kaiserin Josephine* (Zürich, Jan. 18, 1936), the ominous clouds of Nazism led Kálmán to go to Paris in 1939. In 1940 he emigrated to the United States and in 1942 became a naturalized American citizen. During his American sojourn he had some success with the musical *Marinka* (N.Y., July 18, 1945). With World War II over, Kálmán returned to Europe. His last stage work, *Arizona Lady*, was premiered posthumously in Bern on Feb. 14, 1954.
BIBL.: J. Bistron, *E. K.* (Vienna, 1932); R. Oesterreicher, *E. K.: Der Weg eines Komponisten* (Vienna, 1954); V. Kálmán, *Gruss' mir die süssen, die reizenden Frauen: Mein Leben mit E. K.* (Bayreuth, 1966); R. Oesterreicher, *E. K.: Das Leben eines Operettenfürsten* (Vienna, 1988).

Kálmán, Oszkár, Hungarian bass; b. Kis-Szent-Péter, June 18, 1887; d. Budapest, Sept. 18, 1971. He was a student at the Budapest Academy of Music of József Sík. In 1913 he made his debut as Sarastro at the Budapest Opera, where, in 1918, he created Bartók's Duke Bluebeard. After appearances in Hamburg (1926), at the Berlin Kroll Opera (1927), and in Vienna and Barcelona (1927–29), he again sang at the Budapest Opera (1929–54); he also made appearances as a concert artist. Kálmán was particularly admired for his Wagnerian roles.

Kalninš, Alfreds, Latvian organist and composer, father of **Janis Kalninš**; b. Zehsis, Aug. 23, 1879; d. Riga, Dec. 23, 1951. He studied at the St. Petersburg Cons. (1897–1901) with Homilius (organ) and Liadov (composition); he then was organist in various Lutheran churches in Dorpat, Libau, and Riga; he gave recitals in Russia, and was also active as a teacher in Riga. From 1927 to 1933 he lived in New York; he then returned to Riga, where he taught at the Latvian Cons.; was its rector (1944–48). He wrote the first national Latvian opera, *Banuta* (Riga, May 29, 1920); also the operas *Salinieki* (The Islanders; Riga, 1925) and *Dzimtenes atmoda* (The Nation's Awakening; Riga, Sept. 9, 1933); about 200 songs.

BIBL.: J. Vitolinš, *A. K.* (Riga, 1968).

Kalninš, Imants, significant Latvian composer; b. Riga, May 26, 1941. He studied composition with A. Skulte at the Latvian Cons. in Riga, graduating in 1964. In 1959 he directed the choral organization Lachplesis in Lielvarde, then was pianist for a pantomime group in Riga (1962–64) and taught music in Liepaja and later at the Latvian Cons. (1973–80). About 1980 he turned his attention mostly to rock music. His output is innovative, fusing a diversity of styles; his 4th Sym. is scored for jazz ensemble and orch. Other compositions include the operas *Is There Anyone Here?* (1971) and *I Play, I Dance* (1977), the operetta *Quo Vadis My Guitar?* (1971), and the oratorios *In October* (1967), *The Poet and the Mermaid* (1973), and *Morning Drudgery* (1977).

Kalninš, Janis, Latvian-born Canadian organist, conductor, pedagogue, and composer, son of **Alfreds Kalninš**; b. Pernu, Estonia (of Latvian parents), Nov. 3, 1904. He studied piano and organ with his father, then composition with Vitols at the Latvian State Cons. in Riga (1920–24); he also studied conducting with Kleiber in Salzburg, Abendroth in Leipzig, and Blech in Berlin. Returning to Riga, he served as music director of the Latvian National Theater (1923–33) and the Latvian National Opera (1933–44). In 1948 he emigrated to Canada, becoming a naturalized citizen in 1954. From 1948 to 1989 he was organist and choirmaster at St. Paul's United Church in Fredericton, New Brunswick; he served as prof. of music at the Fredericton Teachers' College (1951–71), and was conductor of the Fredericton Civic Orch. (1951–58), the St. John Sym. Orch. (1958–61), and the New Brunswick Sym. Orch. (1961–67). Among his works are the operas *Lolita's Magic Bird* (1933), *Unguni* (1933), *In the Fire* (1934), and *Hamlet* (1935; Riga, Feb. 17, 1936), and the ballets *Autumn* (1936) and *The Nightingale and the Rose* (1936).

Kalomiris, Manolis, distinguished Greek composer and pedagogue; b. Smyrna, Dec. 26, 1883; d. Athens, April 3, 1962. He studied piano with Bauch and Sturm, theory and composition with Grädener, and music history with Mandyczewski at the cons. of the Gesellschaft der Musikfreunde in Vienna (1901–06); he then went to Russia, where he taught piano at a private school in Kharkov. He settled in Athens, where he taught at the Cons. (1911–19); he was founder-director of the Hellenic Cons. (1919–26) and of the National Cons. (1926–48). He was greatly esteemed as a teacher; publ. several textbooks on harmony, counterpoint, and orchestration. Kalomiris was the protagonist of Greek nationalism in music; almost all his works are based on Greek folk-song patterns, and many are inspired by Hellenic subjects. In his harmonies and instrumentation, he followed the Russian school of composition, with a considerable influx of lush Wagnerian sonorities.

WORKS: OPERAS: *O Protomastoras* (The Master-Builder), after Kazantzakis (Athens, March 24, 1916; rev. 1929 and 1940); *To dachtylidi tis manas* (The Mother's Ring; 1917; rev. 1939); *Anatoli* (Sunrise), musical fairy tale, to a libretto by the composer after Cambyssis (1945; rev. 1948); *Ta xotika nera* (The Shadowy Waters), after Yeats (1950; rev. 1952); *Constantinos o Palaeologus*, music legend after Kazantzakis (Athens, Aug. 12, 1962).

Kalter (real name, **Aufrichtig**), **Sabine,** noted Hungarian mezzo-soprano; b. Jaroslaw, March 28, 1889; d. London, Sept. 1, 1957. She studied at the Vienna Academy of Music; she made her debut at the Vienna Volksoper in 1911; she then was a principal member of the Hamburg Opera (1915–35). After being compelled to leave Germany by the Nazis, she settled in London, where she sang at Covent Garden (1935–39); in later years she devoted herself to a concert career, making her last appearance with the Hamburg Radio in 1950. She was also active as a teacher. Her finest roles were Ortrud, Brangäne, and Fricka.

Kamieński, Lucian, Polish composer and pedagogue; b. Gniezno, Jan. 7, 1885; d. Thorn, July 27, 1964. He studied composition with Bruch and musicology with Kretzschmar and Wolf at the Univ. of Berlin (Ph.D., 1910, with the diss. *Die Oratorien von Johann Adolf Hasse*; publ. in Leipzig, 1912); he then was a music critic in Königsberg (until 1919). He taught at the Poznan Academy of Music (1920–39); he also taught musicology at the Univ. of Poznan. After World War II, he taught privately. Among his compositions were the operas *Tabu* (Königsberg, April 9, 1917) and *Dami i huzary* (Poznan, Oct. 2, 1938); also an album of 60 workers' songs to his own words (Berlin, 1905–10), which he issued under the name Dolega-Kamieński.

Kamieński, Maciej, significant Polish composer of Slovak descent; b. probably in Sopron or Magyar-Ovar, between Hungary and Slovakia, Oct. 13, 1734; d. Warsaw, Jan. 25, 1821. He studied composition in Vienna, then settled in Warsaw as a teacher, and brought out the first Polish opera to be premiered in a public theater, *Nesdza uszczęśliwiona* (Poverty Made Happy; July 11, 1778); after its success, he wrote 7 more operas, only 2 of which are extant. He also composed a cantata for the unveiling of the Sobieski monument (Warsaw, Sept. 14, 1788).

Kaminski, Heinrich, eminent German composer; b. Tiengen, Baden, July 4, 1886; d. Ried, Bavaria, June 21, 1946. He studied at the Univ. of Heidelberg with Wolfrum and in Berlin with Kaun, Klatte, and Juon; he settled in Ried (1914), taught a master class at the Prussian Academy of the Arts in Berlin (1930–33), and then returned to Ried. His writing is strictly polyphonic and almost rigid in form; the religious and mystic character of his sacred music stems from his family origins (he was the son of a clergyman); the chief influences in his work were Bach and Bruckner. The Heinrich-Kaminski-Gesellschaft was organized in 1987. Among his works are *Passionspiel* (1920), *Jürg Jenatsch*, opera (Dresden, April 27, 1929), and *Das Spiel vom König Aphelius*, music drama (1946; Göttingen, Jan. 29, 1950).

BIBL.: K. Schleifer, *H. K.* (Kassel, 1945); K. Schleifer and R. Schwarz-Stilling, *H. K.: Werkverzeichnis* (Kassel, 1947); I. Samson, *Das Vokalschaffen von H. K., mit Ausnahme der Opern* (Frankfurt am Main, 1956); A. Suder, ed., *H. K.* (Tutzing, 1986); H. Hartog, *H. K.* (Tutzing, 1987).

Kamionsky, Oscar (Isaievich), Russian baritone; b. Kiev, 1869; d. Yalta, Aug. 15, 1917. He studied with Everard in St. Petersburg and Rossi in Naples, making his debut in Naples in 1891. He sang in Kharkov (1893–94; 1898–99), Kiev (1894–95), and Tiflis (1896–98; 1899–1901); he also appeared in St. Petersburg, Moscow, and other cities as a guest artist. He later sang in Moscow at the Zimin Theater (1905–08; 1913–14), retiring from the stage in 1915. As a singer, he followed the precepts of the Italian school of bel canto. He was famous for his roles as Valentin in *Faust*, Rigoletto, Wolfram in *Tannhäuser*, and other lyrico-dramatic parts.

Kamu, Okko (Tapani), prominent Finnish conductor; b. Helsinki, March 7, 1946. He studied violin at the Sibelius Academy in Helsinki under Onni Suhonen (graduated, 1967). He played in the Helsinki Youth Orch. and founded the Suhonen Quartet (1964). He was a member of the Helsinki Phil. (1965–66) and concertmaster of the orch. of the Finnish National Opera (1966–68); he then was its 3d conductor (1968–69). After winning 1st prize in the Karajan Competition for conductors (1969), he appeared as a guest conductor with the Royal Opera in Stockholm (1969–70); he then was a conductor with the Finnish Radio Sym. Orch. (1970–71), and subsequently its chief conductor (1971–77). He was chief conductor of the Oslo Phil. (1975–79) and of the Helsinki Phil. (1979–90). In 1988 he became principal conductor of the Sjaelland Sym. Orch. in Copenhagen. He also was chief conductor of the Helsingborg Sym. Orch. from 1991. From 1996 to 2000 he was music director of the Finnish National Opera in Helsinki.

Kancheli, Giya (Alexandrovich), Georgian composer; b. Tbilisi, Aug. 10, 1935. He was a student of Tuskiya at the Tbilisi Cons.

(1959–63), where he became a member of the faculty in 1970. From 1984 to 1989 he was first secretary of the Union of Georgian Composers. In 1991 he settled in Berlin. His compositions were honored with prizes by the Soviet (1976) and Georgian (1981) governments. Kancheli's music has been significantly influenced by Georgian melos, and yet he has managed to pursue an eclectic path that is modernistic and accessible at the same time. His works include *The Pranks of Hanum*, musical comedy (1973) and *Music for the Living*, opera (1984; in collaboration with R. Strua); also incidental music for plays and film scores.

Kanitz, Ernest (Ernst), Austrian-American composer and teacher; b. Vienna, April 9, 1894; d. Menlo Park, Calif., April 7, 1978. He changed his first name to Ernest in order to distinguish himself from a homonymous concert manager in Vienna. He studied with Heuberger (1912–14) and Schreker (1914–20) in Vienna; he then taught at the Neues Konservatorium there (1922–38). After the Anschluss (1938), he emigrated to the United States; he taught theory at various colleges, including the Univ. of Southern Calif. in Los Angeles (1945–59) and Marymount College in Palos Verdes, California. (1960–64). He publ. *A Counterpoint Manual: Fundamental Techniques of Polyphonic Music Writing* (Boston, 1948).

WORKS: OPERAS: *Kumana* (1953); *Room No. 12* (1957; Los Angeles, Feb. 26, 1958); *Royal Auction* (1957; Los Angeles, Feb. 26, 1958); *The Lucky Dollar* (1959); *Perpetual* (Los Angeles, April 26, 1961); *Visions at Midnight* (1963; Los Angeles, Feb. 26, 1964); also *Das Hohelied*, oratorio (1921).

Kannen, Günter von, German bass-baritone; b. Rheydt, March 22, 1940. He was a student of Paul Lohmann and Franziska Martienssen. After singing in Kaiserslautern, Bonn, and Karlsruhe, he was a principal member of the Zürich Opera from 1979 to 1990. He also was engaged as Alberich in the *Ring* cycles at the Bayreuth Festival from 1988 to 1992. In 1992 he joined the Berlin State Opera. He also sang in Hamburg, Dresden, Vienna, Salzburg, Paris, Lucerne, Amsterdam, Chicago, and Tokyo. In addition to Alberich, he was known for such roles as Osmin, the Commendatore, Pizarro, Hans Sachs, Klingsor, the Doctor in *Wozzeck*, Cardillac, and La Roche.

Kapp, Eugen (Arturovich), important Estonian composer; b. Astrakhan, May 26, 1908. His father was the significant Estonian composer Artur Kapp (b. Suure-Jaani, Feb. 28, 1878; d. there, Jan. 14, 1952). He graduated from his father's composition class at the Tallinn Cons. (1931), then became a teacher of composition there (1935); after serving as founder-director of the Estonian State Ensemble in Yaroslavl (1941–44), he became a prof. at the Estonian Cons. (1947) and was its director (1952–64). He received the Order of Lenin (1950) and was made a People's Artist of the Estonian SSR (1950) and of the USSR (1956). His operas *Tasuleegid* and *Vabaduse laulik* won Stalin Prizes in 1946 and 1950, respectively, as well as his ballet *Kalevipoeg* in 1952.

WORKS: DRAMATIC: OPERAS: *Tasuleegid* (Flames of Vengeance; Tallinn, July 21, 1945); *Vabaduse laulik* (Freedom's Singer; Tallinn, July 20, 1950); *Talvemuinasjutt* (Winter Fairy Tale; Tartu, Oct. 28, 1958); *Tabamatu* (Elusive Marta; 1960; Tartu, March 19, 1961); *Rembrandt* (March 30, 1975); *Enneolematu ime* (Unheard of Wonder), children's opera (Tallinn, May 8, 1983). OPERETTA: *Assol* (1965). BALLETS: *Kalevipoeg* (1947); *Kullaketrajad* (Goldspinners; 1956).

BIBL.: G. Polyanovsky, *E. K.* (Moscow, 1957).; H. Kyrvits, *E. K.* (Tallinn, 1964).

Kapp, Julius, German writer on music; b. Seelbach, Baden, Oct. 1, 1883; d. Sonthofen, March 18, 1962. He studied in Marburg, Munich, and Berlin (Ph.D. in chemistry, 1907). From 1904 to 1907 he ed. Berlin's *Literarischer Anzeiger*, which he founded; he then was adviser on productions at the Berlin State Opera and ed. of its *Blätter der Staatsoper* (1921–45); he subsequently was an adviser on productions at the Berlin Städtische Oper (1948–54). He wrote significant biographies of Liszt and Wagner.

WRITINGS: *Richard Wagner und Franz Liszt: Eine Freundschaft* (Berlin and Leipzig, 1908); *Arthur Schnitzler* (Berlin, 1909); *Franz Liszt: Eine Biographie* (Berlin and Leipzig, 1909; 20th ed., 1924); *Franz Liszt: Gesammelte Schriften (allgemeine Inhaltsübersicht)* (Leipzig, 1910); *Franz Liszt und die Frauen* (Leipzig, 1910); *Liszt-Brevier* (Leipzig, 1910); *Richard Wagner: Eine Biographie* (Berlin, 1910; 32d ed., 1929); ed. *Der junge Wagner: Dichtungen, Aufsätze, Entwürfe, 1832–1849* (Berlin, 1910); ed. *Franz Liszt: Gesammelte Schriften* (Leipzig, 1910); *Liszt-Brevier* (Leipzig, 1910); *Richard Wagner und die Frauen: Eine erotische Biographie* (Berlin, 1912; 16th ed., 1929; rev. 1951; Eng. tr., 1951, as *The Loves of Richard Wagner*); *Niccolò Paganini: Eine Biographie* (Berlin and Leipzig, 1913; 18th ed., 1954); ed. *Richard Wagner: Gesammelte Schriften und Dichtungen* (Leipzig, 1914); ed. *Richard Wagners gesammelte Briefe, I-II* (Leipzig, 1914–33); ed. *Richard Wagner an Mathilde und Otto Wesendonk* (Leipzig, 1915; 2d ed., 1936); *Berlioz: Eine Biographie* (Berlin and Leipzig, 1917; 2d ed., rev., 1922); *Das Dreigestirn: Berlioz, Liszt, Wagner* (Berlin, 1920); *Giacomo Meyerbeer: Eine Biographie* (Berlin, 1920; 8th ed., rev., 1932); *Franz Schreker: Der Mann und sein Werk* (Munich, 1921); *Das Opernbuch* (Leipzig, 1922; 18th ed., 1928; rev. 1939); *Die Oper der Gegenwart* (Berlin, 1922); *Carl Maria von Weber* (Stuttgart and Berlin, 1922; 15th ed., 1944); ed. *Ludwig van Beethovens sämtliche Briefe* (Leipzig, 1923; rev. ed. of Kastner); ed. *Richard Strauss und die Berliner Oper* (Berlin, 1934); *Geschichte der Staatsoper Berlin* (Berlin, 1937).

Kapp, Richard, American conductor; b. Chicago, Oct. 9, 1936. He studied at Johns Hopkins Univ. (B.A., 1957), then took courses in conducting, composition, and piano at the Staatliche Hochschule für Musik in Stuttgart. Returning to the United States, he studied jurisprudence at N.Y. Univ. (J.D., 1966) and had private lessons with Rosbaud and Halasz in conducting, Simon in piano, and Marlowe in harpsichord. He began his musical career as a répétiteur at the Basel Stadttheater (1960–62); he then was music director of the Opera Theater of the Manhattan School of Music in New York (1963–65). In 1968 he led a concert in New York with a specially assembled group billed as the Philharmonia Virtuosi; he later toured with it in programs of varied repertoire, from Baroque to jazz.

Kapp, Villem, Estonian composer; b. Suure-Jaani, Sept. 7, 1913; d. Tallinn, March 24, 1964. His uncle was the significant Estonian composer Artur Kapp (b. Suure-Jaani, Feb. 28, 1878; d. there, Jan. 14, 1952). He began his training with his uncle, then studied with Eller at the Tallinn Cons. (1939–44); from 1945 to 1964 he was a prof. of composition there. He wrote in an expansive Romantic style rooted in folk song; his opera, *Lembitu* (Tallinn, Aug. 23, 1961), glorifies Estes Lembitu, the leader of the Estonian struggle against the invading Teutonic crusaders in 1217.

BIBL.: H. Tõnson, *V. K.* (Tallinn, 1967).

Kappel, Gertrude, noted German soprano; b. Halle, Sept. 1, 1884; d. Pullach, April 3, 1971. She studied with Nikisch and Noe at the Leipzig Cons. She made her debut in 1903 at the Hannover Opera, where she was a regular member (until 1924); she also sang at London's Covent Garden (1912–14; 1924–26) and the Vienna State Opera (1924–29). She was a principal member of the Bavarian State Opera in Munich (1927–31). She made her Metropolitan Opera debut in New York as Isolde on Jan. 16, 1928, and remained a member until 1936; she also sang with the San Francisco Opera; she returned to Germany, retiring in 1937. Her finest roles were Isolde and Brünnhilde, but she also was admired for her Senta, Sieglinde, Marschallin, and Elektra.

Kapr, Jan, Czech composer; b. Prague, March 12, 1914; d. there, April 29, 1988. He studied with his father, a musician, then composition with Řídký and later with Křička in his master class at the Prague Cons. (1933–40). He was a music producer for the Czech Radio in Prague (1939–46), a music critic (1946–49), and an ed. in music publishing (1950–54); from 1961 to 1970 he taught at the Janáček Academy of Music and Dramatic Arts in Brno. His style of composition is derived from the Czech national school; in his later works he audaciously introduced modernistic serial procedures. Among his works is the opera *Muzikantská pohádka* (Musicians' Fairy Tale; 1962). He publ. a vol. on contemporary music entitled *Konstanty* (The Constants; Prague, 1967).

Karajan, Herbert (Heribert) von, great Austrian conductor; b. Salzburg, April 5, 1908; d. Anif, near Salzburg, July 16, 1989. He was a scion of a cultured family of Greek-Macedonian extraction whose original name was Karajannis. His great-grandfather was Theodor Georg von Karajan (b. Vienna, Jan. 22, 1810; d. there, April 28, 1873), a writer on music; his father was a medical officer who played the clarinet and his brother was a professional organist. Karajan himself began his musical training as a pianist; he took lessons with Franz Ledwinka at the Salzburg Mozarteum. He further attended the conducting classes of the Mozarteum's director, Bernhard Paumgartner. Eventually he went to Vienna, where he pursued academic training at a technical college and took piano lessons from one J. Hofmann; then entered the Vienna Academy of Music as a conducting student in the classes of Clemens Krauss and Alexander Wunderer. On Dec. 17, 1928, he made his conducting debut with a student orch. at the Vienna Academy of Music; shortly afterward, on Jan. 23, 1929, he made his professional conducting debut with the Salzburg Orch. He then received an engagement as conductor of the Ulm Stadttheater (1929–34). From Ulm he went to Aachen, where he was made conductor of the Stadttheater; he subsequently served as the Generalmusikdirektor there (1935–42). On April 9, 1938, he conducted his first performance with the Berlin Phil., the orch. that became the chosen medium of his art. On Sept. 30, 1938, he conducted *Fidelio* at his debut with the Berlin State Opera. After his performance of *Tristan und Isolde* there on Oct. 21, 1938, he was hailed by the *Berliner Tageblatt* as "das Wunder Karajan." His capacity of absorbing and interpreting the music at hand and transmitting its essence to the audience became his most signal characteristic; he also conducted all of his scores from memory, including the entire *Ring des Nibelungen*. His burgeoning fame as a master of both opera and sym. led to engagements elsewhere in Europe. In 1938 he conducted opera at La Scala in Milan and also made guest appearances in Belgium, the Netherlands, and Scandinavia. In 1939 he became conductor of the sym. concerts of the Berlin State Opera Orch.

There was a dark side to Karajan's character, revealing his lack of human sensitivity and even a failure to act in his own interests. He became fascinated by the ruthless organizing solidity of the National Socialist party; shortly after Hitler became chancellor of Germany in 1933, Karajan was recruited to join the Austrian Nazi party in Salzburg, and then formally joined the Germany Nazi party in 1934 in anticipation of his Aachen appointment. He lived to regret these actions after the collapse of the Nazi empire, but he managed to obtain various posts, and in 1947 he was officially denazified by the Allies' army of occupation. His personal affairs also began to interfere with his career. He married the operetta singer Elmy Holgerloef in 1938, but divorced her in 1942 to marry Anita Gütermann. Trouble came when the suspicious Nazi genealogists discovered that she was one-quarter Jewish and suggested that he divorce her. But World War II was soon to end, and so was Nazi hegemony. He finally divorced Gütermann in 1958 to marry the French fashion model Eliette Mouret.

Karajan was characteristically self-assertive and unflinching in his personal relationships and in his numerous conflicts with managers and players. Although he began a close relationship with the Vienna Sym. Orch. in 1948, he left it in 1958. His association as conductor of the Philharmonia Orch. of London from 1948 to 1954 did more than anything to reestablish his career after World War II, but in later years he disdained his relationship with that ensemble. When Wilhelm Furtwängler, the longtime conductor of the Berlin Phil., died in 1954, Karajan was chosen to lead the orch. on its first tour of the United States. However, he insisted that he would lead the tour only on the condition that he be duly elected Furtwängler's successor. Protesters were in evidence for his appearance at N.Y.'s Carnegie Hall with the orch. on March 1, 1955, but his Nazi past did not prevent the musicians of the orch. from electing him their conductor during their visit to Pittsburgh on March 3. After their return to Germany, the West Berlin Senate ratified the musicians' vote on April 5, 1955.

Karajan soon came to dominate the musical life of Europe as no other conductor had ever done. In addition to his prestigious Berlin post, he served as artistic director of the Vienna State Opera from 1956 until he resigned in a bitter dispute with its general manager in 1964. He concurrently was artistic director of the Salzburg Festival (1957–60), and thereafter remained closely associated with it. From 1969 to 1971 he held the title of artistic adviser of the Orchestre de Paris. In the meantime, he consolidated his positions in Berlin and Salzburg. On Oct. 15, 1963, he conducted the Berlin Phil. in a performance of Beethoven's 9th Sym. at the gala concert inaugurating the orch.'s magnificent new concert hall, the Philharmonie. In 1967 he organized his own Salzburg Easter Festival, which became one of the world's leading musical events. In 1967 he re-negotiated his contract and was named conductor-for-life of the Berlin Phil. He made a belated Metropolitan Opera debut in New York on Nov. 21, 1967, conducting *Die Walküre*. He went on frequent tours of Europe and Japan with the Berlin Phil., and also took the orch. to the Soviet Union (1969) and China (1979).

In 1982 Karajan personally selected the 23-year-old clarinetist Sabine Meyer as a member of the Berlin Phil. (any romantic reasons for his insistence were not apparent). The musicians of the orch. rejected her because of their standing rule to exclude women, but also because the majority of the musicians had less appreciation of Fräulein Meyer as an artist than Karajan himself did. A compromise was reached, however, and in 1983 she was allowed to join the orch. on probation. She resigned in 1984 after a year of uneasy coexistence.

In 1985 Karajan celebrated his 30th anniversary as conductor of the Berlin Phil., and in 1988 his 60th anniversary as a conductor. In 1987 he conducted the New Year's Day Concert of the Vienna Phil., which was televised to millions on both sides of the Atlantic. In Feb. 1989 he made his last appearance in the United States, conducting the Vienna Phil. at N.Y.'s Carnegie Hall. In April 1989 he announced his retirement from his Berlin post, citing failing health. Shortly before his death, he dictated an autobiographical book to Franz Endler; it was publ. in an English tr. in 1989.

Through his superlative musical endowments, charismatic and glamorous personality, extraordinary capacity for systematic work, and phenomenal command of every aspect of the great masterworks of the symphonic and operatic repertoire fully committed to memory, Karajan attained legendary stature in his own time. A renowned orchestral technician, he molded the Berlin Phil. into the most glorious musical ensemble of its kind. His interpretations of Beethoven, Wagner, Brahms, Bruckner, Mahler, and Richard Strauss placed him among the foremost conductors in the history of his chosen profession.

BIBL.: E. Haeusserman, *H. v.K. Biographie* (Gütersloh, 1968; new ed., Vienna, 1978); C. Spiel, ed., *Anekdoten um H. v.K.* (Munich, 1968); P. Robinson, *K.* (Toronto, 1975); W. Stresemann, *The Berlin Philharmonic from Bülow to K.* (in Ger. and Eng.; Berlin, 1979); R. Bachmann, *K.: Anmerkungen zu einer Karriere* (Düsseldorf, 1983); H. Kröber, *H. v.K.: Der Magier mit dem Taktstock* (Munich, 1986); R. Vaughan, *H. v.K.: A Biographical Portrait* (N.Y. and London, 1986); H. Götze and W. Simon, eds., *Wo sprache aufhört . . . H. v.K. zum 5. April 1988* (Berlin, 1988); H. Grünewald, *H. v.K. zum Gedenken 1908–1989* (Berlin, 1989); R. Osborne, *Conversations with K.* (Oxford, 1989); R. Bachmann, *K.: Notes on a Career* (N.Y., 1991); W. Stresemann, *Ein seltsamer Mann: Erinnerungen am H. v.K.* (Frankfurt am Main, 1991); F. Endler, *K.: Eine Biographie* (Hamburg, 1992); K. Lang, *The K. Dossier* (London and Boston, 1992); B. Wessling, *H. v.K.: Eine kritische Biographie* (Munich, 1994); F. Endler and K. Fritthum, *K. an der Wiener Oper: Dokumentation einer éra* (Vienna, 1997); R. Osborne, *H. v.K.: A Life in Music* (London, 1998).

Karastoyanov, Assen, Bulgarian composer and teacher; b. Samokov, June 3, 1893; d. Sofia, Sept. 8, 1976. He studied flute at the Sofia Music School (1914–18); subsequently he took courses with Juon (harmony) at the Berlin Hochschule für Musik (1921–22), Dukas (composition) at the École Normale de Musique in Paris (1930–31), and Raphael (composition) at the Leipzig Cons. (1931–32). He taught in Sofia at the Bulgarian State Academy of Music (1933–44), where he was a prof. (1944–58). His works include 7 operettas, including *Michel Strogoff*, after Jules Verne (1937–40).

Karayanis, Plato, American opera administrator; b. Pittsburgh, Dec. 26, 1928. He studied voice at Carnegie-Mellon Univ. in Pittsburgh, opera at the Curtis Inst. of Music in Philadelphia, and opera administration and production technology at the Hamburg State Opera. After singing baritone roles and working as a stage director in Europe, he was made head of the rehearsal dept. at the San Francisco Opera in 1964. From 1965 to 1967 he was assistant stage director and company administrator of the Metropolitan Opera National Co. In 1967 he joined Affiliate Artists, Inc., where he later was executive vice-president. In 1977 he became general director of the Dallas Opera, where his tenure saw the expansion of both the traditional and contemporary repertoires. From 1993 to 1997 he also was president of the board of directors of OPERA America, Inc.

Karayev, Kara (Abulfazogli), Russian composer; b. Baku, Feb. 5, 1918; d. Moscow, May 13, 1982. He studied piano with Sharoyev at the Baku Music Technical School (1930–35) and then composition with Rudolf at the Azerbaijani Cons.; he later took courses in composition with Alexandrov and Shostakovich and instrumentation with Vasilenko at the Moscow Cons. (graduated, 1946). He taught at the Azerbaijani Cons. (from 1946), serving as its director (1949–52). His music is derived mainly from his semi-oriental environment, comprising not only the native Tartar motifs, but also other Asian resources; particularly effective are his theatrical spectacles featuring native dances and choral ensembles. His works include the opera *Fatherland* (1945) and the ballets *7 Beauties* (1952) and *On the Track of Thunder* (1958).

BIBL.: L. Karagicheva, *K. K.* (Baku, 1956).

Karel, Rudolf, Czech composer; b. Pilsen, Nov. 9, 1880; d. in the concentration camp in Terezín, March 6, 1945. He was the last student of Dvořák, with whom he studied in Prague for 1 year during his term at the Prague Cons. (1901–04). In 1914 he went to Russia as a teacher. After the Revolution, he made his way to Irkutsk, Siberia; during the Russian civil war, he became a member of the Czechoslovak Legion and conducted an orch. organized by the legionnaires. He returned to Prague in 1920; from 1923 to 1941, taught at the Prague Cons. As a member of the Czech resistance in World War II, he was arrested by the Nazis in March 1943; he was transferred to Terezín in Feb. 1945, and died there of dysentery shortly before liberation. His music reflects Romantic concepts. He had a predilection for programmatic writing; the national element is manifested by his treatment of old modal progressions; his instrumental writing is rich in sonority and the polyphonic structure is equally strong.

WORKS: DRAMATIC: *Ilseino srdce* (Ilsea's Heart), lyric comedy (1906–09; Prague, Oct. 11, 1924); *Smrt Kmotřička* (Godmother Death), musical fairy tale (1928–33; Brno, Feb. 3, 1933); *Tři vlasy děda Vševěda* (3 Hairs of the Wise Old Man), musical fairy tale (1944–45; arranged by Z. Vostřak; Prague, Oct. 28, 1948); incidental music.

BIBL.: O. Šourek, *R. K.* (Prague, 1947).

Karetnikov, Nikolai, Russian composer; b. Moscow, June 28, 1930; d. there, Oct. 10, 1994. He was a student of Shebalin at the Moscow Cons. (1948–53). He embraced contemporary means of expression in his works, including 12-tone techniques. His advanced scores were not welcomed in official circles, although some of his music was performed abroad. His opera *Til Ulenshpigel* (Till Eulenspiegel; 1985) had to be recorded in secret, which prompted Gerard McBurney on BBC Radio 3 to dub it the first *samizdat* opera. It was finally performed in public in Bielefeld in 1993. He also composed the opera oratorio *Misteriya apostola Pavla* (The Mystery of St. Paul; 1972–87), ballet music, and film scores.

Karkoff, Maurice (Ingvar), prominent Swedish composer and teacher; b. Stockholm, March 17, 1927. He began his training in theory with Blomdahl (1944–47), concurrently studying piano at the Stockholm Musikhögskolan (1945–51) and theory with Larsson (1948–53); he later pursued composition studies with Koch in Stockholm, Holmboe in Copenhagen, Jolivet in Paris, and Vogel in Switzerland. He was music critic of the Stockholm daily *Tidningen* (1962–66); in 1965 he became a teacher of theory and composition at the Stockholm Municipal Music Inst. In 1976 he was awarded the City of Stockholm Prize of Honor, and in 1977 was elected a member of the Royal Swedish Academy of Music in Stockholm. In his music he absorbed many cultures; these are reflected in his compositions, many of which may be described as romantically modernistic and thematically sensitive to exotic resources and coloristic instrumental timbres. Among his many works is the chamber opera *Grandskibbutzen* (The Frontier Kibbutz; 1971–72).

Karkoschka, Erhard, German composer, conductor, and pedagogue; b. Moravská Ostrava, Czechoslovakia, March 6, 1923. He studied composition with Marx at the Stuttgart Hochschule für Musik (1946–53) and musicology with Gerstenberg and Reichert at the Univ. of Tübingen (Ph.D., 1959, with a diss. on Webern's early compositional techniques). He was conductor of the orch. and choir at the Univ. of Hohenheim (1948–68), and in 1958 joined the faculty of the Stuttgart Hochschule für Musik, where he became a prof. in 1964 and director of its electronic music studio in 1973; he retired in 1987. He also founded its Ensemble for New Music (1962), which became an independent ensemble in 1976 under the name Contact-Ensemble. From 1974 to 1980 he was president of the Gesellschaft für Neue Musik. In 1987 he was elected a member of the Free Academy of the Arts in Mannheim. He adoped Webern's serial method of composition, often incorporating electronics and also occasionally resorting to graphic notation in order to achieve greater freedom of resulting sonorities; in his desire to unite the arts, he created various pieces of music sculpture. He also composed the chamber opera *Orpheus? Oder Hadeshöhe* (1990–92).

WRITINGS: *Das Schriftbild der neuen Musik* (1965; Eng. tr., 1972, as *Notations of New Music*); *Analyse neuer Musik* (1976); *Neue Musik-Hören-Verstehen* (1978); with H. Haas, *Hörererziehung mit neuer Musik* (1982).

Karl, Tom, Irish tenor; b. Dublin, Jan. 19, 1846; d. Rochester, N.Y., March 19, 1916. He studied in England with Henry Phillips, and in Italy with Sangiovanni. He sang in Italy for many years, then settled in New York. His remarkable success as Ralph in Pinafore (1879) encouraged him to pursue a career in light opera. With H. Barnabee and W. MacDonald, he formed the light opera company the Bostonians, which had a repertoire of about 150 operas and operettas. After his retirement in 1896, he taught voice in New York and Rochester.

Karpath, Ludwig, Austrian singer and music critic; b. Budapest, April 27, 1866; d. Vienna, Sept. 8, 1936. He was a pupil at the Budapest Cons., studied singing in Vienna, and was a member of the National Opera Co. in the United States (singing minor bass roles; 1886–88). Returning to Vienna, he became an influential music critic; he wrote for the *Neues Wiener Tageblatt* (1894–1921). He publ. *Siegfried Wagner als Mensch und Künstler* (1902) and *Richard Wagner, der Schuldenmacher* (1914).

Karyotakis, Theodore, Greek composer; b. Argos, July 21, 1903; d. Athens, June 14, 1978. He studied with Mitropoulos (composition) and Varvoglis (counterpoint and orchestration) in Athens; concurrently he was enrolled in the law dept. of the Univ. of Athens. He wrote music in a neo-Romantic vein, permeated with euphonious dissonances; several of his works are inspired by Greek folk modes. His works include the opera *Tou fengariou louloudi* (Flower of the Moon; 1953–55).

Kasarova, Vesselina (Ivanova), admired Bulgarian-born Swiss mezzo-soprano; b. Stara Zagora, July 18, 1965. She was a student at the Christina Morfova music gymnasium in Stara Zagora (1979–84), and then pursued her musical education at the National Music Academy in Sofia, where her vocal mentor was Ressa Koleva (diploma, 1989). On April 17, 1988, she made her operatic debut as Rosina at the Bulgarian National Opera in Sofia. In 1989 she won 1st prize in the Neue Stimmen competition in Gütersloh. That same year she made her first appearance at the Zürich Opera as Stéphano in Gounod's *Roméo et Juliette*, and continued on its roster until 1991. After singing Annio in *La clemenza di Tito* at the Salzburg Festival in 1991, she returned there to critical acclaim in 1992 as Tancredi. She made her debut at the Vienna State Opera in 1991 as Rosina, and continued to sing there as a member of the company until 1993. In 1993 she made her first appearance at London's Covent Garden as Rosina, and as Cherubino at the Bavarian State Opera in Munich. From 1993 to 1996 she was a member of the Zürich Opera. She made her first appearance at the Deutsche Oper in Berlin in 1995 as Rossini's Isabella, which role she also portrayed that year at her debut at the Teatro Comunale in Florence. In 1996 she made her debut at the Opéra de la Bastille in Paris as Bellini's Romeo. Her U.S. debut followed in 1997 as Idamante at the Lyric Opera in Chicago. Following an engagement as Angelina in *La Cenerentola* in Pesaro in 1998, she sang Sesto in Munich in 1999. She appeared as a soloist with many leading orchs. and also toured widely as a recitalist.

Kaschmann (Kašman), Giuseppe, Italian baritone; b. Lussimpiccolo, Istria, July 14, 1847; d. Rome, Feb. 7, 1925. He studied in Rome, making his operatic debut in Zagreb in 1869. He then sang the title role in Zajc's *Mislav* at the opening of the Zagreb Opera on Oct. 2, 1870; he made his first appearance in Italy in Turin as Alfonso in *La Favorite* in 1876, and subsequently sang at Milan's La Scala in 1878. He made his Metropolitan Opera debut in New York as Enrico in *Lucia di Lammermoor* on Oct. 24, 1883, returning for the 1895–96 season. He first appeared at the Bayreuth Festival in 1892. In later years he took on buffo roles, making his farewell to the stage in Rome in 1921. His finest roles included Don Giovanni, Amfortas, Wotan, Telramund, Kurwenal, Dr. Bartolo, and Don Pasquale.

Kashin, Daniil Nikitich, Russian composer; b. Moscow, 1769; d. there, Dec. 22, 1841. He was a serf, the property of an aristocratic landowner, Gavril Bibikov, who engaged Sarti to teach him music; he demonstrated his ability by presenting a piano concerto and an overture of his composition in Moscow (March 17, 1790). Bibikov then sent him to Italy for further study; upon his return in 1798, he was given his liberty. On April 10, 1799, he gave in Moscow a monster concert with the participation of 200 executants, including an ensemble of Russian horns; he also presented several of his songs, which became popular. He wrote the operas *Natalya, boyarskaya doch* (Natalia, the Boyar's Daughter; Moscow, Oct. 21, 1801), *Selskiy prazdnik* (The Village Holiday; 1807), *Olga prekrasnaya* (Fair Olga; Moscow, Jan. 14, 1809), and *The One-day Reign of Nourmahal*, after Thomas Moore's *Lalla Rookh* (1817; not perf.). He publ. *Zhurnal octechestvennoy muziki* (Journal of National Music; 1806–09).

Kashperov, Vladimir (Nikitich), Russian composer; b. Tchufarovo, Simbirsk region, Sept. 6, 1826; d. Romantsevo, near Mozhaisk, July 8, 1894. He studied with Voigt and Henselt in St. Petersburg and with Dehn in Berlin (1856), then went to Italy to study singing (1858), remaining there until 1864. He wrote several operas in the Italian style, which were produced in Italy: *Maria Tudor* (Milan, 1859), *Rienzi* (Florence, 1863), and *Consuelo* (Venice, 1865). In 1865 he returned to Russia and taught voice at the Moscow Cons. (1866–72); in 1872 he opened his own school of singing. In Moscow he produced 2 operas with Russian librettos: *The Storm*, after Ostrovsky (1867), and *Taras Bulba*, after Gogol (1893). Even in his Russian works, Kashperov remained faithful to the Italian style of composition, taking Donizetti as a model.

Kasianov, Alexander, Russian composer; b. Bolobonovo, near Nizhny-Novgorod, Aug. 29, 1891; d. there (Gorky), Feb. 13, 1982. He studied composition with Sokolov at the Petrograd Cons. (graduated, 1917); he also studied piano with Liapunov. In 1918 he went to Nizhny-Novgorod, where he organized radio broadcasts; in 1951 he joined the faculty of the Cons. In his compositions, he continued the tradition of early Russian music; his many choral works are quite effective. Among his works are the opera *Stepan Razin* (Gorky, Oct. 29, 1939; rev. version, Gorky, Nov. 14, 1953), *A Partisan Girl* (1941), *On Far North* (1947), and *Ermak* (1957).

BIBL.: N. Ugrumov, *A. K.* (Moscow, 1957).

Kašlík, Václav, Czech conductor, opera producer, and composer; b. Poličná, Sept. 28, 1917; d. Prague, June 4, 1989. He took courses in theory and aesthetics at the Charles Univ. in Prague (1936–39); received training in composition with Karel and A. Hába and in conducting with Doležil and Dědeček at the Prague Cons. (1936–40), completing his studies in conducting in Talich's master classes there (1940–42). From 1941 to 1944 he was assistant director of the National Theater in Prague. He was principal conductor and opera producer in Brno (1944–45). Upon returning to Prague, he was director of the 5th of May Theater (1945–48); subsequently he was an opera producer and conductor with the National Theater; he also conducted at the Smetana Theater (1952–62). In addition to his long association with the National Theater, he was a guest producer in Leningrad, Moscow, Milan, Vienna, London, Geneva, Verona, and Houston. In 1956 he was awarded the Klement Gottwald State Prize and in 1958 was made an Honored Artist by the Czech government. His productions were noteworthy for their use of film, experimental lighting, stereophonic sound, and other modern innovations.

WORKS: DRAMATIC: OPERAS: *Zbojnická balada* (The Brigand's Ballad; 1939–42; Prague, June 17, 1948; rev. 1978; Prague, Oct. 2, 1986); *Křížova cesta* (The Way of the Cross; 1941–45; unfinished); *Krakatit* (Czech TV, March 5, 1961); *La strada* (1980; Prague, Jan. 13, 1982); *Krysar* (Pied Piper; 1983; Plzeň, Oct. 27, 1984). BALLETS: *Don Juan* (1940); *Janošík* (1950); *Pražský karneval* (1954). Also film scores.

Kasparov, Yuri, Armenian composer; b. Moscow, June 8, 1955. He began his music training in childhood. He studied at the Moscow Power Inst. (1972–78), qualifying as an engineer. After further training at a music college (1978–80), he studied with Tchulaki at the Moscow Cons. (1980–84), where he later pursued postgraduate studies with Denisov (1989–91). In 1984 he joined the Central Studio of Documentary Films in Moscow, where he was ed.-in-chief from 1985 to 1989; he was also founder-artistic director of the Moscow Contemporary Music Ensemble from 1990, with which he presented many modern works. In 1985 his first Sym., *Guernica*, won 1st prize in the All-Union Composers Competition. In 1989 his *Ave Maria* for 12 Voices, Violin, Vibraphone, and Organ received 1st prize in the Guido d'Arezzo International Composers Competition in Italy. In his works, Kasparov follows an advanced course reflective of contemporary trends. Among his works is the mono-opera *Nevermore* (1991).

Kaspszyk, Jacek, Polish conductor; b. Biala, Aug. 10, 1952. He received training in theory, composition, and conducting at the Warsaw Cons., graduating in 1975. In 1975 he made his debut at the Warsaw Opera. From 1976 to 1982 he was chief conductor of the Polish Radio National Sym. Orch. in Katowice. He then settled in England, where he made his first appearance at the London Promenade Concerts in 1984. Thereafter he appeared as a guest conductor with the principal British orchs., and also with many orchs. on the Continent. In 1992 he made his debut at the English National Opera in London with *Il Barbiere di Siviglia*. From 1998 he was artistic director of the Warsaw Opera.

Kassern, Tadeusz (Zygfrid), Polish-born American composer; b. Lemberg, March 19, 1904; d. N.Y., May 2, 1957. He studied composition with Soltys and piano with Lalewicz at the Lwów Cons., later with Opienski and Brzostowski at the Poznan Cons.

(1922–26); he also studied law. He went to Paris (1931), then was made cultural attaché at the Polish Consulate in New York (1945). He broke with the communist government in Poland, and remained in New York; he became a naturalized American citizen in 1956. As a composer, he pursued a cosmopolitan trend; although many of his works are inspired by Polish folk music, the idiom and the method are of a general European modern character. Among his works are the operas *The Anointed* (1949–51), *Sun-Up* (1952; N.Y., Nov. 10, 1954), *Comedy of the Dumb Wife* (1953), and *Eros and Psyche* (1954; unfinished).

Kässmayer, Moritz, Austrian violinist, conductor, and composer; b. Vienna, March 20, 1831; d. there, Nov. 9, 1884. He studied with Sechter at the Vienna Cons., then played violin in the orch. of the Vienna Court Opera; he later became ballet conductor there. He wrote a comic opera, *Das Landhaus zu Meudon* (1869).

Kastalsky, Alexander (Dmitrievich), Russian choral conductor and composer; b. Moscow, Nov. 28, 1856; d. there, Dec. 17, 1926. He was a pupil of Tchaikovsky, Taneyev, and Hubert at the Moscow Cons. (1875–81). In 1887 he joined the faculty of Moscow's Synodal School; in 1910 he was appointed director of the school and principal conductor of the choir. In 1911 he took the choir on an extended European tour. In 1918 the Synodal School became a choral academy; in 1923 it merged with the Moscow Cons. Kastalsky was also a teacher of conducting at the Moscow Phil. Inst. (1912–22); in 1923 he was appointed prof. of choral singing at the Moscow Cons. He wrote *Osobennosti narodnorusskoy muzïkalnoy sistemï* (Peculiarities of the Russian Folk Music System; Moscow and Petrograd, 1923; 2d ed., 1961); V. Belaiev ed. his *Osnovï narodnovo mnogogolosiya* (Principles of Folk Polyphony; Moscow and Leningrad, 1948). He was a notable composer of Russian sacred music, into which he introduced modern elements, combining them with the ancient church modes. He composed the opera *Clara Militch* (1907), and incidental music.

Kastle, Leonard (Gregory), American composer and pianist; b. N.Y., Feb. 11, 1929. After attending the Juilliard School of Music in N.Y. (1938–40), he received training in piano from Sheridan and in composition from Szell at the Mannes College of Music in New York (1940–42); he then studied piano with Wittgenstein and Vengerova and also held scholarships in composition with Scalero, Menotti, and Barber at the Curtis Inst. of Music in Philadelphia (1944–50; B.A., 1950); he further attended Columbia Univ. (1947–50), and was a student in conducting with Bamberger in New York (1950–52). He was a visiting prof. of humanities and fine arts at the State Univ. of N.Y. at Albany (1978–88).

WORKS: DRAMATIC: OPERAS: *The Swing* (1954; NBC-TV, June 11, 1956); *Deseret* (1960; NBC-TV, Jan. 1, 1961; rev. for Voices, Piano, and Organ, 1978); *The Pariahs* (1962–66); *The Calling of Mother Ann* (Hancock Shaker Village, Mass., June 21, 1985); *The Journey of Mother Ann* (1986–87; Albany, N.Y., Jan. 22, 1987); *Professor Lookalike and the Children* (1988; Albany, N.Y., May 8, 1989); *The Countess Cathleen* (1995). PLAY WITH MUSIC: *The Birdwatchers* (1980–81).

Kastorsky, Vladimir (Ivanovich), Russian bass; b. Bolshive Soly, March 14, 1871; d. Leningrad, July 2, 1948. He studied with Cotogni and Gabel. He made his debut with Champagner's touring opera company (1894); he became a member of the Maryinsky Theater in St. Petersburg (1899) and later sang with Zimin's opera company in Moscow; he also appeared in Diaghilev's Russian Seasons in Paris and London (1907–08); concurrently he formed a vocal quartet specializing in Russian folk songs, with which he toured abroad. He remained on the operatic stage for nearly 45 years, and appeared in concerts to the end of his life. In addition to his Russian operatic roles, he also was admired as King Marke, Hagen, and Wotan.

Kattnigg, Rudolf, Austrian composer and conductor; b. Oberdorf bei Treffen, April 9, 1895; d. Klagenfurt, Sept. 2, 1955. He went to Vienna and studied law at the Univ. before pursuing training in music at the Academy of Music with Mandyczewski, Löwe, J. Marx, and Krauss (1918–22). From 1928 to 1934 he was director of the Innsbruck Music School. He also was active as a theater conductor, settling in Vienna in 1939. He became best known as an operetta composer, his finest score being *Balkanliebe* or *Die Gräfin von Durazzo* (1937). Other works were the opera *Donna Miranda* (1953), numerous music theater works, including *Der Prinz von Thule* (Basel, Dec. 13, 1936), *Kaiserin Katharina* (Berlin, Feb. 3, 1937), *Balkanliebe* or *Die Gräfin von Durazzo* (Leipzig, Dec. 22, 1937), *Mädels vom Rhein* (Bremen, 1938), *Die Mädel von St. Goar* (Bremen, Feb. 4, 1939), *Hansi fliegt zum Negerkral* (Vienna, Dec. 16, 1942), *Ben Ami* (Vienna, Jan. 18, 1949), and *Rendezvouz um Mitternacht* (Vienna, May 20, 1956), and the ballet *Tarantella* (1942). Also film scores.

Katulskaya, Elena, Russian soprano; b. Odessa, June 2, 1888; d. Moscow, Nov. 20, 1966. She studied privately in Odessa (1904) and St. Petersburg (1905–07) before training with Natalia Iretskaya at the St. Petersburg Cons. (1907–09). She then made her operatic debut as Lakmé at the Maryinsky Theater in St. Petersburg, where she sang until 1911. From 1913 to 1945 she was a principal member of the Bolshoi Theater in Moscow. In 1948 she became a teacher at the Moscow Cons. In 1965 she was made a People's Artist of the USSR. While Katulskaya was particularly esteemed for her roles in Russian operas, she also had success in the Italian and French repertoires.

Katzer, Georg, German composer; b. Habelschwerdt, Silesia, Jan. 10, 1935. He studied with Wagner-Régeny and Zechlin at the Hochschule für Musik in East Berlin (1954–59), then entered the classes of Eisler and Spies at the Akademie der Künste there (1960–63), where he was elected to membership (1979) and became artistic director of its electronic music studio. He served as president of the national section of the International Soc. for Electroacoustic Music (from 1989). In 1981 he received the National Prize for Art of the German Democratic Republic. In his music Katzer is a universalist, applying constructivist principles with lapidary precision. Under the influence of Eisler, he adopted a broad variety of methods, including 12-tone techniques, using his materials for specific purposes accessible to mass audiences.

WORKS: DRAMATIC: *Das Land Bum-Bum*, children's opera (1974); *Schwarze Vögel*, ballet (1974); *Ein neuer Sommernachtstraum*, ballet (1979–80); *Gastmahl oder über die Liebe*, opera (1987; Berlin, April 30, 1988); *Antigone oder die Stadt*, opera (1989).

Kauer, Ferdinand, Moravian-born Austrian conductor and composer; b. Klein-Tajax (baptized), Jan. 18, 1751; d. Vienna, April 13, 1831. As a boy he played organ in a local Jesuit church, then was organist at the Jesuit seminary in Tyrnau, Hungary, where he took courses in philosophy and medicine. He went to Vienna about 1777, where he studied composition with Heidenreich and Zimmermann. He then became a violinist in the orch. of the Theater in der Leopoldstadt about 1781; he was made director of the theater's music school (1789) and later 2d Kapellmeister at the theater, scoring a success with his *Das Donauweibchen* (Jan. 11, 1798); it was subsequently performed all over Europe. After serving as Kapellmeister in Graz (1810–11), he returned to the Leopoldstadt theater; then was Kapellmeister at the Theater in der Josefstadt (1814–18); he subsequently made a precarious living as a 2d violinist in the Leopoldstadt theater orch. (1821–30). He lost almost all of his possessions, including his MSS, in the flood of 1830. Among his compositions were some 200 works for the stage. He publ. *Singschule nach dem neuesten System der Tonkunst* (1790) and *Kurzgefasste Generalbass-Schule für Anfänger* (1800).

BIBL.: K. Manschinger, *F. K.: Ein Beitrag zur Geschichte des Wiener Singspiels um die Wende des 18. Jahrhunderts* (diss., Univ. of Vienna, 1929).

Kauffmann, Leo Justinus, German composer; b. Dammerkirch, Sept. 20, 1901; d. in an air raid in Strasbourg, Sept. 25, 1944. He studied with Erb in Strasbourg and with Jarnach and Abendroth in Cologne. He taught at Cologne's Rheinische Musikschule (1929–32) and worked for the Cologne Radio (1932–33); he later taught at the Strasbourg Cons., serving as its director until his death. He wrote the operas *Die Geschichte vom schönen Annerl* (Strasbourg, June 20, 1942) and *Das Perlenhem* (Strasbourg, 1944).

Kaufmann, Julie, American soprano; b. Iowa, May 20, 1950. She studied at the Univ. of Iowa, the Zürich Opera School, and the Hamburg Hochschule für Musik. Following her operatic debut in Hagen, she sang in various German opera centers before joining the Bavarian State Opera in Munich in 1983. In 1984 she made her debut at London's Covent Garden as Zerlina. She chose Blondchen for her first appearance at the Salzburg Festival in 1987. In 1988 she toured Japan with the Bavarian State Opera, and then sang Woglinde in the staging of the *Ring* cycle in Munich in 1989. In 1991 she was made a Bavarian Kammersängerin. In 1992 she appeared at Milan's La Scala as Zdenka, and then sang Woglinde in Paris in 1994. At the Munich Festival in 1996 she portrayed Handel's Serse. As a concert artist, she sang with leading European orchs. and gave lieder recitals.

Kaufmann, Walter, German-born American conductor, composer, and musicologist; b. Karlsbad, April 1, 1907; d. Bloomington, Ind., Sept. 9, 1984. He studied composition with Schreker in Berlin; he also studied musicology in Prague. In 1935 he traveled to India, where he remained for 10 years; he devoted much time to the study of the Hindu systems of composition; he also appeared as conductor, serving as music director of the Bombay Radio. In 1947 he moved to Nova Scotia and taught piano at the Halifax Cons.; from 1948 to 1957 he was music director of the Winnipeg Sym. Orch. In 1957 he settled in the United States, where he joined the faculty of the Indiana Univ. School of Music in Bloomington. He became a naturalized American citizen in 1964. He wrote *Musical Notations of the Orient* (Bloomington, 1967); *The Ragas of North India* (Bloomington, 1968); *Tibetan Buddhist Chant* (tr. by T. Norbu; Bloomington, 1975); *Involvement with Music: The Music of India* (N.Y., 1976); *Musical References in the Chinese Classics* (Detroit, 1976); *The Ragas of South India* (Bloomington, 1976); *Altinden* (Leipzig, 1981); also valuable articles on Eastern music for American music journals.

WORKS: DRAMATIC: OPERAS: *Der grosse Dorin* (1932); *Der Hammel bringt es an den Tag* (1932); *Esther* (1931–32); *Die weisse Gottin* (1933); *Anasuya*, radio opera (Bombay, Oct. 1, 1938); *The Cloak*, after Gogol (1933–50); *A Parfait for Irene* (Bloomington, Feb. 21, 1952); *The Research* (1951); *The Golden Touch*, children's opera (1953); *Christmas Slippers*, television opera (1955); *Sganarelle* (1955); *George from Paradise* (1958); *Paracelsus* (1958); *The Scarlet Letter*, after Hawthorne (Bloomington, May 6, 1961); *A Hoosier Tale* (Bloomington, July 30, 1966); *Rip van Winkle*, children's opera (1966). BALLETS: *Visages* (1950); *The Rose and the Ring* (1950); *Wang* (1956).

BIBL.: T. Noblitt, ed., *Music East and West: Essays in Honor of W. K.* (N.Y., 1981).

Kaun, Hugo, German composer; b. Berlin, March 21, 1863; d. there, April 2, 1932. He studied at the Berlin Hochschule für Musik (1879–80), then with Oskar Raif (piano) and at the Prussian Academy of Arts with Friedrich Kiel (composition). He was active as a teacher and conductor of the Liederkranz in Milwaukee (1887–1901), then returned to Berlin, becoming a prof. at the Klindworth-Scharwenka Cons. (1922). He publ. *Harmonie- und Modulationslehre* (Leipzig, 1915; 2d ed., 1921); also an autobiography, *Aus meinem Leben* (Berlin, 1932). A cultured composer, he incorporated in his well-crafted works elements of both Brahmsian and Wagnerian idioms. Among his works are the operas *Sappho* (Leipzig, Oct. 27, 1917), *Der Fremde* (Dresden, Feb. 23, 1920), and *Menandra* (staged in Kiel and several other German opera houses simultaneously, Oct. 29, 1925).

BIBL.: W. Altmann, *H. K.* (Leipzig, 1906); R. Schaal, *H. K., 1863–1932, Leben und Werk: Ein Beitrag zur Musik der Jahrhundertwende* (Regensburg, 1946).

Kavrakos, Dimitri, Greek bass-baritone; b. Athens, Feb. 26, 1946. He studied at the Athens Cons. In 1970 he made his operatic debut as Zaccaria in *Nabucco* at the Athens Opera, of which he was a member until 1978. He then made his first appearance in the United States at N.Y.'s Carnegie Hall in Refice's *Cecilia*. On March 7, 1979, he made his Metropolitan Opera debut in New York as the Grand Inquisitor in *Don Carlos*. He made his British debut at the Glyndebourne Festival in 1982 as Mozart's Commendatore, and then his first appearance at London's Covent Garden as Pimen in *Boris Godunov* in 1984. In 1987 he was engaged at the Paris Opéra as the Grand Inquisitor. He sang Silva in *Ernani* at the Rome Opera in 1989. During the 1992–93 season, he appeared as Timur in *Turandot* at the Lyric Opera in Chicago, as Banquo at the Cologne Opera, and as the Commendatore at the Aix-en-Provence Festival. He sang Banquo in Florence in 1995.

Kay, Hershy, American composer, arranger, and orchestrator; b. Philadelphia, Nov. 17, 1919; d. Danbury, Conn., Dec. 2, 1981. He studied cello with Salmond and orchestration with Thompson at the Curtis Inst. of Music in Philadelphia (1936–40); he then went to New York and began a fruitful career as an arranger of Broadway musicals and ballets. He orchestrated a number of Leonard Bernstein's theater works: *On the Town* (1944), *Peter Pan* (incidental music; 1951), *Candide* (1956; revival, 1973), *Mass* (1971), and the Bicentennial pageant *1600 Pennsylvania Avenue* (1976). His last arrangement for Bernstein was *Olympic Hymn* (Baden-Baden, Sept. 23, 1981). He also made many other orchestrations for Broadway, for the N.Y. City Ballet, and for other companies. He completed the orchestration of Robert Kurka's opera *The Good Soldier Schweik* (N.Y., April 23, 1958).

Kay, Ulysses Simpson, eminent black American composer and teacher; b. Tucson, Ariz., Jan. 7, 1917; d. Englewood, N.J., May 20, 1995. He received his early music training at home; on the advice of his uncle "King" Oliver, a leading jazz cornetist and bandleader, he studied piano. In 1934 he enrolled at the Univ. of Arizona at Tucson (Mus.B., 1938); he then went to study at the Eastman School of Music in Rochester, N.Y., where he was a student of Rogers and Hanson (M.M., 1940); he later attended the classes of Hindemith at the Berkshire Music Center in Tanglewood (1941–42). He served in the U.S. Navy (1942–45); he then studied composition with Luening at Columbia Univ. (1946–49); he went to Rome as winner of the American Rome Prize, and was attached there to the American Academy (1949–52). From 1953 to 1968 he was employed as a consultant by Broadcast Music Inc. in New York; was on the faculty of Boston Univ. (1965) and of the Univ. of Calif., Los Angeles (1966–67); in 1968 he was appointed prof. of music at the Herbert H. Lehman College in New York; he was made Distinguished Prof. there in 1972, retiring in 1988. He received honorary doctorates from several American univs. His music followed a distinctly American idiom, particularly in its rhythmic intensity, while avoiding ostentatious ethnic elements; in harmony and counterpoint, he pursued a moderately advanced idiom, marked by prudentially euphonious dissonances; his instrumentation was masterly.

WORKS: DRAMATIC: OPERAS: *The Boor*, after Chekhov (1955; Lexington, Ky., April 3, 1968); *The Juggler of Our Lady* (1956; New Orleans, Feb. 3, 1962); *The Capitoline Venus* (1970; Urbana, Ill., March 12, 1971); *Jubilee* (Jackson, Miss., April 12, 1976); *Frederick Douglass* (1980–85; Newark, April 14, 1991). BALLET: *Dance Calinda* (Rochester, N.Y., April 23, 1941). FILM SCORE: *The Quiet One* (1988).

BIBL.: L. Hayes, *The Music of U. K., 1939–1963* (diss., Univ. of Wisc., 1971); C. Hobson and D. Richardson, *U. K.: A Bio-Bibliography* (Westport, Conn., 1994).

Kazanly, Nikolai (Ivanovich), Russian conductor and composer; b. Tiraspol, Dec. 17, 1869; d. Petrograd, Aug. 5, 1916. He studied in Odessa (1879–83), then went to St. Petersburg, where he entered the composition class of Rimsky-Korsakov at the Cons. (1891–94); he also studied with Balakirev. In 1897 he conducted in western Europe; returning to Russia, he supervised music education in military schools. He wrote an opera, *Miranda* (St. Petersburg, 1910).

Kazarnovskaya, Ljuba, admired Russian soprano; b. Moscow, July 18, 1960. She was 16 when she began vocal training with Nadezhda Malysheva in Moscow; at 19 she enrolled at the Moscow Cons., where she continued her studies with Elena Shumilova. In 1982 she made her formal operatic debut as Tatiana at the Stanislavsky Theater in Moscow. She first sang at the Bolshoi Theater in Moscow in 1983. In 1986 she scored a fine success as Leonora in *La forza del destino* at the Kirov Theater in Leningrad, where she remained as a principal artist until 1989. She also toured with the company abroad, notably as Tatiana at the Paris Opéra and at London's Covent Garden in 1987. In 1989 she was engaged as a soloist in the Verdi *Requiem* at the Salzburg Festival, and subsequently she pursued a successful operatic and concert career in the West. In 1992 she made her North American debut as soloist in the Shostakovich 14th Sym. with the Boston Sym. Orch. Her Metropolitan Opera debut in New York followed later that year, as Tatiana, to critical acclaim. After singing Desdemona there in 1993, she returned to outstanding acclaim in 1994. In 1995 she sang Rimsky-Korsakov's Fevronia during the Kirov company's visit to the Brooklyn Academy of Music. Her engagements also took to her Milan's La Scala, the Vienna State Opera, the Bavarian State Opera in Munich, the Hamburg State Opera, the Teatro Colón in Buenos Aires, and Chicago's Lyric Opera. As a concert artist, she appeared with leading orchs. and at principal festivals. In addition to her esteemed Russian repertoire, she has won notable success as Donna Anna, Vitellia, Marguerite, Amelia, Violetta, Mimi, and Salome.

Kazuro, Stanislaw, Polish composer; b. Teklinapol, near Vilnius, Aug. 1, 1881; d. Warsaw, Nov. 30, 1961. He studied in Warsaw, Paris, and Rome. He was active mainly in Warsaw as a pedagogue and choral conductor; he also publ. several school manuals. His compositions, in an academic style, were chiefly designed for pedagogic purposes; among them are 2 folk operas.

Każyński, Wiktor, Polish pianist, conductor, and composer; b. Vilnius, Dec. 30, 1812; d. St. Petersburg, March 18, 1867. He studied law at the Univ. of Vilnius, and was mostly self-taught in music. From 1836 to 1840 he was organist at Vilnius's Cathedral of St. John; he then went to Warsaw, where he took lessons with Chopin's teacher Elsner. In 1842 he settled in St. Petersburg, where he conducted the orch. of the Alexandrinsky Theater (1845–67). He was one of the first pianists to champion Chopin's works. His own compositions are of little importance, but they are of historical interest as early examples of Polish Romanticism; among them are a melodrama to a Polish libretto, *Żyd wieczny tulacz* (The Wandering Jew; Vilnius, 1842), and a melodrama to a French libretto, *Mąż i żona* (Man and Wife; St. Petersburg, 1848), as well as 7 other works in that genre; also 3 comic operas, including *Antoni i Antosia* (Vilnius, 1840), 4 operettas, and 4 ballets. He also publ. a history of Italian opera (St. Petersburg, 1851; in Polish and in a Russian tr.).

Keene, Christopher, prominent American conductor and music administrator; b. Berkeley, Calif., Dec. 21, 1946; d. N.Y., Oct. 8, 1995. He studied piano as a child, and during his high school years conducted several groups, then attended the Univ. of Calif. at Berkeley (1963–67). In 1965 he made his public debut conducting Britten's *The Rape of Lucretia* in Berkeley; in 1966 he became an assistant conductor at the San Francisco Opera, and in 1967 at the San Diego Opera. In 1968 he made his European debut conducting Menotti's *The Saint of Bleecker Street* at the Spoleto (Italy) Festival. He was music director of the American Ballet Co. (1969–70). On Oct. 18, 1970, he made his N.Y. City Opera debut conducting Ginastera's *Don Rodrigo*, and on Sept. 24, 1971, his Metropolitan Opera debut in New York conducting *Cavalleria rusticana*. He served as co-music director (1971–73), general manager (1973–75), and music director (1975–76) of the Spoleto Festival; he was music director (from 1974) and president (1975–89) of Artpark, the Lewiston, N.Y., summer festival. From 1975 to 1984 he was music director of the Syracuse (N.Y.) Sym. Orch.; he also held that title with the Spoleto Festival U.S.A. in Charleston, S.C. (1977–80), and with the Long Island (N.Y.) Phil. (1979–90). He was artistic supervisor (1982–83) and music director (1983–86) of the N.Y. City Opera, returning there in 1989 as general director. Keene became well known for his championship of rarely heard operas during his years at the N.Y. City Opera. His career was cut short by AIDS-induced lymphoma.

Keenlyside, Simon, English baritone; b. London, Aug. 3, 1959. He studied at St. John's Choir School in Cambridge, took a degree in zoology at the Univ. of Cambridge, and received vocal instruction from John Cameron at the Royal Northern College of Music in Manchester, where he made his operatic debut as Lescaut in 1987. In 1986 he won the Richard Tauber Competition. Following a season with the Hamburg State Opera (1988–89), he joined the Scottish Opera in Glasgow, where he sang Rossini's Figaro in 1991 and Britten's Billy Budd in 1992. In 1989 he made his debut at London's Covent Garden as Silvio, and returned there as Guglielmo in 1995. He sang Gluck's Oreste at the Welsh National Opera in Cardiff in 1991. In 1993 he appeared as Don Giovanni with the Glyndebourne Touring Opera. In 1995 he portrayed Papageno at Milan's La Scala, and returned to Italy in 1997 to sing Don Giovanni. He appeared as Belcore at the Metropolitan Opera in New York in 1996, the same year that he sang Thomas's Hamlet in Geneva. In 1997 he sang Pelléas at the San Francisco Opera. In 1998 he was engaged as Monteverdi's Orfeo in Brussels and in 1999 as Marcello at the Vienna State Opera. He also was active as a lieder artist.

Kegel, Herbert, distinguished German conductor; b. Dresden, July 29, 1920; d. there, Nov. 20, 1990. He studied at the Dresden Staatskapelle's orch. school, where his mentors included Böhm and Blacher (1935–40). In 1946 he became conductor of the Rostock Opera; in 1949 he was engaged as conductor of the Leipzig Radio Choir and Orch.; he was made conductor (1953), Generalmusikdirektor (1958), and chief conductor (1960) of the Leipzig Radio Sym. Orch. From 1975 to 1978 he was a prof. at the Leipzig Hochschule für Musik, and in 1978 became a prof. at the Dresden Hochschule für Musik. From 1977 to 1985 he served as chief conductor of the Dresden Phil. He was regarded as one of the most competent conductors of East Germany, combining a thorough knowledge of his repertoire with a fine sense of effective presentation of the music.

Keil, Alfredo, Portuguese composer and painter of German descent; b. Lisbon, July 3, 1850; d. Hamburg, Oct. 4, 1907. He studied music with António Soares, Oscar de la Cinna, and Ernesto Vieira in Lisbon; he then went to Nuremberg (1868), where he studied music with Kaulbach and painting with Kremling. Returning to Portugal (1870), he pursued a dual career as composer and painter; he devoted his energies to the furtherance of national music. His comic opera, *Susana* (Lisbon, 1883), is generally considered the first substantial work of the Portuguese stage; his song *A Portugueza* (1890) was adopted as the national anthem of Portugal in 1911. He also wrote the operas *Donna Bianca* (Lisbon, March 10, 1888), *Irene* (Turin, March 22, 1893), and *Serrana* (1st perf. in Italian at the Teatro San Carlos, Lisbon, March 13, 1899).

Keilberth, Joseph, distinguished German conductor; b. Karlsruhe, April 19, 1908; d. while conducting a performance of *Tristan und Isolde* at the Nationaltheater in Munich, July 20, 1968. He studied in Karlsruhe, where he became a répétiteur (1925), then Generalmusikdirektor (1935–40) at the State Opera. He was chief conductor of the German Phil. Orch. of Prague (1940–45), and then Generalmusikdirektor of the Dresden Staatskapelle (1945–50). He was chief conductor of the Bamberg Sym. Orch. (1949–68), with which he toured Europe in 1951 and the United States and Latin America in 1954; he was also a conductor at the Bayreuth Festivals (1952–56) and concurrently Generalmusikdirektor of the Hamburg State Phil. Orch. (1950–59), then of the Bavarian State Opera in Munich (1959–68). He was particularly esteemed for his performances of works from the Classical and Romantic Austro-German repertoire.

BIBL.: W.-E. von Lewinski, *J. K.* (Berlin, 1968).

Keiser, Reinhard, important German opera composer; b. Teuchern, near Weissenfels, Jan. 9, 1674; d. Hamburg, Sept. 12, 1739. He received his early musical training from his father, Gottfried Keiser, an organist, and then was sent to Leipzig, where he studied at the renowned Thomasschule directed by Johann Schelle. In 1693 he was in Braunschweig, where he began his career as a composer for the stage. His first opera pastorale, *Der königliche Schäfer oder Basilius in Arcadien*, was performed shortly after his arrival in Braunschweig; in 1694 he produced a Singspiel, *Procris und Cephalus*; there followed another pastorale, *Die wiedergefundenen Verliebten*, in 1695; it was revived in Hamburg in 1699 under the title *Die beständige und getreue Ismene*. In 1694 he was named Cammer-Componist in Braunschweig. In 1695 he went to Hamburg, which became his permanent residence. In 1696 he was engaged as Kapellmeister with the Hamburg Opera; in 1702 he became its codirector, retaining this position until 1707. Hamburg was then the main center of opera productions in Germany, and Keiser worked industriously producing not only his own operas there, but also the stage works of Handel and Mattheson. The number of Keiser's stage works was never calculated with credible precision; the best estimate is that he wrote in Hamburg at least 77 operas and 39 Singspiels and theatrical intermezzi. The subjects of his operas are still predominantly taken from Greek and Roman mythology, as was customary in the Baroque era, but he introduced a decisive innovation by using the German language in his dramatic works; he further made use of popular local themes; he made a concession, however, in resorting to the Italian language in arias. Thus his last opera, *Circe*, produced in Hamburg on March 1, 1734, contains 21 German arias and 23 Italian arias. Keiser also continued the common tradition of having other composers contribute to the music. In his ballets he followed the French *style galant* and effectively used Rococo devices. In so doing he formed a German Baroque idiom national in essence and cosmopolitan in treatment; this aspect of his work influenced his younger contemporaries Bach and Handel. In 1718 Keiser became a guest Kapellmeister to the Duke of Württemberg in Stuttgart. In 1721 he went to Copenhagen to supervise the productions of his operas *Die unvergleichliche Psyche, Ulysses*, and *Der Armenier*. In 1723 he returned to Hamburg, and in 1725 composed 2 operas on subjects connected with Hamburg history and society: *Der Hamburger Jahrmarkt* and *Die Hamburger Schlachtzeit*. In 1728 he became Canonicus minor and Cantor of the Katharinenkirche in Hamburg. Apart from operas, he wrote many sacred works (oratorios, cantatas, Psalms, Passions).

WORKS: DRAMATIC: *Der königliche Schäfer oder Basilius in Arcadien* (Braunschweig, 1693); *Procris und Cephalus*, Singspiel (Braunschweig, 1694); *Die wiedergefundenen Verliebten*, Schäferspiel (Braunschweig, 1695; rev. as *Die beständige und getreue Ismene*, Hamburg, 1699); *Mahumet II*, Trauerspiel (Hamburg, 1696); *Der geliebte Adonis* (Hamburg, 1697); *Die durch Wilhelm den Grossen in Britannien wieder eingeführte Treue* (Hamburg, 1698); *Allerunterthäbigster Gehorsam*, Tantzspiel and Singspiel (Hamburg, Nov. 15, 1698); *Der aus Hyperboreen nach Cymbrien überbrachte güldene Apfel zu Ehren Friedrichs und Hedwig Sophiens zu Holstein* (Hamburg, 1698); *Der bey dem allgemeinen Welt-Friede und dem Grossen Augustus geschlossene Tempel des Janus* (Hamburg, 1699); *Die wunderbahr-errettete Iphigenia* (Hamburg, 1699); *Die Verbindung des grossen Hercules mit der schönen Hebe*, Singspiel (Hamburg, 1699); *Die Wiederkehr der güldnen Zeit* (Hamburg, 1699); *La forza della virtù, oder Die Macht der Tugend* (Hamburg, 1700); *Das höchstpreissliche Crönungsfest Ihrer Kgl. Majestät zu Preussen*, ballet opera (Hamburg, 1701); *Störtebecker und Jödge Michaels* (2 versions; Hamburg, 1701); *Die wunderschöne Psyche*, Singspiel (Hamburg, Oct. 20, 1701); *Circe oder Des Ulisses erster Theil* (Hamburg, 1702); *Penelope oder Des Ulysses ander Theil* (Hamburg, 1702); *Sieg der fruchtbaren Pomona* (Hamburg, Oct. 18, 1702); *Die sterbende Eurydice oder Orpheus erster Theil* (Hamburg, 1702); *Orpheus ander Theil* (Hamburg, 1702); *Neues preussisches Ballet* (Hamburg, 1702); *Die verdammte Staat-Sucht, oder Der verführte Claudius* (Hamburg, 1703); *Die Geburt der Minerva* (Hamburg, 1703); *Die über die Liebe triumphierende Weissheit oder Salomon* (Hamburg, 1703); *Der gestürzte und wieder erhöhte Nebucadnezar, König zu Babylon* (Hamburg, 1704); *Die römische Unruhe oder Die edelmüthige Octavia* (Hamburg, Aug. 5, 1705); *Die kleinmüthige Selbstmörderinn Lucretia oder Die Staats-Thorheit des Brutus*, Trauerspiel (Hamburg, Nov. 29, 1705); *La fedeltà coronata oder Die gekrönte Treue* (Hamburg, 1706); *Masagniello furioso, oder Die Neapolitanische Fischer-Empörung* (Hamburg, June 1706); *La costanza sforzata, Die gezwungene Beständigkeit oder Die listige Rache des Sueno* (Hamburg, Oct. 11, 1706); *Il genio d'Holsatia* (Hamburg, 1706; used as prologue to succeeding work); *Der durchlauchtige Secretarius, oder Almira, Königin von Castilien* (Hamburg, 1706); *Der angenehme Betrug oder Der Carneval von Venedig* (Hamburg, 1707; includes arias by C. Graupner); *La forza dell'amore oder Die von Paris entführte Helena* (Hamburg, 1709); *Die blutdürstige Rache oder Heliates und Olympia* (Hamburg, 1709; with C. Graupner); *Desiderius, König der Langobarden* (Hamburg, July 26, 1709); *Die bis und nach dem Todt unerhörte Treue des Orpheus* (Hamburg, 1709; based on *Die sterbende Eurydice oder Orpheus erster Theil and Orpheus ander Theil*); *La grandezza d'animo oder Arsinoe* (Hamburg, 1710); *Le Bon Vivant oder Die Leipziger Messe* (Hamburg, 1710); *Der Morgen des europäischen Glückes oder Aurora*, Schäferspiel (Hamburg, July 26?, 1710); *Der durch den Fall des grossen Pompejus erhöhte Julius Caesar* (Hamburg, Nov. 1710); *Der hochmüthige, gestürtzte und wieder erhabene Croesus*, dramma musicale (Hamburg, 1710); *Die oesterreichische Grossmuth oder Carolus V* (Hamburg, June 1712); *Die entdeckte Verstellung oder Die geheime Liebe der Diana*, Schäferspiel (Hamburg, April 1712; rev. 1724); *Die wiederhergestellte Ruh oder Die gecrönte Tapferkeit des Heraclius* (Hamburg, June 1712); *L'inganno fedele oder Der getreue Betrug* (Hamburg, Oct. 1714); *Die gecrönte Tugend* (Hamburg, Nov. 15, 1714); *Triumph des Friedens*, serenata (Hamburg, March 1, 1715); *Fredegunda* (Hamburg, March 1715); *L'amore verso la patria oder Der sterbende Cato* (Hamburg, 1715); *Artemisia* (Hamburg, 1715); *Das römische Aprilfest*, Lust- und Tantz-spiel (Hamburg, June 1716); *Das verewigte und triumphirende Ertz-Haus Oesterreich*, serenata (Hamburg, 1716); *Das zerstörte Troja oder Der durch den Tod Helenen versöhnte Achilles* (Hamburg, Nov. 1716); *Die durch Verstellung und Grossmuth über die Grausamkeit siegende Liebe oder Julia* (Hamburg, Feb. 1717); *Die grossmüthige Tomyris* (Hamburg, Feb. 1717); *Der die Festung Siebenburgisch-Weissenburg erobernde und über Dacier triumphirende Kayser Trajanus* (Hamburg, Nov. 1717); *Das bey seiner Ruh und Gebuhrt eines Printzen frolockende Lycien unter der Regierung des Königs Jacobates und Bellerophon* (Hamburg, Dec. 28, 1717); *Die unvergleichliche Psyche* (Copenhagen, April 16, 1722); *Ulysses* (Copenhagen, Oct. 1722); *Der Armenier* (Copenhagen, Nov. 1722); *Die betrogene und nochmahls vergötterte Ariadne* (Hamburg, Nov. 25, 1722; based on the opera by Conradi of 1691); *Sancio oder Die siegende Grossmuth* (1723?); *Das wegen Verbannung der Laudplagen am Geburthstage Herrn Friedrich IV zu Dennemark jauchzende Cimbrien*, serenata (Copenhagen, 1724); *Das frohlockende Gross Britannien*, serenata (Hamburg, June 8, 1724); *Der sich rächende Cupido*, Schäferspiel (Hamburg, 1724; based on *Die entdeckte Verstellung oder Die geheime Liebe der Diana*); *Bretislaus oder Die siegende Beständigkeit* (Hamburg, Jan. 27, 1725); *Der Hamburger Jahrmarkt oder Der glückliche Betrug* (Hamburg, June 27, 1725); *Die Hamburger Schlachtzeit oder Der misslungene Betrug* (Hamburg, Oct. 22, 1725); *Prologus beim Geburths Feste Friderici Ludovici von Hannover*, serenata (Hamburg, Jan. 31, 1726); *Mistevojus König der Obotriten oder Wenden* (Hamburg, 1726); *Der lächerliche Printz Jodelet* (Hamburg, 1726); *Buchhofer der stumme Printz Atis*, intermezzo (Hamburg, 1726); *Barbacola*, intermezzo (Hamburg, 1726; includes music by Lully); *Lucius Verus oder Die siegende Treue* (Hamburg, Oct. 18, 1728; based on *Berenice* by Bronner of 1702); *Der hochmuthige, gestürtzte und wieder erhabene Croesus*, Singspiel (Hamburg, 1730; based on the dramma musicale of 1710); *Jauchzen der Kunste* (1733); *Circe* (Hamburg, March 1, 1734; with arias by other composers). Of these, *Die römische Unruhe oder Die edelmüthige Octavia* was ed. by M. Schneider in the supplement to the Handel *Gesamtausgabe* (Leipzig, 1902);

Der lächerliche Printz Jodelet was ed. by F. Zelle in the *Publikationen der Gesellschaft für Musikforschung* (1892); the 1730 version of *Der hochmüthige, gestürtzte und wieder erhabene Croesus* was ed. by M. Schneider in the Denkmäler Deutscher Tonkunst, vol. 37 (1912). Also *Passions Oratorium* (Hamburg, 1717?), publ. in a modern ed. in the *Geistliche Chormusik*, vol. 10 (Stuttgart, 1963).

BIBL.: H. Leichtentritt, *R. K. in seinen Opern* (diss., Univ. of Berlin, 1901); R. Brenner, *The Operas of R. K. in Their Relationship to the Affektenlehre* (diss., Brandeis Univ., 1968); K. Zelm, *Die Opern R. K.s* (Munich, 1975).

Keldorfer, Robert, Austrian composer; b. Vienna, Aug. 10, 1901; d. Klagenfurt, Sept. 13, 1980. His father was the Austrian conductor and composer Viktor (Josef) Keldorfer (1873–1959). He received his early musical training from his father, then took courses at the Vienna Academy of Music with Prohaska, Springer, and Stöhr (1917–19). From 1930 to 1939 he was director of the Linz Cons., and from 1941 to 1966 director of the Klagenfurt Cons. Among his works are an opera, *Verena* (1951).

Keldysh, Yuri (Vsevolodovich), eminent Russian musicologist; b. St. Petersburg, Aug. 29, 1907; d. Moscow, Dec. 19, 1995. He was a student in music history of Ivanov-Boretsky at the Moscow Cons. (graduated, 1930; candidate degree, 1940; Ph.D., 1947, with the diss. *Khudozhestvennoye mirovozzreniye V. V. Stasova* [The Artistic Views of V. V. Stasov]). From 1930 to 1950 he taught at the Moscow Cons., where he became a prof. in 1948. He again served on its faculty from 1957. From 1950 to 1956 he was a teacher at the Cons. and from 1955 to 1957 was director of the Inst. of Music and Theater in Leningrad. He was ed. of the journal *Sovetskaya muzika* (1957–60) and of the valuable *Muzikalnaya Entsiklopediya* (6 vols., 1973–82). Keldysh was one of the foremost Russian musicologists of the Soviet era, and was the author of numerous articles and books.

WRITINGS (all publ. in Moscow unless otherwise given): *Romansovaya lirika Musorgskovo* (Mussorgsky's Lyrical Songs; 1933); *Russkaya klassicheskaya muzika* (1945; 2d ed., enl., 1960); *Istoriya russkoy muziki* (History of Russian Music; 3 vols., 1947–54); ed. with M. Druskin, *Ocherki po istoril russkoy muziki 1790–1825* (Essays on the History of Russian Music 1790–1825; Leningrad, 1956); *La musique russen en XIXe siècle* (Neuchâtel, 1958); *Russkaya sovetskaya muzika* (1958); ed. *Voprosï muzikoznaniya* (Questions of Musicology; 1960); *Kritika i zhurnalistika: Sbornik statey* (Criticism and Journalism: Collection of Articles; 1963); *Russkaya muzika XVIII veka* (Russian Music of the XVIII Century; 1965); *100 let Moskovskoy konservatorii* (100 Years of the Moscow Conservatory; 1966); *Rakhmaninov i evo vremya* (Rachmaninoff and his Time; 1973).

Kelemen, Milko, significant Croatian composer; b. Podrawska Slatina, March 30, 1924. He was taught to play piano by his grandmother; in 1945, entered the Zagreb Academy of Music, where he studied theory with Šulek; he then went to Paris, where he took courses with Messiaen and Aubin at the Cons. (1954–55); he supplemented his studies at Freiburg im Breisgau with Fortner (1958–60) and then worked on electronic music at the Siemens studio in Munich (1966–68). He taught composition at the Zagreb Cons. (1955–58; 1960–65), the Schumann Cons. in Düsseldorf (1969–73), and the Stuttgart Hochschule für Musik (1973–91). He publ. *Klanglabyrinthe: Reflexionen eines Komponisten über die Neue Musik* (Munich, 1981). As a composer, Kelemen began his career following the trend of European modernism well within academically acceptable lines, but changed his style radically about 1956 in the direction of the cosmopolitan avant-garde, adopting successively or concurrently the techniques of serialism, abstract expressionism, constructivism, and sonorism, making use of electronic sound; he also wrote alternatively valid versions for a single piece.

WORKS: DRAMATIC: *Der Spiegel*, ballet (Paris, Aug. 18, 1960); *Abbandonate*, ballet (Lübeck, Sept. 1, 1964); *Der neue Mieter*, musical scene, after Ionesco (Münster, Sept. 15, 1964); *Der Belagerungszustant*, opera, after Camus (1969–70; Hamburg, Jan. 13, 1970); *Yebell*, action for Soloists and Chamber Ensemble (Munich, Sept. 1, 1972); *Apocalyptica*, multimedia ballet opera (concert perf., Graz, Oct. 10, 1979). Also *Salut au Monde*, oratorio for Soloists, 2 Choruses, Orch., Projections, and Light Actions (1995).

Kelemen, Zoltán, Hungarian bass; b. Budapest, March 12, 1926; d. Zürich, May 9, 1979. He was educated at the Budapest Academy of Music and at the Accademia di Santa Cecilia in Rome. He made his operatic debut in Augsburg (1959). After singing in Wuppertal, he joined the Cologne Opera (1961); he also appeared at Bayreuth (from 1962) and Salzburg (from 1966). On Nov. 22, 1968, he made his Metropolitan Opera debut in New York as Alberich in *Das Rheingold*, a role he repeated for his debut performance at London's Covent Garden (1970). Among his best roles were Osmin, Leporello, the Grand Inquisitor, Dulcamara, Falstaff, and Gianni Schicchi.

Keller, Hans (Heinrich), Austrian-born English writer on music; b. Vienna, March 11, 1919; d. London, Nov. 6, 1985. He received training in violin in Vienna, and then settled in England in 1938 and became a naturalized British subject in 1948. He played in orchs. and string quartets. Keller mastered the English language to an extraordinary degree, and soon began pointing out solecisms and other infractions on the purity of the tongue to native journalists; he wrote articles on film music, and boldly invaded the sports columns in British newspapers, flaunting his mastery of the lingo. In 1947 he founded (with D. Mitchell) the periodical *Music Survey* and was its coed. (1949–52); he joined the music division of the BBC in 1959, retiring in 1979. He originated a system of functional analysis for radio, in which verbal communication was replaced solely by musical examples to demonstrate a composition's structure and thematic development. He publ. several articles expounding the virtues of his ratiocination, among them the fundamental essay "Functional Analysis: Its Pure Application," *Music Review*, XVIII (1957).

WRITINGS (all publ. in London): *Albert Herring* (1947); *Benjamin Britten: The Rape of Lucretia* (1947); *The Need for Competent Film Music Criticism* (1947); ed. with D. Mitchell, *Benjamin Britten: A Commentary on His Works from a Group of Specialists* (1952); *1975 (1984 minus nine)* (1977); *The Great Haydn Quartets: Their Interpretation* (1986); *Criticism* (1987).

Kelley, Edgar Stillman, American composer and teacher; b. Sparta, Wis., April 14, 1857; d. N.Y., Nov. 12, 1944. He studied with F. Merriam (1870–74), then with Clarence Eddy and N. Ledochowsky in Chicago (1874–76); he subsequently took courses at the Stuttgart Cons. with Seifritz (composition), Krüger and Speidel (piano), and Friedrich Finck (organ). Returning to the United States, he served as an organist in San Francisco; he taught piano and theory at various schools and at the N.Y. College of Music (1891–92). He was music critic for the *San Francisco Examiner* (1893–95), lecturer on music for the Univ. Extension of N.Y. Univ. (1896–97), and then acting prof. at Yale Univ. (1901–02). In 1902 he went to Berlin, where he taught piano and theory. From 1910 to 1934 he was dean of the composition dept. of the Cincinnati Cons. He publ. *Chopin the Composer* (N.Y., 1913) and *Musical Instruments* (Boston, 1925). With his wife, Jessie (née Gregg) Stillman Kelley (b. Chippewa Falls, Wis., 1865; d. Dallas, April 3, 1949), a pianist and teacher, he founded the Kelley Stillman Publishing Co., which brought out several of his scores. Although his stage and symphonic works were quite successful when first performed (some critics described him as a natural successor to MacDowell in American creative work), little of his music survived the test of time.

WORKS: DRAMATIC: *Music to Macbeth*, incidental music for Chorus and Orch. (1882–84; San Francisco, Feb. 12, 1885; rev. as the orch. suite *Gaelic March*); *Pompeiian Picnic*, operetta (1887); *Prometheus Bound*, incidental music (1891); *Puritania*, operetta (Boston, June 9, 1892); *Ben-Hur*, incidental music for Solo Voices, Chorus, and Orch. (1899; N.Y., Oct. 1, 1900); *The Pilgrim's Progress*, musical miracle play (1917; Cincinnati May Festival, May 10, 1918).

BIBL.: M. King, *E. S. K.: American Composer, Teacher, and Author* (diss., Florida State Univ., 1970).

Kellogg, Clara (Louise), noted American soprano and operatic impresario; b. Sumterville, S.C., July 9, 1842; d. New Hartford, Conn., May 13, 1916. She received her vocal training in New York from Manzocchi, Errani, and Muzio, making her professional debut there at the Academy of Music as Gilda in *Rigoletto* (Feb. 27, 1861); she then sang in Boston. She sang Marguerite in the N.Y. premiere of *Faust* (Nov. 25, 1863); she made her London debut in the same role on Nov. 2, 1867. In 1872 she organized an opera company with Pauline Lucca, but their rivalry precluded its success. In 1873 she launched an opera enterprise of her own, the English Opera Co., for which she herself sang 125 performances (1874–75). In 1887 she married her manager, Karl Strakosch, nephew of Maurice and Max Strakosch, and retired from the stage. She wrote *Memoirs of an American Prima Donna* (N.Y., 1913).

Kelly, Michael, Irish tenor and composer; b. Dublin, Dec. 25, 1762; d. Margate, Oct. 9, 1826. He studied with Passerini and Rauzzini, then sang in Dublin. He then continued his studies with Fenarole and Aprile in Naples (1779). He sang in Palermo, Livorno, Florence, Bologna, and Venice. He was a member of the Vienna Court Opera (1783–87); a friend of Mozart, he created the roles of Don Curzio and Don Basilio in *Le nozze di Figaro* (May 1, 1786). In 1787 he appeared for the first time at Drury Lane in London, and sang there until his retirement some 30 years later; he also was stage manager at the King's Theatre, Haymarket (1793–1824). He wrote music for 62 stage pieces and many songs. He also had a music shop (1802–11), and then was active in the wine trade. As to the quality of his compositions and wines, Sheridan quipped that he was "a composer of wines and an importer of music." T. Hook prepared his amusing and valuable autobiography and publ. it as *Reminiscences of Michael Kelly, of the King's Theatre, and Theatre Royal, Drury Lane* (London, 1826; ed. by R. Fiske, London, 1975).

BIBL.: S. Ellis, *The Life of M. K., Musician, Actor and Bon Viveur* (London, 1930).

Kelly, Robert, American composer and teacher; b. Clarksburg, W.Va., Sept. 26, 1916. He studied violin with Gardner at the Juilliard School of Music in New York (1935–36); after further violin training at the Cincinnati College of Music (1937–38), he studied composition with Scalero at the Curtis Inst. of Music in Philadelphia (B.M., 1942) and with Elwell at the Eastman School of Music in Rochester, N.Y. (M.M., 1952). From 1946 to 1976 he taught at the Univ. of Ill. at Urbana. His music, while experimental in nature, is skillfully written to utilize traditional forms and structures. Among his works are *Paiyatuma*, ballet (1946), *Tod's Gal*, folk opera (1950; Norfolk, Va., Jan. 8, 1971), and *The White Gods*, opera (Urbana, Ill., July 3, 1966).

Kelterborn, Rudolf, prominent Swiss composer and pedagogue; b. Basel, Sept. 3, 1931. He studied at the Basel Academy of Music with Gustav Güldenstein and Walther Geiser (composition) and Alexander Krannhals (conducting); subsequently took lessons in conducting with Markevitch and in composition with Burkhard in Zürich (1952), Blacher in Salzburg (1953), and Fortner and Bialas at the North West Music Academy in Detmold (1955). He taught at the Basel Academy of Music (1955–60) and at the North West Music Academy (1960–68), then was on the faculty of the Zürich Cons. and Musikhochschule (1968–75; 1980–83). He was ed.-in-chief of the *Schweizerische Musikzeitung* (1969–75) and director of the music division of the Radio D(eutschen und) R(ätoromanischen) S(schweiz) (1974–80); subsequently he was a prof. at the Staatlichen Hochschule für Musik in Karlsruhe (1980–83) and director of (1983–94) and teacher at (1983–96) the Basel Academy of Music. Kelterborn appeared as a guest conductor in performances of his own works; he also lectured in the United States, England, and Japan. He was awarded the composer's prize of the Assn. of Swiss Musicians and the Kunstpreis of the City of Basel in 1984. He publ. *Zum Beispiel Mozart: Ein Beitrag zur musikalischen Analyse* (Basel, 1980; Japanese tr., Tokyo, 1986). In his music, he applies a precisely coordinated serial organization wherein quantitative values of duration form a recurrent series; changes of tempo are also subjected to serialization. Both melody and harmony are derived from a tone row in which the dissonant intervals of the major seventh and minor second are the mainstays.

WORKS: DRAMATIC: OPERAS: *Die Errettung Thebens* (1960–62; Zürich, June 23, 1963); *Kaiser Jovian* (1964–66; Karlsruhe, March 4, 1967); *Ein Engel kommt nach Babylon* (1975–76; Zürich, June 5, 1977); *Der Kirschgarten*, after Chekhov (1979–81; Zürich, Dec. 4, 1984); *Ophelia* (1982–83; Schwetzingen, May 2, 1984); *Die schwarze Spinne*, musical drama (1984). BALLET: *Relations* (1973–74; Bern, Feb. 16, 1975).

BIBL.: D. Larese and F. Goebels, *R. K.* (Amriswiler, 1970).

Kemble, Adelaide, English soprano; b. London, 1814; d. Warsash House, Hampshire, Aug. 4, 1879. She made her debut at a Concert of Ancient Music in London on May 13, 1835. After studies in Paris and Germany, she completed her vocal training with Pasta at Lake Como (1839). In 1839 she sang Norma in Venice, and then appeared in Trieste, Milan, Padua, Bologna, and Mantua with notable success in 1840. In 1841 she returned to London and sang in the English language productions of *Norma, Le nozze di Figaro, La sonnambula*, and *Semiramide* at Covent Garden. In 1843 she retired following her marriage. Her sister, the actress Fanny Kemble, recounted her life in *Record of a Girlhood* (London, 1878).

Kemp, Barbara, German soprano; b. Kochem an der Mosel, Dec. 12, 1881; d. Berlin, April 17, 1959. She studied at the Strasbourg Cons. (1902–05). In 1903 she made her operatic debut as the Priestess in *Aida* in Strasbourg. She then sang in Rostock (1906–08) and Breslau (1908–13) before being engaged as a member of the Berlin Royal (later State) Opera (1913–31); she made her first appearance at the Bayreuth Festival as Senta (1914), and returned there as Kundry (1924–27). She made her Metropolitan Opera debut in New York as Mona Fiordalisa and the Wife in **Max von Schilling**'s *Mona Lisa* (March 1, 1923), and married the composer that same year; she sang there until 1924, and then continued her career in Europe. She later taught voice in Berlin.

BIBL.: O. Bie, *B. K.* (Berlin, 1921).

Kempe, Rudolf, eminent German conductor; b. Niederpoyritz, near Dresden, June 14, 1910; d. Zürich, May 11, 1976. He studied oboe at the Orchestral School of the Dresden Staatskapelle. In 1929 he became 1st oboist of the Gewandhaus Orch. in Leipzig. He made his conducting debut at the Leipzig Opera in 1936. He served in the German army during World War II, then conducted in Chemnitz; he was director of the Opera there (1945–48) and at the Weimar National Theater (1948–49). From 1949 to 1953 he was Generalmusikdirektor of the Dresden Staatskapelle; he then served in an identical capacity with the Bavarian State Opera in Munich (1952–54) and also made appearances in opera in Vienna, in London (Covent Garden), and at the Metropolitan in New York In 1960 Sir Thomas Beecham named him assoc. conductor of the Royal Phil. of London; upon Beecham's death in 1961, he became its principal conductor; from 1963 to 1975, was artistic director as well. He was chief conductor of the Tonhalle Orch. in Zürich (1965–72) and of the Munich Phil. (from 1967); from 1975 he conducted the BBC Sym. Orch. in London. He was a distinguished interpreter of Beethoven, Brahms, Wagner, Bruckner, and Richard Strauss; also conducted lighter scores with equal aplomb.

BIBL.: C. Kempe-Oettinger, *R. K.: Pictures of a Life* (Munich, 1977; Eng. tr., London, 1979).

Kempff, Wilhelm (Walter Friedrich), distinguished German pianist, pedagogue, and composer; b. Juterbog, Nov. 25, 1895; d. Positano, Italy, May 23, 1991. He studied piano with his father, also named Wilhelm Kempff; at the age of 9, he entered the Berlin Hochschule für Musik, where he studied composition with Robert Kahn and piano with Heinrich Barth; he also attended the Univ.

of Berlin. He began his concert career in 1916; in 1918 he made the first of many appearances with the Berlin Phil.; from that time he toured throughout Europe, South America, and Japan, featuring improvisation as part of his programs. From 1924 to 1929 he was director of the Stuttgart Hochschule für Musik; from 1957 he gave annual courses in Positano, Italy. He made his London debut in 1951 and his American debut in New York in 1964. He continued to appear in concerts well past his octogenarian milestone; in 1979 he was a soloist with the Berlin Phil., after having had an association with it for more than 60 years. Kempff epitomized the classic tradition of German pianism; he eschewed flamboyance in his performances of Mozart, Beethoven, Schubert, and other masters. He publ. a book of memoirs, *Unter dem Zimbelstern* (Stuttgart, 1951). Among his compositions were the operas *König Midas* (Königsberg, 1930), *Familie Gozzi* (Stettin, 1934), and *Die Fasnacht von Rottweil* (Hannover, 1937).

BIBL.: B. Gavoty and R. Hauert, *K.* (Monaco and Geneva, 1954).

Keneman, Feodor, Russian pianist and composer of German descent; b. Moscow, April 20, 1873; d. there, March 29, 1937. He studied with Safonov (piano; graduated, 1895) and Ippolitov-Ivanov (composition; graduated, 1897) at the Moscow Cons.; he also with Taneyev (counterpoint) there. From 1899 to 1932 he taught theory at the Moscow Cons. He gave recitals and was the favorite accompanist of Chaliapin, for whom he composed the popular Russian ballad *As the King Went to War* and arranged the folk song *Ei ukhnem!* He toured the United States with Chaliapin (1923–24). He also composed military marches and band pieces.

Kenessey, Jenö, Hungarian conductor and composer; b. Budapest, Sept. 23, 1905; d. there, Aug. 19, 1976. He studied with Lajtha (composition) and Sugár (organ) at the Budapest Cons., Siklós (composition) at the Budapest Academy of Music, and Shalk (conducting) in Salzburg. He was a conductor at the Budapest Opera (1932–65), where he conducted his opera *Arany meg az asszony* (Gold and the Woman; 1942; May 8, 1943) and his ballet *May Festival* (Nov. 29, 1948). His other ballets include *Montmartre* (1930), *Johnny in Boots* (1935), *Mine Is the Bridegroom* (1938), *Perhaps Tomorrow* (1938), *Miraggio* (1938), *The Kerchief* (1951), and *Bihari's Song* (1954).

Kennedy-Fraser, Marjorie (née **Kennedy**), Scottish singer, pianist, and folk-song collector; b. Perth, Oct. 1, 1857; d. Edinburgh, Nov. 22, 1930. She was the daughter of the Scottish tenor David Kennedy (b. Perth, April 15, 1825; d. Stratford, Ontario, Oct. 12, 1886). From the age of 12 she traveled with her father as his accompanist. She then studied voice with Mathilde Marchesi in Milan and Paris; she also took courses in piano with Matthay and in music history with Niecks. Inspired by the example of her father, she became a dedicated collector of folk songs. In 1905 she went to the Outer Hebrides, after which she made a specialty of research in Celtic music. She publ. the eds. *Songs of the Hebrides* (with K. Macleod; 3 vols., London, 1909, 1917, 1921); *From the Hebrides* (Glasgow and London, 1925); *More Songs of the Hebrides* (London and N.Y., 1929); also the handbook *Hebridean Song and the Laws of Interpretation* (Glasgow, 1922). She wrote the libretto for and sang the title role in Bantock's opera *The Seal Woman* (1924). She also publ. the autobiography *A Life of Song* (London, 1928).

Kennedy, (George) Michael (Sinclair), esteemed English music critic and writer on music; b. Manchester, Feb. 19, 1926. He was educated at the Berkhamsted School. In 1941 he joined the staff of the London *Daily Telegraph*, where he was its northern music critic (from 1950), northern ed. (1960–86), and joint chief music critic (1986–89). From 1989 he was music critic of the *Sunday Telegraph*. In 1981 he was made an officer of the Order of the British Empire. In 1997 he became a Commander of the Order of the British Empire. In addition to his perceptive music criticism, he has published a number of valuable biographies and reference works.

WRITINGS: *The Hallé Tradition: A Century of Music* (Manchester, 1960); *The Works of Ralph Vaughan Williams* (London, 1964; rev. 1980); *Portrait of Elgar* (London, 1968; rev. 1982; 3rd ed., 1987); *Elgar: Orchestral Music* (London, 1969), *Portrait of Manchester* (Manchester, 1970); *A History of the Royal Manchester College of Music* (Manchester, 1971); *Barbirolli: Conductor Laureate* (London, 1971); *Mahler* (London, 1974; rev. 1990); ed. *The Autobiography of Charles Hallé, with Correspondence and Diaries* (London, 1976); *Richard Strauss* (London, 1976; rev. 1983; rev. and aug., 1995); ed. *The Concise Oxford Dictionary of Music* (Oxford, 3d ed., 1980; rev. 1995); *Britten* (London, 1981; rev. 1993); *The Hallé 1858–1983* (Manchester, 1983); *Strauss: Tone Poems* (London, 1984); *The Oxford Dictionary of Music* (Oxford, 1985; 2d ed., rev., 1994); *Portrait of Walton* (London, 1989); *Music Enriches All: 21 Years of the Royal Northern College of Music, Manchester* (Manchester, 1994).

Kenny, Yvonne, Australian soprano; b. Sydney, Nov. 25, 1950. She received her training at the New South Wales State Conservatorium of Music in Sydney and at the La Scala Opera School in Milan (1973–74). In 1975 she made her debut in London in a concert perf. as Donizetti's Rosamunda d'Inghilterra. On July 12, 1976, she made her first appearance at London's Covent Garden in the premiere of Henze's *We Come to the River*, and returned there in subsequent years to sing such roles as Mozart's Susanna, Pamina, and Ilia, Verdi's Oscar, Bizet's Micaëla, Handel's Semele, and Puccini's Liù. In 1977 she made her debut at London's English National Opera as Strauss's Sophie. In 1985 she made her first appearance at the Glyndebourne Festival as Ilia. In 1993 she sang Strauss's Madeleine at the Berlin State Opera. She appeared in Purcell's *The Fairy Queen* in London in 1995. In 1997 she portrayed the Marschallin at Covent Garden. Her guest engagements also took her to Paris, Vienna, Hamburg, Munich, Salzburg, Edinburgh, and other music centers. She was also very active as a concert artist. In 1989 she was made a Member of the Order of Australia.

Kerman, Joseph (Wilfred), eminent American musicologist; b. London (of American parents), April 3, 1924. He studied at Univ. College School, London, then at N.Y. Univ. (A.B., 1943), subsequently taking courses with Strunk, Thompson, and Weinrich at Princeton Univ. (Ph.D., 1950, with the diss. *The Elizabethan Madrigal: A Comparative Study*; publ. in New York, 1962); also taught at Westminster Choir College in Princeton, N.J. (1949–51). In 1951 he joined the faculty at the Univ. of Calif. at Berkeley, being made a prof. in 1960; also was chairman of its music dept. (1960–63). After serving as Heather Prof. of Music at the Univ. of Oxford (1971–74), he resumed his professorship at Berkeley. He retired in 1994. In 1977 he became a founding ed. of the journal *19th Century Music*, serving as its coed. until 1989. His various honors included his being made an Honorary Fellow of the Royal Academy of Music in London (1972) and a Fellow of the American Academy of Arts and Sciences (1973). An erudite scholar and provocative critic, Kerman holds an influential position among American musicologists of his generation.

WRITINGS: *Opera as Drama* (N.Y., 1956; rev. 1988); *The Beethoven Quartets* (N.Y. and London, 1967); with H. Janson, *History of Art & Music* (N.Y. and Englewood Cliffs, N.J., 1968); ed. *L. van Beethoven: Autograph Miscellany ("Kafka Sketchbook")* (London, 1970); ed. *W. A. Mozart: Concerto in C, K. 503* (N.Y., 1970; Norton Critical Score); with V. Kerman, *Listen* (N.Y., 1972); *The Music of William Byrd: Vol. I, The Masses and Motets of William Byrd* (London, 1981); *Contemplating Music* (Cambridge, Mass., 1985; publ. in England as *Musicology*, London, 1985); ed. *Music at the Turn of the Century: A "19th-Century Music" Reader* (Berkeley and Oxford, 1990); *Write All These Down: Essays on Music* (Berkeley, 1994).

Kern, Adele, German soprano; b. Munich, Nov. 25, 1901; d. there, May 6, 1980. She received training in Munich. In 1924 she made her operatic debut there as Olympia in *Les Contes d'Hoffmann* at the Bavarian State Opera, singing there until 1926 when she became a member of the Frankfurt am Main Opera. In 1927–28 she toured South America. From 1927 to 1935 she appeared at the Salzburg Festivals. She also sang in Munich, as well as at the Vienna State Opera (1929–30) and the Berlin State Opera (1935–37). She subsequently sang at the Bavarian State Opera (1937–43; 1945–46). As a guest artist, she appeared at London's Covent Garden (1931, 1934), Milan's La Scala, the Rome Opera, and at other European operatic centers. She was especially admired for her Mozart and Richard Strauss roles, among them Despina, Susanna, Zerbinetta, Marzelline, and Sophie.

Kern, Patricia, Welsh mezzo-soprano; b. Swansea, July 4, 1927. She was a student at the Guildhall School of Music in London of Parry Jones (1949–52). In 1952 she made her operatic debut in *Cenerentola* with London's Opera for All group, remaining with it until 1955. In 1959 she made her first appearance with the Sadler's Wells Opera in London as Rusalka, singing there regularly for 10 seasons. In 1967 she made her debut at London's Covent Garden as Zerlina. She made her first appearance in the United States in 1969 in Washington, D.C. She also made guest appearances in Glyndebourne, Stockholm, Spoleto, New York, Chicago, Dallas, and other operatic centers. Among her esteemed roles were Cherubino, Marcellina, Dorabella, Rosina, Ottone, and Isabella.

Kerr, Harrison, American composer; b. Cleveland, Oct. 13, 1897; d. Norman, Okla., Aug. 16, 1978. He studied composition with James H. Rogers and Claus Wolfram in Cleveland, and then continued his training in France with Boulanger (composition) and Philipp (piano) at the American Cons. in Fontainebleau, and with Vidal (composition) and Wolff (conducting). In 1927–28 he was director of music of Greenbriar College in Lewisburg, W.Va., and then was director of music and art at the Chase School in New York (1929–35). In subsequent years, he was active with the American Composers' Alliance and the American Music Center, serving as executive secretary for both organizations. From 1949 to 1960 he was dean of the College of Fine Arts at the Univ. of Okla., where he continued on its faculty as composer-in-residence until 1968. He utilized traditional forms in his works, infusing them with linear chromatic writing and judicious dissonances. Among his works is the opera *The Tower of Kel* (1958–60) and the ballet *Dance Sonata* (1938).

BIBL.: R. Kohlenberg, *H. K.: Portrait of a Twentieth-Century American Composer* (Lanham, Md., 1997).

Kersters, Willem, Belgian composer and teacher; b. Antwerp, Feb. 9, 1929. He studied at the Royal Flemish Cons. of Music in Antwerp, and with Louël (counterpoint), Absil and Quinet (fugue), Poot (composition), and Defossez (conducting) at the Royal Cons. of Music in Brussels. From 1962 to 1994 he taught at the Royal Flemish Cons. of Music. He also taught at the Maastricht Cons. in the Netherlands from 1967 to 1994. In his music, Kersters has made imaginative use of both tonal and atonal resources. He composed the opera *Gansendonk* (1979–82; Antwerp, Sept. 29, 1984) and the ballets *Parwati* (1956), *Triomf van de Geest* (1959), *Halewyn* (1973; Brussels, Jan. 25, 1974), and *Ulenspiegel de Geus* (1975–76).

Kertész, István, noted Hungarian-born German conductor; b. Budapest, Aug. 28, 1929; d. (drowned while swimming in the Mediterranean) Kfar Saba, Israel, April 16, 1973. He studied violin and composition at the Franz Liszt Academy of Music in Budapest, where his principal teachers were Kodály and Weiner; he also received instruction in conducting from Somogyi. He conducted in Györ (1953–55) and at the Hungarian State Opera in Budapest (1955–56); after the unsuccessful Hungarian revolution (1956), he settled in West Germany and became a naturalized citizen; he completed his conducting studies with Previtali at the Accademia di Santa Cecilia in Rome (1958). He was Generalmusikdirektor in Augsburg (1958–63); he made his first appearances as a guest conductor in England in 1960 and in the United States in 1961. In 1964 he became Generalmusikdirektor of the Cologne Opera, a post he retained until his death; he was also principal conductor of the London Sym. Orch. (1965–68), which he led on a world tour (1965). His readings of the Romantic repertoire were especially admired for their warmth and lyricism.

BIBL.: K. Richter, *I. K.* (Augsburg, 1976).

Kessner, Daniel (Aaron), American composer; b. Los Angeles, June 3, 1946. He studied composition with Lazarof at the Univ. of Calif. at Los Angeles (B.A., 1967; M.A., 1968; Ph.D., 1971). In 1970 he was appointed to the faculty of the Calif. State Univ. in Northridge, where he also conducted its New Music Ensemble; he was prof. there from 1980. In 1970 and 1971 he received BMI awards, won the Queen Marie-José International Composition Prize in Geneva in 1972, and in 1974 and 1977 he received NEA grants. Among his works are *The Telltale Heart*, monodrama for Tenor and Chamber Orch. (1975–78), *The Masque of the Red Death*, tale in music, dance, and light for Dancer, Conductor, and 7 Players (1979), and *Texts for Nothing*, musical-literary-theatrical stream for Soprano, Flute, Trombone, Viola, Cello, and Conductor (1980–82).

Ketèlbey, Albert (William), English conductor and composer; b. Birmingham, Aug. 9, 1875; d. Cowes, Isle of Wight, Nov. 26, 1959. Precociously gifted in music, he wrote a piano sonata at the age of 11, and played it at the Worcester Town Hall; Elgar heard it and praised it. At the age of 13 he competed for a Trinity College scholarship in London, and was installed as Queen Victoria Scholar; at 16 he obtained the post of organist at St. John's Church at Wimbledon; at 20 he began tours as the conductor of a musical comedy troupe, then was a theater conductor in London. He became best known for such light orch. pieces as *In a Monastery Garden* (1915), *In a Persian Market* (1920), *In a Chinese Temple Garden* (1923), *Sanctuary of the Heart* (1924), and *In the Mystic Land of Egypt* (1931); he also wrote many smaller pieces under various pseudonyms. His other works include the comic opera *The Wonder Worker* (1900).

Kettenus, Aloys, Belgian violinist and composer; b. Verviers, Feb. 22, 1823; d. London, Oct. 3, 1896. He studied at the Liège Cons. and in Germany. In 1845 he became concertmaster of the Mannheim orch.; in 1855, a member of London's Royal Italian Opera Orch. He wrote an opera, *Stella Monti* (1862).

Ketting, Otto, Dutch composer; b. Amsterdam, Sept. 3, 1935. His father was the Dutch pianist, composer, and conductor Piet Ketting (b. Haarlem, Nov. 29, 1904; d. Rotterdam, May 25, 1984). He studied composition at the Royal Cons. in The Hague (1952–58); he played trumpet in the Residentie Orch., The Hague (1955–60) and taught composition at the Rotterdam Cons. (1967–71) and at the Royal Cons. in The Hague (1971–74). His music represents a valiant effort to adapt Classical modalities to the aesthetics of contemporary musical expression.

WORKS: DRAMATIC: OPERAS: *Dummies* (The Hague, Nov. 14, 1974); *O, Thou Rhinoceros* (Holland Festival, June 2, 1977); *Ithaka* (Amsterdam, Sept. 23, 1986). BALLETS: *Het laatste bericht* (The Last Message; 1962); *Intérieur* (1963); *Barrière* (1963); *The Golden Key* (1964); *Choreostruction* (1963); *Theater Piece* (1973).

Keurvels, Edward (Hubertus Joannes), Belgian conductor and composer; b. Antwerp, March 8, 1853; d. Ekeren, near Antwerp, Jan. 29, 1916. He studied with Peter Benoit at the Vlaamse Music School in Antwerp, becoming conductor of the Nederslandse Schouwburg in 1882; he helped to organize the Nederlands Lyrisch Toneel in 1890, which became the Vlaamse Opera in 1893, and subsequently conducted there regularly, and also led sym. concerts at the Zoological Gardens (from 1896). He wrote an opera, *Parisina* (Antwerp, 1890).

Khachaturian, Karen (Surenovich), Russian composer; b. Moscow, Sept. 19, 1920. His uncle was the brilliant Russian composer of Armenian descent Aram (Ilich) Khachaturian (b. Tiflis, June 6, 1903; d. Moscow, May 1, 1978). He studied at the Moscow Cons. with Litinsky; during World War II, he served in the entertainment division of the Red Army. He resumed studies in 1945 at the Moscow Cons. with Shebalin, Shostakovich, and Miaskovsky, graduating in 1949; he then joined its faculty in 1952. His music follows the general line of socialist realism, nationalist or ethnic in thematic resources and realistic in harmonic and contrapuntal treatment. He composed *An Ordinary Girl*, operetta (1959), *Cipollino*, ballet, after Rodari's fairy tale (Kiev, Nov. 8, 1974), and a number of effective film scores.

BIBL.: M. Uspenskaya, *K. K.* (Moscow, 1956); E. Dolinskaya, *K. K.* (Moscow, 1975).

Khadzhiev, Parashkev, Bulgarian composer; b. Sofia, April 14, 1912. He studied composition with Vladigerov and piano with Stoyanov at the Sofia Cons., graduating in 1936; he then went to Vienna, where he studied composition with Marx (1937), and to Berlin, where he took a course in composition with Thiessen at the Hochschule für Musik (1938–40). Returning to Bulgaria, he occupied various teaching positions.

WORKS: DRAMATIC: OPERAS: *Imalo edno vreme* (Once upon a Time; Sofia, April 11, 1957); *Lud gidiya* (Madcap; Sofia, Nov. 15, 1959); *Albena* (Varna, Nov. 2, 1962); *Jukka nosht* (July Night; 1964; Plovdiv, Feb. 16, 1965); *The Millionaire* (1964; Sofia, March 14, 1965); *Master Woodcarvers* (Sofia, Oct. 9, 1966); *The Knight* (Varna, 1969); *The 3 Brothers and the Golden Apple* (1970; Sofia, Jan. 28, 1971); *The Year 893* (1972; Ruse, March 26, 1973). OPERETTAS: *Delyana* (1952); *Aika* (1955); *Madame Sans-Gêne* (1958); *King Midas Has Ass's Ears* (1976). MUSICAL: *Job Hunters* (1972). BALLET: *Srebarnite pantofki* (The Silver Slippers; 1961; Varna, March 20, 1962).

Khaikin, Boris (Emmanuilovich), prominent Russian conductor; b. Minsk, Oct. 26, 1904; d. Moscow, May 10, 1978. He studied piano with Goedicke and conducting with Saradzhev and Malko at the Moscow Cons. He was a conductor at the Stanislavsky Theater in Moscow (1928–35). From 1936 to 1943 he served as principal conductor of the Maly Theater in Leningrad, from 1943 to 1954, at the Kirov Theater in Moscow, and from 1954 to 1978, at Moscow's Bolshoi Theater. He taught at the Leningrad Cons. (1935–53), then was prof. of conducting at the Moscow Cons. (1954–78). His most famous student was Kirill Kondrashin. He was made a People's Artist of the USSR in 1972. He conducted the premieres of a number of Soviet operas.

Kharitonov, Dimitri, Russian baritone; b. Kuibyshev, Oct. 18, 1958. He studied at the Rimsky-Korsakov College of Music in Leningrad (from 1976), and received training in voice and piano at the Nezhdanova State Cons. in Odessa (1978–84). In 1984 he became principal baritone at the Odessa State Opera. After appearing at the Bolshoi Theater in Moscow (1985–88), he sang Strauss's Jochanaan at the Edinburgh Festival in 1989. His U.S. debut followed in 1990 when he portrayed Sonora in *La Fanciulla del West* at the Lyric Opera in Chicago. In 1991 he sang in San Francisco and Los Angeles. He made his first appearance at the Glyndebourne Festival in 1993 as Prince Yeletsky, and then sang Nabucco in Genoa in 1994.

Khodzha-Einatov, Leon, Russian composer; b. Tiflis, March 23, 1904; d. Leningrad, Nov. 1, 1954. He studied with Spendiarov. In 1927 he went to Leningrad, where he wrote music for the stage. He wrote the opera *Rebellion* (Leningrad, May 16, 1938), and also 3 Armenian operas: *Arshak* (1945), *David Bek* (1951), and *Namus* (1952).

Khokhlov, Pavel (Akinfievich), noted Russian baritone; b. Spassky, Aug. 2, 1854; d. Moscow, Sept. 20, 1919. He studied in Moscow, making his debut with the Bolshoi Theater there as Valentin in *Faust* (March 3, 1879); he remained on its roster until he retired in 1900, and also appeared at the Maryinsky Theater in St. Petersburg (1881; 1887–88). He sang the title role in *Eugene Onegin* at its first professional performance (Moscow, Jan. 23, 1881). His other outstanding roles included Rubinstein's Demon, Boris Godunov, Prince Igor, Don Giovanni, and Wolfram.

BIBL.: S. Durilin, *P. A. K. 1854–1919* (Moscow and Leningrad, 1947); B. Yakovlev, *P. A. K.* (Moscow and Leningrad, 1950).

Khrennikov, Tikhon (Nikolaievich), important Russian music administrator and composer; b. Elets, June 10, 1913. He was the 10th child in the musical family of a provincial clerk; his parents and siblings played the Russian guitar and the mandolin and sang peasant songs. He took piano lessons with a local musician; in 1927 he went to Moscow, where he was introduced to Gnessin, who accepted him as a student in his newly founded musical Technicum; there he studied counterpoint with Litinsky and piano with Ephraim Hellman. After graduation, he entered the Moscow Cons., where he studied composition with Shebalin and piano with Neuhaus (1932–36); he later continued postgraduate work with Shebalin. He developed a mildly modernistic, and technically idiomatic, type of composition which remained his recognizable style throughout his career as a composer. In 1961 he joined the faculty of the Moscow Cons., and was named a prof. in 1966. In the meantime, he became engaged in the political life of the country. He was attached to the music corps of the Red Army and accompanied it during the last months of World War II; in 1947 he joined the Communist Party, and also became a deputy of the Supreme Soviet. In 1948 he was named personally by Stalin as secretary-general of the Union of Soviet Composers, and in 1949 became president of the music section of the All-Union Soc. for Cultural Exchange with Europe and America. He further served as head of the organizing committee for the International Festivals and the Tchaikovsky Competitions in Moscow. He received numerous honors; he was a member of the Soviet delegation to the United States in 1959, was named a Hero of Socialist Labor in 1973, and in 1974 received the Lenin Prize. Amid all this work, he never slackened the tempo of his main preoccupation, that of composition. During his entire career, he was a stout spokesman for Soviet musical policy along the lines of socialist realism. He compromised himself, however, by his vehement condemnation of "formalist" directions in modern music, specifically attacking Stravinsky, Prokofiev, Shostakovich, and, later, also Schnittke and Gubaidulina. But as Soviet aesthetical directions underwent a liberal change, Khrennikov himself became the target of sharp criticism. He defended himself by claiming that he had protected a number of young musicians from attacks by entrenched functionaries of the Soviet musical establishment, and he succeeded in retaining his position as secretary-general of the Union of Soviet Composers until 1991. His compositions express forcefully the desirable qualities of erstwhile Soviet music, a flowing melody suggesting the broad modalities of Russian folk songs, a vibrant and expressive lyricism, and effective instrumental formation.

WORKS: DRAMATIC: *V buryu* (Into the Storm), opera (Moscow, May 31, 1939; rev. version, Moscow, Oct. 12, 1952); *Frol Skobeyev*, comic opera (Moscow, Feb. 24, 1950; rev. as *Bezrodnïy zyat* [The Unrelated Son-in-Law], after the novel by Gorky, Novosibirsk, Dec. 29, 1966); *Mat* (Mother), opera (Moscow, Oct. 26, 1957); *100 Chertey i odna devushka* (100 Devils and a Single Girl), operetta (Moscow, May 16, 1963); *Belaya noch* (White Night), operetta (Moscow, May 23, 1967); *Malchik-velikan* (Boy Giant), children's fairy-tale opera (Moscow, Dec. 19, 1969); *Mnogo shuma . . . iz-za serdets* (Much Ado about . . . Hearts), comic opera (Moscow, March 11, 1972); *Doroteya*, comic opera (Moscow, May 26, 1983); *Zolotoy telyonok* (The Golden Calf), comic opera (Moscow, March 9, 1985); *Golïy korol* (The Naked King), comic opera (Leningrad, May 1988); ballets; incidental music to plays; film scores.

BIBL.: L. Kaltat, *T. K.* (Moscow, 1946); V. Kukharsky, *T. K.* (Moscow, 1957); Y. Kremlev, *T. K.* (Moscow, 1963); I. Martinov, *T. N. K.* (Moscow, 1987).

Khristov, Dobri, Bulgarian choral conductor, pedagogue, and composer; b. Varna, Dec. 14, 1875; d. Sofia, Jan. 23, 1941. He began to teach himself music in his youth. While attending secondary school in Varna, he began to compose. He founded its choir and gained experience as a conductor before being invited to serve as conductor of the choir of Gusla, the town's music soc. After teaching school, he pursued training with Dvořák at the Prague Cons. (1900–03). Following further work as a conductor and teacher in Varna, he settled in Sofia as a teacher in 1907. In 1908 he became chorusmaster of the Opera. In 1922 he became a teacher at the State Academy of Music, where he later was a prof. (1926–33) and director. In 1935 he was made choirmaster of the Alexander Nevsky Memorial Church. In 1928 Khristov was made a member of the Bulgarian Academy of Sciences, the first Bulgarian musician to be so honored. He was the author of *Tekhnicheskiyat stroezh na balgarskata narodna muzika* (The Technical Structure of Bulgarian Folk Music; Sofia, 1928; 2d ed., 1956). His works were principally inspired by Bulgarian folk music. He was especially esteemed for his choral output.

BIBL.: I. Kamburov, *D. K.* (Sofia, 1942); V. Krastev, *D. K.* (Sofia, 1954); idem, ed., *Muzikalno-teoretichno i publitsistichno nasledstvo na D. K.* (Sofia, 1971).

Kiberg, Tina, Danish soprano; b. Copenhagen, Dec. 30, 1958. She received vocal training in Copenhagen. In 1983 she made her debut at the Royal Opera in Copenhagen as Leonora in Nielsen's *Maskarade*, and then returned there as Wagner's Elsa in 1984, Strauss's Marschallin in 1988, Mozart's Countess in 1990, Helene in *Les Vêpres siciliennes* in 1991, Strauss's Ariadne in 1992, and Wagner's Eva in 1996. As a guest artist, she appeared in various European music centers, among them as Elsa at the Vienna State Opera in 1990 and the Opéra de la Bastille in Paris in 1991, and as Elisabeth in *Tannhäuser* at the Bayreuth Festival in 1992, where she returned as Sieglinde in 1995. In 1993 she sang Sieglinde at the Lyric Opera in Chicago, returning there in 1996 in that role and as Freia. She also pursued an active career as a lieder artist and as a soloist with orchs.

Kienzl, Wilhelm, Austrian composer; b. Waizenkirchen, Jan. 17, 1857; d. Vienna, Oct. 3, 1941. He studied in Graz with Johann Buwart and Mortier de Fontaine (piano) and with Ignaz Uhl (violin); also with Mayer-Rémy (composition) at the Univ. there, and then with Krejči at the Univ. of Prague (1876), at the Univ. of Leipzig (1877), with Rheinberger in Munich, with Liszt in Weimar, and at the Univ. of Vienna (Ph.D., 1879, with the diss. *Die musikalische Deklamation*; publ. in Leipzig, 1880). He was director of Amsterdam's German Opera (1883); he conducted in Krefeld before returning to Graz (1884); he then was director of the Steiermärkischer Musikverein there until 1886. He held the post of 1st conductor of the Hamburg Opera (1890–92), then was court conductor in Munich (1892–94). His most successful work was the opera *Der Evangelimann* (Berlin, May 4, 1895). After World War I he wrote the new national anthem of Austria (1918), replacing Haydn's; it was adopted on June 6, 1920, but was dropped on Dec. 13, 1929, in favor of Haydn's melody. He also completed Adolf Jensen's opera *Turandot*. He publ. several books, including an autobiography (1926).

WORKS: DRAMATIC: OPERAS: *Urvasi* (1884; Dresden, Feb. 20, 1886; rewritten 1909); *Heilmar, der Narr* (Munich, March 8, 1892); *Der Evangelimann* (Berlin, May 4, 1895); *Don Quichote*, "musical tragi-comedy" (Berlin, Nov. 18, 1898); *In Knecht Rupprechts Werkstatt*, Weihnachtsmärchenspiel (Graz, Dec. 25, 1907); *Der Kuhreigen (Ranz des Vaches)* (Vienna, Nov. 23, 1911); *Das Testament* (Vienna, Dec. 6, 1916); *Hassan der Schwarmer* (Chemnitz, Feb. 27, 1925); *Sanctissimum* (Vienna, Feb. 14, 1925). SINGSPIEL: *Hans Kipfel* (Vienna, 1926). Also incidental music.

BIBL.: M. Morold, *W. K.* (Leipzig, 1909); H. Sittner, *K.—Rosegger: Eine Künstlerfreundschaft* (Zürich, 1953); I. Samlick-Hagen, *Lehr- und Wanderjahre W. K.s (1874–1897)* (diss., Univ. of Vienna, 1979).

Kiepura, Jan, Polish-American tenor; b. Sosnowiec, May 16, 1902; d. Rye, N.Y., Aug. 15, 1966. He studied in Warsaw and Milan. He made his operatic debut as Faust in Lwów (1924), then appeared in Vienna, Berlin, Milan, Paris, Buenos Aires, and other opera centers. He made his U.S. debut with the Chicago Opera in 1931; he first appeared with the Metropolitan Opera in New York as Rodolfo (Feb. 10, 1938); he sang there until 1939 and again in 1942. He was admired for such roles as Des Grieux and Faust; he also was successful as a film artist and as an operetta singer. He was married to **Martha Eggerth**.

Kiesewetter, Tomasz, Polish composer; b. Sosnowka, Sept. 8, 1911. He studied composition with Rytel and conducting with Bierdiajew at the Warsaw Cons.; during the German occupation in World War II, he was active in resistance groups; after the war, he taught at the Łódz State College of Music. Among his works were *King's Jester*, ballet (1954), and *The Lonely Ones*, operetta (1963).

Kiladze, Grigori, Russian composer; b. Batum, Oct. 25, 1902; d. Tbilisi, April 3, 1962. He studied at the Tiflis Cons. with Ippolitov-Ivanov (1924–27), then at the Leningrad Cons. with Shcherbachev (1927–29). He was an active proponent of ethnic Georgian music in a modern idiom derived thematically from folk melorhythms. He wrote 2 operas on subjects from Caucasian revolutionary history: *Bakhtrioni* (1936) and *Lado Ketzkhoveli* (1941); also *Sinatle*, ballet (1947), and *Childhood and Adolescence of the Leader*, oratorio (1951).

Kilenyi, Edward, Sr., Hungarian-American composer; b. Békésszentràndrás, Jan. 25, 1884; d. Tallahassee, Fla., Aug. 15, 1968. He was the father of the American pianist and teacher Edward Kilenyi Jr. (b. Philadelphia, May 7, 1910). He studied in Budapest, in Szarvas, with Mascagni at Rome's Scuola Nazionale Musicale, and at the Cologne Cons., then settled in the United States (1908), where he completed his training at Columbia Univ. with Rybner and Daniel Gregory Mason (M.A., 1915). He was a teacher of George Gershwin (1919–21). In 1930 he went to Hollywood, where he wrote film scores; he also wrote an opera, *The Cry of the Wolf* (1916).

Killebrew, Gwendolyn, black American mezzo-soprano; b. Philadelphia, Aug. 26, 1939. She studied at Temple Univ. in Philadelphia, and then in New York at the Juilliard School of Music and at the Metropolitan Opera Studio. After winning 1st prize in the Belgian International Vocal Competition, she won a Metropolitan Opera audition and made her operatic debut with the company in New York as Waltraute in *Die Walküre* on Nov. 21, 1967; she made her first appearance at the N.Y. City Opera as Ulrica in *Un ballo in maschera* (Sept. 11, 1971). She was a member of the Deutsche Oper am Rhein in Düsseldorf (from 1976) and also appeared in Munich, Geneva, Salzburg, Bayreuth, and other European opera centers. She made numerous concert, oratorio, and lieder appearances on both sides of the Atlantic. Among her notable operatic roles are Gluck's Orfeo, Azucena, Mistress Quickly, Amneris, Fricka, and Baba the Turk in *The Rake's Progress*.

Killmayer, Wilhelm, German composer; b. Munich, Aug. 21, 1927. He studied conducting and composition with Waltershausen (1945–50); then musicology with Ficker at the Univ. of Munich (1950–53), and composition with Orff (1953). He taught at the Trapp Cons. in Frankfurt am Main (1955–58); he then was ballet conductor at the Bavarian State Opera in Munich (1961–64), and later a prof. at Munich's Staatliche Hochschule für Musik (1973–91).

WORKS: DRAMATIC: OPERAS: *La Buffonata*, ballet opera (1959–60; concert perf., South German Radio, Stuttgart, Oct. 21, 1960; stage perf., Heidelberg, April 30, 1961); *La Tragedia di Orfeo* (1960–61; Munich, June 9, 1961); *Yolimba oder Die Grenzen der Magie* (1962–63; Wiesbaden, March 15, 1964; rev. version, Munich, May 9, 1970); *Une leçon de français* or *Die Französischstunde* (1964; concert perf., South German Radio, Stuttgart, Oct. 20, 1964; stage perf., Stuttgart, Oct. 19, 1966). BALLETS: *Pas de deux classique* (1964; Munich, May 12, 1965); *Encores*, 2 ballet pieces (Munich, May 9, 1970); *Paradies* (1974).

BIBL.: S. Mauser, ed., *Der Komponist W. K.* (Mainz and N.Y., 1992).

Kilpatrick, Jack (Frederick), American composer; b. Stillwater, Okla., Sept. 23, 1915; d. Muskogee, Okla., Feb. 22, 1967. He studied at the Univ. of Redlands, Calif., and at the Catholic Univ. of America in Washington, D.C. Of Cherokee origin, he derived virtually all of his music from Indian folklore, with the pentatonic scale as its foundation. He wrote more than 200 works, including the music dramas *Unto These Hills* (Cherokee, N.C., July 1, 1950),

The Golden Crucible (Pittsburgh, 1959), and *The Blessed Wilderness* (Dallas, April 18, 1959).

Kim, Earl (Eul), American composer and pedagogue of Korean descent; b. Dinuba, Calif., Jan. 6, 1920; d. Cambridge, Mass., Nov. 19, 1998. He commenced piano training at 9, and then studied with Homer Grun; he subsequently studied with Schoenberg (composition and theory) at the Univ. of Calif. at Los Angeles (1939); he then became a student of Bloch at the Univ. of Calif. at Berkeley (1940). His studies were interrupted by service in the U.S. Army Intelligence Service during World War II, after which he returned to Berkeley to study with Sessions (M.A., 1952). After serving as a prof. at Princeton Univ. (1952–67), he was James Edward Ditson Prof. of Music at Harvard Univ. (1967–90). In addition to his activities as a composer and teacher, he made appearances as a pianist and conductor. Among his many honors were the Prix de Paris, a National Inst. of Arts and Letters award, the Brandeis Univ. Creative Arts Award, a Guggenheim fellowship, and an NEA fellowship. His works include the opera *Footfalls* (1981).

Kindermann, August, German bass-baritone; b. Potsdam, Feb. 6, 1817; d. Munich, March 6, 1891. He sang in the chorus of the Berlin Royal Opera, then appeared at the Leipzig theater (1839–46). In 1846 he became a member of the Munich Court Opera, and remained on its roster until his death. He also sang at Bayreuth, where he created the role of Titurel in *Parsifal* (1882).

King, Alec (Alexander) Hyatt, esteemed English bibliographer and musicologist; b. Beckenham, Kent, July 18, 1911; d. March 10, 1995. He was educated at Dulwich College and King's College, Cambridge (B.A., 1933). In 1934 he joined the Dept. of Printed Books of the British Museum; he became superintendent of its music room in 1944, retiring in 1976. He publ. a number of valuable textual and bibliographical studies, including (all publ. in London unless otherwise given) *Handel's Messiah* (exhibition catalog of the British Museum; 1951), *Mozart in Retrospect: Studies in Criticism and Bibliography* (1955; 3d ed., 1970); *Mozart in the British Museum* (1956; 2d ed., 1966), *Henry Purcell 1659?–1695; George Frideric Handel 1685–1759* (exhibition catalog of the British Museum; 1959), *Handel and His Autographs* (1967), *Mozart: A Biography, with a Survey of Books, Editions and Recordings* (1970), and *A Mozart Legacy: Aspects of the British Library Collections* (1984).

BIBL.: O. Neighbour, ed., *Music and Bibliography: Essays in Honour of A. H. K.* (London, 1980).

King, James, American tenor; b. Dodge City, Kansas, May 22, 1925. He studied at the Univ. of Kansas City and also received vocal training from Martial Singher and Max Lorenz. He then went to Europe and made his professional debut as Cavaradossi in Florence (1961); he subsequently sang at the San Francisco Opera (1961), the Berlin Deutsche Oper (1962), the Salzburg Festival (1962), the Bayreuth Festival (1965), the Metropolitan Opera in New York (debut as Florestan, Jan. 8, 1966), London's Covent Garden (1966), and Milan's La Scala (1968). He taught voice at the Indiana Univ. School of Music in Bloomington (from 1984). Among his prominent roles were Lohengrin, Walther von Stolzing, Parsifal, Siegmund, Verdi's Otello, and Pfitzner's Palestrina.

King, Matthew Peter, English composer and music theorist; b. London, c.1773; d. there, Jan. 1823. He composed a number of stage works, several of which became popular in their day. He also publ. *Thorough Bass Made Clear to every Capacity* (London, c.1810) and *A General Treatise on Music, Particularly Harmony or Thoroughbass* (London, 1812). Among his comic operas were *Matrimony* (London, Nov. 20, 1804), *Up All Night, or The Smuggler's Cave* (London, June 26, 1809), and *The Americans* (London, April 27, 1811; in collaboration with Braham). He also composed a grand Romantic opera, *One o'Clock, or The Knight and the Wood Daemon* (London, Aug. 1, 1811; in collaboration with M. Kelly), several musical farces and melodramas, and an oratorio, *The Intercession* (London, June 1, 1816).

Kinkel, Johanna (née **Mockel**), German composer; b. Bonn, July 8, 1810; d. London, Nov. 15, 1858. She studied music in Berlin with Karl Böhmer, and married Gottfried Kinkel, the poet, in 1843. She wrote the operetta *Otto der Schutz* and the well-known song "The Soldier's Farewell." She also publ. *Acht Briefe an eine Freundin über Klavierunterricht* (1852).

Kipnis, Alexander, eminent Russian-born American bass; b. Zhitomir, Feb. 13, 1891; d. Westport, Conn., May 14, 1978. He was the father of the distinguished American harpsichordist and fortepianist Igor Kipnis (b. Berlin, Sept. 27, 1930). He studied conducting at the Warsaw Cons. (graduated, 1912); he later took voice lessons with Ernst Grenzebach at Berlin's Klindworth-Scharwenka Cons. In 1913 he sang at Monti's Operetten Theater and in 1914 at the Filmzauber operetta theater in Berlin. At the outbreak of World War I, he was interned as an enemy alien, but was soon released and made his operatic debut as the hermit in *Der Freischütz* at the Hamburg Opera in 1915; sang there until 1917, then was a member of the Wiesbaden Opera (1917–22). He made his U.S. debut as Pogner with the visiting German Opera Co. in Baltimore on Jan. 31, 1923; he then was a member of the Chicago Civic Opera (1923–32). He also sang regularly at the Berlin Städtische Oper (1922–30), the Berlin State Opera (1932–35), and the Vienna State Opera (1935–38). In 1927 he made his first appearance at London's Covent Garden as Marcel in *Les Huguenots*, and sang there again from 1929 to 1935. He became a naturalized American citizen in 1931. During these years, he made guest appearances at the Bayreuth, Salzburg, and Glyndebourne festivals, as well as at the Teatro Colón in Buenos Aires. On Jan. 5, 1940, he made his belated Metropolitan Opera debut in New York as Gurnemanz, and continued to sing there until 1946; he then devoted himself mainly to teaching. Through the years he appeared as a distinguished concert artist. In addition to his remarkable portrayal of Gurnemanz, he was greatly esteemed for such roles as Sarastro, Rocco, King Marke, Hagen, and Boris Godunov.

Király, Ernö, Hungarian composer and ethnomusicologist; b. Subotica, Yugoslavia, March 16, 1919. He studied trumpet at the Subotica School of Music (1939). In 1953 he became Hungarian folk music ed. for Novi Sad Broadcasting; in 1958 he became head of the folk music dept. at the Vojvodina Museum in Novi Sad. He publ. several books and articles on Hungarian folk music and instruments. As a composer, he was interested in folk music and experimented with new intonational and interpretive structures. Among his works is a children's opera, *A kis torkos* (The Little Glutton; 1962).

Kirchhoff, Walter, German tenor; b. Berlin, March 17, 1879; d. Wiesbaden, March 26, 1951. He studied in Berlin with Eugen Weiss and Lilli Lehmann. He made his operatic debut at the Berlin Royal Opera in 1906 as Faust and continued on its roster until 1920 after it became the Berlin State Opera in 1918; he sang there again in 1923–24, 1928–29, and 1932 and also appeared at the Bayreuth Festival (1911–14) and at Covent Garden in London in 1913 and 1924. He made an acclaimed Metropolitan Opera debut in New York as Loge in *Das Rheingold* on Jan. 28, 1927; remained on its roster until 1931. He was particularly successful in Wagnerian roles.

Kirchner, Leon, distinguished American composer, pedagogue, conductor, and pianist; b. N.Y., Jan. 24, 1919. He began piano lessons when he was 4. In 1928 the family moved to Los Angeles, where he continued his piano training. While attending Los Angeles City College, he began to compose. He studied composition with Schoenberg at the Univ. of Calif. at Los Angeles (1938–39), and then theory with Albert Elkus and Edward Strickland at the Univ. of Calif. at Berkeley (B.A., 1940). In 1942 he had private lessons with Sessions in New York. Following service in the U.S. Army (1943–46), he pursued postgraduate studies with Bloch and Sessions at the Univ. of Calif. at Berkeley (1946; M.A., 1949). In 1946–47 he taught there. He also taught at the San Francisco Cons. of Music. From 1950 to 1954 he was on the faculty of the

Univ. of Southern Calif. at Los Angeles. In 1954 he became the first Luther Brusie Marchant Prof. at Mills College in Oakland, California. In 1961 he joined the faculty of Harvard Univ., where he served as the Walter Bigelow Rosen Prof. of Music from 1966 until his retirement in 1989. He also conducted the Harvard Chamber Players (from 1973) and the Harvard Chamber Orch. (from 1978), and was engaged as a guest conductor and as a pianist with orchs. in the United States and overseas. Kirchner received a Guggenheim fellowship in 1948–49, and again in 1949–50. He won the N.Y. Music Critics Circle Award for his 1st (1950) and 2d (1960) string quartets, and the Pulitzer Prize in Music for his 3d string quartet (1967). In 1962 he was made a member of both the National Inst. of Arts and Letters and the American Academy of Arts and Sciences. In 1994 he received a Kennedy Center Friedheim Award. Kirchner has followed a thoroughly contemporary but independent course as a composer. His finely crafted scores are notable for their linear chromaticism, asymmetric rhythms, and lyricism. Among his many works is the opera *Lily* (1973–76; N.Y., April 14, 1977, composer conducting; also as *Lily* for Soprano, Chamber Orch., and Tape, N.Y., March 11, 1973).

Kirkby, (Carolyn) Emma, admired English soprano; b. Camberley, Feb. 26, 1949. She studied classics at Oxford and received vocal training from Jessica Cash. She made her debut in London in 1974 and then specialized in early music; she was a member of the Academy of Ancient Music, the London Baroque, and the Consort of Musicke. In 1978 she toured the United States, then gave concerts in the Middle East with the lutenist Anthony Rooley (1980–83). She made her operatic debut as Mother Nature in *Cupid and Death* by Gibbons and Locke in Bruges in 1983. In 1989 she made her U.S. operatic debut when she sang Handel's Orlando. In subsequent years, she toured widely in England, appearing at the London Promenade Concerts in works by Charpentier and Monteverdi, and abroad. In 1996 she sang at the Purcell Celebration at the London Barbicon. Her repertoire ranges from the Italian quattrocento to arias by Handel, Mozart, and Haydn. The careful attention she pays to the purity of intonation free from intrusive vibrato has been praised.

Kirkby-Lunn, Louise, English mezzo-soprano; b. Manchester, Nov. 8, 1873; d. London, Feb. 17, 1930. She was a student of J.H. Greenwood in Manchester and of Albert Visetti at the Royal College of Music in London. While still a student, she made her debut as Margaret in Schumann's *Genoveva* at London's Drury Lane Theatre in 1893. After singing minor roles at London's Covent Garden in 1896, she sang with the Carl Rosa Opera Co. until 1899. She then gave concerts until returning to Covent Garden in 1901, where she was a leading singer until 1914, winning particular success as Ortrud, Fricka, Brangäne, Carmen, Amneris, Delilah, and Hérodiade. On Dec. 26, 1902, she made her Metropolitan Opera debut in New York as Ortrud, remaining on its roster for the season; she returned for the 1906–08 seasons, appearing principally as a Wagnerian. After appearing with the British National Opera Co. in London (1919–22), she pursued her concert career.

Kirkendale, (John) Warren, American musicologist; b. Toronto, Aug. 14, 1932. He was educated at the Univs. of Toronto (B.A., 1955) and Vienna (Ph.D., 1961, with the diss. *Fuge und Fugato in der Kammermusik des Rokoko und der Klassik*; publ. in Tuzing, 1966; Eng. tr., 1979). After teaching at the Univ. of Southern Calif. in Los Angeles (1963–67), he was an assoc. prof. (1967–75) and a prof. (1975–83) at Duke Univ. From 1983 to 1992 he was prof. ordinarius of musicology at the Univ. of Regensburg. In 1986 he was made an honorary prof. of the Univ. of Bologna and a member of the Accademico filarmonico of Bologna in 1987. He publ. the books *L'Aria di Fiorenza, id est Il Ballo del Gran Duca* (Florence, 1972) and *The Court Musicians in Florence During the Principate of the Medici, With a Reconstruction of the Artistic Establishment* (Florence, 1993), and also contributed articles to various publications. In 1959 he married the German musicologist, Ursula (née Schottler) Kirkendale (b. Dortmund, Sept. 6, 1932). She was educated at the Univ. of Bonn (Ph.D., 1961). In addition to articles in journals and other publications, she publ. the study *Antonio Caldara: Sein Leben und seine venezianische-römischen Oratorien* (Graz, 1966).

BIBL.: *Musicologia Humana: Studies in Honor of W. and U. K.* (Florence, 1994).

Kirsten, Dorothy, noted American soprano; b. Montclair, N.J., July 6, 1910; d. Los Angeles, Nov. 18, 1992. She studied at the Juilliard School of Music in New York; Grace Moore took an interest in her and enabled her to study with Astolfo Pescia in Rome. With the outbreak of World War II in 1939, she returned to the United States. She became a member of the Chicago Opera Co. (debut as Pousette in *Manon*, Nov. 9, 1940); she made her first appearance in New York as Mimi with the San Carlo Opera Co. (May 10, 1942); she appeared with the Metropolitan Opera in New York in the same role on Dec. 1, 1945; she sang there until 1952, from 1954 to 1957, and from 1960 until her official farewell performance as Tosca (Dec. 31, 1975). Among her finest roles were Manon Lescaut, Cio-Cio-San, Marguerite, Louise (coached by the composer), and Nedda in *Pagliacci*; she also sang in several films, including *The Great Caruso*. She publ. an autobiography, *A Time to Sing* (Garden City, N.Y., 1982).

Kittel, Hermine, Austrian contralto; b. Vienna, Dec. 2, 1879; d. there, April 7, 1948. She was an actress before making her operatic debut in Lemberg in 1897. Following vocal training with Materna in Vienna, she sang in Graz (1899–1900). In 1901 she returned to Vienna as a member of the Court (later State) Opera, where she sang until 1931 and again in 1936. She also appeared at the Bayreuth Festivals (1902, 1908), the Salzburg Festivals (1922, 1925), the Vienna Volksoper (1933–34), Paris, Budapest, Prague, and other European operatic centers. In later years, she devoted herself to teaching voice in Vienna. She was particularly known for her Mozart and Wagner roles.

Kittl, Johann Friedrich (Jan Bedřich), prominent Bohemian composer; b. Castle Worlik, May 8, 1806; d. Lissa, German Poland, July 20, 1868. He studied law at the Univ. of Prague, and took private lessons in piano with Zavora and in composition with Tomaschek. His *Jagdsinfonie* was premiered by Spohr (Kassel, 1839); it subsequently was performed widely in Germany. He was director of the Prague Cons. (1843–65). He was a friend of Liszt, Wagner, and Berlioz. As a symphonic composer, he pointed the way to Dvořák. His works include the operas *Daphnis' Grab* (Prague, 1825; not extant), *Die Franzosen vor Nizza* (Prague, Feb. 19, 1848; written to Wagner's libretto *Bianca und Giuseppe*), *Waldblume* (Prague, 1852), and *Die Bilderstürmer* (Prague, 1854).

BIBL.: W. Neumann, *J. F. K.* (Kassel, 1857); E. Rychnovsky, *J. F. K.* (2 vols., Prague, 1904–05); M. Tarantová, *J. F. K.* (Prague, 1948).

Kiurina, Berta, Austrian soprano; b. Linz, Feb. 19, 1882; d. Vienna, May 3, 1933. She studied voice with Geiringer at the Vienna Cons. She made her operatic debut in Linz in 1904, then sang at the Vienna Court (later State) Opera (1905–22; 1926–27); she made guest appearances in Salzburg, Berlin, and Buenos Aires. A fine coloratura, she excelled in such roles as the Queen of the Night, Desdemona, Gilda, Eva, and the Empress in *Die Frau ohne Schatten*.

Kiurkchiysky, Krasimir, Bulgarian composer; b. Troyan, June 22, 1936. He studied composition with Vladigerov at the Bulgarian State Cons. in Sofia (graduated, 1962); he went to Moscow and took some lessons with Shostakovich. His music reflects Shostakovich's influence in its rhapsodic compactness. Among his compositions is the opera *Yula* (Zagora, 1969).

Kivy, Peter, American musical philosopher; b. N.Y., Oct. 22, 1934. He studied philosophy at the Univ. of Mich. (B.A., 1956; M.A., 1958), music history at Yale Univ. (M.A., 1960), and philosophy at Columbia Univ. (Ph.D., 1966). He joined the faculty of Rutgers Univ. in 1967. His importance to the field of music is in his writings on aesthetics, in which he has revitalized the complex and long-ignored problems of musical analysis as applied to external associations.

WRITINGS: *The Corded Shell: Reflections on Musical Expression* (Princeton, N.J., 1980); *Sound and Semblance: Reflections on Musical Representation* (Princeton, N.J., 1984); *Osmin's Rage: Philosophical Reflections on Opera, Drama and Text* (Princeton, N.J., 1988); *Sound Sentiment: An Essay on the Musical Emotions* (Philadelphia, 1989); *Music Alone: Philosophical Reflections on the Purely Musical Experience* (Ithaca, N.Y., 1990); *The Fine Art of Repetition: Essays on the Philosophy of Music* (Cambridge, 1993).

Klafsky, Katharina (Katalin), famous Hungarian soprano; b. St. Johann, Sept. 19, 1855; d. Hamburg, Sept. 22, 1896. Her nephew was the Austrian musicologist and composer Anton Maria Klafsky (1877–1965). She studied with Marchesi in Vienna and Hey in Berlin, then began her career as a chorus singer in various opera houses. She appeared in minor roles in Salzburg (1875), then was a member of the Leipzig Opera (1876–78); also studied with J. Sucher. In 1882 she attracted attention for her performance in the first London mounting of the *Ring* cycle, then toured with A. Neumann's Wagner company; she was in Bremen (1884) and Vienna (1885). She was a leading member of the Hamburg Opera (1886–95), where she excelled as a Wagnerian; she returned to London (1892, 1894). She married the conductor and composer Otto Lohse in 1893; they toured the United States with the Damrosch Opera Co. (1895–96), then were engaged for the 1896–97 season of the Metropolitan Opera in New York, but she died before her scheduled debut. As one of the outstanding sopranos of her day, she was widely mourned upon her early death.

BIBL.: L. Ordemann, *Aus dem Leben und Wirken von K. K.* (Hameln, 1903).

Klas, Eri, Estonian conductor; b. Tallinn, June 7, 1939. He was a student of Ernesaks at the Tallinn Cons., of Rabinovich at the Leningrad Cons., and of Khaikin at the Bolshoi Theater School in Moscow (1969–72). In 1964 he made his conducting debut with Bernstein's *West Side Story* at the Estonian Opera in Tallinn. From 1969 to 1971 he conducted at the Bolshoi Theater in Moscow, and led the company on tours abroad. In 1975 he became music director of the Estonian Opera. Afer serving as chief conductor of the Royal Opera in Stockholm from 1985 to 1990, he was music director of the Århus Sym. Orch. from 1990 to 1996. In 1991 he made his U.S. debut at the Hollywood Bowl. From 1994 he was a prof. at the Sibelius Academy in Helsinki. He served as chief conductor of the Netherlands Radio Sym. Orch. in Hilversum (from 1996) and as music director of the Tampere Phil. in Finland (from 1998). As a guest conductor, he appeared with major orchs. and operas companies throughout Europe, North America, and the Far East.

Klatzow, Peter (James Leonard), South African composer and teacher; b. Springs, Transvaal, July 14, 1945. After training with Richard Cheery and Aïda Lovell, he obtained a scholarship that allowed him to pursue his training in London at the Royal College of Music (1964–65), where he took courses in piano with Kathleen Long, Angus Morrison, and Frank Merrick, in composition with Bernard Stevens, in orchestration with Gordon Jacob, and in conducting with Sir Adrian Boult; he subsequently completed his studies in Paris with Nadia Boulanger (1965–66). He taught at the Rhodesian College of Music in Salisbury (1966–68) and then was active with the music dept. of the South African Broadcasting Corp. (1968–72). In 1973 he became a prof. of composition at the Univ. of Cape Town. With Robert Grishkoff, he founded the music publishing concern Musications in 1981. He ed. the vol. *Composers in South Africa Today* (Cape Town, 1987). In his compositions, Klatzow generally follows the tonal path but he has not been adverse to utilizing serial and aleatoric procedures in some of his works. Among his works are the opera *The Begger's Opera* (1986) and the ballets *Drie Diere* (1980), *Vespers* (1986), and *Hamlet* (1993).

Klaus, Kenneth Blanchard, American composer; b. Earlville, Iowa, Nov. 11, 1923; d. Baton Rouge, La., Aug. 4, 1980. He studied violin with Burleigh and Krasner, and composition with Philip Greeley Clapp at the Univ. of Iowa (Ph.D., 1950); he also studied meteorology at the Univ. of Chicago and served as a meteorologist in the Army Air Corps during World War II; in 1950 he joined the faculty at Louisiana State Univ. In his works he applied a sui generis synthesis of expanded tonality verging on serialism. In his vocal compositions he modernized the medieval device of "sogetto cavato" by deriving a theme from the vowels of letter names. He publ. *The Romantic Period in Music* (Boston, 1970). Among his compositions are the operas *Tennis Anyone?* (1957) and *Crimson Stones;* also incidental music to *Death of a Salesman* (1954).

Klebanov, Dmitri, outstanding Ukrainian composer; b. Kharkov, July 25, 1907; d. there, June 6, 1987. He studied with Bogatyrev at the Kharkov Inst. for Music and Drama, graduating in 1926. After playing viola in Leningrad (1927–28), he returned to Kharkov as director for several musical comedy theaters and as a teacher at the Cons. (1934–73; prof., 1960; emeritus, 1973). He wrote the Ukrainian State Hymn. Klebanov was president of the local Composer's Union (1945–49).

WORKS: DRAMATIC: OPERAS: *Aistenok*, children's opera (1934); *Single Life* (1947); *Vasily Gubanov* (1966; rev. as *Communist*, 1967); *Red Cossacks* (1971). BALLETS: *Aistenok* (Moscow, 1936); *Svetlana* (Moscow, 1939). OTHER: Musical comedies; film scores.

BIBL.: M. Cherkashina, *D. K.* (1968).

Klebe, Giselher (Wolfgang), German composer and teacher; b. Mannheim, June 28, 1925. He went to Berlin and studied violin, viola, and composition with Kurt von Wolfurt at the Cons. (1940–43) before pursuing his composition studies with Rufer at the Internationales Musikinstitut (1946) and with Blacher (1946–51). He worked in the music division of the Berlin Radio (1946–49), and then taught composition and theory at the North West Music Academy in Detmold from 1957. In 1962–63 he held a fellowship at the Deutsche Akademie in Rome. He was made a member of the Freie Akademie der Künste in Hamburg (1963), the Akademie der Künste in Berlin (1964; president, 1986–89), and the Bayerische Akademie der Schönen Künste in Munich (1978). Klebe has developed an expressive style of composition in which melody, harmony, timbre, and rhythm are complemented by a judicious handling of 12-tone writing.

WORKS: DRAMATIC: *Die Räuber*, opera (1951–56; Düsseldorf, June 3, 1957; rev. 1962); *Die tödlichen Wünsche*, opera (1957–59; Düsseldorf, June 14, 1959); *Die Ermordung Cäsars*, opera (1958–59; Essen, Sept. 20, 1959); *Alkmene*, opera (Berlin, Sept. 25, 1961); *Figaro lässt sich scheiden*, opera buffa (1962–63; Hamburg, June 28, 1963); *Jakobowsky und der Oberst*, comic opera (Hamburg, Nov. 2, 1965); *Das Märchen von der schönen Lilie*, opera (1967–68; Schwetzingen, May 15, 1969); *Das Testament*, ballet-sym. (1970–71; Wiesbaden, April 30, 1971; as Sym. No. 4, Bochum, Jan. 27, 1972); *Ein wahrer Held*, opera (1972–73; Zürich, Jan. 18, 1975); *Das Mädchen aus Domrémy*, opera (1975; Stuttgart, June 19, 1976); *Das Rendezvous*, opera (Hannover, Oct. 7, 1977); *Der jüngste Tag*, opera (1978–79; Mannheim, July 12, 1980); *Die Fastnachtsbeichte*, opera (Darmstadt, Dec. 20, 1983); *Gervaise Macquart* (Düsseldorf, Nov. 10, 1995); *Émile Zola* (1996).

BIBL.: M. Rentzsch, *G. K.: Werkverzeichnis und einführende Darstellung seines Opernschaffens* (diss., Univ. of Münster, 1990).

Klee, Bernhard, respected German conductor: b. Schleiz, April 19, 1936. He studied piano and conducting at the Cologne Hochschule für Musik, then became répétiteur at the Cologne Opera (1957) and the Bern City Theater (1958); he later was an assistant to Sawallisch and a conductor at the Cologne Opera. He was 1st conductor at the opera houses in Salzburg (1962–63), Oberhausen (1963–65), and Hannover (1965–66), then was Generalmusikdirektor in Lübeck (1966–77) and chief conductor of the Hannover Radio Orch. (1976–79). From 1977 to 1987 he was Generalmusikdirektor of the Dusseldorf Sym. Orch.; he served as principal guest conductor of the BBC Phil. in Manchester (1985–

89). In 1991 he returned as chief conductor to the Hannover Radio Orch., which became the Hannover Radio Phil. in 1992. He also served as chief conductor of the Rheinland-Pfalz State Phil. in Ludwigshafen from 1992. In 1995 he was made honorary conductor of the Hannover Radio Orch. and chief conductor of the Staatsphilharmonie Rheinland-Pfalz in Ludwigshafen. Married to **Edith Mathis**, he served as her accompanist in recitals. As a conductor, Klee is particularly admired for his insightful performances of the Austro-German repertoire.

Kleffel, Arno, German composer and conductor; b. Possneck, Sept. 4, 1840; d. Nikolassee, near Berlin, July 15, 1913. He studied with Hauptmann in Leipzig, then conducted theater orchs. and opera in Riga, Cologne, Amsterdam, Berlin, Augsburg, Magdeburg, etc. In 1904 he became conductor of Stern's Gesangverein in Berlin, and in 1910, head of the operatic dept. at the Hochschule für Musik there. He wrote an opera, *Des Meermanns Harfe* (Riga, 1865), and music to Goethe's *Faust*.

Kleiber, Carlos, outstanding German-born Austrian conductor, son of **Erich Kleiber**; b. Berlin, July 3, 1930. He left Nazi Germany with his parents in 1935, eventually settling in South America in 1940. He evinced an early interest in music, but his father opposed it as a career; after studying chemistry in Zürich (1949–50), he turned decisively to music and completed his training in Buenos Aires. In 1952 he became a répétiteur and stage assistant at the Theater am Gärtnerplatz in Munich, making his conducting debut in 1954 with Millöcker's *Gasparone* in Potsdam, where he was active until becoming a répétiteur (1956) and conductor (1958) at the Deutsche Oper am Rhein in Düsseldorf. After conducting at the Zürich Opera (1964–66), he served as 1st conductor at the Württemberg State Theater in Stuttgart (1966–68). From 1968 to 1978 he conducted at the Bavarian State Opera in Munich. In 1966 he made his British debut conducting *Wozzeck* at the Edinburgh Festival; he led performances of *Tristan und Isolde* for his first appearances at the Vienna State Opera in 1973 and at the Bayreuth Festival in 1974, the year in which he made his first appearances at London's Covent Garden and Milan's La Scala with *Der Rosenkavalier*. On Sept. 8, 1977, he made his U.S. debut conducting *Otello* at the San Francisco Opera. His first appearance with a U.S. orch. came in 1978, when he conducted the Chicago Sym. Orch. In 1979 he conducted the Vienna Phil. and in 1982 the Berlin Phil. On Jan. 22, 1988, he made his Metropolitan Opera debut in New York conducting *La Bohème*. In 1989 and 1992 he conducted the New Year's Day Concert of the Vienna Phil. with noteworthy elan. He became a naturalized Austrian citizen in 1980. Kleiber has been accorded accolades from critics, audiences, and his fellow musicians. His brilliant performances reflect his unreserved commitment to the score at hand, his authority, and his mastery of technique. His infrequent appearances, combined with his passion for perfection, have made him a legendary figure among the world's contemporary podium celebrities.

Kleiber, Erich, eminent Austrian conductor, father of **Carlos Kleiber**; b. Vienna, Aug. 5, 1890; d. Zürich, Jan. 27, 1956. He studied at the Prague Cons. and the Univ. of Prague. He made his debut at the Prague National Theater in 1911; then conducted opera in Darmstadt (1912–19), Barmen-Elberfeld (1919–21), Düsseldorf (1921–22), and Mannheim (1922–23). In 1923 he was appointed Generalmusikdirektor of the Berlin State Opera. His tenure was outstanding, both for the brilliant performances of the standard repertoire and for the exciting programming of contemporary works. He conducted the premiere of Berg's *Wozzeck* (Dec. 14, 1925). In 1934, in protest against the Nazi government, he resigned his post and emigrated to South America. He conducted regularly at the Teatro Colón in Buenos Aires from 1936 to 1949. Having first conducted at London's Covent Garden in 1937, he returned there from 1950 to 1953. He then was appointed Generalmusikdirektor once more of the Berlin State Opera in 1954, but resigned in March 1955, before the opening of the season, because of difficulties with the communist regime. He was renowned for his performances of the music of Mozart and Beethoven. He also composed; among his works are a Violin Concerto, Piano Concerto, orch. variations, *Capriccio* for Orch., numerous chamber music works, piano pieces, and songs.

BIBL.: J. Russell, *E. K.: A Memoir* (London, 1957); C. Dillon, *E. K.: A Discogaphy* (Buenos Aires, 1990).

Klein, Bernhard (Joseph), German composer; b. Cologne, March 6, 1793; d. Berlin, Sept. 9, 1832. He went to Paris in 1812 and received some advice from Choron, but he was mainly self-taught; returning to Cologne, he was appointed music director of the Cathedral. In 1818 he settled in Berlin, and from 1820 he taught at the Royal Inst. for Church Music; also taught singing at the Univ. of Berlin, retiring in 1830. He was greatly praised by his Berlin contemporaries for his contrapuntal craftsmanship in sacred works and as a composer of lieder. He composed the operas *Dido* (Berlin, Oct. 15, 1823) and *Ariadne* (Berlin, 1823); also several oratorios, including *Jephtha* (Cologne, 1828) and *David* (Halle, 1830) His stepbrother, Josef Klein (b. Cologne, 1802; d. there, Feb. 10, 1862), was his pupil; he was one of the first composers to set Heine's texts to music.

BIBL.: C. Koch, *B. K.* (diss., Univ. of Rostock, 1902).

Klein, Bruno Oscar, German pianist, organist, teacher, and composer; b. Osnabrück, June 6, 1858; d. N.Y., June 22, 1911. He studied with his father, then with K. Bärmann (piano) at the Munich Cons. In 1878 he settled in the United States, serving as head of the piano dept. at N.Y.'s Convent School of the Sacred Heart (1884–1911); he also was a church organist. He wrote the opera *Kenilworth* (Hamburg, Feb. 13, 1895).

Klein, Fritz Heinrich, Austrian music theorist and composer; b. Budapest, Feb. 2, 1892; d. Linz, July 11, 1977. He took piano lessons with his father; then went to Vienna, where he studied composition with Schoenberg and Berg, and became their devoted disciple. From 1932 to 1957 he taught theory at the Bruckner Cons. in Linz. His most ingenious composition was *Die Maschine* (1921; N.Y., Nov. 24, 1924), subtitled "Eine extonale Selbstsatire" and publ. under the pseudonym "Heautontimorumenos" (i.e., self-tormentor); this work features instances of all kinds of tonal combinations, including a "Mutterakkord," which consists of all 12 different chromatic tones and all 11 different intervals, the first time such an arrangement was proposed. He also publ. an important essay bearing on serial techniques then still in the process of formulation, "Die Grenze der Halbtonwelt," in *Die Musik* (Jan. 1925). He made the vocal score of Berg's opera *Wozzeck*. His compositions include several stage works, among them the opera *Nostradamus*.

Klein, Lothar, German-born Canadian composer; b. Hannover, Jan. 27, 1932. He went to England in 1939 and to the United States in 1941; he studied composition with Fetler at the Univ. of Minnesota (B.A., 1954), then composition with Petrassi at the Berkshire Music Center in Tanglewood (summer, 1956) and orchestration with Dorati in Minneapolis (1956–58). After winning a Fulbright fellowship, he went to Berlin to study composition with Rufer at the Free Univ. and with Blacher at the Hochschule für Musik (1958–60); also with Nono in Darmstadt; he subsequently completed his studies at the Univ. of Minnesota (Ph.D., 1961), serving on its faculty (1962–64). He later taught at the Univ. of Texas at Austin (1964–68); in 1968 he joined the faculty of the Univ. of Toronto, where he was chairman of its graduate music dept. (1971–76). His early music is essentially tonal, aesthetically derived from neo-Romantic procedures; he then experimented with various branches of serialism; also wrote collage pieces embodying elements of all historical periods through linkage of stylistic similarities. Among his works are *Lost Love*, ballet (1950–56), *The Prodigal Son*, dance drama (1966), and *Tale of a Father and Son*, opera (1983).

Klein, Peter, German tenor; b. Zündorf, near Cologne, Jan. 25, 1907; d. Vienna, Oct. 4, 1992. He studied at the Cologne Cons. He made appearances in Düsseldorf, Kaiserslautern, and Zürich; was a member of the Hamburg State Opera (1937–41), then at the Vienna State Opera; he also appeared at Bayreuth (from 1946). In 1947 he first appeared at London's Covent Garden as

Jacquino with the visiting Vienna State Opera; he returned there regularly until 1960. He made his Metropolitan Opera debut in New York on Nov. 21, 1949, as Valzacchi in *Der Rosenkavalier*, remaining on its roster until 1951. From 1956 to 1977 he was head of the opera dept. at the Vienna Cons. His other roles included Basilio, Mime in the *Ring* cycle, the Captain in *Wozzeck*, and Monsieur Taupe in *Capriccio*.

Kleinheinz, Franz Xaver, German conductor and composer; b. Mindelheim (baptized), June 26, 1765; d. Budapest, Jan. 26, 1832. He played in the Munich Orch., and in 1803 went to Vienna to study with Albrechtsberger; then was active in Brünn. He subsequently was a theater conductor in Budapest (1814–15; 1817–24). He wrote the operas *Harald* (Budapest, March 22, 1814) and *Der Käfig* (Budapest, 1816).

Kleinmichel, Richard, German pianist, conductor, and composer; b. Posen, Dec. 31, 1846; d. Charlottenburg, Aug. 18, 1901. He studied with his father, Friedrich Kleinmichel (1827–94), a bandmaster, then at the Leipzig Cons. (1863–66). He was made music director of the Leipzig Theater (1882), and later held similar posts in Danzig and Magdeburg. He wrote the operas *Schloss de l'Orme*, after Prevost's *Manon Lescaut* (Hamburg, Oct. 8, 1883), and *Pfeifer von Dusenbach* (Hamburg, March 21, 1891).

Kleinsinger, George, American composer; b. San Bernardino, Calif., Feb. 13, 1914; d. N.Y., July 28, 1982. He studied with Bauer, Haubiel, and James at N.Y. Univ. (B.A., 1937) and with Jacobi and Wagenaar at the Juilliard Graduate School in New York (1938–40). In 1942 he composed the first of a series of popular melodramas, *Tubby the Tuba*. Also notable was his chamber opera *Shinbone Alley* (N.Y., Dec. 6, 1954), which was based on Don Marquis's popular comic strip *Archy and Mehitabel*.

WORKS: DRAMATIC: MELODRAMAS: *Farewell to a Hero* (1941); *Tubby the Tuba* (1942); *Peewee the Piccolo* (1945); *Pan the Piper* (1946); *The Story of Celeste* (1947); *The Tree that Found Christmas* (1955). CHAMBER OPERA: *Shinbone Alley* (N.Y., Dec. 6, 1954). Also film scores and television music.

Klementyev, Lev (Mikhailovich), Russian tenor; b. St. Petersburg, April 1, 1868; d. Tiflis, Oct. 26, 1910. He appeared in operetta in Kharkov and St. Petersburg, then was a member of the Kiev Opera (1888–89), the Tiflis Opera (1889–90), and Moscow's Bolshoi Theater (from 1892). He was noted for his faithful rendition of Russian operatic roles.

Klemperer, Otto, celebrated German conductor; b. Breslau, May 14, 1885; d. Zürich, July 6, 1973. After early musical training from his mother, he entered the Hoch Cons. in Frankfurt am Main (1901), where he studied piano with Kwast and theory with Knorr; he later received instruction in composition and conducting from Pfitzner in Berlin. He made his debut conducting Max Reinhardt's production of *Orpheus in the Underworld* in Berlin in 1906; on Mahler's recommendation, he then was appointed chorus master and subsequently conductor of the German Theater in Prague; he assisted Mahler in the latter's preparations for the Munich premiere of the *Symphony of a Thousand* in 1910. He became a conductor at the Hamburg Opera in 1910, but was obliged to leave in 1912 as the result of a scandalous liaison with the recently married soprano Elisabeth Schumann. After minor appointments at Barmen (1913–14) and Strasbourg (1914–17), where he was Pfitzner's deputy, he was appointed music director of the Cologne Opera in 1917. While in Cologne, he conducted the German premiere of Janáček's *Kát'a Kabanová*. In 1924 he was named music director of the Wiesbaden Opera. He made his U.S. debut as guest conductor with the N.Y. Sym. Orch. on Jan. 24, 1926. In 1927 he became music director of Berlin's Kroll Opera, where he was given a mandate to perform new works and present repertoire pieces in an enlightened manner. He conducted the world premiere of Hindemith's *Neues vom Tage* (June 8, 1929), as well as the first Berlin performances of Hindemith's *Cardillac*, Stravinsky's *Oedipus Rex*, and Schoenberg's *Die glückliche Hand*; he also conducted the premiere performance of Schoenberg's *Begleitungsmusik* as part of the Kroll concerts. When political and economic pressures forced the Kroll Opera to close in 1931, Klemperer became a conductor at the Berlin State Opera. When the Nazis came to power in 1933 he was compelled to emigrate to the United States. That same year, he became music director of the Los Angeles Phil.; he also appeared as a guest conductor in New York, Philadelphia, and Pittsburgh. His career was disrupted in 1939 when he underwent an operation for a brain tumor. In 1947 he was engaged as conductor at the Budapest State Opera, where he remained until 1950. He made his first appearance as a guest conductor with the Philharmonia Orch. of London in 1951; he was appointed its principal conductor in 1959, and retained that position when the orch.'s manager, Walter Legge, unsuccessfully attempted to disband it in 1964.

Klemperer was accident prone and a manic-depressive all his life. The two sides of his nature were reflected in his conducting styles on either side of World War II. He had earlier been noted for his energetic and hard-driven interpretations, but during his late London years he won great renown for his measured performances of the Viennese classics. He particularly distinguished himself by conducting a memorable series of the Beethoven syms. at the Royal Festival Hall. In the early 1960s he conducted new productions of *Fidelio*, *Die Zauberflöte*, and *Lohengrin* at Covent Garden. His serious and unsentimental readings of Mahler's syms. were largely responsible for the modern critical and popular interest shown in that composer's music. In 1970 he conducted in Jerusalem and accepted Israeli citizenship. Klemperer retired in 1972. He was also a composer. He studied with Schoenberg during the latter's American sojourn, but his compositional style had more in common with that of Pfitzner. He wrote an opera, *Das Ziel* (1915; rev. 1970), a *Missa sacra* (1916), 6 syms. (from 1960), 17 pieces for Voice and Orch. (1967–70), 9 string quartets (1968–70), and about 100 lieder. He publ. *Meine Erinnerungen an Gustav Mahler* (Zürich, 1960; Eng. tr., 1964, as *Minor Recollections*).

BIBL.: P. Heyworth, *Conversations with K.* (London, 1973); C. Osborne and K. Thomson, eds., *K. Stories: Anecdotes, Sayings and Impressions of O. K.* (London, 1980); P. Heyworth, *O. K.: His Life and Times* (2 vols., London, 1983, 1996); M. Anderson, ed., *K. on Music: Shavings from a Musician's Workbench* (London, 1986).

Klenau, Paul (August) von, Danish conductor and composer; b. Copenhagen, Feb. 11, 1883; d. there, Aug. 31, 1946. He studied violin with Hillmer and composition with Malling in Copenhagen; then took lessons in violin with Halir and in composition with Bruch at the Berlin Hochschule für Musik (1902–04). In 1904 he went to Munich, where he studied composition privately with Thuille; in 1908 he moved to Stuttgart, where he became a student of Schillings. He began his conducting career at the Freiburg im Breisgau Opera during the season of 1907–08; from 1909 to 1912 he was conductor at the Stuttgart Court Opera; in 1912 he was conductor of the Bach Soc. in Frankfurt am Main; he then returned to the Freiburg im Breisgau Opera (1913). After World War I, he studied with Schoenberg. From 1920 to 1926 he was conductor of the Danish Phil. Soc. in Copenhagen; concurrently he conducted the Vienna Konzerthausgesellschaft (1922–30). He returned to Copenhagen in 1940.

WORKS: DRAMATIC: OPERAS: *Sulamith*, after the Song of Songs (Munich, Nov. 16, 1913); *Kjartan und Gudrun* (Mannheim, April 4, 1918; rev. version as *Gudrun auf Island*, Hagen, Nov. 27, 1924); *Die Lästerschule*, after Sheridan (Frankfurt am Main, Dec. 25, 1926); *Michael Kolhaas*, after Kleist (Stuttgart, Nov. 4, 1933; new version, Berlin, March 7, 1934); *Rembrandt van Rijn*, libretto by the composer (Berlin and Stuttgart, Jan. 23, 1937); *Elisabeth von England* (Kassel, March 29, 1939; title changed to *Die Königin* after the outbreak of World War II to avoid mentioning England). BALLETS: *Kleine Idas Blumen*, after Hans Christian Andersen (Stuttgart, 1916); *Marion* (Copenhagen, 1920).

Klenovsky, Paul. See **Wood, Sir Henry J(oseph).**

Klička, Josef, Bohemian organist, choral conductor, and composer; b. Klattau, Dec. 15, 1855; d. there, March 28, 1937. He studied with Skuherský in Prague, then conducted various choral societies there; he was prof. of organ at the Prague Cons. (1885–1924) and inspector of music in Bohemia (1906–20). Among his works are the opera *Spanilá mlynářka* (Die Schöne Müllerin; Prague, 1886) and 2 oratorios. His son was the Czech harpist, teacher, and composer Václav Klička (1882–1953).

BIBL.: K. Hoffmeister, *J. K.* (Prague, 1944).

Klima, Alois, Czech conductor; b. Klatovy, Dec. 21, 1905; d. Prague, June 11, 1980. He began his musical training with his father; after taking courses in mathematics and physics at the Univ. of Prague, he studied with Dědeček and Doležil (conducting) and Křička and Řídký (composition) at the Prague Cons. He conducted the radio orchs. in Košice (1936) and Ostrava (1936–38), and then was chief conductor of the Prague Opera Studio (1939–46) and the Prague Radio Sym. Orch. (1950–70); he also was a teacher at the Prague Cons. and Academy of Music.

Klitzsch, Karl Emanuel, German conductor and composer; b. Schönhaide, Oct. 30, 1812; d. Zwickau, March 5, 1889. He lived most of his life in Zwickau, where he was cofounder and conductor of the Music Soc. Under the pen name of Emanuel Kronach, he composed the opera *Juana, oder Ein Tag auf St. Domingo.*

Klobučar, Berislav, Yugoslav conductor; b. Zagreb, Aug. 28, 1924. He was educated at the Zagreb Academy of Music; he studied conducting with Lovro von Matacic and Clemens Krauss. He was conductor at the Zagreb National Theater (1941–51); in 1953 he appeared at the Vienna State Opera; he became a regular conductor there. He was chief conductor of the Graz Phil. and Opera (1961–72); after serving as principal conductor at Stockholm's Royal Theater (1972–81), he was music director of the Orchestre Philharmonique de Nice (1982–88). He also appeared as a guest conductor with the major European and U.S. opera houses.

Klose, Margarete, esteemed German contralto; b. Berlin, Aug. 6, 1902; d. there, Dec. 14, 1968. She studied at the Klindworth-Scharwenka Cons. in Berlin and received vocal training from Bültemann and Marschalk. She made her operatic debut in Ulm in 1927, then sang in Kassel (1928–29) and Mannheim (1929–31). She was a leading member of the Berlin State Opera (1931–49; 1955–61); she also sang at the Bayreuth Festivals (1936–42) and London's Covent Garden (1935, 1937), and was a member of the Berlin Städtische Oper (1949–58). She was particularly praised for her Wagner and Verdi portrayals.

Klughardt, August (Friedrich Martin), German conductor and composer; b. Cöthen, Nov. 30, 1847; d. Rosslau, near Dresden, Aug. 3, 1902. He was a pupil of Blassmann and Reichel in Dresden. From 1867 to 1868 he was a theater conductor in Posen; held similar posts in Neustrelitz (1868–69) and Lübeck (1869). He served as court music director in Weimar (1869–73), where he became a friend of Liszt. He then was music director in Neustrelitz (1873–82) and Dessau (from 1882). Among his works were 4 operas: *Mirjam* (Weimar, 1871), *Iwein* (Neustrelitz, 1879), *Gudrun* (Neustrelitz, 1882), and *Die Hochzeit Mönchs* (Dessau, Nov. 10, 1886).

BIBL.: L. Gerlach, *A. K.: Sein Leben und seine Werke* (Leipzig, 1902).

Klusák, Jan, Czech composer; b. Prague, April 18, 1934. He studied theory with Řídký and Bořkovec at the Prague Academy of Music (1953–57). He wrote a number of works in a neo-Baroque idiom, set in tolerably dissonant counterpoint; he also paid tribute to the ethnic resources of Czech music. He soon succumbed, however, to the Circean lure of cosmopolitan formalism and total serialism, with a well-nigh monastic exercise of tonal egalitarianism.

WORKS: DRAMATIC: OPERAS: *Proces* (The Trial), after Kafka (1966); *Viola* (1984–85); *Zpráva pro akademii* (Report for the Academy), chamber opera, after Kafka (1993–97). BALLET: *Stories from Tapestries* (1988). Also film music.

Kmentt, Waldemar, Austrian tenor; b. Vienna, Feb. 2, 1929. He was a student at the Vienna Academy of Music of Adolf Vogel, Elisabeth Rado, and Hans Duhan; while still a student, he toured the Netherlands and Belgium with a student ensemble of the Academy. In 1950 he made his formal debut as a soloist in Beethoven's 9th Sym. in Vienna, and then appeared as the Prince in *The Love for 3 Oranges* at the Vienna Volksoper in 1951. In the latter year, he became a member of the Vienna State Opera, where he appeared as Jaquino at the reopening of the opera house in 1955. He also sang regularly in Salzburg (from 1955) and Düsseldorf (from 1958), and made guest appearances in Milan, Paris, Rome, Bayreuth, Munich, and other operatic centers. As a concert artist, he sang widely in Europe as well. He acquired a fine reputation for his performances of works from the Austro-German repertoire.

Knaifel, Alexander (Aronovich), Russian composer; b. Tashkent, Nov. 28, 1943. He began his training in the special music school at the Leningrad Cons. (1950–61); after attending the Moscow Cons. (1961–63), he studied composition with Arapov at the Leningrad Cons. (1963–67). In his works, Knaifel employs a variety of modern compositional techniques. His compositions include *Kentervilskoe prividenie* (The Canterville Ghost), chamber opera (1965–66), ballets, and film scores.

Knappertsbusch, Hans, eminent German conductor; b. Elberfeld, March 12, 1888; d. Munich, Oct. 25, 1965. He studied philosophy at the Univ. of Bonn before pursuing musical training with Steinbach and Lohse at the Cologne Cons. (1908–12). He was conductor in Mülheim and served as assistant conductor at the Bayreuth Festivals (1910–12), then conducted in Bochum (1912–13). He was director of opera in Elberfeld (1913–18); he subsequently conducted opera in Leipzig (1918–19) and Dessau (1919–22). In 1922 he became Generalmusikdirektor of the Bavarian State Opera in Munich, a post he held with great distinction until resigning in the face of Nazi pressure in 1936; he then conducted at the Vienna State Opera (1936–45) and was also a conductor with the Vienna Phil. (1937–44). After World War II, he returned to Germany and made his home in Munich. He conducted at the Salzburg Festivals (1947–50; 1954–55) and was a regular guest conductor with the Vienna Phil. (1947–64) and at the Bayreuth Festivals (from 1951). He was one of the great interpreters of the operas of Wagner and Richard Strauss. The authority and spontaneity he brought to such masterworks as *Götterdämmerung* and *Parsifal* were extraordinary.

BIBL.: R. Betz and W. Panofsky, *K.* (Ingolstadt, 1958).

Knecht, Justin Heinrich, German organist, conductor, music theorist, and composer; b. Biberach, Sept. 30, 1752; d. there, Dec. 1, 1817. He was an organist and music director in Biberach from 1771 to the end of his life, traveling only briefly to Stuttgart, where he was court conductor from 1806 till 1808. Despite his provincial field of activity, he attained considerable repute in Germany through his compositions and theoretical writings. He was a follower of the Vogler system of harmony; he taught chord building by thirds up to chords of the eleventh on all degrees of the scale, and publ. several theoretical treatises. He wrote 10 stage works, mostly Singspiels.

BIBL.: E. Kauffmann, *J. H. K.* (Tübingen, 1892); A. Bopp, *J. H. K.* (Biberach, 1917).

Knipper, Lev (Konstantinovich), important Russian composer; b. Tiflis, Dec. 3, 1898; d. Moscow, July 30, 1974. He studied piano with Gnesina and composition with Glière and Zhilyaev at Moscow's Gnessin School; he also took private lessons with Jarnach in Berlin and Julius Weissmann in Freiburg im Breisgau. Under the influence of western European trends, he wrote music in a fairly advanced style of composition, but soon abandoned these experiments and devoted himself to the study of folk music of different nationalities of the Soviet Union. He composed the operas *Severniy veter* (The North Wind; 1929–30; Moscow, March 30, 1930), *Marya* (1936–38), *Aktrisa* (The Actress; 1942), *Na Bay-*

kale (On the Baikal Lake; 1946–48), and *Korenzhizni* (The Source of Life; 1948–49); also ballets.

Knorr, Iwan (Otto Armand), German composer and teacher; b. Mewe, Jan. 3, 1853; d. Frankfurt am Main, Jan. 22, 1916. His family went to Russia when he was 3 years old, returning to Germany in 1868. He entered the Leipzig Cons., where he studied piano with Moscheles, theory with Richter, and composition with Reinecke. In 1874 he returned to Russia, where he taught in Kharkov; he was made head of theoretical studies of the Kharkov division of the Russian Imperial Musical Soc. (1878). He settled in Frankfurt am Main in 1883 as a teacher at the Hoch Cons.; in 1908, became its director. His most distinguished pupils were Cyril Scott, Pfitzner, and Ernst Toch. His works are conceived in a Romantic vein, several inspired by the Ukrainian folk songs that he had heard in Russia. He composed the operas *Dunja* (Koblenz, March 23, 1904), *Die Hochzeit* (Prague, 1907), and *Durchs Fenster* (Karlsruhe, Oct. 4, 1908).

WRITINGS (all publ. in Leipzig): *Aufgaben für den Unterricht in der Harmonielehre* (1903); *Lehrbuch der Fugenkomposition* (1911); *Die Fugen des Wohltemperieten Klaviers in bildlicher Darstellung* (1912; 2d ed., 1926).

BIBL.: M. Bauer, *I. K.: Ein Gedenkblatt* (Frankfurt am Main, 1916).

Knote, Heinrich, distinguished German tenor; b. Munich, Nov. 26, 1870; d. Garmisch, Jan. 12, 1953. He studied with Kirschner in Munich. On May 7, 1892, he made his operatic debut as Georg in Lortzing's *Der Waggenschmied* at the Munich Court Opera, where he soon became a principal singer, continuing on its roster when it became the Bavarian State Opera (1918); he also sang at London's Covent Garden (1901; 1903; 1907–08; 1913). He made his Metropolitan Opera debut in New York as Walther von Stolzing (Dec. 3, 1904), singing there until 1906 and again in 1907–08; he later toured the United States with the German Opera Co. (1923–24). His remarkable Munich career spanned almost half a century; he made his farewell appearance there as Siegfried (Dec. 15, 1931); he subsequently taught voice. He was a greatly esteemed Heldentenor, excelling in such roles as Tannhäuser, Lohengrin, Tristan, and Siegfried.

BIBL.: J. Wagenmann, *Der sechzigjährige deutsche Meistersinger H. K. in seiner stimmbildnerischen Bedeutung und im Vergleich mit anderen Sängern* (Munich, 1930).

Knüpfer, Paul, German bass; b. Halle, June 21, 1865; d. Berlin, Nov. 4, 1920. After attending the Sondershausen Cons., he received vocal lessons from Bernhard Gunzburger. In 1885 he made his operatic debut in Sondershausen, and then was a member of the Leipzig Opera (1887–98) and the Berlin Royal (later State) Opera (1898–1920). Following additional vocal studies with J. Kniese in Bayreuth (1900), he appeared at the Festivals there until 1912. He also sang at London's Covent Garden (1904; 1907–14). Among his finest portrayals were Osmin, Daland, Pogner, Gurnemanz, King Marke, and Baron Ochs.

Knussen, (Stuart) Oliver, prominent English composer and conductor; b. Glasgow, June 12, 1952. Remarkably precocious, he began playing piano as a small boy and showed unusual diligence also in his composition studies, mostly with John Lambert (1963–69) while attending the Central Tutorial School for Young Musicians (1964–67). On April 7, 1968, he made musical headlines when, at the age of 15, he conducted the London Sym. Orch. in the premiere performance of his own 1st Sym., written in an eclectic, but astoundingly effective, modern style. He was awarded fellowships for advanced study with Schuller at the Berkshire Music Center in Tanglewood (1970–73). From 1977 to 1982 he taught composition at the Royal College of Music in London. He served as an artistic director of the Aldeburgh Festivals (from 1983) and as coordinator of contemporary music activities at Tanglewood (1986–93). He served as composer-in-residence of the Philharmonia Orch. in London from 1984. With Steuart Bedford, he served as co-artistic director of the Aldeburgh Festival from 1989. From 1998 he was principal conductor of the London Sinfonietta. In 1994 he was made a Commander of the Order of the British Empire. In his mature works, Knussen has revealed a penchant for experimentation with various styles and for revising scores without surcease, resulting in compositions of great refinement and lucidity. He composed the operas *Where the Wild Things Are* (1979–80; Brussels, Nov. 28, 1980; rev. 1980–83; London, Jan. 9, 1984) and *Higglety Pigglety Pop!* (1983–85; Glyndebourne, Aug. 5, 1985).

Koch, (Sigurd Christian) Erland von, Swedish composer; b. Stockholm, April 26, 1910. His father was the Swedish composer (Richert) Sigurd (Valdemar) von Koch (1879–1919). He studied music with his father, then at the Stockholm Cons. (1931–35); he went to Germany, where he studied composition with Paul Höffer and conducting with Clemens Krauss and Gmeindl (1936–38) and also had piano lessons with Arrau. He subsequently taught at Wohlfart's Music School in Stockholm (1939–53); he also was a sound technician with the Swedish Radio (1943–45); in 1953 he joined the faculty of the Stockholm Musikhögskolan, becoming a prof. in 1968. In 1957 he became a member of the Royal Swedish Academy of Music in Stockholm. In some of his later works, he endeavored to create a curious amalgam of folk motifs with 12-tone rows ("12-tone and folk-tone"). Among his numerous compositions are the children's opera *Pelle svanslös* (Tailless Peter; 1948; Göteborg, Jan. 7, 1949; rev. 1966) and the ballets *Askungen* (Cinderella; 1942; also an orch. suite) and *Samson and Delila* (1963; orch. suite, 1964; rev. 1972); also incidental music for the radio play *Bjälbojarlen*, after Strindberg (Swedish Radio, Jan. 25, 1968).

Koch, Helmut, German conductor; b. Wuppertal-Barmen, April 5, 1908; d. Berlin, Jan. 26, 1975. He studied conducting with Fiedler, Lehmann, and Scherchen. He led workers' choruses for many years; after World War II he was active in East Germany; he was founder-conductor of the Berlin Chamber Orch. (1945), conductor of the Berlin Radio Choir (from 1948), and director of the Berlin Singakademie (from 1963) and also a guest conductor at the Berlin State Opera (from 1960). He was widely known in East Germany for his performances of the music of Handel. He made numerous arrangements of German folk songs.

Kochan, Günter, German composer and teacher; b. Luckau, Oct. 2, 1930. He studied composition with Blacher, Noetel, and Wunsch at the (West) Berlin Hochschule für Musik (1946–50); then attended Eisler's master classes at the (East) Berlin Akademie der Künste of the German Democratic Republic (1950–53). From 1950 to 1991 he taught at the (East) Berlin Hochschule für Musik. In 1965 he was elected to the Akademie der Künste. His music is eminently functional, and in it the formal design is paramount; main subjects are stated repeatedly with utmost clarity; the rhythmic formulas are explicit; there is a distinct affinity with the symphonic processes used by Eisler; polymodal themes abound within starkly dissonant harmonies. Among his works are the opera *Karin Lenz* (1968–70) and the melodrama *Luther* (1981); also *Das Friedensfest oder Die Teilhabe*, oratorio (1978).

Koczalski, Raoul (Raul Armand Georg), Polish pianist and composer; b. Warsaw, Jan. 3, 1884; d. Poznan, Nov. 24, 1948. He was trained by his parents; at the age of 4 he played at a charity concert in Warsaw and was at once proclaimed an "infant phenomenon." He studied with Mikuli in Lemberg, and then with Anton Rubinstein. He performed in Vienna (1892), Russia, Paris, and London (1893); he made nearly 1,000 public appearances before he was 12. His sensational success diminished to some extent as he grew out of the prodigy age, but he was appreciated as a mature pianist, and particularly for his sensitive playing of Chopin. He lived mostly in France, Germany, and Sweden; after World War II he returned to Poland and taught in Poznan and Warsaw. He publ. *Frédéric Chopin: Betrachtungen, Skizzen, Analysen* (Cologne, 1936). His precocity extended to composition as well; he wrote some 50 works before he was 10; he later wrote the operas *Rymond* (Elberfeld, Oct. 14, 1902) and *Die Suhne* (Muhlhausen, 1909).

BIBL.: B. Vogel, *R. K.* (Leipzig and Warsaw, 1896); M. Paruszewska, *Biographical Sketch and the Artistic Career of R. K.* (Poznan, 1936).

Kodalli, Nevit, Turkish conductor and composer; b. Mersin, Jan. 12, 1924. He studied with Necil Kazim Akses at the Ankara Cons., graduating in 1947; he then went to Paris, where he took lessons with Honegger and Boulanger (1948–53). After teaching at the Ankara Cons. (1953–55), he conducted at the Ankara Opera (from 1955). He was a composer at the Ankara State Theater (from 1962). His music preserves the traits of Turkish folk melos, but the harmonic and contrapuntal treatment is in the manner of the French modern school. Among his works are 2 operas (1955, 1963) and an oratorio, *Ataturk* (Ankara, Nov. 9, 1953).

Kodály, Zoltán, renowned Hungarian composer, ethnomusicologist, and music educator; b. Kecskemét, Dec. 16, 1882; d. Budapest, March 6, 1967. He was brought up in a musical family; received his general education at the Archiepiscopal Grammar School in Nagyszombat; at the same time, he took lessons in piano, violin, viola, and cello. He soon began to compose, producing an overture when he was 15; it was performed in Nagyszombat in 1898. He then went to Budapest (1900), where he entered the Univ. as a student of Hungarian and German; he also studied composition with Koessler at the Royal Academy of Music (diplomas in composition, 1904, and teaching, 1905; Ph.D., 1906, with a diss. on the stanzaic structure of Hungarian folk song). He became associated with Bartók, collecting, organizing, and editing the vast wealth of national folk songs; he made use of these melodies in his own compositions. In 1906 he went to Berlin, and in 1907 proceeded to Paris, where he took some lessons with Widor, but it was the music of Debussy that most profoundly influenced him in his subsequent development as a composer. He was appointed a prof. at the Royal Academy of Music in Budapest in 1907. In collaboration with Bartók, he prepared the detailed paper "Az uj egyetemes népdalgyüjtemény tervezete" (A Project for a New Universal Collection of Folk Songs) in 1913. They continued their collecting expeditions until World War I intervened. Kodály wrote music criticism in Budapest (1917–19). In 1919 he was appointed deputy director of the Budapest Academy of Music, but lost his position that same year for political reasons; however, he resumed his teaching there in 1922. In 1923 he was commissioned to write a commemorative work in celebration of the half-century anniversary of the union of Buda, Pest, and Obuda into Budapest. The resulting work, the oratorio *Psalmus hungaricus* (1923), brought him wide recognition. The initial performance in Budapest was followed by numerous productions all over Europe, and also in America. Another major success was his opera *Háry János* (1926); an orch. suite from this work became highly popular in Hungary and throughout the world. His orch. works *Marosszéki táncok* (Dances of Marosszék; 1930; based on a piano work) and *Galántai táncok* (Dances of Galanta; for the 80th anniversary of the Budapest Phil. Soc., 1933) were also very successful. His reputation as one of the most significant national composers was firmly established with the repeated performances of these works. Among his most important subsequent works were the orch. pieces *Variations on a Hungarian Folk Song* "Felszállott a páva," the *Peacock Variations* (for the 50th anniversary of the Amsterdam Concertgebouw Orch., 1939), and the *Concerto for Orchestra* (for the 50th anniversary of the Chicago Sym. Orch., 1941). His great interest in music education is reflected in his numerous choral works, which he wrote for both adults and children during the last 30 years of his life. He also pursued his ethnomusicological studies; from 1940 he was associated with the Hungarian Academy of Sciences, serving as its president (1946–49). He continued to teach at the Academy of Music until 1940, and then gave instruction in Hungarian folk music until 1942; even after his retirement, he taught the latter course there. He toured as a conductor of his own music in England, the United States, and the Soviet Union (1946–47), then throughout western Europe. In succeeding years he held a foremost place in the musical life of his country, receiving many honors; he was awarded 3 Kossuth Prizes (1948, 1952, 1957). He also received foreign honors, being made an honorary member of the Moscow Cons. (1963) and the American Academy of Arts and Sciences (1963); he was also awarded the Gold Medal of the Royal Phil. Soc. of London (1967). An International Kodály Soc. was organized in Budapest in 1975.

As a composer, Kodály's musical style was not as radical as that of Bartók; he never departed from basic tonality, nor did his experiments in rhythm reach the primitivistic power of Bartók's percussive idiom. He preferred a Romantic treatment of his melodic and harmonic materials, with an infusion of Impressionistic elements. All the same, he succeeded in producing a substantial body of music of notable distinction. He was married twice; his first wife, Emma, whom he married in 1910, died in 1958; on Dec. 18, 1959, he married Sarolta Péczely, a student (b. 1940).

WRITINGS: With B. Bartók, *Erdelyi magyarsag: Nepdalok* (The Hungarians of Transylvania: Folk Songs; Budapest, 1923); *A magyar népzene* (Hungarian Folk Music; Budapest, 1937; 2d ed., aug., 1943; 3d ed., aug., 1952 by L. Vargyas; Eng. tr., 1960); with A. Gyulai, *Arany János népdalgyüjteménye* (The Folk Song Collection of János Arany; Budapest, 1953); A. Szöllöy, ed., *A zene mindenkie* (Budapest, 1954; 2d ed., 1975); F. Bónis, ed., *Visszatekintés* (In Retrospect: Budapest, 1964; 2d ed., aug., 1974); *The Selected Writings of Zoltán Kodály* (Budapest, 1974).

WORKS: DRAMATIC: *Notre Dame de Paris*, incidental music for a parody (Budapest, Feb. 1902); *Le Cid*, incidental music for a parody (Budapest, Feb. 1903); *A nagybácsi* (The Uncle), incidental music (Budapest, Feb. 1904); *Pacsirtaszó* (Lark Song), incidental music for Voice and Small Orch. (Budapest, Sept. 14, 1917); *Háry János*, Singspiel (Budapest, Oct. 16, 1926); *Székely fonó* (The Transylvanian Spinning Room), lyrical play (1924–32; Budapest, April 24, 1932); *Czinka Panna*, Singspiel (1946–48; Budapest, March 15, 1948).

BIBL.: A. Molnár, *K. Z.* (Budapest, 1936); B. Szabolcsi and D. Bartha, eds., *Emlékkönyv K. Z. 70. születésnapjára* (Budapest, 1953); L. Eösze, *K. Z. élete és munkassaga* (Z. K.'s Life and Work; Budapest, 1956; Eng. tr., 1962); P. Young, *Z. K.: A Hungarian Musician* (London, 1964); J. Breuer, *K.-kalauz* (Budapest, 1982; Eng. tr., 1990, as *A Guide to K.*); E. Lendvai, *The Workshop of Bartók and K.* (Budapest, 1983); E. Szőnyi, *K. Z. nevelési eszméi* (Budapest, 1984); I. Kecskeméti, *K., the Composer: Brief Studies on the First Half of K.'s Oeuvre* (Kecskemét, 1986); G. Ránki, *Bartók and K. Revisited* (Budapest, 1987); B. Reuer, *Z. K.s Bühnenwerk "Háry János": Beiträge zu seinen volksmusikalischen und literarischen Quellen* (Munich, 1991).

Koechlin, Charles (Louis Eugène), noted French composer, pedagogue, and writer on music; b. Paris, Nov. 27, 1867; d. Le Canadel, Var, Dec. 31, 1950. He studied for a military career, but was compelled to change his plans when stricken with tuberculosis; while recuperating in Algeria, he took up serious music studies; he then entered the Paris Cons. (1890), where he studied with Gédalge, Massenet, Tadou, and Fauré, graduating in 1897. He lived mostly in Paris, where he was active as a composer, teacher, and lecturer; with Ravel and Schmitt, he organized the Société Musicale Indépendante (1909) to advance the cause of contemporary music; with Satie, Roussel, Milhaud, and others, he was a member of the group Les Nouveaux Jeunes (1918–20), a precursor to Les Six. Although he composed prolifically in all genres, he became best known as a writer on music and as a lecturer. He made 3 lecture tours of the United States (1918, 1928, 1937). He became president of the Fédération Musicale Populaire (1937). His pro-communist leanings caused him to promote music for the proletariat during the 1930s; he wrote a number of works "for the people" and also film scores. In spite of the fact that such works as his *Symphonie d'hymnes* (Prix Cressent, 1936) and Sym. No. 1 (Prix Halphan, 1937) won honors, his music made no real impact. Taking Fauré as his model, he strove to preserve the best elements in the French Classical tradition. A skillful craftsman, he produced works of clarity and taste, marked by advanced harmonic and polyphonic attributes.

WRITINGS: *Étude sur les notes de passage* (Paris, 1922); *Précis des règles du contrepoint* (Paris, 1926; Eng. tr., 1927); *Gabriel Fauré* (Paris, 1927; Eng. tr., 1946); *Claude Debussy* (Paris, 1927); *Traité de l'harmonie* (3 vols., Paris, 1927–30); *Étude sur le choral d'école* (Paris, 1929); *Théorie de la musique* (Paris, 1934); *Étude sur l'écriture de la fugue d'école* (Paris, 1934); *Pierre Maurice, musicien* (Geneva, 1938); *Les instruments à vent* (Paris, 1948); *Traité de l'orchestration* (4 vols., Paris, 1954–59).

WORKS (Koechlin orchestrated many of his works well after their original completion. Dates given are those of original, often unorchestrated, versions): DRAMATIC: PASTORALE BIBLIQUE: *Jacob chez Laban* for Soprano, Tenor, Chorus, and Orch. (1896–1908; Paris, May 19, 1925). BALLETS: *La Forêt païenne* (1911–16; Paris, June 17, 1925); *La Divine Vesprée* (1917); *L'Âme heureuse* (1945–47); *Voyages: Film danse* (1947).

BIBL.: R. Orledge, *A Study of the Composer C. K. (1867–1950)* (diss., Univ. of Cambridge, 1973); J. Woodward, *The Theoretical Writings of C. K.* (diss., Univ. of Rochester, 1974); H. Sauget, ed., *Oeuvres de C. K.* (Paris, 1975; a catalog); R. Orledge, *C. K. (1867–1950): His Life and Works* (vol. 1, N.Y., 1989).

Koenemann, Theodore. See **Keneman, Feodor.**

Koenen, Tilly (Mathilde Caroline), Dutch mezzo-soprano; b. Salatiga, Java, Dec. 25, 1873; d. The Hague, Jan. 4, 1941. She studied piano, on which she became a proficient performer, then voice with Cornelia van Zanten. She toured Germany and Austria from 1900 with excellent success; visited the United States in 1909–10 and 1915–16. She was particularly impressive in her interpretations of German Romantic songs; also performed some songs by her compatriots.

Kogan, Pavel, Russian violinist and conductor; b. Moscow, June 6, 1952. He enrolled at Moscow's Central Music School when he was 6, and later pursued his training at the Moscow Cons. with Jankelevitch. After taking 1st prize in the Sibelius Competition in Helsinki in 1970, he toured extensively as a violin virtuoso. In later years, he took up a career as a conductor. In 1988 he became a conductor at the Bolshoi Theater in Moscow. He also conducted the Moscow State Sym. Orch. from 1989, and was principal guest conductor of the Utah Sym. Orch. in Salt Lake City from 1998. His father was the outstanding Russian violinist Leonid (Borisovich) Kogan (b. Dneptropetrovsk, Nov. 14, 1924; d. on the train at the Mytishcha railroad station, Dec. 17, 1982).

Kogoj, Marij, Slovenian composer; b. Trieste, May 27, 1895; d. Ljubljana, Feb. 25, 1956. He was a student of Schreker and Schoenberg in Vienna (1914–18); he then was active as a conductor at the Ljubljana Opera and as a music critic. Although Kogoj's promising career was thwarted in 1932 when he became mentally ill, he was one of the earliest Slovenian composers to experiment with expressionism, as evinced in his opera *Črne maske* (Black Masks; Ljubljana, May 7, 1929).

Köhler, Siegfried, German conductor; b. Freiburg im Breisgau, July 30, 1923. He studied at the local Hochschule für Musik. After conducting opera in provincial German cities, he conducted in Cologne; in 1964 he was named Generalmusikdirektor in Saarbrücken, and in 1974 in Wiesbaden. From 1990 to 1995 he was principal conductor of the Royal Opera in Stockholm. In 1992 he was named Royal Court Conductor of Sweden.

Köhler, Siegfried, German composer, teacher, and administrator; b. Meissen, March 2, 1927; d. Berlin, July 14, 1984. He studied with MacGregor (piano), Hintze (conducting), and Finke (composition) at the Dresden Hochschule für Musik (1946–50) and with Serauky (musicology) and Jahn (art history) at the Univ. of Leipzig (Ph.D., 1955, with the diss. *Die Instrumentation als Mittel musikalischer Ausdrucksgestaltung*). In 1957 he became director of the Berlin International Music Library. After serving as artistic director of the Deutsche Schallplaten (1963–68), he was director of the Dresden Hochschule für Musik (1968–80), where he also was prof. of composition (from 1969). In 1982 he became president of the Assn. of Composers and Music Scholars of the German Democratic Republic. In 1983 he became Intendant of the Dresden State Opera. Among his compositions is the opera *Der Richter von Hohenburg* (1963) and the oratorio *Reich des Menschen* (1962).

BIBL.: G. Schönfelder, *S. K. für Sie porträtiert* (Leipzig, 1984).

Kohoutek, Ctirad, prominent Czech composer, pedagogue, music theorist, and administrator; b. Zábřeh na Moravě, March 18, 1929. He studied at the Brno Cons. with Vilám Petrželka, and with Jaroslav Kvapil at the Janáček Academy of Music there (1949–53); he later attended Lutoslawski's lectures at the Dartington Summer School of Music (1963) and sessions given by Boulez and Ligeti at the Darmstadt summer courses in new music; he obtained his Ph.D. from Palacký Univ. in Olomouc (1973) and his C.Sc. from J. E. Purkyně Univ. in Brno (1980). In 1953 he joined the faculty of the Janáček Academy of Music in Brno (assoc. prof., 1965–80). In 1980 he became assoc. prof. of composition at the Prague Academy of Music, and later that year prof. of composition, which position he retained until 1990. He also served as artistic director of the Czech Phil. (1980–87). In 1988 he was made an Artist of Merit by the Czech government. His music follows the traditions of Central European modernism, well contained within Classical forms but diversified by serial procedures and glamorized by electronic sounds. Among his compositions is the opera *O Kohoutkovi a Slepičce* (About the Cock and Hen; 1988–89). He is the brother of the astronomer Luboš Kohoutek.

Kohs, Ellis (Bonoff), noted American composer and teacher; b. Chicago, May 12, 1916. His mother was a good violinist, and when Kohs learned to play the piano he often accompanied her at home. In 1928 the family moved from San Francisco (following his early musical studies there at the Cons. to New York, where he studied with Adelaide Belser at the Inst. of Musical Art. In 1933 he enrolled at the Univ. of Chicago as a student in composition with Carl Bricken (M.A., 1938). Upon graduation, he proceeded to New York, where he entered the Juilliard School of Music, studying composition with Wagenaar and musical pedagogy with Samaroff. He continued his musical studies at Harvard Univ., with Piston in composition and Leichtentritt and Apel in musicology (1939–41); he also attended a seminar given by Stravinsky at Harvard Univ. in 1940–41. During the summer of 1940, he was a lecturer in music at the Univ. of Wisc. in Madison. From 1941 to 1946 he served in the U.S. Army as a chaplain's assistant and organist, and in the U.S. Air Force as a bandleader. After his discharge from service, he engaged in pedagogical work and in active composition; his teaching posts included Wesleyan Univ. (1946–48), the Kansas City Cons. of Music (1946–47), the College of the Pacific in Stockton, California (1948–50), Stanford Univ. (1950), and the Univ. of Southern Calif. in Los Angeles (1950–85). In his music he pursues the aim of classical clarity; he is particularly adept in variation structures; the rhythmic patterns in his works are often asymmetrical, and the contrapuntal fabric highly dissonant; in some of his works, he makes use of a unifying 12-tone row, subjecting it to ingenious metamorphoses, as revealed in his opera *Amerika*, after the novel by Kafka (1969; abridged concert version, Los Angeles, May 19, 1970; 2 orch. suites, 1986, 1987). A humorous streak is shown in his choral piece *The Automatic Pistol*, to words from the U.S. Army weapons manual, which he composed during his military service. He publ. the useful manuals *Music Theory, a Syllabus for Teacher and Student* (2 vols., N.Y., 1961), *Musical Form: Studies in Analysis and Synthesis* (Boston, 1976), and *Musical Composition: Projects in Ways and Means* (Metuchen, N.J., 1980).

Kókai, Rezsö, Hungarian composer and teacher; b. Budapest, Jan. 15, 1906; d. there, March 6, 1962. He was a student of Koessler (composition) and Emánuel Hegyi (piano) at the Budapest Academy of Music (1925–26), and of W. Gurlitt at the Univ. of Freiburg im Breisgau (Ph.D., 1933, with a diss. on Liszt's early piano music). He taught in Budapest at the National Cons. (1926–34) and at the Academy of Music (from 1929); he also was head of the music dept. of the Hungarian Radio (1945–48). In 1952, 1955, and 1956 he received the Erkel Prize. Among his works are *István király* (King Stephen), scenic oratorio (1942), *A rossz fe-*

leség (The Shrew), dance ballad (1942–45), and *Lészen ágyú* (There Shall be Cannons), radio opera (1951); also music for radio plays and films.

Kokkonen, Joonas, prominent Finnish composer, pianist, pedagogue, and administrator; b. Iisälmi, Nov. 13, 1921; d. Järvenpää, Oct. 2, 1996. He was educated at the Univ. (M.A., 1948) and the Sibelius Academy (piano diploma, 1949) in Helsinki. In addition to appearances as a pianist, he was active as a music critic. He also was a teacher (1950–59) and a prof. (1959–63) of composition at the Sibelius Academy. He served as chairman of the Assn. of Finnish Composers (1965–71), the Nordic Composers Council (1968–71), and of TEOSTO, the Finnish copyright bureau (1968–88). In 1963 he became a member of the Academy of Finland, in 1968 he was awarded the Nordic Council Music Prize, and in 1973 he received the Sibelius Prize of the Wihuri Foundation. After composing in a highly personal dodecaphonic style, Kokkonen developed a compositional idiom marked by an intensive motivic technique and economy of expression tending toward the ascetic in his later works. Among his works is the opera *Viimeiset Kiusaukset* (The Last Temptations; 1973–75; Helsinki, Sept. 2, 1975).

Kollo (real name, **Kollodziejski**), **René,** esteemed German tenor and Intendant, grandson of **(Elimar) Walter Kollo (Kollodziejski)**; b. Berlin, Nov. 20, 1937. He studied with Elsa Varena in Berlin. He made his operatic debut as Oedipus Rex in Braunschweig (1965). He sang in Düsseldorf (1967–71), then with the Vienna State Opera. In 1969 he first appeared at Bayreuth as the Steersman; sang in the centenary *Ring* performances there (1976); he made his Covent Garden debut in London that same year as Siegmund. He made his Metropolitan Opera debut in New York as Lohengrin on Nov. 4, 1976. As a guest artist, he sang in Berlin, Munich, Hamburg, Milan, Salzburg, and other music centers. Among his other roles were Walther von Stolzing, Parsifal, Tamino, and Lensky. From 1996 he was Intendant of the Berlin Metropol-Theater.

BIBL.: I. Fábián, *I. Fábián im Gesprach mit R. K.* (Zürich, 1982).

Kollo (real name, **Kollodziejski**), **(Elimar) Walter,** noted German composer, grandfather of **René Kollo;** b. Neidenburg, Jan. 28, 1878; d. Berlin, Sept. 30, 1940. He studied at the Sondershausen Cons. He began his career writing songs and cabaret music, and also was active as a theater conductor. After working in Königsberg and Stettin, he settled in Berlin and composed several theater pieces before attaining notable success with his musical comedy, *Filmzauber* (Oct. 19, 1912). It soon was performed internationally with great success. Then followed another outstanding score, *Wie einst im Mai!* (Oct. 4, 1913; in collaboration with W. Bredschneider). After composing *Der Juxbaron* (Hamburg, Nov. 14, 1913), Kollo produced a series of remarkably successful Berlin scores, including *Extrablätter* (Oct. 24, 1914; in collaboration with Bredschneider), *Immer feste druff!* or *Gloria Viktoria* (Oct. 1, 1914), *Wenn zwei Hochzeit machen* (Oct. 23, 1915; in collaboration with Bredschneider), *Auf Flügeln des Gesanges* (Sept. 9, 1916; in collaboration with Bredschneider), *Der selige Balduin* (March 31, 1916), *Die tolle Komtess* (Feb. 21, 1917), *Die Gulaschkanone* (Feb. 23, 1917), *Drei alte Schachteln* (Nov. 6, 1917), *Blitzblaues Blut* (Feb. 9, 1918), and *Sterne, die wieder leuchtet* (Nov. 6, 1918). Following the success of *Fräulein Puck* (Munich, June 25, 1919), Kollo resumed composing for the Berlin theaters, producing such successful scores as *Marietta* (Dec. 22, 1923) and *Drei arme kleine Mädels* (April 22, 1927). During this same period, he also composed the music for several highly popular revues, among them *Drunter und Drüber* (1923), which included the hit song "Solang noch Untern Linden." While Kollo continued to compose until his death, he never succeeded in attaining the success of his earlier years.

Kolodin, Irving, prominent American music critic and writer on music; b. N.Y., Feb. 22, 1908; d. there, April 29, 1988. He studied at the Inst. of Musical Art in New York (1930–31). He was music critic for the *N.Y. Sun* (1932–50) and the *Saturday Review* (1947–82); he served as program annotator for the N.Y. Phil. (1953–58) and also taught at N.Y.'s Juilliard School (from 1968).

WRITINGS (all publ. in N.Y. unless otherwise given): *The Metropolitan Opera . . .* (1936; 4th ed., rev., 1966); with Benny Goodman, *The Kingdom of Swing* (1939); ed. *The Critical Composer* (1940); *A Guide to Recorded Music* (Garden City, N.Y., 1941; 2d ed., rev., 1946 as *New Guide to Recorded Music*; 3d ed., rev., 1950); *Mozart on Records* (1942); with C. Burke and E. Canby, *The Saturday Review Home Book of Recorded Music and Sound Reproduction* (1952; 2d ed., 1956); *Orchestral Music* (1955); *The Musical Life* (1958); ed. *The Composer as Listener: A Guide to Music* (1958); *The Continuity of Music: A History of Influence* (1969); *The Interior Beethoven: A Biography of the Music* (1975); *The Opera Omnibus: Four Centuries of Critical Give and Take* (1976); *In Quest of Music* (1980).

Komjáti, Károly, Hungarian composer; Budapest, May 8, 1896; d. there, July 3, 1953. He received training at the Budapest Academy of Music. He then devoted himself to composing light theater works mainly for Budapest. After winning enormous success with his second operetta, *Pillangó főhadnagy* (Lieutenant Butterfly; June 7, 1918), he went on to write such successful works as *A harapós férj* (The Snappy Husband; March 22, 1931; rev. version, May 25, 1949), *Fizessen nagysád* (Jan. 23, 1932), and *Éjfeli tangó* (Feb. 27, 1932). After his *Ein Liebestraum* was premiered in Vienna (Oct. 27, 1933), he resumed composing for the Budapest stage with such scores as *A szegény ördög* (The Poor Devil; Sept. 29, 1934), *Bécsi tavasz* (Nov. 15, 1935), *Antoinette* (Dec. 23, 1937), and *Csicsónénak három lánya* (Oct. 5, 1946).

Komorous, Rudolf, Czech-born Canadian composer, bassoonist, and teacher; b. Prague, Dec. 8, 1931. He studied bassoon at the Prague Cons. (1946–52) before pursuing his training with Karel Pivoňka (bassoon) and Bořkovec (composition) at the Prague Academy of Music (1952–56); later he studied electronic music in Warsaw (1959). After teaching at the Beijing Cons. (1959–61), he returned to Prague as 1st bassoonist in the orch. of the National Theater. In 1961 he was cofounder of Musica Viva Pragensis. In 1969 he emigrated to Canada and in 1974 became a naturalized Canadian citizen. He was a visiting prof. at Macalester College in St. Paul, Minn. (1969–71). In 1971 he joined the faculty of the Univ. of Victoria to teach composition and advanced theory, and also organized its electronic music studio; he then was acting chairman (1975–76) and director (from 1976) of its school of music. He was director of the School for the Contemporary Arts at Simon Fraser Univ. from 1989 to 1994, remaining on the Univ. faculty until his retirement in 1996. In his music Komorous has explored various contemporary paths and byways. In some of his scores he has made use of musical quotations by other composers. His *Sinfony No. 1, Stardust*, makes use of Hoagy Carmichael's famous song. He also composed the opera *Lady Whiterose* (1966) and the chamber opera *No no miya* (Vancouver, Sept. 30, 1988).

Komorzynski, Egon, Austrian musicologist; b. Vienna, May 7, 1878; d. there, March 16, 1963. He took courses at various univs., including those of Berlin, Leipzig, Munich, and Vienna (graduated, 1900). He was a prof. of German language studies and literature at Vienna's Handelsakademie (1904–34); he was also music critic of the *Österreichische Volkszeitung* for 40 years.

WRITINGS: *Emanuel Schikaneder: Ein Beitrag zur Geschichte des deutschen Theaters* (Berlin, 1901; 2d ed., rev., 1951); *Mozarts Kunst der Instrumentation* (Stuttgart, 1906); *Mozart: Sendung und Schicksal eines deutschen Künstlers* (Berlin, 1941; 2d ed., rev., 1955); *Der Vater der Zauberflöte: Emanuel Schikaneders Leben* (Vienna, 1948).

Kondorossy, Leslie, Hungarian-American composer; b. Pressburg, June 25, 1915. He studied at the Academy of Music in Budapest. After World War II, he settled in Cleveland; he continued his studies at Western Reserve Univ., and later studied Japanese music and theater at Tokyo's Sophia Univ.; he was active as a teacher, conductor, and composer. He was especially proficient in producing short operas.

WORKS: DRAMATIC: OPERAS: *Night in the Puszta* (Cleveland, June 28, 1953); *The Voice* (Cleveland, May 15, 1954); *The Pumpkin* (Cleveland, May 15, 1954); *The Midnight Duel*, radio opera (Cleveland, March 20, 1955); *The String Quartet*, radio opera (Cleveland, May 8, 1955); *Unexpected Visitor* (Cleveland, Oct. 21, 1956); *The 2 Imposters* (Cleveland, Oct. 21, 1956); *The Fox* (Cleveland, Jan. 28, 1961); *The Baksis* (1964); *Nathan the Wise* (1964); *The Poorest Suitor*, children's opera (Cleveland, May 24, 1967); *Shizuka's Dance*, children's opera (Cleveland, April 22, 1969); *Kalamona and the 4 Winds*, children's opera (Cleveland, Sept. 12, 1971); *Ruth and Naomi*, church opera (Cleveland, April 28, 1974). BALLETS: *Magic Dance* (1948); *The Ideal* (1950); *King Solomon* (1952). OTHER: *Sacred Fire*, oratorio (1979).

Kondracki, Michal, Russian-American composer; b. Poltava, Oct. 5, 1902. He studied with Statkowski, Melcer, and Szymanowski at the Warsaw Cons. (graduated, 1926), then with Dukas and Boulanger at the Paris École Normale de Musique (until 1931). He was a music critic in Warsaw (1933–39); with the outbreak of World War II (1939), he went to Brazil, then settled in the United States in 1943. Among his works are the opera *Popiliny* (Warsaw, May 4, 1934; not extant) and the ballet *Metropolis* (1929; not extant).

Kondrashin, Kirill (Petrovich), noted Russian conductor; b. Moscow, March 6, 1914; d. Amsterdam, March 7, 1981. He studied piano and theory at the Musical Technicum in Moscow, then took a course in conducting with Khaikin at the Moscow Cons. (1932–36). While still a student, he conducted light opera (1934–37); he then conducted at the Maly Opera Theater in Leningrad (1937–41). In 1943 he received appointment to the staff of the Bolshoi Theater in Moscow, where he conducted a wide repertoire emphasizing Russian operas (until 1956). He received Stalin prizes in 1948 and 1949. In 1969 he was named People's Artist of the USSR. Kondrashin was the first Soviet conductor to appear in the United States (1958), and held numerous subsequent engagements in America, the last being a concert he conducted at the Hollywood Bowl in Feb. 1981. In 1960 he was appointed chief conductor of the Moscow Phil., with which he performed numerous new Soviet works, including Shostakovich's controversial 13th Sym. He also taught at the Moscow Cons. (1950–53; 1972–75). After 1975 he increased his guest engagements outside Russia, and in 1978 decided to emigrate; in 1979 he assumed the post of permanent conductor of the Concertgebouw Orch. in Amsterdam. His conducting style was marked by an effective blend of lyrical melodiousness and dramatic romanticism, without deviating from the prevalent Russian traditions. He publ. a book on the art of conducting (Leningrad, 1970).

Konetzni, Anny, esteemed Austrian soprano, sister of **Hilde Konetzni**; b. Ungarisch-Weisskirchen, Feb. 12, 1902; d. Vienna, Sept. 6, 1968. She studied with Erik Schmedes at the Vienna Cons. and later in Berlin with Jacques Stückgold. She made her operatic debut as a contralto at the Vienna Volksoper in 1925; she soon turned to soprano roles. She sang in Augsburg, Elberfeld, and Chemnitz; she sang with the Berlin State Opera (1931–34) and also appeared with the Vienna State Opera, La Scala in Milan, the Paris Opéra, and London's Covent Garden. She made her Metropolitan Opera debut in New York as Brünnhilde in *Die Walküre* on Dec. 26, 1934; she remained on its roster until the close of the season. After her retirement in 1955, she taught voice in Vienna. She was particularly notable in Wagner and Strauss roles.

Konetzni, Hilde, famous Austrian soprano, sister of **Anny Konetzni**; b. Vienna, March 21, 1905; d. there, April 20, 1980. She studied at the Vienna Cons., and later in Prague with Prochaska-Neumann. She made her operatic debut as Sieglinde in *Die Walküre* in Chemnitz in 1929, then sang at the German Theater in Prague (1932–36). In 1936 she became a member of the Vienna State Opera; she also appeared at Salzburg, La Scala in Milan, Covent Garden in London, South America, and the United States. In 1954 she joined the faculty of the Vienna Academy of Music. She was an outstanding interpreter of Wagner and Strauss.

König, Klaus, German tenor; b. Beuthen, May 26, 1934. He was a student in Dresden of Johannes Kemter. In 1970 he joined the Cottbus City Theater, and in 1973 became a member of the Dessau Landestheater. After singing with the Leipzig City Theater (1978–82), he was a member of the Dresden State Opera (from 1982). In 1984 he made debuts at Milan's La Scala and London's Covent Garden as Tannhäuser, one of his most striking roles. In 1985 he appeared as Tristan at the Théâtre Royal de la Monnaie in Brussels and as Weber's Max at the first performance of the restored Semper Opera House in Dresden. In 1988 he made his U.S. debut as Tannhäuser with the Houston Grand Opera. He also sang opera in Paris, Strasbourg, Madrid, Barcelona, Cologne, Munich, Vienna, and elsewhere in Europe. Among his other roles are Parsifal, Walther von Stolzing, Lohengrin, Don Alvaro, Florestan, Don José, Radames, and Don Carlos. He also appeared throughout Europe as a concert and oratorio artist.

Koning, David, Dutch pianist, choral conductor, and composer; b. Rotterdam, March 19, 1820; d. Amsterdam, Oct. 6, 1876. He studied with Aloys Schmitt in Frankfurt am Main. From 1840 he was conductor of the choral society Felix Meritis in Amsterdam. Although he was active mainly as a piano teacher, he also composed; among his works is a comic opera, *The Fishermaiden*.

Konjovič, Petar, Serbian composer; b. Sombor, May 6, 1882; d. Belgrade, Oct. 1, 1970. He studied at the Prague Cons. with Novák and Stecker. He was director of the Zagreb Opera (1921–26), the national theaters in Osijek, Split, and Novi Sad (1927–33), and again at the Zagreb Opera (1933–39); he then was prof. at the Belgrade Academy of Music (1939–50), where he also served twice as rector. He composed the operas *Vilin Veo* or *Ženidba Miloševa* (The Wedding of Milos; Zagreb, April 25, 1917), *Knez od Zete* (The Duke of Zeta; Belgrade, May 25, 1929), *Koštana* (Zagreb, April 16, 1931), *Sel jaci* (The Peasants; Belgrade, March 3, 1952), and *Otadžbina* (Homeland; 1960).

Kono, Kristo, Albanian composer; b. Korçë, July 17, 1907; d. Tirana, Jan. 22, 1991. After training at the Milan Cons., he returned to Albania and became a prominent figure in the development of a national music. He eventually championed the cause of socialist realism. Kono composed the first Albanian operetta *Agimi* (The Dawn; Korçë, Nov. 22, 1954). Among his other works was the opera *Lulja e kujtimit* (The Flowers of Remembrance; Tirana, Nov. 5, 1961).

Konoye, Hidemarō, Japanese conductor and composer; b. Tokyo, Nov. 18, 1898; d. there, June 2, 1973. A member of an aristocratic Japanese family, he received his education in Japan and in Europe; he attended classes in composition of d'Indy at the Schola Cantorum in Paris; he then took courses with Franz Schreker and Georg Schumann at the Berlin Cons. He made his European debut as a conductor with the Berlin Phil. on Jan. 18, 1924. Returning to Japan, he was principal conductor of the New Sym. Orch. in Tokyo (1926–34), specializing in new works of Japanese, European, and American composers. He conducted in the United States in 1937 and 1957. He was the composer of several orch. pieces based on Japanese subjects; he also orchestrated early Japanese court music for the modern Western orch. He arranged the music of *Madama Butterfly* for the films (inserting many Japanese folk melodies).

Kont, Paul, Austrian composer and teacher; b. Vienna, Aug. 19, 1920. He studied violin with Vittorio Borri and piano with Hans Nast at the Vienna Cons. (1939–40), then took a course in conducting with Josef Krips and Swarowsky (diploma, 1947) and in composition with Josef Lechthaler (diploma, 1948) at the Vienna Academy of Music; he also studied analysis with Josef Polnauer. After attending Fortner's class in Darmstadt (1951), he completed his training with Messiaen, Milhaud, and Honegger in Paris (1952). In 1969 he joined the faculty of the Vienna Academy of Music, where he was a prof. of composition (1980–86). His honors included the Austrian State Prize (1964), the prize of the City of Vienna (1975), the Gold Medal of the City of Vienna (1986), and the Great Honorary Citation of the Austrian Republic (1987).

He adopted a serial method applying the statistical principles of valid recurrences of all musical parameters, including pitch, rhythm, and dynamics. He publ. *Antianorganikum* (Vienna, 1967).

WORKS: DRAMATIC: OPERAS: *Indische Legende* (1950); *Peter und Susanne* (Vienna, June 26, 1959); *Inzwischen* (1953–66; Vienna, Jan. 5, 1967); *Lysistrate* (1957–60); *Plutos* (1975–76; Klagenfurt, Feb. 7, 1977); *Die Paare* (1985–86). BALLETS: *Italia passata* (1967); *Komodie der Unart* (Vienna, Dec. 12, 1978); *Il ballo del mondo* (1980–82); *Arkadien* (1984); *K* (1984; Klagenfurt, Feb. 2, 1985); *Und der Engel sprach . . .* (1991; Vienna, July 9, 1992); *Daphnis und Chloe* (1993; Dresden, Dec. 11, 1994). OTHER: *Traumleben*, musical fairy tale (1958; Salzburg, Dec. 22, 1963); *Celestina*, musical play (1966); other works.

Kontski, Antoine de, famous Polish pianist; b. Krakow, Oct. 27, 1817; d. Ivanichi, near Okulova, Russia, Dec. 7, 1899. He studied with John Field in Moscow (1830), then toured widely; he also taught in Paris (1851–53), Berlin (1853–54), St. Petersburg (1854–67), and subsequently in London. He toured the United States (1883, 1885) and made a world tour when he was nearly 80 (1896–98). He composed 2 piano concertos and various virtuoso and salon pieces for piano; his picturesque *Réveil du lion* was enormously successful for many years, an epitome of Romantic exuberance to the point of being ludicrous. He also composed the light operas *Les Deux Distraits* (London, 1872) and *Le Sultan de Zanzibar* (N.Y., May 8, 1886). His brothers were the Polish violinist and pedagogue Apollinaire de Kontski (1825–1879) and the Polish pianist and teacher Charles de Kontski (1815–1867).

Konwitschny, Franz, esteemed German conductor; b. Fulnek, northern Moravia, Aug. 14, 1901; d. Belgrade, July 28, 1962. He studied violin at the German Musikverein School in Brünn and at the Leipzig Cons. (1923–25); while a student, he played viola and violin in the theater orch. and the Gewandhaus Orch. in Leipzig, subsequently becoming a violist in the Fitzner Quartet in Vienna (1925), and also a teacher at the Volkskonservatorium there. He became répétiteur at the Stuttgart Opera in 1927, rising to chief conductor in 1930; after serving as Generalmusikdirektor in Freiburg im Breisgau (1933–38), he assumed that position with the Frankfurt am Main Opera and Museumgesellschaft concerts in 1938, and then with the Hannover Opera in 1945. He was appointed chief conductor of the Gewandhaus Orch. in 1949; he was also Generalmusikdirektor of the Dresden State Opera (1953–55) and the (East) Berlin State Opera (1955–62). Although he held posts under both the Nazi and communist regimes, he successfully avoided political encounters. He died while on tour and was given a state funeral by the German Democratic Republic; his request for a Requiem Mass was honored, much to the chagrin of the authorities.

BIBL.: H. Sanders, ed., *Vermächtnis und Verpflichtung: Festschrift für F. K.* (Leipzig, 1961).

Konya, Sándor, Hungarian tenor; b. Sarkad, Sept. 23, 1923. He was educated at the Budapest Academy of Music; also studied in Detmold, Rome, and Milan. He made his first professional appearance as Turiddu in Bielefeld in 1951, singing there until 1954; after appearing in Darmstadt (1954–55), he joined the Berlin Städtische Oper in 1955; in 1958 he sang for the first time at the Bayreuth Festival as Lohengrin; he also sang at Milan's La Scala (1960) and the San Francisco Opera (1960–65). On Oct. 28, 1961, he made his Metropolitan Opera debut in New York as Lohengrin; he sang there regularly until 1973. He first appeared at London's Covent Garden in the same role (1963). His most notable roles included Walther von Stolzing, Parsifal, Max, and Don Carlos.

Kopelent, Marek, Czech composer; b. Prague, April 28, 1932. He was a student of Řídký at the Prague Academy of Music (1951–55). From 1956 to 1971 he worked as a music ed. for Supraphon, and from 1965 to 1973 he served as artistic director of the Musica viva Pragensis ensemble. In 1969–70 he was active in Berlin on a Deutscher Akademischer Austauschdienst scholarship. In 1991 he became a prof. of composition at the Prague Academy of Music. In his works, Kopelent has made use of the resources of the multimedia avant-garde.

WORKS: DRAMATIC: *Bludný hlas* (The Wandering Voice) for Actress, Chamber Ensemble, and Film and Light Projection ad libitum (1969–70); *Musica*, comic opera for Soprano, 2 Actors, Flute, Oboe, and Harpsichord (1979); *Lament of Women*, melodrama monologue for Actress, 7 Brass, 4 Women's Voices, and Children's Chorus (1980).

Koppel, Herman D(avid), Danish pianist, teacher, and composer of Polish parentage, father of **Thomas Herman Koppel**; b. Copenhagen, Oct. 1, 1908; d. July 14, 1998. He was a student of Simonson (piano), Bangert (theory), and Hansen (orchestration) at the Copenhagen Cons. (1926–29). He made his debut in 1930 as a concert pianist; toured widely in Europe. He taught at the Royal Inst. of Music for the Blind in Copenhagen (1940–43; 1945–49); he lived in Örebro, Sweden (1943–45), to avoid the Nazi occupation. In 1949 he joined the faculty of the Royal Danish Cons. of Music in Copenhagen; he was a prof. there (from 1955). As a pianist, he performed the music of Nielsen and other 20th-century Danish composers. His early compositions were influenced by Nielsen, Stravinsky, and Bartók, but he eventually developed an individualistic style, marked by rhythmic intensity and melodic expressivity. Among his works is the opera *Macbeth*, (1968; Copenhagen, 1970); also incidental music; music to 29 films.

Koppel, Thomas Herman, Danish composer, son of **Herman D(avid) Koppel**; b. Örebro, Sweden, April 27, 1944. He studied piano and theory with his father at the Royal Danish Cons. of Music in Copenhagen (1963–67). In 1968 he organized in Copenhagen the pop group Savage Rose, and joined the Danish avant-garde in other venturesome activities. He composed the operas *Historien om en moder* (The Story of a Mother), after H. C. Andersen (Copenhagen, Oct. 17, 1965), and *Bérénice* (1968); also the ballet *Triumph of Death* (1971), and *The Emperor's New Clothes*, music for ice ballet (1985–86).

Kopytman, Mark, Russian-born Israeli composer, b. Kamenets-Podolski, Dec. 6, 1929. He began his musical training at the music college (graduated, 1950) and pursued medical studies in Chernovtsy (M.D., 1952); he then studied with Simovitz at the Lwów Academy of Music (M.A., 1955) and with S. Bogatyrev at the Moscow Cons. (Ph.D., 1958). He taught in various Russian music institutes (1955–72), then emigrated to Israel, where he joined the faculty of the Rubin Academy of Music in Jerusalem in 1974, serving as its deputy director (from 1985). He also was a guest prof. at the Hebrew Univ. in Jerusalem (from 1979). In 1985 he was a visiting prof. at the Univ. of Pa. and composer-in-residence at the Canberra School of Music. In 1989 he again was at the Univ. of Pa. His works include the operas *Casa mare* (1966) and *Chamber Scenes from the Life of Susskind von Trinberg* (1983).

Korchmarev, Klimenti (Arkadievich), Russian composer; b. Verkhnedneprovsk, July 3, 1899; d. Moscow, April 7, 1958. He studied at the Odessa Cons. with Maliszewski and Biber (graduated with the gold medal, 1919), then went to Moscow (1923), where he became one of the first Soviet composers to embrace revolutionary themes; he wrote *Leviy marsh* (March on the Left; to words by Mayakovsky) for Chorus and Piano (1923); he then composed the operas *Ivan-Soldat* (Ivan the Soldier; 1925–27; Moscow, April 3, 1927) and *Desyat dney, kotoriye potryasili mir* (10 Days That Shook the World; 1929–31) and the ballet *Krepostnaya balerina* (The Serf Ballerina; Leningrad, Dec. 11, 1927). His other works in this vein included the choral syms. *Oktyabr* (October; 1931) and *Narodi sovetskoy strani* (The Peoples of the Soviet Land; 1935). From 1939 to 1947 he was in Turkmenistan, where he collected native songs; also composed the first native ballet, *Vesyoliy obmanschchik* (The Merry Deceiver). In 1950 he wrote a cantata, *Svobodniy Kitay* (Free China), for which he received a Stalin Prize.

Koréh, Endre, Hungarian bass; b. Sepsiszentgyörgy, April 13, 1906; d. Vienna, Sept. 20, 1960. He was a student of Arpad Palotay in Budapest. In 1930 he made his operatic debut at the Budapest Opera as Sparafucile, and then sang there regularly. In 1948 he became a member of the Vienna State Opera. He also appeared in Salzburg, Glyndebourne, Florence, Paris, Rome, and other European opera centers. On Jan. 22, 1953, he made his Metropolitan Opera debut in New York as Baron Ochs, remaining on its roster until the close of the season. He was best known for his buffo roles, excelling especially in operas by Mozart, Verdi, and Wagner. He also created the role of Caliban in Frank Martin's opera *Der Sturm*, after Shakespeare's *The Tempest* (Vienna, June 17, 1956).

Koreshchenko, Arseni, Russian composer; b. Moscow, Dec. 18, 1870; d. Kharkov, Jan. 6, 1921. He studied piano with Taneyev and composition with Arensky at the Moscow Cons.; later he was an instructor in music theory there. From 1906 to 1919 he taught composition at the Moscow Phil. Inst., then went to Kharkov, where he taught piano and composition at the Academy until his death. He wrote music imitative of Tchaikovsky and Arensky; his songs have a certain obsolete charm. He composed the operas *Belshazzar's Feast* (Moscow, 1892), *The Angel of Death* (1893), and *The House of Ice* (Moscow, Nov. 19, 1900) and the ballet *The Magic Mirror* (Moscow, 1902).

Korn, Peter Jona, German composer, conductor, and pedagogue; b. Berlin, March 30, 1922. He studied at the Berlin Hochschule für Musik (1932–33), with Rubbra in London (1934–36), Wolpe at the Jerusalem Cons. (1936–38), Schoenberg at the Univ. of Calif. at Los Angeles (1941–42), and Eisler and Toch at the Univ. of Southern Calif. in Los Angeles (1946–47); he also studied film composition with Dahl and Rozsa. He was founder-conductor of the New Orch. of Los Angeles (1948–56); he then taught at the Univ. of Calif. at Los Angeles (1964–65). Returning to Germany, he was director of Munich's Richard Strauss Konservatorium from 1967 to 1987. He publ. a book of essays, *Musikalische Unwelt Verschmutzung* (Wiesbaden, 1975). His compositional style is a pragmatic Romanticism marked by polycentric tonality in the framework of strong rhythmic counterpoint. Among his many works is the opera *Heidi in Frankfurt (Das fremde Haus)*, after Johanna Spyri (1961–63; Saarbrücken, Nov. 28, 1978).

BIBL.: N. Düchtel et al., *P. J. K.* (Tutzing, 1989).

Korndorf, Nikolai, Russian composer, conductor, and teacher; b. Moscow, Jan. 23, 1947. He studied composition (M.M., 1970; D.M.A., 1973) and conducting (M.M., 1979) at the Moscow Cons., where he served on the faculty from 1972 until emigrating to Canada in 1991. He composed *MR (Marina and Rainer)*, chamber opera (1989; Munich, May 20, 1994), and . . . *si muove!*, music theater (1993).

Korngold, Erich Wolfgang, remarkable Austrian-born American composer, son of **Julius Korngold**; b. Brünn, May 29, 1897; d. Los Angeles, Nov. 29, 1957. He received his earliest musical education from his father, then studied with Fuchs, Zemlinsky, and Grädener in Vienna. His progress was astounding; at the age of 12, he composed a Piano Trio, which was soon publ., revealing a competent technique and an ability to write in a style strongly influenced by Richard Strauss. About the same time, he wrote (in piano score) a pantomime, *Der Schneemann*; it was orchestrated by Zemlinsky and performed at the Vienna Court Opera (Oct. 4, 1910), creating a sensation. In 1911 Nikisch conducted Korngold's *Schauspiel-Ouvertüre* with the Leipzig Gewandhaus Orch.; that same year, the youthful composer gave a concert of his works in Berlin, appearing also as a pianist; his *Sinfonietta* was conducted by Weingartner and the Vienna Phil. in 1913. Korngold was not quite 19 when his 2 short operas, *Der Ring des Polykrates* and *Violanta*, were produced in Munich. His first lasting success came with the simultaneous premiere in Hamburg and Cologne of his opera *Die tote Stadt* (Dec. 4, 1920). In 1929 he began a fruitful collaboration with the director Max Reinhardt; in 1934 he went to Hollywood to arrange Mendelssohn's music for Reinhardt's film version of *A Midsummer Night's Dream*. He taught at the Vienna Academy of Music (1930–34) before settling in Hollywood, where he distinguished himself as a composer of film scores. He became a naturalized American citizen in 1943. Korngold's music represents the last breath of the Romantic spirit of Vienna; it is marvelously consistent with the melodic, rhythmic, and harmonic style of the judicious modernity of the nascent 20th century. Korngold never altered his established idiom of composition, and was never tempted to borrow modernistic devices, except for some transitory passages in major seconds or an occasional whole-tone scale.

WORKS: DRAMATIC: OPERAS: *Der Ring des Polykrates* and *Violanta* (Munich, March 28, 1916); *Die tote Stadt* (simultaneous premiere, Hamburg and Cologne, Dec. 4, 1920); *Das Wunder der Heliane* (Hamburg, Oct. 7, 1927); *Die Kathrin* (Stockholm, Oct. 7, 1939). PANTOMIME: *Der Schneemann* (Vienna, Oct. 4, 1910). FILM SCORES: *A Midsummer Night's Dream* (1934); *Captain Blood* (1935); *Another Dawn* (1936); *Anthony Adverse* (1936); *Give us this Night* (1936); *The Green Pastures* (1936); *Rose of the Ranch* (1936); *The Prince and the Pauper* (1937); *The Adventures of Robin Hood* (1938); *Juarez* (1939); *The Private Lives of Elizabeth and Essex* (1939); *The Sea Hawk* (1940); *King's Row* (1941); *The Sea Wolf* (1941); *The Constant Nymph* (1942); *Devotion* (1943); *Between Two Worlds* (1944); *Of Human Bondage* (1945); *Deception* (1946); *Escape me Never* (1946); *Magic Fire* (1954).

BIBL.: R. Hoffmann, *E. W. K.* (Vienna, 1923); L. Korngold, *E. W. K.: Ein Lebensbild* (Vienna, 1967); B. Carroll, *E. W. K. 1897–1957: His Life and Works* (Paisley, 1984); J. Korngold, *Die K.s in Wien: Der Musikkritiker und das Wunderkind: Aufzeichnungen* (Zürich, 1991); J. Duchen, *E. W. K.* (London, 1996); B. Carroll, *The Last Prodigy: A Biography of E. W. K.* (Portland, Oregon, 1997).

Korngold, Julius, noted Austrian music critic, father of **Erich Wolfgang Korngold**; b. Brünn, Dec. 24, 1860; d. Los Angeles, Sept. 25, 1945. He was a law student; at the same time, he studied music with Franz Krenn at the Vienna Cons. In 1902 he became music critic of the influential *Neue Freie Presse*, which position he retained until 1934. He was much in the limelight when his son began his spectacular career at the age of 13 as a child composer, and an unfounded suspicion was voiced that Korngold was using his position to further his son's career. He publ. a book on contemporary German opera, *Deutsches Opernschaffen der Gegenwart* (1922). In 1938 he joined his son in the United States.

BIBL.: F. Endler, *J. K. und die "Neu Freie Presse"* (diss., Univ. of Vienna, 1981); J. Korngold, *Die K.s in Wien: Der Musikkritiker und das Wunderkind: Aufzeichnungen* (Zürich, 1991).

Kórodi, Andras, Hungarian conductor; b. Budapest, May 24, 1922; d. Treviso, Sept. 17, 1986. He studied with Ferencsik (conducting) and Lajtha (composition) at the Budapest Academy of Music, where he later taught conducting (1957–82). He was a conductor (1946–63) and principal conductor (1963–86) of the Hungarian State Opera in Budapest, where he led the premieres of many contemporary scores; was also conductor of the Budapest Phil. (1967–86).

Kortekangas, Olli, Finnish composer and teacher; b. Turku, May 16, 1955. He was a student of theory and composition of Rautavaara and Hämeenniemi at the Sibelius Academy in Helsinki (1974–81). In 1977 he was a founding member of the contemporary music society Korvat Auki (Ears Open). Following further training with Schnebel in Berlin (1981–82), he returned to Helsinki and taught at the National Theater Academy (1983–86) and then at the Sibelius Academy. As a composer, Kortekangas has followed an independent course in which he confronts and incorporates various styles and techniques in a stimulating fashion. Among his works are the operas *Short Story* (1979–80; Helsinki, Oct. 15, 1980) and *Grand Hotel* (1984–85; Helsinki, Sept. 12, 1987); also *Memoria*, radiophonic piece (1989); incidental music.

Kósa, György, Hungarian pianist, teacher, and composer; b. Budapest, April 24, 1897; d. there, Aug. 16, 1984. He exhibited a precocious talent for music, and when he was 10 years old studied piano privately with Bartók and then later with him at the Royal

Academy of Music in Budapest (1908–15); he also studied composition with Herzfeld and Kodály (1908–12) and piano with Dohnányi (1915–16) there. He was corépétiteur at the Royal Opera House in Budapest (1916–17); he then toured Europe and North Africa as a pianist (1917–20) and subsequently was a theater conductor in Tripoli (1920–21). He then returned to Budapest as an accompanist (1921); from 1927 to 1960 he was prof. of piano at the Budapest Academy of Music, with the exception of a period during World War II when he was compelled to work as a manual laborer in a war camp. He was actively engaged in the promotion of modern Hungarian music; played both traditional and contemporary scores. He was awarded the Erkel Prize (1955), and was made a Merited Artist (1963) and an Honored Artist (1972) of his homeland. As a composer, he was initially influenced by Bartók, but he later developed an individualistic style of expressionism.

WORKS: DRAMATIC: OPERAS: *A király palástja* (The King's Robe; 1926); *Az két lovagok* (2 Knights), comic opera (1934; Budapest, 1937); *Cenodoxus*, mystery opera (1942); *Anselmus diák* (Student Anselmus; 1945); *A méhek* (The Bees; 1946); *Tartuffe*, comic opera (1951); *Pázmán lovag* (Knight Pázmán), comic opera (1962–63); *Kocsonya Mihály házassága* (The Marriage of Mihály Kocsonya), comic opera (1971); *Kiálts város* (City, Shout!; 1980–81). BALLETS: *Fehér Pierrot* (White Pierrot; 1916; Budapest, 1920); *Phaedra* (1918); *Dávid király* (King David; 1936); *Ének az örök bánatról* (Song about the Everlasting Sorrow; 1955). PANTOMIMES: *Mese a királykisasszonyról* (A Tale of a Princess; 1919); *Laterna Magica* (1922; Budapest, Feb. 23, 1927); *Árva Józsi három csodája* (The 3 Miracles of József Arva; 1932; Budapest, Feb. 26, 1933).

BIBL.: M. Pándi, *K. G.* (Budapest, 1966).

Koschat, Thomas, Austrian bass and composer; b. Viktring, near Klagenfurt, Aug. 8, 1845; d. Vienna, May 19, 1914. He sang in church choirs. He publ. his first vocal quartets in the Carinthian dialect in 1871; they became so successful that he publ. some 100 more. In 1875 he organized the famous Kärnthner Quintett with 4 other singers; their performances were exceedingly popular. His "Liederspiel" *Am Wörthersee* (Vienna, March 22, 1880), containing many of his favorite vocal numbers, had great vogue; he also produced a 4-act "Volksstück mit Gesang," *Die Rosenthaler Nachtigall*, and the Singspiel *Der Bürgermeister von St. Anna* (Vienna, May 1, 1884; given in Italian as *Un colpo di fuoco*).

BIBL.: K. Krobath, *T. K., der Sänger Kärnthners* (Leipzig, 1912).

Koshetz, Nina (Pavlovna), Russian-American soprano; b. Kiev, Dec. 30, 1894; d. Santa Ana, Calif., May 14, 1965. Her father, Paul Koshetz, was a tenor; she began piano study when she was 4 and gave her first recital at 9; she then enrolled at the Moscow Cons. at 11, studying piano with Igumnov and Safonov and voice with Enzo Masetti; she later studied with Félia Litvinne. She toured Russia with Rachmaninoff, of whose songs she was a congenial interpreter; she also toured with Koussevitzky and his orch.; she made her operatic debut as Donna Anna at the Imperial Opera in St. Petersburg (1913); she toured the United States with the Ukrainian National Chorus, under the conductorship of her brother (1920); then settled there. She sang the role of Fata Morgana in the first performance of Prokofiev's *The Love for 3 Oranges* (Chicago, Dec. 30, 1921); subsequently she devoted herself mainly to concert appearances and later taught voice.

Köselitz, Johann Heinrich, German writer and composer; b. Annaberg, Jan. 10, 1854; d. there, Aug. 15, 1918. He studied with Richter at the Leipzig Cons. While in Basel, he formed a close friendship with Nietzsche, from whom he also took lessons in composition; after Nietzsche's death, Köselitz became his literary executor, editing Nietzsche's letters. As a composer, he elaborated the Wagnerian system of Leitmotiv; he used the pen name of Peter Gast for his musical productions, among them the operas *Wilbraum und Siegeheer* (1879), *Scherz, List und Rache* (1881), *Die heimliche Ehe* (Danzig, 1891; publ. in 1901 as *Der Löwe von Venedig*), *König Wenzel* (not produced), and *Orpheus und Dionysos* (not produced); also a festival play, *Walpurgisnacht* (1903).

BIBL.: L. Brieger-Wasservogel, *Peter Gast* (Leipzig, 1906); F. Gotz, *Peter Gast* (Annaberg, 1934).

Košler, Zdeněk, Czech conductor; b. Prague, March 25, 1928; d. there, July 2, 1995. He studied in Prague with Grünfeldová (piano), Jeremiáš and Řídký (theory and composition), and Dědeček (conducting); then took conducting courses with Ančerl, Brock, and Doležil at the Academy of Music (1948–52). He made his conducting debut at the National Theater of Prague with *Il Barbiere di Siviglia* (1951), and conducted there until 1958; he then conducted the Olomouc (1958–62) and Ostrava (1962–66) operas. In 1956 he won 1st prize in the Besançon competition, and in 1963 1st prize in the Mitropoulos competition. He was chief conductor of the Prague Sym. Orch. (1966–67); he also served as Generalmusikdirektor of the Komische Oper in East Berlin (1966–68); then was chief conductor of the Slovak National Theater in Bratislava (1971–79). He was chief conductor of the Prague National Theater from 1980 to 1985, and again from 1989 to 1991. In 1974 he was made an Artist of Merit and in 1984 a National Artist by the Czech government.

Kosma, Joseph, Hungarian-French composer; b. Budapest, Oct. 22, 1905; d. La Roche-Guyon, near Paris, Aug. 7, 1969. He studied at the Budapest Academy of Music, then with Eisler in Berlin (1929). He settled in Paris (1933).

WORKS: DRAMATIC: COMIC OPERAS: *Les Chansons de Bilitis* (1954); *Un Amour électronique* (Paris, 1962); *La Revolté des canuts* (Lyons, 1964); *Les Hussards* (Lyons, Oct. 21, 1969). BALLETS: *Le Rendez-vous* (Paris, June 15, 1945); *Baptiste* (1946); *L'Ecuyère* (1948); *Le Pierrot de Montmartre* (1952). Also film scores to *La Grande Illusion*, *Les Enfants du paradis*, etc. OTHER: *Les Ponts de Paris*, oratorio (1947).

BIBL.: M. Fleuret, ed., *J. K., 1905–1969: Un homme, un musicien* (Paris, 1969).

Kostič, Dušan, Croatian composer; b. Zagreb, Jan. 23, 1925. He studied at the Belgrade Academy of Music (1947–55) and later took a course in conducting with Scherchen in Bayreuth (1955). He was music ed. for Radio Belgrade (1957–59); he then taught at his alma mater (from 1964). He incorporated neoclassical, impressionistic, and serial techniques in his music; he also wrote occasional pieces on national folk themes. His works include the opera buffa *Majstori su prvi ljudi* (Belgrade, April 23, 1962).

Köth, Erika, German soprano; b. Darmstadt, Sept. 15, 1925; d. Speyer, Feb. 20, 1989. She was a student in Darmstadt of Elsa Bank. In 1947 she won 1st prize in a Hessian Radio competition, and then made her debut as Adele in a Darmstadt radio broadcast. In 1948 she made her stage debut as Philine in *Mignon* in Kaiserslautern. After singing in Karlsruhe (1950–53), she appeared with the Bavarian State Opera in Munich (from 1953), the Vienna State Opera (from 1953), and in Berlin (from 1961); she also made appearances at the Salzburg (1955–64) and Bayreuth (1965–68) festivals. In 1956 she was named a Bavarian and in 1970 a Berlin Kammersängerin. She taught at the Cologne Hochschule für Musik (from 1973), and then at the Heidelberg-Mannheim Hochschule für Musik (from 1980). Among her esteemed portrayals were Zerbinetta, the Queen of the Night, Susanna, Constanze, Donna Elvira, Lucia, and Sophie.

BIBL.: K. Adam, *Herzlichst! E. K.* (Darmstadt, 1969).

Kounadis, Arghyris, Greek composer; b. Constantinople, Feb. 14, 1924. He was taken to Athens in his infancy; he studied piano at home and then with S. Farandatos at the Athens Cons. (graduated, 1952) and also studied law at the Univ. of Athens. After studying composition with Papaioannou at Athens's Hellenic Cons. (graduated, 1956), he continued his studies with Fortner in Freiburg im Breisgau (1958–61). In 1963 he joined the faculty of the Freiburg im Breisgau Hochschule für Musik, becoming a prof. there in 1972.

WORKS: DRAMATIC: *Der Gummisarg* (1968); *Die verhexten Notenstander* (1971); *Der Ausbruch* (1975); *Die Bassgeige* (1979; rev. 1987); *Lysistrata*, after Aristophanes (1983); *Der Sandmann* (1986).

Koussevitzky, Serge (Alexandrovich), celebrated Russian-born American conductor; b. Vishny-Volochok, July 26, 1874; d.

Boston, June 4, 1951. His father and his 3 brothers were all amateur musicians. Koussevitzky learned to play the trumpet and took part, with his brothers, in a small wind ensemble, numbering 8 members in all; they earned their living by playing at balls and weddings and occasionally at village fairs. At the age of 14, he went to Moscow; since Jews were not allowed to live there, he became baptized. He then received a fellowship with free tuition at the Musico-Dramatic Inst. of the Moscow Phil. Soc., where he studied double bass with Rambousek; he also studied theory with Blaramberg and Kruglikov. In 1894 he joined the orch. of the Bolshoi Theater, succeeding Rambousek as principal double bass player in 1901, retaining that post until 1905. In the meantime, he became known as a soloist of the first magnitude; he made his public debut in Moscow on March 25, 1901. He garnered great attention with a double bass recital in Berlin on March 27, 1903. To supplement the meager repertoire for his instrument, he arranged various works; also wrote several pieces. With some aid from Glière, he wrote a Double Bass Concerto, which he performed for the first time in Moscow on Feb. 25, 1905. On Sept. 8, 1905, he married Natalie Ushkov, daughter of a wealthy tea merchant family. He soon resigned from the orch. of the Bolshoi Theater; in an open letter to the Russian publication Musical Gazette he explained the reason for his resignation as the economic and artistic difficulties in the orch. He then went to Germany, where he continued to give double-bass recitals; he played the 1st Cello Concerto by Saint-Saëns on the double bass. In 1907 he conducted a student orch. at the Berlin Hochschule für Musik; his first public appearance as a conductor took place on Jan. 23, 1908, with the Berlin Phil. In 1909 he established a publishing house, Editions Russes de Musique; in 1915 he purchased the catalog of the Gutheil Co.; among composers with whom he signed contracts were Scriabin, Stravinsky, Prokofiev, Medtner, and Rachmaninoff; the association with Scriabin was particularly fruitful, and in subsequent years Koussevitzky became the greatest champion of Scriabin's music. In 1909 he organized his own sym. orch. in Moscow, featuring works by Russian composers, but also including classical masterpieces; played many Russian works for the first time, among them Scriabin's *Prometheus*. In the summer of 1910 he took his orch. to the towns along the Volga River in a specially chartered steamboat. He repeated the Volga tour in 1912 and 1914. The outbreak of World War I in 1914 made it necessary to curtail his activities; however, he continued to give his concerts in Moscow; in 1915 he presented a memorial Scriabin program. After the Revolution of 1917 he was offered the directorship of the State Sym. Orch. (former Court Orch.) in Petrograd; he conducted it until 1920; also presented concerts in Moscow, despite the hardships of the revolutionary times. In 1920 he left Russia; went first to Berlin, then to Rome, and finally to Paris, where he organized the Concerts Koussevitzky with a specially assembled orch.; he presented many new scores by French and Russian composers, among them Ravel's orchestration of Mussorgsky's *Pictures at an Exhibition*, Honegger's *Pacific 231*, and several works by Prokofiev and Stravinsky. In 1924 Koussevitzky was appointed the conductor of the Boston Sym. Orch., a position he held with great eminence until 1949. Just as in Russia he championed Russian composers, in France the French, so in the United States he encouraged American composers to write works for him. Symphonic compositions by Copland, Harris, Piston, Barber, Hanson, Schuman, and others were performed by Koussevitzky for the first time. For the 50th anniversary of the Boston Sym. Orch. (1931), he commissioned works from Stravinsky (Symphony of Psalms), Hindemith, Honegger, Prokofiev, Roussel, Ravel (piano concerto), Copland, Gershwin, and others. A highly important development in Koussevitzky's American career was the establishment of the Berkshire Music Center at Tanglewood, Mass. This was an outgrowth of the Berkshire Sym. Festival, organized in 1934 by Henry Hadley; Koussevitzky and the Boston Sym. Orch. presented summer concerts at the Berkshire Festival in 1935 for the first time; since then, the concerts have become an annual institution. The Berkshire Music Center was opened on July 8, 1940, with Koussevitzky as director and Copland as assistant director; among the distinguished guest instructors were Hindemith, Honegger, and Messiaen; Koussevitzky himself taught conducting; he was succeeded after his death by his former student Leonard Bernstein.

Koussevitzky held many honorary degrees: Mus.Doc. from Brown Univ. (1926), Rutgers Univ. (1937), Yale Univ. (1938), Univ. of Rochester (1940), Williams College (1943), and Boston Univ. (1945); LL.D. from Harvard Univ. (1929) and Princeton Univ. (1947). He was a member of the French Legion of Honor and held the Cross of Commander of the Finnish Order of the White Rose. He became a naturalized American citizen on April 16, 1941. His wife died in 1942; he established the Koussevitzky Foundation as a memorial to her, the funds to be used for commissioning works by composers of all nationalities. He married Olga Naoumoff (1901–78), a niece of Natalie Koussevitzky, on Aug. 15, 1947.

As a conductor, Koussevitzky possessed an extraordinary emotional power; in Russian music, and particularly in Tchaikovsky's syms., he was unexcelled; he was capable of achieving the subtlest nuances in the works of the French school; his interpretations of Debussy were notable. As a champion of modern music, he had few equals in his time; his ardor in projecting unfamiliar music before new audiences in different countries served to carry conviction among the listeners and the professional music critics. He was often criticized for the liberties he allowed himself in the treatment of classical masterpieces; undoubtedly his performances of Haydn, Mozart, Beethoven, and other giants of the Austro-German repertoire were untraditional; but they were nonetheless musicianly in the sincere artistry that animated his interpretations.

BIBL.: A. Lourie, *S. A. K. and His Epoch* (N.Y., 1931); H. Leichtentritt, *S. K., The Boston Symphony Orchestra and the New American Music* (Cambridge, Mass., 1946); M. Smith, *K.* (N.Y., 1947).

Kout, Jiří, Czech conductor; b. Novedvory, Dec. 26, 1937. He received training in organ and conducting at the Cons. and the Academy of Music in Prague. In 1964 he became a conductor at the Plzeň Opera. His protest of the Warsaw Pact invasion of his homeland in 1968 led the Czech authorities to ban him from conducting. However, in 1973, he was allowed to resume his career with an engagement at the Prague National Theater. In 1976 he emigrated to West Germany and became a conductor at the Deutsche Oper am Rhein in Düsseldorf. From 1985 to 1991 he was Generalmusikdirektor of the Saarländisches Staatstheater in Saarbrücken; he also appeared as a guest conductor of opera houses in Munich, Berlin, Vienna, Venice, Florence, Paris, Cincinnati, and Los Angeles. From 1991 he was a regular conductor at the Deutsche Oper in Berlin; that same year, he made his Metropolitan Opera debut in New York conducting *Der Rosenkavalier*. In 1993 he conducted *Jenůfa* at London's Covent Garden. In 1993 he became music director of the Leipzig Opera and in 1996 of the St. Gallen Orch. He conducted a *Ring* cycle at the Deutsche Oper in Berlin in 1997. In addition to his idiomatic interpretations of the operas of Smetana, Dvořák, and Janáček, Kout has acquired a distinguished reputation for his performances of operas by Wagner and Strauss.

Koutzen, Boris, Russian-American violinist, teacher, and composer; b. Uman, near Kiev, April 1, 1901; d. Mount Kisco, N.Y., Dec. 10, 1966. He studied violin with Leo Zetlin and composition with Glière at the Moscow Cons. (1918–22). In 1922 he went to the United States and joined the violin section of the Philadelphia Orch. (until 1927); he later played in the NBC Sym. Orch. in New York (1937–45). He was head of the violin dept. at the Philadelphia Cons. (1925–62) and a teacher at Vassar College in Poughkeepsie, N.Y. (1944–66). His music possesses an attractive Romantic flavor in an old Russian manner. He composed an opera, *You Never Know* (1962).

Koval, Marian (Viktorovich), Russian composer; b. Pristan Voznesenya, Olonets district, Aug. 17, 1907; d. Moscow, Feb. 15, 1971. Following training in Nizhny-Novgorod and Petrograd, he studied composition with Gnessin and Miaskovsky at the Moscow Cons. (1925–30). Inspired by the revolutionary ideas of a new collective society, he organized with others a group named Procoll ("Productive Collective"), dedicated to the propaganda of music in its sociological aspects; he was also a member of the Russian Assn. of Proletarian Musicians from 1929 until it was disbanded by the Soviet government in 1931 as being counterproductive. He became known mainly through his choruses and songs on socialist subjects; all of his music is derived from modalities of Russian folk songs and those of the ethnic group of the Urals, to which he belonged. He wrote the operas *Emelian Pugatchev* (Moscow, Nov. 25, 1939) and *Sevastopoltzy* (Perm, Nov. 28, 1946); also *The Wolf and 7 Little Goats*, children's opera (1939).

BIBL.: G. Polyanovsky, *M. K.* (Moscow, 1968).

Kovaříček, František, Czech composer; b. Liteniny, May 17, 1924. He studied with Hlobil at the Prague Cons. and with Řídký at the Prague Academy of Music, graduating in 1952. He was music director of the Czech Radio in Prague (1953–58). From 1966 to 1985 he taught at the Prague Cons., and from 1990 to 1991 was its director. Among his works is the opera *Ukradený mesič* (The Stolen Moon; 1966; Czech Radio, July 1, 1970).

Kovařovic, Karel, noted Czech conductor and composer; b. Prague, Dec. 9, 1862; d. there, Dec. 6, 1920. He studied clarinet, harp, and piano at the Prague Cons. (1873–79); also studied composition privately with Fibich (1878–80). He was harpist in the orch. of Prague's National Theater (1879–85); also was director of Pivoda's Vocal School (1880–1900). In 1900 he was appointed opera director of the National Theater in Prague, a position he held until his death; he also led sym. concerts in Prague. As a conductor, he demonstrated great craftsmanship and established a high standard of excellence in his operatic productions; his interpretations of Dvořák and Smetana were particularly notable; an ardent believer in the cause of Czech music, he promoted national compositions. In his own music, he also made use of national materials, but his treatment was mostly imitative of the French models; the influences of Gounod and Massenet are particularly noticeable. He publ. some of his lighter works under a series of humorously misspelled names of French composers (C. Biset, J. Héral, et al.).

WORKS: DRAMATIC: OPERAS (all 1st perf. in Prague): *Ženichové* (The Bridegrooms; May 13, 1884); *Cesta oknem* (Through the Window; Feb. 11, 1886); *Noc Šimona a Judy* (The Night of Simon and Jude; original title, *Frasquita*; Nov. 5, 1892); *Psohlavci* (The Dog-Heads; April 24, 1898); *Na starém bělidle* (At the Old Bleaching-House; Nov. 22, 1901). BALLETS: *Hashish* (June 19, 1884); *Pohádka o nalezeném štěstí* (A Tale of Found Happiness; Dec. 21, 1886); *Na zaletech* (Flirtation; Oct. 24, 1909).

BIBL.: J. Němeček, *Opera Národního divadla za Karla Kovařovice* (Prague, 1968–69).

Kowalski, Jochen, German countertenor; b. Wachow, Jan. 30, 1954. He studied with Heinz Reeh at the Berlin Hochschule für Musik and with Marianne Fischer-Kupfer. In 1982 he made his debut at the Handel Festival in Halle in Handel's *Mucio Scevola*. He made his first appearance at the Komische Oper in Berlin as Fyodor in *Boris Godunov* in 1983, and subsequently served as a member of the company. In 1987 he sang Ptolomeo in *Giulio Cesare* at the Paris Opéra and Prince Orlovsky at the Vienna State Opera. He appeared as Gluck's Orfeo with the Komische Oper during its visit to London's Covent Garden in 1989. He returned to Covent Garden to sing Prince Orlovsky in 1990 and Farnace in *Mitridate* in 1991. In 1993 he appeared as Ottone in *L'incoronazione di Poppea* at the Salzburg Festival. He was engaged as Britten's Oberon at the Metropolitan Opera in New York in 1996, and returned there as Prince Orlovsky in 1998. Kowalski also sang widely as a concert artist.

Kowalski, Július, Slovak composer; b. Ostrava, Feb. 24, 1912. He studied composition with Rudolf Karel and Alois Hába at the Prague Cons. (1929–33) and subsequently composition with Suk and conducting with Talich at the Master School there (1933–34); he then went to Vienna, where he studied conducting with Clemens Krauss (1939). After World War II, he held administrative and managerial positions in Bratislava. He wrote some microtonal pieces, e.g., Suite for Violin and Viola in the sixth-tone system (1936) and Duo for Violin and Cello in the quarter-tone system (1937), but later composed in a more or less traditional style. His works include the chamber opera *Lampionová slávnost* (The Chinese Lantern Celebration; 1961; Ostrava, 1963).

Kox, Hans, Dutch composer and teacher; b. Arnhem, May 19, 1930. He studied at the Utrecht Cons. and with Badings. After teaching at the Doetinchem Music School (1956–70), he served as a prof. of composition at the Utrecht Cons. In some of his works, he applied a scale of 31 equal intervals, invented by the Dutch physicist Adriaan Fokker. In his series of *Cyclophonies* (1964–79) he experimented with open-end forms. He composed the operas *Dorian Gray* (1972–73; Scheveningen, March 30, 1974; rev. 1976), *Lord Rochester* (1978), and *Das grüne Gesicht* (1991); also *Sjoah*, oratorio (1989).

Koyama, Kiyoshige, Japanese composer; b. Nagano, Jan. 15, 1914. He studied composition with Komei Abe. He wrote a number of works in a Japanese national style, among them *Nomen*, symphonic suite for a Noh play (Tokyo, Dec. 5, 1959), and *Sansho Dayu*, opera (Tokyo, March 29, 1972).

Koželuh (Kozeluch, Koscheluch), Johann Antonín (Jan Evangelista Antonín Tomáš), Bohemian composer, cousin of **Leopold (Jan Antonín) Koželuh (Kozeluch, Kotzeluch)**; b. Welwarn, Dec. 14, 1738; d. Prague, Feb. 3, 1814. He began music studies at school in Welwarn, then was a chorister at the Jesuit College in Breznice; he subsequently studied with J. F. N. Seger in Prague; he then went to Vienna, where he had instruction from Gluck, Gassmann, and Hasse. Upon his return to Prague he became Kapellmeister at St. Vitus's Metropolitan Cathedral (1784–1814). His cousin was one of his pupils. He composed 2 operas: *Alessandro nell'Indie* (Prague, 1769) and *Il Demofoonte* (Prague, 1771); also much sacred music, including 2 oratorios.

BIBL.: R. Fikrle, *Jan Evangelista Antonín K.: Život, dilo a osobnost svatovitsbeho kapelnika* (Prague, 1946).

Koželuh (Kozeluch, Kotzeluch), Leopold (Jan Antonín), Bohemian pianist, teacher, and composer, cousin of **Johann Antonín (Jan Evangelista Antonín Tomáš) Koželuh (Kozeluch, Koscheluch)**; b. Welwarn, June 26, 1747; d. Vienna, May 7, 1818. He began his musical studies in Welwarn, then had instruction with his cousin and with F. X. Dušek in Prague. He also studied law but turned to a career in music after the success he attained with his ballets and pantomimes. In 1778 he went to Vienna, where he established himself as a pianist, teacher, and composer; also was active as a music publisher. In 1792 he was appointed Kammer Kapellmeister and Hofmusik Compositor, succeeding Mozart; he held this position until his death. Although Beethoven referred to him contemptuously in a letter of 1812 as "miserabilis," Koželuh was an excellent pianist and composed about 50 solo sonatas, 22 piano concertos, and about 80 piano trios. His stage works included operas, ballets, and pantomimes, but little of this music is extant; his only extant opera is *Gustav Wasa* (c.1792).

BIBL.: M. Poštolka, *Leopold Koželuh: Život a dilo* (a study of his life and music with summary in Eng. and Ger.; Prague, 1964).

Kozina, Marjan, Slovenian composer and teacher; b. Novo Mesto, June 4, 1907; d. there, June 19, 1966. He studied mathematics at the Univ. and music at the Cons. (1925–27) in Ljubljana, and then was a student of Marx at the Vienna Academy of Music (1927–30) and of Suk at the Prague Cons. (1930–32); he also studied conducting with Malko. He was conductor and director of the music school Maribor Glasbena Matica (1934–39), and then taught at the Belgrade Academy of Music (1939–43). During the Nazi occupation, he took part in the armed resistance movement. After the liberation, he served as director of the Slovene Phil. (1947–50) before teaching composition at the Ljubljana Academy of Music (1950–60). His finely executed scores made circumspect use of modern harmonies, while deriving their melorhythmic essence from native Slovenian folk song patterns. Among his works was the opera *Ekvinokcij* (Equinox; Ljubljana, May 2, 1946); also ballets.

Kozlovsky, Ivan (Semyonovich), Russian tenor; b. Maryanovka, near Kiev, March 24, 1900; d. Moscow, Dec. 21, 1993. He studied at the Kiev Cons. with Lysenko and Muravyova. He made his operatic debut as Faust in Poltava in 1918, then sang in Kharkov (1924) and Sverdlovsk (1925); in 1926 he joined the Bolshoi Theater in Moscow, where he was one of the leading singers until 1954. An artist of imaginative power, Kozlovsky expanded his activities into stage direction, striving to synthesize dramatic action with its musical realization. Apart from operatic performances, he gave recitals in programs of the classical repertoire as well as Russian and Ukrainian songs.

BIBL.: G. Polinovsky, *I. K.* (Moscow, 1945); V. Sletov, *I. K.* (Moscow, 1951); A. Kuznetzova, *I. K.* (Moscow, 1964).

Kraemer, (Thomas Wilhelm) Nicholas, Scottish conductor; b. Edinburgh, March 7, 1945. He was educated at the Dartington College of Arts and at the Univ. of Nottingham (B.Mus., 1967). He was active as a harpsichordist with the Monteverdi Choir and Orch. (1970–80) and the Academy of St. Martin in the Fields (1972–80). In 1978 he founded the Raglan Baroque Players, which ensemble he conducted for over 20 years. From 1980 to 1982 he conducted at Glyndebourne, and from 1980 to 1983 he was music director of Opera 80. He was associate conductor of the BBC Scottish Sym. Orch. in Glasgow from 1983 to 1985. From 1985 to 1990 he was artistic director of the Irish Chamber Orch. in Dublin. In 1985 he became artistic director of the London Bach Orch. He made his first appearance at the English National Opera in London in 1992 conducting *Die Zauberflöte*. His guest appearances as an opera conductor took him to Marseilles, Paris, Geneva, Amsterdam, and other European cities. He was principal conductor (1992–95) and then principal guest conductor (from 1995) of the Manchester Camerata.

Krainik, Ardis (Joan), distinguished American opera administrator; b. Manitowoc, Wis., March 8, 1929; d. Chicago, Jan. 18, 1997. She was educated at Northwestern Univ. (B.S., 1951; postgraduate studies, 1953–54). In 1954 she joined the staff of the Lyric Theater in Chicago, and remained with it after it became the Lyric Opera in 1956. She sang minor roles there until becoming assistant manager in 1960. From 1975 to 1981 she was its artistic administrator. In 1981 she became general director, and proceeded to mold the Lyric Opera into one of the most prestigious opera companies in the world. During her tenure the Civic Opera House was renovated, new scores were commissioned, and a composer-in-residence program was established. In 1996 she oversaw the first complete staging of the *Ring* cycle by the company, but ill health forced her to retire that same year.

Krása, Hans (Johann), Czech composer; b. Prague, Nov. 30, 1899; d. probably in the concentration camp in Auschwitz, Oct. 16(?), 1944. He began playing piano and composing as a child. He later studied with Zemlinsky at the Cons. and at the Deutsche Akademie für Musik und darstellende Kunst in Prague. After working at the Kroll Opera in Berlin (1927), he returned to Prague as répétiteur at the New German Theater. He subsequently became involved in avant-garde artistic circles and devoted much time to composition. Following the German occupation of his homeland, Krása was active at the Prague Jewish orphanage until the Nazis deported him to the Jewish ghetto camp in Theresienstadt in 1942. He continued to compose and to have works performed there. On the night of Oct. 16, 1942, Krása was herded into a railway car by the Nazis and never seen again. It is presumed that he was put to death in the concentration camp in Auschwitz. Krása adopted a neoclassical style of composition enlivened by comedic and grotesque elements. His works include *Die Verlobung in Traum*, opera (Prague, May 18, 1933), *Mládí ve hre*, incidental music to A. Hoffmeister's play (1935), and *Brundibár* (The Bumble Bee), children's opera (1938; rev. version, Theresienstadt camp, Sept. 23, 1943).

BIBL.: J. Karas, *Music in Terezín 1941–1945* (N.Y., 1985).

Krásová, Marta, prominent Czech mezzo-soprano; b. Protivín, March 16, 1901; d. Vráž u Berouna, Feb. 20, 1970. She studied with Olga Borová-Valoušková and Růžena Maturová in Prague, then with Ullanovsky in Vienna. She began her career as a soprano at the Slovak National Theater in Bratislava (1922), but soon turned to mezzo-soprano roles. She made her debut at the Prague National Theater as Azucena (1926), then was one of its principal singers (1928–66); she also made successful guest appearances in Hamburg, Dresden, Madrid, Paris, Moscow, and Warsaw and toured the United States in 1937. In 1935 she married **Karel Boleslav Jirák**; they divorced in 1946. In 1958 she was made a National Artist. She achieved distinction for her roles in Czech operas; was also noted as a Wagnerian singer.

BIBL.: V. Šolín, *M. K.* (Prague, 1960).

Kraus (Trujillo), Alfredo, distinguished Spanish tenor of Austrian descent; b. Las Palmas, Canary Islands, Sept. 24, 1927. He had vocal training with Gali Markoff in Barcelona and Francisco Andrés in Valencia, then completed his studies with Mercedes Llopart in Milan (1955). In 1956 he won 1st prize in the Geneva Competition and made his operatic debut as the Duke of Mantua in Cairo; he also made his European debut in Venice as Alfredo Germont, a role he repeated for his British debut at London's Stoll Theatre in 1957. After he scored a remarkable success in the same role at Lisbon's Teatro São Carlo on March 27, 1958, an international career beckoned. On July 10, 1959, he appeared at London's Covent Garden for the first time as Edgardo in *Lucia di Lammermoor*. His U.S. debut followed at the Chicago Lyric Opera, as Nemorino in *L'elisir d'amore* on Oct. 31, 1962. He made his Metropolitan Opera debut in New York as the Duke of Mantua on Feb. 16, 1966. Thereafter his career took him to most of the major European and North American opera houses. He also toured as a recitalist. In 1996 he celebrated his 40th anniversary on the operatic stage. A consummate artist with a voice of remarkable beauty, he was particularly noted for his portrayals of Rossini's Count Almaviva, Don Ottavio, Ernesto in *Don Pasquale*, Des Grieux, Nadir in *Les Pêcheurs de perles*, and Massenet's Werther.

BIBL.: N. Dentici Bourgoa, *A. K.: Treinta y cinco años de arte en el País Vasco* (Bilbao, 1992).

Kraus, Ernst, outstanding German tenor, father of **(Wolfgang Ernst) Richard Kraus**; b. Erlangen, June 8, 1863; d. Wörthsee, Sept. 6, 1941. He studied in Munich with Schimon-Regan and then in Milan with Cesare Galliera. He made his concert debut at a Kaim Concert in Munich (Jan. 18, 1893), and then his operatic debut in Mannheim on March 26, 1893, as Tamino; he remained on its roster until 1896, and thereafter was a leading member of the Berlin Royal (later State) Opera until 1924. He also was a leading singer with the Damrosch Opera Co. in New York (1896–99) and at the Bayreuth Festivals (1899–1909); he appeared at London's Covent Garden (1900, 1907, 1910). He made his Metropolitan Opera debut in New York on Nov. 25, 1903, as Siegmund in *Die Walküre*, remaining on its roster for a season. After retiring from the Berlin State Opera in 1924, he returned to Munich as a singing teacher. He was one of the foremost Wagnerians of his day, excelling in such roles as Siegfried, Siegmund, and Walther von Stolzing.

Kraus, Felix von, noted Austrian bass; b. Vienna, Oct. 3, 1870; d. Munich, Oct. 30, 1937. He studied philology and music history, took a course in harmony with Bruckner in Vienna, and received training in theory from Mandyczewski at the Univ. of Vienna (Ph.D., 1894, with a diss. on Caldara); also received vocal instruction from C. Van Zanten in Amsterdam and from Stockhausen in Frankfurt am Main. He made his debut in a Vienna concert (1896); he made his operatic debut as Hagen at the Bayreuth Festival (1899), and continued to appear there until 1909, excelling as Gurnemanz, the Landgrave, and King Marke; he sang at London's Covent Garden (1907). In 1908 he became a prof. at the Munich Academy of Music. He married **Adrienne Osborne** (1899).

Kraus, Joseph Martin, important German-born Swedish composer; b. Miltenberg-am-Main, June 20, 1756; d. Stockholm, Dec. 15, 1792. He attended the Jesuit School in Mannheim, then studied law at the univs. of Mainz (1773–74), Erfurt (1775–76), and Göttingen (1777–78). In 1778 he went to Sweden, making his home in Stockholm; in 1780 he was elected a member of the Swedish Academy of Music; in 1781 he was appointed deputy conductor of the Court Orch. His great interest in Swedish culture prompted King Gustavus III to send him to Germany, Austria, Italy, France, and England for study purposes between the years 1782 and 1787. During his travels, he met Gluck and Haydn, both of whom warmly praised his music. In 1788 he was appointed Hovkapellmastare in Stockholm, holding this position until his untimely death from tuberculosis. During his short life (he was almost an exact contemporary of Mozart), he composed several distinguished works for the stage; his operas (to Swedish texts) are estimable achievements, especially *Aeneas i Carthago (Dido och Aeneas)*, which was premiered posthumously in Stockholm on Nov. 18, 1799. He also composed a *Symphonie funebre* and *Begravingskantata* (both 1792) for the assassinated Gustavus III. After Kraus's death, his MSS and letters were deposited in the library of the Univ. of Uppsala. In recent years, a number of his works have been publ. His writings include *Versuch von Schäfergedichten* (Mainz, 1773) and *Etwas von und über Musik fürs Jahr 1777* (Frankfurt am Main, 1778).

WORKS: DRAMATIC: *Azire*, opera (1778; only fragments extant); *Proserpina*, opera (Ulriksdal Castle, June 1781); *Fintbergs Bröllop* (Fintberg's Wedding), comic play with music (Stockholm, Jan. 1788); *Soliman II, eller De tre sultaninnorna*, comic opera (Stockholm, Sept. 22, 1789); *Afventyraren* (The Adventurer), comic play with music (Stockholm, Jan. 30, 1791); *Aeneas i Carthago (Dido och Aeneas)*, opera (Stockholm, Nov. 18, 1799); etc.

BIBL.: F. Silverstolpe, *Biographie af K.* (Stockholm, 1833); K. Schreiber, *Biographie über den Odenwälder Komponisten J. M. K.* (Buchen, 1928); R. Engländer, *J. M. K. und die Gustavianische Oper* (Uppsala and Leipzig, 1943); I. Leux-Henschen, *J. M. K. in seinen Briefen* (Stockholm, 1978); F. Riedel, ed., *J. M. K. und Italien: Beiträge zur Rezeption italienischer Kultur, Kunst und Musik im späten 18. Jahrhundert* (Munich, 1987); B. Van Boer, *Die Werke von J. M. K.: Systematisch-thematisches Werkverzeichnis* (Stockholm, 1988).

Kraus, Otakar, Czech-born English baritone; b. Prague, Dec. 10, 1909; d. London, July 28, 1980. He was a student of Konrad Wallerstein in Prague and of Fernando Carpi in Milan. He made his operatic debut as Amonasro in Brno (1935), then sang in Bratislava. At the outbreak of World War II he went to England, where he sang with the Carl Rosa Opera Co. (1940); he then joined the English Opera Group (1946), creating Tarquinius in Britten's *The Rape of Lucretia*. He sang with the Netherlands Opera (1950–51), created Nick Shadow in Stravinsky's *The Rake's Progress* (Venice, 1951), and subsequently appeared at London's Covent Garden (1951–73), where he created Diomede in Walton's *Troilus and Cressida* (1954) and King Fisher in Tippett's *The Midsummer Marriage* (1955); he also appeared as Alberich at the Bayreuth Festivals (1960–62). After his retirement, he devoted himself to teaching. He was made an Officer of the Order of the British Empire (1973).

Kraus, (Wolfgang Ernst) Richard, German conductor, son of **Ernst Kraus**; b. Berlin, Nov. 16, 1902; d. Walchstadt, April 11, 1978. He studied at the Berlin Hochschule für Musik. After working as a répétiteur at the Berlin State Opera (1923–27), he conducted opera in Kassel (1927–28), Hannover (1928–33), and Stuttgart (1933–37). He served as Generalmusikdirektor of the operas in Halle an der Sale (1937–44) and Cologne (1948–53), and then of the Nordwestdeutsche Phil. in Herford (1963–69). He was particularly admired for his performances of Wagner, Mahler, and R. Strauss.

Krause, Tom, Finnish baritone; b. Helsinki, July 5, 1934. He received his training in Helsinki, Vienna, and Berlin. In 1957 he made his debut as a lieder artist in Helsinki, followed by his operatic debut at the Berlin Städtische Oper as Escamillo in 1959. In 1962 he made his first appearance at the Bayreuth Festival as the Herald in *Lohengrin*, and that same year he became a member of the Hamburg State Opera, where he established a reputation as an interpreter of Mozart, Wagner, and Verdi; he also sang in the premieres there of Krenek's *Der goldene Bock* (June 16, 1964) and Searle's *Hamlet* (title role, March 5, 1968). In 1962 he made his British debut as the Count in *Capriccio* at the Glyndebourne Festival. On Oct. 11, 1967, he made his Metropolitan Opera debut in New York as Count Almaviva, remaining on its roster until 1973. He also sang opera in Chicago, San Francisco, and Houston. He also pursued an extensive concert career which took him to most of the leading music centers of the world. Among his prominent roles were Don Alfonso, Guglielmo, Pizarro, Amonasro, Amfortas, Kurwenal, King Philip II, and Golaud.

Krauss, Clemens (Heinrich), eminent Austrian conductor, great-nephew of **(Marie) Gabrielle Krauss**; b. Vienna, March 31, 1893; d. Mexico City, May 16, 1954. His father was a court figure, and his mother a dancer; of illegitimate birth, he took his mother's maiden name. He was a chorister in the Imperial Choir; then studied piano with Reinhold, composition with Grädener, and theory with Heuberger at the Vienna Cons. (graduated, 1912). He was a chorus master at the Brünn Theater (1912–13), making his conducting debut there with a performance of *Zar und Zimmermann* (Jan. 13, 1913), then was 2d conductor at Riga's German Theater (1913–14) and in Nuremberg (1915–16); after serving as 1st conductor in Stettin (1916–21), he conducted in Graz (1921–22). In 1922 he became Schalk's assistant at the Vienna State Opera; he also taught conducting at the Vienna Academy of Music (1922–24) and was conductor of the Vienna Tonkünstlerkonzerte (1923–27). He was director of the Frankfurt am Main Opera and its Museumgesellschaft concerts (1924–29), and then of the Vienna State Opera (1929–34); he was also conductor of the Vienna Phil. (1930–33). In 1926 he made his first appearance at the Salzburg Festivals, and returned there regularly (1929–34); he also conducted in South America (1927) and was a guest conductor with the N.Y. Phil. and the Philadelphia Orch. (1929); he made his debut at London's Covent Garden in 1934. He was director of the Berlin State Opera (1934–37) and Generalmusikdirektor of the Bavarian State Opera in Munich (1937–44); he also conducted at the Salzburg Mozarteum (1939–45) and appeared with the Vienna Phil. (1944–45). Having been a friend of Hitler and Göring, and a prominent figure in the musical life of the Third Reich, Krauss was held accountable for his actions by the Allied authorities after the end of World War II. There was a strain of humanity in Krauss, however, for he had assisted Jews to escape the clutches of the barbarous Führer's fury. In 1947 he was permitted to resume his career with appearances at the Vienna State Opera; he took it to London that same year. He was a conductor with the Vienna Phil. from 1947, and also served as conductor of its famous New Year's Day Concerts. From 1951 to 1953 he conducted at London's Covent Garden, and in 1953–54 at the Bayreuth Festivals. He died during a visit to Mexico. He was married to **Viorica Ursuleac**, who often appeared in operas under his direction; he also accompanied her in recitals. He was a close friend and collaborator of Richard Strauss, who considered him one of the finest interpreters of his works; he conducted the premieres of *Arabella, Friedenstag, Capriccio* (for which he wrote the libretto), and *Die Liebe der Danae*. Krauss was renowned as a conductor of works by Mozart, Wagner, and Verdi, as well as those by the Viennese waltz composers.

BIBL.: A. Berger, *C. K.* (Graz, 1924; 3d ed., 1929); J. Gregor, *C. K.: Eine musikalische Sendung* (Vienna, 1953); O. van Pander, *C. K. in München* (Munich, 1955); G. Kende and S. Scanzoni, *Der Prinzipal. C. K.: Fakten, Vergleiche, Rückschlüsse* (Tutzing, 1988).

Krauss, (Marie) Gabrielle, esteemed Austrian soprano, great-aunt of **Clemens (Heinrich) Krauss**; b. Vienna, March 24, 1842; d. Paris, Jan. 6, 1906. She studied with Mathilde Marchesi at the Vienna Cons., making her concert debut in Schumann's *Das Paradies und die Peri in Berlin* (1858). She then joined the Vienna

Court Opera, where she made her first important appearance as Mathilde in *Wilhelm Tell* (July 20, 1860); she remained on its roster until 1867. She made her debut at the Théâtre-Italien in Paris as Leonora in *Il Trovatore* (April 6, 1867), becoming a great favorite. The Franco-Prussian War of 1870 compelled her to leave France; she sang in Italy and in Russia. When the new building of the Paris Grand Opéra was opened, she sang Rachel in *La Juive* (Jan. 5, 1875); she remained with the Opéra until 1888, with the exception of the 1885–86 season. She subsequently gave concerts and was active as a teacher. She was greatly admired for her Donna Anna, Leonora, Aida, and roles in Meyerbeer's operas; she also created Catharine of Aragon in Saint-Saëns's *Henry VIII* (1883).

Krauze, Zygmunt, Polish composer and pianist; b. Warsaw, Sept. 19, 1938. He was a student of Sikorski (composition) and Wilkomirska (piano) at the Warsaw State College of Music (M.A., 1964), and then completed his training with Boulanger in Paris (1966–67). In 1966 he took 1st prize as a pianist in the Gaudeamus Competition for interpreters of contemporary music in Holland, and subsequently specialized in the performance of modern works. In 1967 he founded the Warsaw Music Workshop, a new music group that gave over 100 premieres of contemporary scores. In 1970–71 he taught piano at Cleveland State Univ. In 1973–74 he was active in Berlin on a grant from the Deutscher Akademischer Austauschdienst. He became president of the Polish section of the ISCM in 1980. In 1982–83 he served as artistic advisor to IRCAM in Paris. He also lectured extensively on contemporary music in Europe and the United States. In 1987 he was elected president of the ISCM. The French government made him a Chevalier dans l'ordre des arts et les Lettres in 1984. In 1989 he received the Polish Composers Union prize and the prize of the Polish Ministry of Culture and Arts. His compositions include the chamber opera *Die Kleider* or *Der Star* (1981; Mannheim, March 26, 1982).

Krebs (real name, **Miedcke**), **Carl August,** German conductor and composer; b. Nuremberg, Jan. 16, 1804; d. Dresden, May 16, 1880. He studied with the tenor and composer Johann Baptist Krebs (1774–1851), who legally adopted him. He made his debut as a pianist at 6, and then commenced composing at 7. After studies with Schelble, he continued his training with Seyfried in Vienna (1825), then was 3d Kapellmeister at the Kärnthnertortheater there. He subsequently was Kapellmeister in Hamburg (1827–50), where he brought out the operas *Sylvia* (Feb. 4, 1830) and *Agnes* (Oct. 8, 1833; rev. as *Agnes Bernauer*, Dresden, 1858). He succeeded Wagner as Kapellmeister of the Dresden Court Opera (1850), where he remained until 1872, then was director of music of the city's Roman Catholic church. Krebs championed the works of Spontini, Meyerbeer, and the young Wagner. He wrote sacred music, piano pieces, and numerous songs, several of which became well known in his day. He married the mezzo-soprano Aloysia Michalesi (b. Prague, Aug. 29, 1826; d. Dresden, Aug. 5, 1904) in 1850; she made her debut in Brünn in 1843, then sang in Hamburg and Dresden; he retired from opera (1870) and subsequently appeared in concerts and taught. Their daughter Marie Krebs (b. Dresden, Dec. 5, 1851; d. there, June 27, 1900) was a talented pianist who made her debut in Meissen when she was 11; she later toured throughout Europe, becoming quite popular in England and accompanied Vieuxtemps on a concert tour of the United States in 1870.

Krebs, Helmut, German tenor; b. Dortmund, Oct. 8, 1913. He studied at the Berlin Hochschule für Musik. He made his debut at the Berlin Städtische Oper (1938); he then sang with the Düsseldorf Opera (1945–47) and again with the Berlin Städtische Oper. He also sang opera in Hamburg, Munich, Milan, London, Glyndebourne, Edinburgh, and Salzburg; he likewise appeared as an oratorio and concert artist. In 1963 he was made a Berlin Kammersänger. He taught at the Frankfurt am Main Hochschule für Musik (1963–75).

Krein, Alexander (Abramovich), Russian composer; b. Nizhny-Novgorod, Oct. 20, 1883; d. Staraya Ruza, near Moscow, April 21, 1951. At the age of 13, he entered the Moscow Cons. and studied cello; he also studied composition privately with Nikolayev and Yavorsky. He taught at the People's Cons. in Moscow (1912–17); after the Revolution he worked in the music division of the Commissariat of Education and in the Ethnographic Dept. From 1923 he was associated with the productions of the Jewish Drama Theater in Moscow, and wrote music for many Jewish plays. Together with Gnessin, he was a leader of the National Jewish movement in Russia. In general, his style was influenced by Scriabin and Debussy, but he made considerable use of authentic Hebrew material. Among his works were the operas *Zagmuk*, on a revolutionary subject based on an ancient Babylonian tale (Moscow, May 29, 1930) and *Daughter of the People* (1946) and the ballet *Laurencie*, after Lope de Vega (1938). He also composed incidental music to plays, including *The Eternal One* (1923), *Sabbati Zewi* (1924), *Ghetto* (1924), *The People* (1925), and *The Doctor* (1925). His brother, Grigori (Abramovich) Krein (1879–1955), was also a composer; his nephew, Julian (Grigorievich) Krein (b. Moscow, March 5, 1913), is the Russian composer and musicologist.

BIBL.: L. Sabaneyev, *A. K.* (Moscow, 1928; in Russian and German); J. Krein and N. Rogozhina, *A. K.* (Moscow, 1964).

Kreisler, Fritz (Friedrich), great Austrian-born American violinist; b. Vienna, Feb. 2, 1875; d. N.Y., Jan. 29, 1962. His extraordinary talent manifested itself when he was only 4, and it was carefully fostered by his father, under whose instruction he made such progress that at age 6 he was accepted as a pupil of Jacob Dont; he also studied with Jacques Auber until, at 7, he entered the Vienna Cons., where his principal teachers were Hellmesberger, Jr. (violin), and Bruckner (theory); he gave his first performance there when he was 9 and was awarded its gold medal at 10. He subsequently studied with Massart (violin) and Delibes (composition) at the Paris Cons., sharing the premier prix in violin with 4 other students (1887). He made his U.S. debut in Boston on Nov. 9, 1888; he then toured the country during the 1889–90 season with the pianist Moriz Rosenthal, but had only moderate success. Returning to Europe, he abandoned music to study medicine in Vienna and art in Rome and Paris; he then served as an officer in the Austrian army (1895–96). Resuming his concert career, he appeared as a soloist with Richter and the Vienna Phil. on Jan. 23, 1898. His subsequent appearance as a soloist with Nikisch and the Berlin Phil. on Dec. 1, 1899, launched his international career. Not only had he regained his virtuosity during his respite, but he had also developed into a master interpreter. On his 2d tour of the United States (1900–01), both as a soloist and as a recitalist with Hofmann and Gerardy, he took his audiences by storm. On May 12, 1902, he made his London debut as a soloist with Richter and the Phil. Soc. orch.; he was awarded its Gold Medal in 1904. Elgar composed his Violin Concerto for him, and Kreisler gave its premiere under the composer's direction in London on Nov. 10, 1910. At the outbreak of World War I in 1914, Kreisler joined his former regiment, but upon being quickly wounded he was discharged. He then returned to the United States to pursue his career; after the United States entered the war in 1917, he withdrew from public appearances. With the war over, he reappeared in New York on Oct. 27, 1919, and once again resumed his tours. From 1924 to 1934 he made his home in Berlin, but in 1938 he went to France and became a naturalized French citizen. In 1939 he settled in the United States, becoming a naturalized American citizen (1943). In 1941 he suffered a near-fatal accident when he was struck by a truck in New York; however, he recovered and continued to give concerts until 1950.

Kreisler was one of the greatest masters of the violin. His brilliant technique was ably matched by his remarkable tone, both of which he always placed in the service of the composer. He was the owner of the great Guarneri "del Gesu" violin of 1733 and of instruments by other masters. He gathered a rich collection of invaluable MSS; in 1949 he donated the original scores of Brahms's Violin Concerto and Chausson's *Poème* for Violin and

Orch. to the Library of Congress in Washington, D.C. He wrote some of the most popular violin pieces in the world, among them *Caprice viennois, Tambourin chinois, Schön Rosmarin*, and *Liebesfreud*. He also publ. a number of pieces in the classical vein, which he ascribed to various composers (Vivaldi, Pugnani, Couperin, Padre Martini, Dittersdorf, Francoeur, Stamitz, and others). In 1935 he reluctantly admitted that these pieces were his own, with the exception of the first 8 bars from the "Couperin" *Chanson Louis XIII*, taken from a traditional melody; he explained his motive in doing so as the necessity of building up well-rounded programs for his concerts that would contain virtuoso pieces by established composers, rather than a series of compositions under his own, as yet unknown, name. He also wrote the operettas *Apple Blossoms* (N.Y., Oct. 7, 1919) and *Sissy* (Vienna, Dec. 23, 1932), publ. numerous arrangements of early and modern music, and prepared cadenzas for the Beethoven and Brahms violin concertos. He publ. a book of reminiscences of World War I, *Four Weeks in the Trenches: The War Story of a Violinist* (Boston, 1915).

BIBL.: L. Lochner, *F. K.* (N.Y., 1950; 3d ed., rev., 1981); A. Bell, *F. K. Remembered: A Tribute* (Braunton, Devon, 1992).

Kreizberg, Yakov, Russian conductor, brother of **Semyon Bychkov**; b. Leningrad, Oct. 24, 1959. For personal and professional reasons, he assumed the surname of his maternal great-grandfather. Following private training from Musin in Leningrad, he went to the United States in 1976 and studied with Bernstein, Ozawa, and Leinsdorf at the Berkshire Music Center in Tanglewood. He was an assistant to Michael Tilson Thomas at the Los Angeles Phil. Inst. From 1985 to 1988 he was music director of the Mannes College of Music Orch. in New York. In 1986 he won the Stokowski conducting competition in New York. In 1988 he became Generalmusikdirektor of the Niederrheinsichen Sym. Orch. and the Krefeld-Mönchengladbach Opera. He made his debut at the Glyndebourne Festival conducting *Jenůfa* in 1992. In 1994 he conducted *Der Rosenkavalier* at his first appearance at London's Covent Garden. During this period, he also made guest conducting appearances with major European and North American orchs. He was chief conductor of the Komische Oper in Berlin from 1994 and principal conductor of the Bournemouth Sym. Orch. from 1995.

Krejčí, Iša (František), Czech composer and conductor; b. Prague, July 10, 1904; d. there, March 6, 1968. He studied composition with Jirák and Novák and conducting with Talich at the Prague Cons. (graduated, 1929). He conducted at the Bratislava Opera (1928–32), then at the Prague National Theater (1933–34) and at the Prague Radio (1934–45). From 1945 to 1958 he was chief conductor of the Olomouc Opera, then was artistic director of the Prague National Theater (1958–68). His music, in a neoclassical idiom, is distinguished by vivacious rhythms and freely flowing melody; the national Czech element is not ostentatious, but its presence is well marked. He composed the operas *Antigone* (1934) and *Pozdviženi v Efesu* (The Revolt at Ephesus), after Shakespeare's *Comedy of Errors* (1939–43; Prague, Sept. 8, 1946).

Krejčí, Miroslav, Czech composer and teacher; b. Rychnov nad Kněžnou, Nov. 4, 1891; d. Prague, Dec. 29, 1964. He studied piano, organ, and theory at home; subsequently took courses in natural history, geography, and music at the Univ. of Prague (1910–14); he also studied composition privately with Novák (1911–13). He then taught in Prague and Litoměřice (1915–53) and was a prof. at the Prague Cons. (1943–53). His compositions include the operas *Léto* (Summer; 1937; Prague, Dec. 4, 1940) and *Poslední Hejtman* (The Last Captain; 1944; Prague, March 18, 1948).

Krempelsetzer, Georg, German composer; b. Vilsbiburg, April 20, 1827; d. there, June 9, 1871. He was by trade a cloth weaver. He studied music in Munich with Franz Lachner, then became chorus master at theaters in Munich (1865), Görlitz (1868), and Königsberg (1870). He wrote the opera *Der Onkel aus der Lombardei* (1861) and the operettas *Die Franzosen in Gotha, Der Vetter auf Besuch* (1863), *Die Kreuzfahrer* (1865), *Das Orakel in Delphi* (1867), *Die Geister des Weins* (1867), *Aschenbrödel*, and *Rotmantel* (1868).

Kremser, Eduard, Austrian composer; b. Vienna, April 10, 1838; d. there, Nov. 27, 1914. He studied in Vienna. In 1869 he became chorus master of the Männergesangverein there, and also conducted various other choral societies. He wrote the light operas *Der Botschafter* (Vienna, Feb. 25, 1886) and *Der kritische Tag* (Vienna, Dec. 6, 1891), among others. He also ed. *Wiener Lieder und Tänze* (2 vols., 1912, 1913).

BIBL.: H. von Paumgarten, *E. K.* (Vienna, 1915).

Krenek (originally, **Křenek**), **Ernst,** remarkable Austrian-born American composer, whose intellect responded equally to his musical philosophy and his imaginative compositional style; b. Vienna, Aug. 23, 1900; d. Palm Springs, Calif., Dec. 23, 1991. He studied with Schreker at the Vienna Academy of Music (1916–18). Following miltary service (1918), he enrolled at the Univ. of Vienna in 1919 to study philosophy. In 1920 he went to Berlin to continue his studies with Schreker at the Hochschule für Musik. The premiere of Krenek's atonally conceived 2d Sym. (Kassel, June 14, 1923) brought him considerable notoriety. With his so-called "jazz" opera *Jonny spielt auf* (Leipzig, Feb. 10, 1927), Krenek became internationally known via performances of the score around the world. A commission from the Vienna State Opera led to his composing the 12-tone opera *Karl V* (1932–33). After the Nazis assumed control of Germany in 1933, Krenek was declared a degenerate artist and his works were banned. Pressure was brought to bear on the Austrian authorities and the scheduled premiere of *Karl V* in 1934 at the Vienna State Opera was canceled. The opera finally received its premiere in Prague on June 22, 1938. Following the Anschluss of 1938, Krenek emigrated to the United States. In 1945 he became a naturalized American citizen. After teaching at the Malkin Cons. in Boston (1938–39), he taught at Vassar College (1939–42). From 1942 to 1947 he was head of the music dept. at Hamline Univ. in St. Paul, Minn. In 1947 Krenek went to Los Angeles, where he continued to teach. In 1966 he settled in Palm Springs and devoted himself mainly to composing and writing. As a composer, Krenek pursued a modified serial path. After coming into contact with the avant-garde in Darmstadt, he was moved to expand his horizons. In 1957 he embraced total serial writing. In 1970 he adopted the use of rows and serial techniques in a manner which led to a much greater freedom of expression and mastery. Although Krenek was elected to membership in the National Inst. of Arts and Letters (1960) and was awarded honorary titles and degrees from various American institutions, his importance as a composer was most fully realized in Europe. In 1959 he was made an extraordinary member of the Berlin Akademie der Künste. In 1960 he received the Gold Medal of the City of Vienna. He was awarded the Grand Austrian State Prize in 1963. In 1970 he received the Ring of Honor of Vienna, and in 1982 was accorded honorary citizenship of Vienna. In 1986 a composition prize was established in Vienna in his name. His 90th birthday was celebrated by special performances of a number of his scores. Krenek deposited the MS of his autobiography in the Library of Congress in Washington, D.C., in 1950, with the stipulation that it should not be made public until 15 years after his death.

WORKS: DRAMATIC: *Cyrano de Bergerac*, incidental music (1917); *Die Zwingburg,* scenic cantata (1922; Berlin, Oct. 20, 1924); *Napoleon*, incidental music for G. Dietrich's play (1922); *Fiesco*, incidental music for S. Friedrich's play (1922); *Der sprung über den Schatten*, comic opera (1923; Frankfurt am Main, June 9, 1924); *Orpheus und Eurydike*, opera (1923; Kassel, Nov. 27, 1926); *Bluff*, operetta (1924–25; withdrawn); *Mammon*, ballet (1925; Munich, Oct. 1, 1927); *Der vertauschte Cupido*, ballet (Kassel, Oct. 25, 1925); *Das Leben ein Traum*, incidental music for Grillparzer's *La vida es sueño* (Kassel, 1925); *Vom lieben Augustin*, incidental music for Dietzenschmidt's folk play (Kassel, Nov. 28, 1925); *Die Rache des verhöhnten Liebhabers*, incidental music for E. Toller's puppet play (1925; Zürich, 1926); *Das Gotteskind*, incidental music for a radio play (Kassel Radio, 1925); *Der Triumph der Empfindsamkeit*, incidental music for Goethe's play (1925; Kassel, May 9, 1926; suite, 1926–27; Hamburg, Nov. 28, 1927); *Jonny spielt auf*, opera (1926; Leipzig, Feb. 10, 1927); *Ein Sommernachtstraum*, incidental music for Shakespeare's *A Midsummer Night's Dream* (Heidelberg, July 1926); *Der Diktator*, opera (1926; Wiesbaden, May 6, 1928); *Das geheime Königreich*, fairy tale opera (1926–27; Wiesbaden, May 6, 1928); *Marlborough s'en va-t-en guerre*, incidental music for a puppet play after a comedy by M. Archard (Kassel, May 11, 1927); *Schwergewicht, oder Die Ehre der Nation*, operetta (1927; Wiesbaden, May 6, 1928); *Die Kaiserin von Neufundlung*, incidental music for F. Wedekind's play (1927); *Leben des Orest*, opera (1928–29; Leipzig, Jan. 19, 1930); *Kehraus um St. Stephan*, opera (1930); *Herr Reinecke Fuchs*, incidental music for H. Anton's play (1931); *Karl V*, opera (1932–33; Prague, June 22, 1938; rev. 1954; Düsseldorf, May 11, 1958); *Cefalo e Procri*, opera (1933–34; Venice, Sept. 15, 1934); *L'incoronazione di Poppea*, orchestration of Monteverdi's opera (1936; Vienna, Sept. 25, 1937; suite, 1936); *8 Column Line*, ballet (Hartford, Conn., May 19, 1939); *Tarquin*, chamber opera (1940; Poughkeepsie, N.Y., May 13, 1941); *What Price Confidence?*, chamber opera (1945; Saarbrücken, May 22, 1946); *Sargasso*, ballet (1946; N.Y., March 24, 1965; based on the *Symphonic Elegy*); *Dark Waters*, opera (1950–51; Los Angeles, May 2, 1951); *Pallas Athene weint*, opera (1952–53; rev. version, Hamburg, Oct. 17, 1955; also as the *Symphony Pallas Athene*); *The Belltower*, opera (1955–56; Urbana, Ill., March 17, 1957); *Jedermann*, incidental music for Hofmannsthal's play (1960; Salzburg, July 30, 1962; film score, 1961); *Ausgerechnet und verspielt*, television opera (1960–62; Austrian TV, Vienna, July 25, 1962; with entr'acte *Roulette Sestina*, Mannheim, Oct. 15, 1964); *Jest of Cards*, ballet (San Francisco, April 17, 1962; based on *Marginal Sounds* for Chamber Ensemble, 1957); *Alpbach Quintet*, ballet (Alpbach, Austria, Aug. 25, 1962); *Der goldene Bock*, opera (1962–63; Hamburg, June 16, 1964); *Der Zauberspiegel*, television opera (1963; 1965–66; Bavarian TV, Munich, Sept. 6, 1967); *König Oedipus*, incidental music for Sophocles' play (1964; Salzburg, July 27, 1965); *Sardakai, oder Das kommt davon*, opera (1968–69; Hamburg, June 27, 1970); *Flaschenpost vom Paradies, oder Der englische Ausflug*, television play (1972–73; Vienna, March 8, 1974).

WRITINGS: *Über neue Musik: Sechs Vorlesungen zur Einführung in die theoretischen Grundlagen* (Vienna, 1937; rev. ed., N.Y., 1939, as *Music Here and Now*); *Studies in Counterpoint, Based on the Twelvetone Technique* (N.Y., 1940; Ger. tr., Mainz, 1952, as *Zwölfton-Kontrapunkt Studien*); ed. *Hamline Studies in Musicology* (St. Paul, Minn., 1945, 1947); *Selbstdarstellung* (Zürich, 1948; rev. and enl. as "Self-Analysis," *University of New Mexico Quarterly* 23, 1953); *Musik im goldenen Westen* (Vienna, 1949); autobiography (MS, 1950); *Johannes Okeghem* (N.Y., 1953); *De rebus prius factis* (Frankfurt am Main, 1956); *Zur Sprache gebracht* (Munich, 1958); *Tonal Counterpoint in the Style of the 18th Century* (N.Y., 1958); *Gedanken unterwegs: Dokumente einer Reise* (Munich, 1959); *Modal Counterpoint in the Style of the 16th Century* (N.Y., 1959); *Komponist und Hörer* (Kassel, 1964); *Prosa, Drama, Verse* (Munich, 1965); *Exploring Music* (London, 1966); *Horizons Circled: Reflections on My Music* (Berkeley, 1974); *Das musikdramatische Werk* (Vienna, 1974–82); *Im Zweifelsfalle: Aufsätze über Musik* (Vienna, 1984); *Franz Schubert: Ein Porträt* (Tutzing, 1990); C. Zenck, ed., *Ernst Krenek: Die Amerikanischen Tagebücher, 1937–1942: Dokumente aus dem Exil* (Vienna, 1992).

BIBL.: W. Grandi, *Il sistema tonale ed il contrappunto dodecafonico di E. K.* (Rome, 1954); F. Saathen, *E. K.* (Munich, 1959); L. Knessl, *E. K.* (Vienna, 1967); E. Marckhl, *Rede für E. K.* (Graz, 1969); W. Rogge, *E. K.s Opern: Spiegel der zwanziger Jahre* (Wolfenbüttel, 1970); C. Maurer-Zenck, *E. K.: Ein Komponist in Exil* (Vienna, 1980); O. Kolleritsch, ed., *E. K.: Studien zur Wertungsforschung* (Vienna, 1982); S. Cook, *Opera During the Weimar Republic: The Zeitopern of E. K., Kurt Weill, and Paul Hindemith* (Ann Arbor, 1987); G. Bowles, *E. K.: A Bio-Bibliography* (London, 1989); J. Stewart, *E. K.: The Man and His Music* (Berkeley, 1991).

Krenn, Fritz, Austrian bass; b. Vienna, Dec. 11, 1897; d. there, July 17, 1964. He studied at the Vienna Academy of Music. He made his operatic debut as the Herald in *Lohengrin* in Trieste in 1917; he then sang in Vienna at the Volksoper (1917–18) and in Bratislava (1918–19) and subsequently at the Vienna State Opera (1919–25; 1934–42; 1946–59); he also sang with the Berlin State Opera (1927–43), and with Covent Garden in London (1935). He made his Metropolitan Opera debut in New York on Jan. 5, 1951, as Baron Ochs; he then continued his career in Europe. He was highly successful in buffo roles.

Krenn, Werner, Austrian tenor; b. Vienna, Sept. 21, 1943. He sang in the Vienna Boys' Choir; then studied bassoon, and played in the Vienna Sym. Orch. (1962–66); took voice lessons with Elisabeth Rado in Vienna. In 1966 he made his operatic debut in Purcell's *The Fairy Queen* at the Berlin Deutsche Oper, then sang regularly at the Vienna State Opera. He made his English debut as Jaquino with the Scottish Opera (1970). He also appeared frequently as a concert and oratorio singer. He was married to **Helga Dernesch**.

Krenz, Jan, Polish conductor and composer; b. Wloclawek, July 14, 1926. He managed to take music lessons as a boy in Warsaw during the German occupation; after the liberation, he studied composition with Sikorski, conducting with Wilkomirski and Górzyński, and piano with Drzewiecki at the Łódz Academy of Music. In 1948 he became conductor of the Poznan Phil. and Opera; he was made 2d conductor (1950) and conductor (1953) of the Polish Radio National Sym. Orch. in Katowice, which he led on tours of Europe and the Far East; he was its regular conductor until 1956, and then again from 1958 to 1967. From 1967 to 1973 he served as artistic director of the Warsaw Opera; then was Generalmusikdirektor in Bonn (1979–82). His own music, comprised of orch. and vocal works, is audaciously modernistic in its orientation, while preserving a classical form.

Kretschmer, Edmund, German organist and composer; b. Ostritz, Aug. 31, 1830; d. Dresden, Sept. 13, 1908. He studied with Julius Otto (composition) and Johann Schneider (organ) in Dresden, then was its court organist (1863–1901). He was a successful composer; his choral work *Geisterschlacht* won a prize at the Dresden singing festival (1865); his 3-part Mass for Men's Chorus won the Brussels Academy's prize in 1868. He wrote several operas to his own librettos in a Wagnerian manner, at least 2 of which were successful: *Die Folkunger* (Dresden, March 21, 1874) and *Heinrich der Löwe* (Leipzig, Dec. 8, 1877); he also produced 2 light operas: *Der Flüchtling* (Ulm, 1881) and *Schön Rotraut* (Dresden, 1887).

BIBL.: O. Schmid, *E. K.* (Dresden, 1890).

Kreubé, Charles Frédéric, French conductor and composer; b. Luneville, Nov. 5, 1777; d. near St.-Denis, 1846. He studied violin in Paris with R. Kreutzer (1800). He joined the orch. of the Paris Opéra Comique as violinist; from 1816 to 1828 he was 1st conductor. Among his works were 16 operas.

Kreuder, Peter Paul, German composer; b. Aachen, Aug. 18, 1905; d. Salzburg, June 28, 1981. He studied in Munich and in Hamburg. He was active as music director of the Reinhardt theaters in Berlin (1928–30) and at the drama theater in Munich (1930–33). In 1936 he was appointed state music director in Munich. In 1945 he went to Argentina, where he occupied educational posts under the regime of Juan Perón. He wrote an opera, *Der Zerrissene* (Stockholm, 1940), and several operettas. His song *Schön war die Zeit* became extremely popular in Germany. It also served as the title of his autobiography (Munich, 1955).

Kreutz, Arthur, American composer and teacher; b. La Crosse, Wis., July 25, 1906; d. Oxford, Miss., March 11, 1991. He studied at the Univ. of Wisc. and at Columbia Univ. He taught at the latter (1946–52) and at the Univ. of Mississippi (1952–64). Among his works are the operas *Acres of Sky* (Fayetteville, Ark., Nov. 16, 1951), *The University Greys* (Clinton, Miss., March 15, 1954), and *Shorwood Mountain* (Clinton, Miss., Jan. 8, 1959).

Kreutzer, Conradin (originally, **Conrad**), German conductor and composer; b. Messkirch, Baden, Nov. 22, 1780; d. Riga, Dec. 14, 1849. He was a pupil of Johann Baptist Rieger, then entered the Zwiefalten monastery (1789), where he studied organ and theory with Ernst Weinrauch (1792–97). He then studied law at the Univ. of Freiburg (1799–1800) before devoting himself to music. He changed his first name to Conradin in 1799. About 1800 he brought out his first operetta, *Die lächerliche Werbung*, in Freiburg. After a sojourn in Switzerland, he went to Vienna (1804), where he met Haydn and most likely studied with Albrechtsberger. His Singspiel *Jery und Bätely*, after Goethe (May 19, 1810), met with considerable success. He then scored major successes in Stuttgart with the premieres of his operas *Konradin von Schwaben* (March 30, 1812) and *Feodora* (1812). He subsequently served as Kapellmeister there (1812–16), and then held that title in the service of Prince Carl Egon of Furstenberg in Donaueschingen (1818–22). After the success of his opera *Libussa* at Vienna's Kärnthnertortheater (Dec. 4, 1822), he served as its Kapellmeister (1822–27, 1829–32); he was also active in Paris. He was Kapellmeister of Vienna's Theater in der Josefstadt (1833–35), where he achieved his greatest success with *Das Nachtlager von Granada* (Jan. 13, 1834) and *Der Verschwender* (Feb. 20, 1834). After another period as Kapellmeister at the Kärnthnertortheater (1835–40), he served as municipal music director in Cologne (1840–42). He spent much time touring with his daughters Cäcilie and Marie, both of whom were singers. He accompanied the latter to Riga (1848). The success Kreutzer achieved during his lifetime was not sustained after his death. Only *Der Verschwender* is retained in the Austrian repertoire. He was also an effective composer of songs, several of which are still sung in Austria and Germany.

BIBL.: R. Rossmayer, *Konradin K. als dramatischer Komponist* (diss., Univ. of Vienna, 1928); A. Landau, *Das einstimmige Kunstlied C. K.s und seine Stellung zum zeitgenossischen Lied in Schwaben* (Leipzig, 1930); H. Leister, *C. K.s Lieder für Männerchor* (diss., Univ. of Mainz, 1963).

Kreutzer, Rodolphe, famous French violinist, pedagogue, and composer; b. Versailles, Nov. 16, 1766; d. Geneva, Jan. 6, 1831. His brother was the French violinist and composer Jean Nicolas Auguste Kreutzer (b. Versailles, Sept. 3, 1778; d. Paris, Aug. 31, 1832). His father, a wind player, gave him early instruction in music; he began studying violin and composition with Anton Stamitz in 1778. On May 25, 1780, he played a Stamitz violin concerto at the Paris Concert Spirituel, and returned there in May 1784 to play his own 1st Violin Concerto. In 1785 he became a member of the king's music, and soon established a notable reputation as a virtuoso. In 1789 he settled in Paris, where he first gained success as a composer for the theater with his opéra comique *Paul et Virginie* (Jan. 15, 1791). His opéra comique *Lodoiska* (Aug. 1, 1791) was also a success, being accorded an even warmer reception than Cherubini's score of the same name. In 1793 Kreutzer became a prof. at the Inst. National de Musique; when it became the Paris Cons. in 1795, he remained on its faculty, retiring in 1826. Beginning in 1798 he made a number of outstanding concert appearances at the Théâtre Feydeau and the Opéra in Paris, being made solo violin at the latter in 1801; he also became a member of Napoleon's chapel orch. (1802) and of his private orch. (1806). His ballet pantomime *Paul et Virginie* (June 12, 1806) found favor with Paris audiences, as did his ballet *Les Amours d'Antoine et Cléopatre* (March 8, 1808) and his comédie lyrique *Aristippe* (May 24, 1808). In 1810 Kreutzer suffered a broken arm in a carriage accident, which effectively put an end to his career. However, he continued to hold his various positions as a violinist. In 1815 he was made maître de la chapelle du roi. In 1816 he was appointed 2d conductor, and in 1817 1st conductor at the Opéra, retaining this post until 1824, at which time he became director (1824–26). His last opera, *Matilde* (c.1826–27), was refused by the Opéra management. By then in declining health, he spent his remaining years in retirement.

Kreutzer was one of the foremost violinists of his era. With Baillot and Rode, he stands as one of the founders of the French violin school. Beethoven greatly admired his playing, and was moved to dedicate his Violin Sonata, op. 47 (the *Kreutzer*), to him. Kreutzer's most celebrated publication remains the brilliant *42 études ou caprices* (originally 40) for Unaccompanied Violin. He also composed a number of fine violin concertos. His renown as a teacher brought him many students, including his brother, C. Lafont, and Massart. With Rode and Baillot, he publ. *Méthode de violon* (Paris, 1803).

WORKS: DRAMATIC (all 1st perf. in Paris unless otherwise given): *Jeanne d'Arc*, drame historique mêlée d'ariettes (1790); *Paul et Virginie*, opéra comique (1791); *Le Franc breton*, opéra comique (1791; in collaboration with Solié); *Lodoiska*, opéra comique (1791); *Charlotte et Werther*, opéra comique (1792); *Le Siège de Lille*, opéra comique (1792); *Le Déserteur ou La Montagne de Ham*, opera (1793); *Le Congrès des rois*, opéra comique (1793; in collaboration with 11 other composers); *On respire*, comédie mêlée d'ariettes (1795); *Le Brigand*, drame mêlée d'ariettes (1795); *La Journée du 10 août 1792*, opera (1795); *Imogène ou La Gageure indiscrète*, comedie mêlée d'ariettes (1796); *Le Petit Page*, comédie mêlée d'ariettes (1800; in collaboration with N. Isouard); *Flaminius à Corinthe*, opera (1801; in collaboration with N. Isouard); *Astyanax*, opera (1801); *Le Baiser et la quittance*, opéra comique (1803; in collaboration with Boieldieu, Isouard, and Méhul); *Les Surprises ou L'Étourdi en voyage*, opera (1806); *Paul et Virginie*, ballet pantomime (St. Cloud, 1806); *François I ou La Fête mystérieuse*, comédie mêlée d'ariettes (1807); *Les Amours d'Antoine et Cléopatre*, ballet (1808); *Aristippe*, comédie lyrique (1808); *Jadis et aujourd'hui*, opéra comique (1808); *La Fête de Mars*, divertissement pantomime (1809); *Abel*, tragédie lyrique (1810; rev. as *La Mort d'Abel*, 1823); *Le Triomphe du mois de Mars*, ceremonial drama for the King of Rome's birth (1811); *L'Homme sans façon*, opéra comique (1812); *Le Camp de Sobieski*, opéra comique (1813); *Constance et Théodore*, opéra comique (1813); *L'Oriflamme*, opera (1814; in collaboration with Berton, Méhul, and Paër); *Les Béarnais ou Henri IV en voyage*, opéra comique (1814; in collaboration with Boieldieu); *La Perruque et la redingote*, opéra comique (1815; in collaboration with Kreubé); *La Princesse de Babylone*, opera (1815); *L'Heureux Retour*, ballet (1815; in collaboration with Berton and Persuis); *Le Carnaval de Venise*, ballet (1816; in collaboration with Persuis); *Les Dieux rivaux*, opera ballet (1816; in collaboration with Berton, Persuis, and Spontini); *Le Maître et le valet*, opéra comique (1816); *La Servante justifiée ou La Fête de Mathurine*, ballet villageois (1818); *Clari ou La Promesse de mariage*, ballet pantomime (1820); *Blanche de Provence ou La Cour des fées*, opera (1821; in collaboration with Berton, Boieldieu, Cherubini, and Paër); *Le Négociant de Hambourg*, opéra comique (1821); *Le Paradis de Mahomet*, opéra comique (1822; in collaboration with Kreubé); *Ipsiboe*, opera (1824); *Pharamond*, opera (1825; in collaboration with Berton and Boieldieu); *Matilde*, opera (c.1826–27; not perf.).

BIBL.: J. Massart, *L'Art de travailler les études de K.* (Paris, n.d.; Eng. tr., 1926); H. Kling, *R. K.* (Brussels, 1898); J. Hardy, *R. K.* (Paris, 1910).

Křička, Jaroslav, eminent Czech composer and pedagogue; b. Kelc, Moravia, Aug. 27, 1882; d. Prague, Jan. 23, 1969. He studied law in Prague (1900–02); then studied music at the Prague Cons. (1902–05) and in Berlin (1905–06). He was in Ekaterinoslav (1906–09), where he was active as a teacher and conductor; then returned to Prague as a choirmaster; later he was prof. of composition at the Prague Cons. (1918–45), where he also served as rector. His music was influenced by Dvořák and native folk songs.

WORKS: OPERAS: *Hypolita* (1910–16; Prague, Oct. 10, 1917); *Bílý pán* (The White Gentleman), after Oscar Wilde's *The Canterville Ghost* (1927–29; Brno, 1929; rev. 1930; Breslau, Nov. 14, 1931); *Kral Lavra* (King Lawrence; 1936–37; rev. 1938–39; Prague, June 7, 1940); *České jesličky* (The Czech Christmas Manger; 1936–37; rev. 1948; Prague, Jan. 15, 1949); *Jáchym a Juliána* (Joachim and Julia; 1945–48; Opavá, 1951); *Serenáda*, opera buffa (Plzen, 1950); *Kolébka* (The Cradle), musical comedy (1950; Opavá, 1951); *Zahořanský hon* (The Zahorany Hunt; Opavá,

1955). CHILDREN'S OPERAS: *Ogaři* (Country Lads; 1918; Nové Město, Sept. 7, 1919); *Dobře to dopadlo* or *Tlustý pradědeček* (It Turned Out Well or The Fat Great-Grandfather; 1932); *Lupici a detekotyvove* (Robbers and Detectives; 1932; both, Prague, Dec. 29, 1932); also several small operas for children's theater; television opera, *Kalhoty* (A Pair of Trousers; Czech TV, 1962).

BIBL.: J. Dostál, *J. K.* (Prague, 1944).

Krieger, Johann Philipp, eminent German organist, keyboard player, and composer; b. Nuremberg, Feb. 25, 1649; d. Weissenfels, Feb. 6, 1725. His brother was the distinguished German organist and composer Johann Krieger (b. Nuremberg, Dec. 28, 1651; d. Zittau, July 18, 1735). He was a pupil of Johann Dretzel and Gabriel Schütz in Nuremberg, then went to Copenhagen, where he studied organ with the royal organist Johann Schröder and composition with Kaspar Förster. He went to Italy in 1673, continuing his studies in Rome. Krieger was subsequently court musician in Halle (from 1677); when the court moved to Weissenfels in 1680 he went with it as Kapellmeister, retaining that post for the rest of his life. He was particularly important as a composer of sacred cantatas; by introducing madrigal verse for his texts, he came to be regarded as the "father of the new cantata." He wrote more than 2,000 such works, only 74 of which are extant. He also composed some 18 operas, but only arias are extant, along with several librettos.

Krips, Henry (Joseph), Austrian-born Australian conductor, brother of **Josef Krips**; b. Vienna, Feb. 10, 1912; d. Adelaide, Jan. 25, 1987. He studied in Vienna at the Cons. and the Univ. He made his conducting debut at Vienna's Burgtheater in 1932; subsequently he was conductor in Innsbruck (1933–34), Salzburg (1934–35), and Vienna (1935–38). In 1938 he emigrated to Australia and became a naturalized Australian citizen in 1944. He conducted ballet and opera. He was principal conductor of the West Australia Sym. Orch. in Perth (1948–72) and the South Australia Sym. Orch. in Adelaide (1949–72); he also made guest appearances in Europe. He was best known for his performances of light Viennese music.

Krips, Josef, eminent Austrian conductor, brother of **Henry (Joseph) Krips**; b. Vienna, April 8, 1902; d. Geneva, Oct. 13, 1974. He studied at the Vienna Academy of Music and also was a student of Weingartner and Mandyczewski. He was 1st violinist in the Volksoper orch. in Vienna (1918–21); he then became répétiteur and chorus master there, making his conducting debut with *Un ballo in maschera* (1921). In 1924–25 he conducted opera in Aussig an der Elbe, and in 1925–26, in Dortmund; from 1926 to 1933 he was was Generalmusikdirektor in Karlsruhe. In 1933 he became a conductor at the Vienna State Opera; he also was made a prof. at the Vienna Academy of Music. In 1938 he lost these positions, after the annexation of Austria to Germany; he then conducted in Belgrade (1938–39). In 1945 he rejoined the Vienna State Opera as principal conductor; later that year he conducted the first postwar subscription concert of the Vienna Phil., and quickly moved to reestablish the musical life of his native city. In 1947 he appeared with the Vienna State Opera at London's Covent Garden. After leaving the Vienna State Opera in 1950, he served as principal conductor of the London Sym. Orch. until 1954. In 1953 he made his U.S. debut as a guest conductor with the Buffalo Phil., and subsequently was its music director (1954–63); from 1963 to 1970 he was music director of the San Francisco Sym. Orch. He also was a guest conductor of the major opera houses and orchs. of Europe and the United States; he conducted at Chicago's Lyric Opera (1960, 1964), at Covent Garden (1963; 1971–74), and at New York's Metropolitan Opera (1966–67; 1969–70). He excelled in works of the Austro-German repertoire, his interpretations being notable for their authority, insight, warmth, and lyricism. Harrietta Krips ed. and publ. his autobiography (Vienna, 1994).

Kriukov, Vladimir, Russian composer; b. Moscow, July 22, 1902; d. Staraya Rusa, near Moscow, June 14, 1960. His brother was the Russian composer Nikolai Kriukov (1908–1961) who won 2 Stalin prizes for his film scores. He studied composition with Miaskovsky at the Moscow Cons., graduating in 1925. In 1949–50 he was director of the Moscow Phil. Inst.; from 1957 to 1959 he taught composition at the Gnessin Inst. in Moscow. His music is harmoniously and melodiously eclectic, while adhering to an effective Russian style. He composed the operas *Railroad Stationmaster*, after Pushkin (Moscow, Oct. 30, 1940) and *Dmitri Donskoy* (1947).

Krohn, Felix (Julius Theofil), Finnish conductor, teacher, and composer; b. Tampere, May 20, 1898; d. Lahti, Nov. 11, 1963. He studied with his father; later at the Helsinki School of Music and the Hochschule für Musik in Berlin. Returning to Finland in 1922, he was active as a conductor and teacher. He composed the children's opera *Uskollinen sisar* (The Faithful Sister; 1945).

Krohn, Ilmari (Henrik Reinhold), eminent Finnish musicologist; b. Helsinki, Nov. 8, 1867; d. there, April 25, 1960. After studying with Richard Faltin in Helsinki (1885–86), he took courses at the Leipzig Cons. with Papperitz and Reinecke (1886–90); he obtained his M.A. in 1894 and his Ph.D. in 1900 from the Univ. of Helsinki with the diss. *Über die Art und Enstehung der geistlichen Volksmelodien in Finnland* (publ. in Helsinki, 1899); he later studied with Bausznern in Weimar (1909). He lectured at the Helsinki Music Inst. (1900–01; 1905; 1907; 1914–16), the Phil. Orch. School (1900–1901; 1904–14), and the Univ. of Helsinki (1900–18), then was its first prof. of musicology (1918–35); he also taught at the Church Music Inst. (1923–30; 1933–44). He was active in folk music research from 1886, resulting in his valuable compilation of some 7,000 Finnish folk songs in *Suomen kansan sävelmiä* (1898–1933). He founded the Finnish section of the IMS (1910) and was founder (1916) and chairman (1917–39) of the Finnish Musicological Soc. Krohn was also a composer, numbering an opera, *Tuhotulva* (Deluge; 1918; Helsinki, Oct. 25, 1928), and 2 oratorios, *Ikiaartehet* (Eternal Treasures; 1912) and *Voittajat* (Victors; 1935), among his works.

WRITINGS: *Musiikin teorian oppijakso* (Principles of Music Theory; 5 vols., Porvoo: 1, *Rytmioppi* [Rhythm; 1911–14; rev. ed., 1958]; 2, *Säveloppi* [Melody; 1917]; 3, *Harmoniaoppi* [Harmony; 1923]; 4, *Polyfoniaoppi* [Polyphony; 1929]; 5, *Muoto-oppi* [Form; 1937]); *Puhdasvireisen säveltapailun opas* (Guide to Solfège in Natural Tuning; Helsinki, 1911); *Die Sammlung und Erforschung der Volksmusik in Finnland* (Helsinki, 1933); *Die finnische Volksmusik* (Griefswald, 1935); *Liturgisen sävellystyylin opas* (The Liturgical Style of Composition; Porvoo, 1940); *Der Formenbau in den Symphonien von Jean Sibelius* (Helsinki, 1942); *Der lutherische Choral in Finnland* (Åbo, 1944); *Der Stimmungsgehalt in den Symphonien von Jean Sibelius* (2 vols., Helsinki, 1945–46); *Sävelmuistoja elämäni varrelta* (Porvoo, 1951; memoirs); *Anton Bruckners Symphonien: Untersuchung über Formenbau und Stimmungsgehalt* (3 vols., Helsinki, 1955–57).

Krombholc, Jaroslav, esteemed Czech conductor; b. Prague, Jan. 30, 1918; d. there, July 16, 1983. He studied composition with Novák (1937–40) and conducting with Dědeček, Ostrčil, and Talich (1940–41) at the Prague Cons. and its Master School; he also studied quarter tone music with A. Hába and attended V. Nejedlý's classes at the Univ. of Prague. He first gained attention as a composer, winning 1st prize in a Czech Phil. competition with his Suite for Piano and Orch. (1939). He then made his conducting debut at the Prague National Theater (1940); after serving as chief conductor of the Ostrava Opera (1944–45), he rejoined the roster of the Prague National Theater; later was its chief conductor (1968–75), and chief conductor of the Prague Radio Sym. Orch. (1973–78). He also appeared as a guest conductor with leading European opera houses. He was especially renowned for his idiomatic performances of works by Smetana, Dvořák, Janáček, Martinů, and other Czech composers, as well as for his distinguished interpretations of the music of Prokofiev and Shostakovich.

Kroó, György, Hungarian musicologist; b. Budapest, Aug. 26, 1926; d. there, Nov. 12, 1997. He studied violin at the National Cons. and at the Academy of Music in Budapest; he also attended classes in musicology there with Szabolcsi and Bartha. In 1957 he was named head of music education of the Hungarian Radio; in 1960 he became a guest lecturer at the Academy of Music, joining its permanent faculty in 1967; he was chairman of its musicology dept. from 1973; he was a prof. of musicology (from 1975). Among his writings are *Hector Berlioz* (Budapest, 1960), *Bartók Béla szinpadi müvei* (Béla Bartók's Stage Works; Budapest, 1962), *A "szabadito" opera* (The "Rescue" Opera; Budapest, 1966), *Richard Wagner* (Budapest, 1968), *Bartók kalauz* (A Guide to Bartók; Budapest, 1971; Eng. tr., 1974), and *Heilawâc. Négy tanulmány Wagner a Nibelung gyürüjéről* (4 Studies on Wagner's *Ring des Nibelungen*; Budapest, 1983).

Krug, Friedrich, German baritone and composer; b. Kassel, July 5, 1812; d. Karlsruhe, Nov. 3, 1892. He was court music director at Karlsruhe. He wrote the operas *Die Marquise* (Kassel, 1843), *Meister Martin der Kufer und seine Gesellen* (Karlsruhe, 1845), and *Der Nachtwächter* (Mannheim, 1846).

Krug, (Wenzel) Joseph, German composer and conductor, known as **Krug-Waldsee**; b. Waldsee, Nov. 8, 1858; d. Magdeburg, Oct. 8, 1915. He developed precociously, entering the Stuttgart Cons. at 14, studying violin, piano, singing, and theory. He graduated in 1880 and went to Switzerland, where he was active as a teacher in Hofwyl; he then conducted a choral society in Stuttgart (1882–89). He was subsequently chorusmaster in Hamburg (1889–92) and in Nuremberg and Augsburg (from 1894); he then lived in Magdeburg. He composed 4 operas.

Kruis, M. H. van't, Dutch organist and composer; b. Oudewater, March 8, 1861; d. Lausanne, Feb. 14, 1919. He studied in The Hague, then filled various posts as organist and teacher. In 1886 he founded the musical monthly *Het Orgel*. He publ. *Beknopt overzicht der muziekgeschiedenis* (1892). Among his compositions is the opera *De bloem van Island*.

Krull, Annie (Marie Anna), German soprano; b. Rostock, Jan. 12, 1876; d. Schwerin, June 14, 1947. She was a student in Berlin of Hertha Brämer. In 1898 she made her operatic debut in Plauen. From 1901 to 1910 she was a member of the Dresden Court Opera, where she was chosen to create Ulana in Paderewski's *Manru* (May 29, 1901), and Strauss's Diemut in *Feuersnot* (Nov. 21, 1901) and Elektra (Jan. 25, 1909). In 1910 she appeared as Elektra at London's Covent Garden, and then sang in Mannheim (1910–12), Weimar (1912–14), and Schwerin (1914–15).

Krushelnitskaya, Salomea (Ambrosivna), noted Russian soprano; b. Belavyntsy, near Tarnopol, Sept. 23, 1872; d. Lwów, Nov. 16, 1952. As a child she sang in a village choir; after studying voice with Wysocki in Lemberg, she made her debut there in *La Favorite* in 1892, then went to Milan, where she took lessons with Crespi (1893–96). From 1898 to 1902 she was a member of the Warsaw Opera; she then scored a remarkable success as Cio-Cio-San in Brescia (1904). After singing at La Scala in Milan (from 1906) and in Buenos Aires (1906–13), she made her operatic farewell in Naples in 1920; subsequently she devoted herself to concert appearances. She taught at the Lwów Cons. (from 1939). Her voice was of particular beauty, spanning fully 3 octaves. Among her most notable roles were Brünnhilde, Isolde, Elisabeth in *Tannhäuser*, Elsa in *Lohengrin*, Aida, Desdemona, and Elektra. In her concert programs she promoted songs by Ukrainian composers. A collection of articles about her career was publ. in Ukrainian (Lwów, 1956).

Kruyf, Ton de, Dutch composer; b. Leerdam, Oct. 3, 1937. He attended the courses in new music in Darmstadt and studied with Fortner in Heidelberg. His works utilize various contemporary procedures, including serialism. He composed the opera *Spinoza* (Amsterdam, June 15, 1971) and the radio opera *Quauhquauhtinchan in den vreemde* (Quauhquauhtinchan in Foreign Parts; 1971; Hilversum, June 3, 1972); also the ballet *Chronologie II* (1967).

Krygell, Johan Adam, Danish organist and composer; b. Naestved, Sept. 18, 1835; d. Copenhagen, July 27, 1915. He began his career as a painter, but turned his attention to music. He entered the Copenhagen Cons. in 1867, studying organ under G. Matthison-Hansen; he won the Ancker stipend, and spent 1874–75 studying in Germany. Returning to Copenhagen in 1880, he became organist at St. Matthew's Church; he also taught. Among his works are an opera, *Saul* (not produced), and an oratorio.

Kubelík, (Jeroným) Rafael, eminent Czech-born Swiss conductor; b. Býchory, near Kolín, June 29, 1914; d. Lucerne, Aug. 11, 1996. His father was the eminent Czech-born Hungarian violinist Jan Kubelík (b. Michle, near Prague, July 5, 1880; d. Prague, Dec. 5, 1940). He studied violin with his father, and then continued his musical training at the Prague Cons. He made his conducting debut with the Czech Phil. in Prague on Jan. 24, 1934, then was conductor at the National Theater in Brno (1939–41). He was chief conductor of the Czech Phil. from 1942 to 1948, one of the most difficult periods in the history of the orch. and the Czech nation. He refused to collaborate with the Nazi occupation authorities; when the communists took control of the government in 1948, he left the country for the West, vowing not to return until the political situation changed. He appeared as a guest conductor in England and western Europe, then made his U.S. debut with the Chicago Sym. Orch. on Nov. 17, 1949; his success led to his appointment as the orch.'s music director in 1950; however, his inclusion of many contemporary works in his programs and his insistence on painstaking rehearsals antagonized some of his auditors, including members of the Chicago press, causing him to resign his post in 1953. He subsequently was music director at the Royal Opera House at Covent Garden in London (1955–58); his tenure was notable for important productions of *Les Troyens*, *Boris Godunov* (in the original version), and *Jenůfa*. He then was chief conductor of the Bavarian Radio Sym. Orch. in Munich (1961–79). He made his Metropolitan Opera debut in New York as its first music director on Oct. 22, 1973, conducting *Les Troyens*; however, he again became an epicenter of controversy, and soon submitted his resignation. In spite of the contretemps, his artistic integrity remained intact; he continued to appear widely as a guest conductor in western Europe and the United States. In light of his controversial tenure in Chicago, it was ironic that he became an honored guest conductor with that orch. in later years. He retired in 1985. Following the "velvet" revolution that toppled the hard-line communist regime in Czechoslovakia in 1989, Kubelík was invited to return to his free homeland to conduct Smetana's *Má Vlast* at the Prague Spring Festival in 1990. Kubelík was the foremost Czech conductor of his generation; in addition to his idiomatic and authoritative performances of the music of his native country, he was greatly esteemed for his distinguished interpretations of the standard repertoire, which were marked by a pristine musicianship, unfettered by self-indulgence. Kubelík became a naturalized Swiss citizen in 1966. His 2d wife was **Elsie Morison**. He also composed, numbering among his works several operas, including *Veronika* (Brno, April 19, 1947) and *Cornelia Faroli* (Augsburg, 1972).

Kubiak, Teresa (originally, **Tersa Wojtaszek**), Polish soprano; b. Ldzan, Dec. 26, 1937. She studied with Olga Olgina at the Łódz Academy of Music. In 1965 she made her debut as Halk in Monziuszko's opera in Łódz, and then appeared with the Warsaw Opera. She made her U.S. debut in a concert performance of Goldmark's *Die Königen von Saba* in New York (1970); she then appeared with the San Francisco Opera, with the Chicago Lyric Opera, and at the Glyndebourne Festival (1971). In 1972 she made her first appearance at London's Covent Garden as Cio-Cio-San. She made her Metropolitan Opera debut in New York as Liza in *The Queen of Spades* on Jan. 18, 1973; that same year, she appeared at the Vienna State Opera as Elsa. She continued to make occasional appearances at the Metropolitan Opera until her final appearance there as Elisabeth in *Tannhäuser* on Jan. 31, 1987. In 1990 she joined the faculty of the Indiana Univ. School of Music in Bloomington. Among her other roles were Senta, Aida, Tosca, Jenůfa, and many from the 20th-century repertoire.

Kubik, Gail (Thompson), American composer; b. South Coffeyville, Okla., Sept. 5, 1914; d. Covina, Calif., July 20, 1984. He was a student of Samuel Belov (violin), Rogers (composition), and McHose (theory) at the Eastman School of Music in Rochester, N.Y. (B.M., 1934), Scott Willits (violin) and Sowerby (composition) at the American Cons. of Music in Chicago (M.M., 1936), and Piston (composition) at Harvard Univ. (1937–38); he also worked with Boulanger. After teaching at Monmouth (Ill.) College (1934), Dakota Wesleyan Univ. in Mitchell, S. Dak. (1936–37), and at Teachers College at Columbia Univ. (1938–40), he was a staff composer and adviser for NBC in N.Y. (1940–42). In 1942–43 he was director of music for the film bureau of the Office of War Information, and then was a composer-conductor for the U.S. Army Air Force Motion Picture Unit (1943–46). He later was composer-in-residence at Kansas State Univ. (1969), Gettysburg College (1970), and Scripps College in Claremont, California (1970–80). In 1944 and 1965 he held Guggenheim fellowships. He held the American Prix de Rome in 1950–51. In 1952 he received the Pulitzer Prize in Music for his *Symphonie concertante*. He composed much music for films, radio, and television, which exerted a liberating force on his serious scores. The latter were notable for their neoclassical bent in which rhythmic patterns were apt to be stimulatingly asymmetric. Among his works are *A Mirror for the Sky*, folk opera (Eugene, Oreg., May 23, 1939) and *Boston Baked Beans*, opera piccola (1950; N.Y., March 9, 1952).

Kubín, Rudolf, Czech composer and pedagogue; b. Ostrava, Jan. 10, 1909; d. there, Jan. 11, 1973. He was a student at the Prague Cons. (1924–29) of Junek (cello) and A. Hába (composition). In 1929 he became a cellist in the Prague Radio Sym. Orch.; beginning in 1935 he alternated as music director of the Ostrava and Brno sections of the Czech Radio. After World War II, he helped to organize the Ostrava Higher Music Teaching College, of which he served as director in 1953–54; when it became a cons., he was its director also (1958–60). In 1959 the Czech government honored him with the Order of Work. His studies with Hába prompted him to compose several quarter tone pieces early in his career. After pursuing expressionist paths, he took up the cause of socialist realism.

WORKS: DRAMATIC: *Žena, která zdělila muže* (The Woman Who Did Down Men) or *Ženich z prérie* (The Bridegroom from the Prairie), operetta (Prague, March 29, 1930); *Tři mušketýři* (The 3 Musketeers) or *Královnin náhrdelník* (The Queen's Necklace), musical comedy (Prague, April 19, 1931); *Letní noc* (Summer Night), radio opera (Czech Radio, Sept. 26, 1931); *Kavalír* (The Cavalier), operetta (1932); *Cirkus života* (Circus of Life), operetta (Prague, May 15, 1933); *Ta česká muzika, ta srdce pronika* (That Czech Music, it Speaks Straight to the Heart), folk play (1933); *Zasnoubení na paloučku* (A Greenwood Betrothal), folk play (1933); *Zpěv uhlí* (Song of Coal; unfinished; overture, 1936); *Děvčátko z kolonie* (The Girl From the Mining Settlement), operetta (Ostrava, March 22, 1942; rev. version, Ostrava, Sept. 10, 1955); *Naši furianti* (Our Defiant Ones), comic opera (1942–43; rev. version, Ostrava, Sept. 18, 1949); *Selský kníže* (The Village Prince), operetta burlesque (Prague, April 10, 1947); *Koleje mládí* (The Ways of Youth), play (Brno, Sept. 15, 1949); *Pasekáři* (People of the Glades), operetta (1950–51; rev. version, Ostrava, April 30, 1954); *Jiříkovo vidění* (Jiřík's Vision), folk opera (1952; unfinished); *Heva*, folk operetta (1955–64).

BIBL.: V. Grebor, *R. K.: Obraz života a díla* (Ostrava, 1975).

Kučera, Václav, Czech composer and musicologist; b. Prague, April 29, 1929. He studied musicology and aesthetics at the Charles Univ. in Prague (1948–51), and then composition (with Shebalin) and musicology at the Moscow Cons. (1951–56). Returning to Prague, he worked at the Czech Radio (1956–59). After serving as head of contemporary musical studies for the Union of Czech Composers (1959–62), he was head of studies in music aesthetics for the Inst. of Musicology (1962–69). From 1969 to 1983 he served as general secretary of the Union of Czech Composers and Concert Artists. In 1972 he joined the faculty of the Academy of Music and Dramatic Arts as a teacher of contemporary composition, and later was prof. of composition there from 1988. From 1988 to 1990 he was president of the "Prague Spring" International Music Festival. In 1972 he received the Prix d'Italia for his *Lidice* and in 1983 received the prize of the Union of Czech Composers and Concert Artists for his String Quartet, *Consciousness of Continuities*. In 1986 he was made a Merited Artist by the Czech government. After following the precepts of socialist realism in his scores, he developed an advanced compositional style in which he sometimes utilized electronics. Among his books are a study of Mussorgsky (1959) and a theoretical vol. on creative experiments in music (1973).

WORKS: DRAMATIC: *Zbojnický oheň* (Brigand's Fire), dance drama (1958); *Festivalová pohádka* (Festival Fairy Tale), ballet (1959); *Srdce a sen* (Heart and Dream), ballet (1973); *Život bez chyby* (Life without Fault), ballet (1979); also *Lidice*, radio musical-dramatic fresco (1972).

Kücken, Friedrich Wilhelm, German conductor and composer; b. Bleckede, Nov. 16, 1810; d. Schwerin, April 3, 1882. He studied thoroughbass with his brother-in-law, the organist Friedrich Lührss, and piano with Aron and Rettberg in Schwerin; in 1832 he went to Berlin, where he studied counterpoint with Birnbach; from 1841 to 1843 he studied with Sechter in Vienna, and later took courses in orchestration with Halévy and composition with Bordogni. He was Kapellmeister in Stuttgart (1851–61). He wrote the operas *Die Flucht nach der Schweiz* (Berlin, Feb. 26, 1839) and *Der Prätendent* (Stuttgart, April 21, 1847), but he is most noted for his songs.

Kuebler, David, American tenor; b. Detroit, July 23, 1947. He was a student of Thomas Peck in Chicago and of Audrey Field in London. In 1972 he joined the Santa Fe Opera. Following his European debut at the Bern Opera in 1974 as Tamino, he sang for the first time at the Glyndebourne Festival in 1976 as Ferrando. In 1980 he appeared as the Steersman in *Der fliegende Holländer* at the Bayreuth Festival. He made his Metropolitan Opera debut in New York on Feb. 4, 1981, as Tamino. From 1987 to 1990 he again sang at the Glyndebourne Festival. After appearing as Don Ottavio in Rome and Madrid in 1989, he sang at the London Promenade Concerts in 1991 in Dvořák's *The Spectre's Bride*. In 1992 he sang Berlioz's Faust at the Bregenz Festival. He returned to Rome in 1997 to sing Henry in *Les Vêpres siciliennes*. Among his other roles were Idamante, Nemorino, Jacquino, Pinkerton, Rodolfo, and Flamand.

Kuhlau, (Daniel) Friedrich (Rudolph), German-born Danish pianist and composer; b. Ülzen, near Hannover, Sept. 11, 1786; d. Copenhagen, March 12, 1832. He lost an eye in a childhood accident, and studied piano during his recovery; later studied theory and composition with C. F. G. Schwenke, Kantor of Hamburg's Catherinenkirche. He went to Copenhagen in 1810 to avoid conscription into Napoleon's army; he prospered there, being made court chamber musician (1813). He appeared often in concerts, championing the music of Beethoven.

WORKS: DRAMATIC (all 1st perf. in Copenhagen): *Røverborgen* (The Robber's Castle), Singspiel (May 26, 1814); *Trylleharpen* (The Magic Harp), opera (Jan. 30, 1817); *Elisa*, opera (April 17, 1820); *Lulu*, opera (Oct. 29, 1824); *William Shakespeare*, drama (March 28, 1826); *Hugo og Adelheid*, opera (Oct. 29, 1827); *Elverhøj* (The Fairies' Mound), incidental music (Nov. 6, 1828); *Trillingbrødrene, fra Damask* (The Triplet Brothers from Damascus), incidental music (Sept. 1, 1830).

BIBL.: C. Thrane, *F. K.: Zur 100-jährigen Wiederkehr seines Geburtstages* (Leipzig, 1886); K. Graupner, *F. K.* (Leipzig, 1930). D. Fog ed. a thematic and bibliographic catalog (Copenhagen, 1977).

Kuhlmann, Kathleen, American mezzo-soprano; b. San Francisco, Dec. 7, 1950. She studied in San Francisco and at the Chicago Lyric Opera School, making her debut as Maddalena in *Rigoletto* with that company in 1979. She made her European debut in 1980 as Preziosilla in *La forza del destino* at the Cologne Opera; subsequently she appeared at Milan's La Scala (as Meg Page in

Falstaff; Dec. 7, 1980) and at London's Covent Garden (as Ino and Juno in Handel's *Semele*; Nov. 25, 1982). She sang the leading role in *La Cenerentola* at the Glyndebourne Festival in 1983. In 1987 she scored a major success as Falliero in Rossini's *Bianca e Falliero* in its U.S. premiere at the Greater Miami Opera. She made her Metropolitan Opera debut in New York as Charlotte in *Werther* on March 2, 1989. In 1991 she was a soloist in Beethoven's 9th Sym. at the London Promenade Concerts. In 1992 she appeared as Cenerentola at Dresden's Semper Opera. She sang Cornelia in *Giulio Cesare* at the Munich Festival and at the Opéra de la Bastille in Paris in 1997. Among her other notable roles are Isabella in *L'Italiana in Algeri*, Dorabella, Rosina, Arsace in *Semiramide*, Bradamante in *Alcina*, and Carmen.

Kuhn, Gustav, Austrian conductor; b. Turrach, Aug. 28, 1947. He studied conducting at the Salzburg Mozarteum and with Swarowsky at the Vienna Hochschule für Musik; later he had instruction from Maderna and Karajan, completing his education at the Univ. of Salzburg (Ph.D., 1970). He then served as conductor at the Istanbul Opera (1970–73) and 1st conductor at the Dortmund Stadttheater (1975–77). In 1978 he was named a conductor at the Vienna State Opera; he also was chief conductor of the Bern Sym. Orch. and Opera (1979–81); he conducted at the Glyndebourne and Salzburg festivals (1980) and made his U.S. debut at the Chicago Lyric Opera (1981). In 1983 he became Generalmusikdirektor of Bonn, a post he held until being dismissed in 1985 after he physically assaulted the director of the Stadttheater during a dispute. He then served as chief conductor of the Rome Opera (from 1987).

Kuhn, Laura (Diane née **Shipcott)**, spirited American musicologist, editor, teacher, and writer on music; b. San Francisco, Jan. 19, 1953. She studied at Dominican College in San Rafael, Calif. (B.A., 1981) and the Univ. of Calif. at Los Angeles (M.A., 1986; Ph.D., 1992, with the diss. *John Cage's Europeras 1 & 2: The Musical Means of Revolution*); she also had private instruction in San Francisco (1975–82) with John Hudnall (voice) and Robert Hagopian (piano). She was a member of the San Francisco (1980) and Oakland (1980–82) Sym. Choruses; she also appeared as a vocalist in the Daniel Lentz Group (1983–85). She was music critic of Marin County's *Independent Journal* from 1980 to 1982; she also wrote book and record reviews for the *L.A. Times* (1982–87) and *N.Y. Times* (1986–89). From 1986 to 1992 she worked extensively with John Cage on various large-scale works, including his *Europeras 1 & 2* for the Frankfurt am Main Opera and his Harvard lectures as holder of the Charles Eliot Norton Chair in Poetry (publ. as *I-VI*). From 1991 to 1996 she was an assistant prof. at Arizona State Univ. West in Phoenix; she also lectured widely in the United States, South America, and Europe. In 1995 she was appointed secretary of the American Music Center. Upon Cage's death in 1992, she instituted, with long-time Cage associate Merce Cunningham, the John Cage Trust in New York, which she subsequently directed. Kuhn also worked extensively with the seeded Russian-born American lexicographer Nicolas Slonimsky, giving strong editorial assistance to successive editions of his *Baker's Biographical Dictionary of Musicians* (7th and 8th eds., 1984, 1992) and *Music since 1900* (4th and 5th [rev.] eds., 1986, 1994); in 1995 she inherited the editorship of the 9th ed. of *Baker's Biographical Dictionary of Musicians* as well as the 6th ed. of *Music since 1900*. In addition to the present vol., she ed. *Baker's Biographical Dictionary of 20th-Century Classical Musicians* (1997); also *A Pronouncing Pocket Manual of Musical Terms* (5th ed., 1995).

Kühner, Basil, German pedagogue and composer; b. Stuttgart, April 1, 1840; d. Vilnius, Aug. 1911. He studied at the Stuttgart Cons. with Faiszt and Lebert, then studied violin with Massart in Paris, and piano with Henselt in St. Petersburg. He was director of the Tiflis Cons. (1870–76). In 1878 he settled in St. Petersburg, where he established his own music school (1892). He wrote the opera *Taras Bulba* (after Gogol; St. Petersburg, Dec. 24, 1880).

Kuhse, Hanne-Lore, German soprano; b. Schwaan, March 28, 1925. She was educated at the Rostock Cons. and the Stern Cons. in Berlin and later studied in Potsdam. She made her debut in Gera in 1951 as Leonore in *Fidelio*; from 1952 to 1959 she was a member of the Schwerin Opera; then sang at the Leipzig Opera (1959–64). In 1964 she joined the East Berlin State Opera. In 1974 she was appointed prof. at the Hochschule für Musik in East Berlin. In 1954 she was named a Kammersängerin. A versatile artist, she was as stylistically faithful to her roles in Mozart's operas as to the heroic and lyric Wagnerian parts.

Kulenkampff, Gustav, German pianist and composer; b. Bremen, Aug. 11, 1849; d. Berlin, Feb. 10, 1921. He studied with Barth (piano) and Bargiel (composition) in Berlin, then taught in music schools and appeared as a pianist there. He wrote the operas *Der Page* (Bremen, 1890), *Der Mohrenfurst* (Magdeburg, 1892), *Die Braut von Cypern* (Schwerin, 1897), *König Drosselbart* (Berlin, 1899), *Ammarei* (1903), and *Anneliese* (Kassel, 1904).

Kulenty, Hanna, Polish composer; b. Bialystok, March 18, 1961. She studied with Kotonski at the Warsaw Academy of Music (1981–85) and Louis Andriessen at the Royal Cons. of Music at The Hague (1986–88). Following further training in Berlin (1990–91), she settled in the Netherlands in 1992. Her music makes use of various advanced techniques, including an extensive employment of glissandos, toward a personal style of composition she describes as "polyphony of the arcs." She composed the monodrama *Parable of the Seed* for Alto, Flute, Violin, Double Bass, Percussion, and Tape (1985).

Kulka, János, Hungarian conductor; b. Budapest, Dec. 11, 1929. He studied conducting with Ferencsik and Somogyi, and composition with Kodály at the Budapest Academy of Music. He became a répétiteur and choirmaster at the Budapest State Opera (1950) and was a conductor there (1953–57). He conducted at the Bavarian State Opera in Munich (1957–59) and was 1st conductor at the Württemberg State Theater in Stuttgart (1959–61) and the Hamburg State Opera (1961–64). He subsequently was Generalmusikdirektor in Wuppertal (1964–76) and of the North-West German Phil. in Herford (1975–87).

Kullman, Charles, American tenor; b. New Haven, Conn., Jan. 13, 1903; d. there, Feb. 8, 1983. He entered Yale Univ., and sang at the Yale Glee Club; he then took courses at the Juilliard School of Music in New York. After singing with the American Opera Co. in Rochester, N.Y., he went to Berlin, where he made his European debut on Feb. 24, 1931, as Pinkerton in *Madama Butterfly* at the Kroll Opera. He sang at the Berlin State Opera (1932–35); he also appeared at the Vienna State Opera, at the Salzburg Festivals, and at Covent Garden in London (1934–36). On Dec. 19, 1935, he made his debut at the Metropolitan Opera in New York as Gounod's Faust. He remained on the roster of the Metropolitan until 1960. His repertoire comprised over 30 roles. He scored a signal success in the role of Eisenstein in *Die Fledermaus*. From 1956 to 1971 he taught at the Indiana School of Music in Bloomington.

Kunad, Rainer, German composer; b. Chemnitz, Oct. 24, 1936; d. Tübingen, July 17, 1995. He studied with Kurzbach and Hübschmann in Chemnitz, at the Dresden Cons. (1955–56), and with Finke, Gerster, and Schenk at the Leipzig Hochschule für Musik. He worked at the Dresden State Opera (1960–75). After serving as a prof. of composition at the Dresden Hochschule für Musik (1978–84), he settled in West Germany. Kunad was principally influenced by Lutosławski, with some indirect inspiration from Penderecki and Henze. He found his métier as a composer for the theater.

WORKS: DRAMATIC: *Bill Brook*, music theater (Dresden, March 14, 1965); *Old Fritz*, music theater (Dresden, March 14, 1965); *Maître Pathelin, oder Die Hammelkomodie*, opera (Dresden, April 30, 1969); *Sabellicus*, opera (Berlin, Dec. 20, 1974); *Der Eiertanz*, mini-opera (DDR-TV, 1975; 1st stage perf., Tübingen, June 7, 1986); *Litauische Claviere*, opera (Dresden, Nov. 4, 1976); *Vincent*, opera (Dresden, Feb. 22, 1979); *Amphytrion*, musical comedy (Berlin, May 26, 1984); *Der Meister und Margarita*, opera (Karlsruhe, March 9, 1986); *Die Menschen von Babel*, scenic mystery play (1986); *Der verborgene Name*, opera (1990); *Kosmischer Advent*, opera (1991).

BIBL.: S. Kreter, *Alles auf Hoffnung: Bobrowski-Vertonungen von R. K.* (Münster and N.Y., 1994).

Kunc, Jan, Czech composer; b. Doubravice, Moravia, March 27, 1883; d. Brno, Sept. 11, 1976. He studied at the Brno Teachers' Training College, with Janáček at the Brno Organ School (graduated, 1903), and with Novák in Prague (1905–06). He wrote music criticism in Brno (1909–18); he then became an instructor at the Brno Cons. (1919); from 1923 to 1945 he was its director. He lectured at the Masaryk Univ. in Brno (1947–52). While he composed the opera *The Lady from the Seashore* (1919; unfinished), he was best known as a composer of choral music and songs.

Künneke, Eduard, noted German composer; b. Emmerich-am-Rhein, Jan. 27, 1885; d. Berlin, Oct. 27, 1953. He was a student of Bruch at the Berlin Hochschule für Musik. After composing the operas *Robins Ende* (Mannheim, May 5, 1909) and *Coeur-As* (Dresden, Nov. 1913), he found his métier as a composer of light theater works in Berlin. He attracted favorable notice with his Singspiel *Das Dorf ohne Glocke* (April 5, 1919). The success of his operettas *Der Vielgeliebte* (Oct. 17, 1919) and *Wenn Liebe erwacht* (Sept. 3, 1920) was followed by the outstanding reception accorded his *Der Vetter aus Dingsda* (April 15, 1921). It quickly entered the repertoire as a favorite of the German operetta stage, and was heard all over the globe. After bringing out *Die Ehe im Kreise* (Nov. 2, 1921), *Verliebte Leute* (April 15, 1922), and *Casino-Girl* (Sept. 15, 1923), he failed to find success in New York with the pasticcio *The Love Song* (Jan. 13, 1925) and *Mayflowers* (Nov. 24, 1925). In the interim he brought out *Die hellblauen Schwestern* (Berlin, Aug. 22, 1925) with considerable success. After the failure in London of *Riki-Tiki* (April 16, 1926), he again found success with *Lady Hamilton* (Breslau, Feb. 25, 1926). His *Die blonde Liselott* (Altenburg, Dec. 25, 1927) became better known in its revised version as *Liselott* (Berlin, Feb. 17, 1932). After bringing out *Die singende Venus* (Breslau, June 9, 1928) and *Der Tenor der Herzogin* (Prague, Feb. 8, 1931), Künneke composed the opera *Nadja* (Kassel, 1931). Returning to the operetta, he then scored the 2d triumph of his career when he composed *Glückliche Reise* (Berlin, Nov. 23, 1932). It too became a repertoire score of the German operetta stage. Although he never equalled this 2d success, he went on to compose a number of well-crafted scores, including *Die Fahrt in die Jugend* (Zürich, March 26, 1933), *Die lockende Flamme* (Berlin, Dec. 25, 1933), *Klein Dorrit* (Stettin, Oct. 28, 1933), *Liebe ohne Grenzen* (Vienna, March 29, 1934), *Herz über Bord* (Zürich, March 30, 1935), *Die grosse Sünderin* (Berlin, Dec. 31, 1935), *Zauberin Lola* (Dortmund, April 24, 1937), *Hochzeit in Samarkand* (Berlin, Feb. 14, 1938), *Der grosse Name* (Düsseldorf, May 14, 1938), *Die Wunderbare* (Fürth, Jan. 25, 1941), *Traumland* (Dresden, Nov. 15, 1941), and *Hochzeiet mit Erika* (Düsseldorf, Aug. 31, 1949). Künneke also composed film scores, orch. works, and piano pieces.

BIBL.: O. Schneidereit, *E. K. der Komponist aus Dingsda* (Berlin, 1978); V. Karl, *E. K. (1885–1953): Komponistenporträt und Werkverzeichnis* (Berlin, 1995).

Kunz, Alfred (Leopold), Canadian organist, conductor, and composer; b. Neudorf, Saskatchewan, May 26, 1929. After training in composition and conducting at the Royal Cons. of Music of Toronto (1949–55), he pursued his composition studies in Europe; he took his diploma in choral conducting at the Mainz Hochschule für Musik in 1965. He settled in Kitchener, Ontario, where he founded the Kitchener-Waterloo Chamber Music Orch. and Choir in 1959. After serving as organist and choirmaster at Mount Zion Evangelical Lutheran Church (1959–64), he was principal of the Canadian Music Teachers' College in Burlington, Ontario (1965–67) and director of musical activities of the Univ. of Waterloo (1965–79). He also conducted various choral groups, including the German-Canadian Choir from 1965. His extensive output included many choral pieces, piano music, and accordion works. Kunz's style ranged from tonal writing to advanced contemporary usages. He composed *The Damask Drum*, chamber opera (1961), *The Watchful Gods*, operetta (1962), *Moses*, ballet (1965), *Let's Make a Carol*, play with music (1965), and *Ceyx and Alcyone*, opera (1979); also 2 oratorios: *The Big Land* (1967) and *The Creation* (1972).

Kunz, Erich, Austrian bass-baritone; b. Vienna, May 20, 1909; d. there, Sept. 8, 1995. He was a student of Theo Lierhammer and Hans Duhan at the Vienna Academy of Music. In 1933 he made his operatic debut as Osmin in Opava, and then sang in Plauen (1936–37) and Breslau (1937–41). In 1940 he became a member of the Vienna State Opera, and sang with the company during its visit to London's Covent Garden in 1947. He appeared as Beckmesser at the Bayreuth Festival (1943–44; 1951) and as Guglielmo at the Glyndebourne Festival (1948, 1950). On Nov. 26, 1952, he made his Metropolitan Opera debut in New York as Leporello, and remained on its roster until 1954. Kunz was greatly esteemed in buffo roles, as an operetta singer, and as an interpreter of popular Viennese songs. His most successful operatic roles were Papageno, Leporello, Figaro, and Beckmesser.

Kunz, Ernst, Swiss conductor and composer; b. Bern, June 2, 1891; d. Olten, Feb. 7, 1980. He went to Munich to study at the Univ. and with Klose and Kellermann at the Academy of Music; after conducting at the Bavarian Court Opera (1916–18), he pursued his career in his homeland. He wrote in a neo-Romantic style principally influenced by Richard Strauss and Pfitzner.

WORKS: DRAMATIC: OPERAS: *Der Fächer* (1924; Zürich, 1929); *Vreneli ab em Guggisberg* (1935); *Die Bremer Stadtmusikanten* (1937); *Der Traum ein Leben* (1968). SINGSPIEL: *Die Hochzeitsreise* (1960). ORATORIOS: *Vom irdischen Leben* (1931–49), *Weihnachts Oratorium* (1936), *Weisheit des Herzens* (1946), *Einkehr* (1951), and *Psalter und Harfe* (1956).

Kunzen, family of German musicians:

(1) Johann Paul Kunzen, organist and composer; b. Leisnig, Saxony, Aug. 31, 1696; d. Lübeck, March 20, 1757. He studied organ at an early age, being deputized for the Leisnig organist by the age of 9. He later studied various keyboard instruments and violin, and subsequently studied with Kuhnau in Leipzig (1716–18). He played and sang at the Leipzig Opera, and was deputized as organist at the Nikolaikirche; he then was made Kapellmeister in Zerbst (1718). He served as director of the Hamburg Opera (1723–25), then became organist of Lübeck's Marienkirche in 1732. He achieved distinction as a composer and conductor, presenting a noteworthy series of Abendmusiken. Only a few of his compositions are extant.

(2) Adolph Carl Kunzen, organist and composer, son of the preceding; b. Wittenberg, Sept. 22, 1720; d. Lübeck (buried), July 11, 1781. He studied with his father and with W. Lustig in Hamburg, then toured in England with his father (1728–29). He was made Konzertmeister at the Mecklenburg-Schwerin court in 1749; was its Kapellmeister (1752–53). In 1757 he settled in Lübeck as his father's successor as organist of the Marienkirche; he was also active as a composer and conductor, following in his father's footsteps with a distinguished series of Abendmusiken. He wrote 21 oratorios, but only 2 are extant; however, many of his fine songs exist.

(3) Friedrich Ludwig Aemilius Kunzen, composer, son of the preceding; b. Lübeck, Sept. 24, 1761; d. Copenhagen, Jan. 28, 1817. He studied music with his father, then law at the Univ. of Kiel (1781–84). He was active as a keyboard player, concert organizer, and composer in Copenhagen (1784–89), then went to Berlin, where he set up a music shop with Reichert and ed. the journal *Musikalisches Wochenblatt* (1791). He subsequently was made Kapellmeister at the theaters in Frankfurt (1792) and Prague (1794) and finally settled in Copenhagen as Royal Kapellmeister (1795). He also served as director of the oratorio society Det Harmoniske Selskab. He composed a number of fine stage works, as well as cantatas and oratorios.

WORKS: DRAMATIC (all 1st perf. in Copenhagen unless otherwise given): *Holger Danske*, opera (March 31, 1789); *Das Fest der Winzer, oder Die Weinlese*, Singspiel (Frankfurt am Main, May 3, 1793; as *Viinhøsten*, Copenhagen, Dec. 1796); *Festen i Valhal* (Festival in Valhalla), prologue (1796); *Hemmeligheden* (The Secret), Singspiel (Nov. 22, 1796); *Dragedukken* (The Dragon Doll), Singspiel (March 14, 1797); *Erik Ejegod*, opera (Jan. 30, 1798); *Naturens røst* (The Cry of Nature), Singspiel (Nov. 22, 1799); *Min bedste moder* (My Grandmother; May 15, 1800); *Hjemkomsten* (The Homecoming), Singspiel (1802); *Gyrithe* (1807); *Kaerlighed paa landet* (Love in the Country; March 23, 1810); incidental music.

BIBL.: B. Friis, *F. A. K.: Sein Leben und Werk I. Bis zur Oper "Holger Danske" (1761–1789)* (diss., Univ. of Berlin, 1943).

(4) Louise Friederica Ulrica Kunzen, singer, daughter of **Adolph Carl Kunzen**; b. Lübeck, Feb. 15, 1765; d. Ludwigslust, May 4, 1839. She began singing in private concerts in Lübeck when she was 16, then joined the Ludwigslust Court Theater (1787), where she enjoyed a remarkable career until her retirement (1837).

Kupfer, Harry, German opera director and administrator; b. Berlin, Aug. 12, 1935. He was trained at the Hans Otto Theaterhochschule in Leipzig. In 1958 he launched his career as an opera director with his staging of *Rusalka* at the Halle Landestheater. After holding the position of Oberspielleiter at the Stralsund Theater der Werfstadt (1958–62), he was senior resident producer at the Karl-Marx-Stadt Städtische Theater (1962–66). From 1966 to 1972 he was opera director at the Weimar Nationaltheater, and from 1967 to 1972 he was on the faculty of the Franz Liszt Hochschule für Musik in Weimar. He was opera director and chief producer at the Dresden State Opera from 1972 to 1981, where he established himself as one of the leading opera directors of his day through the staging of notable productions of both traditional and contemporary works. In 1978 he garnered acclaim with his thought-provoking staging of *Der fliegender Holländer* at the Bayreuth Festival. He was the chief producer at the Berlin Komische Oper from 1981 to 1994. In 1994 he became opera director at the Komische Oper and also artistic advisor to the Intendant of the Berlin State Opera. He collaborated with Penderecki in preparing the libretto for *Die schwarze Maske* (Salzburg Festival, Aug. 15, 1986). In 1988 he staged a compelling *Ring* cycle at the Bayreuth Festival. His productions have also been mounted at the Berlin State Opera, the Hamburg State Opera, the Vienna State Opera, and at London's Covent Garden. In his most inspired productions, Kupfer fuses the finest elements of the traditional music theater experience with all that is best in contemporary stage direction.

BIBL.: D. Kranz, *"Ich muss Oper machen": Der Regisseur H. K.* (Berlin, 1988); M. Lewin, *H. K.* (Vienna and Zürich, 1988); R. Lummer, *Regie im Theater: H. K.* (Frankfurt am Main, 1989).

Kupferberg, Herbert, American journalist and music critic; b. N.Y., Jan. 20, 1918. He was educated at Cornell Univ. (B.A., 1939) and Columbia Univ. (M.A., 1940; M.S., 1941). From 1942 to 1966 he was on the staff of the *N.Y. Herald Tribune*; he was also music critic of the *Atlantic Monthly* (1962–69) and of the *National Observer* (1967–77). He served as rapporteur for the Twentieth Century Fund's N.Y. task force on cultural exchange with the Soviet Union, which led to the publication of the report *The Raised Curtain* in 1977. Among his writings are *The Mendelssohns: Three Generations of Genius* (N.Y., 1972), *Opera* (N.Y., 1975), and *Amadeus: A Mozart Mosaic* (N.Y., 1986).

Kupferman, Meyer, American composer, clarinetist, and teacher; b. N.Y., July 3, 1926. He attended N.Y.'s High School of Music and Art and then Queens College of the City Univ. of N.Y. (1943–45). He was active as a clarinetist and taught at Sarah Lawrence College (from 1951); he was also composer-in-residence at the Calif. Music Center in Palo Alto (from 1977). With John Yannelli, he founded the recording and publishing company Soundspells Productions in 1986. He publ. the book *Atonal Jazz* (1993). In 1975 he received a Guggenheim fellowship and in 1981 an award from the American Academy and Inst. of Arts and Letters. While he has principally applied serial procedures in his music since 1948, his vast catalog of works is nevertheless highly eclectic, displaying significant examples of neoclassicism, electronic music, and jazz.

WORKS: DRAMATIC: OPERAS: *In a Garden*, after Gertrude Stein (N.Y., Dec. 29, 1949); *Doctor Faustus Lights the Lights*, after Gertrude Stein (1952; rev. 1963); *The Curious Fern* and *Voices for a Mirror* (both perf. in N.Y., June 5, 1957); *Draagenfut Girl*, children's opera (N.Y., May 8, 1958); *The Judgement (Infinities No. 18a)* (1966–67); *Prometheus* (1975–77); *The Proscenium* (1991); *The Waxing Moon* (1993). BALLETS: *Persephone* (1968); *The Possessed* (1974); *O Thou Desire Who Art About to Sing* (1977); *Icarus* (1980).

Kupkovič, Ladislav, Slovak conductor, teacher, and composer; b. Bratislava, March 17, 1936. He studied violin and conducting in Bratislava at the Cons. (1950–55) and at the Academy of Music (1955–61). In 1959–60 he was conductor of the Hungarian Folk Ensemble of Bratislava and then played violin in the Slovak Phil. there (1960–63). In 1963 he organized the chamber ensemble Hudba Dneska (Music of Today). He left Czechoslovakia after the Soviet invasion in 1968 and went to Germany; he was a stipendiary at Berlin's Deutscher Akademischer Austauschdienst (1969–71) and was made a lecturer (1973) and a prof. (1976) of composition at the Hannover Hochschule für Musik. His music utilizes the cosmopolitan resources of ultramodern music. He initiated "walking concerts," in which a group of musicians walk in the streets playing segments of familiar pieces. Within his substantial catalog of works is a Singspiel, *Die Maske* (1986).

Kupper, Annelies (Gabriele), German soprano; b. Glatz, July 21, 1906; d. Haar, near Munich, Dec. 8, 1987. She studied at the Univ. of Breslau, and then taught in that city (1929–35). She made her debut at the Breslau Opera (1935), remaining there until 1937. She then sang in Schwerin (1937–38) and Weimar (1938–39). She was a principal member of the Hamburg State Opera (1940–46) and the Bavarian State Opera in Munich (1946–61); she also sang at Bayreuth, Salzburg, and London's Covent Garden (Chrysothemis, 1953) and appeared as Danae in the first public performance of Richard Strauss's *Die Liebe der Danae* (Salzburg, 1952). She became a teacher at the Munich Academy of Music (1956). In addition to her Mozart and Strauss roles, she became known for her performances of works by contemporary German composers.

Kurka, Robert (Frank), American composer; b. Cicero, Ill., Dec. 22, 1921; d. N.Y., Dec. 12, 1957. He studied violin with Kathleen Parlow and Hans Letz, and composition with Luening and Milhaud, but considered himself autodidact. He received a Guggenheim fellowship (1951–52), and taught at the City College of N.Y., Queens College, and Dartmouth College. His satirical opera, *The Good Soldier Schweik*, after J. Hašek (1952–57; N.Y., April 23, 1958; as a chamber orch. suite, N.Y., Nov. 24, 1952), the composition of which was delayed for years due to problems in clearing rights for the libretto and which existed only as an orchestral suite until 1956, was completed shortly before his untimely death from leukemia and was orchestrated by Hershy Kay. Kurka's music, though quite melodic, makes use of harmonious dissonance, imbuing neoclassical forms with a rhythmic and harmonic intuition reminiscent of Prokofiev and Shostakovich.

Kurpiński, Karol (Kazimierz), prominent Polish conductor and composer; b. Wloszakowice, March 6, 1785; d. Warsaw, Sept. 18, 1857. He studied with his father, Marcian Kurpinski, an organist. In 1797 he became organist in Sarnów, then was a violinist in the private orch. of Feliks Polanowski at his Moszków estate (1800–08); he subsequently was music master to the Rastawiecki family in Lemberg (1808–10). He settled in Warsaw, where he became a theater violinist, then was made deputy conductor of the Opera, and also Kapellmeister of the Polish royal court (1819); he was principal conductor of the Opera (1824–40). He also taught music at the schools of drama (1812, 1817) and voice (1835–40), which he founded. He was founder-ed. of the first

Polish music journal, *Tygodnik Muzyczny* (Music Weekly; 1820–21). As one of the leading Polish composers of his day, he helped to establish the national Polish school. He wrote 24 stage works, including the operas *Jadwiga królowa Polska* (Jadwiga, Queen of Poland; Warsaw, Dec. 23, 1814) and *Zamek na Czorsztynce, czyli Bojomic i Wanda* (The Castle of Czorsztyn, or Bojomic and Wanda; Warsaw, March 5, 1819).

BIBL.: T. Przybylski, *K. K., 1785–1857* (Warsaw, 1975).

Kurt, Melanie, Austrian soprano; b. Vienna, Jan. 8, 1880; d. N.Y., March 11, 1941. She studied piano with Leschetizky at the Vienna Cons. (1887–94), winning the gold medal and Liszt prize; then took vocal lessons from Fannie Mütter in Vienna (1896), but also toured as a pianist (1897–1900). She then made her operatic debut as Elisabeth in *Tannhäuser* (Lübeck, 1902), then sang in Leipzig (1903–04). She then completed her vocal training with Lilli and Marie Lehmann in Berlin. From 1905 to 1908 she sang in Braunschweig, then (1908–12) at the Berlin Royal Opera. She became an outstanding Wagner interpreter and appeared in London (Covent Garden, 1910, 1914), Brussels, Milan, Budapest, etc. When the Deutsches Opernhaus in Charlottenburg was opened in 1912, she was engaged as chief soprano for heroic roles. On Feb. 1, 1915, she made her debut at the Metropolitan Opera in New York as Isolde; she remained on its roster until her contract was terminated with the United States entry into World War I in 1917. After returning to Germany, she appeared at the Berlin Volksoper (1920–25); she also taught there, and later in Vienna. In 1938 she settled in New York. Her roles included Pamina, Beethoven's Leonore, Sieglinde, Brünnhilde, Kundry, and the Marschallin.

Kurth, Ernst, eminent Austrian-born Swiss musicologist; b. Vienna, June 1, 1886; d. Bern, Aug. 2, 1946. He studied with Adler at the Univ. of Vienna (Ph.D., 1908, with the diss. *Der Stil der opera seria von Gluck bis zum Orfeo*; publ. in *Studien zur Musikwissenschaft*, I, 1913); completed his Habilitation at the Univ. of Bern in 1912 with his *Die Voraussetzungen der theoretischen Harmonik und der tonalen Darstellungssystems* (publ. in Bern, 1913). He was made a reader (1920) and a prof. of musicology (1927) there. His principal work, *Grundlagen des linearen Kontrapunkts: Bachs melodische Polyphonie* (Bern, 1917; 5th ed., 1956), profoundly influenced musicology and practical composition, and also introduced the term "linear counterpoint." A companion vol., *Romantische Harmonik und ihre Krise in Wagners Tristan* (Bern, 1920; 3d ed., 1923), is a psychological analysis of Romantic music. His *Musikpsychologie* (Berlin, 1931; 2d ed., 1947) represents a synthesis of his theoretical ideas on musical perception. He also publ. *Anton Bruckner* (2 vols., Berlin, 1925). Lee Rothfarb ed. and tr. *Ernst Kurth: Selected Writings* (Cambridge and N.Y., 1991).

BIBL.: L. Rothfarb, *E. K. as Theorist and Analyst* (Philadelphia, 1988).

Kurz, Selma, noted Austrian soprano; b. Bielitz, Silesia, Nov. 15, 1874; d. Vienna, May 10, 1933. She studied with Johannes Ress in Vienna and Mathilde Marchesi in Paris. She made her first appearance as a mezzo-soprano as Mignon at the Hamburg Opera (May 12, 1895); she then sang in Frankfurt am Main (1896–99). She made her first appearance at the Vienna Court Opera as Mignon (Sept. 3, 1899); after singing lyric-dramatic soprano roles, she turned to coloratura roles; she continued on its roster when it became the State Opera (1918), singing there until her retirement (1927). She made her London debut at Covent Garden as Gilda (June 7, 1904), creating a profound impression; she sang there again in 1905, 1907, and 1924. She appeared as a concert singer in the United States. She was esteemed for such roles as Elizabeth, Eva, Sieglinde, Lucia, and Mimi; also created Zerbinetta in the rev. version of Richard Strauss's *Ariadne auf Naxos* (1916). She married the Austrian gynecologist Josef Halban in 1910; their daughter was the soprano Desi Halban-Kurz (b. Vienna, April 10, 1912).

BIBL.: H. Goldmann, *S. K.* (Bielitz, 1933); D. Halbin and U. Ebbers, *S. K.: Die Sängerin und ihre Zeit* (Stuttgart and Zürich, 1983).

Kurz, Siegfried, German conductor and composer; b. Dresden, July 18, 1930. He studied conducting with Ernst Hintze, composition with Fidelio Finke, and trumpet with Gerd Seifert at the Staatlichen Akademie für Musik und Theater in Dresden (1945–50). From 1949 to 1960 he was conductor of music for dramatic productions at the Dresden State Theater. In 1960 he became a conductor at the Dresden State Opera; in 1975 he was named its music director; in 1979 he also became a prof. of composition at the Dresden Hochschule für Musik. He toured with the Dresden State Orch. to Austria, Japan, and the United States. As a conductor, he was honored with the titles of Staatskapellmeister (1965) and Generalmusikdirektor (1971); as a composer, he received the Kunstpreis and the Nationalpreis of the German Democratic Republic. His compositions combine the principles of Classical lucidity with the dissonant counterpoint of the modern era.

Kusche, Benno, German bass-baritone; b. Freiburg im Breisgau, Jan. 30, 1916. He studied in Karlsruhe with his mother and in Freiburg im Breisgau with Fritz Harlan. He made his operatic debut in Koblenz in 1938, then sang in Augsburg (1939–44); subsequently he became a leading member of the Bavarian State Opera in Munich (1946). He made his debut at London's Covent Garden as Beckmesser (1952); he chose that same role for his Metropolitan Opera debut in New York on Dec. 27, 1971. He was made a Bavarian Kammersänger in 1955. His notable roles included Papageno, Figaro, Leporello, Don Alfonso, and Alberich.

Kusser (or **Cousser**), **Johann Sigismund,** noted German conductor and composer of Hungarian parentage; b. Pressburg (baptized), Feb. 13, 1660; d. Dublin, Nov. 1727. He received his early musical training from his father, Johann Kusser (1626–75), a minister and organist. He lived in Stuttgart as a boy, then spent 8 years in Paris (1674–82), where he became a pupil of Lully. He subsequently was a violin teacher at the Ansbach court (1682–83), then became opera Kapellmeister in Braunschweig (1690). In 1695 he became codirector of the Hamburg Opera, but left the next year and was active in Nuremberg and Augsburg as an opera composer. He was again in Stuttgart from 1700 to 1704 as Ober-Kapellmeister. In 1705 he appeared in London, and in 1709 settled in Dublin, where he was made Chappel-Master of Trinity College in 1717 and Master of the Musick "attending his Majesty's State in Ireland" in 1717. He was greatly esteemed as an operatic conductor; Mattheson, in his *Volkommener Capellmeister*, holds him up as a model of efficiency. Kusser is historically significant for being the mediator between the French and the German styles of composition, and the first to use Lully's methods and forms in German instrumental music. Lully's influence is shown in Kusser's set of 6 suites for Strings, *Composition de musique suivant la méthode française* (Stuttgart, 1682).

WORKS: OPERAS: *Julia* (Braunschweig, 1690); *Cleopatra* (Braunschweig, 1691); *La Grotta di Salzdahl*, divertimento (Braunschweig, 1691); *Ariadne* (Braunschweig, Feb. 15, 1692); *Andromeda* (Braunschweig, Feb. 20, 1692); *Jason* (Braunschweig, Sept. 1, 1692); *Narcissus* (Braunschweig, Oct. 14, 1692); *Porus* (Braunschweig, 1693); *Erindo, oder Dir unsträfliche Liebe*, pastorale play (Hamburg, 1694); *Der grossmüthige Scipio Africanus* (Hamburg, 1694); *Gensericus, als Rom und Karthagens Überwinder* (Hamburg, 1694?; may be by Conradi); *Pyramus und Thisbe getreu und festverbundene Liebe* (Hamburg, 1694?); *Der verliebte Wald* (Stuttgart, 1698); *Erminia* (Stuttgart, Oct. 11, 1698); *The Man of Mode* (London, Feb. 9, 1705).

BIBL.: H. Scholz, *J. S. K.: Sein Leben und seine Werke* (Leipzig, 1911).

Kussevitsky, Serge (Alexandrovich). See **Koussevitzky, Serge (Alexandrovich).**

Kutavičius, Bronislovas, Lithuanian composer; b. Molainiai, near Panevieżys, Sept. 13, 1932. He studied composition with Antanas Račiunas at the Vilnius Cons., graduating in 1964. In 1975 he was appointed to the music faculty at the Arts School in Vilnius.

In his music, he evolves a complex system of varied techniques, impressionistic pointillism, intervallic serialism, and aleatory sonorism, all this intertwined with Lithuanian melorhythms. His compositions include *Doddering Old Man on Iron Mountain*, children's opera ballet (1976), and *The Green Bird*, opera poem (1981); also *Pantheistic Oratorio* for Soprano, Narrator, 4 Men's Voices, and 12 Instruments (1970) and *The Last Pagan Rites*, oratorio for Soprano, Girls' Chorus, Horns, and Organ (1978).

Kuusisto, Ilkka Taneli, Finnish composer, conductor, and administrator; b. Helsinki, April 26, 1933. His father was the Finnish organist and composer Taneli Kuusisto (1905–1988). He studied organ at the Sibelius Academy in Helsinki; also composition with Arre Merikanto and Fougstedt. In 1958 he went to New York to study organ with Seth Bingham; later he continued his studies in Germany and Vienna. Returning to Helsinki, he was a conductor at the City Theater (1965–68; 1971–75); he also was head of the Klemetti Inst. (1969–71); after serving as artistic director of Fazer Music (1981–84), he was general manager of the Finnish National Opera (1984–92).

WORKS: DRAMATIC: OPERAS: *Muumiooppera* (1974); *Miehen kylkiluu* (1977); *Sota valosta* (1980; Helsinki, April 2, 1981); *Jääkäri Stahl* (1981); *Pierrot tai yon salaisuudet* (1991); *Miss Julie* (1994). MUSICALS: *Lumikuningatar* (1979); *Robin Hood* (1987). Also music for plays and films.

Kuznetsova, Maria (Nikolaievna), prominent Russian soprano; b. Odessa, 1880; d. Paris, April 25, 1966. She studied in St. Petersburg with Tartakov. She made her debut in an operatic production at the Cons. there (1904), then was a member of the Maryinsky Theater (1905–13), where she distinguished herself in Russian roles and as Juliette, Elsa, Carmen, and Madama Butterfly. She made guest appearances in Berlin (1908), at the Opéra (1908, 1910, 1912, 1914) and Opéra Comique (1910) in Paris, and at Covent Garden in London (debut as Marguerite in *Faust*, 1909; returned in 1910, 1920). In 1915–16 she sang in Petrograd and in 1916 in Chicago. After the Russian Revolution (1918), she fled to Sweden; she made appearances in Stockholm and Copenhagen (1920), and then toured with her own opera company; she later was artistic adviser of Barcelona's Teatro Liceo.

Kvam, Oddvar S(chirmer), Norwegian composer; b. Oslo, Sept. 9, 1927. He studied at the Oslo Cons. (1943–52), where he took a degree in harmony and counterpoint (1950) and received training in piano and theory; he also obtained a law degree from the Univ. of Oslo (1949); he later studied conducting with Grüner-Hegge (1955–57) and composition with David Monrad Johansen (1964–66) in Oslo, completing his training in composition with Herman Koppel in Copenhagen (1969). He practiced law while devoting much time to composition; was the first composer to hold the influential post of chairman of the Norwegian Arts Council (1985–88). Two of his orch. works, Prologue (1967) and Opening (1974), received awards at the inauguration of the Oslo Concert Hall in 1977. Kvam's compositions tend to be free of tonally based strictures, yet they preserve a feeling of tonality. Among his works are *The Dream of the 13th Hour,* opera (1986), and *The Cabinet*, chamber opera (1989).

Kvandal (real name, **Johansen**), **(David) Johan,** distinguished Norwegian composer and organist; b. Christiania, Sept. 8, 1919. His father was the Norwegian pianist, music critic, and composer David Monrad Johansen (1888–1974). He graduated as a student of organ (under Sandvold) and of conducting at the Oslo Cons., where he also took courses with Tveitt (composition) and Steenberg (counterpoint and composition); he then pursued his composition studies with Marx in Vienna, Boulanger in Paris (1952–54), and Blacher in Berlin (1970). From 1959 to 1974 he was organist of Oslo's Valerengen Church. Kvandal's works are written in a well-crafted neoclassical style but with obeisance to Norway's national musical tradition. His compositions include *Skipper Worse*, television score (1967), and *Mysteries*, opera (1993; Oslo, Jan. 15, 1994).

BIBL.: *Festskrift til J. K. i anledning 70-årsdagen 8. september 1989* (Oslo, 1989).

Kvapil, Jaroslav, significant Czech composer; b. Fryšták, April 21, 1892; d. Brno, Feb. 18, 1958. He studied with Nešvera in Olmütz (1902–06), Janáček at the Brno Organ School (1906–09), and Reger at the Leipzig Cons. (1911–13). He was in the Austrian Army during World War I, then was conductor of the Brno Beseda (1919–47); he then taught at the Janáček Academy of Music there (1947–57). His works show the double influence of Janáček's national and rhapsodic style and Reger's strong polyphonic idiom. Among his compositions is the opera *Pohádka máje* (A Romance in May; 1940–43; Prague, May 12, 1950; rev., Brno, 1955).

BIBL.: L. Kundera, *J. K.* (Prague, 1944).

Kwella, Patrizia, English soprano; b. Mansfield, April 26, 1953. She received vocal training at the Royal College of Music in London. Following her debut at the London Promenade Concerts in 1979, she sang in Aldeburgh, Bath, Edinburgh, Bologna, Warsaw, Salzburg, and other European music centers. In 1983 she made her U.S. debut with the San Diego Sym. Orch., and subsequently appeared with other major U.S. orchs. In 1985 she was engaged to sing for various Bach, Handel, and Scarlatti tercentenary concerts. That same year, she appeared in the premiere of Colin Matthews's *Night's Mask* at the Aldeburgh Festival. Her operatic repertoire includes roles by Monteverdi and Handel, and her concert repertoire ranges from Bach to Britten.

L

La Barbara, Joan (Linda née **Lotz**), American composer and experimental vocalist; b. Philadelphia, June 8, 1947. She learned piano from her grandfather and later sang in church and school choirs, and joined a folk music group. She studied voice with Helen Boatwright at the Syracuse Univ. School of Music (1965–68) and music education at N.Y. Univ. (B.S., 1970); she also studied voice with Phyllis Curtin at the Berkshire Music Center at Tanglewood (summers 1967–68) and with Marion Szekely-Freschl at the Juilliard School in New York. In 1971 she made her debut as a vocalist at N.Y.'s Town Hall with Steve Reich and Musicians, with whom she continued to perform until 1974; also worked with Philip Glass (1973–76). She toured in the United States and Europe; in 1979 she was composer-in-residence in West Berlin under the aegis of the Deutscher Akademischer Austauschdienst; she taught voice and composition at the Calif. Inst. of the Arts in Valencia (1981–86). In 1979 she married **Morton Subotnick**. A champion of contemporary music, she developed her performing talents to a high degree; her vocal techniques include multiphonics and circular breathing, with unique throat clicks and a high flutter to match. Her compositions, often incorporating electronics, effectively exploit her vocal abilities. Among her numerous awards and fellowships are NEA grants (1979, 1982, 1986, 1988, 1989, 1991) and ASCAP and ISCM commissions; also numerous radio commissions. La Barbara has collaborated on interdisciplinary projects with visual artists, including Lita Albuquerque, Judy Chicago, Kenneth Goldsmith, et al.; she has also given numerous first performances of works written for her by American composers, including Robert Ashley, John Cage, Charles Dodge, Morton Feldman, Daniel Lentz et al. In 1993 she appeared in the N.Y. premiere of Subotnick's opera, *Jacob's Room*, and in 1994 in the N.Y. premiere of Robert Ashley's quartet of operas, *Now Eleanor's Idea*.

WORKS: DRAMATIC: *Twelvesong*, radio work (Radio Bremen, Nov. 1, 1977; also for Voice and Tape, Bremen, May 6, 1978); *Erin*, radio work (1980; also for Voice and Tape, Paris, June 21, 1980); *Prologue* to *The Book of Knowing . . . (and) of Overthrowing*, aria for Voice and Tape with Visual Environment and Costumes, based on female creation myths of 6 cultures (1987–88; N.Y., July 6, 1988); *Anima*, film score for Voice, Percussion, Electronic Keyboard Synthesizers, Gamelan, Hand Drums, Cello, and Indigenous Diablo Canyon Sounds (1991; N.Y., Sept. 25, 1992); *The Misfortune of the Immortals*, interactive media opera (1994–95; in collaboration with M. Coniglio and M. Subotnick).

Labarre, Théodore (François-Joseph), eminent French harpist, conductor, and composer; b. Paris, March 5, 1805; d. there, March 9, 1870. He studied privately with Cousineau, Bochsa, and Nadermann, then at the Paris Cons. with Dourlen, Eler, Fétis, and Boieldieu. From 1824 to 1847 he lived alternately in London and Paris, then was a conductor at the Paris Opéra Comique (1847–49). He was made director of the imperial chapel in 1852, and in 1867 a prof. at the Paris Cons. He publ. a *Méthode complète pour la harpe* (Paris, 1844). He wrote operas, ballets, harp pieces, and songs.

Labbette, Dora, English soprano; b. Purley, March 4, 1898; d. there, Sept. 3, 1984. She received training at the Guildhall School of Music in London. From 1917 she was active as an oratorio singer and recitalist. After making her operatic debut as Telaire in Rameau's *Castor et Pollux* in Oxford (1934), she took Beecham's advice and adopted the professional name of Lisa Perli. In 1935 she made her debut at London's Covent Garden as Mimi. In 1937 she made guest appearances in Berlin, Munich, and Dresden, and then sang once more at Covent Garden until 1939. Her final London engagement was as Mimi at the Sadler's Wells Theatre in 1943. Among her other admired roles were Marguerite, Mignon, Desdemona, and Mélisande.

Labey, Marcel, French conductor and composer; b. Le Vésinet, Seine-et-Oise, Aug. 6, 1875; d. Nancy, Nov. 25, 1968. He studied law in Paris, receiving his degree in 1898, then turned his attention to music, studying piano with Delaborde, harmony with Lenormand, and composition with d'Indy at the Paris Schola Cantorum. He taught piano there, and at d'Indy's death (1931), became director; he was also director of the Cesar Franck School (from

1935). He wrote music in a late Romantic style, numbering among his works the opera *Bérengère* (1912; Le Havre, April 12, 1929).

Labia, Fausta, Italian soprano, sister of **Maria Labia**; b. Verona, April 3, 1870; d. Rome, Oct. 6, 1935. She studied with her mother and with Aldighieri. After making her operatic debut as Alice in *Robert le diable* in Verona (1892), she sang in Stockholm (1893–95) and Lisbon (1895–96); she then appeared in various Italian opera centers, including Milan's La Scala and Rome's Teatro Costanzi (1901). She sang in Barcelona (1904–05) and made her last stage appearance in Buenos Aires (1912); she subsequently taught in Rome. In 1907 she married the tenor Emilio Perea. She wrote the method *L'arte del respiro nella recitazione e nel canto* (1936).

Labia, Maria, noted Italian soprano, sister of **Fausta Labia**; b. Verona, Feb. 14, 1880; d. Malcesine del Garda, Feb. 10, 1953. She received her musical education from her mother. Following concert engagements in Milan, Verona, and Padua (1902), and in Russia and Sweden (1903–04), she made her operatic debut as Mimi in Stockholm on May 19, 1905. She scored a remarkable success as Tosca at Berlin's Komische Oper (1907), continuing to sing there until 1911. Among her other notable roles there were Carmen, Thaïs, and Salome. She appeared as Tosca in her debut with the Manhattan Opera on Nov. 9, 1908. After a season there, she continued her career in Europe with engagements in Paris, Vienna, and Milan. She was arrested as a German agent by the Italian authorities in 1916 and spent a year in prison in Ancona. After the close of World War I, she resumed her career in Rome (1919); she subsequently became closely associated with the role of Felice in Wolf-Ferrari's *I quatro rusteghi*, which she sang many times from 1922 until 1936. After teaching at the Warsaw Cons. (1930–34), she gave instruction in Rome and Siena. She wrote *Guardare indietro: Che fatica* (1950).

Labinsky, Andrei (Markovich), Russian tenor; b. Kharkov, July 26, 1871; d. Moscow, Aug. 8, 1941. He went to St. Petersburg, where he joined the chorus of the Maryinsky Theater. Following studies with Gabel, he made his operatic debut at the Maryinsky Theater in 1897, where he sang regularly from 1899 to 1912. In 1907 he created the role of Vsevolod in Rimsky-Korsakov's *Kitezh* there. From 1912 to 1924 he was a member of the Bolshoi Theater in Moscow. He taught at the Moscow Cons. from 1920. His finest roles included Don José, Lohengrin, Berendey in *The Snow Maiden*, Sinodal in *The Demon*, and Sobinin in *A Life for the Czar*.

Lablache, Luigi, famous Italian bass of French and Irish descent; b. Naples, Dec. 6, 1794; d. there, Jan. 23, 1858. He was admitted at 12 to the Cons. della Pietà dei Turchini in Naples, where he studied with Valesi. He commenced his operatic career as a buffo napoletano in Fioravanti's *La Molinara* at the Teatro San Carlino there (1812), then studied in Messina, where he appeared as a buffo; he was made primo basso cantante in Palermo (1813). He gained acclaim at his La Scala debut in Milan as Dandini in Rossini's *La Cenerentola* (1817), and continued to sing there until 1823; he also sang in Rome, Turin, and Venice. He then became a principal member of Barbaja's Vienna opera enterprise (1824); Ferdinand I of Naples made him a member of the royal chapel and the Teatro San Carlo in Naples. He scored a triumphant London debut at the King's Theatre as Geronimo in Cimarosa's *Il matrimonio segreto* (March 30, 1830), and continued to appear there every year until 1852 (1833–34 excepted). He made his Paris debut as Geronimo at the Théâtre-Italien (Nov. 4, 1830), where he was a great favorite until 1851; he created the roles of Sir George Walton in Bellini's *I Puritani* (Jan. 25, 1835), and Marino Faliero (March 12, 1835) and Don Pasquale (Jan. 3, 1843) in Donizetti's operas, ensuring his success with Paris audiences. During one of his stays in England (1836–37), he served as singing teacher to Princess Victoria. He was a principal singer of Gye's company at Covent Garden (1854) until his retirement from the stage owing to ill health (1856). Although he was best known for his buffo roles, he was capable of remarkable serious portrayals as well.

BIBL.: F. Castil-Blaze, *Biographie de L.* (Paris, 1850); G. Widén, *L. L.* (Göteborg, 1897).

La Borde (Laborde), Jean-Benjamin (-François) de, French violinist, composer, and writer on music; b. Paris, Sept. 5, 1734; d. there (guillotined), July 22, 1794. He studied violin with Dauvergne and composition with Rameau. He was chamberlain to Louis XV, and a member of the Compagnie des Fermiers-Généraux; he then withdrew from the court and devoted himself to composition. He wrote about 30 stage pieces, mostly opéras comiques, and many chansons; also an *Essai sur la musique ancienne et moderne* (Paris, 1780); *Mémoires historiques sur Raoul de Coucy [with] recueil de ses chansons en vieux langage, avec la traduction et l'ancienne musique* (Paris, 1781); *Mémoires sur les proportions musicales, le genre énarmonique . . . avec une lettre de l'auteur de l'Essai à M. l'Abbé Roussier* (Paris, 1781).

Labroca, Mario, Italian composer; b. Rome, Nov. 22, 1896; d. there, July 1, 1973. He studied composition with Malipiero and Respighi, and graduated from the Parma Cons. in 1921. He was manager of the Teatro Comunale in Florence (1936–44), artistic director of La Scala in Milan (1947–49), director of the music dept. of the RAI (1949–58), and artistic director of the Teatro La Fenice in Venice (from 1959); he also lectured at the Univ. of Perugia (from 1960). His works include the operas *La Principessa di Perepepe* (Rome, Dec. 11, 1927) and *Le tre figliole di Babbo Pallino* (Rome, Jan. 27, 1928); also many theater and film scores.

Laburda, Jiří, Czech composer; b. Soběslav, April 3, 1931. He received private training in composition from Karel Hába and Zdeněk Hůla and in musicology from Eduard Herzog and took courses in music education and philology at the Charles Univ. in Prague (1952–55); after studies at the Prague Teacher Training College (1957–61), he returned to the Charles Univ., where he took his Ph.D. (1970, with a diss. on Shostakovich's syms.) and subsequently served on its faculty. His works follow along traditional paths with infusions of aleatory and dodecaphonic writing; his vocal and chamber pieces are particularly effective. Among his works are the opera *Red Tape and Rival Divas* (Iowa City, Oct. 17, 1993) and the ballet *Les Petits Riens* (1967; Liberec, March 15, 1986).

Laccetti, Guido, Italian singer and composer; b. Naples, Oct. 1, 1879; d. Cava dei Tirreni, Oct. 8, 1943. He studied at the Naples Cons. From 1925 he taught at the Palermo Cons. His works included the operas *La Contessa di San Remo* (1904), *Hoffmann* (Naples, 1912), *Il miracolo* (Naples, 1915), *Carnasciali* (Rome, 1925), and *La favola dei gobbi* (1935).

Lachenmann, Helmut Friedrich, German composer and pedagogue; b. Stuttgart, Nov. 27, 1935. He was a student of Jürgen Uhde (piano) and J. N. David (theory and counterpoint) at the Stuttgart Staatliche Hochschule für Musik (1955–58), and of Nono (composition) in Venice (1958–60); he then pursued research at the electronic studio at the Univ. of Ghent (1965). He taught theory at the Stuttgart Hochschule für Musik (1966–70), and then music at the Ludwigsburg Pädagogische Hochschule (1970–76). He also served as coordinator of the composition studio at the Darmstadt Internationale Ferienkurse (1972) and led a master class in composition at the Univ. of Basel (1972–73). In 1976 he became a teacher at the Hannover Hochschule für Musik. He also taught at the Ferienkurse in Darmstadt (1978, 1982). From 1981 he taught at the Stuttgart Hochschule für Musik. Among his honors are the cultural prize for music of Munich (1965), the composition prize of Stuttgart (1968), and the Bach prize of Hamburg (1972). He is also a member of the Akademie der Künste in Berlin, the Akademie der Schönen Künste in Munich, and the Freie Akademie der Künste in Mannheim. While producing works based upon structural techniques, he has made it his central aim as a composer to create scores free of societal expectations. His works include *Das Mädchen mit den Schwefelhölzern*, music theater (Hamburg, Jan 26, 1997).

Lachner, family of German musicians, all brothers:

(1) Theodor Lachner, organist and composer; b. Rain-am-Lech, 1788; d. Munich, May 23, 1877. He served as Munich court organist throughout most of his career and was known as a composer of choral music and lieder.

(2) Franz Paul Lachner, conductor and composer; b. Rain-am-Lech, April 2, 1803; d. Munich, Jan. 20, 1890. He studied piano and organ with his father, Anton Lachner, the town organist. He then went to Vienna, where he studied with Sechter and Stadler; he became a close friend of Schubert, and also came to know Beethoven. He was made organist of the Lutheran church (1823), then was assistant conductor (1827–29) and principal conductor (1829–34) of the Kärnthnertortheater. He was conductor of the Mannheim National Theater (1834–36), then court conductor (1836–52) and Generalmusikdirektor (1852–65) in Munich.

WORKS: DRAMATIC: OPERAS: *Die Bürgschaft* (Pest, Oct. 30, 1828); *Alidia* (Munich, April 12, 1839); *Catarina Cornaro* (Munich, Dec. 3, 1841); *Benvenuto Cellini* (Munich, Oct. 7, 1849). Also *Moses*, oratorio (1833).

BIBL.: G. Wagner, *F. L. als Liederkomponist, nebst einem biographischen Teil und dem thematischen Verzeichnis sämtlicher Lieder* (diss., Univ. of Mainz, 1969).

(3) Ignaz Lachner, organist, conductor, and composer; b. Rain-am-Lech, Sept. 11, 1807; d. Hannover, Feb. 24, 1895. He studied with his father and then in Vienna (1824) with his brother Franz, whom he succeeded as organist of the Lutheran church; he was assistant conductor of the Kärnthnertortheater (1825–28) and the Court Opera (1828–31) there. He was court conductor in Stuttgart (1831–36) and Munich (1836–53), conductor of the Hamburg Opera (1853–58), then court conductor in Stockholm (1858–61); he subsequently was principal conductor in Frankfurt am Main (1861–75). He composed the operas *Der Geisterturm* (Stuttgart, 1837), *Die Regenbrüder* (Stuttgart, May 20, 1839), and *Loreley* (Munich, 1846); also Singspiels, other dramatic works; and ballets.

BIBL.: H. Müller, *I. L.: Versuch einer Würdigung, mit Werkverzeichnis* (Celle, 1974).

(4) Vincenz Lachner, organist, conductor, and composer; b. Rain-am-Lech, July 19, 1811; d. Karlsruhe, Jan. 22, 1893. He studied with his father and then with his brothers in Vienna, succeeding Ignaz as organist of the Lutheran church and Franz as conductor of the Kärnthnertortheater (1834) and at the Mannheim National Theater (1836). He conducted the German Opera in London (1842), then became conductor of the Frankfurt am Main Opera (1848); he was pensioned in 1872. From 1884 he taught at the Karlsruhe Cons. As a composer, he was best known for his 4-part male choruses.

Lachnith, Ludwig Wenzel, Bohemian horn player and composer; b. Prague, July 7, 1746; d. Paris, Oct. 3, 1820. He studied violin, harpsichord, and horn, then joined the orch. in Pfalz-Zweibrücken; about 1780 he went to Paris and studied with Rodolphe (horn) and F. A. Philidor (composition). He is known chiefly for his pasticcios; an instance is his oratorio *Saul* (April 6, 1803), with music taken from scores by Mozart, Haydn, Cimarosa, Paisiello, Gossec, and Philidor. He also arranged the music of Mozart's *Die Zauberflöte*, to a libretto reworked by Étienne Morel de Chefdeville, and produced it under the title *Les Mystères d'Isis* (Aug. 20, 1801), justly parodied as *Les Misères d'ici*. In several of his ventures he had the older Kalkbrenner as his collaborator. Among his original works were the operas *L'Heureuse Réconciliation* (June 25, 1785) and *Eugénie et Linval* (1798).

Lacombe, Louis (Trouillon), French pianist and composer; b. Bourges, Nov. 26, 1818; d. Saint-Vaast-la-Hougue, Sept. 30, 1884. He studied piano at the Paris Cons. with Zimmerman, winning the premier prix at the age of 13. After touring through France, Belgium, and Germany, he took courses with Czerny, Sechter, and Seyfried in Vienna. Following another concert tour, he settled in Paris (1839), concentrating on composition. His essay *Philosophie et musique* was publ. posth. (Paris, 1895).

WORKS: DRAMATIC: *L'Amour*, melodrama (Paris, Dec. 2, 1859); *La Madone*, opera (Paris, Jan. 16, 1861); *Le Tonnelier de Nuremberg*, comic opera (perf. as *Meister Martin und seine Gesellen*, Koblenz, March 7, 1897); *Winkelried*, opera (Geneva, Feb. 17, 1892); *La Reine des eaux*, opera (perf. as *Die Korrigane*, Sondershausen, March 12?, 1901); *Der Kreuzritter*, comic opera (Sondershausen, March 21, 1902).

BIBL.: E. Bourdin, *La Musique et les musiciens: L. L.* (Paris, 1882); H. Boyer, *L. L. et son oeuvre* (Paris, 1888); L. Gallet, *Conférence sur L. L. et son oeuvre* (Paris, 1891); E. Jongleux, *Un Grand Musicien méconnu: L. L.* (Bourges, 1935).

Lacome (Lacôme d'Estalenx), Paul (-Jean-Jacques), French composer; b. Le Houga, Gers, March 4, 1838; d. there, Dec. 12, 1920. He studied with José Puig y Absubide, organist in Aire-sur-Adour (1857–60), then went to Paris, where he became known as a composer of operettas, including *Jeanne, Jeannette et Jeannot* (Paris, Oct. 27, 1876) and *Ma Mie Rosette* (Paris, Feb. 4, 1890).

Laderman, Ezra, notable American composer and teacher; b. N.Y., June 29, 1924. He studied at the High School of Music and Art in New York, where he appeared as soloist in the premiere of his 1st Piano Concerto with the school orch. in 1939. He pursued his training in composition with Wolpe in New York (1946–49) and with Gideon at Brooklyn College of the City Univ. of N.Y. (B.A., 1949), and took courses with Leuning and Moore (composition) and Lang (musicology) at Columbia Univ. (M.A., 1952). In 1955, 1958, and 1964 he was awarded Guggenheim fellowships. In 1960–61 he taught at Sarah Lawrence College. After holding the American Prix de Rome (1963–64), he again taught at Sarah Lawrence College (1965–66). From 1971 to 1982 he was composer-in-residence and prof. at the State Univ. of N.Y. in Binghamton. He was also president of the American Music Center (1973–76) and director of the music program of the NEA (1979–82). In 1982–83 he was active at the American Academy in Rome. From 1987 to 1989 he was president of the American Music Council. He was dean of the Yale Univ. School of Music (1989–95), and then was a prof. of music there (from 1995). After composing in a tonal style, Laderman turned to atonal, and later serial writing. Later in his career he came full circle by again exploring the resources of tonality in a synthetic form, utilizing a vast array of techniques and styles.

WORKS: DRAMATIC: OPERAS: *Jacob and the Indians* (1954; Woodstock, N.Y., July 24, 1957); *Goodbye to the Clowns* (1956; N.Y., May 22, 1960); *The Hunting of the Snark*, opera cantata (1958; concert premiere, N.Y., March 26, 1961; stage premiere, N.Y., April 13, 1978); *Sarah* (CBS-TV, Nov. 30, 1958); *Air Raid* (1965); *Shadows Among Us* (1967); *And David Wept*, opera cantata (1970; CBS-TV, April 11, 1971); *The Questions of Abraham*, opera cantata (CBS-TV, Sept. 30, 1973); *Galileo Galilei* (1978; Binghamton, N.Y., Feb. 3, 1979; based on the oratorio *The Trials of Galileo*); *Marilyn* (N.Y., Oct. 6, 1993). MUSICAL COMEDY: *Dominique* (1962). DANCE: Duet for Flute and Dancer (1956); *Dance Quartet* for Flute, Clarinet, Cello, and Dancer (1957); *Esther* for Narrator, Oboe, and String Orch. (1960); *Song of Songs* for Soprano and Piano (1960); *Solos and Chorale* for 4 Mixed Voices (1960). INCIDENTAL MUSIC: *Machinal* (N.Y., April 7, 1960); *The Lincoln Mask* (N.Y., Oct. 30, 1972); numerous film and television scores. ORATORIOS: *The Eagle Stirred* for Soloists, Chorus, and Orch. (1961); *The Trials of Galileo* for Soloists, Chorus, and Orch. (1967; reworked into the opera *Galileo Galilei*); *A Mass for Cain* for Soloists, Chorus, and Orch. (1983).

Ladmirault, Paul (-Émile), French composer and teacher; b. Nantes, Dec. 8, 1877; d. Kerbili en Kamoel, St. Nazaire, Oct. 30, 1944. As a child, he studied piano, organ, and violin; he entered the Nantes Cons. in 1892, winning 1st prize in 1893. He was only 15 when his opera *Gilles de Retz* was staged in Nantes (May 18, 1893); he entered the Paris Cons. in 1895, studying with Tardou (harmony), Fauré (composition), and Gédalge (counterpoint and fugue); he subsequently returned to Nantes, where he taught at the Cons. His *Suite bretonne* (1902–03) and symphonic prelude *Brocéliande au matin* (Paris, Nov. 28, 1909) were extracts from a 2d opera, *Myrdhin* (1902–09), which was never performed; the ballet *La Prêtresse de Koridwen* was premiered at the Paris Opéra (Dec. 17, 1926). Other works included the operetta *Glycère* (Paris, 1928) and incidental music to *Tristan et Iseult* (1929).

Ladurner, Ignace Antoine (François Xavier) (Ignaz Anton Franz Xaver Joseph), Austrian pianist, teacher, and composer of Tirolean descent; b. Aldein, near Bolzano, Aug. 1, 1766; d. Villain, near Massy, March 4, 1839. He studied with his uncle at the Benediktbeuren monastery, and succeeded his father as organist in Algund; he then studied at the Lyceum Gregorianum in Munich. He subsequently became a pianist in the service of Countess Heimhausen in Longeville. In 1788 he settled in Paris, where he became active as a teacher; taught piano at the Paris Cons. (1797–1802); he settled in Villain (1836). He wrote the operas *Wenzel, ou Le Magistrat du peuple* (Paris, April 10, 1793) and *Les Vieux Fous, ou Plus de peur que de mal* (Paris, Jan. 15 or 16, 1796).

La Forge, Frank, American pianist, teacher, and composer; b. Rockford, Ill., Oct. 22, 1879; d. while playing at a dinner given by the Musicians Club in New York, May 5, 1953. He first had piano lessons with his sister; after studies with Harrison Wild in Chicago (1896–1900), he completed his training in Vienna with Leschetizky, Labor, and Navrátil. He was active in Berlin as a soloist, accompanist, and piano teacher. After touring Europe as accompanist to Sembrich, he appeared in the United States with Gadski. Subsequently he was active as accompanist to many of the celebrated artists of the day, gaining distinction for playing his part entirely from memory. In later years, he also was active as a vocal teacher, numbering Marian Anderson, Richard Crooks, and Lawrence Tibbett among his students. He was an accomplished composer of songs, among them "To a Messenger," "I Came with a Song," "Before the Crucifix," "Like a Rosebud," "When Your Dear Hands," and "Song of the Open," and also wrote piano pieces and publ. practical eds. of selections from the vocal repertoire.

La Garde, Pierre de, French composer and baritone; b. near Crécy-en-Brie, Seine-et-Marne, Feb. 1717; d. c.1792. He served as an ordinaire de la chambre du roi and was in charge of the musical education of the children of Louis XV. After serving as assistant conductor at the Paris Opéra (1750–55), he was made compositeur de la chambre du roi in 1756. He later was director of the concerts for the Count of Artois. His most successful stage work was the pastorale héroïque *Aeglé* (Versailles, Jan. 13, 1748). He also wrote the pastorale héroïque *Silvie* (Versailles, Feb. 26, 1749), the opéra ballet *La journée galante* (Versailles, Feb. 25, 1750), the divertissement comique *L'impromptu de la cour de marbe* (Bellevue, Nov. 28, 1751), several notable cantatas and cantatilles, and airs of great popular vogue.

Lagger, Peter, Swiss bass; b. Buchs, Sept. 7, 1930; d. Berlin, Sept. 17, 1979. He studied at the Zürich Cons. and with Hans Duhan in Vienna. In 1953 he made his operatic debut in Graz, and appeared there until 1955; he then sang in Zürich (1955–57), Wiesbaden (1957–59), and Frankfurt am Main (1959–63); from 1963 he was a leading member of the Berlin Deutsche Oper. He made appearances in Hamburg, Vienna, Paris, and Geneva, and also at the Salzburg, Aix-en-Provence, and Glyndebourne festivals. His extensive operatic, concert, and lieder repertoire extended from Bach to Henze.

Lagoanère, Oscar de, French conductor and composer; b. Bordeaux, Aug. 25, 1853; d. Paris, May 23, 1918. He studied at the Paris Cons. with Marmontel, Duprato, and Savard. From 1876 to 1908 he conducted operettas at various theaters in Paris; from 1908 to 1914 he was administrator and director of music at the Théâtre de la Gaîté. He was a prolific composer of operettas, the most successful of which were *Le Cadeau d'Alain* (Paris, Sept. 14, 1902), *L'Habit de César* (Paris, May 14, 1906), *Amour et sport* (Paris, July 28, 1907), and *Un Ménage au violon*.

La Guerre, Élisabeth Jacquet de, French composer, organist, and clavecinist; b. Paris, 1659; d. there, June 27, 1729. A member of a family of professional musicians, she evinced talent at an exceptionally early age. She was favored by the court of Louis XIV, completing her education under the patronage of Mme. de Montespan. She married Marin de La Guerre, organist of several Paris churches. Her works include an opera, *Céphale et Procris* (Paris, March 15, 1694), and a ballet (1691).

BIBL.: C. Cessac, *E. J. de L. G.: Une femme compositeur sous le règne de Louis XIV* (Arles, 1995).

La Houssaye, Pierre (-Nicolas), French violinist and composer; b. Paris, April 11, 1735; d. there, 1818. He studied violin with Pagin, and later in Padua with Tartini. He played in the Court Orch. of Parma; in 1768, went to London with Guglielmi. Returning to Paris, he was concertmaster and conductor of the Concert Spirituel (1777–81), of the Comédie-Italienne (1781–90), then at the Théâtre de Monsieur (1790–1801); he also taught at the Paris Cons. (1795–1802). He publ. an accomplished vol. of *Sei sonate* for Violin and Bass (Paris, c.1774). He also wrote the comic opera *Les Amours de Courcy* (Théâtre de Monsieur, Aug. 22, 1790); his other works are not extant.

Lajarte, Théodore (-Édouard Dufaure de), French writer on music and composer; b. Bordeaux, July 10, 1826; d. Paris, June 20, 1890. He studied at the Paris Cons. with Leborne, then was archivist of the Paris Grand Opéra (1873–90). He wrote some 10 opéras comiques, the most successful being *Le Secret de l'oncle Vincent* (1855), and 2 ballets. However, he is best known for his writings; he also prepared *Airs à danser de Lully à Méhul* (Paris, 1876), *Chefs-d'oeuvre classiques de l'opéra français* (Paris, 1880), and various vocal scores for the Michaelis collection (1880–82).

WRITINGS: *Bibliothèque musicale du théâtre de l'opera: Catalogue historique, chronologique, anecdotique* (2 vols., Paris, 1876–78); *Instruments Sax et fanfares civiles* (Paris, 1867); with A. Bisson, *Grammaire de la musique* (Paris, 1880; 3d ed., 1913); idem, *Petit traité de composition musicale* (Paris, 1881); idem, *Petite encyclopédie musicale* (Paris, 1881–84); *Les Curiosités de l'Opéra* (Paris, 1883).

Lajeunesse, Marie Louise Cecilia Emma. See **Albani, Dame Emma.**

Lajtai, Lajos, Hungarian composer; b. Budapest, April 13, 1900; d. there, Jan. 12, 1966. After training in Budapest and Vienna, he began his career writing various light theater works for the Budapest stage. His first major success came with *A régi nyár* (Once Upon a Time in Summer; June 15, 1928). Among his finest subsequent scores were *Sisters* (March 2, 1929), *Az okos mama* (The Clever Mama; Nov. 26, 1930), *"Ofelsége frakkja* (His Majesty's Overcoat; Sept. 19, 1931; rev. version as *Katinka*, Paris, Feb. 22, 1933), *A régi orfeum* (The Old Time Music Hall; March 12, 1932), and *A Rotschildok* (The Rothschilds; Nov. 25, 1932). After a sojourn in Paris, Lajtai made his home in Sweden to escape the deprivations of World War II.

Lakes, Gary, American tenor; b. Dallas, Sept. 26, 1950. He studied with Thomas Hayward at Southern Methodist Univ. in Dallas and sang in the Dallas Opera Chorus; he also attended the Music Academy of the West in Santa Barbara, California, and pursued extensive vocal training with William Eddy at the Seattle Opera, where he made his professional operatic debut as Froh in 1981. After winning the Heldentenor Foundation competition in New York, he appeared as Florestan in Mexico City (1983), Samson in Charlotte, N.C. (1984), and Siegmund in Act I of *Die Walküre* in Paris (1985) before making his Metropolitan Opera debut in New York as the High Priest in *Idomeneo* (Feb. 4, 1986). In return visits to the Metropolitan Opera, he sang Siegmund, Bacchus, Don José, the Emperor in *Die Frau ohne Schatten*, Erik, Parsifal, and Florestan. In 1991 he sang at the London Promenade Concerts, and returned to London in 1994 to portray Berlioz's Faust. He appeared as Florestan at the Lincoln Center Festival in New York in 1996. He also sang in concerts with major orchs. in the United States and Europe.

Laks, Simon (Szymon), Polish-born French composer; b. Warsaw, Nov. 1, 1901; d. Paris, Dec. 11, 1983. He studied at the Warsaw Cons. (1921–24) with Melcer (conducting) and Statkowski (composition); he went to Paris in 1925, continuing his studies under Rabaud and Vidal at the Cons. He was interned by the Nazis in the Auschwitz and Dachau concentration camps (1941–44), where he was active as a performer and music director; after his liberation, he returned to Paris. He publ. his experiences of his internment as *La Musique d'un autre monde* (Paris, 1948; Eng. tr., 1989). His works include the opera buffa *L'Hirondelle inattendue* (1965).

La Laurencie, (Marie Bertrand) Lionel (Jules), Comte de, important French musicologist; b. Nantes, July 24, 1861; d. Paris, Nov. 21, 1933. After studying law and science, he became a pupil of Léon Reynier (violin) and Alphonse Weingartner (harmony) and of Bougault-Ducoudray at the Paris Cons. In 1898 he became a lecturer at the École des Hautes Études Sociales. He contributed regularly to several music journals. In 1916 he became ed. of Lavignac's *Encyclopédie de la musique et dictionnaire du Conservatoire*, to which he contributed articles on French music of the 17th and 18th centuries. The *Catalogue des livres de musiciens de la bibliothèque de l'Arsénal à Paris*, ed. by L. Laurencie and A. Gastoué, was publ. in 1936.

WRITINGS: *La Légende de Parsifal et la drame musical de Richard Wagner* (1888–94); *España* (1890); *Le Goût musical en France* (1905); *L'Académie de musique et le concert de Nantes* (1908); *Rameau* (1908); *Lully* (1911); *Les Créatures de l'opéra français* (1920; 2d ed., 1930); *L'École française de violon, de Lully à Viotti* (3 vols., 1922–24); *Les Luthistes* (1928); *La Chanson royale en France* (1928); *Inventaire critique du fonds Blancheton à la Bibliothèque du Conservatoire* (2 vols., 1920–31); with Thibault and Mairy, *Chansons du luth et airs du XVI*[e] *siècle* (1931); *Orfée de Gluck* (1934).

BIBL.: *Mélanges de musicologie offerts à M. L. d.l.L.* (Paris, 1933).

La Liberté, (Joseph-François) Alfred, Canadian pianist, teacher, and composer; b. St.-Jean, Quebec, Feb. 10, 1882; d. Montreal, May 7, 1952. After initial training in Canada, he studied at the Stern Cons. in Berlin (1902–06) with Lutzenko (piano), Baeker (harmony), and Klatte (counterpoint and composition). Following a successful recital debut in Montreal in 1906, he met Scriabin in New York in 1907, who suggested that he pursue his piano training with Carreño in Berlin. Subsequently he became Scriabin's student in Brussels. Upon returning to Montreal in 1911, he became active as a teacher and as a champion of Scriabin's music. He also became an advocate of the music of Madtner and Dupré. Among La Liberté's own works was the opera *Soeur Béatrice* (piano score only).

Lalo, Charles, French aesthetician; b. Périgueux, Feb. 24, 1877; d. Paris, April 1, 1953. He studied aesthetics and philosophy in Bayonne, and then at the Univ. of Paris (Ph.D., 1908, with 2 dissertations: *Esquisse d'une esthétique musicale scientifique*; publ. in Paris, 1908; 2d ed., aug., 1939 as *Éléments d'une esthétique*; and *L'Esthétique expérimentale contemporaine*; publ. in Paris, 1908). He lectured at the Univ. of Bordeaux, then taught aesthetics and art history at the Sorbonne in Paris (1933–53); he was also president of the Société Française d'Esthétique.

WRITINGS (all publ. in Paris): *Les Sentiments esthétiques* (1910); *Introduction à l'esthétique* (1912; 4th ed., rev., 1952 as *Notions de philosophie, notions d'esthétique*); *L'Art et la vie sociale* (1921); *La Beauté et l'instinct sexuel* (1922); *L'Art et la morale* (1922); *L'Expression de la vie dans l'art* (1933); *L'Art loin de la vie* (1939); *L'Economie des passions* (1947); *Les Grandes Évasions esthétiques* (1947).

Lalo, Édouard (-Victoire-Antoine), distinguished French composer of Spanish descent, father of **Pierre Lalo**; b. Lille, Jan. 27, 1823; d. Paris, April 22, 1892. He studied violin and cello at the Lille Cons. After his father objected to his pursuing a career as a professional musician, he left home at age 16 to study violin with Habeneck at the Paris Cons.; he also studied composition privately with Schulhoff and Crèvecoeur. He then made a precarious living as a violinist and teacher; also began to compose, producing some songs and chamber music between 1848 and 1860. In the meantime, he became a founding member of the Armingaud Quartet (1855), serving first as a violist and subsequently as 2d violinist. Since his own works met with indifference, he was discouraged to the point of abandoning composition after 1860. However, his marriage to the contralto Bernier de Maligny (1865), who sang many of his songs, prompted him to resume composition. He wrote an opera, *Fiesque*, and sent it to a competition sponsored by the Théâtre-Lyrique in Paris in 1867. It was refused a production, a rebuke that left him deeply embittered. He was so convinced of the intrinsic worth of the score that he subsequently reworked parts of it into various other works, including the 1st *Aubade* for Small Orch., the *Divertissement*, and the Sym. in G minor. Indeed, the *Divertissement* proved a remarkable success when it was introduced at the Concert Populaire (Paris, Dec. 8, 1872). Sarasate then gave the premiere performance of his Violin Concerto (Paris, Jan. 18, 1874), and subsequently of his *Symphonie espagnole* for Violin and Orch. (Paris, Feb. 7, 1875). The latter work, a brilliant virtuoso piece with vibrant Spanish rhythms, brought Lalo international fame. It remains his best-known composition outside his native country. While continuing to produce orch. works, he had not given up his intention to write for the stage. In 1875 he began work on the opera *Le Roi d'Ys*. The major portion of the score was finished by 1881, which allowed extracts to be performed in concerts. However, no theater was interested in mounting a production. While pursuing his work on several orch. pieces, he accepted a commission from the Opéra to write a ballet. Although the resulting work, *Namouna* (Paris, March 6, 1882), failed to make an impression, he drew a series of orch. suites from it, which became quite popular. He finally succeeded in persuading the Paris Opéra Comique to produce *Le Roi d'Ys*. Its premiere on May 7, 1888, was an enormous success. Lalo was rewarded by being made an Officer of the Legion of Honor (1888). While *Le Roi d'Ys* is considered his masterpiece by his countrymen, his instrumental music is of particular importance in assessing his achievement as a composer. His craftsmanship, combined with his originality, places him among the most important French composers of his time.

WORKS: DRAMATIC: *Fiesque*, opera (1866–67; not perf.; parts of the score subsequently used in various other works); *Namouna*, ballet (1881–82; Opéra, Paris, March 6, 1882; also made into a series of orch. suites); *Le Roi d'Ys*, opera (1875–88; Opéra Comique, Paris, May 7, 1888); *Néron*, pantomime with Chorus (1891; Hippodrome, Paris, March 28, 1891; based on *Fiesque* and other works); *La Jacquerie*, opera (1891–92; Monte Carlo, March 9, 1895; Act 1 only; finished by A. Coquard).

BIBL.: M. Dufour, *É. L.* (Lille, 1908); H. Malherbe, *É. L., conférence prononcée . . . 23 décembre, 1920* (Paris, 1921).

Lalo, Pierre, French music critic, son of **Édouard (-Victoire-Antoine) Lalo**; b. Puteaux, Sept. 6, 1866; d. Paris, June 9, 1943. He studied literature and philosophy; he also took courses in modern languages at the École de Chartes and the École Polytechnique. He began writing music criticism for the *Journal des débats* (1896), then was music critic of *Le Temps* (1898–1914). He became known as a caustic critic of Debussy.

WRITINGS: *La Musique* (Paris, 1898–99; a selection of his articles); *Richard Wagner ou le Nibelung* (Paris, 1933); *De Rameau à Ravel: Portraits et souvenirs* (Paris, 1947).

Laloy, Louis, French musicologist and music critic; b. Grey, Haute-Saône, Feb. 18, 1874; d. Dôle, March 3, 1944. He settled in Paris, where he studied at the École Normale Supérieure (1893; agrégé des lettres, 1896; docteur ès lettres, 1904, with the diss. *Aristoxène de Tarente et la musique de l'antiquité*); he also studied with Bordes, Breéille, and d'Indy at the Schola Cantorum (1899–1905). He was cofounder of the *Revue d'Histoire et de Critique Musicale* (1901), the *Mercure musicale* (1905), and the *L'année musicale* (1911); contributed articles to *Revue de Paris,*

Grande Revue, Mercure de France, and *Gazette des Beaux-Arts*. He lectured at the Sorbonne; also was prof. of music history at the Paris Cons. (1936–41).

WRITINGS (all publ. in Paris unless otherwise given): *Jean Philippe Rameau* (1908; 3d ed., 1919); *Claude Debussy* (1909; 2d ed., 1944); *La Musique chinoise* (1910); *The Future of Music* (London, 1910); *La danse à l'Opéra* (1927); *La Musique retrouvée, 1902–1927* (1928); *Une Heure de musique avec Beethoven* (1930); *Comment écouter la musique* (1942).

Lambert, (Leonard) Constant, remarkable English conductor, composer, and writer on music; b. London, Aug. 23, 1905; d. there, Aug. 21, 1951. He won a scholarship to the Royal College of Music in London, where he studied with R. O. Morris and Vaughan Williams (1915–22). His first major score, the ballet *Romeo and Juliet* (1924–25; Monte Carlo, May 4, 1926), was commissioned by Diaghilev. This early association with the dance proved decisive, for he spent most of his life as a conductor and composer of ballets. Of his many ballets, the most striking in craftsmanship was *Horoscope* (1937; London, Jan. 27, 1938, composer conducting); other ballets were *Pomona* (1926; Buenos Aires, Sept. 9, 1927); *Tiresias* (1950–51; London, July 9, 1951, composer conducting). His interest in jazz resulted in such fine scores as *Elegiac Blues* for Orch. (1927), *The Rio Grande* for Piano, Chorus, and Orch. (1927; to a text by S. Sitwell), and the Concerto for Piano and 9 Performers (1930–31). In the meantime, he became conductor of the Camargo Soc. for the presentation of ballet productions (1930). He was made music director of the Vic-Wells Ballet (1931), and remained in that capacity after it became the Sadler's Wells Ballet and the Royal Ballet, until resigning in 1947; he then was made one of its artistic directors (1948), and subsequently conducted it on its first visit to the United States (1949). He also appeared at London's Covent Garden (1937; 1939; 1946–47); he was assoc. conductor of the London Promenade Concerts (1945–46), and then frequently conducted broadcast performances over the BBC. He contributed articles on music to the *Nation* and *Athenaeum* (from 1930) and to the *Sunday Referee* (from 1931). He also penned the provocative book *Music Ho! A Study of Music in Decline* (London, 1934). Lambert was one of the most gifted musicians of his generation. However, his demanding work as a conductor and his excessive consumption of alcohol prevented him from fully asserting himself as a composer in his later years.

BIBL.: R. Shead, *C. L.* (London, 1973; 2d ed., rev., 1987).

Lambert, Juan Bautista, Catalan organist, conductor, and composer; b. Barcelona, 1884; d. there, May 4, 1945. He was a pupil of Pedrell and Morera (composition) and of Pellicer and Malats (piano) at the Barcelona municipal music school. He became conductor of its band, as well as of several others; he also served as organist and choirmaster in various churches and colleges, as well as censor of sacred music for the bishopric (from 1940). Lambert particularly distinguished himself as a composer of Catalan sacred music, producing 3 masses, motets, hymns, and organ pieces. Among his other works were 3 operas and 5 zarzuelas.

Lambert, Lucien, French composer and pianist; b. Paris, Jan. 5, 1858; d. Oporto, Portugal, Jan. 21, 1945. He studied first with his father; after a tour of America and Europe, he returned to Paris to study at the Cons. with Dubois and Massenet, taking the Prix Rossini in 1885 with his cantata *Prométhée enchaîné*. He settled in Portugal in 1914; was a prof. of composition at the Oporto Cons. (1922–37).

WORKS: DRAMATIC: OPERAS: *Brocéliande* (Rouen, Feb. 25, 1893); *Le Spahi* (Paris, Oct. 18, 1897); *La Marseillaise* (Paris, July 14, 1900); *La Flamenca* (Paris, Oct. 31, 1903); *Harald* (1937); *Penticosa; La Sorcière*. BALLETS: *La Roussalka* (Paris, Dec. 8, 1911); *Les Cloches de Porto* (1937). LYRIC COMEDY: *Florette* (1921).

Lammers, Gerda, esteemed German soprano; b. Berlin, Sept. 25, 1915. She studied with L. Mysz-Gmeiner and M. Schwedler-Lohmann at the Berlin Hochschule für Musik. After appearances as a concert and lieder artist (1940–55), she made her operatic debut as Ortlinde at the Bayreuth Festival (1955); that same year she made her first appearance at the Kassel State Theater as Marie in Berg's *Wozzeck*, remaining there for some 15 years. She made an acclaimed debut as Elektra at London's Covent Garden (1957), substituting on short notice for an indisposed Christel Goltz; she returned there as Kundry in 1959. She made her Metropolitan Opera debut in New York as Elektra on March 16, 1962. Her other distinguished roles included Alceste, Medea, Senta, Isolde, and Brünnhilde.

La Montaine, John, American composer and pianist; b. Oak Park, Ill., March 17, 1920. He studied piano with Muriel Parker and Margaret Farr Wilson, then received training in theory in Chicago from Stella Roberts (1935–38); he subsequently took courses in piano with Max Landow and in composition with Hanson and Rogers at the Eastman School of Music in Rochester, N.Y. (B.Mus., 1942); after further training from Rudolph Ganz at the Chicago Musical College (1945), he completed his studies in composition with Wagenaar at the Juilliard School of Music in New York and with Boulanger at the American Cons. in Fontainebleau. From 1950 to 1954 he was the pianist and celesta player in the NBC Sym. Orch. in New York. As a pianist, he often performed his own works. He received a Guggenheim fellowship (1959–60); in 1961 he was a visiting prof. of composition at the Eastman School of Music; in 1962 he served as composer-in-residence at the American Academy in Rome. He received the Pulitzer Prize in Music for his Piano Concerto No. 1 (Washington, D.C., Nov. 25, 1958) in 1959. In 1977 he was a Nixon Distinguished Scholar at Richard Nixon's alma mater, Whittier College, in California. While La Montaine's works incorporate various usages ranging from serialism to jazz, his scores reflect his penchant for accessibility and lyricism.

WORKS: OPERAS: Christmas trilogy on medieval miracle plays: *Novellis, Novellis* (Washington, D.C., Dec. 24, 1961), *The Shephardes Playe* (Washington, D.C., Dec. 27, 1967), and *Erode the Greate* (Washington, D.C., Dec. 31, 1969); *Be Glad, Then, America: A Decent Entertainment from the 13 Colonies*, bicentennial opera (Univ. Park, Pa., Feb. 6, 1976).

Lamote de Grignon, Juan, Catalan conductor and composer, father of **Ricardo Lamote de Grignon y Ribas**; b. Barcelona, July 7, 1872; d. there, March 11, 1949. He studied at the Barcelona Cons., and upon graduation, became prof. (1890) and director (1917) there. He made his debut as a conductor in Barcelona (April 26, 1902). In 1910 he founded the Orquesta Sinfónica of Barcelona, which carried on its activity until 1924; he also was founder-conductor of the Valencia Municipal Orch. (1943–49). He publ. *Musique et musiciens français à Barcelone: Musique et musiciens catalans à Paris* (Barcelona, 1935). He wrote an opera, *Hesperia* (Barcelona, Jan. 25, 1907), and an oratorio, *La Nit de Nadal*.

Lamote de Grignon y Ribas, Ricardo, Catalan cellist, conductor, and composer, son of **Juan Lamote de Grignon**; b. Barcelona, Sept. 23, 1899; d. there, Feb. 5, 1962. He studied cello and composition at the Barcelona Cons. He played cello in the Orquesta Sinfónica of Barcelona, conducted by his father; he then conducted provincial orchs. and became assistant conductor of the municipal band of Barcelona. He publ. a manual, *Síntesis de técnica musical* (Barcelona, 1948). His *Enigmas* for Orch. won the Barcelona Municipal Prize in 1951. Among his other works are the opera *La caperucita verde* and the children's opera *La flor*.

Lamoureux, Charles, noted French conductor and violinist; b. Bordeaux, Sept. 28, 1834; d. Paris, Dec. 21, 1899. He studied at the Paris Cons. with Girard (violin; premier prix, 1852, 1854), Tolbecque (harmony), Leborne (counterpoint and fugue), and Chauvet (composition). In 1850 he became solo violinist in the Théâtre du Gymnase orch., then became a member of the Paris Opéra orch. In 1860 he helped to organize the Séances Populaires de Musique de Chambre; in 1874 he organized the Société Française de l'Harmonie Sacrée; he became known as assistant conductor of the Cons. Concerts (1872–73); he was a conductor of the Paris Opéra (1877–79). He founded the celebrated Concerts Lamoureux (Nouveaux Concerts) on Oct. 23, 1881; he retired as its conductor in 1897, and was succeeded by his son-in-law, Chevillard; he also served as music director of the Opéra (1891–92). More than any other French musician, Lamoureux educated Parisians to appreciate Wagner; he was responsible not only for highly competent performances of Classical masterpieces, but also for presentation of compositions of his contemporaries. However, as a conductor, he had a reputation as an abusive and dictatorial taskmaster; he was so loathed by some of the musicians who performed under him that he carried a pistol for protection.

Lamperti, Francesco, eminent Italian singing teacher, father of **Giovanni Battista Lamperti**; b. Savona, March 11, 1811; d. Cernobbio, May 1, 1892. He studied at the Milan Cons. He was director at the Teatro Filodrammatico in Lodi and tutored many distinguished singers, including Albani, Artôt, both Cruvelis, Campanini, Collini, and Lagrange; he taught at the Milan Cons. (1850–75). He publ. *Guida teorico-pratico-elementare per lo studi del canto; Studi di bravura per soprano; Esercizi giornalieri per soprano o mezzo-soprano; L'arte del canto; Osservazioni e consigli sul trillo; Solfeggi*; etc. His methods and studies in voice production have also appeared in Eng. tr.: *Studies in Bravura Singing for the Soprano Voice* (N.Y., 1875); *A Treatise on the Art of Singing* (London, 1877; rev. ed., N.Y., 1890).

Lamperti, Giovanni Battista, Italian singing teacher, son of **Francesco Lamperti**; b. Milan, June 24, 1839; d. Berlin, March 18, 1910. At the age of 9 he was a choirboy at the Milan Cathedral. He studied piano and voice at the Milan Cons., where he served as accompanist in his father's class. He taught first in Milan, then in Dresden for 20 years, and then in Berlin. Among his pupils were Sembrich, Schumann-Heink, Bispham, and Stagno. He publ. *Die Technik des Bel Canto* (1905; Eng. tr. by T. Baker, N.Y., 1905) and *Scuola di canto* (8 vols. of solfeggi and vocalises); other technical exercises. His pupil W. E. Brown publ. *Vocal Wisdom; Maxims of G. B. Lamperti* (N.Y., 1931; new ed., 1957).

Lampugnani, Giovanni Battista, Italian composer; b. probably in Milan, 1708; d. there, June 12, 1788. He most likely received his training in Milan, where he spent the greater portion of his career. After writing operas for several Italian cities, he was active in London as resident composer at the King's Theater during the 1743–44 season. Returning to Italy, he again composed operas for several cities before taking up the post of harpsichordist at the Teatro Regio Ducale in Milan in 1758. He also became active as a singing teacher. From 1778 he was harpsichordist at the Regio Ducal Teatro alla Scala in Milan. His opera seria style was principally influenced by Hasse, while he followed the path of Galuppi in his comic operas.

WORKS: OPERAS (all are drammi per musica unless otherwise given): *Candace* (Milan, Dec. 26, 1732); *Antigono* (Milan, Dec. 16, 1736); *Arianna e Teseo* (Alessandria, 1737); *Ezio* (Venice, 1737; rev. version, Venice, 1743); *Demofoonte* (Piacenza, Carnival 1738); *Angelica* (Venice, May 11, 1738); *Didone abbandonata* (Padua, June 1739; rev. version, Naples, Jan. 20, 1753); *Adriano in Siria* (Vicenza, May 1740); *Semiramide riconosciuta* (Rome, 1741); *Arsace* (Crema, Sept. 1741); *Farasmene, re di Tracia* (Genoa, Carnival 1743); *Alfonso* (London, Jan. 3, 1744); *Alceste* (London, April 28, 1744); *Semiramide* (Padua, June 1745); *Il gran Tamerlano* (Milan, Jan. 20, 1746); *Tigrane* (Venice, May 10, 1747); *L'Olimpiade* (Florence, Carnival 1748); *Andromaca* (Turin, Dec. 26, 1748); *Artaserse* (Milan, Dec. 26, 1749); *Alessandro sotto le tende di Dario* (Piacenza, 1751); *Vologeso, re de' Patri* (Genoa, Carnival 1752); *Vologeso* (Barcelona, 1753); *Siroe, re di Persia* (London, Jan. 14, 1755); *Il re pastore* (Milan, April 1758); *Le cantatrici*, dramma giocoso (Milan, 1758); *Il conte Chicchera*, dramma giocoso (Milan, 1759); *La contessina*, dramma giocoso (Milan, 1759); *Amor contadino*, dramma giocoso (Venice, Nov. 12, 1760); *Enea in Italia* (Palermo, 1763); *L'illustre villanella*, dramma giocoso (Turin, 1769); also music for pasticcios.

BIBL.: F. Maffei, *G. B. L. (c.1708–1788): Notizie biografiche e un catalogo ragionato della musica* (diss., Univ. of Pisa, 1988).

Lanchbery, John (Arthur), English conductor, composer, and arranger; b. London, May 15, 1923. He held a composition scholarship at the Royal Academy of Music in London (1942–43; 1945–48). He quickly developed a reputation as a ballet conductor in London, where he conducted the Metropolitan Ballet (1948–50), the Sadler's Wells Theatre Ballet (1951–59), and the Royal Ballet at Covent Garden (1960–72). After conducting the Australian Ballet in Melbourne (1972–77), he conducted the American Ballet in New York (1978–80). He also was a guest conductor throughout Europe and the Americas. In addition to his film, radio, and television scores, he also prepared new performing eds. of a number of ballets.

Landau, Siegfried, German-born American conductor and composer; b. Berlin, Sept. 4, 1921. He studied at the Stern Cons. and at the Klindworth-Scharwenka Cons. in Berlin. He continued his studies at the Guildhall School of Music and Drama and at Trinity College of Music in London (1939–40); he pursued conducting studies at the Mannes College of Music in New York (diploma, 1942); he also received conducting lessons from Monteux. In 1946 he became a naturalized American citizen. In 1955 he organized the Brooklyn Philharmonia, which he conducted until 1971; concurrently he was conductor of the Chattanooga Opera Assn. (1960–73) and of the Music for Westchester (later White Plains) Sym. Orch. (1961–81); he likewise served as Generalmusikdirektor of the Westphalian Sym. Orch. (1973–75). He wrote an opera, *The Sons of Aaron* (Scarsdale, N.Y., Feb. 28, 1959), and ballet music.

Landi, Stefano, significant Italian composer; b. Rome, 1586 or 1587; d. there, Oct. 28, 1639. He became a boy soprano at Rome's Collegio Germanico (1595), taking minor orders there (1599); then studied rhetoric and philosophy at the Seminario Romano (1602–07). He subsequently was organist of S. Maria in Trastevere (1610) and a singer at the Oratorio del SS. Crocifisso (1611). He served as maestro di cappella to Marco Cornaro, Bishop of Padua (1618–20), then returned to Rome, where he was made a clericus beneficiatus of St. Peter's and maestro di cappella of the church of the Madonna ai Monti (1624); he was also active as a teacher, and was in the service of Cardinal Maurizio of Savoy and the Barberini family. He became an alto in the papal choir (1629). His opera *Il Sant' Alessio* is important in the history of opera as the first such work to treat the inner life of a human subject and to include true overtures in the form of sinfonias. His sacred music ranges from the stile antico of his 2 masses to the new concertato style of his Vespers Psalms and his Magnificats.

WORKS: OPERAS: *La morte d'Orfeo*, tragicommedia pastorale (Rome?, 1619; publ. in Venice, 1619; libretto ed. by A. Solerti in *Gli albori del melodramma*, III, Milan, 1904); *Il Sant' Alessio*, dramma musicale (Rome, 1631?; publ. in Rome, 1634; libretto ed. by A. della Corte in *Drammi per musica dal Rinuccini allo Zeno*, I, Turin, 1958).

BIBL.: S. Carfagno, *The Life and Dramatic Music of S. L. with a Transliteration and Orchestration of the Opera Sant' Alessio* (diss., Univ. of Calif., Los Angeles, 1960); S. Leopold, *S. L.: Beiträge zur Biographie: Untersuchungen zur weltlichen und geistlichen Vokalmusik* (Hamburg, 1976).

Landon, H(oward) C(handler) Robbins, eminent American musicologist; b. Boston, March 6, 1926. He studied music history and theory with Alfred J. Swan at Swarthmore College, and composition there with Harl McDonald; he also took a course in English literature with W. H. Auden (1943–45); he then enrolled in the musicology class of Geiringer at Boston Univ. (B.Mus., 1947). In 1948 he traveled to Europe and settled in Vienna; in 1949 he founded the Haydn Soc., with a view to preparing a complete ed. of Haydn's works. He also instituted an energetic campaign to locate music MSS that had disappeared or been removed; thus he succeeded in finding the MS of Haydn's Mass No. 13; he also found the MS of the so-called Jena Sym., erroneously ascribed to

Beethoven, and proved that it had actually been composed by Friedrich Witt. In *The Symphonies of Joseph Haydn* (London, 1955; suppl., 1961), he analyzes each sym. and suggests solutions for numerous problems of authenticity; in his new ed. of the syms. (12 vols., Vienna, 1965–68), he carefully establishes the version nearest to the original authentic text. He subsequently publ. his massive study *Haydn: Chronicle and Works* in 5 vols. (Bloomington, Ind., and London): vol. 1, *Haydn: The Early Years, 1732–1765* (1980), vol. 2, *Haydn at Esterháza, 1766–1790* (1978), vol. 3, *Haydn in England, 1791–1795* (1976), vol. 4, *Haydn: The Years of "The Creation," 1796–1800* (1977), and vol. 5, *Haydn: The Late Years, 1801–1809* (1977). In addition to numerous other Haydn studies, he also publ. *The Mozart Companion* (ed. with D. Mitchell; London, 1956; 2d ed., rev., 1965), *Beethoven: A Documentary Study* (London, 1970; 2d ed., rev., 1993 as *Beethoven: His Life, Work, and World*), *Essays on the Viennese Classical Style: Gluck, Haydn, Mozart, Beethoven* (London and N.Y., 1970), *Mozart and the Masons* (London, 1983), *1791: Mozart's Last Year* (London, 1988), *Mozart: The Golden Years* (N.Y., 1989), ed. *The Mozart Compendium* (N.Y., 1990), *Mozart and Vienna, including Selections from Johann Pezzl's "Sketch of Vienna" 1786–90* (N.Y., 1991), *Vivaldi: Voice of the Baroque* (London, 1993), and *Mozart Essays* (London, 1995). He was a lecturer of distinction at various American and British colleges and universities. During his early years in Europe, his wife, Christa Landon (b. Berlin, Sept. 23, 1921; d. Funchal, Madeira, Nov. 19, 1977), joined him as a research partner in the search for rare MSS in libraries, churches, and monasteries. She publ. eds. of works by Haydn, Mozart, and Bach; her ed. of Haydn's piano sonatas (3 vols., Vienna, 1963–66) supersedes the one by Hoboken.

Landormy, Paul (Charles-René), French musicologist, music critic, and composer; b. Issy-les-Moulineaux, Jan. 3, 1869; d. Paris, Nov. 17, 1943. He was an agrégé des lettres of the École Normale in Paris and studied voice with Sbriglia and Plancon. With Rolland, he organized a series of lectures on music history at the École des Hautes Études Sociales (1902) and was founder-director of its acoustic laboratory (1904–07); he became music critic of *La Victoire* (1918), and contributed articles to other publications. Among his compositions were piano pieces and songs.

WRITINGS (all publ. in Paris): *Histoire de la musique* (1910; 3rd ed., 1923); *Brahms* (1920; rev. ed., 1948); *Bizet* (1924); *La Vie de Schubert* (1928); *Albert Roussel* (1938); *Gluck* (1941); *Gounod* (1942); *La Musique française* (3 vols., 1943–44).

Landowski, Marcel (François Paul), eminent French composer and administrator; b. Pont-L'Abbé, Finistère, Feb. 18, 1915. He was the great-grandson of the celebrated Belgian violinist and composer Henri Vieuxtemps (b.Verviers, Feb. 17, 1820; d. Mustapha, Algiers, June 6, 1881), and the son of the sculptor Paul Landowski. He received training in piano from Marguerite Long (1922) and in conducting from Monteux (1932), and was a student at the Paris Cons. (1934–37) of Fauchet (harmony), N. Gallon (fugue), Büsser (composition), and Gaubert (conducting). While rising to eminence as a composer, Landowski also became a prominent administrator. From 1960 to 1965 he was director of the Boulogne-Billancourt Cons., and from 1962 to 1966 he was director of music of the Comédie-Française in Paris. In 1964 he was named inspector-general of music for the Ministry of Cultural Affairs, later serving as its chief of the music service (1966–70) and as director of music, lyric art, and dance (1970–74). In 1974 he became inspector-general of music for the Ministry of Education. From 1977 to 1979 he was director of cultural affairs for the City of Paris. He was president of the Théâtre du Châtelet in Paris from 1980 to 1991. He served as president and director-general of the Editions Salabert in Paris from 1991. In 1950 he received the Grand Prix of the City of Paris for composition. The Société des Auteurs, Compositeurs et Editeurs de Musique awarded him its Grand Prix in 1968 and its Prix Maurice Ravel in 1973. In 1975 Landowski was elected a member of the Académie des Beaux-Arts of the Institut de France, serving as its permanent secretary from 1968 to 1994. In 1987 he was made a Commandeur of the Légion d'honneur. In 1994 he was named Chancelier of the Institut de France. He was the author of *L'orchestre* (with L. Aubert; Paris, 1951), *Honegger* (Paris, 1957), *Batailles pour la musique* (Paris, 1979), and *La Musique n'adoucit pas les moeurs* (Paris, 1990). Landowski's compositions reveal his penchant for eclecticism. While his works are always expertly crafted, his generally accessible style is occasionally made more adventuresome by his utilization of atonal, electronic, and electroacoustic diversions. Some of his piano works were written for his wife, Jacqueline Potier, whom he married in 1941.

WORKS: DRAMATIC: *Le Tour d'une aile de pigeon*, operetta (Paris, April 1, 1938; in collaboration with J.-J. Grünewald); *Les Fleurs de la petite Ida*, ballet (Paris, June 19, 1938); *Clairs-obscurs*, ballet (Paris, Nov. 1938); *Après-midi champêtre*, ballet (Versailles, March 30, 1941); *Les Travaux et les jours*, ballet (1943); *Les Djinns*, ballet (Paris, March 11, 1944); *La Rire de Nils Halerius*, lyric legend (1944–48; Mulhouse, Jan. 19, 1951); *Le Fou*, lyric drama (1948–55; Nancy, Feb. 1, 1956); *Rabelais, François de France*, opera ballet (Tours, July 26, 1953); *Le Ventriloque*, lyric comedy (1954–55; Paris, Feb. 6, 1956); *L'Opéra de Poussière*, lyric drama (1958–62; Avignon, Oct. 25, 1962); *Abîmes*, ballet (Essen, Feb. 12, 1959); *Les Adieux*, lyric drama (Radio Luxembourg, Nov. 1959; 1st stage perf., Paris, Oct. 8, 1960); *Le Leçon d'Anatomie*, ballet (The Hague, 1964; based on the Sym. No. 1); *Le Fantôme de l'Opéra*, ballet (1979; Paris, Feb. 22, 1980); *Les Hauts de Hurlevent*, ballet (Paris, Dec. 28, 1982); *La Sorcière du placard à balais*, children's mini-opera (Sevres, May 2, 1983); *Montségur*, lyric drama (Toulouse, Feb. 1, 1985); *La Vieille Maison*, musical (1987; Nantes, Feb. 25, 1988); *P'tit Pierre et la Sorcière du placard à balais*, children's opera (1991; Colmar, May 7, 1992); *Galina*, opera (Lyons, March 17, 1996); incidental music; film scores. Also the oratorios *Rythmes du Monde* (1939–41; Paris, April 26, 1941), *La Quête sans fin* (1943–44; Paris, March 1945), and *Le Pont de l'espérance* for Soprano, Baritone, Chorus, 2 Dancers, and Orch. (Vaison-la-Romaine, Aug. 8, 1980).

BIBL.: C. Baigneres, *M. L.* (Paris, 1959); A. Golea, *M. L.: L'homme et son oeuvre* (Paris, 1969).

Landré, Guillaume (Louis Frédéric), important Dutch composer, son of **Willem (Guillaume Louis Frédéric) Landré**; b. The Hague, Feb. 24, 1905; d. Amsterdam, Nov. 6, 1968. He took music lessons from his father and from Zagwijn, and then from Pijper in Utrecht, where he also studied law at the Univ. (M.A., 1929). He subsequently was active as a teacher of commercial law and as a music critic in Amsterdam. He was chairman of the Dutch Music Copyright Soc. (1947–58) and president of the Soc. of Netherlands Composers (1950–62). As a composer, he endeavored to revive the spirit and the polyphonic technique of the national Flemish School of the Renaissance in a 20th-century guise, with euphonious dissonances and impressionistic dynamics creating a modern aura. In his later works, he experimented with serial devices. Among his compositions were *De Snoek* (The Pike), comic opera (1934; Amsterdam, March 24, 1938), *Jean Lévecq*, opera after Maupassant (1962–63; Amsterdam, June 16, 1965), and *La Symphonie pastorale*, opera after André Gide (1965–67; Rouen, March 31, 1968).

Landré, Willem (Guillaume Louis Frédéric), Dutch writer on music and composer, father of **Guillaume (Louis Frédéric) Landré**; b. Amsterdam, June 12, 1874; d. Eindhoven, Jan. 1, 1948. He was a pupil of Zweers in Amsterdam. In 1901 he became music critic of the *Oprechte Haarlemsche Courant* in Haarlem; he was music ed. of the *Nieuwe Courant* in The Hague (1901–05), then of the *Nieuwe Rotterdamsche Courant* in Rotterdam (1905–37). He taught theory, composition, and music history at the Rotterdam Cons.; he was ed. of *Caecilia, Het Muziekcollege*. His works include the operas *De Roos van Dekama* (Haarlem, 1897) and *Beatrijs* (The Hague, 1925), as well as incidental music.

Lane, Louis, American conductor; b. Eagle Pass, Texas, Dec. 25, 1923. He studied composition with Kennan at the Univ. of Texas (B.Mus., 1943), Martinů at the Berkshire Music Center in Tanglewood (summer 1946), and Rogers at the Eastman School of Music in Rochester, N.Y. (M.Mus., 1947); he also took a course in opera with Sarah Caldwell (1950). In 1947 he became apprentice conductor to George Szell and the Cleveland Orch.; he subsequently was assistant conductor (1956–60), assoc. conductor (1960–70), and resident conductor (1970–73) there; he also was codirector of the Blossom Festival School (1969–73). He served as music director of the Akron (Ohio) Sym. Orch. (1959–83) and of the Lake Erie Opera Theatre (1964–72). In 1973 he became principal guest conductor of the Dallas Sym. Orch., and later held various positions with it until 1978. From 1977 to 1983 he was coconductor of the Atlanta Sym. Orch.; he then was its principal guest conductor (1983–88) and also was principal guest conductor (1982–83) and principal conductor (1984–85) of the National Sym. Orch. of the South African Broadcasting Corp. in Johannesburg. As a guest conductor, he appeared with major orchs. on both sides of the Atlantic; he also was adjunct prof. at the Univ. of Akron (1969–83), visiting prof. at the Univ. of Cincinnati (1973–75), and artistic adviser and conductor at the Cleveland Inst. of Music (from 1982). In 1971 he received the Mahler Medal and in 1972 the Alice M. Ditson Award; in 1979 he was named a Chevalier of the Order of Arts and Letters of France.

Láng, István, Hungarian composer and teacher; b. Budapest, March 1, 1933. He studied with Viski (1951–56) and Szabó (1956–58) at the Budapest Academy of Music. He pursued his career in Budapest, where he first worked at the Academy of Dramatic and Film Arts (1957–60). From 1966 to 1984 he was municipal consultant to the State Puppet Theater. He taught at the Budapest Academy of Music from 1973. From 1978 to 1990 he also was general secretary of the Assn. of Hungarian Musicians. In 1968 and 1975 he received the Erkel Prize. In 1985 he was made a Merited Artist by the Hungarian government. His music is rooted in euphonious dissonance, without venturing into fashionable ugliness.

WORKS: DRAMATIC: OPERAS: *Bernada háza* (Bernarda's House; 1959); *Pathelin mester* (Master Pathelin; Budapest, 1958); *A nagy drámaíró* (The Great Dramatist), television opera (1960; rev. 1974; Budapest, Feb. 14, 1975); *A gyáva* (The Coward; Budapest, 1968); *Álom a színházról* (A Dream about the Theater), television opera (1979–81; Budapest, March 25, 1984). BALLETS: *Mario és a varázsló* (Mario and the Magician), after Thomas Mann (1962); *Hiperbola* (1963; suite, 1968); *Lebukott* (Nabbed; 1968); *Csillagrатörök* (Starfighters), ballet cantata (1972; rev. 1977).

Lang, Paul Henry, eminent Hungarian-born American musicologist, editor, and teacher; b. Budapest, Aug. 28, 1901; d. Lakeville, Conn., Sept. 21, 1991. He studied bassoon with Wieschendorf, chamber music with L. Weiner, composition with Kodály, and counterpoint with Koessler at the Budapest Academy of Music (graduated, 1922); he then studied musicology with Kroyer and comparative literature with Ernst Curtius and Friedrich Gundorff at the Univ. of Heidelberg (1924) and subsequently studied musicology with Pirro, art history with Henri Focillon, literature with Fernand Baldensperger and Félix Gaiffe, and aesthetics with Victor Basch at the Sorbonne in Paris (degree in literature, 1928). He settled in the United States in 1928, becoming a naturalized American citizen in 1934; he studied musicology with Kinkeldey and French literature and philosophy with James Frederick Mason at Cornell Univ. (Ph.D., 1934, with the diss. *A Literary History of French Opera*). He was an assistant prof. at Vassar College (1930–31); assoc. prof., Wells College (1931–33); visiting lecturer, Wellesley College (1934–35); assoc. prof. of musicology, Columbia Univ. (1933–39; full prof., 1939; prof. emeritus, 1970). He was vice president of the American Musicological Soc. (1947–49) and president of the International Musicological Soc. (1955–58). From 1945 to 1973 he was ed. of the *Musical Quarterly* and from 1954 to 1963, music ed. of the *N.Y. Herald Tribune*. He publ. the valuable and very popular book *Music in Western Civilization* (N.Y., 1941; many subsequent reprints) and the important and comprehensive study *George Frideric Handel* (N.Y., 1966); he also ed. several vols. of articles reprinted from the *Musical Quarterly*, and the anthologies *The Concerto 1800–1900* (N.Y., 1969) and *The Symphony 1800–1900* (N.Y., 1969).

BIBL.: E. Strainchamps and M. Maniates, eds., *Music and Civilization: Essays in Honor of P. H. L.* (N.Y., 1984).

Langdon, Michael (real name, **Frank Birtles**), English bass; b. Wolverhampton, Nov. 12, 1920; d. Hove, Sussex, March 12, 1991. He studied at the Guildhall School of Music in London; subsequently he took voice lessons with Alfred Jerger in Vienna, Maria Carpi in Geneva, and Otakar Kraus in London. In 1948 he joined the chorus at the Royal Opera House, Covent Garden, London; he made his operatic debut there in 1950. In subsequent years, he sang with many of the major opera houses of the world. On Nov. 2, 1964, he made his Metropolitan Opera debut in New York as Baron Ochs. He created several bass roles in operas by Benjamin Britten; he was also noted for his command of the standard operatic repertoire. After his retirement from the stage in 1977, he was director of the National Opera Studio (1978–86). In 1973 he was made a Commander of the Order of the British Empire. He publ. *Notes from a Low Singer* (with R. Fawkes; London, 1982).

Lange-Müller, Peter Erasmus, Danish composer; b. Frederiksberg, Dec. 1, 1850; d. Copenhagen, Feb. 26, 1926. He studied at the Copenhagen Cons. His early compositions show the influence of J. P. E. Hartmann; those of his later period exhibit distinct individuality. Among his works were the operas (all 1st perf in Copenhagen): *Tove* (Jan. 19, 1878); *Spanske studenter* (Oct. 21, 1883); *Fru Jeanna* (Feb. 4, 1891); *Vikingeblod* (April 29, 1900); also incidental music.

BIBL.: J. Clausen, *P. E. L.-M.* (Copenhagen, 1938); H. Bonnen, *P. E. L.-M.* (Copenhagen, 1946).

Langendorff, Frieda, German contralto; b. Breslau, March 24, 1868; d. N.Y., June 11, 1947. She was a student of J. Meyer, M. Mallinger, and A. Iffert. In 1901 she made her operatic debut in Strasbourg. After appearing at Bayreuth (1904), she sang at the German Theatre in Prague (1905–07). On Dec. 7, 1907, she made her Metropolitan Opera debut in New York as Ortrud, remaining on its roster until 1908, and returning in 1910–11. After singing at the Berlin Kroll Opera (1909–11), she gave concerts in the United States (1912–13). From 1914 to 1916 she was a member of the Dresden Court Opera. Among her best roles were Delilah, Azucena, Amneris, and Fricka.

Langer, Suzanne K(atherina), important American philosopher of musical aesthetics; b. N.Y., Dec. 20, 1895; d. Old Lyme, Conn., July 17, 1985. She studied philosophy at Radcliffe College (Ph.D., 1926) and at the Univ. of Vienna, her principal teachers being Whitehead and Cassirer. She held teaching positions at Radcliffe and Columbia Univ., then became a prof. at Conn. College in 1954, retiring in 1962. Her publications center on a philosophy of art derived from a theory of musical meaning, which in turn exemplify a general philosophy of mind. According to her theory, modes of understanding are forms of symbolic transformation, i.e., one understands any phenomenon by constructing an object analogous to it or referring to it. She extended this theory to argue that the patterns of musical form are structurally similar to those of human feelings. She later expanded this into a general theory of the fine arts, her final work suggesting that art criticism might form the basis of a new structure for the behavioral sciences. Her lucid, strong-minded writings are widely considered crucial in understanding musical aesthetics.

WRITINGS: *The Practice of Philosophy* (N.Y., 1930); *Philosophy in a New Key* (Cambridge, Mass., 1942); *Feeling and Form* (N.Y., 1953); *Problems of Art* (N.Y., 1957); *Mind: An Essay in Human Feeling* (3 vols., Baltimore, 1967–72).

Langert, Johann August Adolf, German conductor and composer; b. Coburg, Nov. 26, 1836; d. there, Dec. 27, 1920. He was a theater conductor in Coburg, Mannheim, and Basel. In 1873 he became court conductor at Gotha, retiring in 1897 to his native town. He composed the operas *Die Jungfrau von Orleans* (Coburg, 1861), *Des Sängers Fluch* (Coburg, 1863), *Dona Maria*

(Darmstadt, 1866), *Die Fabier* (Coburg, 1866), *Dornröschen* (Leipzig, 1871), and *Jean Cavallier* (Coburg, 1880; rewritten as *Die Camisarden*, 1887).

Langgaard, Rued (Immanuel), distinguished Danish composer and organist; b. Copenhagen, July 28, 1893; d. Ribe, July 10, 1952. His father, Siegfried Langgaard (1852–1914), a student of Liszt, pursued a career as a pianist, composer, and teacher at the Royal Academy of Music in Copenhagen; his mother, Emma Foss, was a pianist. He began his musical training with his parents, then studied organ with G. Helsted, violin with C. Petersen, and theory with V. Rosenberg in Copenhagen. He made his debut as an organist at age 11; subsequently he was intermittently active as a church organist until becoming organist of Ribe Cathedral (1940). His early works were influenced by Liszt, Gade, Wagner, and Bruckner; following a period in which he was at times highly experimental (1916–24), he returned to his Romantic heritage; however, even in his last period of production, he produced some works with bizarre and polemical overtones. During his lifetime, he was almost totally neglected in official Danish music circles and failed to obtain an important post. A quarter century after he died, his unperformed works were heard for the first time. Among his numerous compositions was the biblical opera *Antikrist* (1921–39; Danish Radio, June 28, 1980).

BIBL.: B. Nielsen, *R. L.s Kompositioner: Annoteret vaerkfortegnelse* (Odense, 1991); idem, *R. L.: Biografi* (Copenhagen, 1993).

Langlé, Honoré (François Marie), French music theorist and composer; b. Monaco, 1741; d. Villiers-le-Bel, near Paris, Sept. 20, 1807. He studied in Naples at the Cons. della Pietà dei Turchini with Cafaro. In 1768 he went to Paris, becoming a singing teacher at the École Royale de Chant et de Déclamation in 1784; he then was a prof. of harmony and librarian at the Paris Cons. (1795–1802). He composed a number of operas, including *Antiochus et Stratonice* (Versailles, 1786) and *Corisandre, ou Les Fous par enchantement* (Paris, March 8, 1791); also other vocal works. He ed. Mengozzi's *Méthode de chant du Conservatoire* (1804; 2d ed., c.1815) and collaborated with Cherubini on his *Méthode de chant*.

WRITINGS (all publ. in Paris): *Traité d'harmonie et de modulation* (1793; 2d ed., 1797); *Traité de la basse sous le chant précédé de toutes les règles de la composition* (c.1798); *Nouvelle méthode pour chiffrer les accords* (1801); *Traité de la fugue* (1805).

Langridge, Philip (Gordon), esteemed English tenor; b. Hawkhurst, Kent, Dec. 16, 1939. He studied violin at the Royal Academy of Music in London and took voice lessons with Bruce Boyce and Celia Bizony. He was active as a violinist but also began to make appearances as a singer from 1962. He first sang at the Glyndebourne Festival in 1964, and made regular appearances there from 1977; he also sang at the Edinburgh Festivals from 1970. He appeared at Milan's La Scala in 1979, then sang for the first time at London's Covent Garden as the Fisherman in Stravinsky's *The Nightingale* in 1983. He made his Metropolitan Opera debut in New York as Ferrando in *Così fan tutte* on Jan. 5, 1985. He was chosen to create the role of Orpheus in Birtwistle's opera *The Mask of Orpheus* at London's English National Opera in 1986. In 1992 he appeared as Stravinsky's Oedipus Rex at the inaugural operatic production at the Saito Kinen Festival in Matsumoto. He portrayed Jupiter in *Semele* at Covent Garden in 1996. After singing Captain Vere in *Billy Budd* at the Metropolitan Opera in 1997, he returned there as Schoenberg's Aron in 1999. He was made a Commander of the Order of the British Empire in 1994. Admired as both an operatic and a concert singer, Langridge maintains an extensive repertoire ranging from the Baroque masters to contemporary works. He is married to **Ann Murray**.

Lankester, Michael (John), English conductor; b. London, Nov. 12, 1944. He studied at the Royal College of Music in London (1962–67). After making his formal conducting debut with the English Chamber Orch. in London (1967), he was a conductor (1969–80) and head of the opera dept. (1975–80) at the Royal College of Music; he also was founder-conductor of Contrapuncti (1967–79) and music director of the National Theatre of Great Britain (1969–74) and of the Surrey Phil. (1974–79). He was assistant conductor (1980–82), assoc. conductor (1982–84), and conductor-in-residence (1984–88) of the Pittsburgh Sym. Orch.; he was also music director of the Hartford (Conn.) Sym. Orch. (from 1986).

Lankow, Anna, noted German contralto and singing teacher; b. Bonn, Jan. 13, 1850; d. there, March 19, 1908. She studied singing in Cologne, Leipzig, and Dresden. She began her career as a concert singer, then was engaged as a contralto in the Weimar Opera. However, because she had been lame since childhood, she was forced to abandon the stage. In 1883 she married the sculptor Paul Pietsch of Berlin; after his death in 1885, she went to New York as a singing teacher, subsequently returning to Germany. She publ. a treatise, *Die Wissenschaft des Kunstgesangs* (1899; in Ger. and Eng.).

Lanza, Mario (real name, **Alfredo Arnold Cocozza**), popular American tenor and actor; b. Philadelphia, Jan. 31, 1921; d. Rome, Oct. 7, 1959. He studied voice in Philadelphia and then attended the Berkshire Music Center in Tanglewood (summer 1942) on a scholarship. Subsequently he was drafted and served in the U.S. Army Air Force, during which time he sang in productions of Frank Loesser's *On the Beam* and was a cast member in the *Winged Victory* show. After his discharge in 1945 he went to New York and pursued further vocal training with Rosati. In 1946 he made an impressive appearance as a concert singer at Chicago's Grant Park. In 1947 he scored a major success as a concert artist at the Hollywood Bowl, and that same year he toured the United States and Europe as a member of the Bel Canto Trio with Frances Yeend and George London. In 1948 he made his only professional appearances on the operatic stage when he appeared in *Madama Butterfly* at the New Orleans Opera. Lanza then went to Hollywood, where he won a starring role in the film *That Midnight Kiss* (1949). Its success led to his appearance in the film *The Toast of New Orleans* (1950), which included his version of the song "Be My Love." His recording of the song sold a million copies and made Lanza a rising star. Then followed his starring role in *The Great Caruso* (1951), a film made memorable by his rendition of the song "The Loveliest Night of the Year." His recording of the song also sold a million copies. Subsequently he starred in the film *Because You're Mine* (1952). His recording of the theme song of the same title likewise sold a million copies. By this time, Lanza's tempermental outbursts, heavy drinking, and overeating had taken a heavy toll. During his filming of *The Student Prince* in 1953, he walked out on the project and only avoided damaging litigation for breach of contract by waiving his rights to the sound track. Ironically, the recording of the sound track preserved some of his finest singing. After starring in one more Hollywood film, *Serenade* (1956), Lanza settled in Rome. He appeared in the film *The 7 Hills of Rome* (1958), which was made in the Eternal City and made memorable by his performance of the song "Arrivederci, Roma." In 1958 he appeared at London's Royal Albert Hall and at the Royal Variety Show, and then toured throughout Europe. His last film appearance was in *For the First Time* (1959). While Lanza's death at only 38 in a Rome hospital was initially attributed to a heart attack, rumors later cropped up that he was murdered on orders of the Mafia after refusing to appear at a mobster-organized concert sponsored by Lucky Luciano.

BIBL.: R. Strait and T. Robinson, *L.: His Tragic Life* (N.Y., 1980).

Laparra, Raoul, French composer and music critic; b. Bordeaux, May 13, 1876; d. in an air raid in Suresnes, near Paris, April 4, 1943. He studied at the Paris Cons. (1890–1903) with Diemer, Fauré, Gédalge, and Lavignac; he won the Grand Prix de Rome with his cantata *Ulysse* (June 27, 1903). He was music critic of *Le Matin*, resigning in 1937 to dedicate himself entirely to composition. He was at his best in music inspired by Spanish subjects.

WORKS: DRAMATIC: OPERAS: *Peau d'âne* (Bordeaux, Feb. 3, 1899); *La Habanera* (Paris, Feb. 26, 1908); *La Jota* (Paris, April 26, 1911); *Le Joueur de viole* (Paris, Dec. 24, 1925); *Las toreras* (Lille, Jan. 17, 1929); *L'Illustre Fregona* (Paris, Feb. 16, 1931). INCIDENTAL MUSIC TO: *El Conquistador*.

Laporte, André, Belgian composer and teacher; b. Oplinter, July 12, 1931. He received training in musicology and philosophy at the Catholic Univ. in Louvain (graduated, 1956), and then was a student of Flor Peeters (organ) and Marinus de Jong (counterpoint) at the Lemmens Inst. in Mechelen (1956–58), where he received the Lemmens-Tinel Prize for organ, piano, and composition (1958); subsequently he attended the courses in new music in Darmstadt (1960–65). In 1963 he joined the staff of the Belgian Radio and Television in Brussels, where he later served as manager of its Phil. Orch. (from 1988). In 1968 he became a teacher of theory and analysis at the Brussels Cons., and then taught composition there from 1988. He also taught composition at the Chapelle Musicale Reine Elisabeth from 1990. In 1971 and 1976 he was awarded the Koopal Prize of the Belgian Ministry of Culture. His oratorio *La vita non è sogno* (Ghent, Sept. 13, 1972) won the Italia Prize in 1976. In 1991 he was made a member of the Belgian Royal Academy. His works also include an opera, *Das Schloss* (1981–85).

Laporte, Joseph de, French writer on the theater and music; b. Belfort, 1713; d. Paris, Dec. 19, 1779. He was a Jesuit abbé.

WRITINGS: *Almanach historique et chronologique de tous les spectacles de Paris*, I (1752); *Calendrier historique de théâtre de l'Opéra et des Comédies Française et Italienne et des Foires*, II (1753); *Les Spectacles de Paris, ou Suite du Calendrier historique et chronologique et des théâtres*, III-XXVII (1754–78; continued by Duchesne and others); with J. Suard, *Nouveaux choix de pièces tirées des anciens Mercures et des autres journeaux*, LX-CVIII (Paris, 1762–64); *L'Esprit de l' "Encyclopédie" ou Choix des articles les plus curieux* (Geneva and Paris, 1768); with J. Clement, *Anecdotes dramatique contenant toutes les pièces de théâtres . . . jusqu'en 1775* (Paris, 1775); with S. Chamfort, *Dictionnaire dramatique contenant l'histoire des théâtres et les règles du genre dramatique* (Paris, 1776).

La Prade, Ernest, American violinist and composer; b. Memphis, Tenn., Dec. 20, 1889; d. Sherman, Conn., April 20, 1969. He studied violin at the Cincinnati College of Music, at the Royal Cons. in Brussels with César Thomson, and in London with J. Jongen (composition). He subsequently taught at the Cincinnati College of Music and was a member of the Cincinnati Sym. Orch. (1909–12), the Belgian and Holbrook Quartets in London (1914–17), and the N.Y. Sym. Orch. (1919–28); in 1929 he joined the staff of NBC; in 1950 he became supervisor of music research there. He wrote a comic opera, *Xantha* (London, 1917), and songs. He publ. *Alice in Orchestralia* (1925), *Marching Notes* (1929), and *Broadcasting Music* (1947).

Laquai, Reinhold, Swiss composer and teacher; b. Zürich, May 1, 1894; d. Oberrieden, Oct. 3, 1957. He studied at the Zürich Cons. and later with Busoni in Berlin. In 1920 he became a teacher at the Zürich Cons. Among his compositions were 2 operas, *Der Schleier der Tanit* and *Die Revisionsreise*.

Larchet, John F(rancis), Irish composer and teacher; b. Dublin, July 13, 1884; d. there, Aug. 10, 1967. He studied in Dublin with Esposito at the Royal Irish Academy of Music before completing his training at the Univ. (Mus.B., 1915; Mus.D., 1917). From 1907 to 1934 he was music director of Dublin's Abbey Theatre. He also was prof. of composition at the Royal Irish Academy of Music (1920–55) and prof. of music at Univ. College, Dublin. He composed orch. works, choral pieces, and songs.

Larmore, Jennifer, highly regarded American mezzo-soprano; b. Atlanta, June 21, 1958. She was a student at Westminster Choir College in Princeton, N.J. (1976–80), and later of John Bullock in Washington, D.C. In 1986 she made her European opera debut as Mozart's Sesto in France. From 1990 she pursued a major career, garnering critical accolades for her portrayal of Rossini's Rosina in Paris, London, and Rome. During the 1992–93 season she sang that role in Berlin, as well as Bellini's Romeo at N.Y.'s Carnegie Hall, Rossini's Angelina in Florence, and Mozart's Dorabella at the Salzburg Festival. In 1993 she made her first appearance at London's Wigmore Hall as a recitalist. She won the Richard Tucker Award in 1994 and gave a recital at Lincoln Center's Walter Reade Theater in New York On Feb. 6, 1995, she made her Metropolitan Opera debut in New York as Rosina. She portrayed Rossini's Elvira at the Los Angeles Opera in 1996, and returned there as Carmen in 1998. In 1999 she sang Handel's *Giulio Cesare* at the Metropolitan Opera. As a soloist with orchs. and as a recitalist, she appeared widely in North America and Europe. Among other operatic roles of note are Monteverdi's Orfeo, Rossini's Arsace and Isabella, and Strauss's Octavian.

La Rosa Parodi, Armando, Italian conductor and composer; b. Genoa, March 14, 1904; d. Rome, Jan. 21, 1977. He studied in Genoa and Milan. He began his career as a conductor in 1929; was active as a guest conductor in Genoa, Milan, Turin, and Rome; in 1963 he was named chief conductor of the RAI Orch. of Rome, a post he held until his death. He composed the operas *Il Mercante e l'avvocato* (1934) and *Cleopatra* (1938).

La Rotella, Pasquale, Italian composer and conductor; b. Bitonto, Feb. 26, 1880; d. Bari, March 20, 1963. He studied in Naples. He was choirmaster at Bari Cathedral (1902–13) and also taught at the Liceo Musicale there (1934–49); he toured Italy as an opera conductor. His works included the operas *Ivan* (Bari, Jan. 20, 1900), *Dea* (Bari, April 11, 1903), *Fasma* (Milan, Nov. 28, 1908), *Corsaresca* (Rome, Nov. 13, 1933), and *Manuela* (Nice, March 4, 1948).

Larrivée, Henri, French bass-baritone; b. Lyons, Jan. 9, 1737; d. Vincennes, Aug. 7, 1802. He sang in the chorus of the Paris Opéra, making his debut there in Rameau's *Castor et Pollux* in 1755. He subsequently distinguished himself in the operas of Gluck, creating the roles of Agamemnon in *Iphigénie en Aulide* (1774), Ubalde in *Armide* (1777), and Orestes in *Iphigénie en Tauride* (1779). Gossec wrote the title role of his opera *Sabinus* (1773) for him. His wife, Marie Jeanne (née Le Miere) Larrivée (b. Sedan, Nov. 29, 1733; d. Paris, Oct. 1786), was a soprano at the Paris Opéra (1750–77); she created the title role of Ernelinde in Philidor's opera of 1767, and also the role of Eponine in *Sabinus*.

L'Arronge, Adolf, German composer and conductor; b. Hamburg, March 8, 1838; d. Berlin, May 25, 1908. He studied at the Leipzig Cons. with R. Genée. He was a theater conductor in Cologne, Danzig, Königsberg, Würzburg, Stuttgart, Budapest, etc. He became director of the Kroll Opera in Berlin in 1866, then of the Lobetheater in Breslau (1874–78). Returning to Berlin, he bought the Friedrich-Wilhelmstädtisches Theater in 1881, and managed it until 1894 as the Deutsches Theater. He brought out many musical farces, Singspiels, etc. at the Wallnertheater, including his comic operas *Das Gespenst* and *Der zweite Jakob*, the "Volksstücke" *Das grosse Los* (1868) and *Mein Leopold*, etc.; also wrote many songs.

Larsen, Jens Peter, distinguished Danish musicologist; b. Copenhagen, June 14, 1902; d. there, Aug. 22, 1988. He studied mathematics and musicology at the Univ. of Copenhagen (M.A., 1928), then joined its staff; he later obtained his Ph.D. there in 1939 with the diss. *Die Haydn-Überlieferung* (publ. in Copenhagen, 1939); retired in 1970. A leading authority on the music of Haydn, he served as general ed. of the critical edition sponsored by the Joseph Haydn Inst. of Cologne from 1955 to 1960; his studies on the music of Handel are also of value. He was the son-in-law of the Danish organist and conductor Mogens Wöldike (1897–1988), with whom he ed. the hymnbook of the Danish Church (1954, 1973).

WRITINGS: *Drei Haydn-Kataloge in Faksimile: Mit Einleitung und erganzenden Themenverzeichnissen* (Copenhagen, 1941; 2d ed., rev., 1979); *Weyses sange: Deres betydning for sangen i hjem, skole og kirke* (Copenhagen, 1942); *Handel's "Messiah": Origins, Composition, Sources* (Copenhagen, 1957; 2d ed., rev., 1972); *Essays on Handel, Haydn, and the Viennese Classical Style* (tr. by U. Kramer; Ann Arbor, 1988).

BIBL.: N. Schiørring, H. Glahn, and C. Hatting, eds., *Festskrift J. P. L.: Studier udgivet af Musikvidenskabeligt institut ved Kbenhavns universitet* (Copenhagen, 1972).

Larsen, Libby (Elizabeth Brown), American composer; b. Wilmington, Del., Dec. 24, 1950. She was a pupil of Argento, Fetler, and Eric Stokes at the Univ. of Minnesota (B.A., 1971; M.A., 1975; Ph.D., 1978). With Stephen Paulus, she founded the Minnesota Composers Forum in Minneapolis in 1973, serving as its managing composer until 1985; she also was composer-in-residence of the Minnesota Orch. (1983–87). Her works have been widely performed in the United States and abroad. One of her most impressive scores, the choral sym. *Coming Forth into Day* (1986), utilizes a text by Jehan Sadat, the widow of the slain leader of Egypt.

WORKS: OPERAS: *The Words upon the Windowpane* (1978); *The Silver Fox*, children's opera (1979); *Tumbledown Dick* (1980); *Clair de lune* (1984); *Frankenstein: The Modern Prometheus* (1989; St. Paul, Minn., May 25, 1990); *Mrs. Dalloway*, chamber opera (1992; Cleveland, July 22, 1993); *Eric Hermannson's Soul* (1997).

Larsén-Todsen, Nanny, Swedish soprano; b. Hagby, Aug. 2, 1884; d. Stockholm, May 26, 1982. She received her training at the Stockholm Cons., in Berlin, and in Milan. In 1906 she made her operatic debut at the Royal Theater in Stockholm as Agathe, where she then was a member from 1907 to 1922. After appearing at Milan's La Scala (1923–24), she made her Metropolitan Opera debut in New York as Brünnhilde in *Götterdämmerung* on Jan. 31, 1925; she remained on its roster until 1927, singing such roles as Isolde, Rachel in *La Juive*, Fricka, Kundry, Elsa, La Gioconda, and Leonore. Returning to Europe, she sang in various opera centers, including London's Covent Garden (1927, 1930) and the Bayreuth Festivals (1927–28; 1930–31). Shortly before the outbreak of World War II in 1939, she became a voice teacher in Stockholm.

Laserna, Blas de, Spanish conductor and composer; b. Corella, Navarre (baptized), Feb. 4, 1751; d. Madrid, Aug. 8, 1816. He was official composer for several theaters; also conductor of the Teatro de la Cruz (1790–1818). He composed the music for Ramon de la Cruz's comedy *El café de Barcelona* (Barcelona, Nov. 4, 1788); also the operas *La gitanilla por amor* (Madrid, 1791; successful) and *Idomeneo* (Madrid, Dec. 9, 1792); incidental music to plays of Calderón, Lope de Vega, Moreto, et al.

BIBL.: J. Gómez, J. de Arrese, and E. Aunós, *El músico B. d.L.* (Corella, 1952).

Larson, Sophia, Austrian soprano; b. Linz, 1954. She studied at the Salzburg Mozarteum and with Ettore Campogalliani. In 1976 she made her operatic debut as Amelia Boccanegra in St. Gallen, and then sang in Ulm (1979–80) and Bremen (1980–83). She also appeared as a guest artist in Hamburg, Stuttgart, and Rome. In 1984 she made her first appearance at the Bayreuth Festival as Gutrune, and returned there to sing Venus in 1987 and Sieglinde in 1989. In 1985 she sang the Duchess of Parma in Busoni's *Doktor Faust* in Bologna. After appearing as Gutrune in Munich, Tosca in Turin, and Isolde in Toronto in 1987, she was a soloist in Britten's *War Requiem* at N.Y.'s Carnegie Hall in 1988. In the latter year, she also appeared as Senta in San Francisco. She sang Els in Schreker's *Der Schatzgräber* at the Holland Festival in 1992. In 1995 she made her British debut as Turandot in London.

Larsson, Lars-Erik (Vilner), important Swedish composer and pedagogue; b. Åkarp, near Lund, May 15, 1908; d. Hälsingborg, Dec. 27, 1986. After passing the organist's examination in Växjö (1924), he studied with Ernst Ellberg (composition) and Olalla Morales (conducting) at the Stockholm Cons. (1924–29); he then completed his training with Berg in Vienna (1929–30) and with Reuter in Leipzig (1930–31). Returning to Stockholm, he was a conductor, composer, and producer with the Swedish Radio (1937–43); he later served as supervisor of its radio orch. (1945–47) and led its chamber orch. (until 1953). He was prof. of composition at the Stockholm Musikshögskolan (1947–59) and director of music at the Univ. of Uppsala (1961–65). His early compositions were in a classical spirit, but with time his idiom became increasingly complex; there are some instances of dodecaphonic procedures in his later compositions. The importance of his works lies in the freedom of application of various techniques without adhering to any current fashion.

WORKS: DRAMATIC: *Prinsessan av Cypern* (The Princess of Cyprus), opera (1930–36; Stockholm, April 29, 1937); *Arresten på Bohus* (The Arrest at Bohus), opera buffa (1938–39); *Linden*, ballet (1958).

Laruette, Jean-Louis, French tenor and composer; b. Paris, March 7, 1731; d. there, Jan. 10, 1792. He made his debut at the Opéra Comique in Paris in 1752. In 1762 he became a member of the Comédie-Italienne when it merged with the Opéra Comique, and sang there with notable success until 1779. Although he specialized in light tenor roles, he was heard in comic roles generally sung by basses. These roles are known to this day as laurettes. His importance as a composer rests upon his contribution to the development of the opéra comique. His wife, Marie-Thérèse (née Villette) Laruette (b. Paris, March 6, 1744; d. there, June 16, 1837), was also a singer who appeared at the Paris Opéra and the Comédie-Italienne (1758–77).

WORKS: OPÉRAS COMIQUES (all 1st perf. in Paris): *Le docteur Sangrado* (Feb. 13, 1758; in collaboration with E. Duni); *L'heureux déguisement, ou La gouvernante supposée* (Aug. 17, 1758); *Le médecin de l'amour* (Sept. 22, 1758); *Cendrillon* (Feb. 21, 1759); *L'ivrogne corrigé, ou Le mariage du diable* (July 24, 1759); *Le depit genereux* (July 16, 1761); *Le guy de chesne, ou La fête des druides* (Jan. 26, 1763); *Les deux compères* (Aug. 4, 1772).

Laschi, Luisa, Italian soprano; b. Florence, *c.*1760; d. *c.*1790. She made an acclaimed debut in Vienna on Sept. 24, 1784, in Cimarosa's *Giannina e Bernardone*. On May 1, 1786, she created the role of the Countess in Mozart's *Le nozze de Figaro* in Vienna. That same year, she married **Domenico Mombelli**, and thereafter sang with him frequently. She appeared in the first Viennese production of Mozart's *Don Giovanni* on May 7, 1788, but later that year she and her husband were dismissed from court service.

Láska, Gustav, Bohemian composer and double bass player; b. Prague, Aug. 23, 1847; d. Schwerin, Oct. 16, 1928. He studied at the Prague Cons. with Hrabe, Kittl, and Krejčí. Following a year of giving double bass concerts, he joined the Court Orch. in Kassel (1868–72), then in Sondershausen (1872–75). He was a theater conductor in Göttingen, Eisleben, and Halberstadt; he played double bass in Berlin. In 1878 he became double bass player in the Court Orch. in Schwerin. Among his works is the opera *Der Kaisersoldat*.

Lassalle, Jean (-Louis), French baritone; b. Lyons, Dec. 14, 1847; d. Paris, Sept. 7, 1909. After training in industrial design and painting, he entered the Paris Cons. to study voice; he also studied privately with Novelli, making his debut as St. Bris in *Les Huguenots* in Liège (1868); then he sang in Lille, Toulouse, The Hague, and Brussels. He made his first appearance at the Paris Opéra in the title role of Rossini's *Guillaume Tell* (June 7, 1872), remaining there for more than 20 years, with extended leaves of absence, during which he toured throughout Europe, Russia, and the United States (debut, Metropolitan Opera, N.Y., Jan. 15, 1892, as Nelusko in *L'Africaine*); he was again on the Metropolitan Opera roster in 1893–94 and 1896–97. He returned to Paris in 1901 and settled there as a singing teacher; in 1903 he became a prof. at the Paris Cons. His repertoire comprised about 60 operas, ranging from Donizetti to Wagner.

Lassen, Eduard, Danish conductor and composer; b. Copenhagen, April 13, 1830; d. Weimar, Jan. 15, 1904. His family moved to Brussels when he was a child. He entered the Brussels Cons., taking the Belgian Prix de Rome (1851). Following a tour through Germany and Italy, he went to Weimar, where Liszt fostered the presentation of his 5-act opera *Landgraf Ludwigs Brautfahrt* (1857). He was court music director in Weimar (1858–95), where he led the world premiere of Saint-Saëns's opera *Samson et Dalila* (Weimar, Dec. 2, 1877). He also wrote the operas *Frauenlob* (Weimar, 1860) and *Der Gefangene* (given in Brussels as *Le Captif*, April 24, 1865) and a ballet, *Diana*; also incidental music.

Lászlò, Magda, Hungarian soprano; b. Marosvársárhely, 1919. She studied at the Budapest Academy of Music and with Irene Stowasser. In 1943 she made her operatic debut at the Budapest Opera, where she sang until 1946. She then became well known via her appearances on the Italian Radio. On Dec. 4, 1949, she created the role of the Mother in Dallapiccola's *Il Prigionero* in a Turin Radio broadcast, and then sang that role in its first stage performance on May 20, 1950, in Florence. Thereafter she sang in various Italian music centers, and also throughout Europe. In 1953 she appeared as Alceste at the Glyndebourne Festival, returning there in 1954 and again in 1962–63. On Dec. 3, 1954, she created the role of Cressida in Walton's *Troilus and Cressida* at London's Covent Garden. She also sang widely as a concert artist. In addition to roles in operas by such contemporary composers as Dallapiccola, Walton, Casella, Malipiero, and Ghedini, she was admired for her portrayals of Handel's Agrippina, Cherubino, Norma, Senta, Isolde, Busoni's Turandot, and Berg's Marie.

Latham, William P(eters), American composer and educator; b. Shreveport, La., Jan. 4, 1917. He studied trumpet at the Cincinnati Cons. of Music (1936–38); he received his B.S. degree in music education from the Univ. of Cincinnati (1938) and continued his studies at the College of Music in Cincinnati (B.M., 1940; M.M., 1941); subsequently he studied composition with Hanson and Elwell at the Eastman School of Music in Rochester, N.Y. (Ph.D., 1951). During World War II, he served in the U.S. Army as a cavalry bandsman and later as an infantry platoon leader in active combat in Germany in 1945. After the war he taught at Iowa State Teacher's College in Cedar Falls (1946–65); he became a prof. at North Texas State Univ. in Denton in 1965, director of graduate studies in music in 1969, and Distinguished Prof. in 1978; he retired in 1984. He excelled as a composer of sacred choruses and band music; in the latter, he boldly experimented with modern techniques, as exemplified by his *Dodecaphonic Set* and, most spectacularly, in *Fusion*, in which he endeavored to translate the process of atomic fusion into musical terms through an ingenious application of asymmetrical rhythms. Among his works is the opera *Orpheus in Pecan Springs* (Denton, Texas, Dec. 4, 1980) and the ballet *A Modern Trilogy* (Cincinnati, April 2, 1941).

Latham-Koenig, Jan, English conductor and pianist; b. London, Dec. 15, 1953. He was a student of Norman del Mar, Kendall Taylor, and Lamar Crowson at the Royal College of Music in London. In 1976 he founded the Koenig Ensemble, and also was active as a concert pianist until 1981. From 1981 to 1986 he was a member of the Cantiere Internazionale d'Artre in Montepulciano. In 1985 he conducted *Giulio Cesare* at the Royal Opera in Stockholm. He first conducted at the English National Opera in London with *Tosca* and at the Wesford Festival with *La straniera* in 1987. In 1988 he conducted the premiere of Bussotti's *L'ispirazione* in Florence. That same year he made his debut at the Vienna State Opera with *Macbeth*, and from 1991 he served as its principal guest conductor. He conducted Weill's *Aufsteig und Fall der Stadt Mahagonny* at the Maggio Musicale Fiorentino in 1990. In 1996 he conducted *Aida* at London's Covent Garden. In 1997 he became music director of the Opéra du Rhin and of the Orchestre Philharmonique in Strasbourg. As a guest conductor, he has appeared with many European and North American orchs. His repertoire is particularly noteworthy for its inclusion of rarely heard scores of the past and of various contemporary works.

Latilla, Gaetano, Italian composer; b. Bari, Jan. 10, 1711; d. Naples, Jan. 15, 1788. He was a child chorister at Bari Cathedral, and then studied at the Cons. di Sant' Onofrio in Naples. After serving as 2d maestro di cappella at Santa Maria Maggiore in Rome (1738–41), he was in Venice as maestro di coro at the Cons. della Pietà (1753–66) and as 2d maestro di cappella at San Marco (1762–70?). About 1774 he returned to Naples. He wrote some 46 operas, but the music to most is not extant. His preserved operas are *Angelica ed Orlando* (Naples, 1735), *Gismòndo* (Naples, 1737; several rev. versions under different titles), *Madama Ciana* (Rome, Feb. 1738), *Siroe* (Rome, Carnival 1740), *Zenobia* (Turin, 1742), *Griselda* (Venice, 1751), *Olimpiade* (Venice, 1752), *Ezio* (Naples, July 10, 1758), *Antigono* (Naples, Aug. 13, 1775), and *Il Temistocle* (n.d.).

Lattuada, Felice, Italian composer; b. Caselle di Morimondo, near Milan, Feb. 5, 1882; d. Milan, Nov. 2, 1962. He studied at the Milan Cons. with Ferroni, graduating in 1911, then was director of the Milan Civic School of Music (1935–62). He wrote an autobiography, *La passione dominate* (Bologna, 1951).

WORKS: DRAMATIC: OPERAS: *La tempesta* (Milan, Nov. 23, 1922); *Sandha* (Genoa, Feb. 21, 1924); *Le Preziose ridicole* (Milan, Feb. 9, 1929); *Don Giovanni* (Naples, May 18, 1929); *La caverna di Salamanca* (Genoa, March 1, 1938); *Caino* (Milan, Jan. 10, 1957). Also film scores.

Laubenthal (real name, **Neumann**), **Horst (Rüdiger),** German tenor; b. Duderstadt, March 8, 1939. He began his studies in Munich and continued his training with **Rudolf Laubenthal,** whose surname he took as his own for his professional career. In 1967 he made his operatic debut as Don Ottavio at the Würzburg Festival, and then was a member of the Württemberg State Theater in Stuttgart from 1968 to 1973. In 1970 he appeared as the Steersman in *Der fliegende Holländer* at the Bayreuth Festival, and in 1972 sang Belmonte at the Glyndebourne Festival. In 1973 he became a member of the Deutsche Oper in Berlin. His guest engagements took him to the Vienna State Opera, the Bavarian State Opera in Munich, the Hamburg State Opera, the Paris Opéra, the Aix-en-Provence Festival, and other music centers. He was especially successful for his roles in Mozart's operas, and was particularly noted for his work as a concert artist.

Laubenthal, Rudolf, German tenor; b. Düsseldorf, March 18, 1886; d. Pöcking, Starnberger See, Oct. 2, 1971. At first he studied medicine in Munich and Berlin; simultaneously he took vocal lessons with Lilli Lehmann. In 1913 he made his debut in Berlin at the Deutsches Opernhaus, and sang there regularly; from 1919 to 1923 he also was engaged by the Bavarian State Opera in Munich. He made his Metropolitan Opera debut in New York as Walther von Stolzing in *Die Meistersinger von Nürnberg* on Nov. 9, 1923; he continued on the company's roster until 1933; he also sang with the Covent Garden Opera in London (1926–30) and made guest appearances in Chicago and San Francisco. In 1937 he retired from the operatic stage. He was primarily noted as a Wagnerian.

Launis (real name, **Lindberg**), **Armas (Emanuel),** Finnish composer; b. Hämeenlinna, April 22, 1884; d. Nice, Aug. 7, 1959. He studied cello and composition at the orch. school of the Helsinki Phil. Soc. (1901–07); after training with Klatte at the Berlin Stern Cons. (1907–08) and with Bauszern in Weimar (1909), he completed his studies with I. Krohn at the Univ. of Helsinki (Ph.D., 1913, with the diss. *Über Art, Entstehung und Verbreitung der Estnisch-Finnischen Runenmelodien*; publ. in Helsinki, 1913). In 1930 he settled in Nice.

WORKS: OPERAS: *Seitsemän veljestäf* (The 7 Brothers; Helsinki, April 11, 1913); *Kullervo* (Helsinki, Feb. 28, 1917); *Aslak Hetta* (Helsinki, 1922); *Noidan laulu* (The Sorcerer's Song; 1932); *Lumottu silkkihuivi* (The Magic Silk Kerchief; 1937); *Jehudith* (1940).

Laurence, Elizabeth, English mezzo-soprano; b. Harrogate, Nov. 22, 1949. She studied at the Trinity College of Music in London, and then pursued a concert career in Europe. In 1986 she sang Stravinsky's Jocasta at the Madrid Opera. She appeared in the premiere of Osborne's *The Electrification of the Soviet Union* at the Glyndebourne Festival in 1987. In 1988 she sang in the rev. version of Boulez's *Le visage nuptial* at Milan's La Scala and appeared as Fricka in *Das Rheingold* in Paris. Her debut at London's Covent Garden followed in 1989 in the British premiere of Berio's *Un re in Ascolto*, where she returned in 1991 to sing in the premiere of Birtwistle's *Gawain*. In 1989 she also sang in the premiere of Höller's *Der Meister und Margarita* in Paris. She was engaged to sing in the premiere of Osborne's *Terrible Mouth* in

London in 1992. In 1993 she sang at the Salzburg Festival, returning there in 1996. In 1998 she appeared in *Lulu* in Paris.

Laurencie, Lionel de la. See **La Laurencie, (Marie Bertrand) Lionel (Jules), Comte de.**

Lauri-Volpi, Giacomo, famous Italian tenor; b. Lanuvio, near Rome, Dec. 11, 1892; d. Valencia, March 17, 1979. He received training in law before turning to vocal studies with Antonio Cotogni at the Accademia di Santa Cecilia in Rome; he completed his vocal training with Enrico Rosati. In 1919 he made his operatic debut under the name Giacomo Rubini in Viterbo as Arturo in *I Puritani*. He sang for the first time under his real name in Rome in 1920 as Des Grieux in *Manon*. In 1922 he made his debut at Milan's La Scala as the Duke of Mantua, and continued to sing there as a great favorite until the outbreak of World War II in 1939. On Jan. 26, 1923, he made his Metropolitan Opera debut in New York as the Duke of Mantua, and subsequently was one of the principal members on its roster until 1933. While at the Metropolitan, he sang Calaf in the U.S. premiere of *Turandot* on Nov. 16, 1926, and also had notable success in such roles as Cavaradossi, Radames, Pollione, Alfredo, Canio, Faust, and Rodolfo. In 1925 and in 1936 he was a guest artist at London's Covent Garden. On Feb. 28, 1928, he appeared as Boito's Nerone at the opening of the new Teatro Reale dell'Opera in Rome. He sang Arnold in the centenary staging of Rossini's *Guillaume Tell* at La Scala in 1929, and also appeared at the Paris Opéra and Opéra Comique that same year. He settled in Burjasot, near Valencia. After World War II ended, he resumed singing in Italy, as well as in Spain. In 1959 he retired from public performances. However, in 1972, when he was in his 80th year, he astounded an audience at a gala performance at Barcelona's Teatro Liceo when he sang *Nessun dorma* from *Turandot*. At the apex of his career, Lauri-Volpi was hailed as one of the foremost lyrico-dramatic tenors of his era. The range and flexibility of his voice, his command of declamation, and his glorious legato, were memorable. He publ. the books *L'equivoco* (Milan, 1938), *Cristalli viventi* (Rome, 1948), *A viso aperto* (Milan, 1953), *Voci parallele* (Milan, 1955), and *Misteri della voce umana* (Milan, 1957).

BIBL.: J. Menéndez, *G. L.-V.* (Madrid, 1990).

Lavagne, André, French composer; b. Paris, July 12, 1913. He studied at the Paris Cons.; he won 1st prize in piano (1933) and Premier 2d Grand Prix de Rome (1938). In 1941 he was appointed inspector of music in Paris schools. He composed the operas *Comme ils s'aiment* (Paris, 1941) and *Corinne* (Enghiens-les-Bains, 1956), as well as several ballets (*Le Pauvre Jongleur, Kermesse* et al.).

Lavagnino, Angelo Francesco, Italian composer; b. Genoa, Feb. 22, 1909; d. Gavi, Aug. 21, 1987. He studied with Renzo Rossi and Vito Frazzi at the Milan Cons., graduating in 1933. From 1948 to 1962 he was a prof. of film music at the Accademia Musicale Chigiana in Siena. Among his compositions was the opera *Malafonte* (Antwerp, 1952).

Lavallée, Calixa, Canadian pianist and composer; b. Vercheres, Quebec, Dec. 28, 1842; d. Boston, Jan. 21, 1891. He first studied with his father, then at the Paris Cons. with Marmontel (piano), and Bazin and Boieldieu *fils* (composition). Returning to Canada, he made tours of his native country and the United States. He took part in the American Civil War; in 1881 he became soloist in the company of Etelka Gerster. He wrote the music to the Canadian national song "O Canada" (Montreal, June 24, 1880; poem by Judge Adolphe B. Routhier). He subsequently settled in Boston, where he became an instructor at the Petersilea Academy. He wrote a comic opera, *The Widow* (Springfield, Ill., March 25, 1882).

BIBL.: E. Lapierre, *C. L.: Musicien national du Canada* (Montreal, 1936).

Lavigna, Vincenzo, Italian composer and teacher; b. Altamura, Feb. 21, 1776; d. Milan, Sept. 14, 1836. He studied at the Cons. di S. Maria di Loreto in Naples, subsequently going to Milan, where he was maestro al cembalo at La Scala (1802–32); he also was prof. of solfeggio at the Milan Cons. (from 1823); he was a teacher of Verdi. He wrote 10 operas, of which his first, *La muta per amore, ossia Il Medico per forza* (Milan, 1803), was his best; also 2 ballets.

BIBL.: G. De Napoli, *La triade melodrammatica altamurana: Giacamo Tritto, V. L., Saverio Mercadante* (Milan, 1931).

La Violette, Wesley, American composer and teacher; b. St. James, Minn., Jan. 4, 1894; d. Escondido, Calif., July 29, 1978. He studied at the Northwestern Univ. School of Music (graduated, 1917) and at the Chicago Musical College (D.Mus., 1925), where he was a member of the faculty (1923–33). After teaching at De Paul Univ. in Chicago (1933–40), where he also was director of De Paul Univ. Press, he taught at the Los Angeles Cons. (from 1946). He also was active as a lecturer on philosophy, religion, and the arts. Among his books were *Music and its Makers* (1938) and *The Crown of Wisdom* (1949), the latter devoted to religious mysticism. His compositions followed generally along traditional pathways, although he was not adverse to atonal usages. Among his works were the operas *Shylock* (1927) and *The Enlightened One* (1935) and the ballet *Schubertiana* (1935).

Lavrangas, Dionyssios, Greek conductor, composer, and pedagogue; b. Argostólion, Oct. 17, 1860?; d. Razata, Cephalonia, July 18, 1941. After studies with N. Serao (violin) and Olivieri and Metaxas-Tzanis (harmony) in Argostólion, he went to Naples to pursue his training with Scarano (harmony and counterpoint) and Ross (piano); he also was a student at the Cons. of San Pietro a Majella there of Rossi and P. Serao (composition). He then went to Paris and had lessons with Dubois (harmony), Anthiome (piano), and Franck (organ); he also took courses at the Cons. there with Delibes and Massenet. After working as a touring opera conductor, he settled in Athens as conductor of the Phil. Soc. (1894–96); he then was founder-conductor of the Elliniko Melodhrama (Greek Opera; 1900–1935). He also was active as a teacher, and served as director of the opera school of the Hellenic Cons. (1919–24). Lavrangas was an important figure in the development of the Ionian school of composition. His works are reflective of French and Italian models.

WORKS: DRAMATIC: OPERAS: *Elda di Vorn* (c.1886; Naples, c. 1890); *La vita è un sogno* (1887; Act 4 rev. as *Mayissa* [The Sorceress], Athens, Oct. 8, 1901); *Galatea* (c.1887); *Ta dyo adelfia* (The 2 Brothers; Athens, April 24, 1900); *O lytrotis* (The Redeemer; 1900–1903; Corfu, Feb. 24, 1934); *Dido* (1906–09; Athens, April 10, 1909); *Mavri petaloudha* (Black Butterfly; Athens, Jan. 25, 1929); *Aida* (c.1928); *Ikaros* (c.1930); *Ena paramythi*, comic opera (1930); *Fakanapas*, comic opera (1935; Athens, Dec. 2, 1950); *Frosso* (1938). OPERETTAS: *I aspri tricha* (The White Hair; Athens, March 22, 1917); *Sporting Club* (Athens, Aug. 4, 1917); *Dhipli Fotia* (Double Flame; Athens, Jan. 10, 1918); *Satore* (n.d.); *O Tragoudistis tou Kazinou* (The Casino Singer; Athens, July 7, 1934; in collaboration with others). OTHER: Ballets.

Lavrovskaya, Elizaveta Andreievna, Russian mezzo-soprano; b. Kashin, Tver district, Oct. 13, 1845; d. Petrograd, Nov. 4, 1919. She studied at the Elizabeth Inst. and the St. Petersburg Cons., making her debut in Gluck's *Orfeo* (1867), then studied with P. Viardot in Paris. She sang opera in St. Petersburg (1868–72; 1879–80) and at the Bolshoi Theater in Moscow (1890); she also appeared as a recitalist. She taught at the Moscow Cons. (from 1888). Tchaikovsky admired her vocal abilities and wrote his 6 songs of op. 27 for her.

Lavry, Marc, Latvian-born Israeli conductor and composer; b. Riga, Dec. 22, 1903; d. Haifa, March 20, 1967. After attending the Riga Cons., he studied with Teichmüller at the Leipzig Cons.; he also received private instruction from Glazunov. He began his career conducting opera and ballet in Latvia and Germany. In 1935 he went to Palestine; he was conductor of the Palestine Folk Opera (1941–47) and then director of the music dept. of the shortwave radio station Kol Zion La Gola (1950–58). In 1952 he visited the United States. His music is imbued with intense feeling for

Jewish folk motifs. Among his works prior to his going to Palestine, the most notable is *Fantastische Suite* for Orch. (1932). He was the composer of the first Palestinian opera in Hebrew to receive a stage performance, *Dan Hashomer* (Dan the Guard; Tel Aviv, Feb. 17, 1945, composer conducting); he also wrote an opera in the form of a series of cantillations with homophonic instrumental accompaniment entitled *Tamar and Judah* (1958; concert perf., N.Y., March 22, 1970); other works include the oratorio *Esther ha'malka* (Queen Esther; 1960).

Lawes, William, important English composer; b. Salisbury (baptized), May 1, 1602; d. in battle at the siege of Chester, Sept. 24, 1645. His brother was the English composer Henry Lawes (b. Dinton, Wiltshire, Jan. 5, 1596; d. London, Oct. 21, 1662). William Lawes most likely commenced his musical studies with his father, then found a patron in Edward Seymour, Earl of Hertford, who enabled him to study with Coperario in London. He became active at the court, being made "musician in ordinary for the lutes and voices" to Charles I in 1635; he joined his monarch's army in 1642, losing his life during the Civil War. He excelled as a composer of both vocal and instrumental music. Of historical significance is the music he wrote for the court masques, occasionally in collaboration with his brother or others.

WORKS: Over 200 songs; also music to Jonson's *Entertainment at Welbeck* (1633); Fletcher's play *The Faithful Shepherdess* (1633); Shirley's masque *The Triumph of Peace* (1634); Davenant's play *Love and Honour* (1634); Davenant's masque *The Triumphs of the Prince d'Amour* (1636); Jonson's play *Epicoene, or The Silent Woman* (1636); W. Cartwright's play *The Royal Slave* (1636); Shirley's play *The Duke's Mistress* (1636); W. Berkeley's play *The Lost Lady* (1637); J. Mayne's play *The City March* (1637); J. Suckling's play *Aglaura* (1637); Beaumont and Fletcher's play *Cupid's Revenge* (1637); Davenant's masque *Britannia triumphans* (1638); Ford's play *The Lady's Trial* (1638); Davenant's play *The Unfortunate Lovers* (1638); Suckling's play *The Goblins* (1638); Suckling's play *The Tragedy of Brennoralt* (1639); H. Glapthorne's play *Argalus and Parthenia* (1639); Cavendish's play *The Country Captain* (1640); Shirley's play *The Cardinal* (1641); J. Denham's play *The Sophy* (1641); R. Brome's play *The Jovial Crew* (1641); etc.

BIBL.: M. Lefkowitz, *W. L.* (London, 1960).

Lawrence, Dorothea Dix, American soprano and folk-song collector; b. N.Y., Sept. 22, 1899; d. Plainfield, N.J., May 23, 1979. She studied with Cesare Stunai, Henry Russell, and Katherine Opdycke in New York. She made her operatic debut as Gounod's Marguerite with the Quebec Opera in Montreal in 1929, then appeared in opera in New York, Philadelphia, and elsewhere. She became active as a folk-song collector, presenting recitals in which she sang American Indian songs in their original languages as well as other folk songs and art songs by established composers; toured Europe as a recitalist (1952–54). She publ. the book *Folklore Songs of the United States* (1959).

Lawrence, Gertrude (real name, **Gertrud Alexandra Dagmar Lawrence Klasen**), English actress, singer, and dancer; b. London, July 4, 1898; d. N.Y., Sept. 6, 1952. She began her career with appearances in British revues (from 1910); she starred in *André Charlot's Revue* in London, with which she made her N.Y. debut (1924). George and Ira Gershwin wrote for her the musicals *Oh, Kay!* (1926) and *Treasure Girl* (1928). After working mainly as an actress in England and the United States, she won great critical acclaim as Liza Elliot in the Kurt Weill and Moss Hart musical play *Lady in the Dark* (1941); her last role was as Anna in the Rodgers and Hammerstein musical *The King and I* (1951). She publ. her autobiography as *A Star Danced* (1945).

BIBL.: R. Aldrich, *G. L. as Mrs. A.* (N.Y., 1954); S. Morley, *G. L.* (London, 1981).

Lawrence, Marjorie (Florence), noted Australian soprano; b. Dean's Marsh, Victoria, Feb. 17, 1907; d. Little Rock, Ark., Jan. 13, 1979. She studied in Melbourne with Ivor Boustead, then in Paris with Cécile Gilly. She made her debut as Elisabeth in *Tannhäuser* in Monte Carlo (1932); then sang at the Paris Opéra (1933–36), gaining success as Donna Anna, Aida, Ortrud, Brangäne, and Brünnhilde. She made her American debut at the Metropolitan Opera in New York on Dec. 18, 1935, as Brünnhilde in *Die Walküre*, where she quickly established herself as a leading Wagnerian on its roster; she also appeared as Alceste, Thaïs, and Salome. She also made guest appearances with the Chicago, San Francisco, St. Louis, and Cincinnati operas. An attack of polio during a performance of *Die Walküre* (1941) interrupted her career. While she never walked again unaided, her determination to return to the operatic stage led to the resumption of her career; her first appearance at the Metropolitan Opera following her illness came on Dec. 27, 1942, when she sang the Venusberg duet in a concert with Melchior, reclining upon a couch. Her last appearance there took place when she sang Venus on April 6, 1944. She continued to make occasional appearances until her retirement in 1952, then devoted herself to teaching. She was a prof. of voice at Tulane Univ. (1956–60) and prof. of voice and director of the opera workshop at Southern Illinois Univ. (from 1960). She publ. an autobiography, *Interrupted Melody, The Story of My Life* (N.Y., 1949), which was made into a film in 1955.

Lawrence (real name, **Cohen**), **Robert,** American conductor; b. N.Y., March 18, 1912; d. there, Aug. 9, 1981. He was educated at Columbia Univ. (M.A., 1934) and the Inst. of Musical Art in New York. From 1939 to 1943 he was a music critic for the *N.Y. Herald Tribune*. During World War II, he served in the U.S. Army in Italy. After conducting opera in Rome (1944–45), he was conductor of the Phoenix (Ariz.) Sym. Orch. (1949–52) and the Ankara Sym. Orch. (1957–58). In 1961 he founded the Friends of French Opera in New York, with which he conducted performances of many rarely heard scores. He later conducted opera in Atlanta and served as head of the opera dept. at the Peabody Cons. of Music in Baltimore. He was the author of the books *The World of Opera* (1958) and *A Rage for Opera* (1971).

Lawton, Jeffrey, English tenor; b. Oldham, 1939. He studied with Elsie Thurston at the Royal Manchester College of Music (1954–58) and with Patrick McGuigan. In 1974 he sang Don Alvaro with the Manchester Opera Co. His professional operatic debut followed in 1981 as Florestan with the Welsh National Opera in Cardiff, where he sang Siegfried in its *Ring* cycle in 1985. His other roles there included those by Berlioz, Strauss, and Janáček. In 1986 he made his first appearance at London's Covent Garden as Siegfried, and returned there as Tristan in 1993. Following engagements in Paris and Brussels as Otello in 1987, he sang Siegmund in Cologne in 1988, returning there as Siegfried in 1989. In the latter year, he portrayed Edmund in Reimann's *Lear* at the English National Opera in London. He sang Shuisky in *Boris Godunov* at Opera North in Leeds and Strauss's Herod at the London Promenade Concerts in 1993. In 1996 he created the role of Pedro in the premiere of MacMillan's *Inés de Castro* in Edinburgh. He also sang widely as a concert artist in Europe.

Lays, François, French tenor; b. La Barthe de Nesthes, Feb. 14, 1758; d. Ingrande, near Angers, March 30, 1831. He studied theology and music at the Guaraison monastery. After settling in Paris, he joined the Opéra in 1780, where he appeared as one of its principal members until 1823. He also was engaged at court concerts and at the Concert Spirituel. From 1795 to 1799 he was prof. of voice at the Cons. He was the principal singer at Napoleon's court from 1801 to 1814. From 1819 to 1826 he taught at the École Royale de Chant et de Déclamation. He publ. *Lays, artiste du théâtre des arts, à ses concitoyens* (Paris, 1793).

Lazar, Filip, Romanian composer and pianist; b. Craiova, May 18, 1894; d. Paris, Nov. 3, 1936. He was a student of Kiriac (theory), Castaldi (harmony and counterpoint), and Saegiu (piano) at the Bucharest Cons. (1907–12), and of Krehl (harmony and composition) and Teichmüller (piano) at the Leipzig Cons. (1913–14). In subsequent years, he made tours as a pianist in Europe and the United States as a champion of modern music. In 1920 he helped to found the Romanian Composers' Soc. In 1928 he founded and served as chairman of the modern music soc. Triton in Paris. He was active as a piano teacher in France and Switzerland from 1928. In 1924 he won the Enesco Prize and in 1931 the prize of the Romanian Radio. His compositions were infused with Romanian folk tunes until he adopted a more adventuresome style in 1928, in which he utilized serial and neoclassical elements. He composed a ballet, *La bouteille de Panurge*, ballet (1918), and an opera cantata, *Les images de Béatrice* (1928).

BIBL.: V. Tomescu, *F. L.* (Bucharest, 1963).

Lazare, Martin, Belgian pianist and composer; b. Brussels, Oct. 27, 1829; d. there, Aug. 6, 1897. He studied in The Hague with van der Does, and at the Paris Cons. with Zimmerman, then traveled to London, Germany, the United States, and Canada. Among his works are the opera *Le Roi de Bohème* (The Hague, 1852) and the operetta *Les Deux Mandarins* (Brussels, 1878).

Lazarev, Alexander, Russian conductor; b. Moscow, July 5, 1945. He was trained in Moscow at the Central Music School and at the Cons., and at the Leningrad Cons. In 1971 he took 1st prize in the Moscow Young Conductors Competition, and then was a prizewinner at the Herbert von Karajan competition in Berlin in 1972. In 1973 he became a conductor at the Bolshoi Theater in Moscow, where he founded the Ensemble of Soloists in 1978 to further the performance of contemporary music. He appeared as both an opera and sym. conductor throughout Europe. From 1987 to 1995 he was chief conductor of the Bolshoi Theater. From 1988 to 1993 he was Generalmusikdirektor of the Duisburg Sym. Orch. From 1992 to 1995 he was principal guest conductor of the BBC Sym. Orch. in London. In 1997–98 he was principal conductor designate, and from 1998 principal conductor of the Royal Scottish National Orch. in Glasgow.

Lazaro, Hippolito, Spanish tenor; b. Barcelona, Aug. 13, 1887; d. Madrid, May 14, 1974. He studied in Milan; then sang operetta in Barcelona. He went to London in 1912, singing at the Coliseum under the name of Antonio Manuele; in 1913 he returned to Italy, where Mascagni chose him to create the role of Ugo in *Parisina* at La Scala in Milan. He made his Metropolitan Opera debut in New York on Jan. 31, 1918, as the Duke of Mantua in *Rigoletto*; he remained on its roster until 1920. In 1921 he created the role of Piccolo Marat in Mascagni's opera in Rome; also the role of Giannetto in *La cena delle beffe* by Giordano at La Scala in 1924. He made guest appearances with the Vienna State Opera, the Budapest Opera, and the Teatro Colón in Buenos Aires. He retired in 1950.

Lazarus, Daniel, French conductor and composer; b. Paris, Dec. 13, 1898; d. there, June 27, 1964. He studied with Diémer, Leroux, and Vidal at the Paris Cons., taking the premier prix in composition (1915). He was conductor of the Théâtre du Vieux Colombier (1921–25), then artistic director of the Paris Opéra Comique (1936–39); later he was chorus master of the Paris Opéra (1946–56), then prof. at the Schola Cantorum in Paris (from 1956). He publ. *Accès à la musique* (Paris, 1960). His compositions include the operas *L'Illustre Magicien* (1924), *La Véritable Histoire de Wilhelm Meister* (1927), *Trumpeldor* (1935), and *La Chambre bleue* (1938); also 3 ballets and incidental music.

Lazarus, Gustav, German pianist and composer; b. Cologne, July 19, 1861; d. Berlin, May 24, 1920. He studied with I. Seiss, G. Jensen, and F. Wüllner. He was a prof. of piano at the Scharwenka Cons. in Berlin (1887–99); in 1899 he became director of the Breslaur Cons. and Seminary in Berlin. He appeared with success as a pianist in Germany, France, and England. He wrote 170 opus numbers, including the operas *Mandanika* (Elberfeld, 1899) and *Das Nest der Zaunkönige*.

Lazzari, (Joseph) Sylvio, Austrian-born French conductor and composer; b. Bozen, Dec. 30, 1857; d. Suresnes, near Paris, June 10, 1944. He was born into a wealthy Austro-Italian family. After extensive travels, he settled in Paris and in 1883 he entered the Cons., where he was a student of Gounod, Guiraud, and Franck. In 1896 he became a naturalized French citizen. He became active as a theater conductor, and also wrote operas and incidental music. His most distinguished work was the tragic opera *La lépreuse* or *L'ensorcelé* (1900–01; Paris, Feb. 7, 1912). His opera *La tour de feu* (1925; Paris, Jan. 28, 1928) was the first to utilize film as an integral part of the score. Other works include the operas *Armor* (1897; Prague, Nov. 7, 1898), *Melaenis* (1913; Mulhouse, March 25, 1927), and *Le sauteriot* (1913–15; Chicago, Jan. 19, 1918); also a pantomime, *Lulu* (Paris, May 1889), and incidental music.

Lazzari, Virgilio, Italian-born American bass; b. Assisi, April 20, 1887; d. Castel Gandolfo, Oct. 4, 1953. He made his stage debut as L'Incognito in Suppe's *Boccaccio* with the Vitale Operetta Co. in 1908, remaining with the company until 1911. After studies with Cotogni in Rome, he made his operatic debut at the Teatro Costanzi there in 1914, then sang in South America. In 1916 he made his U.S. debut as Ramfis in St. Louis. He settled in the United States and became a naturalized American citizen. From 1918 to 1933 he was a member of the Chicago Opera. On Dec. 28, 1933, he made his Metropolitan Opera debut in New York as Pedro in *L'Africaine*; he remained on the roster until 1940, then returned for the 1943–51 seasons. He also sang at the Salzburg Festivals (1934–39) and appeared as Leporello at London's Covent Garden (1939). He became celebrated for his portrayal of Archibaldo in Montemezzi's *L'amore dei tre re*.

Lear, Evelyn (née **Shulman**), outstanding American soprano; b. N.Y., Jan. 8, 1926. She learned to play the piano and the horn before pursuing vocal training with John Yard in Washington, D.C., and with Sergius Kagen at the Juilliard School of Music in New York. She also attended N.Y. Univ. and Hunter College of the City Univ. of N.Y. In 1955 she made her N.Y. recital debut, the same year that she married her 2d husband, **Thomas Stewart.** For professional reasons, however, she retained her first husband's surname of Lear. After obtaining a Fulbright grant, she pursued her studies with Maria Ivogün at the Berlin Hochschule für Musik. On May 17, 1959, she made her operatic debut as Strauss's Composer at the Berlin Städtische Oper. She attracted wide notice when she essayed the role of Lulu in a concert performance in Vienna in 1960, returning there in 1962 to sing the role on stage. In 1961 she created the title role in Klebe's *Alkmene* in Berlin, and in 1963 the role of Jeanne in Egk's *Die Verlobung in San Domingo* in Munich. At the Salzburg Festivals, she appeared as Cherubino (1962–64) and as Fiordiligi (1965). In 1965 she made her first appearance at London's Covent Garden singing Donna Elvira. On March 17, 1967, she made her Metropolitan Opera debut in New York creating the role of Lavinia in Levy's *Mourning Becomes Electra*. In subsequent seasons, she returned to sing Octavian and Berg's Marie (1969), Strauss's Composer (1970), Tosca and Dido (1973), Donna Elvira (1974), Alice Ford (1975), and Countess Geschwitz (1980). She also created the roles of Irma Arkadina in Pasatieri's *The Seagull* in Houston (1974) and Magda in Ward's *Minutes to Midnight* in Miami (1982). On Oct. 15, 1985, she made her farewell appearance at the Metropolitan Opera as the Marschallin. In 1987 she sang Countess Geschwitz in Chicago. Throughout her operatic career, she also pursued a notably successful concert career. She often appeared in both opera and concerts with her husband.

Leborne, Aimé-Ambroise-Simon, French composer; b. Brussels, Dec. 29, 1797; d. Paris, April 2, 1866. He went to France as a child, then studied at the Paris Cons. with Berton and Cherubini; won the 2d Prix de Rome (1818) and then the 1st Prix de Rome (1820). He subsequently was on its faculty, later serving as prof. of counterpoint and fugue (1836–40), then of composition (1840–66); he also was made librarian of the Paris Opéra (1829) and of the Royal Chapel (1834). In 1853 he became a Chevalier of the Légion d'honneur. He ed. a new edition of Catel's *Traité d'harmonie* (Paris, 1848; with numerous additions). He wrote the operas *Les Deux Figaro* (Paris, Aug. 22, 1827; in collaboration with Carafa), *Le Camp du drap d'or* (Paris, Feb. 23, 1828; in collaboration with Baton and Rifaut), and *Cinq ans d'entr'acte and Lequel* (Paris, March 21, 1838).

Lebrun, Franziska (Dorothea née **Danzi**), renowned German soprano; b. Mannheim (baptized), March 24, 1756; d. Berlin, May 14, 1791. She made her debut as Sandrina in Sacchini's *La Contadina in corte in Schwetzingen* (Aug. 9, 1772), then became a prominent member of the Mannheim Court Opera, where she created the countess in Holzbauer's *Günther von Schwarzburg* (Jan. 5, 1777). She made her first appearance in London at the King's Theatre as Ariene in Sacchini's *Creso* (Nov. 8, 1777), then was chosen to sing in Salieri's *Europa riconosciuta* at the opening of Milan's Teatro alla Scala (Aug. 3, 1778). She appeared at the Paris Concert Spirituel (1779) and again in London (1779–81); she also continued to sing with the Court Opera in Mannheim, and later when the court went to Munich and likewise made guest appearances in Vienna and Verona, and later in Naples (1786–87) and Berlin (1789–90). She also composed and publ. 36 sonatas for Violin and Piano. She married the oboist and composer Ludwig August Lebrun (1778), with whom she appeared in concerts.

Lebrun, Louis-Sébastien, French tenor and composer; b. Paris, Dec. 10, 1764; d. there, June 27, 1829. He received training in voice and composition at the maîtrise of Notre Dame in Paris (1771–83). He served as music director of the church of St. Germain-l'Aurerrois before making his operatic debut in 1787 at the Paris Opéra as Polynices in Sacchini's *Oedipe à Colone*. He also appeared at the Concert Spirituel. From 1791 to 1799 he sang at the Théâtre Feydeau before serving as an understudy at the Opéra. In 1803 he became a singing tutor there. In 1807 he was made a tenor and in 1810 chef du chant at Napoleon's chapelle. Lebrun wrote about 15 stage works, the most successful being his operas *Marcelin* (Paris, March 22, 1800) and *Le Rossignol* (Paris, April 23, 1816).

Leça, Armando Lopes, Portuguese choral conductor, folk-song collector, and composer; b. Leça da Palmeira, Aug. 9, 1893; d. Vila Nova de Gaia, Sept. 7, 1977. He studied with Oscar da Silva. He was active as a choral conductor and a collector of native folk songs; he publ. an authoritative ed. of popular Portuguese music (1922; expanded ed. in 2 vols., 1947). Among his compositions were 2 operettas: *Maio florido* (1918) and *Bruxa* (1919).

Lecoq, (Alexandre) Charles, noted French composer; b. Paris, June 3, 1832; d. there, Oct. 24, 1918. He learned to play the flageolet and piano as a youth, and later studied harmony with Crèvecoeur. He then was admitted to the Paris Cons. (1849), where he took courses with Bazin, Halévy, and Benoist; he won 2d prize in counterpoint and was primus accessit in the organ class, but was compelled to leave the Cons. to assist his family (1854). He first gained notice as a composer when he shared a prize with Bizet sponsored by Offenbach for the Théâtre des Bouffes-Parisiens, for the operetta *Le Docteur Miracle* (April 8, 1857). Although he brought out 7 more works for the stage during the next decade, it was only with his *Fleur-de-thé* (Paris, April 11, 1868) that he attained success. After going to Brussels (1870), he scored notable successes with his operettas *Les Cent Vierges* (March 16, 1872), *La Fille de Madame Angot* (Dec. 4, 1872), and *Giroflé-Girofla* (March 24, 1874); they subsequently were performed in Paris with great success, making Lecoq the leading Parisian operetta composer of his day after Offenbach. After returning to Paris, he brought out such popular favorites as *La Petite Mariée* (Dec. 21, 1875), *Le Petit Duc* (Jan. 25, 1878), *Janot* (Jan. 21, 1881), Le Jour et la nuit (Nov. 5, 1881), and *Le Coeur et la main* (Oct. 19, 1882). In subsequent years he continued to write works for the stage, but he failed to equal his previous successes. He also tried his hand at more serious compositional efforts, for example his opera *Plutus* (Paris, March 31, 1886), but was unsuccessful. He was made a Chevalier (1900) and an Officer (1910) of the Légion d'honneur. His music was distinguished by melodic grace, instrumental finish, and dramatic acumen. Among his other operettas, all first perf. in Paris, were *Huis-clos* (Jan. 28, 1859), *Le Baiser à la porte* (March 26, 1864), *Le Barbier de Trouville* (Nov. 19, 1871), *La Marjolaine* (Feb. 3, 1877), *Le Grand Casimir* (Jan. 11, 1879), and *La Princesse des Canaries* (Feb. 9, 1883); also the opéras comiques *L'Égyptienne* (Paris, Nov. 8, 1890), *Yetta* (Brussels, March 7, 1903), and *Le Trahison de Pan* (Aix-les-Bains, 1911), and the ballet *Le Cygne* (Paris, April 20, 1899).

BIBL.: L. Schneider, *Les Maîtres de l'opérette française: Hervé, C. L.* (Paris, 1924); idem, *Une Heure de musique avec C. L.* (Paris, 1930).

Ledger, Philip (Stevens), noted English conductor, organist, harpsichordist, pianist, editor, and arranger; b. Bexhill-on-Sea, Sussex, Dec. 12, 1937. He was educated at King's College, Cambridge, and at the Royal College of Music, London. He served as Master of the Music at Chelmsford Cathedral (1962–65) and as director of music at the Univ. of East Anglia (1965–73), where he served as dean of the School of Fine Arts and Music (1968–71). In 1968 he was named an artistic director of the Aldeburgh Festival; subsequently was engaged as conductor of the Cambridge Univ. Musical Soc. (1973) and director of music and organist at King's College (1974). In 1982 he was appointed principal of the Royal Scottish Academy of Music and Drama in Glasgow. He ed. *The Oxford Book of English Madrigals* (1978) and works of Byrd, Purcell, and Handel. A versatile musician, he is renowned as an elegant performer of early English music. In 1985 he was made a Commander of the Order of the British Empire.

Leduc, Jacques, Belgian composer and teacher; b. Jette, near Brussels, March 1, 1932. He studied music at the Royal Cons. in Brussels and privately with Jean Absil. He was director of the Uccle Academy of Music (1962–83); he was made a prof. of harmony (1968), of counterpoint (1972), and of fugue (1979) at the Royal Cons. in Brussels; he was also director of the Chapelle Musicale Reine Elisabeth (from 1976). He was made a member of the Royal Academy of Sciences, Letters, and Fine Arts of Belgium in 1983. He composed *Nous attendons Sémiramis*, lyric comedy (Belgian TV, Feb. 6, 1973).

Lee, Dai-Keong, Hawaiian composer of Chinese descent; b. Honolulu, Sept. 2, 1915. Following premed training at the Univ. of Hawaii (1933–36), he pursued musical studies with Sessions and Jacobi at the Juilliard Graduate School in New York (1938–41), with Copland at the Berkshire Music Center in Tanglewood (summer 1941), and with Luening at Columbia Univ. (M.A., 1951). He held 2 Guggenheim fellowships (1945, 1951). Lee's works utilize various native elements for the most part, although he has embraced a neoclassical approach in some of his more ambitious scores.

WORKS: DRAMATIC: OPERAS: *The Poet's Dilemma* (N.Y., April 12, 1940); *Open the Gates* (1951); *Phineas and the Nightingale* (1952); *Speakeasy* (N.Y., Feb. 8, 1957); *2 Knickerbocker Tales* (1957); *Ballad of Kitty the Barkeep* (1979; based on *Speakeasy*). MUSICAL PLAYS: *Noa Noa* (1972); *Jenny Lind* (1981; based on *Phineas and the Nightingale*). INCIDENTAL MUSIC: *Teahouse of the August Moon* (1953; orch. suite, 1954). BALLET: *Waltzing Matilda* (1951). Also film scores.

Leech, Richard, American tenor; b. Binghamton, Calif., 1956. During his student years, he made appearances as a baritone and then as a tenor. His professional career began in earnest in 1980. In subsequent years, he sang in Cincinnati, Pittsburgh, Baltimore, Houston, and Chicago. In 1987 he made his European debut as Raoul in *Les Huguenots* at the Berlin Deutsche Oper. He made his first appearance at the N.Y. City Opera as the Duke of Mantua in 1988. In 1990 he made his Metropolitan Opera debut in New York as Gounod's Faust and also sang for the first time at Milan's La Scala as Pinkerton. In the 1991–92 season he made his debut at London's Covent Garden as Raoul. He returned to the Metropolitan Opera in 1994 as Rodolfo. In 1995 he sang Pinkerton at the San Francisco Opera. In 1997 he appeared as Faust at the Metropolitan Opera. He sang Gounod's Roméo at the San Diego Opera in 1998.

Leedy, Douglas, American composer, pianist, and conductor; b. Portland, Oreg., March 3, 1938. He studied at Pomona College (B.A., 1959) and at the Univ. of Calif. at Berkeley (M.A., 1962). He played the horn in the Oakland (Calif.) Sym. Orch. and in the

San Francisco Opera and Ballet orchs. (1960–65); in 1965–66 he held a joint U.S.-Polish government grant for study in Poland. From 1967 to 1970 he was on the faculty of the Univ. of Calif., Los Angeles; from 1973 to 1978 he taught at Reed College in Portland, Oreg. He was conductor of the Oregon Telemann Ensemble, later known as the Harmonie Universelle. From 1984 to 1985 he was music director of the Portland Baroque Orch. His early works cultivated avant-garde methods of electronic application to mixed media, but later he sought to overcome the restrictions of Western music and its equal temperament; for this purpose, he began in 1979 to work with the Carnatic vocalist K. V. Narayanaswamy in Madras, India. Parallel to that, he evinced an interest in early Western music; he ed. *Chansons from Petrucci in Original Notation . . .* in the Musica Sacra et Profana series (1983). He was the author of "A Question of Intonation" in the *Journal of the Conductor's Guild* (fall 1987). Among his compositions is the chamber opera *Sebastian* for Soprano, Baritone, Chamber Ensemble, and Tape, based on documents of J. S. Bach (1971–74); also *Decay*, theater piece for Piano, Wagner Tuba, and Tape (1965), *Teddy Bear's Picnic*, audio-tactile electronic theater piece (1968), and *88 Is Great*, theater piece for many-handed Piano (1968).

Lees (real name, **Lysniansky**), **Benjamin,** distinguished Russian-born American composer and teacher; b. Harbin, Manchuria, Jan. 8, 1924. He was taken to the United States in infancy. At 5 he began piano studies with K. Rodetsky in San Francisco. At 15 he became a piano student of Marguerite Bitter in Los Angeles; he also pursued training in harmony and theory and began to compose. Following studies in theory with Stevens, Dahl, and Kanitz at the Univ. of Southern Calif. in Los Angeles (1945–49), he studied with Antheil (until 1954). In 1954 he held a Guggenheim fellowship and in 1956 a Fulbright fellowship, which enabled him to live in Europe until 1962. In 1966 he held another Guggenheim fellowship. He taught at the Peabody Cons. of Music in Baltimore (1962–64; 1966–68), Queens College of the City Univ. of N.Y. (1964–65), the Manhattan School of Music (1970–72), and the Juilliard School (1973–74). Lees's music possesses an ingratiating quality, modern but not arrogantly so. His harmonies are lucid and are couched in euphonius dissonances. He favors rhythmic asymmetry while the formal design of his works is classical in its clarity. Among his compositions are the operas *The Oracle* (1956), *Medea in Corinth* (1970; London, Jan. 10, 1971), and *The Gilded Cage* (1970–72), and the ballet *Scarlatti Portfolio* (1978; San Francisco, March 15, 1979).

Leeuw, Reinbert de, Dutch composer and conductor, brother of **Ton de Leeuw**; b. Amsterdam, Sept. 8, 1938. He studied at the Amsterdam Cons. In 1963 he was appointed to the faculty of the Royal Cons. of The Hague. A political activist, he collaborated with Louis Andriessen, Mischa Mengelberg, Peter Schat, and Jan van Vlijmen on the anti-American multimedia spectacle *Reconstructie*, produced during the Holland Festival in Amsterdam on June 29, 1969. He further wrote an opera, *Axel* (with Vlijmen; 1977). In later years, he was active as a conductor of contemporary music; he conducted the 1991 premiere of Van Glijmen's opera *Un Malheureux vêtu de Noir*. In 1994 he became director of the Tanglewood Festival of Contemporary Music. He publ. a book about Ives (with J. Bemlef; Amsterdam, 1969) and a collection of 17 articles, *Muzikale anarchie* (Amsterdam, 1973).

Leeuw, Ton (Antonius Wilhelmus Adrianus) de, prominent Dutch composer and teacher, brother of **Reinbert de Leeuw;** b. Rotterdam, Nov. 16, 1926; d. Paris, May 31, 1996. He received training in piano and theory with Toebosch in Breda, and in composition with Badings in Amsterdam (1947–49) and with Messiaen and Hartmann in Paris (1949–50); he studied ethnomusicology with Kunst in Amsterdam (1950–54) and made a study trip to India, Iran, Japan, and the Philippines (1961). After working as director of sound at the Dutch Radio in Hilversum (1954–59), he taught composition at the Amsterdam Cons. (from 1959), where he also was director. From 1962 to 1984 he likewise lectured at the Univ. of Amsterdam. He publ. the book *Muziek van de Twintigste Eeuw* (Music of the Twentieth Century; Utrecht, 1964; 2d ed., 1977). As a composer, he was honored with the Prix Italia (1956), the Prix des Jeunesses Musicales (1961), the Mathijs Vermeulen Prize (1982), and the Johan Wagenaar Prize (1983). In his varied output, Leeuw ranged widely, utilizing both contemporary Western and non-Western means of expression. He developed a personal static style in which his modal writing became increasingly diatonic.

WORKS: DRAMATIC: OPERAS: *Alceste*, television opera (Dutch TV, March 13, 1963); *De droom* (The Dream; 1963; Amsterdam, June 16, 1965); *Antigone* (1991). TELEVISION PLAY: *Litany of Our Time* (1969–70; Dutch TV, Jan 1, 1971). BALLETS: *De Bijen* (The Bees; 1964; Arnhem, Sept. 15, 1965); *Krishna en Radha* (1964).

LeFanu, Nicola (Frances), English composer and teacher; b. Wickham Bishops, Essex, April 28, 1947. She was the daughter of the medical historian William LeFanu and the composer **Elizabeth Maconchy.** Her mother was a major influence on her in her formative years. After initial training in composition with Jeremy Dale Roberts, she pursued her studies at St. Hilda's College, Oxford (B.A., 1968; M.A., 1971) and at the Royal College of Music in London (1968–69). In 1973–74 she held a Harkness fellowship and studied with Earl Kim at Harvard Univ. and Seymour Shifrin at Brandeis Univ. She was active in London as director of music at Francis Holland School (1969–72) and St. Paul's Girls School (1975–77). In 1977 she became a senior lecturer at King's College, Univ. of London. In 1979 she married the Australian composer David Lumsdaine (b. Sydney, Oct. 31, 1931), with whom she served as composer-in-residence at the New South Wales State Conservatorium of Music in Sydney that same year. As a composer, she has won several honors, including the Cobbett Prize (1969), the BBC Composers Prize (1972), and the Leverhulme Award (1989). In her works, she has developed a well-crafted style in which serial techniques are relieved by a deft handling of dramatic and lyrical writing.

WORKS: DRAMATIC: *Anti-World*, music theater (1972); *The Last Laugh*, ballet (1972; London, April 1973); *Dawnpath*, chamber opera (London, Sept. 29, 1977); *The Story of Mary O'Neill*, radiophonic opera (1986; BBC, Jan. 4, 1989); *The Green Children*, children's opera (1990); *Blood Wedding*, opera (1991–92); *The Wildman*, opera (Aldeburgh, June 9, 1995).

Lefébure-Wély, Louis James Alfred, French organist and composer; b. Paris, Nov. 13, 1817; d. there, Dec. 31, 1869. A pupil of his father, he took, at the age of 8, the latter's place as organist of the church of St.-Roch, becoming its regular organist at 14. Entering the Paris Cons. in 1832, he was taught by Benoist (organ), Laurent and Zimmerman (piano), and Berton and Halévy (composition). From 1847 to 1858 he was organist at the Madeleine; then at St. Sulpice. While he wrote an opera, *Les Recruteurs* (1861), his most celebrated piece is the elegant salon piece for piano, the *Monastery Bells*.

Lefebvre, Charles Édouard, French composer; b. Paris, June 19, 1843; d. Aix-les-Bains, Sept. 8, 1917. He studied at the Paris Cons., winning the Premier Grand Prix de Rome in 1870 for his cantata *Le Jugement de Dieu*. He joined the faculty of the Paris Cons. in 1895. Among his works are the operas *Lucrèce* (1877–78), *Le Trésor* (Angers, 1883), *Zaïre* (Lille, 1887), and *Djelma* (Paris, May 25, 1894), and the biblical drama *Judith* (Paris, 1879).

Leffler-Burckhard, Martha, German soprano; b. Berlin, June 16, 1865; d. Wiesbaden, May 14, 1954. She was a student in Dresden of Anna von Meichsner and in Paris of Pauline Viardot-García. In 1888 she made her operatic debut in Strasbourg, and then sang in Breslau (1889–90) and Cologne (1891–92). After a tour of North America (1892–93), she appeared in Bremen (1893–97) and Weimar (1898–99). From 1900 to 1912 she sang in Wiesbaden, and also appeared at London's Covent Garden (1903, 1907) and at the Metropolitan Opera in New York (debut as Brünnhilde in *Die Walküre*, March 4, 1908). She was a member of the Berlin Royal Opera from 1913 to 1918. After singing at the Berlin

Deutsches Opernhaus (1918–19), she taught voice. Among her best-known roles were Leonore, Isolde, the 3 Brünnhildes, Kundry, Ortrud, and Sieglinde.

Le Flem, Paul, French composer, choral conductor, music critic, and teacher; b. Lézardrieux, Côtes-du-Nord, March 18, 1881; d. Trégastel, Côtes-du-Nord, July 31, 1984. He settled in Paris and studied harmony with Lavignac at the Cons. (1899) before completing his training with d'Indy and Roussel at the Schola Cantorum (1904); he also studied philosophy at the Sorbonne. Le Flem wrote perceptive music criticism for *Comoedia* (1921–36), and also served as prof. of counterpoint at the Schola Cantorum (1923–39). In 1924 he became chorus master at the Opéra Comique, and from 1925 to 1939 he distinguished himself as director of the St. Gervais Choir. In 1951 he was awarded the Grand Prix Musical of Paris. From his earliest compositional efforts, Le Flem was influenced by his native Brittany. His later works also owe much to Debussy and d'Indy, and are skillfully written.

WORKS: DRAMATIC: *Endymion et Séléné*, opera (Paris, 1903); *Aucassin et Nicolette*, chante-fable (1908; private perf., Paris, May 19, 1909); *La folie de Lady Macbeth*, ballet (1934); *Le rossignol de St. Malo*, opera (1938; Paris, May 5, 1942); *Les paralytiques volent*, radio score (1938); *La clairière des fées*, opera (1943); *Magicienne de la mer*, opera (1946; Paris, Oct. 29, 1954); *Macbeth*, radio score (1950); *Côte de granit rose*, film score (1954).

BIBL.: G. Bernard-Krauss, *Hundert Jahre französischer Musikgeschichte in Leben und Werk P. L.s* (Frankfurt am Main and N.Y., 1993).

Legge, Walter, influential English recording executive, orchestral manager, and writer on music; b. London, June 1, 1906; d. St. Jean, Cap Ferrat, March 22, 1979. He was an autodidact in music. In 1927 he joined the staff of the Gramophone Co. (His Master's Voice) of London. He became an ardent champion of first-class recording projects, and in 1931 founded a subscription soc. for the purpose of recording unrecorded works. From 1938 he was active with the British Columbia recording label. He also wrote music criticism for the *Manchester Guardian* (1934–38). In 1938–39 he was assistant artistic director of London's Covent Garden. From 1942 to 1945 he was director of music of the Entertainments National Service Assn. In 1945 he founded the Philharmonia Orch. of London, which he managed with notable results as both a recording and concert ensemble until he unsuccessfully attempted to disband it in 1964. In 1953 he married **Elisabeth Schwarzkopf.**

BIBL.: E. Schwarzkopf, ed., *On and Off the Record: A Memoir of W. L.* (London, 1982; 2d ed., 1988); A. Sanders, ed., *W. L.: A Discography* (London, 1985).

Leginska (real name, **Liggins**), **Ethel,** English pianist, teacher, and composer; b. Hull, April 13, 1886; d. Los Angeles, Feb. 26, 1970. She showed a natural talent for music at an early age; the pseudonym Leginska was given to her by Lady Maud Warrender, under the illusion that a Polish-looking name might help her artistic career. She studied piano with Kwast at the Hoch Cons. in Frankfurt am Main, and later in Vienna with Leschetizky. After making her London debut (1907), she toured Europe; on Jan. 20, 1913, she appeared for the first time in America at a recital in New York. Her playing was described as having masculine vigor, dashing brilliance, and great variety of tonal color; however, criticism was voiced against an individualistic treatment of classical works. In the midst of her career as a pianist, she developed a great interest in conducting; she organized the Boston Phil. Orch. (100 players), later the Women's Sym. Orch. of Boston; appeared as a guest conductor with various orchs. in America and in Europe. In this field of activity, she also elicited interest, leading to a discussion in the press of a woman's capability of conducting an orch. While in the United States, she took courses in composition with Rubin Goldmark and Ernest Bloch; she wrote music in various genres, distinguished by rhythmic display and a certain measure of modernism. She married the American composer Emerson Whithorne (1884–1958) in 1907 (divorced in 1916). In 1939 she settled in Los Angeles as a piano teacher. Among her compositions are the operas *The Rose and the Ring* (1932; Los Angeles, Feb. 23, 1957, composer conducting) and *Gale* (Chicago, Nov. 23, 1935, composer conducting).

Legley, Victor, outstanding Belgian composer; b. Hazebrouck, June 18, 1915; d. Ostend, Nov.28, 1994. He studied viola, chamber music, counterpoint, and fugue at the Brussels Cons. (from 1934), then took private lessons in composition with Absil (1941), subsequently winning the Belgian 2d Prix de Rome (1943). He was a violist in the Belgian Radio Sym. Orch. (1936–48), then was a music producer for the Flemish dept. of the Belgian Radio, and later was made head of its serious music broadcasts on its 3d program (1962). He taught at the Brussels Cons. (1949–80). He became a member of the Belgian Royal Academy (1965); he was its president (1972) and chairman of the Société Belge des Auteurs, Compositeurs, et Editeurs (from 1981). In his works, Legley adhered to the pragmatic tenets of modern music, structurally diversified and unconstricted by inhibitions against dissonance. His 2d Violin Concerto was a mandatory work of the 1967 Queen Elisabeth violin competition finals. Other works included the opera *La Farce des deux nus* (Antwerp, Dec. 10, 1966) and the ballet *Le Bal des halles* (1954).

BIBL.: R. Wangermée, *V. L.* (Brussels, 1953).

Legrenzi, Giovanni, celebrated Italian composer; b. Clusone, near Bergamo (baptized), Aug. 12, 1626; d. Venice, May 27, 1690. He was the son of a violinist and composer named Giovanni Maria Legrenzi. In 1645 he became organist at S. Maria Maggiore in Bergamo; in 1651 he was ordained and made resident chaplain there; in 1653 he became 1st organist. In 1656 he was named maestro di cappella of the Accademia dello Spirito Santo in Ferrara. His first opera, *Nino il giusto*, was given in Ferrara in 1662. He left Ferrara in 1665, and in 1671 settled in Venice, where he served as an instructor at the Cons. dei Mendicanti; in 1683 he was its maestro di coro. In 1677 he was maestro of the Oratorio at S. Maria della Fava. In 1681 he became vice maestro of S. Marco; in 1685 he was elected maestro there. Under his regimen the orch. was increased to 34 instrumental parts (8 violins, 11 violettas, 2 viole da braccio, 3 violones, 4 theorbos, 2 cornets, 1 bassoon, and 3 trombones). Legrenzi was a noted teacher; among his pupils were Gasparini, Lotti, and Caldara, as well as his own nephew, Giovanni Varischino. Legrenzi's sonatas are noteworthy, since they served as models of Baroque forms as later practiced by Vivaldi and Bach. His operas and oratorios were marked by a development of the da capo form in arias, and his carefully wrought orch. support of the vocal parts was of historic significance as presaging the development of opera.

WORKS: DRAMATIC: OPERAS: *Nino il giusto* (Ferrara, 1662; not extant); *L'Achille in Sciro* (Ferrara, 1663; not extant); *Zenobia e Radamisto* (Ferrara, 1665); *Tiridate* (based upon the preceding; Venice, 1668; not extant); *Eteocle e Polinice* (Venice, 1675); *La divisione del mondo* (Venice, 1675); *Adone in Cipro* (Venice, 1676; not extant); *Germanico sul Reno* (Venice, 1676); *Totila* (Venice, 1677); *Il Creso* (Venice, 1681); *Antioco il grande* (Venice, 1681); *Il Pausania* (Venice, 1682); *Lisimaco riamato* (Venice, 1682); *L'Ottaviano Cesare Augusto* (Mantua, 1682; not extant); *Giustino* (Venice, 1683); *I due Cesari* (Venice, 1683); *L'anarchia dell'imperio* (Venice, 1684; not extant); *Publio Elio Pertinace* (Venice, 1684; not extant); *Ifianassa e Melampo* (Pratolino, 1685; not extant). ORATORIOS: *Oratorio del giuditio* (Vienna, 1665; not extant); *Gli sponsali d'Ester* (Modena, 1676; not extant); *Il Sedicia* (Ferrara, 1676); *La vendita del core humano* (Ferrara, 1676); *Il Sisara* (Ferrara, 1678; not extant); *Decollatione di S. Giovanni* (Ferrara, 1678; not extant); *La morte del cor penitente* (Vienna, 1705).

BIBL.: P. Fogaccia, *G. L.* (Bergamo, 1954); J. Swale, *A Thematic Catalogue of the Music of G. L.* (diss., Univ. of Adelaide, 1983).

Legros, Joseph, French tenor and composer; b. Monampteuil, Sept. 7, 1739; d. La Rochelle, Dec. 20, 1793. He was a choirboy in Laon, making made his debut at the Paris Opéra in 1764 as Titon in Mondonville's *Titon et l'Aurore*. He subsequently created several roles in operas by Gluck, including Achilles in *Iphigénie* *en Aulide* (1774) and Pylades in *Iphigénie en Tauride* (1779); he also sang in operas by Piccinni, Grétry, and others. He retired from the stage in 1783. He served as director of the Concert Spirituel (1777–90). Legros wrote several operas and a number of songs.

Lehár, Franz (Ferenc), celebrated Austrian composer of Hungarian descent; b. Komárom, Hungary, April 30, 1870; d. Bad Ischl, Oct. 24, 1948. He began his music training with his father, Franz Lehár (1838–98), a military bandmaster. He then entered the Prague Cons. at 12 and studied violin with A. Bennewitz and theory with J. Foerster. In 1885 he was brought to the attention of Fibich, who gave him lessons in composition independently from his studies at the Cons. In 1887 Lehár submitted 2 piano sonatas to Dvořák, who encouraged him in his musical career. In 1888 he became a violinist in a theater orch. in Elberfeld; in 1889 he entered his father's band (50th Infantry) in Vienna, and assisted him as conductor. From 1890 to 1902 Lehár led military bands in Pola, Trieste, Budapest, and Vienna. Although his early stage works were unsuccessful, he gained some success with his marches and waltzes. With *Der Rastelbinder* (Vienna, Dec. 20, 1902), he established himself as a composer for the theater. His most celebrated operetta, *Die lustige Witwe*, was first performed in Vienna on Dec. 30, 1905; it subsequently received innumerable performances throughout the world. From then on Vienna played host to most of his finest scores, including *Der Graf von Luxemburg* (Nov. 12, 1909), *Zigeunerliebe* (Jan. 8, 1910), and *Paganini* (Oct. 30, 1925). For Berlin, he wrote *Der Zarewitsch* (Feb. 21, 1927), *Friederike* (Oct. 4, 1928), and *Das Land des Lächelns* (Oct. 10, 1929; rev. version of *Die gelbe Jacke*). Lehár's last years were made difficult by his marriage to a Jewish woman, which made him suspect to the Nazis. Ironically, *Die lustige Witwe* was one of Hitler's favorite stage works. After World War II, Lehár went to Zürich (1946); then returned to Bad Ischl shortly before his death. Lehár's music exemplifies the spirit of gaiety and frivolity that was the mark of Vienna early in the 20th century; his superlative gift for facile melody and infectious rhythms is combined with genuine wit and irony; a blend of nostalgia and sophisticated humor, undiminished by the upheavals of wars and revolutions, made a lasting appeal to audiences. S. Rourke ed. a thematic index of his works (London, 1985).

WORKS: DRAMATIC (all 1st perf. in Vienna unless otherwise given): OPERETTAS: *Fräulein Leutnant* (1901); *Arabella, die Kubamerin* (1901; unfinished); *Das Club-Baby* (1901; unfinished); *Wiener Frauen (Der Klavierstimmer)* (Nov. 21, 1902; rev. as *Der Schlüssel zum Paradies*, Leipzig, Oct. 1906); *Der Rastelbinder* (Dec. 20, 1902); *Der Göttergatte* (Jan. 20, 1904; rev. as *Die ideale Gattin*, Vienna, Oct. 11, 1913; rev. as *Die Tangokönigin*, Vienna, Sept. 9, 1921); *Die Juxheirat* (Dec. 22, 1904); *Die lustige Witwe* (Dec. 30, 1905); *Peter und Paul reisen im Schlaraffenland (Max und Moritz reisen ins Schlaraffenland)* (Dec. 1, 1906); *Mstislaw der Moderne* (Jan. 5, 1907); *Der Mann mit den drei Frauen* (Jan. 21, 1908); *Das Fürstenkind* (Oct. 7, 1909; rev. as *Der Fürst der Berge*, Berlin, Sept. 23, 1932); *Der Graf von Luxemburg* (Nov. 12, 1909); *Zigeunerliebe* (Jan. 8, 1910; rev. as the opera *Garabonciás diák*, Budapest, Feb. 20, 1943); *Die Spieluhr* (Jan. 7, 1911); *Eva* (Nov. 24, 1911); *Rosenstock und Edelweiss* (Dec. 1, 1912); *Endlich allein* (Jan. 30, 1914; rev. as *Schön ist die Welt*, Berlin, Dec. 3, 1930); *Komm, deutscher Bruder* (Oct. 4, 1914; in collaboration with E. Eysler); *Der Sterngucker* (Jan. 14, 1916; rev. as *La danza delle libellule*, Milan, May 3, 1922; rev. as *Gigolette*, Milan, Oct. 30, 1926); *A Pacsirta (Wo die Lerche singt)* (Budapest, Jan. 1, 1918); *Die blaue Mazur* (May 28, 1920); *Frühling* (Jan. 20, 1922); *Frasquita* (May 12, 1922); *Die gelbe Jacke* (Feb. 9, 1923; rev. as *Das Land des Lächelns*, Berlin, Oct. 10, 1929); *Cloclo* (March 8, 1924); *Paganini* (Oct. 30, 1925); *Der Zarewitsch* (Berlin, Feb. 21, 1927); *Friederike* (Berlin, Oct. 4, 1928); *Das Frühlingsmädel* (Berlin, May 29, 1930); *Giuditta* (Jan. 20, 1934). OPERAS: *Der Kurassier* (1891–92; unfinished); *Rodrigo* (1893; unfinished); *Kukuška* (Leipzig, Nov. 27, 1896; rev. as *Tatjana*, Brünn, Feb. 21, 1905). FILM SCORES: *Die grosse Attraktion* (1931); *Es war einmal ein Walzer* (1932); *Grossfürstin Alexandra* (1934); *Die ganze Welt dreht sich um Liebe* (1936); *Une Nuit à Vienne* (1937).

BIBL.: E. Decsey, *F. L.* (Munich, 1924; 2d ed., 1930); S. Czech, *F. L.: Sein Weg und sein Werk* (Berlin, 1940; new ed., 1957, as *Schon ist die Welt: F. L.s Leben und Werk*); M. von Peteani, *F. L.: Seine Musik, sein Leben* (Vienna, 1950); W. Macqueen-Pope and D. Murray, *Fortune's Favourite: The Life and Times of F. L.* (London, 1953); B. Grun, *Gold and Silver: The Life and Times of F. L.* (London, 1970); M. Schönherr, *F. L.: Bibliographie zu Leben und Werk* (Vienna, 1970); O. Schneidereit, *F. L.: Eine Biographie in Zitaten* (Innsbruck, 1984); C. Marten, *Die Operette als Spiegel der Gesellschaft: F. L.s "Die lustige Witwe": Versuch einer sozialen Theorie der Operette* (Frankfurt am Main and N.Y., 1988); S. Frey, *F. L. oder das schlechte Gewissen der leichten Musik* (Tübingen, 1995).

Lehmann, Lilli, celebrated German soprano, sister of **Marie Lehmann**; b. Würzburg, Nov. 24, 1848; d. Berlin, May 16, 1929. Her father, August Lehmann, was a singer. Her mother, Marie Loew (1807–83), who had sung leading soprano roles and had also appeared as a harpist at the Kassel Opera under Spohr, became harpist at the National Theater in Prague in 1853, and there Lehmann spent her girlhood. At the age of 6 she began to study piano with Cölestin Müller, and at 12 progressed so far that she was able to act as accompanist to her mother, who was her only singing teacher. She made her professional debut in Prague on Oct. 20, 1865, as the 1st Page in *Die Zauberflöte*; then sang in Danzig (1868) and Leipzig (1869–70). In the meantime, she made her first appearance at the Berlin Royal Opera as Marguerite de Valois in *Les Huguenots* (Aug. 31, 1869); she then joined its roster (1870) and established herself as a brilliant coloratura. During the summer of 1875 she was in Bayreuth, and was coached by Wagner himself in the parts of Wöglinde (*Das Rheingold* and *Götterdämmerung*), Helmwige, and the Forest Bird; she created these roles at the Bayreuth Festival the following summer. She then returned to Berlin under a life contract with the Royal Opera; she was given limited leaves of absence, which enabled her to appear in the principal German cities, in Stockholm (1878), in London (debut as Violetta, June 3, 1880), and in Vienna (1882). She made her American debut at the Metropolitan Opera in New York on Nov. 25, 1885, as Carmen; 5 days later she sang Brünnhilde in *Die Walküre*; she then sang virtually all the Wagner roles through subsequent seasons until 1890; her last season there was 1898–99; she also appeared as Norma, Aida, Donna Anna, Fidelio, etc. She sang Isolde at the American premiere of *Tristan und Isolde* (Dec. 1, 1886), and appeared in Italian opera with the De Reszkes and Lassalle during the season of 1891–92. In the meantime, her contract with the Berlin Royal Opera was canceled (1889), owing to her protracted absence, and it required the intervention of Kaiser Wilhelm II to reinstate her (1891). In 1896 she sang the 3 Brünnhildes at the Bayreuth Festival. Her great admiration for Mozart caused her to take an active part in the annual Festivals held at Salzburg (1901–10), where she was artistic director. Her operatic repertoire comprised 170 roles in 114 operas (German, Italian, and French). She possessed in the highest degree all the requisite qualities of a great interpreter; she had a boundless capacity for work, a glorious voice, and impeccable technique; she knew how to subordinate her fiery temperament to artistic taste; on the stage she had plasticity of pose, grace of movement, and regal presence; her ability to project her interpretation with conviction to audiences in different countries was not the least factor in her universal success. Although she was celebrated chiefly as an opera singer, she was equally fine as an interpreter of German lieder; she gave recitals concurrently with her operatic appearances, and continued them until her retirement in 1920; her repertoire of songs exceeded 600. She was also a successful teacher; among her pupils were Geraldine Farrar and Olive Fremstad. On Feb. 24, 1888, in New York she married **Paul Kalisch**, with whom she often sang in opera in subsequent years. They later separated, but never divorced. After her death, Kalisch inherited her manor at Salzkammergut, and remained there until his death in 1946, at the age of 90. Lehmann authored *Meine Gesangskunst* (Berlin,

1902; Eng. tr., 1902, as *How to Sing*; 3d ed., rev. and supplemented, 1924 by C. Willenbücher); *Studie zu Fidelio* (Leipzig, 1904); *Mein Weg*, autobiography (Leipzig, 1913; 2d ed., 1920; Eng. tr., 1914, as *My Path through Life*).

BIBL.: J. Wagenmann, *L. L.s Geheimnis der Stimmbänder* (Berlin, 1905; 2d ed., 1926); L. Andro, *L. L.* (Berlin, 1907).

Lehmann, Liza (Elizabeth Nina Mary Frederica), English soprano and composer; b. London, July 11, 1862; d. Pinner, Sept. 19, 1918. She was the daughter of the painter Rudolf Lehmann and the composer and teacher Amelia Lehmann. She received vocal training from Randegger and Lind in London, and studied composition with Raunkilde in Rome, Freudenberg in Wiesbaden, and MacCunn in London. On Nov. 23, 1885, she made her debut in a recital at a Monday Popular Concert in London, and then sang in concerts throughout Europe. On July 14, 1894, she made her farewell concert appearance at St. James's Hall in London, and later that year she married the painter and composer Herbert Bedford. In 1910 she made a tour of the United States, accompanying herself at the piano in song recitals. In 1911–12 she served as the first president of the Soc. of Women Musicians. In later years she was a prof. of voice at the Guildhall School of Music in London. Her autobiography appeared as *The Life of Liza Lehmann, by Herself* (London, 1919). As a composer, she became best known for her song cycle *In a Persian Garden* for Soprano, Alto, Tenor, Bass, and Piano (1896; London, Jan. 10, 1897), based on selections from Fitzgerald's tr. of the *Rubaiyāt of Omar Khayyām*. Lehmann was the grandmother of **David** and **Stuart Bedford.**

WORKS: DRAMATIC: *Sergeant Brue*, musical farce (London, June 14, 1904); *The Vicar of Wakefield*, romantic light opera (London, Nov. 12, 1906); *The Happy Prince* (1908); *Everyman*, opera (London, Dec. 28, 1915); incidental music.

Lehmann, Lotte, celebrated German-born American soprano; b. Perleberg, Feb. 27, 1888; d. Santa Barbara, Calif., Aug. 26, 1976. She studied in Berlin with Erna Tiedka, Eva Reinhold, and Mathilde Mallinger. She made her operatic debut on Sept. 2, 1910, as the 2d Boy in *Die Zauberflöte* at the Hamburg Opera; her first major role came before that year was out, and she soon was given important parts in Wagner's operas, establishing herself as one of the finest Wagnerian singers. In 1914 she made her first appearance in London as Sophie at Drury Lane. In 1916 she was engaged at the Vienna Opera. Richard Strauss selected her to sing the Composer in the revised version of his *Ariadne auf Naxos* when it was first performed in Vienna (Oct. 4, 1916); then she appeared as Octavian in *Der Rosenkavalier*, and later as the Marschallin, which became one of her most famous roles. She also created the roles of Fäberin (the Dyer's wife) in his *Die Frau ohne Schatten* (Vienna, Oct. 10, 1919) and Christine in his *Intermezzo* (Dresden, Nov. 4, 1924). In 1922 she toured in South America. In 1924 she made her first appearance at London's Covent Garden as the Marschallin, and continued to sing there regularly with great success until 1935; appeared there again in 1938. On Oct. 28, 1930, she made her U.S. debut as Sieglinde with the Chicago Opera, and on Jan. 11, 1934, sang Sieglinde at her Metropolitan Opera debut in New York. She continued to appear at the Metropolitan, with mounting success, in the roles of Elisabeth in *Tannhäuser*, Tosca, and the Marschallin, until her farewell performance as the Marschallin on Feb. 23, 1945. In 1946 she appeared as the Marschallin for the last time in San Francisco. In 1945 she became a naturalized American citizen. She gave her last recital in Santa Barbara, California, on Aug. 7, 1951, and thereafter devoted herself to teaching. Lehmann was universally recognized as one of the greatest singers of the century. The beauty of her voice, combined with her rare musicianship, made her a compelling artist of the highest order. In addition to her unforgettable Strauss roles, she excelled as Mozart's Countess and Donna Elvira, Beethoven's Leonore, and Wagner's Elisabeth, Elsa, and Eva, among others. She publ. a novel, *Orplid mein Land* (1937; Eng. tr., 1938, as *Eternal Flight*); an autobiography, *Anfang und Aufstieg* (Vienna, 1937; in London as *Wings of Song*, 1938; in New York as *Midway in My Song*, 1938); *More Than Singing* (N.Y., 1945); *My Many Lives* (N.Y., 1948); *Five Operas and Richard Strauss* (N.Y., 1964; in London as *Singing with Richard Strauss*, 1964); *Eighteen Song Cycles* (London and N.Y., 1971).

BIBL.: B. Wessling, *L. L. . . . mehr als eine Sängerin* (Salzburg, 1969); B. Glass, *L. L.: A Life in Opera & Song* (Santa Barbara, Calif., 1988); A. Jefferson, *L. L.: 1888–1976: A Centenary Biography* (London, 1988); B. Wessling, *L. L.: "Sie sang, dass es Sterne rührte": Eine Biographie* (Cologne, 1995).

Lehmann, Marie, esteemed German soprano, sister of **Lilli Lehmann;** b Hamburg, May 15, 1851; d. Berlin, Dec. 9, 1931. She received her training from her mother and her sister. On May 1, 1867, she made her operatic debut as Aennchen in Leipzig, and then appeared in Breslau, Cologne, Hamburg, and Prague. She sang with her sister in the first mounting of Wagner's *Ring* cycle at the Bayreuth Festival in 1876, appearing as Wellgunde and Ortlinde. From 1882 to 1896 she was a leading member of the Vienna Court Opera. In later years, she taught voice in Berlin. Among her notable roles were Mozart's Donna Elvira and Donna Anna, Bellini's Adalgisa, and Meyerbeer's Marguerite de Valois.

Lehnhoff, Nikolaus, German opera director; b. Hannover, May 20, 1939. He attended the univs. of Munich and Venice. After gaining experience as an assistant stage director at the Berlin Deutsche Oper, the Bayreuth Festival, and the Metropolitan Opera in New York, he staged his first opera, *Die Frau ohne Schatten*, at the Paris Opéra in 1972. In 1975 he produced *Elektra* at the Lyric Opera of Chicago. His mounting of the *Ring* cycle at the San Francisco Opera (1983–85) and at the Bavarian State Opera in Munich (1987) were notably successful. His stagings of *Kát'a Kabanová* (1988) and *Jenůfa* (1989) at the Glyndebourne Festival were outstanding. In 1989 he produced *Salome* at the Metropolitan Opera. He staged *Idomeneo* at the Salzburg Festival in 1990. In 1991 he produced *Elektra* in Leipzig. After staging *The Makropulos Affair* at the Glyndebourne Festival in 1995, he produced *Palestrina* at London's Covent Garden in 1997. Lehnhoff places great importance upon his collaborations with the finest designers. He is the author of *Es war einmal* (Munich, 1987).

Lehrman, Leonard J(ordan), American composer, pianist, and conductor; b. Ft. Riley, Kansas, Aug. 20, 1949. He received private composition lessons from Siegmeister (1960–70), and also studied with Kim, Del Tredici, Kirchner, and Foss at Harvard Univ. (B.A., 1971) and attended the American Cons. in Fontainebleau (1969). He continued his training at the École Normale de Musique in Paris (1971–72), the Salzburg Mozarteum (1972), with Husa and Palmer at Cornell Univ. (M.F.A., 1975; D.M.A., 1977), and at the Indiana Univ. School of Music in Bloomington (1975–76). Later he studied library and information science at Long Island Univ. (M.A., 1995). After making his debut as a pianist at N.Y.'s Carnegie Recital Hall in 1979, he conducted at the Bremerhaven City Theater (1981–83) before going to Berlin, where he was founder-president of the Jewish Music Theater (1983–86) and a conductor at the Theater des Westens (1983–85). Returning to New York, he became founder-conductor of the Metropolitan Phil. Chorus in 1988. In 1990 he joined the faculty of the Jewish Academy of Fine Arts, which became the Performing Arts Inst. of Long Island in 1993. He served as assoc. ed. of the magazine *Opera Monthly* from 1993.

WORKS: DRAMATIC: OPERAS: *Tales of Malamud*, 2 operas after Malamud: *Idiots First* (completion of Blitzstein's work, 1973; Bloomington, Ind., March 14, 1976) and *Karla* (1974; Bloomington, March 7, 1976); *Sima* (Ithaca, N.Y., Oct. 23, 1976); *Hannah* (Mannheim, May 24, 1980); *The Family Man* (concert perf., Berlin, Jan. 6, 1985; stage perf., N.Y., June 27, 1985); *The Birthday of the Bank* (1988); *New World: An Opera About What Columbus Did to the "Indians"* (1991; Huntington, N.Y., Aug. 11, 1992). MUSICALS: *Growing Up Woman*, chamber musical (1980; Berlin, April 30, 1984); *E. G.: A Musical Portrait of Emma Goldman* (1986; N.Y., May 3, 1987); *Superspy! The Secret Musical* (1988; Paris, July 7, 1989). Also incidental music; cabarets, including *A Blitzstein Cabaret, Memories and Music of Leonard Bernstein, An*

Israel Cabaret, Jewish-American Cabaret, and *The Jewish Woman in Song.*

Leibowitz, René, noted Polish-born French conductor, composer, writer on music, music theorist, and pedagogue; b. Warsaw, Feb. 17, 1913; d. Paris, Aug. 28, 1972. His family settled in Paris in 1926; from 1930 to 1933 he studied in Berlin with Schoenberg and in Vienna with Webern; also studied orchestration with Ravel in Paris (1933). He was active as a conductor from 1937. As a composer, he adopted the 12-tone method of composition, becoming its foremost exponent in France; he had numerous private students, among them Boulez. He publ. the influential books *Schoenberg et son école* (Paris, 1946; Eng. tr., N.Y., 1949) and *Introduction à la musique de douze sons* (Paris, 1949). He also wrote *L'Artiste et sa conscience* (Paris, 1950); *L'Évolution de la musique, de Bach à Schönberg* (Paris, 1952); *Histoire de l'Opéra* (Paris, 1957); with J. Maguire, *Thinking for Orchestra* (N.Y., 1958); with K. Wolff, *Erich Itor Kahn, Un Grand Représentant de la musique contemporaine* (Paris, 1958; Eng. tr., N.Y., 1958); *Schönberg* (Paris, 1969); *Le Compositeur et son double* (Paris, 1971); *Les Fantômes de l'opéra* (Paris, 1973).

WORKS: OPERAS: *La Nuit close* (1949); *La Rumeur de l'espace* (1950); *Ricardo Gonfolano* (1953); *Les Espagnols à Venise,* opera buffa (1963; Grenoble, Jan. 27, 1970); *Labyrinthe,* after Baudelaire (1969); *Todos caerán* (1970–72).

Leichtentritt, Hugo, eminent German-American music scholar; b. Pleschen, Posen, Jan. 1, 1874; d. Cambridge, Mass., Nov. 13, 1951. He studied with J. K. Paine at Harvard Univ. (B.A., 1894); he continued his studies in Paris (1894–95) and at the Berlin Hochschule für Musik (1895–98) and obtained his Ph.D. at the Univ. of Berlin in 1901 with the diss. *Reinhard Keiser in seinen Opern: Ein Beitrag zur Geschichte der frühen deutschen Oper* (publ. in Berlin, 1901); he subsequently taught at the Klindworth-Scharwenka Cons. in Berlin (1901–24) and wrote music criticism for German and American publications. In 1933 he left Germany and became a lecturer on music at Harvard Univ. (until 1940), then taught at Radcliffe College and N.Y. Univ. (1940–44). Although known chiefly as a scholar, he also composed a comic opera, *Der Sizilianer* (Freiburg im Breisgau, May 28, 1920). His MSS are in the Library of Congress in Washington, D.C. Among his many publs. is *Händel* (Berlin and Stuttgart, 1924).

Leider, Frida, outstanding German soprano; b. Berlin, April 18, 1888; d. there, June 4, 1975. She was a student of Otto Schwarz in Berlin before completing her training in Milan. She made her operatic debut in Halle in 1915 as Venus in *Tannhäuser,* then sang at Rostock (1916–18), Königsberg (1918–19), and Hamburg (1919–23). She was engaged by the Berlin State Opera in 1923, and remained on its roster until 1940; she was also highly successful in Wagnerian roles at London's Covent Garden (1924–38) and at the Bayreuth Festivals (1928–38). In 1928 she made her American debut at the Chicago Civic Opera as Brünnhilde in Die *Walküre,* and continued to appear there until 1932, then made her debut at the Metropolitan Opera in New York on Jan. 16, 1933, as Isolde. In 1934 she returned to Germany; she encountered difficulties because her husband, Rudolf Deman, concertmaster of the Berlin State Opera Orch., was Jewish. She was confronted by the Nazis with the demand to divorce him, but refused; he succeeded in going to Switzerland. After the collapse of the Nazi regime (1945), she maintained a vocal studio at the (East) Berlin State Opera until 1952; she also taught at the (West) Berlin Hochschule für Musik from 1948 to 1958. She publ. a memoir, *Das war mein Teil, Erinnerungen einer Opernsängerin* (Berlin, 1959; Eng. tr., N.Y., 1966 as *Playing My Part*). In addition to her celebrated portrayals of Isolde and Brünnhilde, Leider also was acclaimed for her roles of Venus, Senta, Kundry, and the Marschallin. She also was greatly renowned as a concert artist.

Leiferkus, Sergei (Petrovich), Russian baritone; b. Leningrad, April 4, 1946. He was a student of Barsov and Shaposhnikov at the Leningrad Cons. In 1972 he became a member of the Maly Theater in Leningrad, in which city he made his debut at the Kirov Theater in Leningrad as Prince Andrei in *War and Peace* (1977); he subsequently sang there with success. In 1982 he appeared as the Marquis in Massenet's *Griselidis* at the Wexford Festival in England. In 1985 he sang for the first time at the Scottish Opera in Glasgow as Don Giovanni. In 1987 he made his debut at the English National Opera in London as Zurga in *Les Pêcheurs de perles,* the same year he appeared as Eugene Onegin and Tomsky with the Kirov Opera at Covent Garden in London. He also made his U.S. debut that year as soloist in Shostakovich's 13th Sym. with the Boston Sym. Orch. In 1989 he returned to London to make his Wigmore Hall recital debut and his first appearance at the Royal Opera at Covent Garden as Luna; he also sang for the first time at the Glyndebourne Opera as Mandryka and made his U.S. operatic debut at the San Francisco Opera as Telramund. In 1991 he sang Ruprecht in *The Fiery Angel* at the London Promenade Concerts. He made his Metropolitan Opera debut in New York as Iago in 1994, and sang Ruprecht at his first appearance at Milan's La Scala. Following an engagement as Prince Igor at the San Francisco Opera in 1996, he portrayed Telramund and Simon Boccanegra at Covent Garden in 1997. Among his other notable roles are Germont, Amonasro, Prince Igor, Rangoni, Escamillo, and Scarpia.

Leifs, Jón, eminent Icelandic composer, conductor, and administrator; b. Sólheimar, May 1, 1899; d. Reykjavík, July 30, 1968. He entered the Leipzig Cons. in 1916, where he was a student of Graener and Szendrei (composition), Krehl (theory), Paul (harmony and counterpoint), Teichmüller (piano; diploma, 1921), and Lohse and Scherchen (conducting). With the exception of his tenure as music director of the Icelandic National Broadcasting Service in Reykjavík (1935–37), he worked in Germany as a composer and conductor. In 1926 he appeared as a guest conductor of the Hamburg Phil. on a tour of Norway, the Faeroes, and Iceland. After marrying a woman of Jewish descent, the Nazi regime banned Leifs's music in 1937. He and his family were able to flee to Sweden in 1944. In 1945 they settled in Iceland. He became president of the newly organized Soc. of Icelandic Composers. He also was the founder of STEF, an association of composers and copyright owners (1948), and of Islandia Edition (1949), as well as president of the Nordic Council of Composers (1952–54; 1964–66). Leifs publ. the books *Tónlistarhaettir* (Musical Form; Leipzig, 1922) and *Islands künstlerische Anregung* (Reykjavík, 1951). In his compositions, he utilized various resources, ranging from the medieval Icelandic tvisöngur to folk melos. His works include *Galdra-Loftr,* incidental music to the drama (1925; Copenhagen, Sept. 3, 1938; orch. suite, 1925; overture, 1928), and *Baldr,* music drama without words for Chorus, Dancers, and Orch. (1948; Reykjavík, March 24, 1991).

Leigh, Walter, English composer; b. London, June 22, 1905; d. in battle near Tobruk, Libya, June 12, 1942. He was an organ scholar at Christ's College, Cambridge (1922–26), where he studied with Dent; he also took lessons with Darke and later with Hindemith at the Hochschule für Musik in Berlin (1927–29). He was particularly adept in his writing for the theater. Among his works are 2 light operas: *The Pride of the Regiment, or Cashiered for His Country* (Midhurst, Sept. 19, 1931) and *The Jolly Roger, or The Admiral's Daughter* (Manchester, Feb. 13, 1933); also *9 Sharp,* musical revue (London, 1938), and incidental music.

Leighton, Kenneth, English composer and teacher; b. Wakefield, Yorkshire, Oct. 2, 1929; d. Edinburgh, Aug. 24, 1988. He studied classics (1947–50) and composition with Rose (B.Mus., 1951) at Queen's College, Oxford, where he later earned his doctorate in music; he also won the Mendelssohn Scholarship (1951), which enabled him to study with Petrassi in Rome. He was a lecturer at the Univ. of Edinburgh (1956–68); after serving as a lecturer at Worcester College, Oxford (1968–70), he returned to the Univ. of Edinburgh as Reid Prof. of Music (from 1970). He utilized 12-tone procedures while basically adhering to a diatonic style. Among his numerous works is the opera *Columba* (1980; Glasgow, June 16, 1981).

Leinsdorf (real name, **Landauer**), **Erich,** eminent Austrian-born American conductor; b. Vienna, Feb. 4, 1912; d. Zürich, Sept. 11, 1993. He entered a local music school when he was 5; began piano studies with the wife of Paul Pisk at age 8, then continued his piano studies with Paul Emerich (1923–28), and subsequently studied theory and composition with Pisk. In 1930 he took a master class in conducting at the Mozarteum in Salzburg, and then studied for a short time in the music dept. of the Univ. of Vienna; from 1931 to 1933 he took courses at the Vienna Academy of Music, making his debut as a conductor at the Musikvereinsaal upon his graduation. In 1933 he served as assistant conductor of the Workers' Chorus in Vienna; in 1934 he went to Salzburg, where he had a successful audition with Bruno Walter and Toscanini at the Salzburg Festivals, and was appointed their assistant. In 1937 he was engaged as a conductor of the Metropolitan Opera in New York; he made his American debut there conducting *Die Walküre* on Jan. 21, 1938, with notable success; he then conducted other Wagnerian operas, ultimately succeeding Bodanzky as head of the German repertoire there in 1939. In 1942 he became a naturalized American citizen. In 1943 he was appointed music director of the Cleveland Orch.; however, his induction into the U.S. Army in Dec. 1943 interrupted his tenure there. After his discharge in 1944, he once again conducted at the Metropolitan in 1944–45; he also conducted several concerts with the Cleveland Orch. in 1945 and 1946, and made appearances in Europe. From 1947 to 1955 he was music director of the Rochester (N.Y.) Phil. In the fall of 1956 he was briefly music director of the N.Y. City Opera; he then returned to the Metropolitan as a conductor and musical consultant in 1957. He also appeared as a guest conductor in the United States and Europe. In 1962 he received the prestigious appointment of music director of the Boston Sym. Orch., a post he retained until 1969; then he conducted opera and sym. concerts in many of the major music centers of America and in Europe; from 1978 to 1980 he held the post of principal conductor of the (West) Berlin Radio Sym. Orch. He publ. a semiautobiographical and rather candid book of sharp comments, *Cadenza: A Musical Career* (Boston, 1976); also *The Composer's Advocate: A Radical Orthodoxy for Musicians* (New Haven, 1981).

Leisner, David, American guitarist, teacher, and composer; b. Los Angeles, Dec. 22, 1953. He was educated at Wesleyan Univ. (B.A., 1976); received instruction in guitar from John Duarte, David Starobin, and Angelo Gilardino, in interpretation from John Kirkpatrick and Karen Tuttle, and in composition from Richard Winslow; he won 2d prize at the Toronto International Guitar Competition (1975) and a silver medal at the Geneva International Guitar Competition (1981). He made his N.Y. debut in 1979, then toured extensively. He taught guitar at Amherst College (1976–78) and at the New England Cons. of Music in Boston (from 1980). From 1993 he taught at the Manhattan School of Music in New York. He became well known for his programming of contemporary American music at his concerts. His own compositions include an opera, *Fidelity* (Boston, Oct. 20, 1996).

Leite, Antonio (Joaquim) da Silva, Portuguese organist, guitarist, teacher, and composer; b. Oporto, May 23, 1759; d. there, Jan. 10, 1833. He studied in Oporto, becoming mestre de capela at the Cathedral there by 1808. He publ. *Rezumo de todas as regras e preceitos de cantoria assim da musica metrica como da cantochão* (Oporto, 1787) and *Estudo de guitarra* (Oporto, 1796). He wrote the operas *Puntigli per equivico* (Oporto, 1807) and *L'astuzie delle donne* (Oporto, 1807).

Leitner, Ferdinand, noted German conductor; b. Berlin, March 4, 1912; d. Forch, Switzerland, June 1996. He studied composition with Schreker and conducting with Pruwer at the Berlin Hochschule für Musik; he also studied piano with Schnabel and conducting with Muck. He then was active as a pianist until making his debut as a theater conductor in Berlin in 1943. He became conductor of the Württemberg State Theater in Stuttgart in 1947 and was its Generalmusikdirektor (1950–69). He subsequently was chief conductor of the Zürich Opera (1969–84); also of the Residentie Orch. at The Hague (1976–80). From 1986 to 1990 he served as principal conductor of the RAI Orch. in Turin. He was known for his musicianly readings of works by Mozart, Wagner, Bruckner, and Richard Strauss; also conducted a number of modern scores, including premieres of works by Orff and Egk.

Lemeshev, Sergei (Yakovlevich), prominent Russian tenor; b. Knyazevo, near Tver, July 10, 1902; d. Moscow, June 26, 1977. In his youth, he worked at a cobbler's shop in Petrograd, then went to Moscow, where he studied at the Cons. with Raysky, graduating in 1925. He made his operatic debut at Sverdlovsk in 1926, then was a member of the Kharbin Opera in Manchuria (1927–29) and at the Tiflis Opera (1929–31). In 1931 he joined the Bolshoi Theater in Moscow, and gradually created an enthusiastic following; he remained on its roster until 1961 and was particularly admired for his performance of the role of Lensky in *Eugene Onegin*; in 1972, on his 70th birthday, he sang it again at the Bolshoi Theater. Other roles in which he shone, apart from the Russian repertoire, included Faust, Romeo, Werther, Alfredo, and the Duke of Mantua. He also made numerous appearances in solo recitals; he was the first to present an entire cycle of Tchaikovsky's songs in 5 concerts. His autobiography was publ. in Moscow in 1968.

BIBL.: M. Lvov, *S. L.* (Moscow, 1947); E. Grosheva, *S. L.* (Moscow, 1960).

Lemmens-Sherrington (originally, **Sherrington**), **Helen,** noted English soprano; b. Preston, Oct. 4, 1834; d. Brussels, May 9, 1906. When she was 4 her family took her to Rotterdam, where she had vocal training with Verhulst; she then entered the Brussels Cons. (1852). She made her London debut as a concert singer (April 7, 1856); later sang with the English Opera (1860–65) and at Covent Garden (1866), where she appeared as Donna Elvira, Adalgisa, Isabella in *Robert le diable*, and Elisabeth de Valois; however, it was as a concert and oratorio singer that she gained her greatest distinction. She married the eminent Belgian organist, pedagogue, and composer Jacques Nicolas (Jaak Nikolaas) Lemmens (1823–1881) in 1857. After his death, she made her home in Brussels. She continued to make appearances as a singer until 1894, but devoted herself mainly to teaching at the Brussels Cons.; she also taught at the Royal Manchester College of Music (1893–97).

Lemnitz, Tiana (Luise), remarkable German soprano; b. Metz, Oct. 26, 1897; d. Berlin, Feb. 5, 1994. She studied with Hoch in Metz and Kohmann in Frankfurt am Main. She made her operatic debut in Lortzing's *Undine* in Heilbronn (1920), then sang in Aachen (1922–28). Lemnitz subsequently pursued a distinguished career as a member of the Hannover Opera (1928–33), the Dresden State Opera (1933–34), and the Berlin State Opera (1934–57). She also made guest appearances in Vienna, Munich, London's Covent Garden (1936, 1938), and Buenos Aires's Teatro Colón (1936, 1950). Her repertoire included many leading roles in German, Italian, French, and Russian operas. Among her most celebrated portrayals were Pamina, Sieglinde, Desdemona, Micaëla, Octavian, and the Marschallin.

Lemoyne, Jean-Baptiste, French conductor and composer; b. Eymet, Périgord, April 3, 1751; d. Paris, Dec. 30, 1796. He studied with J. G. Graun, Kirnberger, and J. A. P. Schulz at Berlin; he also held a minor post in the service of the Prussian Crown Prince, then went to Warsaw, where he brought out his opera *Le Bouquet de Colette* (1775). Returning to Paris, he brought out an opera, *Électre* (July 2, 1782), pretending to be a pupil of Gluck, an imposture that Gluck did not see fit to expose until the failure of Lemoyne's piece. In his next operas, Lemoyne abandoned Gluck's ideas, copied the style of Piccinni and Sacchini, and produced several successful works, including *Phèdre* (Fontainebleau, Oct. 26, 1786), *Les Prétendus* (Paris, June 2, 1789), and *Nephté* (Paris, Dec. 15, 1789). His son, Gabriel Lemoyne (b. Berlin, Oct, 14, 1772; d. Paris, July 2, 1815), was a pianist and composer; he studied piano with C.-F. Clément and J. F. Edelmann. He wrote 3 opéras comiques.

Lendvai, Ernö, Hungarian musicologist; b. Kaposvár, Feb. 6, 1925; d. Budapest, Jan. 31, 1993. He studied at the Budapest Academy of Music (1945–49). He was made director of the Szombathely Music School (1949) and the Győr Cons. (1954); he was also prof. at the Szeged Cons. (from 1957) and a teacher at the Budapest Academy of Music (1954–56; from 1973). He distinguished himself as a writer on the life and works of Bartók.

WRITINGS: *Bartók stilusa* (Bartók's Style; Budapest, 1955); *Bartók's Dramaturgy: Stage Works and Cantata Profana* (Budapest, 1964); *Toscanini és Beethoven* (Budapest, 1967; Eng. tr., 1966, in *Studia musicologica Academiae scientiarum hungaricae*, VIII); *Bartók költői vilaga* (The Poetic World of Bartók; Budapest, 1971); *Bêla Bartók: An Analysis of His Music* (London, 1971); *Bartók és Kodály harmóniavilága* (The Harmonic World of Bartók and Kodály; Budapest, 1975); *The Workshop of Bartók and Kodály* (Budapest, 1983); *Verdi és a 20. század A Falstaff hangzás-dramaturgiája* (Budapest, 1984).

Lendvai, (Peter) Erwin, Hungarian composer; b. Budapest, June 4, 1882; d. Epsom, Surrey, March 31, 1949. He was a student of Koessler in Budapest and of Puccini in Milan. After teaching at the Jaques Dalcroze school in Hellerau (1913–14), the Hoch Cons. in Frankfurt am Main (1914–19), the Klindworth-Scharwenka Cons. in Berlin (1919–22), and the Volksmusikschule in Hamburg (1923–25), he was active as a choral conductor. He eventually settled in England. He publ. the method *Chorschule*. Among his works was the opera *Elga* (Mannheim, Dec. 6, 1916; rev. 1918).

BIBL.: H. Leichtentritt, *E. L.* (Berlin, 1912).

Lendvay, Kamilló, Hungarian composer, conductor, and teacher; b. Budapest, Dec. 28, 1928. He was a student in composition of Viski at the Budapest Academy of Music (1949–57), and also received lessons in conducting from Somogyi (1953–55). After conducting at the Szeged Opera (1956–57), he returned to Budapest and was music director of the State Puppet Theater (1960–66) and the Hungarian Army Art Ensemble (1966–68); he then was a conductor (1970–72) and subsequently music director (1972–74) of the Municipal Operetta Theater. From 1962 he was active with the Hungarian Radio. In 1973 he joined the faculty of the Academy of Music, where he was head of its theory dept. from 1978. He also served as president of Artisjus, the Hungarian Copyright Office. In 1962, 1964, and 1978 he was awarded the Erkel Prize. He was made a Merited Artist by the Hungarian government in 1981. In 1989 he received the Bartók-Pásztory Award. In his compositions, serial procedures serve as the foundation of his avant-garde explorations.

WORKS: DRAMATIC: *A büvös szék* (The Magic Chair), comic opera (1972); *A tisztességtudó utcalány* (The Respectful Prostitute), opera (1976–78); incidental music for plays; film scores.

Lenepveu, Charles (Ferdinand), French composer and pedagogue; b. Rouen, Oct. 4, 1840; d. Paris, Aug. 16, 1910. While a law student, he took music lessons from Servais, winning 1st prize at Caen in 1861 for a cantata. He entered Ambroise Thomas's class at the Paris Cons. in 1863, and in 1865 took the Grand Prix de Rome with the cantata *Renaud dans les jardins d'Armide* (Paris, Jan. 3, 1866). His comic opera *Le Florentin* also won a prize, offered by the Ministry of Fine Arts (1867), and was performed at the Opéra Comique (Feb. 26, 1874). The grand opera *Velléda* was produced at Covent Garden in London (July 4, 1882), with Adelina Patti in the title role. In 1891 Lenepveu succeeded Guiraud as prof. of harmony at the Cons., and in 1893 again succeeded him as prof. of composition, taking an advanced class in 1894. In 1896 he was elected to Ambroise Thomas's chair in the Academie des Beaux-Arts; was a Chevalier of the Légion d'honneur, and an Officer of Public Instruction.

BIBL.: R. de Saint-Arroman, *C. L.* (Paris, 1898).

Lenya, Lotte (real name, **Karoline Wilhelmine Blamauer),** Austrian-American singer and actress; b. Vienna, Oct. 18, 1898; d. N.Y., Nov. 27, 1981. She received training in classical dance and the Dalcroze method in Zürich (1914–20), where she also worked at the Stadttheater's opera ballet and at the Schauspielhaus. In 1926 she married **Kurt Weill,** and made her debut as a singer in the premiere of his "Songspiel" *Mahagonny* (Baden-Baden, July 17, 1927). She later sang in the first performance of its operatic version as *Aufstieg und Fall der Stadt Mahagonny* (Leipzig, March 9, 1930). She also created the role of Jenny in his *Die Dreigroschenoper* (Berlin, Aug. 31, 1928). In 1933 Lenya and Weill fled Nazi Germany for Paris. During their stay there, she created the role of Anna in his *Die sieben Todsunden der Kleinburger* (June 7, 1933). In 1935 they emigrated to the United States. She created the roles of Miriam in his *The Eternal Road* (N.Y., Jan 7, 1937) and the Duchess in his *The Firebrand of Florence* (N.Y., March 22, 1945). Following Weill's death in 1950, Lenya devoted herself to reviving many of his works for the American stage. She also was active as an actress on stage and in films. Although she was not a professionally trained singer, she adapted herself to the peculiar type of half-spoken, half-sung roles in Weill's works with total dedication.

BIBL.: H. Marx, ed., *Weill-L.* (N.Y., 1976).

Leo, Leonardo (Lionardo Ortensio Salvatore de), important Italian composer; b. San Vito degli Schiavi, near Brindisi, Aug. 5, 1694; d. Naples, Oct. 31, 1744. In 1709 he went to Naples, where he studied with Fago at the Cons. S. Maria della Pietà dei Turchini; his sacred drama *S. Chiara, o L'infedeltà abbattuta* was given there in 1712. In 1713 he was made supernumerary organist in the Viceroy's Chapel; also served as maestro di cappella to the Marchese Stella. His first opera, *Il Pisistrato*, was performed in Naples on May 13, 1714. His first comic opera, *La 'mpeca scoperta*, in the Neapolitan dialect, was given in Naples on Dec. 13, 1723. In all, he wrote some 50 operas, most of them for Naples. Following A. Scarlatti's death in 1725, he was elevated to the position of 1st organist at the viceregal chapel. In 1730 he became provicemaestro of the Royal Chapel; in 1737 vice maestro. He taught as vicemaestro at the Cons. S. Maria della Pietà dei Turchini from 1734 to 1737; from 1741 was primo maestro in succession to his teacher, Fago; he also was primo maestro at the Cons. S. Onofrio from 1739. In Jan. 1744 he became maestro di cappella of the Royal Chapel, but died that same year. Among his famous pupils were Piccinni and Jommelli. Leo's music for the theater (especially his comic operas) is noteworthy; of no less significance were his theoretical works, *Istituzioni o regole del contrappunto* and *Lezione di canto fermo*.

WORKS: OPERAS (all 1st perf. in Naples unless otherwise given): *Il Pisistrato* (May 13, 1714); *Sofonisba* (Jan. 22, 1718); *Caio Gracco* (April 19, 1720); *Arianna e Teseo* (Nov. 26, 1721); *Baiazete, imperator dei Turchi* (Aug. 28, 1722); *Timocrate* (Venice, 1723); *La 'mpeca scoperta*, comic opera (Dec. 13, 1723); *Il Turno Aricino* (with L. Vinci; 1724); *L'amore fedele*, comic opera (April 25, 1724); *Lo pazzo apposta*, comic opera (Aug. 26, 1724); *Zenobia in Palmira* (May 13, 1725); *Il trionfo di Camilla, regina dei Volsci* (Rome, Jan. 8, 1726); *Orismene, ovvero Dalli sdegni l'amore*, comic opera (Jan. 19, 1726); *La semmeglianza de chi l'ha fatta*, comic opera (fall 1726); *Lo matrimonio annascuso*, comic opera (1727); *Il Cid* (Rome, Feb. 10, 1727); *La pastorella commattuta*, comic opera (fall 1727); *Argene* (Venice, Jan. 17, 1728); *Catone in Utica* (Venice, 1729); *La schiava per amore*, comic opera (1729); *Semiramide* (Feb. 2, 1730); *Rosmene*, comic opera (summer 1730); *Evergete* (Rome, 1731); *Demetrio* (Oct. 1, 1732); *Amor da' senno*, comic opera (1733); *Nitocri, regina d'Egitto* (Nov. 4, 1733); *Il castello d'Atlante* (July 4, 1734); *Demofoonte* (Jan. 20, 1735; Act 1 by D. Sarro, Act 2 by F. Mancini, Act 3 by Leo, and intermezzos by G. Sellitti); *La clemenza di Tito* (Venice, 1735); *Emira* (July 12, 1735; intermezzos by I. Prota); *Demetrio* (Dec. 10, 1735; different setting from earlier opera of 1732); *Onore vince amore,* comic opera (1736); *Farnace* (Dec. 19, 1736); *L'amico traditore*, comic opera (1737); *Siface* (Bologna, May 11, 1737; rev. version as *Viriate*, Pistoia, 1740); *La simpatia del sangue*, comic opera (fall 1737); *Olimpiade* (Dec. 19, 1737); *Il conte*, comic opera (1738); *Il Ciro riconosciuto* (Turin, 1739); *Amor vuol sofferenze*, comic opera (fall 1739; rev. version as *La finta frascatana*, Nov. 1744); *Achille in Sciro* (Turin, 1740);

Scipione nelle Spagne (Milan, 1740); *L'Alidoro*, comic opera (summer 1740); *Demetrio* (Dec. 19, 1741; different setting from the earlier operas of 1732 and 1735); *L'ambizione delusa*, comic opera (1742); *Andromaca* (Nov. 4, 1742); *Il fantastico, od Il nuovo Chisciotte*, comic opera (1743; rev. version, fall 1748); *Vologeso, re dei Parti* (Turin, 1744); *La fedeltà odiata*, comic opera (1744); he also contributed to a pasticcio setting of Demetrio (June 30, 1738); he likewise composed prologues, arias, etc., to operas by other composers. A number of operas long attributed to Leo are now considered doubtful. Also serenatas, feste teatrali, and numerous sacred dramas and oratorios.

BIBL.: C. Leo, *L. L. e sua epoca musicale* (Brindisi, 1894); G. Leo, *L. L.: Musicista del secola XVIII e le sue opere musicali* (Naples, 1905); F. Schlitzer, ed., *Tommaso Traetta, L. L., Vincenzo Bellini: Noti e documenti raccolti da F. Schlitzer* (Siena, 1952); G. Pastore, *L. L.* (Galatina, 1957).

León, Tania (Justina), Cuban-born American composer, conductor, pianist, and teacher; b. Havana, May 14, 1943. She studied in Havana at the Carlos Alfredo Peyrellade Cons. (B.A., 1963; M.A. in music education, 1964). In 1967 she went to the United States, where she enrolled at N.Y. Univ. (M.S., 1973) and had conducting lessons with Halasz and at the Berkshire Music Center at Tanglewood with Bernstein and Ozawa. In 1968 she joined the Dance Theatre of Harlem as its first music director, a position she held until 1980; she also organized the Brooklyn Phil. Community Concert Series (1977). She was a guest conductor with several U.S. and European orchs.; in 1992 she conducted the Johannesburg Sym. during the Dance Theatre of Harlem's historic trip to South Africa, when the company became the first multiracial arts troupe to perform and teach there in modern times. Among her many awards were the Young Composer's Prize from the National Council of the Arts, Havana (1966), the Alvin John Award from the Council for Emigrés in the Professions (1971), and the Cintas Award (1974–75); she also was an NEA Fellow (1975). In 1978 she was music director for Broadway's smash musical *The Wiz*, and in 1985 she served as resident composer for the Lincoln Center Inst. in New York; she also joined the composition faculty of Brooklyn College and later was artistic director of the Composers' Forum in New York. She has also held composer and/or conducting residencies in the United States (Cleveland, Seattle, et al.) and in Europe (Italy, Germany, et al.). Her compositions are written in an accessible style, rhythmically vibrant, with some novel piano and percussion effects. Her *Kabiosile* for Piano and Orch. (1988) brings together the rich and disparate elements of her own cultural heritage, combining Afro-Cuban, Hispanic, and Latin jazz elements within a classical Western concerto format. Her ballet *Dougla* (with Geoffrey Holder; 1974) was heard in the Soviet Union during the Dance Theatre of Harlem's 1988 tour.

WORKS: DRAMATIC: *Tones*, ballet (1970; in collaboration with A. Mitchell); *The Beloved*, ballet (1972); *Dougla*, ballet (1974; in collaboration with G. Holder); *Maggie Magalita*, theater piece (1980; in collaboration with W. Kesselman); *The Golden Windows*, theater piece (1982; in collaboration with R. Wilson); *Scourge of Hyacinths*, chamber opera, to a libretto by the composer after a play by Wole Soyinka (1992).

Leoncavallo, Ruggero, noted Italian composer; b. Naples, April 23, 1857; d. Montecatini, Aug. 9, 1919. He attended the Naples Cons. (1866–76), where his teachers were B. Cesi (piano) and M. Ruta and L. Rossi (composition), and then took courses in literature at the Univ. of Bologna (1876–78). His first opera, *Tommaso Chatterton*, was about to be produced in Bologna (1878) when the manager disappeared, and the production was called off. Leoncavallo earned his living playing piano in cafes throughout Europe before going to Paris, where he composed chansonettes and other popular songs. He wrote an opera, *Songe d'une nuit d'été* (after Shakespeare's *Midsummer Night's Dream*), which was privately sung in a salon. He began to study Wagner's scores, and became an ardent Wagnerian; he resolved to emulate the master by producing a trilogy, *Crepusculum*, depicting in epical traits the Italian Renaissance; the separate parts were to be *I Medici, Girolamo Savonarola*, and *Cesare Borgia*. He spent 6 years on the basic historical research; having completed the first part, and with the scenario of the entire trilogy sketched, he returned in 1887 to Italy, where the publisher Ricordi became interested in the project, but kept delaying the publication and production of the work. Annoyed, Leoncavallo turned to Sonzogno, the publisher of Mascagni, whose opera *Cavalleria rusticana* had just obtained a tremendous vogue. Leoncavallo submitted a short opera in a similarly realistic vein; he wrote his own libretto based on a factual story of passion and murder in a Calabrian village, and named it *Pagliacci*. The opera was given with sensational success at the Teatro dal Verme in Milan under the direction of Toscanini (May 21, 1892), and rapidly took possession of operatic stages throughout the world; it is often played on the same evening with Mascagni's opera, both works being of brief duration. Historically, these 2 operas signalized the important development of Italian operatic *verismo*, which influenced composers of other countries as well.

The enormous success of *Pagliacci* did not deter Leoncavallo from carrying on his more ambitious projects. The first part of his unfinished trilogy, *I Medici*, was finally brought out at the Teatro dal Verme in Milan on Nov. 9, 1893, but the reception was so indifferent that he turned to other subjects; the same fate befell his youthful *Tommaso Chatterton* at its production in Rome (March 10, 1896). His next opera, *La Bohème* (Venice, May 6, 1897), won considerable success, but had the ill fortune of coming a year after Puccini's masterpiece on the same story, and was dwarfed by comparison. There followed a light opera, *Zazà* (Milan, Nov. 10, 1900), which was fairly successful, and was produced repeatedly on world stages. In 1894 he was commissioned by the German emperor Wilhelm II to write an opera for Berlin; this was *Der Roland von Berlin*, on a German historic theme; it was produced in Berlin on Dec. 13, 1904, but despite the high patronage it proved a fiasco. In 1906 Leoncavallo made a tour of the United States and Canada, conducting his *Pagliacci* and a new operetta, *La Jeunesse de Figaro*, specially written for his American tour; it was so unsuccessful that he never attempted to stage it in Europe. Back in Italy he resumed his industrious production; the opera *Maia* (Rome, Jan. 15, 1910) and the operetta *Malbrouck* (Rome, Jan. 19, 1910) were produced within the same week; another operetta, *La Reginetta delle rose*, was staged simultaneously in Rome and in Naples (June 24, 1912). In the autumn of that year, Leoncavallo visited London, where he presented the premiere of his *Gli Zingari* (Sept. 16, 1912); a year later he revisited the United States, conducting in San Francisco. He wrote several more operettas, but they made no impression; 3 of them were produced during his lifetime: *La Candidata* (Rome, Feb. 6, 1915), *Goffredo Mameli* (Genoa, April 27, 1916), and *Prestami tua moglie* (Montecatini, Sept. 2, 1916); posthumous premieres were accorded the operetta *A chi la giarettiera?* (Rome, Oct. 16, 1919), the opera *Edipo re* (Chicago, Dec. 13, 1920), and the operetta *Il primo bacio* (Montecatini, April 29, 1923). Another score, *Tormenta*, remained unfinished. Salvatore Allegra collected various sketches by Leoncavallo and arranged from them a 3-act operetta, *La maschera nuda*, which was produced in Naples on June 26, 1925.

BIBL.: R. de Rensis, *Per Umberto Giordano e R. L.* (Siena, 1949).

Leoni, Franco, Italian composer; b. Milan, Oct. 24, 1864; d. London, Feb. 8, 1949. He studied at the Milan Cons. with Dominiceti and Ponchielli. In 1892 he went to London, where he remained until 1917, then lived in France and Italy, eventually returning to England.

WORKS: OPERAS: *Raggio di luna* (Milan, June 5, 1890); *Rip van Winkle* (London, Sept. 4, 1897); *Ib and Little Christina*, "picture in 3 panels" (London, Nov. 14, 1901); *L'oracolo* (London, June 28, 1905); *Tzigana* (Genoa, Feb. 3, 1910); *Le baruffe chiozzotte* (Milan, Jan. 2, 1920); *La terra del sogno* (Milan, Jan. 10, 1920); *Falene* (Milan, 1920). ORATORIOS: *Sardanapalus* (London, 1891); *The Gate of Life* (London, 1891); *Golgotha* (London, 1909).

Leonova, Darya (Mikhailovna), Russian contralto; b. Vyshny-Volochok, March 9, 1829; d. St. Petersburg, Feb. 6, 1896. She stud-

ied singing in St. Petersburg. In 1852 she sang the part of Vanya in Glinka's *A Life for the Czar*, and was greatly praised by Glinka himself; she then sang regularly in St. Petersburg and Moscow (until 1874). In 1875 she went on a concert tour around the world, through Siberia, China, Japan, and America. In 1879 she traveled in southern Russia and the Crimea with Mussorgsky as accompanist; she sang arias from Mussorgsky's operas and his songs. In 1880 she opened a singing school in St. Petersburg, with Mussorgsky acting as coach. She also taught at the Moscow drama school (1888–92). Her memoirs were publ. in *Istorichesky vestnik,* nos. 1–4 (1891). She devoted much of her career to promoting Russian music, creating the roles of the Princess in Dargomyzhsky's *Rusalka* (1856) and the Hostess in Mussorgsky's *Boris Godunov* (1874); her non-Russian roles included Orfeo, Azucena, and Ortrud.
BIBL.: V. Yakovlev, *D. M. L.* (Moscow, 1950).

Leontovich, Mikola (Dmitrovich), prominent Ukrainian composer and teacher; b. Monastïryok, Podolia, Dec. 13, 1877; d. Markovka, near Tulchin, Jan. 25, 1921. He was educated at the seminaries in Stargorod and Kamenets-Podolsky. Although he lacked formal training in music, he was active as a singing teacher in various schools and as a conductor of amateur choirs and orchs. After completing sessions as an external student of the St. Petersburg court chapel choir (1904), he worked with Yavorsky (1909–14); in 1918 he became a teacher at the Lissenko Music and Drama Inst. He also was active with various Ukrainian musical organizations. Leontovich possessed a remarkable talent for arranging Ukrainian folk songs for unaccompanied choral groups. Among his own works were several major unaccompanied choral works, instrumental pieces, and an unfinished opera. A number of collections of his works were publ., as well as a vol. of his writings (Kiev, 1947).
BIBL.: V. Diachenko, *M. D. L.* (Kharkov, 1941); M. Gordichuk, *M. D. L.* (Kiev, 1972).

Leoz, Jesús García, Spanish composer; b. Olite, Navarre, Jan. 10, 1904; d. Madrid, Feb. 25, 1953. He was a cantor in Olite before pursuing his studies in Pamplona; he later received training from del Campo (composition) and Balsa (piano), and finally from Turina (composition), his most significant influence. Leoz's output included zarzuelas and a ballet.
BIBL.: A. Fernández Cid, *J. L.* (Madrid, 1953).

L'Épine, (Francesca) Margherita de, famous Italian soprano; b. c.1683; d. London, Aug. 8, 1746. She began her career at the court in Mantua, then appeared in Venice (1700). She sang in the works of the German composer Jakob Greber at Lincoln's Inn Fields in London; she was also his mistress (from 1702). She joined London's Drury Lane Theatre in 1704, making her first appearance in opera there in Haym's pasticcio *Camillo* in 1706, replacing her archrival, the English soprano Catherine Tofts. When the opera company moved to the Queen's Theatre in 1708, she continued as a leading member with it until 1714. She sang in several works by Handel, creating the roles of Eurilla in his *Il Pastor fido* (Nov. 22, 1712) and Agilea in his *Teseo* (Jan. 10, 1713). She also became associated with the composer Pepusch. She appeared in his works at Drury Lane (1715–17) and at Lincoln's Inn Fields (1718–19), and married him about 1718. In later years she was active mainly as a teacher. She made her last appearance at Drury Lane in 1733. She was the most celebrated soprano on the London stage of her time. Contemporary accounts praise her musical gifts highly but describe her as physically unattractive; indeed, Pepusch dubbed her "Hecate."

Leppard, Raymond (John), eminent English conductor; b. London, Aug. 11, 1927. He studied harpsichord and viola at Trinity College, Cambridge (M.A., 1952), where he also was active as a choral conductor and served as music director of the Cambridge Phil. Soc. In 1952 he made his London debut as a conductor, and then conducted his own Leppard Ensemble. He became closely associated with the Goldsbrough Orch., which became the English Chamber Orch. in 1960. He also gave recitals as a harpsichordist, and was a Fellow of Trinity College and a lecturer on music at his alma mater (1958–68). His interest in early music prompted him to prepare several realizations of scores from that period; while his eds. provoked controversy, they had great value in introducing early operatic masterpieces to the general public. His first realization, Monteverdi's *L'incoronazione di Poppea*, was presented at the Glyndebourne Festival under his direction in 1962. He subsequently prepared performing eds. of Monteverdi's *Orfeo* (1965) and *Il ritorno d'Ulisse in patria* (1972), and of Cavalli's *Messa concertata* (1966), *L'Ormindo* (1967), *La Calisto* (1969), *L'Egisto* (1974), and *L'Orione* (1980). During this period, he made appearances as a guest conductor with leading European opera houses, orchs., and festivals. On Nov. 4, 1969, he made his U.S. debut conducting the Westminster Choir and N.Y. Phil., at which occasion he also appeared as soloist in the Haydn D-major Harpsichord Concerto. In 1973 he became principal conductor of the BBC Northern Sym. Orch. in Manchester, a position he retained until 1980. He made his U.S. debut as an opera conductor leading a performance of his ed. of *L'Egisto* at the Santa Fe Opera in 1974. Settling in the United States in 1976, he subsequently appeared as a guest conductor with the major U.S. orchs. and opera houses. On Sept. 19, 1978, he made his Metropolitan Opera debut in New York conducting *Billy Budd*. He was principal guest conductor of the St. Louis Sym. Orch. (1984–90). From 1987 to 2001 he was music director of the Indianapolis Sym. Orch., thereafter its first conductor laureate. At the invitation of the Prince of Wales, he conducted his ed. of Purcell's *Dido and Aeneas* at London's Buckingham Palace in 1988. He returned there in 1990 to conduct the 90th-birthday concert of the Queen Mother. On Jan. 27, 1991, he conducted a special concert of Mozart's works with members of the N.Y. Phil. and the Juilliard Orch. at N.Y.'s Avery Fisher Hall in Lincoln Center; telecast live to millions via PBS, it re-created a concert given by Mozart in Vienna on March 23, 1783, and celebrated his 235th birthday and the launching of Lincoln Center's commemoration of the 200th anniversary of his death. In 1993 he conducted the Indianapolis Sym. Orch. on a major tour of Europe, visiting London, Birmingham, Frankfurt am Main, Cologne, Düsseldorf, Vienna, Munich, Geneva, and Zürich. In 1994 he was named artist-in-residence at the Univ. of Indianapolis. Leppard was made a Commander of the Order of the British Empire in 1983. As a composer, he produced film scores for *Lord of the Flies* (1963), *Alfred the Great* (1969), *Laughter in the Dark* (1969), *Perfect Friday* (1970), and *Hotel New Hampshire* (1985). He also orchestrated Schubert's "Grand Duo" Sonata and conducted its first performance with the Indianapolis Sym. Orch. (Nov. 8, 1990). Although long associated with early music, Leppard has acquired mastery of a truly catholic repertoire, ranging from Mozart to Britten. His thoughtful views on performance practice are set forth in his book *The Real Authenticity* (London, 1988). T. Lewis ed. the vol. *Raymond Leppard on Music* (White Plains, N.Y., 1993), an anthology of critical and personal writings, with a biographical chronology and discography.

Le Rochois, Marthe, French soprano and teacher; b. Caen, c.1658; d. Paris, Oct. 9, 1728. She was a principal member of the Paris Opéra from 1678 to 1698, and then devoted herself to teaching. She gained distinction for her appearances in Lully's operas, creating major roles in his *Proserpine* (1680), *Persée* (1682), *Amadis* (1684), *Roland* (1685), and *Armide* (1686).

Le Roux, François, French baritone; b. Rennes, Oct. 30, 1955. He studied at the Paris Opéra Studio, his principal mentors being Vera Rosza and Elisabeth Grümmer. After appearing at the Lyons Opera (1980–85), he made his debut at the Paris Opéra as Pelléas. His great success as Pelléas was repeated when he reprised that role in Milan (1986), Vienna (1988), Helsinki (1989), and Cologne (1992). In 1987 he made his first appearance at the Glyndebourne Festival as Ramiro in *L'heure espagnole*. He sang Lescaut in *Manon* at London's Covent Garden in 1988, and returned there in 1991 to create the title role in Birtwistle's *Gawain* and in 1993 to sing Pelléas. In 1996 he appeared as Nick Shadow in Madrid.

Among his other roles were Mozart's Count, Papageno, and Don Giovanni.

Le Roux, Maurice, French conductor, composer, and writer on music; b. Paris, Feb. 6, 1923; d. Avignon, Oct. 19, 1992. He was a student at the Paris Cons. (1944–52) of Philipp and Nat (piano), Fourestier (conducting), and Messiaen (analysis); he also had private instruction in dodecaphonic techniques with Leibowitz. From 1951 he was active with the French Radio and Television in Paris, where he later was music director of its l'Orchestre National de l'ORTF from 1960 to 1968. After serving as musical councillor of the Paris Opéra (1969–73), he was inspector general of music in the Ministry of Culture (1973–88). He utilized serial procedures in his compositions. Among his works were the ballets *Le Petit Prince* (1949) and *Sables* (1956) and incidental music and film scores. He publ. in Paris *Introduction à la musique contemporaine* (1947), *Monteverdi* (1947), *La Musique* (1979), and *Boris Godounov* (1980).

Leroux, Xavier (Henry Napoléon), French composer; b. Velletri, Papal States, Oct. 11, 1863; d. Paris, Feb. 2, 1919. He was a pupil of Dubois and Massenet at the Paris Cons., winning 1st Grand Prix de Rome in 1885. He was appointed a prof. at the Cons. in 1896.

WORKS: THEATER: *Evangeline* (Brussels, Dec. 18, 1885); *Astarté* (Paris, Feb. 15, 1901); *La Reine Fiammette* (Paris, Dec. 23, 1903); *Vénus et Adonis* (Paris, 1897); *William Ratcliff* (Nice, Jan. 26, 1906); *Théodora* (Monte Carlo, March 19, 1907); *Le Chemineau* (Paris, Nov. 6, 1907; *Le Carillonneur* (Paris, March 20, 1913); *La Fille de Figaro* (Paris, March 11, 1914); *Les Cadeaux de Noël* (Paris, Dec. 25, 1915); *1814* (Monte Carlo, April 6, 1918); *Nausithoé* (Nice, April 9, 1920); *La Plus Forte* (Paris, Jan. 11, 1924); *L'Ingénu* (Bordeaux, Feb. 13, 1931).

Lert, Ernst (Josef Maria), Austrian opera Intendant, brother of **Richard (Johanes) Lert**; b. Vienna, May 12, 1883; d. Baltimore, Jan. 30, 1955. He studied at the Univ. of Vienna with G. Adler (Ph.D., 1908). He was a producer and dramaturg in Breslau (1909) and Leipzig (1912–19), then director of the operas in Basel (1919–20) and Frankfurt am Main (1919–23), where he also taught at the Hoch Cons.; from 1923 to 1929 he was producer at La Scala in Milan, and from 1929 to 1931, at the Metropolitan Opera in New York. From 1936 to 1938 he was head of the opera dept. of the Curtis Inst. of Music in Philadelphia. From 1938 to 1953 he was head of the opera dept. of the Peabody Cons. of Music in Baltimore. He wrote *Mozart auf dem Theater* (Berlin, 1918; 4th ed., 1922) and *Otto Lohse* (Leipzig, 1918).

Lert, Richard (Johanes), Austrian conductor and teacher, brother of **Ernst (Josef Maria) Lert**; b. Vienna, Sept. 19, 1885; d. Los Angeles, April 25, 1980. He studied with Heuberger in Vienna; then served as a conductor in Düsseldorf, Darmstadt, Frankfurt am Main, Hannover, and Mannheim. He later was guest conductor with the Berlin State Opera. He emigrated to the United States in 1934 and settled in Pasadena, California, as a conductor and teacher. In 1916 he married the novelist Vicki Baum. He celebrated his 90th birthday in 1975, but continued to be active, conducting summer concerts at Orkney Springs, Va.; also gave courses in conducting.

Leslie, Henry (David), English conductor and composer; b. London, June 18, 1822; d. Llansaintfraid, near Oswestry, Feb. 4, 1896. He was a pupil of Charles Lucas. He was cellist in the Sacred Harmonic Soc., and its conductor from 1853 to 1861. In 1855 he organized (with Heming) an a cappella singing society, which won 1st prize at Paris in 1878. He was also conductor of the Herefordshire Phil. Soc. (1863–89) and principal of the National College of Music (1864–66). He composed the operas *Romance, or Bold Dick Turpin* (1857) and *Ida* (1864), as well as the oratorios *Immanuel* (1853) and *Judith* (1858).

Le Sueur or **Lesueur, Jean François,** eminent French composer and writer on music; b. Drucat-Plessiel, near Abbeville, Feb. 15, 1760; d. Paris, Oct. 6, 1837. At 7 he was a choirboy at Abbeville, and at 14, in Amiens, where he took a course of studies; interrupting his academic education, he became maître de musique at the Cathedral of Seez. He then served as assistant choirmaster at the Church of the Holy Innocents in Paris; during this time, he studied harmony and composition with Abbé Roze. He subsequently was maître de musique at the cathedrals of Dijon (1781), Le Mans (1783), and Tours (1784). He then returned to Paris, serving (upon the recommendation of Grétry) as maître de chapelle at the Holy Innocents. When the competition for the post of maître de chapelle at Notre Dame was announced in 1786, Le Sueur entered it, and won. He organized an orch. for the chief festive days, and brought out masses, motets, services, etc., using a full orch., thus completely transforming the character of the services; he was greatly successful with the congregation, but the conservative clergy strongly objected to his innovations; other critics called his type of musical productions "opéra des gueux" (beggars' opera). He expounded his ideas of effective and descriptive music in a pamphlet, *Essai de musique sacrée ou musique motivée et méthodique, pour la fête de Noël, à la messe de jour* (1787); this evoked an anonymous attack, to which he replied with another publication, *Exposé d'une musique unie, imitative, et particulière à chaque solennité* (1787), reasserting his aim of making church music dramatic and descriptive. He left Notre Dame in 1788. After a sojourn in the country, he returned to Paris and produced 3 successful operas at the Théâtre Feydeau: *La Caverne* (Feb. 16, 1793), which had a popular success, *Paul et Virginie* (Jan. 13, 1794), and *Télémaque* (May 11, 1796). He also composed 10 hymns, written for various revolutionary festivals, which proved popular. He joined the Inst. National de Musique in 1793, the predecessor of the Paris Cons., which was organized in 1795; he subsequently served there as an inspector and a member of the Committee on Instruction. With Méhul, Langlé, Gossec, and Catel, he wrote the *Principes élémentaires de la musique* and the *Solfèges du Conservatoire*. Le Sueur was dismissed in 1802 because of an altercation that occurred following the rejection, by the Opéra, of 2 of his operas in favor of Catel's *Sémiramis*. For 2 years he lived in poverty and suffering, until Napoleon, in 1804, raised him to the highest position attainable by a musician in Paris by appointing him as his maître de chapelle, succeeding Paisiello. His rejected opera *Ossian ou Les Bardes* was then produced (Paris, July 10, 1804) with great applause; his other rejected opera, *La Mort d'Adam* (Paris, March 21, 1809), was a failure. After the restoration of the monarchy, and despite Le Sueur's avowed veneration of Napoleon, the government of Louis XVIII appointed him superintendent and composer to the Chapelle du Roi; he retained his post until 1830; he was also prof. of composition at the Paris Cons. from 1818 until his death, his celebrated pupils numbering Berlioz, Gounod, and Ambroise Thomas. He was made a member of the Institut (1813). His last operas, *Tyrtée* (1794), *Artaxerse* (1797), and *Alexandre à Babylone* (1815), were accepted for performance, but were not produced. His other works include the intermède *L'Inauguration du temple de la Victoire* (Paris, Jan. 20, 1807; in collaboration with L. Loiseau de Persuis) and the opera *Le Triomphe de Trajan* (Paris, Oct. 23, 1807; in collaboration with Persuis); several sacred oratorios (*Debora, Rachel, Ruth et Noémi, Ruth et Booz*). His major theoretical and historical work was his *Exposé d'une musique unie, imitative et particulière à chaque solennité* (4 vols., Paris, 1787). J. Mongredien ed. *Jean-François Le Sueur: A Thematic Catalogue of His Complete Works* (N.Y., 1980).

BIBL.: C. Ducanel, *Mémoire pour J. F. Lesueur* (Paris, 1802); Raoul-Rochette, *Notice historique sur la vie et les oeuvres de J.-F. L. S.* (Paris, 1837); S. de la Madeleine, *Biographie de J.-F. L. S.* (Paris, 1841); W. Buschkotter, *J. F. L. S.* (Halle, 1912); F. Lamy, *J. F. L. S. (1760–1837)* (Paris, 1912).

Lesur, Daniel Jean Yves. See **Daniel-Lesur, Jean Yves.**

Lesure, François (-Marie), distinguished French music librarian, musicologist, and writer; b. Paris, May 23, 1923. He studied at the École des Chartres, the École Pratique des Hautes Études, and the Sorbonne, and musicology at the Paris Cons. A member of the music dept. at the Bibliothèque Nationale (from 1950), he was its chief curator (1970–88). From 1953 to 1967 he headed the Paris office (responsible for Series B) of the Répertoire International des Sources Musicales (RISM), for which he himself ed. *Recueils imprimés: XVIe-XVIIe siècles* (Munich, 1960); *Recueils imprimés: XVIIIe siècle* (Munich, 1964; suppl. in *Notes*, March 1972, vol. 28, pp. 397–418, and the 2 vols. of *Écrits imprimés concernant la musique* (Munich, 1971). He also was a prof. at the Free Univ. of Brussels (1965–77), ed. of the early music series known as Le Pupitre (from 1967), president of the Société Française de Musicologie (1971–74; 1988–91), and prof. at the École Pratique des Hautes Études (from 1973). He ed. such nonserial works as *Anthologie de la chanson parisienne au XVIe siècle* (Monaco, 1953); the report of the 1954 Arras Conference, *La Renaissance dans les provinces du Nord* (Paris, 1956); P. Trichet's *Traité des instruments de musique* (vers 1640) (Neuilly, 1957); 6 vols. of *Chansons polyphoniques* (with A. T. Merrit, Monaco, 1967–72; the 1st 5 vols. constitute the collected works of C. Janequin); a collected ed. of Debussy's writings on music, *Monsieur Croche et autres écrits* (Paris, 1971; Eng. tr., 1977); he ed. a *Catalogue de l'oeuvre de Claude Debussy* (Geneva, 1977); he ed. the letters of Debussy for the period 1884–1918 (Paris, 1980; rev. ed., 1993); he was ed.-in-chief of the complete works of Debussy (from 1986). His own publications include a *Bibliographie des éditions d'Adrian Le Roy et Robert Ballard, 1551–1598* (with G. Thibault, Paris, 1955; suppl. in *Revue de Musicologie*, 1957); *Musicians and Poets of the French Renaissance* (N.Y., 1955); *Mozart en France* (Paris, 1956); *Collection musicale A. Meyer* (with N. Bridgman, Abbeville, 1961); *Musica e società* (Milan, 1966; Ger. tr., 1966, as *Musik und Gesellschaft im Bild: Zeugnisse der Malerei aus sechs Jahrhunderten*; Eng. tr., 1968, as *Music and Art in Society*); *Bibliographie des éditions musicales publiées par Estienne Roger et Michel-Charles Le Cene, Amsterdam, 1696–1743* (Paris, 1969); *Musique et musiciens français du XVIe siècle* (Geneva, 1976, a reprinting in book form of 24 articles orig. publ. 1950–69); *Claude Debussy avant "Pelléas" ou Les Années symbolistes* (Paris, 1992); *Claude Debussy: Biographie critique* (Paris, 1994). He contributed *L'Opéra classique français: 17e et 18e siècles* (Geneva, 1972) and *Claude Debussy* (Geneva, 1975) to the series Iconographie Musicale. For the Bibliothèque Nationale, he prepared a series of exhibition catalogs, most notably one on Berlioz (Paris, 1969).

BIBL.: J.-M. Fauquet, ed., *Musiques, Signes, Images: Liber amicorum F. L.* (Geneva, 1988).

Levasseur, Nicolas (-Prosper), prominent French bass; b. Bresles, March 9, 1791; d. Paris, Dec. 6, 1871. In 1807 he entered the Paris Cons., where he studied in Garat's singing class in 1811. He made his debut as Osman Pacha in Grétry's *La Caravane du Caire* at the Paris Opéra (Oct. 14, 1813). He made his London debut in Mayr's *Adeasia ed Alderano* at the King's Theatre (Jan. 10, 1815), and then returned to the Paris Opéra as an understudy until he made his debut at the Théâtre-Italien as Almaviva (Oct. 5, 1819). He appeared in the premiere of Meyerbeer's *Margherita d'Anjou* at Milan's La Scala (Nov. 14, 1820), and then returned to the Théâtre-Italien. In 1828 he rejoined the Paris Opéra, establishing himself as its principal bass; among the roles he created there were Bertram in *Robert le diable* (1831), Brogni in *La Juive* (1835), Marcel in *Les Huguenots* (1836), and Balthazar in *La Favorite* (1840). He left the Opéra in 1845, but was recalled by Meyerbeer to sing the role of Zacharie in the premiere of *Le Prophète* (1849); he retired from the stage in 1853. He was a prof. at the Paris Cons. (1841–69). He was made a Chevalier de la Légion d'honneur in 1869.

Levasseur, Rosalie (Marie-Rose-Claude-Josèphe), esteemed French soprano; b. Valenciennes, Oct. 8, 1749; d. Neuwied am Rhein, May 6, 1826. She was the illegitimate daughter of Jean-Baptiste Levasseur and Marie-Catherine Tournay, who married when she was 11. She made her debut under the name Mlle. Rosalie in the role of Zaide in Campra's *L'Europe galante* at the Paris Opéra (1766), and continued to appear in minor roles there until 1776. Taking the name Levasseur, she took on major roles, gaining success as Eurydice and Iphigenia. She then was chosen over her rival Sophie Arnould to create the title role in the first Paris staging of Gluck's *Alceste* (1776). She was greatly admired by Gluck, who chose her to create the title roles in his *Armide* (1777) and *Iphigénie en Tauride* (1779); she likewise created roles in works by Philidor, Piccinni, and Sacchini, remaining at the Opéra until 1788. She was the mistress of Count Mercy-Argentau, the Austrian ambassador in Paris, who used his influence to promote her career.

Leveridge, Richard, noted English bass and composer; b. London, c.1670; d. there, March 22, 1758. He first gained notice in London in 1695. After a sojourn in Dublin (1699–1702), he returned to London. He was a member of Handel's company (1712–13), appearing in the premieres of his *Il Pastor fido* and *Teseo*; then sang at Lincoln's Inn Fields (1714–20). He ran a coffeehouse from about 1716. He returned to the stage in 1723. He was principal bass at Lincoln's Inn Fields, and subsequently at Covent Garden; he retired in 1751. He publ. 5 collections of songs (London, 1697–1730). His most popular and enduring song was "The Roast Beef of Old England," which he introduced at his Covent Garden benefit on April 15, 1735. He also wrote works for the stage, including incidental music to *Macbeth* (London, Nov. 21, 1702) and a number of masques.

Levey, William Charles, Irish conductor and composer; b. Dublin, April 25, 1837; d. London, Aug. 18, 1894. His father was the Irish violinist, conductor, teacher, and composer Richard Michael Levey (real name, O'Shaughnessy; b. Dublin, Oct. 25, 1811; d. there, June 28, 1899). He studied with his father, and then with Auber, Thalberg, and Prudent in Paris. He then was a conductor at London's Drury Lane Theatre (1868–74), Covent Garden, and elsewhere. He wrote the operettas *Fanchette* (London, Jan. 4, 1864), *Punchinello* (London, Dec. 28, 1864), and *The Girls of the Period* (London, Feb. 25, 1869), as well as incidental music and pantomimes. His brother, Richard C. Levey (1833–c.1904), was a violinist.

Levi, Hermann, eminent German conductor; b. Giessen, Nov. 7, 1839; d. Munich, May 13, 1900. He was a pupil of Vincenz Lachner in Mannheim (1852–55) and of Hauptmann and Rietz at the Leipzig Cons. (1855–58). He was music director in Saarbrücken (1859–61). After serving as assistant Kapellmeister of the Mannheim National Theater (1861), he was Kapellmeister of the German Opera in Rotterdam (1861–64). He became Hofkapellmeister in Karlsruhe in 1864, and in 1872 was named Hofkapellmeister of the Bavarian Court Opera in Munich; he was made Generalmusikdirektor of the city in 1894, but was compelled by ill health to give up his duties in 1896. He enjoyed great respect among German musicians, and was influential in spreading the Wagnerian gospel. He conducted the first performance of *Parsifal* at Bayreuth (July 26, 1882), and his interpretation received complete approval from Wagner himself, who, for the nonce, repressed his opposition to Jews. Levi conducted the musical program at Wagner's funeral. He was also a friend of Brahms until his championship of Wagner led to an estrangement. He wrote *Gedanken aus Goethes Werken* (1901; 3d ed., 1911).

BIBL.: E. von Possart, *Erinnerungen an H. L.* (Munich, 1901).

Levi, Paul Alan, American composer, teacher, and pianist; b. N.Y., June 30, 1941. After training at Oberlin (Ohio) College (B.A. in music, 1963), he was a composition student of Overton and Persichetti at the Juilliard School in New York (M.M., 1972; D.M.A., 1978); he also attended the Munich Hochschule für Musik (1973–74), held a Deutscher Akademischer Austauschdienst study grant in Germany (1973–74), and took summer courses in new music in Darmstadt (1974). From 1963 he was active as a piano accompanist. He taught at Baruch (1972–73), Queens (1979), and Lehman (1981–82) colleges of the City Univ. of N.Y. In 1979 he joined the faculty of N.Y. Univ.; he also taught at the Manhattan School of Music (from 1992). In 1976 he served as composer-in-residence at the Wolf Trap Farm Park in Vienna, Va. From 1979 to 1982 he was president of the League of Composers.

In 1983–84 he held a Guggenheim fellowship. In 1985 he became a founding partner of Mountain Laurel Music, a production company. In his varied output, Levi has revealed an imaginative handling of instrumentation and setting of vocal texts. His works included *Thanksgiving*, seriocomic opera (N.Y., Nov. 2, 1977), *In the Beginning . . .* , opera parable (1987–95), incidental music to plays, and television and film music.

Levine, James (Lawrence), brilliant American pianist and conductor; b. Cincinnati, June 23, 1943. His maternal grandfather was a cantor in a synagogue; his father was a violinist who led a dance band; his mother was an actress. He began playing the piano as a small child. At the age of 10, he was soloist in Mendelssohn's 2d Piano Concerto at a youth concert of the Cincinnati Sym. Orch.; he then studied music with Walter Levin, 1st violinist in the La Salle Quartet; in 1956 he took piano lessons with Serkin at the Marlboro (Vt.) School of Music; in 1957 he began piano studies with Lhévinne at the Aspen (Colo.) Music School. In 1961 he entered the Juilliard School of Music in New York, and took courses in conducting with Jean Morel; he also had conducting sessions with Wolfgang Vacano in Aspen. In 1964 he graduated from the Juilliard School and joined the American Conductors Project connected with the Baltimore Sym. Orch., where he had occasion to practice conducting with Wallenstein, Rudolf, and Cleva. In 1964–65 he served as an apprentice to Szell with the Cleveland Orch.; he then became a regular assistant conductor with it (1965–70). In 1966 he organized the Univ. Circle Orch. of the Cleveland Inst. of Music; he also led the student orch. of the summer music inst. of Oakland Univ. in Meadow Brook, Mich. (1967–69). In 1970 he made a successful appearance as guest conductor with the Philadelphia Orch. at its summer home at Robin Hood Dell; he subsequently appeared with other American orchs. In 1970 he also conducted the Welsh National Opera and the San Francisco Opera. He made his Metropolitan Opera debut in New York on June 5, 1971, in a festival performance of *Tosca*; his success led to further appearances and to his appointment as its principal conductor in 1973; he then was its music director from 1975 until becoming its artistic director in 1986. From 1973 to 1993 he was music director of the Ravinia Festival, the summer home of the Chicago Sym. Orch., and served in that capacity with the Cincinnati May Festival (1974–78). In 1975 he began to conduct at the Salzburg Festivals; in 1982 he conducted at the Bayreuth Festival for the first time. He conducted his first *Ring* cycle at Bayreuth in 1995, and led another mounting of that tetralogy at the Metropolitan Opera in 1997. In 1997 he received the National Medal of Arts. From 1999 he was also music director of the Munich Phil. He continues to make appearances as a pianist, playing chamber music with impeccable technical precision. But it is as a conductor and an indefatigable planner of the seasons at the Metropolitan Opera that he inspires respect. Unconcerned with egotistical projections of his own personality, he presides over the singers and the orch. with concentrated efficiency.

Levy, Jules, Bulgarian conductor and composer; b. Salonika, June 19, 1930. He studied in Sofia with Stoyanov at the Bulgarian State Cons., graduating in 1957, then was active as a theater conductor. His works include the musicals *The Girl I Was in Love With* (1963), *The World Is Small* (1970), and *The Phone Which . . .* (1975), the ballet *Fair in Sofia* (1968), and the choreographic oratorio *Onward to the Rising World* (1973).

Levy, Marvin David, American composer; b. Passaic, N.J., Aug. 2, 1932. He studied composition with Philip James at N.Y. Univ., and with Luening at Columbia Univ.; he was awarded 2 Guggenheim fellowships (1960, 1964) and 2 American Prix de Rome fellowships (1962–63; 1965). Levy showed a particular disposition toward the musical theater. In his vocal and instrumental writing, he adopted an expressionistic mode along atonal lines, in an ambience of cautiously dissonant harmonies vivified by a nervously asymmetric rhythmic pulse.

WORKS: DRAMATIC: OPERAS: *Sotoba Komachi* (N.Y., April 7, 1957); *The Tower* (Sante Fe, Aug. 2, 1957); *Escorial* (N.Y., May 4, 1958); *Mourning Becomes Electra*, after O'Neill (N.Y., March 17, 1967). MUSICAL: *The Balcony* (1981–87). ORATORIOS: *For the Time Being*, Christmas oratorio (1959); *Masada* for Narrator, Tenor, Chorus, and Orch. (1973; rev. version, Chicago, Oct. 15, 1987).

Lewis, Henry, black American conductor; b. Los Angeles, Oct. 16, 1932; d. N.Y., Jan. 26, 1996. He learned to play piano and string instruments as a child; at the age of 16 he was engaged as a double-bass player in the Los Angeles Phil.; from 1955 to 1959 he played double bass in the 7th Army Sym. Orch. overseas, and also conducted it in Germany and the Netherlands. Returning to the United States, he founded the Los Angeles Chamber Orch.; in 1963 he traveled with it in Europe under the auspices of the State Dept. From 1968 to 1976 he was music director of the New Jersey Sym. Orch. in Newark; he subsequently conducted opera and orch. guest engagements. From 1989 to 1991 he was chief conductor of the Radio Sym. Orch. in Hilversum. He married **Marilyn Horne** in 1960, but they separated in 1976.

Lewis, Keith, New Zealand tenor; b. Methven, Oct. 6, 1950. Following training in New Zealand, he pursued studies at the London Opera Centre. In 1976 he won the Kathleen Ferrier Memorial Scholarship and in 1979 the John Christie Award. He appeared with the Chelsea Opera Group and at the English Bach Festival in 1976. In 1977 he made his debut as Don Ottavio with the Glyndebourne Touring Opera, and then sang that role for his first appearance at the Glyndebourne Festival in 1978. In the latter year he also sang Tebaldo in *I Capuleti e i Montecchi* at London's Covent Garden. After appearing as Tamino at the English National Opera in London in 1982, he made his U.S. debut as Don Ottavio in San Francisco in 1984. In 1989 he sang for the first time at the Salzburg Festival as Berlioz's Faust with the Chicago Sym. Orch. under Solti's direction. In 1993 he appeared as Oedipus Rex in New York. He was engaged as Alwa in *Lulu* at the Berlin State Opera in 1997. As a concert artist, Lewis has appeared with major orchs. on both sides of the Atlantic, principally in works by Bach, Handel, Beethoven, Haydn, Mozart, Berlioz, and Mendelssohn.

Lewis, Richard (real name, **Thomas Thomas**), noted English tenor; b. Manchester, May 10, 1914; d. Eastbourne, Nov. 13, 1990. He studied with T. W. Evans, then with Norman Allin at the Royal Manchester College of Music (1939–41) and at the Royal Academy of Music in London (1945). He made his operatic debut with the Carl Rosa Opera Co. in 1939; from 1947 he sang at the Glyndebourne Festival and at London's Covent Garden. He sang with the San Francisco Opera (1955–60), then appeared there as a guest artist (1962–68). He toured extensively as a concert and oratorio singer. In 1963 he was named a Commander of the Order of the British Empire. His repertoire was extensive, including roles in operas ranging from Monteverdi and Mozart to Schoenberg, Britten, and Tippett.

Ley, Salvador, Guatemalan pianist and composer; b. Guatemala City, Jan. 2, 1907; d. there, March 21, 1985. He studied at the Berlin Hochschule für Musik (1922–30); concurrently he studied piano with Georg Bertram (1922–30) and theory and composition with Klatte (1923–25) and Leichtentritt (1928–29). He was director of the National Cons. in Guatemala City (1934–37; 1944–53); then taught at the Westchester (N.Y.) Cons. (1963–70). Among his works is the opera *Lera* (1959).

Lhérie (real name, **Lévy**), **Paul,** French tenor, later baritone; b. Paris, Oct. 8, 1844; d. there, Oct. 17, 1937. He was a pupil of Obin in Paris. In 1866 he made his operatic debut in the tenor role of Reuben in *Joseph* at the Paris Opéra Comique, where he sang until 1868 and again from 1872. On March 3, 1875, he created the role of Don José there. In 1882 he turned to baritone roles, and in 1884 he appeared as Posa in the rev. version of *Don Carlos* at Milan's La Scala. In 1887 he sang Rigoletto at London's Covent Garden, returning there as Luna and Germont. Following his retirement from the stage in 1894, he was active as a voice teacher in Paris.

Lhotka, Fran, Croatian composer and teacher of Czech descent, father of **Ivo Lhotka-Kalinski**; b. Wožice, Dec. 25, 1883; d. Zagreb, Jan. 26, 1962. He took lessons with Dvořák, Klička, and Stecker in Prague (1899–1905). After teaching in Ekaterinoslav (1908–09), he settled in Zagreb as a member of the Opera orch.; he then was conductor of the Lisinski Chorus (1912–20); subsequently he was a prof. at the Academy of Music (1920–61), where he also served as rector (1923–40; 1948–52). He publ. a harmony manual (Zagreb, 1948). His music followed in the late Romantic style. Among his compositions were the operas *Minka* (Zagreb, 1918) and *The Sea* (Zagreb, 1920) and the ballets *The Devil of the Village* (Zürich, Feb. 18, 1935), *Ballad of Medieval Love* (Zürich, Feb. 6, 1937), and *Luk* (Munich, Nov. 13, 1939).

Lhotka-Kalinski, Ivo, Croatian composer, son of **Fran Lhotka**; b. Zagreb, July 30, 1913; d. there, Jan. 29, 1987. He studied composition with his father and also voice at the Zagreb Academy of Music; after further composition lessons with Pizzetti in Rome (1937–39), he was active as a teacher; he then was prof. of singing at the Zagreb Academy of Music (from 1951), becoming its regional director in 1967. He had a natural flair for stage composition in the folk style; he wrote several brilliant musical burlesques, among them *Analfabeta* (The Illiterate; Belgrade, Oct. 19, 1954); *Putovanje* (The Journey), the first television opera in Yugoslavia (Zagreb, June 10, 1957); *Dugme* (The Button; Zagreb, April 21, 1958); *Vlast* (Authority; Zagreb TV, Oct. 18, 1959); *Svjetleči grad* (The Town of Light; Zagreb, Dec. 26, 1967); also a children's opera, *Velika coprarija* (The Great Sorcerer; 1952).

Liatoshinsky, Boris (Nikolaievich), significant Ukrainian composer and pedagogue; b. Zhitomir, Jan. 3, 1895; d. Kiev, April 15, 1968. He studied jurisprudence at the Univ. of Kiev, simultaneously taking lessons in composition at the Kiev Cons. with Gliere, graduating in 1919. He was an instructor (1919–35) and then a prof. (1935–68) at the Kiev Cons.; he also taught at the Moscow Cons. (1936–37; 1941–43). Liatoshinsky was awarded State Prizes in 1946 and 1952. His style of composition followed the broad outlines of national music, with numerous thematic allusions to folk songs. His works include the operas *The Golden Hoop* (1929; Odessa, March 26, 1930) and *Shchors* (1937; Kiev, Sept. 1, 1938; rev. version, Kiev, Feb. 18, 1970).

BIBL.: I. Boelza, *B. M. L.* (Kiev, 1947); V. Samokhvalov, *B. L.* (Kiev, 1970; 2d ed., 1974).

Licette, Miriam, English soprano; b. Chester, Sept. 9, 1892; d. Twyford, Aug. 11, 1969. She was trained in Milan and Paris, her principal mentors being Marchesi, Jean de Reszke, and Sabbatini. In 1911 she made her operatic debut in Rome as Cio-Cio-San. From 1916 to 1920 she sang with the Beecham Opera Co., and from 1919 to 1929 she appeared in the international seasons at London's Covent Garden. She also was a member of the British National Opera Co. from 1922 to 1928. She won particular praise as a Mozartian. Among her other roles were Eurydice, Gutrune, Eva, Desdemona, Juliette, and Louise.

Lichtenstein, Karl August, Freiherr von, German theater manager, conductor, and composer; b. Lahm, Franconia, Sept. 8, 1767; d. Berlin, Sept. 10, 1845. He was educated in Gotha and Göttingen. After serving in the English army, he entered Hannoverian service and attracted notice as a composer with his comic opera *Glück und Zufall* (Hannover, April 26, 1793). In 1797 he became manager of the Dessau Court Opera, where his opera *Bathmendi* inaugurated the new theater on Dec. 26, 1798. It was there that his most popular work, the Singspiel *Die steinerne Braut*, was premiered on April 25, 1799. Following a sojourn in Leipzig (1799–1800), Lichtenstein went to Vienna as Kapellmeister and artistic director of the Court Theater. In 1806 he resigned his duties to become a minister in the diplomatic service of the Duke of Saxe-Hildburghausen. In 1811 he left the diplomatic service and went to Bamberg, where he was named director of the theater in 1813. After serving as music director in Strasbourg (1814–17), he was again in Bamberg. In 1823 he settled in Berlin, where he was active at the Royal Opera from 1825 until being pensioned in 1832. Besides his operas, Lichtenstein prepared librettos for other composers. He also made translations and arrangements of operas by other composers.

WORKS: OPERAS: *Glück und Zufall*, comic opera (Hannover, April 26, 1793); *Knall und Fall* (Bamberg, 1795); *Bathmendi*, grosse allegorisch-komische Oper (Dessau, Dec. 26, 1798; rev. version, Vienna, April 16, 1801); *Die steinerne Braut*, Singspiel (Dessau, April 25, 1799); *Ende gut, alles gut*, comic opera (Dessau, Oct. 26, 1800); *Mitgefühl*, Liederspiel (Dessau, Oct. 26, 1800); *Der Kaiser als Zimmermann, oder Frauenwerth*, comic opera (Strasbourg, June 22, 1814); *Imago, die Tochter der Zwietracht* (1813–14); *Das Mädchen aus der Fremde*, operetta (Bamberg, 1821); *Die Waldburg* (Dresden, June 11, 1822); *Die Edelknaben, oder Zur guten Stunde*, Singspiel (Berlin, May 27, 1823); *Jerusalem* (Bamberg, 1824); *Singethee und Liedertafel*, Singspiel (Berlin, March 25, 1825); *Die deutschen Herren in Nürnberg* (Berlin, March 1834); *Der Gluthengeist* (n.d.); *Trübsale eines Hofbankiers*, comic opera (1838).

Lickl, Johann Georg, Austrian conductor and composer; b. Korneuburg, Lower Austria, April 11, 1769; d. Fünfkirchen, May 12, 1843. He studied music with the Korneuburg church organist Witzig, then went to Vienna (1785), where he continued his studies with Albrechtsberger and Haydn. He subsequently was active as a teacher and as organist at the Carmelite Church in the Leopoldstadt. He became associated around 1789 with Schikaneder's Freihaus-Theater auf der Wieden, where he contributed numbers to popular Singspiels or wrote entire scores for them. His *Der Brigitten-Kirchtag* (1802) was composed for the new Theater an der Wien, and his comic opera *Slawina von Pommern* (1812) for the Leopoldstadt Theater. He served as regens chori at Fünfkirchen Cathedral (from 1805), producing much sacred music. He publ. arrangements for piano and harmonium of popular classics in *Wiener Salon-Musik*. He had 2 sons: Karl Georg Lickl (b. Vienna, Oct. 28, 1801; d. there, Aug. 3, 1877), a civil servant who became well known as a physharmonica player and composer for the instrument, and Aegidius (Ferdinand) Karl Lickl (b. Vienna, Sept. 1, 1803; d. Trieste, July 22, 1864), who studied with his father, appeared as a pianist, and then settled in Trieste as a teacher, conductor, and composer; he wrote the opera *La disfida Berletta* (1848) and sacred music.

Lidholm, Ingvar (Natanael), prominent Swedish composer; b. Jönköping, Feb. 24, 1921. He studied violin with Hermann Gramms and orchestration with Natanael Berg in Södertälje; then received violin training from Alex Ruunqvist and conducting lessons from Tor Mann at the Stockholm Musikhögskolan (1940–45); he also studied composition with Hilding Rosenberg (1943–45). He was a violinist in the orch. of the Royal Theater in Stockholm (1943–47) and received a Jenny Lind fellowship and pursued his studies in France, Switzerland, and Italy (1947); later he studied in Darmstadt (summer 1949) and with Seiber in England (1954). He served as director of music in Örebro (1947–56) and was director of chamber music for the Swedish Radio (1956–65); after holding the position of prof. of composition at the Stockholm Musikhögskolan (1965–75), he returned to the Swedish Radio as director of planning in its music dept. (1975). In 1960 he was elected a member of the Royal Swedish Academy of Music in Stockholm. He became active in Swedish avant-garde circles, contributing greatly to the formulation of methods and aims of contemporary music. In his works, he applies constructivist methods with various serial algorithms.

WORKS: DRAMATIC: *Cyrano de Bergerac*, incidental music (1947); *Riter*, ballet (1959; Stockholm, March 26, 1960); *Holländarn*, television opera (Swedish TV, Dec. 10, 1967); *Ett drömspel*, opera (1990).

Lidón, José, Spanish organist and composer; b. Béjar, June 2, 1748; d. Madrid, Feb. 11, 1827. He studied at Madrid's Réal Colegio di Niños Cantores. He was organist at Orense Cathedral, then was made 4th organist (1768) and 1st organist (1787) of Madrid's royal chapel; he was master there and rector of the Réal Colegio (1805–27). Among his compositions is an opera, *Glauca y Coriolano* (Madrid, 1791). He also publ. several theoretical works.

Liebe, Eduard Ludwig, German composer; b. Magdeburg, Nov. 19, 1819; d. Chur, Feb. 4, 1900. He studied in Kassel with Spohr and Baldewein, then was a music director at Koblenz, Mainz, and Worms. He went to Strasbourg as a teacher and later taught in London. He wrote an opera, *Die Braut von Azola* (Karlsruhe, 1868).

Liebermann, Lowell, American composer, pianist, and conductor; b. N.Y., Feb. 22, 1961. He began piano lessons at the age of 8, becoming a student of Ada Sohn Segal by age 11; at 14, he began piano and composition lessons with Ruth Schonthal. In 1977 he made his debut at N.Y.'s Carnegie Recital Hall. In 1978 he commenced private composition lessons with Diamond, who continued as his mentor at the Juilliard School in New York from 1979; he also studied there with Lateiner (piano), Halasz (conducting), and Persichetti (composition), taking a B.Mus. (1982), a M.Mus. (1984), and a D.M.A. (1987). In 1986 he won the Victor Herbert/ASCAP Award, and in 1990 the Charles Ives fellowship of the American Academy and Inst. of Arts and Letters and ASCAP's Young Composers Competition. From 1999 to 2001 he was composer-in-residence of the Dallas Sym. Orch. Liebermann's output demonstrates a deft handling of both traditional and modern elements in an accessible style. Among his works is the opera *The Picture of Dorian Gray* (1993–94; Monte Carlo, May 8, 1996).

Liebermann, Rolf, esteemed Swiss opera administrator and composer; b. Zürich, Sept. 14, 1910; d. Paris, Jan. 2, 1999. He studied law at the Univ. of Zürich and received private instruction in music from José Berr (1929–33); he took a conducting course with Scherchen in Budapest (1936), and served as his assistant in Vienna (1937–38); he also had composition studies with Vogel (1940). He was a producer at Radio Zürich (1945–50), then was director of the orch. section of the Schweizerische Rundspruchgesellschaft in Zürich (1950–57); subsequently he was director of music of the North German Radio in Hamburg (1957–59). He was Intendant of the Hamburg State Opera (1959–73), where he pursued a policy of staging numerous 20th-century operas, including specially commissioned works from leading contemporary composers; he then was general administrator of the Paris Opéra (1973–80), bringing enlightened leadership to bear on its artistic policies; he subsequently was recalled to his former post at the Hamburg State Opera in 1985, remaining there until 1988. From 1983 to 1988 he also was director of the International Summer Academy of the Salzburg Mozarteum. He was made a Commandeur de la Légion d'honneur of France in 1975. His autobiography was publ. in English as *Opera Years* (1987). As a composer, he worked mostly in an experimental idiom, sharing the influence of hedonistic eclecticism, French neoclassicism, and Viennese dodecaphony; he became particularly attracted to theatrical applications of modernistic procedures.

WORKS: OPERAS: *Leonore 40/45* (1951–52; Basel, March 25, 1952); *Penelope* (1953–54; Salzburg, Aug. 17, 1954); *The School for Wives* (1954–55; Louisville, Dec. 3, 1955; rev. as *Die Schüle der Frauen*, Salzburg, Aug. 17, 1957); *La Forêt* or *Der Wald* (1985–86; Geneva, April 11, 1987); *Non lieu pour Medea* (1992); *Freispruch für Medea* (Hamburg, Sept. 24, 1995).

BIBL.: I. Scharberth and H. Paris, eds., *R. L. zum 60. Geburtstag* (Hamburg, 1970).

Lieberson, Peter, American composer; b. N.Y., Oct. 25, 1946. His father was the English-American recording executive and composer Goddard Lieberson (b. Hanley, Staffordshire, April 5, 1911; d. N.Y., May 29, 1977). He took a degree in English literature at N.Y. Univ. (1972); after studies with Babbitt, he trained with Wuorinen at Columbia Univ. (M.A. in composition, 1974), then studied Vajrayana Buddhism with Chögyam Trungpa of the Shambhala tradition. After completing his doctoral studies with Martino and Boykan at Brandeis Univ., he taught at Harvard Univ. (1984–88). He then settled in Halifax, Nova Scotia, as international director of Shambhala training, while continuing to pursue his career as a composer. His compositions are written in a well-crafted 12-tone system. Among them is the opera *Ashoka's Dream* (Santa Fe, N.M., July 26, 1997).

Liebling, Estelle, American soprano and pedagogue; b. N.Y., April 21, 1880; d. there, Sept. 25, 1970. She studied with Marchesi in Paris and Nicklass-Kempner in Berlin. She made her operatic debut as Lucia at the Dresden Court Opera; she then appeared at the Stuttgart Opera, the Opéra Comique in Paris, and the Metropolitan Opera in New York (debut Feb. 24, 1902, as Marguerite in *Les Huguenots*); she was again on the Metropolitan's roster in 1903–04. She was a soloist with leading orchs. in the United States, France, and Germany; also with Sousa. From 1936 to 1938 she was a prof. at the Curtis Inst. of Music in Philadelphia; she then settled in New York as a vocal teacher. Her most famous pupil was Beverly Sills. She publ. *The Estelle Liebling Coloratura Digest* (N.Y., 1943). Her brother, Leonard Liebling (b. N.Y., Feb. 7, 1874; d. there, Oct. 28, 1945), was a pianist, music critic, and editor; her uncle, Georg Liebling (b. Berlin, Jan. 22, 1865; d. N.Y., Feb. 7, 1946), was a pianist and composer.

Lierhammer, Theodor, Austrian baritone and teacher; b. Lemberg, Nov. 18, 1866; d. Vienna, Jan. 6, 1937. He was a practicing physician when he began to study singing with Ress in Vienna, Carafa in Milan, and Stockhausen in Frankfurt am Main. He made his debut at Vienna in 1894 in a concert with Fritz Kreisler; he toured Austria and Hungary (1896), Germany (1898), Russia (1899), France and England (1900), and the United States (1904). From 1904 to 1914 he was a prof. of singing at the Royal Academy of Music in London. He served as an army physician during World War I. From 1922 to 1924 he was in London as a singer and teacher; in 1924 he was named prof. of singing at the Academy of Music in Vienna; from 1932 to 1935 he taught at the Austro-American Summer Cons. in Mondsee (Salzburg). One of his American pupils was Roland Hayes.

Ligabue, Ilva, Italian soprano; b. Reggio Emilia, May 23, 1932; d. Palermo, Aug. 19, 1998. She studied at the Milan Cons. and at the opera school of Milan's La Scala, where she made her operatic debut as Marina in Wolf-Ferrari's *I quattro Rusteghi* in 1953. She subsequently sang in other Italian and German music centers. From 1958 to 1961 she appeared at the Glyndebourne Festivals, where she was heard as Alice Ford, Fiordiligi, Donna Elvira, and Anna Bolena. In 1961 she made her U.S. debut as Boito's Margherita. In 1963 she sang with the American Opera Soc. in New York, at the Vienna State Opera, and at London's Covent Garden, returning to the latter in 1974. Her guest engagements took her to many other U.S. and European music centers.

Ligendza, Catarina (real name, **Katarina Beyron**), Swedish soprano; b. Stockholm, Oct. 18, 1937. Her parents sang at Stockholm's Royal Theater; she studied at the Würzburg Cons., in Vienna, and with Greindl in Saarbrücken. She made her debut as Countess Almaviva in Linz (1965); then sang in Braunschweig and Saarbrücken (1966–69); she subsequently became a member of the Deutsche Oper in West Berlin and of the Württemberg State Theater in Stuttgart. In 1970 she sang for the first time at Milan's La Scala and at the Salzburg Easter Festival. She made her Metropolitan Opera debut in New York as Leonore in *Fidelio* on Feb. 25, 1971; that summer she appeared at the Bayreuth Festival; her Covent Garden debut in London followed as Senta in 1972. In subsequent years, she sang in principal operatic centers of Europe before retiring from the operatic stage in 1988. Her other roles included Agathe, Isolde, Brünnhilde, Desdemona, Chrysothemis, and Ariadne.

Ligeti, György (Sândor), eminent Hungarian-born Austrian composer and pedagogue; b. Dicsöszentmárton, Transylvania, May 28, 1923. The original surname of the family was Auer; his great-uncle was the celebrated Hungarian violinist and pedagogue Leopold Auer (b. Veszprém, June 7, 1845; d. Loschwitz, near Dresden, July 15, 1930). He studied composition with Farkas at the Kolozsvar Cons. (1941–43) and privately with Kadosa in Budapest (1942–43); he then continued his training with Veress, Járdányi, Farkas, and Bárdos at the Budapest Academy of Music

(1945–49), where he subsequently was a prof. of harmony, counterpoint, and analysis (from 1950). After the Hungarian revolution was crushed by the Soviet Union in 1956, he fled his homeland for the West; in 1967 he became a naturalized Austrian citizen. He worked at the electronic music studio of the West German Radio in Cologne (1957–58); from 1959 to 1972 he lectured at the Darmstadt summer courses in new music; from 1961 to 1971 he also was a visiting prof. at the Stockholm Musikhögskolan. In 1972 he served as composer-in-residence at Stanford Univ., and in 1973 he taught at the Berkshire Music Center at Tanglewood. From 1973 to 1989 he was a prof. of composition at the Hamburg Hochschule für Musik. He has received numerous honors and awards. In 1964 he was made a member of the Royal Swedish Academy of Music in Stockholm, in 1968 a member of the Akademie der Künste in Berlin, and in 1984 an honorary member of the American Academy and Inst. of Arts and Letters; in 1986 he received the Grawemeyer Award of the Univ. of Louisville; in 1988 he was made a Commandeur in the Ordre National des Arts et Lettres in Paris; in 1990 he was awarded the Austrian State Prize; in 1991 he received the Praemium Imperiale of Japan; in 1993 he won the Ernst von Siemens Music Prize of Munich. In his bold and imaginative experimentation with musical materials and parameters, Ligeti endeavors to bring together all aural and visual elements in a synthetic entity, making use of all conceivable effects and alternating tremendous sonorous upheavals with static chordal masses and shifting dynamic colors. He describes his orch. style as micropolyphony. Among his works is the opera *Le Grand Macabre* (1974–77; Stockholm, April 12, 1978; rev. version, Salzburg, July 28, 1997).

BIBL.: O. Nordwall, *G. L.: Eine Monographie* (Mainz, 1971); P. Griffiths, *G. L.* (London, 1983); E. Restagno, ed., *L.* (Turin, 1985); H. Sabbe, *G. L.: Studien zur kompositorischen Phänomenologie* (Munich, 1987); R. Richart, *G. L.: A Bio-Bibliography* (N.Y., 1990); W. Burde, *G. L.: Eine Monographie* (Zürich, 1993); U. Dibelius, *G. L.: Eine Monographie in Essays* (Mainz and N.Y., 1994).

Liljefors, Ingemar (Kristian), Swedish pianist and composer; b. Göteborg, Dec. 13, 1906; d. Stockholm, Oct. 14, 1981. His father was the Swedish composer and conductor Ruben (Matthias) Liljefors (1871–1936). He studied at the Royal Academy of Music in Stockholm (1923–27; 1929–31) and in Munich (1927–29). He taught piano (1938–43) and harmony (from 1943) at the Stockholm Musikhögskolan. From 1947 to 1963 he was chairman of the Assn. of Swedish Composers. He publ. a manual on harmony from the functional point of view (1937) and one on harmonic analysis along similar lines (1951). His compositions frequently employed elements of Swedish folk music with a later infusion of some modernistic techniques. He composed an opera, *Hyrkusken* (The Coachman; 1951).

Lillo, Giuseppe, Italian composer; b. Galatina, Lecce, Feb. 26, 1814; d. Naples, Feb. 4, 1863. He studied at the Naples Reale Collegio di Musica (later the Cons. di S. Pietro a Majella) with Furno, Lanza, and Zingarelli; in 1846, became a teacher of harmony there; later (1859), a teacher of counterpoint and composition there. He had to retire from active life in 1861 because of mental illness. Among his works are the operas *La moglie per 24 ore ossia L'ammalato di buona salute* (Naples, 1834) and *L'osteria d'Andujar* (Naples, 1840).

Lima, Luis, Argentine tenor; b. Córdoba, Sept. 12, 1948. He was trained in Buenos Aires and at the Madrid Cons. After taking prizes in the Toulouse (1972) and Francisco Viñas (1973) competitions, he took 1st prize in the Lauri-Volpe competition (1973). In 1974 he made his operatic debut as Turiddu in Lisbon, and then appeared throughout Germany. He made his American debut in a concert performance of Donizetti's *Gemma di Vergy* at N.Y.'s Carnegie Hall in 1976. In 1977 he sang for the first time at Milan's La Scala as Donizetti's Edgardo. On March 16, 1978, he made his N.Y. City Opera debut as Alfredo, which role he also chose for his Metropolitan Opera debut in New York on Sept. 20, 1978. He appeared as Cavaradossi at the Teatro Colón in Buenos Aires in 1982. In 1984 he made his debut at London's Covent Garden as Nemorino. He sang Cavaradossi at the Salzburg Easter Festival in 1988; in 1992 he appeared as Don Carlos at the San Francisco Opera. After singing Rodolfo at Covent Garden in 1996, he portrayed Don Carlos at the Metropolitan Opera in 1997. Among his other roles were Berlioz's and Boito's Faust, Verdi's Riccardo, Bizet's Don José, Gounod's Faust and Roméo, and Puccini's Rodolfo.

Limnander de Nieuwenhove, Armand Marie Ghislain, Belgian composer; b. Ghent, May 22, 1814; d. Moignanville, near Paris, Aug. 15, 1892. He studied in Freiburg with Lambillotte and in Brussels with Fétis. In 1835 he became a choral director in Mechelen. He settled in Paris in 1845. His works include a grand opera, *Le Maître-chanteur* (Paris, 1853), and the comic operas *Les Monténégrins* (Paris, 1849), *Le Château de la Barbe-Bleue* (1851), and *Yvonne* (1859).

Lincke, (Carl Emil) Paul, German conductor and composer; b. Berlin, Nov. 7, 1866; d. Klausthal-Zellerfeld, near Göttingen, Sept. 3, 1946. After studies with Rudolf Kleinow in Wittenberge (1880–84), he was active in Berlin as a bassoonist in and later conductor of theater orchs. He also became active as a composer of small operettas and other light theater pieces, scoring his first success with *Venus auf Erden* (June 6, 1897). After a sojourn at the Folies-Bergère in Paris (1897–99), he returned to Berlin and brought out such works as *Frau Luna* (May 1, 1899), *Im Reiche des Indra* (Dec. 18, 1899), *Fräulein Loreley* (Oct. 15, 1900), *Lysistrata* (April 1, 1902; best known for its *Glühwürmchen*-[Glowworm] *Idyll*), *Nakiris Hochzeit* (Nov. 6, 1902), and *Berliner Luft* (Sept. 28, 1904). Among his later works, only *Gri-gri* (Cologne, March 25, 1911) and *Casanova* (Chemnitz, Nov. 5, 1913) attracted much attention. He subsequently devoted himself mainly to conducting and overseeing his own publishing firm, Apollo Verlag. During the Nazi era, Lincke's works were successfully revived and the composer was granted various honors. His new-won fame, however, did not survive the collapse of the Third Reich.

BIBL.: E. Nick, *P. L.* (Hamburg, 1953); O. Schneidereit, *P. L. und die Entstehung der Berliner Operette* (Berlin, 1974).

Lind, Eva, Austrian soprano; b. Innsbruck, June 14, 1965. She received vocal training in Vienna. In 1983 she made her debut as a Flower Maiden in *Parsifal* in Innsbruck. In 1986 she sang Lucia in Basel and at the Vienna State Opera, and also the Italian Singer in *Capriccio* at the Salzburg Festival. She appeared as the Queen of the Night in Paris in 1987. In 1988 she made her British debut as Nannetta at the Glyndebourne Festival. She was engaged as Gounod's Juliet in Zürich in 1990, and in 1993 she sang Weber's Aennechen in Bonn. She appeared as Blondchen in Catania in 1996.

Lind, Jenny (Johanna Maria), famous Swedish soprano, called the "Swedish Nightingale"; b. Stockholm, Oct. 6, 1820; d. Wynds Point, Herefordshire, Nov. 2, 1887. She made her first stage appearance in Stockholm at the age of 10 (Nov. 29, 1830), the same year that she entered the Royal Opera School there, where she studied with C. Craelius and I. Berg; during this period, she also sang in many comedies and melodramas. She continued her studies with A. Lindblad and J. Josephson at the school, and then made her formal operatic debut as Agathe in *Der Freischütz* at the Royal Opera in Stockholm (March 7, 1838); later that year she appeared as Pamina and Euryanthe there, and then as Donna Anna (1839) and Norina (1841). In 1840 she was appointed a regular member of the Royal Swedish Academy of Music, and was also given the rank of court singer. However, she felt the necessity of improving her voice, and went to Paris to study with Manuel García (1841–42). Upon her return to Stockholm, she sang Norma (Oct. 10, 1842); she later appeared there as the Countess in *Le nozze di Figaro*, Anna in *La Sonnambula*, Valentine in *Les Huguenots*, and Anna Bolena. Although Meyerbeer wrote the role of Vielka in his opera *Ein Feldlager in Schlesien* for her, the role was first sung by Tuczec in Berlin (Dec. 7, 1844); Lind first essayed it there on Jan. 4, 1845. She also sang in Hannover, Hamburg, Cologne, Koblenz, Frankfurt am Main, Darmstadt, and Copenhagen. She appeared at the Leipzig Gewandhaus (Dec. 4, 1845) and made her Vienna debut as Norma at the Theater an der Wien (April 22, 1846); she subsequently sang throughout Germany, returning to Vienna as Marie in 1847 and creating a sensation. Lind made a phenomenally successful London debut as Alice in *Robert le diable* at Her Majesty's Theatre in London (May 4, 1847); her appearances in *La Sonnambula* (May 13, 1847) and *La Fille du régiment* (May 27, 1847) were acclaimed; she then created the role of Amalia in Verdi's *I Masnadieri* there (July 22, 1847).

After touring the English provinces, Lind decided to retire from the operatic stage, making her farewell appearance as Norma in Stockholm (April 12, 1848) and as Alice at London's Her Majesty's Theatre (May 10, 1849). If her success in Europe was great, her U.S. concert tour exceeded all expectations in public agitation and monetary reward. Sponsored by P. T. Barnum, she was seen as a natural phenomenon rather than an artist; nonetheless, her outstanding musicality made a deep impression upon the musical public. She made her N.Y. debut on Sept. 11, 1850, subsequently giving 93 concerts in all, her final one in Philadelphia (1851). On Feb. 5, 1852, she married her accompanist, Otto Goldschmidt, in Boston; they returned to Europe, settling permanently in England in 1858. She continued to appear in concert and oratorio performances until her retirement in 1883, when she became prof. of singing at London's Royal College of Music. She also devoted much time to charitable causes. Lind possessed an extraordinary coloratura voice, with a compass reaching high G. She was, without question, one of the greatest vocal artists of her era. A letter written by her, entitled "Jenny Lind's Singing Method," was publ. in *Musical Quarterly* (July 1917).

BIBL.: J. Lyser, *G. Meyerbeer and J. L.* (Vienna, 1847); C. Rosenberg, *J. L. in America* (N.Y., 1851); H. Holland and W. Rockstro, *Memoir of Mme. J. L.-Goldschmidt* (2 vols., 1893); W. Rockstro and O. Goldschmidt, *J. L.-Goldschmidt: A Record and Analysis of the Method of the Late J. L.-Goldschmidt* (London, 1894); T. Norlind, *J. L.* (Stockholm, 1919); R. Maude, *The Life of J. L.* (London, 1926); G. Humphrey, *J. L.* (Philadelphia, 1928); E. Wagenknecht, *J. L.-Goldschmidt* (Boston, 1931); L. Benet, *Enchanting J. L.* (N.Y., 1939); H. Headland, *The Swedish Nightingale: A Biography of J. L.* (Rock Island, Ill., 1940); M. Pergament, *J. L.* (Stockholm, 1945); K. Rotzen and T. Meyer, *J. L.* (Stockholm, 1945); J. Bulman, *J. L.* (London, 1956); G. Schultz, *J. L.: The Swedish Nightingale* (Philadelphia, 1962); A. Dunlop, *The Swedish Nightingale* (N.Y., 1965); W. Ware and T. Lockard Jr., translators and eds., *The Lost Letters of J. L.* (London, 1966); E. Myers, *J. L.: Songbird from Sweden* (Champaign, Ill., 1968).

Lindberg, Oskar (Fredrik), Swedish organist, pedagogue, and composer; b. Gagnef, Feb. 23, 1887; d. Stockholm, April 10, 1955. He became organist in Gagnef when he was 14. At 16 he entered the Stockholm Cons., where he took diplomas as a church musician (1906) and as a music teacher (1908); he also studied composition with Andreas Hallén and Ernst Ellberg. He served as organist at Stockholm's Trefaldighetskyrka (1906–14) and Engelbrektskyrka (1914–55), and also gave recitals. In 1919 he became a teacher of harmony at the Stockholm Cons., where he was a prof. from 1936. In 1926 he was named a member of the Swedish Royal Academy of Music. In his compositions, he pursued a Romantic path in which folk and national elements predominated. He composed an opera, *Fredlös* (1936–42; Stockholm, Nov. 25, 1943).

Lindblad, Adolf Fredrik, esteemed Swedish composer; b. Skänninge, near Stockholm, Feb. 1, 1801; d. Löfvingsborg, near Linköping, Aug. 23, 1878. In his youth he learned to play the flute and the piano, as well as to compose. After studying music formally in Uppsala (1823–25), he completed his training under Zelter in Berlin. He was director of his own music school in Stockholm (1827–61); his pupils included Jenny Lind and members of the royal family. He became a member of the Royal Swedish Academy of Music (1831). Lindblad was a gifted composer of songs; Lind introduced many of them at her concerts, earning him the title of the "Schubert of the North." He wrote some 215 songs (9 vols., Stockholm, 1878–90), including such notable examples as "I dalen" (In the Valley), "En sommardag" (A Summer's Day), and "Aftonen" (Evening); also the opera *Frondörerna* (The Frondists; Stockholm, May 11, 1835).

BIBL.: K. Linder, *Den unge A. F. L. (1801–27)* (diss., Univ. of Uppsala, 1973).

Linde, (Anders) Bo (Leif), Swedish composer, pianist, and music critic; b. Gävle, Jan. 1, 1933; d. there, Oct. 2, 1970. Following initial training with Bengtsson and Bökman, he studied at the Stockholm Musikhögskolan (1948–52) with Larsson (composition) and Wibergh (piano) before pursuing studies in conducting in Vienna (1953–54). He taught theory at the Stockholm Citizens' School (1957–60), and then returned to Gävle as a pianist, music critic, and composer. He composed in a well-crafted style notable for its adherence to classical forms in an accessible idiom. His works include the dramatic scores *Ballet blanc* (1953; Gävle, May 11, 1969) and *Slotts-skoj* (Fun in the Castle), children's opera (1959).

Lindholm, Berit (real name, **Berit Maria Jonsson**), Swedish soprano; b. Stockholm, Oct. 18, 1934. She studied with Britta von Vegesack and Käthe Sundström in Stockholm. She made her debut as Mozart's Countess at the Royal Opera there in 1963. She first appeared at London's Covent Garden as Chrysothemis in *Elektra* (1966), and then sang at the Bayreuth Festival (1967–74). She made her U.S. debut as Brünnhilde with the San Francisco Opera (1972); her Metropolitan Opera debut followed in New York in the same role on Feb. 20, 1975. She became best known for her Wagnerian roles.

Lindpaintner, Peter Joseph von, German conductor and composer; b. Koblenz, Dec. 9, 1791; d. Nonnenhorn, Lake Constance, Aug. 21, 1856. He studied violin and piano in Augsburg, theory in Munich with Winter and Joseph Gratz. In 1812 he became music director of the Isarthor Theater in Munich. From 1819 until his death, he was conductor of the Court Orch. at Stuttgart, where his ability made the orch. famous. His works include 28 operas, including *Der Bergkönig* (Stuttgart, Jan. 30, 1825), *Der Vampyr* (Stuttgart, Nov. 21, 1828), *Die Genueserin* (Vienna, Feb. 8, 1839), and *Lichtenstein* (Stuttgart, Aug. 26, 1846), and 3 ballets (Joko, et al.); also 5 melodramas and 5 oratorios, overture to *Faust*, and incidental music to *Lied von der Glocke*.

BIBL.: R. Nägele, *P. J. von L.: Sein Leben, sein Werk: Ein Beitrag zur Typologie des Kapellmeisters im 19. Jahrhundert* (Tutzing, 1993).

Linley, Thomas, Sr., English harpsichordist, concert director, singing teacher, and composer; b. Badminton, Gloucestershire, Jan. 17, 1733; d. London, Nov. 19, 1795. He began his studies with the Bath Abbey organist Thomas Chilcot, and later studied with William Boyce in London. From the mid-1750s he was active as a concert director and singing teacher in Bath, and also wrote for the London stage from 1767. He was made joint director (with John Stanley) of London's Drury Lane Theatre in 1774; he then continued in that capacity (with Samuel Arnold) from 1786 and was also its joint manager (with his son-in-law, the dramatist Richard Brinsley Sheridan) from 1776. With his son Thomas Linley Jr. he composed the music for Sheridan's comic opera *The Duenna, or The Double Elopement* (1775). He was made a member of the Royal Soc. of Musicians in 1777. Of his 12 children, the following should be noted: Elizabeth Ann Linley (b. Bath, Sept. 5, 1754; d. Bristol, June 28, 1792), soprano; Thomas Linley, Jr. (b. Bath, May 5, 1756; d. [drowned] Grimsthorpe, Aug. 5, 1778), violinist and composer; Mary Linley (b. Bath, Jan. 4, 1758; d. Clifton, Bristol, July 27, 1787), soprano; Ozias Thurston Linley (b. Bath, Aug. 1765; d. London, March 6, 1831), organist and clergyman; William Linley (b. Bath, Feb. 1771; d. London, May 6, 1835), composer. In addition to his dramatic works, he publ. *6 Elegies* (London, 1770) and *12 Ballads* (London, 1780); 14 pieces appeared in *The Posthumous Vocal Works of Mr. Linley and Mr. T. Linley* (London, c.1798).

WORKS: DRAMATIC (all 1st perf. in London): *The Royal Merchant*, opera (Dec. 14, 1767); *The Duenna, or The Double Elopement*, comic opera (Nov. 21, 1775; in collaboration with his son Thomas, Jr.); *Selima and Azor*, comic opera (Dec. 5, 1776); *The Beggar's Opera*, ballad opera (Jan. 29, 1777); *The Camp*, musical entertainment (Oct. 15, 1778); *Zoraida*, tragedy (Dec. 13, 1779); *The Generous Imposter*, comedy (Nov. 22, 1780); *The Gentle Shepherd*, pastoral (Oct. 29, 1781); *The Carnival of Venice*, comic opera (Dec. 13, 1781); *The Spanish Rivals*, musical farce (Nov. 4, 1784); *The Strangers at Home*, comic opera (Dec. 8, 1785); *Love in the East, or Adventures of 12 Hours* (Feb. 25, 1788).

BIBL.: E. Green, *T. L., Richard Brinsley Sheridan, and Thomas Matthews: Their Connection with Bath* (Bath, 1903); C. Black, *The L.s of Bath* (London, 1911; 3d ed., aug., 1971).

Linstead, George (Frederick), Scottish organist, choirmaster, music critic, teacher, and composer; b. Melrose, Jan. 24, 1908; d. Sheffield, Dec. 29, 1974. He wrote an oratorio at the age of 13 and an opera, *Agamemnon*, at 16; he studied with F. Shera in Sheffield; also with E. Bairstow (composition) and James Ching (piano); he was awarded a D.Mus. degree from the Univ. of Durham (1946). He was active as a church organist and choirmaster, as well as a music critic, in Sheffield; he was also a part-time lecturer at the Univ. there (1947–74). Among his compositions were an opera, *Eastward in Eden* (1937), and a ballet, *Hylas*.

Lioncourt, Guy de, French composer and teacher; b. Caen, Dec. 1, 1885; d. Paris, Dec. 24, 1961. He studied Gregorian chant with Gastoué, counterpoint with Roussel, and composition with his uncle, d'Indy, at the Paris Schola Cantorum (graduated, 1916); in 1918 he won the Grand Prix Lasserre with his *La Belle au bois dormant* (1912–15). He became prof. of counterpoint (1914) at the Schola Cantorum; at d'Indy's death in 1931, he became sub-director and prof. of composition. He helped to found the École César Franck in Paris (1935), and then was its director. He publ. an autobiography, *Un Témoignage sur la musique et sur la vie au XXe siècle* (Paris, 1956). His works include the liturgical dramas *Le Mystère de l'Emmanuel* (1924); *Le Mystère de l'Alléluia* (1925–26); *Le Mystère de l'Esprit* (1939–40); also the dramatic score *Jan de la lune* (1915–21).

Lipawsky, Joseph (Josef Lipavský), Bohemian pianist and composer; b. Hohenmauth, Feb. 22, 1769; d. Vienna, Jan. 7, 1810. He studied organ and philosophy in Prague and law in Vienna, where he ultimately settled and enjoyed the friendship of Mozart, who may have given him some instruction. He was house musician for Count Adam Teleky, and also gave public piano concerts. He wrote Singspiels, orch. works, chamber music, and songs, but achieved popular favor primarily as a composer of piano music.

Lipínsky, Carl (Karol Józef), Polish violinist, teacher, and composer; b. Radzyn, Oct. 30, 1790; d. Urlów, near Lemberg, Dec. 16, 1861. His father was a professional musician and gave him his primary education. He met Paganini, who agreed to teach him the violin; in 1835 he visited Leipzig; Schumann was greatly impressed by his playing and dedicated *Carnaval* to him. Lipínsky appeared in London on April 25, 1836, as soloist in his Military Concerto for Violin and Orch.; in 1839 he settled in Dresden as concertmaster of the Court Orch.; Liszt once played at the same concert with him. Among his renowned students were Joachim and Wieniawski. He wrote a comic opera, *Klótnia przez zaklad* (Lemberg, May 27, 1814), and other stage pieces. He also publ. numerous technical violin studies.

Lipkovska, Lydia (Yakovlevna), Russian soprano; b. Babino, Bessarabia, May 10, 1882; d. Beirut, Jan. 22, 1955. She studied with Iretzkaya in St. Petersburg and Vanzo in Milan. She made her debut as Gilda at the St. Petersburg Imperial Opera (1907), singing there until 1908 and again from 1911 to 1913. She appeared in Diaghilev's season in Paris (1909), as well as at the Opéra and the Opéra Comique. Her American debut took place with the Boston Opera on Nov. 12, 1909, when she sang Lakmé; on Nov. 18, 1909, she made her Metropolitan Opera debut in New York as Violetta, singing there until 1911 and in Chicago in 1910–11; she also appeared at London's Covent Garden as Mimi (July 11, 1911). After the Russian Revolution of 1917, she was active in Paris. In 1920 she toured the United States and in 1921–22 appeared at the Chicago Grand Opera. She sang at the Odessa Opera (1941–44) and then returned to Paris. Her last years were spent as a teacher in Beirut.

Lipovšek, Marjana, distinguished Yugoslav mezzo-soprano; b. Ljubljana, Dec. 3, 1946. She received her training in Ljubljana, Graz, and Vienna. In 1979 she became a member of the Vienna State Opera, where she developed a notably successful career. In 1981 she made her first appearance at the Salzburg Festival. In 1982 she sang for the first time at the Hamburg State Opera and at Milan's La Scala. In 1983 she joined the Bavarian State Opera in Munich. She made her London debut as a soloist in *Das Lied von der Erde* with the London Sym. Orch. in 1988, returning to London in 1990 to make her Covent Garden debut as Clytemnestra. On Nov. 25, 1993, she made her North American debut as Fricka in *Die Walküre* at the Lyric Opera of Chicago. In 1995 she made her first appearance at the San Francisco Opera as Brünnhilde, and then sang Clytemnestra in Florence in 1996. She made a major recital tour of the United States in 1998. In addition to her operatic career, Lipovšek has pursued an extensive following as a concert and lieder artist. She has appeared as a soloist with the leading orchs. of Europe and North America, and at many festivals. Among her many roles of note are Gluck's Orfeo, Mistress Quickly, Amneris, Azucena, Brangäne, Orlofsky, Strauss's Composer and Octavian, and Berg's Marie.

Lipp, Wilma, esteemed Austrian soprano; b. Vienna, April 26, 1925. She was a student in Vienna of Sindel, Novikova, Bahr-Mildenburg, and Jerger, and in Milan of Dal Monte. In 1943 she made her operatic debut in Vienna as Rosina, and then was a member of the State Opera there from 1945. She also appeared at the Salzburg Festival from 1948. In 1950 she made her debut at Milan's La Scala as the Queen of the Night, a role she made her own. In 1951 she made her first appearance at London's Covent Garden singing Gilda. In 1953 she sang the Queen of the Night at her debut at the Paris Opéra. She appeared at the Glyndebourne Festival for the first time in 1957 as Constanze. Her U.S. debut followed in 1962 as Nannetta in *Falstaff* at the San Francisco Opera. In 1982 she became a prof. of voice at the Salzburg Mozarteum. She was honored as an Austrian Kammersängerin. Lipp was equally adept in coloratura and lyric roles, ranging from the operas of Mozart to Richard Strauss.

Lipton, Martha, American mezzo-soprano and teacher; b. N.Y., April 6, 1913. She was educated at the Juilliard School of Music in New York. On Nov. 27, 1944, she made her debut as Siebel with the Metropolitan Opera in New York and remained on its roster until 1960; she also sang with the N.Y. City Opera (1944, 1958, 1961) and at the Chicago Lyric Opera (1956). In Europe she sang in Amsterdam and The Hague, and at the Holland and Edinburgh festivals, the Vienna State Opera, and the Paris Opéra; she also made appearances in South America. In 1960 she became a prof. of voice at the Indiana Univ. School of Music in Bloomington. Among her prominent roles were Cherubino, Ulrica, Orlovsky, Herodias, and Octavian. She also appeared extensively as a concert artist.

Lishin, Grigori, Russian composer; b. St. Petersburg, May 5, 1854; d. there, June 27, 1888. He studied piano with his mother. He became a proficient accompanist, and also wrote music criticism. He composed 2 operas, *Don Caesar* (Kiev, 1888) and *Count Nulin* (after Pushkin), to his own librettos. His sentimental ballad *She Laughed* was extremely popular with Russian singers.

Lisinski, Vatroslav (real name, **Ignacije Fuchs**), important Croatian composer; b. Zagreb, July 8, 1819; d. there, May 31, 1854. He was a student of Sojka and Wiesner von Morgenstern in Zagreb. As late as 1847, he went to Prague to study with Pitsch and Kittl. Although he never acquired a solid technique of composition, he was notable in that he tried to establish a national style in dramatic writing. He was the composer of the first Croatian opera, *Ljubav i zloba* (Love and Malice), for which he wrote only the vocal score; it was orchestrated by Wiesner von Morgenstern, and performed in Zagreb on March 28, 1846. His 2d opera, *Porin* (1848–51), also in Croatian, was given many years after his death, in Zagreb, on Oct. 2, 1897.

BIBL.: V. Novák, *V. L.* (Belgrade, 1925); L. Zupanovič, *V. L. (1819–1854), život—djelo—znacenje* (V. L. [1819–1854], Life—Work—Significance; Zagreb, 1969).

Lisitsyan, Pavel (Gerasimovich) (Pogos Karapetovich), Armenian baritone; b. Vladikavkaz, Nov. 6, 1911. He studied in Leningrad. He sang at the Maly Theater there (1935–37); he then was a member of the Armenian Opera Theater in Yerevan (1937–40); in 1940 he joined the Bolshoi Theater in Moscow, remaining on its roster until 1966, but in the interim filled engagements all over Europe, in India, and in Japan; he also made his debut at the Metropolitan Opera in New York as Amonasro (March 3, 1960). From 1967 to 1973 he was on the faculty of the Yerevan Cons. He was best known for his roles in Russian operas.

Lissenko, Nikolai (Vitalievich), significant Ukrainian composer; b. Grinki, near Kremenchug, March 22, 1842; d. Kiev, Nov. 6, 1912. He was the son of a landowner, and grew up in a musical atmosphere; the singing of Ukrainian songs by local peasants produced a lasting impression on him, and determined his future as a national composer. He studied natural sciences at the Univ. of Kiev, graduating in 1864. He was a justice of the peace in the Kiev district (1864–66), then abandoned his nonmusical pursuits and went to Leipzig, where he entered the Cons., and took courses with Richter (theory), Reinecke (piano), and Papperitz (organ). Returning to Russia in 1868, he taught piano at the Kiev Inst. of the Daughters of Nobility; from 1874 to 1876 he studied orchestration with Rimsky-Korsakov in St. Petersburg. As early as 1868 he publ. his first collection of Ukrainian songs (printed in Leipzig); subsequent issues comprised 240 songs in 5 books, arranged according to their categories (Spring Songs, Midsummer Night Songs, Christmas Songs, etc.); he set to music a great number of poems from Kobzar by the Ukrainian poet Shevchenko (5 albums for 2, 3, and 4 Voices; publ. in Kiev, 1870–97). In 1903, on the occasion of the 35th anniversary of the publication of his first collection of Ukrainian songs, Lissenko received a gift of 5,000 rubles from his admirers.

In his pamphlet on the Ukrainian Dumki (1874), Lissenko presented a theory that Ukrainian modes are derived from Greek music, and that antiphonal construction is one of the main features of Ukrainian songs, while the persistence of symmetrical rhythms distinguishes them from Russian songs. In his original compositions, he asserted himself as an ardent Ukrainian nationalist. A complete ed. of his works was publ. in Kiev (20 vols., 1950–59).

WORKS: OPERAS: *Chernomortsy* (Sailors of the Black Sea Fleet; 1870); *Nich pid Rizdvo*, after Gogol's *Christmas Eve Night* (1874; rev. 1877–82; Kharkov, 1883); *Utoplennitsa* (The Drowned Woman), after Gogol's *May Night* (1871–83; Kharkov, 1885); *Koza-Dereza* (The Goat), children's opera (1888; Kiev, April 20, 1901); *Natalka-Poltavka* (Natalie from Poltava), after Kotlarevsky's play (1889; orig. incidental music); *Taras Bulba*, after Gogol (1880–90; Kiev, Dec. 20, 1903; rev. by Liatoshinsky, Kiev, 1937); *Pan Kotsky* (Puss-in-Boots), children's opera (1891); *Zima i vesna, ili Snezhnaya krasavitsa* (Winter and Spring, or The Snow Maiden), children's opera (1892); *Sappho* (1896–1900); *Aeneid* (1910; Kiev, 1911).

List (real name, **Fleissig**), **Emanuel,** noted Austrian-born American bass; b. Vienna, March 22, 1886; d. there, June 21, 1967. He was a boy chorister at the Theater-an-der-Wien. Following voice training with Steger in Vienna, he toured Europe as a member of a comic vocal quartet. He went to the United States and appeared in vaudeville, burlesque, and minstrel shows. After further vocal studies with Zuro in New York, he returned to Vienna in 1920 and in 1922 made his operatic debut as Gounod's Méphistophélès at the Volksoper. He then sang at Berlin's Städtische Oper (1923–25) and State Opera (1925–33), London's Covent Garden (1925; 1934–36), the Salzburg Festivals (1931–35), and the Bayreuth Festival (1933). List made his Metropolitan Opera debut in New York on Dec. 27, 1933, as the Landgrave. While remaining on its roster until 1948, he also appeared in San Francisco and Chicago (1935–37) and gave lieder recitals. He was again on the Metropolitan Opera's roster in 1949–50. In 1952 he returned to Vienna. List was especially admired for the rich vocal resources he brought to such roles as Osmin, the Commendatore, Sarastro, Rocco, King Marke, Hagen, Pogner, Hunding, and Baron Ochs.

List, Kurt, Austrian musicologist, music critic, conductor, record producer, and composer; b. Vienna, June 21, 1913; d. Milan, Nov. 16, 1970. He studied at the Vienna Academy of Music (M.A., 1936) and at the Univ. of Vienna (Ph.D., 1938); he also took private lessons with Berg (1932–35) and Webern (1935–38). He went to the United States in 1938; he became active in the field of recording and wrote music criticism. After World War II he returned to Europe and lived mostly in Italy. He composed 2 unperformed operas, *Der Triumph des Todes* and *Mayerling*, stylistically influenced by Richard Strauss.

Listov, Konstantin, Russian composer; b. Odessa, Sept. 19, 1900; d. Moscow, Sept. 6, 1983. He learned music by ear; he then studied piano in Tsaritsin and in Saratov. In 1923 he went to Moscow and began to write music for the theater. His Red Army song "Tachanka" became immensely popular. He also wrote the opera *Cuba's Daughter* (Voronezh, June 25, 1962), and a sym. in commemoration of the centennial of Lenin (1970).

BIBL.: A. Tishchenko, *K. L.* (Moscow, 1962).

Liszt, Franz (Ferenc; baptized **Franciscus**), greatly celebrated Hungarian pianist and composer, creator of the modern form of the symphonic poem, and innovating genius of modern piano technique; b. Raiding, near Odenburg, Oct. 22, 1811; d. Bayreuth, July 31, 1886. His father was an amateur musician who devoted his energies to the education of his son; at the age of 9, young Liszt was able to play a difficult piano concerto by Ries. A group of Hungarian music lovers provided sufficient funds to finance Liszt's musical education. In 1822 the family traveled to Vienna. Beethoven was still living, and Liszt's father bent every effort to persuade Beethoven to come to young Liszt's Vienna concert on April 13, 1823. Legend has it that Beethoven did come and was so impressed that he ascended the podium and kissed the boy on the brow. There is even in existence a lithograph that portrays the scene, but it was made many years after the event by an unknown lithographer and its documentary value is dubious. Liszt himself perpetuated the legend, and often showed the spot on his forehead where Beethoven was supposed to have implanted the famous kiss. However that might be, Liszt's appearance in Vienna created a sensation; he was hailed by the press as "child Hercules." The link with Beethoven was maintained through Liszt's own teachers: Czerny, who was Beethoven's student and friend and with whom Liszt took piano lessons, and the great Salieri, who was Beethoven's early teacher and who at the end of his life became Liszt's teacher in composition.

On May 1, 1823, Liszt gave a concert in Pest. The announcement of the concert was made in the florid manner characteristic of the period: "Esteemed Gentlemen! High born nobility, valorous army officers, dear audience! I am a Hungarian, and before traveling to France and England, I am happy now to present to my dear Fatherland the first fruits of my training and education." Salieri appealed to Prince Esterházy for financial help so as to enable Liszt to move to Vienna, where Salieri made his residence. "I recently heard a young boy, Francesco Liszt, improvise on the piano," Salieri wrote, "and it produced such a profound impression on me that I thought it was a dream." Apparently Esterházy was sufficiently impressed with Salieri's plea to contribute support.

Under the guidance of his ambitious father, Liszt applied for an entrance examination at the Paris Cons., but its powerful director, Cherubini, declined to accept him, ostensibly because he was a foreigner (Cherubini himself was a foreigner, but was naturalized). Liszt then settled for private lessons in counterpoint from Antoine Reicha, a Parisianized Czech musician who instilled in

Liszt the importance of folklore. Liszt's father died in 1837; Liszt remained in Paris, where he soon joined the brilliant company of men and women of the arts. Paganini's spectacular performances of the violin in particular inspired Liszt to emulate him in creating a piano technique of transcendental difficulty and brilliance, utilizing all possible sonorities of the instrument. To emphasize the narrative Romantic quality of his musical ideas, he accepted the suggestion of his London manager, Frederick Beale, to use the word "recital" to describe his concerts, and in time the term was widely accepted by other pianists.

In his own compositions, Liszt was a convinced propagandist of program music. A true Romantic, he conceived himself as an actor playing the part of his own life, in which he was a child of the Muses. Traveling in Switzerland, he signed his hotel register as follows: "Place of birth—Parnasse. Arriving from—Dante. Proceeding to—Truth. Profession—Musician-philosopher." He was fascinated by a popular contemporary novel that depicted a fictional traveler named Oberman, and he wrote a suite of piano compositions under the general title *Années de pèlerinage*, in which he followed in music the imaginary progressions of Oberman.

Handsome, artistic, a brilliant conversationalist, Liszt was sought after in society. His first lasting attachment was with an aristocratic married woman, the Comtesse Marie d'Agoult; they had 3 daughters, one of whom, Cosima, married Liszt's friend Hans von Bülow before abandoning him for Richard Wagner. D'Agoult was fluent in several European languages and had considerable literary talents, which she exercised under the nom de plume of Daniel Stern. Liszt was 22 when he entered his concubinage with her; she was 28. The growing intimacy between them soon became the gossip of Paris. Berlioz warned Liszt not to let himself become too deeply involved with her. "She possesses a calculated attraction," he told Liszt. "She has a lively spirit, but she lacks true friendship." D'Agoult rapidly established herself as a salon hostess in Paris; she was a constant intermediary between Liszt and his close contemporary Chopin. Indeed, the book on Chopin publ. under Liszt's name after Chopin's early death was largely written by d'Agoult, whose literary French was much superior to Liszt's. His 2d and final attachment was with another married woman, Carolyne von Sayn-Wittgenstein, who was separated from her husband. Her devotion to Liszt exceeded all limits, even in a Romantic age.

Liszt held a clerical title of Abbé, conferred upon him by Pope Pius IX, but his religious affiliations were not limited to the Catholic church. He was also a Freemason and served as a tertiary of the Order of St. Francis. In 1879 he received the tonsure and 4 minor orders (ostuary, lector, exorcist, and acolyte) and an honorary canonry. But he was never ordained a priest, and thus was free to marry if he so wished. When he met an attractive woman in Rome, he said to her, "Under this priestly cloak there beats the passionate heart of a man." He fully intended to marry Sayn-Wittgenstein, but he encountered resistance from the Catholic church, to which they both belonged and which forbade marriage to a divorced woman. His own position as a secular cleric further militated against it. Thus, Liszt, the great lover of women, never married. But the legend of Liszt as a man of fantastic sexual powers persisted even after his death. It found its most repellent expression in a motion picture directed by Ken Russell under the title *Lisztomania*. In it, Liszt was portrayed with a grotesquely extended male organ on which a bevy of scantily dressed maidens obscenely disported themselves.

Liszt's romantic infatuations did not interfere with his brilliant virtuoso career. One of his greatest successes was his triumphant tour in Russia in 1842. Russian musicians and music critics exhausted their flowery vocabulary to praise him as the miracle of the age. Czar Nicholas I himself attended a concert given by Liszt in St. Petersburg, and expressed his appreciation by sending him a pair of trained Russian bears. Liszt acknowledged the imperial honor, but did not venture to take the animals with him on his European tour; they remained in Russia.

Liszt was a consummate showman. In Russia, as elsewhere, he had 2 grand pianos installed on the stage at right angles, so that the keyboards were visible from the right and the left respectively and he could alternate his playing on both. He appeared on the stage wearing a long cloak and white gloves, discarding both with a spectacular gesture. Normally he needed eyeglasses, but he was too vain to wear them in public.

It is not clear why, after all his triumphs in Russia and elsewhere in Europe, Liszt decided to abandon his career as a piano virtuoso and devote his entire efforts to composition. He became associated with Wagner, his son-in-law, as a prophet of "music of the future." Indeed, Liszt anticipated Wagner's chromatic harmony in his works. A remarkable instance of such anticipation is illustrated in his song "Ich möchte hingehen," which prefigures, note for note, Wagner's theme from the prelude to *Tristan und Isolde*. Inevitably, Liszt and Wagner became objects of derision on the part of conservative music critics. A pictorial example of such an attack was an extraordinary caricature entitled "Music of the Future," distributed by G. Schirmer in New York in 1867. It represented Liszt with arms and legs flailing symmetrically over a huge orch. that comprised not only human players but also goats, donkeys, and a cat placed in a cage with an operator pulling its tail. At Liszt's feet there was placed a score marked "Wagner, not to be played much till 1995."

In 1848 Liszt accepted the position of Court Kapellmeister in Weimar. When Wagner was exiled from Saxony, Liszt arranged for the production of his opera *Lohengrin* in Weimar on Aug. 28, 1850; he was also instrumental in supervising performances in Weimar of Wagner's operas *Der fliegende Holländer* and *Tannhäuser*, as well as music by Berlioz and a number of operas by other composers. Liszt was very much interested in the progress of Russian music. In Weimar he received young Glazunov, who brought with him his 1st Sym. He played host to Borodin and Cui, who came to Weimar to pay their respects, and was lavish in his appreciation of their works; he also expressed admiration for Rimsky-Korsakov and Mussorgsky.

In his Weimar years, Liszt aged rapidly. He neglected his physical state, and finally developed double pneumonia and died during his sojourn in Bayreuth at the age of 74.

As a composer, Liszt made every effort to expand the technical possibilities of piano technique; in his 2 piano concertos, and particularly in his *Études d'exécution transcendante*, he made use of the grand piano, which expanded the keyboard in both the bass and the extreme treble. He also extended the field of piano literature with his brilliant transcriptions of operas, among them those by Mozart, Verdi, Wagner, Donizetti, Gounod, Rossini, and Beethoven. These transcriptions were particularly useful at the time when the piano was the basic musical instrument at home.

Although Liszt is universally acknowledged to be a great Hungarian composer, he was actually brought up in the atmosphere of German culture. He spoke German at home, with French as a 2d language. His women companions conversed with him in French, and most of Liszt's own correspondence was in that language. It was not until his middle age that he decided to take lessons in Hungarian, but he never acquired fluency. His knowledge of Hungarian folk songs came through the medium of the popular gypsy dance bands that played in Budapest. He used to refer to himself jocularly as "half gypsy and half Franciscan monk." This self-identification pursued him through his life, and beyond; when the question was raised after his death in Bayreuth regarding the transfer of his body to Budapest, the prime minister of Hungary voiced objection, since Liszt never regarded himself as a purely Hungarian musician.

With the exception of *Don Sanche, ou Le Château d'amour* (1824–25; Paris, Oct. 17, 1825; in collaboration with Paër), Liszt never wrote a full-fledged opera. But he composed several sacred oratorios that were operatic in substance. In his secular works he was deeply conscious of his Hungarian heritage, but he gathered his material mainly from gypsy dances that he heard in public places in Budapest. For his works, see F. Busoni, P. Raabe, et al., eds., *Franz Liszt: Musikalische Werke* (Leipzig, 1907–36), the Liszt Society Publications (London, 1950–), and *Franz Liszt: Neue Ausgabe sämtlicher Werke/New Edition of the Complete Works* (Kassel and Budapest, 1970–).

WRITINGS: *De la fondation Goethe à Weimar* (Leipzig, 1851);

Lohengrin et Tannhäuser de R. Wagner (Leipzig, 1851); *F. Chopin* (Paris, 1852); *Des bohémiens et de leur musique en Hongrie* (Paris, 1859); *Über John Fields Nocturne* (Leipzig, 1859); *R. Schumanns musikalische Haus- und Lebensregeln* (Leipzig, 1860). L. Ramann edited his *Gesammelte Schriften* (Leipzig, 1880–83); a new critical ed. of his writings, under the general editorship of D. Altenburg, began to appear in 1987.

BIBL.: SOURCE MATERIAL: F. Liszt, *Thematisches Verzeichnis der Werke von F. L.* (Leipzig, 1855); idem, *Thematisches Verzeichnis der Werke, Bearbeitungen und Transkriptionen von F. L.* (Leipzig, 1877); E. Waters, *L. Holographs in the Library of Congress* (Washington, D.C., 1979); M. Saffe, *F. L.: A Guide to Research* (N.Y., 1990). BIOGRAPHICAL: J. Christern, *F. L., nach seinem Leben und Werke, aus authentischen Berichten dargestellt* (Hamburg, 1841); G. Schilling, *F. L.: Sein Leben und Werken aus nächster Beschauung* (Stuttgart, 1844); R. de Beaufort, *F. L.: The Story of His Life* (Boston and London, 1866; 2d ed., 1910); J. Schubert, *F. L.s Biographie* (Leipzig, 1871); L. Ramann, *F. L. als Künstler und Mensch* (3 vols., Leipzig, 1880–94; Eng. tr. of vol. 1, 1882); L. Nohl, *F. L.* (Leipzig, 1882–88); R. Pohl, *F. L.* (Leipzig, 1883); B. Vogel, *F. L.: Abriss seines Lebens und Würdigung seiner Werke* (Leipzig, 1898); O. Luning, *F. L.: Ein Apostel der Ideale* (Zürich, 1896); E. Reuss, *F. L.* (Dresden, 1898); R. Louis, *F. L.* (Berlin, 1900); A. von Pozsony, *L. und Hans von Bülow* (Munich, 1900); M.-D. Calvocoressi, *F. L.* (Paris, 1905; Eng. tr. in the *Musical Observer*, N.Y., 1910–11); A. Göllerich, *F. L.* (Berlin, 1908); J. Kapp, *F. L.* (Berlin, 1909; 20th ed., 1924); J. Chantavoine, *L.* (Paris, 1911; 6th ed., 1950); A. Hervey, *F. L. and His Music* (London, 1911); J. Huneker, *F. L.* (N.Y. and London, 1911); H. Thode, *F. L.* (Heidelberg, 1911); P. Bekker, *F. L.* (Bielefeld, 1912); B. Schrade, *F. L.* (Berlin, 1914); K. Grunsky, *F. L.* (Leipzig, 1924); F. Corder, *L.* (London, 1925; 2d ed., 1933); R. Wetz, *F. L.* (Leipzig, 1925); G. de Pourtalès, *La Vie de F. L.* (Paris, 1926; 2d ed., 1950; Eng. tr., 1926); W. Wallace, *L., Wagner and the Princess* (London, 1927); M. Herwegh, *Au banquet des dieux: F. L., Richard Wagner et leurs amis* (Paris, 1931); R. Raabe, *F. L.* (Stuttgart, 1931; 2d ed., rev., 1968); E. Newman, *The Man L.* (London, 1934; 2d ed., 1970); S. Sitwell, *L.* (London, 1934; 3d ed., rev., 1966); R. Bory, *L. et ses enfants: Blandine, Cosima et Daniel* (Paris, 1936); H. Engel, *F. L.* (Potsdam, 1936); Z. Harsányi, *Magyar Rapszódia: F. L.* (Budapest, 1936; Eng. tr., London, 1936, as *Hungarian Melody* and N.Y., 1937, as *Immortal Franz*); A. Hevesy, *L., ou Le Roi Lear de la musique* (Paris, 1936); R. Hill, *L.* (London, 1936; 2d ed., 1949); L. Nowak, *F. L.* (Innsbruck, 1936); B. Ollivier, *L., le musicien passionné* (Paris, 1936); E. von Liszt, *F. L.* (Vienna, 1937); M. Tibaldi Chiesa, *Vita romantica di L.* (Milan, 1937; 2d ed., 1941); P. Raabe, *Wege zu L.* (Regensburg, 1944); A. Pols, *F. L.* (Bloemendaal, 1951); B. Voelcker, *F. L., der grosse Mensch* (Weimar, 1955); W. Beckett, *L.* (London, 1956; 2d ed., 1963); B. Szabolcsi, *L. F. esteje* (The Twilight of F. L.; Budapest, 1956; Eng. tr., 1959); C. Rostand, *L.* (Paris, 1960; Eng. tr., 1972); J. Rousselot, *F. L.* (London, 1960); M. Bagby, *L.'s Weimar* (N.Y., 1961); P. Rehberg and G. Nestler, *F. L.* (Zürich, 1961); K. Hamburger, *L. F.* (Budapest, 1966); E. Haraszti, *F. L.* (Paris, 1967); A. Leroy, *F. L.* (Lausanne, 1967); A. Walker, ed., *F. L.: The Man and His Music* (London, 1970; 2d ed., 1976); idem, *L.* (London, 1971); E. Perényi, *L.: The Artist as Romantic Hero* (Boston, 1974); K. Hamburger, ed., *F. L.: Beiträge von ungarischen Autoren* (Leipzig, 1978); E. Horvath, *F. L.*: vol. 1, *Kindheit, 1811–27* (Eisenstadt, 1978), and vol. 2, *Jugend* (Eisenstadt, 1982); R. Rehberg, *L.: Die Geschichte seines Lebens, Schaffens und Wirkens* (Munich, 1978); B. Gavoty, *L.: Le Virtuose, 1811–1848* (Paris, 1980); D. Legány, *L. and His Country 1869–1873* (Budapest, 1983); A. Walker, *F. L.: Vol. I, The Virtuoso Years, 1811–1847* (London, 1983; rev. ed., 1987); idem, *F. L.: Vol. II, The Weimar Years, 1848–1861* (London, 1989); W. Dömling, *F. L. und seine Zeit* (Laaber, 1986); R. Taylor, *F. L.: The Man and the Musician* (London, 1986); K. Hamburger, *L.* (Budapest, 1987); D. Watson, *L.* (London, 1989); A. Williams, *Portrait of L.: By Himself and His Contemporaries* (Oxford, 1990).

Litaize, Gaston, blind French organist, pedagogue, and composer; b. Ménil-sur-Belvitte, Vosges, Aug. 11, 1909; d. Says, Vosges, Aug. 5, 1991. Following initial training at the Institut National des Jeunes Aveugles in Paris (1926–31), he pursued his studies at the Paris Cons. with Dupré (organ), Caussade (fugue), Büsser (composition), and Emmanuel (music history), taking premiers prix for organ and improvisation (1931), fugue (1933), and composition (1937). In 1938 he won the 2d Prix de Rome and the Prix Rossini with his musical legende *Fra Diavolo*. From 1946 he served as organist at St.-François-Xavier in Paris, and he also made tours as a recitalist in Europe and abroad. He was a prof. at the Institut National des Jeunes Aveugles.

Literes Carrión, Antonio, Spanish composer; b. Arta, Majorca, June 18, 1673?; d. Madrid, Jan. 18, 1747. He was a composer and bass viol player at the Royal Choir School in Madrid under Charles II, Philip V, and Ferdinand VI. In 1693 he was appointed to the royal chapel as bassist. After the fire at the old Alcazar in Madrid on Christmas Eve of 1734, Literes and Nebra were charged with the reconstruction of musical MSS that were damaged or completely burned. They also wrote new music for church services to replace the material destroyed. He wrote an opera, *Los elementos*, and several zarzuelas, including *Accis y Galatea* (Madrid, Dec. 19, 1708). His son, Antonio Literes Montalbo (d. Madrid, Dec. 2, 1768), was a composer and organist under Ferdinand VI.

Litinsky, Genrik, distinguished Russian composer; b. Lipovetz, March 17, 1901; d. Moscow, July 26, 1985. He studied composition with Glière at the Moscow Cons., graduating in 1928; subsequently taught there (1928–43); among his students were Khrennikov, Zhiganov, Arutiunian, and other Soviet composers. In 1945 he went to Yakutsk as an ethnomusicologist; in collaboration with native Siberian composers, he produced the first national Yakut operas, based on authentic folk melorhythms and arranged in contemporary harmonies according to the precepts of socialist realism: *Nurgun Botur* (Yakutsk, June 29, 1947); *Sygy Kyrynastyr* (Yakutsk, July 4, 1947); *Red Shaman* (Yakutsk, Dec. 9, 1967). He wrote 3 Yakut ballets: *Altan's Joy* (Yakutsk, June 19, 1963), *Field Flower* (Yakutsk, July 2, 1947), and *Crimson Kerchief* (Yakutsk, Jan. 9, 1968). He also collected, transcribed, and organized the basic materials of several Soviet Republics; altogether he compiled musical samples from as many as 23 distinct ethnic divisions of folkloric elements. He was in time duly praised by the Soviet authorities on aesthetics, but not until the policy of the Soviet Union itself had changed. In the meantime, Litinsky became the target of unconscionable attacks by reactionary groups within Soviet musical organizations who denounced him as a formalist contaminated by Western bourgeois culture. In one instance, his personal library was ransacked in search of alleged propaganda.

Litolff, Henry Charles, French pianist, conductor, music publisher, and composer; b. London (of an Alsatian father and English mother), Feb. 6, 1818; d. Bois-Colombes, near Paris, Aug. 6, 1891. A precocious pianist, he studied with Moscheles; he made his professional debut in London on July 24, 1832, at the age of 14. An early marriage (at 17) forced him to seek his livelihood in Paris, where he attracted attention with his brilliant concerts; then he became an itinerant musician, traveling in Poland, Germany, and the Netherlands; he was in Vienna during the Revolution of 1848; he became involved, and was compelled to flee. He then settled in Braunschweig. After the termination of his first marriage, he married Julie Meyer (1851), widow of the music publisher Meyer, acquiring the business. Litolff was one of the pioneers in the publication of inexpensive eds. of classical music. He was made Kapellmeister at the court of Saxe-Coburg-Gotha (1855). After divorcing his 2d wife (1858), he became active as a conductor in Paris. In 1860 he married his 3d wife, Comtesse de Larochefoucauld, and also turned his firm over to his adopted son, Theodor Litolff (1839–1912). Following the death of his wife (1870), he married a 15-year-old girl. Besides his business pursuits, he was a prolific composer; 115 of his works were publ., the most famous being the overture *Robespierre* (1856; Paris, Feb. 2, 1870), which carries the idea of programmatic music to its utmost limit, with a vivid description of Robespierre's execution (drumbeats, etc.). He also composed the operas *Die Braut von*

Kynast (Braunschweig, 1847), *Héloïse et Abélard* (Paris, Oct. 17, 1872), and *Les Templiers* (Brussels, Jan. 25, 1886), and the oratorio *Ruth et Boaz* (1869). Of his many character pieces for piano, *Chant de la fileuse* became popular.

BIBL.: T. Blair, *H. C. L. (1818–1891): His Life and Piano Music* (diss., Univ. of Iowa, 1968).

Litta, Giulio, Italian composer; b. Milan, 1822; d. Vedano, near Monza, May 29, 1891. A composer of precocious talent and excellent training, he produced an opera at 20, *Bianca di Santafiora* (Milan, Jan. 2, 1843), followed by 6 more: *Sardanapalo* (Milan, Sept. 2, 1844), *Maria Giovanna* (Turin, Oct. 28, 1851), *Edita di Lorno* (Genoa, June 1, 1853), *Il Viandante* (Milan, April 17, 1873), *Raggio d'amore* (Milan, April 6, 1879), and *Il violino di Cremona* (Milan, April 18, 1882); also an oratorio, *La Passione*.

Litton, Andrew, American conductor; b. N.Y., May 16, 1959. He studied piano with Reisenberg and conducting with Ehrling at the Juilliard School in New York; he also received lessons in conducting from Weller at the Salzburg Mozarteum, Järvi in Hilversum, and Edoardo Müller in Milan. In 1982 he won the BBC/Rupert Foundation International Conductors' Competition; he then was the Exxon-Arts Endowment assistant conductor of the National Sym. Orch. in Washington, D.C. (1982–85), where he subsequently was assoc. conductor (1985–86); he also appeared as a guest conductor in North America and Europe. On March 9, 1989, he made his Metropolitan Opera debut in New York conducting *Eugene Onegin*. In 1988 he assumed the position of principal conductor and artistic adviser of the Bournemouth Sym. Orch., with which he established a fine reputation. In 1994 he took it on its first tour of the United States before concluding his tenure with it that year to become music director of the Dallas Sym. Orch.

Litvinenko-Wohlgemut, Maria (Ivanova), Russian soprano; b. Kiev, Feb. 6, 1895; d. there, April 4, 1966. She was a student of Alexeyeva-Yunevich and Ivanitsky at the Kiev Music Inst. (graduated, 1912). In 1912 she made her operatic debut as Oxana in Gulak-Artemovsky's *The Cossack Beyond the Danube* in Kiev. She was a member of the Petrograd Music Drama Theater (1914–16), the Kharkov Opera (1923–25), and the Kiev Opera (1935–51). From 1946 she taught at the Kiev Cons. In 1936 she was honored as a People's Artist of the USSR. In addition to her portrayals of Russian roles, she was admired for her Aida and Tosca.

BIBL.: A. Polyakov, *M. I. L.-W.* (Kiev, 1956).

Litvinne, Félia (real name, **Françoise-Jeanne Schütz**), noted Russian soprano; b. St. Petersburg, Aug. 31, 1860?; d. Paris, Oct. 12, 1936. She studied in Paris with Barth-Banderoli, Viardot-García, and Maurel; she made her debut there in 1882 at the Théâtre-Italien as Maria Boccanegra; then sang throughout Europe. In 1885 she made her first appearance in the United States with Mapleson's company at N.Y.'s Academy of Music; after singing at the Théâtre Royal de la Monnaie in Brussels (1886–88), at the Paris Opéra (1889), and at Milan's La Scala, in Rome, and in Venice (1890), she appeared at the imperial theaters in St. Petersburg and Moscow (from 1890). She made her Metropolitan Opera debut in New York as Valentine in *Les Huguenots* on Nov. 25, 1896, but remained on the roster for only that season. In 1899 she first appeared at London's Covent Garden as Isolde, and made several further appearances there until 1910. She made her farewell to the operatic stage in Vichy in 1919, but continued to give concerts until 1924. In 1927 she became prof. of voice at the American Cons. in Fontainebleau. Her pupils included Nina Koshetz and Germain Lubin. She publ. her memoirs as *Ma vie et mon art* (Paris, 1933). Her most outstanding roles included Gluck's Alceste, Donna Anna, Aida, Kundry, Brünnhilde, and Selika.

Liuzzi, Fernando, Italian composer and pedagogue; b. Senigallia, Dec. 19, 1884; d. Florence, Oct. 6, 1940. He received training in piano and composition with Fano in Bologna, where he also attended the Univ. (fine arts degree, 1905), and then pursued his studies with Falchi at Rome's Accademia di Santa Cecilia and with Reger and Mottl in Munich. Liuzzi was prof. of theory at the Parma Cons. (1910–17), and also was a teacher of composition at the Naples Cons. (1912–14). After serving as prof. of theory at the Florence Cons. (1917–23), he was prof. of musical aesthetics at the univs. of Florence (1923–27) and Rome (1927–38). With the promulgation of the Fascist racial laws, he went to Belgium in 1939. After a sojourn in New York, he returned to his homeland in 1940. Among his writings were *Estetica della musica* (Florence, 1924) and *Musicista italiani in Francia* (Rome, 1946). His compositions included *L'augellin bel verde*, puppet opera (Rome, 1917), and *Le vergini savie e le vergini folli*, liturgical drama after a 12th-century French MS (Florence, 1930).

Liverati, Giovanni, Italian tenor, conductor, teacher, and composer; b. Bologna, March 27, 1772; d. Florence, Feb. 18, 1846. He studied voice with Giuseppe and Ferdinando Tibaldi in Bologna, then voice with Lorenzo Gibelli and composition with Stanislao Mattei there (1786–90). He was made 1st tenor of the Italian theaters in Barcelona and Madrid (1792), and then Kapellmeister of the Italian Opera in Potsdam (1796) and the Prague National Theater (1799). After teaching voice in Vienna (1805–11), he was music director and composer of the King's Theatre in London (1815–17); he later taught at the Royal Academy of Music there. He returned to Italy about 1835, becoming a prof. at Florence's Accademia di Belle Arti.

WORKS: OPERAS: *Il divertimento in campagna* (Bologna, 1790); *Enea in Cartagine* (Potsdam?, 1796); *La prova generale al teatro* (Vienna?, 1799); *Il convito degli dei* (Vienna, c.1800); *La presa d'Egea* (Vienna, 1809); *Il tempio d'eternità* (Vienna, 1810); *David, oder Goliaths Tod* (Vienna, 1813); *I Selvaggi* (London, 1815); *Gli amanti fanatica* (London, 1816); *Gastone e Bajardo* (London, 1820); *The Nymph of the Grotto* (London, 1829); *Amore e Psiche* (London, 1831).

Ljungberg, Göta (Albertina), Swedish soprano; b. Sundsval, Oct. 4, 1893; d. Lidingö, near Stockholm, June 28, 1955. She studied at the Royal Academy of Music and the Royal Opera School in Stockholm; she later was a student of Mme. Cahier, of Fergusson in London, of Vanza in Milan, and of Bachner and Daniel in Berlin. In 1918 she made her operatic debut as Elsa at the Royal Stockholm Opera, remaining there until 1926; she was a member of the Berlin State Opera (1926–32) and also appeared at London's Covent Garden (1924–29), creating the title role there of Goossens's *Judith* (1929). She made her Metropolitan Opera debut in New York as Sieglinde in *Die Walküre* on Jan. 20, 1932; she remained on the roster until 1935; created the role of Lady Marigold Sandys in Hanson's *Merry Mount* in its first stage production there in 1934. She subsequently taught voice in New York, and later in Sweden. Among her notable roles were Isolde, Brünnhilde, Salome, and Elektra.

Lloyd, David, American tenor; b. Minneapolis, Feb. 29, 1920. He was educated at the Minneapolis College of Music (B.A., 1941) and studied voice with Bonelli at the Curtis Inst. of Music in Philadelphia. On Oct. 13, 1950, he made his operatic debut as David in *Die Meistersinger von Nürnberg* at the N.Y. City Opera, where he sang regularly until 1958; he appeared there again in 1965 and 1976. His other operatic engagements took him to Boston, Washington, D.C., New Orleans, and St. Paul. In 1955 he sang at the Athens Festival and in 1957 at the Glyndebourne Festival. He also pursued an active career as a concert and oratorio singer. He taught at the Univ. of Ill. in Urbana (from 1971) and was director of the Lake George Opera Festival in New York (from 1974). Lloyd was particularly admired for his roles in operas by Mozart, Rossini, and Richard Strauss.

Lloyd, David (John) de, Welsh composer and teacher; b. Skewen, April 30, 1883; d. Aberystwyth, Aug. 20, 1948. He studied at the Univ. College of Wales, Aberystwyth (B.A., 1903; B.Mus., 1905), the Leipzig Cons. (1906–07), and the Univ. of Dublin (Mus.D., 1915). He served as a lecturer (1919–26) and a prof. (1926–48) at the Univ. College of Wales. Among his works were the operas *Gwenllian* (1924) and *Tir na n-og* (1930).

Lloyd, George (Walter Selwyn), English composer and conductor; b. St. Ives, Cornwall, June 28, 1913; d. London, July 3, 1998. He began violin lessons at 5 and commenced composing at 10. He later was a student of Albert Sammons (violin), C. H. Kitson (counterpoint), and Harry Farjeon (composition). In 1933 he attracted notice as a composer with the premiere of his 1st Sym. in Bournemouth, and then had further success with his operas *Iernin* (1933–34) and *The Serf* (1936–38). His career was interrupted when he enlisted in the Royal Marines in 1939. He served on Arctic convoy duty until he was severely shell-shocked in the attack on the HMS *Trinidad* in 1942. Following a long and arduous recuperation, he resumed composition with great earnestness. He was also active as a conductor and served as principal guest conductor and music advisor of the Albany (N.Y.) Sym. Orch. (1989–91). In his compositions, which included the operas *Iernin* (1933–34; Penzance, Nov. 6, 1934), *The Serf* (1936–38; London, Oct. 20, 1938), and *John Socman* (1949–51; Bristol, May 15, 1951), Lloyd embraced an unabashedly Romantic style of pleasurable accessibility.

Lloyd, Jonathan, English composer; b. London, Sept. 30, 1948. He took composition lessons in London with Emile Spira (1963–65), and with Edwin Roxburgh (1965–66) and John Lambert (1966–69) at the Royal College of Music; he also worked with Tristram Cary at the electronic music studio there and then completed his training with György Ligeti at the Berkshire Music Center in Tanglewood (summer 1973). He was composer-in-residence at the Dartington College Theatre Dept. (1978–79). He has produced a number of compositions of considerable and lasting value, distinguished by a variety of forms and styles. His music theater work *Scattered Ruins* (Tanglewood, Aug. 1973) won the Koussevitzky Composition Prize in 1973. Other dramatic scores include *Musices genus*, masque (1974), *The Adjudicator*, "community opera" (1985; Blewbury, April 15, 1986), and *Blackmail*, music for Hitchcock's silent film (1992–93; Paris, March 13, 1993).

Lloyd, Robert (Andrew), esteemed English bass-baritone; b. Southend-on-Sea, March 2, 1940. He studied history at Keble College, Oxford, then voice with Otakar Kraus at the London Opera Centre (1968–69), making his debut at London's Collegiate Theatre as Beethoven's Fernando (1969). He was a member of Sadler's Wells (1969–72) and the Royal Opera at Covent Garden (1972–83) in London; he also made guest appearances in Berlin, Paris, Hamburg, Milan, Munich, San Francisco, Salzburg, and Vienna. On Oct. 26, 1988, he made his Metropolitan Opera debut in New York as Rossini's Basilio. In 1990 he became the first English singer to appear as Boris Godunov at the Kirov Opera in Leningrad. In 1991 he was made a Commander of the Order of the British Empire. Among his best roles are Sarastro, the Commendatore, Oroveso, Banquo, Boris Godunov, King Philip, and Gurnemanz (he appeared as the latter in the Syberberg film version of *Parsifal* in 1981).

Lloyd-Jones, David (Mathias), English conductor; b. London, Nov. 19, 1934. He studied at Magdalen College, Oxford. He appeared as a guest conductor with the leading British opera houses, including Covent Garden, the English National Opera, the Scottish Opera, and the Welsh National Opera; in 1978 he was named music director of the newly organized English National Opera North in Leeds, which was renamed Opera North in 1981; he retained this post until 1990; in 1989 he became artistic adviser of the Guildhall School of Music and Drama in London. He conducted the English premieres of works from the traditional and modern operatic repertoire; he also ed. the full score of Mussorgsky's *Boris Godunov* (1975) and Borodin's *Prince Igor* (1982).

Lloyd Webber, Andrew, Lord Lloyd Webber of Sydmonton, tremendously successful English composer; b. London, March 22, 1948. His father, William Southcombe Lloyd Webber, was the director of the London College of Music and his mother was a piano teacher; further, his brother, Julian Lloyd Webber (b. London, April 14, 1951), grew to become a talented cellist. Inspired and conditioned by such an environment, Lloyd Webber learned to play piano, violin, and horn, and soon began to improvise music, mostly in the style of American musicals. He attended Westminster School in London, then went to Magdalen College, Oxford, the Guildhall School of Music in London, and the Royal College of Music in London. In college he wrote his first musical, *The Likes of Us*, dealing with a philanthropist. In 1967, at the age of 19, he composed the theatrical show *Joseph and the Amazing Technicolor Dreamcoat*, which was performed at St. Paul's Junior School in London in 1968; it was later expanded to a full-scale production (Edinburgh, Aug. 21, 1972), and achieved considerable success for its amalgam of a biblical subject with rock music, French chansonnettes, and country-western songs. In 1970 it was produced in America and in 1972 was shown on television. He achieved his first commercial success with *Jesus Christ Superstar*, an audacious treatment of the religious theme in terms of jazz and rock. It was premiered in London on Aug. 9, 1972, and ran for 3,357 performances. Interestingly, the "rock opera," as it was called, was first released as a record album, which eventually sold 3 million copies. *Jesus Christ Superstar* opened on Broadway on Oct. 12, 1971, even before the London production. There were protests by religious groups against the irreverent treatment of a sacred subject; particularly offensive was the suggestion in the play of a carnal relationship between Jesus and Mary Magdalen; Jewish organizations, on the other hand, protested against the implied portrayal of the Jews as guilty of the death of Christ. The musical closed on Broadway on June 30, 1973, after 720 performances; it received 7 Tony Awards. In 1981 the recording of *Jesus Christ Superstar* was given the Grammy Award for best cast show album of the year. His early musical *Joseph and the Amazing Technicolor Dreamcoat* was revived at the off-Broadway Entermedia Theatre in N.Y.'s East Village on Nov. 18, 1981, and from there moved to the Royale Theater on Broadway. In the meantime, he produced a musical with a totally different chief character, *Evita*, a semi-fictional account of the career of the first wife of Argentine dictator Juan Perón; it was first staged in London on June 21, 1978; a N.Y. performance soon followed, with splendid success. It was followed by the spectacularly successful *Cats*, inspired by T. S. Eliot's *Old Possum's Book of Practical Cats*; it was premiered in London on May 11, 1981, and was brought out in New York in Oct. 1982 with fantastic success; *Evita* and *Joseph and the Amazing Technicolor Dreamcoat* were still playing on Broadway, so that Lloyd Webber had the satisfaction of having 3 of his shows running at the same time. Subsequent successful productions were his *Song and Dance* (London, March 26, 1981) and *Starlight Express* (London, March 19, 1984). His series of commercial successes reached a lucrative apex with the production of *The Phantom of the Opera* (London, Oct. 9, 1986), a gothically oriented melodramatic tale of contrived suspense. On April 17, 1989, his musical *Aspects of Love* opened in London. His musical setting of the 1950 Billy Wilder film *Sunset Boulevard* was first staged in London on July 12, 1993. Apart from popular shows, Lloyd Webber wrote a mini-opera, *Tell Me on a Sunday*, which was produced by BBC Television in 1980. Quite different in style and intent were his *Variations* for Cello and Jazz Ensemble (1978), written for his brother, and his *Requiem Mass* (N.Y., Feb. 24, 1985). He was knighted in 1992 and made a lord in 1997.

BIBL.: G. McKnight, *A. L. W.* (London and N.Y., 1984); J. Mantle, *Fanfare: The Unauthorized Biography of A. L. W.* (London, 1989); M. Walsh, *A. L. W.: His Life and Works* (N.Y., 1989; updated and enl. ed., 1997); H. Mühe, *Die Musik von A. L. W.* (Hamburg, 1993).

Lobe, Johann Christian, German flutist, writer on music, and composer; b. Weimar, May 30, 1797; d. Leipzig, July 27, 1881. He studied with A. E. Müller. He was a flutist (from 1808), later a viola player, in the Weimar Court Orch. until 1842. He also founded a music school, and from 1846 to 1848 he was in Leipzig as ed. of the *Allgemeine musikalische Zeitung*, and from 1855 to 1857 of the *Fliegende Blätter für Musik*; he was also music ed. of *Illustrierte Zeitung*. He championed the cause of Weimar classicism and the German Romantic movement. Among his compositions are the operas (all 1st perf. in Weimar) *Wittekind* (1819), *Die*

Flibustier (1829), *Die Fürstin von Granada* (Sept. 28, 1833), *Der rote Domino* (1835), and *König und Pachter* (1844).

WRITINGS: *Compositionslehre* (1844); *Lehrbuch der musikalischen Komposition* (vol. 1, *Harmony*, 1850; rev. by Kretzschmar, 5th ed., 1884; vol. 2, *Instrumentation*, 3d ed., 1879; vol. 3, *Canon, Fugue, etc.*, 1860; vol. 4, *Opera*, 1867; rev. by Kretzschmar, 1884–87); *Katechismus der Musik* (1851; ed. by W. Neumann, 1949; 7th ed., 1968; Eng. tr., N.Y., 1886); *Musikalische Briefe eines Wohlbekannten* (1852; 2d ed., 1860); *Aus dem Leben eines Musikers* (1859); *Vereinfachte Harmonielehre* (1861); *Consonanzen und Dissonanzen* (1869); *Katechismus der Compositionslehre* (1872; 7th ed., 1902; Eng. tr., 1891); *Handbuch der Musik* (n.d.; ed. by R. Hofmann, 1926).

BIBL.: W. Bode, ed., *Goethes Schauspieler und Musiker: Erinnerungen von Eberwein und L.* (Berlin, 1912).

Locke (also **Lock**), **Matthew,** English composer; b. Exeter, c.1621; d. London, Aug. 1677. He was a chorister at Exeter Cathedral, where he studied with Edward Gibbons, William Wake, and John Lugge. He was in the Netherlands (c.1646–51); at the Restoration he was made private composer-in-ordinary to the king, composer for the wind music, and composer for the band of violins (1660); he was also made organist to the queen (c.1662). He composed the operas *The Siege of Rhodes* (London, 1656; in collaboration with other composers; music not extant), *The Tempest*, after Shakespeare as adapted by Davenant and Dryden (London, 1674; in collaboration with other composers), and *Psyche* (London, March 9, 1675), as well as various other works for the theater, including music to Shirley's masque *Cupid and Death* (March 26, 1653; in collaboration with C. Gibbons; not extant; rev. 1659) and to Shakespeare's *Macbeth* (c.1663–74).

WRITINGS: *Observations upon a Late Book, Entitled, An Essay to the Advancement of Musick, etc., written by Thomas Salmon, M. A. of Trinity College in Oxford: by Matthew Locke* (London, 1672); *The Present Practice of Musick Vindicated against the Exceptions; and New Way of Attaining Musick lately published by Thomas Salmon M. A. etc. by Matthew Locke . . . to which is added Duellum Musicum by John Phillips . . . together with a Letter from John Playford to Mr. T. Salmon by way of Confutation of his Essay* (London, 1673); *Melothesia, or, Certain General Rules for Playing upon a Continued-Bass, with a Choice Collection of Lessons for the Harpsichord and Organ of all Sorts: Never before published* (London, 1673).

BIBL.: E. Fairley, *Studies in the Music of M. L.* (diss., Univ. of Rochester, N.Y., 1941); R. Harding, *A Thematic Catalogue of the Works of M. L. with a Calendar of the Main Events of His Life* (Oxford, 1971).

Lockhart, James (Lawrence), Scottish conductor; b. Edinburgh, Oct. 16, 1930. He studied at the Univ. of Edinburgh and at the Royal College of Music in London. He served as apprentice conductor of the Yorkshire Sym. Orch. (1954–55), assistant conductor at Münster (1955–56), the Bavarian State Opera in Munich (1956–57), Glyndebourne (1957–59), and Covent Garden in London (1959–68). Intercalatorily, he was music director of the Opera Workshop of the Univ. of Texas in Austin (1957–59), and conductor of the BBC Scottish Sym. Orch. in Glasgow (1960–61). From 1968 to 1973 he was music director of the Welsh National Opera in Cardiff; from 1972 to 1980 he served as Generalmusikdirektor of the State Theater in Kassel; from 1981 to 1991 he was Generalmusikdirektor of the Rheinische Phil. in Koblenz and at the Koblenz Opera. He was head of the opera school at the Royal College of Music (1986–92) and director of opera at the London Royal Schools Vocal Faculty (1992–96).

Locklair, Dan (Steven), American composer, organist, and teacher; b. Charlotte, N.C., Aug. 7, 1949. He was educated at Mars Hill (N.C.) College (B.M., 1971), Union Theological Seminary in New York (S.M.M., 1973), and the Eastman School of Music in Rochester, N.Y. (D.M.A., 1982); among his mentors were Robert Baker (1971–73) and David Craighead (1979–80) in organ and Ezra Laderman (1975–77), Samuel Adler (1979), and Joseph Schwantner (1980) in composition. After serving as a church musician in Binghamton, N.Y. (1973–82), he was composer-in-residence and an assoc. prof. of music at Wake Forest Univ. in Winston-Salem, N.C. (from 1982). He received annual ASCAP awards from 1981; in 1989 he won the Barlow International Composition Competition. His works are handsomely wrought within tonal parameters. Among his works are the opera *Good Tidings from the Holy Beast* (Lincoln, Nebr., Dec. 21, 1978) and the ballet *Scintillations* (1986; Winston-Salem, N.C., March 13, 1987).

Lockspeiser, Edward, English writer on music; b. London, May 21, 1905; d. Alfriston, Sussex, Feb. 3, 1973. He went to Paris in 1922, where he studied with Tansman. After studies with Boulanger (1925–26), he returned to London and completed his training at the Royal College of Music (1929–30) with Kitson and Sargent. He was on the staff of the BBC (1942–51). Lockspeiser distinguished himself as a writer on French music.

WRITINGS (all publ. in London unless otherwise given): *Debussy* (1936; 5th ed., rev., 1980); *Berlioz* (1939); *Bizet* (1951); ed. *Lettres inédites de Claude Debussy à André Caplet (1908–1914)* (Monaco, 1957); *The Literary Clef: An Anthology of Letters and Writings by French Composers* (1958); *Debussy et Edgar Poe: Manuscrits et documents inédits* (Monaco, 1961); *Debussy: His Life and Mind* (2 vols., 1962, 1965; 2d ed., rev., 1978); *Music and Painting: A Study in Comparative Ideas from Turner to Schoenberg* (1973).

Lockwood, Normand, American composer and teacher; b. N.Y., March 19, 1906. He studied at the Univ. of Mich. (1921–24), and with Respighi in Rome (1925–26) and Boulanger in Paris (1926–28); he was a Fellow at the American Academy in Rome (1929–31). Upon his return to America, he was an instructor in music at the Oberlin (Ohio) Cons. (1932–43); from 1945 to 1953 he was a lecturer at Columbia Univ., then at Trinity Univ. in San Antonio (1953–55); he later taught at the Univ. of Hawaii and at the Univ. of Oregon (1955–61). In 1961 he was appointed a member of the faculty of the Univ. of Denver; he became prof. emeritus in 1974. Lockwood's compositions are well crafted in an accessible style. He composed the operas *The Scarecrow* (N.Y., May 19, 1945), *Early Dawn* (Denver, Aug. 7, 1961), *The Wizards of Balizar* (Denver, Aug. 1, 1962), *The Hanging Judge* (Denver, March 1964), and *Requiem for a Rich Young Man* (Denver, Nov. 24, 1964); also oratorios, including *Children of God* (1956; Cincinnati, Feb. 1, 1957), *Light out of Darkness* (1957), *Land of Promise* (1960), and *For the Time Being* (1971).

BIBL.: K. Norton, *N. L.: His Life and Music* (Metuchen, N.J., 1993).

Loeffler, Charles Martin (Tornow), outstanding Alsatian-born American composer of German descent; b. Mulhouse, Jan. 30, 1861; d. Medfield, Mass., May 19, 1935. His father was a writer who sometimes used the nom de plume Tornow, which Loeffler later added to his name. When he was a child, the family moved to Russia, where his father was engaged in government work in the Kiev district; later they lived in Debrecen, and in Switzerland. In 1875 Loeffler began taking violin lessons in Berlin with Rappoldi, who prepared him for study with Joachim; he studied theory with Kiel and also took lessons with Bargiel at the Berlin Hochschule für Musik (1874–77). He then went to Paris, where he continued his musical education with Massart (violin) and Guiraud (counterpoint and composition). He was engaged briefly as a violinist in the Pasdeloup Orch.; he then was a member of the private orch. of the Russian Baron Paul von Derwies at his sumptuous residences near Lugano and in Nice (1879–81). When Derwies died in 1881, Loeffler went to the United States, with letters of recommendation from Joachim; he became a naturalized American citizen in 1887. He played in the orch. of Leopold Damrosch in New York in 1881–82. In 1882 he became 2d concertmaster of the newly organized Boston Sym. Orch., but was able to accept other engagements during late spring and summer months; the summers of 1883 and 1884 he spent in Paris, where he took violin lessons with Hubert Léonard. He resigned from the Boston Sym. Orch. in 1903, and devoted himself to composition and farming in Medfield. He was married to Elise Burnett Fay

(1910). After his death she donated to the Library of Congress in Washington, D.C., all of his MSS, correspondence, etc.; by his will, he left the material assets of his not inconsiderable estate to the French Academy and the Paris Cons. He was an officer of the French Academy (1906); a Chevalier in the French Légion d'honneur (1919); a member of the American Academy of Arts and Letters and Mus. Doc. (*honoris causa*), Yale Univ. (1926).

Loeffler's position in American music is unique, brought up as he was under many different national influences, Alsatian, French, German, Russian, and Ukrainian. One of his most vivid scores, *Memories of My Childhood*, written as late as 1924, reflects the modal feeling of Russian and Ukrainian folk songs. But his aesthetic code was entirely French, with definite leanings toward Impressionism; the archaic constructions that he sometimes affected, and the stylized evocations of "ars antiqua," are also in keeping with the French manner. His most enduring work, *A Pagan Poem*, is cast in such a neoarchaic vein. He was a master of colorful orchestration; his harmonies are opulent without saturation; his rhapsodic forms are peculiarly suited to the evocative moods of his music. His only excursion into the American idiom was the employment of jazz rhythms in a few of his lesser pieces. Among his works are the operas *The Passion of Hilarion* (1912–13), *Les Amants jaloux* (1918), and *The Peony Lantern* (c.1919), and incidental music, including *Ouverture pour le T. C. Minstrel Entertainment* (Boston, 1906?), *The Countess Cathleen* (Concord, Mass., May 8, 1924; not extant), and *The Reveller* (Boston, Dec. 22, 1925).

BIBL.: W. Damrosch, *C. M. L.* (N.Y., 1936); H. Colvin, *C. M. L.: His Life and Works* (diss., Univ. of Rochester, 1959); E. Henry, *Impressionism in the Arts and Its Influence on Selected Works of C. M. L. and Charles Tomlinson Griffes* (diss., Univ. of Cincinnati, 1976); E. Knight, *C. M. L.: A Life Apart in American Music* (Urbana, 1993).

Loevendie, Theo, Dutch composer; b. Amsterdam, Sept. 17, 1930. He received training in composition and clarinet at the Amsterdam Cons. (1956–61). He taught at the Haarlem Toonkunst Music School (1960–65) and at the Rotterdam Cons. (from 1968). In 1973 he founded the STAMP concerts for the promotion of contemporary music, ranging from jazz to the avant-garde. His own works reflect his interest in various contemporary styles. Among his compositions is the opera *Naima* (1985) and the chamber opera *Gassir, the Hero* (1990).

Loewe, (Johann) Carl (Gottfried), outstanding German composer of lieder; b. Löbejün, near Halle, Nov. 30, 1796; d. Kiel, April 20, 1869. His father, a schoolmaster and cantor, taught him the rudiments of music. When he was 12 he was sent to the Francke Inst. in Halle, where his attractive manner, excellent high voice, and early ability to improvise brought him to the attention of Jérôme Bonaparte, who granted him a stipend of 300 thalers annually until 1813. His teacher was Türk, the head of the Francke Inst.; after Türk's death in 1813, Loewe joined the Singakademie founded by Naue. He also studied theology at the Univ. of Halle, but soon devoted himself entirely to music. He had begun to compose as a boy; under the influence of Zelter he wrote German ballades, and developed an individual style of great dramatic force and lyrical inspiration; he perfected the genre, and was regarded by many musicians as the greatest song composer after Schubert and before Brahms. His setting of Goethe's *Erlkönig* (1818), which came before the publication of Schubert's great song to the same poem, is one of Loewe's finest creations; other songs that rank among his best are "Edward," "Der Wirthin Töchterlein," "Der Nöck," "Archibald Douglas," "Tom der Reimer," "Heinrich der Vogler," "Oluf," and "Die verfallene Mühle." Loewe was personally acquainted with Goethe, and also met Weber. In 1820 he became a schoolmaster at Stettin, and in 1821 music director there and organist at St. Jacobus Cathedral. He lived in Stettin, except for frequent travels, until 1866, when he settled in Kiel. He visited Vienna (1844), London (1847), Sweden and Norway (1851), and Paris (1857), among other places. Loewe was an excellent vocalist, and was able to perform his ballades in public. He publ. the pedagogic works *Gesang-Lehre, theoretisch und practisch für Gymnasien, Seminarien und Bürgerschulen* (Stettin, 1826; 5th ed., 1854), *Musikalischer Gottesdienst: Methodische Anweisung zum Kirchengesang und Orgelspiel* (Stettin, 1851, and subsequent eds.), and *Klavier- und Generalbass-Schule* (Stettin, 2d ed., 1851). Among his other works are 6 operas: *Die Alpenhütte* (1816), *Rudolf der deutsche Herr* (1825), *Malekadhel* (1832), *Neckereien* (1833), *Die drei Wünsche* (Berlin, Feb. 18, 1834), and *Emmy* (1842). M. Runze ed. a *Gesamtausgabe der Balladen, Legenden, Lieder und Gesange* (17 vols., Leipzig, 1899–1905).

BIBL.: C. Bitter, ed., *Dr. C. L.'s Selbstbiographie* (Berlin, 1870); K. König, *K. L.: Eine aesthetische Beurteilung* (Leipzig, 1884); A. Wellmer, *K. L.: Ein deutscher Komponist* (Leipzig, 1887); M. Runze, *L. redivivus* (Berlin, 1888); A. Bach, *The Art-Ballad: L. and Schubert* (London, 1890; 3d ed., 1891); M. Runze, *Ludwig Giesebrecht und C. L.* (Berlin, 1894); W. Wossidlo, *C. L. als Balladenkomponist* (Berlin, 1894); A. Niggli, *C. L.* (Zürich, 1897); H. Bulthaupt, *C. L., Deutschlands Balladenkomponist* (Berlin, 1898); H. Draheim, *Goethes Balladen in L.s Komposition* (Langensalza, 1905); K. Anton, *Beiträge zur Biographie C. L.s* (Halle, 1912); H. Kleemann, *Beiträge zur Ästhetik und Geschichte der L. schen Ballade* (diss., Univ. of Halle, 1913); O. Altenburg, *C. L.* (Stettin, 1924); H. Engel, *C. L.: Überblick und Würdigung seines Schaffens* (Greifswald, 1934).

Loewe, Sophie (Johanna), German soprano; b. Oldenburg, March 24, 1815; d. Budapest, Nov. 28, 1866. She studied in Vienna with Ciccimarra and in Milan with Lamperti, making her debut as Elisabetta in *Otto mesi in due ore* at Vienna's Kärnthnertortheater in 1832. She sang in London in 1841, the same year she appeared at La Scala in Milan, where she created Donizetti's Maria Padilla; also created Verdi's Elvira in *Ernani* (1844) and Odabella in *Attila* (1846) at the Teatro La Fenice in Venice. She retired from the stage in 1848.

Loewenberg, Alfred, German-born English musicologist; b. Berlin, May 14, 1902; d. London, Dec. 29, 1949. He studied at the Univs. of Berlin and Jena (Ph.D., 1925); he settled in London in 1934. His unique achievement is the compilation of *Annals of Opera: 1597–1940* (Cambridge, 1943; new ed., Geneva, 1955; rev. and corrected, 1978), tabulating in chronological order the exact dates of first performances and important revivals of some 4,000 operas, with illuminating comments of a bibliographical nature. He also publ. *Early Dutch Librettos and Plays with Music in the British Museum* (London, 1947) and *The Theatre of the British Isles, Excluding London: A Bibliography* (London, 1950).

Logar, Mihovil, Croatian composer; b. Rijieka, Oct. 6, 1902. He went to Prague to study with Jirák and then attended Suk's master classes. In 1927 he settled in Belgrade, where he was a prof. of composition at the Academy of Music (1945–72). In his works, he employed a restrained modern idiom.

WORKS: DRAMATIC: OPERAS: *Sablazan u dolini šentflorijansko* (Blasphemy in the Valley of St. Florian; 1937); *Pokondirena tikva* (Middle Class Noblewoman; Belgrade, Oct. 20, 1956); *Četrdesetprva* (The Year of 1941; Sarajevo, Feb. 10, 1961). BALLET: *Zlatna ribica* (The Golden Fish; Belgrade, Nov. 11, 1953).

Logothetis, Anestis, Bulgarian-born Austrian composer of Greek parentage; b. Burgas, Oct. 27, 1921; d. Lainz, Jan. 6, 1994. He went to Vienna in 1942 and studied at the Technischen Hochschule until 1944; then received training in theory and composition from Ratz and Uhl and in piano and conducting from Swarowsky at the Academy of Music, graduating in 1951. In 1952 he became a naturalized Austrian citizen. He worked with Koenig at the electronic music studio of the West German Radio in Cologne (1957). In 1960 and 1963 he was awarded the Theodor Körner Prize; in 1986 he received the honorary gold medal of the city of Vienna. He exhibited in Vienna galleries a series of polymorphic graphs capable of being performed as music by optional instrumental groups. He employed a highly personalized "integrating" musical notation, making use of symbols, signs, and suggestive images, playing on a performer's psychological associations.

WORKS: DRAMATIC: OPERAS: *Daidalia* (1976–78); *Waraus ist der Stein des Sisyphos?* (1982–84). MUSIC THEATER: *Im Gespinst* (1976). MUSICAL RADIO PLAYS: *Anastasis* (1969); *Manratellurium* (1970); *Kybernetikon* (1971–72); *Kerbtierparty* (1972–73); *Sommervögel* or *Schmetterlinge* (1973); *Menetekel* (1974); *Vor! stell! Unk!* (1980); *Bienen' Binom* (1980). BALLETS: *Himmelsmechanik* (1960); *5 Porträts der Liebe* (1960); *Odyssee* (1963).

Logroscino, Nicola Bonifacio, Italian composer; b. Bitonto (baptized), Oct. 22, 1698; d. Palermo, after 1765. He was a pupil of Veneziano and Perugino (1714–27) at the Cons. di S. Maria di Loreto in Naples. From 1728 to 1731 he was organist at Conza (Avellino); he then was active in Naples to about 1756. He subsequently went to Palermo, where he taught at the Ospedale dei Figliuoli Dispersi (c.1758–64). Of his many works, the comic opera *Il Governatore* (Naples, Carnival 1747) and the heroic opera *Giunio Bruto* (Rome, Jan. 1748) are the only 2 in which the music is extant in full.

BIBL.: U. Prota-Giurleo, *N. L.: "il dio dell'opera buffa"* (Naples, 1927). M. Belluci La Salandra, *Triade musicale Bitontina, Brevi cenni biografici di N. B. L., 1698–1760* (Bitonto, 1936).

Löhse, Otto, German conductor and composer; b. Dresden, Sept. 21, 1858; d. Baden-Baden, May 5, 1925. He was a pupil at the Dresden Cons. of Richter (piano), Grützmacher (cello), Draeseke, Kretschmer, and Rischbieter (theory), and Wüllner (conducting). He began his conducting career in Riga (1882) and was 1st conductor there (1889–93). In 1893 he was in Hamburg, where he married Katharina Klafsky. In 1895–96 both artists were members of the Damrosch Opera Co. in New York, with Lohse as conductor. From 1897 to 1904 Löhse conducted opera in Strasbourg; from 1904 to 1911, in Cologne; from 1911 to 1912, at the Théâtre Royal de la Monnaie in Brussels; from 1912 to 1923, at the Leipzig Stadttheater; from 1923 to 1925, in Baden-Baden. He composed an opera, *Der Prinz wider Willen* (Riga, 1890), and songs.

BIBL.: E. Lert, *O. L.* (Leipzig, 1918).

Lombard, Alain, French conductor; b. Paris, Oct. 4, 1940. He was only 9 when he entered Poulet's conducting class at the Paris Cons., making his debut with the Pasdeloup Orch. when he was 11; he later studied with Fricsay. He conducted at the Lyons Opera (1960–64); he won the gold medal at the Mitropoulos Competition in New York (1966) and then was music director of the Miami Phil. (1966–74). He made his Metropolitan Opera debut in New York conducting *Faust* on Dec. 24, 1966, and continued to appear there until 1973. He was chief conductor of the Strasbourg Phil. (1972–83), artistic director of the Opera du Rhin (1974–80), and music director of the Paris Opéra (1981–83). From 1988 to 1995 he was artistic director of the Orchestre National Bordeaux Aquitaine.

Lombardi, Luca, Italian composer and teacher; b. Rome, Dec. 24, 1945. He was educated at the Univ. of Vienna and the Univ. of Rome (graduated with a thesis on Eisler; publ. in Milan, 1978). He also studied composition with Renzi, Lupi, and Porena at the Pesaro Cons. (graduated, 1970). He also was in Cologne to take courses with Zimmermann and Globokar (1968–72) and to attend the courses in new music with Stockhausen, Pousseur, Kagel, Schnebel, and Rzewski (1968–70). After training in electronic music from Eimert in Cologne and Koenig in Utrecht, he studied with Dessau in Berlin (1973). He taught composition at the Pesaro Cons. (1973–78) and the Milan Cons. (1978–93). From 1983 to 1986 he was one of the artistic directors of the Cantiere Internazionale d'Arte in Montepulciano. With W. Gieseler and R. Weyer, he publ. the orchestration treatise *Instrumentation in der Musik des 20. Jahrhunderts* (Celle, 1985). In his compositions, which include the opera *Faust, un travestimento* (1986–90; Basel, Dec. 21, 1991), he pursues an advanced course notable for its eclectic stylistic manifestations.

Lomon, Ruth, Canadian-born American composer, pianist, and teacher; b. Montreal, Nov. 8, 1930. She studied at McGill Univ. in Montreal; in 1960 she went to the United States and continued her training with Frances Judd Cooke and Miklos Schwalb at the New England Cons. of Music in Boston; in 1964 she took a course with Lutosawski at the Dartington Summer School of Music in England; she also attended the Darmstadt summer courses in new music. In 1965 she became a naturalized American citizen. From 1971 to 1983 she was half of the duo-piano team of Lomon and Wenglin, specializing in the performance of works by women composers. Several of her most important works have been inspired by Native American ceremonials. Among her compositions is the chamber opera *The Fisherman and His Soul* (1963); also the mixed media work *Many Moons* for Chamber Orch., Narrator, Mimes, and Dancers (Lexington, Mass., Oct. 14, 1990).

Lonati, Carlo Ambrogio (real name, **Giovanni Ambrogio Leinati**), famous Italian violinist and composer, known as "Il Gobbo della Regina" ("the Queen's hunchback"); b. probably in Milan, c.1645; d. probably there, c.1710. He was a violinist in the Naples royal chapel (1665–67). He went in 1668 to Rome, where he entered the service of Queen Christina of Sweden. Although a hunchback, he was greatly admired as a violinist, hence his sobriquet. He also appeared as a singer; likewise was principal violinist at S. Luigi dei Francesi (1673–74), and concertino violinist at the Oratorio della Stimmate at S. Francesco and the Oratorio del Crocifisso at S. Marcello (1674–75), and at the Oratorio della Pietà at S. Giovanni dei Fiorentini (1675). Having become a close friend of Stradella, he was compelled to leave Rome in 1677 after his friend's notorious conduct became general knowledge. They went to Genoa, but Lonati left the city after Stradella's murder in 1682. He then was in the service of the Mantuan court. He spent his last years in Milan. He was a distinguished composer of operas, cantatas, and instrumental music.

WORKS: OPERAS: *Amor per destino* (Genoa, 1678); *Ariberto e Flavio, regi di Longobardi* (Venice, 1684?); *Enea in Italia* (Milan, 1686; in collaboration with others); *I due germani (fratelli) rivali* (Modena, 1686); *Antico, principe della Siria* (Genoa, 1690); *Scipione africano* (Milan, 1692); *L'Aiace* (Milan, 1694; in collaboration with Magni and Ballarotti); *Aetna festivo* (Milan, 1696; in collaboration with others).

London (real name, **Burnstein**), **George,** esteemed Canadian-born American bass-baritone; b. Montreal, May 5, 1919; d. Armonk, N.Y., March 23, 1985. The family moved to Los Angeles in 1935; there he took lessons in operatic interpretation with Richard Lert; he also studied voice with Hugo Strelitzer and Nathan Stewart. He made his public debut in the opera *Gainsborough's Duchess* by Albert Coates in a concert performance in Los Angeles on April 20, 1941. He appeared as Dr. Grenvil in *La Traviata* on Aug. 5, 1941, at the Hollywood Bowl, and then sang with the San Francisco Opera on Oct. 24, 1943, in the role of Monterone in *Rigoletto*. He took further vocal lessons with Enrico Rosati and Paola Novikova in New York; then, anticipating a serious professional career, he changed his name from the supposedly plebeian and ethnically confining Burnstein to a resounding and patrician London. In 1947 he toured the United States and Europe as a member of the Bel Canto Trio with Frances Yeend, soprano, and Mario Lanza, tenor. His European operatic debut took place as Amonasro at the Vienna State Opera on Sept. 3, 1949. He made his Metropolitan Opera debut in New York in the same role on Nov. 13, 1951; this was also the role he sang at his last Metropolitan appearance on March 10, 1966. From 1951 to 1964 he also sang at the Bayreuth Festivals. On Sept. 16, 1960, he became the first American to sing Boris Godunov (in Russian) at the Bolshoi Theater in Moscow. In 1967 he was stricken with a partial paralysis of the larynx, but recovered sufficiently to be able to perform administrative duties. From 1968 to 1971 he was artistic administrator of the John F. Kennedy Center for the Performing Arts in Washington, D.C.; he was also executive director of the National Opera Inst. from 1971 to 1977. He was general director of the Opera Soc. of Washington, D.C., from 1975 to 1977, when he suffered a cardiac arrest that precluded any further public activities. For several years before his death, he suffered from a grave neurological disease. Among his best roles were Wotan, Don Giovanni, Scarpia, Escamillo, and Boris Godunov.

BIBL.: N. London, *Aria for G.* (N.Y., 1987).

Loomis, Clarence, American pianist, teacher, and composer; b. Sioux Falls, S.Dak., Dec. 13, 1889; d. Aptos, Calif., July 3, 1965. He studied at the American Cons. of Chicago with Heniot Lévy (piano) and Adolph Weidig (composition); subsequently he took lessons with Godowsky in Vienna. Returning to the United States, he held various positions as a music teacher. As a composer, he was mainly successful in writing light operas in a Romantic vein, among them *Yolanda of Cyprus* (London, Ontario, Sept. 25, 1929), *A Night in Avignon* (Indianapolis, July 1932), *The White Cloud* (1935), *The Fall of the House of Usher* (Indianapolis, Jan. 11, 1941), *Revival* (1943), and *The Captive Woman* (1953); he further wrote a comic ballet, *The Flapper and the Quarterback*, first performed in Kyoto, Japan, at the coronation of Emperor Hirohito, Nov. 10, 1928, and *Susanna Don't You Cry*, a stage extravaganza (1939).

Loose, Emmy, Austrian soprano; b. Karbitz, Bohemia, Jan. 22, 1914; d. Vienna, Oct. 14, 1987. She was educated at the Prague Cons.; she then made her debut as Blondchen in *Die Entführung aus dem Serail* in Hannover (1939). From 1941 she sang with the Vienna State Opera; she also appeared at the festivals in Salzburg, Glyndebourne, and Aix-en-Provence, at Milan's La Scala, London's Covent Garden, and in South America. From 1970 she taught at the Vienna Academy of Music. She was admired for her fine soubrette roles in the operas of Mozart and Richard Strauss.

Lopardo, Frank, American tenor; b. N.Y., Dec. 23, 1957. He studied at Queens College and the Juilliard School in New York. In 1984 he made his formal operatic debut in St. Louis as Tamino. In 1988 he was engaged as Belfore in *Il viaggio a Reims* at the Vienna State Opera, Ernesto in *Don Pasquale* in Geneva, Elvino in *La sonnambula* at the Lyric Opera in Chicago, and Tamino in Dallas. After singing Don Ottavio in San Francisco in 1991, he returned there as Lindoro in 1992 and as Tonio in 1993. In the latter year he portrayed Rossini's Count Almaviva at the Metropolitan Opera in New York. He sang Alfredo at London's Covent Garden in 1994, and in 1996 he appeared as Lensky in Paris. In 1997 he returned to Chicago as Tamino. In 1999 he returned to the Metropolitan Opera to sing Rodolfo. In addition to his operatic engagements, Lopardo has also sung with many of the leading orchs.

Lopatnikoff, Nicolai (Nikolai Lvovich), outstanding Russian-born American composer; b. Tallinn, Estonia, March 16, 1903; d. Pittsburgh, Oct. 7, 1976. He studied at the St. Petersburg Cons. (1914–17); after the Revolution he continued his musical training at the Helsinki Cons. with Furuhjelm (1918–20); he then studied with Grabner in Heidelberg (1920) and Toch and Rehberg in Mannheim (1921); concurrently took civil engineering at the Technological College in Karlsruhe (1921–27). He lived in Berlin (1929–33) and London (1933–39) before settling in the United States, becoming a naturalized American citizen in 1944. He was head of theory and composition at the Hartt College of Music in Hartford, Conn., and of the Westchester Cons. in White Plains, N.Y. (1939–45); he then was a prof. of composition at the Carnegie Inst. of Technology (later Carnegie-Mellon Univ.) in Pittsburgh (1945–69). In 1951 he married the poet Sara Henderson Hay. He was elected to the National Inst. of Arts and Letters in 1963. His music is cast in a neoclassical manner, distinguished by a vigorous rhythmic pulse, a clear melodic line, and a wholesome harmonic investment. A prolific composer, he wrote music in all genres; being a professional pianist, he often performed his own piano concertos with orchs. Among his works are the opera *Danton* (1930–32; *Danton Suite* for Orch., Pittsburgh, March 25, 1967) and the ballet *Melting Pot* (1975; Indianapolis, March 26, 1976).

BIBL.: W. Critser, compiler, *The Compositions of N. L.: A Catalogue* (Pittsburgh, 1979).

Lopes-Graça, Fernando, eminent Portuguese composer, musicologist, pianist, and pedagogue; b. Tomar, Dec. 17, 1906; d. Lisbon, Nov. 28, 1994. He took piano lessons at home, then studied with Merea and da Motta (piano), Borba (composition), and de Freitas Branco (theory and musicology) at the Lisbon Cons. (1923–31); he also studied at the Univ. of Lisbon. He taught at the Coimbra music inst. (1932–36). In 1937 he left his homeland for political reasons; went to Paris, where he studied composition and orchestration with Koechlin, and musicology with Masson at the Sorbonne. After the outbreak of World War II (1939), he returned to Lisbon, where he served as a prof. at the Academia de Amadores de Música (1941–54); from 1950 he was director of its chorus, a position he held for 40 years; he also made appearances as a pianist. In his music, he pursued an independent path in which he moved from Portuguese folk traditions to atonality in 1962. His compositions include *La Fièvre du temps*, revue ballet (1938), *D. Duardos e Flérida*, cantata melodrama (1964–69; Lisbon, Nov. 28, 1970), and *Dançares*, choreographic suite (1984). With M. Giacometti, he publ. the 1st vol. of the *Antologia da Música Regional Portuguesa*, the 1st attempt to collect, in a systematic way, the regional songs of Portugal.

WRITINGS: *Sobre a evolução das formas musicais* (Lisbon, 1940; 2d ed., rev., 1959, as *Breve ensaio sobre a evolução das formas musicais*); *Reflexões sobre a música* (Lisbon, 1941); *Introdução à música moderna* (Lisbon, 1941; 3d ed., 1984); *Música e músicos modernos (Aspectos, obras, personalidades)* (Oporto, 1943; 2d ed., 1985); *A música portuguesa e os seus problemas* (3 vols., 1944, 1959, 1973); *Bases teóricas da músicas* (Lisbon, 1944; 2d ed., 1984); *Talia, Euterpe e Terpsicore* (Coimbra, 1945); *Pequena história da música de piano* (Lisbon, 1945; 2d ed., 1984); *Cartas do Abade António da Costa (Introdução e notas)* (Lisbon, 1946; 2d ed., 1973, as *O Abade António da Costa, músico e epistológrafo setecentista*); *Visita aos músicos franceses* (Lisbon, 1948); *Vianna da Motta (Subsídios para uma biografia, incluindo 22 cartas ao autor)* (Lisbon, 1949; 2d ed., 1984); *Béla Bartók (Três apontamentos sobre a sua personalidade e a sua obra)* (Lisbon, 1953); *A Canção popular portuguesa* (Lisbon, 1953; 3d ed., 1981); *Em louvor de Mozart* (Lisbon, 1956; 2d ed., 1984); with T. Borba, *Dicionário de música* (Lisbon, 1956–58); *Musicália* (Baia, 1960; corrected and aug. ed., 1967); *Lieder der Welt, Portugal (Ausgewält und erlautert von . . .)* (Hamburg, 1961); *Nossa companheira música* (Lisbon, 1964); *Páginas escolhidas de crítica e estética musicale* (Lisbon, 1966); *Disto e daquilo* (Lisbon, 1973); *Um artista intervém/Cartas com alguma moral* (Lisbon, 1974); *A caça aos coelhos e outros escritos polémicos* (Lisbon, 1976); *Escritos musicológicos* (Lisbon, 1977); *A música portuguesa e os seus problemas* (Lisbon, 1989).

BIBL.: M. Henriques, *F. L.-G. na música portuguesa contemporanea* (Sacavém, 1956); M. Vieria de Carvalo, *O essencial sobre F. L.-G.* (Lisbon, 1989).

Lopez, Francis(co), French composer; b. Montbéliard, June 15, 1916; d. Paris, Jan. 5, 1995. He studied to be a dentist but after finding success writing songs, he opted for a career as a composer of light works for the French musical theater in Paris. He found an adept librettist and lyricist in Raymond Vincy; they scored an enormous success with their first outing, the operetta *Le Belle de Cadix* (Dec. 24, 1945). They subsequently collaborated on a long series of highly successful works, among them *Andlousie* (Oct. 25, 1947), *Quatre Jours à Paris* (Feb. 28, 1948), *Pour Don Carlos* (Dec. 17, 1950), *Le Chanteur de Mexico* (Dec. 15, 1951), *La Route fleurie* (Dec. 19, 1952), *À la Jamïque* (Jan. 24, 1954), *La Toison d'or* (Dec. 18, 1954), and *Méditerranée* (Dec. 17, 1956). Several of these works became classics and were made into films. Lopez and Vincy continued their collaboration until the latter's death in 1968. Among their later scores were *Maria-Flora* (Dec. 18, 1957), *La Secret de Marco Polo* (Dec. 12, 1959), *Visa pour l'amour* (Dec. 1961), *Cristobal le Magnifique* (Dec. 1963), and *Le Prince de Madrid* (March 4, 1967). In subsequent years, Lopez continued to compose prolifically but only infrequently found the inspiration of his earlier years. His autobiography was publ. as *Flamenco: La gloire et les larmes* (Paris, 1987).

López-Buchardo, Carlos, Argentine composer; b. Buenos Aires, Oct. 12, 1881; d. there, April 21, 1948. He studied piano, violin, and harmony in Buenos Aires and composition with Albert Roussel in Paris. He was founder-director of the National Cons. in Buenos Aires (1924–48) and also founded the school of fine arts at the Univ. of La Plata, where he was a prof. of harmony. His music is set in a vivid style, rooted in national folk song; particularly successful in this respect is his symphonic suite *Escenas argentinas* (Buenos Aires, Aug. 12, 1922). His other works include the opera *El sueño de alma* (Buenos Aires, Aug. 4, 1914; won the Municipal Prize), and 3 lyric comedies: *Madama Lynch* (1932), *La perichona* (1933), and *Amalia* (1935).

López-Cobos, Jesús, distinguished Spanish conductor; b. Toro, Feb. 25, 1940. He took a doctorate in philosophy at the Univ. of Madrid (1964); studied composition at the Madrid Cons. (diploma, 1966) and conducting with Ferrara in Venice, Swarowsky at the Vienna Academy of Music (diploma, 1969), Maag at the Accademia Musicale Chigiana in Siena, and Morel at the Juilliard School of Music in New York. In 1969 he won 1st prize at the Besancon Competition; that same year he conducted at the Prague Spring Festival and at the Teatro La Fenice in Venice; he subsequently was a regular conductor at the Deutsche Oper in West Berlin (1970–75). In 1972 he made his American debut with the San Francisco Opera conducting *Lucia di Lammermoor*, and thereafter appeared as a guest conductor throughout the United States. In 1975 he made his first appearance at London's Covent Garden conducting *Adriana Lecouvreur*. On Feb. 4, 1978, he made his Metropolitan Opera debut in New York conducting the same score. He was Generalmusikdirektor of the Deutsche Oper in West Berlin (1980–90), principal guest conductor of the London Phil. (1982–86), chief conductor of the Orquesta Nacional de España in Madrid (1984–89), and music director of the Cincinnati Sym. Orch. (1986–2001) and of the Lausanne Chamber Orch. (from 1990). To mark the 100th anniversary of the Cincinnati Sym. Orch. in 1995, he conducted it on a tour to Europe. In 1998 he became conductor of the Orchestre Français des Jeunes in Paris.

Lo Presti, Ronald, American composer; b. Williamstown, Mass., Oct. 28, 1933; d. Tempe, Ariz., Oct. 25, 1985. He studied composition with Mennini and Rogers at the Eastman School of Music in Rochester, N.Y. (M.M., 1956); subsequently he was engaged as a clarinet teacher in public schools; in 1964 he was appointed an instructor in theory at Arizona State Univ. in Tempe. He obtained popular success with his orch. score *The Masks* (Rochester, N.Y., May 8, 1955), which was commissioned for the space exhibit at the aerospace building at the Smithsonian Inst. in Washington, D.C. Other works include the opera *The Birthday* (1962; Winfield, Ill. May 1962) and the children's opera *Playback* (Tucson, Ariz., Dec. 18, 1970).

Lorengar, Pilar (real name, **Pilar Lorenza García**), prominent Spanish soprano; b. Saragossa, Jan. 16, 1928; d. Berlin, June 2, 1996. She studied with Angeles Ottein in Madrid, where she made her debut as a mezzo-soprano in zarzuela (1949); after becoming a soprano in 1951, she made her operatic debut as Cherubino at the Aix-en-Provence Festival in 1955. Her first appearance in the United States took place that same year as Rosario in a concert perf. of *Goyescas* in New York. She made her debut at London's Covent Garden as Violetta in 1955, making frequent appearances there from 1964; she also sang at the Glyndebourne Festival (1956–60) and the Berlin Deutsche Oper (from 1958). On Feb. 11, 1966, she made her Metropolitan Opera debut in New York as Donna Elvira. She was named a Kammersängerin of the Berlin Deutsche Oper in 1963, and in 1984 lifetime member of the company on the occasion of her 25th anniversary with it. Her final appearance there was as Tosca on June 9, 1990. She received the Medallo d'Oro de Zaragoza of Saragossa and the Order of Isabella de Catolica (1965), as well as the San Francisco Opera Medal (1989). Among her finest roles were Donna Anna, Fiordiligi, Countess Almaviva, Alice Ford, Eva, and Mélisande.

BIBL.: W. Elsner and M. Busch, *P. L.: Ein Porträt* (Berlin, 1985).

Lorentzen, Bent, Danish composer; b. Stenvad, Feb. 11, 1935. He studied with Knud Jeppesen at the Univ. of Århus and with Holmboe, Jersild, and Hffding at the Royal Danish Cons. of Music in Copenhagen (graduated, 1960), and worked at the Stockholm electronic music studio (1967–68). After teaching at the Århus Cons. (1962–71), he settled in Copenhagen and devoted himself to composition; in 1982 he was awarded a State Grant for Life. Among his honors are the Prix Italia (1970) and 1st prizes in the "Homage to Kazimierz Serocki" International Competition (1984) and the Spittal International Composition Competition (1987). In his music, he employs a variety of quaquaversal techniques, often utilizing highly sonorous effects.

WORKS: DRAMATIC: OPERAS: *Stalten Mette* (Århus, Nov. 17, 1963; rev. 1980); *Die Schlange* (1964; rev. 1974); *Eurydike* (1965; Danish Radio, Dec. 16, 1969); *Die Musik kommt mir äusserst bekannt vor* (Kiel, May 3, 1974); *Eine wundersame Liebesgeschichte* (Munich, Dec. 2, 1979); *Klovnen Toto* (1982); *Fackeltanz* (1986); *The Scatterbrain* (1995); *Pergolesi Hjemmeservice* (Århus, Sept. 1998). INSTRUMENTAL THEATER: *Studies for 2* for Cello or Guitar and Percussion (1967); *Studies for 3* for Soprano Cello or Guitar, and Percussion (1968); *The End* for Cello (1969); *Friisholm*, film (1971); *3 Mobiles* for 3 Different Instruments (1979; rev. 1988).

Lorenz, Alfred (Ottokar), Austrian musicologist, composer, and conductor; b. Vienna, July 11, 1868; d. Munich, Nov. 20, 1939. He studied with Radecke (conducting) and Spitta (musicology) in Berlin. He was a conductor in Königsberg, Elberfeld, and Munich (1894–97), then became a conductor (1898) and later chief conductor (1904) in Coburg; he was made director of its Opera (1917) and was also director of the Musikverein in Gotha (1901–18) and Coburg (1907–20). He then gave up his conducting career and studied musicology with Moritz Bauer at the Univ. of Frankfurt am Main (graduated, 1922); he lectured at the Univ. of Munich from 1923. He made a specialty of Wagnerian research; publ. the comprehensive work *Das Geheimnis der Form bei Richard Wagner* (4 vols., Berlin, 1924–33; 2d ed., 1966); he also publ. *Alessandro Scarlattis Jugendoper* (Augsburg, 1927) and *Abendländische Musikgeschichte im Rhythmus der Generationen* (Berlin, 1928). He composed an opera, *Helges Erwachen* (Schwerin, 1896), and incidental music to various plays.

Lorenz, Max, greatly admired German tenor; b. Düsseldorf, May 17, 1901; d. Salzburg, Jan. 11, 1975. He studied with Grenzebach in Berlin. He made his debut as Walther von der Vogelweide in *Tannhäuser* at the Dresden State Opera (1927) and sang at the Berlin State Opera (1929–44) and the Vienna State Opera (1929–33; 1936–44; 1954). He made his Metropolitan Opera debut in New York as Walther von Stolzing in *Die Meistersinger von Nürnberg* on Nov. 12, 1931; he was again on its roster in 1933–34 and from 1947 to 1950. Lorenz also sang at the Bayreuth Festivals (1933–39; 1952), London's Covent Garden (1934; 1937), the Chicago Opera (1939–40), and the Salzburg Festivals (1953–55; 1961). He was particularly esteemed as a Wagnerian; was also a noted Florestan, Othello, and Bacchus.

BIBL.: W. Herrmann, *M. L.* (Vienna, 1976).

Lorenzani, Paolo, Italian composer; b. Rome, 1640; d. there, Oct. 28, 1713. He was a pupil of Orazio Benevoli at the Vatican. Having failed to obtain Benevoli's position after the latter's death in 1672, he was given the post of maestro di cappella at the Jesuit church, the Gesù, and at the Seminario Romano in Rome in 1675; from 1675 to 1678 he held a similar position at the Messina Cathedral. When Sicily was captured by the French, the Duc de Vivonne, who was the French viceroy, induced Lorenzani to go to Paris (1678); he found favor with Louis XIV, with whose financial support he purchased the post of Surintendant de la musique de la Reyne (1679); he held that post until the queen's death (1683), then was maître de chapelle to the Italian Théatine religious order (1685–87). He produced the Italian pastoral *Nicandro e Fileno* (Fontainebleau, Sept. 1681); having won the support of the Paris faction opposed to Lully, he produced an opera with a French libretto, *Orontée* (Paris, Aug. 23, 1687). This having failed, Lorenzani turned to the composition of motets, which proved his best works; the famous Paris publisher Ballard brought them out in an impressively printed ed. Ballard also publ. a book of Italian airs by Lorenzani. In 1694 Lorenzani returned to Italy, and was appointed maestro di cappella of the Cappella Giulia at the Vatican.

BIBL.: W. Gürtelschmied, *P. L. (1640–1713): Leben, Werk, thematischer Katalog* (diss., Univ. of Vienna, 1975).

Lorenzo Fernândez, Oscar, Brazilian composer and teacher; b. Rio de Janeiro, Nov. 4, 1897; d. there, Aug. 26, 1948. He was a student of João Otaviano (piano and theory) before pursuing his training at the Instituto Nacionale de Música in Rio de Janeiro with Oswald (piano), Nascimento (harmony), and Braga (counterpoint and fugue). In 1924 he joined its faculty as prof. of harmony; he later was founder-director of the Brazilian Cons. (1936–48). His works, derived from Brazilian folk songs, followed along national lines. Among them is the opera *Malazarte* (1931–33; Rio de Janeiro, Sept. 30, 1941; orch. suite, 1941).

Lortzing, (Gustav) Albert, celebrated German composer; b. Berlin, Oct. 23, 1801; d. there, Jan. 21, 1851. His parents were actors, and the wandering life led by the family did not allow him to pursue a methodical course of study. He learned acting from his father, and music from his mother at an early age. After some lessons in piano with Griebel and in theory with Rungenhagen in Berlin, he continued his own studies, and soon began to compose. On Jan. 30, 1823, he married the actress Rosina Regina Ahles in Cologne; they had 11 children. In 1824 he wrote his stage work, the Singspiel *Ali Pascha von Janina, oder Die Franzosen in Albanien*, which, however, was not produced until 4 years later (Münster, Feb. 1, 1828). He then brought out the Liederspiel *Der Pole und sein Kind, oder Der Feldwebel vom IV. Regiment* (1832) and the Singspiel *Szenen aus Mozarts Leben* (Osnabrück, Oct. 11, 1832), which were well received on several German stages. From 1833 to 1844 he was engaged at the Municipal Theater of Leipzig as a tenor; there he launched a light opera, *Die beiden Schützen* (Feb. 20, 1837), which became instantly popular; on the same stage he produced, on Dec. 22, 1837, his undoubted masterpiece, *Zar und Zimmermann, oder Die zwei Peter*. It was performed with enormous success in Berlin (1839), and then in other European music centers. His next opera, *Caramo, oder Das Fischerstechen* (Leipzig, Sept. 20, 1839), was a failure; there followed *Hans Sachs* (Leipzig, June 23, 1840) and *Casanova* (Leipzig, Dec. 31, 1841), which passed without much notice; subsequent comparisons showed some similarities between *Hans Sachs* and *Die Meistersinger von Nürnberg*, not only in subject matter, which was derived from the same source, but also in some melodic patterns; however, no one seriously suggested that Wagner was influenced by Lortzing's inferior work. There followed a comic opera, *Der Wildschütz, oder Die Stimme der Natur* (Leipzig, Dec. 31, 1842), which was in many respects the best that Lortzing wrote, but its success, although impressive, never equaled that of *Zar und Zimmermann*. At about the same time, Lortzing attempted still another career, that of opera impresario, but it was short-lived; his brief conductorship at the Leipzig Opera (1844–45) was similarly ephemeral. Composing remained his chief occupation; he produced *Undine in Magdeburg* (April 21, 1845) and *Der Waffenschmied* in Vienna (May 30, 1846). He then went to Vienna as conductor at the Theater an der Wien, but soon returned to Leipzig, where he produced the light opera *Zum Grossadmiral* (Dec. 13, 1847). The revolutionary events of 1848 seriously affected his position in both Leipzig and Vienna; after the political situation became settled, he produced in Leipzig an opera of a Romantic nature, *Rolands Knappen, oder Das ersehnte Gluck* (May 25, 1849). Although at least 4 of his operas were played at various German theaters, Lortzing received no honorarium, owing to a flaw in the regulations protecting the rights of composers. He was compelled to travel again as an actor, but could not earn enough money to support his large family, left behind in Vienna. In the spring of 1850 he obtained the post of conductor at Berlin's nondescript Friedrich-Wilhelmstadt Theater. His last score, the comic opera *Die Opernprobe, oder Die vornehmen Dilettanten*, was produced in Frankfurt am Main on Jan. 20, 1851, while he was on his deathbed in Berlin; he died the next day. His opera *Regina*, written in 1848, was ed. by Richard Kleinmichel, with the composer's libretto revised by Adolf L'Arronge, and performed in Berlin as *Regina, oder Die Marodeure* on March 21, 1899; the first perf. of the original version in the new critical ed. was given in Gelsenkirchen on March 22, 1998. His Singspiel *Der Weihnachtsabend* was produced in Münster on Dec. 21, 1832. Lortzing also wrote an oratorio, *Die Himmelfahrt Jesu Christi* (Munster, Nov. 15, 1828), and some incidental music to various plays, but it is as a composer of characteristically German Romantic operas that he holds a distinguished, if minor, place in the history of dramatic music. He was a follower of Weber, without Weber's imaginative projection; in his lighter works, he approached the type of French operetta; in his best creations he exhibited a fine sense of facile melody, and infectious rhythm; his harmonies, though unassuming, were always proper and pleasing; his orchestration, competent and effective.

BIBL.: P. Düringer, *A. L.: Sein Leben und Wirken* (Leipzig, 1851); H. Wittmann, *L.* (Leipzig, 1890; 2d ed., 1902); G. Kruse, *A. L.* (Berlin, 1899); idem, *A. L.: Leben und Werk* (Leipzig, 1914; 2d ed., 1947); H. Laue, *Die Operndichtung L.s* (Würzburg, 1932); H. Killer, *A. L.* (Potsdam, 1938); G. Dippel, *A. L.: Ein Leben für das deutsche Musiktheater* (Berlin, 1951); H. Burgmüller, *Die Musen darben: Ein Lebensbild A. L.s* (Berlin, 1955); M. Hoffmann, *G. A. L.: Der Meister der deutschen Volksoper* (Leipzig, 1956); E. Lortzing, *A. L.: Zur Familienchronik L.-L.* (Starnberg, 1963); H. Schirmag, *A. L.: Ein Lebens- und Zeitbild* (Berlin, 1982); I. Capelle, *Chronologisch-thematisches Verzeichnis der Werke von G. A. L.: (LoWV)* (Cologne, 1994); H. Schirmag, *A. L.: Glanz und Elena eines Künstlerlebens* (Berlin, 1995).

Los Angeles (real name, **Gómez Cima**), **Victoria de,** famous Spanish soprano; b. Barcelona, Nov. 1, 1923. She studied at the Barcelona Cons. with Dolores Frau. In 1941 she made her operatic debut as Mimi in Barcelona, but then resumed her training. In 1945 she made her formal operatic debut as Mozart's Countess in Barcelona. After winning 1st prize in the Geneva International Competition in 1947, she sang Salud in *La vida breve* with the BBC in London in 1948. In 1949 she made her first appearance at the Paris Opéra as Marguerite. In 1950 she sang at the Salzburg Festival for the first time. She made her debut at London's Covent Garden as Mimi in 1950, and continued to appear there regularly with notable success until 1961. She also sang at Milan's La Scala from 1950 to 1956. On Oct. 24, 1950, she made her first appearance in the United States in a Carnegie Hall recital in New York. She made her Metropolitan Opera debut in New York as Marguerite on March 17, 1951, and remained on its roster until 1956. In 1957 she sang at the Vienna State Opera, and was again on the roster of the Metropolitan Opera from 1957 to 1961. After making her debut at the Bayreuth Festival as Elisabeth in 1961, she devoted herself principally to a concert career. However, she continued to make occasional appearances in one of her favorite operatic roles, Carmen, during the next 2 decades. Her concert career continued as she entered her 7th decade, highlighted by a well-received recital appearance at N.Y.'s Alice Tully Hall on March 7, 1994. Among her other acclaimed operatic roles were Donna Anna, Rosina, Manon, Nedda, Desdemona, Cio-Cio-San, Violetta, and Mélisande. As a concert artist, she excelled particularly in Spanish and French songs.

Lothar, Mark, German composer; b. Berlin, May 23, 1902; d. Munich, April 6, 1985. He studied with Schreker (composition), Juon (harmony), and Krasselt (conducting) at the Berlin Hochschule für Musik (1919–20), and later with Meiszner (piano) and Wolf-Ferrari (composition). He was active as piano accompanist to the Dutch singer Cora Nerry, whom he married in 1934. Lothar served as director of music at Berlin's Deutsche Theater (1933–34) and Prussian State Theater (1934–44), and at the Bavarian State Theater in Munich (1945–55). In addition to his various dramatic scores, he wrote a number of lieder.

WORKS: DRAMATIC: OPERAS: *Tyll* (Weimar, Oct. 14, 1928); *Lord Spleen* (Dresden, Nov. 11, 1930); *Münchhausen* (Dresden, June 6, 1933); *Das kalte Herz*, radio opera (Berlin Radio, March 24, 1935); *Schneider Wibbel* (Berlin, May 12, 1938); *Rappelkopf* (Munich, Aug. 20, 1958); *Der Glücksfischer* (Nuremberg, March 16, 1962); *Liebe im Eckhaus*, Singspiel (n.d.); *Der widerspenstige Heilige* (Munich, Feb. 8, 1968); *Momo und die Zeitdiebe* (Coburg, Nov. 19, 1978); *La bocca della verità: Hommage à Baldassare Galuppi* (1982); incidental music to many plays and radio dramas; film scores.

BIBL.: A. Ott, ed., *M. L.: Ein Musikerporträt* (Munich, 1968); F. Messmer et al., *M. L.* (Tutzing, 1986).

Lott, Dame Felicity (Ann), distinguished English soprano; b. Cheltenham, May 8, 1947. She studied in London at Royal Holloway College, Univ. of London, and at the Royal Academy of Music. In 1976 she sang at London's Covent Garden in the premiere of Henze's *We Come to the River*; she also appeared there as Anne Trulove in Stravinsky's *The Rake's Progress*, as Octavian in *Der Rosenkavalier*, and in various other roles. She appeared in Paris for the first time in 1976; she made her Vienna debut in 1982 singing the *4 Letze Lieder* of Strauss; in 1984 she was engaged as soloist with the Chicago Sym. Orch. In 1986 she sang at the wedding of the duke and the duchess of York at Westminster Abbey. In 1990 she was made a Commander of the Order of the British Empire. On Sept. 4, 1990, she made her Metropolitan Opera debut in New York as the Marschallin. She chose that same role for her San Francisco Opera debut in 1993. In 1994 she portrayed Strauss's Countess at the Lyric Opera in Chicago, and in 1998 at the Glyndebourne Festival. In 1999 she made her first appearance with the N.Y. Phil. under Previn's direction in excerpts from *Arabella* and *Capriccio*. She was made a Dame Commander of the Order of the British Empire in 1996. Among her finest roles are Pamina, Countess Almaviva, Donna Elvira, Octavian, Arabella, and Anne Trulove.

Lotti, Antonio, eminent Italian organist, pedagogue, and composer; b. probably in Venice, c.1667; d. there, Jan. 5, 1740. He was a student of Legrenzi in Venice by 1683, then became an extra (1687) and regular (1689) singer at S. Marco; he was made assistant to the 2d organist (1690), 2d organist (1692), 1st organist (1704), and primo maestro di cappella (1736). He visited Novara (1711) and later was in Dresden at the crown prince's invitation (1717–19). Lotti was one of the most important composers of the late Baroque and early Classical eras in Italy; his sacred music and madrigals are particularly notable. He was held in great esteem as a pedagogue, numbering among his students Domenico Alberti, Baldassari Galuppi, Michelangelo Gasparini, and Benedetto Marcello. His *Duetti, terzetti e madrigali a più voci*, op. 1 (Venice, 1705), dedicated to Emperor Joseph I, includes the madrigal *In una siepe ombrosa*; it was arranged by Bononcini and presented as his own work in London in 1731, but Lotti successfully defended his authorship in 1732. Much of his music is not extant.

WORKS: DRAMATIC: OPERAS (all 1st perf. in Venice unless otherwise given): *Il trionfo dell'innocenza* (1692); *Tirsi*, dramma pastorale (1696; Act 1 by Lotti); *Sidonio* (1706); *Achille placato*, tragedia per musica (1707); *Le rovine de Troja*, intermezzo (1707); *Dragontana e Policrone*, intermezzo (1707); *Teuzzone* (1707; rev. by G. Vignola as *L'inganno vinto dalla ragione*, Naples, Nov. 19, 1708); *Cortulla e Lardone*, intermezzo (1707); *Il Vincitor generoso* (Jan. 10, 1708); *Il comando non inteso et ubbidito* (Feb. 6, 1709); *La Ninfa Apollo*, scherzo comico pastorale (Feb. 12, 1709; in collaboration with F. Gasparini); *Ama più chi men si crede*, melodramma pastorale (Nov. 20, 1709); *Isacio tiranno* (1710); *Il tradimento traditor di se stesso* (Jan. 17, 1711; rev. by F. Mancini as *Artaserse, re di Persia*, Naples, Oct. 1, 1713); *La forza del sangue* (Nov. 14, 1711); *Porsenna* (1712; rev. by A. Scarlatti, Naples, Nov. 19, 1713); *L'infedeltà punita* (Nov. 12, 1712; in collaboration with C. Pollarolo); *Irene augusta* (1713); *Polidoro*, tragedia per musica (1714); *Ciro in Babilonia* (Reggio Emilia, April 1716); *Costantino* (Vienna, Nov. 19, 1716; in collaboration with others); *Foca superbo* (Dec. 1716); *Alessandro Severo* (Dec. 26, 1716); *Giove in Argo*, melodramma pastorale (Dresden, Oct. 25, 1717); *Ascanio, ovvero Gli odi delusi dal sangue* (Dresden, Feb. 1718); *Teofane* (Dresden, Sept. 13, 1719); *Li quattro elementi*, carosello teatrale (Dresden, Sept. 15, 1719); *Griletta e Serpillo*, intermezzo (n.d.). ORATORIOS: *La Giuditta* (1701); *Il voto crudele* (Vienna, 1712); *Triumphus fidei* (Venice, 1712); *L'umiltà coronata in Esther* (Vienna, c.1714); *Il ritorno di Tobia* (Bologna, 1723); *Gioas, re di Giuda* (Venice, n.d.); *Judith* (Venice, n.d.).

BIBL.: H. Bishop, ed., *Lettres from the Academy of Ancient Music of London to Signor A. L. of Venice with his Answers and Testimonies* (London, 1732); O. Chilesotti, *Sulla lettera-critica di B. Marcello contro A. L.* (Bassano, 1885); C. Spitz, *A. L. in seiner Bedeutung als Opernkomponist* (diss., Univ. of Munich, 1918); R. Holden, *6 Extant Operas of A. L. (1667–1740)* (diss., Univ. of Conn., 1967).

Lourié, Arthur Vincent (real name, **Artur Sergeievich Lure**), Russian-born American composer; b. St. Petersburg, May 14, 1892; d. Princeton, N.J., Oct. 13, 1966). He studied at the St. Petersburg Cons. but gave up formal training after becoming active in various modernistic groups, including the futurists. With the coming of the Bolshevik Revolution in 1917, he was made chief of the music dept. of the Commissariat for Public Instruction in 1918. In 1921 he went to Berlin, where he met Busoni. In 1924 he proceeded to Paris, where he was befriended by Stravinsky. In 1941 he emigrated to the United States and in 1947 became a naturalized American citizen. He was the author of the vol. *Profanation et sanctification du temps* (Paris, 1966). As early as 1915 Lourié experimented with 12-tone techniques in his piano music. He later pursued the practice of stylizing early forms à la Stravinsky. His works include *The Feast During the Plague*, opera ballet (1935; arranged for Soprano, Chorus, and Orch., Boston, Jan. 5, 1945), and *The Blackamoor of Peter the Great*, opera (1961).

BIBL.: D. Gojowy, *A. L. und der Russische Futurismus* (Laaber, 1993).

Love, Shirley, American mezzo-soprano; b. Detroit, Jan. 6, 1940. She studied voice in Detroit with Avery Crew and in New York with Marinka Gurewich and Margaret Harshaw; she then sang with the Baltimore Opera (1962). She first appeared in a minor role at the Metropolitan Opera in New York on Nov. 30, 1963; she subsequently gained experience as a singer with other American opera companies; returned to the Metropolitan in 1970, remaining on its roster until 1984. She also appeared in opera in Europe, sang in concerts with major American orchs., gave recitals, and appeared in musical comedies. Her operatic repertoire included more than 100 roles.

Løveberg, Aase (née **Nordmo**), Norwegian soprano; b. Målselv, June 10, 1923. She was born into a peasant family and spent her childhood on a farm near the Arctic Circle. When she was 19 she went to Oslo, where she studied voice with Haldis Ingebjart. She made her operatic debut in Oslo on Dec. 3, 1948; she then sang in Stockholm, Vienna, Paris, and London. She made her first American appearance as a soloist with the Philadelphia Orch. (Dec. 6, 1957), then pursued her career mainly in Norway, later serving as manager of the Oslo Opera (1978–81).

Løvenskjold, Herman Severin, Norwegian organist and composer; b. Holdensjärnbruk, July 30, 1815; d. Copenhagen, Dec. 5, 1870. At the age of 13 his parents took him to Copenhagen, where he studied music and, in 1836, brought out his ballet *Sylphiden* with much success. After the premiere of his 2d ballet, *Sara*, in 1839, he went to Vienna, where he took some lessons with Seyfried. Returning to Denmark in 1851, he was appointed organist at the Slottskyrka in Christiansborg. He wrote an opera, *Turandot* (Copenhagen, Dec. 3, 1854).

Lover, Samuel, Irish novelist, poet, painter, and composer, grandfather of **Victor (August) Herbert**; b. Dublin, Feb. 24, 1797; d. St. Helier, Jersey, July 6, 1868. He wrote music to several Irish plays, and to many songs; publ. *Songs and Ballads* (London, 1859). Among his most popular songs (some of which are set to old Irish tunes) are "The Angel's Whisper," "Molly Bawn," and "The Low-Backed Car." He also wrote an opera, *Grana Uile, or The Island Queen* (Dublin, Feb. 9, 1832), and devised a very successful musical entertainment, *Irish Evenings* (1844), with which he toured the British Isles and the United States (1846).

BIBL.: B. Bernard, *Life of S. L., R.H.A., Artistic, Literary, and Musical* (London, 1874); A. Symington, *S. L.: A Biographical Sketch* (London, 1880).

Löwe, Ferdinand, noted Austrian conductor; b. Vienna, Feb. 19, 1865; d. there, Jan. 6, 1925. He studied with Dachs, Krenn, and Bruckner at the Vienna Cons.; he then taught piano and choral singing there (1883–96) and was conductor of the Vienna Singakademie (1896–98). In 1897 he became conductor of the Kaim Orch. in Munich, then of the Court Opera in Vienna (1898–1900) and of the Vienna Gesellschaftskonzerte (1900–04). In 1904 he became conductor of the newly organized Vienna Konzertverein Orch., which he made one of the finest instrumental bodies in Europe. He returned to Munich as conductor of the Konzertverein Orch. (1908–14), which comprised members of the former Kaim Orch. From 1918 to 1922 he was head of the Vienna Academy of Music. He was a friend and trusted disciple of Bruckner; he ed. (somewhat liberally) several of Bruckner's works, including his 4th Sym., preparing a new Finale (1887–88); he also made a recomposed version of his unfinished 9th Sym., which he conducted in Vienna with Bruckner's *Te Deum* in lieu of the unfinished Finale (Feb. 11, 1903).

Lualdi, Adriano, Italian composer; b. Larino, March 22, 1885; d. Milan, Jan. 8, 1971. He was a student in Rome of Falchi and in Venice of Wolf-Ferrari. In 1918 he settled in Milan and was active as a music critic and administrator. As a loyal Fascist, he served as director of the Cons. of San Pietro a Majella in Naples (1936–44). After the fall of the Fascist regime, he was forced to withdraw from public life but later resumed his career and was director of the Florence Cons. (1947–56). Lualdi was best known for his dramatic works.

WORKS: DRAMATIC: *Le nozze di Haura*, opera (1908; rev. 1913; Italian Radio, Oct. 19, 1939; stage premiere, Rome, April 18, 1943); *La figlia del re*, opera (1914–17; Turin, March 18, 1922); *Le furie di Arlecchino*, opera (Milan, May 17, 1915; rev. 1925); *Il diavolo nel campanile*, opera (1919–23; Milan, April 21, 1925; rev. 1952; Florence, May 21, 1954); *La grançeola*, opera (Venice, Sept. 10, 1932); *Lumawig e la saetta*, mimodrama (1936; Rome, Jan. 23, 1937; rev. 1956); *Eurydikes diatheke* or *Il testamento di Euridice*, opera (c.1940–62; RAI, Nov. 22, 1962); *La luna dei Caraibi*, opera (1944; Rome, Jan. 29, 1953); *Tre alla radarstratotropojonosferaphonotheca del Luna Park*, satiric radio comedy (c.1953–62).

WRITINGS (all publ. in Milan): *Viaggio musicale in Italia* (1927); *Serate musicali* (1928); *Viaggio musicale in Europa* (1928); *Arte e regime* (1929); *Il rinnovamento musicale italiano* (1931); *Viaggio musicale nel Sud-America* (1934); *L'arte di dirigere l'orchestra* (1940; 3d ed., 1958); *Viaggio musicale nell'URSS* (1941); *Tutti vivi* (1955); *La bilancia di Euripide: 10 libretti d'opera* (1969).

BIBL.: G. Confalonieri, *L'opera di A. L.* (Milan, 1932).

Lubin, Germaine (Léontine Angélique), noted French soprano; b. Paris, Feb. 1, 1890; d. there, Oct. 27, 1979. She studied at the Paris Cons. (1909–12) and with F. Litvinne and Lilli Lehmann. She made her debut at the Paris Opéra Comique in 1912 as Antonio in *Les Contes d'Hoffmann*. In 1914 she joined the Paris Opéra, remaining on its roster until 1944; she also appeared at London's Covent Garden (1937, 1939); in 1938 she became the first French singer to appear at Bayreuth, gaining considerable acclaim for her Wagnerian roles. She continued her career in Paris during the German occupation and was briefly under arrest after the liberation of Paris in 1944, charged with collaboration with the enemy; she was imprisoned for 3 years. After her release, she taught voice. Her most distinguished roles included Alceste, Ariadne, Isolde, Kundry, Donna Anna, Leonore, Brünnhilde, Sieglinde, and the Marschallin.

BIBL.: N. Casanov, *Isolde 39—G. L.* (Paris, 1974).

Lucantoni, Giovanni, Italian composer and singing teacher; b. Rieti, Jan. 18, 1825; d. Paris, May 30, 1902. He studied with his parents, who were both good amateur musicians, then with Giovanni Pacini in Lucca and Nicola Vaccaj in Milan. In 1857 he settled in Paris as a singing teacher; he also lived in London. His vocal compositions were very popular for a time; particularly well known was the vocal duet *Una notte a Venezia*. He also wrote an opera, *Elisa* (Milan, June 20, 1850).

Lucas, Leighton, English conductor and composer; b. London, Jan. 5, 1903; d. there, Nov. 1, 1982. He was trained to be a dancer, and was a member of Diaghilev's Ballets Russes in Paris and in London (1918–21). Then he learned conducting and traveled with various ballet companies. From 1946 he conducted his own orch. He made arrangements of classical pieces for ballet and composed his own ballets, *The Wolf's Ride* (1935), *Death in Adagio*, after Scarlatti (1936), *The Horses* (1945–46), and *Tam O'Shanter* (1972–73).

Lucca, Pauline, famous Austrian soprano of Italian-German parentage; b. Vienna, April 25, 1841; d. there, Feb. 28, 1908. She studied singing in Vienna and sang in the chorus of the Vienna Court Opera. Her professional debut took place in Olmütz as Elvira in *Ernani* on Sept. 4, 1859. Her appearances in Prague as Valentine and Norma (1860) attracted the attention of Meyerbeer, who arranged for her to become a member of Berlin's Royal Opera (1861–72). She made her first appearance at London's Covent Garden as Valentine (July 18, 1863), and sang there until 1867, returning from 1870 to 1872 and in 1882. After singing in the United States (1872–74), she was a leading member of the Vienna Court Opera until retiring from the stage in 1889. In her prime she was regarded as "prima donna assoluta," and her private life and recurring marriages and divorces were favorite subjects of sensational press stories; a curious promotional pamphlet, *Bellicose Adventures of a Peaceable Prima Donna*, was publ. in New York in 1872, presumably to whip up interest in her public appearances, but it concerned itself mainly with a melodramatic account of her supposed experiences during the Franco-Prussian War. Among her finest roles were Cherubino, Selika, Carmen, and Marguerite.

BIBL.: A. Jansen-Mara and D. Weisse-Zehrer, *Die Wiener Nachtigall: Der Lebensweg der P. L.* (Berlin, 1935).

Lucchesi, Andrea, Italian composer; b. Motta di Livenza, near Treviso, May 23, 1741; d. Bonn, March 21, 1801. He studied in Venice, then settled in Bonn as director of a traveling opera troupe (1771). He was made court Kapellmeister and Kurfürstlicher Rat (1774), and then Titularrat (1787); however, after the court left Bonn and the French occupied the city (1794), he was deprived of his positions.

WORKS: DRAMATIC: *L'isola della fortuna* (Venice, 1765); *Le Donne sempre donne* (Venice, Feb. 27, 1767); *Il matrimonio per astuzia* (Venice, Oct. 1771); *Il Giocatore amoroso*, intermezzo (Bonn, 1772); *L'inganno scoperto* (Bonn, 1773); *L'improvisota, ossia La galanteria disturbata* (Bonn, 1773–74); *Ademira* (Venice, May 2, 1784); *L'amore e la misericordia guadagnano il giuoco* (Passua, 1794).

Luchetti, Veriano, Italian tenor; b. Viterbo, March 12, 1939. He studied in Milan and Rome. In 1965 he made his debut as Alfredo at the Wexford Festival, and in 1967 he appeared in Spoleto. In 1971 he sang in *L'Africaine* at the Maggio Musicale Fiorentino, where he returned in 1974 in Spontini's *Agnes von Hohenstaufen*. In 1973 he made his debut at London's Covent Garden as Pinkerton, and made appearances there until 1976. His first appearance at Milan's La Scala took place in 1975 as Foresto in Verdi's *Attila*, and in 1976 he sang Cherubini's Jason in Aix-en-Provence. He was engaged for *I Lombardi* in Verona in 1984. In 1985 he sang Macduff at the Salzburg Festival. After appearing as Foresto at the Vienna State Opera in 1988, he sang Radames in Turin in 1990. He also made many appearances as a soloist with various European orchs., especially in Verdi's *Requiem*.

Luciuk, Juliusz (Mieczyslaw), Polish composer; b. Brzeżnica, Jan. 1, 1927. He studied in Kraków at the Jagiellonian Univ. (graduated in musicology, 1952) and at the State College of Music (diplomas in theory, 1955, and composition, 1956). After further training in composition with Boulanger and Deutsch in Paris (1958–59), he returned to Poland and devoted himself to composition. In 1974 he won 1st prize in the Monaco competition. He received the Golden Cross of Merit of Poland in 1975. In 1983 he was awarded the prize of the City of Kraków. In his extensive output, Luciuk followed a sui generis compositional path.

WORKS: DRAMATIC: *Niobe*, ballet (1962; Gdansk, May 20, 1967); *The Frock*, mimodrama (Wrocław, Oct. 25, 1965); *Brand-Peer Gynt*, mimodrama (Oslo, Sept. 28, 1967); *The Death of Euridice*, ballet (1972; Polish TV, Warsaw, Dec. 27, 1974); *When 5 Years Will Go By: The Legend of Time*, choreodrama (Amsterdam, Oct. 9, 1972); *L'Amour d'Orphée*, opera (1973; Wrocław, Feb. 22, 1980); *Medea*, ballet (Poznan, Oct. 26, 1975); *Demiurgos*, opera (1976; Kraków, April 26, 1990).

Lucký, Štěpán, Czech composer; b. Žilina, Jan. 20, 1919. He was a student at the Prague Cons. (1936–39). During the Nazi occupation, he became active in the resistance and was imprisoned in Budapest before being sent to the concentration camps in Auschwitz and Buchenwald. Following the liberation in 1945, he resumed his training at the master school of the Prague Cons. (graduated, 1947). He also studied musicology and aesthetics at the Charles Univ. in Prague (graduated, 1948; Ph.D., 1990). From 1954 to 1959 he served as artistic director of music broadcasting of Czech-TV. He taught television opera directing at the Prague Academy of Music from 1964 to 1969. In 1972 he was made a Merited Artist by the Czech government. A progressive eye disease hampered his activities from about 1985. His music is couched in a pragmatic contemporary style without circumscription by any particular doctrine or technique. Among his dramatic works is the opera *Půlnoční překvapení* (Midnight's Surprise; 1958–59; Prague, May 15, 1959), 40 feature film scores and over 100 short film scores, and incidental music for plays, radio, and television.

Ludgin, Chester (Hall), American baritone; b. N.Y., May 20, 1925. After service in the U.S. Army (1943–46), he was a student of the American Theatre Wing Professional Training Program (1948–50); he studied voice with Armen Boyajian. He began his career by singing in nightclubs; he made his operatic debut in 1956 as Scarpia with the New Orleans Experimental Opera Theatre of America. In 1957 he became a member of the N.Y. City Opera; he sang leading roles with the San Francisco Opera from 1964; he made his European debut with the Netherlands Opera in 1977. He created major roles in Ward's *The Crucible* (N.Y., 1961), Imbrie's *Angle of Repose* (San Francisco, 1967), and Bernstein's *A Quiet Place* (Houston, 1983); also made successful appearances in productions of Broadway musicals.

Ludikar (real name, **Vyskočil**), **Pavel,** Czech bass-baritone; b. Prague, March 3, 1882; d. Vienna, Feb. 19, 1970. He studied law in Prague; then took piano lessons, acquiring sufficient proficiency to accompany singers, then finally devoted himself to his real profession, that of opera singing; he studied with Lassalle in Paris. He made his operatic debut as Sarastro at the Prague National Theater (1904), then appeared in Vienna, Dresden, and Milan; he was a member of the Boston Civic Opera (1913–14). He made his Metropolitan Opera debut in New York as Timur in *Turandot* on Nov. 16, 1926; he remained on its roster until 1932; he also sang with Hinshaw's touring opera company. He essayed the role of Figaro in *Il Barbiere di Siviglia* more than 100 times in the United States. He created the title role in Krenek's opera *Karl V* (Prague, June 22, 1938).

Ludkewycz, Stanislaus, significant Polish composer and pedagogue; b. Jaroslav, Galicia, Jan. 24, 1879; d. Lwów, Sept. 10, 1979. He studied philosophy at the Univ. of Lemberg, graduating in 1901; he then went to Vienna, where he studied composition with Grädener and Zemlinsky at the Cons. (Ph.D., 1908). He then settled in Lemberg. From 1910 to 1914 he served as director of the Inst. of Music there; he then was recruited in the Austrian Army, and was taken prisoner by the Russians (1915). After the Russian Revolution, he was evacuated to Tashkent; liberated in 1918, he returned to Lemberg; from 1939 to 1972 he was a prof. of composition at the Cons. there. When the city was incorporated in the Ukrainian Soviet Republic after World War II, Ludkewycz was awarded the Order of the Red Banner by the Soviet government (1949). On the occasion of his 100th birthday in 1979, he received the Order of Hero of Socialist Labor. His music followed the precepts of European Romanticism, with the representational, geographic, and folkloric aspects in evidence. Stylistically, the influence of Tchaikovsky was paramount in his vocal and instrumental compositions. His works include an opera, *Dovbush* (1955).

BIBL.: M. Zagaikevycz, *S. L.* (Kiev, 1957); S. Pavlishin, *S. L.* (Kiev, 1974).

Ludwig, Christa, celebrated German mezzo-soprano; b. Berlin, March 16, 1924. She was reared in a musical family. Her father, Anton Ludwig, was a tenor and an operatic administrator, and her mother, Eugenie Besalla, was a mezzo-soprano. She studied with her mother and in Frankfurt am Main with Hüni-Mihacsek. In 1946 she made her debut as Orlovsky there, and continued to sing there until 1952. After appearances in Darmstadt (1952–54), she made her debut at the Salzburg Festival as Cherubino in 1954. In 1954–55 she sang in Hannover. In 1955 she joined the Vienna State Opera, where she became one of its principal artists and was made a Kammersängerin in 1962. In 1959 she made her U.S. debut as Dorabella in Chicago. On Dec. 10, 1959, she made her first appearance at the Metropolitan Opera in New York as Cherubino, and subsequently returned there regularly. Among the many outstanding roles she sang in Vienna and New York were Octavian, the Dyer's Wife, Ortrud, Fricka in *Die Walküre*, the Marschallin, Kundry, Charlotte in *Werther*, Lady Macbeth, Didon in *Les Troyens*, and Strauss's Clytemnestra. In 1966 she sang Brangäne at the Bayreuth Festival and in 1969 made her first appearance at London's Covent Garden as Amneris. In addition to her appearances in other leading operatic centers, she pursued a remarkable career as a soloist with orchs. and as a lieder artist. Her performances of Schubert, Schumann, Brahms, Wolf, Mahler, and Strauss were noteworthy. In 1957 she married **Walter Berry,** but they were divorced in 1970. During their marriage and even afterward, they appeared together in operatic and concert settings. On March 20, 1993, Ludwig gave her last N.Y. recital at Carnegie Hall, and on April 3, 1993, made her farewell appearance at the Metropolitan Opera singing Fricka in *Die Walküre*. Her career closed with concert and operatic farewells in Vienna in 1994. In 1980 she received the Golden Ring of the Vienna State Opera, and in 1981 was made its honorary member. She also was awarded the Silver Rose of the Vienna Phil. in 1980. In 1989 she was honored by the French government as a Chevalier of the Légion d'honneur and as a Commandeur de l'Ordre des Arts et des Lettres. Her autobiography was publ. as *". . . und ich wäre so gern Primadonna geworden"* (Berlin, 1994). Ludwig's fine vocal gifts and compelling musical integrity gained her a distinguished reputation as one of the outstanding operatic and concert artists of her day.

BIBL.: P. Lorenz, *C. L.—Walter Berry: Eine Künstler Biographie* (Vienna, 1968).

Ludwig, Leopold, Austrian conductor; b. Witkowitz, Jan. 12, 1908; d. Lüneburg, April 25, 1979. He studied piano at the Vienna Cons.; then conducted in provincial opera houses. He was made Generalmusikdirektor of the Oldenburg State Theater (1936), then was a conductor at the Vienna State Opera (1939–43), the Berlin Städtische Oper (1943–51), and the Berlin State Opera (1945–51). From 1951 to 1970 he was Generalmusikdirektor of the Hamburg State Opera; he also conducted at the Edinburgh Festivals (1952, 1956), the San Francisco Opera (1958–68), and the Glyndebourne Festival (1959). On Nov. 14, 1970, he made his Metropolitan Opera debut in New York conducting *Parsifal*, and remained on its roster until 1972. He was known as an unostentatious but thoroughly competent interpreter of the Austro-German operatic and symphonic repertoire.

BIBL.: B. Wessling, *L. L.* (Bremen, 1968).

Ludwig, Walther, German tenor; b. Bad Oeynhausen, March 17, 1902; d. Lahr, May 15, 1981. He studied jurisprudence and medicine before deciding on a singing career; he studied voice in Königsberg, where he made his debut in 1928. After singing in Schwerin (1929–32), he was a member of the Berlin Städtische Oper (1932–45). He also made appearances at the Glyndebourne Festival, Milan's La Scala, London's Covent Garden, the Salzburg Festival, and the Vienna State Opera; likewise toured as a concert artist. From 1952 to 1969 he was a prof. at the (West) Berlin Hochschule für Musik. He also completed his medical studies in Berlin (M.D., 1971). He was best known for his Mozart roles.

Ludwig II, King of Bavaria and patron of Wagner; b. Munich, Aug. 25, 1845; d. (suicide) in the Starnberg Lake, June 13, 1886. As crown prince, he conceived an extreme adulation for Wagner, and when he became king, at 19, he declared his intention to sponsor all of Wagner's productions, an event that came at the most difficult time of Wagner's life, beset as he was by personal and financial problems. In sincere gratitude, Wagner spoke of his future plans of composition as "a program for the King." In his total devotion to Wagner, Ludwig converted his castle Neuschwanstein into a "worthy temple for my divine friend," installing in it architectural representations of scenes from Wagner's operas. His bizarre behavior caused the government of Bavaria to order a psychiatric examination, and he was eventually committed to an asylum near the Starnberg Lake. During a walk, he overpowered the psychiatrist escorting him, and apparently dragged him to his death in the lake, and drowned himself, too. Much material on Ludwig II is found in Wagner's bibliography; see also W. Blunt, *The Dream King, Ludwig II of Bavaria* (London, 1970), and C. McIntosh, *The Swan King: Ludwig II of Bavaria* (London, 1982).

Luening, Otto (Clarence), noted American composer, music educator, flutist, and conductor; b. Milwaukee, June 15, 1900; d. N.Y., Sept. 2, 1996. His father, Eugene Luening, was a pianist, conductor, and teacher. After the family moved to Munich in 1912, he studied flute, piano, and theory (with Beer-Walbrunn) at the Akademie der Tonkunst. In 1916 he made his debut as a flutist in Munich. In 1917 he went to Zürich and studied with Jarnach and Andreae at the Cons. (until 1920). He also attended the Univ. there (1919–20) and profited from his association with Busoni. His Sextet (1918) and 1st String Quartet (1919–20) won him recognition as a composer in Europe and the United States. After playing flute in the Tonhalle Orch. and the Opera orch. in Zürich, he went to Chicago in 1920. With Gilbert Wilson, he founded the American Grand Opera Co. in 1922. From 1925 to 1928 he was a faculty member at the Eastman School of Music in Rochester, N.Y. In 1929 he went to New York and conducted on WOR Radio and in the theater. In 1932 he was awarded the David Bispham medal for his opera *Evangeline.* After serving as an assistant prof. at the Univ. of Arizona in Tucson (1932–34), he was head of the music dept. at Bennington (Vt.) College (1934–44). From 1935 to 1937 he was assoc. conductor of the N.Y. Phil. Chamber Orch. He was assoc. prof. and chairman of the music dept. at Barnard College from 1944 to 1948, and then a prof. there from 1948 to 1964. In 1944 he became music director of the Brander Matthews Theater at Columbia Univ., where he conducted the premieres of Menotti's *The Medium* (May 8, 1946), Thomson's *The Mother of Us All* (May 7, 1947), and his own *Evangeline* (May 4, 1948). From 1949 to 1968 he was a prof. of music at Columbia Univ., where he also was a codirector of the Columbia-Princeton Electronic Music Center (1959–80) and music chairman of the School of the Arts (1968–70). From 1971 to 1973 he taught at the Juilliard School in New York. He helped to found the American Composers Alliance in 1937 and was its president from 1945 to 1951. In 1940 he cofounded the American Music Center and was its chairman until 1960. In 1954 he was a founder of Composers Recordings, Inc. Luening received various commissions, grants, awards, and honorary doctorates. He held 3 Guggenheim fellowships (1930–31; 1931–32; 1974–75). In 1952 he was elected to membership in the National Inst. of Arts and Letters. He was composer-in-residence at the American Academy in Rome in 1958, 1961, and 1965. His long and distinguished career in American music is recounted in his autobiography, *The Odyssey of an American Composer* (N.Y., 1980). Although a prolific composer in various genres and styles, Luening's most significant contribution to music rests upon his pioneering work as a composer of electronic music. His flute on tape pieces *Fantasy in Space, Invention in 12 Notes*, and *Low Speed*, all premiered at N.Y.'s Museum of Modern Art on Oct. 28, 1952, were the earliest such works ever written. In collaboration with Vladimir Ussachevsky, he also wrote the first work for tape and orch., the *Rhapsodic Variations* (Louisville, March 20, 1954).

WORKS: DRAMATIC: *Sister Beatrice*, incidental music to Maeterlinck's play (Rochester, N.Y., Jan. 15, 1926); *Evangeline*, opera (1930–32; rev. 1947; N.Y., May 5, 1948, composer conducting); *Blood Wedding*, incidental music to García Lorca's play (Bennington, Vt., Dec. 1, 1940); *Of Identity*, ballet for Organ on Tape (1954; N.Y., Feb. 9, 1955; in collaboration with V. Ussachevsky); *Carlsbad Caverns*, electronic television theme for *Wide, Wide World* (1955; in collaboration with Ussachevsky); *King Lear*, incidental music on tape for Shakespeare's play (1955; in collaboration with Ussachevsky); *Theatre Piece No. 2*, ballet for Narrator, Recorded Soprano, and Instrumental Ensemble (N.Y., April 20, 1956, composer conducting); *Back to Methuselah*, electronic incidental music to Shaw's play (1958; in collaboration with Ussachevsky); *Incredible Voyage*, electronic television score for the series *Twenty-First Century* (1968; in collaboration with Ussachevsky).

BIBL.: R. Hartsock, *O. L.: A Bio-Bibliography* (Westport, Conn., 1991).

Luigini, Alexandre (-Clément-Léon-Joseph), French violinist, conductor, and composer of Italian descent; b. Lyons, March 9, 1850; d. Paris, July 29, 1906. He was the son of Giuseppe Luigini (1820–98), who conducted at the Théâtre-Italien in Paris. He studied at the Paris Cons. with Massart (violin) and Massenet (composition), then became concertmaster at the Grand Théâtre in Lyons (1869), and began his very successful career as a ballet composer with the production of his first stage work, *Le Rêve de Nicette* (Lyons, 1870). In 1877 he became conductor at the Grand Théâtre at Lyons and a prof. of harmony at the Lyons Cons.; after 20 years there, he went to Paris as conductor at the Opéra Comique, where he remained until his death, except during 1903, when he conducted the orch. at the Théâtre-Lyrique. His greatest success as a composer came with the production of the *Ballet égyptien* (Lyons, Jan. 13, 1875); it was inserted, with Verdi's permission, in the 2d act of *Aida* at its performance in Lyons in 1886. In addition to a number of other ballets, he composed the comic operas *Les Caprices de Margot* (Lyons, April 13, 1877) and *Faublas* (Paris, Oct. 25, 1881).

Luisi, Fabio, Italian conductor; b. Genoa, Jan. 17, 1959. He was a student and an assistant of Milan Horvat. After serving on the staff of the Graz Opera (1984–87), he was active as a guest conductor with major opera houses in Austria, Germany, and other European countries. From 1995 to 2000 he was music director of the Niederösterreichisches Tonkünstlerorchester in Vienna. From 1997 he also was artistic director of l'Orchestre de la Suisse Romande in Geneva.

Lukács, Miklós, Hungarian conductor; b. Gyula, Feb. 4, 1905; d. Budapest, Nov. 1, 1986. He took courses with A. Schnabel and Hindemith at the Berlin Hochschule für Musik. He conducted in various German theaters (1930–43), then at the Hungarian State Opera in Budapest (1943–78), where he also served as its director (1944; 1966–78).

Lukáš, Zdeněk, Czech composer; b. Prague, Aug, 21, 1928. He studied at the Prague teachers' inst. and also had lessons with Řídký (composition) and Modr (theory). He was active with the Czech Radio in Plzeň (1953–64) and received instruction from Kabeláč in Prague (1961–70). In his works, he explores various compositional forms. Among his works are the operas *At žije mrtvý* (Long Live the Dead Man; Prague, Dec. 11, 1968), *Domácí karneval* (Domestic Carnival; Prague, March 29, 1969), *Planeta a tiše fialovou září* (Planet with Soft Violet Glow; 1978), *Falkenštejn* (1985), and *Veta za vetu* (Measure for Measure; 1986); also the oratorios *Adam a Eva* (1969) and *Nezabiješ* (Thou Shalt Not Kill; 1971).

Luke, Ray, American composer, conductor, and teacher; b. Forth Worth, Texas, May 30, 1928. He received training in theory at Texas Christian Univ. in Fort Worth (B.M., 1949; M.M., 1950), and in theory and composition at the Eastman School of Music in Rochester, N.Y. (Ph.D., 1960). In 1962 he joined the faculty of Oklahoma City Univ., where he taught for more than 30 years. He also conducted its orch. and opera productions until 1987. From 1963 to 1967 he was music director of the Lyric Theater of Oklahoma in Oklahoma City. He was assoc. conductor of the Oklahoma City Sym. Orch. from 1968 to 1973, and then was its music director and resident conductor in 1973–74. Thereafter he was a frequent guest conductor with it until 1979. His Piano Concerto won 1st prize in the Queen Elisabeth of Belgium International Composition Competition in 1969. In 1978 he won 1st prize in the Rockefeller Foundation/New England Cons. of Music Competition with his opera *Medea* (1978; Boston, May 3, 1979). As a composer, Luke has utilized various contemporary techniques in his works. Other dramatic works include the operas *Drowne's Wooden Image* (1994) and *Mrs. Bullfrog* (1994) and the ballet *Tapestry* (Oklahoma City, May 8, 1975).

Lukomska, Halina, Polish soprano; b. Suchedniów, May 29, 1929. She studied at the Warsaw Academy of Music (graduated, 1954), with Giorgio Favaretto at the Accademia Musicale Chigiana in Siena, and with Toti dal Monte in Venice. In 1956 she captured 1st prize in the 's-Hertogenbosch competition. From 1960 she pursued a concert career that took her all over the world. In 1973 she toured North America as a soloist with the Cleveland Orch. She became especially noted for her performances of contemporary music, including the most daunting of avant-garde scores.

Lully, Jean-Baptiste (originally, **Giovanni Battista Lulli**), celebrated Italian-born French composer; b. Florence, Nov. 28, 1632; d. Paris, March 22, 1687. The son of a poor Florentine miller, he learned to play the guitar at an early age. His talent for singing brought him to the attention of Roger de Lorraine, Chevalier de Guise, and he was taken to Paris in 1646 as a page to Mlle. d'Orléans, a young cousin of Louis XIV. He quickly adapted to the manner of the French court; although he mastered the language, he never lost his Italian accent. There is no truth in the report that he worked in the kitchens, but he did keep company with the domestic servants, and it was while he was serving in Mlle. d'Orléans's court in the Tuileries that he perfected his violin technique. He also had the opportunity to hear the 24 Violons du Roi and was present at performances of Luigi Rossi's *Orfeo* at the Louvre in 1647. When Mlle. d'Orléans suffered political disgrace in 1652 and was forced to leave Paris, Lully was released from her service, and early in 1653 he danced with the young Louis XIV in the ballet *La Nuit*. Shortly thereafter, he was made compositeur de la musique instrumentale du Roi, with joint responsibility for the instrumental music in court ballets. At some time before 1656 he became conductor of Les Petits Violons du Roi, a smaller offshoot of the grand bande. This ensemble was heard for the first time in 1656 in La Galanterie du temps. Thanks to Lully's strict discipline with regard to organization and interpretation, Les Petits Violons soon came to rival the parent ensemble. The 2 groups were combined in 1664.

Lully became a naturalized French citizen in 1661, the same year in which he was appointed surintendant de la musique et compositeur de la musique de la chambre; he also became maître de la musique de la famille royale in 1662. His association with Molière commenced in 1664; he provided Molière with the music for a series of comédies ballets, culminating with *Le Bourgeois Gentilhomme* in 1670. Lully acquired the sole right to form an Académie Royale de Musique in 1672, and thus gained the power to forbid performances of stage works by any other composer. From then until his death he produced a series of tragédies lyriques, most of which were composed to texts by the librettist Philippe Quinault. The subject matter for several of these works was suggested by the king, who was extravagantly praised and idealized in their prologues. Lully took great pains in perfecting these texts, but was often content to leave the writing of the inner voices of the music to his pupils. His monopoly of French musical life created much enmity. In 1674 Henri Guichard attempted to establish an Académie Royale des Spectacles, and their ensuing rivalry resulted in Lully accusing Guichard of trying to murder him by mixing arsenic with his snuff. Lully won the court case that followed, but the decision was reversed on appeal. A further setback occurred when Quinault was thought to have slandered the king's mistress in his text of *Isis* (1677) and was compelled to end his partnership with Lully in disgrace for some time. The king continued to support Lully, however, in spite of the fact that the composer's homosexuality had become a public scandal (homosexuality at the time was a capital offense). Lully's acquisition of titles culminated in 1681, when noble rank was conferred upon him with the title Secrétaire du Roi. In his last years he turned increasingly to sacred music. It was while he was conducting his *Te Deum* on Jan. 8, 1687, that he suffered a symbolic accident, striking his foot with a pointed cane used to pound out the beat. Gangrene set in, and he died of blood poisoning 2 months later.

Lully's historical importance rests primarily upon his music for the theater. He developed what became known as the French overture, with its 3 contrasting slow-fast-slow movements. He further replaced the Italian recitativo secco style with accompanied French recitative. Thus, through the Italian-born Lully, French opera came of age. A complete catalog of his works was ed. by H. Schneider (Tutzing, 1981).

WORKS: DRAMATIC: OPERAS (all are tragédies lyriques unless otherwise given): *Les Fêtes de l'Amour et de Bacchus*, pastorale pastiche (Opéra, Paris, Nov. 15, 1672); *Cadmus et Hermione* (Opéra, Paris, April 27, 1673); *Alceste, ou Le Triomphe d'Alcide* (Opéra, Paris, Jan. 19, 1674); *Thésée* (Saint-Germain, Jan. 12, 1675); *Atys* (Saint-Germain, Jan. 10, 1676); *Isis* (Saint-Germain, Jan. 5, 1677); *Psyché* (Opéra, Paris, April 19, 1678); *Bellérophon* (Opéra, Paris, Jan. 31, 1679); *Proserpine* (Saint-Germain, Feb. 3, 1680); *Persée* (Opéra, Paris, April 18, 1682); *Phaëton* (Versailles, Jan. 9, 1683); *Amadis* (Opéra, Paris, Jan. 18, 1684); *Roland* (Versailles, Jan. 8, 1685); *Armide* (Opéra, Paris, Feb. 15, 1686); *Acis et Galatée*, pastorale héroïque (Anet, Sept. 6, 1686); *Achille et Polyxène* (Opéra, Paris, Nov. 7, 1687; Overture and Act 1 by Lully; Prologue and Acts 2 to 5 by Collasse). BALLETS (all or most music by Lully): *Alcidiane* (Feb. 14, 1658); *La Raillerie* (Louvre, Paris, Feb. 19, 1659); *Xerxes* (Louvre, Paris, Nov. 22, 1660); *Ballet de Toulouze "au mariage du Roy"* (1660); *L'Impatience* (Tuileries, Paris, Feb. 14, 1661); *Les Saisons* (Fontainebleau, July 23, 1661); *Hercule amoureux* (Tuileries, Paris, Feb. 7, 1662); *Les Arts* (Palais Royal, Paris, Jan. 8, 1663); *Les Noces de village* (Vincennes, Oct. 3, 1663); *Les Amours déguisés* (Palais Royal, Paris, Feb. 13, 1664); 5 entrées for *Œdipe* (Fontainebleau, July 21, 1664); *La Naissance de Vénus* (Palais Royal, Paris, Jan. 26, 1665); *Les Gardes* (June 1665); *Ballet de Créquy ou Le Triomphe de Bacchus dans les Indes* (Hôtel de Créqui, Paris, Jan. 9, 1666); *Les Muses* (Saint-Germain, Dec. 2, 1666); *Le Carnaval ou Mascarade de Versailles* (Tuileries, Paris, Jan. 18, 1668); *Flore* (Tuileries, Paris, Feb. 13, 1669); *La Jeunesse* (1669); *Les Jeux pythiens* (Saint-Germain, Feb. 7, 1670); *Ballet des ballets* (Saint-Germain, Dec. 2, 1671); *Le Carnaval* (Opéra, Paris, Oct. 17, 1675); *Le Triomphe de l'amour* (Saint-Germain, Jan. 21, 1681); *Le Temple de la paix* (Fontainebleau, Oct. 20, 1685). BALLETS (music by Lully and others): *La Nuit* (Petit Bourbon, Paris, Feb. 23, 1653); *Les Proverbes* (Louvre, Paris, Feb. 17, 1654; music not extant); *Les Noces de Pelée et de Thétis* (Petit Bourbon, Paris, April 14, 1654); *Le Temps* (Louvre, Paris, Dec. 3, 1654); *Les Plaisirs* (Louvre, Paris, Feb. 4, 1655); *Les Bienvenus* (Compiègne, May 30, 1655; music not extant); *La Révente des habits de ballet* (1655?); *Psyché et la puissance de l'amour* (Louvre, Paris, Jan. 16, 1656; music not extant); *La Galanterie du temps* (Paris, Feb. 19, 1656); *L'Amour malade* (Louvre, Paris, Jan. 17, 1657); *Les Plaisirs trou-*

blés (Louvre, Paris, Feb. 11 or 12, 1657; music not extant); *Mascarade du capitaine* (Palais Royal, Paris, 1664; music not extant). OTHER DRAMATIC WORKS: *L'Impromptu de Versailles*, comedy (Versailles, Oct. 14, 1663); *Le Mariage forcé*, comedy (Louvre, Paris, Jan. 29, 1664); *Les Plaisirs de l'île enchantée*, comédie ballet (Versailles, May 7, 1664); *La Princesse d'Élide*, comédie ballet (Versailles, May 8, 1664); *L'Amour médecin*, comedy (Versailles, Sept. 16, 1665); *La Pastorale comique*, pastorale (Saint-Germain, Jan. 5, 1667); *Le Sicilien, ou L'Amour peintre*, comedy (Saint-Germain, Feb. 10, 1667); *Georges Dandin*, with *Grand divertissement royal de Versailles*, comedy (Versailles, July 18, 1668); *La Grotte de Versailles*, divertissement (Versailles, Aug. 1668); *Monsieur de Pourceaugnac*, comedy (Chambord, Oct. 6, 1669); *Les Amants magnifiques*, comédie ballet (Saint-Germain, Feb. 7, 1670); *Le Bourgeois Gentilhomme*, comédie ballet (Chambord, Oct. 14, 1670); *Psyché*, tragédie ballet (Tuileries, Paris, Jan. 17, 1671); *Idylle sur la paix*, divertissement (Sceaux, July 16, 1685).

BIBL.: H. Guichard, *Requête servant de factums contre B. L.* (Paris, 1673); T. Lajarte, *L.* (Paris, 1878); E. Radet, *L.: Homme d'affaires, propriétaire et musicien* (Paris, 1891); J. Écorcheville, *De L. à Rameau, 1690–1730* (Paris, 1906); H. Prunières, *L.* (Paris, 1909; 2d ed., 1927); L. de La Laurencie, *L.* (Paris, 1911; 2d ed., 1919); H. Prunières, *La Vie illustre et libertine de J.-B. L.* (Paris, 1929); E. Borrel, *J.-B. L.* (Paris, 1949); T. Valensi, *Louis XIV et L.* (Nice, 1952); M.-F. Christout, *Le Ballet de cour de Louis XIV, 1643–1673* (Paris, 1967); H. Ellis, *The Dances of J. B. L. (1632–1687)* (diss., Stanford Univ., 1967); L. Auld, *The Unity of Molière's Comedy-ballets* (diss., Bryn Mawr College, 1968); P. Howard, *The Operas of L.* (diss., Univ. of Surrey, 1974); H. Schneider, *Der Rezeption der L.-Oper im 17. und 18. Jahrhundert in Frankreich* (diss., Univ. of Mainz, 1976); J. Newman, *J.-B. de L. and His Tragédies lyriques* (Ann Arbor, 1979); C. Wood, *J.-B. L. and His Successors: Music and Drama in the "Tragédie en musique," 1673–1715* (diss., Univ. of Hull, 1981); H. Schneider, *Die Rezeption der Opern L.s im Frankreich des Ancien Regime* (Tutzing, 1982); J. Heyer, ed., *J.-B. L. and the Music of the French Baroque: Essays in Honour of James R. Anthony* (Cambridge, 1988); E. Haymann, *L.* (Paris, 1991); P. Beaussant, *L., ou, Le musicien du soleil* (Paris, 1992); M. Couvreur, *J.-B. L.: Musique et dramaturgie au service du Prince* (Brussels, 1992); C. Schmidt, *The livrets of J.-B. L.'s tragédies lyriques: A catalogue raisonné* (N.Y., 1995).

Lumbye, Hans Christian, famous Danish conductor and composer; b. Copenhagen, May 2, 1810; d. there, March 20, 1874. He played in military bands as a youth. In 1839 he formed his own orch. in Copenhagen, soon achieving fame as music director of the Tivoli Gardens there (1843–72). He composed about 400 pieces of dance music, including waltzes, galops, polkas, marches, etc., which earned him the sobriquet of "the Johann Strauss of the North." His 2 sons were also musicians; the elder, Carl (Christian) Lumbye (b. Copenhagen, July 9, 1841; d. there, Aug. 10, 1911), was a violinist, conductor, and composer of dance music; the younger, Georg (August) Lumbye (b. Copenhagen, Aug. 26, 1843; d. there, Oct. 29, 1922), was a conductor and composer; studied at the Paris Cons., then conducted in Copenhagen; wrote operettas, including *Heksefløtjen* (The Witch's Flute; 1869), incidental music, songs, etc.

BIBL.: G. Skjerne, *H. C. L. og hans Samtid* (Copenhagen, 1912; 2d ed., 1946).

Lundquist, Torbjörn Iwan, Swedish composer and conductor; b. Stockholm, Sept. 30, 1920. He received training in musicology at the Univ. of Uppsala, in composition from Wirén, and in conducting from Suitner in Salzburg and Vienna. He then was active as a conductor in Stockholm, and also appeared as a guest conductor throughout Europe. In 1978 he was awarded a government income to pursue composition. In his works, which include the operas *Sekund av evighet* (Moment of Eternity; 1971–74; Stockholm, May 27, 1974) and *Jason and Medea* (1985–89), Lundquist has utilized various styles and techniques, ranging from the traditional to the avant-garde, from jazz to Eastern music.

Lunn, Louise Kirkby. See **Kirkby-Lunn, Louise.**

Lunssens, Martin, Belgian conductor and composer; b. Molenbeek-Saint-Jean, April 16, 1871; d. Etterbeek, Feb. 1, 1944. He studied with Gevaert, Jehin, and Kufferath at the Brussels Cons., gaining the 1st Belgian Prix de Rome in 1895 with the cantata *Callirhoé*; he then became a prof. there. He subsequently was director of the Music Academy at Courtrai (1905–16), at Charleroi (1916–21), at the Louvain Cons. (1921–24), and finally at the Ghent Cons. (from 1924). He was also known as an excellent conductor; he was in charge of the Flemish Opera in Antwerp, where he conducted many Wagner operas. He composed numerous orch. and chamber pieces.

Luria, Juan (real name, **Johannes Lorie**), Polish baritone; b. Warsaw, Dec. 20, 1862; d. in the concentration camp in Auschwitz, 1942. He was a student of Gänsbacher in Vienna. In 1885 he made his operatic debut in Stuttgart. On Dec. 3, 1890, he made his Metropolitan Opera debut in New York as Nevers in *Les Huguenots*, singing there for a season. He subsequently pursued his career in Berlin, Milan, Vienna, Munich, Paris, and other European music centers. In 1893 he sang the role of Wotan at its first performance at Milan's La Scala. From 1914 he taught voice in Berlin. As a Jew, Luria left Germany under the Hitler regime in 1937 and made his way to Holland, where he taught at the conservatories in Amsterdam and The Hague. After the Nazis occupied Holland in 1939, he was unable to flee, and in 1942 was arrested and sent to the Auschwitz concentration camp. Luria was best known as a Wagnerian. He also sang in the premiere of Pfitzner's *Die Rose vom Liebesgarten* (1901).

Lussan, Zélie de, American soprano; b. Brooklyn, Dec. 21, 1862; d. London, Dec. 18, 1949. She was trained in singing by her mother, and made her first public appearance at Chickering Hall in New York (April 2, 1878). In 1885 she joined the Boston Ideal Opera Co., and then went to London, where she made her debut as Carmen with A. Harris's Italian Opera Co. at Covent Garden (July 7, 1888); she subsequently sang with the Carl Rosa Opera Co. and Mapleson's company. She sang Carmen again for her Metropolitan Opera debut in New York on Nov. 26, 1894; after that season, she was on its roster again from 1898 to 1900. She was particularly successful at Covent Garden (1890–93; 1895–1900; 1902–03; 1910). She was called upon to sing Carmen more than 1,000 times during her career; she was also a noted Cherubino, Zerlina, Mignon, and Nedda. Lussan was married to the pianist Angelo Fronani.

Lutyens, (Agnes) Elisabeth, important English composer; b. London, July 9, 1906; d. there, April 14, 1983. She was a daughter of the noted architect Sir Edwin Lutyens, and was brought up in an atmosphere of cultural enlightenment. She studied at the École Normale de Musique in Paris (1922–23) and with H. Darke at the Royal College of Music in London (1926–30). In her vivid autobiography, *A Goldfish Bowl* (London, 1972), she recounted her search for a congenial idiom of musical expression, beginning with the erstwhile fashionable Romantic manner and progressing toward a more individual, psychologically tense writing in an atonal technique using a sui generis dodecaphonic method of composition. In 1969 she was made a Commander of the Order of the British Empire. She was married to **Edward Clark**.

WORKS: DRAMATIC: *The Birthday of the Infanta*, ballet (1932); *The Pit*, dramatic scene for Tenor, Bass, Women's Chorus, and Orch. (Palermo, April 24, 1949); *Penelope*, radio opera (1950); *Infidelio*, chamber opera (1956; London, April 17, 1973); *The Numbered*, opera (1965–67); *Time Off? Not a Ghost of a Chance*, charade (1967–68; London, March 1, 1972); *Isis and Osiris*, lyric drama for 8 Voices and Chamber Orch. (1969); *The Linnet from the Leaf*, musical theater for 5 Singers and 2 Instrumental Groups (1972); *The Waiting Game*, 5 scenes for Mezzo-soprano, Baritone, and Chamber Orch. (1973); *One and the Same*, scena for Soprano, Speaker, and Mimes (1973); *The Goldfish Bowl*, ballad opera (1975); *Like a Window*, extracts from letters of van Gogh (1976).

BIBL.: M. and S. Harries, *A Pilgrim Soul: The Life and Work of E. L.* (London, 1989).

Lutz, (Wilhelm) Meyer, German-born English organist, conductor, and composer; b. Männerstadt, near Kissingen, 1822; d. London, Jan. 31, 1903. He studied music with his father, an organist, and later at Würzburg. In 1848 he settled in England, where he played organ in various churches in Birmingham, Leeds, and London. He conducted theater music in London from 1851, and in 1869 was appointed music director at the Gaiety Theatre, for which he wrote numerous light operas, of which the following were successful: *Faust and Marguerite* (May 16, 1855), *Blonde or Brunette* (May 19, 1862), *Zaida* (1868), *The Miller of Milburg* (April 13, 1872), and *Legend of the Lys* (1873). His popular dance *Pas de quatre* is from the burlesque *Faust Up to Date* (Oct. 30, 1888).

Lux, Friedrich, German conductor and composer; b. Ruhla, Nov. 24, 1820; d. Mainz, July 9, 1895. He studied with his father, a cantor at Ruhla, and at 12 gave an organ concert at Gotha. He then studied with F. Schneider at Dessau, where he remained as music director at the Court Theater (1841–50). From 1851 to 1877 he was conductor at the City Theater in Mainz; from 1867 he also conducted the Oratorio Soc. there. His works include the operas *Das Käthchen von Heilbronn* (Dessau, March 23, 1846), *Der Schmied von Ruhla* (Mainz, March 28, 1882), and *Die Fürstin von Athen* (Frankfurt am Main, 1890). He also publ. transcriptions of Beethoven's syms. (except the 9th) for piano, 4-hands.

BIBL.: A. Reissmann, *F. L.: Sein Leben und seine Werke* (Leipzig, 1888).

Luxon, Benjamin, esteemed English baritone; b. Redruth, March 24, 1937. He studied with Walter Grünner at the Guildhall School of Music in London, then joined the English Opera Group, with which he sang Sid in *Albert Herring* and Tarquinius in *The Rape of Lucretia* on its tour of the Soviet Union (1963). He was chosen by Britten to create the title role in the opera *Owen Wingrave* (BBC-TV, May 16, 1971); he then made his debut at London's Covent Garden as Monteverdi's Ulysses (1972), and subsequently sang there regularly; he also appeared at the festivals in Aldeburgh, Edinburgh, and Glyndebourne (from 1972), and with the English National Opera in London (from 1974). On Feb. 2, 1980, he made his Metropolitan Opera debut in New York as Eugene Onegin. In 1986 he made his first appearance at Milan's La Scala. In 1988 he sang Wozzeck in Los Angeles. In 1992 he appeared as Falstaff at the English National Opera. His last years as a singer were aggravated by increasing deafness. His other roles included Count Almaviva, Don Giovanni, Papageno, Wolfram, and Eisenstein. He also distinguished himself as a concert artist, his repertoire ranging from the standard literature to folk songs. In 1986 he was made a Commander of the Order of the British Empire.

Luzzi, Luigi, Italian composer; b. Olevano di Lomellina, March 28, 1828; d. Stradella, Feb. 23, 1876. He studied medicine at Turin, but later entered the musical profession. He wrote successful songs, as well as an opera, *Tripilla* (Novara, Feb. 7, 1874).

Lvov, Alexei Feodorovich, Russian violinist and composer; b. Reval, June 5, 1798; d. Romano, near Kovno, Dec. 28, 1870. He was the son of the director of the Imperial Court Chapel Choir in St. Petersburg. He received his primary education at home, then attended the Inst. of Road Engineering (graduated in 1818); at the same time he studied violin. In 1827 he was sent to the Turkish front in Bulgaria, then was attached to the court. He wrote the national anthem "God Save the Czar" in 1833, which was first performed in Moscow on the name day of Czar Nicholas I, on Dec. 6 (O.S.; 18 N.S.), 1833; it remained the official anthem until the Revolution of 1917. In 1837 he succeeded his father as director of the St. Petersburg Imperial Court Chapel Choir, remaining there until 1861; in 1839 he organized instrumental classes there. He ed. a collection of services for the entire ecclesiastical year of the Greek Orthodox Church. In 1840 he traveled in Europe; he played his Violin Concerto with the Gewandhaus Orch. in Leipzig (Nov. 8, 1840); Schumann greatly praised his playing. Returning to Russia, he established a series of orch. concerts in St. Petersburg, presenting classical programs. Growing deafness forced him to abandon his activities in 1867. As a composer, he slavishly followed the Italian school. His works include the operas *Bianca und Gaultiero* (Dresden, Oct. 13, 1844), *Ondine* (in Russian; St. Petersburg, Sept. 20, 1847), and *Starosta Boris, or The Russian Muzhik and the French Marauders* (in Russian; St. Petersburg, May 1, 1854).

Lybbert, Donald, American composer and teacher; b. Cresco, Iowa, Feb. 19, 1923; d. Norwalk, Conn., July 26, 1981. He studied at the Univ. of Iowa (B.M., 1946), with Ward and Wagenaar at the Juilliard School of Music in New York (1946–48), with Carter and Luening at Columbia Univ. (M.A., 1950), and with Boulanger in Fontainebleau (1961). From 1954 to 1980 he taught at Hunter College of the City Univ. of N.Y. With F. Davis, he wrote *The Essentials of Counterpoint* (1969). His music was freely atonal for the most part, although he utilized serial procedures in some of his scores. Among his dramatic works are *Monica*, operetta (Amsterdam, Nov. 2, 1952), and *The Scarlet Letter*, opera (1964–67).

Lynn, George, American choral conductor, organist, teacher, and composer; b. Edwardsville, Pa., Oct. 5, 1915; d. Colorado Springs, Colo., March 16, 1989. He was a student of Weinrich (organ), Williamson (conducting), and Harris (composition) at Westminster Choir College in Princeton, N.J. (B.Mus., 1938) and of Thompson (composition) at Princeton Univ. (M.F.A., 1947). He was active as an organist and music director in various churches in New Jersey, California, Pennsylvania, Colorado, and North Carolina. Lynn served as prof. of choral arts at Westminster Choir College (1946–50) and at the Univ. of Colo. (1950–52). From 1963 to 1969 he was music director of the Westminster Choir. In 1971 he was visiting composer-in-residence at the Univ. of New Mexico. He subsequently was prof. of choral arts at the Colorado School of Mines (1971–80), Loretto Heights College (1971–86), and Rice Univ. (1986–87). Lynn composed in a tonal idiom with a strong modal character. Rhythmic variation was indicative of his style and provided a firm foundation for his long melodic lines. Among his works are the operas *The Violinden Tree* (1960) and *From Time to Time* (1962).

M

Maag, (Ernst) Peter (Johannes), eminent Swiss conductor; b. St. Gallen, May 10, 1919. His father, Otto Maag, was the Lutheran minister, philosopher, musicologist, and critic; his mother was a violinist and a member of the Capet Quartet. He attended the univs. of Zürich, Basel, and Geneva, where his principal mentors were Karl Barth and Emil Brunner in theology and Karl Jaspers in philosophy. He also studied piano and theory with Czeslaw Marek in Zürich, and then pursued his training in piano with Cortot in Paris. His conducting mentors were Hoesslin and Ansermet in Geneva. He later profited greatly as an assistant to Furtwängler. He began his career as répétiteur at the Biel-Solothurn theater, where he then served as music director (1943–46). From 1952 to 1955 he held the title of 1st conductor at the Düsseldorf Opera. He was Generalmusikdirektor of the Bonn City Theater from 1955 to 1959. In 1958 he made his first appearance at London's Covent Garden. In 1959 he made his U.S. debut as guest conductor of the Cincinnati Sym. Orch. He was chief conductor of the Vienna Volksoper from 1964 to 1968. On Sept. 23, 1972, he made his Metropolitan Opera debut in New York conducting *Don Giovanni.* He was artistic director of the Teatro Regio in Parma from 1972 to 1974 and of the Teatro Regio in Turin from 1974 to 1976. Thereafter he continued to appear frequently in Italy while continuing to make guest appearances with orchs. and opera houses in Europe, North and South America, and Japan. From 1984 to 1991 he was music director of the Bern Sym. Orch. Maag is particularly esteemed for his remarkable interpretations of the music of Mozart, and also for his efforts to revive forgotten works of the past.

Maas, Joseph, English tenor; b. Dartford, Kent, Jan. 30, 1847; d. London, Jan. 15, 1886. He was a chorister at Rochester Cathedral, where he studied with the organist J. L. Hopkin, and then completed his training with Bodda-Pyne in London and San Giovanni in Milan. In 1871 he made his debut in a concert with Henry Leslie's Choir in London. His operatic debut followed in 1872 as Babil in Dion Boucicault's *Babil and Bijou* at London's Covent Garden. After touring the United States with Clara Kellogg's English Opera Co., he returned to England in 1878 and became principal tenor of the Carl Rosa Opera Co. He was the first to sing the role of Rienzi in England in 1879, and in 1883 he appeared as Lohengrin at Covent Garden. Maas was also active as a concert and oratorio singer. Among his other operatic roles were Des Grieux and Radames.

Ma'ayani, Ami, Israeli composer; b. Ramat-Gan, Jan. 13, 1936. He studied at the New Jerusalem Academy of Music (1951–53), with Ben-Haim (1956–60), and with Ussachevsky at Columbia Univ. in New York (1961–62; 1964–65); he also studied architecture at the Israel Inst. of Technology (B.Sc., 1960) and philosophy at the Univ. of Tel Aviv (M.A., 1973). He composed *The War of the Sons of Light,* opera oratorio (1970–72), and *A Legend of 3 and 4,* ballet (1978).

Maazel, Lorin (Varencove), brilliant American conductor; b. Neuilly, France (of American parents), March 6, 1930. His parents took him to Los Angeles when he was an infant. At a very early age, he showed innate musical ability; he had perfect pitch and could assimilate music osmotically; he began to study violin at age 5 with Karl Moldrem, and then piano at age 7 with Fanchon Armitage. Fascinated by the art of conducting, he went to sym. concerts and soon began to take lessons in conducting with Vladimir Bakaleinikov, who was an assoc. conductor of the Los Angeles Phil.; on July 13, 1938, at the age of 8, he was given a chance to conduct a performance of Schubert's *Unfinished Symphony* with the visiting Univ. of Idaho orch. In 1938 Bakaleinikov was appointed assistant conductor of the Pittsburgh Sym. Orch., and the Maazel family followed him to Pittsburgh. From Bakaleinikov, Maazel quickly learned to speak Russian. On Aug. 18, 1939, he made a sensational appearance in New York conducting the National Music Camp Orch. of Interlochen at the World's Fair, eliciting the inevitable jocular comments (he was compared to a trained seal). Maazel was only 11 when he conducted the NBC Sym. Orch. (1941) and 12 when he led an entire program with the N.Y. Phil. (1942). He survived these traumatic exhibitions, and took academic courses at the Univ. of Pittsburgh. In 1948 he joined the Pittsburgh Sym. Orch. as a violinist, and at the same time was appointed its apprentice conductor. In 1951 he received a Fulbright fellowship for travel in Italy, where he undertook a serious study of Baroque music; he also made his adult debut as a conductor in Catania on Dec. 23, 1953. In 1955 he conducted at the Florence May Festival, in 1957 at the Vienna Festival, and in 1958 at the Edinburgh Festival. In 1960 he became the first American to conduct at the Bayreuth Festival, where he led performances of *Lohengrin*. In 1962 he toured the United States with the Orchestre National de France. On Nov. 1, 1962, he made his Metropolitan Opera debut in New York conducting *Don Giovanni*. From 1965 to 1971 he was artistic director of the Deutsche Oper in West Berlin; from 1965 to 1975 he also served as chief conductor of the (West) Berlin Radio Sym. Orch. He was assoc. principal conductor of the New Philharmonia Orch. of London from 1970 to 1972, and its principal guest conductor from 1976 to 1980. In 1972 he became music director of the Cleveland Orch., a position he held with great distinction until 1982; he was then made conductor emeritus. He led the Cleveland Orch. on 10 major tours abroad, including Australia and New Zealand (1973), Japan (1974), twice in Latin America, and twice in Europe, and maintained its stature as one of the world's foremost orchs. He was also chief conductor of the Orchestre National de France from 1977 to 1982; he then was its principal guest conductor until 1988, and its music director until 1991. In 1980 he became conductor of the famous Vienna Phil. New Year's Day Concerts, a position he retained until 1986. In 1982 he assumed the positions of artistic director and general manager of the Vienna State Opera, the first American to be so honored; however, he resigned these positions in the middle of his 4-year contract in 1984 after a conflict over artistic policies with the Ministry of Culture. He then served as music consultant to the Pittsburgh Sym. Orch. (1984–86); he was its music adviser and principal guest conductor in 1986, becoming its music director that same year. In 1993 he also assumed the post of chief conductor of the Bavarian Radio Sym. Orch. in Munich. In 1994 he again conducted the Vienna Phil. New Year's Day Concert. In 1996 he stepped down as music director of the Pittsburgh Sym. Orch. after a notably distinguished tenure.

Maazel is equally adept as an interpreter of operatic and symphonic scores; he is blessed with a phenomenal memory, and possesses an extraordinary baton technique. He also has composed several scores. He maintains an avid interest in nonmusical pursuits; a polyglot, he is fluent in French, German, Italian, Spanish, Portuguese, and Russian. Maazel was the recipient of many awards; he received an honorary doctorate from the Univ. of Pittsburgh in 1965, the Sibelius Prize in Finland, the Commander's Cross of the Order of Merit from West Germany, and, for his numerous recordings, the Grand Prix de Disque in Paris and the Edison Prize in the Netherlands.

Mabellini, Teodulo, Italian conductor and composer; b. Pistoia, April 2, 1817; d. Florence, March 10, 1897. He studied with Pillotti and Gherardeschi in Pistoia, then was a student at Florence's Istituto Reale Musicale (1833–36). At the age of 19, he produced there an opera, *Matilda a Toledo* (Aug. 27, 1836), which made so favorable an impression that Grand Duke Leopold II gave him a stipend to study with Mercadante at Novara. His 2d opera, *Rolla* (Turin, Nov. 12, 1840), was no less successful; thereupon he wrote many more operas, among them *Ginevra degli Almieri* (Turin, Nov. 13, 1841), *Il Conte di Lavagna* (Florence, June 4, 1843), *I Veneziani a Costantinopoli* (Rome, 1844), *Maria di Francia* (Florence, March 14, 1846), *Il venturiero* (Livorno, Carnival 1851; in collaboration with L. Gordigiani), *Il convito di Baldassare* (Florence, Nov. 1852), and *Fiammetta* (Florence, Feb. 12, 1857). He also wrote several effective oratorios and cantatas: *Eudossia e Paolo* (Florence, 1845), *Etruria* (Florence, Aug. 5, 1849), and *Lo spirito di Dante* (Florence, May 15, 1865). He lived in Florence from 1843 until his death. He conducted the concerts of the Società Filarmonica (1843–59) and taught composition at the Istituto Reale Musicale (1859–87).

BIBL.: M. Giannini, *M. e la musica* (Pistoia, 1899); A. Simonatti, *T. M.* (Pistoia, 1923).

MacArdle, Donald Wales, American musicologist; b. Quincy, Mass., July 3, 1897; d. Littleton, Colo., Dec. 23, 1964. He studied science at the Mass. Inst. of Technology, obtaining an M.S. in chemical engineering; he also took courses at the Juilliard School of Music in New York, and studied musicology at N.Y. Univ. Although he earned his living as an engineer, he devoted much time to scholarly research, mainly to the minutiae of Beethoven's biography; he contributed a number of valuable articles on the subject to the *Musical Quarterly* and other journals. He ed., with L. Misch, *New Beethoven Letters* (Norman, Okla., 1957); he ed. and tr. Schindler's *Biographie von Ludwig van Beethoven*, 3d ed., 1860, as *Beethoven as I Knew Him* (London and Chapel Hill, 1966); he also prepared *An Index to Beethoven's Conversation Books* (Detroit, 1962) and, with S. Pogodda, *Beethoven Abstracts* (Detroit, 1973).

Macbeth, Florence, American soprano; b. Mankato, Minn., Jan. 12, 1891; d. Hyattsville, Md., May 5, 1966. She studied in New York and Paris. In 1913 she made her operatic debut as Rosina in *Il Barbiere di Siviglia* in Braunschweig. On Jan. 14, 1914, she made her American debut with the Chicago Opera Co. and remained on its staff as prima coloratura soprano until 1930; for a season she undertook an American tour with the Commonwealth Opera Co., singing in Gilbert and Sullivan operettas. So melodious and mellifluous were her fiorituras that she was dubbed the "Minnesota Nightingale." In 1947 she married the novelist James M. Cain and settled in Maryland.

MacCunn, Hamish (James), Scottish composer, conductor, and teacher; b. Greenock, March 22, 1868; d. London, Aug. 2, 1916. He won a composition scholarship to the Royal College of Music in London when he was 15, and studied there with Parry, Stanford, and Franklin Taylor (until 1886). He remained in London and served as prof. of harmony at the Royal Academy of Music (1888–94). He also taught composition privately and later at the Guildhall School of Music (from 1912). From 1898 he was also active as a theater conductor. After working with the Carl Rosa Opera Co. and the Moody-Manners Co., he served as principal conductor of the Savoy Theatre (1902–05). Thereafter he conducted at various theaters, and in 1910 and 1915 he was a conductor with the Beecham Opera Co. MacCunn's most important work was the opera *Jeanie Deans* (Edinburgh, Nov. 15, 1894), after Scott's *The Heart of Midlothian*. His other dramatic works include *Diarmid*, opera (London, Oct. 23, 1897), *Breast of Light* (n.d.; unfinished), *The Masque of War and Peace*, masque (London, Feb. 13, 1900), *The Golden Girl*, light opera (Birmingham, Aug. 5, 1905), *Prue*, light opera (n.d.; unfinished), *The Pageant of Darkness and Light*, stage pageant (1908), and *The Sailor and the Nursemaid*, light opera (London, June 27, 1912). He remains best known, however, for the overture "The Land of the Mountain and the Flood" (London, Nov. 5, 1887).

Macdonald, Hugh (John), distinguished English musicologist; b. Newbury, Berkshire, Jan. 31, 1940. He was educated at Pembroke College, Cambridge (B.A., 1961; M.A., 1965; Ph.D., 1969). In 1966 he became a lecturer at the Univ. of Cambridge, then at the Univ. of Oxford in 1971; in 1979 he was a visiting prof. at Indiana Univ. in Bloomington; in 1980 he was named Gardiner Prof. of Music at the Univ. of Glasgow, then was a prof. at Washington Univ. in St. Louis (from 1987). His special field of interest is 19th-century music; he is particularly noted for his studies in French music, and is a leading authority on the life and works of Berlioz; in 1965 he became general ed. of the *New Berlioz Edition*. He publ. *Berlioz: Orchestral Music* (London, 1969), *Skryabin* (London, 1978), and *Berlioz* (London, 1982). He also ed. *Berlioz: Selected Letters* (1995).

MacDonald, Jeanette (Anna), American soprano; b. Philadelphia, June 18, 1903; d. Houston, Jan. 14, 1965. She started a career as a chorus girl and model in New York (1920) and unexpectedly won encomia for her starring role in the musical *The Magic Ring* (1923). She then attained wide recognition as a singing actress via 29 films, especially those in which she paired with Nelson Eddy:

Naughty Marietta (1935), *Rose Marie* (1936), *Maytime* (1937), *The Girl of the Golden West* (1938), *Sweethearts* (1939), *New Moon* (1940), *Bittersweet* (1940), and *I Married an Angel* (1942). She made a belated operatic debut as Juliette in Montreal (May 1944); she also sang in Chicago, but her voice was too small to meet the demands of the large opera halls.

BIBL.: S. Rich, *J. M.: A Pictorial Biography* (Los Angeles, 1973); E. Knowles, *Films of J. M. and Nelson Eddy* (South Brunswick, N.J., 1975); J. Parish, *The J. M. Story* (N.Y., 1976); L. Stern, *J. M.* (N.Y., 1977).

Macfarren, Sir George (Alexander), eminent English composer and pedagogue; b. London, March 2, 1813; d. there, Oct. 31, 1887. He began his studies with his father, George Macfarren, who was a dancing master and dramatist, and with Charles Lucas, then studied composition with C. Potter at the Royal Academy of Music in London (1829–36), where he was a tutor (1834–37), later a prof. (1837–47; 1851–75), and still later its principal (1875–87). He was also a prof. of music at Univ. of Cambridge (1875–87). He was knighted in 1883. Macferren suffered from eye problems from the age of 10. He became totally blind in 1860, but continued to compose by dictating to an amanuensis. He had the great satisfaction of having his early overture *Chevy Chace* performed by Mendelssohn in Leipzig (1843) and by Wagner in London (1855). Macfarren's greatest ambition was to write an opera that would reflect the spirit of England, as the operas of Weber were redolent of the mythical lyricism of German folklore, but he signally failed in this endeavor. His 9 syms. enjoyed transient favor, but attempts at their revival foundered in time. His wife, Natalia Macfarren (née Clarina Thalia Andrae; b. Lübeck, Dec. 14, 1826; d. Bakewell, April 9, 1916), was a singer; she studied with Macfarren and dutifully sang in his operas. She publ. a *Vocal Method and an Elementary Course of Vocalising and Pronouncing the English Language*. His brother, Walter (Cecil) Macfarren (b. London, Aug. 28, 1826; d. there, Sept. 2, 1905), was a pianist and composer.

WORKS: DRAMATIC: OPERAS: *The Prince of Modena* (1833); *El Malhechor* (1837–38); *The Devil's Opera* (London, Aug. 13, 1838); *An Adventure of Don Quixote* (London, Feb. 3, 1846); *King Charles II* (London, Oct. 27, 1849); *Allan of Aberfeldy* (c.1850); *Robin Hood* (London, Oct. 11, 1860); *Jessy Lea*, opera di camera (London, Nov. 2, 1863); *She Stoops to Conquer* (London, Feb. 11, 1864); *The Soldier's Legacy*, opera di camera (London, July 10, 1864); *Helvellyn* (London, Nov. 3, 1864); *Kenilworth* (1880); other stage works. ORATORIOS AND CANTATAS: *The Sleeper Awakened* (London, Nov. 15, 1850); *Lenora* (London, April 25, 1853); *Christmas* (London, May 9, 1860); *St. John the Baptist* (Bristol, Oct. 23, 1873); *The Resurrection* (Birmingham, 1876); *Joseph* (Leeds, 1877); *King David* (Leeds, 1883).

BIBL.: H. Banister, *G. A. M.: His Life, Works and Influence* (London, 1891).

McGegan, Nicholas, English keyboard player, flutist, and conductor; b. Sawbridgeworth, Hertfordshire, Jan. 14, 1950. He studied piano at London's Trinity College of Music (1968) and also learned to play the flute, specializing in the Baroque flute; pursued his education at Corpus Christi College, Cambridge (B.A., 1972), and at Magdalen College, Oxford (M.A., 1976). He was active as a flutist, harpsichordist, fortepianist, and pianist in London, where he was also a prof. of Baroque flute (1973–79) and music history (1975–79) and director of early music (1976–80) at the Royal College of Music. From 1979 to 1984 he was artist-in-residence at Washington Univ. in St. Louis, then became music director of the Philharmonia Baroque Orch. in San Francisco (1985), the Ojai (Calif.) Festival (1988), and the Göttingen Handel Festival (1991). From 1993 to 1995 he was principal conductor of the Drottningholm Court Theater in Stockholm. He also appeared widely in Europe and North America as a guest conductor.

M'Guckin, Barton, Irish tenor; b. Dublin, July 28, 1852; d. Stoke Poges, Buckinghamshire, April 17, 1913. After serving as a choirboy at Armagh Cathedral, he went to Dublin to pursue vocal training and to sing at St. Patrick's Cathedral. In 1874 he made his concert debut in Dublin, and then sang in London in 1875. Following further vocal studies in Milan, he made his operatic debut with the Carl Rosa Opera Co. in Birmingham in 1878, remaining with it until 1887. After touring the United States (1887–88), he returned to England and once more sang with the Carl Rosa Opera Co. (1889–96). In addition to his roles in English operas, M'Guckin was especially admired for his portrayals of Des Grieux, which he introduced to English audiences, and of Wilhelm Meister and Don José.

Mácha, Otmar, Czech composer; b. Ostrava, Oct. 2, 1922. He studied with Hradil (1941–42); then at the Prague Cons. (1943–45), where he subsequently attended Řídký's master class (1945–48). He was active with the Czech Radio (1945–62); then devoted himself to composing; was awarded the State Prize in 1967 and was made a Merited Artist by the Czech government in 1982.

WORKS: DRAMATIC: *Polapená nevěra* (Entrapped Faithlessness), opera (1956–57; Prague, Nov. 21, 1958); *Jezero Ukereve* (Lake Ukereve), opera (1960–63; Prague, May 27, 1966); *Růže pro Johanku (Panichyda za statečné)* (Rose for Jeanne [Homage to the Brave]), dramatic musical fantasy (1971–74); *Svatba na oko* (Feigned Wedding), comic opera (1974–77); *Kolébka pro hříšné panny* (Cradle for Sinful Maidens), musical comedy (1975–76); film scores.

Machabey, Armand, French musicologist; b. Pont-de-Roide, Doubs, May 7, 1886; d. Paris, Aug. 31, 1966. He studied with d'Indy and Pirro; he received his doctorat ès lettres from the Univ. of Paris in 1928 with the diss. *Essai sur les formules usuelles de la musique occidentale (des origines à la fin du XVe siècle)*, publ. in a rev. ed., Paris, 1955, as *Genèse de la tonalité musicale classique*. He was subsequently active as a music historian and essayist; also was one of the eds. of *Larousse de la musique* (Paris, 1957).

WRITINGS (all publ. in Paris unless otherwise given): *Sommaire de la méthode en musicologie* (1930); *Le théâtre musicale en France* (1933); *Précis-manuel d'histoire de la musique* (1942; 2d ed., 1947); *La musique des Hittites* (Liège, 1945); *La Vie et l'oeuvre d'Anton Bruckner* (1945); *Maurice Ravel* (1947); *Traité de la critique musicale* (1947); *Le "bel canto"* (1948); *Portraits de trente compositeurs français* (1950); *Gerolamo Frescobaldi Ferrarensis (1583–1643)* (1952); *La Musique et la médicine* (1952); *La Notation musicale* (1952; 3d ed., rev., 1971 by M. Huglo); *Guillaume de Machaut: La Vie et l'oeuvre musicale* (1955); *Le cantillation manichéene: Notation hypothétique, métrique analogies* (1956); *Notations musicales non modales des XIIe et XIIIe siècle* (1957; 3d ed., aug., 1959); *Problèmes de notation musicale* (1958); *Mélanges musicologiques d'Aristoxène à Hucbald* (1960); *La Musicologie* (1962; 2d ed., 1969); *Embryologie de la musique occidentale* (1963); *La Musique de danse* (1966).

Machado, Augusto (de Oliveira), Portuguese composer; b. Lisbon, Dec. 27, 1845; d. there, March 26, 1924. He was a pupil of Junior, Lami, and D'Almeide in Lisbon, and of Lavignac and Danhauser in Paris. From 1892 to 1908 he was director of the San Carlos Theater in Lisbon; he also taught singing at the Cons. (from 1893), serving as its director (1901–10). Besides numerous operettas, he wrote the operas *A Cruz de oiro* (Lisbon, 1873), *A Maria da Fonte* (Lisbon, 1879), *Lauriane* (Marseilles, Jan. 9, 1883; his most successful work), *Os Dorias* (Lisbon, 1887), *Mario Wetter* (Lisbon, 1898), *Venere* (Lisbon, 1905), and *La Borghesina* (Lisbon, 1909). For the 3d centenary of the death of Camoëns, he wrote the symphonic ode *Camões es os Luziadas* (1880).

Machavariani, Alexei (Davidovich), Russian composer; b. Gory, Sept. 23, 1913. He studied at the Tbilisi Cons., graduating in 1936; he then was on its faculty as a teacher of theory (1940–63) and as a prof. of composition (from 1963). He was made a People's Artist of the USSR in 1958. His music is profoundly infused with Caucasian melorhythms. Among his works are the operas *Deda da shvili* (Mother and Son; 1944; Tbilisi, May 1, 1945) and *Hamlet* (1964) and the ballets *Otello* (1957) and *Knight in a Tiger's Skin* (1965); also *The Day of My Fatherland*, oratorio (1954).

Machlis, Joseph, Latvian-born American writer on music and pedagogue; b. Riga, Aug. 11, 1906; d. N.Y., Oct. 17, 1998. He was taken to the United States as an infant. He studied at the College of the City Univ. of N.Y. (B.A., 1927), and at the Inst. of Musical Art (teacher's diploma, 1927); he also took an M.A. in English literature from Columbia Univ. (1938). He was on the music faculty of Queens College of the City Univ. of N.Y. (1938–74), then on the graduate faculty at the Juilliard School (from 1976). He made English trs. of a number of opera librettos; he publ. several well-written texts: the immensely popular *The Enjoyment of Music* (N.Y., 1955; 7th ed., rev., 1995); *Introduction to Contemporary Music* (N.Y., 1961; 2d ed., 1979); *American Composers of Our Time* (N.Y., 1963); *Getting to Know Music* (N.Y., 1966). He also publ. 5 novels.

Machover, Tod, American cellist, conductor, and composer; b. N.Y., Nov. 24, 1953. He studied composition at the Univ. of Calif. at Santa Cruz (1971–73), Columbia Univ. (1973–74), and the Juilliard School in New York (B.M., 1975; M.M., 1977); among his mentors were Dallapiccola (1973), Sessions (1973–75), and Carter (1975–78); he also studied computer music at the Mass. Inst. of Technology and at Stanford Univ. He was 1st cellist in the orch. of the National Opera of Canada in Toronto (1975–76), guest composer (1978–79) and director of musical research (1980–85) at IRCAM in Paris, and a teacher at the Mass. Inst. of Technology (from 1985), where he also was director of its Experimental Media Facility (from 1986). He ed. the books *Le Compositeur et l'Ordinateur* (Paris, 1981) and *Musical Thought at IRCAM* (London, 1984), and was the author of *Quoi, Quand, Comment? La Recherche Musical* (Paris, 1985; Eng. tr., 1988, as *The Concept of Musical Research*) and *Microcomputers and Music* (N.Y., 1988). Among his honors were the Koussevitzky Prize (1984) and the Friedheim Award (1987). Among his works are the operas *Valis* (Paris, Dec. 2, 1987), *Brain Opera* (N.Y., July 25, 1996), and *Resurrection* (Houston, April 23, 1999).

Macintyre, Margaret, English soprano; b. in India, c.1865; d. London, April 1943. She was a pupil of García in London. In 1885 she made her operatic debut as Mozart's Countess at St. George's Hall in London, and then sang there at Covent Garden (1888–97). She also made appearances in Milan, St. Petersburg, and Moscow. Among her other roles were Donna Elvira, Elisabeth, Senta, and Sieglinde. She also created the role of Rebecca in Sullivan's *Ivanhoe* (1891).

Mackenzie, Sir Alexander (Campbell), distinguished Scottish conductor, educator, and composer; b. Edinburgh, Aug. 22, 1847; d. London, April 28, 1935. A scion of a musical family (there were 4 generations of musicians in his paternal line), he showed musical aptitude as a child. He was sent to Germany, where he studied violin with K. W. Ulrich and theory with Eduard Stein at the Schwarzburg-Sondershausen Realschule (1857–62); returning to England, he studied violin with Sainton, piano with Jewson, and music theory with Charles Lucas at the Royal Academy of Music in London. He subsequently was active in Edinburgh as a violinist and teacher (1865–79). Between 1879 and 1885 he lived in Florence. In 1888 he was elected principal of the Royal Academy of Music in London, holding this post until 1924. From 1892 to 1899 he conducted the concerts of the Phil. Soc. of London. His reputation as an educator and composer was very high among musicians. He was knighted in 1895. As a composer, he was a staunch believer in programmatic music; he introduced national Scottish elements in many of his works; Paderewski gave the first performance of his Scottish Concerto with the Phil. Soc. of London (1897). In 1922 he was made a Knight Commander of the Royal Victorian Order.

WORKS (all 1st perf. in London unless otherwise given): DRAMATIC: OPERAS: *Colomba* (April 9, 1883; rev. version, Dec. 3, 1912); *The Troubadour* (June 8, 1886); *Phoebe*, comic opera (n.d.; not perf.); *His Majesty, or The Court of Vingolia*, comic opera (Feb. 20, 1897); *The Cricket on the Hearth* (1900; June 6, 1914); *The Knights of the Road*, operetta (Feb. 27, 1905); incidental music to plays. ORATORIOS: *The Rose of Sharon* (Norwich Festival, Oct. 16, 1884; rev. 1910); *Bethlehem* (1894; also known as *The Holy Babe*); *The Temptation* (1914).

Mackerras, Sir (Alan) Charles (MacLaurin), eminent American-born Australian conductor; b. Schenectady, N.Y. (of Australian parents), Nov. 17, 1925. He was taken to Sydney, Australia, as an infant; he studied oboe, piano, and composition at the New South Wales State Conservatorium of Music; then was principal oboist in the Sydney Sym. Orch. (1943–46). He subsequently went to London, where he joined the orch. at Sadler's Wells and studied conducting with Michael Mudie; he won a British Council Scholarship in 1947, which enabled him to study conducting with Václav Talich at the Prague Academy of Music. Returning to London in 1948, he was an assistant conductor at Sadler's Wells until 1953; he then was engaged as principal conductor of the BBC Concert Orch. (1954–56); subsequently he appeared as a guest conductor with British orchs. and also had engagements on the Continent. In 1963 he made his debut at London's Covent Garden conducting Shostakovich's *Katerina Izmailova*. From 1966 to 1970 he held the post of 1st conductor at the Hamburg State Opera. In 1970 he became music director at the Sadler's Wells Opera (renamed the English National Opera in 1974), a position he held until 1978. On Oct. 31, 1972, he made his Metropolitan Opera debut in New York conducting Gluck's *Orfeo et Euridice*. From 1976 to 1979 he was chief guest conductor of the BBC Sym. Orch. in London. After serving as chief conductor of the Sydney (Australia) Sym. Orch. (1982–85), he was artistic director of the Welsh National Opera in Cardiff (1987–92). He was principal guest conductor of the Scottish Chamber Orch. in Glasgow (from 1992), of the Royal Phil. in London (from 1993), and of the San Francisco Opera (from 1993). In 1998 he became music director of the Orch. of St. Luke's in New York. He was made a Commander of the Order of the British Empire in 1974, and was knighted in 1979. Mackerras has distinguished himself as an opera conductor by championing the works of Janáček. He has also conducted operas by Handel, Gluck, and J. C. Bach. He likewise is a discriminating interpreter of the orch. repertoire.

BIBL.: N. Phelan, *C. M.: A Musicians' Musician* (London, 1987).

Maclean, Alick (Alexander Morvaren), English composer and conductor; b. Eton, near Windsor, July 20, 1872; d. London, May 18, 1936. His father was the English organist, editor, and composer Alick (Alexander Morvaren) Maclean (b. Cambridge, March 27, 1843; d. London, June 23, 1916). He studied with Joseph Barnby. In 1899 he became music director to Charles Wyndham and in 1911 to the Spa Co. in Scarborough. From 1915 to 1923 he also was a conductor at Chappell's and led the Ballard Concerts at the Queen's Hall in London.

WORKS: DRAMATIC: OPERAS: *Quentin Durward* (1892; Newcastle upon Tyne, Jan. 13, 1920); *Petruccio* (London, June 29, 1895); *The King's Price* (London, April 29, 1904); *Die Liebesgeige* (Mainz, April 15, 1906); *Maître Seiler* (London, Aug. 20, 1909); *Waldidyll* (Mainz, March 23, 1913). OTHER: *The Annunciation*, oratorio (London, 1909).

MacMillan, Sir Ernest (Alexander Campbell), eminent Canadian conductor and composer; b. Mimico, Aug. 18, 1893; d. Toronto, May 6, 1973. He began organ studies with Arthur Blakeley in Toronto at age 8, making his public debut at 10; he continued organ studies with A. Hollins in Edinburgh (1905–08), where he was also admitted to the classes of F. Niecks and W. B. Ross at the Univ. He was made an assoc. (1907) and a fellow (1911) of London's Royal College of Organists, and received the extramural B.Mus. degree from the Univ. of Oxford (1911). He studied modern history at the Univ. of Toronto (1911–14) before receiving piano instruction from Therese Chaigneau in Paris (1914). In 1914 he attended the Bayreuth Festival, only to be interned as an enemy alien at the outbreak of World War I; while being held at the Ruhleben camp near Berlin, he gained experience as a conductor; he was awarded the B.A. degree in absentia by the Univ. of Toronto (1915); his ode, *England*, submitted through the Prisoners of War Education Committee to the Univ. of Oxford, won him his D.Mus. degree (1918). After his release, he returned to Toronto as organist and choirmaster of Timothy Eaton Memorial Church (1919–25). He joined the staff of the Canadian Academy of Music (1920) and remained with it when it became the Toronto Cons. of Music, serving as its principal (1926–42); he was also dean of the music faculty at the Univ. of Toronto (1927–52). He was conductor of the Toronto Sym. Orch. (1931–56) and of the Mendelssohn Choir there (1942–57); he also appeared as guest conductor in North and South America, Europe, and Australia. He served as president of the Canadian Music Council (1947–66) and of the Canadian Music Centre (1959–70). In 1935 he was the first Canadian musician to be knighted, an honor conferred upon him by King George V; he also received honorary doctorates from Canadian and U.S. institutions. He conducted many works new to his homeland, both traditional and contemporary. Among his own compositions are *Snow White*, opera (1907), and *Prince Charming*, ballad opera (1931).

BIBL.: E. Schabas, *Sir E. M.: The Importance of Being Canadian* (Toronto, 1994).

MacMillan, James, Scottish composer and teacher; b. Kilwinning, July 16, 1959. He was a student of Rita McAllister at the Univ. of Edinburgh (1977–81) and then pursued postgraduate studies in composition with Casken at the Univ. of Durham (Ph.D., 1987). He was a lecturer in music at the Univ. of Manchester (1986–88). In 1989 he served as composer-in-residence of the St. Magnus Festival in Orkney. In 1990 he became affiliate composer of the Scottish Chamber Orch. in Glasgow and a teacher at the Royal Scottish Academy of Music and Drama there. In 1991 he was a visiting composer of the Philharmonia Orch. in London. He developed an accessible style of composition that found inspiration in his Roman Catholic faith and Scottish nationalism. His compositions include *Búsqueda*, music theater (Edinburgh, Dec. 6, 1988), *Tourist Variations*, chamber opera (1991), *Inés de Castro*, opera (1992–93; Edinburgh, Aug. 23, 1996), and *Visitatio Sepulchri*, music theater (1992–93; Glasgow, May 20, 1993).

MacNeil, Cornell, noted American baritone; b. Minneapolis, Sept. 24, 1922. While working as a machinist, he appeared on the radio as an actor and sang minor parts on Broadway. He then was a scholarship student of Friedrich Schorr at the Hartt College of Music in Hartford, Conn., and also studied with Virgilio Lazzari and Dick Marzollo in New York and with Luigi Ricci in Rome. On March 1, 1950, he made his professional operatic debut as Sorel in the premiere of Menotti's *The Consul* in Philadelphia. On April 4, 1953, he made his N.Y. City Opera debut as Tonio, and subsequently appeared there regularly. He first sang opera in San Francisco as Escamillo in 1955 and in Chicago as Puccini's Lescaut in 1957. On March 5, 1959, he made his debut at Milan's La Scala as Don Carlo in *Ernani*. On March 21, 1959, he made his Metropolitan Opera debut in New York as Rigoletto, and remained on its roster until 1987. He became particularly successful there in Verdi roles, excelling as Amonasro, Germont, Luna, Iago, and Nabucco. In 1964 he made his debut at London's Covent Garden as Macbeth. His other guest engagements took him to Vienna, Rome, Paris, Geneva, Florence, and other European operatic centers. In addition to his Verdi portrayals, he also had success as Barnaba in *La Gioconda*, the Dutchman in Wagner's opera, and as Scarpia. In the later years of his career, he became well known for his verismo roles.

Maconchy, Dame Elizabeth, significant English composer of Irish descent, mother of **Nicola LeFanu;** b. Broxbourne, Hertfordshire, March 19, 1907; d. Norwich, Nov. 11, 1994. She studied composition with Charles Wood and Vaughan Williams, and counterpoint with C. H. Kitson at the Royal College of Music in London (from 1923); she then pursued further training with Jirák in Prague (1929–30). Returning to England, she devoted herself to composition. She also served as chairman of the Composers Guild of Great Britain (1959–60) and as president of the Soc. for Promotion of New Music (from 1977). In 1977 she was made a Commander and in 1987 a Dame Commander of the Order of the British Empire. Maconchy developed a style peculiarly her own: tonally tense, contrapuntally dissonant, and coloristically sharp in instrumentation.

WORKS: DRAMATIC: *Great Agrippa*, ballet (1933); *The Little Red Shoes*, ballet (1935); *Puck Fair*, ballet (1940); *The Sofa*, opera (1956–57; London, Dec. 13, 1959); *The 3 Strangers*, opera (1958–67; Bishop's Stortford College, June 5, 1968); *The Departure*, opera (1960–61; London, Dec. 16, 1962); *Witnesses*, incidental music (1966); *The Birds*, opera (1967–68; Stortford College, June 5, 1968); *Johnny and the Mohawks*, children's opera (1969; London, March 1970); *The Jesse Tree*, church opera (1969–70; Dorchester Abbey, Oct. 7, 1970); *The King of the Golden River*, opera (Oxford, Oct. 29, 1975).

Macurdy, John, American bass; b. Detroit, March 18, 1929. He studied engineering at Wayne State Univ. in Detroit, and then voice with Avery Crew and Boris Goldovsky. In 1952 he made his operatic debut in New Orleans in *Samson et Dalila*. After singing in Santa Fe, Houston, and Baltimore, he became a member of the N.Y. City Opera in 1959. On Dec. 8, 1962, he made his Metropolitan Opera debut in New York as Tom in *Un ballo in maschera*, and subsequently appeared there regularly. He also sang with other U.S. opera companies, including those of San Francisco and Chicago. In 1973 he appeared as Debussy's Arkel at the Paris Opéra, in 1974 as Beethoven's Pizzaro at Milan's La Scala, and in 1977 as Mozart's Commendatore at the Salzburg Festival. As a concert artist, he was engaged by many orchs. Among his other roles were Sarastro, Hagen, King Marke, Rocco, Pogner, Sparafucile, and Gounod's Méphistophélès.

Madeira, Jean (née **Browning**), American mezzo-soprano; b. Centralia, Ill., Nov. 14, 1918; d. Providence, R.I., July 10, 1972. She studied piano with her mother; at the age of 12, she was piano soloist with the St. Louis Sym. Orch. She took vocal lessons in St. Louis, then studied both piano and voice at the Juilliard School of Music in New York. In 1943 she made her operatic debut as Nancy in *Martha* in Chautauqua, N.Y. In 1948 she joined the Metropolitan Opera in New York, where she sang minor roles. She went to Europe, where she first gained notice as Carmen in Vienna, Aix-en-Provence, and Munich in 1955; she also sang Erda at her Covent Garden debut in London that same year. She then returned to the Metropolitan, where she appeared as Carmen on March 17, 1956; she remained on the Metropolitan's roster until 1971. Her European tours included appearances at the Vienna State Opera, the Bavarian State Opera in Munich, Milan's La Scala, the Paris Opéra, and Bayreuth. She married the conductor, pianist, and composer Francis Madeira (b. Jenkintown, Pa., Feb. 21, 1917) in 1957.

Maderna, Bruno, outstanding Italian-born German conductor, composer, and teacher; b. Venice, April 21, 1920; d. Darmstadt, Nov. 13, 1973. He commenced musical studies at 4, and soon took violin lessons; began touring as a violinist and conductor when he was only 7, appearing under the name Brunetto in Italy and abroad. He studied at the Verdi Cons. in Milan, with Bustini at the Rome Cons. (diploma in composition, 1940), and with Malipiero at the Venice Cons.; he also took a conducting course with Guarnieri at the Accademia Musicale Chigiana in Siena (1941). He then served in the Italian army during World War II, eventually joining the partisan forces against the Fascists. After the war, he studied conducting with Scherchen in Darmstadt. He taught composition at the Venice Cons. (1947–50); he then made his formal conducting debut in Munich (1950). He subsequently became a great champion of the avant-garde; with Berio, he helped to form the Studio di Fonologia in Milan (1954); also with Berio, he was conductor of the RAI's Incontri Musicali (1956–60). He taught conducting and composition in various venues, including Darmstadt (from 1954), the Salzburg Mozarteum (1967–70), the Rotterdam Cons. (from 1967), and the Berkshire Music Center in Tanglewood (1971–72). He was chief conductor of the RAI in Milan from 1971. In 1963 he became a naturalized German citizen. Stricken with cancer, he continued to conduct concerts as long as it was physically possible. He was held in great esteem by composers of the international avant-garde, several of whom wrote special works for him.

WORKS: DRAMATIC: *Don Perlimplin*, radio opera, after García Lorca (1961; RAI, Aug. 12, 1962); *Hyperion*, "lirica in forma di spettacolo" (Venice, Sept. 6, 1964; a composite of *Dimensioni III, Aria de Hyperion*, and tape); *Von A bis Z*, opera (1969; Darmstadt, Feb. 22, 1970); *Oedipe-Roi*, electronic ballet (Monte Carlo, Dec. 31, 1970); *Satyrikon*, opera after Petronius (1972; Scheveningen, the Netherlands, March 16, 1973).

BIBL.: M. Baroni and R. Dalmonte, eds., *B. M.: Documenti* (Milan, 1985); R. Fearn, *B. M.* (Chur and N.Y., 1990).

Madetoja, Leevi (Antti), outstanding Finnish composer; b. Oulu, Feb. 17, 1887; d. Helsinki, Oct. 6, 1947. He was educated at the Univ. of Helsinki (M.A., 1910) and studied composition with Sibelius at the Helsinki Music Inst. (diploma, 1910); he then took courses with d'Indy in Paris (1910–11) and R. Fuchs in Vienna (1911–12) and in Berlin. After serving as deputy conductor of the Helsinki Phil. (1912–14) and as conductor of the Vyborg Music Soc. Orch. (1914–16), he taught at the Helsinki Music Inst. (1916–38); he was also music critic of the *Helsingen Sanomat* (1916–32); he became a lecturer in music at the Univ. of Helsinki (1928). In 1917 he founded the Finnish Musicians' Assn., with which he remained involved until his death. He was awarded a state composer's pension in 1919. He was one of Finland's leading composers; his music for the stage and his symphonic works are particularly notable. He composed the operas *Pohjalaisia* (The Bothnians; 1923; Helsinki, Oct. 25, 1924) and *Juha* (1934; Feb. 17, 1935) and the ballet pantomime *Okon-Fuoko* (Feb. 12, 1930).

BIBL.: K. Tuukkanen, *L. M.* (Helsinki, 1947); *L. M.: Teokset—Works* (1982); K. Karjalainen, *L. M. oopperat Pohjalaisia ja Juha: Teokset, tekstit ja kontekstit* (Helsinki, 1993).

Maes, Jef, Belgian composer; b. Antwerp, April 5, 1905; d. there, June 30, 1996. He studied with N. Distelmans (viola), L. Mortelmans (chamber music), and Karl Candael (harmony, counterpoint, and fugue) at Antwerp's Royal Flemish Cons. of Music. He was a violist in several orchs. in Antwerp; he became a teacher of viola (1932) and director (1952) of the Boom Academy of Music; from 1942 to 1970 he was on the faculty of the Royal Flemish Cons. In his compositions, he continued the traditions of the Belgian national school. His works include *Marise*, opera buffa (1946), *De antikwaar* (The Antique Dealer), television opera (1959; Antwerp TV, March 1963), and *Tu auras nom . . . Tristan*, ballet (1960; Geneva, June 1963; orch. suite, 1963–64).

Maganini, Quinto, American flutist, conductor, arranger, and composer; b. Fairfield, Calif., Nov. 30, 1897; d. Greenwich, Conn., March 10, 1974. He played flute in the San Francisco Sym. (1917–19) and in the N.Y. Sym. (1919–28). He studied flute with Barrère in New York and composition with Boulanger at the American Cons. in Fontainebleau. In 1928–29 he held a Guggenheim fellowship. In 1930 he became conductor of the N.Y. Sinfonietta. In 1932 he organized his own orch., the Maganini Chamber Sym., with which he toured widely. From 1939 to 1970 he was conductor of the Norwalk (Conn.) Sym. Orch. His compositions include *Tennessee's Partner*, opera (WOR Radio, N.Y., May 28, 1942).

Mager, Jörg, German music theorist and pioneer in electronic music; b. Eichstätt, Nov. 6, 1880; d. Aschaffenburg, April 5, 1939. After completing his univ. studies, he became interested in electronic reproduction of sounds; he constructed several instruments capable of producing microtonal intervals by electronic means, which he named Sphärophon, Elektrophon, and Partiturophon; he was also active in visual music for film. He publ. *Vierteltonmusik* (Aschaffenburg, 1916) and *Eine neue Epoche der Musik durch Radio* (Berlin, 1924).

Magini-Coletti, Antonio, Italian baritone; b. Iesi, near Ancona, 1855; d. Rome, July 7, 1912. He launched his career in 1880, and subsequently appeared in various Italian operatic centers, including Milan and Rome. On Dec. 14, 1891, he made his Metropolitan Opera debut in New York as Capulet in *Roméo et Juliette*, singing there until 1892. In subsequent years, he pursued his career in Europe. Among his other roles were Nevers and Amonasro.

Magne, Michel, French composer; b. Lisieux, March 20, 1930; d. (suicide) Cergy-Pontase, Val d'Oise, Dec. 19, 1984. He was mainly self-taught, beginning to compose as a very young man in an ultramodern style; he later took lessons with Plé-Caussade. His film score *Le Pain vivant* (1955) received critical acclaim; he also experimented with electronic music; on May 26, 1955, he conducted in Paris his *Symphonie humaine* for 150 Performers, making use of inaudible "infrasounds" to produce a physiological reaction by powerful low frequencies. He wrote the musical score for Françoise Sagan's ballet *Le Rendez-vous manqué* (1957) and many film scores.

Magnard, (Lucien-Denis-Gabriel-) Albéric, distinguished French composer; b. Paris, June 9, 1865; d. (killed by German soldiers at his home) Baron, Oise, Sept. 3, 1914. He was reared in an intellectual family of means; his father was ed. of *Le Figaro*. He studied with Dubois and Massenet at the Paris Cons. (1886–88; premier prix in harmony, 1888) and with d'Indy (1888–92), and then subsequently taught counterpoint at the Schola Cantorum. He was killed while defending his property during the early days of World War I. He was a composer of high attainments, and his mastery of orchestration was incontestable, but none of his music found a permanent place in the repertoire. His works include the operas *Yolande* (1888–91; Brussels, Dec. 27, 1892), *Guercoeur* (1897–1900; rev. by Guy-Ropartz; Paris, April 24, 1931), and *Bérénice* (1905–09; Paris, Dec. 15, 1911).

BIBL.: M. Boucher, *A. M.* (Lyons, 1919); G. Carrauld, *La Vie, l'oeuvre et la mort d'A. M.* (Paris, 1921); B. Bardet, *A. M., 1865–1914* (Paris, 1966).

Magomayev, (Abdul) Muslim, Azerbaijani conductor and composer; b. Shusha, Sept. 18, 1885; d. Baku, July 28, 1937. He studied at the Gori teachers' seminary (1899–1904); learned to play violin and clarinet, and taught at Lenkoran College (1905–11). He then settled in Baku as an orch. player, conductor, and teacher at the Azerbaijani Theater; he later was associated with the National Commissariat of Enlightenment, becoming artistic director and conductor of the musical theater (1924) and was music director of the Azerbaijani Radio (from 1929). The first version of his opera *Shah Ismail* (1916; Baku, 1919) was mainly made up of improvised songs and dialogue; he later revised it with notated improvisatory sections and added recitatives (1920–23; 1930–32). His second opera, *Nergiz* (1934; Baku, Jan. 1, 1936), was fully notated. He also wrote orch. pieces, incidental music, film scores, and numerous arrangements of folk songs and dances.

BIBL.: G. Ismailova, *M. M.* (Baku, 1975).

Mahler, Gustav, great Austrian composer and conductor; b. Kalischt, Bohemia, July 7, 1860; d. Vienna, May 18, 1911. He attended school in Iglau. In 1875 he entered the Vienna Cons., where he studied piano with Julius Epstein, harmony with Robert Fuchs, and composition with Franz Krenn. He also took academic courses in history and philosophy at the Univ. of Vienna (1877–80). In the summer of 1880 he received his first engagement as a conductor, at the operetta theater in the town of Hall in Upper Austria; subsequently he held posts as theater conductor at Ljubljana (1881), Olmütz (1882), Vienna (1883), and Kassel (1883–85). In 1885 he served as 2d Kapellmeister to Anton Seidl at the Prague Opera, where he gave several performances of Wagner's operas. From 1886 to 1888 he was assistant to Arthur Nikisch in Leipzig. In 1888 he received the important appointment of music director of the Royal Opera in Budapest. In 1891 he was engaged as conductor at the Hamburg Opera; during his tenure there he developed a consummate technique for conducting. In 1897 he received a tentative offer as music director of the Vienna Court Opera, but there was an obstacle to overcome. Mahler was Jewish, and although there was no overt anti-Semitism in the Austrian government, an imperial appointment could not be given to a Jew. Mahler was never orthodox in his religion, and had no difficulty in converting to Catholicism, which was the prevailing faith in Austria. He held this position at the Vienna Court Opera for 10 years; under his guidance, it reached the highest standards of artistic excellence. In 1898 Mahler was engaged to succeed Hans Richter as conductor of the Vienna Phil. Here, as in his direction of opera, he proved a great interpreter, but he also allowed himself considerable freedom in rearranging the orchestration of classical scores when he felt it would redound to greater effect. He also aroused antagonism among the players by his autocratic behavior. He resigned from the Vienna Phil. in 1901, and in 1907 also from the Vienna Court Opera. It was in the latter year that he was diagnosed as suffering from a lesion of the heart. In the meantime, he became immersed in strenuous work as a composer; he confined himself exclusively to composition of symphonic music, sometimes with vocal parts; because of his busy schedule as conductor, he could compose only in the summer months, in a villa on the Worthersee in Carinthia. In 1902 he married Alma Schindler; they had 2 daughters. The younger daughter, Anna Mahler, was briefly married to Ernst Krenek; the elder daughter died in infancy.

Having exhausted his opportunities in Vienna, Mahler accepted the post of principal conductor of the Metropolitan Opera in New York in 1907. He made his American debut there on Jan. 1, 1908, conducting *Tristan und Isolde*. In 1909 he was appointed conductor of the N.Y. Phil. His performances both at the Metropolitan and with the N.Y. Phil. were enormously successful with audiences and N.Y. music critics, but inevitably he had conflicts with the board of trustees in both organizations, which were mostly commanded by rich women. He resigned from the Metropolitan Opera in 1910. The N.Y. newspapers publ. lurid accounts of his struggle for artistic command with the regimen of the women of the governing committee. Alma Mahler was quoted as saying that although in Vienna even the emperor did not dare to order Mahler about, in New York he had to submit to the whims of 10 ignorant women. On Feb. 21, 1911, he conducted his last concert with the N.Y. Phil. and then returned to Vienna. He died shortly thereafter, at the lamentable age of 50, of a severe bacterial infection.

The newspaper editorials mourned Mahler's death, but sadly noted that his N.Y. tenure was a failure. As to Mahler's own compositions, the *N.Y. Tribune* said bluntly, "We cannot see how any of his music can long survive him." His syms. were sharply condemned in the press as being too long, too loud, and too discordant. It was not until the second half of the 20th century that Mahler became fully recognized as a composer, the last great Romantic symphonist. Mahler's syms. were drawn on the grandest scale, and the technical means employed for the realization of his ideas were correspondingly elaborate. The sources of his inspiration were twofold: the lofty concepts of universal art, akin to those of Bruckner, and ultimately stemming from Wagner; and the simple folk melos. of the Austrian countryside, in pastoral moods recalling the intimate episodes in Beethoven's syms. Mahler was not an innovator in his harmonic writing; rather, he brought the Romantic era to a culmination by virtue of the expansiveness of his emotional expression and the grandiose design of his musical structures. Morbid by nature, he brooded upon the inevitability of death; one of his most poignant compositions was the cycle for voice and orch. *Kindertotenlieder*; he wrote it shortly before the death of his little daughter, and somehow blamed himself for this seeming anticipation of his personal tragedy. In 1910 he consulted Sigmund Freud in Leiden, Holland, but the treatment was brief and apparently did not help Mahler to resolve his psychological problems. Unquestionably, he suffered from an irrational feeling of guilt. In the 3d movement of his unfinished 10th Sym., significantly titled *Purgatorio*, he wrote in the margin, "Madness seizes me, annihilates me," and appealed to the devil to take possession of his soul. But he never was clinically insane.

Mahler's importance to the evolution of modern music is very great; the early works of Schoenberg and Berg show the influence of Mahler's concepts. A society was formed in the United States in 1941 "to develop in the public an appreciation of the music of Bruckner, Mahler and other moderns." An International Gustav Mahler Soc. was formed in Vienna in 1955, with Bruno Walter as honorary president. On Mahler's centennial, July 7, 1960, the government of Austria issued a memorial postage stamp of 1 1/2 shillings, with Mahler's portrait. His 2d cousin was Fritz Mahler (b. Vienna, July 16, 1901; d. Winston-Salem, N.C., June 18, 1973), the Austrian conductor and composer.

BIBL.: L. Schiedermair, *G. M.* (Leipzig, 1901); R. Specht, *G. M.* (Berlin, 1913); G. Adler, *G. M.* (Vienna, 1916); H. Redlich, *G. M.: Eine Erkenntnis* (Nuremberg, 1919); A. Roller, *Die Bildnisse G. M.s* (Leipzig, 1922); N. Bauer-Lechner, *Erinnerungen an G. M.* (Vienna, 1923); A. Mahler, *Briefe G. M.s* (Berlin, 1924); W. Hutschenruyter, *G. M.* (The Hague, 1927); G. Engel, *G. M.* (Vienna, 1936; Eng. tr., N.Y., 1957); A. Mahler, *G. M.: Erinnerungen und Briefe* (Amsterdam, 1940; Eng. tr., London, 1946); B. Walter (with E. Krenek), *G. M.* (N.Y., 1941); D. Newlin, *Bruckner-M.-Schoenberg* (N.Y., 1947; 2d ed., rev., 1978); N. Loeser, *G. M.* (Haarlem, 1950); H. Redlich, *Bruckner and M.* (London, 1955; 2d ed., rev., 1963); D. Mitchell, *G. M.: I: The Early Years* (London, 1958; rev. 1980), *G. M.: II: The Wunderhorn Years* (Boulder, Colo., 1976), and *G. M.: III: Songs and Symphonies of Life and Death* (London, 1985); W. Reich, ed., *G. M.: Im eigenen Wort, im Wort der Freunde* (Zürich, 1958); T. Adorno, *M.: Eine musikalische Physiognomik* (Frankfurt am Main, 1960); S. Vestdijk, *G. M.* (The Hague, 1960); N. Cardus, *G. M.: His Mind and His Music* (London, 1965); H. Kralik, *G. M.* (Vienna, 1968); K. Blaukopf, *G. M., oder Zeitgenosse der Zukunft* (Vienna, 1969); H.-L. de La Grange, *G. M.: Chronique d'une vie* (3 vols., Paris, 1973–84; also in Eng.); D. Holbrook, *G. M. and the Courage to Be* (N.Y., 1975); K. Blaukopf, ed., *M.: A Documentary Study* (N.Y., 1976; rev. and enl. ed, 1991, as *M.: His Life, Work and World*); A. Shelley, ed., *G. M. in Vienna* (N.Y., 1976); C. Floros, *G. M.* (3 vols., Wiesbaden, 1977–85); P. Ruzicka, *M.: Eine Herausforderung* (Wiesbaden, 1977); E. Gartenberg, *M.: The Man and His Music* (N.Y., 1978); E. Reilly, *G. M. und Guido Adler: Zur Geschichte einer Freundschaft* (Vienna, 1978; Eng. tr., Cambridge, 1982); B. and E. Vondenhoff, *G. M. Dokumentation* (Tutzing, 1978); D. Cooke, *G. M.: An Introduction to His Music* (London, 1980); H. Eggebrecht, *Die Musik G. M.s* (Munich, 1982); E. Seckerson, *M.: His Life and Times* (N.Y., 1982); H. Blaukopf, ed., and E. Jephcott, tr., *G. M.—Richard Strauss: Correspondence 1888–1911* (London, 1984); D. Greene, *M.: Consciousness and Temporality* (N.Y., 1984); H. Lea, *G. M.: Man on the Margin* (Bonn, 1985); H. Danuser, *G. M.: Das Lied von der Erde* (Munich, 1986); H. Blaukopf, ed., *M.'s Unknown Letters* (Boston, 1987); S. Namenwirth, *G. M.: A Critical Bibliography* (3 vols., Wiesbaden, 1987); K.-J. Müller, *M.: Leben, Werke, Dokumente* (Mainz, 1988); S. Filler, *G. and Alma M.: A Guide to Research* (N.Y., 1989); Z. Roman, *G. M.'s American Years 1907–1911: A Documentary History* (Stuyvesant, N.Y., 1989); H. Danuser, *G. M. und seine Zeit* (Laaber, 1991); H. Danuser, ed., *G. M.* (Darmstadt, 1992); F. Berger, *G. M.: Vision und Mythos: Versuch einer geistigen Biographie* (Stuttgart, 1993); F. Willnauer, *G. M. und die Wiener Oper* (Vienna, 1993); P. Reed, ed., *On M. and Britten: Essays in Honour of Donald Mitchell on his Seventieth Birthday* (Woodbridge, Suffolk, 1995); P. Franklin, *The Life of M.* (Cambridge, 1997); S. Hefling, ed., *M. Studies* (Cambridge, 1997).

Maiboroda, Georgi, Ukrainian composer; b. Pelekhovshchina, near Poltava, Dec. 1, 1913. He studied at the Kiev Cons. with Revutsky, graduating in 1941; from 1952 he taught there. His music tends toward heroically patriotic themes according to the precepts of socialist realism. Among his works are the operas *Milana* (1957), *The Arsenal* (1960), *Taras Shevchenko* (1964), and *Yaroslav the Wise* (1975).

BIBL.: O. Zinkevich, *G. M.* (Kiev, 1973).

Maikl, Georg, Austrian tenor; b. Zell, April 4, 1872; d. Vienna, Aug. 22, 1951. After vocal training in Vienna, he made his operatic debut as Tamino at the Mannheim National Theater in 1899, singing there until 1904. From 1904 to 1944 he was a principal member of the Vienna Court (later State) Opera, where he was particularly noted for his roles in operas by Mozart and Wagner. He also sang in the premiere there of the rev. version of Strauss's *Ariadne auf Naxos* (1916). As a guest artist, he appeared in Salzburg (1906, 1910, 1937). Maikl gave his farewell performance in Pfitzner's *Palestrina* in 1950.

Maillart, Aimé (Louis), French composer; b. Montepellier, March 24, 1817; d. Moulins-sur-Allier, May 26, 1871. He studied at the Paris Cons. with Halévy and Leborne (composition) and with Guérin (violin), winning the Grand Prix de Rome in 1841. He composed the operas (all 1st perf. in Paris) *Gastibelza ou Le Fou de Tolède* (Nov. 15, 1847), *Le Moulin des tilleuls* (1849), *La Croix de Marie* (1852), *Les Dragons de Villars* (Sept. 19, 1856), *Les Pêcheurs de Catane* (Dec. 19, 1860), and *Lara* (March 21, 1864).

Mailman, Martin, American composer, conductor, and teacher; b. N.Y., June 30, 1932. He studied composition with Mennini, Barlow, Rogers, and Hanson at the Eastman School of Music in Rochester, N.Y. (B.M., 1954; M.M., 1955; Ph.D., 1960). He taught at the U.S. Naval School of Music during his naval service (1955–57); after teaching at the Eastman School of Music (1958–59), he was composer-in-residence of Jacksonville, Fla., under a Ford Foundation grant (1959–61). During the summers of 1960–61 and 1983, he taught at the Brevard Music Center; from 1961 to 1966 he was composer-in-residence and prof. of music at East Carolina College; he also taught at West Virginia Univ. (summer 1963). In 1966 he joined the faculty of North Texas State Univ. (later the Univ. of North Texas) in Denton, where he served as Regents Prof. of Music (from 1987) and as composer-in-residence (from 1990). He was active as a guest conductor, composer, and lecturer at more than 80 colleges and univs. In 1982 he won the Queen Marie-Jose Prize for Composition for his Violin Concerto and an NEA grant; in 1983 he received the American Bandmasters Assn./NABIM Award for his *Exaltations* for Band (1981); in 1989 he won the National Band Assn./Band Mans Award and the American Bandmasters Assn./Ostwald Award for his *For Precious Friends Hid in Death's Dateless Night* for Wind Ensemble (1988). Among his numerous other works is the opera *The Hunted* (Rochester, N.Y., April 27, 1959); also *Mirrors*, multimedia theater piece (1986).

Mainzer, Joseph, German singing teacher and musical journalist; b. Trier, Oct. 21, 1801; d. Salford, Lancashire, Nov. 10, 1851. He was a chorister at the Trier Cathedral, then studied music in Darmstadt, Munich, and Vienna. Returning to Trier, he was ordained a priest (1826); taught at the seminary there, and publ. a sight-singing method, *Singschule* (1831). He then abandoned the priesthood. He moved to Brussels (1833), and then to Paris (1834), where he started the short-lived *Chronique Musicale de Paris* (1838). In 1841 he went to London. In 1844 he began publication of the monthly *Mainzer's Musical Times and Singing Circular*, which in 1846 became the enduring *Musical Times*. In 1847 he settled in Manchester as a singing teacher. He mastered the English language to such an extent that he was able to engage in aggressive musical journalism. His methods of self-advertising were quite uninhibited; he arranged singing courses in open-air gatherings, and had pamphlets printed with flamboyant accounts of receptions tendered him.

WRITINGS: *Singschule* (Trier, 1831); *Méthode de chant pour les enfants* (Paris, 1835); *Méthode de chant pour voix d'hommes* (Paris, 1836); *Bibliothèque élémentaire de chant* (Paris, 1836); *Méthode pratique de piano pour enfants* (Paris, 1837); *Abécédaire de chant* (Paris, 1837); *École chorale* (Paris, 1838); *Esquisses musicales, ou Souvenirs de voyage* (Paris, 1838–39); *Cent mélodies enfantines* (Paris, 1840); *Singing for the Million* (London, 1841); *The Musical Athenaeum* (London, 1841); *Music and Education* (London and Edinburgh, 1848).

Mair, Franz, Austrian conductor and composer; b. Weikersdorf, March 15, 1821; d. Vienna, Nov. 14, 1893. He was founder-conductor of the Vienna Schubertbund (1883). He composed music to *Die Jungfrau von Orleans* and other theatrical productions. His reminiscences were publ. as *Aus meinem Leben* (Vienna, 1897).

Maison, René, Belgian tenor; b. Frameries, Nov. 24, 1895; d. Mont-Dore, France, July 15, 1962. He was trained at the Brussels Cons. and the Paris Cons. After making his operatic debut as Rodolfo in *La Bohème* in 1920, he sang in Nice and Monte Carlo. From 1925 he sang in Paris at the Opéra and the Opéra Comique, establishing a reputation as a Wagnerian. He also appeared at the Chicago Opera (1927–32) and the Teatro Colón in Buenos Aires (1934–37). On Feb. 3, 1936, he made his Metropolitan Opera debut in New York as Walther von Stolzing, and remained on its roster until 1943. He later taught voice in New York and Boston. Among his prominent roles were Lohengrin, Loge, Florestan, Samson, Herodes, and Don José.

Maizel, Boris, significant Russian composer; b. St. Petersburg, July 17, 1907; d. Moscow, July 9, 1986. He graduated from the Leningrad Cons. in 1936 in the composition class of Riazanov. During the siege of Leningrad by the Germans in 1942, he was evacuated to Sverdlovsk; in 1944 he settled in Moscow. Among his works are *Snow Queen*, ballet (1940; orch. suite, 1944), *Sombrero*, children's ballet (1959), and *The Shadow of the Past*, opera (1964); also film music.

Majo, Gian Francesco (de), Italian organist and composer, son of **Giuseppe de Majo**, known as **Ciccio di Majo**; b. Naples, March 24, 1732; d. there, Nov. 17, 1770. He received his primary training from his father, and also studied with his uncle Gennaro Manno and his great-uncle Francesco Feo. He was his father's assistant as organista soprannumerario at the royal chapel, being made its 2d organist by 1758. His first opera, *Ricimero re dei Goti* (Parma, 1758), scored a great success in Rome in 1759; his next opera, *Astrea placata* (Naples, June 29, 1760), established his reputation as a composer for the theater. After further studies with Padre Martini (1761–63), he went to Vienna to produce his opera *Alcide negli orti Esperidi* (June 7, 1764) for the coronation of the emperor of the Holy Roman Empire, Joseph II. He then toured widely, returning to his birthplace the year of his death.

WORKS: DRAMATIC: OPERAS: *Ricimero re dei Goti* (Parma, 1758); *Astrea placata* (Naples, June 29, 1760); *Cajo Fabricio* (Naples, Nov. 29, 1760); *L'Almeria* (Livorno, 1761); *Artaserse* (Venice, Jan. 30, 1762); *Catone in Utica* (Turin, Dec. 26, 1762); *Demofoonte* (Rome, Carnival 1764); *Alcide negli orti Esperidi* (Vienna, June 7, 1764); *Ifigenia in Tauride* (Mannheim, Nov. 4, 1764); *Montezuma* (Turin, Carnival 1765); *La constancia dichosa* (Madrid, 1765); *Alessandro nell'Indie* (Mannheim, 1766); *Antigono* (Venice, Dec. 26, 1767); *Antigona* (Rome, Carnival 1768); *Ipermestra* (Naples, Aug. 13, 1768); *Adriano in Siria* (Rome, Carnival 1769); *Didone abbandonata* (Venice, Dec. 26, 1769); *Eumene* (Naples, Jan. 21, 1771; finished by Insanguine and Errichelli). Also arias for 3 London pasticcios: *Ezio* (1764), *Solimano* (1765), and *The Golden Pippin* (Feb. 6, 1773), and many oratorios.

BIBL.: D. DiChiera, *The Life and Operas of G. F. d.M.* (diss., Univ. of Calif., Los Angeles, 1962).

Majo, Giuseppe de, Italian organist and composer, father of **Gian Francesco (de) Majo**; b. Naples, Dec. 5, 1697; d. there, Nov. 18, 1771. He studied with Nicola Fago and Andrea Basso at the Cons. della Pietà dei Turchini in Naples (1706–18). He was organista soprannumerario (1736–37), provicemaestro (1737–44), vicemaestro (1744–45), and maestro (1745–71) at the royal chapel. His most successful stage work was the serenata *Il sogno d'Olimpia* (Naples, Nov. 6, 1747), written to celebrate the birth of the heir apparent.

WORKS: DRAMATIC: *Lo vecchio avaro*, opera buffa (Naples, Carnival 1727); *La Milorda*, opera buffa (Naples, 1728); *La Baronessa, overo Gli equivoci*, opera buffa (Naples, 1729); *Arianna e Teseo*, opera seria (Naples, Jan. 20, 1747); *Il sogno d'Olimpia*, serenata (Naples, Nov. 6, 1747); *Semiramide riconosciuta*, opera seria (Naples, Jan. 20, 1751); *Il Napolitano nelli fiorentini*, farsa (n.d.).

Major (real name, **Mayer**), **(Jakab) Gyula,** Hungarian pianist, choral conductor, and composer; b. Kassa, Dec. 13, 1858; d. Budapest, Jan. 30, 1925. He studied at the Buda Cons., then with

Erkel and Liszt (piano) and Robert Volkmann (composition) at the Academy of Music there (1877–81). He subsequently taught in music schools and teacher-training colleges and also toured in Europe as a pianist; he then returned to Budapest. His music follows the German Romantic tradition with some infusion of original Hungarian folk melos. His works include the operas *Erzsike* (Budapest, Sept. 24, 1901), *Szechy Maria* (1906), and *Mila* (1913). His son was Ervin Major (1901–1967), who was a musicologist and composer.

Makarova, Nina, Russian composer; b. Yurino, Aug. 12, 1908; d. Moscow, Jan. 15, 1976. She studied with Miaskovsky at the Moscow Cons., graduating in 1936. Her early works show a Romantic flair, not without some coloristic touches of French Impressionism. She wrote an opera, *Zoya* (1955). She was married to Aram Khachaturian.

BIBL.: I. Martinov, *N. M.* (Moscow, 1973).

Makedonski, Kiril, Macedonian composer; b. Bitol, Jan. 19, 1925; d. Skopje, June 2, 1984. After completing his academic schooling in Skopje, he studied with Krso Odak at the Zagreb Academy of Music; he later continued his composition studies with Brkanović in Sarajevo, and in Ljubljana with Škerjanc. He was the composer of the first national Macedonian opera, *Goce* (Skopje, May 24, 1954); his second opera was *Tsar Samuil* (Skopje, Nov. 5, 1968). His idiom follows the fundamental vocal and harmonic usages of the Russian national school.

Malanotte, (-Montresor), Adelaide, Italian contralto; b. Verona, 1785; d. Salo, Dec. 31, 1832. She made her debut in 1806 in Verona. She created the title role in Rossini's *Tancredi in Venice* at the Teatro La Fenice in 1813. She retired from the stage in 1821.

Malas, Spiro, American bass-baritone; b. Baltimore, Jan. 28, 1933. He studied voice with Nagy at the Peabody Cons. of Music in Baltimore and with Elsa Baklor and Daniel Ferro in New York; was also coached by Ivor Chichagov. In 1959 he made his operatic debut as Marco in *Gianni Schicchi* in Baltimore, and in 1961 won the Metropolitan Opera Auditions. On Oct. 5, 1961, he made his first appearance at the N.Y. City Opera as Spinellocchio in *Gianni Schicchi*, and continued to sing there regularly. In 1965 he toured Australia with the Sutherland-Williamson International Grand Opera Co. In 1966 he made his debut at London's Covent Garden as Sulpice in *La Fille du régiment*. He sang Assur in *Semiramide* for his first appearance at the Chicago Lyric Opera in 1971. On Oct. 8, 1983, he made his Metropolitan Opera debut in New York as Sulpice, and later appeared as Zuniga in *Carmen*, as Mozart's Bartolo, as Frank in *Die Fledermaus*, and as the sacristan in *Tosca*. He also toured widely as a concert artist. In 1992 he scored a fine success on Broadway in the revival of *The Most Happy Fella*.

Malashkin, Leonid, Russian composer; b. 1842; d. Moscow, Feb. 11, 1902. He was an ardent song collector who publ. the valuable anthology *50 Ukrainian Folksongs*. His original compositions, including the opera *Ilya Murometz* (Kiev, 1879), were not successful.

Maldere, Pierre van, noted South Netherlands violinist, conductor, and composer; b. Brussels, Oct. 16, 1729; d. there, Nov. 1, 1768. In 1746 he became a member of the ensemble of the Royal Chapel of Brussels and was also in the service of Prince Charles of Lorraine, the governor-general of the Netherlands. From 1751 to 1753 he was in Dublin as a violinist, conductor, and composer. He then traveled to Paris (1754). Returning to Brussels, he became director of concerts to Prince Charles (1754); he then was made his valet de chambre (1758). He also conducted at the Brussels Opera, and later was director of the Grand Théâtre there (1762–67). While he composed numerous operas, he excelled primarily as a composer of syms., in which he anticipated the masterpieces of Haydn and Mozart.

WORKS: OPERAS: *Le Déguisement pastoral* (Vienna, July 12, 1756); *Les Amours champêtres* (Vienna, Nov. 5, 1758; not extant); *Les Précautions inutiles* (1760); *Les Soeurs rivals* (1762); *La Bagarre* (Paris, Feb. 10, 1763; not extant); *Le Médecin de l'amour* (Brussels, 1766; not extant); *Le Soldat par amour* (Brussels, Nov. 4, 1766; not extant).

BIBL.: S. Clercx, *P. v.M.: Virtuose et maître des concerts de Charles de Lorraine (1729–1786)* (Brussels, 1948).

Malec, Ivo, Yugoslav-born French composer, conductor, and teacher; b. Zagreb, March 30, 1925. He studied at the Univ. and at the Academy of Music in Zagreb (1945–51). He was director of the Rijeka (Fiume) Opera (1952–53); in 1955 he traveled to Paris, where he met Pierre Schaeffer (1957) and participated in his Groupe de Musique Concrète. In 1959 he settled in Paris and joined the Service de la Recherche de l'ORTF in 1960. He also worked with the Groupe de Recherche Musicale and taught at the Paris Cons. (1972–90). In 1992 he won the Grand Prix national de la musique. From 1956 his music has explored the extremes of timbre and complexity. Among his works is *Operabus*, 2 scenes from the collective opera, to a libretto by Schaeffer (1965); also *Le Roi Lear*, theater score (1967), *Victor Hugo—Un contre tous*, "musical poster" for 2 Actors, Chorus, Orch., and Tape, after Hugo's political texts (Avignon, Aug. 1, 1971), and incidental music.

Malfitano, Catherine, admired American soprano; b. N.Y., April 18, 1948. She received early training at home from her father, a violinist in the Metropolitan Opera orch., and then continued her studies at the Manhattan School of Music (B.A., 1971). In 1972 she made her professional operatic debut as Verdi's Nannetta with the Denver Central City Opera, and then appeared with the Minnesota Opera (1972–73). She made her European debut as Mozart's Susanna at the Holland Festival in 1974. On Sept. 7, 1974, she made her debut at the N.Y. City Opera as Mimi, and remained on its roster until 1979. After making her debut at the Lyric Opera in Chicago as Mozart's Susanna in 1975, she sang that role at her Covent Garden debut in London and his Servilia at her Salzburg Festival debut in 1976. She made her first appearance at the Metropolitan Opera in New York as Gretel on Dec. 24, 1979, returning there in subsequent years in such roles as Violetta, Juliette, Micaëla, and Massenet's Manon. She made her debut at the Vienna State Opera as Violetta in 1982. Following appearances as Berg's Lulu in Munich in 1985 and as Cio-Cio-San at the Berlin Deutsche Oper in 1987, she made her debut at Milan's La Scala as Daphne in 1988. In 1993 she won acclaim as Salome in Salzburg. In 1995 she made her first appearance at the San Francisco Opera as Cio-Cio-San and won accolades as Janáček's Emilia Marty at the Lyric Opera in Chicago. Her outstanding portrayal of Salome at the Metropolitan Opera in 1996 was one of the highlights of the season. In 1998 she was engaged to sing Weill's Jenny in Salzburg and Tosca at the Netherlands Opera in Amsterdam.

Malgoire, Jean-Claude, French oboist, conductor, and musicologist; b. Avignon, Nov. 25, 1940. He studied from 1957 to 1960 at the Paris Cons., where he won 1st prizes in the categories of oboe and chamber music; in 1968 he won the International Prize of Geneva for his performances as an oboist. In 1974 he founded La Grande Écurie et La Chambre du Roy, with the avowed purpose of presenting early French music in historically authentic instrumentation; he toured with this ensemble in Europe, South America, Australia, and the United States. From 1981 he was general director of the Atelier Lyrique in Tourcoing. He also appeared as a guest conductor, leading performances of rarely heard operas in various European music centers.

Malherbe, Charles (-Théodore), French writer on music and composer; b. Paris, April 21, 1853; d. Cormeilles, Eure, Oct. 5, 1911. First he studied law, and was admitted to the bar, but he then took up music under A. Danhauser, A. Wormser, and J. Massenet. After a tour as Danhauser's secretary through Belgium, the Netherlands, and Switzerland in 1880–81 to inspect the music in the public schools, he settled in Paris. In 1896 he was appointed assistant archivist to the Grand Opéra, succeeding Nuitter as archivist in 1899. He ed. *Le Menestrel* and contributed to many leading reviews and musical journals. His collection of musical autographs, which he left to the Paris Cons., was one of the finest private collections in the world. With Saint-Saëns, he ed. an edition of the work of Rameau; he also was ed., with Weingartner, of a complete edition of Berlioz's works. His own works include 4 opéras comiques and a ballet pantomime, *Cendrillon*.

WRITINGS (all publ. in Paris): *L'Œuvre dramatique de Richard Wagner* (with A. Soubies; 1886); *Précis d'histoire de l'Opéra Comique* (with A. Soubies; 1887); *Mélanges sur Richard Wagner* (with A. Soubies; 1891); *Histoire de l'Opéra Comique: La seconde Salle Favart* (with A. Soubies; 2 vols., 1892–93); *Programmes et concerts* (1898); *Auber* (1911).

Malherbe, Edmond Paul Henri, French composer; b. Paris, Aug. 21, 1870; d. Corbeil-Essonnes, Seine-et-Oise, March 7, 1963. He studied at the Paris Cons. with Massenet and Fauré; in 1898 he won the Premier Second Prix de Rome, and in 1899, the Deuxième Premier Grand Prix; he won the Prix Trémont of the Académie des Beaux-Arts (1907, 1913, 1921); in 1950 he received the Grand Prix Musical of the City of Paris. He publ. *L'Harmonie du système musical actuel à demi-tons* (1920) and *Le Tiers-de-ton: Deux Systèmes: Tempéré et non-tempéré* (1900, 1950).

WORKS: DRAMATIC: OPERAS: *Madame Pierre* (1903; Paris, 1912); *L'Avare* (1907); *L'Emeute* (1911; Paris, 1912); *Cléanthis* (1912); *Anna Karénine* (1914); *Le Mariage forcé* (1924); *Néron* (1945); also *L'Amour et Psyché*, lyric tragedy with ballet (1948); *Monsieur de Pourceaugnac*, pantomime with Chorus (1930).

Malibran, María (Felicità née **García)**, famous Spanish mezzo-soprano, daughter of **Manuel (del Popolo Vicente Rodriguez) García**; b. Paris, March 24, 1808; d. Manchester, Sept. 23, 1836. She was taken to Naples, where she sang a child's part in Paër's *Agnese* (1814). She studied voice with her father from the age of 15; she also studied solfeggio with Panseron. She made her debut as Rosina in *Il Barbiere di Siviglia* at the King's Theatre in London (June 7, 1825), then went to New York, where she sang in the same opera in her family's season at the Park Theatre, which commenced on Nov. 29, 1825. She became a popular favorite, singing in *Otello, Tancredi, La Cenerentola, Don Giovanni*, and the 2 operas written for her by her father, *L'Amante astuto* and *La Figlia dell'aria*. She married the French merchant François Eugène Malibran, but he soon became bankrupt, and she returned to Europe without him in 1827. Malibran made her Paris debut as Semiramide at the Théâtre-Italien (April 8, 1828), then alternated her appearances in Paris and London during the 1829–32 seasons. She subsequently went to Italy, singing in Bologna (1832) and Naples (1833); she made her debut at Milan's La Scala as Norma (March 29, 1836). She met the violinist Charles de Béroit in 1829; they lived together until her marriage to Malibran was annulled in 1836, and then were married that same year. Malibran suffered serious injuries when thrown from her horse in 1836; since she was pregnant, complications developed and she lost her life. Her voice was of extraordinary compass, but the medium register had several "dead" tones. She was also a good pianist, and composed numerous nocturnes, romances, and chansonnettes, publ. in album form as *Dernieres pensées*.

BIBL.: I. Nathan, *The Life of Mme. M. M. de Beriot* (London, 1836); A. Pougin, *M. M.: Histoire d'une cantatrice* (Paris, 1911; Eng. tr., London, 1911); A. Flament, *Une Etoile en 1830: La M.* (Paris, 1928); P. Crump, *Musset and M.* (Cambridge, 1932); P. Larionoff, *M. M. e i suoi tempi* (Florence, 1935); A. Flament, *L'Enchanteresse errante, La M.* (Paris, 1937); S. Desternes and H. Chandet, *La M. et Pauline Viardot* (Paris, 1969); C. de Reparaz, *M. M.* (Madrid, 1976); H. Bushnell, *M. M.: A Biography of the Singer* (University Park, 1979); R. Giazotto, *M. M. (1808–1836): Una vita nei nomi di Rossini e Bellini* (Turin, 1986); A. Fitzlyon, *M. M.: Diva of the Romantic Age* (London, 1987).

Malipiero, Francesco, Italian composer, grandfather of **Gian Francesco Malipiero**; b. Rovigio, Jan. 9, 1824; d. Venice, May 12, 1887. He studied with Melchiore Balbi at the Liceo Musicale in Venice. At the age of 18 he wrote an opera, *Giovanna di Napoli*, which was produced with signal success; Rossini praised it. Other operas were *Attila* (Venice, Nov. 15, 1845; renamed *Ildegonda di Borgogna*), *Alberigo da Romano* (Venice, Dec. 26, 1846; his best), and *Fernando Cortez* (Venice, Feb. 18, 1851).

Malipiero, Gian Francesco, eminent Italian composer and teacher, grandson of **Francesco Malipiero**, and uncle of **Riccardo Malipiero**; b. Venice, March 18, 1882; d. Treviso, near Venice, Aug. 1, 1973. His father, Luigi Malipiero, was a pianist and conductor. In 1898 Malipiero enrolled at the Vienna Cons. as a violin student; in 1899 he returned to Venice, where he studied at the Liceo Musicale Benedetto Marcello with Marco Bossi, whom he followed to Bologna in 1904, and took a diploma in composition at the Liceo Musicale G. B. Martini that same year; he subsequently worked as amanuensis to Smareglia, gaining valuable experience in orchestration. He studied briefly with Bruch in Berlin (1908); later went to Paris (1913), where he absorbed the techniques of musical Impressionism, cultivating parallel chord formations and amplified tonal harmonies with characteristic added sixths, ninths, and elevenths. However, his own style of composition was determined by the polyphonic practices of the Italian Baroque. Malipiero was prof. of composition at the Parma Cons. (1921–23); afterwards he lived mostly in Asolo, near Venice. He was made prof. of composition at the Liceo Musicale Benedetto Marcello in Venice (1932), continuing there when it became the Cons. (1940); he was its director (1939–52). He ed. a complete edition of the works of Monteverdi (16 vols., Bologna and Vienna, 1926–42) and many works by Vivaldi, as well as works by other Italian composers. He was made a member of the National Inst. of Arts and Letters in New York in 1949, the Royal Flemish Academy in Brussels in 1952, the Institut de France in 1954, and the Akademie der Künste in West Berlin in 1967.

WORKS: DRAMATIC: OPERAS: *Canossa* (1911–12; Rome, Jan. 24, 1914); *Sogno d'un tramonto d'autunno* (1913–14; concert perf., RAI, Milan, Oct. 4, 1963); *L'Orfeide*, in 3 parts: *La morte della maschere, 7 canzoni*, and *Orfeo* (1918–22; 1st complete perf., Düsseldorf, Nov. 5, 1925; *7 canzoni* [Paris, July 10, 1920] is often perf. separately); *3 commedie goldoniane: La bottega da caffe, Sior Todaro Brontolon*, and *Le baruffe chiozzotte* (1920–22; 1st complete perf., Darmstadt, March 24, 1926); *Filomela e l'Infatuato* (1924–25; Prague, March 31, 1928); *Il mistero di Venezia*, in 3 parts: *Le aquile di aquileia, Il finto Arlecchino*, and *I corvi di San Marco* (1925–28; 1st complete perf., Coburg, Dec. 15, 1932); *Merlino, Maestro d'organi* (1926–27; Rome Radio, Aug. 1, 1934); *Torneo notturno* (1929; Munich, May 15, 1931); *Il festino* (1930; Turin Radio, Nov. 6, 1937); *La favola del figlio cambiato* (1932–33; in German, Braunschweig, Jan. 13, 1934); *Giulio Cesare* (1934–35; Genoa, Feb. 8, 1936); *Antonio e Cleopatra* (1936–37; Florence, May 4, 1938); *Ecuba* (1938; Rome, Jan. 11, 1941); *La vita è sogno* (1940–41; Breslau, June 30, 1943); *I capricci di Callot* (1941–42; Rome, Oct. 24, 1942); *L'allegra brigata* (1943; Milan, May 4, 1950); *Mondi celesti e infernali* (1948–49; RAI, Turin, Jan. 12, 1950; 1st stage perf., Venice, Feb. 2, 1961); *Il Figliuol prodigo* (1952; RAI, Jan. 25, 1953; 1st stage perf., Florence May Festival, May 14, 1957); *Donna Urraca* (1953–54; Bergamo, Oct. 2, 1954); *Il capitan Spavento* (1954–55; Naples, March 16, 1963); *Venere prigioniera* (1955; Florence May Festival, May 14, 1957); *Il marescalco* (1960–68; Treviso, Oct. 22, 1969); *Rappresentazione e festa del Carnasciale e della Quaresima* (1961; concert perf., Venice, April 20, 1962; 1st stage perf., Venice, Jan. 20, 1970); *Don Giovanni* (1962; Naples, Oct. 22, 1963); *Le metamorfosi di Bonaventura* (1963–65; Venice, Sept. 4, 1966); *Don Tartufo bacchettone* (1966; Venice, Jan. 20, 1970); *Gli Eroi di Bonaventura* (1968; Milan, Feb. 7, 1969); *L'Iscariota* (1970; Siena, Aug. 28, 1971); *Uno dei dieci* (1970; Siena, Aug. 28, 1971). BALLETS: *Pantea* (1917–19; Venice, Sept. 6, 1932); *La mascherata delle principesse prigioniere* (1919; Brussels, Oct. 19, 1924); *Stradivario* (1947–48; Florence, June 20, 1949); *Il mondo novo* (1950–51; Rome, Dec. 16, 1951; rev. as *La lanterna magica*, 1955). DIALOGHI: No. 1, *con M. de Falla*, for Orch., No. 2 for 2 Pianos, No. 3, *con Jacopone da Todi*, for Voice and 2 Pianos, No. 4 for Wind Quintet, No. 5 for Viola and Orch., No. 6 for Harpsichord and Orch., No. 7 for 2 Pianos and Orch., and No. 8, *La morte di Socrate*, for Baritone and Small Orch. (all 1956–57).

WRITINGS: *L'orchestra* (Bologna, 1920; Eng. tr., 1920); *Teatro* (Bologna, 1920; 2d ed., 1927); *Oreste e Pilade, ovvero "Le sorprese dell'amicizia"* (Parma, 1922); *I profeti di Babilonia* (Milan, 1924); *Claudio Monteverdi* (Milan, 1929); *Strawinsky* (Venice, 1945; new ed., 1982); *La pietra del bando* (Venice, 1945; new ed., 1990); *Anton Francesco Doni, musico* (Venice, 1946); *Cossí va lo mondo* (Milan, 1946); *L'armonioso labirinto (da Zarlino a Padre Martini, 1558–1774)* (Milan, 1946); *Antonio Vivaldi, il prete rosso* (Milan, 1958); *Il filo d'Arianna (saggi e fantasie)* (Turin, 1966); *Ti co mi e mi co ti (soliloqui di un veneziano)* (Milan, 1966); *Così parlò Claudio Monteverdi* (Milan, 1967); *Di palo in frasca* (Milan, 1967); *Da Venezia lontan* (Milan, 1968); *Maschere della commedia dell'arte* (Bologna, 1969).

BIBL.: F. Alfano, *A. Casella, M. Castelnuovo-Tedesco et al., M. e le sue "Sette canzoni"* (Rome, 1929); F. Ballo, *"I 'Capricci' di Callot" di G. F. M.* (Milan, 1942); M. Bontempelli and R. Cumar, *G. F. M.* (Milan, 1942); G. Scarpa, ed., *L'opera di G. F. M.* (Treviso, 1952); M. Labroca, *M., musicista veneziano* (Venice, 1957; 2d ed., 1967); A. Gianuario, *G. F. M. e l'arte monteverdiana* (Florence, 1973); M. Messinis, ed., *Omaggio a M.* (Florence, 1977); J. Waterhouse, *La musica G. F. M.* (Turin, 1990).

Malipiero, Riccardo, prominent Italian composer, pedagogue, administrator, and writer on music, nephew of **Gian Francesco Malipiero;** b. Milan, July 24, 1914. He received training in piano at the Milan Cons. (diploma, 1932) and in composition at the Turin Cons. (diploma, 1937) before completing his studies in composition in his uncle's master classes in Venice (1937–39). Between 1945 and 1976 he was active as a music critic for various newspapers and magazines. In 1949 he organized the first congress on dodecaphonic music in Milan. From 1969 to 1984 he served as director of the Civico Liceo Musicale in Varese. He also lectured and gave master classes abroad. He was awarded the gold medals of Milan (1977) and Varese (1984) for his services to Italian music. As a composer, Malipiero adopted 12-tone procedures in 1945 but without doctrinaire proclivities. Among his books were *G. S. Bach* (Brescia, 1948), *C. Debussy* (Brescia, 1948; 2d ed., 1958), *Guida alla dodecafonia* (Milan, 1961), and, with G. Severi, *Musica ieri oggi* (6 vols., Rome, 1970).

WORKS: DRAMATIC: *Minnie la Candida*, opera (Parma, Nov. 19, 1942); *La Donna è mobile*, opera buffa (1954; Milan, Feb. 22, 1957); *Battono alla Porta*, television opera (Italian TV, Feb. 12, 1962; 1st stage perf., Genoa, May 24, 1963); *L'ultima Eva*, opera (1992–95).

BIBL.: C. Sartori, *R. M.* (Milan, 1957); P. Franci et al., *Piccolo omaggio a R. M.* (Milan, 1964); C. Sartori and P. Santi, *Due tempi di R. M.* (Milan, 1964).

Maliponte (real name, **Macciaïoli**), **Adriana,** Italian soprano; b. Brescia, Dec. 26, 1938. She was a student of Suzanne Steppen at the Mulhouse Cons. and of Carmen Melis in Como. In 1958 she made her operatic debut as Mimi at Milan's Teatro Nuovo. In 1960 she won the Geneva Competition. After singing Micaëla at the Paris Opéra in 1962, she was chosen to create the role of Sardulla in Menotti's *Le dernier sauvage* at the Paris Opéra Comique in 1963. In 1963 she made her U.S. debut as Leila in *Les Pêcheurs de perles* with the Philadelphia Lyric Opera, and thereafter sang with various U.S. opera companies. In 1970 she made her first appearance at Milan's La Scala as Massenet's Manon. On March 19, 1971, she made her Metropolitan Opera debut in New York as Mimi, and continued to sing there regularly in subsequent years. In 1976 she made her debut at London's Covent Garden as Nedda. She sang at the Vienna State Opera in 1977. In 1986 she appeared as Maria Stuarda in Zürich. In 1990 she portrayed Luisa Miller in Trieste. She appeared in recital at the Salle Gaveau in Paris in 1994. Among her other roles were Gluck's Eurydice, Pamina, Luisa Miller, and Gounod's Juliet.

Mallinger, Mathilde (née **Lichtenegger**), noted Croatian soprano and teacher; b. Agram, Feb. 17, 1847; d. Berlin, April 19, 1920. She was a student in Prague of Gordigiani and Vogl, and in Vienna of Loewy. On Oct. 6, 1866, she made her operatic debut as Norma in Munich, where she was chosen to create the role of Eva in *Die Meistersinger von Nürnberg* (June 21, 1868). On April 6, 1869, she made her first appearance at the Berlin Royal Opera as Elsa, where she continued as one of its principal artists until her retirement in 1882. In 1873 she sang in the United States. She taught voice in Prague (1890–95) and thereafter in Berlin. Among her other distinguished roles were Mozart's Countess, Donna Anna, and Pamina, Beethoven's Leonore, Weber's Agathe, and Wagner's Sieglinde.

Malten (real name, **Müller**), **Therese,** German soprano; b. Insterburg, June 21, 1855; d. Neuzschieren, near Dresden, Jan. 2, 1930. She studied with Gustav Engel in Berlin, making her operatic debut as Pamina at the Dresden Court Opera in 1873, and remained for some 30 years a principal singer on its roster; she also sang in Berlin, Vienna, and London. Wagner heard her and engaged her as Kundry at the premiere of *Parsifal* at Bayreuth in 1882; she continued to sing there until 1894. She was particularly renowned as a Wagnerian, excelling as Elsa, Elisabeth, Eva, Kundry, and Isolde.

Mamiya, Michio, Japanese composer; b. Asahikawa, Hokkaido, June 29, 1929. He was a student of Ikenouchi at the Tokyo National Univ. of Fine Arts and Music. In his works, Mamiya cultivates national Japanese music in modern forms, with inventive uses of dissonant counterpoint and coloristic instrumentation.

WORKS: DRAMATIC: *Mukashi banashi hitokai Tarobê* (A Fable from Olden Times about Tarobê, the Slave Dealer), opera (1959); *Elmer's Adventure*, musical (Tokyo Radio, Aug. 28, 1967); *Narukami*, opera (1974); *Yonagahime and Mimio*, chamber opera (1990).

Mamoulian, Rouben, Russian-born director of operas, musicals, and films; b. Tiflis, Oct. 8, 1897; d. Los Angeles, Dec. 4, 1987. He showed an early interest in theater, founding a drama studio in his native city in 1918; in 1920 he toured England with the Russian Repertory Theater. Later he directed several hit plays in London during a 3-year span. In 1923 he emigrated to the United States to become director of operas and operettas at the George Eastman Theater in Rochester, N.Y. He was an innovator of both stage and screen, using an imaginative and bold blend of all the components of film with the new dimension of sound. He directed the noted early "talkie" *Applause* in 1929, as well as the film version of Gershwin's *Porgy and Bess* in 1935. He was the first director to use a mobile camera in a sound movie, and among the first to use a multiple-channel sound track. He directed the film of the Rodgers and Hammerstein musical *Oklahoma!* (1955), which was the first musical to utilize songs and dance as an integral part of the dramatic flow of the plot.

Mana-Zucca (real name, **Gizella Augusta Zuckermann**), American composer, pianist, and singer; b. N.Y., Dec. 25, 1887; d. Miami Beach, March 8, 1981. She began playing piano as a child and took the name Mana-Zucca as a teenager. In 1902 she played in one of Frank Damrosch's young people's concerts at N.Y.'s Carnegie Hall. After training from Alexander Lambert, she toured as a pianist in Europe from about 1907. She also made some appearances as a singer, attracting notice in Lehár's *Der Graf von Luxemburg* in London in 1919. From 1921 she was active mainly in Florida, where she devoted herself fully to composition. She became best known as a composer of lyrically soaring songs, the most famous being "I Love Life" (1923). Among her other works are the operas *Hypatia* (c.1920) and *The Queue of Ki-Lu*, opera (c.1920) and the ballet *The Wedding of the Butterflies*.

Mancinelli, Luigi, distinguished Italian conductor and composer; b. Orvieto, Feb. 5, 1848; d. Rome, Feb. 2, 1921. He studied organ and cello with his brother, Marino, then was a cellist in the Orvieto cappella and the orch. of the Teatro della Pergola in Florence; he also studied cello with Sbola and composition with Mabellini in Florence. He then was 1st cellist and maestro concertatore at the Teatro Morlacchi in Perugia. In 1874 he made his conducting debut there in *Aida* after the regular conductor was unable to lead the performance owing to a temporarily inebriated condition. He then was called to Rome, where he was conductor of the Teatro Apollo from 1874 to 1881; he subsequently he served as director of the Bologna Cons. On June 18, 1886, he made his London debut conducting a concert performance; in 1887 he conducted at Drury Lane; from 1888 to 1905 he was chief conductor at Covent Garden, and from 1887 to 1893 he conducted opera in Madrid. He joined the roster of the Metropolitan Opera in New York in 1893, and continued to conduct there until 1903. On May 25, 1908, he led the first performance at the newly opened Teatro Colón in Buenos Aires, returning there in 1909, 1910, and 1913. He enjoyed a fine reputation as a competent, dependable, and resourceful opera conductor; naturally, he excelled in the Italian repertoire, but he also conducted Wagner's operas, albeit in dubious Italian translation. From his experience as an opera conductor, he learned the art of composing for the theater; his operas are indeed most effective; of these, *Ero e Leandro* became a favorite.

WORKS: DRAMATIC: OPERAS: *Isora de Provenza* (Bologna, Oct. 2, 1884); *Tizianello* (Rome, June 20, 1895); *Ero e Leandro* (Norwich Festival, Oct. 8, 1896); *Paolo e Francesca* (Bologna, Nov. 11, 1907); *Sogno di una notte d'estate*, after Shakespeare's *Midsummer Night's Dream* (not produced). ORATORIOS: *Isaia* (Norwich, Oct. 13, 1887); *Santa Agnese* (Norwich, Oct. 27, 1905). OTHER: Cinematic cantata, *Giuliano l'Apostata* (Rome, 1920).

BIBL.: L. Arnedo, *L. M. y su opera Hero y Leandro* (Madrid, 1898); G. Orefice, *L. M.* (Rome, 1921); L. Silvestri, *L. M.: Direttore e compositore* (Milan, 1966).

Mancini, Francesco, Italian composer and teacher; b. Naples, Jan. 16, 1672; d. there, Sept. 22, 1737. He became an organ student at the Cons. della Pietà dei Turchini in Naples (1688), where he later was organist (c.1694–1702). He held the post of 1st organist at the royal chapel in Naples (1704–07); subsequently he was its director (1707–08), assistant director (1708–25), and again director (1725–37). He was also director of the Cons. di S. Maria di Loreto in Naples from 1720 until he suffered a stroke in 1735. He was held in high regard as a composer of operas and cantatas, and as a teacher. He also publ. *XII Solos* for Violin or Flute and Basso Continuo, *Which Solos Are Proper Lessons for the Harpsichord* (London, 1724; 2d rev. ed., 1727, by F. Geminiani).

WORKS (all 1st perf. in Naples unless otherwise given): DRAMATIC: OPERAS: *Ariovisto* (Nov. 15, 1702); *Lucio Silla* (Jan. 1703); *La constanza nell'honore* (June 1704); *Gli amanti generosi* (1705); *La Serva favorita* (1705); *Alessandro il Grande in Sidone* (1706); *Turno Aricino* (1708); *Engelberta o sia La forza dell'innocenza* (Nov. 4, 1709; in collaboration with A. Orefici); *Hydaspe (Idaspe) fedele* (London, April 3, 1710); *Mario fuggitivo* (1710); *Selim re d'Ormuz* (Feb. 26, 1712); *Artaserse re di Persia* (Oct. 18, 1713); *Il Gran Mogol* (Dec. 26, 1713); *Il Vincislao* (Dec. 26, 1714); *Alessandro Severo* (Rome, Carnival 1718); *La fortezza al cimento* (1721); *Il Trajano* (Jan. 1723); *Orontea* (Carnival 1729); *Alessandro nelle Indie* (1732); *Don Aspremo* (1733); *Il Demofoonte* (1735; Act 1 by D. Sarro, Act 2 by Mancini, Act 3 by L. Leo). Also several intermezzos, serenatas, and oratorios.

Mandac, Evelyn (Lorenzana), Filipino soprano; b. Malaybalay, Mindanao, Aug. 16, 1945. After training at the Univ. of the Philippines (B.A., 1963), she pursued her studies at the Oberlin (Ohio) College-Cons. of Music and then at the Juilliard School of Music in New York (M.A., 1967). In 1968 she made her formal debut in Orff's *Carmina burana* in Mobile, Ala. Her operatic debut followed as Mimi in Washington, D.C., in 1969. On Dec. 19, 1975, she made her Metropolitan Opera debut in New York as Lauretta in *Gianni Schicchi*, and remained with the company until 1978. She also sang opera in San Francisco, Glyndebourne, Rome, Houston, Geneva, and other cities, and she also toured as a concert artist. Among her roles were Despina, Zerlina, Susanna, Pamina, Juliet, and Mélisande. She also created roles in Pasatieri's *Black Widow* (1972) and *Inez de Castro* (1976).

Mandelbaum, (Mayer) Joel, American composer; b. N.Y., Oct. 12, 1932. He studied with Piston at Harvard Univ. (B.A., 1953), with Fine and Shapero at Brandeis Univ. (M.F.A., 1955), and at Indiana Univ. (Ph.D., 1961, with the diss. *Multiple Division of the Octave and the Tonal Resources of 19-tone Temperament*); he also studied with Dallapiccola at the Berkshire Music Center at Tanglewood and with Blacher at the Berlin Hochschule für Musik. He held a Fulbright fellowship (1957) and was a fellow at the MacDowell Colony (1968). He taught at Queens College of the City Univ. of N.Y. (from 1961), where he served as director of its Aaron Copland School of Music. Many of his compositions reflect his study of microtonal music and the utilization of the Scalatron, an instrument with a color-coordinated keyboard that can be rearranged into divisions of the octave up to and including 31 tones. He composed the operas *The Man in the Man-made Moon* (1955), *The 4 Chaplains* (1956), and *The Dybbuk* (1971; rev. 1978); also light operas, musicals, incidental music, and film scores.

Mandini, Stefano, notable Italian baritone; b. 1750; d. c.1810. He sang in Venice (1775–76) and Parma (1776). With his wife, the soprano Maria Mandini, he made his Vienna debut with the Italian Opera in Cimarosa's *L'italiana in Londra* (May 5, 1783), where they soon established themselves as prominent figures on the operatic stage. Mandini scored a major success as Almaviva in Paisiello's *Il Barbiere di Siviglia* during the 1783–84 season. He sang the role of the Poet in Salieri's *Prima la musica e poi le parole* on Feb. 7, 1786. On May 1, 1786, he created the role of Count Almaviva in Mozart's *Le nozze di Figaro*, his wife taking the role of Marcellina. Mandini remained in Vienna until 1788, and then sang in Paris and Venice (1794–95). In 1795 he once more sang in Vienna. His brother, Paolo Mandini (b. Arezzo, 1757; d. Bologna, Jan. 25, 1842), was a tenor. He studied with Saverio Valente. After making his debut in Brescia (1777), he appeared at Milan's La Scala (1781), and in Turin, Parma, Bologna, and Rome. In 1783–84 he sang under Haydn at Esterháza. On May 6, 1785, he made his Vienna debut in Anfossi's *I viaggiatori felici*. After a sojourn in Venice (1787), he returned to Vienna in 1789.

Mandl, Richard, Austrian composer; b. Prossnitz, May 9, 1859; d. Vienna, April 1, 1918. He studied at the Vienna Cons. and with Delibes at the Paris Cons. He wrote a 1-act comic opera, *Nächtliche Werbung* (Prague, 1888).

Manelli, Francesco, Italian composer; b. Tivoli, Sept. 1594; d. Parma, July 1667. He served as a chorister at the Cathedral of Tivoli from c. 1605, and continued his service there as chapel singer (1609–24); he then was maestro di cappella there (1627–29). He produced an opera, *Gelia*, in Bologna (1630). In 1636 he went to Venice, where he was chapel singer at San Marco (from 1638); from 1645 to his death, he was in the service of the Duke of Parma. In 1637 the Teatro San Cassiano in Venice, the first public opera house in Europe, was opened with Manelli's opera *L'Andromeda*; he wrote several other operas, which enjoyed considerable popularity. All of his scores are lost, but some librettos are preserved. His op. 4, *Musiche varie* (Venice, 1626), a collection of cantatas, arias, canzonette, and ciacone, shows that he had adopted the "parlando" recitative.

Manén, Juan, Catalan violinist and composer; b. Barcelona, March 14, 1883; d. there, June 26, 1971. He received training in solfège and piano at a very early age from his father. At 5, he began to study violin and, at 7, made his public debut as a violinist. At 9, he made his first appearances in America. Following studies with Ibarguren, he made tours of Europe from 1898. He spent some years in Germany, where his orch. compositions were influenced by Wagner and Strauss. After returning to his homeland, he devoted himself principally to composition. Much of his music was redolent of Catalan melorhythms. His writings, all publ. in Barcelona, included *Mis experiencias* (1944), *Variaciones sin tema* (1955), *El violin* (1958), *El jóven artista* (1964), and *Diccionario de celebridades musicales* (1974).

WORKS: DRAMATIC: *Juana de Nápoles*, opera (Barcelona, Jan. 1903); *Acté*, opera (Barcelona, Dec. 3, 1903; rewritten as *Neró i Akté*, Karlsruhe, Jan. 28, 1928); *Der Fackeltanz*, opera (Frankfurt am Main, 1909); *Heros*, opera (n.d.); *Camino del sol*, theater sym.

(Leipzig, 1913); *Don Juan*, tragic comedy (n.d.); *Soledad*, opera (n.d.); *Triana*, ballet (1952).

Manfredini, Vincenzo, Italian composer; b. Pistoia, Oct. 22, 1737; d. St. Petersburg, Aug. 16, 1799. His father was the Italian violinist and composer Francesco Onofrio Manfredini (Pistoia [baptized], June 22, 1684; d. there, Oct. 6, 1762). He was a pupil of his father, and later studied with Perti in Bologna and with Fioroni in Milan. In 1758 he went to Russia, where he was attached to the court (until 1769). He then returned to Italy, living in Bologna and Venice; his former pupil, now Czar Paul I, recalled him to Russia (1798). He publ. *Regole armoniche, o sieno Precetti ragionati* (Venice, 1775; 2d ed., rev. and aug., 1797).

WORKS (all 1st perf. in St. Petersburg unless otherwise given): DRAMATIC: OPERAS: *Semiramide* (1760); *L'Olimpiade* (Moscow, Nov. 24, 1762); *La pupilla* (1763); *La finta ammalata* (1763); *Carlo Magno* (Nov. 24, 1763); *Armida* (Bologna, May 1770); *Artaserse* (Venice, Jan. 1772). BALLETS: *Amour et Psyché* (Moscow, Oct. 20, 1762); *Pygmalion* (Sept. 26, 1763); *Les Amants réchappés du naufrage* (1766); *Le Sculpteur de Carthage* (1766); *La Constance récompensée* (Moscow, 1767).

Mangold, Carl (Ludwig Amand), German conductor and composer, brother of **(Johann) Wilhelm Mangold**; b. Darmstadt, Oct. 8, 1813; d. Oberstdorf im Allgäu, Aug. 5, 1889. He studied at the Paris Cons. with Berton and Bordogni. Returning to Darmstadt, he became a violinist in the Court Orch.; from 1848 to 1869 he was court music director, and also conducted various choral societies there. He wrote an opera, *Tannhäuser*, which was produced in Darmstadt on May 17, 1846, only a few months after the premiere of Wagner's great work; in order to escape disastrous comparisons, the title was changed to *Der getreue Eckart*, and the libretto revised; the new version was produced posthumously in Darmstadt on Jan. 17, 1892. Mangold also wrote 4 more operas, *Das Köhlermädchen, oder Das Tournier zu Linz* (1843), *Die Fischerin* (1845), *Dornröschen* (1848), and *Gudrun* (1851), and several oratorios. Of his choral works, particularly favored was the "concert drama" *Die Hermannsschlacht* (Mainz, 1845).

Mangold, (Johann) Wilhelm, German violinist, conductor, and composer, brother of **Carl (Ludwig Amand) Mangold**; b. Darmstadt, Nov. 19, 1796; d. there, May 23, 1875. He studied with Rinck and Abbé Vogler, then went to Paris for lessons with Cherubini, Méhul, and Kreutzer at the Cons. (1815–18). In 1825 he became a court conductor at Darmstadt; he was pensioned in 1857. Among his works were 3 operas.

Mann, Leslie (Douglas), Canadian composer and clarinetist; b. Edmonton, Alberta, Aug. 13, 1923; d. Balmoral, Manitoba, Dec. 7, 1977. He began to study clarinet at 13 and composition at 15. He was 1st clarinetist of the CBC Winnipeg Orch. (1958) and of the Winnipeg Sym. Orch. (1960–71). His music followed along traditional lines in an accessible manner. Among his works is the chamber opera *The Donkey's Tale* (1971).

Mann, William (Somervell), English music critic, writer on music, and translator; b. Madras, Feb. 14, 1924; d. Bath, Sept. 5, 1989. He studied piano with Kabos and composition with Seiber and also studied at Magdalene College, Cambridge (1946–48), with Patrick Hadley, Hubert Middleton, and Robin Orr. He was on the music staff of the *Times* of London (1948–60) as its chief music critic (1960–82). He made many serviceable Eng. trs. of opera librettos and lieder texts. He publ. *Introduction to the Music of Johann Sebastian Bach* (London, 1950), *Richard Strauss: A Critical Study of the Operas* (London, 1964), and *The Operas of Mozart* (London, 1977).

Manneke, Daan, Dutch composer; b. Kruiningen, Nov. 7, 1939. He was a student of Houet and Toebosch (organ) and of Van Dijk (composition) at the Brabant Cons. (1960–66), and then of D'Hooghe (organ) and de Leeuw (composition) in Amsterdam (1967–73). From 1958 to 1969 he was organist at St. Gertrudes in Bergen op Zoom, and then taught at the Amsterdan Cons. (from 1972). Among his compositions are the opera *De passie van Johannes Mattheus Lanckohr* (1977) and the chamber opera *Jules* (1988).

Mannelli, Carlo, Italian castrato soprano, violinist, and composer; b. Rome, Nov. 4, 1640; d. there, Jan. 6, 1697. He entered the service of Prince Camillo Pamphili as a child, receiving training in voice and violin. He sang in patronal festivities at S. Luigi dei Francesi (1650, 1651), and appeared as Lerino in P. Ziani's opera *Le fortune di Rodope e Damira* (Venice, 1657). In 1660 he became a singer at S. Luigi dei Francesi, where he also was a violinist from 1665. He was its first violinist (1676–82), and then resumed his position as a singer there. From 1659 to 1664 he was also a singer at the Arciconfratenità del Ss. Crocifisso at S. Marcello, where he likewise was a violinist, later serving as its first violin (1668–90). From 1663 he also was a violinist of the Congregazione di S. Cecilia. He was much esteemed as a violinist and composer. His trio sonatas are particularly noteworthy (Rome, 1682, 1692).

Manners, Charles (real name, **Southcote Mansergh**), Irish bass and opera impresario; b. London, Dec. 27, 1857; d. Dundrum, County Dublin, May 3, 1935. He studied in Dublin, then at the Royal Academy of Music in London and in Florence. In 1882 he made his stage debut with the D'Oyly Carte company in London, creating the role of Private Willis in Gilbert and Sullivan's *Iolanthe*. In 1890 he married **Fanny Moody**, with whom he organized the Moody-Manners Opera Co. (1898); it toured widely until its demise in 1916. He retired from active management of its affairs in 1913.

Manning, Jane (Marian), English soprano; b. Norwich, Sept. 20, 1938. She was a student of Greene at the Royal Academy of Music in London (1956–60), of Husler at the Scuola di Canto in Cureglia, Switzerland, and of Frederick Jackson and Yvonne Rodd-Marling in London. In 1964 she made her debut in London singing songs of Webern, Messiaen, and Dallapiccola, and subsequently established herself as a leading proponent of modern music. From 1965 she sang regularly on the BBC, and also toured extensively around the globe. In all, she sang in more than 300 premieres of contemporary scores. In 1988 she founded her own Jane's Minstrels in London, an ensemble devoted to the furtherance of contemporary music. She was active as a lecturer, serving as a visiting prof. at Mills College in Oakland, California (1982–86) and as a lecturer at the Univ. of York (1987). She publ. the book *New Vocal Repertory: An Introduction* (Oxford, 1994). In 1990 she was made a member of the Order of the British Empire. In 1966 she married **Anthony Payne.**

Manning, Kathleen Lockhart, American composer and singer; b. Hollywood, Oct. 24, 1890; d. Los Angeles, March 20, 1951. She was a student of Moszkowski in Paris (1908). She sang in France and England, including an engagement with the Hammerstein Opera Co. in London (1911–12), and later in the United States (1926), but she devoted herself principally to composition. Her output reflected her interest in oriental subjects à la the French impressionists. Among her works is *Operetta in Mozartian Style* (n.d.), *Mr. Wu*, opera (1925–26), and *For the Soul of Rafael*, opera (n.d.).

Mannino, Franco, Italian conductor, pianist, composer, novelist, and playwright; b. Palermo, April 25, 1924. He was a student of Silvestri (piano) and Mortari (composition) at the Accademia di Santa Cecilia in Rome. At 16, he made his debut as a pianist. After the end of World War II, he toured as a pianist in Europe and the United States. He also took up conducting and appeared as a guest conductor throughout Europe, North and South America, and the Far East. In 1968 he founded the Incontri Musicale Romani. From 1969 to 1971 he served as artistic director of the Teatro San Carlo in Naples, where he subsequently was its artistic advisor. He was principal conductor and artistic advisor of the National Arts Centre Orch. in Ottawa from 1982 to 1986, and then was its principal guest conductor from 1986 to 1989. In 1990–91 he was president of the Accademia Filarmonica of Bologna. The Italian Republic gave him its gold medal in 1968 and honored him as Commendatore ordine al merito in 1993. In his compositions, Mannino has generally followed traditional modes of expression with occasional excursions into modernistic practices. In addition to his prolific compositions, he has also written novels, plays, essays, and articles.

WORKS: DRAMATIC: *Mario e il Mago*, azione coreografia (1952; Milan, Feb. 25, 1956); *Vivì*, lyric drama (1955; Naples, March 28, 1957); *La speranza*, melodrama (1956; Trieste, Feb. 14, 1970); *La stirpe di Davide*, tragedy (1958; Rome, April 19, 1962); *La notti della paura*, melodrama (1960; RAI, Rome, May 24, 1963); *Il diavolo in giardino*, comedy (1962; Palermo, Feb. 28, 1963); *Luisella*, drama (1963; Palermo, Feb. 28, 1969); *Il quadro delle meraviglie*, intermezzo ballet (Rome, April 24, 1963); *Il ritratto di Dorian Gray*, drama (1973; Catania, Jan. 12, 1982); *Roma Pagana*, ballet (1978); *Il Principe Felice*, theater piece (1981; Milan, July 7, 1987); *Soltanto il rogo*, drama (1986; Agrigento, Oct. 21, 1987); *Le notte Bianche*, Liederopera (1987; Rome, April 14, 1989); *Le teste Scambiate*, legend (1988); *Anno domini 3000*, opera buffa (1993); film scores.

Manoury, Philippe, French composer; b. Tulle, June 19, 1952. He studied composition with Gérard Condé and Max Deutsch and at the Paris Cons. with Ivo Malec, Claude Ballif, and Michel Philipott (premieres prix in analysis, 1977, and composition, 1978). From 1983 to 1991 he was active with IRCAM in Paris. From 1987 he was also a prof. of composition at the Lyons Cons. He composed the opera *60e Parallèle* (Paris, March 10, 1997). Among his other works were *Puzzle* for 31 Players (1975), String Quartet (1978), *Numéro huit* for 103 Players (1980), *Zeitlauf* for 12 Voices, 13 Players, Electronics, and Tape (1983), *Instantanés III* for 5 Groups of Players (Baden-Baden, May 31, 1985), *Aleph* for 4 Speakers and Orch. (Strasbourg, Sept. 26, 1985; rev. 1987), *Les Livre des claviers* for 6 Percussionists (Strasbourg, Sept. 27, 1988), *La Partition du ciel et de l'enfer* for Orch. (1989), *Prélude* for Orch. (1992), and *Pentaphone* for Orch. (1992).

Manowarda, Josef von, esteemed Austrian bass; b. Kraków, July 3, 1890; d. Berlin, Dec. 24, 1942. He studied in Graz, making his debut there (1911). He sang at the Vienna Volksoper (1915–18) and in Wiesbaden (1918–19), then was a principal member of the Vienna State Opera (1919–42); he also appeared at the Salzburg Festivals (from 1922), the Bayreuth Festivals (1931, 1934, 1939, 1942), and the Berlin State Opera (1934–42); in addition, he taught at the Vienna Academy of Music (1932–35). Among his notable roles were Osmin, King Marke, Gurnemanz, and King Philip; he created the role of the Messenger in Strauss's *Die Frau ohne Schatten* (1919). He also pursued a fine concert career.

Manschinger, Kurt, Austrian conductor and composer; b. Zeil-Wieselburg, July 25, 1902; d. N.Y., Feb. 23, 1968. He studied musicology at the Univ. of Vienna, and at the same time took private lessons with Webern (1919–26). After graduation, he was mainly active as a theatrical conductor in Austria and Germany. His practical acquaintance with operatic production led to his decision to write operas, for which his wife, the singer Greta Hartwig, wrote librettos. Of these his first opera, *Madame Dorette*, was to be performed by the Vienna State Opera, but the Anschluss in 1938 made this impossible. He and his wife fled to London, where they organized an émigré theater, the Lantern. In 1940 they emigrated to America; Manschinger changed his name to Ashley Vernon and continued to compose, earning his living as a musical autographer by producing calligraphic copies of music scores for publishers. Other operas include *The Barber of New York* (N.Y., May 26, 1953), *Grand Slam* (Stamford, Conn., June 25, 1955), *Cupid and Psyche* (Woodstock, N.Y., July 27, 1956), and *The Triumph of Punch* (N.Y., Jan. 25, 1969).

Manski, Dorothée, German-American soprano and teacher; b. Berlin, March 11, 1891; d. Atlanta, Feb. 24, 1967. She studied in Berlin, where she made her debut at the Komische Oper (1911); then sang in Mannheim (1914–20) and Stuttgart (1920–24). She was a member of the Berlin State Opera (1924–27); also sang in Max Reinhardt's productions; then appeared as Isolde at the Salzburg Festival (1933) and the Vienna State Opera (1934). She made her Metropolitan Opera debut in New York as the Witch in *Hänsel und Gretel* on Nov. 5, 1927, and remained on the company's roster until 1941; also sang opera in Philadelphia, Chicago, and San Francisco, and appeared as a concert singer with leading European and U.S. orchs. She was prof. of voice at the Indiana Univ. School of Music in Bloomington (1941–65). Among her other roles were Sieglinde, Venus, Gutrune, Brünnhilde, Freia, and Elsa.

Mansouri, Lotfi (Lotfollah), Iranian-born American opera director and administrator; b. Tehran, June 15, 1929. He studied psychology at the Univ. of Calif., Los Angeles (A.B., 1953). After serving as an assistant prof. on its faculty (1957–60), he was resident stage director of the Zürich Opera (1960–65) and director of dramatics at the Zürich International Opera Studio (1961–65). From 1965 to 1975 he was chief stage director of the Geneva Opera, and from 1967 to 1972 was director of dramatics at the Centre Lyrique in Geneva. In 1976 he became general director of the Canadian Opera Co. in Toronto, remaining there until 1988 when he assumed that position with the San Francisco Opera. His tenure in San Francisco was marked with the major renovation of the opera house in 1996–97, and its gala reopening concert on Sept. 5, 1997. He retired in 2001. In 1992 he was made a Chevalier of l'Ordre des Arts et Lettres of France. Mansouri's opera productions have been staged at many of the leading opera houses of the world, and generally reflect his traditional approach to the art of stage direction.

Mantelli, Eugenia, Italian mezzo-soprano; b. c.1860; d. Lisbon, March 3, 1926. Following her operatic debut as Kalad in *Le Roi de Lahore* in Treviso in 1883, she appeared in Europe and South America. On Nov. 23, 1894, she made her Metropolitan Opera debut in New York as Amneris, remaining on the roster until 1897. She was again on its roster from 1898 to 1900 and in 1902–03. In 1896 she sang Brünnhilde in the French-language production of *Die Walküre* at London's Covent Garden. In 1910 she made her farewell appearance in Lisbon, where she settled. Among her other roles were Urbain, Delilah, Siebel, Ortrud, and Azucena.

Manuel, Roland. See **Roland-Manuel.**

Manziarly, Marcelle de, Russian-born French conductor, pianist, and composer; b. Kharkov, Sept. 13, 1899; d. Ojai, Calif., May 12, 1989. She studied in Paris with Boulanger, in Basel with Weingartner (1930–31), and in New York with Vengerova (1943). She appeared as a pianist and conductor in the United States and taught privately in Paris and New York. Her works extend the boundaries of tonality through such resources and procedures as polytonality, serialism, and atonality. Her compositions include the opera *La Femme en flèche* (1954).

Manzoni, Giacomo, Italian composer, teacher, and writer on music; b. Milan, Sept. 26, 1932. He studied composition with Contilli at the Messina Liceo Musicale (1948–50); he then pursued training at the Milan Cons., where he received diplomas in piano (1954) and composition (1956); he also obtained a degree in foreign languages and literature at the Bocconi Univ. in Milan (1955). He was ed. of *Il Diapason* (1956), music critic of the newspaper *L'Unità* (1958–66), and music ed. of the review *Prisma* (1968); later he was on the editorial staff of the review *Musica/Realtà*. He taught harmony and counterpoint at the Milan Cons. (1962–64; 1968–69; 1974–91) and composition at the Bologna Cons. (1965–68; 1969–74); he also taught at the Scuola di musica in Fiesole (from 1988). In 1982 he was a guest of the Deutscher Akademischer Austauschdienst in Berlin. He contributed articles to Italian and other journals and publications, tr. works of Schoenberg and Adorno into Italian, and publ. the books *Guida all'ascolto della musica sinfonica* (Milan, 1967) and *Arnold Schonberg: L'uomo, l'opera, i testi musicati* (Milan, 1975). Collections of his writings were ed. by C. Tempo (Florence, 1991) and A. De Lisa (Milan, 1994). As a composer, Manzoni has embraced advanced forms of expression. While pursuing a highly individual serial path, he has explored microstructures, macrostructures, and multiphonics with interesting results. He composed the operas *La sentenza*

(1959–60; Bergamo, Oct. 13, 1960), *Atomtod* (1963–64; Milan, March 27, 1965), *Per Massimiliano Robespierre* (1974; Bologna, April 17, 1975), and *Doktor Faustus*, after Thomas Mann (1985–88; Milan, May 16, 1989).

BIBL.: M. Romito, *Le composizioni sinfonico-corali di G. M.* (Bologna, 1982); J. Noller, *Engagement und Form: G. M.s Werk in kulturtheoretischen und musikhistorischen Zusammenhangen* (Frankfurt am Main, 1987); F. Dorsi, *G. M.* (Milan, 1989); *Omaggio a G. M.: 1992 sesant'annil il 26 settembre* (Milan, 1992).

Manzuoli, Giovanni, famous Italian castrato soprano; b. Florence, c.1720; d. there, 1782. He began his operatic career in Florence in 1731. After appearing in Verona (1735), he sang in Naples (until 1748). He appeared in Madrid (1749–52), Parma (1754), Lisbon (1755), and once again in Madrid (1755). He subsequently was active in Italy until 1764. In 1760 he made a visit to Vienna, where he scored a major success. In 1764–65 he appeared to great acclaim at the King's Theatre in London. During his London sojourn, he became friends of the Mozart family. Following further appearances in Verona, Turin, Venice, and Milan, he was made chamber singer to the grand duke of Tuscany in 1768. In 1771 he made his farewell public appearance in Milan.

Mapleson, James Henry, colorful English opera impresario who dubbed himself **Colonel Mapleson**; b. London, May 4, 1830; d. there, Nov. 14, 1901. He was a student at the Royal Academy of Music in London. After playing violin in the orch. of the Royal Italian Opera at Her Majesty's Theatre there (1848–49), he pursued vocal training in Milan with Mazzucato. He sang in Lodi and Verona using the name Enrico Mariani. Returning to London, he sang under his own name in *Masaniello* at Drury Lane in a performance which proved disastrous. He subsequently abandoned his singing aspirations and opened his own musical agency in 1856. In 1858 he served as manager of E. T. Smith's Drury Lane season. He was manager of the Italian Opera at the Lyceum Theatre (1861–62), Her Majesty's Theatre (1862–67), and Drury Lane (1868). In 1869–70 he was comanager with Gye at Covent Garden. He was manager at Drury Lane (1871–76), Her Majesty's Theatre (1877–81; 1887; 1889), and Covent Garden (1885, 1887). Between 1878 and 1897 he also presented operas at N.Y.'s Academy of Music and in other U.S. cities, his ventures fluctuating between success and disaster.

Mapleson was often the subject of news reports on both sides of the Atlantic as a result of his recurrent professional troubles and his conflicts with, and attachments to, various prima donnas. However, he succeeded in producing many operas new to British audiences and also introduced Nilsson, Nordica, and Jean de Reszke to London. He publ. a lively account of his career in *The Mapleson Memoirs* (2 vols., London, 1888; 2d ed., rev., 1966 by H. Rosenthal). His nephew, Lionel Mapleson (b. London, Oct. 23, 1865; d. N.Y., Dec. 21, 1937), became a violinist in the orch. of the Metropolitan Opera in New York in 1889. Soon thereafter he became its librarian, a position he held for 50 years. He amassed an invaluable collection of operatic memorabilia, including turn-of-the-century cylinder recordings of actual Metropolitan Opera performances. In 1985 these recordings were issued by the N.Y. Public Library.

Mara, Gertrud (Elisabeth née **Schmeling)**, famous German soprano; b. Kassel, Feb. 23, 1749; d. Reval, Russia, Jan. 20, 1833. A neglected child, she suffered from disfiguring rickets; her father exhibited her as a violin prodigy in Vienna (1755), and she later played before the queen (1759); she then studied voice with Paradisi. In 1765 she returned to Germany and became a principal singer at Hiller's concerts in Leipzig (1766); she then made her operatic debut in Dresden (1767), but soon returned to Leipzig. She subsequently entered the service of Frederick the Great (1771), singing at the Berlin Royal Opera. Her marriage to the cellist Johann Baptist Mara (1746–1808) brought her grief, for Frederick opposed their union; when the couple tried to leave Leipzig, Frederick had them arrested. However, he eventually consented to their marriage after Gertrud agreed to remain at the Berlin Royal Opera; during this period, she also received instruction in harmony from Kirnberger. In 1779 she finally escaped Berlin, and subsequently sang in other German cities, in the Low Countries, and in Vienna (1780–81); she appeared at the Concert Spirituel in Paris (1782), and again as a rival to Todi (1783). In 1784 she went to London, where she gained renown as a result of her participation in the Handel Commemoration performances; subsequently appeared at the King's Theatre there (1786–91) and also in Turin (1788) and Venice (1789–90; 1792), thereafter mainly in concerts and oratorios in London until 1802, when she and her lover, the flutist and composer Charles Florio, left to tour France, Germany, and Austria; they finally landed in Moscow, but soon separated. Stricken with poverty, she was forced to eke out a meager existence as a teacher. After losing everything in the French destruction of Moscow (1812), she went to Reval as a teacher. In 1819 she made a brief and unsuccessful return to London's King's Theatre, then returned to Reval. During the glory days of her career, her voice ranged from g' to e''.

BIBL.: G. Grosheim, *Das Leben der Künstlerin M.* (Kassel, 1823; reprint, 1972); G. Burkli, *G. E. M.* (Zürich, 1835); R. Kaulitz-Niedeck, *Die M.: Das Leben einer berühmten Sängerin* (Heilbronn, 1929).

Marais, Marin, great French viola da gambist and composer; b. Paris, May 31, 1656; d. there, Aug. 15, 1728. He studied bass viol with Sainte-Colombe and composition with Lully (whom he addresses as teacher in a letter publ. in his first book of pieces for his instrument), then became a member of the royal orch. (1676); he was made Ordinaire de la chambre du Roi in 1679, retiring in 1725. Marais possessed matchless skill as a virtuoso on the viola da gamba, and set a new standard of excellence by enhancing the sonority of the instrument. He also established a new method of fingering, which had a decisive influence on the technique of performance. As a composer, he was an outstanding master of bass viol music, producing 5 extensive collections between 1686 and 1725, numbering some 550 works in all. In his dramatic music, he followed Lully's French manner; his recitatives comport with the rhythm of French verse and the inflection of the rhyme. The purely instrumental parts in his operas were quite extensive; in *Alcione* (Paris, Feb. 18, 1706) he introduced a "tempeste," which is one of the earliest attempts at stage realism in operatic music. His other operas are *Alcide* (Paris, 1693), *Ariane et Bacchus* (Paris, 1696), and *Sémélé* (Paris, 1709). He also publ. 5 books of pieces for viola da gamba (1686–1725), trios (or "symphonies") for violin, flute, and viola da gamba (1692), and a book of trios for violin, viola da gamba, and harpsichord under the title *La Gamme* (1723). An edition of his instrumental works, ed. by J. Hsu, began publication in New York in 1980. He was married in 1676 and had 19 children; his son Roland Marais was also a talented viola da gambist who publ. 2 books of pieces for his instrument with basso continuo (Paris, 1735, 1738) and a *Nouvelle méthode de musique pour servir d'introduction aux acteurs modernes* (Paris, 1711; not extant).

BIBL.: C. Thompson, *M. M., 1656–1728* (diss., Univ. of Michigan, 1956).

Mařák, Otakar, Czech tenor; b. Esztergom, Hungary, Jan. 5, 1872; d. Prague, July 2, 1939. He was a student at the Prague Cons. of Paršova-Zikešová. After making his operatic debut as Faust in Brünn in 1899, he sang in Prague at the Deutsches Theater (1900–01) and the National Theater (1901–07). Following guest engagements in Vienna (1903), Berlin (1906), London (Covent Garden, 1908), and Chicago (1914), he was a principal member of the National Theater in Prague (1914–34). He lost his financial security in a business venture, and went to the United States to seek his fortune. However, he ended up selling newspapers on Chicago streets. After funds were raised for his assistance, he was able to return to Prague to eke out his last days in straitened circumstances. At the zenith of his career, he was dubbed the Czech Caruso. Among his best roles were Turiddu, Canio, and Don José.

Marazzoli, Marco, significant Italian composer; b. Parma, between 1602 and 1608; d. Rome, Jan. 26, 1662. In 1631 he gained the patronage of Cardinal Antonio Barberini in Rome. In 1637 he settled in Rome in the cardinal's service and became a tenor in the Papal Chapel, a position he held until his death; he also was engaged by Cardinal Mazarin in Paris in 1643. He returned to Rome in 1645, and in 1656 he became virtuoso di camera to Queen Christina of Sweden, who held her court in Rome at the time. Marazzoli was a prolific composer of choral music; about 375 of his cantatas and oratorios are extant. His name is also associated with that of Virgilio Mazzocchi; they collaborated on the first comic opera, *Chi soffre, speri* (Rome, Feb. 27, 1639), which was a revision of *Il facone* (Rome, Feb. 1637). His other operas include *L'amore trionfante dello sdegno* (also known as *L'Armida*; Ferrara, Feb. 1641), *Gli amori di Giasone e d' Issifile* (Venice, 1642; not extant), *Le pretensioni del Tebro e del Po* (Ferrara, March 4, 1642), *Il capriccio or Il giudizio della ragione fra la Belta e l'Affetto* (Rome, 1643), *Dal male il bene* (with A. M. Abbatini; Rome, 1653), *Le armi e gli amori* (Rome, 1654), and *La vita humana, ovvero Il trionfo della pietà* (Rome, Jan. 31, 1656).

BIBL.: M. Grace, *M. M. and the Development of the Latin Oratorio* (diss., Yale Univ., 1974).

Marc, Alessandra, accomplished American soprano; b. Berlin, July 29, 1957. She received her training at the Univ. of Maryland. In 1987 she made her operatic debut in Giordano's *La Cene delle Beffe* at the Wexford Festival in England. In 1988 she sang Maria in Strauss's *Friedenstag* at the Santa Fe Opera. During the 1988–89 season, she appeared as Leonora in *La Forza del Destino* at the Greater Miami Opera, as Madame Lidoine in *Les Dialogues des Carmélites* at the Houston Grand Opera, as Strauss's Ariadne at the Washington (D.C.) Concert Opera, and as Aida at the Lyric Opera in Chicago. On Oct. 14, 1989, she made her Metropolitan Opera debut in New York as Aida. In 1992 she sang for the first time at the Philadelphia Opera as Turandot, a role she reprised at the Macerata Festival in 1996. During the 1992–93 season, she made her debut at the Berlin State Opera as Strauss's Ariadne. In 1993 she made her Italian operatic debut at the Rome Opera as Aida. During the 1994–95 season, she appeared for the first time at London's Covent Garden as Turandot. Her other opera engagements included the Vienna State Opera, the San Francisco Opera, the Cologne Opera, the Bavarian State Opera in Munich, and the Hamburg State Opera. Among her other prominent roles are Norma, Sieglinde in *Die Walküre*, and Chrysothemis in *Elektra*. As a concert artist, she has appeared with many of the finest orchs. and festivals in a repertoire ranging from classical standards to Samuel Barber.

Marcel (real name, **Wasself**), **Lucille,** American soprano; b. N.Y., 1885; d. Vienna, June 22, 1921. She studied in N.Y., Berlin, and with J. de Reszke in Paris, where she made her debut as Mallika in *Lakmé* at the Opéra Comique (1903). After marrying **Felix Weingartner** in 1907, she sang the title role in Elektra at its first Viennese staging under his direction (March 24, 1908); she continued to sing at the Court Opera until 1911, then was a member of the Hamburg Opera (1912–14). She made her U.S. debut as Tosca with the Boston Opera Co. (Feb. 14, 1912), and remained on its roster until 1914. After a period in Darmstadt, she settled in Vienna. Her other roles included Eva, Marguerite, Desdemona, and Aida.

Marcello, Benedetto, famous Italian composer and teacher; b. Venice, July 24 or Aug. 1, 1686; d. Brescia, July 24 or 25, 1739. He studied violin with his father, and later took courses in singing and counterpoint with F. Gasparini. Having prepared for a legal career, he accepted a number of distinguished positions in public life: he was made a member of the Grand Council of the Republic (1707), served on the Council of Forty for 14 years, was governor of Pola (1730–37), subsequently camarlingo (chamberlain) of Brescia (1738–39), and was also active as an advocate and magistrate. Adopting the pseudonym Driante Sacreo, he became a member of Rome's Arcadian Academy; he was also elected a member of Bologna's Accademia Filarmonica (1712). His distinguished students included the singer Faustina Bordoni and the composer Baldassare Galuppi. He most likely was the author of *Lettera famigliare d'un accademico filarmonico ed arcade discorsiva sopra un libro di duetti, terzetti e madrigali a piu voci* (Venice, 1705), an anonymous and rather captious critique of Lotti. He publ. a famous satire on Vivaldi and his contemporaries as *Il teatro alla moda, o sia Metodo sicuro e facile per il ben comporre ed eseguire l'opere italiane in musica all'usu moderno* (Venice, c.1720; Eng. tr. by R. Paul, *Musical Quarterly*, July 1948 and Jan. 1949). Marcello was one of the most gifted Italian composers of his time, his mastery ranging from sacred and secular vocal works to instrumental works. Among his works were the oratorios *Il sepolcro* (Venice?, 1705), *Giuditta* (Rome, 1709), *Gioaz* (Vienna, 1726), *Il pianto e il riso delle quattro stagioni* (Venice?, 1731), and *Il trionfo della poesia e della musica* (Venice?, 1733). His brother was the Italian violinist, composer, poet, and painter Alessandro Marcello (b. Venice, Aug. 24, 1669; d. Padua, June 19, 1747).

BIBL.: F. Fontana, *Vita di B. M., patrizio Veneto* (Venice, 1788); F. Caffi, *Della vita e della opera di B. M.* (Venice, 1830); L. Busi, *B. M.* (Bologna, 1884); O. Chilesotti, *Sulla lettera critica di B. M. contro A. Lotti* (Bassano, 1885); E. Fondi, *La vita e l'opera letteraria del musicista B. M.* (Rome, 1909); A. d'Angeli, *B. M.: Vita e opere* (Milan, 1940); G. Tinctori, *L'Arianna di B. M.* (Milan, 1951); E. Selfridge-Field, *The Works of B. and Alessandro M.: A Thematic Catalogue* (Oxford, 1990).

Marchesi (de Castrone), Blanche, French soprano and teacher of Italian-German descent, daughter of **Salvatore Marchesi de Castrone** and **Mathilde** (née **Graumann**) **Marchesi de Castrone**; b. Paris, April 4, 1863; d. London, Dec. 15, 1940. After studying violin, she turned to vocal training with her mother. She began her career singing in private and charity concerts in Paris, and then appeared in Berlin and Brussels in 1895. On June 19, 1896, she made her London debut in a concert and made England her home. In 1900 she made her operatic debut as Brünnhilde in *Die Walküre* in Prague, and then returned to England to sing with the Moody-Manners Co. In 1902 she appeared at London's Covent Garden as Elisabeth, Elsa, and Isolde. For the most part, however, she pursued a career on the concert stage. Later she was also active as a teacher. She made her farewell concert appearance in 1938. She publ. the memoir *A Singer's Pilgrimage* (London, 1923) and the didactic vol. *The Singer's Catechism* (London, 1932).

Marchesi, Luigi (Lodovico), celebrated Italian castrato soprano, known as "Marchesini"; b. Milan, Aug. 8, 1754; d. Inzago, Dec. 14, 1829. He studied horn with his father. After having himself castrated, he pursued vocal training with Alluzzi and Caironi. At age 11, he joined the choir at the Milan Cathedral, where he studied composition with its director Fioroni. He made his debut as Giannetta in Anfossi's *L'Incognita perseguitata* in Rome (1773); he also sang in Treviso (1775), and then was a member of the Munich court (1776–78). He subsequently gained renown as a member of the Teatro San Carlo in Naples (1778–79); he appeared in Florence (1780) and then again in Naples (1780–81). He sang in Milan and also in Turin, where he held the title of musico di corte (1782–98). In 1785 he was engaged by the court of Catherine the Great; on his way to St. Petersburg, he appeared in Sarti's *Giulio Sabino* in Vienna before Emperor Joseph II (Aug. 4, 1785), who ordered a medal be struck in his honor. He made his Russian debut as Rinaldo in Sarti's *Armida e Rinaldo* at the inaugural performance of the Hermitage Theater in St. Petersburg (Jan. 15, 1786). The soprano Luiza-Rosa Todi intrigued against him, however, and despite his successes, he left Russia before the expiration of his contract. He then appeared in Berlin on March 9, 1787, and subsequently scored a London triumph in *Giulio Sabino* on April 5, 1788. He made his last appearance in London on July 17, 1790, and then pursued his career mainly in Italy; he also sang in Vienna again (1798, 1801). He sang in the premiere of Mayr's *Ginevra di Scozia* at the dedicatory performance of the Teatro Nuovo in Trieste on April 21, 1801. He made his farewell stage appearance in Mayr's *Lodoiska* in Milan in May 1805, but sang in public as late as 1820 in Naples. Blessed with a range of

2 1/2 octaves, Marchesi was unsurpassed in the opera seria genre of his era.

Marchesi de Castrone, Mathilde (née **Graumann**), famous German mezzo-soprano and pedagogue, mother of **Blanche Marchesi**; b. Frankfurt am Main, March 24, 1821; d. London, Nov. 17, 1913. She was a student of Ronconi in Frankfurt am Main and of Nicolai in Vienna. After making her debut in a concert in Frankfurt am Main (Aug. 31, 1844), she continued her studies with García in Paris (1844–46; 1848) and in London (1849). She subsequently appeared in concerts in London, Germany, and Holland. Her only operatic appearance was as Rossini's Rosina in Bremen in 1853. In 1852 she married **Salvatore Marchesi de Castrone**. After serving as prof. of voice at the Vienna Cons. (1854–61), she went to Paris as a private teacher and as a concert singer. She subsequently was prof. of voice at the Cologne Cons. (1865–68) and again at the Vienna Cons. (1868–78). Thereafter she taught privately in Vienna until 1881, when she returned to Paris. Following her husband's death, she settled in London. She had many celebrated students, among them Calvé, Eames, Garden, Gerster, Klafsky, Melba, Murska, Nevada, and Sanderson. She publ. the autobiography *Erinnerungen aus meinem Leben* (Vienna, 1877; 4th ed., rev. and aug., 1889 as *Aus meinem Leben*; Eng. tr., 1897, as *Marchesi and Music: Passages from the Life of a Famous Singing Teacher*). She also publ. the manual *10 Singing Lessons* (N.Y., 1910; new ed., 1970, by P. Miller as *Theoretical and Practical Vocal Method*). Her niece was **Dorothea von Ertmann**.

Marchesi de Castrone, Salvatore (full name and title, **Salvatore Marchesi, Cavaliere de Castrone, Marchese della Rajata**), distinguished Italian baritone and teacher, father of **Blanche Marchesi**; b. Palermo, Jan. 15, 1822; d. Paris, Feb. 20, 1908. Of a noble family, he was destined for a government career and studied law in Palermo. However, he turned to music, and took lessons in singing and theory with Raimondi in Palermo, and with Lamperti in Milan. He was involved in the revolutionary events of 1848, and was compelled to leave Italy; he went to New York, where he made his operatic debut as Carlos in *Ernani*. He then studied with Garcia in London. He married **Mathilde Marchesi de Castrone** (née **Graumann**) in 1852, and sang with her in opera on the Continent. From 1854 to 1861, they both taught at the Vienna Cons., and later at the Cologne Cons. (1865–68), and again in Vienna (1868–78). After that they resided in Paris.

Marchetti, Filippo, Italian composer; b. Bolognola, near Camerino, Feb. 26, 1831; d. Rome, Jan. 18, 1902. He was a pupil of Lillo and Conti at the Royal Cons. in Naples. His first opera, *Gentile da Varano* (Turin, Feb. 1856), was extremely well received, and he repeated his success with another opera, *La Demente*, for Turin (Nov. 27, 1856); however, his next opera, *Il Paria*, never reached the stage. He was not discouraged by this and wrote his *Romeo e Giulietta* (Trieste, Oct. 25, 1865), which made little impression until it was mounted at Milan's Teatro Carcano in 1867. He achieved his greatest success with *Ruy-Blas* (La Scala, Milan, April 3, 1869), which was produced also in Germany and England; his remaining operas were *Gustavo Wasa* (La Scala, Feb. 7, 1875) and *Don Giovanni d'Austria* (Turin, March 11, 1880). In 1881 he was appointed president of the Accademia di Santa Cecilia in Rome; then was director of the Liceo Musicale there (1886–1901).

Marchisio, Barbara, Italian contralto and teacher; b. Turin, Dec. 6, 1833; d. Mira, April 19, 1919. She studied with her brother, the composer Antonino Marchisio (1817–1875), and with L. Fabbrica in Turin, making her debut as Adalgisa in *Norma* in Vicenza (1856); she sang Rosina in Madrid that same year. Her sister, Carlotta Marchisio (b. Turin, Dec. 8, 1835; d. there, June 28, 1872), also studied with her brother and with Fabbrica in Turin; made her debut as Norma in Madrid (1856). The 2 sisters first appeared together in Turin in 1858. After singing in Trieste, they made their joint debut at Milan's La Scala in *Semiramide* (Dec. 29, 1858); this opera continued as their vehicle for their joint debut at the Paris Opéra (in French, July 9, 1860) and at Her Majesty's Theatre in London (May 1, 1862). They last appeared together in Rome in 1871. After Carlotta died in childbirth, Barbara continued her career for several more years, appearing in Milan (1872) and Venice (1876). She then devoted herself to teaching, numbering Raisa and dal Monte among her students. Rossini held the Marchisio sisters in the highest esteem.

Marcolini, Marietta, Italian mezzo-soprano; b. Florence, c.1780; place and date of death unknown. By 1800 she was singing in Venice. After appearing in Naples (1803–04), Rome (1807–08), and Milan (La Scala, 1809), she won the esteem of Rossini and created his Ernestina in *Lequivoco stravagante* (1811), Ciro (1812), Clarice in *La pietra del paragone* (1812), Isabella (1813), and the title role in *Sigismondo*. She retired from the operatic stage in 1820.

Marcoux, Vanni (Jean Émile Diogène), remarkable French bass-baritone who was also known as **Vanni-Marcoux;** b. Turin (of French parents), June 12, 1877; d. Paris, Oct. 22, 1962. He received training in law at the Univ. of Turin, and in voice from Taverna and Collino in Turin and from Boyer in Paris. He was only 17 when he made his operatic debut in Turin as Sparafucile. His formal operatic debut followed in 1899 when he sang Frère Laurent in *Roméo et Juliette* in Bayonne. After singing in Nice, Brussels, and The Hague, he distinguished himself at London's Covent Garden (1905–12). In 1908 he made his debut at the Paris Opéra as Méphistophélès. On Jan. 13, 1909, he created the role of Guido Colonna in Février's *Monna Vanna* there. Massenet composed the title role of his opera *Don Quichotte* for Marcoux, who sang in its first Paris staging on Dec. 29, 1910. He appeared as a guest artist at Milan's La Scala (1910), the Boston Opera Co. (1911–12), and the Chicago Grand Opera Co. (1913–14). From 1918 to 1936 he was a principal member of the Paris Opéra Comique. He also sang again in Chicago (1926–32) and at Covent Garden (1937). From 1938 to 1943 he taught at the Paris Cons. In 1940 he retired from the operatic stage, although he made a final appearance as Don Quichotte at the Opéra Comique in 1947. From 1948 to 1951 he served as director of the Grand Théâtre in Bordeaux. Marcoux's outstanding repertoire consisted of over 240 roles, of which the most famous were Don Giovanni, Rossini's Don Basilio, Iago, Boris Godunov, Baron Ochs, Golaud, Scarpia, and Don Quichotte.

Maréchal, Adolphe, Belgian tenor; b. Liège, Sept. 26, 1867; d. Brussels, Feb. 1, 1935. He studied at the Liège Cons. He made his operatic debut in Tournai in 1891, then sang in Rheims, Bordeaux, and Nice; in 1895 he became a member of the Opéra Comique in Paris, where he remained until 1907; during that time, he created the roles of Julien in *Louise* (1901), Alain in *Grisélidis* (1901), and Danielo in *La Reine fiammette* (1903); also Jean in *Le Jongleur de Notre-Dame* at Monte Carlo (1902). In 1902 he appeared at London's Covent Garden as Don José, Des Grieux, and Faust. He retired in 1907 after the loss of his singing voice.

Marenco, Romualdo, Italian composer; b. Novi Ligure, March 1, 1841; d. Milan, Oct. 9, 1907. He played the violin, then the bassoon at the Doria Theater in Genoa, for which he wrote his first ballet, *Lo sbarco di Garibaldi a Marsala*. He studied counterpoint and composition with Taddei, but was mainly self-taught via the manuals of Fenaroli and Mattei. He was director of ballet music at Milan's La Scala (1873–80). He composed some 15 ballets, the most popular being *Sieba* (1878), *Excelsior* (1881), *Amor* (1886), and *Sport* (1897). He also wrote the operas *Lorenzio de' Medici* (Lodi, 1874), *I Moncada* (Milan, 1880), *Le Diablo au corps* (Paris, 1884), and *Strategia d'amore* (Milan, 1896). A posthumous opera, *Federico Struensea*, was produced in Milan in 1908.

BIBL.: S. Cavazza, *R. M.* (Novi Ligure, 1957).

Maretzek (Mareřek), Max, Czech-born American conductor, opera impresario, and composer; b. Brünn, June 28, 1821; d. Staten Island, N.Y., May 14, 1897. He studied medicine and law at the Univ. of Vienna and music with Ignaz von Seyfried. He progressed rapidly, and at the age of 22 conducted his first opera,

Hamlet (Brünn, 1843). He then traveled in Germany, France, and England as a theater conductor and composer of ballet music. In 1848 he settled in New York as conductor and manager of the Italian Opera Co. He presented Adelina Patti for the first time in opera (as Lucia, 1859); in 1876 he staged his own play with music, *Baba*. He conducted his pastoral opera *Sleepy Hollow, or, The Headless Horseman*, after Washington Irving (N.Y., Sept. 25, 1879). As a worldly impresario, he was extremely successful. He traveled to Mexico and Cuba, but lived mostly in New York, and became an American citizen. He publ. a book of reminiscences, *Crotchets and Quavers, or Revelations of an Opera Manager in America* (N.Y., 1855), and its sequel, *Sharps and Flats* (N.Y., 1870).

Margison, Richard (Charles), Canadian tenor; b. Victoria, British Columbia, July 15, 1953. He studied at the Victoria Cons. of Music, graduating in 1980. In 1976 he won the regional Metropolitan Opera auditions, and pursued further studies with Léopold Simoneau. In 1980 he made his first appearance with Pacific Opera Victoria as Count Almaviva, where he continued on its roster until 1983. He made his debut with the Vancouver Opera in 1985 as Lensky, and in 1988 he sang Don Ottavio at the Glimmerglass Opera in Cooperstown, N.Y. In 1989 he made his debut with the Canadian Opera Co. in Toronto as Vitek in the first Canadian production of Janáček's *The Makropulos Affair*. His European operatic debut followed in 1990 when he sang Verdi's Gustavus with the English National Opera in London. That same year he also appeared as Gounod's Faust at the Houston Grand Opera. In 1994 he sang Don Carlos at the San Francisco Opera, returning there in 1997 as Cavaradossi. Among his other fine roles are Alfredo, Edgardo, Rodolfo, Don José, Fenton, and Nemorino. He also sang in oratorio and concert performances throughout Canada.

Margola, Franco, Italian composer and teacher; b. Orzinuovi, near Brescia, Oct. 30, 1908; d. Brescia, March 10, 1992. He studied violin with Romanini and composition with Guerrini, Jachino, Longo, and Casella at the Parma Cons. (diplomas in piano, 1926, and in composition, 1934); he then took a course in advanced theory with Casella at the Accademia di Santa Cecilia in Rome. After serving as director of the Messina Cons. (1938–40), he taught at the conservatories in Cagliari, Bologna, Milan, Rome, and Parma. He publ. a manual, *Guida pratica per lo studio della composizione* (Milan, 1954). Among his compositions is the opera *Il mito di Caino* (Bergamo, 1940).

BIBL.: R. Cresti, *Linguaggio musicale di F. M.* (Milan, 1994).

Maria Antonia Walpurgis, electress of Saxony, daughter of the elector of Bavaria, later Holy Roman Emperor Charles VII; b. Munich, July 18, 1724; d. Dresden, April 23, 1780. She was not only a generous patroness of the fine arts, but a trained musician, pupil of Hasse and Porpora (1747–52). Under the pseudonym E.T.P.A. (Ermelinda Talea Pastorella Arcada, her name as member of the Academy of Arcadians) she produced and publ. 2 Italian operas to her own librettos, and sang in their premieres: *Il trionfo della Fedeltà* (Dresden, 1754) and *Talestri, regina delle Amazoni* (Nymphenburg, near Munich, Feb. 6, 1760). She also wrote texts of oratorios and cantatas for Hasse and Ristori.

BIBL.: C. von Weber, *M. A. W.: Churfürstin zu Sachsen* (2 vols., Dresden, 1857); H. Drewes, *M. A. W. als Komponistin* (Leipzig, 1934).

Mariani, Angelo (Maurizio Gaspare), eminent Italian conductor; b. Ravenna, Oct. 11, 1821; d. Genoa, June 13, 1873. He studied violin with P. Casalini and counterpoint with G. Roberti at the Ravenna Phil. Academy's music school, and also learned to play other instruments. He began his career as bandmaster of the city of Sant' Agata Feltria (1842); became a violinist and violist in the orch. in Rimini (1843). That same year he brought out a concerto and 2 overtures in Macerata, gaining the admiration and friendship of Rossini. He was 1st violinist and maestro concertatore in Messina (1844–45), then made his first appearance in Milan at the Teatro Re conducting Verdi's *I due Foscari* (July 1, 1846), winning the praise of the composer; he subsequently conducted at the Teatro Carcano there, and then conducted at the Copenhagen Court Theater (1847–48). After taking part in the Italian war of independence in 1848, he was compelled to leave his homeland and went to Constantinople. He was conductor at the Pera theater there until 1850. He returned to Italy in 1851, conducting in Messina, then was appointed director and conductor of the Teatro Carlo Felice in Genoa, making his debut conducting *Robert le diable* on May 15, 1852. He led many fine performances there of operas by Rossini, Bellini, Donizetti, Meyerbeer, and Verdi, becoming a close friend of the latter; he also assumed the directorship of the Teatro Comunale in Bologna, making his debut leading *Un ballo in maschera* on Oct. 4, 1860. He conducted the first Italian performances of *Lohengrin* (Nov. 1, 1871) and *Tannhäuser* (Nov. 11, 1872) in Bologna. Stricken with intestinal cancer, he was unable to accede to Verdi's request that he conduct the premiere of *Aida* in Cairo. In spite of his grave illness, he carried out his duties in both Genoa and Bologna until his death. Mariani was one of the foremost Italian operatic conductors of his era, especially esteemed for his authoritative performances of the great masterpieces of the Italian stage. He himself wrote several cantatas, chamber music, songs, and piano pieces.

BIBL.: S. Busmanti, *Cenni su A. M.* (Ravenna, 1887); T. Mantovani, *A. M.* (Rome, 1921); U. Zoppi, *A. M., Giuseppe Verdi e Teresa Stolz in un carteggio inedito* (Milan, 1947).

Mariani, Luciano, Italian bass; b. Cremona, 1801; d. Piacenza, June 10, 1859. He created the role of Oroe in *Semiramide* (1823), Rodolfo in *La sonnambula* (1831), and Alfonso in *Lucrezia Borgia* (1833). His sister, Rosa (b. Cremona, 1799; place and date of death unknown), was also a singer. In 1818 she made her operatic debut in Cremona. In 1823 she created the role of Arsace in *Semiramide*. She appeared at the King's Theatre in London in 1832.

Marin, Ion, Romanian conductor; b. Bucharest, July 8, 1960. He studied at the George Enescu Music School, the Salzburg Mozarteum, the Accademia Musicale Chigiana in Siena, and the International Academy in Nice. In 1981 he became music director of the Transylvania Phil. in Cluj-Napoca. From 1987 to 1991 he served as resident conductor at the Vienna State Opera. He made his first appearance in the British capital as a guest conductor with the London Sym. Orch. in 1991, the same year he made his U.S. debut at the Dallas Opera conducting *L'Elisir d'amore*. In 1992 he conducted *Il Barbiere di Siviglia* at the San Francisco Opera and *Semiramide* at the Metropolitan Opera in New York. As a guest conductor, Marin appeared with many opera companies and orchs. throughout Europe, North America, Australia, and the Far East.

Marini, Ignazio, outstanding Italian bass; b. Tagliuno (Bergamo), Nov. 28, 1811; d. Milan, April 29, 1873. He made his operatic debut most likely in Brescia about 1832. From 1833 to 1847 he was a leading member of Milan's La Scala, where he created the role of Guido in Donizetti's *Gemma di Vergy* (Dec. 26, 1834) and the title role in Verdi's *Oberto, Conte di San Bonifacio* (Nov. 17, 1839). He befriended the youthful Verdi, who added the Cabaletta to Infelice in *Ernani* for him (1844). He later created the title role in Verdi's *Attila* (Venice, March 17, 1846). From 1847 to 1849 he sang at London's Covent Garden, and then in New York from 1850 to 1852. From 1856 to 1863 he appeared in St. Petersburg. Marini was greatly admired for his true basso cantante. Among his other famous roles were Rossini's Mosè and Mustafà, and Bellini's Oroveso. His wife, Antonietta Rainer-Marini, was a noted mezzo-soprano. She created the role of Leonora in Verdi's *Oberto*, as well as the Marchesa in his *Un giorno di regno* (Milan, Sept. 5, 1840).

Marinuzzi, Gino, noted Italian conductor and composer, father of **Gino Marinuzzi;** b. Palermo, March 24, 1882; d. Milan, Aug. 17, 1945. He was a student of Zuelli at the Palermo Cons. He commenced his career conducting at the Teatro Massimo in Palermo, where he conducted the first local performance of *Tristan und Isolde* in 1909. After conducting in various Italian operatic centers, he toured in South America. In 1913 he conducted the first local performance of *Parsifal* at the Teatro Colón in Buenos Aires. From 1915 to 1918 he was director of the Bologna Liceo Musicale. On March 27, 1917, he conducted the premiere of Puccini's *La Rondine* in Monte Carlo. He was artistic director of the Chicago Grand Opera Co. from 1919 to 1921. From 1928 to 1934 he was chief conductor of the Teatro Reale dell'Opera in Rome. In 1934 he conducted at London's Covent Garden. From 1934 to 1944 he conducted at Milan's La Scala, where he served as its superintendent in 1944. Marinuzzi was especially admired as a conductor of the Italian operatic repertoire, but he also won distinction for his performances of Wagner and Strauss. Among his compositions were the operas *Barberina* (Palermo, 1903), *Jacquerie* (Buenos Aires, Aug. 11, 1918), and *Palla de' Mozzi* (Milan, April 5, 1932), a Sym. (1943), and chamber music.

BIBL.: A. Garbelotto, *G. M.* (Ancona, 1965).

Marinuzzi, Gino, Italian conductor and composer, son of **Gino Marinuzzi**; b. N.Y., April 7, 1920; d. Rome, Nov. 6, 1996. He studied at the Milan Cons. with Calace (piano) and Paribeni and Bossi (composition), graduating in 1941. From 1946 to 1951 he was assistant conductor at the Teatro dell'Opera in Rome, and then conducted in other Italian opera houses. He was one of the first Italian composers to explore the potentialities of electronic music; in collaboration with Ketoff, he developed an electronic synthesizer, the "Fonosynth," and was a founder of an electronic studio in Rome. His compositions include a radio opera, *La Signora Paulatim* (Naples, 1966).

Mario, Giovanni Matteo, Cavaliere de Candia, celebrated Italian tenor, known professionally as **Mario**; b. Cagliari, Sardinia, Oct. 17, 1810; d. Rome, Dec. 11, 1883. Born into a noble family, he studied at the Turin military academy and then joined the regiment of which his father was colonel. He eloped with a ballerina to Paris (1836), where he studied voice with Bordogni and Poncharde at the Cons. He made his debut as *Robert le diable* at the Paris Opéra (Dec. 5, 1838). He made his first London appearance as Gennaro in *Lucrezia Borgia* opposite Giulia Grisi's Lucrezia at Her Majesty's Theatre (June 6, 1839); the 2 singers remained intimate, without benefit of marriage, for 22 years. He made his debut at the Théâtre-Italien in Paris as Nemorino (Oct. 17, 1839), and soon became one of its principal members; created the role of Ernesto in *Don Pasquale* there (Jan. 3, 1843). He continued to sing in London at Her Majesty's Theatre until 1846, and then was a leading artist at the Royal Italian Opera at Covent Garden until 1871; he also sang in St. Petersburg (1849–53; 1868–70), New York (1854), and Madrid (1859, 1864). He retired from the stage in 1871, giving farewell appearances in Paris, London, and the United States. Mario's beautiful voice, matched by an exquisite vocal style, handsome figure, and effective acting gifts, made him one of the most renowned operatic singers of his day; he also was greatly esteemed as a concert singer. Among his other roles were the Duke of Mantua, Faust, John of Leyden, Almaviva, Raoul, and Roméo.

BIBL.: L. Engel, *From Mozart to M.* (London, 1886); Mrs. Godfrey Pearce (M.'s daughter) and F. Hird, *The Romance of a Great Singer* (London, 1910); E. Forbes, *M. and Grisi* (London, 1985).

Mario (real name, **Tillotson**), **Queena,** American soprano and teacher; b. Akron, Ohio, Aug. 21, 1896; d. N.Y., May 28, 1951. She went to New York to work as a journalist in order to raise funds to pursue her vocal training with Saenger and Sembrich. On Sept. 4, 1918, she made her operatic debut as Olympia in *Les Contes d'Hoffmann* with the San Carlo Opera Co. in New York. She remained with the company until 1920, and then was a member of the Scotti Grand Opera Co. (1920–22). On Nov. 30, 1922, she made her Metropolitan Opera debut in New York as Micaëla. She remained on its roster until 1938, winning favor for her portrayals of Gilda, Juliette, Marguerite, Nedda, Sophie, and Antonia. She was particularly associated with the role of Gretel, which she sang in the first complete opera to be broadcast on radio by the Metropolitan (Dec. 25, 1931), and also at her farewell appearance with the company (Dec. 26, 1938). Mario also sang with the San Francisco Opera (1923–24; 1929–30; 1932). In 1931 she became a teacher at the Curtis Inst. of Music in Philadelphia. In 1934 she opened her own vocal studio in New York, and in 1942 became a teacher at the Juilliard School of Music there. She wrote 3 mystery novels, including *Murder in the Opera House*. In 1925 she married **Wilfred Pelletier**, but they divorced in 1936.

Mariotte, Antoine, French composer; b. Avignon, Dec. 22, 1875; d. Izieux, Loire, Nov. 30, 1944. He was trained at the Naval Academy. In 1897 he became a pupil of d'Indy at the Schola Cantorum in Paris. In 1899 he was appointed conductor of the sym. concerts at St.-Etienne, Loire; from 1902 to 1919 he taught at the Orléans Cons.; in 1920 he was appointed its director; from 1936 to 1938 he was director of the Paris Opéra Comique.

WORKS: OPERAS: *Salomé* (Lyons, Oct. 30, 1908); *Le Vieux Roi* (Lyons, 1911); *Léontine Soeurs* (Paris, May 21, 1924); *Esther, Princesse d'Israël* (Paris, May 5, 1925); *Gargantua* (1924; Paris, Feb. 13, 1935); *Nele Dooryn* (1940).

Mark, Peter, American conductor; b. N.Y., Oct. 31, 1940. He studied at Columbia Univ. (B.A. in musicology, 1961) and with Jean Morel, Joseph Fuchs, and Walter Trampler at the Juilliard School of Music in New York (M.S., 1963). After serving as principal violist of the Juilliard Orch. (1960–63) and the orch. of the Lyric Opera in Chicago (1964–66), he was assistant principal violist of the Los Angeles Phil. (1968–69). In 1975 he became general director of the Virginia Opera. As a guest conductor, he appeared at the N.Y. City Opera (1981), in Los Angeles (1981), at London's Covent Garden (1982), in Tulsa (1988), Mexico City (1989), Buenos Aires (1989), Orlando (1993), and other opera centers. He also was a guest conductor with various orchs. in the United States and abroad. In 1971 he married **Thea Musgrave**. He was awarded the Rosa Ponselle Gold Medal in 1997.

Märkl, Jun, German conductor; b. Munich, Feb. 11, 1959. He received diplomas in violin and conducting from the Hannover Hochschule für Musik, and then had further studies in conducting with Bakels, Celibidache, Gustav Meier, Bernstein, and Ozawa. In 1989 he was named to the position of first conductor of the Darmstadt State Theater, and of the Mannheim National Theater in 1990. He became Generalmusikdirektor of the Saarland State Theater in Saarbrücken in 1992. From 1994 he served as Generalmusikdirektor of the Mannheim National Theater. As a guest conductor, he appeared with the Berlin State Opera, the Hamburg State Opera, the Bavarian State Opera in Munich, the Royal Opera, Covent Garden, London, and at the Metropolitan Opera in New York.

Markull, Friedrich Wilhelm, German organist, pianist, and composer; b. Reichenbach, near Elbing, Prussia, Feb. 17, 1816; d. Danzig, April 30, 1887. He studied organ and composition with F. Schneider in Dessau. He became a church organist in Danzig (1836), and also conductor of the Gesangverein there; he likewise appeared as a pianist. He wrote 3 operas for Danzig: *Maja und Alpino, oder Die bezauberte Rose* (Dec. 23, 1843), *Der König von Zion* (March 22, 1850), and *Das Walpurgisfest* (Jan. 14, 1855); also 2 oratorios (1845, 1856).

BIBL.: W. Neumann, *F. W. M.* (Kassel, 1857).

Markwort, Johann Christian, German tenor and voice teacher; b. Reisling, near Braunschweig, Dec. 13, 1778; d. Bessungen, near Darmstadt, Jan. 13, 1866. He took courses in theology in Leipzig, then went to Vienna to study voice. He sang opera in Munich and in Liechtenstein, and in 1810 was engaged as choirmaster in Darmstadt. In 1830 he dedicated himself entirely to teaching. He publ. pedagogical books: *Umriss einer Gesammt-Tonwissenschaft überhaupt wie auch einer Sprach- und Tonsatzlehre* (Darmstadt, 1826), *Gesang-, Ton- und Rede-Vortraglehre* (Mainz, 1827), and *Über Klangveredelung der Stimme* (Mainz, 1847).

Marliani, Count Marco Aurelio, Italian composer; b. Milan, Aug. 1805; d. Bologna, May 8, 1849. He studied philosophy, and took some lessons with Rossini in Paris, where he went in 1830. Under Rossini's influence, he wrote several operas, which reached the stage in Paris: *Il Bravo* (Feb. 1, 1834), *Ildegonda* (March 7, 1837), and *La Xacarilla* (Oct. 28, 1839); also a ballet, *La Gypsy* (with A. Thomas; Jan. 28, 1839). He returned to Italy in 1847, producing another opera in Bologna, *Gusmano il Buono* (Nov. 7, 1847). He was involved in the revolutionary struggle of 1848. Wounded in a skirmish near Bologna, he died as a result of his injuries.

Maros, Miklós, Hungarian-born Swedish composer and teacher; b. Pécs, Nov. 14, 1943. His father was the Hungarian composer Rudolf Maros (b. Stachy, Jan. 19, 1917; d. Budapest, Aug. 3, 1982). He studied composition in Budapest with Sugár at the Béla Bartók Cons. (1958–63) and with Szabó at the Franz Liszt Academy of Music (1963–67); he settled in Stockholm, where he continued his training with Lidholm and Ligeti at the Musikhögskolan (1968–72); in 1975 he became a naturalized Swedish citizen. He taught electronic music at the Stockholm Electronic Music Studio (1971–78) and at the Musikhögskolan (1976–80); he also taught privately. In 1972, with his wife, the singer Ilona Maros, he founded the Maros Ensemble, which championed contemporary music. In 1980–81 he held a Deutscher Akademischer Austauschdienst fellowship in West Berlin; in 1982–83 he was composer-in-residence of the Swedish Inst. for National Concerts. In his music, Maros utilizes both traditional and experimental techniques, including electronics. Among his works are *Jag önkar jag vore* (I Wish I Could Be), opera (1971), *Stora grusharpan* (The Huge Gravel-sifter), radio opera (1982), and *Att i denna natt* . . . (In This Night . . .), church opera (1986).

Marpurg, Friedrich, German conductor and composer; b. Paderborn, April 4, 1825; d. Wiesbaden, Dec. 2, 1884. He played the violin and piano as a child, and studied composition later with Mendelssohn and Hauptmann at Leipzig. He became conductor at the Königsberg Theater, then at Sondershausen (1864). He succeeded Mangold as court music director at Darmstadt (1868), then was at Freiburg (1873), Laibach (1875), and Wiesbaden, where he became conductor of the Cäcilienverein. He composed the operas *Musa, der letzte Maurenkönig* (Königsberg, 1855), *Agnes von Hohenstaufen* (Freiburg, 1874), and *Die Lichtensteiner* (not perf.). His great-grandfather was the German music theorist and composer Friedrich Wilhelm Marpurg (1718–95).

Marqués y Garcia, Pedro Miguel, Spanish composer; b. Palma de Mallorca, May 20, 1843; d. there, Feb. 25, 1918. He studied in Paris with Alard and Armingaud, then at the Paris Cons. with Massart (violin) and Bazin (composition), also privately with Berlioz, and in 1867 in Madrid with Monasterio. From 1870 to 1896 he was one of the most successful of the zarzuela composers, his most popular works being *El anillo de hierro* (1878) and *El monaguillo* (1891).

Marriner, Sir Neville, outstanding English conductor; b. Lincoln, April 15, 1924. He studied violin with his father, and then with Frederick Mountney; subsequently he entered the Royal College of Music in London when he was 13, but his studies were interrupted by military service during World War II; after resuming his training at the Royal College of Music, he completed his violin studies in Paris with René Benedetti and took courses at the Cons. He was active as a violinist in chamber music ensembles; he was a prof. of violin at the Royal College of Music (1949–59); joined the Philharmonia Orch. of London as a violinist (1952), and then was principal 2d violinist of the London Sym. Orch. (1956–58). His interest in conducting was encouraged by Pierre Monteux, who gave him lessons at his summer school in Hancock, Maine (1959). In 1958 he founded the Academy of St. Martin-in-the-Fields; served as its director until 1978, establishing an international reputation through recordings and tours. From 1968 to 1978 he also served as music director of the Los Angeles Chamber Orch., then was music director of the Minnesota Orch. in Minneapolis (1978–86). In 1981 he became principal guest conductor of the Stuttgart Radio Sym. Orch.; he was its chief conductor from 1983 to 1989. He appeared as a guest conductor with many of the world's leading orchs. On Sept. 29, 1994, he opened the 1994–95 season of N.Y.'s Carnegie Hall conducting the Academy of St. Martin-in-the-Fields in a program featuring Cecilia Bartoli as the soloist of the evening. The concert was subsequently telecast throughout the United States by PBS. In 1979 he was made a Commander of the Order of the British Empire. He was knighted in 1985. Marriner has proved himself one of the most remarkable conductors of his day. His extensive activities as a chamber music player, orch. musician, and chamber orch. violinist-conductor served as an invaluable foundation for his career as a sym. conductor of the first rank. His enormous repertoire encompasses works from the Baroque era to the great masterworks of the 20th century. In all of his performances, he demonstrates authority, mastery of detail, and impeccable taste.

Marrocco, W(illiam) Thomas, American violinist and musicologist; b. West New York, N.J., Dec. 5, 1909. After initial music studies in the United States, he went to Italy and entered the Cons. di Musica S. Pietro a Majella in Naples, receiving his diploma di Magistero in 1930, then studied violin and musicology at the Eastman School of Music in Rochester, N.Y. (B.M., 1934; M.A., 1940); he earned his Ph.D. at the Univ. of Calif. at Los Angeles with the diss. *Jacopo da Bologna and His Works* (1952; publ. as *The Music of Jacopo da Bologna*, Berkeley, 1954). After teaching at Elmira (N.Y.) College (1936–39) and serving as a visiting lecturer at the Univ. of Iowa (1945–46), he was on the music faculty of the Univ. of Kansas in Lawrence (1946–49); he was prof. of music at the Univ. of Calif. at Los Angeles (1950–77); he also played in the Roth String Quartet. He publ. numerous informative essays dealing with early Italian and American music; ed. vols. 6–9 of *Polyphonic Music of the Fourteenth Century: Italian Secular Music* (Monaco, 1967–78); he also publ. *Fourteenth Century Italian Cacce* (Cambridge, Mass., 1942; 2d ed., rev. and aug., 1961), *Music in America: An Anthology* (with H. Gleason; N.Y., 1964), *Medieval Music* (with N. Sandon; London, 1977), *Inventory of Fifteenth Century Bassedanze, Balli and Balletti in Italian Dance Manuals* (N.Y., 1981), and *Memoirs of a Stradivarius* (N.Y., 1988).

Marschner, Heinrich (August), important German composer; b. Zittau, Saxony, Aug. 16, 1795; d. Hannover, Dec. 14, 1861. He sang in the school choir at the Zittau Gymnasium, and also studied music with Karl Hering. In 1813 he went to Leipzig, where he studied jurisprudence at the Univ. Encouraged by the cantor of the Thomasschule, J. C. Schicht, he turned to music as his main vocation. In 1816 he became a music tutor in Count Zichy's household in Pressburg, and also served as Kapellmeister to Prince Krasatkowitz. In his leisure hours he began to compose light operas; his first opera, *Titus* (1816), did not achieve a performance, but soon he had 2 more operas and a Singspiel produced in Dresden. His first signal success was the historical opera *Heinrich IV und d'Aubigné*, which was accepted by Weber, who was then music director at the Dresden Court Opera, and was produced there on July 19, 1820. In 1817 he was in Vienna, where he was fortunate enough to meet Beethoven. In 1821 Marschner moved to Dresden where his Singspiel *Der Holzdieb* was staged at the Court Opera (Feb. 22, 1825). He expected to succeed Weber as music director at the Court Opera after Weber died in London, but failed to obtain the post. He went to Leipzig, where he became Kapellmeister of the Stadttheater, and wrote for it 2 Romantic operas, in the manner of Weber: *Der Vampyr* (March 29, 1828) and *Der Templer und die Jüdin*, after the famous novel *Ivanhoe* by Sir Walter Scott (Dec. 22, 1829). In 1830 he received the position of Kapellmeister of the Hannover Hoftheater. His most successful opera, *Hans Heiling* (Berlin, May 24, 1833), exhibited the most attractive Romantic traits of his music: a flowing melody, sonorous harmony, and nervous rhythmic pulse; the opera formed a natural transition to the exotic melodrama of Meyerbeer's great stage epics and to Wagner's early lyrical music dramas. Historically important was his bold projection of a continuous dramatic development, without the conventional type of distinct arias separated by recitative. In this respect he was the heir of Weber and a precursor of Wagner.

WORKS: DRAMATIC: OPERAS: *Titus*, opera (1816; not perf.); *Der Kyffhäuserberg*, Singspiel (1816; Zittau, Jan. 2, 1822); *Heinrich IV und d'Aubigné*, opera (1817–18; Dresden, July 19, 1820); *Saidar und Zulima*, romantic opera (Pressburg, Nov. 26, 1818); *Der Holzdieb*, Singspiel (1823; Dresden, Feb. 22, 1825; rev. 1853 as *Geborgt*); *Lukretia*, opera (1820–26; Danzig, Jan 17, 1827); *Der Vampyr*, romantic opera (1827; Leipzig, March 29, 1828); *Der Templer und die Jüdin*, romantic opera (Leipzig, Dec. 22, 1829); *Des Falkners Braut*, comic opera (1830; Leipzig, March 10, 1832); *Hans Heiling*, romantic opera (1831–32; Berlin, May 24, 1833); *Das Schloss am Ätna*, romantic opera (1830–35; Leipzig, Jan. 29, 1836); *Der Bäbu*, comic opera (1836–37; Hannover, Feb. 19, 1838); *Kaiser Adolf von Nassau*, romantic opera (Dresden, Jan 5, 1845); *Austin*, romantic opera (1850–51; Hannover, Jan. 25, 1852); *Sangeskönig Hiarne, oder Das Tyringsschwert*, romantic opera (1857–58; Frankfurt am Main, Sept. 13, 1863). BALLET: *Die stolze Bäuerin* (Zittau, 1810); Also incidental music.

BIBL.: W. Neumann, *H. M.* (Kassel, 1854); E. Danzig, *H. M. in seinen minderbekannten Opern und Liedern* (Leipzig, 1890); M. Wittmann, *H. M.* (Leipzig, 1897); G. Münzer, *H. M.* (Berlin, 1901); C. Preiss, *Templer und Jüdin* (Graz, 1911); H. Gaartz, *Die Opern H. M.s* (Leipzig, 1912); G. Fischer, *M. Erinnerungen* (Hannover, 1918); A. Bickel, *H. M. in seinen Opern* (diss., Univ. of Erlangen, 1929); A. Gnirs, *Hans Heiling* (Karlsbad, 1931); G. Hausswald, *H. M.* (Dresden, 1938); V. Köhler, *H. M.s Bühnenwerke* (diss., Univ. of Göttingen, 1956); A. Dean Palmer, *H. A. M., 1795–1861: His Life and Stage Works* (1980); B. Weber, *H. M.: Königlicher Hoftapellmeisters in Hannover* (Hannover, 1995).

Marsh, Robert C(harles), American music critic; b. Columbus, Ohio, Aug. 5, 1924. He took courses in journalism (B.S., 1945) and philosophy (A.M., 1946) at Northwestern Univ. In 1946–47 he was a Sage fellow at Cornell Univ., where he received training in theory from Robert Palmer. He pursued postgraduate studies at the Univ. of Chicago (1948), and then studied at Harvard Univ. (Ed.D., 1951), where he also attended Hindemith's lectures (1949–50). After attending the Univ. of Oxford (1952–53), he studied musicology with Thurston Dart and theory of criticism with H. S. Middleton at the Univ. of Cambridge (1953–56). He taught social sciences at the Univ. of Ill. (1947–49), was a lecturer in the humanities at Chicago City Junior College (1950–51), and assistant prof. of education at the Univ. of Kansas (1951–52). After serving as visiting prof. of education at the State Univ. of N.Y. (1953–54), he taught the humanities at the Univ. of Chicago (1956–58). He was contributing ed. of *High Fidelity* magazine (1955–66; 1971–77). He served as music critic of the *Chicago Sun-Times* from 1956 to 1991. In addition to his music reviews and books, he contributed articles on music to various literary and philosophical publications. His books on music comprise *Toscanini and the Art of Orchestral Performance* (1956; 2d ed., rev., 1962 as *Toscanini and the Art of Conducting*), *The Cleveland Orchestra* (1967), *Ravinia* (1987), and *James Levine at Ravinia* (1993).

Marshall, Lois (Catherine), prominent Canadian soprano, later mezzo-soprano; b. Toronto, Jan. 29, 1924; d. there, Feb. 19, 1997. She began her vocal training at age 12 with Weldon Kilburn, whom she married in 1968; she also studied lieder interpretation with Emmy Heim (1947–50). She first gained notice as a soloist in Bach's St. Matthew Passion with Sir Ernest MacMillan and the Toronto Sym. Orch. (1947). In 1952 she made her operatic stage debut as the Queen of the Night in Toronto, won the Naumburg Award, and made her N.Y. recital debut. She appeared as a soloist in Beethoven's *Missa solemnis* with Toscanini and the NBC Sym. Orch. in 1953, and subsequently sang with many other important American orchs. She made her London debut in 1956 with Beecham and the Royal Phil., and began a series of world concert tours in 1960; she began singing as a mezzo-soprano in the mid-1970s. Although she gave her official farewell performance at a Toronto concert on Dec. 10, 1982, she made occasional appearances in subsequent years. She was made a Companion of the Order of Canada (1968).

Marshall, Margaret (Anne), Scottish soprano; b. Stirling, Jan. 4, 1949. She studied at the Royal Scottish Academy of Music in Glasgow; she also took voice lessons with Edna Mitchell and Peter Pears in England and with Hans Hotter in Munich. In 1974 she won 1st prize at the International Competition in Munich. She made her London concert debut in 1975; in 1978 she made her operatic debut in Florence as Euridice in *Orfeo*; she then sang the role of the Countess in the 1979 Florence production of *Le nozze di Figaro*, and made her Covent Garden debut in London in the same role in 1980. In 1982 she appeared as Fiordiligi at La Scala in Milan and at the Salzburg Festival. She made her first appearances in the United States in 1980 as a soloist with the Boston Sym. Orch. and N.Y. Phil.; she subsequently made several American tours as a concert artist. In 1988 she made her first appearance at the Vienna State Opera as Mozart's Countess. During the 1991–92 season, she appeared at the Mozart Bicentenary Gala at Covent Garden and also sang Fiordiligi in Salzburg.

Marshall, Robert L(ewis), distinguished American musicologist; b. N.Y., Oct. 12, 1939. After training at Columbia Univ. (A.B., 1960), he studied at Princeton Univ. with Babbitt, Lockwood, Mendel, and Strunk (M.F.A., 1962; Ph.D., 1968, with the diss. *The Compositional Process of J. S. Bach: A Study of the Autograph Scores of the Vocal Works*; publ. in Princeton, 1972). In 1966 he joined the faculty of the Univ. of Chicago, where he served as chairman of the music dept. (1972–77) and then as a prof. (1977–83). He was a prof. at Brandeis Univ. from 1983. From 1977 to 1987 he was general ed. of the series Recent Researches in the music of the Baroque Era. Marshall has particularly distinguished himself in Bach and Mozart studies, and has contributed scholarly articles to various journals. His book *The Music of Johann Sebastian Bach: The Sources, the Style, the Significance* (N.Y., 1989) won the ASCAP–Deems Taylor Award in 1990. His other books include *Mozart Speaks: Views on Music, Musicians, and the World: Drawn from the Letters of Wolfgang Amadeus Mozart and Other Early Accounts* (N.Y., 1991).

Marsick, Armand (Louis Joseph), Belgian conductor, teacher, and composer; b. Liège, Sept. 20, 1877; d. Haine-St.-Paul, April 30, 1959. He was the nephew of the distinguished Belgian violinist Martin (-Pierre-Joseph) Marsick (b. Jupille-sur-Neuse, near Liège, March 9, 1848; d. Paris, Oct. 21, 1924). Armand Marsick studied with his father, Louis Marsick, then took a course in composition with Dupuis at the Liège Cons., with Ropartz at the Nancy Cons., and d'Indy in Paris. After playing 1st violin in the Municipal Théâtre in Nancy, he became concertmaster at the Concerts Colonne in Paris (1898); in 1908 he obtained the position of instructor at the Athens Cons., where he remained until 1921; he was appointed director at the Bilbao Cons. in 1922. He was a prof. at the Liège Cons. (1927–42) and conductor of the Société des Concerts Symphoniques (1927–39). He composed the operas *La Jane* (1903; 1st perf. as *Vendetta corsa*, Rome, 1913; Liège, March 29, 1921), *Lara* (1913; Antwerp, Dec. 3, 1929), and *L'Anneau nuptial* (1920; Brussels, March 3, 1928); also a radio play, *Le Visage de la Wallonie* (1937).

Marteau, Henri, greatly esteemed French-born Swedish violinist and pedagogue; b. Rheims, March 31, 1874; d. Lichtenberg, Bavaria, Oct. 3, 1934. He studied violin with Léonard and Garcin at the Paris Cons. (premier prix, 1892) and began his concert career as a youth; he played in Vienna when he was 10 and in London when he was 14. In 1892, 1893, 1894, 1898, and 1906 he also toured the United States; he gave concerts in Scandinavia, Russia, France, and Germany. In 1900 he was appointed prof. of violin at the Geneva Cons., and in 1908 succeeded Joachim as violin teacher at the Hochschule für Musik in Berlin. He conducted the Göteborg orch. (1915–20) and became a naturalized Swedish citizen (1920); he then taught at the German Academy of Music in Prague (1921–24), the Leipzig Cons. (1926–27), and the Dresden Cons. (from 1928). He was greatly appreciated by musicians of Europe; Reger, who was a personal friend, wrote a violin concerto for him, as did Massenet; his teacher Léonard bequeathed to him his magnificent Maggini violin, once owned by the empress Maria

Theresa. He championed the music of Bach and Mozart. Marteau was also a competent composer. Among his works was an opera, *Meister Schwable* (Plauen, 1921).

BIBL.: B. Marteau, *H. M.: Siegeszug einer Geige* (Tutzing, 1971); G. Weiss, ed., *Der Lehrer und Wegbereiter von H. M., Hubert Léonard* (Tutzing, 1987); K. Bangerter, *H. M. als Komponist im Spiegel der Kritik: Eine Studie zum Begriff der "Einheit" in der Musikkritik um 1900* (Tutzing, 1991).

Martelli, Henri, French composer; b. Santa Fe, Argentina, Feb. 25, 1895; d. Paris, July 15, 1980. He studied law at the Univ. of Paris; simultaneously took courses in fugue and composition with Widor at the Paris Cons. (1912–24). From 1940 to 1944 he was head of orch. and chamber music programs of the French Radio; he was secretary of the Société Nationale de Musique (1945–67) and director of programs there from 1968; from 1953 to 1973, he also was president of the French section of the ISCM. In his compositions, he attempted to re-create the spirit of early French music using modern techniques. Among his works are the operas *La Chanson de Roland* (1921–23; rev. 1962–64; Paris, April 13, 1967) and *Le Major Cravachon* (1958; French Radio, June 14, 1959) and the ballets *La Bouteille de Panurge* (1930; Paris, Feb. 24, 1937) and *Les Hommes de sable* (1951); also 17 radiophonic works (1940–62).

Martin, Frank (Théodore), greatly renowned Swiss composer and pedagogue; b. Geneva, Sept. 15, 1890; d. Naarden, the Netherlands, Nov. 21, 1974. He was the last of 10 children of a Calvinist minister, a descendant of the Huguenots. He studied privately with Joseph Lauber in Geneva (1906–14), who instructed him in the basics of the conservative idiom of Swiss music of the fin de siècle; he then had lessons with Hans Huber and Frederic Klose, who continued to emphasize the conservative foundations of the religious and cultural traditions of the Swiss establishment. However, Martin soon removed himself from the strict confines of Swiss scholasticism, encouraged in this development by Ernest Ansermet. In 1918 Martin went to Zürich and, in 1921, to Rome; he finally settled in Paris in 1923, then the center of modern music. He returned to Geneva in 1926 as a pianist and harpsichordist, taught at the Inst. Jaques-Dalcroze (1927–38), and was founder and director of the Technicum Moderne de Musique (1933–39) and served as president of the Assn. of Swiss Musicians (1942–46). He moved to the Netherlands in 1946; he also taught composition at the Cologne Hochschule für Musik (1950–57). His early music showed the influence of Franck and French impressionists, but soon he succeeded in creating a distinctive style supported by a consummate mastery of contrapuntal and harmonic writing, and a profound feeling for emotional consistency and continuity. Still later he became fascinated by the logic and self-consistency of Schoenberg's method of composition with 12 tones, and adopted it in a modified form in several of his works. He also demonstrated an ability to stylize folk-song materials in modern techniques. In his music, Martin followed the religious and moral precepts of his faith in selecting several subjects of his compositions. In 1944 the director of Radio Geneva asked him to compose an oratorio to be broadcast immediately upon the conclusion of World War II. He responded with *In terra pax* for 5 Soli, Double Chorus, and Orch., which was given its broadcast premiere from Geneva at the end of the war in Europe, May 7, 1945; a public performance followed in Geneva 24 days later. He publ. *Responsabilité du compositeur* (Geneva, 1966); M. Martin ed. his *Un compositeur médite sur son art* (Neuchâtel, 1977).

WORKS: DRAMATIC: *Oedipe-Roi*, incidental music (Geneva, Nov. 21, 1922); *Oedipe à Colone*, incidental music (1923); *Le Divorce*, incidental music (Geneva, April 1928); *Roméo et Juliette*, incidental music (Mézières, June 1, 1929); *Die blaue Blume*, ballet music (1935); *Das Märchen vom Aschenbrodel*, ballet, after *Cinderella* (1941; Basel, March 12, 1942); *La Voix des siècles*, incidental music (Geneva, July 4, 1942); *Ein Totentanz zu Basel im Jahre 1943*, outdoor dance spectacle (Basel, May 27, 1943); *Athalie*, incidental music (1946; Geneva, May 7, 1947); *Der Sturm*, opera, after Shakespeare (1952–55; Vienna, June 17, 1956); *Monsieur de Pourceaugnac*, opera, after Molière (1960; Geneva, April 23, 1963). Also several oratorios: *Le Vin herbé*, secular oratorio in 3 parts (part 1, 1938; Zürich, April 16, 1940; parts 2 and 3, 1940–41; 1st complete perf., Zürich, March 28, 1942), *In terra pax*, oratorio brève for 5 Soloists, 2 Mixed Choruses, and Orch. (1944; radio broadcast, Geneva, May 7, 1945; 1st public perf., Geneva, May 31, 1945), *Golgotha*, passion oratorio for 5 Soloists, Chorus, Organ, and Orch. (1945–48; Geneva, April 29, 1949), *Le Mystère de la Nativité*, Christmas oratorio for 9 Soloists, Mixed Chamber Chorus, Men's Chorus, Mixed Chorus, and Orch. (1957, 1959; Geneva, Dec. 23, 1959), and *Pilate*, oratorio breve for Baritone, Mezzo-soprano, Tenor, Bass, Chorus, and Orch. (RAI, Rome, Nov. 14, 1964).

BIBL.: R. Klein, *F. M.: Sein Leben und Werk* (Vienna, 1960); A. Koelliker, *F. M.: Biographie, les oeuvres* (Lausanne, 1963); B. Billeter, *F. M.: Ein Aussenseiter der neuen Musik* (Frauenfeld, 1970); B. Martin, *F. M. ou la réalité du rêve* (Neuchâtel, 1973); W. Misteli, ed., *F. M.: Né le 15 septembre 1890, décédé le 21 novembre 1974: Liste des oeuvres: Werkverzeichnis* (Zürich, 1981); M. Martin, ed., *Apropos de . . . commentaires de F. M. sur ses oeuvres* (Neuchâtel, 1984); C. King, *F. M.: A Bio-Bibliography* (Westport, Conn., 1990).

Martin, Janis, American mezzo-soprano, later soprano; b. Sacramento, Aug. 16, 1939. She studied in San Francisco and New York, making her operatic debut as Teresa in *La Sonnambula* at the San Francisco Opera in 1960; subsequently sang Marina, Venus, and Meg Page there. On March 25, 1962, she made her first appearance at the N.Y. City Opera as Mrs. Grose in Britten's *The Turn of the Screw*. She won the Metropolitan Opera Auditions, making her debut as Flora in *La Traviata* on Dec. 19, 1962, in New York. After singing for 3 seasons as a mezzo-soprano, she returned to the Metropolitan Opera in 1973 as a soprano and sang such roles as Kundry, Sieglinde, and Berg's Marie in *Wozzeck*. In 1968 she appeared as Magdalene and as Fricka at the Bayreuth Festival. She sang Tosca at the Chicago Lyric Opera in 1971. From 1971 to 1988 she appeared at the Berlin Deutsche Oper. She made her Covent Garden debut in London as Marie in *Wozzeck* in 1973. In 1980 she sang the Woman in *Erwartung* at Milan's La Scala. She appeared as Isolde at the Geneva Opera in 1985. In 1990 she sang Beethoven's Leonore at the Deutsche Opera am Rhein in Düsseldorf. She portrayed Brünnhilde in *Götterdammerung* in Brussels in 1992. In 1996 she was engaged as Orfeo in Rome. Among her other roles are Ortrud, Brangäne, Senta, Elisabeth in *Tännhauser*, Ariadne, and Judith in *Duke Bluebeard's Castle*.

Martin, (Nicolas-) Jean-Blaise, famous French baritone; b. Paris, Feb. 24, 1768; d. Ronzières, Rhone, Oct. 28, 1837. He made his debut at Paris's Théâtre de Monsieur in 1789 in *Le Marquis de Tulipano*. He sang at the Théâtre Feydeau and the Théâtre Favart from 1794 until they were united as the Opéra Comique in 1801, remaining there until 1823; he sang there again in 1826 and 1833. He was also a member of the Imperial (later Royal) Chapel from its founding until 1830. He was a prof. at the Paris Cons. (1816–18; 1832–37). He wrote an opéra comique, *Les Oiseaux de mer* (Paris, 1796). His voice, while essentially baritone in quality, had the extraordinary range of 2 1/2 octaves, E flat to *a'*.

Martin, Riccardo (Hugh Whitfield), American tenor, teacher, and composer; b. Hopkinsville, Ky., Nov. 18, 1874; d. N.Y., Aug. 11, 1952. He received training in composition from MacDowell at Columbia Univ. and in voice from Sbriglia in Paris (1901), Franklin Cannone in Milan, and Vincenzo Lombardi in Florence (1908). In Oct. 1904 he made his operatic debut as Gounod's Faust in Nantes under the name Richard Martin. In 1905 he appeared as Andrea Chénier in Verona under the name Riccardo Martin. After making his U.S. debut as Canio in New Orleans in 1906, he toured with the San Carlo Opera Co. (1906–07). On Nov. 20, 1907, he made his Metropolitan Opera debut in New York as Boito's Faust, remaining on its roster until 1915. During his years with the Metropolitan Opera, he appeared in such roles as Pinkerton, Cavaradossi, Canio, Manrico, Rodolfo, and Turiddu; he also created the roles of Quintus in Horatio Parker's *Mona* (March 14, 1912) and Christian in Walter Damrosch's *Cyrano de Bergerac* (Feb. 27,

1913) while there. In 1910 he appeared as Pinkerton at London's Covent Garden. In 1910–11 and 1912–13 he made appearances with the Boston Grand Opera Co. In 1917–18 he was again on the roster of the Metropolitan Opera, and then sang with the Chicago Grand Opera Co. (1920–22). He also made appearances as a concert artist before settling in New York as a voice teacher. Among his compositions were a ballet, orch. music, and songs. Martin possessed a beautiful spinto voice and dramatic stage gifts, but his career was overshadowed by his celebrated colleague Enrico Caruso.

Martinelli, Caterina, Italian singer; b. Rome, 1589 or 1590; d. Mantua (buried), March 7, 1608. She entered the service of the Gonzaga family in Mantua in 1603, where her talent was appreciated by Monteverdi. After appearing as a singer there in 1608, Monteverdi was prompted to compose the title role of his opera *L'Arianna* for Martinelli. However, she was stricken with smallpox and died before the work could be mounted. Monteverdi was then moved to write his madrigal cycle *Lagrime d'amante al sepolcro dell'amata* in her memory (publ. in his 6th book of madrigals, 1614).

Martinelli, Giovanni, famous Italian tenor; b. Montagnana, Oct. 22, 1885; d. N.Y., Feb. 2, 1969. He sang and played the clarinet in his youth. His potential as a singer was discovered by a bandmaster during Martinelli's military service. In 1908 he first appeared on the operatic stage in Montagnana as the Messenger in *Aida*. He then studied voice with Mandolini in Milan, where he made his concert debut as a soloist in Rossini's *Stabat Mater* on Dec. 3, 1910. His formal operatic debut followed there at the Teatro del Varme as Ernani on Dec. 29, 1910. Puccini was impressed with his vocal gifts and invited Martinelli to sing Dick Johnson in the European premiere of the composer's *La Fanciulla del West* in Rome on June 12, 1911. He subsequently sang that role in various Italian music centers, including Milan's La Scala in 1912. On April 22, 1912, he made his first appearance at London's Covent Garden as Cavaradossi, and sang there again in 1913–14, 1919, and 1937. Martinelli made his lst appearance with the Metropolitan Opera in that same role during the company's visit to Albany, N.Y., on Nov. 18, 1913. His formal debut at the Metropolitan Opera in New York followed as Rodolfo on Nov. 20, 1913, with remarkable success. He rapidly acquired distinction there and, after Caruso's death in 1921, became one of the principal tenors on the Metropolitan Opera roster. He sang there every season until 1943, winning acclaim for his portrayals of such roles as Otello, Radames, Manrico, Eléazar in *La Juive*, Don José, Canio, Faust, Samson, and Andrea Chénier. He also appeared in Boston (1914), San Francisco (1923–39), Chicago (1924–31; 1933–44), St. Louis (1934–41), and Cincinnati (1940–45). In 1944 he returned to the Metropolitan Opera, where he made his farewell appearance as Pollione on March 8, 1945. During the 1945–46 season, he returned to the Metropolitan Opera as a concert artist. After singing in Philadelphia (1945–50), he taught voice in New York while making occasional appearances as a singer. The Metropolitan Opera honored him on the 50th anniversary of his debut with the company with a gala on Nov. 20, 1963. He made his last public appearance as a singer in his 82d year when he sang the Emperor in *Turandot* in Seattle. Martinelli's brilliant vocal and dramatic gifts made him one of the foremost singers of heroic roles of his era.

Martínez, Marianne (Anna Katharina) von, Austrian singer, pianist, and composer; b. Vienna, May 4, 1744; d. there, Dec. 13, 1812. She was the daughter of Nicolò Martínez, who went to Vienna as "gentiluomo" to the papal nuncio. Thanks to his privileged social position in the diplomatic circles in Vienna, her father was able to engage the best instructors for her; Metastasio was put in charge of her education, and he saw that she received lessons in singing, piano, and composition from Porpora and Haydn; she also studied counterpoint with G. Bonno. She appeared as a singer and pianist at the court while still a child, and later performed in aristocratic salons. Her compositions, which included several oratorios, were unremarkable, but are of historical interest as examples of musical composition by a woman of high society who contributed to the artistic life of the Austrian capital during its greatest ascendance on the international scene. Manuscripts of some of her works are preserved in the archives of the Gesellschaft der Musikfreunde in Vienna.

Martínez, Miguel Angel Gomez. See **Gomez Martínez, Miguel Angel.**

Martinez, Odaline de la, Cuban-born American conductor, pianist, and composer; b. Matanzas, Oct. 31, 1949. She emigrated to the U.S. in 1961 and in 1971 became a naturalized American citizen. Following training at Tulane Univ. (B.F.A., 1972), she settled in London and studied composition with Paul Patterson at the Royal Academy of Music (1972–76) and with Reginald Smith Brindle at the Univ. of Surrey (M.M., 1977); she subsequently pursued postgraduate studies in computer music (1977–80). In 1976 she helped organize and was conductor of the chamber ensemble Lontano, with which she toured extensively. In 1981 she also organized the Contemporary Chamber Orch., for which she served as principal conductor. Among her various awards were a Guggenheim fellowship (1980–81) and the Villa-Lobos Medal (1987). Martinez has embraced an inclusive course as a composer in which she utilizes various styles and techniques. Among her works is the opera *Sister Aimee*, on the life of the American evangelist Aimee Semple McPherson (1978–83).

Martini, Jean Paul Egide (real name, **Johann Paul Ágid Schwarzendorf**), German organist, teacher, and composer; b. Freystadt, Upper Palatinate (baptized), Aug. 31, 1741; d. Paris, Feb. 10, 1816. At the age of 10 he enrolled in the Jesuit seminary in Neuburg an der Donau, becoming organist there. He began to tour as an organist in 1758; he went to Nancy in 1760, and was known as Martini il Tedesco. He was in the service of the former king of Poland, Prince Stanislaus Leszcynski, duke of Lorraine, in Lunéville (1761–64), then went to Paris, where he won a prize for a military march for the Swiss Guard; this introduced him into army circles in France; he enlisted as an officer of a Hussar regiment, and wrote more band music. He also composed an opera, *L'Amoureux de quinze ans, ou Le Double Fête*, which was produced with extraordinary success at the Italian Opera in Paris (April 18, 1771). Leaving the army, he became music director to the Prince of Conde, and later to the Comte d'Artois. He purchased the reversion of the office of 1st Intendant of the King's Music, a speculation brought to naught by the Revolution, which caused him to resign in haste his position as conductor at the Théâtre Feydeau, and flee to Lyons in 1792. He then returned to Paris, winning acclaim with the production of his opera *Sappho* (1794). He became Inspector at the Paris Cons. in 1798 and also taught composition there (1800–02). In appreciation of his royalist record, he was given the post of Royal Intendant at the Restoration in 1814, serving as chief director of the Royal Court Orch. until his death. He wrote 13 operas, a Requiem for Louis XVI, Psalms, and other church music, but he is chiefly remembered as the composer of the popular air *Plaisir d'amour*, which was arranged by Berlioz for Voice and Orch.

BIBL.: A Pougin, *J. P. E. M.* (Paris, 1864).

Martinon, Jean, significant French conductor and composer; b. Lyons, Jan. 10, 1910; d. Paris, March 1, 1976. He studied violin at the Lyons Cons. (1924–25) and at the Paris Cons. (1926–29), winning the premier prix, then took lessons in composition with Roussel and d'Indy and in conducting with Munch and Desormière; he obtained his M.A. degree in arts from the Sorbonne (1932). He was in the French army during World War II; he was taken prisoner in 1940 and spent 2 years in a German prison camp (Stalag IX); during imprisonment, he wrote several works of a religious nature, among them *Psalm 136, Musique d'exil ou Stalag IX*, and *Absolve Domine*, in memory of French musicians killed in the war. After his release, he appeared as a conductor with the Pasdeloup Orch. in Paris (1943); he then was conductor of the Bordeaux Sym. Orch. (1943–45), assistant conductor of the Paris Cons. Orch. (1944–46), and assoc. conductor of the London

Phil. (1947–49). After conducting the Radio Eireann Orch. in Dublin (1948–50), he was artistic director of the Lamoureux Orch. in Paris (1950–57). He made his American debut with the Boston Sym. Orch. on March 29, 1957, conducting the U.S. premiere of his 2d Sym. Martinon was artistic director of the Israel Phil. (1958–60) and Generalmusikdirektor of the Düsseldorf Sym. Orch. (1960–66). In 1963 he was appointed music director of the Chicago Sym. Orch.; during the 5 years of his tenure, he conducted about 60 works by American and European composers of the modern school; this progressive policy met opposition from some influential people in Chicago society and in the press, and he resigned in 1968. He subsequently was chief conductor of the Orchestre National de la Radio Television Française in Paris (from 1968) and the Residente Orch. in The Hague (from 1974). As a conductor, he became best known for his idiomatic performances of the French repertoire. His own compositions follow the spirit of French neoclassicism, euphonious in their modernity and expansive in their Romantic élan. Among them is the opera *Hécube*, after Euripides (1949–54; 1st scenic perf., Strasbourg, Nov. 10, 1956), and the ballet *Ambohimanga ou La Cité bleue* (1946; Paris, 1947); also *Le Lis de Sharon*, oratorio (1951; Tel Aviv, 1952).

Martinpelto, Hillevi, Swedish soprano; b. Alvaden, Jan. 9, 1958. She studied at the Royal Opera School in Stockholm. After making her debut as Pamina at the Folksopera in Stockholm, she sang for the first time at the Royal Opera in Stockholm in 1987 as Cio-Cio-San. In 1989–90 she appeared as both Gluck Iphigenias at the Drottningholm Festival. She sang Fiordiligi in Brussels in 1990, and in 1991 reprised that role at the Hamburg State Opera. In 1993 she appeared as Freia in *Das Rheingold* at the Lyric Opera in Chicago, and in 1994 as Donna Anna at the Glyndebourne Festival. In 1997 she sang Agathe at the Royal Opera in Copenhagen. She also appeared as a soloist with many European orchs.

Martinů, Bohuslav (Jan), remarkable Czech-born American composer; b. Polička, Dec. 8, 1890; d. Liestal, near Basel, Aug. 28, 1959. He was born in the bell tower of a church in the village where his father was a watchman. He studied violin with the local tailor when he was 7; from 1906 to 1909 he was enrolled at the Prague Cons., then entered the Prague Organ School (1909), where he studied organ and theory, but was expelled in 1910 for lack of application. He played in the 2d violin section in the Czech Phil. in Prague (1913–14), returning to Polička (1914–18) to avoid service in the Austrian army; after World War I he reentered the Prague Cons. as a pupil of Suk, but again failed to graduate; he also played again in the Czech Phil. (1918–23). In 1923 he went to Paris and participated in progressive musical circles; took private lessons with Roussel. In a relatively short time his name became known in Europe through increasingly frequent performances of his chamber works, ballets, and symphonic pieces; several of his works were performed at the festivals of the ISCM. In 1932 his String Sextet won the Elizabeth Sprague Coolidge Award. He remained in Paris until June 1940, when he fled the German invasion and went to Portugal; he finally reached the United States in 1941 and settled in New York; personal difficulties prevented him from accepting an offer to teach at the Prague Cons. after the liberation of Czechoslovakia in 1945; later he was a visiting prof. of music at Princeton Univ. (1948–51). In 1952 he became a naturalized American citizen. Although Martinů spent most of his life away from his homeland, he remained spiritually and musically faithful to his native country. He composed a poignant tribute to the martyred village of Lidice when, in 1943, the Nazi authorities ordered the execution of all men and boys over the age of 16 to avenge the assassination of the local Gauleiter. Martinů immortalized the victims in a heartfelt lyric work entitled *Memorial to Lidice*. In 1953 he returned to Europe, spending the last 2 years of his life in Switzerland. On Aug. 27, 1979, his remains were taken from Schonenberg, Switzerland, to Polička, Czechoslovakia, where they were placed in the family mausoleum. Martinů's centennial was celebrated in 1990 all over Czechoslovakia. As a musician and stylist, he belonged to the European tradition of musical nationalism. He avoided literal exploitation of Czech or Slovak musical materials, but his music is nonetheless characterized by a strong feeling for Bohemian melorhythms; his stylizations of Czech dances are set in a modern idiom without losing their authenticity or simplicity. In his large works, he followed the neoclassical trend, with some impressionistic undertones; his mastery of modern counterpoint was extraordinary.

WORKS: DRAMATIC: OPERAS: *Voják a tanečnice* (The Soldier and the Dancer; 1926–27; Brno, May 5, 1928); *Les Larmes du couteau* (The Knife's Tears; 1928); *Trois souhaits, ou Les Vicissitudes de la vie*, "opera-film in 3 acts" (1929; Brno, June 16, 1971); *La Semaine de bonté* (1929; unfinished); *Hry o Marii* (The Miracle of Our Lady; 1933–34; Brno, Feb. 23, 1935); *Hlas lesa* (The Voice of the Forest), radio opera (Czech Radio, Oct. 6, 1935); *Divadlo za bránou* (The Suburban Theater), opera buffa (1935–36; Brno, Sept. 20, 1936); *Veselohra na mostě* (Comedy on a Bridge), radio opera (1935; Czech Radio, March 18, 1937; rev. 1950); *Julietta, or The Key to Dreams*, lyric opera (1936–37; Prague, March 16, 1938); *Alexandre bis*, opera buffa (1937; Mannheim, Feb. 18, 1964); *What Men Live By* (Čím člověk žije), pastoral opera after Tolstoy (1951–52; N.Y., May 20, 1955); *The Marriage* (Ženitba), television opera after Gogol (1952; NBC-TV, N.Y., Feb. 7, 1953); *La Plainte contre inconnu* (1953; unfinished); *Mirandolina*, comic opera (1954; Prague, May 17, 1959); *Ariadne*, lyric opera (1958; Gelsenkirchen, March 2, 1961); *Recké pašije* (Greek Passion), musical drama after Kazantzakis (1955–59; Zürich, June 9, 1961). BALLETS: *Noc* (Night), "meloplastic scene" (1913–14); *Stín* (The Shadow; 1916); *Istar* (1918–22; Prague, Sept. 11, 1924); *Who Is the Most Powerful in the World?* (Kdo je na světě nejmocnější), ballet comedy, after an English fairy tale (1922; Brno, Jan. 31, 1925); *The Revolt* (Vzpoura), ballet sketch (1922–23; Brno, Feb. 11, 1928); *The Butterfly That Stamped* (Motýl, ktery dupal), after Kipling (1926); *La Revue de cuisine* (Prague, 1927); *On tourne* (Natáčí se), for a cartoon and puppet film (1927); *Le Raid merveilleux* (Báječný let), "ballet mécanique" for 2 Clarinets, Trumpet, and Strings (1927); *Echec au roi*, jazz ballet (1930); *Špalíček* (The Chapbook), with Vocal Soloists and Chorus (1931; Prague, Sept. 19, 1933; rev. 1940; Prague, April 2, 1949); *Le Jugement de Paris* (1935); *The Strangler* (Uškreovač), for 3 Dancers (New London, Conn., Aug. 15, 1948).

BIBL.: M. Šafránek, *B. M.: The Man and His Music* (N.Y., 1944); J. Löwenbach, *M. pozdravuje domov* (Prague, 1947); M. Šafránek, *B. M.: His Life and Works* (London, 1962); H. Halbreich, *B. M.* (Zürich, 1968); C. Martinů, *Můj život s B. M.* (My Life with B. M.; Prague, 1971); B. Large, *M.* (N.Y., 1975); G. Erismann, *M: Un musicien à l'éveil des sources* (Arles, 1990).

Martín y Soler, (Atanasio Martín Ignacio) Vicente (Tadeo Francisco Pellegrin), distinguished Spanish composer; b. Valencia, May 2, 1754; d. St. Petersburg, Jan. 30, 1806. He was a choirboy in Valencia and a church organist in Alicante before going to Madrid, where he brought out his first work for the stage, the zarzuela *La Madrileña, o Tutor burlado*, most likely in 1776. He then went to Italy, where he became known as Martini lo Spagnuolo. He wrote operas for several theaters there, entering the service of the Infante, the future King Charles IV of Spain, about 1780. With Da Ponte as his librettist, he wrote the opera buffa *Il Burbero di buon cuore*, which was premiered in Vienna to much acclaim on Jan. 4, 1786. It was revived there on Nov. 9, 1789, and included 2 additional arias written expressly for the occasion by Mozart. Martín y Soler and Da Ponte then collaborated on the opera buffa *Una cosa rara, o sia Bellezza ed onestà*, a masterful stage work first given in Vienna on Nov. 17, 1786, and subsequently performed throughout Europe. Mozart used a theme from this popular work in the supper scene of his *Don Giovanni*. Martín y Soler and Da Ponte subsequently collaborated on the successful opera buffa *L'arbore di Diana* (Vienna, Oct. 1, 1787). The composer was then called to St. Petersburg to serve as court composer to Catherine II the Great, who wrote the libretto for his comic opera *Gore bogatyr Kosometovich* (St. Petersburg, Feb. 9, 1789). He then went to London, collaborating again with Da Ponte on the highly successful *La scuola dei maritati* (Jan. 27, 1795) and *L'isola del piacere* (May 26, 1795), both engaging opere buffe. He returned to St. Petersburg in 1796 and was made Imperial Russian Privy Councillor by Paul I in 1798. He was inspector of the Italian Court Theater there (1800–1804).

WORKS: DRAMATIC: OPERAS: *La Madrileña, o Tutor burlado*, zarzuela (Madrid, 1776?); *Ifigenia in Aulide*, opera seria (Naples, Jan. 12, 1779); *Ipermestra*, opera seria (Naples, Jan. 12, 1780); *Andromaca*, opera seria (Turin, Dec. 26, 1780); *Astartea*, opera seria (Lucca, Carnival 1781); *Partenope*, componimento drammatico (Naples, 1782); *L'amor geloso*, azione teatrale comica (Naples, Carnival 1782); *In amor ci vuol destrezza*, opera buffa (Venice, 1782); *Vologeso*, opera seria (Turin, Carnival 1783); *Le burle per amore*, opera buffa (Venice, Carnival 1784); *La Vedova spiritosa*, opera buffa (Parma, Carnival 1785); *Il Burbero di buon cuore*, opera buffa (Vienna, Jan. 4, 1786); *Una cosa rara, o sia Bellezza ed onestà*, opera buffa (Vienna, Nov. 17, 1786); *L'arbore di Diana*, opera buffa (Vienna, Oct. 1, 1787); *Gore bogatyr Kosometovich* (The Unfortunate Hero Kosometovich), comic opera (St. Petersburg, Feb. 9, 1789); *Pesnolyubie* (Beloved Songs), comic opera (St. Petersburg, Jan. 18, 1790); *Il castello d'Atlante*, opera buffa (Desenzano, Carnival 1791); *La scuola dei maritati*, opera buffa (London, Jan. 27, 1795); *L'isola del piacere*, opera buffa (London, May 26, 1795); *Le nozze de' contadini spagnuoli*, intermezzo (London, May 28, 1795); *La festa del villagio*, opera buffa (St. Petersburg, Jan. 26 or 30, 1798). BALLETS: *La bella Arsene* (Naples, 1779 or 1780); *I Ratti Sabini* (Naples, 1779 or 1780); *La Regina di Golconda* (Lucca, 1781); *Cristiano II, rè di Danimarca* (Venice, 1782); *Aci e Galatea* (Parma, 1784); *Didon abandonée* (St. Petersburg, 1792); *L'Oracle* (St. Petersburg, 1793); *Amour et Psyché* (St. Petersburg, 1793); *Tancrède* (St. Petersburg, 1799); *Le Retour de Poliorcete* (St. Petersburg, 1799 or 1800).

Marton, Eva, outstanding Hungarian soprano; b. Budapest, June 18, 1943. She studied with Endre Rösler and Jenö Sipos at the Franz Liszt Academy of Music in Budapest. She made her formal operatic debut as the Queen of Shemakha in *Le Coq d'or* at the Hungarian State Opera there in 1968, remaining on its roster until joining the Frankfurt am Main Opera in 1971; she then became a member of the Hamburg State Opera in 1977. On Feb. 23, 1975, she made her U.S. debut in New York as a soloist in the world premiere of Hovhaness's folk oratorio *The Way of Jesus*; then made her first appearance at the Metropolitan Opera there as Eva in *Die Meistersinger von Nürnberg* on Nov. 3, 1976. After singing at the Bayreuth Festivals (1977–78) and at Milan's La Scala (1978), she scored a notable success as the Empress in *Die Frau ohne Schatten* at the Metropolitan Opera in 1981; thereafter she was one of its most important artists, appearing as Elisabeth in *Tännhauser* (1982), Leonore in *Fidelio* (1983), Ortrud in *Lohengrin* (1984), Tosca (1986), and Lady Macbeth (1988). She first sang Turandot at the Vienna State Opera in 1983; appeared as Elektra there in 1989. In 1987 she made her debut at London's Covent Garden as Turandot, and in 1990 she returned there as Elektra. In 1992 she appeared as Turandot in Chicago and as the Dyer's Wife at the Salzburg Festival. She was engaged as Turandot at the San Francisco Opera in 1993. In 1997 she sang Elektra at the Washington (D.C.) Opera. She sang the Kostelnička in *Jenůfa* at the Hamburg State Opera in 1998. Her appearances as an oratorio and lieder artist were also well received.

BIBL.: C. Wilkens, *E. M.* (Hamburg, 1982).

Marttinen, Tauno (Olavi), Finnish composer, pedagogue, and conductor; b. Helsinki, Sept. 27, 1912. He received training in conducting and composition at the Viipuri Inst. of Music (1920–35), and then was a student of Peter Akimov, Ilmari Hannikainen, and Selim Palmgren at the Sibelius Academy in Helsinki (1935–37); later he studied with Vogel in Switzerland (1958). From 1949 to 1958 he was conductor of the Hämeenlinna City Orch. In 1950 he founded the Hämeenlinna Inst. of Music, serving as its director until 1975. In 1982 he was awarded an honorary prize by the Soc. of Finnish Composers and the Kalevala Soc. He received the 1st Sibelius Award in 1990. After composing in a late Romantic style, Marttinen developed a free serial mode of expression. Later he embraced free tonality before finding renewed creative resources in neo-Baroque and neoclassical styles.

WORKS: DRAMATIC: OPERAS: *Neiti Gamardin talo* (The House of Lady Gamard; 1960–71); *Päällysviitta* (The Cloak; 1962–63); *Kihlaus* (The Engagement; 1964; Helsinki, June 12, 1966); *Apotti ja ikäneito* (The Abbot and the Old Maid; 1965); *Tulitikkuja lainaamassa* (Borrowing Matches; Helsinki, Aug. 20, 1966); *Lea* (1967; Turku, Sept. 19, 1968); *Poltettu oranssi* (Burnt Orange), television opera (1968; Finnish TV, Oct. 6, 1971; 1st stage perf., Helsinki, Nov. 3, 1975); *Mestari Patelin* (Master Patelin; 1969–72; Hämeenlinna, July 31, 1983); *Noitarumpu* (Shaman's Drum; 1974–76); *Psykiatri* (The Psychiatrist; 1974); *Laestadiuksen saarna* (Laestadius's Sermon; 1974–76; Oulu, April 29, 1976); *Meedio* (The Medium), chamber opera (1975–76); *Jaarlin sisar* (The Jarl's Sister; 1977; Hämeenlinna, April 3, 1979); *Faaraon kirje* (Pharaoh's Letter; 1978–80; Tampere, Oct. 18, 1982); *Suuren joen laulu eli Najaadi* (The Song of a Great River; 1980; Kemi, May 2, 1982); *Häät* (The Wedding), chamber opera (1984–85; Helsinki, Jan. 31, 1986); *Noidan kirous* (1987); *Seitsemän veljestä* (7 Brothers; 1989); *Mooses* (1990); *Minna Graucher* (1992). MUSICAL: *Kullanmuru* (The Golden Treasure; 1980). BALLETS: *Tikkaat* (The Ladder; 1955); *Dorian Grayn muotokuva* (The Picture of Dorian Gray; 1969); *Lumikuningatar* (The Snow Queen; 1970); *Beatrice* (1970); *Päivänpäästö* (The Sun Out of the Moon; 1975–77); *Ruma ankanpoikanen* (The Ugly Duckling; 1976, 1982–83).

Marty, Georges-Eugène, French composer and conductor; b. Paris, May 16, 1860; d. there, Oct. 11, 1908. He attended the Paris Cons. (1872–82), winning the Grand Prix de Rome with the cantata *Edith*. In 1894 he was appointed instructor at the Paris Cons., and in 1903 he became conductor of the Société des Concerts du Conservatoire. He wrote 3 operas: *Le Duc de Ferrare*, *Daria*, and *La Grande Mademoiselle*.

Maruzin, Yuri, Russian tenor; b. Perm, Dec. 8, 1947. He received training in Leningrad, where he made his debut in 1972 at the Maly Theater. In 1978 he became a member of the Kirov Opera in Leningrad, with which he toured throughout Europe and North America. In 1987 he sang with the company as Lensky at London's Covent Garden. After appearing as the Czarevich in Rimsky-Korsakov's *The Tale of Czar Sultan* at Milan's La Scala in 1988, he sang Galitsin in *Khovanshchina* at the Vienna State Opera in 1989. He sang Anatol Kuragin in *War and Peace* at the San Francisco Opera and Andrei Khovansky in *Khovanshchina* at the Edinburgh Festival in 1991. In 1992 he appeared as Hermann in *The Queen of Spades* at the Glyndebourne Festival. He sang in *Lady Macbeth of the District of Mtzensk* at the New Israeli Opera in Tel Aviv in 1997. Among his other roles are Don Alvaro, the Duke of Mantua, Don Carlos, Alfredo, Faust, and Pinkerton.

Maryon (-d'Aulby), (John) Edward, English composer; b. London, April 3, 1867; d. there, Jan. 31, 1954. He began to compose early in life; went to Paris, where his first opera, *L'Odalisque*, won the Gold Medal at the Exposition of 1889; however, he regarded the work as immature and destroyed the score. In 1891 he studied with Max Pauer in Dresden; later he took lessons with Wüllner in Cologne. From 1914 to 1919 he was in Montclair, N.J., where he established a cons. with a fund for exchange of music students between England and America; in 1933 he returned to London. He wrote the operas *Paolo and Francesca; La Robe de plume; The Smelting Pot; The Prodigal Son; Werewolf; Rembrandt; Greater Love*; and *Abelard and Heloise*. In his *Werewolf* he applied a curious system of musical symbolism, in which the human part was characterized by the diatonic scale and the lupine self by the whole-tone scale; Maryon made a claim of priority in using the whole-tone scale consistently as a leading motive in an opera. His magnum opus was a grandiose operatic heptalogy under the title *The Cycle of Life*, comprising 7 mystical dramas: *Lucifer, Cain, Krishna, Magdalen, Sangraal, Psyche*, and *Nirvana*. He also wrote a symphonic poem, *The Feather Robe*, subtitled *A Legend of Fujiyama* (1905), which he dedicated to the emperor of Japan; and *Armageddon Requiem* (1916), dedicated to the dead of World War I. After Maryon's death, his complete MSS were donated to the Boston Public Library. Maryon developed a theory of universal art, in which colors were associated with sounds; an outline of this theory was publ. in his *Marcotone* (N.Y., 1915).

Mascagni, Pietro, famous Italian composer; b. Livorno, Dec. 7, 1863; d. Rome, Aug. 2, 1945. His father was a baker who wished him to continue in that trade, but yielded to his son's determination to study music. Thanks to aid from an uncle, he was able to take some music lessons with Soffredini in Livorno and then to attend the Milan Cons., where he studied with Ponchielli and Saladino (1882). However, he became impatient with school discipline, and was dismissed from the Cons. in 1884. He then was active as a double bass player in the orch. of the Teatro dal Verme in Milan. After touring as a conductor with operetta troupes, he taught music in Cerignola, Puglia. He composed industriously; in 1888 he sent the MS of his 1-act opera *Cavalleria rusticana* to the music publisher Sonzogno for a competition, and won 1st prize. The opera was performed at the Teatro Costanzi in Rome on May 17, 1890, with sensational success; the dramatic story of village passion, and Mascagni's emotional score, laden with luscious music, combined to produce an extraordinary appeal to opera lovers. The short opera made the tour of the world stages with amazing rapidity, productions being staged all over Europe and America with never-failing success; the opera was usually presented in 2 parts, separated by an "intermezzo sinfonico" (which became a popular orch. number performed separately). *Cavalleria rusticana* marked the advent of the operatic style known as verismo, in which stark realism was the chief aim and the dramatic development was condensed to enhance the impressions. When, 2 years later, another "veristic" opera, Leoncavallo's *Pagliacci*, was taken by Sonzogno, the 2 operas became twin attractions on a single bill. Ironically, Mascagni could never duplicate or even remotely approach the success of his first production, although he continued to compose industriously and opera houses all over the world were only too eager to stage his successive operas. Thus, his opera *Le Maschere* was produced on Jan. 17, 1901, at 6 of the most important Italian opera houses simultaneously (Rome, Milan, Turin, Genoa, Venice, Verona); it was produced 2 days later in Naples. Mascagni himself conducted the premiere in Rome. But the opera failed to fire the imagination of the public; it was produced in a revised form in Turin 15 years later (June 7, 1916), but was not established in the repertoire even in Italy. In 1902 he made a tour of the United States conducting his *Cavalleria rusticana* and other operas, but, owing to mismanagement, the visit proved a fiasco; a South American tour in 1911 was more successful. He also appeared frequently as a conductor of sym. concerts. In 1890 he was made a Knight of the Crown of Italy; in 1929 he was elected a member of the Academy. At various times he also was engaged in teaching; from 1895 to 1902 he was director of the Rossini Cons. in Pesaro. His last years were darkened by the inglorious role that he had played as an ardent supporter of the Fascist regime, so that he was rejected by many of his old friends. It was only after his death that his errors of moral judgment were forgiven; his centennial was widely celebrated in Italy in 1963. D. Stivender ed. and tr. his autobiography into Eng. (N.Y., 1975).

WORKS: DRAMATIC: OPERAS: *Pinotta* (c.1880; San Remo, March 23, 1932); *Guglielmo Ratcliff* (c.1885; Milan, Feb. 16, 1895); *Cavalleria rusticana* (Rome, May 17, 1890); *L'Amico Fritz* (Rome, Oct. 31, 1891); *I Rantzau* (Florence, Nov. 10, 1892); *Silvano* (Milan, March 25, 1895); *Zanetto* (Pesaro, March 2, 1896); *Iris* (Rome, Nov. 22, 1898; rev. version, Milan, Jan. 19, 1899); *Le Maschere* (simultaneous premiere in Rome, Milan, Turin, Genoa, Venice, and Verona, Jan. 17, 1901); *Amica* (Monte Carlo, March 16, 1905); *Isabeau* (Buenos Aires, June 2, 1911); *Parisina* (Milan, Dec. 15, 1913); *Lodoletta* (Rome, April 30, 1917); *Scampolo* (1921); *Il piccolo Marat* (Rome, May 2, 1921); *Nerone* (Milan, Jan. 16, 1935); *I Bianchi ed i Neri* (1940). OPERETTAS: *Il re a Napoli* (n.d.); *Sí* (Rome, Dec. 13, 1919). OTHER: 2 syms. (1879, 1881); *Poema leopardiano* (for the centenary of G. Leopardi, 1898); Hymn in honor of Admiral Dewey (July 1899); *Rapsodia satanica* for Orch. (music for a film, Rome, July 2, 1917); *Davanti Santa Teresa* (Rome, Aug. 1923); chamber music; choral works; songs; piano pieces.

BIBL.: G. Monaldi, *P. M.: L'Uomo e l'artista* (Rome, 1899); G. Bastianelli, *P. M.: Con nota delle opere* (Naples, 1910); G. Orsini, *L'arte di P. M.* (Milan, 1912); E. Pompei, *P. M.: Nella vita e nell'arte* (Rome, 1912); A. Donno, *M. nel 900 musicale* (Rome, 1935); A. Jeri, *M., 15 Opere, 1000 Episodi* (Milan, 1940); D. Cellamare, *M. e la "Cavalleria" visti da Cerignola* (Rome, 1941); *M. parla* (Rome, 1945); *Comitato nazionale delle onoranze a P. M. nel primo centenario della nascità* (Livorno, 1963); M. Morini, ed., *P. M.* (2 vols., Milan, 1964); G. Gavazzeni, *Discorso per M. nel centenario della nascità* (Rome, 1964); D. Cellamare, *P. M.* (Rome, 1965); R. Iovino, *M: L'avventuroso dell'opera* (Milan, 1987); C. and L. Pini, *M. a quattro mani* (Viareggio, 1992).

Mascheroni, Edoardo, distinguished Italian conductor; b. Milan, Sept. 4, 1852; d. Ghirla, near Varese, March 4, 1941. As a boy, he showed special interest in mathematics and literature; he wrote literary essays for the journal *La Vita Nuova* before he decided to study music seriously; he took lessons with Boucheron in Milan, and composed various pieces. In 1880 he began a career in Brescia as a conductor, and it was in that capacity that he distinguished himself. He was first a theater conductor in Livorno; he then went to Rome, where he established his reputation as an opera conductor at the Teatro Apollo (1884). From 1891 to 1894 he was chief conductor of Milan's La Scala, where Verdi chose him to conduct the premiere of his *Falstaff* (Feb. 9, 1893). After conducting in Germany, Spain, and South America, he continued his career in Italy until retiring about 1925. He wrote 2 operas, *Lorenza* (Rome, April 13, 1901) and *La Perugina* (Naples, April 24, 1909), 2 Requiems, and chamber music. His brother, Angelo Mascheroni (1855–95), was also a conductor.

Masetti, Enzo, Italian composer; b. Bologna, Aug. 19, 1893; d. Rome, Feb. 11, 1961. He studied with Franco Alfano at the Liceo Musicale in Bologna. He devoted his life mainly to film music; from 1942 until his death he was connected with the Centro Sperimentale di Cinematografia in Rome. He publ. *La musica nel film* (Rome, 1950) and composed about 60 film scores. He also wrote several dramatic fables, among them *La fola delle tre ochette* (Bologna, 1928), *La mosca mora* (Bologna, 1930), and *La bella non puo dormire* (Bologna, 1957).

Masini, Angelo, Italian tenor; b. Terra del Sole, near Forli, Nov. 28, 1844; d. Forli, Sept. 26, 1926. He studied with Gilda Minguzzi, making his debut as Pollione in *Norma* in Finale Emilia (1867). He then sang throughout Italy, Spain, and Russia. He was chosen by Verdi to sing in the *Requiem*, appearing under Verdi's direction in London, Paris, and Vienna in 1875. He gave his farewell stage performance in Paris in 1905. Among his finest roles were Count Almaviva, Don Ottavio, Faust, and Radames.

BIBL.: C. Rivalta, *Il tenore A. M. e Faenza* (Faenza, 1927).

Masini, Galliano, Italian tenor; b. Livorno, 1896; d. there, Feb. 15, 1986. He received his training in Milan. In 1923 he made his operatic debut as Cavaradossi in Livorno, and then sang in various Italian music centers. In 1930 he made his first appearance in Rome as Pinkerton, and continued to sing there until 1950. He also sang at Milan's La Scala, in Rio de Janeiro, Buenos Aires, Vienna, and Paris. In 1937–38 he appeared at the Chicago Opera. On Dec. 14, 1938, he made his Metropolitan Opera debut in New York as Edgardo, where he remained on the roster for the season. In subsequent years, he pursued his career in Europe, making his farewell appearance in 1957. Among his other roles were Radames, Rodolfo, Turiddu, and Enzo.

Mason, Edith (Barnes), American soprano; b. St. Louis, March 22, 1893; d. San Diego, Nov. 26, 1973. She studied in Cincinnati, and then with Enrico Bertran and Edmond Clément in Paris. Following her operatic debut in Marseilles (1911), she sang in Boston (1912), Montreal (1912), Nice (1914), and New York (Century Co., 1914–15). On Nov. 20, 1915, she made her Metropolitan Opera debut in New York as Sophie in *Der Rosenkavalier*, remaining on its roster until 1917. After singing in Paris (1919–21), she was a principal member of the Chicago Opera (1921–29). She also sang at Milan's La Scala (1923), was again on the roster of the Metropolitan Opera (1934–36), and appeared at the Salzburg Festival (1935). In 1941 she made her farewell appearance in Chicago as Mimi. She was married twice to **Giorgio Polacco**. Among her other roles were Gilda, Gounod's Marguerite, Thaïs, Elsa, and Cio-Cio-San.

Massa, Juan Bautista, Argentine composer; b. Buenos Aires, Oct. 29, 1885; d. Rosario, March 7, 1938. He studied violin and composition. He became a choral conductor; moved to Rosario, where he was active as a teacher.

WORKS: DRAMATIC: OPERAS: *Zoraide* (Buenos Aires, May 15, 1909); *L'Evaso* (Rosario, June 23, 1922); *La Magdalena* (Buenos Aires, Nov. 9, 1929). OPERETTAS: *Esmeralda* (1903); *Triunfo del corazon* (1910); *La eterna historia* (1911). BALLET: *El cometa* (Buenos Aires, Nov. 8, 1932).

Massa, Nicolò, Italian composer; b. Calice Ligure, Oct. 26, 1854; d. Genoa, Jan. 24, 1894. He studied at the Milan Cons. with Bazzini. He wrote the operas *Aldo e Clarenza* (Milan, April 11, 1878), *Il Conte di Chatillon* (Reggio Emilia, Feb. 11, 1882), *Salammbò* (Milan, April 15, 1886; his most successful), and *Eros* (Florence, May 21, 1895).

Massarani, Renzo, Italian-born Brazilian composer; b. Mantua, March 26, 1898; d. Rio de Janeiro, March 28, 1975. He studied with Respighi at Rome's Accademia di Santa Cecilia (diploma, 1921), then was active as music director of Vittorio Podrecca's puppet theater Il Teatro dei Piccoli and as a music critic. He left Fascist Italy and settled in Rio de Janeiro in 1935, becoming a naturalized Brazilian citizen in 1945; he was active as a music critic. Through the banning of his works during the Mussolini dictatorship, the havoc of World War II, and his own destruction of many scores, much of his output is not extant. His surviving music reveals a composer of considerable talent.

WORKS: DRAMATIC: OPERAS: *Noi due* (c.1921); *La Donna nel pozzo* (1930); *Eliduc* (1938; unfinished). OPERINAS: *Bianco e nero* (Rome, 1921); *Le nozze di Takiu* (Rome, 1927); *Gilbetto e Gherminella* (Rome, 1929); *I dolori della principessa Susina* (Rome, 1929). BALLETS: *Guerin detto il meschino* (1928); *Boe* (Bergamo, 1937).

Massart, Nestor-Henri-Joseph, Belgian tenor; b. Ciney, Oct. 20, 1849; d. Ostend, Dec. 19, 1899. He was an officer in the Belgian army when his remarkable voice attracted the attention of the royal family, through whose influence he was granted a leave of absence for study. He then sang with success in Brussels, Lyons, Cairo, New Orleans, San Francisco, and Mexico.

Massé, Victor (real name, **Félix-Marie**), French composer; b. Lorient, Morbihan, March 7, 1822; d. Paris, July 5, 1884. He was a child prodigy. He was accepted at the Paris Cons. at the age of 12, and studied with Zimmerman (piano) and Halévy (composition). In 1844 he won the Grand Prix de Rome with the cantata *Le Renégat de Tanger*. While in Rome he wrote an Italian opera, *La Favorita e la schiava* (c. 1845; Venice, 1855). After his return, his romances had great vogue, and his first French opera, *La Chambre gothique* (Paris, 1849), was fairly successful. In 1866 he succeeded Leborne as prof. of counterpoint at the Paris Cons.; in 1872 he was elected a member of the Institut de France, as successor to Auber. His most successful light opera was *Les Noces de Jeannette* (Paris, Feb. 4, 1853); his other operas, performed in Paris, include *La Chanteuse voilée* (Nov. 26, 1850), *Galathée* (April 14, 1852), *La Fiancée du Diable* (June 3, 1854), *Miss Fauvette* (Feb. 13, 1855), *Les Saisons* (Dec. 22, 1855), *La Reine Topaze* (Dec. 27, 1856), *Fior d'Aliza* (Feb. 5, 1866), *Le Fils du Brigadier* (Feb. 25, 1867), and *Paul et Virginie* (Nov. 15, 1876). His last opera, *Une Nuit de Cléopatre*, was performed posthumously (Paris, April 25, 1885).

BIBL.: L. Delibes, *Notice sur V. M.* (Paris, 1885); J. Ropartz, *V. M.* (Paris, 1887); H. Delaborde, *Notice sur la vie et les ouvrages de V. M.* (Paris, 1888).

Massenet, Jules (-Émile-Frédéric), famous French composer and pedagogue; b. Montaud, near St.-Etienne, Loire, May 12, 1842; d. Paris, Aug. 13, 1912. He was 6 when he began to study piano with his mother. At 9, he was admitted to the Paris Cons. to study piano and theory. He had to leave the Cons. in 1854 when his father's ill health compelled the family to move to Chambéry. In 1855 he was able to resume his studies at the Cons., where he received instruction in piano from Laurent. In 1858 he made his public debut as a pianist in a Paris recital. In 1859 he won the premier prix for piano at the Cons., where he also pursued training with Reber (harmony), Benoist (organ), and Thomas (composition). In 1863 he won the Grand Prix de Rome with his cantata *David Rizzio*. His first major success as a composer came with the premiere of his oratorio *Marie-Magdeleine* (Paris, April 11, 1873). His next oratorio, *Ève* (Paris, March 18, 1875), won him the Légion d'honneur. His first operatic success came with the premiere of *Le roi de Lahore* at the Paris Opéra on April 27, 1877. The success of his opera *Hérodiade* (Brussels, Dec. 19, 1881) resulted in his being made a Knight of the Order of Leopold of Belgium. He scored a triumph with the first performance of his opera *Manon* at the Paris Opéra on Jan. 19, 1884. This score is generally acknowledged as his finest opera. *Werther*, another distinguished opera, added to his renown when it was premiered at the Vienna Court Opera on Feb. 16, 1892. Equally noteworthy was his opera *Thaïs* (Paris Opéra, March 16, 1894). Among his later operatic efforts, the most important were *Le jongleur de Notre-Dame* (Monte Carlo, Feb. 18, 1902) and *Don Quichotte* (Monte Carlo, Feb. 24, 1910). Of his incidental scores, that for Leconte de Lisle's drama *Les Érinnyes* (Paris, Jan. 6, 1873) was particularly notable. In 1878 Massenet was appointed prof. of composition at the Paris Cons., a position he held with distinction until 1896. He was a highly influential teacher, numbering among his students Bruneau, Charpentier, Pierné, Koechlin, and Schmitt. In 1878 he was elected a member of the Institut of the Académie des Beaux-Arts, ascending to the rank of Grand-Officier in 1900. Massenet wrote an autobiography, *Mes souvenirs* (completed by X. Leroux; Paris, 1912; Eng. tr., 1919, as *My Recollections*). He was one of the leading French opera composers of his era. His operas are the work of a fine craftsman, marked by a distinctive style, sensuous melodiousness, and lyricism which proved immediately appealing to audiences of his day. However, even before his death, developments in the lyric theater had passed him by. In succeeding years, his operas were heard infrequently, and almost disappeared from the active repertoire. Even the celebrated *Meditation* for Violin and Orch. from *Thaïs*, long a favorite concert piece with violinists and audiences, was seldom performed. Today, revivals of *Manon, Werther*, and *Thaïs* have won Massenet new audiences around the world.

WORKS: DRAMATIC: OPERAS: *Esmeralda* (1865; not extant); *La coup du roi de Thulé* (1866?); *La grand'tante* (Paris, April 3, 1867); *Manfred* (1869?; unfinished); *Méduse* (1870; unfinished); *Don César de Bazan* (Paris, Nov. 30, 1872); *L'adorable bel'-boul'* (Paris, April 17, 1874; not extant); *Les templiers* (1875?; not extant); *Bérangère et Anatole* (Paris, Feb. 1876); *Le roi de Lahore* (Paris, April 27, 1877); *Robert de France* (1880?; not extant); *Les Girondins* (1881; not extant); *Hérodiade* (Brussels, Dec. 19, 1881); *Manon* (Paris, Jan. 19, 1884); *Le Cid* (Paris, Nov. 30, 1885); *Esclarmonde* (Paris, May 14, 1889); *Le mage* (Paris, March 16, 1891); *Werther* (Vienna, Feb. 16, 1892); *Thaïs* (Paris, March 16, 1894); *Le portrait de Manon* (Paris, May 8, 1894); *La navarraise* (London, June 20, 1894); *Amadis* (1895?; Monte Carlo, April 1, 1922); *Sapho* (Paris, Nov. 27, 1897; rev. 1909); *Cendrillon* (Paris, May 24, 1899); *Grisélidis* (Paris, Nov. 20, 1901); *Le jongleur de Notre-Dame* (Monte Carlo, Feb. 18, 1902); *Chérubin* (Monte Carlo, Feb. 14, 1903); *Ariane* (Paris, Oct. 31, 1906); *Thérèse* (Monte Carlo, Feb. 7, 1907); *Bacchus* (Paris, May 5, 1909); *Don Quichotte* (Monte Carlo, Feb. 24, 1910); *Roma* (Monte Carlo, Feb. 17, 1912); *Panurge* (Paris, April 25, 1913); *Cléopâtre* (Monte Carlo, Feb. 23, 1914). BALLETS: *Le carillon* (Vienna , Feb. 21, 1892); *Cigale* (Paris, Feb. 4, 1904); *Espada* (Monte Carlo, Feb. 13, 1908). INCIDENTAL MUSIC (all 1st perf. in Paris unless otherwise given): *Les Érinnyes* (Jan. 6, 1873); *Un drame sous Philippe II* (April 14, 1875); *La vie de Bohème* (1876); *L'Hetman* (Feb. 2, 1877); *Notre-Dame de Paris* (June 4, 1879); *Michel Strogoff* (Nov. 17, 1880); *Nana-Sahib* (Dec. 20, 1883); *Théodora* (Dec. 26, 1884); *Le crocodile* (Dec. 21, 1886); *Phèdre* (Dec. 8, 1900); *Le grillon du foyer* (Oct. 1, 1904); *Le manteau du roi* (Oct. 22, 1907); *Perce-Neige et les sept gnomes* (Feb. 2, 1909); *Jérusalem* (Monte Carlo, Jan. 17, 1914). ORATORIOS: *Marie-Magdeleine* (Paris, April 11, 1873); *Ève* (Paris, March 18, 1875); *La Vierge* (Paris, May 22, 1880); *La terre promise* (Paris, March 15, 1900). OTHER: Completion and orchestration of Delibes's opera *Kassya* (Paris, March 24, 1893).

BIBL.: E. de Solenière, *M.: Étude critique et documentaire* (Paris, 1897); C. Fournier, *Étude sur le style de M.* (Amiens, 1905); L. Schneider, *M.: L'homme, le musicien* (Paris, 1908; 2d ed., 1926); H. Finck, *M. and His Operas* (London and N.Y., 1910); O. Séré, *M.* (Paris, 1911); A. Soubies, *M. historien* (Paris, 1913); A. Pougin, *M.* (Paris, 1914); C. Widor, *Notice sur la vie et les travaux de M.* (Paris, 1915); J. Loisel, *Manon de M.: Étude historique et critique* (Paris, 1922); C. Bouvet, *M.* (Paris, 1929); J. d'Udine, *L'art du lied et le mélos de M.* (Paris, 1931); M. Delmas, *M.: Sa vie, ses oeuvres* (Paris, 1932); A. Bruneau, *M.* (Paris, 1935); A. Morin, *J. M. et ses opéras* (Montreal, 1944); N. Boyer, *Trois musiciens français: Gounod, M., Debussy* (Paris, 1946); P. Colson, *M.: Manon* (London, 1947); J. Bruyr, *M.* (Geneva, 1948); idem, *M.: Musicien de la belle époque* (Lyons, 1964); A. Coquis, *J. M.: L'homme et son oeuvre* (Paris, 1965); E. Bouilhol, *M.: Son rôle dans l'évolution du théâtre musicale* (St.-Etienne, 1969); L. Stocker, *The Treatment of the Romantic Literary Hero in Verdi's "Ernani" and in M.'s "Werther"* (diss., Florida State Univ., 1969); J. Harding, *M.* (London, 1970); O. Salzer, *The M. Compendium* (Fort Lee, N.J., 1984); G. Marschall, *M. et la fixation de la forme mélodique française* (Saarbrücken, 1988); D. Irvine, *M.: A Chronicle of His Life and Times* (Portland, Oreg., 1993).

Massol, Eugène Etienne Auguste, French baritone; b. Lodève, Aug. 23, 1802; d. Paris, Oct. 30, 1887. He received training at the Paris Cons. On Nov. 17, 1825, he made his operatic debut in the tenor role of Licinius in Spontini's *La vestale* at the Paris Opéra. After singing secondary tenor roles, he turned with success to baritone roles in the mid-1830s. He created the role of Severus in Donizetti's *Les martyrs* at the Opéra (April 10, 1840). In 1845 he went to Brussels, where he served as director of the Théâtre Royale de la Monnaie (1848–49). In 1846 he made his London debut at Drury Lane. From 1848 to 1850 he sang with the Royal Italian Opera at London's Covent Garden. He was principal baritone of the Paris Opéra from 1850 to 1858. Massol was particularly admired for his portrayals of Alfonso in *La favorite*, Pietro in *Masaniello*, and De Nevers in *Les Huguenots*.

Másson, Áskell, Icelandic composer; b. Reykjavíik, Nov. 21, 1953. He began clarinet lessons at the age of 8. After training at the Reykjavík College of Music, he went to London and studied with Patrick Savill (harmony and counterpoint) and James Blades (percussion). In 1972 he became a composer and instrumentalist with the ballet of the National Theater in Reykjavík. From 1978 to 1983 he worked as a producer for the Icelandic State Radio. He was secretary-general of the Iceland League of Composers (1983–85), then president of STEF, the association of composers and copyright owners (from 1989). Másson's output is generally marked by an intensity and brilliance of expression, complemented by a judicious infusion of lyricism.

WORKS: DRAMATIC: *Eldtröllid* (The Fire Troll), ballet (1974); *Höfudskepnurnar* (The Elements), ballet (1974); *Svart-Hvítt* (Black and White), ballet (1975); *Klakahöllin* (The Ice Palace), opera (1993); incidental music to players; music for radio and television.

Masson, Diego, French conductor; b. Tossa, Spain, June 21, 1935. He studied percussion, harmony, and chamber music at the Paris Cons. (1953–59); he also received training in fugue, counterpoint, and composition from Leibowitz (1955–59), in composition from Maderna (1964), and in conducting from Boulez (1965). In 1966 he founded the Musique Vivante, with which he gave numerous performances of contemporary music. He also was music director of the Marseilles Opera until 1982, and of the Ballet-Théâtre Contemporain in Amiens (from 1968), which removed to Angers in 1972 under his direction as part of the Théâtre-Musical d'Angers.

Masson, Paul-Marie, eminent French musicologist; b. Sète, Hérault, Sept. 19, 1882; d. Paris, Jan. 27, 1954. He studied at the lycée, the arts faculty, and the Lycée Henri IV in Montpellier before going to Paris, where he pursued his education at the Normale Supérieure and concurrently was a student of Rolland and Lefranc at the École des Haute Études (agregation, 1907, with the diss. *La Musique mesurée à l'Antique au XVIe siècle*); after further training with d'Indy and Koechlin (fugue, counterpoint, and composition) at the Schola Cantorum, he completed his education at the Univ. of Paris (docteur ès lettres, 1930, with the diss. *L'opéra de Rameau*; publ. in Paris, 1930). In 1910 he served as chargé de conférences at the Univ. of Grenoble, and also taught the history of French literature and music at the Institut Français in Florence (1910–14). In 1918 he was again at the Institut Français, and then went to Naples, where he founded its Institut Français in 1919. He taught music history at the Sorbonne in Paris from 1931 to 1952. In 1951 he founded the Institut de Musicologie of the Univ. of Paris. In 1937 he was elected vice president of the Société Française de Musicologie, and in 1949 was elected its president. He contributed numerous articles to journals and publ. the book *Berlioz* (Paris, 1923). He also composed.

BIBL.: *Mélanges d'histoire et d'esthétique musicale offertes à P.-M. M.* (Paris, 1955).

Masterson, Valerie, English soprano; b. Birkenhead, June 3, 1937. She studied at the Matthay School of Music in Liverpool and the Royal College of Music in London; also in Milan. She made her debut as Frasquita in *Carmen* at the Salzburg Landestheater in 1963; she then sang with the D'Oyly Carte Opera Co. in London (1966–70) and became a member of the Sadler's Wells Opera in London in 1970; from 1974 she sang at Covent Garden in London. She made her debut at the Paris Opéra as Marguerite (1978); made her U.S. debut as Violetta with the San Francisco Opera (1980). As a guest artist, she appeared in opera and concert around the world. In 1988 she was made a Commander of the Order of the British Empire.

Mastilović, Danica, Yugoslav soprano; b. Negotin, Nov. 7, 1933. She was a pupil of Nikola Cvejić in Belgrade; while still a student, she sang with the Belgrade Operetta Theater (1955–59); in 1959 she made her formal operatic debut as Tosca at the Frankfurt am Main Opera, where she sang until 1969. Her guest appearances took her to Hamburg, Vienna, Munich, Bayreuth, Paris, and London. In 1963 she made her first U.S. appearance at the Chicago Lyric Opera as Abigaille, and on Nov. 25, 1975, her Metropolitan Opera debut in New York as Elektra. In 1973 she made her first appearance at London's Covent Garden as Elektra. In 1978–79 she was again on the roster of the Metropolitan Opera. She became principally known for her roles in operas by Verdi, Wagner, and Strauss.

Masur, Kurt, eminent German conductor; b. Brieg, Silesia, July 18, 1927. He received training in piano and cello at the Breslau Music School (1942–44); then studied conducting with H. Bongartz and took courses in piano and composition at the Leipzig Hochschule für Musik (1946–48). In 1948 he commenced his career with appointments as répétiteur and conductor at the Halle Landestheater; held the title of 1st conductor at the Erfurt City Theater (1951–53) and at the Leipzig City Theater (1953–55). He was conductor of the Dresden Phil. (1955–58), Generalmusikdirektor of the Mecklenburg State Theater in Schwerin (1958–60), and senior director of music at the Komische Oper in East Berlin (1960–64). In 1967 he returned to the Dresden Phil. as its music director, a position he retained until 1972. In 1970 he assumed the time-honored position of Gewandhauskapellmeister of Leipzig, where he served as music director of the Gewandhaus Orch. with notable distinction. He also made extensive tours with his orch. in Europe and abroad. In 1973 he made his British debut as a guest conductor with the New Philharmonia Orch. of London;

his U.S. debut followed in 1974 as a guest conductor with the Cleveland Orch. On Oct. 9, 1981, he conducted the Beethoven 9th Sym. at the gala opening of the new Gewandhaus in Leipzig. In 1988 he was named principal guest conductor of the London Phil. In the autumn of 1989, during the period of political upheaval in East Germany, Masur played a major role as peacemaker in Leipzig. In 1990 he was appointed music director of the N.Y. Phil., which position he assumed in 1991 while retaining his title in Leipzig until 1998. On Dec. 7, 1992, he conducted the N.Y. Phil. in a performance of Dvořák's *New World* Symphony as part of the orch.'s 150th anniversary concert, which was televised live throughout the United States by PBS. In 1997 he was named honorary conductor of the Gewandhaus Orch. and was a Commandeur of the Légion d'honneur of France. From 2000 he was principal conductor of the London Phil. While he has earned a reputation as a faithful guardian of the hallowed Austro-German repertoire, he frequently programs contemporary scores as well.

BIBL.: D. Härtwig, *K. M.* (Leipzig, 1975); A. Fritzsch and M. Simon, *Der Gewandhauskapellmeister K. M.* (Leipzig, 1987).

Masurok, Yuri (Antonovich), Polish-born Russian baritone; b. Krasnik, July 18, 1931. He studied at the Lwów Inst. and the Moscow Cons.; won prizes in singing competitions in Prague (1960), Bucharest (1961), and Montreal (1967); in 1964 he made his debut as Eugene Onegin at the Bolshoi Theater in Moscow, where he later sang Prince Andrei in Prokofiev's *War and Peace*. He made his London debut at Covent Garden in 1975 as Anckarström, the same role he chose for his U.S. debut with the San Francisco Opera in 1977. In 1979 he sang Escamillo in Zeffirelli's production of *Carmen* at the Vienna State Opera, and also appeared there as Scarpia and Luna. In 1989 he portrayed Eugene Onegin in Barcelona, a role he reprised in Milwaukee in 1992. In 1991 he became a member of the Mannheim National Theater. In 1996 he sang Scarpia in Moscow. His other roles include Rossini's Figaro, Giorgio Germont, and Rodrigo in *Don Carlos*.

Matačić, Lovro von, noted Slovenian conductor; b. Sušak, Feb. 14, 1899; d. Zagreb, Jan. 4, 1985. He studied with Herbst and Nedbal at the Vienna Cons.; he later worked under Brechner at the Cologne Opera, where he made his debut in 1919; he then conducted in Ljubljana (1924–26), Belgrade (1926–32), and Zagreb (1932–38). He was chief conductor of the Belgrade Opera (1938–42), then conducted at the Vienna Volksoper (1942–45); subsequently he was Generalmusikdirektor of the Dresden State Opera (1956–58) and also conducted at the (East) Berlin State Opera. He was chief conductor of the Frankfurt am Main Opera (1961–65), the Zagreb Phil. (1970–80), and the Monte Carlo Opera (1974–78). His guest conducting engagements included appearances in Europe, the United States, and South America.

Matěj, Josef, Czech composer; b. Brušperk, Feb. 19, 1922; d. there, March 28, 1992. He learned to play the trombone from his father; studied composition with Hlobil at the Prague Cons. (1942–47) and Řídký and Janáček at the Prague Academy of Musical Arts (1947–51). His early works are characterized by folksong inflections of the Lachian region of his birth; after 1960 he introduced into his works some coloristic oriental elements; also made discreet use of dodecaphonic techniques. His works include the opera *Čtyřicet dní hory Musa Dagh* (40 Days of Musa Dagh Mountain; 1979–82).

Materna, Amalie, remarkable Austrian soprano; b. St. Georgen, Styria, July 10, 1844; d. Vienna, Jan. 18, 1918. She was first a church singer. She married the actor Karl Friedrich, with whom she sang in light opera. She made her debut in Graz in 1865, and in 1869 she first sang at the Vienna Court Opera as Selika, remaining on its staff until 1894. Her dramatic talent, powerful voice, and beauteous features attracted the notice of Wagner, who selected her for the role of Brünnhilde in the first Bayreuth Festival of 1876; the following year she sang at the Wagner festival in London, under the composer's direction, and also sang in Wagner festivals in New York, Chicago, and Cincinnati. From 1882 to 1891 she sang regularly at Bayreuth. Her American opera debut took place on Jan. 5, 1885, as Elisabeth in *Tannhäuser* during the first season of German opera at the Metropolitan Opera in New York. In 1894 she became a member of Walter Damrosch's German company in New York. In 1902 she returned to Vienna and opened a singing studio.

Mather, (James) Bruce, Canadian composer, pianist, and teacher; b. Toronto, May 9, 1939. He studied at the Royal Cons. of Music of Toronto (1952–57) and at the Univ. of Toronto (B.Mus., 1959), his principal mentors being Alberto Guerrero, Earle Moss, and Uninsky in piano and Ridout, Morawetz, and Weinzweig in theory and composition. During the summers of 1957–58, he also attended the Aspen (Colo.) Music School. He then studied at the Paris Cons. (1959–61) with Milhaud (composition), Plé-Caussade (counterpoint and fugue), Messiaen (analysis), and Lévy (piano). Following further training in composition with Leland Smith and Roy Harris at Stanford Univ. (M.A., 1964), he returned to the Univ. of Toronto to take his D.Mus. in 1967. In 1969 he studied conducting with Boulez in Basel. After teaching at the Brodie School of Music and Dance and at the Univ. of Toronto (1964–66), he taught at McGill Univ. in Montreal from 1966. As a pianist, he won approbation as an interpreter of contemporary scores. He appeared in duo piano concerts with his wife, Pierrett LePage. In 1979 he won the Jules Léger Prize for his *Musique pour Champigny*. In 1987 he was one of the winners of the Micheline Coulombe Saint-Marcoux prize for his *Barbaresco*. In his music, Mather has utilized various contemporary modes of expression, ranging from serialism to microtonality. He has displayed a special affinity in composing chamber and vocal pieces. He composed the opera *La Princesse Blanche* (1993; Montreal, Feb. 2, 1994).

Mathias, William (James), prominent Welsh composer and teacher; b. Whitland, Nov. 1, 1934; d. Menai Bridge, July 29, 1992. He was a student of Ian Parrott at Univ. College of Wales, Aberystwyth (B.Mus., 1956); in 1957 he went to London to continue his training with Lennox Berkeley (composition) and Peter Katin (piano) at the Royal Academy of Music, where he was made a Fellow in 1965. Upon returning to his homeland, he received his D.Mus. from the Univ. of Wales (1966). From 1959 to 1968 he lectured at Univ. College of North Wales, Bangor. In 1968–69 he taught at the Univ. of Edinburgh. In 1969 he rejoined the faculty of Univ. College of North Wales, where he then was a prof. and head of the music dept. from 1970 to 1988. From 1972 he also served as artistic director of the North Wales Music Festival in St. Asaph. In 1968 he received the Bax Soc. Prize and in 1981 the John Edwards Memorial Award. In 1985 he was made a Commander of the Order of the British Empire. In his music, Mathias followed a basically tonal path notable for its craftsmanship, adept handling of instrumental and vocal forces, and euphonious appeal. Among his many works is the opera *The Servants* (Cardiff, Sept. 15, 1980); also *Culhwch and Olwen*, entertainment (1966), *As You Like It*, incidental music to Shakespeare's play (1967), and *Jonah: A Musical Morality* (Guildford, July 6, 1988).

Mathis, Edith, admired Swiss soprano; b. Lucerne, Feb. 11, 1938. She received her training at the Lucerne Cons. and from Elisabeth Bosshart in Zürich. In 1956 she made her operatic debut as the 2d boy in *Die Zauberflöte* in Lucerne. From 1959 to 1962 she sang at the Cologne Opera. In 1960 she appeared at the Salzburg Festival, which led to engagements in Vienna and Munich. From 1960 to 1975 she appeared with the Hamburg State Opera, and in 1962 made her debut at Glyndebourne as Cherubino. From 1963 she also sang at the Berlin Deutsche Oper. On Jan. 19, 1970, she made her Metropolitan Opera debut in New York as Pamina, remaining on its roster until 1974. She sang for the first time at London's Covent Garden in 1970 as Mozart's Susanna, returning there until 1972. Her frequent Munich engagements led to her being made a Kammersängerin in 1980. She appeared as the Marschallin in Bern in 1990. In addition to her operatic appearances, she won notable distinction as a concert and lieder artist. She married **Bernhard Klee**, with whom she often appeared. Her other memorable operatic roles were Zerlina, Zdenka, Nannetta, Mélisande, the Marschallin, Sophie, and Arabella.

Matsudaira, Yoriaki, Japanese composer; b. Tokyo, March 27, 1931. His father was the Japanese composer Yuritsune Matsudaira (b. Tokyo, May 5, 1907). He studied biology at the Tokyo Metropolitan Univ. (1948–57); as a composer, he was autodidact. In 1958 he became a teacher of physics and biology at Rikkyo Univ. in Tokyo. He was also active with the composing collective Group 20.5, which he founded to promote contemporary music. In his output, Matsudaira has followed an avant-garde path in which he has utilized serialism, aleatory, tape, and electronics. His works include *Sara*, opera (Tokyo, Nov. 12, 1960) and *Ishikawa no iratsume*, dance drama (Tokyo, July 1964). He publ. the book *Conpyuta to ongaku* (Computers in Music; Tokyo, 1972).

Matsumura, Teizo, Japanese composer and pedagogue; b. Kyoto, Jan. 15, 1929. He was orphaned at an early age. After lessons from Tsuneharu Takahashi (piano) and Toshio Nagahiro (harmony), he settled in Tokyo in 1949 to pursue his training with Ikenouchi (harmony, counterpoint, and composition) and Ifukube (composition). Between 1950 and 1955 his life was seriously threatened by tuberculosis. During his convalescence, he began to compose and in 1955 won 1st prize in the NHK-Mainichi Music Competition with his *Introduction and Allegro Concertante* for Orch. From 1970 to 1987 he was prof. of composition at the National Univ. of Fine Arts and Music. In 1994 he won the Mainichi Art Prize and the Grand Prize of the Kyoto Music Awards. Matsumura rebelled early on against dodecaphonism, the then-prevailing musical ideology in Japan. Instead, he pursued an independent course in which he combined the use of Western instruments and forms with the rich inheritance of Asian culture. Among his notable works were his Sym. (1965) and his *Prélude pour orchestre* (1968), the latter winning the Otaka Prize. He also composed *Flute of Devil's Passion*, mono-opera (1965), *Silence*, opera (1980–93; Tokyo, Nov. 3, 1993), and incidental music and film scores.

Matsushita, Shinichi, Japanese composer; b. Osaka, Oct. 1, 1922; d. there, Dec. 25, 1990. He graduated in mathematics from the Kyushu Univ. in Fukuoka in 1947; concurrently he studied music. In 1958 he went to work in an electronic music studio in Osaka; he taught both mathematics and music at the Univ. of Osaka City. In his music, he followed cosmopolitan modernistic techniques, mostly of a functional, pragmatic nature. His works include the radio operas *Comparing Notes on a Rainy Night* (1960) and *Amayo* (1960).

Mattei, Tito, Italian pianist, conductor, and composer; b. Campobasso, near Naples, May 24, 1841; d. London, March 30, 1914. He studied with Parisi, Conti, and Thalberg, making such rapid progress that at the age of 11 he obtained a nominal appointment as "professore" of the Accademia di Santa Cecilia in Rome. He received a gold medal for playing before Pope Pius XI, and was appointed pianist to the king of Italy. About 1865 he settled in London, where he was active principally as an opera conductor. He composed the operas *Maria di Gand* (London, 1880), *The Grand Duke* (London, 1889), and *La Prima Donna* (London, 1889) and the ballet *The Spider and the Fly* (London, 1893).

Mattfeld, Julius, American librarian, organist, and musicographer; b. N.Y., Aug. 8, 1893; d. there, July 31, 1968. He studied at the N.Y. German Cons. In 1910 he joined the staff of the N.Y. Public Library; he resigned in 1926 to become music librarian of NBC (until 1929); he then was librarian of CBS and was also organist of the Fordham Lutheran Church in New York (1915–32). He publ. *A Hundred Years of Grand Opera in New York, 1825–1925* (1927) and *A Handbook of American Operatic Premieres, 1731–1962* (Detroit, 1963).

Mattheson, Johann, famous German composer, music theorist, and lexicographer; b. Hamburg, Sept. 28, 1681; d. there, April 17, 1764. He received a thorough education in the liberal arts at the Johanneum; he acquired proficiency in English, Italian, and French; he studied music there with the Kantor, Joachim Gerstenbuttel. He received private musical instruction studying keyboard music and composition with J. N. Hanff; he also took singing lessons and learned to play the violin, gamba, oboe, flute, and lute. At a very early age he began to perform as an organist in the churches of Hamburg; he also sang in the chorus at the Hamburg Opera. He graduated from the Johanneum in 1693, and concurrently took courses in jurisprudence. He then served as a page at the Hamburg court of Graf von Güldenlöw, who held the title of Vice-König of Norway. He made his debut as a singer in a female role with the Hamburg Opera during its visit to Kiel in 1696; from 1697 to 1705 he was a tenor with the Hamburg Opera, conducted rehearsals, and also composed works for it. He befriended Handel in 1703; together they journeyed to Lübeck to visit Buxtehude, who was about to retire as organist, and to apply for his post. The unwritten requirement for the job was marriage to one of Buxtehude's five daughters, whose attractions seemed dubious; both Mattheson and Handel declined the opportunity. In 1704 a violent quarrel broke out between Mattheson and Handel during a performance of Mattheson's opera *Cleopatra* at the Hamburg Opera. Mattheson sang the principal male role of Antonius while Handel acted as conductor from the keyboard in the capacity of maestro al cembalo. Upon the conclusion of his role on stage, Mattheson asked Handel to let him assume the position at the keyboard, since he was the composer. Handel refused and an altercation ensued. The dispute was finally decided by a duel, during which Mattheson broke his sword on a metal button of Handel's coat, or so at least the most credible report of the episode went. They were, however, soon reconciled and remained friends. In 1704 Mattheson became the tutor of Cyrill Wich, the son of Sir John Wich, British envoy at Hamburg. In 1706 he became secretary to Sir John; when the younger Wich became ambassador in 1715, he retained Mattheson as secretary, a position he held for most of his life. During this period Mattheson diligently studied English politics, law, and economics, thereby adding to his many other accomplishments. In 1715 he assumed the post of music director of the Hamburg Cathedral. He composed much sacred music for performance there, including many oratorios. In 1719 he also became Kapellmeister to the court of the duke of Holstein. Growing deafness compelled him to resign his post at the Cathedral in 1728. In 1741 he was given the title of legation secretary to the duke of Holstein, and was made counsel in 1744.

Mattheson's output as a composer was substantial, but little of his music has survived. Of his major compositions, only the MSS of one of his operas, *Cleopatra* (modern ed., by G. Buelow in *Das Erbe deutscher Musik*, 69, 1975), and one of his oratorios, *Das Lied des Lammes* (modern ed. by B. Cannon, Madison, Wis., 1971), are extant. The bulk of his MSS, kept in the Hamburg Stadtbibliothek, were destroyed during the hideous "fire-storm" bombing of Hamburg during World War II. However, most of his numerous literary writings are preserved. Outstanding among his books is *Der vollkommene Capellmeister* (1739), an original theoretical treatise on the state of music in his era. Also valuable are his *Grosse General-Bass-Schule* (1731; based on his earlier work *Exemplarische Organisten-Probe*, 1719) and *Kleine General-Bass-Schule* (1735). Of great historical value is his biographical dictionary, *Grundlage einer Ehren-Pforte . . .* (1740), which contains 149 entries. Many of the entries on musicians of his own time were compiled from information provided by the subjects themselves, and several prepared complete autobiographical accounts for his lexicon.

WRITINGS (all publ. in Hamburg): *Das neu-eröffnete Orchestre, oder gründliche Anleitung, wie ein "galant homme" einen vollkommenen Begriff von der Hoheit und Würde der edlen Musik erlangen möge* (1713); *Das beschützte Orchestre* (1717); *Exemplarische Organisten-Probe im Artikel vom General-Bass* (1719; publ. in an enl. ed. as *Grosse-General-Bass-Schule, oder: Der exemplarischen Organisten-Probe zweite, verbesserte und vermehrte Auflage*, 1731); *Réflexions sur l'éclaircissement d'un problème de musique pratique* (1720); *Das forschende Orchester* (1721); *Melotheta, das ist der grundrichtige, nach jetziger neuesten Manier angeführte Componiste* (1721–22); *Critica musica*

(1722–25); *Der neue gottingische, aber viel schlechter, als die alten lacedämonischen urtheilende Ephorus* (1727); *Der musicalische Patriot* (1728); *De eruditione musica, ad virum plurimum reverendum, amplissimum atque doctissimum, Joannes Christophorum Krüsike* (1732); *Kleine General-Bass-Schule* (1735); *Kern melodischer Wissenschaft* (1737); *Gültige Zeugnisse über die jüngste Matthesonisch-Musicalische Kern-Schrift* (1738); *Der vollkommene Capellmeister, das ist gründliche Anzeige aller derjenigen Sachen, die einer wissen, können und vollkommen inne haben muss, der eine Capelle mit Ehren und Nützen verstehen will* (1739; facsimile reprint, Kassel, 1954; rev. Eng. tr. by E. Harriss, 1980); *Grundlage einer Ehren-Pforte, woran die tüchtigsten Capellmeister, Componisten, Musikgelehrten, Tonkünstler, etc. Leben, Werke, Verdienste, etc., erscheinen sollen* (1740; new ed., with addenda, by M. Schneider, Berlin, 1910); *Die neuste Untersuchung der Singspiele, nebst beygefügter musicalischen Geschmacksprobe* (1744); *Das erläuterte Selah, nebst einigen andern nützlichen Anmerkungen und erbaulichen Gedanken über Lob und Liebe* (1745); *Behauptung der himmlischen Musik aus den Gründen der Vernunft, Kirchen-Lehre und heiligen Schrift* (1747); *Matthesons Mithridat wider den Gift einer welschen Satyre, genannt: La Musica* (by S. Rosa; 1749); *Matthesons bewährte Panacea, als eine Zugabe zu seinem musicalischen Mithridat, erste Dosis* (1750); *Wahrer Begriff der harmonischen Lebens. Der Panacea zwote Dosis* (1750); *Sieben Gespräche der Weisheit und Musik samt zwo Beylagen: Als die dritte Dosis der Panacea* (1751); *Philologisches Tresespiel, als ein kleiner Beytrag zur kritischen Geschichte der deutschen Sprache* (1752); *Plus ultra, ein Stüchwerk von neuer und mancherley Art* (4 vols., 1754, 1755, 1755, 1756); *Georg Friederich Händels Lebensbeschreibung* (German tr. of J. Mainwaring's biography; 1761); etc.

WORKS (all 1st perf. in Hamburg unless otherwise given): DRAMATIC: OPERAS: *Die Plejades oder Das Sieben-Gestirne* (1699); *Der edelmüthige Porsenna* (1702); *Victor, Hertzog der Normannen* (pasticcio; Act 1 by Schiefferdecker; Act 2 by Mattheson; Act 3 by Bronner; 1702); *Die unglückselige Cleopatra* (1704); *Le Retour du siècle d'or* (Holstein, 1705); *Boris Goudenow* (1710); *Die geheimen Begebenheiten Henrico IV* (1711); he also prepared a German version of Orlandini's *Nero* (1723), with additions. ORATORIOS: *Die heylsame Geburth und Menschwerdung unsers Herrn und Heylandes Jesu Christi* (1715); *Die gnädige Sendung Gottes des Heiligen Geistes* (1716); *Chera, oder Die Leidtragende und getröstete Wittwe zu Nain* (1716); *Der verlangte und erlangte Heiland* (1716); *Der Altonaische Hirten-Segen, nebst einer Passions-Andacht über den verlassenen Jesum* (1717); *Der reformirende Johannes* (1717); *Der für die Sünde der Welt gemartete und sterbende Jesus* (1718); *Der aller-erfreulichste Triumph oder Der überwindende Immanuel* (1718); *Die glücklich-streitende Kirche* (1718); *Die göttliche Vorsorge über alle Creaturen* (1718); *Die Frucht des Geistes* (1719); *Christi Wunder-Wercke bey den Schwachgläubigen* (1719); *Die durch Christi Auferstehung bestägte Auferstehung aller Todten* (1720); *Das gröste Kind* (1720); *Der Blut-rünstige Kelter-Treter und von der Erden erhöhete Menschen-Sohn* (1721); *Das irrende und wieder zu recht gebrachte Sünde-Schaaf* (1721); *Die Freudenreiche Geburt und Menschwerdung unsers Herrn und Heilandes Jesu Christi* (1721); *Der unter den Todten gesuchte, und unter den lebendigen gefundene Sieges-Fürst* (1722); *Das Grosse in dem Kleinen, oder Gott in den Herzen eines gläubigen Christen* (1722); *Das Lied des Lammes* (1723); *Der liebreiche und gedultige David* (1723); *Der aus dem Löwen-Graben befreyte, himmlische Daniel* (1725); *Das gottseelige Geheimnis* (1725); *Der undanckbare Jerobeam* (1726); *Der gegen seine Brüder barmherzige Joseph* (1727); *Das durch die Fleischwerdung des ewigen Wortes erfüllte Wort der Verheissung* (1727). He also composed his own funeral oratorio, *Das fröhliche Sterbelied*.

BIBL.: L. Meinardus, *M. und seine Verdienste um die deutsche Tonkunst*, in Waldersee's *Sammlung musikalischer Vorträge* (Leipzig, 1879); H. Schmidt, *J. M.: Ein Förderer der deutschen Tonkunst, im Lichte seiner Werke* (diss., Univ. of Munich, 1897); B. Cannon, *J. M.: Spectator in Music* (New Haven, 1947); W. Braun, *J. M. und die Aufklärung* (diss., Univ. of Halle, 1952); H. Marx, *J. M.* (Hamburg, 1982); G. Buelow and H. Marx, eds., *New M. Studies* (Cambridge, 1984).

Matthus, Siegfried, German composer; b. Mallenuppen, April 13, 1934. He studied composition with Wagner-Régeny at the Deutsche Hochschule für Musik (1952–58) and with Eisler at the Deutsche Akademie der Künste (1958–60) in East Berlin. In 1964 he was appointed a composer and dramatist at the (East) Berlin Komische Oper. In 1972 he became a member of the presidium of the Deutsche Akademie der Künste.

WORKS: DRAMATIC: OPERAS: *Lazarillo vom Tormes* (1960–63; Karl-Marx-Stadt, May 26, 1964); *Der letzte Schuss* (1966–67; Berlin, Nov. 5, 1967); *Noch ein Löffel Gift, Liebling?* (1971–72; Berlin, April 16, 1972); *Omphale* (1972–73; Weimar, Aug. 29, 1976); *Die Weisse von Liebe und Tod des Cornet Christoph Rilke*, opera vision (1983–84; Dresden, May 12, 1985); *Judith* (Berlin, Sept. 28, 1985); *Eine Opernvision* (1985); *Mirabeau* (1989); *Desdemona und ihre Schwestern*, opera monologues (1991; Schwetzingen, May 12, 1992); *Farinelli* (1998). OTHER: *Laudate pacem*, oratorio (1974), and *Unter dem Holunderstrauch*, scene after Kleist for Soprano, Tenor, and Orch. (1976).

Mattila, Karita (Marjatta), Finnish soprano; b. Somero, Sept. 5, 1960. She was a pupil of Liisa Linko-Malmio and Kim Borg at the Sibelius Academy in Helsinki and of Vera Rozsa in London. In 1982 she made her operatic debut as Mozart's Countess at the Finnish National Opera in Helsinki; after winning the Singer of the World Competition in Cardiff in 1983, she appeared as a soloist with many of the world's major orchs. In 1983 she sang Fiordiligi at the Munich Festival and also made her U.S. debut as Donna Elvira in Washington, D.C.; in 1986 she made her first appearance at London's Covent Garden as Fiordiligi. In 1989 she appeared as Ilia in *Idomeneo* at the San Francisco Opera. On Oct. 24, 1990, she made her Metropolitan Opera debut in New York as Donna Elvira, and returned there in 1993 as Eva. She also sang at the Salzburg Festival in the latter year. In 1995 she sang Lisa in *The Queen of Spades* at the Metropolitan Opera, and in 1996 returned to San Francisco as Elsa. After singing that role and Chrysothemis at Covent Garden in 1997, she was engaged as Jenůfa in Hamburg in 1998. In 1999 she returned to the Metropolitan Opera as Emilia Grimaldi. In addition to her Mozart roles, she also became well known as a Wagnerian.

Matzenauer, Margarete, celebrated Hungarian soprano and contralto; b. Temesvár, June 1, 1881; d. Van Nuys, Calif., May 19, 1963. Her father was a conductor and her mother a soprano; she grew up in favorable musical surroundings, and began to study singing at an early age, first in Graz, then in Berlin, and finally in Munich. In 1901 she joined the staff of the Strasbourg Opera, then sang contralto roles at the Munich Court Opera (1904–11); she also sang at Bayreuth in 1911. She made her American debut as Amneris in *Aida* at the Metropolitan Opera in New York (Nov. 13, 1911) and remained one of its leading members until 1930; in the interim, she sang in opera in Germany and South America. She gave her farewell concert recital in Carnegie Hall, N.Y., in 1938, and settled in California. She had one of the most remarkable singing careers of her day; she sang both soprano and contralto roles until 1914, and thereafter concentrated on contralto roles. Among her many outstanding roles were Brünnhilde, Venus, Isolde, Fricka, Ortrud, Eboli, Azucena, Leonora, and Laura in *La Gioconda*.

Mauceri, John (Francis), American conductor; b. N.Y., Sept. 12, 1945. He studied with Gustav Meier at Yale Univ. (B.A., 1967; M.Phil., 1972) and with Maderna, Colin Davis, Ozawa, and Bernstein at the Berkshire Music Center at Tanglewood (summer 1971). He conducted the Yale Univ. Sym. Orch. (1968–74); subsequently he appeared widely as a guest conductor of opera, musical theater, and sym. orchs. He was music director of the Washington (D.C.) Opera (1980–82), the American Sym. Orch. in New York (1984–87), the Scottish Opera in Glasgow (1987–93), and the Hollywood Bowl Orch. (from 1990).

Maupin, infamous French soprano; b. 1670; d. Provence, 1707. She was the daughter of the secretary to the count of Armagnac. In 1690 she made her operatic debut as Pallas in Lully's *Cadmus et Hermione* at the Paris Opéra, where she continued to sing until 1705. She possessed a remarkable voice of great beauty, which was complemented by her physical attributes. Her life outside the theater was as exciting as any role she played on the stage. A penchant for donning men's clothing gave rise to situations in which she defended herself in duels. Her sexual appetite led to various bisexual encounters. For many years she was the mistress of the elector of Bavaria. Her notorious life served as the basis of Gautier's novel *Mademoiselle Maupin, double amour* (Paris, 1835–36).

BIBL.: G. Letainturier-Fradin, *La M. (1670–1707): Sa vie, ses duels, ses aventures* (Paris, 1904).

Maurel, Victor, famous French baritone; b. Marseilles, June 17, 1848; d. N.Y., Oct. 22, 1923. He studied singing at the Paris Cons., making his debut in *Guillaume Tell* in Marseilles (1867). He made his first appearance at the Paris Opéra as De Nevers in *Les Huguenots* in 1868, then sang in Italy, Spain, England, and Russia; in 1873 he made an American tour. Returning to Paris, he was on the staff of the Opéra (1879–94). He made his debut at the Metropolitan Opera in New York on Dec. 3, 1894, as Iago in *Otello*; he sang there until 1896, then returned in 1898–99. He was a member of the Opéra Comique in Paris until 1904. In 1909 he emigrated to the United States, where he remained until his death; in his last years he was active as a stage designer in New York. He created the role of Iago in Verdi's *Otello* (Milan, Feb. 5, 1887) and the title role in *Falstaff* (Milan, Feb. 9, 1893); he also distinguished himself in Wagnerian roles. He publ., in Paris, several monographs on the aesthetics of singing and also autobiographical reminiscences, among them *Le Chant removè par la science* (1892), *Un Problème d'art* (1893), *L'Art du chant* (1897), and *Dix ans de carrière* (1897).

Maurer, Ludwig (Wilhelm), German violinist and composer; b. Potsdam, Feb. 8, 1789; d. St. Petersburg, Oct. 25, 1878. He studied with K. Haack. A precocious child musician, he appeared in concerts at the age of 13. At 17 he went to Russia, remaining there for 10 years, giving concerts and serving as house musician to Russian aristocrats. From 1817 until 1832 he traveled in Europe, and was successful as a violinist in Berlin and in Paris. He was in Russia again (1832–45), then lived in Dresden, eventually returning to St. Petersburg. He produced 2 operas in Hannover, *Der neue Paris* (Jan. 27, 1826) and *Aloise* (Jan. 16, 1828); he also wrote many stage pieces in Russia. With Aliabiev and Verstovsky, he contributed the music to Chmelnitsky's comedy *A Novel Prank, or Theatrical Combat* (1822). His 2 sons, Vsevolod (1819–92), a violinist, and Alexis, a cellist, remained in Russia.

Maurice, Alphons, German composer; b. Hamburg, April 14, 1862; d. Dresden, Jan. 27, 1905. He studied with Dessoff, Krenn, and Grädener at the Vienna Cons. He wrote the operas *Josepha, Schatz*, and *Der Wundersteg*.

Maurice, Pierre, Baron de, Swiss composer; b. Allaman, Nov. 13, 1868; d. Geneva, Dec. 25, 1936. He attended the Geneva Cons., then for a short time studied at Stuttgart, finishing his musical education with Lavignac and Massenet at the Paris Cons. He composed the operas *Die weisse Flagge* (Kassel, 1903), *Misê brun* (Stuttgart, 1908), *Lanval* (Weimar, 1912), *Kalif Storch* (not perf.), *Andromède* (1923), *Le Mystère de la Nativité* (1933), et al.; also a biblical drama, *La Fille de Jephthé* (Geneva, 1899).

BIBL.: M. Maurice, *P. M.* (Geneva, 1938).

Mauro, Ermanno, Italian-born Canadian tenor; b. Trieste, Jan. 20, 1939. He emigrated to Canada in 1958 and became a naturalized Canadian citizen in 1963; after vocal training with Jean Létourneau in Edmonton, he entered the Royal Cons. Opera School in Toronto in 1964 and studied with George Lambert, Herman Geiger-Torel, and Ernesto Barbini. In 1962 he made his operatic debut as Manrico in Edmonton; after appearances in opera productions at the Royal Cons. in Toronto and with the Canadian Opera Co., he sang at London's Covent Garden (1967–72). On Feb. 3, 1975, Mauro made his debut at the N.Y. City Opera, remaining with the company until 1979; on Jan. 6, 1978, he made his Metropolitan Opera debut in New York as Canio, and returned there as Cavaradossi in 1986 and as Turiddu in 1989. After singing Manrico in Brussels in 1984, he appeared as Otello in Dallas in 1985 and as Calaf at the Deutsche Oper in Berlin in 1987. In 1990 he portrayed Manrico in Zürich, and in 1992 Turiddu at the Teatro Colón in Buenos Aires. He sang Loris in *Fedora* in Montreal in 1995. Among his other roles are Ernani, Des Grieux, Alfredo, Faust, Pinkerton, and Rodolfo.

Maw, (John) Nicholas, distinguished English composer and teacher; b. Grantham, Lincolnshire, Nov. 5, 1935. After studies with Berkeley (composition) and Steinitz (theory) at the Royal Academy of Music in London (1955–58), he held a French government scholarship for further training in Paris with Deutsch and Boulanger (1958–59). In 1959 he was awarded the Lili Boulanger Prize. He taught at the Royal Academy of Music (1964–66), and then was fellow commoner (composer-in-residence) at Trinity College, Cambridge (1966–70). He was a lecturer in music at the Univ. of Exeter, Devon (1972–74), and also served as composer-in-residence of the South Bank Summer Music series in London (1973). In 1984–85 and 1989 he was a visiting prof. of music at the Yale School of Music. From 1989 he was a prof. of music at the Milton Avery Graduate School of the Arts at Bard College in Annandale-on-Hudson, N.Y. In his music, Maw pursued a personal compositional path that utilized neoclassical and late Romantic elements before finding fulfillment in a style notable for its expansive lyrical qualities. His works include the operas *One-Man Show* (London, Nov. 12, 1964; rev. 1966 and 1970), *The Rising of the Moon* (1967–70; Glyndebourne, July 19, 1970), and *Sophie's Choice* (1999–2000); also incidental music; film scores.

Maxakova, Mariya (Petrovna), Russian mezzo-soprano; b. Astrakhan, April 8, 1902; d. Moscow, Aug. 11, 1974. She was a student of Maximilian Maxakov, whom she married. After singing in Astrakhan, she appeared at Moscow's Bolshoi Theater in 1923. From 1925 to 1927 she sang at the Leningrad Academy Opera. In 1927 she became a member of the Bolshoi Theater, where she sang until 1953. She also appeared as a concert artist. In addition to her distinguished Russian roles, she won particular notice for her Ortrud, Delilah, and Carmen.

BIBL.: M. Lvov, *M. P. M.* (Moscow and Leningrad, 1947).

Maxwell Davies, Sir Peter. See **Davies, Sir Peter Maxwell.**

Maxwell, Donald, Scottish baritone; b. Perth, Dec. 12, 1948. He studied at the Univ. of Edinburgh. In 1977 he made his operatic debut as Morton in Musgrave's *Mary, Queen of Scots* with the Scottish Opera in Glasgow, where he subsequently sang many roles. In 1982 he made his first appearance with the Welsh National Opera in Cardiff as Anckarström, and later toured with the company as Falstaff to Paris, Tokyo, and Milan. He made his debut at London's Covent Garden in the British premiere of Sallinen's *The King Goes Forth to France* in 1987, returning there in 1990 as Gunther. He portrayed Wozzeck at the English National Opera in London in 1990 and at Opera North in Leeds in 1993. In 1996 he appeared in *Lulu* at the Glyndebourne Festival. His other roles include Rossini's Figaro, Pizzaro, Don Carlos, Iago, Rigoletto, Golaud, and Scarpia.

Mayer, (Benjamin) Wilhelm, Austrian pianist, pedagogue, and composer who used the pseudonym **W. A. Rémy**; b. Prague, June 10, 1831; d. Graz, Jan. 22, 1898. He studied with C. Pietsch, and also took a degree in law (1856). In 1862 he became conductor of the Graz Musical Soc. resigning in 1870 to apply himself to pedagogy. He taught both piano and composition, and achieved great renown, numbering among his pupils Busoni, Rezniček, and Weingartner. He wrote a concert opera, *Das Waldfräulein* (Graz, 1876).

Mayer, William (Robert), American composer; b. N.Y., Nov. 18, 1925. He was a student of Richard Donovan and Herbert Baumgartner at Yale Univ. (B.A., 1949), of Sessions at the Juilliard School of Music in New York (summer 1949), of Salzer at the Mannes College of Music in New York (1949–52), and of Izler Solomon (conducting) at the Aspen (Colo.) Music School (summer 1960). In 1966 he held a Guggenheim fellowship. In 1980 he was secretary of the National Music Council. He received the National Inst. for Musical Theater Award in 1983.

WORKS: DRAMATIC: *The Greatest Sound Around*, children's opera (1954); *Hello World!*, children's opera (N.Y., Nov. 10, 1956); *The Snow Queen*, ballet (1963); *One Christmas Long Ago*, opera (Philadelphia, Dec. 12, 1964); *Brief Candle*, "micro-opera" (1964); *A Death in the Family*, opera (Minneapolis, March 11, 1983); *A Sobbing Pillow of Man* (N.Y., Dec. 7, 1995).

Maynor, Dorothy (Leigh), noted black American soprano and music educator; b. Norfolk, Va., Sept. 3, 1910; d. West Chester, Pa., Feb. 19, 1996. She was educated at the Hampton Inst. (B.S., 1933). She began her career singing in various choirs, and later toured with the inst.'s famous chorus in Europe; she subsequently studied at Westminster Choir College and with William Kamroth and John Alan Haughton in New York. After a successful appearance at the Berkshire Music Festival at Tanglewood in 1939, she made her Town Hall debut in New York on Nov. 19, 1939. In subsequent years, she toured widely in the United States and Europe as a concert singer, appearing with leading orchs. She founded the Harlem School of the Arts in 1963 to provide music education for underprivileged children, and served as its executive director until her retirement in 1979.

BIBL.: W. Rogers, *D. M. and the Harlem School of the Arts: The Diva and the Dream* (Lewiston, N.Y., 1993).

Mayr, (Johannes) Simon (Giovanni Simone), outstanding German composer; b. Mendorf, Bavaria (of Italian parents), June 14, 1763; d. Bergamo, Dec. 2, 1845. He first studied music with his father, a schoolteacher and organist, and he sang in a church choir and played organ. In 1774 he entered the Jesuit college in Ingolstadt, and in 1781 he began a study of theology at the Univ. of Ingolstadt. In 1787 a Swiss Freiherr, Thomas von Bassus, took him to Italy to further his musical education; in 1789 he commenced studies with Carlo Lenzi in Bergamo; he then was sent to Ferdinando Bertoni in Venice. He began his career as a composer of sacred music; his oratorios were performed in Venice. After the death of his patron, Count Presenti, in 1793, he was encouraged by Piccinni and Peter von Winter to compose operas. His first opera, *Saffo o sia I riti d'Apollo Leucadio*, was performed in Venice in 1794. He gained renown with his opera *Ginevra di Scozia* (Trieste, April 21, 1801), and it remained a favorite with audiences; also successful were his operas *La rosa bianca e la rosa rossa* (Genoa, Feb. 21, 1813) and *Medea in Corinto* (Naples, Nov. 28, 1813). In 1802 he became maestro di cappella at S. Maria Maggiore in Bergamo, and in 1805 he reorganized the choir school of the Cathedral as the Lezioni Caritatevoli di Musica and assumed its directorship; intractable cataracts, which led to total blindness in 1826, forced him to limit his activities to organ playing. In 1822 he founded the Societa Filarmonica of Bergamo. Mayr's operas, while reflecting the late Neapolitan school, are noteworthy for their harmonization and orchestration, which are derived from the German tradition. After 1815 he devoted most of his time to composing sacred music, which totals some 600 works in all. He was also an eminent pedagogue. Donizetti was his pupil.

WORKS: DRAMATIC: OPERAS: *Saffo o sia I riti d'Apollo Leucadio*, dramma per musica (Venice, Feb. 17, 1794); *La Lodoiska*, dramma per musica (Venice, Jan. 26, 1796; rev. for Milan, Dec. 26, 1799); *Un pazzo ne fa cento [I Rivali delusi; La Contessa immaginaria]*, dramma giocoso (Venice, Oct. 8, 1796); *Telemaco nell'isola di Calipso*, dramma per musica (Venice, Jan. 16, 1797); *Il segreto*, farsa (Venice, Sept. 24, 1797); *L'intrigo della lettera [Il pittore astratto]*, farsa (Venice, fall 1797); *Avviso ai maritati*, dramma giocoso (Venice, Jan. 15, 1798); *Lauso e Lidia*, dramma per musica (Venice, Feb. 14, 1798); *Adriano in Siria*, dramma per musica (Venice, April 23, 1798); *Che originali [Il trionfo della musica; Il fanatico per la musica: La musicomania]*, farsa (Venice, Oct. 18, 1798); *Amor ingegnoso*, farsa (Venice, Dec. 27, 1798); *L'ubbidienza per astuzia*, farsa (Venice, Dec. 27, 1798); *Adelaide di Gueselino*, dramma per musica (Venice, May 1, 1799); *Labino e Carlotta*, farsa (Venice, Oct. 9, 1799); *L'Avaro*, farsa (Venice, Nov. 1799); *L'accademia di musica*, farsa (Venice, fall 1799); *Gli sciti*, dramma per musica (Venice, Feb. 1800); *La Locandiera*, farsa (Vicenza, spring 1800); *Il caretto del venditore d'aceto*, farsa (Venice, June 28, 1800); *L'Imbroglione e il castiga-matti*, farsa (Venice, fall 1800); *L'equivoco, ovvero Le bizzarie dell'amore*, dramma giocoso (Milan, Nov. 5, 1800); *Ginevra di Scozia [Ariodante]*, dramma serio eroico per musica (Trieste, April 21, 1801; inaugural perf. at the Teatro Nuovo there); *Le due giornate [Il Portatore d'acqua]*, dramma eroicomico per musica (Milan, Aug. 18, 1801); *I Virtuosi [I Virtuosi a teatro]*, farsa (Venice, Dec. 26, 1801); *Argene*, dramma eroico per musica (Venice, Dec. 28, 1801); *Elisa, ossia Il monte S. Bernardo*, dramma sentimentale per musica (Malta, 1801); *I misteri eleusini*, dramma per musica (Milan, Jan. 6, 1802); *I castelli in aria, ossia Gli Amanti per accidente*, farsa (Venice, May 1802); *Ercole in Lidia*, dramma per musica (Vienna, Jan. 29, 1803); *Gl'intrighi amorosi*, dramma giocoso (Parma, Carnival 1803); *Le finte rivali*, melodramma giocoso (Aug. 20, 1803); *Alonso e Cora*, dramma per musica (Milan, Dec. 26, 1803; rev. as *Cora* for Naples, 1815); *Amor non ha ritegno [La fedeltà delle vedove]*, melodramma eroicomico (Milan, May 18, 1804); *I due viaggiatori*, dramma giocoso (Florence, summer 1804); *Zamori, ossia L'Eroe dell'Indie*, dramma per musica (Piacenza, Aug. 10, 1804; inaugural perf. at the Nuovo Teatro Communale); *Eraldo ed Emma*, dramma eroico per musica (Milan, Jan. 8, 1805); *Di locanda in locanda e sempre in sala*, farsa (June 5, 1805); *L'amor coniugale [Il custode di buon cuore]*, dramma giocoso (Padua, July 26, 1805); *La rocca di Frauenstein*, melodramma eroicomico (Venice, Oct. 26, 1805); *Gli Americani [Idalide]*, melodramma eroico (Venice, Carnival 1806); *Palmira, o sia Il trionfo della virtù e dell'amore*, dramma per musica (Florence, fall 1806); *Il piccolo compositore di musica*, farsa (Venice, 1806); *Nè l'un, nè l'altro*, dramma giocoso (Milan, Aug. 17, 1807); *Belle ciarle e tristi fatti [L'imbroglio contro l'imbroglio]*, dramma giocoso (Venice, Nov. 1807); *Adelasia e Aleramo*, melodramma serio (Milan, Dec. 25, 1807); *I cherusci*, dramma per musica (Rome, Carnival 1808); *Il vero originale*, burletta per musica (Rome, Carnival 1808); *La finta sposa, ossia Il Barone burlato*, dramma giocoso (Rome, spring 1808); *Il matrimonio per concorso*, dramma giocoso (Bologna, Carnival 1809); *Il ritorno di Ulisse*, azione eroica per musica (Venice, Carnival 1809); *Amor non soffre opposizione*, dramma giocoso (Venice, Carnival 1810); *Raùl di Créqui*, melodramma serio (Milan, Dec. 26, 1810); *Il sacrifizio d'Ifigenia [Ifigenia in Aulide]*, azione seria drammatica per musica (Brescia, Carnival 1811); *L'amor figliale [Il Disertore]*, farsa sentimentale (Venice, Carnival 1811); *La rosa bianca e la rosa rossa [Il trionfo dell'amicizia]*, melodramma eroica (Genoa, Feb. 21, 1813); *Medea in Corinto*, melodramma tragico (Naples, Nov. 28, 1813); *Tamerlano*, melodramma serio (Milan, Carnival 1813); *Elena [Elena e Costantino]*, dramma eroicomico per musica (Naples, Carnival 1814); *Atar, o sia Il serraglio d'Ormus*, melodramma serio (Genoa, June 1814); *Le due duchesse, ossia La caccia dei lupi [Le due amiche]*, dramma semiserio per musica (Milan, Nov. 7, 1814); *La Figlia dell'aria, ossia La vendetta di Giunone*, dramma per musica (Naples, Lent 1817); *Nennone e Zemira*, dramma per musica (Naples, March 22, 1817); *Amor avvocato*, commedia per musica (Naples, spring 1817); *Lanassa*, melodramma eroico (Venice, Carnival 1818); *Alfredo il grande*, melodramma serio (Rome, Feb. 1818); *Le Danaide [Danao]*, melodramma serio (Rome, Carnival 1819); *Fedra*, melodramma serio (Milan, Dec. 26, 1820); *Demetrio*, dramma per musica (Turin, Carnival 1824). ORATORIOS: *Iacob a Labano fugiens* (Venice, 1791); *Sisara* (Venice, 1793); *Tobia, o Tobiae matrimonium* (Venice, 1794); *La Passione* (Forli, 1794); *David in spelunca Engaddi* (Venice, 1795); *Il sacrifizio di Iefte* (Forli; year unknown); *Samuele* (Bergamo, 1821); *S. Luigi Gonzaga* (Bergamo, 1822); also the sacred dramas *Ifigenia in Tauride* (Florence, spring 1817) and *Atalia* (Naples, Lent 1822).

WRITINGS: In addition to his *Breve notizie storiche della vita e delle opere di Giuseppe Haydn* (Bergamo, 1809) and *Regolamento delle Lezioni Caritatevoli di musica* (Bergamo, 1822), many other writings remain in MS.

BIBL.: G. Calvi, *Musica sacra di S. M.* (Milan, 1848); G. Finazzi, *Per la solenne inaugurazione del monumento eretto alla memoria del celebre maestro G. S. M. nella basilica di S. Maria Maggiore in Bergamo* (Bergamo, 1853); F. Alborghetti and M. Galli, *Gaetano Donizetti e G. S. M.: Notizie e documenti* (Bergamo, 1875); C. Schmidl, *Cenni biografici su G. S. M.* (Trieste, 1901); C. Scotti, *G. S. M.: Discorso* (Bergamo, 1903); L. Schiedermair, *Beiträge zur Geschichte der Oper um die Wende des 18. und 19. Jahrhunderts: S. M.* (2 vols., Leipzig, 1907, 1910); A. Gazzaniga, *Il Fondo musicale M. della biblioteca civica di Bergamo* (Bergamo, 1963); J. Allitt, *G. S. M.* (Shaftesbury, 1989; rev. Italian ed., 1995).

Mayuzumi, Toshirō, eminent Japanese composer; b. Yokohama, Feb. 20, 1929; d. Kawasaki, April 10, 1997. He was a student of Ikenouchi and Ifukube at the Tokyo National Univ. of Fine Arts and Music (1945–51) and of Aubin at the Paris Cons. (1951–52). With Akutagawa and Dan, he organized the contemporary music group Ars Nova Japonica, Sannin no Kai (Group of 3). In 1959 and 1962 he won the Otaka Prize, and in 1964 the Mainichi Music Prize. His style of composition embodied sonorous elements from Japanese and other Asian traditions, modified serial techniques, and electronic sounds, all amalgamated in a remarkably effective manner.

WORKS: DRAMATIC: *Bugaku*, ballet (1962; N.Y., March 20, 1963); *The Bible*, film score (1965); *Kinkakuji* (The Temple of the Golden Pavilion), opera (Berlin, June 23, 1976); *The Kabuki*, ballet (1985); incidental music; dance dramas.

Mazas, Jacques-Féréol, French violinist, teacher, and composer; b. Lavaur, Tarn, Sept. 23, 1782; d. Bordeaux, Aug. 25, 1849. He was a pupil of Baillot at the Paris Cons., winning 1st prize as violinist (1805). He then played in the orch. of the Italian Opera in Paris. He toured Europe (1811–27), then was a teacher in Orléans (from 1831), and director of a music school in Cambrai (1837–41). He spent the last years of his life in Bordeaux. He wrote a method for violin (new ed. by J. Hrímalý) and numerous valuable studies. Among his compositions were 3 operas, one of which, *Le Kiosque*, was performed in Paris in 1842.

Mazzolani, Antonio, Italian composer; b. Ruina, near Ferrara, Dec. 26, 1819; d. Ferrara, Jan. 25, 1900. He studied with Zagagnoni (composition) and Lodi (piano). He wrote the operas *Gismonda* (Ferrara, May 17, 1854) and *Enrico Charlis* (Ferrara, Nov. 25, 1876), but was most popular in Italy for his choruses with extensive soli.

Mazzoleni, Ester, Italian soprano; b. Sebenico, March 12, 1883; d. Palermo, May 17, 1982. After vocal studies, she made her operatic debut in Rome in 1906 as Leonora in *Il Trovatore*. From 1908 to 1917 she appeared at Milan's La Scala, where she sang such roles as Spontini's Giulia and Cherubini's Médée. She also sang Aida at Verona (1913) and appeared in many other Italian opera centers. Her guest engagements also took her to various European opera houses. Among her other roles were Norma, Elisabeth de Valois, and Lucrezia Borgia.

Mazura, Franz, Austrian bass-baritone; b. Salzburg, April 21, 1924. He studied in Detmold. He made his operatic debut in Kassel (1949); he later appeared at the opera houses of Mainz, Braunschweig, and Mannheim. In 1963 he made his first appearance at the Berlin Städtische Oper and in 1967 at the Hamburg State Opera; he also sang at the Bayreuth Festival (from 1971). In 1979 he sang Dr. Schön in the premiere of the 3-act version of *Lulu* in Paris, which role he also sang at his Metropolitan Opera debut in New York (Dec. 12, 1980). In addition to the Wagnerian repertoire, he sang Pizzaro in *Fidelio*, Jochanaan in *Salome*, and Moses in Schoenberg's *Moses und Aron*.

Mazzucato, Alberto, Italian violinist, composer, and writer on music; b. Udine, July 28, 1813; d. Milan, Dec. 31, 1877. He first studied mathematics, then turned to music, his teacher being Bresciano in Padua, where his first opera, *La Fidanzata di Lammermoor*, was given (Feb. 24, 1834). He subsequently wrote 8 more operas: *Don Chisciotte* (Milan, April 26, 1836), *Esmeralda* (Mantua, Feb. 10, 1838; his most successful stage work), *I Corsari* (Milan, Feb. 15, 1840), *I due sergenti* (Milan, Feb. 27, 1841), *Luigi V, re di Francia* (Milan, Feb. 25, 1843), *Hernani* (Genoa, Dec. 26, 1843), *Alberico da Romano* (Padua, 1847), and *Fede* (not perf.). Verdi's ascendance soon put him into the shade. He joined the faculty of the Milan Cons. in 1839, and from 1872 until his death was its director. From 1859 to 1868 he was concertmaster in the orch. of La Scala, Milan. He wrote for the *Gazzetta Musicale di Milano* (1845–56), and then was its ed. (1856–58). He publ. *Trattato d'estetica musicale*.

McArthur, Edwin, American conductor, pianist, and pedagogue; b. Denver, Sept. 24, 1907; d. N.Y., Feb. 24, 1987. He studied piano in Denver and with Rosina Lhévinne in New York. He toured widely as a piano accompanist to various celebrated artists of the day, becoming well known as accompanist to Kirsten Flagstad. In 1938 he made his debut as an opera conductor in Chicago, and then appeared with the San Francisco Opera in 1939. On April 1, 1940, he made his Metropolitan Opera debut in New York conducting *Tristan und Isolde*, remaining on its roster until 1941. From 1945 to 1950 he was director of the St. Louis Municipal Opera. He was conductor of the Harrisburg (Pa.) Sym. Orch. from 1950 to 1974. He also served as director of the opera dept. at the Eastman School of Music in Rochester, N.Y. (1967–72) before devoting himself to private teaching. McArthur was the author of the book *Flagstad: A Personal Memoir* (N.Y., 1965).

McCabe, John, esteemed English pianist, music educator, and composer; b. Huyton, April 21, 1939. He learned to play piano, violin, and cello as a child; he studied with Proctor Gregg (composition) at the Univ. of Manchester and with Pitfield (composition) and Green (piano) at the Royal Manchester College of Music; he later took courses at the Munich Academy of Music (1964–65) and also studied privately there with Genzmer. He was pianist-in-residence at Univ. College, Cardiff (1965–67), then settled in London as a pianist, excelling in the music of Haydn and contemporary composers. He was director of the London College of Music from 1983 to 1990. In 1985 he was made a Commander of the Order of the British Empire.

WORKS: DRAMATIC: *The Lion, the Witch, and the Wardrobe*, children's opera (1968; Manchester, April 29, 1969); *This Town's a Corporation Full of Crooked Streets*, entertainment for Speaker, Tenor, Children's Chorus, Mixed Chorus, and Instrumental Ensemble (1969); *Notturni ed Alba*, ballet (1970); *The Teachings of Don Juan*, ballet (Manchester, May 30, 1973); *The Play of Mother Courage*, chamber opera (Middlesbrough, Oct. 3, 1974); *Mary Queen of Scots*, ballet (1975; Glasgow, March 3, 1976).

BIBL.: S. Craggs, *J. M.: A Bio-Bibliography* (N.Y., 1991).

McCormack, John, famous Irish-born American tenor; b. Athlone, June 14, 1884; d. "Glena," Booterstown, County Dublin, Sept. 16, 1945. In 1902 he became a member of the Palestrina Choir of Dublin's Cathedral, where he received lessons from the choirmaster, Vincent O'Brien. In 1903 he won the gold medal in the tenor section of the Feis Ceoil (National Music Festival) in Dublin, and began making concert appearances there. He first sang in the United States at the St. Louis Exposition in 1904; that same year he commenced making recordings. After vocal studies with Vincenzo Sabatini in Milan (1905), he made his operatic debut under the name Giovanni Foli in the role of Fritz in *L'Amico Fritz* in Savona (Jan. 13, 1906); he then went to London, where he began appearing in concerts in 1907; he made his Covent Garden debut as Turiddu (Oct. 15, 1907), and subsequently sang there during the 1908–14 summer seasons in such roles as Edgardo, the Duke in *Rigoletto*, Rodolfo, Count Almaviva in *Il Barbiere di Siviglia*, Pinkerton, Gounod's Romeo, Cavaradossi, and Elvino. He made his U.S. operatic debut as Alfredo in *La Traviata* at the Manhattan Opera House (Nov. 10, 1909), a role he also chose for his Metropolitan Opera debut in New York (Nov. 29, 1910), remaining on the company's roster until 1911 and returning from 1912 to 1914 and from 1917 to 1919; he also sang with the Chicago Opera (1910–11). After making his formal concert debut at the Manhattan Opera House (Nov. 18, 1909), McCormack devoted much of his time to a concert career, which he furthered through his many recordings. After World War I, he made few appearances in opera, giving his last performance as Gritzko in Mussorgsky's *The Fair at Sorochinsk* in Monte Carlo on March 25, 1923. He applied for American citizenship in 1914; this action, coupled with his strong support of the Irish cause, cost him the support of the British public during World War I. He became a naturalized American citizen in 1919. After an absence of 10 years, he made a triumphant return to England at a Queen's Hall Concert in London in 1924. In subsequent years he pursued a far-flung concert career with enormous success, although his vocal powers began to wane about 1930. He bade his farewell to the United States in Buffalo on March 17, 1937. He gave his last concert in London at the Royal Albert Hall on Nov. 27, 1938. At the outbreak of World War II (1939), he came out of retirement to aid the Red Cross; he sang on the radio and continued to make recordings until 1942. He received a number of honors, including being made a Papal Count by Pope Pius XI in 1928. McCormack was an incomparable recitalist, his repertoire ranging from the works of the great masters to popular Irish songs and ballads.

BIBL.: P. Key, *J. M.: His Own Life Story* (Boston, 1918); L. Strong, *J. M.* (London, 1941); L. McCormack (his widow), *I Hear You Calling Me* (Milwaukee, 1949); L. MacDermott Roe, *J. M.: The Complete Discography* (London, 1956; 2d ed., 1972); R. Foxall, *J. M.* (London, 1963); G. Ledbetter, *The Great Irish Tenor* (London, 1977).

McCoy, Seth, black American tenor and teacher; b. Sanford, N.C., Dec. 17, 1928; d. Rochester, N.Y., Jan. 22, 1997. He studied at the North Carolina Agricultural and Technical College (graduated, 1950), then pursued vocal training with Pauline Thesmacher at the Cleveland Music School Settlement and with Antonia Lavanne in New York. He first gained notice as a soloist with the Robert Shaw Chorale (1963–65), with which he toured throughout the United States and South America; later he appeared with the Bach Aria Group (1973–80); he also was a soloist with such leading U.S. orchs. as the N.Y. Phil., Boston Sym. Orch., Chicago Sym. Orch., and Los Angeles Phil. In 1978 he made his European debut at the Aldeburgh Festival. On Feb. 17, 1979, he made his Metropolitan Opera debut in New York as Tamino. His London debut was as soloist in Bach's Christmas Oratorio in 1986. He taught at the Eastman School of Music in Rochester, N.Y. (from 1982).

McCracken, James (Eugene), remarkable American tenor; b. Gary, Ind., Dec. 16, 1926; d. N.Y., April 29, 1988. After working at the Roxy Theatre in New York, he sang at Radio City Music Hall and appeared in minor roles on Broadway; following formal vocal studies with Wellington Ezekiel, he made his operatic debut as Rodolfo with the Central City Opera in Colorado (1952). On Nov. 21, 1953, he made his first appearance at the Metropolitan Opera in New York as Parpignol; he continued to sing minor roles there until he decided to try his fortune in Europe in 1957. After further vocal training with Marcello Conati in Milan, he joined the Zürich Opera in 1959 and proved himself in major roles there. He soon gained wide recognition for his portrayal of Verdi's Otello, a role he sang to great acclaim at the Metropolitan Opera on March 10, 1963; he remained on its roster until quitting the company in a dispute with the management in 1978. In 1983 he returned to the Metropolitan Opera as a participant in its Centennial Gala; he rejoined its roster in 1984, singing there with distinction until his death. He also appeared as a guest artist with major U.S. and European opera houses, and as a soloist with leading orchs. He often made joint appearances with his wife, **Sandra Warfield**. In addition to Otello, he won renown as Canio, Florestan, Don José, Radames, Samson in Saint-Saëns's opera, and Bacchus in Strauss's *Ariadne auf Naxos*. With his wife, he publ. the memoir *A Star in the Family* (ed. by R. Daley; N.Y., 1971).

McCreesh, Paul, remarkable English conductor and music scholar; b. London, May 24, 1960. He received his education at the Univ. of Manchester, where he specialized in music, performance, and musicology (Mus.B., 1981). While still a student there, he formed his own chamber choir and period-instrument ensemble. In 1982 he founded the Gabrieli Consort and Players in London, which he molded into an outstanding choral and period-instrument ensemble, known for its extraordinary technical expertise and refinement. He conducted his ensemble throughout England, on British radio and television, and on tours abroad. As both an interpreter and music scholar, McCreesh has brought insight and erudition to his handling of works from the Venetian High Renaissance and Baroque eras. While he sometimes provokes controversy, he always elicits respect and often accolades for his imaginative performances.

McDaniel, Barry, American baritone; b. Lyndon, Kansas, Oct. 18, 1930. He was a student at the Juilliard School of Music in New York and of Alfred Paulus and Hermann Reutter at the Stuttgart Hochschule für Musik. In 1953 he made his recital debut in Stuttgart. After appearing in opera in Mainz (1954–55), Stuttgart (1957–59), and Karlsruhe (1960–62), he was a principal member of the Deutsche Opera in Berlin (from 1962). On Jan. 19, 1972, he made his Metropolitan Opera debut in New York as Pelléas, remaining on the roster for that season. His guest engagements took him to most of the leading opera houses and festivals. He also appeared widely as a concert artist and recitalist. His expansive repertoire ranged from early music to contemporary scores.

McDermott, Vincent, American composer and teacher; b. Atlantic City, N.J., Sept. 5, 1933. He studied with Rochberg at the Univ. of Pa. (B.F.A. in composition, 1959; Ph.D. in music history and theory, 1966) and took a course in music history at the Univ. of Calif. at Berkeley (M.A., 1961); he also received instruction in composition from Milhaud and Stockhausen. He studied the tabla at the Ali Akbar Khan College in Oakland, California (1973), and the Javanese gamelan at the Akademi Seni Karawitan Indonesia in Surakarta (1971, 1978). He taught at the Hampton Inst. in Virginia (1966–67), at the Wisconsin Cons. of Music in Milwaukee (1967–77), and at Lewis and Clark College in Portland, Oreg. (from 1971); in 1980 he held the directorship of the Venerable Showers of Beauty gamelan. His music draws freely upon both Western and Eastern elements.

WORKS: DRAMATIC: *A Perpetual Dream*, chamber opera (1978); *Spirits among the Spires*, chamber opera (1987); *The King of Bali*, opera (Portland, Oreg., April 20, 1990); *Mata Hari*, chamber opera (1994; Dallas, April 21, 1995).

McFerrin, Robert, black American baritone; b. Marianna, Ariz., March 19, 1921. He studied at Fisk Univ. in Nashville, Chicago Musical College (B.M., 1948), and Kathryn Turney Long School in N.Y. In 1949 he appeared in Weill's *Lost in the Stars*, in Still's *Troubled Island* (with the N.Y. City Opera), and as Amonasro in *Aida* (with Mary Cardwell Dawson's National Negro Opera Co.); he joined the New England Opera Co. in 1950, creating roles in Marc Connelly's play *The Green Pastures* (N.Y., 1951; music by Hall Johnson) and *My Darlin' Aida* (1952), a version of Verdi's opera set in the time of the Confederacy. He won the Metropolitan Auditions of the Air in 1953; he became the first black male to join the company, making his debut on Jan. 27, 1955, as Amonasro. After singing in Naples at the Teatro San Carlo, he sang the role of Porgy (played by Sidney Poitier) in the film version of Gershwin's *Porgy and Bess* (1959); he also sang on the recording. He toured internationally, giving recitals of arias, art songs, and spirituals. His son is the gifted vocalist and conductor Bobby (Robert) McFerrin (b. N.Y., March 11, 1950).

McGlinn, John, American conductor; b. Philadelphia, Sept. 18, 1953. His academic and musical studies led him to pursue an intensive investigation of the scores of the American musical theater. As a result, he dedicated himself to restoring the classic

American musicals to their pristine state via original orchestrations and texts. In 1985 he won critical accolades when he conducted the Jerome Kern Centennial Festival at N.Y.'s Carnegie Hall. In subsequent years, he returned there with major success and also appeared as a guest conductor with various major North American orchs. His recordings were especially valuable in documenting America's golden era on Broadway. He occasionally appeared as an opera conductor as well. In 1988 he made his first appearance in London leading the London Sym. Orch.'s 70th birthday concert in honor of Leonard Bernstein. His championship of Jerome Kern, George Gershwin, Cole Porter, Vincent Youmans, and Richard Rodgers has been particularly notable.

McGurty, Mark, remarkably gifted American composer whose music possesses an aura of new classicism; b. Newark, N.J., April 28, 1955. He studied at the Juilliard School in New York, where his major teachers were Diamond and Carter. He also took lessons in violin with Frank Scocozza, piano with Frances Goldstein, and conducting with Abraham Kaplan. However, he did not at once pursue the occupation of a professional composer or performer, but had to earn a living elsewhere. He was manager of the Orquesta Filarmónica de Caracas in Venezuela (1979–83); concurrently he was active as an instructor at the Simon Bolivar Univ. in Caracas, and occasional director for the Opera Nacional of Caracas. His next engagement was with the Opera of the Dominican Republic. In 1985 he moved to California, where he worked on the production of recordings for the Pacific Sym. Orch. During all these years, he was intensely working on a number of compositions for theater, orch., and chamber ensembles. In all cases, he favors complex ensembles of variegated instruments marked by a resilient rhythmic beat while the flow of governing melody is never muted. Among his works are the ballets *The Castle*, after Kafka (1974), and *Journey to the Land of the Tarahumaras* (1975).

McIntire, Dennis K(eith), diligent American music historian and lexicographer; b. Indianapolis, June 25, 1944. As a lexicographer, he was an autodidact, being mainly inspired by the example of the great Samuel Johnson. His precocious self-assurance was such that at the age of 12 he undertook a systematic attack on imperfections in reference books, beginning with misinformative vols. such as *The Lincoln Library of Essential Information*. After 10 years of badgering its eds., he was made an assistant and research ed. of the aforesaid encyclopedia in 1967. His fascination for reference books spurred him on to consume virtually the entire contents of several voluminous standard sources, among them *Baker's Biographical Dictionary of Musicians*, *Grove's Dictionary of Music and Musicians*, and even the monumental *Encyclopaedia Britannica*. Appalled by the surprising percentage of errors in such dignified reference publications, he undertook a systematic correspondence with their eds., suggesting corrections and additions. In the meantime, he undertook a thorough study of 20th century European history at Indiana Univ., but managed to depart the halls of academe without a devastating critique of any deficiencies in instruction. He continued to fulfill editorial duties all the while. His capacity of total recall and indefatigability in corresponding with far corners of the musical world enabled him to make valuable additions to the 7th and 8th eds. of *Baker's Biographical Dictionary of Musicians* (1984, 1992), and also contributed material to Slonimsky's *Supplement to Music since 1900* (1986) and the 5th ed. of *Music since 1900* (1994). He also lent assistance to *The Concise Oxford Dictionary of Opera* (1979), *The Oxford Dictionary of Music* (1985; 2d ed., 1994), *The New Everyman Dictionary of Music* (1988), the French edition of *Baker's Biographical Dictionary of Musicians* (1995), and *The Hutchinson Encyclopedia of Music* (1995); he served as an adviser and contributor to *The New Grove Dictionary of American Music* (1986), was co-consultant ed. (with D. Cummings) of the 12th ed. of the *International Who's Who in Music* (1990), and subsequently was a contributing ed. to the 13th to 15th eds. (1992–96). He was a contributor to *The New Grove Dictionary of Opera* (1992). From 1996 to 1998 he was a member of the editorial advisory board of the *Encyclopaedia Britannica*. He served as assoc. ed. of *Baker's Biographical Dictionary of 20th Century Classical Musicians* (1997), and then of the present dictionary. McIntire was also consultant ed. of the *International Authors and Writers Who's Who* (15th to 17th eds., 1997–2001) and the *International Who's Who in Poetry and Poets' Encyclopaedia* (8th to 10th eds., 1997–2001), and was a contributor to *The New Grove Dictionary of Music and Musicians* (rev. ed., 2001).

McIntyre, Sir Donald (Conroy), esteemed New Zealand bass-baritone; b. Auckland, Oct. 22, 1934. He studied at the Guildhall School of Music in London. He made his operatic debut as Zaccaria in *Nabucco* with the Welsh National Opera in Cardiff (1959), then was a member of the Sadler's Wells Opera in London (1960–67). In 1967 he made his debut as Pizzaro at Covent Garden in London; that same year he made his first appearance at the Bayreuth Festival as Telramund, returning there annually until 1981; he sang Wotan there during the centenary *Ring* production in 1976. On Feb. 15, 1975, he made his Metropolitan Opera debut in New York as Wotan. He made guest appearances with many of the leading opera houses of the world. He appeared as Prospero in the British premiere of Berio's *Un re in ascolto* in London and as Wotan in *Die Walküre* in Amsterdam in 1989. In 1990 he sang Hans Sachs in Wellington. He portrayed Gurnemanz in Antwerp in 1996 and King Marke at the Los Angeles Opera in 1997. In 1998 he sang Count Waldner in *Turandot* at the San Francisco Opera. In 1977 he was made an Officer of the Order of the British Empire, and in 1985 a Commander of the Order of the British Empire. In 1992 he was knighted. His other roles include Kaspar in *Der Freischütz*, Attila, Klingsor, Amfortas, the Dutchman, Golaud, and Escamillo.

McKellar, Kenneth, Scottish tenor; b. Paisley, June 23, 1927. He took a course in philology at the Univ. of Aberdeen and received a B.S. degree, then studied voice at the Royal College of Music in London. He subsequently sang with the Carl Rosa Opera Co. in London and later toured the United States as a concert singer. He was also a fine interpreter of traditional Scottish ballads, which he included in his concert programs.

McLaughlin, Marie, Scottish soprano; b. Hamilton, Lanarkshire, Nov. 2, 1954. She studied at Notre Dame College of Education and with Joan Alexander in Glasgow, and later at the London Opera Centre and the National Opera Studio. In 1978 she made her debut as Tatiana at the Aldeburgh Festival, and as Anna Gomez in *The Consul* at the English National Opera in London. Her debut at London's Covent Garden followed in 1980 as Barbarina, where she subsequently sang such roles as Susanna, Zerlina, Nannetta, and Britten's Tytania. After singing Ilia in Rome in 1982 and Marzelline in Berlin in 1984, she was engaged as Micaëla at the Glyndebourne Festival in 1985. On Dec. 10, 1986, she made her debut at the Metropolitan Opera in New York as Marzelline. Her first appearance at the Salzburg Festival was as Susanna in 1987. In 1988 she sang Adina at Milan's La Scala and in 1990 Zerlina at the Vienna Festival. Following an engagement as Despina in Geneva and a tour to Japan with the Royal Opera, Covent Garden, as Susanna in 1992, she sang Weill's Jenny at the Opéra de la Bastille in Paris in 1995. In 1996 she appeared as Donna Elvira in Lausanne.

McNair, Sylvia, highly talented American soprano; b. Mansfield, Ohio, June 23, 1956. She studied with Margarita Evans at Wheaton (Ill.) College (B.M., 1978) and with Virginia MacWatters (1978–80), John Wustman (1978–82), and Virginia Zeani (1980–82) at the Indiana Univ. School of Music in Bloomington (M.M., 1982). She made her formal concert debut as a soloist in *Messiah* with the Indianapolis Sym. Orch. (1980). Her operatic debut followed as Sandrina in Haydn's *L'Infedeltà delusa* at N.Y.'s Mostly Mozart Festival (1982). In 1984 she created the title role in Kelterborn's opera *Ophelia* at her European debut at the Schwetzingen Festival, and immediately thereafter sang the role at Berlin's Deutsche Oper. In 1990 she was honored with the Marian Anderson Award. In 1993 she sang Poppea at the Salzburg Festival. On Nov. 27,

1994, she made her Alice Tully Hall recital debut in New York. In 1996 she sang Britten's Tytania at the Metropolitan Opera in New York. She was engaged as Pamina at the Salzburg Festival in 1997. In 1998 she created the role of Blanche Dubois in Previn's *A Streetcar Named Desire* at the San Francisco Opera. She portrayed Cleopatra in *Giulio Cesare* at the Metropolitan Opera in 1999. Her extensive repertoire ranges from Monteverdi to contemporary composers.

Meader, George, American tenor; b. Minneapolis, July 6, 1888; d. Los Angeles, Dec. 19, 1963. He studied law at the Univ. of Minnesota (graduated, 1908) and concurrently took vocal lessons with Anna Schoen-René, then studied with Pauline Viardot-García in Paris. He made his operatic debut as the Steersman in *Der fliegende Holländer* in Leipzig (1911), then was a member of the Stuttgart Opera until 1919. Returning to America in 1919, he gave recitals before making his operatic debut with the Metropolitan Opera in New York as Victorin in Korngold's *Die tote Stadt* (Nov. 19, 1921); he left the Metropolitan in 1931 and sang in operetta; was particularly successful in Jerome Kern's *Cat and the Fiddle*.

Meale, Richard (Graham), notable Australian composer and teacher; b. Sydney, Aug. 24, 1932. He received training in piano, clarinet, harp, and theory at the New South Wales State Conservatorium of Music in Sydney (1946–55). As a composer, he was autodidact. In 1960 he received a Ford Foundation grant and studied non-Western music at the Inst. of Ethnomusicology at the Univ. of Calif. at Los Angeles. From 1961 to 1969 he was on the music staff of the Australian Broadcasting Corp. He was also active as a pianist and conductor of contemporary music. From 1969 to 1988 he taught at the Elder Conservatorium of Music at the Univ. of Adelaide. In 1974 he received a senior fellowship in composition from the state government of South Australia. He was awarded an Australian Creative Fellowship in 1989. In 1971 he was made a Member of the Order of the British Empire, and in 1985 a Member of the Order of Australia. By the 1960s, Meale was recognized as one of Australia's principal avant-garde composers. His visit to France and Spain, as well as his study of Japanese ritual and theater music, was influential in his development as a composer. By the close of the 1970s, Meale made a profound change of course and became one of Australia's leading composers of the neo-Romantic persuasion. Among his works are the operas *Voss* (1979–86; Adelaide, March 1, 1986) and *Mer de Glace* (1986–91; Sydney, Oct. 3, 1991) and ballets.

Mechem, Kirke (Lewis), American composer, conductor, and lecturer on music; b. Wichita, Kansas, Aug. 16, 1925. He was a pupil of Harold Schmidt, Leonard Ratner, and Sandor Salgo at Stanford Univ. (B.A., 1951) and of Walter Piston, Randall Thompson, and A. Tillman Merritt at Harvard Univ. (M.A., 1953). After serving as director of music at Menlo College in California (1953–56) and as a teacher and conductor at Stanford Univ. (1953–56), he was active in Vienna (1956–57; 1961–63). He was composer-in-residence at the Univ. of San Francisco's Lone Mountain College (1964–65; 1966–72) and a teacher and conductor at San Francisco State College (1965–66). In his works he adopts a candidly euphonious method of composition, not shirking resolvable dissonances and circumtonal patterns, but faithfully observing basic tonality. He became well known as a composer of choral works and instrumental pieces. His opera *Tartuffe*, after Molière (1977–80; San Francisco, May 27, 1980), proved an immediate success at its premiere and was subsequently performed more than 100 times. He also composed the opera *John Brown* (1988–89).

Medek, Ivo, Czech composer; b. Brno, July 20, 1956. He received training in computers and structural mechanics at the Technical Univ. in Brno, and in composition from Alois Piňos at the Janáček Academy of Music and Dramatic Art in Brno (M.A., 1989; Ph.D., 1997), where he was an assistant prof. from 1990. His output includes dramatic, orch., chamber, vocal, electroacoustic, and multimedia scores. With Piňos and Miloš Štědroň, he wrote the collaborative operas *Věc Cage aneb Anály avantgardy dokořán* (The Cage Affair, or the Avant-Garde Chronicles Flung Open; Brno, Oct. 6, 1995) and *Anály předchůdců avantgardy aneb Setkání slovansksých velikánů* (Annals of the Predecessors of the Avant-Garde, or the Meeting of the Slavonic Giants; Brno, Oct. 1997). Among his other works are *Pangea* for Clarinet, Violin, and Piano (1991), *Světy bez hranic I.* (Worlds Without Borders I.), audiovisual piece (1993), *Adam a Eva*, oratorio (1994), *Fests* for 3 Percussionists and Piano (1994), *Variace na štěstí* (Variations on Happiness) for Electrophonic Violin, Percussion, and Tape (1994), and *Persephonia* for Percussionist and String Orch. (1995).

Medek, Tilo, German composer; b. Jena, Jan. 22, 1940. He went to Berlin and studied musicology at Humboldt Univ., attended the Deutsche Hochschule für Musik, and received training in composition from Wagner-Régeny at the Deutsche Akademie der Künste. Thereafter he devoted himself to composition, numbering among his works the operas *Einzug* (1969) and *Katharina Blum* (1984–91; Bielefeld, April 20, 1991), the Singspiels *Icke und die Hexe Yu* (1971) and *Appetit auf Frühkirschen* (1971), and the ballet *David und Goliath* (1972).

Meder, Johann Valentin, German singer, organist, and composer; b. Wasungen, near Meiningen (baptized), May 3, 1649; d. Riga, July 1719. He studied theology in Leipzig and Jena. After serving as a court singer in Gotha (1671), Bremen (1672–73), Hamburg (1673), Copenhagen (1674), and Lübeck (1674), he was Kantor at the Reval Gymnasium (1674–80). From 1687 to 1698 he was Kapellmeister at St. Marien in Danzig, then was Kantor at Königsberg Cathedral, and subsequently in Riga (from 1700). He composed the opera *Die beständige Argenia* (Reval, 1680) and the oratorio *Passion* (1700).

Medinš, family of prominent Latvian musicians, all brothers:

(1) Jāzeps Medinš, conductor and composer; b. Kaunas, Feb. 13, 1877; d. Riga, June 12, 1947. He studied at the Riga Music Inst. (graduated, 1896), where he later was a teacher and director. He was a conductor at the Riga Theater (1906–11), the Baku Opera (1916–22), and the Latvian National Opera in Riga (1922–25); he later taught piano at the Riga Cons. (1945–47). He composed the operas *Vaidelote* (The Priestess; 1922–24; Riga, 1927) and *Zemdegi* (The Zemdegs Family; 1947; completed by M. Zarinš).

BIBL.: M. Zālīte, *J. M.* (Riga, 1951).

(2) Jākabs Medinš, conductor, teacher, and composer; b. Riga, March 22, 1885; d. there, Nov. 27, 1971. He studied at the Riga Music Inst. (graduated, 1905) and at the Berlin Hochschule für Musik (1910–14). He taught at the Jelgava Teachers' Inst. (1921–44), and was director of the People's Cons. there (1921–41); he later taught choral conducting at the Riga Cons. (1944–71), serving as its rector (1949–51). He wrote an autobiography, *Silueti* (Silhouettes; Riga, 1968).

(3) Jānis Medinš, conductor and composer; b. Riga, Oct. 9, 1890; d. Stockholm, March 4, 1966. He studied at the Riga Music Inst. (graduated, 1909). He was a violist and conductor at the Latvian Opera in Riga (1913–15), then a military bandmaster in St. Petersburg (1916–20). He conducted at the Latvian National Opera (1920–28); subsequently he was chief conductor of the Latvian Sym. Orch. (1928–44) and was also a prof. at the Riga Cons. (1929–44). As the Soviet army approached his homeland (1944), he went to Germany; then settled in Stockholm (1948). He wrote an autobiography, *Toni un pustoni* (Tones and Semitones; Stockholm, 1964). He distinguished himself as a composer of both vocal and instrumental works. His *Mīlas uzvara* (Love's Victory; 1935) was the first Latvian ballet. He also composed the operas *Uguns un nakts* (Fire and Night; 1st written as 2 operas, 1913–19; Riga, May 26, 1921; rev. as a single opera, 1924), *Dievi un cilvēki* (Gods and Men; Riga, May 23, 1922), *Sprīdītis* (Tom Thumb; Riga, 1927), and *Luteklīte* (The Little Darling), children's opera (Riga, 1939).

Medlam, Charles, English conductor and cellist; b. Port-au-Prince, Trinidad, Sept. 10, 1949. He studied cello in London, and with Gendron at the Paris Cons. He also studied in Salzburg with Harnoncourt. After playing in the resident string quartet at the Chinese Univ. in Hong Kong, he settled in England. In 1978 he cofounded London Baroque, a chamber orch., which he conducted in many early music performances. In 1990 he conducted *Dido and Aeneas* at the Paris Opéra, and in 1991 he made his debut at the Salzburg Festival. In 1993 he conducted at the London Promenade Concerts. His large repertoire of orch. and vocal music includes scores by Monteverdi, Lully, Charpentier, Blow, Scarlatti, Handel, Bach, Purcell, and Rameau.

Meester, Louis de, Belgian composer; b. Roeselare, Oct. 28, 1904; d. Ghent, Dec. 12, 1987. He was mainly autodidact as a composer. After serving as director of the Meknes Cons. in French Morocco (1933–37), he returned to Belgium and studied with Absil. From 1945 to 1961 he worked for the Belgian Radio. He was director of the Inst. for Psychoacoustics and Electronic Music at the Univ. of Ghent from 1961 to 1969.

WORKS: DRAMATIC: *Van een trotse vogel*, musical comedy (1948); *La Grande Tentation de Saint Antoine*, opera buffa (1957; Antwerp, Nov. 11, 1961); *2 is te weining, 3 is te veel* (2 is too little, 3 is too much), opera (1966; Palermo, June 13, 1969); *Paradijsgeuzen* (Beggars in Heaven), opera (1966; Ghent, March 26, 1967); incidental music.

Méfano, Paul, French composer; b. Basra, Iraq, March 6, 1937. He studied at the Paris Cons. with Dandelot, Messiaen, Martenot, and Milhaud and attended seminars of Boulez, Stockhausen, and Pousseur in Basel. He received a grant from the Harkness Foundation for residence in the United States (1966–68) and in Berlin (1968–69). In his music, he pursues a constructivist style, with an emphasis on rhythmic percussion and electronic sound; the influences of Stravinsky and Varèse are particularly in evidence. He composed the opera *Micromegas* for 4 Singers, Narrator, 3 Actors, 10 Instruments, and Tape, after Voltaire (1979).

Mehta, Zubin, notable Indian conductor; b. Bombay, April 29, 1936. His first mentor was his father, the Indian violinist and conductor Mehli Mehta (b. Bombay, Sept. 25, 1908). He received training in violin and piano in childhood, and at 16 had his first taste of conducting when he led a rehearsal of the Bombay Sym. Orch. He studied medicine in Bombay but the lure of music compelled him to abandon his medical training to pursue musical studies at the Vienna Academy of Music. While playing double bass in its orch., he found a conducting mentor in Swarowsky. During the summers of 1956 and 1957, he also studied conducting with Carlo Zecchi and Alceo Galliera at the Accademia Musicale Chigiana in Siena. In 1957 he made his professional conducting debut with the Niederösterreichisches Tonkünstlerorchester in Vienna. He won the 1st Royal Liverpool Phil. conducting competition in 1958, and then served for a season as its assistant conductor. In the summer of 1959 he attended the Berkshire Music Center in Tanglewood, where he took 2d prize in conducting. He made his North American debut conducting the Philadelphia Orch. in 1960. Later that year his successful appearances with the Montreal Sym. Orch. led to his appointment as its music director in 1961. That same year he also became assoc. conductor of the Los Angeles Phil. His London debut came later in 1961 when he appeared as a guest conductor with the Royal Phil. In 1962 he became music director of the Los Angeles Phil. while retaining his Montreal post until 1967. He made his first appearance at the Salzburg Festival in 1962. He first conducted opera in Montreal in 1964 when he led a performance of *Tosca*. On Dec. 29, 1965, he made his Metropolitan Opera debut in New York conducting *Aida*. In 1966 he conducted for the first time at Milan's La Scala. He was named music advisor of the Israel Phil. in 1968. His success with that ensemble led to his appointment as its music director in 1977 and as its music director for life in 1981. He led it on major tours of Europe, North and South America, and the Far East. In 1977 he made his debut at London's Covent Garden conducting *Otello*. During his tenure in Los Angeles, Mehta was glamorized in the colorful Hollywood manner. This glamorization process was abetted by his genuine personableness and his reputation as a bon vivant. As a conductor, he secured the international profile of the Los Angeles Phil. through recordings and major tours. He became particularly known for his effulgent and expansive readings of the Romantic repertoire, which he invariably conducted from memory. His success in Los Angeles led the management of the N.Y. Phil. to appoint him as music director in 1978 with the hope that he could transform that ensemble in the wake of the austere Boulez tenure. Although Mehta served as music director of the N.Y. Phil. until 1991, he was unable to duplicate the success he attained in Los Angeles. Critics acknowledged his abilities but found his interpretations often indulgent and wayward. On July 7, 1990, Mehta served as conductor of the 3 tenors extravaganza in Rome with Carreras, Domingo, and Pavarotti in a concert telecast live to the world. He returned to the N.Y. Phil. for its 150th anniversary concert on Dec. 7, 1992, when he conducted a performance of *Till Eulenspiegels lustige Streich*. On July 16, 1994, he was conductor of the Carreras, Domingo, and Pavarotti reunion when he led the Los Angeles Phil. in a concert again telecast live around the globe. In 1995 he was appointed Generalmusikdirektor of the Bavarian State Opera in Munich, which post he assumed in 1998. In 1997 he received the Great Silver Medal of Austria.

BIBL.: M. Bookspan and R. Yockey, *Z.: The Z. M. Story* (N.Y., 1978).

Méhul, Etienne-Nicolas, famous French composer; b. Givet, Ardennes, June 22, 1763; d. Paris, Oct. 18, 1817. His father apprenticed him to the old blind organist of the Couvent des Récollets in Givet, after which he went to Lavaldieu, where he studied with the German organist Wilhelm Hansen, director of music at the monastery there. In 1778 he went to Paris, where he continued his musical studies with Jean-Frédéric Edelmann. His first opera to receive a performance was *Euphrosine, ou Le Tyran corrigé* (Théâtre Favart, Paris, Sept. 4, 1790); another opera, *Alonso et Cora* (later known as *Cora*), was staged at the Paris Opéra on Feb. 15, 1791. His next opera, *Adrien*, was in rehearsal by the end of 1791, but the revolutionary turmoil prevented a performance; it finally received its premiere at the Paris Opéra on June 4, 1799. His opera *Stratonice* was given at the Théâtre Favart in Paris on May 3, 1792, and was highly successful. Then followed his opera *Le Jeune Sage et le vieux fou*, which was performed at the same theater on March 28, 1793. In 1793 Méhul became a member of the Inst. National de Musique, which had been organized by the National Convention under the revolutionary regime. He composed a number of patriotic works during these turbulent years of French history, including the popular *Chant du départ* (1st perf. publicly on July 4, 1794). He also continued to compose for the theater, shrewdly selecting subjects for his operas allegorically suitable to the times. In 1794 he was awarded an annual pension of 1,000 francs by the Comédie-Italienne. In 1795 he became one of the 5 inspectors of the newly established Cons., and was also elected to the Institut. He became a member of the Légion d'honneur in 1804. Between 1795 and 1807 Méhul composed 18 operas, some of which were written in collaboration with other composers. His greatest opera from this period is the biblical *Joseph* (Opéra Comique, Feb. 17, 1807); its success in Paris led to performances in Germany, Austria, Hungary, Russia, the Netherlands, Belgium, Switzerland, England, Italy, and America. Also noteworthy is his *Chant national du 14 juillet 1800*, an extensive work calling for 2 choirs with an additional group of high voices and orchestral forces. Apart from operas, he composed several syms. In spite of poor health, he continued to teach classes at the Paris Cons.; among his students was Hérold. His last opera was *La Journée aux aventures*, which was given at the Opéra Comique on Nov. 16, 1816. Although Méhul's operas practically disappeared from the active repertoire, his contribution to the operatic art remains of considerable historical importance. Beethoven, Weber, and Mendelssohn were cognizant of some of his symphonic works, which included 4 well-crafted syms.

WORKS: DRAMATIC (all 1st perf. in Paris): OPERAS: *Euphrosine, ou Le Tyran corrigé* (Sept. 4, 1790; rev. as *Euphrosine et Coradin*); *Alonso et Cora* (Feb. 15, 1791; later known as *Cora*); *Stratonice*

(May 3, 1792); *Le Jeune Sage et le vieux fou* (March 28, 1793); *Horatius Coclès* (Feb. 18, 1794); *Le Congrès des rois* (Feb. 26, 1794; in collaboration with 11 other composers); *Mélidore et Phrosine* (May 6, 1794); *Doria, ou La Tyrannie détruite* (March 12, 1795); *La Caverne* (Dec. 5, 1795); *La Jeunesse d'Henri IV* (May 1, 1797; later known as *Le Jeune Henri*); *La Prise du pont de Lodi* (Dec. 15, 1797); *Adrien, empéreur de Rome* (June 4, 1799; later known as *Adrien*); *Ariodant* (Oct. 11, 1799); *Epicure* (March 14, 1800; in collaboration with Cherubini); *Bion* (Dec. 27, 1800); *L'Irato, ou L'Emporté* (Feb. 17, 1801); *Une Folie* (April 5, 1802); *Le Trésor supposé, ou Le Danger d'écouter aux portes* (July 29, 1802); *Joanna* (Nov. 23, 1802); *Héléna* (March 1, 1803); *Le Baiser et la quittance, ou Une Aventure de garnison* (June 18, 1803; in collaboration with Boieldieu, R. Kreutzer, and Nicolo); *L'Heureux malgré lui* (Dec. 29, 1803); *Les 2 Aveugles de Tolède* (Jan. 28, 1806); *Uthal* (May 17, 1806); *Gabrielle d'Estrées, ou Les Amours d'Henri IV* (June 25, 1806); *Joseph* (Feb. 17, 1807); *Amphion, ou Les Amazones* (Dec. 17, 1811; later known as *Les Amazones, ou La Fondation de Thèbes*); *Le Prince troubadour* (May 24, 1813); *L'Oriflamme* (Feb. 1, 1814; overture by Méhul; remainder in collaboration with H.-M. Berton, R. Kreutzer, and Paër); *La Journée aux aventures* (Nov. 16, 1816); *Valentine de Milan* (Nov. 28, 1822); the opera *Lausus* and the opéra ballet *L'Amour et Psyché* are considered doubtful works in the Méhul canon. BALLETS: *Le Jugement de Paris* (March 5, 1793; with music by Gluck, Haydn, and others); *La Dansomanie* (June 14, 1800; with music by Mozart and others); *Daphnis et Pandrose* (Jan. 14, 1803; with music by Gluck, Haydn, and others); *Persée et Andromède* (June 8, 1810; with music by Haydn, Paër, and Steibelt). He also composed several pieces of incidental music.

BIBL.: A. Quatremère de Quincy, *Funérailles de M. M., Institut Royal de France* (Paris, 1817); P. Vieillard, *M.: Sa vie et ses oeuvres* (Paris, 1859); A. Pougin, *M.: Sa vie, son génie, son caractère* (Paris, 1889; 2d ed., 1893); R. Brancour, *M.* (Paris, 1912).

Meier, Johanna, American soprano; b. Chicago, Feb. 13, 1938. She was a scholarship student at the Manhattan School of Music in New York. She made her debut with the N.Y. City Opera in 1969 as the Countess in Strauss's *Capriccio*; she continued to appear there regularly until 1979; she made her Metropolitan Opera debut in New York as Strauss's Ariadne on April 9, 1976, and subsequently appeared there regularly; she also sang opera in Chicago, Cincinnati, Pittsburgh, Seattle, and Baltimore. In Europe, she had guest engagements in opera in Zürich, Vienna, Hamburg, Berlin, and Bayreuth; she also appeared in concerts.

Meier, Jost, Swiss composer and conductor; b. Solothurn, March 15, 1939. He studied cello, conducting, and composition at the Bern Cons., and completed his training in composition with Frank Martin in the Netherlands. From 1969 to 1979 he was chief conductor of the Biel Orch. and Theater. After conducting in Basel (1980–83), he was active as a guest conductor throughout Europe. He also taught at the Basel Academy of Music and the Zürich Cons. His compositions follow the precepts of the second Viennese school. Among his works are the operas *Sennetuntschi* (Freiburg, April 23, 1983), *Der Drache* (Basel, May 24, 1985), *Der Zoobär* (Zürich, June 11, 1987), *Augustin* (Basel, April 21, 1988), and *Dreyfus—Die Affäre* (Berlin, May 8, 1994).

Meier, Waltraud, outstanding German mezzo-soprano; b. Würzburg, Jan. 9, 1956. She was a student of Dietger Jacob in Cologne. In 1976 she made her operatic debut as Lola in *Cavalleria rusticana* at the Würzburg Opera, where she was engaged until 1978. In 1980 she appeared as Fricka at the Teatro Colón in Buenos Aires. From 1980 to 1983 she was a member of the Dortmund Opera, and then sang in Hannover (1983–84). In 1983 she made her debut at the Bayreuth Festival, where she won acclaim for her portrayal of Kundry. After singing Brangäne at the Paris Opéra in 1984, she made her first appearance at London's Covent Garden in 1985 as Eboli, returning there as Kundry in 1988. From 1985 to 1988 she sang in Stuttgart. On Oct. 9, 1987, she made her debut at the Metropolitan Opera in New York as Fricka. From 1988 to 1992 she was engaged as Waltraute at Bayreuth. In 1990 she sang Venus at the Hamburg State Opera, Marguerite at the Théâtre du Châtelet in Paris, and Ortrud at the Teatro São Carlos in Lisbon. She appeared as Isolde at Bayreuth in 1993 and 1995. In 1994 she sang Sieglinde at the Vienna State Opera and at Milan's La Scala. After an engagement as Carmen at the Metropolitan Opera in 1996, she sang Beethoven's Leonore in Chicago and appeared in an all-Wagner concert in London at the Royal Festival Hall in 1998. Meier has been honored as a Kammersängerin of both the Bavarian State Opera in Munich and the Vienna State Opera.

Meili, Max, Swiss tenor; b. Winterthur, Dec. 11, 1899; d. Zürich, March 17, 1970. He was a student of P. Deutsch in Winterthur and of F. von Kraus in Munich. He pursued an active concert career in Europe, becoming known as an interpreter of early music. In 1933 he helped to found the Schola Cantorum Basiliensis. In 1955 he founded and subsequently served as director of the Collegium Cantorum Turicense.

Meinardus, Ludwig (Siegfried), German conductor, composer, and writer on music; b. Hooksiel, Oldenburg, Sept. 17, 1827; d. Bielefeld, July 10, 1896. He was a pupil at the Leipzig Cons., and also studied in Berlin, in Weimar (with Liszt), and with Marx in Berlin. From 1853 to 1865 he was conductor of the Singakademie at Glogau, then was a teacher at the Dresden Cons.; from 1874 to 1887 he lived in Hamburg as a composer and critic, then went to Bielefeld. He wrote a kind of autobiography, *Ein Jugendleben* (2 vols., 1874); other writings include *Rückblick auf die Anfänge der deutschen Oper* (1878), *Mattheson und seine Verdienste um die deutsche Tonkunst* (1879), *Mozart: Ein Künstlerleben* (1882), *Die deutsche Tonkunst im 18.–19. Jahrhundert* (1887), *Klassizität und Romantik in der deutschen Tonkunst* (1893), and *Eigene Wege* (1895). Among his compositions were 2 operas and 6 oratorios, including *Luther in Worms* (Leipzig, 1876), his most successful score.

BIBL.: C. Kleinschmidt, *L. M., 1827–1896: Ein Beitrag zur Geschichte der ausgehenden musikalischen Romantik* (Wilhelmshaven, 1985).

Meitus, Yuli (Sergievich), eminent Ukrainian composer; b. Elizavetgrad, Jan. 28, 1903. He studied piano at a local music school, where he soon began to compose. Later he moved to Kharkov, where he composed music to theatrical productions on contemporary revolutionary subjects. In 1924 he wrote a melodeclamation commemorating the death of Lenin, and in 1930 he composed a symphonic suite, *Dneprostroy*, on the subject of the building of the hydroelectric station on the Dnieper River; in the score he included a number of percussion instruments representing various mechanical aspects of the project. During the Russian Civil War (1918–20), he wrote the opera *Perekop*, on the subject of the protracted struggle between the red and white armies on the Crimean Peninsula (Kiev, Jan. 20, 1939). When Russia was invaded by the Nazi armies (1941), Meitus was forced to move to Turkestan in Central Asia. There he produced the operas *Gaidamaki* (Ashkhabad, Oct. 15, 1943) and *Leili and Medzhiun* (Ashkhabad, Nov. 2, 1946). Returning to the Ukraine, he produced the operas *The Young Guard* (Kiev, Nov. 7, 1947), *Dawn over the River Dvina* (Kiev, July 5, 1955), *Stolen Happiness* (Lvov, Galicia, Sept. 10, 1960), and *The Daughter of the Wind* (Odessa, Oct. 24, 1965). There followed *The Brothers Ulyanov* (Ufa, Nov. 25, 1967), on the subject of the family of Lenin, whose real name was Ulyanov (Lenin's brother was executed by hanging for participation in a conspiracy to kill the Czar). Other operas include *Makhtunkuli*, on Turkmenian themes (Ashkhabad, Dec. 29, 1962); *Yaroslav the Wise*, on the rule of an early Russian chieftain (Donetsk, March 3, 1973); *Richard Sorge*, on the life of a German Soviet agent working in Nazi circles in Tokyo (Lvov, 1976); *Ivan the Terrible* (1980–82); and *Maria Volkonskaya*, on the wife of one of the Decembrist rebels against Czar Nicholas I; she followed her husband to his Siberian exile (1986–89). Apart from operas, which constitute his main contribution to Soviet music, Meitus composed a number of instrumental works, which were invariably connected with themes of socialist structures; in this connection, he joined the Assn. of Revolutionary Ukrainian Composers. It was only when such proletarian groups were disbanded by the Soviet government in 1932 that Meitus devoted himself mainly to opera. He also composed a considerable number of choruses and solo songs to Russian and Ukrainian words. Stylistically, most of his music follows the tenets of socialist realism, observing clear tonality but freely using dissonant harmonies when necessary for dramatic effect; he also applied considerable variety in asymmetrical meters and rhythms, especially in his works based on Turkmenian themes.

BIBL.: L. Arkhimovich and I. Mamchur, *Y. M.* (Moscow, 1983).

Melani, family of Italian musicians, of whom the most important were the following 3 brothers:

(1) Jacopo Melani, organist and composer; b. Pistoia, July 6, 1623; d. there, Aug. 19, 1676. He became organist (1645) and maestro di cappella (1657) of Pistoia Cathedral. He excelled as a composer of comic operas, which included *Il potesta di Colognole* (Florence, 1657; also known as *La Tancia*), *Ercole in Tebe* (Florence, July 8, 1661), *Il Girello* (Rome, 1668), and *Enea in Italia* (Pisa, 1670).

(2) Atto Melani, alto and composer; b. Pistoia, March 31, 1626; d. Paris, 1714. He was a pupil of Luigi Rossi and Marc'Antonio Pasqualini in Rome. In 1664 he visited Paris, where he won the esteem of Queen Anne and Mazarin; while singing in opera there, he also secretly served as a diplomatic courier. After Mazarin's death, he entered the service of Cardinal Giulio Rospigliosi and became enmeshed in papal politics; in 1679 he returned to Paris, where he was active in politics. He composed various vocal pieces.

(3) Alessandro Melani, composer; b. Pistoia, Feb. 4, 1639; d. Rome, Oct. 1703. He sang at Pistoia Cathedral (1650–60) and then served as maestro di cappella in Orvieto and Ferrara. In 1667 he succeeded his brother Jacopo as maestro di cappella of Pistoia Cathedral, but later that year went to Rome to take up that position at S. Maria Maggiore; in 1672 he obtained the same position at S. Luigi dei Francesi, which he held until his death. He composed the operas *L'empio punito* (Rome, 1669), *Il trionfo della continenza considerato in Scipione Africano* (Fano, 1677), *Le reciproche gelosie* (Siena, 1677), *Roberto ovvero Il Carceriere di se medesimo* (Florence, 1681), and *Ama chi t'ama* (Siena, 1682); he also collaborated with B. Pasquini and A. Scarlatti on the opera *S. Dinna* (Rome, 1687). His other works include oratorios, motets, and cantatas.

Melartin, Erkki (Gustaf), Finnish composer; b. Käkisälmi, Feb. 7, 1875; d. Pukinmäki, Feb. 14, 1937. He was a pupil of Wegelius at the Helsinki Music Inst. and of Robert Fuchs in Vienna. He taught theory at the Helsinki Music Inst. (1898; 1901–07); he succeeded Wegelius as director in 1911, and remained at this post until 1936. His compositions are marked by a lyrical strain, with thematic materials often drawn from Finnish folk songs. They include the operas *Aino* (1907; Helsinki, Dec. 10, 1909) and *Sininen helmi* (The Blue Pearl), a ballet (1930), and incidental music.

Melba, Dame Nellie (Helen Porter née **Mitchell Armstrong),** famous Australian soprano; b. Burnley, near Richmond, May 19, 1861; d. Sydney, Feb. 23, 1931. Her father, who had decided objections to anything connected with the stage, was nevertheless fond of music and proud of his daughter's talent. When she was only 6 years old he allowed her to sing at a concert in the Melbourne Town Hall, but would not consent to her having singing lessons; instead, she was taught piano, violin, and harp, and even had instruction in harmony and composition. As she grew older she frequently played the organ in a local church, and was known among her friends as an excellent pianist, while all the time her chief desire was to study singing. Not until after her marriage in 1882 to Captain Charles Armstrong was she able to gratify her ambition, when she began to study with a local teacher, Cecchi; her first public appearance as a singer was on May 17, 1884, in a benefit concert in Melbourne. The next year her father received a government appointment in London, and she accompanied him, determined to begin an operatic career. She studied with Mathilde Marchesi in Paris. Melba gave her first concert in London (June 1, 1886). Her debut as Gilda at the Théâtre Royal de la Monnaie in Brussels (Oct. 13, 1887) created a veritable sensation; the famous impresario Augustus Harris immediately engaged her for the spring season at London's Covent Garden, where she appeared on May 24, 1888, as Lucia, to only a half-full house. However, she scored a major success at the Paris Opéra as Ophelia in Thomas's *Hamlet* (May 8, 1889); she then sang with great success in St. Petersburg (1891), Milan (La Scala, 1893; immense triumph over a carefully planned opposition), Stockholm and Copenhagen (Oct. 1893), New York (Metropolitan Opera, as Lucia, Dec. 4, 1893), and Melbourne (Sept. 27, 1902). From her first appearance at Covent Garden she sang there off and on until 1914; besides being one of the most brilliant stars of several seasons at the Metropolitan Opera in New York, she also sang with Damrosch's Opera Co. (1898) and at Hammerstein's Manhattan Opera (1906–07 and 1908–09), and made several transcontinental concert tours of the U.S. Bemberg wrote for her *Elaine* (1892), and Saint-Saëns, *Hélène* (1904), in both of which she created the title roles. In 1915 she began teaching at the Albert Street Conservatorium in Melbourne; returned to Covent Garden for appearances in 1919, 1923, and a farewell performance on June 8, 1926. Then she returned to Australia and retired from the stage. Melba was by nature gifted with a voice of extraordinary beauty and belllike purity; through her art she made this fine instrument perfectly even throughout its entire extensive compass and wonderfully flexible, so that she executed the most difficult fioriture without the least effort. As an actress she did not rise above the conventional, and for this reason she was at her best in parts demanding brilliant coloratura (Gilda, Lucia, Violetta, Rosina, Lakmé et al.). On a single occasion she attempted the dramatic role of Brünnhilde in *Siegfried* (Metropolitan Opera, N.Y., Dec. 30, 1896), and met with disaster. In 1918 she was created a Dame Commander of the Order of the British Empire. She was a typical representative of the golden era of opera; a prima donna assoluta, she exercised her powers over the public with perfect self-assurance and a fine command of her singing voice. Among her other distinguished roles were Mimi, Else, Nedda, Aida, Desdemona, and Marguerita. As a measure of Melba's universal popularity, it may be mentioned that her name was attached to a delicious dessert (Peach Melba) and also to Melba toast, patented in 1929 by Bert Weil. A film based on her life was produced in 1953 with Patrice Munsel as Melba. She wrote an autobiography, *Melodies and Memories* (London, 1925).

BIBL.: A. Murphy, *M.: A Biography* (London, 1909); P. Colson, *M.: An Unconventional Biography* (London, 1931); J. Wechsberg, *Red Plush and Black Velvet: The Story of M. and Her Times* (Boston, 1961); G. Hutton, *M.* (Melbourne, 1962); J. Hetherington, *M.* (London, 1967); W. Moran, *N. M.: A Contemporary Review* (Westport, Conn., 1985); T. Radic, *M.: The Voice of Australia* (Melbourne and London, 1986).

Melcer (-Szczawiński), Henryk, esteemed Polish pianist, conductor, teacher, and composer; b. Kalisch, Sept. 21, 1869; d. Warsaw, April 18, 1928. He was a pupil of Noszkowski (composition) and Strobl (piano) at the Warsaw Music Inst. (graduated, 1890); after touring Russia as an accompanist, he received further piano training from Leschetizky in Vienna. After successful concert tours of Russia, Germany, and France, he taught at the Helsinki Cons. (1895–96) and was a prof. at the Lemberg Cons. (1896–99); he was director of the Łódz music society (1899–1902) and director-conductor of the Łódz Phil. (from 1902) and conductor of the Warsaw Phil. (1910–12) and Opera (1915–16). He subsequently taught at the Warsaw Cons. (from 1919), serving as head of piano studies (until 1928), orchestration (1925–26), and composition (1925–28). His works include 2 operas: *Protasilas i Laodamia* (1902; Paris, 1925) and *Marja* (Warsaw, Nov. 16, 1904).

BIBL.: J. Reiss, *H. M.* (Warsaw, 1949).

Melchior, Lauritz (real name, **Lebrecht Hommel**), celebrated Danish-born American tenor; b. Copenhagen, March 20, 1890; d.

Santa Monica, Calif., March 18, 1973. He studied with Paul Bang at the Royal Opera School in Copenhagen, making his operatic debut in the baritone role of Silvio in *Pagliacci* at the Royal Theater there (April 2, 1913); continued on its roster while studying further with Vilhelm Herold, and then made his tenor debut as Tannhäuser (Oct. 8, 1918). In 1921 he went to London to continue his training with Beigel, and then studied with Grenzebach in Berlin and Bahr-Mildenburg in Munich. On May 24, 1924, he made his Covent Garden debut in London as Siegmund, returning there regularly from 1926 to 1939. He was in Bayreuth in 1924 to study with Kittel; made his first appearance at the Festspielhaus there as Siegfried on July 23, 1924, and continued to make appearances there until 1931. On Feb. 17, 1926, he made his Metropolitan Opera debut in New York as Tannhäuser, and quickly established himself as one of its principal artists; with the exception of the 1927–28 season, he sang there regularly until his farewell performance as Lohengrin on Feb. 2, 1950. In 1947 he became a naturalized American citizen. After the close of his operatic career, Melchior appeared on Broadway and in films; also continued to give concerts. He was accorded a preeminent place among the Wagnerian Heldentenors of his era.

BIBL.: H. Hanse, *L. M.: A Discography* (Copenhagen, 1965; 2d ed., 1972); S. Emmons, *Tristanissimo: The Authorized Biography of Heroic Tenor L. M.* (N.Y., 1990).

Melik-Pashayev, Alexander (Shamilievich), noted Russian conductor; b. Tiflis, Oct. 23, 1905; d. Moscow, June 18, 1964. He studied with N. Tcherepnin at the Tiflis Cons. He was pianist and concertmaster of the Tiflis Opera orch. (1921–24), and then its conductor. After conducting studies with Gauk at the Leningrad Cons. (graduated, 1930), he returned to the Tiflis Opera as chief conductor (1930–31); then conducted at Moscow's Bolshoi Theater, later serving as its chief conductor (1953–62). He was highly esteemed for his interpretations of Russian operas. He was awarded 2 Stalin prizes (1942, 1943) and was made a People's Artist of the USSR (1951).

Melikyan, Romanos Hovakimi, Armenian composer; b. Kiziyar, northern Caucasus, Dec. 1, 1883; d. Yerevan, March 30, 1935. He studied at the Rostov College of Music (graduated, 1905), then with Ippolitov-Ivanov, Taneyev, and Yavorsky in Moscow (1905–07) and subsequently with Kalafati and Steinberg at the St. Petersburg Cons. (1910–14). He founded the Tiflis Music League (1908); he became director of music at the Armenian House of Culture in Moscow (1918), then founded the Yerevan Cons. (1923); he was also founder-director of the Yerevan Theater of Opera and Ballet (1933). He was a major figure in Armenian music circles; as a composer, he was highly regarded for his songs and folk song arrangements.

BIBL.: G. Geodakyan, *R. M.* (Yerevan, 1960); K. Tordjyan, *R. M.* (Yerevan, 1960).

Melis, Carmen, Italian soprano; b. Cagliari, Aug. 14, 1885; d. Longone al Segrino, Dec. 19, 1967. She was a student of Teresina Singer and Carlo Carignani in Milan, of Cotogni in Rome, and of Jean de Reszke in Paris. In 1905 she made her operatic debut in Novara, and then sang in Naples (1906) and Russia (1907). On Nov. 26, 1909, she made her U.S. debut as Tosca at the Manhattan Opera in New York, and then appeared in Boston, Chicago, and other U.S. cities. In 1913 she made her first appearance at London's Covent Garden. She later sang at Milan's La Scala, and sang regularly at the Rome Opera. Following her retirement in 1935, she taught voice. Among her most impressive roles were Musetta, Thaïs, Nedda, Zazà, Mistress Ford, Fedora, and the Marschallin.

Mellers, Wilfrid (Howard), English musicologist and composer; b. Leamington, Warwickshire, April 26, 1914. He studied at the Univ. of Cambridge (B.A., 1936; M.A., 1939); he was a pupil in composition of Wellesz and Rubbra and received his D.Mus. from the Univ. of Birmingham (1960). He was a lecturer in music at Downing College, Cambridge (1945–48); after serving as a staff tutor in the extramural dept. at the Univ. of Birmingham (1948–59), he served as Andrew W. Mellon Prof. of Music at the Univ. of Pittsburgh (1960–63); he then was prof. of music at the Univ. of York (1964–81). In 1982 he was made an Officer of the Order of the British Empire. Among his numerous writings are *Music and Society: England and the European Tradition* (London, 1946), *Studies in Contemporary Music* (London, 1947), *François Couperin and the French Classical Tradition* (London, 1950; 2d ed., rev., 1987), *Music in the Making* (London, 1952), *Romanticism and the 20th Century* (London, 1957; 2d ed., rev., 1988), *Music in a New Found Land: Themes and Developments in the History of American Music* (London, 1964; 2d ed., rev., 1987), *Harmonious Meeting: A Study of the Relationship between English Music, Poetry and Theatre, c.1600–1900* (London, 1965), *Caliban Reborn: Renewal in Twentieth-Century Music* (N.Y., 1967), *The Masks of Orpheus: Seven Stages in the Story of European Music* (Manchester, England, and Wolfeboro, N.H., 1987), *Le Jardin Retrouvé: Homage to Federico Mompou* (1989), *Vaughan Williams and the Vision of Albion* (London, 1989), *Percy Grainger* (Oxford, 1992), and *Francis Poulenc* (Oxford, 1994).

WORKS: DRAMATIC: OPERAS: *The Tragicall History of Christopher Marlowe* (1952); *The Shepherd's Daughter*, chamber opera (1953–54); *Mary Easter*, ballad opera (1957). MONODRAMA: *The Ancient Wound* (Victoria, British Columbia, July 27, 1970).

Mellnäs, Arne, Swedish composer and teacher; b. Stockholm, Aug. 30, 1933. He entered the Stockholm Musikhögskolan in 1953, where he studied composition with Koch, Larsson, Blomdahl, and Wallner (1958–61). He also was a student of Blacher at the Berlin Hochschule für Musik (1959) and of Deutsch in Paris (1961). After further training with Ligeti in Vienna (1962), he worked at the San Francisco Tape Music Center (1964). He made Stockholm the center of his activities, where he taught at the Citizen's School (1961–63) and at the Musikhögskolan (from 1963). From 1983 to 1996 he also served as chairman of the Swedish section of the ISCM. In 1984 he was elected a member of the Royal Swedish Academy of Music. He was awarded the Atterberg Prize in 1994. Mellnäs is one of Sweden's most innovative composers, and has done much to advance the cause of contemporary music in his homeland.

WORKS: DRAMATIC: *Minibuff*, opera (1966); *Kaleidovision*, television ballet (1969); *Erik den helige*, church opera (1975; Stockholm, May 18, 1976); *Spöket på Canterville*, opera (Umeå, April 25, 1981); *Dans på rosor*, opera buffa (1984); *Doktor Glas*, opera (1987–90).

Melnikov, Ivan (Alexandrovich), noted Russian baritone; b. St. Petersburg, March 4, 1832; d. there, July 8, 1906. He was a choirboy in school. He was engaged in trade, and for a time served as inspector of Volga boats; he began to study seriously late in life; he took lessons with Lomakin (1862), then went to Italy, where he studied with Repetto. He made his operatic debut as Riccardo in *I Puritani* in St. Petersburg (Oct. 6, 1867), where he sang regularly until his farewell performance in Prince Igor in 1890, then taught voice. He created the title role in Mussorgsky's *Boris Godunov* (St. Petersburg, Feb. 8, 1874). He was particularly esteemed for his portrayals of roles in operas by Glinka, Borodin, and Tchaikovsky.

Melton, James, American tenor; b. Moultrie, Ga., Jan. 2, 1904; d. N.Y., April 21, 1961. He studied with Gaetano de Luca in Nashville and Enrico Rosati in New York and then with Michael Raucheisen in Berlin. He began his career on the radio; he made his concert debut in New York on April 22, 1932, and his operatic debut as Pinkerton in *Madama Butterfly* in Cincinnati on June 28, 1938. On Dec. 7, 1942, he appeared for the first time with the Metropolitan Opera in New York as Tamino in *Die Zauberflöte*; remained on its roster until 1950; he also toured the United States as a concert singer and later appeared in films.

Membrée, Edmond, French composer; b. Valenciennes, Nov. 14, 1820; d. Chateau Damont, near Paris, Sept. 10, 1882. He studied at the Paris Cons. with Alkan and Zimmerman (piano) and Carafa (composition). Among his compositions were the operas *François Villon* (Paris, April 20, 1857), *L'Esclave* (Paris, July 17,

1874), *Les Parias* (Paris, Nov. 13, 1876), and *La Courte Echelle* (Paris, 1879).

BIBL.: L. Mention, *Un Compositeur valenciennois: E. M.* (Paris, 1908).

Mendelsohn, Alfred, Romanian composer, conductor, and teacher; b. Bucharest, Feb. 17, 1910; d. there, May 9, 1966. He was a student of Schmidt and Marx (composition) and of Lach and Wellesz (music history) in Vienna (1927–31). Returning to Bucharest, he completed his training with Jora (composition) at the Cons. (1931–32). He taught harmony (1932–36) and was director (1936–40) at the E. Massini Cons. From 1946 to 1954 he was assistant music director of the Romanian Opera. From 1949 until his death he also was a prof. at the Cons. In 1945 he received the Enesco Prize and in 1949 was awarded the Romanian Academy Prize. While his music primarily reflects the influence of the Romantic Viennese School, he also probed the potentialities of motivic structures, suggesting the serial concepts of modern constructivists while remaining faithful to basic tonalitarianism.

WORKS: DRAMATIC: *Imnul iubirii* (The Love Hymn), dramatic sym. (1946); *Harap-Alb* (The White Moor), ballet (1948; Bucharest, March 30, 1949); *Meşterul Manole*, lyric drama (1949); *Călin*, choreographic poem (1956; Bucharest, May 2, 1957); *Anton Pann*, operetta (1961); *Michelangelo*, opera (1964; Timişoara, Sept. 29, 1968); *Spinoza*, lyric scene (1966). Also *Horia*, heroic oratorio for Soloists and Orch. (1954–56); *1907*, oratorio for Soloists, Chorus, and Orch. (1956; Bucharest, March 21, 1957); *Pentru Marele Octombrie*, oratorio for Soloists, Chorus, and Orch. (Bucharest, Nov. 3, 1960).

Mendelssohn (-Bartholdy), (Jacob Ludwig) Felix, famous German composer, pianist, and conductor; b. Hamburg, Feb. 3, 1809; d. Leipzig, Nov. 4, 1847. He was a grandson of the philosopher Moses Mendelssohn and the son of the banker Abraham Mendelssohn; his mother was Lea Salomon; the family was Jewish, but upon its settlement in Berlin the father decided to become a Protestant and added Bartholdy to his surname. Mendelssohn received his first piano lessons from his mother, and then subsequently studied piano with Ludwig Berger and violin with Carl Wilhelm Henning and Eduard Rietz; he also had regular lessons in foreign languages and in painting (he showed considerable talent in drawing with pastels); he also had piano lessons with Marie Bigot in Paris, where he went with his father for a brief stay in 1816. His most important teacher in his early youth was Carl Friedrich Zelter, who understood the magnitude of Mendelssohn's talent. In 1821 Zelter took him to Weimar and introduced him to Goethe, who took considerable interest in the boy after hearing him play. Zelter arranged for Mendelssohn to become a member of the Singakademie in Berlin in 1819 as an alto singer; on Sept. 18, 1819, his 19th Psalm was performed by the Akademie. In 1825 Mendelssohn's father took him again to Paris to consult Cherubini on Mendelssohn's prospects in music; however, he returned to Berlin, where he had better opportunities for development. Mendelssohn was not only a precocious musician, both in performing and in composition; what is perhaps without a parallel in music history is the extraordinary perfection of his works written during adolescence. He played in public for the first time at the age of 9, on Oct. 28, 1818, in Berlin, performing the piano part of a trio by Wölffl. He wrote a remarkable octet at the age of 16; at 17 he composed the overture for the incidental music to Shakespeare's *A Midsummer Night's Dream*, an extraordinary manifestation of his artistic maturity, showing a mastery of form equal to that of the remaining numbers of the work, which were composed 15 years later. He proved his great musicianship when he conducted Bach's St. Matthew Passion in the Berlin Singakademie on March 11, 1829, an event that gave an impulse to the revival of Bach's vocal music. In the spring of 1829 Mendelssohn made his first journey to England, where he conducted his Sym. in C minor (seated, after the fashion of the time, at the keyboard); later he performed in London the solo part in Beethoven's *Emperor* Concerto. He then traveled through Scotland, where he found inspiration for the composition of his overture *Fingal's Cave (Hebrides)*, which he conducted for the first time during his 2d visit to London, on May 14, 1832; 10 days later he played in London the solo part of his G minor Concerto and his *Capriccio brillante*. He became a favorite of the English public; Queen Victoria was one of his most fervent admirers; altogether he made 10 trips to England as a pianist, conductor, and composer. From 1830 to 1832 he traveled in Germany, Austria, Italy, and Switzerland, and also went to Paris. In May 1833 he led the Lower-Rhine Music Festival in Düsseldorf, then conducted at Cologne in June 1835. He was still a very young man when, in 1835, he was offered the conductorship of the celebrated Gewandhaus Orch. in Leipzig; the Univ. of Leipzig bestowed upon him an honorary degree of Ph.D. Mendelssohn's leadership of the Gewandhaus Orch. was of the greatest significance for the development of German musical culture; he engaged the violin virtuoso Ferdinand David as its concertmaster, which soon became the most prestigious symphonic organization in Germany. On March 28, 1837, he married Cécile Charlotte Sophie Jeanrenaud of Frankfurt am Main, the daughter of a French Protestant clergyman. Five children (Carl, Marie, Paul, Felix, and Elisabeth) were born to them, and their marriage was exceptionally happy. At the invitation of King Friedrich Wilhelm IV, Mendelssohn went in 1841 to Berlin to take charge of the music of the court and in the Cathedral; he received the title of Royal Generalmusikdirektor, but residence in Berlin was not required. Returning to Leipzig in 1842, he organized the famous "Conservatorium." Its splendid faculty comprised, besides Mendelssohn (who taught piano, ensemble playing, and later composition), Schumann, who taught classes in piano and composition, Hauptmann, in music theory, David, in violin, Becker, in organ, and Plaidy and Wenzel, in piano. The Conservatorium was officially opened on April 3, 1843. The financial nucleus of the foundation was a bequest from Blumner of 20,000 thaler, left at the disposal of the king of Saxony for the promotion of the fine arts. Mendelssohn made a special journey to Dresden to petition the King on behalf of the Leipzig Cons. During his frequent absences, the Gewandhaus Concerts were conducted by Hiller (1843–44) and Gade (1844–45). In the summer of 1844 he conducted the Phil. Concerts in London; this was his 8th visit to England; during his 9th visit he conducted the first performance of his oratorio *Elijah* in Birmingham, on Aug. 26, 1846. It was in England that the "Wedding March" from Mendelssohn's music to *A Midsummer Night's Dream* began to be used to accompany the bridal procession; the performance of the work was for the marriage of Tom Daniel and Dorothy Carew at St. Peter's Church, Tiverton, on June 2, 1847; the organist was Samuel Reay. It became particularly fashionable, however, when it was played at the wedding of the Princess Royal in 1858. He made his 10th and last visit to England in the spring of 1847; this was a sad period of his life, for his favorite sister, Fanny, died on May 14, 1847. Mendelssohn's own health began to deteriorate, and he died at the age of 38. The exact cause of his early death is not determined; he suffered from severe migraines and chills before he died, but no evidence could be produced by the resident physicians for either a stroke or heart failure. The news of his death produced a profound shock in the world of music, not only in Germany and England, where he was personally known and beloved, but in distant America and Russia as well. Mendelssohn societies were formed all over the world; in America the Mendelssohn Quintette Club was founded in 1849. A Mendelssohn Scholarship was established in England in 1856; its first recipient was Arthur Sullivan.

Mendelssohn's influence on German, English, American, and Russian music was great and undiminishing through the years; his syms., concertos, chamber music, piano pieces, and songs became perennial favorites in concerts and at home, the most popular works being the overture *Die Hebriden* or *Fingals Höhle* (The Hebrides or Fingal's Cave), overture, op. 26 (1830; London, May 14, 1832), the ubiquitously played Violin Concerto in E minor, op. 64 (1844; Leipzig, March 13, 1845; Ferdinand David, soloist, composer conducting), *Lieder ohne Worte* (Songs without Words) for Piano: 8 books, opp. 19 (1829–30), 30 (1833–34), 38 (1836–37), 53 (1839–41), 62 (1842–44), 67 (1843–45), 85 (1834–

45), 102 (1842–45), and the afore-mentioned "Wedding March" from the incidental music to *A Midsummer Night's Dream*, op.61 (1842; Potsdam, Oct. 14, 1843). Professional music historians are apt to place Mendelssohn below the ranks of his great contemporaries Schumann, Chopin, and Liszt; in this exalted company Mendelssohn is often regarded as a phenomenon of Biedermeier culture. A barbaric ruling was made by the Nazi regime to forbid performances of Mendelssohn's music as that of a Jew; his very name was removed from music history books and encyclopedias publ. in Germany during that time. This shameful episode was of but a transitory nature, however; if anything, it served to create a greater appreciation of Mendelssohn's genius following the collapse of the infamous 3d Reich.

WORKS: DRAMATIC: *Ich, J. Mendelssohn . . .* , Lustspiel (1820); *Die Soldatenliebschaft*, comic opera (1820; Wittenberg, April 28, 1962); *Die beiden Pädagogen*, Singspiel (1821; Berlin, May 27, 1962); *Die wandernden Komödianten*, comic opera (1822; dialogue not extant); *Der Onkel aus Boston oder Die beiden Neffen*, comic opera (1823; Berlin, Feb. 3, 1824; dialogue not extant); *Die Hochzeit des Camacho*, op. 10, opera (1825; Berlin, April 29, 1827; dialogue not extant); *Die Heimkehr aus der Fremde*, op. 89, Liederspiel (1829, written for the silver wedding anniversary of Mendelssohn's parents, perf. at their home, Berlin, Dec. 26, 1829); *Der standhafte*, incidental music to Calderón's play (1833); *Trala. A frischer Bua bin i* (1833); *Ruy Blas*, incidental music to Hugo's play (1839); *Antigone*, op. 55, incidental music to Sophocles' play (Potsdam, Oct. 28, 1841); *A Midsummer Night's Dream*, op. 61, incidental music to Shakespeare's play (1842; Potsdam, Oct. 14, 1843); *Oedipus at Colonos*, op. 93, incidental music to Sophocles' play (Potsdam, Nov. 1, 1845); *Athalie*, op. 74, incidental music to Racine's play (Berlin-Charlottenburg, Dec. 1, 1845); *Lorelei*, op. 98, opera (begun in childhood but unfinished; *Ave Maria*, a vintage chorus, and finale to Act I only; Birmingham, Sept. 8, 1852). ORATORIOS: *St. Paul*, op. 36 (1834–36; Düsseldorf, May 22, 1836, composer conducting); *Elijah*, op. 70 (1846; Birmingham, Aug. 26, 1846, composer conducting); *Christus*, op. 97 (unfinished; Boston, May 7, 1874).

BIBL.: COLLECTED EDITIONS, SOURCE MATERIAL: The first collected ed. of his works, *F. M.-B.: Werke: Kritisch durchgesehene Ausgabe*, was ed. by Julius Rietz and publ. by Breitkopf & Härtel (Leipzig, 1874–77); this ed. omits a number of works, however. A new ed. of the complete works, the *Leipziger Ausgabe der Werke F. M.-B.s*, began publication in Leipzig in 1960 by the Internationale Felix-Mendelssohn-Gesellschaft. Breitkopf & Härtel publ. a *Thematisches Verzeichnis im Druck erschienener Compositionen von F. M.-B.* (Leipzig, 1846; 2d ed., 1853; 3d ed., 1882). Other sources include: M. Schneider, *M.-Archiv der Staatsbibliothek Stiftung Preussischer Kulturbesitz* (Berlin, 1965); R. Elvers, *F. M.-B.: Dokumente seines Lebens: Ausstellung zum 125. Todestag* (Berlin, 1972); P. Krause, *Autographen, Erstausgaben und Frühdrucke der Werke von F. M.-B. in Leipziger Bibliotheken und Archiven* (Leipzig, 1972); E. Klessmann, *Die M.s: Bilder aus einer deutschen Familie* (Zürich, 1990); R. Todd, ed., *M. Studies* (Cambridge, 1992). BIOGRAPHICAL: W. Lampadius, *F. M.-B.: Ein Denkmal für seine Freunde* (Leipzig, 1848; Eng. tr., with additional articles by others, N.Y., 1865; 2d greatly aug. Ger. ed., as *F. M.-B.: Ein Gesammtbild seines Lebens und Wirkens*, Leipzig, 1886); L. Stierlin, *Biographie von F. M.-B.* (Zürich, 1849); W. Neumann, *F. M.-B.: Eine Biographie* (Kassel, 1854); A. Reissmann, *F. M.-B.: Sein Leben und seine Werke* (Berlin, 1867; 3d ed., rev., 1893); H. Barbedette, *F. M.-B.: Sa vie et ses oeuvres* (Paris, 1868); C. Mendelssohn-Bartholdy, *Goethe und F. M.-B.* (Leipzig, 1871; Eng. tr., London, 1872; 2d ed., 1874); S. Hensel, *Die Familie M. 1729–1847, nach Briefen und Tagebüchern* (3 vols., Berlin, 1879; 18th ed., 1924; Eng. tr., 2 vols., London, 1881); J. Sittard, *F. M.-B.* (Leipzig, 1881); W. Rockstro, *M.* (London, 1884; rev. ed., 1911); E. David, *Les M.-B. et Robert Schumann* (Paris, 1886); J. Eckardt, *Ferdinand David und die Familie M.-B.* (Leipzig, 1888); J. Hadden, *M.* (London, 1888; 2d ed., 1904); S. Stratton, *M.* (London, 1901; 6th ed., 1934); V. Blackburn, *M.* (London, 1904); E. Wolff, *F. M.-B.* (Berlin, 1906; 2d ed., rev., 1909); C. Bellaigue, *M.* (Paris, 1907; 4th ed., 1920); J. Hartog, *F. M.-B. en zijne werken* (Leyden, 1908); P. de Stoecklin, *M.* (Paris, 1908; 2d ed., 1927); M. Jacobi, *F. M.-B.* (Bielefeld, 1915); W. Dahms, *M.* (Berlin, 1919; 9th ed., 1922); C. Winn, *M.* (London, 1927); J. Cooke, *F. M.-B.* (Philadelphia, 1929); S. Kaufmann, *M.: A Second Elijah* (N.Y., 1934; 2d ed., 1936); J. Petitpierre, *Le Mariage de M. 1837–1847* (Lausanne, 1937; Eng. tr. as *The Romance of the M.s*, London, 1947); B. Bartels, *M.-B.: Mensch und Werk* (Bremen, 1947); K. Wörner, *F. M.-B.: Leben und Werk* (Leipzig, 1947); P. Radcliffe, *M.* (London, 1954; 2d ed., rev., 1967); H. Worbs, *F. M.-B.* (Leipzig, 1956; 2d ed., 1957); idem, *F. M.-B.: Wesen und Wirken im Spiegel von Selbstzeugnissen und Berichten der Zeitgenossen* (Leipzig, 1958); H. Jacob, *F. M. und seine Zeit: Bildnis und Schicksal eines Meisters* (Frankfurt am Main, 1959–60; Eng. tr., 1963); E. Werner, *M.: A New Image of the Composer and His Age* (N.Y., 1963; 2d ed., rev. and aug., Zürich, 1980); K.-H. Köhler, *F. M.-B.* (Leipzig, 1966; 2d ed., rev., 1972); S. Grossmann-Vendrey, *F. M.-B. und die Musik der Vergangenheit* (Regensburg, 1969); M. Hurd, *M.* (London, 1970); W. Reich, *F. M. im Spiegel eigener Aussagen und zeitgenössischer Dokumente* (Zürich, 1970); H. Kupferberg, *The M.s: Three Generations of Genius* (N.Y., 1972); G. Marek, *Gentle Genius: The Story of F. M.* (N.Y., 1972); P. Ranft, *F. M. B.: Eine Lebenschronik* (Leipzig, 1972); Y. Tiénot, *M.: Musicien complet* (Paris, 1972); W. Blunt, *On Wings of Song: A Biography of F. M.* (N.Y., 1974); H. Worbs, *M.-B.* (Hamburg, 1974); D. Jenkins and M. Visocchi, *M. in Scotland* (London, 1978); M. Moshansky, *M.* (Tunbridge Wells, 1982); G. Schuhmacher, ed., *F. M.-B.* (Darmstadt, 1982); W. Konold, *F. M.B. und seine Zeit* (Laaber, 1984); R. Elvers, ed., *F. M.: A Life in Letters* (London, 1989); R. Todd, ed., *M. and His World* (Princeton, 1991); E. Donner, *F. M. B.: Aus der Partitur eines Musikerlebens* (Düsseldorf, 1992); A. Richter, *M.: Leben, Werke, Dokumente* (Mainz, 1994). CRITICAL, ANALYTICAL: F. Zander, *Über M.s Walpurgisnacht* (Königsberg, 1862); F. Edwards, *The History of M.'s Oratorio "Elijah"* (London, 1896; 2d ed., 1900); R. Werner, *F. M.-B. als Kirchenmusiker* (Frankfurt am Main, 1930); T. Armstrong, *M.'s "Elijah"* (London, 1931); P. Young, *Introduction to the Music of M.* (London, 1949); J. Werner, *M.'s "Elijah": A Historical and Analytical Guide to the Oratorio* (London, 1965); C. Dahlhaus, ed., *Das Problem M.* (Regensburg, 1974); A. Kurzhals-Reuter, *Die Oratorien F. M. B.s: Untersuchungen zur Quellenlage, Entstehung, Gestaltung und Überlieferung* (Tutzing, 1978); R. Todd, *M.'s Musical Education: A Study and Edition of His Exercises in Composition* (Cambridge, 1982); J. Finson and R. Todd, eds., *M. and Schumann: Essays on Their Music and Its Context* (Durham, 1984); R. Todd, ed., *M. Studies* (Cambridge, 1992).

Mennini, Louis (Alfred), American composer and music educator; b. Erie, Pa., Nov. 18, 1920. He studied at the Oberlin (Ohio) Cons. (1939–42), then served in the U.S. Army Air Force (1942–45); he subsequently studied composition with Rogers and Hanson at the Eastman School of Music, Rochester, N.Y. (B.M., 1947; M.M., 1948). He was a prof. at the Univ. of Texas (1948–49), then was a prof. of composition at the Eastman School of Music, receiving his doctorate in composition from the Univ. of Rochester in 1961. After serving as dean of the School of Music at the North Carolina School of the Arts in Winston-Salem (1965–71), he became chairman of the music dept. at Mercyhurst College in Erie, Pa., in 1973, where he founded the D'Angelo School of Music and D'Angelo Young Artist Competition. In 1983 he founded the Virginia School of the Arts in Lynchburg, serving as its head until his retirement in 1988. His music is pragmatic and functional, with occasional modernistic touches. Among his works are *The Well,* opera (Rochester, N.Y., May 8, 1951), and *The Rope*, chamber opera, after Eugene O'Neill (Tanglewood, Aug. 8, 1955). His brother was the eminent American composer and music educator Peter Mennin (real name, Mennini; b. Erie, Pa., May 17, 1923; d. N.Y., June 17, 1983).

Menotti, Gian Carlo, remarkable Italian composer; b. Cadegliano, July 7, 1911. He was the 6th of 10 children. He learned the rudiments of music from his mother, and began to compose as a child, making his first attempt at an opera, entitled *The Death of*

Pierrot, at the age of 10. After training at the Milan Cons. (1924–27), he studied with Scalero at the Curtis Inst. of Music in Philadelphia (1927–33). Although Menotti associated himself with the cause of American music, and spent much of his time in the United States, he retained his Italian citizenship. As a composer, he is unique on the American scene, being the first to create American opera possessing such an appeal to audiences as to become established in the permanent repertoire. Inheriting the natural Italian gift for operatic drama and an expressive singing line, he adapted these qualities to the peculiar requirements of the American stage and to the changing fashions of the period; his serious operas have a strong dramatic content in the realistic style stemming from the Italian verismo. He wrote his own librettos, marked by an extraordinary flair for drama and for the communicative power of the English language; with this is combined a fine, though subdued, sense of musical humor. Menotti made no pretensions at extreme modernism, and did not fear to approximate the successful formulas developed by Verdi and Puccini; the influence of Mussorgsky's realistic prosody is also in evidence, particularly in recitative. When dramatic tension required a greater impact, Menotti resorted to atonal and polytonal writing, leading to climaxes accompanied by massive dissonances. His first successful stage work was *Amelia Goes to the Ball*, an opera buffa in 1 act (originally to an Italian libretto by the composer, as *Amelia al ballo*), staged at the Academy of Music, Philadelphia, on April 1, 1937. This was followed by another comic opera, *The Old Maid and the Thief*, commissioned by NBC, first performed on the radio, April 22, 1939, and on the stage, by the Philadelphia Opera Co., on Feb. 11, 1941. Menotti's next operatic work was *The Island God*, produced by the Metropolitan Opera, N.Y., on Feb. 20, 1942, with indifferent success; but with the production of *The Medium* (N.Y., May 8, 1946), Menotti established himself as one of the most successful composer-librettists of modern opera. The imaginative libretto, dealing with a fraudulent spiritualist who falls victim to her own practices when she imagines that ghostly voices are real, suited Menotti's musical talent to perfection; the opera had a long and successful run in New York, an unprecedented occurrence in the history of the American lyric theater. A short humorous opera, *The Telephone*, was first produced by the N.Y. Ballet Soc., Feb. 18, 1947, on the same bill with *The Medium*; these 2 contrasting works were subsequently staged all over the United States and in Europe, often on the same evening. Menotti then produced *The Consul* (Philadelphia, March 1, 1950), his finest tragic work, describing the plight of political fugitives vainly trying to escape from an unnamed country but failing to obtain the necessary visa from the consul of an anonymous power; very ingeniously, the author does not include the title character in the cast, since the consul never appears on the stage but remains a shadowy presence. *The Consul* exceeded Menotti's previous operas in popular success; it had a long run in New York, and received the Pulitzer Prize in music. On Christmas Eve, 1951, NBC presented Menotti's television opera *Amahl and the Night Visitors*, a Christmas story of undeniable poetry and appeal; it became an annual television production every Christmas for many years thereafter. His next opera was *The Saint of Bleecker Street*, set in a N.Y. locale (N.Y., Dec. 27, 1954); it won the Drama Critics' Circle Award for the best musical play of 1954, and the Pulitzer Prize in music for 1955. A madrigal ballet, *The Unicorn, the Gorgon and the Manticore*, commissioned by the Elizabeth Sprague Coolidge Foundation, was first presented at the Library of Congress, Washington, D.C., Oct. 21, 1956. His opera *Maria Golovin*, written expressly for the International Exposition in Brussels, was staged there on Aug. 20, 1958. In 1958 he organized the Festival of 2 Worlds in Spoleto, Italy, staging old and new works; in 1977 he inaugurated an American counterpart of the festival in Charleston, S.C. In many of the festival productions Menotti acted also as stage director. In the meantime, he continued to compose; he produced in quick succession *Labyrinth*, a television opera to his own libretto (N.Y., March 3, 1963); *Death of the Bishop of Brindisi*, dramatic cantata with the text by the composer (Cincinnati, May 18, 1963); *Le Dernier Sauvage*, opera buffa, originally with an Italian libretto by Menotti, produced at the Opéra Comique in Paris in a French tr. (Oct. 21, 1963; produced in Eng. at the Metropolitan Opera, N.Y., Jan. 23, 1964); *Martin's Lie*, chamber opera to Menotti's text (Bath, England, June 3, 1964); *Help, Help, the Globolinks!*, "an opera in 1 act for children and those who like children" to words by Menotti, with electronic effects (Hamburg, Dec. 19, 1968); *The Most Important Man*, opera to his own libretto (N.Y., March 12, 1971); *The Hero*, comic opera (Philadelphia, June 1, 1976); *The Egg*, a church opera to Menotti's own libretto (Washington Cathedral, June 17, 1976); *The Trial of the Gypsy* for Treble Voices and Piano (N.Y., May 24, 1978); *Miracles* for Boy's Chorus (Fort Worth, April 22, 1979); *La loca*, opera to Menotti's own libretto dealing with a mad daughter of Ferdinand and Isabella (San Diego, June 3, 1979); *A Bride from Pluto*, children's opera (Washington, D.C., April 14, 1982); *The Boy Who Grew Too Fast*, opera for young people (Wilmington, Del., Sept. 24, 1982); *The Wedding*, opera (Seoul, Sept. 16, 1988); *Singing Child*, children's opera (Charleston, S.C., May 31, 1993). Among Menotti's nonoperatic works are the ballets *Sebastian* (1944) and *Errand into the Maze* (N.Y., Feb. 2, 1947); 2 piano concertos: No. 1 (Boston, Nov. 2, 1945) and No. 2 (Miami, June 23, 1982); *Apocalypse*, symphonic poem (Pittsburgh, Oct. 19, 1951); Violin Concerto (Philadelphia, Dec. 5, 1952, Zimbalist soloist); *Triplo Concerto a Tre*, triple concerto (N.Y., Oct. 6, 1970); *Landscapes and Remembrances*, cantata to his own autobiographical words (Milwaukee, May 14, 1976); First Symphony, subtitled *The Halcyon* (Philadelphia, Aug. 4, 1976); Nocturne for Soprano, String Quartet, and Harp (N.Y., Oct. 24, 1982); Double Bass Concerto (N.Y. Phil., Oct. 20, 1983, James VanDemark, soloist, Zubin Mehta conducting); *For the Death of Orpheus* for Tenor, Chorus, and Orch. (Atlanta, Nov. 8, 1990). He also wrote a number of *pièces d'occasion* such as *Trio for a House-Warming Party* for Piano, Cello, and Flute (1936); *Variations on a Theme by Schumann*; *Pastorale* for Piano and Strings; *Poemetti per Maria Rosa* (piano pieces for children); etc. He is also the author of the librettos for Samuel Barber's operas *Vanessa* (Metropolitan Opera, N.Y., Jan. 15, 1958) and *A Hand of Bridge* (1959); also wrote a play without music, *The Leper* (Tallahassee, April 22, 1970).

Menotti's last years were plagued with disputes over his role as an artistic director. In 1991 a major dispute arose between the composer and the director of the Spoleto Festival USA in Charleston, but ultimately Menotti retained control. However, in 1993 he announced that he was taking the festival away from Charleston, but the city's mayor intervened and Menotti lost control of his festival. That same year he was named artistic director of the Rome Opera, but again conflicts over artistic policy between the composer and the superintendent led to Menotti's dismissal in 1994. However, he continued to be associated with the Festival in Spoleto.

BIBL.: J. Gruen, *M.: A Biography* (N.Y., 1978); J. Ardoin, *The Stages of M.* (Garden City, N.Y., 1985).

Mentzner, Susanne, American mezzo-soprano; b. Philadelphia, Jan. 21, 1957. She was a student of Norma Newton at the Juilliard School in New York. After making her operatic debut as Albina in *La donna del lago* at the Houston Grand Opera in 1981, she made appearances at the Washington (D.C.) Opera, the Lyric Opera in Chicago, the Opera Co. of Philadelphia, and the N.Y. City Opera. In 1983 she made her European operatic debut as Cherubino at the Cologne Opera, where she returned as Massenet's Cendrillon. She made her first appearance at London's Covent Garden as Rosina in 1985, where she later sang Giovanna Seymour in 1988 and Dorabella in 1989. In 1988 she portrayed Adalgisa in Monte Carlo. She made her Metropolitan Opera debut in New York on Jan. 4, 1989, as Cherubino. That same year, she was engaged as Octavian at the Théâtre des Champs-Elysées in Paris. She appeared as Annius in *La clemenza di Tito* at Milan's La Scala in 1990. During the 1992–93 season, she sang Offenbach's Nicklausse and Strauss's Composer and Octavian at the Metropolitan Opera. Following an engagement as Geneviève in *Pelléas et Mélisande* at the Palais Garnier in Paris in 1997, she returned to the Metropolitan Opera as Cherubino in 1998.

Mercadante, (Giuseppe) Saverio (Raffaele), important Italian composer and teacher; b. Altamura, near Bari (baptized), Sept. 17, 1795; d. Naples, Dec. 17, 1870. He was born out of wedlock, and was taken to Naples when he was about 11. In 1808 he was enrolled in the Collegio di San Sebastiano. He had no means to pay for his tuition; besides, he was over the age limit for entrance, and was not a Neapolitan. To gain admission he had to change his first Christian name and adjust his place and date of birth. He studied solfeggio, violin, and flute; he also took classes in figured bass and harmony with Furno and counterpoint with Tritto; subsequently he studied composition with the Collegio's director, Zingarelli (1816–20). He began to compose while still a student. In 1818 he composed 3 ballets, and the success of the 3d, *Il flauto incantato*, encouraged him to try his hand at an opera. His first opera, *L'apoteosi d'Ercole*, had a successful premiere in Naples on Jan. 4, 1819. He wrote 5 more operas before *Elisa e Claudio*, produced at La Scala in Milan on Oct. 30, 1821, which established his reputation. Other important operas were *Caritea, regina di Spagna* (Venice, Feb. 21, 1826), *Gabriella di Vergy* (Lisbon, Aug. 8, 1828), *I Normanni a Parigi* (Turin, Feb. 7, 1832), *I Briganti* (Paris, March 22, 1836), *Il giuramento* (Milan, March 10, 1837; considered his masterpiece), *Le due illustri rivali* (Venice, March 10, 1838), *Elena da Feltre* (Naples, Dec. 26, 1838), *Il Bravo* (Milan, March 9, 1839), *La Vestale* (Naples, March 10, 1840; one of his finest), *Il Reggente* (Turin, Feb. 2, 1843), *Leonora* (Naples, Dec. 5, 1844), *Orazi e Curiazi* (Naples, Nov. 10, 1846; a major success in Italy), and *Virginia* (Naples, April 7, 1866; his last opera to be perf., although composed as early as 1845; its premiere was delayed for political reasons). Mercadante wrote about 60 operas in all, for different opera houses, often residing in the city where they were produced; thus he lived in Rome, Bologna, and Milan; he also spent some time in Vienna (where he composed 3 operas in 1824) and in Spain and Portugal (1826–31). From 1833 to 1840 he was maestro di cappella at the Cathedral of Novara. About that time he suffered the loss of sight in one eye, and in 1862 he became totally blind. In 1839 Rossini offered him the directorate of the Liceo Musicale in Bologna, but he served in that post only a short time; in 1840 he was named director of the Naples Cons. in succession to his teacher Zingarelli. Mercadante's operas are no longer in the active repertoire, but they are historically important, and objectively can stand comparison with those of his great compatriots Rossini, Bellini, and Donizetti.

WORKS: DRAMATIC: OPERAS: *L'apoteosi d'Ercole*, dramma per musica (Teatro San Carlo, Naples, Jan. 4, 1819); *Violenza e costanza, ossia I falsi monetari*, dramma giocoso (Teatro Nuovo, Naples, Jan. 19, 1820; also known as *Il castello dei spiriti*); *Anacreonte in Samo*, dramma per musica (Teatro San Carlo, Naples, Aug. 1, 1820); *Il geloso ravveduto*, melodramma buffo (Teatro Valle, Rome, Oct. 1820); *Scipione in Cartagine*, melodramma serio (Teatro Argentina, Rome, Dec. 26, 1820); *Maria Stuarda regina di Scozia [Maria Stuart]*, dramma serio (Teatro Comunale, Bologna, May 29, 1821); *Elisa e Claudio, ossia L'amore protetto dall'amicizia*, melodramma semiserio (Teatro alla Scala, Milan, Oct. 30, 1821); *Andronico*, melodramma tragico (Teatro La Fenice, Venice, Dec. 26, 1821); *Il posto abbandonato, ossia Adele ed Emerico*, melodramma semiserio (Teatro alla Scala, Milan, Sept. 21, 1822); *Amleto*, melodramma tragico (Teatro alla Scala, Milan, Dec. 26, 1822); *Alfonso ed Elisa*, melodramma serio (Teatro Nuovo, Mantua, Dec. 26, 1822); *Didone abbandonata*, dramma per musica (Teatro Regio, Turin, Jan. 18, 1823); *Gli sciti*, dramma per musica (Teatro San Carlo, Naples, March 18, 1823); *Costanzo ed Almeriska*, dramma per musica (Teatro San Carlo, Naples, Nov. 22, 1823); *Gli Amici di Siracusa*, melodramma eroico (Teatro Argentina, Rome, Feb. 7, 1824); *Doralice*, dramma semiserio (Kärnthnertortheater, Vienna, Sept. 18, 1824); *Le nozze di Telemaco ed Antiope*, azione lirica (Kärnthnertortheater, Vienna, Nov. 5, 1824; in collaboration with others); *Il Podestà di Burgos, ossia Il Signore del villaggio*, melodramma semiserio (Kärnthnertortheater, Vienna, Nov. 20, 1824; 2d version as *Il Signore del villaggio*, in Neapolitan dialect, Teatro Fondo, Naples, May 28, 1825); *Nitocri*, melodramma serio (Teatro Regio, Turin, Dec. 26, 1824); *Ipermestra*, dramma tragico (Teatro San Carlo, Naples, c.1824); *Erode, ossia Marianna*, dramma tragico (Teatro La Fenice, Venice, Dec. 27, 1825); *Caritea, regina di Spagna [Donna Caritea], ossia La morte di Don Alfonso re di Portogallo*, melodramma serio (Teatro La Fenice, Venice, Feb. 21, 1826); *Ezio*, dramma per musica (Teatro Regio, Turin, Feb. 2, 1827); *Il montanaro*, melodramma comico (Teatro alla Scala, Milan, April 16, 1827); *La testa di bronzo, ossia La capanna solitaria*, melodramma eroico comico (private theater of Barone di Quintella, Lisbon, Dec. 3, 1827); *Adriano in Siria*, dramma serio (Sao Carlos, Lisbon, Feb. 24, 1828); *Gabriella di Vergy*, melodramma serio (Sao Carlos, Lisbon, Aug. 8, 1828); *La rappresaglia*, opera buffa (Cadiz, Nov. 20?, 1829); *Don Chisciotte [alle nozze di Gamaccio]*, opera buffa (Cadiz, c.1829); *Francesca da Rimini*, melodramma (Madrid, c.1830); *Zaira*, melodramma tragico (Teatro San Carlo, Naples, Aug. 31, 1831); *I Normanni a Parigi*, tragedia lirica (Teatro Regio, Turin, Feb. 7, 1832); *Ismalia, ossia Amore e morte*, melodramma serio fantastico (Teatro alla Scala, Milan, Oct. 27, 1832); *Il Conte di Essex*, melodramma (Teatro alla Scala, Milan, March 10, 1833); *Emma d'Antiochia*, tragedia lirica (Teatro La Fenice, Venice, March 8, 1834); *Uggero il danese*, melodramma (Teatro Riccardi, Bergamo, Aug. 11, 1834); *La gioventù di Enrico V*, melodramma (Teatro alla Scala, Milan, Nov. 25, 1834); *I due Figaro*, melodramma buffo (1st confirmed perf., Madrid, Jan. 26, 1835); *Francesca Donato, ossia Corinto distrutta,* melodramma semiserio (Teatro Regio, Turin, Feb. 14, 1835); *I Briganti*, melodramma (Théâtre-Italien, Paris, March 22, 1836); *Il giuramento*, melodramma (Teatro alla Scala, Milan, March 10, 1837; also known as *Amore e dovere*); *Le due illustri rivali*, melodramma (Teatro La Fenice, Venice, March 10, 1838); *Elena da Feltre*, dramma tragico (Teatro San Carlo, Naples, Dec. 26, 1838); *Il Bravo [La Veneziana]*, melodramma (Teatro alla Scala, Milan, March 9, 1839); *La Vestale*, tragedia lirica (Teatro San Carlo, Naples, March 10, 1840); *La Solitaria delle Asturie, ossia La Spagna ricuperata*, melodramma (Teatro La Fenice, Venice, March 12, 1840); *Il proscritto*, melodramma (Teatro San Carlo, Naples, Jan. 4, 1842); *Il Reggente*, dramma lirico (Teatro Regio, Turin, Feb. 2, 1843); *Leonora*, melodramma semiserio (Teatro Nuovo, Naples, Dec. 5, 1844); *Il Vascello de Gama*, melodramma romantico (Teatro San Carlo, Naples, March 6, 1845); *Orazi e Curiazi*, tragedia lirica (Teatro San Carlo, Naples, Nov. 10, 1846); *La Schiava saracena, ovvero Il campo di Gerosolima*, melodramma tragico (Teatro alla Scala, Milan, Dec. 26, 1848); *Medea*, tragedia lirica (Teatro San Carlo, Naples, March 1, 1851); *Statira*, tragedia (Teatro San Carlo, Naples, Jan. 8, 1853); *Violetta*, melodramma (Teatro Nuovo, Naples, Jan. 10, 1853); *Pelagio*, tragedia lirica (Teatro San Carlo, Naples, Feb. 12, 1857); *Virginia*, tragedia lirica (Teatro San Carlo, Naples, April 7, 1866). BALLETS: *Il Servo balordo o La disperazione di Gilotto* (Teatro San Carlo, Naples, Feb. 1, 1818); *Il Califfo generoso* (Teatro Fondo, Naples, 1818); *Il flauto incantato o Le convulsioni musicali* (Teatro San Carlo, Naples, Nov. 19, 1818; rev. version for Teatro alla Scala, Milan, Jan. 12, 1828); *I Portoghesi nelle Indie o La conquista di Malacca* (Teatro San Carlo, Naples, May 30, 1819; in collaboration with Gallenberg).

BIBL.: W. Neumann, *S. M.* (Kassel, 1855); R. Colucci, *Biografia di S. M.* (Venice, 1867); O. Serena, *I musicisti altamurani . . . in occasione del centenario di S. M.* (Altamura, 1895); A. Pomè, *Saggio critico sull'opera musicale di S. M.* (Turin, 1925); G. de Napoli, *La triade melodrammatica altamurana: Giacomo Tritto, Vincenzo Lavigna, S. M.* (Milan, 1931); G. Solimene, *La patria e i genitori di M.* (Naples, 1940); B. Notarnicola, *S. M.: Biografia critica* (Rome, 1945; 3d ed., rev., 1951, as *S. M. nella gloria e nella luce: Verdi non ha vinto M.*); F. Schlitzer, *M. e Cammarano* (Bari, 1945); A. Sardone, *M., le due patrie e "La gran madre Italia"* (Naples, 1954); S. Palermo, *S. M.: Biografia, epistolario* (Fasano, 1985).

Méric-Lalande, Henriette (Clémentine), French soprano; b. Dunkirk, 1798; d. Chantilly, Sept. 7, 1867. She studied with her father, who was the director of a provincial opera company, making her debut in Nantes in 1814. After vocal studies with García in Paris, she made her first appearance there on April 3, 1823, in Castil-Blaze's pasticcio *Les Folies amoureuses*, then continued her training with Bonfichi and Banderali in Milan and took part in the Venice premiere of Meyerbeer's *Il Crociatto in Egitto* (March 7, 1824). She created Bianca in Bellini's *Bianca e Gernando* (Naples, May 30, 1826), Imogene in *Il Pirata* (Milan, Oct. 27, 1827), and Alaide in *La Straniera* (Milan, Feb. 14, 1829), even though Bellini himself declared that she was "incapable of delicate sentiment." She made her London debut in *Il Pirata* at the King's Theatre (April 17, 1830) and appeared in Rossini's *Semiramis* (1831). She retired shortly after creating the title role in Donizetti's *Lucrezia Borgia* (Milan, Dec. 26, 1833).

Mêriel, Paul, French composer; b. Mondonbleau, Loire-et-Cher, Jan. 4, 1818; d. Toulouse, Feb. 24, 1897. As a boy, he earned his living playing the violin in theater orchs., and then later studied with Napoleão in Lisbon. He produced a comic opera, *Cornelius l'argentier*, in Amiens, and then settled in Toulouse, where he brought out a grand opera, *L'Armorique* (1854), and the comic opera *Les Précieuses ridicules* (1877).

Merighi, Antonia Margherita, Italian soprano; b. c.1680; d. before 1764. She was in the service of the Dowager Grand Duchess Violante Beatrice of Tuscany. After making appearances in Venice (1717–21; 1724–26; 1732–33), Bologna (1719, 1727), Naples (1721–24; 1728–29), Parma (1725), Florence (1725), and Turin (1726), she was engaged by Handel for London, where she created the role of Matilde in his *Lotario* at her debut on Dec. 2, 1729. She also created the roles of Rosmira in his *Partenope* (Feb. 24, 1730) and Erissena in his *Poro* (Feb. 2, 1731). After singing again in Florence (1732) and Modena (1735), she returned to London to sing with the Opera of the Nobility (1736–37). In 1737–38 she was a member of Heidegger's company. In 1740 she appeared in Munich, and then retired to Bologna.

Merikanto, Aarre, Finnish composer and teacher, son of **(Frans) Oskar Merikanto**; b. Helsinki, June 29, 1893; d. there, Sept. 29, 1958. He studied composition with Melartin at the Helsinki Music Inst., then in Leipzig with Reger (1912–14) and with Vasilenko in Moscow (1915–16). In 1936 he joined the faculty at the Sibelius Academy in Helsinki, and in 1951 succeeded Palmgren as head of the dept. of composition there; he held this post until his death. Like his father, he wrote on themes of Finnish folklore, but some of his early works reveal Russian and French traits. He composed the opera *Juha* (1920–22; Finnish Radio, Helsinki, Dec. 3, 1958; 1st stage perf., Lahti, Oct. 28, 1963).

Merikanto, (Frans) Oskar, Finnish composer, conductor, and organist, father of **Aarre Merikanto**; b. Helsinki, Aug. 5, 1868; d. Hausjärvi-Oiti, Feb. 17, 1924. After preliminary study in his native city, he studied at the Leipzig Cons. (1887–88) and in Berlin (1890–91). Returning to Finland, he became organist of St. John's Church, and from 1911 to 1922 was conductor of the National Opera in Helsinki. He wrote manuals for organ playing. He wrote the first opera in Finnish, *Pohjan Neiti* (The Maid of the North; 1899; Vyborg, June 18, 1908); also the operas *Elinan surma* (Elina's Death; Helsinki, Nov. 17, 1910) and *Regina von Emmeritz* (Helsinki, Jan. 30, 1920) as well as numerous songs, many of which became popular in his homeland.

BIBL.: Y. Suomalainen, *O. M.* (Helsinki, 1950).

Merli, Francesco, Italian tenor; b. Milan, Jan. 27, 1887; d. there, Dec. 12, 1976. He studied with Borghi and Negrini in Milan. He made his first appearance at Milan's La Scala as Alvaro in Spontini's *Fernando Cortez* (1916), and subsequently sang there regularly until 1942; he also appeared at the Teatro Colón in Buenos Aires; between 1926 and 1930 he sang at Covent Garden in London. He made his debut at the Metropolitan Opera in New York as Radamés in *Aida* on March 2, 1932; then returned to Italy. He retired from the stage in 1948 and was active mainly as a voice teacher.

Mermet, Auguste, French composer; b. Brussels, Jan. 5, 1810; d. Paris, July 4, 1889. He was a student of Le Sueur and Halévy. After bringing out his opera *La Banniere du Roi* (Versailles, April 1835), he won success in Paris with his operatic spectacles *Le Roi David* (June 3, 1846) and *Roland à Roncevaux* (Oct. 3, 1864). His *Jeanne d'Arc* was the first work to be premiered at the Salle Garnier (April 5, 1876), the new Paris opera house which had opened on Jan. 5, 1875. Although popular in his day, none of his operas entered the standard repertoire.

Merola, Gaetano, Italian-American conductor and opera manager; b. Naples, Jan. 4, 1881; d. while conducting a performance of the San Francisco Sym. Orch. at Sigmund Stern Grove in San Francisco, Aug. 30, 1953. He studied at the Naples Cons. He went to the United States in 1899, and was appointed assistant conductor at the Metropolitan Opera in New York; he also conducted the Henry Savage English Opera in New York (1903) and at the Manhattan Opera; subsequently he became music director and manager of the San Francisco Opera in 1923, where he remained until his death; also conducted opera in Los Angeles (1924–32).

Merrem-Nikisch, Grete, German soprano; b. Düren, July 7, 1887; d. Kiel, March 12, 1970. She studied with Schulz-Dornburg in Cologne and Marie Hedmondt at the Leipzig Cons. In 1910 she made her operatic debut at the Leipzig Opera, where she sang until 1913. In 1911 she made her first appearance at the Berlin Royal Opera, where she was a member (1913–18), and then of its successor, the State Opera (1918–30). She was known for her lyric roles, and for her Eva and Sophie. She also sang in Dresden, where she appeared in the premieres of *Die toten Augen* (1916), *Intermezzo* (1924), and *Cardillac* (1926). From 1918 she likewise pursued a fine career as a lieder artist. In later years, she taught at the Univ. of Kiel. In 1914 she married the eldest son of Arthur Nikisch.

Merrill, Robert, noted American baritone; b. N.Y., June 4, 1917. He first studied voice with his mother, Lillian Miller Merrill, a concert singer; subsequently took lessons with Samuel Margolis. He began his career as a popular singer on the radio; he then made his operatic debut as Amonasro in Trenton, N.J., in 1944. After winning the Metropolitan Opera Auditions of the Air in New York, he made his debut there with the Metropolitan Opera on Dec. 15, 1945, as Germont. He remained on the roster of the Metropolitan Opera until 1976, and was again on its roster in 1983–84; he also gave solo recitals. In 1961 he made his European operatic debut as Germont in Venice; sang that same role at his Covent Garden debut in London in 1967. He became a highly successful artist through many radio, television, and film appearances and gave recitals and sang with the major American orchs.; he also starred in *Fiddler on the Roof* and other popular musicals. Among his numerous roles were Don José, Iago, Figaro, Rigoletto, Ford, and Scarpia. He was briefly married to **Roberta Peters**. He publ. 2 autobiographical books, *Once More from the Beginning* (N.Y., 1965) and *Between Acts* (N.Y., 1977). In 1993 he was awarded the National Medal of Arts.

Merriman, Nan (Katherine-Ann), American mezzo-soprano; b. Pittsburgh, April 28, 1920. She studied with Alexia Bassian in Los Angeles. She made her operatic debut as La Cieca in *La Gioconda* with the Cincinnati Summer Opera in 1942; from 1943 she sang with Toscanini and the NBC Sym. Orch.; she also appeared in opera at Aix-en-Provence, Edinburgh, and Glyndebourne. She retired in 1965. Her best operatic roles were Gluck's Orfeo, Maddalena in *Rigoletto*, Dorabella in *Così fan tutte*, Emilia in *Otello*, Baba the Turk in *The Rake's Progress*, and Meg in *Falstaff*.

Merritt, Chris (Allan), American tenor; b. Oklahoma City, Sept. 27, 1952. Following studies at Oklahoma City Univ. and the Santa Fe Opera, he made his formal operatic debut in 1978 as Rossini's Lindoro at the Salzburg Landestheater. In 1981 he made his first appearance at the N.Y. City Opera as Bellini's Arturo, and from 1981 to 1984 he sang at the Augsburg Opera. He made his debut at the Paris Opéra as Aaron in *Mosè in Egitto* in 1983. Following his debut at London's Covent Garden as James in *La donna del Lago* in 1985, he appeared as Rossini's Arnoldo at Milan's La Scala in 1988. He sang Gluck's Admète at the Lyric Opera in Chicago in 1990. In 1995 he sang the role of Aron in Schoenberg's *Moses und Aron* in Amsterdam. He sang in the premiere of Henze's

Venus und Adonis in Munich in 1997. As a concert artist, Merritt has appeared with many major orchs. While he has been most notably successful in operas by Rossini, Bellini, and Donizetti, he has also been admired for his portrayals of Idomeneo, Aeneas, and Rodolfo.

Mertens, Joseph, Belgian conductor and composer; b. Antwerp, Feb. 17, 1834; d. Brussels, June 30, 1901. He was 1st violinist at the opera orch. in Brussels, a violin teacher at the Cons., and conductor of the Flemish Opera there (1878–89). He then was inspector of the Belgian music schools, and finally director of the Royal Theater at The Hague. He composed a number of Flemish and French operettas and operas which had local success: *De zwaarte Kapitein* (The Hague, 1877), *De Vrijer in de strop* (1866), *La Méprise* (1869), *L'Egoïsa* (1873), *Thécla* (1874), and *Liederik l'intendent* (1875).

Mertke, Eduard, German pianist and composer; b. Riga, June 17, 1833; d. Cologne, Sept. 25, 1895. He studied with S. von Lützau (piano) and Agthe (theory), appearing in public as a child pianist. He toured Russia and Germany, and in 1869 was appointed to the faculty of the Cologne Cons., where he continued to teach until his death. He wrote the operas *Lisa, oder Die Sprache des Herzens* (Mannheim, Feb. 24, 1872), *Resi vom Hemsensteig*, and *Kyrill von Thessalonica*.

Messager, André (Charles Prosper), celebrated French composer and conductor; b. Montiuçon, Allier, Dec. 30, 1853; d. Paris, Feb. 24, 1929. He studied at the École Niedermeyer in Paris with Gigout, Fauré, and Saint-Saëns (composition), A. Lassel (piano), and C. Loret (organ). In 1874 he became organist at St.-Sulpice. He was active as a conductor at the Folies-Bergère, where he produced several ballets. After conducting at Brussels's Eden-Théâtre (1880), he returned to Paris as organist of St. Paul-St. Louis (1881) and as maître de chapelle at Ste. Marie-des-Baugnolles (1882–84). He subsequently was music director at the Opéra Comique (1898–1903); he also managed the Grand Opera Syndicate at London's Covent Garden (1901–07). He was conductor of the Concerts Lamoureux (1905) and music director of the Paris Opéra (1907–14) and was also conductor of the Société des Concerts da Conservatoire from 1908 until 1919; under the auspices of the French government, he visited the United States with that orch., giving concerts in 50 American cities (1918); he also toured Argentina (1916). Returning to Paris, he again conducted at the Opéra Comique; he led a season of Diaghilev's Ballets Russes in 1924. As a conductor, Messager played an important role in Paris musical life; he conducted the premiere of *Pelléas et Mélisande* (1902), the score of which Debussy dedicated to him. His initial steps as a composer were auspicious; his Sym. (1875) was awarded the gold medal of the Société des Compositeurs and performed at the Concerts Colonne (Jan. 20, 1878); his dramatic scene *Don Juan et Haydée* (1876) was awarded a gold medal by the Academy of St. Quentin. He wrote several other works for orch. (*Impressions orientals, Suite funambulesque*, etc.) and some chamber music, but he was primarily a man of the theater. His style may be described as enlightened eclecticism; his music was characteristically French, and more specifically Parisian, in its elegance and gaiety. He was honored in France; in 1926 he was elected to the Académie des Beaux Arts. He was married to Hope Temple (real name, Dotie Davis; 1858–1938), who was the author of numerous songs. His stage works (1st perf. in Paris unless otherwise given) included *François les-Bas-Bleus* (Nov. 8, 1883; score begun by F. Bernicat and completed after his death by Messager), *La Fauvette du temple* (Nov. 17, 1885), *La Béarnaise* (Dec. 12, 1885), *Le Bourgeois de Calais* (April 6, 1887), *Isoine* (Dec. 26, 1888), *La Basoche* (May 30, 1890; greatly acclaimed), *Madame Chrysanthème* (Jan. 26, 1893; to a story similar to Puccini's *Madame Butterfly*, produced 11 years later, but Puccini's dramatic treatment eclipsed Messager's lyric setting), *Le Chavalier d'Harmental* (May 5, 1896), *Véronique* (Dec. 10, 1898), *Les Dragons de l'impératrice* (Feb. 13, 1905), *Fortunio* (June 5, 1907), *Béatrice* (Monte Carlo, March 21, 1914), and *Monsieur Beaucaire* (Birmingham, April 7, 1919). Other stage works were *Le Mart de la Reine* (Dec. 18, 1889), *Mies Dollar* (Jan. 22, 1893), *La Fiancée en loterie* (Feb. 15, 1896), *Les Pittes Michu* (Nov. 18, 1897), *La Petite Fonctionnaire* (May 14, 1921), and *Passionnément* (Jan. 15, 1926). His ballets included *Fleur d'oranger* (1878), *Les Vins de France* (1879), *Mignons et villains* (1879), *Les Deux Pigeons* (1886), *Scaramouche* (1891), *Amants éternels* (1893), *Le Chevalier aux fleurs* (1897), *Le Procès des roses* (1897), and *Une Aventure de la guimard* (1900). He also wrote incidental music.

BIBL.: H. Février, *A. M.: Mon maître, mon ami* (Paris, 1948); M. Augé-Laribé, *A. M.: Musicien de théâtre* (Paris, 1951); J. Wagstaff, *A. M.: A Bio-Bibliography* (N.Y., 1991).

Messchaert, Johannes (Martinus), Dutch baritone; b. Hoorn, Aug. 22, 1857; d. Zürich, Sept. 9, 1922. He studied violin, then changed to singing, studying with Stockhausen in Frankfurt am Main and Wüllner in Munich. He began his career as a choral conductor in Amsterdam, then appeared as a singer of the German repertoire. He was prof. of voice at the Berlin Königliche Hochschule für Musik (1911–20) and at the Zürich Cons. (1920–22).

BIBL.: F. Martienssen, *J. M.: Ein Beitrag zum Verständnis echter Gesangskunst* (Berlin, 1914; 2d ed., 1920).

Messiaen, Olivier (Eugène Prosper Charles), outstanding French composer and pedagogue; b. Avignon, Dec. 10, 1908; d. Clichy, Hauts-de-Seine, April 27, 1992. A scion of an intellectual family (his father was a translator of English literature; his mother, Cécile Sauvage, a poet), he absorbed the atmosphere of culture and art as a child. A mystical quality was imparted by his mother's book of verses *L'Âme en bourgeon*, dedicated to her as yet unborn child. He learned to play piano; at the age of 8 he composed a song, *La Dame de Shalott*, to a poem by Tennyson. At the age of 11 he entered the Paris Cons., where he attended the classes of Jean and Noël Gallon, Dupré, Emmanuel, and Dukas, specializing in organ, improvisation, and composition; he carried 1st prizes in all these depts. After graduation in 1930, he became organist at the Trinity Church in Paris. He taught at the École Normale de Musique and at the Schola Cantorum (1936–39). He also organized, with Jolivet, Baudrier, and Daniel-Lesur, the group La Jeune France, with the aim of promoting modern French music. He was in the French army at the outbreak of World War II in 1939; he was taken prisoner and spent 2 years in a German prison camp in Görlitz, Silesia; there he composed his *Quatuor pour la fin du temps*; he was repatriated in 1941 and resumed his post as organist at the Trinity Church in Paris. He was prof. of harmony and analysis at the Paris Cons. (from 1948). He also taught at the Berkshire Music Center in Tanglewood (summer 1948) and in Darmstadt (1950–53). Young composers seeking instruction in new music became his eager pupils; among them were Boulez, Stockhausen, Xenakis, and others who were to become important composers in their own right. He received numerous honors; he was made a Grand Officier de la Légion d'Honneur and was elected a member of the Institut de France, the Bavarian Academy of the Fine Arts, the Accademia di Santa Cecilia in Rome, the American Academy of Arts and Letters, and other organizations. He married **Yvonne Loriod** in 1961.

Messiaen was one of the most original of modern composers; in his music, he made use of a wide range of resources, from Gregorian chant to oriental rhythms. A mystic by nature and Catholic by religion, he strove to find a relationship between progressions of musical sounds and religious concepts; in his theoretical writing, he postulated an interdependence of modes, rhythms, and harmonic structures. Ever in quest of new musical resources, he employed in his scores the Ondes Martenot and exotic percussion instruments; a synthesis of these disparate tonal elements found its culmination in his grandiose orch. work *Turangalîla-Symphonie*. One of the most fascinating aspects of Messiaen's innovative musical vocabulary was the phonetic emulation of bird song in several of his works; in order to attain ornithological fidelity, he made a detailed study notating the rhythms and pitches of singing birds in many regions of several countries. The municipal council of Parowan, Utah, where Messiaen wrote his work

Des canyons aux étoiles, glorifying the natural beauties of the state of Utah, resolved to name a local mountain Mt. Messiaen on Aug. 5, 1978. On Nov. 28, 1983, his opera, *St. François d'Assise*, was premiered, to international acclaim, at the Paris Opéra.

WRITINGS: *20 leçons de solfèges modernes* (Paris, 1933); *20 leçons d'harmonie* (Paris, 1939); *Technique de mon langage musical* (2 vols., Paris, 1944; Eng. tr., 1957, as *The Technique of My Musical Language*).

BIBL.: B. Gavoty, *Musique et mystique: Le "Cas" M.* (Paris, 1945); V. Zinke-Bianchini, *O. M.: Notice biographique, catalogue détaillé des oeuvres éditées* (Paris, 1946); C. Rostand, *O. M.* (Paris, 1958); A. Goléa, *Rencontres avec O. M.* (Paris, 1961); C. Samuel, *Entretiens avec O. M.* (Paris, 1967); R. Johnson, *M.* (Berkeley, Calif., 1975); R. Nichols, *M.* (London, 1975; 2d ed., 1985); C. Bell, *O. M.* (Boston, 1984); P. Griffiths, *O. M. and the Music of Time* (London, 1985); A. Michaely, *Die Musik O. M.s: Untersuchungen zum Gesamtschaffen* (Hamburg, 1987); T. Hirsbrunner, *O. M.: Leben und Werk* (Laaber, 1988); J. Boivin, *La classe de M.* (Paris, 1995); P. Hill, ed., *The M. Companion* (Portland, Oreg., 1995).

Messner, Joseph, Austrian organist, conductor, and composer; b. Schwaz, Tirol, Feb. 27, 1893; d. St. Jakob Thurn, near Salzburg, Feb. 23, 1969. He studied at the Univ. of Innsbruck; after his ordination (1918), he took courses in organ and composition with Friedrich Klose at the Munich Akademie der Tonkunst. In 1922 he was appointed Cathedral organist in Salzburg; from 1926 to 1967 he led the concerts at the Salzburg Cathedral; at the same time, he gave a seminar in church music at the Mozarteum there. He wrote 4 operas: *Hadassa* (Aachen, March 27, 1925), *Das letzte Recht* (1932), *Ines* (1933), and *Agnes Bernauer* (1935).

Mestres-Quadreny, Josep (Maria), Spanish composer; b. Manresa, March 4, 1929. He studied composition with Taltabull at the Univ. of Barcelona (1950–56). In 1960 he collaborated in the founding of Música Abierta, an organization of avant-garde musical activity; later he joined composers Xavier Benguerel, Joaquim Homs, and Josep Soler in founding the Conjunt Català de Másica Contemporània, for the propagation of Catalan music. In his music, he consciously attempts to find a counterpart to Abstract Expressionism in art, as exemplified by the paintings of Miró; for this purpose he applies serial techniques and aleatory procedures.

WORKS: DRAMATIC: OPERA: *El Ganxo* (1959). BALLETS: *Roba i ossos* (1961); *Petit diumenge* (1962); *Vegetació submergida* (1962). MUSIC THEATER: *Concert per a representar* for 6 Voices, 6 Instrumentalists, and Tape (1964); *Suite bufa* for Ballerina, Mezzo-soprano, Piano, and Electronic Sound (1966).

Metastasio, Pietro (real name, **Antonio Domenico Bonaventura Trapassi**), famous Italian poet and opera librettist; b. Rome, Jan. 3, 1698; d. Vienna, April 12, 1782. He was the son of a papal soldier named Trapassi, but in his professional career assumed the Greek tr. of the name, both Trapassi (or Trapassamento) and Metastasio meaning transition. He was a learned classicist. He began to write plays as a young boy, and also studied music with Porpora. He achieved great fame in Italy as a playwright. In 1729 he was appointed court poet in Vienna by Emperor Charles VI. He wrote 27 opera texts, which were set to music by Handel, Gluck, Mozart, Hasse, Porpora, Jommelli, and many other celebrated composers; some of them were set to music 60 or more times. His librettos were remarkable for their melodious verse, which naturally suggested musical associations; the libretto to the opera by Niccolo Conforto, *La Nitteti* (1754; Madrid, Sept. 23, 1756), was on the same subject as *Aida*, anticipating the latter by more than a century. Metastasio's complete works were publ. in Paris (12 vols., 1780–82) and Mantua (20 vols., 1816–20); they were ed. by F. Gazzani (Turin, 1968) and by M. Fubino (Milan, 1968); see also A. Wotquenne, *Alphabetisches Verzeichnis der Stücke in Versen . . . von Zeno, Metastasio und Goldoni* (Leipzig, 1905).

BIBL.: S. Mattei, *Memorie per servire alla vita del M.* (Colle, 1785); C. Burney, *Memoirs of the Life and Letters of the Abate M.* (London, 1796); M. Zito, *Studio su P. M.* (Naples, 1904); E. Leonardi, *Il melodramma del M.* (Naples, 1909); L. Russo, *P. M.* (Pisa, 1915; 2d ed., rev., 1921–45, as *M.*); A. della Corte, *L'estetica musicale di P. M.* (Turin, 1922); A. Vullo, *Confronto fra i melodrammi di Zeno e M.* (Agrigento, 1935); B. Brunelli, ed., *Tutte le opere di P. M.* (Milan, 1943–54); M. Muraro, *M. e il mondo musicale* (Florence, 1986); C. Maeder, *M., l'Olimpiade e l'opera del Settecento* (Bologna, 1993).

Methfessel, Albert Gottlieb, German composer; b. Stadtilm, Thuringia, Oct. 6, 1785; d. Heckenbeck, near Gandersheim, March 23, 1869. From 1832 until 1842 he was court composer at Braunschweig, then retired on a pension. Among his works was the opera *Der Prinz von Basra,* the oratorio *Das befreite Jerusalem,* and part-songs, publ. in his *Liederbuch, Liederkranz*, and other collections. His brother, Friedrich Methfessel (1771–1807), publ. songs with guitar accompaniment.

Métra, (Jules-Louis-) Olivier, French composer; b. Le Mans, June 2, 1830; d. Paris, Oct. 22, 1889. An actor's son, he became an actor himself as a boy. He was first taught music by E. Roche, then was a pupil of Elwart at the Paris Cons. (1849–54). He played violin, cello, and double bass at Paris theaters, then conducted at various dance halls, the masked balls at the Opéra Comique (1871), the orch. at the Folies-Bergère (1872–77), the balls at the Théâtre Royal de la Monnaie, Brussels (1874–76), and, finally, the balls at the Paris Opéra. At the Folies-Bergère he produced 19 operettas and ballet divertissements. At the Opéra he produced the ballet *Yedda* (Paris, Jan. 17, 1879). His waltzes, mazurkas, polkas, quadrilles, etc., were extremely popular.

Metternich, Josef, German baritone; b. Hermuhlheim, near Cologne, June 2, 1915. He studied in Berlin and Cologne. After singing in the opera choruses in Bonn and Cologne, he made his operatic debut as Tonio at the Berlin Städtische Opera in 1945. In 1951 he sang the Dutchman at his first appearance at London's Covent Garden. On Nov. 21, 1953, he made his Metropolitan Opera debut in New York as Carlo in *La forza del destino*, and remained on its roster until 1956. In 1954 he became a member of the Bavarian State Opera in Munich, where he created the role of Johannes Kepler in Hindemith's *Die Harmonie der Welt* in 1957. His guest engagements took him to Cologne, Hamburg, Vienna, Milan, Edinburgh, and other European music centers. In 1963 he sang Kothner in *Die Meistersinger von Nürnberg* at the reopening of the National Theater in Munich. He retired from the operatic stage in 1971. From 1965 he was a prof. at the Cologne Hochschule für Musik. Among his other roles were Kurwenal, Wolfram, Amfortas, Amonasro, Jochanaan, and Scarpia.

Metzger, Heinz-Klaus, German writer on music; b. Konstanz, Feb. 6, 1932. He studied at the Staatliche Musikhochschule in Freiburg im Breisgau (1949–52), then studied composition with Deutsch in Paris and musicology in Tübingen (1952–54). He qualified in 1956 at the Akademie für Tonkunst in Darmstadt, where he later was active in the Darmstadt summer courses. His theoretical, philosophical, and cultural writings on modern and avant-garde music were influenced by Adorno, who recognized his talent. Metzger cofounded the journal *Musik-Konzepte* with Rainer Riehn in 1977. His relationship with Bussotti led to his remarkable studies of music considered unanalyzable by other writers, by composers including Bussotti, Schnebel, and Kagel. He also wrote extensively on Cage's *Europeras 1 & 2.*

Metzger-Lattermann, Ottilie, German contralto; b. Frankfurt am Main, July 15, 1878; d. in the concentration camp in Auschwitz, Feb. 1943. She was a pupil of Selma Nicklass-Kempner and Emanuel Reicher in Berlin. In 1898 she made her operatic debut in Halle, and then appeared in Cologne (1900–03), at the Bayreuth Festivals (1901–12), the Hamburg Opera (1903–15), and the Dresden Court Opera (1915–18), and its successor, the State Opera (1918–21). In 1910 she was the first to sing Herodias in *Salome* in London under Beecham's direction. She made guest appearances in Berlin, Vienna, Munich, and other European cities, and in 1923 she toured the United States with the German Opera Co. As a Jew, she was forced to leave Germany in 1935 and went to Brussels, where she taught voice. In 1942 she was arrested by the Nazi henchmen and was sent to Auschwitz.

Metzmacher, Ingo, German conductor; b. Hannover, Nov. 10, 1957. He received training in piano and conducting in Hannover, Salzburg, and Cologne. After serving as pianist in the Ensemble Modern (1981–84), he concentrated his energies on a conducting career. In 1985 he made his debut as an opera conductor with *Le nozze di Figaro* at the Frankfurt am Main Opera. In subsequent seasons, he appeared as a guest conductor with major European opera houses. In 1997 he became Generalmusikdirektor of the Hamburg State Opera and chief conductor of the Hamburg State Phil. Orch.

Meulemans, Arthur, eminent Belgian composer; b. Aarschot, May 19, 1884; d. Brussels, June 29, 1966. He was a student of Tinel at the Lemmens Inst. in Mechelen (1900–06), and then was a prof. there until 1914. In 1916 he founded the Limburg School for organ and song in Hasselt, serving as its director until 1930. He subsequently settled in Brussels, where he was a conductor with the Belgian Radio (1930–42). In 1954 he became president of the Royal Flemish Academy of Fine Arts. Meulemans composed a prodigious body of music, excelling especially as a composer of orch. works. He also composed the operas *Vikings* (1919), *Adriaen Brouwer* (1926), and *Egmont* (1944), and also oratorios.

BIBL.: M. Boereboom, *A. M.* (Kortrijk, 1951); *Aan Meester A. M. bij zijn tachtigs verjaardag* (Antwerp, 1964).

Meyer, Ernst Hermann, German musicologist and composer; b. Berlin, Dec. 8, 1905; d. there, Oct. 8, 1988. His father was a medical doctor of artistic interests who encouraged him to study music; he took piano lessons with Walter Hirschberg and played in chamber music groups. During the economic disarray in Germany in the 1920s, Meyer was obliged to do manual labor in order to earn a living. In 1926 he was able to enroll in the Univ. of Berlin, where he studied musicology with Wolf, Schering, Blume, Hornbostel, and Sachs; in 1928 he had additional studies with Besseler at the Univ. of Heidelberg, obtaining his Ph.D. in 1930 with the diss. *Die mehrstimmige Spielmusik des 17. Jahrhunderts in Nord- und Mitteleuropa* (publ. in Kassel, 1934). In 1929 he met Eisler, who influenced him in the political aspect of music. In 1930 he joined the German Communist party. He conducted workers' choruses in Berlin and composed music for the proletarian revue *Der rote Stern*. He also attended classes on film music given by Hindemith. In 1931 he took a course in Marxism-Leninism with Hermann Duncker at the Marxist Workers' School in Berlin. He also began a detailed study of works by modern composers; in his own works, mostly for voices, he developed a style characteristic of the proletarian music of the time, full of affirmative action in march time adorned by corrosive discords, and yet eminently singable. When the Nazis bore down on his world with a different march, he fled to London, where, with the help of Alan Bush, he conducted the Labour Choral Union. During World War II, he participated in the Chorus of the Free German Cultural Union in London and wrote propaganda songs; of these, "Radio Moskau ruft Frau Kramer" was widely broadcast to Germany. In 1948 he went to East Berlin, where he was a prof. and director of the musicological inst. of the Humboldt Univ. until 1970. He was acknowledged as one of the most persuasive theoreticians of socialist realism in music; he founded the periodical *Musik und Gesellschaft*, which pursued the orthodox Marxist line. He publ. *English Chamber Music: The History of a Great Art from the Middle Ages to Purcell* (London, 1946; in Ger. as *Die Kammermusik Alt-Englands*, East Berlin, 1958; new ed., rev., 1982, with D. Poulton as *Early English Chamber Music*); *Das Werk Beethovens und seine Bedeutung für das sozialistisch-realistische Gegenwartsschaffen* (East Berlin, 1970); and the autobiographical *Kontraste-Konflikte* (East Berlin, 1979). A Festschrift was publ. in his honor in Leipzig in 1973. Among his compositions was the opera *Reiter der Nacht* (1969–72; Berlin, Nov. 17, 1973); also film music.

BIBL.: K. Niemann, *E. H. M.: Für Sie porträtiert* (Leipzig, 1975); M. Hansen, ed., *E. H. M.: Das kompositorische und theoretische Werk* (Leipzig, 1976).

Meyer, Kerstin (Margareta), Swedish mezzo-soprano; b. Stockholm, April 3, 1928. She studied at the Royal Academy of Music (1948–50) and at the Opera School (1950–52) in Stockholm, also at the Accademia Musicale Chigiana in Siena and at the Salzburg Mozarteum. In 1952 she made her operatic debut as Azucena at the Royal Theater in Stockholm, where she subsequently sang regularly; she also made guest appearances in numerous European opera centers and toured widely as a concert artist. In 1960 she made her first appearance at London's Covent Garden as Dido in the English-language production of *Les Troyens*. On Oct. 29, 1960, she made her Metropolitan Opera debut in New York as Carmen, remaining on its roster until 1963; she also appeared at the Bayreuth Festivals (1962–65). In 1963 she was made a Royal Swedish Court Singer. Following her retirement, she served as director of the Opera School in Stockholm (1984–94). In 1985 she was made an honorary Commander of the Order of the British Empire. She excelled particularly in contemporary operas, most notably in the works of Schuller, Searle, Henze, Maw, and Ligeti; among her standard portrayals were Orfeo, Dorabella, Fricka, Octavian, and Clytemnestra.

Meyer, Krzysztof, remarkable Polish composer and teacher; b. Kraków, Aug. 11, 1943. He commenced piano lessons when he was 5. At 11 he began to take lessons in theory and composition with Wiechowicz. He pursued his training at the Kraków College of Music with Penderecki (composition diploma, 1965) and Fraczkiewicz (theory diploma, 1966). He also studied in Fontainebleau and Paris with Boulanger in 1964, 1966, and 1968. From 1965 to 1967 he was a pianist with the contemporary music group MW-2. He was prof. of theoretical subjects at the Kraków College of Music from 1966 to 1987, and was also head of its theory dept. from 1972 to 1975. From 1985 to 1989 he was president of the Union of Polish Composers. He was prof. of composition at the Cologne Hochschule für Musik from 1987. In addition to his various articles on contemporary music, he publ. the first monograph on the life and works of Shostakovich in Poland (Kraków, 1973; 2d ed., 1986; Ger. tr., 1980; new ed., enl., Paris, 1994, and Bergish Gladbach, 1995). He prepared his own version of Shostakovich's unfinished opera *The Gamblers* (1980–81; Wuppertal, Sept. 9, 1984). His 3d Sym. won 1st prize in the Young Polish Composers' Competition in 1968. In 1970 he won the Grand Prix of the Prince Pierre of Monaco composers' competition for his opera *Cyberiada*. He received awards from the Polish Ministry of Culture and Art in 1973 and 1975. In 1974 his 4th Sym. won 1st prize in the Szymanowski Competition in Warsaw. In 1984 he received the Gottfried von Herder Prize of Vienna. In 1987 he was made a member of the Freien Akademie der Künste in Mannheim. He received the annual award of the Union of Polish Composers in 1992. As a composer, he abandoned the early influence of Penderecki and Boulanger and pursued his own advanced course without ever transcending the practical limits of instrumental and vocal techniques or of aural perception. His scores are the product of a rare musical intelligence and acoustical acuity.

WORKS: DRAMATIC: *Cyberiada*, fantastic comic opera (1967–70; Act. 1, Polish-TV, May 12, 1971; 1st complete perf., Wuppertal, May 11, 1986); *Hrabina* (The Countess), ballet (1980; Poznan, Nov. 14, 1981); *Igroki* (The Gamblers), completion of Shostakovich's opera (1980–81; Wuppertal, Sept. 9, 1984); *Klonowi bracia* (The Maple Brothers), children's opera (1988–89; Poznan, March 3, 1990).

Meyerbeer, Giacomo (real name, **Jakob Liebmann Beer**), famous German composer; b. Vogelsdorf, near Berlin, Sept. 5, 1791; d. Paris, May 2, 1864. He was a scion of a prosperous Jewish family of merchants. He added the name Meyer to his surname, and later changed his first name for professional purposes. He began piano studies with Franz Lauska, and also received some instruction from Clementi. He made his public debut in Berlin when he was 11. He then studied composition with Zelter (1805–07), and subsequently with B. A. Weber. It was as Weber's pupil that he composed his first stage work, the ballet pantomime *Der Fischer und das Milchmädchen*, which was produced at the Berlin Royal Theater (March 26, 1810). He then went to Darmstadt to continue his studies with Abbé Vogler until late 1811; one of his fellow pupils was Carl Maria von Weber. While under Vogler's tutelage, he composed the oratorio *Gott und die Natur* (Berlin, May 8, 1811) and also the operas *Der Admiral* (1811; not perf.) and *Jephthas Gelübde* (Munich, Dec. 23, 1812). His next opera, *Wirth und Gast, oder Aus Scherz Ernst* (Stuttgart, Jan. 6, 1813), was not a success; revised as *Die beyden Kalifen* for Vienna, it likewise failed there (Oct. 20, 1814). However, he did find success in Vienna as a pianist in private musical settings. In Nov. 1814 he proceeded to Paris, and in Dec. 1815 to London. He went to Italy early in 1816, and there turned his attention fully to dramatic composition. His Italian operas—*Romilda e Costanza* (Padua, July 19, 1817), *Semiramide riconosciuta* (Turin, March 1819), *Emma di Resburgo* (Venice, June 26, 1819), *Margherita d'Angiù* (Milan, Nov. 14, 1820), *L'Esule di Granata* (Milan, March 12, 1821), and *Il Crociato in Egitto* (Venice, March 7, 1824)—brought him fame there, placing him on a par with the celebrated Rossini in public esteem. The immense success of *Il Crociato in Egitto* in particular led to a successful staging at London's King's Theatre (July 23, 1825), followed by a triumphant Paris production (Sept. 25, 1825), which made Meyerbeer famous throughout Europe. To secure his Paris position, he revamped *Margherita d'Angiù* for the French stage as *Margherita d'Anjou* (March 11, 1826). He began a long and distinguished association with the dramatist and librettist Eugène Scribe in 1827 as work commenced on the opera *Robert le diable*. It was produced at the Paris Opéra on Nov. 21, 1831, with extraordinary success.

Numerous honors were subsequently bestowed upon Meyerbeer: he was made a Chevalier of the Légion d'honneur and a Prussian Hofkapellmeister in 1832, a member of the senate of the Prussian Academy of Arts in 1833, and a member of the Institut de France in 1834. He began work on what was to become the opera *Les Huguenots* in 1832; set to a libretto mainly by Scribe, it was accorded a spectacular premiere at the Opéra on Feb. 29, 1836. Late in 1836 he and Scribe began work on a new opera, *Le Prophète*. He also commenced work on the opera *L'Africaine* in Aug. 1837, again utilizing a libretto by Scribe; it was initially written for the famous soprano Marie-Cornélie Falcon; however, after the loss of her voice, Meyerbeer set the score aside; it was destined to occupy him on and off for the rest of his life. In 1839 Wagner sought out Meyerbeer in Boulogne. Impressed with Wagner, Meyerbeer extended him financial assistance and gave him professional recommendations. However, Wagner soon became disenchanted with his prospects and berated Meyerbeer in private, so much so that Meyerbeer was compelled to disassociate himself from Wagner. The ungrateful Wagner retaliated by giving vent to his anti-Semitic rhetoric.

Meyerbeer began work on *Le Prophète* in earnest in 1838, completing it by 1840. However, its premiere was indefinitely delayed as the composer attempted to find capable singers. On May 20, 1842, *Les Huguenots* was performed in Berlin. On June 11, 1842, Meyerbeer was formally installed as Prussian Generalmusikdirektor. From the onset of his tenure, disagreement with the Intendant of the Royal Opera, Karl Theodor von Küstner, made his position difficult. Finally, on Nov. 26, 1848, Meyerbeer was dismissed from his post, although he retained his position as director of music for the royal court; in this capacity he composed a number of works for state occasions, including the opera *Ein Feldlager in Schlesien*, which reopened the opera house on Dec. 7, 1844, following its destruction by fire. The leading role was sung by Jenny Lind, one of Meyerbeer's discoveries. It had a modicum of success after its first performance in Vienna under the title *Vielka* in 1847, although it never equaled the success of his Paris operas. In 1849 he again took up the score of *Le Prophète*. As he could find no tenor to meet its demands, he completely revised the score for the celebrated soprano Pauline Viardot-García. With Viardot-García as Fidès and the tenor Gustave Roger as John of Leyden, it received a brilliant premiere at the Opéra on April 16, 1849, a success that led to Meyerbeer's being made the 1st German Commandeur of the Légion d'honneur. His next opera was *L'Étoile du nord*, which utilized music from *Ein Feldlager in Schlesien*; its first performance at the Opéra Comique on Feb. 16, 1854, proved an outstanding success. Equally successful was his opera *Le Pardon de Ploërmel* (Opéra Comique, April 4, 1859). In 1862 he composed a special work for the London World Exhibition, the *Fest-Ouverture im Marschstyl*, and made a visit to England during the festivities. In the meantime, work on *L'Africaine* had occupied him fitfully for years; given Scribe's death in 1861 and Meyerbeer's own failing health, he was compelled to finally complete it. In April 1864 he put the finishing touches on the score and rehearsals began under his supervision. However, he died on the night of May 2, 1864, before the work was premiered. His body was taken to Berlin, where it was laid to rest in official ceremonies attended by the Prussian court, prominent figures in the arts, and the public at large. Fétis was subsequently charged with making the final preparations for the premiere of *L'Africaine*, which was given at the Paris Opéra to notable acclaim on April 28, 1865.

Meyerbeer established himself as the leading composer of French grand opera in 1831 with *Robert le diable*, a position he retained with distinction throughout his career. Indeed, he became one of the most celebrated musicians of his era. Although the grandiose conceptions and stagings of his operas proved immediately appealing to audiences, his dramatic works were more than mere theatrical spectacles. His vocal writing was truly effective, for he often composed and tailored his operas with specific singers in mind. Likewise, his gift for original orchestration and his penchant for instrumental experimentation placed his works on a high level. Nevertheless, his stature as a composer was eclipsed after his death by Wagner. As a consequence, his operas disappeared from the active repertoire, although revivals and several recordings saved them from total oblivion in the modern era.

WORKS: DRAMATIC: OPERAS: *Jephthas Gelübde* (Munich, Dec. 23, 1812); *Wirth und Gast, oder Aus Scherz Ernst*, Lustspiel (Stuttgart, Jan. 6, 1813; rev. as *Die beyden Kalifen*, Vienna, Oct. 20, 1814; later known as *Alimelek*); *Das Brandenburger Tor*, Singspiel (1814; not perf.); *Romilda e Costanza*, melodramma semiserio (Padua, July 19, 1817); *Semiramide riconosciuta*, dramma per musica (Turin, March 1819); *Emma di Resburgo*, melodramma eroico (Venice, June 26, 1819); *Margherita d'Angiù*, melodramma semiserio (Milan, Nov. 14, 1820; rev. as *Margherita d'Anjou*, Paris, March 11, 1826); *L'Almanzore* (1821; not perf.); *L'Esule di Granata*, melodramma serio (Milan, March 12, 1821); *Il Crociato in Egitto*, melodramma eroico (Venice, March 7, 1824); *Robert le diable*, grand opéra (Paris, Nov. 21, 1831); *Les Huguenots*, grand opéra (Paris, Feb. 29, 1836); *Ein Feldlager in Schlesien*, Singspiel (Berlin, Dec. 7, 1844; later known as *Vielka*); *Le Prophète*, grand opéra (Paris, April 16, 1849); *L'Étoile du nord*, opéra comique (Paris, Feb. 16, 1854; much of the music based on *Ein Feldlager in Schlesien*); *Le Pardon de Ploërmel*, opéra comique (Paris, April 4, 1859; also known as *Le Chercheur du trésor* and as *Dinorah, oder Die Wallfahrt nach Ploërmel*); *L'Africaine*, grand opéra (Paris, April 28, 1865; originally known as *Vasco da Gama*). He also left a number of unfinished operas in various stages of development. OTHER: *Der Fischer und das Milchmädchen, oder Viel Lärm um einen Kuss (Le Passage de la rivière, ou La Femme jalouse; Le Pêcheur et la laitière)*, ballet pantomime (Berlin, March 26, 1810); *Gli amori di Teolinda (Thecelindens Liebschaften)*, monodrama (Genoa, 1816); *Das Hoffest von Ferrara*, masque (Berlin, Feb. 28, 1843); *Struensee*, incidental music for a drama by Michael Beer, Meyerbeer's brother (Berlin, Sept. 19, 1846); etc. ORATORIO: *Gott und die Natur* (Berlin, May 8, 1811).

BIBL.: A. Morel, *Le Prophète: Analyse critique de la nouvelle partition de G. M.* (Paris, 1849); E. Lindner, *M.s "Prophet" als Kunstwerk beurtheilt* (Berlin, 1850); E. de Mirecourt, *M.* (Paris, 1854); A. de Lasalle, *M.: Sa vie et le catalogue de ses oeuvres* (Paris, 1864); A. Pougin, *M.: Notes biographiques* (Paris, 1864); H. Blaze de Bury, *M. et son temps* (Paris, 1865); H. Mendel, *G. M.* (Berlin, 1868); J. Schucht, *M.s Leben und Bildungsgang* (Leipzig, 1869); A. Body, *M. aux eaux de Spa* (Brussels, 1885); A. Kohut, *M.* (Leipzig, 1890); E. Destranges, *L'Œuvre théâtral de M.* (Paris, 1893); J. Weber, *M.: Notes et souvenirs d'un de ses secrétaires* (Paris, 1898); H. de Curzon, *M.: Biographie critique* (Paris, 1910); H. Eymieu, *L'Œuvre de M.* (Paris, 1910); L. Dauriac, *M.* (Paris, 1913; 2d ed.,

1930); J. Kapp, *G. M.* (Berlin, 1920; 8th ed., rev., 1932); H. Strelitzer, *M.s deutsche Jugendopern* (diss., Univ. of Münster, 1920); R. Haudek, *Scribes Operntexte für M.: Eine Quellenuntersuchung* (diss., Univ. of Vienna, 1928); J. Cooke, *M.* (Philadelphia, 1929); H. Becker, *Der Fall Heine-M.: Neue Dokumente revidieren ein Geschichtsurteil* (Berlin, 1958); idem, ed., *G. M.: Briefwechsel und Tagebücher* (4 vols., Berlin, 1960–85); C. Frese, *Dramaturgie der grossen Opern G. M.s* (Berlin, 1970); H. Becker, *G. M. in Selbstzeugnissen und Bilddokumenten* (Reinbek, 1980); H. and G. Becker, *G. M.: Ein Leben in Briefen* (Wilhelmshaven, 1983; Eng. tr., 1989); S. Segalini, *M.: Diable ou prophète?* (Paris, 1985); H. and G. Becker, *G. M.: Weltbürger der Musik* (Wiesbaden, 1991); R. Zimmermann, *G. M.: Eine Biographie nach Dokumenten* (Berlin, 1991).

Meyerowitz, Jan (Hans-Hermann), German-born American composer and teacher; b. Breslau, April 23, 1913; d. Colmar, France, Dec. 15, 1998. In 1927 he went to Berlin, where he studied with Gmeindl and Zemlinsky at the Hochschule für Musik. Compelled to leave Germany in 1933, he went to Rome, where he took lessons in advanced composition with Respighi and Casella, and in conducting with Molinari. In 1938 he moved to Belgium and later to southern France, where he remained until 1946; he then emigrated to the United States, becoming a naturalized American citizen in 1951. He married the French singer Marguerite Fricker in 1946. He held a Guggenheim fellowship twice (1956, 1958). He taught at the Berkshire Music Center in Tanglewood (summers 1948–51) and at Brooklyn (1954–61) and City (1962–80) Colleges of the City Univ. of N.Y. He publ. a monograph on Schoenberg (Berlin, 1967) and *Der echte judische Witz* (Berlin, 1971). His music is imbued with expansive emotionalism akin to that of Mahler; in his works for the theater, there is a marked influence of the tradition of 19th-century grand opera. His technical idiom was modern, enlivened by a liberal infusion of euphonious dissonance, and he often applied the rigorous and vigorous devices of linear counterpoint.

WORKS: DRAMATIC: OPERAS: *Simoon* (1948; Tanglewood, Aug. 2, 1950); *The Barrier*, after Langston Hughes (1949; N.Y., Jan. 18, 1950); *Eastward in Eden*, later renamed *Emily Dickinson* (Detroit, Nov. 16, 1951); *Bad Boys in School* (Tanglewood, Aug. 17, 1953); *Esther*, after Langston Hughes (Urbana, Ill., May 17, 1957); *Port Town*, after Langston Hughes (Tanglewood, Aug. 4, 1960); *Godfather Death* (N.Y., June 2, 1961); *Die Doppelgängerin*, after Gerhart Hauptmann, later renamed *Winterballade* (1966; Hannover, Jan. 29, 1967).

Meyrowitz, Selmar, German conductor; b. Bartenstein, April 18, 1875; d. Toulouse, March 24, 1941. He studied at the Leipzig Cons., and later with Max Bruch in Berlin. In 1897 he became assistant conductor at the Karlsruhe Opera under Mottl, with whom he went to America as conductor at the Metropolitan Opera in New York (1903); he subsequently conducted at the Prague National Theater (1905–06), the Berlin Komische Oper (1907–10), the Munich Opera (1912–13), and the Hamburg Opera (1913–17). After appearing as a guest conductor with the Berlin Phil., he conducted at the Berlin Radio and the State Opera (1924–33); also toured with the German Grand Opera Co. in the United States (1929–31); settled in France (1933).

Mézeray, Louis (-Charles-Lazare-Costard) de, French baritone, conductor, and composer; b. Braunschweig, Nov. 25, 1810; d. Asnières, near Paris, April 1887. As a young man, he conducted theater orchs. in Strasbourg and elsewhere. At 17 he obtained the post of conductor at the Liège Theater, and at 20 he became conductor at the Court Theater in The Hague, where he brought out his heroic opera *Guillaume de Nassau*; subsequently he studied with Reicha in Paris. He again traveled as a theater conductor in France, and also appeared as a baritone. Finally, in 1843, he became chief conductor at the Grand Théâtre in Bordeaux, and brought the standard of performance there to a very high level.

Miča, František Adam, Moravian composer; b. Jaroměřice nad Rokytnou, Jan. 11, 1746; d. Lemberg, March 19, 1811. He studied law in Vienna, where he was active in government service. As a composer, he won the esteem of Emperor Joseph II and Mozart. His works include the Singspiel *Adrast und Isidore, oder Die Nachtmusik* (Vienna, April 26, 1781).

Michaelides, Solon, Greek conductor, musicologist, and composer; b. Nicosia, Nov. 25, 1905; d. Athens, Sept. 9, 1979. He studied at London's Trinity College of Music (1927–30) before pursuing his training in Paris with Boulanger (harmony, counterpoint, and fugue) and Maize and Cortot (piano) at the École Normale de Musique (1930–34), and with Labey (conducting) and Lioncourt (composition) at the Schola Cantorum. In 1934 he founded the Limassol Cons. in Cyprus, for which he served as director until 1956. He also taught music at its Lanitis Communal High School (1941–56). From 1957 to 1970 he was director of the Salonica State Cons. He also was director-general and principal conductor of the Salonica State Orch. from 1959 to 1970. As a guest conductor, he appeared in Europe and the United States. Among his compositions were *Nausicaa*, ballet (1950), *Ulysses*, opera (1951; rev. 1972–73), and incidental music for Greek tragedies.

WRITINGS: *Synchroni angliki moussiki* (Modern English Music; Nicosia, 1939); *I kypriaki laiki moussiki* (Cypriot Folk Music; Nicosia, 1944; 2d ed., 1956); *Harmonia tis synchronis moussikis* (Harmony of Contemporary Music; Limassol, 1945); *The Neo-Hellenic Folk-Music* (Limassol, 1948); *I neo-elleniki moussiki* (Neo-Hellenic Music; Nicosia, 1952); *The Music of Ancient Greece: An Encyclopedia* (London, 1978).

Michaels-Moore, Anthony, English baritone; b. Essex, April 8, 1957. He studied with Denis Matthews at the Univ. of Newcastle (B.A., 1978), at the Royal Scottish Academy of Music and Drama in Glasgow, and with Eduardo Asquez and Neilson-Taylor. After winning the Pavarotti Competition in 1985, he appeared with Opera North in Leeds in 1986. In 1987 he made his debut at London's Covent Garden in *Jenůfa* and at the English National Opera in London as Zurga in *Les Pêcheurs de perles*. He made his U.S. debut with the Opera Co. of Philadelphia in 1989 as Guglielmo. In 1992 he created the role of Don Fernando in the stage premiere of Gerhard's *The Duenna* in Madrid. Following an engagement as Posa with Opera North in 1993, he sang Licinius in *La Vestale* at Milan's La Scala that year. In 1994 he was engaged as Figaro at the Vienna State Opera and as Sharpless at the Opéra de la Bastille in Paris. In 1995 he sang Simon Boccanegra at Covent Garden. He made his Metropolitan Opera debut in New York as Marcello on Dec. 28, 1996. In 1997 he portrayed Macbeth at Covent Garden. In 1999 he sang Enrico in *Lucia di Lammermoor* at the Metropolitan Opera. Among his other roles are Escamillo, Hamlet, Falke, Belcore, Lescaut, Onegin, and Scarpia.

Michalsky, Donal, American composer and teacher; b. Pasadena, Calif., July 13, 1928; d. in a fire at his home in Newport Beach, Calif., Dec. 31, 1975. After clarinet training in his youth, he studied with Stevens (theory) and Dahl (orchestration) at the Univ. of Southern Calif. at Los Angeles (Ph.D., 1965) and on a Fulbright scholarship with Fortner in Freiburg im Breisgau (1958). From 1960 until his tragic death he was a prof. of composition at Calif. State College in Fullerton. His music was marked by robust dissonant counterpoint, often in dodecaphonic technique, and yet permeated with a lyric and almost Romantic sentiment. Among his works was the opera *Der arme Heinrich*, the unfinished MS of which was destroyed in the fire that took his life.

Micheau, Janine, French soprano; b. Toulouse, April 17, 1914; d. Paris, Oct. 18, 1976. She studied in Toulouse and at the Paris Cons. In 1933 she made her operatic debut in *Louise* at the Paris Opéra Comique, where she was a distinguished member until 1956. In 1937 she made her debut at London's Covent Garden as Micaëla. She made her U.S. debut as Mélisande in San Francisco in 1938, a role she subsequently sang with remarkable success on both sides of the Atlantic. In 1939 she appeared for the first time at the Teatro Colón in Buenos Aires. From 1940 to 1956 she was a member of the Paris Opéra. Among her other esteemed roles were Pamina, Juliet, Violetta, Gilda, Zerbinetta, Sophie, and Anne Trulove.

Michel, Paul-Baudouin, Belgian composer; b. Haine-St.-Pierre, Sept. 7, 1930. He studied humanities at the Mons Cons., then took courses in composition with Absil at the Queen Elisabeth Music Chapel in Brussels (1959–62) and in conducting at the Royal Cons. in Brussels; attended summer courses in Darmstadt with Ligeti, Boulez, Maderna, and Messiaen. He was later appointed director of the Academy of Music in Woluwe-St.-Lambert. His music adheres to the doctrine of precisely planned structural formations in a highly modern idiom. Among his works is the ballet *Pandora* (1961) and the opera *Jeanne la Folle* (1983–87).

Micheletti, Gaston, French tenor; b. Tavaco, Corsica, Jan. 5, 1892; d. Ajaccio, May 21, 1959. He was a student at the Paris Cons. In 1922 he made his operatic debut as Gounod's Faust in Rheims. In 1925 he became a member of the Paris Opéra Comique, where he remained a principal artist for 2 decades. He also made guest appearances in Brussels, Nice, and Monte Carlo. In later years, he was active as a voice teacher in Paris and then in Ajaccio. Among his admired roles were Don José, Des Grieux, and Werther.

Middleton, Robert (Earl), American composer and teacher; b. Diamond, Ohio, Nov. 18, 1920. He was educated at Harvard Univ. (B.A., 1948; M.A., 1954); he also studied composition with Boulanger at the Longy School of Music (1941–42) and piano with Beveridge Webster at the New England Cons. of Music in Boston (1941–42) and with K. U. Schnabel (1946–49). While holding the John Knowles Paine Traveling Fellowship from Harvard Univ. (1948–50), he pursued his composition studies with Boulanger in Paris. In 1965–66 he held a Guggenheim fellowship. After teaching at Harvard Univ. (1950–53), he joined the faculty of Vassar College in 1953, where he was a prof. from 1966 to 1985 and chairman of the music dept. from 1973 to 1976. He publ. *Harmony in Modern Counterpoint* (Boston, 1967). He displayed a deft handling of genres and forms throughout his basically conservative course as a composer. Among his works are the operas *Life Goes to a Party* (1947; Tanglewood, Aug. 12, 1948) and *The Nightingale is Guilty* (1953; Boston, March 1954) and the opera concerto *Command Performance* (1958–60; rev. 1987–88).

Mielke, Antonia, German soprano; b. Berlin, c.1852; d. there, Nov. 15, 1907. At first she sang chiefly coloratura roles, but gradually assumed the great dramatic parts, for which she was particularly gifted. She sang the Wagner heroines at the Metropolitan Opera in New York during the season of 1890–91 (succeeding Lilli Lehmann); she also toured the United States in concert recitals. Returning to Germany, she continued her operatic career until 1902, when she settled in Berlin as a teacher.

Miereanu, Costin, Romanian-born French composer and teacher; b. Bucharest, Feb. 27, 1943. He studied in Bucharest at the School of Music (B.M., 1960) and the Cons. (M.F.A., 1966), and then attended the summer courses in new music given by Stockhausen, Ligeti, and Karkoschka in Darmstadt (1967–68). In 1968 he settled in France and in 1977 became a naturalized French citizen. He pursued training in musical semiotics at the École des Hautes Études en Sciences Sociales in Paris (D.M.A., 1978) and in the liberal arts at the Univ. of Paris (Ph.D., 1979). In 1978 he joined the faculty of the Univ. of Paris. He also was associated with Editions Salabert (from 1981), and taught at the Sorbonne in Paris (from 1982) and at the summer courses in new music in Darmstadt (from 1982). His music represents a totality of the cosmopolitan avant-garde: semiotics, structuralism, serialism, electronic sound, aleatory, musical-verbal theater, etc. He composed *L'Avenir est dans les oeufs*, opera (1980), *La Porte du paradis*, lyric fantasy (1989–91), and film scores.

Migenes-Johnson, Julia, American soprano; b. N.Y., March 13, 1945. She studied at the High School of Music and Art in New York, and while still a student sang in a televised concert performance of Copland's *The 2nd Hurricane* under Bernstein's direction; she then appeared in *West Side Story* and *Fiddler on the Roof* on Broadway. On Sept. 29, 1965, she made her operatic debut at the N.Y. City Opera as Annina in *The Saint of Bleecker Street*, then pursued training in Vienna, where she sang at the Volksoper; she also studied with Gisela Ultmann in Cologne. In 1978 she made her first appearance at the San Francisco Opera as Musetta. Her Metropolitan Opera debut in New York took place on Dec. 10, 1979, as Jenny in *The Rise and Fall of the City of Mahagonny*. In 1983 she sang with the Vienna State Opera. She gained international acclaim for her sultry portrayal of Carmen in Francesco Rosi's film version of Bizet's opera in 1984. In 1985 she returned to the Metropolitan Opera as Berg's Lulu. She won accolades for her compelling performances as Strauss's Salome.

Mignone, Francisco (Paulo), eminent Brazilian composer and pedagogue; b. São Paulo, Sept. 3, 1897; d. Rio de Janeiro, Feb. 20, 1986. He studied with his father; then took courses in piano, flute, and composition at the São Paulo Cons. (graduated, 1917), then studied with Ferroni at the Milan Cons. (1920). Returning to Brazil, he taught at the São Paulo Cons. (1929–33); he was appointed to the faculty of the Escola Nacional de Música in Rio de Janeiro (1933), and taught there until 1967. His music shows the influence of the modern Italian school of composition; his piano pieces are of virtuoso character; his orchestration shows consummate skill. In many of his works he employs indigenous Brazilian motifs, investing them in sonorous modernistic harmonies not without a liberal application of euphonious dissonances.

WORKS: DRAMATIC: OPERAS: *O Contractador dos diamantes* (Rio de Janeiro, Sept. 20, 1924); *O inocente* (Rio de Janeiro, Sept. 5, 1928); *O Chalaca* (1972). OPERETTA: *Mizú* (1937). BALLETS: *Maracatú de Chico-Rei* (Rio de Janeiro, Oct. 29, 1934); *Quadros amazónicos* (Rio de Janeiro, July 15, 1949); *O guarda chuva* (São Paulo, 1954).

BIBL.: B. Kiefer, *F. M.* (Porto Alegre, 1984).

Migot, Georges, significant French composer; b. Paris, Feb. 27, 1891; d. Levallois, near Paris, Jan. 5, 1976. He began taking piano lessons at the age of 6 and entered the Paris Cons. in 1909; after preliminary courses in harmony, he studied composition with Widor, counterpoint with Gédalge, and music history with Emmanuel, then orchestration with d'Indy and organ with Gigout and Guilmant. Before completing his studies at the Paris Cons., he was mobilized into the French army, was wounded at Longuyon in 1914, and was released from military service. In 1917 he presented in Paris a concert of his own works; received the Lily Boulanger Prize in 1918. He competed twice for the Prix de Rome in 1919 and 1920, but failed to win and abandoned further attempts to capture it. In the meantime, he engaged in a serious study of painting; in fact, he was more successful as a painter than as a composer in the early years of his career; he exhibited his paintings in Paris art galleries in 1917, 1919, 1923, and subsequent years. He also wrote poetry; virtually all of his vocal works are written to his own words. In his musical compositions, he endeavored to recapture the spirit of early French polyphony, thus emphasizing the continuity of national art in history. His melodic writing is modal, often with archaic inflections, while his harmonic idiom is diatonically translucid; he obtains subtle coloristic effects through unusual instrumental registration. Profoundly interested in the preservation and classification of early musical instruments, he served as curator of the Instrumental Museum of the Paris Cons. (1949–61). He wrote *Essais pour une esthétique générale* (Paris, 1920; 2d ed., 1937); *Appoggiatures résolues et non résolues* (Paris, 1922–31); *Jean-Philippe Rameau et le génie de la musique française* (Paris, 1930); *Lexique de quelques termes utilisés en musique* (Paris, 1947); 2 vols. of poems (Paris, 1950, 1951); *Matériaux et inscriptions* (Toulouse, 1970); *Kaléidoscope et miroirs ou les images multipliées et contraires* (autobiography; Toulouse, 1970).

WORKS: DRAMATIC: *Hagoromo*, symphonie lyrique et chorégraphique (Monte Carlo, May 9, 1922); *Le Rossignol en amour*, chamber opera (1926–28; Geneva, March 2, 1937); *Cantate d'amour*, concert opera (1949–50); *La Sulamite*, concert opera (1969–70); *L'Arche*, polyphonie spatiale (1971; Marseilles, May 3,

1974). ORATORIOS: *La Passion* (1939–46; Paris, July 25, 1957); *L'Annonciation* (1943–46); *La Mise au tombeau* (1948–49); *La Résurrection* (1953; Strasbourg, March 28, 1969).

BIBL.: L. Vallas, *G. M.* (Paris, 1923); P. Wolff, *La Route d'un musicien: G. M.* (Paris, 1933); M. Pinchard, *Connaissance de G. M., musicien français* (Paris, 1959); M. Honegger, ed., *Catalogue des oeuvres musicales de G. M.* (Strasbourg, 1977); C. Latham, ed. and tr., *G. M.: The Man and His Work* (Strasbourg, 1982).

Miguez, Leopoldo (Américo), Brazilian conductor and composer; b. Rio de Janeiro, Sept. 9, 1850; d. there, July 6, 1902. He studied with Nicolau Ribas in Oporto, Portugal, then was active with a publishing firm and as a conductor in Rio de Janeiro, where he championed the cause of Wagner. He was director of the Instituto Nacional de Música there (1890–1902). He pursued Wagnerian ideas in his theater works, which included the operas *Pele amor!* (Rio de Janeiro, 1897) and *Os Saldunes* (Rio de Janeiro, Sept. 20, 1901).

Mihalovich, Edmund von (Ödön Péter József de), Hungarian composer; b. Fericsancze, Sept. 13, 1842; d. Budapest, April 22, 1929. He studied with Mosonyi in Pest and with Hauptmann in Leipzig, and also took lessons with Peter Cornelius in Munich. From 1887 to 1919 he taught at the Academy of Music in Budapest. Although he remained wholly committed to the German school of composition throughout his life, he did support the efforts of Bartók, Kodály, and Weiner in their search for a distinct national school. His works include the operas *Hagbart und Signe* (1867–74; Dresden, March 12, 1882), *Wieland der Schmied* (1876–78), *König Fjalar* (1880–84; unfinished), *Eleane* (1885–87; Budapest, Feb. 16, 1908), *Toldi szerelme* (Toldi's Love; 1880–90; Budapest, March 18, 1893; rev. 1893–94; Budapest, Feb. 28, 1895), and *A tihanyi visszhang* (The Echo of Tichany; 1903; unfinished).

Mihalovici, Marcel, significant Romanian-born French composer; b. Bucharest, Oct. 22, 1898; d. Paris, Aug. 12, 1985. After studies with Bernfeld (violin), Cuclin (harmony), and Cremer (counterpoint) in Bucharest (1908–19), he settled in Paris and completed his training with d'Indy (composition), Saint Requier (harmony), Gastoué (Gregorian chant), and Lejeune (violin) at the Schola Cantorum (1919–25). With Martinů, Conrad Beck, and Harsányi, he founded the "École de Paris" of emigrants. In 1932 he helped to organize the contemporary music society Triton. He became a naturalized French citizen in 1955. In 1964 he was elected a member of the Institut de France. His wife was **Monique Haas**. Mihalovici's music presents a felicitous synthesis of French and Eastern European elements, tinted with a roseate impressionistic patina and couched in euphoniously dissonant harmonies.

WORKS: DRAMATIC: OPERAS: *L'Intransigeant Pluton* (1928; Paris, April 3, 1939); *Phèdre* (1949; Stuttgart, June 9, 1951); *Die Heimkehr* (Frankfurt am Main, June 17, 1954); *Krapp ou La Dernière Bande*, after Samuel Beckett (1959–60; Bielefeld, Feb. 25, 1961); *Les Jumeaux*, opera buffa (1962; Braunschweig, Jan. 23, 1963). BALLETS: *Une Vie de Polichinelle* (1923); *Le Postillon du Roy* (1924); *Divertimento* (1925); *Karagueuz*, marionette ballet (1926); *Thésée au labyrinthe* (1956; Braunschweig, April 4, 1957; rev. version as *Scènes de Thésée*, Cologne, Oct. 15, 1958); *Alternamenti* (1957; Braunschweig, Feb. 28, 1958); *Variations* (Bielefeld, March 28, 1960). Also incidental music for plays.

BIBL.: G. Beck, *M. M.: Esquisse biographique* (Paris, 1954).

Mihály, András, Hungarian composer, conductor, administrator, and teacher; b. Budapest, Nov. 6, 1917; d. there, Sept. 19, 1993. He was a student of Adolf Schiffer (cello) and of Leó Weiner and Imre Waldbauer (chamber music) at the Budapest Academy of Music. He also received private instruction in composition from Pál Kadosa and István Strasser. After playing 1st cello in the orch. of the Budapest Opera (1946–48), he was general secretary of the Opera (1948–50). From 1950 to 1978 he taught chamber music at the Budapest Academy of Music. He also was a music reader with the Hungarian Radio (1962–78). From 1978 to 1986 he was director of the Hungarian State Opera in Budapest, and then of the student orch. at the Budapest Academy of Music (from 1986). In 1952, 1954, and 1964 he received the Erkel Prize, and in 1955 was awarded the Kossuth Prize. He was made a Merited Artist (1969) and an Outstanding Artist (1974) by the Hungarian government. Among his works was the opera *Együtt és egyedül* (Together and Alone; 1964–65; Budapest, Nov. 5, 1966); also incidental music for plays and films.

BIBL.: J. Kárpáti, *M. A.* (Budapest, 1965).

Mikhailova, Maria (Alexandrovna), Russian soprano; b. Kharkov, June 3, 1866; d. Moscow, Jan. 18, 1943. She studied in St. Petersburg, and then in Paris and Milan. In 1892 she made her debut at the Imperial Opera in St. Petersburg as Marguerite de Valois in *Les Huguenots*; she remained a member there until 1912. On Oct. 29, 1895, she created the role of Electra in Taneyev's *Oresteia*. She visited Tokyo in 1907. She made over 300 recordings, achieving a considerable reputation through the gramophone alone.

Mikhailovich, Maxim (Dormidontovich), Russian bass; b. Koltsovka, near Kazan, Aug. 25, 1893; d. Moscow, March 30, 1971. He studied in Kazan with Oshustovich and in Moscow with Osipov. After appearing as a soloist with Moscow's All-Union Radio (1930–32), he sang with Moscow's Bolshoi Theater (from 1932). He was admired for his many portrayals in Russian operas. In 1940 he was made a People's Artist of the USSR.

BIBL.: V. Endrzheyevsky and E. Osipov, *M. M.* (Moscow, 1957).

Miki, Minoru, Japanese composer; b. Tokushima, March 16, 1930. He studied with Ifukube and Ikenouchi at the National Univ. of Fine Arts and Music in Tokyo (1951–55). He was a founder of the Nihon Ongaku Shūdan (Pro Musica Nipponia; 1964), an ensemble dedicated to performing new music for traditional Japanese instruments; he later served as its artistic director. He lectured at the Tokyo College of Music; was founder-director of UTAYOMI-ZA (1986), a musical opera theater.

WORKS: DRAMATIC: OPERAS: *Mendori Teishu* (A Henpecked Husband), chamber opera (1963); *Shunkin-shō* (Tokyo, 1975); *An Actor's Revenge* (London, 1979); *Toge no muko ni naniga aruka*, choral opera (1983); *Utayomizaru*, musical opera (1983); *Joruri* (St. Louis, 1985); *At the Flower Garden*, mini-opera (1985); *Wakahime* (1991); *Orochi-den* (1992); *Shizuka and Yoshitsume* (1993). CHAMBER MUSICAL: *Yomigaeru* (1992). BALLET: *From the Land of Light* (1987).

Miksch, Johann Aloys, esteemed Bohemian baritone and teacher; b. Georgental, July 19, 1765; d. Dresden, Sept. 24, 1845. He was a choirboy in Dresden, then a singer at the Court Church (from 1786); he was a baritone in the Italian Opera of Dresden (from 1797). He was chorus master of the German Opera (from 1820), being pensioned in 1831. He was greatly renowned as a teacher, numbering among his pupils Schröder-Devrient.

BIBL.: A. Kohut, *J. M.* (Leipzig, 1890).

Mila, Massimo, Italian writer on music; b. Turin, Aug. 14, 1910; d. there, Dec. 26, 1988. He studied literature at the Univ. of Turin; after graduation, he became a regular contributor to many Italian musical publications; he was music critic of *L'Espresso* (1955–68) and of *La Stampa* (1968–74). He taught music history at the Turin Cons. (1953–73) and at the Univ. of Turin (from 1960). Among his writings was *Il melodramma di Verdi* (Bari, 1933), *W. A. Mozart* (Turin, 1945), *"I vespri siciliani" di Verdi* (Turin, 1973), and *Lettura del Don Giovanni di Mozart* (Turin, 1988).

BIBL.: G. Pestelli, ed., *Il melodramma italiano dell'ottocento: Studi e ricerche per M. M.* (Turin, 1977).

Milanov, Zinka (née **Kunc**), famous Croatian-American soprano; b. Zagreb, May 17, 1906; d. N.Y., May 30, 1989. She studied at the Zagreb Academy of Music, then with Milka Ternina, Maria Kostrenčić, and Fernando Carpi. She made her debut as Leonora in *Il Trovatore* in Ljubljana (1927); subsequently she was principal soprano of the Zagreb Opera (1928–35), where she sang in over

300 performances in Croatian. After appearing at Prague's German Theater (1936), she was invited by Toscanini to sing in his performance of the Verdi *Requiem* at the Salzburg Festival (1937). She then made her Metropolitan Opera debut in New York as Verdi's Leonora on Dec. 17, 1937; she was one of the outstanding members on its roster (1937–41; 1942–47; 1950–66); she gave her farewell performance there as Maddalena in *Andrea Chénier* on April 13, 1966. In addition to appearing in San Francisco and Chicago, she also sang at Buenos Aires's Teatro Colón (1940–42), Milan's La Scala (1950), and London's Covent Garden (1966–67). Her brother was **Božidar Kunc**. She married Predrag Milanov in 1937, but they were divorced in 1946; she then married Ljubomir Ilic in 1947. Blessed with a voice of translucent beauty, she became celebrated for her outstanding performances of roles in operas by Verdi and Puccini.

Milde, Hans Feodor von, Austrian baritone; b. Petronell, April 13, 1821; d. Weimar, Dec. 10, 1899. He studied with F. Hauser and M. García. He was a life member of the Weimar Court Opera, and created the role of Telramund in *Lohengrin* (1850). His wife, Rosa Agthé Milde (b. Weimar, June 25, 1827; d. there, Jan. 26, 1906), also sang in Weimar (1845–67), where she created the role of Elsa in *Lohengrin*.

BIBL.: N. von Milde, *P. Cornelius. Briefe . . . an F. und R. v.M.* (Weimar, 1901).

Mildenberg, Albert, American composer; b. Brooklyn, Jan. 13, 1878; d. there (N.Y.), July 3, 1918. He was a member of a musical family. He studied piano with his mother, then took lessons with Rafael Joseffy (piano) and Bruno Oscar Klein (composition). In 1905 he went to Rome, where he studied with Sgambati; later he studied in Paris with Massenet. Returning to America, he became dean of the music dept. of Meredith College in Raleigh, N.C. He wrote a number of songs, many of them to his own texts and also wrote his own opera librettos. His style was in the Italian tradition; Massenet commended his gift of melody. His light opera *The Wood Witch* was produced in New York on May 25, 1903; another comic opera, *Love's Locksmith*, was given in New York in 1912.

Milder-Hauptmann, (Pauline) Anna, prominent German soprano; b. Constantinople, Dec. 13, 1785; d. Berlin, May 29, 1838. She was the daughter of an Austrian diplomatic official. In Vienna she attracted the notice of Schikaneder. He recommended her to Tomaselli and Salieri, who taught her opera singing. She made her debut as Juno in Süssmayr's *Der Spiegel von Arkadien* in Vienna on April 9, 1803, and soon became so well regarded as an artist and singer that Beethoven wrote the role of Fidelio for her (Vienna, Nov. 20, 1805). After a tour in 1808 she was made prima donna assoluta at the Berlin court. In 1810 she married a Vienna merchant, Hauptmann. In 1812 she went to Berlin, where she created a sensation, particularly as Gluck's heroines (in *Iphigénie en Tauride, Alcestis*, and *Armida*). She left Berlin in 1829, then sang in Russia, Sweden, and Austria. Mendelssohn chose her as a soloist in his revival of Bach's St. Matthew Passion in Berlin (1829). She made her farewell appearance in Vienna in 1836. Her voice was so powerful that Haydn reportedly said to her: "Dear child, you have a voice like a house."

Mildmay, (Grace) Audrey (Louise St. John), English soprano; b. Herstmonceux, Dec. 19, 1900; d. London, May 31, 1953. She studied in London with Johnstone Douglas and in Vienna with Jani Strasser. In 1927–28 she toured North America as Polly Peachum in *The Beggar's Opera*, and then returned to England as a member of the Carlo Rosa Opera Co. (1928–31). In 1931 she married John Christie, with whom she helped to found the Glyndebourne Festival in 1934. She sang there from 1934 to 1936 and again in 1938–39. In 1939 she appeared at the Sadler's Wells Theatre in London. She retired from the operatic stage in 1943. Mildmay was cofounder of the Edinburgh Festival with Rudolf Bing in 1947. Her finest roles were Susanna, Zerlina, and Norina.

Miles, Philip Napier, English composer and conductor; b. Shirehampton, Jan. 21, 1865; d. King's Weston, near Bristol, July 19, 1935. He studied in London with Parry and Dannreuther. He organized the Shirehampton Choral Soc. on his own estate and conducted festivals in various localities in England. He wrote the operas *Westward Ho!* (London, Dec. 4, 1914), *Fire Flies* (Clifton, Oct. 13, 1924; on the same program with his opera *Markheim*), *Good Friday, Demeter*, and *Queen Rosamond*.

Miletić, Miroslav, Croatian violinist and composer; b. Sisak, Aug. 22, 1925. He studied in Zagreb, where he organized the renowned Pro Arte String Quartet, specializing in performances of modern music. His works include the operas *Hasanaginica* and *Der Fall Ruženka*; also *Auvergnanski Senatori*, radio opera (1957), and *Vision,* television ballet (1958).

Milford, Robin (Humphrey), English composer and teacher; b. Oxford, Jan. 22, 1903; d. Lyme Regis, Dec. 29, 1959. He was a student of Holst, Vaughan Williams, and R. O. Morris at the Royal College of Music in London. Thereafter he was active as a composer and teacher. He was best known for his chamber music, choral pieces, and songs. He also composed an opera, *The Scarlet Letter* (1959), a ballet, *The Snow Queen* (1946), and the oratorio *The Pilgrim's Progress* (1932).

BIBL.: I. Copley, *R. M.* (London, 1985).

Milhaud, Darius, eminent French composer; b. Aix-en-Provence, Sept. 4, 1892; d. Geneva, June 22, 1974. He was the descendant of an old Jewish family, settled in Provence for many centuries. His father was a merchant of almonds; there was a piano in the house, and Milhaud improvised melodies as a child; he then began to take violin lessons. He entered the Paris Cons. in 1909, almost at the age limit for enrollment; he studied with Berthelier (violin), Lefèvre (ensemble), Leroux (harmony), Gédalge (counterpoint), Widor (composition and fugue), and d'Indy (conducting); he played violin in the student orch. under Dukas. He received 1st "accessit" in violin and counterpoint, and 2d in fugue; won the Prix Lepaulle for composition. While still a student, he wrote music in a bold modernistic manner; became associated with Satie, Cocteau, and Claudel. When Claudel was appointed French minister to Brazil, he engaged Milhaud as his secretary; they sailed for Rio de Janeiro early in 1917; he returned to Paris (via the West Indies and N.Y.) shortly after the armistice of Nov. 1918. Milhaud's name became known to a larger public as a result of a newspaper article by Henri Collet in *Comoedia* (Jan. 16, 1920), grouping him with 5 other French composers of modern tendencies (Auric, Durey, Honegger, Poulenc, and Tailleferre) under the sobriquet Les Six, even though the association was stylistically fortuitous. In 1922 he visited the United States; he lectured at Harvard Univ., Princeton Univ., and Columbia Univ.; appeared as pianist and composer in his own works; in 1925 he traveled in Italy, Germany, Austria, and Russia; returning to France, he devoted himself mainly to composition and teaching. At the outbreak of World War II in 1939, he was in Aix-en-Provence; in July 1940 he went to the United States; he taught at Mills College in Oakland, Calif. In 1947 he returned to France; was appointed prof. at the Paris Cons., but continued to visit the United States as conductor and teacher almost annually, despite arthritis, which compelled him to conduct while seated; he retained his post at Mills College until 1971, then settled in Geneva. Exceptionally prolific from his student days, he wrote a great number of works in every genre; he introduced a modernistic type of music drama, "opéra à la minute," and also the "miniature symphony." He experimented with new stage techniques, incorporating cinematic interludes and also successfully revived the Greek type of tragedy with vocal accompaniment. He composed works for electronic instruments, and demonstrated his contrapuntal skill in such compositions as his 2 String Quartets (No. 14 and No. 15), which can be played together as a string octet. He was the first to exploit polytonality in a consistent and deliberate manner; applied the exotic rhythms of Latin America and the West Indies in many of his lighter works; of these, his *Saudades do Brasil* are particularly popular; Brazilian movements are also found in his *Scaramouche* and *Le Boeuf sur le toit*; in some of his works he drew upon the resources of jazz. His ballet *La Création du monde* (1923), portraying the Creation in terms of Negro cosmology, constitutes the earliest example of the use of the blues and jazz in a symphonic score, anticipating Gershwin in this respect. Despite this variety of means and versatility of forms, Milhaud succeeded in establishing a style that was distinctly and identifiably his own; his melodies are nostalgically lyrical or vivaciously rhythmical, according to mood; his instrumental writing is of great complexity and difficulty, and yet entirely within the capacities of modern virtuoso technique; he arranged many of his works in several versions.

WORKS: DRAMATIC: OPERAS: *La Brebis égarée*, "roman musical" (1910–15; Paris, Dec. 10, 1923); *Le Pauvre Matelot*, "complainte en trois actes" (1926; Paris, Dec. 12, 1927); *Les Malheurs d'Orphée* (Brussels, May 7, 1926); *Esther de Carpentras*, opéra bouffe (1925; Paris, Feb. 1, 1938); 3 "minute operas": *L'Enlèvement d'Europe* (Baden-Baden, July 17, 1927), *L'Abandon d'Ariane*, and *La Délivrance de Thésée* (Wiesbaden, April 20, 1928); *Christophe Colomb* (Berlin, May 5, 1930); *Maximilien* (Paris, Jan. 4, 1932); *Médée* (Antwerp, Oct. 7, 1939); *Bolivar* (1943; Paris, May 12, 1950); *Le Jeu de Robin et Marion*, mystery play after Adam de la Halle (Wiesbaden, Oct. 28, 1951); *David* (Jerusalem, June 1, 1954); *La Mère coupable*, to a libretto by Madeleine Milhaud, after Beaumarchais (Geneva, June 13, 1966); *Saint Louis, Roi de France*, opera oratorio (1970–71; Rio de Janeiro, April 14, 1972). INCIDENTAL MUSIC: *Agamemnon* (1913; Paris, April 16, 1927); *Les Choéphores* (concert version, Paris, June 15, 1919; stage version, Brussels, March 27, 1935); *Les Euménides* (1922; Antwerp, Nov. 27, 1927); *Jeux d'enfants*, 3 children's plays: *A propos de bottes* (1932), *Un Petit Peu de musique* (1933), and *Un Petit Peu d'exercise* (1937). BALLETS: *L'Homme et son désir* (Paris, June 6, 1921); *Le Boeuf sur le toit* (Paris, Feb. 21, 1920); *Les Mariés de la Tour Eiffel* (Paris, June 19, 1921; in collaboration with Honegger, Auric, Poulenc, and Tailleferre); *La Création du monde* (Paris, Oct. 25, 1923); *Salade*, "ballet chanté" (Paris, May 17, 1924); *Le Train bleu*, "danced operetta" (Paris, June 20, 1924); *Polka* for the ballet *L'Éventail de Jeanne*, in homage to the music patroness Jeanne Dubost (Paris, June 16, 1927; in collaboration with Ravel, Ibert, Roussel et al.); *Jeux de printemps* (Washington, D.C., Oct. 30, 1944); *The Bells*, after Poe (Chicago, April 26, 1946); *'adame Miroir* (Paris, May 31, 1948); *Vendange* (1952; Nice, April 17, 1972); *La Rose des vents* (1958); *La Branche des oiseaux* (1965).

WRITINGS: *Études* (essays; Paris, 1926); *Notes sans musique* (autobiography; Paris, 1949; Eng. tr., London, 1952, as *Notes without Music*); *Entretiens avec Claude Rostand* (Paris, 1952); *Ma vie heureuse* (Paris, 1973).

BIBL.: G. Augsbourg, *La Vie de D. M. en images* (Paris, 1935); G. Beck, *D. M.: Étude suivie du catalogue chronologique complet* (Paris, 1949; supplement, 1957); J. Roy, *D. M.* (Paris, 1968); A. Braga, *D. M.* (Naples, 1969); C. Palmer, *M.* (London, 1976); P. Collaer, *D. M.* (Geneva and Paris, 1982; Eng. tr., 1988); F. Bloch, *D. M., 1892–1974* (Paris, 1992); A. Lunel, *Mon ami D. M.: Inédits* (Aix-en-Provence, 1992); H. Malcomess, *Die opéras minute von D. M.* (Bonn, 1993); J. Roy, *Le groupe des six: Poulenc, M., Honegger, Auric, Tailleferre, Durey* (Paris, 1994).

Millard, Harrison, American composer; b. Boston, Nov. 27, 1829; d. there, Sept. 10, 1895. He sang in the chorus of the Handel and Haydn Soc. as a child, then went to Italy to study voice. He was a concert tenor for several years, and made tours in England with the Irish soprano Catherine Hayes. Returning to America in 1854, he became a vocal instructor, first in Boston, then (from 1856) in New York. He publ. about 350 songs as well as an opera, *Deborah*, to an Italian libretto (not perf.). He also set to music *Uncle Tom's Cabin* by Harriet Beecher Stowe.

Miller, Jonathan (Wolfe), English opera director; b. London, July 21, 1934. He studied the natural sciences at St. John's College, Cambridge, taking his M.D. degree in 1959. However, his abiding interest in the arts led him to pursue work in television and the theater. Turning to opera direction, he attracted notice with his staging of Alexander Goehr's *Arden Must Die* with the New Opera Co. in 1974. From 1974 to 1981 he was an opera director with the Kent Opera, where his stagings of *Così fan tutte, Orfeo, Falstaff*, and *Evgeny Onegin* were highly praised; he also worked regularly with the English National Opera in London, winning special acclaim for his stagings of *Rigoletto* (1982) and *The Mikado* (1986). In 1991 he staged *Le nozze di Figaro* at the Vienna Festival and *Káťa Kabanová* at the Metropolitan Opera in New York. His *Manon Lescaut* was produced at Milan's La Scala in 1992. He mounted *Così fan tutte* at London's Covent Garden in 1995. In 1997 he staged *Ariadne auf Naxos* in Florence.

BIBL.: M. Romain, *A Profile of J. M.* (Cambridge, 1992).

Miller, Mildred, American soprano; b. Cleveland, Dec. 16, 1924. Her parents came from Germany; the original family name was Müller. She studied at the Cleveland Inst. of Music (B.M., 1946), then with Sundelius at the New England Cons. of Music in Boston (diploma, 1948). In 1949 she went to Germany; she sang with the Stuttgart Opera and with the Bavarian State Opera in Munich. In 1950 she married the American pilot Wesley W. Posvar. Returning to the United States, she made her debut with the Metropolitan Opera in New York as Cherubino (Nov. 17, 1951); she remained there until 1975 and also appeared widely as a concert singer. She was founder-artistic director of the Pittsburgh Opera Theater (from 1978).

Millico, (Vito) Giuseppe, Italian castrato soprano, singing teacher, and composer; b. Terlizzi, near Bari, Jan. 19, 1737; d. Naples, Oct. 2, 1802. After singing at the St. Petersburg Imperial Court (1758–65), he was active in Italy. He became a friend of Gluck and created the role of Paris in his *Paride ed Elena* (Vienna, Nov. 3, 1770). Following appearances in London (1772–73) and Paris (1774), Millico sang in Zweibrücken and Mannheim. In 1780 he returned to Italy and became virtuoso di camera of the Naples royal chapel. Among his works were several operas and cantatas, as well as many arias, canzonettas, and duets.

BIBL.: M. Belluci La Salandria, *V. G. M.* (Baris, 1951).

Milligan, Harold Vincent, American organist, writer on music, and composer; b. Astoria, Oreg., Oct. 31, 1888; d. N.Y., April 12, 1951. He studied with Carl and Noble. He was a church organist in Portland, Oreg., before going to New York in 1907; he then taught organ at various schools and colleges; he was church organist in New Jersey and New York; he also lectured on American music. He ed. 4 vols. of 18th-century American songs and, with G. Souvaine, *The Opera Quiz Book* (N.Y., 1948) and wrote a biography of Stephen Foster (N.Y., 1920) and *Stories of Famous Operas* (N.Y., 1950; 2d ed., rev., 1955). He composed 2 children's operettas, *The Outlaws of Etiquette* (1914) and *The Laughabet* (1918); incidental music.

Millo, Aprile (Elizabeth), talented American soprano; b. N.Y., April 14, 1958. Her father was a tenor and her mother a soprano; after living in Europe, Millo's family moved to Los Angeles when she was 11; during her high school years, she studied voice with her parents and augmented her training by listening to recordings of the great divas. In 1977 she won 1st place in the San Diego Opera competition, received the Geraldine Farrar Award, and sang in the opening concert of the new opera center there. In 1978 she won 1st prize in the Concorso Internazionale di Voci Verdiane in Busseto and received the Montserrat Caballe Award at the Francisco Vinas competition in Barcelona. In 1981 she sang with the N.Y. City Opera and also joined the Metropolitan Opera's Young Artists Development Program; she later studied with Rita Patane. On Jan. 4, 1983, she made her first appearance at La Scala in Milan as Elvira in *Ernani*, a role she repeated with the Welsh National Opera in 1984. She made her Metropolitan Opera debut in New York as Amelia in *Simon Boccanegra* on Dec. 3, 1984, substituting for the ailing Anna Tomowa-Sintow. In 1985 she received the Richard Tucker Award. Subsequently she appeared at the Metropolitan Opera in such roles as Elisabetta in *Don Carlos*, Liù in *Turandot*, Luisa Miller, Leonora in *Il Trovatore*, Desdemona in *Otello*, and Aida. She also sang in concert performances with the Opera Orch. of N.Y., appearing as Giselda in *I Lombardi alla prima crociata* (1986) and as Lida in *La battaglia di Legnano* (1987). In 1992 she made her San Francisco Opera debut as Maddalena, a role she later sang at the Metropolitan Opera and in Rome in 1996.

Millöcker, Carl, Austrian conductor and composer; b. Vienna, April 29, 1842; d. Baden, near Vienna, Dec. 31, 1899. His father was a jeweler, and Millöcker was destined for that trade, but showed irrepressible musical inclinations and learned music as a child. He played the flute in a theater orch. at 16, and later took courses at the Cons. of the Gesellschaft der Musikfreunde in Vienna. Upon the recommendation of Franz von Suppé, he received a post as theater conductor in Graz (1864). In 1866 he returned to Vienna, and from 1869 to 1883 was 2d conductor of the Theater an der Wien. He suffered a stroke in 1894, which left him partially paralyzed. As a composer, Millocker possessed a natural gift for melodious music; although his popularity was never as great as that of Johann Strauss or Lehár, his operettas captured the spirit of Viennese life.

WORKS: DRAMATIC: OPERETTAS (all 1st perf. in Vienna unless otherwise given): *Der tote Gast* (Graz, Dec. 21, 1865); *Die lustigen Binder* (Graz, Dec. 21, 1865); *Diana* (Jan. 2, 1867); *Die Fraueninsel* (Budapest, 1868); *Drei Paar Schuhe* (Jan. 5, 1871); *Wechselbrief und Briefwechsel, or Ein nagender Wurm* (Aug. 10, 1872); *Ein Abenteuer in Wien* (Jan. 20, 1873); *Das verwunschene Schloss* (March 30, 1878); *Gräfin Dubarry* (Oct. 31, 1879); *Apajune der Wassermann* (Dec. 18, 1880); *Die Jungfrau von Belleville* (Oct. 29, 1881); *Der Bettelstudent* (Dec. 6, 1882; his most successful work; popular also in England and America as *Student Beggar*; N.Y., Oct. 29, 1883); *Gasparone* (Jan. 26, 1884); *Der Feldprediger* (Oct. 31, 1884); *Der Vice-Admiral* (Oct. 9, 1886); *Die sieben Schwaben* (Oct. 29, 1887); *Der arme Jonathan* (Jan. 4, 1890; new version by Hentschke and Rixner, 1939); *Das Sonntagskind* (Jan. 16, 1892); *Der Probekuss* (Dec. 22, 1894); *Nordlicht, oder Der rote Graf* (Dec. 22, 1896).

Mills, Erie, American soprano; b. Granite City, Ill., June 22, 1953. She attended the National Music Camp in Interlochen, Mich., then studied voice with Karl Trump at the College of Wooster, Ohio, with Grace Wilson at the Univ. of Ill., and with Elena Nikolaidi. In 1979 she made her professional operatic debut as Ninette in *The Love for 3 Oranges* at the Chicago Lyric Opera; on Oct. 13, 1982, she made her first appearance with the N.Y. City Opera as Cunegonde in *Candide*, and subsequently sang there regularly; she made her Metropolitan Opera debut in New York as Blondchen in *Die Entführung aus dem Serail* on Nov. 26, 1987. She also made guest appearances with the Cincinnati Opera, Cleveland Opera, San Francisco Opera, Minnesota Opera, Opera Soc. of Washington, D.C., Santa Fe Opera, Houston Grand Opera, Hamburg State Opera, La Scala in Milan, and Vienna State Opera. On March 17, 1989, she made her N.Y. recital debut. On Oct. 5, 1992, she sang Orazio in the U.S. premiere of Handel's *Muzio* in New York. She portrayed Zerlina in Milwaukee in 1996. Among her other prominent roles are Rossini's Rosina, Donizetti's Lucia, Offenbach's Olympia, Johann Strauss's Adele, and Richard Strauss's Zerbinetta.

Milnes, Sherrill (Eustace), distinguished American baritone; b. Downers Grove, Ill., Jan. 10, 1935. He learned to play piano and violin at home, then played tuba in a school band; after a period as a medical student at North Central College in Naperville, Ill., he turned to music; he subsequently studied voice with Andrew White at Drake Univ. in Des Moines and with Hermanus Baer at Northwestern Univ. He sang in choral performances under Margaret Hillis in Chicago, then was a member of the chorus at the Santa Fe Opera, where he received his first opportunity to sing minor operatic roles. In 1960 he joined Boris Goldovsky's Boston opera company and toured widely with it. He met Rosa Ponselle in Baltimore in 1961, and she coached him in several roles; he first appeared with the Baltimore Civic Opera as Gérard in *Andrea Chénier* in 1961. He made his European debut as Figaro in *Il Barbiere di Siviglia* at the Teatro Nuovo in Milan on Sept. 23, 1964, then made his first appearance at the N.Y. City Opera on Oct. 18, 1964, singing the role of Valentin in *Faust*. His Metropolitan Opera debut in New York followed in the same role on Dec. 22, 1965. He rose to a stellar position at the Metropolitan, being acclaimed for both vocal and dramatic abilities; he also sang with other opera houses in the United States and Europe. His notable roles included Don Giovanni, Escamillo, the Count di Luna, Tonio, Iago, Barnaba, Rigoletto, and Scarpia. In later years he became active as a conductor, and also taught at the Yale Univ. School of Music.

Milveden, (Jan) Ingmar (Georg), Swedish composer, organist, and musicologist; b. Göteborg, Feb. 15, 1920. He studied cello and organ, then took a course in composition with Sven Svensson and in musicology with C.A. Moberg at the Univ. of Uppsala (graduated, 1945; Fil.lic., 1951; Ph.D., 1972, with the diss. *Zu den liturgischen "Hystorie" in Schweden. Liturgie- und choralgeschichtliche Untersuchungen*). He was organist at Uppsala's St. Per's Church (1967–78); he lectured at the Univ. of Stockholm (1970–73) and at the Univ. of Uppsala (1972–86). He distinguished himself as a composer of church music, numbering among his works the church opera *Vid en Korsväg* (1971; Lund, Nov. 30, 1974).

Minghetti, Angelo, Italian tenor; b. Bologna, Dec. 6, 1889; d. Milan, Feb. 10, 1957. He began his career in 1911, and then sang in various Italian music centers. After appearing in Rio de Janeiro (1921), he was a member of the Chicago Opera (1922–24). In 1923 he made his debut at Milan's La Scala as Rodolfo, and sang there until 1932. He also was a guest artist at Buenos Aires's Teatro Colón (1924) and London's Covent Garden (1926; 1930; 1933–34).

Mingotti, Pietro, Italian opera impresario; b. Venice, c.1702; d. Copenhagen, April 28, 1759. His brother, Angelo Mingotti (b. c.1700; d. after 1767), was also an opera impresario who organized his opera troupe in Prague about 1732. In the meantime, Pietro founded his own opera troupe and from 1736 to 1740 the two brothers worked together in Graz. During the next 10 years, they continued to work together occasionally but frequently also toured with their own troupes in Germany and Austria. By 1746 **Regina** (née **Valentini**) **Mingotti** had joined Pietro's troupe and was briefly his wife. In 1747 Gluck became his music director, appearing with the troupe in Dresden and Copenhagen, and in 1748 in Hamburg. Pietro settled with his troupe in Copenhagen in 1748 under contract to the Danish court. Sarti became his music director in 1752. The decline in his fortunes compelled Pietro to ask that his contract with the court be dissolved in 1755. He lost everything when the court seized his assets to pay off his debts, and he spent his last days in poverty.

BIBL.: E. Müller, *Die M.schen Opernunternehmungen: 1732 bis 1756* (Leipzig, 1915); idem, *Angelo und P. M.* (Dresden, 1917).

Mingotti, Regina (née **Valentini**), Italian soprano; b. Naples, Feb. 16, 1722; d. Neuburg an der Donau, Oct. 1, 1808. She may have been the sister of the Italian composer Michelangelo Valentini. After training at a convent in Grätz in Silesia, she was a member of **Pietro Mingotti**'s opera troupe by 1746. Her first known appearance with the troupe was in *Il tempio di Melpomene* in Hamburg on Jan. 31, 1747. She married Mingotti, but they soon parted company. In 1747 she so impressed the Saxon court in Dresden that she became a member of the court musical establishment and received training from Porpora. Her rivalry with Bordoni became celebrated. After singing in Naples, Prague, and Madrid (1751–53), she appeared in Paris and London (1754–55). With Giardini, she was comanager of the King's Theatre in London (1756–57; 1763–64). Her feuds with Vaneschi there were also notorious. Mingotti had her greatest success in breeches roles, where her gifts as an actress were put to particularly good use.

Minkowski, Marc, French conductor; b. Paris, Oct. 4, 1962. He was educated at the Royal Cons. of Music at The Hague and at the Monteux conducting school in the United States. In 1984 he founded Les Musiciens du Louvre in Paris, with which he championed early music. In 1991 he conducted Gluck's *Iphigénie en Tauride* at London's Covent Garden. After conducting Lully's *Phaëton* at the Lyons Opera in 1993, he conducted Handel's

Ariodante at the Welsh National Opera in Cardiff and Handel's *Agrippina* at the Semper Opera in Dresden in 1994. In 1995 he led a performance of Purcell's *Dido and Aeneas* at the Houston Grand Opera. After conducting Mozart's *Idomeneo* at the Opéra de la Bastille in Paris and Gluck's *Orfeo ed Euridice* at the Netherlands Opera in Amsterdam in 1996, he conducted Mozart's *Die Entführung aus dem Serail* at the Salzburg Festival in 1997. Minkowski served as music director of the Flanders Opera and Sym. Orch. in Belgium from 1997.

Minoja, Ambrogio, Italian composer and singing teacher; b. Ospitaletto Lodigiano, near Piacenza, Oct. 22, 1752; d. Milan, Aug. 3, 1825. He studied music in Lodi and Naples, and then served as maestro al cembalo at La Scala in Milan and at the Teatro Canobbiano there from 1780 to 1802. In 1814 he became censor of the Milan Cons., holding that position until his death. As an instructor of high repute, he publ. books of solfeggi and *Lettere sopra il canto* (Milan, 1812). He composed the operas *Tito nelle Gallie* (La Scala, Milan, Dec. 26, 1786) and *Olimpiade* (Rome, Dec. 26, 1787).

Minter, Drew, American countertenor; b. Washington, D.C., Jan. 11, 1955. He studied at Indiana Univ. and with Marcy Lindheimer, Myron McPherson, Rita Streich, and Erik Werba. After singing with many early music ensembles, he made his stage debut as Handel's Orlando at the St. Louis Baroque Festival in 1983; in subsequent years he appeared in performances of early operas in Boston, Brussels, Los Angeles, Omaha, and Milwaukee; he also sang in the U.S. premiere of Judith Weir's *A Night at the Chinese Opera* at the Santa Fe (N.M.) Opera in 1989. In 1992 he was engaged as Handel's Ottone at the Göttingen Festival. He sang Endymion in Cavalli's *Calisto* at the Glimmerglass Opera in New York in 1996. He is best known for his roles in operas by Monteverdi, Handel, and Landi.

Minton, Yvonne (Fay), noted Australian mezzo-soprano; b. Sydney, Dec. 4, 1938. She studied with Marjorie Walker in Sydney and with Henry Cummings and Joan Cross in London; she won the Kathleen Ferrier Prize and the 's Hertogenbosch Competition (both 1961). She sang the role of Maggie Dempster in the premiere of Maw's *One Man Show* (London, 1964); she made her Covent Garden debut in London as Lola in *Cavalleria rusticana* (1965), and subsequently sang there regularly; she also sang at the Cologne Opera (from 1969) and at the Bayreuth Festivals (from 1974). She made her first appearance in the United States in Chicago (1970); she made her Metropolitan Opera debut in New York as Octavian in *Der Rosenkavalier* on March 16, 1973; she also appeared in concerts with the Chicago Sym. Orch. In 1983 she retired from the operatic stage, but continued her concert career. She resumed an active career in 1990 with an engagement in Florence. In 1994 she made her debut at the Glyndebourne Festival as Madame Larina in *Eugene Onegin*. In 1980 she was made a Commander of the Order of the British Empire. Among her finest roles were Gluck's Orfeo, Cherubino, Sextus in *La clemenza di Tito*, Dorabella, Waltraube, Fricka, Dido, and Brangäne; she also created the role of Thea in Tippett's *The Knot Garden* (1970) and sang the role of the Countess in the first perf. of the complete version of Berg's *Lulu* (1979).

Mirecki, Franz (Franciszek Wincenty), Polish composer, pianist, and singing teacher; b. Kraków (baptized), March 31, 1791; d. there, May 29, 1862. He first studied with his father, making his debut as a pianist at the age of 9; later he was a student of Hummel in Vienna (1814) and of Cherubini in Paris (1817). He was active as a singing teacher, conductor, and composer in Milan (1822–38) and Genoa (1826–38) and also conducted an Italian opera company on a tour of Portugal, England, and France (1825–26). He returned to Kraków in 1838, running his own school until 1841; he also served as director of the local Opera (1844–47). Among his works were the operas *Cyganie* (The Gypsies; Warsaw, May 23, 1822), *Evandro in Pergamo* (Genoa, Dec. 26, 1824), *I due forzati* (Lisbon, March 7, 1826), *Cornelio Bentivoglio* (Milan, March 18, 1844), and *Nocleg w Apeninach* (A Night in the Apennines; Kraków, April 11, 1845).

Miricioiu, Nelly, Romanian soprano; b. Adjud, March 31, 1952. She studied in Bucharest and Milan. Following her operatic debut in *Iaşi* in 1974 as the Queen of the Night, she sang with the Braşov Opera (1975–78). In 1981 she made her British debut as Tosca with the Scottish Opera in Glasgow, and then made her first appearance at London's Covent Garden in 1982 as Nedda. She subsequently was engaged to sing in San Francisco, San Diego, Rome, Hamburg, Milan, and other music centers. In 1988 she appeared as Rossini's Armida in Amsterdam. She sang Violetta in Philadelphia in 1992. In 1996 she portrayed Elisabeth in *Don Carlos* in Brussels. Among her other roles were Lucia di Lammermoor, Manon Lescaut, Marguerite, Cio-Cio-San, and Mimi.

Mirouze, Marcel, French composer and conductor; b. Toulouse, Sept. 24, 1906; d. in an automobile accident in Aude, Aug. 1, 1957. He studied with Büsser at the Paris Cons. He conducted the Paris Radio Orch. (1935–40) and in Monte Carlo (1940–43). He wrote an opera, *Geneviève de Paris*, for the 2,000th anniversary of the founding of the city of Paris; it was produced first as a radio play with music in 1952, and then on stage in Toulouse in the same year. He also composed 2 ballets: *Paul et Virginie* (1942) and *Les Bains de mer* (1946).

Miry, Karel, Belgian composer; b. Ghent, Aug. 14, 1823; d. there, Oct. 3, 1889. He studied violin with Jean Andries and composition with Martin Joseph Mergal at the Ghent Cons. In 1857 he was engaged as a prof. of harmony and counterpoint there, and in 1871 as assistant director. From 1875 he was inspector of music in the municipal schools of Ghent, and from 1881, inspector of state-supported music schools. As a composer, he cultivated the national Flemish style. He wrote 18 operas and operettas to French and Flemish librettos. His opera *Boucherd d'Avesnes* was first staged in Ghent on Feb. 5, 1864, obtaining considerable success, but he owes his fame to the patriotic song *De Vlaamse Leeuw*, which he wrote at the age of 22, and which became the Flemish anthem of Belgium.

Misón, Luis, Spanish flutist, oboist, conductor, and composer; b. probably in Barcelona, date unknown; d. Madrid, Feb. 13, 1776. He was a flutist in the Royal Chapel and the Royal Opera, Madrid (from 1748), becoming conductor there in 1756. He composed stage music; was one of the first to introduce the "tonadilla escénica," a sort of miniature comic opera that developed from the musical interludes in early Spanish plays. He also wrote "sainetes" (dramatic dialogues) and zarzuelas.

Missa, Edmond (Jean Louis), French organist and composer; b. Rheims, June 12, 1861; d. Paris, Jan. 29, 1910. He studied with Massenet at the Paris Cons., receiving an honorable mention for the Prix de Rome in 1881. He then served as organist at St. Thomas d'Aquin. He wrote a number of operas, including *Babette* (London, Oct. 22, 1900) and *Muguette*, based on Ouida's *Two Little Wooden Shoes* (Paris, March 18, 1903).

Mitchell, Donald (Charles Peter), eminent English writer on music and publishing executive; b. London, Feb. 6, 1925. He studied at Dulwich College in London (1939–42) and with A. Hutchings and A. E. F. Dickinson at the Univ. of Durham (1949–50). After noncombatant wartime service (1942–45), he founded (1947) and then became coed. (with Hans Keller) of *Music Survey* (1949–52). From 1953 to 1957 he was London music critic of the *Musical Times*. In 1958 he was appointed music ed. and adviser of Faber & Faber, Ltd.; in 1965 he became managing director, and in 1976 vice chairman; he became chairman in 1977 of its subsidiary, Faber Music. He also ed. *Tempo* (1958–62); he was on the music staff of the *Daily Telegraph* (1959–64); in 1963–64 he served as music adviser to Boosey & Hawkes, Ltd. From 1971 to 1976 he was prof. of music, and from 1976 visiting prof. of music, at the Univ. of Sussex; in 1973 he was awarded by it an honorary M.A. degree and received his doctorate in 1977 from the Univ. of Southampton with a diss. on Mahler. He lectured widely in the

United Kingdom, United States, and Australia; he contributed articles to the *Encyclopaedia Britannica* and other reference publications. As a music scholar, he made a profound study, in Vienna and elsewhere, of the life and works of Gustav Mahler and was awarded in 1961 the Mahler Medal of Honor by the Bruckner Soc. of America and in 1987 the Mahler Medal of the International Gustav Mahler Soc. His major work is a Mahler biography: vol. 1, *Gustav Mahler: The Early Years* (London, 1958; rev. ed., 1980); vol. 2, *The Wunderhorn Years* (London, 1976); vol. 3, *Songs and Symphonies of Life and Death* (London, 1985). His other publications include: ed. with H. Keller, *Benjamin Britten: A Commentary on All His Works from a Group of Specialists* (London, 1952); *W. A. Mozart: A Short Biography* (London, 1956); with H. C. Robbins Landon, *The Mozart Companion* (N.Y., 1956; 2d ed., 1965); *The Language of Modern Music* (London, 1963; 3d ed., 1970); ed. and annotated Alma Mahler's *Gustav Mahler: Memories and Letters* (London, 1968; 3d ed., rev., 1973); ed. with J. Evans, *Benjamin Britten, 1913–1976: Pictures from a Life* (London, 1978); *Britten and Auden in the Thirties* (London, 1981); *Benjamin Britten: Death in Venice* (Cambridge, 1987); *Cradles of the New: Writings on Music, 1951–1991* (1995).

BIBL.: P. Reed, ed., *On Mahler and Britten: Essays in Honour of D. M. on his Seventieth Birthday* (Woodbridge, Suffolk, 1995).

Mitchell, Leona, talented black American soprano; b. Enid, Okla., Oct. 13, 1948. She was one of 15 children; her father, a Pentecostal minister, played several instruments by ear; her mother was a good amateur pianist. She sang in local church choirs, then received a scholarship to Oklahoma City Univ., where she obtained her B.Mus. degree in 1971. She made her operatic debut in 1972 as Micaëla in *Carmen* with the San Francisco Spring Opera Theater. She then received the $10,000 Opera America grant (1973), which enabled her to study with Ernest St. John Metz in Los Angeles. On Dec. 15, 1975, she made her Metropolitan Opera debut in New York as Micaëla; subsequently she sang there as Pamina in *Die Zauberflöte* and Musetta in *La Bohème*; she won critical acclaim for her portrayal of Leonora in *La forza del destino* in 1982. In 1987 she appeared as Massenet's Salome in Nice. She sang the 3 leading soprano roles in Puccini's *Trittico* at the Paris Opéra Comique in 1988. She sang Verdi's Elvira in Parma in 1990. In 1992 she appeared as Aida with the New Israeli Opera. She portrayed Strauss's Ariadne in Sydney in 1997.

Mitchinson, John (Leslie), English tenor and educator; b. Blackrod, Lancashire, March 31, 1932. He studied at the Royal Manchester College of Music (graduated, 1955). In 1953 he became a founding member of the BBC Northern Singers. After singing in a concert performance of *Don Giovanni* with the Chelsea Opera Group in 1955, he made his stage debut as Jupiter in Handel's *Semele* with the Handel Opera Soc. He sang with the Sadler's Wells Opera (1972–74), and its successor, the English National Opera (1974–78) in London, and then with the Welsh National Opera in Cardiff (1978–82). From 1987 to 1992 he was senior lecturer at the Royal Northern College of Music in Manchester, and then was head of vocal studies at the Welsh College of Music and Drama in Cardiff from 1992. Among his operatic roles, he won particular success as Florestan, Tristan, and Peter Grimes. He was especially well known for his appearances as a soloist with the principal British orchs.

Mitropoulos, Dimitri, celebrated Greek-born American conductor and composer; b. Athens, March 1, 1896; d. after suffering a heart attack while rehearsing Mahler's 3d Sym. with the orch. of the Teatro alla Scala, Milan, Nov. 2, 1960. He studied piano with Wassenhoven and harmony with A. Marsick at the Odeon Cons. in Athens; he wrote an opera after Maeterlinck, *Soeur Béatrice* (1918), performed at the Odeon Cons. (May 20, 1919); in 1920, after graduation from the Cons., he went to Brussels, where he studied composition with Gilson; in 1921 he went to Berlin, where he took piano lessons with Busoni at the Hochschule für Musik (until 1924); concurrently was répétiteur at the Berlin State Opera. He became a conductor of the Odeon Cons. orch. in Athens (1924); was its coconductor (1927–29) and principal conductor (from 1929); he was also prof. of composition there (from 1930). In 1930 he was invited to conduct a concert of the Berlin Phil.; when the soloist Egon Petri became suddenly indisposed, Mitropoulos substituted for him as soloist in Prokofiev's Piano Concerto No. 3, conducting from the keyboard (Feb. 27, 1930). He played the same concerto in Paris in 1932 as a pianist-conductor, and later in the United States. His Paris debut as a conductor (1932) obtained a spontaneous success; he conducted the most difficult works from memory, which was a novelty at the time; he also led rehearsals without a score. He made his American debut with the Boston Sym. Orch. on Jan. 24, 1936, with immediate acclaim; that same year he was engaged as music director of the Minneapolis Sym. Orch.; there he frequently performed modern music, including works by Schoenberg, Berg, and other representatives of the atonal school; the opposition that naturally arose was not sufficient to offset his hold on the public as a conductor of great emotional power. He resigned from the Minneapolis Sym. Orch. in 1949 to accept the post of conductor of the N.Y. Phil.; he shared the podium with Stokowski for a few weeks, and in 1950 became music director. In 1956 Leonard Bernstein was engaged as assoc. conductor with Mitropoulos, and in 1958 succeeded him as music director. With the N.Y. Phil., Mitropoulos continued his policy of bringing out important works by European and American modernists; he also programmed modern operas (*Elektra, Wozzeck*) in concert form. A musician of astounding technical ability, Mitropoulos became very successful with the general public as well as with the musical vanguard whose cause he so boldly espoused. While his time was engaged mainly in the United States, Mitropoulos continued to appear as guest conductor in Europe; he also appeared on numerous occasions as conductor at the Metropolitan Opera in New York (debut conducting *Salome*, Dec. 15, 1954) and at various European opera theaters. He became a naturalized American citizen in 1946. As a composer, Mitropoulos was one of the earliest among Greek composers to write in a distinctly modern idiom. Among his works was the opera *Soeur Béatrice* (1918; Odeon Cons., Athens, May 20, 1919); also incidental music to *Electra* (1936) and *Hippolytus* (1937).

BIBL.: S. Arfanis, *The Complete Discography of D. M.* (Athens, 1990); W. Trotter, *Priest of Music: The Life of D. M.* (Portland, Oreg., 1995).

Mitterwurzer, Anton, famous Austrian baritone; b. Sterzing, April 12, 1818; d. Döbling, near Vienna, April 2, 1876. He studied with his uncle, Johann Gänsbacher. After serving as chorister at St. Stephen's, Vienna, he sang in Austrian provincial theaters. In 1839 he was engaged by the Dresden Court Opera, and remained there until he was pensioned in 1870. He was particularly notable in Wagnerian roles.

Mittler, Franz, Austrian composer and pianist; b. Vienna, April 14, 1893; d. Munich, Dec. 28, 1970. He studied in Vienna with Heuberger and Prohaska and later in Cologne with Steinbach and Friedberg. From 1921 to 1938 he lived in Vienna as a pianist and accompanist; in 1939 he settled in New York. He wrote an opera, *Rafaella* (Duisburg, 1930).

BIBL.: D. Mittler Battipaglia, *F. M.: Composer, Pedagogue and Practical Musician* (diss., Univ. of Rochester, 1974).

Miyagi (real name, **Wakabe**), **Michio,** Japanese koto player, teacher, and composer; b. Kobe, April 7, 1894; d. in a railroad accident in Kariya, near Tokyo, June 25, 1956. He was given the surname of Suga in infancy; he became blind at age 7; he studied the koto with Nakajima Kengyō II and made his debut when he was 9. He went to Inchon (1908) to teach the koto and shakuhachi; then taught in Seoul. After receiving his certificate as a koto player with highest honors, he was given the professional name of Nakasuga; he was known as Michio Miyagi from 1913. He settled in Tokyo (1917); with Seiju Yoshida, he founded the New Japanese Music Movement (1920); he became a lecturer (1930) and a prof. (1937) at the Tokyo Music School and taught at the National Univ. of Fine Arts and Music (from 1950). He wrote more than 1,000 works for koto and other Japanese instruments as well as an opera, *Kariteibo* (1924).

BIBL.: E. Kikkawa, *Miyagi Michio den* (The Life of M. M.; Tokyo, 1962).

Miyoshi, Akira, Japanese composer and teacher; b. Tokyo, Jan. 10, 1933. He joined the Jiyû-Gakuen children's piano group at the age of 3, graduating at the age of 6. He studied French literature; in 1951 he began to study music with Hirai, Ikenouchi, and Gallois-Montbrun, who was in Tokyo at the time. He obtained a stipend to travel to France and took lessons in composition with Challan and again with Gallois-Montbrun (1955–57); upon his return to Japan he resumed his studies in French literature at the Univ. of Tokyo, obtaining a degree in 1961. In 1965 he was appointed instructor at the Toho Gakuen School of Music in Tokyo. Among his works are the poetical dramas *Happy Prince* (1959) and *Ondine* (1959).

Mlynarski, Emil (Simon), Polish violinist, conductor, and composer; b. Kibarty, July 18, 1870; d. Warsaw, April 5, 1935. He studied at the St. Petersburg Cons. (1880–89), taking up both the violin, with Leopold Auer, and piano, with Anton Rubinstein; he also took a course in composition with Liadov. He embarked on a career as a conductor; in 1897 he was appointed principal conductor of the Warsaw Opera, and concurrently conducted the concerts of the Warsaw Phil. (1901–05); from 1904 to 1907 he was director of the Warsaw Cons. He achieved considerable success as a conductor in Scotland, where he was principal conductor of the Scottish Orch. in Glasgow (1910–16). Returning to Warsaw, he was director of the Opera (1918–29) and Cons. (1919–22). After teaching conducting at the Curtis Inst. of Music in Philadelphia (1929–31), he returned to Warsaw. He composed an opera, *Noc letnia* (Summer Night; 1914; Warsaw, March 29, 1924).

BIBL.: A. Wach, *Zycie i twórczoć Emila M.ego* (Life and Works of E. M.; diss., Univ. of Kraków, 1953); J. Mechanisz, *E. M.: W setna rocznice urodzin (1870–1970)* (Warsaw, 1970).

Mödl, Martha, esteemed German mezzo-soprano, later soprano; b. Nuremberg, March 22, 1912. She studied at the Nuremberg Cons. and in Milan. She made her operatic debut as Hansel in Nuremberg (1942), then sang in Düsseldorf (1945–49) and at the Hamburg State Opera (1947–55), appearing in soprano roles from 1950 with notable success. She sang at London's Covent Garden (1949–50; 1953; 1959; 1966); she appeared as Kundry at the resumption of the Bayreuth Festival productions in 1951, and continued to sing there regularly until 1967 and sang Leonore in the first performance at the rebuilt Vienna State Opera in 1955. On March 2, 1957, she made her Metropolitan Opera debut in New York as Brünnhilde in *Götterdämmerung*, remaining on the roster there until 1960; was again a member of the Hamburg State Opera (1956–75). In 1981 she sang in the premiere of Cerha's *Baal* in Salzburg. She was made both a German and an Austrian Kammersängerin. Among her finest mezzo-soprano roles were Dorabella, Carmen, Eboli, Octavian, the Composer, and Marie in *Wozzeck*; as a soprano, she excelled as Brünnhilde, Isolde, Gutrune, Venus, and Sieglinde.

BIBL.: W. Schafer, *M. M.* (Hannover, 1967).

Moffo, Anna, noted American soprano; b. Wayne, Pa., June 27, 1932. She is of Italian descent. She studied voice at the Curtis Inst. of Music in Philadelphia and later went to Italy on a Fulbright fellowship and studied at the Accademia di Santa Cecilia in Rome. She made her debut as Norina in Spoleto in 1955, and, progressing rapidly in her career, was engaged at La Scala in Milan, at the Vienna State Opera, and in Paris. She made her U.S. debut as Mimi with the Chicago Lyric Opera in 1957; on Nov. 14, 1959, she made her debut at the Metropolitan Opera in New York as Violetta, obtaining a gratifying success; she sang regularly at the Metropolitan and other major opera houses in the United States and Europe until she suffered a vocal breakdown in 1974; she then resumed her career in 1976, but then abandoned it a few years later. In her prime, she became known for her fine portrayals of such roles as Pamina, the 4 heroines in *Les Contes d'Hoffmann*, Gilda, Massenet's Manon, Mélisande, Juliet, Luisa Miller, and Gounod's Marguerite.

Mohaupt, Richard, German composer; b. Breslau, Sept. 14, 1904; d. Reichenau, Austria, July 3, 1957. He studied with J. Prüwer and R. Bilke. He began his musical career as an opera conductor and also gave concerts as a pianist. After the advent of the Nazi regime in 1933, he was compelled to leave Germany because his wife was Jewish; he settled in New York in 1939, and continued to compose; was also active as a teacher. In 1955 he returned to Europe.

WORKS: DRAMATIC: OPERAS: *Die Wirtin von Pinsk* (Dresden, Feb. 10, 1938); *Die Bremer Stadtmusikanten* (Bremen, June 15, 1949); *Double Trouble* (Louisville, Dec. 4, 1954); *Der grüne Kakadu* (Hamburg, Sept. 16, 1958). BALLETS: *Die Gaunerstreiche der Courasche* (Berlin, Aug. 5, 1936); *Max und Moritz*, dance burlesque (1945; Karlsruhe, Dec. 18, 1950); *Lysistrata* (1946; rev. for Orch. as *Der Weiberstreik von Athen*, 1955); *The Legend of the Charlatan*, mimodrama (1949). Also incidental music.

Mojsisovics (-Mojsvár), Roderich, Edler von, Austrian composer; b. Graz, May 10, 1877; d. there, March 30, 1953. He studied with Degner in Graz, with Wüllner and Klauwell at the Cologne Cons., and with Thuille in Munich. He conducted a choral group in Brünn (1903–07); he then taught in various Austrian towns. He became director of the Graz Steiermärkische Musikverein (1912); it became the Graz Cons. in 1920, and he remained as director until 1931; from 1932 to 1935 he taught music history at the Univ. of Graz; then lectured at the Trapp Cons. in Munich (1935–41) and at the Mannheim Hochschule für Musik (1941–44); he returned to teach at the Graz Cons. from 1945 to 1948. He publ. *Bach-Probleme* (Würzburg, 1931). As a composer, he followed Regerian precepts. Among his stage works were 5 operas, a melodrama, and a musical comedy.

BIBL.: K. Haidmayer, *R. v.M.: Leben und Werk* (diss., Univ. of Graz, 1951).

Molchanov, Kirill (Vladimirovich), Russian composer; b. Moscow, Sept. 7, 1922; d. there, March 14, 1982. He was attached to the Red Army Ensemble of Song and Dance during World War II; after demobilization, he studied composition with Anatoly Alexandrov at the Moscow Cons., graduating in 1949. From 1973 to 1975 he served as director of the Bolshoi Theater in Moscow and accompanied it on its American tour in 1975. He was primarily an opera composer; his musical style faithfully followed the precepts of socialist realism. His most successful work, the opera *The Dawns Are Quiet Here*, to his own libretto depicting the Russian struggle against the Nazis, was first performed at the Bolshoi Theater on April 11, 1975. It became the melodramatic event of the year, accompanied by an unabashed display of tearful emotion; however, its American performance during the visit of the Bolshoi Theater to New York in June 1975 met with a disdainful dismissal on the part of the critics. His other operas were *The Stone Flower* (Moscow, Dec. 2, 1950), *Dawn* (1956), *Romeo, Juliet, and Darkness* (1963), *The Unknown Soldier* (1967), and *A Woman of Russia* (1969).

BIBL.: Y. Korev, *K. M.* (Moscow, 1971).

Moldovan, Mihai, Romanian composer; b. Dej, Nov. 5, 1937; d. Medgidia, Sept. 11, 1981. He studied with Toduţa and Comes at the Cluj Cons. (1956–59) and with Vancea, Vieru, and Jora at the Bucharest Cons. (1959–62). He was active in various branches of Romanian radio and television. His music fuses a Romanian ethos with modern harmonic textures. His works include the operas *Trepte ale istoriei* (1972) and *Micul prinţ* (1977–78).

Moldoveanu, Vasile, Romanian tenor; b. Konstanza, Oct. 6, 1935. He was a student of Badescu in Bucharest, where he made his operatic debut in 1966 as Rinuccio. In 1972 he made his first appearance in Stuttgart as Edgardo, and then sang Alfredo at the Vienna State Opera and Rodolfo at the Bavarian State Opera in Munich in 1976. In 1977 he sang at the Deutsche Oper in Berlin and at the Chicago Lyric Opera, and on May 19 of that year he made his Metropolitan Opera debut in New York as Rodolfo. He appeared as Don Carlos at the Hamburg State Opera in 1978, and sang that role at his debut at London's Covent Garden in 1979. His later engagements took him to Zürich (1980), Monte Carlo (1982), Nice (1988), Rome (1990), and other European music centers.

Molina, Antonio (Jesus), Filipino conductor, music administrator, and composer; b. Manila, Dec. 26, 1894; d. there, Jan. 29, 1980. He studied at the S. Juan de Letran College and at the Univ. of the Philippines Cons.; he became a teacher at the latter (1925) and was also active as a conductor; he was director of the Centro Escolar Univ. Cons. (1948–71) and founder-director of a string group, Rondalla Ideal. Among his works was the lyric drama *Ritorna Vincitor* (Manila, March 10, 1918) and the zarzuelas *Panibuglo* (Manila, April 16, 1918) and *Ang Ilaw* (Manila, Nov. 23, 1918).

Molinari, Bernardino, eminent Italian conductor; b. Rome, April 11, 1880; d. there, Dec. 25, 1952. He studied with Falchi and Renzi at Rome's Liceo di Santa Cecilia (graduated, 1902). He was artistic director of Rome's Augusteo Orch. (1912–43); he also conducted throughout Europe and South America. In 1928 he made his American debut with the N.Y. Phil., which he conducted again during the 1929–30 and 1930–31 seasons; he also appeared with other American orchs. He was head of the advanced conducting class at Rome's Accademia di Santa Cecilia (from 1936), serving as a prof. there (from 1939). Molinari championed the modern Italian school, and brought out many works by Respighi, Malipiero, and other outstanding Italian composers. He publ. a new ed. of Monteverdi's *Sonata sopra Sonata Maria* (1919) and concert transcriptions of Carissimi's oratorio *Giona*, Vivaldi's *Le quattro stagioni* et al. He also orchestrated Debussy's *L'Isle joyeuse*.

BIBL.: E. Mucci, *B. M.* (Lanciano, 1941).

Molinari-Pradelli, Francesco, Italian conductor; b. Bologna, July 4, 1911; d. Marano di Castenaso, Aug. 7, 1996. He studied with d'Ivaldi and Nordio in Bologna, and with Molinari at the Accademia di Santa Cecilia in Rome. In 1938 he launched his career as a conductor; in 1939 he appeared for the first time as an opera conductor, leading *L'elisir d'amore* in Bologna. He conducted at Milan's La Scala from 1946; he made his first appearance at London's Covent Garden in 1955, at the San Francisco Opera in 1957, and at the Vienna State Opera in 1959. On Feb. 7, 1966, he made his Metropolitan Opera debut in New York conducting *Un ballo in maschera*, and remained on the company's roster until 1973. He was also active as a pianist. He was best known as an interpreter of the Italian operatic repertoire.

Moll, Kurt, outstanding German bass; b. Buir, near Cologne, April 11, 1938. He learned to play the guitar and cello and sang in a school choir in his youth, then studied voice at the Cologne Hochschule für Musik and with Emmy Müller. After singing minor roles at the Cologne Opera (1958–61), he sang in Aachen (1961–63), Mainz (1963–66), and Wuppertal (1966–69); he subsequently pursued a career of great distinction, appearing regularly in Hamburg, Bayreuth, Salzburg, Vienna, Paris, Milan, and London. He made his U.S. debut as Gurnemanz at the San Francisco Opera in 1974; on Sept. 18, 1978, came his Metropolitan Opera debut in New York, in which he essayed the role of the Landgrave; he subsequently appeared there regularly. He made his first appearance at the Chicago Lyric Opera as Daland in 1983. In 1984 he toured Japan with the Hamburg State Opera. He portrayed Osmin at London's Covent Garden in 1987, and then sang Gurnemanz at the San Francisco Opera in 1988. In 1990 he was engaged as the Commendatore at the Metropolitan Opera, and returned there in 1992 as Gurnemanz. He sang Pogner at the Munich Festival in 1997. He also sang widely as a concert artist and recitalist; made his North American recital debut at N.Y.'s Carnegie Hall in 1984. Among his other notable roles are the Commendatore, Sarastro, King Marke, Pogner, Nicolai's Falstaff, and Baron Ochs.

Mombelli, Domenico, Italian tenor and composer; b. Villanova, Feb. 17, 1751; d. Bologna, March 15, 1835. He made appearances throughout Italy from 1780. In 1786 he married **Luisa Laschi**, and sang with her in Vienna until 1788. After her death, he married Vincenza Vigarnò. She wrote the libretto for Rossini's first opera, *Demetrio e Polibio*, and her husband created its role of Demetrio (Rome, May 18, 1812). In 1816 he retired from the operatic stage and then was active as a voice teacher in Florence and Bologna.

Monaco, Mario del. See **Del Monaco, Mario.**

Moncayo García, José Pablo, Mexican composer and conductor; b. Guadalajara, June 29, 1912; d. Mexico City, June 16, 1958. He studied with Chávez at the Mexico City Cons. From 1932 he was a member of the Mexico Sym. Orch.; he was conductor of the National Sym. Orch. (1949–52). In company with Ayala, Contreras, and Galindo (also pupils of Chávez), he formed the so-called Grupo de Los Cuatro for the purpose of furthering the cause of Mexican music. Among his works was the opera *La mulata de Córdoba* (Mexico City, Oct. 23, 1948).

Mondonville, Jean-Joseph Cassanéa de (de Mondonville was his wife's maiden name), distinguished French violinist, conductor, and composer; b. Narbonne (baptized), Dec. 25, 1711; d. Belleville, near Paris, Oct. 8, 1772. He played in the Holy Week program at the Concert Spirituel in Paris (1734). After appearing at the Concert de Lille, he returned to Paris, where he was made violinist at the royal chapel and chamber (1739). He wrote motets for the Concert Spirituel. He was made sous-maître of the royal chapel (1740); he became intendant of the "musique de la chapelle" in Versailles (1744) and was music director of the Concert Spirituel (1755–62). He composed numerous stage works and oratorios.

BIBL.: J.-J. Galibert, *J.-J. C. d.M.* (Narbonne, 1856); F. Hellouin, *M.: Sa vie et son oeuvre* (Paris, 1903).

Mongini, Pietro, admired Italian tenor; b. Rome, Oct. 29, 1828; d. Milan, April 27, 1874. He commenced his career as a bass, and then appeared as a tenor in Genoa by 1853. In 1855 he made his debut in Paris at the Théâtre-Italien as Edgardo in *Lucia di Lammermoor*. On March 11, 1858, he made his first appearance at Milan's La Scala as Arnold in *Giullaume Tell*. His London debut followed on April 25, 1859, at Drury Lane as Elvino in *La Sonnambula*. He subsequently appeared at Her Majesty's Theatre in London. On Oct. 24, 1868, he made his debut at London's Covent Garden as Gennaro in *Lucrezia Borgia*. On Dec. 24, 1871, he created the role of Radamès in *Aida* in Cairo. Among his other notable roles were Alvaro, John of Leyden, and Manrico.

Moniuszko, Stanislaw, famous Polish composer; b. Ubiel, Minsk province, Russia, May 5, 1819; d. Warsaw, June 4, 1872. In 1827 his family went to Warsaw, where he studied piano and music with August Freyer; he continued his training with Dominick Stefanowica in Minsk and with Rungenhagen in Berlin (1837). He went to Vilnius in 1840, where he served as organist at St. John's. He gained attention as a composer when he publ. vol. 1 of his *Śpiewnik domowy* (Songbook for Home Use; 1843), garnering the support of various Polish figures in the arts, and also winning the admiration of Glinka, Dargomizhsky, and Cui in Russia. On Jan. 1, 1848, a concert performance of the 2-act version of his opera *Halka* was given for the first time in Vilnius; after he expanded it to 4 acts, it was staged in Warsaw on Jan. 1, 1858, scoring a great success. He then settled in Warsaw (1859), becoming conductor of opera at the Grand Theater. He continued to compose for the stage, and also taught at the Music Inst. (from 1864). He publ. *Pamietnik do nauki harmonii* (Textbook on Harmony; 1871). Moniuszko holds a revered place in Polish music history as the outstanding composer of opera in his era; he also excelled as a composer of songs. A complete ed. of his works commenced publication in Krakow in 1965.

WORKS: DRAMATIC: OPERAS: *Halka* (1846–47; 2-act version, concert perf., Vilnius, Jan. 1, 1848; 4-act version, 1857; Warsaw, Jan. 1, 1858); *Sielanka* (Idyll; c.1848); *Bettly* (Vilnius, May 20, 1852); *Flis* (The Raftsman; Warsaw, Sept. 24, 1858); *Rokiczana* (1858–59); *Hrabina* (The Countess; 1859; Warsaw, Feb. 7, 1860); *Verbum nobile* (Warsaw, Jan. 1, 1860); *Straszny dwór* (The Haunted

Manor; 1861–64; Warsaw, Sept. 18, 1865); *Paria* (1859–69; Warsaw, Dec. 11, 1869); *Trea* (1872; unfinished). OPERETTAS: *Nocleg w Apeninach* (A Night's Lodging in the Apennines; Vilnius, 1839); *Ideal czyli Nowa Precioza* (Ideal or The New Preciosa; Vilnius, 1840); *Karmaniol czyli Francuzi lubi zartować* (Carmagnole or The French Like Joking; 1841); *Zólta szlafmyca* (The Yellow Nightcap; 1841); *Nowy Don Quichot czyli Sto szanlestw* (The New Don Quixote or 100 Follies; 1841; Lemberg, 1849); *Loteria* (The Lottery; Minsk, Nov. 1843); *Cyganie* (The Gypsies; 1850; Vilnius, May 20, 1852; rev. as *Jawnuta*, Warsaw, June 5, 1860); *Beata* (1871; Warsaw, Feb. 2, 1872). Also incidental music to 14 plays; ballets.

BIBL.: A. Walicki, *S. M.* (Warsaw, 1873); A. Poliński, *M.* (Kiev, 1914); H. Opieński, *S. M.: Zycie i dziela* (S. M.: Life and Works; Lwów, 1924); S. Niewiadomski, *S. M.* (Warsaw, 1928); F. Kecki, *A Catalogue of Musical Works of M. Karlowicz and S. M.* (Warsaw, 1936); W. Rudziński, *S. M.* (Kraków, 1954; 4th ed., 1972); J. Prosnack, *S. M.* (Kraków, 1964; 2d ed., 1969); W. Rudziński and M. Stokowska, eds., *S. M.: Listy zebrane* (S. M.: Collected Letters; Kraków, 1969); K. Mazur, *Pierwodruki S.a M.* (The Editions of M.'s Works; Warsaw, 1970).

Monk, Meredith (Jane), American composer, singer, and filmmaker; b. Lima, Peru (of American parents), Nov. 20, 1942. She studied eurythmics from an early age. She was educated at Sarah Lawrence College (B.A., 1964), then was a pupil in voice of Vicki Starr, John Devers, and Jeanette Lovetri, in composition of Ruth Lloyd, Richard Averee, and Glenn Mack, and in piano of Gershon Konikow. She pursued an active and diverse career as a singer, filmmaker, director, choreographer, recording artist, and composer. In 1968 she organized the House in N.Y., a company devoted to interdisciplinary approaches to the arts; in 1978 she founded there her own vocal chamber ensemble, with which she toured widely in the United States and abroad. In 1972 and 1982 she held Guggenheim fellowships; received various ASCAP awards and many commissions; in 1995 she was awarded a MacArthur fellowship. Her unique soprano vocalizations employ a wide range of ethnic and avant-garde influences. As one of the first and most natural of performance artists, she developed a flexible, imaginative theatrical style influenced by dream narrative and physical movement.

WORKS: DRAMATIC: *Juice*, theater cantata for 85 Voices, Jew's Harp, and 2 Violins (1969); *Key*, album of invisible theater for Voice, Electric Organ, Vocal Quartet, Percussion, and Jew's Harp (1970–71); *Vessel*, opera epic for 75 Voices, Electric Organ, Dulcimer, and Accordion (1971); *Education of the Girlchild*, opera for 6 Voices, Electric Organ, and Piano (1972–73); *Quarry*, opera for 38 Voices, 2 Pump Organs, 2 Soprano Recorders, and Tape (1976).

BIBL.: D. Jowitt, ed., *M. M.* (Baltimore, 1997).

Monleone, Domenico, Italian opera composer; b. Genoa, Jan. 4, 1875; d. there, Jan. 15, 1942. He studied at the Milan Cons. From 1895 to 1901 he was active as a theater conductor in Amsterdam and in Vienna. He attracted attention by producing in Amsterdam (Feb. 5, 1907) an opera, *Cavalleria rusticana*, to a libretto by his brother Giovanni, on the same subject as Mascagni's celebrated work; after its first Italian performance (Turin, July 10, 1907), Mascagni's publisher, Sonzogno, brought a lawsuit against Monleone for infringement of copyright. Monleone was forced to change the title; his brother rewrote the libretto, and the opera was produced as *La Giostra dei falchi* (Florence, Feb. 18, 1914). Other operas were *Una novella di Boccaccio* (Genoa, May 26, 1909), *Alba eroica* (Genoa, May 5, 1910), *Arabesca* (Rome, March 11, 1913; won 1st prize at the competition of the City of Rome), *Suona la ritrata* (Milan, May 23, 1916), *Il mistero* (Venice, May 7, 1921), *Fauvette* (Genoa, March 2, 1926), and *La ronda di notte* (Genoa, March 6, 1933); also an opera in Genovese dialect, *Scheuggio Campann-a* (Genoa, March 12, 1928). For some of his works he used the pseudonym W. di Stolzing.

Monpou, (François Louis) Hyppolite, French organist and composer; b. Paris, Jan. 12, 1804; d. Orléans, Aug. 10, 1841. He became a choirboy at Paris's St.-Germain-l'Auxerrois at age 5, then went to Notre Dame when he was 9. He entered Choron's École Royale et Speciale de Chant at age 13. Choron sent him to the Tours Cathedral to study organ; he became its organist (1819). He soon returned to Paris, where he became master accompanist at the Académie Royale. He studied harmony with Fétis at Choron's Academy (1822), then became a teacher of singing and maître de chapelle at the College of St. Louis (1825); subsequently he was made organist at St. Thomas d'Aquin, St. Nicolas des Champs, and the Sorbonne (1827). He was notably successful as a composer of some 75 songs. His opera *Le Planteur* (Paris, March 1, 1839) also proved a popular success. Other operas (all 1st perf. in Paris) were *Les Deux Reines* (Aug. 6, 1835), *Le Luthier de Vienne* (June 30, 1836), *Le Piquillo* (Oct. 31, 1837), *Un Conte d'autrefois* (Feb. 28, 1838), *Perugina* (Dec. 20, 1838), *La Chaste Suzanne* (Dec. 27, 1839), *La Reine Jeanne* (Oct. 13, 1840), *Lambert Simnel* (Sept. 1, 1843; completed by A. Adam), and *L'Orfèvre* (unfinished).

Monsigny, Pierre-Alexandre, noted French composer; b. Fauquembergues, near St.-Omer, Oct. 17, 1729; d. Paris, Jan. 14, 1817. He was educated at the Jesuit college in St.-Omer, where he also received instruction in violin. Upon his father's death, he abandoned his studies in order to support his family; he took a job in the Paris offices of the receiver-general of the Clergé de France (1749). Several years later he was befriended by the duke of Orléans, who encouraged him to pursue his musical career. After studying for 5 months with the double-bass player Gianotti, he successfully brought out his first opera, *Les Aveux indiscrets* (Théâtre de la Foire St.-Germain, Feb. 7, 1759). In quick succession, and with increasing success, the same theater brought out 3 more of Monsigny's operas: *Le Maître en droit* (Feb. 23, 1760), *Le Cadi dupé* (Feb. 4, 1761), and *On ne s'avise jamais de tout* (Sept. 14, 1761). The members of the Comédie-Italienne, alarmed at the rising prestige of the rival enterprise, succeeded in closing it, by exercise of vested privilege, and took over its best actors. Thereafter Monsigny wrote most of his works for the Théâtre-Italien and the private theaters of the duke of Orléans, having become the latter's maître d'hôtel in 1768. After scoring a triumph with his *Félix, ou L'Enfant trouvé* (Fontainebleau, Nov. 10, 1777), he abruptly abandoned his career as a composer for the theater. His patron died in 1785 and the new duke abolished Monsigny's job, but retained him as inspector of the canals of Orléans. With the coming of the Revolution, he lost his post. He obtained a pension from the Opéra Comique (1798) and served as inspector of musical education from 1800 until the post was abolished in 1802. His last years were relieved by several pensions; he was made a Chevalier of the Légion d'honneur (1804) and was elected to Grétry's chair in the Institut de France (1813). Monsigny possessed an uncommon and natural melodic invention, and sensibility in dramatic expression, but his theoretical training was deficient; still, his works attained the foremost rank among the precursors of the French comic operas.

WORKS: DRAMATIC (all 1st perf. in Paris unless otherwise given): *Les Aveux indiscrets*, opéra comique (Feb. 7, 1759); *Le Maître en droit*, opéra comique (Feb. 23, 1760); *Le Cadi dupé*, opéra comique (Feb. 4, 1761); *On ne s'avise jamais de tout*, opéra comique (Sept. 14, 1761); *Le Roy et le fermier*, comédie (Nov. 22, 1762); *Le Nouveau Monde*, divertissement (1763; not perf.); *Rose et Colas*, comédie (March 8, 1764); *Le Bouquet de Thalie*, prologue (Bagnolet, Dec. 25, 1764); *Aline, reine de Golconde*, ballet héroïque (April 15, 1766); *Philémon et Baucis*, comédie (Bagnolet, 1766); *L'Isle sonnante*, opéra comique (Bagnolet, June 5, 1767); *Le Déserteur*, drame (March 6, 1769); *La Rosière de Salency*, comédie (Fontainebleau, Oct. 25, 1769; in collaboration with Philidor, Blaise, and Swieten); *Pagamin de Monègue*, opéra comique (c.1770; not perf.); *Le Faucon*, opéra comique (Fontainebleau, Nov. 2, 1771); *La Belle Arsène*, comédie féerie (Fontainebleau, Nov. 6, 1773; rev. for Paris, Aug. 14, 1775); *Félix, ou L'Enfant trouvé*, comédie (Fontainebleau, Nov. 10, 1777); *Robin et Marion* (n.d.; not perf.).

BIBL.: A. Quatremère de Quincy, *Notice historique sur la vie et les ouvrages de M. de M.* (Paris, 1818); P. Hédouin, *Notice historique sur P.-A. de M.* (Paris, 1821); F. de Ménil, *Les Grands Musiciens du Nord: M.* (Paris, 1893); A. Pougin, *M. et son temps* (Paris, 1908); P. Druilhe, *M.: Sa vie et son oeuvre* (Paris, 1955).

Montagnana, Antonio, Italian bass who flourished from 1730 to 1750. After singing in Rome (1730) and Turin (1731), he was engaged by Handel for his London opera company at the King's Theatre, where he created the roles of Varo in *Ezio* (Jan. 15, 1732), Altomaro in *Sosarme, Rè di Media* (Feb. 15, 1732), and Zoroastro in *Orlando* (Jan. 27, 1733). He also sang in Handel's oratorios, being the first to sing Abinoam and the Chief Priest of Israel in *Deborah* (March 17, 1733) and Abner in *Athalia* (July 10, 1733). From 1733 to 1737 he was a member of the Opera of the Nobility in London. He then appeared with Heidegger's company at the King's Theatre, where he created the roles of Handel's Gustavo in *Faramondo* (Jan. 3, 1738) and Ariodante in *Serse* (April 15, 1738). From 1740 he was a member of the royal chapel in Madrid.

Montagu-Nathan, M(ontagu) (real name, **Montagu Nathan**), English writer on music; b. Banbury, Sept. 17, 1877; d. London, Nov. 15, 1958. He legally changed his name to Montagu Montagu-Nathan on March 17, 1909. He studied in Birmingham, then took violin lessons with Ysaije in Brussels, with Heermann in Frankfurt am Main, and with Wilhelmj in London. He appeared as a violinist in Belfast and Leeds, but soon abandoned concerts in favor of music journalism. He learned the Russian language and wrote several books on Russian music. He also wrote monographs on Glinka (London, 1916; 2d ed., 1921), Mussorgsky (London, 1916), and Rimsky-Korsakov (London, 1916).

Montague, Stephen (Rowley), American composer and pianist; b. Syracuse, N.Y., March 10, 1943. Following studies in piano, conducting, and composition at Florida State Univ. (B.M., 1965; M.M., 1967), he pursued his education at Ohio State Univ. (D.M.A., 1972) and worked at the Studio for Experimental Music at the Polish Radio in Warsaw on a Fulbright scholarship (1972–74). In 1974 he made London the center of his activities, but also toured widely as a pianist championing contemporary music. From 1985 he also toured with the pianist Philip Mead in the duo known as Montague/Mead Piano Plus. In 1980 he helped organize the Electro-Acoustic Music Assn. of Great Britain. In 1992 and 1995 he was a guest prof. at the Univ. of Texas at Austin. From 1993 he was a visiting guest prof. at the Royal College of Music in London, and chairman of the SPNM (Soc. for the Promotion of New Music) of Great Britain. In 1995–96 he was also composer-in-residence with the Orch. of St. John's Smith Square in London. Montague's extensive output includes various electroacoustic pieces and acoustic scores.

WORKS: DRAMATIC: *Largo con moto*, graphic/text piece for Dancer and Tape (London, March 15, 1975); *Criseyde*, theater piece for Soprano Playing Ocarina, Slide, and Tape (Mexico City, Oct. 19, 1976); *Into the Sun*, ballet for 4-Channel Tape, Percussion, and Prepared Piano (Manchester, Oct. 31, 1977); *The West of the Imagination*, music for a television drama/documentary series (1986).

Monte, Toti dal. See **Dal Monte, Toti.**

Montéclair, Michel Pignolet de (real name, **Michel Pignolet**), distinguished French composer, teacher, and music theorist; b. Andelot, Haute-Marne (baptized), Dec. 4, 1667; d. Aumont, Sept. 22, 1737. He became a pupil at the Langres Cathedral choir school (1676), where he was taught by the choirmaster, Jean-Baptiste Moreau. He was maître de la musique to the Prince of Vaudémont, whom he followed to Italy. He went to Paris (1687), and later added the name of the fortress in his birthplace, "Montéclair," to his own. With Fedeli, he introduced the double bass to the Paris Opéra orch., where he played from 1699 until 3 months before his death. He was also active as a teacher, his students including François Couperin's daughters. Among his works were *Les Festes de l'été*, opera ballet (Paris Opéra, June 12, 1716) and *Jephté*, tragédie lyrique (Paris Opéra, Feb. 28, 1732).

WRITINGS (all publ. in Paris): *Nouvelle méthode pour apprendre la musique* (1709); *Leçons de musique divisées en quatre classes* (c.1709); *Méthode facile pour apprendre à jouer du violon* (1711–12); *Petite méthode pour apprendre la musique aux enfans et même aux personnes plus avencées en âge* (c.1735); *Principes de musique* (1736).

BIBL.: E. Voillard, *Essai sur M.* (Paris, 1879).

Montemezzi, Italo, eminent Italian opera composer; b. Vigasio, near Verona, Aug. 4, 1875; d. there, May 15, 1952. He was a pupil of Saladino and Ferroni at the Milan Cons., and graduated in 1900; his graduation piece, conducted by Toscanini, was *Cantico dei Cantici*, for Chorus and Orch. He then devoted himself almost exclusively to opera. In 1939 he went to the United States; he lived mostly in California; in 1949 he returned to Italy. Montemezzi's chief accomplishment was the maintenance of the best traditions of Italian dramatic music, without striving for realism or overelaboration of technical means. His masterpiece in this genre was the opera *L'amore dei tre re* (Milan, April 10, 1913), which became a standard work in the repertoire of opera houses all over the world. Other operas were *Giovanni Gallurese* (Turin, Jan. 28, 1905), *Hellera* (Turin, March 17, 1909), *La nave* (libretto by Gabriele d'Annunzio; Milan, Nov. 1, 1918), *La notte di Zoraima* (Milan, Jan. 31, 1931), and *L'incantesimo* (NBC, Oct. 9, 1943, composer conducting).

BIBL.: L. Tretti and L. Fiumi, eds., *Omaggio a I. M.* (Verona, 1952).

Monteux, Pierre, celebrated French-born American conductor; b. Paris, April 4, 1875; d. Hancock, Maine, July 1, 1964. He studied at the Paris Cons. with Berthelier (violin), Lavignac (harmony), and Lenepveu (composition), receiving 1st prize for violin (1896). He began his career as a violist in the Colonne Orch. in Paris, where he later was chorus master; he also was a violist in the orch. of the Opéra Comique in Paris. He then organized his own series, the Concerts Berlioz, at the Casino de Paris (1911); that same year, he also became conductor for Diaghilev's Ballets Russes, where his performances of modern ballet scores established him as one of the finest technicians of the baton. He led the premieres of Stravinsky's *Petrouchka, Le Sacre du printemps*, and *Le Rossignol*, Ravel's *Daphnis et Chloé,* and Debussy's *Jeux*. Monteux conducted at the Paris Opéra (1913–14), founded the Société des Concerts Populaires in Paris (1914), and appeared as guest conductor in London, Berlin, Vienna, Budapest, and other music centers. In 1916–17 he toured the United States with the Ballets Russes. In 1917 he conducted the Civic Orch. Soc., N.Y., and from 1917 to 1919 at the Metropolitan Opera there. In 1919 he was engaged as conductor of the Boston Sym. Orch., holding this post until 1924; from 1924 to 1934 he was assoc. conductor of the Concertgebouw Orch. in Amsterdam, and from 1929 to 1938 he was principal conductor of the newly founded Orch. Symphonique de Paris. From 1936 to 1952 he was conductor of the reorganized San Francisco Sym. Orch. He became a naturalized American citizen in 1942. He appeared as a guest conductor with the Boston Sym. Orch. from 1951, and also accompanied it on its first European tour in 1952, and then again in 1956; likewise he was again on the roster of the Metropolitan Opera (1953–56). In 1961 (at the age of 86) he became principal conductor of the London Sym. Orch., retaining this post until his death.

Monteux was married in 1927 to Doris Hodgkins (b. Salisbury, Maine, 1895; d. Hancock, Maine, March 13, 1984), an American singer who cofounded in 1941 the Domaine School for Conductors and Orchestral Players in Hancock, Maine, of which Monteux was director. She publ. 2 books of memoirs, *Everyone Is Someone* and *It's All in the Music* (N.Y., 1965). After Monteux's death, she established the Pierre Monteux Memorial Foundation. As an interpreter, Monteux endeavored to bring out the inherent essence of the music, without imposing his own artistic personality; unemotional and restrained in his podium manner, he nonetheless succeeded in producing brilliant performances in an extensive repertoire ranging from the classics to the 20th century.

Monteverdi, Claudio (Giovanni Antonio), great Italian composer, brother of **Giulio Cesare Monteverdi**; b. Cremona (baptized), May 15, 1567; d. Venice, Nov. 29, 1643. His surname is also rendered as Monteverde. He was the son of a chemist who practiced medicine as a barber-surgeon. He studied singing and theory with Marc' Antonio Ingegneri, maestro di cappella at the Cathedral of Cremona, and also learned to play the organ. He acquired the mastery of composition at a very early age. He was only 15 when a collection of his 3-part motets was publ. in Venice; there followed several sacred madrigals (1583) and canzonettas (1584). In 1589 he visited Milan, and made an appearance at the court of the duke of Mantua; by 1592 he had obtained a position at the court in the service of Vincenzo I as "suonatore" on the viol (viola da gamba) and violin (viola da braccio). He came into contact with the Flemish composer Giaches de Wert, maestro di cappella at the Mantuan court, whose contrapuntal art greatly influenced Monteverdi. In 1592 Monteverdi publ. his 3d book of madrigals, a collection marked by a considerable extension of harmonic dissonance. In 1595 he accompanied the retinue of the Duke of Mantua on forays against the Turks in Austria and Hungary, and also went with him to Flanders in 1599. He married Claudia de Cattaneis, one of the Mantuan court singers, on May 20, 1599; they had 2 sons; a daughter died in infancy. In 1601 he was appointed maestro di cappella in Mantua following the death of Pallavicino. The publication of 2 books of madrigals in 1603 and 1605 further confirmed his mastery of the genre. Having already composed some music for the stage, he now turned to the new form of the opera. *L'Orfeo*, his first opera, was given before the Accademia degli Invaghiti in Mantua in Feb. 1607. In this pastoral, he effectively moved beyond the Florentine model of recitative-dominated drama by creating a more flexible means of expression; the score is an amalgam of monody, madrigal, and instrumental music of diverse kinds. In 1607 Monteverdi was made a member of the Accademia degli Animori of Cremona. He suffered a grievous loss in the death of his wife in Cremona on Sept. 10, 1607. Although greatly depressed, he accepted a commission to compose an opera to celebrate the marriage of the heir apparent to the court of Mantua, Francesco Gonzaga, to Margaret of Savoy. The result was *L'Arianna*, to a text by Rinuccini, presented in Mantua on May 28, 1608. Although the complete MS has been lost, the extant versions of the *Lamento d'Arianna* from the score testify to Monteverdi's genius in expressing human emotion in moving melodies. In 1614 he prepared a 5-part arrangement of his 6th book of madrigals, also publ. separately (Venice, 1623). He further wrote 2 more works for wedding celebrations, the prologue to the pastoral play *L'Idropica* (not extant) and the French-style ballet *Il ballo delle ingrate*. His patron, Duke Vincenzo of Mantua, died in 1612, and his successor, Francesco, did not retain Monteverdi's services. However, Monteverdi had the good fortune of being called to Venice in 1613 to occupy the vacant post of maestro di cappella at San Marco, at a salary of 300 ducats, which was raised to 400 ducats in 1616. His post at San Marco proved to be the most auspicious of his career, and he retained it for the rest of his life. He composed mostly church music, but did not neglect the secular madrigal forms. He accepted important commissions from Duke Ferdinando of Mantua. His ballet *Tirsi e Clori* was given in Mantua in 1616. In 1619 he publ. his 7th book of madrigals, significant in its bold harmonic innovations. In 1624 his dramatic cantata, *Il combattimento di Tancredi e Clorinda*, after Tasso's *Gerusalemme liberata*, was performed at the home of Girolamo Mocenigo, a Venetian nobleman. The score is noteworthy for the effective role played by the string orch. Other works comprised intermedi for the Farnese court in Parma. A great inconvenience was caused to Monteverdi in 1627 when his son Massimiliano, a medical student, was arrested by the Inquisition for consulting books on the *Index Librorum Prohibitorum*; he was acquitted. In 1630 Monteverdi composed the opera *Proserpina rapita* for Venice; of it only 1 trio has survived. Following the plague of 1630–31, he wrote a mass of thanksgiving for performance at San Marco (the *Gloria* is extant); in 1632 he took Holy Orders. His *Scherzi musicali* for 1 and 2 Voices was publ. in 1632. Then followed his *Madrigali guerrieri et amorosi*, an extensive retrospective collection covering some 30 years, which was publ. in 1638. In 1637 the first public opera houses were opened in Venice, and Monteverdi found a new outlet there for his productions. His operas *Il ritorno d'Ulisse in patria* (1640), *Le nozze d'Enea con Lavinia* (1641; not extant), and *L'incoronazione di Poppea* (1642) were all given in Venice. (Research by Alan Curtis suggests that the latter opera owes its final form to Francesco Sacrati.) The extant operas may be considered the first truly modern operas in terms of dramatic viability. Monteverdi died at the age of 76 and was accorded burial in the church of the Frari in Venice. A commemorative plaque was erected in his honor, and a copy remains in the church to this day.

Monteverdi's place in the history of music is of great magnitude. He established the foundations of modern opera conceived as a drama in music. For greater dynamic expression, he enlarged the orch., in which he selected and skillfully combined the instruments accompanying the voices. He was one of the earliest, if not the first, to employ such coloristic effects as string tremolo and pizzicato; his recitative assumes dramatic power, at times approaching the dimensions of an arioso. In harmonic usage he introduced audacious innovations, such as the use of the dominant seventh-chord and other dissonant chords without preparation. He is widely regarded as having popularized the terms "prima prattica" and "secunda prattica" to demarcate the polyphonic style of the 16th century from the largely monodic style of the 17th century, corresponding also to the distinction between "stile antico" and "stile moderno." For this he was severely criticized by the Bologna theorist Giovanni Maria Artusi, who publ. in 1600 a vitriolic pamphlet against Monteverdi, attacking the "musica moderna" that allowed chromatic usages in order to achieve a more adequate expression.

In addition to various eds. of his works in separate format, G. F. Malipiero edited a complete ed. as *Claudio Monteverdi: Tutte le opere* (16 vols., Asolo, 1926–42; 2d ed., rev., 1954; vol. 17, supplement, 1966). All of these are now being superseded by 2 new complete eds.: one, by the Fondazione Claudio Monteverdi, began publishing in 1970; the other, ed. by B. B. de Surcy, began issuing simultaneously critical and facsimile eds. in 1972.

WORKS: DRAMATIC: *L'Orfeo*, opera, designated "favola in musica" (Mantua, Feb. 1607; publ. in Venice, 1609); *L'Arianna*, opera (Mantua, May 28, 1608; not extant except for various versions of the *Lament*); *In ballo delle ingrate*, ballet (Mantua, 1608; publ. in *Madrigali guerrieri et amorosi*, Venice, 1638); *Prologue to L'Idropica*, comedy with music (Mantua, June 2, 1608; not extant); *Tirsi e Clori*, ballet (Mantua, 1616; publ. in *Concerto: Settimo libro*, Venice, 1619); *Le nozze di Tetide*, favola marittima (begun 1616 but unfinished; not extant); *Andromeda*, opera (begun c.1618 but unfinished; libretto extant); *Apollo*, dramatic cantata (unfinished; not extant); *Il combattimento di Tancredi e Clorinda* (Venice, 1624; publ. in *Madrigali guerrieri et amorosi*, Venice, 1638); *La finta pazza Licori* (composed for Mantua, 1627; never perf.; not extant); *Gli amori di Diana e di Endimione* (Parma, 1628; not extant); *Mercurio e Marte*, torneo (Parma, 1628; not extant); *Proserpina rapita*, opera (Venice, 1630; only 1 trio extant); *Volgendo il ciel*, ballet (Vienna, c.1636; publ. in *Madrigali guerrieri et amorosi*, Venice, 1638); *Il ritorno d'Ulisse in patria*, opera (Venice, 1640); *Le nozze d'Enea con Lavinia*, opera (Venice, 1641; not extant); *La vittoria d'Amore*, ballet (Piacenza, 1641; not extant); *L'incoronazione di Poppea*, opera (Venice, 1642).

BIBL.: S. Davari, *Notizie biografiche del distinto maestro di musica C. M.* (Mantua, 1884); G. Sommi Picenardi, *C. M. a Cremona* (Milan, 1896); L. Schneider, *Un Précurseur de la musique italienne aux XVIe et XVIIe siècles: C. M.: L'Homme et son temps* (Paris, 1921); H. Prunières, *La Vie et l'oeuvre de C. M.* (Paris, 1924; Eng. tr., 1926; 2d French ed., 1931); G. Malipiero, *C. M.* (Milan, 1929); K. Müller, *Die Technik der Ausdrucksdarstellung in M.s monodischen Frühwerken* (Berlin, 1931); H. Redlich, *C. M.: Ein formgeschichtlicher Versuch* (Berlin, 1932); W. Kreidler, *Heinrich Schütz und der Stile Concitato von C. M.* (Stuttgart, 1934); O. Tiby, *C. M.* (Turin, 1944); D. de' Paoli, *C. M.* (Milan, 1945); H. Redlich, *C. M.: Leben und Werk* (Olten, 1949; Eng. tr. and rev., London, 1952); L. Schrade, *M.: Creator of Modern Music* (London, 1950); M. le Roux, *C. M.* (Paris, 1951); C. Sartori, *M.* (Brescia,

1953); A. Abert, *C. M. und das musikalische Drama* (Lippstadt, 1954); R. Roche, *M.* (Paris, 1959); W. Osthoff, *Das dramatische Spätwerk C. M.s* (Tutzing, 1960); D. Arnold, *M.* (London, 1963; rev. ed., 1990); R. Tellart, *C. M.: L'Homme et son oeuvre* (Paris, 1964); D. Arnold, *M. Madrigals* (London, 1967); G. Barblan et al., *C. M. nel quarto centenario della nascita* (Turin, 1967); E. Santoro, *La famiglia e la formazione di C. M.: Note biografiche con documenti inediti* (Cremona, 1967); D. Arnold and N. Fortune, eds., *The M. Companion* (London, 1968; 2d ed., rev., 1985, as *The New M. Companion*); N. Anfuso and A. Gianuario, *Preparazione alla interpretazione della Poiésis M.ana* (Florence, 1971); D. Stevens, *M.: Sacred, Secular and Occasional Music* (Rutherford, N.J., 1978); D. de' Paoli, *M.* (Milan, 1979); D. Stevens, ed. and tr., *The Letters of C. M.* (London, 1980; rev. ed., 1995); S. Leopold, *C. M. und seine Zeit* (Laaber, 1982; Eng. tr., 1991, as *M.: Music in Transition*); J. Whenham, *Duet and Dialogue in the Age of M.* (Ann Arbor, 1982); P. Fabbri, *M.* (Turin, 1985 Eng. tr., 1994); G. Tomlinson, *M. and the End of the Renaissance* (Oxford, 1986); D. Kiel and K. Adams, *C. M.: A Guide to Research* (N.Y., 1989); E. Chafe, *M.'s Tonal Language* (N.Y., 1992); I. Fenlon and P. Miller, *The Song of the Soul: Understanding Poppea* (Chicago, 1992); A. Gianuario, *L'estetica di C. M. attraverso quattro sue lettere* (Sezze Romano, 1993); R. Tellart, *C. M.* (Paris, 1997).

Monteverdi, Giulio Cesare, Italian organist, composer, and writer on music, brother of **Claudio (Giovanni Antonio) Monteverdi**; b. Cremona (baptized), Jan. 31, 1573; d. Salò, Lake Garda, during the plague of 1630–31. In 1602 he entered the service of the duke of Mantua, where his famous brother was maestro di cappella. He composed the music for the 4th intermedio in Guarini's play *L'Idropica*, which was performed for the wedding celebration of the Mantuan heir apparent, Francesco Gonzaga, and Margaret of Savoy in 1608. His opera *Il rapimento di Proserpina* was given in Casale Monferrato in 1611. In 1620 he was named maestro di cappella of the Cathedral in Salo. He publ. a collection of 25 motets under the title *Affetti musici, ne quali si contengono motetti a 1–4 et 6 voci, per concertarli nel basso per l'organo* (Venice, 1620). A madrigal for 3 Voices and Continuo (1605) and 2 pieces in his brother's *Scherzi musicali* (Venice, 1607) are extant. He contributed to the collection *Scherzi musicali* an important *Dichiaratione*, in which he expounded at length the musical ideas of his brother and gave a vigorous reply to the attacks on Monteverdi by Artusi; an Eng. tr. is found in O. Strunk, *Source Readings in Music History* (N.Y., 1950).

Montgomery, Kenneth (Mervyn), Irish conductor; b. Belfast, Oct. 28, 1943. He received his formal musical education at the Royal College of Music in London; he studied conducting in Siena with Celibidache, and in London with Boult and also had instruction with Pritchard and Schmidt-Isserstedt. In 1964 he joined the conducting staff of the Glyndebourne Festival; in 1966 he conducted at the Sadler's Wells Opera in London. In 1970 he became assistant conductor of the Western Orch. Soc. at Bournemouth; in 1972, its assoc. conductor; in 1973 he was appointed music director of the Bournemouth Sinfonietta. He was music director of the Glyndebourne Touring Opera (1975–76). From 1976 to 1980 he was principal conductor of the Netherlands Radio; in 1981 he became chief conductor of its Groot Omroep Koor. He was music director of Opera Northern Ireland in Belfast from 1985 to 1997.

Monti, family of Italian musicians:

(1) Anna Maria Monti, singer; b. Rome, 1704; d. probably in Naples, after 1727. She was only 13 when she made her debut in the 2d comedienne's role in the Piscopo-De Falco dialect opera *Lo mbruoglio d'ammore* at the Teatro dei Fiorentini in Naples, where she sang until 1727.

(2) Laura Monti, singer, sister of the preceding; b. probably in Rome, afer 1704; d. Naples, 1760. After appearing in comic roles at the Teatro Nuovo in Naples, she sang at the royal theater S. Bartolomeo in that city (1733–35), where she created roles in operas by Hasse, Leo, and Pergolesi, including the latter's Serpina in *La Serva padrona* (1733). She was active at the court until her retirement around 1746.

(3) Marianna Monti, soprano, cousin of the two preceding; b. Naples, 1730; d. there, 1814. She made her debut in the Trinchera-Conforto opera *La finta vedova* at the Teatro dei Fiorentini in 1746. She sang there and at the Teatro Nuovo until 1759, and also appeared in concerts under the patronage of the Marchese di Gerace. From 1760 to 1780 Monti was the outstanding prima buffa in Naples, creating numerous roles in operas by Cimarosa, Jommelli, Logroscino, Paisiello, Piccinni, and Sacchini. Her last years were blighted by poverty until she was granted a royal pension in 1812.

(4) Gaetano Monti, organist and composer, brother of the preceding; b. Naples, c.1750; d. probably there, c.1816. He was organista straordinario at the Philippine Tesoro di S. Gennaro in Naples from 1776 to about 1788. He wrote a number of operas, many with roles composed especially for his sister. His most successful stage works were *Le donne vendicate* (Naples, Oct. 17, 1781; also known as *Il gigante*) and *Lo studente* (Naples, 1783; not extant).

Monticelli, Angelo Maria, Italian castrato soprano; b. Milan, c.1712; d. Dresden, 1764. He made his first stage appearance in Rome about 1730. After singing in Venice, Milan, and Florence, he was a principal member of the King's Theatre in London (1741–44; 1746). In subsequent years, he was active in various European music centers until settling in Dresden about 1755.

Montsalvatge, (Bassols) Xavier, Spanish composer, music critic, and teacher; b. Gerona, March 11, 1911. He settled in Madrid and studied at the Cons. His mentors in composition were Morera and Pahissa. He was active as a teacher and as a music critic, writing for the newspaper *La Vanguardia* (1960–72) and serving as ed. of the newspaper *Destino* (1962–70). His autobiography was publ. in Barcelona in 1987. Montsalvatge composed in a well-crafted tonal style in which he occasionally made use of bracing dissonance. His works include *El gato con botas*, magic opera (1948), *Una voce in off*, opera (1961), incidental music, and film scores.

BIBL.: M. Valls, *X. M.* (Barcelona, 1969); E. Franco, *X. M.* (Madrid, 1975); R. Paine, *Hispanic Traditions in Twentieth-Century Catalan Music with Particular Reference to Gerhard, Mompou, and M.* (N.Y. and London, 1989).

Monza, Carlo, Italian composer; b. Milan, c.1735; d. there, Dec. 19, 1801. He studied with G. A. Fioroni and most likely received instruction from G. B. Sammartini, whom he succeeded as organist (1768) and then as maestro di cappella (1775) at Milan's ducal court. He also held the position of maestro di cappella at the churches of S. Maria Segreta, S. Giovanni in Conca, and the Chiesa della Rosa there. He later became maestro di cappella at Milan Cathedral (1787), but retained his position at the ducal court. Illness ended his tenure at the former (1793), and the French occupation (1796) at the latter. He was a skillful composer of both operas and sacred music.

WORKS: OPERAS: *Olimpiade* (Milan, May 1753); *Sesostri re d'Egitto* (Milan, Dec. 26, 1759); *Achille in Sciro* (Milan, Feb. 4, 1764); *Temistocle* (Milan, Jan. 1, 1766); *Oreste* (Turin, Carnival 1766); *Demetrio* (Rome, Jan. 3, 1769); *Adriano in Siria* (Naples, Nov. 4, 1769); *Germanico in Germania* (Rome, Jan. 7, 1770); *La Lavandara astuta*, pasticcio (Milan, July 2, 1770); *Nitteti* (Milan, Jan. 22, 1771); *Aristo e Temira* (Bologna, May 1771); *Berenice* (Turin, 1771?); *Antigono* (Rome, Carnival 1772); *Il (finto) cavalier parigino* (Milan, Sept. 3, 1774); *Alessandro nelle Indie* (Bologna, Jan. 1775); *Cleopatra* (Turin, Dec. 26, 1775); *Caio Mario* (Venice, Ascension Fair 1777); *Attilio Regolo* (1777; not perf.); *Ifigenia in Tauride* (Milan, Jan. 1784); *Enea in Cartagine* (Alessandria, Oct. Fair 1784); *Erifile* (Turin, Dec. 26, 1785).

Moody, Fanny, English soprano; b. Redruth, Cornwall, Nov. 23, 1866; d. Dundrum, County Dublin, July 21, 1945. She studied with Charlotte Sainton-Dolby, making her debut in a memorial concert for her teacher at Prince's Hall in London (1885). She made her operatic debut as Arline in *The Bohemian Girl* with the Carl Rosa Opera Co. in Liverpool (1887), and subsequently was the company's principal soprano until 1898; she married the Irish bass and impresario Charles Manners (1890), with whom she founded the Moody-Manners Opera Co. (1898), and thereafter toured widely with it until it was disbanded (1916). Among her best roles were Gounod's Marguerite and Juliet and Verdi's Leonora and Santuzza.

Moór, Emanuel, Hungarian pianist, inventor, and composer; b. Kecskemét, Feb. 19, 1863; d. Mont Pélerin, near Montreux, Switzerland, Oct. 20, 1931. He studied in Budapest and Vienna. He toured the United States from 1885 to 1887 as director of the Concerts Artistiques, for which he engaged Lilli Lehmann, Ovide Musin, and other celebrated artists, and also acted as their accompanist. He then lived in London, Lausanne, and Munich. He invented the Moór-Duplex piano, consisting of a double keyboard with a coupler between the two manuals (an octave apart). With the introduction of this piano, a new technique was made possible, facilitating the playing of octaves, tenths, and even chromatic glissandos. Some piano manufacturers (Steinway, Bechstein, Bösendorfer) put the Moór mechanism into their instruments. His 2d wife, Winifred Christie (b. Stirling, Feb. 26, 1882; d. London, Feb. 8, 1965), an English pianist, aided him in promoting the Moór keyboard, and gave many performances on it in Europe and the United States. She publ. (in collaboration with her husband) a manual of technical exercises for the instrument.

WORKS: OPERAS: *La Pompadour* (Cologne, Feb. 22, 1902); *Andreas Hofer* (Cologne, Nov. 9, 1902); *Hochzeitsglocken* (Kassel, Aug. 2, 1908; in London as *Wedding Bells*, Jan. 26, 1911); *Der Goldschmied von Paris* (n.d.); *Hertha* (unfinished).

BIBL.: M. Pirani, *E. M.* (London, 1959).

Moor (real name, **Mohr**), **Karel,** Czech conductor, composer, and writer; b. Bělohrad, Dec. 26, 1873; d. Prague, March 30, 1945. He studied at the Prague Cons. and in Vienna. From 1900 to 1923 he was active as a theatrical director and conductor in Bohemia and Serbia; he then lived mainly in Prague. He achieved his first success as a composer with the operetta *Pan profesor v pekle* (Mr. Professor in Hell), produced in Brünn in 1908; his other operas, *Hjördis* (1899; rev. 1901; Prague, Oct. 22, 1905) and *Viy*, after Gogol's fantastic tale (1901; Prague, July 14, 1903), were also successful. A facile writer, he publ. an autobiography in the form of a novel as *Karl Martens* (Prague, 1906), a vol. of reminiscences, *Vzpomínsky* (Pilsen, 1917), and a semifictional book, *V dlani osudu* (In the Hands of Fate; Nový Bydžov, 1947).

Moore, Carman (Leroy), versatile black American composer, conductor, teacher, and writer on music; b. Lorain, Ohio, Oct. 8, 1936. He studied with Martin Morris (horn), Peter Brown (cello), and Cecil Isaacs (conducting) at the Oberlin (Ohio) College-Cons. of Music; after further studies at Ohio State Univ. (B.M., 1958), he went to New York, where he studied at the Juilliard School of Music with Persichetti and Berio (B.M., 1966); he completed his studies with Wolpe (1967). He helped to launch the Soc. of Black Composers in 1968 and taught at Manhattanville College (1969–71), Yale Univ. (1969–71), and Queens (1970–71) and Brooklyn (1972–74) Colleges of the City Univ. of N.Y. He presented concerts with his own group, Carman Moore and Ensemble, which he transformed into the Skymusic Ensemble in 1985. In addition to writing music criticism, he publ. a biography of Bessie Smith as *Somebody's Angel Child* (1970) and a textbook on teaching popular music (1980). In his compositions, he makes imaginative use of various genres, ranging from jazz to the avant-garde.

WORKS: DRAMATIC: OPERAS: *The Masque of Saxophone's Voice* (1981); *Gethsemane Park* (1998). MUSIC THEATER: *Wild Gardens of the Loup Garou* (1983); *Distraughter, or The Great Panda Scanda* (1983); *Paradise Re-Lost* (1987). MUSICALS: *Franklin and Eleanor* (1989); *Journey to Benares* (1997). BALLETS: *A Musical Offering* (1962); *Catwalk* (1966); *Tryst* (1966); *They Tried to Touch* (1986); *La Dea delle Acque* (Milan, March 29, 1988). DANCE PIECE: *Shipwreck* (1989). INTERMEDIA: *Broken Suite* for Instrumental Ensemble (1969); *The Illuminated Workingman* for 11 Instruments and Tape (1971); *American Themes and Variations* for Narrator and Instrumental Ensemble (1980); *Sky Dance/Sky Time* for Instrumental Ensemble, Dance Ensemble, and Sculpture (1984); *The Persistence of Green* for Dance, Dance Projections, and Instrumental Ensemble (N.Y., April 16, 1988); *The Magical Turn About Town* for Instrumental Ensemble (N.Y., July 18, 1989); *Tales of Exile* for Dancers and Instrumental Ensemble (N.Y., July 15, 1989); *Magic Circle* for Dancer, Projections, and Instrumental Ensemble (N.Y., Dec. 28, 1989).

Moore, Dorothy Rudd, black American composer; b. New Castle, Del., June 4, 1940. She studied with Mark Fax at Howard Univ. (B.Mus., 1963), with Boulanger at the American Cons. at Fontainebleau (1963), and with Chou Wen-chung in New York (1965). She then taught at the Harlem School of the Arts (1965–66), N.Y. Univ. (1969), and Bronx Community College (1971); she also appeared as a singer in New York and wrote poetry. In 1968 she helped to found the Soc. of Black Composers. She is married to the cellist Kermit Moore, who has given premiere performances of her works. Her works include the opera *Frederick Douglass* (1979–85).

Moore, Douglas (Stuart), distinguished American composer and pedagogue; b. Cutchogue, N.Y., Aug. 10, 1893; d. Greenport, Long Island, July 25, 1969. After initial musical training in New York, he studied with D.S. Smith and Horatio Parker at Yale Univ. (B.A., 1915; B.M., 1917). He composed several univ. and popular songs, including the football song "Good Night, Harvard," which became a favorite among the Yale student body. After serving in the U.S. Navy, he studied organ with Tournemire and composition with d'Indy and Boulanger in Paris. He was organist at the Cleveland Museum of Art (1921–23) and at Adelbert College, Western Reserve Univ. (1923–25). During this period he pursued training with Ernest Bloch. In 1925 he received a Pulitzer traveling scholarship, which enabled him to study in Europe. From 1926 to 1962 he taught at Barnard College and at Columbia Univ., serving as chairman of the latter's music dept. from 1940 to 1962. In 1934 he held a Guggenheim fellowship. In 1951 he won the Pulitzer Prize in music for his opera *Giants in the Earth*. His opera *The Ballad of Baby Doe* won the N.Y. Music Critics' Circle Award in 1958. In 1941 he was elected to the National Inst. of Arts and Letters, and in 1951 to the American Academy of Arts and Letters. He was the author of the books *Listening to Music* (1932; 2d ed., aug., 1937) and *From Madrigal to Modern Music: A Guide to Musical Style* (1942). Moore was a fine musical craftsman who applied his technical mastery to American subjects in his operas and symphonic scores. He achieved popular success with his operas *The Devil and Daniel Webster* (N.Y., May 18, 1939) and *The Ballad of Baby Doe* (Central City, Colo., July 7, 1956).

WORKS: DRAMATIC: OPERAS: *Jesse James* (1928; unfinished); *White Wings*, chamber opera (1935; Hartford, Conn., Feb. 9, 1949); *The Headless Horseman*, high school opera (1936; Bronxville, N.Y., March 4, 1937); *The Devil and Daniel Webster*, folk opera (1938; N.Y., May 18, 1939); *The Emperor's New Clothes*, children's opera (1948; N.Y., Feb. 19, 1949; rev. 1956); *Giants in the Earth* (1949; N.Y., March 28, 1951; rev. 1963); *The Ballad of Baby Doe*, folk opera (Central City, Colo., July 7, 1956); *Gallantry*, soap opera (1957; N.Y., March 19, 1958); *The Wings of the Dove* (N.Y., Oct. 12, 1961); *The Greenfield Christmas Tree*, Christmas entertainment (Baltimore, Dec. 8, 1962); *Carrie Nation* (Lawrence, Kansas, April 28, 1966). MUSICAL COMEDY: *Oh, Oh, Tennessee* (1925). CHILDREN'S OPERETTA: *Puss in Boots* (1949; N.Y., Nov. 18, 1950). BALLET: *Greek Games* (1930). INCIDENTAL MUSIC TO: plays and for the films *Power in the Land* (1940), *Youth Gets a Break*, and *Bip Goes to Town* (1941).

Moore, Earl Vincent, American music educator and composer; b. Lansing, Mich., Sept. 27, 1890; d. La Jolla, Calif., Dec. 29, 1987. He studied at the Univ. of Mich. (B.A., 1912; M.A., 1915) and later in Europe with Widor, Holst, Boult, Heger, and others. He was an organist and teacher of theory at the Univ. of Mich. (1914–23), and then director of its School of Music, while continuing to teach (was a prof. there, 1923–46); from 1946 to 1960 he was dean of the School of Music. In 1939–40 he was national director of the WPA Music Project. From 1960 to 1970 he was chairman of the music dept. at the Univ. of Houston. He was a founder-member of the National Assn. of Schools of Music and its president from 1936 to 1938. He composed parts of the Michigan Union Operas and other pieces, but is most famous at the Univ. of Mich. as composer of the football song *Varsity*.

Moore, Gerald, renowned English piano accompanist; b. Watford, July 30, 1899; d. Penn, Buckinghamshire, March 13, 1987. He first studied with Wallis Bandey at the local music school; after the family went to Canada in 1913, he continued his studies with Michael Hambourg, then made appearances as a solo recitalist and accompanist; following his return to England (1919), he completed his training with Mark Hambourg. He began recording in 1921 and first gained distinction as accompanist to John Coates in 1925; he subsequently achieved well-nigh legendary fame as the preeminent accompanist of the day, appearing with such celebrated singers as Kathleen Ferrier, Dietrich Fischer-Dieskau, Elisabeth Schwarzkopf, Janet Baker, and others. He retired from the concert platform in 1967 but continued to make recordings. He was made a Commander of the Order of the British Empire (1954) and was made an honorary D.Litt. by the Univ. of Sussex (1968) and Mus.D. by the Univ. of Cambridge (1973). As a witty account of his experiences at the piano, he publ. a sort of autobiography, *The Unashamed Accompanist* (London, 1943; rev. 1957), followed by an even more unzipped opus, *Am I Too Loud? Memoirs of an Accompanist* (London, 1962), and concluding with a somewhat nostalgic vol., *Farewell Recital: Further Memoirs* (London, 1978), and a rip-roaring sequel, *Furthermoore [sic]: Interludes in an Accompanist's Life* (London, 1983). Of a purely didactic nature are his books *Singer and Accompanist: The Performance of 50 Songs* (London, 1953), *The Schubert Song Cycles* (London, 1975), and *"Poet's Lore" and Other Schumann Cycles and Songs* (London, 1984).

Moore, Grace, popular American soprano; b. Nough, near Del Rio, Tenn., Dec. 5, 1898; d. in an airplane crash near Copenhagen, Jan. 26, 1947. She studied at the Wilson Greene School of Music in Chevy Chase, Md., and with Marafioti in New York; she first appeared in musical comedy in New York (1921–26), then continued her studies in Antibes with Richard Berthelemy. Upon returning to America, she made her operatic debut as Mimi at the Metropolitan Opera in New York (Feb. 7, 1928), and sang there off and on until 1946; made successful appearances also at the Paris Opéra Comique (1928), Covent Garden, London (1935), and other European centers; she also sang with the Chicago City Opera (1937) and appeared in several films, including *One Night of Love* (1934). She publ. an autobiography, *You're Only Human Once* (1944). Her finest roles were Mimi, Tosca, Louise, Fiora, and Manon.

Moore, Jerrold Northrop, American editor and writer on music; b. Paterson, N.J., March 1, 1934. He studied at Swarthmore College (B.A., 1955) and Yale Univ. (M.A., 1956; Ph.D., 1959). He taught English at the Univ. of Rochester (1958–61), then was curator of historical sound recordings at Yale Univ. (1961–70). He wrote the authoritative biography *Edward Elgar: A Creative Life* (1984) and was also an editor of the complete critical ed. of Elgar's works (from 1981). His other publications include *Elgar: A Life in Photographs* (1972), *Elgar on Record: The Composer and the Gramophone* (1974), *A Voice in Time: The Gramophone of Fred Gaisberg* (1976; U.S. ed. as *A Matter of Records*), *Music and Friends: Letters to Adrian Boult* (1979), *Spirit of England: Edward Elgar in His World* (1984), *Elgar and His Publishers: Letters of a Creative Life* (2 vols., 1987), *Edward Elgar: Letters of a Lifetime* (1990), and *Vaughan Williams: A Life in Photographs* (1992).

Moore, Mary (Louise) Carr, American composer and teacher; b. Memphis, Tenn., Aug. 6, 1873; d. Inglewood, Calif., Jan. 9, 1957. Her father was a cavalry officer in the U.S. Army who sang; her mother authored several theater dramas; her uncle, John Harraden Pratt, was an organist; after the family went to California (1885), she studied composition with her uncle and singing with H. B. Pasmore in San Francisco. She began her career as a teacher, composer, and singer; she sang the lead role in her first operetta, *The Oracle* (San Francisco, March 19, 1894), but soon devoted herself fully to teaching and composition. She taught in Lemoore, California (1895–1901), and in Seattle (1901–15), where she founded the American Music Center (1909); after teaching in San Francisco (1915–26), she went to Los Angeles as an instructor at the Olga Steeb Piano School (1926–43) and was prof. of theory and composition at Chapman College (1928–47); she was a founder of the Calif. Soc. of Composers (1936–38) and the Soc. of Native Composers (1938–44). As a composer, she devoted herself mainly to writing vocal works, particularly operas on American themes; her most important score was *Narcissa, or The Cost of Empire* (Seattle, April 22, 1912), which was awarded the David Bispham Memorial Medal.

WORKS: OPERAS: *The Oracle* (San Francisco, March 19, 1894); *Narcissa, or The Cost of Empire* (1909–11; Seattle, April 22, 1912); *The Leper* (1912); *Memories* (Seattle, Oct. 31, 1914); *Harmony* (San Francisco, May 25, 1917); *The Flaming Arrow, or The Shaft of Ku'pish-ta-ya* (1919–20; San Francisco, March 27, 1922); *David Rizzio* (1927–28; Los Angeles, May 26, 1932); *Los rubios* (Los Angeles, Sept. 10, 1931); *Legende provençale* (1929–35); *Flutes of Jade Happiness* (1932–33; Los Angeles, March 2, 1934).

BIBL.: C. Smith and C. Richardson, *M. C. M., American Composer* (Ann Arbor, 1989).

Moorhead, John, Irish violinist and composer; b. in Ireland, c.1760; d. (suicide) near Deal, March 1804. After studying music in Ireland, he became a theater musician in England. In 1798 he joined the orch. at London's Covent Garden, but became insane and had to be committed in 1802. After his release, he became a navy bandmaster. Then, following a relapse in 1804, he took his own life. He wrote 14 stage works, including the comic operas *Il Bondocani, or The Caliph Robber* (Covent Garden, Nov. 15, 1800; in collaboration with Attwood), *The Cabinet* (Covent Garden, Feb. 9, 1802; in collaboration with Braham, Corri, Davy, and Reeve), and *Family Quarrels* (Covent Garden, Dec. 18, 1802; in collaboration with Braham and Reeve).

Mooser, R(obert) Aloys, Swiss writer on music; b. Geneva, Sept. 20, 1876; d. there, Aug. 24, 1969. He was the great-grandson of the noted Swiss organist and organ builder (Jean Pierre Joseph) Aloys Mooser (b.Niederhelfenschwyl, June 27, 1770; d. Fribourg, Dec. 19, 1839). His mother was a Russian, and he acquired the knowledge of the Russian language in childhood. He studied with his father and Otto Barblan in Geneva. In 1896 he went to St. Petersburg, where he served as organist at the French church, wrote music criticism for the *Journal de St. Petersbourg*, and made an extensive study of Russian music in the archives. He took courses with Balakirev and Rimsky-Korsakov. In 1909 he returned to Geneva and wrote music criticism for the periodical *La Suisse* (1909–62); he was also founder, ed., and publisher of the periodical *Dissonances* (1923–46). His reviews were collected in the vols. *Regards sur la musique contemporaine: 1921–1946* (Lausanne, 1946); *Panorama de la musique contemporaine: 1947–1953* (Geneva, 1953); *Aspects de la musique contemporaine: 1953–1957* (Geneva, 1957); and *Visage de la musique contemporaine, 1957–1961* (Paris, 1962). He wrote the following books on Russian music: *Contribution à l'histoire de la musique russe: L'Opéra comique française en Russie au XVIIIe siècle* (Geneva, 1932; 2d ed., 1954); *Violonistes-compositeurs italiens en Russie au XVIIIe siècle* (Milan, 1938–50); *Opéras, intermezzos, ballets, cantates, oratorios joués en Russie durant le XVIIIe siècle* (Geneva, 1945; 3d ed., 1964); *Annales de la musique et des musiciens en Russie au XVIIIe siècle* (of prime importance; 3 vols., Geneva, 1948–51).

Morales, Melesio, Mexican composer; b. Mexico City, Dec. 4, 1838; d. San Petro de los Pinos, May 12, 1908. He began to compose salon music for piano and soon acquired sufficient technique to write for the stage. He produced 2 operas, *Romeo y Julieta* (Mexico City, Jan. 27, 1863) and *Ildegonda* (Mexico City,

Dec. 27, 1865), then went to France and Italy for additional study. Returning to Mexico, he taught and composed. His orch. fantasy, *La locomotiva*, was performed at the opening of the Mexico-Puebla railway (Nov. 16, 1869); it anticipated Honegger's *Pacific 231* by more than 50 years. He later produced 2 more operas: *Gino Corsini* (Mexico City, July 14, 1877) and *Cleopatra* (Mexico City, Nov. 14, 1891). Despite his passionate advocacy of national music, he followed conventional Italian models in his own works.

Moralt, Rudolf, esteemed German composer, nephew of **Richard (Georg) Strauss**; b. Munich, Feb. 26, 1902; d. Vienna, Dec. 16, 1958. He studied in Munich at the Univ. and the Academy of Music, his principal teachers being Courvoisier and Schmid-Lindner. After serving as répétiteur at the Bavarian State Opera in Munich (1919–23), he was conductor at the Kaiserslautern Stadtische Oper (1923–28; 1932–34) and music director of the German Theater in Brno (1932–34); he then conducted opera in Braunschweig (1934–36) and Graz (1937–40); subsequently he was a principal conductor at the Vienna State Opera (1940–58) and also appeared as a guest conductor in Europe. In addition to his natural affinity for the music of his uncle, he also conducted fine performances of Mozart, Wagner, Johann Strauss, and Pfitzner.

Moran, Robert (Leonard), American composer; b. Denver, Jan. 8, 1937. He studied piano and went to Vienna in 1957 and took lessons in 12-tone composition with Apostel. Returning to America, he enrolled at Mills College in Oakland, California, where he attended seminars of Berio and Milhaud (M.A., 1963); he completed his training with Haubenstock-Ramati in Vienna (1963) and also painted in the manner of Abstract Expressionism. He was active in avant-garde music circles; with Howard Hersh, he was founder and codirector of the San Francisco Cons.'s New Music Ensemble; he was composer-in-residence at Portland (Oreg.) State Univ. (1972–74) and at Northwestern Univ. (1977–78), where he led its New Music Ensemble; he also appeared extensively as a pianist in the United States and Europe in programs of contemporary music. In his compositions, he combines the "found art" style with aleatory techniques; some of his works are in graphic notation animated by a surrealistic imagination.

WORKS: DRAMATIC: OPERAS: *Let's Build a Nut House*, chamber opera in memory of Paul Hindemith (San Jose, April 19, 1969); *Divertissement No. 3: A Lunchbag Opera* for Paper Bags and Instruments (BBC-TV, 1971); *Metamenagerie*, department store window opera (1974); *Hitler: Geschichten aus der Zukunft* (1981); *Erlösung dem Erlöser*, music drama for Tape Loops and Performers (1982); *The Juniper Tree*, children's opera (1985; in collaboration with P. Glass); *Desert of Roses* (Houston, Feb. 1992); *The Dracula Diaries*, chamber opera (Houston, March 18, 1994). BALLETS: *Spin Again* for Amplified Harpsichord(s) and Electric Keyboards (1980); *Chorale Variations: 10 Miles High over Albania* for 8 Harps (1983). OTHER DRAMATIC: *Durch Wüsten und Wolken* for Shadow Puppets and Instruments (1975); *Marketmenagerie* for Children and Musique Concrète (1975); *Es war einmal*, children's show for Film, Slides, and Musique Concrete (1976); *Music for Gamelan*, incidental music (1978); *Am 29. 11. 1780* for Tape and Dancers (1979).

Moran-Olden (real name, **Tappenhorn**), **Fanny,** German soprano; b. Oldenburg, Sept. 28, 1855; d. Berlin, Feb. 13, 1905. She studied with Haas in Hannover and Götze in Dresden, making her concert debut at the Leipzig Gewandhaus (1877). She made her operatic debut under the name Fanny Olden as Norma in Dresden (1878), then sang at the Frankfurt am Main Opera (1878–84), the Leipzig City Theater (1884–91), and the Munich Court Opera (1891–95). She made her Metropolitan Opera debut in New York on Nov. 28, 1888, as Valentine in *Les Huguenots*; she was on its roster until 1889 and again in 1900–01. In 1896 she toured Europe. After retiring from the stage (1902), she taught voice at Berlin's Klindworth-Scharwenka Cons. She married the tenor Karl Moran (1879) and the baritone Theodor Bertram (1897).

Morawski-Dĕbrowa, Eugeniusz, Polish composer and pedagogue; b. Warsaw, Nov. 2, 1876; d. there, Oct. 23, 1948. He was a student of Noskowski at the Warsaw Music Inst., and then of Gédalge (counterpoint) and Chevillard (orchestration) in Paris. In 1930 he became director of the Poznan Cons. From 1932 to 1939 he was director and prof. of composition at the Warsaw Cons. His music followed the precepts of late Romanticism, He wrote the operas *Aspazja, Lilla Weneda*, and *Salammbô*; also ballets.

Mordden, Ethan, American writer on music; b. Heavensville, Pa., Jan. 27, 1949. He studied piano at an early age; was educated in Quaker schools, including Friends Academy in Locust Valley, N.Y.; then studied at the Univ. of Pa. (B.A. in history, 1969). He worked as a musical director and coach in New York (1971–74), then was assistant ed. of *Opera News* (1974–76); he also was a visiting fellow at Yale Univ. (1980). He is a regular contributor to the *New Yorker* and won a National Magazine Award in 1989; he also wrote for the *N.Y. Times* and *Christopher Street*, among other publications. In addition to his numerous books on music, film, and theater, he publ. fiction on gay life, especially the *Buddies Trilogy* (*I've a Feeling We're Not in Kansas Anymore* [1985], *Buddies* [1986], and *Everybody Loves You* [1988]).

WRITINGS: *Better Foot Forward: The Story of America's Musical Theatre* (1976); *Opera in the Twentieth Century* (1978); *That Jazz!: An Idiosyncratic Social History of the American Twenties* (1978); *The Splendid Art of Opera: A Concise History* (1980); *The Hollywood Musical* (1983); *Demented: The World of the Opera Diva* (1985); *Opera Anecdotes* (1986); *A Guide to Opera Recordings* (1987).

Moreau, Jean-Baptiste, French composer; b. Angers, 1656; d. Paris, Aug. 24, 1733. He was a chorister at Angers Cathedral, then maître de musique at the cathedrals of Langres (1681–82) and Dijon. By Jan. 1687 he was in Paris, where he was introduced at the French court by the Dauphine, and also commissioned by Louis XIV to write several divertissements, among them *Les Bergers de Marly* (1687). He won great success with his musical interludes (recitatives and choruses) for Racine's *Esther* (1698) and *Athalie* (1691), and performed at the school for young noblewomen at St.-Cyr, where he was musicien ordinaire; he also wrote music for Racine's *Cantiques spirituels*, for performance at St.-Cyr. His success at court was marred by his dissolute habits; however, he was greatly esteemed as a teacher of singing and composition; among his pupils were Monteclair, J. F. Dandrieu, Clérambault, and the singers Louise Couperin and his own daughter Marie-Claude Moreau. The music to *Esther* and *Athalie*, and the *Cantiques spirituels*, were publ. in the music supplement to P. Mesnard's *Œuvres de J. Racine* (Paris, 1873).

Moreau, Léon, French composer; b. Brest, July 13, 1870; d. Paris, April 11, 1946. He studied at the Paris Cons., winning the Grand Prix de Rome in 1899. Among his works were the operas *Myriade* and *Pierrot décoré*.

Moreira, Antônio Leal, Portuguese composer; b. Abrantes, 1758; d. Lisbon, Nov. 21, 1819. He studied with João de Sousa Carvalho at the Lisbon Seminario Patriarcal, becoming his assistant in 1775. In 1787 he was appointed mestre de capela of the royal chapel, then served as music director of the Italian Opera Theater (1790–93) and the Teatro San Carlo (1793–1800) in Lisbon. He composed numerous stage works; his opera buffa *Il disertore francese* was given at the Turin Carnival in 1800.

Morel, Auguste-François, French composer; b. Marseilles, Nov. 26, 1809; d. Paris, April 22, 1881. He lived in Paris from 1836 to 1850, then returned to Marseilles, and became director of the Cons. He wrote the opera *Le Jugement de Dieu* (1860).

Morel, Jean (Paul), French-American conductor and pedagogue; b. Abbeville, Jan. 10, 1903; d. N.Y., April 14, 1975. He was a student of Philipp (piano), N. Gallon (theory), Emmanuel (music history), Pierné (composition), and Hahn (lyric repertoire) in Paris. From 1921 to 1936 he taught at the American Cons. in Fontainebleau. He conducted the Orchestre National (1936–39) and the Orchestre Symphonique de Paris (1938). In 1939 he emigrated to the United States. He taught at Brooklyn College of the City Univ. of N.Y. (1940–43). From 1949 to 1971 he was a teacher and conductor at the Juilliard School of Music in New York, where he proved influential in producing a generation of musicians. On Nov. 12, 1944, he made his debut at the N.Y. City Opera conducting *La Traviata*. He made his Metropolitan Opera debut in New York on Dec. 21, 1956, conducting *La Périchole*. He remained on the roster there until 1962, and then returned for the 1967–68 and 1969–71 seasons.

Morell, Barry, American tenor; b. N.Y., March 30, 1927. He received his training in New York. On March 26, 1955, he made his first appearance at the N.Y. City Opera as Pinkerton. He chose that same role for his Metropolitan Opera debut in New York on Nov. 1, 1958, and continued to make occasional appearances there until 1979. As a guest artist, he also sang in Europe and South America. He was best known for his roles in Italian opera.

Morelli (real name, **Zanelli**), **Carlo,** Chilean baritone; b. Valparaiso (of an Italian father and a Chilean mother), Dec. 25, 1897; d. Mexico City, May 12, 1970. He studied voice in Bologna with Angelo Queize and in Florence with Leopoldo Mugnone. He sang at La Scala, Milan (1922) and toured South America (1925–31). He made his first U.S. appearence with the Chicago Opera in 1932; he made his debut at the Metropolitan Opera in New York on Dec. 21, 1935, as Marcello; he remained there until 1940, then sang with the San Carlo Opera at the City Center, N.Y. (1940–49). In 1949 he settled in Mexico.

Morena (real name, **Meyer**), **Berta,** noted German soprano; b. Mannheim, Jan. 27, 1878; d. Rottach-Egern, Oct. 7, 1952. Her buxom beauty attracted the attention of the famous painter von Lenbach, who persuaded her to study voice with Sophie Röhr-Brajnin and Aglaja von Orgeni in Munich; after additional training with Regina de Sales, she made her operatic debut as Agathe in *Der Freischütz* at the Munich Court Opera (1898); she remained on its roster until 1927. She made her American debut with the Metropolitan Opera in New York as Sieglinde (March 4, 1908), remaining on its roster until 1909; she then returned from 1910 to 1912 and in 1924–25. She was regarded in Germany as an intelligent and musicianly singer, excelling particularly in Wagnerian roles, including Elisabeth, Elsa, Eva, Isolde, and the 3 Brünnhildes.

BIBL.: A. Vogl, *B. M. und ihre Kunst* (Munich, 1919).

Morera, Enrique (Enric), Spanish composer; b. Barcelona, May 22, 1865; d. there, March 11, 1942. As a child, he was taken to Argentina, and studied in Buenos Aires; he then took courses at the Brussels Cons. Returning to Barcelona, he studied piano with Albéniz and harmony with Felipe Pedrell. In 1895 he founded the choral society Catalunya Nova, which he conducted until 1909; he then taught at the Escuela Municipal de Música in Barcelona (1910–28). He was an ardent propagandist of Catalan music, and wrote a number of songs to Catalan words; he also collected 193 melodies of popular origin. His opera *Emporium*, originally to a Catalan text, was performed first in Italian (Barcelona, Jan. 20, 1906); he wrote more than 50 other stage works (lyric comedies, zarzuelas, operettas, intermezzos, etc.).

BIBL.: I. Iglesias, *Enric M.* (Barcelona, 1921); J. Pena, *Enric M.* (Barcelona, 1937).

Morère (real name, **Couladère**), **Jean,** French tenor; b. Toulouse, Oct. 6, 1836; d. Paris, Feb. 1887. He studied with Paul Laget in Toulouse, making his debut as *Manrico* at the Paris Opéra in 1861, where he sang until 1869. He created the title role in Verdi's *Don Carlos* there in 1867, and also appeared in Brussels at the Théâtre Royal de la Monnaie (1865–66; 1869–70). He suffered a mental derangement in the wake of the Franco-Prussian War in 1871.

Moreschi, Alessandro, Italian castrato soprano; b. Montecompatri, near Rome, Nov. 11, 1858; d. Rome, April 21, 1922. He studied with Capocci in Rome, and from 1883 to 1913 sang at the Vatican's Sistine Chapel. The last of the castrati, he had a voice of such purity and beauty that he was nicknamed "l'angelo di Roma."

Mori, Frank (Francis), English conductor and composer; b. London, March 21, 1820; d. Chaumont, France, Aug. 2, 1873. He was educated by his father, the English violinist and music publisher Nicolas Mori (1796–1839). He wrote light music, including the operetta *The River-Sprite* (London, Feb. 9, 1865), which was fairly successful.

Moriani, Napoleone, outstanding Italian tenor; b. Florence, March 10, 1806; d. there, March 4, 1878. He studied with C. Ruga, making his operatic debut in Pacini's *Gli Arabi nelle Gallie* in Pavia in 1833. He then sang throughout Italy, garnering great praise for his interpretations of Bellini, Donizetti, and Verdi; he created the role of Enrico in Donizetti's *Maria di Rudenz* in Venice in 1838, and that of Carlo in *Linda di Chamounix* in Vienna in 1842. He sang in Madrid (1844–46) and London (1844–45) and made his Paris debut at the Théâtre-Italien (1845), where he returned in 1849–50 before appearing again in Madrid. He retired from the stage in 1851. Having sung so many death-laden tenor roles, he became known as "il tenore della bella morte."

Mörike, Eduard, German conductor; b. Stuttgart, Aug. 16, 1877; d. Berlin, March 14, 1929. He was a great-nephew of the poet Eduard Friedrich Mörike. He studied at the Leipzig Cons. with Ruthard and Sitt, and received private piano instruction from Siloti. In 1899 he went to the United States and made appearances as a pianist. After working as a coach at the Metropolitan Opera in New York, he returned to Germany and conducted in various theaters. From 1906 to 1909 he was an assistant conductor at the Bayreuth Festivals. He held the post of 1st conductor at the Deutsches Opernhaus in Berlin from 1912 to 1922, and also made appearances as a guest conductor with the Berlin Phil. He subsequently was active as a conductor in Europe and the United States. From 1924 until his death he was chief conductor of the Dresden Phil.

Morison, Elsie (Jean), Australian soprano; b. Ballarat, Aug. 15, 1924. She studied with Clive Carey at the Melbourne Cons. She made her London debut at the Royal Albert Hall in London in 1948, then sang with the Sadler's Wells Opera (1948–54) and at Covent Garden (1953–62). She married **Rafael Kubelik** in 1963. Her roles included Pamina, Susanna, Marzelline, Micaëla, and Anne Trulove.

Morlacchi, Francesco (Giuseppe Baldassare), prominent Italian conductor and composer; b. Perugia, June 14, 1784; d. Innsbruck, Oct. 28, 1841. He studied with his uncle, the Cathedral organist L. Mazzetti, and with Luigi Caruso in Perugia, then with Zingarelli in Loreto (1803–04) and Padre Mattei at Bologna's Liceo Filarmonica (1805), where he received his diploma of "maestro compositore" for the cantata *Il tempio della gloria*, written in honor of Napoleon's coronation as King of Italy. He demonstrated his contrapuntal skill by composing a *Miserere à 16* (1807). He first gained success as a composer for the stage with his operas *La Principessa per ripiego* (Rome, autumn 1809) and *Le Danaidi* (Rome, Feb. 11, 1810). He then was called to Dresden as deputy Kapellmeister of the Italian Opera in 1810, being made Kapellmeister for life in 1811; he retained the latter title until the Italian Opera was closed in 1832. During these years, he wrote some of his most successful stage works, among them *Il nuovo barbiere di Siviglia* (Dresden, May 1816), *La simplicetta di Pirna* (Dresden, Aug. 1817), *La gioventu di Enrico* (Dresden, Oct. 4, 1823), *Il Colombo* (Genoa, June 28, 1828), and *Il Rinnegato* (Dresden, March 1832); he also wrote a Requiem upon the death of King Friedrich August I of Saxony (1827). In later years he divided his time between Dresden and Italy. Stricken with tuberculosis in 1839, he died on his way to his homeland.

BIBL.: G. Ricci des Ferres-Cancani, *F. M.: Un maestro italiano alla corte di Sassonia (1785–1841)* (Florence, 1956); B. Brumana and G. Ciliberti, eds., *F. M. e la musica del suo tempo (1785–1841)* (Florence, 1986).

Moross, Jerome, American composer; b. N.Y., Aug. 1, 1913; d. Miami, July 25, 1983. He studied at the Juilliard School of Music in New York (1931–32) and at N.Y. Univ. (graduated, 1932). He became associated with various ballet groups and wrote a number of scores for the dance, most of them on American subjects, all of them in a vivid folklike manner. In 1940 he went to Hollywood as an arranger; collaborated with Copland on the score for *Our Town*. He held 2 Guggenheim fellowships (1947, 1948). His first film score was *Close Up* (1948); his other film scores included *The Cardinal, The Proud Rebel*, and *The Big Country*. For Broadway he wrote music for *Parade* (1935). His works for the dance included *Paul Bunyan* (1934), *American Patterns* (1937), *Frankie and Johnny* (1938), *Guns and Castanets* (1939), *The Eccentricities of Davy Crockett* (1946), and *Robin Hood* (1946). He also wrote the operas *Susanna and the Elders* (1940), *Willie the Weeper* (1945), *The Golden Apple* (1948–50), *Gentleman, Be Seated!* (1955–56; N.Y., Oct. 10, 1963), and *Sorry, Wrong Number* (1977); also a ballet suite, *The Last Judgment* (1953).

Morris, James (Peppler), outstanding American bass-baritone; b. Baltimore, Jan. 10, 1947. After studies with a local teacher, he won a scholarship to the Univ. of Maryland; concurrently he received invaluable instruction from Rosa Ponselle, then continued his studies with Frank Valentino at the Peabody Cons. of Music in Baltimore (1966–68). He made his debut as Crespel in *Les Contes d'Hoffmann* with the Baltimore Civic Opera (1967). After further training with Nicola Moscona at the Philadelphia Academy of Vocal Arts (1968–70), he made his Metropolitan Opera debut in New York as the King in *Aida* on Jan. 7, 1971; he appeared with the Opera Orch. of N.Y. and sang widely in Europe. In 1975 he scored a notable success as Don Giovanni at the Metropolitan. Although closely associated with the Italian and French repertoires, he appeared as Wotan in *Die Walküre* at the Baltimore Civic Opera in 1984; subsequently he sang that role in the San Francisco Opera's *Ring* cycle in 1985, eliciting extraordinary critical acclaim. In 1986 he appeared at the Salzburg Festival as Mozart's Guglielmo and Figaro. In 1990 he sang Méphistophélès in Cincinnati and at the Metropolitan Opera, where he also appeared as Wotan, and as the Wanderer in *Siegfried* at London's Covent Garden. He portrayed Wotan at the Lyric Opera in Chicago in 1993 and 1996. In 1995 he sang that role at the San Francisco Opera, and returned there in 1997 as Scarpia. After singing Iago at the Metropolitan Opera in 1995, he returned there as Mozart's Figaro in 1997. His other esteemed roles include Count Almaviva, Philip II, the Dutchman, the 4 villains in *Les Contes d'Hoffmann*, Timur in *Le Roi de Lahore*, Scarpia, and Claggart in *Billy Budd*. In 1987 he married **Susan Quittmeyer**.

Morris, Joan (Clair), American mezzo-soprano; b. Portland, Oreg., Feb. 10, 1943. She studied voice with Lyle Moore at Gonzaga Univ. (1963–65), and received training in speech and voice from Clifford Jackson, first at the American Academy of Dramatic Arts (diploma, 1968), and then privately (1968–73); she also had private instruction from Frederica Schmitz-Svevo in New York (1968–74). In 1975 she married **William Bolcom**, with whom she subsequently appeared regularly in concerts. Morris became notably successful as an interpreter of both serious scores and popular music, ranging from the early American period to works by Bolcom. In 1983 she was featured in the PBS-TV special *Fascinating Rhythms*. In 1987 she appeared at Weill Recital Hall at N.Y.'s Carnegie Hall. From 1981 she taught at the Univ. of Mich.

Mortari, Virgilio, Italian composer and pedagogue; b. Passirana di Lainate, near Milan, Dec. 6, 1902; d. Rome, Sept. 6, 1993. He began his training at the Milan Cons. with Bossi and Pizzetti, and then completed his studies at the Parma Cons. (composition diploma, 1928). After appearances as a pianist, he taught composition at the Venice Cons. (1933–40). From 1940 to 1973 he was a prof. of composition at the Rome Cons. He also served as superintendent of the Teatro La Fenice in Venice from 1955 to 1959. With A. Casella, he wrote the book *Le tecnica dell'orchestra contemporanea* (Milan, 1947; 2d ed., 1950). Mortari completed Mozart's unfinished score *L'Oca del Cairo* (Salzburg, Aug. 22, 1936). Among his own works were the operas *Secchi e Sberlecchi* (1927), *La scuola delle moglie* (1930; rev. 1959), *La Figlia del diavolo* (Milan, March 24, 1954), and *Il contratto* (1964), and the ballets *L'allegro piazetta* (1945) and *Specchio a tre luci* (1973).

Mortelmans, Ivo (Oscar), Belgian conductor, teacher, and composer, son of **Lodewijk Mortelmans**; b. Antwerp, May 19, 1901; d. Ostend, Aug. 20, 1984. He studied at the Antwerp Cons.; upon graduation he taught academic subjects and theory in Berchem (1925–66), Deurne (1939–70), and Mortsel (1946–67). He was also active as an opera conductor. He wrote an oratorio, *Eeuwig vlecht de bruid haar kroon* (1964), and numerous other choral works, both sacred and secular.

Mortelmans, Lodewijk, Belgian conductor, teacher, and composer, father of **Ivo (Oscar) Mortelmans**; b. Antwerp, Feb. 5, 1868; d. there, June 24, 1952. He was a chorister in the Dominican Church; he then studied with Benoit in Antwerp. In 1889 he won the 2d Belgian Prix de Rome; gained 1st prize with his cantata Lady Macbeth in 1893; he then taught at the Antwerp Cons. from 1902. In 1921 he made a tour in the United States. He was director of the Antwerp Cons. from 1924 to 1933. His finest creations were his songs to Flemish texts, which prompted Gilson to call him the "Prince of the Flemish song." He composed the opera *De kinderen der Zee* (Antwerp, 1920).

BIBL.: J. Broeckx, *L. M.* (Antwerp, 1945).

Mortier, Gerard, provocative Belgian opera administrator; b. Ghent, Nov. 25, 1943. He received training in law and journalism at the Univ. of Ghent. From 1968 to 1972 he was an administrative assistant at the Flanders Festival. After serving as artistic planner at the Deutsche Oper am Rhein in Düsseldorf (1972–73), he was assistant administrator at the Frankfurt am Main Opera (1973–77). From 1977 to 1979 he was director of artistic planning at the Hamburg State Opera, and then technical program consultant to the Paris Opéra (1979–81). In 1981 he became general director of the Théâtre Royal de la Monnaie in Brussels, where he raised standards to a new high but provoked much controversy. In 1992 he became artistic director of the Salzburg Festival and proceeded to implement a radical transformation of every facet of the festival's operations. In spite of the storm of controversy he engendered, he successfully carried out his grand plan to make the festival a viable and creative music center for the dawning of the 21st century.

Mosca, Giuseppe, Italian composer, brother of **Luigi Mosca**; b. Naples, 1772; d. Messina, Sept. 14, 1839. He studied with Fenaroli at the Cons. of S. Maria di Loreto in Naples. He was engaged as répétiteur at the Théâtre-Italien, Paris (1803–10), then was music director at the Teatro Carolino in Palermo (1817–20) and later was director of music at a Messina theater (1827). He wrote 42 operas, ballets, and other stage pieces.

Mosca, Luigi, Italian composer, brother of **Giuseppe Mosca**; b. Naples, 1775; d. there, Nov. 30, 1824. He was a pupil of Fenaroli. He served as maestro al cembalo at Naples's Teatro San Carlo and also primo maestro di canto at the Cons. (from 1813). He wrote 16 operas, of which *I Pretendenti delusi* (Milan, Sept. 7, 1811) was the most successful.

Moscona, Nicola, Greek bass; b. Athens, Sept. 23, 1907; d. Philadelphia, Sept. 17, 1975. He studied at the Athens Cons. with Elena Teodorini. He sang opera in Greece and Eygpt, then was engaged to sing at the Metropolitan Opera in New York, and made a successful American debut there as Ramfis in *Aida* (Dec. 13, 1937); remained on its roster until 1962. He then went to Philadelphia, where he taught at the Academy of Vocal Arts.

Mosel, Ignaz Franz von, Austrian composer, conductor, and writer on music; b. Vienna, April 1, 1772; d. there, April 8, 1844. He was the first conductor of the musical festivals given by Vienna's Gesellschaft der Musikfreunde at the imperial riding school (1812–16); he pioneered the use of the baton in Vienna. He was vice director of the 2 Court Theaters (1820–29), then principal custos of the Imperial Library (1829–44). He was ennobled and made a Hofrat. He composed *Die Feuerprobe*, Singspiel (April 28, 1811), *Salem*, lyric tragedy (March 5, 1813), and *Cyrus und Astyages*, heroic opera (June 13, 1818); also much incidental music. All of these works were first perf. at the Vienna Court Opera.

WRITINGS (all publ. in Vienna): *Versuch einer Ästhetik des musikalischen Tonsatzes* (1813); *Über das Leben und die Werke des Anton Salieri* (1827); *Geschichte der k.k. Hofbibliothek in Wien* (1835); *Über die Original-Partitur des Requiems von W. A. Mozart* (1839).

Moser, Edda (Elisabeth), prominent German soprano, daughter of **Hans Joachim Moser**; b. Berlin, Oct. 27, 1938. She studied with Hermann Weissenborn and Gerty König at the Berlin Cons. She made her debut as Kate Pinkerton at the Berlin Städtische Oper (1962); after singing in the Würzburg Opera chorus (1962–63), she sang opera in Hagen and Bielefeld; subsequently appeared with the Frankfurt am Main Opera (1968–71) before joining the Vienna State Opera; she also sang in Berlin, Salzburg, Hamburg, and other major music centers. She made her U.S. debut as Wellgunde in *Das Rheingold* at the Metropolitan Opera in New York on Nov. 22, 1968, and later appeared there as Donna Anna, the Queen of the Night, and Liù. Her last appearance there was in 1984. She maintained an extensive repertoire, singing both coloratura and lyrico-dramatic roles, being equally successful in standard and contemporary works; also sang widely as a concert artist.

Moser, Hans Joachim, eminent German musicologist, father of **Edda (Elisabeth) Moser**; b. Berlin, May 25, 1889; d. there, Aug. 14, 1967. He studied violin with his father, the noted German violin pedagogue and music scholar Andreas Moser (b. Semlin an der Donau, Nov. 29, 1859; d. Berlin, Oct. 7, 1925), then took courses in musicology with Kretzschmar and Wolf at the Univ. of Berlin, with Schiedermair at the Univ. of Marburg, and with Riemann and Schering at the Univ. of Leipzig; he also studied voice with Oskar Noë and Felix Schmidt, and took courses in composition with H. van Eyken, Robert Kahn, and G. Jenner; he received his Ph.D. from the Univ. of Rostock in 1910 with the diss. *Die Musikergenossenschaften im deutschen Mittelalter*. Returning to Berlin, he was active as a concert singer (bass-baritone); he then served in the German army during World War I. He subsequently completed his Habilitation at the Univ. of Halle in 1919 with his *Das Streichinstrumentenspiel im Mittelalter* (publ. in A. Moser's *Geschichte des Violinspiels*, Berlin, 1923; 2d ed., rev. and enl., 1966–67). In 1919 he joined the faculty of the Univ. of Halle as a Privatdozent of musicology, and then became a reader there in 1922; he then was a reader at the Univ. of Heidelberg from 1925 to 1927; he was honorary prof. at the Univ. of Berlin from 1927 to 1934, and also served as director of the State Academy for Church and School Music in Berlin from 1927 to 1933; he received the degree of doctor of theology at Königsberg in 1931. He retired from his public positions in 1934 but continued his musicological pursuits in Berlin; he later served as head of the Reichsstelle für Musik-Bearbeitungen from 1940 to 1945. After World War II, he resumed teaching by accepting appointments as a prof. at the Univ. of Jena and the Hochschule für Musik in Weimar in 1947; he then served as director of the Berlin Cons. from 1950 until 1960. Moser was an outstanding music historian and lexicographer; his numerous writings are notable for their erudition. However, his unquestionable scholarship was marred by his ardent espousal of the Nazi racial philosophy; so ferocious was his anti-Semitism that he excluded Mendelssohn from his books publ. during the 3d Reich. He served as ed. of a projected complete edition of Weber's works (Augsburg and Leipzig, 1926–33), but it remains unfinished. Other works he ed. include *Luthers Lieder, Werke*, XXXV (Weimar, 1923; with O. Albrecht and H. Lucke); *Minnesang und Volkslied* (Leipzig, 1925; 2d ed., enl., 1933); *Das Liederbuch des Arnt von Aich* (Kassel, 1930; with E. Bernoulli); *Das deutsche Sololied und die Ballade, Das Musikwerk*, XIV (1957; Eng. tr., 1958); *Heinrich Schütz: Italienische Madrigale, Neue Ausgabe sämtlicher Werke*, XXII (Kassel, 1962). He also contributed countless articles to various German music journals; likewise wrote novels, short stories, and a comedy. He also tried his hand at composing, producing the school opera *Der Reisekamerad*, choruses, and songs. He arranged operas by Handel and Weber; wrote an entirely new libretto for Weber's Euryanthe and produced it under the title *Die sieben Raben* (Berlin, March 5, 1915).

WRITINGS: *Technik der deutschen Gesangskunst* (Berlin, 1911; 3d ed., 1955, with Oskar Noë); *Geschichte der deutschen Musik* (3 vols., Stuttgart and Berlin, 1920, 1922, and 1924; 2d ed., enl., 1968); *Musikalisches Wörterbuch* (Leipzig and Berlin, 1923); *Paul Hofhaimer: Ein Lied- und Orgelmeister des deutschen Humanismus* (Stuttgart and Berlin, 1929; 2d ed., enl., 1966); *Die Ballade* (Berlin, 1930); *Die Epochen der Musikgeschichte im Überblick* (Stuttgart and Berlin, 1930; 2d ed., 1956); *Die mehrstimmige Vertonung des Evangeliums* (2 vols., Leipzig, 1931 and 1934); *Musiklexikon* (Berlin, 1932–35; 2d ed., 1943, withdrawn; 3d ed., 1951; 4th ed., 1955; supplement, 1963); *Corydon: das ist: Geschichte des mehrstimmigen Generalbass-Liedes und des Quodlibets im deutschen Barock* (2 vols., Braunschweig, 1933); *Die Melodien der Luther-Lieder* (Leipzig and Hamburg, 1935); *Johann Sebastian Bach* (Berlin, 1935; 2d ed., 1943); *Tönende Volksaltertümer* (Berlin, 1935); *Heinrich Schütz: Sein Leben und Werk* (Kassel, 1936; 2d ed., rev., 1954; Eng. tr., 1959); *Lehrbuch der Musikgeschichte* (Berlin, 1936; 13th ed., 1959); *Das deutsche Lied seit Mozart* (Berlin and Zürich, 1937; 2d ed., rev., 1968); *Die Musikfibel* (Leipzig, 1937); *Kleine deutsche Musikgeschichte* (Stuttgart, 1938; 4th ed., 1955); *Allgemeine Musiklehr* (Berlin, 1940); *Christoph Willibald Gluck* (Stuttgart, 1940); *Kleines Heinrich-Schütz-Buch* (Kassel, 1940; Eng. tr., 1967); *Carl Maria von Weber* (Leipzig, 1941; 2d ed., 1955); *George Friedrich Händel* (Kassel, 1941; 2d ed., 1952); *Goethe und die Musik* (Leipzig, 1949); *Lebensvolle Musikerziehung* (Vienna, 1952); *Musikgeschichte in hundert Lebensbildern* (Stuttgart, 1952); *Die evangelische Kirchenmusik in Deutschland* (Berlin, 1953); *Musikästhetik* (Berlin, 1953); *Die Musikleistung der deutschen Stämme* (Vienna, 1954); *Die Tonsprachen des Abendlandes* (Berlin and Darmstadt, 1954); *Dietrich Buxtehude* (Berlin, 1957); *Musik in Zeit und Raum* (Berlin, 1960; collected essays); *Bachs Werke: Ein Führer für Musikfreunde* (Kassel, 1964); etc.

BIBL.: *Festgabe für H. J. M.* (Kassel, 1954).

Moser, Rudolf, Swiss composer, conductor, violist, and teacher; b. Niederuzwyl, Jan. 7, 1892; d. in a mountain-climbing accident in Silvaplana, Aug. 20, 1960. He studied musicology with Nef and received training in theology at the Univ. of Basel. After further studies with Reger, Sitt, and Klengel at the Leipzig Cons. (1912–14), he completed his training with Huber in Basel and Lauber in Geneva. He settled in Basel, where he conducted the Cathedral Choir, played viola in a string quartet, and taught at the Cons. He composed the Singspiel *Die Fischerin* (1935) and a dance play, *Der Rattenfänger* (1950).

BIBL.: H. Buchli, *R. M.* (Zürich, 1964).

Moser, Thomas, American tenor; b. Richmond, Va., May 27, 1945. After training at the Richmond (Va.) Professional Inst., he studied at the Curtis Inst. of Music in Philadelphia; he later pursued vocal training with Martial Singher, Gérard Souzay, and Lotte Lehmann. In 1974 he was a winner in the Metropolitan Opera auditions; he then joined the Graz Landestheater in 1975. In 1976 he appeared as Mozart's Belmonte with the Bavarian State Opera in Munich. From 1977 he sang with the Vienna State Opera, where he appeared as Mozart's Tamino, Ottavio, Titus, and Idomeneo, Strauss's Flamand and Henry, and Gluck's Achilles. He made his first appearance with the N.Y. City Opera in 1979 as Titus. In 1983 he sang at the Salzburg Festival, returning there in 1984 to create the role of the tenor in Berio's *Un re in ascolto*. In 1985 he made his debut at Milan's La Scala as Tamino. In 1986 he sang for the first time at the Rome Opera as Achilles. In 1988 he appeared in the title role of Schubert's *Fierrabras* at the Theater an der Wien. In 1992 he sang the Emperor in *Die Frau ohne Schatten* in Geneva. He portrayed Palestrina during the visit to New York of the Royal Opera of London in 1997. In 1998 he was engaged as Florestan in Chicago. As a concert artist, he appeared with leading North American and European orchs. His expansive operatic and concert repertoire ranges from early music to the cosmopolitan avant-garde.

Moshinsky, Elijah, Australian opera and theater producer; b. Shanghai, Jan. 8, 1946. He was educated at the Univ. of Melbourne (B.A.) and at St. Anthony's College, Oxford. He began his career as a theater producer, overseeing plays of Shakespeare for BBC-TV and for plays at the National Theatre in London. In 1975 he produced his first opera at London's Covent Garden with a staging of *Peter Grimes*, and returned there with such productions as *Lohengrin* (1977), *The Rake's Progress* (1979), *Macbeth* (1981), *Tannhäuser* (1984), *Otello* (1986), *Die Entführung aus dem Serail* (1987), *Attila* (1994), and a revival of *Lohengrin* (1997). In 1980 he worked for the first time at the Metropolitan Opera in New York when he staged *Un ballo in maschera*. He oversaw the British stage premiere of Ligeti's *Le Grand Macabre* at the English National Opera in London in 1981. In 1983 he produced *Un ballo in maschera* at the Australian Opera in Sydney. His staging of *La Bohème* was seen at the Scottish Opera in Glasgow in 1988. In 1998 he produced *Lohengrin* at the Metropolitan Opera. In his productions, Moshinsky upholds the traditional approach to stagecraft.

Moskowa, Joseph Napoléon Ney, Prince de la, French statesman and composer; b. Paris, May 8, 1803; d. St.-Germain-en-Laye, July 25, 1857. He was the eldest son of Michel Ney, Duc d'Elchingen and Prince de la Moskowa, and revealed a talent for music as child. He was made a member of the Chambre de Paris (1831), and later served as brigadier general under Napoleon III. With A. Adam, he organized the Société de Concerts de Musique Vocale, Religieuse et Classique (1843), which presented works of the Renaissance, Baroque, and Classical periods at his palace. The society publ. 11 vols. of these works as *Recueil des morceaux de musique ancienne*. He composed 2 comic operas: *Le Cent-Suisse* (Paris, June 7, 1840) and *Yvonne* (Paris, March 16, 1855).

Mosolov, Alexander (Vasilievich), Russian composer; b. Kiev, Aug. 11, 1900; d. Moscow, July 12, 1973. He fought in the Civil War in Russia (1918–20) and was wounded and decorated twice with the Order of the Red Banner for heroism. After the war he studied composition with Glière in Kiev, then studied harmony and counterpoint with Glière, composition with Miaskovsky, and piano with Prokofiev and Igumnov at the Moscow Cons. (1922–25). He played his 1st Piano Concerto in Leningrad on Feb. 12, 1928. In his earliest works, he adopted modernistic devices; wrote songs to texts of newspaper advertisements. His ballet *Zavod* (Iron Foundry; Moscow, Dec. 4, 1927) attracted attention because of the attempt to imitate the sound of a factory at work by shaking a large sheet of metal. However, Mosolov's attempt to produce "proletarian" music by such means elicited a sharp rebuke from the official arbiters of Soviet music. On Feb. 4, 1936, he was expelled from the Union of Soviet Composers for staging drunken brawls and behaving rudely to waiters in restaurants. He was sent to Turkestan to collect folk songs as a move toward his rehabilitation. After settling in Moscow in 1939, he continued to make excursions to collect folk songs in various regions of Russia.

WORKS: DRAMATIC: OPERAS: *Geroy* (The Hero; 1927; Baden-Baden, July 15, 1928); *Plotina* (The Dam; 1929); *The Signal* (1941); *Maskarad* (Masquerade; 1940). MUSICAL COMEDY: *Friedrich Barbarossa*. ORATORIOS: *M. I. Kalinin* (1940); *Moscow* (1948).

Mosonyi, Mihály (real name, **Michael Brand**), noted Hungarian composer; b. Boldogasszonyfalva, Sept. 4, 1814; d. Pest, Oct. 31, 1870. He learned to play wind instruments and the organ in childhood. He went to Magyaróvár as a church officer when he was 15, and taught himself music by copying Hummel's piano exercises. He then proceeded to Pressburg (c.1832), where he studied piano and theory with Károly Turányi; after serving as a piano teacher in the household of Count Péter Pejachevich in Rétfalu (1835–42), during which time he honed his compositional skills through diligent study of Reicha's theoretical works, he settled in Pest as a teacher of piano and composition. He first attracted notice as a composer when his overture was premiered in April 1843. It was followed by his 1st Sym. and a Piano Concerto, the latter anticipating Liszt in the formulation of cyclic development. His first work to adopt Hungarian idioms was his 2d Sym. (Pest, March 30, 1856). Liszt became his friend in 1856 and encouraged him in his work, proposing to produce his German Romantic opera *Kaiser Max auf der Martinswand* (1856–57); the score was never performed. Mosonyi's espousal of Hungarian nationalism led him to abandon his real name in 1859, adopting one that honored his birthplace, the county of Mosen. In his compositions, he gave increasing attention to Hungarian elements, producing his *Hódolat Kazinczy Ferenc szellemenek* (Homage to Kazinczy; 1860) for Piano (later orch.), a Hungarian rhapsody, and *Gyász hangok Széchenyi István halálára* (Funeral Music for Széchenyi; 1860) for Piano (later orch.), which employs the so-called Hungarian ostinato. His 2d opera, *Szép Ilonka* (Pretty Helen), was premiered at the National Theater in Pest on Dec. 19, 1861, but made little impact. His last opera, *Álmos* (1862), was not performed in his lifetime; its first performance took place at Budapest's Royal Hungarian Opera on Dec. 6, 1934.

BIBL.: K. Abrányi, *Mosonyi Mihály élet és jellemrajza* (M. M., His Biography and Character; Pest, 1872); J. Káldor, *Michael M.* (Dresden, 1936); F. Bonis, *Mosonyi Mihály* (Budapest, 1960).

Moss, Lawrence (Kenneth), American composer and teacher; b. Los Angeles, Nov. 18, 1927. He studied at the Univ. of Calif. at Los Angeles (B.A., 1949), at the Eastman School of Music in Rochester, N.Y. (M.A., 1950), and with Kirchner at the Univ. of Southern Calif. in Los Angeles (Ph.D., 1957); he held a Fulbright scholarship (1953–54), 2 Guggenheim fellowships (1959–60; 1968–69), and 3 NEA grants (1975, 1977, 1980). He taught at Mills College (1956–59) and Yale Univ. (1960–68), then was a prof. and director of the composition dept. at the Univ. of Maryland at College Park (from 1969); in 1986 he was composer-in-residence at the Rockefeller Center in Bellagio, Italy. His style of composition tends toward polycentric tonality, with sporadic application of serial techniques and electronic sounds.

WORKS: DRAMATIC: OPERAS: *The Brute*, comic opera (1960; Norfolk, Conn., July 15, 1961); *The Queen and the Rebels* (1989). THEATER: *Unseen Leaves* for Soprano, Oboe, Tapes, Slides, and Lights (Washington, D.C., Oct. 20, 1975); *Nightscape* for Soprano, Flute, Clarinet, Violin, Percussion, Dancer, Tape, and Slides (1978); *Dreamscape* for Dancer, Tape, and Lights (1980); *Images* for Clarinet, Tape, and Dancer (1981); *Rites* for Tape, Slides, Lights, and Dancers (1983); *Song to the Floor* for Dancer and Tape (1984); *That Gong-Tormented Sea* for Tape and Dance (1985); *Lesbia's Sparrow* for Singer, Tape, and Dancer (1985); *Incidental Music* for Percussion and Mime/Dancer (1986); *Blackbird* for Clarinet, Mime/Dancer, and Tape (1987); *Summer Night on the Yogahenney River* for Soprano, Dancer, and Tape (1989).

Mottl, Felix (Josef), celebrated Austrian conductor; b. Unter-Sankt Veit, near Vienna, Aug. 24, 1856; d. Munich, July 2, 1911. After preliminary studies at a seminary, he entered the Vienna Cons. and studied with Door (piano), Bruckner (theory), Dessoff (composition), and Hellmesberger (conducting), graduating with high honors. In 1876 he acted as one of the assistants at the first Wagner festival at Bayreuth. In 1881 he succeeded Dessoff as court conductor at Karlsruhe, and in 1893 he was appointed Generalmusikdirektor there. He conducted *Tristan und Isolde* at the Bayreuth Festival in 1886, led a Wagner concert in London in 1894, and conducted the premiere of part I of Berlioz's *Les Troyens à Carthage, La Prise de Troie* (in German; Karlsruhe, 6, 1890). After conducting at London's Covent Garden (1898–1900), he made his Metropolitan Opera debut in New York conducting *Die Walküre* on Nov. 25, 1903. Engaged to conduct *Parsifal* there, he withdrew after protests from the Wagner family over copyright violations. In 1903 he became Generalmusikdirektor of the Munich Court Opera; he was conductor of the Vienna Phil. (1904–07). His long intimate relationship with **Zdenka Fassbender** was legalized in marriage on his deathbed. He ed. vocal scores of the works of Wagner. Among his own works were 4 operas: *Agnes Bernauer* (Weimar, 1880), *Graf Eberstein* (Karlsruhe, 1881), *Fürst und Sänger* (1893), and *Rama*.

Mouret, Jean-Joseph, noted French composer; b. Avignon, April 11, 1682; d. Charenton, Dec. 20, 1738. He is believed to have received his musical training at the Notre Dame des Doms choir school in Avignon. After settling in Paris (1707), he became maître de musique to the marshal of Noailles; within a year or so, he was made surintendant de la musique at the Sceaux court. He was director of the Paris Opéra orch. (1714–18) and became composer-director at the New Italian Theater (1717), remaining there for 2 decades. He was also made an ordinaire du Roy as a singer in the king's chamber (1720), and served as artistic director of the Concert Spirituel (1728–34), where he brought out many of his cantatas, motets, and cantatilles. In 1718 he was granted a royal privilege to publ. his own music. Stricken with a mental disorder in 1737, he was placed in the care of the Fathers of Charity in Charenton in 1738. Among his most successful works were the opéra ballet *Les Fêtes ou Le Triomphe de Thalie* (Paris, Aug. 14, 1714), the comédie lyrique *Le Mariage de Ragonde et de Colin ou La Veillée de village* (Sceaux, Dec. 1714), and various divertissements for the Italian theater.

BIBL.: R. Viollier, *J.-J. M.: Le musicien des grâces* (Paris, 1950).

Moussorgsky, Modest (Petrovich). See **Mussorgsky, Modest (Petrovich)**.

Moyzes, Alexander, Slovak composer and teacher, son of **Mikuláš Moyzes**; b. Kláštor pod Znievom, Sept. 4, 1906; d. Bratislava, Nov. 20, 1984. He studied conducting with Ostrcil, composition with Karel and Šin, and organ with Wiedermann at the Prague Cons. (1925–28), then studied in Novák's master class there (1929–30). He taught at the Bratislava Academy of Music and Drama (from 1929) and was chief music adviser to the Bratislava Radio and a prof. at the Bratislava Cons. (from 1941); he became a prof. of composition at the Bratislava College of Musical Arts (1949), serving as its rector (1965–71). He won the State Prize (1956) and was made an Artist of Merit (1961) and a National Artist (1966). His music uses the melodic resources of Slovak folk songs; his Sym. No. 1 is the first national Slovak sym. Among his works is the opera *Udatný kráľ* (The Brave King; 1966; Bratislava, 1967).

BIBL.: L. Burlas, *A. M.* (Bratislava, 1956).

Moyzes, Mikuláš, Slovak composer and teacher, father of **Alexander Moyzes**; b. Zvolenská, Slatina, Dec. 6, 1872; d. Prešov, April 2, 1944. He was a nonresident student at the Budapest Academy of Music, then was a music teacher and organist in various Slovak towns; he settled in Prešov as a teacher (1908). He was a leading figure in the development of Slovak national music, numbering among his works the melodramas *Siroty* (Orphans; 1921), *Lesná panna* (Maid of the Woods; 1922), and *Čertova rieka* (The Devil's River; 1940).

BIBL.: Z. Bokesová, *Sedemdesiatročný M. M.* (M. M. at 70; Bratislava, 1942).

Mozart, Wolfgang Amadeus (baptismal names, **Johannes Chrysostomus Wolfgangus Theophilus**), supreme Austrian genius of music whose works in every genre are unsurpassed in lyric beauty, rhythmic variety, and effortless melodic invention; b. Salzburg, Jan. 27, 1756; d. Vienna, Dec. 5, 1791. He was the son of the German-born Austrian composer, violinist, and music theorist (Johann Georg) Leopold Mozart (b. Augsburg, Nov. 14, 1719; d. Salzburg, May 28, 1787), brother of the Austrian pianist and teacher Maria Anna Mozart (b. Salzburg, July 30, 1751; d. there, Oct. 29, 1829), and father of the Austrian pianist and composer Franz Xaver Wolfgang Mozart (b. Vienna, July 26, 1791; d. Carlsbad, July 29, 1844). He and his sister, tenderly nicknamed Nannerl, were the only 2 among the 7 children of Anna Maria and Leopold Mozart to survive infancy. Mozart's sister took harpsichord lessons from her father, and Mozart as a very young child eagerly absorbed the sounds of music. He soon began playing the harpsichord himself, and later studied the violin. Leopold was an excellent musician, but he also appreciated the theatrical validity of the performances that Wolfgang and Nannerl began giving in Salzburg. On Jan. 17, 1762, he took them to Munich, where they performed before the elector of Bavaria. In Sept. 1762 they played for Emperor Francis I at his palace in Vienna. The family returned to Salzburg in Jan. 1763, and in June 1763 the children were taken to Frankfurt am Main, where Wolfgang showed his skill in improvising at the keyboard. In Nov. 1763 they arrived in Paris, where they played before Louis XV and where Wolfgang's first compositions were printed. In April 1764 they proceeded to London, where Wolfgang played for King George III. In London he was befriended by Johann Christian Bach, who gave exhibitions improvising 4-hands at the piano with the child Mozart. By that time Mozart had tried his ability in composing serious works; he wrote 2 syms. for a London performance, and the MS of another very early sym., purportedly written by him in London, was discovered in 1980. Leopold wrote home with undisguised pride: "Our great and mighty Wolfgang seems to know everything at the age of 7 that a man acquires at the age of 40." Knowing the power of publicity, he diminished Wolfgang's age, for at the time the child was fully 9 years old. In July 1765 they journeyed to the Netherlands, then set out for Salzburg, visiting Dijon, Lyons, Geneva, Bern, Zürich, Donaueschingen, and Munich on the way. Arriving in Salzburg in Nov. 1766, Wolfgang applied himself to serious study of counterpoint under the tutelage of his father. In Sept. 1767 the family proceeded to Vienna, where Wolfgang began work on an opera, *La finta semplice*; his 2d theater work was a Singspiel, *Bastien und Bastienne*, which was produced in Vienna at the home of Dr. Franz Mesmer, the protagonist of the famous method of therapy by "animal magnetism," which became known as Mesmerism. On Dec. 7, 1768, Mozart led a performance of his *Missa solemnis* in C minor before the royal family and court at the consecration of the Waisenhauskirche. Upon Mozart's return to Salzburg in Jan. 1769, Archbishop Sigismund von Schrattenbach named him his Konzertmeister; however, the position was without remuneration. Still determined to broaden Mozart's artistic contacts, his father took him on an Italian tour. The announcement for a concert in Mantua on Jan. 16, 1770, just a few days before Mozart's 14th birthday, was typical of the artistic mores of the time: "A Symphony of his own composition; a harpsichord concerto, which will be handed to him, and which he will immediately play prima vista; a Sonata handed him in like manner, which he will provide with variations, and afterwards repeat in another key; an Aria, the words for which will be handed to him and which he will immediately set to music and sing himself, accompanying himself on the harpsichord; a Sonata for harpsichord on a subject given him by the leader of the violins; a Strict Fugue on a theme to be selected, which he will improvise on the harpsichord; a Trio in which he will execute a violin part all' improvviso; and, finally, the latest Symphony by himself."

Legends of Mozart's extraordinary musical ability grew; it was reported, for instance, that he wrote out the entire score of *Miserere* by Allegri, which he had heard in the Sistine Chapel at the Vatican only twice. Young Mozart was subjected to numerous tests by famous Italian musicians, among them Giovanni Sammartini, Piccini, and Padre Martini; he was given a diploma as an elected member of the Accademia Filarmonica in Bologna after he had passed examinations in harmony and counterpoint. On Oct. 10, 1770, the Pope made him a Knight of the Golden Spur. He was commissioned to compose an opera, *Mitridate, rè di Ponto*, which was performed in Milan on Dec. 26, 1770; Mozart himself conducted 3 performances of this opera from the harpsichord. After a short stay in Salzburg, they returned to Milan in 1771, where he composed the serenata *Ascanio in Alba* for the wedding festivities of Archduke Ferdinand (Oct. 17, 1771). He returned to Salzburg late in 1771; his patron, Archbishop Schrattenbach, died about that time, and his successor, Archbishop Hieronymus Colloredo, was indifferent to Mozart as a musician. Once more Mozart went to Italy, where his newest opera, *Lucio Silla*, was performed in Milan on Dec. 26, 1772. He returned to Salzburg in March 1773, but in July of that year he went to Vienna, where he became acquainted with the music of Haydn, who greatly influenced his instrumental style. Returning to Salzburg once more, he supervised the production of his opera *Il Rè pastore*, which was performed on April 23, 1775.

In March 1778 Mozart visited Paris again for a performance of his "Paris" Sym. at a Concert Spirituel. His mother died in Paris on July 3, 1778. Returning to Salzburg in Jan. 1779, he resumed his duties as Konzertmeister and also obtained the position of court organist at a salary of 450 gulden. In 1780 the Elector of Bavaria commissioned from him an opera seria, *Idomeneo*, which was successfully produced in Munich on Jan. 29, 1781. In May 1781 Mozart lost his position with the archbishop in Salzburg and moved to Vienna, which became his permanent home. There he produced the operatic masterpiece *Die Entführung aus dem Serail*, staged at the Burgtheater on July 16, 1782, with excellent success. On August 4, 1782, he married Constanze Weber, the sister of Aloysia Weber, with whom he had previously been infatuated. Two of his finest syms.—No. 35 in D major, "Haffner," written for the Haffner family of Salzburg, and No. 36 in C major, the "Linz"—date from 1782 and 1783, respectively. From this point forward Mozart's productivity reached extraordinary dimensions, but despite the abundance of commissions and concert appearances, he was unable to earn enough to sustain his growing family. Still, melodramatic stories of Mozart's abject poverty are gross exaggerations. He apparently felt no scruples in asking prosperous friends for financial assistance. Periodically he wrote to Michael Puchberg, a banker and a brother Freemason (Mozart joined the Masonic fraternity in 1784), with requests for loans (which he never repaid); invariably Puchberg obliged, but usually granting smaller amounts than Mozart requested.

In 1785 Mozart completed a set of 6 string quartets, which he dedicated to Haydn. Haydn himself paid a tribute to Mozart's genius; Mozart's father quoted him as saying, "Before God and as an honest man I tell you that your son is the greatest composer known to me either in person or by name." On May 1, 1786, Mozart's great opera buffa, *Le nozze di Figaro*, was produced in Vienna, obtaining a triumph with the audience; it was performed in Prague early in 1787 with Mozart in attendance. It was during that visit that Mozart wrote his 38th Sym., in D major, known as the "Prague" Sym.; it was in Prague, also, that his operatic masterpiece *Don Giovanni* was produced, on Oct. 29, 1787. It is interesting to note that at its Vienna performance the opera was staged under the title *Die sprechende Statue*, unquestionably with the intention of sensationalizing the story; the dramatic appearance of the statue of the Commendatore, introduced by the ominous sound of trombones, was a shuddering climax to the work. In Nov. 1787 Mozart was appointed Kammermusicus in Vienna as a successor to Gluck, albeit at a smaller salary: he received 800 gulden per annum as against Gluck's salary of 2,000 gulden. The year 1788 was a glorious one for Mozart and for music history; it was the year when he composed his last 3 syms.: No. 39 in E-flat major; No. 40 in G minor; and No. 41 in C major, known under the name "Jupiter." In the spring of 1789 Mozart went to Berlin; on the way he appeared as soloist in one of his piano concertos before the Elector of Saxony in Dresden, and also played the organ at the Thomaskirche in Leipzig. His visits in Potsdam and Berlin were marked by his private concerts at the court of Friedrich Wilhelm II; the king commissioned from him a set of 6 string quartets and a set of 6 piano sonatas, but Mozart died before completing these commissions. Returning to Vienna, he began work on his opera buffa *Così fan tutte,* first performed in Vienna on Jan. 26, 1790. In Oct. 1790 Mozart went to Frankfurt am Main for the coronation of Emperor Leopold II. Returning to Vienna, he saw Haydn, who was about to depart for London. In 1791, during his last year of life, he completed the score of *Die Zauberflöte*, with a German libretto by Schikaneder. It was performed for the first time on Sept. 30, 1791, in Vienna. There followed a mysterious episode in Mozart's life; a stranger called on him with a request to compose a Requiem; the caller was an employee of Count Franz von Walsegg, who intended to have the work performed as his own in memory of his wife. Mozart was unable to finish the score, which was completed by his pupil Süssmayr, and by Eybler.

The immediate cause of Mozart's death at the age of 35 has been the subject of much speculation. A detailed examination of his medical history is found in P. Davies, "Mozart's Illnesses and Death–1: The Illnesses, 1756–90" and "2: The Last Year and the Fatal Illness," *Musical Times* (Aug. and Oct. 1984). Almost immediately after the sad event, myths and fantasies appeared in the press, the most persistent being that Mozart had been poisoned by Salieri out of professional jealousy; this particularly morbid piece of invention gained circulation in European journals and the story was further elaborated upon by a report that Salieri confessed his unspeakable crime on his deathbed in 1825. Pushkin used the tale in his drama *Mozart and Salieri*, which Rimsky-Korsakov set to music in his opera of the same title; a fanciful dramatization of the Mozart-Salieri rivalry was made into a successful play, *Amadeus*, by Peter Shaffer, which was produced in London in 1979 and in New York in 1980; it subsequently gained wider currency through its award-winning film version of 1984. The notion of Mozart's murder also appealed to the Nazis; in the ingenious version propagated by some German writers of the Hitlerian persuasion, Mozart was a victim of a double conspiracy of Masons and Jews who were determined to suppress the flowering of racial Germanic greatness; the Masons, in this interpretation, were outraged by his revealing of their secret rites in *Die Zauberflöte*, and allied themselves with plutocratic Jews to prevent further spread of his dangerous revelations. Another myth related to Mozart's death that found its way into the majority of Mozart biographies and even into respectable reference works was that a blizzard raged during his funeral and that none of his friends could follow his body to the cemetery; this story is easily refuted by the records of the Vienna weather bureau for the day (see N. Slonimsky, "The Weather at Mozart's Funeral," *Musical Quarterly*, Jan. 1960). In fact, the funeral, paid for by Baron Gottfried van Swieten, took place on Dec. 6, 1791. Among those in attendance from the musical world were Albrechtsberger, Hüttenbrenner, and, of course, Salieri. On Dec. 10, 1791, a Requiem Mass was held in his memory at St. Michael's, at which time the completed portions of his own Requiem were performed.

The universal recognition of Mozart's genius during the 2 centuries since his death has never wavered among professional musicians, amateurs, and the general public. In his music, smiling simplicity was combined with somber drama, lofty inspiration was contrasted with playful diversion, profound meditation alternated with capricious moodiness, and religious concentration was permeated with human tenderness. Mozart is also the only great composer to have a town named after him—the town of Mozart, in the province of Saskatchewan, Canada, lying between Synyard and Elfros on a CPR main line that skirts the south end of Big Quill Lake. It consists of 2 elevators, a covered curling rink, a Centennial hall, a co-op store, and a handful of well-kept homes. A local recounts that the town was named in the early 1900s by one Mrs. Lunch, the wife of the stationmaster, who was reportedly a talented musician and very well thought of in the community. She not only named the town Mozart but also brought about the naming of the streets after other, equally famous musicians: Chopin, Wagner, and Liszt.

The variety of technical development in Mozart's works is all the more remarkable considering the limitations of instrumental means in his time. The vocal technique displayed in his operas is amazing in its perfection; to be sure, the human voice has not changed since Mozart's time, but he knew how to exploit vocal resources to the utmost. This adaptability of his genius to all available means of sound production is the secret of the eternal validity of his music, and the explanation of the present popularity of minifestivals, such as the N.Y. concert series advertised as "Mostly Mozart."

In the list of Mozart's works given below, the K. numbers represent the system of identification established by L. von Köchel in his *Chronologisch-thematisches Verzeichnis sämtlicher Tonwerke Wolfgang Amade Mozarts* (Leipzig, 1862; 6th ed., rev. by F. Giegling, A. Weinmann, and G. Sievers, Wiesbaden, 1964); the rev. K. numbers of the 6th ed. are also included.

WORKS: DRAMATIC: *Apollo et Hyacinthus*, K.38, Latin intermezzo (Salzburg Univ., May 13, 1767); *La finta semplice*, K.51;

46a, opera buffa (Archbishop's palace, Salzburg, May 1?, 1769); *Bastien und Bastienne*, K.50; 46b, Singspiel (Franz Mesmer's residence, Vienna, Sept.?-Oct.? 1768); *Mitridate, rè di Ponto*, K.87; 74a, opera seria (Regio Ducal Teatro, Milan, Dec. 26, 1770); *Ascanio in Alba*, K.111, festa teatrale (Regio Ducal Teatro, Milan, Oct. 17, 1771); *Il sogno di Scipione*, K.126, serenata (Archbishop's palace, Salzburg, May? 1772); *Lucio Silla*, K.135, opera seria (Regio Ducal Teatro, Milan, Dec. 26, 1772); *La finta giardiniera*, K.196, opera buffa (Munich, Jan. 13, 1775; also produced as a Singspiel, *Die verstellte Gärtnerin*, Augsburg, May 1, 1780); *Il Rè pastore*, K.208, dramma per musica (Archbishop's palace, Salzburg, April 23, 1775); *Semiramis*, K.Anh. 11; 315e, duodrama (not extant); *Thamos, König in Ägypten*, K.345; 336a, music for Gebler's play; *Zaide*, K.344; 336b, Singspiel (unfinished; dialogue rewritten and finished by Gollmick, with overture and finale added by Anton André, Frankfurt am Main, Jan. 27, 1866); *Idomeneo, rè di Creta*, K.366, opera seria (Hoftheater, Munich, Jan. 29, 1781); *Die Entführung aus dem Serail*, K.384, Singspiel (Burgtheater, Vienna, July 16, 1782); *L'oca del Cairo*, K.422, opera buffa (unfinished); *Lo Sposo deluso*, K.430; 424a, opera buffa (unfinished); *Der Schauspieldirektor*, K.486, Singspiel (Schönbrunn Palace, Heitzing [suburb of Vienna], Feb. 7, 1786); *Le nozze di Figaro*, K.492, opera buffa (Burgtheater, Vienna, May 1, 1786); *Il dissoluto punito, ossia Il Don Giovanni*, K.527, opera buffa (National Theater, Prague, Oct. 29, 1787); *Così fan tutte, ossia La scuola degli amanti*, K.588, opera buffa (Burgtheater, Vienna, Jan. 26, 1790); *Die Zauberflöte*, K.620, Singspiel (Theater auf der Wieden, Vienna, Sept. 30, 1791); *La clemenza di Tito*, K.621, opera seria (National Theater, Prague, Sept. 6, 1791). Also *Die Schuldigkeit des ersten Gebots*, K.35, sacred drama (1767; part 1 by Mozart, part 2 by Michael Haydn, part 3 by Adlgasser; Salzburg, March 12, 1767). ORATORIOS: *La Betulia liberata*, K.118; 74c (1771); *Davidde penitente*, K.469 (1785; music from the *Missa* in C minor, K.427; 417a, 2 arias excepted).

BIBL.: COLLECTED EDITIONS, SOURCE MATERIAL: The standard thematic catalog is L. von Köchel, ed., *Chronologisch-thematisches Verzeichnis sämtlicher Tonwerke W. Amade M.s* (Leipzig, 1862; 3d ed., extensively rev. by A. Einstein, Leipzig, 1937; reprint, with supplement, Ann Arbor, 1947; 6th ed., a major revision, by F. Giegling, A. Weinmann, and G. Sievers, Wiesbaden, 1964; the 6th ed. contains a rev. K. numbering system; further supplementary material is found in the *M.-Jahrbuch 1971–2*, as prepared by P. van Reijen). See also C. Eisen, *New M. Documents* (Stanford, 1991). CORRESPONDENCE: L. Nohl, *M.s Briefe nach den Originalen herausgegeben* (Salzburg, 1865; Eng. tr. by Lady Wallace, London, 1866; 2d Ger. ed., aug., Leipzig, 1877); H. de Curzon, *Nouvelles lettres des dernières années de la vie de M.* (Paris, 1898); K. Storck, *M.s Briefe in Auswahl* (Stuttgart, 1906); A. Leitzmann, *M.s Briefe ausgewählt* (Leipzig, 1910); M. Weigel, *M.s Briefe* (Berlin, 1910); H. Leichtentritt, *M.s Briefe* (Berlin, 1912); L. Schiedermair, *Die Briefe W. A. M.s und seiner Familie: Erste kritische Gesamtausgabe* (5 vols., Munich and Leipzig, 1914); E. Anderson, ed. and tr., *Letters of M. and His Family* (3 vols., London and N.Y., 1938; 2d ed., rev. by A. Hyatt King and M. Carolan, 1966; 3d ed., rev. by S. Sadie and F. Smart, 1985); E. Müller von Asow, ed., *Gesamtausgabe der Briefe und Aufzeichnungen der Familie M.* (5 vols., Berlin, 1942); W. Bauer, O. Deutsch, and J. Eibl, eds., *M.: Briefe und Aufzeichnungen* (7 vols., Kassel, 1962–75). BIOGRAPHICAL: I. Arnold, *M.s Geist: Seine kurze Biographie und ästhetische Darstellung* (Erfurt, 1803); idem, *Galerie der berühmtesten Tonkünstler des 18. und 19. Jahrhunderts . . . W. A. M. und Joseph Haydn: Versuch einer Parallele* (Erfurt, 1810; 2d ed., 1816); Stendhal, *Lettres . . . sur le célèbre compositeur Haydn: Suivies d'une vie de M. et considérations sur Métastase* (Paris, 1814; 2d ed., rev., as *Vies de Haydn, de M. et de Métastase*; Eng. tr., 1972); P. Lichtenthal, *Cenni biografici intorno al celebre maestro W. A. M.* (Milan, 1816); G. von Nissen, *Biographie W. A. M.s nach Originalbriefen* (Leipzig, 1828); A. Oulibicheff, *Nouvelle biographie de M., suivie d'un aperçu sur l'histoire générale de la musique* (3 vols., Moscow, 1843; Ger. tr. by L. Gantter, Stuttgart, 1859; Russian tr. by M. Tchaikovsky, Moscow, 1890); E. Holmes, *The Life of M.* (London, 1845; 2d ed., 1878); O. Jahn, *W. A. M.* (4 vols., Leipzig, 1856–59; 2d ed., 1867; Eng. tr. by P. Townsend, London, 1882; Ger. revisions by H. Deiters, 3d ed., 1891–93, and 4th ed., 1905–07; exhaustively rewritten and rev. by H. Abert as *W. A. M.: Neu bearbeitete und erweiterte Ausgabe von Otto Jahns "M.," 2 vols., Leipzig, 1919–21*; further revision by A. A. Abert, 2 vols., Leipzig, 1955–56); L. Nohl, *M.* (Leipzig, 1863; 2d ed., aug., as *M.s Leben*, 1877; Eng. tr. by Lady Wallace, London, 1877; 3d Ger. ed., rev. by P. Sakolowski, Berlin, 1906); C. Pohl, *M. und Haydn in London* (Vienna, 1867); L. Nohl, *M. nach den Schilderungen seiner Zeitgenossen* (Leipzig, 1880); G. Nottebohm, *M.iana* (Leipzig, 1880); V. Wilder, *M., L'Homme et l'artiste* (Paris, 1880; 4th ed., 1889; Eng. tr., London, 1908); L. Meinardus, *M.: Ein Künstlerleben* (Leipzig, 1882); F. Gehring, *M.* (London, 1883; 2d ed., 1911); L. Klasen, *W. A. M.: Sein Leben und seine Werke* (Vienna, 1897); O. Fleischer, *M.* (Berlin, 1899); R. Procházka, *M. in Prag* (Prague, 1899; rev. and aug. ed. by P. Nettl as *M. in Böhmen*, Prague, 1938); E. Breakspeare, *M.* (London, 1902); E. Prout, *M.* (London, 1903); L. Mirow, *M.s letzte Lebensjahre: Eine Künstlertragödie* (Leipzig, 1904); C. Belmonte, *Die Frauen im Leben M.s* (Augsburg, 1905); C. Bellaigue, *M.* (Paris, 1906); F. Lentner, *M.s Leben und Schaffen* (Innsbruck, 1906); H. von der Pfordten, *M.* (Leipzig, 1908); K. Storck, *M.: Sein Leben und Schaffen* (Stuttgart, 1908); W. Flower, *Stray Notes on M. and His Music* (Edinburgh, 1910); L. Schmidt, *W. A. M.* (Berlin, 1912); T. de Wyzewa and G. de Saint-Foix, *W. A. M.: Sa vie musicale et son oeuvre de l'enfance à la pleine maturité* (5 vols., Paris, 1912–46; vols. 3–5 by Saint-Foix alone); A. Schurig, *W. A. M.: Sein Leben und sein Werk* (2 vols., Leipzig, 1913; 2d ed., 1923; French tr., 1925); H. de Curzon, *M.* (Paris, 1914; 2d ed., 1927); E. Engel, *W. A. M.* (Vienna, 1914); J. Kreitmeier, *W. A. M.: Eine Charakterzeichnung des grossen Meisters nach literarischen Quellen* (Düsseldorf, 1919); L. Schiedermair, *M.: Sein Leben und seine Werke* (Munich, 1922; 2d ed., rev., 1948); E. Blümml, *Aus M.s Freundes und Familien Kreis* (Vienna, 1923); O. Keller, *W. A. M.* (Berlin, 1926); B. Paumgartner, *M.* (Berlin, 1927; 10th ed., 1993); D. Hussey, *W. A. M.* (London, 1928; 2d ed., 1933); M. Morold, *M.* (Vienna, 1931); R. Tenschert, *M.* (Leipzig, 1931); M. Davenport, *M.* (N.Y., 1932); H. Ghéon, *Promenades avec M.* (Paris, 1932; 7th ed., 1948; Eng. tr. as *In Search of M.*, London, 1934); S. Sitwell, *M.* (N.Y., 1932); R. Haas, *W. A. M.* (Potsdam, 1933; 2d ed., 1950); E. Schmid, *W. A. M.* (Lübeck, 1934; 3d ed., 1955); J. Talbot, *M.* (London, 1934); E. Blom, *M.* (London, 1935; 3d ed., rev. by J. Westrup, 1975); A. Boschot, *M.* (Paris, 1935; 2d ed., 1949); C. Perriolat, *M.: Révélateur de la beauté artistique* (Paris, 1935); A. Kolb, *M.* (Vienna, 1937); W. Turner, *M.: The Man and His Works* (London and N.Y., 1938; 3d ed., 1966); I. Gyomai, *Le Coeur de M.* (Paris, 1939); W. Goetz, M.: *Sein Leben in Selbstzeugnissen, Briefen und Berichten* (Berlin, 1941); E. Komorzynski, *M.* (Berlin, 1941; Vienna, 1955); G. Schaeffner, *W. A. M.* (Bern, 1941); A. Albertini, *M.: La vita, le opere* (Milan, 1942); E. Valentin, *Wege zu M.* (Regensburg, 1942); A. Einstein, *M.: His Character, His Work* (N.Y., 1945; Ger. ed., 1947; 4th ed., 1960); P. Espil, *Les Voyages de Chérubin, ou L'Enfance de M.* (Bayonne, 1946); M. Mila, *W. A. M.* (Turin, 1946); E. Valentin, *M.* (Hameln, 1947); R. Tenschert, *W. A. M.* (Salzburg, 1951; Eng. tr., London, 1952); M. Kenyon, *M. in Salzburg* (London, 1952); K. Röttger, *W. A. M.* (Stuttgart, 1952); M. Brion, *M.* (Paris, 1955); J. Dalchow, *W. A. M.s Krankheiten, 1756–1763* (Bergisch Gladbach, 1955); N. Medici di Marignano and R. Hughes, *A M. Pilgrimage: Being the Travel Diaries of Vincent and Mary Novello in the Year 1829* (London, 1955); A. Ostoja, *M. e l'Italia* (Bologna, 1955); E. Schenk, *W. A. M.: Eine Biographie* (Vienna and Zürich, 1955; 2d ed., rev., 1975; Eng. tr. in an abr. ed. as *M. and His Times*, N.Y., 1959); G. Barblan and A. Della Corte, *M. in Italia* (Milan, 1956); C. Fusero, *M.* (Turin, 1956); F. Hadamowsky and L. Nowak, *M.: Werk und Zeit* (Vienna, 1956); J. Burk, *M. and His Music* (N.Y., 1959); J. and B. Massin, *W. A. M.: Biographie, histoire de l'oeuvre* (Paris, 1959; 2d ed., 1970); C. Haldane, *M.* (London, 1960); O. Deutsch, *M.: Die Dokumente seines Lebens, gesammelt und erläutert* (Kassel, 1961; Eng. tr. as *M.: A Documented Biography*, Palo Alto, Calif., 1965; 2d ed., 1966; supplement, 1978); S. Sadie, *M.* (London, 1965); C. Bär, *M.: Krankheit, Tod, Begräbnis* (Kassel, 1966; rev. ed., 1972); A. Hyatt King, *M.: A Biography with a Survey of Books, Editions and Recordings* (London, 1970); M. Levey, *The Life and Death of M.* (London, 1971); H. Schuler, *Die Vorfahren W. M.s* (Essen, 1972); A. Hutchings, *M.: The Man, the Musician* (London and N.Y., 1976); W. Hildesheimer, *M.* (Frankfurt am Main, 1977; Eng. tr., 1979); I. Keys, *M.: His Life in His Music* (St. Albans, 1980); J. Féron, *M.: L'Avenir d'un enfant prodige* (Paris, 1983); G. Gruber, *M. und die Nachwelt* (Salzburg, 1985; Eng. tr. as *M. and Posterity,* Boston, 1994); K. Pahlen, *Das M.-Buch: Chronik von Leben und Werk* (Zürich, 1985); P. Autexier, *M.* (Paris, 1987); V. Braunbehrens, *M. in Wien* (Munich, 1986; Eng. tr. as *M. in Vienna, 1781–1791,* N.Y., 1990); J. Hocquard, *M.: L'Amour, la mort* (Paris, 1987); P. Young, *M.* (N.Y., 1987); H. C. Robbins Landon, *1791: M.'s Last Year* (London, 1988); P. Davies, *M. in Person: His Character and Health* (Westport, Conn., 1989); H. C. Robbins Landon, *M.: The Golden Years* (N.Y., 1989); W. Ritter, *Wurde M. ermordet?: Eine psychologische Studie* (Frankfurt am Main, 1989); V. Braunbehrens and K.-H. Jürgens, *M.: Lebensbilder* (Bergisch Gladbach, 1990); G. Carli Ballola and R. Parenti, *M.* (Milan, 1990); H. Gärtner, *Folget der Heissgeliebten: Frauen um M.* (Munich, 1990); B. Hamann, *Nichts als Musik im Kopf: Das Leben von W. A. M.* (Vienna, 1990); H. Kröplin, *W. A. M., 1756–1791: Eine Chronik* (Wiesbaden, 1990); K. Küster, *M.: Eine musikalische Biographie* (Stuttgart, 1990; Eng. tr. as *M.: A Musical Biography,* 1996); H. C. Robbins Landon, *The M. Compendium* (N.Y., 1990); R. Mann, *W. A. M.: Triumph und frühes Ende: Biographie* (Berlin, 1990); M. Becker, *M.: Sein Leben und seine Zeit in Texten und Bildern* (Frankfurt am Main, 1991); B. Cormican, *M.'s Death—M.'s Requiem: An Investigation* (Belfast, 1991); N. Elias, *M.: Zur Sociologie eines Genies* (Frankfurt am Main, 1991; Eng. tr. as *M.: Portrait of a Genius,* Berkeley, 1993); G. Knepler, *W. A. M.: Annäherungen* (Berlin, 1991; Eng. tr. as *W. A. M.,* Cambridge, 1994); H. C. Robbins Landon, *M. and Vienna* (N.Y., 1991); D. Leonhart, *M.: Liebe und Geld: Ein Versuch zu seiner Person* (Munich, 1991); M. Publig, *M.: Ein unbeirrbares Leben: Biographie* (Munich, 1991); M. Remus, *M.* (Stuttgart, 1991); W. Stafford, *The M. Myths: A Critical Reassessment* (Stanford, 1991); J. Hocquard, *M., de l'ombre à la lumière* (Paris, 1993); R. Angermüller, *Delitiae Italiae: M.s Reisen in Italien* (Bad Honnef, 1994); V. Braunbehrens, *M.: Ein Lebensbild* (Munich, 1994); W. Siegmund Schultze, *W. A. M.: Ideal-Idol-Idee* (Trier, 1994); M. Solomon, *M.: A Life* (N.Y., 1994); N. Wenborn, *M.* (N.Y., 1994); D. Nardo, *M.* (San Diego, 1997); A. Steptoe, *M.* (N.Y., 1997); R. Halliwell, *The M. Family: Four Lives in a Social Context* (Oxford, 1998); J. Rosselli, *The Life of M.* (Cambridge, 1998). CRITICAL AND ANALYTICAL: OPERA: A. Oulibicheff, *M.s Opern: Kritische Erläuterungen* (Leipzig, 1848); C. Gounod, *Le Don Juan de M.* (Paris, 1890; Eng. tr., 1895); A. Farinelli, *Don Giovanni: Note critiche* (Turin, 1896); A. Weltner, *M.s Werke und die Wiener Hoftheater: Statistisches und Historisches* (Vienna, 1896); K. Söhle, *M. Dramatisches Zeitbild* (Leipzig, 1907); E. Dent, *M.'s Operas: A Critical Study* (London, 1913; 2d ed., 1947); H. Cohen, *Die dramatische Idée in M.s Operntexten* (Berlin, 1916); H. von Waltershausen, *Die Zauberflöte* (Munich, 1920); O. Beer, *M. und das Wiener Singspiel* (Vienna, 1932); F. Brukner, *Die Zauberflöte: Unbekannte Handschriften und seltene Drucke aus der Frühzeit der Oper* (Vienna, 1934); P. Stefan, *Die Zauberflöte: Herkunft, Bedeutung, Geheimnis* (Vienna, 1937); P. Jouve, *Le Don Juan de M.* (Freiburg, 1942; 3d ed., Paris, 1948; Eng. tr., London, 1957); L. Conrad, *M.s Dramaturgie der Oper* (Würzburg, 1943); C. Benn, *M. on the Stage* (London, 1946; 2d ed., 1947); S. Levarie, *M.'s "Le nozze di Figaro": A Critical Analysis* (Chicago, 1952); D. Lauener, *Die Frauengestalten in M.s Opern* (Zürich, 1954); A. Greither, *Die sieben grossen Opern M.s: Versuche über das Verhältnis der Texte zur Musik* (Heidelberg, 1956; 2d ed., enl., 1970); B. Brophy, *M. the Dramatist: A New View of M., His Operas and His Age* (London and N.Y., 1964; new ed., 1988); A. Rosenberg, *Die Zauberflöte: Geschichte und Deutung* (Munich, 1964); R. Moberly, *Three M. Operas: Figaro, Don Giovanni, The Magic Flute* (London, 1967; N.Y., 1968); E. Batley, *A Preface to The Magic Flute* (London, 1969); A. Abert, *Die Opern M.s* (Wolfenbüttel, 1970; Eng. tr. in *The New Oxford History of Music,* vol. 7, London, 1973); H. Eggebrecht, *Versuch über die Wiener Klassik: Die Tanzszene in M.s "Don Giovanni"* (Wiesbaden, 1972); S. Kunze, *Don Giovanni vor M.: Die Tradition der Don Giovanni-Opern im italienischen Buffo-Theater des 18. Jahrhunderts* (Munich, 1972); W. Mann, *The Operas of M.* (London, 1977); F. Noske, *The Signifier and the Signified: Studies in the Operas of M. and Verdi* (The Hague, 1977); C. Osborne, *The Complete Operas of M.* (London, 1978); C. Gianturco, *M.'s Early Operas* (London, 1982); W. Allanbrook, *Rhythmic Gesture in M.: Le nozze di Figaro and Don Giovanni* (Chicago and London, 1984); S. Kunze, *M.s Opern* (Stuttgart, 1984); S. Henze-Döhring, *Opera seria, Opera buffa und M.s Don Giovanni: Zur Gattungskonvergenz in der italienischen Oper des 18. Jahrhunderts* (Laaber, 1986); J. Hocquard, *La Clemenza di Tito K. 621* (n.p., 1986); J. Kaiser, *Who's Who in M.'s Operas: From Alfonso to Zerlina* (London, 1986); B. Blomhert, *The Harmoniemusik of "Die Entführung aus dem Serail" by W. A. M.: Study about its Authenticity and Critical Edition* (The Hague, 1987); S. Corse, *Opera and the Uses of Language: M., Verdi, and Britten* (London and Toronto, 1987); J. Kristek, ed., *M.'s Don Giovanni in Prague* (Prague, 1987); T. Bauman, *W. A. M.: Die Entführung aus dem Serail* (Cambridge, 1988); T. Carter, *W. A. M.: Le Nozze di Figaro* (Cambridge, 1988); A. Steptoe, *The M.-Da Ponte Operas: The Cultural and Musical Background to Le nozze di Figaro, Don Giovanni, and Così fan tutte* (Oxford, 1988); D. Heartz, *M's Operas* (Berkeley, 1990); P. Branscombe, *W. A. M.: Die Zauberflöte* (Cambridge, 1991); J. Eckelmeyer, *The Cultural Context of M.'s Magic Flute: Social, Aesthetic, Philosophical* (Lewiston, N.Y., 1991); C. Ford, *Così? Sexual Politics in M.'s Operas* (Manchester, 1991); J. Rice, *W. A. M.: La Clemenza di Tito* (Cambridge, 1991); P. Alcalde, *Strukturierung und Sinn: Die dramatische Funktion der musikalische Form in Da Pontes und M.s Don Giovanni* (Frankfurt am Main, 1992); N. Till, *M. and the Enlightenment: Truth, Virtue and Beauty in M.s Operas* (London, 1992); J. Rushton, ed., *W. A. M.: Idomeneo* (Cambridge, 1993); B. Brown, *W. A. M.: Così fan tutte* (Cambridge, 1995); J. Hocquard, *Les opéras de M.* (Paris, 1995); P. Adlung, *M.s Opera seria "Mitridate, rè de Ponto"* (Eisenach, 1996); W. Willaschek, *M. Theater: Vom "Idomeneo" bis zur "Zauberflöte"* (Stuttgart, 1996).

Mraczek (Mraček), Joseph Gustav, Czech composer, violinist, conductor, and teacher; b. Brünn, March 12, 1878; d. Dresden, Dec. 24, 1944. He received his first instruction from his father, the cellist Franz (František) Mraček (1842–98); he was a chorister in various churches in Brünn before going to Vienna, where he studied with Hellmesberger, Stocker, and Löwe at the Cons. From 1897 to 1902 he was concertmaster at the Stadttheater in Brünn, then taught violin at the Cons. there (1898–1919). He settled in Dresden and conducted the Phil. (1919–24) and taught composition at the Cons. (from 1919).

WORKS: OPERAS: *Der glaserne Pantoffel* (Brünn, 1902); *Der Traum* (Brünn, Feb. 26, 1909); *Aebelö* (Breslau, 1915); *Ikdar* (Dresden, 1921); *Herrn Dürers Bild oder Madonna am Wiesenzaun* (Hannover, Jan. 29, 1927); *Der Liebesrat* (not perf.); *Der arme Tobias* (1936).

BIBL.: E. Müller, *J. G. M.* (Dresden, 1917).

Mravina (original name, **Mravinskaya**), **Evgeniya (Konstantinovna),** noted Russian soprano; b. St. Petersburg, Feb. 16, 1864; d. Yalta, Oct. 25, 1914. She studied in St. Petersburg with Pryanishnikov, and later with Désirée d'Artôt in Berlin, and then sang in Italy. After returning to Russia, she joined the Maryinsky Theater in St. Petersburg in 1886, remaining on its roster until 1900. In 1891–92 she toured in England, France, Belgium, and Germany. She had the privilege of going over the part of Marguerite in *Faust* with Gounod, and the part of Mignon in the opera of that name by Thomas with the composer himself. She gave brilliant renditions of Italian soprano roles, and also was greatly praised in Russia for her performances of the Russian operatic parts. She retired from the operatic stage in 1900 but continued to appear in recital.

BIBL.: A. Grigorieva, *E. K. M.* (Moscow, 1970).

Mravinsky, Evgeni (Alexandrovich), eminent Russian conductor; b. St. Petersburg, June 4, 1903; d. there (Leningrad), Jan.

19, 1988. He studied biology at the Univ. of St. Petersburg, then joined the Imperial Ballet as a pantomimist and rehearsal pianist; in 1924 he enrolled in the Leningrad Cons., where he studied conducting with Gauk and Malko, graduating in 1931; he also had courses in composition with Shcherbachev. He then was conductor of the Leningrad Theater of Opera and Ballet (1932–38). In 1938 he was appointed principal conductor of the Leningrad Phil., which position he held with imperious authority for 50 years. Mravinsky represented the best of the Soviet school of conducting, in which technical precision and fidelity to the music were combined with individual and even Romantic interpretations. He was especially noted for his fine performances of Tchaikovsky's operas, ballets, and syms.; he gave first performances of several syms. of Prokofiev and Shostakovich and also conducted works by Bartók and Stravinsky. In 1973 he was awarded the order of Hero of Socialist Labor.

Mshvelidze, Shalva (Mikhailovich), Russian ethnomusicologist, teacher, and composer; b. Tiflis, May 28, 1904; d. there (Tbilisi), March 4, 1984. He studied with Bagrinovsky at the Tiflis Cons., graduating in 1930, and with Shcherbachev, Tyulin, Steinberg, and Ryazanov at the Leningrad Cons. He was made a teacher (1929) and a prof. (1942) at the Tbilisi Cons. He was a leading figure in Georgian music.

WORKS: DRAMATIC: OPERAS: *Legend of Tariel* (Tbilisi, Feb. 25, 1946; rev. 1966); *The Grandmaster's Right Hand* (Tbilisi, June 3, 1961); *Widow of a Soldier* (1967); *Aluda Ketelauri* (1972). Also incidental music; film scores; 2 oratorios: *Caucasiana* (1949) and *The Legacy of Posterity*, for the centennial of Lenin's birth (1970).

BIBL.: V. Donadze, *S. M.* (Tbilisi, 1946); A. Shaverzashvili, *Fugi S. M.* (Tbilisi, 1964); A. Tsulukidze, *S. M.* (Tbilisi, 1964).

Muck, Karl, eminent German conductor; b. Darmstadt, Oct. 22, 1859; d. Stuttgart, March 3, 1940. He received his first musical instruction from his father; then studied piano with Kissner in Würzburg; later he pursued academic studies (classical philology) at the univs. of Heidelberg and Leipzig (Ph.D., 1880). He also attended the Leipzig Cons., and shortly before graduation made a successful debut as pianist with the Gewandhaus Orch. However, he did not choose to continue a pianistic career, but obtained a position as chorus master at the municipal opera in Zürich; his ability soon secured him the post of conductor there. In subsequent years, he was a theater conductor in Salzburg, Brünn, and Graz; there Angelo Neumann, impresario of a traveling opera company, heard him, and engaged him as conductor for the Landestheater in Prague (1886), and then as Seidl's successor for his traveling Wagner Co. It was during those years that Muck developed his extraordinary qualities as a masterful disciplinarian and faithful interpreter possessing impeccable taste. In 1889 he conducted the Wagner tetralogy in St. Petersburg, and in 1891, in Moscow. In 1892 he was engaged as first conductor at the Berlin Royal Opera, and also frequently conducted sym. concerts of the Royal Chapel there. From 1894 to 1911 he led the Silesian Music Festivals; in 1899 he conducted the Wagner repertoire at London's Covent Garden. He also appeared, with outstanding success, in Paris, Rome, Brussels, Madrid, Copenhagen, and other European centers. In 1901 he was selected to conduct the performances of *Parsifal* at Bayreuth; he appeared there regularly until 1930. Muck was one of the conductors of the Vienna Phil. (1904–06), then was conductor of the Boston Sym. Orch. (1906–08) before returning to Berlin as Generalmusikdirektor. He returned to America in 1912 and again assumed the post of conductor of the Boston Sym. Orch.; he held that post with the greatest distinction until the United States entered World War I in 1917. Muck's position then became controversial; a friend of Kaiser Wilhelm II, he saw no reason to temper his ardent German nationalism, nor was he inclined to alter certain aspects of his private life. Protests were made against his retention as conductor, but despite the efforts to defend him by Major Higginson, the founder of the Boston Sym. Orch., Muck's case proved hopeless. In order to avoid prosecution under the Mann Act, he subsequently submitted to being arrested at his home on March 25, 1918, as an enemy alien and was interned until the end of the war. In 1919 he returned to Germany; he conducted the Hamburg Phil. from 1922 until his retirement in 1933. Muck was one of the foremost conductors of his era. A consummate musician, endowed with a masterful technique, he was renowned for his authoritative performances of the revered Austro-German repertoire. His sympathies were wide, however, and he programmed such contemporary musicians as Mahler, Debussy, Sibelius, and even Schoenberg and Webern at his concerts. His penchant for stern disciplinarianism and biting sarcasm made him a feared podium figure for the musicians who played under him, but the results he obtained were exemplary.

BIBL.: N. Stücker, *K. M.* (Graz, 1939).

Mueller (Müller) von Asow, Erich H(ermann), noted German musicologist; b. Dresden, Aug. 31, 1892; d. Berlin, June 4, 1964. He studied with Riemann and Schering at the Univ. of Leipzig (Ph.D., 1915, with the diss. *Die Mingottischen Opernunternehmungen, 1732–1756*; publ. in Dresden, 1917, as *Angelo und Pietro Mingotti: Ein Beitrag zur Geschichte der Oper im XVIII. Jahrhundert*). During World War I he was active as a military bandmaster. After serving as assistant director of Leipzig's Neue Theater, he was artistic director of Dresden's international festival for modern music (1917–18); he was director of the Wernow Theater (1918–19) and then was active as a music critic in Berlin and Dresden; he joined the staff of Dresden's Pädagogium der Tonkunst (1926), serving as its director (1927–33). He went to Austria (1936); was briefly under arrest by the Gestapo (1943); returned to Germany in 1945, where he founded the Internationales Musiker-Brief-Archiv in Berlin.

WRITINGS: *Joseph Gustav Mraczek* (Dresden, 1917); *Die Musiksammlung der Bibliothek zu Kronstadt* (Kronstadt, 1930); *Dresdner Musikstätten* (Dresden, 1931); *Egon Kornauth: Ein Bild von Leben und Schaffen des mährischen Komponisten* (Vienna, 1941); *Max Reger und seine Welt* (Berlin, 1944); *Richard Strauss: Thematisches Verzeichnis* (3 vols., Vienna and Wiesbaden, 1959–74; completed by A. Ott and F. Trenner); also ed. numerous vols.

Muench, Gerhart, German-born Mexican pianist, teacher, and composer; b. Dresden, March 23, 1903; d. Tacambaro, Dec. 9, 1988. He studied piano with his father, a prof. at the Dresden Cons.; he gave a public piano recital in Dresden at the age of 9. His auspicious career was halted by the Nazi takeover in Germany; Muench was drafted into the German army, but was discharged in 1944 as physically unfit. He went to the United States in 1947. In 1953 he settled in Mexico City and taught at the Univ. Nacional. In his piano recitals he introduced the new music of Stockhausen, Boulez, Pousseur, and others to Mexican audiences. Among his works is the chamber opera *Tumulus Veneris* (1950).

Mugellini, Bruno, Italian composer; b. Potenza, Dec. 24, 1871; d. Bologna, Jan. 15, 1912. He studied with Busi and Martucci in Bologna. After appearing as a concert pianist in Italy, he was appointed prof. of piano at the Liceo Musicale in Bologna (1898), succeeding Martucci as its director in 1911. He wrote an opera, *Catullo*.

Mugnone, Leopoldo, noted Italian conductor; b. Naples, Sept. 29, 1858; d. there, Dec. 22, 1941. He studied with Cesi and Serrao at the Naples Cons.; he began to compose as a young student; when he was 16, he produced a comic opera, *Don Bizarro e le sue figlie* (Naples, April 20, 1875); other operas were *Il Biricchino* (Venice, Aug. 11, 1892; fairly successful) and *Vita Brettone* (Naples, March 14, 1905). He also composed an attractive Neapolitan song, *La Rosella*, and other light music. But it was as a fine opera conductor that Mugnone achieved fame; his performances of Italian stage works possessed the highest degree of authority and an intense musicianly ardor. He also brought out Wagner's music dramas in Italy; conducted the first performances of Mascagni's *Cavalleria rusticana* (Rome, May 17, 1890) and Puccini's *Tosca* (Rome, Jan. 14, 1900).

Mul, Jan, Dutch organist, choral conductor, and composer; b. Haarlem, Sept. 20, 1911; d. Overveen, near Haarlem, Dec. 30, 1971. He was a student of H. Andriessen and Dresden in Amsterdam, and of the Roman Catholic School of Church Music in Utrecht. From 1931 to 1960 he was an organist and choral conductor in Overveen. He also was music ed. of the Amsterdam daily *De Volkskrant*. He orchestrated Dresden's opera *François Villon* from the vocal score (Amsterdam, June 12, 1958) and Sweelinck's *Keyboard Variations on an Old Song* (Amserdam, June 12, 1963). Mul composed some fine sacred choral music, as well as the operas *De Varkenshoeder* (The Swineherd; Amsterdam, June 25, 1953) and *Bill Clifford* (Hengelo, Oct. 5, 1964).

Mulder, Ernest Willem, Dutch composer, conductor, and teacher; b. Amsterdam, July 21, 1898; d. there, April 12, 1959. He was a pupil of Schulz (piano) and Zweers (composition) at the Amsterdam Toonkunst cons., where he later was a prof. of theory and composition. From 1938 to 1947 he lectured at the Univ. of Utrecht. He also was director of the Bussum Music School and conductor of the Toonkunst Musical Soc. Among his works is the opera *Dafne* (1932–34).

Muldowney, Dominic (John), English composer; b. Southampton, July 19, 1952. He received his training from Harvey at the Univ. of Southampton, Birtwistle in London, and Rands and Blake at the Univ. of York (1971–74). In 1976 he became music director of the National Theatre in London. He composes within tonal parameters with a penchant for adventuresome harmonic explorations.

WORKS: DRAMATIC: *An Heavyweight Dirge*, music theater (1971); *Klavier-Hammer*, music theater (1973); *Da Capo al Fine*, ballet (1975); *The Earl of Essex's Galliard*, music theater (1975–76); *Macbeth*, ballet (1979); *Carmen*, ballet (1984–85); incidental music; film scores.

Mulè, Giuseppe, Italian composer and pedagogue; b. Termini, Imerese, Sicily, June 28, 1885; d. Rome, Sept. 10, 1951. He studied at the Palermo Cons., graduating as a cellist as well as in composition. In 1922 he was engaged as director of the Palermo Cons. (until 1925), and in 1925 succeeded Respighi as director of the Accademia di Santa Cecilia in Rome; he remained there until 1943. He wrote mostly for the stage, and was particularly successful in providing suitable music for revivals of Greek plays. He composed numerous operas in the tradition of the Italian verismo: *La Baronessa di Carini* (Palermo, April 16, 1912), *La Monacella della fontana* (Trieste, Feb. 17, 1923), *Dafni* (Rome, March 14, 1928), *Liola* (Naples, Feb. 2, 1935), *Taormina* (San Remo, 1938), and *La zolfara* (Rome, 1939); also the oratorio *Il Cieco di Gerico* (1910).

Müller, Adolf, Jr., Austrian composer and conductor, son of **Adolf Müller Sr.**; b. Vienna, Oct. 15, 1839; d. there, Dec. 14, 1901. After completing his education in Vienna, he was engaged as a theater conductor in the provinces. He was conductor of the German Opera at Rotterdam (1875–83), then at the Theater an der Wien, where his father had directed before him. He produced a number of operas, including *Heinrich der Goldschmidt* (Magdeburg, 1867), *Waldmeisters Brautfahrt* (Hamburg, Feb. 15, 1873), and *Van Dyke* (Rotterdam, 1877), and the Viennese operettas *Der Hofnarr* (Nov. 20, 1886; his greatest success), *Der Teufels Weib* (Nov. 22, 1890), *Der Millionen-Onkel* (Nov. 5, 1892), *General Gogo* (Feb. 1, 1896), and *Der Blondin von Namur* (Oct. 15, 1898).

Müller, Adolf, Sr. (real name, **Matthias Schmid**), Austrian conductor and composer, father of **Adolf Müller Jr.**; b. Tolna, Oct. 7, 1801; d. Vienna, July 29, 1886. He was orphaned at an early age and reared by an aunt. He studied with Joseph Rieger, the Brünn Cathedral organist, and with Joseph von Blumenthal in Vienna. After appearances as a singer and actor, he became a prolific composer for the Viennese theater. He was conductor of the Theater an der Wien (1828–78) and also conducted at the Leopoldstadt Theater. He wrote almost 600 scores for the stage, some sacred music, chamber pieces, and about 400 songs.

BIBL.: A. Bauer, *Die Musik Adolph M.s in den Theaterstücken Johann Nestroys* (diss., Univ. of Vienna, 1935).

Müller, August Eberhard, German organist and composer; b. Nordheim, Hannover, Dec. 13, 1767; d. Weimar, Dec. 3, 1817. He studied keyboard playing with his father, Matthäus Müller, an organist. After receiving instruction in harmony and composition from J. C. F. Bach in Bückeburg, he studied law in Göttingen (1786). He was an organist at various churches at Magdeburg and Leipzig. In 1800 he became assistant to Johann Adam Hiller at the Thomasschule in Leipzig, and succeeded him as Kantor there in 1804; he also was music director of the Thomaskirche and Nikolaikirche. In 1810 he became court conductor in Weimar. He wrote a Singspiel, *Der Polterabend* (Weimar, 1813 or 1814). He publ. a practical piano method (1805; actually the 6th ed. of G. Löhlein's *Clavier-Schule*, rev. by Müller; Kalkbrenner's method is based on it; Czerny publ. the 8th ed. in 1825) and a method for the flute. He also publ. cadenzas for, and a guide to the interpretation of, Mozart's concertos, and arranged piano scores of Mozart's operas, which were very popular in his time.

BIBL.: G. Haupt, *A. E. M.'s Leben und Klavierwerke* (Leipzig, 1926).

Müller, Maria, Austrian soprano; b. Leitmeritz, Jan. 29, 1898; d. Bayreuth, March 13, 1958. She studied with Erik Schmedes in Vienna and Max Altglass in New York. She made her operatic debut as Elsa in Linz in 1919, then sang at the German Theater in Prague (1921–23) and at the Bavarian State Opera in Munich (1923–24). On Jan. 21, 1925, she made her Metropolitan Opera debut in New York as Sieglinde, remaining on its roster until 1935. In 1926 she joined the Berlin Städtische Oper. From 1927 to 1943 she sang at the Berlin State Opera. She also sang at the Wagner festivals in Bayreuth (1930–44) and in Salzburg.

Müller, Peter, German composer; b. Kesselstadt, near Hanau, June 9, 1791; d. Langen, Aug. 29, 1877. He taught music at various schools in Germany. In 1839 he became pastor at Staden. His opera (after Bulwer-Lytton), *Die letzten Tage von Pompeii*, was produced at Darmstadt on Dec. 25, 1853.

Müller, Sigfrid Walther, German composer; b. Plauen, Jan. 11, 1905; d. in a Russian prison camp in Baku, Nov. 2, 1946. He studied at the Leipzig Cons. with Karg-Elert and Martienssen; also church music and organ with Straube. He taught at the Leipzig Cons. (1929–32) and at the Hochschule für Musik in Weimar (1940–41), then was in the German army on the eastern front. His output comprised 62 opus numbers, including the opera *Schlaraffenhochzeit* (Leipzig, 1937).

Müller, Wenzel, prominent Austrian conductor and composer; b. Tyrnau, Moravia, Sept. 26, 1767; d. Baden, near Vienna, Aug. 3, 1835. He studied with the Kornitz schoolmaster, learning to play all the instruments of the orch. and beginning to compose as a child; he continued his studies at the Raigern Benedictine foundation, where he received further instruction from its choirmaster, Maurus Haberbauer, and then completed his studies with Dittersdorf in Johannisberg. In 1782 he became 3d violinist in Waizhofer's theater company in Brünn, attracting notice with his successful Singspiel *Das verfehlte Rendezvouz, oder Die weiblichen Jäger*. After a concert tour with the Willmann family (1786), he settled in Vienna as Kapellmeister at the Leopoldstädter-Theater. His first success as a composer there came with his Singspiel *Das Sonnenfest der Braminen* (Sept. 9, 1790), which was followed by such popular stage works as *(Kaspar) Der Fagottist, oder Die Zauberzither* (June 8, 1791), *Die Schwestern von Prag* (March 11, 1794), *Das lustige Beilager* (Feb. 14, 1797), *Die zwölf schlafenden Jungfrauen* (Oct. 12, 1797), and *Die Teufelsmühle am Wienerberg* (Nov. 12, 1799). After serving as Kapellmeister at Prague's German Opera (1807–13), he returned to the Leopoldstädter-Theater as Kapellmeister in 1815; among the subsequent popular scores he wrote for it were *Tankredi* (April 25, 1817), *Der verwunschene Prinz* (March 3, 1818), *Aline, oder Wien in einem andern Weltteil* (Oct. 9, 1822), *Der Barometermacher auf der Zauberinsel* (Dec. 18, 1823), *Die gefesselte Phantasie* (Jan. 8, 1828), and *Der Alpenkönigund der Menschenfeind* (Oct. 17, 1828). His daughter was **Therese Grünbaum**. Müller was the most successful composer of light stage works for the Vienna theater of his day, and several of his works remain a part of the Austrian repertoire. A prolific composer, he produced some 250 theatrical pieces alone.

BIBL.: W. Krone, *W. M.: Ein Beitrag zur Geschichte der komischen Oper* (Berlin, 1906); L. Raab, *W. M.: Ein Tonkünstler Altwiens* (Baden, 1928).

Müller-Reuter, Theodor, German conductor and composer; b. Dresden, Sept. 1, 1858; d. there, Aug. 11, 1919. He studied piano with Alwin Wieck in Dresden and Clara Schumann in Frankfurt am Main, and also took lessons in composition with E. J. Otto and Meinardus in Dresden. He taught piano at the Strasbourg Cons. (1879–87), and at Dresden, and then conducted the Concert Soc. in Krefeld (1893–1918), returning to Dresden shortly before his death. He wrote the operas *Ondolina* (Strasbourg, 1883) and *Der tolle Graf* (Nuremberg, 1887). He also publ. *Lexikon der deutschen Konzert-Literatur* (Leipzig, 1909; supplement, 1921) and a vol. of reminiscences and essays, *Bilder und Klänge des Friedens: Musikalische Erinnerungen und Aufsätze* (Leipzig, 1919).

Müller von Kulm, Walter, Swiss composer; b. Kulm, Aug. 31, 1899; d. Arlesheim, near Basel, Oct. 3, 1967. He studied in Aarau and at the conservatories and in Basel and Zürich, and took courses in musicology, philosophy, and psychology at the Univ. of Basel. He was director of the Basel Cons. (1947–64). He publ. the manual *Grundriss der Harmonielehre* (Basel, 1948). Among his works were the opera *Der Erfinder* (1944), a ballet, *Die blaue Blume* (1936), and the oratorios *Vater unser* (1945) and *Petrus* (1960).

Mullings, Frank (Coningsby), distinguished English tenor; b. Walsall, March 10, 1881; d. Manchester, May 19, 1953. He studied voice in Birmingham. He made his operatic debut in Coventry in 1907 as Faust; he then sang Tristan in London in 1913, and performed the role of Otello in Manchester in 1916. In 1919 he was the first to sing Parsifal in English, at Covent Garden in London. From 1922 to 1926 he was the principal dramatic tenor of the British National Opera Co., and appeared with it as Apollo in the first performance, in 1924, of Rutland Boughton's *Alkestis*. He taught at the Birmingham School of Music (1927–46) and at the Royal Manchester College of Music (1944–49). His other roles included Siegfried, Tannhäuser, Canio, and Radames.

Munsel, Patrice (Beverly), American soprano; b. Spokane, Wash., May 14, 1925. She studied in New York with William Herman and Renato Bellini. She won an audition at the Metropolitan Opera and made a successful debut there on Dec. 4, 1943, in the role of Philine in Thomas's *Mignon*, being the youngest singer to appear there to that time; she remained on the staff until 1958, excepting the 1945–46 season. She subsequently made several European tours. Her best roles were Gilda, Lucia, Rosina, Violetta, and Lakme. She portrayed Melba in a film of Melba's life (1953) and also made successful appearances in operetta and in Broadway musicals.

Muradeli, Vano (Ilyich), Russian composer; b. Gori, Georgia, April 6, 1908; d. Tomsk, Siberia, Aug. 14, 1970. As a child he improvised songs, accompanying himself on the mandolin; he studied with Barchudarian and Bagrinsky at the Tiflis Cons. (graduated, 1931) and with Shekhter and Miaskovsky at the Moscow Cons. (graduated, 1934). His early compositions were influenced by his native folk music; he wrote a *Georgian Suite* for Piano (1935) and incidental music to plays on Caucasian subjects. His first important work was a sym. in memory of the assassinated Soviet dignitary Kirov (Moscow, Nov. 28, 1938); his 2d Sym. (1946) received a Stalin prize. The performance of his opera *Great Friendship* (Moscow, Nov. 7, 1947) gave rise to an official condemnation of modernistic trends in Soviet music, culminating in the resolution of the Central Committee of the Communist Party of Feb. 10, 1948, which described the opera as "chaotic, inharmonious, and alien to the normal human ear." His reputation was rehabilitated by his subsequent works, which included the opera *October* (Moscow, April 22, 1964).

Muratore, Lucien, prominent French tenor and teacher; b. Marseilles, Aug. 29, 1876; d. Paris, July 16, 1954. He studied at the Marseilles Cons., graduating with honors in 1897, but began his career as an actor. Later he studied opera at the Paris Cons. He made his operatic debut at the Paris Opéra Comique on Dec. 16, 1902, as the King in Hahn's *La Carmélite*, with extraordinary success. Muratore also sang in the premieres of several operas by Massenet: *Ariane* (1906), *Bacchus* (1909), and *Roma* (1912); Février's *Monna Vanna* (1909), and Giordano's *Siberia* (1911), et al. In 1913 he made his American debut with the Boston Opera Co.; on Dec. 15, 1913, he sang Faust with the Chicago Opera Co. In 1914 he joined the French army, then returned to the Chicago Grand Opera (1915–19; 1920–22). In 1922 he went back to France; for 7 years he served as mayor of the town of Biot. He was married 3 times; his first 2 marriages (to Marguerite Beriza, a soprano, and to **Lina Cavalieri**) ended in divorce; his 3d wife was Marie Louise Brivaud. Among his finest roles were Faust, Don José, and Des Grieux.

Murio-Celli, Adelina, Italian soprano, teacher, and composer; b. Breslau, 1836; d. N.Y., April 10, 1900. She studied with Louis Ponchard, G. Bordogni, and G. Roger at the Paris Cons. After appearances in major European opera houses, she married E. Ravin d'Elpeux, the French vice consul to the United States, in 1867 and retired from the operatic stage. Settling in New York, she was active as a voice teacher, numbering Eleanora de Cisneros and Emma Juch among her outstanding pupils. She composed some instrumental works and vocal pieces, the best known of which was the song *The Soldier's Bride*.

Muro, Bernardo de, Italian tenor; b. Tempio Pausanio, Sardinia, Nov. 3, 1881; d. Rome, Oct. 27, 1955. He studied at the Accademia di Santa Cecilia in Rome and with Alfredo Martinio. He made his operatic debut as Turiddu at Rome's Teatro Costanzi in 1910; in 1911 he appeared at Milan's La Scala as Folco in Mascagni's *Isabeau* and returned there in the title role of *Don Carlos* in 1912, then sang in various Italian music centers, winning admiration for his portrayal of Otello; he also appeared in Europe and South America. After marrying the American soprano Barbara Wait, he toured in the United States with minor opera companies; following his retirement from the stage (1943), he devoted himself to teaching. He never became a star in the operatic firmament, yet knowledgeable critics regarded him as worthy of comparison with Caruso, both in the carrying force of his natural voice and in emotional appeal. He wrote an autobiographical vol., *Quandro ero Folco* (Milan, 1956).

Murphy, Suzanne, Irish soprano; b. Limerick, Aug. 15, 1941. She received vocal training from Veronica Dunne at the Dublin College of Music (1973–76). After making her operatic debut in *La Cenerentola* at the Irish National Opera in Dublin, she was engaged as Constanze at the Welsh National Opera in Cardiff in 1976. She subsequently sang such roles there as Gilda, Norma, Leonora, Elisabeth de Valois, Violetta, Amelia Boccanegra, and Musetta. In 1985 she sang Norma in Munich. In 1987 she made her first appearance at the Vienna State Opera as Elettra. She sang Alice Ford during the Welsh National Opera's tour to New York and Milan in 1989. In 1991 she portrayed Elettra at the London Promenade Concerts, and in 1992 she appeared as Tosca with the English National Opera in London. She was engaged as Leonore in Belfast in 1996.

Murray, Ann, Irish mezzo-soprano; b. Dublin, Aug. 27, 1949. She studied at the Royal Manchester College of Music and in London. In 1974 she made her operatic debut as Alceste at Glasgow's Scottish Opera, and then appeared regularly at London's English National Opera; in 1976 she made her Covent Garden debut in London as Cherubino, and subsequently sang there frequently. On Oct. 18, 1985, she made her Metropolitan Opera debut in New York as Sextus in *La clemenza di Tito*. In 1990 she scored a notable success as Berlioz's Beatrice with the English National

Opera. In 1994 she appeared as Giulio Cesare in Munich. She appeared as Xerxes at the Lyric Opera in Chicago in 1995. In 1997 she sang Giulio Cesare at Covent Garden. She also sang as a guest artist with various opera houses and festivals at home and abroad, and likewise pursued a notably successful career as a concert artist. Among her finest roles are Handel's Xerxes, Mozart's Dorabella and Zerlina, and Strauss's Composer. Her husband is **Philip Langridge**.

Murray, Bain, American composer and teacher; b. Evanston, Ill., Dec. 26, 1926; d. Cleveland, Jan. 16, 1993. He was a student of Elwell at Oberlin (Ohio) College (A.B., 1951), of Thompson and Piston at Harvard Univ. (A.M., 1952), and of Boulanger in Paris. He taught at Harvard Univ. (1954–55), Oberlin College (1955–60), and Cleveland State Univ. (from 1960), where he was head of its theory and composition dept. (from 1966). His works included *The Legend*, opera oratorio (1986; Cleveland, May 8, 1987), *Mary Stuart: A Queen Betrayed*, opera (Cleveland, March 1, 1991), and *Peter Pan*, ballet.

Murray, William, American baritone; b. Schenectady, N.Y., March 13, 1935. He studied at Adelphi Univ. In 1956 he received a Fulbright scholarship and continued his training in Rome. After making his operatic debut as Count Gil in *Il segreto di Susanna* in Spoleto in 1956, he sang in Detmold, Braunschweig, Munich, Frankfurt am Main, Amsterdam, and Salzburg. In 1969 he became a member of the Deutsche Oper in Berlin, where he was made a Kammersanger. In 1970 he created the title role in Dallapiccola's *Ulisse* at Milan's La Scala. In 1973 he sang in the premiere of Nabokov's *Love's Labours Lost* in Brussels. Among his other roles were Don Giovanni, Rigoletto, Don Carlo, Wolfram, Macbeth, and Scarpia.

Murska, Ilma di, Croatian soprano; b. Zagreb, Jan. 4, 1836; d. Munich, Jan. 14, 1889. She studied with Mathilde Marchesi in Vienna and Paris, making made her debut in Florence (1862). After a European tour, she was engaged at the Vienna Court Opera. She made her London debut as Lucia (May 11, 1865) and was favorably received there until 1873; she toured America (debut as Amina in New York, Oct. 7, 1873) and Australia (1873–76), and was again in London in 1879. She was greatly admired for the quality of her voice and stage presence, but her voice and health deteriorated so rapidly that reviewers were embarrassed by her pathetic vocal display at her last N.Y. appearance (Dec. 29, 1887). She taught unsuccessfully at the National Cons. there (1888) and then returned to Germany, where she died in poverty. She also composed a few works. Her life was filled with turbulence and a fabricated background: 2 marriages, an illegitimate daughter whose legitimacy was established by fabricating a 3d marriage, lawsuits with opera companies, and injudicious advice from friends. Learning of her death, her daughter, with whom she was living, committed suicide.

Musgrave, Thea, remarkable Scottish composer; b. Barnton, Midlothian, May 27, 1928. She pursued preliminary medical studies at the Univ. of Edinburgh, and concurrently studied with Mary Grierson (musical analysis) and Hans Gál (composition and counterpoint), receiving her B.Mus. (1950) and winning the Donald Tovey Prize, then studied privately and at the Paris Cons. with Boulanger (1952–54); she later was a scholarship student of Copland at the Berkshire Music Center in Tanglewood (summer 1959). She taught at the Univ. of London (1958–65), then was a visiting prof. of composition at the Univ. of Calif. at Santa Barbara (1970); she also lectured at various other U.S. and English univs.; likewise made appearances as a conductor on both sides of the Atlantic. She held 2 Guggenheim fellowships (1974–75; 1982). In 1971 she married **Peter Mark**. She was named Distinguished Prof. of Music at Queens College in New York in 1987. At the outset of her career, she followed the acceptable modern style of composition, but soon the diatonic lyricism of the initial period of her creative evolution gave way to increasingly chromatic constructions, eventually systematized into serial organization. She described her theatrical works as "dramatic abstracts" in form, because even in the absence of a programmatic design, they revealed some individual dramatic traits. Appreciated by critics and audiences alike, her compositions enjoy numerous performances in Europe and America.

WORKS: DRAMATIC: OPERAS: *The Abbott of Drimock*, chamber opera (London, 1955); *The Decision* (1964–65; London, Nov. 30, 1967); *The Voice of Ariadne* (1972–73; Aldeburgh, June 11, 1974); *Mary, Queen of Scots* (1976; Edinburgh, Sept. 6, 1977); *A Christmas Carol* (Norfolk, Va., Dec. 7, 1979); *An Occurrence at Owl Creek Bridge*, radio opera (1981; London, Sept. 14, 1982); *Harriet, the Woman Called Moses* (Norfolk, Va., March 1, 1985); *Simon Bolivar* (1994; Norfolk, Va., Jan. 20, 1995). BALLETS: *A Tale for Thieves* (1953); *Beauty and the Beast* (London, Nov. 19, 1969); *Orfeo* (1975; BBC-TV, March 17, 1977; as *Orfeo II* for Flute and Strings, Los Angeles, March 28, 1976; as *Orfeo I* for Flute and Tape, Chichester, July 5, 1976).

BIBL.: D. Hixon, *T. M.: A Bio-Bibliography* (Westport, Conn., 1984).

Mussorgsky, Modest (Petrovich), great Russian composer; b. Karevo, March 21, 1839; d. St. Petersburg, March 28, 1881. He received his first instruction on the piano from his mother, and at the age of 10 he was taken to St. Petersburg, where he had piano lessons with Anton Herke, remaining his pupil until 1854. In 1852 he entered the cadet school of the Imperial Guard. He composed a piano piece entitled *Porte enseigne Polka*, which was publ. (1852); after graduation (1856), he joined the regiment of the Guard. In 1857, he met Dargomyzhsky, who introduced him to Cui and Balakirev; he also became friendly with the critic and chief champion of Russian national music, Vladimir Stasov. These associations prompted his decision to become a professional composer. He played and analyzed piano arrangements of works by Beethoven and Schumann, and Balakirev helped him to acquire a knowledge of form. He tried to write music in classical style, but without success; his inner drive was directed toward "new shores," as Mussorgsky expressed it. The liquidation of the family estate made it imperative for him to take a paying job. He became a clerk in the Ministry of Communications (1863), being dismissed 4 years later. During this time, he continued to compose, but his lack of technique compelled him time and again to leave his various pieces unfinished. He eagerly sought professional advice from his friends Stasov (for general aesthetics) and Rimsky-Korsakov (for problems of harmony), and to the very end of his life he regarded himself as being only half educated in music, and constantly acknowledged his inferiority as a craftsman. But he yielded to no one in his firm faith in the future of national Russian music. When a group of composers from Bohemia visited St. Petersburg in 1867, Stasov publ. an article in which he for the first time referred to the "mighty handful of Russian musicians" pursuing the ideal of national art. The expression was picked up derisively by some journalists, but it was accepted as a challenge by Mussorgsky and his comrades-in-arms, Balakirev, Borodin, Cui, and Rimsky-Korsakov, the "mighty 5" of Russian music. In 1869 he once more entered government service, this time in the forestry dept. He became addicted to drink, and had epileptic fits; he died a week after his 42d birthday.

The significance of Mussorgsky's genius did not become apparent until some years after his death. Most of his works were prepared for publication by Rimsky-Korsakov, who corrected some of his harmonic crudities, and reorchestrated the symphonic works. Original versions of his music were preserved in MS, and eventually publ. But despite the availability of the authentic scores, his works continue to be performed in Rimsky-Korsakov's eds., made familiar to the whole musical world. In his dramatic works, and in his songs, Mussorgsky draws a boldly realistic vocal line, in which inflections of speech are translated into a natural melody. His first attempt in this genre was an unfinished opera, "The Marriage," to Gogol's comedy; here he also demonstrated his penetrating sense of musical humor. His ability to depict tragic moods is revealed in his cycle of 4 songs *Songs and Dances of Death* (1875–77); his understanding of intimate poetry is shown in the children's songs. His greatest work is the opera *Boris Go-*

dunov (to Pushkin's tragedy), which has no equal in its stirring portrayal of personal destiny against a background of social upheaval. In it, Mussorgsky created a true national music drama, without a trace of the Italian conventions that had theretofore dominated the operatic works by Russian composers. He wrote no chamber music, perhaps because he lacked the requisite training in contrapuntal technique. Of his piano music, the set of pieces *Pictures at an Exhibition* (actually *Kartinki s vistavki*, suite, 1874; comprised of *Promenade, Gnomus, Il vecchio castello, Tuileries, Bydlo, Ballet des poussins dans leurs coques, Deux juifs, l'un riche et l'autre pauvre, Limoges—Le Marché, Catacombae, Cum mortuis in lingua mortua, La Cabane sur des pattes de poule*, and *La Grande Porte de Kiev*; French titles by Mussorgsky) is remarkable for its vivid representation of varied scenes (it was written to commemorate his friend, the painter Victor Hartmann, whose pictures were the subjects of the music); the work became famous in the brilliant orchestration of Ravel (1922). Although Mussorgsky was a Russian national composer, his music influenced many composers outside Russia, and he came to be regarded as the most potent talent of the Russian national school. The paintings of Hartmann that inspired *Pictures at an Exhibition* were reproduced by Alfred Frankenstein in his article on the subject in the *Musical Quarterly* (July 1939); he also brought out an illustrated ed. of the work (1951). A collected ed. of Mussorgsky's works was compiled by P. Lamm (8 vols., Moscow, 1928–34; 1939). A complete ed. of his works in 34 vols. began publ. in Mainz in 1992.

WORKS: OPERAS: *Salammbô* (1863–66; unfinished); *Zhenitba* (The Marriage), comic opera (1868; only Act 1 completed; St. Petersburg, April 1, 1909; completed and orchestrated by A. Tcherepnin; Essen, Sept. 14, 1937); *Boris Godunov* (1st version, with 7 scenes, 1868–69; Leningrad, Feb. 16, 1928; 2d version, with prologue and 4 acts, 1871–72, rev. 1873; St. Petersburg, Feb. 8, 1874; rev. and reorchestrated by Rimsky-Korsakov, 1896; St. Petersburg, Dec. 10, 1896; another ed. By Buketoff, N.Y., Dec. 19, 1997); *Khovanshchina* (1872–80; completed and orchestrated by Rimsky-Korsakov; St. Petersburg, Feb. 21, 1886); *Sorochinskaya yarmarka* (The Fair at Sorochinsk), comic opera (1874–80; completed by Cui, Liadov, Karatigin, and others; Moscow, Oct. 21, 1913; also arranged and orchestrated by N. Tcherepnin; Monte Carlo, March 17, 1923).

BIBL.: The Russian literature on Mussorgsky is extensive. A collection of letters and documents was publ. by A. Rimsky-Korsakov (Moscow, 1932); materials, largely taken from this vol., were tr. and ed. by J. Leyda and S. Bertensson as *The M. Reader* (N.Y., 1947). See also V. Stasov, *M.* (St. Petersburg, 1881); V. Baskin, *M.* (Moscow, 1887); P. d'Alheim, *M.* (Paris, 3d ed., 1896); M. Olénine-d'Alheim, *Le Legs de M.* (Paris, 1908); M. D. Calvocoressi, *M.* (Paris, 1907; 2d French ed., 1911; Eng. tr., London, 1919); M. Montagu-Nathan, *M.* (London, 1916); O. von Riesemann, *M.* (Munich, 1925; in Eng., N.Y., 1935); R. Godet, *En marge de Boris Godunov* (Paris, 1927); K. von Wolfurt, *M.* (Stuttgart, 1927); I. Glebov, *M.* (Leningrad, 1928); H. van Dalen, *M.* (The Hague, 1930); V. Fedorov, *M.* (Paris, 1935); M. Tibaldi Chiesa, *M.* (Milan, 1935); C. Barzel, *M.* (Paris, 1939); G. Orlov, *Chronicle of the Life and Works of M.* (Moscow, 1940); G. Gavazzeni, *M. e la musica russa dell' 800* (Florence, 1943); M.D. Calvocoressi, *M.* (completed by G. Abraham, London, 1946; 2d ed., rev., 1974); R. Hofmann, *M.* (Paris, 1952); M. D. Calvocoressi, *M. M., His Life and Works* (London, 1956; ed. by G. Abraham; a completely different book from the earlier ones by Calvocoressi); V. Serov, *M. M.* (N.Y., 1968); L. Hübsch, *M. M.: Bilder einer Ausstellung* (Munich, 1978); R. Oldani, *New Pespectives on M.'s Boris Godunov* (diss., Univ. of Michigan, 1978); M. Schandert, *Das Problem der originalen Instrumentation des Boris Godunov von M. P. M.* (Hamburg, 1979); E. Reilly, *A Guide to M.: A Scorography* (N.Y., 1980); M. Brown, ed., *M.: In Memoriam 1881–1981* (Ann Arbor, 1982); A. Orlova, *M.'s Days and Works: A Biography in Documents* (Ann Arbor, 1983); C. Emerson, *Boris Godunov: Transpositions of a Russian Theme* (Bloomington and Indianapolis, 1986); R. Taruskin, *M.: Eight Essays and an Epilogue* (Princeton, 1993); C. Emerson and R. Oldani, *M. M. and Boris Godunov: Myths, realities, reconsiderations* (Cambridge, 1994); E. Kuhn, *M. M.: Zugaenge zu Leben und Werk* (Berlin, 1994).

Mustafà, Domenico, Italian castrato soprano and composer; b. Sterpara, near Perugia, April 14, 1829; d. Montefalco, near Perugia, March 18, 1912. He entered the Sistine Chapel Choir in Rome in 1848, being the last castrato employed there. He later served as its maestro di cappella (until 1895). Among his compositions were much sacred music and various songs.

BIBL.: A. De Angelis, *D. M. e la Cappella Sistina* (Bologna, 1926).

Muti, Riccardo, greatly talented Italian conductor; b. Naples, July 28, 1941. His father was a physician who possessed a natural Neapolitan tenor voice; after receiving instruction in violin and piano from his father, Riccardo studied composition with Napoli and Rota at the Cons. di Musica San Pietro a Majella in Naples, taking a diploma in piano; then studied conducting with Votto and composition with Bettinelli at the Verdi Cons. in Milan; he also attended a seminar in conducting with Ferrara in Venice (1965). After winning the Guido Cantelli Competition in 1967, he made his formal debut with the RAI in 1968, then conducted in several of the major Italian music centers. His success led to his appointment as principal conductor of the Teatro Comunale in Florence in 1970; he also conducted at the Maggio Musicale Fiorentino, becoming its artistic director in 1977. In the meantime, he began his advancement to international fame with guest conducting appearances at the Salzburg Festival in 1971 and with the Berlin Phil. in 1972. He made his U.S. debut with the Philadelphia Orch. on Oct. 27, 1972. In 1973 he conducted at the Vienna State Opera, and that same year became principal conductor of the New Philharmonia Orch. in London (it resumed its original name of Philharmonia Orch. in 1977). In 1974 he conducted the Vienna Phil. and in 1977 appeared at London's Covent Garden. His successful appearances with the Philadelphia Orch. led to his appointment as its principal guest conductor in 1977. In 1979 he was also named music director of the Philharmonia Orch. In 1980 he succeeded Eugene Ormandy as music director of the Philadelphia Orch., and subsequently relinquished his posts in London and Florence in 1982. In 1986 he became music director of Milan's La Scala, but retained his Philadelphia position. Muti announced his resignation as music director of the Philadelphia Orch. in 1990, but agreed to serve as its laureate conductor from 1992. His brilliance as a symphonic conductor enabled him to maintain, and even enhance, the illustrious reputation of the Philadelphia Orch. established by Stokowski and carried forward by Ormandy. Unlike his famous predecessors, he excels in both the concert hall and the opera pit. His tenure at La Scala has been notable for his raising artistic standards to a memorable level of achievement.

BIBL.: J. Kurnick, ed., *R. M.: Twenty Years in Philadelphia* (Philadelphia, 1992).

Muzio, Claudia (real name, **Claudina Muzzio**), oustanding Italian soprano; b. Pavia, Feb. 7, 1889; d. Rome, May 24, 1936. She studied with Casaloni in Turin and Viviani in Milan. She made her operatic debut as Manon in Arezzo (Jan. 15, 1910), then sang in Turin (1911; 1914–15), at Milan's La Scala (1913–14), and at London's Covent Garden (1914). She made her Metropolitan Opera debut in New York as Tosca (Dec. 4, 1916), remaining on its roster until 1922; she created the role of Giorgetta in Puccini's *Il tabarro* there (Dec. 14, 1918). In 1922 she made her first appearance with the Chicago Opera as Aida, and continued to sing there regularly until 1932; she also sang in South America and again at La Scala (1926–27); after returning to the Metropolitan (1933–34), she pursued her career mainly in Rome. She was one of the most gifted dramatic sopranos of her time, excelling in such roles as Desdemona, Mimi, Santuzza, Margherita in *Mefistofele*, Violetta, and Madeleine de Coigny.

BIBL.: H. Barnes, *C. M.: A Biographical Sketch and Discography* (Austin, Texas, 1947).

Muzio, (Donnino) Emanuele, Italian conductor and composer; b. Zibello, Aug. 24, 1821; d. Paris, Nov. 27, 1890. He began his studies with Ferdinando Provesi, then studied piano with Margherita Barezzi (Verdi's 1st wife), and composition with Verdi himself, becoming one of the very few pupils Verdi ever had. In 1850 he was engaged as conductor of the Théâtre du Cirque in Brussels, and later traveled to England and America. He settled in Paris in 1875 as a singing teacher, numbering Carlotta Patti and Clara Louise Kellogg among his pupils. He wrote several operas: *Giovanna la pazza* (Brussels, April 8, 1851), *Claudia* (Milan, Feb. 7, 1853), *Le due regine* (Milan, May 17, 1856), and *La Sorrentina* (Bologna, Nov. 14, 1857).

BIBL.: A. Belforti, *E. M., l'unico alievo di Giuseppe Verdi* (Fabriano, 1895); L. Garibaldi, ed., *Giuseppe Verdi nelle lettere di E. M. ed Antonio Barezzi* (Milan, 1931).

Myers, Rollo (Hugh), English music critic and writer on music; b. Chislehurst, Kent, Jan. 23, 1892; d. Chichester, Jan. 1, 1985. He was educated at Balliol College, Oxford, and at the Royal College of Music in London. From 1919 to 1934 he was the Paris music correspondent of *The Times* and the *Daily Telegraph* of London. He was on the staff of the BBC in London from 1935 to 1944. After serving as music officer of the British Council in Paris (1944–45), he returned to London as ed. of *The Chesterian* (from 1947) and of *Music Today* (from 1949).

WRITINGS (all publ. in London unless otherwise given): *Modern Music: Its Aims and Tendencies* (1923); *Music in the Modern World* (1939; 2d ed., rev., 1948); *Debussy* (1948); *Erik Satie* (1948); *Introduction to the Music of Stravinsky* (1950); *Ravel: Life and Works* (1960); ed. *Twentieth Century Music* (1960; 2d ed., aug., 1968); ed. and tr., *Richard Strauss and Romain Rolland: Correspondence* (1968); *Emmanuel Chabrier and his Circle* (1969); *Modern French Music* (Oxford, 1971).

Mysliveček (Mysliweczek; Misliveček), Josef, famous Bohemian composer, called "Il divino Boemo" and "Il Venatorini" in Italy; b. Ober-Sárka, near Prague, March 9, 1737; d. Rome, Feb. 4, 1781. His father was a miller. He was a pupil at the Normalschule of the Dominicans of St. Jilgi (1744–47) and the Jesuit Gymnasium (1748–53), where he received his first instruction in music; he also sang in the choir of St. Michal under Felix Benda. He then was apprenticed as a miller, being made a master miller in 1761. He also pursued his musical studies, taking courses in counterpoint with František Habermann and organ with Josef Seger. In 1760 he publ. anonymously a set of 6 sinfonias, named after the first 6 months of the year. Determined upon a career as a composer, he went to Venice in 1763 to study the art of operatic writing with Giovanni Pescetti. His first opera, *Medea*, was produced in Parma in 1764. While in Parma, he met the singer Lucrezia Aguiari, who became his mistress in the first of his many romantic liaisons. He was commissioned to write another opera, *Il Bellerofonte*, for the Teatro San Carlo in Naples, where it was performed with considerable success on Jan. 20, 1767. This led to other commissions from Italian theaters. His opera *Ezio* (Naples, June 5, 1775) and his oratorio *Isacco figura del Redentore* (Florence, March 10, 1776) were successfully performed in Munich in 1777; his career was blunted, however, by syphilis and disfiguring facial surgery. He returned to Italy but never regained his social standing. He succumbed at the age of 43. Mysliveček was one of the most significant Bohemian composers; his operas and oratorios were frequently performed and publ. in his lifetime. Mozart expressed admiration of his talent.

WORKS: DRAMATIC: OPERAS: *Medea* (Parma, 1764); *Il Bellerofonte* (Naples, Jan. 20, 1767); *Farnace* (Naples, Nov. 4, 1767); *Il trionfo di Clelia* (Turin, Dec. 26, 1767); *Il Demofoonte* (Venice, Jan. 1769); *L'Ipermestra* (Florence, March 28, 1769); *La Nitteti* (Bologna, spring 1770); *Montezuma* (Florence, Jan. 23, 1771); *Il gran Tamerlano* (Milan, Dec. 26, 1771); *Il Demetrio* (Pavia, Jan. 25, 1773); *Erifile* (Munich, 1773); *Romolo ed Ersilia* (Naples, Aug. 13, 1773); *La clemenza di Tito* (Venice, Dec. 26, 1773); *Antigona* (Turin, Carnival 1774); *Atide* (Padua, June 1774); *Artaserse* (Naples, Aug. 13, 1774); *Il Demofoonte* (Naples, Jan. 20, 1775); *Ezio* (Naples, June 5, 1775); *Merope* (Naples, 1775); *Adriano in Siria* (Florence, fall 1776); *Las Calliroe* (Naples, May 30, 1778); *L'Olimpiade* (Naples, Nov. 4, 1778); *La Circe* (Venice, May 1779); *Il Demetrio* (Naples, Aug. 13, 1779); *Armida* (Milan, Dec. 26, 1779); *Medonte* (Rome, Jan. 1780); *Antigono* (Rome, April 1780). ORATORIOS: *La famiglia di Tobia* (Padua, 1769); *Adamo ed Eva* (Florence, May 24, 1771); *Giuseppe riconosciuto* (Padua, 1771); *La Passione di Gesu Cristo* (Prague, 1773); *La liberazione d'Israele* (1775); *Isacco figura del Redentore* (Florence, March 10, 1776).

BIBL.: H. Wilkemann, *Joseph Mysliweczek als Opernkomponist* (diss., Univ. of Vienna, 1915); J. Čeleda, *J. M., tvůrce pražského nářečí hudebniho rokoka tereziánského* (J. M.: Creator of the Prague Dialect of Theresian Musical Rococo; Prague, 1946); R. Pečman, *J. M. und sein Opernepilog* (Brno, 1970).

Mysz-Gmeiner, Lula (née **Gmeiner**), noted Hungarian contralto; b. Kronstadt, Transylvania, Aug. 16, 1876; d. Schwerin, Aug. 7, 1948. She studied violin in her native town, and singing in Berlin with Etelka Gerster and Lilli Lehmann. She made her concert debut in Berlin in 1899; then traveled in Europe as a concert singer; she was greatly praised for her interpretations of German lieder. She was a prof. at the Berlin Hochschule für Musik (1920–45), numbering among her students Peter Anders and Elisabeth Schwarzkopf.

Myszuga, Alexander, Polish tenor of Ukrainian descent; b. Nowy Witków, near Lemberg, June 7, 1853; d. Schwarzwald, near Freiburg im Breisgau, March 9, 1922. He studied voice in Lemberg, Milan, and Paris, adopting the name Filippi for his stage appearances in Italy. He sang in Italy, Vienna, and Prague in both lyrical and dramatic roles in French and Italian operas. He was also noted for singing tenor parts in Polish operas. In later years he taught voice in Kiev and Stockholm.

Jeannine Altmeyer as Brünnhilde

Marian Anderson

Olaf Bär outside opera house

Teresa Berganza in costume for *Carmen*

Isobel Buchanan

Montserrat Caballé

Emma Calvé

José Carreras in costume for *Werther*

Enrico Caruso with paintbrush and pallette

Feodor Chalíapin

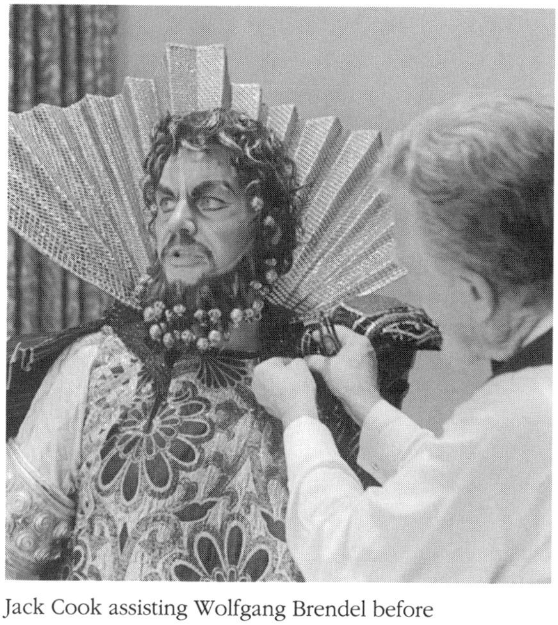

Jack Cook assisting Wolfgang Brendel before *Samson et Dalila*

Emmy Destinn in *Mignon*

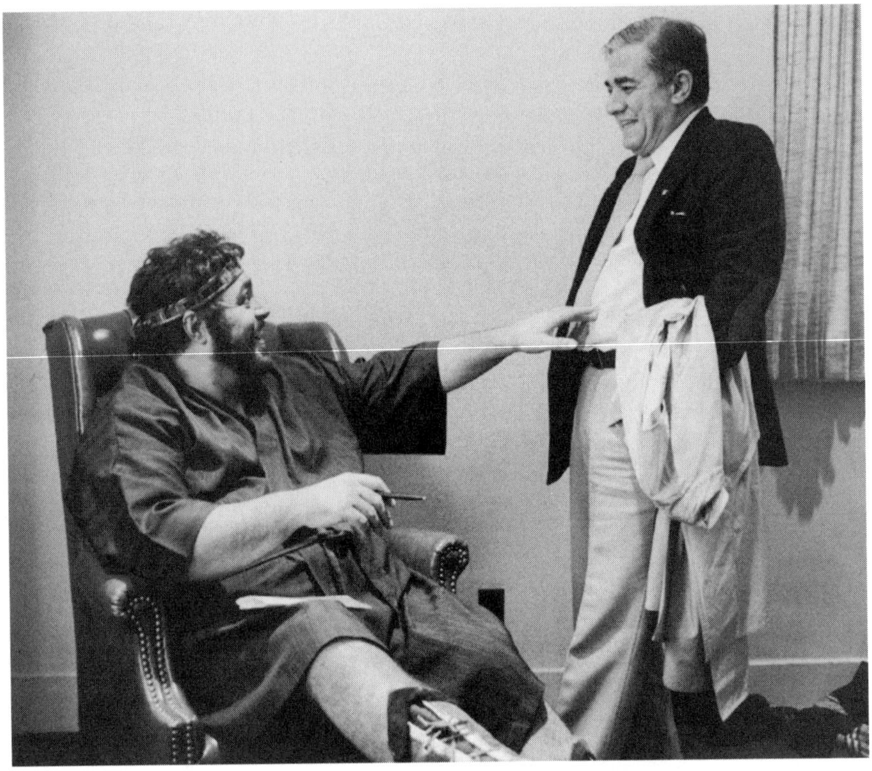

Giuseppe Di Stefano with Luciano Pavarotti (seated) before *Aida*

Plácido Domingo as Don José in *Carmen*

Emma Eames

Maria Ewing in costume for *Werther*

Geraldine Farrar

Mary Garden

Tito Gobbi during rehearsal of *Falstaff*

Nancy Gustafson preparing for *Das Rheingold*

Joan Hammond as Rusalka

Cynthia Haymon in costume as Bess

Raimund Herinex in costume for *Billy Budd*

Elizabeth Schwarzkopf and Hans Hotter

Anne Howells as Dorabella in *Così fan tutte*

Walter Hyde as Siegmund in *Die Walküre*

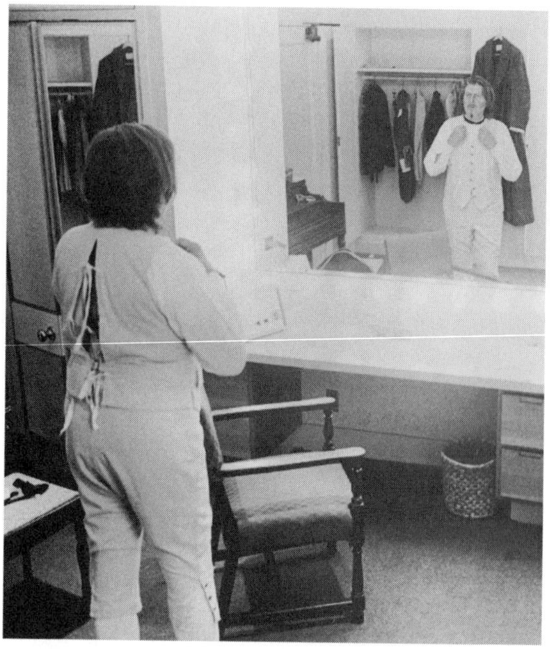

Richard Lewis dressing for *Billy Budd*

Jenny Lind

Franz Mazura (l.) and dresser before a performance of *Das Rheingold*

Marie McLaughlin

Robert Merrill singing at the White House

Luciano Pavarotti costumed as Radames

Ashley Putnam with David Angler

Susan Quittmeyer in costume for *Così fan tutte*

Forbes Robinson in *Billy Budd*

Beverly Sills and Justino Díaz rehearsing *The Siege of Corinth*

Anna Steiger in costume for *L'heure Espagnole*

Thomas Stewart

Joan Sutherland with Richard Bonynge

Birgitta Svenden preparing for *Das Rheingold*

Giuseppe Taddei as
Gianni Schicchi

Eric Tappy as the emperor Nero in
L'incoronazione di Poppea

Richard Tauber (l.) and Franz Lehár

Helen Traubel rehearses

Tatiana Troyanos after a performance of *Cavalleria rusticana*

Shirley Verrett as Norma

Galina Vishnevskaya in rehearsal for *Aida*

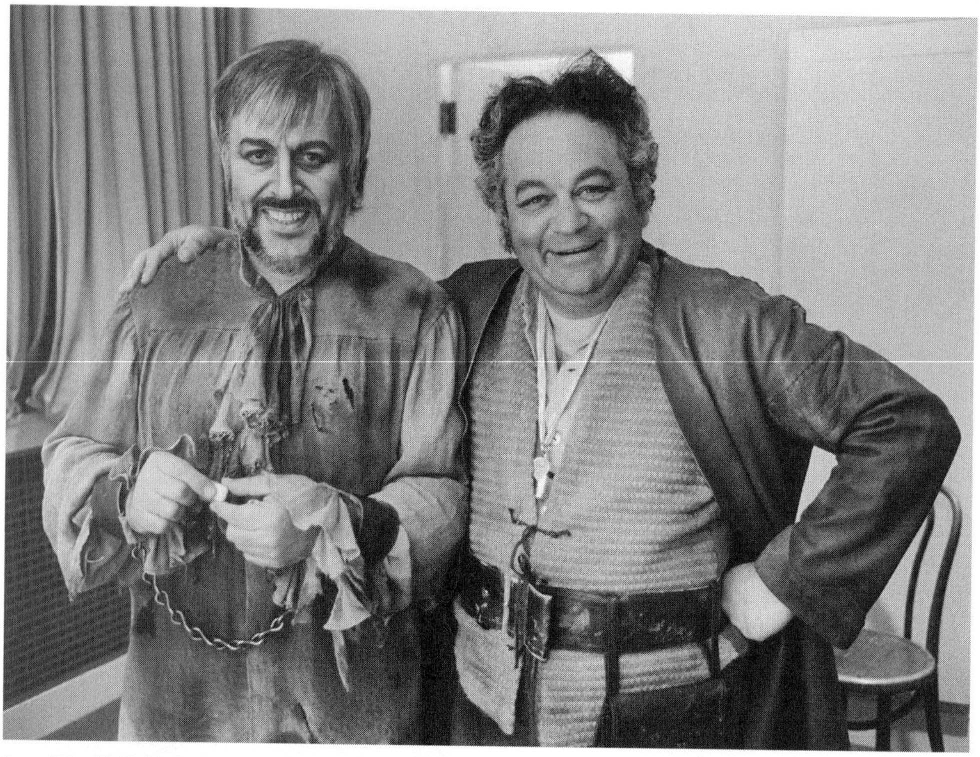
Spas Wenkoff (l.) and Marius Rintzler in costume for *Fidelio*

Willard White as Porgy

Marilyn Zschau backstage before *Tosca*

N

Nabokov, Nicolas (Nikolai), distinguished Russian-born American composer; b. near Lubcha, April 17, 1903; d. N.Y., April 6, 1978. He was a scion of a distinguished Russian family; his uncle was a liberal member of the short-lived Duma (Russian parliament); the famous writer Vladimir Nabokov was his 1st cousin. Nabokov received his early education with Rebikov in St. Petersburg and in Yalta; after taking courses at the Stuttgart Cons. (1920–22), he continued his studies with Juon and Busoni at the Berlin Hochschule für Musik (1922–23); he finally moved to Paris, where he was introduced to Diaghilev, who commissioned him to write his first major score, the ballet oratorio *Ode: Méditation sur la majesté de Dieu* (1927), for the Ballets Russes. In 1933 he went to the United States, and in 1939 became a naturalized American citizen; he taught at Wells College in Aurora, N.Y. (1936–41) and at St. John's College in Annapolis (1941–44); after working for the U.S. government in Berlin (1944–47), he taught at the Peabody Cons. of Music in Baltimore (1947–52). From 1951 to 1963 he was secretary-general of the Congress for Cultural Freedom; he then served as artistic director of the Berlin Music Festivals (1963–68) and lectured on aesthetics at the State Univ. of N.Y. at Buffalo (1970–71) and at N.Y. Univ. (1972–73). He was elected to membership in the National Inst. of Arts and Letters in 1970. In addition to writing articles for various periodicals, he wrote a book of essays, *Old Friends and New Music* (Boston, 1951), and the vols. *Igor Stravinsky* (Berlin, 1964) and *Bagazh: Memoirs of a Russian Cosmopolitan* (N.Y., 1975). In his music, he adopted a cosmopolitan style, with an astute infusion of fashionable bitonality; in works of Russian inspiration, he reverted to melorhythms of Russian folk songs.

WORKS: DRAMATIC: OPERAS: *The Holy Devil* (1954–58; Louisville, April 16, 1958; rev. version as *Der Tod des Grigorij Rasputin*, Cologne, Nov. 27, 1959); *Love's Labour's Lost* (1970–73; Brussels, Feb. 7, 1973). BALLETS: *Ode: Méditation sur la majesté de Dieu*, ballet oratorio (1927; Paris, June 6, 1928); *La vie de Polichinelle* (Paris, 1934); *Union Pacific* (Philadelphia, April 6, 1934); *The Last Flower* (1941); *Don Quixote* (1966); *The Wanderer* (1966).

Nachbaur, Franz (Ignaz), German tenor; b. Giessen, near Friedrichshafen, March 25, 1830; d. Munich, March 21, 1902. He studied with Pischek in Stuttgart and Lamperti in Milan, making his debut in Passau (1857). He then sang in Basel (1857), Hannover (1859–60), Prague (1860–63), and Darmstadt (1863–68). He made his first appearance at the Munich Court Opera on June 24, 1867, in Flotow's *Alessandro Stradella*; subsequently he was one of its principal members, and was chosen to create the roles of Walther von Stolzing in *Die Meistersinger von Nürnberg* (June 21, 1868) and Froh in *Das Rheingold* (Sept. 22, 1869). He made his London debut in *Euryanthe* at Drury Lane (1882). He gave his farewell performance at the Munich Court Opera as Chapelou in Adam's *Le Postillon de Longjumeau* on Oct. 13, 1890, his 1,001st appearance there.

Nagano, Kent (George), talented American conductor; b. Morro Bay, Calif. (of Japanese-American parents), Nov. 22, 1951. He studied at the Univ. of Oxford (1969), with Grosvenor Cooper at the Univ. of Calif. at Santa Cruz (B.A., 1974), at San Francisco State Univ. (M.M., 1976), and at the Univ. of Toronto; he also had instruction in conducting from Laszlo Varga in San Francisco. He was associated with Sarah Caldwell's Opera Co. of Boston (1977–79) and was made music director of the Berkeley (Calif.) Sym. Orch. (1978) and of the Ojai (Calif.) Music Festival (1984). While working as an assistant conductor with the Boston Sym. Orch., he was called upon to substitute for Ozawa at the last moment and led a notably successful performance of Mahler's 9th Sym. without benefit of rehearsal (Nov. 30, 1984). In 1985 he was the first corecipient (with Hugh Wolff) of the Affiliate Artist's Seaver Conducting Award. He subsequently appeared as a guest conductor with various orchs. on both sides of the Atlantic. From 1989 to 1998 he was chief conductor of the Opéra de Lyon. In 1991 he also was named principal conductor designate of the Hallé Orch. in Manchester, serving as its principal conductor from 1994 to 1998. In 1992 he made his San Francisco Opera debut conducting Milhaud's *Christoph Colomb*. He was made an Officier in the Order of Arts and Letters of France in 1993.

Naldi, Giuseppe, Italian bass; b. Bologna, Feb. 2, 1770; d. Paris, Dec. 14, 1820. After making his debut in Milan in 1789, he made appearances throughout Italy. He sang in Lisbon (1803–06) before making his London debut at the King's Theatre in Guglielmi's *Le due nozza ed un sol marito* (April 15, 1806). He continued to sing in London until 1818, where he was the first to appear as Mozart's Don Alfonso (1811), Papageno (1811), Figaro (1812), and Leporello (1817), and as Rossini's Figaro (1818). Naldi was killed in a freak accident in Manuel García's Paris apartment when a steam cooker exploded and the lid struck him in the head. His daughter, Caroline Naldi (1809–76), was a singer who appeared in operas by Rossini and Bellini in Paris (1819–24).

Nantier-Didiée, Constance (Betzy Rosabella), French mezzo-soprano; b. St. Denis, Ile de Bourbon, Nov. 16, 1831; d. Madrid, Dec. 4, 1867. She was a pupil of Duprez at the Paris Cons., where she took the premier prix in opera in 1849. In 1850 she made her stage debut in Mercadante's *La Vestale* at the Teatro Carignano in Turin. After appearing at the Salle Ventadour (1851) and the Théâtre-Italien (1852) in Paris, she made her debut at Covent Garden in London as the Chevalier de Gondi in Donizetti's *Maria di Rohan* (May 3, 1853), remaining there for 3 seasons. She also toured Spain in 1854 and North America in 1855–56. From 1856 to 1858 she once again at the Théâtre-Italien. She then resumed her association with Covent Garden, appearing as Urbain in *Les Huguenots* in the inaugural production of its new theater on May 15, 1858. She continued to sing there until 1864. On Nov. 10, 1862, she created the role of Preziosilla in *La forza del destino* in St. Petersburg.

Napoli, Gennaro, Italian composer and teacher, father of **Jacopo Napoli**; b. Naples, May 19, 1881; d. there, June 28, 1943. He was a student of d'Arienzo and de Nardis at the Royal Cons. in Naples. In 1906 he won the Pensionato Nazionale per la Musica. He taught composition in Naples at the Liceo Musicale (1912–15) and at the Royal Cons. (from 1915), where he served as assistant director (from 1926). He ed. *L'Arte Pianistica* and publ. *Bassi imitati e fugati* (1915). Among his compositions were *Jacopo Ortis*, opera, and *Armida abbandonata*, dramatic scene (1906).

Napoli, Jacopo, Italian composer, son of **Gennaro Napoli**; b. Naples, Aug. 26, 1911; d. Ascea Marina, Oct. 20, 1994. He studied at the Cons. San Pietro a Majella in Naples, with his father and S. Cesi; he was subsequently appointed to the faculty, and eventually was its director (1954–62) and subsequently was director of the Milan Cons. (1962–72) and then of the Rome Cons. (1972–76). He specialized in opera, often with a Neapolitan background, which gave him the opportunity to use Neapolitan songs in his scores. His operas include *Il Malato immaginario* (Naples, 1939), *Miseria e nobilità* (Naples, 1945), *Un curioso accidente* (Bergamo, 1950), *Masaniello* (1951; won a prize of La Scala, Milan), *I Peccatori* (1954), *Il tesoro* (Rome, 1958), *Il rosario* (Brescia, 1962), *Il povero diavolo* (Trieste, 1963), and *Il Barone avaro* (Naples, 1970).

Nápravník, Eduard (Francevič), celebrated Czech-born Russian conductor; b. Býšt, near Hradec Králové, Aug. 24, 1839; d. Petrograd, Nov. 23, 1916. He began his musical training with Půhonný, the village school master, and then with his uncle, Augustin Svoboda, in Dašice; subsequently he went to Prague, where he took courses with Blažek and Pitsch at the Organ School; after further studies at the Maydl Inst. (1856–61), he joined its faculty; he also received instruction in orchestration from Kittl. He then was engaged to conduct the private orch. of the Russian nobleman Yussupov in St. Petersburg (1861–63); after serving as répétiteur and organist at the Imperial Opera, he was named its 2d conductor in 1867; he subsequently was its chief conductor from 1869 until his death. He also was the conductor of the concerts of the St. Petersburg branch of the Russian Musical Soc. (1869–81), the Red Cross Concerts (1869–87), and the Patriotic Concerts (1871–87). He became greatly renowned as a thorough musician, possessing a fabulous sense of pitch and rhythm and exceptional ability as a disciplinarian. His reputation and influence were very great in Russian operatic affairs; Dostoyevsky, in one of his novels, uses Nápravník's name as a synonym for a guiding spirit. Nápravník conducted premieres of operas by Tchaikovsky, Mussorgsky, Dargomyzhsky, N. Rubinstein, and Rimsky-Korsakov, and also introduced many non-Russian works to his adopted homeland. His interpretations of the Russian repertoire established a standard emulated by other Russian conductors, yet he was deficient in emotional inspiration; his performances of symphonic works were regarded as competent but not profound. He was himself a composer of several operas in the Russian style, imitative of Tchaikovsky; one of them, *Dubrovsky* (St. Petersburg, Jan. 15, 1895), has become part of the active repertoire in Russia. His other operas, all premiered in St. Petersburg, were *Nizhegorotzy* (Jan. 8, 1869), *Harold* (Nov. 23, 1886), and *Francesca da Rimini* (Dec. 9, 1902).

BIBL.: P. Weymarn, *E. F. N.* (St. Petersburg, 1881); N. Findeisen, *E. F. N.* (St. Petersburg, 1898); V. Walter, *E. F. N.: Ksoletiyu yevo artisticheskoy deyatelnosti 1863–1913* (St. Petersburg, 1914); V. Nápravník, *E. F. N. i ego sovrem enniki* (Leningrad, 1991).

Nash, Heddle, admired English tenor; b. London, June 14, 1896; d. there, Aug. 14, 1961. He was a chorister at Westminster Abbey in London. After training in London, he studied with Borgatti in Milan, where he made his operatic debut at the Teatro Carcano as Rossini's Count Almaviva in 1924. Returning to London, he sang the Duke of Mantua at his first appearance at the Old Vic Theatre in 1925. From 1926 to 1929 he appeared with the British National Opera Co. In 1929 he made his debut at Covent Garden as Don Ottavio, singing there until 1939. During World War II, he appeared with the Carl Rosa Opera Co. In 1947–48 he again sang at Covent Garden. In 1957–58 he appeared with the New Opera Co. He was greatly esteemed for his roles in operas by Mozart and Rossini. Among his other distinguished roles were David in *Die Meistersinger von Nürnberg*, Gounod's Faust, and Rodolfo. He also was a notable concert singer, winning particular renown for his interpretation of Elgar's Gerontius. His son, John Heddle Nash (b. London, March 30, 1928; d. there, Sept. 29, 1994), was a baritone who sang at the Sadler's Wells Theatre and with the Carl Rosa Opera Co.

Nasolini, Sebastiano, Italian composer; b. Piacenza, c.1768; d. probably in Naples, c.1816. He most likely studied at the ducal chapel in Venice. He was maestro al cembalo at the S. Pietro theater in Trieste (1787–90), and also maestro di cappella at the Cathedral of S. Giusto there (1788–90), then was mainly active in Venice as a composer for the theater. He was a highly successful composer of popular stage works; among his extant operas are *La morte di Semiramide* (Padua, Oct. 1790), *La morte di Cleopatra* (Vicenza, June 22, 1791), *Merope* (Venice, Jan. 21, 1796), *Il Medico di Lucca* (Venice, 1797), *Gli umori contrarii* (Venice, June 1798), *Il trionfo di Clelia* (Milan, Dec. 26, 1798), and *Achille* (Modena, June 23, 1806). He also composed pasticcios, oratorios, and cantatas.

BIBL.: E. de Giovanni, *Giuseppe Nicolini e S. N.* (Piacenza, 1927); C. Anguissola, *Geminiano Giacomelli e S. N.: Musicisti placentini* (Piacenza, 1935).

Nastasijevič, Svetomir, Serbian composer; b. Gornje Milanovec, April 1, 1902; d. Belgrade, Aug. 17, 1979. He studied engineering and architecture; at the same time, he learned to play the violin; wrote music criticism and publ. 2 manuals on theory. His works include the music drama *Medjuluško blago* (The Treasure of the Medjuluzje; Belgrade, March 4, 1937) and *Durad Brankovič*, national opera from medieval Serbian history (Belgrade, June 12, 1940), in which he adopted the Wagnerian system of leitmotifs.

Natanson, Tadeusz, Polish composer and pedagogue; b. Warsaw, Jan. 26, 1927; d. Wrocław, Nov. 10, 1990. He studied composition with K. Wilkomirski, P. Perkowski, and S. Poradowski at the Wrocław Academy of Music (1952–56); he was on its faculty (from 1957), and also taught at the Warsaw Academy of Music (from 1977), where he received his Ph.D. (1977; with a diss. on music therapy as a function of music). He also taught at the Univ. of Silesia in Cieszyn (from 1983), where he served as head of the Inst. for Music Therapy (from 1984). His works include *Quo Vadis*, ballet pantomime (1970), and *Tamango*, opera (1972).

Nathan, Isaac, English-born Australian composer of Polish-Jewish descent; b. Canterbury, 1790; d. Sydney, Jan. 15, 1864. He studied singing and composition with D. Corri in London. He collaborated with Byron on the *Hebrew Melodies* (1815–19), his most successful effort. He served as music librarian to George IV, and also maintained a music publishing business. In 1841 he moved to Australia, where he continued his enterprises. He also continued to compose, being the first to write operas in Australia. Among his works were the comic operas *Sweethearts and Wives* (London, July 7, 1823) and *The Alcaid, or The Secrets of the Office* (London, July 14, 1824); also the operatic farce, *The Illustrious Stranger, or Married and Buried* (London, Oct. 1, 1827), and the opera, *Don John of Austria* (Sydney, May 3, 1847). He publ. *An Essay on the History and Theory of Music, and on the Qualities, Capabilities and Management of the Human Voice* (1823; 2d ed., 1836, as *Musurgia Vocalis*) and *Memoirs of Madame Malibran de Bériot* (1836).

BIBL.: C. Berti, *I. N.: Australia's First Composer* (Sydney, 1922); O. Phillips, *I. N.: Friend of Byron* (London, 1940); C. Mackerras, *The Hebrew Melodist: A Life of I. N.* (Sydney, 1963).

Nathan, Montagu. See **Montague-Nathan, M(ontagu).**

Nattiez, Jean-Jacques, learned French-born Canadian musicologist; b. Amiens, Dec. 30, 1945. He studied piano privately while pursuing musical training at the Amiens Cons. Following further studies in Aix-en-Provence (L.Litt. in modern languages, 1967; Licentiate in linguistics, 1968; M.Litt. in modern languages, 1968), he studied in Paris (Certificat d'aptitude pédagogique à l'enseignement secondaire, 1970; Ph.D., 1973, with a diss. on musical semiology). He also received instruction in conducting from Jacques Clément in Montreal, Fernand Quattrochi and Pierre Dervaux in Nice, and Charles Bruck in Hancock, Maine. He settled in Canada, becoming a naturalized Canadian citizen in 1975. In 1970 he became a prof. at the Univ. of Montreal, where he taught musicology (from 1972) and also was director of the Groupe de recherches en sémiologie musicale (1974–80). From 1980 to 1985 he was coed. of the *Canadian University Music Review/Revue de musique des universités canadiennes*. With Pierre Boulez, he became coed. of the series Musique/Passé/Présent of Paris in 1981. From 1984 to 1987 he was music director of the Joliette-Lanaudière Sym. Orch. In 1988 he was elected to membership in the Royal Soc. of Canada and was awarded the Dent Medal of the Royal Musical Assn. of England. In 1990 he was made a Member of the Order of Canada. Nattiez is a foremost authority on musical semiotics. His study *Fondements d'une sémiologie de la musique* (Paris, 1975; rev. and expanded, 1987, as *Musicologie générale et sémiologie*) is notable for its erudite investigation of structural linguistics as applied to musical analysis.

WRITINGS: *Fondements d'une sémiologie de la musique* (Paris, 1975; rev. and expanded, 1987, as *Musicologie générale et sémiologie*); *Tétralogies "Wagner, Boulez, Chéreau," essai sur l'infidélite* (Paris, 1983); *Proust musicien* (Paris, 1989); *Il discorso musicale, Per una semiologia della musica* (Turin, 1987); *De la sémiologie à la musique* (Montreal, 1988); ed. *Pierre Boulez, John Cage: Correspondance et documents* (vol. 1, Basel, 1990); *Wagner adrogyne: Essai sur l'interprétation* (Paris, 1990); *Le combat de Chronos et d'Orphée Essais* (Paris, 1993).

Naudin, Emilio, Italian-born French tenor; b. Parma (of French parents), Oct. 23, 1823; d. Boulogne-sur-Mer, May 5, 1890. He was a pupil of Panizza in Milan, making his debut in Pacini's *Saffo in Cremona* (1843). He appeared in Vienna, St. Petersburg, London, Madrid, and Paris (from 1862, at the Théâtre-Italien). He created the role of Vasco da Gama in *L'Africaine* (in accordance with a stipulation in Meyerbeer's will). He retired in 1879.

Naumann, Emil, German music scholar and composer, grandson of **Johann Gottlieb Naumann**; b. Berlin, Sept. 8, 1827; d. Dresden, June 23, 1888. He was a pupil of Schnyder von Wartensee in Frankfurt am Main, and then of Mendelssohn in Leipzig (1842); he studied at the Leipzig Cons. (1843–44), and later took courses at the Univ. of Bonn. He received his Ph.D. at the Univ. of Berlin in 1867 with the dissertation *Das Alter der Psalmengesänge*. In 1850 he became Hofkirchen-Musikdirektor in Berlin. In 1873 he was made a lecturer in music history at the Dresden Cons. In his works he faithfully followed the methods of his revered teacher Mendelssohn, without ever attaining the melodic grace and harmonic lucidity that made Mendelssohn's music a perennial art. Naturally, he opposed Wagner's innovations and wrote critically about "the music of the future." His works included *Judith*, opera (Dresden, 1858), *Die Muhlenhexe*, Singspiel (Berlin, 1861), and *Loreley*, grand opera (Berlin, 1889); also *Christus der Friedensbote*, oratorio (Dresden, 1848).

WRITINGS: *Über Einführung des Psalmengesanges in die evangelische Kirche* (Berlin, 1856); *Die Tonkunst in ihren Beziehungen zu den Formen und Entwickelungsgesetzen alles Geisteslebens* (2 vols., Berlin, 1869–70); *Ludwig van Beethoven: Zur hundertjährigen Geburtstagsfeier* (Berlin, 1871); *Deutsche Tondichter von Sebastian Bach bis auf die Gegenwart* (Berlin, 1871; 6th ed., 1895); *Nachklänge: Eine Sammlung von Vorträgen und Gedenkblättern* (Berlin, 1872); *Deutschlands musikalische Heroen in ihrer Rückwirkung auf die Nation* (Berlin, 1873); *Italienische Tondichter von Palestrina bis auf die Gegenwart* (Berlin, 1874–75; 2d ed., 1883); *Das goldene Zeitalter der Tonkunst in Venedig* (Berlin, 1876); *Musikdrama oder Oper? Eine Beleuchtung der Bayreuther Bühnenfestspiele* (Berlin, 1876); *Zukunftsmusik und die Musik der Zukunft* (Berlin, 1877); *Darstellung eines bisher unbekannt gebliebenen Stylgesetzes im Aufbau des classischen Fugenthemas* (Berlin, 1878); *Illustrierte Musikgeschichte* (2 vols., Berlin and Stuttgart, 1880–85; Eng. tr. by F. Ouseley, 1882–86; 10th Ger. ed., 1934, by E. Schmitz); *Der moderne musikalische Zopf* (Berlin, 1880).

Naumann, Johann Gottlieb, distinguished German composer and conductor, grandfather of **Emil Naumann;** b. Blasewitz, near Dresden, April 17, 1741; d. Dresden, Oct. 23, 1801. Another grandson was the German organist, conductor, and composer (Karl) Ernst Naumann (b. Freiberg, Saxony, Aug. 15, 1832; d. Jena, Dec. 15, 1910). He received his first instruction in music at the Dresden Kreuzschule. In 1757 the Swedish violinist Anders Weström took him to Italy, where he received valuable instruction from Tartini in Padua, Padre Martini in Bologna, and Hasse in Venice. His intermezzo *Il tesoro insidiato* was premiered in Venice on Dec. 28, 1762. In 1764 he returned to Dresden, where he was appointed 2d church composer to the court; in 1765 he was named chamber composer. He made return trips to Italy (1765–68; 1772–74), where he brought out several operas. In 1776 he was appointed Kapellmeister in Dresden. In 1777 he visited Stockholm at the invitation of Gustavus III, and was charged with reorganizing the Hofkapelle. His most popular opera, *Cora och Alonzo*, received its first complete performance in Stockholm during the consecration of the New Opera House on Sept. 30, 1782. Another important opera, *Gustaf Wasa*, was premiered there on Jan. 19, 1786, and was considered the Swedish national opera for many years. In 1785–86 he visited Copenhagen, where he carried out some reforms at the Hofkapelle and court opera. He composed the opera *Orpheus og Eurydike* for the Danish king's birthday, and it was premiered in Copenhagen on Jan. 31, 1786. He was named Oberkapellmeister for life in Dresden in 1786. At the request of Friedrich Wilhelm II, he made several visits to Berlin, where his operas *Medea in Colchide* (Oct. 16, 1788) and *Protesilao* (Jan. 26, 1789) were premiered at the Royal Opera. He also wrote masses, cantatas, oratorios, and lieder.

WORKS: DRAMATIC (all 1st perf. at the Kleines Kurfürstliches Theater in Dresden unless otherwise given): *Il tesoro insidiato*, intermezzo (Teatro San Samuele, Venice, Dec. 28, 1762); *Li creduti spiriti*, opera buffa (Teatro San Cassiano, Venice, Carnival 1764; in collaboration with 2 other composers); *L'Achille in Sciro*, opera seria (Teatro San Cecilia, Palermo, Sept. 5, 1767); *Alessandro nelle Indie*, opera seria (1768; unfinished); *La clemenza di*

Tito, opera seria (Feb. 1, 1769); *Il villano geloso*, opera buffa (1770); *Solimano*, opera seria (Teatro San Benedetto, Venice, Carnival 1773); *L'isola disabitata*, azione per musica (Venice, Feb. 1773); *Armida*, opera seria (Teatro Nuovo, Padua, June 13, 1773); *Ipermestra*, opera seria (Teatro San Benedetto, Venice, Feb. 1, 1774); *La villanella incostante*, opera buffa (Teatro San Benedetto, Venice, fall 1773); *L'Ipocondriaco*, opera buffa (March 16, 1776); *Amphion*, prologue and opera ballet (Royal Theater, Stockholm, Jan. 1, 1778); *Elisa*, opera seria (April 21, 1781); *Cora och Alonzo*, opera seria (New Opera House, Stockholm, Sept. 30, 1782); *Osiride*, opera seria (Oct. 27, 1781); *Tutto per amore*, opera buffa (March 5, 1785); *Gustaf Wasa*, lyric tragedy (New Opera House, Stockholm, Jan. 19, 1786); *Orpheus og Eurydike*, opera seria (Royal Theater, Copenhagen, Jan. 31, 1786); *La reggia d'Imeneo*, festa teatrale (Oct. 21, 1787); *Medea in Colchide*, opera seria with ballet (Royal Opera, Berlin, Oct. 16, 1788); *Protesilao*, opera seria with ballet and choruses (Royal Opera, Berlin, Jan. 26, 1789; in collaboration with J. F. Reichardt); *La dama soldato*, opera buffa (March 30, 1791); *Amore giustificato*, festa teatrale (May 12, 1792); *Aci e Galatea ossia I ciclopi amanti*, opera buffa (April 25, 1801). ORATORIOS (all performed in Dresden unless otherwise given): *La passione di Gesù Cristo* (Padua, 1767); *Isacco, figura del Redentore* (1772); *S. Elena al calvario* (1775); *Giuseppe riconosciuto* (1777); *Il ritorno del figliolo prodigo* (1785); *La morte d'Abel* (1790); *Davide in Terebinto, figura del Salvatore* (1794); *I Pellegrini al sepolcro* (1798); *Il ritorno del figliolo prodigo* (1800); *Betulia liberata* (1805).

BIBL.: A. Meissner, *Bruckstücke zur Biographie J. G. N.'s* (2 vols., Prague, 1803–4; 2d ed., Vienna, 1814); F. Mannstein, *Vollständiges Verzeichnis aller Kompositionen des Kurfürstlich Sächsischen Kapellmeisters N.* (Dresden, 1841); G. Schweizer, *Biographie von J. G. N.* (3 vols., Zürich, 1843–45); M. Nestler, *Der kursächsische Kapellmeister N. aus Blasewitz* (Dresden, 1901); R. Englander, *J. G. N. als Opernkomponist (1741–1801)* (Leipzig, 1922).

Nava, Gaetano, Italian vocal pedagogue; b. Milan, May 16, 1802; d. there, March 31, 1875. He was taught by his father, Antonio Maria Nava (1775–1826) and Pollini, then at the Milan Cons. from 1817 to 1824 by Orlandi, Ray, Piantanida, and Frederici. From 1837 he was a prof. of solfeggio at the Cons., and of choral singing, from 1848. He wrote a great number of excellent solfeggi and vocalises, as well as *Metodo pratico di vocalizzazione*.

Navarrini, Francesco, distinguished Italian bass; b. Citadella, 1853; d. Milan, Feb. 23, 1923. He studied with Giuseppe Felix and Carlo Boroni in Milan, making his debut as Alfonso in *Lucrezia Borgia* in Ferrara in 1876. From 1883 to 1900 he was a member of La Scala in Milan, where he created the role of Lodovico in Verdi's *Otello* (Feb. 5, 1887); he then toured in England, France, and Russia. He made his first American appearance in 1902 as a member of Mascagni's traveling opera co. A giant of a man (he measured 6 and a half feet), he imposed his presence in heroic and buffo bass roles, including roles in Wagner's operas.

Navarro, (Luis Antonio) García, Spanish conductor; b. Chiva, April 30, 1941. He was educated at the Valencia Cons., where he studied oboe; also took courses at the Madrid Cons. He then went to Vienna to study conducting with Hans Swarowsky, Karl Oesterreicher, and Reinhold Schmid; he also took composition lessons with Alfred Uhl. In 1967 he won 1st prize at the conducting competition in Besançon. He was music director of the Valencia Sym. Orch. (1970–74), then was assoc. conductor of the Noordhollands Phil. in Haarlem (1974–78), and music director of Lisbon's Portuguese Radio Sym. Orch. (1976–78) and National Opera at the São Carlos Theater (1980–82). In 1979 he made his debut as an opera conductor at London's Covent Garden, and then appeared for the first time in the United States in 1980. He was principal guest conductor of the Stuttgart Radio Sym. Orch. (1984–87), the Vienna State Opera (1987–91), and the Tokyo Phil. (from 1992). He was Generalmusikdirektor of the Württemberg State Theater in Stuttgart from 1987 to 1991. From 1991 to 1993 he was music director of the Barcelona Sym. Orch. In 1992 he became permanent guest conductor of the Deutsche Oper in Berlin. He served as music director and artistic director of the Teatro Real in Madrid from 1997.

Nazareth, Daniel, Indian conductor; b. Bombay, June 8, 1948. He received training in piano and theory in Bombay and London, and then studied composition and conducting in Vienna and with Bernstein at the Berkshire Music Center in Tanglewood. He appeared as a guest conductor with various orchs. in Europe, and made his debut as an opera conductor with *Così fan tutte* in Spoleto in 1977. From 1982 to 1985 he was chief conductor of the Berlin Sym. Orch. In 1988 he became music director of the Teatro San Carlo in Naples. He was chief conductor of the sym. orch. of the Mitteldeutschen Radio in Leipzig from 1992 to 1996.

Neblett, Carol, American soprano; b. Modesto, Calif., Feb. 1, 1946. She studied voice privately with William Vennard, then with Lotte Lehmann and Pierre Bernac at the Univ. of Southern Calif. in Los Angeles; quitting school before graduating (1965), she toured as a soloist with the Roger Wagner Chorale, then made her operatic debut as Musetta with the N.Y. City Opera (March 8, 1969). She garnered wide public exposure when she appeared as Thaïs with the New Orleans Opera (1973), choosing to disrobe at the close of Act 1; subsequently she made debuts with the Chicago Lyric Opera (Chrysothemis in *Elektra*, 1975), the Dallas Civic Opera (Antonia in *Les Contes d'Hoffmann*, 1975), the Vienna State Opera (1976), and London's Covent Garden (1977); she also sang widely as a soloist with U.S. orchs. On March 8, 1979, she made her Metropolitan Opera debut in New York as Senta. She made occasional appearances there in subsequent years, and also sang with various opera houses in North America and Europe. In 1975 she married **Kenneth Schermerhorn**.

Nebra (Blasco), José (Melchor de), Spanish composer; b. Catalayud, Zaragoza (baptized), Jan. 6, 1702; d. Madrid, July 11, 1768. He studied with his father, José (Antonio) Nebra (b. La Hoy [baptized], Nov. 23, 1672; d. Cuenca, Dec. 4, 1748), maestro de cappella of Cuenca Cathedral (1729–48). He became principal organist of the royal chapel and of the Descalzas Reales Convent in Madrid (1724), where he was made deputy director of the royal chapel and head of the royal choir school (1751). Together with Literes, he was engaged to reconstruct and compose new music when the archives of the Royal Chapel were destroyed in the fire of 1734. He was a prolific composer, numbering among his works about 20 operas.

Nechayev, Vasily, Russian pianist and composer; b. Moscow, Sept. 28, 1895; d. there, June 5, 1956. He studied at the Moscow Cons. with Goldenweiser (piano), graduating in 1917; he then took composition lessons with Vasilenko. In 1925 he joined the staff of the Moscow Cons. He made a systematic study of the folk songs of the Ural region and made arrangements of folk songs of other lands. He composed the operas *7 Princesses*, after Maeterlinck (1923), and *Ivan Bolotnikov* (1930).

Nedbal, Oskar, distinguished Czech violist, conductor, and composer; b. Tábor, Bohemia, March 26, 1874; d. (suicide) Zagreb, Dec. 24, 1930. He was a pupil of Bennewitz (violin), Knittl and Stecker (theory), and Dvořák (composition) at the Prague Cons., where he graduated in 1892. From 1891 to 1906 he played viola in the famous Bohemian String Quartet; from 1896 to 1906 he conducted the Czech Phil.; from 1906 to 1918 he was conductor of the Tonkünstler-Orch. in Vienna; later he was director of the Slovak National Theater in Bratislava (1923–30) and a conductor with the Radio there (1926–30). He was a notable interpreter of Czech music, and also was admired for his fine performances of the standard repertory.

WORKS: DRAMATIC: OPERA: *Sedlák Jakub* (Peasant Jacob; 1919–20; Brno, Oct. 13, 1922; rev. version, Bratislava, Dec. 15, 1928). OPERETTAS: *Die keusche Barbora* (Vienna, Oct. 7, 1911); *Polenblut* (Vienna, Oct. 25, 1913); *Die Winzerbraut* (Vienna, Feb. 11, 1916); *Die schöne Saskia* (Vienna, Nov. 16, 1917); *Eriwan* (Vienna, Nov. 29, 1918). BALLETS: *Pohádka o Honzovi* (Legend of Honza; Prague, Jan. 24, 1902); *Z pohádky do pohádky* (From Fairy Tale to Fairy

Tale; Prague, Jan. 25, 1908); *Princezna Hyacinta* (Prague, Sept. 1, 1911); *Des Teufels Grossmutter* (Vienna, April 20, 1912); *Andersen* (Vienna, March 1, 1914).

BIBL.: J. Květ, *O. N.* (Prague, 1947); M. Šulc, *O. N.* (Prague, 1959); A. Buchner, *O. N.: Život a dílo* (O. N.: Life and Works; Prague, 1976).

Neefe, Christian Gottlob, German composer and conductor; b. Chemnitz, Feb. 5, 1748; d. Dessau, Jan. 26, 1798. He studied music in Chemnitz with Wilhelmi, the city organist, and with C. G. Tag, the cantor of Hohenstein. He began to compose when he was 12, and studied the textbooks of Marpurg and C. P. E. Bach. He studied law at the Univ. of Leipzig (1769–71); he subsequently continued his studies in music with A. Hiller; he then succeeded Hiller as conductor of Seyler's traveling opera troupe (1776). In 1779 he became conductor of the Grossmann-Hellmuth opera enterprise in Bonn. Neefe's name is especially honored in music history because about 1780 Beethoven was his pupil in piano, organ, figured-bass practice, and composition in Bonn; there is evidence that Neefe realized the greatness of Beethoven's gift even as a child. In 1782 he was named court organist. After the Grossmann theater closed in 1784, he devoted himself mainly to teaching as a means of support. The theater was reopened in 1789, and Neefe served as its stage director until 1794, when the French army occupied Bonn and the theater was closed again. He then moved to Dessau, becoming music director of its theater in 1796. His autobiography, *Lebenslauf von ihm selbst geschrieben*, dated 1782, was revised by F. Rochlitz for publ. in the *Allgemeine musikalische Zeitung* (1798–99; Eng. tr. in P. Nettl, *Forgotten Musicians*, N.Y., 1951).

WORKS: DRAMATIC: *Die Apotheke*, comic opera (Berlin, Dec. 13, 1771); *Amors Guckkasten*, operetta (Leipzig, May 10, 1772); *Die Einsprüche*, operetta (Leipzig, Oct. 16, 1772); *Zemire und Azor* (Leipzig, March 5, 1776; not extant); *Heinrich und Lyda*, Singspiel (Berlin, March 26, 1776); *Die Zigeuner* (Frankfurt am Main, Nov. 1777); *Sophonisbe*, monodrama (Mannheim, Nov. 3, 1778); *Adelheit von Veltheim*, opera (Frankfurt am Main, Sept. 23, 1780).

BIBL.: A. Becker, *C. G. N. und die Bonner Illuminaten* (Bonn, 1969).

Neel, (Louis) Boyd, English-born Canadian conductor; b. Blackheath, Kent, July 19, 1905; d. Toronto, Sept. 30, 1981. He studied at the Royal Naval College in Dartmouth; after taking medical courses at Caius College, Cambridge (B.A., 1926; M.A., 1930), he studied theory and orchestration at the Guildhall School of Music in London (1931). In 1932 he organized the Boyd Neel Orch., which gave its first performance in London on June 22, 1933; it quickly gained a fine reputation, excelling in performances of contemporary British music; he also played Baroque works. He commissioned Britten's *Variations on a Theme of Frank Bridge* and conducted its premiere at the Salzburg Festival in 1937. He remained active with his ensemble until 1952; he also appeared as a conductor with various English orchs. and theaters. He conducted at the Sadler's Wells Theatre (1945–47) and with the D'Oyly Carte Opera (1948–49) and was also conductor of the Robert Mayer Children's Concerts (1946–52). After serving as founder-conductor of the Hart House Orch. in Toronto (1954–71), with which he made many tours, he conducted the Mississauga Sym. Orch. (1971–78); he was also dean of the Royal Cons. of Music of Toronto (1953–71). He became a naturalized Canadian citizen in 1961. He was made a Commander of the Order of the British Empire (1953) and an Officer of the Order of Canada (1973). His book, *The Story of an Orchestra* (London, 1950), recounted his years with the Boyd Neel Orch.

Nef, Albert, Swiss conductor and composer; b. St. Gallen, Oct. 30, 1882; d. Bern, Dec. 6, 1966. He studied at the Leipzig Cons. and with Kretzschmar at the Univ. of Berlin (Ph.D., 1906). From 1907 he was an opera conductor in Lübeck, Neustrelitz, and Rostock; from 1912 he was in Bern, and was conductor of the Orch. Society there from 1922; from 1920 he was president of the Swiss Stage Artists' Alliance. He was the author of *Das Lied in der deutschen Schweiz Ende des 18. und am Anfang des 19. Jahrhunderts* (1909), also of *50 Jahre Berner Theater* (Bern, 1956). He composed a Singspiel, *Graf Strapinski* (Bern, 1928). His brother was the Swiss musicologist Karl Nef (1873–1935).

Negrea, Marţian, Romanian composer and teacher; b. Vorumloc, Feb. 10, 1893; d. Bucharest, July 13, 1973. He studied with Timotei Popovici (theory and harmony) at the Andréien Seminary in Sibiu (1910–14) and of Mandyczewski (harmony, counterpoint, and music history) and Franz Schmidt (composition) at the Vienna Academy of Music (1918–21). He was a prof. of harmony at the Cluj Cons. (1921–41) and the Bucharest Cons. (1941–63). In his music, Negrea sought a balance between post-Romantic and Impressionist elements, to which he brought an infusion of folk melodies. Among his works is the opera *Marin Pescarul* (Marin the Fisherman; 1933; Cluj, Oct. 3, 1934).

Negri, Gino, Italian composer; b. Milan, May 25, 1919; d. Cernusco Montevecchia, July 19, 1991. He studied at the Milan Cons. with Renzo Bossi and Paribeni, graduating in 1942. In 1959 he was appointed artistic director of the Teatro del Popolo in Milan. He wrote a number of light operas, all to his own librettos, among them *Vieni qui, Carla* (Milan, Feb. 28, 1956), *Massimo* (Milan, April 12, 1958), *Il tè delle tre* (Como, Sept. 12, 1958), *Il Circo Max* (Venice, Sept. 23, 1959), and *Publicità, ninfa gentile* (Milan, 1970).

Negri, Maria Rosa, Italian mezzo-soprano; b. c.1715; d. Dresden, Aug. 4, 1760. She became a member of the Dresden Court Opera in 1730, and subsequently sang in a number of Hasse's operas. From 1733 to 1736 she also sang in several operas by Handel in London. Her sister, Maria Caterina Negri, was a contralto. After training from Pasi, she sang in Prague, Venice, and Naples. She also sang in operas by Handel in London (1733–37) before pursuing her career mainly in Italy.

Negri, Vittorio, Italian conductor, record producer, and musicologist; b. Milan, Oct. 16, 1923. He was educated at the Milan Cons., graduating with a degree in composition and conducting in 1946. He began his professional career at the Salzburg Mozarteum, working with Bernhard Paumgartner; he then served as a guest conductor of the Orch. del Teatro alla Scala in Milan, the Orchestre National de France in Paris, the Dresden State Orch., and the Boston Sym. Orch. and also made festival appearances in Salzburg, Montreux, Monte Carlo, and Versailles.

Neidlinger, Gustav, noted German bass-baritone; b. Mainz, March 21, 1910; d. Bad Ems, Dec. 26, 1991. He studied at the Frankfurt am Main Cons. In 1929 he made his operatic debut in Mainz, where he was a member of the Opera (1931–34). After singing with the Plauen Opera (1934–35), he was a member of the Hamburg Opera (1936–50). In 1950 he became a member of the Stuttgart Opera. In 1952 he made his first appearance at the Bayreuth Festival, where he won renown as Alberich; among his other distinguished roles there were Kurwenal, Telramund, Klingsor, and Hans Sachs. He was made a German Kammersänger in 1952. In 1953 he sang at Milan's La Scala, and from 1956 he appered with the Vienna State Opera. In 1963 he made his debut at London's Covent Garden as Telramund. On Nov. 17, 1972, he made his Metropolitan Opera debut in New York as Alberich, but remained on the roster for only one season. He continued to sing in Europe until his retirement in 1977.

Neikrug, Marc (Edward), American pianist and composer; b. N.Y., Sept. 24, 1946. He was a student of Klebe at the Northwest Music Academy in Detmold (1964–68), of Schuller at the Berkshire Music Center in Tanglewood, and at the State Univ. of N.Y. at Stony Brook (M.M., 1971). In 1972 he was composer-in-residence at the Marlboro (Vt.) Music Festival. From 1975 he toured extensively in duo concert appearances with Pinchas Zukerman. From 1978 to 1986 he was a consultant on contemporary music to the St. Paul (Minn.) Chamber Orch. As a composer, Neikrug has produced both tonal and atonal scores. Among his works are the operas *Through Roses* (1979–80) and *Los Alamos* (Berlin, Oct. 1, 1988).

Neitzel, Otto, German pianist, conductor, music critic, and composer; b. Falkenburg, Pomerania, July 6, 1852; d. Cologne, March 10, 1920. He was a pupil at Kullak's Academy in Berlin, and also studied at the Univ. (Ph.D., 1875). He then made a concert tour, as pianist, with Pauline Lucca and Sarasate, and in 1878 became conductor of the Musikverein at Strasbourg, where (1879–81) he also conducted at the City Theater. From 1881 to 1885 he taught at the Moscow Cons., then at the Cologne Cons. From 1887 he was also critic for the *Kölnische Zeitung*. He visited the United States in 1906–07 as a lecturer, pianist, and conductor; in 1919, became a member of the Academy of Arts in Berlin. He wrote *Führer durch die Oper des Theaters der Gegenwart* (3 vols., 1890–93; 4th ed., 1908). Among his compositions were the operas *Die Barbarina* (Wiesbaden, Nov. 15, 1905) and *Der Richter von Kaschau* (Darmstadt, March 31, 1916).

Nejedlý, Vít, Czech composer, conductor, and musicologist, son of **Zdeněk Nejedlý**; b. Prague, June 22, 1912; d. Dukla, Slovakia, Jan. 1, 1945. He was a student of Svěceny and Jeremías (composition) and Talich (conducting) at the Charles Univ. in Prague, obtaining his Ph.D. in musicology in 1936. From 1936 to 1938 he was a répétiteur and conductor at the Olomouc Theater. After the Nazi occupation of his homeland in 1939, he fled to the Soviet Union and served as an ed. of Czech programs for Radio Moscow's foreign broadcasts. In 1943 he joined the Czech contingent of the Red Army. Among his works were *The Dying*, melodrama (1933) and *Tkalci* (The Weavers), opera (1938; unfinished; completed by J. Hanuš; Plzeň, May 7, 1961).

BIBL.: J. Plavec, *Vzpominky na Víta Nejedlého* (Memories of V. N.; Prague, 1948); J. Jiránek, *V. N.* (Prague, 1959).

Nejedlý, Zdeněk, Czech musicologist and politician, father of **Vít Nejedlý**; b. Litomyšl, Feb. 10, 1878; d. Prague, March 9, 1962. He studied in Prague with Fibich, and took courses with Jaroslav Goll (history) and Hostinský (aesthetics) at the Charles Univ., where he qualified in 1900. He was an archivist at the National Museum (1899–1909) and joined the staff of the Charles Univ. (1905), serving as a reader (1908–19) and prof. (1919–39) in musicology. He joined the Czech Communist Party in 1929; after the Nazi occupation of his country (1939), he went to the Soviet Union and was a prof. of history at the Univ. of Moscow. After the liberation of Czechoslovakia (1945), he returned to Prague; was minister of education (1948–53) and deputy premier (1953).

WRITINGS (all publ. in Prague): *Zdenko Fibich, zakladatel scénického melodramu* (Zdenko Fibich, Founder of the Scenic Melodrama; 1901); *Katechismus estetiky* (A Manual of Aesthetics; 1902); *Dějinv české hudby* (A History of Czech Music; 1903); *Dějiny předhusitského v Čechách* (A History of Pre-Hussite Song in Bohemia; 1904; 2d ed., 1954, as *Dějiny husitského zěpvu*); *Počátky husitského zěpvu* (The Beginnings of Hussite Song; 1907; 2d ed., 1954–55, as *Dějiny husitského zpěvu*); *Zpěvohry Smetanovy* (Smetana's Operas; 1908; 3d ed., 1954); *Josef Bohuslav Foerster* (1910); *Dějiny husitského spěvu za válek husitských* (A History of Hussite Song during the Hussite Wars; 1913; 2d ed., 1955–56, as *Dějiny husitského zpěvu*); *Gustav Mahler* (1913; 2d ed., 1958); *Richard Wagner* (1916; 2d ed., 1961); *Všeobecné dějiny hudby, I: O původy hudby, Antika* (A General History of Music, 1: Origin and Antiquity; 1916–30); *Vitězslav Novák* (1921; articles and reviews); *Otakara Hostinského estetika* (Otakar Hostinsky's Aesthetics; 1921); *Smetaniana* (1922); *Bedřich Smetana* (4 vols., 1924–33; 2d ed., 1950–54); *Zdeňka a Fibicha milostný denik* (Zdenka Fibich's Erotic Diary; 1925; 2d ed., 1949); *Otakar Ostrčil, Vzrůst a uzrání* (Otakar Ostrčil: Growth and Maturity; 1935; 2d ed., 1949); *Sovětská hudba* (Soviet Music; 1936–37); *Otakar Hostinský* (1937; 2d ed., 1955); *Kritiky* (2 vols., 1954, 1965).

BIBL.: J. Teichmann, *Z. N.* (Prague, 1938); V. Pekárek, *Z. N.* (Prague, 1948); J. Jiránek, *Z. N.* (Prague, 1952); A. Sychra, *Estetika Z.a Nejedlého* (Z. N.'s Aesthetics; Prague, 1956); F. Cervinka, *Z. N.* (Prague, 1959); *Z. N.: Doba—život—dilo* (Z. N.: Times—Life—Work; Prague, 1975); M. Ransdorf, *Z. N.* (Prague, 1988).

Nelhybel, Vaclav, Czech-born American composer and conductor; b. Polanka nad Odrou, Sept. 24, 1919; d. there, March 22, 1996. He studied composition and conducting with Řídký at the Prague Cons. (1938–42) and musicology at the Univ. of Prague (1938–42); in 1942 he went to Switzerland and took courses in medieval and Renaissance music at the Univ. of Fribourg. He was affiliated with the Swiss Radio (1946–50), then was music director of Radio Free Europe in Munich (1950–57). In 1957 he settled in the United States, becoming a naturalized American citizen in 1962; he subsequently evolved energetic activities as a lecturer and guest conductor at American colleges and high schools. As a composer, he was especially notable for his fine pieces for symphonic band. His harmonic idiom was of a freely dissonant texture, with melorhythmic components gravitating toward tonal centers. Among his works are *A Legend*, opera (1953–54), *Everyman*, medieval morality play (Memphis, Oct. 30, 1974), and *The Station*, opera (1978); also the ballets *In the Shadow of a Lime Tree* (1946) and *The Cock and the Hangman* (Prague, Jan. 17, 1947).

Nelson, John (Wilton), American conductor; b. San Jose, Costa Rica (of American parents), Dec. 6, 1941. He studied at Wheaton (Ill.) College and with Morel at the Juilliard School of Music in New York. He was music director of the Indianapolis Sym. Orch. (1976–87), the Caramoor Festival in Katonah, N.Y. (1983–90), and the Opera Theatre of St. Louis (1985–91). In 1998 he became music director of the Ensemble Orchestral de Paris.

Nelson, Judith (Anne née **Manes**), American soprano; b. Chicago, Sept. 10, 1939. She studied at St. Olaf College in Northfield, Minn. She sang with music groups of the Univ. of Chicago and the Univ. of Calif. at Berkeley; she made her operatic debut as Drusilla in Monteverdi's *L'incoronazione di Poppea* in Brussels in 1979. She appeared widely as a soloist and recitalist. Although she is particularly noted for her performances of Baroque music, she also introduced compositions by American and English composers.

Nelson, Ron(ald Jack), American composer and teacher; b. Joliet, Ill., Dec. 14, 1929. He studied composition with Hanson, Rogers, Mennini, and Barlow at the Eastman School of Music in Rochester, N.Y. (B.Mus., 1952; M.Mus., 1953; D.M.A., 1956) and with Aubin at the École Normale de Musique in Paris on a Fulbright grant (1955). In 1956 he joined the faculty of Brown Univ. in Providence, R.I., where he was chairman of the music dept. (1963–73) and a prof. (1968–93). In addition to numerous commissions, he received a Ford Foundation fellowship (1963), a Howard Foundation grant (1965–66), NEA grants, and the John Philip Sousa Medal of Honor (1994). His widely known scores are stylistically diverse and generally accessible. They include *Dance in Ruins*, ballet (1954), *The Birthday of the Infanta*, opera (1955–56), and *Hamaguchi*, opera (1981); also *What Is Man?*, oratorio for Soprano, Baritone, Narrator, Chorus, and Orch. (1964).

Nelsson, Woldemar, Russian-born German conductor; b. Kiev, April 4, 1938. His father, a conductor, gave him violin lessons in Kiev; after conducting studies at the Novosibirsk Cons., he attended master classes at the Moscow Cons. and the Leningrad Cons. He won 1st prize in the All-Union Conducting Competition in Moscow (1971), then became assistant to Kondrashin and the Moscow Phil.; he also appeared as a guest conductor throughout the Soviet Union. In 1977 he emigrated to West Germany, where he served as Generalmusikdirektor of the Kassel State Theater (1980–87). From 1980 he was a regular conductor at the Bayreuth Festivals. In 1990 he became chief conductor of the Royal Opera and Orch. in Copenhagen.

Németh, Mária, Hungarian soprano; b. Körmend, March 13, 1897; d. Vienna, Dec. 28, 1967. She studied with Georg Anthes and Géza Laszló in Budapest, Giannina Russ in Milan, Fernando De Lucia in Naples, and Felicie Kaschowska in Vienna. She made her operatic debut as Sulamith in *Königin von Saba* in Budapest in 1923. In 1924 she became a member of the Vienna State Opera, where she remained until 1946; she also made appearances at Covent Garden in London, La Scala in Milan, Munich, Rome, Paris, and Salzburg. She sang both lyric and coloratura roles during her career, excelling as the Queen of the Night, Aida, Donna Anna, and Tosca, among others.

Némethy, Ella, Hungarian mezzo-soprano; b. Sátoraljaujhely, April 5, 1895; d. Budapest, June 14, 1961. She studied at the Budapest Academy of Music and with Panizza in Milan. In 1919 she made her operatic debut as Delilah at the Budapest Opera, where she remained as one of its principal artists until 1948. She was especially known as a Wagnerian, garnering particular success as Brünnhilde, Isolde, and Kundry.

Nepomuceno, Alberto, important Brazilian composer; b. Fortaleza, July 6, 1864; d. Rio de Janeiro, Oct. 16, 1920. He studied in Rome, Berlin, and Paris, returning to Brazil in 1895. In 1902 he was appointed director of the Instituto Nacional de Música in Rio de Janeiro, remaining only for a few months; he returned to this post in 1906, holding it until 1916. In 1910 he conducted Brazilian music at the International Exposition in Brussels. In some of his music he introduced thematic material from Brazilian folk music. His works include the operas *Artemis* (Rio de Janeiro, June 14, 1898), *O Garatuja* (Rio de Janeiro, Oct. 26, 1904), and *Abul* (1899–1905; Buenos Aires, June 30, 1913).

Neri, Giulio, Italian bass; b. Turilla di Siena, May 21, 1909; d. Rome, April 21, 1958. He studied with Ferraresi in Florence. He made his operatic debut at the Teatro delle Quattro Fontane in Rome in 1935, then sang at the Teatro Reale dell'Opera in Rome, where he soon established himself as a principal bass; he also made guest appearances at La Scala in Milan, Florence, Venice, London, and Munich. An outstanding Verdi interpreter, he was equally distinguished as a Wagnerian.

Nerini, Emile, French composer; b. Colombes, near Paris, Feb. 2, 1882; d. Paris, March 22, 1967. Son of a piano manufacturer, he studied with Decombes, Diémer, Lenepveu, and Caussade at the Paris Cons. Among his works were 4 lyric dramas: *Manoël* (Paris, May 11, 1905), *Le Soir de Waterloo* (Paris, April 17, 1910), *L'Epreuve dernière* (Monte Carlo, March 16, 1912), and *Mazeppa* (Bordeaux, 1925); also *Mademoiselle Sans-Gêne*, operetta (1944; Bordeaux, 1966).

Nessi, Giuseppe, Italian tenor; b. Bergamo, Sept. 25, 1887; d. Milan, Dec. 16, 1961. He studied at the Bergamo Cons. with Vezzani and Melli. In 1910 he made his operatic debut as Alfredo in Saluzzo. From 1921 to 1959 he was a valued member of Milan's La Scala, where he excelled in comprimario roles. He also sang in other Italian opera centers and at London's Covent Garden (1927–37). Among his most notable roles were Bardolfo, Spoletta, Missail, and Goro. He also created the roles of Gobrias in *Nerone* (1924) and Pong in *Turandot* (1926).

Nessler, Victor E(rnst), Alsatian composer; b. Baldenheim, Jan. 28, 1841; d. Strasbourg, May 28, 1890. He studied in Strasbourg, where he produced his first opera, *Fleurette* (1864), then continued his studies in Leipzig with M. Hauptmann, being made chorusmaster at the Stadttheater (1870) and later at the Carola-Theater. He established his reputation as a composer for the theater with his opera *Der Rattenfänger von Hameln* (Leipzig, March 19, 1879). An even greater success was achieved by his opera *Der Trompeter von Säkkingen* (Leipzig, May 4, 1884), which entered the repertoire of many European opera houses. In both operas Nessler adroitly appealed to the Romantic tastes of the German audiences, even though from a purely musical standpoint these productions offered little originality. His other operas premiered in Leipzig were *Dornröschens Brautfahrt* (1867), *Irmingard* (1876), *Der wilde Jäger* (1881), and *Otto der Schütz* (1886); his last opera was *Die Rose von Strassburg* (Munich, 1890). He also wrote the operettas *Die Hochzeitsreise* (1867), *Nachtwächter und Student* (1868), and *Am Alexandertag* (1869).

Nesterenko, Evgeni (Evgenievich), distinguished Russian bass; b. Moscow, Jan. 8, 1938. He went to Leningrad to pursue training in architectural engineering at the Structural Inst. (graduated, 1961) and in voice with Lukanin at the Cons. In 1963 he made his operatic debut as Prince Gremin at the Maly Theater in Leningrad, where he sang until 1967. From 1967 to 1971 he was a member of the Kirov Opera and Ballet Theater in Leningrad. In 1970 he captured 1st prize in the Tchaikovsky Competition in Moscow. In 1971 he became a member of the Bolshoi Theater in Moscow, with which he toured as Boris Godunov to Milan's La Scala (1973), the Vienna State Opera (1974), and N.Y.'s Metropolitan Opera (1975). In 1978 he made his debut at London's Covent Garden as Don Basilio. In subsequent years, he appeared as a guest artist with many European opera houses. His festival appearances took him to Verona (1978, 1985, 1989, 1991), Bregenz (1986), and Orange (1990). In 1993 he appeared as Verdi's Attila in Antwerp. He also toured widely as a concert artist. Among his various honors are the People's Artist of the USSR (1976), the Vercelli Prize (1981), the Lenin Prize (1982), and the Verona Prize (1986). Among his other outstanding roles are Ruslan, Kutuzov, King Philip, Zaccaria, and Méphistophélés.

Nestyev, Izrail (Vladimirovich), Russian musicologist; b. Kerch, April 17, 1911. He received training in theory and composition at the Moscow Cons. (graduated, 1937), and then pursued postgraduate studies there with Ferman (1940; degree, 1946). From 1945 to 1948 he was ed. of music broadcasting in the USSR. He was on the staff of *Sovetskaya muzika* from 1949 to 1959. He also taught at the Moscow Cons. (from 1956) and was a senior research fellow at the Inst. of the History of the Arts in Moscow (from 1960), which awarded him his Ph.D. in 1971 for his study on Bartók (publ. in Moscow, 1969). His major work was a biography of Prokofiev (Moscow, 1946; Eng. tr., N.Y., 1946; rev. ed., Moscow, 1957; Eng. tr., Stanford, Calif., 1960, with a foreword by N. Slonimsky; new ed. rev. and aug., Moscow, 1973).

Nettl, Paul, eminent Czech-born American musicologist; b. Hohenelbe, Bohemia, Jan. 10, 1889; d. Bloomington, Ind., Jan. 8, 1972. He studied jurisprudence (Jur.D., 1913) and musicology (Ph.D., 1915) at the German Univ. of Prague; from 1920 to 1937 he was on its faculty. In 1939 he emigrated to the United States; he became a naturalized American citizen (1945). After teaching at Westminster Choir College and in New York and Philadelphia, he was a prof. of musicology at Indiana Univ. in Bloomington (1946–59); he remained a part-time teacher there until 1963. Among his numerous writings were *Musik und Tanz bei Casanova* (Prague, 1924), *Mozart in Böhmen*, after Prochazka's *Mozart in Prag* (Prague, 1938), *The Story of Dance Music* (N.Y., 1947), *Casanova und seine Zeit* (Esslingen, 1949), *Goethe und Mozart: Eine Betrachtung* (Esslingen, 1949), *The Other Casanova* (N.Y., 1950), *Mozart and Masonry* (N.Y., 1957), *Beethoven und seine Zeit* (Frankfurt am Main, 1958), *Georg Friedrich Handel* (Berlin, 1958), *Mozart und der Tanz* (1960), and *The Dance in Classical Music* (N.Y., 1963). His son is the distinguished Czech-born American ethnomusicologist Bruno Nettl (b.Prague, March 14, 1930).

BIBL.: T. Atcherson, *Ein Musikwissenschaftler in zwei Welten: Die musikwissenschaftlen und literarischen Arbeiten von P. N.* (Vienna, 1962).

Neubauer, Franz Christoph, Czech violinist and composer; b. Melnik, March 21, 1750; d. Bückeburg, Oct. 11, 1795. He was taught violin by the village schoolmaster. He led a wandering life. He produced an operetta, *Ferdinand und Yariko*, in Munich (1784), then proceeded to Vienna, where he met Mozart and Haydn. From 1790 to 1794 he served as Kapellmeister to Prince Weilburg; in 1795 he succeeded Johann Christoph Friedrich Bach as court Kapellmeister at Bückeburg.

Neuendorff, Adolph (Heinrich Anton Magnus), German-American conductor, impresario, and composer; b. Hamburg, June 13, 1843; d. N.Y., Dec. 4, 1897. He went to New York in 1854 and studied violin with Matzka and Weinlich, and piano with Schilling. He appeared both as a concert violinist and pianist and gave violin concerts in Brazil in 1861. In 1864 he went to Milwaukee, then a center of German music, and served as music director of the German theater; he subsequently moved to New York, where he conducted German opera, including the first

American performances of *Lohengrin* (April 3, 1871) and *Die Walküre* (April 2, 1877). In 1878–79 he conducted the N.Y. Phil., and from 1884 to 1889 he was in Boston and became the first conductor of the Music Hall Promenade Concerts (later Boston Pops); he then conducted the Emma Juch Grand Opera Co. (1889–91). He then followed his wife, the singer Georgine von Januschowsky, to Vienna, where she was prima donna and he a conductor at the Hofoper (1893–95). Returning to New York, he served as director of music at Temple Emanu-El (1896) and as conductor at the Metropolitan Opera (1897). He wrote the comic operas *Der Rattenfänger von Hameln* (1880), *Don Quixote* (1882), *Prince Waldmeister* (1887), and *The Minstrel* (1892).

Neuhaus, Rudolf, German conductor and pedagogue; b. Cologne, Jan. 3, 1914; d. Dresden, March 7, 1990. He first studied violin; then took conducting lessons with Hermann Abendroth, and also studied theory with Philipp Jarnach at the Cologne Hochschule für Musik (1932–34). He was music director of the Landestheater in Neustrelitz (1934–44), then was conductor of the Landestheater in Schwerin (1945–50), serving as its Generalmusikdirektor from 1950 to 1953. In 1953 he joined the Dresden State Opera, where he was deputy Generalmusikdirektor until 1975. From 1953 he was a member of the faculty of the Dresden Hochschule für Musik; in 1959, was named prof. there.

Neuhold, Günter, Austrian conductor; b. Graz, Nov. 2, 1947. He studied at the Graz Hochschule für Musik (M.A., 1969) and pursued advanced training in conducting with Ferrara in Rome and Swarowsky in Vienna. He won several prizes in conducting competitions, among them 1st prizes in Florence (1976), San Remo (1976), and Salzburg (1977), 2d prize in Vienna (1977), and 3d prize in Milan (1977). From 1972 to 1980 he conducted in various German opera houses, and also led performances at the Salzburg Festival (1978, 1980, 1983, 1986). From 1981 to 1986 he was music director of the Teatro Regio in Parma, where he also served as chief conductor of the Orch. Sinfonica dell'Emilia Romagna "Arturo Toscanini." He was chief conductor of the Royal Phil. Orch. of Flanders in Antwerp from 1986 to 1990, with which he toured Europe. From 1989 to 1995 he was Generalmusikdirektor of the Badisches State Theater in Karlsruhe, where he oversaw a Richard Strauss cycle and Wagner's *Ring* cycle. In 1995 he became Generalmusikdirektor and artistic director of the Theater der Freien Hansestadt in Bremen. As a guest conductor, he appeared with the Vienna Phil., the Vienna Sym. Orch., the Dresden State Orch., the Vienna State Opera, the Deutsche Oper in Berlin, the Teatro alla Scala in Milan, the Opera Co. of Philadelphia, and many others.

Neukomm, Sigismund, Ritter von, Austrian pianist, conductor, writer on music, and composer; b. Salzburg, July 10, 1778; d. Paris, April 3, 1858. He began his musical studies when he was 7, with Franz Xaver Weissauer, the Salzburg Cathedral organist, then studied theory with Michael Haydn; he also took courses in philosophy and mathematics at the Univ. there, being made honorary organist of the Univ. church (c.1792) and chorus master of the court theater (1796). He continued his studies in Vienna with Joseph Haydn (1797–1804), after which he was active as a teacher. After serving as conductor of the German Theater in St. Petersburg (1804–08), he went to Paris, where he befriended Cherubini, Gossec, Grétry, Monsigny, and other prominent musicians. He was pianist to Prince Talleyrand, in which capacity he went to the Congress of Vienna (1814), where his Requiem in C minor in memory of Louis XVI was given (Jan. 21, 1815); that same year he was ennobled by Louis XVII and was made Chevalier of the Légion d'honneur. He was taken to Rio de Janeiro by the duke of Luxembourg (1816), and became active at the court of John VI of Portugal; after the outbreak of the revolution (1821), he accompanied John VI to Lisbon, and then returned to Paris. After again serving Talleyrand, he traveled widely (from 1826); he visited England in 1829, and thereafter made frequent trips between London and Paris. Many of his articles appeared in the *Revue et Gazette Musicale de Paris*. His autobiography was publ. as *Esquisses biographiques de Sigismond Neukomm* (Paris, 1859). Elisabeth Neukomm (1789–1816), his sister, gained fame in Vienna as a soprano. A prolific composer, he produced over 1,300 works, including *Die Nachtwächter*, intermezzo (Vienna, 1804), *Die neue Oper oder Der Schauspieldirektor*, intermezzo (Vienna, 1804), *Alexander am Indus*, opera (St. Petersburg, Sept. 27, 1804), *Musikalische Malerei*, farce (Moscow, May 1, 1806), *Arkona*, melodrama (Würzburg, Sept. 21, 1808), and *Niobé*, tragédie lyrique (Montbéliard, 1809); also incidental music to plays; oratorios.

BIBL.: R. Angermüller, *S. N.: Werkverzeichnis, Autobiographie, Beziehung zu seinen Zeitgenossen* (Munich, 1977).

Neumann, Angelo, Austrian tenor and opera administrator; b. Vienna, Aug. 18, 1838; d. Prague, Dec. 20, 1910. He began a mercantile career, but deserted it after taking vocal lessons from Stilke-Sessi. After making his debut in Berlin in 1859, he sang in Kraków, Oldenburg, Pressburg, Danzig, and at the Vienna Court Opera (1862–76). From 1876 to 1882 he was manager of the Leipzig Opera, then gathered together a traveling company for producing Wagner operas, journeying as far as Italy. From 1882 to 1885 he was manager of the Bremen Opera, then until his death, of the Prague Deutsches Theater. He publ. *Erinnerungen an Richard Wagner* (1907; Eng. tr. by E. Livermore, 1908).

Neumann, Václav, prominent Czech conductor; b. Prague, Sept. 29, 1920; d. Vienna, Sept. 2, 1995. He studied violin with J. Micka and conducting with Pavel Dědeček and Metod Doležil at the Prague Cons. (1940–45). While still a student, he was active as a chamber-music player; he became a founding member of the Smetana Quartet (1945); that same year he was made 1st violist of the Czech Phil., making his conducting debut in 1948. He was chief conductor of the Karlovy Vary Sym. Orch. (1951–54) and of the Brno Sym. Orch. (1954–56); he then conducted at East Berlin's Komische Oper (1956–64), and concurrently was conductor of Prague's FOK Sym. Orch. From 1964 to 1968 he held the post of 2d conductor of the Czech Phil. in Prague; during that same period, he was the conductor of the Gewandhaus Orch. and Generalmusikdirektor of the Opera in Leipzig; he then held the latter post at the Württemberg State Theater in Stuttgart (1969–72). He was chief conductor of the Czech Phil. (1968–90), touring widely with it in Europe and abroad.

Neumann, Věroslav, Czech composer and music educator; b. Citoliby, near Louny, May 27, 1931. He studied with Řídký at the Prague Academy of Music (1950–54). Thereafter he was active as a composer and teacher, working in both professional and amateur circles, and with young people. In 1991 he was appointed director of the Prague Cons. and made it his goal to restore that once venerable institution to its pre-communist days of educational distinction. In his works, Neumann has developed an accessible style with touches of leavening wit. These include *Opera o komínku* (Chimney Opera; 1965–66), *Glorie*, radio opera (1970), and *Příběh se starou lenoskou* (Story of an Old Armchair), comic opera (1987).

Neumann, Wolfgang, Austrian tenor; b. Waiern, June 20, 1945. He received training in Essen and Duisburg. In 1973 he made his operatic debut as Weber's Max in Bielefeld, and sang there until 1978. Following appearances in Augsburg (1978–80), he sang at the Mannheim National Theater from 1980. As a guest artist, he was engaged in Hamburg, Munich, Vienna, Zürich, Bologna, Florence, and other European music centers. In 1984 he made his first appearance in the United States in Dallas as Tannhäuser. He made his Metropolitan Opera debut in New York on Feb. 20, 1988, as Siegfried. In 1990 he sang Rienzi in a concert perf. at the Teatro Colón in Buenos Aires. His portrayal of Tannhäuser at the Bayreuth Festival in 1995 proved memorable. Among his other roles were Tristan, Lohengrin, Erik, Loge, the Emperor in *Die Frau ohne Schatten*, the Drum Major in *Wozzeck*, the Cardinal in *Mathis der Maler*, and Schoenberg's Aron.

Nevada (real name, **Wixom**), **Emma,** noted American soprano, mother of **Mignon (Mathilde Marie) Nevada**; b. Alpha, near Nevada City, Calif., Feb. 7, 1859; d. Liverpool, June 20, 1940. She studied from 1877 with Marchesi in Vienna. She made her operatic debut as Amina at London's Her Majesty's Theatre (May 17, 1880), then sang in the leading Italian music centers, including Milan's La Scala (1881). Her first appearance in Paris was at the Opéra Comique, May 17, 1883, as Zora in F. David's *Perle du Bresil*. During the 1884–85 season she was a member of Col. Mapleson's company at the Academy of Music in New York, singing on alternate nights with Patti. She sang in Chicago at the Opera Festival in 1885, and again in 1889. She then sang mostly in Europe; she retired in 1910.

Nevada, Mignon (Mathilde Marie), American soprano, daughter of **Emma Nevada**; b. Paris (of American parents), Aug. 14, 1886; d. Long Melford, England, June 25, 1971. She studied with her mother. She made her operatic debut at Rome's Teatro Costanzi as Rosina in *Il Barbiere di Siviglia* in 1907, then sang a season at the Teatro San Carlos in Lisbon; after a season at the Pergola Theater in Florence, she made her London debut at Covent Garden as Ophelia (Oct. 3, 1910), and sang there in subsequent seasons; she also appeared at the Théâtre Royal de la Monnaie in Brussels, and at La Scala in Milan (1923). During World War II, she engaged in war work at Liverpool, England; from 1954 she lived in London.

Nevin, Arthur (Finley), American composer and pedagogue; b. Edgeworth, Pa., April 27, 1871; d. Sewickley, Pa., July 10, 1943. He received musical training at home, mainly from his father, then at the New England Cons. of Music in Boston (1889–93); in 1893 he went to Berlin, where he studied piano with Klindworth and composition with Boise and Humperdinck. Returning to the United States, he devoted himself to teaching, research, composition, and conducting; he lived with the Blackfoot Indians in Montana (summers 1903, 1904), and later wrote and lectured on his experiences. He was a prof. of music at the Univ. of Kansas (1915–20) and director of the municipal music dept. of Memphis, Tenn. (1920–22); he settled in Sewickley as a private teacher (1926). His works include *A Night in Yaddo Land*, masque (1900), *Poia*, opera (Berlin, April 23, 1910), and *A Daughter of the Forest*, opera (Chicago, Jan. 5, 1918). His brother, Ethelbert (Woodbridge) Nevin (b. Edgeworth, Pa., Nov. 25, 1892; d. New Haven, Conn., Feb. 17, 1901) was also a composer who excelled in popular piano pieces and songs.

Neway, Patricia, American soprano; b. N.Y., Sept. 30, 1919. She was educated at Notre Dame College for women and received vocal instruction from Morris Gesell, who later became her husband. She made her stage debut as Fiordiligi at the Chautauqua Festival in 1946. After several appearances in minor roles, she achieved her first significant success as Magda Sorel in Menotti's opera *The Consul* (Philadelphia, March 1, 1950); she created the role of the Mother in another Menotti opera, *Maria Golovin*, at the Brussels World's Fair (Aug. 20, 1958). Her repertoire also included parts in operas by Berg and Britten.

Newlin, Dika, American writer on music and composer; b. Portland, Oreg., Nov. 22, 1923. She studied piano and theory at Michigan State Univ. (B.A., 1939) and at the Univ. of Calif. at Los Angeles (M.A., 1941) and later took courses at Columbia Univ. in New York (Ph.D., 1945, with the diss. *Bruckner-Mahler-Schoenberg*; publ. in N.Y., 1947; 2d ed., rev., 1978); concurrently she received instruction in composition from Farwell, Schoenberg, and Sessions, and in piano from Serkin and A. Schnabel. She taught at Western Maryland College (1945–49), Syracuse Univ. (1949–51), Drew Univ. (1952–65), North Texas State Univ. (1965–73), and Virginia Commonwealth Univ. (from 1978). She ed. and tr. several books by and about Schoenberg and also publ. *Schoenberg Remembered: Diaries and Recollections, 1938–1976* (N.Y., 1980). Her compositions follow the Schoenbergian idiom and include 3 operas.

BIBL.: T. Albrecht, ed., *D. Caecilia: Essays for D. N., November 22, 1988* (Kansas City, Mo., 1988).

Newman, Ernest (real name, **William Roberts**), renowned English music critic and writer on music; b. Everton, Lancashire, Nov. 30, 1868; d. Tadworth, Surrey, July 7, 1959. He was educated at Liverpool College and the Univ. of Liverpool; while employed as a bank clerk (1889–1904), he pursued various studies on his own and began to publ. books on music; assumed his *nom de plume* to symbolize an "earnest new man." In 1904 he accepted an instructorship in Birmingham's Midland Inst., and took up music as a profession; in 1905–06 he was in Manchester as critic of the *Guardian*; from 1906 to 1918 he was in Birmingham as critic for the *Daily Post*; in 1919–20 he was in London as critic for the *Observer*; from 1920 to 1958 he was on the staff of the *London Sunday Times*; from 1923 he was also a contributor to the *Glasgow Herald*; in 1924–25 he was guest critic of the *N.Y. Evening Post*. One of the best equipped and most influential of English music critics, Newman continued to write his regular column in the *Sunday Times* in his 90th year.

WRITINGS (all publ. in London unless otherwise given): *Gluck and the Opera* (1895); *A Study of Wagner* (1899); *Wagner* (1904); *Musical Studies* (1905; 3d ed., 1914); *Elgar* (1906); *Hugo Wolf* (1907); *Richard Strauss* (1908); *Wagner as Man and Artist* (1914; 2d ed., 1924); *A Musical Motley* (1919); *The Piano-Player and Its Music* (1920); *Confessions of a Musical Critic* (1923); *Solo Singing* (1923); *A Musical Critic's Holiday* (1925); *The Unconscious Beethoven* (1927); *What to Read on the Evolution of Music* (1928); *Stories of the Great Operas* (3 vols., 1929–31); *Fact and Fiction about Wagner* (1931); *The Man Liszt* (1934); *The Life of Richard Wagner* (4 vols., 1933, 1937, 1941, 1946); *Opera Nights* (1943; U.S. ed. as *More Stories of Famous Operas*); *Wagner Nights* (1949; U.S. ed. as *The Wagner Operas*); *More Opera Nights* (1954; U.S. ed. as *17 Famous Operas*); *From the World of Music: Essays from "The Sunday Times"* (selected by F. Aprahamian; London, 1956); *More Musical Essays* (2d selection from the *Sunday Times*, London, 1958); *Testament of Music* (selected essays; 1962); *Berlioz, Romantic Classic* (ed. by P. Heyworth; 1972).

BIBL.: H. van Thal, ed., *Fanfare for E. N.* (London, 1955); V. Newman, *E. N.: A Memoir by His Wife* (London, 1963).

Nezhdanova, Antonina (Vasilievna), distinguished Russian soprano; b. Krivaya Balka, near Odessa, June 16, 1873; d. Moscow, June 26, 1950. She studied at the Moscow Cons. (graduated, 1902). She made her operatic debut as Antonida in *A Life for the Czar* in Moscow (1902); shortly thereafter she became a principal member of the Bolshoi Theater there, remaining on its roster for almost 40 years; she also appeared in other Russian music centers, as both an opera singer and a concert singer; she sang Gilda in Paris (1912). She taught at the Stanislavsky Opera Studio and the Bolshoi Theater Opera Studio (from 1936) and was prof. of voice at the Moscow Cons. (from 1943). Her husband was **Nikolai Golovanov**. She was made a People's Artist of the USSR (1936). She was notably successful in lyric, coloratura, and dramatic roles, her range extending to high G; in addition to Antonida, she excelled as Tatiana, Marguerite, Marfa, Lakme, and Juliette. Her memoirs were publ. posthumously in Moscow (1967).

BIBL.: M. Lvov, *A. V. N.* (Moscow, 1952); G. Polyanovsky, *A. N.* (Moscow, 1970).

Nibelle, Adolphe-André, French composer; b. Gien, Loiret, Oct. 9, 1825; d. Paris, March 11, 1895. He wrote numerous operettas for Paris, the most successful being *Le Loup-Garou* (1858), *Les Filles du lac* (1858), *L'Arche-Marion* (1868), *La Fontaine de Berny* (1869), *Le 15 août* (1869), *Les Quatre Cents Femmes d'Ali-Baba* (1872), and *L'Alibi* (1873); also publ. *Heures musicales* (24 songs).

Nicholls, Agnes, English soprano; b. Cheltenham, July 14, 1877; d. London, Sept. 21, 1959. She studied singing with Visetti at the Royal College of Music in London. She made her operatic debut in Manchester on Nov. 20, 1895, as Dido in a revival of Purcell's opera. From 1901 to 1924 she sang with the Denhof, Beecham, and British National Opera companies. On July 15, 1904, she married the eminent Irish conductor and composer Sir (Herbert) Hamilton Harty (b. Hillsborough, County Down, Dec. 4, 1879; d. Brighton, Feb. 19, 1941). She was quite successful in Wagnerian roles; in 1908 she sang Sieglinde in *Die Walküre* at Covent Garden in London under the direction of Hans Richter.

Nicholson, Sir Sydney (Hugo), English organist, music educator, and composer; b. London, Feb. 9, 1875; d. Ashford, Kent, May 30, 1947. He was educated at Oxford, the Royal College of Music in London, and in Frankfurt am Main. He served as organist of the Lower Chapel, Eton (1900–04), acting organist of Carlisle Cathedral (1904–08), and organist of Manchester Cathedral (1908–19) and of Westminster Abbey, London (1919–28). Nicholson then founded the School of English Church Music, which became the Royal School of Church Music in 1945. In 1938 he was knighted. He composed a comic opera, *The Mermaid* (1928), and an opera for boy's voices, *The Children of the Chapel* (1934). He publ. *Church Music: A Practical Handbook* (London, 1920), *A Manual of English Church Music* (with G. Gardner; London, 1923; 2d ed., 1936), and *Quires and Places where they sing* (London, 1932; 2d ed., 1942).

Nicolai, (Carl) Otto (Ehrenfried), famous German composer and conductor; b. Königsberg, June 9, 1810; d. Berlin, May 11, 1849. He studied piano at home, and in 1827 went to Berlin, where he took lessons in theory with Zelter; he also took courses with Bernhard Klein at the Royal Inst. for Church Music. On April 13, 1833, he made his concert debut in Berlin as a pianist, singer, and composer. He then was engaged as organist to the embassy chapel in Rome by the Prussian ambassador, Bunsen. While in Italy, he also studied counterpoint with Giuseppe Baini. In 1837 he proceeded to Vienna, where he became a singing teacher and Kapellmeister at the Kärnthnertortheater. In 1838 he returned to Italy; on Nov. 26, 1839, he presented in Trieste his first opera, *Rosmonda d'Inghilterra*, given under its new title as *Enrico II*. His 2d opera, *Il Templario*, was staged in Turin on Feb. 11, 1840. In 1841 he moved to Vienna, where he was appointed court Kapellmeister in succession to Kreutzer. Nicolai was instrumental in establishing sym. concerts utilizing the musicians of the orch. of the Imperial Court Opera Theater; on March 28, 1842, he conducted this ensemble featuring Beethoven's 7th Sym.; this became the inaugural concert of the celebrated Vienna Phil. In 1848 he was appointed Kapellmeister of the Royal Opera in Berlin. On March 9, 1849, his famous opera *Die lustigen Weiber von Windsor*, after Shakespeare, was given at the Berlin Royal Opera; it was to become his only enduring creation. Nicolai died 2 months after its production. In 1887 Hans Richter, then conductor of the Vienna Phil., inaugurated an annual "Nicolai-Konzert" in his memory, and it became a standard occasion.

WORKS: OPERAS: *Enrico II* (original title, *Rosmonda d'Inghilterra*; Trieste, Nov. 26, 1839); *Il Templario* (Turin, Feb. 11, 1840; rev. as *Der Tempelritter*, Vienna, Dec. 20, 1845); *Gildippe ed Odoardo* (Genoa, Dec. 26, 1840); *Il proscritto* (Milan, March 13, 1841; rev. as *Die Heimkehr des Verbannten*, Vienna, Feb. 3, 1846); *Die lustigen Weiber von Windsor* (Berlin, March 9, 1849).

BIBL.: H. Mendel, *O. N.: Eine Biographie* (Berlin, 1866; 2d ed., 1868); B. Schröder, ed., *O. N.: Tagebücher nebst biographischen Ergänzungen* (Leipzig, 1892); G. Kruse, *O. N.s musikalische Aufsätze* (Regensburg, 1913); W. Altmann, ed., *O. N.: Briefe an seinen Vater* (Regensburg, 1924); W. Altmann, ed., *O. N.: Ein Künstlerleben* (Berlin, 1911); W. Jerger, ed., *O. N.: Briefe an die Wiener Philharmoniker* (Vienna, 1942); U. Konrad, *O. N., 1810–1849; Studien zu Leben und Werk* (Baden-Baden, 1986).

Nicolescu, Marianna, Romanian soprano; b. Gavjani, Nov. 28, 1948. After studies in Romania, she pursued training at the Cons. Statale di Musica di St. Cecilia in Rome and with Elizabeth Schwarzkopf and Rodolfo Celletti. She made her debut in a television concert in Milan in 1972. Following an engagement as Beatrice di Tenda in Venice in 1975, she appeared in Florence as Violetta in 1976. On April 18, 1978, she made her Metropolitan Opera debut in New York as Nedda. She made her first appearance at Milan's La Scala in the premiere of Berio's *La vera storia* in 1982, and made return visits there in 1987, 1988, and 1993. In 1984 she sang Donna Elvira at the Rome Opera. From 1986 to 1993 she made appearances at the Bavarian State Opera in Munich and at the Munich Festival. In 1990 she was engaged as Elettra at the Salzburg Festival. She sang Donizetti's Queen Elizabeth in Monte Carlo in 1992. In 1995 she returned to Munich as Anna Bolena.

Nicolini (real name, **Ernest Nicolas**), French tenor; b. Saint-Malo, Feb. 23, 1834; d. Pau, Jan. 19, 1898. He studied at the Paris Cons. In July 1857 he made his operatic debut in Halévy's *Les Mousquetaires de la Reine* at the Paris Opéra Comique, and then sang there until 1859. He subsequently studied in Italy, where he adopted the name Nicolini and appeared at Milan's La Scala in 1859–60. Returning to Paris, he was a member of the Théâtre-Italien (1862–69); on May 29, 1866, he made his debut at London's Covent Garden as Edgardo opposite Patti's Lucia. He returned to London to sing at Drury Lane (1871) and at Covent Garden (1872–84); he toured Europe, the United States, and South America with Patti, marrying her on Aug. 10, 1886. That same year he bade his farewell to the operatic stage as Almaviva in *Il Barbiere di Siviglia* at Drury Lane. Among his finest roles were Roméo and Faust.

Nicolini (real name, **Nicolo Grimaldi**), renowned Italian castrato alto; b. Naples (baptized), April 5, 1673; d. there, Jan. 1, 1732. He studied with Provenzale in Naples, making his debut there as a page in his La Stellidaura vendicata (1685), then entered the Cappella del Tesoro di S. Gennaro at Naples Cathedral (1690) and the Naples Royal Chapel (1691). He appeared in opera in Naples (1697–1724) and also in Venice (1700–1731), being made a Knight of the Order of San Marco (1705). He made his London debut at the Queen's Theatre in Haym's arrangement of A. Scarlatti's *Pirroe Demetrio* (Dec. 14, 1708), and subsequently was its leading singer until 1712; he created Handel's Rinaldo (Feb. 24, 1711). He returned to London to create Handel's Amadigi (May 25, 1715), singing there until 1717. He then pursued his career in his homeland, remaining active until his death. At the zenith of his career, he was held in the highest esteem by his contemporaries, being celebrated for his remarkable vocal gifts and dramatic abilities.

Nicolini, Giuseppe, Italian composer; b. Piacenza, Jan. 29, 1762; d. there, Dec. 18, 1842. He studied with his father, Omobono Nicolini, organist and maestro di cappella in Piacenza. Following vocal instruction from Filippo Macedone, he studied composition at the Cons. di S. Onofrio in Naples with Insanguine. During the first two decades of the 19th century, Nicolini enjoyed great popularity as a composer for the theater, bringing out some 50 operas in all. However, with the ascendancy of Rossini, he abandoned the theater and in 1819 was made maestro di cappella at Piacenza Cathedral. He died in poverty, long forgotten by his contemporaries. In addition to his operas, he wrote some orch. pieces, chamber music, and many sacred works. Piacenza finally honored its native son by naming the Liceo Musicale after him in 1914.

BIBL.: E. de Giovanni, *G. N. e Sebastiano Nasolini* (Piacenza, 1927).

Niculescu, Stefan, Romanian composer and teacher; b. Moreni, July 31, 1927. He was a student of Jora (harmony and counterpoint), Rogalski (orchestration), and Andricu (composition) at the Bucharest Cons. (1951–59), of Kagel at the Siemens Studio in Munich (1966), and of Ligeti, Stockhausen, and Karkoschka at the summer courses in new music in Darmstadt (1966–68). After serving as head of research at the Bucharest Inst. of the Arts (1960–63), he taught at the Bucharest Cons. (1963–87). He was director of the International Festival of New Music in Bucharest from 1990. In addition to his various articles on music, he publ. a vol. of reflections on music (Bucharest, 1980). He first composed in a stringent adherence to serial dictates before adopting a more freely inspired personal mode of expression in which he utilized aleatory and diatonic harmony while remaining true to nontonal precepts. He later enhanced his works with enriched melodic and harmonic elements. Among his compositions are *Cartea cu "Apo-*

Iodor," opera (Cluj-Napoca, April 13, 1975), and *Le Prince né des larmes*, ballet (1982).

Niedermeyer, (Abraham) Louis, Swiss composer; b. Nyon, April 27, 1802; d. Paris, March 14, 1861. He was a pupil in Vienna of Moscheles (piano) and Forster (composition), and, in 1819, of Fioravanti in Rome and Zingarelli in Naples. He lived in Geneva as an admired song composer, and settled in Paris in 1823, where he brought out 4 unsuccessful operas: *La casa nel bosco* (May 28, 1828), *Stradella* (March 3, 1837), *Marie Stuart* (Dec. 6, 1844), and *La Fronde* (May 2, 1853). He then bent his energies to sacred composition, and reorganized Choron's Inst. for Church Music as the École Niedermeyer, which eventually became a flourishing inst. with government subvention; he also founded (with d'Ortigue) a journal for church music, *La Maitrise* (1857–61); they also publ. *Traité théorique et pratique de l'accompagnement du plain-chant* (Paris, 1857; 2d ed., 1876; Eng. tr., N.Y., 1905).

BIBL.: A. Niedermeyer, *L. N.: Son oeuvre et son école* (Paris, n.d.); M. Galerne, *L'École N.* (Paris, 1928).

Nielsen, Alice, American soprano; b. Nashville, Tenn., June 7, 1868?; d. N.Y., March 8, 1943. She sang in a church choir in Kansas City, then joined the Burton Stanley Opera Co., where she sang in operettas; she made her debut as a grand-opera singer in Naples as Marguerite in *Faust* (Dec. 6, 1903); she made her first American appearance in New York (Nov. 10, 1905). In 1908 she toured with the San Carlo Co. in the United States; she then achieved the status of a prima donna with the Boston Opera Co. (1909–13) and also sang concurrently with the Metropolitan Opera in New York. She eventually settled in New York as a singing teacher.

Nielsen, Carl (August), greatly significant Danish composer; b. Sortelung, near Nørre-Lyndelse, June 9, 1865; d. Copenhagen, Oct. 3, 1931. He received violin lessons in childhood from his father and the local schoolteacher and played 2d violin in the village band, and later in its amateur orch. After studying cornet with his father, he played in the Odense military orch. (1879–83), serving as its signal horn and alto trombone player; he also taught himself to play piano. While in Odense, he began to compose, producing several chamber pieces, then received financial assistance to continue his training at the Royal Cons. in Copenhagen, where he studied violin with Tofte, theory with J. P. E. Hartmann and Orla Rosenhoff, and music history with Gade and P. Matthison-Hansen (1884–86). He was a violinist in Copenhagen's Royal Chapel Orch. (1889–1905); in the interim he achieved his first success as a composer with his *Little Suite* for Strings (1888); he then continued private studies with Rosenhoff. In 1901 he was granted an annual pension. He was conductor of the Royal Theater (1908–14) and the Musikföreningen (1915–27) in Copenhagen; he also appeared as a guest conductor in Germany, the Netherlands, Sweden, and Finland; he taught theory and composition at the Royal Cons. (1916–19), being appointed its director a few months before his death. The early style of Nielsen's music, Romantic in essence, was determined by the combined influences of Gade, Grieg, Brahms, and Liszt, but later on he experienced the powerful impact of modern music, particularly in harmony, which in his works grew more and more chromatic and dissonant, yet he reserved the simple diatonic progressions, often in a folksong manner, for his major climaxes; in his orchestration, he applied opulent sonorities and colorful instrumental counterpoint; there are instances of bold experimentation in some of his works, as, for example, the insertion of a snare-drum solo in his 5th Sym., playing independently of the rest of the orch.; he attached somewhat mysterious titles to his 3d and 4th syms. (*Expansive* and *Inextinguishable*). Nielsen is sometimes described as the Sibelius of Denmark, despite obvious dissimilarities in idiom and sources of inspiration; while the music of Sibelius is deeply rooted in national folklore, both in subject matter and melodic derivation, Nielsen seldom drew on Danish popular modalities; Sibelius remained true to the traditional style of composition, while Nielsen sought new ways of modern expression. It was only after his death that Nielsen's major works entered the world repertoire; festivals of his music were organized on his centennial in 1965, and his syms. in particular were played and recorded in England and America, bringing him belated recognition as one of the most important composers of his time. In 1988 Queen Margrethe II dedicated the Carl Nielsen Museum in Odense. His writings include *Levende musik* (Copenhagen, 1925; Eng. tr., London, 1953, as *Living Music*) and *Min fynske barndom* (Copenhagen, 1927; Eng. tr., London, 1953, as *My Childhood*). A new ed. of his works commenced publication in Copenhagen in 1994 as *The New Carl Nielsen Edition*.

WORKS (all 1st perf. in Copenhagen unless otherwise given): DRAMATIC: *Saul og David*, opera (1898–1901; Nov. 28, 1902); *Maskarade*, opera (1904–06; Nov. 11, 1906); *Snefrid*, melodrama (1893; April 10, 1894; rev. 1899); incidental music to A. Munch's *En aften paa Giske* (1889; Jan. 15, 1890), G. Wied's *Atalanta* (Dec. 19, 1901), Drachmann's *Hr. Oluf han rider*— (Master Oluf Rides—; Oct. 9, 1906), L. Holstein's *Tove* (1906–08; March 20, 1908), L. Nielsen's *Willemoes* (1907–08; Feb. 7, 1908), O. Benzon's *Foraeldre* (Feb. 9, 1908), J. Aakjaer's *Ulvens søn* (Århus, Nov. 14, 1909), A. Oehlenschlaeger's *Hagbarth og Signe* (June 4, 1910) and *Sankt Hansaftenspil* (June 3, 1913), Christiansen's *Faedreland* (1915; Feb. 5, 1916), H. Rode's prologue to the Shakespeare Memorial Celebrations (Elsinore, June 24, 1916), J. Sigurjónsson's *Løgneren* (Feb. 15, 1918), Oehlenschlaeger's *Aladdin*, op. 34 (1918–19; Feb. 15 and 22, 1919), Rode's *Moderen*, op. 41 (1920; Jan. 30, 1921), Christiansen's *Cosmus* (1921–22; Feb. 25, 1922), H. Bergstedt's *Ebbe Skammelsen* (June 25, 1925), S. Michaelis's *Amor og Digteren*, op. 54 (Odense, Aug. 12, 1930), and N. Grundtvig's *Paaske-aften* (April 4, 1931).

BIBL.: H. Seligmann, *C. N.* (Copenhagen, 1931); T. Meyer and F. Schandorf Petersen, *C. N.: Kunstneren og mennesket* (2 vols., Copenhagen, 1947–48); I. Møller and T. Meyer, eds., *C. N.s breve i udvalg og med kommentarer* (Copenhagen, 1954); J. Balzer, ed., *C. N. i hundredåret for hans fødsel* (Copenhagen, 1965; Eng. tr., 1965); J. Fabricius, *C. N. 1865–1931: A Pictorial Biography* (Copenhagen, 1965); D. Fog and T. Schousboe, *C. N.: kompositioner: En bibliografi* (Copenhagen, 1965); R. Simpson, *Sibelius and N.: A Centenary Essay* (London, 1965); T. Schousboe, ed., *C. N.: Dagboger og brevvesling med Anna Marie Carl Nielsen* (2 vols., Copenhagen, 1983); M. Miller, *C. N.: A Guide to Research* (N.Y., 1987); J. Jensen, *C. N.: Danskeren: Musikbiografi* (Copenhagen, 1991); M. Miller, ed., *The N. Companion* (Portland, Oreg., 1995); J. Lawson, *C. N.* (London, 1997).

Nielsen, Inga, Danish soprano; b. Holbaek, June 2, 1946. She received training at the Vienna Academy of Music and at the Stuttgart Hochschule für Musik. Following her operatic debut in Gelsenkirchen in 1973, she sang in Münster (1974–75) and Bern (1975–77). From 1978 to 1983 she was a member of the Frankfurt am Main Opera. In 1980 she sang at the N.Y. City Opera. She created the role of Minette in Henze's *The English Cat* at the Schwetzingen Festival in 1983. After singing Donna Anna in Stuttgart in 1984, she appeared at the Wexford Festival in 1986 as Amenaide in *Tancredi*. Her debut at London's Covent Garden followed in 1987 as Constanze, a role she also sang at the Salzburg Festival that year. In 1990 she appeared as Christine in the Italian premiere of Strauss's *Intermezzo* in Bologna. In 1992 she sang Gilda in Oslo, and then returned to Covent Garden as Ursula in Hindemith's *Mathis der Maler* in 1995. She appeared as Chrysothemis in Amsterdam in 1996 and sang at the Vienna Festival in 1997. She married **Robert Hale**.

Nielsen, (Carl Henrik) Ludolf, Danish violist, conductor, and composer; b. Nørre-Tvede, Jan. 29, 1876; d. Copenhagen, Oct. 16, 1939. He was a pupil of V. Tofte (violin), A. Orth (piano), Bondesen (harmony), and O. Malling and J. P. E. Hartmann (composition) at the Copenhagen Cons. (1896–98), then was a violist at the Tivoli and violist and deputy conductor at the Palekoncerter. He won the Ancker stipend and traveled in Germany, Austria, and Italy (1907); he later played in the Bjørvig Quartet and subsequently was conductor of the musical society Euphrosyne (1914–20). His music represents an expansive late Romantic style.

Among his works were the operas *Isbella* (Copenhagen, Oct. 8, 1915), *Uhret* (The Clock; 1911–13), and *Lola* (1917–20), and the ballets *Lackschmi* (1921; Copenhagen, March 4, 1922) and *Rejsekammeraten* (1928); also incidental music to plays; music for radio.

Nielsen, Riccardo, Italian composer and administrator; b. Bologna, March 3, 1908; d. Ferrara, Jan. 30, 1982. He studied with Casella and Gatti. He served as director of the Teatro Comunale in Bologna (1946–50). In 1952 he became director of the Liceo Musicale (later Cons.) in Ferrara. In his early works, he was influenced by Casella. He later wrote in a 12-tone idiom, which eventually evolved into a post-Webern style. His works include *L'incuba*, monodrama (1948), and *La via di Colombo*, radio opera (1953).

Nielsen, Svend, Danish composer and teacher; b. Copenhagen, April 20, 1937. He studied theory with Holmboe at the Royal Danish Cons. of Music in Copenhagen (graduated, 1967). After advanced composition studies with Nørgård, he taught at the Jutland Cons. of Music in Århus. Among his works is the chamber opera *Bulen* (1968).

Nielsen, Tage, Danish composer, pedagogue, and administrator; b. Copenhagen, Jan. 16, 1929. He received training in music and French at the Univ. of Copenhagen (M.A., 1955). In 1951 he joined the music dept. of Radio Denmark, where he was program secretary (from 1954) and later program ed. and deputy head of the dept. (from 1957). In 1963 he became director of the Jutland Academy of Music in Århus, where he was prof. of theory and music history from 1964. From 1983 to 1989 he was director of the Accademia di Danimarca in Rome. He served as managing director of the Soc. for the Publication of Danish Music from 1989 to 1993. In 1992 he received the Schierbeck Prize. His stylistic development proceeded through neoclassicism, expressionism, the Danish New Simplicity mode, to neo-Romanticism. Among his numerous works is the opera *Laughter in the Dark* (1986–91; Elsinore, May 6, 1995).

Niemann, Albert, greatly respected German tenor; b. Erxleben, near Magdeburg, Jan. 15, 1831; d. Berlin, Jan. 13, 1917. He began his career as an actor and dramatist. He joined the Dessau Opera (1849), where he sang in the chorus and appeared in minor roles, then had lessons with F. Schneider and Nusch. He sang in Halle from 1852 to 1854, then in Hannover; he then went to Paris, where he studied with Duprez. In 1866 he was engaged at the Berlin Royal Opera, remaining on its roster until 1888. Wagner thought highly of him, and asked him to create the role of Tannhäuser in Paris (March 13, 1861) and of Siegmund at the Bayreuth Festival (Aug. 14, 1876). From 1886 to 1888 he was a member of the Metropolitan Opera in New York; his debut there was in his star role as Siegmund (Nov. 10, 1886); then he sang Tristan at the American premiere of *Tristan und Isolde* (Dec. 1, 1886) and Siegfried in *Götterdämmerung* (Jan. 25, 1888) there. He publ. *Erinnerungen an Richard Wagner* (Leipzig, 1907; Eng. tr., 1908); his correspondence with Wagner was ed. by W. Altmann (Berlin, 1924).

BIBL.: R. Sternfeld, *A. N.* (Berlin, 1904).

Nikisch, Arthur, famous Austrian conductor of Moravian and Hungarian descent; b. Lébényi Szent-Miklós, Oct. 12, 1855; d. Leipzig, Jan. 23, 1922. His father was head bookkeeper to Prince Lichtenstein. Nikisch attended the Vienna Cons., studying with Dessoff (composition) and Hellmesberger (violin), graduating in 1874. While still a student, he had the honor of playing among the first violins under Wagner's direction at the laying of the cornerstone of the Bayreuth Theater (1872). He was at first engaged as a violinist in the Vienna Court Orch. (1874–77), then was chorusmaster (1877–78), 2d conductor (1878–79), and 1st conductor (1879–89) of the Leipzig City Theater. In 1889 he was engaged as conductor of the Boston Sym. Orch., with excellent success, remaining at this post until 1893. Returning to Europe, he was music director of the Budapest Opera (1893–95); he also conducted the Phil. Concerts there; from 1895 he was conductor of the Gewandhaus Orch. in Leipzig, and of the Berlin Phil. From 1897 he was in constant demand as a visiting conductor, and made a number of extended tours with the Berlin Phil.; he directed many of the concerts of the London Phil. Soc., and works of Wagner and Richard Strauss at Covent Garden; in 1912 he made a tour of the United States with the London Sym. Orch. From 1902 to 1907 he was director of studies at the Leipzig Cons.; in 1905–06, general director of the Leipzig City Theater. As a sym. conductor, he possessed an extraordinary Romantic power of musical inspiration; he was the first of his profession to open the era of "the conductor as hero," exercising a peculiar magnetism on his audiences equal to that of virtuoso artists; his personal appearance, a poetic-looking beard and flowing hair, contributed to his success. His son Mitja Nikisch (b. Leipzig, May 21, 1899; d. Venice, Aug. 5, 1936) was an excellent pianist; he toured South America in 1921; made his U.S. debut in New York, Oct. 23, 1923.

BIBL.: F. Pfohl, *A. N. als Mensch und als Künstler* (Leipzig, 1900; 2d ed., 1925); E. Segnitz, *A. N.* (Leipzig, 1920); H. Chevalley, ed., *A. N.: Leben und Wirken* (Berlin, 1922; 2d ed., 1925); A. Dette, *A. N.* (Leipzig, 1922).

Nikolov, Lazar, Bulgarian composer; b. Burgas, Aug. 26, 1922. He studied composition with Vladigerov at the Bulgarian State Cons. in Sofia (1942–47); in 1961 he joined its faculty. An experimenter by nature, Nikolov was one of the few composers in Bulgaria who adopted modern procedures of composition, melodically verging on atonality and harmonically on polytonality. Among his works are *Prometheus Bound*, chamber opera (1963–69; Ruse, March 24, 1974), and *Uncles,* opera (1975).

Nilsson, (Märta) Birgit, greatly renowned Swedish soprano; b. Vastra Karups, May 17, 1918. She studied with Joseph Hislop at the Royal Academy of Music in Stockholm. She made her debut as Agathe in *Der Freischütz* at the Royal Theater in Stockholm (1946), gaining her first success as Verdi's Lady Macbeth (1947); she then sang major roles in operas by Wagner, Puccini, and Strauss with increasing success. She first appeared as Brünnhilde in *Gotterdämmerung* in Stockholm during the 1954–55 season, and sang this role in the *Ring* cycle for the first time in Munich during the same season; she likewise appeared at the Vienna State Opera (1954) and at the Bayreuth Festival (1954), to which she returned regularly from 1959 to 1970. On Aug. 9, 1956, she made her U.S. debut at the Hollywood Bowl, then sang Brünnhilde in *Die Walküre* at the San Francisco Opera (Oct. 5, 1956); subsequently she made her first appearance at London's Covent Garden (1957). She made her long-awaited Metropolitan Opera debut in New York as Isolde on Dec. 19, 1959. Nilsson was universally acclaimed as one of the greatest Wagnerian dramatic sopranos of all time. After an absence of 5 years, she returned to the Metropolitan Opera for a gala concert on Nov. 4, 1979. She then rejoined the co., appearing as Elektra in 1980. She retired from the operatic stage in 1982. In addition to her brilliant Wagnerian roles, she excelled as Beethoven's Leonore, Puccini's Turandot, and Strauss's Salome and Elektra. She publ. *Mina minnesbilder* (Stockholm, 1977; Eng. tr., 1981, as *My Memoirs in Pictures*).

Nilsson, Christine (real name **Kristina Törnerhjelm**), admired Swedish soprano; b. Sjoabol, near Vaxjo, Aug. 20, 1843; d. Stockholm, Nov. 22, 1921. Her teachers were Baroness Leuhausen, and F. Berwald in Stockholm; with him she continued study in Paris, and on Oct. 27, 1864, made her debut, as Violetta in *La Traviata*, at the Théâtre-Lyrique, where she was engaged for 3 years. After successful visits to London, she was engaged from 1868 to 1870 at the Paris Opéra, then made long tours with Strakosch in America (1870–72), and sang in the principal continental cities. In 1872 she married Auguste Rouzaud (d. 1882); her 2d husband (married 1887) was the Spanish count Angel Vallejo y Miranda. She revisited America in the winters of 1873, 1874, and 1883, making her debut on the opening night of the Metropolitan Opera House in New York on Oct. 22, 1883, as Marguerite in *Faust*. Her voice was not powerful, but it was brilliant. She excelled as Marguerite and Mignon.

BIBL.: B. Carlsson, *K. N.* (Stockholm, 1922); T. Norlind, *K. N.*

(Stockholm, 1923); H. Headland, *C. N.: The Songbird of the North* (Rock Island, Ill., 1943).

Nilsson, Sven, Swedish bass; b. Gävle, May 11, 1898; Stockholm, March 1, 1970. He studied with Gillis Bratt and Hjaldis Ingebjarth in Stockholm, and then with Ivar Andresen in Dresden (1928–30). From 1930 to 1944 he was a member of the Dresden State Opera, where he became well known for his Mozart and Wagner portrayals, and also sang in the premieres of Strauss's *Arabella* (1933) and *Daphne* (1938). He likewise sang Wagner in Zoppot from 1934 to 1942. In 1946 he became a member of the Royal Theater in Stockholm, where he appeared until his death. On Nov. 9, 1950, he made his Metropolitan Opera debut in New York as Daland, remaining there on the roster for a season. His guest engagements also took him to London, Milan, Amsterdam, Brussels, Barcelona, and other European music centers. Among his other roles were Osmin, Sarastro, Pogner, and Baron Ochs.

Nilsson, Torsten, Swedish organist, choirmaster, teacher, and composer; b. Höör, Jan. 21, 1920. He studied church music and pedagogy at the Stockholm Musikhögskolan (1938–42); he also had instruction in organ from Alf Lindner and in organ and composition from Anton Heiller in Vienna (1961, 1965). He was organist in Köping (1943–53), Hälsingborg (1953–62), and at the Oscar Church in Stockholm (1962–79); he also was conductor of the Oscar Motet Choir. He taught theory at the Stockholm Citizen's School (1962–73) and liturgical singing at the Stockholm Theological Inst. (1964–70) and the Univ. of Uppsala (1966–70). He excels in liturgical works; in his organ music he introduces many innovations, such as static tone-clusters and specified periods of thematic improvisation.

WORKS: DRAMATIC: CHURCH OPERA ORATORIOS: *Ur jordens natt* (Out of the Night of the Earth) for Improvising Soli and Vocal Groups, with Organ (Stockholm, April 12, 1968); *Dantesvit* (Dante Suite) for Soli, Vocal Group, Percussion, Organ, Harpsichord, and Tape (Stockholm, April 23, 1969); *Skapelse* (The Creation) for Narrator, Chorus, Organ, and Instruments (Stockholm, May 11, 1970); *Ur jordens natt. Del 2* (Out of the Night of the Earth, Part 2; Stockholm, April 12, 1974); *Den sista natten* (The Last Night) for 2 Actors, Mixed and Children's Chorus, Flute, Harp, Organ, and Percussion (Stockholm, Nov. 25, 1973). OPERA: *Malin: Pictures of History* for Chorus and Archaeological Instruments (1987; Nashville, Tenn., April 8, 1988).

Nimsgern, Siegmund, German bass-baritone; b. Stiring-Wendel, Jan. 14, 1940. He was a student in Saarbrücken of Sibylle Fuchs, Jakob Stämpfli, and Paul Lohmann. In 1965 he made his debut as a concert artist; his operatic debut followed in 1967 when he appeared as Lionel in Tchaikovsky's *The Maid of Orleans* in Saarbrücken, where he sang until 1971. In 1970 he made his Salzburg Festival debut. From 1971 to 1974 he was a member of the Deutsche Oper am Rhein in Düsseldorf. He made his British debut in 1972 as a soloist in *La Damnation de Faust*. In 1973 he made his first appearance at London's Covent Garden as Amfortas, and he also made debuts as Milan's La Scala and the Paris Opéra. In 1974 he made his U.S. debut as Jochanaan at the San Francisco Opera. He made his Metropolitan Opera debut in New York as Pizarro on Oct. 2, 1978, and returned there as Jochanaan in 1981. From 1983 to 1985 he appeared as Wotan at the Bayreuth Festivals. Among his other roles were Telramund, Alberich, Günther, the Dutchman, Macbeth, Iago, and Luna.

Nin-Culmell, Joaquín (María), Cuban-American composer, pianist, and teacher; b. Berlin, Sept. 5, 1908. His father was the Spanish-born Cuban pianist and composer Joaquín Nin (y Castellanos) (b. Havana, Sept. 29, 1879; d. there, Oct. 24, 1949). He went to Paris and studied piano at the Schola Cantorum and composition with Dukas at the Cons. From 1930 to 1935 he pursued training in composition with Falla in Granada. He also continued piano studies with Cortot and Viñes. In 1938 he emigrated to the United States, where he taught at Williams College in Williamstown, Mass. (1940–50) and the Univ. of Calif. at Berkeley (1950–74). He ed. and annotated the Spanish Choral Tradition (1975 et seq.), a series devoted to secular music of the Renaissance. His own music exhibits Spanish influence in its basic lyricism and vital rhythmic energy, but it combines these elements with 20th century harmonies in transparent textures that are essentially homophonic and tonal. His works include *Yerma*, incidental music to García Lorca's play (1956), *El burlador de Sevilla*, ballet (1957–65), *La Celestina*, opera (1965–85), *Le rêve de Cyrano*, ballet (1978), and *Cymbeline*, incidental music to Shakespeare's play (1980).

Nishimura, Akira, Japanese composer; b. Osaka, Sept. 8, 1953. He studied with Ikenouchi, Yashiro, and Mamiya at the Tokyo National Univ. of Fine Arts and Music (1973–80). He taught at the Tokyo College of Music and served on the board of the Japanese Composers Soc. In 1993–94 he was composer-in-residence of the Kanazawa Orch. Ensemble. He won the Queen Elisabeth of Belgium International Music Competition (1977), the Dallapiccola Composition Award (1977), and the Otaka Prize (1988, 1992, 1993). His energetic and colorfully chromatic music explores the universe of sound and its transfigurations, with a special affinity for percussion. His works include *Hot Rain in August*, television opera (1986).

Nissen, Hans Hermann, distinguished German bass-baritone; b. Zippnow, near Marienwerder, West Prussia, May 20, 1893; d. Munich, March 28, 1980. He studied with Julius von Raatz-Brickmann in Berlin, where he made his concert debut (1920), then made his operatic debut as the Caliph in *Der Barbier von Bagdad* at the Berlin Volksoper (1924); subsequently he joined the Bavarian State Opera in Munich (1925). In 1930 he went to the United States, where he was a member of the Chicago Civic Opera (until 1932); on Nov. 23, 1938, he made his debut with the Metropolitan Opera in New York as Wotan and remained with it for a season. He then rejoined the Bavarian State Opera in Munich, retiring in 1967. He remained in Munich as a voice teacher.

Nixon, Marni (née **Margaret Nixon McEathron**), American soprano; b. Altadena, Calif., Feb. 22, 1930. She studied with Carl Ebert at the Univ. of Southern Calif. in Los Angeles, Jan Popper at Stanford Univ., and Boris Goldovsky and Sarah Caldwell at the Berkshire Music Center at Tanglewood. She pursued a multifaceted career: she sang on the sound track of the films *The King and I*, *West Side Story*, and *My Fair Lady*, and also starred in her own children's program on television; she appeared in musical comedy and opera and was a soloist with major orchs. in the United States and abroad. She taught at the Calif. Inst. of the Arts (1969–71) and the Music Academy of the West in Santa Barbara (from 1980).

Nixon, Roger, American composer and teacher; b. Tulare, Calif., Aug. 8, 1921. He studied clarinet with a local teacher; in 1940, attended a seminar in composition with Bliss at the Univ. of Calif. at Berkeley, and in 1941, with Bloch. From 1942 to 1946 he was in the U.S. Army; he returned in 1947 to Berkeley, where he studied with Sessions (M.A., 1949; Ph.D., 1952); in the summer of 1948 he took private lessons with Schoenberg. In 1960 he joined the faculty of San Francisco State College (later Univ.), where he retired as prof. emeritus in 1991. A prolific composer, Nixon writes in a consistent modern idiom anchored in fluctuating tonality and diversified by atonal protuberances. His music is marked by distinctly American melorhythms; his miniature opera *The Bride Comes to Yellow Sky* (Charleston, Ill., Feb. 20, 1968; rev. version, San Francisco, March 22, 1969) is an exemplar of adroit modernistic Westernism fashioned in a nonethnomusicological manner.

Niyazi (real name, **Taghi-zade-Khadzhibekov**), Russian conductor and composer; b. Tiflis, Aug. 20, 1912; d. Baku, Aug. 2, 1984. His father was the composer Zulfugar Khadzhibekov. He studied music in Moscow, Yerevan, and Baku. From 1937 to 1965 he served, off and on, as conductor of the Azerbaijani Ballet. In 1961 he was named principal conductor of the Leningrad Theater of Opera and Ballet. He conducted a number of first performances of works by Azerbaijani composers. Among his works are *Hosrov and Shirin*, opera (1942), and *Chitra*, ballet, after Rabindranath Tagore (1961).

BIBL.: E. Abasova, *N.* (Baku, 1965).

Noble, Dennis (William), English baritone; b. Bristol, Sept. 25, 1899; d. Jávea, Spain, March 14, 1966. He was trained as a chorister at Bristol Cathedral. In 1924 he made his operatic debut at London's Covent Garden as Marullo in *Rigoletto*, and then sang there until 1938 and again in 1947. He also appeared with the British National Opera Co. and the Carl Rosa Opera Co. In 1931 he was soloist in the premiere of Walton's *Belshazzar's Feast* in Leeds. In 1936–37 he appeared in Cleveland. In addition to his various French and Italian roles, he also sang in many contemporary British operas.

Noda, Ken, American pianist and composer; b. N.Y., Oct. 5, 1962. He studied piano with Adele Marcus at the Juilliard School in New York, and also had lessons in composition with Sylvia Rabinof and Thomas Pasatieri. In 1977 he made his professional debut as a soloist with the Minnesota Orch. in Minneapolis, followed by his London debut as soloist with the English Chamber Orch. in 1979. After further studies with Barenboim in Paris (1979–83), he made appearances on both sides of the Atlantic until 1990. In 1991 he became musical assistant to the artistic director, artistic administration, at the Metropolitan Opera in New York. He again appeared in public as a pianist in 1997. Among his works were several operas, song cycles, and piano pieces.

Noelte, A. Albert, German-American music pedagogue and composer; b. Starnberg, March 10, 1885; d. Chicago, March 2, 1946. He went to the United States in 1901 and studied music and literature in Boston; in 1908 he returned to Germany, but frequently visited the United States; in 1931 he settled there and was appointed a prof. at Northwestern Univ. in Evanston, Ill. He earned a fine reputation as a teacher; many American scholars and composers were his pupils. Among his works was the opera *François Villon* (1920).

Noni, Alda, Italian soprano; b. Trieste, April 30, 1916. After studies in piano and voice in Trieste, she pursued vocal training in Vienna. In 1937 she made her operatic debut as Rossini's Rosina in Ljubljana, and then sang in Zagreb, Belgrade, and Trieste. She was a member of the Vienna State Opera (1942–44), where she sang the role of Zerbinetta at Strauss's 80th birthday celebration in 1944. In 1946 she appeared as Norina in London. In 1949 she sang with the Glyndebourne Opera at the Edinburgh Festival, and then appeared at Glyndebourne (1950; 1952–54). From 1949 to 1953 she also sang at Milan's La Scala. Among her notable roles were Despina, Papagena, Zerlina, Nannetta, Clorinda in *La Cenerentola*, and Oscar.

Nono, Luigi, remarkable Italian composer who earned a prominent and controversial place in the history of modern music through his consistent devotion to social problems; b. Venice, Jan. 29, 1924; d. there, May 8, 1990. He became a student at the Venice Cons. (1941), where he received instruction in composition with Malipiero (1943–45); he also studied law at the Univ. of Padua (graduated, 1946), and later had advanced harmony and counterpoint lessons with Maderna and Scherchen. He joined the Italian Communist Party while the country was still under the dictatorship of Mussolini, and was an active participant in the Italian Resistance Movement against the Nazis. In 1975 he was elected to the Central Committee of the Communist Party, and remained a member until his death. Although his works were extremely difficult to perform and practically all were devoted to leftist propaganda, he found support among a number of liberal composers and performers. At the end of his life, he acquired an enormous reputation as a highly original composer in the novel technical idiom as well as a fearless political agitator. In his technique of composition, he followed the precepts of Schoenberg without adhering to the literal scheme of dodecaphonic composition. As a resolutely "engaged" artist, Nono mitigated the antinomy between the modern idiom of his music and the conservative Soviet ideology of socialist realism by his militant political attitude and his emphasis on revolutionary subjects in his works, so that even extreme dissonances may be dialectically justified as representing the horrors of Fascism. He made several visits to Russia, the last in 1988, but his works were rarely performed there because of the intransigence of his idiom. He made use of a variety of techniques: serialism, "sonorism" (employment of sonorities for their own sake), aleatory and concrete music, and electronics. Perhaps his most militant composition, both politically and musically, is the opera *Intolleranza 1960*, utilizing texts by Brecht, Eluard, Sartre, and Mayakovsky. The work is a powerful protest against imperialist policies and social inequities. At its premiere in Venice on April 13, 1961, a group of neo-Fascists showered the audience with leaflets denouncing Nono for his alleged contamination of Italian music by alien doctrines, and even making a facetious allusion to his name as representing a double negative. His other dramatic works include *Der rote Mantel*, ballet (Berlin, Sept. 20, 1954), *A Floresta é jovem e cheja de vida*, oratorio to texts from declarations by the Vietnam guerrilla fighters (1966), and *Al gran sole carico d'amore*, opera (1974). Nono was married to Schoenberg's daughter, Nuria, in 1955; they separated on friendly terms after several years; they had 2 daughters. Nuria settled in her father's last residence in Los Angeles, while Nono traveled widely in Europe. He died of a liver ailment at the age of 66.

BIBL.: J. Stenzl, ed., *L. N.: Texte: Studien zu seiner Musik* (Zürich, 1975); F. Spangemacher, *L. N.: Die elektronische Musik* (Regensburg, 1983); C. Henius, *Schnebel, N., Schönberg, oder, Die wirkliche und die erdachte Musik: Essays und autobiographisches* (Hamburg, 1993); M. Taibon, *L. N. und sein Musiktheater* (Vienna, 1993).

Norberg-Schulz, Elizabeth, Norwegian soprano; b. Oslo, Jan. 1959. She studied at the Accademia di Santa Cecilia in Rome, the Pears-Britten School in Snape, and with Schwarzkopf in Zürich. After singing Britten's *Les Illuminations* in Snape in 1981, she was active as a concert and lieder artist. She also appeared at Milan's La Scala, touring with the company to Japan in 1988 as Musetta. In 1989 she sang Barbarina at the Rome Opera and Ilia at the Maggio Musicale Fiorentino. After portraying Pamina in Salzburg in 1991, she returned there as Servilia in 1992, the same year she sang Norina in Naples. In 1994 she made her debut at London's Covent Garden as Liù. Her Metropolitan Opera debut followed in New York on Nov. 10, 1995, as Verdi's Oscar. She appeared as Cimarosa's Carolina in Rome in 1996. In 1998 she sang Adele at the Metropolitan Opera.

Nordgren, Pehr Henrik, Finnish composer; b. Saltvik, Jan. 19, 1944. He studied composition with Kokkonen and musicology at the Univ. of Helsinki, and composition and traditional Japanese music at the Tokyo Univ. of Arts and Music (1970–73). In his works, he utilizes traditional and advanced harmonies and both Western and traditional Japanese instruments. They include *Den svarte munken* (The Black Monk), chamber opera (1981; Stockholm, March 20, 1984), and *Alex*, television opera (1983; Helsinki, Sept. 6, 1986).

Nordica (real name, **Norton**), **Lillian,** distinguished American soprano; b. Farmington, Maine, Dec. 12, 1857; d. Batavia, Java, May 10, 1914. She studied with John O'Neill at the New England Cons. of Music in Boston (graduated, 1876), then with Marie Maretzek in New York (1876), where she made her formal debut as soloist with Gilmore's Grand Boston Band (Sept. 30, 1876); she toured with it in the United States and later in Europe (1878). After coaching from Francois Delsarte and Emilio Belari in Paris, she studied with Antonio Sangiovanni at the Milan Cons., who suggested she adopt the stage name Nordica. It was under that name that she made her operatic debut as Donna Elvira at the Teatro Manzoni there (March 8, 1879). In St. Petersburg, she sang for Czar Alexander II a week before he was assassinated in March 1881. After making appearances in several German cities, she went to Paris to study with Giovanni Sbriglia (1881–82); she made her Paris debut on July 22, 1882, as Marguerite, at the Opéra. On Jan. 22, 1883, she married Frederick A. Gower. With him she returned to America and made her American debut as Marguerite with Mapleson's company at N.Y.'s Academy of Music on Nov. 26, 1883. In 1884 she began proceedings for divorce from her first husband, but he mysteriously disappeared while attempting to cross the English Channel in a balloon. She made her debut at Covent Garden in London on March 12, 1887, as Violetta and sang there again in 1898, 1899, and 1902. She first sang at the Metropolitan Opera in New York on Dec. 18, 1891, as Valentine in *Les Huguenots*. She was heard for the first time as Isolde at the Metropolitan on Nov. 27, 1895, scoring an overwhelming success. From then on she sang chiefly Wagnerian roles; she continued to appear off and on at the Metropolitan until 1909, when she began to make extended concert tours. Her farewell appearance was at a concert in Melbourne on Nov. 25, 1913. In 1896 she married the Hungarian tenor Zoltan Doeme, from whom she was divorced in 1904; in 1909 she married the banker George W. Young in London. She died while on a trip around the world.

BIBL.: I. Glackens, *Yankee Diva: L. N. and the Golden Days of Opera* (N.Y., 1963).

Nordin, Lena, Swedish soprano; b. Visby, Feb. 18, 1956. She studied at the Malmö Musikhögskolan and the Stockholm Musikhögskolan, and in Salzburg, Florence, and Siena. In 1984 she attracted notice with her performance of Rameau's Aricie at the Swedish Baroque Festival. In 1986 she made her debut at the Royal Opera in Stockholm as Luisa Miller and in 1987 she was awarded the Birgit Nilsson Prize. In subsequent years, she appeared at the Royal Opera in such roles as Cleopatra, Donna Anna, Constanze, Maria Stuarda, Marguerite, and Sophie. Her portrayal of Norma there in 1997 was acclaimed. That same year, she was awarded the Jussi Björling Prize. As a guest artist, she sang in Copenhagen, Wexford, London, Dresden, Moscow, and other European cities. She also toured as a concert artist in Europe and the United States.

Nordoff, Paul, American composer and music therapist; b. Philadelphia, June 4, 1909; d. Herdecke, Germany, Jan. 18, 1977. He studied piano with Olga Samaroff at the Philadelphia Cons. (B.M., 1927; M.M., 1932) and composition with Rubin Goldmark at the Juilliard School of Music in New York (1928–33); he later received the degree of Bachelor of Music Therapy at Combs College (1960). In 1993–94 and 1935–36 he held Guggenheim fellowships. He taught composition at the Philadelphia Cons. (1937–42), Michigan State College (1945–49), and Bard College (1949–59). From 1959 he devoted himself mainly to music therapy for handicapped children, publishing many works with C. Robbins concerning music therapy, with particular emphasis on handicapped children. Among his compositions are the operas *Mr. Fortune* (1936–37; rev. 1956–57) and *The Sea Change* (1951), the operetta *The Masterpiece* (1940; Philadelphia, Jan. 24, 1941), and the ballets *Every Soul Is a Circus* (1937), *Salem Shore* (1943), and *Tally Ho* (1943).

Norena, Eidé (real name, **Kaja Andrea Karoline Hansen-Eidé**), Norwegian soprano; b. Horten, April 26, 1884; d. Lausanne, Nov. 19, 1968. She studied voice with Ellen Gulbranson in Christiania, later in Weimar, London, and Paris; she was a pupil of Raimund von Zur Mühlen. She began her career as a concert singer in Scandinavia. She made her operatic debut as Amor in Gluck's *Orfeo* in Christiania (1907), subsequently singing at the National Theater there (1908–18). After appearances at Stockholm's Royal Theater, she sang at La Scala in Milan (1924), Covent Garden in London (1924–25; 1930–31; 1934; 1937), and at the Paris Opéra (1925–37). She was a member of the Chicago Opera (1926–28) and from 1933 to 1938, of the Metropolitan Opera in New York (made her debut as Mimi, on Feb. 9, 1933); she toured the United States in concert. Among her finest roles were Mathilde in *Guillaume Tell*, Violetta, Marguerite in *Les Huguenots*, the 3 heroines in *Les Contes d'Hoffmann*, and Desdemona.

Nørgård, Per, prominent Danish composer and pedagogue; b. Gentofte, near Copenhagen, July 13, 1932. He began piano lessons when he was 8; in 1949 he became a private composition pupil of Holmboe; after entering the Royal Danish Cons. of Music in Copenhagen (1952), he continued his training with Holmboe there and also took courses with Høffding (theory), Koppel (piano), and Jersild (solfège), passing his examinations in theory, composition, and pedagogy (1955); following further studies with Boulanger in Paris (1956–57) he was awarded the Lily Boulanger Prize in 1957. He was a music critic for Copenhagen's *Politiken* (1958–62) and also taught at the Odense Cons. (1958–60); after teaching at the Royal Danish Cons. of Music in Copenhagen (1960–65), he joined the faculty of the Århus Cons. in 1965, where he was made prof. of composition in 1987. In 1988 he was awarded the Henrik-Steffens-Preis of Germany. In 1995 he was made an honorary member of the ISCM, the first Dane ever to be accorded that distinction. In 1996 he received the Léonie Sonning Music Prize of Denmark. After a period of adolescent emulation of Sibelius, Nørgård plunged into the mainstream of cosmopolitan music making, exploring the quasi-mathematical serial techniques based on short tonal motifs, rhythmic displacement, metrical modulation, pointillism, graphic notation, and a "horizontal" invariant fixing certain notes to specific registers; then shifted to a pointillistically impressionistic colorism evolving in a tonal bradykinesis.

WORKS: DRAMATIC: OPERAS: *The Labyrinth* (1963; Copenhagen, Sept. 2, 1967); *Gilgamesh* (1971–72; Århus, May 4, 1973); *Siddharta* (1977–79; Stockholm, March 18, 1983); *The Divine Tivoli*, chamber opera (1982). BALLETS: *Le Jeune Homme à marier* (1964; Danish TV, April 2, 1965; 1st stage perf., Copenhagen, Oct. 15, 1967); *Tango Chicane* (Copenhagen, Oct. 15, 1967); Trio for 3 Dancers and Percussion (Paris, Dec., 1972).

BIBL.: A. Beyer, ed., *The Music of P. N.: Fourteen Interpretive Essays* (Brookfield, Vt., 1996).

Nørholm, Ib, Danish composer, organist, and teacher; b. Copenhagen, Jan. 24, 1931. He studied theory with Holmboe, music history with Hjelmborg, and form and analysis with Bentzon and Høffding at the Royal Danish Cons. of Music in Copenhagen (1950–54), passing his examinations in theory and music history (1954), organ and teaching (1955), and sacred music (1956). He was active as a music critic (1956–64) and was a church organist in Elsinore (1957–63) and then at Copenhagen's Bethlemskirken (from 1964); he also taught part-time at the Royal Danish Cons. of Music in Copenhagen (from 1961) and at the Odense Cons.; he subsequently taught theory at the Royal Danish Cons. of Music in Copenhagen (from 1973). His musical idiom is permeated with Scandinavian lyricism, even when he introduces modernistic devices. Among his works are *Invitation to a Beheading*, opera after Nabokov (1965, Danish TV, Oct. 10, 1967), *The Young Park*, chamber opera (Århus, Oct. 14, 1970), *The Garden Wall*, choral opera (1976), and *The Revenge of the Truth*, chamber opera (1985).

Norman, Jessye, exceptionally gifted black American soprano; b. Augusta, Ga., Sept. 15, 1945. She received a scholarship to study at Howard Univ. in Washington, D.C. (1961), where she had vocal lessons from Carolyn Grant; she continued her training at the Peabody Cons. of Music in Baltimore and at the Univ. of Mich., where her principal teachers were Pierre Bernac and Elizabeth Mannion. She won the Munich Competition (1968), and then made her operatic debut as Elisabeth in *Tannhäuser* at the Berlin Deutsche Oper (1969); she appeared in the title role of *L'Africaine* at Florence's Maggio Musicale (1971), and the following year sang Aida at Milan's La Scala and Cassandra in *Les Troyens* at London's Covent Garden; subsequently she made major recital debuts in London and New York (1973). After an extensive concert tour of North America (1976–77), she made her U.S. stage debut as Jocasta in *Oedipus rex* and as Purcell's Dido on a double bill with the Opera Co. of Philadelphia on Nov. 22, 1982. She made her Metropolitan Opera debut in New York as Cassandra on Sept. 26, 1983. In 1986 she appeared as soloist in Strauss's *Vier letzte Lieder* with the Berlin Phil. during its tour of the United States. On Sept. 20, 1989, she was the featured soloist with Zubin Mehta and the N.Y. Phil. in its opening concert of its 148th season, which was telecast live to the nation by PBS. In 1992 she sang

Jocasta at the opening operatic production at the new Saito Kinen Festival in Matsumoto. On Sept. 20, 1995, Norman was again the featured soloist with the N.Y. Phil., this time under Kurt Masur's direction, in a gala concert telecast live to the nation by PBS making the opening of the orch.'s 53d season. In 1996 she appeared as Emilia Marty at the Metropolitan Opera.

Norman's extraordinary repertory ranges from Purcell to Richard Rodgers; she commended herself in Mussorgsky's songs, which she performed in Moscow in the original Russian; in her recitals she gave performances of the classical German repertory as well as contemporary masterpieces, such as Schoenberg's *Gurrelieder* and the French moderns, which she invariably performed in the original tongue. This combination of scholarship and artistry contributed to her consistently successful career as one of the most versatile concert and operatic singers of her time.

Norman, (Fredrik Vilhelm) Ludvig, notable Swedish conductor and composer; b. Stockholm, Aug. 28, 1831; d. there, March 28, 1885. He studied piano and composition at the Leipzig Cons. with Moscheles, Hauptmann, and Rietz (1848–52). Returning to Stockholm, he taught at the Cons. (1858–61). In 1861 he became conductor of the Royal Opera, a position he held with great distinction until 1878. He introduced many works to the Swedish public, among them operas by Wagner, Verdi, Gounod, and Bizet. He married the violinist Wilma Neruda in 1864 (separated, 1869).

Norrington, Sir Roger (Arthur Carver), scholarly English conductor; b. Oxford, March 16, 1934. He was educated at Clare College, Cambridge, and the Royal College of Music in London; was active as a tenor. In 1962 he founded the Schütz Choir in London, with which he first gained notice as a conductor. From 1966 to 1984 he was principal conductor of the Kent Opera, where he produced scores by Monteverdi utilizing his own performing eds. He served as music director of the London Baroque Players (from 1975) and the London Classical Players (from 1978); he also was principal conductor of the Bournemouth Sinfonietta (1985–89). On April 2, 1989, he made an auspicious N.Y. debut at Carnegie Hall conducting Beethoven's 8th and 9th syms. In 1990 he became music director of the Orch. of St. Luke's in New York, which post he held until 1994. In 1980 he was made an Officer of the Order of the British Empire; in 1990, a Commander of the Order of the British Empire; in 1996 he was knighted. In 1990 he conducted *Die Zauberflöte* at the Promenade Concerts in London. In 1997 he conducted Mozart's *Mitridate* in Salzburg, where he also became chief conductor of its Camerata Academica that year. In 1998 he also became chief conductor of the Stuttgart Radio Sym. Orch.

Norrington entered controversy by insisting that the classical tempo is basic for all interpretation. He also insisted that Beethoven's metronome markings, not usually accepted by performers, are in fact accurate reflections of Beethoven's inner thoughts about his own music. He obtained numerous defenders of his ideas (as one critic put it, "inspired literalism") for the interpretation of classical music, which aroused sharp interest as well as caustic rejection. However that might be, his performances, especially in the United States, received a great deal of attention, and he was particularly praised for the accuracy and precision of his interpretations.

North, Alex, gloriously gifted American composer and conductor with a predilection for uniquely colored film music; b. Chester, Pa., Dec. 4, 1910; d. Pacific Palisades, Calif., Sept. 8, 1991. His father, a blacksmith, was an early immigrant from Russia. North studied piano and theory at the Curtis Inst. of Music in Philadelphia, and later studied on scholarship at the Juilliard School of Music in New York, where he took courses in composition (1929–32). A decisive change in his life came with his decision to go to Russia as a technology specialist at a time when Russia was eager to engage American technicians. He became fascinated with new Russian music and received a scholarship to attend the Moscow Cons., where he studied composition with Anton Weprik and Victor Bielyi (1933–35). He also was music director of the propaganda group of German Socialists called "Kolonne Links" (Column to the Left!). He mastered the Russian language and acquired a fine reputation in Russia as a true friend of Soviet music. Returning to the United States, he took additional courses in composition with Copland (1936–38) and Toch (1938–39). In 1939 he conducted 26 concerts in Mexico as music director of the Anna Sokolow Dance Troupe; during his stay in Mexico City, he had some instruction from Silvestre Revueltas. In 1942 North entered the U.S. Army; promoted to captain, he became responsible for entertainment programs in mental hospitals. He worked closely with the psychiatrist Karl Menninger in developing a theatrical genre called "psychodrama," which later became an accepted mode of psychological therapy. During his army years, North also worked with the Office of War Information, composing scores for over 25 documentary films. During all these peregrinations he developed a distinct flair for theater music, while continuing to produce estimable works in absolute forms. His concerto, *Revue* for Clarinet and Orch., was performed by Benny Goodman in New York under the baton of Leonard Bernstein on Nov. 18, 1946. He further expanded his creative talents to write a number of modern ballets. The result of these multifarious excursions into musical forms was the formation of a style peculiarly recognizable as the specific art of North. His concentrated efforts, however, became directed mainly toward the art of film music, a field in which he triumphed. John Huston stated in 1986 that "it is the genius of Alex North to convey an emotion to the audience"; other directors praised North's cinemusical abilities in similar terms. Among the writers with whom he worked were Tennessee Williams, John Steinbeck, and Arthur Miller. But no success is without disheartening frustration. North was commissioned to write the score for *2001: A Space Odyssey*, on which he worked enthusiastically. But much to his dismay, the director, Stanley Kubrick, decided to replace it by a pasticcio that included such commonplaces as Strauss's *The Blue Danube Waltz*. North refused to be downhearted by this discomfiture and used the discarded material for his 3d Sym. He was nominated 15 times for an Academy Award for Best Film Music, but it was not until 1986 that the Academy of Motion Picture Arts and Sciences finally awarded him an Oscar for lifetime achievement. Among his outstanding scores are *A Streetcar Named Desire* (1951), *Death of a Salesman* (1951), *The Bad Seed* (1956), *The Rainmaker* (1956), *The Sound and the Fury* (1959), *Spartacus* (1960), *Who's Afraid of Virginia Woolf?* (1966), *The Shoes of the Fisherman* (1968), *Shanks* (1973), *Bite the Bullet* (1975), *Dragonslayer* (1981), *Under the Volcano* (1984), *Prizzi's Honor* (1985), *The Penitent* (1986), and *Good Morning, Vietnam* (1988). His song "Unchained Melody" (1955) became a popular hit in its rendition by the Righteous Brothers.

WORKS: DRAMATIC: BALLETS: *Ballad in a Popular Style*, for Anna Sokolow (1933); *Case History* (1933); *War Is Beautiful* (1936); *Slaughter of the Innocents* (N.Y., Nov. 14, 1937); *American Lyric*, for Martha Graham (N.Y., Dec. 26, 1937); *Inquisition* (1938); *Lupe* (1940); *Design for 5* (1941); *Exile* (Mansfield, March 3, 1941); *Golden Fleece*, for Hanya Holm (Mansfield, March 17, 1941); *Clay Ritual* (Hartford, Conn., May 20, 1942); *Intersection* (1947); *A Streetcar Named Desire* (Montreal, Oct. 9, 1952); *Daddy Long Legs Dream Ballet* (1955; for Fred Astaire and Leslie Caron in the film *Daddy Long Legs*); *Mal de siècle* (Brussels, July 3, 1958). CHILDREN'S OPERA AND THEATER: *The Hither and Thither of Danny Dither* (1941); *Little Indian Drum* for Narrator and Orch. (N.Y., Oct. 19, 1947).

Norup, Bent, Danish baritone; b. Hobro, Dec. 7, 1936. He received vocal training in Copenhagen from Kristan Rils, in Munich from Karl Schmitt-Walter, and in New York from Herta Sperber. In 1970 he made his operatic debut in Copenhagen as Kurwenal, where he subsequently sang at the Royal Theater. He also made guest appearances in Hamburg, Berlin, Düsseldorf, Paris, Vienna, and the United States. His concert engagements took him to leading music centers of the world. Among his roles of note were Hans Sachs, Wotan, Telramund, Klingsor, Amfortas, Jochanaan, Iago, and Scarpia.

Noske, Frits (Rudolf), Dutch musicologist; b. The Hague, Dec. 13, 1920; d. Ariolo, Switzerland, Sept. 15, 1993. He studied cello and theory at the Amsterdam Cons. and at the Royal Cons. in The Hague (1940–45), then pursued musicological training with Bernet Kempers and Smits van Waesberghe at the Univ. of Amsterdam (Ph.D., 1954, with the diss. *La Mélodie française de Berlioz à Duparc*; publ. in Amsterdam, 1954; Eng. tr., rev., 1970); he also had lessons with Masson at the Sorbonne in Paris (1949–50). He taught music history at the Amsterdam Cons. and at the Bussum Toonkunst Music School and was librarian at the Amsterdam Music Library (1951–54), and subsequently its director (1954–68); he also was a reader in musicology at the Univ. of Leiden (1965–68) and prof. of musicology at the Univ. of Amsterdam (from 1968).

WRITINGS: *Forma formans: Een strutuuranalytische methode, toegepast op de instrumentale muziek van Jan Pieterszoon Sweelinck* (Amsterdam, 1969; Eng. tr., rev., 1976, in the *International Review of the Aesthetics and Sociology of Music*, 7); *The Signifier and the Signified: Studies in the Operas of Mozart and Verdi* (The Hague, 1977); *Sweelinck* (Oxford, 1988); *Saints and Sinners: The Latin Musical Dialogue in the Seventeenth Century* (Oxford, 1992).

Noskowski, Zygmunt, significant Polish conductor and composer; b. Warsaw, May 2, 1846; d. there, July 23, 1909. He studied at the Warsaw Music Inst., then became an instructor in a school for the blind, and devised a music notation for the blind. He subsequently studied composition with Kiel in Berlin. After a brief period of professional activities in Western Europe, he returned to Warsaw and was director of the Music Soc. (1881–1902); in 1888 he was appointed a prof. at the Warsaw Cons., and later was director of the Warsaw Phil. (1905–08) and Opera (1907–09). He wrote the operas *Livia Quintilla* (Lemberg, Feb. 1, 1898), *Wyrok* (The Judgement; Warsaw, Nov. 15, 1906), and *Zemsta za mur graniczny* (Revenge for the Boundary Wall), after A. Fredro's *Zemsta* (Warsaw, 1909).

BIBL.: A. Sutkowski, *Z. N.* (Kraków, 1957); W. Wrónski, *Materialy z życia i twórczości Z. N.ego* (Kraków, 1960).

Noté, Jean, Belgian baritone; b. Tournai, May 6, 1859; d. Brussels, April 1, 1922. He studied at the Ghent Cons., making his debut in a concert in Ghent in 1883. He then sang opera in Lille, Brussels, Lyons, Marseilles, etc. He made his N.Y. Metropolitan Opera debut on Dec. 3, 1908, as Escamillo. In 1913 he joined the Paris Opéra, and remained on its roster until his death. Among his finest roles were Hamlet, Beckmesser, Rigoletto, and Wolfram.

Nottara, Constantin, Romanian violinist, conductor, teacher, and composer; b. Bucharest, Oct. 13, 1890; d. there, Jan. 19, 1951. He studied with Klenck (violin), Kiriac (theory), and Castaldi (composition) at the Bucharest Cons. (1900–07), with Enesco and Bethelier (violin) in Paris (1907–09), and with Klinger (violin) and Schatzenhalz (composition) at the Berlin Royal Academy (1909–13). His career was centered in Bucharest, where he was a violinist in the Phil. (1905–07; 1918–20) and 1st violinist in a string quartet (1914–33). From 1916 to 1947 he taught at the Cons. He also was a conductor with the Municipal Orch. (1929–32) and the Radio Sym. Orch. (1933–38).

WORKS: DRAMATIC: *Iris*, drama (1926; Moravska Ostrava, Nov. 13, 1931); *La drumul mare* (In the Highway), opera (1931; Cluj-Napoca, Oct. 3, 1934); *Cu dragostea nu se glumeşte* (Love is Not a Joke), comic opera (1940; Bucharest, Feb. 8, 1941); *Ovidiu* (Ovid), opera (1941–43; unfinished; completed by W. Berger); *Se face ziuă* (At Dawn), opera (1943); ballets.

Nouguès, Jean, French composer; b. Bordeaux, April 25, 1875; d. Auteuil, Aug. 28, 1932. He showed remarkable precocity as a composer, having completed an opera, *Le Roi du Papagey*, before he was 16. After regular study in Paris, he premiered his opera *Yannha* at Bordeaux in 1897. The next 2 operas, *Thamyris* (Bordeaux, 1904) and *La Mort de Tintagiles* (Paris, 1905), were brought out without much success; but after the production of his spectacular *Quo Vadis?* (libretto by H. Cain, after Sienkiewicz's famous novel; Nice, Feb. 9, 1909), he suddenly found himself famous. The work was given in Paris on Nov. 26, 1909, and in New York on April 4, 1911; it had numerous revivals in subsequent years. His later operas, not nearly so successful, included *L'Auberge rouge* (Nice, Feb. 21, 1910), *La Vendetta* (Marseilles, 1911), *L'Aiglon* (Rouen, Feb. 2, 1912), and *Le Scarabée bleu* (1931).

Nourrit, Adolphe, celebrated French tenor, son of **Louis Nourrit**; b. Montpellier, March 3, 1802; d. (suicide) Naples, March 8, 1839. He studied voice with the elder Manuel García. At the age of 19, he made his debut as Pylaides in Gluck's *Iphigénie en Tauride* at the Paris Opéra (Sept. 10, 1821), with excellent success. He soon became known in Paris as one of the finest tenors of his generation, and famous opera composers entrusted him with leading roles at the premieres of their works; thus, he appeared in the title role of Meyerbeer's *Robert le diable* (Paris, Nov. 21, 1831) and as Raoul in *Les Huguenots* (Paris, Feb. 29, 1836), in the title role in Rossini's *Le Comte Ory* (Paris, Aug. 20, 1828) and as Arnold in his *Guillaume Tell* (Paris, Aug. 3, 1829), as Masaniello in Auber's *La Muette de Portici* (Paris, Feb. 29, 1828), as Eléazar in Halévy's *La Juive* (Paris, Feb. 23, 1835), and others. He then traveled in Italy in Dec. 1837, and was particularly successful in Naples. His career seemed to be assured, but despite all these successes, vocal problems and a liver ailment led to depression, and he killed himself by jumping from the roof of his lodging in Naples.

BIBL.: M. Quicherat, *A. N.: Sa vie* (3 vols., Paris, 1867); E. Boutet de Monvel, *Un Artiste d'autrefois, A. N.* (2 vols., Paris, 1903); H. Pleasants, ed. and annotator, *The Great Tenor Tragedy: The Last Days of A. N. as Told (Mostly) by Himself* (Portland, Oreg., 1995).

Nourrit, Louis, French tenor, father of **Adolphe Nourrit**; b. Montpellier, Aug. 4, 1780; d. Brunoy, Sept. 23, 1831. He was a pupil of Garat at the Paris Cons. On March 3, 1805, he made his debut at the Paris Opéra as Renaud in Gluck's *Armide*. He sang there regularly thereafter, serving later as its principal tenor from 1812 until his retirement in 1826.

Novák, Jan, Czech composer; b. Nová Říše na Morave, April 8, 1921; d. Ulm, Germany, Nov. 17, 1984. He studied composition with Petrželka at the Brno Cons. (1940–46; interrupted by the Nazi occupation) and Bořkovec at the Prague Academy of Musical Arts (1946–47), then with Copland at the Berkshire Music Center at Tanglewood (summer 1947) and Martinů in New York (1947–48). He subsequently made his home in Brno; being outside his homeland at the time of the Soviet invasion (1968), he chose not to return, and went to Denmark before settling in Rovereto, Italy (1970), where he taught piano at the municipal music school. Predictably, his works ceased to be performed in his native land until the Communist regime collapsed in 1989. His early music is influenced by Martinů; with the Concertino for Wind Quintet (1957) and the *Capriccio* for Cello and Orch. (1958), he adopted jazz elements; beginning in 1958 he applied dodecaphonic techniques, and after 1960 his interest in all things Latin and vocal almost completely dominates his output.

WORKS: DRAMATIC: *Svatební Košile* (The Specter's Bride), ballet ballad (1954; Plzeň, 1955); *Komedie o umučenie a slavném vzkříšení Pána a spasitele našeho Ježíše Krista* (Play of the Passion and Glorious Resurrection of the Lord Our Savior Jesus Christ; Brno, 1965); *Dulcitius*, lyric drama (1977); *Aesopia*, fable cantata with introit and exit (1981; version for 2 Pianos and Orch. as *Aesopia minora*).

Novák, Johann Baptist (Janez Krstnik), Slovenian composer; b. Ljubljana, c. 1756; d. there, Jan. 29, 1833. He served as a government clerk and at the same time studied music. In 1799–1800 he was conductor, and from 1808 to 1829, music director, of the Phil. Soc. in Ljubljana; he also gave concerts as a singer and violinist. A close contemporary of Mozart, he composed in a Mozartean manner. His historical importance lies in his incidental music to T. Linhart's play *Ta veseli dan, ali Matiček se ženi* (A Happy Day, or Matiček Is Getting Married; 1790), which is based on

Beaumarchais's comedy that served for Mozart's great opera *Le nozze di Figaro*. Novák later renamed his work *Figaro*. His music forms a striking parallel to Mozart's procedures and yet contains some original traits.

Novák, Vítězslav (Augustín Rudolf), eminent Czech composer and pedagogue; b. Kamenitz, Dec. 5, 1870; d. Skuteč, July 18, 1949. He studied in Jindřichův Hradec with Vilím Pojman; he subsequently won a scholarship to study law at the Univ. of Prague, but concentrated his studies on music at the Prague Cons., where he received instruction in piano from Jiránek, harmony from Knittl, and counterpoint from Strecker; he later attended Dvořák's master class there. After graduating in 1892, he continued to study piano until 1896 and also remained a student of philosophy at the Univ. until 1895. He then taught privately and was active as a folk-song collector; through such orch. works as *V tatrách* (In the Tatra Mountains; 1902), *Slovácká svita* (Slovak Suite; 1903), and *O věčne touzé* (Eternal Longing; 1903–05), the cantata *Bouře* (The Storm; 1910), and the piano tone poem *Pan* (1910), he acquired a notable reputation as a composer; he devoted himself to teaching, serving as a prof. at the Prague Cons. (1909–39). His importance as a composer was enhanced in later years by such works as the *Podzimni symfonie* (Autumn Sym.; 1931–34) and *Jihočeská svita* (South Bohemian Suite) for Orch. (1936–37). He was honored with the title of National Artist of the Czech Republic in 1945. The first vol. of his unfinished autobiography, *O sobě a jiných*, was publ. in Prague in 1946. Novák's earliest works followed the general line of German Romanticism; Brahms was so impressed with them that he recommended Novák to his own publisher, Simrock. Novák's interest in folk music made a substantial impact on his music, although he rarely incorporated original folk material in his compositions. His late works espoused patriotic themes.

WORKS (all 1st perf. in Prague unless otherwise given): DRAMATIC: *Zvikovský rarášek* (The Imp of Zvikov), comic opera (1913–14; Oct. 10, 1915); *Karlštejn*, opera (1914–15; Nov. 18, 1916); *Lucerna* (The Lantern), musical fairy tale (1919–22; May 13, 1923); *Dědův odkaz* (Old Man's Bequest; 1922–25; Brno, Jan. 16, 1926); 2 ballet pantomimes: *Signorina Gioventu* (1926–28; Feb. 10, 1929) and *Nikotina* (Feb. 10, 1929); incidental music to F. Rachlik's *Žižka* (1948).

BIBL.: Z. Nejedlý, *V. N.: Studie a kritiky* (Prague, 1921); A. Srba, ed., *V. N.: Studie a vzpominky* (Prague, 1932; supplements, 1935, 1940); A. Hába, *V. N.: K 70. narozeninám* (Prague, 1940); V. Štěpán, *N. a Suk* (Prague, 1945); K. Hoffmeister, *Tvorba V. a N. a z let 1941–1948* (Prague, 1949); V. Lébl, *V. N.: Zivot a dilo* (Prague, 1964); idem, *V. N.* (Prague, 1968; in Eng.); K. Padrta and B. Štědroň, eds., *Národni umelec V. N., Studie a vzpominsky k 100. vyroci narozeni* (Studies and Reminiscences on the 100th Anniversary of V. N.'s Birth; České Budějovice, 1972).

Novello, Clara (Anastasia), outstanding English soprano; b. London, June 10, 1818; d. Rome, March 12, 1908. Her father was the English organist, conductor, editor, music publisher, and composer Vincent Novello (1781–1861), and her brother the prominent English music publisher (Joseph) Alfred Novello (1810–1896). Having studied piano and singing in London, she entered the Paris Institution de Musique Religieuse in 1829, but returned home the following year because of the revolution. She won the approbation of Rossini, and became his friend for life. After a successful concert debut on Oct. 22, 1832, at Windsor, she was engaged for the Phil. Society, the Antient Concerts, and the principal festivals. In 1837 Mendelssohn engaged her for the Gewandhaus concerts in Leipzig. Following additional studies in Milan (1839), she made her operatic debut as Rossini's Semiramide in Bologna (1841); she sang with great success in the principal Italian cities. On Nov. 22, 1843, she married Count Gigliucci, withdrawing to private life for several years; she reappeared in 1850, singing in concert and opera (chiefly in England and Italy). After her farewell appearance in London in 1860, she retired to Rome. Schumann greatly admired her, and coined the term Novelette for some of his pieces as an affectionate homage to her.

BIBL.: V. Gigliucci, *C. N.'s Reminiscences, compiled by her daughter* (London, 1910; with memoir by A. Coleridge); A. Mackenzie-Grieve, *C. N., 1818–1908* (London, 1955).

Novello-Davies (real name, **Davies**), **Clara,** Welsh singer, choral conductor, and composer; b. Cardiff, April 7, 1861; d. London, March 1, 1943. Her father (who was also her first teacher) called her "Clara Novello" after the celebrated singer of that name, and she adopted the combined name professionally. She sang at concerts; in 1881 she turned to choral conducting; she organized a Royal Welsh Ladies' Choir, with which she traveled with fine success in Great Britain, France, America, and South Africa; at the World's Fair in Chicago (1893) and at the Paris Exposition (1900) the chorus was awarded 1st prize. She was commended by Queen Victoria (1894) and by King George V and Queen Mary (1928). She publ. a number of successful songs ("A Voice from the Spirit Land," "The Vigil," and "Comfort"); authored *You Can Sing* and an autobiography, *The Life I Have Loved* (London, 1940). Her son, Ivor Novello (real name, David Ivor Davies) (b. Cardiff, Jan. 15, 1893; d. London, March 6, 1951), was a composer, playwright, and actor; at his mother's request, he wrote the popular World War I song "Till the Boys Come Home (Keep the Home Fires Burning"; 1914); he wrote musical comedies and revues, and was also active as an actor; after working as a playwright, he resumed composing for the stage; his most successful musical was *The Dancing Years* (London, March 23, 1939).

BIBL.: S. Wilson, *I.* (London, 1975).

Novotná, Jarmila, Czech soprano; b. Prague, Sept. 23, 1907; d. N.Y., Feb. 9, 1994. She studied with Destinn in Prague and made her operatic debut as Mařenka in *The Bartered Bride* there (1925), then continued her studies in Milan. She sang in Berlin (from 1928) and was a member of the Vienna State Opera (1933–38), where she gained distinction as Octavian; she also created the title role in Lehar's Giuditta (1934). She made her American debut at San Francisco as Madama Butterfly (Oct. 18, 1939); she first sang at the Metropolitan Opera in New York as Mimi in *La Bohème* on Jan. 5, 1940; she remained on its roster until 1951 and was there again from 1952 to 1956; she also appeared in films and on Broadway. Her other fine roles included Pamina, Donna Elvira, Violetta, Mélisande, and various roles in Czech operas. She was the author of *Byla jsem stastná* (Prague, 1991).

Nowowiejski, Felix, Polish organist, conductor, and composer; b. Wartenburg, Feb. 7, 1877; d. Poznan, Jan. 18, 1946. He studied in Berlin with Bussler at the Stern Cons., with Bruch at the Königliche Musikakademie, and with Friedlaender, Ballermann, and Dessoir at the Univ.; he also received some instruction from Dvořák in Prague and won the Paderewski Prize in 1903. He was director of the Kraków Music Soc. (1909–14) and a prof. at the Poznan Cons. (1920–27). A competent composer, he followed the line of German Romanticism. His works include the operas *Emigranci* (The Emigrants; 1917) and *Legenda Baltyku* (Baltic Legend; Poznan, 1924) and several ballets.

BIBL.: J. Boehm, *F. N.* (Olsztyn, 1968).

Nozzari, Andrea, Italian tenor; b. Vertrova, near Bergamo, 1775; d. Naples, Dec. 12, 1832. He studied with Petrobelli in Bergamo, making his operatic debut in 1794. He then made appearances in Rome, Milan, and Paris; he was a principal tenor in Naples (1811–25), where he created tenor roles in several operas of Rossini. He then retired and taught singing.

Nucci, Leo, prominent Italian baritone; b. Castiglione dei Pepuli, near Bologna, April 16, 1942. He studied with Giuseppe Marchesi and Ottaviano Bizzarri. He made his operatic debut as Rossini's Figaro in Spoleto (1967). After singing in the chorus of Milan's La Scala (1969–75), he attracted attention with his portrayal of Schaunard in *La Bohème* at Venice's Teatro La Fenice (1975); he then was engaged as a member of La Scala, where he appeared as Rossini's Figaro, Rodrigo in *Don Carlos*, Miller in *Luisa Miller*, Marcello, and Sharpless. In 1978 he made his first appearance at the Vienna State Opera and at London's Covent Garden; he made his Metropolitan Opera debut in New York as Renato in *Un ballo* *in maschera* on Feb. 22, 1980. He first sang at the Paris Opera and the Chicago Lyric Opera in 1981. In 1985 he appeared as Rigoletto in Wiesbaden. In 1991 he sang Iago in concert performances of *Otello* in Chicago and New York. He was engaged as Dulcamara in Turin in 1994, and in 1996 as Rossini's Figaro in Verona. He also sang in San Francisco, Berlin, Rome, Hamburg, and Geneva.

Nyman, Michael (Laurence), notable English composer; b. London, March 23, 1944. He studied with Alan Bush at the Royal Academy of Music in London (1961–65) and with Thurston Dart at King's College, London (B.Mus., 1967). From 1968 to 1978 he was active as a music critic for *The Spectator, The New Statesman*, and *The Listener*. In 1977 he founded his own Michael Nyman Band. He publ. the important study *Experimental Music: Cage and Beyond* (1974; 2d ed., 1995). Nyman became particularly well known for his many fine film scores, which included *Drowning by Numbers* (1988), *The Cook, the Thief, His Wife and Her Lover* (1989), *Monsieur Hire* (1989), *The Hairdresser's Husband* (1990), *Prospero's Books* (1991), *The Piano* (1992), *Carrington* (1994), *The Diary of Anne Frank* (1995), and *The Ogre* (1996). In his output, he attempts to bridge the chasm between art music and popular music.

WORKS: DRAMATIC: OPERAS: *The Kiss* (Channel 4 TV, London, Oct. 13, 1984); *The Man Who Mistook his Wife for a Hat*, after Oliver Sacks (London, Oct. 27, 1986); *Vital Statistics* (London, June 3, 1987); *Orpheus' Daughter* (Rotterdam, Dec. 13, 1988); *La princese de Milan* (Avignon, July 24, 1991); *Letters, Riddles, and Writs* (BBC TV, Nov. 10, 1991).

Nystedt, Knut, esteemed Norwegian choral conductor, organist, pedagogue, and composer; b. Christiania, Sept. 3, 1915. He studied organ with Sandvold, conducting with Fjeldstad, and composition with Per Steenberg and Brustad at the Oslo Cons. (1931–43), then pursued training with Ernest White (organ) and Copland (composition) in New York (1947). From 1946 to 1982 he was organist at Oslo's Torshov Church; he also was a prof. of choral conducting at the Oslo Cons. (1964–85). In 1950 he founded Det Norske Solistokor (the Norwegian Soloist Choir), which he conducted for the first time in Oslo on May 23, 1951; in subsequent years he developed it into one of the finest choral groups in the world, conducting it in a comprehensive literature with a special regard for contemporary scores. In 1960 he conducted it for the first time in the United States; he later led it on tours of Japan, Korea, Hong Kong, and Thailand (1978), China (1982), and Israel (1984, 1988). On March 18, 1990, he conducted his farewell concert as its conductor in Oslo. In 1966 he was made a Knight of the Order of St. Olav; in 1978 he was awarded the Spellemannsprisen; in 1980 he received the music prize of the Norwegian Council for Cultural Affairs. He is an outstanding composer of choral music, including *Nådevegen*, oratorio for Soli, Chorus, and Orch. (1943–46); his orch. works have also won approbation both at home and abroad. He also composed *Med krone og stjerne* (With Crown and Star), Christmas opera (1971), and *Salomos hoysang* (The Song of Songs), church opera (1989).

Nystroem, Gösta, Swedish composer; b. Silvberg, Oct. 13, 1890; d. Särö, near Göteborg, Aug. 9, 1966. He studied piano, harmony, and composition with his father, then piano and harmony with Lundberg and Bergenson in Stockholm; he took courses at the Cons. there (1913–14), and also studied composition with Hallén; after further training in Copenhagen and Germany, he went to Paris (1920) and studied composition and instrumentation with d'Indy and Sabaneyev and conducting with Chevillard and subsequently wrote music criticism in Göteborg (1932–47). After following neo-Baroque practices, he developed an independent mode of composition. Among his works are *De Blinda* (The Blind), radio drama (1949), *Ungersvennen och de sex prinsessorna* (The Young Lad and the 6 Princesses), ballet (1951), and *Herr Arnes penningar* (Sir Arne's Hoard), opera (Swedish Radio, Nov. 26, 1959); also incidental music.

O

Oberlin, Russell (Keys), American countertenor; b. Akron, Ohio, Oct. 11, 1928. He studied at the Juilliard School of Music in New York, graduating in 1951. In 1952 he joined the N.Y. Pro Musica Antiqua, appearing as a soloist in works from the medieval and Renaissance periods; in 1960 he sang the role of Oberon in Britten's *A Midsummer Night's Dream* at Covent Garden, London. In 1966 he joined the faculty at Hunter College in New York.

Oboussier, Robert, Swiss composer; b. Antwerp (of Swiss parents), July 9, 1900; d. (stabbed to death by his roommate) Zürich, June 9, 1957. He studied at the Zürich Cons. with Andreae and Jarnach (composition), then with Ochs (conducting) at the Berlin Hochschule für Musik. He then lived in Florence (1922–28); he was music ed. of the *Deutsche Allgemeine Zeitung*, but in 1939 political conditions in Germany impelled him to leave for Switzerland; in 1942 he became director of the Central Archive of Swiss Music, and in 1948 of Suisa (the Swiss assn. of writers, composers, and publishers). Of cosmopolitan background, Oboussier combined in his music the elements of both Germanic and Latin cultures. Among his compositions was the opera *Amphitryon* (1948–50; Berlin, March 13, 1951). He publ. *Der Sänger* (with others; Berlin, 1934; 2d ed., rev., 1959) and *Die Sinfonien Beethovens* (Berlin, 1937); also a collection of critical reviews, *Berliner Musik-Chronik 1930–38* (1969).

Obraztsova, Elena (Vasilievna), outstanding Russian mezzo-soprano; b. Leningrad, July 7, 1937. Her father was an engineer who played the violin. She studied at the Leningrad Cons., graduating in 1964. She made her operatic debut as Marina in *Boris Godunov* at Moscow's Bolshoi Theater (1963). In 1970 she won 1st prize at the Tchaikovsky Competition in Moscow. She made her first tour of the United States with the Bolshoi troupe in June-July 1975; on Oct. 12, 1976, she made her Metropolitan Opera debut in New York as Amneris in Verdi's *Aida*. She appeared in recital in New York in 1987, and was also invited to sing again at the Metropolitan Opera after an absence of some 10 years. In 1973 she was named a National Artist of the R.S.F.S.R. and in 1976 she was awarded the Lenin prize. She possessed a remarkably even tessitura, brilliant in all registers; her roles included virtually the entire Russian operatic repertoire, and such standard roles as Norma, Carmen, Eboli, and Delilah.

Obukhova, Nadezhda (Andreievna), Russian mezzo-soprano; b. Moscow, March 6, 1886; d. Feodosiya, Aug. 14, 1961. She studied with Masetti at the Moscow Cons., graduating in 1912. She made her operatic debut at the Bolshoi Theater there in 1916 as Pauline in *The Queen of Spades*; she remained on its roster until 1948. In addition to the Russian repertoire, she was noted for her portrayals of Carmen, Delilah, Amneris, and Fricka. She was greatly esteemed in Russia; in 1943 she was awarded the State Prize of the USSR.

BIBL.: E. Grosheva, *N. O.* (Moscow, 1953).

Očenáš, Andrej, Slovak composer; b. Selce, near Banská Bystrica, Jan. 8, 1911. He studied composition with Alexander Moyzes at the Bratislava Academy of Music, graduating in 1937, then took a course with Novák at the Prague Cons., graduating in 1939. He worked at the Czech Radio in Bratislava (1939–50) and was music deputy to the regional director of broadcasting there (1956–62); he taught at the Bratislava Cons. (1943–73), serving as director from 1950 to 1954. His music is imbued with a Slovak ethos.

WORKS: DRAMATIC: *At the Brigand's Ball* (1941); *Year in a Village*, musical play (Bratislava, Dec. 11, 1948); *Highlander's Songs*, ballet (1954–56); *The Romance of the Rose*, stage sym. for Narrator, Soloists, Chorus, and Orch. (1969–71).

Ochman, Wieslaw, Polish tenor; b. Warsaw, Feb. 6, 1937. He studied in Kraków, Bytom, and Warsaw. He made his operatic debut as Edgardo in *Lucia di Lammermoor* in Bytom (1959), appearing there regularly until 1963; he then sang in Kraków and Warsaw. He subsequently made debuts at Berlin's Deutsche Oper (1966), the Hamburg State Opera (1967), the Chicago Lyric Opera (1972), the San Francisco Opera (1972), the Paris Opéra (1974), and the Vienna State Opera (1975); he made his Metropolitan Opera debut in New York as Arrigo in *Les Vêpres siciliennes* (March 12, 1975). In 1982 he returned to the Metropolitan Opera as Grigori in *Boris Godunov*. He sang Idomeneo in San Francisco in 1989. In 1996 he portrayed Grigori at the Berlin State Opera. Among his best known roles were those in Mozart's operas as well as Count Almaviva, Ernesto, the Duke of Mantua, and Cavaradossi.

Ochs, Siegfried, German choral conductor and composer; b. Frankfurt am Main, April 19, 1858; d. Berlin, Feb. 5, 1929. He entered the Berlin Hochschule für Musik (1877), where his mentors were F. Kiel (theory), Joachim (ensemble playing), and Adolf Schulze (choral singing); later he continued private studies with Kiel and Barth, and also attended the Univ. In 1882 he organized in Berlin a choral union under his own name, working in close collaboration with the Berlin Phil.; it was known as the Phil. Choir from the 1887–88 season until being merged with the chorus of the Berlin Hochschule fur Musik (1920), where Ochs served as director of the oratorio dept. He publ. *Der deutsche Gesangverein* (4 vols., Berlin, 1923–28) and *Über die Art, Musik zu Hören* (Berlin, 1926), as well as an autobiography, *Geschehenes, Gesehenes* (Leipzig, 1922). Among his works were a comic opera, *Im Namen des Gesetzes* (Hamburg, Nov. 3, 1888), and 2 operettas.

BIBL.: K. Singer, *S. O.: Der Bergrunder des Philharmonischen Chors* (Berlin, 1933).

O'Connell, Charles, American conductor and recording executive; b. Chicopee, Mass., April 22, 1900; d. N.Y., Sept. 1, 1962. He studied at the Catholic School and College of the Holy Cross (B.A., 1922) and also had instruction in organ from Widor in Paris. From 1930 to 1944 he was head of the artist and repertoire dept. of the RCA Victor Red Seal label, then music director of Columbia Masterworks (1944–47). His publs. included *The Victor Book of the Opera* (1937).

Odak, Krsto, Croatian composer and teacher; b. Siverić, Dalmatia, March 20, 1888; d. Zagreb, Nov. 4, 1965. He studied composition with P. Hartmann in Munich (1912–13) and with Novák in his master class at the Prague Cons. (1919–22). Upon his return to Yugoslavia, he was prof. of composition at the Zagreb Academy of Music, retiring in 1961. Among his works were *Dorica pleše*, opera (Dorica Dances; Zagreb, April 16, 1934), *Majka Margarita* (Mother Margaret), radio opera (Zagreb, March 25, 1955), incidental music, and film scores.

Oddone Sulli-Rao, Elisabetta, Italian composer; b. Milan, Aug. 13, 1878; d. there, March 3, 1972. She studied at the Milan Cons. She composed a one-act opera, *A gara colle rondini* (Milan, 1920), and a children's opera, *Petruccio e il cavallo cappuccio* (Milan, 1916) and also several oratorios. She did some valuable work on dissemination of Italian folk songs and publ. *Canzoniere popolare italiano, Canzoncine per bimbi, Cantilene popolari dei bimbi d'Italia*, etc.

O'Dwyer, Robert, English-Irish composer and conductor; b. Bristol, Jan. 27, 1862; d. Dublin, Jan. 6, 1949. He was a conductor of the Carl Rosa Opera Co. in London and on tour (1891), then with the Arthur Rousbey Opera Co. in England and Ireland (1892–99); in 1899 he became music director at the Univ. of Ireland in Dublin; from 1914 to 1939 he was prof. of music there. He was music director (from 1901) of the Gaelic League choir, for which he arranged many Irish songs. He wrote one of the earliest operas with a Gaelic text, *Eithne* (Dublin, May 16, 1910). He left a book in MS, *Irish Music and Its Traditions*.

Oelze, Christiane, German soprano; b. Cologne, Oct. 9, 1963. She studied in Cologne and received vocal instruction from Schwarzkopf. After winning the Hugo Wolf Competition in 1987, she appeared as a concert artist. In 1990 she made her operatic debut in Ottawa as Despina. She sang Constanze in Salzburg and Anne Trulove at the Glyndebourne Festival in 1991, and in 1993 she appeared in London. In 1994 she made her U.S. debut with the Atlanta Sym. Orch. She sang Zerlina at London's Covent Garden in 1996, and in 1997 she returned to Salzburg as Mitridate. She has pursued a highly successful career as a soloist with the world's major orchs. and as a lieder artist. Among her other operatic roles are Pamina, Marzelline, Zdenka in *Arabella*, and Regina in *Mathis der Maler*.

Oestvig, Karl (Aagaard), Norwegian tenor; b. Christiania, May 17, 1889; d. there (Oslo), July 21, 1968. He studied in Cologne. He made his operatic debut at the Stuttgart Opera in 1914; he remained on its roster until 1919; he was then a member of the Vienna State Opera (1919–27), where he created the role of the Emperor in Strauss's *Die Frau ohne Schatten* in 1919; he also sang at the Berlin State Opera (until 1926) and the Städtische Oper (1927–30), and made concert tours of Europe and North America. He retired from the stage in 1932 and devoted himself to teaching; accepted the post of director of the Oslo Opera (1941) during the Nazi occupation of Norway, an action that brought him disgrace after the liberation. He was married to the soprano Maria Rajdl. Among his finest roles were Walther von Stolzing, Lohengrin, and Parsifal.

Offenbach, Jacques (Jacob), famous French composer of German descent; b. Cologne, June 20, 1819; d. Paris, Oct. 5, 1880. He was the son of a Jewish cantor, whose original surname was Eberst; Offenbach was the town where his father lived. He studied violin before taking up the cello when he was 9. After training with Joseph Alexander and Bernhard Breuer in Cologne, he settled in Paris (1833). Following cello studies with Vaslin at the Cons. (1833–34), he played in the orch. of the Opéra Comique; he also received further instruction from Louis Norblin and Halévy. He then pursued a career as a soloist and chamber music artist (from 1838) and subsequently was a conductor at the Théâtre-Français (1850–55). His *Chanson de Fortunio* for Musset's *Chandelier* (1850) proved tremendously popular. In 1855 he ventured to open his own theater, the Bouffes-Parisiens, at the Salle Marigny; late that year it moved to the Salle Choiseul, where he scored his first great success with the operetta *Orphée aux enfers* (Oct. 21, 1858). His *La Belle Hélène* (Variétés, Dec. 17, 1864) proved to be one of his most celebrated works, soon taken up by theatrical enterprises all over the world. Having abandoned the management of the Bouffes-Parisiens in 1866, he nevertheless continued to write for the stage. His *La Vie parisienne* (Palais Royal, Oct. 31, 1866), *La Grande-Duchesse de Gérolstein* (Variétés, April 12, 1867), and *La Périchole* (Variétés, Oct. 6, 1868) were notably successful. In 1873 he took over the management of the Théâtre de la Gaîté, where he brought out his rev. version of *Orphée aux enfers* as an opéra féerique (Feb. 7, 1874). In 1876 he undertook a tour of the United States, describing his impressions in *Notes d'un musicien en voyage* (Paris, 1877) and *Offenbach en Amérique* (Paris, 1877; Eng. tr., 1877, as *Offenbach in America*; republ. as *Orpheus in America*, Bloomington, Ind., 1957). His only grand opera, the masterpiece *Les Contes d'Hoffmann*, remained unfinished at his death; recitatives were added by E. Guiraud with the famous barcarolle from Offenbach's *Die Rheinnixen* (1864), in which the tune was used for a ghost song; the completed score was premiered at the Opéra Comique in Paris (Feb. 10, 1881) with instantaneous success, and subsequently was performed on both sides of the Atlantic. Offenbach was a master of the operetta; his music is characterized by an abundance of flowing, rollicking melodies, seasoned with ironic humor, suitable to the extravagant burlesque of the situations. His irreverent treatment of mythological characters gave Paris society a salutary shock; his art mirrored the atmosphere of precarious gaiety during the 2d Empire.

WORKS: DRAMATIC (all 1st perf. in Paris unless otherwise given): *L'Alcôve* (April 24, 1847); *Le Trésor à Mathurin* (May 1853; rev. as *Le Mariage aux lanternes*, Oct. 10, 1857); *Pépito* (Oct. 28, 1853); *Luc et Lucette* (May 2, 1854); *Oyayaie, ou La Reine des îles* (June 26, 1855); *Entrez, messieurs, mesdames* (July 5, 1855); *Les Deux Aveugles* (July 5, 1855); *Une Nuit blanche* (July 5, 1855); *Le Rêve d'une nuit d'été* (July 30, 1855); *Le Violoneux* (Aug. 31, 1855); *Madame Papillon* (Oct. 3, 1855); *Paimpol et Périnette* (Oct. 29, 1855); *Ba-ta-clan* (Dec. 29, 1855); *Élodie, ou Le Forfait nocturne* (Jan. 19, 1856); *Le Postillon en gage* (Feb. 9, 1856); *Trombalcazar, ou Les Criminels dramatiques* (April 3, 1856); *La Rose de Saint-Flour* (June 12, 1856); *Les Dragées du baptême* (June 18, 1856); *Le "66"* (July 31, 1856); *Le Savetier et le financier* (Sept. 23, 1856); *La Bonne d'enfants* (Oct. 14, 1856); *Les Trois Baisers du diable* (Jan. 15, 1857); *Croquefer, ou Le Dernier des paladins* (Feb. 12, 1857); *Dragonette* (April 30, 1857); *Vent du soir, ou L'Horrible Festin* (May 16, 1857); *Une Demoiselle en lôterie* (July 27, 1857); *Les Deux Pêcheurs* (Nov. 13, 1857); *Mesdames de la Halle* (March 3, 1858); *La Chatte métamorphosée en femme* (April 19, 1858); *Orphée aux enfers* (Oct. 21, 1858; rev. version, Feb. 7, 1874); *Un Mari à la porte* (June 22, 1859); *Les Vivandières de la grande armée* (July 6, 1859); *Geneviève de Brabant* (Nov. 19, 1859; rev. version, Dec. 26, 1867; 2d rev. version, Feb. 25, 1875); *Le Carnaval des revues* (Feb. 10, 1860); *Daphnis et Chloé* (March 27, 1860); *Barkouf* (Dec. 24, 1860); *La Chanson de Fortunio* (Jan. 5, 1861); *Le Pont des soupirs* (March 23, 1861; rev. version, May 8, 1868); *M. Choufleuri restera chez lui le . . .* (May 31, 1861); *Apothicaire et perruquier* (Oct. 17, 1861); *Le Roman comique* (Dec. 10, 1861); *Monsieur et Madame Denis* (Jan. 11, 1862); *Le Voyage de MM. Dunanan père et fils* (March 23, 1862); *Les Bavards or Bavard et bavarde* (Bad Ems, June 11, 1862); *Jacqueline* (Oct. 14, 1862); *Il Signor Fagotto* (Bad Ems, July 11, 1863); *Lischen et Fritzchen* (Bad Ems, July 21, 1863); *L'Amour chanteur* (Jan. 5, 1864); *Die Rheinnixen* (Vienna, Feb. 4, 1864); *Les Géorgiennes* (March 16, 1864); *Jeanne qui pleure et Jean qui rit* (Bad Ems, July 1864); *Le Fifre enchanté, ou Le Soldat magicien* (Bad Ems, July 9, 1864); *La Belle Hélène* (Dec. 17, 1864); *Coscoletto, ou Le Lazzarone* (Bad Ems, July 24, 1865); *Les Refrains des bouffes* (Sept. 21, 1865); *Les Bergers* (Dec. 11, 1865); *Barbe-bleue* (Feb. 5, 1866); *La Vie parisienne* (Oct. 31, 1866); *La Grande-Duchesse de Gérolstein* (April 12, 1867); *La Permission de dix heures* (Bad Ems, July 9, 1867); *La Leçon de chant* (Bad Ems, Aug. 1867); *Robinson Crusoé* (Nov. 23, 1867); *Le Chateau à Toto* (May 6, 1868); *L'Île de Tulipatan* (Sept. 30, 1868); *La Périchole* (Oct. 6, 1868; rev. version, April 25, 1874); *Vert-vert* (March 10, 1869); *La Diva* (March 22, 1869); *La Princesse de Trébizonde* (Baden-Baden, July 31, 1869; rev. version, Paris, Dec. 7, 1869); *Les Brigands* (Dec. 10, 1869); *La Romance de la rose* (Dec. 11, 1869); *Mam'zelle Moucheron* (c.1870; rev. version by Delibes, May 10, 1881); *Boule de neige* (Dec. 14, 1871; rev. version of *Barkouf*); *Le Roi Carotte* (Jan. 15, 1872); *Fantasio* (Jan. 18, 1872); *Fleurette, oder Näherin und Trompeter* (Vienna, March 8, 1872); *Der schwarze Korsar* (Vienna, Sept. 21, 1872); *Les Braconniers* (Jan. 29, 1873); *Pomme d'api* (Sept. 4, 1873); *La Jolie Parfumeuse* (Nov. 29, 1873); *Bagatelle* (May 21, 1874); *Madame l'archiduc* (Oct. 31, 1874); *Whittington* (London, Dec. 26, 1874); *Les Hannetons* (April 22, 1875); *La Boulangère à des écus* (Oct. 19, 1875); *Le Créole* (Nov. 3, 1875); *Le Voyage dans la lune* (Nov. 26, 1875); *Tarte à la crème* (Dec. 14, 1875); *Pierrette et Jacquot* (Oct. 13, 1876); *La Boîte au lait* (Nov. 3, 1876); *Le Docteur Ox* (Jan. 26, 1877); *La Foire Saint-Laurent* (Feb. 10, 1877); *Maître Péronilla* (March 13, 1878); *Madame Favart* (Dec. 28, 1878); *La Marocaine* (Jan. 13, 1879); *La Fille du tambour-major* (Dec. 13, 1879); *Belle Lurette* (Oct. 30, 1880; completed by Delibes); *Les Contes d'Hoffmann* (Feb. 10, 1881; completed by Guiraud). VAUDEVILLES AND INCIDENTAL MUSIC: *Pascal et Chambord* (March 2, 1839); *Le Brésilien* (May 9, 1863); *Le Gascon* (Sept. 2, 1873); *La Haine* (Dec. 3, 1874). BALLETS: *Arlequin barbier* (July 5, 1855); *Pierrot clown* (July 30, 1855); *Polichinelle dans le monde* (Sept. 19, 1855); *Les Bergers de Watteau* (June 24, 1856); *Le Papillon* (Nov. 26, 1860); much other dance music.

BIBL.: E. de Mirecourt, *Les Contemporains: Auber, O.* (Paris, 1869); Argus, *Célébrites dramatiques: J. O.* (Paris, 1872); A. Martinet, *O.: Sa vie et son oeuvre* (Paris, 1887); P. Bekker, *J. O.* (Berlin, 1909); R. Northcott, *J. O.: A Sketch of His Life and a Record of His Operas* (London, 1917); E. Rieger, *O. und seine Wiener Schule* (Vienna, 1920); L. Schneider, *O.* (Paris, 1923); R. Brancour, *O.* (Paris, 1929); A. Henseler, *Jakob O.* (Berlin, 1930); S. Kracauer, *J. O. und das Paris seiner Zeit* (Amsterdam, 1937; 2d ed., 1962; Eng. tr., 1937); S. Sitwell, *La Vie Parisienne: A Tribute to O.* (London, 1937); J. Brindejont-Offenbach, *O.: Mon grand-père* (Paris, 1940); A. Decaux, *O.: Roi du Second Empire* (Paris, 1958; 3d ed., 1975); A. Silbermann, *Das imaginäre Tagebuch des Herrn J. O.* (Berlin, 1960); O. Schneidereit, *J. O.* (Leipzig, 1966); P. Jacob, *J. O. in selbtstzeugnissen und Bilddokumenten* (Hamburg, 1969); R. Pourvoyeur, *J. O.: Essay in Toengepaste Muziek- en Toneelsociologie* (Brussels, 1977); A. Faris, *J. O.* (London, 1980); P. Gammond, *O.: His Life and Times* (Tunbridge Wells, 1980; 2d ed., rev., 1986); J. Harding et al., *O., 1819–1880: A Tribute* (London, 1980); R. Pourvoyeur, *O.: Idillio e Parodia* (Turin, 1980); T. Groepper, *Aspekte der O.iade: Untersuchungen zu den Libretti der grossen Operetten O.s* (Frankfurt am Main and N.Y., 1990); C. Dufresne, *J. O., ou, La gaîté parisienne* (Paris, 1992); R. Pourvoyeur, *O.* (Paris, 1994).

Ogden, Will (Wilbur Lee), American composer and teacher; b. Redlands, Calif., April 19, 1921. He studied at the Univ. of Wisc. in Madison (B.M., 1942) and at Hamline Univ. in St. Paul, Minn. (M.A., 1947); after graduate studies at the Univ. of Calif. at Berkeley (1949–50) and at Indiana Univ. in Bloomington (1950–52), he went to Paris on a Fulbright grant and attended the École Normale de Musique (1952–53); returning to the United States, he obtained his Ph.D. in 1955 from Indiana Univ. with the diss. *Series and Structure: An Investigation into the Purpose of the Twelve-Note Row in Selected Works of Schoenberg, Webern, Krenek, and Leibowitz*; his teachers in the United States included Krenek, Sessions, Bukofzer, Apel, and P. Nettl, and in Paris, Leibowitz. He taught at the Univ. of Texas in Austin (1947–50), at St. Catherine College in St. Paul, Minn. (1954–55), and at Illinois Wesleyan Univ. in Bloomington (1956–65); he then became a prof. at the Univ. of Calif. at San Diego (1966), where he served as founder-chairman of its music dept. (1966–71). He retired in 1991. His compositions display an effective utilization of serial procedures. Among his works is the chamber opera *The Awakening of Sappho* (1976–80).

Ogura, Roh, Japanese composer and teacher; b. Kitakyūshu, Jan. 19, 1916; d. Kamakura, Aug. 26, 1990. He studied with Fukai, Sugawara, and Ikenouchi, and then engaged in teaching. His compositions included the opera *Neta* (1957).

Ohana, Maurice, French composer and pianist; b. Casablanca (of Spanish parents), June 12, 1914; d. Paris, Nov. 13, 1992. He studied piano with Frank Marshall in Barcelona and with Lazare Lévy at the Paris Cons. and also had lessons in counterpoint with Daniel-Lesur at the Schola Cantorum in Paris (1937–40). Following service in the British Army during World War II, he completed his training with Casella at Rome's Accademia di Santa Cecilia (1944–46), then settled in Paris. In 1981 he was made a Commandeur des Arts et Lettres. He won the Prix National de Musique (1975) and the Honegger (1982) and Ravel (1985) prizes.

WORKS: DRAMATIC: OPERAS: *Syllabaire pour Phèdre* (1967; Paris, Feb. 5, 1968); *Autodafé* (Lyons, May 23, 1972); *Trois contes de l'Honorable Fleur* (Avignon, July 16, 1978); *La Célestine* (1982–86; Paris, June 13, 1988). RADIOPHONIC SCORES: *Les Hommes et les autres* (1955); *Histoire véridique de Jacotin* (1961); *Hélène* (1963); *Les Héraclides* (1964); *Iphigénie en Tauride* (1965); *Hippolyte* (1965–66); film music. Also *Récit de l'ano zéro*, scenic oratorio (1958–59).

BIBL.: N. Quist, *M. O.* (diss., Univ. of Heidelberg, 1973).

O'Hara, Geoffrey, Canadian-born American composer; b. Chatham, Ontario, Feb. 2, 1882; d. St. Petersburg, Fla., Jan. 31, 1967. He settled in the United States in 1904 and became a naturalized American citizen in 1919. He studied with Homer Norris and J. Vogler, then acted in vaudeville as a pianist, singer, and composer; he wrote the song "Your Eyes Have Told Me" for Caruso. In 1913 he was appointed an instructor in American Indian music as part of a program of the Dept. of the Interior; in 1917 he became an army song leader and was instructor in community singing at Teachers College, Columbia Univ. (1936–37). He wrote the operettas *Peggy and the Pirate* (1927), *Riding Down the Sky* (1928), *The Count and the Co-ed* (1929), and *The Smiling Six-pence* (1930); also about 300 songs, some of which were extremely popular.

Ohms, Elisabeth, Dutch soprano; b. Arnhem, May 17, 1888; d. Marquardstein, Oct. 16, 1974. She studied in Amsterdam, Frankfurt am Main, and Berlin. She made her operatic debut in Mainz in 1921; in 1922 she joined the Bavarian State Opera in Munich, of which she was a principal member until 1936; she also sang at La Scala in Milan (1927–29), Covent Garden in London (1928–29, 1935), and the Bayreuth Festival (1931). On Jan. 17, 1930, she made her debut with the Metropolitan Opera in New York as Brünnhilde; she remained on its roster until 1932. She excelled in Wagner's operas; among her finest roles were Brünnhilde, Kundry, Venus, and Isolde.

Olczewska, Maria (real name, **Marie Berchtenbreitner**), prominent German mezzo-soprano; b. Ludwigsschwaige bei Donauwörth, near Augsburg, Aug. 12, 1892; d. Klagenfurt, Austria, May 17, 1969. She studied with Karl Erler in Munich. She began her career singing in operetta and made her operatic debut in Krefeld (1915), then appeared in Leipzig (1916–20) and Hamburg (1920–23), also in Vienna (1921–23). She was a favorite at London's Covent Garden in Wagnerian roles (1924–32); she also sang in Munich (1923–25) and again in Vienna (1925–30); she likewise appeared in Chicago (1928–32). She made her Metropolitan Opera debut in New York as Brängane on Jan. 16, 1933, remaining on its roster until 1935. From 1947 to 1969 she taught at the Vienna Academy of Music. She had a powerful voice, which made it possible for her to master the Wagner roles, but she was also excellent in dramatic parts, such as Carmen. Furthermore, she had a genuine talent as a stage actress. She was married for a time to **Emil Schipper**.

Oldman, C(ecil) B(ernard), English librarian and bibliographer; b. London, April 2, 1894; d. there, Oct. 7, 1969. He studied at Exeter College, Oxford. In 1920 he received an appointment in the Dept. of Printed Books in the British Museum in London; from 1948 to 1959, was Principal Keeper. In 1952 he was made a Companion of the Order of the Bath and in 1958 a Commander of the Royal Victorian Order. He was an authority on Haydn, Mozart, and Beethoven bibliographical matters; annotated the letters of Constanze Mozart to J. A. André in E. Anderson's *The Letters of Mozart and His Family* (3 vols., London, 1938; 2d ed., rev., 1966 by A. Hyatt King and M. Carolan; 3d ed., rev., 1985 by S. Sadie and F. Smart).

Oldmixon, Mrs. (Georgina née **Sidus)**, English-American soprano; b. Oxford, c.1767; d. Philadelphia, Feb. 3, 1835. She made her debut under the name of Miss George at London's Haymarket Theatre on June 2, 1783. Following contention with Elizabeth Billington, she settled in the United States and became a member of the Wignell and Reinagle enterprise in Philadelphia, where she made her first appearance on May 14, 1793. After a sojourn in New York, she returned to Philadelphia, where she gave her farewell performance in a benefit on Feb. 19, 1814. She subsequently ran her own Female Academy.

Olenin, Alexander, Russian composer, brother of **Marie (Alexeievna) Olénine d'Alheim**; b. Istomino, Riazan district, June 13, 1865; d. Moscow, Feb. 15, 1944. He studied with P. Pabst and with Erdmannsdörfer. He lived most of his life in Moscow. He wrote an opera in a folk style, *Kudeyar* (Moscow, Nov. 26, 1915).

Olénine d'Alheim, Marie (Alexeievna), Russian soprano, sister of **Alexander Olenin**; b. Istomino, Riazan district, Oct. 2, 1869; d. Moscow, Aug. 27, 1970. She studied in Russia and later in Paris, where she made her debut in 1896. Through her brother she met Stasov, Balakirev, and Cui, and became interested in Russian vocal music. In 1893 she married the French writer Pierre d'Alheim (1862–1922), tr. of the text of *Boris Godunov*; together they organized, in Moscow and in Paris, numerous concerts and lectures on Russian music, particularly on Mussorgsky. She was an outstanding interpreter of Russian songs; publ. a book, *Le Legs de Mussorgsky* (Paris, 1908). In 1935 she settled in Paris as a voice teacher; in 1949 she joined the French Communist Party and in 1959 she returned to Russia.

Olitzka, Rosa, German-American contralto and teacher, aunt of **Walter Olitzki**; b. Berlin, Sept. 6, 1873; d. Chicago, Sept. 29, 1949. She studied with Julius Hey in Berlin and with Désirée Artôt in Paris. She sang at Berlin (1891), then was engaged at the Hannover Opera (1892–93), at Covent Garden in London (1894), and in New York with the German Opera Co. (1895–97); she was also with the Metropolitan Opera (1895–97; 1899–1901). After a season with the Chicago Grand Opera (1910–11), she made guest appearances in opera and concert in Europe and North America; later taught voice in Chicago.

Olitzki, Walter, German-American baritone, nephew of **Rosa Olitzka**; b. Hamburg, March 17, 1903; d. Los Angeles, Aug. 2, 1949. He received his training in Germany, where he developed his career. On Dec. 2, 1939, he appeared as Beckmesser at the Metropolitan Opera in New York, where he remained until 1947. He specialized in Wagnerian roles.

Oliver, Stephen (Michael Harding), English composer; b. Liverpool, March 10, 1950; d. London, April 29, 1992. He was a student at Worcester College, Oxford (1968–72), receiving training from Leighton (composition) and Sherlaw Johnson (electronic music). Oliver revealed a special talent for composing dramatic scores.

WORKS: DRAMATIC: *Slippery Soules*, Christmas drama (Oxford, Dec. 1969; rev. 1976; orchestrated version, London, Dec. 12, 1988); *The Duchess of Malfi* (1971; rev. version, Santa Fe, N. Mex., Aug. 5, 1978); *3 Instant Operas: Paid Off, Time Flies*, and *Old Haunts* (1973); *Sufficient Beauty* (1973); *Past Tense* (1973); *Cadenus Observ'd* (1974; London, Jan. 26, 1975); *Perseverance* (1974); *Tom Jones* (1974–75; Snape, April 6, 1976); *Bad Times* (London, June 24, 1975); *The Great McPorridge Disaster* (1976); *The Waiter's Revenge*, short opera (Nottingham, June 15, 1976); *Il Giardino*, short opera (Batignano, July 27, 1977; Eng. version as *The Garden*, London, April 17, 1980); *A Stable Home*, short opera (1977); *The Girl and the Unicorn* (London, Dec. 9, 1978); *The Dreaming of the Bones* (1979); *Jacko's Play*, short opera (1979); *A Man of Feeling*, short opera (London, Nov. 17, 1980); *Nicholas Nickelby*, incidental music (London, June 1980); *The Lord of the Rings*, incidental music (1981); *Euridice*, after Peri's score of 1600 (London, March 4, 1981); *Sasha* (1982; Banff, April 7, 1983); *Peter Pan*, incidental music (London, Dec. 16, 1982); *Blondel*, musical (Bath, Sept. 5, 1983); *Britannia Preserv'd*, masque (Hampton Court, May 30, 1984); *The Ring* (Manchester, May 31, 1984); *La Bella e la bestia* (Batignano, July 26, 1984; Eng. version as *Beauty and the Beast*, London, June 21, 1985); *Exposition of a Picture* (London, June 24, 1986); *Mario ed il mago* (Batignano, Aug. 5, 1988; Eng. version as *Mario and the Magician*); *Tables Meet* (London, May 1990); *Timon of Athens* (London, May 17, 1991); *L'Oca del Cairo* (Batignano, July 30, 1991).

Olivero, Magda (Maria Maddalena), remarkable Italian soprano; b. Saluzzo, near Turin, March 25, 1912. She studied at the Turin Cons. She made her operatic debut as Lauretta in *Gianni Schicchi* in Turin in 1933, then sang in the Italian provinces. She temporarily retired from the stage when she married in 1941, but resumed her career in 1951; she made successful appearances at La Scala in Milan, and in Paris and London. On Nov. 4, 1967, she made her U.S. debut in Dallas in the title role of Cherubini's *Médée*; she was 63 years old when she made her first appearance with the Metropolitan Opera in New York, on April 3, 1975, as Tosca; on Dec. 5, 1977 she gave a highly successful recital in a program of Italian art songs at Carnegie Hall, N.Y. Among her other notable operatic roles were Violetta, Fedora, Liù, Suor Angelica, and Minnie; she was praised mainly for her dramatic penetration of each character and her fine command of dynamic nuances.

d'Ollone, Max(imilien-Paul-Marie-Félix), French conductor, writer on music, and composer; b. Besançon, June 13, 1875; d. Paris, May 15, 1959. He studied with Lavignac, Massenet, and Lenepveu at the Paris Cons.; received the Grand Prix de Rome in 1897 with his cantata *Frédégonde*. He was active as an opera conductor in Paris and the French provinces. He wrote the books *Le langage musical* (Paris and Geneva, 1952) and *Le Théâtre lyrique et le public* (Paris, 1955). He wrote 5 operas: *Le Retour* (Angers, Feb. 13, 1913), *Les Uns et les autres* (Paris, Nov. 6, 1922), *L'Arlequin* (Paris, Dec. 24, 1924), *George Dandin* (Paris, March 19, 1930), and *La Samaritaine* (Paris, June 25, 1937); *Fantaisie* for Piano and Orch. (1899); *Dans la cathédrale* for Orch. (1906).

Olsen, Poul Rovsing, Danish composer and ethnomusicologist; b. Copenhagen, Nov. 4, 1922; d. there, July 2, 1982. He studied law at the Univ. of Århus (1940–42) and at the Univ. of Copenhagen (1942–48); concurrently, he studied harmony and counterpoint with Jeppesen and piano with Christiansen at the Copenhagen Cons. (1943–46); he later studied composition with Boulanger and analysis with Messiaen in Paris (1948–49). Between 1958 and 1963 he took part in ethnomusicological expeditions to Arabia, India, Greece, and eastern Greenland and wrote numerous valuable papers on the folklore and musical cultures of the areas he visited. He worked until 1960 for the Danish Ministry of Education as a legal expert on music copyright and served as chairman of the Danish Soc. of Composers (1962–67); he taught ethnomusicology at the Univ. of Lund, Sweden (1967–69), and subsequently at the Univ. of Copenhagen. He was president of the International Council of Traditional Music (formerly the International Folk Music Council) from 1977 until his death. He was a music critic for the newspapers *Morgenbladet* (1945–46), *Information* (1949–54), and *Berlingske Tidende* (1954–74). Much of his music embodies materials of non-European cultures, reflecting the influence of his travels. His *Elegy* for Organ (1953) is the first serial work written by a Danish composer.

WRITINGS: *Musiketnologi* (Copenhagen, 1974); with J. Jenkins, *Music and Musical Instruments in the World of Islam* (London, 1976).

WORKS: DRAMATIC: OPERAS: *Belisa*, after García Lorca (1964; Copenhagen, Sept. 3, 1969); *Usher*, after Poe (1980). BALLETS: *Ragnarök* (Twilight of the Gods; 1948; Copenhagen, Sept. 12, 1960); *La Création* (1952; Copenhagen, March 10, 1961); *Brylluppet* (The Wedding; 1966; Copenhagen, Sept. 15, 1969); *Den Fremmede* (The Stranger; 1969; Copenhagen, July 17, 1972).

O'Mara, Joseph, Irish tenor; b. Limerick, July 16, 1861; d. Dublin, Aug. 5, 1927. He studied with Moretti in Milan. On Feb. 4, 1891, he made his debut as Sullivan's Ivanhoe at the Royal English Opera House in London. After further training from Perini and Edwin Holland, he toured under the auspices of Augustus Harris. From 1902 to 1908 he was the principal tenor of the Moody-Manners Opera Co. In 1910 he became a member of Beecham's Co. at London's Covent Garden. From 1912 to 1924 he was director of his own O'Mara Grand Opera Co., with which he often appeared in leading roles.

Oncina, Juan, Spanish tenor; b. Barcelona, April 15, 1925. He was a student in Oran, Algeria, and of Mercedes Caspir in Barcelona. In 1946 he made his Italian operatic debut as Count Almaviva in Bologna, and subsequently appeared with leading Italian opera houses. From 1952 to 1961 he also sang at the Glyndebourne Festivals. While he was best known for his roles in operas by Mozart, Rossini, and Donizetti, he also appeared in operas by Verdi and Puccini.

Onégin, (Elisabeth Elfriede Emilie) Sigrid (née **Hoffmann**), noted German contralto; b. Stockholm (of a German father and a French mother), June 1, 1889; d. Magliaso, Switzerland, June 16, 1943. She studied in Frankfurt am Main with Resz, in Munich with E. R. Weiss, and with di Ranieri in Milan. She made her first public appearance, under the name Lilly Hoffmann, in Wiesbaden, Sept. 16, 1911, in a recital, accompanied by the Russian pianist and composer Eugene Onégin (real name, Lvov; b. St. Petersburg, Oct. 10, 1883; d. Stuttgart, Nov. 12, 1919; he was a grandnephew of Alexis Lvov, composer of the Russian czarist hymn). She married him on May 25, 1913; after his death she married a German doctor, Fritz Penzoldt (Nov. 20, 1920). She made her first operatic appearance as Carmen in Stuttgart on Oct. 10, 1912 and made her first appearance in London in 1913; she was a member of the Bavarian State Opera in Munich (1919–22). On Nov. 22, 1922, she made her Metropolitan Opera debut in New York as Amneris, continuing on its roster until 1924. She subsequently sang in Berlin (1926–31), at London's Covent Garden (1927), the Salzburg Festivals (1931–32), in Zürich (1931–35), and at the Bayreuth Festivals (1933–34). She made her last appearances in the United States as a recitalist in 1938. Among her most distinguished roles were Gluck's Orfeo, Eboli, Fidès, Erda, Lady Macbeth, Fricka, Waltraute, and Brangäne.

BIBL.: F. Penzoldt, *Alt-Rhapsodie: S. O., Leben und Werk* (Magdeburg, 1939; 3d ed., 1953).

O'Neill, Dennis (James), Welsh tenor; b. Pontardulais, Feb. 25, 1948. He studied at the Univ. of Sheffield and at the Royal Northern College of Music in Manchester. In 1973 he made his debut in *Ivan Susanin* at the Wexford Festival, and then sang with the State Opera of South Australia (1974–76) and subsequently with the Scottish Opera in Glasgow. In 1979 he sang Alfredo with the Welsh National Opera in Cardiff and Flavio at London's Covent Garden. He appeared as the Italian Singer in *Der Rosenkavalier* at the Glyndebourne Festival in 1980. After singing at the Vienna State Opera and the Hamburg State Opera in 1981, he made his U.S. debut as Edgardo at the Dallas Opera in 1983. In 1984 he sang at the San Francisco Opera, in 1985 at the Lyric Opera in Chicago, and in 1986 at the Paris Opéra. His first appearance with the Metropolitan Opera was as Alfredo during a tour by the company in 1986. In 1987 he returned to the Metropolitan Opera to make his house debut in New York. In 1992 he sang at the Bavarian State Opera in Munich. He was engaged as Radamès at Covent Garden in 1994, and he returned there in 1997 as Macduff.

O'Neill, Norman (Houstoun), English conductor and composer; b. London, March 14, 1875; d. there, March 3, 1934. He was a direct descendant of John Wall Callcott; his father was a painter. He studied in London with Arthur Somervell (1890–93), and later with Knorr in Frankfurt am Main (1893–97). Returning to London in 1899, he married the pianist Adine Rückert (1875–1947). He wrote incidental music for the Haymarket Theatre, of which he was music director from 1908 to 1919 and again 1920 to 1934; from 1924 to 1934 he taught at the Royal Academy of Music in London. He also composed 3 ballets.

BIBL.: D. Hudson, *N. O.: A Life of Music* (London, 1945).

Onslow, (André) Georges (Louis), noted French composer of English descent; b. Clermont-Ferrand, July 27, 1784; d. there, Oct. 3, 1853. He was the grandson of the 1st Lord Onslow. He studied in London with Hüllmandel, Dussek, and Cramer (piano) and in Paris with Reicha (composition). He wrote 3 comic operas, produced in Paris: *L'Alcalde de la Vega* (Aug. 10, 1824), *Le colporteur, ou L'enfant du bûcheron* (Nov. 22, 1827), and *Guise, ou Les états de Blois* (Sept. 8, 1837). However, these works failed to maintain interest, and Onslow's real achievement was the composition of a great number of chamber works, in which he demonstrated an uncommon mastery of counterpoint. He was struck by a stray bullet during a hunting expedition in 1829 and became deaf in one ear; his Quintet No. 15, subtitled *Le Quintette de la balle* (Quintet of the Bullet), was the musical rendering of this episode.

BIBL.: L. Halévy, *Notice sur O.* (Paris, 1855); C. Vulliamy, *The O. Family, 1528–1874* (London, 1953); C. Nobach, *Untersuchungen zu G. O.s Kammermusik* (Basel, 1985).

Opie, Alan (John), English baritone; b. Redruth, Cornwall, March 22, 1945. He received training at London's Guildhall School of Music and Drama, and at the London Opera Centre. In 1969 he made his operatic debut as Papageno at the Sadler's Wells Opera in London, where he was its principal bass in 1973–74 and its successor, the English National Opera from 1974 to 1996. He made his U.S. operatic debut as Tony in *Help, Help, the Globolinks!* at the Santa Fe Opera in 1970. In 1971 he sang for the first time at London's Covent Garden in *Il Barbiere di Siviglia*, where his later appearances included Hector in *King Priam* (1985), Mangus in *The Knot Garden* (1988), Falke (1989), Sharpless (1993), and Faninal (1995). He made his debut at the Glyndebourne Festival as Sid in *Albert Herring* in 1985, and returned there as Mozart's Figaro in 1991 and as Britten's Balstrode in 1992. In 1994 he sang the latter role at the Metropolitan Opera in New York, and in 1997 he returned there as Sharpless. On Oct. 2, 1996, he created the title role in Berio's *Outis* at Milan's La Scala.

Opieński, Henryk, Polish conductor, music scholar, teacher, and composer; b. Kraków, Jan. 13, 1870; d. Morges, Switzerland, Jan. 21, 1942. He studied with Zeleński in Kraków, with d'Indy in Paris, and with H. Urban in Berlin, then went to Leipzig, where he studied musicology with Riemann and conducting with Nikisch. In 1907 he was appointed an instructor at the Warsaw Musical Soc.; from 1908 to 1912 he conducted the Warsaw Opera; in 1912 he went again to Germany, where he took his degree of Ph.D. (Univ. of Leipzig, 1914). He spent the years of World War I in Morges, Switzerland; returning to Poland, he was director of the Poznan Cons. (1919–26), then settled again in Morges. He publ. several books and essays on Chopin (Lemberg, 1910; 2d ed., 1922); he also ed. the collected letters of Chopin in Polish, German, French, and Eng. (1931); other writings include a history of Polish music (Warsaw, 1912; 2d ed., 1922); *La Musique polonaise* (Paris, 1918; 2d ed., 1929); a monograph on Paderewski (Lemberg, 1910; 2d ed., 1928; Fr. tr., Lausanne, 1928; 2d ed., 1948); a valuable monograph on Moniuszko (Warsaw, 1924). His own compositions include 2 operas: *Maria* (1904; Poznan, April 27, 1923) and *Jakub lutnista* (Jacob the Lutenist; 1916–18; Poznan, Dec. 21, 1927); also *The Prodigal Son*, oratorio (1930); many songs.

BIBL.: A. Forenerod, *H. O.* (Lausanne, 1942).

Orchard, William (Arundel), English-born Australian pianist, conductor, and composer; b. London, April 13, 1867; d. during a voyage in the South Atlantic off the coast of South Africa (23°49'S; 9°33'E), April 17, 1961. He studied in London and Durham. In 1903 he went to Australia and lived in Sydney, where he was active as a conductor and music educator; he served as director of the New South Wales State Cons. (1923–34) and later taught at the Univ. of Tasmania. He wrote an opera, *The Picture of Dorian Gray*. He also publ. 2 books on Australian music: *The Distant View* (Sydney, 1943) and *Music in Australia* (Melbourne, 1952).

Ordonez or **Ordoñez, Carlos d',** Austrian composer of Spanish descent; b. Vienna, April 19, 1734; d. there, Sept. 6, 1786. He was employed as a clerk, but studied violin and performed successfully at chamber music concerts. He wrote numerous Singspiels and much instrumental music, some of which was publ. during his lifetime. His Singspiel *Diesmal hat der Mann den Willen* was performed in Vienna on April 22, 1778; his marionette opera *Alceste* was introduced by Haydn in Esterhaz on Aug. 30, 1775. Ordoñez developed an excellent metier, and several of his syms. possessed enough merit to be misattributed to Haydn.

BIBL.: A. Brown, *Carlo d'Ordoñez (1734–1786): A Thematic Catalogue* (Detroit, 1978).

Orefice, Antonio, Italian composer who flourished in the first half of the 18th century. His comic opera in Neapolitan dialect, *Patrò Calienno de la Costa* (Naples, Teatro dei Fiorentini, Oct. 1, 1709), was the first such work given on a public stage in Naples. With Mancini and Albinoni, he composed the opera seria *Engelberta, ossia La forza dell'innocenza* (Naples, Nov. 4, 1709). His 7 arias from *Le finte zingare* (1717) are the earliest extant music from a comic opera in Neapolitan dialect.

Orefice, Giacomo, Italian pianist, music critic, teacher, and composer; b. Vicenza, Aug. 27, 1865; d. Milan, Dec. 22, 1922. He studied piano with Busi and composition with Mancinelli at the Bologna Liceo Musicale (diploma, 1885). He taught at the Milan Cons. (1909–22) and was also active as a music critic. He publ. the study *Luigi Mancinelli* (Rome, 1921) and ed. Monteverdi's *Orfeo* (Milan, 1909) and Rameau's *Platée*. As a composer of operas, he followed in the verismo school.

WORKS: DRAMATIC: OPERAS: *L'oasi* (Bologna, 1885); *Mariska* (Turin, Nov. 19, 1889); *Consuelo* (Bologna, Nov. 27, 1895); *Il Gladiatore* (Madrid, March 20, 1898); *Chopin* (Milan, Nov. 25, 1901); *Cecilia* (Vicenza, Aug. 16, 1902); *Il Mosè* (Genoa, Feb. 18, 1905); *Il pane d'altrui* (Venice, Jan. 19, 1907); *Radda* (Milan, Oct. 25, 1912); *I Castello dei sogni* (not perf.). BALLET: *La soubrette* (Milan, 1907).

BIBL.: A. Bassi, *G. O.: Tradizione e avanguardia nel melodramma del primo '900* (Padua, 1987).

Orff, Carl, outstanding German composer and music educator; b. Munich, July 10, 1895; d. there, March 29, 1982. He took courses with Beer-Walbrunn and Zilcher at the Munich Academy of Music (graduated, 1914); later he had additional instruction from Heinrich Kaminski in Munich. He was a conductor at the Munich Kammerspiele (1915–17); after military service during World War I (1917–18), he conducted at the Mannheim National Theater and the Darmstadt Landestheater (1918–19); later he was conductor of Munich's Bach Soc. (1930–33). Orff initiated a highly important method of musical education, which was adopted not only in Germany but in England, America, and Russia. It stemmed from the Günther School for gymnastics, dance, and music, founded in Munich in 1924 by Orff with Dorothee Günther with the aim of promoting instrumental playing and understanding of rhythm among children. He commissioned the piano manufacturer Karl Maendler to construct special percussion instruments that would be extremely easy to play; these "Orff instruments" became widely adopted in American schools. Orff's ideas of rhythmic training owe much to the eurhythmics of Jaques-Dalcroze, but he simplified them to reach the elementary level; as a manual, he compiled a set of musical exercises, *Schulwerk* (1930–35; rev. 1950–54). He also taught composition at the Munich Staatliche Hochschule für Musik (1950–55). As a composer, Orff sought to revive the early monodic forms and to adapt them to modern tastes by means of dissonant counterpoint, with lively rhythm in asymmetrical patterns, producing a form of "total theater." His most famous score is the scenic oratorio *Carmina Burana* (Frankfurt am Main, June 8, 1937), with words (in Latin and German) drawn from 13th-century student poems found in the Benediktbeuren monastery in Bavaria ("Burana" is the Latin adjective of the locality). His other works include *Der Mond*, opera, after a fairy tale by Grimm (1937–38; Munich, Feb. 5, 1939; rev. 1945; Munich, Nov. 26, 1950); *Die Kluge*, opera, after a fairy tale by Grimm (1941–42; Frankfurt am Main, Feb. 20, 1943); *Catulli Carmina*, scenic cantata after Catullus (Leipzig, Nov. 6, 1943); *Die Bernauerin*, musical play (1944–45; Stuttgart, June 15, 1947); *Antigonae*, musical play after Sophocles (1947–48; Salzburg, Aug. 9, 1949); *Trionfo di Afrodite* (1950–51; 3d part of a triology under the general title *Trionfi*, the 1st and 2d parts being *Carmina Burana* and *Catulli Carmina*; Milan, Feb. 13, 1953); *Astutuli*, opera ballet (1945–46; Munich, Oct. 20, 1953); *Comoedia de Christi Resurrectione*, Easter cantata (1955; Munich, March 31, 1956); *Oedipus der Tyrann*, musical play after Sophocles (1957–58; Stuttgart, Dec. 11, 1959); *Ludus de nato infante mirificus*, Nativity play (Stuttgart, Dec. 11, 1960); *Prometheus*, opera (1963–67; Stuttgart, March 24, 1968); *Rota* for Voices and Instruments, after the canon *Sumer is icumen in*, composed as a "salute to youth" for the opening ceremony of the Munich Olympics (1972); *De temporum fine comoedia*, stage play (1969–71; Salzburg, 1973). He further wrote a dance play, *Der Feuerfarbene* (1925); *Präludium* for Orch. (1925); Concertino for Wind Instruments and Harpsichord (1927); *Entrata* for Orch., based on melodies of William Byrd (1928; rev. 1940); *Festival Music* for Chamber Orch. (1928); *Bayerische Musik* for Small Ensemble (1934); *Olympischer Reigen* for Various Instruments (1936); 3 stage works after Monteverdi: *Klage der Ariadne* (Karlsruhe, 1925; rev. version, Gera, 1940), *Orpheus* (Mannheim, April 17, 1925; 2d version, Munich, Oct. 13, 1929; 3d version, Dresden, Oct. 4, 1940), and *Tanz der Spröden* (Karlsruhe, 1925; rev. version, Gera, 1940). In 1984 the Carl Orff Foundation was organized.

BIBL.: W. Trittenhoff, *O.-Schulwerk: Einführung* (Mainz, 1930); A. Liess, *C. O.: Idee und Werk* (Zürich, 1955; 2d ed., rev., 1977; Eng. tr., 1966); K. Ruppel, G. Sellner, and W. Thomas, *C. O., ein Bericht in Wort und Bild* (Mainz, 1955; 2d ed., rev., 1960; Eng.

tr., 1960); I. Kiekert, *Die musikalische Form in den Werken C. O.s* (Regensburg, 1957); M. Devreese-Papgnies, *Sur les traces du Schulwerk de C. O.: Méthodologie pour l'usage des instruments d'orchestre scolaire* (Brussels, 1968); F. Willnauer, ed., *Prometheus: Mythos, Drama, Musik: Beiträge zu C. O.s Musikdrama nach Aischylos* (Tübingen, 1968); U. Klement, *Das Musiktheater C. O.s: Untersuchungen zu einem bürgerlichen Kunstwerk* (diss., Univ. of Leipzig, 1969); G. Keetman, *Elementaria: Erster Umgang mit dem O.Schulwerk* (Stuttgart, 1970; Eng. tr., 1974); R. Münster, ed., *C. O.: Das Bühnenwerk* (Munich, 1970); H. Wolfgart, ed., *Das O.- Schulwerk im Dienste der Erziehung und Therapie behinderter Kinder* (Berlin, 1971); W. Thomas, *C. O.: De temporum fine comoedia . . . eine Interpretation* (Tutzing, 1973); G. Orff, *The O. Music Therapy* (London, 1980); U. Klement, *Das Musiktheater C. O.s* (Leipzig, 1982); H. Leuchtmann, *C. O.: Ein Gedenkbuch* (Tutzing, 1985); G. Orff-Büchtemann, *Mein Vater und ich: Erinnerungen an C. O.* (Munich, 1992); A. Fassone, *C. O.* (Lucca, 1994).

Orgeni, Aglaja (real name, **Anna Maria von Görger St. Jorgen**), respected Hungarian soprano and teacher; b. Roma Szombat, Dec. 17, 1841; d. Vienna, March 15, 1926. She was a pupil of Pauline Viardot-García at Baden-Baden, making her debut on Sept. 28, 1865, as Amina, at the Berlin Royal Opera. She made her first appearance in London on April 7, 1866, as Violetta, at Covent Garden; she later sang in Vienna, Dresden, Berlin, Copenhagen, etc. From 1886 she taught singing at the Dresden Cons. She was made a Royal Professor in 1908, the first case of the title being conferred on a woman. In 1914 she settled in Vienna. Among her distinguished pupils were Erika Wedekind and Edyth Walker. She was held in high esteem for such roles as Agathe in *Der Freischütz*, Marguerite in *Faust*, Leonora in *Il Trovatore*, and Valentine in *Les Huguenots*.

BIBL.: E. Brand, *A. O.* (Munich, 1931).

Orlandini, Giuseppe Maria, prominent Italian composer; b. Florence, March 19, 1675; d. there, Oct. 24, 1760. He most likely received his musical training in Florence. He served as maestro di cappella at the court of Tuscany during most of his career, and also held that position in Florence at the Cathedral (1732–60) and at S. Michele (1734–57). His *Serpilla e Bacocco* was one of the most celebrated stage works of the 18th century.

WORKS: DRAMATIC: OPERAS: *Artaserse* (Naples, 1708; additional music by F. Mancini); *L'amor generoso* (Pratolino, 1708; additional music by R. Cerruti); *L'odio e l'amore* (Genoa, 1709); *La fede tradita e vendicata* (Genoa, 1709); *Ataulfo re de'Goti, ovvero La forza della virtù* (Rome, Carnival 1712); *L'innocenza difesa* (Ferrara, 1712); *Teuzzone* (Ferrara, 1712); *Carlo, rè d'Alemagna* (Bologna, Oct. 28, 1713); *Nerone fatto Cesare* (Venice, Carnival 1715; in collaboration with others); *Amore e maestà* (Florence, 1715; rev. as *Arsace*, London, Jan. 1, 1721); *I veri amici* (Naples, Nov. 26, 1715); *Griselda, ovvero La virtù al cimento* (Brescia, Carnival 1716); *La Merope* (Bologna, Oct. 24, 1717); *Lucio Papirio* (Naples, Dec. 11, 1717; additional music by F. Feo); *Antigona* (Venice, Carnival 1718; rev. as *La fedeltà coronata*, Bologna, 1727); *Le amazoni vinte da Ercole* (Reggio Emilia, April 1718); *Ifigenia in Tauride* (Venice, Carnival 1719); *Il carciere di se stesso* (Turin, Dec. 26, 1719); *Paride* (Venice, Carnival 1720); *Il Farasmene* (Bologna, Nov. 1720; rev. as *L'amor tirannico,* Pesaro, Carnival 1722); *Nerone* (Hamburg, 1720); *Nino* (Rome, Jan. 7, 1722; with additional music by A. Tinazzoli, Pesaro, Carnival 1723); *Semiramide* (Turin, Carnival 1722); *Ormisda* (Bologna, 1722); *Alessandro Severo* (Milan, Jan. 1723); *L'Oronta* (Milan, Jan. 1724); *Berenice* (Venice, Carnival 1725); *Adelaide* (Genoa, Carnival 1726; with additional music by others, Mantua, Carnival 1731); *La fida ninfa* (Venice, 1730); *Massimiano* (Venice, Carnival 1731); *Ifigenia in Aulide* (Florence, Carnival 1732); *Temistocle* (Florence, Carnival 1737); *Le nozze di Perseo e Andromeda* (Florence, 1738); *Arianna* (Florence, Jan. 1739); *Venceslao* (Florence, Dec. 26, 1741); *Vologeso re de'Parti* (Florence, Jan. 1742); *Lo scialacquatore* (Florence, 1744). INTERMEZZOS: *Madama Dulcinea e il cuoco del Marchese del Bosco, ovvero La preziosa ridicola* (Rome, 1712); *Lisetta e Delfo* (Rome, Carnival 1713); *Il Marito giocatore e la moglie becchatona* (Venice, Jan. 1719; best known as *Serpilla e Bacocco*); *Melinda e Tiburzio* (Venice, Carnival 1721; rev. as *La Donna nobile*, Venice, Carnival 1730); *Il bottegaro gentiluomo, ovvero Larinda e Vanesio* (Florence, Carnival 1721); *L'Ammalato immaginario* (Florence, Carnival 1725); *Un vecchio innamorato* (Florence, Carnival 1732); *Porsugnacco e Grilletta* (Milan, 1727); *Grullo e Moschetta* (Venice, Carnival 1725); *Il Marito geloso* (St. Petersburg, 1734); *Balbo e Dalisa* (Rome, Carnival 1740) OTHER: 8 oratorios (only librettos extant).

Orr, Robin (Robert Kemsley), Scottish composer, organist, and teacher; b. Brechin, June 2, 1909. He studied at the Royal College of Music in London (1926–29), and then was an organ scholar at Pembroke College, Cambridge (Mus.B., 1932); he subsequently took his Mus.B. (1938) and Mus.D. (1950) at the Univ. of Cambridge; he also studied composition with Casella at the Accademia Musicale Chigiana in Siena (1934) and with Boulanger in Paris (1938). He was director of music at Sidcot School in Somerset (1933–36), and then was an assistant lecturer at the Univ. of Leeds (1936–38). From 1938 to 1941, and again from 1945 to 1951, he was organist and director of music at St. John's College, Cambridge. From 1947 to 1956 he was a lecturer at the Univ. of Cambridge, and from 1950 to 1956 he was a prof. at the Royal College of Music in London. After serving as the Gardiner prof. of music at the Univ. of Glasgow from 1956 to 1965, he was prof. of composition at the Univ. of Cambridge from 1965 to 1976. From 1962 to 1976 he served as the first chairman of the Scottish Opera in Glasgow. He was director of the Welsh National Opera in Cardiff from 1977 to 1983. In 1972 he was made a Commander of the Order of the British Empire. As a composer, Orr has been particularly adept at investing traditional forms with an individual voice of distinction.

WORKS: DRAMATIC: *A Winter's Tale*, incidental music to Shakespeare's play (1947); *Oedipus et Colonus*, incidental music to Sophocles' play (1950); *Deirdre of the Sorrows*, incidental music (1951); *Full Circle*, opera (Perth, April 10, 1968); *Hermiston*, opera (Edinburgh, Aug. 27, 1975); *On the Razzle*, comic opera (1986; Glasgow, June 27, 1988).

Orrego-Salas, Juan (Antonio), distinguished Chilean composer and musicologist; b. Santiago, Jan. 18, 1919. He studied composition at the National Cons. (1936–43) and architecture at the Catholic Univ. (graduated, 1943) in Santiago. In the meantime, he became a teacher of music history at the Univ. of Chile and in 1938 founder-conductor of the Catholic Univ. Chorus. After receiving a Rockefeller Foundation grant and a Guggenheim fellowship, he studied musicology with Lang and Herzog at Columbia Univ. (1944–45), and composition with Thompson at Princeton Univ. (1945–46) and Copland at the Berkshire Music Center in Tanglewood (summer 1946). Upon returning to Santiago in 1947, he became prof. of composition at the Univ. of Chile; he also resumed his post as conductor of the Catholic Univ. Chorus. In 1949 he became ed. of the *Revista Musical Chilena* and in 1950 music critic of the newspaper *El Mercurio*. In 1953 he was made Distinguished Prof. of composition at the Univ. of Chile. In 1954 he received a 2d Guggenheim fellowship and revisited the United States. Upon returning to Santiago, he was director of the Instituto de Extension Musical until 1956. He then became the first director of the music dept. at the Catholic Univ. while continuing to teach at the Univ. of Chile. In 1961 he became a prof. at the Indiana Univ. School of Music in Bloomington, where he was founder-director of its Latin American Music Center. From 1975 to 1980 he also was chairman of its composition dept. He retired as prof. emeritus in 1987. In addition to monographs on composers, Orrego-Salas publ. numerous articles in journals in the United States, England, and Latin America. In 1956 and 1958 he won the Olga Cohen prize for composition. He was made a corresponding member of the Chilean Academy of Fine Arts in 1971. In 1988 the OAS awarded him the Inter-American Gabriela Mistral Cultural Prize. In 1992 the Chilean government honored him with the Premio Nacional de Arte. As a composer, Orrego-Salas has revealed himself as a refined craftsman and an assured master of neoclassical techniques.

WORKS: DRAMATIC: *Juventud*, ballet (Santiago, Nov. 19, 1948; based on Handel's *Solomon*); *El Retablo del rey pobre*, opera oratorio (1950–52; 1st stage perf., Bloomington, Ind., Nov. 10, 1990); *Umbral del sueño*, ballet (Santiago, Aug. 8, 1951); *La Veta del diablo*, film score (1953); *Caleta olvidada*, film score (1959); *The Tumbler's Prayer*, ballet (concert perf., Santiago, Nov. 1960; stage perf., Santiago, Oct. 1961); *Versos del ciego*, incidental music (Santiago, June 1961); *Widows*, opera (1987–90); *The Goat That Couldn't Sneeze*, musical comedy (Bloomington, Ind., Oct. 25, 1992). Also *The Days of God*, oratorio for Soprano, Alto, Tenor, Baritone, Chorus, and Orch. (1974–76; Washington, D.C., Nov. 2, 1976).

Osborne (real name, **Eisbein**), **Adrienne,** American contralto; b. Buffalo, Dec. 2, 1873; d. Zell am Ziller, Austria, June 15, 1951. She studied with August Götze and Max Stagemann in Leipzig and later with **Felix von Kraus**, whom she married in 1899. She sang at the Leipzig City Theater; in 1908 she settled in Munich, where she received the rank of Royal Chamber Singer. After the death of her husband in 1937, she went to Zell am Ziller.

Osborne, Nigel, English composer and teacher; b. Manchester, June 23, 1948. He received training in composition from Leighton and in 12-tone procedures from Wellesz at the Univ. of Oxford (B.Mus., 1970), and then worked in Warsaw with Rudziński and at the Polish Radio Experimental Studio (1970–71). In 1976 he became a lecturer in music at the Univ. of Nottingham. In 1990 he became prof. of music at the Univ. of Edinburgh. His *7 Words* won the International Opera Prize of the Radio Suisse Romande in 1971, his *Heaventree* received the Gaudeamus Prize in 1973, and his *I Am Goya* was honored with the Radcliffe Award in 1977. Osborne's works are in a thoroughly contemporary style pointing the way to postmodernism. They include the operas *Hell's Angels* (1985; London, Jan. 4, 1986), *The Electrification of the Soviet Union* (1986–87; Glyndebourne, Oct. 5, 1987), *Terrible Mouth* (1992), and *Sarajevo* (1993–94).

Osborn-Hannah, Jane, American soprano; b. Wilmington, Ohio, July 8, 1873; d. N.Y., Aug. 13, 1943. After vocal instruction from her mother, she studied with Marchesi and Sbriglia in Paris and with Sucher in Berlin. In 1904 she made her operatic debut as Elisabeth in *Tannhäuser* in Leipzig, and sang there until 1907. After appearances in Dresden, Munich, and Berlin, she sang at London's Covent Garden in 1908. On Jan. 5, 1910, she made her Metropolitan Opera debut in New York as Elisabeth, and continued on its roster for the 1910–11 season. She also was a member of the Chicago Grand Opera (1910–14). While she was best known as a Wagnerian, she also sang such roles as Desdemona, Cio-Cio-San, and Nedda with conviction.

Osten, Eva von der, German soprano; b. Insel, Aug. 19, 1881; d. Dresden, May 5, 1936. She studied with August Iffert and Marie Söhle in Dresden. She made her operatic debut as Urbain in *Les Huguenots* in Dresden in 1902 and was a principal member of the Dresden Court (later State) Opera until 1927, where she created the role of Octavian in *Der Rosenkavalier* in 1911; she also appeared at London's Covent Garden (1912–14) and in the United States with the German Opera Co. (1923–24). After her retirement from the stage, she became a producer of opera in Dresden. She was married to **Friedrich Plaschke**. Among her other outstanding roles were Kundry, Isolde, Senta, Ariadne, and Tosca.

Osterc, Slavko, Slovenian composer and teacher; b. Veržej, June 17, 1895; d. Ljubljana, May 23, 1941. He began his training with Beran in Maribor, then studied at the Prague Cons. (1925–27); he subsequently taught at Ljubljana's Cons. and Academy of Music. He experimented with various techniques, including quarter tone writing.

WORKS: DRAMATIC: OPERAS: *Salome* (1919–30); *Krst pri Savici* (Baptism at the Savica; 1921); *Iz komične opere* (1928); *Krog s kredo* (The Chalk Circle; 1928–29); *Medea* (1930); *Dandin v vicah* (Dandin in Purgatory; 1930). BALLETS: *Iz Satanovega dnevnika* (From Satan's Diary; 1924); *Maska rdeče smrti* (The Masque of the Red Death; 1930); *Illusions* (1938–40); *Illegitimate Mother* (1940).

Osthoff, Helmuth, distinguished German musicologist, father of **Wolfgang Osthoff**; b. Bielefeld, Aug. 13, 1896; d. Würzburg, Feb. 9, 1983. He studied music in Bielefeld and in Münster. He served in the German army during World War I; after the Armistice he resumed his studies at the Univ. of Münster (1919), and later (1920–22) took courses with Wolf, Kretzschmar, and Schünemann at the Univ. of Berlin, where he received his Ph.D. in 1922 with the diss. *Der Lautenist Santino Garsi da Parma: Ein Beitrag zur Geschichte der oberitaliensischen Lautenmusik der Spätrenaissance* (publ. in Leipzig, 1926). He subsequently studied conducting with Brecher, composition with Klatte, and piano with Kwast at Berlin's Stern Cons. (1922–23). From 1923 to 1926 he served as répétiteur at the Leipzig Opera; in 1926 he became assistant lecturer to Arnold Schering in the dept. of musicology at the Univ. of Halle; in 1928 he was appointed chief assistant to Schering in the dept. of music history at the Univ. of Berlin; completed his Habilitation there in 1932 with his treatise *Die Niederländer und das deutsche Lied 1400–1640* (publ. in Berlin, 1938). In 1938 he became a prof. and director of the inst. of musicology at the Univ. of Frankfurt am Main, positions he held until his retirement in 1964. He was especially noted for his astute studies of Renaissance music. His other publications include *Adam Krieger; Neue Beiträge zur Geschichte des deutschen Liedes in 17. Jahrhundert* (Leipzig, 1929; 2d ed., 1970); *Johannes Brahms und seine Sendung* (Bonn, 1942); *Josquin Desprez* (2 vols., Tutzing, 1962–65). A Festschrift was publ. in Tutzing in 1961 to honor his 65th birthday, a 2d in 1969 for his 70th birthday (contains a bibliography of his writings), and a 3d in 1977 for his 80th birthday.

Osthoff, Wolfgang, German musicologist, son of **Helmuth Osthoff**; b. Halle, March 17, 1927. He studied piano and theory at the Frankfurt am Main Staatliche Hochschule für Musik (1939–43); he then took lessons in conducting with Kurt Thomas (1946–47). He subsequently studied musicology with his father at the Univ. of Frankfurt am Main (1947–49) and with Georgiades at the Univ. of Heidelberg (1949–54); he received his Ph.D. there in 1954 with the diss. *Das dramatische Spätwerk Claudio Monteverdis* (publ. in Tutzing, 1960). He taught at the Univ. of Munich (1957–64) and completed his Habilitation there in 1965 with his *Theatergesang und darstellende Musik in der italienischen Renaissance* (publ. in Tutzing, 1969). He became a lecturer at the Univ. of Munich in 1966. In 1968 he was named a prof. of musicology at the Univ. of Würzburg. In addition to many scholarly articles dealing with music history from the 15th to the 19th century, he also contributed to many music reference works. With R. Wiesend, he ed. *Bach und die italienische Musik (Bach e la musica italiana)* (Venice, 1987). He publ. the vol. *St. George und "Les deux Musiques"— Tönende und vertonte Dichtung im Einklang und Widerstreit* (Stuttgart, 1989).

BIBL.: M. Just and R. Wiesend, eds., *Liedstudien: W. O. zum 60. Geburtstag* (Tutzing, 1989).

Östman, Arnold, Swedish conductor; b. Malmö, Dec. 24, 1939. He received training in art history at the Univ. of Lund and in music history at the univs. of Paris and Stockholm. From 1969 to 1979 he was artistic director of the Vadstena Academy, where he attracted notice with his productions of operas of the 17th and 18th centuries. He then was artistic director of the Drottningholm Court Theater in Stockholm from 1980 to 1992, where he mounted performances of early operas utilizing period instruments, costumes, and stagings. He also appeared frequently with the Cologne Opera, taking its productions of *Il matrimonio segreto* on tour to London (1983) and Washington, D.C. (1986). In 1984 he conducted *Don Giovanni* at London's Covent Garden. In 1985 he conducted *Le Siège de Corinthe* at the Paris Opéra. He conducted *Lucio Silla* at the Vienna State Opera in 1990. Östman also appeared as a guest conductor with various European orchs. While he has become best known for his performances of early operas, he has also commissioned and conducted the premieres of many contemporary works.

Ostrčil, Otakar, eminent Czech conductor and composer; b. Smichov, near Prague, Feb. 25, 1879; d. Prague, Aug. 20, 1935. He studied languages at the Univ. of Prague, and then taught at a school in Prague (until 1919); at the same time, he took courses in piano with Adolf Mikeš (1893–95) and studied composition privately with Fibich (1895–1900). From 1908 to 1922 he conducted the amateur orch. assn. in Prague; also conducted opera there (from 1909); in 1920 he succeeded Karel Kovařovic as principal conductor at the Prague National Theater; also taught conducting at the Prague Cons. (1926–29). In his compositions, Ostrčil continued the Romantic tradition of Czech music, with some modern elaborations revealing the influence of Mahler.

WORKS: OPERAS: *Vlasty skon* (The Death of Vlasta; 1900–03; Prague, Dec. 14, 1904); *Kunálovy oči* (Kunala's Eyes; Prague, Nov. 25, 1908); *Poupě* (The Bud; 1909–10; Prague, Jan. 25, 1911); *Legenda z Erinu* (The Legend of Erin; 1913–19; Brno, June 16, 1921); *Honzovo království* (Honza's Kingdom; 1928–33; Brno, May 26, 1934).

BIBL.: Z. Nejedlý, *O. O.: Vzrůst a uzrání* (O. O.: Development and Maturity; Prague, 1935); J. Bartos, *O. O.* (Prague, 1936).

O'Sullivan, Denis, American baritone; b. San Francisco, April 25, 1868; d. Columbus, Ohio, Feb. 1, 1908. He was a student of Ugo Talbot and Karl Formes in San Francisco, Vannuccini in Florence, Stanley and Shakespeare in London, and Sbriglia in Paris. Following an engagement at a London concert in 1895, he made his operatic debut as Ferrando in *Il trovatore* with the Carl Rosa Co. in Dublin on Aug. 25, 1895. He was notably successful as the hero in Stanford's *Shamus O'Brien* (London, March 2, 1896). From 1897 to 1899 he sang on both sides of the Atlantic.

Otescu, Ion (Nonna), Romanian conductor, teacher, and composer; b. Bucharest, Dec. 15, 1888; d. there, March 25, 1940. He was a student of Kiriac (theory) and Castaldi (composition) at the Bucharest Cons. (1903–07), and then completed his training in composition in Paris with d'Indy at the Schola Cantorum and with Widor at the Cons. (1908–11). Returning to Budapest, he was a teacher of harmony and composition (1913–40) and director (1918–40) of the Cons. He also was a conductor of the National Theater (1921–39) and the Bucharest Phil. (from 1927). In 1920 he helped to organize the Soc. of Romanian Composers, serving as its vice chairman until his death. In 1913 he won the Enesco Prize and in 1928 the National Prize for composition. Otescu's music followed along traditional lines with infusions of folk and French elements.

WORKS: DRAMATIC: *Buby*, musical comedy (1903); *Ileana Cosinzeana*, ballet (1918; to a libretto by Queen Marie of Romania); *Rubinul miraculos*, ballet (1919); *Iderim*, opera (1920); *De la Matei cetire*, opera buffa (1926–38; completed by A. Stroe; Cluj, Dec. 27, 1966).

Ott, David, American composer and teacher; b. Crystal Falls, Mich., July 5, 1947. He studied at the Univ. of Wisc., Platteville (B.S. in music education, 1969); after training in piano with Alfonso Montecino at the Indiana Univ. School of Music (M.M., 1971), he took courses in theory and composition at the Univ. of Kentucky (D.M.A., 1982). He taught at Houghton (N.Y.) College (1972–75), the Univ. of Kentucky, Lexington (1976–77), Catawba College, Salisbury, N.C. (1977–78), Pfeiffer College, Misenheimer, N.C. (1978–82), and DePauw Univ., Greencastle, Ind. (from 1982); he also was active as an organist and conductor. In 1991 he became composer-in-residence of the Indianapolis Sym. Orch. His works include *Lucinda Hero*, opera (1985), and *Visions: The Isle of Patmos*, ballet (1988).

Ottani, Bernardo, Italian composer, brother of **Gaetano Ottani**; b. Bologna, Sept. 8, 1736; d. Turin, April 26, 1827. He was a pupil of Padre Martini. In 1765 he was elected a member of the Accademia Filarmonica in Bologna. He was made maestro di cappella at the basilica of S. Giovanni in Monte in Bologna in 1769, and later held similar appointments in that city at the church of S. Luca and at the Collegio degli Ungheri. In 1779 he became maestro di cappella at Turin Cathedral. Ottani wrote 13 operas, including *L'amore senza malizia* (Venice, Carnival 1767–68), *Le virtuose ridicole* (Dresden, Carnival 1769), and *L'amore industrioso* (Dresden, Nov. 21, 1769). He also wrote much sacred music.

Ottani, Gaetano, Italian tenor, brother of **Bernardo Ottani**; place and date of birth unknown; d. Turin, 1808. After singing in Bologna (1747) and Lucca (1748), he appeared in Turin in 1750, where he served as primo uomo at the court opera from 1754 to 1768. He also sang in Milan in 1752 and in 1770. In addition to his career as a tenor, Ottani was active as a landscape painter.

Otter, Anne Sofie von, outstanding Swedish mezzo-soprano; b. Stockholm, May 9, 1955. She began her training at the Stockholm Musikhögskolan; then studied with Erik Werba in Vienna and Geoffrey Parsons in London, and later with Vera Rozsa. In 1982 she joined the Basel Opera; in 1984 she sang at the Aix-en-Provence Festival. She made her first appearance at London's Covent Garden in 1985 as Cherubino; that same year, she made her U.S. debut as soloist in Mozart's C-minor Mass with the Chicago Sym. Orch. In 1987 she sang at La Scala in Milan and at the Bavarian State Opera in Munich. In 1988 she appeared as Cherubino at the Metropolitan Opera in New York. In 1989 she made her first appearance at the Salzburg Festival as Marguerite in *La Damnation de Faust* with Solti and the Chicago Sym. Orch. In 1992 she returned to Salzburg to sing Ramiro. In 1996 she sang in the Metropolitan Opera Gala, and returned there in 1997 as Mozart's Sesto. On May 6, 1998, she made her Carnegie Hall recital debut in New York. She sang widely as a soloist with major orchs. and as a recitalist. Her other operatic roles include Gluck's Orfeo, Mozart's Idamantes and Dorabella, Tchaikovsky's Olga, and R. Strauss's Octavian. Otter was acclaimed for her extraordinary vocal mastery, from opera to lieder.

Ottman, Robert W(illiam), American music theorist and pedagogue; b. Fulton, N.Y., May 3, 1914. He studied theory with Rogers at the Eastman School of Music in Rochester, N.Y. (M.Mus., 1943). He served in U.S. Army infantry (1943–46), then took lessons in composition with Alec Rowley at Trinity College of Music in London; in 1946 he was engaged as a lecturer in music at North Texas State Univ., from which he also received his Ph.D. (1956); he became prof. emeritus in 1980. Among his writings is *Music for Sight Singing* (Englewood Cliffs., N.J., 1956; 3d ed., 1986), with P. Kreuger, *Basic Repertoire for Singers* (San Antonio, 1959), and *More Music for Sight Singing* (1981).

Otto, Lisa, German soprano; b. Dresden, Nov. 14, 1919. She was educated at the Hochschule für Musik in Dresden. She made her operatic debut as Sophie in 1941 at the Landestheater in Beuthen. In 1945–46 she sang at the Nuremberg Opera. She was a member of the Dresden State Opera (1946–51), then joined the Berlin Städtische Oper (1952); she also sang in Salzburg (from 1953), and made tours of the United States, South America, and Japan. She was made a Kammersängerin in 1963. She became best known for her roles in Mozart's operas.

Ötvos, Gabor, Hungarian-born German conductor; b. Budapest, Sept. 21, 1935. He began his training at the Franz Liszt Academy of Music in Budapest. Following the abortive Hungarian Revolution in 1956, he pursued studies in Venice and Rome. In 1958 he became a conductor at the Teatro Verdi in Trieste, and served as its music director in 1960–61. From 1961 to 1967 he was chief conductor of the Hamburg Sym. Orch. He held the title of 1st conductor and deputy Generalmusikdirektor of the Frankfurt am Main Opera from 1967 to 1972. In 1969 he made his debut with the N.Y. City Opera. On Oct. 27, 1971, he made his first appearance with the Metropolitan Opera in New York conducting *Carmen*, returning there in 1973 and 1974. From 1972 to 1981 he was Generalmusikdirektor of Augsburg. He served as chief conductor of the Royal Danish Opera in Copenhagen from 1981 to 1990. From 1998 he was principal conductor of the Orquesta Filarmónica in Santiago, Chile.

Oudin, Eugène (Espérance), American baritone of French descent; b. N.Y., Feb. 24, 1858; d. London, Nov. 4, 1894. He studied law at Yale Univ. He made his debut in New York, on Aug. 30, 1886, in an operetta. On Jan. 31, 1891, he created the role of Ivanhoe in London in Arthur Sullivan's opera of that name, and won immediate acclaim. He remained in England most of his life, but also made several appearances in Europe, including Russia. He scored notable successes in Wagnerian roles, especially Wolfram and Telramund.

Oudrid (y Segura), Cristóbal, Spanish conductor and composer; b. Badajoz, Feb. 7, 1825; d. while conducting a rehearsal at the Teatro Real in Madrid, March 12, 1877. He studied music with his father, acquiring his craft by arranging works of Haydn and Mozart for wind instruments. In 1844 he went to Madrid, where he conducted Italian opera (from 1867) and was director of the Teatro Real (from 1870). He showed a decided talent for writing melodious zarzuelas, among them *Buenas noches, Señor Don Simon* (Madrid, April 16, 1852), *El postillon de la Rioja* (Madrid, June 7, 1856), and *El último mono* (Madrid, May 30, 1859).

Ouseley, Sir Frederick (Arthur) Gore, English organist, pianist, music theorist, and composer; b. London, Aug. 12, 1825; d. Hereford, April 6, 1889. He was the son of Sir Gore Ouseley, ambassador to Persia and Russia. He studied classics and theology with James Joyce, vicar of Dorking (1840–43). He inherited his father's title of baronet (1844) and his considerable wealth, then completed his education at Christ Church, Oxford (B.A., 1846; M.A., 1849; D.Mus., 1854). He was ordained a priest in 1849. He was curate at St. Barnabas, Pimlico (1849–51); he founded the College of St. Michael and All Angels, Tenbury (1854), serving as warden and vicar of the new parish; he was also made precentor of Hereford Cathedral (1855), and later canon residentiary there (1886); likewise he was prof. of music at the Univ. of Oxford (1855–89). He was a fine organist, and excelled in fugal improvisation. Among his compositions are an opera, *L'isola disabitata* (1834), and 2 oratorios. He publ. *A Treatise on Harmony* (1868), *A Treatise on Counterpoint, Canon, and Fugue, based on Cherubini* (1869), and *A Treatise on Musical Form and General Composition* (1875). He left his fine music library to St. Michael's College, Tenbury.

BIBL.: F. Havergal, *Memorials of F. A. G. O., Bart.* (London, 1889); F. Joyce, *Life of Rev. Sir F. A. G. O., Bart., etc.* (London, 1896); W. Shaw, ed., *Sir F. O. and St Michael's, Tenbury: A Chapter in the History of English Church Music and Ecclesiology* (Birmingham, 1988).

Ovchinnikov, Viacheslav, Russian conductor and composer; b. Voronezh, May 29, 1936. He studied composition with Khrennikov at the Moscow Cons., graduating in 1962; also studied conducting with Lev Ginzburg; upon graduation he conducted various orchs. in Moscow and on Soviet radio and television. His works include *Sulamith*, ballet (1962), and *On the Dawn of Misty Youth*, opera (1974–78); also scores for films, including *War and Peace* (1961–67).

Overton, Hall (Franklin), American pianist, teacher, and composer; b. Bangor, Mich., Feb. 23, 1920; d. N.Y., Nov. 24, 1972. He studied piano at the Chicago Musical College and counterpoint at the Juilliard School of Music in New York (1940–42). He served in the U.S. Army overseas (1942–45). After World War II, he studied composition with Persichetti at the Juilliard School of Music, graduating in 1951; he also took private lessons with Riegger and Milhaud. At the same time, he filled professional engagements as a jazz pianist and contributed articles to the magazine *Jazz Today*. He was awarded 2 Guggenheim fellowships (1955, 1957). He taught at Juilliard (1960–71), the New School for Social Research in New York (1962–66), and at the Yale Univ. School of Music (1970–71). His works include the operas *The Enchanted Pear Tree*, after Boccaccio's *Decameron* (N.Y., Feb. 7, 1950), *Pietro's Petard* (N.Y., June 1963), and *Huckleberry Finn*, after Mark Twain (N.Y., May 20, 1971).

Owen, Richard, American lawyer, judge, and composer; b. N.Y., Dec. 11, 1922. He graduated from Dartmouth College in 1947 and from Harvard Law School in 1950; subsequently he served as a senior trial attorney, and then was appointed to the bench by President Nixon to the U.S. District Court in New York (1974). In between he attended night school at the Mannes School of Music, took courses in harmony and counterpoint with Vittorio Giannini and Robert Starer, and attended the Berkshire Music Center at Tanglewood. He wrote several operas deeply influenced by Puccini and Menotti, including *Dismissed with Prejudice* (1956), *A Moment of War* (1958), *A Fisherman Called Peter* (1965), *Mary Dyer* (dealing with a woman Quaker who was hanged in Boston on June 1, 1660; N.Y., June 12, 1976, with Owen's wife singing the title role), *The Death of the Virgin* (N.Y., March 31, 1983), *Abigail Adams* (N.Y., March 18, 1987), and the children's opera *Tom Sawyer* (N.Y., April 2, 1989).

Ozawa, Seiji, famous Japanese conductor; b. Fenytien, China (of Japanese parents), Sept. 1, 1935. His father was a Buddhist, his mother a Christian. The family returned to Japan in 1944, at the end of the Japanese occupation of Manchuria. Ozawa began to study piano; at 16, he enrolled at the Toho School of Music in Tokyo, where he studied composition and conducting; one of his teachers, Hideo Saito, profoundly influenced his development as a musician; he graduated in 1959 with 1st prizes in composition and conducting. By that time he had already conducted concerts with the NHK (Japan Broadcasting Corp.) Sym. Orch. and the Japan Phil.; upon Saito's advice, he went to Europe; to defray his expenses, he became a motor-scooter salesman for a Japanese firm, and promoted the product in Italy and France. In 1959 he won 1st prize at the international competition for conductors in Besançon, and was befriended by Charles Munch and Eugène Bigot; he then studied conducting with Bigot in Paris. Munch arranged for Ozawa to go to the United States and to study conducting at the Berkshire Music Center in Tanglewood; in 1960 he won its Koussevitzky Prize, and was awarded a scholarship to work with Karajan and the Berlin Phil. Bernstein heard him in Berlin and engaged him as an assistant conductor of the N.Y. Phil. On April 14, 1961, he made his first appearance with the orch. at Carnegie Hall; later that year he accompanied Bernstein and the orch. on its tour of Japan. In 1962 he was invited to return as a guest conductor of the NHK Sym. Orch., but difficulties arose between him and the players, who objected to being commanded in an imperious manner by one of their own countrymen; still, he succeeded in obtaining engagements with other Japanese orchs., which he conducted on his periodic visits to his homeland.

After serving as sole assistant conductor of the N.Y. Phil. (1964–65), Ozawa's career advanced significantly; from 1964 to 1968 he was music director of the Ravinia Festival, the summer home of the Chicago Sym. Orch.; in 1969 he served as its principal guest conductor; from 1965 to 1969 he also was music director of the Toronto Sym. Orch., which he took to England in 1965. From 1970 to 1976 he was music director of the San Francisco Sym. Orch., and then its music adviser (1976–77); he took it on an extensive tour of Europe in 1977, garnering exceptional critical acclaim. Even before completing his tenure in San Francisco, he had begun a close association with the Boston Sym. Orch.; with Schuller, he became co-artistic director of its Berkshire Music Center in 1970; in 1972 he assumed the post of music adviser of the Boston Sym. Orch., and in 1973 he became its music director, and sole artistic director of the Berkshire Music Center, an astonishing event in American music annals, marking the first time an Asian musician was chosen solely by his merit to head the Boston Sym. Orch., which was for years since its foundation the exclusive preserve of German, and later French and Russian, conductors. In 1976 Ozawa took the Boston Sym. Orch. on a tour of Europe; in 1978 he escorted it to Japan, where those among Japanese musicians who had been skeptical about his abilities greeted his spectacular ascendance with national pride. Another unprecedented event took place in the spring of 1979, when Ozawa traveled with the Boston Sym. Orch. to the People's Republic of China on an official cultural visit; in Aug. 1979 Ozawa and the orch. went on a tour of European music festivals. The centennial of the Boston Sym. Orch. in 1981 was marked by a series of concerts, under Ozawa's direction, which included appearances in 14 American cities and a tour of Japan, France, Germany, Austria, and England. On Sept. 24, 1991, he conducted the Saito Kinen Orch. of Japan at its first appearance in the United States at N.Y.'s Carnegie Hall. One Sept. 5, 1992, he inaugurated the Saito Kinen Festival in Matsumoto. He made his Metropolitan Opera debut in New York on Dec. 4, 1992, conducting *Eugene Onegin*. In 1994 the Boston Sym. Orch.'s new concert hall at Tanglewood was named the Seiji Ozawa Hall in his honor.

After Ozawa consolidated his music directorship of the Boston Sym. Orch., he retained that position for more than 25 years. His last years at its helm did not equal his early success, but he contrived to demonstrate his capacity for interpretations of occasional brilliance. He was married twice: first to the Japanese pianist Kyoko Edo, and 2d, to a Eurasian, Vera Ilyan. He received an honorary doctorate in music from the Univ. of San Francisco in 1971, and one from the New England Cons. of Music in Boston in 1982. His career was the subject of the documentary film *Ozawa*, which was telecast by PBS in 1987.

P

Pablo (Costales), Luís (Alfonso) de, eminent Spanish composer and teacher; b. Bilbao, Jan. 28, 1930. He commenced his musical training in Fuenterrabía when he was 8. After settling in Madrid, he pursued the study of law at the Universidad Complutense (graduated, 1952) while continuing his musical training on his own. In 1958 he joined the Nueva Música group. In 1959 he organized the Tiempo y Música group, with which he presented concerts of contemporary chamber music until 1963. He founded the Forum Musical in 1963 for the purpose of giving concerts of contemporary music. In 1964 he served as the artistic organizer of the first gathering of the Música Contemporánea of Madrid. He founded the new music group Alea and the first electroacoustic music laboratory in Spain in 1965. In 1967 he was in Berlin as a guest of the Deutscher Akademischer Austauschdienst. In 1968 he founded Alea, Música electronica libre, a group that presented performances of live electroacoustic music. He became a prof. of contemporary music analysis at the Madrid Cons. in 1971. With José Luis Alexanco, he served as codirector of the Encuentros de Arts in Pamplona in 1972. In 1973 he was the Visiting Slee Prof. at the State Univ. of N.Y. at Buffalo, and in 1974 he was a prof. of contemporary music analysis at the Univs. of Ottawa and Montreal. In subsequent years, he lectured widely on contemporary music in Spain and abroad. He became president of the Spanish section of the ISCM in 1981. In 1983 he was made director of the Centro para la Difusión de la Música Contemporánea of the Ministry of Culture. In 1994 he was composer-in-residence at the Spanish Academy in Rome. In 1973 the French government honored him with the title of Chevalier des Arts et des Lettres, and in 1986 it bestowed upon him the Médaille d'Officier de l'Ordre des Arts et des Lettres. In 1986 King Juan Carlos of Spain presented him with the Medalla de Oro al Mérito en las Bellas Artes españolas. He was made a full member of the Real Academia de Bellas Artes de San Fernando of Madrid and a corresponding member of the Academy of Granada in 1988. In 1991 he was awarded the Premio Nacional de Música by the Ministry of Culture, and in 1993 he was awarded its diploma of the Consejo Internacional de la Música. In his compositions, he has demonstrated a remarkable versatility in handling various techniques. All the while, he has remained true to himself by finding his own compositional path in which each score becomes a thoroughly new adventure in sound. This is so whether he utilizes traditional instruments or ranges into other sound worlds, such as electronic manifestations.

WORKS: DRAMATIC: *Per diversos motivos* for 2 Actors, Soprano, 12 Voices, and Piano (1969); *Berceuse* for Actor, Soprano, 3 Flutes, 2 Percussionists, and Hammond Organ (1973–74; Buffalo, Jan. 26, 1975); *Sólo un paso* for Actor and Flute (Bremen Radio, May 1974); *Very Gentle* for Soprano, Countertenor, and 2 Instrumentalists (Royan, April 3, 1974); *Kiu*, opera (1979–82; Madrid, April 16, 1983); *El viajero indiscreto*, opera (1984–88; Madrid, March 12, 1990); *Llanto*, ballet (1987); *La madre invita a comer*, opera (1992; Venice, June 19, 1993); incidental music; film scores.

BIBL.: T. Marco, *L. d. P.* (Madrid, 1976); J. García del Busto, *L. d. P.* (Madrid, 1979); idem, *Escritos sobre L. d. P.* (Madrid, 1987).

Pacchiarotti, Gasparo, famous Italian castrato soprano; b. Fabriano, near Ancona (baptized), May 21, 1740; d. Padua, Oct. 28, 1821. He studied with Bertoni at San Marco in Venice, where he was principal soloist (1765–68). He then was primo uomo in Palermo (1770–71) before singing in Naples (1771–76). After appearing throughout Italy, he was engaged for the inaugural operation productions at Milan's La Scala (Aug.-Sept. 1778). He sang at the King's Theatre in London (1778–80), returning there 1781–84; he also appeared at the Tuileries before the French court (1782). Having served as primo uomo at Venice's Teatro S. Benedetto (1784–91), he once more sang in London (1791), appearing in concert as well as opera. He sang in the inaugural season at Venice's Teatro La Fenice (1792–93) before retiring to his estate in Padua. He later sang for Napoleon in Padua (1796) and at Bertoni's funeral at San Marco (June 28, 1814). Pacchiarotti was acclaimed as the greatest castrato of his day, his voice ranging from c′ to B flat. A. Calegari publ. *Modi generali del canto premessi alle maniere parziali onde adornace o rifiorice le nude o semplici melodie o cantilene giusta il metodo di Gasparo Pacchiarotti* (Milan, 1836).

BIBL.: G. Pacchiarotti (his adopted son), *Cenni biografici intorno a G. P.* (Padua, 1844); R. Sassi, *Un celebre musico fabrianese, G. P. (col testamento)* (Fabriano, 1935).

Pacchierotti, Ubaldo, Italian composer and conductor; b. Cervarese-Croce (Padua), Oct. 30, 1875; d. Milan, April 18, 1916. He studied at the Cons. S. Pietro a Majella in Naples, then conducted in Livorno and Buenos Aires. Among his works were the operas *La lampada* (Buenos Aires, 1899), *L'albatro* (Milan, 1905), *Eidelberga mia!* (Genoa, Feb. 27, 1908), and *Il Santo* (Turin, 1913).

Pacini, Andrea, Italian castrato alto and composer; b. Lucca, c.1690; d. there, March 1764. He made his debut in Albinoni's *Astarto* in Venice in 1708, and returned to sing there (1714–16; 1726). He also appeared in Naples (1713–14; 1722–23), Turin (1719), and Genoa (1720). In 1721 he was elected to membership in the Accademia Filarmonica in Bologna, in which city he sang in 1722. From 1720 to 1730 he was virtuoso to Prince Antonio of Parma. On Oct. 31, 1724, he made his London debut creating the title role in Handel's *Tamerlano*. Handel also wrote the role of Unulfo for him. Following appearances in Florence (1725–26; 1731–32) and Parma (1729), he was active as a priest.

Pacini, Giovanni, Italian composer; b. Catania, Feb. 17, 1796; d. Pescia, Dec. 6, 1867. He was a pupil of Marchesi and Padre Mattei at Bologna, and of Furlanetto at Venice. His first opera was *Don Pomponio* (1813; not perf.), followed by *Annetta e Lucinda* (Milan, Oct. 17, 1813); by 1835 he had produced over 40 operas on various Italian stages, when the failure of *Carlo di Borgogna* (Feb. 21, 1835) at Venice temporarily checked the flow of dramatic composition. He went to Viareggio, near Lucca, and established a very successful school of music, for which he wrote several short treatises, *Corso teoretico-pratico di lezioni di armonia* (Milan, c.1844), and *Cenni storici sulla musica e trattato di contrappunto* (Lucca, 1864), and built a private theater. Later he removed the school to Lucca. In 1840 Pacini, who prided himself on rapid work, wrote his dramatic masterpiece, *Saffo*, in 28 days (Naples, Nov. 29, 1840). Forty more operas followed to 1867, the best of which were *Medea* (Palermo, Nov. 28, 1843), *La Regina di Cipro* (Turin, Feb. 7, 1846), and *Niccolò de Lapi* (1857; Florence, Oct. 29, 1873). He also wrote numerous oratorios. He excelled in melodic invention, although his early style prompted Rossini to exclaim, "God help us if he knew music: no one could resist him." He was also an active contributor to several musical papers. He publ. memoirs as *Le mie memorie artistiche* (Florence, 1865; enl.by Cicconetti, 1872; rev. by F. Magnani, 1875). His brother, Emilio Pacini (b. 1810; d. Neuilly, near Paris, Dec. 2, 1898), was a distinguished librettist.
BIBL.: M. Davini, *Il maestro G. P.* (Palermo, 1927).

Paciorkiewicz, Tadeusz, Polish composer and organist; b. Sierpc, Oct. 17, 1916. He studied organ with Rutkowski at the Warsaw Cons. (graduated, 1942) and composition with Sikorski at the Łódz State College of Music (graduated, 1951). He taught in music schools in Plock (1945–49) and Łódz (1949–59); he also taught at the Warsaw State College of Music (from 1954), becoming a permanent faculty member (1959); he was dean of its composition, theory, and conducting dept. (1963–69), and then its rector (1969–71). His works include *Ushico*, radio opera (1962), *The Maiden from the Dormer Window*, opera (1964), and *Ligea*, radio opera (1967); also the ballet *Warsaw Legend* (1959) and the oratorio *De Revolutionibus* for 4 Solo Voices, Reciter, Boy's Chorus, Chorus, Organ, and Orch. (1972).

Pacius, Fredrik (Friedrich), significant German-born Finnish conductor, teacher, and composer; b. Hamburg, March 19, 1809; d. Helsinki, Jan. 8, 1891. He studied violin with Spohr and composition with Hauptmann in Kassel. After playing violin in Stockholm's Royal Chapel (1828–34), he settled in Helsinki (1835) as a lecturer at the Univ., being promoted to prof. (1860); he also founded a choral society (1835) and regular sym. concerts (1845). Pacius is acknowledged as the father of Finnish music. His works owe much to the German Romanticists, especially Spohr and Mendelssohn, and to Finnish folk music. His setting of J. Runeberg's Swedish poem *Vart land* became the Finnish national anthem in 1843; it was set to Finnish words as *Maamme* in 1848. He also wrote the first Finnish opera, *Kung Karls jakt* (to a Swedish libretto; Helsinki, March 24, 1852), as well as the opera *Loreley* (Helsinki, April 28, 1887) and incidental music to *Prinsessan af Cypern* (1860), both to Swedish texts.
BIBL.: M. Colan-Beaurain, *F. P.* (Helsinki, 1921); O. Andersson, *Den unge P. och musiklivet i Helsingfors på 1830-talet* (Helsinki, 1938); J. Rosas, *F. P. som tonsättare* (Turku, 1949).

Paderewski, Ignacy (Jan), celebrated Polish pianist and composer; b. Kurylowka, Podolia (Russian Poland), Nov. 18, 1860; d. N.Y., June 29, 1941. His father was an administrator of country estates; his mother died soon after his birth. From early childhood Paderewski was attracted to piano music; he received some musical instruction from Peter Sowinski, who taught him 4-hand arrangements of operas. His first public appearance was in a charity concert at the age of 11, when he played piano with his sister. His playing aroused interest among wealthy patrons, who took him to Kiev. He was then sent to Warsaw, where he entered the Cons., learned to play trombone, and joined the school band. He also continued serious piano study; his teachers at the Warsaw Cons. were Schlözer, Strobl, and Janotha. In 1875 and 1877 he toured in provincial Russian towns with the Polish violinist Cielewicz; in the interim periods, he took courses in composition at the Warsaw Cons., and upon graduation in 1878 was engaged as a member of the piano faculty there. In 1880 he married a young music student named Antonina Korsak, but she died 9 days after giving birth to a child, on Oct. 10, 1880. In 1882 he went to Berlin to study composition with Kiel; there he met Anton Rubinstein, who gave him encouraging advice and urged him to compose piano music. He resigned from his teaching job at the Warsaw Cons. and began to study orchestration in Berlin with Heinrich Urban. While on a vacation in the Tatra Mountains (which inspired his *Tatra Album* for piano), he met the celebrated Polish actress Modjeska, who proposed to finance his further piano studies with Leschetizky in Vienna. Paderewski followed this advice and spent several years as a Leschetizky student. He continued his career as a concert pianist. On March 3, 1888, he gave his first Paris recital, and on Nov. 10, 1888, played a concert in Vienna, both with excellent success. He also began receiving recognition as a composer. Anna Essipova (who was married to Leschetizky) played his piano concerto in Vienna under the direction of Hans Richter. Paderewski made his London debut on May 9, 1890. On Nov. 17, 1891, he played for the first time in New York, and was acclaimed with an adulation rare for pianists; by some counts he gave 107 concerts in 117 days in New York and other American cities and attended 86 dinner parties; his wit, already fully developed, made him a social lion in wealthy American salons. At one party, it was reported, the hostess confused him with a famous polo player who was also expected to be a guest, and greeted him effusively. "No," Paderewski is supposed to have replied, "he is a rich soul who plays polo, and I am a poor Pole who plays solo." American spinsters beseeched him for a lock of his luxurious mane of hair; he invariably obliged, and when his valet observed that at this rate he would soon be bald, he said, "Not I, my dog." There is even a story related by a gullible biographer that Paderewski could charm beasts by his art and that a spider used to come down from the ceiling in Paderewski's lodgings in Vienna and sit at the piano every time Paderewski played a certain Chopin etude. Paderewski eclipsed even Caruso as an idol of the masses. In 1890 he made a concert tour in Germany; he also toured South America, South Africa, and Australia. In 1898 he purchased a beautiful home, the Villa Riond-Bosson on Lake Geneva, Switzerland; in 1899 he married Helena Gorska, Baroness von Rosen. In 1900, by a deed of trust, Paderewski established a fund of $10,000 (the original trustees were William Steinway, Henry Lee Higginson, and William Mason), the interest from which was to be used for triennial prizes given "to composers of American birth without distinction as to age or religion" for works in the categories of syms., concertos, and chamber music. In 1910, on the occasion of the centennial of Chopin's birth, Paderewski donated $60,000 for the construction of the Chopin Memorial Hall in Warsaw; in the same year, he contributed $100,000 for the erection of the statue of King Jagiello in Warsaw, on the quinquecentennial of his victory over the Teutonic Knights in 1410. In 1913 he purchased a ranch in Paso Robles in California.

Although cosmopolitan in his culture, Paderewski remained a great Polish patriot. During the First World War he donated the entire proceeds from his concerts to a fund for the Polish people caught in the war between Russia and Germany. After the establishment of the independent Polish state, Paderewski served as its representative in Washington; in 1919 he was named prime minister of the Polish Republic, the first musician to occupy such a post in any country at any period. He took part in the Versailles Treaty conference; it was then that Prime Minister Clemenceau of France welcomed Paderewski with the famous, if possibly apocryphal, remark: "You, a famous pianist, a prime minister! What a comedown!" Paderewski resigned his post on Dec. 10, 1919. He reentered politics in 1920 in the wake of the Russian invasion of Poland that year, when he became a delegate to the League of Nations; he resigned on May 7, 1921, and resumed his musical career. On Nov. 22, 1922, he gave his first concert after a hiatus of many years at Carnegie Hall in New York. In 1939 he made his last American tour. Once more during his lifetime Poland was invaded, this time by both Germany and Russia. Once more Paderewski was driven to political action. He joined the Polish government-in-exile in France and was named president of its parliament on Jan. 23, 1940. He returned to the United States on Nov. 6, 1940, a few months before his death. At the order of President Roosevelt, his body was given state burial in Arlington National Cemetery, pending the return of his remains to Free Poland. While his body was buried at Arlington National Cemetery, his heart was buried in Brooklyn and finally entombed at the Shrine of Our Lady of Czestochowa in Doylestown, Pa., in 1986. His body was finally removed from Arlington National Cemetery and returned to Free Poland, where a Mass and state burial was accorded him at the St. John the Baptist Cathedral in Warsaw on July 5, 1992, with President Bush of the United States and President Walesa of Poland in attendance. Paderewski received many honors. He held the following degrees: Ph.D. from the Univ. of Lemberg (1912); D.Mus. from Yale Univ. (1917); Ph.D. from the Univ. of Kraków (1919); D.C.L. from the Univ. of Oxford (1920); LL.D. from Columbia Univ. (1922); Ph.D. from the Univ. of Southern Calif. (1923); Ph.D. from the Univ. of Poznan (1924); and Ph.D. from the Univ. of Glasgow (1925). He also held the Grand Cross of the French Legion of Honor (1922). A postage stamp with his picture was issued in Poland in 1919, and 2 postage stamps honoring him in the series "Men of Liberty" were issued in the United States in 1960.

As an artist, Paderewski was a faithful follower of the Romantic school, which allowed free, well-nigh improvisatory declensions from the written notes, tempi, and dynamics; judged by contemporary standards of precise rendering of the text, Paderewski's interpretations appear surprisingly free, but this very personal freedom of performance moved contemporary audiences to ecstasies of admiration. Also, Paderewski's virtuoso technique, which astonished his listeners, has been easily matched by any number of pianists of succeeding generations. Yet his position in the world of the performing arts remains undiminished by the later achievements of younger men and women pianists. As a composer, Paderewski also belongs to the Romantic school. At least one of his piano pieces, the *Menuet in G* (a movement of his set of *6 Humoresques de concert*), achieved enormous popularity. His other compositions, however, never sustained a power of renewal and were eventually relegated to the archives of unperformed music. His opera *Manru* (1897–1900), dealing with folk life in the Tatra Mountains, was produced in Dresden on May 29, 1901, and was also performed by the Metropolitan Opera in New York on Feb. 14, 1902.

BIBL.: F. Buffen, *I. P.* (N.Y., 1891); C. Tretbar, *P.: A Biographical Sketch* (N.Y., 1892); H. Finck, *P. and His Art* (N.Y., 1895); A. Nossig, *P.* (Leipzig, 1901); E. Baughan, *I. P.* (London, 1908); A. Chybiński, *P.* (Warsaw, 1910); S. Popielowna, *I. P.* (Tarnow, 1919); F. Martens, *P.* (N.Y., 1923); B. Sidorowicz, *I. P.* (Poznan, 1924); J. Cooke, *P.* (Philadelphia, 1928); H. Opieński, *I. J. P.* (Warsaw, 1928; 3d ed., rev. and aug., 1960); C. Philips, *P.* (N.Y., 1933); R. Landau, *I. P.: Musician and Statesman* (N.Y., 1934); *P.'s Diamond Anniversary* (N.Y., 1936); M. Lawton, *The P. Memoirs* (to 1914 only; N.Y., 1938); E. Ligocki, *Homage to P.* (Edinburgh, 1941); A. Gronowicz, *P.: Pianist and Patriot* (Edinburgh, 1943); B. Sarrazin, *Imageries de P.* (Annonay, 1945); A. Baumgartner, *La Vérité sur le prétendu drame P.* (Geneva, 1948); S. Giron, *Le Drame P.* (Geneva, 1948); A. Strakacz, *P. as I Knew Him* (New Brunswick, N.J., 1949); C. Kellogg, *P.* (N.Y., 1956); J. Cieplinski, *I. P.* (N.Y., 1960); R. and P. Hume, *The Lion of Poland: The Story of P.* (N.Y., 1962); R. Halski, *P.* (London, 1964); W. Dulaba, *I. P.* (Kraków, 1966); A. Zamoyski, *P.* (N.Y., 1982); J. Hoskins, *I. J. P., 1860–1941: A Biographical Sketch and a Selective List of Reading Materials* (Washington, D.C., 1984); E. Lipmann, *P., l'idole des années folles* (Paris, 1984); M. Perkowska, *Diariusz koncertowy I.ego J.a. P.ego* (Kraków, 1990).

Padilla y Ramos, Mariano, Spanish baritone; b. Murcia, 1842; d. Auteuil, near Paris, Nov. 23, 1906. He studied with Mabellini and Ronconi in Florence, making his debut in Messina. He sang in opera with great success in Italy, Austria, Germany, and Russia. In 1869 he married **Désirée Artôt**.

Paër, Ferdinando, significant Italian composer; b. Parma, June 1, 1771; d. Paris, May 3, 1839. He studied with Francesco Fortunati and Gaspare Ghiretti in Parma, producing his first stage work, the prose opera *Orphée et Euridice*, there in 1791. On July 14, 1792, he was appointed honorary maestro di cappella to the court of Parma, bringing out his opera *Le astuzie amorose* that same year at the Teatro Ducale there. His finest work of the period was *Griselda, ossia La virtù al cimento* (Parma, Jan. 1798). In 1797 he was appointed music director of the Kärnthnertortheater in Vienna. While there, he made the acquaintance of Beethoven, who expressed admiration for his work. It was in Vienna that he composed one of his finest operas, *Camilla, ossia Il sotteraneo* (Feb. 23, 1799). Another fine opera was his *Achille* (Vienna, June 6, 1801). After a visit to Prague in 1801, he accepted the appointment of court Kapellmeister in Dresden. Three of his most important operas were premiered there: *I Fuorusciti di Firenze* (Nov. 27, 1802), *Sargino, ossia L'Allievo dell'amore* (May 26, 1803), and *Leonora, ossia L'amore conjugale* (Oct. 3, 1804), a work identical in subject with that of Beethoven's *Fidelio* (1805). In 1806 he resigned his Dresden post and accepted an invitation to visit Napoleon in Posen and Warsaw. In 1807 Napoleon appointed him his maître de chapelle in Paris, where he also became director of the Opéra Comique. Following the dismissal of Spontini in 1812, he was appointed director of the Théâtre-Italien. One of his most successful operas of the period, *Le Maître de chapelle* (Paris, March 29, 1821), remained in the repertoire in its Italian version until the early years of the 20th century. Paër's tenure at the Théâtre-Italien continued through the vicissitudes of Catalani's management (1814–17) and the troubled joint directorship with Rossini (1824–27). After his dismissal in 1827, he was awarded the cross of the Légion d'honneur in 1828; he was elected a member of the Inst. of the Académie des Beaux Arts in 1831. He was appointed director of music of Louis Philippe's private chapel in 1832. Paër was one of the most important Italian composers of opera in his era. His vocal writing was highly effective, as was his instrumentation. Nevertheless, his operas have disappeared from the active repertoire. His *Leonora*, however, was revived and recorded in the 1970s by the Swiss conductor Peter Maag.

BIBL.: T. Masse and A. Deschamps, *De MM. P. et Rossini* (Paris, 1820); F. Paër, *M. P.: Ex-directeur du Théâtre-Italien, a MM les dilettans* (Paris, 1827); C. de Colobrano, *Funerailles de F. P.* (Paris, 1893).

Paganelli, Giuseppe Antonio, Italian composer; b. Padua, March 6, 1710; d. probably in Madrid, c.1762. He was employed as a harpsichordist in an Italian opera company. He was in Venice (1732), then at Bayreuth (1737–38). In 1755 he went to Madrid.

His *Divertisement de le Beau Sexe* (6 sonatas) was ed. by G. Tagliapietra (Milan, 1936). In addition to 11 operas, he composed a number of instrumental works that were popular in his day.

BIBL.: E. Schenk, *G. A. P.* (Salzburg, 1928).

Pagliughi, Lina, American-born Italian soprano; b. N.Y., May 27, 1907; d. Rubicone, Oct. 2, 1980. She was encouraged to pursue a career as a singer by Tetrazzini; she studied voice in Milan with Manlio Bavagnoli. She made her operatic debut at the Teatro Nazionale in Milan as Gilda in 1927, then made appearances throughout Italy; sang at La Scala in Milan in 1930, and continued to make appearances there until 1947; she then sang with the RAI until her retirement in 1956. She was married to the tenor Primo Montanari. She was best known for her roles in operas by Rossini, Bellini, and Donizetti.

Pahissa, Jaime, Catalan-born Argentine writer on music, teacher, and composer; b. Barcelona, Oct. 7, 1880; d. Buenos Aires, Oct. 27, 1969. He was a practicing architect for 4 years before turning to music as a profession and studied composition with Morera in Barcelona. He associated himself with the Catalan nationalist movement in art, obtaining his first important success in 1906 with the Romantic opera *La presó de Lledida* (The Prison of Lérida), which had 100 consecutive performances in Barcelona; it was later revised and produced in Barcelona on Feb. 8, 1928, as *La Princesa Margarita*, again obtaining a notable success. Other operas produced in Barcelona were *Gala Placidía* (Jan. 15, 1913) and *Marianela* (March 31, 1923). In 1935 Pahissa emigrated to Argentina, settling in Buenos Aires, where he continued to compose; he also established himself as a teacher and writer. He publ. in Buenos Aires *Espíritu y cuerpo de la música* (1945), *Los grandes problemas de la música* (1945; 2d ed., 1954), *Vida y obra de Manuel de Falla* (1947; Eng. tr., 1954), and *Sendas y cumbres de la música española* (1955).

Paik, Nam June, innovative avant-garde Korean-American composer and visual arts; b. Seoul, July 20, 1932. He studied first at the Univ. of Tokyo, then took courses in theory with Georgiades in Munich and with Fortner in Freiburg im Breisgau; he then attended the summer courses in new music in Darmstadt (1957–61) and worked at the Cologne Electronic Music Studio (1958–60). In his showings, he pursues the objective of total art as the sum of integrated synesthetic experiences, involving all sorts of mundane actions: walking, talking, dressing, undressing, drinking, smoking, moving furniture, etc. Paik attracted attention at his duo recitals with the topless cellist Charlotte Moorman, at which he acted as a surrogate cello, with his denuded spinal column serving as the fingerboard for Moorman's cello bow, while his bare skin provided an area for intermittent pizzicati. About 1963 Paik began experimenting with videotape as a medium for sounds and images; his initial experiment in this field was *Global Groove*, a high-velocity collage of intermingled television bits, which included instantaneous commercials, fragments from news telecasts, and subliminal extracts from regular programs, subjected to topological alterations. His works include *Opéra sextronique* (1967) and *Opéra électronique* (1968); also the video works *Video Buddha* (1974), *VIDEA* (1980), *The More the Better* (1988), *My Faust/The Stations* (1988–91), and *Video Opera* (1993).

Paine, John Knowles, prominent American composer and pedagogue; b. Portland, Maine, Jan. 9, 1839; d. Cambridge, Mass., April 25, 1906. His father ran a music store, and conducted the band in Portland. He studied organ, piano, harmony, and counterpoint with Hermann Krotzschmar, then took courses with K. Haupt (organ), W. Wieprecht (orchestration and composition), and others in Berlin (1858–61); concurrently he appeared as an organist and pianist in Germany and England. He settled in Boston, becoming organist of the West Church (1861). He joined the faculty of Harvard Univ. (1862), where he also was organist at its Appleton Chapel; was prof. of music at Harvard (1875–1906), the first to hold such a position at a U.S. univ.; he was made a member of the National Inst. of Arts and Letters (1898), and was awarded the honorary degrees of M.A. from Harvard (1869) and Mus.D. from Yale (1890). He greatly distinguished himself as a teacher, serving as mentor to J. A. Carpenter, F. S. Converse, A. Foote, E. B. Hill, D. G. Mason, W. Spalding, and many others. He publ. *The History of Music to the Death of Schubert* (Boston, 1907).

WORKS: DRAMATIC: *Il pesceballo*, comic opera (1862; music not extant); *Azara*, grand opera (1883–98; concert perf., Boston, May 7, 1903); incidental music to Sophocles' *Oedipus tyrannus* (1880–81; Cambridge, Mass., May 17, 1881; rev. 1895) and to Aristophanes' *The Birds* (1900; Cambridge, May 10, 1901).

BIBL.: J. Schmidt, *The Life and Works of J. K. P.* (Ann Arbor, Mich., 1980).

Paisiello, Giovanni, famous Italian composer; b. Roccaforzata, near Taranto, May 9, 1740; d. Naples, June 5, 1816. He studied at the Jesuit school in Taranto, and then at the Cons. di S. Onofrio in Naples (1754–63). He began his career as an opera composer by writing works for the Marsigli-Rossi Theater in Bologna in 1764. He settled in Naples in 1766, and proceeded to write over 40 operas during the next decade. Outstanding works from this period include *Le finte contesse* (Rome, Feb. 1766), *L'idolo cinese* (Naples, 1767), and *La Frascatana* (Venice, 1774). In 1776 he was invited to Russia, where he was appointed maestro di cappella to the empress Catherine II in St. Petersburg. He composed one of his most celebrated operas there, *Il Barbiere di Siviglia* (Sept. 26, 1782), which remained popular in Italy until the appearance of Rossini's masterpiece in 1816. In 1783 Ferdinand IV of Naples made him compositore della musica de' drammi. In 1784 he left Russia for Naples, making a stop in Vienna, where he brought out one of his finest scores, *Il Re Teodoro in Venezia* (Aug. 23, 1784). His success in Naples led to his additional appointment in 1787 as maestro della real camera, in which capacity he was responsible for secular music at the court. Between 1784 and 1799 he composed several noteworthy operas, including *Le gare generose* (Naples, 1786), *L'amore contrastato* (Naples, 1788), *Nina, o sia La Pazza per amore* (Caserta, June 25, 1789), and *I Zingari in fiera* (Naples, Nov. 21, 1789). After Republican troops took control of Naples in Jan. 1799, Paisiello was named maestro di cappella nazionale by the new government on May 4, 1799. However, with the return of the Royalists in June 1799, he fell into disfavor with the court; he was eventually granted a pardon, and restored to his posts on July 7, 1801. Ferdinand subsequently allowed him to serve as Napoleon's maitre de chapelle in Paris from April 1802 until his return to Naples in Aug. 1804. He was made a member of the Légion d'honneur in 1806. He was further honored with membership in the Institut, taking the place of the deceased Haydn in 1809. After Joseph Bonaparte became king of Naples in 1806, Paisiello was appointed director of secular and sacred music at the court; he continued to hold these positions under Joachim Murat, Joseph's successor as king (1808–15); he also served as one of the directors of the new college of music (1807–13). In 1815 Ferdinand returned to the throne, and Paisiello lost all of his posts with the exception of that of maestro della real cappella.

Paisiello's success as a composer of comic operas equaled that of Piccini and Cimarosa. He was extraordinarily prolific; his operas alone number over 90, a few of which have been revived in the 20th century. Although he employed instrumental effects that were rare in Italy, he avoided the over-elaborate numbers in his operas that marked the works of many of his contemporaries, obtaining his results by melodic invention, and by the grace, beauty, and dramatic faithfulness of his conceptions.

BIBL.: J. Le Sueur, *Notice sur P.* (Paris, 1816); Quatremère de Quincy, *Notice historique de P.* (Paris, 1817); G. de Dominicis, *Saggio su la vita del Cavalier Don G. P.* (Moscow, 1818); F. Schizzi, *Della vita e degli studi di G. P.* (Milan, 1833); C. Pupino, *P.* (Naples, 1908); S. Panareo, *P. in Russia* (Trani, 1910); U. Prota-Giurleo, *P. ed i suoi primi trionfi a Napoli* (Naples, 1925); A. Cametti, *P. e la corte di Vienna* (Rome, 1929); G. Speziale, *G. P.* (Naples, 1931); E. Faustini-Fasini, *L'ultima opera di P., I pittagorici* (Taranto, 1937); idem, *Opere teatrali, oratori e cantate di G. P.* (Bari, 1940); A. Ghislanzoni, *G. P.: Valutazioni critiche ret-*

tificate (Rome, 1969); J. Hunt, *G. P.: His Life as an Opera Composer* (N.Y., 1975); M. Robinson and U. Hoffmann, *G. P.: A Thematic Catalogue of His Music* (2 vols., Stuyvesant, N.Y., 1991, 1994).

Paladilhe, Emile, French composer; b. Montpellier, June 3, 1844; d. Paris, Jan. 6, 1926. He entered the Paris Cons. in 1853, where he was a pupil of Marmontel (piano), Benoist (organ), and Halevy (counterpoint); he won 1st prize for piano and organ in 1857, and the Grand Prix de Rome in 1860 with the cantata *Le Czar Ivan IV* (Paris Opéra, 1860). He brought out the comic opera *Le Passant* in Paris (April 24, 1872), followed by *L'Amour africain* (May 8, 1875), *Suzanne* (Dec. 30, 1878), *Diana* (Feb. 23, 1885), the opera *Patrie* (Dec. 20, 1886), and *Les Saintes Maries de la mer*, a sacred lyric drama (Montpellier, 1892). In 1892 he succeeded Guiraud as member of the Institut de France.

Palazzesi, Matilde, Italian soprano; b. Montecarotto, March 1, 1802; d. Barcelona, July 3, 1842. She studied with Giacomo Solarto in Pesaro, making her debut in the title role of Rossini's *Zelmira* in 1824 in Dresden. She sang with the Italian Opera there until 1833, then appeared at La Scala in Milan and other Italian opera houses. She went to Barcelona, where she sang at the Opera from 1841. She was a leading interpreter of Mozart, Rossini, Bellini, Donizetti, and Spontini.
BIBL.: B. Padovano, *M. P.* (1953).

Palester, Roman, Polish composer; b. Śniatyń, Dec. 28, 1907; d. Paris, Aug. 25, 1989. After training in piano from Soltysowa at the Lwów Cons., he entered the Warsaw Cons. in 1925 and studied composition with Sikorski. He subsequently pursued the study of art history at the Univ. of Warsaw. In 1931 he obtained diplomas in composition and theory. After dividing his time between Poland and France, he taught at the Warsaw Cons. from the end of World War II until 1948, when he settled in Paris. In 1981 he was reinstated as a member of the Polish Composers Union. In his music, he was particularly influenced by French music but sought to preserve elements of Polish folk melos in the thematic structure of his scores. Harmonically he did not choose to transcend the limit of enhanced tonality. His works include the operas *Zywe kamienie* (The Living Stones; 1944; unfinished) and *La Mort de Don Juan* (1959–60), and the ballet *Piesn o ziemi* (Song of the Earth; 1937).

Palisca, Claude V(ictor), esteemed American musicologist; b. Fiume, Yugoslavia, Nov. 24, 1921. He was taken to the United States as a child and in 1929 he became a naturalized American citizen. He was a student of Rathaus (composition) at Queens College of the City Univ. of N.Y. (B.A., 1943), and of Piston and Thompson (composition) and Kinkeldey, Gombosi, and Davison (musicology) at Harvard Univ. (M.A., 1948; Ph.D., 1954, with the diss. *The Beginnings of Baroque Music: Its Roots in Sixteenth-century Theory and Polemics*). In 1949–50 he held a John Knowles Paine Traveling fellowship, and then studied in Italy on a Fulbright grant (1950–52). From 1953 to 1959 he taught at the Univ. of Ill. in Urbana. He was assoc. prof. (1959–64) and prof. (1964–80) of the history of music at Yale Univ., where he then was the Henry L. and Lucy G. Moses Prof. of Music from 1980 until being made a prof. emeritus in 1992. He also served as chairman of the music dept. (1969–75), and later as director of its graduate studies (1987–92). From 1966 he was ed. of the Yale Music Theory Translation Series. In 1971–72 he was president of the American Musicological Soc. In 1960–61 and 1981–82 he held Guggenheim fellowships. In 1972–73 he was a senior fellow of the NEH. He became a member of the American Academy of Arts and Sciences in 1986 and of the Accademia filarmonica of Bologna in 1987. In 1991 he was made an honorary member of the American Musicological Soc. His numerous writings include *Girolamo Mei: Letters on Ancient and Modern Music to Vincenzo Galilei and Giovanni Bardi* (Rome, 1960; 2d ed., 1977), *Baroque Music* (Englewood Cliffs, N.J., 1968; 3d ed., 1991), *Humanism in Italian Renaissance Musical Thought* (New Haven, 1985), *The Florentine Camerata: Documentary Studies and Translations* (New Haven, 1989), and *Studies in the History of Italian Music and Music Theory* (Oxford, 1994).
BIBL.: N. Baker and B. Hanning, *Musical Humanism and Its Legacy: Essays in Honor of C. V. P.* (Stuyvesant, N.Y., 1992).

Pallandios, Menelaos, Greek composer and pedagogue; b. Piraeus, Feb. 11, 1914. He studied with Mitropoulos in Athens and with Casella in Rome. In 1936 he became an instructor at the Athens Cons., and in 1962 was appointed its director. In 1969 he was elected to the Athens Academy. He wrote music to several ancient Greek tragedies, endeavoring to re-create the classical modes in modern investiture. His works include the opera *Antigone* (1942) and the ballets *Pombi ston Aheronta* (Procession Towards Acheron; 1942), *Prosefhi se archaeo nao* (Prayer in the Ancient Temple; 1942), *Electra* (1944), *Penthesilea* (1944), *3 Archaic Suites* (1949), and *Greek Triptych* (1960); also incidental music to Greek dramas; film scores.
BIBL.: M. Pallandios, ed., *M. G. P., moussourgos* (Athens, 1968).

Pallavicino, Carlo, Italian composer; b. Salo, near Brescia, date unknown; d. Dresden, Jan. 29, 1688. He served as an organista ai concerti at S. Antonio in Padua in 1665–66, and in 1673–74 was maestro dei concerti there. He became a vice Kapellmeister at the Dresden court in 1667; he was named Kapellmeister in 1672. In 1674 he was named maestro di coro of the Ospedale degli Incurabili in Venice. In succeeding years he became one of the leading opera composers in Venice. In 1685 he accepted an invitation from the elector Johann Georg III of Saxony to resume his former post as Dresden Kapellmeister. On Jan. 1, 1687, he assumed his duties as director of theater and chamber music. Thirteen of his operas are extant.

Palló, Imre, Hungarian-American conductor and teacher; b. Budapest, May 15, 1941. He was a student of Kodály at the Budapest Academy of Music and of Swarowsky at the Vienna Academy of Music. After conducting in Europe, he made his U.S. debut as a guest conductor with the National Sym. Orch. in Washington, D.C., in 1973. He subsequently conducted at the N.Y. City Opera. From 1976 to 1991 he was music director of the Hudson Valley Phil. in Poughkeepsie, N.Y. He also held the post of 1st conductor of the Frankfurt am Main Opera from 1987. In 1994 he joined the faculty of the Indiana Univ. School of Music in Bloomington.

Palma, Athos, Argentine composer and teacher; b. Buenos Aires, June 7, 1891; d. Miramar, Jan. 10, 1951. He studied with C. Troiani (piano) and other teachers in Buenos Aires; in 1904, went to Europe, returning to Buenos Aires in 1914. There he was busily engaged as a teacher. He publ. *Teoría razonada de la música* (5 vols., n.d.) and *Tratado completo de armonía* (1941). His music follows the Italian tradition, although the subject matter is derived from South American history and literature. Among his works are the operas *Nazdah* (Buenos Aires, June 19, 1924) and *Los Hijos del Sol* (Buenos Aires, Nov. 10, 1928).
BIBL.: N. Lamuraglia, *A. P.: Vida, arte, educación* (Buenos Aires, 1954).

Palmer, Felicity (Joan), admired English soprano; b. Cheltenham, April 6, 1944. She received her training at the Guildhall School of Music in London (1962–67) and from Marianne Schech at the Munich Hochschule für Musik. She first sang in the John Alldis Choir and the Purcell Consort in London. In 1970 she won the Kathleen Ferrier Memorial Scholarship and made her formal debut in Purcell's *Dioclesian* at London's Queen Elizabeth Hall. She made her operatic debut as Dido with the Kent Opera in 1971. In 1973 she made her U.S. operatic debut as Mozart's Countess with the Houston Grand Opera. In 1975 she made her first appearance with the English National Opera in London as Pamina. She continued to make regular appearances in opera in London in subsequent years. She also pursued a highly successful career as a soloist with orchs. and as a recitalist. In 1973, 1977, and 1984 she toured Europe as soloist with the BBC Sym. Orch. After singing opera in Bern (1977), Frankfurt am Main (1978), and Zürich (1980), she made her Glyndebourne debut as Florence in *Albert*

Herring in 1985. In 1986 she appeared as Kabanicha in *Kát'a Kabanová* at the Chicago Lyric Opera. In 1987 she sang in the first perf. of Testi's *Riccardo III* at Milan's La Scala. She made her debut at the Salzburg Festival in 1988 as a soloist in *Messiah*. In 1992 she sang the title role in the stage premiere of Roberto Gerhard's *The Duenna* in Madrid. She portrayed Clytemnestra at Covent Garden in 1997. Palmer's operatic and concert repertoire is notable for its range, from early music to the avant-garde. In 1993 she was made a Commander of the Order of the British Empire.

Palmgren, Selim, eminent Finnish composer and teacher; b. Björneborg, Feb. 16, 1878; d. Helsinki, Dec. 13, 1951. He studied piano and composition at the Helsinki Cons. (1895–99), then went to Berlin, where he continued his piano studies with Ansorge, Berger, and Busoni. Returning to Finland, he became active as a choral conductor in Helsinki (1902–04); from 1909 to 1912 he was director of the Music Soc. in Turku. In 1921 he made a tour of the United States as a pianist; from 1923 to 1926 he taught piano and composition at the Eastman School of Music in Rochester, N.Y.; he then returned to Helsinki and became a prof. of harmony and composition at the Sibelius Academy in 1936, remaining there until his death. He was married to the Finnish soprano Maikki Pakarinen in 1910, after her divorce from Armas Järnefelt. He publ. *Minusta tuli muusikko* (Helsinki, 1948). He excelled in piano compositions, often tinged with authentic Finnish colors; some of his pieces are marked by effective impressionistic devices, such as whole-tone scales and consecutive mild dissonances. Among his piano miniatures, *May Night* enjoyed considerable popularity with music students and their teachers. He also composed the operas *Daniel Hjort* (Turku, April 15, 1910; rev. version, Helsinki, 1938) and *Peter Schlemihl*.

Pampani, Antonio Gaetano, Italian composer; b. Modena, c.1705; d. Urbino, Dec. 1775. He was a student of Salviati in Urbino. From 1726 to 1734 he was maestro di cappella at Fano Cathedral. He served as director of the chorus and orch. at the Ospedaletto orphanage in Venice from 1749 to 1764. In 1767 he was made maestro di cappella at Urbino Cathedral. He composed some 18 stage works, mainly opere serie (1730–68).

Pampanini, Rosetta, Italian soprano; b. Milan, Sept. 2, 1896; d. Corbola, Aug. 2, 1973. She studied with Emma Molajoli in Milan. She made her operatic debut as Micaëla in Rome in 1920, then continued her vocal studies; in 1925 she joined La Scala in Milan, remaining on its roster until 1937, with the exception of the 1931–33 seasons; she also sang at Covent Garden in London (1928, 1929, 1933) and in Chicago (1931–32). After retiring in 1942 she taught voice. She was particularly admired for her Puccini roles, most notably Manon, Cio-Cio-San, and Mimi.

Pandolfini, Angelica, Italian soprano, daughter of **Francesco Pandolfini**; b. Spoleto, Aug. 21, 1871; d. Lenno, July 15, 1959. She studied with Jules Massart in Paris. She made her debut as Marguerite in 1894 in Modena; after singing in the Italian provinces, she appeared at La Scala in Milan (1897–99; 1906). She created the title role in *Adriana Lecouvreur* at the Teatro Lirico in Milan in 1902; she retired from the stage in 1908. She was best known for her convincing portrayals of verismo roles.

Pandolfini, Francesco, Italian baritone, father of **Angelica Pandolfini**; b. Termini Imerese, Palermo, Nov. 22, 1836; d. Milan, Feb. 15, 1916. He studied with Ronconi and Vannuccini in Florence, making his debut in Gemma di Vergy in Pisa in 1859; then sang throughout Italy. In 1871 he appeared with notable success at La Scala in Milan, creating the role of Arnoldo in *I Lituani* by Ponchielli there in 1874. He also sang at Covent Garden in London (1877, 1882). He retired from the stage in 1890.

Panerai, Rolando, Italian baritone; b. Campi Bisenzio, near Florence, Oct. 17, 1924. He studied at the Florence Cons. with Frazzi and also with di Armani and Tess in Milan. After winning 1st prize in the voice competition in Spoleto, he made his debut as Faraone in *Mosè in Egitto* in Naples (1947); in 1951 he joined La Scala in Milan; also sang at Covent Garden in London, the Vienna State Opera, and the Salzburg Festivals. He specialized in the Italian repertoire.

Panizza, Ettore, Argentine conductor and composer of Italian descent; b. Buenos Aires, Aug. 12, 1875; d. Milan, Nov. 27, 1967. He studied at the Milan Cons., graduating in 1898 with prizes for piano and composition. From 1907 to 1914 and again in 1924 he conducted at London's Covent Garden. He made his first appearance at the Teatro Colón in Buenos Aires (1908), conducting there regularly from 1921. He joined the roster of Milan's La Scala (1916), serving as assistant to Toscanini (1921–29); he was a regular conductor there (1930–32; 1946–48) and also conducted at the Chicago Civic Opera (1922–24) and N.Y.'s Metropolitan Opera (1934–42). He publ. an autobiography, *Medio siglo de vida musical* (Buenos Aires, 1952). His compositions include the operas *Il Fidanzato del mare* (Buenos Aires, Aug. 15, 1897), *Medio evo latino* (Genoa, Nov. 17, 1900), *Aurora* (Buenos Aires, Sept. 5, 1908), and *Bisanzio* (Buenos Aires, July 25, 1939).

Pannain, Guido, distinguished Italian musicologist and composer; b. Naples, Nov. 17, 1891; d. there, Sept. 6, 1977. He studied composition with C. de Nardis at the Naples Cons. (graduated, 1914). He was prof. of music history at the Naples Cons. (1915–61); he also wrote music criticism. As a musicologist, he devoted much of his time to the study of Neapolitan music. Among his compositions were the operas *L'Intrusa* (1926; Genoa, 1940), *Beatrice Cenci* (Naples, Feb. 21, 1942), and *Madame Bovary* (Naples, April 16, 1955).

WRITINGS: *La teoria musicale di Giovanni Tinctoris* (Naples, 1913); *Le origini della scuola musicale napoletana* (Naples, 1914); *Le origini e lo sviluppo dell'arte pianistica in Italia dal 1500 fino al 1730 circa* (Naples, 1917); *Lineamenti di storia della musica* (Naples, 1922; 9th ed., rev., 1970); *Musica e musicisti in Napoli nel secolo XIX* (Naples, 1922); *Musicisti dei tempi nuovi* (Milan, 1932; Eng. tr., 1932, as *Modern Composers*; 2d Italian ed., 1954); with A. della Corte, *Storia della musica* (Turin, 1936; 4th ed., 1964); *Il Conservatorio di musica di S. Pietro in Maiella* (Florence, 1942); *La vita del linguaggio musicale* (Milan, 1947; 2d ed., 1956); *Ottocento musicale italiano: Saggi e note* (Milan, 1952); *L'opera e le opere ed altri scritti di letteratura musicale* (Milan, 1958); *Giuseppe Verdi* (Turin, 1964); *Richard Wagner: Vita di un artista* (Milan, 1964).

Panseron, Auguste-Mathieu, French singing teacher and composer; b. Paris, April 26, 1795; d. there, July 29, 1859. His father, who orchestrated many operas for Grétry, taught him until he entered the Paris Cons. in 1804, where he studied under Gossec, Levasseur, and Berton, winning the Prix de Rome in 1813. After study in Bologna, Rome, Naples, Vienna (with Salieri), and Munich, he returned to Paris in 1818, where he taught singing, was an accompanist at the Opéra Comique, and wrote 4 1-act operas. He became a prof. of solfège at the Cons. in 1826, of vocalization in 1831, and of singing in 1836. From 1825 to 1840 he brought out some 200 romances. He also composed church music, but attained real eminence as a vocal teacher and as a writer of instructive works on singing.

Pantaleoni, Adriano, Italian baritone, brother of **Romilda Pantaleoni**; b. Udine, Oct. 7, 1837; d. there, Dec. 18, 1908. He studied in Udine and Milan. He was a principal member of La Scala in Milan (1871–77; 1896), and also sang in London and the United States (1879). After his retirement, he taught voice in Udine and Trieste. He was particularly noted for his roles in Verdi's operas.

Pantaleoni, Romilda, Italian soprano, sister of **Adriano Pantaleoni**; b. Udine, 1847; d. Milan, May 20, 1917. She studied with Prati, Rossi, and Lamperti in Milan, making her debut at the Teatro Carcano in Milan in Foroni's *Margherita* in 1868. She then sang in Turin and at La Scala in Milan, where she created the role of Desdemona in Verdi's *Otello* in 1887 and Tigrana in Puccini's *Edgar* in 1889.

Panula, Jorma, Finnish conductor, pedagogue, and composer; b. Kauhajoki, Aug. 10, 1930. He studied in Helsinki at the School of Church Music and with Leo Funtek at the Sibelius Academy (1948–53); he then pursued conducting studies with Dean Dixon in Lund (1953), and with Albert Wolff (1957) and Franco Ferrara (1958) in Hilversum. He conducted theater orchs. in Lahti (1953–55), Tampere (1955–58), and Helsinki (1958–62); after conducting the Finnish National Opera (1962–63), he conducted the Turku Phil. (1963–65), the Helsinki Phil. (1965–72), the Århus Sym. Orch. in Denmark (1972–75), and the Espoo City Orch. (1986–88); he also appeared as a guest conductor throughout Europe and in North America. He served as a prof. of conducting at the Sibelius Academy (from 1972), the Stockholm Musikhögskolan (1980–86), and the Copenhagen Royal Danish Cons. of Music (1986–91). Among his works are 2 folk operas: *Jaakko Ilkka* (1978) and *Jokiooppera* (The River Opera; 1982); also *Vallan Miehet* (Men of Power), television opera (1987); musicals; scores for films, radio, and television.

Panzéra, Charles (Auguste Louis), noted Swiss-born French baritone and teacher; b. Geneva, Feb. 16, 1896; d. Paris, June 6, 1976. He studied at the Paris Cons. He made his operatic debut as Albert in *Werther* at the Paris Opéra Comique in 1919, then gave concerts in Europe and America; he also taught at the Juilliard School of Music in New York. In 1949 he was appointed a prof. at the Paris Cons. He excelled in the interpretation of French songs. He publ. *L'Art de chanter* (Paris, 1945), *L'Amour de chanter* (Paris, 1957), *L'Art vocal: 30 leçons de chant* (Paris, 1959), and *Votre voix: Directives générales* (Paris, 1967).

Paoli, Antonio (real name, **Ermogene Imleghi Bascaran**), Puerto Rican tenor; b. Ponce, April 14, 1871; d. San Juan, Aug. 24, 1946. He studied in Spain and at the Milan Cons. In 1899 he made his operatic debut as Arnold in Rossini's *Guillaume Tell* at the Paris Opéra. After appearances in Caracas, Havana, and New York (1901), he toured the United States with Mascagni's opera troupe (1902) and then pursued his career in Europe and South America. From 1928 he taught at the Univ. of Puerto Rico. Among his best roles were Verdi's Manrico and Otello, Meyerbeer's Vasco da Gama, and Saint-Saëns's Samson.

Papandopulo, Boris, Croatian conductor and composer; b. Bad Honnef am Rhein, Feb. 25, 1906; d. Zagreb, Oct. 17, 1991. He studied in Zagreb and Vienna. Returning to his homeland, he was active as a conductor and composer; in 1959 he was appointed conductor of the National Theater in Zagreb; from 1964 to 1968 he conducted in Split and Rijeka; he later filled engagements as a guest conductor in Yugoslavia. His operas and most of his instrumental works were written in a national Croatian idiom; but he also experimented with the 12-tone techniques, as exemplified by his pointedly titled *Dodekafonski concert* for 2 Pianos (1961).

WORKS: DRAMATIC: OPERAS: *Amiftrion* (Zagreb, Feb. 17, 1940); *Sunčanica* (The Sun Girl; Zagreb, June 13, 1942); *Rona* (Rijeka, May 25, 1955); *Marulova Pisan* (Marul's Song; Split, Aug. 14, 1970); *Madame Buffault* (1972). BALLETS: *Zlato* (Gold; Zagreb, May 31, 1930); *Žetva* (The Harvest; Sarajevo, March 25, 1950); *Intermezzo* (Sarajevo, May 25, 1953); *Beatrice Cenci* (Gelsenkirchen, 1959); *Gitanella* (1965); *Doktor Atom: Qu + H^3 + H^2 = He^4 + n + 9* (Rijeka, Oct. 29, 1966); *Ljudi u hotelu* (People in a Hotel; Vienna, May 27, 1967); *Teuta* (1973).

Pape, René, German bass-baritone; b. Dresden, Sept. 4, 1964. After singing in the Dresden Kreuzchor (1974–81), he pursued vocal training at the Dresden Hochschule für Musik. In 1987 he made his debut as the Speaker in *Die Zauberflöte* at the Berlin State Opera, where he also sang Capellio in 1993. In 1994 he appeared as Hunding in Philadelphia and as Masetto at the Bavarian State Opera in Munich. He portrayed Rocco, Ramfis, and Fafner in Berlin in 1995, and then was engaged as Sarastro in Bonn in 1996. In 1997 he sang Pope Pius IV in *Palestrina* and King Heinrich in *Die Meistersinger von Nürnberg* at London's Covent Garden.

Papi, Gennaro, Italian-American conductor; b. Naples, Dec. 21, 1886; d. N.Y., Nov. 29, 1941. He received training in piano, organ, violin, and theory at the Naples Cons. (graduated, 1904). He was a chorus master at S. Severo (1906), Warsaw (1909–10), Turin (1911), and London's Covent Garden (1911–12). After serving as Toscanini's assistant on a tour of Argentina (1912), Toscanini made him his assistant at the Metropolitan Opera in New York. On April 29, 1915, he made his debut there conducting *Rigoletto*. He was on the conducting roster there from 1916 to 1926, and again from 1935 until his death. He also conducted at Chicago's Ravinia Festival (1916–31) and Civic Opera (1925–32).

Pappano, Antonio, Italian-born American conductor; b. London, Dec. 30, 1959. He went to the United States and pursued training in piano with Norma Verrilli, in composition with Arnold Franchetti, and in conducting with Gustav Meier. After working as a répétiteur and assistant conductor in several opera houses, he conducted at the Norwegian Opera in Oslo, the English National Opera in London, the Royal Opera, Covent Garden, London, the San Francisco Opera, the Lyric Opera in Chicago, the Théâtre du Châtelet in Paris, and the Berlin State Opera. From 1992 he served as music director of the Théâtre Royal de la Monnaie in Brussels. In 1993 he made an acclaimed debut at the Vienna State Opera when he conducted on short notice a performance of *Siegfried*. He conducted *Eugene Onegin* at his Metropolitan Opera debut in New York on Jan. 13, 1997. In 1998 he was made principal guest conductor of the Israel Phil. He was engaged to conduct *Lohengrin* at the Bayreuth Festival in 1999. As a guest conductor, Pappano appeared with the Orchestre de Paris, the Chicago Sym. Orch., the Cleveland Orch., the Orch. of La Scala in Milan, the Berlin Phil., the Los Angeles Phil., the London Sym. Orch., and the Philharmonia Orch. in London.

Paradies (originally **Paradisi**), **(Pietro) Domenico,** Italian composer and harpsichordist; b. Naples, 1707; d. Venice, Aug. 25, 1791. He was a pupil of Porpora. He brought out several operas in Italy, then, in 1746, he went to London, where he earned a living mainly as a teacher of harpsichord playing, but also produced several operas, including *Fetonte* (London, Jan. 17, 1747) and *La forza d'amore* (London, Jan. 19, 1751). He publ. *12 sonate di gravicembalo* (London, 1754). Toward the end of his life he returned to Italy. Some of his MSS are preserved in the Fitzwilliam Museum at Cambridge. His sonatas were brought out by G. Benvenuti and D. Cipollini in Milan (1920).

Paradis, Maria Theresia von, noted Austrian pianist, organist, singer, and composer; b. Vienna, May 15, 1759; d. there, Feb. 1, 1824. She was the daughter of Josef von Paradis, the imperial court secretary. She studied piano with L. Koželuh, singing with Richter, singing and dramatic composition with Salieri, dramatic composition with Vogler, and theory with Friberth. She appeared in concerts in Vienna (from c.1775). She was blind from her 5th year; Mesmer became interested in her condition and attempted to cure her, without effect (1777–78). She set out on a major concert tour in 1783, visiting Salzburg, Frankfurt am Main, Mainz, and other cities; in 1784 she arrived in Paris, where she was highly praised for her appearances as both a keyboard artist and a singer at the Concert Spirituel; Mozart composed a concerto for her. She went to London in late 1784 and appeared at court and in public concerts. She returned to Vienna in 1786, and continued to make tours until founding her own music inst. there (1808). Her friend and librettist Johann Riedinger invented a notation system for her, and she became a skilled composer. Much of her music is not extant. Among her compositions were *Ariadne und Bacchus*, melodrama (Laxenburg, June 20, 1791), *Der Schulkanditat*, landliches Singspiel (Vienna, Dec. 5, 1792), and *Rinaldo und Alcine, Die Insel der Verführung*, comic opera (Prague, June 30, 1797).

Paranov, Moshe (Morris Perlmutter), American pianist, conductor, and music educator; b. Hartford, Conn., Oct. 28, 1895; d. West Hartford, Conn., Oct. 7, 1994. He began his musical studies as a child and sang in synagogues. At 14 he commenced piano playing in theaters and hotels. He was 17 when he made his formal debut as a pianist in Hartford. He pursued training in piano with Julius Hartt and Harold Bauer, and in composition with Ernest Bloch and Rubin Goldmark. After making his N.Y. recital debut as a pianist at Aeolian Hall in 1920, he made appearances as a soloist with orchs. and as a recitalist. With Hartt and others, he founded a music school in Hartford in 1920 as Julius Hartt, Moshe Paranov, and Associated Teachers, which soon became the Hartt School of Music. In 1934 Paranov became its director and proceeded to develop it into one of the finest schools of its kind. After it became a part of the Univ. of Hartford in 1957, he continued to preside over the school until 1971. He also served as music director of WTIC Radio in Hartford (1938–49), and as conductor of the Hartt Opera Theater, the Hartford Sym. Orch. (1947–53), and the Brockton (Mass.) Sym. Orch. (1954–64). His 95th birthday was marked by a special celebration at the Univ. of Hartford on May 16, 1991, at which occasion he conducted a sprightly rendition of Offenbach's overture to *Orpheus in the Underworld*. An endowed chair was also created in his honor to further his efforts in promoting music education.

Parelli (real name, **Paparella**), **Attilio,** Italian conductor and composer; b. Monteleone d'Orvieto, near Perugia, May 31, 1874; d. there, Dec. 26, 1944. He studied at the Accademia di Santa Cecilia in Rome, graduating in 1899. He held various posts as a conductor in Italy and France; he went to the United States as assistant conductor to Campanini at the Manhattan Opera in New York (1906); he also conducted for the Chicago Grand Opera Co. In 1925 he returned to Europe. He wrote the operas *Hermes* (Genoa, Nov. 8, 1906), *I dispettosi amanti* (Philadelphia, March 6, 1912), and *Fanfulla* (Trieste, Feb. 11, 1921).

Parepa-Rosa, Euphrosyne (née **Parepa de Boyescu**), prominent Scottish soprano; b. Edinburgh, May 7, 1836; d. London, Jan. 21, 1874. Her father was Baron Georgiades de Boyescu of Bucharest, and her mother the soprano Elizabeth Seguin. After studying with her mother, she made her debut as Amina in *La Sonnambula* in Malta (1855), then sang in Italy, Madrid, and Lisbon. She made her first London appearance as Elvira in *I Puritani* with the Royal Italian Opera at the Lyceum Theatre (May 21, 1857); she appeared at Covent Garden and Her Majesty's Theatre (1859–65), becoming a great favorite of the English public; also sang in Germany. She then toured the United States with Theodore Thomas's orch. and with Carl Rosa (1865). She married Rosa in 1867, and together they formed an opera company in which she starred as the principal soprano. She returned to Covent Garden (1872), but illness forced her to give up her career the following year. Her husband founded the Parepa-Rosa Scholarship at the Royal Academy of Music in her memory.

Pareto, Graziella (Graciela), Spanish soprano; b. Barcelona, March 6, 1888; d. Rome, Sept. 1, 1973. She studied with Vidal in Milan. She made her operatic debut as Micaëla in Barcelona in 1906 then sang at the Teatro Colón in Buenos Aires, in Turin, and in St. Petersburg. In 1914 she appeared at La Scala in Milan; she subsequently sang at Covent Garden in London (1920), in Chicago (1923–25), and in Salzburg (1931). Among her prominent roles were Rosina, Ophelia, Marguerite de Valois, Violetta, and Norina.

Paribeni, Giulio Cesare, Italian music critic, teacher, and composer; b. Rome, May 27, 1881; d. Milan, June 13, 1960. He studied at the Univ. of Rome and at the Liceo di S. Cecilia of Rome. He was first a conductor, then, from 1911 to 1915, head of the publishing firm of Sonzogno; from 1914 he was a teacher of composition and harmony at the Royal Cons. in Milan. From 1922 he was an opera critic of *L'Ambrosiano* in Milan. He was the author of *Storia e teoria della antica musica greca* (Milan, 1912) and *Muzio Clementi* (Milan, 1921).

Pâris, Alain, French conductor and writer on music; b. Paris, Nov. 22, 1947. He had a conducting course with Dervaux at the École Normal de Musique in Paris (Licence de concert, 1967), where he also was a student of Dandelot (1965–68); he then studied conducting with Fourestier. In 1968 he won 1st prize in the Besançon conducting competition; subsequently appeared as a guest conductor with various French orchs. In 1976–77 he was assistant conductor of the Orchestre de Capitole de Toulouse. In 1980 he organized the Ensemble à Vent in Paris, which he led in programs of rarely heard works as well as premiere performances of many contemporary scores. From 1983 to 1987 he was permanent conductor of the Opéra du Rhin in Strasbourg. From 1986 to 1989 he was a prof. of conducting at the Strasbourg Cons. As a guest conductor, he appeared throughout Europe. He publ. the *Dictionnaire des interprètes et de l'interprétation musicale au XXe siècle* (Paris, 1982; 4th ed., rev., 1995) and *Les Livrets d'opéra* (Paris, 1991); he also made French translations of the *New Oxford Companion to Music* (Paris, 1988) and *Baker's Biographical Dictionary of Musicians* (Paris, 1995).

Parker, Horatio (William), eminent American composer and pedagogue; b. Auburndale, Mass., Sept. 15, 1863; d. Cedarhurst, N.Y., Dec. 18, 1919. He studied piano with John Orth, theory with Emery, and composition with Chadwick in Boston, and then went to Germany, where he took courses in organ and composition with Rheinberger in Munich (1882–85); under his tutelage he wrote a cantata, *King Trojan* (1885). Returning to the United States, he settled in New York and taught at the cathedral schools of St. Paul and St. Mary (1886–90), at the General Theological Seminary (1892), and at the National Cons. of Music (1892–93). He was organist and choirmaster at St. Luke's (1885–87), St. Andrew's (1887–88), and the Church of the Holy Trinity (1888–93); in 1893 he went to Boston as organist and choirmaster at Trinity Church, remaining there until 1902. He attracted attention with the first performance of his oratorio *Hora novissima* (N.Y., May 3, 1893), in which he demonstrated his mastery of choral writing, while his harmonic and contrapuntal style remained securely tied to German practices. In 1894 he was engaged as a prof. of theory at Yale Univ.; in 1904 he became dean of its School of Music, and remained there until his death. Many American composers received the benefit of his excellent instruction, among them Charles Ives, who kept his sincere appreciation of Parker's teaching long after he renounced Parker's conservative traditions. In 1895 he founded the New Haven Sym. Orch., which he conducted until 1918. Parker conducted performances of his works in England in 1900 and 1902, and received an honorary degree of Mus.Doc. at Cambridge Univ. in 1902. Returning to the United States, he served as organist and choirmaster at the collegiate church of St. Nicholas in Boston from 1902 to 1910. He continued to compose industriously, without making any concessions to the emerging modern schools of composition; his choral works are particularly notable. In 1911 his opera *Mona* won the $10,000 prize offered by the Metropolitan Opera in New York, and was produced there on March 14, 1912; he also won a prize offered by the National Federation of Women's Clubs for his 2d opera, *Fairyland*, which was produced in Los Angeles on July 1, 1915. Neither of the operas possessed enough power to survive in the repertoire. Other dramatic works included incidental music to *The Eternal Feminine* for Chorus and Orch. (1903–04; New Haven, Nov. 7, 1904; not extant) and *The Prince of India* for Voice, Chorus, and Orch. (1905; N.Y., Sept. 24, 1906); also *Cupid and Psyche,* a masque (New Haven, June 16, 1916), *The Legend of St. Christopher*, dramatic oratorio for Solo Voices, Chorus, and Orch. (1897; N.Y., April 15, 1898), and *Morven and the Grail*, oratorio for Solo Voices, Chorus, and Orch. (Boston, April 13, 1915).

BIBL.: G. Chadwick, *H. P.* (New Haven, 1921); W. Kearns, *H. P. 1863–1919: A Study of His Life and Music* (diss., Univ. of Illinois, 1965).

Parker, William, American baritone; b. Butler, Pa., Aug. 5, 1943; d. N.Y., March 29, 1993. He took German language and literature courses at Princeton Univ. (B.A., 1965); after singing in the U.S. Army Chorus in Washington, D.C., he pursued serious vocal training with Bernac and Ponselle. He won 1st prize in the Toulouse Competition and the special Poulenc Prize in the Paris Competition; he then gained wide recognition in 1979 when he took 1st prize in the Kennedy Center-Rockefeller Foundation International Competition for Excellence in the Performance of American Music. In subsequent years, Parker acquired a fine reputation as a concert singer; he also sang with various opera companies in the

United States and abroad. He was especially admired for his cultured approach to art song interpretation and for his advocacy of contemporary American music. After contracting AIDS, he commissioned a number of composers to contribute selections to *The AIDS Quilt Songbook*. With the baritones Kurt Ollman, William Sharp, and Sanford Sylvan, he gave the premiere of the cycle at N.Y.'s Alice Tully Hall in 1992. Parker continued to make appearances until his last public concert in Minneapolis on Jan. 1, 1993.

Parmeggiani, Ettore, Italian tenor; b. Rimini, Aug. 15, 1895; d. Milan, Jan. 28, 1960. He was a pupil of Mandolini in Milan, making his operatic debut there in 1922 at the Teatro dal Verme as Cavaradossi. In 1927 he made his first appearance at Milan's La Scala as Max in *Der Freischütz*, and continued to sing there for a decade. In addition to his Wagnerian roles, he appeared in the premieres of Mascagni's *Nerone* (1935) and Respighi's *Lucrezia* (1937) there. In 1936 he also sang in the premiere of Malipiero's *Giulio Cesare* in Genoa. In later years, he taught voice in Milan and led the claque at La Scala.

Parrott, Andrew, esteemed English conductor; b. Walsall, March 10, 1947. He studied at the Univ. of Oxford, where he pursued research into the performing practices of 16th- and 17th-century music. In 1973 he founded the Taverner Choir, and subsequently the Taverner Consort and Players. He conducted Monteverdi's *Vespers* at London's Promenade Concerts in 1977; gave the first performance in London of Bach's B-minor Mass with period instruments; also presented in authentic style the St. Matthew Passion and the "Brandenburg" Concertos. He appeared as a guest conductor with the English Chamber Orch., the London Bach Orch., and the Concerto Amsterdam. In 1987 he made his first appearance at the Salzburg Festival conducting Monteverdi's *Vespers*. In 1989 he became artistic director of Kent Opera. In 1993 he made his debut at London's Covent Garden conducting *Die Zauberflöte*. With H. Keyte, he ed. *The New Oxford Book of Carols* (Oxford, 1992).

Parrott, (Horace) Ian, English composer, teacher, and writer on music; b. London, March 5, 1916. At 12 he began lessons in harmony with Benjamin Dale. Following studies at the Royal College of Music in London (1932–34), he completed his education at New College, Oxford (D.Mus., 1940; M.A., 1941). From 1940 to 1945 he saw service in the Royal Signals. He was a lecturer at the Univ. of Birmingham from 1947 to 1950. From 1950 to 1983 he was the Gregynog Prof. of Music at the Univ. College of Wales in Aberystwyth. In his music, Parrott remained faithful to the tonal tradition. In a number of his works, he was inspired by the culture of Wales.

WRITINGS: *Pathways to Modern Music* (1947); *A Guide to Musical Thought* (1955); *Method in Orchestration* (1957); *The Music of "An Adventure"* (1966); *The Spiritual Pilgrims* (1969); *Elgar* (1971); *Rosemary Brown: Music from Beyond* (1977); *Cyril Scott and His Piano Music* (1992); *The Crying Curlew: Peter Warlock: Family & Influences: Centenary 1994* (1994).

WORKS: OPERAS: *The Sergeant-Major's Daughter*, burlesque opera (1942–43); *The Black Ram* (1951–53; Aberystwyth, March 9, 1966); *Once Upon a Time*, comic opera (1959; Christchurch, New Zealand, Dec. 3, 1960); *The Lady of Flowers*, chamber opera (1981; Colchester, Sept. 17, 1982).

Parry, Sir C(harles) Hubert H(astings), eminent English composer, pedagogue, and writer on music; b. Bournemouth, Feb. 27, 1848; d. Rustington, Oct. 7, 1918. While attending a preparatory school in Twyford, near Winchester, he began piano lessons with a local organist. He then had training in piano, harmony, and counterpoint with Edward Brind, the organist at Highnam Church. In 1861 he entered Eton, where he became active in its musical society. During this time, he also had composition lessons with George Elvey, organist at St. George's Chapel, Windsor. In 1866 he took his B.Mus. exercise at New College, Oxford, with his cantata *O Lord, Thou hast cast us out*. In 1867 he entered Exeter College, Oxford, to study law and history. During the summer of that year, he pursued training in instrumentation and composition with Pierson in Stuttgart. After graduating from Exeter College in 1870, he had a few lessons with Sterndale Bennett. Between 1873 and 1877 he was engaged in business in London, but he also pursued training in piano with Dannreuther (from 1873) and in composition with Macfarren (1875–77). In 1875 Grove made him subeditor of his *Dictionary of Music and Musicians*, to which Parry contributed a number of the major articles. In 1883 he was named prof. of music history at the newly organized Royal College of Music in London and was awarded an honorary Doc.Mus. from Trinity College, Cambridge. In 1884 he was elected Choragus at the Univ. of Oxford, where he received an honorary doctorate. In 1894 Parry was elevated to the directorship of the Royal College of Music, a position he retained with distinction for the rest of his life. He also served as the Heather Prof. of Music at the Univ. of Oxford from 1900 to 1908. In 1898 he was knighted and in 1905 he was made a Commander of the Royal Victorian Order. Parry secured his reputation as a composer with his distinguished choral ode *At a Solemn Music: Blest Pair of Sirens* (1887). There followed a series of ethical choral works in which he attempted to build upon the British choral tradition. His coronation anthem "I was glad" (1902) is a masterwork in the genre. Also notable is his "Ode on the Nativity" (1910). His unison song "Jerusalem" (1916) quickly established itself as a national song. Among his other fine works are his *Songs of Farewell* and his collections of *English Lyrics*. In his orchestral music, Parry played a significant role in the fostering of the British symphonic tradition. While his orchestral works owe much to the German Romanticists, particularly Mendelssohn, Schumann, and Brahms, he nevertheless developed a personal style notable for its fine craftsmanship and mastery of diatonic writing. His 5 syms. reveal a growing assurance in handling large forms. He also wrote some effective incidental music and fine chamber pieces.

WRITINGS (all publ. in London unless otherwise given): *Studies of the Great Composers* (1887); *The Art of Music* (1893; enl. ed., 1896, as *The Evolution of the Art of Music*); *Summary of the History and Development of Medieval and Modern European Music* (1893; 2d ed., 1904); *The Music of the Seventeenth Century*, vol. 3 of *The Oxford History of Music* (1902); *Johann Sebastian Bach* (1910); *Style in Musical Art* (1911); *Instinct and Character* (c.1915–18; MS); H. Colles, ed., *College Addresses* (1920).

WORKS: DRAMATIC: OPERA: *Guenever* (1886). BALLET: *Proserpine* (London, June 25, 1912). INCIDENTAL MUSIC TO: Aristophanes' *The Birds* (Cambridge, Nov. 27, 1883; rev. 1903); Aristophanes' *The Frogs* (Oxford, Feb. 24, 1892; rev. version, Oxford, Feb. 19, 1909); S. Ogilvie's *Hypatia* (London, Jan. 2, 1893; orch. suite, London, March 9, 1893); P. Craigie's *A Repentance* (London, Feb. 28, 1899); Aeschylus's *Agamemnon* (London, Nov. 16, 1900); Aristophanes' *The Clouds* (Oxford, March 1, 1905); Aristophanes' *The Acharnians* (Oxford, Feb. 21, 1914).

BIBL.: C. Graves, *H. P.: His Life and Works* (2 vols., London, 1926); J. Dibble, *C. H. H. P.: His Life and Music* (Oxford, 1992).

Parry, Joseph, Welsh composer; b. Merthyr Tydfil, May 21, 1841; d. Penarth, near Cardiff, Feb. 17, 1903. His parents emigrated to America, but he returned to Britain. He won Eisteddfod prizes for songs, and entered the Royal Academy of Music in 1868, studying under Bennett, Garcia, and Steggall; he received his Mus.Bac. degree from Cambridge in 1871. He was prof. of music at the Univ. of Wales in Aberystwyth (1873–79). After receiving his Mus.D. from Cambridge (1878), he ran his own music school in Swansea (1881–88); subsequently he lectured at the Univ. College of South Wales and Monmouthshire in Cardiff. In addition to his dramatic works, he wrote some 400 hymn tunes, the most celebrated being "Aberystwyth" (1877). He also ed. and harmonized *Cambrian Minstrelsie* (6 vols., Edinburgh, 1893).

WORKS: DRAMATIC: OPERAS: *Blodwen* (Aberdare, 1878); *Virginia* (Aberdare, 1883); *Arianwen* (Cardiff, 1890); *Sylvia* (Cardiff, 1895); *King Arthur* (1897); *Ceridwen* (Liverpool, 1900); *The Maid of Cefn Ydfa* (Cardiff, 1902). ORATORIOS: *The Prodigal Son* (Chester, 1866); *Emmanuel* (London, 1880); *Saul of Tarus* (Rhyl and Cardiff, 1892).

BIBL.: E. Evans et al., *Cofiant Dr. J. P.* (Cardiff and London, 1921).

Partridge, Ian (Harold), English tenor; b. Wimbledon, June 12, 1938. He was a chorister at New College, Oxford, and a music scholar at Clifton College before pursuing his training in London at the Royal College of Music and the Guildhall School of Music. He commenced his career as a piano accompanist while singing in the Westminster Cathedral Choir (1958–62). In 1958 he made his formal debut as a singer in Bexhill, and from 1962 he pursued a solo career. In 1969 he made his debut at London's Covent Garden as Iopas in *Les Troyens*. He appeared as a soloist with many major orchs. in England and abroad, gave many recitals, and sang on radio and television. In 1989 he made his debut at the Salzburg Festival in Bach's St. John Passion. In 1991 he was made a Commander of the Order of the British Empire. His sister, Jennifer Partridge (b. New Malden, June 17, 1942), is a pianist who has often served as his accompanist.

Pasatieri, Thomas, talented American composer; b. N.Y., Oct. 20, 1945. He began to play the piano by spontaneous generation, and picked up elements of composition, particularly vocal, by a similar subliminal process; between the ages of 14 and 18 he wrote some 400 songs. He persuaded Boulanger to take him as a student by correspondence between Paris and New York when he was 15; at 16 he entered the Juilliard School of Music in New York, where he became a student of Giannini and Persichetti; he also took a course with Milhaud in Aspen, Colo., where his first opera, *The Women*, to his own libretto, was performed when he was only 19. It became clear to him that opera was his natural medium, and that the way to achieve the best results was by following the evolutionary line of Italian operatic productions characterized by the felicity of *bel canto*, facility of harmonic writing, and euphonious fidelity to the lyric and dramatic content of the subject. In striving to attain these objectives, Pasatieri ran the tide of mandatory inharmoniousness; while his productions were applauded by hoi polloi, they shocked music critics and other composers; one of them described Pasatieri's music as "a stream of perfumed urine." This attitude is akin to that taken by some toward Giannini and Menotti (interestingly, all 3 are of Italian genetic stock). From 1967 to 1969 Pasatieri taught at the Juilliard School; he then was engaged at the Manhattan School of Music (1969–71); from 1980 to 1983 he was Distinguished Visiting Prof. at the Univ. of Cincinnati (Ohio) College-Cons. of Music.

WORKS: OPERAS: *The Women* (Aspen, Aug. 20, 1965); *La Divina* (N.Y., March 16, 1966); *Padrevia* (N.Y., Nov. 18, 1967); *Calvary* (Seattle, April 7, 1971); *The Trial of Mary Lincoln*, television opera (Boston, Feb. 14, 1972); *Black Widow* (Seattle, March 2, 1972); *The Seagull*, after Chekhov (Houston, March 5, 1974); *Signor Deluso*, after Molière's *Sganarelle* (Vienna, Va., July 27, 1974); *The Penitentes* (Aspen, Aug. 3, 1974); *Inez de Castro* (Baltimore, April 1, 1976); *Washington Square*, after Henry James (Detroit, Oct. 1, 1976); *Three Sisters*, after Chekov (1979; Columbus, Ohio, March 13, 1986); *Before Breakfast* (N.Y., Oct. 9, 1980); *The Goose Girl*, children's opera (Fort Worth, Texas, Feb. 15, 1981); *Maria Elena* (Tucson, April 8, 1983).

Pasero, Tancredi, noted Italian bass; b. Turin, Jan. 11, 1893; d. Milan, Feb. 17, 1983. He studied in Turin. He made his operatic debut in 1917 as Rodolfo in *La Sonnambula* in Vicenza; from 1924 to 1930 he sang at the Teatro Colón in Buenos Aires; in 1926 he joined La Scala in Milan, remaining on its roster until 1952. He made his Metropolitan Opera debut in New York on Nov. 1, 1929, as Alvise in *La Gioconda*; continued on its roster until 1933. He also had guest engagements at London's Covent Garden (1931) and the Paris Opéra (1935). His repertoire was extensive and included Italian, German, French, and Russian operas; he excelled in Verdi's operas, and made a distinctive appearance as Mussorgsky's Boris Godunov.

BIBL.: C. Clerico, *T. P.: Voce verdiana* (Scomegna, 1985).

Pashchenko, Andrei (Filippovich), Russian composer; b. Rostov, Aug. 15, 1883; d. Moscow, Nov. 16, 1972. He studied with Wihtol and Steinberg at the St. Petersburg Cons., graduating in 1917. He occupied various clerical positions; he was librarian of the St. Petersburg Court Orch. (from 1911), remaining with it when it became the State Orch. (1917) and the Leningrad Phil. (1924); left his post in 1931; in 1961 he went to live in Moscow. An exceptionally fertile composer, he wrote some 14 operas and 15 syms.; the style of his music is a natural continuation of the traditions of the Russian national school; in his later works he allowed a certain influx of impressionistic harmonies and unresolved dissonant combinations.

WORKS: OPERAS: *Eagles in Revolt* (Leningrad, Nov. 7, 1925); *King Maximilian* (1927); *The Black Cliff* (Leningrad, June 12, 1931); *The Pompadours* (1939); *Jester Balakirev* (1949); *The Capricious Bride* (1956); *Radda and Loyko* (1957); *Nila Snishko* (1961); *The Great Seducer* (1966); *Woman, This Is the Devil* (1966); *African Love* (1966); *The Horse in the Senate* (1967); *Portrait* (1968); *Master and Margarita* (1971).

BIBL.: Y. Meylikh, *A. F. P.* (Leningrad, 1960).

Pashkevich, Vasily (Alexeievich), Russian violinist and composer; b. c.1740; d. St. Petersburg, March 20, 1797. In 1763 he was admitted as a violinist to the 2d court orch. in St. Petersburg. His Russian opera *A Carriage Accident* was performed in St. Petersburg on Nov. 7, 1779; in 1782 he presented 2 comic operas in Russian: *The Miser* (Moscow) and *The Pasha of Tunis* (St. Petersburg). In 1783 he became a violinist in the first court orch. In 1786 was commissioned by Catherine the Great to write a comic Russian opera, *Fevey*, for which the empress herself wrote the libretto. It was produced in St. Petersburg on April 19, 1786, and Pashkevich received an award of 1,000 rubles. He was then made chief of ball music at the Imperial Palace and concertmaster of the first court orch. (1786); he received the honorary rank of colonel. In 1790 he collaborated with Sarti and Canobbio on another Russian opera to a text of Catherine the Great, *The Early Reign of Oleg*, which was first produced at the palace, and publicly performed in St. Petersburg on Nov. 2, 1790. In collaboration with Martin y Soler, he wrote still another comic opera to a text by the empress, *Fedul and His Children* (perf. at the palace, Jan. 27, 1791; publicly, St. Petersburg, March 2, 1791). His Mass according to the Russian Orthodox liturgy was publ. in Moscow in 1796.

Pasini, Laura, Italian soprano; b. Gallarate, Jan. 28, 1894; d. Rome, Sept. 30, 1942. She studied piano with Appiano at the Milan Cons., and made her debut as a pianist in Rome in 1912. After vocal training from Pietro at the Accademia di Santa Cecilia in Rome, she made her operatic debut as Zerlina in *Fra Diavolo* at Milan's Teatro Eden in 1921. She sang in Rome (1922–23), at Milan's La Scala (1923–26; 1930–31) and Buenos Aires's Teatro Colón (1925), and in Turin (1925–27), Salzburg (1931), and Florence (1933) before settling in Cagliari as a voice teacher.

Pasini (-Vitale), Lina, Italian soprano; b. Rome, Nov. 8, 1872; d. there, Nov. 23, 1959. She studied in Rome. She made her operatic debut in 1893 as Cecilia in Cilea's *Tilda* at the Teatro dal Verme in Milan, then sang at La Scala in Milan, Turin, the Teatro Colón in Buenos Aires, Rome, and Naples; retired from the stage in 1928. She married the conductor Edoardo Vitale in 1897. At the height of her career, she was widely regarded as one of the finest Wagnerian sopranos on the Italian stage. Her sister, Camilla Pasini (b. Rome, Nov. 6, 1875; d. there, Oct. 29, 1935), was also a soprano; she studied in Rome and created the role of Musetta in *La Bohème* (Turin, Feb. 1, 1896); she retired from the stage in 1905.

Paskalis, Kostas, Greek baritone; b. Levadia, Sept. 1, 1929. He received training in voice in Athens, where he concurrently took courses in piano and composition at the Cons. In 1951 he made his operatic debut as Rigoletto at the National Opera in Athens, where he sang until 1958. In 1958 he made his debut at the Vienna State Opera as Renato, and continued to appear there regularly until 1979. He made his British debut as Macbeth at the Glyndebourne Festival in 1964. On Feb. 17, 1965, he made his Metropolitan Opera debut in New York as Carlo in *La forza del destino*. He made occasional appearances there until 1975. In 1965–66 he sang in Rome. In 1966 he appeared as Pentheus in the premiere of *The Bassarids* at the Salzburg Festival. In 1967 he made his first appearance at Milan's La Scala as Valentin. He first sang at London's Covent Garden in 1969 as Macbeth, returning there in 1971–72. From 1988 he was director of the National Opera in Athens. Among his other roles were Don Giovanni, Donizetti's Alfonso, Posa, Nabucco, Iago, and Escamillo.

Pasquini, Bernardo, eminent Italian organist, harpsichordist, pedagogue, and composer; b. Massa di Valdinievole, near Lucca, Dec. 7, 1637; d. Rome, Nov. 21, 1710. He settled in Rome (1650), where he studied with Vittori and Cesti. He was organist at Chiesa Nuova (1661–63), S. Maria Maggiore (1663), S. Maria in Aracoeli (1664–1710), and S. Luigi dei Francesi (1673–75); was also first organist at the Oratory of SS. Crocifisso (1664–85). He served as harpsichordist and music director to Prince Giambattista Borghese, and was the teacher of Della Ciaja, Durante, and G. Muffat. In 1706 he became a member of the Arcadian Academy. Although greatly esteemed as a keyboard player, little of his music was publ. in his lifetime; many of his vocal works are lost. He excelled as a composer of keyboard suites and variations.

WORKS (all 1st perf. in Rome unless otherwise given): DRAMATIC: OPERAS: *La sincerità con la sincerità, overo Il Tirinto* (Ariccia, 1672); *La forza d'amore* (Rome, 1672; rev. as *Con la forza d'amor si vince amore*, Pratolino, near Florence, 1679); *L'amor per vendetta, overo L'Alcasta* (Jan. 27, 1673); *Tespolo tutore* (1675); *La Donna ancora è fidele* (Carnival 1676); *La caduta del regno dell'Amazzoni* (1678); *Dov'è è pietà* (Carnival 1679); *L'Idalma, overo Chi la duca la vince* (Carnival 1680); *Il Lisimaco* (Carnival 1681); *La Tessalonica* (Jan. 31, 1683); *L'Arianna* (Carnival 1685); *Santa Dinna* (Carnival 1687; in collaboration with A. Melani and A Scarlatti); *L'Eudossia* (Feb. 6, 1692). ORATORIOS: *L'Agar* (March 17, 1675); *L'Assuero* (April 15, 1675); *Sant'Alessio* (1676); *Sant'Agnese* (1677); *Sant'Eufrasia* (c.1677); *Salutazione angelica* (Messina, 1681); *Divae clarae triumphus* (March 20, 1682); *L'idolatria di Salomone* (1686); *I fatti di Mosè nel deserto* (Modena, 1687); *Il martirio dei santi* (Modena, 1687); *L'Abramo* (Palermo, 1688); *La sete di Christo* (1689); *La caduta di Salomone* (Florence, 1693); *L'Ismaele* (Florence, 1693); *David trionfante contro Goliath* (Florence, 1694).

BIBL.: V. Virgili, *B. P.* (Pescia, 1908); A. Bonaventura, *B. P.* (Ascoli Piceno, 1923); E. Luin, *B. P. e il suo tricentenario* (Rome, 1939); G. Crain, *The Operas of B. P.* (diss., Yale Univ., 1965).

Pasta, Giuditta (Maria Costanza née **Negri)**, famous Italian soprano; b. Saronno, near Milan, Oct. 28, 1797; d. Blevio, Lake Como, April 1, 1865. She studied with Asioli at the Milan Cons. and with Giuseppe Scappa, making her debut in his *Le tre Eleonore* at the Teatro degli Accademici Filodrammatici in Milan (1815). She then made her Paris debut in Paër's *Il Principe di Taranto* (1816) and her London debut as Telemachus in Cimarosa's *Penelope* at the King's Theatre (Jan. 11, 1817). After further studies with Scappa, she sang in Venice, Padua, Rome, Brescia, Trieste, and Turin. She then returned to Paris and made a sensational appearance as Desdemona in Rossini's *Otello* at the Théâtre-Italien (June 5, 1821), her voice being acclaimed as a vocal phenomenon and her dramatic abilities without equal. She continued to sing there, appearing in the premiere of Rossini's *Il viaggio a Reims* (June 19, 1825); she also sang in London from 1824. She created the title role in Pacini's *Niobe* at Naples's Teatro San Carlo (Nov. 19, 1826). After singing in Vienna (1829), she created the title role in Donizetti's *Anna Bolena* (Milan, Dec. 26, 1830) and Amina in Bellini's *La Sonnambula* (Milan, March 6, 1831); she then created the title role in Bellini's *Norma* at Milan's La Scala (Dec. 26, 1831) and Beatrice di Tenda in Venice (March 16, 1833). After appearances in London (1837) and St. Petersburg (1840), she virtually abandoned the stage due to the wretched condition of her voice. At the apex of her career, she astounded her auditors by the range of her voice, which encompassed A in the low register to D in the high treble; combined with her rare dramatic gifts, she had few equals on the operatic stage.

BIBL.: M. Ferranti-Giulini, *G. P. e i suoi tempi* (Milan, 1935).

Patachich, Iván, Hungarian composer; b. Budapest, June 3, 1922. He studied with Albert Siklós, János Viski, and Ferenc Szabó at the Budapest Academy of Music. After working as a theater conductor, he became music director of the Budapest Film Studio in 1952; he established the electronic music studio EXASTUD (Experimentum Auditorii Studii) in Budapest in 1971.

WORKS: DRAMATIC: OPERAS: *Theomachia* (1962); *Fuente ovajuna* (1969); *Brave New World* (1988–89). BALLETS: *Fekete-fehér* (Black and White; 1958); *Bakaruhában* (Sunday Romance; 1963); *Mngongo and Mlaba* (1965); *Studio sintetico* (1973). PANTOMIME: *Möbius tér* (Mobius Space; 1980).

Pataky, Kálmán, Hungarian tenor; b. Alsolenda, Nov. 14, 1896; d. Los Angeles, March 3, 1964. He studied in Budapest. In 1922 he made his operatic debut as the Duke of Mantua at the Budapest Opera, where he subsequently appeared regularly. From 1926 he also sang at the Vienna State Opera. He made guest appearances at the Paris Opéra (1928), the Glyndebourne Festival (1936), the Salzburg Festival (1936), and at Milan's La Scala. He also appeared frequently at the Teatro Colón in Buenos Aires. After the Anschluss in Austria in 1938, he sang mainly in Hungary. After World War II, he settled in the United States. Pataky was admired for his Mozart roles, particularly his Belmonte, Ottavio, and Tamino. He was a fine concert artist. Strauss dedicated several of his lieder to him.

BIBL.: V. Somogyi and I. Molnár, *P. K.* (Budapest, 1968).

Patanè, Giuseppe, Italian conductor; b. Naples, Jan. 1, 1932; d. (fatally stricken while conducting *Il Barbiere di Siviglia* at the Bavarian State Opera) Munich, May 30, 1989. He was a son of Franco Patane (1908–68), a conductor. He studied at the Cons. S. Pietro a Majella in Naples and made his debut as a conductor at the age of 19, when he led a performance of *La Traviata* at the Teatro Mercadante in Naples. He was subsequently 2d conductor at the Teatro San Carlo in Naples (1951–56); he became principal conductor of the Linz Landestheater in 1961, and in 1962 to 1968 was a conductor of the Deutsche Oper in Berlin; he further filled engagements at La Scala in Milan, at the Vienna State Opera, and in Copenhagen. On Oct. 18, 1975, he made his Metropolitan Opera debut in New York conducting *La Gioconda*. In 1982 he was appointed co-principal conductor of the American Sym. Orch. in New York, remaining at this post until 1984; he then was chief conductor of the Mannheim National Theater (from 1987) and of the Munich Radio Orch. (from 1988).

Patey, Janet (Monach née **Whytock)**, greatly esteemed Scottish contralto; b. London, May 1, 1842; d. Sheffield, Feb. 28, 1894. She studied with Wass, making her debut under the name Ellen Andrews in Birmingham in 1860; she then continued her studies with Mrs. Sims Reeves and Ciro Pinsuti. In 1866 she married the baritone John (George) Patey (b. Stonehouse, Devon, 1835; d. Falmouth, Dec. 4, 1901); he studied in Paris and Milan, and then made his London debut (1858); he appeared in light roles at Covent Garden and the Italian Opera at the Lyceum Theatre. The 2 then traveled extensively together, both at home and overseas. She became duly recognized as the leading British contralto by 1870. She made a tour of the United States in 1871.

Paton, Mary Ann, distinguished Scottish soprano; b. Edinburgh, Oct. 1802; d. Bulcliffe Hall, Chapelthorpe, July 21, 1864. Of a musical family, she sang in concerts as a child, making her first operatic appearance as Susanna in *Le nozze di Figaro* (London, Aug. 3, 1822). She sang the part of Rezia in the premiere of Weber's *Oberon* in London (April 12, 1826) and was praised by Weber himself. She had a very fine voice, and could sing lyric and coloratura parts with equal brilliance. She was married to the tenor Joseph Wood.

BIBL.: J. Wood, *Memoir of Mr. and Mrs. Wood* (Philadelphia, 1840).

Patorzhinsky, Ivan (Sergeievich), noted Ukrainian bass; b. Petrovo-Svistunovo, March 3, 1896; d. Kiev, Feb. 22, 1960. He studied at the Ekaterinoslav Cons., graduating in 1922. From 1925 to 1935 he was a member of the Kharkov Opera, and from 1935 to 1960 of the Kiev Opera. He also pursued a concert career. From 1946 he taught at the Kiev Cons. In 1944 he was made a People's Artist of the USSR. Patorzhinsky was the leading Ukrainian bass of his day, excelling particularly in roles in Ukrainian operas. He also was a fine Don Basilio, Boris Godunov, and Méphistophélès.

BIBL.: M. Stefanovich, *I. S. P.* (Moscow, 1960).

Patterson, Annie Wilson, Irish organist, folk song collector, writer on music, and composer; b. Lurgan, Oct. 27, 1868; d. Cork, Jan. 16, 1934. She studied organ with Robert Stewart at the Royal Irish Academy of Music; she also studied at the Royal Univ. of Ireland (Mus.B., B.A., 1887; Mus.D., 1889). She held several posts as an organist before being made organist at Cork's Shandon Church (1904); she was named to the chair of Irish music at the Univ. College, Cork (1924). She organized the Feis Ceoil (Irish Music Festival), held annually from 1897. Among her compositions were 2 operas, *The High-King's Daughter* and *Oisin*.

WRITINGS (all publ. in London): *The Story of Oratorio* (1902); *Schumann* (1903; 2d ed., rev., 1934); *The Profession of Music* (1926); *Great Minds in Music* (1926); *The Music of Ireland* (1926).

Patti, family of prominent Italian singers:

(1) Salvatore Patti, tenor; b. Catania, 1800; d. Paris, Aug. 21, 1869. He was 2d tenor at Palermo's Teatro Carolino (1825–26). After singing throughout Sicily, Italy, and Spain, he settled in New York (1844), where he became active as an opera manager. His wife was the soprano Caterina Chiesa Barilli-Patti (b. Rome, date unknown; d. there, Sept. 6, 1870); she studied with her first husband, Barilli; she created the role of Eleanora in Donizetti's *L'assedio di Calais* (Naples, Nov. 19, 1836); she later sang in New York before retiring to Rome. She had 4 children by her first husband, all of whom became singers; she had 3 daughters by her 2d husband.

(2) Amalia Patti, singer; b. Paris, 1831; d. there, Dec. 1915. She appeared in opera and concert in the United States until marrying **Maurice Strakosch**.

(3) Carlotta Patti, soprano; b. Florence, Oct. 30, 1835; d. Paris, June 27, 1889. She studied with her parents and with Henri Herz in Paris, making her concert debut in New York (1861). She sang opera at the Academy of Music there (1862), but due to lameness decided to pursue a concert career. She toured in the United States and Europe. After marrying the cellist Ernest de Munck in 1871, she settled in Paris as a voice teacher.

(4) Adelina (Adela Juana Maria) Patti, greatly celebrated soprano; b. Madrid, Feb. 19, 1843; d. Craig-y-Nos Castle, near Brecon, Wales, Sept. 27, 1919. She was taken to New York (1844), where she began study with her half brother, Ettore Barilli, and made her first public appearance at a charity concert at Tripler's Hall when she was 7. She then toured the United States as a child prodigy with her brother-in-law **Maurice Strakosch**, and with Ole Bull; she later toured with Gottschalk (1857). As the "little Florinda," she made her formal debut as Lucia in New York on Nov. 24, 1859; her European debut followed at London's Covent Garden as Amina in *La Sonnambula* on May 16, 1861. She was hailed as the true successor of Grisi, and subsequently returned to Covent Garden each season for the next 25 years. She sang in Berlin (1861), then in Brussels, Amsterdam, and The Hague (1862); she appeared as Amina at the Théâtre-Italien in Paris (Nov. 19, 1862), a role she sang at Vienna's Karlstheater (1863). She made her first tour of Italy in 1865–66. She married the Marquis de Caux in Paris in 1868; soon after their divorce in 1885 she married the tenor **Nicolini**; after his death in 1898 she married the Swedish nobleman Baron Rolf Cederstrom in 1899. Patti made her first appearance at Milan's La Scala as Violetta on Nov. 3, 1877. She returned to the United States for a concert tour in 1881–82, then sang in opera there under the auspices of J. H. Mapleson during the next 3 seasons, earning as much as $5,000 per performance. In 1886–87 she again toured the United States under the auspices of H. E. Abbey, who presented her at the Metropolitan Opera in New York in the spring of 1887, and then again in 1890 and 1892; her final tour of the United States followed in 1903. She made her last appearance at Covent Garden in 1895; her operatic farewell took place in Nice in 1897. Her official farewell concert was given at London's Albert Hall on Dec. 1, 1906. Her last public appearance was at a benefit concert for the Red Cross in that same hall on Oct. 20, 1914. Patti was one of the greatest coloraturas of the 19th century. Although her voice was not one of great power, it possessed a wide range, wonderful flexibility, and perfect evenness. In addition to Amina and Lucia, she was renowned for such roles as Zerlina, Rosina, Norina, Elvira, Martha, Adina, and Gilda; she was also esteemed as Aida and Gounod's Marguerite.

BIBL.: T. de Grave, *Le Biographie d'A. P.* (Paris, 1865); G. de Charnace, *A. P.* (Paris, 1868); G. Dalmazzo, *A. P.'s Life* (London, 1877); L. Lauw, *Fourteen Years with A. P.* (London, 1884); H. Klein, *The Reign of P.* (N.Y., 1920); J. Cone, *A. P.: Queen of Hearts* (Portland, Oreg., 1993).

Pattiera, Tino, Croatian tenor; b. Čavtat, near Ragusa, June 27, 1890; d. there, April 24, 1966. He studied at the Vienna Academy of Music with Ranieri. In 1915 he joined the Dresden Court (later State) Opera, where he was a principal member of the company until 1941; he also sang with the Berlin State Opera (1924–29) and was a guest artist in Chicago, Vienna, Budapest, Paris, Prague, and other music centers. He gave his farewell concert in Dresden in 1948; from 1950 he taught voice at the Vienna Academy of Music. He was most renowned for the lyric roles in Verdi's operas.

Patzak, Julius, distinguished Austrian tenor; b. Vienna, April 9, 1898; d. Rottach-Egern, Bavaria, Jan. 26, 1974. He studied musicology and conducting with Adler, Schmidt, and Mandyczewski at the Univ. of Vienna; was autodidact as a singer. He made his operatic debut as Radamès in Reichenberg (1923). After singing in Brno (1927–28), he was a principal member of the Bavarian State Opera in Munich (1928–45) and the Vienna State Opera (1945–59); he first appeared at London's Covent Garden as Tamino (1938), returning there with the visiting Vienna State Opera (1947), and then singing there regularly (1951–54). He was a teacher at the Vienna Academy of Music and the Salzburg Mozarteum; he retired from the stage in 1966. Patzak was noted for his roles in Mozart's operas, but he became best known for his compelling portrayals of Beethoven's Florestan and Pfitzner's Palestrina.

Pauer, Jiří, Czech composer and arts administrator; b. Libušín, near Kladno, Feb. 22, 1919. He studied composition with Otakar Šin; then with Alois Hába at the Prague Cons. (1943–46) and with Bořkovec at the Prague Academy of Musical Arts (1946–50). He occupied various administrative posts with the Ministry of Education and Culture and with the Czech Radio; he was artistic director of the Opera of the National Theater in Prague (1953–55; 1965–67; 1979–89) and also taught at the Prague Academy. He was director of the Czech Phil. from 1958 to 1980. His music followed the pragmatic precepts of socialist realism in its modern application, broadly lyrical and tensely dramatic by turns.

WORKS: DRAMATIC: OPERAS: *Žvanivý Slimejš* (Prattling Snail; 1949–50; Prague, April 5, 1958); *Zuzana Vojířová* (1954–57; Prague, May 11, 1958); *Červená Karkulka* (Little Red Riding Hood; 1959; Olomouc, 1960); *Manželské kontrapunkty* (Marital Counterpoints; 1961; 3 operatic satirical sketches, Ostrava, 1962; 2d version as 5 satires, Liberec, 1967); *Zdravý nemocný* (The Imaginary Invalid), after Molière (1966–69; Prague, May 22, 1970). MONODRAMA: *Labutí píseň* (The Swan Song; 1973). BALLET: *Ferda Mravenec* (Ferdy the Ant; 1975).

Paul, Thomas (Warburton), distinguished American bass; b. Chicago, Feb. 22, 1934. He studied with Howard Swan and Robert Gross at Occidental College in Los Angeles (B.A., 1956), then took courses in conducting with Jean Morel and Frederic Waldman at the Juilliard School of Music in New York; he also studied voice privately in New York. He made his vocal debut in Handel's *Belshazzar* at Carnegie Hall in New York on April 10, 1961. He sang with the N.Y. City Opera (1962–71; debut Oct. 4, 1962), and with other U.S. opera companies. He made his European debut in Zürich on April 3, 1976, in a performance of Bach's St. Matthew

Passion. In 1980 he made his recital debut in New York. He made many appearances as a soloist with the major North American orchs. He was a visiting prof. (1971–74) and prof. (from 1974) at the Eastman School of Music in Rochester, N.Y., and also taught at the Aspen (Colo.) Music School. His finest roles included Boris Godunov, Figaro, and Méphistophélès.

Paulli, Holger Simon, Danish violinist, conductor, and composer; b. Copenhagen, Feb. 22, 1810; d. there, Dec. 23, 1891. He studied violin with Schall and Wexschall, and at the age of 12, entered the court orch. in Copenhagen, then was its concertmaster (1849–63) and principal conductor (1863–83). In 1866 he was appointed codirector, with Gade and Hauptmann, of the newly founded Copenhagen Cons. He was an admirer of Wagner, and conducted the first performances in Denmark of *Lohengrin* (1870) and *Die Meistersinger von Nürnberg* (1872). He composed a Singspiel, *Lodsen* (The Pilot), which was produced in Copenhagen on Sept. 25, 1851; also some ballet music.

Paulus, Stephen (Harrison), American composer; b. Summit, N.J., Aug. 24, 1949. He studied with Paul Fetler and Dominick Argento at the Univ. of Minnesota (B.M., 1971; M.M., 1974; Ph.D., 1978). In 1973 he founded the Minnesota Composers Forum in Minneapolis with Libby Larsen, and was managing composer until 1984. He served as composer-in-residence of the Minnesota Orch. (1983–87), the Santa Fe Chamber Music Festival (1986), the Atlanta Sym. Orch. (1988–92), the Dale Warland Singers (1991–92), and the Aspen (Colo.) Music Festival (1992). In 1987 his Violin Concerto No. 1 won the Kennedy Center Friedheim 3d Prize. In 1983 he held a Guggenheim fellowship. Paulus has demonstrated fine craftsmanship in both vocal and instrumental writing.

WORKS: OPERAS: *The Village Singer* (1977; St. Louis, June 9, 1979); *The Postman Always Rings Twice* (1981; St. Louis, June 19, 1982; also an orch. suite, Minneapolis, July 26, 1986); *The Woodlanders* (1984; St. Louis, June 13, 1985); *Harmoonia*, children's opera (1991); *The Woman at Otowi Crossing* (St. Louis, June 15, 1995).

Pauly, Rosa (Rose née **Pollak)**, noted Hungarian soprano; b. Eperjes, March 15, 1894; d. Kfar Shmaryahn, near Tel Aviv, Dec. 14, 1975. She studied voice with Rosa Papier in Vienna, and made her operatic debut at the Vienna State Opera as Desdemona in Verdi's *Otello* in 1918. She subsequently sang in Hamburg, Cologne, and Mannheim. From 1927 to 1931 she was a member of the Kroll Opera in Berlin; also of the Vienna State Opera (1929–35); in 1934 she sang the challenging role of Elektra in Strauss's opera in Salzburg, gathering encomiums; in 1935 she appeared at La Scala in Milan. She made her American debut as Elektra in a concert performance with the N.Y. Phil. on March 21, 1937; she sang it again at her first appearance with the Metropolitan Opera in New York on Jan. 7, 1938; she appeared there until 1940 and also sang at the Teatro Colón in Buenos Aires in 1939. In 1946 she went to Palestine, and devoted herself to teaching in Tel Aviv. She was esteemed for her roles in the operas of Mozart, Verdi, and Wagner, but most particularly for her compelling portrayals of such Strauss roles as Elektra, the Dyer's Wife, and Helena.

Paumgartner, Bernhard, eminent Austrian musicologist and conductor; b. Vienna, Nov. 14, 1887; d. Salzburg, July 27, 1971. He was a son of the pianist Hans Paumgartner (1843–96) and the mezzo-soprano Rosa Papier. He learned to play the horn, violin, and piano in his youth; he began to conduct while still in school. After receiving a doctorate in law from the Univ. of Vienna (1911), he studied musicology privately with Adler. He was répétiteur at the Vienna Court Opera (1911–12), then was director of the Salzburg Mozarteum (from 1917), which he headed until 1938, and again from 1945 to 1959; he was also closely associated with the Salzburg Festival from its founding (1920), serving as its president (1960–71). He also composed: he wrote the operas *Die Höhle von Salamanca* (Dresden, 1923) and *Rossini in Neapel* (Zürich, March 27, 1936), various other stage pieces, including several ballets.

WRITINGS: *Mozart* (Berlin, 1927; 10th ed., 1993); *Franz Schubert: Eine Biographie* (Zürich, 1943; 3d ed., 1960); *Johann Sebastian Bach: Leben und Werk, I: Bis zur Berufung nach Leipzig* (Zürich, 1950); *Erinnerungen* (Salzburg, 1969); G. Croll, ed., *Bernhard Paumgartner: Vorträge und Essays* (Salzburg, 1972).

BIBL.: E. Preussner, ed., *Wissenschaft und Praxis: Eine Festschrift zum 70. Geburtstag von B. P.* (Zürich, 1957); G. Croll, ed., *B. P.* (Salzburg and Munich, 1971).

Paunović, Milenko, Serbian composer; b. Šajkaš, Nov. 28, 1889; d. Belgrade, Oct. 1, 1924. He studied in Leipzig with Reger and Riemann. He became a choral conductor in Novi Sad. In his music, which included several music dramas to his own texts, he followed Wagnerian concepts.

Pavarotti, Luciano, greatly renowned Italian tenor; b. Modena, Oct. 12, 1935. His father, a baker by trade, sang in the local church choir; Luciano learned to read music and began singing with the boy altos; he later joined his father in the choir, and also sang in the chorus of the local Teatro Comunale and the amateur Chorale Gioacchino Rossini. To prepare himself for a career as a schoolteacher, he attended the local Scuola Magistrale; then taught in an elementary school, augmenting his income by selling insurance. In the meantime, he began vocal studies with Arrigo Polo in Modena (1955), then went to Mantua, where he continued his training with Ettore Campogalliani (1960). He made his operatic debut as Rodolfo in *La Bohème* at the Teatro Municipale in Reggio Emilia on April 29, 1961. He obtained his first major engagement when he appeared as the Duke of Mantua at the Teatro Massimo in Palermo (March 15, 1962). His first important appearance outside his homeland was as Edgardo with the Netherlands Opera in Amsterdam (Jan. 18, 1963). On Feb. 24, 1963, he made his Vienna State Opera debut as Rodolfo, a role he also sang for his first appearance at London's Covent Garden (Sept. 21, 1963). On Feb. 15, 1965, he made his U.S. debut as Edgardo opposite Joan Sutherland's Lucia with the Greater Miami Opera. After his first appearance at Milan's La Scala as Alfredo (April 28, 1965), he made a summer tour of Australia with the Sutherland Williamson International Grand Opera Co., a venture featuring the celebrated diva. He subsequently scored his first triumph on the operatic stage when he essayed the role of Tonio in *La Fille du régiment* at Covent Garden (June 1, 1966); with insouciant aplomb, he tossed off the aria *Pour mon âme*, replete with 9 successive high Cs, winning an ovation. He was dubbed the "King of the High Cs," and a brilliant international career beckoned. He made his debut at the San Francisco Opera as Rodolfo (Nov. 11, 1967), a role he chose for his first appearance at the Metropolitan Opera in New York (Nov. 23, 1968). In subsequent seasons, he became a mainstay at both houses, and also appeared regularly with other opera houses on both sides of the Atlantic. He also made frequent appearances in solo recitals and concerts with orchs. In 1977 he starred as Rodolfo in the first "Live from the Met" telecast by PBS. In 1978 he made an acclaimed solo recital debut at the Metropolitan Opera, which was also telecast by PBS. In 1980 he founded the Opera Co. of Philadelphia/Luciano Pavarotti International Voice Competition. On Oct. 22, 1983, he was one of the featured artists at the Metropolitan Opera Centennial Gala. In 1984 he gave a concert before 20,000 admirers at N.Y.'s Madison Square Garden, which was also seen by millions on PBS. He celebrated the 25th anniversary of his operatic debut by singing his beloved Rodolfo at the Teatro Comunale in Modena on April 29, 1986. In 1988 he sang Nemorino at the Berlin Deutsche Oper, eliciting thunderous applause and no less than 15 curtain calls. On Jan. 9, 1989, he appeared in concert with the N.Y. City Opera orch. in a special program at Avery Fischer Hall at N.Y.'s Lincoln Center for the Performing Arts, which was televised live by PBS. In 1990 he appeared at the Bolshoi Theater in Moscow. On July 7, 1990, he made an unprecedented concert appearance with fellow tenors José Carreras and Plácido Domingo in Rome in an extravaganza telecast to the world. In subsequent years, the "three tenors" appeared in concert in various cities around the globe. Pavarotti celebrated the 30th anniversary of his career with a special concert at London's Hyde Park on July 30, 1991, which was telecast throughout Europe and overseas. On July 26, 1993, he gave a concert before some 500,000 people in N.Y.'s Central Park, which was seen by countless others via a live telecast by PBS. He celebrated the 25th anniversary of his debut at the Metropolitan Opera on Sept. 27, 1993, singing Otello in the first act of Verdi's opera in a live radio broadcast heard around the world. On July 6, 1994, he again appeared with Carreras and Domingo in concert in Los Angeles, an event telecast live around the globe. On Nov. 22, 1998, he celebrated the 30th anniversary of his Metropolitan Opera debut in a gala performance with the company.

The most idolized tenor since Caruso, Pavarotti made such roles as Nemorino in *L'elisir d'amore*, Riccardo in *Un ballo in maschera*, Fernando in *La Favorite*, Manrico in *Il Trovatore*, Cavaradossi in *Tosca*, and Radames in *Aida*, as well as the ubiquitous Rodolfo, virtually his own. Indeed, through recordings and television appearances, he won an adoring global following, which he retained into his sixth decade. His autobiography was publ. as *Pavarotti: My Own Story* (with W. Wright; Garden City, N.Y., 1981).

BIBL.: M. Mayer, *Grandissimo P.* (Garden City, N.Y., 1986; with career chronology and discography by G. Fitzgerald); A. Pavarotti and W. Dallas, *P.: Vivere con L.* (Trento, 1992; Eng. tr., 1992, as *P.: Life with L.*); C. Bonvicini, *The Tenor's Son: My Days with P.* (N.Y., 1993); L. Magiera, *P.: Mythos, Methode und Magie* (Zürich, 1993); E. Ruggieri, *P.* (Paris, 1993).

Pavesi, Stefano, Italian composer; b. Casaletto Vaprio, near Crema, Jan. 22, 1779; d. Crema, July 28, 1850. He was a pupil of Piccinni in Naples (1795–97) and of Fenaroli there at the Cons. di S. Onofrio, later S. Maria di Loreto (1797–99). After being expelled for his revolutionary sentiments, he was deported to Marseilles, joined Napoleon's army, and fought in the Italian campaign. He then completed his vocal training with Gazzaniga, whom he succeeded as maestro di cappella at Crema Cathedral (1818–50). From 1826 to 1830 Pavesi also served as music director of the Vienna Court Opera. He composed about 70 operas, winning notable success with *La fiera* (Florence, 1804), *La festa della rosa* (Venice, May 21, 1808), *Ser Marcantonio* (Milan, Sept. 26, 1810), and *Fenella, ovvero La muta Portici* (Venice, Feb. 5, 1831). Among his other compositions were sacred pieces, songs, and 6 harpsichord sonatas.

BIBL.: F. Sanseverino, *Notizie intorno alla vita e alle opere del Maestro S. P.* (Milan, 1851).

Pazovsky, Ariy (Moiseievich), Russian conductor; b. Perm, Feb. 2, 1887; d. Moscow, Jan. 6, 1953. He received violin training as a child, and then was a student of Krasnokutsky and Auer at the St. Petersburg Cons. (1897–1904). After conducting provincial opera companies (1905–08), he was conductor of Zimin's opera company in Moscow (1908–10), and then conducted in Kharkov, Odessa, and Kiev. He was music director of the Petrograd People's Opera (1916–18). After conducting at Moscow's Bolshoi Theater (1923–24; 1925–28), he conducted in Baku, Sverdlovsk, Kharkov, and Kiev (1926–36). He was artistic director of Leningrad's Kirov Theater (1936–43), and then of the Bolshoi Theater (1943–48). In 1940 he was made a People's Artist of the USSR. He publ. *Zapiski dirizhora* (The Writings of a Conductor; Moscow, 1966).

Pearce, S(tephen) Austen, English-American organist and composer; b. Brompton, Kent, Nov. 7, 1836; d. Jersey City, N.J., April 9, 1900. He studied at the Univ. of Oxford (Mus.B., 1859; Mus.D., 1864). In 1872 he settled in America, where he taught vocal music at Columbia College in New York: he also taught at the Peabody Inst. in Baltimore. He wrote an opera, *La Belle Americaine*, and a dramatic oratorio, *Celestial Visions*. He compiled *A Pocket Dictionary of Musical Terms* in 21 languages (N.Y., 1889).

Pearlman, Martin, noted American conductor, harpsichordist, and composer; b. Chicago, May 21, 1945. He received training in composition, violin, piano, and theory in his youth. Following studies in composition with Husa at Cornell Univ. (B.A., 1967), he pursued training in harpsichord with Leonhardt on a Fulbright scholarship in the Netherlands (1967–68). He subsequently took his M.M. in composition under Wyner at Yale Univ. (1971), and also studied with Ralph Kirkpatrick (harpsichord) and Arel (electronic music). In 1972 he won the Erwin Bodky Award and in 1974 he was a prize winner in the Bruges Competition. In 1973 he founded and became music director of Banchetto Musicale, the first permanent Baroque orch. established in North America. In 1992 it was renamed Boston Baroque. From 1976 to 1981 he taught at the Univ. of Mass. in Boston, and also at Brandeis Univ. in 1980–81. As a harpsichordist, Pearlman has become well known for his performances of the Couperin family and of D. Scarlatti. As a conductor, he has led numerous period instrument performances and has given the American premieres of many Baroque and Classical scores, including those of Bach, Handel, Rameau, Mozart, and Beethoven. He has also appeared as a guest conductor of modern instrument groups and sym. orchs., as well as of Baroque ensembles. In 1995 he made his Kennedy Center debut in Washington, D.C., conducting Handel's *Semele*. Pearlman has prepared performing eds. of Monteverdi's *L'incoronazione di Poppea*, Purcell's *Comical History of Don Quixote*, and Mozart's *Lo sposo deluso*. He has also prepared a complete ed. of the keyboard music of Armand-Louis Couperin.

Pears, Sir Peter (Neville Luard), renowned English tenor; b. Farnham, June 22, 1910; d. Aldeburgh, April 3, 1986. He began his career as temporary organist at Hertford College, Oxford (1928–29), then was director of music at the Grange School, Crowborough (1930–34). He was a scholarship student at the Royal College of Music in London (1933–34); concurrently he sang in the BBC Chorus, and then was a member of the BBC Singers (1934–38) and the New English Singers (1936–38). During this period, he received vocal instruction from Elena Gerhardt and Dawson Freer. In 1936 he also met Benjamin Britten; they gave their first joint recital in 1937, and thereafter remained lifelong personal and professional companions. After singing in the Glyndebourne Chorus (1938), he accompanied Britten to the United States (1939); he continued his vocal training with Thérèse Behr and Clytie Hine-Mundy. In 1942 he returned to England with Britten, making his stage debut that same year in the title role of *Les Contes d'Hoffmann* at London's Strand Theatre. In 1943 he joined the Sadler's Wells Opera Co., gaining fame when he created the title role in Britten's *Peter Grimes* (June 7, 1945). In 1946 he became a member of the English Opera Group, and thereafter greatly distinguished himself in operas by Britten; among the roles he created were Albert Herring, the Male Chorus in *The Rape of Lucretia*, Captain Vere in *Billy Budd*, Essex in *Gloriana*, Quint in *The Turn of the Screw*, Flute in *A Midsummer Night's Dream* (was colibrettist with the composer), the Madwoman in *Curlew River*, Sir Philip Wingrave in *Owen Wingrave*, and Aschenbach in *Death in Venice*. It was in the latter role that he made his Metropolitan Opera debut in New York on Oct. 18, 1974. He was one of the founders of the Aldeburgh Festival (1948), serving as a director and as a teacher of master classes until his death. Pears also sang in several first performances of Britten's nonoperatic works, including the *Serenade* for Tenor, Horn, and Strings, the *Michelangelo Sonnets*, and the *War Requiem*. He also excelled in the works of other English composers, among them Elgar, Holst, Vaughan Williams, and Walton, as well as those by Schütz, Bach, Mozart, Schubert, and Schumann. He was made a Commander of the Order of the British Empire in 1957, and was knighted in 1978. P. Reed ed. and annotated *The Travel Diaries of Peter Pears, 1936–1978* (Woodbridge, 1995).

BIBL.: M. Thorpe, ed., *P. P.: A Tribute on His 75th Birthday* (London, 1985); C. Headington, *P. P.: A Biography* (London and Boston, 1993).

Pease, James, American bass-baritone; b. Indianapolis, Jan. 9, 1916; d. N.Y., April 26, 1967. He studied at the Curtis Inst. of Music in Philadelphia. In 1941 he made his operatic debut as Gounod's Méphistophélès at the Philadelphia Opera. On May 9, 1946, he made his first appearance at the N.Y. City Opera as Sparafucile, where he sang until 1953 and again in 1959–60 and 1967. From

1952 to 1959 he also was a member of the Hamburg State Opera. As a guest artist, Pease appeared at London's Covent Garden, the Zürich Opera, the San Francisco Opera, the Chicago Lyric Opera, and other opera centers. Among his best roles were Don Giovanni, Figaro, King Marke, Hans Sachs, and Baron Ochs.

Pechner, Gerhard, German-American baritone; b. Berlin, April 15, 1903; d. N.Y., Oct. 21, 1969. He studied in Berlin, making his debut there in 1927. After singing at the German Theater in Prague (1933–39), he emigrated to the United States. In 1940 he made his U.S. debut as Mozart's Bartolo at the San Francisco Opera. On Nov. 27, 1941, he made his Metropolitan Opera debut in New York as the Notary in *Der Rosenkavalier*, and remained on its roster until 1965. In 1966–67 he was again on its roster. Pechner was especially admired for such roles as Alberich, Beckmesser, Melitone in *La forza del destino*, and the Sacristan in *Tosca*.

Pederzini, Gianna, noted Italian mezzo-soprano; b. Vò di Avio, Feb. 10, 1903; d. Rome, March 12, 1988. She studied with De Lucia in Naples. She made her operatic debut as Preziosilla in 1923 in Messina; in 1930 she joined La Scala in Milan, where she sang until 1943; she also appeared in Rome (1939–52), at Covent Garden, London (1931), and at the Teatro Colón in Buenos Aires (1937–39; 1946–47). She returned to La Scala in 1956–57, creating the role of the Prioress in Poulenc's *Dialogues des Carmélites*. She was an outstanding interpreter of roles in Rossini's operas; was also greatly admired for her interpretation of Carmen.

Pedrell, Carlos, Uruguayan composer, nephew of **Felipe Pedrell**; b. Minas, Oct. 16, 1878; d. Montrouge, near Paris, March 3, 1941. He studied in Madrid with his uncle, and later went to Paris, where he took lessons with d'Indy and Breville at the Schola Cantorum. Returning to South America, he was inspector of music in the Buenos Aires schools. He lectured at the Univ. of Tucumán. In 1921 he went to Paris, where he remained for the rest of his life. His works are cast in the French style, but the rhythmic elements are related to Spanish and South American sources; his songs, with richly developed accompaniments, are the best among his works. He also composed the operas *Ardid de Amor* (Buenos Aires, June 7, 1917) and *Cuento de Abril*; *La Guitare* (Madrid, 1924), and the ballets *La Rose et le gitan* (Antwerp, 1930) and *Alleluia* (Buenos Aires, 1936).

Pedrell, Felipe, eminent Spanish musicologist and composer, uncle of **Carlos Pedrell**; b. Tortosa, Feb. 19, 1841; d. Barcelona, Aug. 19, 1922. He became a chorister at Tortosa Cathedral when he was about 7, receiving instruction from Juan Antonio Nin y Serra. In 1873 he went to Barcelona as deputy director of the Light Opera Co., where he produced his first opera, *L'ultimo Abenzeraggio* (April 14, 1874). After a visit to Italy (1876–77) and a sojourn in Paris, he settled in Barcelona (1881), where he devoted himself mainly to musicological pursuits. In 1882 he founded the journals *Salterio Sacro-Hispano* and *Notas Musicales y Literarias*, both of which ceased publication in 1883. He then was founder–ed. of the important journal *La Illustración Musical Hispano-Americana* (1888–96). During this period, he worked on his operatic masterpiece, the trilogy *Los Pirieneos/Els Pirineus* (1890–91), and also publ. the book *Por nuestra música* (1891), which served as its introduction and as a plea for the creation of a national lyric drama based on Spanish folk song. In 1894 he went to Madrid, where he was named prof. of choral singing at the Cons. and prof. of advanced studies at the Ateneo; he was also elected a member of the Royal Academy of Fine Arts. Upon his return to Barcelona (1904), he devoted himself to writing, teaching, and composing. Among his outstanding pupils were Albéniz, Falla, Granados, and Gerhard. Although Pedrell was admired as a composer by his contemporaries, his music has not obtained recognition outside his homeland. His lasting achievement rests upon his distinguished as a musicologist, in which he did much to restore interest in both historical and contemporary Spanish sacred music.

WRITINGS: *Gramática musical or manual expositivo de la teoria del solfeo, en forma de diálogo* (Barcelona, 1872; 3d ed., 1883); *Las sonatas de Beethoven* (Barcelona, 1873); *Los músicos españoles en sus libros* (Barcelona, 1888); *Por nuestra música* (Barcelona, 1891); *Diccionario técnico de la música bibliográfico de músicos y escritores de música españoles, portugueses y hispano-amerianos antiguos y modernos* (Barcelona, 1895–97); *Emporio cientifico e histórico de organografia musical española antigua* (Barcelona, 1901); *Prácticas preparatorias de instrumentación* (Barcelona, 1902); *La cançó popular catalana* (Barcelona, 1906); *Documents pour servir à l'histoire de théâtre musical: La Festa d'Elche ou le drame lyrique liturgique espagnol* (Paris, 1906); *Musicalerias* (Valencia, 1906); *Catàlech de la Biblioteca musical de la Diputació de Barcelona* (Barcelona, 1909); *Músicos contemporáneos y de otros tiempos* (Paris, 1910); *Jornadas de arte* (Paris, 1911; memoirs and articles, 1841–1902); *La lirica nacionalizada* (Paris, 1913); *Tomás Luis de Victoria Abulense* (Valencia, 1918); *P. Antonio Eximeno* (Madrid, 1920); *Jornados postreras* (Valls, 1922; autobiography); *Musiquerias* (Paris, n.d.; autobiography).

EDITIONS: *Hispaniae schola musical sacra* (Barcelona, 1894–98); *Teatro lirico español anterior al siglo XIX* (La Coruña, 1897–98); *T. L. de Victoria: Opera omnia* (Leipzig, 1902–13); *El organista litúrgico español* (Barcelona, 1905); *Antologia de organistas clásicos españoles* (Madrid, 1908); *Cancionero musical popular español* (Valls, 1918–22; 2d ed., 1936); with H. Anglès, *Els madrigals i la missa de difunts d'en Brudieu* (Barcelona, 1921).

BIBL.: G. Tebaldini, *F. P. ed il dramma lirico spagnuolo* (Turin, 1897); R. Mitjana, *La música contemporanea en España y F. P.* (Málaga, 1901); H. de Curzon, *F. P. et "Les Pyrénées"* (Paris, 1902); L. Vilalba Muñoz, *F. P.: Semblanza y biografia* (Madrid, 1922); F. Bonastre, *F. P.: Acotaciones a una idea* (Tarragona, 1977).

Pedrollo, Arrigo, Italian composer and pedagogue; b. Montebello Vicentino, Dec. 5, 1878; d. Vicenza, Dec. 23, 1964. He studied at the Milan Cons. (1891–1900); at his graduation he wrote a sym., which was performed by Toscanini. He was the director of the Istituto Musicale in Vicenza (1920–30), then a prof. of composition at the Milan Cons. (1930–41); from 1942 to 1959 he was director of the Vicenza Cons. In 1914 he won the Sonzogno competition with his opera *Juana*. His other operas include *Terra promessa* (Cremona, 1908), *La Veglia* (Milan, Jan. 2, 1920), *L'Uomo che ride* (Rome, March 6, 1920), *Maria di Magdala* (Milan, 1924), *Delitto e castigo*, after Dostoyevsky (Milan, Nov. 16, 1926), *L'Amante in trappola* (Verona, Sept. 22, 1936), and *Il Giglio di Ali* (1948).

Pedrotti, Carlo, eminent Italian conductor and composer; b. Verona, Nov. 12, 1817; d. there (suicide), Oct. 16, 1893. He studied with Domenico Foroni in Verona, where he first gained success as a composer with his opera *Lina* (May 2, 1840). After serving as conductor of the Italian Opera in Amsterdam (1841–45), he returned to Verona, where he was active as a teacher, opera coach, and conductor at the Teatro Filarmonico and at the Teatro Nuovo, where he brought out his finest opera, *Tutti in maschera* (Nov. 4, 1856). In 1868 he was called to Turin as director of the Liceo Musicale and as director and conductor of the Teatro Regio, where he reorganized the musical life of the city; he also founded and conducted the weekly series of Concerti Popolari, in which he presented the Italian premieres of many historical and contemporary works. In 1882 he went to Pesaro as the first director of the newly founded Liceo Musicale, a position he held until ill health compelled him to resign in 1893; that same year he took his own life by drowning himself in the Adige River. Although Pedrotti excelled as a composer of opera buffa, his importance today rests upon his work as a conductor.

BIBL.: T. Mantovani, *C. P.* (Pesaro, 1894).

Peellaert, Augustin-Philippe (-Marie-Ghislain), South Netherlands composer; b. Bruges, March 12, 1793; d. Brussels, April 16, 1876. He studied in Paris with Momigny. In 1832 he became a member of the executive board of the Brussels Cons. He wrote several operas, of which the following were produced in Brussels: *L'Heure du rendez-vous* (1821), *Agnes Sorel* (Aug. 30, 1823), *Le Barmècide* (1824), *Teniers ou La Noce flamande* (Feb. 21, 1825),

L'Exilé (1827), *Faust* (1834), *Le Coup de pistolet* (1836), and *Louis de Male* (1838). His autobiography appeared as *Cinquante ans de souvenirs* (Brussels, 1867).

Peerce, Jan (real name, **Jacob Pincus Perelmuth**), noted American tenor; b. N.Y., June 3, 1904; d. there, Dec. 15, 1984. He played the violin in dance bands, and sang at various entertainment places in New York. In 1932 he was engaged as a singer at Radio City Music Hall in New York. He made his operatic debut in Philadelphia as the Duke of Mantua in *Rigoletto* (May 14, 1938), and gave his first solo recital in New York on Nov. 7, 1939. His lyrical voice attracted attention, and he was engaged by the Metropolitan Opera in New York; he made his debut there as Alfredo in *La Traviata* on Nov. 29, 1941; he sang also the parts of Cavaradossi in *Tosca*, Rodolfo in *La Bohème*, and Gounod's Faust; he remained on the staff of the Metropolitan until 1966, appearing again in 1967–68. He continued to make occasional appearances until his retirement in 1982. He was the brother-in-law of **Richard Tucker**.

BIBL.: A. Levy, *The Bluebird of Happiness: The Memoirs of J. P.* (N.Y., 1976).

Peiko, Nikolai, Russian composer; b. Moscow, March 25, 1916. He studied with Litinsky, Rakov, and Miaskovsky at the Moscow Cons. (1933–40). After graduation, he was commissioned to collect folk-song materials in the remote Yakutsk district of Siberia, and produced *Suite on a Yakutsk Theme* for Orch. (1941); he then investigated Bashkir folk music and composed a Bashkir opera, *Aikhylu* (1943). Returning to Moscow, he taught at the Cons. (1942–59); he also taught at the Gnessin Musical Inst. His music faithfully follows the precepts of socialist realism, national in thematic derivation and realistic in social content. His 1st and 5th syms. are inspired by the heroism and suffering of the war of 1941–45; his 4th Sym. depicts the glory of the 1917 Soviet Revolution. He also composed the opera *Aikhylu*, on a Bashkir subject (1943; rev. 1953), and the ballets *Spring Winds*, on a Tatar subject (1950), and *Jeanne d'Arc* (1957).

BIBL.: G. Grigorieva, *N. P.* (Moscow, 1965).

Pelemans, Willem, Belgian composer; b. Antwerp, April 8, 1901; d. Brussels, Oct. 28, 1991. He studied music history at the Malines Cons. A highly prolific composer, he adopted an attractive idiom of writing music in a Romantic manner.

WORKS: DRAMATIC: *La Rose de Bakawali*, chamber opera (1938); *Het tinnen soldaatje*, musical play, after Andersen (1945); *Floris en Blancefloer*, lyric drama (1947); *Le Combat de la vierge et du diable*, chamber opera (1949); *De mannen van Smeerop* (1952); *De nozem en de nimf*, chamber opera (1960). BALLETS: *Miles gloriosus* (1945); *Herfstgoud* (1959); *Pas de quatre* (1969). ORATORIO: *De wandelende jood* (1929).

Pélissier, Marie, French singer; b. 1707; d. Paris, March 21, 1749. She made her debut at the Paris Opéra in 1722. After marrying the theater impresario Pélissier in 1725, she appeared at his theater in Rouen until it went bankrupt. Returning to Paris, she was a principal singer at the Académie Royale (1726–34; 1735–41), where she created roles in numerous works, including Rameau's Aricia in *Hippolyte et Aricie* (1733), Emilie in *Les Indes galantes* (1735), Telaïre in *Castor et Pollux* (1737), and Iphis in both *Les fêtes d'Hébé* (1739) and *Dardanus* (1739).

Pellegrini, Valeriano, Italian castrato soprano and composer; b. Verona, date unknown; d. after 1729. He was in the service of the elector palatine in Düsseldorf from about 1705 until 1716. He also was active in London, where he made his concert debut on April 9, 1712, and was principal castrato at the Queen's Theatre, where he created Handel's Mirtillo in *Il pastor fido* (Nov. 22, 1712) and Teseo (Jan. 10, 1713). From 1716 he pursued his career in Italy. He spent his last years in Rome as a priest.

Pelletier, (Louis) Wilfred, noted Canadian conductor and music educator; b. Montreal, June 20, 1896; d. N.Y., April 9, 1982. His father, a baker by trade, was an amateur musician who gave Pelletier his primary instruction; at the age of 14, he played piano in the orch. of the National Theatre in Montreal; in 1915 he won the Prix d'Europe and went to Paris, where he studied piano with Philipp, composition with Widor, and opera repertoire with Bellaigue. In 1917 he returned to America and was engaged as rehearsal pianist at the Metropolitan Opera in New York; in 1921 he was appointed an assistant conductor there; from 1928 to 1950 he was a principal conductor there, specializing in the French repertoire; in 1936 he founded the popular Metropolitan Opera Auditions of the Air. He also was active as a conductor in Canada; from 1935 to 1951 he was conductor of the Société des Concerts Symphoniques de Montréal, and from 1951 to 1966, of the Orchestre Symphonique de Québec. From 1943 to 1961 he served as director of the Cons. de Musique in Montreal. In 1968 he was made a Companion of the Order of Canada. He was married consecutively to **Queena Mario** (1925–36) and **Rose Bampton** (from 1937). He publ. an autobiographical sketch, *Une Symphonie inachevée* (Quebec, 1972).

BIBL.: C. Huot, *W. P.: Un grand homme, une grande oeuvre* (Montreal, 1996).

Pembaur, Joseph, Sr., Austrian composer and teacher, father of **Karl Maria Pembauer**; b. Innsbruck, May 23, 1848; d. there, Feb. 19, 1923. He studied at the Vienna Cons. with Bruckner and in Munich with Rheinberger and others. In 1874 he was appointed director of the Innsbruck Music School, retiring in 1918. His son was the Austrian pianist Joseph Pembauer Jr. (1875–1950). Among his works was the opera *Der Bauer von Langwall* (Innsbruck, May 2, 1898).

Pembaur, Karl Maria, Austrian organist and conductor, son of **Joseph Pembauer, Sr.**; b. Innsbruck, Aug. 24, 1876; d. Dresden, March 6, 1939. He studied with his father, then with Rheinberger at the Munich Academy of Music. In 1901 he went to Dresden, where he became court organist and choral conductor; he also conducted at the Dresden Opera. He wrote the Singspiel *Seien Sie vorsichtig*. He publ. *Drei Jahrhunderte Kirchenmusik am sächsischen Hofe* (Dresden, 1920). His brother was the Austrian pianist Joseph Pembauer Jr. (1875–1950).

Penderecki, Krzysztof, celebrated Polish composer, pedagogue, and conductor; b. Debica, Nov. 23, 1933. He went to Kraków, where he attended the Jagellonian Univ. Following private composition lessons with Skolyszewski, he studied theory with Malawski and Wiechowicz at the State Higher School of Music (1955–58). In 1958 he joined its faculty as a lecturer in composition, later serving as a prof. (from 1972) and as rector (1972–87). He also lectured at the Essen Folkwang-Hochschule (1966–68) and was a prof. at Yale Univ. (1973–78). In later years he also was active as a conductor. In 1988 he became principal guest conductor of the North German Radio Sym. Orch. in Hamburg, and also served as music director of the Casals Festival in San Juan. In 1995 he conducted the Sinfonia Varsovia on a tour of the United States. Penderecki's rapid ascent as one of the most original composers of his time prompted many honors to come his way. In 1959 he won the 1st, 2d, and 3d prizes in the Competition of Young Polish Composers. His *Threnos* received the UNESCO Prize in 1961. In 1967 his *St. Luke Passion* won the Prix Italia, and in 1968 his *Dies Irae* won another Prix Italia. He received the award of the Union of Polish Composers in 1970. In 1977 he was honored with the Gottfried von Herder Prize of the F.v.S. Foundation in Hamburg. In 1983 he won the Sibelius Prize of the Wihouri Foundation and the Polish State Prize. He was honored with the Premio Lorenzo Magnifico in 1985. In 1992 he received the Grawemeyer Award of the Univ. of Louisville.

After a few works of an academic nature, he developed a hyper-modern technique of composition in a highly individual style, in which no demarcation line is drawn between consonances and dissonances, tonal or atonal melody, traditional or innovative instrumentation; an egalitarian attitude prevails toward all available resources of sound. While his idiom is naturally complex, he does not disdain tonality, even in its overt triadic forms. In his creative evolution, he has bypassed orthodox serial procedures; his music follows an athematic course, in constantly varying metrical and rhythmic patterns. He utilizes an entire spectrum of modern sonorities, expanding the domain of tone to unpitched elements, making use of such effects as shouting, hissing, and verbal ejaculations in vocal parts, at times reaching a climax of aleatory glossolalia; tapping, rubbing, or snapping the fingers against the body of an instrument; striking the piano strings with mallets, etc. For this he designed an optical notation, with symbolic ideograms indicating the desired sound; thus, a black isosceles triangle denotes the highest possible pitch; an inverted isosceles triangle, the lowest possible pitch; a black rectangle for a sonic complex of white noise within a given interval; vertical lines tied over by an arc for arpeggios below the bridge of a string instrument; wavy lines of varying amplitudes for extensive vibrato; curvilinear figures for aleatory passages; dots and dashes for repetitions of a pattern; sinusoidal oscillations for quaquaversal glissandos; etc. He applies these modern devices to religious music, including masses in the orthodox Roman Catholic ritual. Penderecki's most impressive and most frequently performed works is his *Tren pamieci ofiarom Hiroszimy* (Threnody for the Victims of Hiroshima) for 52 Strings (1959–60), rich in dynamic constrasts and ending on a tone cluster of 2 octavefuls of icositetraphonic harmony.

WORKS: DRAMATIC: OPERAS: *The Devils of Loudun* (1968–69; Hamburg, June 20, 1969); *Paradise Lost* (1976–78; Chicago, Nov. 29, 1978); *Die schwarze Maske* (1984–86; Salzburg, Aug. 15, 1986); *Ubu rex*, opera buffa (1990–91; Munich, July 6, 1991). ORATORIO: *Dies irae*, oratorio for Soprano, Tenor, Bass, Chorus, and Orch. (1966–67; Kraków, April 14, 1967). OTHER: *2 Scenes and Finale from the Opera Die schwarze Maske* for Soprano, Mezzo-soprano, Chorus, and Orch. (Poznan, Nov. 6, 1988).

Penherski, Zbigniew, Polish composer; b. Warsaw, Jan. 26, 1935. He studied composition with Stefan Poradowski at the Poznan Cons. (1955–56) and with Tadeusz Szeligowski at the Warsaw Cons. (1956–59). His works include the operas *Girls Through Will* (1961), *The Little Prince* (1962), *Samson Put on Trial* (1967; Warsaw, Sept. 23, 1969), *Mice* (1971–72), *The Fall of Peryn* (1972; Poznan, Oct. 6, 1974), *Edgar, Son of Walpor* (1982), and *The Island of the Roses* (1989).

Pentenrieder, Franz Xaver, German composer; b. Kaufbeuren, Bavaria, Feb. 6, 1813; d. Munich, July 17, 1867. He studied with Kalcher and Stunz, then became conductor at the Munich Court Opera. He wrote a successful opera, *Die Nacht zu Paluzzi* (Munich, Oct. 2, 1840; perf. widely in Germany), and a comic opera, *Das Haus ist zu verkaufen* (Leipzig, 1846). As a result of an accident, he became insane, and spent the last few years of his life in an asylum.

Pentland, Barbara (Lally), Canadian composer and teacher; b. Winnipeg, Jan. 2, 1912. After taking piano lessons at a Montreal boarding school, she went to New York and studied with Jacobi and Wagenaar at the Juilliard School of Music (1936–39); she also took courses with Copland at the Berkshire Music Center in Tanglewood (summers 1941–42). She was an instructor at the Toronto Cons. (1943–49) and the Univ. of British Columbia in Vancouver (1949–63). In her compositions, she adopts a pragmatic method of cosmopolitan modernism, employing dissonant linear counterpoint and dodecaphonic melodic structures within the framework of Classical forms. She composed *Beauty and the Beast*, ballet pantomine (1940), and *The Lake*, chamber opera (1952; Vancouver, March 3, 1954).

BIBL.: S. Eastman and T. McGee, *B. P.* (Toronto, 1983).

Pepöck, August, Austrian composer; b. Gmunden, May 10, 1887; d. there, Sept. 5, 1967. He studied in Vienna with Heuberger and R. Fuchs. He was active as a conductor of theater music in various provincial towns in Germany; he subsequently lived mostly in Vienna. He scored great success with his operettas *Mädel ade!* (Vienna, Oct. 5, 1930) and *Der Reiter de Kaiserin* (Vienna, April 30, 1941).

Pepusch, John Christopher (Johann Christoph), German-born English composer; b. Berlin, 1667; d. London, July 20, 1752. He was taught by Klingenberg (theory) and Grosse (organ). He had a position at the Prussian court in 1681–97, then went to Holland. He was in London by 1704, where he was active as a violist and harpsichordist at Drury Lane Theatre, later as a composer, adapting Italian airs to English operas and adding recitatives and songs. In 1710 he founded (with Needler, Gates, Galliard, and others) the Academy of Ancient Music, famous for the revival of 16th-century compositions. Having received the D.Mus. degree from Oxford in 1713, he served as music director to James Brydges (later the Duke of Chandos) at Cannons. He wrote the masques *Venus and Adonis* (1715), *Apollo and Daphne* (1716), and *The Death of Dido* (1716), the ode *The Union of the Three Sister-Arts* (for St. Cecilia's Day; 1723), and also arranged music to the ballad operas *The Beggar's Opera, Polly*, and *The Wedding*. In 1730 a fortune brought him by marriage with the singer Marguerite de l'Epine rendered him independent. From 1737 until his death he was organist of the Charterhouse. Pepusch was a learned, though conservative, musician who enjoyed high renown in England. His various odes and cantatas and his instrumental concertos and sonatas are of slight importance, and his name is preserved in music history mainly for his original music and some arranged numbers in *The Beggar's Opera*. He publ. a *Treatise on Harmony* (London, 1730; 2d ed., rev., 1731).

BIBL.: J. Williams, *The Life, Work and Influence of J. C. P.* (diss., Univ. of York, 1976).

Peragallo, Mario, Italian composer; b. Rome, March 25, 1910; d. there, Nov. 23, 1996. He was a student of Casella. In his early works, he followed the line of Italian traditionalism, characterized by modern but euphonious polyphony; later he adopted a radical quasi-dodecaphonic idiom, with frequent reversions to diatonic structures. Among his works were the operas *Ginevra degli Almieri* (Rome, Feb. 13, 1937), *Lo stendardo di S. Giorgio* (Genoa, 1941), *La collina* (Venice, 1947), *La Gita in campagna* (Milan, March 24, 1954), and *La parrucca dell'imperatore* (Spoleto, 1959).

Peralta, Angela, Mexican soprano, known as "the Mexican Nightingale"; b. Puebla, July 6, 1845; d. Matzatlán, Aug. 30, 1883. She made her debut in *Il Trovatore* in Mexico City at the age of 15. In 1862, at age 17, she made her Italian debut as Lucia; she sang in Havana, New York, and Madrid. She then barnstormed throughout Mexico as the organizer of her own opera company, presenting operas by Donizetti, Bellini, and Verdi; she also appeared in the premieres of several Mexican operas, including Melesio Morales's *Ildegonda* (Jan. 27, 1866) and *Gino Corsini* (July 14, 1877) and Aniceto Ortega's *Guatimotzin* (Sept. 13, 1871). She made her last appearance in *Il Trovatore* (May 23, 1883), succumbing on tour to yellow fever, but not before marrying, on her deathbed, one of her many devotees.

Peranda, Marco Gioseppe, important Italian composer; b. Rome or Macerata, c.1625; d. Dresden, Jan. 12, 1675. He was taken by Christoph Bernhard to Dresden, where he was an alto in the chapel of the heir to the electorate. He sang with the chapel after it was incorporated into the court (1656), then was made vice Kapellmeister (1661), Kapellmeister (1663), and 1st Hofkapellmeister (1672). Although a Roman Catholic at a Lutheran court, he earned the greatest esteem. He was a distinguished composer of sacred concertos and motets, and influenced many of his German contemporaries.

WORKS: DRAMATIC: OPERAS: *Dafne* (Dresden, Sept. 3, 1671; in collaboration with G. A. Bontempi); *Jupiter und Io* (Dresden, Jan. 16, 1673; in collaboration with Bontempi; only libretto extant). ORATORIOS: *Historia von der Geburt des Herrn Jesu Christi* (Dresden, Dec. 25, 1668; not extant); *Historia des Leidens und Sterbens unsers Hernn . . . Jesu Christi nach dem Evangelisten St. Marcum* (Dresden, March 20, 1668); *Il sacrificio de Jefte* (Bologna, 1675; only text extant).

Perera, Ronald (Christopher), American composer and teacher; b. Boston, Dec. 25, 1941. He studied composition with Kirchner at Harvard Univ. (B.A., 1963; M.A., 1967) and then traveled on its John Knowles Paine Traveling Fellowship to study electronic music and computer composition with Koening at the Univ. of Utrecht (1967–68); he also studied privately in the United States with Thompson in choral music and electronic music with Davidovsky. After teaching at Syracuse Univ. (1968–70), he served as director of the Dartmouth College Electronic Music Studio (1970–71); he then taught theory, composition, and electronic music at Smith College in Northampton, Mass. (from 1971) and was also active as a visiting scholar at the Columbia-Princeton Electronic Music Center (1975–76). With Appleton, he ed. *The Development and Practice of Electronic Music* (1975). He received annual ASCAP awards from 1972, and in 1978 and 1988 grants from the NEA. His works include *The Yellow Wallpaper*, chamber opera (Northampton, Mass., May 17, 1989), and *S.*, opera (1995).

Pérez, David or **Davide,** significant Italian composer; b. Naples (of Spanish descent), 1711; d. Lisbon, Oct. 30, 1778. He studied counterpoint and composition with Mancini, Veneziano, and Galli at the Cons. di S. Maria di Loreto in Naples (1722–33). Between 1735 and 1752 he produced some 19 operas, establishing himself as a leading opera composer in his day. He served as vice maestro di cappella of the Royal Chapel Palatine in Palermo (1738–39) and as maestro di cappella in Palermo (1741–48); he then was called to Lisbon (1752) as maestro di cappella and music master to the royal princesses, duties he retained for the rest of his life. He continued to compose until his last days, even though he was stricken with blindness. He was a master of the opera seria, being acclaimed as a worthy rival of Hasse and Jommelli.

WORKS: DRAMATIC: OPERAS: *La nemica amante* (Naples, Nov. 4, 1735); *Li travestimenti amorosi*, opera buffa (Naples, July 10, 1740); *Il Siroe* (Naples, Nov. 4, 1740); *L'eroismo di Scipione* (Palermo, 1741); *Demetrio* (Palermo, June 13, 1741; 2d version, Lisbon, 1766); *Astartea* (Palermo, 1743); *Medea* (Palermo, 1744); *Alessandro nell'Indie* (Genoa, Carnival 1744; 2d version, Lisbon, March 31, 1755); *Merope* (Genoa, Carnival 1744); *L'isola incantata* (Palermo, 1746); *Artaserse* (Florence, 1748); *La clemenza di Tito* (Naples, 1749); *Vologeso* (Vienna, 1750); *Il Farnace* (Rome, 1750); *Andromaca* (Vienna, 1750); *Semiramide* (Rome, 1750); *Ezio* (Milan, Carnival 1751); *La Didone* (Genoa, 1751); *La Zenobia* (Milan, 1751); *Demofoonte* (Lisbon, 1752); *Adriano in Siria* (Lisbon, 1752); *L'Eroe cinese* (Lisbon, June 6, 1753); *Olimpiade* (Lisbon, 1753); *L'Impermestra* (Lisbon, 1754); *Lucio Vero* (Verona, 1754); *Solimano* (Lisbon, Carnival 1757); *Enea in Italia* (Lisbon, 1759); *La Berenice* (Verona, Carnival 1762); *Giulio Cesare* (Lisbon, 1762); *L'isola disabitata* (Lisbon, 1767); *Il Cinese* (Lisbon, 1769); *Creusa in Delfo* (Lisbon, Carnival 1774); *Il ritorno di Ulisse in Itaca* (Lisbon, 1774); *L'Eroe coronato* (Lisbon, 1775); *La pace fra la Virtù e la Bellezza* (Lisbon, Dec. 17, 1777). Also *Il martirio di S. Bartolomeo*, oratorio.

BIBL.: E. Soares, *D. P.: Subsidios para a biografia' do celébre mestre de musica da camera de D. José* (Lisbon, 1935); P. Jackson, *The Operas of D. P.* (diss., Stanford Univ., 1967).

Pérez Casas, Bartolomeo, Spanish conductor and composer; b. Lorca, near Murcia, Jan. 24, 1873; d. Madrid, Jan. 15, 1956. He studied at the Madrid Cons. He played the clarinet in various military bands; he also was a bandmaster. He then established himself in Madrid as a teacher at the Cons.; from 1915 to 1936 he conducted the Orquesta Filarmónica de Madrid. He wrote a lyric drama, *Lorenzo*; *A mi tierra*.

Perfall, Karl, Freiherr von, German composer and conductor; b. Munich, Jan. 29, 1824; d. there, Jan. 14, 1907. He took music lessons with Hauptmann in Leipzig (1848–49). He became conductor of the Munich Liedertafel (1850), and founded the Oratorio Soc. (1854); in 1864 he was appointed Intendant of the court music and abandoned his activities as a conductor. From 1867 to 1893 he was Intendant of the National Theater in Munich. Of his operas (all produced in Munich), *Raimondin* (March 27, 1881; rev. as *Melusine*, 1885) and *Junker Heinz* (April 9, 1886; rev. as *Jung Heinrich*, 1901) were successful. He publ. *25 Jahre Münchener Hoftheater-Geschichte* (1892; covering the period from 1867), *Ein Beitrag zur Geschichte des königlichen Theaters in Munchen 25 November 1867–25 November 1892* (1894), and *Die Entwickelung des modernen Theaters* (1899).

Pergament, Moses, Finnish-born Swedish music critic and composer; b. Helsinki, Sept. 21, 1893; d. Gustavsberg, near Stockholm, March 5, 1977. He studied violin at the St. Petersburg Cons. and conducting at Berlin's Stern Cons. In 1915 he settled in Sweden and became a naturalized Swedish citizen (1918); from 1923 to 1966 he was active as a music critic in Swedish newspapers; he publ. 4 books on music. His musical style was initially circumscribed by Russian paradigms; later he was influenced by Sibelius; still later he adopted some modernistic procedures. Several of his compositions reflect an ancestral strain of Jewish melos.

WORKS: DRAMATIC: OPERAS: *Himlens hemlighet* (The Secret of Heaven), chamber opera (1952); *Eli*, radio opera (1958; Swedish Radio, March 19, 1959); *Abrams Erwachen*, opera oratorio (1970–73). BALLETS: *Krelantems and Eldeling* (1920–28); *Vision* (1923). ORATORIO: *De sju dödssynderna* (The 7 Deadly Sins; 1963). Also incidental music and film scores.

Perger, Richard von, Austrian composer and conductor; b. Vienna, Jan. 10, 1854; d. there, Jan. 11, 1911. He studied cello and theory. After serving in the Austrian army during the campaign in Bosnia (1878), he received a stipend and took lessons with Brahms (1880–82). He was director of the Rotterdam Cons. (1890–95). Returning to Vienna, he conducted the Gesellschaftskonzerte, and from 1899 to 1907 he was director of the Vienna Cons. His music bears unmistakable evidence of the profound influence of Brahms. Among his works are the text and music of a comic opera, *Der Richter von Granada* (Cologne, 1889), a Singspiel, *Die 14 Nothhelfer* (Vienna, 1891), and a musical fairy tale, *Das stählerne Schloss* (Vienna, 1904). He also publ. a biography of Brahms (1908; new ed. by Hernried, 1934). His *Geschichte der K. K. Gesellschaft der Musikfreunde in Wien* was publ. posthumously (1912).

Pergolesi, Giovanni Battista, remarkable Italian composer; b. Jesi, near Ancona, Jan. 4, 1710; d. Pozzuoli, near Naples, March 16, 1736. The original family name was Draghi; the name Pergolesi was derived from the town of Pergola, where Pergolesi's ancestors lived. He was the only surviving child of his parents, 3 others having died in infancy. His childhood seems to have been plagued by ill health; a later caricature depicts him as having a deformed leg. He first studied music with Francesco Santi, the maestro di cappella of the Jesi Cathedral; he also studied violin with Francesco Mondini. He then was given a stipend by the Marchese Cardolo Maria Pianetti, which enabled him to enter the Cons. dei Poveri di Gesù Cristo in Naples, where he studied violin with Domenico de Matteis and composition with Gaetano Greco, its maestro di cappella, Leonardo Vinci, and Francesco Durante. He became highly proficient as a violinist, playing at the Conservatorio and throughout Naples. His first work to be performed was the dramma sacro *Li prodigi della divina grazia nella conversione di S. Guglielmo Duca d'Aquitania*, which was given by the Cons. at the monastery of S. Agnello Maggiore in 1731. He graduated shortly thereafter, and received a commission for his first opera, *La Salustia* (Naples, Jan. 1732). He then became maestro di cappella to Prince Ferdinando Colonna Stigliano, equerry to the Viceroy of Naples, in 1732. His *Lo Frate 'nnamorato* (Naples, Sept. 27, 1732) proved highly successful. In Dec. 1732 he composed several sacred works for performance at the church of S. Maria della Stella as a votive offering following a series of severe earthquakes in Naples. He was next commissioned to write an opera seria to celebrate the birthday of the empress on Aug. 28, 1733; however, the premiere of the resulting *Il Prigionier superbo* was delayed until Sept. 5, 1733; it contained the 2-act intermezzo *La Serva padrona*, which became his most celebrated stage work. He was named deputy to the maestro di cappella of Naples in 1734. During a brief sojourn in Rome, his Mass in F major was performed at the church of S. Lorenzo in Lucina (May 16, 1734).

After returning to Naples, Pergolesi became maestro di cappella to Marzio Domenico IV Carafa, the duke of Maddaloni. For the birthday of the king's mother, he was commissioned to write the opera *Adriano in Siria*; it was premiered, without success, in Naples on Oct. 25, 1734, with the intermezzo *La Contadina astuta* (subsequently staged under various titles). He then was commissioned to write an opera for Rome's Teatro Tordinona, resulting in his unsuccessful opera seria *L'Olimpiade* (Jan. 8 or 9, 1735). His last popular success for the stage was the commedia musicale *Il Flaminio* (Naples, 1735). By 1735 his health had seriously declined, most likely from tuberculosis. Early in 1736 he went to the Franciscan monastery in Pozzuoli, where he soon died at the age of 26. He was buried in the common grave adjacent to the cathedral. Following his death, his fame spread rapidly through performances of *La Serva padrona* and several other stage works. The Paris revival of the work in 1752 precipitated the so-called querelle des bouffons between the partisans of the Italian and French factions. His fame was further increased by performances of the *Salve regina* in C minor and the *Stabat Mater* in F minor.

The chaotic entanglement of spurious, doubtful, and authentic works attributed to Pergolesi was unraveled in M. Paymer's *G. B. P.: A Thematic Catalogue of the Opera Omnia with an Appendix Listing Omitted Compositions* (N.Y., 1976). *The Opera Omnia*, ed. by F. Caffarelli (5 vols., Rome, 1939–42), is most unreliable; it is being replaced by a critical ed., the first vol. of which appeared in 1985.

BIBL.: C. de Rosa, Marchese di Villarosa, *Lettera biografica intorno alla patria ed all vita di G. B. P. celebre compositore di musica* (Naples, 1831; 2d ed., 1843); F. Villars, *La Serva padrona, Son apparition à Paris en 1752, son influence, son analyse* (Paris, 1863); G. Annibaldi, *Alcune delle notizie più importanti intorno al P. recentemente scoperte: Il P. in Pozzuoli: Vita intima* (Jesi, 1890); E. Faustini-Fasini, *G. B. P. attraverso i suoi biografi e le sue opere* (Milan, 1900); G. Radiciotti, *G. B. P.: Vita, opere ed influenza su l'arte* (Rome, 1910; 2d ed., rev., 1935; Ger. tr., Zürich, 1954); A. Della Corte, *G. B. P.* (Turin, 1936); R. Giraldi, *G. B. P.* (Rome, 1936); F. Schlitzer, *G. B. P.* (Turin, 1940); S. Luciani, ed., *G. B. P. (1710–1736): Note e documenti* (Siena, 1942); E. Luin, *Fortuna e influenza della musica di P. in Europa* (Siena, 1943); A. Dunning, *Count Unico Wilhelm van Wassenaer (1692–1766); A Master Unmasked; or, The P.-Ricciotti Puzzle Solved* (Buren, 1980); F. Degrada, ed., *Studi P.ani/P. Studies* (2 vols., N.Y., 1986, 1988); M. Paymer and H. Williams, *G. B. P.: A Guide to Research* (N.Y., 1989).

Peri, Jacopo, significant Italian composer, called "Il Zazzerino" for his abundant head of hair; b. Rome, Aug. 20, 1561; d. Florence, Aug. 12, 1633. He was descended from a noble Florentine family. At an early age he went to Florence, where he entered the convent of Ss. Annunziata in 1573 and became a singer; he also studied music with Cristofano Malvezzi. He was organist at the Badia (1579–1605) and a singer at S. Giovanni Battista (by 1586). He entered the service of the Medici court of Grand Duke Ferdinando I (1588), and was also in the service of the Mantuan court (from the early 1600s). The Florentine Camerata met at the home of Count Giovanni de' Bardi in the 1580s, and it is likely that Peri participated in its activities. As early as 1583 he collaborated with other composers in writing music for the intermedi to Giovanni Fedini's dramatic comedy *Le due Persilie*. In the 1590s the home of Jacopo Corsi became the meeting place for many Florentine musicians, poets, and philosophers, and Peri undoubtedly attended, for Corsi collaborated with him in setting Ottavio Rinuccini's pastoral *Dafne* to music. The first known performance of this work was a private one in Florence in 1598. Later versions were given in 1599, 1600, and 1605. *Dafne* is generally recognized as the first opera in monodic style (i.e., vocal soli supported by instruments), which was termed *stile rappresentativo*. Peri's next opera was *Euridice*, again to a text by Rinuccini; some of the music was rewritten by Caccini for the first performance, which was given for the wedding of Maria de' Medici and Henri IV of France at the Palazzo Pitti in Florence (Oct. 6, 1600). He composed the opera *Tetide* (libretto by Cini) for Mantua in 1608, but it was not performed. His next opera, *Adone* (libretto by Cicognini), was finished by 1611; a performance scheduled for Mantua in 1620 never took place. Another work of the period, *La liberazione di Tirreno e d'Arnea* (Florence, Feb. 6, 1617), may be by Peri; it is also possible that he collaborated with M. da Gagliano on the score, or it may be totally the work of Gagliano. Peri collaborated with Marco da Gagliano on the opera *Lo sposalizio di Medoro e Angelica*. It was given in honor of the election of Emperor Ferdinand III at the Palazzo Pitti on Sept. 25, 1619. He also composed the role of Clori for the opera *La Flora*, the remainder of the music being by Gagliano. It was first performed in honor of the wedding of Margherita de' Medici and Duke Odoardo Farnese of Parma at the Palazzo Pitti on Oct. 14, 1628. Peri also collaborated with Gagliano on 3 oratorios, *La benedittione di Jacob* (Florence, Sept. 23, 1622), *Il gran natale di Christo salvator nostro* (Florence, Dec. 27, 1622), and *La celeste guida, o vero L'Arcangelo Raffaello* (Florence, Jan. 5, 1624), but these works are not extant. In addition to individual songs publ. in various collections of the time, he also brought out *La varie musiche . . . for 1 to 3 Voices, con alcune spirituali in ultimo, per cantare, harpsichord, chitarrone, ancora la maggior parte di esse per sonare semplicemente, organ* (Florence, 1609; 2d ed., 1619).

BIBL.: G. Corazzini, *J. P. e la sua famiglia* (Florence, 1895); F. Ghisi, *Alle fonti della monodia: Due nuove brani della 'Dafne'* (Milan, 1940); T. Carter, *J. P. (1561–1633): His Life and Works* (diss., Univ. of Birmingham, 1980).

Perick (real name, **Prick**), **Christof,** German conductor; b. Hamburg, Oct. 23, 1946. He was a student in Hamburg of Brückner-Rüggeberg. After serving as an assistant conductor at the Hamburg State Opera, he conducted at the operas in Trier (1970–72) and Darmstadt (1972–74). He was Generalmusikdirektor in Saarbrücken (1974–77) and Karlsruhe (1977–84), and also held the title of 1st conductor at the Deutsche Oper in Berlin (1977–84). He was music director (1991–94) and music advisor (from 1994) of the Los Angeles Chamber Orch. In 1993 he became Generalmusikdirektor of the Niedersächsische State Theater and Orch. in Hannover. Perick appeared as a guest conductor of opera and sym. throughout Europe and North America.

Périer, Jean (Alexis), French baritone; b. Paris, Feb. 2, 1869; d. there, Nov. 3, 1954. He studied at the Paris Cons., obtaining the premier prix for singing (1892). He made his debut at the Paris Opéra Comique as Monostatos in *Die Zauberflöte* on Dec. 16, 1892; was engaged there until 1894, and again from 1900 to 1920. He created the role of Pélleas at the premiere of Debussy's opera (1902), and sang the leading tenor parts in several other premieres of French operas; he sang at N.Y.'s Manhattan Opera House (1908). A talented comedian, Périer also appeared in variety shows in Paris. He publ. an instructive album, *Mes exercises, tirés des chansons populaires de France* (Paris, 1917).

Perkins, John MacIvor, American composer and teacher; b. St. Louis, Aug. 2, 1935. He studied at Harvard Univ. (B.A., 1958), at the New England Cons. of Music in Boston (B.Mus., 1958), with Boulanger in Paris and Gerhard and Rubbra in London (1958–59), and at Brandeis Univ. (M.F.A., 1962). After teaching at the Univ. of Chicago (1962–65) and at Harvard Univ. (1965–70), he was assoc. prof. of music (from 1970) and chairman of the music dept. (1970–75) at Washington Univ. in St. Louis. In 1966 he received an American Academy and National Inst. of Arts and Letters award. His works include *Divertimento*, chamber opera (1958), and *Andrea del Sarto*, operatic monologue (1981).

Perkowski, Piotr, Polish composer and pedagogue; b. Owecczacze, Ukraine, March 17, 1901; d. Otwock, near Warsaw, Aug. 12, 1990. He studied composition with Statkowski at the Warsaw Cons. (1923–25), then took private lessons with Szymanowski in Warsaw and with Roussel in Paris. He was director of the Toruń Cons. (1936–39); he taught composition at the Warsaw Cons. (1946–51; 1954–73) and was artistic director of the Kraków Phil. (1949–51) and dean of the Music Academy in Wrocław (1951–55); he served as councilor for cultural development for the city of Warsaw (1965–74). In his earlier years, he followed the fashionable cosmopolitan trend of absolute music without reference to national or general programmatic subjects, but under the influence of social changes he began introducing concrete, historic, and pictorial representations. Among his compositions were the opera *Garlands* (Warsaw, 1962) and the ballets *Swantewit* (1930; rev. 1945–47; Poznan, June 19, 1948), *Rhapsody* (1949), *Fantasia* (1950), *Clementine* (1960–63), and *Balladyna* (1960–64; Warsaw, 1965).

Perlea, Jonel, Romanian-born American conductor, teacher, and composer; b. Ograda, Dec. 13, 1900; d. N.Y., July 29, 1970. He studied piano and composition in Munich (1918–20) and conducting in Leipzig (1920–23). He made his conducting debut in Bucharest in 1919 and held posts as a conductor in Leipzig (1922–23) and Rostock (1923–25); he then conducted the Bucharest Opera (1929–32; 1934–36) and the Bucharest Radio Orch. (1936–44), of which he was a founder. He led conducting classes at the Bucharest Cons. (1941–44); during the last year of World War II, he was interned in a German concentration camp. After the war, he conducted opera in Rome (1945–47); in 1950 he conducted at La Scala in Milan. He made his American debut at the Metropolitan Opera in New York on Dec. 1, 1949, conducting *Tristan und Isolde*; appeared at the San Francisco Opera and the Lyric Opera of Chicago; from 1955 to 1970 he was conductor of the Conn. Sym. Orch. He taught conducting at the Manhattan School of Music from 1952 until shortly before his death. Perlea became a naturalized American citizen in 1960. He suffered a heart attack in 1957 and a stroke in 1958, as a result of which he lost the use of his right arm, but he continued to conduct with his left hand.

Pernet, André, French bass; b. Rambervillers, Jan. 6, 1894; d. Paris, June 23, 1966. He studied at the Paris Cons. with Gresse. He made his operatic debut in 1921 in Nice; he was a principal member of the Paris Opéra (1928–45) and appeared there again in 1948; he also sang at the Paris Opéra Comique (1931–48). His most notable roles included Don Giovanni, Boris Godunov, and Méphistophélès; he also sang in many contemporary operas.

Pernerstorfer, Alois, Austrian bass-baritone; b. Vienna, June 3, 1912; d. there, May 12, 1978. He took courses with Lierhammer and Josef Krips at the Vienna Academy of Music. In 1936 he made his operatic debut as Biterolf in Graz, where he sang until 1939. He was a member of the Volksoper (1939–45) and State Opera (from 1945) in Vienna. He also sang in Zürich (1947–51), and at the Salzburg Festivals (from 1948), the Glyndebourne Festival (1951), and the Metropolitan Opera in New York (debut as Sparafucile, Nov. 15, 1951). He was known for such roles as Figaro, Leporello, King Marke, Alberich, Pogner, and Baron Ochs.

Perron (real name, **Pergamenter**), **Karl,** noted German bass-baritone; b. Frankenthal, June 3, 1858; d. Dresden, July 15, 1928. He studied with Hey in Berlin, Hasselbasch in Munich, and Stockhausen in Frankfurt am Main, making his debut as Wolfram in 1884 in Leipzig, where he sang until 1891. He then joined the Dresden Court (later State) Opera, remaining on its roster until 1924; during his tenure there he created the roles of Jochanaan in *Salome*, Orest in *Elektra*, and Baron Ochs in *Der Rosenkavalier*; he also appeared at the Bayreuth Festivals (1889–1904), where he was acclaimed for his fine performances of Wotan and King Marke.

Perry, George Frederick, English violinist, organist, and composer; b. Norwich, 1793; d. London, March 4, 1862. He was a choirboy at the Cathedral in Norwich. He moved to London in 1822, and became director of music at the Haymarket Theatre, then organist of the Quebec Chapel. From 1832 to 1848 he served as concertmaster of the Sacred Harmonic Soc. Orch. and from 1846 as organist at Trinity Church, Gray's Inn Rd.

WORKS: DRAMATIC: OPERAS: *Morning, Noon and Night* (London, Sept. 9, 1822); *Family Jars* (London, Aug. 26, 1822). ORATORIOS: *The Death of Abel* (Norwich, 1816); *Elijah and the Priests of Baal* (Norwich, March 12, 1819); *The Fall of Jerusalem* (London, Feb. 20, 1832); *Belshazzar's Feast* (London, Feb. 10, 1836); *Hezekiah* (1847).

Perry, Janet, American soprano; b. Minneapolis, Dec. 27, 1944. She received piano and violin lessons at home, and appeared in local young people's theater productions; then studied voice with Eufemia Giannini Gregory at the Curtis Inst. of Music in Philadelphia (B.M., 1967). In 1969 she made her operatic debut as Zerlina at the Linz Landestheater, remaining on its roster until 1971; following guest appearances at the Gärtnerplatztheater in Munich and at the Cologne Opera, she became a member of the Bavarian State Opera in Munich. She further made guest appearances in opera and concert in Hamburg, Düsseldorf, Paris, Zürich, Vienna, Berlin, Glyndebourne, and Salzburg. In 1983 she made her formal U.S. debut as Despina in Washington, D.C. Among her most successful roles were Susanna, Pamina, Constanze, Gilda, and Sophie.

Perry, Julia (Amanda), black American composer; b. Lexington, Ky., March 25, 1924; d. Akron, Ohio, April 29, 1979. After studying at the Westminster Choir College in Princeton, N.J. (M.Mus., 1948), she took a course in composition with Dallapiccola at the Berkshire Music Center in Tanglewood (summer 1951); she then took composition lessons, intermittently, with Boulanger in Paris and again with Dallapiccola in Italy (1952–56); she also attended classes in conducting in Siena (1956–58). She received 2 Guggenheim fellowships and an award from the National Inst. of Arts and Letters. Among her works were the operas *The Bottle* (n.d.), *The Cask of Amontillado* (N.Y., Nov. 20, 1954), *The Selfish Giant*, opera ballet (1964), and *3 Warnings* (n.d.).

Persen, John, Norwegian composer; b. Porsanger, Norwegian Lapland, Nov. 9, 1941. He studied composition with Finn Mortensen at the Oslo Cons. (1968–73). From 1974 to 1976 he was president of Ny Musikk, the Norwegian section of the ISCM. His music follows the lines of the cosmopolitan avant-garde, with a mixture of jazz, rock, sonorism, and special effects (*ČSV* requires 2 pistol shots to be heard at the end of the work). Persen is a nationalistic Lapp from the extreme polar north; some titles of his compositions are political in their allusions. Among his works is the opera *Under Kors og Krone* (Under Cross and Crown; 1978–85), based on a revolt of the Lapp population against the authorities in the late 19th century.

Persiani, Fanny (née **Tacchinardi**), renowned Italian soprano and singing teacher and daughter of **Nicola (Niccolò) Tacchinardi**, known as "La Persiani"; b. Rome, Oct. 4, 1812; d. Neuilly-sur-Seine, May 3, 1867. She studied with her father, and performed at an early age in his small training theater in Florence. After marrying the composer Giuseppe Persiani in 1830, she made her professional debut as Fournier-Gorre's Francesca da Rimini in Livorno in 1832. Following successful appearances in Venice and Milan, she gained distinction as a leading performer of roles in operas by Bellini and Donizetti, creating the title role in Donizetti's *Lucia di Lammermoor* in Naples in 1835; she also sang in her husband's operas, including *Ines de Castro*. She made her first appearance in Paris at the Théâtre-Italien in 1837, and continued to sing there with brilliant success until 1850. She made her London debut at the King's Theatre in *La Sonnambula* in 1838, remaining a favorite there, and later at Covent Garden, until 1849; she also sang in Vienna (1837, 1844). After singing at the Italian Opera in St. Petersburg (1850–52), she settled in Paris as a voice teacher. Blessed with a small but beautiful coloratura voice, she had few equals in her day.

BIBL.: Chaudesaigues, *Madame P.* (Paris, 1839); P. Ciarlantini, *Giuseppe Persiani e F. Tacchinardi: Due Protagonisti del Melodramma Romantico* (Ancona and Bologna, 1988).

Persiani, Giuseppe, Italian composer; b. Recanati, Sept. 11, 1799; d. Paris, Aug. 13, 1869. As a youth he played violin in theater orchs. in Rome and Naples, where he studied with Zingarelli and Tritto. In 1830 he married the soprano Fanny Tacchinardi, who became famous as "La Persiani"; her illustrious name completely eclipsed his, yet he was a notable composer whose dramatic opera *Ines de Castro*, produced in Naples on Jan. 27, 1835, scored great success and was performed all over Europe. The celebrated soprano Malibran sang the title role, and Czerny wrote a piano paraphrase on themes of the opera. Persiani's other operas were *Attila* (Parma, Jan. 31, 1827), *Il Solitario* (Milan, April 26, 1829), *Il Fantasma* (Paris, Dec. 14, 1843), and *Eufemio di Messina* (Lucca, Sept. 20, 1829; perf. also under the alternative titles *La distruzione di Catania* and *I Saraceni a Catania*).

BIBL.: P. Ciarlantini, *G. P. e Fanny Tacchinardi: Due Protagonisti del Melodramma Romantico* (Ancona and Bologna, 1988).

Persichetti, Vincent (Ludwig), remarkable American composer and pedagogue whose finely amalgamated instrumental and symphonic music created an image of classical modernity; b. Philadelphia, June 6, 1915; d. there, Aug. 13, 1987. His father was a native of Abruzzi, Italy, who emigrated to the United States in 1894. His mother was of German descent, hailing from Bonn. Persichetti's middle name was given to him not to honor Beethoven but to commemorate his maternal grandfather who owned a saloon in Camden, N.J. He studied piano, organ, double bass, tuba, theory, and composition as a youth; began his career as a professional musician when he was only 11 years old; he became a church organist at 15. He took courses in composition with Russell King Miller at the Combs Cons. (Mus.B., 1936); he then served as head of the theory and composition dept. there; concurrently he studied conducting with Reiner at the Curtis Inst. of Music (diploma, 1938) and piano with Samaroff and composition with Nordoff at the Philadelphia Cons. (M.Mus., 1941; D.Mus., 1945); he also studied composition with Harris at Colorado College. From 1941 to 1947 he was head of the theory and composition dept. of the Philadelphia Cons.; in 1947 he joined the faculty of the Juilliard School of Music in New York; in 1963 he was named chairman of the composition dept. there. In 1952 he became director of music publishing of Elkan-Vogel, Inc. With F. Schreiber, he wrote a biography of William Schuman (N.Y., 1954). He publ. a valuable manual, *Twentieth Century Harmony: Creative Aspects and Practice* (N.Y., 1961). His music is remarkable for its polyphonic skill in fusing the ostensibly incompatible idioms of Classicism, Romanticism, and stark modernism, while the melodic lines maintain an almost Italianate diatonicism in a lyrical manner. The skillful concatenation of ostensibly mutually exclusive elements created a style that was characteristically Persichetti's. He was not interested in program music or in any kind of descriptive tonal works (exceptionally, he wrote a piece of background music for the Radio City Music Hall organs which was performed in 1969). His significance for American music, therefore, is comprised in his 9 syms., and, most particularly, in his 12 piano sonatas and 6 piano sonatinas. Although he stood far from the turmoil of musical politics, he unexpectedly found himself in the center of a controversy when he was commissioned by the 1973 Presidential Inauguration Committee to write a work for narrator and orch. for a perf. at President Richard Nixon's 2d inauguration. Persichetti selected the text of a speech by President Abraham Lincoln, his 2d inaugural address, but, surprisingly, objections were raised by certain groups to the passionate denunciation of war in the narrative, at a time when the Vietnam War was very much in the news. The scheduled performance by the Philadelphia Orch. was hurriedly canceled, and the work's premiere was deferred to a performance by the St. Louis Sym. Orch. on Jan. 25, 1973. In 1987 Persichetti contracted a cancer of the lungs, but even when racked by disease he continued to work on his last opus, *Hymns and Responses for the Church Year, Vol. II.* He requested that his body be donated to medical science. His devoted wife suffered a stroke and died on Thanksgiving Day in the same year. Her monograph on her husband (1960) remains unpublished. Among Persichetti's many works is the opera *Parable XX: The Sibyl* (1976; Philadelphia, April 13, 1985).

BIBL.: D. and J. Patterson, *V. P.: A Bio-Bibliography* (Westport, Conn., 1988).

Perti, Giacomo or **Jacopo Antonio**, greatly significant Italian composer; b. Crevalcore, near Bologna, June 6, 1661; d. Bologna, April 10, 1756. He began to study music with his uncle, Lorenzo Perti, and with Rocco Laurenti, and later took lessons in counterpoint with Petronio Franceschini. As early as 1678 he had a Mass performed at the church of S. Tomaso al Mercato. In 1679 he collaborated on the opera *Atide*, to which he contributed the score for the 3d act. In 1681 he was elected a member of the Accademia Filarmonica, of which he was 5 times the principe (in 1719 was named censor). He then went to Parma, where he continued his studies with Giuseppe Corso. In 1689 he had his opera *Dionisio Siracusano* performed in Parma, and another opera, *La Rosaura*, in Venice. In 1690 he succeeded his uncle as maestro di cappella at the Cathedral of S. Pietro in Bologna. In 1696 he became maestro di cappella of S. Petronio, a position he held until his death. He also held similar positions at S. Domenico (1704–55; deputized for Alberti from 1734) and at S. Maria in Galliera (1706–50). Emperor Charles VI made him a royal councillor in 1740. His students included G. B. Martini and Giuseppe Torelli.

WORKS: DRAMATIC: OPERAS: *Atide* (Bologna, June 23, 1679; incomplete; in collaboration with others); *Marzio Coriolano* (Venice, Jan. 20, 1683); *Oreste in Argo* (Modena, Carnival 1685); *L'incoronazione di Dario* (Bologna, Jan. 13, 1686); *La Flavia* (Bologna, Feb. 16, 1686); *Dionisio Siracusano* (Parma, Carnival 1689); *La Rosaura* (Venice, 1689); *Brenno in Efeso* (Venice, 1690); *L'inganno scoperto per vendetta* (Venice, Carnival 1690 or 1691); *Il Pompeo* (Genoa, Carnival 1691); *Furio Camillo* (Venice, Carnival 1692); *Nerone fatto Cesare* (Venice, 1693); *La forza della virtù* (Bologna, May 25, 1694); *Laodicea e Berenice* (Venice, 1695); *Penelope la casta* (Rome, Jan. 25, 1696); *Fausta restituita all'impero* (Rome, Jan. 19, 1697); *Apollo geloso* (Bologna, Aug. 16, 1698); *Ariovisto* (Milan, Sept. 1699; in collaboration with others); *La prosperità di Elio Sejano* (Milan, Carnival 1699; in collaboration with others); *Dionisio rè di Portogallo* (Pratolino, Sept. 1707); *Il fratricida innocente* (Bologna, May 19, 1708); *Ginevra principessa di Scozia* (Pratolino, fall 1708); *Berenice regina d'Egitto* (Pratolino, Sept. 1709); *Rodelinda regina de' Longobardi* (Pratolino, fall 1710); *Lucio vero* (Bologna, spring 1717); *Rosinde ed Emireno* (undated). ORATORIOS: *S. Serafina [I due gigli porporati nel martirio de S. Serafina e S. Sabina]* (Bologna, 1679); *Abramo vincitore* (Venice, 1683); *Mosè* (Modena, 1685); *Oratorio della passione di Cristo* (Bologna, 1685); *La beata Imelde Lambertini* (Bologna, 1686); *Agar* (Bologna, 1689); *La passione del Redentore* (Bologna, 1694); *S. Galgano* (Bologna, 1694); *Cristo al limbo* (Bologna, 1698); *La sepoltura di Cristo* (Bologna, 1704); *S. Giovanni* (Bologna, 1704); *Gesù al sepolcro* (Bologna, 1707); *S. Petronio* (Bologna, 1720); *L'amor divino [I conforti di Maria vergine addolorata]* (Bologna, 1723); also several undated oratorios.

BIBL.: L. Mancini, *J. A. P.* (Bologna, 1813); G. Vecchi, ed., *La musica barocca a Bologna . . . G. A. P.* (Bologna, 1961).

Pertile, Aureliano, noted Italian tenor; b. Montagnana, Nov. 9, 1885; d. Milan, Jan. 11, 1952. He studied with Orefice and Fugazzola. He made his operatic debut in *Martha* in Vicenza in 1911, then sang in Naples (1914), at Milan's La Scala (1916), and the Teatro Colón in Buenos Aires (1918); he made his Metropolitan Opera debut in New York as Cavaradossi in *Tosca* (Dec. 1, 1921). He then returned to La Scala, where he gained renown for his portrayal of Faust in *Mefistofele* (1922); he was a leading tenor there until 1937 and also appeared at London's Covent Garden (1927–31); he retired from the stage (1946); he taught at the Milan Cons. (from 1945). He was esteemed for such roles as Andrea Chénier, Manrico, Radames, Canio, and Don Alvaro; he created Boito's Nerone and Mascagni's Nerone.

Pescetti, Giovanni Battista, Italian composer; b. Venice, c.1704; d. there, March 20, 1766. He was the grandson of C. F. Pollarolo. Following his training with Lotti, he became active as an opera composer, frequently collaborating with Galuppi. In 1736 he went to London as director of the Opera of the Nobility, where he commenced a rivalry with Handel. Pescetti's opera *Demetrio*, first performed in Venice in 1732, was given in London in a revised version on Feb. 12, 1737. His success was short-lived, and from 1738 he prepared various pasticcios. He returned to Venice about

1745, where he wrote a number of works for the stage. In 1762 he became 2d organist at San Marco. He wrote about 25 operas in all, as well as sacred music and instrumental pieces.

Peskó, Zoltán, Hungarian-born Italian conductor and composer; b. Budapest, Feb. 15, 1937. He studied at the Budapest Academy of Music (graduated, 1962); he also took courses in composition with Petrassi and in conducting with Ferrara in Italy, and in conducting with Boulez in Switzerland (1963–66). He was assistant conductor to Maazel and the Deutsche Oper and Berlin Radio Sym. Orch. in the Western sector (1966–69), then conducted at the Berlin State Opera in East Berlin (1969–73); he also served on the faculty at the Berlin Hochschule für Musik (1969–72). From 1974 to 1976 he was chief conductor of the Teatro Comunale in Bologna; subsequently he was chief conductor of Venice's Teatro La Fenice (1976–77) and Milan's Orchestra Sinfonica della RAI (1978–82). From 1996 to 1999 he was chief conductor of the Deutsche Oper am Rhein in Düsseldorf.

Pesonen, Olavi, Finnish composer and teacher; b. Helsinki, April 8, 1909. He studied with Ilmari Krohn and Leevi Madetoja at the Univ. of Helsinki (M.A., 1932) and also took courses with Arthur Willner in Vienna and Seiber in London, and studied organ with Ramin in Leipzig. He then devoted himself to teaching and composing in Helsinki. His works follow along traditional lines. They include *Havahtuminen* (Awakening), melodrama for Narrator and Orch. (1936), and *Huutokauppa* (Auction), music to A. Leinonen's play (1949).

Pessard, Émile (-Louis-Fortuné), French composer; b. Paris, May 29, 1843; d. there, Feb. 10, 1917. He studied at the Paris Cons. with Bazin (harmony), Laurent (piano), Benoist (organ), and Carafa (composition), winning the 1st harmony prize in 1862, and the Grand Prix de Rome in 1866 with the cantata *Dalila* (1866). In 1881 he was appointed prof. of harmony at the Paris Cons. He enjoyed considerable regard as a composer of fine songs. As a student, Debussy copied Pessard's song *Chanson d'un fou*, and the MS in Debussy's handwriting was publ. erroneously as Debussy's own.

WORKS: OPERAS (all 1st perf. in Paris): *La Cruche cassée* (Feb. 1870); *Don Quichotte* (Feb. 13, 1874); *Le Char* (Jan. 18, 1878); *Le Capitaine Fracasse* (July 2, 1878); *Tabarin* (Jan. 12, 1885); *Tartarin sur les Alpes* (Nov. 17, 1888); *Les Folies amoureuses* (April 15, 1891); *Une Nuit de Noël* (1893); *Mam'zelle Carabin* (Nov. 3, 1893); *La Dame de trèfle* (May 13, 1898); *L'Armée des vierges* (Oct. 15, 1902); *L'Epave* (Feb. 17, 1903).

Peters (real name, **Petermann**), **Roberta,** outstanding American soprano; b. N.Y., May 4, 1930. She studied voice with William Pierce Hermann. At the age of 20, she made her operatic debut with the Metropolitan Opera in New York as Zerlina in *Don Giovanni* on Nov. 17, 1950, as a substitute on short notice; she subsequently remained on its roster for more than 40 years. She also sang with the opera companies of San Francisco and Chicago, at Covent Garden in London, at the Salzburg Festivals, and at the Vienna State Opera. In 1998 she was awarded the National Medal of Arts. She was one of the leading coloratura sopranos of her generation; she also appeared with success on television, films, and in musical comedies. She was briefly married to **Robert Merrill**. With Louis Biancolli, she wrote *A Debut at the Met* (1967).

Petersen, Wilhelm, German composer and teacher; b. Athens, March 15, 1890; d. Darmstadt, Dec. 18, 1957. He studied in Germany and worked as a theater conductor and served in the German army during World War I; in 1922 he settled in Darmstadt as a teacher. He wrote the opera *Der goldne Topf* (Darmstadt, March 29, 1941). He was highly regarded in Darmstadt as a musician and pedagogue. In 1972 a Wilhelm Petersen Society was founded to memorialize his work.

BIBL.: A. Petersen, *W. P.: Skizze seines Wesens und Lebens* (Darmstadt, 1962).

Peterson-Berger, (Olof) Wilhelm, esteemed Swedish music critic, teacher, and composer; b. Ullånger, Feb. 27, 1867; d. Östersund, Dec. 3, 1942. He studied with J. Dente and O. Bolander at the Stockholm Cons. (1886–89), then in Dresden with Scholtz (piano) and Kretzschmar (composition). He eventually settled in Stockholm, where he became active as a pedagogue and music critic of *Dagens Nyheter* (1896–1908; 1910–20; 1921–30). His opera *Arnljot* was one of the finest Swedish operas in the national tradition.

WORKS: DRAMATIC: *Sveagaldrar*, festival play for the silver jubilee of the accession of Oscar II (1897); 4 music dramas (all 1st perf. in Stockholm): *Ran* (1899–1900; May 20, 1903), *Arnljot* (1907–09; April 13, 1910), *Domedagsprofeterna* (The Prophets of Doom; 1912–17; Feb. 21, 1919), and *Adils och Elisiv* (1921–24; Feb. 27, 1927); *Lyckan* (Luck), fairy opera (Stockholm, March 27, 1903).

WRITINGS: *Svensk Musikkultur* (1911); *Richard Wagner som kulturföreteelse* (Richard Wagner as a Phenomenon of Civilization; 1913; Ger. tr., 1917, as *Richard Wagner als Kulturerscheinung*). A selection of his essays was publ. in Stockholm in 2 vols. (1923); another, in one vol., in Östersund (1951). His reminiscences were publ. posthumously (Uppsala, 1943).

BIBL.: B. Carlberg, *W. P.-B.* (Stockholm, 1950); S. Beite, *W. P.-B.: En känd och okänd tondiktare* (Östersund, 1965); G. Norell, *W. P.-B. och dikten* (vol. 1, Arboga, 1991).

Petit, Raymond, French music critic and composer; b. Neuilly-sur-Seine, July 6, 1893; d. Annemasse, Haute-Savoie, Sept. 25, 1976. He studied with Tournemire in Paris, then devoted himself mainly to music criticism. Among his works is the opera *La Sulamithe*.

Petkov, Dimiter, Bulgarian composer and conductor; b. Smolyan, May 4, 1919. He studied composition with Veselin Stoyanov at the State Academy of Music in Sofia, graduating in 1950, then went to Moscow for postgraduate studies in theory at the Cons. (1952–54). He taught theory at the State Academy of Music in Sofia (1949–52; 1954–58) and was director of the National Opera Theater; he later served as president of the Union of Bulgarian Composers (1972–80). His works include *The Winding Path*, children's operetta (1956; Michailovgrad, Oct. 29, 1975), and *Restless Hearts*, musical comedy (1960).

BIBL.: E. Pavlov, *D. P.* (Sofia, 1987).

Petkov, Dimiter, noted Bulgarian bass; b. Sofia, March 5, 1938. He received training at the Sofia Academy of Music. In 1964 he made his operatic debut in Sofia as Ramfis. In 1968 he appeared as Osmin at the Glyndebourne Festival, and returned there in 1970 as Gremin. From 1972 to 1986 he made regular appearances at the Vienna State Opera, where he returned in 1990. He also sang in Chicago (1980), Bologna (1980–83; 1988), Milan's La Scala (1981, 1984, 1989), N.Y.'s Carnegie Hall (1982, 1984, 1989), Naples (1984, 1991), Florence (1986–89; 1991), Paris (1986; 1988; 1990–93), Rome (1987, 1992), Berlin (1988–93), Dallas (1989, 1993), and Strasbourg (1996). His concert engagements took him to the world's principal music centers. While he was most admired for his Russian roles, particularly Boris Godunov, Ivan Susanin, and Ivan Khovansky, he also had success in operas by Rossini, Bellini, Donizetti, Gounod, and Verdi.

Petrassi, Goffredo, outstanding Italian composer and teacher; b. Zagarolo, near Rome, July 16, 1904. He went to Rome and had private piano lessons with Bastini, then commenced the study of harmony with Donato (1925); he subsequently entered the Cons. di Santa Cecilia (1928), where he studied composition with Bustini (diploma, 1932) and organ with Germani (diploma, 1933). He taught at the Accademia di Santa Cecilia (1934–36), where he also received instruction from Molinari; he was general director of Venice's Teatro La Fenice (1937–40). After teaching composition at the Cons. di Santa Cecilia (1939–59), he taught again at the Accademia di Santa Cecilia (1959–74); he also taught at Siena's Accademia Musicale Chigiana (1966–67). He publ. the vol. *Autoritratto* (Rome, 1991). Despite the late beginning, Petrassi acquired a solid technique of composition; the chief influence in his music was that of Casella; later he became interested in 12-tone procedures.

WORKS: DRAMATIC: OPERAS: *Il Cordovano* (1944–48; Milan, May 12, 1949; rev. 1958; Milan, Feb. 18, 1959); *La morte dell'aria* (1949–50; Rome, Oct. 24, 1950). BALLETS: *La follia di Orlando* (1942–43; Milan, April 12, 1947); *Il ritratto di Don Chisciotte* (1945; Paris, Nov. 21, 1947). OTHER: *Coro di morti*, dramatic madrigal for Men's Chorus, Brass, Double Basses, 3 Pianos, and Percussion (Venice, Sept. 28, 1941); *Beatitudines*, chamber oratorio for Baritone and 5 Instruments, in memory of Martin Luther King, Jr. (Fiuggi, July 17, 1969); *Orationes Christi* for Chorus, Brass, 8 Violins, and 8 Cellos (1974–75; Rome, Dec. 6, 1975).

BIBL.: J. Weissmann, *G. P.* (Milan, 1957; 2d ed., 1980); C. Annibaldi, *G. P.: Catalogo delle opere e bibliografia* (Milan, 1971); G. Zosi, *Ricerca e sintesi nell'opera di G. P.* (Rome, 1978); E. Restagno, ed., *P.* (Turin, 1986); S. Sablich et al., *A G. P., per i suoi 90 anni* (Milan, 1994; in Italian and Eng.).

Petrauskas, Kipras, Lithuanian tenor, brother of **Mikas Petrauskas**; b. Vilnius, Nov. 23, 1885; d. there, Jan. 17, 1968. He studied with his brother. He appeared in his brother's opera *Birute* (Vilnius, Nov. 6, 1906); he then was a singer at the Imperial Opera in St. Petersburg (1911–20) and also appeared in Berlin, Paris, and Milan, and made a tour of the United States. He returned to Lithuania before World War II. In 1950 he received the Stalin Prize.

Petrauskas, Mikas, Lithuanian composer, brother of **Kipras Petrauskas;** b. Kaunas, Oct. 19, 1873; d. there, March 23, 1937. He studied organ with his father and was a student at the St. Petersburg Cons. of Rimsky-Korsakov. During the abortive revolution in 1905, he was implicated in political activities and imprisoned. After his release, he brought out the opera *Birute* (Vilnius, Nov. 6, 1906). In 1907 he went to the United States. He settled in Boston in 1914, where he founded the Lithuanian Cons. and brought out the operas *The Devil Inventor* (May 20, 1923) and *Egle, Queen of the Snakes* (May 30, 1924; he sang the role of the King of the Snakes). In 1930 he returned to Lithuania.

Petrella, Clara, Italian soprano; b. Greco Milanese, March 28, 1918; d. Milan, Nov. 19, 1987. She studied with her sister, Micaela Oliva, and with Giannina Russ in Milan. She made her operatic debut in 1939 as Liù at the Teatro Puccini in Milan, then sang in several provincial Italian theaters. She made her first appearance at La Scala in Milan in 1941, becoming a principal member of the company in 1947; she also sang in Rome and Naples; in addition, she appeared in concerts. She was particularly noted for her performances of contemporary operas by Italian composers.

Petrella, Errico, noted Italian composer; b. Palermo, Dec. 10, 1813; d. Genoa, April 7, 1877. He studied at the age of 8 with the violinist Del Giudice in Naples and then at the Cons. there, becoming a free boarder when he was 11; his teachers included Bellini, Furno, Ruggi, and Zingarelli. While still a student, he received a commission to write his first opera, *Il Diavolo color di rosa* (July 1829), for Naples's Teatro della Fenice; it proved a success, but led him to be expelled from the Cons. for showing such daring at his age; nevertheless, he continued to receive private instruction from Ruggi. After producing 5 more operas during the next decade, he devoted himself mainly to teaching singing. In 1851 he was named music director of Naples's Teatro Nuovo, where he successfully produced his opera *Le precauzioni* (May 20, 1851); his next opera, *Elena di Tolosa* (Teatro del Fondo, Naples, Aug. 12, 1852), proved even more successful, prompting him to compose his first serious opera, *Marco Visconti* (Teatro San Carlo, Naples, Feb. 9, 1854), which scored a brilliant success and spread his name throughout Italy; it also led to the production of his best-known serious opera, *Jone* (La Scala, Milan, Jan. 26, 1858). His greatest notoriety came with his opera *I promessi sposi* (Lecco, Oct. 2, 1869). Petrella was the last representative of the old Neapolitan school. He was at his best in buffo works, for his serious operas could not compete with the dramatic masterpieces of Verdi.

BIBL.: G. Carotti, *Cenni biografici e ritratto di E. P.* (Turin, 1877); F. Guardione, *Di E. P. e della traslazion e della salma da Genova a Palermo* (Palermo, 1908); G. Cosenza, *Vita e opere di E. P.* (Rome, 1909); G. Siciliano, *Di E. P.: Musicista palermitano* (Palermo, 1913).

Petrelli, Eleanora (née **Wigstrom**), Swedish soprano; b. Simtuna, April 9, 1835; d. Chicago, Feb. 21, 1904. While touring Finland as a member of a small theatrical company, she married a wealthy Russian named Petrov, and Italianized her married name to Petrelli. She studied in Milan with Lamperti, and in Paris with Viardot-García. After her husband died in 1869, she virtually abandoned the stage, but continued to give concerts in Russia, Germany, and Scandinavian countries. In 1886 she settled in Stockholm, but soon went to Chicago, where she established a school for vocal culture. She publ. a number of songs.

Petridis, Petros (John), eminent Turkish-born Greek composer; b. Nigdé, July 23, 1892; d. Athens, Aug. 17, 1977. He studied in Constantinople at the American Robert College; he received instruction in piano from Hegey and in harmony from Selvelli; he then went to Paris and read law at the Sorbonne and political science at the École Libre des Sciences Politiques (1911–14); later he studied with Wolff (1914) and Roussel (1919). He became a naturalized Greek citizen (1913); subsequently he was a music critic for English, American, and Greek publications, dividing his time between Paris and Athens. His use of Byzantine modalities, adorned with contemporary harmonies, reveals the influence of Greek culture. Among his works were *Zefyra*, opera (1923–25; rev. 1958–64), *Iphigenia in Tauris*, incidental music to Euripides' play (Athens, Oct. 15, 1941), and *O pramateftis* (The Pedlar), ballet (1941–43; Athens, May 6, 1944); also *Hayos Pavlos*, oratorio for Narrator, Soloists, Chorus, and Orch. (1950; Athens, June 29, 1951).

Petrobelli, Pierluigi, prominent Italian musicologist; b. Padua, Oct. 18, 1932. He studied composition with Pedrollo at Padua's Liceo Musicale and musicology with Ronga at the Univ. of Rome (arts degree, 1957). Upon receiving a Fulbright grant, he continued his studies with Lockwood, Mendel, and Strunk at Princeton Univ. (M.A., 1961), and also took courses at Harvard Univ. and the Univ. of Calif., Berkeley. He was librarian-archivist at Parma's Istituto di Studi Verdiani (1964–69); he became a lecturer (1968) and later a reader in music history at the Univ. of Parma; he was named librarian of the Pesaro Cons. (1970). He received his libera docenza in 1972, and then served as a lecturer in music (1973–77) and reader in musicology (1977–80) at King's College, London. In 1980 he was made director of the Istituto di Studi Verdiani in Parma; from 1981 to 1983 he served as prof. of music history at the Univ. of Perugia, then was a prof. at the Univ. "La Sapienza" of Rome (from 1983). With W. Rhem, he ed. the critical edition of Mozart's *Il Re pastore* for the *Neue Mozart Ausgabe*. Among his writings is *Music in the Theater: Essays on Verdi and Other Composers* (Princeton, N.J., 1994).

Petrov, Andrei (Pavlovich), Russian composer; b. Leningrad, Sept. 2, 1930. He studied composition at the Leningrad Cons. with Evlakhov, graduating in 1954. In 1957 he joined the Communist Party. In his music he follows the general precepts of socialist realism, ethnic in thematic material, euphonious in harmony, energetic in rhythm, stimulating in modalities, optimistic in contemporary philosophy, and realistic in treatment.

WORKS: DRAMATIC: OPERA: *Peter the First* (Leningrad, 1975). BALLETS: *The Magic Apple Tree* (Leningrad, Nov. 8, 1953); *The Station Master*, after Pushkin (Leningrad, May 9, 1955); *The Shore of Hope* (1959); *The Creation of the World* (1971); *Pushkin* (1979). MUSICAL: *We Want to Dance* (1967).

Petrov, Ivan (Ivanovich), prominent Russian bass; b. Irkutsk, Feb. 29, 1920. He studied with A. Mineyev at the Glazunov Music College in Moscow (1938–39). He then joined the Kozlovsky opera group; he became a soloist with the Moscow Phil. in 1941. In 1943 he joined the staff of the Bolshoi Theater in Moscow; his most celebrated interpretation was in the title role of *Boris Go-*

dunov, inviting comparisons with Chaliapin. He made several tours as a member of the Opera of the Bolshoi Theater in Europe, Japan, and the United States.

BIBL.: I. Nazarenko, *I. P.* (Moscow, 1957).

Petrov, Osip (Afanasievich), celebrated Russian bass; b. Elizavetgrad, Nov. 15, 1807; d. St. Petersburg, March 11, 1878. He joined the Zhurakhovsky opera troupe and made his debut in Cavos's *The Cossack Poet* in Elizavetgrad (1826); he received instruction from Cavos. In 1830 Lebedev, the director of the St. Petersburg Imperial Opera, heard him sing with an inferior company at a fair in Kursk, and immediately engaged him. Petrov made his debut in St. Petersburg as Sarastro that same year. The enormous compass of his voice, its extraordinary power and beautiful quality, combined with consummate histrionic skill, secured for him recognition as one of the greatest of Russian bassos. He appeared on the stage for the last time on March 10, 1878, on the eve of his death. He created the roles of Susanin in Glinka's *Life for the Czar* (1836), Ruslan in *Ruslan and Ludmila* (1842), the Miller in Dargomyzhsky's *Rusalka* (1856), and Varlaam in Mussorgsky's *Boris Godunov* (1874).

BIBL.: E. Lastotchkina, *O. P.* (Moscow, 1950).

Petrova-Vorobieva, Anna, Russian contralto; b. St. Petersburg, Feb. 14, 1817; d. there, April 26, 1901. She was a student of Antonio Sapienza and Cavos in St. Petersburg, and also received some training from Glinka. Following her operatic debut as Pippo in *La gazza ladra*, she sang with the St. Petersburg Opera (1835–50), where she created the roles of Vanya in *A Life for the Czar* (1836) and Ratmir in *Ruslan and Ludmila* (1842). Glinka subsequently added the aria *In the Monastery* to his latter opera to showcase her vocal talent. Her husband was **Osip Petrov**.

Petrovics, Emil, Hungarian composer; b. Zrenjanin, Yugoslavia, Feb. 9, 1930. He went to Budapest (1941) and studied at the Academy of Music with Sugár (1949–51), Viski (1951–52), and Farkas (1952–57). He was director of the Petőfi Theater (1960–64) and taught at the Academy of Music (from 1969); he served as director of the Hungarian State Opera (1986–90). His opera *C'est la guerre* (1961) was awarded the Kossuth Prize in 1966.

WORKS: DRAMATIC: OPERAS: *C'est la guerre* (Budapest Radio, Aug. 17, 1961; 1st stage perf., Budapest, March 11, 1962); *Lysistrate*, after Aristophanes (1962; rev. 1971); *Bün es bűnhődés* (Crime and Punishment), after Dostoyevsky (Budapest, Oct. 26, 1969). BALLET: *Salome* (1978). ORATORIOS: *Jónás könyve* (The Book of Jonah; 1966); *Ott essem el én* (Let Me Die There) for Men's Chorus and Orch. (1972).

Petrželka, Vilém, noted Czech composer and pedagogue; b. Královo Pole, near Brünn, Sept. 10, 1889; d. Brno, Jan. 10, 1967. He studied with Janáček at the Brno Organ School (1905–08) and in 1910 became his assistant at the school; subsequently he took private lessons in Prague with Vítězslav Novák. He taught at the Phil. Society School in Brno (1914–19), and in 1919 became a prof. at the newly formed Brno Cons. In his compositions, he continued the national tradition of modern Moravian music; he was mainly influenced by Janáček, but expanded his resources and on occasion made use of jazz rhythms, quarter tones, and other modernistic procedures. His works include *Námořník Mikuláš* (Mariner Nicholas), symphonic drama for Narrator, Soli, Chorus, Organ, Jazz Band, and Orch. (1928; Brno, Dec. 9, 1930), and *Horník Pavel* (The Miner Paul), opera (1935–38).

BIBL.: L. Firkušný, *V. P.* (Prague, 1946).

Petyrek, Felix, Czech composer and teacher; b. Brünn, May 14, 1892; d. Vienna, Dec. 1, 1951. After training with Godowsky and Sauer (piano), he studied with Schrecker (composition) and Adler (musicology) at the Univ. of Vienna (graduated, 1919). He taught at the Salzburg Mozarteum (1919–21), the Berlin Hochschule für Musik (1921–23), the Athens Odeon Athenon (1926–30), the Stuttgart Cons. (1930–39), the Cons. and Univ. in Leipzig (1939–49), and the Vienna Academy of Music (1949–51). In his melodic writing, he adopted the scale of alternating whole tones and semitones as a compromise between tonality and atonality. His works include *Die arme Mutter und der Tod*, musical fairy play (1923), *Der Garten des Paradieses*, opera (1923–41; Leipzig, Nov. 1, 1942), and pantomimes.

Petzoldt, Richard (Johannes), German musicologist; b. Plauen, Nov. 12, 1907; d. Leipzig, Jan. 14, 1974. He studied at the Univ. of Berlin, where his teachers were Abert, Schering, Moser, Sachs, Hornbostel, Schünemann, and Blume; received his Ph.D. in 1933 with the diss. *Die Kirchenkompositionen und weltlichen Kantaten Reinhard Keisers* (publ. in Düsseldorf, 1935). He ed. the *Allgemeine Musikalische Zeitung* (1935–39) and the periodical *Musik in der Schule* (1949–59). He was a prof. of music history at the Univ. of Leipzig (1952–67). His publs. include *Beethoven* (Leipzig, 1938; 2d ed., 1947); *Schubert* (Leipzig, 1940; 2d ed., 1947); *Schumann* (Leipzig, 1941; 2d ed., 1947); *Mozart* (Wiesbaden, 1948; 2d ed., 1965); *Johann Sebastian Bach und Leipzig* (Leipzig, 1950); *Die Oper in ihrer Zeit* (Leipzig, 1956); iconographies of Bach (Leipzig, 1950; 2d ed., 1970), Verdi (Leipzig, 1951), Beethoven (Leipzig, 1952; 7th ed., rev., 1968), Schubert (Leipzig, 1953), Tchaikovsky (Leipzig, 1953), Handel (Leipzig, 1954; 2d ed., 1960), Glinka (Leipzig, 1955), Schumann (Leipzig, 1956), Mozart (Leipzig, 1956; 3d ed., 1961), *Beethoven* (Leipzig, 1970; 2d ed., 1973), and *Schütz* (Kassel, 1972).

Peyser, Joan (née **Gilbert**), American musicologist, editor, author, and journalist; b. N.Y., June 12, 1931. She played piano in public at 13; she majored in music at Barnard College (B.A., 1951); studied musicology with Lang at Columbia Univ. (M.A., 1956). She then devoted herself mainly to musical journalism; enlivened the music pages of the Sunday *N.Y. Times* with book reviews and breezy colloquies with composers; she wrote scripts for the television series *The World of Music*; she acted as musical adviser to the N.Y. City Board of Education. She publ. the popular book *The New Music: The Sense Behind the Sound* (N.Y., 1971; 2d ed., rev., 1981 as *Twentieth Century Music: The Sense Behind the Sound*); she created considerable excitement in the music world with her biography *Boulez: Composer, Conductor, Enigma* (N.Y., 1976); trying to penetrate the eponymous enigma, she undertook a journey to the interior of France, where she interviewed family and friends of her subject, with a fervor suggesting that Boulez was indeed the 4th B of music. From 1977 to 1984 she was ed. of the *Musical Quarterly*, the first woman to occupy this position; during her tenure, she attempted to veer away from the prevalent musicological sesquipedalianism toward plain diction. Among her other publs. are *The Orchestra: Origins and Transformations* (N.Y., 1986), *Leonard Bernstein: A Biography* (N.Y., 1987), and *The Memory of All That: The Life of George Gershwin* (N.Y., 1993).

Pfeiffer, Georges-Jean, French composer; b. Versailles, Dec. 12, 1835; d. Paris, Feb. 14, 1908. He began his career as a pianist, then was active as a music critic in Paris. He succeeded his father as a partner in the piano firm of Pleyel, Wolff & Cie. Among his works were *Le Capitaine Roche*, operetta (1862), *L'Enclume*, opera (Paris, 1884), and *Le Légataire universel*, comic opera (Paris, July 6, 1901).

Pfitzner, Hans (Erich), eminent German composer and conductor; b. Moscow (of German parents), May 5, 1869; d. Salzburg, May 22, 1949. He studied piano with James Kwast and composition with Iwan Knorr at the Hoch Cons. in Frankfurt am Main; in 1899 he eloped with Kwast's daughter and took her to England, where they were married. In 1892–93 he taught piano and theory at the Koblenz Cons.; he then served as assistant conductor of the Municipal Theater in Mainz (1894–96); from 1897 to 1907 he was on the faculty of the Stern Cons. in Berlin; concurrently he conducted at the Theater Westens (1903–06). During the 1907–08 season he led the renowned Kaim Concerts in Munich. From 1908 to 1918 he was in Strasbourg as municipal music director and also served as dean at the Strasbourg Cons.; from 1910 to 1916 he conducted at the Strasbourg Opera. During the 1919–20 season he was music director of the Munich Konzertverein; from 1920 to 1929 he led a master class at the Berlin Academy of Arts; from 1929 to 1934 he taught composition at the Akademie der Tonkunst in Munich. Being of certified German stock, though born in Russia, Pfitzner was favored by the Nazi authorities, and became an ardent supporter of the Third Reich; he reached the nadir of his moral degradation in dedicating an overture, *Krakauer Begrüssung*, to Hans Frank, the murderous Gauleiter of occupied Poland in 1944. After the collapse of Hitler's brief millennium, Pfitzner had to face the Denazification Court in Munich in 1948; owing to his miserable condition in both body and soul, he was exonerated. He was taken to a home for the aged in Munich, and later was transferred to Salzburg, where he died in misery. Eventually, his body was honorably laid to rest in a Vienna cemetery.

In his better days, Pfitzner was hailed in Germany as a great national composer. He presented a concert of his works in Berlin on May 12, 1893, with excellent auguries. After the premiere of his opera *Der arme Heinrich* in Mainz on April 2, 1895, the critics, among them the prestigious Humperdinck, praised the work in extravagant terms. Even more successful was his opera *Palestrina*, making use of Palestrina's themes, written to his own libretto, which was conducted by Bruno Walter at its first performance on June 12, 1917, in Munich. The Pfitzner Soc. was formed in Munich as early as 1904, and a Hans Pfitzner Assn. was established in Berlin in 1938, with Furtwängler as president. Although Pfitzner's music is traditional in style and conservative in harmony, he was regarded as a follower of the modern school, a comrade-in-arms of his close contemporary Richard Strauss. Very soon, however, his fame began to dwindle; there were fewer performances of his operas and still fewer hearings of his instrumental works; he himself bitterly complained of this lack of appreciation of his art. It was a miserable end for a once important and capable musician.

WORKS: DRAMATIC: OPERAS: *Der arme Heinrich* (1891–93; Mainz, April 2, 1895); *Die Rose vom Liebesgarten* (1897–1900; Elberfeld, Nov. 9, 1901); *Das Christ-Elflein* (Munich, Dec. 11, 1906); *Palestrina* (1911–15; Munich, June 12, 1917). INCIDENTAL MUSIC: *Das Fest auf Solhaug*, after Ibsen (Mainz, Nov. 28, 1890); *Das Käthchen von Heilbronn*, after Kleist (Berlin, Oct. 19, 1905); *Gesang der Barden* for *Die Hermannsschlacht*, after Kleist (1906).

WRITINGS: *Gesammelte Schriften* (2 vols., Augsburg, 1926, 1929; containing Pfitzner's vicious pamphlets against modern ideas about music, including *Futuristengefahr*, dedicated against Busoni [1917], and *Neue Aestetik der musikalischen Impotenz*, denouncing the critic Paul Bekker); *Über musikalische Inspiration* (Berlin, 1940); *Philosophie und Dichtung in meinem Leben* (Berlin, 1944); *Eindrücke und Bilder meines Lebens* (Hamburg, 1947); W. Abendroth, ed., *Reden, Schriften, Briefe* (Berlin, 1955).

BIBL.: P. Cossmann, *H. P.* (Munich, 1904); R. Louis, *H. P.s "Rose vom Liebesgarten"* (Munich, 1904); C. Wandrey, *H. P.* (Leipzig, 1922); E. Kroll, *H. P.* (Munich, 1924); W. Lütge, *H. P.* (Leipzig, 1924); E. Valentin, *H. P.: Werk und Gestalt eines Deutschen* (Regensburg, 1939); H. Rutz, *H. P.: Musik zwischen den Zeiten* (Vienna, 1949); K. Müller, *In memoriam H. P.* (Vienna, 1950); H. Rectanus, *Leitmotivik und Form in den musikdramatischen Werken H. P.s* (Würzburg, 1967); W. Dietz, *H. P.s Lieder: Versuch einer Stilbetrachtung* (Regensburg, 1968); W. Abendroth and K.-R. Danler, eds., *Festschrift aus Anlass des 100. Geburtstags und des 20. Todestags H. P.s* (Munich, 1969); W. Osthoff, ed., *Symposium H. P. (1981: Berlin, Germany)* (Tutzing, 1984); R. Ermen, *Musik als Einfall: H. P.s Position im ästhetischen Diskurs nach Wagner* (Aachen, 1986); E. Wamlek-Junk, *H. P. und Wien: Sein Briefwechsel mit Victor Junk und andere Dokumente* (Tutzing, 1986); J. Williamson, *The Music of H. P.* (Oxford, 1992); W. Osthoff, ed., *Symposium H. P. (1989; Hamburg, Germany)* (Tutzing, 1994).

Philidor (real name, **Danican**), family of famous French musicians:

(1) Michel Danican; b. Dauphiné, c.1600; d. Paris, Aug. 1659. He is the earliest known member of the family, although he never used the name Philidor. He went to Paris about 1620. By 1651 he was in the service of King Louis XIII as a member of the grande écurie (military band), in which he played the oboe, cromorne, and trompette marine.

(2) Jean Danican; b. probably in Dauphiné, c.1620; d. Versailles, Sept. 8, 1679. He most likely was a younger brother or son of **Michel Danican (1)**. He adopted the name Philidor about 1659, and by 1657 was in the royal service. In 1659 he became a phiphre marine. He was also a composer.

(3) André Danican Philidor (l'aîné), son of **Jean Danican (2)**; b. Versailles, c.1647; d. Dreux, Aug. 11, 1730. In 1659 he entered the grande écurie, succeeding **Michel Danican (1)**; in it he played the cromorne, trompette marine, and drums. He subsequently played the oboe, bassoon, and bass cromorne in the royal chapel and chambre du roi. In 1684 King Louis XIV appointed him royal music librarian, a position he held until his death. During his long tenure, he acquired operas, ballets, sacred music, partbooks, etc. from various periods of French history for the collection. A large portion of this collection eventually passed to St. Michael's College, Tenbury. It was sold at auction in London in 1978, and passed to the Bibliothèque Nationale in Paris and the Bibliothèque Municipale in Versailles. The latter library already housed 35 vols. of the royal collection. The Paris Cons. library once housed 59 vols., but through various misfortunes its collection was reduced to 34 vols. Additional vols. are housed in other library collections. Philidor continued to serve as a musician in the royal chapel until 1722, and in the royal service until 1729. By his first wife he had 16 children, and by his 2d, 5. His most famous son was **François-André Danican Philidor (7).**

WORKS: OPÉRAS BALLETS: *Le Canal de Versailles* (Versailles, July 16, 1687); *Le Mariage de la couture avec la grosse Cathos* (Versailles, 1687?); *La Princesse de Crète* (Marly, 1700?); *La Mascarade du roi de la Chine* (Marly, 1700); *La Mascarade du vaisseau marchand* (Marly, Feb. 18, 1700); *La Mascarade de la noce village* (Marly, 1700).

(4) Jacques Danican Philidor (le cadet), son of **Jean Danican (2)** and younger brother of **André Danican Philidor (l'aîné) (3)**; b. Paris, May 6, 1657; d. Versailles, May 27, 1708. In 1668 he became a phiphre in the grande écurie, and subsequently played the cromorne and trompette marine. In 1683 he became a musicien ordinaire de la chapelle, and played the oboe and bassoon. In 1690 he became a member of the chambre du roi. He composed airs, dance music, and marches (only the last are extant). Of his 12 children, 4 became musicians.

(5) Anne Danican Philidor, son of **André Danican Philidor (l'aîné) (3)**; b. Paris, April 11, 1681; d. there, Oct. 8, 1728. In 1698 he became an oboist in the grande écurie. In 1704 he became a member of the royal chapel, and in 1712 of the chambre du roi. He founded the famous Paris concert series known as the Concert Spirituel, which was launched on March 18, 1725; it was disbanded in 1790. He also founded the short-lived Concerts Français (1727–33). Among his works were *L'Amour vainqueur*, pastoral (Marly, Aug. 9, 1697), *Diane et Endymion*, pastoral (Marly, 1698), and *Danae*, opera (Marly, 1701).

(6) Pierre Danican Philidor, son of **Jacques Danican Philidor (le cadet) (4)**; b. Paris, Aug. 22, 1681; d. there, Sept. 1, 1731. In 1697 he became a member of the grande écurie, in 1704 an oboist in the royal chapel, and in 1712 a flutist in the chambre du roi. A pastoral he composed in 1697 was given in Marly and Versailles.

(7) François-André Danican Philidor, the greatest in the line of musicians in the family, the youngest son of **André Danican Philidor (l'aîné) (3)**; b. Dreux, Sept. 7, 1726; d. London, Aug. 31, 1795. He was a page boy in the royal chapel in Versailles, where he studied music with the maître de chapelle, André Campra. It was also at that time that he learned to play chess. A motet by him was performed in the royal chapel when he was 12. In 1740 he went to Paris, where he supported himself by copying and teaching. His interest in chess continued; he gained distinction as an outstanding player by defeating a number of celebrated chess masters of the day. He publ. a fundamental treatise on chess, *L'Analyze des échecs* (London, 1749; rev. ed., 1777, as *Analyse du jeu des échecs*; there were more than 100 eds. of this book and several trs.). As a member of the St. James Chess Club in London, he gave lectures and demonstrations as a master; a famous chess opening was named after him. In the meantime, he began a successful career as a composer for the theater. His first success was *Le Maréchal ferrant* (Paris, Aug. 22, 1761), which was accorded numerous performances. His *Le Sorcier* (Paris, Jan. 2, 1764) was also a triumph. Although *Tom Jones* (Paris, Feb. 27, 1765) was an initial failure, it enjoyed great popularity after its libretto was revised by Sedaine and performed on Jan. 30, 1766. The same fate attended his *Ernelinde, princesse de Vorvège* when it was first given at the Paris Opéra on Nov. 24, 1767. It was subsequently revised by Sedaine and performed most successfully as *Ernelinde* in Versailles on Dec. 11, 1773. Philidor continued to compose for the stage until his death, but he allowed his love for chess to take more and more of his time. He made frequent trips to London after 1775 to play at the St. James Chess Club. Philidor was one of the finest early composers of opéra comique. Although his scores are often hampered by poor librettos, his orch. writing is effective. He was an inventive composer, and introduced the novelty of a vocal quartet a cappella (in *Tom Jones*). He wrote sacred music as well. His choral work, the *Carmen saeculare*, after Horace, proved most successful at its premiere in London on Feb. 26, 1779. Other vocal works include 12 ariettes périodiques.

BIBL.: G. Allen, *The Life of P., Musician and Chess Player* (Philadelphia, 1858; 2d ed., 1863; reprint, 1971; 3d ed., 1865); G.-E. Bonnet, *P. et l'évolution de la musique française au XVIIIe siècle* (Paris, 1921); C. Carroll, *F.-A. D.-P.: His Life and Dramatic Art* (diss., Florida State Univ., 1960).

Philip, Achille, French composer and teacher; b. Arles, Oct. 12, 1878; d. Béziers, Hérault, Oct. 12, 1959. He studied at the Paris Cons. with Guilmant (organ) and d'Indy (composition). From 1905 to 1950 he taught organ at the Schola Cantorum in Paris. He wrote an opera, *L'Or du Menhir* (Rouen, 1934).

Phillipps, Adelaide, English contralto; b. Stratford-on-Avon, Oct. 26, 1833; d. Karlsbad, Oct. 3, 1882. Her family took her to America as a child. She was trained as a dancer, and made her first appearance at the Tremont Theater in Boston on Jan. 12, 1842, in a variety show. She also displayed an early gift as a vocalist, and was introduced to Jenny Lind, who encouraged her to study singing. Accordingly she was sent to London, where she took lessons with Manuel García, making her operatic debut in Brescia (1853). She continued to sing in Italy under the name Signorina Filippi until 1855, when she returned to Boston to appear in light opera in English. Her first major appearance on the grand opera stage in America was as Azucena in Verdi's *Il Trovatore* (N.Y., March 17, 1856). After a long and successful tour in Europe (1861–62), she sang with the Boston Ideal Opera Co. from 1879 to 1881. She was advised to go to Karlsbad for her health in 1882, but died shortly after her arrival there.

BIBL.: A. Waterston, *A. P.: A Record* (Boston, 1883).

Phillips, Burrill, American composer and teacher; b. Omaha, Nov. 9, 1907; d. Berkeley, Calif., June 22, 1988. He studied music with Edwin Stringham in Denver; then with Hanson and Rogers at the Eastman School of Music in Rochester, N.Y. (B.M., 1932; M.M., 1933). He taught at the Eastman School of Music (1933–49; 1965–66), the Univ. of Ill. in Urbana (1949–64), the Juilliard School in New York (1968–69), and Cornell Univ. (1972–73). His early music was cast in a neoclassical style; later he incorporated free serial techniques. Among his works are the operas *Don't We All* (1947; Rochester, N.Y., May 9, 1949) and *The Unforgiven* (1981), and the ballets *Katmanusha* (1932–33), *Play Ball* (Rochester, N.Y., April 29, 1938), *Step into My Parlor* (1942), and *La piñata* (1969); also incidental music.

Phillips, Henry, English bass; b. Bristol, Aug. 13, 1801; d. London, Nov. 8, 1876. He sang as a boy soprano at the Harrowgate theater about 1807, and then proceeded to London and sang in the chorus at Drury Lane. After studying as a baritone with Broadhurst, he sang in the chorus of the English Opera House before completing his training with Smart. In 1824 he sang Artabanes in Arne's *Artaxerxes* at Covent Garden, and then garnered notable success as Caspar in *Der Freischütz* at the English Opera House that same year. In 1825 he became principal bass of the Concert of Ancient Music. He also toured as an opera and concert singer, making a visit to the United States in 1844–45. On Feb. 25, 1863, he gave his farewell concert in London, and then was active as a teacher in Birmingham and later in Dalston. He publ. *The True Enjoyment of Angling, with Music to the Songs* (1843), *Hints on Declamation* (1848), and *Musical and Personal Recollections during Half a Century* (1864).

Phillips, Montague (Fawcett), English composer and pedagogue; b. London, Nov. 13, 1885; d. Esher, Jan. 4, 1969. He studied with F. Corder at the Royal Academy of Music in London and subsequently taught there. He wrote a light opera, *The Rebel Maid* (London, March 12, 1921), which enjoyed some success.

Piazzolla, Astor, fiery Argentine bandoneón player, bandleader, composer, and arranger; b. Mar del Plata, March 11, 1921; d. Buenos Aires, July 5, 1992. He was taken to New York in 1924, where he took up the bandoneón when he was 12. Upon settling in Buenos Aires in 1937, he began a career as a bandoneón player and arranger; he also pursued training with Ginastera, and later was a scholarship student in Paris of Boulanger (1954–55). Upon his return to Buenos Aires, he organized his own band, and in 1960 founded the innovative Quinteto Nuevo Tango. From 1974 to 1985 he made his home in Paris, then returned to his homeland. Piazzolla was a master of the modern tango, embracing an avant-garde style incorporating classical and jazz elements with a piquant touch of modern dissonances. His other works included operas, theater music, and film scores.

BIBL.: C. Kuri, *P.: La música límite* (Buenos Aires, 1992).

Piccaver (real name, **Peckover**), **Alfred,** English tenor; b. Long Sutton, Lincolnshire, Feb. 15, 1884; d. Vienna, Sept. 23, 1958. He studied at the Metropolitan School in New York. He made his operatic debut as Roméo in Prague in 1907, then continued his studies there and in Milan. In 1910 he deputized at the Vienna Court (later State) Opera in the Italian season; he remained in Vienna as a leading lyric tenor until 1937. His repertoire included Don José, Florestan, Walther von Stolzing, Lensky, and Andrea Chénier; he also took part in the first Austrian performance of *La Fanciulla del West* in 1913. He appeared in Chicago (1923–25); in 1924 he sang Cavaradossi and the Duke of Mantua at Covent Garden in London. From 1937 to 1955 he taught voice in London; he then returned to Vienna to attend the opening of the new building of the Staatsoper; he remained in Vienna as a voice teacher until his death.

Picchi, Mirto, Italian tenor; b. Florence, March 15, 1915; d. there, Sept. 25, 1980. He was a pupil in Florence of Giuseppe Armani and Giulia Tess. After making his operatic debut as Radamès in Milan in 1946, he sang in various Italian music centers. In 1947–48 he sang at London's Cambridge Theatre, appearing as Rodolfo, Cavaradossi, and the Duke of Mantua. In 1949 he appeared with the Glyndebourne company as Verdi's Riccardo during its visit to Edinburgh. In 1952 he sang at London's Covent Garden. In 1957 he appeared at Milan's La Scala, where he gave his farewell appearance as Don Basilio in 1974. Picchi was especially known for his roles in contemporary operas.

Piccinni, (Vito) Niccolò (Marcello Antonio Giacomo), significant Italian composer; b. Bari, Jan. 16, 1728; d. Passy, near Paris, May 7, 1800. His father was a violinist at Bari's Basilica di San Nicola, and his maternal uncle was **Gaetano Latilla**. His precocity manifested itself at an early age; thanks to Muzio Gaeta, archbishop of Bari, he was able at 14 to enter Naples's Cons. di S. Onofrio, where he studied with Leo and Durante. Upon graduation (1754), he commenced his career as a composer for the stage with his comic opera *Le Donne dispettose* (Naples, 1754). His theatrical instinct led him to select librettos rich in dramatic content; his melodic invention was fresh, and his arias were written in a pleasing style eminently suited to the voice; he elaborated the conventional climactic scenes so that dramatic interest was sustained to the end; he varied the tempos and the harmonies in the ensembles, which further contributed to the general effect. His *Zenobia* (Naples, Dec. 18, 1756) was his first attempt at a serious opera. After several other operas for Naples, he received a commission to write an opera for Rome, *Alessandro nelle Indie* (Jan. 21, 1758); it was followed by his comic opera *La Cecchina, ossia La buona figliuola* (Rome, Feb. 6, 1760), which proved a great success at home and abroad. In subsequent years he wrote prolifically for the stage, producing well over 100 operas for the major Italian theaters. Making his home in Naples, he served as 2d maestro di cappella at the Cathedral, was active as an organist in convents, and taught singing. Piccinni's fortunes in Rome declined with the rise of Anfossi, his former pupil and protégé, in 1773. However, he still found success in Naples with a 2d *Alessandro nelle Indie* (Jan. 12, 1774) and *I Viaggiatori* (1775). In 1776 he was called to Paris by the French court, where his presence precipitated the "querelle célèbre" between the "Gluckists" and "Piccinnists." Piccinni's first French opera, *Roland* (Jan. 27, 1778), won considerable success. He then served as director of an Italian troupe in Paris (1778–79). Although he was promised by the Paris Opéra that his *Iphigénie en Tauride* would be produced before Gluck's masterpiece on the same subject, it was not given until Jan. 23, 1781, some 2 years after the Gluck premiere. While it was fairly successful, he gained his only major success with the opera *Didon* (Fontainebleau, Oct. 16, 1783), the same year in which he finally was granted a pension by the French court. In 1784 he was appointed maître de chant at the École Royale de Chant et de Déclamation Lyrique in Paris. In spite of their rivalry, Piccinni held the highest regard for Gluck; indeed, he suggested that an annual memorial concert be given in Gluck's memory, but financial support was not forthcoming. Upon the death of another rival, Sacchini, Piccinni spoke in homage at his funeral. With the coming of the French Revolution, Piccinni lost his post as maître de chant and his pension. In 1791 he returned to Naples; upon his daughter's marriage to a French Jacobite, he was placed under house arrest in 1794; he finally gained freedom in 1798 and returned to Paris, where he obtained a partial restoration of his pension; his appointment as 6th inspector at the Cons. came when he was too ill to pursue an active life. Piccinni demonstrated a remarkable facility in writing both comic and serious operas. His historical importance rests upon his establishment of the Italian operatic style as the model for his French and German successors. His son Luigi (Lodovico) Piccinni (b. 1764; d. Passy, July 31, 1827) was also a composer; he studied with his father and then wrote operas for Paris and several Italian cities; he was Kapellmeister to the Swedish court in Stockholm (1796–1801), then taught singing. Piccinni had another son, who in turn sired an illegitimate son, Louis Alexandre (Luigi Alessandro) Piccinni (b. Paris, Sept. 10, 1779; d. there, April 24, 1850), who also became a composer; studied piano with Haussmann and composition with Le Sueur; he also received some instruction from his grandfather and was active as an accompanist and rehearsal pianist in several Parisian theaters, and also as a conductor; he taught in various French cities, serving as director of the Toulouse music school (1840–44); he wrote numerous works for the theater.

BIBL.: P. Ginguene, *Notice sur la vie et les ouvrages de Nicolas P.* (Paris, 1801); G. le Brisoys Desnoiresterres, *La Musique française au XVIIIe siècle: Gluck et P. 1774–1800* (Paris, 1872); E. Thoinan, *Notes bibliographiques sur la guerre musicale des Gluckistes et P.stes* (Paris, 1878); H. de Curzon, *Les Dernières Années de P. a Paris* (Paris, 1890); J. Popovici, *La buona figliuola von Nicola P.* (Vienna, 1920); A. della Corte, *P.: Settecento italiano* (Bari, 1928); P. La Rotella, *N. P.: Commemorato nel II centenario della nascità* (Bari, 1928); N. Pascazio, *L'Uomo P. e la "Querelle célèbre"* (Bari, 1951).

Pichl, Wenzel (Václav), Bohemian violinist and composer; b. Bechin, Sept. 23, 1741; d. Vienna, Jan. 23, 1805. He studied violin with the local Kantor, Jan Pokorný, and composition with Seger in Prague. He was made 1st violinist of the Vienna court theater (c.1770). He served as music director and Kammerdiener (valet) to Archduke Ferdinando d'Este, the Austrian governor of Lombardy, in Milan (1777–96), and then in Vienna. He wrote some 900 works, including 13 operas.

Pickett, Philip, esteemed English recorder player, conductor, and teacher; b. London, Nov. 17, 1950. He was initiated into the world of early wind instruments by Anthony Baines and David Munrow, and subsequently made that field his specialty. He mastered the recorder and learned to play other early instruments, including the shawm, crumbhorn, and rackett. He appeared as recorder soloist with the leading British ensembles. He also founded and directed the New London Consort, which he conducted throughout Europe. From 1972 he served as prof. of recorder at the Guildhall School of Music in London. In 1997 he became music director of the new Globe Theater in London. As both performer and conductor, Pickett brings erudition and mastery to his vast early music repertoire.

Pick-Mangiagalli, Riccardo, Italian pianist and composer; b. Strakonice, Bohemia, July 10, 1882; d. Milan, July 8, 1949. He was of mixed Italian and Bohemian parentage; studied at the Cons. Giuseppe Verdi in Milan with Appiani (piano) and Ferroni (composition). He began his career as a successful concert pianist, but later turned exclusively to composition. In 1936 he succeeded Pizzetti as director of the Cons. Giuseppe Verdi, and held this post until his death.

WORKS: DRAMATIC: OPERAS: *Basi e Bote* (1919–20; Rome, March 3, 1927); *Casanova a Venezia* (Milan, Jan. 19, 1929; orch. suite as *Scene carnevalesche*, Milan, Feb. 6, 1931); *L'Ospite inatteso* (Milan-Turin-Genoa Radio, Oct. 25, 1931); *Il notturno romantico* (Rome, April 25, 1936). DANCE: *Il salice d'oro*, ballet (1911–12; Milan, 1914); *Sumitra* (1917; Frankfurt am Main, 1922); *Mahit*, ballet fable (Milan, March 20, 1923); *La Berceuse* (San Remo, Feb. 21, 1933); *Variazioni coreografiche* (San Remo, April 13, 1935).

Picka, František, Czech organist, conductor, and composer; b. Strašice, near Hořovice, May 12, 1873; d. Prague, Oct. 18, 1918. Of a musical family, he received a solid education in Prague. He held several posts as a chorus master and opera conductor. His opera, *Malíř Reiner* (The Painter Reiner), was produced in Prague (April 28, 1911).

Picker, Tobias, American composer; b. N.Y., July 18, 1954. He was a student of Wuorinen at the Manhattan School of Music (B.M., 1976) and of Carter at the Juilliard School (M.M., 1978) in New York. From 1985 to 1987 he served as composer-in-residence of the Houston Sym. Orch. In addition to various awards and commissions, he held a Guggenheim followship in 1981. In his music, Picker has generally used serial techniques without abandoning tonality. His works include the operas *Emmeline* (1996) and *Fantastic Mr. Fox* (Los Angeles, Dec. 9, 1998).

Pierné, (Henri-Constant-) Gabriel, noted French composer, conductor, and organist; b. Metz, Aug. 16, 1863; d. Ploujean, near Morlaix, July 17, 1937. He studied at the Paris Cons. (1871–82), where his teachers were Marmontel (piano), Franck (organ), and Massenet (composition); he won 1st prizes for piano (1879), counterpoint and fugue (1881), and organ (1882); he was awarded the Grand Prix de Rome (1882) with the cantata *Edith*; he succeeded Franck as organist at Ste.-Clotilde (1890), where he remained until 1898. He was assistant conductor (1903–10) and conductor (1910–34) of the Concerts Colonne. Pierné was elected a member of the Académie des Beaux-Arts in 1925. His music reveals the hand of an expert craftsman.

WORKS: DRAMATIC: OPERAS: *La Coupe enchantée* (Royan, Aug. 24, 1895; rev. version, Paris, Dec. 26, 1905); *Vendée* (Lyons, March 11, 1897); *La Fille de Tabarin* (Paris, Feb. 20, 1901); *On ne badine pas avec l'amour* (Paris, May 30, 1910); *Sophie Arnould*, lyric comedy, based on episodes from the life of the famous singer (Paris, Feb. 21, 1927). BALLETS AND PANTOMIMES: *Le Collier de saphirs* (1891); *Les Joyeuses Commères de Paris* (1892); *Bouton d'or* (1893); *Le Docteur Blanc* (1893); *Salomé* (1895); *Cydalise et le chèvre-pied* (1919; Paris, Jan. 15, 1923; as an orch. suite, 1926);

Impressions de Music-Hall, "ballet à l'Américaine" (Paris, April 6, 1927); *Giration* (1934); *Fragonard* (1934); *Images*, "divertissement sur un thème pastoral" (Paris, June 19, 1935). ORATORIOS: *La Croisade des enfants* for Chorus of Children and Adults (Paris, Jan. 18, 1905); *Les Enfants à Bethléem* for Soloists, Children's Chorus, and Orch. (Amsterdam, April 13, 1907); *Les Fioretti de St. François d'Assise* (1912).

BIBL.: G. Masson, *G. P.: Musicien lorrain* (Nancy and Metz, 1987).

Pierson (real name, **Pearson**), **Henry Hugo (Hugh),** English composer; b. Oxford, April 12, 1815; d. Leipzig, Jan. 28, 1873. He was educated at Trinity College, Cambridge; in 1839 he went to Germany, where he took courses in music with Rinck and Reissiger, also with Tomaschek in Prague. He entered the circle of Mendelssohn in Leipzig. After a brief term as Reid Prof. of music at the Univ. of Edinburgh (1844–45), he returned to Germany, where he remained for the rest of his life. He married Caroline Leonhardt, who wrote the German librettos for his operas. He changed his name from the original form Pearson to Pierson in order to secure proper pronunciation by Germans; he used the pen name Edgar Mansfeldt for his publ. music. His music reflects the profound influence of Schumann. He won wide acceptance in Germany with his incidental music to part 2 of Goethe's *Faust*, the symphonic poem *Macbeth*, works for men's choruses, and lieder.

WORKS: DRAMATIC: OPERAS: *Der Elfensieg* (Brünn, 1845); *Leila* (Hamburg, Feb. 22, 1848); *Contarini oder Die Verschwörung zu Padua* (1853; Hamburg, April 16, 1872; as *Fenice*, Dessau, April 24, 1883); also incidental music to part 2 of Goethe's *Faust* (Hamburg, March 25, 1854) and to Shakespeare's *As You Like It* (Leipzig, Jan. 17, 1874) and *Romeo and Juliet* (1874). ORATORIOS: *Jerusalem* (Norwich Festival, Sept. 23, 1852); *Hezekiah* (Norwich Festival, 1869; unfinished).

Pijper, Willem, renowned Dutch composer and pedagogue; b. Zeist, Sept. 8, 1894; d. Leidschendam, March 18, 1947. He received a rudimentary education from his father, an amateur violinist; then went to the Toonkunst School of Music in Utrecht, where he studied composition with Johan Wagenaar and piano with Mme. H. J. van Lunteren-Hansen (1911–16). From 1918 to 1923 he was music critic of *Utrecht Dagblad*, and from 1926 to 1929, coed. of the monthly *De Muziek*. He taught theory at the Amsterdam Cons. (from 1918), and was a prof. of composition there from 1925 to 1930; he served as director of the Rotterdam Cons. from 1930 until his death. In his music, Pijper continued the Romantic tradition of Mahler, and also adopted the harmonic procedures of the modern French School. He postulated a "germ-cell theory," in which an opening chord or motif is the source of all succeeding harmonic and melodic development; he also cultivated the scale of alternating whole tones and semitones, regarding it as his own, not realizing that it was used abundantly by Rimsky-Korsakov (in Russian reference works it is termed the Rimsky-Korsakov scale); the "Pijper scale," as it became known in the Netherlands, was also used by Anton von der Horst and others. During the German bombardment of Rotterdam in May 1940, nearly all of Pijper's MSS were destroyed by fire, including the unpubl. reduced scoring of his large 2d Sym. (restored in 1961 by Pijper's student Karel Mengelberg); also destroyed was the unpubl. *Divertimento* for Piano and Strings.

WORKS: DRAMATIC: OPERAS: *Halewijn* (1932–33; Amsterdam, June 13, 1933; rev. 1934); *Merlijn* (1939–45; incomplete; Rotterdam, June 7, 1952). INCIDENTAL MUSIC TO: Sophocles's *Antigone* (1920; rev. 1922 and 1926); Euripides's *Bacchantes* (1924) and *The Cyclops* (1925); Shakespeare's *The Tempest* (1930); Vondel's *Phaëton* (1937).

BIBL.: W. Kloppenburg, *Thematisch-bibliografische Catalogus van de Werken van W. P.* (Assen, 1960).

Pilarczyk, Helga (Käthe), German soprano; b. Schöningen, March 12, 1925. She studied piano and aspired to a concert career, then took voice lessons and sang in operetta. She found her true vocation in opera; she made her debut at Braunschweig in 1951 and was a member of the Hamburg State Opera from 1953 until 1968. She made a specialty of modern music; she sang Schoenberg's dramatic monologue *Erwartung*, and the leading parts in Berg's *Wozzeck* and Lulu as well as in works by Stravinsky, Prokofiev, Dallapiccola, Honegger, Krenek, and others. She appeared as a guest artist at the Bavarian State Opera in Munich, the Vienna State Opera, La Scala in Milan, the Paris Opéra, Covent Garden in London, and the Metropolitan Opera in New York (debut, Feb. 19, 1965, as Marie in *Wozzeck*). She publ. an interesting essay, "Kann man die moderne Oper singen?" (Hamburg, 1964).

Pilotti-Schiavonetti, Elisabetta, Italian soprano; b. place and date of birth unknown; d. Hannover, May 5, 1742. She married the oboist Giovanni Schiavonetti and entered the service of the dowager electress Sophia of Hannover, whom she also served in England. On Nov. 22, 1710, she made her first London appearance with the Queen's Theatre company in Mancini's *Idaspe fedele*. She then created the roles of Armida in *Rinaldo* (Feb. 24, 1711), Amarilli in *Il pastor fido* (Nov. 12, 1712), Medea in *Teseo* (Jan. 21, 1713), and Melissa in *Amadigi di Gaula* (May 25, 1715), all by Handel. By 1715 she was in the service of the princess of Wales. In 1726 she sang in Stuttgart. She settled in Hannover in 1728.

Pimsleur, Solomon, Austrian-American pianist and composer; b. Paris (of Austrian-Jewish parents), Sept. 19, 1900; d. N.Y., April 22, 1962. He was taken to the United States in 1903. He studied piano privately and majored in Eng. literature at Columbia Univ. in New York (M.A., 1923), where he also received instruction in composition from Daniel Gregory Mason. He was a fellowship student of Rubin Goldmark at the Juilliard School of Music in New York (1926), and then studied at the Salzburg Mozarteum. Returning to the United States, he was active as a pianist and lecturer. He also ran his own artists agency and production company. His compositions followed along Romantic lines, and included an unfinished opera *The Diary of Anne Frank*.

Pini-Corsi, Antonio, noted Italian baritone; b. Zara, Dalmatia, June 1858; d. Milan, April 22, 1918. He made his debut as Dandini in *La Cenerentola* in Cremona (1878), then sang throughout Italy. Verdi chose him to create the role of Ford in *Falstaff* at La Scala in Milan in 1893. He also sang at Covent Garden in London (1894–96, 1902–03). On Dec. 27, 1899, he made his Metropolitan Opera debut in New York as Masetto, remaining on its roster until 1901; he returned for the 1909–14 seasons. He was one of the great buffo singers of his day, being famous for his portrayals of Dr. Bartolo, Leporello, Don Pasquale, and others.

Pinkham, Daniel (Rogers, Jr.), esteemed American composer, organist, choral conductor, and teacher; b. Lynn, Mass., June 5, 1923. He received training in organ and harmony from Carl Pfatteicher at the Phillips Academy in Andover, Mass., before pursuing his studies with Merritt, Piston, Davison, and Copland at Harvard Univ. (A.B., 1943; M.A., 1944). He also received instruction in harpsichord from Aldrich and Landowska, and in organ from Biggs. He likewise attended the composition courses given by Honegger and Barber at the Berkshire Music Center in Tanglewood, and then studied with Boulanger. Pinkham taught at Simmons College in Boston, Boston Univ., and Dartington Hall in Devon, England. In 1957–58 he was a visiting lecturer at Harvard Univ. In 1958 he became music director of the King's Chapel in Boston. He also taught at the New England Cons. of Music in Boston from 1959. In 1950 he held a Fulbright fellowship and in 1962 received a Ford Foundation fellowship. He was awarded honorary Mus.D. degrees from Westminster Choir College in Princeton, N.J. (1979), the New England Cons. of Music (1993), and Ithaca College (1994). In 1990 he was named composer of the year by the American Guild of Organists. In his prolific output as a composer, Pinkham has demonstrated a fine capacity for producing versatile scores. The formal design of his music is compact and contrapuntally cohesive. The rhythmic element is often propulsive while he occasionally introduces modernistic devices without disrupting the tonal fabric of his scores. His works include theater works, chamber operas, and some 20 documentary film scores.

BIBL.: K. Deboer and J. Ahouse, *D. P.: A Bio-Bibliography* (Westport, Conn., 1988).

Pinnock, Trevor (David), outstanding English harpsichordist and conductor; b. Canterbury, Dec. 16, 1946. He became a chorister at Canterbury Cathedral when he was 7; after receiving instruction in piano and organ, he served as a church organist; at 19 he entered the Royal College of Music in London, where he took courses in organ and later harpsichord. While still a student, he organized the Gailliard Harpsichord Trio (1966); he also toured Europe with the Academy of St. Martin-in-the Fields. In 1973 he founded the English Concert, an ensemble devoted to the performance of early music on original instruments; through numerous tours and recordings, his ensemble acquired an international reputation; toured North America with it for the first time in 1983. He also pursued a distinguished career as a harpsichord virtuoso. On Sept. 27, 1988, he made his Metropolitan Opera debut in New York conducting *Giulio Cesare*. In 1989 he founded the Classical Band of N.Y., which he led in performances of the Classical repertoire from Haydn to Mendelssohn on period instruments until resigning unexpectedly in 1990. In 1991 he was named artistic director and principal conductor of the National Arts Centre Orch. in Ottawa. In 1995 he conducted it on a critically acclaimed tour of Europe. In 1996 he stepped down from his post but served as its artistic advisor during the 1996–97 season. In 1992 he was made a Commander of the Order of the British Empire.

Piňos, Alois Simandl, Czech composer and teacher; b. Vyškov, Oct. 2, 1925. He studied forestry at the Univ. of Brno (graduating in 1953), music with Petrželka at the Brno Cons. (1948–49) and at the Janáček Academy of Music in Brno with Kvapil and Schaeffer (1949–53); he attended the summer courses of new music at Darmstadt (1965) and an electronic music seminar in Munich (1966). In 1953 he joined the faculty of the Janáček Academy of Music in Brno. In 1967 he founded in Brno a modern music group, with which he produced a number of works by the local avant-garde, some composed collectively.

WORKS: DRAMATIC: OPERAS: *The Criers*, chamber opera (1970); *The Cage Affair, or the Avant-Garde Chronicles Flung Open* (Brno, Oct. 6, 1995; in collaboration with I. Medek and M. Štědron); *Annals of the Predecessors of the Avant-Garde, or the Meeting of the Slavonic Giants* (Brno, Oct. 1997; in collaboration with I. Medek and M. Štědron). AUDIOVISUAL: *The Lattice* for Piano and Film (1970); *The Genesis* for Chamber Orch. and Film (1970); *Static Music* for Tape and Slides (1970).

Pinsuti, Ciro, Italian singing teacher and composer; b. Sinalunga, near Florence, May 9, 1829; d. Florence, March 10, 1888. His talent developed so rapidly that at 11 he was elected an honorary member of the Accademia Filarmonica of Rome. Taken to England soon after by Henry Drummond, he studied piano under C. Potter and violin under Blagrove; he returned to Bologna in 1845, and studied at the Liceo, also privately with Rossini, soon becoming assistant teacher of a piano class. In 1848 he returned to England, where he was appointed a prof. of singing at London's Royal Academy of Music in 1856. He divided his time between London and Italy. He brought out an opera, *Il Mercante di Venezia*, at Bologna (Nov. 9, 1873), another, *Mattia Corvino*, at Milan (1877), and a 3d, *Margherita*, at Venice (1882). In 1871 he represented Italy at the opening of the London Exhibition, for which he composed the hymn *O people of this favoured land*. As a recipient of the order of the Italian Crown, he was styled "Cavaliere" Pinsuti. Besides his operas, he wrote some 250 songs to Eng. and Italian texts.

Pinto, Alfredo, Italian-Argentine pianist, conductor, and composer; b. Mantua, Oct. 22, 1891; d. Buenos Aires, May 26, 1968. He studied piano with Longo and composition with De Nardis in Naples. He then went to Buenos Aires, where he became active as a pianist and conductor. He wrote the operas *La última esposa, o Sheherazade* and *Gualicho* (Buenos Aires, 1940).

Pinza, Ezio (baptized **Fortunio**), celebrated Italian bass; b. Rome, May 18, 1892; d. Stamford, Conn., May 9, 1957. The family moved to Ravenna when he was an infant; he studied engineering. He began to study voice at the age of 18 with Ruzza and Vizzani at the Bologna Cons. He made his operatic debut as Oroveso in *Norma* in Soncino (1914); after military service in World War I, he resumed his career, making his first important appearance as Comte Des Grieux in Rome (1920), then sang at La Scala in Milan (1922–24); he was selected by Toscanini for the leading part in the premiere of Boito's *Nerone* (May 1, 1924). He made his American debut at the Metropolitan Opera in New York as Pontifex Maximus in Spontini's *La Vestale* (Nov. 1, 1926), and remained on its staff until 1947; he also appeared in San Francisco, Chicago, and other cities in the United States; he also sang in Europe and in South America. His most celebrated roles were Méphistophélès in Gounod's *Faust*, Don Giovanni, and Boris Godunov. In 1949 he appeared as a musical comedy star in *South Pacific*, and immediately became successful in this new career; also appeared in films.

BIBL.: R. Magidoff, ed., *E. P.: An Autobiography* (N.Y., 1958).

Pipkov, Lubomir, noted Bulgarian composer, son of **Panayot Pipkov**; b. Lovec, Sept. 19, 1904; d. Sofia, May 9, 1974. He studied piano and composition with his father; entered the Sofia Music School (1919); he completed his training with Boulanger and Dukas (composition) and Lefebure (piano) at the Paris École Normale de Musique (1926–32). Returning to Bulgaria, he occupied several administrative posts, including the directorship of the National Theater in Sofia (1944–47). His style of composition is determined by the inherent asymmetry of Bulgarian folk songs; there is a similarity in his compositions with those of Bartók, resulting from common sources in Balkan and Macedonian music; his harmonic investiture is often polytonal or polymodal. His works included the operas *Yaninite devet bratya* (The 9 Brothers of Yanina; 1929–37; Sofia, Sept. 19, 1937), *Momchil* (1939–44; Sofia, April 24, 1948), and *Antigone 43* (1961–62; Ruse, Dec. 23, 1963); also *Oratorio for Our Time* (Plovdiv, Dec. 18, 1959).

BIBL.: K. Iliev, *L. P.* (Sofia, 1958); L. Koen, *L. P.* (Sofia, 1968).

Pipkov, Panayot, Bulgarian composer, father of **Lubomir Pipkov**; b. Plovdiv, Dec. 2, 1871; d. Sofia, Aug. 25, 1942. He studied violin before attending the Milan Cons. (1893–95). After conducting in Rusa, he settled in Sofia in 1905. In addition to his musical career, he also pursued acting and literary activities. He composed 2 children's operettas.

Pirogov, Alexander (Stepanovich), noted Russian bass; b. Novoselki, July 4, 1899; d. Bear's Head Island, June 26, 1964. He studied voice at the Moscow Phil. Inst., and simultaneously attended classes in history and philology at the Univ. of Moscow. In 1924 he joined the Bolshoi Theater in Moscow, remaining on its roster until 1954. He specialized in the Russian operatic repertoire; his performance of the role of Boris Godunov received a prize in 1949; also notable were his interpretations of Méphistophélès in *Faust* and Don Basilio in *Il Barbiere di Siviglia*. His 2 brothers, Grigori (1885–1931) and Mikhail (1887–1933), were also notable basses.

Pironkoff, Simeon, Bulgarian composer; b. Lom, June 18, 1927. He took courses in violin, conducting (with A. Dimitrov), and composition (with P. Khadzhiev) at the Bulgarian State Cons. in Sofia (graduated, 1952). He was active as a composer and conductor at Sofia's Youth Theater (1951–61) and served as secretary of the Bulgarian Composer's Union (1966–69). He received the Gottfried von Herder Prize of the Univ. of Vienna (1985). His music is rhythmically animated, harmonically tense, melodically modal, and instrumentally coloristic. His works include the operas *A Good Woman from Szechwan* (1965), *The Motley Bird* (1979), and *Ah, You, My Dream . . .* (1985), and the oratorio *The Life and the Sufferings of the Sinful Sofronii* for Narrator, Tenor, Chorus, and Orch. (1976); also film and theater music.

Pirrotta, Nino (Antonino), eminent Italian musicologist; b. Palermo, June 13, 1908; d. there, Jan. 15, 1998. He studied at the

Cons. Vincenzo Bellini in Palermo, then received a diploma in organ and organ composition at the Florence Cons. (1930) and a liberal arts degree at the Univ. of Florence (1931). He was a lecturer in music history and a librarian at the Palermo Cons. (1936–48); he was chief librarian at the Santa Cecilia Cons. in Rome (1948–56) and was also a visiting prof. at Princeton Univ. (1954–55), the Univ. of Calif., Los Angeles (summer 1955), and Columbia Univ. (1955). He then was a prof. at Harvard Univ. (1956–72), where he also was chairman of the music dept. (1965–68); subsequently he was prof. of music history at the Univ. of Rome (1972–83). He was made a member of the American Academy of Arts and Sciences (1967) and an honorary member of the American Musicological Soc. (1980). An erudite scholar of wide interests, Pirrotta greatly distinguished himself in the study of Renaissance polyphony and Baroque opera. In addition to his important books, he ed. *The Music of Fourteenth-century Italy* in the Corpus Mensurabilis Musicae series (1954–64), and contributed valuable articles to music journals and other publications.

WRITINGS: With E. Li Gotti, *Il Sacchetti e la tecnica musicale del trecento italiano* (Florence, 1935); *Il codice estense lat.568 e la musica francese in Italia al principio del '400* (Palermo, 1946); *Li due Orfei: Da Poliziano a Monteverdi* (Turin, 1969; 2d ed., 1975; Eng. tr., 1981); *Music and Culture in Italy from the Middle Ages to the Baroque: A Collection of Essays* (Cambridge, Mass., and London, 1984); *Musica tra Medioevo e Rinascimento* (Turin, 1984); *Scelte poetiche di musicisti: Teatro, poesia e musica da Willaert a Malipiero* (Venice, 1987); *Don Giovanni's Progress: A Rake Goes to the Opera* (N.Y., 1994).

BIBL.: F. Della Seta and F. Piperno, eds., *In Cantu et in sermone: For N. P. on His 80th Birthday* (Florence, 1989).

Pisari, Pasquale, esteemed Italian bass and composer; b. Rome, 1725; d. there, March 27, 1778. He was a pupil of Giovanni Biordi. In 1752 he was taken into the papal chapel, being a fine bass singer. He wrote most of his sacred works for it, and the MSS are preserved in the archives of the papal chapel. They include several masses, motets, 2 Te Deums for 8 Voices, and one Te Deum for 4 Voices (his most remarkable work); also a Dixit in 16 parts, for 4 Choirs, and a series of motets for the entire year, written for the Lisbon Court. Padre Martini called Pisari the "Palestrina of the 18th century."

Pisaroni, Benedetta (Rosmunda), Italian soprano, later contralto; b. Piacenza, May 16, 1793; d. there, Aug. 6, 1872. After training in Milan, she made her operatic debut in Mayr's *La rosa biana e la rosa rossa* in Bergamo in Aug. 1813. Upon the advice of Rossini, she turned to contralto roles and sang in Padua (1814), Bologna (1815), and Venice (1816). After singing in the premiere of Meyerbeer's *Romilda e Costanza* (Padua, July 19, 1817), she was called to Naples to create the roles of Zomira in *Riccardo e Zoraide* (Dec. 13, 1818), Andromache in *Ermione* (March 27, 1819), and Malcolm in *La donna del lago* (Sept. 24, 1819), all by Rossini. She appeared as Malcolm in Rome in 1823 and at Milan's La Scala in 1824, and then made her Paris debut as Arsace at the Théâtre-Italien in 1827. In 1829 she sang at the King's Theatre in London. Following further engagements at La Scala in 1831, she retired from the operatic stage.

Pischek, Johann Baptist (Jan Křtitel Pišek), Bohemian tenor; b. Mšeno, Oct. 13, 1814; d. Sigmaringen, Feb. 16, 1873. He was trained in the law before taking up music. In 1835 he made his operatic debut in Prague. From 1840 to 1848 he toured throughout Germany, appearing in both opera and concert. He served as court singer to the King of Württemberg in Stuttgart from 1844 to 1863. In 1845 he made his London debut, and sang with the Phil. Society there in 1845, 1846–47, 1849, and 1853. In 1849 he gave a command performance before Queen Victoria and Prince Albert.

Pisk, Paul A(madeus), Austrian-born American composer, pedagogue, and musicologist; b. Vienna, May 16, 1893; d. Los Angeles, Jan. 12, 1990. He studied piano with J. Epstein, composition with Schreker and Schoenberg, and orchestration with Hellmesberger in Vienna; he studied musicology with Adler at the Univ. of Vienna (Ph.D., 1916, with the diss. *Das Parodieverfahren in den Messen des Jacobus Gallus*) and later studied at the Vienna Cons. (graduated, 1919). From 1922 to 1934 he taught at the Volkshochschule Volksheim in Vienna; in 1925–26 he was instructor in theory at the New Vienna Cons.; from 1931 to 1933 he lectured at the Austro-American Cons. in Mondsee, near Salzburg. He also wrote music criticism for the Socialist newspaper *Wiener Arbeiterzeitung*; with Paul Stefan, he founded the progressive music journal *Musikblätter des Anbruch*. He was closely associated with Schoenberg, Berg, and Webern, and espoused the tenets of the New Vienna School, adopting in many of his own works the methods of 12-tone composition. As the dark cloud of ignorance and barbarity fell on Germany and approached Austria, Pisk left Vienna and emigrated to the United States (1936); he became a naturalized American citizen (1941). He occupied with great honor teaching posts at the Univ. of Redlands, Calif. (1937–51), the Univ. of Texas in Austin (1951–63), and Washington Univ. in St. Louis (1963–72); he also gave courses at summer sessions at the Univ. of Calif., Los Angeles (1966), the Univ. of Cincinnati (1969), and Dartmouth College (1972). In 1973 he settled in Los Angeles. His 90th birthday was celebrated by his many disciples and admirers in 1983. He continued to compose prolifically, accumulating an impressive catalogue of works, mostly chamber music, but also *Schattenseite*, monodrama (1931), and *American Suite*, ballet (Redlands, Calif., Feb. 19, 1948). He wrote (with H. Ulrich) *History of Music and Musical Style* (N.Y., 1963); ed. masses by Jacobus Gallus for Denkmäler der Tonkunst in Österreich. A Festschrift, *Paul A. Pisk: Essays in His Honor*, ed. by J. Glowacki, was publ. in 1966.

Pistocchi, Francesco Antonio Mamiliano, noted Italian singer, teacher, and composer, known as **Il Pistocchino**; b. Palermo, 1659; d. Bologna, May 13, 1726. A precocious child, he sang in public at age 3 and publ. his first work, *Capricci puerilli*, when he was 8. He made appearances as a singer in Bologna's cappella musicale at S. Petronio (from 1670), where he was permanently engaged as a soprano (1674–75), then toured as a contralto with great success in his homeland and in Germany. He was in the service of the Parma court (1686–95), then was Kapellmeister to the Margrave of Brandenburg in Ansbach (1696–99). After a sojourn in Vienna (1699–1700), he returned to Bologna, and once more sang in the cappella musicale at S. Petronio (1701–08); he was made virtuoso di camera e di cappella to Prince Ferdinando of Tuscany (1702). He was active as a singing teacher, his notable pupils being Antonio Bernacchi, Annibale Pio Fabri, and G. B. Martini. Having been elected to membership in the Accademia Filarmonica (1687), he served as its principe (1708, 1710); he took Holy Orders (1709); became honorary chaplain to the Elector Palatine Johann Wilhelm (1714); and was made a member of the Congregation of the Oratory in Forli (1715).

WORKS: DRAMATIC: OPERAS: *Il Leandro* (Venice, May 15, 1679; 2d version, Venice, Jan. 1682); *Il Narciso* (Ansbach, March 1697); *Le pazzie d'amore e dell'interesse* (Ansbach, June 16, 1699); *Le risa di Democrito* (Vienna, Feb. 17, 1700); *I Rivali generosi* (Reggio Emilia, April 1710; in collaboration with C. Monari and G. Cappelli). ORATORIOS: *Sant'Adriano* (Modena, 1692); *Maria vergine addolorata* (Ansbach, 1698); *Il sacrificio di Gefte* (Bologna, 1720); *I Pastori al Presepe* (Bologna, Dec. 25, 1721); *Davide* (Bologna, March 19, 1721).

Pistor, Gotthelf, German tenor; b. Berlin, Oct. 17, 1887; d. Cologne, April 4, 1947. He began his career as an actor in Berlin. Following vocal training from Luria, he made his operatic debut in Nuremberg in 1923. He had engagements in Würzburg (1924–25), Darmstadt (1925–27), and Magdeburg (1928–29) before serving as a principal member of the Cologne Opera (from 1929). He also made guest appearances at the Bayreuth Festival (1925; 1927–31), at the Zoppot Festivals (1930–38), and in San Francisco (1931). In his last years, he taught voice in Cologne. Pistor was esteemed for such Wagnerian roles as Tristan, Parsifal, Siegfried, and Siegmund.

Pitt, Percy, English conductor and composer; b. London, Jan. 4, 1870; d. there, Nov. 23, 1932. He studied with Jadassohn and Reinecke at the Leipzig Cons. and with Rheinberger at the Akademie der Tonkunst in Munich. Returning to England in 1893, he pursued his career in London; he was musical advisor (1902–07) and musical director (1907–24) of the Grand Opera Syndicate at Covent Garden; he was the first English conductor to appear at Covent Garden (1907), returning there in 1909–10 and 1919–20; he was artistic director of the British National Opera Co. (1922–24) and musical advisor to the BBC (1922–24), serving as the latter's musical director (1924–30). He wrote stage music.

BIBL.: J. Chamier, *P. P. of Covent Garden and the BBC* (London, 1938).

Pittaluga, Gustavo, Spanish composer; b. Madrid, Feb. 8, 1906. He studied law at the Univ. of Madrid and composition with Oscar Esplá. He was a member of the Grupo de los 8 in Madrid and of the Paris group of modern musicians, Triton (1935); from 1936 to 1939 he was a member of the staff of the Spanish Embassy in Washington, D.C. (for the Loyalist government), then settled in the United States, where he was active with the film library at the Museum of Modern Art in New York (1941–43). Among his compositions were *La Romería de los Cornudos*, ballet (1933), and *El Loro*, zarzuela (1933).

Pittman-Jennings, David, American baritone; b. Duncan, Okla., Dec. 13, 1946. He studied voice with Elisabeth Parham and took his B.M. cum laude in oboe (1969) at the Univ. of Oklahoma, and then his master's degree in vocal performance (1974) at California State Univ. in Northridge. He continued vocal training with Parham in Los Angeles, San Francisco, and Paris until 1998. In 1977 he made his operatic debut as Mozart's Count at the Graz Opera, where he sang until 1979. From 1979 to 1982 he sang at the Bremen Opera. In 1982 he appeared as Fernando at the Paris Opéra. Following his debut as a soloist in Mahler's *Lieder eines fahrenden Gesellen* in Bordeaux in 1983, he made his recital debut in Nice in 1984. From 1984 to 1986 he sang at the Netherlands Opera in Amsterdam. In 1987 he was engaged as Wozzeck at the Opéra du Rhin in Strasbourg, a role he sang in Parma in 1989. In the latter year, he also portrayed Schoenberg's Moses in Lyons. After singing Germont at the Frankfurt am Main Opera in 1991, he made his first appearance at the Vienna State Opera in 1992 as Mandryka, a role he reprised at the Semper Opera in Dresden in 1994. In the latter year, he also was engaged as Pizzaro at the Berlin State Opera, as Don Alfonso at the Hamburg State Opera, and as Renato at the Bavarian State Opera in Munich. In 1995 he again portrayed Wozzeck at the Teatro Colón in Buenos Aires and Schoenberg's Moses at the Netherlands Opera, and then repeated the latter role at the Salzburg Festival in 1996. In 1997 he appeared as Wozzeck at the Spoleto Festival U.S.A. in Charleston, S.C., and as Mandryka at the Santa Fe Opera. He sang Jochanaan at the Berlin State Opera and Scarpia in Verona in 1998, and then Rigoletto at the Leipzig Opera and Frank in *Die tote stadt* at the Teatro Colón in 1999. As a concert artist, he sang with many orchs. in Europe in an expansive repertoire ranging from Bach, Haydn, Beethoven, and Berlioz to Hindemith, Dallapiccola, Walton, and Zender.

Pitzinger, Gertrude, Bohemian contralto; b. Mährisch-Schönberg, Aug. 15, 1904. She studied music with Joseph Marx at the Vienna Academy of Music, and voice with various teachers. After several concert tours in central Europe, she went to the United States and gave a N.Y. recital on Jan. 17, 1938, with excellent success. She specialized in German lieder; her repertoire included some 400 songs. She taught singing at the Hochschule für Musik in Frankfurt am Main (1960–73).

Pixis, Johann Peter, German pianist, teacher, and composer; b. Mannheim, Feb. 10, 1788; d. Baden-Baden, Dec. 22, 1874. Of a musical family (his father and his brother were musicians), he received his primary education at home. After touring with his brother (1796), he returned to Mannheim to study composition; he continued his studies with Albrechtsberger in Vienna (1806). He went to Paris in 1823, where he established himself as a teacher. In 1840 he settled in Baden-Baden as a teacher. Among his works were the operas *Almazinde, oder Die Höhle Sesam* (Vienna, April 11, 1820) and *Bibiana, oder Die Kapelle im Walde* (Aachen, Oct. 8, 1829).

BIBL.: L. Schiwietz, *J. P. P.* (Frankfurt am Main and N.Y., 1994).

Pizzetti, Ildebrando, eminent Italian composer and teacher; b. Parma, Sept. 20, 1880; d. Rome, Feb. 13, 1968. He studied piano with his father, Odvardo Pizzetti, in Parma and composition with Tebaldini at the Parma Cons., graduating in 1901. He was on the faculty of the Parma Cons. (1907–08); then of the Florence Cons. (1908–24), where he became director in 1917; from 1924 to 1936 he was director of the Milan Cons.; he then taught at the Accademia di Santa Cecilia in Rome (1936–58); from 1947 to 1952 he was also its president. In 1914 he founded (with G. Bastianelli) in Florence a modernistic periodical, pointedly named *Dissonanza*, to promote the cause of new music. In 1930 he made a trip to the United States to attend the performance of his *Rondo veneziano*, conducted by Toscanini with the N.Y. Phil.; in 1931 Pizzetti conducted his opera *Fra Gherardo* at the Teatro Colón in Buenos Aires. Pizzetti's music represents the Romantic trend in 20th century Italy; in his many works for the theater, he created the modern counterpart of medieval mystery plays; the mystical element is very strong in his own texts for his operas. He employed astringent chromatic harmony, but the mainstream of his melody flows along pure diatonic lines.

WORKS: DRAMATIC: OPERAS: *Fedra* (1909–12; Milan, March 20, 1915); *Debora e Jaele* (1915–21; Milan, Dec. 16, 1922); *Lo straniero* (1922–25; Rome, April 29, 1930); *Fra Gherardo* (1925–27; Milan, May 16, 1928); *Orséolo* (1931–35; Florence, May 4, 1935); *L'Oro* (1938–42; Milan, Jan. 2, 1947); *Vanna Lupa* (1947–49; Florence, May 4, 1949); *Ifigenia* (RAI, Oct. 3, 1950; 1st stage perf., Florence, May 9, 1951); *Cagliostro* (RAI, Nov. 5, 1952; 1st stage perf., Milan, Jan. 24, 1953); *La figlia di Iorio* (Naples, Dec. 4, 1954); *Assassinio nella cattedrale*, after T. S. Eliot (1957; Milan, March 1, 1958); *Il calzare d'argento* (Milan, March 23, 1961); *Clitennestra* (1961–64; Milan, March 1, 1965). INCIDENTAL MUSIC TO: G. d'Annunzio's *La nave* (1905–07; Rome, March 1908) and *La Pisanella* (Paris, June 11, 1913); F. Belcare's *La sacra rappresentazione di Abram e d'Isaac* (1915–17; Florence, June 1917; expanded into an opera, 1925; Turin, March 11, 1926); Aeschylus' *Agamemnon* (Syracuse, April 28, 1930); Sophocles' *Le trachiniae* (1932; Syracuse, April 26, 1933); Sophocles' *Edipo a Colono* (Syracuse, April 24, 1936); *La festa delle Panatenee* (1935; Paestum, June 1936); Shakespeare's *As You Like It* (Florence, May 1938).

WRITINGS: *La musica dei Greci* (Rome, 1914); *Musicisti contemporanei* (Milan, 1914); *Intermezzi critici* (Florence, 1921); *Paganini* (Turin, 1940); *Musica e dramma* (Rome, 1945); *La musica italiana dell' 800* (Turin, 1947).

BIBL.: R. Fondi, *I. P. e il dramma musicale italiano d'oggi* (Rome, 1919); G. Tebaldini, *I. P. nelle memorie* (Parma, 1931); G. Gatti, *I. P.* (Turin, 1934; 2d ed., 1955; Eng. tr., 1951); G. Gavazzeni, *Tre studi su P.* (Como, 1937); V. Bucchi, L. Dallapiccola et al., *Firenze a I. P.* (Florence, 1947); G. Gavazzeni, *Altri studi pizzettiani* (Bergamo, 1956); M. la Morgia, ed., *La citta d'annunziana a I. P.: Saggi e note* (Pescara, 1958); B. Pizzetti, ed., *I. P.: Cronologia e bibliografia* (Parma, 1980).

Pizzi, Pier Luigi, distinguished Italian opera producer and designer; b. Milan, June 15, 1930. He was a student of architecture at the Milan Polytechnic. In 1952 he began his career as an opera designer with a production of *Don Giovanni* in Genoa. In 1959 he staged Handel's *Orlando* in Florence and acquired a notable reputation as a producer of Baroque stage works. He produced Verdi's *I due Foscari* (1979) and Gluck's *Alceste* (1989) and *Armide* (1996) at Milan's La Scala, Rameau's *Hippolyte et Aricie* in Aix-en-Provence (1983), Bellini's *Capuleti e i Montecchi* at London's Covent Garden (1984), and *Don Carlos* in Vienna (1989). In 1990 he oversaw the production of Berlioz's *Les Troyens* at the gala opening of the Opéra de la Bastille in Paris. After staging *Otello* in Chicago in 1992, he produced the first modern staging of Traetta's *Buova d'Antona* in Venice in 1993. In 1997 he produced Verdi's *Macbeth* in Verona. Pizzi's productions and designs reveal him as a master of stagecraft.

Pizzini, Carlo Alberto, Italian composer; b. Rome, March 22, 1905; d. there, Sept. 9, 1981. He studied with Respighi at the Accademia di Santa Cecilia in Rome, graduating in 1929; later he was an administrator there and with the RAI. His works include *Dardanio*, opera (Rome, 1928); also theater, film, and radio music.

Plaichinger, Thila, Austrian soprano; b. Vienna, March 13, 1868; d. there, March 17, 1939. She studied with Gänsbacher at the Vienna Cons. and with Dustmann and Mampe-Babbnigg. In 1893 she made her operatic debut in Hamburg. She was a principal member of the Strasbourg Opera (1894–1901) and of the Berlin Royal Opera (1901–14). In 1904 and 1910 she was a guest artist at London's Covent Garden, and also appeared in Munich, Dresden, and Vienna. Among her finest roles were Isolde, Brünnhilde, Ortrud, Venus, and Elektra.

Plançon, Pol (-Henri), famous French bass; b. Fumay, June 12, 1851; d. Paris, Aug. 11, 1914. He was destined by his parents for a commercial career in Paris, but showed a natural vocal ability, and began to study singing with Sbriglia and Duprez. He made his operatic debut as St.-Bris in *Les Huguenots* in Lyons (1877), then appeared for the first time in Paris as Colonna in Duprat's *Petrarque* at the Théâtre de la Gaîté (Feb. 11, 1880). After a season in Monte Carlo, he made a highly successful appearance at the Paris Opéra as Méphistophélès in Gounod's *Faust* (June 23, 1883); he sang that role more than 100 times during his 10 seasons at the Opéra, and was regarded as unrivaled in his dramatic delivery and vocal power. On June 3, 1891, he sang Méphistophélès for his debut at London's Covent Garden, singing there every subsequent season until 1904. His American debut took place at the Metropolitan Opera in New York on Nov. 29, 1893, as Jupiter in Gounod's *Philemon et Baucis*. He then resigned from the Paris Opéra and remained a member of the Metropolitan Opera until his retirement in 1908. He had an imposing physique, mobile features, and an innate acting ability. His repertoire consisted of about 50 roles in French, Italian, German, and Eng. In some operas he sang more than one part, as in *Roméo et Juliette* (Capulet and Friar), *Aida* (Ramfis and the King), *Les Huguenots* (St.-Bris and Marcel), etc. Of Wagnerian roles, he sang the Landgrave, King Heinrich, and Pogner.

Planquette, (Jean-) Robert, French composer; b. Paris, July 31, 1848; d. there, Jan. 28, 1903. He studied at the Paris Cons. with Duprato. He wrote chansonnettes and "saynètes" for cafés-concerts in Paris, then composed a one-act operetta, *Paille d'avoine* (Paris, March 12, 1874), and others. He achieved his first great success with the production of *Les Cloches de Corneville*, a comic opera in 3 acts, at the Folies-Dramatiques (Paris, April 19, 1877); it was performed for the 1,000th time there in 1886, and became one of the most popular works of its genre; in Eng., it was given as *The Chimes of Normandy* (N.Y., Oct. 22, 1877; London, Feb. 23, 1878). Other operettas were *Le Chevalier Gaston* (Monte Carlo, Feb. 8, 1879), *Rip Van Winkle* (London, Oct. 14, 1882; very successful), *Nell Gwynne* (London, Feb. 7, 1884), *Surcouf* (Paris, Oct. 6, 1887; in Eng. as *Paul Jones*, London, Jan. 12, 1889), *La Cocarde tricolore* (Paris, Feb. 12, 1892), *Le Talisman* (Paris, Jan. 20, 1893), *Panurge* (Paris, Nov. 22, 1895), and *Mam'zelle Quat'Sous* (Paris, Nov. 5, 1897). A posthumous operetta, *Le Paradis de Mahomet* (orchestrated by Louis Ganne), was produced at the Variétés in Paris on May 15, 1906.

Plantade, Charles-Henri, French composer; b. Pontoise, Oct. 14, 1764; d. Paris, Dec. 18, 1839. As a child, he studied singing and the cello in the Royal School for the "pages de musique," and afterward took lessons with Honoré Langlé (theory), Hüllmandel (piano), and Petrini (harp). In 1797 he became a singing teacher at the Campan Inst. at St.-Denis, where Hortense de Beauharnais, the future queen of the Netherlands, was his pupil. He subsequently was in the service of Queen Hortense as her representative in Paris; he was a prof. at the Paris Cons. from 1799 to 1807, and again in 1815–16 and from 1818 to 1828. From 1812 to 1815 he also held the post of singing master and stage director at the Paris Opéra. He received the ribbon of the Légion d'honneur from Louis XVIII (1814); from 1816 he was music master of the Royal Chapel. Losing his various positions after the revolution of 1830, he retired to Batignolles. He wrote several operas, of which *Le Mari de circonstances* (Paris, March 18, 1813) was the most successful; other operas for Paris included *Les 2 Soeurs* (May 22, 1792), *Les Souliers mordores* (May 18, 1793), *Au plus brave la plus belle* (Oct. 5, 1794), *Palma, ou Le Voyage en Grèce* (Aug. 22, 1797), *Romagnesi* (Sept. 3, 1799), *Le Roman* (Nov. 12, 1800), *Zoé, ou La Pauvre Petite* (July 3, 1800), *Lisez Plutarque* (spring 1800), and *Bayard à la ferté, ou Le Siège de Mezières* (Oct. 13, 1811). His son, Charles-François Plantade (b. Paris, April 14, 1787; d. there, May 26, 1870), was also a composer; he studied at the Paris Cons. and worked in the Ministry of Fine Arts; he wrote romances, chansons, and chansonettes.

Plantinga, Leon (Brooks), American musicologist; b. Ann Arbor, Mich., March 25, 1935. He studied at Calvin College (B.A., 1957), Michigan State Univ. (M.Mus., 1959), and Yale Univ. (Ph.D., 1964, with the diss. *The Musical Criticism of Robert Schumann in the "Neue Zeitschrift für Musik"*). He taught there from 1963, being made a prof. (1974), acting chairman (1978–79), and chairman (1979–86) of its music dept. In 1985 he received the ASCAP-Deems Taylor Award for his study *Romantic Music: A History of Musical Style in Nineteenth-Century Europe*.

WRITINGS: *Schumann as Critic* (New Haven, Conn., and London, 1967); *Muzio Clementi: His Life and Music* (London, 1977); *Romantic Music: A History of Musical Style in Nineteenth-Century Europe* (N.Y. and London, 1984); *Anthology of Romantic Music* (N.Y. and London, 1984).

Plaschke, Friedrich (real name, **Bedřich Plaške**), Czech bass-baritone; b. Jaroměr, Jan. 7, 1875; d. Prague, Nov. 20, 1951. He studied with Leontine von Döttcher and Ottilie Sklenář-Mala in Prague, and then with Karl Scheidemantel in Dresden. He made his operatic debut with the Dresden Court (later State) Opera as the Herald in *Lohengrin* in 1900; he was on its roster until 1939; during his tenure there, he created the following roles in operas by Richard Strauss: Pöschel in *Feuersnot*, the 1st Nazarene in *Salome*, Da-Ud in *Die ägyptische Helena*, Count Waldner in *Arabella*, and Sir Morosus in *Die schweigsame Frau*. He made many guest appearances at Vienna and Munich; also sang at Bayreuth, at Covent Garden in London, and in the United States with the German Opera Co. in 1923–24.

Plasson, Michel, French conductor; b. Paris, Oct. 2, 1933. He received training in piano from Lazare-Lévy, and then studied percussion at the Paris Cons., where he took the premier prix. In 1962 he won 1st prize in the Besançon conducting competiton, and then studied conducting in the United States with Leinsdorf, Monteux, and Stokowski. From 1966 to 1968 he was music director of the Théâtre de Metz. In 1968 he became conductor of the Théâtre du Capitole in Toulouse, where he served as its music and general director from 1973 to 1982. In 1974 he became music director of the Orchestre du Capitole in Toulouse, which became the Orchestre National du Capitole in 1980. He took the orch. on various tours of Europe and North America. As a guest conductor, he appeared with many of the major orchs. and opera houses of the world. In 1987 he became principal guest conductor of the Tonhalle Orch. in Zürich. In 1994 he became music director of the Dresden Phil.

Platania, Pietro, Italian composer; b. Catania, April 5, 1828; d. Naples, April 26, 1907. He studied with P. Raimondi at the Naples Cons. He was director of the Palermo Cons. (1863–82), and later maestro di cappella at Milan (from 1882), and also director of the Naples Cons. (1885–1902). Rossini and Verdi considered him an excellent contrapuntist. His compositions included the operas *Matilde Bentivoglio* (Palermo, 1852), *Piccarda Donati* (Palermo,

March 3, 1857), *La vendetta slava* (Palermo, Feb. 4, 1865), and *Spartaco* (Naples, March 29, 1891).

BIBL.: F. Guardione, *P. P.* (Milan, 1908).

Plath, Wolfgang, German musicologist; b. Riga, Latvia, Dec. 27, 1930; d. Augsburg, March 19, 1995. He studied musicology at the Free Univ. of Berlin with Gerstenberg, and later at the Univ. of Tübingen (Ph.D., 1958, with the diss. *Das Klavierbüchlein für Wilhelm Friedemann Bach*). In 1960 he was named coed. (with Wolfgang Rehm) of the *Neue Mozart-Ausgabe*. His studies of Mozart autographs and texts are valuable; he contributed important articles to the *Mozart-Jahrbuch*.

Platti, Giovanni Benedetto, Italian composer; b. Padua, July 9, 1697; d. Würzburg, Jan. 11, 1763. In 1722 he went to Würzburg, where he was active as an instrumentalist, tenor, singing teacher, and composer at the court of the bishops until at least 1761. His works included the opera *Arianna* (Würzburg, 1729) and 2 oratorios.

Pleasants, Henry, American music critic and writer on music; b. Wayne, Pa., May 12, 1910. He was educated at the Philadelphia Musical Academy and the Curtis Inst. of Music in Philadelphia. From 1930 to 1942 he was music critic of the *Philadelphia Evening Bulletin*, and then central European music correspondent of the *N.Y. Times* from 1945 to 1955. From 1950 to 1964 he was also active with the U.S. Foreign Service. In 1967 he became the London music critic of the *International Herald Tribune* and the London ed. of *Stereo Review*. He was active as a guest lecturer throughout the United States and England, and also appeared on radio and television programs of the BBC, as well as those in North America and Europe. His writings appeared in many leading American and English music magazines, and he also was a contributor to the *Encyclopaedia Britannica* and *The New Grove Dictionary of Music and Musicians*. As a tr. and ed., he publ. *Vienna's Golden Years of Music 1850–1900* (writings of Hanslick: 1950); *The Musical Journeys of Louis Spohr* (1961), *The Musical World of Robert Schumann* (1965), *The Music Criticism of Hugo Wolf* (1979), and *Piano and Song* (by Friedrich Wieck; 1988).

WRITINGS (all publ. in N.Y.): *The Agony of Modern Music* (1955); *Death of a Music? The Decline of the European Tradition and the Rise of Jazz* (1961); *The Great Singers from the Dawn of Opera to Our Own Time* (1966; 3d ed., rev. and enl., 1985); *Serious Music, and All That Jazz* (1969); *The Great American Popular Singers* (1974); *Opera in Crisis: Tradition, Present, Future* (1989); *The Great Tenor Tragedy: The Last Days of Adolphe Nourrit as Told (Mostly) by Himself* (Portland, Oreg., 1995).

Pleyel, Ignace Joseph (Ignaz Josef), eminent Austrian-French pianist, piano manufacturer, music publisher, and composer; b. Ruppertsthal, near Vienna, June 18, 1757; d. on his estate near Paris, Nov. 14, 1831. He was the 24th of 38 children in the impoverished family of a schoolteacher; however, he received sufficient education, including music lessons, to qualify for admittance to the class of Wanhal. Thanks to the generosity of Count Ladislaus Erdödy, he became Haydn's pupil and lodger in Eisenstadt (c.1772–77), and then was enabled to go to Rome. In 1783 he became 2d Kapellmeister at the Strasbourg Cathedral; he was advanced to the rank of 1st Kapellmeister in 1789, but lost his position during the turbulent times of the French Revolution. He conducted the "Professional Concerts" in London during the 1791–92 season, and honored his teacher Haydn by playing a work of Haydn at his opening concert (Feb. 13, 1792). After several years he returned to Strasbourg to liquidate his estate, and in 1795 he went to Paris, where he opened a music store which was in business until 1834, and in 1807 founded a piano factory, which manufactured famous French pianos; the firm eventually became known as Pleyel et Cie., and continued to prosper for over a century and a half. The name Pleyel is mainly known through his piano manufacture, but he was a prolific and an extremely competent composer. His productions are so close in style to those of Haydn that specialists are still inclined to attribute certain works in Haydn's catalogues to Pleyel. Among his works were *Die Fee Urgele* for puppet theater (Eszterház, Nov. 1776) and the opera *Ifigenia in Aulide* (Naples, May 30, 1785). His son was the French pianist, piano manufacturer, and composer (Joseph Stephen) Camille Pleyel (b. Strasbourg, Dec. 18, 1788; d. Paris, May 4, 1855).

BIBL.: L. de Fourcaud, *La Salle P.* (Paris, 1893); R. Benton, *Ignace P.: A Thematic Catalogue of His Compositions* (N.Y., 1977).

Plishka, Paul (Peter), American bass; b. Old Forge, Pa., Aug. 28, 1941. He studied at Montclair, N.J., State College. From 1961 to 1965 he was a member of the Paterson (N.J.) Lyric Opera; in 1965 he joined the Metropolitan Opera National Co., and sang with it on tour. On June 27, 1967, he made his Metropolitan Opera debut in a concert performance at the Botanical Garden in the Bronx as the Uncle-Priest in *Madama Butterfly*; he first sang on the Metropolitan's stage as the Monk in *La Gioconda* on Sept. 21, 1967; he has remained on its roster, most notably in such roles as King Marke, Leporello, Varlaam, Oroveso, Pimen, Gounod's Méphistophélès, and Henry VIII in *Anna Bolena*. In 1992 he celebrated his 25th anniversary at the Metropolitan Opera in an acclaimed appearance as Falstaff. In 1993 he won critical accolades as Philip II at the Seattle Opera. In 1997 he portrayed Mozart's Dr. Bartolo at the Metropolitan Opera. He has also appeared as a concert singer with many of the major U.S. orchs.

Plotnikov, Eugene, Russian conductor; b. Odessa, Aug. 29, 1877; d. N.Y., Sept. 28, 1951. He studied at the Moscow Cons. He was a coach and assistant conductor at the Moscow Opera; he also conducted at the Paris Opéra (1921). In 1922 he settled in the United States; he conducted Russian operas in New York and other American cities.

Plowright, Rosalind (Anne), English mezzo-soprano, later soprano; b. Worksop, May 21, 1949. She was a student of F. R. Cox at the Royal Manchester College of Music, where she made her operatic debut in the college's first British production of J. C. Bach's *Temistocle* in 1968. In 1975 she made her first appearance with the English National Opera in London as Page in *Salome*, and as Agathe with the Glyndebourne Touring Opera. In 1979 she won the Sofia International Competition and sang Miss Jessel in *The Turn of the Screw* at the English National Opera. She made her debut at London's Covent Garden as Ortlinde in 1980. In 1981 she sang at the Frankfurt am Main Opera and at the Bavarian State Opera in Munich. In 1982 she made her U.S. debut as a soloist with Muti and the Philadelphia Orch., and then her U.S. operatic debut in *Il Corsaro* in San Diego. In 1983 she appeared at Milan's La Scala, the Edinburgh Festival, and in San Francisco. She sang Aida at Covent Garden in 1984, and appeared at the Deutsche Oper in Berlin. In 1986 she sang Senta at Covent Garden. In 1987 she appeared as Gluck's Alceste at La Scala. In 1990 she made her debut at the Vienna State Opera as Amelia. She was engaged as Tosca at the English National Opera in 1994, and in 1996 she portrayed Santuzza at the Berlin State Opera. She also toured widely as a soloist with orchs. and as a recitalist. Among her other operatic roles were Médée, Rossini's Desdemona, Norma, Ariadne, and Maddalena in *Andrea Chénier*.

Plush, Vincent, remarkable Australian composer; b. Adelaide, April 18, 1950. He studied piano, organ, and voice before embarking on regular courses at the Univ. of Adelaide (B.M., 1971), where his principal instructors in composition were Andrew McCredie and Richard Meale. From 1973 to 1980 he taught at the New South Wales State Conservatorium of Music in Sydney. In 1976 he founded the Seymour Group, an ensemble devoted to the performance of contemporary music. In 1981 he joined the staff of the Australian Broadcasting Commission (A.B.C.) in Sydney. From his earliest independent activities as a lecturer, radio commentator, and conductor, Plush dedicated his efforts to the promotion of Australian music. Thanks to a generous Harkness fellowship, he was able to spend a couple of years at Yale Univ., conducting interviews with a number of American composers for its Oral History Project; he also worked at the Univ. of Minnesota

(1981), and participated in an Australian Arts Festival in Minneapolis (1982). He then spent a year at the Center for Music Experiment and the Computer Music Facility at the Univ. of Calif. at San Diego. Returning to Australia in 1983, he became composer-in-residence for the A.B.C., where he inaugurated a series of radio broadcasts pointedly entitled "Mainstreet U.S.A.," dedicated to new American music. A firm believer in the authentic quality of Australian folk music, he organized in Sydney the whimsically named ensemble Magpipe Musicians, which gave performances of native music in schools and art galleries, on the radio, in the concert hall, at country festivals, citizenship ceremonies, railway openings, and suchlike events, public and private. Their programs were deliberately explorative, aggressive, and exhortatory, propagandistic of new ideas, often with a decided revolutionary trend. The titles of Plush's own works often pay tribute to revolutionary or heroic events, e.g., *On Shooting Stars—Homage to Victor Jara* (a Chilean folksinger murdered by the fascistic Chilean police), *Bakery Hill Rising* (memorializing the suppression of the rebellion of Australian gold miners in 1854), *Gallipoli Sunrise* (commemorating the sacrificial attempt at capturing the Gallipoli Straits in World War I, during which thousands of Australians perished), and *The Ludlow Lullabies* (recalling the brutal attack on striking coal miners in the region of Ludlow, Colo., in 1914). The musical setting of each of these works varies from astutely homophonic to acutely polyphonic, according to the requirements of the subject.

WORKS: DRAMATIC: *Australian Folksongs*, musical theater piece for Baritone and Ensemble (Sydney, July 19, 1977); *The Maitland and Morpeth String Quartet* for Narrator and String Quartet (Sydney, April 1, 1979; rev. 1985); *Facing the Danger* for Narrator and Instruments, after the poem *Say No* by Barbara Berman (1982; Las Vegas, Jan. 18, 1983); *Grody to the Max* for "Val"– (i.e., San Fernando "Valley Girl") Speaker and Trumpeter (1983); *The Wakefield Chronicles*, pageant for Narrator, Solo Trumpet and Trombone, and Ensemble, after Edward Gibbon Wakefield (Adelaide, March 5, 1986); *The Muse of Fire* for Narrator, Baritone, Trumpet, Flute, Piano, Chorus, 2 Brass Bands, Children's Chorus, and Organ, after Andrew Torning (1986–87). Also *All Ears*, radiophonic composition for Voices (Radio 2MBS-FM, Sydney, March 16, 1985), and *The Muse of Fire*, pageant for Voices and Instruments (Penrith, New South Wales, Oct. 17, 1987).

Pocci, Franz, Graf von, German writer on music and composer; b. Munich, March 7, 1807; d. there, May 7, 1876. Possessing versatile talents, he wrote plays with music for a puppet theater in Munich, for which he also designed the scenery. He was at his best in pieces for children (*Blumenlieder, Bildertöne für Klavier, Soldatenlieder, Jägerlieder, Alte und neue Kinderlieder*, etc.). His 2 piano sonatas were praised by Schumann for their poetic expression and fine Romantic spirit. An opera, *Der Alchymist*, was produced in Munich (1840). His grandson F. Pocci publ. a collection, *Franz Poccis Lustiges Komödienbüchlein* (Munich, 1921).

BIBL.: H. Holland, *Zur Erinnerung an F. P.* (Munich, 1877); K. Pastor, *F. P. als Musiker* (diss., Univ. of Munich, 1932).

Poděšt, Ludvík, Czech composer; b. Dubňany, Dec. 19, 1921; d. Prague, Feb. 27, 1968. He was a student of Kvapil (composition) at the Brno Cons. (1945–48) and of Racek and B. Štědroň (musicology) at the Univ. of Brno (Ph.D., 1949). After working at the Brno Radio (1947–51), he was music director of the Vit Nejedlý Army Artistic Ensemble (1953–56) and head of the music dept. of the Czech TV (1958–60). His works include the operas *Tři apokryfy* (3 Apocryphas; 1957–58) and *Hrátky s čertem* (Frolics with the Devil; 1957–60; Liberec, Oct. 12, 1963).

Poglietti, Alessandro, eminent Italian organist, teacher, and composer; place and date of birth unknown; d. at the hands of the Turks during the siege of Vienna, July 1683. He served as court and chamber organist in the Vienna Kapelle of Emperor Leopold I (from 1661). He was one of the outstanding keyboard composers of his era. His compositions included the opera *Endimione festeggiante* (Göttweig, Jan. 12, 1677).

Poise, (Jean Alexandre) Ferdinand, French composer; b. Nîmes, June 3, 1828; d. Paris, May 13, 1892. He studied at the Paris Cons. with A. Adam and Zimmerman, taking the 2d Grand Prix de Rome in 1852.

WORKS: DRAMATIC: OPÉRAS COMIQUES (all 1st perf. in Paris): *Bonsoir, voisin* (Sept. 18, 1853); *Le Thé de Polichinelle* (March 4, 1856); *Le roi Don Pèdre* (Sept. 30, 1857); *Le Jardinier galant* (March 4, 1861); *Le corricolo* (Nov. 28, 1868); *Les deux billets* (Feb. 19, 1870); *Les trois souhaits* (Oct. 29, 1873); *La surprise de l'amour* (Oct. 31, 1877); *L'amour médicin* (Dec. 20, 1880). ORATORIO: *Cécile* (Dijon, 1888).

Poissl, Johann Nepomuk, Freiherr von, German composer; b. Haukenzell, Lower Bavaria, Feb. 15, 1783; d. Munich, Aug. 17, 1865. He was educated in Straubing, Munich, and at the Univ. of Landshut (1800); he settled in Munich (1805), and studied composition with Danzi and Abbé Vogler. In 1811 he met Weber, who became a champion of his works. As a composer for the theater, he won his most notable successes with *Athalia* (June 3, 1814) and *Der Wettkampf zu Olympia oder Die Freunde* (April 21, 1815); nevertheless, he was dogged by poverty until being made assistant superintendent of court music in 1823; he was also named director of the Court Theater (1825). His opera *Die Prinzessin von Provence* was first performed at the reopening celebrations of the rebuilt Nationaltheater (Jan. 23, 1825), and remains his best-known achievement. He was replaced as director of the Court Theater (1833), but was retained as director of court music until his dismissal in 1847, when he was made 1st chamberlain. His final years were marked by illness and poverty. Poissl was an important link in the development of German opera between the eras of Mozart and Weber.

WORKS: DRAMATIC: OPERAS (all first perf. in Munich unless otherwise given): *Die Opernprobe*, comic opera (Feb. 23, 1806); *Antigonus*, serious opera (Feb. 12, 1808); *Ottaviano in Sicilia*, dramma eroico (June 30, 1812); *Aucassin und Nicolette*, Singspiel (March 28, 1813); *Athalia*, grand opera (June 3, 1814); *Der Wettkampf zu Olympia oder Die Freunde*, grand opera (April 21, 1815); *Die wie mir oder Alle betrügen*, comic opera (1816; not perf.); *Nittetis*, grand opera (Darmstadt, June 29, 1817); *Issipile*, grand opera (1818; not perf.); *La rappresaglia*, opera semiseria (April 7, 1820); *Die Prinzessin von Provence*, magical opera (Jan. 23, 1825); *Der Untersberg*, Romantic opera (Oct. 30, 1829); *Zaide*, Romantic-tragic opera (Nov. 9, 1843). INCIDENTAL MUSIC TO: Heyden's *Renata* (Munich, Oct. 12, 1823), von Schenk's *Belisar* (Munich, Feb. 23, 1826) and *Kaiser Ludwigs Traum* (Munich, March 27, 1826), and Kleist's *Hermannschlacht* (1826). ORATORIOS: *Judith* (1824); *Der Erntetag* (Munich, April 4, 1835).

BIBL.: E. Reipschlager, *Schubaur, Danzi und P. als Opernkomponisten* (diss., Univ. of Rostock, 1911).

Polacco, Giorgio, Italian conductor; b. Venice, April 12, 1873; d. N.Y., April 30, 1960. He studied in St. Petersburg, at Venice's Liceo Benedetto Marcello, and at the Milan Cons. He became assistant conductor at London's Covent Garden (1890), then conducted in Europe and South America; he appeared in the United States for the first time for Tetrazzini's debut in San Francisco (1905); he toured the United States with the Savage Opera Co. (1911). He made his Metropolitan Opera debut in New York with *Manon Lescaut* (Nov. 11, 1912), remaining on its roster until 1917; he conducted the Chicago Grand Opera (1918–19; 1921) and in Boston (1927); he was principal conductor of the Chicago Civic Opera (1922–30). He was married twice to the soprano Edith (Barnes) Mason.

Polaski, Deborah, American soprano; b. Richmond Center, Wisc., Sept. 26, 1949. She studied in Cincinnati and Graz. After making her operatic debut in Gelsenkirchen in 1976, she sang in Munich, Hamburg, Karlsruhe, Mannheim, and other German cities in such roles as Leonore, Sieglinde, Isolde, and Berg's Marie. In 1986 she appeared as Elektra in Oslo and as Chrysothemis in Geneva, and in 1988 as Senta at Milan's La Scala. While her portrayal of Brünnhilde at the Bayreuth Festival was cooly received in 1988, she triumphed there in that role in 1991 and 1995. In

1990 she sang Brünnhilde in Cologne and Elektra in Spoleto. Following an engagement as the *Walküre* Brünnhilde at London's Covent Garden in 1994, she sang Elektra upon her return there in 1997. Her appearance as Brünnhilde in the Berlin mounting of the *Ring* cycle in 1996 brought her further accolades.

Poleri, David (Samuel), American tenor; b. Philadelphia, Jan. 10, 1921; d. in a helicopter accident in Hanalei, Hawaii, Dec. 13, 1967. He studied at the Philadelphia Academy of Vocal Arts, the Berkshire Music Center in Tanglewood, and with Alberto Sciarretti. In 1945 he sang with the Philadelphia Orch. In 1949 he made his operatic debut as Gounod's Faust with Gallo's San Carlo Opera on a tour in Chicago. He subsequently was a guest artist with various opera companies and a soloist with various orchs. in the United States. He also sang at the Edinburgh Festivals (1951, 1955) and at London's Covent Garden (1956). In 1954 he created the role of Michele in Menotti's *The Saint of Bleecker Street*. In 1955 he appeared as Cavaradossi on NBC-TV.

Polgar, Tibor, Hungarian-born Canadian composer, conductor, pianist, and teacher; b. Budapest, March 11, 1907. He was a pupil of Kodály at the Budapest Academy of Music (composition diploma, 1925), and earned a degree in philosophy (1931). He was active as a performer and composer with the Hungarian Radio, later serving as its artistic director (1948–50). From 1962 to 1964 he was assoc. conductor of the Philharmonia Hungarica in Marl kreis Recklinghausen; he then emigrated to Canada and became a naturalized citizen (1969). He conducted the Univ. of Toronto Sym. Orch. (1965–66), and later was on the staff of the Univ.'s opera dept. (1970–75); he also taught at the Royal Cons. of Music of Toronto (1966–68); he then taught orchestration at York Univ. in Toronto (1976–77). His works include the operas *Kérök* (The Suitors; 1954), *The Troublemaker* (1968), *The Glove* (1973), and *A Strange Night* (1978–88); also the musical satire *A European Lover* (1965).

Poliakov, Valeri(an), Russian composer and conductor; b. Orel, Oct. 24, 1913; d. Kishinev, Jan. 17, 1970. He studied clarinet and composition in Kharkov (1928–34). In 1935 he joined the staff of the Kiev Opera; in 1937 he was appointed head of the music dept. of the Moldavian Music Theater in Kishinev, and taught at a music school there until 1940; he then taught in Armenia (1941–45) and Riga (1945–51). He was music ed. and conductor of the Moldavian Radio (1951–54); he conducted the dance ensemble Zhok (1955–57) and the jazz band Bukuria (1965–66); he also taught at the Kishinev Cons. (1961–70). In 1960 he was made an Honored Artist of the Moldavian SSR. His works include the opera *Where?* (1969) and the ballets *Iliana, An Ancient Tale* (1936), *Legend of the Architect* (1959), and *Eternity* (1961).

Polignac, Armande de, French composer; b. Paris, Jan. 8, 1876; d. Neauphle-le-Vieux, Seine-et-Oise, April 29, 1962. She studied with Fauré and d'Indy. She composed the operas *Morgane* and *L'Hypocrite sanctifie*; also *Judith de Béthulie*, dramatic scene (Paris, March 23, 1916), *La Source lointaine*, Persian ballet (Paris, 1913), *Les 1,001 Nuits*, Arabian ballet (Paris, 1914), *Chimères*, Greek ballet (Paris, June 10, 1923), *Urashima*, Japanese ballet, and *La Recherche de la verité*, Chinese ballet for Small Orch.

Polívka, Vladimír, Czech pianist and composer; b. Prague, July 6, 1896; d. there, May 11, 1948. He studied piano at the Prague Cons., and took lessons in composition from Vítězslav Novák at the Master School there (1912–18). He traveled in Europe, America, and Japan with the violinist Jaroslav Kocián; from 1923 to 1930 he taught piano in Chicago. In 1938 he returned to Prague and taught at the Cons.; he was chairman of Pritomnost, an association for contemporary music. He publ. several collections of children's pieces, collaborated on a book about Smetana (Prague, 1941), and wrote a book of travels, describing his world tour (Prague, 1945). Among his works were *Polobůh* (The Demigod), opera (1930), *A Ballad of a Deaf-Mute*, melodrama (1936), and incidental music.

Polko, Elise (née **Vogel**), German singer and writer; b. Leipzig, Jan. 13, 1822; d. Munich, May 15, 1899. She studied with Manuel García in Paris, She married a railway engineer, Eduard Polko, under whose name she became professionally known. She publ. a number of semifictional stories about music which became astonishingly popular in Germany during her lifetime.

WRITINGS: *Musikalische Märchen* (3 vols., 1852; also Eng. tr.); *Faustina Hasse* (2 vols., 1860); *Alte Herren* (1865); *Verklungene Akkorde* (1868); *Erinnerungen an Felix Mendelssohn-Bartholdy* (1868; Eng. tr, 1869); *Nicolò Paganini und die Geigenbauer* (1876); *Vom Gesange* (1876); *Aus der Künstlerwelt* (1878); *Der Klassiker der Musik* (1880); *Meister der Tonkunst* (1897).

Pollak, Anna, English mezzo-soprano of Austrian descent; b. Manchester, May 1, 1912; d. Hythe, Kent, Nov. 28, 1996. She studied in the Netherlands and in Manchester. Following appearances as an actress and singer in musical comedy and operetta, she studied voice with Joan Cross. In 1945 she made her operatic debut as Dorabella at the Sadler's Wells Opera in London, where she was one of its leading artists until 1962. In 1952 she made her first appearance at the Glyndebourne Festival as Dorabella and at London's Covent Garden as Cherubino. Between 1962 and her retirement in 1968 she was a guest artist at the Sadler's Wells Opera. In 1962 she was made an Officer of the Order of the British Empire. She created the role of Bianca in Britten's *The Rape of Lucretia* (1946) and the title role in Berkeley's *Ruth* (1956).

Pollak, Egon, esteemed Czech-born Austrian conductor; b. Prague, May 3, 1879; d. there (of a heart attack while conducting a performance of *Fidelio*), June 14, 1933. He studied with Knittl at the Prague Cons. He was chorus master at the Prague Deutsches Theater (1901–05); he conducted opera in Bremen (1905–10), Leipzig (1910–12), and Frankfurt am Main (1912–17); he also conducted in Paris and at London's Covent Garden (1914). He led Wagner's *Ring* cycle at the Chicago Grand Opera (1915–17); he was able to leave the United States with the Austrian diplomatic legation as the United States entered World War I (1917). He was Generalmusikdirektor of the Hamburg Opera (1917–31); he also conducted in Rio de Janeiro and at Buenos Aires's Teatro Colón (1928); he appeared at the Chicago Civic Opera (1929–32) and in Russia (1932); he led performances of the ensemble of the Vienna State Opera in Cairo and Alexandria (1933). He was a distinguished interpreter of the operas of Wagner and Richard Strauss.

Pollarolo, (Giovanni) Antonio, Italian composer, son of **Carlo Francesco Pollarolo**; b. Brescia (baptized), Nov. 12, 1676; d. Venice, May 30, 1746. He studied with his father, for whom he began substituting as vice maestro di cappella at Venice's San Marco (1702). He was named to that position (1723), and was acting primo maestro (1733–36) and then primo maestro (1740–46); he was also maestro di coro at the Ospedale degl'Incurabili (from 1716). He wrote about 12 operas, but only *I tre voti* (Vienna, 1724) is extant; he also wrote some sacred music, including oratorios.

Pollarolo, Carlo Francesco, prominent Italian organist and composer, father of **(Giovanni) Antonio Pollarolo**; b. c.1653; d. Venice, Feb. 7, 1723. His father, Orazio Pollarolo, was organist in Brescia at the parish church of Ss. Nazaro e Celso and at the cathedral, and it is likely that Carlo Francesco studied with him. After serving as organist at the Congregazione dei Padri della Pace and substituting for his father at the cathedral, he was named his father's successor at the latter (1676). He was elected capo musico there (1680), and also held a similar post with the Accademia degli Erranti (1681–89). He then went to Venice, where he was elected 2d organist at San Marco (1690). He became its vice maestro di cappella (1692), a position he held until his son Antonio succeeded him (1702); he was also music director of the Ospedale degl'Incurabili. He composed about 85 operas, many of which are not extant; among those surviving are *Il Roderico* (1686), *Onorio in Roma* (Venice, 1692), *La forza della virtù* (Venice, 1693), *Il Faramondo* (Venice, 1699), *Semiramide* (Venice, 1713), *Ario-*

dante (Venice, 1716), and *Astinome* (Rome, 1719). He also wrote oratorios and many other sacred works.

BIBL.: O. Termini, *C. F. P.: His Life, Time, and Music with Emphasis on the Operas* (diss., Univ. of Southern Calif., 1970).

Pollini, Bernhard (real name, **Baruch Pohl**), German tenor, later baritone, and opera impresario; b. Cologne, Dec. 16, 1838; d. Hamburg, Nov. 27, 1897. He made his debut as Arturo in *I Puritani* in Cologne in 1857, and later sang baritone roles in an Italian opera troupe, of which he subsequently became manager and artistic director. He then undertook the management of the Italian opera at St. Petersburg and Moscow. In 1874 he became director of the Hamburg City Theater; in 1876 he also became manager of the Altona Theater and in 1894 of the Thalia Theater in Hamburg.

Pollini, Francesco (Giuseppe), Italian pianist, singer, and composer of Slovenian birth; b. Laibach, March 25, 1762; d. Milan, Sept. 17, 1846. He was a pupil of Mozart (who dedicated a violin rondo to him) at Vienna, and later of Zingarelli at Milan, where he was appointed a prof. of piano shortly after the opening of the Cons. (1809). He was the first to write piano music on 3 staves, a method imitated by Liszt, Thalberg, and others; a specimen of this style is one of his *32 Esercizi in forma di toccata*, op. 42 (1820), a central melody surrounded by passagework for both hands. He publ. *Metodo per clavicembalo* (Milan, 1811). Among his compositions is an opera buffa, *La cassetta nei boschi* (Milan, Feb. 25, 1798).

Pololáník, Zdeněk, Czech composer; b. Brno, Oct. 25, 1935. Following training with Vladimír Malacka and František Suchý, he was a student of Josef Černocký (organ) at the Cons. (graduated, 1957) and of Vilém Petrželka and Theodor Schafer (composition) at the Janáček Academy of Music (graduated, 1961) in Brno. Thereafter, he devoted himself fully to composing. In his music, Pololáník reveals an assured handling of form, structure, color, and unusual instrumental combinations.

WORKS: DRAMATIC: MELODRAMA: *Malá mytologická cvičení* (Small Mythological Exercises; 1991). MUSICAL-LITERARY DRAMAS: *Císařův mim* (The Emperor's Mime Artist; 1994); *Pražská legenda* (Prague Legend; 1995). BALLETS: *Mechanismus* (Mechanism; 1964); *Popelka* (Cinderella; 1966); *Pierot* (About; 1976; orch. suite, 1977); *Sněhová královna* (Snow Queen; 1978); *Paní mezi stíny* (Lady Among Shadows; 1984). Also much incidental music and numerous radio, television, and film scores. ORATORIOS: *Sheer hash sheereem* (Song of Songs) for Soli, Chorus, and Orch. (1970; orch. suite, 1975); *Cinderella of Nazareth*, chamber oratorio for Medium Voice and Synthesizer (1991); *First One Must Carry the Cross*, chamber oratorio for Medium Voice and Synthesizer (1992); *God is Love*, chamber oratorio for Medium Voice and Synthesizer (1993).

Ponchielli, Amilcare, celebrated Italian composer; b. Paderno Fasolaro, near Cremona, Aug. 31, 1834; d. Milan, Jan. 15, 1886. He studied with his father, a shopkeeper and organist at the village church, and entered the Milan Cons. as a nonpaying student when he was 9; his mentors included Pietro Ray (theory), Arturo Angeleri (piano), Felice Frasi (composition), and Alberto Mazzucato (music history, aesthetics, and composition). While a student there he collaborated on the operetta *Il sindaco babbeo* (Milan Cons., March 1851) and also wrote the sym. *Scena campestre* (1852). After his graduation (1854), he went to Cremona as a church organist. He was named assistant to Ruggero Manna, director of Cremona's Teatro Concordia (1855), where he brought out his opera *I promessi sposi* (Aug. 30, 1856). He was conductor of the municipal bands in Piacenza (1861–64) and Cremona (from 1864), where he also conducted opera; he continued to pursue his interest in composing for the theater. He finally achieved notable success with the revised version of his *I promessi sposi* (Milan, Dec. 4, 1872), which was subsequently performed throughout Italy; his *La Gioconda* (Milan, April 8, 1876) secured his reputation. He was prof. of composition at the Milan Cons. in 1880 and again from 1881; he also served as maestro di cappella at Bergamo's S. Maria Maggiore (1881–86). He married **Teresina Brambilla** in 1874. His birthplace was renamed Paderno Ponchielli in his honor. *La Gioconda* remains his only work to have acquired repertoire status; it includes the famous ballet number *Dance of the Hours*. In addition to his numerous stage works, he composed many band pieces, vocal chamber music, chamber works, and piano pieces.

BIBL.: A. Mandelli, *Le distrazioni di A. P.* (Cremona, 1897); G. Cesari, *A. P. nell'arte del suo tempo: Ricordi e carteggi* (Cremona, 1934); U. Rolandi, *Nel centenario ponchielliano: A. P. librettista* (Como, 1935); G. De Napoli, *A. P. (1834–1886): La vita, le opere, l'epistolario, le onoranze* (Cremona, 1936); A. Damerini, *A. P.* (Turin, 1940); N. Albarosa et al., eds., *A. P. 1834–1886: Saggio e ricerche nel 1507 anniversario della nascità* (Casalmorano, 1984); L. Sirch, *Catalogo tematico delle musiche di A. P.* (Cremona, 1989).

Poné, Gundaris, Latvian-born American conductor and composer; b. Riga, Oct. 17, 1932; d. Kingston, N.Y., March 15, 1994. In 1944 his family went to Germany, where he studied violin. In 1950 he emigrated to the United States, becoming a naturalized American citizen in 1956. He studied violin and composition at the Univ. of Minnesota (B.A., 1954; M.A., 1956; Ph.D., 1962). In 1966 he made his conducting debut in New York, and subsequently appeared as a guest conductor in the United States and in Europe; he served as music director of the Music in the Mountains Festivals (from 1981). His compositions captured 1st prizes in the Concorso Internazionale "Citta di Trieste" (1981), the Kennedy Center Friedheim Awards Competition (1982), the International Louisville Orch. Competition (1984), the International Hambach Prize Competition (1985), and the International Georges Enesco Competition (1988). His concern as a composer was to develop a musical language capable of communicating with the general audience while maintaining the high intellectual standards of contemporary composition. Among his works was the opera *Rosa Luxemburg* (1968).

Pongrácz, Zoltán, Hungarian composer and teacher; b. Diószeg, Feb. 5, 1912. He studied with Kodály at the Budapest Academy of Music (1930–35); he then took lessons in conducting from Nilius in Vienna (1935–38) and Krauss in Salzburg (1941). He served as director of the music dept. of Hungarian Radio in Budapest (1943–44) and then conducted the Debrecen Phil. (1946–49). He taught composition at the Debrecen Cons. (1947–58) and electronic composition at the Budapest Academy of Music (from 1975). His works include the operas *Odysseus and Nausikaa* (1949–50; Debrecen, 1960) and *The Last Station* (1983), and the ballet *The Devil's Present* (1936).

Poniatowski, Józef (Michal Xsawery Franciszek Jan), Prince of Monte Rotondo, Polish tenor and composer; b. Rome, Feb. 20, 1816; d. Chislehurst, England, July 3, 1873. He was a member of the Polish nobility; his uncle was a marshal in Napoleon's army. He studied in Florence, and appeared on the stage as a tenor. He then wrote operas (to Italian and French librettos). In 1848 he went to Paris and was elevated to the rank of Senator by Napoleon III; after the fall of the 2d Empire, he went to England. In addition to operas, he also composed the popular ballad, *The Yeoman's Wedding Song*.

WORKS: OPERAS: *Giovanni da Procida* (Florence, Nov. 25, 1838); *Don Desiderio, ossia Il disperato per eccesso di buon cuore* (Pisa, Dec. 26, 1840); *Ruy Blas* (Lucca, Sept. 2, 1843); *Bonifazio de' Geremei* (Rome, Nov. 28, 1843); *La sposa d'Abido* (Venice, Feb. 1845); *Malek-Adel* (Genoa, June 26, 1846); *Esmeralde* (Florence, June 26, 1847); *Pierre de Médicis* (Paris, March 9, 1860); *Au travers du mur* (Paris, May 9, 1861); *L'Aventurier* (Paris, Jan. 26, 1865); *La Contessina* (Paris, April 28, 1868); *Gelmina* (London, June 4, 1872).

Ponnelle, Jean-Pierre, notable French opera designer and producer; b. Paris, Feb. 19, 1932; d. Munich, Aug. 11, 1988. He received his education at the Sorbonne in Paris. In 1952 he gained early recognition as a designer with the premiere of Henze's *Boul-*

evard Solitude in Hannover. His first opera production followed in 1962 in Düsseldorf with his staging of *Tristan und Isolde*, and he subsequently worked in Berlin, Hamburg, Munich, Stuttgart, and other German music centers. In 1968 he brought out *Il Barbiere di Siviglia* at the Salzburg Festival, where he later worked regularly. In 1973 he produced *L'Italiana in Algeri* at the Metropolitan Opera in New York, returning there to oversee such productions as *Der fliegende Holländer* (1979), *Idomeneo* (1982), *La clemenza di Tito* (1984), *Le nozze di Figaro* (1985), and *Manon* (1986). He also worked at London's Covent Garden, where he produced *Don Pasquale* (1973), *Aida* (1984), and *L'Italiana in Algeri* (1988). In 1981 he produced *Tristan und Isolde* at the Bayreuth Festival. He also made many film productions of his stagings. Ponnelle was one of the most creative and influential opera designers and producers of his time. While he could be controversial, there was no denying his genius in the art of stagecraft.

BIBL.: I. Fabian, *J.-P. P.* (Zürich, 1983).

Pons, Charles, French composer; b. Nice, Dec. 7, 1870; d. Paris, March 16, 1957. He studied organ, and earned his living as a church organist in his youth, then turned to theater music, and produced a long series of operas: *L'Epreuve* (Nice, 1904), *Laura* (Paris, 1906), *Mourette* (Marseilles, 1909), *Le Voile du bonheur* (Paris, April 26, 1911), *Françoise* (Lyons, 1913), *Loin du bal* (Paris, 1913), *Les Fauves* (Paris, 1917), *Le Drapeau* (Paris, 1918), *Le Passant de Noël* (Nice, 1935), and *L'Envol de la Marseillaise* (Marseilles, 1947).

Pons, Juan, Spanish baritone; b. Ciutadela, Aug. 8, 1946. He received his training in Barcelona, where he commenced his career as a tenor at the Teatro Liceo. In 1979 he made his first appearance at London's Covent Garden as Alfio in *Cavalleria rusticana*. On Jan. 4, 1983, he made his Metropolitan Opera debut in New York as Conte di Luna in *Il trovatore*, and also appeared that same year as Massenet's Hérode in Barcelona and as Donizetti's Tonio at the Paris Opéra. After singing Amonasro in Vienna in 1984, he appeared as Rigoletto and Sharpless at Milan's La Scala in 1985. In 1987 he portrayed Verdi's Falstaff at the Bavarian State Opera in Munich, and in 1988 sang Germont at the Lyric Opera in Chicago. He again appeared as Falstaff in 1989 at the San Francisco Opera and at the Rome Opera. In 1992 he sang Tonio in Philadelphia and Conte di Luna in Madrid. He was engaged as Tonio in Los Angeles in 1996.

Pons, Lily (Alice Josephine), glamorous French soprano; b. Draguignan, April 12, 1898; d. Dallas, Feb. 13, 1976. She studied piano as a child; took voice lessons with Alberti di Gorostiaga. She made her debut as an opera singer in Mulhouse in 1927 in the title role in *Lakmé*; he sang in provincial theaters in France, then was engaged at the Metropolitan Opera in New York, and sang Lucia at her debut there on Jan. 3, 1931, with excellent success; she remained on its roster until 1944 (again from 1945 to 1958; on Dec. 14, 1960, she made a concert appearance there). While in New York, she continued vocal studies with Maria Gay and Giovanni Zenatello. Her fame as an extraordinary dramatic singer spread rapidly; she was engaged to sing at the Grand Opéra and the Opéra Comique in Paris, at Covent Garden in London, the Teatro Colón in Buenos Aires, in Mexico, and in Cuba. She went to Hollywood and appeared in films, among them *That Girl from Paris* (1936) and *Hitting a New High* (1938). During World War II, she toured the battlefronts of North Africa, India, China, and Burma; received numerous honors. So celebrated did she become that a town in Maryland was named Lillypons in her honor. She was married twice (divorced both times) to the publisher August Mesritz, and once to **André Kostelanetz**. She possessed an expressive coloratura voice, which she used with extraordinary skill. In addition to Lakmé, she won great renown for her portrayals of Philine in *Mignon*, Gilda, Marie in *La Fille du régiment*, Rosina, Olympia in *Les Contes d'Hoffmann*, and Amina in *La Sonnambula*.

Ponselle (real name, **Ponzillo**), **Carmela,** American mezzo-soprano and teacher, sister of **Rosa (Melba) Ponselle**; b. Schenectady, N.Y., June 7, 1892; d. N.Y., June 13, 1977. She began to study singing rather late in life. She made her professional debut as Amneris in New York in 1923, a role she also sang at her Metropolitan Opera debut there on Dec. 5, 1925; she remained on its roster until 1928 and was reengaged for the seasons 1930–35; she then devoted most of her time to teaching.

Ponselle (real name, **Ponzillo**), **Rosa (Melba),** brilliant American soprano, sister of **Carmela Ponselle**; b. Meriden, Conn., Jan. 22, 1897; d. Green Spring Valley, Md., May 25, 1981. Her parents, who emigrated to the United States from southern Italy, gave her, with a prescient hope, the middle name Melba. Her father owned a grocery store in Meriden; she studied music with her mother, an amateur singer, and sang in a local church choir. Her older sister, Carmela, also learned to sing, and the 2 sisters, billed under their real name, Ponzillo, as "Italian Girls," sang in vaudeville shows in Pittsburgh and in New York. Later she took voice lessons in New York with William Thorner, who became her manager; he introduced her to Caruso, who in turn arranged for her audition at the Metropolitan Opera. She made a fine impression, and was engaged for a debut on Nov. 15, 1918, in the role of Leonora in *La forza del destino*, opposite Caruso, who sang the male lead of Don Alvaro. She was immediately successful, and the critics, including the usually skeptical James Huneker, praised her. She subsequently sang at the Metropolitan Opera a rich assortment of Italian roles. She was equally successful in London when she appeared at Covent Garden as Norma (May 28, 1929). In 1936 she was married to Carl Jackson, son of the former mayor of Baltimore, who built for her a magnificent villa at Green Spring Valley, near Baltimore; she divorced him in 1950. She made her last appearance at the Metropolitan Opera in New York as Carmen on Feb. 15, 1937. After her retirement, she became active in social affairs. Her 80th birthday was celebrated in 1977 at her estate, with a multitude of friends and itinerant celebrities in attendance.

BIBL.: E. Aloi, *My Remembrances of R. P.* (N.Y., 1994); J. Drake, *R. P.: A Centenary Biography* (Portland, Oreg., 1997); M. Phillips-Matz, *R. P.: American Diva* (Boston, 1997).

Pontoglio, Cipriano, Italian composer; b. Grumello del Piano, Dec. 25, 1831; d. Milan, Feb. 22, 1892. He was a pupil of Antonio Cagnoni in Milan, and P. Serrao in Naples, then opened a music school in Milan. He composed 5 operas: *Lamberto Malatesta* (Pavia, 1857), *Tebaldo Brusato* (Brescia, 1865; rewritten as *L'Assedio di Brescia*, Rome, June 15, 1872), *La Schiava greca* (Bergamo, 1868), *La notte di natale* (Bergamo, Aug. 29, 1872), and *Edoardo Stuart* (Milan, May 21, 1887).

Poole, Elizabeth, English mezzo-soprano; b. London, April 5, 1820; d. Langley, Buckinghamshire, Jan. 14, 1906. She made her debut at Drury Lane in London in 1834, and then sang in Italian opera in the United States (appearing with Malibran). Until her retirement in 1870, she was immensely popular as a ballad singer. Balfe wrote for her " 'Tis gone, the past is all a dream," which she introduced into *The Bohemian Girl*.

Poot, Marcel, remarkable Belgian composer; b. Vilvoorde, near Brussels, May 7, 1901; d. Brussels, June 12, 1988. He received his first musical training from his father, continued his studies with Gilson (1916), then studied at the Brussels Cons. with Sevenants, Lunssens, and de Greef (1916–20), and at the Royal Flemish Cons. of Antwerp with Lodewijk Mortelmans (1921–23). In 1925, with 7 other Gilson pupils, he founded the Groupe des Synthétistes, dedicated to propaganda of new musical ideas (the group disbanded in 1930). Also in 1925, Poot was cofounder, with Gilson, of *La Revue Musicale Belge*, to which he contributed until its dissolution in 1938. He was on the staff of the Brussels Cons. from 1938 to 1966, and was its director from 1949 until his retirement. The most striking element of his music is its rhythmic vivacity; his harmony is well within the tonal sphere. His Piano Concerto (1959) was a compulsory work for finalists of 1960 Queen Elisabeth piano competition, won by Malcolm Frager. Other works include the chamber opera *Moretus* (1943; Brussels, 1944) and the ballets *Paris et les 3 divines* (1933), *Camera* (1937), *Pygmalion* (1952); also incidental music and 2 oratorios: *Le Dit du routier* (1943) and *Icare* (1945).

Popovici, Doru, Romanian composer; b. Reşiţa, Feb. 17, 1932. He studied at the Bucharest Cons. with Constantinescu, Negrea, Andricu, Rogalski, Jora, and Vancea (1950–55) and attended the summer courses in new music in Darmstadt. His works include the operas *Prometeu* (1958; Bucharest, Dec. 16, 1964), *Mariana Pineda*, after García Lorca (Bucharest, Dec. 22, 1966), *Interogateriul din zori* (Bucharest, Feb. 6, 1975), and *Noaptea cea mai lungă* (Bucharest, March 30, 1978).

Popp, Lucia, esteemed Czech-born Austrian soprano; b. Uhorška Veš, Nov. 12, 1939; d. Munich, Nov. 16, 1993. She studied at the Bratislava Academy of Music (1959–63) and in Prague, her principal mentor being Anna Prosenč-Hřusková. After singing at the Bratislava Opera, she went to Vienna and appeared as Barbarina at the Theater an der Wien (1963); that same year she joined the Vienna State Opera, where she established herself as a principal member; she also became a favorite at the Salzburg Festivals. In 1966 she made her first appearance at London's Covent Garden as Oscar; then made her Metropolitan Opera debut in New York in one of her finest roles, the Queen of the Night, on Feb. 19, 1967. She sang with many of the world's leading opera houses, and also won distinction as a gifted concert and lieder artist. In 1979 she was made an Austrian Kammersängerin, and was awarded the Silver Rose of the Vienna Phil. She won accolades for her roles in operas by Mozart and Strauss, especially Pamina, Despina, Zerlina, Susanna, Zdenka, Sophie, and the Countess, as well as the Queen of the Night. For some years she was married to **György Fischer**. In 1986 she married **Peter Seiffert**.

Poradowski, Stefan (Boleslaw), Polish composer and pedagogue; b. Włocławek, Aug. 16, 1902; d. Poznan, July 9, 1967. He studied composition with Opieński at the Poznań Cons. (1922–26), then took private lessons with Rezniček in Berlin (1929). Returning to Poland, he taught composition and theory at the Poznan Cons. (1930–39; 1945–67); he also gave courses (from 1956) at the Wrocław Cons. He publ. *Nauka harmonii* (Science of Harmony; Poznan, 1931; 5th ed., rev., 1964), *Ogólne wiadomołci z akustyki* (General Knowledge on Acoustics; Poznan, 1947), and *Sztuka pisania kanonów* (Art of Writing Canons; Poznan, 1965). His compositions include *Odkupienie* (Redemption), passion play for Mezzo-soprano, Chorus, and Orch. (1939–41), and *Plomienie* (Flames), opera (1961–66).

Porpora, Nicola (Antonio), famous Italian composer and singing teacher; b. Naples, Aug. 17, 1686; d. there, March 3, 1768. The son of a bookseller, he entered the Cons. dei Poveri at Naples at the age of 10 and studied with Gaetano Greco, Matteo Giordano, and Ottavio Campanile. Porpora's first opera, *Agrippina*, was presented at the Royal Palace of Naples (Nov. 4, 1708); Cardinal Grimani attended the performance and wrote a libretto on the same subject for Handel. This episode gave rise to the incorrect statement (by Fétis and others) that Handel heard Porpora's opera in Rome in 1710. Porpora produced in Naples 2 more operas: *Flavio Anicio Olibrio* (1711) and *Basilio, re d'oriente* (June 24, 1713). From 1711 until 1725, he held the title of maestro di cappella to Philip, landgrave of Hesse-Darmstadt. He gained a great reputation as a singing teacher, and numbered among his pupils the famous castrati Farinelli, Caffarelli, Antonio Uberti (who called himself "Porporino" out of respect for his teacher), and Salimbeni. Metastasio, who wrote librettos for several of Porpora's operas, was also his pupil. Porpora's career as a singing teacher was divided between Naples and Venice. In Naples he taught at the conservatories of Sant' Onofrio (1715–22, 1760–61) and Santa Maria di Loreto (1739–41, 1760–61); in Venice he gave lessons at the Ospedali degli Incurabili (1726–33, 1737–38), the Ospedali della Pietà (1742–46), and the Ospedaletto (1746–47). In 1718 Porpora collaborated with D. Scarlatti in the writing of the opera *Berenice, regina d'Egitto*, produced in Rome (1718). At about this time he succeeded in obtaining support from the Austrian court. His opera *Temistocle* was produced in Vienna on the Emperor's birthday (Oct. 1, 1718); his next opera, *Faramondo*, was staged in Naples (Nov. 19, 1719). He continued to write operas for theaters in Naples and Rome: *Eumene* (Rome, 1721), *Adelaide* (Rome, 1723), *Semiramide, regina dell'Assiria* (Naples, 1724), and *Didone abbandonata* (his 1st opera to a libretto by Metastasio; Reggio Emilia, 1725). In 1726 he settled in Venice. Among the operas he wrote during the next 8 years were *Meride e Selinunte* (Venice, 1726), *Siroe, re di Persia* (Milan, 1726), *Semiramide riconosciuta* (Venice, 1729), *Mitridate* (Rome, 1730), *Tamerlano* (Turin, 1730), *Poro* (Turin, 1731), *Germanico in Germania* (Rome, 1732), and *Issipile* (Rome, 1733). In 1733 he applied for the post of maestro di cappella at San Marco in Venice, but failed to obtain it. In the same year he was engaged by the directors of the Opera of the Nobility in London (organized as a rival company to that of Handel). For this venture Porpora wrote 5 operas: *Arianna in Nasso* (Dec. 29, 1733), *Enea nel Lazio* (May 11, 1734), *Polifemo* (Feb. 1, 1735), *Ifigenia in Aulide* (May 3, 1735), and *Mitridate* (Jan. 24, 1736; a different score from the earlier opera of the same title). For a while he competed successfully with Handel, but soon the Opera of the Nobility began to falter, and Porpora left London on the eve of the company's collapse. From 1747 to 1751, he was in Dresden as singing teacher to the electoral princess. There he became Hasse's competitor for the position of music director. Although Hasse conducted Porpora's "pastoral drama" *Filandro* (Dresden, July 18, 1747), their relationship was made difficult by the intrigues of Hasse's wife, the singer Faustina Bordoni. In 1751 Porpora left Dresden for Vienna, where he became the teacher of Haydn, who paid for his lessons by serving Porpora as accompanist and personal helper. Porpora returned to Naples in 1758. His last stage work, *Il trionfo di Camilla*, was given in Naples on May 30, 1760, with little success. In addition to his varied and numerous stage works, Porpora wrote sacred oratorios and secular cantatas and serenatas.

BIBL.: F. Walker, A *Chronology of the Life and Works of N. P.* (Cambridge, 1951); E. Sutton, *The Solo Vocal Works of N. P.: An Annotated Thematic Index* (diss., Univ. of Minnesota, 1974).

Porrino, Ennio, Italian composer and teacher; b. Cagliari, Sardinia, Jan. 20, 1910; d. Rome, Sept. 25, 1959. He studied at the Accademia di Santa Cecilia in Rome with Mulè, and later took a course with Respighi (1932–35). He subsequently taught in Rome, Venice, and Naples; from 1956 he was director of the Cagliari Cons. His works included the operas *Gli orazi* (Milan, 1941), *L'organo di bambu* (Venice, 1955), and *I shardana* (Naples, 1959), and the ballets *Proserpina* (Florence, 1938), *Altair* (Naples, 1942), *Mondo tondo* (Rome, 1949), and *La bambola malata* (Venice, 1959); also *Il processo di Cristo*, oratorio (1949).

Porsile, Giuseppe, Italian composer; b. Naples, May 5, 1680; d. Vienna, May 29, 1750. He studied in Naples at the Cons. dei Poveri di Gesù Cristo with Ursino, Giordano, and Greco. He then served as vice maestro di cappella at the Spanish chapel in Naples. In 1695 he went to Spain to organize the music chapel of King Charles II in Barcelona; he subsequently served Charles III. When Charles III was elected Holy Roman Emperor as Charles VI, with the seat in Vienna, Porsile followed him there. On Dec. 17, 1720, he became court composer. He continued to serve the court after Charles VI died in 1740, being granted an honorary stipend; he was pensioned on April 1, 1749. Most of his stage works were written for the court of Vienna.

WORKS (all 1st perf. in Vienna unless otherwise given): DRAMATIC: OPERAS: *Il ritorno di Ulisse alla patria* (Naples, 1707); *Il giorno natalizio dell'imperatrice Amalia Wilhelmina* (April 21, 1717); *La Virtù festeggiata* (July 10, 1717); *Alceste*, festa teatrale (Nov. 19, 1718); *Meride e Selinunte*, dramma per musica (Aug. 28, 1721); *Il tempo fermato*, componimento da camera (Oct. 15, 1721); *La Virtù e la Bellezza in lega*, serenata (Oct. 15, 1722); *Il giorno felice*, componimento da camera (Aug. 28, 1723); *Componimento a due voci* (Aug. 28, 1725); *Spartaco*, dramma per musica (Feb. 21, 1726); *Il tempio di Giano, chiuso da Cesare Au-*

gusto, componimento per musica (Oct. 1, 1726); *La clemenza di Cesare*, servizio di camera (Oct. 1, 1727); *Telesilla*, festa teatrale (Nov. 19, 1729); *Scipione Africano, Il maggiore*, festa di camera (Oct. 1, 1730); *Dialogo tra il Decoro e la Placidezza*, festa di camera (July 26, 1732); *Dialogo*, pastorale a cinque voci (Aug. 28, 1732); *Dialogo tra la Prudenza e la Vivacita*, festa di camera (Oct. 15, 1732); *La Fama accresciuta dalla Virtù*, festa di camera (Oct. 15, 1735); *Sesostri, re d'Egitto, ovvero Le feste d'Iside*, dramma per musica (Carnival 1737); *Il giudizio rivocato*, festa di camera (Oct. 15, 1737). ORATORIOS: *Sisara* (March 23, 1719); *Tobia* (March 14, 1720); *Il zelo di Nathan* (1721); *L'anima immortale creata e redenta per il cielo* (Feb. 26, 1722); *Il trionfo di Giuditta* (Feb. 18, 1723); *Il sacrifizio di Gefte* (March 9, 1724); *Mosè liberato dal Nilo* (March 1, 1725); *Assalone nemico del padre amante* (March 14, 1726); *L'estaltazione de Salomone* (March 6, 1727); *L'ubbidienza a Dio* (March 9, 1730); *Due re, Roboamo e Geroboamo* (Feb. 23, 1731); *Giuseppe riconosciuto* (March 12, 1733); *La madre de' Maccabei* (March 14, 1737)

Porter, Andrew (Brian), brilliant English writer on music; b. Cape Town, South Africa, Aug. 26, 1928. He studied music at Diocesan College in Cape Town, then went to England and continued his education at Univ. College, Oxford; he became a proficient organist. In 1949 he joined the staff of the Manchester Guardian, then wrote music criticism for the *Financial Times* of London (1953–74); he also served as ed. of the *Musical Times* of London (1960–67). In 1972 he became the music critic of the *New Yorker*. In 1992 he became the chief music critic of *The Observer* in London, a post he held until 1997. He was made a corresponding member of the American Musicological Soc. in 1993. A polyglot, a polymath, and an uncommonly diversified intellectual, Porter expanded his interests far beyond the limited surface of purely musical studies; he mastered German, Italian, and French; made an exemplary tr. into Eng. of the entire text of *Der Ring des Nibelungen*, taking perspicuous care for the congenial rendition of Wagner's words and melodic inflections; his tr. was used to excellent advantage in the performance and recording of the cycle by the conductor Reginald Goodall with the English National Opera. Porter also tr. texts of Verdi's operas, Mozart's *Die Zauberflöte*, and some French operas. His mastery of English prose and his unostentatious display of arcane erudition make him one of the most remarkable music critics writing in the English language. Selections from his reviews have been publ. in *A Musical Season* (N.Y., 1974), *Music of Three Seasons, 1974–1977* (N.Y., 1978), *Music of Three More Seasons, 1977–1980* (N.Y., 1981), *Musical Events: A Chronicle, 1980–1983* (N.Y., 1987), and *Musical Events: A Chronicle, 1983–1986* (N.Y., 1989); he also was coed. of *Verdi's Macbeth: A Sourcebook* (N.Y., 1983).

Portugal or **Portogallo** (real name, **Ascenção** or **Assumpção**), **Marcos Antônio (da Fonseca),** prominent Portuguese composer; b. Lisbon, March 24, 1762; d. Rio de Janeiro, Feb. 7, 1830. A pupil at the ecclesiastical seminary at Lisbon, he continued his musical education with composition lessons from João de Souza Carvalho. Between 1784 and 1791 he wrote for Lisbon 17 stage works, mostly ephemeral. His reputation was made in Italy, where, with the exception of a short visit to Lisbon, he lived from 1792 to 1800, bringing out some 21 operas for various Italian theaters. Upon his return to Lisbon (1800), he was made mestre de capela of the royal chapel and director of the Teatro San Carlos. His *Il Filosofo seducente, ossia Non irritar le donne* (Venice, Dec. 27, 1798) was selected by Napoleon for opening the Théâtre-Italien at Paris in 1801. In 1807 the royal family fled to Brazil before the French invasion; Portugal remained until the Treatro San Carlos was closed in 1810, and then followed the court to Rio de Janeiro, where he served as mestre de capela of the royal chapel and master of music to the future John VI. The royal theater of Sao João, after its inauguration in 1813, produced several new operas by him. In that year he became director of the new Cons. at Vera Cruz, jointly with his brother Simão. He visited Italy in 1815, returned to Rio de Janeiro, and passed his last years there as an invalid. His masterpiece is *Fernando nel Messico* (Venice, Jan. 16, 1798; written for the famous English singer Elizabeth Billington; produced in London, in Italian, March 31, 1803); other Italian operas that had a favorable reception were *Demofoonte* (Milan, Feb. 8, 1794) and *Le Donne cambiate* (Venice, Oct. 22, 1797). Of his Portuguese operas, *A Castanheira* (The Chestnut Seller), produced in Lisbon in 1787, enjoyed considerable popular success.

BIBL.: M. Carvalhães, *M. P. na sua musica dramatica* (Lisbon, 1910).

Pospíšil, Juraj, Slovak composer and teacher; b. Olomouc, Jan. 14, 1931. He received training in piano, organ, and theory at the Olomouc School of Music (1949–50). After studying composition with Petrželka at the Janáček Academy of Music and Drama in Brno (1950–52), he completed his studies in composition with Moyzes and Cikker at the Bratislava Academy of Music and Drama (1952–55). From 1955 to 1991 he lectured on theory and composition at the Bratislava Cons. In 1988 he received an award from the Union of Slovak Composers. Pospíšil developed a compositional style which owed much to the Second Viennese School while paying homage to Slovak tradition. His works include *Inter arma*, cycle of 3 operas (1969–70), and *Manon Lescaut*, scenic drama (1993).

Potter, A(rchibald) J(ames), Irish composer and teacher; b. Belfast, Sept. 22, 1918; d. Greystones, July 5, 1980. He received training under W. Vale at the choir school of All Saints, Margaret Street, in London (1929–33), DGA. Fox at Clifton College in Bristol (1933–36), and Vaughan Williams at the Royal College of Music in London (1936–38); later he took his D.Mus. at the Univ. of Dublin (1953). From 1955 to 1973 he was a prof. of composition at the Royal Irish Academy of Music in Dublin. His output followed in the path of tradition and opted for Romantic qualities. Among his compositions were *Patrick*, television opera (1962; RTE, March 17, 1965), and *The Wedding*, opera (1979; Dublin, June 8, 1981); also the ballets *Careless Love* (1959; Dublin, April 12, 1960) and *Caitlín Bhocht* (1963; Radio Ireland, June 27, 1964).

Poueigh, Jean (Marie-Octave-Géraud), French composer and writer on music; b. Toulouse, Feb. 24, 1876; d. Olivet, Loiret, Oct. 20, 1958. After music study in his native city, he entered the Paris Cons. as a student of Caussade, Lenepveu, and Fauré; he also received advice from d'Indy; he settled in Paris. He harmonized and ed. a number of folk songs of Languedoc and Gascogne in *Les Chansons de France* (1907–09), *3 chansons des Pays d'Oc*, and *14 chansons anciennes*; also ed. the collection *Chansons populaires des Pyrénées françaises* (vol. 1, 1926). Under the pen name of Octave Séré, he publ. *Musiciens français d'aujourd'hui* (Paris, 1911; 7th ed., 1921); he contributed numerous articles to various French periodicals. His original compositions include the operas *Les Lointains* (1903), *Le Meneur de louves* (1921), *Perkin*, a Basque legend (Bordeaux, Jan. 16, 1931), *Le Roi de Camargue* (Marseilles, May 12, 1948), and *Bois-brule* (1956), and 3 ballets: *Funn* (1906), *Frivolant* (Paris, May 1, 1922), and *Chergui*, Moroccan ballet.

Poulenc, Francis (Jean Marcel), brilliant French composer; b. Paris, Jan. 7, 1899; d. there, Jan. 30, 1963. He was born into a wealthy family of pharmaceutical manufacturers; his mother taught him music in his childhood; at 16 he began taking formal piano lessons with Ricardo Viñes. A decisive turn in his development as a composer occurred when he attracted the attention of Erik Satie, the arbiter elegantiarum of the arts and social amenities in Paris. Deeply impressed by Satie's fruitful eccentricities in the then-shocking manner of Dadaism, Poulenc joined an ostentatiously self-descriptive musical group called the Nouveaux Jeunes. In a gratuitous parallel with the Russian Five, the French critic Henri Collet dubbed the "New Youths" Le Groupe de Six, and the label stuck under the designation Les Six. The 6 musicians included, besides Poulenc: Auric, Durey, Honegger, Milhaud, and Tailleferre. Although quite different in their styles of composition and artistic inclinations, they continued collective participation in various musical events. Poulenc served in the French army (1918–

21), and then began taking lessons in composition with Koechlin (1921–24). An excellent pianist, Poulenc became in 1935 an accompanist to the French baritone Pierre Bernac, for whom he wrote numerous songs. Compared with his fortuitous comrades-in-six, Poulenc appears a classicist. He never experimented with the popular devices of "machine music," asymmetrical rhythms, and polyharmonies as cultivated by Honegger and Milhaud. Futuristic projections had little interest for him; he was content to follow the gentle neoclassical formation of Ravel's piano music and songs. Among his other important artistic contacts was the ballet impresario Diaghilev, who commissioned him to write music for his Ballets Russes. Apart from his fine songs and piano pieces, Poulenc revealed himself as an inspired composer of religious music, of which his choral works *Stabat Mater* and *Gloria* are notable. He also wrote remarkable music for the organ, including a concerto that became a minor masterpiece. A master of artificial simplicity, he pleases even sophisticated listeners by his bland triadic tonalities, spiced with quickly passing diaphonous discords.

WORKS: DRAMATIC: OPERAS: *Les Mamelles de Tirésias*, opéra bouffe (1944; Paris, June 3, 1947); *Dialogues des Carmélites*, religious opera (1953–56; Milan, Jan. 26, 1957); *La Voix humaine*, monodrama for Soprano (1958; Paris, Feb. 6, 1959). BALLETS: *La Baigneuse de Trouville and Discours de Général*, 2 movements for *Les Mariés de la Tour Eiffel*, ballet farce (Paris, June 18, 1921; other movements by members of Les Six, except for Durey); *Les Biches*, with Chorus (1923; Monte Carlo, Jan. 6, 1924); *Pastourelle*, 9th movement of an 11-movement collective ballet, *L'Eventail de Jeanne* (1927; 1st perf. of orch. version, Paris, March 4, 1929; movements by Roussel, Ravel, Ibert, Milhaud et al.); *Aubade*, choreographic concerto for Piano and 18 Instruments (private perf., Paris, June 18, 1929; public perf., London, Dec. 19, 1929); *Les Animaux modèles* (1940–41; Paris, Aug. 8, 1942).

WRITINGS: *Emmanuel Chabrier* (Paris, 1961); *Moi et mes amis* (Paris, 1963; Eng. tr., London, 1978 as *My Friends and Myself*); *Journal de mes mélodies* (Paris, 1964); S. Buckland, tr. and ed., *Francis Poulenc: Selected Correspondence, 1915–1963: Echo and Source* (1991).

BIBL.: C. Rostand, *F. P.: Entretiens avec Claude Rostand* (Paris, 1954); H. Hell, *P.: Musicien français* (Paris, 1958); J. Roy, *F. P.* (Paris, 1964); P. Bernac, *F. P.: The Man and His Songs* (London, 1977); K. Daniel, *F. P.: His Artistic Development and Musical Style* (N.Y., 1982); F. Bloch, *F. P.* (Paris, 1984); M. Rosenthal, *Satie, Ravel, P.: An Intimate Memoir* (Madras and N.Y., 1987); G. Keck, *F. P.: A Bio-Bibliography* (Westport, Conn., 1990); W. Mellers, *F. P.* (Oxford, 1994); J. Roy, *Le groupe des six: P., Milhaud, Honegger, Auric, Tailleferre, Durey* (Paris, 1994); R. Machart, *P.* (Paris, 1995); C. Schmidt, *The Music of F. P. (1899–1963): A Catalogue* (Oxford, 1995).

Pound, Ezra (Loomis), greatly significant American man of letters and amateur composer; b. Hailey, Idaho, Oct. 30, 1885; d. Venice, Nov. 1, 1972. He was educated at Hamilton College (Ph.B., 1905) and the Univ. of Pa. (M.A., 1906). He went to England, where he established himself as a leading experimental poet and influential critic. He also pursued a great interest in early music, especially that of the troubadours, which led him to try his hand at composing. With the assistance of George Antheil, he composed the opera *Le Testament*, after poems by François Villon (1923; Paris, June 19, 1926); it was followed by a 2d opera, *Calvacanti* (1932), and a 3d, left unfinished, based on the poetry of Catullus. In 1924 he settled in Rapallo. Although married to Dorothy Shakespear, daughter of one of Yeats's friends, he became intimate with the American violinist Olga Rudge; Rudge bore him a daughter in 1925 and his wife bore him a son in 1926. Through the influence of Rudge, his interest in music continued, and he became a fervent champion of Vivaldi; he also worked as a music reviewer and ran a concert series with Rudge, Inverno Musicale. A growing interest in economic history and an inordinate admiration for the Fascist dictator Benito Mussolini led Pound down the road of political obscurantism. During World War II, he made many broadcasts over Rome Radio on topics ranging from literature to politics. His condemnation of Jewish banking circles in America and the American effort to defeat Fascism led to his arrest by the Allies after the collapse of Il Duce's regime. In 1945 he was sent to a prison camp in Pisa. In 1946 he was sent to the United States to stand trial for treason, but was declared insane and confined to St. Elizabeth's Hospital in Washington, D.C. Finally, in 1958, he was released and allowed to return to Italy, where he died. Among his writings on music is *Antheil and the Treatise on Harmony* (1924). The uncatalogued collection of Pound's musical MSS at Yale Univ. includes various musical experiments, including rhythmic and melodic realizations of his poem *Sestina: Altaforte*. Among the composers who have set his poems to music are Copland, Luytens, and Berio.

BIBL.: S. Adams, *E. P. and Music* (diss., Univ. of Toronto, 1974); R. Schafer, ed., *E. P. and Music* (N.Y., 1977).

Pountney, David (Willoughby), English opera director; b. Oxford, Sept. 10, 1947. He received his education at Radley College and at the Univ. of Cambridge. In 1967 he staged his first opera, A. Scarlatti's *Il trionfo dell'onore*, with the Cambridge Opera Soc. In 1971 he produced *The Rake's Progress* at Glasgow's Scottish Opera, and in 1972 at the Netherlands Opera in Amsterdam. He first directed opera in the United States in 1973 when he mounted *Macbeth* at the Houston Grand Opera. From 1975 to 1980 he served as director of productions at the Scottish Opera; in collaboration with the Welsh National Opera in Cardiff, he produced a celebrated cycle of Janáček's operas. In 1977 he oversaw the production of the premiere of Blake's *Toussaint* at the English National Opera in London, and in 1980 he was responsible for the staging of the premiere of Glass's *Satyagraha* at the Netherlands Opera. Pountney garnered critical accolades during his tenure as director of productions at the English National Opera from 1982 to 1993. His productions have also been staged in Berlin, Rome, Paris, Chicago, and N.Y. Pountney's imaginative approach to opera production aims to create a total theater experience, running the gamut from the purely visual to the psychological.

Pourtalès, Guy (Guido James) de, French writer on music; b. Berlin, Aug. 4, 1881; d. Lausanne, June 12, 1941. He studied in Bonn, Berlin, and Paris, then was in the French army during World War I. He then settled in Paris as a music critic. He publ. *La Vie de Franz Liszt* (1925), *Chopin, ou Le Poète* (1927; 2d ed., 1946; Eng. tr., London, 1930 as *Chopin: A Man of Solitude*), *Wagner: Histoire d'un artiste* (1932; 2d ed., rev. and aug. 1942), and *Berlioz et l'Europe romantique* (1939).

Pousseur, Henri (Léon Marie Thérèse), radical Belgian composer and pedagogue; b. Malmédy, June 23, 1929. He studied at the Liège Cons. (1947–52) and the Brussels Cons. (1952–53) and had private lessons in composition from Souris and Boulez. Until 1959, he worked in the Cologne and Milan electronic music studios, where he came in contact with Stockhausen and Berio; he was a member of the avant-garde group of composers "Variation" in Liège. He taught music in various Belgian schools (1950–59) and was founder (1958) and director of the Studio de Musique Electronique APELAC in Brussels, from 1970 a part of the Centre de Recherches Musicales in Liège; he gave lectures at the summer courses of new music in Darmstadt (1957–67), Cologne (1966–68), Basel (1963–64), the State Univ. of N.Y. in Buffalo (1966–69), the Liège Cons. (1970–94), and the Univ. of Liège (1983–94). In his music he tries to synthesize all the expressive powers of which man, as a biological species, Homo sapiens (or even Homo insipiens), is capable in the domain of art (or nonart); the technological resources of the subspecies Homo habilis (magnetic tape, electronics/synthesizers, aleatory extensions, the principle of indeterminacy, glossolalia, self-induced schizophasia) all form part of his rich musical (or nonmusical) vocabulary for multimedia (or nullimedia) representations. The influence of his methods (or nonmethods) of composition (or noncomposition) is pervasive. He publ. *Fragments théoriques I. Sur la musique experimentale* (Brussels, 1970).

WORKS: DRAMATIC: *Electre*, "musical action" (1960); *Votre Faust*, aleatory "fantasy in the manner of an opera" for 5 Actors,

Vocal Quartet, 12 Musicians, and Tapes, for which the audience decides the ending (1961–67; Milan, 1969; concert version as *Portail de Votre Faust* for 4 Voices, Tape, and 12 Instruments; in collaboration with Michel Butor); *Mnemosyne I*, monody, after Hölderlin, for Solo Voice, or Unison Chorus, or one Instrument (1968), and *II*, an instrumental re-creation of *Mnemosyne I*, with ad libitum scoring (1969); *Die Erprobung des Petrus Herbraicus*, chamber opera (Berlin, Sept. 12, 1974); *Leçons d'enfer*, musical theater (Metz, Nov. 14, 1991).

Pownall, Mary Ann, English actress, singer, and composer; b. London, Feb. 1751; d. Charleston, S.C., Aug. 11, 1796. She was known first as **Mrs. James Wrightson** (her 1st husband was a prompter in a London theater). She made her debut in 1770 in *The Recruiting Officer* in London, and then, from 1776 to 1788, she was a Vauxhall favorite. In 1792 she first appeared in Boston with the Old American Co., of which she was a leading artist; later she sang in subscription concerts in New York, and joined John Henry's N.Y. Co. She composed the text and music of numerous songs, including "Advice to the Ladies of Boston," "Washington" (in honor of George Washington), and "Primroses." Some of her songs were publ. in *Six Songs for the Harpsichord* (in collaboration with J. Hewitt; 1794) and *Kisses Sued For* (1795).

Pozdro, John (Walter), American composer and pedagogue; b. Chicago, Aug. 14, 1923. He began training in piano and theory at an early age with Nina Shafran, and later studied piano with Edward Collins at the American Cons. of Music in Chicago (1941–42). After serving in military intelligence in the U.S. Army, he pursued his training with Robert Delaney at Northwestern Univ., taking B.M. and M.M. (1949) degrees. He completed his studies with Hanson, Rogers, and Barlow at the Eastman School of Music in Rochester, N.Y. (Ph.D. in composition, 1958). In 1950 he joined the faculty of the Univ. of Kansas in Lawrence, becoming chairman of theory and composition in 1961; from 1958 to 1968 he also chaired its Annual Symposium of Contemporary Music. He retired from teaching in 1992. In 1993 he served as guest composer for the International Carillon Congress in Berkeley, where he was awarded the Univ. of Calif. at Berkeley Medal for distinguished service in music. His music is inherently pragmatic, with tertian torsion resulting in the formation of tastefully enriched triadic harmony, and with asymmetric rhythms enhancing the throbbing pulse of musical continuity. Among his works are *Hello, Kansas!*, musical play (Lawrence, Kansas, June 12, 1961), and *Malooley and the Fear Monster*, "family opera" (1976; Lawrence, Kansas, Feb. 6, 1977).

Pratella, Francesco Balilla, Italian music critic, musicologist, and composer; b. Lugo di Romagna, Feb. 1, 1880; d. Ravenna, May 17, 1955. He studied with Ricci-Signorini, then at the Liceo Rossini in Pesaro with Cicognani and Mascagni. He taught in Cesana (1908–09) and was director of the Istituto Musicale in Lugo (1910–29), and of the Liceo Musicale Giuseppe Verdi in Ravenna (1927–45). He joined the Italian futurist movement in 1910 (Russolo's manifesto of 1913 was addressed to "Balilla Pratella, grande musicista futurista"), and in 1913 wrote his first composition in a "futurist" idiom, the choral work *Musica futurista*, renamed *Inno alla vita* (1912; rev. 1933). After World War I, he broke with futurism.

WORKS: DRAMATIC: OPERAS: *Lilia* (1903; Lugo, Nov. 13, 1905); *La Sina d'Vargöun* (1906–08; Bologna, Dec. 4, 1909); *L'Aviatore Dro* (1911–14; Lugo, Nov. 4, 1920); *La ninnananna della bambola*, children's opera (1920–22; Milan, May 21, 1923); *La leggenda di San Fabiano* (1928–32; Bologna, Dec. 9, 1939); *L'uomo* (1934–49); *Dono primaverile*, comedy with music (Bologna, Oct. 17, 1923). Also incidental music.

WRITINGS: *Cronache e critiche dal 1905 al 1917* (Bologna, 1918); *L'evoluzione della musica: Dal 1910 al 1917* (Milan, 1918–19); *Saggio di gridi, canzoni, cori e danze del popolo italiano* (Bologna, 1919); *Luci ed ombre: per un musicista italiano ignorato in Italia* (Rome, 1933); *Scritti vari di pensiero, di arte, di storia musicale* (Bologna, 1933); *Autobiografia* (Milan, 1971).

BIBL.: A. Ghigi, *F. B. P.* (Ravenna, 1930); *F. B. P.: Appunti biografici e bibliografici* (Ravenna, 1931); R. Payton, *The Futurist Musicians: F. B. P. and Luigi Russola* (diss., Univ. of Chicago, 1974).

Pratt, Silas Gamaliel, American composer; b. Addison, Vt., Aug. 4, 1846; d. Pittsburgh, Oct. 30, 1916. Both his parents were church singers. The family moved to Chicago when he was a child, and he received his primary music education there; at 22 he went to Berlin, where he studied piano with Kullak and theory with Kiel (1868–71). He then returned to Chicago, where he served as organist of the Church of the Messiah. In 1872 he established the Apollo Club. In 1875 he went to Germany once more, where he studied orchestration with Heinrich Dorn, and also took some piano lessons with Liszt. On July 4, 1876, he conducted in Berlin his *Centennial Overture*, dedicated to President Grant; he also conducted at the Crystal Palace in London, when President Grant was visiting there; another work that he presented in London was *Homage to Chicago March*. Returning to Chicago, he conducted his opera *Zenobia, Queen of Palmyra* (to his own libretto) in concert form, on June 15, 1882 (stage perf., Chicago, March 26, 1883; N.Y., Aug. 21, 1883). The opera was received in a hostile manner by the press, partly owing to the poor quality of the music, but mainly as a reaction to Pratt's exuberant and immodest proclamations of its merit in advance of the production. Undaunted, Pratt unleashed a vigorous campaign for native American opera; he organized the Grand Opera Festival of 1884, which had some support. The following year he visited London again, and conducted there his symphonic work *The Prodigal Son* (Oct. 5, 1885). Returning to Chicago, he revised his early lyric opera *Antonio*, renamed it *Lucille*, and produced it on March 14, 1887. In 1888 he moved to New York, where he presented, during the quadricentennial of the discovery of America, his opera *The Triumph of Columbus* (in concert form, Oct. 12, 1892); he also produced a scenic cantata, *America*, subtitled *4 Centuries of Music, Picture, and Song* (Nov. 24, 1894; with stereopticon projections). He also publ. a manual, *Pianist's Mental Velocity* (N.Y., 1903). In 1906 he settled in Pittsburgh, where he established the Pratt Inst. of Music and Art, and remained its director until his death. Pratt was a colorful personality; despite continuous and severe setbacks, he was convinced of his own significance. The story of his salutation to Wagner at their meeting—"Herr Wagner, you are the Silas G. Pratt of Germany"—may be apocryphal, but is very much in character.

Predieri, family of Italian musicians:

(1) Giacomo (Maria) Predieri, organist, cornett player, and composer; b. Bologna, April 9, 1611; d. there, 1695. He was active as a cornett player in Bologna's municipal instrumental ensemble. He was also a singer at S. Petronio (1636–57), where he was vice maestro di cappella (1650–57); he was organist at the cathedral of S. Pietro (1679–93). He was a founding member of the Accademia Filarmonica (1666), and in 1693 was made its principe. He had 2 nephews who studied with him and pursued careers in music:

(2) Antonio Predieri, singer; b. Bologna, c.1650; d. there, 1710. He began his career as a tenor in F. Bassani's *L'inganno trionfato* (1673), then sang opera in various Italian cities. He was also in the service of the dukes of Mantua (1684–87) and Parma (1687–99?), and also sang at the church of the Steccata in Parma (1689–96). He was made a member of Bologna's Accademia Filarmonica in 1685.

(3) Giacomo Cesare Predieri, singer and composer; b. Bologna, March 26, 1671; d. there, 1753. He studied with G. P. Colonna, and became a member of Bologna's Accademia Filarmonica as a singer in 1688, being promoted to composer in 1690; he also served as its principe (1698, 1707, 1711), and was maestro di cappella at the cathedral of S. Pietro (1696–1742). He wrote many sacred works, including 11 oratorios (only 1 extant). He had a nephew who was also a musician.

(4) Luca Antonio Predieri, violinist and composer; b. Bologna, Sept. 13, 1688; d. there, 1767. He studied violin with Abondio Bini and Tommaso Vitali, and counterpoint with his uncle, as well as with Angelo Predieri (b. Bologna, Jan. 14, 1655; d. there, Feb. 27, 1731), the singer and composer, and Giacomo Antonio Perti. He was an instrumentalist at the church of S. Petronio; he became a member of the Accademia Filarmonica with the rank of composer (1716), serving as its principe (1723). He was maestro di cappella at S. Paolo (1725–29), Madonna della Galliera (1726), Arciconfraternità della Vita (1727), and the cathedral of S. Pietro (1728–31). He went to Vienna (1737), where he served as vice maestro (1739–41) and maestro (1741–51) at the court chapel; he returned to Bologna (1765). He wrote 31 operas, of which the following are extant: *Gli auguri spiegati* (Laxenburg, May 3, 1738), *La pace tra la virtù e la bellezza* (Vienna, Oct. 15, 1738), *Perseo* (Vienna, Nov. 4, 1738), *Astrea placata, ossia La felicità della terra* (Vienna, Aug. 28, 1739), and *Zenobia* (Vienna, Aug. 28, 1740). He distinguished himself as a composer of sacred music; of his 7 oratorios, only *Il sacrificio d'Abramo* (Vienna, 1738) and *Isacco figura del Redentore* (Vienna, Feb. 12, 1740) are extant.

BIBL.: R. Ortner, *L. A. P. und sein Wiener Opernschaffen* (Vienna, 1971).

Prégardien, Christoph, German tenor; b. Limburg an der Lahn, Jan. 18, 1956. He gained experience as a member of the cathedral boy's choir and later the cathedral choir in his native city. He studied voice with Martin Gründler at the Frankfurt am Main Hochschule für Musik (graduated, 1983) and with Carla Castellani in Milan. In 1978 he won the Federal Republic of Germany vocal competition in Berlin. He sang opera in Frankfurt am Main, Stuttgart, Hamburg, Antwerp, Karlsruhe, Ghent, and other European cities, becoming well known for his roles in Baroque and Classical operas. As a concert and lieder artist, he appeared in major European music centers with notable success. In 1989 he gave a series of early music concerts in London, returning there in 1993 to make his Wigmore Hall recital debut. In 1997 he gave a London recital to mark the bicentenary of Schubert's birth. Prégardien has won particular praise for his interpretations of works by Schütz, Bach, Handel, Buxtehude, Haydn, and Mozart.

Prêtre, Georges, prominent French conductor; b. Waziers, Aug. 14, 1924. He studied at the Douai Cons., then at the Paris Cons.; he also received instruction in conducting from Cluytens. He made his debut as a conductor at the Marseilles Opera in 1946; subsequently he had guest engagements in Lille, Casablanca, and Toulouse, then was music director of the Paris Opéra Comique (1955–59); he subsequently conducted at the Paris Opéra (from 1959), where he served as music director (1970–71). In 1959 he made his U.S. debut at the Chicago Lyric Opera; in 1961 he appeared for the first time in London. On Oct. 17, 1964, he made his first appearance at the Metropolitan Opera in New York, conducting *Samson et Dalila*. He appeared as a guest conductor with many of the major opera houses and orchs. of the world in succeeding years. He also served as principal guest conductor of the Vienna Sym. Orch. (1986–91).

Previn, André (George) (real name, **Andreas Ludwig Priwin**), brilliant German-born American pianist, conductor, and composer; b. Berlin, April 6, 1929. He was of Russian-Jewish descent. He showed an unmistakable musical gift as a child; his father, a lawyer, was an amateur musician who gave him his early training; they played piano, 4-hands, together at home. At the age of 6, he was accepted as a pupil at the Berlin Hochschule für Musik, where he studied piano with Breithaupt; as a Jew, however, he was compelled to leave school in 1938. The family then went to Paris; he continued his studies at the Cons., Dupré being one of his teachers. In 1939 the family emigrated to America, settling in Los Angeles, where his father's cousin, Charles Previn, was music director at Universal Studios in Hollywood. He took lessons in composition with Joseph Achron, Toch, and Castelnuovo-Tedesco. He became a naturalized American citizen in 1943. Even before graduating from high school, he obtained employment at MGM; he became an orchestrator there and later one of its music directors; he also became a fine jazz pianist. He served in the U.S. Army (1950–52); stationed in San Francisco, he took lessons in conducting with Monteux, then music director of the San Francisco Sym. During these years, he wrote much music for films; he received Academy Awards for his arrangements of *Gigi* (1958), *Porgy and Bess* (1959), *Irma la Douce* (1963), and *My Fair Lady* (1964). Throughout this period he continued to appear as a concert pianist. In 1962 he made his formal conducting debut with the St. Louis Sym. Orch., and conducting soon became his principal vocation. From 1967 to 1969 he was conductor-in-chief of the Houston Sym. Orch. In 1968 he assumed the post of principal conductor of the London Sym. Orch., retaining it with distinction until 1979; he then was made its conductor emeritus. In 1976 he became music director of the Pittsburgh Sym. Orch., a position he held with similar distinction until a dispute with the management led to his resignation in 1984. He had already been engaged as music director of the Royal Phil. of London in 1982, a position he held from 1985 to 1987; he then served as its principal conductor from 1987 to 1992, and thereafter was its Conductor Laureate. Previn also accepted appointment as music director of the Los Angeles Phil., after resigning his Pittsburgh position; he formally assumed his duties in Los Angeles in 1985, but gave up this position in 1990 after disagreements with the management over administrative procedures. During his years as a conductor of the London Sym. Orch., he took it on a number of tours to the United States, as well as to Russia, Japan, South Korea, and Hong Kong. He also took the Pittsburgh Sym. Orch. on acclaimed tours of Europe in 1978 and 1982. He continued to compose popular music, including the scores for the musicals *Coco* (1969) and *The Good Companions* (1974); with words by Tom Stoppard, he composed *Every Good Boy Deserves Favour* (1977), a work for Actors and Orch. His first opera, *A Streetcar Named Desire*, was mounted in San Francisco on Sept. 19, 1998, Previn conducting. He ed. the book *Orchestra* (Garden City, N.Y., 1979); he also publ. *André Previn's Guide to Music* (London, 1983) and the autobiographical *No Minor Chords: My Days in Hollywood* (N.Y., 1991). He was married four times (and divorced thrice): to the jazz singer Betty Bennett, to the jazz poet Dory Langdon (who made a career of her own as composer and singer of pop songs), to the actress Mia Farrow, and in 1982 to Heather Hales. In 1996 he was made an honorary knight by Queen Elizabeth II of England.

BIBL.: E. Greenfield, *A. P.* (N.Y., 1973); M. Bookspan and R. Yockey, *A. P.: A Biography* (Garden City, N.Y., 1981); H. Ruttencutter, *P.* (London, 1985).

Previtali, Fernando, prominent Italian conductor; b. Adria, Feb. 16, 1907; d. Rome, Aug. 1, 1985. He studied cello, piano, and composition at the Turin Cons.; he then was Gui's assistant at the Maggio Musicale Fiorentino (1928–36). He was chief conductor of the Rome Radio orch. (1936–43; 1945–53); he also conducted at Milan's La Scala and at other major Italian opera houses. From 1953 to 1973 he was chief conductor of the Orchestra Sinfonica dell'Accademia Nazionale di Santa Cecilia in Rome, which he led on tours abroad. On Dec. 15, 1955, he made his U.S. debut as a guest conductor with the Cleveland Orch. Previtali became well known for his advocacy of contemporary Italian composers, and conducted the premieres of numerous operas and orch. works. He was also a composer; he wrote the ballet *Allucinazioni* (Rome, 1945), choral works, chamber music, etc. He publ. *Guida allo studio della direzione d'orchestra* (Rome, 1951).

Prévost, Eugène-Prosper, French conductor and composer; b. Paris, April 23, 1809; d. New Orleans, Aug. 19, 1872. He studied at the Paris Cons. with Le Sueur, winning the Grand Prix de Rome in 1831 with the cantata *Bianca Capello*. He conducted theatrical music in Le Havre (1835–38), then went to New Orleans, where he conducted until 1862. He was active in Paris (1862–67) before returning to New Orleans as a singing master. He produced several operas in Paris, of which *Cosimo* (Opéra Comique, Oct. 13, 1835) was the most successful; another, *Blanche et Rene*, was given in New Orleans in 1861. He also wrote oratorios and masses.

Prey, Claude, French composer; b. Fleury-sur-Andelle, Eure, May 30, 1925. After studies at the Sorbonne in Paris and with

Milhaud and Messiaen at the Paris Cons., he pursued his training with Mignone in Rio de Janeiro (1953–54) and with Frazzi in Siena before completing his studies at Laval Univ. in Quebec. In 1963 he won the Prix Italia. He devoted himself principally to composing dramatic scores.

WORKS: DRAMATIC: *Le Phénix*, opera (1957); *Lettres perdues*, radiophonic opera (1960); *La Dictée*, lyric monodrama (1961); *Le Coeur révélateur*, chamber opera (1962); *L'Homme occis*, opera (1963); *Jonas*, opera oratorio (1964; 1st stage perf., Lyons, Dec. 2, 1969); *Donna mobile I*, opera (1965; Avignon, July 15, 1972); *La Noirceur du lait*, "opéra test" (1967); *On veut la lumière? Allons-y!*, opera parody (1969); *Fêtes de la faim*, opera (1969); *Jeu de l'oie*, opera (1970); *Théâtrophonie*, opera (1971); *Donna mobile II*, "opéra kit" (1972); *Les liaisons dangereuses*, "opéra épistolaire" (1973); *Young libertad*, "opéra study" (1975); *Les Trois Langages*, children's opera (1978); *Utopopolis*, "opéra chanson(s)" (1980); *L'Escalier de Chambord*, opera (1981); *Scenarios VII*, opera (1982); *Lunedi blu*, "opéra flash" (1982); *Paulina*, chamber opera (1983); *O comme eau*, madrigal opera (1984); *Paysages pacifiques*, "mélo cycle" (1986); *Le Rouge et le Noir*, opera (1989); *Sommaire soleil*, "mélo(d)rama" (1991); *Parlons fric!* (1992); *Sitôt le septuor*, opera (1994).

Prey, Hermann, outstanding German baritone; b. Berlin, July 11, 1929; d. Munich, July 22, 1998. He studied with Günther Baum and Harry Gottschalk at the Berlin Hochschule für Musik; he won 1st prize in a vocal competition organized by the U.S. Army (1952), and that same year made his operatic debut as the 2d prisoner in *Fidelio* in Wiesbaden. After appearing in the United States, he joined the Hamburg State Opera (1953); he also sang in Vienna (from 1956), Berlin (from 1956), and in Salzburg (from 1959). In 1959 he became a principal member of the Bavarian State Opera in Munich; made his Metropolitan Opera debut in New York as Wolfram (Dec. 16, 1960); he appeared for the first time in England at the Edinburgh Festival (1965), and later sang regularly at London's Covent Garden (from 1973). He also appeared as a soloist with the major orchs. and as a recitalist; likewise he starred in his own Munich television show. In 1982 he became a prof. at the Hamburg Hochschule für Musik. His autobiography was publ. as *Premierenfieber* (1981; Eng. tr., 1986, as *First Night Fever: The Memoirs of Hermann Prey*). Among his finest operatic roles were Count Almaviva, Papageno, Guglielmo, and Rossini's Figaro; he also sang a number of contemporary roles. As a lieder artist, he distinguished himself in Schubert, Schumann, and Brahms.

Preyer, Gottfried von, Austrian organist and composer; b. Hausbrunn, March 15, 1807; d. Vienna, May 9, 1901. He studied with Sechter in Vienna. In 1835 he became organist of the Lutheran Church in Vienna, and, in 1838, prof. of music theory at the Vienna Cons., of which he was director from 1844 to 1848. In 1853 he became music director at St. Stephen's; he was pensioned in 1876. He wrote 3 operas and the oratorio *Noah*.

Prianishnikov, Ippolit (Petrovich), Russian baritone; b. Kerch, Aug. 26, 1847; d. Petrograd, Nov. 11, 1921. He joined the Russian Imperial Navy, and later began to study voice, first at the St. Petersburg Cons. (1873–75), then in Italy, where he became a student of Ronconi in Milan. He made his debut in Milan in 1876. Returning to Russia, he joined the Maryinsky Theater in St. Petersburg in 1878, remaining there until 1886. He then went to Tiflis (1886–89) and Moscow (1892–93), where he sang and produced opera. In later years he also taught voice. Among his students were Bolshakov, Nikolai Figner, and Mravina.

Přibyl, Vilém, Czech tenor; b. Náchod, April 10, 1925; d. Brno, July 13, 1990. After making his debut with an amateur opera company in Hradec Králové (1952), he pursued vocal instruction there with Jakoubková (1952–62); he sang at the opera in Ústí nad Labem (1960) and at the Janáček Opera in Brno (1960); he also received further training from Vavrdová at the Brno Academy of Music. He gained notable success with his portrayal of Dalibor with the Prague National Theater Opera during its visit to the Edinburgh Festival (1964); he then appeared in various European music centers; he also taught at the Janáček Academy of Arts in Brno (from 1969). In 1969 he was made an Artist of Merit and in 1977 a National Artist by the Czech government. His repertoire included Lohengrin, Radames, and Otello, as well as roles in operas by Prokofiev, Martinů, and Shostakovich; he was especially esteemed for his roles in operas by Janáček.

Price, (Mary Violet) Leontyne, remarkably endowed black American soprano; b. Laurel, Miss., Feb. 10, 1927. She was taught piano by a local woman, and also learned to sing. On Dec. 17, 1943, she played piano and sang at a concert in Laurel. She went to Oak Park High School, graduating in music in 1944; she then enrolled in the College of Education and Industrial Arts in Wilberforce, Ohio, where she studied voice with Catherine Van Buren; she received her B.A. degree in 1948, and then was awarded a scholarship at the Juilliard School of Music in New York; there she received vocal training from Florence Page Kimball, and also joined the Opera Workshop under the direction of Frederic Cohen. Virgil Thomson heard her perform the role of Mistress Ford in Verdi's opera *Falstaff* and invited her to sing in the revival of his opera *4 Saints in 3 Acts* in 1952. She subsequently performed the role of Bess in Gershwin's *Porgy and Bess* on a tour of the U.S. (1952–54) and in Europe (1955). On Nov. 14, 1954, she made a highly acclaimed debut as a concert singer in New York. On Dec. 3, 1954, she sang at the first performance of Samuel Barber's *Prayers of Kierkegaard* with the Boston Sym. Orch., conducted by Charles Munch. On Jan. 23, 1955, she performed Tosca on television, creating a sensation both as an artist and as a member of her race taking up the role of an Italian diva. Her career was soon assured without any reservations. In 1957 she appeared with the San Francisco Opera; on Oct. 18, 1957, she sang Aida, a role congenial to her passionate artistry. In 1958 she sang Aida with the Vienna State Opera under the direction of Herbert von Karajan; on July 2, 1958, she sang this role at Covent Garden in London and again at La Scala in Milan in 1959, becoming the first black woman to sing with that most prestigious and most fastidious opera company. On Jan. 27, 1961, she made her first appearance with the Metropolitan Opera in New York in the role of Leonora in *Il Trovatore*. A series of highly successful performances at the Metropolitan followed: Aida on Feb. 20, 1961; Madama Butterfly on March 3, 1961; Donna Anna on March 25, 1961; Tosca on April 1, 1962; Pamina on Jan. 3, 1964; Cleopatra in the premiere of Samuel Barber's opera *Antony and Cleopatra* at the opening of the new Metropolitan Opera House at Lincoln Center in New York on Sept. 16, 1966. On Sept. 24, 1973, she sang Madama Butterfly at the Metropolitan once more. On Feb. 7, 1975, she appeared there in the title role of *Manon Lescaut*; and on Feb. 3, 1976, she sang Aida, a role she repeated for her farewell performance in opera in a televised production broadcast live from the Metropolitan Opera in New York by PBS on Jan. 3, 1985. She then continued her concert career, appearing with notable success in the major music centers. She was married in 1952 to **William Warfield** (who sang Porgy at her performances of *Porgy and Bess*), but separated from him in 1959; they were divorced in 1973. She received many honors during her remarkable career; in 1964 President Johnson bestowed upon her the Medal of Freedom, and in 1985 President Reagan presented her with the National Medal of Arts.

BIBL.: H. Lyon, *L. P.: Highlights of a Prima Donna* (N.Y., 1973); R. Steins, *L. P., Opera Superstar* (Woodbridge, Conn., 1993).

Price, Dame Margaret (Berenice), outstanding Welsh soprano; b. Blackwood, near Tredegar, South Wales, April 13, 1941. She commenced singing lessons when she was 9; she then won the Charles Kennedy Scott scholarship of London's Trinity College of Music at 15, and studied voice with Scott for 4 years. After singing in the Ambrosian Singers for 2 seasons, she made her operatic debut as Cherubino with the Welsh National Opera (1962); she then sang that same role at her Covent Garden debut in London (1963). She made her first appearance at the Glyndebourne Festival as Constanze in *Die Entführung aus dem Serail* (1968); she then made her U.S. debut as Pamina at the San Francisco Opera (1969); and subsequently sang Fiordiligi at the Chicago Lyric Opera (1972). In 1973 she sang at the Paris Opéra, later joining its cast during its U.S. tour in 1976, eliciting extraordinary praise from the public and critics for her portrayal of Desdemona; she made an auspicious Metropolitan Opera debut in New York in that same role on Jan. 21, 1985. In 1987 she was engaged as Norma at Covent Garden. After appearing as Adriana Lecouvreur in Bonn in 1989, she sang Amelia Grimaldi in a concert performance of *Simon Boccanegra* at the Royal Festival Hall in London in 1990. During the 1993–94 season she sang in *Ariadne auf Naxos* at the Berlin State Opera. She also toured widely as a concert singer. Her other notable roles include Donna Anna, Aida, Adriana Lecouvreur, and Strauss's Ariadne. Price's voice is essentially a lyric soprano, but is capable of technically brilliant coloratura. She was made a Commander of the Order of the British Empire in 1982. In 1992 she was made a Dame Commander of the Order of the British Empire.

Priestman, Brian, English conductor and music educator; b. Birmingham, Feb. 10, 1927. He received his training at the Univ. of Birmingham (B.Mus., 1950; M.A., 1952) and the Brussels Cons. (diploma, 1952). After serving as founder-conductor of the Opera da Camera and the Orch. da Camera in Birmingham, he was music director of the Royal Shakespeare Theatre at Stratford-upon-Avon (1960–63). He conducted the Edmonton (Alberta) Sym. Orch. (1964–68) and the Baltimore Sym. Orch. (1968–69), and then was music director of the Denver Sym. Orch. (1970–78). He also was principal conductor of the New Zealand National Orch. in Wellington (1973–76) and music director of the Florida Phil. (1977–80). From 1980 to 1986 he was principal conductor of the Cape Town Sym. Orch., prof. and chairman of the music dept. at the Univ. of Cape Town, and director of the South African College of Music. He was principal guest conductor of the Malmö Sym. Orch. (1988–90). In 1992 he became artist-in-residence, prof., and director of orch. studies at the Univ. of Kansas at Lawrence.

Prigozhin, Lucian (Abramovich), Russian composer; b. Tashkent, Aug. 15, 1926. He received training in piano and theory in Tashkent, and then completed his studies with Shcherbachev, Evlakhov, and Kochurov at the Leningrad Cons. He became a convinced modernist in his music, introducing the concept of "supplementary tones" in the 12-tone method of composition by allowing members of the tone-row to permutate freely. However, he preserved the basic tonality even when he no longer used the key signatures. Among his works are *Doctor Aybolit* (Ay! It Hurts!), children's radio opera (1956), *Circle of Hades*, ballet (1964; orch. suite, 1965), *Malchish-Kibalchish*, children's radio opera (1969), and *Robin Hood*, opera (1972); also film music and *Snowstorm*, chamber oratorio (1968).

BIBL.: E. Ruchyevskaya, *L. P.* (Moscow, 1977).

Pringsheim, Klaus, German conductor and composer; b. Feldafing, near Munich, July 24, 1883; d. Tokyo, Dec. 7, 1972. A scion of a highly cultured family, he studied mathematics with his father, a prof. at the Univ. of Munich, and physics with Röntgen, the discoverer of X-rays. His twin sister, Katherine, was married to Thomas Mann. In Munich, Pringsheim took piano lessons with Stavenhagen and composition with Thuille. In 1906 he went to Vienna and was engaged as assistant conductor of the Court Opera, under the tutelage of Mahler, who took him as a pupil in conducting and composition, a relationship that developed into profound friendship. Mahler recommended him to the management of the German Opera in Prague; Pringsheim conducted there from 1909 to 1914, then was engaged as conductor and stage director at the Bremen Opera (1915–18) and music director of the Max Reinhardt theaters in Berlin (1918–25). In 1923–24 he conducted in Berlin a Mahler cycle of 8 concerts, featuring all of Mahler's syms. and songs with orch. In 1927 he became the music critic of the socialist newspaper *Vorwärts*. A turning point in Pringsheim's life came in 1931 with an invitation to teach music at the Imperial Academy of Music in Tokyo, where he taught until 1937; several of his Japanese students became prominent composers. From 1937 to 1939 Pringsheim served as music adviser to the Royal Dept. of Fine Arts in Bangkok, Thailand. In 1939 he returned to Japan; he was briefly interned in 1944 as an opponent of the Axis policies. In 1946 he went to California; after some intermittent activities, he returned to Japan in 1951; he was appointed director of the Musashino Academy of Music in Tokyo; he continued to conduct and also wrote music reviews for English-language Tokyo newspapers. As a composer, Pringsheim followed the neo-Romantic trends, deeply influenced by Mahler. His compositions include a *Concerto for Orchestra* (Tokyo, Oct. 13, 1935); *Yamada Nagasama*, Japanese radio opera (1953); Concertino for Xylophone and Orch. (1962); *Theme, Variations, and Fugue* for Wind Orch. (his last composition, 1971–72); and a curious album of 36 2-part canons for Piano (1959). A chapter from his theoretical work *Pythagoras, die Atonalität und wir* was publ. in *Schweizerische Musikzeitung* (1957). His reminiscences, "Mahler, My Friend," were publ. posthumously in the periodical *Composer* (1973–74). Pringsheim was a signatory of a letter of protest by surviving friends of Mahler against the film *Death in Venice*, after a novel of Thomas Mann, in which the central character, a famous writer who suffers a homosexual crisis, was made to resemble Mahler.

Pritchard, Sir John (Michael), distinguished English conductor; b. London, Feb. 5, 1921; d. Daly City, Calif., Dec. 5, 1989. He studied violin with his father, and then continued his musical training in Italy, returning to England to serve in the British army during World War II. In 1947 he joined the staff of the Glyndebourne Festival Opera as a répétiteur; he became chorus master and assistant to Fritz Busch in 1948; he conducted there regularly from 1951, serving as its music director (1969–77). He made his first appearance at London's Covent Garden in 1952. He was principal conductor of the Royal Liverpool Phil. (1957–63) and the London Phil. (1962–66), touring widely abroad with the latter. In 1963 he made his U.S. debut as a guest conductor with the Pittsburgh Sym. Orch.; he also conducted at the Chicago Lyric Opera (1969) and the San Francisco Opera (1970). On Oct. 25, 1971, he made his Metropolitan Opera debut in New York conducting *Così fan tutte*. As a guest conductor, he appeared with many of the world's leading opera houses and orchs. He was chief conductor of the Cologne Opera (1978–89). In 1979 he became chief guest conductor of the BBC Sym. Orch. in London, and subsequently was made its chief conductor in 1982. He was also joint music director of the Opera National in Brussels (1981–89), and served as the 1st music director of the San Francisco Opera (1986–89). In 1962 he was made a Commander of the Order of the British Empire, and was knighted in 1983. Pritchard was esteemed for his unpretentious but assured command of a vast operatic and symphonic repertory, extending from the Baroque masters to the leading composers of the present era.

BIBL.: H. Conway, *Sir J. P.: His Life in Music* (London, 1993).

Proch, Heinrich, Austrian conductor and composer; b. Bohmisch-Leipa, July 22, 1809; d. Vienna, Dec. 18, 1878. He studied law and at the same time took violin lessons. He became conductor of the Josephstadt Theater in Vienna in 1837, and from 1840 to 1870, conducted at the Vienna Court Opera. He wrote many songs that were popular for a time; his set of variations for coloratura soprano, with flute obbligato, was particularly well known; he also brought out in Vienna a comic opera, *Ring und Maske* (Dec. 4, 1844), and 3 1-act operas: *Die Blutrache* (Dec. 5, 1846), *Zweiter und dritter Stock* (Oct. 5, 1847), and *Der gefährliche Sprung* (Jan. 5, 1849).

Procter, (Mary) Norma, English contralto; b. Cleethorpes, Feb. 15, 1928. She studied voice with Roy Henderson and Alec Redshaw. She made her debut in Handel's *Messiah* at Southwark Cathedral in 1948; she soon established herself as an outstanding concert singer; in 1961 she made her operatic debut at London's Covent Garden as Gluck's Orpheus.

Prod'homme, J(acques)-G(abriel), industrious French librarian and music critic; b. Paris, Nov. 28, 1871; d. Neuilly-sur-Seine, near Paris, June 18, 1956. He studied philology and music history at the Paris École des Hautes Études Sociales (1890–94), then became a writer on musical and other subjects in the socialist publications, among them *La Revue Socialiste, Droits de l'Homme*, and *Messidor*. An ardent believer in the cause of peace, he ed. in Munich the *Deutsche-französische Rundschau*, dedicated to the friendship between the French and German peoples (1899–1902). His hopes for peace were shattered by 2 devastating world wars within his lifetime. Back in Paris, he founded, with Dauriac and Écorcheville, the French section of the IMS (1902), serving as its secretary (1903–13); with La Laurencie, he founded the French Musicological Soc. (1917), serving as its secretary (1917–20) and vice president (1929–36). He was curator of the library and archivist of the museum at the Paris Opéra (1931–40); he was also librarian at the Paris Cons. (1934–40). He was made a Chevalier of the Légion d'honneur (1928). With others, he tr. Wagner's prose works (13 vols., 1907–25); also Wagner's music dramas (1922–27) and Beethoven's conversation books (1946).

WRITINGS (all publ. in Paris): *Le Cycle Berlioz*, in 2 vols.: *La Damnation de Faust* (1896) and *L'Enfance du Christ* (1899); with C. Bertrand, *Guides analytiques de l'Anneau du Nibelung. Crépuscule des dieux* (1902); *Hector Berlioz 1803–1869: Sa vie et ses oeuvres* (1905; 2d ed., rev., 1913); *Les Symphonies de Beethoven (1800–1827)* (1906; 15th ed., 1938); *Paganini* (1907; 2d ed., 1927; Eng. tr., 1911); *Franz Liszt* (1910); with A. Dandelot, *Gounod 1818–93: Sa vie et ses oeuvres d'après des documents inédits* (2 vols., 1911); *Ecrits de musiciens (XVe-XVIIIe siècles)* (1912); *Richard Wagner et la France* (1921); *La jeunesse de Beethoven, 1770–1800* (1921; 2d ed., 1927); *L'Opéra, 1669–1925* (1925); *Pensées sur la musique et les musiciens* (1926); *Beethoven raconté par ceux qui l'ont vu* (1927); *Mozart raconté par ceux qui l'ont vu 1756–1791* (1928); *Schubert raconté par ceux qui l'ont vu* (1928); with E. Crauzat, *Paris qui disparaît: Les Menus plaisirs du roi; L'Ecole royale et le Conservatoire de Paris* (1929); *Wagner raconté par ceux qui l'ont vu* (1929); *Les Sonates pour piano de Beethoven, 1782–1823* (1937; 2d ed., rev., 1950); *L'Immortelle bien-aimée de Beethoven* (1946); *Gluck* (1948); *François-Joseph Gossec, 1734–1829* (1949).

Profeta, Laurenciu, Romanian composer; b. Bucharest, Jan. 12, 1925. He studied with Constantinescu and Mendelsohn (harmony, counterpoint, and composition) at the Bucharest Cons. (1945–49) and with Messner (composition) at the Moscow Cons. (1954–56). He pursued his career in Bucharest, where he was assistant director of the Romanian Radio (1948–52). From 1952 to 1960 he was director of the music dept. of the Ministry of Culture. He was secretary of the Romanian National Committee of the International Music Council from 1960 to 1970. From 1968 he was also secretary of the Union of Composers and Musicologists, serving as a member of its directory council from 1990. It awarded him its prize 8 times (1968, 1969, 1976, 1979, 1980, 1986, 1990, 1993). In his music, Profeta has followed in the path of neoclassicism while utilizing various contemporary elements in his scores.

WORKS: DRAMATIC: *The Captain's Wife*, ballet (1946); *The Prince and the Pauper*, ballet (Bucharest, Sept. 15, 1967); *The Wistful Mariner*, ballet (1976); *The Hours of the Sea*, dance piece (1979); *The Triumph of Love*, ballet (1983); *Peter Pan's Story*, children's comic opera (Bucharest, Dec. 20, 1984); *Rica*, ballet (1986); *Hershale*, musical (1989); *The Loosers*, musical (Bucharest, Oct. 22, 1990); *Of the Carnival*, ballet (1991); *Maria Tănase*, musical (1992); *Turandot*, musical (1992); *Eva Now*, musical (1993); film scores. Also *The Happening in the Garden*, oratorio for Soloists, Reciter, Children's Chorus, and Orch. (1958).

Prohaska, Carl, Austrian composer, father of **Felix Prohaska**; b. Mödling, near Vienna, April 25, 1869; d. Vienna, March 28, 1927. He studied piano with Anna Assmayr in Vienna and with d'Albert in Berlin and composition with Franz Krenn and musicology with Mandyczewski in Vienna. In 1908 he joined the faculty of the Vienna Academy of Music, where he taught piano and theory. He wrote an opera, *Madeleine Guinard*, and an oratorio, *Frühlingsfeier* (1913).

Prohaska, Felix, Austrian conductor, son of **Carl Prohaska**; b. Vienna, May 16, 1912; d. there, March 29, 1987. He received his primary music education at home with his father, then studied piano with Steuermann and theory with Kornauth, Gál, et al. He served as répétiteur at the Graz Opera (1936–39); he conducted opera in Duisburg (1939–41) and in Strasbourg (1941–43), then was 1st conductor of the Vienna State Opera (1945–55) and the Frankfurt am Main Opera (1955–61). He again conducted at the Vienna State Opera (1964–67); he conducted at the opera in Hannover (1965–74), and also served as director of the Hochschule für Musik there (1961–75).

Prohaska, Jaro(slav), Austrian bass-baritone; b. Vienna, Jan. 24, 1891; d. Munich, Sept. 28, 1965. He sang in the Wiener Sängerknaben, and studied voice with Otto Müller in Vienna. He made his operatic debut in Lübeck in 1922, then sang in Nuremberg (1925–31). In 1932 he joined the Berlin State Opera, remaining on its roster until 1953; he also made many appearances at the Bayreuth Festivals (1933–44), where he excelled in such roles as Hans Sachs, Wotan, and the Dutchman. He was director of the West Berlin Hochschule für Musik (1947–59), where he also directed its opera school (1952–59).

Prokina, Elena, Russian soprano; b. Odessa, Jan. 16, 1964. Following training in Odessa, she studied at the Theater Inst. and at the Cons. in Leningrad. In 1988 she became a member of the Kirov Opera in Leningrad, with which she appeared in many Russian roles both at home and on tours abroad. In 1994 she made her first appearance at London's Covent Garden as Kát'a Kabanová, and also sang Tatiana at the Glyndebourne Festival and in Monte Carlo, and Donna Anna in Los Angeles. In 1995 she returned to Covent Garden as Desdemona and to Los Angeles as Lina in *Steffelio*, and also appeared as Amelia Boccanegra in Zürich. She sang in recital at London's Wigmore Hall in 1997. In 1998 she was engaged as Kát'a Kabanová in Dallas and as Violetta in Zürich.

Prokofiev, Sergei (Sergeievich), great Russian composer, creator of new and original formulas of rhythmic, melodic, and harmonic combinations that became the recognized style of his music; b. Sontsovka, near Ekaterinoslav, April 27, 1891; d. Moscow, March 5, 1953. His mother was born a serf in 1859, 2 years before the emanicipation of Russian serfdom, and she assumed (as was the custom) the name of the estate where she was born, Sontsov. Prokofiev was born on that estate on April 27, 1891, although he himself erroneously believed that the date was April 23; the correct date was established with the discovery of his birth certificate. He received his first piano lessons from his mother, who was an amateur pianist; he improvised several pieces, and then composed a children's opera, *The Giant* (1900), which was performed in a domestic version. Following his bent for the theater, he put together 2 other operas, *On Desert Islands* (1902) and *Ondine* (1904–07); fantastic subjects obviously possessed his childish imagination. He was 11 years old when he met the great Russian master Taneyev, who arranged for him to take systematic private lessons with Glière, who became his tutor at Sontsovka during the summers of 1903 and 1904 and by correspondence during the intervening winter. Under Glière's knowledgeable guidance in theory and harmony, Prokofiev composed a sym. in piano version and still another opera, *Plague*, based upon a poem by Pushkin. Finally, in 1904, at the age of 13, he enrolled in the St. Petersburg Cons., where he studied composition with Liadov and piano with Alexander Winkler; later he was accepted by no less a master than Rimsky-Korsakov, who instructed him in orchestration. He also studied conducting with Nikolai Tcherepnin, and form with Wihtol. Further, he entered the piano class of Anna Essipova. During the summers, he returned to Sontsovka or traveled in the Caucasus and continued to compose, already in quite an advanced style; the Moscow publisher Jurgenson accepted his first work, a piano sonata, for publication; it was premiered in Moscow on

March 6, 1910. It was then that Prokofiev made his first visit to Paris, London, and Switzerland (1913); in 1914 he graduated from the St. Petersburg Cons., receiving the Anton Rubinstein Prize (a grand piano) as a pianist-composer with his Piano Concerto No. 1, which he performed publicly at the graduation concert. Because of audacious innovations in his piano music (he wrote one piece in which the right and left hands played in different keys), he was described in the press as a "futurist," and because of his addiction to dissonant and powerful harmonic combinations, some critics dismissed his works as "football music." This idiom was explicitly demonstrated in his *Sarcasms and Visions fugitives*, percussive and sharp, yet not lacking in lyric charm. Grotesquerie and irony animated his early works; he also developed a strong attraction toward subjects of primitive character. His important orch. work, the *Scythian Suite* (arr. from music written for a ballet, *Ala and Lolly*, 1915), draws upon a legend of ancient Russian sun-worship rituals. While a parallel with Stravinsky's *Le Sacre du printemps* may be drawn, there is no similarity between the styles of the 2 works. The original performance of the *Scythian Suite*, scheduled at a Koussevitzky concert in Moscow, was canceled on account of the disruption caused by war, which did not prevent the otherwise intelligent Russian music critic Sabaneyev, blissfully unaware that the announced premiere had been canceled, from delivering a blast of the work as a farrago of atrocious noises. (Sabaneyev was forced to resign his position after this episode.) Another Prokofiev score, primitivistic in its inspiration, was the cantata *Seven, They Are Seven*, based upon incantations from an old Sumerian religious ritual. During the same period, Prokofiev wrote his famous *Classical Symphony* (1916–17), in which he adopted with remarkable acuity the formal style of Haydn's music. While the structure of the work was indeed classical, the sudden modulatory shifts and subtle elements of grotesquerie revealed decisively a new modern art.

After conducting the premiere of his *Classical Symphony* in Petrograd on April 21, 1918, Prokofiev left Russia by way of Siberia and Japan for the United States (the continuing war in Europe prevented him from traveling westward). He gave concerts of his music in Japan and later in the United States, playing his first solo concert in New York on Oct. 29, 1918. Some American critics greeted his appearance as the reflection of the chaotic events of Russia in revolution, and Prokofiev himself was described as a "ribald and Bolshevist innovator and musical agitator." "Every rule in the realm of traditional music writing was broken by Prokofiev," one N.Y. writer complained. "Dissonance followed dissonance in a fashion inconceivable to ears accustomed to melody and harmonic laws." Prokofiev's genteel *Classical Symphony* struck some critics as "an orgy of dissonant sound, an exposition of the unhappy state of chaos from which Russia suffers." One N.Y. critic indulged in the following: "Crashing Siberians, volcano hell, Krakatoa, sea-bottom crawlers. Incomprehensible? So is Prokofiev." But another critic issued a word of caution, suggesting that "Prokofiev might be the legitimate successor of Borodin, Mussorgsky, and Rimsky-Korsakov." The critic was unintentionally right; Prokofiev is firmly enthroned in the pantheon of Russian music.

In 1920 Prokofiev settled in Paris, where he established an association with Diaghilev's Ballets Russes, which produced his ballets *Chout* (a French transliteration of the Russian word for buffoon), *Le Pas d'acier* (descriptive of the industrial development in Soviet Russia), and *L'Enfant prodigue*. In 1921 Prokofiev again visited the United States for the production of the opera commissioned by the Chicago Opera Co., *The Love for 3 Oranges*. In 1927 he was invited to be the pianist for a series of his own works in Russia. He gave a number of concerts in Russia again in 1929, and eventually decided to remain there. In Russia he wrote some of his most popular works, including the symphonic fairy tale *Peter and the Wolf*, staged by a children's theater in Moscow, the historical cantata *Alexander Nevsky*, the ballet *Romeo and Juliet*, and the opera *War and Peace*.

Unexpectedly, Prokofiev became the target of the so-called proletarian group of Soviet musicians who accused him of decadence, a major sin in Soviet Russia at the time. His name was included in the official denunciation of modern Soviet composers issued by reactionary Soviet politicians in 1948. He meekly confessed that he had been occasionally interested in atonal and polytonal devices during his stay in Paris, but insisted that he had never abandoned the ideals of classical Russian music. Indeed, when he composed his 7th Sym., he described it specifically as a youth sym., reflecting the energy and ideals of new Russia. There were also significant changes in his personal life. He separated from his Spanish-born wife, the singer Lina Llubera, the mother of his 2 sons, and established a companionship with Myra Mendelson, a member of the Young Communist League. She was a writer and assisted him on the libretto of his *War and Peace*. He made one final attempt to gain favor with the Soviet establishment by writing an opera based on a heroic exploit of a Soviet pilot during the war against the Nazis. But this, too, was damned by the servile communist press as lacking in true patriotic spirit, and the opera was quickly removed from the repertory. Prokofiev died suddenly of heart failure on March 5, 1953, a few hours before the death of Stalin. Curiously enough, the anniversary of Prokofiev's death is duly commemorated, while that of his once powerful nemesis is officially allowed to be forgotten. O. Prokofiev tr. and ed. his *Soviet Diary, 1927, and Other Writings* (London, 1991).

WORKS: DRAMATIC: OPERAS: *Maddalena* (1912–13, piano score only; orchestrated by Edward Downes, 1978; BBC Radio, March 25, 1979; 1st stage perf., Graz, Nov. 28, 1981; U.S. premiere, St. Louis, June 9, 1982); *The Gambler*, after Dostoyevsky (1915–16; rev. 1927; Brussels, April 29, 1929); *The Love for 3 Oranges*, after Gozzi (1919; Chicago, Dec. 30, 1921); *The Fiery Angel* (1919; 2 fragments perf., Paris, June 14, 1928; 1st complete concert perf., Paris, Nov. 25, 1954; 1st stage perf., Venice, Sept. 14, 1955); *Semyon Kotko* (1939; Moscow, June 23, 1940); *Betrothal in a Convent*, after Sheridan's *Duenna* (1940; Leningrad, Nov. 3, 1946); *War and Peace*, after Tolstoy (1941–52; concert perf. of 8 of the original 11 scenes, Ensemble of Soviet Opera of the All-Union Theatrical Society, Oct. 16, 1944; concert perf. of 9 of the original 11 scenes with scenes 6 and 8 omitted, Moscow Phil., June 7, 1945; stage perf. of Part I [*Peace*] with new Scene 2, Maly Theater, Leningrad, June 12, 1946; "final" version of 11 scenes, Prague, June 25, 1948; another "complete" version, Leningrad, March 31, 1955; rev. version in 13 scenes with cuts, Moscow, Nov. 8, 1957; 13 scenes with a choral epigraph, Moscow, Dec. 15, 1959); *A Tale about a Real Man* (1947–48; private perf., Leningrad, Dec. 3, 1948; public perf., Bolshoi Theater, Moscow, Oct. 8, 1960). BALLETS: *Buffoon* (1920; Paris, May 17, 1921); *Trapeze* (1924; music used in his Quintet); *Le Pas d'acier* (1924; Paris, June 7, 1927); *L'Enfant prodigue* (1928; Paris, May 21, 1929); *Sur le Borysthène* (1930; Paris, Dec. 16, 1932); *Romeo and Juliet* (1935–36; Brno, Dec. 30, 1938); *Cinderella* (1940–44; Moscow, Nov. 21, 1945); *A Tale of the Stone Flower* (1948–50; Moscow, Feb. 12, 1954). INCIDENTAL MUSIC TO: *Egyptian Nights* (1933); *Boris Godunov* (1936); *Eugene Onegin* (1936); *Hamlet* (1937–38; Leningrad, May 15, 1938). FILM MUSIC: *Lt. Kijé* (1933); *The Queen of Spades* (1936); *Alexander Nevsky* (1938); *Lermontov* (1941); *Tonya* (1942); *Kotovsky* (1942); *Partisans in the Ukrainian Steppes* (1942); *Ivan the Terrible* (1942–45).

BIBL.: I. Nestyev, *S. P.* (Moscow, 1946; Eng. tr., N.Y., 1946; enl. Russian ed., Moscow, 1957; Eng. tr. with a foreword by N. Slonimsky, Stanford, Calif., 1961); M. Sabinina, *S. P.* (Moscow, 1958); C. Samuel, *P.* (Paris, 1960; Eng. tr., 1971); F. Streller, *P.* (Leipzig, 1960); M. Hofmann, *P.* (Paris, 1963); H. Brockhaus, *S. P.* (Leipzig, 1964); L. and E. Hanson, *P., The Prodigal Son* (London, 1964); M. Rayment, *P.* (London, 1965); L. Danko, *S. S. P.* (Moscow, 1966); S. Morozov, *P.* (Moscow, 1967); V. Serov, *S. P., A Soviet Tragedy* (N.Y., 1968); R. McAllister, *The Operas of S. P.* (diss., Cambridge Univ., 1970); I. Martynov, *P.* (Moscow, 1974); D. Appel, ed., and G. Daniels, tr., *P. by P.: A Composer's Memoir* (Garden City, N.Y., 1979); V. Blok, ed., *S. P.: Materials, Articles, Interviews* (London, 1980); H. Robinson, *The Operas of S. P. and Their Russian Literary Sources* (diss., Univ. of Calif., Berkeley, 1980); M. Nesteyeva, *S. S. P.* (Moscow, 1981); N. Savkina, *S. S. P.* (Moscow, 1982; Eng.

tr., Neptune City, N.J., 1984); D. Gutman, *P.* (London, 1988); C. Samuel, *P.* (Paris, 1995).

Prošev, Toma, Yugoslav conductor, teacher, and composer; b. Skopje, Nov. 10, 1931. He studied with Škerjanc at the Ljubljana Academy of Music, graduating in composition in 1960, then made a musical pilgrimage to Boulanger in Paris (1964). Upon returning to his homeland, he was active as a conductor, teacher, and composer. His music is moderately modern and includes the operas *Paučina* (The Cobweb; 1957) and *Mali princ* (The Little Prince; 1966), and the ballets *Okviri i odjeci* (Frames and Echoes; 1961), *Pesma nad pesmama* (Song of Songs; 1967), and *Relacije* (Relaxations; 1969). He also composed 4 oratorios: *Jama* (The Pit; 1961), *Skopje* (1965), *Sunce prastare zemlje* (Sun of the Ancient Country; 1967), and *Prouka* (The Message; 1968).

Protschka, Josef, Czech-born German tenor; b. Prague, Feb. 5, 1944. He studied philology and philosophy at the Univ. of Tübingen and the Univ. of Bonn, and pursued vocal instruction with Erika Köth and Peter Witsch at the Cologne Hochschule für Musik. In 1977 he made his operatic debut in Giessen, and then sang in Saarbrücken (1978–80). From 1980 to 1987 he was a leading member of the Cologne Opera. In 1985 he sang Pisandro in the Monteverdi-Henze version of *Il ritorno d'Ulisse* at the Salzburg Festival, and he also appeared at the Vienna State Opera. Following engagements at Milan's La Scala and in Dresden in 1986, and Florence and Zürich in 1987, he sang the title role in Schubert's *Fierrabras* at the Vienna Festival in 1988. In 1989 he sang Florestan at the Hamburg State Opera, which role he also chose for his debut at London's Covent Garden in 1990. He made his U.S. debut in 1991 as soloist in *Das Lied von der Erde* with the Houston Sym. Orch. In subsequent seasons, he appeared with many of the world's major opera houses, festivals, and orchs., and also toured as a lieder artist. He served as a prof. at the Cologne Hochschule für Musik's Aachen division and at the Royal Cons. of Music in Copenhagen. In addition to the critical accolades he has won for his roles in operas by Mozart and Wagner, he is much esteemed for his interpretations of the lieder of Schubert and Mendelssohn.

Provenzale, Francesco, noted Italian composer and teacher; b. Naples, c.1626; d. there, Sept. 6, 1704. By the early 1650s he was active as a composer of operas in Naples, and thus became the first major figure of the so-called Neapolitan school. In 1663 he began teaching at the Cons. S. Maria di Loreto; that same year was made its chief maestro, a position he retained until 1675. He then was director of the music staff at the cons. of S. Maria della Pietà dei Turchini from 1675 to 1701. He also served as maestro di cappella to the city of Naples from 1665; he held a similar post to the treasury of S. Gennaro from 1686 to 1699. In 1680 he was named maestro onorario, without pay, to the viceregal court under its maestro di cappella P.A., Ziani. After Ziani's death in 1684, A. Scarlatti was named his successor, and Provenzale resigned in protest at being passed over by the court authorities. He returned briefly to court service in 1688 as maestro di cappella di camera. Finally, in 1690, he was renamed maestro onorario with a salary of 19 ducats a month.

WORKS: OPERAS: *Il Ciro* (Naples, 1653); *Il Theseo, o vero L'incostanza trionfante* (Naples, 1658); *Il Schiavo di sua moglie* (Naples, 1671); *La colomba ferita*, sacred opera (Naples, Sept. 18, 1672); *La Fenice d'Avila Teresa di Giesù*, sacred opera (Naples, Nov. 6, 1672); *La Stellidaura vendicata* (Naples, Sept. 2, 1674; also known as *Difendere l'offensore, ovvero La Stellidaura vendicata*). The opera *Il martirio di S. Gennaro* (Naples, Nov. 6, 1664) may be by Provenzale. The operas *Xerse* (Naples, 1655?) and *Artemisia* (Naples, 1657?), often listed as original works by Provenzale, may be adaptations by Cavalli.

Prunières, Henry, eminent French musicologist; b. Paris, May 24, 1886; d. Nanterre, April 11, 1942. He studied music history with Rolland at the Sorbonne (1906–13), receiving his doctorat ès lettres from the Univ. of Paris in 1913 with the diss. *L'Opéra italien en France avant Lulli* (publ. in Paris, 1913); he also wrote a supplementary diss. in 1913, *La Ballet de cour en France avant Benserade et Lully*, publ. in Paris in 1914. From 1909 to 1914 he was an instructor at the École des Hautes Études Sociales in Paris; in 1920 he founded the important journal *La Revue Musicale*, of which he was ed.-in-chief until 1939; he was head of the French section of the ISCM. He was general editor of a complete ed. of Lully's works (10 vols., Paris, 1930–39).

WRITINGS (all publ. in Paris): *Lully* (1910; 2d ed., 1927); *La Musique de la chambre et de l'écurie* (1912); *La Vie et l'oeuvre de Claudio Monteverdi* (1924; Eng. tr., 1926; 2d French ed., 1931); *La Vie illistre et libertine de Jean-Baptiste Lully* (1929); *Cavalli et l'opéra vénitien au XVIIe siècle* (1931); *Nouvelle histoire de la musique* (2 vols., 1934, 1936; Eng. tr., 1943).

Prüwer, Julius, Austrian conductor; b. Vienna, Feb. 20, 1874; d. N.Y., July 8, 1943. He studied piano with Friedheim and Moriz Rosenthal, and theory with R. Fuchs and Krenn; he also profited greatly by his friendly association with Brahms. He studied conducting with Hans Richter. Prüwer began his career as a conductor in Bielitz; he then conducted at the Cologne Opera (1894–96) and at the Breslau Opera (1896–1923), where he distinguished himself by conducting numerous new works. From 1924 to 1933 he conducted popular concerts of the Berlin Phil. In 1933 he was compelled to leave Germany owing to the barbarous racial laws of the Nazi regime; he conducted in Russia and in Austria; he eventually reached New York, where he remained until his death.

Pryor, Arthur (Willard), American trombonist, conductor, and composer; b. St. Joseph, Mo., Sept. 22, 1870; d. Long Branch, N.J., June 18, 1942. He began his professional career in 1889 as a performer on the slide trombone. When Sousa formed his own band in 1892, he hired Pryor as his trombone soloist; from 1895 until he left to form his own band in 1903, Pryor was assistant conductor for Sousa. Pryor's Band gave its first major concert at the Majestic Theatre in New York on Nov. 15, 1903, but beginning in 1904 it initiated a series of summer outdoor concerts at Asbury Park, Coney Island, and other amusement parks. From 1903 to 1909 it made 6 coast-to-coast tours. Unlike Sousa, who had little to do with "canned music," Pryor was quick to take advantage of the developing recording industry; he made some 1,000 acoustic recordings before 1930. He also entered upon a series of commercial radio broadcasts. He composed about 300 works, including operettas, ragtime and cakewalk tunes, and novelties such as *The Whistler and His Dog*, Pryor's best-known work. He was a charter member of ASCAP in 1914 and of the American Bandmasters Assn. in 1929. In 1933 he retired to Long Branch.

BIBL.: D. Frizane, *A. P. (1870–1942) American Trombonist, Bandmaster, Composer* (diss., Univ. of Kansas, 1984).

Przybylski, Bronisław Kazimierz, Polish composer and teacher; b. Łódź, Dec. 11, 1941. He was a student of Franciszek Wesolowski (theory diploma, 1964) and Tomasz Kiesewetter (composition diploma, 1969) at the Łódz State College of Music, of Szabelski in Katowice, and of Haubenstock-Ramati at the Vienna Hochschule für Musik (1975–76). From 1964 he taught at the Łódz State College of Music. Among his works are *Miriam*, ballet (1985), *The Strange Adventures of Mr. Hare*, musical fairy tale (1985), *Wawelski Smok*, ballet (1987), and *3 Cheers for the Elephant*, musical fairy tale (1989).

Ptaszyńska, Marta, Polish composer and percussionist; b. Warsaw, July 29, 1943. She studied piano and timpani at the Music Lyceum in Warsaw (1957–62); then took courses in composition with Dobrowolski and Rudziński at the Warsaw Cons. (1962–68), and worked out problems of electronic music with Kotoński in his studio; she had supplementary practice in percussion at the Poznan Cons. (1963–67); in 1969 she traveled to Paris, where she had lessons with Boulanger. In 1972 she received a grant from the Kosciuszko Foundation to travel to the United States, and studied percussion at the Cleveland Inst. of Music (until 1974). From 1974 to 1977 she taught percussion at Bennington (Vt.) College; in 1977 she became an instructor in composition at the Univ. of Calif., Berkeley. She played with the "Percussions de Strasbourg" and was a composer and percussionist at the Claremont

Music Festival in California. Her music is entirely free of any strictures, whether academically traditional or fashionably modern. Being a virtuoso drummer, she naturally gives a prominent place to percussion in her scores; she also makes use of stereophony by spatial separation of players or groups of instruments. Her compositions include *Oscar from Alva*, television opera (1972), and *Helio, centricum, musicum*, multimedia spectacle for Voices, Dancers, and Instrumentalists (1973); also *Chant for All the People on Earth*, oratorio (1969).

Puccini, family of Italian musicians:

(1) Giacomo Puccini, composer; b. Celle di Val di Roggia, Lucca (baptized), Jan. 26, 1712; d. Lucca, May 16, 1781. He studied with Caretti in Bologna, then pursued his career in Lucca, where he was organist at S. Martino (1739–72) and director of the Cappella Palatina (1739–81). He became a member of Bologna's Accademia Filarmonica (1743). He was a talented composer of vocal music and also wrote a number of dramatic pieces for the Lucca municipal elections.

(2) Antonio (Benedetto Maria) Puccini, composer, son of the preceding; b. Lucca, July 30, 1747; d. there, Feb. 10, 1832. He received financial assistance from the Lucca authorities to study in Bologna with Caretti and Zanardi; while there, he married the organist Caterina Tesei, then returned to Lucca, where he was substitute organist for his father at S. Martino (from 1772). He was his father's successor as director of the Cappella Palatina (1781–1805); he became a member of Bologna's Accademia Filarmonica (1771). His output reveals a composer of solid technique and expressivity in vocal writing.

(3) Domenico (Vencenzo Maria) Puccini, composer, son of the preceding; b. 1772; d. Lucca, May 25, 1815. After musical training with his parents, he studied with Mattei in Bologna and Paisiello in Naples. He then returned to Lucca as director of the Cappella di Camera (1806–09) and of the municipal chapel (1811–15). He was notably successful as a composer of comic operas.

WORKS: OPERAS: *Le frecce d'amore*, opera pastorale (c.1800); *L'Ortolanella, o La Moglie capricciosa*, farsa buffa (Lucca, 1800); *Il Quinto Fabio*, opera seria (Livorno, 1810); *La scuola dei tutori*, farsa (Lucca, 1813); *Il Ciarlatano, ossia I finti savoiardi*, atto buffo (Lucca, 1815).

(4) Michele Puccini, teacher and composer, son of the preceding; b. Lucca, Nov. 27, 1813; d. there, Jan. 23, 1864. He studied with his grandfather Antonio Puccini and others in Lucca, and completed his training with Pillotti in Bologna and Donizetti and Mercadante in Naples. He then returned to Lucca as a teacher at the Istituto Musicale Pacini, serving as its director (from 1862); he was also organist at S. Martino. He became well known as a teacher. Among his works are 2 operas, *Antonio Foscarini* (n.d.) and *Giambattista Cattani, o La rivoluzione degli Straccioni* (Lucca, 1844).

(5) Giacomo (Antonio Domenico Michele Secondo Maria) Puccini, celebrated composer, son of the preceding; b. Lucca, Dec. 22, 1858; d. Brussels, Nov. 29, 1924. He was the 5th of 7 children of Michele Puccini, who died when Giacomo was only 5; his musical training was thus entrusted to his uncle, Fortunato Magi, a pupil of his father; however, Giacomo showed neither inclination nor talent for music. His mother, determined to continue the family tradition, sent him to the local Istituto Musicale Pacini, where Carlo Angeloni—its director, who had also studied with Michele Puccini—became his teacher. After Angeloni's untiring patience had aroused interest, and then enthusiasm, in his pupil, progress was rapid and he soon became a proficient pianist and organist. He began serving as a church organist in Lucca and environs when he was 14, and began composing when he was 17. After hearing *Aida* in Pisa in 1876, he resolved to win laurels as a dramatic composer. Having written mainly sacred music, it was self-evident that he needed further training after graduating from the Istituto (1880). With financial support from his granduncle, Dr. Nicolao Ceru, and a stipend from Queen Margherita, he pursued his studies with Antonio Bazzini and Amilcare Ponchielli at the Milan Cons. (1880–83). For his graduation, he wrote a *Capriccio sinfonico*, which was conducted by Faccio at a Cons. concert, eliciting unstinting praise from the critics. In the same year, Ponchielli introduced Puccini to the librettist Fontana, who furnished him the text of a 1-act opera; in a few weeks the score was finished and sent to the Sonzongo competition. It did not win the prize, but on May 31, 1884, *Le villi* was produced at the Teatro dal Verme in Milan, with gratifying success. Ricordi, who was present, considered the work sufficiently meritorious to commission the young composer to write a new opera for him; but 5 years elapsed before this work, *Edgar* (3 acts; text by Fontana), was produced at La Scala in Milan (April 21, 1889), scoring only a moderate success. By this time Puccini had become convinced that, in order to write a really effective opera, he needed a better libretto than Fontana had provided. Accordingly, he commissioned Domenico Oliva to write the text of *Manon Lescaut*; during the composition, however, Puccini and Ricordi practically rewrote the entire book, and in the publ. score Oliva's name is not mentioned. With *Manon Lescaut* (4 acts), first produced at the Teatro Regio in Turin on Feb. 1, 1893, Puccini won a veritable triumph, which was surpassed by his next work, *La Bohème* (4 acts; text by Illica and Giacosa), produced at the same theater on Feb. 1, 1896. These 2 works not only carried their composer's name throughout the world, but also have found and maintained their place in the repertoire of every opera house. With fame came wealth, and in 1900 he built at Torre del Lago, where he had been living since 1891, a magnificent villa. His next opera, *Tosca* (3 acts; text by Illica and Giacosa), produced at the Teatro Costanzi in Rome on Jan. 14, 1900, is Puccini's most dramatic work; it has become a fixture of the standard repertoire, and contains some of his best-known arias. At its premiere at La Scala on Feb. 17, 1904, *Madama Butterfly* (2 acts; text by Illica and Giacosa) was hissed. Puccini thereupon withdrew the score and made some slight changes (division into 3 acts, and addition of the tenor aria in the last scene). This revised version was greeted with frenzied applause in Brescia on May 28 of the same year. Puccini was now the acknowledged ruler of the Italian operatic stage, his works rivaling those of Verdi in the number of performances. The first performance of *Madama Butterfly* at the Metropolitan Opera in New York (Feb. 11, 1907) took place in the presence of the composer, whom the management had invited especially for the occasion. It was then suggested that he write an opera on an American subject, the premiere to take place at the Metropolitan. He found his subject when he witnessed a performance of Belasco's *The Girl of the Golden West*; he commissioned C. Zangarini and G. Civinini to write the libretto, and in the presence of the composer the world premiere of *La Fanciulla del West* occurred, amid much enthusiasm, at the Metropolitan on Dec. 10, 1910; while it never equaled the success of his *Tosca* or *Madama Butterfly*, it had various revivals over the years. Puccini then brought out *La Rondine* (3 acts; Monte Carlo, March 27, 1917) and the 3 1-act operas *Il Tabarro* (after Didier Gold's *La Houppelande*), *Suor Angelica*, and *Gianni Schicchi* (all 1st perf. at the Metropolitan Opera, Dec. 14, 1918). His last opera, *Turandot* (after Gozzi), was left unfinished; the final scene was completed by Franco Alfano and performed at La Scala on April 25, 1926.

BIBL.: A. Bruggemann, *Madama Butterfly e l'arte di G. P.* (Milan, 1904); W. Dry, *G. P.* (London, 1906); F. Torrefranca, *G. P. e l'opera internazionale* (Turin, 1912); A. Weismann, *G. P.* (Munich, 1922); A. Bonaventura, *G. P.: L'Uomo, l'artista* (Livorno, 1924); A. Fraccaroli, *La vita di G. P.* (Milan, 1925); G. Marotti and F. Pagni, *G. P. intimo* (Florence, 1926); G. Adami, *Epistolario di G. P.* (Milan, 1928; Eng. tr., London, 1931); A. Neisser, *P.* (Leipzig, 1928); F. Salerno, *Le Donne pucciniane* (Palermo, 1928); R. Merlin, *P.* (Milan, 1930); R. Specht, *P.* (Berlin, 1931; Eng. tr., N.Y., 1933); W. Maisch, *P.s musikalische Formgebung* (Neustadt, 1934); G. Adami, *P.* (Milan, 1935; Ger. tr., 1943); K. Fellerer, *G. P.* (Potsdam, 1937); V. Seligman, *P. among Friends* (correspondence; N.Y., 1938); F. Thiess, *P.: Versuch einer Psychologie seiner Musik* (Berlin, 1947); A. Bonaccorsi, *G. P. e i suoi antenati musicali* (Milan, 1950); G. Marek, *P.: A Biography* (N.Y., 1951); D. del Fiorentino, *Immortal Bohemian: An Intimate Memoir of G. P.* (N.Y., 1952); A. Machard, *Une Vie d'amour: P.* (Paris, 1954); L. Ricci, *P. interprete di se stesso* (Milan, 1954); V. Terenzio, *Ritratto di P.* (Bergamo, 1954); M. Carner, *P.* (London, 1958; 2d ed., rev., 1974); E. Greenfield, *P.: Keeper of the Seal* (London, 1958); C. Sartori, *P.* (Milan, 1958); C. Paladini, *G. P.* (Florence, 1961); W. Ashbrook, *The Operas of P.* (N.Y., 1968; 2d ed., rev., 1985); D. Amy, *G. P.* (Paris, 1970); A. Monnosi, *P. a tu per tu* (Pisa, 1970); G. Tarozzi, *P.: La fine del bel canto* (Milan, 1972); N. Galli, *P. e la sua terra* (Lucca, 1974); G. Magri, *P. e le sue rime* (Milan, 1974); I. Lombardi, *P., ancora da scoprire* (Lucca, 1976); E. Siciliani, *P.* (Milan, 1976); W. Weaver, *P.: The Man and His Music* (N.Y., 1977); C. Casini, *G. P.* (Turin, 1978); L. Pinzauti, *P.* (Milan, 1978); H. Greenfield, *P.* (N.Y., 1980); C. Osborne, *The Complete Operas of P.* (London, 1981); A. Bottero, *Le Donne di P.* (Lucca, 1984); M. Carner, *Tosca* (Cambridge, 1985); E. Krause, *P.* (Leipzig, 1985); D. Martino, *Metamorfosi del femminino nei libretti per P.* (Turin, 1985); A. Groos and R. Parker, *G. P.: "La Bohème"* (Cambridge, 1986); J. DiGaetani, *P. the Thinker: The Composer's Intellectual and Dramatic Development* (Bern and N.Y., 1987); G. Musco, *Musica e teatro in G. P.* (vol. 1, Cortona, 1989); L. Fairtile, *G. P.: A Guide to Research* (Levittown, Pa., 1998).

Pucitta, Vincenzo, Italian composer; b. Civitavecchia, 1778; d. Milan, Dec. 20, 1861. He studied with Fenaroli in Naples, then traveled through Europe. He was successful as an opera composer in Italy, Austria, France, and England. He wrote about 30 operas, of which the best were *La burla fortunata* (Venice, April 9, 1804) and *La Vestale* (London, May 3, 1810).

Puente, Giuseppe Del, Italian baritone; b. Naples, Jan. 30, 1841; d. Philadelphia, May 25, 1900. He first studied cello at the Naples Cons. but later began to cultivate his voice, making his operatic debut at Iasi. He was then engaged for the Teatro San Carlo in Naples, and for appearances in France, Germany, Russia, Spain, and England (made his Covent Garden debut in 1873, and became very popular there). His first American engagement was under Strakosch at the N.Y. Academy of Music in 1873–74; he became a member of the first Metropolitan Opera season in New York and sang the role of Valentin in the inaugural performance of *Faust* on Oct. 22, 1883; he remained on its roster for the seasons of 1883–84, 1891–92, and 1894–95. In 1885 he returned to the N.Y. Academy of Music under Mapleson's management, taking part in the American premiere of *Manon* on Dec. 23 of that year; he was also a member of the opera troupes of Patti and Hinrichs; with the latter's company, he sang in the American premiere of *Cavalleria rusticana* (Philadelphia, Sept. 9, 1891). He married the mezzo-soprano Helen Dudley Campbell.

Puget, Paul-Charles-Marie, French composer; b. Nantes, June 25, 1848; d. Paris, March 14, 1917. He studied at the Paris Cons. with Marmontel (piano) and Massé (composition), winning 1st Grand Prix de Rome in 1873 with the cantata *Mazeppa*. He wrote much theater music. His opera *Beaucoup de bruit pour rien*, after Shakespeare (Paris, March 24, 1899), had a moderately good reception.

Pugnani, (Giulio) Gaetano (Gerolamo), celebrated Italian violinist and composer; b. Turin, Nov. 27, 1731; d. there, July 15, 1798. He studied violin with G. B. Somis. When he was 10, he was allowed to play in the last chair of the 2d violins in the orch. of Turin's Teatro Regio; he officially became a member of the orch. on April 19, 1748. In 1749, on a royal stipend, he went to Rome to study with Ciampi, and later toured in Europe as a concert violinist. Pugnani was particularly successful in London, where he played concerts with J. C. Bach; from 1767 to 1769 he also served as conductor at the King's Theatre, where he brought out his successful opera *Nanetta e Lubino* (April 8, 1769). He then returned to Turin, where he was appointed concertmaster of the King's Music and of the orch. of the Teatro Regio in 1770. He was named general director of instrumental music in 1776; in 1786 he served as supervisor of military music. He made, from 1780 to 1782, a concert tour of Europe, which included a visit to Russia. He was also active as a teacher of the violin. His students included Viotti, Conforti, Bruni, and Polledro. His style of composition approximated that of Tartini. Fritz Kreisler publ. an arrangement for violin and piano of a piece, purportedly by Pugnani, titled *Preludio e Allegro e Tempo di Minuetto*, but this proved to be by Kreisler himself.

WORKS: DRAMATIC: *Nanetta e Lubino*, opera buffa (London, April 8, 1769); *Issea*, favola pastorale (Turin, 1771); *Tamas Kouli-Kan nell'India*, dramma per musica (Turin, Feb. 1, 1772; not extant); *Aurora*, festa per musica (Turin, 1775; not extant); *Adone e Venere*, opera seria (Naples, Nov. 1784); *Achille in Sciro*, dramma per musica (Turin, Jan. 15, 1785); *Demofoonte*, dramma per musica (Turin, Dec. 26, 1787); *Demetrio a Rodi*, festa per musica (Turin, 1789); also *Correso e Calliroe*, balleto eroico (1792; not extant), ballet music to Gluck's *Orfeo* (not extant), and an oratorio, *Betulia liberata*.

BIBL.: G. Rangoni, *Essai sur le goût de la musique . . . Saggio sul gusto della musica col carattere de' tre celebri sonatori di violino i signori Nardini, Lolli, e P.* (Livorno, 1790); F. Fayolle, *Notices sur Corelli, Tartini, Gaviniès, P. et Viotti* (Paris, 1810); A. Bertolotti, *G. P. e altri musici alla corte di Torino nel secolo XVIII* (Milan, 1892); A. Della Corte, *Notizie di G. P.* (Turin, 1931); E. von Zschinsky-Troxler, *G. P.* (Berlin, 1939).

Puig-Roget, Henriette, French organist, pianist, teacher, and composer; b. Bastia, Jan 9, 1910; d. Paris, Nov. 24, 1992. She studied with Philipp (piano), Dupré (organ), J. Gallon (harmony), Tournemire (chamber music), Emmanuel (music history), and Büsser (composition) at the Paris Cons., winning premiers prix in 1926 and 1930. In 1933 she won the Premier 2d Prix de Rome. From 1934 to 1979 she was organist at l'Oratoire du Louvre in Paris. She also pursued an active career as a pianist until 1975. She was "chef de chant" at the Paris Opéra (1937–40; 1946–57) and then was prof. of piano accompaniment and score reading at the Paris Cons. (1957–79). She wrote many piano books for children; also the ballet *Cathérinettes* (1937).

Purcell, Daniel, English organist and composer, brother of **Henry Purcell**; b. London, c.1660; d. there (buried), Nov. 26, 1717. He became organist of Magdalen College, Oxford, in 1688. He took his brother's place as a dramatic composer in 1695, and was organist of St. Andrew's, Holborn, from 1713. He supplied scores of incidental music to over 40 plays.

Purcell, Henry, great English composer, brother of **Daniel Purcell**; b. London, 1659; d. Dean's Yard, Westminster, Nov. 21, 1695. His parentage remains a matter of dispute, since documentary evidence is lacking. His father may have been Henry Purcell (d. Westminster, Aug. 11, 1664), a singer, who was named a "singing-man" and Master of the Choristers at Westminster Abbey (1661) and a Gentleman of the Chapel Royal (1661), where he became a musician-in-ordinary for the lutes and voices (1662). It is possible that his father was Thomas Purcell (d. Westminster, July 31, 1682), a singer and composer, who most likely was the brother of the elder Henry Purcell; Thomas became a Gentleman of the Chapel Royal (1661), where he was admitted to the private music for lutes, viols, and voices (1662); with Pelham Humfrey, he served as composer for the violins (from 1672); that same year he was made marshal of the Corp. of Music and a musician-in-ordinary in the King's Private Musick. Whatever the case, the young Henry Purcell became a chorister of the Chapel Royal under Cooke and Humfrey (1669), and also received instruction from Blow; when his voice broke (1673), he was appointed Assistant Keeper of the Instruments; was named composer-in-ordinary for the violins (1677). He became Blow's successor as organist of Westminster Abbey (1679) and one of the 3 organists of the Chapel Royal (1682); he was named organ maker and keeper of the king's instruments (1683). His first printed work was a song in Playford's *Choice Ayres* (vol. 1, 1675); vol. 2 (1679) contains other songs and an elegy on the death of Matthew Locke. In 1680 he publ. one of his finest instrumental works, the *Fantasias* for Strings; in that same year he began writing odes and welcome songs; although their texts are almost invariably stupid or bombastic, he succeeded in clothing them in some of his finest music; his incidental music for the stage also dates from that year. He wrote the anthem "My Heart is Inditing" for the coronation of King James II (1685). With *Dido and Aeneas* (1689) he produced the first great English opera. In the remaining years of his life he devoted much time to composition for the theater; he also wrote some outstanding sacred music.

Purcell lies in the north aisle of Westminster Abbey, and his burial tablet well expresses contemporary estimation of his worth: "Here lyes Henry Purcell, Esq.; who left this life, and is gone to that blessed place where only his harmony can be exceeded." His church music shows him to be an original melodist, and a master of form, harmony, and all contrapuntal devices; his music for the stage is equally rich in invention, dramatic instinct, and power of characterization; his chamber works surpass those of his predecessors and contemporaries. A complete ed. of Purcell's works was issued by the Purcell Soc. (London, 1878–1965; 2d ed., rev., 1974–81).

WORKS: DRAMATIC: OPERA: *Dido and Aeneas* (London, 1689). SEMI-OPERAS: *The Prophetess, or The History of Dioclesian* (London, 1690); *King Arthur, or The British Worthy* (London, 1691); *The Fairy Queen* (London, 1692); *The Indian Queen* (London, 1695; final masque by D. Purcell); *The Tempest, or The Enchanted Island* (c.1695). INCIDENTAL MUSIC TO: N. Lee's *Theodosius, or The Force of Love* (1680); T. D'Urfey's *Sir Barnaby Whigg, or No Wit Like a Woman's* (1681); Tate's *The History of King Richard II (The Sicilian Usurper)*, after Shakespeare (1681); Beaumont and Fletcher's *The Double Marriage* (c.1682–85); Lee's *Sophonisba, or Hannibal's Overthrow* (c.1685); D'Urfey's *A Fool's Preferment, or The 3 Dukes of Dunstable*, after Fletcher's *Noble Gentleman* (1688); Dryden's *Amphitryon, or The Two Sosias* (1690); E. Settle's *Distressed Innocence, or The Princess of Persia* (1690); T. Southerne's *Sir Anthony Love, or The Rambling Lady* (1690); Lee's *The Massacre of Paris* (1690); C. D'Avenant's *Circe* (c.1690); *The Gordian Knot Unty'd* (1691); Dryden and R. Howard's *The Indian Emperor, or The Conquest of Mexico* (1691); Southerne's *The Wives' Excuse, or Cuckolds Make Themselves* (1691); Dryden's *Cleomenes, the Spartan Hero* (1692); W. Mountfort and J. Bancroft's *Henry the 2d, King of England* (1692); J. Crowne's *Regulus* (1692); Dryden's *Aureng-Zebe* (c.1692); Dryden and Lee's *Oedipus* (c.1692); T. Shadwell's *The Libertine* (c.1692); D'Urfey's *The Marriage-Hater Match'd* (1692); Shadwell's *Epsom Wells* (1693); W. Congreve's *The Double Dealer* (1693); Fletcher's *Rule a Wife and Have a Wife* (1693); T. Wright's *The Female Vertuosos*, after Molière's *Les Femmes savantes* (1693); Southerne's *The Maid's Last Prayer, or Any Rather than Fail* (1693); Congreve's *The Old Bachelor* (1693); D'Urfey's *The Richmond Heiress, or A Woman Once in the Right* (1693); Dryden's *Love Triumphant, or Nature Will Prevail* (1694); E. Ravenscroft's *The Canterbury Guests, or A Bargain Broken* (1694); Southerne's *The Fatal Marriage, or The Innocent Adultery* (1694); Crowne's *The Married Beau, or The Curious Impertinent* (1694); Shadwell's *Timon of Athens*, after Shakespeare (1694); Dryden's *Tyrannic Love, or The Royal Martyr* (1694); D'Urfey's *The Virtuous Wife, or Good Luck at Last* (c.1694); Dryden's *The Spanish Friar, or The Double Discovery* (1694–95); D'Urfey's *The Comical History of Don Quixote* (1694–95); A. Behn's *Abdelazer, or The Moor's Marriage* (1695); *Bonduca, or The British Heroine*, after Beaumont and Fletcher (1695); Southerne's *Oroonoko* (1695); Norton's *Pausanias, the Betrayer of His Country* (1695); T. Scott's *The Mock Marriage* (1695); R. Gould's *The Rival Sisters, or The Violence of Love* (1695).

BIBL.: W. Cummings, *P.* (London, 1881; 3d ed., 1911; abr. ed., 1923); J. Runciman, *P.* (London, 1909); D. Arundell, *H. P.* (London, 1927); H. Dupre, *P.* (Paris, 1927; Eng. tr., 1928); A. Holland, *H. P.: The English Musical Tradition* (London, 1932; 2d ed., 1948); J. Westrup, *P.* (London, 1937; 4th ed., rev., 1980); S. Demarquez, *P.: La Vie, l'oeuvre* (Paris, 1951); R. Sietz, *H. P.: Zeit, Leben, Werk* (Leipzig, 1956); I. Holst, ed., *H. P. (1659–1695): Essays on His Music* (London, 1959); R. Moore, *H. P. and the Restoration Theatre* (London, 1961); M. Laurie, *P.'s Stage Works* (diss., Cambridge Univ., 1962); F. Zimmerman, *H. P., 1659–1695: An Analytical Catalogue of His Music* (London, 1963); idem, *H. P., 1659–1695: His Life and Times* (London, 1967; 2d ed., rev., 1983); I. Spink, *English Song: Dowland to P.* (London, 1974); F. Zimmerman, *H. P. 1659–1695: Melodic and Intervallic Indexes to His Complete Works* (Philadelphia, 1975); K. Rohrer, *"The Energy of English Words": A Linguistic Approach to H. P.'s Methods of Setting Texts* (diss., Princeton Univ., 1980); A. Hutchings, *P.* (London, 1982); C. Price, *H. P. and the London Stage* (Cambridge, 1984); E. Harris, *H. P.'s Dido and Aeneas* (Oxford, 1987); F. Zimmerman, *H. P.: A Guide to Research* (N.Y., 1988); M. Campbell, *H. P.: Glory of His Age* (London, 1993); M. Burden, ed., *The P. Companion* (London, 1994); M. Duffy, *H. P.* (London, 1994); R. King, *H. P.* (London, 1994); M. Adams, *H. P.: The Origins and Development of his Musical Style* (Cambridge, 1995); P. Holman, *H. P.* (Oxford, 1995); J. Keates, *P.: A Biography* (London, 1995); C. Price, ed., *P. Studies* (Cambridge, 1995); B. Wood, ed., *A P. Anthology* (Oxford, 1995).

Putnam, Ashley (Elizabeth), American soprano; b. N.Y., Aug. 10, 1952. She studied flute at the Univ. of Mich., eventually turning to voice (B.M., 1974; M.M., 1975). After graduating, she was an apprentice with the Santa Fe Opera Co. In 1976 she made her operatic debut in the title role of Donizetti's *Lucia di Lammermoor* with the Virginia Opera Assn. in Norfolk. After winning 1st prize in the Metropolitan Opera Auditions and receiving the Weyerhauser Award (1976), she made her European debut as Musetta in Puccini's *La Bohème* at the Glyndebourne Festival (1978). On Sept. 15, 1978, she won accolades as Violetta in her N.Y. City Opera debut. In 1986 she made her first appearance at London's Covent Garden as Jenůfa. She sang Donna Elvira at her Metropolitan Opera debut in New York in 1990. In 1995 she appeared as Wagner's Eva at the Cleveland Opera. She portrayed Thomson's St. Theresa I at the Houston Grand Opera in 1996. As a concert artist, she appeared with leading U.S. and European orchs., and also gave recitals.

Pylkkänen, Tauno Kullervo, Finnish composer; b. Helsinki, March 22, 1918; d. there, March 13, 1980. He studied composition with Palmgren, Madetoja, and Ranta at the Helsinki Academy of Music (1937–40); he also studied musicology at the Univ. of Helsinki (M.A., 1941). He worked at the Finnish Broadcasting Co. (1942–61) and was artistic director of the Finnish National Opera (1960–70); he lectured on opera history at the Sibelius Academy (from 1967). He was primarily an opera composer; his idiom was basically Romantic, with sporadic excursions into modernity.

WORKS: DRAMATIC: OPERAS: *Bathsheba Saarenmaalla* (Bathsheba at Saarenmaa; 1940; rev. 1958); *Mare ja hanen poikansa* (Mare and Her Son; 1943); *Simo Hurtta* (1948); *Sudenmorsian* (The Wolf's Bride), radio opera (1950); *Varjo* (The Shadow; 1952); *Ikaros* (1956–60); *Opri and Oleksi* (1957); *Vangit* (The Prisoners; 1964); *Tuntematon sotilas* (The Unknown Soldier; 1967). BALLET: *Kaarina Maununtytär* (Kaarina, Maunu's Daughter; 1960).

Pyne, Louisa (Fanny), English soprano; b. Aug. 27?, 1832; d. London, March 20, 1904. She was a student of G. Smart. At the age of 10, she made her debut with her sister Susannah in London. In 1849 she made her operatic debut as Bellini's Amina in Boulogne. Returning to London, she appeared at the Princess's Theatre that same year. She also sang at the Haymarket and Royal Italian Opera at Covent Garden, garnering critical accolades at the latter in 1851 for her portrayal of the Queen of the Night. In 1854 she sang in opera in New York, and then toured the United States with her sister and the tenor William Harrison. In 1857 she and Harrison founded the Pyne-Harrison Opera Co. in London. It gave regular performances at Covent Garden (1859–64), with Pyne taking leading roles in premieres of scores by Balfe, Benedict, and Wallace. In 1868 she married the baritone Frank Bodda and subsequently taught voice.

Q

Quadri, Argeo, Italian conductor; b. Como, March 23, 1911. He studied piano, composition, and conducting at the Milan Cons. (graduated, 1933), then conducted opera throughout Italy. In 1956 he became a conductor at Covent Garden in London. He was a regular conductor at the Vienna State Opera (1957–75).

Quarenghi, Guglielmo, Italian cellist and composer; b. Casalmaggiore, Oct. 22, 1826; d. Milan, Feb. 3, 1882. He was a pupil at the Milan Cons. (1839–42). From 1850 he was 1st cello in the orch. at La Scala, and in 1851 became a prof. of cello at the Cons. From 1879 to 1881 he was maestro di cappella at the Milan Cathedral. He publ. *Metodo di violoncello* (Milan, 1876). He composed an opera *Il di di San Michele* (Milan, 1863).

Queler, Eve (née **Rabin**), American conductor; b. N.Y., Jan. 1, 1936. She studied in New York with Bamberger at the Mannes College of Music, and took courses at the Hebrew Union School of Education and Sacred Music; after studying with Rosenstock on a Martha Baird Rockefeller Fund grant, she continued her training with Susskind and Slatkin in St. Louis and with Markevitch and Blomstedt in Europe. She made her conducting debut with *Cavalleria rusticana* in Fairlawn, N.J. (1966), then devoted herself mainly to conducting operas in concert with her own Opera Orch. of N.Y. (from 1967). She led performances of rarely heard operas on both sides of the Atlantic, and also gave the U.S. premieres of many works, ranging from Donizetti to Richard Strauss. She also appeared as a guest conductor with several North American orchs. Queler was the first American woman to conduct such esteemed ensembles as the Philadelphia Orch., the Cleveland Orch., and the Montreal Sym. Orch.

Quilico, Gino, Canadian bartione, son of **Louis Quilico**; b. N.Y., April 29, 1955. He received training from his parents, and then from James Craig and Constance Fischer at the Univ. of Toronto Opera Dept. On June 8, 1977, he made his operatic debut as Mr. Gobineau in *The Medium* with the COMUS Music Theatre in Toronto. In 1978 he sang Papageno in Milwaukee. He first appeared with the Canadian Opera Co. in 1979 singing Escamillo. Following additional studies at the École d'art lyrique of the Paris Opéra (1979–80), he made his debut with the company in Damase's *L'Héritière* in 1980 and sang with it for 3 seasons. In 1982 he made his British debut with the Scottish Opera at the Edinburgh Festival. He made his first appearance at London's Covent Garden as Gounod's Valentin in 1983. That same year he sang Massenet's Lescaut at his debut with the Opéra de Montréal, a role he also chose for his Metropolitan Opera debut in New York in 1987. In 1988 he appeared as Dandini at the Salzburg Festival. He sang Riccardo in *I Puritani* in Rome in 1990. In 1991 he appeared in Corigliano's *The Ghosts of Versailles* at the Metropolitan Opera. In 1994 he was engaged as Gluck's Oreste at the Vienna Festival. He portrayed Iago in Cologne in 1996. Among his other roles are Monteverdi's Orfeo, Don Giovanni, Dr. Malatesta, and Posa.

BIBL.: R. Mercer, *The Q.s: Louis, G. & Lina: An Operatic Family* (Oakville, Ontario, 1991).

Quilico, Louis, notable Canadian baritone and teacher of Italian and French-Canadian descent, father of **Gino Quilico**; b. Montreal, Jan. 14, 1925. He was a solo chorister in the St.-Jacques Church choir in Montreal and began his vocal studies with Frank Rowe. After training with Teresa Pediconi and Riccardo Stracciani at the Cons. de Santa Cecilia in Rome (1947–48), he returned to Montreal to study at the Cons. (1948–52) with Lina Pizzolongo (b. Montreal, Jan. 25, 1925; d. Toronto, Sept. 21, 1991), who became his wife in 1949, and with Singher. He completed his training at the Mannes College of Music in New York (1952–55) with Singher and Emil Cooper. In 1954 he made his professional operatic stage debut with the Opera Guild of Montreal as Rangoni. In 1955 he won the Metropolitan Opera Auditions of the Air, but made his U.S. debut with the N.Y. City Opera on Oct. 10, 1955, as Germont. He made his European debut at the Spoleto Festival as Donizetti's Duca d'Alba in 1959. In 1960 he made his first appearance at London's Covent Garden as Germont, and sang there until 1963. In 1962 he sang for the first time at Moscow's Bolshoi Theater as Rigoletto. He made his debut at the Paris Opéra as Verdi's Rodrigo in 1963. In subsequent seasons, he sang regularly in Europe and with the Canadian Opera Co. On Feb. 10, 1972, Quilico made his Metropolitan Opera debut in New York as Golaud, and thereafter sang there regularly. In 1991 he revealed a lighter touch when he sang Tony in *The Most Happy Fella* at the N.Y. City Opera. That same year he appeared as Rigoletto at the Opéra de Montréal, a role he essayed over 500 times. From 1970 to 1987 he taught at the Univ. of Toronto, and from 1987 to 1990 at the McGill Cons. in Montreal. In 1965 he received the Prix de musique Calixa-Lavallee and in 1974 he was made a Commander of the Order of Canada.

BIBL.: R. Mercer, *The Q.s: L., Gino & Lina: An Operatic Family* (Oakville, Ontario, 1991).

Quilter, Roger, English composer; b. Brighton, Nov. 1, 1877; d. London, Sept. 21, 1953. He received his primary education at Eton College; then studied with Iwan Knorr at the Hoch Cons. in Frankfurt am Main. He was particularly noted for his fine settings of Shakespeare's poems. His works included *As You Like It*, incidental music to Shakespeare's play (1922), and *Julia*, light opera (London, Dec. 3, 1936).

BIBL.: T. Hold, *The Walled-in Garden: A Study of the Songs of R. Q.* (Rickmansworth, 1978); M. Pilkington, *Gurney, Ireland, Q. and Warlock* (London, 1989).

Quinault, Jean-Baptiste-Maurice, French singer, actor, and composer; b. Verdun, Sept. 9, 1687; d. Gien, Aug. 30, 1745. He was an actor at the Théâtre Francais (1712–28) and at the Comédie Française in Paris until 1734. He set to music about 20 intermedes, ballets, etc., and also produced a grand ballet, *Les Amours des deesses* (Paris, Aug. 9, 1729).

Quinault, Philippe, French dramatist, poet, and librettist; b. Paris, June 3, 1635; d. there, Nov. 26, 1688. He was Lully's librettist from 1671 to 1676.

BIBL.: G. Crapelet, *Notice sur la vie et les ouvrages de Q.* (Paris, 1824); E. Richter, *P. Q.: Sein Leben, seine Tragödien, seine Bedeutung für das Theater Frankreichs und des Auslandes* (Leipzig, 1910); E. Gros, *P. Q.: Sa vie et son oeuvre* (Paris, 1926); J. Buijtendorp, *P. Q.: Sa vie, ses tragédies et ses tragi-comédies* (Amsterdam, 1928).

Quinet, Marcel, Belgian composer and teacher; b. Binche, July 6, 1915; d. Woluwé-St. Lambert, Brussels, Dec. 16, 1986. He studied at the conservatories of Mons and Brussels with Léon Jongen, Raymond Moulaert, and Marcel Maas (1934–43); he also took private composition lessons with Jean Absil (1940–45). In 1945 he won the Belgian Grand Prix de Rome with his cantata *La Vague et le Sillon*. He was on the staff of the Brussels Cons. (1943–79) and also taught at the Chapelle Musicale Reine Elisabeth (1956–59; 1968–71; 1973–74). In 1978 he was made a member of the Académie Royale de Belgique. His music is moderately modernistic in the amiable manner of the French school, with some euphoniously dissonant excrescences. His works included *Les 2 Bavards*, chamber opera (1966), and *La Nef des fous*, ballet (1969).

Quiroga, Manuel, Spanish violinist and composer; b. Pontevedra, April 15, 1890; d. there, April 19, 1961. He studied at the Royal Cons. in Madrid and at the Paris Cons. He toured in Europe and in the United States with great success. After suffering a street accident in New York in 1937 during one of his American tours, he was compelled to abandon public appearances; he then retired to Pontevedra. He composed a "sainete," *Los amos del barrio* (Madrid, Sept. 7, 1938).

Quittmeyer, Susan, American mezzo-soprano; b. N.Y., Oct. 27, 1953. She studied at the Illinois Wesleyan Univ. School of Music (1971–75) and at the Manhattan School of Music (1975–77). In 1978 she made her operatic debut as Chloe in *The Tree of Chastity* at the Opera Theatre in St. Louis. Her debut as a soloist came in 1981 when she sang in Beethoven's 9th Sym. with the San Francisco Sym. under Slatkin's direction. She made her recital debut at N.Y.'s Carnegie Recital Hall in 1985. On Dec. 21, 1987, she made her Metropolitan Opera debut in New York as Nicklausse in *Les Contes d'Hoffmann*, and continued to make appearances there until 1994. She portrayed Mozart's Annius at the Bavarian State Opera in Munich in 1986, returning there as Cherubino in 1989. After appearing as Handel's Sextus at the Paris Opéra in 1987, she sang Cherubino and Zerlina at the Vienna State Opera in 1989. In 1992 she sang Cherubino at the Opéra de la Bastille in Paris and Marina at the San Francisco Opera. She appeared as Idamante at the Salzburg Festival in 1994. Following an engagement as Fricka in *Das Rheingold* at the Dallas Opera in 1998, she sang Nicklausse at the Florida Grand Opera in Miami in 1999. She also appeared as a soloist with various orchs. In 1987 she married **James Morris**.

Quivar, Florence, black American mezzo-soprano; b. Philadelphia, March 3, 1944. She studied at the Philadelphia Musical Academy, the Salzburg Mozarteum, and with Luigi Ricci in Rome. She was a member of the Juilliard Opera Theater in New York; subsequently she launched a successful concert career, appearing as soloist with the N.Y. Phil., the Cleveland Orch., the Philadelphia Orch., the Chicago Sym. Orch., and the Boston Sym. Orch. She made her Metropolitan Opera debut in New York as Marina in *Boris Godunov* on Oct. 10, 1977; she then sang there regularly, appearing in such roles as Jocasta in *Oedipus Rex*, Isabella in *L'Italiana in Algeri*, Fides in *Le Prophète*, Eboli in *Don Carlos*, Marfa in *Khovanshchina*, and Serena in *Porgy and Bess*. In 1983 she made her first appearance at the Salzburg Festival as a soloist in Mahler's 3d Sym. with Mehta and the Israel Phil. She made her first operatic appearance there in 1989 as Ulrike. In 1991 she was a soloist in the *Gurrelieder* at the Promenade Concerts in London. She appeared at the Metropolitan Opera Gala in 1996.

R

Raabe, Peter, German conductor and writer on music; b. Frankfurt an der Oder, Nov. 27, 1872; d. Weimar, April 12, 1945. He studied with Bargiel at the Berlin Hochschule für Musik and later continued his training at the Univ. of Jena (Ph.D., 1916). In 1894 he began a career as a theater conductor; from 1899 to 1903 he conducted the Netherlands Opera in Amsterdam, and from 1903 to 1907, the Volks-Symphonie-Konzerte in Munich; in 1907 he became court conductor in Weimar; in 1910 he was appointed curator of the Liszt Museum in Weimar; from 1920 to 1934 he was Generalmusikdirektor in Aachen. In 1935 he became head of the Reichsmusikkammer and the Deutscher Tonkünstlerverein; in these offices he was called upon to perform administrative tasks for the Nazi regime, including the racial restrictions of musicians. His coworkers presented him with *Von deutscher Tonkünst: Festschrift zu Peter Raabes 70. Geburtstag* (Leipzig, 1942; 2d ed., rev., 1944). Raabe died just before the total collapse of the 3d Reich, which he tried to serve so well. He left some scholarly and valuable writings, among them *Grossherzog Carl Alexander und Liszt* (Leipzig, 1918), *Franz Liszt: Leben und Schaffen* (2 vols., Stuttgart, 1931; rev. ed. 1968 by his son Felix), *Die Musik im dritten Reich* (Regensburg, 1935), *Kulturwille im deutschen Musikleben* (Regensburg, 1936), *Deutsche Meister* (Berlin, 1937), *Wege zu Weber* (Regensburg, 1942), *Wege zu Liszt* (Regensburg, 1943), and *Wege zu Bruckner* (Regensburg, 1944).

Raaff, Anton, esteemed German tenor; b. Gelsdorf, near Bonn (baptized), May 6, 1714; d. Munich, May 28, 1797. He studied with Ferrandini in Munich and Bernacchi in Bologna. He sang in Italy, then in Bonn, in Vienna, and at various German courts (1742–52), in Lisbon (1752–55), Madrid (1755–59), and Naples, returning in 1770 to Germany, where he was attached to the court of the elector Karl Theodor at Mannheim. In 1778 he went to Paris with Mozart. From 1779 he was in Munich. Mozart wrote the role of Idomeneo for him, and also the aria *Se al labbro mio non credi*, K. 295.

BIBL.: H. Freiberger, *A. R. (1714–1797): Sein Leben und Wirken* (Cologne, 1929).

Raalte, Albert van, Dutch conductor; b. Amsterdam, May 21, 1890; d. there, Nov. 23, 1952. He studied at the Cologne Cons. with Bram Eldering (violin) and Baussnern (theory) and later in Leipzig with Nikisch and Reger. He was a theater conductor in Brussels (1911) and Leipzig (1912; 1914–15), then at the Dutch National Opera in The Hague; he formed his own opera enterprise there. He remained in the Netherlands during the German occupation; he conducted the radio orch. at Hilversum; he was sent to a concentration camp as a person with Jewish associations; after the liberation in 1945, he returned to his post at Hilversum, building the radio orch. to a high degree of efficiency.

Rabaud, Henri (Benjamin), noted French conductor, pedagogue, and composer; b. Paris, Nov. 10, 1873; d. there, Sept. 11, 1949. His father was Hippolyte Rabaud (1839–1900), prof. of cello at the Paris Cons., where Henri studied with Gédalge and Massenet (1893–94); he won the Premier Grand Prix de Rome in 1894 with his cantata *Daphné*. In 1908 he became conductor at the Paris Opéra and at the Opéra Comique; from 1914 to 1918 he was director of the Opéra. In 1918–19 he was engaged to conduct the Boston Sym. Orch.; he then was appointed director of the Paris Cons. in 1922; he held this post until 1941.

WORKS: DRAMATIC: OPERAS: *La Fille de Roland* (Paris, March 16, 1904); *Le Premier Glaire* (Béziers, 1908); *Marouf, savetier du Caire* (Paris, May 15, 1914); *Antoine et Cléopâtre*, after Shakespeare (1916–17); *L'Appel de la mer* (Paris, April 10, 1924); *Le Miracle des loups* (Paris, Nov. 14, 1924); *Rolande et le mauvais garçon* (1933; Paris, May 28, 1934); *Le Jeu de l'amour et du hasard* (1948; Monte Carlo, 1954); incidental music and film scores.

BIBL.: M. d'Ollone, *H. R.: Sa vie et son oeuvre* (Paris, 1958).

Racek, Jan, Czech musicologist; b. Bučovice, June 1, 1905; d. Brno, Dec. 5, 1979. He studied with Helfert at the Univ. of Brno (Ph.D., 1929, with the diss. *Idea vlasti, nāroda a slávy v dile B. Smetany* [The Idea of the Fatherland, Nation, and Glory in the Works of B. Smetana]; publ. in Brno, 1933; 2d ed., aug., 1947); later he received a D.Sc. degree (1957). He was director of the music archives of the Moravian Regional Museum (1930–48) and also was a lecturer at the Univ. of Brno (from 1939) and prof. and director of the Brno dept. of ethnography and folk music of the Czech Academy of Sciences (1948–70). He served as ed. of the journal *Musikologie* and as general ed. of Musica Antiqua Bohemica.

WRITINGS: *Leoš Janáček* (Olomouc, 1938); *Slohové problémy italské monodie* (Problems of Style in Italian Monody; Prague and Brno, 1938; Ger. tr., 1965); ed. with L. Firkušný, *Janáčkovy feuilletony z Lidové Noviny* (Janáček's Feuilletons in the Lidové Noviny; Brno, 1938; 2d ed., rev., 1958, as *Leoš Janáček: Fejetony z Lidových Noviny*; Ger. tr., 1962); *Leoš Janáček a současni moravšti skladatelé* (Leoš Janáček and Contemporary Moravian Composers; Brno, 1940); *Ceská hudba od nejstaršich dob do počátku 19. stoleti* (Czech Music from the Earliest Times to the Beginning of the 19th Century; Prague, 1949; 2d ed., aug., 1958); *Ruská hudba: Od nejstaršich dob az po velkou řijnovou revoluci* (Russian Music from the Earliest Times up to the Great Revolution; Prague, 1953); *Beethoven a české země* (Beethoven in Bohemia and Moravia; Brno, 1964).

Rachmaninoff, Sergei (Vassilievich), greatly renowned Russian-born American pianist, conductor, and composer; b. probably in Oneg, April 1, 1873; d. Beverly Hills, March 28, 1943. He was of a musical family; his grandfather was an amateur pianist, a pupil of John Field; his father also played the piano; Rachmaninoff's *Polka* was written on a theme improvised by his father; his mother likewise played piano, and it was from her that he received his initial training at their estate, Oneg, near Novgorod. After financial setbacks, the family estate was sold and he was taken to St. Petersburg, where he studied piano with Vladimir Demiansky and harmony with Alexander Rubets at the Cons. (1882–85); acting on the advice of his cousin, Alexander Siloti, he enrolled as a piano student of Nikolai Zverev at the Moscow Cons. (1885); he then entered Siloti's piano class and commenced the study of counterpoint with Taneyev and harmony with Arensky (1888). He met Tchaikovsky, who appreciated his talent and gave him friendly advice. He graduated as a pianist (1891) and as a composer (1892), winning the gold medal with his opera *Aleko*, after Pushkin. Then followed his Prelude in C-sharp Minor (1892); publ. that same year, it quickly became one of the most celebrated piano pieces in the world. His 1st Sym., given in Moscow (1897), proved a failure, however. Discouraged, Rachmaninoff destroyed the MS, but the orch. parts were preserved; after his death, the score was restored and performed in Moscow (1945). In the meantime, Rachmaninoff launched a career as a piano virtuoso; he also took up a career as a conductor, joining the Moscow Private Russian Orch. (1897). He made his London debut in the triple capacity of pianist, conductor, and composer with the Phil. Soc. (1899). Although he attempted to compose after the failure of his 1st Sym., nothing significant came from his pen. Plagued by depression, he underwent treatment by hypnosis with Nikolai Dahl, and then began work on his 2d Piano Concerto. He played the first complete performance of the score with Siloti conducting in Moscow (Nov. 9, 1901); this concerto became the most celebrated work of its genre written in the 20th century, and its singular charm has never abated since; it is no exaggeration to say that it became a model for piano concertos by a majority of modern Russian composers, and also of semipopular virtuoso pieces for piano and orch. written in America. On May 12, 1902, Rachmaninoff married his cousin Natalie Satina; they spent some months in Switzerland, then returned to Moscow. After conducting at Moscow's Bolshoi Theater (1904–06), he decided to spend most of his time in Dresden, where he composed his 2d Sym., one of his most popular works. Having composed another major work, his 3d Piano Concerto, he took it on his first tour of the United States in 1909. His fame was so great that he was offered the conductorship of the Boston Sym. Orch., but he declined; the offer was repeated in 1918, but once again he declined. He lived in Russia from 1910 until after the Bolshevik Revolution of Oct. 1917, at which time he left Russia with his family, never to return. From 1918 until 1939 he made annual tours of Europe as a pianist and also of the United States (from 1918 until his death), where he spent much of his time; he also owned a villa in Lucerne (1931–39), and it was there that he composed one of his most enduring scores, the *Rhapsody on a Theme of Paganini* (1934). In 1932 he was awarded the Gold Medal of the Royal Phil. Soc. of London. After the outbreak of World War II (1939), he spent his remaining years in the United States. He became a naturalized American citizen a few weeks before his death, having made his last appearance as a pianist in Knoxville, Tenn., on Feb. 15, 1943.

Among Russian composers, Rachmaninoff occupies a very important place. The sources of his inspiration lie in the Romantic tradition of 19th-century Russian music; the link with Tchaikovsky's lyrical art is very strong; melancholy moods prevail and minor keys predominate in his compositions, as in Tchaikovsky's; but there is an unmistakable stamp of Rachmaninoff's individuality in the broad, rhapsodic sweep of the melodic line, and particularly in the fully expanded sonorities and fine resonant harmonies of his piano writing; its technical resourcefulness is unexcelled by any composer since Liszt. Despite the fact that Rachmaninoff was an émigré and stood in avowed opposition to the Soviet regime (until the German attack on Russia in 1941 impelled him to modify his stand), his popularity never wavered in Russia; after his death, Russian musicians paid spontaneous tribute to him. Rachmaninoff's music is much less popular in Germany, France, and Italy; on the other hand, in England and America it constitutes a potent factor on the concert stage.

WORKS: OPERAS: *Esmeralda* (1888; introduction to Act 1 and fragment of Act 3 only completed); *Aleko*, after Pushkin's *Tsigani* (The Gypsies; 1892; Moscow, May 9, 1893); *The Miserly Knight*, op. 24, after Pushkin (1903–05; Moscow, Jan. 24, 1906); *Francesca da Rimini*, op. 25, after Dante's *Inferno* (1900; 1904–05; Moscow, Jan. 24, 1906); *Monna Vanna*, after Maeterlinck (1907; piano score of Act 1 and sketches of Act 2 only completed; Act 1 orchestrated by I. Buketoff; concert perf., Saratoga, N.Y., Aug. 11, 1984).

BIBL.: I. Lipayev, *S. R.* (Saratov, 1913); V. Belaiev, *S. R.* (Moscow, 1924; Eng. tr. in *Musical Quarterly*, July 1927); O. von Riesemann, *R.'s Recollections* (N.Y., 1934); W. Lyle, *R.: A Biography* (London, 1939); A. Solovtsov, *S. R.* (Moscow, 1947); J. Culshaw, *S. R.* (London, 1949); V. Seroff, *R.* (N.Y., 1950); A. Alexeyev, *S. R.* (Moscow, 1954); S. Bertensson and J. Leyda, *S. R.: A Lifetime in Music* (N.Y., 1956; 2d ed., 1965); Y. Keldish, *R. and His Time* (Moscow, 1973); R. Threlfall, *S. R.: His Life and Music* (London, 1973); V. Bryantseva, *S. V. R.* (Moscow, 1976); G. Norris, *R.* (London, 1976; 2d ed., rev., 1993); R. Walker, *R.: His Life and Times* (Tunbridge Wells, 1980); R. Threlfall and G. Norris, *Catalogue of the Compositions of S. R.* (London, 1982); R. Palmieri, *S. V. R.: A Guide to Research* (London and N.Y., 1985); C. Poivre D'Arvor, *R., ou, La Passion au bout des doigts* (Monaco, 1986); M. Biesold, *S. R., 1873–1943: Zwischen Moskau und New York: Eine Künstlerbiographie* (Weinheim, 1991); B. Nikitin, *S. R.: Dve zhizni* (Moscow, 1993).

Račiūnas, Antanas, significant Lithuanian composer and pedagogue; b. Užliašiai, near Panevėzys, Sept. 17, 1905; d. Kaunas, April 3, 1984. He studied composition with J. Gruodis at the Kaunas Cons. (graduated, 1933) and with Boulanger and Koechlin in Paris (1936–39). He taught at the Kaunas Cons. (1933–36; 1939–49) and the Vilnius Cons. (1949–59). In 1965 he was made a People's Artist of the Lithuanian SSR. He wrote and produced the first opera in Lithuanian, *3 Talismen* (Kaunas, March 19, 1936), and 3 other operas, *Amber Shore* (1940), *Marite* (1953), and *Sun City* (1965); also *Liberated Lithuania*, oratorio (1945).

Radford, Robert, esteemed English bass; b. Nottingham, May 13, 1874; d. London, March 3, 1933. He was educated at London's Royal Academy of Music, taking voice lessons with Alberto Randegger. He made his operatic debut at Covent Garden in London in 1904 as the Commendatore in *Don Giovanni*; he later sang Hagen and Hunding in the first English *Ring* cycle under Richter in London (1908). In 1921 he became a founder, with Beecham, of the British National Opera Co.; later he became its director. In

1929 he was appointed to the faculty of his alma mater. His fame as an opera singer was great in England; in addition to singing opera, he greatly distinguished himself as a concert artist. His daughter, Winifred Radford (b. London, Oct. 2, 1901; d. Cheltenham, April 15, 1993), was a singer and teacher. She was closely associated with Bernac and Poulenc.

Radicati, Felice Alessandro, Italian violinist, teacher, and composer; b. Turin, 1775; d. when thrown from his carriage in Bologna, March 19, 1820. He was a pupil of Pugnani. He was a violinist in the Turin cappella until 1798. After marying **Teresa Bertinotti** in 1801, the couple toured Germany, Austria, Holland, England, and Portugal. He was again a member of the Turin cappella (1814–15) before settling in Bologna as concertmaster and director of the orch., as maestro di cappella at S. Petronio, and as prof. of violin at the Cons. As a composer of chamber music, he was hailed as the restorer of the string quartet in Italy.

WORKS: OPERAS: *Il sultano generoso* (*c.*1805); *Coriolano* (Amsterdam, 1809); *Fedra* (London, March 5, 1811); *L'intrigo fortunato* (1815); *Castore e Polluce* (Bologna, May 27, 1815); *Blondello ossia Riccardo Cuor di Leone* (Turin, 1816); *La lezione singolare ossia Un giorno a Parigi* (*c.*1819); *I due prigiorneri* (*c.*1820); *Il medico per forza* (*c.*1820).

BIBL.: C. Pancaldi, *Cenni intorno F. R.* (Bologna, 1828).

Radnai, Miklós, Hungarian composer; b. Budapest, Jan. 1, 1892; d. there, Nov. 4, 1935. He studied violin, piano, and composition at the Budapest Academy of Music; he continued his composition studies with Mottl in Munich (1911). In 1925 he was appointed director of the Budapest Opera. He wrote a textbook on harmony and contributed critical essays to publications. He wrote an opera, *Az infánsnő születésnapja*, and a ballet, *The Birthday of the Infanta*, after Oscar Wilde (Budapest, April 26, 1918).

Radó, Aladár, Hungarian composer; b. Budapest, Dec. 26, 1882; d. in battle near Belgrade, Sept. 7, 1914. He studied in Budapest and Berlin. He wrote 2 operas: *The Black Knight* (1911) and *Golem* (1912).

Radoux, Jean-Théodore, Belgian composer and pedagogue, father of **Charles Radoux-Rogier**; b. Liège, Nov. 9, 1835; d. there, March 20, 1911. He studied composition with Daussoigne-Mehul at the Liège Cons., winning the Belgian Prix de Rome with the cantata *Le Juif errant* (1859), then went to Paris for additional study with Halévy. He was prof. of bassoon at the Liège Cons. (from 1856), serving as its director (from 1872). He wrote monographs on Daussoigne-Méhul (1882) and Vieuxtemps (1891); also *La Musique et les Ecoles nationales* (1896), all publ. in Brussels. Among his compositions were the operas *Le Béarnais* (Liège, March 14, 1866) and *La Coupe enchantée* (Brussels, 1872) and the oratorio, *Cain* (1877).

Radoux-Rogier (real name, **Radoux**), **Charles,** Belgian pedagogue, writer on music, and composer, son of **Jean-Théodore Radoux**; b. Liège, July 30, 1877; d. there, April 30, 1952. He studied with his father at the Liège Cons., winning the Belgian Prix de Rome with his cantata *Geneviève de Brabant* (1907); he was made a prof. of harmony there (1905); he wrote music criticism and was active in folk-song research and served as inspector of music education (1930–42). His compositions included 2 operas: *Les Sangliers des Ardennes* (1905) and *Oudelette* (Brussels, April 11, 1912).

Raff, (Joseph) Joachim, greatly renowned Swiss pedagogue and composer; b. Lachen, near Zürich, May 27, 1822; d. Frankfurt am Main, June 24, 1882. He was educated at the Jesuit Gymnasium in Schwyz. He was a schoolteacher in Rapperswill (1840–44), but pursued an interest in music. He sent some of his piano pieces to Mendelssohn (1843), who recommended them for publication; having met Liszt in Basel (1845), he received his encouragement and assistance in finding employment; later he was his assistant in Weimar (1850–56), where he became an ardent propagandist of the new German school of composition, He then went to Wiesbaden as a piano teacher and composer, where he married the actress Doris Genast. He subsequently was director of the Hoch Cons. in Frankfurt (1877–82), where he also taught composition; students flocked from many countries to study with him, including Edward MacDowell. Raff was a composer of prodigious fecundity, and a master of all technical aspects of composition. He wrote 214 opus numbers that were publ., and many more that remained in MS. In spite of his fame, his music fell into lamentable desuetude after his death. He publ. *Die Wagnerfrage: Wagners letzte künstlerische Kundgebung im Lohengrin* (Braunschweig, 1854).

WORKS: OPERAS: *König Alfred* (1848–50; Weimar, March 9, 1851; rev. 1852; Weimar, 1853); *Samson* (1853–57); *Die Parole* (1868); *Dame Kobold*, comic opera (1869; Weimar, April 9, 1870); *Benedetto Marcello* (1877–78); *Die Eifersüchtigen*, comic opera (1881–82).

BIBL.: A. Schäfer, *Chronologisch-systematisches Verzeichnis der Werke J. R.s* (Wiesbaden, 1888); H. Raff, *J. R.: Ein Lebensbild* (Regensburg, 1925); J. Kälin and A. Marty, *Leben und Werk des Komponisten J. R.* (Zürich, 1972); M. Römer, *J. J. R. (1822–1882)* (Wiesbaden, 1982).

Ragin, Derek Lee, American countertenor; b. West Point, N.Y., June 17, 1958. He was a student at the Oberlin College-Cons. of Music. In 1983 he made his operatic debut in Innsbruck in Cesti's *Tito*, and in 1984 he made his London recital debut at Wigmore Hall. On Sept. 27, 1988, he made his Metropolitan Opera debut in New York as Nirenus in *Giulio Cesare*. His first appearance in Salzburg took place in 1990 when he sang Gluck's Orfeo. In 1992 he portrayed Britten's Oberon in St. Louis. He appeared in Hasse's *Attilio regolo* in Dresden in 1997. Among his other roles are Handel's Flavio, Saul, and Tamerlano. His engagements as an oratorio singer and recitalist have taken him to many of the world's leading music centers.

Rahbari, Alexander (Ali), Iranian-born Austrian conductor; b. Varamin, May 26, 1948. After studying violin at the Tehran Cons., he went to Vienna to study conducting and composition at the Academy of Music, his principal mentors being Swarowsky, Osterreicher, and Einem. He was active as a violinist and conductor in Tehran, where he later was chief conductor of the Opera. In 1977 he went to Austria, becoming a naturalized Austrian citizen. After winning the Besançon conducting competition and a medal at the Geneva competition in 1978, he was invited to appear as a guest conductor with the Berlin Phil. in 1979; thereafter he appeared as a guest conductor throughout Europe. In 1989 he became chief conductor of the Belgian Radio and TV Phil. in Brussels.

Raichev, Alexander, prominent Bulgarian composer and pedagogue; b. Lom, April 11, 1922. He studied composition with Vladigerov at the Bulgarian State Cons. in Sofia (1943–47), then took courses in composition with Kodály and Viski and in conducting with Ferencsik at the Budapest Academy of Music (1949–50); returning to Sofia, he taught at the Bulgarian State Cons. (from 1950), where he also served as rector (1972–79). His music makes use of innovative techniques that breathe new life into traditional genres and forms.

WORKS: DRAMATIC: OPERAS: *The Bridge* (Ruse, Oct. 2, 1965); *Your Presence* (Sofia, Sept. 5, 1969); *Alarm* (Sofia, June 14, 1974); *Khan Asparouch* (Ruse, March 9, 1981). OPERETTA: *The Nightingale of Orchid* (Sofia, March 7, 1963). BALLETS: *A Haidouk Epic* (Sofia, Feb. 13, 1953); *The Spring of the White-legged Maiden* (Sofia, Feb. 26, 1978). ORATORIOS: *Friendship* (1954); *Dimitrov Is Alive* (1954); *October 50* (1967); *Bulgaria—White, Green, Red* (1977); *Oratorio Meeting* (1984).

Raichl, Miroslav, Czech composer; b. Náchod, Feb. 2, 1930; d. Pardubice, Jan. 11, 1998. He studied composition with Bořkovec at the Prague Academy of Music, graduating in 1953. He subsequently devoted himself mainly to teaching and administrative work in the Union of Czechoslovak Composers. Among his works was the opera *Fuente Ovejuna*, after Lope de Vega (1957; Prague,

1959), and *Farewell Elegy*, concertant aria for Soprano and Chamber Orch. (1981–82).

Raida, Karl Alexander, German composer; b. Paris (of German parents), Oct. 4, 1852; d. Berlin, Nov. 26, 1923. He studied at the conservatories of Stuttgart and Dresden. He was conductor from 1878 to 1892 at the Viktoria Theater in Berlin, where he founded the Akademie für Dramatischen Gesang (1882) and the Gesellschaft der Opernfreunde (1887); from 1895 to 1897 he served as director of the new Deutsches Theater in Munich. He was a successful composer of light operas, operettas, ballets, farces, etc.

Raimann, Rudolf, Hungarian composer; b. Veszprem, May 7, 1861; d. Vienna, Sept. 26, 1913. He entered the service of Prince Esterházy as music director. He wrote an opera, *Enoch Arden*, after Tennyson (Budapest, May 8, 1894), and about 12 operettas for Vienna, including *Das Waschermädel* (April 19, 1905), *Paula macht alles* (March 27, 1909), *Die Frau Gretl* (April 7, 1911), and *Unser Stammhalter* (Nov. 15, 1912).

Raimondi, Gianni, Italian tenor; b. Bologna, April 13, 1923. He was a student of Gennaro Barra-Carcacciolo and Ettore Campogalliani. In 1947 he made his operatic debut as the Duke of Mantua in Bologna, and then sang in other Italian opera centers. In 1953 he made appearances at the Stoll Theatre in London, at the Paris Opéra, and in Monte Carlo. In 1955 he joined Milan's La Scala. He made his U.S. debut in San Francisco in 1957. In 1959 he appeared in Vienna. In 1960 he sang in Munich. On Sept. 29, 1965, he made his Metropolitan Opera debut in New York as Rodolfo, remaining on its roster until 1969. From 1969 to 1977 he sang at the Hamburg State Opera. He became well known for his roles in Rossini's operas, and also had success as Alfredo, Cavaradossi, Faust, Pollione, and Edgardo.

BIBL.: D. Rubboli, *G. R..: Felicemente tenore* (Parma, 1992).

Raimondi, Ignazio, Italian violinist, conductor, and composer; b. Naples, *c*.1735; d. London, Jan. 14, 1813. He studied violin with Emanuele Barbella, then played in the orch. of the Teatro San Carlo in Naples (1759–62). He then was active in Amsterdam as a violinist and conductor. He settled in London (1780). Among his works was the opera *La Muta* (Paris, Nov. 12, 1789).

Raimondi, Pietro, inventive Italian composer; b. Rome, Dec. 20, 1786; d. there, Oct. 30, 1853. He studied with La Barbara and Tritto at the Cons. della Pietà de' Turchini in Naples. In 1807 he brought out an opera buffa, *Le bizzarie d'amore*, at Genoa; it was followed by about 60 other dramatic works and 22 ballets, for whose production he traveled from place to place (Florence, Naples, Rome, Messina, Milan, etc.). He was director of the royal theaters at Naples (1824–32) and a prof. at the Palermo Cons. (1834–52); in 1852 he became maestro di cappella at St. Peter's in Rome. Raimondi was a contrapuntist of remarkable skill, and many of his fugues were designed to be combined with others to form complex musical structures. His most astounding combinatorial feat, however, was the sacred trilogy *Giuseppe (Joseph)*, comprising 3 oratorios (*Potifar, Giuseppe, Giacobbe*), performed at the Teatro Argentina in Rome, Aug. 7, 1852, at first separately, and then simultaneously, the ensemble of 400 musicians on the stage and in the orch. presenting a most striking effect and arousing great curiosity among professional musicians.

BIBL.: F. Cicconetti, *Memorie intorno a P. R.* (Rome, 1867).

Raimondi, Ruggero, notable Italian bass; b. Bologna, Oct. 3, 1941. He was a student of Pediconi (1961–62) and Piervenanzi (1963–65) at the Cons. di Santa Cecilia in Rome. In 1964 he made his operatic debut as Colline in Spoleto, and then sang at the Teatro La Fenice in Venice until 1969. In 1964 he made his first appearance in Rome as Procida. In 1968 he made his debut at Milan's La Scala as Timur in *Turandot*, and his London debut in a concert perf. of Donizetti's *Lucrezia Borgia*. He sang Don Giovanni at the Glyndebourne Festival in 1969. In 1970 he made his first appearance at the Salzburg Festival as a soloist in the Verdi *Requiem*. On Sept. 14, 1970, he made his Metropolitan Opera debut in New York as Silva in *Ernani*, and subsequently made regular appearances there. He made his first appearance at London's Covent Garden as Verdi's Fiesco on Feb. 23, 1972. In 1978 he returned to the Salzburg Festival to make his operatic bow as Philip in *Don Carlos*. He sang at the Paris Opéra in 1979. In 1982 he appeared as Don Quichotte at the Vienna State Opera. In 1987 he sang Mozart's Count Almaviva in Chicago. He appeared in the opening concert at the new Opéra de la Bastille in Paris in 1989. In 1990 he sang Attila at Covent Garden. In 1992 he appeared as Scarpia in Rome. He returned to Covent Garden in 1994 as Rossini's Mosè. In 1996 he sang Iago in Salzburg. Raimondi's vocal resources are ably complemented by his stage deportment. Among his other distinguished roles are Boris Godunov, Méphistophélès, Sparafucile, Oroveso, and Ramfis.

Raisa, Rosa (real name, **Raisa** or **Rose Burschstein**), outstanding Polish soprano; b. Bialystok, May 23, 1893; d. Los Angeles, Sept. 28, 1963. In order to escape the horrors of anti-Semitic persecution, she fled to Naples at the age of 14; on Lombardi's advice she entered the Cons. San Pietro a Majella, where she studied under Barbara Marchisio. She made her operatic debut as Leonora in Verdi's *Oberto, Conte di San Bonifacio* in Parma on Sept. 6, 1913; she then sang 2 seasons at the Teatro Costanzi in Rome. In 1914 she made her first appearance at Covent Garden in London. She sang with increasing success in Rio de Janeiro, Montevideo, São Paulo, and Milan. In 1920 she married the baritone Giacomo Rimini, with whom she founded a singing school in Chicago in 1937. Raisa was one of the finest dramatic sopranos of her day, excelling in the Italian repertoire; she created the title role in Puccini's *Turandot* at Milan's La Scala (April 25, 1926), her husband taking the role of Ping.

Raitio, Väinö (Eerikki), Finnish composer; b. Sortavala, April 15, 1891; d. Helsinki, Sept. 10, 1945. He studied in Helsinki with Melartin and Furuhjelm and in Moscow with Ilyinsky; also in Berlin (1921) and Paris (1925–26). From 1926 to 1932 he taught at the Viipuri Music Inst. His music is programmatic in the Romantic manner, but there is a more severe strain in his pieces derived from Finnish legends. He was one of the earliest Finnish composers to embrace modern compositional techniques, being mainly influenced by Scriabin, German expressionism, and French Impressionism.

WORKS: DRAMATIC: OPERAS: *Jephtan tytär* (Jephtha's Daughter; 1929; Helsinki, 1931); *Prinsessa Cecilia* (1933; Helsinki, 1936); *Väinämöinen kosinta* (Väinämöinen's Courtship; 1935); *Lyydian kuningas* (The King of Lydia; 1937; Helsinki, 1955); *Kaksi kuningatarta* (2 Queens; 1937–40; Helsinki, 1945). BALLET: *Vesipatsas* (Waterspout; 1929).

Rajičić, Stanojlo, Serbian composer and pedagogue; b. Belgrade, Dec. 16, 1910. He studied composition (diplomas, 1934 and 1935) with Karel and Suk and piano (diploma, 1935) with Alois Sima at the Prague Cons., then attended piano master classes of Hoffmeister in Prague and of Walter Kerschbaumer in Vienna. From 1937 to 1977 he was prof. of composition at the Belgrade Academy of Music. In 1950 he was elected a corresponding member and in 1958 a fellow of the Serbian Academy of Sciences and Arts, serving as secretary of its dept. of visual and musical arts (from 1964); he also was elected a member of the Slovenian Academy of Sciences and Arts (1975). He received the Serbian State Prize (1968), the Gottfried von Herder Prize of Vienna (1975), and the Vuk Prize (1986). His early compositions are set in a radical idiom of atonal music, verging on dodecaphony, but later he adopted a national style derived from melorhythms of Serbian folk songs.

WORKS: DRAMATIC: OPERAS: *Simonida* (1956; Sarajevo, May 24, 1957); *Karadjordje* (1973; Belgrade, June 26, 1977); *Dnevnik jednog ludaka* (The Diary of a Madman; 1977; Belgrade, April 4, 1981); *Bele noći* (White Nights; 1983; Belgrade, April 14, 1985). BALLET: *Pod zemljom* (Under the Earth; 1940).

Ralf, Oscar (Georg), Swedish tenor, brother of **Torsten (Ivar) Ralf**; b. Malmö, Oct. 3, 1881; d. Kalmar, April 3, 1964. He studied with Forsell (1902–04) and Gillis Bratt (from 1905), and in Berlin and Munich. He began his career as a singer at Stockholm's Oscarsteatern, an operetta theater (1905–15); completing his studies with Bratt, he made his operatic debut as Siegmund at the Royal Opera in 1918; he was a principal member of the company until 1940 and also appeared as Siegmund at Bayreuth in 1927. He was best known for his roles in operas by Wagner and Verdi. He publ. an autobiography, *Tenoren han går i Ringen* (The Tenor Goes into the Ring; Stockholm, 1953).

Ralf, Torsten (Ivar), Swedish tenor, brother of **Oscar (Georg) Ralf**; b. Malmö, Jan. 2, 1901; d. Stockholm, April 27, 1954. He studied at the Stockholm Cons. and with Hertha Dehmlow in Berlin. He made his operatic debut as Cavaradossi in Stettin (1930); then sang in Chemnitz (1932–33) and Frankfurt am Main (1933–35). He was a member of the Dresden State Opera (1935–44), where he created the role of Apollo in Strauss's *Daphne* in 1938; he was made a Kammersänger in 1936. He sang at London's Covent Garden (1935–39; 1948) and at the Teatro Colón in Buenos Aires (1946); he made his Metropolitan Opera debut in New York as Lohengrin on Nov. 26, 1945, and remained on its roster until 1948. He was best known for such roles as Walther von Stolzing, Tannhäuser, Parsifal, Otello, and Radames.

Rameau, Jean-Philippe, great French composer, organist, and music theorist; b. Dijon (baptized), Sept. 25, 1683; d. Paris, Sept. 12, 1764. His father was organist of St. Étienne in Dijon. He learned to play the harpsichord as a small child, and from age 10 to 14 attended the Jesuit Collège des Godrans in Dijon, where he took up singing and composing instead of concentrating on his academic studies. At 18 his father sent him to Milan, where he stayed for only a brief time before joining the orch. of a traveling French opera troupe as a violinist. In Jan. 1702 he received a temporary appointment as organist at Avignon Cathedral; in May 1702 he became organist at Clermont Cathedral. By 1706 he was in Paris, where he publ. his 1st *Livre de pièces de clavecin*; was active there as a church organist until 1708. He succeeded his father as organist at Notre Dame Cathedral in Avignon in 1709, and then became organist to the Jacobins in Lyons in July 1713. He was organist at Clermont Cathedral from 1715 to 1723, where he wrote his famous *Traité de l'harmonie* (Paris, 1722). This epoch-making work, though little understood at the time, attracted considerable attention and roused opposition, so that when he settled definitely in Paris (1723) he was by no means unknown. The fact that he failed in 1727 in a competition for the position of organist at St.-Vincent-de-Paul did not injure his reputation, for it was generally known that Marchand (probably out of jealousy) had exerted his powerful influence in favor of Daquin, who was in every respect inferior to Rameau. In 1732 he became organist at Ste.-Croix-de-la-Bretonnerie, and soon was recognized as the foremost organist in France. In 1726 appeared his *Nouveau système de musique théorique*, an introduction to the *Traité*. The leading ideas of his system of harmony are (1) chord building by thirds; (2) the classification of a chord and all its inversions as one and the same, thus reducing the multiplicity of consonant and dissonant combinations to a fixed and limited number of root chords; and (3) his invention of a fundamental bass (basse fondamentale), which is an imaginary series of root tones forming the real basis of the varied chord progressions employed in a composition. The stir that these novel theories occasioned, and his reputation as the foremost French organist, by no means satisfied Rameau's ambition; his ardent desire was to bring out a dramatic work at the Opéra. He had made a modest beginning with incidental music to Alexis Piron's comedy *L'Endriague* in 1723. After contributing further incidental music to Piron's comedies *L'Enrôlement d'Arlequin* (1726) and *La Robe de dissension, ou Le Faux Prodigue* (1726), he became music master to the wife of the "fermier-général" La Pouplinière; the latter obtained from Voltaire a libretto for *Samson*, which Rameau set to music, but it was rejected on account of its biblical subject. A 2d libretto, by Abbé Pellegrin, was accepted, and *Hippolyte et Aricie* was produced at the Opéra in 1733; its reception was cool, despite undeniable superiority over the operas of Lully and his following. Rameau considered abandoning composing any further works for the theater, but the persuasions of his friends, who also influenced public opinion in his favor, were effective; in 1735 he brought out the successful opéra ballet *Les Indes galantes*, and in 1737 his masterpiece, *Castor et Pollux*, a work that for years held its own beside the operas of Gluck. A career of uninterrupted prosperity commenced. Rameau was recognized as the leading theorist of the time, and his instruction was eagerly sought. For the next 30 years his operas dominated the French stage. He was named Compositeur du cabinet du roy in 1745, and was ennobled 4 months before his death.

From the beginning of his dramatic career Rameau roused opposition, and at the same time found ardent admirers. The 1st war of words was waged between the "Lullistes" and the "Ramistes." This had scarcely been ended by a triumphant revival of *Pygmalion* in 1751 when the production of Pergolesi's *La Serva padrona* (1752) caused a more prolonged and bitter controversy between the adherents of Rameau and the "Encyclopédistes," a struggle known as "La Guerre des Bouffons," in which Rameau participated by writing numerous essays defending his position. Practically the same charges were made against him as would be made a century later against Wagner: unintelligible harmony, lack of melody, preponderance of discords, noisy instrumentation, etc. But when 25 years later the war between Gluckists and Piccinnists was raging, Rameau's works were praised as models of beauty and perfection. It is a matter for regret that Rameau was indifferent to the quality of his librettos; he relied so much upon his musical inspiration that he never could be brought to a realization of the importance of a good text; hence the inequality of his operas. Nevertheless, his operas mark a decided advance over Lully's in musical characterization, expressive melody, richness of harmony, variety of modulation, and expert and original instrumentation.

WRITINGS: (all publ. in Paris): *Traité de l'harmonie reduite à ses principes naturels* (1722; Eng. tr., 1737; modern ed. in Eng. tr. by P. Gossett, 1971); *Nouveau système de musique théorique* (1726); *Dissertation sur les différentes méthodes d'accompagnement pour le clavecin ou pour l'orgue* (1732); *Génération harmonique ou Traité de musique théorique et pratique* (1737; modern ed. in Eng. tr. by D. Hayes in *Rameau's "Génération harmonique,"* diss., Stanford Univ., 1974); *Mémoire où l'on expose les fondements du Système de musique théorique et pratique de M. Rameau* (1749); *Démonstration du principe de l'harmonie* (1750); *Nouvelles réflexions de M. Rameau sur sa Démonstration du principe de l'harmonie* (1752); *Observations sur notre instinct pour la musique* (1754); *Erreurs sur la musique dans l'Encyclopédie* (1755–56); *Suite des erreurs sur la musique dans l'Encyclopédie* (1756); *Prospectus, où l'on propose au public, par voye de souscription, un code de musique pratique, composé de sept méthodes* (1757); *Réponse de M. Rameau à MM. les éditeurs de l'Encyclopédie* (1757); *Nouvelles réflexions sur le principe sonore* (1758–59); *Code de musique pratique, ou Méthodes pour apprendre la musique . . . avec de nouvelles réflexions sur le principe sonore* (1760); *Lettre à M. d'Alembert sur ses opinions en musique* (1760); *Origine des sciences, suivie d'une controverse sur le même sujet* (1762); also *Vérités intéressantes* (unfinished MS). For a complete edition, see E. Jacobi, ed., *Jean-Philippe Rameau: Complete Theoretical Writings* (Rome, 1967–72).

WORKS: DRAMATIC (all 1st perf. at the Paris Opéra unless otherwise given): OPERAS: *Samson*, tragédie en musique (1733; not perf.; not extant); *Hippolyte et Aricie,* tragédie en musique (Oct. 1, 1733); *Les Indes galantes,* opéra ballet (Aug. 23, 1735); *Castor et Pollux*, tragédie en musique (Oct. 24, 1737); *Les Fêtes d'Hébé (Les Talents lyriques),* opéra ballet (May 21, 1739); *Dardanus,* tragédie en musique (Nov. 19, 1739); *La Princesse de Navarre,* comédie ballet (Versailles, Feb. 23, 1745); *Platée (ou Junon jalouse),* comédie lyrique (Versailles, March 31, 1745); *Les Fêtes de Polymnie,* opéra ballet (Oct. 12, 1745); *Le Temple de la gloire,* opéra ballet (Versailles, Nov. 27, 1745); *Les Fêtes de l'Hymen et de l'Amour, ou Les Dieux d'Egypte*, ballet-héroïque (Versailles, March 15, 1747); *Zaïs,* ballet-héroïque (Feb. 29, 1748); *Pygmalion*, acte de ballet (Aug. 27, 1748); *Les Surprises de l'Amour*, divertissement (Versailles, Nov. 27, 1748); *Naïs*, pastorale-héroïque (April 22, 1749); *Zoroastre*, tragédie en musique (Dec. 5, 1749); *Linus*, tragédie en musique (not perf.; greater portion of music not extant); *La Guirlande, ou Les Fleurs enchantées*, acte de ballet (Sept. 21, 1751); *Acante et Céphise, ou La Sympathie*, pastorale-héroïque (Nov. 18, 1751); *Daphnis et Eglé*, pastorale-héroïque (Fontainebleau, Oct. 30, 1753); *Lysis et Délie*, pastorale (1753; not perf.; music not extant); *Les Sybarites*, acte de ballet (Fontainebleau, Nov. 13, 1753); *La Naissance d'Osiris, ou La Fête Pamilie*, acte de ballet (Fontainebleau, Oct. 12, 1754); *Anacréon*, acte de ballet (Fontainebleau, Oct. 23, 1754; rev. version to different text, May 31, 1757); *Le Procureur dupé sans le savoir*, opéra comique en vaudevilles (private perf., 1758 or 1759; music not extant); *Les Paladins*, comédie ballet (Feb. 12, 1760); *Abaris, ou Les Boréades*, tragédie lyrique (1st perf. in concert form in London, April 19, 1975; 1st stage perf. in Aix-en-Provence, July 21, 1982). BALLETS: *Nélée et Myrthis (Les Beaux Jours de l'amour)*, *Zéphyre (Les Nymphes de Diane)*, and *Io* (none publicly performed). OTHER: He also contributed music, in collaboration with others, to the following comedies by A. Piron: *L'Endriague* (Feb. 3, 1723); *L'Enrôlement d'Arlequin* (Feb. 1726); *La Robe de dissension, ou Le Faux Prodigue* (Sept. 7, 1726); *Les Jardins de l'Hymen, ou La Rose* (1726; March 5, 1744); *Les Courses de Tempé* (Aug. 30, 1734); also the intermède en musique *Aruéris* (Dec. 15, 1762).

BIBL.: BIOGRAPHICAL: C. Poisot, *Notice biographique sur J.-P. R.* (Paris, 1864); T. Nisard, *Monographie de J.-P. R.* (Paris, 1867); R. Garraud, *R.* (Paris, 1876); H. Grigne, *R.* (Dijon, 1876); A. Pougin, *R.* (Paris, 1876); L. de La Laurencie, *R.* (Paris, 1908); L. Laloy, *R.* (Paris, 1908); Y. Tiénot, *J.-P. R.: Esquisse biographique, suivie d'un tableau chronologique comprenant une liste complète des oeuvres de R.* (Paris, 1954); H. Charlier, *J.-P. R.* (Lyons, 1955); P. Berthier, *Réflexions sur l'art et la vie de J.-P. R. (1683–1764)* (Paris, 1957); C. Girdlestone, *J.-P. R.: His Life and Work* (London, 1957; 2d ed., rev., 1969); J. Malignon, *R.* (Paris, 1960); C. Kintzler, *J.-P. R.: Splendeur et naufrage de l'esthétique du plaisir à l'age classique* (Paris, 1983).

WORKS: G. Graf, *J.-P. R. in seiner Oper Hippolyte et Aricie: Eine musikkritische Würdigung* (Wädenswil, 1927); P.-M. Masson, *L'Opéra de R.* (Paris, 1930); E. Ahnell, *The Concept of Tonality in the Operas of J.-P. R.* (diss., Univ. of Illinois, 1958); G. Seefrid, *Die Airs de danse in den Bühnenwerken von J.-P. R.* (Wiesbaden, 1969); M. Terey-Smith, *J.-P. R.: "Abaris ou les Boréades": A Critical Edition* (diss., Eastman School of Music, 1971); P. Rice, *The Fontainebleau Operas of J.-P. R.: A Critical Study* (diss., Univ. of Victoria, Canada, 1981); C. Dill, *Monstrous Opera: R. and the Tragic Tradition* (Princeton, 1998). THEORIES: P. Estève, *Nouvelle découverte du principe de l'harmonie, avec un examen de ce que M. R. a publié sous le titre de Démonstration de ce principe* (Paris, 1752); J. Le Rond d'Alembert, *Éléments de musique théorique et pratique selon les principes de M. R.* (Paris, 1752; 2d ed., 1762); F. Marpurg, *Versuch über die musikalische Temperatur, nebst einem Anhang über den R.- und Kirnbergerschen Grundbass* (Breslau, 1776); M. Keane, *The Theoretical Writings of J.-P. R.* (diss., Catholic Univ. of America, 1961); J. Krehbiel, *Harmonic Principles of J.-P. R. and His Contemporaries* (diss., Indiana Univ., 1964); D. Hayes, *R.'s "Génération harmonique ou Traité de musique théorique et pratique"* (diss., Stanford Univ., 1974); E. Verba, *A Hierarchic Interpretation of the Theories and Music of J.-P. R.* (diss., Univ. of Chicago, 1979); E. Haeringer, *L'esthétique de l'opéra en France au temps de J.-P. R.* (Oxford, 1990); T. Christensen, *R. and Musical Thought in the Enlightenment* (Cambridge, 1993).

Ramey, Samuel (Edward), outstanding American bass; b. Colby, Kansas, March 28, 1942. He attended Kansas State Univ., and then studied voice with Arthur Newman at Wichita State Univ. (B.Mus., 1968). After singing with the Grass Roots Opera Co. in Raleigh, N.C. (1968–69), he continued his studies with Armen Boyajian in New York. On March 11, 1973, he made his professional operatic debut as Zuniga in *Carmen* at the N.Y. City Opera, where he rose to prominence as its principal bass. In 1976 he made his first appearance at the Glyndebourne Festival as Mozart's Figaro. Following debuts at the Lyric Opera in Chicago and at the San Francisco Opera as Colline in 1979, he sang for the first time at Milan's La Scala and at the Vienna State Opera as Mozart's Figaro in 1981. From 1981 to 1989 he appeared in various Rossini roles in Pesaro. In 1982 he made his debut at London's Covent Garden as Mozart's Figaro, and then portrayed Mosè at the Paris Opéra in 1983. On Jan. 19, 1984, he made a brilliant debut at the Metropolitan Opera in New York as Argante in Handel's *Rinaldo*. That same year, he sang the role of Mozart's Figaro for the soundtrack recording of the award-winning film *Amadeus*. His first appearance at the Salzburg Festival came in 1987 when he sang Don Giovanni. He returned to the Metropolitan Opera in such roles as Bartók's Bluebeard in 1989, Don Basilio in 1992, and Boris Godunov in 1997. He also returned to the Lyric Opera in Chicago as Boris Godunov in 1994, and as Méphistophélès at the San Francisco Opera in 1995 and at the Vienna State Opera in 1997.

Ran, Shulamit, Israeli pianist and composer; b. Tel Aviv, Oct. 21, 1949. She studied piano with Miriam Boskovich and Emma Gorochov and composition with Ben-Haim and Boskovich, then was a scholarship student at the America-Israel Cultural Foundation and the Mannes College of Music in New York (graduated, 1967), her mentors being Reisenberg (piano) and Dello Joio (composition); she continued piano studies with Dorothy Taubman and composition training with Ralph Shapey (1976). She made tours of the United States and Europe as a pianist; she was artist-in-residence at St. Mary's Univ. in Halifax, Nova Scotia (1972–73), then taught at the Univ. of Chicago. She held a Guggenheim fellowship (1977) and was a visiting prof. at Princeton Univ. (1987). From 1991 to 1997 she was composer-in-residence of the Chicago Sym. Orch. Her Sym. No. 1 (1989–90; Philadelphia, Oct. 19, 1990) won the Pulitzer Prize in Music in 1991 and 1st prize in the Kennedy Center Friedheim awards in 1992. Among her other works is the opera *Between Two Worlds: The Dybbuk* (1994–95; Chicago, June 20, 1997).

Ranalow, Frederick (Baring), Irish baritone; b. Dublin, Nov. 7, 1873; d. London, Dec. 8, 1953. He became a chorister at St. Paul's Cathedral in London when he was 10. After training with Randegger at the Royal Academy of Music in London, he pursued a successful career as an oratorio singer. He also appeared with the Beecham Opera Co., winning praise for his Mozart's Figaro. In 1920 he sang Captain Macheath in Austin's revival of *The Beggar's Opera*, a role he sang on some 1,600 occasions.

Ranczak, Hildegard, Czech soprano; b. Vitkovice, Dec. 20, 1895; d. Munich, Feb. 19, 1987. She studied at the Vienna Cons. She made her operatic debut in Düsseldorf in 1918 and remained there until 1923; she then sang in Cologne (1923–25) and Stuttgart (1925–27). In 1927 she joined the Bavarian State Opera in Munich, where she appeared until 1944; she sang there again from 1946 to 1949; she also sang at Covent Garden in London, the Paris Opéra, the Rome Opera, and the Berlin State Opera. She created the role of Clairon in Richard Strauss's *Capriccio* in 1942.

Randegger, Alberto, Jr., Italian violinist and composer, nephew of **Alberto Randegger, Sr.**; b. Trieste, Aug. 3, 1880; d. Milan, Oct. 7, 1918. He accompanied his uncle to London and appeared as a violinist at an orch. concert conducted by the latter. After taking courses at the Royal Cons. of Music, he lived in Milan. He composed a short opera, *L'ombra di Werther* (Trieste, 1899).

Randegger, Alberto, Sr., Italian conductor, organist, teacher, and composer, uncle of **Alberto Randegger, Jr.**; b. Trieste, April 13, 1832; d. London, Dec. 18, 1911. He studied piano and composition in Italy. After working as a music director in Italian theaters, he settled in London (1854) and gained distinction as a conductor, singing teacher, and composer; he was also organist at St. Paul's in Regent's Park (1854–70). He conducted at the Wolverhampton (from 1868) and Norwich (1881–1905) festivals, with the Carl Rosa Opera Co. (1879–85), at Drury Lane and Covent Garden (1887–98), and at the Queen's Hall (1895–97); he was a prof. of singing at the Royal Academy of Music (from 1868) and later at the Royal College of Music. He publ. the manual *Singing* (London, 1893). His compositions include the operas *Bianca Ca-*

pello (Brescia, 1854) and *The Rival Beauties* (Leeds, 1864); also a dramatic cantata, *Fridolin* (1873).

Randle, Thomas, American tenor; b. Los Angeles, Dec. 21, 1958. He received vocal training in Los Angeles, and then pursued a career as a soloist with major orchs. in North America and Europe. In 1988 he made his operatic debut as Tamino with the English National Opera in London, and in 1989 he sang in *The Fairy Queen* at the Aix-en-Provence Festival. After appearing as Tamino at the Glyndebourne Festival in 1991, he returned to the English National Opera in 1992 to create the role of Dionysius in Buller's *Bakxai*. In 1994 he sang in the premiere of Schat's *Symposium* with the Netherlands Opera in Amsterdam. He was engaged as Idomeneo at the Scottish Opera in Glasgow in 1996. Throughout these years, he continued to appear frequently in concerts.

Rangström, (Anders Johan) Ture, prominent Swedish conductor, music critic, and composer; b. Stockholm, Nov. 30, 1884; d. there, May 11, 1947. He studied counterpoint with Johan Lindegren in Stockholm (1903–04), then went to Berlin, where he took courses in singing with Hey and in composition with Pfitzner (1905–06); he continued his vocal training with Hey in Munich (1906–08). He was a music critic for Stockholm's *Svenska Dagbladet* (1907–09), the *Stockholms Dagblad* (1910–14; 1927–30), and the *Nya Dagligt Allehanda* (1938–42); he was conductor of the Göteborg Sym. Orch. (1922–25), and thereafter made guest conducting appearances in Scandinavia. His music is permeated with a lyrical sentiment, and his forms are rhapsodic; in his syms. he achieves great intensity by concentrated development of the principal melodic and rhythmic ideas; his songs are also notable.

WORKS: OPERAS: *Kronbruden* (The Crown Bride; 1915–16; 1st perf. in German as *Die Kronbraut,* Stuttgart, Oct. 21, 1919; 1st perf. in Swedish, Göteborg, March 25, 1936); *Middelalderlig* or *Medeltida* (1917–18; Göteborg, May 11, 1921); *Gilgamesj* (1943–44; unfinished; completed and orchestrated by J. Fernström; Stockholm, Nov. 20, 1952).

BIBL.: A. Helmer and S. Jacobsson, *T. R.: Life and Work* (Stockholm, 1987).

Ránki, György, noted Hungarian composer; b. Budapest, Oct. 30, 1907. He studied composition with Kodály at the Budapest Academy of Music (1926–30) and ethnomusicology with Schaeffner in Paris (1938–39); he then devoted himself to composition. He won the Erkel (1952, 1957) and Kossuth (1954) prizes; in 1963 he was made a Merited Artist by the government and received the Bartók-Pásztory award (1987). He won distinction as a composer of both serious and popular works.

WORKS: DRAMATIC: *King Pomádé's New Clothes*, comic opera (1953–67); *The Tragedy of Man*, "mystery opera" (1970); *The Boatman of the Moon*, "opera-fantasy" (1979); *Terminal*, music drama (1988); also *3 Nights*, musical tragedy (1961), an operetta, much other theater music, numerous film scores, and *1944*, oratorio for Baritone, Chorus, and Chamber Orch. (1967).

Rankin, Nell, American mezzo-soprano; b. Montgomery, Ala., Jan. 3, 1926. She studied voice with Jeanne Lorraine at the Birmingham Cons. of Music and continued her training with Karin Branzell in New York (1945–49). In 1949 she made her operatic debut as Ortrud in *Lohengrin* at the Zürich Opera, of which she later became an active member; in 1950–51 she sang at the Basel Opera, and in 1951 appeared at La Scala, Milan. In 1951 she won the Metropolitan Opera Auditions of the Air and made her debut with it in New York on Nov. 22, 1951, as Amneris; she then sang at Covent Garden in London (1953–54) and at the San Francisco Opera (1955). Subsequently she appeared at the Teatro Colón in Buenos Aires, in Mexico, and in Europe. Her best roles were Carmen, Azucena, Ortrud, Santuzza, and Maddalena.

Rankl, Karl, Austrian-born English conductor and composer; b. Gaaden, near Vienna, Oct. 1, 1898; d. Salzburg, Sept. 6, 1968. He was a pupil of Schoenberg and Webern in Vienna; from them he acquired a fine understanding of the problems of modern music. He occupied various positions as a chorus master and an opera coach in Vienna; he served as assistant to Klemperer at the Kroll Opera in Berlin (1928–31), then conducted opera in Graz (1932–37) and at the German Theater in Prague (1937–39). At the outbreak of World War II, he went to England and later became a naturalized subject; he was music director at Covent Garden in London (1946–51), the Scottish National Orch. in Glasgow (1952–57), and the Elizabethan Opera Trust in Sydney (1958–60). He composed an opera, *Deirdre of the Sorrows* (1951), which won the Festival of Britain prize but was not perf.; also an oratorio, *Der Mensch*.

Rappold, Marie (née **Winterroth**), English soprano; b. London, c.1873; d. Los Angeles, May 12, 1957. The family moved to America when she was a child. She studied with Oscar Saenger in New York; she made her Metropolitan Opera debut there as Sulamith in *Die Königen von Saba* (Nov. 22, 1905) and remained on its roster until 1909; she then went to Europe. She was married to Dr. Julius Rappold, but divorced him and married **Rudolf Berger** in 1913. She had another period of singing at the Metropolitan Opera (1910–20) and later appeared in Chicago (1927–28); she then settled in Los Angeles as a teacher.

Raskin, Judith, noted American soprano; b. N.Y., June 21, 1928; d. there, Dec. 21, 1984. She studied at Smith College, graduating in 1949; she took private voice lessons with Anna Hamlin in New York. Her stage career received an impetus on July 7, 1956, when she sang the title role in Douglas Moore's folk opera *The Ballad of Baby Doe*, premiered in Central City, Colo. In 1957 she became a member of the NBC-TV Opera; in 1959 she joined the N.Y. City Opera. She made her Metropolitan Opera debut in New York on Feb. 23, 1962, as Susanna in *Le nozze di Figaro*; she sang there until 1972. She taught at the Manhattan School of Music and the 92d Street "Y" School of Music in New York from 1975 and also at the Mannes College of Music there from 1976.

Rasmussen, Karl Aage, Danish composer, conductor, and teacher; b. Kolding, Dec. 13, 1947. He took courses in music history, theory, and composition at the Århus Cons. (graduated, 1971), where his principal mentors were Nrgård and Gudmundsen-Holmgreen. He taught at the Funen Cons. (1970–72); in 1971 he joined the faculty of the Århus Cons. as a lecturer, becoming a docent in 1979 and a prof. in 1988; he also was a docent at the Royal Danish Cons. of Music in Copenhagen (1980–82). From 1973 to 1988 he was active with the Danish Radio; in 1975 he founded a chamber ensemble, the Elsinore Players, and in 1978 the NUMUS Festival, serving as its artistic director until 1985 and again from 1987 to 1990; in 1986 he founded the Danish Piano Theater. From 1987 to 1990 he was chairman of the Danish Arts Foundation. In addition to monographs on composers, he wrote much music criticism and contributed articles on music history to periodicals in his homeland and abroad. His music follows the cosmopolitan trends of pragmatic hedonism within neoclassical formal structures.

WORKS: DRAMATIC: *Crapp's Last Tape*, opera (1967); *Jephta*, opera (1977); *Majakovskij*, scenic concert piece (1978); *The Story of Jonah*, musical radio play (1981); *Our Hoffmann*, musical play (1986); *The Sinking of the Titanic*, opera (1993; Jutland, May 4, 1994).

Rasse, François (Adolphe Jean Jules), Belgian violinist, conductor, teacher, and composer; b. Helchin, near Ath, Jan. 27, 1873; d. Brussels, Jan. 4, 1955. He studied violin with Ysaÿe at the Brussels Cons., winning the Belgian Grand Prix de Rome in 1899. From 1925 to 1938 he was director of the Liège Cons. Among his works are the operas *Déidamia* (1905) and *Soeur Béatrice* (1938), and the ballet *Le maître à danser* (1908).

Rastrelli, Joseph (Gioseffo or **Giuseppe),** eminent Italian conductor and composer; b. Dresden, April 13, 1799; d. there, Nov. 15, 1842. He 1st studied with his father, then received instruction in violin from Poland and in harmony from Fiedler in Dresden, and in counterpoint with Padre Mattei in Bologna (1814). Returning to Dresden (1817), he gained success with his opera *La Schiava circassa* (1820); that same year, he became a violinist in the royal chapel. He was made deputy music director at the Court Theater (1829), and was appointed royal music director (1830).

WORKS: DRAMATIC: OPERAS (all 1st perf. in Dresden unless otherwise given): *La distruzione di Gerusalemme* (Ancona, 1816); *La Schiava circassa* (1820); *Le Donne curiose* (1821); *Velleda* (1822); *Amina* (Milan, 1824); *Salvator Rosa, oder Zwey Nächte in Rom* (July 22, 1832); *Bertha von Bretagne* (1835); *Die Neuvermählten* (1839); *Il trionfo di Nabucco il grande* (n.d.). BALLET: *Der Raub Zetulbeus* (*c.*1836–37).

Rathaus, Karol, Polish-born American pedagogue and composer; b. Tarnopol, Sept. 16, 1895; d. N.Y., Nov. 21, 1954. He studied at the Vienna Academy of Music and the Univ. of Vienna (Ph.D., 1922) and in Berlin (1920–21; 1922–23). In 1932 he went to Paris, and in 1934 to London. In 1938 he settled in the United States, becoming a naturalized American citizen in 1946. After a brief stay in Hollywood in 1939, during which he wrote some film scores, he settled in New York; in 1940 he was appointed to the faculty of Queens College. He was highly respected as a teacher of composition. His own music, however, never attracted large audiences; always noble in purpose and design and masterly in technique, it reveals a profound feeling for European neo-Romanticism. In 1952 he rev. and ed. the orch. score to Mussorgsky's *Boris Godunov* on a commission from the Metropolitan Opera, which gave the new version on March 6, 1953.

WORKS: DRAMATIC: OPERA: *Fremde Erde* (Berlin, Dec. 10, 1930; also as a symphonic interlude, 1950). BALLETS: *Der letzte Pierrot* (1926; Berlin, May 7, 1927); *Le Lion amoureux* (1937). INCIDENTAL MUSIC: *Uriel Acosta* (1930; orch. suite, 1933; rev. 1947). FILM MUSIC: 17 scores, including *The Brothers Karamazov* (1931), *The Dictator* (1934), *Dame de pique* (1937), *Let Us Live* (1939), and *Out of Evil* (1950).

Ratner, Leonard Gilbert, American musicologist and composer; b. Minneapolis, July 30, 1916. He studied composition with Schoenberg at the Univ. of Calif. at Los Angeles, and musicology with Bukofzer and Elkus at the Univ. of Calif. at Berkeley (Ph.D., 1947). He also had composition lessons with Bloch and F. Jacobi. In 1947 he was appointed to the staff of Stanford Univ.; held a Guggenheim fellowship in 1962–63. Among his works is the chamber opera *The Necklace.*

WRITINGS: *Music: The Listener's Art* (N.Y., 1957); *Harmony: Structure and Style* (N.Y., 1962); *Classic Music: Expression, Form, and Style* (N.Y., 1979); *Romantic Music: Sound and Syntax* (N.Y., 1992).

BIBL.: W. Allanbrook, J. Levy, and W. Mahrt, eds., *Conventions in Eighteenth- and Nineteenth-Century Music: Essays in Honor of L. G. R.* (Stuyvesant, N.Y., 1992).

Rattle, Sir Simon (Denis), brilliant English conductor; b. Liverpool, Jan. 19, 1955. He began playing piano and percussion as a child; appeared as a percussionist with the Royal Liverpool Phil. when he was 11, and was a percussionist in the National Youth Orch.; he also took up conducting in his youth, and was founder-conductor of the Liverpool Sinfonia (1970–72); concurrently he studied at the Royal Academy of Music in London (1971–74). After winning 1st prize in the John Player International Conductors' Competition (1974), he was assistant conductor of the Bournemouth Sym. Orch. and Sinfonietta (1974–76); he made his first tour of the United States conducting the London Schools Sym. Orch. (1976). In 1977 he conducted at the Glyndebourne Festival, then was assistant conductor of the Royal Liverpool Phil. (1977–80) and the BBC Scottish Sym. Orch. in Glasgow (1977–80). He made his first appearance as a guest conductor of a U.S. orch. with the Los Angeles Phil. in 1979; he was its principal guest conductor (from 1981) and also appeared as a guest conductor with other U.S. orchs., as well as with those in Europe. In 1980 he became principal conductor of the City of Birmingham Sym. Orch.; he led it on its first tour of the United States in 1988, the same year in which he made his U.S. debut as an opera conductor leading *Wozzeck* in Los Angeles. In 1990 he made his debut at London's Covent Garden conducting *The Cunning Little Vixen*. He was named music director of the City of Birmingham Sym. Orch. in 1991, a post he held until 1998. In 1987 he was made a Commander of the Order of the British Empire. He was knighted in 1994.

BIBL.: N. Kenyon, *S. R.: The Making of a Conductor* (London, 1987).

Rauchenecker, Georg Wilhelm, German violinist, conductor, teacher, and composer; b. Munich, March 8, 1844; d. Elberfeld, July 17, 1906. He studied violin with Joseph Walter, then filled various posts as a theater violinist in France. He then lived in Switzerland. In 1889 he established a music school in Elberfeld, and conducted an orch. society there until his death.

WORKS: OPERAS (all 1st perf. in Elberfeld unless otherwise given): *Die letzten Tage von Thule* (1889); *Ingo* (1893); *Don Quixote* (1897); *Sanna* (1898); *Zlatorog* (1903); *Der Florentiner* (Strasbourg, 1910).

Raupach, Hermann Friedrich, German harpsichordist, conductor, and composer; b. Stralsund, Dec. 21, 1728; d. St. Petersburg, Dec. 1778. In 1755 he went to St. Petersburg as deputy harpsichordist in the Court Orch., and subsequently served as Kapellmeister and court composer (1758–62); he then was active mainly in Hamburg and Paris until 1768. In Paris he met Mozart, who used several movements of his violin sonatas in his own early keyboard concertos (K.37, 39, and 41). Upon his return to St. Petersburg in 1768, Raupach again became deputy harpsichordist in the Court Orch.; in 1770 he was once more named Kapellmeister. His opera *Alcesta* (St. Petersburg, 1758) was one of the 1st operas on a Russian text. He also wrote the operas *The New Monastery* (1759), *Siroe* (St. Petersburg, 1760), and *The Good Soldiers* (St. Petersburg, Feb. 29, 1780), as well as ballet scenes in operas by Traetta.

Rautavaara, Einojuhani (Eino Juhani), prominent Finnish composer and pedagogue; b. Helsinki, Oct. 9, 1928. He took up piano lessons at 17 in Turku, and then went to Helsinki to study musicology at the Univ. (M.A., 1953). He also studied composition with Merikanto at the Sibelius Academy (1951–53), where he was awarded his diploma (1957). In 1955–56 he pursued his training with Persichetti at the Juilliard School of Music in New York, and with Sessions and Copland at the Berkshire Music Center in Tanglewood (summers, 1956–57). Following further training with Vogel in Ascona, Switzerland (1957), he completed his studies with Petzold in Cologne (1958). From 1957 to 1959 he taught at the Sibelius Academy. He was acting general manager of the Helsinki Phil. from 1959 to 1961. In 1965–66 he was principal of the Käpylä Music School in Helsinki. In 1966 he joined the faculty of the Sibelius Academy as a lecturer in composition, a position he held until 1976. He also held the Finnish State title of Arts Prof. from 1971 to 1976. From 1976 to 1988 he was prof. of composition at the Sibelius Academy. He served on the music panel of the Finnish Arts Council from 1989 to 1991. His autobiography, *Omakuva* (Self-Portrait), was publ. in 1989. In 1961 he was honored with the Arnold Bax Medal, in 1965 he received the International Sibelius Prize of the Wihuri Foundation in Helsinki, and in 1985 he won the Finnish State music prize. In 1975 he was made a member of the Royal Swedish Academy of Music in Stockholm and in 1983 he received an honorary doctorate from the Univ. of Oulu. An eclectic composer, Rautavaara has employed various musical techniques over the years, ranging the gamut from Gregorian chant to the 12-tone method and aleatory.

WORKS: DRAMATIC: OPERAS: *Kaivos* (The Mine; 1957–58; Finnish TV, April 10, 1963); *Apollo contra Marsyas*, comic opera-musical (1970; Helsinki, Aug. 30, 1973); *Runo 42, "Sammon ryöstö"* (The Abduction of Sampo), choral opera (1974–81; Helsinki, April 8, 1983); *Thomas* (1984–85; Joensuu, June 21, 1985); *Vincent* (1986–87; Helsinki, May 17, 1990); *Auringon talo* (The House of the Sun), chamber opera (1990; Lappeenranta, April 25, 1991); *Aleksis Kivi* (Savonlinna, July 10, 1997). MYSTERY PLAY: *Marjatta matala neiti* (Marjatta, the Lowly Maiden; 1975; Espoo, Sept. 3, 1977). BALLET: *Kiusaukset* (The Temptations; 1969; Helsinki, Feb. 8, 1973).

Rautio, Nina, Russian soprano; b. Bryansk, Sept. 21, 1957. She was trained at the Leningrad Cons. From 1981 to 1987 she appeared at the Leningrad State Theater. In 1987 she joined the Bolshoi Theater in Moscow, with which she toured widely in Russia and Eastern Europe. In 1991 she sang Tatiana with the company during its visit to the Metropolitan Opera in New York, and also appeared as Oksana in Rimsky-Korsakov's *Christmas Eve* during its engagement at the Edinburgh Festival. During the 1992–93 season she sang Lisa in *The Queen of Spades* at the Opéra de la Bastille in Paris. She was engaged as Aida at the Berlin State Opera in the 1994–95 season. On Oct. 3, 1995, she made her debut at the Metropolitan Opera in New York as Aida, a role she then sang in Verona in 1996.

Rauzzini, Venanzio, Italian castrato soprano, harpsichordist, teacher, and composer; b. Camerino, near Rome (baptized), Dec. 19, 1746; d. Bath, April 18, 1810. He studied in Rome, where he made his debut in Piccinni's *Il finto astrologo* (Feb. 7, 1765). He then was in the service of the Elector Max Joseph III in Munich (1766–72), during which period he commenced his career as a composer for the theater; also sang in Venice and Vienna. He was primo uomo in Mozart's *Lucio Silla* (Milan, Dec. 26, 1772) and in Paisiello's *Sismano nel Mogol* (Milan, Jan. 30, 1773); Mozart wrote his famous motet *Exsultate, jubilate* for him (1773). After singing in Venice (1773–74), Padua (1773), and Turin (1774), he went to London as a leading member of the King's Theatre (1774–77); the revised version of his most successful opera, *Piramo e Tisbe*, was produced there on March 16, 1775. He subsequently was active mainly in Bath as a performer, teacher, and concert manager; also made visits to London. Among his most famous pupils were Mrs. Billington, John Braham, Michael Kelly, and Nancy Storace.

WORKS (all 1st perf. in London unless otherwise given): DRAMATIC: OPERAS: *Piramo e Tisbe* (Munich, 1769; rev. version, March 16, 1775); *L'Eroe cinese* (Munich, 1771; rev. version, March 16, 1782); *Le ali d'amore* (Feb. 29, 1776; rev. version, March 13, 1777); *L'omaggio di paesani al signore del contado* (June 5, 1781; only Act 2 by Rauzzini); *Creusa in Delfo* (April 29, 1783); *Alina, o sia La Regina di Golconda* (March 18, 1784); *La Vestale, o sia L'amore protetto dal cielo* (May 1, 1787). PASTICCIOS: *Armida* (Nov. 19, 1774); *La Sposa fedele* (Oct. 31, 1775); *Didone* (Nov. 11, 1775); *The Duenna or Double Elopement* (Nov. 21, 1775); *Astarto* (Nov. 2, 1776); *Ezio* (Nov. 17, 1781); *The Village Maid* (n.d.). Also incidental music.

Ravasenga, Carlo, Italian composer; b. Turin, Dec. 17, 1891; d. Rome, May 6, 1964. He studied violin, piano, and composition in Turin, then became active as a teacher and music ed. He wrote the operas *Una tragedia fiorentina*, after Oscar Wilde (Turin, 1916), and *Il giudizio di Don Giovanni* (1916).

Ravel, (Joseph) Maurice, great French composer; b. Ciboure, Basses-Pyrénées, March 7, 1875; d. Paris, Dec. 28, 1937. His father was a Swiss engineer, and his mother of Basque origin. The family moved to Paris when he was an infant. He began to study piano at the age of 7 with Henri Ghis and harmony at 12 with Charles-René. After further piano studies with Emile Descombes, he entered the Paris Cons. as a pupil of Eugène Anthiôme in 1889; he won 1st medal (1891), and passed to the advanced class of Charles de Bériot and also studied harmony with Emile Pessard. He left the Cons. in 1895 and that same year completed work on his song *Un Grand Sommeil noir*, the *Menuet antique* for Piano, and the *Habanera* for 2 Pianos (later included in the *Rapsodie espagnole* for Orch.); these pieces, written at the age of 20, already reveal great originality in the treatment of old modes and of Spanish motifs; however, he continued to study; in 1897 he returned to the Cons. to study with Fauré (composition) and Gédalge (counterpoint and orchestration); his well-known *Pavane pour une infante défunte* for Piano was written during that time (1899). On May 27, 1899, he conducted the premiere of his overture *Shéhérazade* in Paris; some elements of this work were incorporated in his song cycle of the same name (1903). In 1901 he won the 2d Prix de Rome with the cantata *Myrrha*, but ensuing attempts to win the Grand Prix de Rome were unsuccessful; at his last try (1905) he was eliminated in the preliminaries, and so was not allowed to compete; the age limit then set an end to his further effort to enter. Since 6 prizes all went to pupils of Lenepveu, suspicion of unfair discrimination was aroused; Jean Marnold publ. an article, "Le Scandale du Prix de Rome," in the *Mercure de France* (June 1905) in which he brought the controversy into the open; this precipitated a crisis at the Cons.; its director, Théodore Dubois, resigned, and Fauré took his place. By that time, Ravel had written a number of his most famous compositions, and was regarded by most French critics as a talented disciple of Debussy. No doubt Ravel's method of poetic association of musical ideas paralleled that of Debussy; his employment of unresolved dissonances and the enhancement of the diatonic style into pandiatonicism were techniques common to Debussy and his followers, but there were important differences: whereas Debussy adopted the scale of whole tones as an integral part of his musical vocabulary, Ravel resorted to it only occasionally; similarly, augmented triads appear much less frequently in Ravel's music than in Debussy's; in his writing for piano, Ravel actually anticipated some of Debussy's usages; in a letter addressed to Pierre Lalo and publ. in *Le Temps* (April 9, 1907), Ravel pointed out that at the time of the publication of his piano piece *Jeux d'eau* (1902) Debussy had brought out only his suite *Pour le piano*, which had contained little that was novel. In Paris, elsewhere in France, and soon in England and other European countries, Ravel's name became well known, but for many years he was still regarded as an ultramodernist. A curious test of audience appreciation was a "Concert des Auteurs Anonymes" presented by the Société Independante de Musique on May 9, 1911; the program included Ravel's *Valses nobles et sentimentales*, a set of piano pieces in the manner of Schubert; yet Ravel was recognized as the author. Inspired evocation of the past was but one aspect of Ravel's creative genius; in this style are his *Pavane pour une infante défunte, Le Tombeau de Couperin*, and *La Valse*; luxuriance of exotic colors marks his ballet *Daphnis et Chloé*, his opera *L'Heure espagnole*, the song cycles *Shéhérazade* and *Chansons madécasses*, and his virtuoso pieces for Piano "Miroirs" and "Gaspard de la nuit"; other works are deliberately austere, even ascetic, in their pointed classicism: the piano concertos, the Piano Sonatina, and some of his songs with piano accompaniment. His association with Diaghilev's Ballets Russes was most fruitful; for Diaghilev he wrote one of his masterpieces, *Daphnis et Chloé*; another ballet, *Boléro*, commissioned by Ida Rubinstein and performed at her dance recital at the Paris Opéra on Nov. 22, 1928, became Ravel's most spectacular success as an orch. piece.

Ravel never married, and lived a life of semiretirement, devoting most of his time to composition; he accepted virtually no pupils, although he gave friendly advice to Vaughan Williams and to others; he was never on the faculty of any school. As a performer, he was not brilliant; he appeared as a pianist only in his own works, and often accompanied singers in programs of his songs; although he accepted engagements as a conductor, his technique was barely sufficient to secure a perfunctory performance of his music. When World War I broke out in 1914, he was rejected for military service because of his frail physique, but he was anxious to serve; his application for air service was denied, but he was received in the ambulance corps at the front; his health gave way, and in the autumn of 1916 he was compelled to enter a hospital for recuperation. In 1922 he visited Amsterdam and Venice, conducting his music; in 1923 he appeared in London; in 1926 he went to Sweden, England, and Scotland; in 1928 he made an American tour as a conductor and pianist; in the same year he received the degree of D.Mus. honoris causa at the Univ. of Oxford. In 1929 he was honored by his native town by the inauguration of the Quai Maurice Ravel. Shortly afterward, he began to experience difficulties in muscular coordination, and suffered from attacks of aphasia, symptoms indicative of a cerebral malady; he underwent brain surgery on Dec. 19, 1937, but it was not successful; he died 9 days later.

WORKS: DRAMATIC: OPERAS: *L'Heure espagnole*, opera (1907–09; Paris, May 19, 1911); *L'Enfant et les sortilèges*, fantaisie lyrique (1920–25; Monte Carlo, March 21, 1925). BALLETS: *Ma Mère l'Oye*

(1911; Paris, Jan. 21, 1912; based on the piano work with additional material); *Daphnis et Chloé* (1909–12; Paris, June 8, 1912); *Adélaïde, ou Le Langage des fleurs* (Paris, April 22, 1912; based on the *Valses nobles et sentimentales*); *Le Tombeau de Couperin* (Paris, Nov. 8, 1920; based on the piano work); *La Valse* (Paris, Dec. 12, 1920); *Boléro* (Paris, Nov. 22, 1928).

BIBL.: Roland-Manuel, *M. R. et son oeuvre* (Paris, 1914; 2d ed., rev., 1926; Eng. tr., 1941); W.-L. Landowski, *M. R.: Sa vie, son oeuvre* (Paris, 1938; 2d ed., 1950); Roland-Manuel, *À la gloire de R.* (Paris, 1938; 2d ed., 1948; Eng. tr., 1947); V. Jankélévitch, *M. R.* (Paris, 1939; 2d ed., 1956; Eng. tr., 2d ed., 1959); R. Wild, ed., *M. R. par quelques-uns de ses familiers* (Paris, 1939); M. Goss, *Boléro: The Life of M. R.* (N.Y., 1940); H. Jourdan-Morhange, *R. et nous* (Geneva, 1945); N. Demuth, *R.* (London, 1947); A. Machabey, *M. R.* (Paris, 1947); F. Onnen, *M. R.* (Stockholm, 1947); R. Malipiero, *M. R.* (Milan, 1948); L.-P. Fargue, *M. R.* (Paris, 1949); J. Bruyr, *M. R. ou Le Lyrisme et les sortilèges* (Paris, 1950); L. La Pegna, *R.* (Brescia, 1950); W. Tappolet, *M. R.: Leben und Werk* (Olten, 1950); V. Perlemuter and H. Jourdan-Morhange, *R. d'après R.* (Lausanne, 1953; Eng. tr., 1988, as *R. according to R.*); V. Seroff, *M. R.* (N.Y., 1953); M. Gerar and R. Chalupt, eds., *R. au miroir de ses lettres* (Paris, 1956); J. van Ackere, *M. R.* (Brussels, 1957); J. Geraedts, *R.* (Haarlem, 1957); R. de Fragny, *M. R.* (Lyons, 1960); R. Myers, *R.: Life and Works* (London, 1960); H. Stuckenschmidt, *M. R.: Variationen über Person und Werk* (Frankfurt am Main, 1966; Eng. tr., 1969); P. Petit, *R.* (Paris, 1970); A. Orenstein, *R.: Man and Musician* (N.Y., 1975; new ed., 1991); R. Nichols, *R.* (London, 1977); M. Marnat, ed., *M. R.: L'Hommage de La Revue musicale, décembre 1938* (Lyons, 1987); R. Nichols, *R. Remembered* (London and Boston, 1987); M. Rosenthal, *Satie, R., Poulenc: An Intimate Memoir* (Madras and N.Y., 1987); T. Hirsbrunner, *M. R.: Sein Leben, sein Werk* (Laaber, 1989); A. Orenstein, ed., *R.: Correspondance, écrits et entretiens* (Paris, 1989; Eng. tr., 1989, as *A R. Reader*); R. Beyer, *Organale Satztechniken in den Werken von Claude Debussy und M. R.* (Wiesbaden, 1992).

Rea, John (Rocco), Canadian composer and teacher; b. Toronto, Jan. 14, 1944. He studied at Wayne State Univ. in Detroit (B.Mus., 1967). Following training in composition with Weinzweig and Ciamaga at the Univ. of Toronto (M.Mus., 1969), he studied with Babbitt and Westergaard at Princeton Univ. (Ph.D., 1978). In 1973 he became a teacher of composition and theory at McGill Univ. in Montreal, where he also was dean of the faculty of music (1986–91). He was composer-in-residence in Mannheim in 1984 and of the Incontri music festival in Terra di Siena in 1991. In his music, Rea has explored various genres and styles, and has utilized both Western and non-Western elements in a number of his scores. Among his works are *The Days/Les Jours*, ballet (1969; suite, Toronto, July 11, 1974), *The Prisoners Play*, opera (Toronto, May 12, 1973), and *Com-possession*, "daemonic afterimages in the theatre of transitory states" (1980).

Read, Gardner, eminent American composer, pedagogue, and writer on music; b. Evanston, Ill., Jan. 2, 1913. He studied at Northwestern Univ. (1930–32), with Hanson and Rogers at the Eastman School of Music in Rochester, N.Y. (B.M., 1936; M.M., 1937), with Pizzetti in Rome on a Cromwell Traveling Fellowship (1938–39), and with Copland at the Berkshire Music Center in Tanglewood (summer 1941). In 1936 he won 1st prize in the American Composers' Contest of the N.Y. Phil. for his 1st Sym. and in 1943 he won the Paderewski Prize for his 2d Sym. After teaching at the St. Louis Inst. of Music (1941–43) and the Kansas City Cons. (1943–45), he was head of the Cleveland Inst. of Music (1944–48). He subsequently was prof. of music and composer-in-residence at the Boston Univ. School for the Arts (1948–78). He publ. *Thesaurus of Orchestral Devices* (1953), *Music Notation: A Manual of Modern Practice* (1964), *Contemporary Instrumental Techniques* (1976), *Modern Rhythmic Notation* (1978), *Style and Orchestration* (1979), *Source Book of Proposed Music Notation Reform* (1987), *20th-Century Microtonal Notation* (1990), *Compendium of Modern Instrumental Techniques* (1993), and *Pictographic Score Notation* (1995). As a composer, Read has produced a substantial body of works notable for their mastery of orchestration and form. Among his works is the opera *Villon* (1965–67) and *The Prophet*, oratorio (1960; Boston, Feb. 23, 1977); also incidental music.

Reardon, John, American baritone; b. N.Y., April 8, 1930; d. Santa Fe, N. Mex., April 16, 1988. He studied at Rollins College (B.Mus., 1952), then took voice lessons with Martial Singher and Margaret Harshaw. He made his first appearance with the N.Y. City Opera on Oct. 16, 1954, as Falke in *Die Fledermaus*. He made his Metropolitan Opera debut in New York on Sept. 28, 1965, as Count Tomsky in Tchaikovsky's *Queen of Spades*, remaining on its roster until 1977. He mastered an extensive repertoire, which included several roles in modern operas.

Rebel, family of French musicians:

(1) Jean Rebel, singer; place and date of birth unknown; d. Versailles, before Feb. 29, 1692. He was a tenor in the private chapel of Louis XIV by 1661, singing there until his death; he was also a secular singer at the court. He had 2 children who became prominent musicians.

(2) Anne-Renée Rebel, singer; b. Paris (baptized), Dec. 6, 1663; d. Versailles, May 5, 1722. She began singing at the court when she was about 10, and shortly thereafter took solo roles there; was held in high esteem by the king.

(3) Jean-Féry Rebel (le père), violinist, harpsichordist, conductor, and composer; b. Paris (baptized), April 18, 1666; d. there, Jan. 2, 1747. He began playing the violin at an early age, winning the approbation of the king and Lully when he was only 8. He was 1st violin at the Académie Royale de Musique (1699–1700). He joined the king's 24 Violons (1705), gaining the right of succession to half of the office of chamber composer to the court (1718), which was held by his brother-in-law, Lalande. He was granted the title as well (1726), and also was active at the Académie Royale de Musique in various capacities, being made its maître de musique (1716); he conducted at the Concert Spirituel (1734–35). He was held in high regard by his contemporaries. Among his works was the opera *Ulysse* (Paris, Jan. 23, 1703).

(4) François Rebel (le fils), violinist, theorbist, conductor, theater director, and composer, son of the preceding; b. Paris, June 19, 1701; d. there, Nov. 7, 1775. He began music studies at an early age, joining the orch. of the Académie Royale de Musique at age 13. He gained the right of succession to his father's position in the king's 24 Violons when he was 16. He soon became a close associate of François Francoeur, who collaborated with him on several stage works. He was royal chamber composer (1727–55) and surintendant and maître of the royal chamber music (1733–75); he was inspecteur général (1743–53) and codirector (with Francoeur; 1757–67) of the Académie Royale de Musique; returned as its administrateur général (1772). In all, he wrote 18 stage works with Francoeur.

Reber, (Napoléon-) Henri, French composer; b. Mulhouse, Oct. 21, 1807; d. Paris, Nov. 24, 1880. He studied with Reicha and Le Sueur at the Paris Cons., becoming a prof. of harmony there in 1851. He succeeded Halévy as prof. of composition in 1862 (being succeeded in turn by Saint-Saëns in 1880), and was also inspector of the branch conservatories from 1871. He publ. *Traité d'harmonie* (Paris, 1862; 2d ed., 1889, ed. by T. Dubois).

WORKS: DRAMATIC: COMIC OPERAS (all 1st perf. at the Opéra Comique, Paris): *La Nuit de Noël* (Feb. 9, 1848); *Le Père Gaillard* (Sept. 7, 1852); *Les Papillotes de Monsieur Benoist* (Dec. 28, 1853); *Les Dames-capitaines* (June 3, 1857). BALLET: *Le Diable amoureux* (Sept. 23, 1840; in collaboration with F. Benoist).

BIBL.: C. Saint-Saëns, *Notice sur N. H. R.* (Paris, 1881).

Redlich, Hans F(erdinand), Austrian-born English conductor, musicologist, and composer; b. Vienna, Feb. 11, 1903; d. Manchester, Nov. 27, 1968. He studied piano and composition, but devoted his energies mainly to writing biographical and analytical books on composers; he was only 16 when he publ. an essay on Mahler. After taking courses at the Univs. of Vienna and Munich, he obtained his Ph.D. at the Univ. of Frankfurt am Main with the diss. *Das Problem des Stilwandels in Monteverdis Madrigalwerk* (publ. in Berlin, 1931; 2d ed., aug., 1932, as *Claudio Monteverdi: I. Das Madrigalwerk*). He conducted opera in Mainz (1925–29), then lived in Mannheim. In 1939 he emigrated to England and in 1947 became a naturalized British subject. From 1941 to 1955 he conducted the Choral and Orch. Soc. in Letchworth and also was a lecturer for the extramural depts. of the Univs. of Cambridge and Birmingham. From 1955 to 1962 he was a lecturer at the Reid School of Music at the Univ. of Edinburgh, then was at the Univ. of Manchester (1962–68).

WRITINGS: *Gustav Mahler: Eine Erkenntnis* (Nuremberg, 1919); *Richard Wagner: Tristan und Isolde, Lohengrin, Parsifal* (London, 1948; 3d ed., 1951); *Claudio Monteverdi: Leben und Werk* (Olten, 1949; Eng. tr., 1952); *Bruckner and Mahler* (London, 1955; 2d ed., rev., 1963); *Alban Berg: Versuch einer Würdigung* (Vienna, 1957; condensed Eng. version, 1957, as *Alban Berg: The Man and His Music*).

Reed, H(erbert) Owen, American composer and music educator; b. Odessa, Mo., June 17, 1910. He was educated at the Univ. of Missouri (theory and composition, 1929–33), Louisiana State Univ. (B.M. in theory, 1934; M.M. in composition, 1936; B.A. in French, 1937), and at the Eastman School of Music in Rochester, N.Y. (Ph.D. in composition, 1939), where his mentors included Hanson, Rogers, and McHose. He pursued further studies at the Berkshire Music Center in Tanglewood (summer 1942) with Martinů, Copland, and Bernstein and in Colorado Springs (summer 1947) with Roy Harris. Subsequently he studied folk music in Mexico (1948–49; 1960), the Caribbean (1976), and Scandinavia (1977), and also Native American music in Arizona. In 1939 he joined the faculty of Michigan State Univ., where he was chairman of its theory and composition dept. until 1967; he then was chairman of music composition from 1967 until his retirement as prof. emeritus in 1976. In 1948–49 he held a Guggenheim fellowship and in 1960 a Huntington Foundation fellowship. His textbooks have been widely used. In his compositions, Reed generally has followed a tonal course with later diversions into nontonal pathways.

WRITINGS: *A Workbook in the Fundamentals of Music* (1947); *Basic Music* (1954); *Basic Music Workbook* (1954); *Composition Analysis Chart* (1958); with P. Harder, *Basic Contrapuntal Technique* (1964); *Basic Contrapuntal Workbook* (1964); with J. Leach, *Scoring for Percussion and the Instruments of the Percussion Section* (1969; rev. ed., 1979); with R. Sidnell, *The Materials of Music Composition* (3 vols., 1978, 1980, in progress).

WORKS: DRAMATIC: *The Masque of the Red Death*, ballet-pantomime (1936); *Michigan Dream*, renamed *Peter Homan's Dream*, folk opera (East Lansing, Mich., May 13, 1955; rev. 1959); *Earth Trapped*, chamber dance opera (1960; East Lansing, Mich., Feb. 24, 1962); *Living Solid Face*, chamber dance opera (1974; Brookings, S. Dak., Nov. 28, 1976); *Butterfly Girl and Mirage Boy*, chamber opera (East Lansing, Mich., May 1980). Also *A Tabernacle for the Sun*, oratorio for Contralto, Chorus, Speaking Men's Chorus, and Orch. (1963).

Reed, Lou(is) Alan, American rock singer, guitarist, and songwriter; b. N.Y., March 2, 1942. He studied piano in his childhood, taking up the guitar in high school; after graduating from Syracuse Univ., he read books, wrote poetry, essayed journalism, vocalized to guitar accompaniment, and finally found his niche improvising variously with such psychedelically inclined groups as the Primitives and the Warlocks. In 1966 he recruited a British musician of similarly educated background, John Cale, and together they formed the short-lived (1965–70) but highly influential group the Velvet Underground. They attracted Andy Warhol, who hired them for his N.Y. multimedia organization the Factory, then toured under the auspices of his "Exploding Plastic Inevitable." However, the aesthetic of the Velvet Underground was closer to the earthy films of Paul Morrissey than to Warhol's deadpan irony, and it did not take long before the group separated from Warhol. The group produced 4 studio albums before its demise. Reed left the group in 1970, and began exploring different aspects of his musical personality: there was the accessible hard rock and balladry of *Transformer* (1972, including his biggest hit, "Walk on the Wild Side," a satire on life at Warhol's Factory), *Rock 'n' Roll Animal* (1974), *Coney Island Baby* (1976), *Blue Mask* (1981), *New Sensations* (1984), and *Magic and Loss* (1992); 2 brilliant concept albums, the harrowing *Berlin* (1973) and the streetwise *New York* (1989); and an unadulterated, utterly anarchistic display of uninhibited white noise, *Metal Machine Music* (1975). Reed and Cale reunited after some 20 years to compose the suite *Songs for Drella*, in memory of Warhol (1989); they in turn joined with Sterling Morrison and Maureen "Mo" Tucker, other former members of the Underground, for a European reunion tour in 1993. In 1996 Reed provided music for the final work in Robert Wilson's trilogy of operas, *Time Rocker*. Reed is also an avid photographer and poet, and is currently writing a novel.

BIBL.: D. Clapton, *L. R. and the Velvet Underground* (London, 1982).

Reeves, (John) Sims, English tenor; b. Shooter's Hill, Kent, Sept. 26, 1818; d. Worthing, London, Oct. 25, 1900. He learned to play several instruments, and had lessons with J. B. Cramer (piano) and W. H. Callcott (harmony). He made his debut as a baritone in *Guy Mannering* in Newcastle upon Tyne (Dec. 14, 1838); he also studied further and sang minor tenor roles at London's Drury Lane (1841–43) and studied in Paris under Bordogni and in Milan under Mazzucato, appearing at La Scala in 1846 as Edgardo in *Lucia di Lammermoor*. He sang Faust in the 1st British performance of Berlioz's *La Damnation de Faust* under the composer's direction (1848), then was a member of Her Majesty's Theatre in London (from 1848); he also sang at the leading festivals. He retired in 1891, but reappeared in concerts in 1893. He made a successful tour of South Africa in 1896. He publ. *Sims Reeves; His Life and Recollections Written by Himself* (London, 1888), *My Jubilee, or Fifty Years of Artistic Life* (London, 1889), and *Sims Reeves on the Art of Singing* (London, 1900).

BIBL.: H. Edwards, *The Life and Artistic Career of S. R.* (London, 1881); C. Pearce, *S. R.: Fifty Years of Music in England* (London, 1924).

Refice, Licinio, Italian conductor, teacher, and composer; b. Patrica, near Rome, Feb. 12, 1883; d. while conducting his sacred play *Santa Cecilia* in Rio de Janeiro, Sept. 11, 1954. He studied organ and composition at Rome's Liceo di Santa Cecilia (diploma, 1910); after being ordained (1910), he taught at Rome's Scuola Pontificia Superiore di Musica Sacra (1910–50) and was maestro di cappella at S. Maria Maggiore (1911–47); he toured Europe and North and South America as a conductor. He composed the operas *Cecilia* (1922–23; Rome, 1934) and *Margherita da Cortona* (Milan, 1938), as well as 4 oratorios: *La Cananea* (1910), *Maria Magdalena* (1914), *Martyrium S. Agnetis Virginis* (1919), and *Trittico Francescano* (1926).

BIBL.: E. Mucci, *L. R.* (Assisi, 1955); T. Onofri and E. Mucci, *Le composizioni di L. R.* (Assisi, 1966).

Regamey, Constantin, Swiss pianist and composer; b. Kiev (of a Swiss father and a Russian mother), Jan. 28, 1907; d. Lausanne, Dec. 27, 1982. He went to Poland in 1920 and took piano lessons with Turczyński (1921–25); he then turned to linguistics and took courses in Sanskrit at the Univ. of Warsaw and later at L'École des Hautes Études in Paris, graduating in 1936. Returning to Poland, he taught Sanskrit at the Univ. of Warsaw (1937–39); concurrently he ed. periodicals on contemporary music. He was interned by the Germans during World War II, but managed to escape to Switzerland in 1944. He received an appointment to teach Slavic and oriental languages at the Univ. of Lausanne; he also gave courses in Indo-European linguistics at the Univ. of Fribourg. However, he did not abandon his musical activities; he served as coed. of the *Revue Musicale de Suisse Romande* (1954–62); he was president of the Assn. of Swiss Composers (1963–68) and a member of the executive board of the ISCM (1969–73). In 1978 he became partially paralyzed; he dictated the last pages of his last work, *Visions*, to Jean Balissat, a fellow composer, who also orchestrated the work. As a composer, he adopted free serial methods, without a doctrinaire adherence to formal dodecaphony. In 1963 he moderated his modernity and wrote music using free, often composite, techniques. Among his works were *Don Robott*, opera (1970), and *Mio, mein Mio*, fairy tale opera, after Bächli and Lindgren (1973).

WRITINGS: *Musique du XX*e *siècle: Présentation de 80 oeuvres pour orchestre de chambre* (Lausanne and Paris, 1966).

BIBL.: H. Jaccard, *Initiation à la musique contemporaine: Trois compositeurs vaudois: Raffaele d'Alessandro, C. R., Julien-François Zbinden* (Lausanne, 1955).

Rehfuss, Heinz (Julius), German-born Swiss, later American, bass-baritone; b. Frankfurt am Main, May 25, 1917; d. Buffalo, June 27, 1988. He studied with his father, Carl Rehfuss (1885–1946), a singer and teacher, and with his mother, Florentine Rehfuss-Peichert, a contralto. The family moved to Neuchâtel, and Rehfuss became a naturalized Swiss citizen. He made his professional debut in opera at Biel-Solothurn in 1938, then sang with the Lucerne Stadttheater (1938–39) and at the Zürich Opera (1940–52). He subsequently was active mainly in Europe and in America; he became a naturalized American citizen; he taught voice at the Montreal Cons. in 1961; in 1965 was on the faculty of the State Univ. of N.Y. at Buffalo; in 1970 he was a visiting prof. at the Eastman School of Music in Rochester, N.Y. He also toured in Asia, giving vocal recitals in India and Indonesia. He was successful mainly in dramatic roles, such as Don Giovanni and Boris Godunov.

Rehm, Wolfgang, German musicologist; b. Munich, Sept. 3, 1929. He studied with Gurlitt and Zenck at the Univ. of Freiburg im Breisgau (Ph.D., 1952, with the diss. *Das Chansonwerk von Gilles Binchois*); he also studied theory and piano at the Hochschule für Musik in Freiburg im Breisgau. In 1954 he joined the publishing firm of Barenreiter in Kassel, eventually becoming chief ed.; he held that position until 1982. In 1960 he was named coed. (with Wolfgang Plath) of the *Neue Mozart-Ausgabe*, serving as chief ed. from 1981 to 1994.

Reich, Willi, Austrian-born Swiss music critic and musicologist; b. Vienna, May 27, 1898; d. Zürich, May 1, 1980. He studied at the Univ. of Vienna, receiving his Ph.D. (1934) with the diss. *Padre Martini als Theoretiker und Lehrer* and also studied privately with Berg and Webern. He ed. a modern music magazine, *23—Eine Wiener Musikzeitschrift* (1932–37). In 1938 he settled in Switzerland; in 1948 he became music critic of the *Neue Zürcher Zeitung*; in 1961, became a naturalized Swiss citizen. In addition to editing numerous documentary vols., he publ. the studies *Wozzeck: A Guide to the Words and Music of Alban Berg* (N.Y., 1932), *Alban Berg* (Vienna, 1937), *Romantiker der Musik* (Basel, 1947), *Alexander Tscherepnin* (Bonn, 1961; 2d ed., 1970), *Alban Berg: Leben und Werk* (Zürich, 1963; Eng. tr., 1965), and *Arnold Schönberg oder der konservative Revolutionär* (Vienna, 1968; Eng. tr., 1971, as *Schoenberg: A Critical Biography*).

Reicha, Antoine (-Joseph) (Antonín or **Anton Rejcha**), distinguished Czech-born French music theorist, pedagogue, and composer; b. Prague, Feb. 26, 1770; d. Paris, May 28, 1836. His father died when he was only 10 months old, and he eventually was adopted by his uncle, who gave him lessons in violin and piano; he also studied flute. The family settled in Bonn in 1785, where Antoine played violin and flute, his fellow musicians including Beethoven and C. G. Neefe. Having acquired a knowledge of composition, he conducted his 1st Sym. in Bonn in 1787. After attending the Univ. there, in the wake of the French invasion, in 1794, he went to Hamburg, where he was active there as a teacher of piano, harmony, and composition; he also devoted part of his time to composing. In 1799 he went to Paris to establish himself as a composer for the theater, but found success only with 2 of his syms., an overture, and some scenes italiennes. In 1801 he went to Vienna, and then to Bonn, where he had made the acquaintance of Haydn and the 2 became good friends; he received instruction from Albrechtsberger and Salieri. His friendship with Beethoven grew apace, and Prince Lobkowitz commissioned Reicha to write the opera *L'Ouragan* (*c.*1801). The empress Marie Therese then was moved to commission him to compose the opera *Argina, regina di Granata*, which was given at the Imperial Palace in a private performance with the empress taking a prominent role (c.1802). In 1808 he settled in Paris; although his operas *Cagliostro* (Nov. 27, 1810), *Natalie* (July 13, 1816), and *Sapho* (Dec. 16, 1822) failed to make an impression, Reicha gained prominence as a music theorist and teacher; in 1818 he was appointed prof. of counterpoint and fugue at the Paris Cons. Among those who studied with him either privately or at the Cons. were Baillot, Habeneck, Rode, Berlioz, Liszt, and Franck. His *Cours de composition musicale, ou Traité complet et raisonné d'harmonie pratique* (Paris, c.1817) was adopted by the Cons.; his most significant publication was the *Traité de haute composition musicale* (Paris, 1824–26). In 1829 he became a naturalized French citizen. He was made Chevalier of the Légion d'honneur in 1831. In 1835 he succeeded Boieldieu as a member of the Académie. He dictated his autobiography, *Notes sur Antoine Reicha*, to his student Henri Blanchard about 1824. As a composer, he remains best known for his chamber music. He also wrote a great deal of orch. music, including at least 17 syms. and numerous concertos.

WRITINGS: *Practische Beispiele: Ein Beitrag zur Geistescultur des Tonsetzers . . . begleitet mit philosophisch-practischen Anmerkungen* (1803); *Sur la musique comme art purement sentimental* (c.1813); *Traité de mélodie* (Paris, 1814; ed. by C. Czerny as *Vollständiges Lehrbuch der musikalischen Composition*, II, Vienna, 1832); *Petit traité d'harmonie pratique à 2 parties*, op. 84 (Paris, c.1814); *Cours de composition musicale, ou Traité complet et raisonné d'harmonie pratique* (Paris, c.1817; ed. by C. Czerny as *Vollständiges Lehrbuch*, I, Vienna, 1832); *Traité de haute composition musicale* (Paris, 1824–26; ed. by C. Czerny as *Vollständiges Lehrbuch*, III-IV, Vienna, 1832); *À messieurs les membres de l'Académie des beaux-arts à l'Institut de France* (Paris, 1831); *Art du compositeur dramatique, ou Cours complet de composition vocale* (Paris, 1833; ed. by C. Czerny as *Die Kunst der dramatischen Composition*, Vienna, 1833).

BIBL.: E. Bücken, *Anton R.: Sein Leben und seine Kompositionen* (Munich, 1912); M. Emmanuel, *Antonín R.* (Paris, 1937); O. Šotolová, *Antonín Rejcha: A Biography and Thematic Catalogue* (Prague, 1990).

Reichardt, Johann Friedrich, prominent German composer and writer on music, father of **Luise Reichardt**; b. Königsberg, Nov. 25, 1752; d. Giebichenstein, near Halle, June 27, 1814. He received his initial musical training from his father, the lutenist Johann Reichardt (c.1720–80), becoming proficient as a violinist, lutenist, and singer; he also studied with J. F. Hartknoch, C. G. Richter, F. A. Veichtner, and others. After attending the Univ. of Königsberg (1768–71), he traveled widely; he received some instruction from Kirnberger in Berlin and from Homilius in Dresden and also briefly attended the Univ. of Leipzig. He was active as a government official for a year, and then was appointed Kapellmeister of the Royal Opera in Berlin by Frederick the Great in 1775. In 1783 he founded the Concert Spirituel in Berlin, where he brought out several of his own compositions; he traveled widely while retaining his royal appointment. After the death of Frederick the Great in 1786, Reichardt's star rose under the new king, Friedrich Wilhelm II. In collaboration with Goethe, he produced the successful Singspiel *Claudine von Villa Bella* (Berlin, July 29, 1789). Dissension at the Royal Opera, however, led the king to give Reichardt a leave of absence for 3 years, with full pay, in 1790. He again traveled widely; among the cities he visited was Paris (1792). His sympathies for the French Revolution led his Berlin enemies to persuade Friedrich Wilhelm to dismiss him without pay in 1794. He then settled at his estate in Giebichenstein. In 1796 Friedrich Wilhelm pardoned him and named him director of the Halle salt mines. With the French invasion of 1806, he fled with his family to north Germany; upon his return in 1807, he found that his estate had been destroyed; shortly afterward, Jérôme Bonaparte called him to Kassel as directeur général des théâtres et de son orchestre, but he renewed his travels in 1808. In 1809 he returned to Giebichenstein, where he eked out a living by writing and composing. His most significant contribution as a composer rests upon his more than 1,500 songs. He is generally regarded as the finest lieder composer before Schubert. His stage works are important for their movement away from the opera seria conventions. As a writer on music, he was a pioneering figure in music journalism. His 1st wife was Juliane (née Benda) Reichardt (b. Potsdam, May 4, 1752; d. there, May 11, 1783), the daughter of Franz Benda; she married Reichardt in 1776; a fine pianist, she also publ. a number of songs.

BIBL.: H. Schletter, *J. F. R.: Sein Leben und seine musikalische Tätigkeit* (Augsburg, 1865); C. Lange, *J. F. R.* (Halle, 1902); M. Faller, *J. F. R. und die Anfänge der musikalischen Journalistik* (Kassel, 1929); P. Sieber, *J. F. R. als Musikästhetiker: Seine Anschauungen über Wesen und Wirkung der Musik* (Strasbourg, 1930); F. Flössner, *Beiträge zur R.-Forschung* (Frankfurt am Main, 1933); E. Neuss, *Das Giebichensteiner Dichterparadies: J. F. R. und die Herberge der Romantik* (Halle, 1949); W. Salmen, *J. F. R.* (Freiburg, 1963); N. Reich, *A Translation and Commentary of Selected Writings of J. F. R.* (diss., N.Y. Univ., 1973).

Reichardt, Luise, German singing teacher and composer, daughter of **Johann Friedrich Reichardt**; b. Berlin, April 11, 1779; d. Hamburg, Nov. 17, 1826. She settled about 1813 in Hamburg, where she was active as a singing teacher; she also conducted a women's chorus that became the core of the Hamburg Singverein in 1819. She wrote over 90 choruses and songs, both sacred and secular. Selections of her works were publ. by G. Rheinhardt (Munich, 1922) and N. Reich (N.Y., 1978).

BIBL.: M. Brandt, *Leben der L. R.* (Karlsruhe, 1858; 2d ed., 1865).

Reicher-Kindermann, Hedwig, esteemed German soprano; b. Munich, July 15, 1853; d. Trieste, June 2, 1883. She was a daughter of the baritone August Kindermann (b. Potsdam, Feb. 6, 1817; d. Munich, March 6, 1891). She began her career as a contralto but later sang soprano. She first sang in the chorus of the Munich Court Opera (1870–71), making her debut at Karlsruhe in 1871. She appeared in Berlin (1874) and Munich (1875), and also sang at the opening of Bayreuth in 1876; she then sang in Hamburg (1877) and Vienna (1878). The impresario Neumann engaged her for his Wagner troupe in Leipzig from 1880, and she successfully performed the roles of Fricka, Isolde, Brünnhilde, Waltraute, and Erda. She was married to the playwright Emanuel Reicher, and adopted the hyphenated name Reicher-Kindermann in her professional activities. Her early death was lamented.

Reichmann, Theodor, noted German baritone; b. Rostock, March 15, 1849; d. Marbach, May 22, 1903. He studied in Berlin and Prague, and after further training with Lamperti in Milan, made his operatic debut in Magdeburg (1869). Following appearances in Rotterdam, Strasbourg, and Hamburg, he sang in 1874 in Munich, where he became a member of the Court Opera in 1875; he also sang at the Bayreuth Festivals (1882–1902), where he was esteemed for his portrayal of Amfortas, which he created. In 1882 he made his London debut as Wotan; his Covent Garden debut followed as Telramund on June 11, 1884. He was a member of the Vienna Court Opera (1883–89). He made his Metropolitan Opera debut in New York as the Dutchman on Nov. 27, 1889, and remained on its roster until 1893; he then rejoined the Vienna Court Opera, singing there until his death. He gave his farewell performance in Munich as Hans Sachs on Aug. 11, 1902.

Reina, Domenico, Italian tenor; b. Lugano, 1797; d. there, July 29, 1843. He studied with Boile in Milan, making his debut in 1829 at La Scala in Milan as Ilio in Rossini's *Zelmira*; while there, he created Arturo in Bellini's *La Straniera* and Tamas in Donizetti's *Gemma di Vergy*. He was greatly admired for his performances of the lyrico-dramatic tenor parts in the operas of Rossini, Bellini, and Donizetti.

Reichwein, Leopold, Austrian conductor, teacher, and composer; b. Breslau, May 16, 1878; d. (suicide) Vienna, April 8, 1945. He was a theater conductor in Breslau, Mannheim, and Karlsruhe, then was on the staff of the Vienna Opera (1913–21), music director of the Gesellschaft der Musikfreunde in Vienna (1921–26), and music director in Bochum (1926–38); he returned to Vienna in 1938; he conducted at the State Opera and taught conducting at the Academy of Music. He wrote the operas *Vasantasena* (Breslau, 1903) and *Die Liebenden von Kandahar* (Breslau, 1907) and also incidental music to Goethe's *Faust*.

Reid, Cornelius L., American voice teacher and music scholar; b. Jersey City, N.J., Feb. 7, 1911. He was a member of the Trinity Church Choir in N.Y. (1920–25), and studied with Frederick Kurzweil and Ruth Kirch-Arndt at the N.Y. College of Music (1945–48); studied voice privately with George Mead (1929), Marie Wagner (1929–30), and Douglas Stanley (1934–37), and had coaching from Frieda Hempel (1930) and Povla Frijsh (1932–40). He taught voice privately in New York (from 1934); also taught at Marymount College (1940–41) and at the General Theological Seminary there (1946–49); he conducted various performing groups (1939–45) and gave master classes and lectures throughout the United States. Reid authored 3 books defining his Functional Vocal training: *Bel Canto: Principles and Practices* (Boston, 1950), *The Free Voice* (N.Y., 1965), and *Voice: Psyche and Soma* (N.Y., 1975); also compiled the important *Dictionary of Vocal Terminology* (N.Y., 1984).

Reimann, Aribert, German composer, pianist, and teacher; b. Berlin, March 4, 1936. He studied at the Berlin Hochschule für Musik (1955–60) with Otto Rausch (piano), Blacher (composition), and Pepping (counterpoint), and also took courses in musicology at the Univ. of Vienna (1958). In 1963 he received the Prix de Rome and studied at the Villa Massimo in Rome. In 1957 he made his debut as a pianist, becoming particularly known in later years as a sensitive accompanist. From 1971 he was a member of the Berlin Akademie der Künste. He also was a prof. at the Hamburg Hochschule für Musik (1974–83), and later at the Berlin Hochschule der Künste (1983). In 1976 he was made a member of the Bayerische Akademie der Schönen Künste in Munich and in 1985 of the Hamburg Freien Akademie der Künste. In 1986 he won the Prix de la composition musicale of the Prince Pierre Foundation of Monaco. He received the Frankfurt am Main music award in 1991. After adhering to the precepts of the 2d Viennese School of composition, he abandoned orthodox serialism in favor of a compositional style in which linear elements were occasionally complemented by lyrical effusions.

WORKS: DRAMATIC: OPERAS: *Ein Traumspiel* (1963–64; Kiel, June 20, 1965); *Melusine* (1970; Schwetzingen, April 29, 1971); *Lear* (1976–78; Munich, July 9, 1978); *Die Gespenstersonate* (1983; Berlin, Sept. 25, 1984); *Troades* (1985; Munich, July 7, 1986); *Das Schloss* (1989–91; Berlin, Sept. 2, 1992); *Melusine* (Munich, Oct. 19, 1997). BALLETS: *Stoffreste* (1957; Essen, 1959); *Die Vogelscheuchen* (1969–70; Berlin, Oct. 7, 1970; orch. suite, 1970). POÈME VISUEL: *Chacun sa chimère* for Tenor and Orch. (1981; Düsseldorf, April 17, 1982).

Reimers, Paul, German-American tenor; b. Lunden, Schleswig-Holstein (of Danish parents), March 14, 1878; d. N.Y., April 14, 1942. He studied in Hamburg, where he made his stage debut as Max in *Der Freischütz* (1902); after further training with George Henschel in Scotland, Raimund von Zur Mühlen in London, and Jean Criticos in Paris, he devoted himself to a concert career; he sang widely in Europe. In 1913 he went to America, gave programs of German lieder, and also performed songs of the modern French school. From 1924 he taught at the Juilliard School of Music in New York.

Reinagle, Alexander, prominent English-born American pianist, teacher, impresario, and composer; b. Portsmouth (of Austrian parents) (baptized), April 23, 1756; d. Baltimore, Sept. 21, 1809. He studied in Edinburgh with Rayner Taylor, and in London for a time; he also visited Lisbon and other continental cities. From his correspondence he appears to have been a close friend of C. P. E. Bach. He went to New York early in 1786, settling in the same year in Philadelphia, where he taught, managed subscription concerts (also in N.Y.), and was active as a singer, pianist, conductor, and composer. In 1787 he introduced 4-hand piano music to America. He was associated, possibly as harpsichordist, with the Old American Co., and took part in its 1788–89 season in New York. In 1790 he was engaged as music director of a stock company for the production of plays and comic operas, with Thomas Wignell as general director; he also built the New Theatre, which opened on Feb. 2, 1793, with Reinagle acting as composer, singer, and director. He also managed a company in Baltimore (from 1794). Among his works were incidental music to *The Sicilian Romance* (1795), *The Witches of the Rock*, pantomime (1796), and various English plays.

Reinecke, Carl (Heinrich Carsten), renowned German pianist, composer, conductor, and pedagogue; b. Altona, June 23, 1824; d. Leipzig, March 10, 1910. He was a pupil of his father, a music teacher. His 1st concert tour was to Denmark and Sweden in 1843; he then went to Leipzig, learned much through meetings with Mendelssohn and Schumann, made a 2d tour through North Germany, and was from 1846 to 1848 court pianist to Christian VIII at Copenhagen. After spending some years in Paris, he became a teacher at the Cologne Cons. in 1851; he was music director at Barmen (1854–59) and Breslau (1859–60), and (1860–95) conductor of the Gewandhaus Concerts in Leipzig. At the same time he was a prof. of piano and composition at the Leipzig Cons., where he taught from 1860; was its director from 1897 until his retirement in 1902. An eminent pianist, he excelled as an interpreter of Mozart, made concert tours almost yearly, and was enthusiastically welcomed in England, the Netherlands, Scandinavia, Switzerland, and throughout Germany; among his pupils were Grieg, Riemann, Sinding, Arthur Sullivan, Karl Muck, and Cosima Wagner. As a conductor, composer, and teacher of composition, Reinecke was the leader in Leipzig for over 35 years; his numerous works, in every genre, are classic in form and of refined workmanship. Altogether he wrote some 300 opus numbers.

WORKS: DRAMATIC: *König Manfred,* opera (Wiesbaden, July 26, 1867); *Ein Abenteuer Händels oder Die Macht des Liedes*, Singspiel (Schwerin, 1874); *Auf hohen Befehl*, comic opera (Hamburg, Oct. 1, 1886); *Der Gouverneur von Tours*, comic opera (Schwerin, 1891); also 5 musical fairy tales for Soloists, Chorus, and Piano: *Nussknacker und Mausekönig, Schneewittchen, Dornröschen, Aschenbrödel*, and *Die wilden Schwäne*, and the oratorio, *Belsazar*.

WRITINGS: *Was sollen wir spielen?* (1886); *Zur Wiederbelebung der Mozartschen Clavier-Concerto* (1891); *Die Beethovenschen Clavier-Sonaten: Briefe an eine Freundin* (1895; Eng. tr., 1898; 9th Ger. ed., 1924); *Und manche liebe Schatten steigen auf: Gedenkblätter an berühmte Musiker* (1900; 2d ed., 1910); *Meister der Tonkunst* (1903); *Aus dem Reich der Tone* (1907).

BIBL.: W. von Wasielewski, *C. R.: Ein Künstlerbild* (Leipzig, 1892); E. Segnitz, *C. R.* (Leipzig, 1900); M. Steinitzer, *Das Leipziger Gewandhaus im neuen Heim unter C. R.* (Leipzig, 1924); N. Topusov, *C. R.: Beiträge zu seinem Leben und seiner Symphonik* (Sofia, 1943).

Reiner, Fritz (Frigyes), eminent Hungarian-born American conductor; b. Budapest, Dec. 19, 1888; d. N.Y., Nov. 15, 1963. He studied piano with Thomán and composition with Koessler at the Royal Academy of Music in Budapest; concurrently he took courses in jurisprudence at the Univ. of Budapest. In 1909 he made his debut in Budapest conducting *Carmen*. In 1910–11 he conducted at the Laibach Landestheater. He was conductor of the Volksoper in Budapest (1911–14) and of the Court (later State) Opera in Dresden (1914–21); he also conducted in Hamburg, Berlin, Vienna, Rome, and Barcelona. In 1922 he was engaged as music director of the Cincinnati Sym. Orch.; he was naturalized as an American citizen in 1928. In 1931 he became a prof. of conducting at the Curtis Inst. of Music in Philadelphia; among his students were Leonard Bernstein and Lukas Foss. In 1936–37 he made guest appearances at London's Covent Garden; between 1935 and 1938 he was a guest conductor at the San Francisco Opera; from 1938 to 1948 he was music director of the Pittsburgh Sym. Orch., then was a conductor at the Metropolitan Opera in New York until 1953. He achieved the peak of his success as a conductor with the Chicago Sym. Orch., which he served as music director from 1953 to 1962, and which he brought up to the point of impeccably fine performance in both Classical and modern music. His striving for perfection created for him the reputation of a ruthless master of the orch.; he was given to explosions of temper, but musicians and critics agreed that it was because of his uncompromising drive toward the optimum of orch. playing that the Chicago Sym. Orch. achieved a very high rank among American symphonic organizations.

BIBL.: P. Hart, *R. R.: A Biography* (Evanston, Ill., 1994).

Reiner, Karel, prominent Czech composer and pianist; b. Žatec, June 27, 1910; d. Prague, Oct. 17, 1979. He studied law at the German Univ. in Prague (Dr.Jur., 1933) and musicology at the Univ. of Prague; he attended Suk's master classes (1931) and A. Hába's courses in microtonal music (1934–35) at the Prague Cons. He was associated with E. Burian's improvisational theater in Prague (1934–38). Unable to leave central Europe when the Nazis invaded Czechoslovakia, he was detained at Terezín, and later sent to the concentration camps of Dachau and Auschwitz, but survived, and after liberation resumed his activities as a composer and pianist. His earliest works were atonal and athematic; in 1935–36 he wrote a *Suite* and a *Fantasy* for quarter tone piano, and a set of 5 quarter-tone songs; after 1945 he wrote mostly traditional music, then returned to ultramodern techniques. Among his works were *Pohádka o zakleté píseň* (Tale of an Enchanted Song), opera (1949), *Schustermärchen*, fairy tale opera (1972), and *Jednota* (Unity), ballet (1933).

Reinhardt, Delia, German soprano; b. Elberfeld, April 27, 1892; d. Arlesheim, near Basel, Oct. 3, 1974. She studied with Strakosch and Hedwig Schako at the Hoch Cons. in Frankfurt am Main. She made her operatic debut in Breslau in 1913. In 1916 she joined the Munich Court (later Bavarian State) Opera, where she sang until 1923. She made her debut at the Metropolitan Opera in New York on Jan. 27, 1923, as Sieglinde, then sang at the Berlin State Opera (1924–33); she also made guest appearances at Covent Garden in London (1924–27; 1929). She was married to **Gustav Schützendorf**, and later to **Georges Sébastian**. Among her outstanding roles were Desdemona, Elsa, and Eva.

Reinhardt, Heinrich, Austrian composer; b. Pressburg, April 13, 1865; d. Vienna, Jan. 31, 1922. He studied with Bruckner and Mocker in Vienna. He was music critic for several newspapers. Among his works, the operetta *Das süsse Mädel* was his greatest success.

WORKS: DRAMATIC: OPERETTAS: *Das süsse Mädel* (Vienna, Oct. 25, 1901); *Der liebe Schatz* (Vienna, Oct. 30, 1902); *Der General-Konsul* (Vienna, Jan. 28, 1904); *Krieg im Frieden* (Vienna, Jan. 20, 1906); *Die süssen Grisetten* (Vienna, 1907); *Ein Märchen für alles* (Munich, 1908); *Die Sprudelfee* (Vienna, 1909); *Napoleon und die Frauen* (Vienna, April 28, 1911); *Prinzessin Gretl* (Berlin, 1914); *Der Gast des Königs* (Vienna, Jan. 9, 1916); *Die erste Frau* (Munich, 1918). OPERAS: *Die Minnekönigin; Der Schuster von Delft*.

Reining, Maria, noted Austrian soprano; b. Vienna, Aug. 7, 1903; d. there, March 11, 1991. She studied at a business school, and was employed in the foreign exchange dept. of a Vienna bank before taking up singing. In 1931 she made her debut at the Vienna State Opera, remaining on its roster until 1933, then sang in Darmstadt (1933–35) and at the Bavarian State Opera in Munich (1935–37). In 1937 she rejoined the Vienna State Opera, continuing on its roster, with interruptions, until 1958; she also appeared at the Salzburg Festivals (1937–41); Toscanini engaged her to sing Eva in *Die Meistersinger von Nürnberg* in Salzburg under his direction in 1937; she also sang the role of the Marschallin in *Der Rosenkavalier* and the title role in *Arabella* by Richard Strauss.

She was equally successful in soubrette roles and as a dramatic soprano. In 1938 she appeared with the Covent Garden Opera in London and with the Chicago Opera; in 1949, as the Marschallin with the N.Y. City Opera. She also sang at La Scala in Milan, and toured as a concert singer. In 1962 she became a prof. of singing at the Mozarteum in Salzburg.

Reinmar (real name, **Wochinz**), **Hans,** distinguished Austrian baritone; b. Vienna, April 11, 1895; d. Berlin, Feb. 7, 1961. He studied at the Vienna Academy of Music and in Milan. He made his operatic debut in 1919 in Olomouc as Sharpless, then sang in Nuremberg, Zürich, Dresden, and Hamburg; he was a member of the Berlin Städtische Oper (1928–45; 1952–61), the Bavarian State Opera in Munich (1945–46; 1950–57), the Berlin State Opera (1948–52), and the Berlin Komische Oper (1952–61); he also sang at the festivals in Bayreuth and Salzburg. He excelled in dramatic roles in Italian operas.

Reinthaler, Karl (Martin), German organist, conductor, and composer; b. Erfurt, Oct. 13, 1822; d. Bremen, Feb. 13, 1896. He studied with G. A. Ritter and Marx in Berlin, and for 3 years in Rome. He taught singing at the Cologne Cons. (1853–57), then was organist at Bremen Cathedral (from 1858) and conductor of the Singakademie (1858–90). He was made a member of the Berlin Academy (1882) and a Royal Prof. (1888). His works include the operas *Edda* (Bremen, 1875) and *Käthchen von Heilbronn* (Frankfurt and Main, 1881), and the oratorio *Jephtha* (London, 1856).

Reise, Jay, American composer and teacher; b. N.Y., Feb. 9, 1950. He studied composition with Jimmy Giuffre (1968–70), and pursued his education at Hamilton College (A.B. in English literature, 1972) and the Univ. of Pa. (M.A. in music composition, 1975). He also studied with Messiaen, Davidovsky, Earle Brown, and Schuller at Tanglewood (summers 1975–77), where he won the Koussevitzky Prize in composition in 1975, and later pursued training in Carnatic (South Indian) rhythm with Adrian L'Armand (1989–92). After teaching at Kirkland College (1976–78) and Hamilton College (1978–80), he joined the faculty of the Univ. of Pa., where he became a prof. of composition. In 1978 and 1984 he held N.E.A. fellowships, in 1980 a Guggenheim fellowship, and in 1998 a Bellagio fellowship. Reise composed the first "operafilm," *Devil in the Flesh* (1998–2000); also *Rasputin*, opera (N.Y., Sept. 17, 1988), and *The Selfish Giant*, choreographic tone poem (London, Dec. 4, 1997).

Reiser, Alois, Czech-American composer; b. Prague, April 6, 1887; d. Los Angeles, April 4, 1977. He studied composition with Dvořák; he also took cello lessons and toured Europe; he later emigrated to the United States and played cello with the Pittsburgh Sym. Orch. and the N.Y. Sym. Orch. From 1918 to 1929 he was engaged as a theater conductor in New York; in 1929 he settled in Hollywood, where he worked as a composer and conductor at film studios. His works adhere to the established style of European Romanticism; typical of these are *Slavic Rhapsody*, which he conducted in Los Angeles on March 8, 1931, and *Erewhon*, which he conducted there on Jan. 24, 1936. He composed a Cello Concerto, which he performed in Los Angeles on March 23, 1933; also a considerable amount of chamber music. He wrote an opera, *Gobi*, in which he painted in tones the great Asian desert; it had its first and last performance in New York on July 29, 1923, and even then only in concert excerpts.

Reiss, Albert, German tenor; b. Berlin, Feb. 22, 1870; d. Nice, June 19, 1940. He was an actor before his voice was discovered by Pollini, after which he studied with Wilhelm Vilmar in Berlin, and later with Beno Stolzenburg and Julius Lieban. He made his operatic debut in Königsberg as Ivanov in *Zar und Zimmermann* (Sept. 28, 1897), then sang in various German towns; on Dec. 23, 1901, he made his American debut at the Metropolitan Opera in New York in the minor roles of the Sailor and the Shepherd in *Tristan und Isolde*; he remained on its roster until 1920; he won distinction there as David in *Die Meistersinger von Nürnberg* and Mime in the *Ring* cycle. In 1919 he returned to Berlin and sang at the Volksoper (1923–25). In 1938 he retired from the stage and lived in Nice.

Reissiger, Carl Gottlieb, noted German conductor and composer; b. Belzig, near Wittenberg, Jan. 31, 1798; d. Dresden, Nov. 7, 1859. His father, Christian Gottlieb Reissiger, was the Belzig organist and choirmaster. He studied piano and composition with Schicht at the Leipzig Thomasschule (1811–18), then theory with Salieri in Vienna (1821–22) and voice and composition with Winter in Munich (1822). Weber conducted the premiere of his opera *Didone abbandonata* at the Dresden Court Opera (Jan. 31, 1824). After teaching composition in Berlin (1825–26), he was called to Dresden as director of the Court Opera in 1826; he was named Hofkapellmeister in 1828, and was in charge of sacred music and chamber music, as well as the Court Opera, until his death. He was highly esteemed by his contemporaries as a conductor; he built upon the foundation laid by Weber and made the Dresden Court Opera the premiere opera house of Germany. He was a prolific composer, writing with great facility but with little originality. His *Danses brillantes pour le pianoforte or Webers letzter Gedanke* (1822) was very popular, as was his melodrama *Yelva* (1827).

BIBL.: W. Neumann, *K. G. R.* (Kassel, 1854); K. Kreiser, *C. G. R.: Sein Leben nebst einigen Beitragen zur Geschichte des Konzertwesens in Dresden* (diss., Univ. of Leipzig, 1918).

Reizen, Mark (Osipovich), notable Russian bass; b. Zaytsevo, July 3, 1895; d. Moscow, Nov. 25, 1992. He was a pupil of Bugamelli at the Kharkov Cons. In 1921 he made his operatic debut as Pimen at the Kharkov Opera. After singing at the Kirov Theater in Leningrad (1925–30), he was a principal member of the Bolshoi Theater in Moscow (1930–54). As a guest artist, he sang with the Paris Opéra, the Berlin State Opera, the Dresden State Opera, et al.; he also toured widely as a concert artist. In 1985 he returned to the Bolshoi Theater to celebrate his 90th birthday, appearing as Gremin in *Evgeny Onegin*. He publ. a vol. of autobiographical notes (Moscow, 1980). Reizen possessed a voice of remarkable beauty, ably complemented by his assured stage deportment. Among his finest portrayals were Mozart's Don Basilio, Gounod's Méphistophélès, Boris Godunov, Philip II, Dosifey, and Ivan Susanin.

Reizenstein, Franz (Theodor), German-born English pianist, teacher, and composer; b. Nuremberg, June 7, 1911; d. London, Oct. 15, 1968. He studied piano with Leonid Kreutzer and composition with Hindemith at the Hochschule für Musik in Berlin (1930–34); with the advent of the anti-Semitic Nazi regime, he went to England; he entered the Royal College of Music in London and studied with Lambert and Vaughan Williams (1934–36), then took private piano lessons with Solomon (1938–40). He was an instructor in piano at the Royal Academy of Music in London (1958–68), and from 1962 until his death, at the Royal Manchester College of Music. He wrote music of fine neo-Romantic quality, including the radio operas *Men against the Sea* (1949) and *Anna Kraus* (1952); also *Genesis*, oratorio (1958).

Rekašius, Antanas, Lithuanian composer; b. Pauvandene, Telsiu, July 24, 1928. He studied composition with Juzeliunas at the Lithuanian State Cons. in Vilnius (1954–59). He taught at the J. Gruodis Music School in Kaunas (1959–69). His music is cast in a highly advanced idiom incorporating aleatory and sonoristic techniques. Among his works was the opera-oratorio *The Ballad of Light* (1969) and the ballets *The Light of Happiness* (1959), *The Smouldering Cross* (1963), *Passions* (1968), and *A Little Humming Fly*, children's ballet (1969).

Remedios, Alberto, English tenor; b. Liverpool, Feb. 27, 1935. He studied in Liverpool with Edwin Francis and later in London with Clive Carey at the Royal College of Music. He made his operatic debut as Tinca in *Il tabarro* at the Sadler's Wells Opera in London in 1957; he made his first appearance at Covent Garden in London as Dimitri in *Boris Godunov* in 1965 he sang at the Frankfurt am Main Opera (1968–70). He made his U.S. debut with the San Francisco Opera in 1973; he made his Metropolitan Opera debut in New York as Bacchus in *Ariadne auf Naxos* on March 20, 1976. In 1983 he appeared as Walther von Stolzing at the Scottish Opera in Glasgow. He was engaged as a soloist in Schoenberg's *Gurre-Lieder* in Melbourne in 1988. In 1993 he portrayed Tristan in Nashville. He was highly successful as Lohengrin, Siegfried, and Siegmund; he showed fine lyrical talent as Faust in Gounod's opera, and a dramatic flair in Verdi's Otello.

Remenkov, Stefan, Bulgarian composer; b. Silistra, April 30, 1923. He studied piano with Nenov and composition with Vladigerov and Stoyanov at the Bulgarian State Cons. in Sofia, graduating in 1950; later he took a course with Khachaturian at the Moscow Cons. Among his works are *The Unvanquished*, ballet (1960), *The Errors Are Ours*, operetta (1966), and 2 children's operettas: *Ghanem* (1967) and *The Prince and the Pauper* (1973).

Renaud (real name, **Cronean**), **Maurice (Arnold),** distinguished French baritone; b. Bordeaux, July 24, 1861; d. Paris, Oct. 16, 1933. He studied at the Paris Cons. and the Brussels Cons., then sang at the Théâtre Royal de la Monnaie in Brussels (1883–90) and at the Opéra Comique in Paris (1890–91). He made his 1st appearance at the Paris Opéra as Nelusko on July 17, 1891, remaining on its roster until 1902. He then made guest appearances there until 1914, and was also a member of the Monte Carlo Opera (1891–1907). He made his U.S. debut in New Orleans on Jan. 4, 1893; he sang at London's Covent Garden (1897–99; 1902–04), at the Manhattan Opera in New York (1906–07; 1909–10), and again in Brussels (1908–14). He made his Metropolitan Opera debut in New York as Rigoletto on Nov. 24, 1910, remaining on the company's roster until 1912. His finest roles included Athanaël in *Thaïs,* Coppelius, Dapertutto, and Dr. Miracle in *Les Contes d'Hoffmann,* Nevers in *Les Huguenots,* Lescaut in *Manon,* Herod in *Hérodiade*, and Saint-Saëns's *Henry VIII*. His non-French roles included Don Giovanni, Wolfram, Jack Rance, Telramund, and Beckmesser. He was among the most convincing dramatic artists of his era.

Rendall, David, English tenor; b. London, Oct. 11, 1948. He studied at the Royal Academy of Music in London and at the Salzburg Mozarteum. In 1975 he made his operatic debut with the Glyndebourne Touring Opera as Ferrando, and then sang for the first time at London's Covent Garden as the Italian Singer in *Der Rosenkavalier*. In 1976 he made his debut at the Glyndebourne Festival as Ferrando. Following his first appearance at the English National Opera in London in 1976 as Leicester in *Maria Stuarda*, he made regular appearances there until 1992. In 1978 he portrayed Rodolfo at the N.Y. City Opera and Don Ottavio at the San Francisco Opera. He sang Ernesto in *Don Pasquale* at his Metropolitan Opera debut in New York on Feb. 28, 1980. In 1983 he appeared as Berlioz's Faust in Lyons. He returned to the Glyndebourne Festival as Tom Rakewell in 1989. In 1992 he sang Don Antonio in the first stage production of Gerhard's *The Duenna* in Madrid. In 1996 he was engaged as Hoffmann in Genoa.

Rendano, Alfonso, Italian pianist, teacher, and composer; b. Carolei, near Cosenza, April 5, 1883; d. Rome, Sept. 10, 1931. He studied in Caserta and then at the Naples Cons. (1863). After making his debut as a pianist in 1864, he pursued training with Thalberg in Naples (1866–67), with Mathias in Paris (1867), and with Reinecke and Richter at the Leipzig Cons. (1868). He successfully toured in Europe. After teaching at the Naples Cons. (1883) and at his own piano school (1883–86), he settled in Rome to teach privately. Rendano was the inventor of the pedale indipendente, which became known as the pedale Rendano. This 3d pedal was placed between the standard 2 pedals of the piano with the intention of prolonging the vibration of single sounds or chords. He composed an opera, *Consuelo* (Turin, May 25, 1902).

BIBL.: G. Puccio, *A. R.* (Rome, 1937).

Rennert, Günther, leading German opera producer and administrator; b. Essen, April 1, 1911; d. Salzburg, July 31, 1978. He was educated in Munich, Berlin, and Halle. From 1935 to 1939 he worked in Wuppertal, in Frankfurt am Main (with Walter Felsenstein), and in Mainz, then was chief producer in Königsberg (1939–42), at the Berlin Städtische Oper (1942–44), and at the Bavarian State Opera in Munich (1945). In 1946 he became Intendant of the Hamburg State Opera, a post he held until 1956; he then worked as a guest producer with several major opera houses, including La Scala in Milan and the Metropolitan Opera in New York. From 1967 to 1976 he was Intendant of the Bavarian State Opera in Munich. Through the consistent successes of his operatic productions in several cities under changing circumstances, Rennert acquired a reputation as one of the most competent members of his profession.

BIBL.: W. Schafer, *G. R.: Regisseur in dieser Zeit* (Bremen, 1962).

Rescigno, Nicola, American conductor; b. N.Y., May 28, 1916. He studied law in Rome before pursuing a career in music. In 1943 he made his conducting debut at the Brooklyn Academy of Music. In 1954 he cofounded the Lyric Theatre in Chicago, serving as its artistic director until 1956. In 1957 he cofounded the Dallas Civic Opera, where he served as music director until 1981, and of its successor, the Dallas Opera, until 1992. During his long tenure in Dallas, he conducted many premieres. He also was on the roster of the Metropolitan Opera in New York (1978–82), and appeared as a guest conductor of opera companies throughout North and South America and in Europe.

Resnik, Regina, American soprano, later mezzo-soprano; b. N.Y., Aug. 30, 1922. She studied in New York. She made her concert debut at the Brooklyn Academy of Music (Oct. 27, 1942); she sang in opera in Mexico (1943), won an annual audition at the Metropolitan Opera in New York in 1944, and appeared there as Leonora in *Il Trovatore* (Dec. 6, 1944); she continued to sing there regularly, turning to mezzo-soprano roles in 1955. In 1953 she appeared in Bayreuth as Sieglinde; she made her Covent Garden debut in London as Carmen in 1957, and sang there until 1972. She remained on the roster of the Metropolitan Opera until 1974. She was active as an opera producer from 1971. Among her finest roles were Mistress Quickly, Marina, Amneris, Herodias, and Clytemnestra. She also created the role of the Countess in Barber's *Vanessa* (1958).

Respighi, Ottorino, eminent Italian composer and teacher; b. Bologna, July 9, 1879; d. Rome, April 18, 1936. He studied violin with F. Sarti and composition with L. Torchi and G. Martucci at Bologna's Liceo Musicale (1891–1900). In 1900 he went to Russia, and played 1st viola in the orch. of the Imperial Opera in St. Petersburg; there he took lessons with Rimsky-Korsakov, which proved a decisive influence in Respighi's coloristic orchestration. From 1903 to 1908 he was active as a concert violinist; he also played the viola in the Mugellini Quartet of Bologna. In 1913 he was engaged as a prof. of composition at Rome's Liceo (later Cons.) di Santa Cecilia; in 1924, was appointed its director, but resigned in 1926, retaining only a class in advanced composition; subsequently he devoted himself to composing and conducting. He was elected a member of the Italian Royal Academy on March 23, 1932. In 1925–26 and again in 1932 he made tours of the United States as a pianist and a conductor. Respighi's style of composition is a highly successful blend of songful melodies with full and rich harmonies; he was one of the best masters of modern Italian music in orchestration. His power of evocation of the Italian scene and his ability to sustain interest without prolixity is incontestable. Although he wrote several operas, he achieved his greatest success with 2 symphonic poems, *Le fontane di Roma* and *I pini di Roma*, each consisting of 4 tone paintings of the Roman landscape; a great innovation for the time was the insertion of a phonograph recording of a nightingale into the score of *I pini di Roma*. His wife, Elsa Olivieri Sangiacomo Respighi (b. Rome, March 24, 1894; d. there, March 17, 1996), was his pupil; she wrote a fairy opera, *Fior di neve*; the symphonic poem *Serenata di maschere*; and numerous songs; she was also a concert singer. She publ. a biography of her husband.

WORKS: DRAMATIC: OPERAS: *Re Enzo* (Bologna, March 12, 1905); *Semirama*, lyric tragedy (Bologna, Nov. 20, 1910); *Marie-Victoire* (1913–14; not perf.); *La bella dormente nel bosco* or *La bella addormentata nel bosco*, musical fairy tale (1916–21; Rome, April 13, 1922); *Belfagor*, lyric comedy (1921–22; Milan, April 26, 1923); *La campana sommersa*, after Hauptmann's *Die versunkene Glocke* (1923–27; Hamburg, Nov. 18, 1927); *Maria Egiziaca*, mystery play (1929–32; N.Y., March 16, 1932); *La fiamma* (1930–33; Rome, Jan. 23, 1934); a free transcription of Monteverdi's *Orfeo* (Milan, March 16, 1935); *Lucrezia* (1935; Milan, Feb. 24, 1937). BALLETS: *La Boutique fantasque*, on themes by Rossini (London, June 5, 1919); *Scherzo veneziano* (Rome, Nov. 27, 1920); *Belkis, Regina di Saba* (1930–31; Milan, Jan. 23, 1932).

BIBL.: R. de Rensis, *O. R.* (Turin, 1935); E. Respighi, *O. R.: Dati biografici ordinati* (Milan, 1954; abridged Eng. tr., 1962); *O. R.: Catalogo delle opere* (Milan, 1965); E. Battaglia, ed., *O. R.* (Turin, 1985); D. Bryant, ed., *Il Novecento musicale italiano: Tra neoclassicismo e neogoticismo: Atti del convegno di studi promosso dalla Fondazione Giorgio Cini per il 50° anniversario della scomparsa di O. R.* (Florence, 1988).

Rethberg, Elisabeth (real name, **Lisbeth Sattler**), outstanding German-American soprano; b. Schwarzenberg, Sept. 22, 1894; d. Yorktown Heights, N.Y., June 6, 1976. She studied at the Dresden Cons. and with Otto Watrin. She made her operatic debut as Arsena in *Der Zigeunerbaron* at the Dresden Court Opera (1915) and continued to sing there when it became the State Opera in 1918. She then made her U.S. debut as Aida at the Metropolitan Opera in New York on Nov. 22, 1922, remaining one of its most celebrated artists until her farewell performance there in that same role on March 6, 1942. She subsequently embarked on a grand concert tour with Ezio Pinza in the United States, Europe, and Australia; their close association resulted in a lawsuit for alienation of affection brought by Pinza's wife against her, but the court action was not pursued. Throughout her operatic career, Rethberg sang in many of the major music centers in Italy; she also appeared at the Salzburg Festivals and at London's Covent Garden (1925; 1934–39). She excelled in both the German and Italian repertoires; among her memorable roles were Mozart's Countess, Donna Anna, Pamina, Constanze, and Donna Elvira; Verdi's Aida, the 2 Leonoras, Amelia, Desdemona, and Maria Boccanegra; and Wagner's Eva, Elisabeth, Sieglinde, and Elsa; she also created the title role in Strauss's *Die ägyptische Helena* (Dresden, June 6, 1928). Rethberg was married twice: first to Ernst Albert Dormann, and then to George Cehanovsky, whom she married in 1956.

BIBL.: H. Henschel and E. Friedrich, *E. R.: Ihr Leben und Künstlertum* (Schwarzenberg, 1928).

Reuling, (Ludwig) Wilhelm, German conductor and composer; b. Darmstadt, Dec. 22, 1802; d. Munich, April 19, 1879. He studied with Rinck and Seyfried, then was a theater conductor in Vienna (1829–54). He composed 37 operas and operettas, and 17 ballets, produced mostly in Vienna.

Reuss, August, German composer and teacher; b. Liliendorf bei Znaim, Moravia, March 6, 1871; d. Munich, June 18, 1935. He was a pupil of Thuille in Munich; after a brief activity as conductor in Augsburg (1906) and Magdeburg (1907), he lived in Berlin, then in Munich, where he taught at the Trapp Cons. (1927–29) and at the Akademie der Tonkünst (1929–35). His works, all in a late Romantic style, included an opera, *Herzog Philipps Brautfahrt* (Graz, 1909).

Reuss-Belce, Luise, Austrian soprano; b. Vienna, Oct. 24, 1860; d. (found dead in a refugee train) Aibach, Germany, March 5, 1945. She studied voice in Vienna. She made her operatic debut as Elsa in *Lohengrin* in Karlsruhe (1881), then sang in Bayreuth (1882) and in Wiesbaden (1896–99); her subsequent appearances were at Covent Garden in London (1900) and at the Metropolitan Opera in New York, where she made her debut as Brünnhilde in *Die Walküre* (Feb. 11, 1902); she then sang in Dresden (1903–11). In 1885 she married Eduard Reuss (b. N.Y., Sept. 16, 1851; d. Dresden, Feb. 18, 1911), a music pedagogue; after his death she moved to Berlin, where she established a singing school. In 1913 she was appointed stage manager at the festival opera performances in Nuremberg; she was the first woman to occupy such a post in Germany.

Reuter, Rolf, German conductor; b. Leipzig, Oct. 7, 1926. He studied at the Academy for Music and Theater in Dresden. He conducted in Eisenach (1951–55), then was Generalmusikdirektor in Meiningen (1955–61). In 1961 he became a conductor at the Leipzig Opera, and subsequently served as its Generalmusikdirektor (1963–78). He was chief conductor of the Weimar State Orch. (1979–81). From 1981 to 1994 he was chief conductor and music director of the Komische Oper in East Berlin.

Reutter, Hermann, outstanding German composer and pedagogue; b. Stuttgart, June 17, 1900; d. Heidenheim an der Brenz, Jan. 1, 1985. He studied with Franz Dorfmüller (piano), Ludwig Mayer (organ), Karl Erler (voice), and Walter Courvoisier (composition) at the Munich Academy of Music (1920–23). He began his career as a pianist in 1923 and made numerous concert tours with the singer Sigrid Onegin (1930–35), including 7 separate tours in the United States. He taught composition at the Stuttgart Hochschule für Musik (1932–36); after serving as director of the Berlin Staatliche Hochschule für Musik (1936–45), he became a teacher of lieder and composition at the Stuttgart Staatliche Hochschule für Musik (1952), serving as its director (1956–66); he then was prof. of music at the Munich Academy of Music. As a composer, Reutter followed the traditional line of German neo-Classicism, in which the basic thematic material, often inspired by German folk music, is arranged along strong contrapuntal lines, wherein a dissonant intervallic fabric does not disrupt the sense of immanent tonality. He excelled particularly in stage music and songs. He brought out an anthology of contemporary art songs, *Das zeitgenössische Lied* (4 vols., Mainz, 1969).

WORKS: OPERAS: *Saul* (Baden-Baden, July 15, 1928; rev. version, Hamburg, Dec. 21, 1947); *Der verlorene Sohn* (Stuttgart, March 20, 1929; rev. as *Die Rückkehr des verlorenen Sohnes*, Dortmund, 1952); *Doktor Johannes Faust* (1934–36; Frankfurt am Main, May 26, 1936; rev. version, Stuttgart, 1955); *Odysseus* (1940–42; Frankfurt am Main, Oct. 7, 1942); *Der Weg nach Freundschaft: Ballade der Landstrasse* (Göttingen, Jan. 25, 1948); *Don Juan und Faust* (Stuttgart, June 11, 1950); *Die Witwe von Ephesus* (1953; Cologne, June 23, 1954); *Die Brücke von San Luis Rey* (Frankfurt am Main Radio, June 20, 1954); *Hamlet* (Stuttgart, 1980); also *Der Tod des Empedokles*, scenic concerto (1965; Schwetzingen, May 29, 1966).

BIBL.: H. Lindlar, ed., *H. R.: Werk und Wirken: Festschrift der Freunde* (Mainz, 1965).

Rey, Cemal Reshid, Turkish pianist, conductor, teacher, and composer; b. Jerusalem, Sept. 24, 1904; d. Istanbul, Oct. 7, 1985. Of a distinguished family (his father was a poet and also served twice as minister of the interior in the Turkish government), he went to Paris at age 9 to study composition with Laparra, then continued his studies at the Geneva Cons.; returning to Paris, he took courses in piano with Long, composition with Fauré, and conducting with Derosse. In 1923 he settled in Constantinople and taught at the Cons.; from 1949 to 1969 he was principal conductor of the Istanbul Radio Orch. His works are imbued with Turkish melorhythms, and many have Turkish subjects. Among them are the operas *Yann Marek* (1922), *Sultan Cem* (1923), *Zeybek* (1926), *Tchelebi* (1945), and *Benli Hürmüz* (1965); also the operetta *Yaygara* (1969).

Rey, Jean-Baptiste, French conductor and composer, brother of **Louis-Charles-Joseph Rey**; b. Tarn-et-Garonne, Dec. 18, 1734; d. Paris, July 15, 1810. He studied at Toulouse and became a theater conductor in the provinces. In 1776 he settled in Paris as conductor of the Opéra, being named director of its orch. in 1781; he was also made master of the musique de chambre to Louis XVI (1779). He conducted at the Concert Spirituel (1781–86), served as prof. of harmony at the Cons. (1799–1801), and was named maître de chapelle to Napoleon in 1804. He taught according to the principles of Rameau and became embroiled in an academic controversy with the followers of the more modern method of Catel. He played an important role in producing operas by Gluck, Grétry. Among his own works was the opera *Diane et Endymion* (Paris, 1791). He also arranged operas by others.

Rey, Louis-Charles-Joseph, French composer and cellist, brother of **Jean-Baptiste Rey**; b. Lauzerte, Oct. 26, 1738; d. Paris, May 12, 1811. He was trained as a cellist, and was in the orch. of the Paris Opéra from 1767 until 1806; he also played in the orch. of the royal chapel (from 1772). He composed some stage pieces and chamber music.

Reyer (real name, **Rey**), **(Louis-Etienne-) Ernest,** French composer; b. Marseilles, Dec. 1, 1823; d. Le Lavandou, near Hyères, Jan. 15, 1909. An ardent admirer of Wagner, he added the German suffix *-er* to his real name. He entered a Marseilles music school when he was 6. He was sent to Algiers in 1839 to work in a government dept. with an uncle, where he composed a Solemn Mass (for the arrival of the French governor in Algiers; perf. 1847) and publ. several songs. He definitely embarked upon a musical career in 1848, studying in Paris with his aunt, **Louise Farrenc**. In 1866 he became librarian at the Opéra, and followed d'Ortigue as music critic of the *Journal des Débats* (1866–98); his collected essays were publ. in 1875 as *Notes de musique*; also in *Quarante ans de musique* (posthumous, 1909). He was elected to David's chair in the Institut in 1876, was made a Chevalier of the Légion d'honneur in 1872, and received the Grande-Croix in 1906. Although Reyer was an avowed admirer of Wagner, his music did not betray specific Wagnerian influences; both in form and in harmonic progressions, Reyer adhered to the Classical French school of composition, with a certain tendency toward exoticism in his choice of librettos. His reputation as a composer for the theater was securely established with his operas *Sigurd* (Brussels, Jan. 7, 1884) and *Salammbô* (Brussels, Feb. 10, 1890). Other works were *Le Sélam*, "symphonie orientale," but actually an opera (Paris, April 5, 1850), *Maître Wolfram*, opera (Paris, May 20, 1854), *Sacountalâ*, ballet pantomime (Paris, July 14, 1858), *La Statue*, opéra comique (Paris, April 11, 1861; rev. Paris, Feb. 27, 1903), and *Erostrate*, opera (in German, Baden-Baden, Aug. 21, 1862; in French, Paris, Oct. 16, 1871).

BIBL.: A. Jullien, *E. R.: Sa vie et ses oeuvres* (Paris, 1909); H. Roujon, *Notice sur la vie et les travaux de E. R.* (Paris, 1911); H. de Curzon, *E. R.: Sa vie et ses oeuvres* (Paris, 1923).

Reynolds, Anna, English mezzo-soprano; b. Canterbury, Oct. 4, 1931. She studied piano at the Royal Academy of Music in London, then went to Italy for vocal lessons. She made her operatic debut in Parma in 1960 as Suzuki; subsequently she sang in Vicenza (1961), Rome (1964), Spoleto (1966), Trieste (1967), and Venice (1969), and at La Scala in Milan (1973). She made her first appearance in England at Glyndebourne in 1962; she sang at Covent Garden in London in 1967 and also at Bayreuth (1970–76). She made her Metropolitan Opera debut in New York as Flosshilde in *Das Rheingold* on Nov. 22, 1968, and returned there in 1975. She also sang widely as a concert artist and recitalist.

Řezáč, Ivan, Czech composer; b. Řevnice, Nov. 5, 1924; d. Prague, Dec. 26, 1977. He studied piano with Rauch and composition with Šín, Janeček, and Dobiáš at the Prague Academy, graduating in 1953; later he joined its faculty, becoming its vice dean in 1961. In his music, he follows the type of optimistic lyricism made popular by Shostakovich. Among his works is the opera *Pan Theodor Mundstock* (Mr. Theodor Mundstock; 1974).

Rheinberger, Joseph (Gabriel), eminent German organist, conductor, composer, and pedagogue; b. Vaduz, Liechtenstein, March 17, 1839; d. Munich, Nov. 25, 1901. He played piano and organ as a child, then took regular lessons in organ with J. G. Herzog, piano with J. E. Leonhard, and composition with J. H. Maier at the Munich Cons.; subsequently he studied composition with Franz Lachner. From 1864 to 1877 he served as principal conductor of the Munich Choral Soc., being named Hofkapellmeister in 1877. In 1859 he succeeded his teacher Leonhard as prof. of piano at the Munich Cons., and also taught composition there. His loyalty to the cultural and musical institutions in Munich earned him many honors from the Bavarian government; King Ludwig II made him Knight of St. Michael; in 1894 he was given the rank of "Zivilverdienstorden," the equivalent of nobility, and in 1899 he was made Dr.Phil. honoris causa by the Univ. of Munich. Rheinberger's reputation as a teacher of organ was without equal during his lifetime, and students flocked to him from all parts of the world. As a composer, he created a number of works remarkable for their dignity, formal perfection, and consummate technical mastery, if not their inventive power. His organ sonatas are unquestionably among the finest productions of organ literature. Among his works for the stage were *Die sieben Raben*, romantic opera (Munich, 1869), *Des Türmers Töchterlein*, comic opera (Munich, 1873), and incidental music. See H.-J. Irmen, *Joseph Rheinberger: Thematisches Verzeichnis seiner Kompositionen* (Regensburg, 1975).

BIBL.: T. Kroyer, *J. R.* (Regensburg, 1916); H. Wagner and H.-J. Irmen, eds., *J. G. R.: Briefe und Dokumente seines Leben* (Vaduz, 1982).

Rhené-Baton (real name, **René Baton**), French conductor and composer; b. Courseulles-sur-Mer, Calvados, Sept. 5, 1879; d. Le Mans, Sept. 23, 1940. He studied piano at the Paris Cons. and theory privately with Gédalge. He began his conducting career as a chorus master at the Opéra Comique in Paris, then conducted various concert groups in Angers and Bordeaux. From 1916 to 1932 he was principal conductor of the Concerts Pasdeloup in Paris.

Rhodes, Jane (Marie Andrée), French mezzo-soprano; b. Paris, March 13, 1929. Following vocal studies, she made her debut as Marguerite in *La Damnation de Faust* in Nancy in 1953, which role she also chose for her first appearance at the Paris Opéra in 1958. On Nov. 15, 1960, she made her Metropolitan Opera debut in New York as Carmen, returning to sing Salome in 1962. In 1961 she appeared at the Aix-en-Provence Festival and in 1968 at the Paris Opéra Comique; also sang in various other French operatic centers, and in Buenos Aires and Tokyo. In 1966 she married **Roberto Benzi**. In addition to her French roles, Rhodes also essayed the roles of Tosca and Renata in Prokofiev's *The Fiery Angel*.

Rhodes, Phillip (Carl), American composer and teacher; b. Forest City, N.C., June 6, 1940. He studied composition with Iain Hamilton at Duke Univ. (B.A., 1962) and took courses in composition with Martino and Powell and in theory with Schuller and Perle at Yale Univ. (M.M., 1963). He was composer-in-residence in Cicero, Ill. (1966–68), and Louisville (1969–72); he taught at Amherst College (1968–69), the Univ. of Louisville (1969–72), and Carleton College in Northfield, Minn. (from 1974), where he was composer-in-residence and the Andrew W. Mellon Prof. of the Humanities. From 1985 to 1987 he served as president of the College Music Soc. His works include the operas *The Gentle Boy* (1979–80; rev. version, Tallahassee, June 12, 1987) and *The Magic Pipe* (1989) and the ballet *About Faces* (1970).

Ribáry, Antal, Hungarian composer; b. Budapest, Jan. 8, 1924. He studied composition with Rezső Kokai at the Budapest Academy of Music (1943–47) and later took lessons with Ferenc Szabó. His works include the operas *Lajos Király Válik* (The Divorce of King Louis; 1959) and *Liliom* (1960), the ballet *Fortunio* (1969), and the oratorio *La Paques à New York* (1987).

Ricci, Federico, Italian composer, brother of **Luigi Ricci**; b. Naples, Oct. 22, 1809; d. Conegliano, Dec. 10, 1877. He studied with Zingarelli, Bellini, and his brother Luigi at the Naples Cons. (1818–29). He gained notable success as a composer for the theater with his opera *La prigione di Edimburgo* (Trieste, March 13, 1838); it was followed by the successful operas *Luigi Rolla* (Florence, March 30, 1841) and *Corrado d'Altamura* (Milan, Nov. 16, 1841). Having established his reputation, he never again was able to duplicate these successes, and in subsequent years devoted himself mainly to composing comic operas. In 1853 he was made maître de chapelle of the imperial theaters in St. Petersburg, but this post only involved supervising the vocal classes at the Cons.

In 1869 he went to Paris, where he found success with his opera bouffe *Une Folie a Rome* (Jan. 30, 1869). He retired to Conegliano in 1876.

BIBL.: L. de Rada, *I fratelli R.* (Florence, 1878).

Ricci, Luigi, Italian composer, brother of **Federico Ricci**; b. probably in Naples, June 8(?), 1805; d. Prague, Dec. 31, 1859. He enrolled at the Naples Cons. when he was 9, his principal teachers being Furno and Zingarelli; he also studied privately with Generali. His 1st opera, *L'Impresario in angustie*, was performed at the Cons. in his 18th year; he scored a major success with his opera *Chiara di Rosembergh* (Milan, Oct. 11, 1831), composed for the diva Giuditta Grisi; his *Un avventura di Scaramuccia* proved a popular favorite when premiered there (March 8, 1834). In 1836 he was appointed maestro di cappella in Trieste, where he also became maestro concertatore at the Teatro Grande; after the twins Fanny and Lidia Stolz joined its roster in 1843, Ricci became closely associated with them—indeed, so closely that he began living with them during his tenure as director of the Odessa Opera (1844–45). Returning to Trieste, he finally married Lidia in 1849 but did not abandon his intimacy with Fanny; Lidia bore him a daughter, Adelaide (1850–71), who became a singer at the Paris Théâtre-Italien (1868–69); Fanny bore him a son, also named Luigi (1852–1906), who became a composer. After he produced his last opera, *Il Diavolo a quattro* (Trieste, May 15, 1859), a mental derangement manifested itself, and he was sent to an asylum in Prague, where he spent the remaining months of his life.

BIBL.: V. dal Torso, *L. R.* (Trieste, 1860); F. de Villars, *Notices sur L. et Federico R., suivies d'une analyse critique de "Crispino e la comare"* (Paris, 1866); L. de Rada, *I fratelli R.* (Florence, 1878).

Ricciarelli, Katia, Italian soprano; b. Rovigo, Jan. 18, 1946. She studied at the Venice Cons. She made her operatic debut as Mimi in Mantua in 1969; after winning the Giuseppe Verdi Award for Young Singers in Parma (1970) and the New Verdi Voices Contest (1971), she pursued a successful career in the major Italian music centers. She made her U.S. debut as Lucrezia in *I due Foscari* in Chicago (1972); her first appearance at London's Covent Garden was as Mimi (1974), a role she also chose for her Metropolitan Opera debut in New York (April 11, 1975). In 1979 she made her debut in recital at the Salzburg Festival. In 1985 she sang Desdemona in Zeffirelli's film version of Verdi's *Otello*. In 1985–86 she sang Rossini roles in Pesaro, returning there in 1988. She appeared as Desdemona at the Metropolitan Opera and at Covent Garden in 1990. In 1997 she sang Handel's Agrippina in Palermo. Among her other fine roles were Amelia Boccanegra, Suor Angelica, Luisa Miller, and Elisabeth de Valois.

Ricciotti, Carlo, Italian violinist and operatic impresario; b. c.1681; d. The Hague, July 13, 1756. He settled in The Hague, where he became director of a French opera company. *Six Concerti armonici*, long attributed to Pergolesi, were later attributed to Ricciotti; still later they were confirmed to be the work of Count Unico van Wassenaer.

Riccius, Karl August, German violinist, conductor, and composer; b. Bernstadt, July 26, 1830; d. Dresden, July 8, 1893. He studied in Dresden with Wieck, and in Leipzig with Mendelssohn, Schumann, and Ferdinand David. In 1847 he became violinist in the Dresden Court Orch., and later also conductor. He wrote a comic opera, *Es spukt* (Dresden, 1871), several ballets, and music to various plays. His uncle was the German conductor, music critic, and composer August Ferdinand Riccius (1819–1886).

Richter, Ferdinand Tobias, German-born Austrian organist and composer; b. Würzburg (baptized), July 22, 1651; d. Vienna, Nov. 3, 1711. He was court and chamber organist in Vienna from 1683, where he enjoyed a great reputation as a theorist and teacher. Among his compositions were 20 operas, 4 oratorios and other sacred works, and music for Jesuit school plays.

Richter, Hans (Johann Baptist Isidor), celebrated Austro-Hungarian conductor; b. Raab, Hungary, April 4, 1843; d. Bayreuth, Dec. 5, 1916. He was born into a musical family; his father, Anton Richter, was a composer and Kapellmeister at Raab Cathedral, and his mother, Josefine (née Czasensky) Richter, was an opera singer and vocal teacher. Richter was blessed with perfect pitch and was only 4 when he began piano lessons with his mother; he soon received instruction in organ and timpani, and also began to sing. In 1854 he was taken to Vienna to pursue academic studies at the Piaristengymnasium; he also was accepted as a chorister in the Imperial Chapel, where he sang until 1858. He then studied at the Cons. of the Gesellschaft der Musikfreunde (1858–62); his principal mentors there were Kleinecke (horn), Heissler (violin), Ramesch (piano), J. Hellmesberger (orchestral training), and Sechter (theory and composition). He continued his training with Kleinecke as an external student until 1865. In addition, he learned to play virtually every instrument in the orch., the harp excepted. While still attending to his studies, he gained experience as a player in various opera orchs. before serving as a horn player in the orch. of Vienna's Kärtnerthortheater (1862–66). In the meantime, he made his professional debut as a conductor in a concert in Raab on Sept. 19, 1865. Upon the recommendation of Heinrich Esser, Wagner invited Richter to Tribschen in 1866 to prepare the fair copy of his score to the opera *Die Meistersinger von Nürnberg*. Wagner was so satisfied with Richter's work that he secured the young musician's appointment as chorus master and répétiteur at the Munich Court Opera. Richter prepared the chorus for the premiere of *Die Meistersinger*, which was conducted by Han von Bülow on June 21, 1868. Later that year he was appointed court music director in Munich, but was dismissed from his post the following year after a dispute with the royal authorities over aspects of the staging of the premiere of *Das Rheingold*. With Wagner's approval, Richter conducted instead the Brussels premiere (in French) of *Lohengrin* on March 22, 1870, with notable success. In 1871 Richter became conductor of the Opera and Phil. concerts in Budapest, where he won distinction as both an operatic and symphonic conductor. In 1874 he was made the director of the Opera. In 1875 he was called to Vienna to assume the post of 1st Kapellmeister of the Court Opera, a position he retained until 1900. From 1875 to 1882, and again from 1883 to 1898, he was conductor of the Vienna Phil. At Wagner's invitation, he went to Bayreuth in 1876 to conduct the first complete staging of the *Ring* cycle at the opening of the Festival: *Das Rheingold* on Aug. 13, *Die Walküre* on Aug. 14, *Siegfried* on Aug. 16, and *Götterdammerung* on Aug. 17. In May 1877 Wagner invited Richter to share his conducting duties at the Royal Albert Hall in London. That same year Richter was made Vize-Hofkapellmeister of the Court Chapel in Vienna. In 1879 he returned to London to conduct a series of Orchestral Festival Concerts, which he subsequently led as the annual Richter Concerts from 1880 to 1902. In 1882 Richter conducted the first British performances of *Die Meistersinger* (May 30) and *Tristan und Isolde* (June 20) at the Theatre Royal, Drury Lane, London. His debut at London's Covent Garden followed on June 4, 1884, when he conducted *Die Meistersinger*. In 1884 he became conductor of the Gesellschaft der Musikfreunde in Vienna, a post he held until 1890. From 1885 to 1909 he was conductor of the Birmingham Triennial Music Festival. In 1887 he returned to Bayreuth, and between 1892 and 1912 conducted notable performances at 11 festivals there. In 1893 Richter accepted the conductorship of the Boston Sym. Orch., but was compelled to withdraw his acceptance when he learned from the Viennese authorities that he would lose his pension. Instead, he was made Imperial Hofkapellmeister that year, a title he retained until 1900. In 1895 Richter made his first appearance as a guest conductor with the Hallé Orch. in Manchester, and subsequently served as its conductor from 1899 to 1911. From 1903 to 1910 he conducted seasons of German opera at Covent Garden, and in 1908 conducted the first English-language performances of the *Ring* cycle there. On June 9, 1904, he conducted the inaugural concert of the London Sym. Orch., and then served as its principal conductor until 1911. After making his home in Bayreuth, Richter conducted his farewell performance at the Festival there with *Die Meistersinger* on Aug. 19, 1912. In addition to the honors bestowed upon him in his homeland, he was also honored in England with honorary doctorates in music by the univs. of Oxford (1885) and Manchester (1902), and was made an Honorary Member, 4th class (1904) and Honorary Commander (1907) of the Royal Victorian Order. Richter's unstinting devotion to the composer's intentions, communicated via a flawless conducting technique, resulted in performances of great commitment and authority. He invariably conducted all his scores from memory. While his association with Wagner rendered his performances of the master of Bayreuth's works as authoritative, he also won great renown for his interpretations of Beethoven. He further distinguished himself as an outstanding champion of Mozart, Brahms, Bruckner, Tchaikovsky, Dvořák, and Elgar.

BIBL.: C. Fifield, *True Artist and True Friend: A Biography of H. R.* (Oxford, 1993).

Richter, Nico (Max), Dutch composer; b. Amsterdam, Dec. 2, 1915; d. there, Aug. 16, 1945. He studied conducting with Scherchen and directed a student orch.; in Feb. 1942 he was arrested by the Nazis as a member of the Dutch Resistance, and spent 3 years in the Dachau concentration camp, which fatally undermined his health; he died shortly after liberation. Among his works were the chamber opera *Amorijs* (1937) and the ballet *Kannitverstan*.

Rickards, Steven, accomplished American countertenor; b. Pottstown, Pa., Sept. 19, 1955. He was a student of Russel Oberlin at Oberlin (Ohio) College (1976), of Elizabeth Mannion and Paul Matthen at Indian Univ. (B.Mus.Ed., 1979; M.M., 1984), of Sir Peter Pears at the Britten-Pears School in Aldeburgh (1981), at the Guildhall School of Music and Drama in London (diplomas in singing, 1982, and opera performance, 1983), and of Roy Delp at Florida State Univ. in Tallahassee (1989–93). While still a student, he was chosen to create the role of Marat in the premiere of Eaton's *Danton and Robespierre* in Bloomington, Ind., in 1979. He won the countertenor prize at the 's-Hertogenbosch Competition and 2d prize at the Royal Tunbridge Wells Competition in 1982, and then took 2d prize at the Oratorio Soc. of N.Y. Competition in 1985. In 1985 he sang Egeo in the U.S. premiere of Handel's *Teseo* in Boston and created the role of Trinculo in the premiere of Eaton's *The Tempest* at the Santa Fe Opera. From 1985 to 1989 he sang with Chanticleer throughout the United States and Europe. He portrayed Apollo in Britten's *Death in Venice* with the Opera Co. of Philadelphia in 1988. After appearing as Medarse in the U.S. premiere of Handel's *Siroe* in New York in 1990, he sang Alcandro in Hasse's *L'Olimpiade* at the Semper Opera in Dresden in 1992. He commissioned and gave the first performance of Ladislav Kubik's *Der Weg* in 1993 in Prague. In 1997 he sang St. Francis Xavier in Zipoli's *San Ignacio de Loyola* in Boston. From 1997 to 1999 he toured with Hillier's Theatre of Voices. In addition to his esteemed interpretations of Buxtehude, Bach, Handel, Purcell, and Dowland, Rickards has won distinction for his performances of scores by contemporary composers, among them Britten and Pärt.

Rickenbacher, Karl Anton, Swiss conductor; b. Basel, May 20, 1940. He received his training at the Berlin Städtisches Cons. (1962–66); his mentors in conducting were Karajan and Boulez. After serving as an assistant conductor at the Zürich Opera (1966–69), he was conductor of the Freiburg im Breisgau Opera (1969–74). From 1976 to 1985 he was Generalmusikdirektor of the Westhphalian Sym. Orch. in Recklinghausen. He also served as principal conductor of the BBC Scottish Sym. Orch. in Glasgow from 1977 to 1980. In 1983 he appeared for the first time as a guest conductor with the Berlin Phil. and at the Deutsche Oper in Berlin. In 1987 he made his debuts as a guest conductor with the Royal Phil. and the Philharmonia Orch. in London. After making his first appearances in the United States during the 1987–88 season, he was a guest conductor with many European and North American orchs. His repertoire embraces the classical, romantic, and modern repertoires.

Ridder, Anton de, Dutch tenor; b. Amsterdam, Feb. 13, 1929. He studied voice at the Amsterdam Cons. with Herman Mulder (1947–49) and with Jan Keyzer (1951–56). From 1956 to 1962 he was on the roster of the Karlsruhe Opera, then sang at the Gärtnerplatz State Theater in Munich (1962–66). In 1965 he joined the Komische Oper in West Berlin. In 1969 he took part in the Salzburg Festival; he also sang in Vienna and Hamburg. In 1972 he appeared at the Edinburgh Festival. He sang Florestan at the Glyndebourne Festival in 1979. In 1985 he again appeared at the Salzburg Festival. He was equally adept at lyric and dramatic tenor parts.

Ridderbusch, Karl, admired German bass; b. Recklinghausen, May 29, 1932; d. Wels, near Linz, June 21, 1997. He was a student of Rudolf Schock at the Duisburg Cons. and of Clemens Kaiser-Breme in Essen. In 1961 he made his operatic debut in Münster. After singing in Essen (1963–65), he appeared with the Deutsche Oper am Rhein in Düsseldorf (from 1965). In 1967 he made his debut at the Bayreuth Festival as Titurel, and sang there regularly until 1976. He appeared for the first time in Paris in 1967. On Nov. 21, 1967, he made his Metropolitan Opera debut in New York as Hunding, and returned there as Hans Sachs in 1976. In 1968 he appeared for the first time in Vienna and at the Salzburg Easter Festival. In 1971 he made his debut at London's Covent Garden. He also sang with many other leading opera houses and toured widely as a concert singer. He was especially noted for his Wagnerian roles. In addition to those already noted, he excelled as King Marke, Fafner, Hagen, and Daland. Among his esteemed non-Wagnerian roles were Rocco, Boris Godunov, Baron Ochs, and the Doktor in *Wozzeck*.

Rider-Kelsey, Corinne (née **Rider**), American soprano and teacher; b. near Batavia, N.Y., Feb. 24, 1877; d. Toledo, Ohio, July 10, 1947. She studied with Helen Rice at the Oberlin (Ohio) College-Cons. of Music, then with L. Torrens in Rockford, Ill., where she made her recital debut (1897); after further training with Toedt and his wife in New York, she became successful as a concert singer. She made her debut as a soloist in Handel's *Messiah* in St. Louis (Nov. 24, 1904); she made her operatic debut as Micaëla at London's Covent Garden (July 2, 1908), but soon abandoned the opera stage to devote herself to a concert career. In 1926 she married the violinist and composer Lynnel Reed; they settled in Toledo, where she was active as a singer and a teacher.

BIBL.: L. Reed, *Be Not Afraid: Biography of Madame R. K.* (N.Y., 1955).

Ridout, Godfrey, Canadian composer, teacher, conductor, and writer on music; b. Toronto, May 6, 1918; d. there, Nov. 24, 1984. He studied at the Toronto Cons. with Charles Peaker (organ and counterpoint), Ettore Mazzoleni (conducting), Weldon Kilburn (piano), and Healey Willan (composition). He served on the faculties of the Toronto Cons. (from 1940) and the Univ. of Toronto (from 1948), retiring in 1982. He also was music director of the Eaton Operatic Soc. (1949–58), director of the Composers, Authors, and Publishers Assn. of Canada (1966–73), and a program annotator for the Toronto Sym. (1973–84). With T. Kenins, he ed. the vol. *Celebration* (Toronto, 1984). In his music, Ridout charted an eclectic path notable for its accessible style. His works include *La Prima Ballerina*, ballet (1966; Montreal, Oct. 26, 1967), and *The Lost Child*, television opera (1976).

Riegel, Kenneth, American tenor; b. Womelsdorf, Pa., April 29, 1938. He studied at the Manhattan School of Music in New York and also at the Metropolitan Opera Studio. He made his operatic debut as the Alchemist in Henze's opera *König Hirsch* with the Santa Fe Opera in 1965, then sang with the Cincinnati Opera, the Houston Opera, the N.Y. City Opera, and others. On Oct. 22, 1973, he made his debut with the Metropolitan Opera in New York as Iopas in *Les Troyens*. In 1977 he appeared at the Vienna State Opera, in 1978 at the Paris Opéra, in 1979 at Milan's La Scala, in 1981 at the Hamburg State Opera, in 1983 at the Deutsche Oper in Berlin, and in 1985 at London's Covent Garden. In 1988 he was engaged at the Bavarian State Opera in Munich, in 1992 in Salzburg, and in 1996 in Florence. He also toured as a concert artist.

Rieger, Fritz, German conductor; b. Oberaltstadt, June 28, 1910; d. Bonn, Sept. 29, 1978. He was educated at the Prague Academy of Music, taking courses in piano with Langer, composition with Finke, and conducting with Szell. He conducted at the German Opera Theater in Prague (1931–38), the Bremen Opera (1939–41), and the Mannheim National Theater (1947–49). From 1949 to 1966 he was Generalmusikdirektor of the Munich Phil.; he also conducted at the Bavarian State Opera in Munich. In 1972–73 he was chief conductor of the Melbourne Sym. Orch.; he also gave guest performances in Japan. In his programs, he gave considerable prominence to modern music.

Rieti, Vittorio, Italian-born American composer and teacher; b. Alexandria, Egypt, Jan. 28, 1898; d. N.Y., Feb. 19, 1994. He studied with Frugatta in Milan, then took courses with Respighi and Casella in Rome, where he lived until 1940, when he emigrated to the United States; he became a naturalized American citizen on June 1, 1944. He taught at the Peabody Cons. of Music in Baltimore (1948–49), Chicago Musical College (1950–53), Queens College in New York (1958–60), and N.Y. College of Music (1960–64). His style of composition represents an ingratiating synthesis of cosmopolitan modern tendencies.

WORKS: DRAMATIC: OPERAS: *Orfeo tragedia* (1928; withdrawn); *Teresa nel bosco* (1933; Venice, Sept. 15, 1934); *Don Perlimplin* (1949; Urbana, Ill., March 30, 1952); *Viaggio d'Europa*, radio opera (1954); *The Pet Shop* (1957; N.Y., April 14, 1958); *The Clock* (1959–60); *Maryam the Harlot* (1966). BALLETS: *L'Arca di Noe* (1923; only orch. suite extant); *Robinson et Vendredi* (1924); *Barabau* (London, Dec. 11, 1925); *Le Bal* (Monte Carlo, May 1929); *David triomphant* (Paris, May 1937); *Hippolyte* (1937); *The Night Shadow* (1941; N.Y., Feb. 1946); *Waltz Academy* (Boston, Oct. 1944); *The Mute Wife* (N.Y., Nov. 1944); *Trionfo di Bacco e Arianna*, ballet-cantata (1946–47; N.Y., Feb. 1948); *Native Dancer* (1959; based on the Sym. No. 5); *Conundrum* (1961); *A Sylvan Dream* (1965; Indianapolis, Oct. 1, 1982); *Scenes Seen* (1975; Indianapolis, March 25, 1976); *Verdiana* (1983; Indianapolis, Feb. 16, 1984); *Indiana* (1984; Indianapolis, Sept. 14, 1985); *Kaleidoscope* (1987; Indianapolis, April 30, 1988).

BIBL.: F. Ricci, *V. R.* (Naples, 1987).

Rietz, (August Wilhelm) Julius, German cellist, conductor, music editor, and composer; b. Berlin, Dec. 28, 1812; d. Dresden, Sept. 12, 1877. He was of a musical family: his father was a court musician, and his brother was a friend of Mendelssohn. Julius studied cello and played in theater orchs. in Berlin. In 1834 he became 2d conductor of the Düsseldorf Opera, and from 1847 to 1854 he was chief conductor of the Leipzig Opera; from 1848 to 1860 he served as chief conductor of the Leipzig Gewandhaus Orch. In 1860 he became Hofkapellmeister in Dresden, being named Generalmusikdirektor in 1874; he was also artistic director of the Cons. there (from 1870). A scholarly musician and competent conductor, Rietz was also an excellent music ed.; he prepared for publication the complete edition of Mendelssohn's works for Breitkopf & Härtel (1874–77), and also ed. Mozart's operas and syms., Beethoven's overtures, etc. As a composer, he followed the musical style of Mendelssohn.

BIBL.: H. Zimmer, *J. R.* (diss., Univ. of Berlin, 1943).

Rigel, Henri-Jean, French pianist, teacher, and composer, son of **Henri (Heinrich) Joseph Riegel**; b. Paris, May 11, 1772; d. Abbeville, Dec. 16, 1852. After receiving lessons in piano and composition from his father, he entered the École Royale de Chant (1784), where he was made a sous-maître de solfège (1785); his works were given at the Concert Spirituel (from 1787). He taught at the Paris Cons. (1795–97), then accompanied Napoleon on his expedition to Egypt (1798), where he served as music director of the new French Theater in Cairo (until 1800). Upon his return to Paris (1800), he became active as a piano teacher and accompanist. Napoleon made him pianiste de la musique particulière de l'Empereur et Roi, and he also acquired distinction as a composer. He wrote numerous works, including 2 comic operas, *Les Deux Meuniers* (Cairo, 1799) and *Le Duel nocturne* (Paris, Dec. 23, 1805). Many of his works are lost.

Righetti-Giorgi, Geltrude, outstanding Italian contralto; b. Bologna, 1793; d. there, 1862. She studied in Bologna, making her debut there (1814) under the name Righetti. After her marriage to the lawyer Giorgi (1815), she retired from the stage, only to be convinced of her vocal gifts by Rossini. She subsequently distinguished herself in his operas, creating Rosina in his *Il Barbiere di Siviglia* (1816) and the title role in his *La Cenerentola* (1817). She continued to sing regularly until 1822, making her last appearance in 1836.

Righini, Vincenzo, Italian tenor, conductor, singing teacher, and composer; b. Bologna, Jan. 22, 1756; d. there, Aug. 19, 1812. He was a choirboy at Bologna's S. Petronio, making his debut in Parma (1775). He then became a member of Bustelli's opera company in Prague (1776), the same year that he wrote for it his 1st opera, *Il Convitato di pietra*, which proved successful. He abandoned his singing career and went to Vienna as a singing master to Princess Elisabeth of Württemberg and director of the Italian Opera (1780). From 1787 to 1793 he was Kapellmeister at the Mainz electoral court. In 1788 he married the contralto Anna Maria Lehritter (1762–93). In 1793 he became court Kapellmeister and director of the Italian Opera in Berlin, where he was an influential figure. In 1793 he married the singer Henriette Kneisel (1767–1801); they divorced in 1800. After the Italian Opera was dissolved in the wake of war in 1806, he bided his time until the royal theater was reorganized in 1811, after which he and B. A. Weber shared the duties of Kapellmeister. In 1812 he returned to his homeland. In addition to his operas, Righini wrote a number of successful instrumental works and songs.

WORKS: DRAMATIC: *Il Convitato di pietra, ossia Il Dissoluto punito*, dramma tragicomico (Prague, 1776; as *Das steinerne Gastmahl, oder Der Ruchlose*, Vienna, 1777); *La bottega del café*, commedia giocosa (Prague, 1778); *La Vedova scaltra*, dramma giocoso (Prague, 1778); *Armida*, dramma (Vienna, 1782; rev. Berlin, 1799); *L'incontro inaspettato*, dramma giocoso (Vienna, 1785; as *Die unvermutete Zusammenkunft*, Berlin, 1793); *Il Demogorgone, ovvero Il Filosofo confuso*, opera buffa (Vienna, 1786); *Antigono*, dramma serio (Mainz, 1788); *Alcide al bivio*, azione teatrale (Koblenz, 1790; rev. as a cantata, Vienna, 1804); *Vasco di Gama*, opera (Berlin, 1792; pasticcio in collaboration with others); *Enea nel Lazio*, dramma eroi-tragico (Berlin, 1793); *Il trionfo d'Arianna*, dramma (Berlin, 1793); *Atalante e Meleagro*, festa teatrale (Berlin, 1793); *La Gerusalemme liberata, ossia Arminda al campo de' franchi*, dramma (Berlin, 1799); *Tigrane*, dramma eroico (Berlin, 1800); *Minerva belebet die Statue des Dädalus*, pantomimischer Tanz (Berlin, 1802); *La selva incantata*, opera (Berlin, 1803); also an oratorio, *Der Tod Jesu* (1790).

Rihm, Wolfgang (Michael), German composer and teacher; b. Karlsruhe, March 13, 1952. He received training in composition with Eugen Velte at the Karlsruhe Hochschule für Musik (1968–72), with Stockhausen in Cologne (1972–73), and with Klaus Huber in Freiburg im Breisgau (1973–76). He also studied with Fortner and Searle, and received training in musicology with Eggebrecht in Freiburg im Breisgau. From 1970 he attended the summer courses in new music in Darmstadt, and then taught there from 1978. He taught at the Karlsruhe Hochschule für Musik (1973–78). After teaching in Munich (1981), he returned to the Karlsruhe Hochschule für Musik as a prof. (from 1985). In his music, Rihm embraced an atonal, post-expressionist path with occasional infusions of tonal writing.

WORKS: DRAMATIC: *Faust und Yorick*, chamber opera (1976; Mannheim, April 29, 1977); *Jakob Lenz*, chamber opera (1977–78; Hamburg, March 8, 1979); *Tutuguri*, ballet (1981–82; Berlin, Nov. 12, 1982); *Die Hamletmaschine*, music theater (1983–86; Mannheim, April 4, 1987); *Oedipus*, music theater (1986–87; Berlin, Oct. 4, 1987); *Die Eroberung von Mexico*, music theater (1987–91; Hamburg, Feb. 9, 1992); *Medea-Spiel*, dance theater (1988–89; Salzburg, April 6, 1989); *Séraphin*, music theater (Frankfurt am

Main, Sept. 7, 1994). Also *Konzertarie*, "telepsychogramm" for Mezzo-soprano and Orch. (1975; Rome, June 28, 1989), and *Andere Schatten*, musical scene for Soprano, Mezzo-soprano, Baritone, Speaker, Chorus, and Orch. (Frankfurt am Main, Sept. 6, 1985).

BIBL.: R. Urmetzer, *W. R.* (Stuttgart, 1988).

Riisager, Knudåge, prominent Danish composer; b. Port Kunda, Estonia, March 6, 1897; d. Copenhagen, Dec. 26, 1974. He went to Copenhagen and studied theory and composition with Otto Malling and Peder Gram, and violin with Peder Mller (1915–18). He also took courses in political science at the Univ. (1916–21; graduated, 1921) before pursuing musical studies with Roussel and Le Flem in Paris (1921–23), and later with Grabner in Leipzig (1932). He held a civil service position in Denmark (1925–50) and was chairman of the Danish Composers' Union (1937–62) and director of the Royal Danish Cons. (1956–67). A fantastically prolific composer, he wrote music in quaquaversal genres, but preserved a remarkable structural and textural consistency while demonstrating an erudite sense of modern polyphony. He also had a taste for exotic and futuristic subjects. He publ. a collection of essays, *Det usynlige mønster* (The Unseemly Monster; Copenhagen, 1957), and a somewhat self-deprecatory memoir, *Det er sjovt at vaere lille* (It Is Amusing to Be Small; Copenhagen, 1967).

WORKS (all 1st perf. in Copenhagen unless otherwise given): DRAMATIC: OPÉRA BUFFA: *Susanne* (1948; Jan. 7, 1950). BALLETS: *Benzin* (1927; Dec. 26, 1930); *Cocktails-Party* (1929); *Tolv med Posten* (12 by the Mail), after H. C. Andersen (1939; Feb. 21, 1942); *Slaraffenland* (Fool's Paradise; 1940; Feb. 21, 1942; originally an orch. piece, 1936); *Qarrtsiluni*, on Eskimo themes (Feb. 21, 1942; originally an orch. piece, 1938); *Fugl fønix* (Phoenix; 1944–45; May 12, 1946); *Étude*, based on Czerny's studies (1947; Jan. 15, 1948); *Månerenen* (The Moon Reindeer; 1956; Nov. 22, 1957); *Stjerner* (1958); *Les Victoires de l'Amour* (1958; March 4, 1962); *Fruen fra havet* (Lady from the Sea; 1959; N.Y., April 20, 1960); *Galla-Variationer* (1966; March 5, 1967); *Ballet Royal* (May 31, 1967); *Svinedrengen* (The Swineherd; Danish TV, March 10, 1969).

Riley, Terry (Mitchell), significant American composer and performer; b. Colfax, Calif., June 24, 1935. He studied piano with Duane Hampton at San Francisco State College (1955–57) and composition with Seymour Shifrin and William Denny at the Univ. of Calif. at Berkeley (M.A., 1961). In 1967 he was a creative assoc. at the Center for Creative and Performing Arts at the State Univ. of N.Y. in Buffalo. In 1970 he was initiated in San Francisco as a disciple of Pandit Pran Nath, the north Indian singer, and followed him to India. From 1971 to 1980 he was assoc. prof. at Mills College in Oakland, California. In 1979 he held a Guggenheim fellowship. In his music, Riley explores the extremes of complexity and gymnosophistical simplicity. Among his compositions is the chamber opera *The Saint Adolf Ring* (1992).

BIBL.: W. Mertens, *American Minimal Music: La Monte Young, T. R., Steve Reich, Philip Glass* (London, 1991).

Rimini, Giacomo, Italian baritone and teacher; b. Verona, March 22, 1888; d. Chicago, March 6, 1952. He was trained at the Verona Cons. After making his operatic debut in Verona (1910), he sang in various Italian opera houses. In 1916 he joined the Chicago Opera. He also appeared at London's Covent Garden in 1933. In 1920 he married **Rosa Raisa**. They opened a singing school in Chicago in 1937.

Rimsky-Korsakov, Andrei (Nikolaievich), Russian musicologist, son of **Nikolai (Andreievich) Rimsky-Korsakov**; b. St. Petersburg, Oct. 17, 1878; d. there (Leningrad), May 23, 1940. He studied philology at the Univ. of St. Petersburg and later at the univs. of Strasbourg and Heidelberg (Ph.D., 1903). Returning to Russia, he devoted his energies to Russian music history. In 1915 he began the publication of an important magazine, *Musikalny Sovremennik* (The Musical Contemporary), but the revolutionary events of 1917 forced suspension of its publication. He wrote a major biography of his father (5 vols., Moscow, 1933–46; vol. 5 ed. by his brother, Vladimir Rimsky-Korsakov); he also ed. the 3d to 5th eds. of his father's autobiography (Moscow, 1926, 1932, 1935) and publ. a study of Maximilian Steinberg (Moscow, 1928). He was married to **Julia Weissberg**. His nephew was Georgi (Mikhailovich) Rimsky-Korsakov (b. St. Petersburg, Dec. 26, 1901; d. there [Leningrad), Oct. 10, 1965).

Rimsky-Korsakov, Nikolai (Andreievich), great Russian composer, father of **Andrei (Nikolaievich) Rimsky-Korsakov**; b. Tikhvin, near Novgorod, March 18, 1844; d. Liubensk, near St. Petersburg, June 21, 1908. He remained in the country until he was 12 years old, then in 1856 entered the Naval School in St. Petersburg, graduating in 1862. He took piano lessons as a child with provincial teachers, and later with a professional musician, Théodore Canillé, who introduced him to Balakirev; he also met Cui and Borodin. In 1862 he was sent on the clipper *Almaz* on a voyage that lasted 2 1/2 years; returning to Russia in the summer of 1865, he settled in St. Petersburg, where he remained most of his life. During his travels he maintained contact with Balakirev, and continued to report to him the progress of his musical composition. He completed his 1st Sym. (which was also the earliest significant work in this form by a Russian composer), and it was performed under Balakirev's direction on Dec. 31, 1865, at a concert of the Free Music School in St. Petersburg. In 1871 Rimsky-Korsakov was engaged as a prof. of composition and orchestration at the St. Petersburg Cons., even though he was aware of the inadequacy of his own technique. He remained on the faculty until his death, with the exception of a few months in 1905, when he was relieved of his duties as prof. for his public support of the rebellious students during the revolution of that year. As a music educator, Rimsky-Korsakov was of the greatest importance to the development and maintenance of the traditions of the Russian national school; among his students were Glazunov, Liadov, Arensky, Ippolitov-Ivanov, Gretchaninov, N. Tcherepnin, Maximilian Steinberg, Gnessin, and Miaskovsky. Stravinsky studied privately with him from 1903.

In 1873 Rimsky-Korsakov abandoned his naval career, but was appointed to the post of inspector of the military orchs. of the Russian navy, until it was abolished in 1884. From 1883 to 1894 he was also assistant director of the Court Chapel and led the chorus and the orch. there. Although he was not a gifted conductor, he gave many performances of his own orch. works; made his debut at a charity concert for the victims of the Volga famine in St. Petersburg on March 2, 1874 in a program that included the 1st performance of his 3d Sym. From 1886 until 1900 he conducted the annual Russian Sym. concerts organized by the publisher Belaieff; in June 1889 he conducted 2 concerts of Russian music at the World Exposition in Paris; in 1890 he conducted a concert of Russian music in Brussels; he led a similar concert there in 1900. His last appearance abroad was in the spring of 1907, when he conducted in Paris 2 Russian historic concerts arranged by Diaghilev; in the same year he was elected corresponding member of the French Academy, to succeed Grieg. These activities, however, did not distract him from his central purpose as a national Russian composer. His name was grouped with those of Cui, Borodin, Balakirev, and Mussorgsky as the "Mighty 5," and he maintained an intimate friendship with most of them; at Mussorgsky's death he collected his MSS and prepared them for publication, and he also revised Mussorgsky's opera *Boris Godunov*; it was in Rimsky-Korsakov's version that the opera became famous. Later some criticism was voiced against Rimsky-Korsakov's reduction of Mussorgsky's original harmonies and melodic lines to an academically acceptable standard. He had decisive influence in the affairs of the Belaieff publishing firm and helped publish a great number of works by Russian composers of the St. Petersburg group; only a small part of these sumptuously printed scores represents the best in Russian music, but culturally Rimsky-Korsakov's solicitude was of great importance. Although he was far from being a revolutionary, he freely expressed his disgust at the bungling administration of czarist Russia; he was particularly indignant about the attempts of the authorities to alter Pushkin's lines in his own last opera, *The Golden Cockerel*, and refused to compromise. He died, of angina pectoris, with the situation still unresolved. The opera was produced posthumously, with the censor's changes, and the original text was not restored until the revolution of 1917.

Rimsky-Korsakov was one of the greatest masters of Russian music. His source of inspiration was Glinka's operatic style; he made use of both the purely Russian idiom and coloristic oriental melodic patterns; such works as his symphonic suite *Scheherazade* and *The Golden Cockerel* represent Russian orientalism at its best. In the purely Russian style, the opera *Snow Maiden* and the *Russian Easter Overture* are outstanding examples. The influence of Wagner and Liszt in his music was small; only in his opera *The Legend of the Invisible City of Kitezh* are there perceptible echoes from *Parsifal*. In the art of orchestration Rimsky-Korsakov had few equals; his treatment of instruments, in solo passages and in ensemble, was invariably idiomatic. In his treatise on orchestration he selected only passages from his own works to demonstrate the principles of practical and effective application of registers and tone colors. Although an academician in his general aesthetics, he experimented boldly with melodic progressions and ingenious harmonies that pointed toward modern usages. He especially favored the major scale with the lowered submediant and the scale of alternating whole tones and semitones (which in Russian reference works came to be termed as "Rimsky-Korsakov's scale"; in the score of his opera ballet *Mlada* there is an ocarina part tuned in this scale); in *The Golden Cockerel* and *Kashchei the Immortal* he applied dissonant harmonies in unusual superpositions; but he set for himself a definite limit in innovation, and severely criticized Richard Strauss, Debussy, and d'Indy for their modernistic practices.

Among his pedagogical works, the book on harmony (St. Petersburg, 1884; numerous subsequent eds. in Russian; in Eng., N.Y., 1930) is widely used in Russian music schools. He also publ. a book on orchestration (2 vols., St. Petersburg, 1913; ed. by Maximilian Steinberg; also available in French and in Eng.), and his collected articles were publ. in 1911, ed. by M. Gnessin. His autobiography (posthumous, 1909; 5th ed. by his son Andrei, supplemented and annotated, 1935), is a valuable document of the most important period of Russian music; it is publ. also in Eng. (N.Y., 1924; new ed., 1942), in French (Paris, 1938), etc. A complete ed. of Rimsky-Korsakov's works was begun in Moscow in 1946, edited by A. Rimsky-Korsakov and others; 49 vols. were publ. by 1970.

WORKS: OPERAS: *The Maid of Pskov* (1868–72; St. Petersburg, Jan. 13, 1873; 2d version, 1876–77; 3d version, 1891–92; St. Petersburg, April 18, 1895); *May Night* (1878–79; St. Petersburg, Jan. 21, 1880); *Snow Maiden* (1880–81; St. Petersburg, Feb. 10, 1882; 2d version, c.1895); *Mlada*, opera ballet (1889–90; St. Petersburg, Nov. 1, 1892); *Night before Christmas* (St. Petersburg, Dec. 10, 1895); *Sadko* (1894–96; Moscow, Jan. 7, 1898); *Mozart and Salieri* (1897; Moscow, Dec. 7, 1898); *Boyarynia Vera Sheloga* (originally the prologue to the 2d version of *The Maid of Pskov*; Moscow, Dec. 27, 1898); *The Tsar's Bride* (1898; Moscow, Nov. 3, 1899); *The Tale of Tsar Saltan* (Moscow, Nov. 3, 1900); *Servilia* (1900–1901; St. Petersburg, Oct. 14, 1902); *Kashchei the Immortal* (Moscow, Dec. 25, 1902); *The Commander* (1902–03; St. Petersburg, Oct. 16, 1904); *The Legend of the Invisible City of Kitezh* (1903–05; St. Petersburg, Feb. 20, 1907); *The Golden Cockerel* (1906–07; Moscow, Oct. 7, 1909). ARRANGEMENTS AND EDITIONS: He ed. a collection of 100 Russian folk songs, op. 24 (1876); harmonized 40 folk songs. After Dargomyzhsky's death, he orchestrated his posthumous opera *Kamennyi gost* (The Stone Guest); also orchestrated Borodin's *Prince Igor*; his greatest task of musical reorganization was the preparation for publication and performance of Mussorgsky's works; he reharmonized the cycle *Songs and Dances of Death* and the symphonic picture *Night on Bald Mountain*; orchestrated the opera *Khovanshchina*; rev. *Boris Godunov* (in melody and harmony, as well as in orchestration).

BIBL.: N. van Gilse van der Pals, *R.-K.* (Leipzig, 1914); M. Montagu-Nathan, *R.-K.* (London, 1916); N. van Gilse van der Pals, *R.-K.s Opernschaffen* (Leipzig, 1929); A. Rimsky-Korsakov, *R.-K.* (5 fascicles; Moscow, 1933, 1935, 1936, 1937, 1946; last vol. ed. by V. Rimsky-Korsakov); I. Markevitch, *R.-K.* (Paris, 1935); A. Solovtzov, *R.-K.* (Moscow, 1948; 2d ed., 1957); G. Abraham, *R.-K.: A Short Biography* (London, 1949); I. Kunin, *N. A. R.-K.* (Moscow, 1979); G. Seaman, *N. A. R.-K.: A Guide to Research* (N.Y., 1988).

Rinaldo di (da) Capua, Italian composer; b. Capua or Rome, c.1705; d. probably in Rome, c.1780. He came from the vicinity of Naples and seems to have been active chiefly in Rome, where Burney knew him in 1770, and where most of his operas were given (others were produced in Florence, Venice, London, and Paris). His career as a dramatic composer probably began in 1737. Thereafter he produced about 30 theatrical works with varying success, among them *Ciro riconosciuto* (Rome, Jan. 19, 1737), *Vologeso re de' Parti* (Rome, Carnival 1739), and *La Zingara* (Paris, June 19, 1753), his best work. He also composed numerous oratorios.

BIBL.: R. Bostian, *The Works of R. d. C.* (diss., Univ. of North Carolina, 1961).

Rinuccini, Ottavio, great Italian poet and librettist; b. Florence, Jan. 20, 1562; d. there, March 28, 1621. He was born into a family of the nobility and became a prominent courtier. He commenced writing verses for court entertainments about 1579, and was also active in the Accademia Fiorentina and the Accademia degli Alterati, taking the name "Il Sonnacchioso" (the somnolent one). He collaborated with Bardi in preparing intermedi for the wedding of the grand duke Ferdinando I (1589). Corsi and Peri then set his pastoral *Dafne* to music, which work is generally recognized as the 1st opera in the monodic style (Florence, 1598). Rinuccini's *Euridice*, with music by Peri, was performed in 1600, and another setting, by Caccini, in 1602. He also wrote the libretto of Monteverdi's *Arianna* (1608). These texts were republ. by A. Solerti in vol. 2 of *Gli albori del melodramma* (Milan, 1905) and by A. Della Corte, *Drammi per musica dal Rinuccini allo Zeno* (Turin, 1958).

BIBL.: F. Meda, *O. R.* (Milan, 1894); A. Civita, *O. R. ed il sorgere del melodramma in Italia* (Mantua, 1900); F. Raccamadoro-Ramelli, *O. R.: Studio biografico e critico* (Fabriano, 1900); A. Solerti, *Le origini del melodramma* (Turin, 1903); A. Della Corte, *O. R. librettista* (Turin, 1925); M. Schild, *Die Musikdramen O. R.s* (Würzburg, 1933).

Riotte, Philipp Jakob, German conductor and composer; b. St. Wendel, Saar, Aug. 16, 1776; d. Vienna, Aug. 20, 1856. He studied with André in Offenbach. In 1808 he settled in Vienna, where he conducted at the Theater an der Wien and produced there 48 works of his own, including operas and ballets. He was the author of the "tone picture" *Die Schlacht bei Leipzig* for Piano, which achieved extraordinary popularity in Germany.

BIBL.: G. Spengler, *Der Komponist P. J. R.* (diss., Univ. of Saarbrücken, 1973).

Ristori, Giovanni Alberto, Italian composer; b. probably in Bologna, 1692; d. Dresden, Feb. 7, 1753. He received his education from his father, a violinist in an Italian opera company, with whom he went to Dresden (1715) and obtained the post of director of the Polish chapel in Warsaw. He then was appointed chamber organist to the court of Saxony (1733), church composer (1746), and assistant conductor (1750). He wrote a number of operas for the Italian Opera in Dresden. His *Calandro*, staged at Pillnitz, near Dresden, on Sept. 2, 1726, was one of the earliest Italian comic operas produced in Germany, and so possesses historical significance beyond its intrinsic worth. Other operas produced in Dresden and in court theaters near Dresden were *Cleonice* (Aug. 15, 1718), *Un pazzo ne fà cento, ovvero Don Chisciotte* (Feb. 2, 1727), *Arianna* (Aug. 7, 1736), *Le Fate* (Aug. 10, 1736), etc. He also wrote oratorios, cantatas, and masses. Many of his MSS were destroyed during the siege of Dresden (1760) and the bombing of the city in World War II.

BIBL.: C. Mengelberg, *G. A. R.* (Leipzig, 1916).

Ritchie, Margaret (Willard), English soprano; b. Grimsby, June 7, 1903; d. Ewelme, Oxfordshire, Feb. 7, 1969. She studied at the Royal College of Music in London and with Plunket Greene, Agnes Wood, and Henry Wood. She established herself as a prominent concert artist early in her career, and also was the principal soprano of Frederick Woodhouse's Intimate Opera Co. Later she sang with the Sadler's Wells Opera in London (1944–47), at the Glyndebourne Festivals (1946–47), with the English Opera Group (from 1947), and at Covent Garden in London. From 1960 she taught voice in Oxford. She created the roles of Lucia in *The Rape of Lucretia* (1946) and of Miss Wordsworth in *Albert Herring* (1947). As a concert artist, she was much admired for her Schubert lieder recitals.

Ritter, Alexander, German violinist, conductor, composer, and poet; b. Narva, Estonia (of German parents), June 27, 1833; d. Munich, April 12, 1896. He was taken to Dresden in 1841, where he studied violin with Franz Schubert (namesake of the great composer), concertmaster of the Dresden Opera; he then studied at the Leipzig Cons. (1849–51) with Ferdinand David (violin) and E. F. Richter (theory). In 1854 he married Wagner's niece Franziska Wagner and settled in Weimar, where he entered into a close association with Liszt, Bülow, Cornelius, Raff, and others; he was 2d Konzertmeister in the orch. there (until 1856). He was conductor at the opera in Stettin (1856–58), where his wife was engaged as a soprano; he then lived in Dresden (1858–60), Schwerin (1860–62), and Würzburg (1863–82). When Bülow became conductor at the Hofkapelle in Meiningen (1882), Ritter followed him there and was made 2d Konzertmeister of the orch.; after Bülow's departure from Meiningen in 1886, Ritter moved to Munich. He wrote 2 operas, *Der faule Hans* (Munich, Oct. 15, 1885) and *Wem die Krone?* (Weimar, June 8, 1890), to his own librettos, and several symphonic poems in an intensely Romantic manner. Ritter's significance derives, however, not from his well-made but ephemeral compositions, but from his profound influence on young Richard Strauss; it was Ritter who encouraged Strauss in the creation of a new type of philosophical tone poem along the lines of "Musik als Ausdruck" (music as expression), a modern development of the art of Liszt, Wagner, and Berlioz. Ritter wrote the poem printed in the score of *Tod und Verklärung*.

Ritter, Peter, German cellist, violinist, conductor, and composer; b. Mannheim, July 2, 1763; d. there, Aug. 1, 1846. He studied violin and cello with his father, and then completed his theoretical studies under Abbé Vogler. He entered the Mannheim Court Orch. as a cellist in 1783, becoming its concertmaster in 1801, and in 1803 its conductor. He brought out in Mannheim his 1st opera, *Der Eremit auf Formentera* (Dec. 14, 1788; text by the celebrated poet A. von Kotzebue), which attained considerable vogue in Germany; some 20 more operas and Singspiels followed, but were not successful. In 1787 he married the famous actress Katharina Baumann (to whom Schiller had proposed), and in 1790 both were employed at the Hoftheater; his wife retired on a pension in 1819, and Ritter himself in 1823. Besides his operas, he wrote an oratorio, *Das verlorene Paradies* (1819).

BIBL.: W. Schulze, *P. R.* (Berlin, 1895); G. Schmidt, *P. R.* (diss., Univ. of Munich, 1924).

Ritter (real name, **Bennet**), **Théodore,** French pianist and composer; b. Nantes, April 5, 1841; d. Paris, April 6, 1886. He was a pupil of Liszt. He made successful European tours, and also publ. numerous solo pieces for piano, of which *Les Courriers* was a favorite. His operas, *Marianne* (Paris, 1861) and *La Dea risorta* (Florence, 1865), were unsuccessful.

Rivier, Jean, French composer and pedagogue; b. Villemonble, July 21, 1896; d. La Penne sur Huveaune, Nov. 6, 1987. His early musical training was interrupted by his enlistment in the French army during World War I. His health was severely damaged as a result of mustard gas, and it was only after a long recuperation that he was able to enter the Paris Cons. in 1922 to study with Emmanuel (music history), J. Gallon (harmony), and Caussade (counterpoint and fugue; premier prix, 1926). He also studied cello with Bazelaire. In subsequent years, he was active with various contemporary music societies in Paris, including Triton, of which he was president (1936–40). From 1948 to 1966 he taught composition at the Paris Cons. In 1970 he was awarded the Grand Prix for music of the City of Paris. He formed a style of composition in which he effectively combined elements of French Classicism and Impressionism. Among his works was the opera *Vénitienne* (Paris, July 8, 1937) and the oratorio *Christus Rex* for Contralto, Chorus, and Orch. (1966).

Rizzi, Carlo, Italian conductor; b. Milan, July 19, 1960. He took courses in piano, conducting, and composition at the Milan Cons., and then studied conducting with Delman in Bologna (1984) and Ferrara at the Accademia Musicale Chigiana in Siena (1985). In 1982 he made his debut conducting Donizetti's *L'Ajo nell'imbarazzo, o Don Gregorio* at Milan's Angelicum. In 1985 he was 1st prize winner in the new Toscanini conducting competition in Parma, where he then conducted *Falstaff*; subsequently he conducted throughout Italy. In 1988 he made his British debut at the Buxton Festival conducting *Torquato Tasso*, and in 1989 conducted *Il Barbiere di Siviglia* at the Australian Opera in Sydney and *Don Pasquale* at the Netherlands Opera in Amsterdam. He conducted *La Cenerentola* at London's Covent Garden in 1990. He was chosen to conduct *Il Trovatore* at the opening of the restored Teatro Carlo Felice in Genoa in 1991. In 1992 he made his first appearance at the Deutsche Oper in Berlin conducting *L'Italiana in Algeri*. Rizzi served as music director of the Welsh National Opera in Cardiff from 1992. In 1993 he made his first appearance in the United States as a guest conductor of the Chicago Sym. Orch. at the Ravinia Festival in Chicago. On Oct. 29, 1993, he made his Metropolitan Opera debut in New York conducting *La Bohème*.

Robbin, Catherine, Canadian mezzo-soprano; b. Toronto, Sept. 28, 1950. She studied at the Royal Cons. of Music in Toronto (B.A., 1977), and with Jacob Hamm and Phyliss Mailing in Vancouver, Audrey Langford in London, Ré Koster in Canada, and Sir Peter Pears in England. In 1972 she made her professional debut as a soloist in *Messiah* with the St. Catharines Sym. Orch. In 1978 she won the Caplet Award at the Concours international de chant in Paris and the Silver Medal at the Concours international in Geneva, and in 1979 the Gold Award in the Benson & Hedges International Competition for Concert Singers. In 1979 she sang Britten's Lucretia at the Aldeburgh Festival and in 1981 she made her N.Y. recital debut. She subsequently devoted herself principally to a career as a concert and oratorio singer with engagements in leading North American and European music centers. Her later operatic appearances included Tchaikovsky's Olga at the Lyons Opera (1984), and various Handelian roles, among them Cleone in Washington, D.C., and New York (1985), Orlando at the London Promenade Concerts (1989), and Rinaldo in Blackheath (1996). While her concert and oratorio performances have been especially successful in the Baroque repertoire, she has also won acclaim for her Mahler and Elgar.

Robertson, David, American conductor and composer; b. Santa Monica, Calif., July 19, 1958. He received training in horn, viola, conducting, and composition; in 1976 he became a student at the Royal Academy of Music in London and also attended the Hilversum conducting courses in 1979 and 1980, and concurrently studied privately with Kondrashin before attending the master class given by Kubelik in Lucerne in 1981. In 1980 he took 2d prize at the Nicolai Malko Competition in Copenhagen, and then was an assistant at the Deutsche Oper am Rhein in Düsseldorf in 1981. He was a resident conductor of the Jerusalem Sym. Orch. from 1985 to 1987. In 1992 he became music director of the Ensemble InterContemporain in Paris. In 1997 he won the Seaver/NEA conductors award. In addition to conducting contemporary scores in Paris, Robertson appeared as a guest conductor of the traditional repertoire with various European orchs. and in various opera houses. His compositions include an unfinished operatic trilogy: part 1, *Dangerous Children* (1989–90).

Robertson, Stewart (John), Scottish conductor and pianist; b. Glasgow, May 22, 1948. He studied at the Royal Scottish Academy of Music in Glasgow (1965–69), the Univ. of Bristol (1969–70), the Vienna Academy of Music (1975), and the Salzburg Mozarteum (1977). His conducting mentors were Suitner and Swarowsky; he also studied piano with Denis Matthews. In 1968–69 he was assistant chorus master of Glasgow's Scottish Opera and of the Edinburgh Festival. After serving as chorus master of the London City Singers (1970–72), he conducted at the Cologne Opera (1972–75). In 1975–76 he was music director of the Tanz Forum at the Zürich Opera, and then of the Scottish Opera Touring Co. (1976–79). From 1979 to 1982 he was music director of the Hidden Valley Chamber Orch. in California. From 1980 to 1988 he was assoc. conductor and director of the apprentice artists program of the Des Moines Metro Opera. In 1984–85 he was music director of the Mid-Columbia Sym. Orch., and in 1985–86 assistant conductor of the Oakland (Calif.) Sym. Orch. He subsequently was music director of the Santa Fe (N.M.) Sym. Orch. (from 1986), the Glimmerglass Opera in New York (from 1987), and the Florida Grand Opera (from 1998).

Robeson, Paul (Bustill), great black American bass and actor; b. Princeton, N.J., April 9, 1898; d. Philadelphia, Jan. 23, 1976. He first studied law (B.A., 1919, Rutgers Univ.; LL.B, 1923, Columbia Univ.). When his talent for singing and acting was discovered, he appeared in plays in the United States and England. He acted the part of the Emperor Jones in Eugene O'Neill's play and of Porgy in the Negro folk play by Du Bose and Dorothy Heyward. In 1925 he gave his first Negro spiritual recital in New York; he then toured in Europe. In 1927 he scored an enormous success in the musical *Show Boat*, becoming deservedly famous for his rendition of "Ol' Man River." In 1930 he appeared in the title role of Shakespeare's *Othello* in London. Returning to the United States, he continued to give recitals, but his outspoken admiration for the Soviet regime from the 1940s on interfered with the success of his career. In 1952 he was awarded the International Stalin Peace Prize ($25,000). During the summer of 1958, he made an extensive European tour. He continued to sing abroad until he was stricken with ill health and returned to the United States in 1963. His autobiography was publ. as *Here I Stand* (London, 1958).

BIBL.: E. Robeson, *P. R., Negro* (N.Y., 1930); S. Graham, *P. R.: Citizen of the World* (N.Y., 1946); M. Seton, *P. R.* (London, 1958); E. Hoyt, *P. R.: The American Othello* (London, 1967); D. Gilliam, *P. R., All American* (N.Y., 1977); P. Dean, *P. R.* (Garden City, N.Y., 1978); S. Robeson, *The Whole World in His Hands: A Pictorial Biography of P. R.* (Secaucus, N.J., 1981); L. Davis, *A P. R. Research Guide* (Westport, Conn., 1983); C. Bell, *P. R.'s Last Days in Philadelphia* (Bryn Mawr, 1986).

Robin, Mado, French soprano; b. Yseures-sur-Creuse, near Tours, Dec. 29, 1918; d. Paris, Dec. 10, 1960. She studied voice with Giuseppe Podestà. She then began her career as a concert artist; she made her operatic debut in 1945 as Gilda at the Paris Opéra and also sang at the Opéra Comique; she made guest appearances in Brussels, Liège, and San Francisco. She was best known for her performances in the roles of Lakmé and Lucia.

Robinson, Anastasia, English soprano, later contralto; b. in Italy, c.1692; d. Southampton, April 1755. She was the daughter of the portrait painter Thomas Robinson. After studying music with Croft and singing with Sandoni and Lindelheim, she began her career singing in private concerts at her father's home in London. Handel wrote the soprano part of his *Ode for Queen Anne's Birthday* (1714) for her and she made her operatic debut with his company in London in the pasticcio *Creso* on Jan. 27, 1714. She subsequently sang in several of Handel's operas, creating the role of Oriana in his *Amadigi di Gaula* on May 25, 1715. After his company was disbanded in 1717, she turned to contralto roles and appeared at London's Drury Lane in 1719–20. She then was a member of Handel's Royal Academy of Music (1720–24), where she created the roles of Elmira in *Floridante* (Dec. 9, 1721), Matilda in *Ottone, Rè di Germania* (Jan. 12, 1723), Teodata in *Flavio, Rè di Longobardi* (May 14, 1723), and Cornelia in *Giulio Cesare in Egitto* (Feb. 20, 1724). In 1724 she retired from the stage and married the Earl of Peterborough, who did not publicly acknowledge their marriage until 1735.

Robinson, Earl (Hawley), American composer; b. Seattle, July 2, 1910; d. in an automobile accident there, July 20, 1991. He studied with George McKay at the Univ. of Wash. (B.M. and teaching diploma, 1933), and then went to New York (1934), where he completed his training with Copland and Eisler; he was also active with the Workers Laboratory Theater and the Composers Collective of the Pierre Degeyter Club; it was during this period that he first gained notice via his topical songs. He won a Guggenheim fellowship (1942) and was active in Hollywood as a composer for films until he was blacklisted during the McCarthy era; he then returned to New York and served as head of the music dept. at Elisabeth Irwin High School (1958–65). The film *The House I Live In* (1946) was inspired by his song of that title (1942), which won him an Academy Award in 1947.

WORKS: DRAMATIC: MUSIC DRAMA: *Song of Atlantis* (1983). FOLK OPERAS: *Sandhog* (1951–54); *David of Sassoon* (1978). MUSICALS: *Processional* (1938); *Sing for Your Supper* (1939); *1 Foot in America* (1962); *Earl Robinson's America* (1976); *Listen for the Dolphin*, children's musical (1981). BALLET: *Bouquet for Molly* (1949). Also film scores.

Robinson, Faye, prominent black American soprano; b. Houston, Nov. 2, 1943. She studied at Bennett College in Greensboro, N.C., Texas Southern Univ. in Houston, and North Texas State Univ. in Denton. After winning 1st prize in the San Francisco Opera Auditions, she made her debut as Micaëla in *Carmen* at the N.Y. City Opera on Sept. 2, 1972; she was on its roster until 1979. She appeared with opera companies in Houston, Philadelphia, Pittsburgh, San Diego, and Washington, D.C.; she also sang widely in Europe and appeared frequently at the Aix-en-Provence Festival from 1974; she was a guest artist with the Paris Opéra, the Vienna State Opera, the Hamburg State Opera, the Frankfurt am Main Opera, the Bavarian State Opera in Munich, and others. She was also active as a concert artist. Her operatic roles include Donna Anna, Pamina, Constanze, Elvira in I Puritani, Gilda, Liù, Violetta, the 4 principal soprano roles in *Les Contes d'Hoffmann*, and Gounod's Juliette; she also sang in the premiere of Tippett's *The Mask of Time* (Boston, April 5, 1984).

Robinson, (Peter) Forbes, English bass; b. Macclesfield, May 21, 1926; d. London, May 13, 1987. He studied at Loughborough College, then went to Italy and took courses at the La Scala Opera School in Milan. He made his professional debut as Monterone at Covent Garden in London in 1954; he later sang at the Aldeburgh Festival and the Edinburgh Festival, and with the English Opera Group, the English National Opera, the Teatro Colón in Buenos Aires, and the Zürich Opera. He had an extensive repertoire; his roles included Figaro, Boris Godunov, Don Giovanni, King Philip, Claggart in *Billy Budd*, and Tippett's King Priam, a role he created in 1962; he also appeared widely as a concert artist.

Robinson, Michael Finlay, English musicologist; b. Gloucester, March 3, 1933. He was educated at the Univ. of Oxford (B.A., 1956; B.Mus., 1957; M.A., 1960; Ph.D., 1963, with the diss. *Neapolitan Opera, 1700–1780)*. He taught at the Royal Scottish Academy of Music in Glasgow (1960–61), the Univ. of Durham (1961–65), and McGill Univ. in Montreal (1965–70). In 1970 he joined the faculty of the Univ. of Wales College in Cardiff, where he was senior lecturer (1975–91) and prof. (1991–94), and head of the music dept. (1987–94). He publ. *Opera Before Mozart* (1966), *Naples and Neapolitan Opera* (1972), and a thematic catalog of the works of Paisiello (2 vols., 1990, 1993).

Robson, Christopher, Scottish countertenor; b. Falkirk, Dec. 9, 1953. He attended the Cambridge College of Arts and Technology (1970–72) and the Trinity College of Music in London (1972–73), and also received vocal instruction from Paul Esswood and Helga Moth. He was a member of various groups, among them the London Oratory Choir (1974–80), the Monteverdi Choir (1974–84), the Westminster Cathedral Choir (1980–85), the King's Consort (1981–86), and the New London Consort (from 1986). In 1976 he made his formal debut in a concert performance of Handel's *Samson* in London, and in 1979 his stage debut as Argones in Handel's

Sosarme in Birmingham. He made his first appearance at London's Covent Garden as Athamas in Handel's *Semele* in 1988. During the 1992–93 season, he sang Tolomeo in Handel's *Giulio Cesare* with the Scottish Opera in Glasgow. In the 1993–94 season, he appeared as Arsamenes in Handel's *Xerxes* at the English National Opera in London, a role he reprised during the 1995–96 season at the Lyric Opera in Chicago. He was engaged as Prince Orlovsky at the Bavarian State Opera in Munich in the 1997–98 season.

Rocca, Lodovico, Italian composer; b. Turin, Nov. 29, 1895; d. there, June 25, 1986. He studied with Orefice at the Milan Cons. and also attended the Univ. of Turin. From 1940 to 1966 he was director of the Turin Cons. He composed the operas *La morte di Frine* (1917–20; Milan, April 24, 1937), *In terra di leggenda* (1922–23; Milan, Sept. 28, 1933), *Il Dibuk* (1928–30; Milan, March 24, 1934), *Monte Ivnor* (1936–38; Rome, Dec. 23, 1939), and *L'uragano* (1942–51 Milan, Feb. 8, 1952).

BIBL.: M. Bruni, *L. R.* (Milan, 1963).

Rochberg, George, significant American composer and teacher; b. Paterson, N.J., July 5, 1918. He took courses in counterpoint and composition with Weisse, Szell, and Mannes at the Mannes College of Music in New York (1939–42); after military service during World War II, he took courses in theory and composition with Scalero and Menotti at the Curtis Inst. of Music in Philadelphia (B.Mus., 1947); he also studied at the Univ. of Pa. (M.A., 1948). He taught at the Curtis Inst. of Music (1948–54) and was in Rome on Fulbright and American Academy fellowships (1950). In 1951 he became music ed. of the Theodore Presser Co. in Philadelphia, and soon after was made its director of publications. In 1960 he joined the faculty of the Univ. of Pa. as chairman of the music dept., a position he held until 1968; he then continued on its faculty as a prof. of music, serving as Annenberg Prof. of the Humanities from 1979 until his retirement in 1983. He held 2 Guggenheim fellowships (1956–57; 1966–67) and was elected to membership in the American Academy and Inst. of Arts and Letters (1985) and was made a fellow of the American Academy of Arts and Sciences (1986) he was awarded honorary doctorates from the Univ. of Pa. (1985) and the Curtis Inst. of Music (1988). He publ. the study *The Hexachord and Its Relation to the Twelve-Tone Row* (Bryn Mawr, Pa., 1955). A collection of his writings was ed. by W. Bolcom as *The Aesthetics of Survival: A Composer's View of Twentieth-century Music* (Ann Arbor, 1984). In his style, he pursues the ideal of tonal order and logically justifiable musical structures; the most profound influence he experienced was that of Schoenberg and Webern; many of his early works follow the organization in 12 different notes; more recently, he does not deny himself the treasures of the sanctified past, and even resorts to overt quotations in his works of recognizable fragments from music by composers as mutually unrelated as Schutz, Bach, Mahler, and Ives, treated by analogy with the "objets trouvés" in modern painting and sculpture. Among his works are *The Confidence Man*, opera, after Melville (Santa Fe, July 31, 1982), *Phaedra*, monodrama for Mezzo-soprano and Orch. (1974–75; Syracuse, N.Y., Jan. 9, 1976), and incidental music to Ben Jonson's play *The Alchemist* (1965; N.Y., Oct. 13, 1968).

BIBL.: J. Dixon, *G. R.: A Bio-Bibliographic Guide to His Life and Works* (Stuyvesant, N.Y., 1991).

Rode, Wilhelm, German bass-baritone; b. Hannover, Feb. 17, 1887; d. Icking, near Munich, Sept. 2, 1959. He studied in Hannover. He made his operatic debut in 1908 as the Herald in *Lohengrin* in Erfurt, then sang in Bremerhaven (1912–14), Breslau (1914–21), and Stuttgart (1921–22). He was a leading member of the Bavarian State Opera in Munich (1922–30), the Vienna State Opera (1930–32), and the Deutsches Opernhaus in Berlin (1932–45), where he also served as Intendant (1935–45); he also appeared at London's Covent Garden and in other European opera houses. A member of the Nazi party, he was compelled to give up his career at the close of World War II. He became best known for his roles in Wagner's operas.

Röder, Martin, German composer and singing teacher; b. Berlin, April 7, 1851; d. Boston, June 7, 1895. After studying music in Berlin, he went to Milan, where he organized the Società del Quartetto Corale (1875), giving performances of vocal quartets. He then was a singing teacher in Berlin (1881–87), in Dublin (1887–92), and at the New England Cons. of Music in Boston (from 1892). He wrote 3 operas, including *Vera* (Hamburg, Nov. 1, 1881), and also publ. *Studi, critici, raccolti* (Milan, 1881) and *Dal Taccuino di un direttore di orchestra* (1881; Ger. tr. as *Aus dem Tagebuche eines wandernden Kapellmeisters*, 1884).

Rodgers, Joan, English soprano; b. Whitehaven, Nov. 4, 1956. After pursuing studies in Russian at the Univ. of Liverpool, she studied music at the Royal Northern College of Music in Manchester. In 1981 she was awarded the Kathleen Ferrier Memorial Scholarship, and then made her professional operatic debut at the Aix-en-Provence Festival in 1982 as Pamina. In 1983 she made first appearances in London with the English National Opera as the Wood Nymph in *Rusalka* and at Covent Garden as the Princess in *L'Enfant et les sortilèges*. She made her debut at the Glyndebourne Festival in 1989 as Mozart's Susanna, and then was soloist in Mahler's 4th Sym. at the Promenade Concerts in London. Her first appearance in Salzburg followed in 1991 when she sang at a Mozart Matinée. In 1992 she sang Handel's Cleopatra at the Scottish Opera in Glasgow, and also appeared as Mozart's Susanna in Florence. In 1995 she sang Mélisande with Opera North in Leeds. She returned to the Glyndebourne Festival in 1997 to sing Handel's Theodora. As a recitalist and a soloist with orchs., her engagements took her to the principal music centers of Europe. In 1988 she married **Paul Daniel**.

Rodolphe, Jean Joseph (actually, **Johann Joseph Rudolph**), Alsatian horn player, violinist, and composer; b. Strasbourg, Oct. 14, 1730; d. Paris, Aug. 12?, 1812. He studied horn with his father, Theodor Peter Rudolph, and took violin lessons with J. M. Leclair (c.1745); he was also a violinist in Bordeaux and Montpellier. He was in Parma as a violinist in the ducal orch. by 1754, where he received instruction in counterpoint from Traetta (from 1758). As a chamber virtuoso, became a member of the Stuttgart Court Orch. (c.1760), where he completed his studies with Jommelli. With the choreographer J. G. Noverre, he brought out several ballets. He appeared in Paris as a horn virtuoso at the Concert Spirituel in 1764, but continued to work in Stuttgart until returning to Paris in 1767 as a member of Prince Conti's orch.; he became a violinist and hornist in the Opéra orch. and later was active at the royal chapel. He befriended the young Mozart during the latter's visit to Paris in 1778. From 1784 until the Revolution, Rodolphe taught composition at the École Royale de Chant et de Déclamation; later he was prof. of solfège at the Paris Cons. (1798–1802). He publ. *Solfège ou Nouvelle méthode de musique* (Paris, 1784; 2d ed., rev., 1790) and *Théorie d'accompagnement et de composition* (Paris, c.1785).

WORKS: DRAMATIC: OPERAS: *Le Mariage par capitulation*, opéra comique (Paris, Dec. 3, 1764); *L'Aveugle de Palmire*, opéra comique (Paris, March 5, 1767); *Isménor*, opéra ballet (Versailles, Nov. 17, 1773). BALLETS: *Renaud et Armide* (Stuttgart, Feb. 11, 1761); *Psyche et l'Amour* (Stuttgart, Feb. 11, 1762); *Médée et Jason* (Ludwigsburg, Feb. 11, 1763; rev. by Noverre, Paris, Jan. 30, 1780); *Apollon et Daphne* (Kassel, *c*.1764; in collaboration with Deller); *Télèphe et Isménie ou La Mort d'Eurite* (Kassel, 1768; in collaboration with Deller); *Apelle et Campaspe* (Paris, Oct. 1, 1776).

Rodrigo, Joaquín, noted Spanish composer and teacher; b. Sagunto, Valencia, Nov. 22, 1901. He lost his sight as a child but revealed an innate talent for music and was sent to Paris, where he studied with Dukas at the Schola Cantorum; he returned to Madrid in 1939, where the Manuel de Falla chair was created for him at the Univ. in 1947. His music is profoundly imbued with Spanish melorhythms; his *Concierto de Aranjuez* for Guitar and Orch. (1939) became famous. Other works include *Pavana real*, ballet (1955), *El hijo fingido*, zarzuela (1964), and *La azuzena de Quito*, opera (1965).

BIBL.: F. Sopeña, *J. R.* (Madrid, 1946; 2d ed., rev., 1970); V. Vaya Pia, *J. R.: Su vida y su obra* (Madrid, 1977); V. Kamhi de Rodrigo, *De la mano de J. R.: Historia de nuestra vida* (Madrid, 1986; Eng. tr., 1992, as *Hand in hand with J. R.: My Life at the Maestro's Side*).

Rodriguez, Robert Xavier, American composer; b. San Antonio, June 28, 1946. He studied with Hunter Johnson and Kent Kennan at the Univ. of Texas in Austin (B.M., 1967; M.M., 1969), Stevens and Dahl at the Univ. of Southern Calif. in Los Angeles (D.M.A., 1975), Druckman at the Berkshire Music Center in Tanglewood, and Boulanger in Paris; he also attended master classes given by Maderna and Carter. He taught at the Univ. of Southern Calif. (1973–75) and at the Univ. of Texas in Dallas (from 1975); held a Guggenheim fellowship (1976) and was composer-in-residence of the Dallas Sym. Orch. (1982–85).

WORKS: DRAMATIC: OPERAS: *Le Diable amoureux* (1978; orch. suite, 1978); *Suor Isabella* (1982; Boston, May 3, 1984); *Tango*, chamber opera (1985); *Monkey See, Monkey Do*, children's opera (1986); *Frida* (1990); *The Old Majestic* (1991). BALLETS: *Estampie* (1980); *Meta-4* (1993). Also *Scrooge*, concert scene from *A Christmas Carol* for Bass-baritone, Chorus, and Orch. (El Paso, Texas, Dec. 9, 1994).

Rodríguez de HitaAntonio, Spanish composer; b. c.1724; d. Madrid, Feb. 21, 1787. From 1740 to 1757 he was maestro de capilla at Palencia Cathedral, where he publ. a book of advice to his pupils, *Consejos que a sus discípulos da don Antonio Rodríguez de Hita*. Then he held that title at the Convent of the Incarnation in Madrid. From 1768 he collaborated with the dramatist Ramón de la Cruz in a series of notable stage works impregnated with Spanish atmosphere; the best are the zarzuelas *Las segadoras de Vallecas* (Madrid, Sept. 13, 1768) and *Las labradoras de Murcia* (Madrid, Sept. 16, 1769). He also composed the Spanish opera *La Briseida* (Madrid, July 10, 1768).

Rodzinski, Artur, eminent Polish-born American conductor; b. Spalato, Dalmatia, Jan. 1, 1892; d. Boston, Nov. 27, 1958. He studied jurisprudence at the Univ. of Vienna; at the same time, he took lessons in piano with Sauer, composition with Schreker, and conducting with Schalk. He made his conducting debut in Lwów in 1920; subsequently he conducted at the Warsaw Opera. In 1926 he was appointed assistant conductor to Stokowski with the Philadelphia Orch.; concurrently he was head of the opera and orch. depts. at the Curtis Inst. of Music; in 1929 he was appointed conductor of the Los Angeles Phil.; after 4 seasons there, he was engaged as conductor of the Cleveland Orch., where he introduced the novel custom of presenting operas in concert form; on Jan. 31, 1935, he conducted the American premiere of Shostakovich's controversial opera *Lady Macbeth of the District of Mtzensk*. He became a naturalized American citizen in 1932. In 1943 he received his most prestigious appointment as conductor of the N.Y. Phil., but his independent character and temperamental ways of dealing with the management forced him to resign amid raging controversy in the middle of his 4th season (Feb. 3, 1947); almost immediately he was engaged as conductor of the Chicago Sym. Orch., but there, too, a conflict rapidly developed, and the management announced after a few months of the engagement that his contract would not be renewed, stating as a reason that his operatic ventures using the orch. were too costly. After these distressing American experiences, Rodzinski conducted mainly in Europe; in the autumn of 1958 he received an invitation to conduct at the Lyric Opera in Chicago, but after 3 performances of *Tristan und Isolde* (Nov. 1, 7, and 10), a heart ailment forced him to cancel his remaining appearances; he died in a Boston hospital.

BIBL.: H. Rodzinski, *Our Two Lives* (N.Y., 1976).

Rogatis, Pasqual de. See **De Rogatis, Pascual.**

Rogel, José, Spanish composer; b. Orihuela, Alicante, Dec. 24, 1829; d. Cartagena, Feb. 25, 1901. At a very early age he was taught music by the organist J. Cascales, and at 10 composed a Mass, which he conducted himself. After he finished his law studies in Valencia, he studied counterpoint with Pascual Pérez Cascón. He subsequently conducted at various theaters in Madrid, and in 1854 began his unusually successful career as a composer of zarzuelas, of which he wrote 81 (some in collaboration). Among the best are *El Joven Telémaco, Las Amazones del Tormes, El Rey Midas, Los Infiernos de Madrid, Genoveva de Brabante*, and *Pablo y Virginia*.

Roger, Gustave-Hippolyte, famous French tenor; b. La Chapelle St.-Denis, near Paris, Dec. 17, 1815; d. Paris, Sept. 12, 1879. He was a pupil of Blès Martin at the Paris Cons., making his debut as Georges in Halévy's *L'Éclair* at the Paris Opéra Comique in 1838. He then was at the Paris Opéra (from 1848), where he created the role of the Prophète in Meyerbeer's opera (1849); later he toured in Germany. While he was hunting in the fall of 1859, the accidental discharge of his gun injured his right arm so severely that it had to be amputated. An artificial arm proved ineffective, and he was obliged to retire from the stage in 1861. From 1868 until his death he was a prof. of singing at the Paris Cons. He publ. his memoirs as *Le Carnet d'un ténor* (Paris, 1880).

BIBL.: A. Laget, *G.-H. R.: Notice biographique* (Paris, 1865).

Roger, Victor, French composer and music critic; b. Montpellier, July 22, 1853; d. Paris, Dec. 2, 1903. He studied at the École Niedermeyer in Paris. He composed some 30 operettas, of which the following were brought out in Paris with considerable success: *Joséphine vendue par ses soeurs* (March 20, 1886), *Oscarine* (Oct. 15, 1888), *Le Fétiche* (March 13, 1890), *Samsonnet* (Nov. 26, 1890), *Miss Nicol-Nick* (Jan. 23, 1895), *Sa Majesté l'Amour* (Dec. 24, 1896), *L'Auberge du Tohu-Bohu* (Feb. 10, 1897), *Les Fêtards* (Oct. 28, 1897), *L'Agence Crook et Cie* (Jan. 22, 1898), *La Petite Tâche* (March 26, 1898), and *Le Jockey malgré lui* (Dec. 4, 1902). After his death, 3 completely finished scores were found: *La Fille de Fra Diavolo, La Princesse de Babylone*, and *Adélaïde*.

Roger-Ducasse, Jean (-Jules Aimable), French composer and teacher; b. Bordeaux, April 18, 1873; d. Le-Taillan-Médoc, near Bordeaux, July 19, 1954. He studied at the Paris Cons. with Fauré (composition), Pessard (harmony), Gédalge (counterpoint), and de Bériot. In 1902 he won the 2d Prix de Rome for the cantata *Alcyone*. In 1909 he was appointed inspector of singing in the Paris schools; subsequently he was a prof. of ensemble at the Paris Cons.; from 1935 to 1940 he taught composition there; he then retired to Bordeaux. His first work to be played in public was a *Petite suite* for Orch. (Paris, March 5, 1898). He adopted a pleasing style of Impressionism; his symphonic pieces enjoyed considerable success, without setting a mark for originality. Among his works were *Orphée*, mimodrama (1913; St. Petersburg, Jan. 31, 1914), and *Cantegril*, comic opera (1930; Paris, Feb. 9, 1931). His autobiography was publ. in *L'Écran des musiciens* (1930).

BIBL.: L. Ceillier, *R.-D.* (Paris, 1920); *Catalogue de l'oeuvre de R.-D.* (Bordeaux, 1955).

Rogers, Bernard, distinguished American composer and pedagogue; b. N.Y., Feb. 4, 1893; d. Rochester, N.Y., May 24, 1968. He began piano lessons when he was 12; after leaving school at 15, he was employed in an architectural firm while training in architecture at Columbia Univ.; he subsequently received instruction in theory from Hans van den Berg, composition from Farwell, and harmony and composition from Bloch in Cleveland; returning to New York, he continued his studies with Goetschius at the Inst. of Musical Art (1921); later he held a Guggenheim fellowship (1927–29), which made it possible for him to train with Bridge in England and Boulanger in Paris. He first won recognition as a composer with his orch. work *To the Fallen* (1918; N.Y., Nov. 13, 1919), on the strength of which he received a Pulitzer Traveling Scholarship. He taught at the Cleveland Inst. of Music (1922–23), the Hartt School of Music in Hartford, Conn. (1926–27), and the Eastman School of Music in Rochester, N.Y. (1929–67), where he also served as chairman of the composition dept. In 1947 he was elected to membership in the National Inst. of Arts and Letters. Other works include the following operas (all 1st perf. in Rochester, N.Y.): *Deirdre* (1922), *The Marriage of Aude* (May 22, 1931), *The Warrior* (1944; N.Y., Jan. 11, 1947), *The Veil* (Bloomington, Ind., May 18, 1950), and *The Nightingale* (1954); also 2 oratorios: *The Passion* (1942; Cincinnati, May 12, 1944) and *The Light of Man* (1964). He publ. a valuable manual, *The Art of Orchestration* (N.Y., 1951).

BIBL.: F. Koch, *Reflections on Composing: Four American Composers: Elwell, Shepherd, R., Cowell* (Pittsburgh, 1983).

Rogers, Nigel (David), English tenor, conductor, and teacher; b. Wellington, Shropshire, March 21, 1935. He studied at King's College, Cambridge (1953–56), in Rome (1957), in Milan (1958–59), and with Hüsch at the Munich Hochschule für Musik (1959–64). He became a singer with the Studio der frühen Musik in Munich in 1961 and later acquired a fine reputation as an interpreter of Baroque music. He was a prof. of singing at the Royal College of Music in London (from 1978) and founded the vocal ensemble Chiaroscuro for the performance of Italian Baroque music (1979).

Rogister, Jean (François Toussaint), Belgian violist, pedagogue, and composer; b. Liège, Oct. 25, 1879; d. there, March 20, 1964. He studied violin, viola, horn, and composition at the Liège Cons.; he was head of the viola classes there (1900–45) and at the Brussels Cons. (1945–48) and played in various orchs.; he was also founder of the Liège Quartet (1925), with which he toured extensively. His style of composition followed the precepts of Franck, but upon occasion he introduced into his music some modernistic impressionistic sonorities. Among his works are the lyric drama *Lorsque minuit sonna* (1930) and the oratorio *The Bells* for Soprano and 8 Instruments, after Edgar Allan Poe (1924).

BIBL.: J. Servais, *J. R.: Un Musicien du coeur* (1972).

Rögner, Heinz, German conductor; b. Leipzig, Jan. 16, 1929. He studied piano with Hugo Steuer, viola with Gutschlicht, and conducting with Egon Bölsche at the Hochschule für Musik in Leipzig. He was a conductor at the German National Theater in Weimar (1951–54), then led the opera school at the Hochschule für Musik in Leipzig (1954–58). From 1958 to 1962 he was chief conductor of the Great Radio Orch. in Leipzig; from 1962 to 1973 he was Generalmusikdirektor of the State Opera in East Berlin. In 1973 he became chief conductor of the (East) Berlin Radio Sym. Orch. and also appeared as a guest conductor in Europe. He served as music director of the Yomiuri Nippon Sym. Orch. in Tokyo (1985–91).

Rogowski, Ludomir (Michal), Polish composer and conductor; b. Lublin, Oct. 3, 1881; d. Dubrovnik, March 14, 1954. He was a student of Noskowski (composition) and Mlynarski (conducting) at the Warsaw Cons., and then of Nikisch and Riemann in Leipzig. In 1909 he went to Vilnius as director of the Organ School. He also founded the Vilnius Sym. Orch. in 1910. From 1912 to 1914 he was a theater conductor in Warsaw. In 1926 he settled in Dubrovnik. In 1938 he was awarded the Polish State Music Prize.

WORKS: DRAMATIC: OPERAS: *Tamara* (1918); *Un Grand Chagrin de la petite Ondine* (1919); *La Sérénade inutile* (1921); *Królewicz Marko* (1930). BALLETS: *Bajka* (1922); *Kupala* (1925).

Roig, Gonzalo, Cuban conductor and composer; b. Havana, July 20, 1890; d. there, June 13, 1970. He played violin in theater orchs. In 1922 he organized the Orquesta Sinfónica de la Habana. He wrote zarzuelas, among which *Cecilia Valdés* enjoyed considerable success. In 1912 he wrote the song "Quiereme mucho," which became a popular hit.

Rokitansky, Hans, Freiherr von, Austrian bass; b. Vienna, March 8, 1835; d. Schloss Laubegg, Styria, Nov. 2, 1909. He received his training in Bologna and Milan. After making his concert debut in London in 1856, he made his operatic debut at the Théâtre-Italien in Paris in 1857 as Oroveso. He sang in Prague from 1862 to 1864. From 1864 to 1893 he was a member of the Vienna Court Opera, and then taught at the Vienna Cons. from 1894. Among his finest roles were Sarastro, Leporello, Caspar, Heinrich, and the Landgrave. His brother, Victor, Freiherr von Rokitansky (b. Vienna, July 9, 1836; d. there, July 17, 1896), was a singer and composer of songs who taught at the Vienna Cons. (1871–80).

Roland-Manuel (real name, **Roland Alexis Manuel Lévy**), French composer and writer on music; b. Paris, March 22, 1891; d. there, Nov. 1, 1966. He was a pupil of Roussel and d'Indy; he also studied privately with Ravel. In 1947 he became a prof. at the Paris Cons. In his compositions, he adopted the French neoclassical style, close to Roussel's manner; however, he became best known as a perspicacious critic, publishing, in Paris, 3 vols. on Ravel: *Maurice Ravel et son oeuvre* (1914; 2d ed., rev., 1926; Eng. tr., 1941), *Maurice Ravel et son oeuvre dramatique* (1928), and *À la gloire Maurice Ravel* (1938; 2d ed., 1948; Eng. tr., 1947); also monographs on Satie (1916), Honegger (1925) and Falla (1930).

WORKS: DRAMATIC: *Isabelle et Pantalon*, opéra-bouffe (Paris, Dec. 11, 1922); *Le Diable amoureux*, light opera (1929); *L'Écran des jeunes filles*, ballet (Paris, May 16, 1929); *Elvire*, ballet on themes of Scarlatti (Paris, Feb. 8, 1937). Also *Jeanne d'Arc*, oratorio (1937).

Rolandi, Gianna, gifted American soprano; b. N.Y., Aug. 16, 1952. Her first contact with opera came through her mother, herself a singer, and by the age of 15 she had already become acquainted with much of the operatic repertoire. She then enrolled at the Curtis Inst. of Music in Philadelphia (B.M., 1975). While still a student there, she was contracted to sing at the N.Y. City Opera, with which she made an impressive debut as Olympia in *Les Contes d'Hoffmann* (Sept. 11, 1975). On Dec. 26, 1979, she made her Metropolitan Opera debut in New York as Sophie in *Der Rosenkavalier*. In 1981 she made her European debut at the Glyndebourne Festival singing Zerbinetta. In 1982 she sang the title role in a televised production of *Lucia di Lammermoor* with the N.Y. City Opera, receiving flattering notices from the press. She scored an outstanding success as Bianca in Rossini's *Bianca e Falliero* at its U.S. premiere at the Greater Miami Opera in 1987. In 1989 she appeared as Cimarosa's Curiazio at the Rome Opera. In 1993 she sang Despina in Chicago. In 1996 she toured the United States as a soloist with the BBC Sym. Orch. of London. She was married to **Andrew Davis**.

Rolfe Johnson, Anthony, English tenor and conductor; b. Tackley, Nov. 5, 1940. He was a student of Ellis Keeler at the Guildhall School of Music in London, and later of Vera Rozsa. He gained experience singing in the chorus and appearing in small roles at the Glyndebourne Festivals between 1972 and 1976. In 1973 he made his formal operatic debut with the English Opera Group in *Iolanta*. In 1978 he made his first appearance with the English National Opera in London as Don Ottavio. He sang Tamino with the Welsh National Opera in Cardiff in 1979. In 1983 he appeared as Aschenbach at Glasgow's Scottish Opera. In 1987 he made his first appearance at the Salzburg Festival in Schmidt's *Das Buch mit sieben Siegeln*. On Dec. 22, 1988, he made his debut at London's Covent Garden as Jupiter in Handel's *Semele*. In 1990 he returned to the Salzburg Festival to sing his first operatic role there, Monteverdi's Orfeo. From 1990 he served as director of singing at the Britten-Pears School in Snape, but also continued his singing career. In 1994 he appeared as Peter Grimes in the reopening of the Glyndebourne Festival and sang Aschenbach at the Metropolitan Opera in New York. As a concert artist, he received many engagements with leading orchs. in Europe and North America. In 1997 he made his debut as a conductor with *Orfeo* in St. Louis.

Rolland, Romain, famous French author and musicologist; b. Clamecy, Nièvre, Jan. 29, 1866; d. Vézelay, Yonne, Dec. 30, 1944. He was educated in Paris at the École Normale Supérieure (1886–89), the École de Rome (1889–91), and the Sorbonne (doctorat ès lettres, 1895, with the diss. *Les Origines du théâtre lyrique moderne: L'Histoire de l'opéra en Europe avant Lully et Scarlatti*; publ. in Paris, 1895; 4th ed., 1936). He then was a prof. of music history at the École Normale Supérieure until becoming the first prof. of music history at the Sorbonne (1903); he was also director of the École des Hautes Sociales (1903–09). In 1900 he organized the first international congress for the history of music in Paris, and read a paper on *Les Musiciens italiens en France sous Mazarin et "l'Orfeo" de Luigi Rossi* (publ. 1901); with J. Combarieu, he ed. the transactions and the papers read as *Documents, mémoires et voeux* (1901). In 1901 he founded, with J. Combarieu (ed.), P. Aubry, M. Emmanuel, L. Laloy, and himself as principal contributors, the fortnightly *Revue d'Histoire et Critique Musicales*. From 1913 he resided in Switzerland, but in 1938 returned to France and took up his residence at Vézelay.

Rolland's writings exhibit sound scholarship, broad sympathy, keen analytical power, well-balanced judgment, and intimate acquaintance with the musical milieu of his time. The book by which he is most widely known is *Jean-Christophe*, a musical novel remarkable for its blending of historical accuracy, psychological and aesthetic speculation, subtle psychological analysis, and romantic interest; it won him the Nobel Prize in literature (1915). The 1st vol. was publ. in 1905, the last (10th) in 1912 (Eng. tr., N.Y., 1910–13). Rolland's other works include *Paris als Musikstadt* (1904; in Strauss's series *Die Musik*; rewritten and publ. in French as *Le Renouveau in Musiciens d'aujourd'hui*); *Beethoven* (Paris, 1903; 3d ed., 1927, as *La Vie de Beethoven*; Eng. tr., 1969); *La Vie de Haendel* (Paris, 1906; 2d ed., 1910; Eng. tr., 1916; rev. and enl. by F. Raugel, 1974); *Voyage musical au pays du passé* (1920; Eng. tr., 1922); *Beethoven: Les Grandes Époques créatrices* (4 vols., Paris, 1928–45; Eng. tr., 1964); *Goethe et Beethoven* (1930; Eng. tr., 1931); *Beethoven: Le Chant de la Résurrection* (1937); essays in various journals he collected and publ. in 2 vols. as *Musiciens d'autrefois* (1908; 6th ed., 1919; Eng. tr., 1915) and *Musiciens d'aujourd'hui* (1908; 8th ed., 1947; Eng. tr., 1914).

BIBL.: P. Seippel, *R. R.: L'Homme et l'oeuvre* (Paris, 1913); S. Zweig, *R. R.: Der Mann und das Werk* (Frankfurt am Main, 1921; Eng. tr., N.Y., 1921); J. Bonnerot, *R. R.: Sa vie, son oeuvre* (Paris, 1921); E. Lerch, *R. R. und die Erneuerung der Gesinnung* (Munich, 1926); M. Lob, *Un Grand Bourguignon, R. R.* (Auxerre, 1927); C. Sénéchal, *R. R.* (Paris, 1933); M. Doisy, *R. R.* (Brussels, 1945); R. Argos, *R. R.* (Paris, 1950); W. Starr, *A Critical Bibliography of the Published Writings of R. R.* (Evanston, Ill., 1950); J. Robichez, *R. R.* (Paris, 1961); E. Bondeville, *R. R. à la recherche de l'homme dans la création artistique* (Paris, 1966).

Roller, Alfred, influential Austrian stage designer and painter; b. Vienna, Oct. 2, 1864; d. there, June 21, 1935. He studied painting at the Vienna Academy. Roller became closely associated with Mahler at the Vienna Court Opera. With Gustav Klimt, Egon Schiele, Oskar Kokoschka, et al., he founded the Vienna Sezession, a group of artists whose ideals were at variance with the established orthodoxy of the day. His ideal as a stage designer was to integrate the elements of space, color, and light in an effort to harmonize stage decors with the music and stage action. His slogan, "space, not pictures," embodied his attempt to discard naturalism in opera productions in favor of a new symbolism. In his production of *Tristan und Isolde* (1903), which inaugurated his 30-year tenure as chief designer at the Vienna Opera, he allowed a different color to symbolize the mood of each act. The subtle lighting effects he achieved prompted one reviewer to declare "here is the conception of the music of light." His Wagner productions, which continued with the first 2 parts of the *Ring* cycle, set new standards throughout Europe. They also had a strong influence on later productions at Bayreuth. In his production of *Don Giovanni* (1905), he introduced his "Roller towers," focal points in a stylized stage picture which, remaining on stage throughout the opera, served different purposes as the action progressed. He was also active in Berlin, Salzburg, and Bayrueth. He designed the Dresden premiere productions of *Elektra* (1909) and *Der Rosenkavalier* (1911). His subtle and harmonious use of color was also in evidence for the premiere production of *Die Frau ohne Schatten* (Vienna, 1919). Roller taught at the Vienna School of Arts and Crafts for 25 years.

Röllig, Carl Leopold, German glass-harmonica player, inventor, and composer; b. Hamburg, *c.*1735; d. Vienna, March 4, 1804. He was music director of Ackermann's theater company in Hamburg (1764–69; 1771–72). After taking up the glass harmonica about 1780, he toured widely. He invented the Orphika (*c.*1795) and the Xänorphika (1801), pianos with bows instead of hammers. He settled in Vienna (1791). He wrote a comic opera, *Clarisse* (Hamburg, Oct. 10, 1771), and various pieces for glass harmonica, including 4 concertos. He publ. *Über die Harmonika* (Berlin, 1787), *Versuch einer musikalischen Intervallentabelle* (Leipzig, 1789), *Orphica, ein musikalisches Instrument erfunden von C.L. Röllig* (Vienna, 1795), and *Versuch einer Anleitung zur musikalischen Modulation durch mechanische Vortheile* (Vienna, 1799); his *Miscellanea, figurierter Kontrapunkt* remains in MS.

Rollin, Jean, French composer; b. Paris, Aug. 3, 1906; d. Bayeux, Calvados, Aug. 30, 1977. He studied composition at the Paris Cons. with N. Gallon, and musicology with Pirro and Masson. His works included *Gringoue*, opera (1965).

Roman, Stella (real name, **Florica Vierica Alma Stela Blasu**), Romanian-American soprano; b. Cluj, March 25, 1904; d. N.Y., Feb. 12, 1992. She was a student of Pfeiffer in Cluj, Cosma, Vulpescu, and Pessione in Bucharest, Narducci and Poli-Randaccio in Milan, and Baldassare-Tedeschi and Ricci in Rome. In 1932 she made her operatic debut in Piacenza. In 1940 she made her first appearance at Milan's La Scala as the Empress in *Die Frau ohne Schatten*. On Jan. 1, 1941, she made her Metropolitan Opera debut in New York as Aida. She remained on its roster until 1950, becoming best known for such roles as Gioconda, Amelia, Leonora in *Il Trovatore*, Desdemona, and Tosca.

Romani, Carlo, Italian composer, nephew of **Pietro Romani**; b. Avelino, May 24, 1824; d. Florence, March 4, 1875. He studied with Palafuti (piano) and Picchianti (composition), and then completed his studies under his uncle. He set to music the recitatives of *Der Freischütz* for its 1st Italian performance (Florence, Feb. 3, 1843). He composed the operas (all produced in Florence): *Tutti amanti* (1847), *Il Mantello* (1852), *I Baccanali di Roma* (1854), and *Ermellina ossia Le Gemme della corona* (1865); also an oratorio, *San Sebastiano* (1864).

Romani, Felice, renowned Italian librettist; b. Genoa, Jan. 31, 1788; d. Moneglia, Jan. 28, 1865. He was educated at the Univ. of Pisa. He wrote about 100 librettos for Mayr, Winter, Vaccai, Rossini, Bellini, Donizetti, Pacini, Ricci, et al.

BIBL.: F. Regli, *Elogio a F. R.* (Turin, 1865); L. Lianovosani, *Saggio bibliografico relativo ai melodrammi di F. R.* (Milan, 1878); E. Branca (R.'s wife), *F. R. ed i più riputati maestri di musica del suo tempo* (Turin, 1882); C. Paschetto, *F. R.* (Turin, 1907); M. Rinaldi, *F. R.* (Rome, 1965).

Romani, Pietro, Italian conductor, teacher, and composer, uncle of **Carlo Romani**; b. Rome, May 29, 1791; d. Florence, Jan. 11, 1877. He studied with Fenaroli, and then became conductor at the Teatro della Pergola in Florence; he also taught singing at the Istituto Musicale there. He wrote 2 operas, *Il Qui pro quo* (Rome, 1817) and *Carlo Magno* (Florence, 1823), and ballet music, but he is remembered chiefly for his aria *Manca un foglio*, for Bartolo in *Il Barbiere de Siviglia*, which he wrote for the production of the opera in Florence in 1816 as a substitute for Rossini's original aria *A un dottor della mia sorte*, which presented some vocal difficulties. Romani's aria was long retained in many productions of the opera.

Romberg, Andreas Jakob, German violinist and composer, cousin of **Bernhard Heinrich Romberg**; b. Vechta, near Munster, April 27, 1767; d. Gotha, Nov. 10, 1821. He was the son of the clarinetist and violinist Gerhard Heinrich Romberg (b. Aug. 8, 1745; d. Nov. 14, 1819). He studied with his father, then made his debut at age 7 in Münster with his cousin; the 2 subsequently toured (with their fathers) to Frankfurt am Main (1782) and Paris (1784, 1785). They played in the Bonn electoral orch. from 1790 until the French invasion of 1793 compelled them to flee to Hamburg; after playing in the opera orch. at the Ackermann Theater, they set out on a tour of Italy (1795–96). They also visited Vienna in 1796 and were befriended by Haydn; then returned to Italy. After another sojourn in Paris (1801), Andreas Romberg settled in Hamburg and devoted himself mainly to composition; he was then called to Gotha as court Kapellmeister (1815). He had 2 sons: Heinrich Maria (b. Paris, April 4, 1802; d. Hamburg, May 2, 1859) became concertmaster of the St. Petersburg Imperial Opera orch. (1827) and later served as its music director; Ciprian Friedrich (b. Hamburg, Oct. 28, 1807; d. there, Oct. 14, 1865) was 1st cellist of the St. Petersburg German Opera orch. (1835–45).

WORKS: OPERAS: *Der blaue Ungeheuer* (1790–93; not perf.); *Die Macht der Musik* (1791; not perf.); *Die Nebelkappen* (1793; unfinished); *Der Rabe* (Hamburg, April 7, 1794); *Don Mendoza* (Paris, 1802; in collaboration with B. H. Romberg); *Point de bruit* (Paris, 1810); *Die Ruinen zu Paluzzi* (Hamburg, Dec. 27, 1811); *Die Grossmut des Scipio* (Gotha, 1816).

BIBL.: K. Stephenson, *A. R.: Ein Beitrag zur Hamburger Musikgeschichte* (Hamburg, 1938).

Romberg, Bernhard Heinrich, German cellist and composer, cousin of **Andreas Jakob Romberg**; b. Dinklage, Nov. 11, 1767; d. Hamburg, Aug. 13, 1841. He was the son of the bassoonist and cellist Bernhard Anton Romberg (b. Münster, March 6, 1742; d. there, Dec. 14, 1814), who played in the orch. of the Prince-Bishop of Münster (1776–1803). Bernhard Heinrich began his career in Munster when he appeared with his cousin at age 7. They toured with their fathers thereafter, making visits to Frankfurt am Main (1782) and Paris (1784, 1785); after playing in the Bonn electoral orch. (1790–93), they fled in the face of the French invasion and went to Hamburg, where they were members of the opera orch. at the Ackermann Theater. They then toured Italy (1795–96) and visited Vienna (1796), where they became friends of Haydn. After further travels in Italy and another visit to Paris (1801), the cousins pursued separate careers. Bernhard Heinrich visited Spain in 1801. He served as prof. of cello at the Paris Cons. (1801–03), then joined the Berlin Royal Court Orch. (1805). He visited Russia in 1807 and England in 1814; he was Berlin Hofkapellmeister (1816–19). In 1820 he went to Hamburg, which he made his home with the exception of another Berlin sojourn (1826–31); he also made extensive tours as a virtuoso. He publ. *Méthode de violoncelle* (Berlin, 1840). He had 2 children who pursued musical careers: Bernhardine (b. Hamburg, Dec. 14, 1803; d. there, April 26, 1878), a concert singer, and Karl (b. Moscow, Jan. 16, 1811; d. Hamburg, Feb. 6, 1897), a cellist in the St. Petersburg German Opera orch. (1830–42).

WORKS: DRAMATIC: *Der Schiffbruch*, operetta (1791; not perf.); *Die wiedergefundene Statue*, opera (c.1792; not perf.); *Don Mendoza*, opera (Paris, 1802; in collaboration with A. Romberg); *Ulisse und Circe*, opera (Berlin, July 27, 1807); *Rittertreue*, opera (Berlin, Jan. 31, 1817); *Daphne und Agathokles*, ballet (Berlin, 1818); *Alma*, opera (Copenhagen, May 15, 1824); also incidental music.

BIBL.: H. Schäfer, *B. R.: Sein Leben und Wirken* (diss., Univ. of Bonn, 1931).

Romberg, Sigmund, famous Hungarian-born American composer; b. Nagykanizsa, July 29, 1887; d. N.Y., Nov. 9, 1951. He studied at the Univ. of Bucharest and in Vienna (with Heuberger). In 1909 he went to the United States as an engineer and later became a naturalized American citizen; he settled in New York in 1913 and devoted himself to composing for the theater. He composed over 70 operettas, including *The Midnight Girl* (Feb. 23, 1914), *The Blue Paradise* (with E. Eysler; N.Y., Aug. 5, 1915), *Maytime* (N.Y., Aug. 16, 1917), *Blossom Time* (on Schubert's melodies; N.Y., Sept. 29, 1921), *The Rose of Stamboul* (March 7, 1922), *The Student Prince* (N.Y., Dec. 2, 1924), *The Desert Song* (N.Y., Nov. 30, 1926), *My Maryland* (N.Y., Sept. 12, 1927), *The New Moon* (Sept. 19, 1928), and *Up in Central Park* (N.Y., Jan. 27, 1945).

BIBL.: E. Arnold, *Deep in My Heart* (N.Y., 1949); J. Koegel, *The Film Operettas of S. R.* (thesis, Calif. State Univ., 1984).

Ronald, Sir Landon (real name, **Landon Ronald Russell**), English pianist, conductor, and composer; b. London, June 7, 1873; d. there, Aug. 14, 1938. He was a son of the composer Henry Russell and brother of the impresario Henry Russell. He entered the Royal College of Music in London, where he studied composition with Parry and also attended the classes of Stanford and Parratt. He first embarked on a concert career as a pianist, but soon turned to conducting light opera and summer sym. concerts; was conductor of the New Sym. Orch. of London (1909–14) and of the Scottish Orch. in Glasgow (1916–20). He served as principal of the Guildhall School of Music and Drama in London (1910–38). Ronald was knighted in 1922. He composed an operetta, *A Capital Joke*, a ballet, *Britannia's Realm* (1902; for the coronation of King Edward VII), and a scenic spectacle, *Entente cordiale* (1904; to celebrate the triple alliance of Russia, France, and England); also about 300 songs. He publ. 2 autobiographical books: *Variations on a Personal Theme* (London, 1922) and *Myself and Others* (London, 1931).

Roncaglia, Gino, Italian musicologist and composer; b. Modena, May 7, 1883; d. there, Nov. 27, 1968. He studied composition with Sinigaglia, then devoted himself to musical biography.

WRITINGS: *Giuseppe Verdi* (Naples, 1914; 2d ed., rev., 1940, as *L'ascensione creatice di Giuseppe Verdi*; 3d ed., 1951); *La Rivoluzione musicale italiana* (Milan, 1928); *Rossini l'olimpico: Vita e opere* (Milan, 1946; 2d ed., 1953); *Invito alla musica* (Milan, 1946; 4th ed., 1958); *Invito all' opera* (Milan, 1949; 4th ed., 1958); *La Cappella musicale del Duomo di Modena* (Florence, 1957); *Galleria verdiana: Studi e figure* (Milan, 1959).

Ronconi, family of Italian musicians:

(1) Domenico Ronconi, tenor and singing teacher; b. Lendinara, near Rovigo, July 11, 1772; d. Milan, April 13, 1839. He made his debut in Venice (1797). After singing in St. Petersburg (1801–05), he returned to Italy and appeared at Milan's La Scala (1808), where he was chosen to create roles in operas by Mosca, Orlandi, and Lamberti. He then sang at the Italian Opera in Vienna (1809) and in Paris (1810). After further appearances in Italy, he was a member of the Munich Hof- und Nationaltheater (1819–29); then returned to his homeland and opened his own singing school in Milan. He had 3 sons who became musicians.

(2) Giorgio Ronconi, baritone; b. Milan, Aug. 6, 1810; d. Madrid, Jan. 8, 1890. He studied with his father, making his debut as Valdeburgo in *La Straniera* in Pavia (1831). He then went to Rome, where he sang in the premieres of Donizetti's *Il Furioso all'isola di San Domingo* and *Torquato Tasso* in 1833; subsequently he sang in the premieres of that composer's *Il campanello* in Naples (1836), *Pia de' Tolomei* in Venice (1837), *Maria di Rudez* in Venice (1838), *Maria Padilla* in Milan (1841), and *Maria di Rohan* in Vienna (1843). From 1839 he sang at Milan's La Scala, where he was chosen by Verdi to create the title role in *Nabucco* (1842). In 1842 he made his London debut at Her Majesty's Theatre, and later made frequent appearances at Covent Garden (1847–66); he also sang in St. Petersburg (1850–60). After a sojourn in New York (1866–72), he went to Granada and founded his own singing school, then was prof. of singing at the Madrid Cons. (from 1874). Although his voice was mediocre, he won distinction for his dramatic abilities.

(3) Felice Ronconi, singing teacher; b. Venice, 1811; d. St. Petersburg, Sept. 10, 1875. He received his musical training from his father. He was active as a singing teacher in Würzburg, Frankfurt am Main, Milan, and St. Petersburg. He wrote a method on the teaching of singing and also some songs.

(4) Sebastiano Ronconi, baritone; b. Venice, May 1814; d. Milan, Feb. 6, 1900. He studied with his father, making his debut as Torquato Tasso in Lucca (1836). He later sang throughout Europe and the United States, and spent his last years teaching voice in Milan.

Ronga, Luigi, eminent Italian musicologist; b. Turin, June 19, 1901; d. Rome, Sept. 11, 1993. After obtaining an arts degree from the Univ. of Turin, he went to Dresden to pursue his training in musicology. In 1930 he received his libera docenza. In 1926 he became a prof. at the Palermo Cons. In 1930 he settled in Rome, where he was a teacher at the Accademia di Santa Cecilia and at the Pontifico Istituto di Musica Sacra. He then was a lecturer (1938–50) and subsequently a prof. (1950–71) at the Univ. of Rome. He was ed. of *Rassegna musicale* (1928–29) and *Rivista musicale italiana* (1954–55).

WRITINGS: *Per la critica wagneriana* (Turin, 1928); *Gerolamo Frescobaldi, organista vaticano, nella storia della musica strumentale* (Turin, 1930); *Lezioni di storia della musica* (2 vols., Rome, 1933, 1935; new ed., 1991); *Rossini* (Florence, 1939); *Lineamenti del romanticismo musicale* (Rome, 1943); *La musica nell'antichità* (Rome, 1945); *Claude Debussy e l'impressionismo musicale* (Rome, 1946); *Il dramma musicale di Richard Wagner* (Rome, 1947); *Arte e gusto nella musica, dell'ars nova a Debussy* (Milan, 1956); *Bach, Mozart, Beethoven: Tre problemi critici* (Venice, 1956); *The Meeting of Poetry and Music* (N.Y., 1956); *La musica nell'età barocca* (Rome, 1959); *Il linguaggio musicale romantico* (Rome, 1960); *L'esperienza storica della musica* (Bari, 1960); *Introduzione a "La Diana schernita" di Cornacchioli* (Rome, 1961); *La musica europa nella seconda metà dell'Ottocento* (Rome, 1961); *Storia della musica* (2 vols., Rome, 1962–63).

BIBL.: *Scritti in onore di L. R.* (Milan and Naples, 1973).

Rongé, Jean-Baptiste, Belgian composer and translator; b. Liège, April 1, 1825; d. there, Oct. 28, 1882. He was a pupil at the Liège Cons., winning the 2d Belgian Prix de Rome (1851). He wrote occasional cantatas and other pieces. A meeting with the poet André van Hasselt directed his interests toward literary work, and in collaboration they tr. into French many standard operas. After van Hasselt's death (1874), Rongé returned to composing, producing a comic opera, *La Comtesse d'Albany* (Liège, 1877).

Ronnefeld, Peter, German conductor and composer; b. Dresden, Jan. 26, 1935; d. Kiel, Aug. 6, 1965. He studied with Blacher in Berlin and Messiaen in Paris. After winning the Hilversum conducting competition in 1955, he was assistant conductor at the Vienna State Opera (1958–61); he served as chief conductor at the Theater der Stadt Bonn (1961–63); he then was Generalmusikdirektor in Kiel from 1963 until his death. As a conductor, he specialized in modern music, but he also excelled in the Romantic repertoire; his own opera, *Die Ameise* (Düsseldorf, Oct. 21, 1961), had a fine reception. He also wrote a chamber opera, *Nachtausgabe* (Salzburg, 1956); 2 ballets, *Peter Schlemihl* (1955–56) and *Die Spirale* (1961); Concertino for Flute, Clarinet, Horn, Bassoon, and Strings (1950); *Sinfonie '52* (1952); *Rondo* for Orch. (1954); *2 Episodes* for Chamber Orch. (1956); cantata, *Quartar* (1958); chamber music; songs.

Ronzi de Begnis (originally, **Ronzi**), **Giuseppina,** notable Italian soprano; b. Milan, Jan. 11, 1800; d. Florence, June 7, 1853. She married **Giuseppe de Begnis** in 1816, and that same year made her operatic debut in Bologna. She then appeared in Genoa, Florence, and Bergamo. In 1818 she sang Ninetta in *La gazza ladra* in Pesaro under Rossini's direction, and soon acquired a fine reputation for her performances in his operas. In 1819 she went to Paris with her husband, where she sang Rosina opposite his Don Basilio in the first production there of Rossini's *Il Barbiere di Siviglia* at the Théâtre-Italien on Oct. 26 of that year. She and her husband continued to appear in Paris until 1821, when they proceeded to London. She made her debut there at the King's Theatre on May 19, 1821, singing Fiorilla opposite her husband's Don Geronio in Rossini's *Il turco in Italia*. She continued to sing with her husband until they were separated in 1825, and she subsequently pursued her career in Naples, where she created roles in Mercadante's *Zaira* (1831) and Donizetti's *Fausta* (1832), *Sancia di Castiglia* (1832), *Buondelmonte* (1834), and *Roberto Devereux* (1837). Donizetti also chose her to create the title role in his *Gemma di Vergy* at Milan's La Scala on Dec. 26, 1834. In 1843 she returned to London to sing Norma in an English-language staging at Covent Garden. In addition to her Italian portrayals, she had marked success in Mozartian roles.

Roocroft, Amanda, English soprano; b. Coppull, Feb. 9, 1966. She was a student of Barbara Robotham at the Royal Northern College of Music in Manchester. After winning the Kathleen Ferrier Prize in 1988, she made her formal operatic debut in 1990 as Sophie at the Welsh National Opera in Cardiff, and then appeared as Pamina with the Glyndebourne Touring Opera. In 1991 she made her first appearance at London's Covent Garden as Pamina, and also was engaged as Fiordiligi at the Glyndebourne Festival. She portrayed the latter role in Paris, Amsterdam, and Lisbon in 1992, and then at the Bavarian State Opera in Munich in 1993. In 1993 she also appeared as Ginevra in *Ariodante* at the English National Opera in London, and then returned to the Glyndebourne Festival as Donna Anna and to Munich as Amelia Boccanegra in 1994. She sang Fiordiligi upon her return to Covent Garden in 1995. After singing in recital at London's Wigmore Hall in 1997, she once again returned to the Glyndebourne Festival as Kát'a Kabanová in 1998.

Roos, Robert de, Dutch composer; b. The Hague, March 10, 1907; d. there, March 18, 1976. He was a student of Wagenaar (composition) at the Royal Cons. of Music in The Hague. After further studies in Paris (1926–34) with Koechlin, Roland-Manuel, and Milhaud (composition), Philipp (piano), and Monteux (conducting), he completed his training in his homeland with Dresden. He was a cultural attaché at the Dutch embassy in Paris (1947–56), and then was first secretary for press and cultural affairs for the Dutch embassies in Caracas (1957–62), London (1962–67), and Buenos Aires (1967). Among his works were *Kaartspel* (Card Game), ballet (1930), and *Landelijke Comedie* (Pastoral Comedy), dance pantomime (1937–39); also Chamber oratorio (1928) and incidental music.

Roosevelt, J(oseph) Willard, American composer, pianist, and teacher; b. Madrid, Jan. 16, 1918. He was the grandson of President Theodore Roosevelt. He studied at Harvard (1936–38), at the Longy School of Music in Cambridge, Mass. (1936–38; 1940–41), with Boulanger in Paris and Gargenville (1938–39), at the N.Y. College of Music (composition and piano diplomas, 1947), and at the Hartt College of Music in Hartford, Conn. (B.Mus., 1959; M.Mus., 1960). In addition to his appearances as a pianist, he lectured on music at Columbia Univ. (1961), Fairleigh-Dickinson Univ. (1964–67), and the N.Y. College of Music (1967–68). Among his compositions is the opera *And the Walls Came Tumbling Down* (1974–76).

Rootering, Jan-Hendrik, German bass; b. Wedingfeld, March 18, 1950. He first studied with his father, a voice teacher, and then at the Hamburg Hochschule für Musik. In 1980 he made his operatic debut as Colline at the Hamburg State Opera, and then sang there regularly. He also appeared at the Bavarian State Opera in Munich from 1982, and was made a Bavarian Kammersänger in 1989. In 1983 he portrayed King Marke in Frankfurt am Main. On Jan. 15, 1987, he made his Metropolitan Opera debut in New York as the Landgrave, and subsequently sang such roles there as Claggart, Sparafucile, and Pogner (1993). In 1987 he was engaged as Orestes in Geneva, Sarastro at London's Covent Garden, and Marcel in *Les Huguenots* at the Deutsche Oper in Berlin. He sang Gurnemanz at the Opéra de la Bastille in Paris in 1997. He also sang as a soloist with orchs. and as a recitalist. Among his other roles were Fasolt, Falstaff, and Baron Ochs.

Rootham, Cyril (Bradley), English organist, teacher, and composer; b. Bristol, Oct. 5, 1875; d. Cambridge, March 18, 1938. He studied music with his father, Daniel Rootham (1837–1922); he won classical and musical scholarships at St. John's College, Cambridge (B.A., 1897; Mus.B., 1900; M.A., 1901; Mus.Doc., 1910) and finished at the Royal College of Music in London under Stanford, Parratt, and Barton. He was organist (from 1901) and a lecturer (from 1913) at St. John's College, Cambridge; also conductor of the Univ. Musical Soc. there (1912–36). His career as a composer was very much bound to the musical life of Cambridge. He brought out his opera, *The 2 Sisters*, there on Feb. 14, 1922.

Ropartz, Joseph Guy (Marie), French conductor, teacher, and composer; b. Guingamp, Côtes-du-Nord, June 15, 1864; d. Lanloup-par-Plouha, Côtes-du-Nord, Nov. 22, 1955. He entered the Paris Cons. as a pupil of Dubois and Massenet, then took lessons in organ and composition from Franck, who remained his chief influence in composition. From 1894 to 1919 he was director of the Cons. and conductor of the sym. concerts at Nancy; from 1919 to 1929 he conducted the Municipal Orch. and was director of the Cons. in Strasbourg.

WORKS: DRAMATIC: OPERA: *Le Pays* (1910; Nancy, Feb. 1, 1912). BALLETS: *Prélude dominical et 6 pièces à donner pour chaque jour de la semaine* (1929); *L'Indiscret* (1931). INCIDENTAL MUSIC TO: *Pêcheur d'Islande* (1891); *Oedipe à Colonne* (1914).

BIBL.: F. Lamy, *J. G.-R.: L'homme et l'oeuvre* (Paris, 1948); L. Kornprobst, *J. G.-R.* (Strasbourg, 1949); *Livre du centenaire de J. G.-R.* (Paris, 1966).

Rorem, Ned, brilliant American composer, pianist, and writer; b. Richmond, Ind., Oct. 23, 1923. His father, C. Rufus Rorem, was a medical economist, and his mother, Gladys Miller Rorem, was a civil rights activist. Following piano lessons as a youth, he entered the American Cons. in Chicago in 1938 to study harmony with Sowerby. After further training with Nolte at Northwestern Univ. (1940–42) and Scalero at the Curtis Inst. of Music in Philadelphia (1942–44), he went to New York and received private lessons in orchestration from Virgil Thomson (1944) and then pursued training in composition with Wagenaar at the Juilliard School of Music (B.S., 1946; M.S., 1948). During the summers of 1946 and 1947 he studied with Copland at the Berkshire Music Center in Tanglewood. In 1949 he went to Paris, where he rapidly absorbed French musical culture and mastered the French language. After a sojourn in Morocco (1949–51), he lived in Paris until 1957, where he found a patroness in Vicomtesse Noailles and moved in the circle of modern French composers. In 1951 he received a Fulbright fellowship and in 1957 a Guggenheim fellowship. From 1959 to 1961 he was composer-in-residence at the State Univ. of N.Y. at Buffalo. In 1965 he became a prof. of composition at the Univ. of Utah, where he later was composer-in-residence (until 1967). He received an award from the National Inst. of Arts and Letters in 1968. In 1971 and 1975 he received ASCAP-Deems Taylor awards for his outstanding achievements as a writer. In 1976 he won the Pulitzer Prize in music for his *Air Music* for Orch. In 1978 he received a 2d Guggenheim fellowship. In 1980 he became a teacher of composition at the Curtis Inst. of Music. In 1980, 1982, 1985, and 1990 he served as composer-in-residence at the Santa Fe Chamber Music Festival. Rorem is one of America's most distinguished and original compositional craftsmen. A born linguist, he has a natural feeling for vocal line and for prosody of text. He is without question one of the finest composers of art songs America has produced. An elegant stylist in French as well as in English, he has publ. various books recounting with gracious insouciance his encounters in Paris and New York.

WORKS: DRAMATIC: OPERAS: *Cain and Abel* (1946); *A Childhood Miracle* (1952; N.Y., May 10, 1955); *The Robbers* (1956; N.Y., April 14, 1958); *Miss Julie* (N.Y., Nov. 4, 1965; rev. 1978; N.Y., April 5, 1979); *3 Sisters Who Are Not Sisters* (1968; Philadelphia, July 24, 1971); *Bertha* (1968; N.Y., Nov. 26, 1973); *Fables*, 5 short operas (1970; Martin, Tenn., May 21, 1971); *Hearing* (1976; N.Y., March 15, 1977; arranged from a song cycle, 1966). MUSICAL COMEDY: *The Ticklish Acrobat* (1958). BALLETS: *Lost in Fear* (1945); *Death of the Black Knight* (1948); *Ballet for Jerry* (1951); *Melos* (1951); *Dorian Gray* (1952); *Early Voyagers* (1959); *Excursions* (1965). ORATORIOS: *An American Oratorio* for Tenor, Chorus, and Orch. (1984; Pittsburgh, Jan. 4, 1985); *Goodbye My Fancy*, oratorio for Alto, Baritone, Chorus, and Orch. (1988; Chicago, Nov. 8, 1990). Also incidental music.

WRITINGS: (all publ. in N.Y.): *The Paris Diary of Ned Rorem* (1966; reprint, 1983, with *The New York Diary*, as *The Paris and New York Diaries*); *The New York Diary* (1967; reprint, 1983, with *The Paris Diary of Ned Rorem*, as *The Paris and New York Diaries*); *Music from the Inside Out* (1967); *Music and People* (1968); *Critical Affairs: A Composer's Journal* (1970); *Pure Contraption: A Composer's Essays* (1973); *The Final Diary, 1961–1972* (1974; reprint, 1983, as *The Later Diaries of Ned Rorem*); *An Absolute Gift: A New Diary* (1977); *Setting the Tone: Essays and a Diary* (1983); *The Nantucket Diary of Ned Rorem, 1973–1985* (1987); *Settling the Score: Essays on Music* (1988); *Knowing When to Stop: A Memoir* (1994).

BIBL.: A. McDonald, *N. R.: A Bio-Bibliography* (Westport, Conn., 1989).

Rosa, Carl (real name, **Karl August Nikolaus Rose**), German violinist, conductor, and opera impresario; b. Hamburg, March 22, 1842; d. Paris, April 30, 1889. At 12 he made tours as a violinist in England, Denmark, and Germany; he studied further in the conservatories of Leipzig (1859) and Paris. He was concertmaster at Hamburg (1863–65), and gave a concert at the Crystal Palace in London (March 10, 1866). He toured in the United States with Bateman, meeting Euphrosyne Parepa and marrying her in New York in 1867. They organized an English opera company and toured America until 1871, then returned to London. After his wife's death in 1874, he produced opera in English in various London theaters, forming the Carl Rosa Opera Co. (1875), which gave regular performances at the Theatre Royal at Drury Lane (from 1883). Following Rosa's death, the company became notably successful as a touring enterprise, being granted the title of the Royal Carl Rosa Opera Co. by Queen Victoria in 1893. It remained active until 1958.

Rosbaud, Hans, eminent Austrian conductor; b. Graz, July 22, 1895; d. Lugano, Dec. 29, 1962. He studied at the Hoch Cons. in Frankfurt am Main. He was director of the Hochschule für Musik in Mainz (1921–30) and also conducted the City Orch. there. He served as 1st Kapellmeister of the Frankfurt am Main Radio and of the Museumgesellschaft concerts (1928–37), then was Generalmusikdirektor in Münster (1937–41) and in Strasbourg (1941–44); subsequently he was appointed Generalmusikdirektor of the Munich Phil. (1945). In 1948 he became chief conductor of the Sym. Orch. of the Southwest Radio in Baden-Baden, and in 1957, music director of the Tonhalle Orch. in Zürich. He particularly distinguished himself as a conductor of modern works. He conducted the first performance of Schoenberg's *Moses und Aron* (concert perf., Hamburg, 1954); he also conducted its first stage performance (Zürich, 1957).

BIBL.: J. Evans, *H. R.: A Bio-Bibliography* (N.Y., 1992).

Rosell, Lars-Erik, Swedish composer, teacher, and organist; b. Nybro, Aug. 9, 1944. He studied organ (1962–68) and then was a composition student of Ingvar Lidholm at the Stockholm Musikhögskolan (1968–72); he then taught counterpoint there (from 1973). He was also active as an organist, becoming well known for his advocacy of contemporary scores. In his music, he often requires improvisation from performers.

WORKS: DRAMATIC: OPERAS: *Nattesang*, chamber opera (Copenhagen, Dec. 15, 1974); *Tillfalligt avbrott*, chamber opera (Stockholm, Dec. 12, 1981); *Amedée*, chamber opera (1983–85); *Illusionisten* (1994–95; Stockholm, Sept. 26, 1996). OTHER: *Efter syndafallet*, dramatic scene for Soprano, Alto, Baritone, and Instrumental Ensemble, after Arthur Miller's play *After the Fall* (Stockholm, Feb. 15, 1973); *Visiones prophetae*, biblical scene for Soloists, 3 Choruses, Wind Orch., Harp, Organ, and 2 Double Basses (Lund, June 27, 1974); *Ordens kalla*, scenic cantata (Stockholm, Nov. 7, 1980).

Rosen, Charles (Welles), erudite American pianist, teacher, and writer on music; b. N.Y., May 5, 1927. He began piano studies when he was only 4. Between the ages of 7 and 11 he studied at the Juilliard School of Music in New York, and then took piano lessons with Moriz Rosenthal and Hedwig Kanner-Rosenthal (1938–44). He continued his training with the latter (1944–52) and also received lessons in theory and composition from Karl Wiegl. He concurrently studied music history at Princeton Univ.

(B.A., 1947; M.A., 1949), where he took his Ph.D. in Romance languages in 1951. In 1951 he made his debut in New York, and subsequently appeared as a soloist with major orchs. and as a recitalist. He was assistant prof. of modern languages at the Mass. Inst. of Technology (1953–55). In 1971 he became prof. of music at the State Univ. of N.Y. at Stony Brook. In 1976–77 he also was the Ernest Bloch Prof. of Music at the Univ. of Calif. at Berkeley. As a pianist, Rosen has garnered notable distinction for his insightful interpretations of Bach, Beethoven, and Debussy, and for his traversal of such 20th-century composers as Schoenberg, Webern, Boulez, and Carter. He has contributed brilliant articles on various subjects to various publications. In 1972 he received the National Book Award for his distinguished vol. *The Classical Style: Haydn, Mozart, Beethoven* (N.Y., 1971). His subsequent books included *Arnold Schoenberg* (N.Y., 1975), *Sonata Forms* (N.Y., 1980; 2d. ed., rev., 1988), *Frontiers of Meaning: Three Informal Lectures on Music* (N.Y., 1994), and *The Romantic Generation* (Cambridge, Mass., 1995).

Rosen, Jerome (William), American clarinetist, teacher, and composer; b. Boston, July 23, 1921. He studied at New Mexico State Univ. in Las Cruces, and with William Denny and Sessions at the Univ. of Calif. at Berkeley (M.A., 1949); then, as recipient of a Ladd Prix de Paris, he went to Paris, where he continued his studies with Milhaud and also obtained a diploma as a clarinetist (1950). Upon his return to the United States, he became a teacher at the Univ. of Calif. at Davis (1952), was made an assoc. prof. (1957) and a prof. (1963), and also served as director of its electronic music studio; he was made prof. emeritus (1988).

WORKS: DRAMATIC: OPERA: *Emperor Norton of the U.S.A.* (1990). CHAMBER OPERA: *Calisto and Melibea* (1978; Davis, Calif., May 31, 1979). MUSICAL PLAY: *Emperor Norton Lives!* (1976). DANCE SATIRES: *Search* (1953); *Life Cycle* (1954).

Rosenberg, Hilding (Constantin), important Swedish composer and teacher; b. Bosjökloster, Ringsjön, Skåne, June 21, 1892; d. Stockholm, May 19, 1985. He studied piano and organ in his youth, and then was active as an organist. He went to Stockholm in 1914 to study piano with Andersson, then studied composition with Ellberg at the Stockholm Cons. (1915–16) and later took a conducting course there. He made trips abroad from 1920, then studied composition with Stenhammer and conducting with Scherchen. He was a répétiteur and assistant conductor at the Royal Opera in Stockholm (1932–34); he also appeared as a guest conductor in Scandinavia and later in the United States (1948), leading performances of his own works; likewise he was active as a teacher, numbering Bäck, Blomdahl, and Lidholm among his students. Rosenberg was the foremost Swedish composer of his era. He greatly influenced Swedish music by his experimentation and stylistic diversity, which led to a masterful style marked by originality, superb craftsmanship, and refinement.

WORKS: DRAMATIC: OPERAS: *Resa till Amerika* (Journey to America; Stockholm, Nov. 24, 1932; orch. suite, Stockholm, Sept. 29, 1935); *Spelet om St. Örjan*, children's opera (1937; rev. 1941); *Marionetter* (1938; Stockholm, Feb. 14, 1939; 2 suites for Small Orch., 1926; overture and dance suite, 1938); *De två konungadöttrarna* (The 2 Princesses), children's opera (Swedish Radio, Stockholm, Sept. 19, 1940); *Lycksalighetens ö* (The Isle of Bliss; 1943; Stockholm, Feb. 1, 1945; *Vindarnas musik* for Orch. from the opera, 1943); *Josef och hans bröder* (Joseph and His Brothers), opera oratorio, after Thomas Mann (1946–48; Swedish Radio, Stockholm: part 1, May 30, 1946; part 2, Dec. 19, 1946; part 3, Sept. 9, 1947; part 4, Jan. 23, 1948; *Partita* for Orch. from the opera oratorio, 1948); *Kaspers fettisdag* (Kasper's Shrove Tuesday), chamber opera (1953; Swedish Radio, Stockholm, Feb. 28, 1954); *Porträtett* (The Portrait), radio opera after Gogol (1955; Swedish Radio, Stockholm, March 22, 1956; rev. 1963); *Hus med dubbel ingång* (The House with 2 Doors), lyric comedy after Calderón (1969; Stockholm, May 24, 1970). BALLETS: *Eden* (1946; based on the Concerto No. 1 for Strings, 1946); *Salome* (1963; Stockholm, Feb. 28, 1964; based on the *Metamorfosi sinfoniche Nos. 1* and *2*, 1963); *Sönerna* (The Sons; Swedish TV, Stockholm, Dec. 6, 1964; based on the *Metamorfosi sinfoniche No. 3*, 1964); *Babels torn* (The Tower of Babel; 1966; Swedish TV, Stockholm, Jan. 8, 1968; based on the Sym. for Wind and Percussion, 1966). PANTOMIME: *Yttersta domen* (The Last Judgment; 1929; not perf.; 2 preludes and 2 suites for Orch. from the pantomime, 1929). MELODRAMAS: *Prometheus och Ahasverus* (Swedish Radio, Stockholm, April 27, 1941); *Djufars visa* (Djufar's Song; Swedish Radio, Stockholm, Dec. 18, 1942; suite for Orch. from the melodrama, 1942). INCIDENTAL MUSIC TO: Plays and films. ORATORIOS: *Den heliga natten* (The Holy Night; Swedish Radio, Stockholm, Dec. 27, 1936); *Perserna* (The Persians; 1937; not perf.); *Huvudskalleplats* (Calvary), for Good Friday (Swedish Radio, Stockholm, April 15, 1938; rev. 1964–65); *Svensk lagsaga* (Swedish Radio, Stockholm, Feb. 24, 1942); *Hymnus* (1965; Swedish Radio, Stockholm, July 24, 1966).

BIBL.: M. Pergament, *H. R., a Giant of Modern Swedish Music* (Stockholm, 1956); P. Lyne, *H. R.: Catalogue of Works* (Stockholm, 1970).

Rosenhain, Jacob (also, **Jakob** or **Jacques**), German pianist and composer; b. Mannheim, Dec. 2, 1813; d. Baden-Baden, March 21, 1894. He was a child prodigy, making his debut in Frankfurt am Main when he was 8; he studied with Kalliwoda, Jakob Schmitt, and Schnyder von Wartensee. In 1837 he went to Paris and London, and continued to travel until 1870, when he settled as a teacher in Baden-Baden. Among his works were the operas *Der Besuch im Irrenhause* (Frankfurt am Main, Dec. 29, 1834), *Le Démon de la nuit* (Paris, March 17, 1851), and *Le Volage et jaloux* (Baden-Baden, Aug. 3, 1863) His brother Eduard Rosenhain (b. Mannheim, Nov. 16, 1818; d. Frankfurt am Main, Sept. 6, 1861) was also a noteworthy pianist and teacher.

BIBL.: E. Kratt-Harveng, *Jacques R., Komponist und Pianist: Ein Lebensbild* (Baden-Baden, 1891).

Rosenshein, Neil, American tenor; b. N.Y., Nov. 27, 1947. He studied at Wilkes College in Wilkes-Barre, Pa. (1967), and with Jennie Tourel and others at N.Y.'s Juilliard School (1969). He made his operatic debut as Count Almaviva in *Il Barbiere di Siviglia* in Cocoa Beach, Fla. (1972); his first appearance in Europe was as Tom Rakewell in *The Rake's Progress* with the Netherlands Opera in Amsterdam (1982). He made frequent appearances with the major U.S. and European opera houses thereafter, and also sang with the leading orchs. On June 2, 1986, he made his Covent Garden debut in London as Lensky in *Eugene Onegin*. He made his Metropolitan Opera debut in New York as Alfredo in *La Traviata* on Nov. 19, 1987. In 1988 he sang in the premiere of Argento's *The Aspern Papers* in Dallas. On Dec. 19, 1991, he created the role of Leon in Corigliano's *The Ghosts of Versailles* at the Metropolitan Opera. In 1994 he appeared in Santa Fe as Cavaradossi. Among his other roles are Belmonte in *Die Entführung aus dem Serail*, Tamino in *Die Zauberflöte*, Oberon, Werther, Alfred in *Die Fledermaus*, Alfonso in Korngold's *Violanta*, and the title role in Stravinsky's *Oedipus Rex*.

Rosenstock, Joseph, Polish-born American conductor; b. Kraków, Jan. 27, 1895; d. N.Y., Oct. 17, 1985. He studied in Kraków and at the Vienna Cons. and received instruction from Franz Schreker. He was assistant conductor at the Stuttgart Opera (1919–20) and a conductor (1920–22) and Generalmusikdirektor (1922–25) at the Darmstadt Opera; he then was Generalmusikdirektor at the Wiesbaden Opera (1927–29). On Oct. 30, 1929, he made his Metropolitan Opera debut in New York conducting *Die Meistersinger von Nürnberg*; returning to Germany, he became Generalmusikdirektor at the Mannheim National Theater in 1930. As a Jew, he was removed from his post by the Nazis in 1933; he then conducted the Jüdisches Kulturbund in Berlin until 1936. He went to Tokyo to become conductor of the Nippon Phil. (1936); as an alien, he lost his post and was removed to Karuizawa with the Japanese attack on Pearl Harbor in 1941; after his liberation in 1945 he returned to Tokyo to help reorganize musical life under the U.S. occupation forces. In 1946 he settled in the United States; he became a naturalized citizen in 1949. He became a conductor at the N.Y. City Opera in 1948, and subsequently was its general director (1952–56); after serving as music director of the Cologne Opera (1958–60), he conducted at the Metropolitan Opera in New York (1960–69). His wife was **Herta Glaz**.

Rosenthal, Harold (David), English music editor and critic; b. London, Sept. 30, 1917; d. there, March 19, 1987. He received his B.A. degree from Univ. College, London, in 1940. In 1950 he launched, with the Earl of Harewood, the magazine *Opera* and was its ed. (1953–86). He was archivist of the Royal Opera House in London (1950–56). Rosenthal contributed to many European and American music journals, and also wrote numerous biographical entries on singers for *The New Grove Dictionary of Music and Musicians* (1980). In 1983 he was made an Officer of the Order of the British Empire. His publications, all publ. in London, included *Sopranos of Today* (1956), *Two Centuries of Opera at Covent Garden* (1958), ed. with J. Warrack, *The Concise Oxford Dictionary of Opera* (1964; 2d ed., rev., 1979), and *Covent Garden: A Short History* (1967). He wrote an autobiography, *My Mad World of Opera* (1982).

Rosenthal, Manuel (Emmanuel), French composer and conductor; b. Paris (of a French father and a Russian mother), June 18, 1904. He studied violin and composition at the Paris Cons. (1918–23); he also took some lessons with Ravel. He was coconductor of the Orchestre National de la Radiodiffusion in Paris from 1934 until his mobilization as an infantryman at the outbreak of World War II in 1939; after being held as a prisoner of war in Germany (1940–41), he was released and returned to France, where he became active in the Résistance. After the liberation, he served as chief conductor of the French Radio orch. (1944–47); he made his first tour of the United States in 1946; in 1948 he was appointed instructor in composition at the College of Puget Sound in Tacoma, Wash. In 1949 he was engaged as conductor of the Seattle Sym. Orch.; he was dismissed summarily for moral turpitude in Oct. 1951 (the soprano who appeared as soloist with the Seattle Sym. Orch. under the name of Mme. Rosenthal was not his legal wife). In 1962 he was appointed prof. of conducting at the Paris Cons.; he was conductor of the Liège Sym. Orch. (1964–67). He made his belated Metropolitan Opera debut in New York on Feb. 20, 1981, conducting a triple bill of Ravel's *L'Enfant et les sortilèges*, Poulenc's *Les Mamelles de Tirésias*, and Satie's *Parade*; he returned there in subsequent seasons with notable success. Rosenthal publ. the books *Satie, Ravel, Poulenc: An Intimate Memoir* (Madras and N.Y., 1987) and *Musique dorable* (Paris, 1994). In 1992 he received the Grand Prix for music of the City of Paris.

WORKS: DRAMATIC: *Rayon des soieries*, comic opera (1926–28); *Un baiser pour rien*, ballet (1928–29); *Les Bootleggers*, musical comedy (1932; Paris, May 2, 1933); *La Poule noire*, musical comedy (1934–37; Paris, 1937); *Gaîté parisienne*, ballet after Offenbach (Monte Carlo, April 5, 1938); *Que le diable l'emporte*, ballet (1948); *Les Femmes au tombeau*, lyric drama (1956); *Hop, signor!*, lyric drama (1957–61).

BIBL.: D. Saudinos, *M. R., une vie* (Paris, 1992).

Rosing, Vladimir, Russian-American tenor and opera director; b. St. Petersburg, Jan. 23, 1890; d. Los Angeles, Nov. 24, 1963. He studied voice with Jean de Reszke. He made his operatic debut in St. Petersburg in 1912 and gave a successful series of recitals in programs of Russian songs in London between 1913 and 1921. In 1923 he was appointed director of the opera dept. at the Eastman School of Music in Rochester, N.Y.; he founded an American Opera Co., which he directed in a series of operatic productions in the English language. In 1939 he went to Los Angeles as organizer and artistic director of the Southern Calif. Opera Assn.

BIBL.: R. Rosing, *V. R.: Musical Genius, an Intimate Biography* (Manhattan, Kansas, 1993).

Rösler, Endre, Hungarian tenor; b. Budapest, Nov. 27, 1904; d. there, Dec. 13, 1963. He studied in Budapest and with De Lucia and Garbin in Italy. In 1927 he made his operatic debut as Alfredo at the Budapest Opera, where he was a principal member for some 30 years. Subsequently he sang comprimario roles there. At the apex of his career he appeared as a guest artist with other European opera houses and also pursued a concert career. From 1953 until his death he taught at the Budapest Academy of Music. He was especially esteemed for his roles in Mozart's operas.

BIBL.: P. Varnai, *R. E.* (Budapest, 1969).

Rösler, or **Rössler, Johann Joseph (Jan Josef),** Bohemian pianist and composer; b. Banska Stiavnica, Aug. 22, 1771; d. Prague, Jan. 28, 1813. He studied music with his father, then was a composer for Prague's Nostitz Theater, where he brought out the opera *Elisene, Prinzessin von Bulgarien* (Oct. 18, 1807), the 1st original stage work to be produced there. He went to Vienna (1805) and was active at the Court Theater; he was also in the service of Countess Lobkowitz.

Rosner, Arnold, American composer and teacher; b. N.Y., Nov. 8, 1945. He studied mathematics at the State Univ. of N.Y. at Buffalo, and composition with Leo Smit, Allen Sapp, and Lejaren Hiller (Ph.D., 1972). He subsequently taught at various schools, including Kingsborough Community College (from 1983). His music is couched formally in a neoclassical idiom, but he freely admits melodic, harmonic, and contrapuntal methods of the modern school of composition. Among his works is the opera *The Chronicle of 9* (1984).

Ross, Walter (Beghtol), American composer; b. Lincoln, Nebr., Oct. 3, 1936. He studied music at the Univ. of Nebr., receiving an M.Mus. in 1962, then composition with Robert Palmer and conducting with Husa at Cornell Univ. (D.M.A., 1966). In 1967 he was appointed to the music faculty of the Univ. of Virginia. Much of his music is inspired by American themes. Among his works is the opera *In the Penal Colony* (1972).

Rosseau, Norbert (Oscar Claude), Belgian composer; b. Ghent, Dec. 11, 1907; d. there, Nov. 1, 1975. He played violin as a child; his family emigrated to Italy in 1921, and he studied piano with Silvestri and composition with Respighi at the Accademia di Santa Cecilia in Rome (1925–28). His early works are cast in a traditional style of European modernism; later he halfheartedly experimented with dodecaphony and electronics.

WORKS: DRAMATIC: OPERAS: *Sicilenne* (1947); *Les Violons du prince* (1954). BALLET: *Juventa* (1957). ORATORIOS: *Inferno*, after Dante (1940); *Maria van den Kerselare*, Flemish oratorio (1952); *Il Paradiso terrestre*, after Dante (1968).

Rossellini, Renzo, Italian composer and teacher; b. Rome, Feb. 2, 1908; d. Monte Carlo, May 14, 1982. He studied composition in Rome with Setaccioli and Sallustio and also took courses in orchestration with Molinari. In 1940 he was appointed prof. of composition at the Rome Cons., and in 1956 at the Accademia di Santa Cecilia in Rome. In 1973 he was named artistic director at the Opera at Monte Carlo. He publ. 2 books of autobiographical content, *Pagine di un musicista* (Bologna, 1964) and *Addio del passato* (Milan, 1968).

WORKS: DRAMATIC: OPERAS: *Alcassino e Nicoletta* (1928–30); *La guerra* (Rome, Feb. 25, 1956); *Il vortice* (Naples, Feb. 8, 1958); *Uno sguardo del ponte* (Rome, March 11, 1961); *L'Avventuriere* (Monte Carlo, Feb. 2, 1968); *La Reine morte* (Monte Carlo, 1973). BALLETS: *La danza di Dâssine* (San Remo, Feb. 24, 1935); *Poemetti pagani* (Monte Carlo, 1963); *Il Ragazzo e la sua ombra* (Venice, 1966). Also film music.

Rossi, Abbate Francesco, Italian composer; b. Bari, c.1645; d. date unknown. He was a canon in Bari in 1680. He composed the operas *Bianca di Castiglia* (Milan, 1674), *Il Sejano moserno della Tracia* (Venice, 1680), *La pena degli occhi and La Clorilda* (both Venice, 1688), and *Mitrane* (Venice, 1689); also an oratorio, *La Caduta degli angeli*.

Rossi, Giovanni (Gaetano), Italian composer; b. Borgo S. Donnino, Parma, Aug. 5, 1828; d. Genoa, March 30, 1886. He studied at the Milan Cons., and from 1852 was maestro concertatore at the Teatro Regio in Parma. He was also organist at the court chapel and deputy singing master at the Cons., becoming deputy composition master (1853), composition master and vice director

(1856), and director (1864) of the Cons. He then was director of the Teatro Carlo Felice in Genoa (1874–86), and also of the Genoa Liceo Musicale (1874–86). Among his compositions were the operas *Elena di Taranto* (Parma, 1852), *Giovanni Giscala* (Parma, 1855), *Nicolò de Lapi* (Parma, 1865), and *La Contessa d'Altenberg* (Borgo S. Donnino, 1871); also an oratorio, *Le sette parole*, and an overture, *Saulo*.

Rossi, Giulio, Italian bass; b. Rome, Oct. 27, 1865; d. Milan, Oct. 9, 1931. He had a tenor voice until he was 19, when an unintentional plunge into the Tiber in Dec. induced an illness, after which his voice lowered to the range of basso profondo. He then began vocal study under Oreste Tomassoni, making his debut at Parma, Oct. 20, 1887. In 1889 he toured South America with Adelina Patti, and made 2 tours of Mexico and California with Luisa Tetrazzini. He made his Metropolitan Opera debut in New York as the King in *Aida* on Nov. 16, 1908, remaining on its roster until 1919.

Rossi, Lauro, Italian composer; b. Macerata, Feb. 19, 1810; d. Cremona, May 5, 1885. He was a pupil of Furno, Zingarelli, and Crescentini at Naples, bringing out a comic opera, *Le Contesse villane*, there (1829) with fair success. He was assistant director at the Teatro Valle in Rome (1831–33). With his 10th opera, *La casa disabitata o I falsi monetari*, produced at La Scala, Milan, Aug. 11, 1834, he won a veritable triumph; it made the rounds of Italy and was given in Paris. In 1835 he went to Mexico as conductor and composer to an Italian opera troupe; when it folded, he set up his own opera company, becoming its director in 1837, and going to Havana (1840) and New Orleans (1842), returning to Italy in 1843. He brought out a new opera, *Il Borgomastro di Schiedam* (Milan, June 1, 1844), with indifferent success; his opera *Il Domino nero* (Milan, Sept. 1, 1849) fared a little better. His most successful opera was *La Contessa di Mons* (Turin, Jan. 31, 1874). He wrote 29 operas in all. In 1850 he was given the post of director of the Milan Cons., and in 1870 he succeeded Mercadante as director of the Naples Cons.. He resigned in 1878, and retired to Cremona in 1880.

Rossi-Lemeni, Nicola, Italian bass; b. Constantinople (of an Italian father and a Russian mother), Nov. 6, 1920, d. Bloomington, Ind., March 12, 1991. He was educated in Italy; studied law and planned a diplomatic career. In 1943 he decided to become a professional singer, but World War II interfered with his plans, and his debut as Varlaam in Venice did not take place until May 1, 1946. He first sang in the United States as Boris Godunov with the San Francisco Opera (Oct. 2, 1951); he sang at the Metropolitan Opera in New York in 1953–54. In 1980 he joined the faculty of Indiana Univ. in Bloomington. He married **Virginia Zeani** in 1958. Besides the regular operatic repertoire, he sang a number of roles in modern works, such as Wozzeck.

Rossini, Gioacchino (Antonio), great Italian opera composer possessing an equal genius for shattering melodrama in tragedy and for devastating humor in comedy; b. Pesaro, Feb. 29, 1792; d. Paris, Nov. 13, 1868. He came from a musical family; his father served as town trumpeter in Lugo and Pesaro and played brass instruments in provincial theaters and his mother sang opera as seconda donna. When his parents traveled, he was usually boarded in Bologna. After the family moved to Lugo, his father taught him to play the horn; he also had a chance to study singing with a local canon. Later the family moved to Bologna, where he studied singing, harpsichord, and music theory with Padre Tesei; he also learned to play the violin and viola. Soon he acquired enough technical ability to serve as maestro al cembalo in local churches and at occasional opera productions. He studied voice with the tenor Matteo Babbini. In 1806 he was accepted as a student at the Liceo Musicale in Bologna, where he studied singing and solfeggio with Gibelli, cello with Cavedagna, piano with Zanotti, and counterpoint with Padre Mattei. He also began composing. On Aug. 11, 1808, his cantata *Il pianto d'Armonia sulla morte d'Orfeo* was performed at the Liceo Musicale in Bologna and received a prize. About the same time he wrote his 1st opera, *Demetrio e Polibio*. In 1810 he was commissioned to write a work for the Teatro San Moise in Venice; he submitted his opera *La cambiale di matrimonio*, which won considerable acclaim. His next production was *L'equivoco stravagante*, produced in Bologna in 1811. There followed a number of other operas: *L'inganno felice* (Venice, 1812), *Ciro in Babilonia* (Ferrara, 1812), and *La scala di seta* (Venice, 1812). In 1812 he obtained a commission from La Scala of Milan; the resulting work, *La pietra del paragone*, was a fine success. In 1813 he produced 3 operas for Venice: *Il Signor Bruschino, Tancredi*, and *L'Italiana in Algeri*; the last became a perennial favorite. The next 3 operas, *Aureliano in Palmira* (Milan, 1813), *Il Turco in Italia* (Milan, 1814), and *Sigismondo* (Venice, 1814), were unsuccessful. By that time Rossini, still a very young man, had been approached by the famous impresario Barbaja, the manager of the Teatro San Carlo and the Teatro Fondo in Naples, with an offer for an exclusive contract, under the terms of which Rossini was to supply 2 operas annually for Barbaja. The 1st opera Rossini wrote for him was *Elisabetta, regina d'Inghilterra*, produced at the Teatro San Carlo in Naples in 1815; the title role was entrusted to the famous Spanish soprano Isabella Colbran, who was Barbaja's favorite mistress. An important innovation in the score was Rossini's use of *recitativo stromentato* in place of the usual *recitativo secco*. His next opera, *Torvaldo e Dorliska*, produced in Rome in 1815, was an unfortunate failure. Rossini now determined to try his skill in composing an opera buffa, based on the famous play by Beaumarchais *Le Barbier de Seville*; it was an audacious decision on Rossini's part, since an Italian opera on the same subject by Paisiello, *Il Barbiere di Siviglia*, originally produced in 1782, was still playing with undiminished success. To avoid confusion, Rossini's opera on this subject was performed at the Teatro Argentina in Rome under a different title, *Almaviva, ossia L'inutile precauzione*. Rossini was only 23 years old when he completed the score, which proved to be his greatest accomplishment and a standard opera buffa in the repertoire of theaters all over the world. Rossini conducted its 1st performance in Rome on Feb. 20, 1816, but if contemporary reports and gossip can be trusted, the occasion was marred by various stage accidents that moved the unruly Italian audience to interrupt the spectacle with vociferous outcries of derision; however, the next performance scored a brilliant success. For later productions he used the title *Il Barbiere di Siviglia*. Strangely enough, the operas he wrote immediately afterward were not uniformly successful: *La Gazzetta*, produced in Naples in 1816, passed unnoticed; the next opera, *Otello*, also produced in Naples in 1816, had some initial success but was not retained in the repertoire after a few sporadic performances. There followed *La Cenerentola* and *La gazza ladra*, both from 1817, which fared much better. But the following 7 operas, *Armida, Mosè in Egitto, Ricciardo e Zoraide, Ermione, La Donna del lago, Maometto II*, and *Zelmira*, produced in Naples between 1817 and 1822, were soon forgotten; only the famous *Prayer* in *Mosè in Egitto* saved the opera from oblivion. The prima donna assoluta in all these operas was Isabella Colbran; after a long association with Barbaja, she went to live with Rossini, who finally married her on March 16, 1822. This event, however, did not result in a break between the impresario and the composer; Barbaja even made arrangements for a festival of Rossini's works in Vienna at the Kärnthnertortheater, of which he became a director. In Vienna Rossini met Beethoven. Returning to Italy, he produced a fairly successful mythological opera, *Semiramide* (Venice, 1823), with Colbran in the title role. Rossini then signed a contract for a season in London with Giovanni Benelli, director of the Italian opera at the King's Theatre. Rossini arrived in London late in 1823 and was received by King George IV. He conducted several of his operas, and was also a guest at the homes of the British nobility, where he played piano as an accompanist to singers, at very large fees. In 1824 he settled in Paris, where he became director of the Théâtre-Italien. For the coronation of King Charles X he composed *Il viaggio a Reims*, which was performed in Paris under his direction on June 19, 1825. He used parts of this *pièce d'occasion* in his opera *Le Comte Ory*. In Paris he met Meyerbeer, with whom he established an excellent relationship. After the expiration of his contract with the Théâtre-Italien, he was given the nominal titles of "Premier Compositeur du Roi" and "Inspecteur Général du Chant en France" at an annual salary of 25,000 francs. He was now free to compose for the Paris Opéra; there, on Oct. 9, 1826, he produced *Le Siège de Corinthe*, a revised French version of *Maometto II*. Later he also revised the score of *Mosè in Egitto* and produced it at the Paris Opéra in French as *Moïse et Pharaon* on March 26, 1827. There followed *Le Comte Ory* (Aug. 20, 1828). In May 1829 Rossini was able to obtain an agreement with the government of King Charles X guaranteeing him a lifetime annuity of 6,000 francs. In return, he promised to write more works for the Paris Opéra. On Aug. 3, 1829, his *Guillaume Tell* was given its premiere at the Opéra; it became immensely popular.

At the age of 37, Rossini stopped writing operas. The French revolution of July 1830, which dethroned King Charles X, invalidated his contract with the French government. Rossini sued the government of King Louis Philippe, the successor to the throne of Charles X, for the continuation of his annuity; the incipient litigation was settled in 1835. In 1832 Rossini met Olympe Pélissier, who became his mistress; in 1837 Rossini legally separated from Colbran. She died in 1845, and on Aug. 16, 1846, Rossini married Pélissier. From 1836 to 1848 they lived in Bologna, where Rossini served as consultant to the Liceo Musicale. In 1848 they moved to Florence; in 1855 he decided to return to Paris, where he was to remain for the rest of his life. His home in the suburb of Passy became the magnet of the artistic world. Rossini was a charming, affable, and gregarious host; he entertained lavishly; he was a great gourmet, and invented recipes for Italian food that were enthusiastically adopted by French chefs. His wit was fabulous, and his sayings were eagerly reported in the French journals. He did not abandon composition entirely during his last years of life; in 1867 he wrote a *Petite messe solennelle*; as a token of gratitude to the government of the 2d Empire he composed a *Hymne à Napoleon III et à son vaillant peuple*; of great interest are the numerous piano pieces, songs, and instrumental works which he called *Péchés de vieillesse*, a collection containing over 150 pieces.

What were the reasons for Rossini's decision to stop writing operas? Rumors flew around Paris that he was unhappy about the cavalier treatment he received from the management of the Paris Opéra, and he spoke disdainfully of yielding the operatic field to "the Jews" (Meyerbeer and Halévy), whose operas captivated the Paris audiences. The report does not bear the stamp of truth, for Rossini was friendly with Meyerbeer until Meyerbeer's death in 1864. Besides, he was not in the habit of complaining; he enjoyed life too well. He was called "Le Cygne de Pesaro" (The Swan of Pesaro, his birthplace). The story went that a delegation arrived from Pesaro with a project of building a monument to Rossini; the town authorities had enough money to pay for the pedestal, but not for the statue itself. Would Rossini contribute 10,000 francs for the completion of the project? "For 10,000 francs," Rossini was supposed to have replied, "I would stand on the pedestal myself." *Se non è vero è ben trovato*. He had a healthy sense of self-appreciation, but he invariably put it in a comic context. While his mother was still living, he addressed his letters to her as "Mother of the Great Maestro."

The circumstance that Rossini was born on a leap-year day was the cause of many a bon mot on his part. On Feb. 29, 1868, he decided to celebrate his 19th birthday, for indeed, there had been then only 19 leap years since his birth. He was superstitious; like many Italians, he stood in fear of Friday the 13th. He died on Nov. 13, 1868, which was a Friday. In 1887 his remains were taken to Florence for entombment in the Church of Santa Croce.

Rossini's melodies have been used by many composers as themes for various works: Respighi utilized Rossini's *Quelques riens* in his ballet *La Boutique fantasque*, and other themes in his orch. suite *Rossiniana*. An opera entitled *Rossini in Neapel* was written by Bernhard Paumgartner. Britten made use of Rossini's music in his orch. suites *Soirées musicales* and *Matinées musicales*. The most famous arrangement of any of Rossini's compositions is the afore-mentioned *Prayer* from *Mosè in Egitto*, transcribed for violin by Paganini.

A complete ed. of the works of Rossini, the *Quaderni rossiniani, a cura della Fondazione Rossini*, began publication in Pesaro in 1954.

WORKS: OPERAS: *Demetrio e Polibio*, opera seria (1808; Teatro Valle, Rome, May 18, 1812); *La cambiale di matrimonio*, farsa (Teatro San Moisè, Venice, Nov. 3, 1810); *L'equivoco stravagante*, opera buffa (Teatro del Corso, Bologna, Oct. 26, 1811); *L'inganno felice*, farsa (1811; Teatro San Moisè, Venice, Jan. 8, 1812); *Ciro in Babilonia, ossia La caduta di Baldassare*, dramma con cori or oratorio (Teatro Municipale, Ferrara, March 1812); *La scala di seta*, farsa (Teatro San Moisè, Venice, May 9, 1812); *La pietra del paragone*, melodramma giocoso or opera buffa (Teatro alla Scala, Milan, Sept. 26, 1812); *L'occasione fa il ladro, ossia Il cambio della valigia*, burletta per musica (Teatro San Moisè, Venice, Nov. 24, 1812); *Il Signor Bruschino, ossia Il Figlio per azzardo*, farsa giocosa (1812; Teatro San Moise, Venice, Jan. 1813); *Tancredi*, opera seria or melodramma eroico (1812–13; Teatro La Fenice, Venice, Feb. 6, 1813); *L'Italiana in Algeri*, melodramma giocoso (Teatro San Benedetto, Venice, May 22, 1813); *Aureliano in Palmira*, opera seria or dramma serio (Teatro alla Scala, Milan, Dec. 26, 1813); *Il Turco in Italia*, opera buffa or dramma buffo (Teatro alla Scala, Milan, Aug. 14, 1814); *Sigismondo*, opera seria or dramma (Teatro La Fenice, Venice, Dec. 26, 1814); *Elisabetta, regina d'Inghilterra*, dramma (Teatro San Carlo, Naples, Oct. 4, 1815); *Torvaldo e Dorliska*, dramma semiserio (Teatro Valle, Rome, Dec. 26, 1815); *Il Barbiere di Siviglia*, opera buffa or commedia (1st perf. as *Almaviva, ossia L'inutile precauzione*, Teatro Argentina, Rome, Feb. 20, 1816); *La Gazzetta, ossia Il matrimonio per concorso* (subtitle does not appear in the 1st printed libretto), opera buffa (Teatro dei Fiorentini, Naples, Sept. 26, 1816); *Otello, ossia Il Moro di Venezia*, opera seria or dramma (Teatro del Fondo, Naples, Dec. 4, 1816); *La Cenerentola, ossia La bontà in trionfo*, dramma giocoso (1816–17; Teatro Valle, Rome, Jan. 25, 1817); *La gazza ladra*, melodramma or opera semiseria (Teatro alla Scala, Milan, May 31, 1817); *Armida*, opera seria or dramma (Teatro San Carlo, Naples, Nov. 11, 1817); *Adelaide di Borgogna, ossia Ottone, re d'Italia*, dramma (Teatro Argentina, Rome, Dec. 27, 1817); *Mosè in Egitto*, azione tragico-sacra or oratorio (Teatro San Carlo, Naples, March 5, 1818); *Adina, o Il Califfo di Bagdad*, farsa (1818; Teatro São Carlos, Lisbon, June 22, 1826); *Ricciardo e Zoraide*, dramma, opera seria, or opera semiseria (Teatro San Carlo, Naples, Dec. 3, 1818); *Ermione*, azione tragica (Teatro San Carlo, Naples, March 27, 1819); *Eduardo* [later *Edoardo*] *e Cristina*, dramma (Teatro San Benedetto, Venice, April 24, 1819); *La Donna del lago*, melodramma or opera seria (Teatro San Carlo, Naples, Sept. 24, 1819); *Bianca e Falliero, ossia Il consiglio dei tre*, opera seria (Teatro alla Scala, Milan, Dec. 26, 1819); *Maometto II*, dramma or opera seria (Teatro San Carlo, Naples, Dec. 3, 1820); *Matilde Shabran* [later *Matilde di Shabran*], *ossia Bellezza e Cuor di Ferro*, opera semiseria (1820–21; Teatro Apollo, Rome, Feb. 24, 1821); *Zelmira*, dramma or opera seria (1821–22; Teatro San Carlo, Naples, Feb. 16, 1822); *Semiramide*, melodramma tragico or opera seria (1822–23; Teatro La Fenice, Venice, Feb. 3, 1823); *Il viaggio a Reims, ossia L'albergo del Giglio d'Oro*, cantata scenica (Théâtre-Italien, Paris, June 19, 1825); *Le Siège de Corinthe*, grand opera (rev. of *Maometto II*; Opéra, Paris, Oct. 9, 1826); *Moise et Pharaon, ou Le Passage de la Mer Rouge*, grand opera (rev. of *Mosè in Egitto*; Opéra, Paris, March 26, 1827); *Le Comte Ory*, opera-comique (utilizing numbers from *Il viaggio a Reims*; Opéra, Paris, Aug. 20, 1828); *Guillaume Tell*, grand opera (1828–29; Opéra, Paris, Aug. 3, 1829).

BIBL.: A valuable source is the *Bollettino del Centro Rossiniano di Studi* (Pesaro, 1955–60; 1967–). Also G. Righetti-Giorgi, *Cenni di una donna già cantante sopra il maestro R.* (Bologna, 1823); G. Carpani, *Le Rossiniane, ossia Lettere musico-teatrali* (Padua, 1824); Stendhal, *Vie de R.* (Paris, 1824; many subsequent eds. and trs.; Eng. tr. as *Life of R.*, tr. and ed. by R. Coe, London and N.Y., 1956; 2d ed., 1970); J. A. Wendt, *R.'s Leben und Treiben* (Leipzig, 1824); J.-L. d'Ortigue, *De la guerre des dilettanti, ou De la Révolution opérée par R. dans l'opéra français, et des rapports qui existent entre la musique, la littérature et les arts* (Paris, 1830); A. Zanolini, *Biografia di G. R.* (Paris, 1836; also later eds.); L. and M. Escudier, *R.: Sa vie et ses oeuvres* (Paris, 1854); E. de Mirecourt,

R. (Paris, 1855); A. Aulagnier, *G. R.: Sa vie et ses oeuvres* (Paris, 1864); A.-J. Azevedo, *G. R.: Sa vie ses oeuvres* (Paris, 1864); F. Hiller, *Plaudereien mit R.*, vol. 2 of *Aus dem Tonleben unserer Zeit* (Leipzig, 1868); H. Edwards, *Life of* R. (London, 1869; reissued in a condensed version as *R. and His School*, London, 1881); C. Montrond, *R.: Étude biographique* (Lille, 1870); F. Mordani, *Della vita privata di G. R.: Memorie inedite* (Imola, 1871); A. Pougin, *R.: Notes, impressions, souvenirs, commentaires* (Paris, 1871); G. Vanzolini, *Della vera patria di G. R.* (Pesaro, 1873); L. Silvestri, *Della vita e delle opere di G. R. . . .* (Milan, 1874); C. Magnico, *R. e Wagner, o La musica italiana e la musica tedesca* (Genoa, 1875); G. de Sanctis, *G. R.: Appunti di viaggio* (Rome, 1878); J. Sittard, *G. A. R.* (Leipzig, 1882); C. Thrane, *R. og operaen* (Copenhagen, 1885); V. Camaiti, *G. R.: Notizie biografiche, artistiche e aneddotiche* (Florence, 1887); R. Gandolfi, *G. R.* (Florence, 1887); G. Mazzatinti, *Lettere inedite di G. R.* (Imola, 1890); A. Allmäyer, *Undici lettere di G. R. pubblicate per la prima volta . . .* (Siena, 1892); A. Kohut, *R.* (Leipzig, 1892); G. Mazzatinti, *Lettere inedite e rare di G. R.* (Imola, 1892); E. Michotte, *Souvenirs: Une Soirée chez R. à Beau-Sejour (Passy) 1858 . . .* (Brussels, n.d. [after 1893]; Eng. tr. by H. Weinstock, Chicago, 1968); E. Checchi, *R.* (Florence, 1898); A. Maffei, *R.* (Florence, 1898); G. Mazzatinti and F. and G. Manis, *Lettere di G. R.* (Florence, 1902); L. Dauriac, *R.: Biographie critique* (Paris, 1906); E. Michotte, *Souvenirs: La Visite de R. Wagner à R. (Paris, 1860): Détails inédits et commentaires* (Paris, 1906; Eng. tr. by H. Weinstock, Chicago, 1968); E. Corradi, *G. R.* (Rome, 1909); F. Cowen, *R.* (London and N.Y., 1912); G. Fara, *Genio e ingegno musicale: G. R.* (Turin, 1915); N. Morini, *La casa di R. in Bologna* (Bologna, 1916); L. Neretti, *I due inni patriottici di G. R.* (Florence, 1918); F. Vatielli, *R. e Bologna* (Bologna, 1918); H. de Curzon, *R.* (Paris, 1920; 2d ed., 1930); R. Fauchois, *R.* (Lyons, 1922); G. Radiciotti, *Il Barbiere di Siviglia: Guida attraverso la commedia e la musica* (Milan, 1923); G. Gatti, *Le "Barbier de Séville" de R.* (Paris, 1926); G. Biamonti, *Guglielmo Tell* (Rome, 1929); G. Radiciotti, *G. R.: Vita documenta, opere ed influenza su l'arte* (3 vols., Tivoli, 1927–29); idem, *Aneddoti rossiniani autentici* (Rome, 1929); H. de Curzon, *Une Heure avec R.* (Paris, 1930); A. Bonaventura, *R.* (Florence, 1934); G. Derwent, *R. and Some Forgotten Nightingales* (London, 1934); H. Gerigk, *R.* (Potsdam, 1934); F. Toye, *R.: A Study in Tragi-Comedy* (London and N.Y., 1934); H. Faller, *Die Gesangskoloratur in R.s Opern und ihre Ausführung* (Berlin, 1935); G. Monaldi, *Gli Uomini illustri: G. R. nell'arte, nella vita, negli aneddoti* (Milan, n.d. [1936]); L. D'Amico, *R.* (Turin, 1939); R. Bacchelli, *G. R.* (Turin, 1941; 2d ed., 1945); F. Bonavia, *R.* (London, 1941); A. Fraccaroli, *R.* (Milan, 1941; 4th ed., 1944); G. Roncaglia, *R. l'olimpico* (Milan, 1946; 2d ed., 1953); G. Brigante Colonna, *Vita di R.* (Florence, 1947); K. Pfister, *Das Leben R.s: Gesetz und Triumph der Oper* (Vienna and Berlin, 1948); C. van Berkel, *G. R.* (Haarlem, 1950); F. Bonafé, *R. et son oeuvre* (Le-Puy-en-Velay, 1955); U. Gozzano, *R.: Il romanzo dell'opera* (Turin, 1955); L. Rognoni, *R., con un'appendice comprendente lettere, documenti, testimonianze* (Parma, 1956; 3d ed., 1977); R. Bacchelli, *R. e esperienze rossiniane* (Milan, 1959); P. Ingerslev-Jensen, *R.* (Copenhagen, 1959); F. Schlitzer, *Un piccolo carteggio inedito di R. con un impresario italiano a Vienna* (Florence, 1959); V. Viviani, ed., *I libretti di R.* (Milan, 1965); A. Bonaccorsi, ed., *G. R.* (Florence, 1968); F. d'Amico, *L'opera teatrale di G. R.* (Rome, 1968); H. Weinstock, *R.: A Biography* (N.Y., 1968); P. Gossett, *The Operas of R.: Problems of Textual Criticism in Nineteenth-Century Opera* (diss., Princeton Univ., 1970); N. Till, *R.: His Life and Times* (Tunbridge Wells, 1983); A. Camosci, *G. R. dai ritratti e dalle scritture* (Rome, 1985); P. Mioli, *Invito all'ascolto di G. R.* (Milan, 1986); R. Osborne, *R.* (London, 1986; rev. ed., 1993); R. Bacchelli, *Vita di R.* (Florence, 1987); A Bassi, *G. R.* (Padua, 1992); A. Kendall, *G. R.: The Reluctant Hero* (London, 1992); C. Osborne, *The Bel Canto Operas of R., Donizetti, and Bellini* (Portland, Oreg., 1994).

Rössl-Majdan, Hildegard, Austrian contralto; b. Moosbierbaum, Jan. 21, 1921. She was educated at the Vienna Academy of Music. In 1946 she launched her career as a concert singer; she also appeared at the Vienna State Opera, Milan's La Scala, London's Covent Garden, and other European opera houses; she sang at the festivals in Salzburg, Edinburgh, and Aix-en-Provence and later was active as a voice teacher.

Rossum, Frederik (Leon Hendrik) van, Belgian composer and teacher of Dutch descent; b. Elsene, Brussels, Dec. 5, 1939. He took Belgian citizenship when he was 18; he studied composition with Souris and Quinet at the Brussels Cons. (1956–62) and won a Premier Grand Prix de Rome for his *Cantate de la Haute Mer* (1965). He taught piano at the Brussels Cons. (1965–68), then became prof. of counterpoint at the Liège Cons. (1968); he served as prof. of analysis at the Brussels Cons. (from 1971) and also was director of the Watermael-Bosvoorde Academy of Music. Among his works is *De soldaat Johan*, television opera (1975–76).

Rostropovich, Mstislav (Leopoldovich), famous Russian cellist and conductor; b. Baku, March 27, 1927. A precocious child, he began cello studies with his father, the Russian cellist Leopold Rostropovich (1892–1942), at an early age; he also had piano lessons from his mother. In 1931 the family moved to Moscow, where he made his debut when he was 8. He continued his training at the Central Music School (1939–41), then studied cello with Kozolupov and composition with Shebalin and Shostakovich at the Moscow Cons. (1943–48); he subsequently studied privately with Prokofiev. He won the International Competition for Cellists in Prague in 1950, and the next year made his first appearance in the West in Florence. A phenomenally successful career ensued. He made his U.S. debut at N.Y.'s Carnegie Hall in 1956, winning extraordinary critical acclaim. He became a teacher (1953) and a prof. (1956) at the Moscow Cons., and also a prof. at the Leningrad Cons. (1961). A talented pianist, he frequently appeared as accompanist to his wife, **Galina Vishnevskaya**, whom he married in 1955. In 1961 he made his first appearance as a conductor. As his fame increased, he received various honors, including the Lenin Prize in 1963 and the Gold Medal of the Royal Phil. Soc. of London in 1970. In spite of his eminence and official honors, however, he encountered difficulties with the Soviet authorities, owing chiefly to his spirit of uncompromising independence. He let the dissident author Aleksandr Solzhenitsyn stay at his dacha near Moscow, protesting the Soviet government's treatment of the Nobel prize winner for literature in a letter to Pravda in 1969. Although the letter went unpubl. in his homeland, it was widely disseminated in the West. As a result, Rostropovich found himself increasingly hampered in his career by the Soviet Ministry of Culture. His concerts were canceled without explanation, as were his wife's engagements at the Bolshoi Theater. Foreign tours were forbidden, as were appearances on radio, television, and recordings. In 1974 he and his wife obtained permission to go abroad, and were accompanied by their 2 daughters. He made a brilliant debut as a guest conductor with the National Sym. Orch. in Washington, D.C. (March 5, 1975), a success that led to his appointment as its music director in 1977. Free from the bureaucratic annoyances of the USSR, he and his wife publicized stories of their previous difficulties at home in Russia. Annoyed by such independent activities, the Moscow authorities finally stripped them both of their Soviet citizenship as "ideological renegades." The Soviet establishment even went so far as to remove the dedication to Rostropovich of Shostakovich's 2d Cello Concerto. The whole disgraceful episode ended when the Soviet government, chastened by perestroika, restored Rostropovich's citizenship in Jan. 1990, and invited him to take the National Sym. Orch. to the USSR. Besides conducting the American orch. there, Rostropovich appeared as soloist in Dvořák's Cello Concerto. His return to Russia was welcomed by the populace as a vindication of his principles of liberty. A symbolic linguistic note: the difficult-to-pronounce first name of Rostropovich, which means "avenged glory," is usually rendered by his friends and admirers as simply Slava, that is, "glory."

Rostropovich is duly recognized as one of the greatest cellists of the century, a master interpreter of both the standard and the contemporary literature. To enhance the repertoire for his instrument, he commissioned and premiered numerous scores, includ-

ing works by Prokofiev, Shostakovich, Britten, Piston, and Foss. As a conductor, he proved himself an impassioned and authoritative interpreter of the music of the Russian national and Soviet schools of composition. He organized the 1st Rostropovich International Cello Competition in Paris in 1981 and the Rostropovich Festival in Snape, England, in 1983. He was made an Officer of the French Légion d'honneur in 1982, and received an honorary knighthood from Queen Elizabeth II of England in 1987.
BIBL.: T. Gaidamovich, *M. R.* (Moscow, 1969).

Rosvaenge (real name, **Rosenving-Hansen**), **Helge,** esteemed German tenor; b. Copenhagen (of German parents), Aug. 29, 1897; d. Munich, June 19, 1972. He studied in Copenhagen and Berlin. He made his operatic debut as Don José in Neustrelitz in 1921, then sang in Altenburg (1922–24), Basel (1924–26), and Cologne (1926–29). He distinguished himself as a member of the Berlin State Opera (1929–44); he also sang in Vienna and Munich. He appeared at the Salzburg (1933, 1937) and Bayreuth (1934, 1936) festivals; he made his debut at London's Covent Garden as Florestan in 1938. After World War II he again sang in Berlin and Vienna; made a concert tour of the United States in 1962. In his prime, he was compared to Caruso as a practitioner of bel canto. He excelled in the operas of Mozart and was also noted for his portrayals of Radames, Manrico, Huon, and Calaf. He publ. the autobiographical booklets *Skratta Pajazza* (*Ridi, Pagliaccio*; Copenhagen, 1945); *Mach es besser, mein Sohn* (Leipzig, 1962); and *Leitfaden für Gesangsbeflissene* (Munich, 1964).
BIBL.: F. Tassie, *H. R.* (Augsburg, 1975).

Rota (real name, **Rinaldi**), **Nino,** brilliant Italian composer; b. Milan, Dec. 3, 1911; d. Rome, April 10, 1979. He was a precocious musician; at the age of 11 he wrote an oratorio that had a public performance, and at 13 composed a lyric comedy in 3 acts, *Il Principe porcaro*, after Hans Christian Andersen. He entered the Milan Cons. in 1923, and took courses with Delachi, Orefici, and Bas; after private studies with Pizzetti (1925–26), he studied composition with Casella at the Accademia di Santa Cecilia in Rome, graduating in 1930; he later went to the United States, and enrolled in the Curtis Inst. of Music in Philadelphia, studying composition with Scalero and conducting with Reiner (1931–32). Returning to Italy, he entered the Univ. of Milan to study literature, gaining a degree in 1937. He taught at the Taranto music school (1937–38), then was a teacher (from 1939) and director (1950–78) at the Bari Liceo Musicale. His musical style demonstrates a great facility, and even felicity, with occasional daring excursions into the forbidding territory of dodecaphony. However, his most durable compositions are related to his music for the cinema; he composed the sound tracks of a great number of films of the Italian director Federico Fellini covering the period from 1950 to 1979.
WORKS: DRAMATIC: OPERAS: *Il Principe porcaro* (1925); *Ariodante* (Parma, Nov. 5, 1942); *Torquemada* (1943; rev. version, Naples, Jan. 24, 1976); *I 2 timidi*, radio opera (Italian Radio, 1950; stage version, London, March 17, 1952); *Il cappello di paglia di Firenzi* (1946; Palermo, April 2, 1955); *La scuola di guida* (Spoleto, 1959); *Lo scoiattolo in gamba* (Venice, Sept. 16, 1959); *La notte di un nevrastenico*, opera buffa (concert version, Turin, July 9, 1959; stage version, Milan, Feb. 8, 1960); *Aladino e la lampada magica* (Naples, Jan. 14, 1968); *La visita meravigliosa*, after H.G. Wells (Palermo, Feb. 6, 1970); *Napoli milionaria* (Spoleto, June 22, 1977). BALLETS: *La rappresentazione di Adamo ed Eva* (Perugia, Oct. 5, 1957); *La strada* (after the 1954 Fellini film of the same name; Milan, 1965; rev. 1978); *La Molière imaginaire* (Paris, 1976). FILM SCORES: Many, including the following for films by Fellini: *Lo sceicco bianco* (*The White Sheik*; 1950); *I vitelloni* (1953); *La strada* (1954); *Il bidone* (1955); *Notti di Cabiria* (1957); *La dolce vita* (1959); part of *Boccaccio 70* (1962); *Otto de mezza* (*8 1/2*; 1963); *Giulietta degli spiriti* (*Juliet of the Spirits*; 1965); *Satyricon* (1969); *The Clowns* (1971); *Fellini Roma* (1972); *Amarcord* (1974); *Casanova* (1977); *Orchestra Rehearsal* (1979). ORATORIOS: *L'infanzia di S. Giovanni Battista* (1923); *Mysterium Catholicum* (1962); *La vita di Maria* (1970); *Roma capomunni* (1972); *Rabelaisiana* (1978).

Roters, Ernst, German composer; b. Oldenburg, July 6, 1892; d. Berlin, Aug. 25, 1961. He was a student of Moritz Mayer-Mahr (piano), Leichtentritt (theory), and Georg Schumann (composition) at Berlin's Klindworth-Scharwenka Cons., and then devoted himself mainly to composition. He wrote an opera, *Die schwarze Kammer* (Darmstadt, 1928), incidental music to plays, and radio scores.

Rothenberger, Anneliese, esteemed German soprano; b. Mannheim, June 19, 1924. After vocal study in with Erika Müller at the Mannheim Hochschule für Musik, she made her operatic debut in Koblenz in 1943. From 1946 to 1957 and again from 1958 to 1973 she was a member of the Hamburg State Opera; she also had engagements in Düsseldorf, Salzburg, Edinburgh, and Aix-en-Provence. In 1958 she joined the Vienna State Opera she also sang at La Scala in Milan and in Munich. On Nov. 18, 1960, she made a notable debut at the Metropolitan Opera in New York as Zdenka in *Arabella*, and remained on its roster until 1966. She was one of the most versatile singers of her generation, capable of giving congenial renditions of soprano roles in operas of Mozart and Verdi. She also gave excellent performances of the challenging role of Marie in Berg's *Wozzeck*. She further distinguished herself in the even more demanding role of Lulu in Berg's opera. She publ. an autobiography, *Melodie meines Lebens* (Munich, 1972).

Rother, Artur (Martin), German conductor; b. Stettin, Oct. 12, 1885; d. Aschau, Sept. 22, 1972. He studied piano and organ with his father and also attended the Univs. of Tübingen and Berlin. In 1906 he became a répétiteur at the Wiesbaden Opera and was an assistant at the Bayreuth Festivals (1907–14). From 1927 to 1934 he was Generalmusikdirektor in Dessau; in 1938 he went to Berlin as a conductor at the Deutsches Opernhaus, where he remained until 1958; he was also chief conductor of the Berlin Radio (1946–49).

Rothier, Léon, French bass and teacher; b. Rheims, Dec. 26, 1874; d. N.Y., Dec. 6, 1951. He studied at the Paris Cons. with Crosti (singing), Lherie (opéra comique), and Melchissedec (opera), winning 1st prizes in all 3 classes upon graduation. He made his operatic debut as Jupiter in Gounod's *Philemon et Baucis* at the Opéra Comique in Paris in 1899, remaining there until 1903; he then was active in Marseilles (1903–07), Nice (1907–09), and Lyons (1909–10). On Dec. 10, 1910, he made his American debut at the Metropolitan Opera in New York as Méphistophélès; he remained on its roster until 1939 and then devoted himself to recitals. He taught at the Volpe Inst. in New York (from 1916) and privately after his retirement from the stage.

Rothmüller, (Aron) Marko, Croatian baritone and teacher; b. Trnjani, Dec. 31, 1908; d. Bloomington, Ind., Jan. 20, 1993. He studied in Zagreb, then took lessons in singing with Franz Steiner in Vienna, and also had lessons in composition with Alban Berg. He made his operatic debut as Ottokar in *Der Freischütz* at the Schiller Theater in Hamburg-Altona in 1932 and was a member of the opera in Zagreb (1932–34) and Zürich (1935–47); he was with the Covent Garden Opera in London (1939; 1948–55). He sang with the N.Y. City Opera (1948–52) and also at the Glyndebourne and Edinburgh festivals (1949–52); he made his debut at the Metropolitan Opera in New York on Jan. 22, 1959, as Kothner in *Die Meistersinger von Nürnberg*; appeared there again in 1960 and 1964. He taught at the Indiana Univ. School of Music in Bloomington from 1955 to 1979. He was distinguished in Wagnerian roles and also sang leading roles in modern works, including Wozzeck in Berg's opera. He wrote some chamber music and songs. Rothmüller publ. an interesting vol., *Die Musik der Juden* (Zürich, 1951; Eng. tr., London, 1953; 2d ed., rev., 1967).

Röttger, Heinz, German conductor and composer; b. Herford, Westphalia, Nov. 6, 1909; d. Dessau, Aug. 26, 1977. He studied in Munich at the Academy of Music (1928–31) and took courses in musicology at the Univ. (Ph.D., 1937, with the diss. *Das Formproblem bei Richard Strauss*; publ. in Berlin, 1937). He served as music director of the Stralsund City Theater (1948–51), Generalmusikdirektor in Rostock (1951–54), and chief conductor of the Dessau Landestheater (from 1954). His works include the operas *Bellmann* (1946), *Phaëton* (1957), *Der Heiratsantrag* (1959), *Die Frauen von Troja* (1961), *Der Weg nach Palermo* (1965), and *Spanisches Capriccio* (1976), and the ballets . . . *und heller wurde jeder Tag* (1964) and *Der Kreis* (1964).

Rouleau, Joseph (Alfred Pierre), admired Canadian bass and teacher; b. Matane, Quebec, Feb. 28, 1929. He went to Montreal and studied with Édouard Woolley and Albert Cornellier, and then at the Cons. with Martial Singher (1949–52). In 1951 he made a concert tour of eastern Canada. After further training with Mario Basiola and Antonio Narducci in Milan (1952–54), he made his first major appearance in opera as Colline at the New Orleans Opera in 1955. In 1956 he sang Verdi's King Philip II in Montreal. On April 23, 1957, he made his debut at London's Covent Garden as Colline, and continued to make appearances there for some 20 seasons. He made his first appearance at the Paris Opéra as Raimondo in 1960. In 1965–66 he toured Australia with Joan Sutherland's operatic enterprise. In 1967 he sang Basilio with the Canadian Opera Co., and returned there as Ramfis in 1968. In the latter year, he also made his debut at the N.Y. City Opera as Méphistophélès. In subsequent years, he sang with various North American and European opera companies. He also was engaged as a soloist with leading orchs. on both sides of the Atlantic. On April 13, 1984, he made his Metropolitan Opera debut in New York as the Grand Inquisitor. His esteemed portrayal of Boris Godunov in Montreal in Feb. 1988 was telecast by the CBC. From 1980 he taught at the Montreal Cons. In 1967 he won the Prix de musique Calixa-Lavallée. He was made an Officer of the Order of Canada in 1977. In 1990 he was awarded the Prix Denise-Pelletier.

Rouse, Mikel (Michael Joseph), formidably original American composer; b. St. Louis, Jan. 26, 1957. His father was a state trooper and his mother a social (case) worker. He attended the Kansas City Art Inst. where he studied music, art, and filmmaking (graduated, 1977), and the Cons. of Music at the Univ. of Missouri at Kansas City. He moved to New York in 1979, where he further studied African and other world musics as well as the Schillinger method of composition. He formed his own contemporary chamber ensemble, Mikel Rouse Broken Consort, consisting of keyboard, electric guitar/bass, woodwinds, and percussion, with which he toured and produced numerous recordings. He has become most widely known for his trilogy of operas, beginning with *Failing Kansas* (1994; N.Y., Feb. 2, 1995), inspired by Truman Capote's chilling *In Cold Blood*, which explores his technique of counterpoetry, an artful manipulation of multiple unpitched and pitched voices in strict metric counterpoint, which enables him to explore the complex, overlapping harmonies of meaning and emotion embedded in his masterful librettos as these correspond to the equally complex and overlapping harmonies of the music "bed" on which they lie. Other works that explore this technique include *Living Inside Design* (1994; a collection of extended spoken songs) and *Autorequiem* (1994) for strings, percussion, and voice. The second work in the trilogy is the critically acclaimed *Dennis Cleveland* (N.Y., Oct. 29, 1996), the first-ever talk-show opera in which Rouse himself appears as the obsequious and omnipresent host. The third and final work is the in-progress *The End of Cinematics*, a commission from N.Y.'s Brooklyn Academy of Music and in collaboration with video artist John Jesurun, based upon four "retro-songs" and involving an elaborate use of real-time film.

Composers are usually elevated by terms applied to their work that manage to enter common musical parlance. Rouse has not one but two, and both of his own devising: the above-mentioned counterpoetry, and totalism, denotative of certain compositional tendencies among composers coming of professional age at the end of the 20th century. Both terms are well developed by the N.Y. critic Kyle Gann in the closing chapters of his book *American Music in the 20th Century* (N.Y., 1998). Rouse's other works include *Quorum* (1984), the first piece of its kind for sequencer and used in Ulysses Dove's choreographic work, *Vespers*, presented by the Alvin Ailey American Dance Theater in 1987.

Rousseau, Jean-Jacques, great Swiss-born French philosopher and author; b. Geneva, June 28, 1712; d. Ermenonville, near Paris, July 2, 1778. Without other musical training besides desultory self-instruction, Rousseau made his debut as a music scholar at the age of 29, reading a paper before the Académie in Paris (1724), which was received and publ. as a *Dissertation sur la musique moderne* (1743). His opera *Les Muses galantes* had only 1 private representation, at the house of La Pouplinière in 1745; his revision of the intermezzo *La Reine de Navarre* (by Voltaire and Rameau) was a failure in Paris, but his opera *Le Devin du village* (Fontainebleau, Oct. 18, 1752; Paris Opéra, March 1, 1753) was very successful and remained in the repertoire for 75 years. In the meantime, his musical articles for the *Encyclopédie* had evoked scathing criticism from Rameau and others; improved by revision and augmentation, they were republ. as his *Dictionnaire de musique* (Geneva, 1767; the existence of this ed. cannot be proved; 1st known ed., Paris, 1768). In 1752 commenced the dispute, known as the "guerre des bouffons," between the partisans of French and Italian opera; Rousseau sided with the latter, publ. a *Lettre à M. Grimm au sujet des remarques ajoutées à sa lettre sur Omphale* (1752), followed by the caustic *Lettre sur la musique française* (1753; to which the members of the Opéra responded by burning him in effigy and excluding him from the theater) and *Lettre d'un symphoniste de l'Académie royale de musique à ses camarades* (1753). He wrote 2 numbers for the melodrama *Pygmalion* (1770; Paris, Oct. 30, 1775). Publ. posthumously were 6 new arias for *Le Devin du village*, and a collection of about 100 romances and duets, *Les Consolations des misères de ma vie* (1781), and fragments of an opera, *Daphnis et Chloé* (1780). His writings on music are included in the *Oeuvres complètes de Jean-Jacques Rousseau* (4 vols., 1959–69); for his letters, see R. Leigh, ed., *Correspondance complète Jean-Jacques Rousseau* (18 vols., 1965–73).

BIBL.: A. Jensen, *J.-J. R.: Fragments inédits, recherches biographiques* (Paris, 1882); A. Jansen, *J.-J. R. als Musiker* (Berlin, 1884); A. Pougin, *J.-J. R., Musicien* (Paris, 1901); E. Istel, *J.-J. R. als Komponist seiner lyrischen Szene "Pygmalion"* (Leipzig, 1901); E. Schütte, *J.-J. R.: Seine Persönlichkeit und sein Stil* (Leipzig, 1910); J. Tiersot, *J.-J. R.* (Paris, 1912); E. Faguet, *R. artiste* (Paris, 1913); A. Sells, *The Early Life of R.: 1712–40* (London, 1929); R. Gerin, *J.-J. R.* (Paris, 1930); M. Moffat, *R. et le théâtre* (Paris, 1930); A. Pochon, *J.-J. R., musiciens et le critique* (Montreux, 1940); J. Senelier, *Bibliographie générale des oeuvres de J.-J. R.* (Paris, 1949); P. Gülke, *R. und die Musik, oder, Von der Zuständigkeit des Dilettanten* (Wilhelmshaven, 1984).

Rousseau, Marcel (-Auguste-Louis), French composer, son of **Samuel-Alexandre Rousseau**; b. Paris, Aug. 18, 1882; d. there, June 11, 1955. He studied with his father, then entered the Paris Cons. as a student of Lenepveu; he won the Deuxième Premier Grand Prix de Rome with the cantata *Maia* (1905); he later added his father's first name to his own, and produced his works as Samuel-Rousseau. In 1947 he was elected to the Académie des Beaux-Arts.

WORKS: DRAMATIC: OPERAS (all 1st perf. in Paris): *Tarass Boulba* (Nov. 22, 1919); *Le Hulla* (March 9, 1923); *Le Bon Roi Dagobert* (Dec. 5, 1927); *Kerkeb* (April 6, 1951). BALLETS: *Promenade dans Rome* (Paris, Dec. 7, 1936); *Entre 2 rondes* (Paris, April 27, 1940).

Rousseau, Samuel-Alexandre, French conductor, teacher, and composer, father of **Marcel (-Auguste-Louis) Rousseau**; b. Neuve-Maison, Aisne, June 11, 1853; d. Paris, Oct. 1, 1904. He studied at the Paris Cons. with Franck (organ) and Bazin (composition), winning the Grand Prix de Rome with the cantata *La Fille de Jephté* (1878) and the Prix Cressent with the comic opera *Dianora* (Paris, Opéra Comique, Dec. 22, 1879). His opera *Mérowig* was awarded the Prize of the City of Paris, and was performed in concert form at the Grand Théâtre there on Dec. 12, 1892. In 1892 he was appointed conductor at the Théâtre-Lyrique in Paris. He was for 10 years chorus master at the Société des Concerts du Cons., and also taught harmony at the Paris Cons. On June 8, 1898, his lyric drama *La Cloche du Rhin* was staged at the Paris Opéra with considerable success, but had only 9 performances in all; this was followed by the music dramas *Milia* (Opéra Comique, 1904) and *Léone* (Opéra Comique, March 7, 1910).

Roussel, Albert (Charles Paul Marie), outstanding French composer and teacher; b. Tourcoing, April 5, 1869; d. Royan, Aug. 23, 1937. Orphaned as a child, he was educated by his grandfather, mayor of his native town, and after the grandfather's death, by his aunt. He studied academic subjects at the Collège Stanislas in Paris and music with the organist Stoltz; he then studied mathematics in preparation for entering the Naval Academy; at the age of 18 he began his training in the navy; from 1889 to Aug. 1890 he was a member of the crew of the frigate *Iphigénie*, sailing to Indochina. This voyage was of great importance to Roussel, since it opened for him a world of oriental culture and art, which became one of the chief sources of his musical inspiration. He later sailed on the cruiser *Dévastation*; he received a leave of absence for reasons of health, and spent some time in Tunis; he was then stationed in Cherbourg, and began to compose there. In 1893 he was sent once more to Indochina. He resigned from the navy in 1894 and went to Paris, where he began to study music seriously with Gigout. In 1898 he entered the Schola Cantorum in Paris as a pupil of d'Indy; continued this study until 1907, when he was already 38 years old, but at the same time he was entrusted with a class in counterpoint, which he conducted at the Schola Cantorum from 1902 to 1914; among his students were Satie, Golestan, Le Flem, Roland-Manuel, Lioncourt, and Varèse. In 1909 Roussel and his wife, Blanche Preisach-Roussel, undertook a voyage to India, where he became acquainted with the legend of the queen Padmavati, which he selected as a subject for his famous opera-ballet. His choral sym. *Les Evocations* was also inspired by this tour. At the outbreak of World War I in 1914, Roussel applied for active service in the navy but was rejected, and volunteered as an ambulance driver. After the Armistice of 1918, he settled in Normandy and devoted himself to composition. In the autumn of 1930 he visited the United States.

Roussel began his work under the influence of French Impressionism, with its dependence on exotic moods and poetic association. However, the sense of formal design asserted itself in his symphonic works; his Suite (1926) signalizes a transition toward neoclassicism; the thematic development is vigorous, and the rhythms are clearly delineated, despite some asymmetrical progressions; the orchestration, too, is in the Classical tradition. Roussel possessed a keen sense of the theater; he was capable of fine characterization of exotic or mythological subjects, but also knew how to depict humorous situations in lighter works. N. Labelle ed. a *Catalogue raisonné de l'oeuvre d'Albert Roussel* (Louvain-la-Neuve, 1992).

WORKS: (all 1st perf. in Paris unless otherwise given): DRAMATIC: *Le marchand de sable qui passe*, incidental music (Le Havre, Dec. 16, 1908); *Le festin de l'araignée*, ballet-pantomime (1912; April 3, 1913); *Padmâvatî*, opera-ballet (1914–18; June 1, 1923); *La naissance de la lyre*, lyric opera (1923–24, July 1, 1925); *Sarabande*, ballet music (June 16, 1927); *Bacchus et Ariane*, ballet (1930; May 22, 1931; 2 orch. suites: No. 1, April 2, 1933; No. 2, Feb. 2, 1934); *Le testament de la tante Caroline*, opéra-bouffe (1932–33; Olomouc, Nov. 14, 1936); *Aenéas*, ballet (Brussels, July 31, 1935); Prelude to Act 2 of *Le quatorze juillet*, incidental music (July 14, 1936); *Elpénor* for Flute and String Quartet, radio music (n.d.).

BIBL.: L. Vuillemin, *A. R. et son oeuvre* (Paris, 1924); A. Hoérée, *A. R.* (Paris, 1938); N. Demuth, *A. R.: A Study* (London, 1947); R. Bernard, *A. R.: Sa vie, son oeuvre* (Paris, 1948); M. Pincherle, *A. R.* (Geneva, 1957); B. Deane, *A. R.* (London, 1961); A. Surchamp, *A. R.* (Paris, 1967); R. Follet, *A. R.: A Bio-Bibliography* (Westport, Conn., 1988).

Rousselière, Charles, French tenor; b. St. Nazaire, Jan. 17, 1875; d. Joue-les-Tours, May 11, 1950. He studied at the Paris Cons. He made his operatic debut in 1900 as Samson at the Paris Opéra, where he sang until 1912; he also sang with the Monte Carlo Opera (1905–14), creating roles in Mascagni's *Amica*, Saint-Saëns's *L'Ancêtre*, and Fauré's *Pénélope*; he also sang the role of Julien in Charpentier's opera at its first performance at the Opéra Comique in Paris. He made his debut at the Metropolitan Opera in New York as Romeo on Nov. 26, 1906, but remained on its roster for only 1 season. He made guest appearances at La Scala in Milan, the Teatro Colón in Buenos Aires, in Palermo, etc.

Rousset, Christophe, remarkable French harpsichordist and esteemed conductor; b. Avignon, April 12, 1961. Following training with André Raynaud and Huguette Dreyfus at the Schola Cantorum in Paris, he was a student of Kenneth Gilbert before completing his studies with Bob van Asperen (harpsichord), the Kuijken brothers and Lucy van Dael (chamber music), and Leonhardt (interpretation) at the Royal Cons. of Music at The Hague (soloist diploma, 1983). In 1983 he took 1st prize in the Bruges harpsichord competition, and then launched a global career. From 1992 he also was active with his own Les Talens Lyriques ensemble. In 1999 he was a guest conductor of the N.Y. Collegium Vocal Ensemble and Orch. Rousset has won critical accolades for his extraordinary command of the harpsichord repertory. He particularly excels in the music of the French school, giving particularly outstanding performances of Couperin and Rameau.

Rovere, Agostino, Italian bass; b. Monza, 1804; d. N.Y., Dec. 10, 1865. He studied in Milan, making his debut in 1826 in Pavia. He was a leading singer at La Scala in Milan (1831–44; 1846–47; 1856–57), and also appeared in Vienna (1839; 1842–45), where he created the role of Boisfleury in Donizetti's *Linda di Chamounix*; he also sang at Covent Garden in London (1847–48). He was most famous for his buffo roles, excelling as Leporello, Bartolo, and Dulcamara.

Rovetta, Giovanni, Italian composer; b. Venice, c.1595; d. there, Oct. 23, 1668. He pursued his career in his native city, being closely associated with San Marco. He was a boy treble, and later an instrumentalist (1615–17); in 1623 he was made a bass singer, and soon thereafter a priest. After serving as assistant maestro di cappella (1627–44), he succeeded Monteverdi (in 1644) as maestro di cappella, a post he held until his death. He was a fine composer of both sacred and secular works. Among his output were the operas *Ercole in Lidia* (1645) and *Argiope* (1649).

Roxburgh, Edwin, English composer, oboist, conductor, and teacher; b. Liverpool, Nov. 6, 1937. He studied composition with Howells at the Royal College of Music in London, with Nono and Dallapiccola in Italy, and with Boulanger in France; completed his education at St. John's College, Cambridge. He was principal oboist in the Sadler's Wells Opera orch. in London (1964–67), then prof. of composition and founder-director of the 20th-century performance studies dept. at the Royal College of Music (from 1967); he also appeared as an oboist and was conductor of the 20th Century Ensemble of London. With L. Goossens, he publ. *The Oboe* (London, 1976). He composed a number of finely crafted orch., chamber, and vocal works, his idiomatic writing for woodwinds being particularly admirable. Among his works are the opera *Abelard* and the ballet *The Tower* (1964); also *The Rock*, oratorio for Soloists, Chorus, Children's Chorus, and Orch. (1979).

Roy, Klaus George, Austrian-born American composer, writer, and program annotator; b. Vienna, Jan. 24, 1924. He went to the United States in 1940 and became a naturalized American citizen in 1944. He studied at Boston Univ. with Geiringer (B.Mus., 1947) and at Harvard Univ. with Davison, Kinkeldey, Merritt, and Piston (M.A., 1949). In 1945–46 he served as an officer in education and information with U.S. Army General Headquarters in Tokyo. From 1948 to 1957 he was employed as a librarian and instructor at Boston Univ.; he also wrote music criticism for the *Christian Science Monitor* (1950–57). From 1958 to 1988 he was program annotator and ed. of the Cleveland Orch. and also taught at the

Cleveland Inst. of Art (from 1975) and served as adjunct prof. at the Cleveland Inst. of Music (1986–94), which bestowed upon him an honorary doctorate in music (1987). A perspicacious collection of his writings appeared as *Not Responsible for Lost Articles: Thoughts and Second Thoughts from Severance Hall (1958–1988)* (Cleveland, 1993). He writes compositions in a variety of genres, all extremely pleasing to the ear. Among his works is *Zoopera: The Enchanted Garden* (Cleveland, Sept. 2, 1983).

Royer, Joseph-Nicolas-Pancrace, French composer; b. Turin, c.1705; d. Paris, Jan. 11, 1755. He was a native of Burgundy, and settled in Paris in 1725. He was maître de musique at the Opéra (1730–33), and then maître de musique des enfans de France (1734), serving with Matho; he obtained the latter's reversion as chantre de la musique de la chambre du roi (1735). In 1748 he became director of the Concert Spirituel; in 1753 he obtained the reversion of maître de musique de la chambre du roi from Rebel and Bury; that same year was named director and composer at the Opéra.

WORKS: DRAMATIC (all 1st perf. in Paris unless otherwise given): *Le Fâcheux Veuvage*, opéra comique (Aug. 1725); *Crédit est mort*, opéra comique (Feb. 19, 1726); *Pyrrhus,* tragédie-lyrique (Oct. 26, 1730); *Zaïde, reine de Granade,* opéra-ballet (Sept. 3, 1739); *Le Pouvoir de l'amour,* opéra ballet (April 23, 1743); *Almasis* (Versailles, Feb. 26, 1748); *Myrtil et Zélie*, pastorale-héroïque (Versailles, June 20, 1750); *Prométhée et Pandore,* opera (n.d.; not perf.).

Rôze, Marie (real name **Hippolyte Ponsin**), French soprano and pedagogue, mother of **Raymond Rôze**; b. Paris, March 2, 1846; d. there, June 21, 1926. She studied at the Paris Cons. with Mocker and later with Auber, winning 2 prizes in 1865. She made her debut at the Opéra Comique in the title role of Hérold's *Marie* (Aug. 16, 1865), singing there for 3 seasons. She then appeared at the Paris Opéra as Marguerite in Gounod's *Faust* (Jan. 2, 1879). She made her London debut as Marguerite (1872), and continued to sing in England for many years. She visited America twice, in 1877–78 and 1880–81. In 1874 she married an American bass, Julius E. Perkins, who died the following year. In 1890 she settled in Paris as a teacher.

Rôze, Raymond, English composer, son of **Marie Rôze**; b. London, 1875; d. there, March 31, 1920. He studied at the Brussels Cons., where he won 1st prize;. He wrote overtures and incidental music to many plays. In 1913 he organized at Covent Garden a season of opera in English, during which he conducted his own opera *Joan of Arc* (Oct. 31, 1913); another opera, *Arabesque*, was produced at the Coliseum in London in 1916.

Rozkošný, Josef Richard, Czech composer; b. Prague, Sept. 21, 1833; d. there, June 3, 1913. He studied painting and music in Prague, his teachers being Tomaschek (piano) and Kittl (composition). His songs and choruses became popular, and he successfully attempted the composition of operas to Czech librettos; 8 operas were produced in Prague, among them: *Svatojanské proudy* (The Rapids of St. John; Oct. 3, 1871), *Popelka* (Cinderella; May 31, 1885), and *Černé jezero* (The Black Lake; Jan. 6, 1906).

Rozsnyai, Zoltán, Hungarian conductor; b. Budapest, Jan. 29, 1927; d. San Diego, Sept. 10, 1990. He was educated at the Franz Liszt Academy of Music, where his teachers included Bartók, Kodály, and Dohnányi; he also took courses at the Technical Univ. and at the Pazmany Peter Univ. of Sciences in Budapest; he completed his musical training at the Univ. of Vienna. He was conductor of the Phil. Orch. in Miskolc (1948–50), then conducted the Debrecen Opera (1950–53); he later led several Hungarian orchs. He left Hungary after the abortive revolution of 1956 and went to the United States. In 1957 he organized the Philharmonia Hungarica; toured with it in 1958. He was an assistant conductor of the N.Y. Phil. (1962–63); then was music director of the Cleveland Phil. (1965–68) and the San Diego Sym. (1967–71). In 1976 he became music director of the Golden State Opera Co. in Los Angeles; in 1978 he became music director of the Knoxville (Tenn.) Sym. Orch., a post he retained until 1985.

Różycki, Ludomir, Polish composer and pedagogue; b. Warsaw, Nov. 6, 1884; d. Katowice, Jan. 1, 1953. He was a student of his father and Zawirski (piano), and of Noskowski (composition) at the Warsaw Cons., graduating with honors in 1903; he then completed his training with Humperdinck in Berlin (1905–08). In 1908 went to Lemberg as conductor at the Opera and as a piano teacher at the Cons. After another Berlin sojourn (1914–20), he went to Warsaw as conductor of the Opera. In 1926 he helped to found the Polish Composers Union and served as its first president. From 1930 to 1945 he was a prof. at the Warsaw Cons., and then from 1945 at the Katowice Cons. He was highly regarded in Poland as a national composer of stature; his style of composition was a successful blend of German, Russian, and Italian ingredients, yet the Polish characteristics were not obscured by the cosmopolitan harmonic and orch. dress.

WORKS: DRAMATIC: OPERAS: *Boleslaw smialy* (Boleslaw the Bold; 1908; Lemberg, Feb. 11, 1909); *Meduza* (1911; Warsaw, Oct. 22, 1912); *Eros i Psyche* (1916; in German, Breslau, March 10, 1917); *Casanova* (1922; Warsaw, June 8, 1923); *Beatrix Cenci* (1926; Warsaw, Jan. 30, 1927); *Mlyn diabelski* (The Devilish Mill; 1930; Poznan, Feb. 21, 1931). OPERETTA: *Lili chce spiewac* (Lile Wants to Sing; 1932; Poznan, March 7, 1933). BALLETS: *Pan Twardowski* (1920; Warsaw, May 9, 1921); *Apollo i dziewczyna* (Apollo and the Maiden; 1937).

BIBL.: A. Wieniawski, *L. R.* (Warsaw, 1928); M. Kaminski, *L. R.* (Katowice, 1951); J. Kański, *L. R.* (Kraków, 1955).

Rubbra, (Charles) Edmund, notable English composer and teacher; b. Northampton, May 23, 1901; d. Gerard's Cross, Feb. 13, 1986. His parents were musical, and he was taught to play the piano by his mother. He left school when he was 14 and was employed in various factories; at the same time, he continued to study music by himself, and attempted some composition; he received a scholarship to study composition at Reading Univ. in 1920, and then entered the Royal College of Music in London in 1921, taking courses with Holst (composition), R. O. Morris (harmony and counterpoint), and Evlyn and Howard Jones (piano); he also received some instruction from Vaughan Williams there before completing his studies in 1925. He taught at the Univ. of Oxford (1947–68) and at the Guildhall School of Music and Drama in London (from 1961). In 1960 he was made a Commander of the Order of the British Empire. He compensated for a late beginning in composition by an extremely energetic application to steady improvement of his technique; he finally elaborated a style of his own, marked by sustained lyricism and dynamic Romanticism; his harmonic language often verged on polytonality. His works include the opera *Bee-Bee-Bei* (1933) and the ballet *Prism* (1938). He publ. the books *Holst: A Monograph* (Monaco, 1947), *Counterpoint: A Survey* (London, 1960), and *Casella* (London, 1964).

BIBL.: R. Grover, *The Music of E. R.* (Aldershot, 1993).

Rubens, Paul (Alfred), English composer; b. London, April 29, 1875; d. Falmouth, Feb. 5, 1917. He was educated at the Univ. of Oxford. In 1899 he contributed some numbers to the famous musical revue *Floradora*, a success that induced him to devote himself to the composition of light operas. The following stage works by him were produced: *Lady Madcap* (1904), *Miss Hook of Holland* (1907), *My Mimosa Maid* (1908), *Dear Little Denmark* (1909), *The Balkan Princess* (1910), and *The Sunshine Girl* (1912).

Rubin, Marcel, Austrian composer; b. Vienna, July 7, 1905; d. there, May 12, 1995. He studied piano with Richard Robert, theory of composition with Richard Stöhr, and counterpoint and fugue with Franz Schmidt at the Vienna Academy of Music; he simultaneously attended courses in law. In 1925 he went to Paris, where he took private lessons with Milhaud. He was back in Vienna in 1931 to complete his studies in law, and in 1933 received his degree of Dr. Juris. After the Nazi Anschluss of Austria in 1938, Rubin, being a non-Aryan, fled to Paris, but was interned as an enemy alien; after France fell in 1940 he made his way to Marseilles. Convinced that only the communists could efficiently oppose fascism, he became a member of the illegal Austrian Communist Party in exile; in 1942 he went to Mexico and remained there until 1946; he returned to Vienna in 1947. His music followed the modernistic models of Parisianized Russians and Russianized French, with a mandatory hedonism in "new simplicity." Although he studied works of Schoenberg, Berg, and Webern with great assiduity and wrote articles about them, he never adopted the method of composition with 12 tones in his own music. Among his works is the comic opera *Kleider machen Leute* (1966–69; Vienna, Dec. 14, 1973); also *Die Stadt*, dance piece (1932; rev. 1980), and *Licht über Damaskus*, oratorio for 4 Soloists, Chorus, Organ, and Orch. (1987–88).

BIBL.: H. Krones, *M. R.* (Vienna, 1975).

Rubini, Giovanni Battista, celebrated Italian tenor; b. Romano, near Bergamo, April 7, 1794; d. there, March 3, 1854. His teacher was Rosio of Bergamo. After an auspicious debut in Pavia (1814), he appeared in Naples (1815–25), where he profited from further study with Nozzari. On Oct. 6, 1825, he sang in Paris, where he scored his 1st triumphs in Rossini's operas at the Théâtre-Italien. His performances of the leading parts in the operas of Bellini and Donizetti were also very successful, and there is reason to believe that Rubini's interpretations greatly contributed to the rising fame of both of those composers. Between 1831 and 1843 he sang in Paris and London; in 1843 he undertook a tour with Liszt, traveling with him in the Netherlands and Germany; in the same year he sang in Russia with tremendous acclaim; he visited Russia again in 1844, then returned to Italy, where he bought an estate near his native town, and remained there until his death; for some years he gave singing lessons. He publ. *12 lezioni di canto moderno per tenore o soprano* and an album of 6 songs, *L'addio*.

BIBL.: C. Traini, *Il cigno di Romano: G. B. R.* (Romano, 1954).

Rubinstein, Anton (Grigorievich), renowned Russian pianist, conductor, composer, and pedagogue; b. Vykhvatinetz, Podolia, Nov. 28, 1829; d. Peterhof, near St. Petersburg, Nov. 20, 1894. He was of a family of Jewish merchants who became baptized in Berdichev in July 1831. His mother gave him his 1st lessons in piano; the family moved to Moscow, where his father opened a small pencil factory. A well-known Moscow piano teacher, Alexandre Villoing, was entrusted with Rubinstein's musical education, and was in fact his only piano teacher. In 1839 Villoing took him to Paris, where Rubinstein played before Chopin and Liszt. He remained there until 1841, then made a concert tour in the Netherlands, Germany, Austria, England, Norway, and Sweden, returning to Russia in 1843. Since Anton's brother Nikolai evinced a talent for composition, the brothers were taken in 1844 to Berlin, where, on Meyerbeer's recommendation, Anton studied composition, with Dehn. He subsequently made a tour through Hungary with the flutist Heindl. He returned to Russia in 1848 and settled in St. Petersburg. There he enjoyed the enlightened patronage of the grand duchess Helen, and wrote 3 Russian operas: *Dmitri Donskoy* (1852), *The Siberian Hunters* (1853), and *Thomas the Fool* (1853). In 1854, with the assistance of the Grand Duchess, Rubinstein undertook another tour in western Europe. He found publishers in Berlin, and gave concerts of his own works in London and Paris, exciting admiration as both composer and pianist; on his return in 1858 he was appointed court pianist and conductor of the court concerts. He assumed the direction of the Russian Musical Soc. in 1859, and in 1862 founded the Imperial Cons. in St. Petersburg, remaining its director until 1867. For 20 years thereafter he held no official position; from 1867 until 1870 he gave concerts in Europe, winning fame as a pianist 2d only to Liszt. During the season of 1872–73, he made a triumphant American tour, playing in 215 concerts, for which he was paid lavishly; he appeared as a soloist and jointly with the violinist Wieniawski. He produced a sensation by playing without the score, a novel procedure at the time. Returning to Europe, he elaborated a cycle of historical concerts, in programs ranging from Bach to Chopin; he usually devoted the last concert of a cycle to Russian composers. In 1887 he resumed the directorship of the St. Petersburg Cons., resigning again in 1891, when he went to Dresden. He returned to Russia the year of his death.

In 1890 he established the Rubinstein Prize, an international competition open to young men between 20 and 26 years of age. Two prizes of 5,000 francs each were offered, 1 for composition, the other for piano. Quinquennial competitions were held in St. Petersburg, Berlin, Vienna, and Paris.

Rubinstein's role in Russian musical culture was of the greatest importance. He introduced European methods into education, and established high standards of artistic performance. He was the 1st Russian musician who was equally prominent as composer and interpreter. According to contemporary reports, his playing possessed extraordinary power (his octave passages were famous) and insight, revealed particularly in his performance of Beethoven's sonatas. His renown as a composer was scarcely less. His *Ocean Symphony* was one of the most frequently performed orch. works in Europe and America; his piano concertos were part of the standard repertoire; his pieces for Piano Solo, *Melody in F, Romance*, and *Kamennoi Ostrow*, became perennial favorites. After his death, his orch. works all but vanished from concert programs, as did his operas, with the exception of *The Demon*, which is still perf. in Russia. His brother was the prominent Russian pianist, conductor, teacher, and composer Nikolai (Grigorievich) Rubinstein (b. Moscow, June 14, 1835; d. Paris, March 23, 1881).

WORKS: DRAMATIC: OPERAS: *Dmitri Donskoy* (1849–50; St. Petersburg, April 30, 1852); *The Siberian Hunters* (1852; Weimar, 1854); *Stenka Razin* (1852; unfinished); *Hadji-Abrek* (1852–53; 1st perf. as *Revenge*, St. Petersburg, 1858); *Thomas the Fool* (St. Petersburg, May 23, 1853); *Das verlorene Paradies* (1856; Düsseldorf, 1875); *Die Kinder der Heide* (1860; Vienna, Feb. 23, 1861); *Feramors* (1862; Dresden, Feb. 24, 1863); *Der Thurm zu Babel* (1869; Königsberg, 1870); *The Demon* (1871; St. Petersburg, Jan. 25, 1875); *Die Makkabäer* (1874; Berlin, April 17, 1875); *Nero* (1875–76; Hamburg, Nov. 1, 1879); *The Merchant Kalashnikov* (1877–79; St. Petersburg, March 5, 1880); *Sulamith* (1882–83; Hamburg, Nov. 8, 1883); *Unter Räubern* (Hamburg, Nov. 8, 1883); *Der Papagei* (Hamburg, Nov. 11, 1884); *The Careworn One* (1888; St. Petersburg, Dec. 3, 1889); *Moses* (1885–91; Prague, 1892); *Christus* (1887–93; Bremen, 1895). BALLET: *The Vine* (1882).

WRITINGS: *Memoirs* (St. Petersburg, 1889; Eng. tr. as *Autobiography of Anton Rubinstein*, Boston, 1890); *Music and Its Representatives* (Moscow, 1891; Eng. tr., N.Y., 1892; also publ. as *A Conversation on Music*); *Leitfaden zum richtigen Gebrauch des Pianoforte-Pedals* (Leipzig, 1896; French tr., Brussels, 1899); *Gedankenkorb, Litterarischer Nachlass* (Stuttgart, 1896); *Die Meister des Klaviers* (Berlin, 1899).

BIBL.: A. McArthur, *A. R.* (London, 1889); E. Zabel, *A. R.* (Leipzig, 1892); L. Martinov, *Episodes de la vie de R.* (Brussels, 1895); A. Soubies, *A. R.* (Paris, 1895); E. Wessel, *Some Explanations, Hints and Remarks of A. R. from His Lessons in the St. Petersburg Cons.* (St. Petersburg, 1901; Ger. tr., Leipzig, 1904); N. Findeisen, *A. R.* (Moscow, 1907); La Mara, *A. R., Musikalische Studienkopfe* (vol. 3, 7th ed., Leipzig, 1909; separately, Leipzig, 1911); N. Bernstein, *A. R.* (Leipzig, 1911); A. Hervey, *A. R.* (London, 1913); L. Barenboym, *A. G. R.*, vol. 1 (Moscow, 1957).

Rubinstein, Beryl, American pianist, teacher, and composer; b. Athens, Ga., Oct. 26, 1898; d. Cleveland, Dec. 29, 1952. He studied piano with his father and Alexander Lambert; he toured the United States as a child (1905–11), then went to Berlin to study with Busoni and Vianna da Motta. He was appointed to the faculty of the Cleveland Inst. of Music in 1921 and became its director in 1932. He wrote an opera, *The Sleeping Beauty*, to a libretto by John Erskine (Juilliard School of Music, N.Y., Jan. 19, 1938); also transcriptions from Gershwin's *Porgy and Bess*.

Rudel, Julius, prominent Austrian-born American conductor; b. Vienna, March 6, 1921. Following training at the Vienna Academy of Music, he emigrated to the United States in 1938 and became a naturalized American citizen in 1944. He completed his studies at the Mannes School of Music in New York. In 1943 he joined the staff of the N.Y. City Opera as a répétiteur. On Nov. 25, 1944, he made his conducting debut there with *Der Zigeunerbaron*, and subsequently remained closely associated with it. From 1957 to 1979 he served as its music director. During his innovative tenure, he programmed an extensive repertoire of standard, nonstandard, and contemporary operas. He made a special effort to program operas by American composers. He also was music director of the Caramoor Festival in Katonah, N.Y., and the Wolf Trap Farm Park for the Performing Arts in Vienna, Virginia. He was the first music director of the Kennedy Center in Washington, D.C. (1971–74). On. Oct. 7, 1978, he made his Metropolitan Opera debut in New York conducting *Werther*, and continued to make occasional appearances there in subsequent years. He also appeared as a guest conductor of operas in San Francisco, Chicago, London, Paris, Berlin, Munich, Milan, Hamburg, and Buenos Aires. After serving as music director of the Buffalo Phil. from 1979 to 1985, he concentrated on a career as a guest conductor around the world. In 1969 the Julius Rudel Award for young conductors was established in his honor.

Ruders, Poul, Danish composer; b. Ringsted, March 27, 1949. He began piano and organ lessons in childhood, and later pursued training in organ at the Royal Danish Cons. of Music in Copenhagen (graduated, 1975). Although he had a few orchestration lessons there, he was mainly autodidact as a composer. From 1975 he was active as a Lutheran church organist and choirmaster. Later he devoted much time to composition and guest lecturing. In 1991 he was a guest lecturer at Yale Univ. He received the Charles Heidseick Award of the Royal Phil. Soc. of London in 1991. In his music, Ruders has been particularly cognizant of all styles of music, from the Baroque to the popular genres. His works are notable for their startling juxtapositions and superimpositions of various styles and techniques. Among his compositions are the operas *Tycho* (1985–86; Århus, May 16, 1987) and *The Handmaid's Tale* (1998).

Rüdinger, Gottfried, German composer; b. Lindau, Aug. 23, 1886; d. Gauting, near Munich, Jan. 17, 1946. He was a student in theology; he took courses in composition with Reger at the Leipzig Cons. (1907–09). In 1910 he settled in Munich and began teaching privately; he taught at the Academy of Music there from 1920. He composed industriously in many genres; he brought out a "peasant play-opera," *Die Tegernseer im Himmel*, and several children's operas, including *Benchtesgadener Sagenspiel, Musikantenkomödie*, and *König Folkwart*.

Rudnicki, Marian (Teofil), Polish conductor and composer; b. Kraków, March 7, 1888; d. Warsaw, Dec. 31, 1944. He conducted operetta in Kraków (1916–19) and later at the Warsaw Municipal Opera. He wrote mostly theater music.

Rudnytsky, Antin, Polish-American pianist, conductor, and composer; b. Luka, Galicia, Feb. 7, 1902; d. Toms River, N.J., Nov. 30, 1975. He studied piano with Schnabel and Petri, composition with Schreker, and musicology with Curt Sachs in Berlin; he received his Ph.D. at the Univ. of Berlin in 1926. In 1927 he went to Russia, where he conducted opera in Kharkov and Kiev; then was conductor of the Lwów Opera (1932–37). In 1937 he emigrated to the United States; he toured with his wife, the singer Maris Sokil, as her piano accompanist. He composed an opera, *Dovbush* (1937), and some ballet music.

Rudolf, Max, eminent German-born American conductor and teacher; b. Frankfurt am Main, June 15, 1902; d. Philadelphia, Feb. 28, 1995. He began his musical training when he was 7. He studied cello with Maurits Frank, piano with Eduard Jung, and composition with Bernhard Sekles, and also learned to play the organ and the trumpet. In 1921–22 he attended the Univ. of Frankfurt am Main. In 1922 he became a répétiteur at the Freiburg im Breisgau Opera, where he made his conducting debut in 1923. After working as a répétiteur at the Darmstadt Opera (1923–25), he returned there to hold its post of 1st conductor from 1927 to 1929. From 1929 to 1935 he conducted at the German Theater in Prague. In 1929–30 he appeared as a guest conductor of the Berlin Phil. In 1935 he went to Göteborg, where he made appearances as a conductor with both the radio orch. and the orch. society. In 1940 he emigrated to the United States and in 1945 became a naturalized American citizen. He conducted the New Opera Co. in New York before joining the staff of the Metropolitan Opera in New York in 1945. On Jan. 13, 1946, he made his first appearance as a conductor at the Metropolitan Opera in a Sunday night concert. His formal debut followed on March 2, 1946, when he conducted *Der Rosenkavalier*. From 1950 to 1958 he served as artistic administrator of the Metropolitan Opera, and also was active as a conductor there. In 1958 he became music director of the Cincinnati Sym. Orch., a position he retained with distinction until 1969. In 1966 he led it on a world tour and in 1969 on a major tour of Europe. He also served as music director of the Cincinnati May Festival in 1963 and again from 1967 to 1970. From 1970 to 1973 he was head of the opera and conducting depts. at the Curtis Inst. of Music in Philadelphia. In 1973–74 he was principal conductor of the Dallas Sym. Orch., and he also returned to the Metropolitan Opera as a conductor during this time. In 1976–77 he was music advisor of the New Jersey Sym. Orch. In subsequent years, he made occasional appearances as a guest conductor with American orchs. From 1983 he again taught at the Curtis Inst. of Music. In 1988 he received the 1st Theodore Thomas Award for his services to music. He publ. the widely used vol. *The Grammar of Conducting: A Comprehensive Guide to Baton Technique and Interpretation* (N.Y., 1950; 3d. ed., 1994, with the assistance of Michael Stern). As was to be expected, Rudolf displayed a mastery of baton technique. In his interpretations, he excelled in unmannered performances of the great Austro-German masterpieces.

Rudziński, Witold, Polish composer and pedagogue; b. Siebież, Lithuania, March 14, 1913. He studied with Szeligowski at the Vilnius Cons. (1928–36) and attended the Univ. of Vilnius (1931–36); he went to Paris, where he took composition lessons with Boulanger and Koechlin (1938–39); upon his return, he taught at the Vilnius Cons. (1939–42) and the Łódz Cons. (1945–47); he settled in Warsaw and served as director of the Opera (1948–49) and as a prof. at the Cons. (from 1957). He wrote a biography of Moniuszko (2 vols., Kraków, 1955, 1961), a study on the technique of Bartók (Kraków, 1965), and an exposition on musical rhythm (2 vols., 1987), among other works.

WORKS: DRAMATIC: OPERAS: *Janko muzykant* (Janko the Musician; 1948–51; Bytom, June 20, 1953); *Komendant Paryza* (The Commander of Paris; 1955–58; Poznan, 1960); *Odprawa posłów greckich* (The Departure of Greek Emissaries; Kraków, 1962); *Sulamita* (The Shulamite; 1964); *The Yellow Nightcap* (1969); *Chlopi* (The Peasants; 1972; Warsaw, June 30, 1974); *The Ring and the Rose* (1982). ORATORIOS: *Gaude Mater Polonia* for Narrator, 3 Soloists, Chorus, and Orch. (1966); *Lipce* for Chorus and Chamber Orch. (1968).

Rudzinski, Zbigniew, Polish composer and teacher; b. Czechowice, Oct. 23, 1935. After attending the Univ. of Warsaw (1956), he pursued training in composition with Perkowski at the Warsaw Academy of Music (diploma, 1960); he completed his studies in Paris and the Netherlands. He served as chief of the music dept. of the Warsaw Documentary Film Studio (1960–67), then was a prof. (from 1973) of composition at the Chopin Academy of Music in Warsaw, where he also was vice rector (1981–83). His works include the chamber opera *Manekiny* (The Mannequins; Wrocław, Oct. 29, 1981).

Ruffo, Titta (real name, **Ruffo Cafiero Titta**), famous Italian baritone; b. Pisa, June 9, 1877; d. Florence, July 5, 1953. He found it convenient to transpose his first and last names for professional purposes. He studied with Persichini at the Accademia di Santa Cecilia in Rome, then with Casini in Milan. He made his operatic debut in Rome as the Herald in *Lohengrin* (1898), then sang in South America; returning to Italy, he appeared in all the principal theaters; he also sang in Vienna, Paris, and London. He made his American debut in Philadelphia as Rigoletto (Nov. 4, 1912) with the combined Philadelphia-Chicago Opera Co., and then sang in Chicago (1912–14; 1919–27); his first appearance with the Metropolitan Opera was as Figaro in *Il Barbiere di Siviglia* (N.Y., Jan. 19, 1922). He left the Metropolitan in 1929 and returned to Rome. In 1937 he was briefly under arrest for opposing the Mussolini regime; he then went to Florence, where he remained until his death. His memoirs appeared as *La mia parabola* (Milan, 1937; rev. 1977, by his son). A renowned dramatic artist, he excelled in roles from Verdi's operas and was also an outstanding Figaro, Hamlet, Tonio, and Scarpia.

BIBL.: M. Barrenechea, *T. R.: Notas de psicologia artistica* (Buenos Aires, 1911); A. Farkas, ed., *T. R.: An Anthology* (Westport, Conn., 1984).

Ruggi, Francesco, Italian composer; b. Naples, Oct. 21, 1767; d. there, Jan. 23, 1845. He studied at the Cons. di S. Loreto in Naples under Fenaroli. He became a prof. of composition at the Cons. di San Pietro a Majella. Among his works were the operas *L'ombra di Nino* (Naples, 1795), *La Guerra aperta* (Naples, 1796), and *Sofi tripponi* (Milan, 1804).

Rung, Frederik, Danish conductor, teacher, and composer; b. Copenhagen, June 14, 1854; d. there, Jan. 22, 1914. He studied with his father, the Danish conductor and composer Henrik Rung (1807–71), succeeding him as conductor of the Cecilia Soc. (1871). He founded its Madrigalkoret (1887), which won considerable renown, and was also 2d conductor (1884–1908) and chief conductor (from 1908) at the Royal Theater in Copenhagen. He taught at the Copenhagen Cons. (1881–93). Among his works were the operas *Det hemmelige Selskab* (The Secret Party; Copenhagen, Feb. 9, 1888) and *Den trekantede Hat* (The 3-cornered Hat; Copenhagen, Nov. 7, 1894).

Rungenhagen, Carl Friedrich, German conductor and composer; b. Berlin, Sept. 27, 1778; d. there, Dec. 21, 1851. He was a pupil of Benda. In 1815 became 2d conductor of the Singakademie, succeeding Zelter in 1833 as 1st conductor. He was a member of the Berlin Academy, and a teacher in the School of Composition. Among his works were 4 operas and 3 oratorios.

Runnicles, Donald, Scottish conductor; b. Edinburgh, Nov. 16, 1954. He was educated at the univs. of Edinburgh and Cambridge, and also studied at the London Opera Centre. In 1980 he became a répétiteur at the Mannheim National Theater, where he then was a conductor (1984–87), then was conductor in Hannover (1987–89). From 1989 to 1992 he was Generalmusikdirektor in Freiburg im Breisgau. He also conducted at the Metropolitan Opera in New York (from 1988), the San Francisco Opera (from 1990), the Vienna State Opera (from 1990), and the Glyndebourne Festival (from 1991). In 1992 he became music director of the San Francisco Opera. In 1994 he scored an outstanding success at the Edinburgh Festival conducting Mahler's 8th Sym. On Sept. 5, 1997, he conducted the gala reopening performance at the renovated San Francisco Opera house. Runnicles conducts left-handed.

Ruolz-Montchal, Henri (-Catherine-Camille), Comte de, French composer; b. Paris, March 5, 1808; d. there, Sept. 30, 1887. He was a pupil of Berton, Lesueur, Paër, and Rossini. He won some success as a composer, but the loss of his family fortune in 1840 induced him to abandon music and devote himself to the more practical study of chemistry. His dramatic works included *Attendre et courir* (with F. Halévy; 1830), *Lara* (Naples, Nov. 22, 1835), and *La Vendetta* (Paris, 1839).

Rusconi, Gerardo, Italian composer; b. Milan, Feb. 1, 1922; d. there, Dec. 23, 1974. He studied at the Parma Cons. He began his career as a composer by writing light music for the stage, radio, and the films, then undertook more serious genres of music. His works include *L'appuntamento*, opera (1971).

Rushton, Julian (Gordon), English musicologist; b. Cambridge, May 22, 1941. He studied at the Guildhall School of Music and Drama in London (1959–60), Trinity College, Cambridge (B.A., 1963), and Magdalen College, Oxford (B.Mus., 1965; M.A., 1967; Ph.D., 1970, with the diss. *Music and Drama at the Academie royale de musique, Paris, 1774–1789*). He taught at the Univ. of East Anglia (1968–74) and at the Univ. of Cambridge (1974–81); was West Riding Prof. of Music and head of the music dept. at the Univ. of Leeds (from 1982). He ed. *W. A. Mozart: Don Giovanni* (Cambridge, 1981) and *W. A. Mozart: Idomeneo* (Cambridge, 1993) and publ. *The Musical Language of Berlioz* (Cambridge, 1983) and *Classical Music: A Concise History* (London, 1986).

Russell, Lillian (real name, **Helen Louise Leonard**), colorful American soprano and actress; b. Clinton, Iowa, Dec. 4, 1861; d. Pittsburgh, June 6, 1922. She studied with L. Damrosch in N.Y., where she sang in the chorus for a production of *H.M.S. Pinafore* in 1879. In the following year she was engaged by the entertainer and manager Tony Pastor for the vaudeville circuit, assuming the stage name of Lillian Russell. Her 1st success came in 1881, when she starred in *The Grand Mogul* (also known as *The Snake Charmer*) in New York; she subsequently starred in *Polly, or The Pet of the Regiment* (1885), *Pepita, or The Girl with the Glass Eyes* (1886), *The Queen's Mate* (1888), *Poor Jonathan* (1890), *La Cigale* (1891), *Princess Nicotine* (1893), *An American Beauty* (1896), and *Whirl-i-gig* (1899). She toured England and the United States in a burlesque company with Joe Weber and Lew Fields (1899–1904); after her last stage appearance, in *Hokey-pokey* (1912), she remained in the limelight by writing a syndicated newspaper column and lecturing on the vaudeville circuit.

BIBL.: P. Morell, *L. R.: The Era of Plush* (N.Y., 1940); J. Burke, *Duet in Diamonds: The Flamboyant Saga of L. R. and Diamond Jim Brady in America's Gilded Age* (N.Y., 1972).

Russo, William (Joseph), American composer and teacher; b. Chicago, June 25, 1928. He studied privately with Lennie Tristano (composition and improvisation, 1943–46), John J. Becker (composition, 1953–55), and Karel B. Jirák (composition and conducting, 1955–57). He was a trombonist and chief composer-arranger with the Stan Kenton Orch. (1950–54), then worked with his own groups in New York and London. He taught at the School of Jazz in Lenox, Mass. (summers, 1956–57), and at the Manhattan School of Music (1958–61). In 1965 he joined the faculty of Columbia College in Chicago; he also was a Distinguished Visiting Prof. of Composition at the Peabody Inst. in Baltimore (1969–71), a teacher at Antioch College (1971–72), and composer-in-residence of the city and county of San Francisco (1975–76). He publ. *Composing for the Jazz Orchestra* (Chicago, 1961; 2d ed., 1973), *Jazz: Composition and Orchestration* (Chicago, 1968; 2d ed., 1974), and *Composing Music: A New Approach* (Chicago, 1988). Russo's expertise as a composer-arranger has led him to create a number of remarkable third-stream scores.

WORKS: DRAMATIC: OPERAS: *John Hooton* (1961; BBC, London, Jan. 1963); *The Island* (1963); *Land of Milk and Honey* (1964); *Antigone* (1967); *Aesop's Fables*, rock opera (N.Y., Aug. 17, 1972); *A General Opera* (1976); *The Payoff*, cabaret opera (Chicago, Feb. 16, 1984); *A Cabaret Opera* (1985; alternate forms as *The Alice B. Toklas Hashish Fudge Review*, N.Y., Dec. 8, 1977; Paris Lights, N.Y., Jan. 24, 1980, and *The Shepherds' Christmas*, Chicago, Dec. 1979); *Dubrovsky* (1988); *The Sacrifice* (1990). BALLETS: *The World of Alcina* (1954; rev. 1962); *Les Deux Errants* (Monte Carlo, April 1956); *The Golden Bird* (Chicago, Feb. 17, 1984); other stage pieces; film music. OTHER: *Talking to the Sun*, song cycle theater piece (Chicago, March 5, 1989).

Rust, Giacomo, Italian composer; b. Rome, 1741; d. Barcelona, 1786. He studied at the Turchini Cons. in Naples and with Rinaldo di Capua in Rome. In 1763 he composed his first opera for Venice, where many of his subsequent operas were premiered. In 1777 he was called to Salzburg as court Kapellmeister, but ill health compelled him to give up his post within a few months and he returned to Italy to continue his productive career as an opera composer. In 1783 he became maestro di cappella at the Barcelona Cathedral, but continued to compose until his death. In all, he wrote some 30 dramatic scores.

Rutini, Giovanni Marco, Italian composer; b. Florence, April 25, 1723; d. there, Dec. 22, 1797. He studied with Leo (composition), Fago (harpsichord), and Pagliarulo (violin) at the Cons. della Pietà dei Turchini in Naples (1739–44). In 1748 he went to St. Petersburg, where he served as harpsichord teacher to the future Catherine II and conductor of Count Sheremetev's private orch. After returning to his homeland in 1761, he brought out a number of operas, winning particular notice for his *I matrimoni in maschera* (Cremona, 1763) and *L'Olandese in Italia* (Florence, 1765). In 1769 he became maestro di cappella to the duke of Modena. Although Rutini won accolades as a composer for the theater during his lifetime, his historical significance rests on his harpsichord music. His influence on the development of keyboard music may be discerned in the works of Haydn, Mozart, Beethoven, and Clementi.

BIBL.: G. Balducci, *La figura e l'opera di G.M. R.* (diss., Univ. of Florence, 1964).

Rutter, John (Milford), well-known English conductor and composer; b. London, Sept. 24, 1945. He was educated at Clare College, Cambridge (B.A., 1967; Mus.B., 1968; M.A., 1970), where he was later director of music (1975–79); among his teachers was David Willcocks, with whom he coedited several choral collections, including 3 in the Carols for Choirs series (Oxford, 1970–80); he also taught through the Open Univ. (1975–88). In 1981 he founded the Cambridge Singers, subsequently conducting them in an extensive repertoire; in 1990 he conducted their Carnegie Hall debut in New York; in 1984 he established Collegium Records, a label dedicated to their performances. His compositions and arrangements are numerous and accessible, and feature an extensive catalog of choral works that are frequently performed in Britain and the United States. His works include 2 children's operas: *Bang!* (1975) and *The Piper of Hamelin* (1980).

Ruyneman, Daniel, Dutch composer; b. Amsterdam, Aug. 8, 1886; d. there, July 25, 1963. He began his study of music relatively late. He received training in piano from De John and in composition from Zweers at the Amsterdam Cons. (1913–16). In 1918 he was a cofounder of the Nederlansche Vereeniging voor Moderne Scheppende Toonkunst, which became the Dutch section of the ISCM in 1922. In 1930 he organized the Netherlands Soc. for Contemporary Music, serving as president until 1962; he ed. its journal, *Maandblad voor Hedendaagse Muziek* (1930–40), until it was suppressed during the Nazi occupation of the Netherlands; he was general secretary of the ISCM (1947–51). Ruyneman made a special study of Javanese instruments and introduced them in some of his works. He was naturally attracted to exotic subjects with mystic connotations and coloristic effects; he also worked on restoration of early music; in 1930 he orchestrated fragments of Mussorgsky's unfinished opera *The Marriage*, and added his own music for the missing acts of the score. His own works include the operas *De gebroeders Karamasoff* (1928) and *Le Mariage* (1930) as well as incidental music, *De Clown*, "psycho-symbolic" play (1915).

BIBL.: A. Petronio, *D. R. et son oeuvre* (Liège, 1922).

Rydl, Kurt, Austrian bass; b. Vienna, Oct. 8, 1947. He received vocal training in Vienna and Moscow. In 1973 he made his operatic debut as Wagner's Daland in Stuttgart. He became a member of the Vienna State Opera in 1976, where he sang such roles as Osmin, Rocco, King Marke, the Landgrave, Hagen, Méphistophélès, Zaccaria, and King Philip II. As a guest artist, he sang at the Salzburg Festival (1985; 1987–90), Barcelona (1990), Milan's La Scala (1990–91), Florence (1992), and London's Covent Garden (1995, 1997).

Ryelandt, Joseph, Belgian composer and teacher; b. Bruges, April 7, 1870; d. there, June 29, 1965. He studied composition with Edgar Tinel. Thanks to a personal fortune (he was a baron), he did not have to earn a living by his music. He was director of the Bruges Cons. (1924–45) and a teacher at the Ghent Cons. (1929–39). He lived a very long life and composed much music. His works include *La Parabole des vierges*, spiritual drama (1894), and *Sainte Cécile*, lyrical drama (1902); also 5 oratorios: *Purgatorium* (1904), *De Komst des Heren* (1906–07), *Maria* (1910), *Agnus Dei* (1913–15), and *Christus Rex* (1921–22).

Rypdal, Terje, Norwegian composer and jazz and rock guitarist; b. Oslo, Aug. 23, 1947. He took up the piano at age 5 and the guitar at 13; subsequently he studied musicology at the Univ. of Oslo and was a composition student of Mortensen at the Oslo Cons. (1970–72) and of George Russell, who introduced him to his Lydian Concept of tonal organization. Rypdal was active as a performer with his own pop band, the Vanguards, and later with his group, Dreams; he also worked with Russell's sextet and big band. In 1969 he became a member of the Jan Garbarek Quartet. His long association with jazz and rock had significant impact upon his approach to composition. Whether composing in a serial or tonal mode, Rypdal's music relfects a penchant for utilizing late romantic, jazz, and avant-garde elements. Among his works are the operas *Orfeus* (1971) and *Freden* (1976); also incidental music.

Rysanek, Leonie, distinguished Austrian soprano; b. Vienna, Nov. 14, 1926; d. there, March 7, 1998. She studied at the Vienna Cons. with Rudolf Grossmann, whom she later married. She made her operatic debut as Agathe in *Der Freischütz* in Innsbruck in 1949, then sang at Saarbrücken (1950–52). She first attracted notice when she appeared as Sieglinde at the Bayreuth Festival in 1951; she became a member of the Bavarian State Opera in Munich in 1952, and went with it to London's Covent Garden in 1953, where she sang Danae; in 1954 she joined the Vienna State Opera; she also sang in various other major European opera houses. On Sept. 18, 1956, she made her U.S. debut as Senta at the San Francisco Opera and later made a spectacular appearance at the Metropolitan Opera in New York on Feb. 5, 1959, when she replaced Maria Callas in the role of Lady Macbeth in Verdi's opera on short notice; she continued to sing there with notable distinction for some 35 years. She received the Lotte Lehmann Ring from the Vienna State Opera in 1979. In 1984 she toured Japan with the Hamburg State Opera. In 1986 she appeared as Kostelnika in *Jenůfa* in San Francisco. She sang Kabanicha in *Kat'á Kabanová* in Los Angeles in 1988. In 1990 she appeared as Herodias at the Deutsche Opera in Berlin. In 1992 she sang the Countess in *The Queen of Spades* in Barcelona, a role she repeated for her farewell appearance at the Metropolitan Opera on Jan. 2, 1996. Her younger sister Lotte Rysanek (b. Vienna, March 18, 1928) attained a fine reputation in Vienna as a lyric soprano.

BIBL.: P. Dusek and P. Schmidt, *L. R.: 40 Jahre Operngeschichte* (Hamburg, 1990).

Rytel, Piotr, Polish composer and teacher; b. Vilnius, Sept. 20, 1884; d. Warsaw, Jan. 2, 1970. He studied with Michalowski and Noskowski at the Warsaw Cons.; in 1911 he was appointed a prof. of piano, and in 1918 a prof. of harmony there. He was director of the Sopot State College of Music (1956–61). His works include the operas *Ijola* (1927; Warsaw, Dec. 14, 1929), *Koniec Mesjasza* (1935–36), *Krzyzowcy* (1940–41), and *Andrzej z Chelmna* (1942–43), and the ballets *Faun i Psyche* (1931) and *Śląski pierścień* (The Silesian Ring; 1956).

Rzewski, Frederic (Anthony), American pianist, teacher, and composer; b. Westfield, Mass., April 13, 1938. He studied counterpoint with Thompson and orchestration with Piston at Harvard Univ. (B.A., 1958) and continued his studies with Sessions and Babbitt at Princeton Univ. (M.F.A., 1960), then received instruction from Dallapiccola in Florence on a Fulbright scholarship (1960–61) and from Carter in Berlin on a Ford Foundation grant (1963–65). With Curran and Teitelbaum, other similarly futuroscopic musicians, he founded the M.E.V. (Musica Elettronica Viva) in Rome in 1966; he was active as a pianist in various avant-garde settings and played concerts with the topless cellist Charlotte Moorman; he also devoted much time to teaching. In 1977 he became prof. of composition at the Liège Cons. As a composer, he pursues the shimmering distant vision of optimistic, positivistic anti-music. He is furthermore a granitically overpowering piano technician, capable of depositing huge boulders of sonoristic material across the keyboard without actually wrecking the instrument. Among his works are *The Persians*, music theater (1985), *Chains*, 12 television operas (1986), and *The Triumph of Death*, stage oratorio (1987–88).

S

Sabata, Victor de. See **De Sabata, Victor.**

Sacchini, Antonio (Maria Gasparo Gioacchino), prominent Italian composer; b. Florence, June 14, 1730; d. Paris, Oct. 6, 1786. He entered the Cons. of Santa Maria di Loreto at Naples as a violin pupil of Nicola Fiorenza; he also received instruction in singing from Gennaro Manna and in harpsichord, organ, and composition from Francesco Durante. His intermezzo *Fra Donato* was performed at the Cons. in 1756; his comic opera *Olimpia* was given at the Teatro dei Fiorentini in 1758, the same year in which he became maestro di cappella straordinario at the Cons.; he was made secondo maestro in 1761. His opera seria, *Olimpiade*, scored a remarkable success at its Padua premiere on July 9, 1763; it subsequently was performed throughout Italy. During a stay in Rome, he produced several comic operas, including *Il finto pazzo per amore* (1765), *La Contadina in corte* (1766), and *L'isola d'amore* (1766). In 1768 he was named director of the Cons. dell'Ospedaletto in Venice; he also made a visit to Germany, where he brought out the operas *Scipione in Cartagena* (Munich, Jan. 8, 1770), *Calliroe* (Stuttgart, Feb. 11, 1770), and *L'Eroe cinese* (Munich, April 27, 1770). In 1772 he went to London, where he acquired a notable reputation; among the operas produced there were *Tamerlano* (May 6, 1773), *Montezuma* (Feb. 7, 1775), *Erifile* (Feb. 7, 1778), *L'Amore soldato* (May 4, 1778), *L'Avaro deluso, o Don Calandrino* (Nov. 24, 1778), and *Enea e Lavinia* (March 25, 1779). In 1781 he received an invitation from Marie Antoinette, through the "intendant des menus-plaisirs," to go to Paris. His name was already known in France, since his opera *L'isola d'amore*, arranged as *La Colonie* ("comic opera imitated from the Italian"), had been produced in Paris on Aug. 16, 1775; upon his arrival he was forthwith commissioned to write 3 works at a fee of 10,000 francs each. For this purpose he adapted his Italian opera *Armida e Rinaldo* (Milan, 1772) to a French text as *Renaud*, "tragédie lyrique" in 3 acts (produced at the Académie Royale de Musique, Feb. 25, 1783), and his opera *Il Cidde* (Rome, 1764) as *Chimène* (Fontainebleau, Nov. 18, 1783); the 3d opera, *Dardanus*, was a new work; it was staged at the Trianon at Versailles, Sept. 18, 1784, in the presence of Louis XVI and Marie Antoinette. In Paris Sacchini found himself in unintended rivalry with Piccinni as a representative of Italian music in the famous artistic war against the proponents of the French operas of Gluck; Sacchini's most successful opera, however, was to the French text *Œdipe à Colonne*, first presented at Versailles (Jan. 4, 1786) and produced at the Paris Opéra (Feb. 1, 1787) after Sacchini's death. It held the stage for half a century, and there were sporadic revivals later on. His last opera, also to a French libretto, *Arvire et Evelina*, was left unfinished, and was produced posth. (Paris Opéra, April 29, 1788; 3d act added by J. B. Rey). Sacchini found his métier as a composer of serious operas, but his works were nonetheless typical products of the Italian operatic art of his time, possessing melodious grace but lacking in dramatic development. Among his other compositions were 8 oratorios.

BIBL.: U. Prota-Giurleo, *S. non nacque a Pozzuoli* (Naples, 1952); F. Schlitzer, *A. S.: Schede e appunti per una sua storia teatrale* (Siena, 1955); U. Prota-Giurleo, *S. a Napoli* (Naples, 1956); idem, *S. fra Piccinisti e Gluckisti* (Naples, 1957); E. Thierstein, *Five French Operas of S.* (diss., Univ. of Cincinnati, 1974).

Sacco, P(atrick) Peter, American composer, tenor, and teacher; b. Albion, N.Y., Oct. 25, 1928. He was born into a musical family and began touring as a child pianist and boy soprano at an early age. Following studies at the Eastman Preparatory School in Rochester, N.Y. (1941–44), he pursued training with Vivian Major and William Willett at the State Univ. of N.Y. at Fredonia (B.M., 1950). During military service, he continued his studies with Wolfgang Niederste-Schee in Frankfurt am Main (1950–52). After his discharge, he completed his training with Barlow, Rogers, and Hanson at the Eastman School of Music in Rochester, N.Y. (M.M., 1954; D.Mus., 1958). From 1959 until his retirement in 1980 he taught at San Francisco State Univ. He also pursued an active career as a concert artist. In his music, Sacco adhered to traditional harmony but developed an ingenious chromatic method of expression. His works include the chamber opera *Mr. Vinegar* (1966–67; Redding, Calif., May 12, 1967) and 3 oratorios: *Jesu*

(Grand Rapids, Mich., Dec. 3, 1956), *Midsummer Dream Night* (San Francisco, June 15, 1961), and *Solomon* (San Francisco, Dec. 12, 1976).

Sachse, Leopold, German-American bass, opera producer, and administrator; b. Berlin, Jan. 5, 1880; d. Englewood, N.J., April 3, 1961. He studied at the Cologne Cons.; then in Vienna. In 1902 he joined the Strasbourg Opera as a baritone, then was Intendant in Münster (1907), Halle (1914–19), and at the Hamburg Opera (1922–33), where he produced a number of contemporary works. He was forced to leave his homeland by the Nazis and settled in the United States; he was a producer at the Metropolitan Opera in New York (1935–55), taught stage technique at the Juilliard Graduate School in New York (1936–43), and was a stage director at the N.Y. City Opera (from 1945). He founded his own Opera in English Co. (1951).

Sack (real name, **Weber**), **Erna,** German soprano; b. Berlin, Feb. 6, 1898; d. Mainz, March 2, 1972. She studied in Prague and with O. Daniel in Berlin. She made her operatic debut as a contralto at the Berlin Städtische Oper (1925), then turned to coloratura soprano roles and sang in Bielefeld (1930–32), Wiesbaden (1932–34), and Breslau (1934–35); subsequently, in 1935, she joined the Dresden State Opera, where she was chosen to create the role of Isotta in Strauss's *Die schweigsame Frau*; she appeared with the company as Zerbinetta under Strauss's direction during its visit to London's Covent Garden in 1936. In 1937 she sang opera in Chicago and made a concert tour of the United States; she also appeared in opera in Milan, Paris, Vienna, Salzburg, and other major European music centers. After World War II, she made an extensive world tour as a concert singer (1947–52) and gave concerts in the United States (1954–55). In 1966 she settled in Wiesbaden.

Sacrati, Francesco, Italian composer; b. Parma (baptized), Sept. 17, 1605; d. probably in Modena, May 20, 1650. He was one of the earliest composers for the opera theaters that opened in Venice after 1637; he was also a pioneer of opera buffa before the rise of the Neapolitan school. He wrote an opera, *La Delia*, for the opening of the Teatro Crimani dei Santi Giovanni e Paolo in Venice (Jan. 20, 1639); there followed *La finta pazza* (Teatro Novissimo, Venice, Jan. 14, 1641), also one of the earliest Italian operas performed in Paris (Salle du Petit Bourbon, Dec. 14, 1645). Other operas by Sacrati were *Bellerofonte* (Venice, 1642), *L'Ulisse errante* (Venice, 1644), and *L'isola d'Alcina* (Bologna, 1648). All of his operas are lost. In 1649 he became maestro di cappella to the Modena court. Research by A. Curtis suggests that Sacrati played a major role in preparing the final form of Monteverdi's last opera, *L'incoronazione di Poppea*.

Sadai, Yizhak, Bulgarian-born Israeli composer and teacher; b. Sofia, May 13, 1935. He emigrated to Israel in 1949 and studied with Haubenstock-Ramati and Boscovich at the Tel Aviv Academy of Music (1951–56). In 1966 he joined the music staff of the Univ. of Tel Aviv. Among his works is the opera *Trial* (1979).

Sadie, Stanley (John), eminent English writer on music and lexicographer; b. London, Oct. 30, 1930. He studied music privately with Bernard Stevens (1947–50) and then with Dart, Hadley, and Cudworth at Cambridge (B.A. and Mus.B., 1953; M.A., 1957; Ph.D., 1958, with the diss. *British Chamber Music, 1720–1790*). He was on the staff of Trinity College of Music in London (1957–65); from 1964 to 1981 he was a music critic on the staff of the *Times* of London. In 1967 he became the ed. of the *Musical Times*, a position he retained until 1987. A distinguished scholar, he wrote the following monographs (all publ. in London): *Handel* (1962), *Mozart* (1966), *Beethoven* (1967; 2d ed., 1974), *Handel* (1968), and *Handel Concertos* (1972); he also publ. numerous articles in British and American music journals. With Arthur Jacobs, he ed. *The Pan Book of Opera* (London, 1964; rev. ed. as *Opera: A Modern Guide*, N.Y., 1972; new ed., 1984). In 1969 he was entrusted with the formidable task of preparing for publication, as ed.-in-chief, a completely new ed. of *Grove's Dictionary of Music and Musicians*; after 11 years of labor, *The New Grove Dictionary of Music and Musicians* was publ. in London in 1980. He also ed. *The New Grove Dictionary of Musical Instruments* (1984) and was coed., with H. Wiley Hitchcock, of *The New Grove Dictionary of American Music* (4 vols., 1986). With A. Hicks, he ed. the vol. *Handel Tercentenary Collection* (Ann Arbor, 1988). He also ed. *The Grove Concise Dictionary of Music* (1988; U.S. ed., 1988, as *The Norton/Grove Concise Encyclopedia of Music*), *The New Grove Dictionary of Opera* (4 vols., 1992), and *Wolfgang Amadé Mozart: Essays on His Life and His Music* (1995). He served as ed. of the Master Musicians series from 1976. In 1981 he received the honorary degree of D.Litt. from the Univ. of Leicester and was made an honorary member of the Royal Academy of Music, London. In 1982 he was made a Commander of the Order of the British Empire. In 1978 he married the American cellist and writer on music Julie Anne Sadie (b. Eugene, Oreg., Jan. 26, 1948).

Saenger, Oscar, American singing teacher; b. Brooklyn, Jan. 5, 1868; d. Washington, D.C., April 20, 1929. He sang in church as a boy, and studied voice with J. Bouhy at the National Cons. in New York, where he taught (1889–97). He made his operatic debut with the Hinrichs Grand Opera Co. in 1891; after a brief tour in Germany and Austria he returned to America and devoted himself entirely to teaching. Among his students were many well-known singers, including Marie Rappold, Paul Althouse, and Mabel Garrison.

Saeverud, Harald (Sigurd Johan), prominent Norwegian composer, father of **Ketil Hvoslef** (real name, **Saeverud**); b. Bergen, April 17, 1897; d. Siljustøl, March 27, 1992. He studied theory at the Bergen Music Academy with B. Holmsen (1915–20) and with F. E. Koch at the Hochschule für Musik in Berlin (1920–21); he took a course in conducting with Clemens Krauss in Berlin (1935). In 1953 he received the Norwegian State Salary of Art (a government life pension for outstanding artistic achievement). He began to compose very early, and on Dec. 12, 1912, at the age of 15, conducted in Bergen a program of his own symphonic pieces. His music was permeated with characteristically lyrical Scandinavian Romanticism, with Norwegian folk melos as its foundation; his symphonic compositions are polyphonic in nature and tonal in essence, with euphonious dissonant textures imparting a peculiarly somber character.

WORKS: DRAMATIC: *The Rape of Lucretia*, incidental music to Shakespeare's play (1935; also a *Lucretia Suite* for Orch., 1936); *Peer Gynt*, incidental music to Ibsen's play (1947; Oslo, March 2, 1948; also as 2 orch. suites and a piano suite); *Olav og Kari*, dance scene (1948); *Ridder Blåskjeggs mareritt* (Bluebeard's Nightmare), ballet (Oslo, Oct. 4, 1960).

BIBL.: C. Baden, *H. S. 80 år* (Oslo, 1977).

Saeverud, Ketil. See **Hvoslef, Ketil.**

Sagaev, Dimiter, Bulgarian composer and teacher; b. Plovdiv, Feb. 27, 1915. He was a student of Stoyanov and Vladigerov at the Bulgarian State Cons. in Sofia (graduated, 1940), where he then taught. His music is Romantic in essence and national in its thematic resources. Among his works are the operas *Under the Yoke* (1965) and *Samouil* (1975) and the ballets *The Madara Horseman* (1960) and *Orpheus* (1978); also the oratorios *In the Name of Freedom* (1969) and *The Artist* (1987); incidental music.

Sahl, Michael, American composer; b. Boston, Sept. 2, 1934. He studied at Amherst College (B.A., 1955), with Sessions and Babbitt at Princeton Univ. (M.F.A., 1957), with Dallapiccola on a Fulbright Fellowship in Florence (1957), and with Citkowitz, Foss, and Copland. From 1963 he wrote various film scores. After serving as a creative associate at the State Univ. of N.Y. at Buffalo (1965), he was pianist and music director for Judy Collins (1968–69), and then music director WBAI-FM in New York (1972–73). He collaborated with Eric Salzman on a number of music theater pieces, including the opera *Civilizations and its Discontents* (1977), which won the Prix Italia in 1980. They also wrote the book *Making Changes: A Practical Guide to Vernacular Harmony* (1977). In his output, he developed a populist style in which elements of art music and popular music combine to produce a refreshing synergy.

WORKS: DRAMATIC: *Biograffiti* (N.Y., Dec. 14, 1974; in collaboration with E. Salzman); *The Conjuror* (N.Y., June 1, 1975; in collaboration with E. Salzman); *Stauf* (N.Y., May 25, 1976; final version, Philadelphia, Sept. 20, 1987; in collaboration with E. Salzman); *Civilization and its Discontents* (N.Y., May 19, 1977; rev. as a radio opera, 1980; in collaboration with E. Salzman); *An Old-Fashioned Girl* (N.Y., May 19, 1977); *Noah* (N.Y., Feb. 10, 1978; in collaboration with E. Salzman); *The Passion of Simple Simon* (N.Y., Feb. 1, 1979; rev. as a radio opera, 1980; in collaboration with E. Salzman); *Boxes* (1982–83; in collaboration with E. Salzman); *Dream Beach* (N.Y., March 20, 1988); *Body Language* (1995–96).

Saikkola, Lauri, Finnish violinist and composer; b. Vyborg, March 31, 1906. He studied violin at the local music school (1919–28) and composition privately with Akimov and Funtek (1930–34). He was a violinist in the Viipuri (Vyborg) Phil. (1923–34) and the Helsinki Phil. (1934–65). His extensive compositional output followed along traditional lines. His works include *Taivaaseen menija*, radio opera (1950), *Ristin,* opera (1957–58), and *The Master's Snuff Box*, chamber opera (1970).

Saint-Foix, (Marie-Olivier-) Georges (du Parc Poulain), Comte de, eminent French musicologist; b. Paris, March 2, 1874; d. Aix-en-Provence, May 26, 1954. He studied law at the Sorbonne and concurrently attended classes in theory with d'Indy and had violin lessons (diploma, 1906) at the Schola Cantorum in Paris. His principal, and most important, publ. was *Wolfgang-Amédée Mozart, sa vie musicale et son oeuvre, de l'enfance à la pleine maturité* (5 vols., Paris, 1912–46; vols. 1–2 with T. de Wyzewa); also publ. *Les Symphonies de Mozart* (Paris, 1932; 2d ed., 1948; Eng. tr., London, 1947).

Saint-Georges, Joseph Boulogne, Chevalier de, noted West Indian violinist and composer; b. near Basse Terre, Guadeloupe, c.1739; d. Paris, June 9?, 1799. He was the son of a wealthy Frenchman and a black slave, and was reared in Santo Domingo. He went to Paris with his father in 1749 (his mother joined them in 1760); as a youth he studied boxing and fencing, and became one of the leading fencers of Europe; he also studied music with Jean-Marie Leclair *l'aîné* and with François Gossec (1763–66); the latter dedicated his op. 9 string trios to him. In 1769 he became a violinist in the orch. of the Concert des Amateurs, becoming its director in 1773; after it was disbanded in 1781, he founded his own Concert de la Loge Olympique, for which Haydn composed his set of Paris syms.; it was disbanded in 1789. He also continued his activities as a fencer, and visited London in this capacity in 1785 and 1789. In 1791 he became a captain in the National Guard in Lille and soon was charged with organizing a black regiment, the Legion Nationale des Américains et du Midi (among his 1,000 troops was the father of Dumas *père*); when the venture proved of little success, he was relieved of his duties and later imprisoned for 18 months; after living on St. Dominique, he returned to Paris about 1797. His works include the operas (all 1st perf. in Paris): *Ernestine* (July 19, 1777), *La Chasse* (Oct. 12, 1778), *L'Amant anonyme* (March 8, 1780), *Le Droit du seigneur* (n.d.), *La Fille garçon* (Aug. 18, 1787), *Le Marchand de marrons* (1788), and *Guillaume tout coeur* (1790).

BIBL.: E. Derr, *J. B., C. de S.-G.: Black Musician and Athlete in Galant Paris* (Ann Arbor, 1972).

Saint-Huberty, Mme. de (real name, **Antoinette Cécile Clavel**), French soprano; b. Strasbourg, Dec. 15, 1756; d. (murdered) London, July 22, 1812. She studied with J. B. Lemoyne in Warsaw. After singing in Strasbourg, she went to Paris and appeared as Melissa in Gluck's *Armide* (1777); she was a leading singer at the Opéra (1781–90), where she sang in the premiere of Piccinni's *Didon* (1783); she also created Hypermnestra in Salieri's *Les Danaïdes* (1784) and the title roles in Edelmann's *Ariane dans l'isle de Naxos* (1782), Sacchini's *Chimène* (1783), and Lemoyne's *Phédre* (1786). With the coming of the Revolution, she left France in the company of the Count of Antraigues; they were married in 1790. When her husband was imprisoned by Napoleon in Italy in 1797, she assisted in his rescue; they finally settled in London, where they were both murdered by a servant.

BIBL.: E. de Goncourt, *Mme. S.-H.* (1885).

Saint-Lubin, Léon de, violinist and composer; b. Turin, July 5, 1805; d. Berlin, Feb. 13, 1850. After filling various positions as a theater violinist, he pursued further studies with Spohr. He was concertmaster at the Josephstadt Theater in Vienna (1823–30), then at the Königstadt Theater in Berlin (1830–47). He composed 2 operas, *König Branors Schwert* and *Der Vetter des Doctor Faust.*

Saint-Saëns, (Charles-) Camille, celebrated French composer; b. Paris, Oct. 9, 1835; d. Algiers, Dec. 16, 1921. His widowed mother sent him to his great-aunt, Charlotte Masson, who taught him to play piano. He proved exceptionally gifted, and gave a performance in a Paris salon before he was 5; at 6 he began to compose; at 7 he became a private pupil of Stamaty; so rapid was his progress that he made his pianistic debut at the Salle Pleyel on May 6, 1846, playing a Mozart concerto and a movement from Beethoven's C minor Concerto, with Orch. After studying harmony with Pierre Maleden, he entered the Paris Cons., where his teachers were Benoist (organ) and Halévy (composition). He won the 2d prize for organ in 1849, and the 1st prize in 1851. In 1852 he competed unsuccessfully for the Grand Prix de Rome, and failed again in a 2d attempt in 1864, when he was already a composer of some stature. His *Ode à Sainte Cécile* for Voice and Orch. was awarded the 1st prize of the Société Sainte-Cécile (1852). On Dec. 11, 1853, his 1st numbered sym. was performed; Gounod wrote him a letter of praise, containing a prophetic phrase regarding the "obligation de devenir un grand maitre." From 1853 to 1857 Saint-Saëns was organist at the church of Saint-Merry in Paris; in 1857 he succeeded Léfebure-Wély as organist at the Madeleine. This important position he filled with distinction, and soon acquired a great reputation as virtuoso on the organ and a master of improvisation. He resigned in 1876, and devoted himself mainly to composition and conducting; he also continued to appear as a pianist and organist. From 1861 to 1865 he taught piano at the École Niedermeyer; among his pupils were André Messager and Gabriel Fauré. Saint-Saëns was one of the founders of the Société Nationale de Musique (1871), established for the encouragement of French composers, but withdrew in 1886 when d'Indy proposed to include works by foreign composers in its program. In 1875 he married Marie Truffot; their 2 sons died in infancy; they separated in 1881, but were never legally divorced; Madame Saint-Saëns died in Bordeaux on Jan. 30, 1950, at the age of 95. In 1891 Saint-Saëns established a museum in Dieppe (his father's birthplace), to which he gave his MSS and his collection of paintings and other art objects. On Oct. 27, 1907, he witnessed the unveiling of his own statue (by Marqueste) in the court foyer of the opera house in Dieppe. He received many honors: in 1868 he was made a Chevalier of the Légion d'honneur; in 1884, Officer; in 1900, Grand-Officer; in 1913, Grand-Croix (the highest rank). In 1881 he was elected to the Institut de France; he was also a member of many foreign organizations; he received an honorary Mus.D. degree at the Univ. of Cambridge. He visited the United States for the first time in 1906; he was a representative of the French government at the Panama-Pacific Exposition in 1915 and conducted his choral work *Hail California* (San Francisco, June 19, 1915), written for the occasion. In 1916, at the age of 81, he made his first tour of South America and continued to appear in public as conductor of his own works almost to the time of his death. He took part as conductor and pianist in a festival of his works in Athens in May 1920. He played a program of his piano pieces at the Saint-Saëns museum in Dieppe on Aug. 6, 1921. For the winter he went to Algiers, where he died.

The position of Saint-Saëns in French music was very important. His abilities as a performer were extraordinary; he aroused the admiration of Wagner during the latter's stay in Paris (1860–61) by playing at sight the entire scores of Wagner's operas; curiously, Saint-Saëns achieved greater recognition in Germany than in France during the initial stages of his career. His most famous opera, *Samson et Dalila*, was produced in Weimar (1877) under the direction of Eduard Lassen, to whom the work was suggested by Liszt; it was not performed in France until nearly 13 years later, in Rouen. He played his 1st and 3d piano concertos for the first time at the Gewandhaus in Leipzig. Solidity of contrapuntal fabric, instrumental elaboration, fullness of sonority in orchestration, and a certain harmonic saturation are the chief characteristics of his music, qualities that were not yet fully exploited by French composers at the time, the French public preferring the lighter type of music. However, Saint-Saëns overcame this initial opposition, and toward the end of his life was regarded as an embodiment of French traditionalism. The shock of the German invasion of France in World War I made him abandon his former predilection for German music, and he wrote virulent articles against German art. He was unalterably opposed to modern music, and looked askance at Debussy; he regarded later manifestations of musical modernism as outrages, and was outspoken in his opinions. That Saint-Saëns possessed a fine sense of musical characterization, and true Gallic wit, is demonstrated by his ingenious suite *Carnival of the Animals*, which he wrote in 1886 but did not allow to be publ. during his lifetime. He also publ. a book of elegant verse (1890). For a complete list of his works, see the Durand *Catalogue général et thématique des oeuvres de Saint-Saëns* (Paris, 1897; rev. ed., 1909).

WORKS: DRAMATIC (all 1st perf. in Paris unless otherwise given): OPERAS: *La Princesse jaune* (June 12, 1872); *Le Timbre d'argent* (Feb. 23, 1877); *Samson et Dalila* (Weimar, Dec. 2, 1877); *Étienne Marcel* (Lyons, Feb. 8, 1879); *Henry VIII* (March 5, 1883); *Proserpine* (March 16, 1887); *Ascanio* (March 21, 1890); *Phryné* (May 24, 1893); *Frédégonde* (Dec. 18, 1895); *Les Barbares* (Oct. 23, 1901); *Hélène* (Monte Carlo, Feb. 18, 1904); *L'Ancêtre* (Monte Carlo, Feb. 24, 1906); *Déjanire* (Monte Carlo, March 14, 1911). BALLET: *Javotte* (Lyons, Dec. 3, 1896). INCIDENTAL MUSIC TO: *Antigone* (Nov. 21, 1893); *Parysatis* (Béziers, Aug. 17, 1902); *Andromaque* (Feb. 7, 1903); *La Foi* (Monte Carlo, April 10, 1909); *On ne badine pas avec l'amour* (Feb. 8, 1917). FILM SCORE: *L'Assassinat du Duc de Guise* (Nov. 16, 1908). ORATORIOS: *Oratorio de Noël* for Solo Voices, Chorus, String Quartet, Harp, and Organ, op. 12 (1858); *Le Déluge* for Solo Voices, Chorus, and Orch., op. 45 (1875; Paris, March 5, 1876).

WRITINGS (all publ. in Paris unless otherwise given): *Notice sur Henri Reber* (1881); *Harmonie et mélodie* (1885; 9th ed., 1923); *Charles Gounod et le "Don Juan" de Mozart* (1893); *Problèmes et mystères* (1894; rev. ed., aug., 1922, as *Divagations sérieuses*); *Portraits et souvenirs* (1899; 3d ed., 1909); *Essai sur les lyres et cithares antiques* (1902); *Quelques mots sur "Prosperpine"* (Alexandria, 1902); *École buissonnière: Notes et souvenirs* (1913; abr. Eng. tr., 1919); *Notice sur Le Timbre d'argent* (Brussels, 1914); H. Bowie, ed., *On the Execution of Music, and Principally of Ancient Music* (San Francisco, 1915); *Au courant de la vie* (1916); *Germanophile* (1916); *Les idées de M. Vincent d'Indy* (1919); F. Rothwell, tr., *Outspoken Essays on Music* (London and N.Y., 1922).

BIBL.: C. Bellaigue, *M. C. S.-S.* (Paris, 1889); C. Kit and P. Loanda, *Musique savante: Sur la musique de M. S.-S.* (Lille, 1889); Blondel, *C. S.-S. et son cinquantenaire artistique* (Paris, 1896); O. Neitzel, *C. S.-S.* (Berlin, 1899); E. Solenière, *C. S.-S.* (Paris, 1899); E. Baumann, *Les Grandes Formes de la musique: L'Oeuvre de S.-S.* (Paris, 1905; new ed., 1923); L. Auge de Lassus, *S.-S.* (Paris, 1914); J. Bonnerot, *C. S.-S.* (Paris, 1914; 2d ed., 1922); J. Montargis, *C. S.-S.* (Paris, 1919); J. Chantavoine, *L'Oeuvre dramatique de C. S.-S.* (Paris, 1921); A. Hervey, *S.-S.* (London, 1921); W. Lyle, *C. S.-S.: His Life and Art* (London, 1923); G. Servières, *S.-S.* (Paris, 1923; 2d ed., 1930); A. Dandelot, *S.-S.* (Paris, 1930); J. Handschin, *C. S.-S.* (Zürich, 1930); J. Langlois, *C. S.-S.* (Moulins, 1934); R. Dumanine, *Les Origines normandes de C. S.-S.* (Rouen, 1937); R. Fauchois, *La Vie et l'oeuvre prodigieuse de C. S.-S.* (Paris, 1938); J. Chantavoine, *C. S.-S.* (Paris, 1947); J. Harding, *S.-S. and His Circle* (London, 1965).

Sala, Nicola, Italian teacher, music theorist, and composer; b. Tocco-Gaudio, near Benevento, April 7, 1713; d. Naples, Aug. 31, 1801. He was a pupil of Fago, Abos, and Leo at the Cons. della Pietà de' Turchini in Naples (1732–40); he apparently taught there for many years, serving as secondo maestro (1787–93) and primo maestro (1793–99). He publ. the celebrated theoretical work *Regole del contrappunto prattico* (3 vols., 1794; reprinted by Choron in Paris, 1808, as *Principii di composizione delle scuole d'Italia*). He brought out several operas: *Vologeso* (Rome, 1737), *La Zenobia* (Naples, Jan. 12, 1761), *Demetrio* (Naples, Dec. 12, 1762), *Merope* (Naples, Aug. 13, 1769), and an oratorio, *Giuditta* (1780).

Salazar, Manuel, Costa Rican tenor; b. San José, Jan. 3, 1887; d. there, Aug. 6, 1950. He was trained in Italy and New York. In 1913 he made his operatic debut in Vicenza as Edgardo, and then sang in various Italian opera houses. After appearing in Havana (1917), he toured North America with the San Carlo Opera Co. On Dec. 31, 1921, he made his Metropolitan Opera debut in New York as Alvaro, and remained on its roster until 1923. Among his other roles were Radames, Andrea Chénier, and Canio.

Saldoni, Baltasar, Spanish composer and lexicographer; b. Barcelona, Jan. 4, 1807; d. Madrid, Dec. 3, 1889. He was a pupil of Mateo Ferrer in Montserrat and of Francisco Queralt in Barcelona; he completed his studies with Carnicer in Madrid (1829). In 1830 he became prof. of voice training and singing at the Madrid Cons. In 1826 he produced in Madrid his light opera *El triunfo del amor* and the Italian operas *Saladino e Clotilde* (1833), *Ipermestra* (Jan. 20, 1838), and *Cleonice regina di Siria* (Jan. 24, 1840); he also wrote the zarzuelas *La corte de Mónaco* (Feb. 16, 1857) and *Los maridos en las mascaras* (Barcelona, Aug. 26, 1864). His magnum opus as a scholar was the *Diccionario biográfico-bibliográfico de efemérides de músicos españoles*, in 4 vols. (Madrid, 1868–81), to which was added a supplementary vol. in the form of a chronology of births and deaths of Spanish musicians, with exhaustive biographical notes. This monumental compilation, upon which Saldoni worked nearly 40 years, contains (inevitably) a number of errors, but in the absence of other musicographical works on Spanish musicians, it still retains considerable documentary value.

Sales (de Sala), Pietro Pompeo, esteemed Italian composer; b. Brescia, c.1729; d. Hanau, Nov. 21, 1797. After attending the Univ. of Innsbruck, he began his career as a conductor of an Italian opera company; he traveled with it in various European cities. He served as director of the court chapel of Prince-Bishop Joseph, Landgrave of Hessen-Darmstadt, in Augsburg and Dillingen an der Donau (1756–68), then was director of the court chapel of the Trier Elector Clemens Wenzeslaus, Prince-Bishop of Augsburg, in Ehrenbreitstein am Rhein (1768–86); he subsequently was active at the elector's court in Koblenz, which was disrupted twice during the French Revolutionary wars; he fled the French for the 3d time in 1797 and made his way to Hanau, dying shortly afterward. He was a distinguished representative of the Italian style.

WORKS: DRAMATIC: OPERAS: *Le nozze di Amore e di Norizia* (Munich, 1765); *Antigona in Tebe* (Padua, 1767); *L'Antigono* (Munich, 1769); *Achille in Sciro* (Munich, 1774); *Il Re pastore* (n.d.). SINGSPIEL: *L'isola disabitata* (Augsburg, 1758); also *Massanissa, oder Die obsiegende Treu*, Jesuit drama (Innsbruck, 1752), and *Le Cinesi*, componimento drammatico (Augsburg, 1757). ORATORIOS: *Oratorio per la festa del Santo Natale* (Augsburg, 1756); *Giefte* (Mannheim, 1762); *Passion* (Ehrenbreitstein, 1772); *Giuseppe riconosciuto* (Ehrenbreitstein, 1780); *Gioas re di Giuda* (Ehrenbreitstein, 1781); *La Betulia liberata* (Ehrenbreitstein, 1783); *Affectus amantis* (Ehrenbreitstein, 1784); *Sant'Elena* (Koblenz, 1791).

BIBL.: F. Collingnon, *P. P. S.* (diss., Univ. of Bonn, 1923).

Salêza, Albert, French tenor; b. Bruges, near Bayonne, Oct. 18, 1867; d. Paris, Nov. 26, 1916. He studied with Bax and Obin at the Paris Cons., making his debut as Mylio in *Le Roi d'Ys* at the Paris Opéra Comique on July 19, 1888. After appearances in

Rouen, Bordeaux, and Nice, he returned to Paris to make his debut at the Opéra as Mathôs in Reyer's *Salammbô* on May 16, 1892. He sang in the posthumous premiere of Franck's *Hulda* in Monte Carlo (March 4, 1894), and then in the premiere of Lefebvre's *Djelma* at the Paris Opéra (May 25, 1894). He made his first appearance at London's Covent Garden as Gounod's Roméo on May 10, 1898, and continued to sing there until 1902; he made his Metropolitan Opera debut in New York in the same role on Dec. 2, 1898; he was on its roster until 1901, and again in 1904–05; he also sang regularly in Paris until 1911, when he joined the faculty of the Cons. He was especially noted for such roles as Gounod's Faust, John of Leyden, Raoul in *Les Huguenots*, Edgardo in *Lucia di Lammermoor*, the Duke of Mantua, Rigoletto, Tannhäuser, Don José, Siegmund, and Otello.

Salieri, Antonio, famous Italian composer and teacher; b. Legnago, near Verona, Aug. 18, 1750; d. Vienna, May 7, 1825. He studied violin and harpsichord with his brother, Francesco, then continued violin studies with the local organist, Giuseppe Simoni. He was orphaned in 1765; subsequently he was taken to Venice, where he studied thoroughbass with Giovanni Pescetti, deputy maestro di cappella of San Marco, and singing with Ferdinando Pacini, a tenor there. Florian Gassmann took Salieri to Vienna in 1766 and provided for his musical training and a thorough education in the liberal arts; there he came into contact with Metastasio and Gluck, the latter becoming his patron and friend. His first known opera, *La Vestale* (not extant), was premiered in Vienna in 1768. His comic opera, *Le Donne letterate*, was successfully performed at the Burgtheater in Jan. 1770. The influence of Gluck is revealed in his first major production for the stage, *Armida* (June 2, 1771). Upon the death of Gassmann in 1774, Salieri was appointed his successor as court composer and conductor of the Italian Opera. After Gluck was unable to fulfill the commission for an opera to open the Teatro alla Scala in Milan, the authorities turned to Salieri; his *L'Europa riconosciuta* inaugurated the great opera house on Aug. 3, 1778. While in Italy, he also composed operas for Venice and Rome. He then returned to Vienna, where he brought out his Lustspiel, *Der Rauchfangkehrer* (April 30, 1781). With Gluck's encouragement, Salieri set his sights on Paris. In an effort to provide him with a respectful hearing, Gluck and the directors of the Paris Opéra advertised Salieri's *Les Danaides* (April 26, 1784) as a work from Gluck's pen; following a number of performances, it was finally acknowledged as Salieri's creation. Returning to Vienna, he composed 3 more stage works, including the successful *La grotta di Trofonio* (Oct. 12, 1785). His French opera *Les Horaces* (Paris, Dec. 7, 1786) proved a failure. However, his next French opera, *Tarare* (Paris Opera, June 8, 1787), was a triumphant success. After Da Ponte revised and tr. Beaumarchais's French libretto into Italian and Salieri thoroughly recomposed the score, it was given as *Axur, re d'Ormus* (Vienna, Jan. 8, 1788), and then performed throughout Europe to great acclaim. Salieri was appointed court Kapellmeister in Vienna in 1788, and held that position until 1824; however, he did not conduct operatic performances after 1790. He continued to compose for the stage until 1804, his last major success being *Palmira, regina di Persia* (Oct. 14, 1795).

Salieri's influence on the musical life of Vienna was considerable. From 1788 to 1795 he was president of the Tonkunstler-Sozietat, the benevolent society for musicians founded by Gassmann in 1771; he was its vice president from 1795; he was also a founder of the Gesellschaft der Musikfreunde. He was widely celebrated as a pedagogue, his pupils including Beethoven, Hummel, Schubert, Czerny, and Liszt. He was the recipient of numerous honors, including the Gold Medallion and Chain of the City of Vienna; he was also a Chevalier of the Légion d'honneur and a member of the French Institut. Salieri's eminence and positions in Vienna earned him a reputation for intrigue; many unfounded stories circulated about him, culminating in the fantastic tale that he poisoned Mozart; this tale prompted Pushkin to write his drama *Mozart and Salieri*, which subsequently was set to music by Rimsky-Korsakov; a contemporary dramatization of the Mozart-Salieri rivalry, Peter Shaffer's *Amadeus*, was successfully produced in London in 1979 and in New York in 1980; it later obtained even wider circulation through the award-winning film version of 1984. Salieri was a worthy representative of the traditional Italian school of operatic composition. He was a master of harmony and orchestration. His many operas are noteworthy for their expressive melodic writing and sensitive vocal treatment. All the same, few held the stage for long, and all have disappeared from the active repertoire.

BIBL.: I. von Mosel, *Über das Leben und die Werke des A. S.* (Vienna, 1827); W. Neumann, *A. S.* (Kassel, 1855); G. Magnani, *A. S.: Musicista legnaghese* (Legnago, 1934); A. Della Corte, *Un Italiano all'estero: A. S.* (Turin and Milan, 1937); R. Angermüller, *A. S.: Sein Leben und seine weltlichen Werke unter besonderer Berücksichtingung seiner "grossen" Opern* (diss., Univ. of Salzburg, 1970; publ. in 3 vols., Munich, 1971–74); V. Braunbehrens, *S.: Ein Musiker im Schatten Mozarts* (Munich, 1989; Eng. tr., 1992, as *Maligned Master: The Real Story of A. S.*); J. Rice, *A. S. and Viennese Opera, 1770–1800* (Chicago, 1998).

Salignac, Thomas (real name, **Eustace Thomas**), French tenor, opera director, and teacher; b. Générac, near Nîmes, March 19, 1867; d. Paris, 1945. He studied in Marseilles and with Duvernoy at the Paris Cons. In 1893 he became a member of the Paris Opéra Comique. On Dec. 11, 1896, he made his debut at the Metropolitan Opera in New York as Don José, remaining on its roster for that season and again from 1898 to 1903. He also sang at London's Covent Garden (1897–99; 1901–04) and again at the Paris Opéra Comique (1905–14). He sang in the premieres of operas by Laparra, Leroux, Milhaud, and Widor, and in the private premiere of Falla's *El retablo de Maese Pedro* (1923). In 1913–14 he was director of the Nice Opera, and later of an opéra comique company which toured North America in 1926. He was founder-ed. of the journal *Lyrica* (1922–39), and a teacher at the American Cons. in Fontainebleau (1922–23) and at the Paris Cons. (from 1924).

Salimbeni, Felice, Italian castrato soprano; b. Milan, c.1712; d. Ljubljana, Aug. 1751. He was a student of Porpora. Following his operatic debut in Hasse's *Caio Fabrizio* (Rome, 1731), he sang widely in Italy. He also sang in Vienna, was a court singer in Berlin (1745–50), and won particular success in Hasse's operas in Dresden.

Sallinen, Aulis, prominent Finnish composer; b. Salmi, April 9, 1935. He studied under Merikanto and Kokkonen at the Sibelius Academy in Helsinki (1955–60). He was managing director of the Finnish Radio Sym. Orch. in Helsinki (1960–70); he also taught at the Sibelius Academy (1963–76) and held the government-bestowed title of Professor of Arts for Life (from 1981), the first such appointment. In 1979 he was made a member of the Royal Swedish Academy of Music in Stockholm. With Penderecki, he was awarded the Withuri International Sibelius Prize in 1983. In his music, he uses modern techniques, with a prevalence of euphonious dissonance and an occasional application of serialism.

WORKS: DRAMATIC: OPERAS: *Ratsumies* (The Horseman; 1973–74; Savonlinna, July 17, 1975); *Punainen viiva* (The Red Line; 1976–78; Helsinki, Nov. 30, 1978); *Kuningas lähtee Ranskaan* (The King Goes Forth to France; 1983; Savonlinna, July 7, 1984; in Eng., London, April 1, 1987); *Kullervo* (1986–88; Los Angeles, Feb. 25, 1992); *The Palace* (1993; Savonlinna, July 26, 1995). BALLETS: *Variations sur Mallarmé* (1967; Helsinki, 1968); *Midsommernatten* (Atlanta, March 29, 1984; based on the Sym. No. 3); *Himlens hemlighet* (Secret of Heavens; Swedish TV, Oct. 20, 1986; based on the syms. Nos. 1, 3, and 4).

Salmenhaara, Erkki (Olavi), Finnish composer and musicologist; b. Helsinki, March 12, 1941. He studied at the Sibelius Academy in Helsinki with Kokkonen (diploma, 1963), then went to Vienna, where he took lessons with Ligeti (1963); he then pursued his education with Tawaststjerna at the Univ. of Helsinki (Ph.D., 1970), where he taught (from 1963). He was chairman of the Society of Finnish Composers (1974–76). His music is often inspired by literary works; he favors unusual combinations of instruments, including electronics, and makes use of serial techniques in dense, fastidious sonorities. Among his works is the opera *Portugalin nainen* (The Woman of Portugal; 1970–72; Helsinki, Feb. 4, 1976).

Salmhofer, Franz, Austrian conductor, operas administrator, and composer; b. Vienna, Jan. 22, 1900; d. there, Sept. 22, 1975. He studied composition with Schreker and Schmidt at the Vienna Academy of Music and musicology with Guido Adler at the Univ. of Vienna. In 1929 he became conductor at the Vienna Burgtheater, for which he composed incidental music, ballets, and operas; he resigned in 1939; from 1945 to 1955 he was director at the Vienna State Opera, then was director of the Vienna Volksoper (1955–63). In 1923 he married the pianist Margit Gál.

WORKS: DRAMATIC: OPERAS: *Dame im Traum* (Vienna, Dec. 26, 1935); *Iwan Sergejewitsch Tarassenko* (Vienna, March 9, 1938); *Das Werbekleid* (Salzburg, Dec. 5, 1943); *Dreikönig* (1945; Vienna, 1970). BALLETS: *Das lockende Phantom* (1927); *Der Taugenichts in Wien* (1930); *Österreichische Bauernhochzeit* (1933); *Weihnachtsmarchen* (1933). Also incidental music to about 300 plays.

Salminen, Matti, notable Finnish bass; b. Turku, July 7, 1945. He studied at the Sibelius Academy in Helsinki and with Luigi Rossi in Rome. In 1966 he joined the Finnish National Opera in Helsinki, where he sang his first major role, Verdi's Philip II, in 1969. From 1972 to 1979 he was principal bass of the Cologne Opera. In 1973 he sang Fafner at Milan's La Scala and Glinka's Ivan Susanin in Wexford. He made his first appearance at London's Covent Garden as Fasolt in 1974. From 1975 he sang at the Savonlinna Festival. In 1976 he made his debut at the Bayreuth Festival as Hunding. On Jan. 9, 1981, he made his Metropolitan Opera debut in New York as King Marke. He appeared as Boris Godunov in Zürich in 1985. In 1990 he sang Hunding at the Metropolitan Opera, a role he repeated in 1997 to great acclaim. During the 1992–93 season, he was engaged as King Philip at the Deutsche Oper in Berlin. After singing Fasolt at the Lyric Opera in Chicago in 1996, he portrayed Fafner at the Metropolitan Opera in 1997. His performances in operas by Mozart, Wagner, and Verdi have been much admired.

BIBL.: P. Tuomi-Nikula, *Kuningasbasso: M. S.* (Porvoo, 1994).

Saloman, Siegfried, composer; b. Tondern, Schleswig, Oct. 2, 1816; d. Stockholm, July 22, 1899. He studied composition with J. P. Hartmann in Copenhagen, and violin with Lipinski in Dresden. He lived in Copenhagen for many years and produced 2 operas there, *Tordenskjold I Dynekilen* (May 23, 1844) and *Diamantkorset* (The Diamond Cross; March 20, 1847); he toured Russia and the Netherlands (1847–50); he married the singer Henriette Nissen, and traveled with her; in 1859 they settled in Russia. One of his operas, to a German libretto, was produced in Russian as *Karpatskaya roza* in Moscow, Jan. 7, 1868; several other operas were produced in Stockholm, where he went in 1879 after the death of his wife.

Salomon, Johann Peter, German violinist, impresario, and composer; b. Bonn (baptized), Feb. 20, 1745; d. London, Nov. 25, 1815. He was a member of the Electoral orch. at Bonn (1758–62); after a successful concert tour he was engaged as concertmaster and composer to Prince Heinrich of Prussia at Rheinsberg (1764). When the orch. was disbanded (c.1780), Salomon went to Paris and then to London, where he settled in 1781. He made his debut at Covent Garden on March 23 of that year; he began promoting concerts in 1783, introducing syms. by Haydn and Mozart in 1786. In 1790 he went to Italy to engage singers for the Italian Opera in London, and from there went to Vienna, where he saw Haydn and persuaded him to accept an engagement in London. At Salomon's behest Haydn wrote the works familiarly known as his "Salomon Symphonies"; it is through his association with Haydn's 2 visits to England, in 1790–91 and 1794–95, that Salomon's name remains in the annals of music. He was a founder of the Phil. Soc. in London (1813), conducting its first concert on March 8, 1813. His own works are of merely antiquarian interest and include the operas *Les Recruteurs* (Rheinsberg, 1771), *Le Séjour du bonheur* (Berlin, March 5, 1773), *Titus* (Rheinsberg, 1774), *La Reine de Golconde* (Rheinsberg, 1776), and *Windsor Castle, or The Fair Maid of Kent* (Covent Garden, London, April 6, 1795; in collaboration with R. Spofforth); he also wrote an oratorio, *Hiskias* (1779).

Salomon, (Naphtali) Siegfried, Danish cellist and composer; b. Copenhagen, Aug. 3, 1885; d. there, Oct. 29, 1962. He studied with Rudinger, Malling, and Bondesen at the Copenhagen Cons. (1899–1902), Klengel in Leipzig, and Le Flem in Paris. Returning to Copenhagen, he was principal cellist in the Tivoli Orch. (from 1903) and a cellist in the Royal Orch. (1907–56). He also pursued a solo career. He wrote an opera, *Leonora Christina* (1926).

Saltzmann-Stevens, Minnie, American soprano; b. Bloomington, Ill., March 17, 1874; d. Milan, Jan. 25, 1950. She studied voice with Jean De Reszke in Paris. She made her operatic debut as Brünnhilde in the English version of the *Ring* at London's Covent Garden in 1909; she continued to sing there until 1913 and also appeared at the Bayreuth Festivals of 1911 and 1913. From 1911 to 1914 she sang with the Chicago Grand Opera. Her other roles included Kundry, Isolde, and Sieglinde.

Salva, Tadeáš, Slovak composer; b. Lúčky, near Ruzonberok, Oct. 22, 1937; d. Bratislava, Jan. 3, 1995. Following early training with Viliam Kostka, he studied cello, accordion, and piano at the Žilina Cons. (1953–58). During this time, he also took composition lessons with Zimmer in Bratislava. He continued his composition studies with Moyzes and Cikker at the Bratislava Academy of Music and Drama (1958–60). Subsequently he completed his composition training with Szabelski in Katowice and Lutoslawski in Warsaw. From 1965 to 1968 he was head of the music dept. of the Czech Radio in Košice. He then was a dramaturg for the Czech TV in Bratislava (1965–77) and the Slovak Folk Artistic Ensemble (1977–88). In his music, Salva embraced sonorism with occasional excursions into aleatory procedures. Among his works are *Margita a Besná*, television opera (1971), *The Weeping*, radio opera (1977), and *Reminiscor*, ballet opera (1982).

Salvayre, Gaston (Gervais-Bernard), French composer; b. Toulouse, June 24, 1847; d. St. Ague, near Toulouse, May 17, 1916. He was a pupil at the Toulouse Cons., then entered the Paris Cons., studying organ with Benoist and composition with Ambroise Thomas. After failing to win the Prix de Rome for 5 consecutive years, he finally obtained it in 1872 with the cantata *Calypso*. He subsequently devoted himself mainly to composition and also wrote music criticism for *Gil Blas*. He was made a Chevalier of the Légion d'honneur in 1880.

WORKS: DRAMATIC: OPERAS: *Le Bravo* (Paris, April 18, 1877); *Richard III* (in Italian as *Riccardo III*, St. Petersburg, Dec. 21, 1883; in French, Nice, Jan. 29, 1891); *La Dame de Monsoreau* (Paris, Jan. 30, 1888); *Solange* (Paris, March 10, 1909); *Egmont* (Paris, Dec. 6, 1886). BALLETS: *Le Fandango* (Paris, Nov. 26, 1877); *La Fontaine des fées* (Paris, 1899); *L'Odalisque* (Paris, 1905); also *Calypso*, dramatic scene (1872).

Salvi, Lorenzo, Italian tenor; b. Ancona, May 4, 1810; d. Bologna, Jan. 16, 1879. He made his debut at the Teatro San Carlo in Naples in 1830, then sang at La Scala in Milan (1839–42); during his tenure there, he created the title role in Verdi's *Oberto*; also the role of Riccardo in *Giorno di regno*. He made guest appearances at Covent Garden in London (1847–50) and in New York. He became particularly known for his roles in operas by Bellini and Donizetti.

Salvini-Donatelli, Fanny (real name, **Francesca Lucchi**), Italian soprano; b. Florence, 1815; d. Milan, June 1891. She made her debut at the Teatro Apollo in Venice as Rosina in 1839, then sang throughout Italy; she also appeared in Vienna (1842) and in London at Drury Lane (1858) and likewise appeared in various other European music centers; she retired from the stage in 1859 but briefly resumed her career in 1865. She created the role of Violetta in *La Traviata* in 1853 in Venice and distinguished herself in other Verdi operas.

Salzman, Eric, versatile American composer, writer, editor, director/producer, and pioneer of new music theater; b. N.Y., Sept. 8, 1933. His maternal grandfather, Louis Klenetzky, was a song-and-dance performer in the Yiddish theater and his mother, Frances Klenett Salzman, a founder-director of a children's music-theater company. He studied composition and theory in New York with Mark Lawner while still in high school, then composition at Columbia Univ. with Luening, Ussachevsky, Mitchell, and Beeson (B.A., 1954) and at Princeton Univ. with Sessions, Babbitt, Kim, and Cone (M.F.A., 1956); in addition, he took courses in musicology with Strunk, Mendel, and Pirotta. In 1956–58 he was in Rome on a Fulbright fellowship for study with Petrassi at the Accademia di Santa Cecilia and also attended courses of Stockhausen, Scherchen, Maderna, and Nono at Darmstadt (summer 1957). Returning to the United States, he was a music critic for the *N.Y. Times* (1958–62) and the *N.Y. Herald Tribune* (1964–66); from 1984 to 1991 he was ed. of the *Musical Quarterly* and from 1962 to 1964 and again from 1968 to 1972 music director of the Pacifica Radio station WBAI-FM in N.Y., where he founded the Free Music Store. He taught at Queens College of the City Univ. of N.Y. (1966–68) and also lectured at N.Y. Univ., Yale Univ., Brooklyn College, Hunter College, Instituto Torquato di Tella in Buenos Aires, the Banff Centre for the Arts et al. He founded and was artistic director, in New York, of the Electric Ear (at Electric Circus; 1967–68), New Image of Sound (1968–71), Quog Music Theater (1970–82), and Music Theater/New York (from 1993); he also was founder and artistic director of the American Music Theater Festival in Philadelphia (1983–94); his works for Quog Music Theater include *Ecolog*, music theater work for television (1971; in collaboration with J. Cassen; also a live version), *Helix* for Voice, Percussion, Clarinet, and Guitar (1972), *Voices*, a capella radio opera (1972), *Saying Something* (1972–73), and *Biograffiti* (1972–73; N.Y., Dec. 14, 1974). From 1975 to 1990 he produced and directed some 2 dozen recordings (2 receiving Grammy Award nominations, a Prix Italia, and an Armstrong Award), featuring works by Weill, Partch, and Bolcom et al., as well as his own music; also produced numerous programs for public radio.

Salzman is the composer, author, and/or adaptor of more than 24 music-theater works; in all capacities, he merges the most advanced techniques in mixed media with ideas and forms derived from popular music and theater. He made a significant reconstruction and adaptation for the American Music Theater Festival of the long-unperformed Gershwin/Kaufman *Strike Up the Band* (1984) and the Kurt Weill/Alan Jay Lerner *Love Life* (1990), and a translation/adaptation of a French music-theater piece, *Jumelles*, by James Giroudon, Pierre Alain Jaffrennou, and Michel Rostain (as *The Silent Twins*, London Opera Festival, June 17, 1992). In 1994 he commenced work on *La Prière du Loup* or *Wolfman Prayer*, a new music theater piece commissioned by the National Theater in Quimper, France, and first performed there on March 31, 1997. In 1999 he commenced work on *Abel Gance à New York* with the Quèbec writer Francis Godin, to a bilingual libretto and including the use of both new (live holograms) and old (silent films of Gance) technologies. His writings include *Twentieth Century Music: An Introduction* (Englewood Cliffs, N.J., 1967; 3d ed., rev., 1988; tr. into Spanish, Portuguese, Hungarian, and Japanese), *Making Changes: A Practical Guide to Vernacular Harmony* (with M. Sahl; N.Y., 1977), and *The New Music Theater* (Oxford, 2000); also numerous extended articles on new music theater, including "Opera is Dead . . . Long Live Opera," special opera issue of *BBC Music Magazine* (Nov. 1996). Salzman is also a seasoned and enthusiastic ornithologist and has contributed writings on natural history to various publs. He is married to the environmentalist Lorna Salzman, with whom he has twin daughters, Eva, a poet resident in England, and Stephanie, a music-theater and pop song lyricist and composer.

WORKS: DRAMATIC: *The Peloponnesian War*, mime-dance theater piece (1967–68; in collaboration with D. Nagrin); *Wiretap* for Tape (1968); *Feedback*, multimedia participatory environmental work for Live Performers, Visuals, and Tape (1968; in collaboration with S. Vanderbeek); *The Nude Paper Sermon* for Actor, Renaissance Consort, Chorus, and Electronics, after Stephen Wade and John Ashbery (1968–69); *Can Man Survive?*, environmental multi-media piece for the centennial of the American Museum of Natural History (1969–71); *The Conjurer*, music theater work (1975; in collaboration with M. Sahl); *Accord*, music theater piece for Accordion (1975); *Stauf*, music theater piece, after *Faust* (1976; rev. 1987; in collaboration with M. Sahl); *Civilization and Its Discontents*, music theater comedy (1977; in collaboration with M. Sahl); *Noah*, music theater miracle (N.Y., Feb. 10, 1978; in collaboration with M. Sahl); *The Passion of Simple Simon* (1979; in collaboration with M. Sahl); *Boxes*, music theater piece (1982–83; in collaboration with M. Sahl); *Big Jim & the Small-time Investors*, music theater piece, after N. Jackson (1985–86; rev. 1990); *Toward a New American Opera*, mixed-media piece (1985); *The Last True Words of Dutch Schultz*, to a libretto by V. Vasilevski (1995–97; Amsterdam, Dec. 6, 1997); *La Prière du Loup* or *Wolfman Prayer*, music theater (1994–97; Quimper, France, March 31, 1997).

Samara, Spiro (Spyridon Filiskos), Greek composer; b. Corfu, Nov. 29, 1861; d. Athens, March 25, 1917. He was a pupil of Enrico Stancampiano in Athens, and later of Delibes at the Paris Cons. He won considerable success with his first opera, *Flora mirabilis* (Milan, May 16, 1886), and devoted himself almost exclusively to dramatic composition. Other operas were *Medgè* (Rome, 1888), *Lionella* (Milan, 1891), *La Martyre* (Naples, May 23, 1894), *La furia domata* (Milan, 1895), *Istoria* (Milan, 1903; as *La biondinetta*, Gotha, 1906), *Mademoiselle de Belle-Isle* (Genoa, Nov. 9, 1905), *Rhea* (Florence, April 11, 1908), and *La guerra in tempo di guerra* (Athens, 1914).

Saminsky, Lazare, Russian-American composer, conductor, and writer on music; b. Valegotsulova, near Odessa, Nov. 8, 1882; d. Port Chester, N.Y., June 30, 1959. He studied mathematics and philosophy at the Univ. of St. Petersburg, and composition with Rimsky-Korsakov and Liadov and conducting with N. Tcherepnin at the St. Petersburg Cons. (graduated, 1910). He emigrated to the United States in 1920, settling in New York; in 1923 he was a cofounder of the League of Composers; he served as music director of Temple Emanu-El in New York (1924–56), where he founded the annual Three Choirs Festival (1926). He was married to an American writer, Lillian Morgan Buck, who died in 1945; in 1948 he married the American pianist Jennifer Gandar. He wrote an autobiography, *Third Leonardo* (MS, 1959). In his compositions, he followed the Romantic tradition; Hebrew subjects and styles play an important part in some of his music.

WORKS: DRAMATIC: *The Gagliarda of a Merry Plague*, opera ballet (1924; N.Y., Feb. 22, 1925); *The Daughter of Jephta*, opera ballet (1928); *Julian, the Apostate Caesar*, opera (1933–38).

WRITINGS: *Music of Our Day* (N.Y., 1932; 2d ed., rev. and aug., 1939); *Music of the Ghetto and the Bible* (N.Y., 1934); *Living Music of the Americas* (N.Y., 1949); *Physics and Metaphysics of Music and Essays on the Philosophy of Mathematics* (The Hague, 1957); *Essentials of Conducting* (N.Y., 1958).

BIBL.: D. de Paoli et al., *L. S.: Composer and Civic Worker* (N.Y., 1930).

Sammarco, (Giuseppe) Mario, Italian baritone; b. Palermo, Dec. 13, 1868; d. Milan, Jan. 24, 1930. He studied singing with Antonio Cantelli, making a successful debut as Valentine in Faust in Palermo (1888); he then sang in Brescia, Madrid, Lisbon, Brussels, Moscow, Warsaw, Berlin, and Vienna. After his London appearance as Scarpia in Tosca at Covent Garden in 1904, he sang there every season until the outbreak of World War I in 1914. He made his American debut as Tonio (Feb. 1, 1908) at the Manhattan Opera House in New York; from 1910 to 1913 he sang with the Chicago Grand Opera; he retired from the operatic stage in 1919 and later settled in Milan as a teacher. He was one of the finest verismo singers of his time.

Sammartini, Giovanni Battista, significant Italian composer and pedagogue, brother of **Giuseppe (Francesco Gaspare Melchiorre Baldassare) Sammartini**; b. probably in Milan, 1700 or 1701; d. there, Jan. 15, 1775. It is likely that he studied music with his father, Alexis Saint-Martin, a French oboist who settled in Italy. In 1728 he became maestro di cappella of the Congregation of the SS. Entierro in Milan, which met at the Jesuit church of S. Fedele; he held this position most of his life. He also held similar positions with various other churches in Milan, and was active as a composer of sacred music and as an organist. In 1768 he became maestro di cappella to the ducal chapel at S. Gottardo; he was a founder-member of Milan's philharmonic society. A noted teacher, he taught at the Collegio de' Nobili from 1730. His most famous pupil was Gluck, who studied with him from about 1737 to 1741. Sammartini's historical importance rests upon his contribution to the development of the Classical style; his large body of syms. (68 in all), concertos, and other works for orch. are noteworthy for their extensive thematic development and evolution of sonata form. The earliest known dated syms., in 3-movement form, are credited to him. However, the claim that he composed a 4-movement sym. in 1734 lacks confirmation. See B. Churgin, ed., *The Symphonies of G. B. S.* (Cambridge, Mass., 1968–). He also composed the following works for the theater: *Memet*, opera (Lodi, 1732), *L'ambizione superata dalla virtù*, opera (Milan, Dec. 26, 1734), *L'Agrippina, moglie di Tiberio*, opera (Milan, Jan. 1743), *La gara dei geni*, introduzione e festa da ballo (Milan, May 28, 1747), and *Il trionfo d'amore*, ballet (Milan, 1773); also the oratorio *Gesù bambino adorato dalli pastori* (Milan, Jan. 11, 1726). Many other works attributed to him are doubtful or spurious.

BIBL.: N. Jenkins and B. Churgin, *Thematic Catalogue of the Works of G. B. S.: Orchestral and Vocal Music* (Cambridge, Mass., 1976).

Sammartini, Giuseppe (Francesco Gaspare Melchiorre Baldassare), Italian oboist and composer, brother of **Giovanni Battista Sammartini**, called "il Londinese" after settling in London; b. Milan, Jan. 6, 1695; d. London, Nov. 1750. He most likely studied oboe with his father, Alexis Saint-Martin, who settled in Italy. By 1720 he was a member of the orch. of the Teatro Regio Ducal in Milan. In 1728 he went to London, where he established himself as a virtuoso oboist; he also played in the opera orch. at the King's Theatre. From 1736 until his death he was music master to the wife and children of the prince of Wales. He composed a considerable number of instrumental works; his vocal music includes an aria and a sinfonia for the oratorio *La calunnia delusa* (Milan, 1724), a pasticcio by several Italian composers. He may also have composed the masque *The Judgement of Paris* (c.1740), which is usually attributed to Arne.

Samosud, Samuil (Abramovich), prominent Russian conductor and teacher; b. Tiflis, May 14, 1884; d. Moscow, Nov. 6, 1964. He studied cello at the Tiflis Cons. (graduated, 1906). After playing cello in various orchs., he went to St. Petersburg, where he was a conductor at the Maryinsky Theater (1917–19) and artistic director of the Maly Theater (1918–36); he then settled in Moscow and was artistic director of the Bolshoi Theater (1936–43), the Stanislavsky-Nemirovich-Danchenko Music Theater (1943–50), and the Moscow Phil. and the All-Union Radio orch. (1953–57); he also taught conducting at the Leningrad Cons. (1929–36), becoming a prof. in 1934. In 1937 he was made a People's Artist of the USSR. He conducted premieres of a number of works by Soviet composers, including Shostakovich's opera *The Nose* (1930) and Prokofiev's 7th Sym. (1952).

Samuel, Adolphe (-Abraham), Belgian composer and teacher, father of **Eugène Samuel-Holeman**; b. Liège, July 11, 1824; d. Ghent, Sept. 11, 1898. He was educated at the Liège Cons. and the Brussels Cons., winning the Belgian Grand Prix de Rome (1845). He taught harmony at the Brussels Cons. (1850–70), and in 1871 was appointed director of the Ghent Cons. He publ. *Cours d'accompagnement de la basse chiffrée* (Brussels, 1849), *Cours d'harmonie pratique* (Brussels, 1861), and *Livre de lecture musicale* (Paris, 1886). Among his works are 5 operas: *Il a rêvé* (1845), *Giovanni da Procida* (1848), *Madeleine* (1849), *Les Deux Prétendants* (1851), and *L'Heure de la retraite* (1852).

BIBL.: E. Mathieu, *Notice sur A. S.* (Brussels, 1922).

Samuel, Léopold, Belgian composer; b. Brussels, May 5, 1883; d. there, March 10, 1975. He studied with Edgar Tinel at the Brussels Cons. and took courses in Berlin, winning the Belgian Prix de Rome with his cantata *Tycho-Brahé* (1911). He later served as inspector of music education in Belgium (1920–45) and was made a member of the Belgian Royal Academy (1958). His works follow in a late Romantic style, with pronounced impressionistic elements. Among his works were the operas *Ilka* (1919) and *La Sirène au pays des hommes* (1937).

Samuel-Holeman, Eugène, Belgian pianist, conductor, and composer, son of **Adolphe (-Abraham) Samuel**; b. Brussels, Nov. 3, 1863; d. there, Jan. 25, 1942. After studying piano and theory at the Ghent Cons., he was active as a pianist and conductor, pursuing his career primarily in France. He wrote an opera, *Un vendredi saint en Zélande,* and a monodrama, *La jeune fille à la fenêtre* (1904).

Samuel-Rousseau, Marcel. See **Rousseau, Marcel.**

Sances, Giovanni Felice, Italian singer, teacher, and composer; b. Rome, c. 1600; d. Vienna (buried), Nov. 12, 1679. After serving several patrons, he was called to Vienna as a singer in the court chapel in 1636; in 1649 he was named assistant Kapellmeister, and subsequently was Kapellmeister (1669–76). He played a significant role in the cultivation of Italian dramatic music at the Viennese court. He composed the operas *Ermiona* (Padua, April 11, 1636), *I trionfi d'Amore* (Prague, July 2, 1648), *La Roselmina fatta canara* (Vienna, Feb. 1662), *Mercurio esploratore* (Vienna, Feb. 21, 1662), *Apollo deluso* (Vienna, June 9, 1669), and *Aristomene Messenio* (Vienna, Dec. 22, 1670).

BIBL.: P. Webhofer, *G. F. S. (ca. 1600–1679): Biographisch-bibliographische Untersuchung und Studie über sein Motettenwerk* (Innsbruck, 1965).

Sânchez de Fuentes, Eduardo, important Cuban composer and educator; b. Havana, April 3, 1874; d. there, Sept. 7, 1944. He studied music with Ignacio Cervantes and Carlos Anckermann. He occupied an influential position in the artistic affairs of Cuba. He wrote 5 operas and many other works, but is known outside Cuba chiefly by his popular song *Tú*, which he publ. at the age of 18. His operas (all 1st perf. in Havana) were *El náufrago*, after Tennyson's *Enoch Arden* (1900; Jan. 31, 1901), *La dolorosa* (April 23, 1910), *Doreya* (1917; Feb. 7, 1918), *El caminante* (1921), and *Kabelia*, after a Hindu legend (June 22, 1942).

WRITINGS (all publ. in Havana): *El folklore en la música cubana* (1923); *Folklorismo* (1928); *Viejos ritmos cubanos* (1937).

BIBL.: M. Guiral, *Un gran musicógrafo y compositor cubano: E. S. d. F.* (Havana, 1944); O. Martínez, *E. S. d. F.: In Memoriam* (Havana, 1944).

Sandberger, Adolf, eminent German musicologist; b. Würzburg, Dec. 19, 1864; d. Munich, Jan. 14, 1943. He studied composition in Würzburg and Munich (1881–87) and musicology in Munich and Berlin (1883–87); he obtained his Ph.D. in 1887 at the Univ. of Würzburg with the diss. *Peter Cornelius* (publ. in Leipzig, 1887) and completed his Habilitation in 1894 at the Univ. of Munich with his *Beiträge zur Geschichte der Bayerischen Hofkapelle unter Orlando di Lasso* (vols. 1 and 3 publ. in Leipzig, 1894–95; vol. 2 not publ.). In 1889 he was appointed head of the music dept. at the Bavarian Hofbibliothek in Munich; he also was a reader (1900–04) and a prof. (1904–30) at the Univ. of Munich. He was ed. of the Denkmäler der Tonkunst in Bayern (1900–31) and the *Neues Beethoven-Jahrbuch* (1924–42); with F. Haberl, he also ed. Breitkopf & Härtel's monumental edition of the complete works of Lassus (1894–1927). Sandberger was one of the most important teachers of musicology in Germany; he formulated the basic principles of 20th-century musical bibliography. Among his writings were *Emmanuel Chabriers Gwendoline* (Munich, 1898), *Über* *zwei ehedem Wolfgang Mozart zugeschriebene Messen* (Munich, 1907), and *Ausgewählte Aufsätze zur Musikgeschichte* (Munich, 1921–24). He was also a composer, including in his works 2 operas.

BIBL.: T. Kroyer, ed., *Festschrift zum 50. Geburtstag A. S.* (Munich, 1918).

Sanderling, Kurt, eminent German conductor, father of **Thomas Sanderling**; b. Arys, Sept. 9, 1912. Following private studies, he joined the Berlin Städtische Oper as a répétiteur (1931). Being Jewish, he left Nazi Germany and made his way to the Soviet Union (1936); he was a conductor with the Moscow Radio Orch. (1936–41) and the Leningrad Phil. (1941–60). He then was chief conductor of the (East) Berlin Sym. Orch. (1960–77). From 1964 to 1967 he was chief conductor of the Dresden State Opera. He also filled a number of engagements as a guest conductor in Western Europe and America.

BIBL.: H. Bitterlich, *K. S.: Für Sie portratiert* (Leipzig, 1987).

Sanderling, Thomas, German conductor, son of **Kurt Sanderling;** b. Novosibirsk, Russia, Oct. 2, 1942. He studied at the Leningrad Cons. and at the Hanns Eisler Hochschule für Musik in East Berlin. In 1962 he made his conducting debut with the (East) Berlin Sym. Orch. After serving as music director in Sondershausen (1963–64) and Reichenbach (1964–66), he was music director in Halle (from 1966). In 1978 he became permanent guest conductor of the (East) Berlin State Opera. In 1979 he made a highly successful debut at the Vienna State Opera conducting *Die Zauberflöte*, and subsequently was engaged by many major opera houses and orchs. in Europe and abroad. From 1984 to 1986 he was artistic director of the Amsterdam Phil. He was music director of the Osaka Sym. Orch. from 1992.

Sanderson, Sibyl, American soprano; b. Sacramento, Calif., Dec. 7, 1865; d. Paris, May 15, 1903. She was educated in San Francisco, where her musical talent attracted attention; taken to Paris by her mother at the age 19, she studied at the Cons. with Massenet, Sbriglia, and Mathilde Marchesi. Massenet was charmed with her voice and her person and wrote the leading part in Esclarmonde for her; she created it at the Opéra Comique, on May 14, 1889. The role of Thaïs (Paris Opera, March 16, 1889) was also written by Massenet for her. Other French composers were equally enchanted with her; Saint-Saëns wrote *Phryné* for her (1893). She made her American debut at the Metropolitan Opera in New York as Manon (Jan. 16, 1895), but had little success with the American public. In 1897 she married a wealthy Cuban, Antonio Terry, who died in 1899.

Sandi, Luis, Mexican conductor, teacher, and composer; b. Mexico City, Feb. 22, 1905. He studied violin with Rocabruna (1923–30) and composition with Campa and Mejía (1925–31) at the National Cons. of Mexico City. He conducted a chorus at the Cons. (1922–35); in 1937 he founded the Coro de Madrigalistas and conducted it until 1965. He was a prof. of music in primary schools (1924–32) and chief of the Music Section of the Secretariat of Public Education (1933–65). He publ. *Introducción al estudio de la música: Curso completo* (Mexico City, 1923; 2d ed., 1956) and a collection of articles as *De música y otras cosas* (Mexico City, 1969). His works include the operas *Carlota* (Mexico City, Oct. 23, 1948) and *La señora en su balcón* (1964), and the ballets *Día de difuntos* (1938), *Bonampak* (1948; Mexico City, Nov. 2, 1951), and *Coatlicue* (1949).

Sandström, Sven-David, Swedish composer and teacher; b. Borensberg, Oct. 30, 1942. He studied art history and musicology at the Univ. of Stockholm (1963–67) and attended composition classes with Lidholm at the Stockholm Musikhögskolan (1967–72); he also took special courses in advanced techniques of composition with Norgard and Ligeti. In 1981 he joined the faculty of the Stockholm Musikhögskolan. In 1983 he served as chairman of the Swedish section of the ISCM. In his early works he made use of quarter-tone tuning. Later he turned to tonal and modal writing.

WORKS: DRAMATIC: *Stark såsom döden* (Strong like Death), church opera (Stockholm, April 18, 1978); *Hasta o älskade brud* (Hasta, O Beloved Bride), chamber opera (1978); *Kejsaren Jones* (Emperor Jones), after O'Neill (1980); *Ett drömspel* (The Dreamplay), incidental music to Strindberg's play (1980); *Amos*, church opera (1981); *Slottet det vita*, opera (1981–82; Stockholm, Feb. 12, 1987); *Admorica*, ballet (1985); *Den elfte gryningen*, ballet (Stockholm, Nov. 4, 1988); ballet music (1991); *Staden*, opera (1996; Stockholm, Sept. 12, 1998); *Sankt Göran och draken*, stage music (1998).

Sandunova, Elizaveta Semyonovna, prominent Russian mezzo-soprano who was known as **Uranova**; b. St. Petersburg, c.1772; d. Moscow, Dec. 3, 1826. She was a student of Martín y Soler, Paisiello, and Sarti in St. Petersburg. In 1790 she made her operatic debut in Martín y Soler's *Arbore di Diana* in St. Petersburg, and then sang at the imperial theaters there from 1791 to 1794. She took the professional name of Uranova by order of Catherine II in honor of the discovery of the planet Uranus. After marrying the actor Sila Sandunov in 1794, they appeared together at the Petrovsky Theater in Moscow. They were divorced in 1810 and in 1813 Uranova returned to St. Petersburg, where she made frequent appearances until her retirement from the stage in 1823.

Sangiovanni, Antonio, celebrated Italian singing teacher; b. Bergamo, Sept. 14, 1831; d. Milan, Jan. 6, 1892. He studied at the Milan Cons. where, in 1854, he was appointed prof. of singing. Two generations of Italian and foreign singers were his pupils.

Sanjust, Filippo, Italian stage designer and opera director; b. Rome, Sept. 9, 1925; d. there, Nov. 29, 1992. He studied architecture in Rome and at Princeton Univ. before turning to stage design. In 1958 Visconti chose him as designer for his staging of *Don Carlos* at London's Covent Garden, and thereafter they collaborated successfully on various productions, including *Il Trovatore* at Covent Garden (1964) and *Le nozze di Figaro* in Rome (1964) and at the Metropolitan Opera in New York (1968). Henze chose Sanjust as designer for the premieres of his *Der junge Lord* in Berlin in 1965 and for his *The Bassarids* at the Salzburg Festival in 1966. From 1969 Sanjust combined work as a stage designer with opera directing. Among his most distinguished productions were *Ariadne auf Naxos* (1976) and *Falstaff* (1980) in Vienna, *L'incoronazione di Poppea* (1979) in Brussels, and *Simon Boccanega* (1980) at Covent Garden.

Santi, Nello, Italian conductor; b. Adria, Sept. 22, 1931. He studied at the Padua Liceo Musicale and with Coltro and Pedrollo. In 1951 he made his debut conducting *Rigoletto* in Padua, and then conducted in various Italian opera houses. From 1958 he was a regular conductor at the Zürich Opera. In 1960 he made his first appearance at London's Covent Garden conducting *La Traviata*. That same year he made his debuts at the Vienna State Opera and the Salzburg Festival. He made his Metropolitan Opera debut in New York on Jan. 25, 1962, conducting *Un ballo in maschera*. He remained on its roster until 1965, and then conducted there regularly from 1976. As a guest conductor, he led operatic performances in Milan, Paris, Berlin, Munich, Florence, Naples, Geneva, and other European music centers. He also appeared as a guest conductor with many European orchs. In 1986 he became chief conductor of the Basel Radio Sym. Orch. In 1988 he conducted *Aida* in the first arena production in London at Earl's Court. He has won particular distinction for his performances of the Italian operatic repertoire.

Santini, Gabriele, Italian conductor; b. Perugia, Jan. 20, 1886; d. Rome, Nov. 13, 1964. After studies in Perugia and Bologna, he conducted opera in Rio de Janeiro, Buenos Aires, New York, and Chicago. From 1925 to 1929 he was Toscanini's assistant at La Scala in Milan, then was a conductor (1929–33) and artistic director (1944–47) at the Rome Opera.

Santley, Sir Charles, noted English baritone; b. Liverpool, Feb. 28, 1834; d. Hove, near London, Sept. 22, 1922. He studied with Nava in Milan, making his operatic debut as Dr. Grenville in *La Traviata* in Pavia (1857), then continued his training with García in London, where he sang for the first time as Adam in Haydn's *Creation* on Nov. 16, 1857. His British operatic debut followed as Hoël in *Dinorah* at Covent Garden in a production mounted by the Pyne-Harrison Co. (Oct. 1, 1859); he continued to sing with the company until 1863, creating many roles in English operas under its auspices. In 1862 he appeared with the Royal Italian Opera at Covent Garden; that same year he became a member of Mapleson's company at Her Majesty's Theatre, winning renown for his portrayal of Valentine in 1863; he left the company in 1870. After singing at the Gaiety Theatre and touring in the United States as a concert artist (1871), he sang with the Carl Rosa Opera Co. (1875–77); subsequently he devoted himself to oratorio and concert appearances. He sang in Australia (1889–90) and again in the United States (1891). On May 23, 1911, he made his farewell appearance at Covent Garden but came out of retirement in 1915 to sing at a concert for Belgian war refugees. In 1887 he was made a Commander of the Order of St. Gregory by Pope Leo XIII, and in 1907 he was knighted by King Edward VII. He publ. some songs under the pseudonym Ralph Betterton; he also publ. *Student and Singer* (London, 1892; reminiscences), *The Singing Master* (2 parts, London, 1900), *The Art of Singing and Vocal Declamation* (London, 1908), and *Reminiscences of My Life* (London, 1909).

BIBL.: J. Levien, *Sir C. S.* (London, 1930).

Santoliquido, Francesco, Italian composer; b. San Giorgio a Cremano, Naples, Aug. 6, 1883; d. Anacapri, Aug. 26, 1971. He studied at the Liceo di Santa Cecilia in Rome and graduated in 1908; in 1912 he went to live in Hammamet, a village in Tunisia, spending part of each year in Rome; in 1933 he made his home in Anacapri. Many of his compositions contain melodic inflections of Arabian popular music. He publ. *Il Dopo-Wagner, Claudio Debussy e Richard Strauss* (Rome, 1909; 2d ed., 1922); also books of verse; he wrote short stories in Eng. His 3d wife was the pianist and teacher Ornella (née Puliti) Santoliquido (b. Florence, Sept. 4, 1906; d. there, Nov. 11, 1977); she studied with Brugnoli; after receiving her diploma at the Florence Cons., she continued her training with Casella in Rome and Cortot in Paris; she was a teacher at the Rome Cons. (1939–71), played in chamber-music concerts, and became an advocate of contemporary music.

WORKS: DRAMATIC: OPERAS: *La Favola di Helga* (Milan, Nov. 23, 1910); *Ferhuda* (Tunis, Jan. 30, 1919); *L'Ignota* (1921; not perf.); *La porta verde*, musical tragedy (Bergamo, Oct. 15, 1953). BALLET: *La Bajadera dalla maschera gialla* (1917).

Santoro, Claudio, distinguished Brazilian composer, conductor, and teacher; b. Manáos, Nov. 23, 1919; d. Brasília, March 27, 1989. He studied at the Rio de Janeiro Cons. and received training from Guerra and Koellreutter. In 1946 he held a Guggenheim fellowship. In 1947 he received a French scholarship and pursued his studies in Paris with Boulanger and Eugène Bigot. He was awarded the Lili Boulanger Prize in 1948. In 1965 he held a Ford Foundation scholarship and was active in Berlin. From 1970 to 1978 he taught at the Univ. of Heidelberg-Mannheim. In 1979 he settled in Brasília, where he was a conductor at the Univ. and of the orch. of the National Theater until his death. He also appeared as a guest conductor in South America and Europe. In his earliest works, he composed mainly in the 12-tone manner. After a period in which he wrote in an accessible style, he returned to advanced techniques, including aleatory. His works include the ballets *A fábrica* (1947), *Anticocos* (1951), *O café* (1953), *Icamiabas* (1959), *Zuimaaluti* (1960), and *Prelúdios* (1962).

BIBL.: V. Mariz, *C. S.* (Rio de Janeiro, 1994).

Santos, (José Manuel) Joly Braga, Portuguese conductor and composer; b. Lisbon, May 14, 1924; d. there, July 18, 1988. He studied composition with Luis de Freitas Branco at the Lisbon Cons. (1934–43), conducting with Scherchen at the Venice Cons. (1948), electronic music at the Gavessano (Switzerland) Acoustic Experimental Studio (1957–58), and composition with Mortari at the Rome Cons. (1959–60). He conducted the Oporto Radio Sym. Orch. (1955–59); subsequently he was active as a guest conductor. His music represents a felicitous fusion of Portuguese Renaissance modalities and folk rhythms.

WORKS: DRAMATIC: OPERAS: *Viver ou morrer* (To Live or to Die), radio opera (1952); *Mérope* (Lisbon, May 15, 1959); *Trilogia das Barcas* (1969; Lisbon, May, 1970). BALLETS: *Alfama* (1956); *A nau Catrineta* (1959); *Encruzilhada* (1968).

Sanzogno, Nino, Italian conductor and composer; b. Venice, April 13, 1911; d. Milan, May 4, 1983. He studied at the Venice Cons. (graduated, 1932), pursuing his training with Malipiero (composition) in Venice and Scherchen (conducting) in Brussels. He began his career as a violinist in the Guarneri Quartet. In 1937 he became conductor at the Teatro La Fenice in Venice, and he also conducted the Gruppo Strumentale Italiano (1938–39). In 1939 he made his first appearance at Milan's La Scala, returning there as a conductor in subsequent years. In 1955 he conducted Cimarosa's *Il Matrimonio segreto* at the first performance given at Milan's Piccola Scala. He took the company to the Edinburgh Festival in 1957. As a guest conductor, he appeared with principal Italian, European, and North and South American opera houses. In addition to his performances of works from the standard repertoire, he became particularly known for his advocacy of contemporary composers, among them Petrassi, Malipiero, Milhaud, Berio, Hartmann, and Poulenc.

Sapelnikov, Vasili, Russian pianist and composer; b. Odessa, Nov. 2, 1867; d. San Remo, March 17, 1941. He was a pupil of L. Brassin and Sophie Menter at the St. Petersburg Cons.; in 1888 made his debut at Hamburg with Tchaikovsky's First Piano Concerto, under the composer's direction, he then made tours throughout Europe; after living in Russia (1916–22), he settled in the West. Among his works is an opera, *Der Khan und sein Sohn*.

Saporiti (real name, **Codecasa**), **Teresa,** Italian soprano; b. c.1763; d. Milan, March 17, 1869. She joined Pasquale Bondini's Italian company in 1782 and appeared with it in Leipzig, Dresden, and Prague, often being obliged to appear in male costume and take on castrati roles. The success of Bondini's production of *Le nozze di Figaro* in Prague in 1786 prompted him to request an opera from Mozart for the following year; the part of Donna Anna in *Don Giovanni* was written with Saporiti's voice in mind: the taxing coloratura in her aria in the 2d act indicates that Mozart had a high opinion of her ability. She then appeared in Venice (1788–89) and at Milan's La Scala (1789); later in Bologna, Parma, and Modena. By 1795 she was prima buffa assoluta in Gennaro Astarita's company in St. Petersburg; she sang in Astarita's own comic operas, as well as in revivals of Cimarosa's *Italiana in Londra* and Paisiello's *Il Barbiere di Siviglia*. She then fell into total oblivion. If the dates of her life can be believed, she lived to about the age of 105.

Sarabia, Guillermo, Mexican baritone; b. Mazatlán, Aug. 30, 1936; d. Amsterdam, Sept. 19, 1985. He studied with Herbert Graf, Ria Ginster, Dusolina Giannini, and Carl Ebert in Zürich at the Opera Studio and Cons. After making his operatic debut as Doktor Faust in Detmold (1965), he sang in various German opera houses. On May 5, 1973, he made his Metropolitan Opera debut in New York as Amonasro. In 1976 he made his first appearance at the N.Y. City Opera as the Dutchman. His guest appearances took him to Vienna, Berlin, London, Paris, and Milan. He made his last appearance in the United States as Falstaff with Solti and the Chicago Sym. Orch. in 1985, shortly before his death. Among his other roles were Pizzaro, Rigoletto, Scarpia, and Wozzeck.

Saradzhev, Konstantin, Armenian conductor and pedagogue; b. Derbent, Oct. 8, 1877; d. Yerevan, July 22, 1954. He studied violin with Hřimalý at the Moscow Cons. (graduated, 1898). After further training with Ševčík in Prague (1900), he studied conducting with Nikisch in Leipzig (1904–08). He began his conducting career in Moscow, where he championed the cause of Soviet composers. From 1922 to 1935 he also was prof. of conducting at the Cons. He then settled in Yerevan, where he was artistic director of the Opera and Ballet Theater. He also was director of the Cons. (from 1939) and principal conductor of the

Phil. (1941–44). In 1946 he was made a People's Artist of the Armenian SSR.

Sargeant, Winthrop, prominent American music critic; b. San Francisco, Dec. 10, 1903; d. Salisbury, Conn., Aug. 15, 1986. He studied violin in San Francisco with Arthur Argiewicz and with Lucien Capet in Paris and took composition lessons with Albert Elkus in San Francisco and with Carl Prohaska in Vienna. He played the violin in the San Francisco Sym. Orch. (1922–24), the N.Y. Sym. Orch. (1926–28), and the N.Y. Phil. (1928–30). He then devoted himself to musical journalism; he was on the editorial staff of *Musical America* (1931–34), was music critic of the *Brooklyn Daily Eagle* (1934–36) and served as music ed. of *Time* magazine (1937–39); he also wrote essays on various subjects for *Time* (1939–45); he subsequently was roving correspondent for *Life* magazine (1945–49) and music critic for the *New Yorker* (1947–72), continuing as a contributor to the latter until his death. He evolved a highly distinctive manner of writing: professionally solid, stylistically brilliant, and ideologically opinionated; he especially inveighed against the extreme practices of the cosmopolitan avant-garde. He publ. *Divas: Impressions of Today's Sopranos* (N.Y., 1973).

Sargent, Sir (Harold) Malcolm (Watts), eminent English conductor; b. Stamford, Lincolnshire, April 29, 1895; d. London, Oct. 3, 1967. He studied organ at the Royal College of Organists in London, then was articled to Keeton, organist of Peterborough Cathedral (1912–14); he subsequently served in the infantry during World War I. He made his first major conducting appearance on Feb. 3, 1921, in Leicester, leading the Queen's Hall Orch. of London in his own composition, *Allegro impetuoso: An Impression on a Windy Day*. He then went to London, where he conducted the D'Oyly Carte Opera Co. and Diaghilev's Ballets Russes; from 1928 he was conductor-in-chief of the Royal Choral Soc. From 1929 to 1940 he was conductor of the Courtauld-Sargent Concerts in London. He toured Australia in 1936, 1938, and 1939, and Palestine in 1937. He was conductor-in-chief and musical adviser of the Hallé Orch. of Manchester (1939–42), then was principal conductor of the Liverpool Phil. (1942–48). In 1945 he made his American debut with the NBC Sym. Orch. in New York; then made appearances in Europe, Australia, and Japan. He was knighted in 1947. From 1950 to 1957 he was chief conductor of the BBC Sym. Orch. in London; he led this ensemble on several European tours. From 1948 to 1966 he also served as chief conductor of the London Promenade Concerts. He took the London Phil. on an extensive Far Eastern tour in 1962; he also led the Royal Phil. to the Soviet Union and the United States in 1963. His performances of the standard repertoire were distinguished for their precision and brilliance; he championed the music of Elgar, Vaughan Williams, Walton, and other English composers throughout his career. A commemorative stamp with his portrait was issued by the Post Office of Great Britain on Sept. 1, 1980.

BIBL.: C. Reid, *M. S.: A Biography* (London, 1968).

Sargon, Simon, Indian-born American pianist and composer; b. Bombay (of Sephardic, Russian-Jewish, and Indian descent), April 6, 1938. He took private piano lessons with Horszowski and studied theory at Brandeis Univ. (B.A., 1959) and composition with Persichetti at the Juilliard School of Music in New York (M.S., 1962); he also took a course with Milhaud at the Aspen (Colo.) School of Music. He was a teacher at Sarah Lawrence College in Bronxville, N.Y. (1965–68), at the Rubin Academy of Music in Jerusalem (1971–74), where he served as head of the voice dept., and at Hebrew Univ. in Jerusalem (1973–74). In 1974 he was appointed music director at Temple Emanu-El in Dallas.

WORKS: DRAMATIC: *Thirst*, chamber opera, after Eugene O'Neill (Jerusalem, Dec. 17, 1972); *A Voice Still and Small*, children's musical play (Dallas, Dec. 6, 1981); *Saul, King of Israel*, opera (1990). Also *Not by Might*, oratorio (Dallas, Dec. 16, 1979).

Sari, Ada (real name, **Jadwiga Szajerowa**), Polish soprano; b. Wadowice, near Kraków, June 29, 1886; d. Ciechocinek, July 12, 1968. She studied in Milan. After appearances in Rome, Naples, Trieste, and Parma, she joined the Warsaw Opera; she made extensive tours in Europe, South America, and the United States; she later taught voice in Warsaw.

Sárközy, István, Hungarian composer and teacher; b. Erzsébetfalva, Nov. 26, 1920. He was a student of Farkas and Szatmári, and of Kodály and Viski at the Budapest Academy of Music. From 1957 to 1960 he was ed.-in-chief for music with Editio Musica Budapest. In 1959 he became a teacher of theory at the Budapest Academy of Music.

WORKS: DRAMATIC: *Az új traktorállomás* (The New Tractor Station), ballet (1949); *Liliomfi*, musical play (1950); *Szelistyei asszonyok* (The Women of Szelistye), opera (1951); folk dance plays; incidental music.

Sarro (or **Sarri**), **Domenico Natale**, Italian composer; b. Trani, Apulia, Dec. 24, 1679; d. Naples, Jan. 25, 1744. He settled in Naples and studied at the Cons. di S. Onofrio. From 1704 to 1707 he was vice maestro di cappella at the court; in 1725 he became its vice maestro, and in 1735 assumed the duties of maestro di cappella when Mancini fell ill; upon Mancini's death in 1737, Sarro formally assumed the post. From 1728 he was also maestro di cappella of the city. Sarro was one of the principal Neapolitan composers of his day. His output includes 28 secular operas, as well as several sacred operas and oratorios.

Sarti, Giuseppe, noted Italian composer, nicknamed "Il Domenichino"; b. Faenza (baptized), Dec. 1, 1729; d. Berlin, July 28, 1802. He took music lessons in Padua with Valotti; when he was 10, he went to Bologna to continue his studies with Padre Martini. Returning to Faenza, he was organist at the Cathedral (1748–52); in 1752 he was appointed director of the theater in Faenza; that same year his first opera, *Pompeo in Armenia*, was performed. His next opera, *Il Re pastore*, was staged in Venice in 1753 with great success. Toward the end of 1753 he went to Copenhagen as a conductor of Pietro Mingotti's opera troupe. His work impressed the king of Denmark, Frederik V, and in 1755 he was named court Kapellmeister. He subsequently was made director of the Italian Opera, but it was closed in 1763; he then was appointed director of court music. In 1765 he was sent by the king to Italy to engage singers for the reopening of the Opera, but Frederik's death aborted the project. Sarti remained in Italy, where he served as maestro di coro at the Pietà Cons. in Venice (1766–67). In 1768 he returned to Copenhagen, where he resumed his duties as director of the royal chapel; from 1770 to 1775 he was conductor of the court theater. He then returned to Italy with his wife, the singer Camilla Passi, whom he had married in Copenhagen. He became director of the Cons. dell'Ospedaletto in Venice in 1775. In 1779 he entered the competition for the position of maestro di cappella at Milan Cathedral, winning it against a number of competitors, including Paisiello. By this time his prestige as a composer and as a teacher was very high. Among his numerous pupils was Cherubini. In 1784 he was engaged by Catherine the Great as director of the Imperial chapel in St. Petersburg. On his way to Russia, he passed through Vienna, where he was received with honors by the emperor Joseph II; he also met Mozart, who quoted a melody from Sarti's opera *Fra i due litiganti* in *Don Giovanni*. His greatest success in St. Petersburg was *Armida e Rinaldo* (Jan. 26, 1786), remodeled from an earlier opera, *Armida abbandonata*, originally performed in Copenhagen in 1759; the leading role was sung by the celebrated Portuguese mezzo-soprano Luiza Todi, but she developed a dislike of Sarti, and used her powerful influence with Catherine the Great to prevent his reengagement. However, he was immediately engaged by Prince Potemkin, and followed him to southern Russia and Moldavia during the military campaign against Turkey; on the taking of Ochakov, Sarti wrote an ode to the Russian liturgical text of thanksgiving, and it was performed in Jan. 1789 at Jassy, Bessarabia, with the accompaniment of cannon shots and church bells. Potemkin offered him a sinecure as head of a singing school in Ekaterinoslav, but Sarti did not actually teach there. After Potemkin's death in 1791, his arrangements with Sarti were honored by the court of St. Petersburg; in 1793 he was reinstated as court composer and was named director of a conservatory. Sarti's operas enjoyed considerable success during his lifetime but sank into oblivion after his death. He was an adept contrapuntist, and excelled in polyphonic writing; his *Fuga a otto voci* on the text of a Kyrie is notable. He was also astute in his adaptation to political realities. In Denmark he wrote Singspiels in Danish, and in Russia he composed a Requiem in memory of Louis XVI in response to the great lamentation at the Russian Imperial Court at the execution of the French king (1793). He also composed an offering to the emperor Paul, whose daughters studied music with Sarti. After Paul's violent death at the hands of the palace guard, Sarti decided to leave Russia, but died in Berlin on his way to Italy. In 1796 Sarti presented to the Russian Academy of Sciences an apparatus to measure pitch (the so-called St. Petersburg tuning fork).

WORKS: DRAMATIC: *Pompeo in Armenia*, dramma per musica (Faenza, Carnival 1752); *Il Re pastore*, dramma per musica (Venice, Carnival 1753); *Vologeso*, dramma per musica (Copenhagen, Carnival 1754); *Antigono*, dramma per musica (Copenhagen, Oct. 14, 1754; some arias by other composers); *Ciro riconosciuto*, dramma per musica (Copenhagen, Dec. 21, 1754); *Arianna e Teseo*, dramma per musica (Copenhagen, Carnival 1756); *Anagilda*, dramma per musica (Copenhagen, fall 1758); *Armida abbandonata*, dramma per musica (Copenhagen, 1759; later version as *Armida e Rinaldo*, St. Petersburg, Jan. 26, 1786); *Achille in Sciro*, dramma per musica (Copenhagen, 1759); *Andromaca*, dramma per musica (Copenhagen, 1759?); *Filindo*, pastorale eroica (Copenhagen, 1760); *Astrea placata*, festa teatrale (Copenhagen, Oct. 17, 1760); *La Nitteti*, dramma per musica (Copenhagen, Oct. 12, 1760); *Issipile*, dramma per musica (Copenhagen, 1760?); *Alessandro nell'Indie*, dramma per musica (Copenhagen, 1761); *Semiramide*, dramma per musica (Copenhagen, fall 1762); *Didone abbandonata*, dramma per musica (Copenhagen, winter 1762); *Narciso*, dramma pastorale (Copenhagen, Carnival 1763); *Cesare in Egitto*, dramma per musica (Copenhagen, fall 1763); *Il naufragio di Cipro*, dramma pastorale (Copenhagen, 1764); *Il gran Tamerlano*, tragedia per musica (Copenhagen, 1764); *Ipermestra*, dramma per musica (Rome, Carnival 1766); *La Giardiniera brillante*, intermezzo (Rome, Jan. 3, 1768); *L'Asile de l'amour*, dramatic cantata (Copenhagen, July 22, 1769); *La Double Méprise, ou, Carlile et Fany*, comédie mêlée d'ariettes (Copenhagen, July 22, 1769); *Soliman den Anden*, Singspiel (Copenhagen, Oct. 8, 1770); *Le Bal*, opéra comique (Copenhagen, 1770); *Il tempio d'eternità*, festa teatrale (Copenhagen, 1771); *Demofoonte*, dramma per musica (Copenhagen, Jan. 30, 1771); *Tronfølgen i Sidon*, lyrisk tragicomedia (Copenhagen, April 4, 1771); *Il Re pastore*, dramma per musica (Copenhagen, 1771; a different score from the one of 1753); *La clemenza di Tito*, dramma per musica (Padua, June 1771); *Deucalion og Pyrrha*, Singspiel (Copenhagen, March 19, 1772); *Aglae, eller Støtten*, Singspiel (Copenhagen, Feb. 16, 1774); *Kierlighedsbrevene*, Singspiel (Copenhagen, March 22, 1775); *Farnace*, dramma per musica (Venice, 1776); *Le gelosie villane (Il Feudatario)*, dramma giocoso (Venice, Nov. 1776); *Ifigenia*, dramma per musica (Rome, Carnival 1777); *Medonte re di Epiro*, dramma per musica (Florence, Sept. 8, 1777); *Il Militare bizzarro*, dramma giocoso (Venice, Dec. 27, 1777); *Olimpiade*, dramma per musica (Florence, 1778); *Scipione*, dramma per musica (Mestre, fall 1778); *I contratempi*, dramma giocoso (Venice, Nov. 1778); *Adriano in Siria*, dramma per musica (Rome, Dec. 26, 1778); *L'ambizione delusa*, intermezzo (Rome, Feb. 1779); *Mitridate a Sinope*, dramma per musica (Florence, fall 1779); *Achille in Sciro*, dramma per musica (Florence, fall 1779); *Siroe*, dramma per musica (Turin, Dec. 26, 1779); *Giulio Sabino*, dramma per musica (Venice, Jan. 1781); *Demofoonte*, dramma per musica (Rome, Carnival 1782; a different score from the one of 1771); *Didone abbandonata*, dramma per musica (Padua, June 1782; a different score from the one of 1762); *Alessandro e Timoteo*, dramma per musica (Parma, April 6, 1782); *Fra i due litiganti il terzo gode*, dramma giocoso (Milan, Sept. 14, 1782; subsequently perf. under various titles); *Attalo re di Bitinia*, dramma per musica (Venice, Dec. 26, 1782); *Idalide*, dramma per musica (Milan, Jan. 8, 1783); *Erifile*, dramma per musica (Pavia, Carnival 1783); *Il trionfo della pace*, dramma per musica (Mantua, May 10, 1783); *Olimpiade*, dramma per musica (Rome, 1783; a different score from the one of 1778); *Gli Amanti consolati*, dramma giocoso (St. Petersburg, 1784); *I finti eredi*, opera comica (St. Petersburg, Oct. 30, 1785); *Armida e Rinaldo*, dramma per musica (St. Petersburg, Jan. 26, 1786; based upon *Armida abbandonata* of 1759); *Castore e Polluce*, dramma per musica (St. Petersburg, Oct. 3, 1786); *Zenoclea*, azione teatrale (1786; not performed); *Alessandro nell'Indie*, dramma per musica (Palermo, winter 1787; a different score from the one of 1761); *Cleomene*, dramma per musica (Bologna, Dec. 27, 1788); *The Early Reign of Oleg*, Russian opera to a libretto by Catherine the Great (St. Petersburg, Oct. 22, 1790; in collaboration with V. Pashkevich); *Il trionfo d'Atalanta* (1791; not performed); *Andromeda*, dramma per musica (St. Petersburg, Nov. 4, 1798); *Enea nel Lazio*, dramma per musica (St. Petersburg, Oct. 26, 1799); *La Famille indienne en Angleterre*, opera (St. Petersburg, 1799); *Les Amours de Flore et de Zéphire*, ballet anacréontique (Gatchina, Sept. 19, 1800).

BIBL.: G. Pasolini, *G. S.* (Faenza, 1883); C. Rivalta, *G. S.: Musicista faentino del secolo XVIII* (Faenza, 1928); F. Samory, *A G. S. nel 2° centenario di sua nascita* (Faenza, 1929).

Sartori, Claudio, eminent Italian music scholar and bibliographer; b. Brescia, April 1, 1913; d. Milan, March 11, 1994. He received an arts degree in 1934 from the Univ. of Pavia with a thesis in music history; then studied with Gerold at the Univ. of Strasbourg and with Vittadini at the Pavia Cons. He served as an assistant librarian at the Bologna Cons. (1938–42); in 1943 he was appointed prof. of Italian literature there; in 1967 he assumed a similar professorship at the Milan Cons. He founded and became director of the Ufficio Ricerche Musicali in 1965; its aim was to conduct a thorough codification of Italian musical sources, providing information on all MSS and publ. music in Italy before 1900, on all publ. librettos in Italy down to 1800, and on all literature on music in Italy. In addition to this invaluable compilation, he also served as ed.-in-chief of *Dizionario Ricordi della musica e dei musicisti* (Milan, 1959). In 1983 he was made a corresponding member of the American Musicological Soc.

WRITINGS: *Il R. Conservatorio di Musica G. B. Martini di Bologna* (Florence, 1942); *Bibliografia delle opere musicali stampate da Ottaviano Petrucci* (Florence, 1948; later continued as "Nuove conclusive aggiunte alla 'Bibliografia del Petrucci,'" *Collectanea Historiae Musicae*, I, 1953); *Bibliografia della musica strumentale italiana stampata in Italia fino al 1700* (2 vols., Florence, 1952 and 1968); *Monteverdi* (Brescia, 1953); *Catalogo delle musiche della Cappella del Duomo di Milano* (Milan, 1957); *Riccardo Malipiero* (Milan, 1957); *Casa Ricordi 1808–1958* (Milan, 1958); *Dizionario degli editori musicali italiani* (Florence, 1958); *Giacomo Puccini a Monza* (Monza, 1958); *Puccini* (Milan, 1958); ed. *Puccini Symposium* (Milan, 1959); *Assisi: La Cappella della Basilica di S. Francesco: Catalogo del fondo musicale nella Biblioteca comunale di Assisi* (Milan, 1962); ed. *L'enciclopedia della musica* (Milan, 1963–64); *Commemorazione di Ottaviano de' Petrucci* (Fossombrone, 1966); *Giacomo Carissimi: Catalogo delle opere attribuite* (Milan, 1975); ed., with F. Lesure, *Bibliografia della musica italiana vocale profana pubblicata dal 1500 al 1700* (Geneva, 1978).

Sartorio, Antonio, important Italian composer; b. Venice, 1630; d. there, Dec. 30, 1680. His first opera, *Gl' amori infruttuosi di Pirro*, was performed in Venice on Jan. 4, 1661; his second opera, *Seleuco* (Venice, Jan. 16, 1666), established his reputation. In 1666 he went to Germany to take up the post of Kapellmeister to Duke Johann Friedrich of Braunschweig-Lüneburg, who maintained his court in Hannover. He held this post until 1675, but continued to make regular visits to Venice to oversee productions of his operas. It was in Venice that he brought out his most famous opera, *L'Adelaide*, on Feb. 19, 1672. He returned to Venice permanently in 1675; in 1676 he was appointed vice maestro di cappella at San Marco, a position he held until his death. Sartorio was a leading representative of the Venetian school of opera; his operas are notable for their arias, which he composed in a varied and effective manner.

WORKS: OPERAS (all 1st perf. in Venice unless otherwise given): *Gl'amori infruttuosi di Pirro* (Jan. 4, 1661); *Seleuco* (Jan. 16, 1666); *La prosperità d'Elio Seiano* (Jan. 15, 1667); *La caduta d'Elio Seiano* (Feb. 3, 1667); *L'Ermengarda regina de' Longobardi* (Dec. 26, 1669); *L'Adelaide* (Feb. 19, 1672); *L'Orfeo* (Dec. 14, 1672); *Massenzio* (Jan. 25, 1673); *Alcina* (c.1674; not perf.); *Giulio Cesare in Egitto* (Dec. 17, 1676); *Antonino e Pompeiano* (1677); *L'Anacreonte tiranno* (1677); *Ercole su'l Termodonte* (1678); *I duo tiranni al soglio* (Jan. 15, 1679); *La Flora* (music completed by M. A. Ziani; Carnival 1681).

Sass, Marie Constance, Belgian soprano; b. Oudenaarde, Jan. 26, 1834; d. Auteuil, near Paris, Nov. 8, 1907. She studied with Gevaert in Ghent, Ugalde in Paris, and Lamperti in Italy, making her operatic debut as Gilda in Venice (1852). She then went to Paris, where she sang at the Théâtre-Lyrique (1859) and at the Opéra (from 1860), where she was the first Paris Elisabeth in the controversial mounting of *Tannhäuser* (1861) and where she created the roles of Selika in *L'Africaine* (1865) and Elisabeth de Valois in *Don Carlos* (1867); subsequently she appeared at Milan's La Scala (1869–70). During her Paris years, she made appearances under the name Marie Sax until a lawsuit was brought against her by Adolphe Sax; thereafter she reverted to her real name, also using the name Sasse. She was married to **Castelmary** (1864–67). After retiring from the stage in 1877, she taught voice. Sass died in abject poverty.

Sass, Sylvia, Hungarian soprano; b. Budapest, July 21, 1951. She was a student of Olga Revghegyi at the Budapest Academy of Music; later in her career she received some lessons from Callas. In 1971 she made her operatic debut as Frasquita at the Hungarian State Opera in Budapest, where she subsequently sang many major roles. In 1972 she appeared as Violetta at the Bulgarian State Opera in Sofia. She made her first appearance at the Hamburg State Opera as Fiodiligi in 1975, the same year she made her debut at Glasgow's Scottish Opera as Desdemona. In 1976 she sang Giselda at her debut at London's Covent Garden and appeared as Violetta in Aix-en-Provence. On March 12, 1977, she made her Metropolitan Opera debut in New York as Tosca. In 1979 she appeared in recital at London's Wigmore Hall. In subsequent years, she sang in opera and concert in many major music centers. Among her other operatic roles were Donna Elvira, Countess Almaviva, Donna Anna, Lady Macbeth, Turandot, Salome, and Bartók's Judith. Her concert repertoire extended from Bach to Messiaen.

Satie, Erik (Alfred-Leslie), celebrated French composer who elevated his eccentricities and verbal virtuosity to the plane of high art; b. Honfleur, May 17, 1866; d. Paris, July 1, 1925. He received his early musical training from a local organist, Vinot, who was a pupil of Niedermeyer; at 13 he went to Paris, where his father was a music publisher, and received instruction in harmony from Taudou and in piano from Mathias; however, his attendance at the Cons. was only sporadic between 1879 and 1886. He played in various cabarets in Montmartre; in 1884 he publ. a piano piece which he numbered, with malice aforethought, op. 62. His whimsical ways and Bohemian manner of life attracted many artists and musicians; he met Debussy in 1891; he joined the Rosicrucian Society in Paris in 1892 and began to produce short piano pieces with eccentric titles intended to ridicule modernistic fancies and Classical pedantries alike. Debussy thought highly enough of him to orchestrate 2 numbers from his piano suite *Gymnopédies* (1888). Satie was almost 40 when he decided to pursue serious studies at the Paris Schola Cantorum, taking courses in counterpoint, fugue, and orchestration with d'Indy and Roussel (1905–8). In 1898 he had moved to Arcueil, a suburb of Paris; there he held court for poets, singers, dancers, and musicians, among whom he had ardent admirers. Milhaud, Sauguet, and Désormière organized a group, which they called only half-facetiously "École d'Arcueil," in honor of Satie as master and leader. But Satie's eccentricities were not merely those of a Parisian poseur; rather, they were adjuncts to his aesthetic creed, which he enunciated with boldness and total disregard for professional amenities (he was once brought to court for sending an insulting letter to a music critic). Interestingly enough, he attacked modernistic aberrations just as assiduously as reactionary pedantry, publishing "manifestos" in prose and poetry. Although he was dismissed by most serious musicians as an uneducated person who tried to conceal his ignorance of music with persiflage, he exercised a profound influence on the young French composers of the first quarter of the 20th century; moreover, his stature as an innovator in the modern idiom grew after his death, so that the avant-garde musicians of the later day accepted him as inspiration for their own experiments; thus "space music" could be traced back to Satie's *musique d'ameublement*, in which players were stationed at different parts of a hall playing different pieces in different tempi. The instruction in his piano piece *Vexations*, to play it 840 times in succession, was carried out literally in New York on Sept. 9, 1963, by a group of 5 pianists working in relays overnight, thus setting a world's record for duration of any musical composition. When critics accused Satie of having no idea of form, he publ. *Trois Morceaux en forme de poire*, the eponymous pear being reproduced in color on the cover; other pieces bore self-contradictory titles, such as *Heures séculaires et instantanées* and *Crépuscule matinal de midi*; other titles were *Pièces froides, Embryons desséchés, Prélude en tapisserie, Préludes flasques (pour un chien), Descriptions automatiques*, etc. In his ballets, he introduced jazz for the first time in Paris; at the performance of his ballet *Relâche* (Nov. 29, 1924), the curtain bore the legend "Erik Satie is the greatest musician in the world; whoever disagrees with this notion will please leave the hall." He publ. a facetious autobiographical notice as *Mémoires d'un amnésique* (1912); N. Wilkins tr. and ed. *The Writings of Erik Satie* (London, 1980).

WORKS: DRAMATIC: *Geneviève de Brabant*, marionette opera (1899); *Le Piège de Méduse*, lyric comedy (1913); *Parade*, ballet (Paris, May 18, 1917); *Mercure*, ballet (Paris, June 15, 1924); *Relâche*, ballet (Paris, Nov. 29, 1924). Also incidental music to *Le Fils de étoiles* (1891; prelude reorchestrated by Ravel, 1913), *Le Prince de Byzance* (1891), *Le Nazaréen* (1892), *La Porte heroïque du ciel* (1893), and *Pousse l'Amour* (1905).

BIBL.: P.-D. Templier, *E. S.* (Paris, 1932); R. Myers, *E. S.* (London, 1948); A. Rey, *E. S.* (Paris, 1974; rev. ed., 1995); G. Wehmeyer, *E. S.* (Berlin, 1974); V. Lajoinie, *E. S.* (Lausanne, 1985); A. Gillmor, *E. S.* (Boston, 1988); R. Orledge, *S. the Composer* (Cambridge, 1990); N. Perloff, *Art and the Everyday: Popular Entertainment and the Circle of E. S.* (Oxford, 1991); O. Volta, *S. et la danse* (Paris, 1992); G. Wehmeyer, *E. S.: Bilder und Dokumente* (Munich, 1992); R. Orledge, *S. Remembered* (Portland, Oreg., 1995).

Satoh, Sômei, Japanese composer; b. Sendai, Jan. 19, 1947. Born into a musical family, he was self-educated in composition. In the late 1960s he began experimenting in music, producing multimedia scores. In 1983–84 he lived in New York on a Rockefeller Foundation scholarship. His music, ethereally static and subtly metered in the non-Western tradition, seeks to reproduce the inner voices of elements and beings. His works include *Stabat Mater*, operatic oratorio for Soprano and Chorus (1987).

Satter, Gustav, Austrian pianist and composer; b. Rann, Slovenia, Feb. 12, 1832; place and date of death unknown. He studied in Vienna and Paris. He undertook a pianistic tour in the United States and Brazil (1854–60) with surprising success; went back to Paris, where Berlioz warmly praised his music. He then lived in Vienna, Dresden, Hannover, and Stockholm. Among his works was the opera *Olanthe*.

BIBL.: Anonymous (most likely Satter), *The Life and Works of G. S.* (Macon, Ga., 1879).

Satz, Ilya, Russian composer; b. Chernobyl, Kiev Oblast, April 30, 1875; d. Moscow, Dec. 24, 1912. He studied cello in Kiev, then took lessons in composition with Taneyev in Moscow. He traveled in Europe in 1900, then made a tour as a cellist through

Siberia. He returned to Moscow in 1903; in 1905 he became music director of the Studio of the Moscow Art Theater, and wrote incidental music for new plays, including Maeterlinck's *Blue Bird* and Andreyev's *A Man's Life*; he also composed ballet music for Salome's dance; the ballet *The Goat-Footed (The Dance of the Satyrs)* was reorchestrated and prepared for performance by Glière. Satz had a talent for the grotesque; a lack of technique prevented his development into a major composer. A memorial vol., *Ilya Satz*, with articles by Glière and several members of the Moscow Art Theater, was publ. in Moscow in 1923.

Sauguet, Henri (real name, **Jean Pierre Poupard**), French composer; b. Bordeaux, May 18, 1901; d. Paris, June 22, 1989. He assumed his mother's maiden name as his own. He was a pupil of Vaubourgois in Bordeaux and of Canteloube in Montauban. In 1922 he went to Paris, where he studied with Koechlin; he became associated with Satie, and formed a group designated as the École d'Arcueil (from the locality near Paris where Satie lived). In conformity with the principles of utilitarian music, he wrote sophisticated works in an outwardly simple manner; his first conspicuous success was the production of his ballet *La Chatte* by Diaghilev in 1927. He was elected a member of the Académie des Beaux Arts in 1976. He was the author of *La Musique, ma vie* (Paris, 1990).

WORKS: DRAMATIC: OPERAS: *Le Plumet du colonel* (Paris, April 24, 1924); *La Chartreuse de Parme* (1927–36; Paris, March 16, 1939; rev. 1968); *La Contrebasse* (1930; Paris, 1932); *La Gageure imprévue* (1942; Paris, July 4, 1944); *Les Caprices de Marianne* (Aix-en-Provence, July 20, 1954); *Le Pain des autres* (1967–74); *Boule de suif* (Lyons, 1978); *Tistou les pouces verts* (Paris, 1980). BALLETS: *La Chatte* (Monte Carlo, April 30, 1927); *Paul et Virginie* (Paris, April 15, 1943); *Les Mirages* (Paris, Dec. 15, 1947); *Cordelia* (Paris, May 7, 1952); *L'As de coeur* (1960); *Paris* (1964); *L'Imposteur ou Le Prince et le mendiant* (1965).

BIBL.: M. Schneider, *H. S.* (Paris, 1959); F.-Y. Bril, *H. S.* (Paris, 1967); D. Austin, *H. S.: A Bio-Bibliography* (N.Y., 1991).

Saunders, Arlene, American soprano and teacher; b. Cleveland, Oct. 5, 1935. She studied at Baldwin-Wallace College and in New York. She made her operatic debut as Rosalinde with the National Opera Co. in 1958; she won the Vercelli Vocal Competition and made her European debut as Mimi at Milan's Teatro Nuovo in 1961; that same year, she appeared as Giorgetta in *Il Tabarro* at the N.Y. City Opera. In 1964 she joined the Hamburg State Opera, where she subsequently sang regularly and was made a Kammersängerin in 1967; she also appeared as Pamina at the Glyndebourne Festival (1966), as Louise at the San Francisco Opera (1967), as the creator of the title role in Ginastera's *Beatrice Cenci* at the Opera Soc. in Washington, D.C. (Sept. 10, 1971), as Eva in her Metropolitan Opera debut in New York (April 2, 1976), and as Minnie at London's Covent Garden (1980); in 1985 she made her farewell appearance in opera as the Marschallin at the Teatro Colón in Buenos Aires. She taught at Rutgers, the State Univ. of New Jersey (from 1987), and at the Abraham Goodman School in New York (from 1987). Among her other roles were Sieglinde, Nedda, Desdemona, Tosca, and Santuzza.

Savage, Henry W(ilson), American impresario; b. New Durham, N.H., March 21, 1859; d. Boston, Nov. 29, 1927. He started in business as a real estate operator in Boston, where he took control of the Castle Square Opera House by default in 1894; he founded his own company there to present opera in English in 1895, and subsequently gave performances in Chicago, New York, and other cities; with Maurice Grau, he produced opera in English at the Metropolitan Opera in New York (1900). His Henry Savage Grand Opera Co. toured throughout the United States with an English-language production of Parsifal in 1904–05; he subsequently made successful tours with Puccini's *Madama Butterfly* (1906) and *La fanciulla del West* (1911), and Lehár's *Die lustige Witwe* (1907).

Saville, Frances, American soprano; b. San Francisco, Jan. 6, 1863; d. Burlingame, Calif., Nov. 8, 1935. She went early to Australia, where she made her debut in oratorio; continued her studies in Paris with Marchesi. In 1892 she made her operatic debut in Brussels; she also appeared with the Carl Rosa Co. in England, at the Opéra Comique in Paris, and in Vienna, Berlin, St. Petersburg, Warsaw, etc. On Nov. 18, 1895, she made her debut as Juliette at the Metropolitan Opera in New York, on whose roster she remained through that season and again in 1899–1900; she also sang with the Vienna Court Opera (1899–1903).

Savine, Alexander, Serbian-American conductor, teacher, and composer; b. Belgrade, April 26, 1881; d. Chicago, Jan. 19, 1949. He studied in Belgrade with S. Mokranjac, and later studied voice at the Vienna Cons. with Pauline Lucca. He was an opera conductor in Berlin (1905–07), taught voice at the Musical Academy in Winnipeg, Canada (1908–12), settled in the United States, and was director of the opera dept. at the Inst. of Musical Art in New York (1922–24); in 1929 he moved to Chicago. In 1914 he married **Lillian Blauvelt**. He wrote the opera *Xenia* (Zürich, May 29, 1919).

Sawallisch, Wolfgang, eminent German conductor; b. Munich, Aug. 26, 1923. He began piano study when he was 5; he later pursued private musical training with Ruoff, Haas, and Sachse in Munich before entering military service during World War II (1942), then completed his musical studies at the Munich Hochschule für Musik. In 1947 he became répétiteur at the Augsburg Opera, making his conducting debut there in 1950; then was Generalmusikdirektor of the opera houses in Aachen (1953–58), Wiesbaden (1958–60), and Cologne (1960–63); he also conducted at the Bayreuth Festivals (1957–61). From 1960 to 1970 he was chief conductor of the Vienna Sym. Orch.; he made his first appearance in the United States with that ensemble in 1964; he also was Generalmusikdirektor of the Hamburg State Phil. (1961–73). From 1970 to 1980 he was chief conductor of the Orchestre de la Suisse Romande in Geneva; from 1971 he also served as Generalmusikdirektor of the Bavarian State Opera in Munich, where he was named Staatsoperndirektor in 1982. In 1990 he was named music director of the Philadelphia Orch, which position he assumed in 1993. That same year, he took it on an acclaimed tour of China. He appeared as a guest conductor with a number of the world's major orchs. and opera houses. A distinguished representative of the revered Austro-German tradition, he has earned great respect for his unostentatious performances; he has also made appearances as a sensitive piano accompanist to leading singers of the day. His autobiography appeared as *Im Interesse der Deutlichkeit: Mein Leben mit der Musik* (Hamburg, 1988). He also publ. *Kontrapunkt—Herausforderung Musik* (Hamburg, 1993).

BIBL.: H. Krellmann, ed., *Stationen eines Dirigenten, W. S.* (Munich, 1983).

Saxton, Robert (Louis Alfred), English composer and teacher; b. London, Oct. 8, 1953. He was a student of Elisabeth Lutyens (1970–74), of Robin Holloway at St. Catherine's College, Cambridge (1972–75; B.A.), of Robert Sherlaw Johnson at Worcester College, Oxford (1975–76; B.Mus.), and of Luciano Berio (1976–77). In 1979 he became a teacher at the Guildhall School of Music in London, where he headed its composition dept. from 1990. His music reveals fine craftsmanship and harmonic invention. Among his works is the opera *Caritas* (1990–91; Huddersfield, Nov. 1991).

Sayão, Bidú (Balduina de Oliveira), noted Brazilian soprano; b. Niteroi, near Rio de Janeiro, May 11, 1902; d. Rockport, Maine, March 12, 1999. She studied with Elena Teodorini in Rio de Janeiro, and then with Jean de Reszke in Vichy and Nice. Returning to Brazil, she gave her first professional concert in Rio de Janeiro in 1925; in 1926 she sang the role of Rosina in *Il Barbiere di Siviglia* at the Teatro Municipal there. She made her American debut on Dec. 29, 1935, in a recital in New York. On Feb. 13, 1937, she sang Manon at her Metropolitan Opera debut in New York, earning enthusiastic reviews; she remained on its roster until 1952. She retired in 1958. Her finest performances were in lyric roles in bel canto operas; especially memorable were her interpretations of Violetta, Gilda, and Mimi. She also showed her versatility in coloratura parts, such as Lakme; in France, she was described as "a Brazilian nightingale." She also sang vocal parts in several works of her great compatriot Villa-Lobos. She was a recipient of numerous honors from European royalty, and of the Palmes Academiques from the French government; in 1972 she was decorated a Commandante by the Brazilian government.

Saygun, Ahmed Adnan, Turkish teacher and composer; b. Izmir, Sept. 7, 1907; d. Istanbul, Jan. 6, 1991. He studied composition in Paris with Borrel at the Cons. and with Le Flem and d'Indy at the Schola Cantorum; returning to Turkey in 1931, he taught at the Istanbul Cons. (1936–39); he accompanied Bartók on a music-ethnological trip through Anatolia (1936). From 1964 he taught composition at the State Cons. in Ankara and from 1972 at the Istanbul State Cons. He wrote operas, including *Tasbebek* (Ankara, Dec. 27, 1934) and *Kerem* (1947; Ankara, March 1, 1953); also the oratorio *Yunus Emre* (Ankara, May 25, 1946).

Saylor, Bruce (Stuart), American composer and teacher; b. Philadelphia, April 24, 1946. He studied composition with Weisgall and Sessions at the Juilliard School of Music in New York (B.Mus., 1968; M.S., 1969). In 1969–70 he held a Fulbright grant and pursued his training with Petrassi at the Accademia di Santa Cecilia in Rome. In 1970 he entered the Graduate School of the City Univ. of N.Y. and studied composition with Perle and theory with Salzer, taking his Ph.D. in 1978. He taught at Queens College of the City Univ. of N.Y. (1970–76) and at N.Y. Univ. (1976–79). In 1979 he returned to Queens College, where he became a prof. at the Aaron Copland School of Music. He also served on the faculty of the Graduate School of the City Univ. of N.Y. from 1983. From 1992 to 1994 he was composer-in-residence of the Lyric Opera of Chicago, which gave the premiere of his opera *Orpheus Descending* on June 10, 1994. He received grants from the NEA (1976, 1978), the Ives scholarship (1976) and an award (1983) from the American Academy and Inst. of Arts and Letters, a Guggenheim fellowship (1982–83), and the Ingram Merrill Foundation Award (1991). He is married to the mezzo-soprano Constance Beavon, who has performed many of his vocal works.

WORKS: DRAMATIC: *My Kinsman, Major Molineux*, opera (Pittsburgh, Aug. 28, 1976); *Cycle*, dance piece (Chilmark, Mass., July 27, 1978; rev. version, Chilmark, Mass., July 24, 1980); *Inner World Out*, dance piece (Chilmark, Mass., Aug. 30, 1978); *Wildfire*, dance piece (Chilmark, Mass., Aug. 29, 1979; rev. version as *Wildfire II*, N.Y., April 2, 1985); *The Waves*, 3 dramatic monologues for Mezzo-soprano and 5 Instruments (Chilmark, Mass., Aug. 27, 1981; rev. version, Paris, Nov. 18, 1985); *Spill*, dance piece (N.Y., May 10, 1984); *Voices from Sandover*, incidental music (N.Y., May 23, 1989); *Orpheus Descending*, opera (Chicago, June 10, 1994).

Sbriglia, Giovanni, Italian tenor and singing teacher; b. Naples, June 23, 1829; d. Paris, Feb. 20, 1916. He made his debut at the Teatro San Carlo in Naples in 1853 and was heard in Italy by Maretzek, the impresario, who engaged him for a season at the Academy of Music in New York, where Sbriglia appeared with Adelina Patti (1860). He then made a grand tour of the United States with Parodi and Adelaide Phillipps, and also sang in Mexico and Havana. He returned to Europe in 1875 and settled in Paris, where he became a highly successful vocal teacher. Jean, Joséphine, and Edouard de Reszke studied with him when they were already professional artists; he trained the baritone voice of Jean de Reszke, enabling him to sing tenor roles. Pol Plançon, Nordica, and Sibyl Sanderson were among his pupils.

Scacciati, Bianca, Italian soprano; b. Florence, July 3, 1894; d. Brescia, Oct. 15, 1948. She studied in Milan. She made her operatic debut there as Marguerite in *Faust* in 1917. She rapidly asserted herself as one of the most impressive dramatic sopranos in Italy; she sang for many seasons at La Scala in Milan and also made successful appearances at Covent Garden in London, at the Paris Opéra, and at the Teatro Colón in Buenos Aires. She was particularly noted for her interpretation of the title role in Puccini's *Turandot*.

Scalchi, Sofia, celebrated Italian mezzo-soprano; b. Turin, Nov. 29, 1850; d. Rome, Aug. 22, 1922. She studied with Boccabadati, making her debut at Mantua in 1866 as Ulrica in Verdi's *Un ballo in maschera*. She then sang throughout Italy. She appeared in concert in London (Sept. 16, 1868) and at Covent Garden (Nov. 5, 1868) as Azucena, obtaining enormous success; she continued to appear there regularly until 1889, and also sang in St. Petersburg (1872–81; 1889–90). On Dec. 20, 1882, she made her U.S. debut as Arsaces in *Semiramide* at N.Y.'s Academy of Music; she then was engaged for the first performance at the Metropolitan Opera, where she sang Siebel in *Faust* on Oct. 22, 1883; she was again on its roster in 1891–92 and from 1893 to 1896, and then retired from the operatic stage. Her voice had a range of 2 1/2 octaves; it was essentially a contralto voice, but with so powerful a high register that she successfully performed soprano parts. Among her other roles were Fidès, Ortrud, Amneris, Emilia, and Mistress Quickly.

Scalzi, Carlo, Italian castrato soprano who flourished from 1719 to 1738. He sang in Venice (1719–21; 1724–25), Reggio and Modena (1720), Genoa (1722–23; 1733), Parma (1725), Naples (1726–27; 1730), where he created Hasse's *Ezio*, and Rome (1728–29; 1731–32). Handel then called him to London, where he made his first appearance in the pasticcio *Semiramide riconosciuta* (Oct. 30, 1733). Handel composed the role of Alceste in *Arianna in Creta* (Jan. 26, 1734) for him, and he also appeared in other works by that composer until the end of 1734. In 1737–38 he again sang in Venice.

Scarabelli, Diamante Maria, Italian soprano who flourished from 1695 to 1718. She was born in Bologna, where she first gained distinction (1696–97; 1699; 1700; 1708–09; 1718). She also made many appearances in Venice (1695; 1703; 1707–12; 1714–16), and sang in Milan (1699), Pavia and Genoa (1705), Ferrara (1715), and Padua (1718). She was in the service of the duke of Mantua (1697–1708), Cardinal Grimani, viceroy of Naples (1709), and the duke of Modena (1715). Scarabelli was greatly esteemed for her roles in operas by Caldara, Handel, Lotti, Orlandini, and C. F. Pollarolo.

Scaria, Emil, outstanding Austrian bass; b. Graz, Sept. 18, 1838; d. Blasewitz, near Dresden, July 22, 1886. He studied with Netzer in Graz and Lewy in Vienna, making his debut as St. Bris in *Les Huguenots* in Pest (1860); following additional training with García in London, he sang in Dessau (1862–63), Leipzig (1863–65), and Dresden (from 1865), where he won notable distinction by singing both bass and baritone roles. After appearing as a guest artist at the Vienna Court Opera (1872–73), he sang there regularly as one of its leading artists until his death. He also sang with Angelo Neumann's company; while appearing in *Die Walküre* with the company in London in May 1882, he suffered a mental breakdown; however, he appeared in public 2 days later in *Siegfried*, and then sang Gurnemanz in the first mounting of *Parsifal* at the Bayreuth Festival on July 26, 1882. He continued to make tours with Neumann's company, returned to Bayreuth in 1883, and made a concert tour of the United States in 1884. In early 1886 he suffered a relapse and shortly thereafter died insane. He was hailed as one of the greatest Wagnerians of his time.

Scarlatti, (Pietro) Alessandro (Gaspare), important Italian composer, father of **(Giuseppe) Domenico Scarlatti**; b. Palermo, May 2, 1660; d. Naples, Oct. 22, 1725. Nothing is known concerning his musical training. When he was 12, he went with his 2 sisters to Rome, where he found patrons who enabled him to pursue a career in music. His first known opera, *Gli equivoci nel sembiante*, was performed there in 1679. By 1680 he was maestro di cappella to Queen Christina of Sweden, whose palace in Rome served as an important center for the arts. He also found patrons in 2 cardinals, Benedetto Pamphili and Pietro Ottoboni, and served as maestro di cappella at S. Gerolamo della Carità. From 1684 to 1702 he was maestro di cappella to the viceroy at

Naples. During these years he composed prolifically, bringing out numerous operas and oratorios. In addition, he served as director of the Teatro San Bartolomeo, where he conducted many of his works. His fame as a composer for the theater soon spread, and many of his works were performed in the leading music centers of Italy; one of his most popular operas, *Il Pirro e Demetrio* (Naples, Jan. 28, 1694), was even performed in London. His only confirmed teaching position dates from this period, when he served for 2 months in the spring of 1689 as a faculty member of the Cons. di Santa Maria di Loreto. Tiring of his exhaustive labors, he was granted a leave of absence and set out for Florence in June 1702; Prince Ferdinando de' Medici had been one of his patrons for some years in Florence, and Scarlatti hoped he could find permanent employment there. When this did not materialize, he settled in Rome and became assistant maestro di cappella at S. Maria Maggiore in 1703; he was promoted to maestro di cappella in 1707. One of his finest operas, *Il Mitridate Eupatore*, was performed in Venice in 1707. Since the Roman theaters had been closed from 1700, he devoted much of his time to composing serenatas, cantatas, and oratorios. In late 1708 he was again appointed maestro di cappella to the viceroy at Naples. His most celebrated opera from these years, *Il Tigrane*, was given in Naples on Feb. 16, 1715. His only full-fledged comic opera, *Il trionfo dell'onore*, was performed in Naples on Nov. 26, 1718. Scarlatti's interest in purely instrumental music dates from this period, and he composed a number of conservative orch. and chamber music pieces. Having again obtained a leave of absence from his duties, he went to Rome to oversee the premiere of his opera *Telemaco* (1718). His last known opera, *La Griselda*, was given there in Jan. 1721. From 1722 until his death he lived in retirement in Naples, producing only a handful of works. Scarlatti was the foremost Neapolitan composer of the late Baroque era in Italy.

WORKS: DRAMATIC: OPERAS (all are drammas and were 1st perf. in Naples unless otherwise given): *Gli equivoci nel sembiante* (1st perf. publicly, Rome, Feb. 5, 1679; later perf. as *L'errore innocente*, Bologna, 1679, and as *L'amor non vuole inganni*, Linz, Carnival 1681); *L'honestà negli amori* (Rome, Feb. 6, 1680); *Tutto il mal non vien per nuocere*, commedia (Rome, 1681; later perf. as *Dal male il bene*, Naples, 1687); *Il Pompeo* (Rome, Jan. 25, 1683); *La Guerriera costante* (Rome, Carnival 1683); *L'Aldimiro o vero Favor per favore* (Nov. 6, 1683); *La Psiche o vero Amore innamorato* (Dec. 21, 1683); *Olimpia vendicata* (Dec. 23, 1685); *La Rosmene o vero L'infedeltà fedele*, melodramma (Rome, Carnival 1686); *Clearco in Negroponte* (Dec. 21, 1686); *La Santa Dinna*, commedia (Rome, Carnival 1687; only Act 3 by Scarlatti); *Il Flavio* (Nov. 14?, 1688); *L'Anacreonte tiranno*, melodramma (Feb. 9, 1689); *L'Amazzone corsara [guerriera] o vero L'Alvilda* (Nov. 6, 1689); *La Statira* (Rome, Jan. 5, 1690); *Gli equivoci in amore o vero La Rosaura*, melodramma (Rome, Dec. 1690); *L'humanità nelle fiere o vero Il Lucullo* (Feb. 25, 1691); *La Teodora Augusta* (Nov. 6, 1692); *Gerone tiranno di Siracusa* (Dec. 22, 1692); *L'Amante doppio o vero Il Ceccobimbi*, melodramma (April 1693); *Il Pirro e Demetrio* (Jan. 28, 1694; later perf. as *La forza della fedeltà*, Florence, 1712); *Il Bassiano o vero Il maggior impossibile*, melodramma (1694); *La santa Genuinda, o vero L'innocenza difesa dall'inganno*, dramma sacro (Rome, 1694; only Act 2 by Scarlatti); *Le nozze con l'inimico o vero L'Analinda*, melodramma (1695; later perf. as *L'Analinda overo Le nozze col nemico*, Florence, Carnival 1702); *Nerone fatto Cesare*, melodramma (Nov. 6, 1695); *Massimo Puppieno*, melodramma (Dec. 26, 1695); *Penelope la casta* (Feb. 23?, 1696); *La Didone delirante*, opera drammatica (May 28, 1696); *Comodo Antonino* (Nov. 18, 1696); *L'Emireno o vero Il consiglio dell'ombra*, opera drammatica (Feb. 2, 1697); *La caduta de' Decemviri* (Dec. 15, 1697); *La Donna ancora è fedele* (1698); *Il Prigioniero fortunato* (Dec. 14, 1698); *Gl'inganni felici* (Nov. 6, 1699; later perf. as *L'Agarista ouvero Gl'inganni felici*, with the intermezzo *Brenno e Tisbe*, Florence, Carnival 1706); *L'Eraclea* (Jan. 30, 1700); *Odoardo*, with the intermezzo *Adolfo e Lesbina* (May 5, 1700); *Dafni*, favola boschereccia (Aug. 5, 1700; later perf. as *L'amore non viene dal caso*, Jesi, Carnival 1715); *Laodicea e Berenice* (April 1701); *Il pastor[e] di Corinto*, favola boschereccia (Aug. 5, 1701); *Tito Sempronio Gracco*, with the intermezzo *Bireno e Dorilla* (Carnival? 1702); *Tiberio imperatore d'Oriente* (May 8, 1702); *Il Flavio Cuniberto* (Pratolino, Sept.? 1702); *Arminio* (Pratolino, Sept. 1703); *Turno Aricino* (Pratolino, Sept. 1704); *Lucio Manlio l'imperioso* (Pratolino, Sept. 1705); *Il gran Tamerlano* (Pratolino, Sept. 1706); *Il Mitridate Eupatore*, tragedia (Venice, Carnival 1707); *Il trionfo della libertà*, tragedia (Venice, Carnival 1707); *Il Teodosio* (Jan. 27, 1709); *L'amor volubile e tiranno* (May 25, 1709; later perf. as *La Dorisbe o L'amor volubile e tiranno*, Rome, Carnival 1711, and as *La Dorisbe*, Genoa, 1713); *La Principessa fedele* (Feb. 8, 1710); *La fede riconosciuta*, dramma pastorale (Oct. 14, 1710); *Giunio Bruto o vero La caduta dei Tarquini* (1711; not perf.; only Act 3 by Scarlatti); *Il Ciro* (Rome, Carnival 1712); *Scipione nelle Spagne*, with the intermezzo *Pericca e Varrone* (Jan. 21, 1714); *L'amor generoso*, with the intermezzo *Despina e Niso* (Oct. 1, 1714); *Il Tigrane o vero L'egual impegno d'amore e di fede* (Feb. 16, 1715); *Carlo re d'Allemagna* (Jan. 30, 1716); *La virtù trionfante dell'odio e dell'amore* (May 3, 1716); *Telemaco* (Rome, Carnival 1718); *Il trionfo dell'onore*, commedia (Nov. 26, 1718); *Il Cambise* (Feb. 4, 1719); *Marco Attilio Regolo*, with the intermezzo *Leonzio e Eurilla* (Rome, Carnival 1719); *La Griselda* (Rome, Jan. 1721). Several operas attributed to him are now considered doubtful. A complete edition of his operas began to appear in the Harvard Publications in Music series in 1974. SERENATAS: *Diana ed Endimione* (c.1680–85); *Serenata in honor of James II of England* (Rome, 1688); *Il genio di Partenope, la gloria del Sebeto, il piacere di Mergellina* (Naples, Jan. 1696); *Venere, Adone e Amore* (Naples, July 15, 1696); *Il trionfo delle stagioni* (Naples, July 26, 1696); *Venere ed Amore* (c.1695–1700); *Clori, Lidia e Filli* (c.1700); *Clori, Dorino e Amore* (Naples, May 2, 1702); *Venere e Adone: Il giardino d'amore* (c.1702–5); *Endimione e Cintia* (Rome, 1705); *Amore e Virtù ossia Il trionfo della virtù* (Rome, 1706); *Clori e Zeffiro* (Rome, 1706?); *Fileno, Niso e Doralbo: Serenata a Filli* (Rome, 1706?); *Sole, Urania e Clio: Le Muse Urania e Clio lodano le bellezze di Filli* (Rome, 1706?); *Venere, Amore e Ragione: Il ballo delle ninfe: Venere, havendo perso Amore, lo ritrova fra le ninfe e i pastori dei Sette Colli* (Rome, 1706); *Cupido e Onestà: Il trionfo dell'Onestà* (Rome, Sept. 1709); *Le glorie della Bellezza del Corpo e dell'Anima* (Naples, Aug. 28, 1709); *Pace, Amore e Provvidenza* (Naples, Nov. 4, 1711); *Il genio austriaco* (Naples, June 21, 1712); *Il genio austriaco: Zefiro, Flora, il Sole, Partenope e il Sebeto* (Naples, Aug. 28, 1713); *Serenata in honor of the Vicereine, Donna Barbara d'Erbenstein* (Naples, Dec. 4, 1715); *La gloria di Primavera: Primavera, Estate, Autunno, Inverno e Giove* (Vienna, April 1716?); *Partenope, Teti, Nettuno, Proteo e Glauco* (Naples, 1716); *Filli, Clori e Tirsi* (Naples, 1718?); *La virtù negli amori: La Notte, il Sole, Lanso, Lisa, Toante e Agave* (Rome, Nov. 16, 1721); *Erminia, Tancredi, Polidoro e Pastore* (Naples, June 13, 1723); *Diana, Amore, Venere* (undated). ORATORIOS: An edition of his oratorios commenced publication in Rome in 1964.

BIBL.: E. Dent, *A. S.: His Life and Works* (London, 1905; 2d ed., rev., 1960, by F. Walker); C. van den Borren, *A. S. et l'esthétique de l'opéra napolitain* (Brussels and Paris, 1921); A. Lorenz, *A. S.s Jugendoper* (Augsburg, 1927); O. Tilby, *La Famiglia S.: Nuove ricerche e documenti* (Rome, 1947); M. Fabbri, *A. S. e il Principe Ferdinando de' Medici* (Florence, 1961); C. Morey, *The Late Operas of A. S.* (diss., Indiana Univ., 1965); D. Poultney, *The Oratorios of A. S.: Their Lineage, Milieu, and Style* (diss., Univ. of Michigan, 1968); R. Pagano, L. Bianchi, and G. Rostirolla, *A. S.* (Turin, 1972); D. Grout, *A. S.: An Introduction to His Operas* (Berkeley, 1979); W. Holmes, *La Statira by Pietro Ottoboni and A. S.: The Textual Sources, with a Documentary Postscript* (N.Y., 1983); F. D'Accone, *The History of a Baroque Opera: A. S.'s "Gli equivoci nel sembiante"* (N.Y., 1985); R. Pagano, *S.: A. e Domenico: Due vite in una* (Milan, 1985); U. Schachet-Pape, *Das Messenschaffen von A. S.* (Frankfurt am Main and N.Y., 1993); C. Vidali, *A. and D. S.: A Guide to Research* (N.Y., 1993).

Scarlatti, (Giuseppe) Domenico, famous Italian composer, harpsichordist, and teacher, son of **(Pietro) Alessandro (Gaspare) Scarlatti**; b. Naples, Oct. 26, 1685; d. Madrid, July 23, 1757.

Nothing is known about his musical training. On Sept. 13, 1701, he was appointed organist and composer at the Royal Chapel in Naples, where his father was maestro di cappella. The 2 were granted a leave of absence in June 1702, and they went to Florence; later that year Domenico returned to Naples without his father, and resumed his duties. His first opera, *Ottavia ristituita al trono*, was performed in Naples in 1703. He was sent to Venice by his father in 1705, but nothing is known of his activities there. In 1708 he went to Rome, where he entered the service of Queen Maria Casimira of Poland; he remained in her service until 1714, and composed a number of operas and several other works for her private palace theater. He became assistant to Bai, the maestro di cappella at the Vatican, in 1713; upon Bai's death the next year, he was appointed his successor; he also became maestro di cappella to the Portuguese ambassador to the Holy See in 1714. During his years in Rome, he met such eminent musicians as Corelli and Handel. Mainwaring relates the unconfirmed story that Scarlatti and Handel engaged in a friendly contest, Scarlatti being judged the superior on the harpsichord and Handel on the organ. He resigned his positions in 1719; by 1724 he was in Lisbon, where he took up the post of mestre at the patriarchal chapel. His duties included teaching the infanta Maria Barbara, daughter of King John V, and the king's younger brother, Don Antonio. In 1728 Maria Barbara married the Spanish crown prince Fernando, and moved to Madrid. Scarlatti accompanied her, remaining in Madrid for the rest of his life. In 1724 he visited Rome, where he met Quantz; in 1725 he saw his father for the last time in Naples; in 1728 he was in Rome, where he married his first wife, Maria Caterina Gentili. In 1738 he was made a Knight of the Order of Santiago. When Maria Barbara became queen in 1746, he was appointed her maestro de cámera. His last years were spent quietly in Madrid; from 1752 until 1756, Antonio Soler studied with him. So closely did he become associated with Spain that his name eventually appeared as Domingo Escarlatti.

Scarlatti composed over 500 single-movement sonatas for solo keyboard. Although these works were long believed to have been written for the harpsichord, the fact that Maria Barbara used pianos in her residences suggests that some of these works were written for that instrument as well; at least 3 were written for the organ. His sonatas reveal his gifts as one of the foremost composers in the "free style" (a homophonic style with graceful ornamentation, in contrast to the former contrapuntal style). He also obtained striking effects by the frequent crossing of hands, tones repeated by rapidly changing fingers, etc. His other works included operas and oratorios.

WORKS: OPERAS: *Ottavia ristituita al trono*, melodramma (Naples, Carnival 1703); *Giustino*, dramma per musica (Naples, Dec. 19, 1703; in collaboration with Legrenzi); *Irene*, dramma per musica (Naples, Carnival 1704; a complete revision of the opera by Pollarolo); *Silvia*, dramma pastorale (Rome, Jan. 27, 1710); *Tolomeo e Alessandro, ovvero La corona disprezzata*, dramma per musica (Rome, Jan. 19, 1711); *Orlando, ovvero La gelosa pazzia*, dramma (Rome, Carnival 1711); *Tetide in Sciro*, dramma per musica (Rome, Jan. 10, 1712); *Ifigenia in Aulide*, dramma per musica (Rome, Jan. 11, 1713); *Ifigenia in Tauri*, dramma per musica (Rome, Feb. 15, 1713); *Amor d'un ombra e gelosia d'un'aura*, dramma per musica (Rome, Jan. 20, 1714; rev. version as *Narciso*, London, May 30, 1720); *Ambleto*, dramma per musica (Rome, Carnival 1715); *La Dirindina*, farsetta per musica (1715; intermezzo for the preceding work; not perf.); *Intermedi pastorali*, intermezzo in Ambleto (Rome, Carnival 1715); *Berenice, regina d'Egitto, ovvero Le gare d'amore e di politica*, dramma per musica (Rome, Carnival 1718; in collaboration with Porpora).

BIBL.: A. Longo, *D. S. e la sua figura nella storia della musica* (Naples, 1913); S. Sitwell, *A Background for D. S.* (London, 1935); C. Valabrega, *Il Clavicembalista D. S., il suo secolo, la sua opera* (Modena, 1937; 2d ed., rev., 1955); S. Luciani, *D. S.* (Turin, 1939); R. Kirkpatrick, *D. S.* (Princeton and London, 1953; 3d ed., rev., 1968); A. Basso, *La formazione storica ed estetica della storia di D. S.* (diss., Univ. of Turin, 1957); B. Ife, *D. S.* (Sevenoaks, England, 1985); R. Pagano, *S.: Alessandro e D.: Due vite in una* (Milan, 1985); P. Williams, ed., *Bach, Handel, and S.: Tercentenary Essays* (Cambridge, 1985); M. Boyd, *D. S.: Master of Music* (London, 1986); C. Vidali, *A. and D. S.: A Guide to Research* (N.Y., 1993).

Scarlatti, Giuseppe, Italian composer, grandson of **(Pietro) Alessandro (Gaspare)** and nephew of **(Giuseppe) Domenico Scarlatti**; b. Naples, c.1718; d. Vienna, Aug. 17, 1777. He was in Rome in 1739, and later in Lucca, where he married Barbara Stabili, a singer (1747); he went to Vienna in 1757. He wrote 31 operas, produced in Rome, Florence, Lucca, Turin, Venice, Naples, Milan, and Vienna; of these the most successful was *L'isola disabitata* (Venice, Nov. 20, 1757). Another Giuseppe Scarlatti (a nephew of Alessandro Scarlatti), whose name appears in some reference works, was not a musician.

Scarmolin, (Anthony) Louis, Italian-American composer; b. Schio, July 30, 1890; d. Union City, N.J., July 13, 1969. He went to the United States as a boy; he graduated from the N.Y. College of Music in 1907, served in the U.S. Army during World War I, then lived in Union City, N.J. He wrote 6 operas and several symphonic poems and overtures.

Schack, Benedikt (Emanuel), Bohemian-born Austrian tenor and composer; b. Mirotitz (baptized), Feb. 7, 1758; d. Munich, Dec. 10, 1826. He began his training with his father, a school teacher; after further studies in Staré Sedlo and Svatá Hora, he continued his training as a chorister at the Prague Cathedral (1773–75), then went to Vienna, where he received lessons in singing from Karl Frieberth, and also studied medicine and philosophy. He became Kapellmeister to Prince Heinrich von Schönaich-Carolath in Silesia in 1780; he became a member of Schikaneder's traveling theater troupe in 1786, and went with it to Vienna, where he was its principal tenor at the Freihaus-Theater auf der Wieden (from 1789). He was a close friend of Mozart, who wrote the role of Tamino for him; his wife, Elisabeth (née Weinhold) Schack, appeared as the 3d Lady in the first perf. of *Die Zauberflöte*. If contemporary accounts are to be trusted, it was Schack who sang passages from the Mozart Requiem for the dying composer. After a sojourn in Graz (1793–96), he went to Munich as a member of the Hoftheater; having lost his voice, he was pensioned about 1814. Mozart wrote piano variations (K. 613) on an aria from Schack's opera *Die verdeckten Sachen*. Among Schack's theatrical pieces, the following were performed in Vienna: *Der dumme Gärtner aus dem Gebirge* (July 12, 1789), *Die wiener Zeitung* (Jan. 12, 1791), *Die Antwort auf die Frage* (Dec. 16, 1792), and *Die beiden Nannerin* (July 26, 1794).

Schadewitz, Carl, German choral conductor, teacher, and composer; b. St. Ingbert, Jan. 23, 1887; d. Reppendorf, near Kitzingen, March 27, 1945. He studied in Würzburg, where he was active for most of his life as a choral conductor and teacher. He was a prolific composer; his works include a musical fairy tale, *Johannisnacht*, a "Romantic" oratorio, *Kreislers Heimkehr*, and an opera, *Laurenca*. Among his songs, the cycle *Die Heimat* (1934) is outstanding.

BIBL.: A. Maxsein, *C. S.* (Würzburg, 1954).

Schaefer, Theodor, Czech composer and teacher; b. Telč, Jan. 23, 1904; d. Brno, March 19, 1969. He studied with Kvapil at the Brno Cons. (1922–26) and with Novák at the Prague Cons. (1926–29). Upon graduation, he taught at the Palacký Univ. at Olomouc, the Brno Cons. (1948–59), and at the Janáček Academy of Music in Brno (1959–69). He was an advocate of a so-called diathematic principle of constructing themes using fragments of preceding thematic units. Among his works are *Maugli*, children's opera (1932), and *Legenda o štěstí* (Legend of Happiness), ballet (1952).

Schaeffer, Boguslaw (Julien), outstanding Polish composer, pianist, pedagogue, writer on music, stage manager, and playwright; b. Lwów, June 6, 1929. He studied violin in Opole, then went to Kraków, where he took courses in composition with Malawski at the State High School of Music and in musicology with Jachimecki at the Jagiello Univ. (1949–53); he later received instruction in advanced techniques from Nono (1959). In 1963 he became prof. of composition at the Kraków Cons.; he served as prof. of composition at the Salzburg Mozarteum (from 1986). In 1967 he founded the periodical *Forum Musicum*, devoted to new music; in addition to his writings on music, he was active as a playwright from 1955; he was the most widely performed playwright in Poland from 1987 to 1995, winning an award at the Wrocław Festival of Contemporary plays in 1987 and in 5 subsequent years. All of his plays were publ. in 3 vols. and were translated into 16 languages. As a composer, he received many awards, and numerous concerts of his works were presented in Poland and abroad. In 1995 he was made an honorary member of the Polish Soc. of Contemporary Music. He is married to **Mieczyslawa Janina Hanuszewska-Schaeffer**. Their son, Piotr (Mikolaj) Schaeffer (b. Kraków, Oct. 1, 1958), is a music journalist. Schaeffer's earliest compositions (*19 Mazurkas* for Piano, 1949) were inspired by the melorhythms of Polish folk songs, but he made a decisive turn in 1953 with his *Music for Strings: Nocturne*, which became the first serial work by a Polish composer; he devised a graphic and polychromatic optical notation indicating intensity of sound, proportional lengths of duration, and position of notes in melodic and contrapuntal lines, with the components arranged in binary code; he also wrote music in the "third stream" style, combining jazz with classical procedures. In 1960 he invented topophonical music in a tone-color passacaglia form in his *Topofonica* for 40 Instruments. In 1966 he created so-called idiomatic music by using various stylistic categories, including early jazz, neoclassicism, entertainment music, and indeterminate music (e.g., *Howl*). In 1967 he introduced his own rhythmic system, built on metric-tempo proportions. In 1970 he began using synthesizers and computers. Many of his chamber scores, such as *Quartet 2+2*, utilize indeterminacy. He experimented by introducing ideas of philosophers such as Heraclitus, Spinoza, Bergson, and Heidegger in his music called *Heraklitiana, Spinoziana* et al. In his music for and with actors, he uses mixed media procedures. With his *Missa elettronica* (1975), he charted a bold course in sacred music. Schaeffer is regarded as one of the foremost composers of microtonal scores. *Three Short Pieces* for Orch. (1951) and *Music* for String Quartet (1954) are notable examples of his early microtonal works in which he uses a 24-tone row with 23 different microtonal intervals. In 1979 he introduced a new kind of instrumentation in which the disposition of instruments totally changes many times, thus utilizing various changing orchs.; in his Organ Concerto the disposition of instruments changes 53 times. Each of his orch. works and concertos follows this new disposition, sometimes very specifically, as in his *Musica ipsa* (1962). In his orch. works, he utilizes precisely calculated textures. Many of his works are inspired by paintings and literature. There are great influences of his theatrical praxis on his music. He uses electronic and computer media in a free and poetic manner.

WORKS: DRAMATIC: *TIS-MW–2*, metamusical audiovisual spectacle for Actor, Mime, Ballerina, and 5 Musicians (1962–63; Kraków, April 25, 1964); *TIS GK*, stage work (1963); *Audiences I-V* for Actors (1964); *Howl*, monodrama for Narrator, 2 Actors, Ensemble of Instrumentalists, and Ensemble of Performers, after Allen Ginsberg (1966; Warsaw, March 1, 1971); *Quartet* for 4 Actors (1966; Athens, Sept. 15, 1979); *Hommage à Czyzewski* for Ensemble of Stage and Musical Performers (1972); *Vaniniana* for 2 Actors, Soprano, Piano, Cello, and Electronic Sources (1978; Lecce, Oct. 24, 1985); *Teatrino fantastico* for Actor, Violin, and Piano, with Multimedia and Tape (Brussels, Nov. 17, 1983); *Liebesblicke*, opera (1990). PLAYS (WITH ORIGINAL MUSIC): *Anton Webern* (1955); *Eskimos' Paradise* (1964; the same as his *Audience III*); *Scenario* for 3 Actors (1970); *Mroki* (Darknesses; 1979); *Zorza* (Dawn; 1981); *Grzechy starosci* (Sins of Old Age; 1985); *Kaczo* for 2 Actors and an Actress (1987); *Ranek* (Daybreak; 1988).

WRITINGS: *Maly informator muzyki XX wieku* (Little Lexicon of Music of the 20th Century; Kraków, 1958; new ed., 1987); *Nowa muzyka, problemy wspólczesnej techniki kompozytorskiej* (New Music: Problems of Contemporary Technique in Composing; Kraków, 1958; new ed., 1969); *Klasycy dodekafonii* (Classics of Dodecaphonic Music; 2 vols., Kraków, 1961, 1964); *Leksykon kompozytorów XX wieku* (Lexicon of 20th-century Composers; 2 vols., Kraków, 1963, 1965); *W kręgu nowej muzyki* (In the Sphere of New Music; Kraków, 1967); *Dźwieki i znaki* (Sounds and Signs: Introduction to Contemporary Composition; Warsaw, 1969); *Muzyka XX wieku, Twórcy i problemy* (Music of the 20th Century, Composers and Problems; Kraków, 1975); *Wstęp do kompozycji* (Introduction to Composition; in Polish and Eng.; Kraków, 1976); *Dzieje muzyki* (History of Music; Warsaw, 1983); *Dzieje kultury muzycznej* (History of Music Culture; Warsaw, 1987); *Kompozytorzy XX wieku* (Composers of the 20th Century; 2 vols., Kraków, 1988, 1990).

BIBL.: J. Hodor and B. Pociej, *B. S. and His Music* (Glasgow, 1975); L. Stawowy, *B. S.: Leben, Werk, Bedeutung* (Innsbruck, 1993).

Schaeffer, Pierre, French acoustician, composer, and novelist; b. Nancy, Aug. 14, 1910; d. Aix-en-Provence, Aug. 19, 1995. Working in a radio studio in Paris, he conceived the idea of arranging a musical montage of random sounds, including outside noises. On April 15, 1948, he formulated the theory of *musique concrète*, which was to define such random assemblages of sounds. When the magnetic tape was perfected, Schaeffer made use of it by rhythmic acceleration and deceleration, changing the pitch and dynamics and modifying the nature of the instrumental timbre. He made several collages of elements of "concrete music," among them *Concert de bruits* (1948) and (with P. Henry) *Symphonie pour un homme seul* (1950); he also created an experimental opera, *Orphée 53* (1953). He incorporated his findings and ideas in the publ. *A la recherche de la musique concrète* (Paris, 1952) and in *Traité des objects sonores* (Paris, 1966). Eventually he abandoned his acoustical experimentations and turned to literature. He publ. both fictional and quasi-scientific novels, among them *Traité des objets musicaux* (1966); *Le Gardien de volcan* (1969); *Excusez-moi si je meurs* (1981); *Prélude, Chorale et Fugue* (1983).

BIBL.: M. Pierret, *Entretiens avec P. S.* (Paris, 1969); S. Brunet, *P. S.* (Paris, 1970).

Schafer, R(aymond) Murray, Canadian composer, writer, and educator; b. Sarnia, Ontario, July 18, 1933. After obtaining his Licentiate from the Royal Schools of Music (1952), he studied with Alberto Guerrero (piano), Greta Kraus (harpsichord), Arnold Walter (musicology), and John Weinzweig (composition) at the Royal Cons. of Music of Toronto (1952–55). He pursued studies in languages, literature, and philosophy on his own, and then lived in Vienna (1956–57). After receiving some lessons from Peter Racine Fricker in England, he returned to Toronto in 1961 and served as director of the Ten Centuries Concerts. From 1963 to 1965 he was artist-in-residence at Memorial Univ., and from 1965 to 1975 taught at Simon Fraser Univ. In 1972 he founded the World Soundscape Project for the purpose of exploring the relationship between people and their acoustic world. As the self-styled "father of acoustic ecology," he campaigned against the "sonic sewers" of modern urban life caused by noise pollution. In 1974 he held a Guggenheim fellowship and in 1987 received the Glenn Gould Award. In addition to his many books on music, he also wrote literary works and was active as a visual artist. Over the years, Schafer has utilized various contemporary techniques in his compositions. His explorations into ancient and modern languages, literature, and philosophy are reflected in many of his works. In his later scores, he made use of Eastern philosophy and religion.

WRITINGS: *British Composers in Interview* (London, 1963); *The Composer in the Classroom* (Toronto, 1965); *Ear Cleaning: Notes for an Experimental Music Course* (Toronto, 1967); *The New Soundscape* (Toronto, 1969); *The Book of Noise* (Vancouver, 1970); *When Words Sing* (Scarborough, Ontario, 1970); *The Public of the Music Theatre: Louis Riel—A Case Study* (Vienna, 1972); *The Rhinoceros in the Classroom* (London, 1975); *E. T. A. Hoffmann and Music* (Toronto, 1975); *Creative Music Education* (N.Y., 1976); ed. and commentator, *Ezra Pound and Music: The Complete Criticism* (N.Y., 1977); *On Canadian Music* (Bancroft, Ontario, 1984); *Dicamus et Labyrinthos: A Philologist's Notebook*

(Bancroft, Ontario, 1984); *The Thinking Ear: Complete Writings on Music Education* (Toronto, 1986); *Patria and the Theatre of Confluence* (Indian River, Ontario, 1991).

WORKS: DRAMATIC: *Loving* or *Toi*, opera (1963–65; 1st complete perf., Toronto, March 11, 1978); *Patria*, cycle of 12 musical/theatrical pieces (1966-in progress); *Jonah*, theater piece (1979); *Apocalypsis*, musical/theatrical pageant (London, Oct. 28, 1980).

Schäffer, August, German composer; b. Rheinsberg, Aug. 25, 1814; d. Baden-Baden, Aug. 7, 1879. He was a pupil, from 1833, of Mendelssohn in Berlin, where he spent most of his life. His humorous duets and quartets won great popularity; he also composed the operas *Emma von Falkenstein* (Berlin, 1839), *José Riccardo* (Hannover, 1857), and *Junker Habakuk* (Hannover, 1861).

Schalk, Franz, noted Austrian conductor; b. Vienna, May 27, 1863; d. Edlach, Sept. 2, 1931. He studied with Bruckner at the Vienna Cons.; after making his debut in Liberec (1886), he conducted in Reichenbach (1888–89), Graz (1889–95), and Prague (1895–98), and at the Berlin Royal Opera (1899–1900). He subsequently concentrated his activities in Vienna, where he conducted at the Court Opera (from 1900); when it became the State Opera in 1918, he was named its director; after sharing that position with R. Strauss (1919–24), he was sole director until 1929. He was a regular conductor with the Vienna Phil. from 1901 until his death; he also was conductor of the Gesellschaft der Musikfreunde (1904–21). On Dec. 14, 1898, he made his Metropolitan Opera debut in New York conducting *Die Walküre*, but remained on the roster for only that season. He also conducted *Ring* cycles at London's Covent Garden in 1898, 1907, and 1911; likewise he conducted at the Salzburg Festivals. He devoted part of his time to teaching conducting in Vienna. A champion of Bruckner, he ed. several of his syms., even recomposing his 5th Sym. While Schalk's eds. were well-intentioned efforts to obtain public performances of Bruckner's scores, they are now totally discredited. L. Schalk ed. his *Briefe und Betrachtungen* (Vienna, 1935). His brother, the Austrian pianist, teacher, and writer Josef Schalk (b. Vienna, March 24, 1857; d. there, Nov. 7, 1900), also defended Bruckner's music; publ. *Anton Bruckner und die moderne Musikwelt* (1885).

Schall, Claus Nielsen, Danish violinist and composer; b. Copenhagen, April 28, 1757; d. there, Aug. 9, 1835. He became a dancer at the Royal Theater in 1772; he was made a member of the court chapel in 1775 and became répétiteur and director of the ballet at the Royal Theater in 1776. After touring in Europe, he returned to Copenhagen as Konzertmeister of the Opera in 1792; he was made composer to the Royal Ballet in 1795 and served as music director of the Opera (1818–34). He wrote 6 Singspiels, of which the following (all 1st perf. in Copenhagen) were the most successful: *Claudine af Villa Bella* (Jan. 29, 1787), *Kinafarerne* (March 2, 1792), *Domherren i Milano* (March 16, 1802), and *De tre Galninger* (March 19, 1816). He also wrote some 20 ballets.

BIBL.: J. Friedrich, *C. S. als dramatischer Komponist* (diss., Univ. of Breslau, 1930).

Scharrer, August, German composer and conductor; b. Strasbourg, Aug. 18, 1866; d. Weiherhof, near Fürth, Oct. 24, 1936. After studies in Strasbourg and Berlin, he was a theater conductor in Karlsruhe (1897–98) and Regensburg (1898–1900); from 1914 to 1931 he conducted the Phil. Soc. of Nuremberg. He wrote an opera, *Die Erlösung* (Strasbourg, Nov. 21, 1895), and overtures.

Scharwenka, (Ludwig) Philipp, Polish-German composer and pedagogue, brother of **(Franz) Xaver Scharwenka**; b. Samter, Posen, Feb. 16, 1847; d. Bad Nauheim, July 16, 1917. He studied with Wüerst and Dorn at the Kullak Academy of Music in Berlin; in 1868 he was appointed teacher of composition there. With his brother Xaver, he founded in 1881 the Scharwenka Cons. in Berlin; together they made an American trip in 1891; in 1893 the Scharwenka Cons. was amalgamated with the Klindworth Cons., and the resulting Klindworth-Scharwenka Cons. acquired an excellent reputation for its teaching standards. He was also an accomplished composer.

Scharwenka, (Franz) Xaver, Polish-German pianist, composer, and pedagogue, brother of **(Ludwig) Philipp Scharwenka**; b. Samter, Posen, Jan. 6, 1850; d. Berlin, Dec. 8, 1924. He studied with Kullak and Wüerst at the Kullak Academy of Music in Berlin, graduating in 1868; then joined its faculty. He made his debut in Berlin in 1869, and then made regular tours from 1874; he also presented chamber music concerts in Berlin from 1881. With his brother, he founded the Scharwenka Cons. in Berlin in 1881; in 1891 he went to the United States and opened a N.Y. branch of his Cons.; he appeared as soloist in his own Piano Concerto (N.Y., Jan. 24, 1891). Returning to Berlin in 1898, he became codirector of the newly amalgamated (1893) Klindworth-Scharwenka Cons.; in 1914 he established his own course of master classes for piano. As a composer, he was undoubtedly superior to his brother, although both were faithful imitators of Schumann and other German Romantics. Among his works was an opera, *Mataswintha* (Weimar, Oct. 4, 1896). He also publ. technical studies for piano, and a book of memoirs, *Klänge aus meinem Leben: Erinnerungen eines Musikers* (Leipzig, 1922).

Schat, Peter, significant Dutch composer; b. Utrecht, June 5, 1935. He was a student of Baaren at the Utrecht Cons. (1952–58), of Seiber in London (1959), and of Boulez in Basel (1960–62). Settling in Amsterdam, he was active with the Studio for Electro-Instrumental Music (from 1967), and with the Amsterdam Electric Circus (from 1973). After teaching at the Royal Cons. of Music in The Hague (1974–83), he devoted himself fully to composition. In his early works, he followed a diligent serialist path. Later he combined serial and tonal elements in his works. Finally, he experimented with a method of 12 tonalities related only to each other as formulated in his "tone clock" (1982). In his "tone clock," Schat distinguishes between 12 trichords, one being the natural trichord, which are interrelated through their steering principle. This expansive harmonic and melodic method points the way to a new tonal system. He explained his system in the book *De Toonklok: Essays en gesprekken over muziek* (Amsterdam, 1984; Eng. tr., 1993).

WORKS: DRAMATIC: *Labyrint*, a kind of opera (1964; Amsterdam, June 23, 1966); *Reconstructie*, a morality (Amsterdam, June 29, 1969; in collaboration with L. Andriessen, R. de Leeuw, M. Mengelberg, and J. van Vlijmen); *Het vijde seizoen* (The 5th Season), music theater (1973); *Houdini*, circus opera (1974–76; Amsterdam, Sept. 29, 1977); *I Am Houdini*, ballet (1976); *Aap verslaat de knekelgeest* (Monkey Subdues the White-Bone Demon), strip opera (1980); *Symposion*, opera (1989; Amsterdam, April 29, 1994).

Schech, Marianne, German soprano; b. Geitau, Jan. 18, 1914. She was educated in Munich. She made her operatic debut in Koblenz in 1937, then sang in Munich (1939–41), Düsseldorf (1941–44), and at the Dresden State Opera (1944–51); she also sang with the Bavarian State Opera in Munich. In 1956 she was named a Kammersängerin. On Jan. 22, 1957, she made her debut at the Metropolitan Opera in New York as Sieglinde in *Die Walküre*; she also made guest appearances in London, Vienna, and Hamburg. She retired from the stage in 1970 and devoted herself mainly to teaching.

Scheff, Fritzi, famous Austrian soprano; b. Vienna, Aug. 30, 1879; d. N.Y., April 8, 1954. She studied with her mother, the singer Anna Jäger; after further training with Schröder-Hanfstängl in Munich, she completed her studies at the Frankfurt am Main Cons. She made her operatic debut as Martha in Frankfurt am Main (1896), and soon adopted her mother's maiden name of Scheff for professional purposes. After singing at the Munich Court Opera (1897–1900), she made her Metropolitan Opera debut in New York as Marzellina in *Fidelio* (Dec. 28, 1900), and remained on its roster until 1903; concurrently she sang at London's Covent Garden. She later shifted to light opera, and it was in this field that she became famous. She created the role of Fifi in Victor Herbert's operetta *Mlle. Modiste* (Trenton, N.J., Oct. 7, 1905); her singing of Fifi's waltz song "Kiss Me Again" became a hallmark of her career. She also found success as a dramatic actress, becoming particularly well known for her appearance in Arsenic and Old Lace. Her 3 marriages (to Baron Fritz von Bardeleben, the American writer John Fox Jr. and the singer George Anderson) ended in divorce.

Scheibe, Johann Adolf, German music theorist and composer; b. Leipzig, May 3, 1708; d. Copenhagen, April 22, 1776. He was the son of the organ builder Johann Scheibe (b. Saxony, c.1680; d. Leipzig, Sept. 3, 1748), in whose workshop he lost his right eye when he was 8. He commenced the study of keyboard instruments at age 6; after attending the school of the Nicolaikirche, he entered the Univ. of Leipzig as a law student in 1725, but was compelled to give up his studies when the family's financial condition changed for the worse. He subsequently devoted himself to music, being mainly autodidact; failing to obtain organ posts at the Nicolaikirche in Leipzig (1729; Bach was one of the adjudicators), in Prague and Gotha (1735), and in Sondershausen and Wolfenbüttel (1736), he went to Hamburg as a music critic and composer (1736); he brought out his *Der critische Musikus*, which includes his famous attack on Bach (No. 6, 1737). After serving as Kapellmeister to Margrave Friedrich Ernst of Brandenburg-Culmbach, the governor of Holstein (1739–40), he was made Kapellmeister at the court of King Christian VI in Copenhagen in 1740; with the accession of King Frederik V in 1747, Scheibe was pensioned and settled in Sønderborg, where he devoted himself to running a music school for children. In 1766 he once again resumed a relationship with the Danish court, serving as a composer for it until his death. The major portion of his compositional output, which includes the Singspiel *Thusnelde* (libretto publ. in Leipzig and Copenhagen, 1749), is not extant. He is therefore primarily known as an important music theorist of his era.

WRITINGS: *Compendium musices theoretico-practicum, das ist Kurzer Begriff derer nötigsten Compositions-Regeln* (c.1730; publ. by P. Benary in *Die deutsche Kompositionslehre des 18. Jahrhunderts*, Leipzig, 1961); *Der critische Musikus* (vol. 1, Hamburg, 1738; vol. 2, Hamburg, 1740; complete ed., Leipzig, 1745); *Beantwortung der unparteiischen Anmerkungen über eine bedenkliche Stelle in dem sechsten Stücke des critischen Musicus* (Hamburg, 1738; reprint in *Der critische Musikus*, Leipzig, 1745); *Eine Abhandlung von den musicalischen Intervallen und Geschlechtern* (Hamburg, 1739); *Thusnelde, ein Singspiel in vier Aufzügen, mit einem Vorbericht von der Möglichkeit und Beschaffenheit guter Singspiele begleitet* (Leipzig and Copenhagen, 1749); *Abhandlung vom Ursprunge und Alter der Musik, insonderheit der Vokalmusik* (Altona and Flensburg, 1754); *Über die musikalische Composition, erster Theil: Die Theorie der Melodie und Harmonie* (Leipzig, 1773).

BIBL.: K. Storch, *S.s Anschauungen von der musikalische Historie, Wissenschaft und Kunst* (diss., Univ. of Leipzig, 1923); E. Rosenkaimer, *J. A. S. als Verfasser des Critischen Musikus* (Bonn, 1929); I. Willheim, *J. A. S.: German Musical Thought in Transition* (diss., Univ. of Illinois, 1963); G. Skapski, *The Recitative in J.A. S.'s Literary and Musical Work* (diss., Univ. of Texas, 1963).

Scheidemantel, Karl, noted German baritone; b. Weimar, Jan. 21, 1859; d. there, June 26, 1923. He was a pupil of Bodo Borchers, and sang at the court theater in Weimar (1878–86); he also studied voice with Julius Stockhausen in the summers of 1881–83. He was a member of the Dresden Court Opera from 1886 to 1911 and also sang at the Munich Court Opera (1882), London's Covent Garden (debut as Wolfram, June 14, 1884), the Vienna Court Opera (1890), and Milan's La Scala (1892). From 1911 to 1920 he was a prof. at the Grossherzogliche Musikschule in Weimar; from 1920 to 1922 he was director of the Landestheater in Dresden. He publ. *Stimmbildung* (1907; 4th ed. as *Gesangsbildung*, 1913; in Eng., 1910); he also ed. a collection of songs, *Meisterweisen* (1914). Among his finest roles were Hans Sachs, Kurwenal, Amfortas, Klingsor, Telramund, Pizarro, and Scarpia; he also created the roles of Kunrad in *Feuersnot* (Dresden, Nov. 21, 1901) and Faninal in *Der Rosenkavalier* (Dresden, Jan. 26 1911).

BIBL.: P. Trede, *K. S.* (Dresden, 1911).

Scheidl, Theodor, Austrian baritone and teacher; b. Vienna, Aug. 3, 1880; d. Tübingen, April 22, 1959. He was trained in Vienna. After making his debut there at the Volksoper in *Lohengrin* (1910), he sang in Olmütz (1911–12) and Augsburg (1913). He was a member of the Stuttgart Opera (1913–21) and of the Berlin State Opera (1921–32). He also appeared at the Bayreuth Festivals, most notably as Klingsor (1914), Amfortas (1924–25), and Kurwenal (1927). In 1932 he joined the German Theater in Prague. In 1937 he became a prof. of voice at the Munich Hochschule für Musik. He settled in Tübingen as a teacher in 1944.

Scheidt, family of German singers, all siblings:

(1) Selma vom Scheidt, soprano; b. Bremen, Sept. 26, 1874; d. Weimar, Feb. 19, 1959. She was a pupil of Heinrich Böllhoff in Hamburg, and later of Theodor Bertram. In 1891 she made her operatic debut as Agathe in Elberfeld. After singing in Essen (1892–94) and Düsseldorf (1894–95), she appeared in Aachen, Bonn, and Berlin. In 1900 she joined the Weimar Opera, where she sang for some 25 years.

(2) Julius vom Scheidt, baritone; b. Bremen, March 29, 1877; d. Hamburg, Dec. 10, 1948. He made his operatic debut in Cologne in 1899, and sang there until 1916. After appearing at the Berlin Deutsches Opernhaus (1916–24), he sang at the Hamburg Opera (1924–30). He subsequently taught voice.

(3) Robert vom Scheidt, baritone; b. Bremen, April 16, 1879; d. Frankfurt am Main, April 10, 1964. He studied at the Cologne Cons. In 1897 he made his operatic debut at the Cologne Opera, singing there until 1903. From 1903 to 1912 he sang at the Hamburg Opera, and in 1904 at the Bayreuth Festival. He was a member of the Frankfurt am Main Opera from 1912 to 1940, singing in the premieres of Schreker's *Die Gezeichneten* (1918) and *Der Schatzgräber* (1920), and of Egk's *Die Zaubergeige* (1935).

Scheinpflug, Paul, German violinist, conductor, and composer; b. Loschwitz, near Dresden, Sept. 10, 1875; d. Memel, March 11, 1937. He studied violin with Rappoldi and composition with Draeseke at the Dresden Cons. In 1898 he went to Bremen as concertmaster of the Phil. and conductor of the Liederkranz; he then was conductor of the Königsberg Musikverein (1909–14); he conducted the Blüthner Orch. in Berlin (1914–19) and was music director in Duisburg (1920–28) and of the Dresden Phil. (1929–33). Among his works is the opera *Das Hofkonzert* (1922).

Schelble, Johann Nepomuk, German singer, conductor, pedagogue, and composer; b. Hüfingen, May 16, 1789; d. there, Aug. 6, 1837. He studied with Weisse in Donaueschingen, Volger in Darmstadt, and Krebs in Stuttgart, where he then sang as a tenor and baritone at the court and opera (1808–14); he also was a teacher at the Royal Musical Inst. (from 1812). From 1814 to 1816 he was in Vienna and became a close friend of Beethoven; he settled in Frankfurt am Main, where he founded the Cacilien-Verein (1818), and sang at the Frankfurt am Main theater (1817–19). His methods for teaching the musical rudiments and training the sense of absolute pitch were much admired; he enjoyed the esteem of many musicians of his time; Mendelssohn paid tribute to him in his correspondence. In addition to various didactic works, he also composed vocal and chamber music.

BIBL.: K. Lang, *Die Gehörsentwicklungs-Methode von S.* (Braunschweig, 1873); O. Bormann, *J. N. S. 1789–1837* (diss., Univ. of Frankfurt am Main, 1926).

Schelle, Michael, American composer and teacher; b. Philadelphia, Jan. 22, 1950. He studied theater at Villanova Univ. (B.A., 1971), then pursued musical training at Butler Univ. (B.M., 1974), at the Hartt School of Music of the Univ. of Hartford (M.M., 1976), with Copland (1976–77), and with Argento at the Univ. of Minnesota (Ph.D., 1980). From 1979 he taught at Butler Univ., where he also was composer-in-residence from 1981. He received grants from the NEA, the Rockefeller Foundation, BMI, ASCAP et al., and in 1989 was named distinguished composer of the year by the Music Teachers National Assn. Many major American orchs. have commissioned and premiered his scores, including those of Indianapolis, Detroit, Buffalo, Cleveland, Seattle, Milwaukee, and Cincinnati. He was also a guest composer at Capital Univ. in Columbus, Ohio (1991), the Univ. of Southern Calif. in Los Angeles (1994), and Sam Houston State Univ. in Huntsville, Texas (1995), among others. His works include the chamber opera *Soap Opera* (1988; Indianapolis, June 9, 1989).

Schenck, Andrew (Craig), American conductor; b. Honolulu, Jan. 7, 1941; d. Baltimore, Feb. 19, 1992. He was educated at Harvard Univ. (B.A., 1962) and Indiana Univ. (Mus.M., 1968); pursued training in conducting with Bernstein at the Berkshire Music Center in Tanglewood, Monteux in Hancock, Maine, and in Germany on a Fulbright scholarship (1962–63), subsequently winning 1st prize in the Besançon conducting competition. He was assistant conductor of the Honolulu Sym. Orch. (1970–73) and the Baltimore Sym. Orch. (1973–80), and then founder-music director of the Baltimore Chamber Opera (1980–84). After serving as a resident conductor of the San Antonio Sym. Orch. (1986–88), he was music director of the Nassau (N.Y.) Sym. Orch. and the Atlantic Sinfonietta of N.Y. Schenck made a special effort to program American music at his concerts, both with his own orchs. and as a guest conductor with the Pittsburgh Sym. Orch., the Chicago Sym. Orch., the London Sym. Orch. et al.

Schenck, Pyotr, Russian pianist, conductor, and composer; b. St. Petersburg, Feb. 28, 1870; d. Perkiarvy, Finland, July 5, 1915. He studied piano and theory at the St. Petersburg Cons. He gave concerts as a pianist, then devoted himself to conducting; he appeared in several European countries. His music was entirely under the influence of Tchaikovsky. Among his works were the operas *Acteya* (concert perf., St. Petersburg, Dec. 3, 1899, composer conducting) and *The Miracle of Roses* (St. Petersburg, Oct. 7, 1913); also ballet music.

Schenk, Erich, eminent Austrian musicologist; b. Salzburg, May 5, 1902; d. Vienna, Oct. 11, 1974. He studied theory and piano at the Salzburg Mozarteum and musicology with Sandberger at the Univ. of Munich (Ph.D., 1925, with the diss. *Giuseppe Antonio Paganelli: Sein Leben und seine Werke*; publ. in Salzburg, 1928); he completed his Habilitation at the Univ. of Rostock in 1929 with his *Studien zur Triosonate in Deutschland nach Corelli* and subsequently founded its musicology dept. (1936). From 1940 until his retirement in 1971 he was a prof. of musicology at the Univ. of Vienna. He was particularly esteemed for his studies of Baroque and Classical music. In 1947 he revived the Denkmäler der Tonkunst in Österreich series, overseeing its progress until 1972. In 1955 he also took over the valuable *Studien zur Musikwissenschaft*. Festschrifts honored him on his 60th (Vienna, 1962) and 70th (Kassel, 1975) birthdays.

WRITINGS: *Johann Strauss* (Potsdam, 1940); *Musik in Kärnten* (Vienna, 1941); *Beethoven zwischen den Zeiten* (Bonn, 1944); *950 Jahre österreichische Musik* (Vienna, 1946); *Kleine wiener Musikgeschichte* (Vienna, 1946); *W. A. Mozart: Eine Biographie* (Vienna, 1955; Eng. tr., 1960, as *Mozart and His Time*; 2d Ger. ed., aug., 1975, as *Mozart: Sein Leben, seine Welt*); *Ausgewählte Aufsätze: Reden und Vorträge* (Vienna, 1967); ed. *Beethoven-Studien* (Vienna, 1970).

Schenk, Johann Baptist, Austrian composer and teacher; b. Wiener-Neustadt, Nov. 30, 1753; d. Vienna, Dec. 29, 1836. He received elementary instruction in music as a small child, and then studied with the Baden choirmaster Anton Stoll; he learned to play violin and keyboard instruments, and began composing in his youth. In 1773 he went to Vienna, where he took courses in counterpoint and composition with Wagenseil. In 1778 he established his reputation with the performance of a Mass, and in 1780 he began composing for the theater, winning notable success with his *Der Dorfbarbier*. In 1793 Beethoven took surreptitious lessons from him while studying formally with Haydn.

WORKS: DRAMATIC (all Singspiels and 1st perf. in Vienna unless otherwise given): *Der Schatzgräber*, opera (1780; not perf.); *Der Dorfbarbier*, comedy (June 18, 1785; as a Singspiel, Oct. 30, 1796); *Die Weinlese* (Oct. 12, 1785); *Die Weihnacht auf dem Lande* (Dec. 14, 1786); *Im Finstern ist nicht gut tappen* (Oct. 12, 1787); *Das unvermutete Seefest* (Dec. 9, 1789); *Das Singspiel ohne Titel*, operetta (Nov. 4, 1790); *Der Erntekranz* (July 9, 1791); *Achmet und Almanzine* (July 17, 1795); *Die Jagd* (May 7, 1799); *Der Fassbinder* (Dec. 17, 1802).

BIBL.: F. Staub, *J. S. Eine Skizze seines Lebens* (Wiener-Neustadt, 1901); E. Rosenfeld (-Roemer), *J. B. S. als Opernkomponist* (diss., Univ. of Vienna, 1921); F. Rieger, *J. S.: Ein Altmeister des deutschen Singspiels* (St. Pölten, 1944).

Schenk, Otto, Austrian opera producer and actor; b. Vienna, June 12, 1930. He studied at the Reinhardt Seminar and at the Univ. of Vienna. In 1952 he began his career as an actor, and in later years became particularly known for his portrayal of the jailer Frosch in *Die Fledermaus*. In 1957 he produced his first opera, *Die Zauberflöte*, at the Salzburg Landestheater. His productions of *Dantons Tod* and *Lulu* at the Vienna Festival in 1962 secured his reputation, and in 1963 he conquered audiences at the Salzburg Festival with *Die Zauberflöte*. In 1964 he oversaw a production of *Jenůfa* at the Vienna State Opera, where he was made resident producer in 1965. In 1968 he staged *Tosca* for his first production at the Metropolitan Opera in New York, and subsequently produced there *Fidelio* (1970), *Tannhäuser* (1977), *Les Contes d'Hoffmann* (1981), *Arabella* (1982), and the *Ring* cycle (1986–91). His other productions included *Le nozze di Figaro* at Milan's La Scala (1974) and *Un ballo in maschera* at London's Covent Garden (1975). His productions followed along traditional lines with a preference for naturalistic settings.

Schenker, Heinrich, outstanding Austrian music theorist; b. Wisniowczyki, Galicia, June 19, 1868; d. Vienna, Jan. 13, 1935. He studied jurisprudence at the Univ. of Vienna (Dr.Jur., 1890); concurrently took courses with Bruckner at the Vienna Cons. He composed some songs and piano pieces; Brahms liked them sufficiently to recommend Schenker to his publisher Simrock. For a while Schenker served as accompanist of the baritone Johannes Messchaert; he then returned to Vienna and devoted himself entirely to the development of his theoretical research; he gathered around himself a group of enthusiastic disciples who accepted his novel theories, among them Otto Vrieslander, Hermann Roth, Hans Weisse, Anthony van Hoboken, Oswald Jonas, Felix Salzer, and John Petrie Dunn. He endeavored to derive the basic laws of musical composition from a thoroughgoing analysis of the standard masterworks. The result was the contention that each composition represents a horizontal integration, through various stages, of differential triadic units derived from the overtone series. By a dialectical manipulation of the thematic elements and linear progressions of a given work, Schenker succeeded in preparing a formidable system in which the melody is the "Urlinie" (basic line), the bass is "Grundbrechung" (broken ground), and the ultimate formation is the "Ursatz" (background). The result seems as self-consistent as the Ptolemaic planetary theory of epicycles. Arbitrary as the Schenker system is, it proved remarkably durable in academia; some theorists even attempted to apply it to modern works lacking in the triadic content essential to Schenker's theories.

WRITINGS: *Ein Beitrag zur Ornamentik als Einführung zu Ph.E. Bachs Klavierwerke* (Vienna, 1904; 2d ed., rev., 1908; Eng. tr. in *Music Forum*, 4, 1976); *Neue musikalische Theorien und Fantasien*: 1. *Harmonierlehre* (Stuttgart, 1906; Eng. tr., ed. by O. Jonas, Chicago, 1954); 2. *Kontrapunkt* in 2 vols., *Cantus Firmus und zweistimmiger Satz* (Vienna, 1910), and *Drei- und mehrstimmiger Satz, Übergänge zum freien Satz* (Vienna, 1922); Eng. tr. of both vols. by J. Thymn, N.Y., 1987; 3. *Der freie Satz* (Vienna, 1935; new ed. by O. Jonas, 1956; Eng. tr. by E. Oster, 1979); *Beethovens Neunte Sinfonie* (Vienna, 1912; Eng. tr., ed. by J. Rothgeb, New Haven, 1992); *Der Tonwille* (a periodical, 1921–24); *Beethovens Fünfte Sinfonie* (Vienna, 1925); *Das Meisterwerk in der Musik* (3 vols., Vienna, 1925, 1926, 1930); *Fünf Urlinie-Tafeln*

(Vienna, 1932; 2d ed., rev., 1969 as *Five Graphic Music Analyses by F. Salzer*); *Johannes Brahms: Oktaven und Quinten* (Vienna, 1933).

BIBL.: O. Jonas, *Das Wesen des musikalischen Künstwerks* (Vienna, 1934; 2d ed., rev., 1973 as *Einführung in die Lehre H. S.s*; Eng. tr., 1982); L. Laskowski, ed., *H. S.: An Annotated Index to His Analyses of Musical Works* (N.Y., 1978); A. Forte and S. Gilbert, *An Introduction to S.ian Analysis* (London, 1982); F.-E. von Cube, *The Book of the Musical Artwork: An Interpretation of the Musical Theories of H. S.* (Lewiston, N.Y., 1988); H. Siegel, ed., *S. Studies* (Cambridge, 1989); A. Cadwallader, ed., *Trends in S.ian Research* (N.Y., 1990); D. Neumeyer and S. Tepping, *A Guide to S.ian Analysis* (Englewood Cliffs, N.J., 1992).

Schering, Arnold, eminent German music historian; b. Breslau, April 2, 1877; d. Berlin, March 7, 1941. His father was a merchant; the family moved to Dresden, where Schering began to take violin lessons with Blumner. In 1896 he went to Berlin, where he studied violin with Joachim, hoping to start a concert career; he organized a tour with the pianist Hinze-Reinhold, but soon gave up virtuoso aspirations, and in 1898 entered classes in musicology with Fleischer and Stumpf at the Univ. of Berlin, then took courses with Sandberger at the Univ. of Munich and with Kretzschmar at the Univ. of Leipzig, obtaining his Ph.D. in 1902 with the diss. *Geschichte des Instrumental- (Violin-) Konzerts bis A. Vivaldi* (publ. in Leipzig, 1905; 2d ed., 1927); he subsequently completed his Habilitation there in 1907 with his *Die Anfänge des Oratoriums* (publ. in an aug. ed. as *Geschichte des Oratoriums*, Leipzig, 1911). He devoted himself to teaching and musical journalism; from 1904 to 1939 he was ed. of the *Bach-Jahrbuch*. From 1909 to 1923 he taught at the Leipzig Cons.; from 1915 to 1920 he was prof. of the history and aesthetics of music at the Univ. of Leipzig; then was prof. of music at the Univ. of Halle (1920–28); subsequently he was prof. of musicology at the Univ. of Berlin (1928–41). In 1928 he became president of the Deutsche Gesellschaft für Musikwissenschaft. In his voluminous publications, he strove to erect an infallible system of aesthetic principles derived from musical symbolism and based on psychological intuition, ignoring any contradictions that ensued from his axiomatic constructions. In his book *Beethoven in neuer Deutung*, publ. in 1934 at the early dawn of the Nazi era, he even attempted to interpret Beethoven's music in terms of racial German superiority, alienating many of his admirers. But in his irrepressible desire to establish an immutable sequence of historic necessity, he compiled an original and highly informative historical tabulation of musical chronology, *Tabellen zur Musikgeschichte*, which was publ. in 1914 and went through several eds.

WRITINGS: *Musikalische Bildung und Erziehung zum musikalischen Hören* (Leipzig, 1911; 4th ed., 1924); *Tabellen zur Musikgeschichte* (Leipzig, 1914; 4th ed., 1934; 5th ed., 1962, by H. J. Moser); *Aufführungspraxis alter Musik* (Berlin, 1931); *Geschichte der Musik in Beispielen* (Leipzig, 1931; 2d ed., 1954; Eng. tr., 1950); *Beethoven in neuer Deutung* (Berlin, 1934); *Beethoven und die Dichtung* (Berlin, 1936); *Johann Sebastian Bachs Leipziger Kirchenmusik* (Leipzig, 1936; 2d ed., 1954); *Von grossen Meistern der Musik* (Leipzig, 1940); *Das Symbol in der Musik* (ed. by W. Gurlitt; Berlin, 1941); *Über Kantaten J. S. Bachs* (ed. by F. Blume; Berlin, 1942; 2d ed., 1950); *Vom musikalischen Künstwerk* (ed. by F. Blume; Berlin, 1949; 2d ed., 1951); *Humor, Heldentum, Tragik bei Beethoven* (Strasbourg, 1955).

BIBL.: H. Osthoff, ed., *Festschrift A. S. zum 60. Geburtstag* (Berlin, 1937).

Scherman, Thomas (Kielty), American conductor; b. N.Y., Feb. 12, 1917; d. there, May 14, 1979. He was a son of Harry Scherman, founder and president of the Book-of-the-Month Club; he attended Columbia Univ. (B.A., 1937), then studied piano with Vengerova, theory with Weisse, and conducting with Bamberger, Rudolf, and Klemperer, whose assistant he became in conducting a chamber orch. composed of European refugees at the New School for Social Research in New York (1939–41). He subsequently served in the U.S. Army (1941–45), reaching the rank of captain in the Signal Corps. In 1947 he became assistant conductor of the National Opera in Mexico City; that same year, he organized in New York the Little Orch. Soc. for the purposes of presenting new works, some of them specially commissioned, and of reviving forgotten music of the past; he also gave performances of operas in concert versions. He terminated the seasons of the Little Orch. Soc. in 1975, but organized the New Little Orch. Soc. to present children's concerts; these he continued to lead until his death.

Schermerhorn, Kenneth (de Witt), American conductor; b. Schenectady, N.Y., Nov. 20, 1929. He studied conducting with Richard Burgin at the New England Cons. of Music in Boston (graduated, 1950); he also took courses at the Berkshire Music Center at Tanglewood, where he won the Koussevitzky Prize. His first important engagement was as conductor of the American Ballet Theater in New York (1957–67); he also was assistant conductor of the N.Y. Phil. (1960–61). He was music director of the New Jersey Sym. Orch. in Newark (1963–68) and the Milwaukee Sym. Orch. (1968–80), then was general music director of the American Ballet Theater in New York (from 1982) and also music director of the Nashville (Tenn.) Sym. Orch. (from 1983) and the Hong Kong Phil. (1984–88). In 1975 he married **Carol Neblett**.

Schibler, Armin, Swiss composer; b. Breuzlingen, Nov. 20, 1920; d. Zürich, Sept. 7, 1986. He went to Zürich and studied with Frey and Müller, and then with Burkhard (1942–45). After further training in England (1946), he attended the summer courses in new music in Darmstadt (1949–53) and profited from studies with Fortner, Krenek, Leibowitz, and Adorno. He taught music at the Zürich Real- und Literargymnasium from 1944. His music represented an eclectic synthesis of various 20th-century compositional techniques.

WORKS: DRAMATIC: OPERAS: *Der spanische Rosenstock*, opera (1947–50; Bern, April 9, 1950); *Der Teufel im Winterpalais*, opera (1950–53); *Das Bergwerk von Falun*, opera (1953); *Die späte Sühne*, chamber opera (1953–54); *Die Füsse im Feuer*, opera (Zürich, April 25, 1955); *Amadeus und der graue Bote*, chamber opera (1982–85); *Schlafwagen Pegasus*, chamber opera (1982–85). BALLETS: *Der Raub des Feuers* (1954); *Die Gefangene*, chamber ballet (1957); *Ein Lebenslauf*, chamber ballet (1958); *Selene und Endymion* (1959–60); *Die Legende von der drei Liebespfändern* (1975–76); *La Naissance d'Eros* (1985). OTHER STAGE WORKS: *Blackwood & Co.*, musical burlesque (1955–58; Zürich, June 3, 1962); *La Folie de Tristan*, music theater (1980); *Antonie und die Trompete*, chamber musical (1981) *Königinnen von Frankreich*, musical chamber-comedy (1982–85); *Sansibar oder Die Rettung*, music theater (1984–86). RADIO PIECES: *Das kleine Mädchen mit den Schwefelhölzchen*, melodrama (1955; rev. 1965); *Orpheus: Die Unwiederbringlichkeit des Verlorenen* (1967–68); *The Point of Return* (1971–72); *. . . später als du denkst* (1973); *. . . der da geht . . .* (1974); *Epitaph auf einen Mächtigen* (1974–75). ORATORIOS: *Media in vita* for 4 Soloists, Mixed Chorus, Men's Chorus, and Orch. (1958–59); *Der Tod Enkidus* for Choruses and Orch. (1970–72); *Der Tod des Einsiedlers* for Soloists, Chorus, and Chamber Ensemble (1975); *Messe für die gegenwärtige Zeit* for 2 Soloists, Youth Chorus, 2 Pianos, and Jazz-rock Group (1979–80); *De Misterio* for Speaking Voice, Man's Voice, and Orch. (1982).

BIBL.: K. Wörner, *A. S.: Werk und Persönlichkeit* (Amriswil, 1953); H.-R. Metzger, *A. S., 1920–1986* (2 vols., Zürich, 1990–91).

Schick, George, Czech-American conductor; b. Prague, April 5, 1908; d. N.Y., March 7, 1985. He studied at the Prague Cons. He was assistant conductor at the Prague National Theater from 1927 until 1938. He settled in the United States in 1939; was conductor of the San Carlo Opera (1943); from 1948 to 1950 he was conductor of the Little Sym. of Montreal; from 1950 to 1956 he was assoc. conductor of the Chicago Sym. Orch. He was a conductor at the Metropolitan Opera in New York (1958–69), then served as president of the Manhattan School of Music in New York (1969–76).

Schick, Margarete (Luise née **Hamel)**, noted German soprano; b. Mainz, April 26, 1773; d. Berlin, April 29, 1809. Her father was the bassoonist J. N. Hamel. After keyboard and vocal training, the elector of Mainz ennabled her to continue her vocal studies with Domonicus Steffani in Würzburg; returning to Mainz, she sang at the electoral court while pursuing further studies with Righini; she made her stage debut there in 1791. She settled in Berlin in 1793 as a court chamber and theater singer and also sang at the National Theater (from 1794). She especially excelled in operas by Gluck and Mozart; her most celebrated role was Gluck's Iphigenia, but she also was admired for Mozart's Susanna and Zerlina. Her contemporaries regarded her as the equal of the famous Mara. In 1791 she married the violinist Ernst Schick.

BIBL.: K. von Levezow, *Leben und Kunst der Frau M. L. S., geboren Hamel* (Berlin, 1809).

Schickele, Peter, American composer and musical humorist; b. Ames, Iowa, July 17, 1935. He was educated at Swarthmore College (B.A., 1957) and studied composition with Harris in Pittsburgh (1954), Milhaud at the Aspen (Colo.) School of Music (1959), and Persichetti and Bergsma at the Juilliard School of Music in New York (M.S., 1960). After serving as composer-in-residence to the Los Angeles public schools (1960–61), he taught at Swarthmore College (1961–62) and at the Juilliard School of Music (from 1962). He rocketed to fame at N.Y.'s Town Hall on April 24, 1965, in the rollicking role of the roly-poly character P. D. Q. Bach, the mythical composer of such outrageous travesties as *The Civilian Barber, Gross Concerto for Divers Flutes* (featuring a Nose Flute and a Wiener Whistle to be eaten during the perf.), *Concerto for Piano vs. Orchestra, Iphigenia in Brooklyn, The Seasonings, Pervertimento for Bagpipes, Bicycles & Balloons, No-No Nonette, Schleptet, Fuga Meshuga, Missa Hilarious, Sanka Cantata, Fantasie-Shtick*, and the opera *The Abduction of Figaro* (Minneapolis, April 24, 1984). He publ. *The Definitive Biography of P. D. Q. Bach (1807–1742?)* (N.Y., 1976). In 1967 he organized a chamber-rock-jazz trio known as Open Window, which frequently presented his serious compositions; among these are several orch. works, vocal pieces, film and television scores, and chamber music. In later years, he was host of his own radio program, "Schickele Mix."

Schidlowsky, León, Chilean composer; b. Santiago, July 21, 1931. He studied in Santiago at the National Cons. (1940–47), and also took courses in philosophy and psychology at the Univ. of Chile (1948–52), and had private lessons in composition with Focke and in harmony with Allende-Blin; he then went to Germany for further studies (1952–55). Returning to Chile, he organized the avant-garde group Agrupación Tonus for the propagation of new techniques of composition. He taught at the Santiago Music Inst. (1955–63) and served as prof. of composition at the Univ. of Chile (1962–68), then held a Guggenheim fellowship (1968). In 1969 he emigrated to Israel, where he was appointed to the faculty of the Rubin Academy of Music. In his music, he adopts a serial technique, extending it into fields of rhythms and intensities; beginning in 1964, he super-added aleatory elements, using graphic notation. Among his works is the opera *Die Menschen* (1970); also *Rabbi Akiba*, scenic fantasy for Narrator, 3 Soloists, Children's and Mixed Choruses, and Orch. (1972), and *Silvestre Revueltas*, oratorio for Narrator, 9 Voices, and Chamber Orch. (1994).

BIBL.: W. Elias, *L. S.* (Tel Aviv, 1978).

Schiedermair, Ludwig, eminent German musicologist; b. Regensburg, Dec. 7, 1876; d. Bensberg, near Cologne, April 30, 1957. He studied in Munich with Sandberger and Beer-Walbrunn and received his Ph.D. at the Univ. of Erlangen in 1901 with the diss. *Die Künstlerische Bestrebungen am Hofe des Kurfürsten Ferdinand Maria von Bayern*; he studied further with Riemann at the Univ. of Leipzig and with Kretzschmar at the Univ. of Berlin; he completed his Habilitation in 1906 at the Univ. of Marburg with his *Simon Mayr: Beiträge zur Geschichte der Oper um die Wende des 18. und 19. Jahrhunderts* (publ. in Leipzig, 1907–10), where he then taught (1906–11); he then went to the Univ. of Bonn (1911), where he was a reader (1915–20) and a prof. (1920–45). He was founder-director of the Beethoven Archives in Bonn; he was made president of the Deutsche Gesellschaft für Musikwissenschaft (1937) and chairman of the music section of the Deutsche Akademie (1940). A Festschrift was publ. in honor of his 60th (Berlin, 1937) and 80th (Cologne, 1956) birthdays.

WRITINGS: *Gustav Mahler* (Leipzig, 1901); *Bayreuther Festspiele im Zeitalter des Absolutismus* (Leipzig, 1908); *Die Briefe Mozarts und seiner Familie* (5 vols., Munich, 1914; vol. 5 is an iconography); *W. A. Mozarts Handschrift* (Bückeburg, 1919; facsimiles); *Einführung in das Studium der Musikgeschichte* (Munich, 1918; new ed., Bonn, 1947); *Mozart* (Munich, 1922; 2d ed., Bonn, 1948); *Der junge Beethoven* (Leipzig, 1925; 4th ed., 1970); *Beethoven: Beiträge zum Leben und Schaffen* (Leipzig, 1930; 3d ed., 1943); *Die deutsche Oper* (Leipzig, 1930); *Die Gestaltung weltanschaulicher Ideen in der Vokalmusik Beethovens* (Leipzig, 1934); *Musik am Rheinstron* (Cologne, 1947); *Musikalische Begegnungen: Erlebnis und Erinnerung* (Cologne, 1948); *Deutsche Musik im Europäischen Raum* (Münster, 1954).

Schiedermayer, Johann Baptist, German organist and composer; b. Pfaffenmünster, Bavaria, June 23, 1779; d. Linz, Jan. 6, 1840. He served as Linz Cathedral organist. He wrote *Theoretisch-praktische Chorallehre zum Gebrauch beim katholischen Kirchenritus* (1828), and composed the Singspiels *Wellmanns Eichenstämme* (Linz, 1815), *Das Gluck ist kugelrund* (Linz, 1816), and *Die Rückkehr ins Vaterhaus* (Linz, 1816).

Schieferdecker, Johann Christian, German organist and composer; b. Teuchern, near Weissenfels, Nov. 10, 1679; d. Lübeck, April 5, 1732. He studied at the Thomasschule (1692–97) and Univ. (1697–1702) in Leipzig. In 1706 he became Buxtehude's deputy at Lübeck's St. Marienkirche. On Jan. 23, 1707, he succeeded Buxtehude as organist and parish clerk; as the successful applicant, he was required to marry Buxtehude's daughter, Anna Margareta (Sept. 5, 1707), a requirement declined by Mattheson and Handel. The Abendmusiken, which had achieved wide respect under Tunder and Buxtehude, were continued under his supervision until 1730. His works for these concerts are lost. He also wrote several operas.

Schierbeck, Poul (Julius Ouscher), distinguished Danish organist, pedagogue, and composer; b. Copenhagen, June 8, 1888; d. there, Feb. 9, 1949. He studied composition with Nielsen and Laub; also received instruction from Paul Hellmuth, Henrik Knudsen, and Frank van der Stucken. He was organist at Copenhagen's Skovshoved Church (1916–49) and a teacher of composition and instrumentation at the Royal Danish Cons. of Music (1931–49). In 1947 he was made a member of the Royal Swedish Academy of Music in Stockholm. His works include the opera *Fête galante* (1923–30; Copenhagen, Sept. 1, 1931).

BIBL.: O. Mathisen, *P. S.* (diss., Univ. of Copenhagen, 1972).

Schifrin, Lalo (Boris), Argentine-American pianist, conductor, and composer; b. Buenos Aires, June 21, 1932. He studied music at home with his father, the concertmaster of the Teatro Colón orch. and subsequently studied harmony with Juan Carlos Paz; he won a scholarship to the Paris Cons. in 1950, where he received guidance from Koechlin, and took courses with Messiaen. He became interested in jazz, and represented Argentina at the International Jazz Festival in Paris in 1955; returning to Buenos Aires, he formed his own jazz band, adopting the bebop style. In 1958 he went to New York, and later was pianist with Dizzy Gillespie's band (1960–62); he composed for it several exotic pieces, such as "Manteca," "Con Alma," and "Tunisian Fantasy," based on Gillespie's "Night in Tunisia." In 1963 he wrote a ballet, *Jazz Faust*. In 1964 he went to Hollywood, where he rapidly found his métier as composer for the films and television; among his scores are *The Liquidator* (1966), *Cool Hand Luke* (1967), *The Fox* (1967), *The Amityville Horror* (1978), *The Sting II* (1983), and *Bad Medicine* (1985). He also experimented with applying the jazz idiom to religious texts, as, for instance, in his *Jazz Suite on Mass Texts* (1965). He achieved his greatest popular success with the theme-motto for the television series *Mission: Impossible* (1966–73), in 5/4 time, for which he received 2 Grammy awards. His adaptation of modern techniques into mass media placed him in the enviable position of being praised by professional musicians. His oratorio *The Rise and Fall of the Third Reich*, featuring realistic excerpts and incorporating an actual recording of Hitler's speech in electronic amplification, was brought out at the Hollywood Bowl on Aug. 3, 1967. He served as music director of the newly organized Paris Phil from 1988.

Schikaneder, Emanuel (Johannes Joseph), prominent Austrian actor, singer, dramatist, theater director, and composer; b. Straubing, Sept. 1, 1751; d. Vienna, Sept. 21, 1812. He studied at Regensburg's Jesuit Gymnasium, where he was a chorister at the cathedral. He became an actor with F. J. Moser's troupe about 1773, then its director (1778); he met Mozart in Salzburg in 1780. In 1783 he became lessee of Vienna's Kärnthnertortheater until 1784; he was a member of the National Theater (1785–86), then organized his own theater company. Following a sojourn as director of the Regensburg Court Theater (1787–89), he returned to Vienna to assume the directorship of the Freihaus-Theater; he gave up his management duties in 1799, but remained the theater's artistic director until it closed in 1801. He persuaded Mozart to set his play *Die Zauberflöte* to music; with Schikaneder as Papageno, it was first performed on Sept. 30, 1791. In 1801 he opened the Theater an der Wien, but then sold it in 1806; after a period as director of the Brünn theater, he returned to Vienna. He suffered several financial setbacks over the years and died insane. He wrote roughly 100 plays and librettos.

BIBL.: E. von Komorzynski, *E. S.: Ein Beitrag zur Geschichte des deutschen Theaters* (Berlin, 1901; 2d ed., rev., 1951); idem, *Der Vater der Zauberflöte: E. S.s Leben* (Vienna, 1948; 2d ed., 1990).

Schillinger, Joseph (Moiseievich), Russian-born American music theorist and composer; b. Kharkov, Aug. 31, 1895; d. N.Y., March 23, 1943. He studied at the St. Petersburg Cons. with Tcherepnin, Wihtol, and others. He was active as a teacher, conductor, and administrator in Kharkov (1918–22), Moscow, and Leningrad (1922–28). In 1928 he emigrated to the United States and became a naturalized American citizen in 1936; he settled in New York as a teacher of music, mathematics, and art history as well as his own system of composition based on rigid mathematical principles; he taught at the New School for Social Research, N.Y. Univ., and Columbia Univ. Teachers College; he also gave private lessons. Among his pupils were Tommy Dorsey, Vernon Duke, George Gershwin, Benny Goodman, Oscar Levant, and Glenn Miller. Schillinger publ. a short vol. of musical patterns, *Kaleidophone: New Resources of Melody and Harmony* (N.Y., 1940). L. Dowling and A. Shaw ed. and publ. his magnum opus, *The Schillinger System of Musical Composition* (2 vols., N.Y., 1941; 4th ed., 1946); this was followed by *The Mathematical Basis of the Arts* (N.Y., 1948) and *Encyclopedia of Rhythm* (N.Y., 1966). Schillinger was also a composer; his works include *March of the Orient* for Orch. (Leningrad, May 12, 1926); *First Airphonic Suite* for Theremin and Orch. (Cleveland, Nov. 28, 1929; Leo Theremin soloist); *North-Russian Symphony* (1930); *The People and the Prophet*, ballet (1931); piano pieces; songs; etc.

BIBL.: D. Augestine, *Four Theories of Music in the United States, 1900–1950: Cowell, Yasser, Partch, S.* (diss., Univ. of Texas, 1979).

Schillings, Max von, German composer and conductor; b. Duren, April 19, 1868; d. Berlin, July 24, 1933. While attending the Gymnasium at Bonn, he studied violin with O. von Königslow, and piano and composition with K. J. Brambach. He then entered the Univ. of Munich, where he studied law, philosophy, literature, and art. He became associated with Richard Strauss, and under his influence decided to devote himself entirely to music. In 1892 he was engaged as assistant stage director at the Bayreuth Festival; in 1902 he became chorus master. He went to Stuttgart in 1908 as assistant to the Intendant at the Royal Opera, and then was its Generalmusikdirektor (1911–18); upon the inauguration of its new opera theater, he was ennobled as von Schillings; was Intendant of the Berlin State Opera (1919–25). He made several visits as a conductor to the United States. In 1923 he married **Barbara Kemp**. As a composer, he trailed in the path of Wagner, barely avoiding direct imitation. His works include the operas *Ingwelde* (Karlsruhe, Nov. 13, 1894), *Der Pfeifertag* (Schwerin, Nov. 26, 1899; rev. 1931), *Moloch* (Dresden, Dec. 8, 1906), and *Mona Lisa* (Stuttgart, Sept. 26, 1915).

BIBL.: R. Louis, *M. S.* (Leipzig, 1909); A. Richard, *M. S.* (Munich, 1922); W. Raupp, *M. v.S.: Der Kampf eines deutschen Künstlers* (Hamburg, 1935); J. Geuenich and K. Strahn, eds., *Gedenkschrift M. v.S. zum 100. Geburtstag* (Düren, 1968).

Schimon, Adolf, Austrian pianist, singing teacher, and composer; b. Vienna, Feb. 29, 1820; d. Leipzig, June 21, 1887. He studied with Berton, Halévy, and others at the Paris Cons.; he studied the Italian method in Florence, bringing out his opera *Stradella* there in 1846. He was maestro al cembalo at Her Majesty's Theatre in London (1850–53), then at the Italian Opera in Paris (1854–59). In 1858 Flotow brought out Schimon's comic opera *List um List at Schwerin*. He taught singing at the Leipzig Cons. (1874–77) and in Munich (1877–86). He married **Anna Schimon-Regan** in 1872.

Schimon-Regan, Anna, distinguished German soprano; b. Aich, near Karlsbad, Sept. 18, 1841; d. Munich, April 18, 1902. In 1859 she had her first singing lessons from Mme. Schubert in Karlsbad; the next year her aunt, **Caroline Unger**, took her to Florence and taught her until 1864. She was then engaged at the court opera in Hannover (1864–67); during the winter of 1867–68 she sang in Berlioz's concerts in St. Petersburg. She made her first visit to England in 1869, appearing in concerts with Unger; she gave song recitals there every winter until 1875. In 1872 she married **Adolf Schimon**, and settled in Munich.

Schindelmeisser, Louis (Ludwig Alexander Balthasar), German conductor and composer; b. Königsberg, Dec. 8, 1811; d. Darmstadt, March 30, 1864. He studied with Marx and Gährich in Berlin, then with his stepbrother, Heinrich Dorn, in Leipzig (1831), where he was befriended by Wagner. After conducting in Salzburg, Innsbruck, Graz, Berlin (1837), Pest (1838–47), Hamburg, Frankfurt am Main, and Wiesbaden, he was Hofkapellmeister in Darmstadt (from 1853).

WORKS: DRAMATIC: OPERAS: *Peter von Szapáry* (Budapest, Aug. 8, 1839); *Malwina* (Budapest, 1841); *Der Rächer*, after Corneille's *Le Cid* (Budapest, April 4, 1846); *Melusine* (Darmstadt, 1861). BALLET: *Diavolina*.

Schiørring, Nils, Danish musicologist; b. Copenhagen, April 8, 1910. He studied musicology with Abrahamsen and Larsen at the Univ. of Copenhagen (M.A., 1933); concurrently he took lessons in cello from L. Jensen. He completed his musicological training at the Univ. of Copenhagen (Ph.D., 1950, with the diss. *Det 16. og 17. århundredes verdslige danske visesang*; publ. in Copenhagen, 1950). He worked at the Copenhagen Music History Museum (1932–53); also wrote music criticism and served as ed. of *Dansk musiktidsskrift* (1943–45) and *Dansk årbog for musikforskning* (with S. Sorensen; from 1961). In 1950 he joined the faculty of the Univ. of Copenhagen, retiring in 1980.

WRITINGS (all publ. in Copenhagen): *Billeder fra 125 aars musikliv (1827–1952)* (1952); *Selma Nielsens Viser* (1956); *Allemande og fransk ouverture* (1957); *Musikkens vije* (1959; 2d ed., 1964); ed. with S. Kragh-Jacobsen, *August Bournonville: Lettres à la maison de son enfance* (1969–70); with N. Jensen, *Deutsch-dänische Begegnungen um 1800: Künst, Dichtung, Musik* (1974); *Musikkens Historie i Danmark* (1978).

Schiøtz, Aksel (Hauch), famous Danish tenor, baritone, and pedagogue; b. Roskilde, Sept. 1, 1906; d. Copenhagen, April 19, 1975. His father was an architect, and he urged Schiøtz to follow an academic career; accordingly, he enrolled at the Univ. of Copenhagen in language studies (M.A., 1929). He also studied singing, first at the Danish Royal Opera School in Copenhagen, and later with John Forsell in Stockholm. He made his concert debut in 1938; his operatic debut followed in 1939 as Ferrando in *Così fan tutte* at the Royal Danish Theater in Copenhagen, and he soon gained wide recognition as a Mozartian and as a lieder artist. In 1946 he made appearances in England; in 1948 he visited the United States. His career was tragically halted when he developed a brain tumor in 1950, which led to an impairment of his speech; however, he regained his capacities as a singer and gave concerts as a baritone. From 1955 to 1958 he taught voice at the Univ. of Minnesota; from 1958 to 1961 he was a prof. of voice at the Royal Cons. of Music and the Univ. of Toronto; from 1961 to 1968, at the Univ. of Colo., and from 1968 at the Royal Danish School of Educational Studies in Copenhagen. In 1977 a memorial fund was formed in the United States to preserve his memory by granting scholarships in art songs. He publ. *The Singer and His Art* (N.Y., 1969).

BIBL.: G. Schitz, *Kunst og Kamp: Gerd og A. S.* (Copenhagen, 1951).

Schipa, Tito (Raffaele Attilio Amadeo), famous Italian tenor; b. Lecce, Jan. 2, 1888; d. N.Y., Dec. 16, 1965. He studied with A. Gerunda in Lecce and with E. Piccoli in Milan, and began his career as a composer of piano pieces and songs, then turned to singing, and in 1910 made his operatic debut at Vercelli in *La Traviata*. After numerous appearences in Europe, he was engaged by the Chicago Opera (1919–32); he made his first appearance with the Metropolitan Opera in New York on Nov. 23, 1932, as Nemorino in *L'elisir d'amore*; continued to sing with the Metropolitan until 1935, then again in 1941. Schipa made extensive tours of Europe and South America, as well as in the United States. He retired from the operatic stage in 1954, but continued to give concerts until late in life. Among his greatest roles were Des Grieux in *Manon*, the Duke of Mantua, Don Ottavio, and Werther. He wrote an operetta, *La Principessa Liana* (1935); a Mass (1929); several songs; also wrote a book, *Si confessi* (Genoa, 1961). His autobiography appeared in 1993.

Schipper, Emil (Zacharias), Austrian bass-baritone; b. Vienna, Aug. 19, 1882; d. there, July 20, 1957. He studied in Vienna and with Guarino in Milan. He made his operatic debut at the German Theater in Prague in 1904 as Telramund, then sang in Linz (1911–12), at the Vienna Volksoper (1912–15), the Bavarian Court (later State) Opera (1916–22), and the Vienna State Opera (1922–28); he also made guest appearances at Covent Garden in London (1924–28), in Chicago (1928–29), and in Salzburg (1930; 1935–36). His finest roles were in operas by Wagner and R. Strauss. He was married to **Maria Olczewska**.

Schippers, Thomas, greatly gifted American conductor; b. Kalamazoo, Mich., March 9, 1930; d. N.Y., Dec. 16, 1977. He played piano in public at the age of 6, and was a church organist at 14. He studied piano at the Curtis Inst. of Music in Philadelphia (1944–45) and privately with Olga Samaroff (1946–47); subsequently he attended Yale Univ., where he took some composition lessons from Hindemith. In 1948 he won 2d prize in the contest for young conductors organized by the Philadelphia Orch. He then took a job as organist at the Greenwich Village Presbyterian Church in New York; he joined a group of young musicians in an enterprise called the Lemonade Opera Co., and conducted this group for several years. On March 15, 1950, he conducted the N.Y. premiere of Menotti's opera *The Consul*; he also conducted the television premiere of his *Amahl and the Night Visitors* (N.Y., Dec. 24, 1951). On April 9, 1952, he made his first appearance at the N.Y. City Opera conducting Menotti's *The Old Maid and the Thief*, remaining on its roster until 1954. On March 26, 1955, he led the N.Y. Phil. as guest conductor. On Dec. 23, 1955, he made his debut at the Metropolitan Opera in New York conducting *Don Pasquale*; he conducted there regularly in subsequent seasons. From 1958 to 1976 he was associated with Menotti at the Spoleto Festival of Two Worlds. Other engagements included appearances with the N.Y. Phil., which he accompanied in 1959 to the Soviet Union as an alternate conductor with Leonard Bernstein. In 1962 he conducted at La Scala the premiere of Manuel de Falla's cantata *Atlántida*. In 1964 he conducted at the Bayreuth Festival. He was a favorite conductor for new works at the Metropolitan Opera; he conducted the first performance of Menotti's opera *The Last Savage* and the opening of the new home of the Metropolitan with Samuel Barber's *Antony and Cleopatra* (Sept. 16, 1966); he also conducted the first production at the Metropolitan of the original version of Mussorgsky's *Boris Godunov* (1974). In 1970 he was appointed music director of the Cincinnati Sym. Orch., one of the few American-born conductors to occupy a major sym. orch. post; he was also a prof. at the Univ. of Cincinnati College-Cons. of Music (from 1972). There was an element of tragedy in his life. Rich, handsome, and articulate, he became a victim of lung cancer, and was unable to open the scheduled season of the Cincinnati Sym. Orch. in the fall of 1977; in a grateful gesture the management gave him the title of conductor laureate; he bequeathed a sum of $5,000,000 to the orch. His wife died of cancer in 1973. When he conducted *La forza del destino* at the Metropolitan Opera on March 4, 1960, the baritone Leonard Warren collapsed and died on the stage.

Schirmer, Ulf, German conductor; b. Eschenhausen, near Bremen, Jan. 8, 1959. He received training in composition from Ligeti and in conducting from Horst Stein and Dohnányi. After working as a répétiteur at the Mannheim National Theater (1980), he was named to that position at the Vienna State Opera (1981). He was assistant to Maazel (1982) and Stein (1983) at the Bayreuth Festival, and then conducted at the Vienna State Opera (1984–86), where he subsequently served as 1st conductor (1986–88). From 1988 to 1991 he was Generalmusikdirektor in Wiesbaden. He appeared as a guest conductor at the Salzburg Festival (1989), with the Vienna Phil. (1992), at Milan's La Scala (1993), and with the Berlin Phil. (1993), among others. From 1995 to 1999 he was chief conductor of the Danish National Radio Sym. Orch. in Copenhagen.

Schiuma, Alfredo, Argentine composer; b. Buenos Aires, July 1, 1885; d. there, July 24, 1963. He studied with Romaniello in Buenos Aires, and later established his own music school there. He wrote several operas in a singable Italianate idiom for Buenos Aires: *Amy Robsart*, based on Walter Scott's novel *Kenilworth* (April 24, 1920), *La Sirocchia* (April 23, 1922), *Tabaré* (Aug. 6, 1925), *Las virgenes del sol* (June 20, 1939), and *La infanta* (Aug. 12, 1941).

Schläger, Hans, Austrian composer; b. Felskirchen, Dec. 5, 1820; d. Salzburg, May 17, 1885. He was a pupil of Preyer at Vienna. He was chorus master of the Männergesangverein (1844–61), then Kapellmeister of the Salzburg Cathedral, and director of the Mozarteum, resigning on his marriage to Countess Zichy in 1867. He wrote the operas *Heinrich und Ilse* (Salzburg, 1869) and *Hans Haidekukuk* (Salzburg, 1873).

Schlick, Barbara, admired German soprano; b. Würzburg, July 21, 1943. She studied at the Würzburg Hochschule für Musik, with Lohmann in Wiesbaden, and with Wesselmann in Essen. In 1966 she joined Adolf Scherbaum's Baroque ensemble as a soloist, and began to sing widely in Europe. In 1972 she toured North America as soloist with Paul Kuentz and his chamber orch. In subsequent years, she appeared as a concert artist and established a strong reputation as an exponent of early music. From 1979 she also sang in Baroque and Classical operas, appearing in Munich, Göttingen, Bern, St. Gallen, and Hamburg. She also taught at the Würzburg Hochschule für Musik.

Schlösser, Louis, German conductor and composer; b. Darmstadt, Nov. 17, 1800; d. there, Nov. 17, 1886. He was pupil of Rinck at Darmstadt, of Seyfried, Mayseder, and Salieri at Vienna, and of Le Sueur and Kreutzer at the Paris Cons. He was court conductor in Darmstadt. His works include the operas *Granada* (Vienna, 1826), *Das Leben ein Traum* (1839), *Die Jugend Karls II. von Spanien* (1847), *Die Braut des Herzogs* (1847), and *Benvenuto Cellini*, and the operetta, *Kapitan Hector*. He also composed a melodrama, *Die Jahreszeiten*, music to *Faust*, and various ballets and entr'actes. His son was the German pianist, teacher, and composer (Karl Wilhelm) Adolf Schlösser (1830–1913).

Schlosser, Max, distinguished German tenor; b. Amberg, Oct. 17, 1835; d. Utting am Ammersee, Sept. 2, 1916. He sang in Zürich, St. Gallen, and Augsburg, but then decided to become a baker. Still, he did not abandon hopes for a stage career. He met Bülow, who entrusted him with the role of David at the premiere of *Die Meistersinger von Nürnberg* in Munich in 1868; he remained a member of the Munich Court Opera until his retirement in 1904. He also sang at Bayreuth and made guest appearances with Neumann's traveling opera company. He was principally known for his fine performances of the Wagnerian repertoire.

Schlusnus, Heinrich, eminent German baritone; b. Braubach am Rhein, Aug. 6, 1888; d. Frankfurt am Main, June 18, 1952. He studied voice in Frankfurt am Main and Berlin. He made his operatic debut as the Herald in *Lohengrin* at the Hamburg Opera on Jan. 1, 1914; he was then on its roster for the 1914–15 season; he subsequently sang in Nuremberg (1915–17), then was a leading member of the Berlin Royal (later State) Opera, remaining there until 1945; he also appeared in Chicago (1927–28), Bayreuth (1933), and Paris (1937). He was renowned as a lieder artist.

BIBL.: E. von Naso and A. Schlusnus, *H. S.: Mensch und Sänger* (Hamburg, 1957).

Schlüter, Erna, German contralto, later soprano; b. Oldenburg, Feb. 5, 1904; d. Hamburg, Dec. 1, 1969. She made her operatic debut as a contralto in Oldenburg in 1922. Turning to soprano roles, she sang in Mannheim (1925–30) and Düsseldorf (1930–40). From 1940 to 1956 she was a member of the Hamburg State Opera. On Nov. 26, 1947, she made her Metropolitan Opera debut in New York as Isolde, remaining on the roster for one season. In 1948 she appeared at the Salzburg Festival as Beethoven's Leonore. She also made guest appearances at London's Covent Garden, the Vienna State Opera, in Amsterdam, and in Brussels. Her most famous role was Elektra.

Schmid, Ernst Fritz, eminent German musicologist; b. Tübingen, March 7, 1904; d. Augsburg, Jan. 20, 1960. He studied violin, viola, and viola d'amore at the Munich Academy of Music; he took private lessons in theory and conducting, then studied musicology at the Univs. of Munich (with Sandberger), Freiburg im Breisgau (with Gurlitt), Tübingen (with Hasse), and Vienna (with Haas, Orel et al.); he received his Ph.D. from the Univ. of Tübingen in 1929 with the diss. *Carl Philipp Emanuel Bach und seine Kammermusik* (publ. in Kassel, 1931); he completed his Habilitation as a Privatdozent in musicology at the Univ. of Graz in 1934 with his *Joseph Haydn: Ein Buch von Vorfahren und Heimat des Meisters* (publ. in Kassel, 1934). He became a prof. at the Univ. of Tübingen in 1935 and also founded the Schwabisches Landesmusikarchiv; he left Tübingen in 1937 to devote himself to private research. During World War II he served in the German army. In 1948 he founded the Mozartgemeinde, and in 1951 the German Mozartgesellschaft. In 1954 he became academic director of the Neue Mozart Ausgabe; from 1955 he oversaw the publ. of the new critical ed. of Mozart's complete works, the *Neue Ausgabe Sämtlicher Werke*. In addition to his valuable research on Mozart, he discovered the private music collection of Emperor Franz II in Graz in 1933; this important collection is now housed in Vienna's Nationalbibliothek.

WRITINGS: *Wolfgang Amadeus Mozart* (Lübeck, 1934; 3d ed., 1955); *Die Orgeln der Abtei Amorbach* (Buchen, 1938); ed. *Ein schwäbisches Mozartbuch* (Lorch and Stuttgart, 1948); *Musik am Hofe der Fürsten von Löwenstein-Wertheim-Rosenberg, 1720–1750* (Würzburg, 1953); *Musik an den schwäbischen Zollernhöfen der Renaissance* (Kassel, 1962).

BIBL.: W. Fischer et al., eds., *In memoriam E. F. S., 1904–1960: Ein Gedenkblatt für seine Angehörigen und Freunde* (Recklinghausen, 1961).

Schmid, Heinrich Kaspar, German composer and teacher; b. Landau an der Isar, Bavaria, Sept. 11, 1874; d. Munich, Jan. 8, 1953. He studied with Thuille and Bussmeyer at the Munich Academy of Music (1899–1903). In 1903 he went to Athens, where he taught music at the Odeon; in 1905 he returned to Munich and was on the faculty of the Academy of Music until 1921; he then was director of the Karlsruhe Cons. (1921–24) and of the Augsburg Cons. (1924–32). His eyesight failed him and he was totally blind during the last years of his life. As a composer, he followed the Romantic tradition of the Bavarian School; he wrote a great number of lieder, and composed Singspiels in a folklike manner.

BIBL.: H. Roth, *H. K. S.* (Munich, 1921).

Schmidt, Andreas, German baritone; b. Düsseldorf, June 30, 1960. He studied with Ingeborg Reichelt in Düsseldorf and with Fischer-Dieskau in Berlin. In 1984 he made his operatic debut as Dr. Malatesta at the Deutsche Oper in Berlin. After making his first appearance at London's Covent Garden as Valentin in 1986, he returned to Berlin to create the title role in Rihm's *Oedipus* in 1987. In 1990 he created the role of Ryuji in Henze's *Das verratene Meer* in Berlin and sang Olivier in *Capriccio* in Salzburg. He was engaged as Lysiart in *Euryanthe* at the Aix-en-Provence Festival in 1993. On Nov. 18, 1996, he made his N.Y. recital debut. In 1997 he sang in the Brahms centenary concert at London's Wigmore Hall. As a soloist with orchs. and as a lieder artist, he has sung throughout the world. Among his other operatic roles are Mozart's Count, Don Giovanni, Papageno, and Guglielmo, Posa, Amfortas, Wolfram, and Méphistophélès.

Schmidt, Gustav, German conductor and composer; b. Weimar, Sept. 1, 1816; d. Darmstadt, Feb. 11, 1882. He studied with Hummel, Eberwein, and Lobe in Weimar and with Mendelssohn in Leipzig, then conducted opera in Brünn (1841–44), Würzburg (1845), Frankfurt am Main (1846; 1851–61), Wiesbaden (1849), Leipzig (1864–76), and Mainz; he was court Kapellmeister in Darmstadt (from 1876). He was a determined champion of Wagner and Berlioz. He wrote the operas *Prinz Eugen* (Frankfurt am Main, 1847), *Weibertreue or Die Weiber von Weinsberg* (Weimar, 1858), *La Réole* (Breslau, 1863), and *Alibi* (Weimar, 1880).

Schmidt, Johann Christoph, German organist and composer; b. Hohnstein, near Pirna, Aug. 6, 1664; d. Dresden, April 13, 1728. He entered the Dresden court chapel as a chorister in 1676, where he received training from Christoph Bernhard. After serving as an instrumentalist in the Court Orch., he became master of the choristers in 1687 and 2d organist in 1692. In 1694 he went to Italy to complete his training. Upon his return to Dresden, he was made deputy Kapellmeister and chamber organist (1696). In 1698 he was promoted to principal Kapellmeister, pursuing his duties in Kraków and Warsaw as well as in Dresden, since he was responsible for the music for both the Saxon electoral and Polish courts. He also served as Kapellmeister for the Protestant and Catholic church music at the court, turning over his duties for the Catholic church music to J. D. Heinichen in 1717. Under Schmidt's leadership, the Dresden Court Orch. became one of the most celebrated in Europe. He wrote an opera seria, *Latona in Delo* (n.d.) and a divertissement, *Les Quatre Saisons* (Dresden, Sept. 23, 1719).

Schmidt, Johann Philipp Samuel, German composer; b. Königsberg, Sept. 8, 1779; d. Berlin, May 9, 1853. He settled in Berlin, where he studied with J. G. Naumann and then took a government position; also devoted much time to performing, writing on music, and composing. He wrote several operas, including *Das Fischermädchen* (1818).

Schmidt, Joseph, Romanian tenor; b. Bavideni, Bukovina, March 4, 1904; d. Zürich, Nov. 16, 1942. He studied at the Berlin Cons. In 1928 he began his career as a radio singer and won great popularity in Germany. In 1933 he went to Belgium; in 1938 he was briefly in America, then settled in Switzerland, where he died in an internment camp. His voice was regarded as of great lyric expressiveness, but because of his height (he stood only 4 feet, 10 inches in height), he was unable to appear in opera.

BIBL.: A. Fassbind, *J. S.: Ein Lied Geht um die Welt: Spuren einer Legende* (Zürich, 1992).

Schmidt, Ole, Danish conductor and composer; b. Copenhagen, July 14, 1928. He studied at the Royal Danish Cons. of Music in Copenhagen (1947–55) and received training in conducting from Albert Wolff, Celibidache, and Kubelik. From 1959 to 1965 he was conductor of the Royal Danish Opera and Ballet in Copenhagen. After serving as chief conductor of the Hamburg Sym. Orch. (1970–71), he was a guest conductor of the Danish Radio Sym. Orch. in Copenhagen (from 1971). He also appeared as a guest conductor throughout Europe. Following his first appearance as a guest conductor of the BBC Sym. Orch. in London in 1977, he appeared as a guest conductor of all the BBC regional orchs. From 1979 to 1985 he was chief conductor of the Århus Sym. Orch. In 1980 he made his U.S. debut as a guest conductor of the Oakland (Calif.) Sym. Orch. From 1986 to 1989 he was chief guest conductor of the Royal Northern College of Music in Manchester, England. In 1989–90 he was interim conductor of the Toledo (Ohio) Sym. Orch.

WORKS: DRAMATIC: *Bag taeppet*, ballet (Copenhagen, Oct. 9, 1954); *Feber*, ballet (Copenhagen, Oct. 8, 1957); *Chopiniana*, ballet (Copenhagen, Feb. 2, 1958); *Ballet* (1959; Copenhagen, April 27, 1961); *Udstilling*, opera (Copenhagen, Dec. 5, 1969); *Jeanne d'Arc*, music for C. T. Dreyer's silent film of 1927 (Los Angeles, May 27, 1983); *Dyrefabler og Fabeldyr*, musical fairy tale (Copenhagen, April 26, 1987); *Harald og Tine*, musical (Århus, Sept. 9, 1988).

Schmidt, Trudeliese, German mezzo-soprano; b. Saarbrücken, Nov. 7, 1941. She received her training in Saarbrücken and Rome. In 1965 she made her operatic debut as Hansel in Saarbrücken. In 1969 she became a member of the Deutsche Oper am Rhein in Düsseldorf. From 1971 she appeared in various German music centers, and in 1974 toured Japan with the Bavarian State Opera of Munich. She sang Dorabella at the Glyndebourne Festival in 1976. In subsequent years, she appeared in leading European music centers. In 1985 she was a soloist in Mozart's *Coronation Mass* with Karajan and the Vienna Phil. at a special concert at the Vatican in Rome for Pope John Paul II. She was engaged as Fatima in *Oberon* at Milan's La Scala in 1989. In 1990 she sang Strauss's Composer in Barcelona. She appeared at the Munich Festival in 1997. Among her prominent roles are Cherubino, Rossini's Isabella, Weber's Fatima, and Strauss's Octavian and Composer.

Schmidt, Wolfgang, German tenor; b. Kassel, Aug. 19, 1956. He was a student of Martin Gründler at the Frankfurt am Main Hochschule für Musik. After appearances with the Pocket Opera in Nuremberg, he sang at the Court Theater in Bayreuth (1982–84), in Kiel (1984–86), and in Dortmund (1986–89). In 1989 he sang Wagner's Erik at the Bregenz Festival, and that same year he joined the Deutsche Oper am Rhein in Düsseldorf. In 1991 he was engaged by the Salzburg Festival and the Vienna State Opera. He portrayed Tannhäuser at the Bayreuth Festival in 1992. On April 22, 1993, he made his Metropolitan Opera debut in New York as Siegfried, a role he reprised at Bayreuth in 1994 and at Milan's La Scala in 1997. He also appeared widely as a concert artist.

Schmidt-Görg, Joseph, eminent German musicologist; b. Rüdinghausen, near Dortmund, March 19, 1897; d. Bonn, April 3, 1981. He studied musicology with Schiedermair and Schmitz at the Univ. of Bonn (Ph.D., 1926, with the diss. *Die Messen des Clemens non Papa*; completed his Habilitation there in 1930 with his *Die Mitteltontemperatur*). He became Schiedermair's assistant in the Beethoven Archives in Bonn in 1927; he later served as director of the archives (1946–72) and concurrently lectured on musicology at the Univ. of Bonn (1930–65). On his 70th birthday he was presented with a Festschrift under the friendly Latin title *Colloquium amicorum* (Bonn, 1967), containing a catalogue of his writings. His publs. include *Unbekannte Manuskripte zu Beethovens weltlicher und geistlicher Gesangsmusik* (Bonn, 1928), *Katalog der Handschriften des Beethoven-Hauses und Beethoven-Archivs Bonn* (Bonn, 1935), *Nicolas Gombert: Leben und Werk* (Bonn, 1938), and *Ludwig van Beethoven* (with H. Schmidt; Bonn, 1969; Eng. tr., N.Y., 1970).

Schmidt-Isserstedt, Hans, respected German conductor; b. Berlin, May 5, 1900; d. Holm-Holstein, near Hamburg, May 28, 1973. He studied composition with Schreker at the Berlin Hochschule für Musik; he also took courses at the Univs. of Berlin, Heidelberg, and Münster. In 1923 he became a répétiteur at the Wuppertal Opera; after conducting opera in Rostock (1928–31) and Darmstadt (1931–33), he held the post of 1st conductor at the Hamburg State Opera (1935–43); he then joined the Deutsche Oper in Berlin, where he was made Generalmusikdirektor in 1944. In 1945 he was mandated by the British occupation authorities with the direction of the music section of the Hamburg Radio; he organized the North German Radio Sym. Orch., which he led with notable distinction until his retirement in 1971; he was also chief conductor of the Stockholm Phil. (1955–64). He appeared widely as a guest conductor and also conducted at Covent Garden in London and at the Bavarian State Opera in Munich. He was especially admired for his cultured performances of the Austro-German repertoire.

Schmitt, Aloys, German pianist and composer, father of **Georg Aloys Schmitt**; b. Erlenbach, Aug. 26, 1788; d. Frankfurt am Main, July 25, 1866. He studied composition with André at Offenbach. In 1816 he went to Frankfurt am Main, where he remained all his life with the exception of short stays in Berlin and Hannover (1825–29). He composed 4 operas: *Der Doppelgänger* (Hannover, 1827), *Valeria* (Mannheim, 1832), *Das Osterfest zu Paderborn* (Frankfurt am Main, 1843), and *Die Tochter der Wüste* (Frankfurt am Main, 1845), as well as 2 oratorios, *Moses* and *Ruth*, but he is principally known and appreciated for his numerous piano compositions. His brother, Jacob Schmitt (1803–1853), was a pianist, teacher, and composer.

BIBL.: H. Henkel, *Leben und Wirken von Dr. A. S.* (Frankfurt am Main, 1873).

Schmitt, Georg Aloys, German pianist, conductor, and composer, son of **Aloys Schmitt**; b. Hannover, Feb. 2, 1827; d. during a rehearsal in Dresden, Oct. 15, 1902. He studied with his father; after theory training from Vollweiler in Heidelberg, he toured Europe as a pianist; subsequently he devoted himself mainly to theatrical conducting. He was court conductor at Schwerin (1857–92), and in 1893 was appointed director of the Mozartverein in Dresden, which had a multitudinous choral ensemble (some 1,400 members) and its own orch. He wrote 3 operas; he also ed. and completed Mozart's Mass in C minor (1901). His uncle, Jacob Schmitt (1803–53), was a pianist, teacher, and composer.

Schmitt-Walter, Karl, German baritone; b. Gernersheim am Rhein, Dec. 23, 1900; d. Kreuth, Oberbayern, Jan. 14, 1985. He studied in Nuremberg and Munich. He made his operatic debut in 1921 in Oberhausen, then sang in Nuremberg, Saarbrücken, and Dortmund; he was a member of the Wiesbaden Opera (1929–34), the Berlin Deutsche Oper (1934–50), and the Bavarian State Opera in Munich (1950–61); he also sang at Bayreuth and Salzburg. In 1957 he became a prof. of voice at the Munich Academy of Music.

Schmitz, Eugen, German musicologist; b. Neuburg an der Donau, Bavaria, July 12, 1882; d. Leipzig, July 10, 1959. He studied musicology with Sandberger and Kroyer at the Univ. of Munich (Ph.D., 1905, with the diss. *Der Nürnberger Organist Johann Staden: Beiträge zur Würdigung seiner musikgeschichtlichen Stellung*; extracts publ. in Leipzig, 1906), then completed his Habilitation there in 1909 with his *Beiträge zur Geschichte der italienischen Kammerkantate im 17. Jahrhundert* (publ. in Leipzig, 1914, as *Geschichte der Kantate und des geistlichen Konzerts I. Theil: Geschichte der weltlichen Solokantate*; 2d ed., 1955, as *Geschichte der weltlichen Solokantate*). He taught music at the Dresden Technische Hochschule (1916–39). From 1939 to 1953 he was director of the Musikbibliothek Peters in Leipzig.

WRITINGS: *Hugo Wolf* (Leipzig, 1906); *Richard Strauss als Musikdramatiker: eine ästhetische-kritische Studie* (Munich, 1907); *Richard Wagner* (Leipzig, 1909; 2d ed., 1918); *Harmonielehre als Theorie: Aesthetik und Geschichte der musikalischen Harmonik*

(Munich, 1911); *Palestrina* (Leipzig, 1914; 2d ed., 1954); *Musikästhetik* (Leipzig, 1915; 2d ed., 1925); *Orlando di Lasso* (Leipzig, 1915; 2d ed., 1954); *Klavier, Klaviermusik und Klavierspiel* (Leipzig, 1919); *Richard Wagner: Wie wir ihn heute sehen* (Dresden, 1937); *Schuberts Auswirkung auf die deutsche Musik bis zu Hugo Wolf und Bruckner* (Leipzig, 1954); *Unverwelkter Volksliedstil: J. A. P. Schulz und seine "Lieder im Volkston"* (Leipzig, 1956).

Schmöhe, Georg, German conductor; b. Gummersbach, Feb. 16, 1939. He studied at the Berlin Hochschule für Musik and the Milan Cons., and also received training from Karajan, Celibidache, Ferrara, and Blacher. He was a conductor in Bern (1964–65), Essen (1965–67), Wuppertal (1967–70), Kiel (1970–73), and Düsseldorf (1973–74). From 1974 to 1980 he was Generalmusikdirektor in Bielefeld, and from 1978 to 1982 he was chief conductor of the Caracas Sym. Orch. He was chief conductor of the Nüremberg Sym. Orch. from 1989 to 1992. From 1992 he was Generalmusikdirektor of the Kassel State Theater. He also was a guest conductor with opera houses and orchs. in Europe.

Schnebel, Dieter, eminent German composer; b. Lahr, March 14, 1930. At 10, he began piano lessons with Wilhelm Siebler. After further piano instruction from Wilhelm Resch in Villingen (1945–49), he studied theory and music history with Erich Doflein at the Freiburg im Breisgau Hochschule für Musik (1949–52). He also attended the summer courses in new music in Darmstadt beginning in 1950. He completed his studies at the Univ. of Tübingen (1952–56), where he took courses in theology, philosophy, and musicology, receiving his doctorate with a thesis on Schoenberg's dynamics. From 1963 to 1970 he taught religion in Frankfurt am Main, and then religion and music in Munich from 1970 to 1976. He also devoted increasing attention to his career as a composer. In 1976 he was a prof. of experimental music and musicology at the Berlin Hochschule für Musik. In 1991 he was made a member of the Berlin Akademie der Künste. The complex construction of his early works gave way in 1968 to the simpler forms intended for wider audiences; in 1984 he began a "third period" of major forms as collections of traditions and innovation, first the mass (*Miss [Dahlemer Messe]*), then the symphony (*Sinfonie X*) and opera (*Majakovskis Tod*; Venice, Sept. 1996). Among his writings are *Mauricio Kagel: Musik, Theater, Film* (1970), *Denkbare Musik: Schriften 1952–72* (1972), *MO-NO: Musik zum Lesen* (1973), and *Anschläge-Ausschläge: Texte zur Neuen Musik* (1994). In his music, Schnebel follows a conceptually sophisticated and highly avant-garde course in which he makes use of such unusual materials as vocal noise, breath, and graphics.

WORKS: MUSIC THEATER: *ki-no (Räume 1)* (1963–67; Munich, July 10, 1967); *Maulwerke* (1968–74; Donaueschingen, Oct. 20, 1974); *Körper-Sprache* (1979–80; Metz, Nov. 20, 1980); *Jowaegerli (Tradition IV, 1)* (1982–83; Baden-Baden, June 26, 1983); *Zeichen-Sprache* (1987–89; Berlin, April 12, 1989); *Chili (Tradition IV, 2)* (1989–91; Hamburg, May 12, 1991).

BIBL.: H.-K. Metzger and R. Riehn, eds., *D. S.* (Munich, 1980); W. Grünzweig, G. Schröder, and M. Supper, eds., *S. 60.* (Hofheim, 1990).

Schnéevoigt, Georg (Lennart), prominent Finnish conductor; b. Vyborg, Nov. 8, 1872; d. Malmö, Nov. 28, 1947. He received training in cello in Helsinki, with Karl Schröder in Sondershausen, and with Julius Klengel in Leipzig. He then continued his musical studies in Brussels, Dresden, and with Robert Fuchs in Vienna. Returning to Helsinki, he served as principal cellist in the Phil. (1895–98; 1899–1903) and as a cello teacher at the Music Inst. In 1901 he launched his conducting career in Riga. From 1904 to 1908 he was conductor of the Kaim Orch. in Munich. After conducting the Kiev Sym. Orch. (1908–09), he was conductor of the Riga Sym. Orch. (1912–14). He also conducted the Helsinki Sym. Orch. (1912–14); in 1914 it merged with Kajanus's Helsinki Phil. to form the Helsinki City Orch. with Schnéevoigt as coconductor (1916–32). From 1932 to 1941 Schnéevoigt was its sole conductor. He also was conductor of the Stockholm Konsertförening (1915–21), founder-conductor of the Christiania (later Oslo) Phil. (1919–27), conductor in Düsseldorf (1924–26), of the Los Angeles Phil. (1927–29), and of the Riga Opera (1929–32). Subsequently he conducted in Malmö. In 1907 he married the pianist and teacher Sigrid Ingeborg Sundgren (b. Helsinki, June 17, 1878; d. Stockholm, Sept. 14, 1953). She studied at the Helsinki Music Inst. (1886–94) and with Busoni in Berlin (1894–97). From 1901 she taught at the Helsinki Music Inst. She also appeared as a soloist with orchs., often under the direction of her husband, and as a recitalist.

Schneider, Georg Abraham, German horn player, oboist, conductor, and composer; b. Darmstadt, April 19, 1770; d. Berlin, Jan. 19, 1839. He studied with J. W. Magnold in Darmstadt, where he became a member of the court chapel in 1787; later he took courses in theory and composition with J. G. Portmann. In 1795 he joined the Rheinsberg Court Orch., then settled in Berlin and became a member of the royal chapel in 1803. He founded a series of subscription concerts in 1807 and the Musikalische Übungsakademie zur Bildung der Liebhaber in 1818; he also was conductor of the Reval theater (1813–16). He was made music director of Berlin's royal theater in 1820 and then its Kapellmeister in 1825; he taught at the music school of the royal theater and at the Prussian Academy of Arts. Among his works are the operettas *Die Orakelspruch, Aucassin und Nicolette, Die Verschworenen, Der Traum*, and *Der Währwolf*; also 13 ballets, music to numerous plays and melodramas, and 2 oratorios.

BIBL.: A. Meyer-Hanno, *G. A. S. und seine Stellung im Musikleben Berlins* (Berlin, 1965).

Schneider, Hortense (Caroline-Jeanne), French soprano; b. Bordeaux, April 30, 1833; d. Paris, May 6, 1920. Following her debut as Inès in *La favorite* in Agen (May 15, 1853), she went to Paris and joined the Bouffes-Parisiens in 1855. She sang at the Variétés (1856–58) and the Palais-Royal (1858–64), and then scored a remarkable success when Offenbach chose her to create the title role in his *La belle Hélène* (Dec. 17, 1864). Her popularity increased when she created the title roles in his *La Grande Duchessse de Gérolstein* (April 12, 1867) and *La Périchole* (Oct. 6, 1868). She then appeared in London (1868–69) and St. Petersburg (1872). Her career off the stage was a colorful one, more than a match for the roles she played on stage.

BIBL.: M. Rouff and T. Casevitz, *H. S.: La vie de fête sous le Second Empire* (Paris, 1931).

Schneider, Peter, Austrian conductor; b. Vienna, March 26, 1939. He received training in conducting from Swarowsky at the Vienna Academy of Music. In 1959 he made his debut conducting Handel's *Giulio Cesare* at the Salzburg Landestheater. He was named to the position of 1st conductor at the Heidelberg Theater in 1961, and at the Deutsche Oper am Rhein in Düsseldorf in 1968. From 1978 to 1985 he was Generalmusikdirektor in Bremen. He conducted at the Bayreuth Festival for the first time in 1981, and led a *Ring* cycle there in 1987. From 1985 to 1987 he was Generalmusikdirektor of the Mannheim National Theater. He was a conductor with the Vienna State Opera during its visit to London's Covent Garden and Tokyo in 1986. From 1993 to 1998 he was Generalmusikdirektor of the Bavarian State Opera in Munich. As a guest conductor, he appeared with various opera companies in Europe and the United States.

Schneider-Trnavský, Mikuláš, Slovak choral conductor and composer; b. Trnava, May 24, 1881; d. Bratislava, May 28, 1958. He studied in Budapest, Vienna, and Prague. He was choirmaster of the cathedral of St. Mikuláš in Trnava (1909–58) and was named a National Artist in 1956. He publ. several valuable collections of Slovak folk songs, arranged with piano accompaniment: *Sbierka slovenských ludových piesní* (2 vols., 1905–10); *Sbierka slovenských národných piesní* (5 sections, Bratislava, 1930; new ed., Prague, 1935–40); *50 Slovakische Volkslieder* (Bratislava, 1943). He also publ. a book of memoirs, *Usmevy a slzy* (Smiles and Tears; Bratislava, 1959). Among his compositions is *Bellarosa*, operetta (1941).

BIBL.: J. Samko, *M. S.-T.-phol'ad na život a dielo* (Bratislava, 1965).

Schneitzhoeffer, Jean, French composer; b. Toulouse, Oct. 13, 1785; d. Paris, Oct. 4, 1852. He studied with Catel at the Paris Cons. After serving as timpanist at the Paris Opéra (1815–23), he was appointed chef du chant there; from 1831 to 1850 he was in charge of choral classes at the Paris Cons. He composed several ballet scores for the Paris Opéra, of which *La Sylphide* (1832), which he wrote for the famous dancer Maria Taglioni, became a perennial favorite. His other ballets are *Proserpine* (1818), *Zémire et Azor* (1824), and *Mars et Venus*.

Schnittke, Alfred (Garrievich), prominent Russian composer of German descent; b. Engels, near Saratov, Nov. 24, 1934; d. Hamburg, Aug. 3, 1998. He studied piano in Vienna (1946–48), where his father was a correspondent of a German-language Soviet newspaper; he then took courses in composition with Golubev and in instrumentation with Rakov at the Moscow Cons. (1953–58); after serving on its faculty (1962–72), he devoted himself fully to composition. He pursued many trips abroad, and in 1981 was a guest lecturer at the Vienna Hochschule für Musik and Darstellende Künst. In 1981 he was elected a member of the Bayerische Akademie der Schönen Künste. In 1985 he survived a serious heart attack. In 1988 and again in 1991 he suffered debilitating strokes. After writing in a conventional manner, he became acutely interested in the new Western techniques, particularly in serialism and "sonorism," in which dynamic gradations assume thematic significance; soon he became known as one of the boldest experimenters in modernistic composition in Soviet Russia.

WORKS: DRAMATIC: OPERAS: *Odinnadtsataya Zapoved* (The 11th Commandment; 1962; unfinished); *Historia von D. Johann Fausten* (1989–93); *Zhizn's idiotom* (Life With an Idiot; 1990–91; Amsterdam, April 13, 1992); *Gesualdo* (1993–94; Vienna, May 26, 1995); *Historia von D. Johann Fausten* (1994; Hamburg, June 22, 1995). BALLETS: *Labirinti* (Labyrinths; 1971; Leningrad, June 7, 1978); *Zhyoltïy zvuk* (Yellow Sound), after Kandinsky (Saint Bomme, France, 1974); *Sketches*, after Gogol (1984; Moscow, Jan. 16, 1985; in collaboration with E. Denisov, S. Gubaidulina, and G. Rozhdestvensky); *Peer Gynt*, after Ibsen (1986; Hamburg, Jan. 1989). Also incidental music to plays and many film scores. ORATORIO: *Nagasaki* for Mezzo-soprano, Chorus, and Orch. (1958).

BIBL.: D. Shulgin, *Gody neizvestnosti A. S.: Besedy s kompozitorom* (Moscow, 1993).

Schnoor, Hans, distinguished German writer on music; b. Neumünster, Oct. 4, 1893; d. Bielefeld, Jan. 15, 1976. He studied with Riemann and Schering at the Univ. of Leipzig, where he received his Ph.D. with the diss. *Das Buxheimer Orgelbuch* in 1919. He was a music critic in Dresden and Leipzig (1922–26), then music ed. of the *Dresdner Anzeiger* (1926–45). He was an authority on the life and music of Weber.

WRITINGS: *Musik der germanischen Völker im XIX. und XX. Jahrhundert* (Breslau, 1926); with G. Kinsky and R. Haas, *Geschichte der Musik in Bildern* (Leipzig, 1929; Eng. tr., 1930); *Weber auf dem Welttheater* (Dresden, 1942; 4th ed., 1963); *Weber: Ein Lebensbild aus Dresdner Sicht* (Dresden, 1947); *400 Jahre deutscher Musikkultur: Zum Jubiläum der Staatskapelle und zur Geschichte der Dresdner Oper* (Dresden, 1948); *Geschichte der Musik* (1953); *Weber: Gestalt und Schöpfung* (Dresden, 1953; 2d ed., rev., 1974); *Oper, Operette, Konzert: Ein praktisches Nachschlagsbuch* (Gutersloh, 1955); ed. *Bilderatlas zur Musikgeschichte* (Brussels, 1960; 2d ed., 1963); *Harmonie und Chaos* (Munich, 1962); *Musik und Theater ohne eigene Dach* (Hagen, 1969); *Die Stunde des Rosenkavalier* (Munich, 1969).

Schnorr von Carolsfeld, Ludwig, greatly admired German tenor; b. Munich, July 2, 1836; d. Dresden, July 21, 1865. He was the son of the noted painter Julius Schnorr von Carolsfeld. After studies with J. Otto in Dresden and at the Leipzig Cons., he was engaged by Eduard Devrient for the Karlsruhe Opera in 1854; he became its principal tenor in 1858, then was the leading tenor at the Dresden Court Opera (from 1860). Wagner chose him to create the role of Tristan in *Tristan und Isolde* (Munich, June 10, 1865); his wife, **Malvina Schnorr von Carolsfeld** (née **Garrigues**), sang Isolde. He was also an outstanding Tannhäuser, and won accolades as an oratorio and lieder artist as well. His death at the age of 29 was widely lamented.

BIBL.: C. Garrigues, *Ein ideales Sängerpaar: L. S.v.C. und Malvina Schnorr von Carolsfeld* (Copenhagen, 1937).

Schnorr von Carolsfeld, Malvina (née **Garrigues**), esteemed German soprano; b. Copenhagen, Dec. 7, 1825; d. Karlsruhe, Feb. 8, 1904. She studied with García in Paris, making her operatic debut in *Robert le diable* in Breslau (1841), and singing there until 1849. After appearances in Coburg, Gotha, and Hamburg, she joined the Karlsruhe Opera in 1854. Wagner chose her to create the role of Isolde in *Tristan und Isolde* (Munich, June 10, 1865), with her husband, **Ludwig Schnorr von Carolsfeld**, singing Tristan. Following his untimely death at the age of 29, she quit the operatic stage and became a convert to spiritualism. She publ. a vol. of poems by her husband and herself in 1867.

BIBL.: C. Garrigues, *Ein ideales Sängerpaar: Ludwig Schnorr von Carolsfeld und M. S.v.C.* (Copenhagen, 1937).

Schnyder von Wartensee, (Franz) Xaver, significant Swiss composer; b. Lucerne, April 18, 1786; d. Frankfurt am Main, Aug. 27, 1868. He had piano lessons at age 16 with P. Heggli, then taught himself to play the double bass, cello, clarinet, viola, and timpani; in 1811 he went to Vienna, where he met Beethoven and studied composition with J. C. Kienlen. After teaching at Pestalozzi's Inst. in Yverdun (1816–17), he settled in Frankfurt am Main. He played recitals on the glass harmonica and piano, taught, composed, and founded the Liederkranz (1828). He founded the Schnyder von Wartensee Foundation in 1847, which sponsored competitions in the sciences and assisted in the publ. of scientific and artistic works. Among his compositions was the opera *Ubaldo* (1811–12; only 1 chorus extant) and the operetta *Heimweh und Heimkehr* (1854; Zürich, Dec. 14, 1855).

BIBL.: *Lebenserinnerungen von X. S. v. W.* (Zürich, 1887; new ed. by W. Schuh, Berlin, 1940).

Schoberlechner, Franz, Austrian pianist and composer; b. Vienna, July 21, 1797; d. Berlin, Jan. 7, 1843. He studied with Hummel in Vienna, making his debut in Hummel's 2d Concerto (1809), written for him; he then continued his training with E. A. Förster. On a pianistic tour to Italy, he produced his opera *I Virtuosi teatrali* at Florence (1814), and the next year became maestro di cappella to the Duchess of Lucca, producing there a 2d opera, *Gli Arabi nelle Gallie* (1816); in 1820 returned to Vienna, where he brought out an opera in German, *Der junge Onkel* (Jan. 14, 1823). He made a trip to Russia in 1823, and there married the singer Sophie dall'Occa (1807–63), with whom he made further tours to Italy and Vienna. He purchased a villa in Florence in 1831, and retired to it some years later.

Schobert, Johann, important composer; b. probably in Silesia, c.1735; d. Paris, Aug. 28, 1767 (with his entire family, except 1 child, from eating poisonous mushrooms). About 1760 he settled in Paris, where he entered the service of the Prince de Conti. His works show the general characteristics of the Mannheim School, although it cannot be proved that he ever was in that city. Mozart was significantly influenced by him, and reworked and incorporated movements of his scores into his own sonatas and piano concertos. Other works include the opéra comique *Le Garde-chasse et le braconnier* (Paris, Jan. 18, 1766).

Schock, Rudolf (Johann), German tenor; b. Duisburg, Sept. 4, 1915; d. Duren-Gürzenich, Nov. 13, 1986. He studied in Cologne, Hannover, and with Robert von der Linde and Laurenz Hofer in Berlin. At the age of 18, he joined the chorus of the Duisburg Opera. In 1937 he made his operatic debut in Braunschweig, where he sang until 1940. After singing in Hannover (1945) and at the Berlin State Opera (1946), he was a member of the Hamburg State Opera (1947–56), with which company he visited the Edinburgh Festival (1952). In 1948 he made his first appearance at the Salzburg Festival as Idomeneo and in 1951 his debut at the Vienna State Opera. In 1959 he made his Bayreuth Festival debut as Walther von Stolzing. He also appeared in operetta. Among his other roles were Tamino, Florestan, Max in *Der Freischütz*, and

Bacchus in *Ariadne auf Naxos*. His autobiography was publ. as *Ach ich hab' in meinerm Herzen* (Berlin and Munich, 1985).

Schoeck, Othmar, eminent Swiss pianist, conductor, and composer; b. Brunnen, Sept. 1, 1886; d. Zürich, March 8, 1957. He was the son of the painter Alfred Schoeck; he went to Zürich, where he took courses at the Industrial College before pursuing musical training with Attenhofer, Freund, Hegar, and Kempter at the Cons. (from 1905); after further studies with Reger in Leipzig (1907–08), he returned to Zürich and conducted the Aussersihl Men's Chorus (1909–15), the Harmonie Men's Chorus (1910–11), and the Teachers' Chorus (1911–17); he then was conductor of the St. Gallen sym. concerts (1917–44). Schoeck was one of the most significant Swiss composers of his era; he won his greatest renown as a masterful composer of songs, of which he wrote about 400. He also was highly regarded as a piano accompanist and a conductor. Among his many honors were an honorary doctorate from the Univ. of Zürich (1928), the 1st composer's prize of the Schweizerische Tonkünstlerverein (1945), and the Grand Cross of Merit and Order of Merit of the Federal Republic of Germany (1956). In 1959 the Othmar Schoeck Gesellschaft was founded to promote the performance of his works.

WORKS: DRAMATIC: OPERAS: *Don Ranudo de Colibrados*, op. 27 (1917–18; Zürich, April 16, 1919); *Venus*, op. 32 (1919–20; Zürich, May 10, 1922); *Penthesilea*, op. 39 (1924–25; Dresden, Jan. 8, 1927); *Massimilla Doni*, op. 50 (1934–35; Dresden, March 2, 1937); *Das Schloss Dürande*, op. 53 (1938–39; Berlin, April 1, 1943); other stage works.

BIBL.: W. Vogel, *Wesenszüge von O. S.s Liedkunst* (Zürich, 1950); idem, *Thematisches Verzeichnis der Werke von O. S.* (Zürich, 1956); F. Kienberger, *O. S.: Eine Studie* (Zürich, 1975); S. Tiltmann-Fuchs, *O. S.s Liederzyklen für Singstimme und Orchester* (Regensburg, 1976); D. Puffet, *The Song Cycles of O. S.* (Stuttgart and Bern, 1982).

Schoemaker, Maurice, Belgian composer; b. Anderlecht, near Brussels, Dec. 27, 1890; d. Brussels, Aug. 24, 1964. He studied harmony with Théo Ysaÿe, counterpoint with Michel Brusselmans, fugue with Martin Lunssens, and composition and orchestration with Paul Gilson. He was one of 8 Gilson pupils to form, in 1925, the Groupe des Synthétistes, whose aim was to promote modern music. He held administrative posts in various Belgian musical organizations.

WORKS: DRAMATIC: OPERAS: *Swane* (1933); *Arc-en-ciel* (1937); *De Toverviool* (1954). RADIO PLAYS: *Sire Halewijn* (1935); *Médée la magicienne* (1936); *Philoctetes* (1942). BALLETS: *Breughel-Suite* (1928); *Pan* (1937).

Schoenberg (originally, **Schönberg**), **Arnold (Franz Walter),** great Austrian-born American composer whose new method of musical organization in 12 different tones related only to one another profoundly influenced the entire development of modern techniques of composition; b. Vienna, Sept. 13, 1874; d. Los Angeles, July 13, 1951. He studied at the Realschule in Vienna; learned to play the cello, and also became proficient on the violin. His father died when Schoenberg was 16; he took a job as a bank clerk to earn a living; an additional source of income was arranging popular songs and orchestrating operetta scores. Schoenberg's first original work was a group of 3 piano pieces, which he wrote in 1894; it was also about that time that he began to take lessons in counterpoint from Alexander Zemlinsky, whose sister he married in 1901. He also played cello in Zemlinsky's instrumental group, Polyhymnia. In 1897 Schoenberg wrote his 1st String Quartet, in D major, which achieved public performance in Vienna on March 17, 1898. About the same time, he wrote 2 songs with piano accompaniment which he designated as op. 1. In 1899 he wrote his first true masterpiece, *Verklärte Nacht*, set for string sextet, which was first performed in Vienna by the Rosé Quartet and members of the Vienna Phil. on March 18, 1902. It is a fine work, deeply imbued with the spirit of Romantic poetry, with its harmonic idiom stemming from Wagner's modulatory procedures; it remains Schoenberg's most frequently performed composition, known principally through its arrangement for string orch. About 1900 he was engaged as conductor of several amateur choral groups in Vienna and its suburbs; this increased his interest in vocal music. He then began work on a choral composition, *Gurre-Lieder*, of monumental proportions, to the translated text of a poem by the Danish writer Jens Peter Jacobsen. For grandeur and opulence of orchestral sonority, it surpassed even the most formidable creations of Mahler or Richard Strauss; it calls for 5 solo voices, a speaker, 3 men's choruses, an 8-part mixed chorus, and a very large orch. Special music paper of 48 staves had to be ordered for the MS. He completed the first 2 parts of *Gurre-Lieder* in the spring of 1901, but the composition of the remaining section was delayed by 10 years; it was not until Feb. 23, 1913, that Franz Schreker was able to arrange its complete performance with the Vienna Phil. and its choral forces.

In 1901 Schoenberg moved to Berlin, where he joined E. von Wolzogen, F. Wedekind, and O. Bierbaum in launching an artistic cabaret, which they called Überbrettl. He composed a theme song for it with trumpet obbligato, and conducted several shows. He met Richard Strauss, who helped him to obtain the Liszt Stipendium and a position as a teacher at the Stern Cons. He returned to Vienna in 1903 and formed friendly relations with Gustav Mahler, who became a sincere supporter of his activities; Mahler's power in Vienna was then at its height, and he was able to help him in his career as a composer. In March 1904 Schoenberg organized with Alexander Zemlinsky the Vereinigung Schaffender Tonkünstler for the purpose of encouraging performances of new music. Under its auspices he conducted on Jan. 26, 1905, the first performance of his symphonic poem *Pelleas und Melisande*; in this score occurs the first use of a trombone glissando. There followed a performance on Feb. 8, 1907, of Schoenberg's *Kammersymphonie*, op. 9, with the participation of the Rosé Quartet and the wind instrumentalists of the Vienna Phil.; the work produced much consternation in the audience and among critics because of its departure from traditional tonal harmony, with chords built on fourths and nominal dissonances used without immediate resolution. About the same time, he turned to painting, which became his principal avocation. In his art, as in his music, he adopted the tenets of Expressionism, that is, freedom of personal expression within a self-defined program. Schoenberg's reputation as an independent musical thinker attracted to him such progressive-minded young musicians as Alban Berg, Anton von Webern, and Egon Wellesz, who followed Schoenberg in their own development. His 2d String Quartet, composed in 1908, which included a soprano solo, was his last work that carried a definite key signature, if exception is made for his Suite for Strings, ostentatiously marked as in G major, which he wrote for school use in America in 1934. On Feb. 19, 1909, Schoenberg completed his piano piece op. 11, no. 1, which became the first musical composition to dispense with all reference to tonality. In 1910 he was appointed to the faculty of the Vienna Academy of Music; in 1911 he completed his important theory book *Harmonielehre*, dedicated to the memory of Mahler; it comprises a traditional exposition of chords and progressions, but also offers illuminating indications of possible new musical developments, including fractional tones and melodies formed by the change of timbre on the same note. In 1911 he went again to Berlin, where he became an instructor at the Stern Cons. and taught composition privately. His *5 Orchesterstücke*, first perf. in London on Sept. 3, 1912, under Sir Henry Wood's direction, attracted a great deal of attention; the critical reception was that of incomprehension, with a considerable measure of curiosity. The score was indeed revolutionary in nature, each movement representing an experiment in musical organization. In the same year, Schoenberg produced another innovative work, a cycle of 21 songs with instrumental accompaniment, entitled *Pierrot Lunaire*, and consisting of 21 "melodramas," to German texts translated from verses by the Belgian poet Albert Giraud. Here he made systematic use of *Sprechstimme*, with a gliding speech-song replacing precise pitch (not an entire innovation, for Engelbert Humperdinck had applied it in his incidental music to Rosmer's play *Königskinder* in 1897). The work was given, after some 40 rehearsals, in Berlin on Oct. 16, 1912, and the reaction was startling, the purblind critics drawing upon the strongest invective in their vocabulary to condemn the music.

Meanwhile, Schoenberg made appearances as conductor of his works in various European cities (Amsterdam, 1911; St. Petersburg, 1912; London, 1914). During World War I he was sporadically enlisted in military service; after the Armistice he settled in Mödling, near Vienna. Discouraged by his inability to secure performances for himself and his associates in the new music movement, he organized in Vienna, in Nov. 1918, the Verein für Musikalische Privataufführungen (Society for Private Musical Performances), from which critics were demonstratively excluded, and which ruled out any vocal expression of approval or disapproval. The organization disbanded in 1922. About that time, Schoenberg began work on his Suite for Piano, op. 25, which was to be the first true 12-tone piece consciously composed in that idiom. In 1925 he was appointed prof. of a master class at the Prussian Academy of Arts in Berlin. With the advent of the beastly Nazi regime, the German ministry of education dismissed him from his post as a Jew. As a matter of record, Schoenberg had abandoned his Jewish faith in Vienna on March 25, 1898, by being baptized in the Protestant Dorotheer Community (Augsburger Konfession); 35 years later, horrified by the hideous persecution of Jews at the hands of the Nazis, he was moved to return to his ancestral faith and was reconverted to Judaism in Paris on July 24, 1933. With the rebirth of his hereditary consciousness, he turned to specific Jewish themes in works such as *Survivor from Warsaw* and *Moses und Aron*. Although Schoenberg was well known in the musical world, he had difficulty obtaining a teaching position; he finally accepted the invitation of Joseph Malkin, founder of the Malkin Cons. of Boston, to join its faculty. He arrived in the United States on Oct. 31, 1933. After teaching in Boston for a season, he moved to Hollywood. In 1935 he became a prof. of music at the Univ. of Southern Calif. in Los Angeles, and in 1936 accepted a similar position at the Univ. of Calif. at Los Angeles, where he taught until 1944, when he reached the mandatory retirement age of 70. On April 11, 1941, he became a naturalized American citizen. In 1947 he received the Award of Merit for Distinguished Achievements from the National Inst. of Arts and Letters. In the United States he changed the original spelling of his name from Schönberg to Schoenberg.

In 1924 Schoenberg's creative evolution reached the all-important point at which he found it necessary to establish a new governing principle of tonal relationship, which he called the "method of composing with 12 different notes related entirely to one another." This method was adumbrated in his music as early as 1914, and is used partially in his *5 Klavierstücke*, op. 23, and in his *Serenade*, op. 24; it was employed for the first time in its integral form in the Piano Suite, op. 25 (1924); in it, the thematic material is based on a group of 12 different notes arrayed in a certain prearranged order; such a tone row was henceforth Schoenberg's mainspring of thematic invention; development was provided by the devices of inversion, retrograde, and retrograde inversion of the basic series; allowing for transposition, 48 forms were obtainable in all, with counterpoint and harmony, as well as melody, derived from the basic tone row. Immediate repetition of thematic notes was admitted; the realm of rhythm remained free. As with most historic innovations, the 12-tone technique was not the creation of Schoenberg alone but was, rather, a logical development of many currents of musical thought. Josef Matthias Hauer rather unconvincingly claimed priority in laying the foundations of the 12-tone method; among others who had elaborated similar ideas at about the same time with Schoenberg was Jef Golyscheff, a Russian émigré who expounded his theory in a publication entitled "12 Tondauer-Musik." Instances of themes consisting of 12 different notes are found in the *Faust* Symphony of Liszt and in the tone poem *Also sprach Zarathustra* of Richard Strauss in the section on Science. Schoenberg's great achievement was the establishment of the basic 12-tone row and its changing forms as foundations of a new musical language; using this idiom, he was able to write music of great expressive power. In general usage, the 12-tone method is often termed "dodecaphony," from Greek dodeca, "12," and phone, "sound." The tonal composition of the basic row is devoid of tonality; an analysis of Schoenberg's works shows that he avoided using major triads in any of their inversions, and allowed the use of only the 2d inversion of a minor triad. He deprecated the term "atonality" that was commonly applied to his music. He suggested, only half in jest, the term "atonicality," i.e., absence of the dominating tonic. The most explicit work of Schoenberg couched in the 12-tone idiom was his *Klavierstück*, op. 33a, written in 1928–29, which exemplifies the clearest use of the tone row in chordal combinations. Other works that present a classical use of dodecaphony are *Begleitungsmusik zu einer Lichtspielszene*, op. 34 (1929–30); Violin Concerto (1934–36); and Piano Concerto (1942). Schoenberg's disciples Berg and Webern followed his 12-tone method in general outlines but with some personal deviations; thus, Berg accepted the occasional use of triadic harmonies, and Webern built tone rows in symmetric groups. Other composers who made systematic use of the 12-tone method were Egon Wellesz, Ernst Krenek, René Leibowitz, Roberto Gerhard, Humphrey Searle, and Luigi Dallapiccola. As time went on, dodecaphony became a lingua franca of universal currency; even in Russia, where Schoenberg's theories were for many years unacceptable on ideological grounds, several composers, including Shostakovich in his last works, made use of 12-tone themes, albeit without integral development. Ernest Bloch used 12-tone subjects in his last string quartets, but he refrained from applying inversions and retrograde forms of his tone rows. Stravinsky, in his old age, turned to the 12-tone method of composition in its total form, with retrograde, inversion, and retrograde inversion; his conversion was the greatest artistic vindication for Schoenberg, who regarded Stravinsky as his most powerful antagonist, but Schoenberg was dead when Stravinsky saw the light of dodecaphony.

Schoenberg's personality was both heroic and egocentric; he made great sacrifices to sustain his artistic convictions, but he was also capable of engaging in bitter polemics when he felt that his integrity was under attack. He strongly opposed the claims of Hauer and others for the priority of the 12-tone method of composition, and he vehemently criticized in the public press the implication he saw in Thomas Mann's novel *Doktor Faustus*, in which the protagonist was described as the inventor of the 12-tone method of composition; future historians, Schoenberg argued, might confuse fiction with facts, and credit the figment of Mann's imagination with Schoenberg's own discovery. He was also subject to superstition in the form of triskaidecaphobia, the fear of the number 13; he seriously believed that there was something fateful in the circumstance of his birth on the 13th of the month. Noticing that the title of his work *Moses und Aaron* contained 13 letters, he crossed out the 2d "a" in Aaron to make it 12. When he turned 76 and someone remarked facetiously that the sum of the digits of his age was 13, he seemed genuinely upset, and during his last illness in July 1951, he expressed his fear of not surviving July 13; indeed, he died on that date. Schoenberg placed his MSS in the Music Division of the Library of Congress in Washington, D.C.; the remaining materials were deposited after his death at the Schoenberg Inst. at the Univ. of Southern Calif. in Los Angeles. Schoenberg's centennial in 1974 was commemorated worldwide. A journal of the Schoenberg Institute began publ. in 1976, under the editorship of Leonard Stein.

Schoenberg's personality, which combined elements of decisive affirmation and profound self-negation, still awaits a thorough analysis. When he was drafted into the Austrian armed forces during World War I (he never served in action, however) and was asked by the examiner whether he was the "notorious" modernist composer, he answered, "Someone had to be, and I was the one." He could not understand why his works were not widely performed. He asked a former secretary to Serge Koussevitzky why the Boston Sym. Orch. programs never included any of his advanced works; when the secretary said that Koussevitzky simply could not understand them, Schoenberg was genuinely perplexed. "Aber, er spielt doch Brahms!" he said. To Schoenberg, his works were the natural continuation of German Classical music. Schoenberg lived in Los Angeles for several years during the period when Stravinsky was also there, but the two never made artistic contact. Indeed, they met only once, in a downtown food market, where they greeted each other, in English, with a formal handshake. Schoenberg wrote a satirical canon, *Herr Modernsky*, obviously aimed at Stravinsky, whose neoclassical works ("ganz wie Papa Bach") Schoenberg lampooned. But when Schoenberg was dead, Stravinsky said he forgave him in appreciation of his expertise in canonic writing.

In his private life, Schoenberg had many interests; he was a fairly good tennis player, and also liked to play chess. In his early years in Vienna, he launched several theoretical inventions to augment his income, but none of them ever went into practice; he also designed a set of playing cards. The MSS of arrangements of Viennese operettas and waltzes he had made in Vienna to augment his meager income were eventually sold for large sums of money after his death. That Schoenberg needed money but was not offered any by an official musical benefactor was a shame. After Schoenberg relocated to Los Angeles, which was to be his final destination, he obtained successful appointments as a prof. at the Univ. of Southern Calif. and eventually at the Univ. of Calif., Los Angeles. But there awaited him the peculiar rule of age limitation for teachers, and he was mandatorily retired when he reached his seventieth year. His pension from the Univ. of Calif., Los Angeles, amounted to $38 a month. His difficulty in supporting a family with growing children became acute and eventually reached the press. He applied for a grant from the munificent Guggenheim Foundation, pointing out that since several of his own students had received such awards, he was now applying for similar consideration, but the rule of age limitation defeated him there as well. It was only after the Schoenberg case and its repercussions in the music world that the Guggenheim Foundation canceled its offensive rule. Schoenberg managed to square his finances with the aid of his publishing income, however, and, in the meantime, his children grew up. His son Ronald (an anagram of Arnold) eventually became a city judge, an extraordinary development for a Schoenberg!

WORKS: DRAMATIC: *Erwartung*, monodrama, op. 17 (1909; Prague, June 6, 1924, Gutheil-Schoder mezzo-soprano, Zemlinsky conducting); *Die glückliche Hand*, drama with music, to Schoenberg's own libretto, op. 18 (1910–13; Vienna, Oct. 14, 1924, Stiedry conducting); *Von Heute auf Morgen*, opera, op. 32 (1928–29; Frankfurt am Main, Feb. 1, 1930, W. Steinberg conducting); *Moses und Aron*, biblical drama, to Schoenberg's own libretto (2 acts composed 1930–32; 3d act begun in 1951, but not completed; radio perf. of Acts 1 and 2, Hamburg, March 12, 1954, Rosbaud conducting; stage perf., Zürich, June 6, 1957, Rosbaud conducting). Also the oratorio *Die Jakobsleiter*, begun in 1917 but left unfinished; a performing version was prepared by Winfried Zillig, and given for the first time in Vienna on June 16, 1961.

WRITINGS: *Harmonielehre* (Vienna, 1911,; 3d ed., rev., 1922; abr. Eng. tr., 1947, as *Theory of Harmony*; complete Eng. tr., 1978); *Models for Beginners in Composition* (N.Y., 1942; 3d ed., rev., 1972, by L. Stein); *Style and Idea* (N.Y., 1950; enl. ed. by L. Stein, London, 1975); *Structural Functions of Harmony* (N.Y., 1954; 2d ed., rev., 1969, by L. Stein); *Preliminary Exercises in Counterpoint*, ed. by L. Stein (London, 1963); *Fundamentals of Musical Composition*, ed. by L. Stein (London, 1967); also numerous essays in German and American publs.

BIBL.: COLLECTED WORKS: SOURCE MATERIAL: J. Rufer and his successors are preparing a complete ed. of his works, *A. S.: Sämtliche Werke* (Mainz, 1966–). Rufer also compiled an annotated catalogue, *Das Werk A. S.s* (Kassel, 1959; Eng. tr., 1962; 2d Ger. ed., rev., 1975). I. Vojtch ed. vol. 1 of the *Gesammelte Schriften* (Frankfurt am Main, 1976). See also the following: *A. S.: Mit Beiträgen von Alban Berg, Paris von Gütersloh . . .* (essays by 11 admirers; Munich, 1912); E. Wellesz, *A. S.* (Leipzig, 1921; Eng. tr., rev., London, 1925); E. Stein, *Praktischer Leitfaden zu S.s Harmonielehre* (Vienna, 1923); P. Stefan, *A. S.: Wandlung, Legende, Erscheinung, Bedeutung* (Vienna, 1924); *A. S. zum 60. Geburtstag* (articles by friends and pupils; Vienna, 1934); H. Wind, *Die Endkrise der bürgerlichen Musik und die Rolle A. S.s* (Vienna, 1935); M. Armitage, ed., *A. S.* (N.Y., 1937); R. Leibowitz, *S. et son école* (Paris, 1947; Eng. tr., 1949); D. Newlin, *Bruckner, Mahler, S.* (N.Y., 1947; rev. ed., 1978); H. Stuckenschmidt, *A. S.* (Zürich, 1951; 2d ed., rev., 1957; Eng. tr., 1959); K. Wörner, *Gotteswort und Magie* (Heidelberg, 1959; Eng. tr., rev., 1963, as *S.'s "Moses and Aron"*); M. Kassler, *The Decision of A. S.'s Twelve-Note-Class-System and Related Systems* (Princeton, 1961); G. Perle, *Serial Composition and Atonality: An Introduction to the Music of S., Berg and Webern* (Berkeley, 1962; 5th ed., rev., 1982); J. Meyerowitz, *A. S.* (Berlin, 1967); B. Boretz and E. Cone, eds., *Perspectives on S. and Stravinsky* (Princeton, 1968); A. Payne, *S.* (London, 1968); W. Reich, *A. S., oder Der konservative Revolutionär* (Vienna, 1968; Eng. tr., 1971); R. Leibowitz, *S.* (Paris, 1969); D. Rexroth, *A. S. als Theoretiker der tonalen Harmonik* (Bonn, 1971); J. Maegaard, *Studien zur Entwicklung des dodekaphonen Satzes bei A. S.* (Copenhagen, 1972); E. Freitag, *A. S. in Selbstzeugnissen und Bilddokumenten* (Reinbek, 1973); H. Stuckenschmidt, *S.: Leben, Umwelt, Werk* (Zürich, 1974; Eng. tr., 1976, as *S.: His Life, World and Work*); C. Rosen, *A. S.* (N.Y., 1975); M. Macdonald, *S.* (London, 1976); D. Newlin, *S. Remembered: Diaries and Recollections (1938–76)* (N.Y., 1980); W. Bailey, *Programmatic Elements in the Works of A. S.* (Ann Arbor, 1983); W. Jakobik, *A. S.: Die Verräumlichte Zeit* (Regensburg, 1983); J. Hahl-Koch, ed., *A. S./Wassily Kandinsky: Letters, Pictures and Documents* (London, 1984); P. Franklin, *The Idea of Music: S. and Others* (London, 1985); G. Bauer, *A Contextual Approach to S.'s Atonal Works: Self Expression, Religion, and Music Theory* (diss., Wash. Univ., 1986); J. Brand, C. Hailey, and D. Harris, eds., *The Berg-S. Correspondence* (N.Y., 1986); E. Smaldone, *Linear Analysis of Selected Posttonal Works of A. S.: Toward an Application of Schenkerian Concepts to Music of the Posttonal Era* (diss., City Univ. of N.Y., 1986); J. Smith, *S. and His Circle: A Viennese Portrait* (N.Y., 1986); J. and J. Christensen, *From A. S.'s Literary Legacy: A Catalog of Neglected Items* (Warren, Mich., 1988); G. Beinhorn, *Das Groteske in der Musik: A. S.s Pierrot Lunaire* (Pfaffenweiler, 1989); G. Biringer, *Registral and Temporal Influences on Segmentation and Form in S.'s Twelve-Tone Music* (diss., Yale Univ., 1989); E. Haimo, *S.'s Serial Odyssey: The Evolution of his Twelve-Tone Method, 1914–1928* (Oxford, 1990); A. Ringer, *A. S.: The Composer as Jew* (Oxford, 1990); M. Sichardt, *Die Entstehung der Zwölftonmethode A. S.s* (Mainz, 1990); A. Trenkamp and J. Suess, eds., *Studies in the S.ian Movement in Vienna and the United States: Essays in Honor of Marcel Dick* (Lewiston, N.Y., 1990); W. Thomson, *S.'s Error* (Philadelphia, 1991); J. Dunsby, *S.: Pierrot lunaire* (Cambridge, 1992); B. Meier, *Feschichtliche Signaturen der Musik bei Mahler, Strauss und S.* (Hamburg, 1992); S. Milstein, *A. S.: Notes, Sets, Forms* (Cambridge, 1992); N. Nono-Schoenberg, ed., *A. S., 1874–1951: Lebensgeschichte in Begegnungen* (Klagenfurt, 1992); W. Frisch, *The Early Works of A. S., 1893–1908* (Berkeley, 1993); C. Sterne, *A. S.: The Composer as Numerologist* (Lewiston, N.Y., 1993); C.-S. Mahnkopf, *Gestalt und Stil: S.s Erste Kammersymphonie und ihr Umfeld* (Kassel and N.Y., 1994).

Schoen-René, Anna, German-American singing teacher; b. Koblenz, Jan. 12, 1864; d. N.Y., Nov. 13, 1942. She studied singing with Pauline Viardot-García. She appeared in opera before settling in the United States, where she taught in Minneapolis and then at the Juilliard School of Music in New York. She publ. a book of memoirs, *America's Musical Heritage* (N.Y., 1941).

Schöffler, Paul, distinguished German bass-baritone; b. Dresden, Sept. 15, 1897; d. Amersham, Buckinghamshire, Nov. 21, 1977. He studied in Dresden, Berlin, and Milan. In 1925 he made his operatic debut at the Dresden State Opera as the Herald in *Lohengrin*; he continued on its roster until 1938, then was a member of the Vienna State Opera until 1965. He also sang at London's Covent Garden (1934–39; 1949–53), the Bayreuth Festivals (1943–44; 1956), and the Salzburg Festivals (1938–41; 1947; 1949–65). He made his Metropolitan Opera debut in New York on Jan. 26, 1950, as Jochanaan in *Salome*; he continued to sing there, with interruptions, until 1956, returning there in 1963 to sing one of his finest roles, Hans Sachs; he remained on its roster until 1965, when he went to England. His other notable roles included Figaro, Don Giovanni, the Dutchman, Kurwenal, Scarpia, and Hindemith's Cardillac and Mathis der Maler; he also created the role of Jupiter in the first stage perf. of Strauss's *Die Liebe der Danae* (1952) and Einem's Danton (1947).

BIBL.: H. Christian, *P. S.: Versuch einer Würdigung* (Vienna, 1967).

Scholl, Andreas, remarkable German countertenor; b. Eltville, near Wiesbaden, Nov. 10, 1967. He became a member of the Kiedricher Chorbuben in Eltville when he was 7. He pursued vocal training with René Jacobs at the Scholar Cantorum Basilienses (1987–93), and was active as a soloist in oratorio and cantata performances. In 1992 he scored a notable success as a recitalist when he substituted on short notice for Jacobs in Paris. Thereafter he was engaged to sing with the principal early music orchs. and at leading festivals. In 1996 he appeared with the Collegium Vocale at the London Promenade Concerts. In 1997 he made his Wigmore Hall debut in London, the same year he was engaged to sing in Handel's *Solomon* at the Barbican in London. In 1998 he made an auspicious stage debut as Bertarido in Handel's *Rodelinda* at the Glyndebourne Festival. In addition to his outstanding interpretations of Handel, he has won notable distinction for his Bach and Vivaldi.

Schollum, Robert, Austrian composer, writer on music, and teacher; b. Vienna, Aug. 22, 1913; d. there, Sept. 30, 1987. He was a student at the Vienna Academy of Music and at the New Vienna Cons. He also received training from Marx and Lustgarten (theory and composition), Lafite (piano and organ), and Nilius (conducting). From 1959 to 1982 he taught voice at the Vienna Academy of Music. He was president of the Austrian Composers Union from 1965 to 1970, and again in 1983. In 1961 he was awarded the Austrian State Prize for composition and in 1971 the prize of the City of Vienna. After World War II, the influence of impressionism on his music was replaced by dodecaphony, aleatory, and timbre display. His compositions included *Der Tote Mann*, musical comedy (1936–38); *Mirandolina*, musical comedy (1950); *Der Biedermann Elend*, opera (1962).

WRITINGS (all publ. in Vienna unless otherwise given): *Musik in der Volksbildung* (1962); *Egon Wellesz* (1964); *Die Wiener Schule: Entwicklung und Ergebnis* (1969); with J. Fritz et al., *Das kleine Wiener Jazzbuch* (Salzburg, 1970); *Singen als menschliche Kundgebung: Einführung in die Arbeit mit den "Singblattern zur Musikerziehung"* (1970); *Das Österreichische Lied des 20. Jahrhunderts* (Tutzing, 1977); *Vokale Aufführungspraxis* (1983).

Scholz, Bernhard E., German conductor, pedagogue, and composer; b. Mainz, March 30, 1835; d. Munich, Dec. 26, 1916. He studied with H. Esser and H. Pauer in Mainz, S. Dehn in Berlin, and A. Sangiovanni in Milan. After teaching in Munich and conducting in Zürich and Nuremberg, he was assistant court Kapellmeister in Hannover (1859–65); he then conducted the Cherubini Soc. in Florence (1865–66); he led the concerts of the Breslau Orch. Soc. (1871–82), and in 1883 succeeded Raff as director of the Hoch Cons. in Frankfurt am Main. He retired in 1908. His works include the operas *Carlo Rosa* (Munich, 1858), *Ziethen'sche Husaren* (Breslau, 1869), *Morgiane* (Munich, 1870), *Golo* (Nuremberg, 1875), *Der Trompeter von Säkkingen* (Wiesbaden, 1877), *Die vornehmen Wirte* (Leipzig, 1883), *Ingo* (Frankfurt am Main, 1898), *Anno 1757* (Berlin, 1903), and *Mirandolina* (Darmstadt, 1907).

WRITINGS: Ed. *S. W. Dehns Lehre vom Contrapunkt, dem Canon und der Fuge* (Berlin, 2d ed., 1883); *Wohin treiben wir?* (Frankfurt am Main, 1897); *Musikalisches und Persönliches* (Stuttgart, 1899); *Die Lehre vom Kontrapunkt und der Nachahmung* (Leipzig, 1904); *Verklungene Weisen* (Mainz, 1911).

Schönbach, Dieter, German composer; b. Stolp-Pommern, Feb. 18, 1931. He studied at the Freiburg im Briesgau Hochschule für Musik with Bialas and Fortner (1949–59). He was music director of the Bochum theater (1959–73). His style of composition is quaquaversal. He wrote the first genuine multimedia opera, *Wenn die Kälte in die Hütten tritt, um sich bei den Frierenden zu wärmen, weiss einer "Die Geschichte von einem Feuer"* (Kiel, 1968).

Schönberg, Arnold (Franz Walter). See **Schoenberg (Schönberg), Arnold (Franz Walter).**

Schonberg, Harold C(harles), eminent American music critic; b. N.Y., Nov. 29, 1915. He studied at Brooklyn College (B.A., 1937) and at N.Y. Univ. (M.A., 1938). He served in the army (1942–46), then was on the staff of the *N.Y. Sun* (1946–50); he was appointed to the music staff of the *N.Y. Times* in 1950 and was senior music critic from 1960 until 1980. In 1971 he was the first music critic to be honored with the Pulitzer Prize in criticism. In his concert reviews and feature articles, he reveals a profound knowledge of music and displays a fine journalistic flair without assuming a posture of snobbish aloofness or descending to colloquial vulgarity. His intellectual horizon is exceptionally wide; he is well-versed in art, and can draw and paint; he is a chess aficionado and covered knowledgeably the Spassky-Fischer match in Reykjavík in 1972 for the *N.Y. Times*. He publ. in New York: *Chamber and Solo Instrument Music* (1955); *The Collector's Chopin and Schumann* (1959); *The Great Pianists* (1963; 2d ed., rev., 1987); *The Great Conductors* (1967); *Lives of the Great Composers* (1970; 2d ed., 1981); *Facing the Music* (1981); *The Glorious Ones: Classical Music's Legendary Performers* (1985); *Horowitz: His Life and Music* (1992).

Schöne, Lotte (real name, **Charlotte Bodenstein**), admired Austrian-born French soprano; b. Vienna, Dec. 15, 1891; d. Paris, Dec. 22, 1977. She studied in Vienna. She made her debut at the Vienna Volksoper in 1912, and continued to appear there until 1917; she then sang at the Vienna Court (later State) Opera (1917–26); also at the Berlin Städtische Oper (1926–33); she made many appearances at the Salzburg Festivals (1922–35). After leaving Germany in 1933, she went to Paris, became a naturalized French citizen, and made guest appearances at the Opéra and the Opéra Comique; she was compelled to go into hiding during the Nazi occupation, but resumed her career after the liberation, and sang in Berlin in 1948; she retired in 1953. Among her many notable roles were Cherubino, Papagena, Susanna, Despina, Pamina, Zerlina, Sophie, Mimi, Liù, and Mélisande.

Schöne, Wolfgang, German baritone; b. Bad Gandersheim, Feb. 9, 1940. He received his vocal training at the Hochschules für Musik in Hannover and Hamburg (diploma, 1969), his principal teacher being Naan Pöld. He took prizes in competitions in Berlin, Bordeaux, 's-Hertogenbosch, and Rio de Janeiro, and was active as a concert artist. In 1970 he launched his operatic career with engagements at the Württemberg State Opera in Stuttgart, the Hamburg State Opera, and the Vienna State Opera. In 1973 he became a member of the Württemberg State Opera, where he was honored as a Kammersänger. In 1984 he sang Don Giovanni at the reopening of the Stuttgart Opera. In 1990 he was engaged as the Count in *Capriccio* at the Salzburg Festival. He portrayed Dr. Schön at the Théâtre du Châtelet in Paris in 1992. In 1997 he appeared as Amfortas at the Opéra de la Bastille in Paris. As a concert singer, he garnered extensive engagements in Europe and the Americas, appearing with many notable orchs. and as a recitalist. Among his operatic roles are Don Giovanni, Guglielmo, Count Almaviva, Eugene Onegin, Wolfram, Amfortas, Golaud, Mandryka, and Tom in Henze's *The English Cat*, which role he created at the Schwetzingen Festival in 1983.

Schönherr, Max, Austrian conductor, musicologist, and composer; b. Marburg an der Drau, Nov. 23, 1903; d. Mödling, near Vienna, Dec. 13, 1984. He studied with Hermann Frisch in Marburg and Roderich von Mojsisovics at the Graz Cons. and later studied musicology at the Univ. of Vienna (Ph.D., 1970). After conducting at the Graz Landestheater (1924–28), he settled in Vienna as a conductor with the Theater an der Wien and Stadttheater (1929–33), the Volksoper (1933–38), and the Austrian Radio (1931–68), where he won distinction for his idiomatic readings of light Viennese scores. He composed much light music in a stylish manner, and also made effective arrangements of scores by the Viennese Strausses et al. He publ. *Carl Michael Ziehrer: Sein Werk, sein Leben, seine Zeit* (Vienna, 1974), *Lanner, Strauss, Ziehrer: Synoptic Handbook of the Dances and Marches* (Vienna, 1982), and with E. Brixel, *Karl Komzák: Vater, Sohn, Enkel: Ein Beitrag zur Rezeptionsgeschichte der Österreichischen Popularmusik* (Vienna, 1989). A Lamb ed. the vol. *Unterhaltungsmusik aus Österreich: Max Schönherr in seinen Erinnerungen und Schriften (Light Music from Austria: Reminiscences and Writings of Max Schönherr)* (in Ger. and Eng., N.Y., 1992).

Schønwandt, Michael, Danish conductor; b. Copenhagen, Sept. 10, 1953. After training in musicology at the Univ. of Copenhagen (B.Mus., 1975), he studied conducting and composition at the Royal Academy of Music in London (1975–77). In 1977 he made his conducting debut in Copenhagen, and subsequently appeared as a guest conductor with various European orchs. After conducting opera at the Royal Danish Theater in 1979, he appeared as a guest conductor at London's Covent Garden, the Paris Opéra, and the Stuttgart Opera. In 1981 he became music director of the Collegium Musicum in Copenhagen. He was also principal guest conductor of the Théâtre Royal de la Monnaie in Brussels (1984–87), the Nice Opera (1987–91), and the Danish Radio Sym. Orch. in Copenhagen (from 1989). From 1990 he was permanent conductor at the Vienna State Opera and, from 1992, music director of the Berlin Sym. Orch.

Schoop, Paul, Swiss-American composer; b. Zürich, July 31, 1909; d. Los Angeles, Jan. 1, 1976. He studied piano in Paris with Cortot and Casadesus, and in Berlin with Schnabel; also composition with Dukas in Paris, and with Hindemith and Schoenberg in the United States. He settled in Los Angeles, and wrote music for films; he also composed a comic opera, *The Enchanted Trumpet* and ballet scores for productions of his sister, Trudi Schoop, a modern dancer.

Schorr, Friedrich, renowned Hungarian-American bass-baritone; b. Nagyvarád, Sept. 2, 1888; d. Farmington, Conn., Aug. 14, 1953. He studied law at the Univ. of Vienna, and also took private lessons in singing. He appeared with the Chicago Grand Opera (1912), then was a member of the opera companies in Graz (1912–16), Prague (1916–18), Cologne (1918–23), and of the Berlin State Opera (1923–31); he also sang Wotan at Bayreuth (1925–31), and appeared at London's Covent Garden (1925–33). He made his Metropolitan Opera debut in New York as Wolfram on Feb. 14, 1924, and continued as a member until his farewell performance as the Wanderer in *Siegfried* on March 2, 1943. Schorr is generally recognized as the foremost Wagnerian bass-baritone of his era; he also sang roles in operas by Beethoven, Strauss, Verdi, and Puccini, and appeared in the United States premieres of Krenek's *Jonny Spielt Auf* (Daniello; 1929) and Weinberger's *Schwanda* (title role; 1931) at the Metropolitan Opera.

Schott, Anton, German tenor; b. Schloss Staufeneck, June 24, 1846; d. Stuttgart, Jan. 6, 1913. He was in the Prussian army. After the Franco-Prussian War, he sang at the Munich Opera (1871) and the Berlin Opera (1872–75), then in London and in Italy. He made his U.S. debut at the Metropolitan Opera in New York as Tannhäuser (Nov. 17, 1884), and was on its roster until 1885, and again in 1886–87. He excelled as an interpreter of Wagnerian roles. He publ. a polemical brochure, *Hie Welf, hie Waibling* (1904).

Schrade, Leo, eminent German musicologist; b. Allenstein, Dec. 13, 1903; d. Spéracèdès, Alpes-Maritimes, Sept. 21, 1964. He studied with Hermann Halbig at the Univ. of Heidelberg (1923–27), with Sandberger at the Univ. of Munich, and with Kroyer at the Univ. of Leipzig (Ph.D., 1927, with the diss. *Die ältesten Denkmäler der Orgelmusik als Beitrag zu einer Geschichte der Toccata*; publ. in Münster, 1928); he completed his Habilitation in 1929 at the Univ. of Königsberg. He taught at the Univs. of Königsberg (1928–32) and Bonn (from 1932). In 1937 he emigrated to the United States; he was on the faculty of Yale Univ. (1938–58), where he taught music history; in 1958 he was appointed to the music faculty of the Univ. of Basel. He was also the Charles Eliot Norton Lecturer at Harvard Univ. in 1962–63. He was founder-ed. of the Yale Studies in the History of Music and the Yale Collegium Musicum series (1947–58) and was coed. of the *Journal of Renaissance and Baroque Music* (1946–47), *Annales musicologiques* (1953–64), and the *Archiv für Musikwissenschaft* (1958–64); he served as an ed. of the series Polyphonic Music in the Fourteenth Century (vols. 1–3, 1956; vol. 4, 1958).

WRITINGS: *Beethoven in France: The Growth of an Idea* (New Haven, 1942); *Monteverdi: Creator of Modern Music* (N.Y., 1950; 2d ed., 1964); *Bach: The Conflict Between the Sacred and the Secular* (N.Y., 1954); *W. A. Mozart* (Bern and Munich, 1964); *Tragedy in the Art of Music* (Cambridge, Mass., 1964).

BIBL.: *Musik und Geschichte: L. S. zum sechzigsten Geburtstag* (Cologne, 1963; Eng. tr., 1965, as *Music and History: L. S. on the Occasion of His 60th Birthday*); *L. S. in memoriam* (Bern and Munich, 1966); E. Lichtenhahn, ed., *L. S.: De scientia musicae studia atque orationes* (Bern and Stuttgart, 1967); W. Arlt et al., eds., *Gattungen der Musik in Einzeldarstellungen: Gedenkschrift für L. S.* (Bern and Munich, 1973).

Schramm, Hermann, German tenor; b. Berlin, Feb. 7, 1871; d. Frankfurt am Main, Dec. 14, 1951. He made his operatic debut in Breslau in 1895 as Gomez in Kreutzer's *Die Nachtlager von Granada*. From 1896 to 1900 he sang at the Cologne Opera. In 1899 he appeared at London's Covent Garden and at the Bayreuth Festival (debut as David). From 1900 to 1933 he was a member of the Frankfurt am Main Opera, where he created the role of the chancellor in Schreker's *Der Schatsgräber* (1920). Schramm was hailed as the finest David and Mime of his era.

Schramm, Margit, German soprano; b. Dortmund, July 21, 1935; d. Munich, May 12, 1996. She was educated at the Dortmund Cons., and made her debut at Saarbrücken in 1956. She sang in Koblenz (1957–58), in Munich at the Gärtnerplatz State Theater (1959–64), in Berlin at the Theater des Westens (1965–66), and in the municipal theaters in Dortmund (1967). In 1968 she joined the ensemble of the State Theater in Wiesbaden. Her repertoire of German and Austrian operettas was vast and impressive.

Schreier, Peter (Max), esteemed German tenor and conductor; b. Meissen, July 29, 1935. He sang in the Dresdner Kreuzchor. He gained a taste for the theater when he appeared as one of the 3 boys in *Die Zauberflöte* at Dresden's Semper Opera House (1944). He received private vocal lessons from Polster in Leipzig (1954–56), and then with Winkler in Dresden; he also took courses at the Hochschule für Musik there (1956–59); concurrently he worked at the studio of the Dresden State Opera, where he appeared as Paolino in *Il Matrimonio segreto* (1957); he made his official debut there as the 1st Prisoner in *Fidelio* (1959), and went on to become a regular member of the company in 1961. In 1963 he joined the Berlin State Opera, and became one of its principal artists; he also made guest appearances with opera houses throughout Eastern Europe and the Soviet Union; likewise sang in London (debut as Ferrando with the visiting Hamburg State Opera, 1966) and at the Salzburg Festivals (from 1967), the Vienna State Opera (from 1967), the Metropolitan Opera in New York (debut as Tamino, Dec. 25, 1967), La Scala in Milan (1969), and the Teatro Colón in Buenos Aires (1969). His roles in Mozart's operas brought him critical acclaim; he was also a distinguished oratorio and lieder artist, excelling in a repertoire that ranged from Bach to Orff. In 1970 he launched a second, equally successful career as a conductor. In 1964 he was honored with the title of Kammersänger. He publ. the book *Aus meiner Sicht: Gedanken und Erinnerungen* (ed. by M. Meier; Vienna, 1983).

BIBL.: G. Schmiedel, *P. S.: Für Sie portratiert* (Leipzig, 1976); W.-E. von Lewinski, *P. S.: Interviews, Tatsachen, Meinungen* (Munich, 1992).

Schreker, Franz, eminent Austrian conductor, pedagogue, and composer; b. Monaco (of Austrian parents), March 23, 1878; d. Berlin, March 21, 1934. His father, the court photographer, died when he was 10; the family went to Vienna, where he studied with Arnold Rosé; he also received instruction in composition from Robert Fuchs at the Cons. (1892–1900). He first gained notice as a composer with his pantomime *Der Geburtstag der Infantin* (Vienna, Aug. 1908); that same year he founded the Phil. Chorus, serving as its conductor until 1920. He won great distinction with his opera *Der ferne Klang* (Frankfurt am Main, Aug. 18, 1912); outstanding among his later operas were *Die Gezeichneten* (Frankfurt am Main, April 25, 1918) and *Der Schatzgräber* (Frankfurt am Main, Jan. 21, 1920). After teaching composition at the Vienna Academy of Music (1912–20), he settled in Berlin as director of the Hochschule für Musik. Being of Jewish birth, he became a target of the rising Nazi movement; in 1931 he withdrew from performance his opera *Christophorus* in the face of Nazi threats; his last opera, *Der Schmied von Gent*, was premiered in Berlin on Oct. 29, 1932, in spite of Nazi demonstrations. Schreker was pressured into resigning his position at the Hochschule für Musik in 1932, but that same year he was given charge of a master class in composition at the Prussian Academy of Arts; he lost this position when the Nazis came to power in 1933. Shortly afterward, he suffered a major heart attack, and spent the remaining months of his life in poor health and reduced circumstances. As a composer, Schreker led the neo-Romantic movement in the direction of Expressionism, emphasizing psychological conflicts in his operas; in his harmonies, he expanded the basically Wagnerian sonorities to include many devices associated with Impressionism. He exercised considerable influence on the German and Viennese schools of his time, but with the change of direction in modern music toward economy of means and away from mystical and psychological trends, Schreker's music suffered a decline after his death.

WORKS: DRAMATIC: OPERAS (all but the 1st to his own librettos): *Flammen* (c.1900; concert perf., Vienna, April 24, 1902); *Der ferne Klang* (1901–10; Frankfurt am Main, Aug. 18, 1912); *Das Spielwerk und die Prinzessin* (1909–12; Frankfurt am Main and Vienna, March 15, 1913; rev. as *Das Spielwerk*, 1916; Munich, Oct. 30, 1920); *Die Gezeichneten* (1913–15; Frankfurt am Main, April 25, 1918); *Der Schatzgräber* (1915–18; Frankfurt am Main, Jan. 21, 1920); *Irrelohe* (1919–23; Cologne, March 27, 1924); *Christophorus, oder Die Vision einer Oper* (1924–27; Freiburg im Breisgau, Oct. 1, 1978); *Der singende Teufel* (1924–28; Berlin, Dec. 10, 1928); *Der Schmied von Gent* (1929–32; Berlin, Oct. 29, 1932). PANTOMIME: *Der Geburtstag der Infantin* for Strings (Vienna, Aug. 1908; rev. as *Spanisches Fest* for Orch., 1923). DANCE ALLEGORY: *Der Wind* for Clarinet and Piano Quartet (1908). BALLET: *Rokoko* (1908; rev. as *Ein Tanzspiel*, 1920).

BIBL.: P. Bekker, *F. S.: Studie zur Kritik der modernen Oper* (Berlin, 1919; 2d ed., 1983); R. Hoffmann, *F. S.* (Leipzig and Vienna, 1921); J. Kapp, *F. S.: Der Mann und sein Werk* (Munich, 1921); F. Bayerl, *F. S.s Opernwerk* (Erlangen, 1928); *S.-Heft* (Berlin, 1959); G. Neuwirth, *F. S.* (Vienna, 1959); H. Bures-Schreker, *El caso S.* (Buenos Aires, 1969; rev. Ger. tr. with H. Stuckenschmidt and W. Oehlmann as *F. S.*, Vienna, 1970); G. Neuwirth, *Die Harmonik in der Oper "Der ferne Klang" von F. S.* (Regensburg, 1972); F. Heller, ed., *Arnold Schönberg—F. S.: Briefwechsel* (Tutzing, 1974); O. Kolleritsch, ed., *F. S. am Beginn der neuen Musik, Studien zur Wertungsforschung*, XI (Graz, 1978); R. Ermen, ed., *F. S. (1878–1934) zum 50. Todestag* (Aachen, 1984); M. Brzoska, *F. S.s Oper "Der Schatzgräber"* (Stuttgart, 1988); C. Hailey, *F. S.: His Life, Times, and Music* (Cambridge, 1993).

Schröder, Hanning, German composer; b. Rostock, July 4, 1896; d. Berlin, Oct. 16, 1987. He was a medical student; concurrently he took violin lessons with Havemann in Berlin and composition with Weismann in Freiburg im Breisgau, then took a course in musicology with W. Gurlitt. In 1929 he married the musicologist Cornelia Auerbach (b. Breslau, Aug. 24, 1900); they remained in Germany under the Nazi regime, but were barred from professional work for their act of human charity in giving shelter to a Jewish couple in their Berlin apartment. After the fall of the Third Reich, they resumed their careers. Among his works is *Hänsel und Gretel*, children's Singspiel (Berlin, Dec. 23, 1952).

Schrøder, Jens, Danish conductor; b. Bielsko, Poland, Nov. 6, 1909; d. Ålborg, Aug. 10, 1991. He studied at the Prague Academy of Music. After conducting in various Danish cities, he was chief conductor of the Municipal Theater (1942–75) and the Sym. Orch. (1942–80) in Ålborg; he also was a guest conductor with the Danish Radio Sym. Orch. and the Royal Danish Orch. in Copenhagen. In 1980 he was made a Knight of the Dannebrog Order (1st Grade) for his services to Danish music.

Schröder-Devrient, Wilhelmine, celebrated German soprano; b. Hamburg, Dec. 6, 1804; d. Coburg, Jan. 26, 1860. She received early training for the stage from her father, Friedrich Schröder (1744–1816), a baritone, and from her mother, Antoinette Sophie Bürger, a well-known actress; she herself played children's parts and was an actress until her 17th year. After the death of her father, she followed her mother to Vienna, where she studied with Mozatti. She made her operatic debut at the Kärnthnertortheater in Vienna on Jan. 20, 1821, as Pamina, then sang Agathe in *Der Freischütz* under Weber's direction (Vienna, March 7, 1822). When *Fidelio* was revived in Vienna in 1822, she sang Leonore in the presence of Beethoven (Nov. 3, 1822). In 1822 she sang in Dresden, and then was a member of its court opera from 1823 to 1847, where she received additional training from the chorus master, Aloys Mieksch. She also made guest appearances in Berlin (1828), Paris (1830–32), and London (1832–33; 1837); she likewise won renown as a concert artist, continuing to make appearances in this capacity in Germany until 1856. She was one of the great singing actresses of her era, numbering among her many fine roles Donna Anna, Euryanthe, Norma, Rossini's Desdemona, Amina, and Lady Macbeth. Wagner held her in high esteem and chose her to create the roles of Adriano Colonna in *Rienzi* (Dresden, Oct. 20, 1842), Senta in *Der fliegende Holländer* (Dresden, Jan. 2, 1843), and Venus in *Tannhäuser* (Dresden, Oct. 19, 1845). She was married 3 times: her first husband was the actor Karl Devrient, whom she divorced in 1828; her 2d husband, a Saxon officer named Von Doring, cheated her out of her earnings, and she likewise divorced him; her 3d husband was the Livonian baron Von Bock, whom she married in 1850. A purported autobiography, publ. anonymously in many eds. since about 1870 as *Aus den Memoiren einer Sängerin or Memoires d'une chanteuse allemande*, is in fact a pornographic fantasy whose real author is unknown. A novel based on her life by Eva von Baudissin, *Wilhelmine Schröder-Devrient: Der Schicksalsweg einer grossen Künstlerin*, was publ. in Berlin in 1937.

BIBL.: C. von Glümer, *Erinnerungen an W. S.-D.* (Leipzig, 1862); A. von Wolzogen, *W. S.-D.* (Leipzig, 1863); C. Hagemann, *W. S.-D.* (Berlin, 1904; 2d ed., 1947); J. Bab, *Die D.s* (Berlin, 1932).

Schröder-Feinen, Ursula, German soprano; b. Gelsenkirchen, July 21, 1936. She studied voice with Maria Helm in Gelsenkirchen, and took courses at the Essen Folkwangschule. She sang in the chorus of the Gelsenkirchen Opera (1958), where she made her operatic debut as Aida in 1961, and remained on its roster until 1968, then sang with the Deutsche Opera am Rhein in Düsseldorf (1968–72). On Dec. 4, 1970, she made her Metropolitan Opera debut in New York as Chrysothemis in *Elektra*; she also sang at Bayreuth, Salzburg, Milan, and Berlin. She retired in 1979. Schröder-Feinen was a versatile singer whose repertoire included major dramatic roles in German and Italian opera.

Schröter, family of German musicians:

(1) Johann Friedrich Schröter, oboist and teacher; b. Eilenburg, 1724; d. Kassel, 1811. He began his career as an oboist in Count Brühl's regiment. In 1766 he went to Leipzig, where he nurtured his children's musical careers; he also took them on tours of Germany, the Netherlands, and England (1771–c.1773). He later was a court musician and teacher in Hanau (1779–86) and Kassel. His 4 children were:

(2) Corona (Elisabeth Wilhelmine) Schröter, soprano, actress, and composer; b. Guben, Jan. 14, 1751; d. Ilmenau, Aug. 23, 1802. She began her musical training with her father, becoming proficient as a keyboard player, guitarist, and singer; she continued her studies with Hiller in Leipzig, where she sang in his Grand Concerts from 1765; later she became active as an actress in amateur productions there. She won the admiration of Goethe, who arranged for her to be made a Kammersängerin to the Duchess Anna Amalia in Weimar in 1776; she also appeared as an actress at the amateur court theater, frequently taking roles opposite Goethe in his own dramas. When the court theater became a professional ensemble in 1783, she devoted herself to singing, teaching, poetry, drawing, and painting. Her association with the court ended about 1788. She settled in Ilmenau about 1801. She created the title role in and wrote music for Goethe's Singspiel *Die Fischerin* (1782); she also wrote other stage music and publ. *25 Lieder in Musik gesetzt* for Voice and Piano (Weimar, 1786; includes one of the earliest settings of Goethe's *Der Erlkönig* from *Die Fischerin*) and (16) *Gesänge* for Voice and Piano (Weimar, 1794).

BIBL.: H. Düntzer, *Charlotte von Stein und C. S.: Eine Vertheidigung* (Stuttgart, 1876); P. Pasig, *Goethe und Ilmenau mit einer Beigabe: Goethe und C. S.* (Ilmenau, 1902); H. Stümcke, *C. S.* (Bielefeld, 1904; 2d ed., 1926).

(3) Johann Samuel Schroeter, pianist and composer; b. probably in Guben, c.1752; d. London, Nov. 1, 1788. He commenced musical studies with his father, and about 1763 became a pupil of Hiller in Leipzig, where he sang in Hiller's concerts and later was active as a pianist (from 1767). He went to London with his family, then settled there; he was organist at the German Chapel before being made music master to Queen Charlotte in 1782 in succession to J. S. Bach. He eventually entered the service of the prince of Wales (later King George IV). He publ. 12 concertos for Keyboard and Strings (London, 6 c.1774 and 6 c.1777), various sonatas and other chamber pieces, and some vocal music. His widow became attached to Haydn during Haydn's stay in London (1790–91), and sent him many impassioned letters, of which copies made by Haydn are extant.

(4) (Johann) Heinrich Schröter, violinist and composer; b. Warsaw, c.1760; d. probably in Paris, after 1782. He first made an impression as a soloist in a Dittersdorf violin concerto in Leipzig (1770). After appearing in concerts with his family in London, he went with his father to Hanau in 1779; he gave concerts with his sister Marie in Frankfurt am Main (1780) and in Leipzig (1782) before disappearing from the musical scene. His extant works comprise 6 violin duets (London, c.1772), 6 Duo concertans for 2 Violins (Paris, c.1785), and 6 string trios (London and Paris, c.1786).

(5) Marie Henriette Schröter, singer; b. Leipzig, 1766; d. probably in Karlsruhe, after 1804. She studied with her father and gave concerts in Leipzig; she went with her father to Hanau, where she became a court music teacher when she was only 13. She was a Kammersängerin at the Darmstadt court until 1804.

Schryock, Buren, American composer and conductor; b. Sheldon, Iowa, Dec. 13, 1881; d. San Diego, Jan. 20, 1974. At the age of 7, he moved to West Salem, Oreg., where he studied music and played organ in a church. He occupied various teaching posts in Michigan, Texas, Nebraska, and California and was conductor of the San Diego Sym. Orch. (1913–20) and the San Diego Opera (1920–36). His works include the operas *Flavia* (1930–46), *Mary and John* (1948), *Nancy and Arthur* (1951), *Malena and Nordico* (1954), and *Tanshu and Sanchi* (1955).

Schubaur, Johann Lukas, German physician and composer; b. Lechfeld (baptized), Dec. 23, 1749; d. Munich, Nov. 15, 1815. He was the son of the painter Ignatius Schubaur, but was orphaned quite young and reared in the Zwiefalten monastery. After attending school in Augsburg, he studied at the Neuburg an der Donau theological seminary, where he received a thorough grounding in music; he then went to Vienna and studied music while earning his livelihood by giving piano lessons and composing short pieces; he took his medical degree in Ingolstadt, and then began his practice at the Barmherzige Brüder hospital in Neuburg an der Donau in 1775; shortly thereafter, he settled in Munich, where he became court physician and president of the medical commission. A dilettante composer, he won notable success with only one score, his Singspiel *Die Dorfdeputierten* (Munich, May 8, 1783); his other Singspiels, all produced in Munich, were *Melide oder Der Schiffer* (Sept. 24, 1782), *Das Lustlager* (1784), and *Die treuen Köhler* (Sept. 29, 1786).

BIBL.: E. Reipschläger, *S., Danzi und Poissl als Opernkomponisten* (diss., Univ. of Rostock, 1911).

Schubert, Ferdinand (Lukas), Austrian teacher and composer, brother of **Franz (Peter) Schubert**; b. Lichtenthal, near Vienna, Oct. 18, 1794; d. Vienna, Feb. 26, 1859. He began his musical training with his father. After taking instruction at Vienna's Normalhauptschule (1807–08), he taught at his father's school. He was an assistant teacher (1810–16) and a teacher (1816–24) at the Alsergrund orphanage, then headmaster (1824–51) and director (1851–59) of the Normalhauptschule. He was devoted to his brother and took charge of his MSS after his death. He wrote 2 Singspiels.

Schubert, Franz (Peter), great Austrian composer, a supreme melodist and an inspired master of lieder, brother of **Ferdinand (Lukas) Schubert**; b. Vienna, Jan. 31, 1797; d. there, Nov. 19, 1828. He studied violin with his father, a schoolmaster, and received instruction on the piano from his brother Ignaz; in addition, he took lessons in piano, organ, singing, and theory with Holzer, the choirmaster. In 1808 he became a member of the Vienna Imperial Court chapel choir, and also entered the Stadtkonvict, a training school for court singers, where he studied music with the Imperial Court organist Wenzel Ruzicka and with the famous court composer Salieri. He played violin in the school orch. and conducted it whenever an occasion called for it. He began composing in school, works including the unfinished Singspiel *Der Spiegelritter*. His first song, "Hagars Klage," is dated March 30, 1811. In 1813 he left the Stadtkonvict, but Salieri, evidently impressed by his talent, continued to give him instruction. He further attended a training college for teachers in Vienna, and then became an instructor at his father's school. Although very young, he began writing works in large forms; between 1813 and 1816 he composed 5 syms., 4 masses, several string quartets, and also some stage music. He also wrote his first opera, *Des Teufels Lustschloss*. It was then that he wrote some of his most famous lieder. He was only 17 when he wrote "Gretchen am Spinnrade," and only 18 when he composed the overpowering dramatic song "Erlkönig." The prodigious facility that Schubert displayed is without equal; during the year 1815 he composed about 140 songs; on a single day, Oct. 15, he wrote 8 lieder. He became friendly with the poets Johann Mayrhofer and Franz von Schober, and set a number of their poems to music. In 1817 he lodged with Schober and his widowed mother, arranging to pay for his keep from his meager resources. It was then that he met the noted baritone Johann Michael Vogl, who put many of Schubert's songs on his concert programs. Outstanding lieder from this period include the "3 Harfenspieler," "Der Wanderer," "Der Tod und das Mädchen," "Ganymed," "An die Musik," and "Die Forelle." During the summer of 1818, he served as music tutor to the family of Count Esterházy at Zélesz in Hungary. On March 1, 1818, his Overture in C major, "in the Italian style," became his first orch. work to be accorded a public performance in Vienna. On June 14, 1820, his Singspiel *Die Zwillingsbrüder* was performed at the Kärnthnertortheater in Vienna. On Aug. 19, 1820, a score of his incidental music for the play *Die Zauberharfe* was heard at the Theater an der Wien; this score contains an overture that became subsequently popular in concert performances under the name *Rosamunde Overture*, although it was not composed for the score to the play *Rosamunde, Fürstin von Zypern*, which was produced at the Theater an der Wien more than 3 years later, on Dec. 20, 1823. Although Schubert still had difficulties in earning a living, he formed a circle of influential friends in Vienna, and appeared as a pianist at private gatherings; sometimes he sang his songs, accompanying himself at the keyboard; he was also able to publ. some of his songs. A mystery is attached to his most famous work, begun in 1822, the Sym. in B minor, known popularly as the "Unfinished" Sym. Only 2 movements are known to exist, with portions of the 3d, a Scherzo, in sketches. What prevented him from finishing it? Speculations are as rife as they are worthless, particularly since he was usually careful in completing a work before embarking on another composition. In 1823 he completed his masterly song cycle *Die schöne Müllerin*; in 1824 he once again spent the summer as a private tutor in Count Esterházy's employ in Zélesz. In 1827 he wrote another remarkable song cycle, *Die Winterreise*. On March 26, 1828, he presented in Vienna a public concert of his works. From that year, which proved to be his last, date several masterpieces, including the 2 books of songs collectively known as the *Schwanengesang*. His health was frail, and he moved to the lodgings of his brother Ferdinand. On the afternoon of Nov. 19, 1828, Schubert died, at the age of 31. For a thorough account of his illness, see E. Sams's "Schubert's Illness Re-examined," *Musical Times* (Jan. 1980). There is no incontrovertible evidence that Schubert died of syphilis.

Schubert is often described as the creator of the genre of strophic lieder; this summary description is chronologically untenable, since Zelter wrote strophic lieder a generation before him. Goethe, whose poems were set to music by Zelter, Beethoven, and Schubert, favored Zelter's settings. What Schubert truly created was an incomparably beautiful florilegium of lieder typifying the era of German Romantic sentiment and conveying deeply felt emotions, ranging from peaceful joy to enlightened melancholy, from philosophic meditation to throbbing drama; the poems he selected for his settings were expressive of such passing moods. He set to music 72 poems by Goethe, 47 by Mayrhofer, 46 by Schiller, 44 by Wilhelm Muller, 28 by Matthison, 23 by Hölty, 22 by Kosegarten, 13 by Körtner, 12 by Schober, and 6 by Heine.

WORKS: In the list of Schubert's works given below, the D. numbers are those established by O. Deutsch (with D. Wakeling) in his *Schubert: Thematic Catalogue of All His Works in Chronological Order* (London, 1951; in Ger. as *Franz Schubert: Thematisches Verzeichnis seiner Werke in chronologischer Folge* . . . , publ. in the *Neue Ausgabe sämtlicher Werke of Schubert* in a rev. ed. in 1978). DRAMATIC: *Der Spiegelritter*, D.11, Singspiel (1811–12; unfinished; only the Overture and Act 1 completed; 1st perf. by the Swiss Radio, Dec. 11, 1949); *Des Teufels Lustschloss*, D.84, opera (1813–15; 2 versions; Vienna, Dec. 12, 1879); *Adrast*, D.137, opera (1817–19; unfinished; Vienna, Dec. 13, 1868); *Der vierjährige Posten*, D.190, Singspiel (1815; Dresden, Sept. 23, 1896); *Fernando*, D.220, Singspiel (1815; Vienna, April 13, 1907); *Claudine von Villa Bella*, D.239, Singspiel (1815; unfinished; only the Overture and Act 1 completed; Vienna, April 26, 1913); *Die Freunde von Salamanka*, D.326, Singspiel (1815; Halle, May 6, 1928); *Die Bürgschaft*, D.435, opera (1816; unfinished; only Acts 1 and 2 completed; Vienna, March 7, 1908); *Die Zauberharfe*, D.644, melodrama (1820; Theater an der Wien, Vienna, Aug. 19, 1820); *Die Zwillingsbrüder*, D.647, Singspiel (1819; Kärnthnertortheater, Vienna, June 14, 1820); *Sakuntala*, D.701, opera (1820; only sketches for Acts 1 and 2; these 1st perf. in Vienna, June 12, 1971); Duet and Aria for Hérold's *Das Zauberglöckchen (La Clochette)*, D.723 (1821; Vienna, June 20, 1821); *Alfonso und Estrella*, D.732, opera (1821–22; Weimar, June 24, 1854); *Die Verschworenen (Der häusliche Krieg)*, D.787, Singspiel (1823; Vienna, March 1, 1861); *Rüdiger*, D.791, opera (1823; sketches only; these 1st perf. in Vienna, Jan. 5, 1868); *Fierabras*, D.796, opera (1823; Karlsruhe, Feb. 9, 1897); *Rosamunde, Fürstin von Zypern*, D.797, incidental music to the play by H. von Chézy (1823; Theater an der Wien, Vienna, Dec. 20, 1823); *Der Graf von Gleichen*, D.918, opera (1827; sketches only); *Der Minnesänger*, D.981, Singspiel (date unknown; unfinished; not extant).

BIBL.: COLLECTED EDITIONS: SOURCE MATERIAL: The first complete critical edition of his works, *F. S.s Werke: Kritisch durchgesehene Gesamtausgabe*, edited by E. Mandyczewski (assisted by Brahms, Brüll, Hellmesberger, J. N. Fuchs et al.), was publ. by Breitkopf & Härtel (40 vols. in 21 series, Leipzig, 1884–97). A new and exhaustive critical edition, *F. S.: Neue Ausgabe sämtlicher Werke*, ed. by W. Durr, A. Feil, C. Landon et al., is being publ. under the sponsorship of the Internationalen Schubert-Gesellschaft (Kassel, 1964–). The standard thematic catalogue is by O. Deutsch and D. Wakeling, *S.: Thematic Catalogue of All His Works in Chronological Order* (London, 1951; in Ger. as *F. S.: Thematisches Verzeichnis seiner Werke in chronologischer Folge* . . . , publ. in the *Neue Ausgabe sämtlicher Werke of Schubert* in a rev. ed. in 1978). BIOGRAPHICAL: H. Kreissle von Hellborn, *F. S.: Eine biographische Skizze* (Vienna, 1861; 2d ed., greatly enl. as *F. S.*, 1865; Eng. tr., London, 1866); A. Reissmann, *F. S.: Sein Leben und seine Werke* (Berlin, 1873); H. Frost, *F. S.* (London, 1881; 2d ed., 1923); M. Friedlaender, *Beiträge zur Biographie F. S.s* (Berlin, 1887; new ed. as *F. S.: Skizze seines Lebens und Wirken*, Leipzig, 1928); A. Niggli, *S.* (Leipzig, 1890); H. Ritter, *F. S.* (Bamberg, 1896); R. Heuberger, *F. S.* (Berlin, 1902; 3d ed., rev., 1920, by H. von der Pforten); M. Zenger, *F. S.s Wirken und Erdenwallen* (Langensalza, 1902); O. Deutsch, *S.-Brevier* (Berlin, 1905); W. Klatte, *S.* (Berlin, 1907); L.-A. Bourgault-Ducoudray, *S.* (Paris, 1908; new ed., 1926); H. Antcliffe, *S.* (London, 1910); W. Dahms, *S.* (Berlin, 1912); O. Deutsch, ed., *F. S.: Die Dokumente seines Lebens und Schaffens* (in collaboration, 1st with L. Scheibler, then with W. Kahl and G. Kinsky; it was planned as a comprehensive work in 3 vols. containing all known documents, pictures, and other materials, arranged in chronological order, with a thematic catalogue; only 2 vols. publ.: vol. 3, *Sein Leben in Bildern*, Munich, 1913; vol. 2, part 1, *Die Dokumente seines Lebens*, Munich, 1914, which appeared in an Eng. tr. by Eric Blom as *S.: A Documentary Biography*, London, 1946, and in an American ed. as *The S. Reader: A Life of F. S. in Letters and Documents*, N.Y., 1947; a 2d Ger. ed., enl., was publ. in the *Neue Ausgabe sämtlicher Werke* in 1964); K. Kobald, *S. und Schwind* (Zürich, 1921); O. Bie, *F. S.: Sein Leben und sein Werk* (Berlin, 1925; Eng. tr., 1928); E. Bethge, *F. S.* (Leipzig, 1928); H. Eulenberg, *S. und die Frauen* (Hellerau, 1928); N. Flower, *F. S.* (London and N.Y., 1928; new ed., 1949); A. Glazunov, *S.* (Leningrad, 1928); K. Kobald, *F. S. und seine Zeit* (Zürich, 1928; Eng. tr., 1928; new Ger. ed., 1948); G. Kruse, *F. S.* (Bielefeld, 1928); P. Landormy, *La Vie de S.* (Paris, 1928); J.-G. Prod'homme, *S.* (Paris, 1928); idem, *S. raconté par ceux qui l'ont vu* (Paris, 1928); P. Stefan, *F. S.* (Berlin, 1928; new ed., Vienna, 1947); A. Weiss, *F. S.* (Vienna, 1928); R. Bates, *F. S.* (London, 1934); W. Vetter, *F. S.* (Potsdam, 1934); G. Schünemann, *Erinnerungen an S.* (Berlin, 1936); A. Orel, *Der junge S.* (Vienna, 1940); A. Kolb, *F. S.: Sein Leben* (Stockholm, 1941); K. Höcker, *Wege zu S.* (Regensburg, 1942); B. Paumgartner, *F. S.* (Zürich, 1943; 2d ed., 1947); R. Tenschert, *Du holde Kunst: Ein kleiner S.-Spiegel* (Vienna, 1943); A. Hutchings, S. (London, 1945; 4th ed., rev., 1973); W. and P. Rehberg, *F. S.* (Zürich, 1946); C. Weingartner, *F. S.* (Alten, 1947); R. Schauffler, *F. S.: The Ariel of Music* (N.Y., 1949); A. Einstein, *S.: A Musical Portrait* (N.Y., 1951; Ger. ed., 1952); H. Rutz, *S.: Dokumente seines Lebens und Schaffens* (Munich, 1952); H. Goldschmidt, *F. S.* (Berlin, 1954; 5th ed., 1964); P. Mies, *F. S.* (Leipzig, 1954); O. Deutsch, ed., *S.: Die Erinnerungen seiner Freunde* (Leipzig, 1957; Eng. tr. as *S.: Memoirs by His Friends*, N.Y., 1958; 3d Ger. ed., 1974); M. J. E. Brown, *S.: A Critical Biography* (London, 1958; 2d ed., 1961); F. Hug, *F. S.: Leben und Werk eines Frühvollendeten* (Frankfurt am Main, 1958); L. Kusche, *F. S.: Dichtung und Wahrheit* (Munich, 1962); K. Kobald, *F. S.* (Vienna, 1963); A. Kolb, *S.* (Gütersloh, 1964); J. Bruyr, *F. S.: L'Homme et son oeuvre* (Paris, 1965); F. de Eaubonne and M.-R. Hofmann, *La Vie de S.* (Paris, 1965); W. Marggraf, *F. S.* (Leipzig, 1967); J. Reed, *S.: The Final Years* (London, 1972); J. Wechsberg, *S.* (N.Y., 1977); H. Fröhlich, *S.* (Munich, 1978); H. Osterheld, *F. S.: Schicksal und Persönlichkeit* (Stuttgart, 1978); P. Gammond, *S.* (London, 1982); E. Hilmar, *F. S. in seiner Zeit* (Vienna, 1985); G. Marek, *S.* (N.Y., 1985); C. Osborne, *S. and his Vienna* (London, 1985); J. Reed, *S.* (London, 1987); F. Hilmar, *S.* (Graz, 1989); E. Krenek, *F. S.: Ein Portrat* (Tutzing, 1990); P. Gülke, *F. S. und seine Zeit* (Laaber, 1991); M. Schneider, *S.* (Paris, 1994); E. McKay, *F. S.: A Biography* (Oxford, 1996); W. Bodendorff, *Wer war F. S.?: Eine Biographie* (Augsburg, 1997); B. Newbould, *S.: The Music and the Man* (Berkeley, 1997). CRITICAL, ANALYTICAL: R. Krott, *Die Singspiele S.s* (diss., Univ. of Vienna, 1921); H. Therstappen, *Die Entwicklung der Form bei S.* (Leipzig, 1931); G. Abraham, ed., *The Music of S.* (N.Y., 1947); W. Vetter, *Der Klassiker S.* (2 vols., Leipzig, 1953); E. Norman-McKay, *The Stage-works of S., Considered in the Framework of Austrian Biedermeier Society* (diss., Univ. of Oxford, 1962–63); T. Georgiades, *S.: Musik und Lyrik* (Göttingen, 1967); M. Citron, *S.'s Seven Complete Operas: A Musico-dramatic Study* (diss., Univ. of North Carolina, 1971); G. Cunningham, *F. S. als Theaterkomponist* (diss., Univ. of Freiburg, 1974); E. Badura-Skoda and P. Branscombe, eds., *S. Studies: Problems of Style and Chronology* (Cambridge, 1982); L. Minchin, *S. in English* (London, 1982); W. Frisch, *S.: Critical and Analytical Studies* (Lincoln, Nebr., 1986); W. Thomas, *S.-Studien* (Frankfurt am Main and N.Y., 1990); C. Gibbs, ed., *The Cambridge Companion to S.* (Cambridge, 1997); B. Newbould, ed., *S. Studies* (Brookfield, Vt., 1998).

Schubert, Louis, German violinist, singing teacher, and composer; b. Dessau, Jan. 27, 1828; d. Dresden, Sept. 17, 1884. He went to St. Petersburg at the age of 17, then was concertmaster of the City Theater in Königsberg for 6 years; eventually he settled in Dresden, and became a singing teacher. He publ. a *Gesang-Schule in Liedern*, opp. 18 and 23 to 24 (Leipzig, c.1868). He composed the operettas *Aus Sibirien* (Königsberg, 1856), *Die Rosenmädchen* (Königsberg, 1860), *Die Wahrsagerin* (Dresden, 1864), *Wer ist der Erbe?* (Dresden, 1865), and *Die beiden Geizigen* (Altenburg, 1879), and the opera *Faustina Hasse* (Altenburg, 1879).

Schubert, Richard, German tenor; b. Dessau, Dec. 15, 1885; d. Oberstaufen, Oct. 12, 1959. He studied with Rudolf von Milde. In 1909 he made his operatic debut as a baritone in Strasbourg. Following further training from Milde and Hans Nietan in Dresden, he turned to tenor roles and sang in Nuremberg (1911–13) and Wiesbaden (1913–17). From 1917 to 1935 he was a member of the Hamburg Opera, where he became well known for his Wagnerian roles. He also created the role of Paul in Korngold's *Die tote Stadt* there in 1920. As a guest artist, he sang at the Vienna State Opera (1920–29) and in Chicago (1921–22).

Schuch, Ernst von, eminent Austrian conductor; b. Graz, Nov. 23, 1846; d. Kötzschenbroda, near Dresden, May 10, 1914. He studied law in Graz, where he also received instruction in music from Eduard Stolz, and served as director of the Musikverein; he then went to Vienna, where he completed his training in law at the Univ. and also continued his musical studies with Otto Dessoff. He began his career as a violinist. After serving as music director of Lobe's theater in Breslau (1867–68), he conducted in Würzburg (1868–70), Graz (1870–71), and Basel (1871). In 1872 he was called to Dresden as conductor of Pollini's Italian Opera; that same year he was named Royal Music Director at the Court Opera, and then Royal Kapellmeister in 1873, sharing his duties with Julius Rietz until 1879 and with Franz Wüllner until 1882, when he became sole Royal Kapellmeister. In addition to his exemplary performances at the Court Opera, he also distinguished himself as conductor of the concerts of the Königliche Kapelle from 1877. In 1889 he was named Dresden's Generalmusikdirektor, and in 1897 was ennobled by Emperor Franz Joseph of Austria-Hungary. He appeared widely as a guest conductor in Europe; his only visit to the United States was in 1900, when he led concerts in New York. During his long tenure, Schuch conducted 51 world premieres at the Dresden Court Opera, including Strauss's *Feuersnot* (Nov. 21, 1901), *Salome* (Dec. 9, 1905), *Elektra* (Jan. 25, 1909), and *Der Rosenkavalier* (Jan. 26, 1911); he was also the first conductor to perform Puccini's operas and Mascagni's *Cavalleria rusticana* in Germany. In his concert programs, he likewise conducted many works by contemporary composers. In 1875 he married the Hungarian soprano Clementine Procházka (b. Odenburg, Feb. 12, 1850; d. Kötzschenbroda, June 8, 1932); she studied with Mathilde Marchesi at the Vienna Cons., then was principal coloratura soprano at the Dresden Court Opera (1873–1904), where she took the name Schuch-Proska after her marriage. On June 4, 1884, she made her debut at London's Covent Garden as Eva in *Die Meistersinger von Nürnberg*; she also sang in Vienna and Munich. Her other notable roles included Blondchen, Zerlina, Amina, Aennchen, and Violetta. Their daughter Liesel von Schuch (b. Dresden, Dec. 12, 1891; d. there, Jan. 10, 1990) was also a coloratura soprano at the Dresden Court (later State) Opera (1914–35); she then taught voice at the Dresden Hochschule für Musik (until 1967).

BIBL.: P. Sakolowski, *E. v. S.* (Leipzig, 1901); F. von Schuch, *Richard Strauss, E. v. S. und Dresdens Oper* (Dresden, 1952; 2d ed., 1953).

Schüchter, Wilhelm, German conductor; b. Bonn, Dec. 15, 1911; d. Dortmund, May 27, 1974. He studied conducting with Abendroth and composition with Jarnach at the Cologne Hochschule für Musik. He then conducted opera at Würzburg (1937–40), and served as assistant to Karajan in Aachen (1940–42); he also conducted at the Berlin Städtische Oper (1942–43). In 1947 he was appointed to the post of 1st conductor of the North German Radio Sym. Orch. in Hamburg. After serving as principal guest conductor of the NHK Sym. Orch. in Tokyo (1958–61), he settled in Dortmund as Generalmusikdirektor in 1962; he was named artistic director of its Städtische Oper in 1965, and conducted the inaugural production at its new opera house in 1966. He acquired a fine reputation as a Wagnerian interpreter.

Schudel, Thomas (Michael), American-born Canadian composer and teacher; b. Defiance, Ohio, Sept. 8, 1937. He studied composition with Marshal Barnes, and received training in bassoon at Ohio State Univ. (B.Sc., 1959; M.A., 1961); he then studied composition with Bassett and Finney at the Univ. of Mich. (D.M.A., 1971). In 1964 he joined the faculty of the Univ. of Regina in Saskatchewan; he also was principal bassoonist in the Regina Sym. Orch. (1964–67; 1968–70); he became a naturalized Canadian citizen in 1974. In 1972 his Sym. No. 1 (1971; Trieste, Oct. 20, 1972) won 1st prize in the City of Trieste International Competition for symphonic composition. His works also include the children's operetta *The Enchanted Cat* (1992).

Schuh, Willi, eminent Swiss music critic and musicologist; b. Basel, Nov. 12, 1900; d. Zürich, Oct. 4, 1986. He studied music in Aarau with Kutschera and Wehrli, in Bern with Papst, and in Munich with Courvoisier and Beer-Walbrunn. He took courses in art history and musicology in Munich with Sandberger and in Bern with Kurth; in 1927 he received his Ph.D. from the Univ. of Bern with the diss. *Formprobleme bei Heinrich Schütz* (publ. in Leipzig, 1928). In 1928 he was engaged as music critic of the *Neue Zürcher Zeitung* and was its music ed. from 1944 until 1965; he was also ed.-in-chief of the *Schweizerische Musikzeitung* (1941–68). He also taught music history and harmony in Winterthur, in St. Gall, and at the Zürich Cons. He was made an honorary member of the Schweizerischer Tonkünstlerverein in 1969 and of the Schweizerische Musikforschende Gesellschaft in 1971. He was an ed. of the *Schweizer Musikerlexikon* (Zürich, 1964). Several of his writings were republished in *Kritiken und Essays* (4 vols.: vol. 1, *Über Opern von Richard Strauss*, Zürich, 1947; vol. 2, *Zeitgenössische Musik*, Zürich, 1947; vol. 3, *Schweizer Musik der Gegenwart*, Zürich, 1948; vol. 4, *Von neuer Musik*, Zürich, 1955); also *Umgang mit Musik: Über Komponisten, Libretti und Bilder* (Zürich, 1970; 2d ed., 1971). He was the ed. of *Die Briefe Richard Wagners an Judith Gautier* (Zürich, 1936); *Ferruccio Busoni: Briefe an seine Frau* (Zürich, 1936); *Hugo von Hofmannsthal's Beethoven* (Vienna, 1937; 2d ed., 1949); with H. Ehinger and E. Refardt, *Schweizer Musikbuch* (Zürich, 1939); *Richard Strauss: Betrachtungen und Erinnerungen* (Zürich, 1949; Eng. tr., 1955; 2d Swiss ed., rev., 1957); *Hugo von Hofmannsthal: Briefwechsel* (Zürich, 1952; Eng. tr., 1961; 4th Swiss ed., rev., 1970); *Richard Strauss: Briefe an die Eltern* (Zürich, 1954); *Igor Strawinsky: Leben und Werk, von ihm selbst* (Zürich and Mainz, 1957); *Richard Strauss und Stefan Zweig: Briefwechsel* (Frankfurt am Main, 1957; Eng. tr., 1977, as *A Confidential Matter: The Letters of Richard Strauss and Stefan Zweig 1931–1935*); with G. Kende, *Richard Strauss und Clemens Krauss: Briefwechsel* (Munich, 1963; 2d ed., 1964); *Richard Strauss und Willi Schuh: Briefwechsel* (Zürich, 1969). His publ. writings include *Othmar Schoeck* (Zürich, 1934); *In memoriam Richard Strauss* (Zürich, 1949); *Danae oder Die Vernunftheirat* (Frankfurt am Main, 1952); *Renoir und Wagner*

(Zürich, 1959); *Ein paar Erinnerungen an Richard Strauss* (Zürich, 1964); *Hugo von Hofmannsthal und Richard Strauss: Legende und Wirklichkeit* (Munich, 1964); *Der Rosenkavalier: Vier Studien* (Olten, 1968); *Richard Strauss: Jugend und frühe Meisterjahre: Lebenschronik 1864–98* (the authorized biography; Zürich, 1976; Eng. tr., 1982, as *Richard Strauss: A Chronicle of the Early Years 1864–98*).

Schüler, Johannes, German conductor; b. Vietz, Neumark, June 21, 1894; d. Berlin, Oct. 3, 1966. He received his training at the Berlin Hochschule für Musik. After conducting opera in Gleiwitz (1920–22), Königsberg (1922–24), and Hannover (1924–28), he was music director in Oldenburg (1928–32) and Essen (1933–36). From 1936 to 1949 he conducted at the Berlin State Opera, where he was granted the titles of Staatskapellmeister and Generalmusikdirektor. He then was Generalmusikdirektor in Hannover from 1949 to 1960, where he conducted a number of contemporary operas.

Schuller, Gunther (Alexander), significant American composer, conductor, and music educator; b. N.Y., Nov. 22, 1925. He was of a musical family; his paternal grandfather was a bandmaster in Germany before emigrating to America; his father was a violinist with the N.Y. Phil. He was sent to Germany as a child for a thorough academic training; returning to New York, he studied at the St. Thomas Choir School (1938–44); he also received private instruction in theory, flute, and horn. He played in the N.Y. City Ballet orch. (1943), then was 1st horn in the Cincinnati Sym. Orch. (1943–45) and the Metropolitan Opera orch. in New York (1945–49). At the same time, he became fascinated with jazz; he played the horn in a combo conducted by Miles Davis; also began to compose jazz pieces. He taught at the Manhattan School of Music in New York (1950–63), the Yale Univ. School of Music (1964–67), and the New England Cons. of Music in Boston, where he greatly distinguished himself as president (1967–77). He was also active at the Berkshire Music Center at Tanglewood as a teacher of composition (1963–84), head of contemporary-music activities (1965–84), artistic codirector (1969–74), and director (1974–84). In 1984–85 he was interim music director of the Spokane (Wash.) Sym. Orch., then was director of its Sandpoint (Idaho) Festival. In 1986 he founded the Boston Composers' Orch. In 1988 he was awarded the 1st Elise L. Stoeger Composer's Chair of the Chamber Music Soc. of Lincoln Center in New York. In 1975 he organized Margun Music to make available unpubl. American music. He founded GunMar Music in 1979. In 1980 he organized GM Recordings. He publ. the manual *Horn Technique* (N.Y., 1962; 2d ed., 1992) and the very valuable study *Early Jazz: Its Roots and Musical Development* (3 vols., N.Y., 1968 et seq.). A vol. of his writings appeared as *Musings* (N.Y., 1985). In his multiple activities, he tried to form a link between serious music and jazz; he popularized the style of "cool jazz" (recorded as Birth of the Cool). In 1957 he launched the slogan "third stream" to designate the combination of classical forms with improvisatory elements of jazz as a synthesis of disparate, but not necessarily incompatible, entities, and wrote fanciful pieces in this synthetic style; in many of these, he worked in close cooperation with John Lewis of the Modern Jazz Quartet. As part of his investigation of the roots of jazz, he became interested in early ragtime and formed, in 1972, the New England Cons. Ragtime Ensemble; its recordings of Scott Joplin's piano rags in band arrangement were instrumental in bringing about the "ragtime revival." In his own works he freely applied serial methods, even when his general style was dominated by jazz. He received honorary doctorates in music from Northwestern Univ. (1967), the Univ. of Ill. (1968), Williams College (1975), the New England Cons. of Music (1978), and Rutgers Univ. (1980). In 1967 he was elected to membership in the National Inst. of Arts and Letters, and in 1980 to the American Academy and Inst. of Arts and Letters. In 1989 he received the William Schuman Award of Columbia Univ. In 1991 he was awarded a MacArthur Foundation grant. In 1994 he won the Pulitzer Prize in music for his orch. work, *Of Reminiscences and Reflections* (1993), composed in memory of his wife who died in 1992.

WORKS: DRAMATIC: OPERAS: *The Visitation* (Hamburg, Oct. 12, 1966); *The Fisherman and His Wife*, children's opera (Boston, May 7, 1970); *A Question of Taste* (Cooperstown, N.Y., June 24, 1989). BALLET: *Variants* for Jazz Quartet and Orch. (1960; N.Y., Jan. 4, 1961). FILM SCORES: *Automation* (1962); *Journey to the Stars* (1962); *Yesterday in Fact* (1963). TELEVISION SCORES: *Tear Drop* (1966); *The 5 Senses*, ballet (1967). ORATORIO: *The Power within Us* for Baritone, Narrator, Chorus, and Orch. (1971).

BIBL.: N. Carnovale, *G. S.: A Bio-Bibliography* (Westport, Conn., 1987).

Schultz, Svend (Simon), Danish composer, pianist, and conductor; b. Nykøbing Falster, Dec. 30, 1913. He received training in piano and composition at the Copenhagen Cons. (1933–38), where his principal mentor was Schierbeck. After serving as music critic for *Politiken* (1942–49), he was a choral conductor with the Danish Radio in Copenhagen (from 1949). He also appeared as a pianist and conductor of his own works throughout Europe. His music is neoclassical in style and is characterized by simplicity of form and a cumulative rhythmic drive.

WORKS: DRAMATIC: OPERAS: *Bag kulisserne* (Behind the Scenes; 1946; Copenhagen, May 26, 1949); *Solbadet* (The Sunbath; 1947; Århus, Nov. 26, 1949); *Kaffehuset* (The Coffee House; 1948); *Høst* (Harvest; 1950); *Bryllupsrejsen* (The Honeymoon; 1951); *Hyrdinden og skorstensfejeren* (The Shepherdess and the Chimney Sweep), puppet opera (1953); *Tordenvejret* (The Thunderstorm; 1954); *Hosekraemmeren* (The Stocking Peddler; 1955; rev. 1985; Århus, May 4, 1990); *The Marionettes*, puppet opera (1957); *Dommer Lynch* (Judge Lynch; 1959); *Konen i muddergrøften* (The Woman in the Muddy Ditch), comic television opera (1964; Danish TV, April 18, 1965); *Lykken og forstanden*, children's opera (1973). CHAMBER OPERETTA: *Den kåde Donna* (Copenhagen, Aug. 30, 1957). MUSICAL CHURCH PLAY: *Eva* (1968). ORATORIO: *Job* (1945).

Schultze, Norbert, German composer; b. Braunschweig, Jan. 26, 1911. He studied piano, conducting, and composition at the Cologne Staatliche Hochschule für Musik; after studying theatrical arts in Cologne and Munich (1931), he was active as an actor and composer in a student cabaret, *Vier Nachrichter*, in Munich (1931–32); he then conducted opera in Heidelberg (1932–33) and Darmstadt (1933–34); later he was a composer for stage, films, and television; he was head of his own music publishing business (from 1953). He wrote the operas *Schwarzer Peter* (Hamburg, 1936) and *Das kalte Herz* (Leipzig, 1943), the television opera, *Peter der dritte* (1964), the operetta, *Regen in Paris* (Nuremberg, 1957), and 3 pantomimes: *Struwwelpeter* (Hamburg, 1937), *Max und Moritz* (Hamburg, 1938), and *Maria im Walde* (Vienna, 1940). However, his chief claim to fame was a sentimental song, *Lili Marleen* (1938), which became immensely popular during World War II among both German and Allied soldiers after it was broadcast from German-occupied Belgrade in 1941; it was tr. into 27 languages. For some of his works he used the names Frank Norbert, Peter Kornfeld, and Henri Iversen.

Schulz, Johann Philipp Christian, German conductor and composer; b. Langensalza, Feb. 1, 1773; d. Leipzig, Jan. 30, 1827. He studied with Engel and Schicht in Leipzig, and from 1810 was conductor of the Gewandhaus concerts and the Singakademie there; he became music director of the Univ. of Leipzig in 1818. He wrote an overture to Klingemann's *Faust* and other stage music.

Schuman, Patricia, American soprano; b. Los Angeles, Feb. 4, 1954. She studied at the Univ. of Calif. at Santa Cruz. After appearances in San Francisco, Houston, New York, Paris, Venice, and Washington, D.C., she sang Dorabella and Zerlina at the Théâtre Royal de la Monnaie in Brussels in 1983. In 1986 she sang in the U.S. premiere of *Il viaggio a Reims* in St. Louis. She was engaged to sing Poppea at the Théâtre du Châtelet in Paris in 1989. On Sept. 27, 1990, she made her debut at the Metropolitan Opera in New York as Donna Elvira. That same year, she also appeared as Blanche in Poulenc's *Dialogues des Carmélites* in Seattle. In 1992 she portrayed Donna Elvira at her debut at London's Covent Garden. She sang in *La clemenza di Tito* at the Salzburg Festival in 1997.

Schuman, William (Howard), eminent American composer, music educator, and administrator; b. N.Y., Aug. 4, 1910; d. there, Feb. 15, 1992. He began composing at 16, turning out a number of popular songs; he also played in jazz groups. He took courses at N.Y. Univ.'s School of Commerce (1928–30) before turning decisively to music and taking private lessons in harmony with Max Persin and in counterpoint with Charles Haubiel (1931) in New York. After attending summer courses with Wagenaar and Schmid at N.Y.'s Juilliard School (1932–33), he pursued his education at Teacher's College of Columbia Univ. (B.S., 1935; M.A., 1937); he also studied conducting at the Salzburg Mozarteum (summer 1935) and composition with Harris, both at the Juilliard School (summer 1936) and privately (1936–38). He came to the attention of Koussevitzky, who conducted the premieres of his *American Festival Overture* (1939), 3d Sym. (1941; received the 1st N.Y. Music Critics' Circle Award), *A Free Song* (1943; received the 1st Pulitzer Prize in music), and the Sym. for Strings (1943); Rodzinski conducted the premiere of his 4th Sym. (1942). After teaching at Sarah Lawrence College (1935–45), he served as director of publications of G. Schirmer, Inc. (1945–52) and as president of the Juilliard School of Music (1945–62), where he acquired a notable reputation as a music educator; he subsequently was president of Lincoln Center for the Performing Arts in New York (1962–69). He was chairman of the MacDowell Colony (from 1973) and the first chairman of the Norlin Foundation (1975–85). The recipient of numerous honors, he held 2 Guggenheim fellowships (1939–41), was elected a member of the National Inst. of Arts and Letters (1946) and the American Academy of Arts and Letters (1973), was awarded the gold medal of the American Academy and Inst. of Arts and Letters (1982), won a 2d, special Pulitzer Prize (1985), and received the National Medal of Arts (1987) and a Kennedy Center Honor (1989). Columbia Univ. established the William Schuman Award in 1981, a prize of $50,000 given to a composer for lifetime achievement; fittingly, Schuman was its first recipient. His music is characterized by great emotional tension, which is maintained by powerful asymmetric rhythms; the contrapuntal structures in his works reach a great degree of complexity and are saturated with dissonance without, however, losing the essential tonal references. In several of his works, he employs American melorhythms, but his general style of composition is cosmopolitan, exploring all viable techniques of modern composition.

WORKS: DRAMATIC: OPERA: *The Mighty Casey* (1951–53; Hartford, Conn., May 4, 1953; rev. as the cantata *Casey at the Bat*, Washington, D.C., April 6, 1976). BALLETS: *Undertow* (N.Y., April 10, 1945); *Night Journey* (Cambridge, Mass., May 3, 1947); *Judith* (1949; Louisville, Jan. 4, 1950); *Voyage for a Theater* (N.Y., May 17, 1953; withdrawn); *The Witch of Endor* (N.Y., Nov. 2, 1965; withdrawn). FILM SCORES: *Steeltown* (1941); *The Earth Is Born* (1959).

BIBL.: C. Rouse, *W. S.: Documentary* (N.Y., 1980).

Schumann, Elisabeth, celebrated German-born American soprano; b. Merseburg, June 13, 1888; d. N.Y., April 23, 1952. She studied in Dresden, Berlin, and Hamburg. She made her operatic debut at the Hamburg Opera on Sept. 2, 1909, as the Shepherd in *Tannhäuser*; she remained on its roster until 1919. In the meantime, she made her American debut at the Metropolitan Opera in New York on Nov. 20, 1914, as Sophie in *Der Rosenkavalier*, one of her most famous roles; she sang there only one season (1914–15). From 1919 to 1938 she was a principal member of the Vienna State Opera. In 1921 she made a concert tour of the United States with Richard Strauss. After the Anschluss in 1938, she settled in the United States and taught at the Curtis Inst. of Music in Philadelphia. She became a naturalized American citizen in 1944. She publ. *German Song* (London, 1948). Among her finest roles were Blondchen, Zerlina, Susanna, Adele, and Sophie; she also was renowned as an incomparable lieder artist.

BIBL.: G. Puritz, *E. S.: A Biography* (London, 1993).

Schumann, Robert (Alexander), great German composer of surpassing imaginative power whose music expressed the deepest spirit of the Romantic era; b. Zwickau, June 8, 1810; d. Endenich, near Bonn, July 29, 1856. He was the 5th and youngest child of a Saxon bookseller, who encouraged his musical inclinations. At the age of 10 he began taking piano lessons from J. G. Kuntzsch, organist at the Zwickau Marienkirche. In 1828 he enrolled at the Univ. of Leipzig as studiosus juris, although he gave more attention to philosophical lectures than to law. In Leipzig he became a piano student of Friedrich Wieck, his future father-in-law. In 1829 he went to Heidelberg, where he applied himself seriously to music; in 1830 he returned to Leipzig and lodged in Wieck's home; he also took a course in composition with Heinrich Dorn. His family life was unhappy; his father died at the age of 53 of a nervous disease not distinctly diagnosed, and his sister Emily committed suicide at the age of 19. Of his 3 brothers, only one reached late middle age. Schumann became absorbed in the Romantic malaise of *Weltschmerz*; his idols, the writers and poets Novalis, Kleist, Byron, Lenau, and Hölderin, all died young and in tragic circumstances. He hoped to start his music study with Carl Maria von Weber, who also died unexpectedly. Schumann wrote plays and poems in the Romantic tradition and at the same time practiced his piano playing in the hope of becoming a virtuoso pianist. He never succeeded in this ambition; ironically, it was to be his beloved bride, Clara (Josephine) Schumann (née Wieck) (b. Leipzig, Sept. 13, 1819; d. Frankfurt am Main, May 20, 1896), who would become a famous concert pianist, with Schumann himself often introduced to the public at large as merely her husband. His own piano study was halted when he developed an ailment in the index and middle fingers of his right hand. He tried all the fashionable remedies of the period, allopathy, homeopathy, and electrophysical therapy; in addition, he used a mechanical device to lift the middle finger of his right hand, but it only caused him harm. His damaged fingers exempted him from military service; the medical certificate issued in 1842 stated that the index and middle fingers of his right hand were affected so that he was unable to pull the trigger of a rifle. Schumann had a handsome appearance; he liked the company of young ladies, and enjoyed beer, wine, and strong cigars; this was in sharp contrast with his inner disquiet; as a youth, he confided to his diary a fear of madness. He had auditory hallucinations that caused insomnia; he also suffered from acrophobia. When he was 23 years old, he noted sudden onsets of inexpressible angst, momentary loss of consciousness, and difficulty in breathing. He called his sickness a pervasive melancholy, a popular malaise of the time. He thought of killing himself. What maintained his spirits then was his great love for Clara, 9 years his junior; he did not hesitate to confess his psychological perturbations to her. Her father must have surmised the unstable character of Schumann, and resisted any thought of allowing Clara to become engaged to him; the young couple had to go to court to overcome Wieck's objections, and were finally married on Sept. 12, 1840, the day before Clara turned 21. In 1843, when Schumann and Clara already had 2 daughters, Wieck approached him with an offer of reconciliation. Schumann gladly accepted the offer, but the relationship remained only formal.

Whatever inner torment disturbed Schumann's mind, it did not affect the flowering of his genius as a composer. As a young man he wrote music full of natural beauty, harmonious and melodious in its flow; his compositions are remarkably free from the somber and dramatic qualities that characterize the music of Beethoven and his Romantic followers. His very first opus number was a set of variations on the notes A, B, E, G, G, which spelled the name of Countess Meta von Abegg, to whom he was also poetically attached. And, incidentally, it was Ernestine's adoptive father, an amateur flutist, who gave him the theme for his remarkable set of variations for Piano titled *Etudes symphoniques*.

As Schumann's talent for music grew and he became recognized as an important composer, he continued his literary activities. In 1834 he founded, with J. Knorr, L. Schunke, and Wieck, a progressive journal, *Neue Zeitschrift für Musik*, in which he militated against the vapid mannerisms of fashionable salon music and other aspects of musical stagnation. He wrote essays, signing them with the imaginary names of Florestan, Eusebius, or Meister Raro. (Eusebius was the name of 3 Christian saints; etymologically, it is a compound of the Greek components *eu*, "good," and *sebiai*, "to worship." *Florestan* is obviously "one in a state of flowering"; *Raro* is "rare"; he also noticed that the juxtaposition of the names Clara and Robert would result in the formation of Raro: ClaRARObert.) As early as 1831, Schumann, in the guise of Eusebius, hailed the genius of Chopin in an article in the *Allgemeine Musikalische Zeitung*; it was signed only by his initials, and in an editorial note, he was identified merely as a young student of Prof. Wieck; but the winged phrase became a favorite quotation of biographers of both Chopin and Schumann, cited as Schumann's discovery of Chopin's talent. Actually, Chopin was a few months older than Schumann, and had already started on a brilliant concert career, while Schumann was an unknown. One of the most fanciful inventions of Schumann was the formation of an intimate company of friends, which he named Davidsbundler to describe the sodality of David, dedicated to the mortal struggle against Philistines in art and to the passionate support of all that was new and imaginative. He immortalized this society in his brilliant piano work *Davidsbündlertänze*. Another characteristically Romantic trait was Schumann's attachment to nocturnal moods, nature scenes, and fantasies; the titles of his piano pieces are typical: *Nachtstücke, Waldszenen*, and *Fantasiestücke*, the last including the poetic *Warum?* and the explosive *Aufschwung*. A child at heart himself, he created in his piano set of exquisite miniatures, *Kinderszenen*, a marvelous musical nursery that included the beautifully sentimental dream piece "Traumerei." Parallel with his piano works, Schumann produced some of his finest lieder, including the song cycles to poems by Heine (op. 24) and Eichendorff (op. 39), *Die Frauenliebe und Leben* (op. 42), and *Dichterliebe*, to Heine's words (op. 48). In 1841, in only 4 days, he sketched out his First Sym., in B-flat major, born, as he himself said, in a single "fiery hour." He named it the *Spring* Sym. It was followed in rapid succession by 3 string quartets (op. 41), the Piano Quintet (op. 44), and the Piano Quartet (op. 47). To the same period belongs also his impassioned choral work *Das Paradies und die Peri*. Three more syms. followed the *Spring* Sym. within the next decade, and also a Piano Concerto, a masterpiece of a coalition between the percussive gaiety of the solo part and songful paragraphs in the orch.; an arresting hocketus occurs in the finale, in which duple meters come into a striking conflict with the triple rhythm of the solo part.

In 1843 Schumann was asked by Mendelssohn to join him as a teacher of piano, composition, and score reading at the newly founded Cons. in Leipzig. In 1844 he and Clara undertook a concert tour to Russia; in the autumn of 1844 they moved to Dresden, remaining there until 1850. To this period belong his great C major Sym. (1846), the Piano Trio (1847), and the opera *Genoveva* (1848). In 1847 he assumed the conducting post of the Liedertafel, and in 1848 organized the Chorgesang-Verein in Dresden. In 1850 he became town music director in Düsseldorf, but his disturbed condition manifested itself in such alarming ways that he had to resign the post, though he continued to compose. In 1853 he completed a violin concerto. Joachim, in whose care Schumann left the work, thought it was not worthy of his genius, and ruled that it should not be performed until the centennial of Schumann's death. The concerto was first performed in Berlin on Nov. 26, 1937.

Schumann's condition continued to deteriorate. On Feb. 27, 1854, he threw himself into the Rhine, but was rescued. On March 4, 1854, he was placed, at his own request, in a sanatorium at Endenich, near Bonn, remaining there until the end of his life. Strangely, he did not want to see Clara, and there were months when he did not even inquire about her and the children. But Brahms was a welcome visitor, and Schumann enjoyed his company during his not infrequent periods of lucidity. According to Schumann's own account during his confinement in Endenich in 1855, he contracted syphilis in 1831 and was treated with arsenic. See F. Franken, "Robert Schumann in der Irrenanstalt Endenich," *Robert Schumanns letzte Lebensjahre: Protokoll einer Krankheit, Archiv Blätter 1* (Berlin, March 1994).

WORKS: DRAMATIC: *Der Corsar*, opera (1844; unfinished; only a chorus and sketch for an air completed); *Genoveva*, opera, op. 81 (1847–49; Leipzig, June 25, 1850); *Manfred*, incidental music to Byron's play, op. 115 (1848–49; Leipzig, June 13, 1852).

BIBL.: COLLECTED WORKS: SOURCE MATERIAL: A complete edition of his works, *R. S.: Werke*, was ed. by Clara Schumann et al. and publ. by Breitkopf & Härtel (34 vols., Leipzig, 1881–93; supplement ed. by Brahms, 1893). His *Gesammelte Schriften über Musik und Musiker* is a collection of his articles from *Neue Zeitschrift für Musik* (4 vols., Leipzig, 1854; Eng. tr., London, 1877; 5th Ger. ed., rev. by M. Kreisig, 1914). A judicious selection from the complete writings, ed. by H. Simon, was publ. under the same title as the original edition (3 vols., Leipzig, 1888–89). A selection of Schumann's critical reviews, tr. into Eng. by P. Rosenfeld, was publ. in New York in 1946. The R.-S.-Gesellschaft began the publication of the *Sammelbände der R.-S.-Gesellschaft* in Leipzig in 1961. See also H. Drinker, *Texts of the Vocal Works of R. S. in English Translation* (N.Y., 1947), and L. Minchin, *S. in English: Four Famous Song-Cycles in Singable English Verse* (London, 1981). A thematic catalogue was prepared by A. Dörffel, *Thematisches Verzeichniss sämmtlicher in Druck erschienenen Werke R. S.s* (Leipzig, 1860; 4th ed., 1868). See also K. Hofmann, *Die Erstdrucke der Werke von R. S.* (Tützing, 1979). BIOGRAPHICAL: W. von Wasielewski, *R. S.* (Dresden, 1858; Eng. tr., Boston, 1871; aug. Ger. ed., 1906); A. Reissmann, *R. S.: Sein Leben und seine Werke* (Berlin, 1865; 3d ed., 1879; Eng. tr., London, 1886); A. Niggli, *R. S.* (Basel, 1879); P. Spitta, *Ein Lebensbild R. S.s* (Leipzig, 1882); W. von Wasielewski, *S.iana* (Bonn, 1883); J. Fuller-Maitland, *S.* (London, 1884; new ed., 1913); H. Reimann, *R. S.s Leben und Werke* (Leipzig, 1887); R. Batka, *S.* (Leipzig, 1893); H. Abert, *R. S.* (Berlin, 1903; 3d ed., 1918); A. Paterson, *S.* (London, 1903; rev. ed., 1934); L. Schneider and M. Mareschal, *S.: Sa vie et ses oeuvres* (Paris, 1905); C. Mauclair, *S.* (Paris, 1906); M.D. Calvocoressi, *S.* (Paris, 1912); M. Wieck, *Aus dem Kreise Wieck-S.* (Dresden, 1912; 2d ed., 1914); W. Dahms, *S.* (Berlin, 1916); F. Niecks, *R. S.: A Supplementary and Corrective Biography* (London, 1925); R. Pitrou, *La Vie intérieure de R. S.* (Paris, 1925); E. Schumann, *Erinnerungen* (Stuttgart, 1925; Eng. tr., London, 1927); V. Basch, *S.* (Paris, 1926); idem, *La Vie douloureuse de S.* (Paris, 1928; Eng. tr., N.Y., 1931); H. Tessmer, *R. S.* (Stuttgart, 1930); E. Schumann, *R. S.: Ein Lebensbild meines Vaters* (Leipzig, 1931); M. Beaufils, *S.* (Paris, 1932); C. Valabrega, *S.* (Modena, 1934); W. Gertler, *R. S.* (Leipzig, 1936); W. Korte, *R. S.* (Potsdam, 1937); E. Bücken, *R. S.* (Cologne, 1940); W. Boetticher, *R. S.: Einführung in Persönlichkeit und Werk* (Berlin, 1941); R. Schauffler, *Florestan: The Life and Work of R. S.* (N.Y., 1945); J. Chissell, *S.* (London, 1948; 5th ed., rev., 1989); R. Sutermeister, *R. S.: Sein Leben nach Briefen, Tagebüchern und Erinnerungen des Meisters und seiner Gattin* (Zürich, 1949); K. Wörner, *R. S.* (Zürich, 1949); A. Coeuroy, *R. S.* (Paris, 1950); E. Müller, *R. S.* (Olten, 1950); M. Brion, *S. et l'âme romantique* (Paris, 1954; in Eng. as *S. and the Romantic Age*, London, 1956); P. and W. Rehberg, *R. S.: Sein Leben und sein Werk* (Zürich, 1954); H. Moser and E. Rebling, eds., *R. S.: Aus Anlass seines 100. Todestages* (Leipzig, 1956); A. Boucourechliev, *S.* (Paris, 1957; Eng. tr., 1959); P. Young, *Tragic Muse: The Life and Works of R. S.* (London, 1957; 2d ed., enl., 1961); K. Laux, *R. S.* (Leipzig, 1972); T. Dowley, *S.: His Life and Times* (Tunbridge Wells, 1982); P. Sutermeister, *R. S.: Eine Biographie nach Briefen, Tagebuchern und Erinnerungen von R. und Clara S.* (Tubingen, 1982); R. Taylor, *R. S.: His Life and Work* (London, 1982); H. Köhler, *R. S.: Sein Leben und Wirken in den Leipziger Jahren* (Leipzig, 1986); U. Rauchfleisch, *R. S., Leben und Werk: Eine Psychobiographie* (Stuttgart, 1990); B. Meier, *R. S.* (Reinbeck bei Hamburg, 1995); J. Daverio, *R. S.: Herald of a "New Poetic Age"* (N.Y., 1997). CRITICAL, ANALYTICAL: L. Mesnard, *Un Successeur de Beethoven: Étude sur R. S.* (Paris, 1876); F. Jansen, *Die Davidsbündler: Aus R. S.s Sturm- und*

Drangperiode (Leipzig, 1883); M. Katz, *Die Schilderung des musikalischen Eindrucks bei S.* (Giessen, 1910); I. Hirschberg, *R. S.s Tondichtungen balladischen Charakters* (Langensalza, 1913); F. Schnapp, *Heinrich Heine und R. S.* (Hamburg, 1924); P. Frenzel, *R. S. und Goethe* (Leipzig, 1926); K. Wagner, *R. S. als Schuler und Abiturient* (Zwickau, 1928); M. Ninck, *S. und die Romantik in der Musik* (Heidelberg, 1929); G. Minotti, *Die Geheimdokumente der Davidsbündler* (Leipzig, 1934); I. Forger, *R. S. als Kritiker: Ein Beitrag zur Geschichte der musikalischen Kritik und zum S.-Problem* (diss., Univ. of Munster, 1948); G. Abraham, ed., *S.: A Symposium* (London, 1952); H. Homeyer, *Grundbegriffe der Musikanschauung R. S.s: Ihr Wesen, ihre Bedeutung und Funktion in seinem literarischen Gesamtwerk* (diss., Univ. of Münster, 1956); H. Pleasants, *The Musical World of R. S.* (N.Y., 1965); L. Plantinga, *S. As Critic* (New Haven, 1967); T. Brown, *The Aesthetics of R. S.* (N.Y., 1968); A. Walker, ed., *R. S.: The Man and His Music* (London, 1972; 2d ed., rev., 1976); H.-P. Fricker, *Die musikkritischen Schriften R. S.s: Versuch eines literaturwissenschaftlichen Zugangs* (Bern, 1983); J. Finson and R. Todd, eds., *Mendelssohn and S.: Essays on their Music and its Context* (Durham, N.C., 1984); R. Kapp, *Studien zum Spätwerk R. S.s* (Tutzing, 1984); F. Otto, *R. S. als Jean-Paul-Leser* (Frankfurt am Main, 1984); B. Borchard, *R. S. und Clara Wieck: Bedingungen künstlerischer Arbeit in der ersten Hälfte des 19. Jahrhunderts* (Weinheim, 1985); D. Fischer-Dieskau, *R. S.: Das Vokalwerk* (Munich, 1985); B. Meissner, *Geschichtsrezeption als Schaffenkorrelat: Studien zum Musikgeschichtsbild R. S.s* (Bern, 1985); P. Ostwald, *S.: Music and Madness* (London, 1985); R. Larry Todd, *S. and His World* (Princeton, N.J., 1994).

Schumann, Walter, American composer; b. N.Y., Oct. 8, 1913; d. Minneapolis, Aug. 21, 1958. He studied law and music at the Univ. of Southern Calif. in Los Angeles. He became associated with radio shows and composed music for films; also wrote an opera, *John Brown's Body* (Los Angeles, Sept. 21, 1953). He contributed the famous ominously syncopated theme to the television show *Dragnet*, based on the initial 3 notes of the minor scale.

Schumann-Heink, Ernestine (née **Rössler**), famous Austrian-born American contralto and mezzo-soprano; b. Lieben, near Prague, June 15, 1861; d. Los Angeles, Nov. 17, 1936. Her father was an officer in the Austrian army; her mother, an Italian amateur singer. In 1872 she was sent to the Ursuline Convent in Prague, where she sang in the church choir; after lessons from Marietta von Leclair in Graz, she made her first public appearance there as soloist in Beethoven's 9th Sym. (1876); she made her operatic debut at the Dresden Court Opera (Oct. 15, 1878) as Azucena, where she sang until 1882; she also continued her studies with Karl Krebs, Franz Wüllner, and others. From 1883 to 1897 she was a member of the Hamburg Opera; she appeared with the company on its visit to London's Covent Garden in 1892, where she sang Erda, Fricka, and Brangäne. She was a regular singer at the Bayreuth Festivals from 1896 to 1914 and appeared at Covent Garden (1897–1901); she also sang with the Berlin Royal Opera. She made her U.S. debut as Ortrud in Chicago on Nov. 7, 1898, a role she chose for her Metropolitan Opera debut in New York on Jan. 9, 1899; she canceled her contract with the Berlin Royal Opera in order to remain a member of the Metropolitan Opera (until 1903; then appeared intermittently until 1932); she created the role of Clytemnestra in *Elektra* (Dresden, Jan. 25, 1909); she made her last operatic appearance as Erda at the Metropolitan on March 11, 1932. She became a naturalized American citizen in 1908. During the last years of her life, she was active mainly as a teacher. Her operatic repertoire included about 150 parts; her voice, of an even quality in all registers, possessed great power, making it peculiarly suitable to Wagnerian roles. She was married in 1882 to Ernst Heink of Dresden, from whom she was later divorced; in 1893 she married the actor Paul Schumann in Hamburg; he died in 1904; she assumed the names of both Schumann and Heink. Her 3d husband was a Chicago lawyer, William Rapp Jr., whom she married in 1905 and then subsequently divorced (1914).

BIBL.: M. Lawton, *S.-H., The Last of the Titans* (N.Y., 1928); J. Howard, *Madame E. S.-H.: Her Life and Times* (Sebastopol, Calif., 1990).

Schunk, Robert, German tenor; b. Neu-Isenburg, Jan. 5, 1948. He was a pupil of Martin Grundler at the Frankfurt Hochschule für Musik. In 1973 he made his operatic debut as Jack in *The Midsummer Marriage* in Karlsruhe, where he sang until 1975; he then appeared in Bonn (1975–77), Dortmund (1977–79), and at the Bayreuth Festivals (from 1977), where he was heard as Siegmund, Melot, Erik, and Walther in *Tannhäuser*. As a guest artist, he appeared in operas in Hamburg, Munich, Vienna, Cologne, Berlin, Geneva, Chicago, and San Francisco. He made his debut at the Metropolitan Opera in New York as Florestan on Dec. 10, 1986. In 1987 he sang for the first time at London's Covent Garden as the Emperor in *Die Frau ohne Schatten*. His other roles include Don Carlos, Weber's Max, Hoffmann, Walther von Stolzing, and Parsifal.

Schürer, Johann Georg, prominent German composer; b. probably in Raudnitz, Bohemia, c.1720; d. Dresden, Feb. 16, 1786. He settled in Dresden about 1746, where he first gained notice as composer and music director of an opera troupe at the Zwinger; in 1748 he was made Kirchencompositeur to the court, a position he held with distinction until his retirement in 1780. His mastery of contrapuntal writing is revealed in his numerous sacred compositions, which include the oratorios *Il Figliuol Prodigo* (1747), *Isacco figura del Redentore* (1748), and *La Passione di Jesu Christo* (n.d.). He also wrote the operas *Astrea placata ovvero La felicità della terra* (Warsaw, Oct. 7, 1746), *La Galatea* (Dresden, Nov. 8, 1746), *L'Ercole sul Termodonte* (Dresden, Jan. 9, 1747), *Doris* (Dresden, Feb. 13, 1747), and *Calandro* (Dresden, Jan. 20, 1748).

BIBL.: R. Haas, *J. G. S. (1720–1786): Ein Beitrag zur Geschichte der Musik in Dresden* (Dresden, 1915).

Schurmann, (Eduard) Gerard, pianist, conductor, and composer of Dutch and Hungarian descent; b. Kertosono, Dutch East Indies, Jan. 19, 1924. His father was an employee at a sugar factory in Java; his mother was a pianist who had studied with Bartók at the Budapest Academy of Music. As war clouds gathered over southeastern Asia, Schurmann was sent to England in 1937; he went to school in London, and after matriculation joined the Royal Air Force, serving in aircrews on active flying duty. While still in uniform, he gave piano recitals; he studied piano with Kathleen Long and composition with Alan Rawsthorne. During his travels in Italy, he took lessons in conducting with Ferrara. The government of the Netherlands offered him the position of cultural attaché at the Dutch Embassy in London; being fluent in the Dutch language, which was his mother tongue in the Dutch East Indies, he accepted. Later, he moved to the Netherlands, where he was active with the radio in Hilversum. He developed a successful career in London as a pianist, conductor, and composer. In 1981 he settled in Hollywood, where he became active as a film composer; he also traveled widely as a guest conductor, presenting a comprehensive repertory ranging from Haydn to contemporary composers, including his own works. The structure of Schurmann's music is asymptotic toward tonality; melodic progressions are linear, with the fundamental tonic and dominant often encasing the freely atonal configurations, while dodecaphony assumes the adumbrative decaphonic lines, with 2 notes missing in the tone row. The harmonic texture is acrid, acerbic, and astringent; the styptic tendency is revealed in his predilection for dissonant minor seconds and major sevenths treated as compound units; yet after the needed tension is achieved, the triadic forms are introduced as a sonic emollient. Thanks to this versatility of application, Schurmann achieves a natural felicity in dealing with exotic subjects; his proximity to gamelan-like pentatonicism during his adolescence lends authentic flavor to his use of pentatonic scales; remarkable in his congenial treatment is the set *Chuench'i*, to Eng. trs. of 7 Chinese poems. On the other hand, his intimate knowledge of Eng. music and history enables him to impart a true archaic sentiment to his opera cantata based on the medieval poem *Piers Plowman* (Gloucester Cathedral, Aug. 22, 1980). Schurmann is self-critical in regard to works of his which he deems imperfect; thus, he destroyed his Piano Concerto, which he had played under prestigious auspices with the London Sym. Orch. conducted by Sir Adrian Boult in Cambridge in April 1944.

Schürmann, Georg Caspar, eminent German composer; b. Idensen, near Hannover, 1672 or 1673; d. Wolfenbüttel, Feb. 25, 1751. He went to Hamburg, where he became a male alto at the Opera and in various churches when he was 20; after appearing with the Hamburg Opera at the Braunschweig court of Duke Anton Ulrich of Braunschweig-Lüneburg in 1697, the duke engaged him as solo alto to the court; he was also active as a conductor at the Opera and at the court church. After the duke sent him to Italy for further training (1701–2?), he was loaned to the Meiningen court as Kapellmeister and composer; in 1707 he resumed his association with the Braunschweig-Wolfenbüttel court, where he was active as a composer and conductor for the remainder of his life. Schurmann was a leading opera composer during the Baroque era. He wrote over 40 operas, only 3 of which survived in their entirety after their Braunschweig premieres: *Heinrich der Vogler* (part I, Aug. 1, 1718; part II, Jan. 11, 1721), *Die getreue Alceste* (1719), and *Ludovicus Pius, oder Ludewig der Fromme* (1726). He was also a noted composer of sacred music.

BIBL.: G. Schmid, *Die frühdeutsche Oper und die musikdramatische Kunst G. C. S.s* (2 vols., Regensburg, 1933–34).

Schuster, Bernhard, German music publisher and composer; b. Berlin, March 26, 1870; d. there, Jan. 13, 1934. After studies in piano, organ, and violin, he was active as a theater conductor. In 1901 he founded the fortnightly review *Die Musik*, which from its inception ranked with the foremost musical journals of Germany; he was its ed.-in-chief until 1933. In 1905 he founded the publishing house Schuster und Loeffler (Berlin and Leipzig), which brought out a number of important works on music (the business was acquired by the Stuttgart Deutsche Verlags-Anstalt in 1922). He wrote the operas *Der Jungbrunnen* (Karlsruhe, 1920) and *Der Dieb des Glucks* (Wiesbaden, March 10, 1923).

Schuster, Joseph, distinguished German conductor and composer; b. Dresden, Aug. 11, 1748; d. there, July 24, 1812. After initial training with his father, a Dresden court musician, and J. G. Schürer, he pursued his studies on a scholarship in Italy with Girolamo Pera (1765–68). After serving as a church composer in Dresden (1772–74), he returned to Italy and completed his studies with Padre Martini in Bologna. He wrote operas for Venice and Naples, and was named honorary maestro di cappella to the King of Naples. Settling in Dresden in 1781, he was active as a conductor at the court church and theater; with Seydelmann, he shared the duties of Kapellmeister to the elector from 1787. Schuster assumed a leading position at the Dresden court, both as a conductor and as a composer. Of his some 20 works for the stage, the Singspiel *Der Alchymist oder Der Liebesteufel* (Dresden, March 1778) won great popularity in Germany. His Padua String Quartet in C major (1780) was formerly attributed to Mozart.

Schützendorf, family of German musicians, all brothers:

(1) Guido Schützendorf, bass; b. Vught, near 's-Hertogenbosch, the Netherlands, April 22, 1880; d. in Germany, April 1967. He studied at the Cologne Cons. He sang with the German Opera Co., with which he toured the United States (1929–30); he also sang under the name **Schützendorf an der Mayr.**

(2) Alfons Schützendorf, bass-baritone; b. Vught, May 25, 1882; d. Weimar, Aug. 1946. He studied in Cologne and with Borgatti in Milan. He sang at the Bayreuth Festivals (1910–12) and at London's Covent Garden (1910); he taught at the Essen Folkwangschule (1927–31) and in Berlin (from 1932). He was esteemed for such roles as Wotan, Klingsor, and Telramund.

(3) Gustav Schützendorf, baritone; b. Cologne, 1883; d. Berlin, April 27, 1937. He studied at the Cologne Cons. and in Milan. He made his operatic debut as Don Giovanni in Düsseldorf (1905); after singing in Berlin, Wiesbaden, and Basel, he was a member of the Bavarian Court Opera (later State Opera) in Munich (1914–20) and the Berlin State Opera (1920–22); he made his Metropolitan Opera debut in New York as Faninal on Nov. 17, 1922, and remained on its roster until 1935. He married **Grete Stückgold** in 1929.

(4) Leo Schützendorf, bass-baritone; b. Cologne, May 7, 1886; d. Berlin, Dec. 31, 1931. He studied with D'Arnals in Cologne. He made his operatic debut in Düsseldorf (1908); he sang in Krefeld (1909–12), Darmstadt (1913–17), Wiesbaden (1917–19), and Vienna (1919–20) and at the Berlin State Opera (1920–29), where he created the role of Wozzeck (Dec. 14, 1925); among his other roles were Faninal, Beckmesser, and Boris Godunov.

Schwanenberg, Johann Gottfried, German keyboard player, music theorist, and composer; b. probably in Wolfenbüttel, c.1740; d. Braunschweig, March 29, 1804. He studied with G. C. Schurmann and Ignazio Fiorillo in Wolfenbüttel; after continuing his training in Venice on a court stipend with Hasse, Gaetano Latilla, and Giuseppe Saratelli (1756–61), he returned to the Braunschweig court as Kapellmeister (1762–1802). He was praised by his contemporaries as both a keyboard virtuoso and as a composer. In one of his theoretical papers, he argues for the deletion of H from the German musical scale. He produced 14 operas to Italian librettos, all 1st perf. in Braunschweig, including *Adriano in Siria* (Aug. 1762), *Solimano* (Nov. 4, 1762), and *Antigono* (Feb. 2, 1768).

Schwarz, Hanna, German mezzo-soprano; b. Hamburg, Aug. 15, 1943. She studied in Hamburg, Hannover, and Essen. In 1970 she made her operatic debut as Maddalena in *Rigoletto* in Hannover. In 1973 she became a member of the Hamburg State Opera. She sang with the Bavarian State Opera in Munich for the first time in 1974. In 1975 she made her debut at the Bayreuth Festival as Flosshilde in *Das Rheingold*, and continued to sing there during the next decade. In 1977 she made her U.S. debut as Fricka in *Das Rheingold* at the San Francisco Opera, and also appeared as Preziosilla at the Paris Opéra. In 1978 she sang Cherubino at the Deutsche Oper in Berlin. On Feb. 24, 1979, she appeared as Countess Geschwitz in the first complete performance of *Lulu* at the Paris Opéra. That same year she also made her debut at the Salzburg Festival as a soloist in Beethoven's 9th Sym. In 1980 she sang for the first time at London's Covent Garden as Waltraute and returned to the Salzburg Festival to sing Juana in a concert performance of Krenek's *Karl V*. In 1992 she made her first operatic stage appearance at the Salzburg Festival when she sang Herodias. She was engaged as Fricka and Waltraute at the Bayreuth Festival in 1995, and that same year she sang in the premiere of Schnittke's *Historia von D. Johann Fausten* in Hamburg. In 1996 she appeared as Herodias and Fricka at the Metropolitan Opera in New York. As a concert artist, she sang widely in Europe and North America.

Schwarz, Joseph, German baritone; b. Riga, Oct. 10, 1880; d. Berlin, Nov. 10, 1926. He studied in Berlin with Alexander Heinemann, and then continued his training at the Vienna Cons. In 1900 he made his operatic debut in *Aida* in Linz. Following engagements in Riga, Graz, and St. Petersburg, he sang in Vienna, principally at the Volksoper and then at the Court Opera (1909–15). From 1915 he was a principal member of the Berlin Royal (later State) Opera. He also sang at the Chicago Opera (1921–25) and at London's Covent Garden as Rigoletto (1924).

Schwarz, Paul, Austrian tenor; b. Vienna, June 30, 1887; d. Hamburg, Dec. 24, 1980. He sang in Bielitz and Vienna (1909–12). From 1923 to 1933 he was a member of the Hamburg Opera, where he gained success in buffo roles. He made guest appearances in Berlin, Paris, Amsterdam, and London (Covent Garden debut as Monostatos, 1936). During World War II, he lived in the United States. After the war, he resumed his career in Europe, singing until 1949.

Schwarz, Vera, Austrian soprano; b. Zagreb, July 10, 1889; d. Vienna, Dec. 4, 1964. She studied voice and piano in Vienna, where she appeared in operettas. She went to Hamburg in 1914 and to Berlin in 1917; she toured in South America. In 1939 she went to Hollywood, where she became a vocal instructor; in 1948 she returned to Austria; gave courses at the Mozarteum in Salzburg. Her best roles were Carmen and Tosca.

Schwarzkopf, Dame (Olga Maria) Elisabeth (Friederike), celebrated German-born English soprano; b. Jarotschin, near Posen, Dec. 9, 1915. She studied with Lula Mysz-Gmeiner at the Berlin Hochschule für Musik; she made her operatic debut as a Flower Maiden in Parsifal at the Berlin Städtische Oper (April 17, 1938), then studied with Maria Ivogun while continuing on its roster, appearing in more important roles from 1941. In 1942 she made her debut as a lieder artist in Vienna, and also sang for the first time at the State Opera there as Zerbinetta, remaining on its roster until the Nazis closed the theater in 1944. Having registered as a member of the German Nazi Party in 1940, Schwarzkopf had to be de-Nazified by the Allies after the end of World War II. In 1946 she rejoined the Vienna State Opera and appeared as Donna Elvira during its visit to London's Covent Garden in 1947; she subsequently sang at Covent Garden regularly until 1951. In 1947 she made her first appearance at the Salzburg Festival as Susanna; she also sang regularly at Milan's La Scala (1948–63). Furtwängler invited her to sing in his performance of the Beethoven 9th Sym. at the reopening celebrations of the Bayreuth Festival in 1951. She then created the role of Anne Trulove in Stravinsky's *The Rake's Progress* in Venice on Sept. 11, 1951. On Oct. 25, 1953, she gave her first recital at N.Y.'s Carnegie Hall; she made her U.S. operatic debut as the Marschallin with the San Francisco Opera on Sept. 20, 1955. On Oct. 13, 1964, she made her belated Metropolitan Opera debut in New York in the same role, continuing on its roster until 1966. In 1975 she made a farewell tour of the United States as a concert singer. She married **Walter Legge** in 1953 and became a naturalized British subject. She ed. his memoir, *On and Off the Record* (N.Y., 1982; 2d ed., 1988). In 1992 she was made a Dame Commander of the Order of the British Empire. In addition to her acclaimed Mozart and Strauss roles, she was also admired in Viennese operetta. As an interpreter of lieder, she was incomparable.

BIBL.: A. Sanders and J. Steane, *E. S.: A Career on Record* (Portland, Oreg., 1996).

Schweitzer, Anton, German composer; b. Coburg (baptized), June 6, 1735; d. Gotha, Nov. 23, 1787. He was a chorister, and later played viola in Hildburghausen; after study with J. F. Kleinknecht in Bayreuth, he returned to Hildburghausen as Kammermusicus, and following further training in Italy (1764–66), he returned once more to Hildburghausen as court Kapellmeister. In 1769 he became conductor of Seyler's opera troupe, which was engaged by the Weimar court in 1771. He produced his successful Singspiel *Die Dorfgala* there (June 30, 1772), which was followed by the successful *Alkeste* (May 28, 1773), the first through-composed grand opera to a German libretto, the text being by C. M. Wieland. After fire destroyed the Weimar theater in 1774, he accompanied Seyler's troupe to Gotha, where he subsequently was director of the ducal chapel from 1778 until his death. Among his other stage works were *Rosamunde,* Singspiel (Mannheim, Jan. 20, 1780), *Die Wahl des Herkules,* lyric drama (Weimar, Sept. 4, 1773), and the melodrama *Pygmalion*, after Rousseau (Weimar, May 13, 1772; not extant). He also wrote many ballets.

BIBL.: J. Maurer, *A. S. als dramatischer Komponist* (Leipzig, 1912).

Schwertsik, Kurt, Austrian composer, horn player, and teacher; b. Vienna, June 25, 1935. He studied composition with Marx and Schiske at the Vienna Academy of Music (1949–57), where he also received training in horn. From 1955 to 1959 he played horn in the Niederösterreichisches Tonkünstlerorchester in Vienna. With Cerha, he founded the new music ensemble die reihe in Vienna in 1958. He continued his training with Stockhausen in Darmstadt and Cologne (1959–62), and held a bursary with the Austrian Cultural Inst. in Rome (1960–61). From 1962 to 1968 he again played horn in the Niederösterreichisches Tonkünstlerorchester. He also studied analysis with Polnauer (1964–65). While serving as a visiting teacher of composition at the Univ. of Calif. at Riverside (1966), he pursued his studies in analysis with Jonas. In 1968 he became a horn player in the Vienna Sym. Orch. He also taught composition at the Vienna Cons. from 1979. A skillful and imaginative composer, he explores in his works many new paths in synthesizing the traditional with the contemporary.

WORKS: DRAMATIC: *Der lange Weg zur grossen Mauer*, opera (1974; Ulm, May 13, 1975); *Walzerträume (. . . als das Tanzen noch geholfen hat)*, ballet (1976; Cologne, Feb. 16, 1977; also as the ballet or set of 3 orch. suites, *Wiener Chronik 1848*, 1976–77); *Ur-Faust*, music to Goethe's play (1976; Mattersburg, Feb. 2, 1977); *Kaiser Joseph und die Bahnwärters-Tochter*, music to Herzmanovsky-Orlando's play (1977); *Das Märchen von Fanferlieschen Schönefusschen*, opera (1982; Stuttgart, Nov. 24, 1983); *Macbeth*, dance theater (Heidelberg, Feb. 10, 1988); *Die verlorene Wut*, Singspiel (ORF, Dec. 26, 1989); *Das Friedensbankett*, operetta (1990); *Frida Kahlo*, ballet (1991; Bremen, Feb. 8, 1992); *Ulrichslegende*, music for an opera (1992); *Café Museum oder die Erleuchtung*, opera (Deutschlandsberg, Oct. 9, 1993); *Nietzsche*, ballet (1994); *Der ewige Frieden*, operetta (1994; Bonn, Jan. 8, 1995).

Sciarrino, Salvatore, Italian composer; b. Palermo, April 4, 1947. He was 12 when he began to compose under the tutelage of Antonino Titione; he also received some guidance from Evangelisti. After studies with Turi Belfiore (1964), he attended Evangelisti's electronic music sessions at the Accademia di Santa Cecilia in Rome (1969). He taught at the Milan Cons. (from 1974); he also served as artistic director of the Teatro Comunale in Bologna (1977–80). His music reveals an innovative approach to traditional forms; in some works he utilizes aleatoric procedures.

WORKS: OPERAS: *Amore e Psiche* (Milan, March 2, 1973); *Aspern* (Florence, June 8, 1978); *Cailles en sarchophage* (Venice, Sept. 26, 1979); *Vanitas* (Milan, Dec. 11, 1981); *Lohengrin* (Milan, Jan. 15, 1983); *Perseo e Andromeda* (1990; Stoccardo, Jan. 27, 1991).

Scio, Julie-Angélique, French soprano; b. Lille, 1768; d. Paris, July 14, 1807. She launched her career in 1786 under the name Mlle. Grécy. After appearances in Montpellier, Avignon, and Marseilles, she married the violinist Etienne Scio (1766–1796) and settled with him in Paris. In 1792 she made her first appearance at the Opéra Comique, and then became a principal member of the Opéra, where she created the title role in Cherubini's *Médée* (March 13, 1797) and the role of Constance in his *Les Deux journées* (March 14, 1800). She also won distinction in operas by Berton, Dalayrac, and Le Sueur.

Sciutti, Graziella, Italian soprano, opera producer, and teacher; b. Turin, April 17, 1927. She received her training at the Accademia di Santa Cecilia in Rome. In 1951 she made her debut as Lucy in Menotti's *The Telephone* at the Aix-en-Provence Festival. In 1954 she sang for the first time at the Glyndebourne Festival as Rosina, and she returned there until 1959. She sang Carolina in *Il Matrimonio segreto* at the opening of the Piccola Scala in Milan in 1955. From 1956 she appeared at La Scala in Milan. She made her debut at London's Covent Garden in 1956 as Oscar, and made appearances there until 1962. In 1958 she made her first appearance at the Salzburg Festival as Despina, and continued to sing there until 1966. In 1961 she made her U.S. debut as Susanna at the San Francisco Opera. After her career as a soubrette exponent ended, she devoted herself to producing opera in Glyndebourne, at Covent Garden, in New York, Chicago, and other opera centers. From 1986 she also ran her own music academy in Florence.

Scontrino, Antonio, prominent Italian double bass player, teacher, and composer; b. Trapani, May 17, 1850; d. Florence, Jan. 7, 1922. He studied at the Palermo Cons., becoming a virtuoso on the double bass and giving concerts. He went to Munich for a special study of German music at the Musikschule (1872–74). After various engagements as an orch. player and teacher, he settled in Florence in 1892, and taught composition at the Reale Istituto Musicale. He composed the operas *Matelda* (Milan, June

19, 1879), *Il Progettista* (Rome, Feb. 8, 1882), *Il sortilegio* (Turin, June 21, 1882), *Gringoire* (Milan, May 24, 1890), and *La Cortigiana* (Milan, Jan. 30, 1896); also incidental music to Gabriele d'Annunzio's *Francesca da Rimini* (Rome, Dec. 12, 1901).

BIBL.: *A. S. nella vita e nell'arte* (Trapani, 1935).

Scott, Cyril (Meir), remarkable English composer; b. Oxton, Cheshire, Sept. 27, 1879; d. Eastbourne, Dec. 31, 1970. He was a scion of a cultural family; his father was a classical scholar, his mother a fine amateur musician. Having displayed a natural penchant for music as a child, he was sent to Frankfurt am Main at age 12 to study with Uzielli and Humperdinck, remaining there for a year and a half before returning to England; he once again went to Frankfurt am Main in 1895 to study piano and theory with Iwan Knorr. In 1898 he went to Liverpool as a teacher. In 1900 Hans Richter conducted Scott's *Heroic Suite*, in Liverpool and Manchester; also in 1900, his 1st Sym. was played in Darmstadt; his overture *Pelléas and Mélisande* was performed in Frankfurt am Main. His 2d Sym. (1902) was given at a Promenade Concert in London on Aug. 25, 1903. (It was later converted into *3 Symphonic Dances*.) His setting of Keats's *La Belle Dame sans merci* for Baritone, Chorus, and Orch. was premiered in London in 1916. His opera *The Alchemist* (1917), for which he wrote his own libretto, was premiered in Essen on May 28, 1925. In 1920 Scott traveled to the United States and played his 1st Piano Concerto with the Philadelphia Orch. under Stokowski (Nov. 5, 1920). However, Scott acquired fame mainly as a composer of some exotically flavored piano pieces, of which *Lotus Land* became a perennial favorite; Fritz Kreisler arranged it for violin and piano, and played it repeatedly at his concerts. Among his other works are: 2 more operas, *The Saint of the Mountain* (1925) and *Maureen O'Mara* (1946), and 3 ballets, *The Incompetent Apothecary* (1923), *Karma* (1926), and *The Masque of the Red Death* (1932); From his early youth, Scott was attracted to occult sciences, and was a believer in the reality of the supernatural; he publ. books and essays on music as a divinely inspired art, and inveighed violently against jazz as the work of Satan. Among his books, all publ. in London, are *The Philosophy of Modernism in Its Connection with Music* (1917), *The Initiate Trilogy* (1920, 1927, 1935), *My Years of Indiscretion* (1924), *The Influence of Music on History and Morals: A Vindication of Plato* (1928), *Music: Its Secret Influence through the Ages* (1933; aug. ed., 1958), *An Outline of Modern Occultism* (1935), *The Christian Paradox* (1942), and an autobiographical vol., *Bone of Contention* (1969); also 2 books on medical matters: *Medicine, Rational and Irrational* (1946) and *Cancer Prevention* (1968).

BIBL.: A. Hull, *C. S.: Composer, Poet and Philosopher* (London, 1918; 3d ed., 1921).

Scott, Tom (Thomas Jefferson), American folksinger and composer; b. Campbellsburg, Ky., May 28, 1912; d. N.Y., Aug. 12, 1961. He studied violin with an uncle. He played in dance bands and also wrote songs; he then went to Hollywood, where he took theory lessons with Antheil; he subsequently studied with Harrison Kerr and Riegger. His works include the opera *The Fisherman* (1956).

Scotti, Antonio, celebrated Italian baritone; b. Naples, Jan. 25, 1866; d. there, Feb. 26, 1936. He studied with Ester Trifari-Paganini in Naples. He made his operatic debut in Naples (March 1889) as Cinna in Spontini's *La Vestale*, then sang elsewhere in Italy, Russia, Spain, and South America. He made his London debut at Covent Garden on June 8, 1899, as Don Giovanni, and appeared in the same role with the Metropolitan Opera in New York (Dec. 27, 1899). He remained with the Metropolitan for 33 years; he made his farewell appearance on Jan. 20, 1933. He also toured in America with his own company. He possessed great histrionic ability, and was especially noted for his dramatic roles (Scarpia, Rigoletto, Falstaff, Don Giovanni, and Iago).

Scotto, Renata, famous Italian soprano; b. Savona, Feb. 24, 1933. She commenced music study in Savona at age 14; when she was 16, she went to Milan for vocal training with Emilio Ghirardini, then with Merlini, and finally with Mercedes Llopart. She made her debut as Violetta in Savona in 1952. After winning a national vocal competition in 1953, she made her formal debut as Violetta at Milan's Teatro Nuovo, then joined Milan's La Scala, where she sang secondary roles until being called upon to replace Maria Callas as Amina during the company's visit to the Edinburgh Festival in 1957. She made her U.S. debut at the Chicago Lyric Opera on Nov. 2, 1960, as Mimi, a role she also chose for her Metropolitan Opera debut in New York on Oct. 13, 1965. She scored a brilliant success with her portrayal of Mimi in the Metropolitan Opera production of *La Bohème* in the "Live from Lincoln Center" telecast on PBS (March 15, 1977); thereafter she was a stellar figure in the U.S. opera scene; she also toured widely as a recitalist. In later years, she was active as an opera director. She sang her final performance there as Cio-Cio-San in 1987. In 1995 she sang the Marshallin at the Spoleto Festival U.S.A. in Charleston, S.C. Among her other fine roles were Lucia, Gilda, Elena in *I Vespri Siciliani*, Norma, Manon Lescaut, and Luisa Miller. She publ. the book *Scotto: More than a Diva* (with O. Riva; N.Y., 1984).

BIBL.: B. Tosi, *R. S.: Voce di due mondi* (Venice, 1990).

Scovotti, Jeanette, American soprano; b. N.Y., Dec. 5, 1936. She received her training in New York at the High School of Music and Art, and at the Juilliard School of Music. She began her career singing in concerts. In 1960 she appeared as Despina with the New England Opera Theater in Boston. After singing at the Santa Fe Opera, she appeared as Blondchen at the San Francisco Opera. On Nov. 15, 1962, she made her Metropolitan Opera debut in New York as Adele, and remained on its roster until 1966. She also appeared at the Teatro Colón in Buenos Aires (1963–65). From 1966 to 1977 she sang with the Hamburg State Opera. In 1977 she appeared in the U.S. premiere of Glinka's *Ruslan and Ludmila* in Boston. Among her other roles of note were Zerlina, Rosina, Gilda, Lucia, Aminta in *Die schweigsmae Frau*, the Italian Singer in *Capriccio*, and the title role in Krenek's *Sardakai*.

Scribe, (Augustin) Eugène, famous French dramatist and librettist; b. Paris, Dec. 24, 1791; d. there, Feb. 20, 1861. He was a scholarship student at the Collège Ste.-Barbe in Paris. After training in the law, he turned to the theater, being made a member of the Académie Française (1836). He was closely associated as a librettist with Meyerbeer, but also wrote librettos for Auber, Bellini, Donizetti, Gounod, Halévy, Offenbach, Verdi, and others. See *Eugène Scribe: Oeuvres complètes* (76 vols., Paris, 1874–85).

BIBL.: N. Arvin, *E. S.* (N.Y., 1924); K. Pendle, *E. S. and French Opera of the 19th Century* (Ann Arbor, 1979).

Sculthorpe, Peter (Joshua), eminent Australian composer and teacher; b. Launceston, Tansmania, April 29, 1929. He studied at the Univ. of Melbourne Conservatorium of Music (B.Mus., 1951) and with Wellesz and Rubbra at Wadham College, Oxford (1958–60). In 1963 he joined the faculty of the Univ. of Sydney, where he later served as prof. of composition. He also was composer-in-residence at Yale Univ. while on a Harkness Fellowship (1966–67) and a visiting prof. at the Univ. of Sussex (1972–73). In 1970 he was made a Member and in 1977 an Officer of the Order of the British Empire. He was awarded the Silver Jubilee Medal in 1977. In 1980 he received an honorary doctor of letters degree from the Univ. of Tasmania, and in 1989 he received the same from the Univ. of Sussex; that same year he also received an honorary doctor of music degree from the Univ. of Melbourne. He was elected a fellow of the Australian Academy of the Humanities in 1991. Schulthorpe rejected such modern compositional methods as atonality and serialism to pursue an independent course. He has found inspiration in aboriginal Australian music, as well as in the music of Asia, particularly Japanese and Balinese music. In all of his music, one finds a discerning musicianship, mastery of resources, and inventiveness.

WORKS: DRAMATIC: *Sun Music*, ballet (Sydney, Aug. 2, 1968; based on the *Sun Music* series); *Rites of Passage*, theater piece (1972–73); *Quiros*, television opera (ABC National TV, July 1, 1982).

BIBL.: M. Hannan, *P. S.: His Music and Ideas 1929–*

1979 (Brisbane, 1982); D. Hayes, *P. S.: A Bio-Bibliography* (Westport, Conn., 1993).

Searle, Humphrey, distinguished English composer, teacher, and writer on music; b. Oxford, Aug. 26, 1915; d. London, May 12, 1982. He studied classical literature at Oxford (1933–37) and music at the Royal College of Music in London (1937), where his teachers were John Ireland and R. O. Morris. In 1937 he went to Vienna, where he took private lessons with Webern; this study proved to be a decisive influence in Searle's own compositions, which are imbued with the subtle coloristic processes peculiar to the 2d Viennese School of composition. He served in the British Army during World War II, and was stationed in Germany in 1946. Returning to London, he engaged in various organizations promoting the cause of modern music. He was honorary secretary of the Liszt Soc. (1950–62); he was an adviser on music for the Sadler's Wells Ballet (1951–57). In 1964–65 he was composer-in-residence at Stanford Univ. in California; after serving as a prof. at the Royal College of Music in London (1965–76), he was composer-in-residence at the Univ. of Southern Calif. in Los Angeles (1976–77). In 1968 he was made a Commander of the Order of the British Empire. Although Searle's method of composing included some aspects of the 12-tone method, he did not renounce tonal procedures, and sometimes applied purely national English melodic patterns. As a writer, he became particularly well known for his writings on Liszt.

WORKS: DRAMATIC: OPERAS: *The Diary of a Madman* (Berlin, Oct. 3, 1958); *The Photo of the Colonel* (Frankfurt am Main, June 3, 1964); *Hamlet* (1964–68; Hamburg, March 5, 1968). BALLETS: *Noctambules* (1956); *The Great Peacock* (1957–58); *Dualities* (1963).

WRITINGS (all publ. in London): *The Music of Liszt* (1954; 2d ed., 1966); *Twentieth Century Counterpoint* (1954); *Ballet Music: An Introduction* (1958; 2d ed., rev., 1973); with R. Layton, *Twentieth-Century Composers 3: Britain, Scandinavia and the Netherlands* (1972).

Sébastian, Georges (real name, **György Sebestyén**), Hungarian-born French conductor; b. Budapest, Aug. 17, 1903; d. Le Hauteville, Yvelines, April 12, 1989. He studied with Bartók, Kodály, and Weiner at the Budapest Academy of Music (graduated, 1921), then received instruction in conducting from Walter in Munich (1922–23). He conducted at the Hamburg Opera (1924–25) and with the Leipzig Gewandhaus Orch. (1925–27). After serving as principal conductor at Berlin's Städtische Oper (1927–31), he went to Moscow as music director of the Radio and as a conductor with the Phil. In 1938 he went to the United States; he was conductor of the Scranton (Pa.) Phil. (1940–45); he also conducted in South America. In 1946 he settled in Paris, where he conducted at the Opéra and the Opéra Comique; he also appeared with the Orchestre National de France. Sébastian became well known for his championship of the Romantic repertoire. He conducted complete cycles of the Bruckner and Mahler syms. in France.

Šebor, Karl, Bohemian conductor and composer; b. Brandeis, Aug. 13, 1843; d. Prague, May 17, 1903. He was a pupil of Kittl, then conductor of the National Opera (1864–67) and military bandmaster in Vienna (from 1871). He wrote Czech operas (all 1st produced in Prague): *The Templars in Moravia* (Oct. 19, 1864), *Drahomira* (1867), *The Hussite's Bride* (Sept. 28, 1868), *Blanka* (1870), and *The Frustrated Wedding* (Oct. 25, 1879).

Sechter, Simon, famous Austrian organist, pedagogue, and composer; b. Friedberg, Bohemia, Oct. 11, 1788; d. Vienna, Sept. 10, 1867. In 1804 he went to Vienna, where he studied with L. Koželuh and Hartmann, then was a piano and singing teacher at the Inst. for the Blind (1810–25). He also was assist. (1824–25) and principal (from 1825) Hoforganist, and likewise served as prof. of thoroughbass and counterpoint at the Cons. (1851–63). He won his greatest renown as a teacher, numbering among his best-known pupils Henselt, Bruckner, Vieuxtemps, and Thalberg; Schubert took a lesson from him (Nov. 4, 1828) shortly before his untimely death. Although he was a master contrapuntist, his output is unknown outside his homeland. Among his more than 8,000 works were 3 operas: *Ezzeline, die unglückliche Gegangene aus Deli-Katesse* (1843; not perf.), *Ali Hitsch-Hatsch* (1843; Vienna, Nov. 12, 1844), and *Melusine* (1851; not perf.); also 2 oratorios: *Die Offenbarung Johannes* (1838–45) and *Sodoms Untergang* (1840).

WRITINGS: *Die Grundsätze der musikalischen Komposition*: I, *Die richtige Folge der Grundharmonien* (Leipzig, 1853), II, *Von den Gesetzen des Taktes in der Musik; Vom einstimmigen Satz; Die Kunst, zu einer gegebenen Melodie die Harmonie zu finden* (Leipzig, 1853), and III, *Vom drei- und zweistimmigen Satze; Rhythmische Entwürfe; Vom strengen Satze, mit Kurzen Andeutungen des freien Satzes; Vom doppelten Contrapunkte* (Leipzig, 1854).

BIBL.: C. Pohl, *S. S.* (Vienna, 1868); J. Markus, *S. S.: Biographisches Denkmal* (Vienna, 1888); G. Capellen, *Ist das System S. S.s ein geeigneter Ausgangspunkt für die theoretische Wagnerforschung?* (Leipzig, 1902).

Seckendorff, Karl Siegmund, Freiherr von, German writer and composer; b. Erlangen, Nov. 26, 1744; d. Ansbach, April 26, 1785. He studied literature and jurisprudence at the Univ. of Erlangen. He was an officer in the Austrian army (1761–74), then in the diplomatic service in Weimar (1776–84); shortly before his death, he was appointed Prussian ambassador in Ansbach (1784). At Weimar he was on close terms with Goethe, who allowed him to write music for a number of his poems before their publ. (*Der Fischer, Der König in Thule*, etc.); in these songs, Seckendorff caught the characteristic inflections of folk melodies.

WORKS: DRAMATIC: *Lila*, Liederspiel (Weimar, 1776); *Le marché (La foire) du village*, ballet comique (1776); *Proserpina*, monodrama (Weimar, 1778); *Die Laune des Verliebten* (Weimar, May 20, 1779; not extant); *Jery und Bätely*, Singspiel (Weimar, July 12, 1780; not extant); *Der Geist der Jugend*, comédie ballet (Weimar, Jan. 30, 1782; not extant); *Der Blumenraub*, operetta (1784); *Die Empfindsamkeit* (n.d.).

BIBL.: V. Knab, *K. S. v. S. (1774–1785): Ein Beitrag zur Geschichte des deutschen volkstümlichen Liedes und der Musik am weimarischen Hof im 18. Jahrhundert* (diss., Univ. of Bonn, 1914).

Secunda, Sholom, Russian-born American composer; b. Alexandria, near Kherson, Sept. 4, 1894; d. N.Y., June 13, 1974. His family went to the United States in 1907. He took music lessons with Goetschius and Bloch at the Inst. of Musical Art in New York, graduating in 1917. He became a naturalized American citizen in 1923. In 1932 he became a founder of the Soc. of Jewish Composers, Publishers and Songwriters, which was absorbed by Broadcast Music, Inc. in 1940. From 1916 to 1973 he was associated with the Yiddish Theater in New York, for which he wrote over 40 operettas; most of these hardly made any impression outside ethnic circles, but one song, "Bei mir bist du schön," from the operetta *I Would if I Could* (1933), made an unexpected splash even among gentiles, and was sung, in the original Yiddish, by the Andrews Sisters, Rudy Vallee, Judy Garland, and Kate Smith, becoming one of the most popular songs worldwide. Secunda sold the copyright in 1937 for $30; he regained it in 1961, but never made any appreciable sum of money from it; a legal hassle with the author of the lyrics, Jacob Jacobs, further depleted Secunda's income. Other songs from his operettas were often taken as traditional; among these, "Dona, Dona, Dona," from the operetta *Esterke* (1940), was recorded by Joan Baez. He also wrote some Jewish service music.

BIBL.: V. Secunda, *Bei Mir Bist Du Schön: The Story of S. S.* (N.Y., 1982).

Secunde, Nadine, American soprano; b. Independence, Ohio, Dec. 21, 1953. She studied at the Oberlin College-Cons. of Music, with Margaret Harshaw at the Indiana Univ. School of Music in Bloomington, and in Germany as a Fulbright scholar. From 1980 to 1985 she was a member of the Wiesbaden State Theater. In 1985 she made her debut as Kát'a Kabanová at the Cologne

Opera, where she remained as a principal member. She sang Elsa at the Bayreuth Festival in 1987, and returned there in 1988 as Sieglinde in the *Ring* cycle. In 1988 she appeared as Elsa at London's Covent Garden and as Elisabeth at the Lyric Opera in Chicago. She portrayed Berlioz's Cassandre in Los Angeles in 1991. In 1994 she sang Elisabeth in Munich, returning there in 1997 to sing in the premiere of Henze's *Venus und Adonis*. Her other roles include Agathe, Chrysothemis, and Ariadne.

Seedo, (Sidow or **Sydow**), German composer; b. c.1700; d. probably in Prussia, c.1754. He was active at London's Drury Lane (1731–34), where he contributed music to several stage pieces. About 1736 he went to Potsdam to work with the Royal Band.

Seefried, Irmgard, outstanding German soprano; b. Köngetried, Bavaria, Oct. 9, 1919; d. Vienna, Nov. 24, 1988. She received her early musical instruction from her father, then studied voice at the Augsburg Cons., graduating in 1939. She made her professional operatic debut as the Priestess in *Aida* at the Aachen Stadttheater (Nov. 8, 1940); her first appearance at the Vienna State Opera followed as Eva in *Die Meistersinger von Nürnberg* (May 2, 1943); Richard Strauss chose her for the role of the Composer in *Ariadne auf Naxos* at his 80th birthday celebration there (1944). She subsequently sang in Salzburg, Edinburgh, Berlin, Paris, London, and Buenos Aires. On Nov. 20, 1953, she made her Metropolitan Opera debut in New York as Susanna in *Le nozze di Figaro*. She was made a Kammersängerin of the Vienna State Opera in 1947; she was named an honorary member in 1969. In 1948 she married Wolfgang Schneiderhan.

BIBL.: F. Fassbind, *Wolfgang Schneiderhan, I. S.: Eine Künstler- und Lebensgemeinschaft* (Bern, 1960).

Seeger, Horst, German musicologist; b. Erkner, near Berlin, Nov. 6, 1926. He began his training at the Berlin Hochschule für Musik (1950–55); he then studied musicology at Humboldt Univ. in Berlin, where he received his Ph.D. in 1958 with the diss. *Komponist und Folklore in der Musik des 20. Jahrhunderts*. He was chief dramaturg of the (East) Berlin Komische Oper (1960–73); from 1973 to 1983 he served as Intendant of the Dresden State Opera. His books include *Wolfgang Amadeus Mozart* (Leipzig, 1956); *Kleines Musiklexikon* (Berlin, 1958); *Joseph Haydn* (Leipzig, 1961); *Der kritische Musikus: Musikkritiken aus zwei Jahrhunderten* (Leipzig, 1963); *Musiklexikon* (Leipzig, 1966); *Wir und die Musik* (Berlin, 1968); *Opern-Lexikon* (Berlin, 1978; 3d ed., rev., 1987).

Segerstam, Leif (Selim), Finnish conductor and composer; b. Vaasa, March 2, 1944. He studied violin and conducting (diplomas in both, 1963) and also took courses in composition with Fougstedt, Kokkonen, and Englund at the Sibelius Academy in Helsinki. He then was a student of Persinger (violin), Overton and Persichetti (composition), and Morel (conducting) at the Juilliard School of Music in New York, where he took his diploma (1964) and postgraduate diploma (1965); in the summer of 1964 he also attended Susskind's conducting course at the Aspen (Colo.) Music School. After conducting at the Finnish National Opera in Helsinki (1965–68), he became a conductor at the Royal Theater in Stockholm in 1968; he was made its principal conductor in 1970 and its music director in 1971. In 1972–73 he held the post of 1st conductor at the Deutsche Oper in Berlin. In 1973–74 he was general manager of the Finnish National Opera. He was chief conductor of the Austrian Radio Sym. Orch. in Vienna (1975–82) and the Finnish Radio Sym. Orch. in Helsinki (1977–87), and also was Generalmusikdirector of the State Phil. in Rheinland-Pfalz (1983–89). From 1989 to 1995 he was chief conductor of the Danish National Radio Sym. Orch. in Copenhagen. In 1995 he became music director of the Royal Theater in Stockholm. He became prof. of conducting at the Sibelius Academy in Helsinki in 1997. In 1999 he was awarded the Nordic Council Music Prize. In 2001 he will become music director of the Finnish National Opera in Helsinki. Segerstam is one of the most prolific composers of his era. He composes in what he describes as a "freely pulsative" style. Among his works are 8 violin concertos (1967–93); 2 piano concertos (1977, 1981); 19 syms. (1977–94); 8 cello concertos (1981–93); a series of *Thoughts* for Orch. (1987–96); 27 string quartets (1962–90); 4 string trios (1977–91); many other chamber pieces; piano music; organ pieces; many songs.

Seibel, Klauspeter, German conductor; b. Offenbach, May 7, 1936. He received training in Nuremberg and Munich. Following his conducting debut at Munich's Gärtnerplatz State Theatre in 1957, he conducted opera in Freiburg im Breisgau (1963–65), Lübeck (1965–67), Kassel (1967–71), and Frankfurt am Main (1971–75). In 1975 he became Generalmusikdirektor in Freiburg im Breisgau, a position he retained until 1981. He also served as music director of the Nuremberg Sym. Orch. (from 1975). From 1987 to 1995 he was Generalmusikdirektor in Kiel. In 1995 he became music director of the Louisiana Phil. in New Orleans and in 1997 Generalmusikdirektor of the Frankfurt am Main Opera.

Seiber, Mátyás (György), significant Hungarian-born English composer; b. Budapest, May 4, 1905; d. in an automobile accident in Kruger National Park, Johannesburg, South Africa, Sept. 24, 1960. Of a musical family, he learned to play the cello at home; he later entered the Budapest Academy of Music, where he studied composition with Kodály (1919–24). During the following years, he traveled as a member of a ship's orch. on a transatlantic liner; he visited Russia as a music journalist. From 1928 to 1933 he taught composition at the Frankfurt am Main Hoch Cons.; he was the cellist in the Lenzewski Quartet, which specialized in modern music, then was again in Budapest. The catastrophic events in Germany and the growing Nazi influence in Hungary forced him to emigrate to England in 1935, where he quickly acquired a group of loyal disciples; he was cofounder of the Soc. for the Promotion of New Music (1942) and founder-conductor of the Dorian Singers (1945); he taught at Morely College (from 1942). His early music followed the national trends of the Hungarian School; later he expanded his melodic resources to include oriental modes and also jazz, treated as folk music; by the time he arrived in England, he had added dodecaphony to his oeuvre, though he used it in a very personal, lyrical manner, as in his cantata *Ulysses* for Tenor, Chorus, and Orch., after James Joyce (1946–47; London, May 27, 1949) and his 3d String Quartet, *Quartetto Lirico (*1948–51). His works also include *Eva spielt mit Puppen*, opera (1934), 2 operettas, and *The Invitation*, ballet (London, Dec. 30, 1960); also over 25 film scores, including Orwell's *Animal Farm*. He publ. the books *Schule für Jazz-Schlagzeug* (Mainz, 1929) and *The String Quartets of Béla Bartók* (London, 1945).

Seidel, Friedrich Ludwig, German organist, conductor, and composer; b. Treuenbrietzen, June 1, 1765; d. Charlottenburg, May 5, 1831. He studied with Benda in Berlin, then served as organist of the Marienkirche (from 1792); he became assistant conductor at the National Theater in 1801, and was named music director of the royal chapel in 1808 and court Kapellmeister in 1822, being pensioned in 1830. He composed the Singspiel *Claudine von Villa Bella*, several operas, 3 ballets, incidental music, and other dramatic works.

Seidel, Jan, Czech composer; b. Nymburk, Dec. 25, 1908. He was first attracted to architecture and graphic art; he attended Alois Hába's classes in quarter-tone composition at the Prague Cons. (1936–40), then took private lessons in theory with J. B. Foerster for a more traditional musical training. He was a composer, conductor, and pianist in E. F. Burian's Theater, acted as artistic adviser to the recording firm Esta (1938–45) and the Gramophone Corp. (1945–53), was chief of the Opera of the National Theater (1958–64), then served as dramatic adviser there. In 1976 he was made a National Artist by the Czech government. His String Quartet No. 2 with Narrator (1940) is in the quarter tone system, but most of his music is based on folk-song tradition according to the doctrine of socialist realism. He composed an opera, *Tonka Šibenice* (Tonka the Gallows; 1964).

Seidl, Anton, famous Hungarian conductor; b. Pest, May 7, 1850; d. N.Y., March 28, 1898. He studied at the Univ. and at the Cons.

in Leipzig, then was engaged by Hans Richter as chorus master at the Vienna Court Opera. Richter in turn recommended him to Wagner to assist in preparing the score and parts of the *Ring* tetralogy for the Bayreuth Festival of 1876. Returning to Leipzig, he was 1st conductor of its Opera (1879–82); in 1882 he was engaged by the impresario Angelo Neumann for a grand tour of Wagner's operas. From 1883 he conducted the Bremen Opera; in 1885 he was engaged to conduct the German opera repertoire at the Metropolitan Opera in New York. He made his American debut with *Lohengrin* there (Nov. 23, 1885), then conducted the American premieres of *Die Meistersinger von Nürnberg* (Jan. 4, 1886), *Tristan und Isolde* (Dec. 1, 1886), *Siegfried* (Nov. 9, 1887), and the *Ring* cycle (March 4–11, 1889). In 1891 he was engaged as conductor of the N.Y. Phil., and led it until his death (of ptomaine poisoning). Seidl was an excellent technician of the baton and established a standard of perfection rare in American orch. playing of that time; he introduced many unfamiliar works by German composers and conducted the premiere of Dvořák's *New World* Sym. (N.Y., Dec. 15, 1893). He married the Austrian soprano Auguste Kraus (b. Vienna, Aug. 28, 1853; d. Kingston, N.Y., July 17, 1939); after vocal studies with Marchen, she made her operatic debut at the Vienna Court Opera in 1877, where she sang minor roles; then sang in Leipzig (1881–82), where she subsequently became a member of Neumann's Wagnerian company and married Seidl; she sang at Her Majesty's Theatre in London in 1882 and then made her Metropolitan Opera debut in New York as Elisabeth in *Tannhäuser* under her husband's direction, remaining on its roster until 1888. Among her best known roles were Elsa, Eva, Siegliende, and Gutrune.

BIBL.: H. Krehbiel, *A. S.* (N.Y., 1898); H. Finck, ed., *A. S.: A Memorial by His Friends* (N.Y., 1899).

Seidl, Arthur, German writer on music; b. Munich, June 8, 1863; d. Dessau, April 11, 1928. He studied with Spitta and Bellermann in Berlin; he completed his training at the Univ. of Leipzig (Ph.D., 1887, with the diss. *Vom Musikalisch-Erhabenen: Prolegomena zur Ästhetik der Tonkunst*; publ. in 1887; 2d ed., 1907). He was music critic of Munich's *Neueste Nachrichten* (1899–1903).

WRITINGS: *Zur Geschichte des Erhabenheitsbegriffs seit Kant* (1889); *Hat Richard Wagner eine Schule hinterlassen?* (1892); with W. Klatte, *Richard Strauss: Eine Charakterstudie* (1896); *Moderner Geist in der deutschen Tonkunst* (1901; 2d ed., 1913); *Wagneriana* (3 vols., 1901–02); *Moderne Dirigenten* (1902); *Kunst und Kultur* (1902); *Die Hellerauer Schulfeste und die "Bildungsanstalt Jaques-Dalcroze"* (1912); *Straussiana* (1913); *Ascania: Zehn Jahre in Anhalt* (1913); *Richard Wagners "Parsifal"* (1914); *Neue Wagneriana* (3 vols., 1914); *Hans Pfitzner* (1921); *Neuzeitliche Tondichter und zeitgenössische Tonkünstler* (2 vols. 1926).

BIBL.: L. Frankenstein, *A. S.* (Regensburg, 1913); B. Schuhmann, ed., *Musik und Kultur. Festschrift zum 50. Geburtstag A. S.s* (1913).

Seiffert, Peter, German tenor; b. Düsseldorf, Jan. 4, 1954. He was educated at the Robert Schumann Hochschule für Musik in Düsseldorf. After appearing at the Deutsche Oper am Rhein in Düsseldorf, he sang at the Deutsche Oper in Berlin (from 1982) and at the Bavarian State Opera in Munich (from 1983). In 1984 he first appeared at the Vienna State Opera and at Milan's La Scala. In 1988 he made his debut at London's Covent Garden as Parsifal. He portrayed Strauss's Emperor during the Bavarian State Opera's visit to the new Nagoya Opera House in Japan in 1992. That same year, he was engaged as Narraboth in Salzburg. In 1993 he sang Tamino at the Metropolitan Opera in New York. He portrayed Florestan in London in 1995. In 1996 he was engaged as Walther von Stolzing at the Bayreuth Festival. As a concert artist, he sang with various orchs. on both sides of the Atlantic. His other operatic roles include Faust, Lensky, Lohengrin, Erik, and Jenik. In 1986 he married **Lucia Popp**.

Seinemeyer, Meta, admired German soprano; b. Berlin, Sept. 5, 1895; d. Dresden, Aug. 19, 1929. She studied with Nikolaus Rothmühl and Ernst Grenzebach in Berlin. She made her operatic debut there in *Orphée aux enfers* at the Deutsches Opernhaus (1918), where she continued to sing until 1925; she also toured the United States with the German Opera Co. (1923–24), then was a member of the Dresden State Opera (from 1925); she also appeared in South America (1926), at the Vienna State Opera (1927), and at London's Covent Garden (1929). She married the conductor Frieder Weissmann on her deathbed. Her voice possessed a silken quality and a natural expressiveness; she was particularly esteemed for her roles in operas by Wagner, Verdi, Puccini, and Strauss.

Sekles, Bernhard, German conductor, composer, and teacher; b. Frankfurt am Main, March 20, 1872; d. there, Dec. 8, 1934. He studied with Knorr and Uzielli at the Hoch Cons. in Frankfurt am Main, where he became a prof. of theory in 1896. From 1923 to 1933 he was director of the Cons. His compositions include the operas *Scheherazade* (Mannheim, Nov. 2, 1917) and *Die zehn Küsse* (1926), and the ballets *Der Zwerg und die Infantin* (1913) and *Die Hochzeit des Faun* (1921).

Selby, Bertram Luard, English organist, composer, and teacher; b. Ightham, Kent, Feb. 12, 1853; d. Winterton, Dec. 26, 1918. He studied with Reinecke and Jadassohn at the Leipzig Cons., then filled various organ positions in London. He was organist at the Rochester Cathedral. Among his works were 2 operas: *The Ring* (1886) and *Adela* (1888); also a successful operetta ("duologue"), *Weather or no* (London, Aug. 10, 1896; produced in Germany as *Das Wetterhäuschen*).

Sellars, Peter, provocative American theater producer; b. Pittsburgh, Sept. 27, 1957. His fascination with the stage began at age 10, when he began working with a puppet theater; he then attended Harvard Univ., where his bold theatrical experiments resulted in his expulsion from student theater groups. He gained wide notice when he produced Gogol's *The Inspector General* for the American Repertory Theater in Cambridge, Mass., in 1980. During the 1981–82 season, he staged a highly controversial mounting of Handel's *Orlando*, in which the protagonist is depicted as an astronaut. In 1983 he became director of the Boston Shakespeare Co. and in 1984 of the American National Theater Co. at the Kennedy Center in Washington, D.C. In 1987, at the Houston Grand Opera, he produced John Adam's opera *Nixon in China*, which he then mounted in other U.S. cities and at the Holland Festival in 1988; that same year, he jolted the Glyndebourne Festival with his staging of Nigel Osborne's *Electrification of the Soviet Union*. He oversaw the Los Angeles Festival in 1990. That same year he became artistic advisor of the Boston Opera Theatre. In 1991 he mounted the premiere of Adams's *The Death of Klinghoffer* in Brussels, and in 1992 Messiaen's *St. François d'Assise* at the Salzburg Festival. His staging of *Pelléas et Mélisande* in Amsterdam in 1993 concentrated on the contemporary themes of sex and violence. His *Pelléas et Mélisande* was then mounted at the Los Angeles Opera in 1995. In 1997 he returned to the Salzburg Festival to produce Ligeti's *Le Grand Macabre*. In 1998 he was awarded the Erasmus Prize of the Netherlands.

Selvaggi, Rito, Italian composer and pedagogue; b. Noicattaro di Bari, May 22, 1898; d. Zoagli (Genoa), May 19, 1972. He studied piano and composition at the Liceo Musicale in Pesaro, and later took lessons with Busoni. He was a prof. at the Parma Cons. (1934–38), then director of the Palermo Cons. (1938–58) and the Pesaro Cons. (1959–68). He composed the operas *Maggiolata veneziana* (Naples, 1929) and *Santa Caterina de Siena* (1947), the music drama *Eletta* (1947), and the oratorio *Estasi francescana* (1926).

Sembach (real name, **Semfke**), **Johannes,** German tenor; b. Berlin, March 9, 1881; d. Bremerhaven, June 20, 1944. He studied in Vienna and with Jean de Reszke in Paris. In 1900 he made his operatic debut at the Vienna Court Opera. From 1905 to 1913 he was a member of the Dresden Court Opera, where he appeared as a Wagnerian and also created the role of Aegisthus in Strauss's *Elektra* (1909). On Nov. 26, 1914, he made his Metropolitan Opera debut in New York as Parsifal, remaining on its roster until

1917; he was again on its roster during the 1920–22 seasons. His guest engagements also took him to London, Paris, and South America. In 1925 he settled in Berlin as a voice teacher.

Semet, Théophile (-Aimé-Emile), French composer; b. Lille, Sept. 6, 1824; d. Corbeil, near Paris, April 15, 1888. He studied with Halévy in Paris, where he was a percussionist in the Opéra orch. He wrote popular songs before producing the following operas for Paris: *Nuits d'Espagne* (Dec. 30, 1857), *Gil Blas* (March 23, 1860), *Ondine* (Jan. 7, 1863), and *La Petite Fadette* (Sept. 11, 1869).

Semkow, Jerzy, prominent Polish conductor; b. Radomsko, Oct. 12, 1928. He studied at the Univ. of Kraków (1946–50) and at the Leningrad Cons. (1951–55). After serving as assistant conductor of the Leningrad Phil. (1954–56), he conducted at Moscow's Bolshoi Theater (1956–58); he also continued his training with Kleiber in Prague, Serafin in Rome, and Walter in Vienna. He was artistic director and chief conductor of the Warsaw National Opera (1959–62), then was chief conductor of the Royal Danish Theater in Copenhagen (1966–76). In 1968 he made his U.S. debut as a guest conductor of the Boston Sym. Orch. He served as music director of the St. Louis Sym. Orch. (1976–79), artistic director of the RAI orch. in Rome (1979–83), and music adviser and principal conductor of the Rochester (N.Y.) Phil. (1985–89). His guest conducting engagements took him all over the world. He is especially admired for his performances of Polish and Russian scores, particularly of works from the late Romantic era.

Sendrey, Alfred. See **Szendrei, Aladár.**

Sénéchal, Michel, French tenor and teacher; b. Tavery, Feb. 11, 1927. He received training at the Paris Cons. After making his operatic debut in Brussels in 1950, he won the Geneva International Competition in 1952 and subsequently sang regularly at the Opéra and the Opéra Comique in Paris. In 1966 he made his first appearance at the Glyndebourne Festival as Ravel's Gonzalve. From 1972 to 1988 he sang at the Salzburg Festival. In 1980 he became director of the opera school at the Paris Opéra. He sang the villains in *Les Contes d'Hoffmann* at his Metropolitan Opera debut in New York on March 8, 1982. In 1985 he created the role of Pope Leo X in Boehmer's *Docteur Faustus* at the Paris Opéra. He was best known for his character roles.

Senesino (real name, **Francesco Bernardi**), celebrated Italian castrato alto who took his professional name from his birthplace; b. Siena, c.1680; d. probably there, c.1759. He began his career in Venice (1707–08). After singing in Bologna (1709) and Genoa (1709, 1712), he again appeared in Venice (1713–14), then sang in Naples (1715–16). In 1717 he was called to the Dresden court, where he was a prominent singer until he was dismissed for unconscionable behavior during a rehearsal in 1720. Handel heard him during a visit to Dresden, and engaged him for the Royal Academy of Music opera productions in London, where Senesino made his debut at the King's Theatre on Nov. 19, 1720. He remained with the company until 1728, although his arrogance caused bitter disputes with Handel. After singing in Venice (1729), he was reengaged by Handel and Heidegger for the new Academy opera productions in London (1730–33). Senesino's dislike for Handel prompted him to lend his support to the Opera of the Nobility, with which he was associated from 1733 to 1736. After appearances in Florence (1737–39), he retired from the operatic stage (1740). Although Senesino was personally disagreeable to many of his colleagues, there was no denying the greatness of his vocal abilities; indeed, in spite of their disagreements, Handel wrote no fewer than 17 roles for him.

Senilov, Vladimir, Russian composer; b. Viatka, Aug. 8, 1875; d. Petrograd, Sept. 18, 1918. He was a student of jurisprudence at the Univ. of St. Petersburg; he went to Leipzig, where he studied with Hugo Riemann (1895–1901); returning to Russia, he studied composition with Rimsky-Korsakov and Glazunov at the St. Petersburg Cons., graduating in 1906. His works include a lyric drama, *Vasili Buslayev*, and an opera, *Hippolytus*, after Euripides.

Serafin, Tullio, eminent Italian conductor; b. Rottanova de Cavarzere, Venice, Sept. 1, 1878; d. Rome, Feb. 2, 1968. He studied at the Milan Cons. He made his conducting debut in Ferrara in 1898. In 1901 Toscanini engaged him as one of his assistant conductors at La Scala in Milan. He was principal conductor of La Scala (1909–14; 1917–18). From 1924 to 1934 he was a conductor at the Metropolitan Opera in New York. In 1934 he became chief conductor and artistic director of the Rome Opera, a post he retained until 1943; he then was engaged as artistic director of La Scala (1946–47). From 1956 to 1958 he conducted at the Chicago Lyric Opera; in 1962 he was named artistic adviser of the Rome Opera. He was especially authoritative in the Italian operatic repertoire. As an artistic adviser, he helped launch the careers of Maria Callas and several other noted artists. He publ. (with A. Toni) 2 vols. on the history of Italian opera, *Stile, tradizioni e convenzioni del melodramma italiano del Settecento e del l'Ottocento* (Milan, 1958–64).

BIBL.: T. Celli and G. Pugliese, *T. S.: Il patriarca del melodramma* (Venice, 1985).

Serauky, Walter (Karl-August), eminent German musicologist; b. Halle, April 20, 1903; d. there, Aug. 20, 1959. He studied musicology in Halle and with Schering at the Univ. of Leipzig (Ph.D., 1929, with the diss. *Die musikalische Nachahmungsästhetik im Zeitraum von 1700 bis 1850*; publ. in Münster, 1929); he completed his Habilitation in 1932 at the Univ. of Halle, where he subsequently served as a prof. (from 1940), then was director of the musicological inst. at the Univ. of Leipzig (from 1949), a post he shared with Besseler (from 1956). He contributed valuable essays to various German publications; also publ. *Samuel Scheidt in seinen Briefen* (Halle, 1937) and *G. F. Händel: Sein Leben, sein Werk* (Kassel and Leipzig, 1956–58).

Şerban, Andrei, Romanian theater and opera producer; b. Bucharest, June 21, 1943. He received training at the Theater Inst. in Bucharest. He began his career as a producer of plays in his homeland, where he attracted notice with his staging of *Ubu Roi* in 1966. In 1970 he went to New York to work with the experimental theater group La Mama, where his production of *The Cherry Orchard* in 1972 was produced to much critical acclaim. In 1980 he made his debut as an opera producer with *Eugene Onegin* at the Welsh National Opera in Cardiff. He staged *Turandot* in Los Angeles and at London's Covent Garden in 1984, and returned to Covent Garden to produce *Fidelio* in 1985 and *Prince Igor* in 1990. From 1990 to 1993 he was artistic director of the National Theater in Bucharest. He produced *Les Contes d'Hoffmann* at the Vienna State Opera in 1993. After staging *Lucia di Lammermoor* at the Opéra de la Bastille in Paris in 1995, he produced *Thaïs* in Nice in 1997. His opera productions reflect his long and successful career in the legitimate theater.

Sereni, Mario, Italian baritone; b. Perugia, March 25, 1928. He studied at the Accademia di Santa Cecilia in Rome; also in Siena with Mario Basiola. He made his debut at the Florence May Festival in 1953, and then sang throughout Italy. In 1956 he sang at the Teatro Colón in Buenos Aires. He made his Metropolitan Opera debut in New York on Nov. 9, 1957, as Gérard in *Andrea Chénier*; subsequently he sang there for some 2 decades in such roles as Amonasro, Belcore, Germont, Marcello, and Sharpless; he also sang in London, Vienna, Milan, Chicago, Houston, Dallas, and other opera centers.

Seroen, Berthe, Belgian-born Dutch soprano and teacher; b. Mechelen, Nov. 27, 1882; d. Amsterdam, April 17, 1957. She was trained at the Brussels Cons. After giving concerts in Belgium and France, she made her operatic debut in Antwerp in 1908 at the Flemish Opera as Elisabeth in *Tannhäuser*. She later sang at the Théâtre Royal de la Monnaie in Brussels. In 1914 she settled in Holland and pursued a career as a concert artist. She taught at the Rotterdam Cons. (from 1927), and at the conservatories in Amsterdam and Utrecht (from 1937). Seroen was particularly admired for her performances of contemporary Dutch and French art songs.

Seroff, Victor, Russian-born American writer on music; b. Batumi, Caucasus, Oct. 14, 1902; d. N.Y., May 10, 1979. He studied law at the Univ. of Tiflis, then took piano lessons with Moriz Rosenthal in Vienna and Theodore Szanto in Paris. He eventually settled in New York and became a naturalized American citizen.

WRITINGS (all publ. in N.Y.): *Dmitri Shostakovich: The Life and Background of a Soviet Composer* (1943); *The Mighty Five: The Cradle of Russian National Music* (1948); *Rachmaninoff* (1950); *Maurice Ravel* (1953); *Debussy, Musician of France* (1956); *Hector Berlioz* (1967); *Prokofiev: A Soviet Tragedy* (1968); *Mussorgsky* (1968); *Franz Liszt* (1970).

BIBL.: M. Werner, *To Whom It May Concern: The Story of V. I. S.* (N.Y., 1931).

Serov, Alexander (Nikolaievich), important Russian music critic and composer; b. St. Petersburg, Jan. 23, 1820; d. there, Feb. 1, 1871. He studied law, and also took cello lessons with Karl Schuberth. He became a functionary in the Ministry of Justice and served in St. Petersburg (1840–45), Simferopol, Crimea (1845–48), and Pskov (1848–51). He never took lessons in composition, except a correspondence course in counterpoint with Joseph Hunke, but achieved a certain mastery in harmony and orchestration by studying the classics. In 1851 he began writing critical articles on music, and soon became an important figure in Russian journalism; in 1856 he became ed. of the *Musical and Theatrical Monitor*. In 1858 he made his first trip abroad, visiting Germany and Bohemia; the following year he made another German visit, and also traveled in Austria and Switzerland; during this journey he met Wagner, whose ardent admirer he became and remained to the end of his career. He expounded Wagner's ideas in Russian publications and engaged in bitter polemics with those who did not subscribe to his views, including his old friend and schoolmate Vladimir Stasov. He started very late in the field of composition; inspired by the performance of a biblical play, *Judith*, by an Italian troupe at St. Petersburg in 1861, he resolved to write an opera on this subject, essaying an Italian libretto, but later deciding on a Russian text. *Judith* was produced in St. Petersburg on May 28, 1863, with excellent success, but although Serov intended to emulate Wagner in the music, the style of *Judith* was closer to Meyerbeer. Quite different was Serov's 2d opera, *Rogneda*, written on a Russian subject, in a distinctly national idiom, with plentiful use of Russian folk songs. *Rogneda* was staged in St. Petersburg on Nov. 8, 1865, and won a spectacular success; the czar Alexander II attended a subsequent performance and granted Serov an annual stipend of 1,000 rubles for it. He then began the composition of another Russian opera, *Vrazhya sila* (Malevolent Power), but death (as a result of heart failure) overtook him when the 5th act was still incomplete; the opera was finished by N. T. Soloviev and produced in St. Petersburg on May 1, 1871. All 3 operas of Serov retain their popularity in Russia but are unknown elsewhere. Serov wrote further an *Ave Maria* for Adelina Patti (1868) and incidental music to *Nero*. A selection from his writings was publ. in 4 vols. (St. Petersburg, 1892–95). In 1863 Serov married a Cons. pupil, Valentina Bergmann (1846–1924), who was the first Russian woman to compose operas: *Uriel Acosta* (Moscow, 1885) and *Ilya Murometz* (Moscow, March 6, 1899; with Chaliapin in the title role). She helped to ed. and publ. Serov's posthumous works, wrote essays, and publ. a book of memoirs (St. Petersburg, 1914) under the name Valentina Serova.

BIBL.: G. Khubov, *The Life of A. N. S.* (Moscow, 1950).

Serpette, (Henri Charles Antoine) Gaston, French composer and music critic; b. Nantes, Nov. 4, 1846; d. Paris, Nov. 3, 1904. He studied with Ambroise Thomas at the Paris Cons., taking the Premier Grand Prix de Rome in 1871 with the cantata *Jeanne d'Arc*. From 1874 he produced in Paris a steady progression of light operas, of which the following enjoyed a modicum of success: *La branche cassée* (Jan. 23, 1874), *Le manoir du Pic-Tordu* (May 28, 1875), *Le moulin du vert-galant* (April 12, 1876), *La petite muette* (Oct. 3, 1877), *Le petit chaperon rouge* (Oct. 10, 1885), *Adam et Eve* (Oct. 6, 1886), *Le demoiselle du téléphone* (May 2, 1891), and *Shakespeare* (Nov. 23, 1899).

Serra, Luciana, Italian soprano; b. Genoa, Nov. 4, 1942. She was a student of Michele Casato at the Genoa Cons. In 1966 she made her operatic debut in Cimarosa's *Il Convito* at the Hungarian State Opera in Budapest. From 1969 to 1976 she was a member of the Tehran Opera. In 1980 she made her first appearance at London's Covent Garden as Olympia in *Les Contes d'Hoffmann*. She sang Lucia at the Hamburg State Opera in 1982 and at Milan's La Scala in 1983. Following her U.S. debut as Violetta in Charleston in 1983, she sang Lakmé at the Lyric Opera in Chicago that same year. She portrayed the Queen of the Night at the Vienna State Opera in 1988. In 1992 she was engaged as Zerlina in *Fra Diavolo* at La Scala. She sang Olympia in Genoa in 1996. Among her other roles were Adina, Ophelia, Rosina, Norina, Elvira in *I Puritani*, and Hanna Glawari.

Serrano y Ruiz, Emilio, Spanish conductor, teacher, and composer; b. Vitoria, March 13, 1850; d. Madrid, April 8, 1939. He studied at the Madrid Cons., and taught piano and composition there (1870–1920); he also conducted sym. concerts in Madrid. He wrote 5 operas: *Mitridates* (Madrid, 1882), *Doña Juana la Loca* (Madrid, 1890), *Irene de Otranto* (Madrid, Feb. 17, 1891), *Gonzalo de Córdoba* (Madrid, Dec. 6, 1898), and *La Maja de Rumbo* (Buenos Aires, Sept. 24, 1910); also a zarzuela, *La bejarana* (in collaboration with F. Alonso).

Serrao, Paolo, Italian pedagogue and composer; b. Filadelfia, Catanzaro, 1830; d. Naples, March 17, 1907. He studied with Mercadante at the Naples Cons., and taught there from 1863. His first opera to be performed was *Pergolesi* (Naples, July 19, 1857), followed by *La duchessa di Guisa* (Naples, Dec. 6, 1865) and *Il figliuol prodigo* (Naples, April 23, 1868); he also composed an oratorio, *Gli Ortonesi in Scio* (1869).

Servais, François (Franz Matheiu), French composer and conductor; b. St. Petersburg, c.1847; d. Asnieres, near Paris, Jan. 14, 1901. It was claimed for him that he was an illegitimate son of Liszt and Princess Carolyne Sayn-Wittgenstein, but nothing in her voluminous correspondence with Liszt indicates that she was an expectant mother. However it might be, he was adopted by the famous Belgian cellist, teacher, and composer (Adrien-) François Servais (1807–1866), and assumed his name. He studied cello with Kufferath at the Brussels Cons., and won the Belgian Prix de Rome in 1873 with the cantata *La mort du Tasse*. He founded the Concerts d'Hiver in Brussels. He was a champion of Wagner, several of whose operas he introduced to Brussels. He wrote an opera, *L'Apollonide*, later titled *Iön* (Karlsruhe, 1899).

BIBL.: E. Michotte, *Au souvenir de F. S.* (Paris, 1907).

Sessions, Roger (Huntington), eminent American composer and teacher; b. Brooklyn, Dec. 28, 1896; d. Princeton, N.J., March 16, 1985. He studied music at Harvard Univ. (B.A., 1915); he took a course in composition with Parker at the Yale School of Music (B.M., 1917); he then took private lessons with Bloch in Cleveland and New York; this association was of great importance for Sessions; his early works were strongly influenced by Bloch's rhapsodic style and rich harmonic idiom verging on polytonality. He taught theory at Smith College (1917–21), then was appointed to the faculty of the Cleveland Inst. of Music, first as assistant to Bloch, then as head of the dept. (1921–25). He lived mostly in Europe from 1926 to 1933, supporting himself on 2 Guggenheim fellowships (1926, 1927), an American Academy in Rome fellowship (1928), and a Carnegie Foundation grant (1931); he also was active with Copland in presenting the Copland-Sessions Concerts of contemporary music in New York (1928–31), which played an important cultural role at that time. His subsequent teaching posts included Boston Univ. (1933–35), the New Jersey College for Women (1935–37), Princeton Univ. (1935–44), and the Univ. of Calif. at Berkeley (1944–53); he returned to Princeton as Conant Professor of Music in 1953 and as codirector of the Columbia-Princeton Electronic Music Center in New York in 1959; subsequently he taught at the Juilliard School of Music in New York (1965–85); he also was Bloch Prof. at Berkeley (1966–67) and Norton Prof. at Harvard Univ. (1968–69). In 1938 he was elected a member of the National Inst. of Arts and Letters, in 1953 of the American Academy of Arts and Letters, and in 1961 of the American Academy of Arts and Sciences. In 1974 he received a special citation of the Pulitzer Award Committee "for his life's work as a distinguished American composer." In 1982 he was awarded a 2d Pulitzer Prize for his Concerto for Orch. (1979–81). In his compositions, Sessions evolved a remarkably compact polyphonic idiom, rich in unresolvable dissonances and textural density, and yet permeated with true lyricism. In his later works, he adopted a *sui generis* method of serial composition. The music of Sessions is decidedly in advance of his time; the difficulty of his idiom, for both performers and listeners, creates a paradoxical situation in which he is recognized as one of the most important composers of the century, while actual performances of his works are exasperatingly infrequent.

WORKS: DRAMATIC: OPERAS: *Lancelot and Elaine* (1910); *The Fall of the House of Usher* (1925; unfinished); *The Trial of Lucullus* (Berkeley, April 18, 1947); *Montezuma* (1941–63; West Berlin, April 19, 1964). INCIDENTAL MUSIC TO: L. Andreyev's *The Black Maskers* (Northampton, Mass., June 1923; orch suite, 1928; Cincinnati, Dec. 5, 1930); Volkmüller's *Turandot* (Cleveland, May 8, 1925).

WRITINGS: *The Musical Experience of Composer, Performer, Listener* (Princeton, N.J., 1950); *Harmonic Practice* (N.Y., 1951); *Reflections on the Music Life in the United States* (N.Y., 1956); *Questions about Music* (Cambridge, Mass., 1970); E. Cone, ed., *Roger Sessions on Music: Collected Essays* (Princeton, N.J., 1979); A. Olmstead, ed., *Correspondence of Roger Sessions* (Ithaca, N.Y., 1992).

BIBL.: C. Mason, *A Comprehensive Analysis of R. S.'s Opera Montezuma* (diss., Univ. of Ill., Urbana, 1982); F. Prausnitz, *R. S.: A Critical Biography* (London, 1983); R. Meckna, *The Rise of the American Composer-Critic: Aaron Copland, R. S., Virgil Thomson, and Elliott Carter in the Periodical "Modern Music," 1924–1946* (diss., Univ. of Calif., Santa Barbara, 1984); A. Olmstead, *R. S. and his Music* (Ann Arbor, 1985); idem, *Conversations with R. S.* (Boston, 1986).

Séverac, (Marie-Joseph-Alexandre) Déodat de, French composer; b. Saint Félix de Caraman en Lauragais, Haute-Garonne, July 20, 1872; d. Céret, Pyrénées-Orientales, March 24, 1921. He studied piano with his father, a painter and music lover, then in Toulouse at the Dominican College of Sorèze, at the Univ. (law), and at the Cons. (1893–96); he also took courses with d'Indy and Magnard (composition), Blanche Selva and Albéniz (piano), Guilmant (organ), and Bordes (choral conducting) at the Paris Schola Cantorum. After completing his training (1907), he divided his time between Paris and his native town, devoting himself mainly to composition. His works are notable for their Gallic refinement.

WORKS: DRAMATIC: OPERAS: *Le Coeur du moulin* (1903–08; Paris, Dec. 8, 1909); *Héliogabale* (Béziers, Aug. 21, 1910); *La Fille de la terre* (Coursan, July 1913); *Le Roi pinard* (1919). INCIDENTAL MUSIC TO: L. Damard's *Le Mirage* (1905); M. Navarre's *Muguetto* (Tarn, Aug. 13, 1911); E. Verhaeren's *Hélène de Sparthe* (Paris, May 5, 1912).

BIBL.: *Centenaire D. d. S.* (Paris, 1972).

Seydelmann, Franz, German composer; b. Dresden, Oct. 8, 1748; d. there, Oct. 23, 1806. He was the son of Franciscus Seydelmann, a tenor in the Dresden electoral Kapelle, where he received instruction in music from J. C. Weber, J. G. Schürer, and J. G. Naumann; he accompanied Naumann on a study tour of Italy (1765–68). Returning to Dresden, he was named church composer (1772) and Kapellmeister (1787) at the court. His most successful works for the theater were 2 operas buffa, *Il Mostro ossia Da gratitudine amore* (1785) and *Il Turco in Italia* (1788); thereafter he devoted himself mainly to writing sacred music.

WORKS: DRAMATIC (all 1st perf. in Dresden unless otherwise given): OPERAS: *La Serva scaltra* (1773); *Arsene* or *Die schöne Arsene* (March 3, 1779); *Das tartarische Gesetz* (c.1779); *Der lahme Husar* (Leipzig, July 17, 1780); *Der Kaufmann von Smyrna* (c.1780); *Der Soldat* (1783); *Il capriccio corretto* (1783); *La Villanella di Misnía* (1784; in Ger. as *Das sächsische Bauermädchen*, Frankfurt am Main, 1791); *Il Mostro ossia Da gratitudine amore* (1785); *Il Turco in Italia* (1788); *Amore per oro* (1790). ORATORIOS: *La Betulia liberata* (1774); *Gioas rè di Giuda* (1776); *La morte d'Abele* (1801).

BIBL.: R. Cahn-Speyer, *F. S. als dramatischer Komponist* (Leipzig, 1909).

Seyfried, Ignaz (Xaver), Ritter von, Austrian conductor, teacher, and composer; b. Vienna, Aug. 15, 1776; d. there, Aug. 27, 1841. He was a close friend of Mozart, and had some piano lessons with him; he studied also with Koželuh and Albrechtsberger. In 1797 he became conductor at Schikaneder's Freihaus-Theater in Vienna, then was conductor of the Theater an der Wien (1801–27). He was an extremely prolific composer, and some of his Singspiels were very successful; one of them, *Die Ochsenmenuette*, based on Haydn's music (Vienna, Dec. 31, 1823), gave rise to the well-known anecdote about Haydn's composing an *Ox Minuet* for a butcher and receiving an ox as a gift. Seyfried he also wrote the opera *Der Wundermann am Rheinfall* (Vienna, Oct. 26, 1799), which elicited praise from Haydn. He further wrote numerous melodramas, ballets, and oratorios. He publ. *Albrechtsberger's Sämmtliche Schriften* (1826), *Preindl's Wiener Tonschule* (1827), and *Ludwig van Beethoven's Studien im Generalbasse, Contrapuncte und in der Compositions-Lehre* (1832).

BIBL.: A. Schmidt, *Denksteine: Biographien von I. R. v. S. . . .* (Vienna, 1848); B. von Seyfried, *I. Ritter von S.: Thematisch-bibliographisches Verzeichnis: Aspekte der Biographie und des Werkes* (Frankfurt am Main and N.Y., 1990).

Seymour, John Laurence, American composer; b. Los Angeles, Jan. 18, 1893; d. San Francisco, Feb. 1, 1986. He studied piano at the Univ. of Calif. at Berkeley (B.A. in music, 1917; M.A. in Slavic languages, 1919); he received instruction in piano and theory from Fannie Charles Dillon and in violin from Leila Fagge; he then took courses in composition with Pizzetti and Bohgen in Italy and with d'Indy in Paris (1923–28); he later obtained his Ph.D. in English literature in 1940 from the Univ. of Calif. at Berkeley with the diss. *Drama and Libretto*. He lectured there on opera and drama (1928–36), and also served as chairman of the theater dept. of Sacramento Junior College; he later was a librarian at Southern Utah College in Cedar City (1969–85). His opera, *In the Pasha's Garden*, was premiered at the Metropolitan Opera in New York on Jan. 24, 1935, and won the David Bispham Memorial Award.

WORKS: DRAMATIC: OPERAS: *Les précieuses ridicules* (1920); *In the Pasha's Garden* (1934; N.Y., Jan. 24, 1935); *Ramona* (Provo, Utah, Nov. 11, 1970); *Ollanta, el Jefe Kolla* (1977). OPERETTAS: *Bachelor Belles* (1922); *Hollywood Madness* (1936); *The Devil and Tom Walker* (1942). MUSICALS: *Ming Toy* (1949); *The Lure and the Promise* (1960).

Shade, Ellen, American soprano; b. N.Y., Feb. 17, 1944. She studied with Talma at Hunter College of the City Univ. of N.Y., and with Tito Capobianco and Cornelius Reid. Following an apprenticeship at the Santa Fe Opera (1968–69), she made her operatic debut as Liù in Frankfurt am Main in 1972. That same year, she made her U.S. operatic debut as Micaëla in Pittsburgh. She then sang in Houston, Dallas, Santa Fe, New Orleans, Milwaukee, and Cincinnati. On April 21, 1976, she made her debut at the Metropolitan Opera in New York as Wagner's Eva. That same year, she sang for the first time at London's Covent Garden as Emma in *Khovanshchina*, and returned there in 1978 to create the role of Eve in Penderecki's *Paradise Lost*. In 1981 she made her debut at the N.Y. City Opera as Donna Elvira. She first appeared at the Salzburg Festival in Einem's *Der Prozess* in 1988, and also sang Kát'a Kabanová in Geneva that year. In 1992 she portrayed Strauss's Empress in Amsterdam and Salzburg. She was engaged as Arabella at Covent Garden in 1996. As a soloist, she appeared with many orchs. in North America and Europe.

Shallon, David, Israeli conductor; b. Tel Aviv, Oct. 15, 1950. He studied composition and conducting with Sheriff, then completed his conducting studies with Swarowsky at the Vienna Academy of Music (1973–75). He was an assistant to Bernstein in Europe (1974–79), and also made appearances as a guest conductor with major European orchs. and opera houses. Shallon led the premiere of Gottfied von Einem's controversial opera *Jesu Hochzeit* in Vienna in 1980. He made his U.S. debut as a guest conductor with the San Francisco Sym. in 1980. From 1987 to 1993 he was Generalmusikdirektor of the Düsseldorf Sym. Orch. He was music director of the Jerusalem Sym. Orch. from 1993, and of the Orchestre Philharmonique du Luxembourg from 1997.

Shankar, Ravi, famous Indian sitarist, teacher, and composer; b. Varanasi, Uttar Pradesh, April 7, 1920. He revealed a notable talent as a musician and dancer in childhood. After some training from his brother, Uday Shankar, he accompanied him to Paris in 1930 to further his education. Returning to India, he pursued his musical training with Ustad Allauddin Khan in Maihar (1936). After World War II, Shankar became active as a performer. He also served as director of the instrumental ensemble of All-India Radio from 1949 to 1956. In 1956–57 he toured Europe and the United States, and subsequently performed extensively in both East and West. In 1962 he became founder-director of the Kinnara School of Music in Bombay. His numerous sitar recitals in the West did much to foster an appreciation for Indian music. He publ. a memoir, *My Music, My Life* (N.Y., 1968). E. Barnett ed. *Ravi Shankar: Learning Indian Music, a Systematic Approach* (1981). His own compositions include *Ghanashyam* (A Broken Branch), opera ballet (1989); also several ballets and film scores, including the trilogy *Pather Panchali* (1955), *Aparajito* (1956), and *Apur Sansar* (1959); television music. In 1997 he was awarded the Praemium Imperiale of Japan and in 1998 the Polar Prize of the Royal Swedish Academy of Music.

Shaporin, Yuri (Alexandrovich), significant Russian composer; b. Glukhov, Ukraine, Nov. 8, 1887; d. Moscow, Dec. 9, 1966. He studied law, and graduated from the Univ. of St. Petersburg in 1912; he also studied at the St. Petersburg Cons. with Sokolov (composition), graduating in 1918. He wrote theatrical music in Leningrad; he moved to Moscow in 1936, where he served as a prof. at the Cons. (from 1939). His masterpiece is the opera *Polina Gyebl* (1925; rev. and enl. as *The Decembrists*, 1925–53; Moscow, June 23, 1953), which occupied him for over 30 years. Other works include 80 theater scores, much film music, and an oratorio, *A Tale of the Battle for the Russian Land* for Solo Voices, Chorus, and Orch. (Moscow, April 18, 1944).

BIBL.: E. Grosheva, *Y. A. S.* (Moscow, 1957); I. Martynov, *Y. S.* (Moscow, 1966).

Shaw, George Bernard, famous Irish dramatist; b. Dublin, July 26, 1856; d. Ayot St. Lawrence, England, Nov. 2, 1950. Before winning fame as a playwright, he was active as a music critic in London, writing for the *Star* under the name of "Corno di Bassetto" (1888–89) and for the *World* (1890–94). In 1899 he publ. *The Perfect Wagnerite*, a highly individual socialistic interpretation of *The Ring of the Nibelung*. His criticisms from the *World* were reprinted as *Music in London* (3 vols., 1932; new ed., 1950); those from the *Star* as *London Music in 1888–89* (London and N.Y., 1937); selected criticisms were ed. by E. Bentley (N.Y., 1954). Shaw's play *Arms and the Man* was made into an operetta, *The Chocolate Soldier*, by Oskar Straus (1908); his *Pygmalion* was converted into a highly successful musical comedy under the title *My Fair Lady*, with a musical score by Frederick Loewe (1956).

Shaw, Martin (Edward Fallas), English organist and composer; b. London, March 9, 1875; d. Southwold, Sussex, Oct. 24, 1958. He was a pupil at the Royal College of Music in London; he played organ in various churches in London. In 1900 he founded the Purcell Operatic Soc. in London. He was made an Officer of the Order of the British Empire in 1955. He composed the operas *Mr. Pepys* (London, Feb. 11, 1926) and *The Thorn of Avalon* (1931); also incidental music; sacred works; some 100 songs; etc. He publ. *The Principles of English Church Music Composition* (London, 1921) and *Up to Now* (autobiography; London, 1929). Among his eds., all publ. in London, are *Songs of Britain* (with F. Kidson; 1913), *The English Carol Book* (with P. Dearmer; 1913–19), *The League of Nations Song Book* (with P. Dearmer; 1921), *Songs of Praise* (with P. Dearmer and R. Vaughan Williams; 1925; 2d ed., aug., 1931), and *The Oxford Book of Carols* (1928; 25th ed., rev., 1964). His brother, Geoffrey (Turton) Shaw (1879–1943), was the English organist, music educator, and composer.

BIBL.: E. Routley, *M. S.: A Centenary Appreciation* (London, 1975).

Shaw, Mary (née **Postans**), English contralto; b. Lea, Kent, 1814; d. Hadleigh Hall, Suffolk, Sept. 9, 1876. She studied at the Royal Academy of Music in London (1828–31), and then with Sir George Smart. Under the name Mary Postans, she made a successful debut in London (1834); the next year she married the painter Alfred Shaw and thereafter appeared as Mary Shaw. In 1838 she sang with the Leipzig Gewandhaus Orch. under Mendelssohn's direction; her operatic debut followed as Imelda in the premiere of Verdi's first opera, *Oberto, conte di San Bonifacio*, at Milan's La Scala (Nov. 17, 1839); in 1842 she sang at London's Covent Garden and at Drury Lane. In 1844, at the height of her success, her husband went insane; the shock affected her vocal cords, so that she was unable to sing. Some time later she remarried and went to live in the country.

Shawe-Taylor, Desmond (Christopher), eminent Irish music critic; b. Dublin, May 29, 1907; d. Wimborne, Nov. 1, 1995. He was educated at Oriel College, Oxford (1926–30). Through the years he contributed literary and musical criticism to various newspapers and periodicals. After service in World War II, he was engaged as music critic of the *New Statesman* in 1945, retaining his post until 1958; from 1950 to 1958 he also served as phonograph record reviewer for the *Observer*. In 1958 he was named music critic of the *Sunday Times*; he retired in 1983; he also was a guest critic for the *New Yorker* (1973–74). He was made a Commander of the Order of the British Empire in 1965. His writings are notable for their unostentatious display of wide learning. He publ. the vol. *Covent Garden for the World of Music Series* (London, 1948); also, with Edward Sackville-West, *The Record Guide* (London, 1951, and later rev. eds.). He contributed a number of insightful biographies of singers to *The New Grove Dictionary of Music and Musicians* (1980).

Shchedrin, Rodion (Konstantinovich), brilliant Russian composer; b. Moscow, Dec. 16, 1932. His father was a music theorist and writer. After piano lessons in childhood, he attended the music and then choral schools (1948–51) attached to the Moscow Cons.; he subsequently took courses in piano with Yakov Flier and composition with Yuri Shaporin at the Cons. (1951–55), where he subsequently taught (1965–69). Following graduation, he achieved great recognition within the accepted Soviet establishment; he wrote about current trends in Soviet music in official publications; he held several significant posts within the Composer's Union, including chairman of the Russian Federation section (from 1974); he received many awards, and was made a People's Artist of the USSR (1981). In 1964, 1968, and 1986 he visited the United States on cultural exchange programs. His music has wide appeal, artfully employing numerous pseudo-modernistic devices; particularly interesting among his compositions are the aleatoric 2d Sym., the prepared encore for the 1st Piano Concerto, and his ballets *Anna Karenina* and *Carmen Suite*, which incorporate music by earlier composers (Tchaikovsky and Bizet, respectively). He was married to the ballerina Maya Plisetskaya, for whom he wrote several ballets.

WORKS (all 1st perf. in Moscow unless otherwise given): DRAMATIC: OPERAS: *Not for Love Alone* (Dec. 25, 1961; version for Chamber Orch., 1971); *Dead Souls*, after Gogol (1976; June 7, 1977); *Lolita* (Stockholm, Dec. 14, 1994). BALLETS: *The Little Humpback Horse* (1955; March 4, 1960); *Carmen Suite* (April 20, 1967); *Anna Karenina* (1971; June 10, 1972); *The Seagull* (1979; rev. 1980). Also incidental music to plays and film scores.

Shcherbachev, Vladimir (Vladimirovich), Russian composer; b. Warsaw, Jan. 24, 1889; d. Leningrad, March 5, 1952. He studied at the St. Petersburg Cons. with Maximilian Steinberg and Liadov, graduating in 1914. From 1924 to 1931 he was a prof. of composition at the Leningrad Cons. He wrote an opera, *Anna Kolosova* (1939); also music for films.

BIBL.: G. Orlov, *V. V. S.* (Leningrad, 1959).

Shebalin, Vissarion (Yakovlevich), Russian composer; b. Omsk, June 11, 1902; d. Moscow, May 28, 1963. He studied at the Moscow Cons. with Miaskovsky (1923–28), then began teaching there; in 1935 he was appointed prof. of composition there; from 1942 to 1948 he was its director. On Feb. 10, 1948, by resolution of the Central Committee of the Communist Party, he was condemned (along with Shostakovich, Prokofiev, Miaskovsky, and others) for adhering to a "decadent formalism" in composition, but these strictures were removed in a corrective declaration of May 28, 1958, "restoring the dignity and integrity of Soviet composers." In addition to his original compositions, Shebalin also completed Mussorgsky's unfinished opera *The Fair at Sorochinsk*, using only Mussorgsky's own material (Leningrad, Dec. 21, 1931; version with supplementary materials, Moscow, March 19, 1952).

WORKS: DRAMATIC: OPERAS: *The Taming of the Shrew*, after Shakespeare (concert version, Oct. 1, 1955; stage version, Kuibishev, May 25, 1957); *Sun over the Steppe* (Moscow, June 9, 1958). BALLETS: *Festival* (1958; unfinished); *Reminiscences of a Bygone Day* (1961). MUSICAL COMEDY: *Bridegroom from the Embassy* (Sverdlovsk, Aug. 1, 1942).

Shekhter, Boris (Semyonovich), Russian composer and teacher; b. Odessa, Jan. 20, 1900; d. Moscow, Dec. 16, 1961. After studies at the Odessa Cons. (graduated, 1922), he entered the Moscow Cons., studying composition with Vasilenko and Miaskovsky (graduated, 1929). In 1940 he became a prof. at the Ashkhabad Cons. Among his works were the operas *1905 god* (The Year 1905; 1935; rev. 1955; in collaboration with A. Davidenko), *Yusup i Akhmet* (1941; Ashkhabad, June 12, 1942; in collaboration with A. Kuliyev), and *Pushkin v Mikhailovskom* (1955).

Shelton, Lucy (Alden), American soprano; b. Pomona, Calif., Feb. 25, 1944. She studied at Pomona College (B.A., 1965) and with Gladys Miller at the New England Cons. of Music in Boston (M.M., 1968); she completed her training with DeGaetani at the Aspen (Colo.) School of Music. While a member of the Jubal Trio, she shared in winning the Naumburg Competition in 1977, and then won it on her own in 1980. She sang with the Waverly Consort, the N.Y. Pro Musica, and the 20th Century Consort of the Smithsonian Institution, and also pursued a career as a touring solo artist. In 1989 she sang the role of Jenifer in the Thames TV production of Tippett's *Midsummer Marriage* in England. While she has become closely associated with the performance of contemporary music, her repertoire ranges across the entire spectrum of music.

Sheng, Bright, remarkable Chinese composer; b. Shanghai, Dec. 6, 1955. He began piano lessons when he was 5; after graduating from high school, he worked as a pianist and timpanist in a dance company in Chinhai, near Tibet, where he began to study Chinese folk music. After China's Cultural Revolution, he entered the Shanghai Cons. (1976), where he earned an undergraduate degree in composition. In 1982 he followed his parents to the United States, where he attended Queens College at the City Univ. of N.Y. and Columbia Univ.; his teachers included Chou-Wen Chung, Davidovsky, Perle, and Weisgall. Sheng received numerous awards, both in China and the United States, including NEA grants, a Guggenheim fellowship, and awards from the American Academy and Inst. of Arts and Letters. His works have been championed by such eminent artists as Peter Serkin, who commissioned his *MY SONG* (1988), and Gerard Schwarz, who has given many premiere performances of his orch. pieces. His *H'UN (Lacerations): In Memoriam 1966–1976* was the 1st runner-up for the 1989 Pulitzer Prize in music. Sheng appeared throughout the United States as a lecturer. After serving as composer-in-residence of the Chicago Lyric Opera, for which he wrote the opera *The Song of Majnun* (1992) with a libretto by Andrew Porter on an Islamic legend, he held that post with the Seattle Sym. Orch. (1992–94). He also orchestrated Leonard Bernstein's *Arias and Barcarolles*, which received its premiere performance under the direction of Leonard Slatkin in New York on Dec. 6, 1990. Like so many refugees of China's cultural upheaval, Sheng strives to find the personal means to integrate the disparate musical styles of China and the West.

Shenshin, Alexander (Alexeievich), Russian conductor, teacher, and composer; b. Moscow, Nov. 18, 1890; d. there, Feb. 14, 1944. He studied philology at the Univ. of Moscow; he later took music lessons with Gretchaninoff and Glière. He subsequently taught music in Moscow, and also conducted occasional sym. concerts. His music is cast in a style reminiscent of Liadov; the elements of exotic musical patterns are noticeable. He composed an opera, *O T'ao* (1925), and 2 ballets: *Ancient Dances* (1933) and *Story of Carmen* (1935).

BIBL.: V. Belaiev, *A. A. S.* (Moscow, 1929).

Shere, Charles, American writer on music and composer; b. Berkeley, Calif., Aug. 20, 1935. He was reared on a small farm in Sonoma County, where he attended high school and learned to play wind instruments; after graduating from the Univ. of Calif. at Berkeley with a degree in English (1960), he studied composition with Erickson privately and at the San Francisco Cons. of Music, and also studied conducting with Samuel (1961–64); he also studied art, on which he later wrote and lectured extensively. From 1964 to 1967 he was music director of Berkeley's KPFA-FM; he also was active at San Francisco's KQED-TV (1967–73), an instructor at Mills College in Oakland (1973–84), and art and music critic for the Oakland *Tribune* (1972–88). He was co-founder, publisher, ed., and a major contributor to *EAR*, a monthly new-music tabloid magazine. He is married to Lindsey Remolif Shere, the famed pastry chef of Chez Panisse in Berkeley. Shere describes his early compositions, many notated in open form and scored for unspecified or variable ensembles, as "rural and contemplative rather than urban and assertive in nature"; his later works utilize more conventional notation, his shift from pen-and-ink to computer-generated notation coinciding with a greater use of rhythmic conventions, as in the ostinatos in the finales of his *Symphony in 3 Movements* (1988), Concerto for Violin with Harp, Percussion, and Small Orchestra (1985), and *Sonata: Bachelor Machine* (1989). Among his publications are *Even Recently Cultural HIstory, Five Lectures for the 1980s* (Lebanon, New Hampshire, 1995), *Thinking Sound Music: The Life and Work of Robert Erickson* (Berkeley, 1995), and *Everbest Ever: Letters from Virgil* (Berkeley, 1995). Among his other compositions are the operas *The Box of 1914* (1980; San Francisco, Jan. 29, 1981) and *The Bride Stripped Bare by Her Bachelors, Even* (partial perf., Oakland, Dec. 1, 1984); also *Ladies Voices*, chamber opera for 3 Sopranos and 6 Instruments (Berkeley, Oct. 30, 1987).

Sheridan, Margaret, Irish soprano; b. Castlebar, County Mayo, Oct. 15, 1889; d. Dublin, April 16, 1958. She was a student of William Shakespeare at the Royal Academy of Music in London (1909–11) and of Alfredo Martino in Italy. In 1918 she made her operatic debut in *La Bohème* in Rome. She sang at London's Covent Garden (1919; 1925–26; 1928–30) but pursued her career principally in Italy. In 1931 she settled in Dublin as a singing teacher. She was esteemed for her roles in Puccini's operas.

Sheriff, Noam, Israeli conductor, composer, and pedagogue; b. Tel Aviv, Jan. 7, 1935. He studied composition with Ben-Haim (1949–57), conducting with Markevitch at the Salzburg Mozarteum (1955), philosophy at the Hebrew Univ. in Jerusalem (1955–59), and composition with Blacher at the Berlin Hochschule für Musik (1960–62). In 1955 he won the 1st Josef Krips prize of the Israel Phil. conducting competition. He returned there in 1959 and won the conducting competition outright. In the meantime, he was founder-conductor of the Hebrew Univ. Sym. Orch. (1955–59). From 1963 to 1983 he taught composition, orchestration, and conducting at the Rubin Academies of Music in Jerusalem and Tel

Aviv. He was music director of the Kibbutz Chamber Orch. from 1970 to 1982, and also was assoc. conductor of the Israel Chamber Orch. (1971–73). From 1983 to 1986 he taught orchestration at the Cologne Hochschule für Musik, and then was on the faculty of the Rubin Academy of Music in Jerusalem (1986–88). In 1989 he became music director of the Israel Sym. Orch., Rishon LeZion. He also was a prof. at the Univ. of Tel Aviv's Rubin Academy of Music from 1991, where he was head of the orch. conducting dept. In his music, Sheriff has adroitly fused Western and Eastern elements in scores made notable by their command of orchestration and form. Among his works are *Destination 5*, ballet music (1961), *Psalms of Jerusalem*, ballet (1982), *The Sorrows of Job*, opera (1990), and *Gesualdo*, chamber opera (1996).

Shibata, Minao, Japanese composer; b. Tokyo, Sept. 29, 1916; d. there, Feb. 2, 1996. He studied science at the Univ. of Tokyo (graduated, 1939) and music with Saburo Moroi (1940–43). From 1959 to 1969 he taught at the Tokyo National Univ. of Fine Arts and Music. His works include *Strada a Roma*, radio opera (1961), and *Forgotten Boys,* opera (1990).

Shicoff, Neil, American tenor; b. N.Y., June 2, 1949. He began vocal training with his father, a cantor; then studied at the Juilliard School in New York. After singing Narroboth in Salome in Washington, D.C., he appeared as Ernani at the Cincinnati May Festival in 1975. On Oct. 15, 1976, he made his Metropolitan Opera debut in New York as Rinuccio in *Gianni Schicchi*, returning there in subsequent seasons as the Duke in *Rigoletto*, Rodolfo, Werther, Hoffmann, Romeo, Massenet's Des Grieux, and Lensky. He also sang at London's Covent Garden (debut as Pinkerton, 1978), the Chicago Lyric Opera (debut as Rodolfo, 1979), the San Francisco Opera (debut as Edgardo, 1981), and the Paris Opéra (debut as Romeo, 1981). In 1988 he sang Macduff in the BBC production of *Macbeth*. In 1990 he made his debut in Barcelona as Hoffmann. In 1993 he appeared at Covent Garden as Pinkerton. In 1997 he returned to the Metropolitan Opera as Lensky. He portrayed Don Carlos at the Opéra de la Bastille in Paris in 1998. He also toured as a concert artist. In 1978 he married the soprano Judith Haddon.

Shield, William, English violinist and composer; b. Swalwell, County Durham, March 5, 1748; d. Brightling, Sussex, Jan. 25, 1829. He was taught by his father, a singing master, on whose death he was apprenticed to a shipbuilder; he then took lessons in music with Charles Avison at Newcastle upon Tyne. He played violin in various small theaters in the neighborhood, and in 1772 settled in London as violinist at the King's Theatre; from 1773 to 1791 he played the viola there. He produced his first comic opera, *A Flitch of Bacon*, at the Haymarket Theatre on Aug. 17, 1778; it was followed by a great number of theatrical pieces. He held the post of composer to Covent Garden from 1778 to 1791, then traveled in France and Italy, returning to Covent Garden in 1792; he retained this position until 1797. He was appointed Master of the King's Music in 1817, and was the last to compose court odes in 1818. He wrote about 40 light operas, pantomines, musical farces, ballad operas, etc. He also publ. *An Introduction to Harmony* (1800) and *The Rudiments of Thoroughbass* (1815).

Shimizu, Osamu, Japanese composer; b. Osaka, Nov. 4, 1911; d. Tokyo, Oct. 29, 1986. He studied traditional Japanese instruments; he also took courses in theory and composition with Hashimoto and Hosokawa at the Tokyo Music School (1936–39). He was active in the music dept. of Tokyo Radio; also wrote articles on music.

WORKS: DRAMATIC: OPERAS: *The Tale of the Mask-Maker Shuzenji* (Osaka, Nov. 4, 1954); *The Charcoal Princess* (Osaka, Nov. 1, 1956); *The Man Who Shoots at the Blue Sky* (Osaka, Nov. 26, 1956); *Gauche, the Violoncellist* (Osaka, Oct. 11, 1957); *The Singing Skeleton* (Osaka, March 15, 1962); *Shunkan, the Exile* (Osaka, Nov. 18, 1964); *The Merciful Poet*, operetta (1965); *Muko Erabi* (The Marriage Contest), comic opera (Los Angeles, Oct. 3, 1968); *Daibutsu-Kaigen* (The Great Image of Buddha), historic opera on the inauguration of the bronze statue of Buddha on April 9, A.D. 752 (Tokyo, Oct. 2, 1970); *Ikuta Gawa* (The River Ikuta; Tokyo, Nov. 10, 1971). BALLETS: *The Sun* (1955); *The Crane* (1956); *The Earth* (1957); *Araginu* (1958); *Fire in the Field* (1962); *Love Poems* (1966).

Shira, Francesco, Italian conductor, singing teacher, and composer; b. Malta, Aug. 21, 1808; d. London, Oct. 15, 1883. He studied at the Milan Cons. with Basili. He brought out his first opera, *Elena e Malvina*, at La Scala in Milan (Nov. 17, 1832), on the strength of which he was engaged as conductor of the Teatro São Carlos in Lisbon (1833–42); he also taught at the Lisbon Cons. In 1842, after a brief sojourn in Paris, he became conductor for the English Opera at the Princess's Theatre in London; he then conducted at Drury Lane in London (1844–47); in 1848 he went over to Covent Garden, then returned to Drury Lane in 1852. In later years he made a high reputation as a singing teacher, without abandoning composition. He wrote the operas *Niccolò de' Lapi* (London, 1863), *Selvaggia* (Venice, Feb. 20, 1875), and *Lia* (Venice, 1876).

Shirai, Mitsuko, notable Japanese soprano and mezzo-soprano; b. Nagano, May 28, 1942. Following training in Japan, she went to Germany and completed her vocal studies with Schwarzkopf. She won first prizes in vocal competitions in Vienna, Zwickau, 's-Hertogenbosch, Athens, and Munich (1973–76), and soon acquired a distinguished reputation as a lieder artist in tours of the globe with Hartmut Höll as her accompanist. She also appeared as a soloist with orchs. on both sides of the Atlantic. In 1987 she made her stage debut as Despina at the Frankfurt am Main Opera. In 1989 she made her N.Y. debut at Carnegie Hall in Ravel's *Shéhérazade*. Shirai's extraordinary vocal range allowed her enormous scope in her choice of repertoire. In addition to the great masters of the Austro-German lied, she sang scores by Berlioz, Lili Boulanger, Loeffler, Schoeck, Hindemith, Prokofiev, Malipiero, Carillo, and others. Her operatic roles included works by Mozart, Wagner, Hugo Wolf, and Dukas.

Shirinsky, Vasili (Petrovich), Russian violinist, conductor, teacher, and composer; b. Ekaterinodar, Jan. 17, 1901; d. Mamontovka, near Moscow, Aug. 16, 1965. He studied violin with D. Krein and composition with Miaskovsky at the Moscow Cons., then played in orchs.; in 1923 he joined the Moscow Cons. Quartet as 2d violin. Concurrently, he was active as conductor with the Moscow Radio Orch. (1930–32) and the Opera Theater Orch. (1932–36); he was a teacher (1939–49) and a prof. (1949–65) at the Moscow Cons. In 1944 he was made a People's Artist of the R.S.F.S.R. He wrote 2 operas, *Pyer i Lyus* (1943–46) and *Ivan the Terrible* (1951–54); incidental music for theatrical plays; film scores; choruses. His music adheres to the principles of socialist conservatism, emphasizing playability and tonal coherence; it was met with appreciation by the Soviet critics, but its performances were few and far between. His brother, Sergei Shirinsky (b. Ekaterinodar, July 18, 1903; d. Moscow, Oct. 18, 1974), was a cellist, who promoted in his programs the cause of Soviet music; he also made arrangements of various works by Classical and Romantic composers.

Shirley, George (Irving), black American tenor and teacher; b. Indianapolis, April 18, 1934. He was educated at Wayne State Univ. in Detroit, and then received vocal training from Thelmy Georgi in Washington, D.C. and Cornelius Reid in New York. He made his operatic debut as Eisenstein in *Die Fledermaus* with the Turnau Opera Players in Woodstock, N.Y. (1959). In 1960 he won the American Opera Auditions and in 1961 the Metropolitan Opera Auditions; following appearances in Europe, he made his Metropolitan Opera debut in New York as Ferrando on Oct. 24, 1961, and continued to sing there until 1973, as well as with other U.S. opera companies; in addition, he sang at Glyndebourne, Covent Garden in London, and La Scala in Milan. He created the role of Romilayu in Kirchner's *Lily* (N.Y., April 14, 1977). In 1992 he was made the Joseph Edgar Maddy Distinguished Univ. Prof. of Music at the Univ. of Mich. In 1993 he appeared as Edrisi in Szymanowski's *King Roger* in Buffalo. He portrayed Strauss's Herod in Detroit in 1996.

Shirley-Quirk, John (Stanton), distinguished English baritone; b. Liverpool, Aug. 28, 1931. He studied voice with Roy Henderson, and at the same time took courses in chemistry and physics at the Univ. of Liverpool. He made his operatic debut as the Doctor in *Pelléas et Mélisande* at the Glyndebourne Festival (1961); he then was a leading member of the English Opera Group (1964–76), where he became well known for his roles in Britten's operas; he created all 7 baritone roles in Britten's *Death in Venice* (June 16, 1973). In 1973 he sang at London's Covent Garden, then made his Metropolitan Opera debut in New York as the Traveler in *Death in Venice* on Oct. 18, 1974. On July 7, 1977, he created the role of Lev in Tippett's *The Ice Break* at Covent Garden. He also toured widely as a concert artist. In 1975 he was made a Commander of the Order of the British Empire.

Shishov, Ivan, Russian composer; b. Novocherkassk, Oct. 8, 1888; d. Moscow, Feb. 6, 1947. He studied composition with Koreshchenko at the Phil. So. in Moscow, and also took courses in choral polyphony with Kastalsky and in form and orchestration with G. Conus, graduating in 1914. He subsequently conducted choral groups and taught at the Moscow Cons. (1925–31). He wrote the opera *Painter Serf* (Moscow, March 24, 1929).

Shnitke, Alfred. See **Schnittke, Alfred.**

Shostakovich, Dmitri (Dmitrievich), great Russian composer, whose style and idiom of composition largely defined the nature of new Russian music; b. St. Petersburg, Sept. 25, 1906; d. Moscow, Aug. 9, 1975. He was the father of the Russian conductor Maxim Shostakovich (b. Leningrad, May 10, 1938). He was a member of a cultured Russian family; his father was an engineer employed in the government office of weights and measures; his mother was a professional pianist. Shostakovich grew up during the most difficult period of Russian revolutionary history, when famine and disease decimated the population of Petrograd. Of frail physique, he suffered from malnutrition; Glazunov, the director of the Petrograd Cons., appealed personally to the Commissar of Education, Lunacharsky, to grant an increased food ration for Shostakovich, essential for his physical survival. At the age of 9, he commenced piano lessons with his mother; in 1919 he entered the Petrograd Cons., where he studied piano with Nikolayev and composition with Steinberg; he graduated in piano in 1923, and in composition in 1925. As a graduation piece, he submitted his 1st Sym., written at the age of 18; it was first performed by the Leningrad Phil. on May 12, 1926, under the direction of Malko, and subsequently became one of Shostakovich's most popular works. He pursued postgraduate work in composition until 1930. His 2d Sym., composed for the 10th anniversary of the Soviet Revolution in 1927, bearing the subtitle *Dedication to October* and ending with a rousing choral finale, was less successful despite its revolutionary sentiment. He then wrote a satirical opera, *The Nose*, after Gogol's whimsical story about the sudden disappearance of the nose from the face of a government functionary; here Shostakovich revealed his flair for musical satire; the score featured a variety of modernistic devices and included an interlude written for percussion instruments only. *The Nose* was premiered in Leningrad on Jan. 12, 1930, with considerable popular acclaim, but was attacked by officious theater critics as a product of "bourgeois decadence," and quickly withdrawn from the stage. Somewhat in the same satirical style was his ballet *The Golden Age* (1930), which included a celebrated dissonant *Polka*, satirizing the current disarmament conference in Geneva. There followed the 3d Sym., subtitled *May First* (Leningrad, Jan. 21, 1930), with a choral finale saluting the International Workers' Day. Despite its explicit revolutionary content, it failed to earn the approbation of Soviet spokesmen, who dismissed the work as nothing more than a formal gesture of proletarian solidarity. Shostakovich's next work was to precipitate a crisis in his career, as well as in Soviet music in general; it was an opera to the libretto drawn from a short story by the 19th-century Russian writer Leskov, entitled *Lady Macbeth of the District of Mtzensk*, and depicting adultery, murder, and suicide in a merchant home under the czars. It was premiered in Leningrad on Jan. 22, 1934, and was hailed by most Soviet musicians as a significant work comparable to the best productions of Western modern opera. But both the staging and the music ran counter to growing Soviet puritanism; a symphonic interlude portraying a scene of adultery behind the bedroom curtain, orchestrated with suggestive passages on the slide trombones, shocked the Soviet officials present at the performance by its bold naturalism. After the Moscow production of the opera, *Pravda*, the official organ of the Communist party, publ. an unsigned (and therefore all the more authoritative) article accusing Shostakovich of creating a "bedlam of noise." The brutality of this assault dismayed Shostakovich; he readily admitted his faults in both content and treatment of the subject, and declared his solemn determination to write music according to the then-emerging formula of "socialist realism." His next stage production was a ballet, *The Limpid Brook* (Leningrad, April 4, 1935), portraying the pastoral scenes on a Soviet collective farm. In this work he tempered his dissonant idiom, and the subject seemed eminently fitting for the Soviet theater; but it, too, was condemned in *Pravda*, this time for an insufficiently dignified treatment of Soviet life. Having been rebuked twice for 2 radically different theater works, Shostakovich abandoned all attempts to write for the stage, and returned to purely instrumental composition. But as though pursued by vengeful fate, he again suffered a painful reverse. His 4th Sym. (1935–36) was placed in rehearsal by the Leningrad Phil., but withdrawn before the performance when representatives of the musical officialdom and even the orch. musicians themselves sharply criticized the piece. Shostakovich's rehabilitation finally came with the production of his 5th Sym. (Leningrad, Nov. 21, 1937), a work of rhapsodic grandeur, culminating in a powerful climax; it was hailed, as though by spontaneous consensus, as a model of true Soviet art, classical in formal design, lucid in its harmonic idiom, and optimistic in its philosophical connotations. The height of his rise to recognition was achieved in his 7th Sym. He began its composition during the siege of Leningrad by the Nazis in the autumn of 1941; he served in the fire brigade during the air raids, then flew from Leningrad to the temporary Soviet capital in Kuibishev, on the Volga, where he completed the score, which was premiered there on March 1, 1942. Its symphonic development is realistic in the extreme, with the theme of the Nazis, in mechanical march time, rising to monstrous loudness, only to be overcome and reduced to a pathetic drum dribble by a victorious Russian song. The work became a musical symbol of the Russian struggle against the overwhelmingly superior Nazi war machine; it was given the subtitle *Leningrad Symphony*, and was performed during World War II by virtually every orch. in the Allied countries. Ironically, in later years Shostakovich intimated that the sym. had little or nothing to do with the events of the siege of Leningrad but actually with the siege of Russia in the grip of the dehumanizing and tyrannical Stalinist regime. After the tremendous emotional appeal of the *Leningrad Symphony*, the 8th Sym., written in 1943, had a lesser impact; the 9th, 10th, and 11th syms. followed (1945, 1953, 1957) without attracting much comment; the 12th Sym. (1960–61), dedicated to the memory of Lenin, aroused a little more interest. But it was left for his 13th Sym. (Leningrad, Dec. 18, 1962) to create a controversy that seemed to be Shostakovich's peculiar destiny; its vocal 1st movement for solo bass and men's chorus, to words by the Soviet poet Yevtushenko, expressing the horror of the massacre of Jews by the Nazis during their occupation of the city of Kiev, and containing a warning against residual anti-Semitism in Soviet Russia, met with unexpected criticism by the chairman of the Communist Party, Nikita Khrushchev, who complained about the exclusive attention in Yevtushenko's poem to Jewish victims, and his failure to mention the Ukrainians and other nationals who were also slaughtered. The text of the poem was altered to meet these objections, but the 13th Sym. never gained wide acceptance. There followed the remarkable 14th Sym. (1969), in 11 sections, scored for voices and orch., to words by Federico García Lorca, Apollinaire, Rilke, and the Russian poet Kuchelbecker. Shostakovich's 15th Sym., his last (premiered in Moscow under the direction of his son Maxim on Jan. 8, 1972), demonstrated his undying spirit of innovation; the score is set in the key of C major, but it contains a dodecaphonic passage and literal allusions to motives from Rossini's *William Tell Overture* and the Fate Motif from Wagner's *Die Walküre*. Shostakovich's adoption, however limited, of themes built on 12 different notes, a procedure that he had himself condemned as anti-musical, is interesting both from the psychological and sociological standpoint; he experimented with these techniques in several other works; his first explicit use of a 12-tone subject occurred in his 12th String Quartet (1968). Equally illuminating is his use in some of his scores of a personal monogram, D.S.C.H. (for D, Es, C, H in German notation, i.e., D, E-flat, C, B). One by one, his early works, originally condemned as unacceptable to Soviet reality, were returned to the stage and the concert hall; the objectionable 4th and 13th syms. were publ. and recorded; the operas *The Nose* and *Lady Macbeth of the District of Mtzensk* (renamed *Katerina Izmaylova*, after the name of the heroine) had several successful revivals.

Shostakovich excelled in instrumental music. Besides the 15 syms., he wrote 15 string quartets, a String Octet, Piano Quintet, 2 piano trios, Cello Sonata, Violin Sonata, Viola Sonata, 2 violin concertos, 2 piano concertos, 2 cello concertos, 24 preludes for Piano, 24 preludes and fugues for Piano, 2 piano sonatas, and several short piano pieces; also choral works and song cycles. What is most remarkable about Shostakovich is the unfailing consistency of his style of composition. His entire oeuvre, from his first work to the last (147 opus numbers in all), proclaims a personal article of faith. His idiom is unmistakably of the 20th century, making free use of dissonant harmonies and intricate contrapuntal designs, yet never abandoning inherent tonality; his music is teleological, leading invariably to a tonal climax, often in a triumphal triadic declaration. Most of his works carry key signatures; his metrical structure is governed by a unifying rhythmic pulse. Shostakovich is equally eloquent in dramatic and lyric utterance; he has no fear of prolonging his slow movements in relentless dynamic rise and fall; the cumulative power of his kinetic drive in rapid movements is overwhelming. Through all the peripeties of his career, he never changed his musical language in its fundamental modalities. When the flow of his music met obstacles, whether technical or external, he obviated them without changing the main direction. In a special announcement issued after Shostakovich's death, the government of the USSR summarized his work as a "remarkable example of fidelity to the traditions of musical classicism, and above all, to the Russian traditions, finding his inspiration in the reality of Soviet life, reasserting and developing in his creative innovations the art of socialist realism, and in so doing, contributing to universal progressive musical culture." His honors, both domestic and foreign, were many: the Order of Lenin (1946, 1956, 1966), People's Artist of the USSR (1954), Hero of Socialist Labor (1966), Order of the October Revolution (1971), honorary Doctor of the Univ. of Oxford (1958), Laureate of the International Sibelius Prize (1958), and Doctor of Fine Arts from Northwestern Univ. (1973). He visited the United States as a delegate to the World Peace Conference in 1949, as a member of a group of Soviet musicians in 1959, and to receive the degree of D.F.A. from Northwestern Univ. in 1973. A postage stamp of 6 kopecks, bearing his photograph and an excerpt from the Leningrad Symphony, was issued by the Soviet Post Office in 1976 to commemorate his 70th birthday. A collected edition of his works was publ. in Moscow (42 vols., 1980–).

WORKS: DRAMATIC: OPERAS: *The Nose*, op. 15 (1927–28; Leningrad, Jan. 12, 1930); *Lady Macbeth of the District of Mtzensk*, op. 29 (1930–32; Leningrad, Jan. 22, 1934; rev. as *Katerina Izmaylova*, op. 114, 1956–63; Moscow, Jan. 8, 1963); *The Gamblers* (1941–42; unfinished; Leningrad, Sept. 18, 1978). OPERETTA: *Moskva, Cheryomushki*, op. 105 (1958; Moscow, Jan. 24, 1959). BALLETS: *The Golden Age*, op. 22 (Leningrad, Oct. 26, 1930); *Bolt*, op. 27 (Leningrad, April 8, 1931); *The Limpid Brook*, op. 39 (Leningrad, April 4, 1935). INCIDENTAL MUSIC TO: *The Bedbug*, op. 19 (Moscow, Feb. 13, 1929); *The Shot*, op. 24 (Leningrad, Dec. 14, 1929; not extant); *Virgin Soil*, op. 25 (Leningrad, May 9, 1930; not extant); *Rule, Britannia!*, op. 28 (Leningrad, May 9, 1931); *Conditionally Killed*, op. 31 (Leningrad, Oct. 20, 1931); *Hamlet*, op. 32 (Moscow, March 19, 1932); *The Human Comedy*, op. 37 (Moscow, April 1, 1934); *Hail, Spain*, op. 44 (Leningrad, Nov. 23, 1936); *King Lear*, op. 58a (1940; Leningrad, March 24, 1941); *Native Country*, op. 63 (Moscow, Nov. 7, 1942); *Russian River*, op. 66 (Moscow, Dec. 1944); *Victorious Spring*, op. 72 (1945; Moscow, May 1946). FILM SCORES: *New Babylon*, op. 18 (1928–29); *Alone*, op. 26 (1930–31); *Golden Mountains*, op. 30 (1931); *Counterplan*, op. 33 (1932); *The Tale of the Priest and His Worker Blockhead*, op. 36 (1933–34; unfinished; rev. as a comic opera by S. Khentova, 1980); *Love and Hatred*, op. 38 (1934); *The Youth of Maxim*, op. 41 (1934); *Girl Friends*, op. 41a (1934–35); *The Return of Maxim*, op. 45 (1936–37); *Volochayev Days*, op. 48 (1936–37); *The Vyborg District*, op. 50 (1938); *Friends*, op. 51 (1938); *The Great Citizen*, op. 52 (1937); *The Man with a Gun*, op. 53 (1938); *The Great Citizen*, op. 55 (1938–39); *The Silly Little Mouse*, op. 56 (1939; unfinished); *The Adventures of Korzinkina*, op. 59 (1940; not extant); *Zoya*, op. 64 (1944); *Simple People*, op. 71 (1945); *The Young Guard*, op. 75 (1947–48); *Pirogov*, op. 76 (1947); *Michurin*, op. 78 (1948); *Encounter at the Elbe*, op. 80 (1948); *The Fall of Berlin*, op. 82 (1949); *Belinsky*, op. 85 (1950); *The Unforgettable Year 1919*, op. 89 (1951); *Song of the Great Rivers (Unity)*, op. 95 (1954); *The Gadfly*, op. 97 (1955); *The First Echelon*, op. 99 (1955–56); *Five Days—Five Nights*, op. 111 (1960); *Hamlet*, op. 116 (1963–64); *A Year is a Lifetime*, op. 120 (1965); *Sofia Perovskaya*, op. 132 (1967); *King Lear*, op. 137 (1970).

BIBL.: V. Seroff, *D. S.: The Life and Background of a Soviet Composer* (N.Y., 1943); M. Sahlberg-Vatchnadze, *S.* (Paris, 1945); I. Martinov, *D. S.* (Moscow, 1946; 2d ed., 1956; Eng. tr., 1947); L. Danilevich, *D. S.* (Moscow, 1958); M. Sabinina, *D. S.* (Moscow, 1959); H. Brockhaus, *D. S.* (Leipzig, 1962; 2d ed., abr., 1963); K. Laux, *D. S.: Chronist seines Volkes* (Berlin, 1966); G. Orlov, *D. S.* (Leningrad, 1966); L. Danilevich, ed., *D. S.* (Moscow, 1967); G. Ordzhonokidze, ed., *D. S.* (Moscow, 1967); N. Kay, *S.* (London, 1971); P. Buske, *D. S.* (Berlin, 1975); L. Tretyakova, *D. S.* (Moscow, 1976); M. MacDonald, *D. S.: A Complete Catalogue* (London, 1977); S. Khentova, *S. v Petrograde-Leningrade* (Leningrad, 1979; 2d ed., 1979); M. Shaginyan, *D. S.* (Moscow, 1979); S. Volkov, ed., *Testimony: The Memoirs of D. S.* (London and N.Y., 1979); N. Lukyanova, *D. D. S.* (Moscow, 1980); D. and L. Sollertinsky, *Pages from the Life of D. S.* (N.Y., 1980); D. Hulme, *D. S.: Catalogue, Bibliography and Discography* (Muir of Ord, 1982; 2d ed., 1991); C. Norris, ed., *S.: The Man and His Music* (London, 1982); E. Roseberry, *S.: His Life and Times* (Tunbridge Wells and N.Y., 1982); F. Streller, *D. S.* (Leipzig, 1982); J. Devlin, *S.* (Borough Green, 1983); D. Gojowy, *D. S. mit Selbstzeugnissen und Bilddokumenten* (Reinbek bei Hamburg, 1983); I. MacDonald, *The New S.* (Boston, 1990); G. Wolter, *D. S., eine sowjetische Tragödie: Rezeptionsgeschichte* (Frankfurt am Main, 1991); E. Wilson, *S.: A Life Remembered* (London, 1994); D. Fanning, ed., *S. Studies* (Cambridge, 1995).

Shuard, Amy, English soprano; b. London, July 19, 1924; d. there, April 18, 1975. She studied at London's Trinity College of Music. Her principal vocal instructors were Ivor Warren, Ernst Urbach, Gustav Sachs, and Eva Turner. In 1948 she gave a series of lecture-recitals in South Africa, and then made her operatic debut as Aida in Johannesburg in 1949. Returning to London, she sang at the Sadler's Wells Opera until 1955. From 1954 to 1974 she was a principal member of London's Covent Garden. She also sang in Italy, Vienna, Bayreuth, San Francisco, and Buenos Aires. In 1966 she was made a Commander of the Order of the British Empire. Her most acclaimed role was Turandot, but she also won admiration for her Brünnhilde, Sieglinde, Lady Macbeth, Santuzza, Elektra, Káta Kabanová, and Jenůfa.

Sibelius, Jean (Johan Julius Christian), great Finnish composer whose music, infused with the deeply felt modalities of national folk songs, opened a modern era of Northern musical art; b. Hämeenlinna, Dec. 8, 1865; d. Järvenpää, Sept. 20, 1957. The family name stems from a Finnish peasant named Sibbe, traced back to the late 17th century; the Latin noun ending was commonly added among educated classes in Scandinavia. Sibelius was the son of an army surgeon; from early childhood, he showed a natural affinity for music. At the age of 9 he began to study piano; he then took violin lessons with Gustaf Levander, a local bandmaster. He learned to play violin well enough to take part in amateur performances of chamber music. In 1885 he enrolled at the Univ. of Helsingfors (Helsinki) to study law, but abandoned it after the first semester. In the fall of 1885, he entered the Helsingfors Cons., where he studied violin with Vasiliev and Csillag; he also took courses in composition with Wegelius. In 1889 his String Quartet was performed in public, and produced a sufficiently favorable impression to obtain for him a government stipend for further study in Berlin, where he took lessons in counterpoint and fugue with Albert Becker. Later he proceeded to Vienna for additional musical training, and became a student of Robert Fuchs and Karl Goldmark (1890–91). In 1892 he married Aino Järnefelt. From then on, his destiny as a national Finnish composer was determined; the music he wrote was inspired by native legends, with the great Finnish epic *Kalevala* as a prime source of inspiration. On April 28, 1892, his symphonic poem *Kullervo*, scored for soloists, chorus, and orch., was first performed in Helsingfors. There followed one of his most remarkable works, the symphonic poem entitled simply *En Saga*, that is, "a legend"; in it he displayed to the full his genius for variation forms, based on a cumulative growth of a basic theme adorned but never encumbered with effective contrapuntal embellishments. From 1892 to 1900 he taught theory of composition at the Helsingfors Cons. In 1897 the Finnish Senate granted him an annual stipend of 3,000 marks. On April 26, 1899, he conducted in Helsingfors the premiere of his 1st Sym. He subsequently conducted the first performances of all of his syms., the 5th excepted. On July 2, 1900, the Helsingfors Phil. gave the first performance of his most celebrated and most profoundly moving patriotic work, *Finlandia*. Its melody soon became identified among Finnish patriots with the aspiration for national independence, so that the czarist government went to the extreme of forbidding its performances during periods of political unrest. In 1901 Sibelius was invited to conduct his works at the annual festival of the Allgemeiner Deutscher Tonkünstlerverein at Heidelberg. In 1904 he settled in his country home at Järvenpää, where he remained for the rest of his life; he traveled rarely. In 1913 he accepted a commission for an orch. work from the American music patron Carl Stoeckel, to be performed at the 28th annual Festival at Norfolk, Conn. For it he contributed a symphonic legend, *Aalotaret* (Nymphs of the Ocean; later rev. as *The Oceanides*). He took his only sea voyage to America to conduct its premiere on June 4, 1914; on that occasion he received the honorary degree of Mus.D. from Yale Univ. Returning to Finland just before the outbreak of World War I, Sibelius withdrew into seclusion, but continued to work. He made his last public appearance in Stockholm, conducting the premiere of his 7th Sym. on March 24, 1924. He wrote 2 more works after that, including a score for Shakespeare's *The Tempest* and a symphonic poem, *Tapiola*; he practically ceased to compose after 1927. At various times, rumors were circulated that he had completed his 8th Sym., but nothing was forthcoming from Järvenpää. One persistent story was that Sibelius himself decided to burn his incomplete works. Although willing to receive journalists and reporters, he avoided answering questions about his music. He lived out his very long life as a retired person, absorbed in family interests; in some modest ways he was even a *bon vivant*; he liked his cigars and his beer, and he showed no diminution in his mental alertness. Only once was his peaceful life gravely disrupted; this was when the Russian Army invaded Finland in 1940; Sibelius sent an anguished appeal to America to save his country, which by the perverse fate of world politics became allied with Nazi Germany. But after World War II, Sibelius cordially received a delegation of Soviet composers who made a reverential pilgrimage to his rural retreat. Honors were showered upon him; festivals of his music became annual events in Helsinki; in 1939 the Helsinki Cons. was renamed the Sibelius Academy in his honor; a postage stamp bearing his likeness was issued by the Finnish government on his 80th birthday; special publications—biographical, bibliographical, and photographic—were publ. in Finland. Artistically, too, Sibelius attained the status of greatness rarely vouchsafed to a living musician; several important contemporary composers paid him homage by acknowledging their debt of inspiration to him, Vaughan Williams among them. Sibelius was the last representative of 19th-century nationalistic Romanticism. He stayed aloof from modern developments, but he was not uninterested in reading scores and listening to performances on the radio of works of such men as Schoenberg, Prokofiev, Bartók, and Shostakovich.

The music of Sibelius marked the culmination of the growth of national Finnish art, in which Pacius was the protagonist, and Wegelius a worthy cultivator. Like his predecessors, he was schooled in the Germanic tradition, and his early works reflect German lyricism and dramatic thought. He opened a new era in Finnish music when he abandoned formal conventions and began to write music that seemed inchoate and diffuse but followed a powerful line of development by variation and repetition; a parallel with Beethoven's late works has frequently been drawn. The thematic material employed by Sibelius is not modeled directly on known Finnish folk songs; rather, he re-created the characteristic melodic patterns of folk music. The prevailing mood is somber, even tragic, with a certain elemental sweep and grandeur. His instrumentation is highly individual, with long songful solo passages, and with protracted transitions that are treated as integral parts of the music. His genius found its most eloquent expression in his syms. and symphonic poems; he wrote relatively little chamber music, and only in his earlier years. His only opera, *The Maid in the Tower* (1896), to a text in Swedish, was never publ. He wrote some incidental music for the stage; the celebrated *Valse triste* was written in 1903 for *Kuolema*, a play by Arvid Järnefelt, brother-in-law of Sibelius.

WORKS: DRAMATIC: OPERA: *Jungfrun i tornet* (The Maid in the Tower; Helsinki, Nov. 7, 1896). INCIDENTAL MUSIC TO: Overture, op. 10, and Suite, op. 11, to *Karelia* (Helsinki, Nov. 13, 1893); *King Kristian II*, op. 27, for a play by A. Paul (Helsinki, Feb. 28, 1898, composer conducting); *Kuolema* (Death) for Strings and Percussion, op. 44, for a play by Arvid Järnefelt (Helsinki, Dec. 2, 1903, composer conducting); *Pelléas et Mélisande*, op. 46, for Maeterlinck's play (Helsinki, March 17, 1905, composer conducting); *Belshazzar's Feast*, op. 51, for a play by H. Procopé (Helsinki, Nov. 7, 1906, composer conducting); *Svanevhit* (Swanwhite), op. 54, for Strindberg's play (Helsinki, April 8, 1908, composer conducting); *Ödlan* (The Lizard) for Violin and String Quintet, op. 8, for a play by M. Lybeck (1909; Helsinki, April 6, 1910, composer conducting); *Jedermann* for Chorus, Piano, Organ, and Orch., op. 83, for Hofmannsthal's play (Helsinki, Nov. 5, 1916); *The Tempest*, op. 109, for Shakespeare's play (1925; Copenhagen, March 16, 1926). OTHER: *Näcken* (The Watersprite), 2 songs with Piano Trio, for a play by Wennerberg (1888); *The Language of the Birds*, wedding march for A. Paul's play *Die Sprache der Vögel* (1911); *Scaramouche*, op. 71, "tragic pantomime" after the play by P. Knudsen and M. Bloch (1913; Copenhagen, May 12, 1922).

BIBL.: R. Newmarch, *J. S.: A Finnish Composer* (Leipzig, 1906); E. Furuhjelm, *J. S.: Hans tondikting och drag ur hans liv* (Borgå, 1916); W. Niemann, *J. S.* (Leipzig, 1917); C. Gray, *S.* (London, 1931; 2d ed., 1945); K. Ekman, *J. S.: En konstnärs liv och personlighet* (Stockholm, 1935; Eng. tr., 1935, as *J. S.: His Life and Personality*; 4th Swedish ed., 1959); B. de Törne, *S.: A Close-Up* (London, 1937); R. Newmarch, *J. S.: A Short History of a Long Friendship* (Boston, 1939; 2d ed., 1945); B. Sandberg, *J. S.* (Helsinki, 1940); E. Arnold, *Finlandia: The Story of S.* (N.Y., 1941; 2d ed., 1951); S. Levas, *J. S. ja hänen Ainolansa* (Helsinki, 1945; 2d ed., 1955); M. Similä, *Sibeliana* (Helsinki, 1945); B. de Törne, *S., i närbild och samtal* (Helsinki, 1945; 2d ed., 1955); G. Abraham, ed., *S.: A Symposium* (London, 1947; 2d ed., 1952); I. Hannikainen, *S. and the Development of Finnish Music* (London, 1948); N.-E. Ringbom, *S.* (Stockholm, 1948; Eng. tr., Norman, Okla., 1954); V. Helasvuo, *S. and the Music of Finland* (Helsinki, 1952; 2d ed., 1957); O. Anderrson, *J. S. i Amerika* (Åbo, 1955); L. Solanterä, *The Works of J. S.* (Helsinki, 1955); H. Johnson, *J. S.* (N.Y., 1959); E. Tanzberger, *J. S.: Eine Monographie* (Wiesbaden, 1962); F. Blum, *J. S.: An International Bibliography on the Occasion of the Centennial Celebrations, 1965* (Detroit, 1965); R. Layton, *S.* (London, 1965; 3d ed., rev., 1983); E. Tawaststjerna, *J. S.* (5 vols., Helsinki, 1965–88; Eng. tr. by R. Layton, 1976–); R. Layton, *The World of S.* (London, 1970); B. James, *The Music of J. S.* (East Brunswick, N.J., London, and Mississauga, Ontario, 1983); E. Salmenhaara, *J. S.* (Helsinki, 1984); F. Dahlström, *The Works of J. S.* (Helsinki, 1987); K. Kilpeläinen, *The J. S. Musical Manuscripts at Helsinki University Library: A Complete Catalogue* (Wiesbaden, 1991); E. Tawaststerjna, *J. S.: Aren 1865–1893* (Helsinki, 1992); G. Schlüter, *The Harold E. Johnson J. S. Collection at Butler University: A Complete Catalogue* (Indianapolis, 1993); G. Goss, *J. S. and Olin Downes: Music, Friendship, Criticism* (Boston, 1995).

Siboni, Erik (Anthon Valdemar), Danish organist, teacher, and composer of Italian parentage, son of **Giuseppe (Vincenzo Antonio) Siboni**; b. Copenhagen, Aug. 26, 1828; d. Frederiksberg, Feb. 11, 1892. He studied with J. P. E. Hartmann, then with Moscheles and Hauptmann at Leipzig and with Sechter at Vienna. He returned to Copenhagen, and in 1865 became organist and prof. of piano at the Søro Academy. He retired in 1883. Among his works were 2 operas: *Loreley* (Copenhagen, 1859) and *Carl den Andens flugt* (Flight of Charles II; Copenhagen, 1861).

Siboni, Giuseppe (Vincenzo Antonio), Italian tenor and singing teacher, father of **Erik (Anthon Valdemar) Siboni**; b. Forlì, Jan. 27, 1780; d. Copenhagen, March 28, 1839. He made his operatic debut in Rimini when he was only 17. Following appearances in Florence (1797), Bologna (1798), Genoa (1800), and at Milan's La Scala (1805), he became a principal singer at the King's Theatre in London in 1806, where he was chosen to create roles in several operas by Paër. He continued to sing in Italy, and also fulfilled engagements in Paris, Vienna, Prague, and St. Petersburg. In 1819 he settled in Copenhagen, where he was made director of singing at the Royal Theater and founded the Royal Cons. in 1821.

Siciliani, Alessandro, Italian conductor and composer; b. Florence, June 5, 1952. He received training in piano, conducting, and composition at the Milan Cons. and the Accademia di Santa Cecilia in Rome, his principal conducting mentor being Ferrara. He conducted opera throughout Italy, including Rome, Naples, and Palermo; he also conducted opera in Barcelona, Marseilles, Nice, Liège, New York, Philadelphia, and New Orleans. In 1988 he conducted for the first time at the Metropolitan Opera in New York, leading the double bill of *Cavalleria Rusticana* and *Pagliacci*; also appeared as a symphonic conductor with leading orchs. throughout Europe, the United States, and the Far East. In 1988 he became principal guest conductor of the Teatro Colón in Buenos Aires, and of the Teatro Municipal in São Paulo. He was music advisor (1991–92) and music director (from 1992) of the Columbus (Ohio) Sym. Orch. Among his compositions are a ballet, *L'Amour Peintre*, and an oratorio, *Giona*.

Sieber, Ferdinand, Austrian singing teacher and composer; b. Vienna, Dec. 5, 1822; d. Berlin, Feb. 19, 1895. He studied with Ronconi, and after a brief period of singing in opera, he was a singing teacher in Dresden (1848–54) and in Berlin. He publ. the treatises *Die Kunst des Gesangs* (with a supplement, *50 Vocalisen und Solfeggien*), *Vollständiges Lehrbuch der Gesangskunst für Lehrer und Schüler* (1858; 3d ed., 1878), *Katechismus der Gesangskunst* (1862 and many subsequent eds.), *Die Aussprache des Italienischen im Gesang* (1860; 2d ed., 1880), and *Handbuch des deutschen Liederschatzes* (1875), containing a catalogue of 10,000 songs arranged according to vocal range. He also composed many songs.

Siegmeister, Elie, significant American composer and teacher, whose works reflected the national moods and preoccupations from early social trends to universal concepts; b. N.Y., Jan. 15, 1909; d. Manhasset, N.Y., March 10, 1991. He took piano lessons as a youth with Emil Friedberger; in 1925 he entered Columbia Univ. and studied theory and composition with Seth Bingham (B.A., 1927); he also took private lessons in counterpoint with Riegger; after training with Boulanger in Paris (1927–32), he received instruction in conducting from Stoessel at the Juilliard School of Music in New York (1935–38). He was active with the Composers Collective of N.Y., for which he wrote songs under the name L. E. Swift; was a founder of the American Composers Alliance in 1937; he was founder-conductor of the American Ballad Singers (1939–46), which he led in performances of American folk songs. He felt strongly that music should express the social values of the people; in his early songs, he selected texts by contemporary American poets voicing indignation at the inequities of the modern world; he also gave lectures and conducted choruses at the revolutionary Pierre Degeyter (composer of the *Internationale*) Club in New York. As a result of his multiple musical experiences, Siegmeister developed an individual style of composition ranging from the populist American manner to strong modernistic sonorities employing a sort of euphonious dissonance with intervallic stress on minor seconds, major sevenths, and minor ninths. In his syms. and chamber music, he organized this dissonant idiom in self-consistent modern formulations, without, however, espousing any of the fashionable doctrines of composition, such as dodecaphony. The subject matter of his compositions, especially in the early period, was marked by a strongly national and socially radical character, exemplified by such works as *American Holiday, Ozark Set, Prairie Legend, Wilderness Road*, and *Western Suite*, the last achieving the rare honor of being performed by Toscanini. Siegmeister did not ignore the homely vernacular; his Clarinet Concerto is a brilliant realization of jazz, blues, and swing in a classically formal idiom. Siegmeister achieved an important position as an educator; he taught at Brooklyn College (1934), the New School for Social Research (1937–38), the Univ. of Minnesota (1948), and Hofstra Univ. (1949–76), where he also was composer-in-residence (from 1966); in 1976 he became prof. emeritus. He received numerous commissions and awards; held a Guggenheim fellowship in 1978 and in 1990 was elected a member of the American Academy and Inst. of Arts and Letters. In accepting this honor, he stated his *profession de foi* as first formulated in 1943: "My aim is to write as good music as I can that will at the same time speak the language of all our people."

WORKS: DRAMATIC: OPERAS: *Darling Corie* (1952; Hempstead, N.Y., Feb. 18, 1954); *Miranda and the Dark Young Man* (1955; Hartford, Conn., May 9, 1956); *The Mermaid of Lock No. 7* (Pittsburgh, July 20, 1958); *Dublin Song* (St. Louis, May 15, 1963; rev. version as *The Plough and the Stars*, Baton Rouge, La., March 16, 1969); *Night of the Moonspell* (Shreveport, La., Nov. 14, 1976); *The Marquesa of O* (1982); *Angel Levine* (N.Y., Oct. 5, 1985); *The Lady of the Lake* (N.Y., Oct. 5, 1985). OTHER DRAMATIC: *Doodle Dandy of the USA*, play with music (N.Y., Dec. 26, 1942); *Sing Out, Sweet Land*, musical (Hartford, Conn., Nov. 10, 1944); *Fables from the Dark Woods*, ballet (Shreveport, April 25, 1976). Also incidental music; film scores, including *They Came to Cordura* (1959).

WRITINGS: Ed. with O. Downes, *A Treasury of American Song* (N.Y., 1940; 3d ed., 1984); *The Music Lover's Handbook* (N.Y., 1943; rev., 1973, as *The New Music Lover's Handbook*; new ed., 1983); *Work and Sing* (N.Y., 1944); *Invitation to Music* (Irvington-on-Hudson, 1961); *Harmony and Melody* (2 vols., Belmont, Calif., 1965–66).

Siegmund-Schultze, Walther, German musicologist; b. Schweinitz, July 6, 1916; d. Halle, March 6, 1993. He studied musicology with Arnold Schmitz at the Univ. of Breslau (Ph.D., 1940, with the diss. *Mozarts Vokal- und Instrumentalmusik in ihren motivisch-thematischen Beziehungen*); he completed his Habilitation at the Univ. of Halle with his *Untersuchungen zum Brahms Stil und Brahms Bild* in 1951. In 1954 he became a lecturer at the Univ. of Halle; in 1956 he was made a prof. of musicology, director of the musicological faculty, and dean of the philosophy faculty. He was noted for his studies of 18th-century music; his analysis of the styles of Bach, Handel, and Mozart is interesting as an example of Marxist theories applied to music.

WRITINGS: *Die Musik Bachs* (Leipzig, 1953); *Georg Friedrich Händel: Leben und Werk* (Leipzig, 1954; 3d ed., 1962); *Mozarts*

Melodik und Stil: Eine Studie (Leipzig, 1957); *Lehrbriefe für das Fernstudium: Die Musik der Klassik* (Halle, 1964); *Georg Friedrich Händel: Thema mit 20 Variationen* (Halle, 1965); *Die Hauptvertreter der bürgerlichen Musikkultur im 20. Jahrhundert* (Halle, 1966–67); *Johannes Brahms: Eine Biographie* (Leipzig, 1966; 2d ed., 1974); *Die Musik der sozialistischen Länder (ausser DDR)* (Halle, 1967); *Ziele und Aufgaben der sozialistischen Musikerziehung* (Leipzig, 1967; 3d ed., 1975); *Die Bach-Händel-Epoche* (Halle, 1968); *Das Musikschaffen der DDR* (Halle, 1969); *Ludwig van Beethoven: Eine Biographie* (Leipzig, 1975; 2d ed., 1977); *Johann Sebastian Bach* (Leipzig, 1976); *Wolfgang Amadeus Mozart, 1756–1791: Eine kleine Biographie gewidmet allen Freunden von Michaelstein im Mozartjahr 1991* (Michaelstein, 1991); *Wolfgang Amadeus Mozart: Ideal-Idol-Idee* (Trier, 1994).

Siehr, Gustav, noted German bass; b. Arnsberg, Sept. 17, 1837; d. Munich, May 18, 1896. He studied with Heinrich Dorn and Julius Krause, making his debut in 1863 in Neustrelitz. He then sang in Prague (1865–70), Wiesbaden (1870–81), and at the Munich Court Opera (1881–96). He also appeared at the Bayreuth Festivals, where he created the role of Hagen in *Götterdämmerung* (Aug. 17, 1876). He was particularly distinguished as a Wagnerian interpreter.

Siems, Margarethe, outstanding German soprano; b. Breslau, Dec. 30, 1879; d. Dresden, April 13, 1952. She studied with Orgeni. She made her debut at the Prague May Festival in 1902, and that same year joined the Prague Opera; in 1908 she joined the Dresden Court (later State) Opera, where she was a leading dramatic coloratura soprano until 1920; Strauss chose her to create the roles of Chrysothemis in *Elektra* (Jan. 25, 1909) and the Marschallin in *Der Rosenkavalier* (Jan. 26, 1911) there, and also Zerbinetta in *Ariadne auf Naxos* in Stuttgart (Oct. 25, 1912). In 1913 she made her London debut at Covent Garden. She retired from the operatic stage in Breslau in 1925 but continued to sing in concerts; she taught at the Berlin Cons. (1920–26), and then in Dresden and Breslau. In addition to her roles in Strauss's operas, she gained renown for her performances in the operas of Bellini, Donizetti, Verdi, and Wagner.

Siepi, Cesare, admired Italian bass; b. Milan, Feb. 10, 1923. He studied at the Milan Cons. He made his operatic debut as Sparafucile in Schio, near Vicenzo (1941); he appeared as Zaccaria in *Nabucco* in Verona (1945) and at his La Scala debut in Milan (1946), where he was a principal artist until 1958; he also appeared with the company during its 1950 visit to London's Covent Garden, where he was a regular singer from 1962 to 1973. On Nov. 6, 1950, he made his Metropolitan Opera debut in New York as Philip II in *Don Carlos*, remaining on its roster until 1973; also sang in other major opera houses on both sides of the Atlantic. An esteemed cantante artist, he excelled in the operas of Mozart and Verdi.

Sierra, Roberto, Puerto Rican composer; b. Vega Baja, Oct. 9, 1953. He began musical training at the Puerto Rico Cons. of Music and at the Univ. of Puerto Rico (graduated, 1976); then pursued studies in London at the Royal College of Music and the Univ. (1976–78), at the Inst. of Sonology in Utrecht (1978), and with Ligeti at the Hamburg Hochschule für Musik (1979–82). He was assist. director (1983–85) and director (1985–86) of the cultural activities dept. at the Univ. of Puerto Rico, then dean of studies (1986–87) and chancellor (1987–89) at the Puerto Rico Cons. of Music. From 1989 to 1992 he was composer-in-residence at the Milwaukee Sym. Orch. In 1992 he became an assistant prof. at Cornell Univ. His works include *El Mensajero de Plata*, chamber opera (1984), and *El Contemplado*, ballet (1987); also *Bayoán*, oratorio for Soprano, Baritone, and Orch. (1991; N.Y., Oct. 14, 1994).

Siface. See **Grossi, Giovanni Francesco**.

Sigismondi, Giuseppe, Italian librarian, historian, singing teacher, and composer; b. Naples, Nov. 13, 1739; d. there, May 10, 1826. He studied law (degree, 1759), and also received instruction in singing, figured bass, and counterpoint, taking lessons with Durante and later with Porpora (1761–67). He wrote comedies for an amateur theater company, and also composed 2 stage pieces, but he became best known as a singing teacher. He also served as archivist-librarian at the Pietà dei Turchini Cons. (from 1794). He prepared a 4 vol. MS, *Apoteosi della musica del regno di Napoli in tre ultimi transundati secoli* (1820), which was reworked and publ. by Villarosa as *Memorie dei compositori di musica del regno di Napoli* (Naples, 1840).

Sigurbjörnsson, Thorkell, prominent Icelandic composer, pedagogue, and administrator; b. Reykjavík, July 16, 1938. He studied at the Reykjavík College of Music (1948–57), then had lessons in composition with R. G. Harris at Hamline Univ. in St. Paul, Minn. (B.A., 1959), and in electronic music with Hiller and composition with Gaburo at the Univ. of Illinois in Urbana (M.M., 1961), then attended sessions in Nice and Darmstadt (1962). Returning to Reykjavík, he founded the modern group Musica Nova; he taught at the Reykjavík College of Music (from 1962), becoming a full prof. in 1969 and also was active with the Icelandic State Radio (1966–69). In 1973 he was a creative assoc. at the State Univ. of N.Y. at Buffalo, and in 1975 was a research musician at the Univ. of Calif. in La Jolla. He served as secretary (1969–85) and president (1985–88) of the Icelandic Soc. of Composers. In addition to his work as a composer, pedagogue, and broadcaster, he also appeared as a pianist and conductor. Among his works were *Composition in 3 Scenes*, chamber opera (1964), *Apaspil*, children's opera (1966), *Rabbi*, children's opera (1968), and *Thorgeirsboli* (The Bull-man), ballet (1971).

Sigwart, Botho (real name, **Sigwart Botho, Count of Eulenburg**), German pianist, musicologist, and composer; b. Berlin, Jan. 10, 1884; d. from wounds received in battle, Galicia, June 2, 1915. He was the son of the German diplomat and poet Count Phillip of Eulenburg. He studied piano in Vienna and musicology at the Univ. of Munich (Ph.D., 1907, with the diss. *Erasmus Widmann*); he completed his studies with Reger in Leipzig (1908–09). In 1909 he married the concert singer Helene Staegemann. He wrote several melodramas.

Siklós (real name, **Schönwald**), **Albert,** Hungarian cellist, musicologist, pedagogue, and composer; b. Budapest, June 26, 1878; d. there, April 3, 1942. He changed his name to Siklós in 1910. He studied law, and later took courses with Koessler at the Budapest Academy of Music, graduating in 1901; he taught at the Academy from 1910, and gradually became one of its most respected teachers. He was a prolific composer, but few of his works were publ., and there were virtually no performances outside Hungary. Among his works were the operas *Knight Fulkó* (1896) and *The House of Moons* (1926; Budapest, Dec. 21, 1927) and the ballet *The Mirror* (Budapest, March 28, 1923). He publ. a number of instructive books; also a music dictionary (1923).

Sikorski, Tomasz, Polish composer and pianist; b. Warsaw, May 19, 1939; d. there, Nov. 13, 1988. His father was the Swiss-born Polish composer and pedagogue Kazimierz Sikorski (1895–1986). He studied piano with Drzewiecki and composition with his father at the Warsaw Cons., then took lessons with Boulanger in Paris. As a pianist, he emphasized new music in his programs. His own compositions were in an advanced idiom. They include the radio opera *Przygody Sindbada zeglaraza* (The Adventures of Sinbad the Sailor; 1971).

Silja, Anja, remarkable German soprano; b. Berlin, April 17, 1935. Her grandmother was the singer Paula Althof; at the age of 8, she began vocal training with her grandfather, Egon van Rijn; gave a solo recital in Berlin at the age of 10. In 1956 she sang Rosina at the Berlin Städtische Opera; after appearing at the Braunschweig State Theater (1956–58), she sang at the Württemberg State Theater in Stuttgart (1958), at the Frankfurt am Main Opera (1960–63), and at the Bayreuth Festivals (from 1965). In 1968 she made her U.S. debut as Senta with the Chicago Lyric Opera; her Metropolitan Opera debut followed in New York as Leonore in *Fidelio* on Feb. 26, 1972. In subsequent years, she made appearances with leading North American and European opera houses; she also sang in concerts with major orchs. She later was also active as an opera producer. However, she continued to make appearances in opera. In 1995 she gave a stunning portrayal of Janaček's Elina Makropulos at the Glyndebourne Festival and at the London Proms. The breadth of her repertoire is commanding. Wagner's grandson Wieland coached her in the Wagnerian roles, among them Elisabeth, Elsa, Eva, and Senta, which she performed at Bayreuth. She also sang the roles of Salome and Elektra in Strauss's operas, of Marie and Lulu in Berg's operas, and of the sole character in Schoenberg's *Erwartung*. As a matter of course, she mastered the majority of standard soprano roles. She married **Christoph von Dohnányi**, under whose baton she sang in both operatic and concert settings.

Silk, Dorothy (Ellen), English soprano; b. King's Norton, Worcestershire, May 4, 1883; d. Alvechurch, Worcestershire, July 30, 1942. She studied in Birmingham and with Johannes Ress in Vienna. She pursued a fine career as a concert artist, appearing in London and at major English festivals. She also made forays into opera. In addition to her performances of works by English composers, she programmed the music of Schütz and other rarely heard composers.

Sills, Beverly (real name, **Belle Miriam Silverman**), celebrated American soprano and opera administrator; b. N.Y., May 25, 1929. At the age of 3, she appeared on the radio under the cute nickname "Bubbles," and won a prize at a Brooklyn contest as "the most beautiful baby of 1932." At 4, she joined a Saturday morning children's program, and at 7 she sang in a movie. At 10 she had a part on the radio show *Our Gal Sunday*. Her natural thespian talent and sweet child's voice soon proved to be valuable financial assets. She did a commercial advertising Rinso White soap, and appeared on an early television program, *Stars of the Future*. She began formal vocal studies with Estelle Liebling when she was 7; she also studied piano with Paolo Gallico; in Public School 91 in Brooklyn she was voted most "likely to succeed." In 1947 she made her operatic debut as Frasquita in *Carmen* with the Philadelphia Civic Opera; she then toured with several opera companies, and sang with the San Francisco Opera (1953) and the N.Y. City Opera (1955), quickly establishing herself at the latter as one of its most valuable members. She extended her repertoire to embrace modern American operas, including the title role of Douglas Moore's *The Ballad of Baby Doe*; she also sang in the American premiere of Luigi Nono's avant-garde opera *Intolleranza 1960*. She was a guest singer at the Vienna State Opera and in Buenos Aires in 1967, at La Scala in Milan in 1969, and at Covent Garden in London and the Deutsche Oper in Berlin in 1970. She made her first appearance with the Metropolitan Opera as Donna Anna in a concert production of *Don Giovanni* on July 8, 1966, at the Lewisohn Stadium in New York; her formal debut with the Metropolitan took place at Lincoln Center in New York as Pamira in *Le Siège de Corinthe* on April 7, 1975. At the height of her career, she received well-nigh universal praise, not only for the excellence of her voice and her virtuosity in coloratura parts, but also for her intelligence and erudition, rare among the common run of operatic divas. She became general director of the N.Y. City Opera in 1979, and made her farewell performance as a singer in 1980. She showed an uncommon administrative talent; during her tenure with the N.Y. City Opera, she promoted American musicians and broadened the operatic repertoire. In 1988 she retired from her post with the N.Y. City Opera. In 1994 she was named chairwoman of Lincoln Center. In her personal life, she suffered a double tragedy; one of her 2 children was born deaf, and the other autistic. In 1972 she accepted the national chairmanship of the Mothers' March on Birth Defects. She publ. *Bubbles: A Self-portrait* (N.Y., 1976; 2d ed., rev., 1981, as *Bubbles: An Encore*) and *Beverly: An Autobiography* (N.Y., 1987). She received honorary doctorates from Harvard Univ., N.Y. Univ., and the Calif. Inst. of the Arts. On Nov. 22, 1971, she was the subject of a cover story in *Time*. In 1980 she was awarded the U.S. Presidential Medal of Freedom. In 1998 she was inducted into the National Women's Hall of Fame. Her most notable roles included Cleopatra in Handel's *Giulio Cesare*, Lucia, Elisabeth in *Roberto Devereux*, Anna Bolena, Elvira in *I puritani*, and Maria Stuarda.

BIBL.: M. Kerby, *B. S.: America's Own Opera Star* (N.Y., 1989); B. Paolucci, *B. S.* (N.Y., 1990).

Silva, (David) Poll da, French composer; b. St.-Esprit, near Bayonne, March 28, 1834; d. Clermont, Oise, May 9, 1875. He went to Paris as a youth, and was encouraged by Halévy to study music and compose despite his incipient blindness; his mother, who was an educated musician, wrote out his compositions from dictation. His works include 3 operas and 2 oratorios.

Silva, Oscar da, Portuguese pianist, teacher, and composer; b. Paranhos, near Oporto, April 21, 1870; d. Oporto, March 6, 1958. He studied at the Lisbon Cons.; in 1892 he went to Leipzig, where he had lessons with Reinecke and Clara Schumann. Returning to Portugal in 1910, he devoted himself mainly to teaching, acquiring a very high reputation as a piano pedagogue. From 1932 to 1952 he lived in Brazil, then returned to Portugal. He wrote an opera, *Dona Mecia* (Lisbon, July 4, 1901).

BIBL.: A. Pinto, *Musica moderna portuguesa e os seus representantes* (Lisbon, 1930).

Silver, Charles, French composer; b. Paris, April 16, 1868; d. there, Oct. 10, 1949. He studied with Dubois and Massenet at the Paris Cons., winning the Grand Prix de Rome in 1891 with the cantata *L'Interdit*. He wrote the operas *La Belle au bois dormant* (Marseilles, 1902), *Le Clos* (Paris, 1906), *Myriane* (Nice, 1913), *La Mégère apprivoisée* (Paris, Jan. 30, 1922), *La Grand'-mère* (Oct. 7, 1930), and *Quatre-vingt-treize* (Paris, Jan. 24, 1936).

Silver, Sheila, talented, prolific, and original American composer; b. Seattle, Wash., Oct. 3, 1946. She studied at the Univ. of Wash. in Seattle (1964–65), then went to Paris for a course at the Inst. for European Studies (1966–67); she returned to the United States to earn her B.A. degree at the Univ. of Calif. at Berkeley (1968), and then enrolled at the Paris Cons. (1968). She further took courses at the Hochschule für Musik in Stuttgart, where her mentors were Ligeti and Karkoschka. Shuttling back to the United States once more, she studied with Shifrin, Berger, and Shapero at Brandeis Univ., completing her Ph.D. in composition there in 1976; she also attended the summer courses in new music in Darmstadt (1970), and studied with Druckman at the Berkshire Music Center at Tanglewood (summer 1972). There followed a number of grants that enabled her to travel to London and to Italy, where she was awarded the Prix de Rome at the American Academy. The list of awards she has received is most impressive. In 1979 she was appointed instructor in composition at the State Univ. of N.Y. at Stony Brook. During all of her peregrinations, she continued to compose productively; her mature style may be described as enlightened dissonance devoid of ostensible disharmonies. Among her works is the opera *The Thief of Love*, after a Bengali tale (1986).

Silveri, Paolo, Italian baritone; b. Ofena, near Aquila, Dec. 28, 1913. He studied in Milan and at the Accademia di Santa Cecilia in Rome. In 1939 he made his operatic debut as Schwarz in *Die Meistersinger von Nürnberg*. After singing bass roles, he turned to baritone roles after successfully appearing as Germont in Rome in 1944. In 1946 he sang Marcello, Scarpia, and Rossini's Figaro with the Teatro São Carlo of Naples during its visit to London's Covent Garden. He continued to sing at Covent Garden until 1952, both with the resident company and with the visiting La Scala company of Milan as Rigoletto, Count Luna, Amonasro, and Iago. He sang Don Giovanni and Renato with the Glyndebourne company during its visit to the Edinburgh Festival (1948, 1949). From 1949 to 1955 he sang regularly at La Scala. On Nov. 20, 1950, he made his Metropolitan Opera debut in New York as Don Giovanni. He remained on its roster until 1953, singing such roles as Tonio, Marcello, Germont, Escamillo, Rigoletto, and Scarpia. He then pursued his career in Europe. In 1959 he sang the tenor role of Otello in Dublin but then resumed his career as a baritone.

His farewell performance took place at the Camden Festival in 1967 as Donizetti's Israele. From 1970 he taught voice in Rome.

Silvestri, Constantin, esteemed Romanian-born English conductor and composer; b. Bucharest, June 13, 1913; d. London, Feb. 23, 1969. He studied piano as a child, making his debut at age 10; after taking courses in piano and composition (with Jora) at the Bucharest Cons., he was active as a pianist. In 1930 he made his debut as a conductor with the Bucharest Radio Sym. Orch.; he was a conductor with the Bucharest Opera (from 1935) and music director of the Bucharest Phil. (1947–53); he also taught conducting at the Bucharest Cons. (from 1948). In 1956 he went to Paris, and in 1957 settled in England, becoming a naturalized British subject in 1967. In 1961 he became principal conductor of the Bournemouth Sym. Orch., which he led with distinction until his death; he took it on a European tour in 1965. In 1963 he made his debut at London's Covent Garden conducting *Khovanshchina*. He was an impassioned if sometimes willful interpreter of the classics. He composed mostly in small forms in an unpretentious, neo-Baroque manner.

Simándy, József, noted Hungarian tenor; b. Budapest, Sept. 18, 1916; d. there, March 4, 1997. Following studies with Emilia Posszert (1943–45), he completed his training at the Budapest Academy of Music. After singing in the Budapest Opera chorus (1940–45), he was a member of the Szeged Opera (1945–47). In 1947 he joined the Budapest Opera, where he distinguished himself in lyric, heroic, and spinto roles. He also sang at the Bavarian State Opera in Munich from 1956 to 1960. His guest engagements took him to many of the major European music centers. From 1978 he was a prof. at the Budapest Academy of Music. In 1953 he received the Kossuth Prize, and in 1962 he was made a Meritorious Artist and in 1964 an Outstanding Artist by the Hungarian government. Among his outstanding portrayals were Florestan, Lohengrin, Don Carlos, Otello, Walther von Stolzing, Don José, Cavaradossi, Des Grieux, and Turiddu. He also was renowned for his roles in operas by Ferenc Erkel.

Simeonov, Konstantin (Arsenievich), Russian conductor; b. Koznakovo, June 20, 1910; d. Kiev, Jan. 3, 1987. He began a career as a singer, then studied conducting at the Leningrad Cons. with Alexander Gauk. He subsequently appeared as a guest conductor throughout the Soviet Union; he served as chief conductor of the Ukrainian Theater of Opera and Ballet in Kiev (1961–66), then occupied a similar post at the Kirov Theater of Opera and Ballet in Leningrad (1966–75); he resumed his Kiev post in 1975. He also appeared as a guest conductor abroad.

Simionato, Giulietta, outstanding Italian mezzo-soprano; b. Forlì, May 12, 1910. She studied with Locatello and Palumbo in Rovigo; she won the bel canto competition in Florence in 1933, and then returned there to sing in the premiere of Pizzetti's *Orsèolo* (May 5, 1935). In 1939 she joined Milan's La Scala, remaining on its roster as one of its principal artists until 1966. In 1947 she made her British debut as Cherubino at the Edinburgh Festival; her first appearance at London's Covent Garden followed, as Adalgisa in 1953. In 1954 she made her U.S. debut at the Chicago Lyric Opera. On Oct. 26, 1959, she made her first appearance at the Metropolitan Opera in New York as Azucena; she sang there again in 1960 and 1962. She gave her farewell stage performance as Servilia in *La clemenza di Tito* at Milan's Piccola Scala in 1966. A distinguished coloratura artist, Simionato excelled in the operas of Rossini, Donizetti, Bellini, and Verdi.

BIBL.: J.-J. Hanine Vallaut, *G. S.: Come Cenerentola divenne regina* (n.p., 1987).

Simmons, Calvin (Eugene), gifted black American conductor; b. San Francisco, April 27, 1950; d. (drowned) Connery Pond, east of Lake Placid, N.Y., Aug. 21, 1982. He was the son of a longshoreman and a gospel singer. He joined the San Francisco Boys' Choir at age 11, where he received conducting lessons from its conductor, Madi Bacon; he then went to the Cincinnati College-Cons. of Music, where he studied conducting with Max Rudolf (1968–70); when Rudolf was appointed to the faculty of the Curtis Inst. of Music in Philadelphia, Simmons joined him there (1970–72); he also took piano lessons with Serkin. He served as a rehearsal pianist and assistant conductor under Adler at the San Francisco Opera (1968–75), where he made his formal debut conducting *Hänsel und Gretel* in 1972. In 1975 he made his British debut at the Glyndebourne Festival. He was assistant conductor of the Los Angeles Phil. and music director of the Young Musicians Foundation orch. (1975–78). In 1979 he was appointed music director of the Oakland (Calif.) Sym. Orch. Before his tragic death in a canoeing accident, he appeared as a guest conductor with increasing success throughout North America. He made his Metropolitan Opera debut in New York in 1978 and his N.Y. City Opera debut in 1980.

Simon, Anton, French pianist, conductor, and composer; b. Paris, Aug. 5, 1850; d. St. Petersburg, Feb. 1, 1916. He studied piano at the Paris Cons., and in 1871 went to Moscow, where he became active as a piano teacher. He wrote the operas *Rolla* (Moscow, April 29, 1892), *The Song of Triumphant Love* (Moscow, Dec. 14, 1897), and *The Fishermen* (Moscow, March 7, 1899); also a mimodrama, *Esmeralda* (1902), and 2 ballets: *The Stars* (1898) and *Living Flowers* (1900, c.1910).

Simon, James, German musicologist and composer; b. Berlin, Sept. 29, 1880; d. in the Auschwitz concentration camp about Oct. 14, 1944. He studied piano with Ansorge and composition with Bruch in Berlin. From 1907 to 1919 he taught at the Klindworth-Scharwenka Cons. in Berlin. He left Germany shortly after the advent of the Nazi regime in 1933, and lived in Zürich, then moved to Amsterdam, where the Hitlerite wave engulfed him after the Nazi invasion of the Netherlands. He was deported to Theresienstadt on April 5, 1944, and from there, on Oct. 12, 1944, was sent to Auschwitz, where he was put to death a few days later. His opera, *Frau im Stein*, was premiered in Stuttgart in 1925.

Simon, Stephen (Anthony), American conductor; b. N.Y., May 3, 1937. He studied piano with Joel Rosen; he then enrolled at the Yale Univ. School of Music and also took courses in choral conducting with Hugh Ross and Julius Herford. In 1963 he became music director of the Westchester Orch. Soc.; from 1970 to 1974 he was music director of the Handel Soc. in New York, and then of the Handel Festival in Washington, D.C. (from 1977).

Simoneau, Léopold, eminent Canadian tenor, pedagogue, and administrator; b. St.-Flavien, near Quebec City, May 3, 1916. He was a student of Émile Larochelle in Quebec City (1939–41) and of Salvator Issaurel in Montreal (1941–44). In 1941 he made his operatic debut as Hadji in *Lakmé* with the Variétés lyriques in Montreal. In 1943 he sang Don Curzio at the Montreal Festival. After winning the Prix Archambault in 1944, he studied with Paul Althouse in New York (1945–47). He also pursued his career, winning extraordinary success as Ferrando and Tamino in Montreal in 1945. During this period, he also sang in the United States. In 1949 he made his Paris debut as Mireille at the Opéra Comique; he continued to sing there, as well as at the Opéra, until 1954. In 1953 he made his first appearance at Milan's La Scala. In 1954 he sang with the Vienna State Opera on its visit to London. He soon acquired a notable reputation as a Mozartian. He also sang widely in the United States and Canada as a soloist with the leading orchs. and as a recitalist. On Oct. 18, 1963, he made his Metropolitan Opera debut in New York as Ottavio, but remained on its roster for only that season. In 1964 he chose Ottavio as his farewell to the operatic stage at the Place de arts in Montreal. He sang for the last time in public as a soloist in *Messiah* with the Montreal Sym. Orch. on Nov. 24, 1970. From 1963 to 1967 he taught at the Montreal Cons. In 1967 he became deputy head of the music division of the Ministry of Cultural Affairs of Quebec. In 1971 he served as the first artistic director of the Opéra du Quebec. He taught at the San Francisco Cons. of Music from 1972, and also at the Banff School of Fine Arts from 1973 to 1976. In 1982 he settled in Victoria, British Columbia, and founded Canada Opera Piccola. In 1946 he married **Pierrette Alarie.** In 1959 they were the first recipients of the Prix de musique Calixa-Lavallée. In 1971 he was made an Officer of the Order of Canada. The French government made him an Officier of the Ordre des Arts des Lettres in 1990.

BIBL.: R. Maheu, *Pierrette Alarie, L. S.: Deux voix, un art* (Montreal, 1988).

Simon-Girard, Juliette, French soprano; b. Paris, May 8, 1859; d. Nice, Dec. 1959. She made her debut at the Folies-Dramatiques in Paris, where she created the principal role in *Les Cloches de Corneville*s on April 19, 1877, then sang at the premieres of *La Fille du Tambour-major* (1879), *Fanfan la tulipe* (1882), and many other operettas; she became particularly successful in Offenbach's repertoire. She married the tenor Nicolas Simon, known as Simon-Max (1855–1923); she divorced him in 1894, and married the comedian Huguenet, then retired to Nice.

Simonis, Jean-Marie, Belgian composer; b. Mol, Nov. 22, 1931. He studied composition with Stekke, Souris, Louel, and Quinet, and conducting with Defossez at the Brussels Cons.; he taught there (from 1969) and at the Uccles Academy of Music (from 1971). Among his works is the radio opera *Gens de maison* (1962).

Simonov, Yuri (Ivanovich), prominent Russian conductor; b. Saratov, March 4, 1941. He received training in violin at a Saratov music school, where he made his debut as a conductor of the school orch. when he was only 12. He pursued his studies with Kramarov (viola) and Rabinovich (conducting) at the Leningrad Cons. (1956–68), where he made his formal conducting debut as a student in 1963. In 1966 he won 1st prize in the USSR conducting competition and in 1968 took 1st prize in the Accademia di Santa Cecilia conducting competition in Rome. He was conductor of the Kislovodsk Phil. (1967–69) and assistant conductor to Mravinsky and the Leningrad Phil. (1968–69). In 1969 he made his debut at the Bolshoi Theater in Moscow conducting *Aida*. From 1970 to 1985 he was chief conductor of the Bolshoi Theater, where he established a notable reputation for his idiomatic performances of the Russian masterworks. He also restored Wagner's operas to the active repertoire after a hiatus of some 40 years. He conducted the company on acclaimed tours abroad, including visits to Paris, Vienna, New York (Metropolitan Opera, *War and Peace*, 1975), Milan, Washington, D.C., and Japan. During these years, he also appeared as a conductor with the leading Russian orchs. at home and on tours abroad. In 1982 he made his first appearance with a Western opera company when he made his debut at London's Covent Garden with *Eugene Onegin*. He returned to Covent Garden in 1986 to open the season with *La Traviata*. He also appeared with most of the major British orchs. During the 1991–92 season, he conducted the Junge Deutsche Philharmonie and the Buenos Aires Phil. on tours of Europe. He made his debut at the Hamburg State Opera conducting *Don Carlos* during the 1992–93 season. In 1994 he became music director of the Orchestre National de Belgique in Brussels.

Sinclair, Monica, English mezzo-soprano; b. Evercreech, Somerset, March 23, 1925. She studied voice with Marcus Thomson and piano with Harold Craxton at the Royal Academy of Music (1942–44), and voice with Arnold Smith, piano with Olive Bloom, and accompaniment with Charles Lofthouse at the Royal College of Music (1944–48) in London. In 1948 she made her operatic debut as Suzuki with the Carl Rosa Opera Co., a role she also chose for her debut at London's Covent Garden in 1949, where she sang until 1967. In 1954 she appeared as Ragonde in *Le Comte Ory* with the Glyndebourne company during its visit to the Edinburgh Festival, and she continued to make appearances with the Glyndebourne company until 1960. She also made frequent appearances with the Handel Opera Soc. On March 14, 1972, she made her Metropolitan Opera debut in New York as Berkenfield in *La Fille du régiment*. She was best known for her roles in operas by Lully, Mozart, Rossini, and Strauss.

Sinding, Christian (August), celebrated Norwegian composer; b. Kongsberg, Jan. 11, 1856; d. Oslo, Dec. 3, 1941. He studied first with L. Lindeman in Norway, then at the Leipzig Cons. (1874–78) with Schradieck (violin), Jadassohn (theory), and Reinecke (orchestration); a government stipend enabled him to continue his studies in Germany, and he spent 2 years (1882–84) in Munich, Berlin, and Dresden; there he wrote his first opera, *Titandros*, much influenced by Wagner. On Dec. 19, 1885, he gave a concert of his works in Oslo; during another stay in Germany, his Piano Quintet was played in Leipzig, with Brodsky and Busoni among the performers (Jan. 19, 1889); Erika Lie-Nissen played his Piano Concerto in Berlin (Feb. 23, 1889). He publ. a number of piano pieces in Germany; of these, *Frühlingsrauschen* became an international favorite. His opera to a German text, *Der heilige Berg* (1914), was not successful. In 1915 he received a life pension of 4,000 crowns "for distinguished service"; on his 60th birthday (1916), the Norwegian government presented him with a purse of 30,000 crowns, a mark of appreciation for "the greatest national composer since Grieg." He was invited by George Eastman to teach at the Eastman School of Music in Rochester, N.Y., during the academic season 1921–22; after this journey, he lived mostly in Oslo. He continued to compose, and toward the end of his life wrote in larger forms; his 3d Sym. was conducted by Nikisch with the Berlin Phil. in 1921, and his 4th Sym. was performed on his 80th birthday in Oslo (1936). His works aggregate to 132 opus numbers. Most of his music is of a descriptive nature; his lyric pieces for piano and his songs are fine examples of Scandinavian Romanticism, but the German inspiration of his formative years is much in evidence; he was chiefly influenced by Schumann and Liszt. He also composed the operas *Titandros* (1884; not perf) and *Der heilige Berg* (1912; Dessau, April 19, 1914).

Singer, George, Czech-born Israeli conductor and composer; b. Prague, Aug. 6, 1908; d. Tel Aviv, Sept. 30, 1980. He studied piano at the Prague Academy of Music with Schulhoff and composition with Zemlinsky. He made his first appearance as an opera conductor in Prague in 1926. In 1930 he received an engagement at the Hamburg Opera, returning to Prague in 1934. When the Nazis invaded Czechoslovakia in 1939, he, being Jewish, was compelled to take refuge in Tel Aviv, where he established himself favorably as a conductor. He also accepted engagements as a conductor in Russia and in the United States, where he led the N.Y. City Opera in 1968. Back in Israel, he gave performances of several works of local composers. He was known for his phenomenal facility in sight-reading, performing works perfectly at first reading on the piano and conducting every nuance of an orch. score. He composed some orch pieces.

Singher, Martial (Jean-Paul), noted French baritone and pedagogue; b. Oloron-Ste. Marie, Aug. 14, 1904; d. Santa Barbara, Calif., March 10, 1990. He received his education as a public-school teacher in Dax, and at the École Normale de Toulouse and the École Normale Supérieure de St. Cloud. He then studied voice with André Gresse at the Paris Cons. (premier prix for singing, 1929; premier prix for opera and opéra comique singing, 1930; Grand Prix Osiris de l'Institute de France, 1930); he also studied voice with Juliette Fourestier. He made his operatic debut in Amsterdam as Orestes in *Iphigénie en Tauride* on Nov. 14, 1930, then joined the Paris Opéra, remaining with it until 1941; he also sang at the Opéra Comique. On Jan. 10, 1940, he married Margareta Busch, daughter of the conductor Fritz Busch. He went to the United States in 1941; he made his Metropolitan Opera debut in New York on Dec. 10, 1943, as Dapertutto in *Les Contes d'Hoffmann*; subsequently he sang the roles of the Count in *Le nozze di Figaro*, Lescaut in *Manon*, and all 4 baritone roles in *Les Contes d'Hoffmann*; remained on the roster, with some interruptions, until 1959. He also sang with the leading orchs. of the United States, and appeared widely in song recitals. He was on the faculty of the Mannes College of Music in New York (1951–62) and the Curtis Inst. of Music in Philadelphia (1955–68); he then was director of the voice and opera dept., and was the opera producer at the Music Academy of the West in Santa Barbara (1962–81). His students included Donald Gramm, John Reardon, James King, Louis Quilico, Judith Blegen, Benita Valente, and Jeannine Altmeyer. He was a particularly distinguished interpreter of the French operatic and song repertoire. He wrote a book useful to vocalists aspiring to an operatic career, *An Interpretive Guide to Operatic Arias: A Handbook for Singers, Coaches, Teachers, and Students* (1983).

Singleton, Alvin (Elliot), black American composer; b. N.Y., Dec. 28, 1940. He took courses in composition and music education at N.Y. Univ. (B.M., 1967), then continued his study of composition with Powell and Wyner at Yale Univ. (M.M.A., 1971). He received a Fulbright fellowship to study with Petrassi in Rome at the Accademia di Santa Cecilia (1971–72), and in 1981 was awarded an NEA grant. From 1985 to 1988 he served as composer-in-residence of the Atlanta Sym. Orch.; in 1988 he was appointed composer-in-residence at Spelman College in Atlanta. Among his works is the opera *Dream Sequence '76* (1976); also *Necessity Is a Mother*, wordless drama (1981).

Sinico, Francesco, Italian organist, choirmaster, teacher, and composer; b. Trieste, Dec. 12, 1810; d. there, Aug. 18, 1865. He studied with G. Farinelli. He was an organist and conductor in various churches. In 1843 he established his own singing school in Trieste, providing excellent training for choral singing. He produced his opera *I Virtuosi di Barcellona* in 1841. His son, Giuseppe Sinico (b. Trieste, Feb. 10, 1836; d. there, Dec. 31, 1907), continued the popular singing classes at the Sinico School in Trieste; wrote several operas, which he produced there: *Marinella* (Aug. 26, 1854), *I Moschettieri* (March 26, 1859), *Aurora di Nevers* (March 12, 1861), *Alessandro Stradella* (Lugo, Sept. 19, 1863), and *Spartaco* (Nov. 20, 1886). He publ. *Breve metodo teoricopratico di canto elementare*.

BIBL.: *Una famiglia triestina di musicisti "I S."* (Trieste, 1932).

Sinopoli, Giuseppe, distinguished Italian conductor and composer; b. Venice, Nov. 2, 1946. He studied organ and harmony as a youth in Messina, then took courses in harmony and counterpoint at the Venice Cons.; he also studied medicine at the Univ. of Padua (degree in psychiatry, 1971) while concurrently studying composition privately with Donatoni in Paris; he then took a course in conducting with Swarowsky at the Vienna Academy of Music. He organized the Bruno Maderna Ensemble in 1975, and conducted it in performances of contemporary music; he was also active as a teacher. After a successful engagement as a guest conductor at the Teatro La Fenice in Venice in 1976, he appeared at the Deutsche Oper in Berlin (1980), the Hamburg State Opera (1980), and the Vienna State Opera (1982). On May 3, 1983, he made his Covent Garden debut in London, conducting *Manon Lescaut*; his Metropolitan Opera debut followed in New York on March 11, 1985, when he led a performance of *Tosca*. He served as chief conductor of the Orchestra dell'Accademia Nazionale di Santa Cecilia in Rome (1983–87). He also was principal conductor of the Philharmonia Orch. of London (1984–94). In 1990 he became Generalmusikdirektor of the Deutsche Oper in Berlin, but abruptly resigned that same year after disagreements with its intendant, Götz Friedrich. In 1992 he became chief conductor of the Dresden State Orch. and Opera. His training as a psychiatrist led him to probe deeply into the scores he conducted, often resulting in startlingly revealing but controversial interpretations. As a composer, he pursues contemporary modes of expression. Among his works is the opera *Lou Salome* (Munich, May 10, 1981; also 2 suites: No. 1 for Soli, Chorus, and Orch., 1981, and No. 2 for Orch., 1985).

Siohan, Robert (-Lucien), French conductor, composer, and writer on music; b. Paris, Feb. 27, 1894; d. there, July 16, 1985. He studied at the Paris Cons. (1909–22). In 1929 he founded the Concerts Siohan, which he conducted until 1936; was chorus master at the Paris Opéra (1931–46); from 1948 to 1962 he was an instructor in solfège and sight-reading at the Paris Cons.; subsequently served as inspector-general of music in the Ministry of Culture. He received his doctorate at the Sorbonne in Paris in 1954 with the diss. *Théories nouvelles de l'homme* (publ. as *Horizons sonores*, Paris, 1956). Among his compositions is the opera *Le saut dans les etoiles* (1926–27). He publ. *Stravinsky* (Paris, 1959; Eng. tr., London, 1966) and *Histoire du public musical* (Lausanne, 1967).

Siqueira, José (de Lima), Brazilian conductor and composer; b. Conceição, June 24, 1907. After training in saxophone and trumpet from his father, he studied with Paulo Silva, Francisco Braga, and Burle Marx at the National School of Music in Rio de Janeiro; much later he studied with Aubin, Bigot, Chailley, and Messiaen in Paris (1954). In 1940 he founded the Orquesta Sinfónica Brasileira in Rio de Janeiro, for which he served as music director until 1944. In 1948 he founded the Orquesta Sinfónica de Rio de Janeiro. He also appeared as a guest conductor abroad. His compositions include *A compadecida*, opera (1959; Rio de Janeiro, Dec. 20, 1961), *Gimba*, drama (1960), and *O carnaval Caricoa*, theater piece (1965); also *Candomblé*, oratorio (Rio de Janeiro, Dec. 20, 1957).

Širola, Božidar, distinguished Croatian musicologist and composer; b. Žakanj, Dec. 20, 1889; d. Zagreb, April 10, 1956. He studied mathematics and physics at the Univ. of Zagreb. After training in composition from Ivan Zajc, he studied musicology with Robert Lach at the Univ. of Vienna (Ph.D., 1921, with the diss. *Das istrische Volkslied*). He taught mathematics and physics in Zagreb secondary schools, and also was active as a lecturer, critic, ethnomusicologist, and organologist. From 1935 to 1941 he was director of the secondary school of music at the Zagreb Academy of Music, and then was director of the Ethnographic Museum. After Tito consolidated his control of Yugoslavia in 1945, Širola devoted himself to private research. He was a noted authority on Croatian folk music. As a composer, he became best known for his operas and songs.

WRITINGS (all publ. in Zagreb): *Pregled povijesti hrvatske muzike* (Survey of the History of Croatian Music; 1922); with M. Gavazzi, *Muzikološki rad Etnografskog muzeja u Zagrebu* (Musicological Works of the Ethnographic Museum in Zagreb; 1931); *Fućkalice: Sviraljke od kore svježeg drveta* (Fućkalice: Wind Instruments Made From the Bark of Green Wood; 1932); *Sopile i zurle* (Sopilas and Zurlas; 1932); *Sviraljke s udarnim jezičkom* (Wind Instruments with a Beating Reed; 1937); *Hrvatska narodna glazba* (Croatian Folk Music; 1940; 2d ed., 1942); *Hrvatska umjetnička glasba: Odabrana poglavlja iz povijesti hrvatske glazbe* (Croatian Art Music: Selected Chapters of a History of Croatian Music; 1942).

WORKS: DRAMATIC: OPERAS: *Stanac* (1915); *Citara i bubanj* (The Cittern and the Drum; 1929); *Grabancijaš* (The Student of the Black Arts; 1935); *Mladi gospodin* (The Young Gentleman; 1940); *Kameni svatovi* (The Stone Wedding Guests; 1954). MELODRAMAS: *Iz Danteova "Ruja"* (From Dante's "Paradiso"; 1912); *Putnik* (The Traveller; 1919); *Otmica* (The Abduction; 1922); *Šuma Striborova* (1923); *Kameni svatovi* (1935). OPERETTAS: *Z Griča na Trešnjevku* (1931); *Mecena* (1934). Also ballets and incidental music.

Sistermans, Anton, Dutch bass; b. 's-Hertogenbosch, Aug. 5, 1865; d. The Hague, March 18, 1926. He studied with Stockhausen in Frankfurt am Main, and from 1895 gave concerts in Europe. His only appearance in opera was as Pogner (Bayreuth, 1899). From 1904 to 1915 he taught singing at Berlin's Klindworth-Scharwenka Cons.

Sitsky, Larry, Australian pianist, teacher, and composer; b. Tientsin, China (of Russian parents), Sept. 10, 1934. He was improvising on the piano and writing music by the age of 10; in 1951 his family went to Australia, where he studied piano with Winifred Burston and composition with Raymond Hanson at the New South Wales State Conservatorium of Music in Sydney (1951–55); after further piano training with Petri in San Francisco (1958–61), he taught piano at the Queensland State Conservatorium (1961–65), then was head of keyboard studies (1966–78) and composition and musicology (from 1981) at the Canberra School of Music. He undertook official exchange visits as a composer to Russia (1977) and to the People's Republic of China (1983), where he was the first composer from the West to make an official visit since the 1950s; he also appeared as a pianist in China (1945–51). In

1989–90 he was composer-in-residence at the Univ. of Cincinnati College-Cons. of Music. He specializes in late Romantic and early-20th-century scores, showing preference for the music of Busoni. He publ. *Busoni and the Piano: The Music, the Writings, the Recordings: A Complete Survey* (Westport, Conn., 1986), *The Classical Reproducing Piano Roll: A Catalogue-Index* (2 vols., Westport, Conn., 1990), and *Music of the Repressed Russian Avant-Garder, 1900–1929* (Westport, Conn., 1994); he also made transcriptions and ed. some of Busoni's scores for publication. Sitsky's own music is advanced, although it makes no systematic use of particular devices.

WORKS: OPERAS: *Fall of the House of Usher* (Hobart Festival, Aug. 1965); *Lenz* (1969–70; Sydney, March 1974); *The Fiery Tales*, after Chaucer and Boccaccio (1975); *Voices in Limbo*, radio opera (1977); *The Golem* (1980; Sydney, Oct. 14, 1993; orch. extracts as *Songs and Dances* and *9 Orchestral Interludes*, 1984).

Skilton, Charles Sanford, American composer and teacher; b. Northampton, Mass., Aug. 16, 1868; d. Lawrence, Kansas, March 12, 1941. He first studied in Germany; after graduating from Yale Univ. (B.A., 1889), he studied in New York with Harry Rowe Shelley (organ) and Dudley Buck (composition), then at the Berlin Hochschule für Musik with Bargiel (1891–93). From 1893 to 1896 he was director of music at the Salem (N.C.) Academy and College, and conducted the local orch. there; he then filled a similar post at the State Normal School in Trenton, N.J. (1897–1903); in 1903 he was engaged as a prof. of organ and theory at the Univ. of Kansas, Lawrence, where he remained most of his life. He made a detailed study of Indian music, and introduced Indian motifs into the traditional forms of the suite and fantasy. His opera *Kalopin* (1927) received the David Bispham Memorial Medal in 1930; other works include the operas *The Sun Bride* (NBC, April 17, 1930) and *The Day of Gayomair* (1936), and *The Guardian Angel*, oratorio (1925).

BIBL.: J. Howard, *C. S. S.* (N.Y., 1929); J. Smith, *C. S. S. (1868–1941), Kansas Composer* (thesis, Univ. of Kansas, 1979).

Sklavos, George, Greek composer and teacher; b. Brailov, Romania (of Greek parents), Aug. 20, 1888; d. Athens, March 19, 1976. He studied with Armand Marsick at the Athens Cons., where he was an instructor (1913–68). He devoted himself chiefly to the musical theater.

WORKS: DRAMATIC: OPERAS: *Niovi* (1919); *Lestenisa* (1923; Athens, March 14, 1947); *Kassiani* (1929–36; Athens, Oct. 30, 1959); *Krino st' akroyali* (Lily at the Seashore; 1937–41); *Amphitryon* (1955–60); *St' Ai Yorghi to panyghiri* (At St. George's Fair; 1961–62). Also incidental music.

Skovhus, Bo(je), admired Danish baritone; b. Århus, May 22, 1962. He received his training at the Århus Cons. (1982–86), the Royal Opera Academy in Copenhagen (1986–88), and with Oren Brown in New York. In 1988 he made his operatic debut as Don Giovanni at the Vienna Volksoper, a role he reprised for his first appearance at the Royal Opera in Copenhagen in 1990. In 1991 he made his debut at the Vienna State Opera as Silvio and at the Hamburg State Opera as Guglielmo. Following debuts as Billy Budd at the Cologne Opera in 1992 and as Mozart's Almaviva at the Bavarian State Opera in Munich in 1994, he portrayed Don Giovanni at his first appearance at the Deutsche Oper in Berlin in 1995. In 1997 he sang for the first time at London's Covent Garden as Guglielmo, at the Opéra de la Bastille in Paris as Danilo, and at the San Francisco Opera as Almaviva. After singing Billy Budd at the Houston Grand Opera in 1998, he made his Metropolitan Opera debut on Dec. 24 of that year as Eisenstein. His first engagement at the Dresden State Opera followed in 1999 as Don Giovanni. As a soloist, he appeared with the Berlin Phil., the Chicago Sym. Orch., the Vienna Sym. Orch., the Boston Sym. Orch., the Cleveland Orch., and many others. His recital engagements took him to the principal music centers on both sides of the Atlantic. Among his other roles are Hamlet, Eugene Onegin, Wolfram, Strauss's Olivier, and Wozzeck.

Skram, Knut, Norwegian baritone; b. Saebo, Dec. 18, 1937. He was educated in Montana and studied voice with George Buckee, in Wiesbaden with Paul Lohmann, in Rome with Luigi Ricci, and in Copenhagen with Kristian Riis. In 1964 he made his operatic debut at the Norwegian Opera in Oslo as Amonasro. After winning 1st prize in the Munich International Competition in 1967, he made his debut at the Glyndebourne Festival as Mozart's Guglielmo in 1969, where he made return visits until 1976. From 1978 he sang at the Spoleto Festival. In 1979 he made his U.S. debut as Papageno with the Kentucky Opera in Louisville. He portrayed Eugene Onegin in Lyons in 1984. During the Berlin State Opera's tour of Japan in 1987, he was engaged as Jochanaan. In 1988 he sang Pizzaro in Buenos Aires and Scarpia in Moscow. He appeared as Hans Sachs in Nice in 1992. In 1996 he sang the Wanderer in *Siegfried* in Oslo. As a concert artist, he appeared frequently as a lieder interpreter.

Škroup, František Jan, prominent Bohemian conductor and composer, brother of **Jan Nepomuk Škroup**; b. Osice, near Pardubice, June 3, 1801; d. Rotterdam, Feb. 7, 1862. He received his musical training from his father, the teacher and composer Dominik Josef Skroup (1766–1830). He studied law in Prague. In 1827 he became assistant conductor, and in 1837 principal conductor, at the Estates Theater, Prague, and remained at that post until 1857; he put into performance several Wagner operas for the first time in Prague. He wrote several operas to Czech librettos, which he conducted in Prague: *Drátenik* (The Tinker; Feb. 2, 1826), *Oldřich a Božena* (Dec. 14, 1828), *Libušin snatek* (Libusa's Marriage; April 11, 1835; rev. 1849; April 11, 1850), *Die Geisterbraut* (Nov. 17, 1836), *Drahomira* (Nov. 20, 1848), and *Der Mergeuse* (Nov. 29, 1851). In 1860 he went to Rotterdam as conductor of a German opera troupe. He also scored a success as a composer with his incidental music to Josef Tyl's play *Fidlovačka* (Prague, Dec. 21, 1834), which includes the song *Kde domov můj* (Where Is My Home?); the latter became so famous that it was mistaken for a folk song and the first part of it was made into the Czech national anthem in 1918.

BIBL.: J. Plavec, *F. S.* (Prague, 1946).

Škroup, Jan Nepomuk, Bohemian conductor, teacher, and composer, brother of **František Jan Škroup**; b. Osice, near Pardubice, Sept. 15, 1811; d. Prague, May 5, 1892. He studied at the Prague Gymnasium, then conducted various orch. concerts and theater productions and served as choirmaster in churches and monasteries in Prague, and was choirmaster at St. Vitus Cathedral (1848–87). He wrote the operas *Svédové v Praze* (The Swedish Girl in Prague; 1844), *Der Liebesring* (1860), and *Vineta* (1861); also incidental music.

Skrowaczewski, Stanislaw, eminent Polish-born American conductor and composer; b. Lwów, Oct. 3, 1923. He composed an orch. overture at the age of 8, played a piano recital at 11, and performed Beethoven's 3d Piano Concerto at 13, conducting the orch. from the keyboard. He studied composition and conducting at the Lwów Cons. and also physics, chemistry, and philosophy at the Univ. of Lwów. The oppressive Nazi occupation of Poland interrupted his studies, and an unfortunate bomb exploded in the vicinity of his house, causing an injury to his hands that interfered with his further activities as a concert pianist. After World War II, he went to Kraków to study composition with Palester and conducting with Bierdiajew. In 1947 he received a French government scholarship which enabled him to study composition with Boulanger and conducting with Kletzki in Paris. He then conducted the Wroclaw Orch. (1946–47), the State Silesian Phil. in Katowice (1949–54), the Kraków Phil. (1954–56), and the National Phil. in Warsaw (1956–59). In 1956 he won 1st prize in the international conducting competition in Rome. On Dec. 4, 1958, he made his American debut as a guest conductor of the Cleveland Orch., scoring an impressive success. In 1960 he was named music director of the Minneapolis Sym. Orch. (renamed the Minnesota Orch. in 1968), and asserted his excellence both as a consummate technician of the baton and a fine interpreter of the classic and modern repertoire. In 1966 he became a naturalized

American citizen. In the interim, he appeared as a guest conductor throughout the world. As an opera conductor, he made his Metropolitan Opera debut in New York on Jan. 8, 1970, with *Die Zauberflöte*. In 1979 he resigned as music director of the Minnesota Orch., and was made its conductor emeritus. He was principal conductor and musical adviser of the Hallé Orch. in Manchester from 1984 to 1990; he also served as music adviser of the St. Paul (Minn.) Chamber Orch. (1987–88). His own compositions include the ballet *Ugo and Parisina* (1949); also theater and film music.

Skuherský, František Zdeněk (Xavier Alois), Bohemian conductor, teacher, music theorist, and composer; b. Opočno, July 31, 1830; d. Budweis, Aug. 19, 1892. He first studied medicine, then had music lessons with Kittl in Prague. From 1854 to 1866 he was in Innsbruck, where he conducted the Musikverein. In 1866 he went to Prague as director of the Organ School; he also was choirmaster at St. Hastal's and at the Holy Trinity, director of the court chapel, and a teacher of music theory at the Czech Univ. (from 1882). In 1890 he retired. Among his outstanding pupils were J. F. Foerster and Janáček. Skuherský was a leading figure in the reform of church music in his homeland. He publ. several texts on music theory (in Prague): *O formách hudebních* (Musical Form; 1873; 2d ed., 1884), *Nauka o hudební komposici* (Theory of Musical Composition; 4 vols., 1880–84), and *Nauka o harmonii na vědeckém základě ve formě nejjednodušší* (Theory of Harmony on a Scientific Basis in the Simplest Form; 1885). His works included the operas *Samo* (1854; unfinished), *Der Apostat* (rev. as *Vladimir, bohů zvolenec* [Vladimir, the Gods's Chosen One], Prague, Sept. 27, 1863), *Der Liebesring* (Innsbruck, 1861; Czech version as *Lora*, Prague, April 13, 1868), *Der Rekrut* (Czech version as *Rektor a generál* [Rector and General], Prague, March 28, 1873), and *Smrt krále Václava* (King Wenceslas's Death; 1868; unfinished).

Slatkin, Leonard (Edward), prominent American conductor; b. Los Angeles, Sept. 1, 1944. His father was the American violinist and conductor Felix Slatkin (b. St. Louis, Dec. 22, 1915; d. Los Angeles, Feb. 8, 1963). He received musical training in his youth, studying violin, viola, piano, and conducting, as well as composition with Castelnuovo-Tedesco; after attending Indiana Univ. (1962) and Los Angeles City College (1963), he received valuable advice from Susskind at the Aspen (Colo.) Music School (1964); he then studied conducting with Morel at the Juilliard School of Music in New York (Mus.B., 1968). In 1968 he joined the St. Louis Sym. Orch. as assistant conductor to Susskind, and was successively named assoc. conductor (1971), assoc. principal conductor (1974), and principal guest conductor (1975). He made his European debut in London as a guest conductor with the Royal Phil. in 1974. He was music adviser of the New Orleans Phil. (1977–80) and also music director of the Minnesota Orch. summer concerts (from 1979). In 1979 he became music director of the St. Louis Sym. Orch.; he took it on a major European tour in 1985. In 1990 he became music director of the Great Woods Performing Arts Center in Mansfield, Mass., the summer home of the Pittsburgh Sym. Orch., and in 1991 of the Blossom Music Center, the summer home of the Cleveland Orch. On Oct. 10, 1991, he made his Metropolitan Opera debut in New York conducting *La Fanciulla del West*. In 1992 he was awarded the Elgar Medal. He was named music director designate of the National Sym. Orch. in Washington, D.C., in 1994. After completing his tenure with the St. Louis Sym. Orch. in 1996, he thereafter served as its laureate conductor. In 1996 he assumed his new post as music director of the National Sym. Orch. On Oct. 24, 1997, he led it in the opening of its refurbished concert hall at the Kennedy Center. From 1997 he also was principal guest conductor of the Philharmonia Orch. in London. He appeared widely as a guest conductor of major orchs., both in North America and Europe, demonstrating particular affinity for works of the 19th and 20th centuries.

Slezak, Leo, famous Austrian tenor; b. Mährisch-Schönberg, Moravia, Aug. 18, 1873; d. Egern am Tegernsee, Bavaria, June 1, 1946. He studied with Adolf Robinson; as a youth he sang in the chorus of the Brünn Opera, making his operatic debut there as Lohengrin (March 17, 1896), one of his finest roles. He appeared with the Berlin Royal Opera (1898–99); in 1901 he became a member of the Vienna Opera, where he was active until 1926; also performed frequently in Prague, Milan, and Munich. He made his London debut with marked acclaim as Lohengrin, May 18, 1900, at Covent Garden; not satisfied with his vocal training, he went to Paris, where he studied with Jean de Reszke in 1907. He appeared in America for the first time as Otello with the Metropolitan Opera in New York (Nov. 17, 1909); he remained with the company until 1913. He returned to the Vienna Opera as a guest artist, making his farewell appearance in *Pagliacci* on Sept. 26, 1933. Slezak also toured widely as a recitalist of impeccable taste; also made some appearances in films. He was a man of great general culture, and possessed an exceptionally sharp literary wit, which he displayed in his reminiscences, *Meine sämtlichen Werke* (1922) and *Der Wortbruch* (1927); both were later combined in a single vol. (1935; Eng. tr. as *Songs of Motley: Being the Reminiscences of a Hungry Tenor*, London, 1938); he also publ. *Der Rückfall* (1940). A final book of memoirs, *Mein Lebensmärchen*, was publ. posthumously (1948). His son, the film actor Walter Slezak, publ. Slezak's letters, *Mein lieber Bub. Briefe eines besorgten Vaters* (Munich, 1966), and *What Time's the Next Swan?* (N.Y., 1962), alluding to the possibly apocryphal story of the swan failing to arrive in time during one of his father's performances as Lohengrin, thus prompting the non-Wagnerian query from the hapless hero.

BIBL.: L. Kleinenberger, *L. S.* (Munich, 1910).

Slobodskaya, Oda, esteemed Russian soprano; b. Vilnius, Dec. 10, 1888; d. London, July 29, 1970. She studied at the St. Petersburg Cons. She made her operatic debut as Lisa in *The Queen of Spades* at the Maryinsky Theater there in 1917. She also sang the regular repertoire there, including the roles of Marguerite in *Faust* and *Aida*. She emigrated in 1922; she sang in Paris, at La Scala in Milan, and in Buenos Aires; eventually she settled in London; she sang Venus in *Tannhäuser* at Covent Garden in 1932. She developed an active career in England, establishing herself as an authoritative interpreter of Russian songs in recital; she also joined the faculty of the Guildhall School of Music and proved a sympathetic and effective voice teacher.

BIBL.: M. Leonard, *S.: A Biography of O. S.* (London, 1978).

Slonimsky, Nicolas (Nikolai Leonidovich), legendary Russian-born American musicologist of manifold endeavors, uncle of **Sergei (Mikhailovich) Slonimsky**; b. St. Petersburg, April 27, 1894; d. Los Angeles, Dec. 25, 1995. A self-described failed *wunderkind*, he was given his first piano lesson by his illustrious maternal aunt Isabelle Vengerova, on Nov. 6, 1900, according to the old Russian calendar. Possessed by inordinate ambition, aggravated by the endemic intellectuality of his family of both maternal and paternal branches (novelists, revolutionary poets, literary critics, university professors, translators, chessmasters, economists, mathematicians, inventors of useless artificial languages, Hebrew scholars, speculative philosophers), he became determined to excel beyond common decency in all these doctrines; as an adolescent he wrote out his future biography accordingly, setting down his death date as 1967, but survived. He enrolled in the St. Petersburg Cons. and studied harmony and orchestration with 2 pupils of Rimsky-Korsakov, Kalafati and Maximilian Steinberg; he also tried unsuccessfully to engage in Russian journalism. After the Revolution he made his way south; he was a rehearsal pianist at the Kiev Opera, where he took some composition lessons with Glière (1919), then was in Yalta (1920), where he earned his living as a piano accompanist to displaced Russian singers, and as an instructor at a dilapidated Yalta Cons.; thence he proceeded to Turkey, Bulgaria, and Paris, where he became secretary and piano-pounder to Serge Koussevitzky. In 1923 he went to the United States; he became coach in the opera dept. of the Eastman School of Music in Rochester, N.Y., where he took an opportunity to study some more composition with the visiting prof. Selim Palmgren, and conducting with Albert Coates;

in 1925 he was again with Koussevitzky in Paris and Boston, but was fired for insubordination in 1927. He learned to speak polysyllabic English and began writing music articles for the *Boston Evening Transcript* and the *Christian Science Monitor*; he ran a monthly column of musical anecdotes of questionable authenticity in *Etude* magazine; he taught theory at the Malkin Cons. in Boston and at the Boston Cons. and conducted the Pierian Sodality at Harvard Univ. (1927–29) and the Apollo Chorus (1928–30). In 1927 he organized the Chamber Orch. of Boston with the purpose of presenting modern works; with it he gave first performances of works by Charles Ives, Edgar Varèse, Henry Cowell, and others. He became a naturalized American citizen in 1931. In 1931–32 he conducted special concerts of modern American, Cuban, and Mexican music in Paris, Berlin, and Budapest under the auspices of the Pan-American Assn. of Composers, producing a ripple of excitement; he repeated these programs at his engagements with the Los Angeles Phil. (1932) and at the Hollywood Bowl (1933), which created such consternation that his conducting career came to a jarring halt. From 1945 to 1947 he was, by accident (the head of the dept. had died of a heart attack), lecturer in Slavonic languages and literatures at Harvard Univ. In 1962–63 he traveled in Russia, Poland, Yugoslavia, Bulgaria, Romania, Greece, and Israel under the auspices of the Office of Cultural Exchange at the U.S. State Dept., as a lecturer in native Russian, ersatz Polish, synthetic Serbo-Croatian, Russianized Bulgarian, Latinized Romanian, archaic Greek, passable French, and tolerable German. Returning from his multinational travels, he taught variegated musical subjects at the Univ. of Calif., Los Angeles; was irretrievably retired after a triennial service (1964–67), ostensibly owing to irreversible obsolescence and recessive infantiloquy; but, disdaining the inexorable statistics of the actuarial tables, continued to agitate and even gave long-winded lecture-recitals in institutions of dubious learning. In 1987 he received a Guggenheim fellowship. In 1991 he was inducted as an honorary member of the American Academy and Inst. of Arts and Letters for his manifold contributions to music. As a composer, he cultivated miniature forms, usually with a gimmick, e.g., *Studies in Black and White* for Piano (1928; orchestrated as *Piccolo Divertimento*; Los Angeles Phil. New Music Group, Oct. 17, 1983) in "mutually exclusive consonant counterpoint," a song cycle, *Gravestones*, to texts from tombstones in an old cemetery in Hancock, N.H. (1945), and *Minitudes*, a collection of 50 quaquaversal piano pieces (1971–77). His only decent orch. work is *My Toy Balloon* (1942), a set of variations on a Brazilian song, which includes in the score 100 colored balloons to be exploded *fff* at the climax. He also conjured up a *Möbius Strip-Tease*, a perpetual vocal canon notated on a Möbius band to be revolved around the singer's head; it had its first and last performance at the Arrière-Garde Coffee Concert at UCLA, on May 5, 1965, with the composer officiating at the piano non-obbligato. A priority must be conceded to him for writing the earliest singing commercials to authentic texts from the *Saturday Evening Post* advertisements, among them "Make This a Day of Pepsodent," "No More Shiny Nose," and "Children Cry for Castoria" (1925). More "scholarly," though no less defiant of academic conventions, is his *Thesaurus of Scales and Melodic Patterns* (1947), an inventory of all conceivable and inconceivable tonal combinations, culminating in a mind-boggling "Grandmother Chord" containing 12 different tones and 11 different intervals. Beset by a chronic itch for novelty, he coined the term "pandiatonicism" (1937), which, *mirabile dictu*, took root and even got into reputable reference works, including the 15th ed. of the *Encyclopaedia Britannica*. In his quest for trivial but not readily accessible information, he blundered into the muddy field of musical lexicography; he publ. *Music since 1900*, a chronology of musical events, which actually contains some beguiling serendipities (N.Y., 1937; 5th ed., rev., 1994); he took over the vacated editorship (because of the predecessor's sudden death during sleep) of Thompson's *International Cyclopedia of Music and Musicians* (4th to 8th eds., 1946–58) and accepted the editorship of the 5th, 6th, 7th, and 8th eds. of the prestigious *Baker's Biographical Dictionary of Musicians* (N.Y., 1958, 1978, 1984, 1992). He also abridged this venerable vol. into *The Concise Baker's Biographical Dictionary of Musicians* (N.Y., 1988). In 1978 he mobilized his powers of retrospection in preparing an autobiography, *Failed Wunderkind*, subtitled *Rueful Autopsy* (in the sense of self-observation, not dissection of the body); the publishers, deeming these titles too lugubrious, renamed it *Perfect Pitch* (N.Y., 1988). He also translated Boris de Schloezer's biography of Scriabin from the original Russian (Berkeley and Los Angeles, 1987), which was followed by his *Lectionary of Music*, a compendium of articles on music (N.Y., 1988). His other writings include *Music of Latin America* (N.Y., 1945; also in Spanish, Buenos Aires, 1947); *The Road to Music*, ostensibly for children (N.Y., 1947); *A Thing or Two about Music* (N.Y., 1948; inconsequential; also lacking an index); *Lexicon of Musical Invective*, a random collection of pejorative reviews of musical masterpieces (N.Y., 1952); numerous articles for encyclopedias; also a learned paper, *Sex and the Music Librarian*, valuable for its painstaking research; the paper was delivered by proxy, to tumultuous cachinnations, at a symposium of the Music Library Assn., at Chapel Hill, N.C., Feb. 2, 1968. R. Kostelanetz ed. a collection of his writings as *Nicolas Slonimsky: The First Hundred Years* (N.Y., 1994). His much-lamented death, just 4 months before his 102d birthday, brought to a close one of the most remarkable careers in the annals of 20th-century music.

Slonimsky, Sergei (Mikhailovich), greatly talented Russian composer, nephew of **Nicolas (Nikolai Leonidovich) Slonimsky**; b. Leningrad, Aug. 12, 1932. A member of a highly intellectual family (his father was a well-known Soviet author; his paternal grandfather, an economist, the author of the first book on Karl Marx in the Russian language; his father's maternal uncle was a celebrated Russian ed. and literary critic; his father's maternal aunt was the noted piano teacher Isabelle Vengerova), he studied at the Leningrad Cons., taking composition with Boris Arapov and Orest Evlakhov (graduated, 1955) and piano with Vladimir Nilsen (graduated, 1956); he also took courses in musicology with F. Rubtzov (folk music) and N. Uspensky (polyphonic analysis). While a student, he wrote a fairy-tale suite, *Frog-Princess*, and in 1951 composed a string quartet on Russian folk motifs. In 1959 he was appointed to the faculty of the Leningrad Cons. For further study of folk music he traveled into the countryside, in the rural regions of Pskov and Novgorod. Concurrently, he explored the technical modalities of new music, in the tradition of Soviet modernism, evolving a considerable complexity of texture in a framework of dissonant counterpoint, while safeguarding the tonal foundation in triadic progressions. Some of his works, such as his opera *Virineya*, represent a contemporary evolution of the Russian national school of composition, broadly diatonic and spaciously songful; his other works tend toward ultramodern practices, including polytonality, microtonality, dodecaphony, tone-clusters, amplified sound, prepared piano, electronic sonorism, aleatory proceedings, and spatial placement of instruments. His Concerto for Orch. employs electronically amplified guitars and solo instruments; even more advanced is his *Antiphones* for String Quartet, employing nontempered tuning and an "ambulatory" setting, in which the players are placed in different parts of the hall and then walk, while playing, en route to the podium; the piece is especially popular at modern music festivals. A prolific composer, he has written 10 syms. and a remarkably varied catalogue of chamber music pieces which he produces with a facility worthy of Rossini. He also has an easy hand with choral works. Although his natural impulse tends towards the newest sound elements, he proves remarkably successful in gathering and transforming folk motifs and rhythms, as in his Novgorod choruses, composed for the American Festival of Soviet Music of 1988. The most unusual subject, for a Soviet composer, was an opera based on the life and death of the Catholic queen of Scotland, Mary Stuart. *Mary Stuart* was first performed in Kuibishev on Oct. 1, 1983, and then subsequently performed in Leningrad and in Leipzig (1984). It was then selected for a gala production at the Edinburgh Festival in Scotland, where it was given on Aug. 22, 1986, by the Leningrad Opera in a performance in the Russian language. The score utilizes authentic Scottish folk songs, suitably arranged in modern harmonies, as well as original themes in the pentatonic scale. The opera received the prestigious Glinka Prize in 1983. Slonimsky encountered considerable difficulties in producing his chamber opera, *The Master and Margarita*, after a novel by Bulgakov, because the subject had to do with mystical religious events. The Soviet authorities delayed its production for nearly 15 years. Finally, with a liberal change in the political climate, the opera was performed, first in East Germany, and, eventually and to considerable acclaim, in Leningrad, on Dec. 1, 1989. Practically all of Slonimsky's music, including the operas, has been publ. Apart from his work as a composer and teacher, he contributes music criticism to Russian magazines; he also publ. a valuable analytic survey of the symphonies of Prokofiev (Leningrad, 1976).

WORKS: DRAMATIC: OPERAS: *Virineya* (Leningrad, Sept. 30, 1967); *The Master and Margarita*, chamber opera, after Bulgakov (1973; Leningrad, Dec. 1, 1989); *Mary Stuart*, opera ballad (1978–80; Kuibishev, Jan. 31, 1981); *Hamlet* (1992). BALLET: *Icarus* (1962–69; Moscow, May 29, 1971). Also incidental music and film scores.

BIBL.: A. Milka, *S. S.* (Leningrad, 1976).

Smallens, Alexander, Russian-born American conductor; b. St. Petersburg, Jan. 1, 1889; d. Tucson, Ariz., Nov. 24, 1972. He was taken to the United States as a child; became a American naturalized citizen in 1919. He studied at the Inst. of Musical Art and the College of the City of N.Y. (B.A., 1909), then took courses at the Paris Cons. (1909). He was assistant conductor of the Boston Opera (1911–14); he accompanied the Anna Pavlova Ballet Co. on a tour of South America (1915–18), then was on the staff of the Chicago Opera (1919–23) and of the Philadelphia Civic Opera (1924–31); from 1927 to 1934 he was assist. conductor of the Philadelphia Orch., and from 1947 to 1950 he was music director at Radio City Music Hall in New York. In 1934 he conducted the premiere of Gershwin's *Porgy and Bess* in Boston; he conducted it on a European tour in 1956. He retired in 1958.

Smareglia, Antonio, talented Italian composer; b. Pola, Istria, May 5, 1854; d. Grado, Istria, April 15, 1929. He was trained in engineering before turning to music; he studied composition with Franco Faccio at the Milan Cons. (1873–77), who became an early champion of his works. He first attracted notice with his opera *Preziosa* (Milan, Nov. 19, 1879); he wrote his finest opera for Trieste, *Nozze istriane* (March 28, 1895). In 1903 he was stricken with blindness and was soon reduced to poverty; through the intervention of the Tartini Cons. in Trieste, which made him honorary artistic director in 1921, and the local industrialist Carlo Sai, his fortunes were mended and he was able to present several of his operatic and orch. works. He also engaged in private teaching. After the onset of his blindness, he continued to compose with the assistance of an amanuensis.

WORKS: DRAMATIC: OPERAS: *Preziosa* (Milan, Nov. 19, 1879); *Bianca di Cervia* (Milan, Feb. 7, 1882); *Re Nala* (Venice, Feb. 9, 1887; destroyed by the composer); *Il vassallo di Szigeth* (1st perf. as *Der Vasall von Szigeth*, Vienna, Oct. 4, 1889; 1st perf. in Italian, Pola, Oct. 4, 1930); *Cornil Schut* (1st perf. as *Cornelius Schut*, Prague, May 20, 1893; 1st perf. in Italian, Trieste, Feb. 17, 1900; rev. as *Pittori fiamminghi*, Trieste, Jan. 21, 1928); *Nozze istriane* (Trieste, March 28, 1895); *La falena* (Venice, Sept. 4, 1897); *Oceàna* (Milan, Jan. 22, 1903); *Abisso* (Milan, Feb. 9, 1914). Also *Caccia lontana*, melodramatic scene (Milan, Aug. 10, 1875).

BIBL.: G. Zuccoli, *A. S.* (Trieste, 1922); G. Nacamuli, *A. S.* (Trieste, 1930); A. Smareglia, *Vita ed arte di A. S.: Un capitolo di storia del teatro lirico italiano* (Lugano, 1932; 2d ed., 1936); M. Smareglia, *A. S. nella storia del melodramma italiano: Accolta di critiche musicali e di altri documenti* (Pola, 1934); V. Levi, *Nozze istriane: Nel centenario della nascita di A. S.* (Trieste, 1954); S. Benco, *Ricordi di A. S.* (Duino, 1968).

Smetana, Bedřich, great Bohemian composer; b. Leitomischl, March 2, 1824; d. Prague, May 12, 1884. His talent manifested itself very early, and although his father had misgivings about music as a profession, he taught his son violin; Bedřich also had piano lessons with a local teacher, making his first public appearance at the age of 6 (Oct. 14, 1830). After the family moved to Jindrichův Hradec in 1831, he studied with the organist František Ikavec; he continued his academic studies in Jihlava and Německý Brod, then entered the Classical Grammar School in Prague in 1839; he also had piano lessons with Jan Batka, and led a string quartet for which he composed several works. His lack of application to his academic studies led his father to send him to the gymnasium in Pilsen, but he soon devoted himself to giving concerts and composing. He met a friend of his school days there, Kateřina Kolářová, whom he followed to Prague in 1843; he was accepted as a theory pupil of Kolářová's piano teacher, Josef Proksch, at the Music Inst. To pay for his lessons, Bedřich Kittl, director of the Prague Cons., recommended Smetana for the position of music teacher to the family of Count Leopold Thun. He took up his position in Jan. 1844, and for 3 1/2 years worked earnestly in the count's service; he also continued to study theory and to compose. Bent on making a name for himself as a concert pianist, Smetana left the count's service in the summer of 1847 and planned a tour of Bohemia; however, his only concert in Pilsen proved a financial disaster, and he abandoned his tour and returned to Prague, where he eked out a meager existence. He wrote to Liszt, asking him to find a publisher for his op. 1, the *6 Characteristic Pieces* for piano; Liszt was impressed with the score, accepted Smetana's dedication, and found a publisher. In 1848 Smetana established a successful piano school, and on Aug. 27, 1849, he married Kolářová. In 1850 he became court pianist to the abdicated emperor Ferdinand. His reputation as a pianist, especially as an interpreter of Chopin, grew, but his compositions made little impression. The death of his children and the poor health of his wife (who had tuberculosis) affected him deeply; he set out for Sweden in 1856; gave a number of successful piano recitals in Göteborg, where he remained. He soon opened his own school, and also became active as a choral conductor. His wife joined him in 1857, but the cold climate exacerbated her condition; when her health declined, they decided to return to Prague (1859), but she died en route, in Dresden, on April 19, 1859. Stricken with grief, Smetana returned to Göteborg. Before his wife's death, he had composed the symphonic poems *Richard III* and *Valdštýnův tabor* (Wallenstein's Camp); he now began work on a 3d, *Hakan Jarl*. On July 10, 1860, he married Betty Ferdinandi, which proved an unhappy union. During Smetana's sojourn in Sweden, Austria granted political autonomy to Bohemia (1860), and musicians and poets of the rising generation sought to establish an authentic Bohemian voice in the arts. Agitation for the erection of a national theater in Prague arose; although earlier attempts to write operas in a Bohemian vein had been made by such composers as František Škroup and Jiří Macourek, their works were undistinguished. Smetana believed the time was ripe for him to make his mark in Prague, and he returned there in May 1861. However, when the Provisional Theater opened on Nov. 18, 1862, its administration proved sadly unimaginative, and Smetana contented himself with the conductorship of the Hlahol Choral Soc., teaching, and writing music criticism. In his articles he condemned the poor musical standards prevailing at the Provisional Theater. In 1862–63 he composed his first opera, *Braniboři v Čechách* (The Brandenburgers in Bohemia), conducting its successful premiere at the Provisional Theater on Jan. 5, 1866. His next opera, *Prodaná nevěsta* (The Bartered Bride), proved a failure at its premiere in Prague under his direction on May 30, 1866, but eventually it was accorded a niche in the operatic repertoire at home and abroad. Smetana became conductor of the Provisional Theater in 1866. He immediately set out to reform its administration and to raise its musical standards. For the cornerstone laying of the National Theater on May 16, 1868, he conducted the first performance of his tragic opera *Dalibor*, which was criticized as an attempt to Wagnerize the Bohemian national opera. In 1871, when there was talk of crowning Emperor Franz Josef as king of Bohemia, Smetana considered producing his opera *Libuše* for the festivities; however, no coronation took place and the work was withheld. Hoping for a popular success, he composed the comic opera *Dvě* *vdovy* (The 2 Widows), which proved to be just that at its premiere under his direction on March 27, 1874. Smetana's success, however, was short-lived. By the autumn of 1874 he was deaf and had to resign as conductor of the Provisional Theater. In spite of the bitter years to follow, marked by increasingly poor health, family problems, and financial hardship, he continued to compose. Between 1874 and 1879 he produced his 6 orch. masterpieces collectively known as *Má Vlast* (My Country): *Vyšehrad* (referring to a rock over the river Vltava, near Prague, the traditional seat of the ancient kings of Bohemia), *Vltava* (The Moldau), *Šárka* (a wild valley, near Prague, depicting the legendary story of the maiden Sarka), *Z českych luhüv a hájü* (From Bohemia's Woods and Fields), *Tábor* (the medieval town in southern Bohemia, the seat of the Hussites, and thus the traditional symbol of freedom and religion; the work is based on the chorale *Ye Who Are God's Warriors*), and *Blaník* (the mountain that served as a place of refuge for the Hussites; the previously mentioned chorale serves as the foundation of the work). From 1876 dates his famous String Quartet in E minor, subtitled *Z mého života* (From My Life), which he described as a "remembrance of my life and the catastrophe of complete deafness." His opera *Hubička* (The Kiss) was successfully premiered in Prague on Nov. 7, 1876. It was followed by the opera *Tajemství* (The Secret), which was heard for the first time on Sept. 18, 1878. For the opening of the new National Theater in Prague on June 11, 1881, his opera *Libuše* was finally given its premiere performance. The ailing Smetana attended the opening night and was accorded sustained applause. His last opera, *Čertova stěna* (The Devil's Wall), was a failure at its first hearing in Prague on Oct. 29, 1882. By this time Smetana's health had been completely undermined by the ravages of syphilis, the cause of his deafness. His mind eventually gave way and he was confined to an asylum. At his death in 1884, the nation was plunged into a state of mourning. The funeral cortege passed the National Theater as Smetana was carried to his final resting place in the Vyšehrad cemetery.

Smetana was the founder of the Czech national school of composition, and it was through his efforts that Czech national opera came of age. The centenary of his death in 1984 was marked by numerous performances of his music in Czechoslovakia and a reaffirmation of his revered place in the history of his nation.

WORKS: OPERAS (all 1st perf. in Prague): *Braniboři v Čechách* (The Brandenburgers in Bohemia; 1862–63; Jan. 5, 1866, composer conducting); *Prodaná nevěsta* (The Bartered Bride; 1863–66; May 30, 1866, composer conducting; 2 revs., 1869; final version, 1869–70; Sept. 25, 1870, composer conducting); *Dalibor* (1865–67; May 16, 1868, composer conducting; rev. 1870); *Libuše* (1869–72; June 11, 1881, A. Čech conducting); *Dvě vdovy* (The 2 Widows; March 27, 1874, composer conducting; final version, 1877; March 15, 1878, Čech conducting); *Hubička* (The Kiss; Nov. 7, 1876, Čech conducting); *Tajemství* (The Secret; Sept. 18, 1878, Čech conducting); *Čertova stěna* (The Devil's Wall; 1879–82; Oct. 29, 1882, Čech conducting); *Viola* (sketches begun in 1874; fragment from 1883–84 only).

BIBL.: K. Teige, *Příspěvky k životopisu a umělecké činnosti mistra B.a Smetany, I: Skladby Smetanovy* (S.'s Works; Prague, 1893) and II: *Dopisy Smetanoy* (S.'s Letters; Prague, 1896); O. Hostinský, *B. S. a jeho boj o moderni českou hudbu* (S. and His Struggle for Modern Czech Music; Prague, 1901; 2d ed., 1941); W. Ritter, *S.* (Paris, 1907); Z. Nejedlý, *Zpěvohry Smetanovy* (S.'s Operas; Prague, 1908; 3d ed., 1954); V. Balthasar, *B. S.* (Prague, 1924); V. Helfert, *Tvůrči rozvoj B.a Smetany* (S.'s Creative Development; Prague, 1924; 3d ed., 1953; Ger. tr., 1956); Z. Nejedlý, *B. S.* (4 vols., Prague, 1924–33; 2d ed., 7 vols., 1950–54; additional vol. as *S.: Dobá zrání* [S.: The Period of Maturity], Prague, 1962); J. Tiersot, *S.* (Paris, 1926); F. Bartoş, *B. S.* (Prague, 1940); J. Teichman, *B. S.: Život a dilo* (S.: Life and Work; Prague, 1944); P. Pražák, *Smetanovy zpěvohry* (S.'s Operas; Prague, 1948); M. Malý, *B. S.* (Prague, 1954; Eng. tr., 1956); H. Boese, *Zwei Urmusikanten: S.—Dvořák* (Zürich, 1955); B. Karásek, *B. S.* (Prague, 1966; Eng. tr., 1967); C. Thörnqvist, *S. in Göteborg, 1856–1862* (in Eng.; Göteborg, 1967); B. Large, *S.* (N.Y., 1970); J. Clapham, *S.* (London, 1972); H. Séguardtová, *B. S.* (Leipzig, 1985); G. Erismann, *S.: L'éveilleur* (Arles, 1993).

Smirnov, Dmitri (Alexeievich), outstanding Russian tenor; b. Moscow, Nov. 19, 1882; d. Riga, April 27, 1944. He sang in a church choir as a youth, then studied voice with Dodonov and others in Moscow. On Feb. 3, 1903, he made his debut as Gigi in Esposito's *Camorra* at Moscow's Hermitage Theater. In 1904 he was accepted as a member of the Bolshoi Theater there, but interrupted his career by traveling to Paris and Milan for further voice training. Returning to Moscow in 1906, he sang again at the Bolshoi Theater; from 1910 he appeared also with the Maryinsky Opera Theater in St. Petersburg. During the same period, he took part in the famous Russian Seasons in Paris. On Dec. 30, 1910, he made his debut at the Metropolitan Opera in New York in the role of the Duke of Mantua in *Rigoletto*, remaining with the company until 1912; he then sang with the Boston Opera (1911); after a tour of Latin America, he appeared at London's Drury Lane (1914) and other European theaters. Although he lived mostly abroad, he revisited Russia in 1926 and 1928 as a guest artist. He later appeared mostly in solo recitals; he was also active as a voice teacher; he taught at the Athens Cons. and in Riga. In Russia he was regarded as one of the finest lyric tenors of his time, often compared to Caruso; as a bel canto singer, he was praised by Russian and European critics. Apart from the Russian repertoire, in which he excelled, he made a deep impression in such lyrico-dramatic roles as Faust, Don José, Canio, and Rodolfo.

Smirnov, Dmitri, Russian composer; b. Minsk, Nov. 2, 1948. After training in Frunze, he studied at the Moscow Cons. (1967–72) with Nikolai Sidelnikov (composition), Edison Denisov (orchestration), and Yuri Kholopov (analysis). He also received private instruction from Philip Gershkovich. From 1973 to 1980 he was an ed. with the publishing firm Soviet Composer. In 1993 he became a prof. and composer-in-residence at the Univ. of Keele in England. In 1972 he married **Elena Firsova.** While thoroughly grounded in various contemporary styles and techniques, Smirnov has found great inspiration in the tonal world of late Romanticism. He has also been much influenced by the poetry and painting of William Blake, and has set a number of his works to music. His works include the operas *Tiriel* (1983–85; Freiburg im Breisgau, Jan. 28, 1989) and *The Lamentations of Thel* (1985–86; London, June 9, 1989); also film scores.

Smit, Leo, American pianist and composer; b. Philadelphia, Jan. 12, 1921. He studied piano with Vengerova at the Curtis Inst. of Music in Philadelphia (1930–32) and took lessons in composition with Nabokov (1935). He made his debut as a pianist at Carnegie Hall in New York in 1939, then made tours of the United States; he also taught at Sarah Lawrence College (1947–49), at the Univ. of Calif. at Los Angeles (1957–63), and at the State Univ. of N.Y. at Buffalo (from 1962); likewise he served as director of the Monday Evening Concerts in Los Angeles (1957–63) and as composer-in-residence at the American Academy in Rome (1972–73) and at Brevard Music Center (1980). His style of composition is neoclassical, marked by a strong contrapuntal fabric; the influence of Stravinsky, with whom he had personal contact, is particularly pronounced here. His works include the operas *The Alchemy of Love* (1969) and *Magic Water* (1978), the melodrama *A Mountain Eulogy* (1975), and the ballets *Yerma* (1946) and *Virginia Sampler* (N.Y., March 4, 1947; rev. 1960).

Smith, David Stanley, American conductor, music educator, and composer; b. Toledo, Ohio, July 6, 1877; d. New Haven, Conn., Dec. 17, 1949. He studied with Horatio Parker at Yale Univ., graduating in 1900. He then took courses in composition with Thuille in Munich and Widor in Paris. Upon his return to the United States, he obtained a Mus.B. degree at Yale (1903) and was appointed an instructor at the Yale Univ. School of Music; in 1916 he became a prof. there; in 1920 he was appointed dean of the School of Music, retiring in 1946. He was conductor of the New Haven Sym. Orch. from 1920 to 1946. In 1910 he was elected a member of the National Inst. of Arts and Letters. His compositions were cast in a conservative mold. They include the opera *Merrymount* (1914).

BIBL.: E. Goode, *D. S. S. and his Music* (diss., Univ. of Cincinnati, 1978).

Smith, Gregg, American conductor and composer; b. Chicago, Aug. 21, 1931. He studied composition with Leonard Stein, Lukas Foss, and Ray Moreman and conducting with Fritz Zweig at the Univ. of Calif. at Los Angeles (M.A., 1956). In 1955 in Los Angeles he founded the Gregg Smith Singers, a chamber choir, with which he toured and recorded extensively; from 1970, was active with it in New York. He also taught at Ithaca College, the State Univ. of N.Y. at Stony Brook, the Peabody Cons. of Music in Baltimore, Barnard College, and the Manhattan School of Music in New York. His repertoire extends from early music to works by contemporary American composers. He ed. the Gregg Smith Choral Series. He wrote much vocal music, including 2 operas.

Smith, Hale, black American composer; b. Cleveland, June 29, 1925. He studied piano with Dorothy Price and composition with Marcel Dick at the Cleveland Inst. of Music (B.Mus., 1950; M.Mus., 1952); he went to New York in 1958 and was active as a music ed. for publishers, as a jazz arranger, and as a teacher; later he was a prof. at the Univ. of Conn. in Storrs (1970–84). His output is remarkable for its utilization of serial procedures with jazz infusions; he wrote musical scores for Dizzy Gillespie, Ahmad Jamal, Eric Dolphy, and Abby Lincoln, and worked in various capacities for Quincy Jones, Clark Terry, Oliver Nelson, Miriam Makeba, and Hugh Masekela. His works include the chamber opera *Blood Wedding* (1953).

BIBL.: M. Breda, *H. S.: Biographical and Analytical Study of the Man and His Music* (diss., Univ. of Southern Miss., Harrisburg, 1975).

Smith, Jennifer, English soprano; b. Lisbon, July 13, 1945. Following training at the Lisbon Cons., she pursued vocal studies with Winifred Radford in London, Pierre Bernac in London and Paris, and Hans Keller in London. In 1966 she made her operatic debut as Carissimi's Jeptha in Lisbon, and then sang in other European cities and in England. In 1979 she appeared as Mozart's Countess at the Welsh National Opera in Cardiff. She portrayed Alphise in the first stage performance of Rameau's *Les Boréades* in Aix-en-Provence in 1982. In 1988 she sang Cybele in the first U.S. performance of Lully's *Atys* in New York. She appeared as the Queen of the Night in London in 1989. In 1992 she was engaged as Iphigénie in Gluck's *Iphigénie en Tauride* at the English Bach Festival at London's Covent Garden. In 1995 she sang Elettra in Lisbon. Her concert engagements took her to major European music centers. Among her other important portrayals were roles in operas by Marais, Mondonville, and Purcell.

Smith, John Christopher (real name, **Johann Christoph Schmidt**), German-born English organist and composer; b. Ansbach, 1712; d. Bath, Oct. 3, 1795. His father, Johann Christoph Schmidt, went to London in 1716 as Handel's treasurer and chief copyist; the son followed in 1720, and received a few lessons from Handel about 1725; after lessons from Pepusch, he studied with Thomas Roseingrave. He wrote his first opera, *Ulysses*, in 1733; after its failure, he gave up the theater. Following a sojourn abroad (1746–48), he became organist at the Foundling Hospital in London in 1754, where he directed the annual performance of *Messiah* (1759–68). He scored a success with his opera *The Enchanter of Love and Magic* (1760), but thereafter devoted himself to composing oratorios; with Stanley, he oversaw the Lenten performances of oratorios at Covent Garden (1760–74). He settled in Bath, where he was active as a teacher; upon his father's death in 1763, he was bequeathed his father's large Handel collection, which, after being granted a royal pension by King George III (1772), he bequeathed to the king; it is now housed in the Royal Music Library at the British Museum.

WORKS: (all 1st perf. in London unless otherwise given): DRAMATIC: OPERAS: *Ulysses* (April 16, 1733); *Rosalinda* (Jan. 4, 1740); *The Seasons* (1740; not perf.); *Issipile* (1743; not perf.); *Il ciro riconosciuto* (1745; not perf.); *Dario* (1746; not perf.); *Artaserse* (1748; unfinished); *The Fairies* (Feb. 3, 1755); *The Tempest* (Feb. 11, 1756); *The Enchanter of Love and Magic* (Dec. 13, 1760); *Medea* (1760–61; unfinished). ORATORIOS: *David's Lamentation over Saul and Jonathan* (1738; Feb. 22, 1740); *Paradise Lost* (1757–58; Feb. 29, 1760); *Judith* (1758; not perf.); *Feast of Darius* (1761–62; not perf.; based on the opera *Dario*); *Rebecca* (March 16, 1764); *Nabal* (March 16, 1764); *Jehosaphat* (1764; not perf.); *Gideon* (Feb. 10, 1769; based on the *Feast of Darius* and works by Handel); *Redemption* (1774; not perf.).

BIBL.: [W. Coxe], *Anecdotes of George Frederick Handel and J. C. S.* (London, 1799).

Smith (real name, **Vielehr**), **Julia (Frances),** American pianist, composer, and writer on music; b. Denton, Texas, Jan. 25, 1911; d. N.Y., April 27, 1989. She studied at North Texas State Univ. (graduated, 1930), then took courses in piano with Carl Friedberg and received instruction in composition at the Juilliard School of Music in New York (diploma, 1939); she also studied at N.Y. Univ. (M.A., 1933; Ph.D., 1952). She was the pianist of the all-women Orchestrette of N.Y. (1932–39); she made tours of the United States, Latin America, and Europe; taught at the Hartt School of Music in Hartford, Conn. (1941–46).

WRITINGS: *Aaron Copland: His Work and Contribution to American Music* (N.Y., 1955); *Master Pianist: The Career and Teaching of Carl Friedberg* (N.Y., 1963); *Directory of American Women Composers* (Indianapolis, 1970).

WORKS: OPERAS: *Cynthia Parker* (1938; Denton, Feb. 16, 1940; rev. 1977); *The Stranger of Manzano* (1943; Dallas, May 6, 1947); *The Gooseherd and the Goblin* (1946; N.Y., Feb. 22, 1947); *Cockcrow* (1953; Austin, Texas, April 22, 1954); *The Shepherdess and the Chimney Sweep* (1963; Fort Worth, Texas, Dec. 28, 1967); *Daisy* (Miami, Nov. 3, 1973).

Smith, Leland (Clayton), American bassoonist, clarinetist, teacher, computer music publisher, and composer; b. Oakland, Calif., Aug. 6, 1925. He was a student of Milhaud (composition) at Mills College in Oakland, Calif. (1941–43; 1946–47), of Sessions (composition) and Bukofzer (musicology) at the Univ. of Calif. at Berkeley (M.A., 1948), and of Messiaen at the Paris Cons. (1948–49). After teaching at the Univ. of Calif. at Berkeley (1950–51), Mills College (1951–52), and the Univ. of Chicago (1952–58), he joined the faculty of Stanford Univ. in 1958 and was a prof. there from 1968 until his retirement in 1992. He was one of the founders and director of Stanford's computer music center, and he also served as an advisor to IRCAM in Paris. He pioneered in the development of a computer music publishing system he named SCORE. In 1971 he published what is believed to have been the first score ever printed entirely by a computer without added hand work. Since that time, he has perfected his system to such a high level of excellence that most of the principal music publishers of the world have chosen his SCORE system for their prestige publications. He later worked on projects to use his SCORE system and the Internet for complete music distribution systems. In addition to his lectures on the use of computers in both composing and printing, he publ. the *Handbook of Harmonic Analysis* (1963). In his compositions, Smith has traversed a modern course in which serial procedures are often utilized with occasional excursions into explorations of computer-generated sounds. His works include the opera *Santa Claus* (Chicago, Dec. 9, 1955).

Smith, Patrick J(ohn), American music critic, author, and editor; b. N.Y., Dec. 11, 1932. He was educated at Princeton Univ. (A.B., 1955). He then pursued a career as a music critic, contributing articles to *High Fidelity, Musical America*, *Musical Quarterly*, and the *Musical Times*. From 1965 to 1985 he was book ed. of *Musical America*; also served as N.Y. music correspondent to the *Times* of London. He was president of the Music Critics Assn. (1977–81) and director of the Opera-Musical Theater Program of the NEA (from 1985). From 1988 to 1998 he was ed.-in-chief of *Opera News,* then ed.-at-large. He publ. *The Tenth Muse, A Historical*

Study of the Opera Libretto (N.Y., 1970) and *A Year at the Met* (N.Y., 1983).

Smith Brindle, Reginald, English composer, teacher, and writer on music; b. Bamber Bridge, Lancashire, Jan. 5, 1917. He studied architecture before serving as a captain in the Royal Engineers (1940–46). He then studied music at the Univ. College of North Wales in Bangor (1946–49; B.Mus.; later Mus.D.), and subsequently with Pizzetti at the Accademia di Santa Cecilia in Rome (1949–52; composition diploma). He also studied privately with Dallapiccola in Florence (1949; 1952–53). From 1956 to 1961 he was active with the RAI. In 1957 he joined the faculty of the Univ. College of North Wales, serving as a prof. there from 1967 to 1970. From 1970 to 1985 he was prof. of music at the Univ. of Surrey in Guildford. In addition to his many articles in journals, he publ. the books *Serial Composition* (1966), *Contemporary Percussion* (1970), *The New Music* (1975), and *Musical Composition* (1980). He utilized serial techniques in his scores until about 1970, all the while varying his style. Thereafter his path proved ever more eclectic as he refined his personal idiom of musical expression. Among his works is the opera *The Death of Antigone* (1969).

Smither, Howard E(lbert), distinguished American musicologist; b. Pittsburg, Kansas, Nov. 15, 1925. He studied at Hamline Univ. in St. Paul, Minn. (A.B., 1950), and at Cornell Univ. with Grout and Austin (M.A., 1952; Ph.D., 1960, with the diss. *Theories of Rhythm in the Nineteenth and Twentieth Centuries, with a Contribution to the Theory of Rhythm for the Study of Twentieth Century Music*); he also attended classes of Rudolf von Ficker at the Univ. of Munich (1953–54). He taught at the Oberlin Cons. of Music (1955–60), the Univ. of Kansas (1960–63), and Tulane Univ. (1963–68); in 1968 he was appointed a prof. of music at the Univ. of North Carolina at Chapel Hill; he served as president of the American Musicological Soc. (1981–82). His major work is the valuable study *A History of the Oratorio* (3 vols., Chapel Hill, 1977–87).

Smyth, Dame Ethel (Mary), eminent English composer; b. London, April 22, 1858; d. Woking, Surrey, May 8, 1944. She became a pupil of Reinecke and Jadassohn at the Leipzig Cons. in 1877, but soon turned to Heinrich von Herzogenberg for her principal training, following him to Berlin; her String Quintet was performed in Leipzig in 1884. She returned to London in 1888; presented her orchestral *Serenade* (April 26, 1890) and an overture, *Antony and Cleopatra* (Oct. 18, 1890). Her prestige as a composer rose considerably with the presentation of her *Mass* for Solo Voices, Chorus, and Orch. at the Albert Hall (Jan. 18, 1893). After that she devoted her energies to the theater. Her first opera, *Fantasio*, to her own libretto in German, after Alfred de Musset's play, was premiered in Weimar on May 24, 1898; this was followed by *Der Wald* (Berlin, April 9, 1902), also to her own German libretto; it was premiered in London in the same year, and then performed in New York by the Metropolitan Opera on March 11, 1903. Her next opera, *The Wreckers*, was her most successful work; written originally to a French libretto, *Les Naufrageurs*, it was first performed in a German version as *Strandrecht* (Leipzig, Nov. 11, 1906); the composer herself tr. it into Eng., and it was staged in London on June 22, 1909; the score was revised some years later, and produced at Sadler's Wells, London, on April 19, 1939. She further wrote a comic opera, *The Boatswain's Mate* (London, Jan. 28, 1916); a one-act opera, described as a "dance-dream," *Fête galante* (Birmingham, June 4, 1923); and the opera *Entente cordiale* (Bristol, Oct. 20, 1926). Her music never overcame the strong German characteristics, in the general idiom as well as in the treatment of dramatic situations on the stage. At the same time, she was a believer in English national music and its potentialities. She was a militant leader for woman suffrage in England, for which cause she wrote "The March of the Women" (1911), the battle song of the WSPU After suffrage was granted, her role in the movement was officially acknowledged; in 1922 she was made a Dame Commander of the Order of the British Empire. She publ. a number of books in London, mostly autobiographical in nature: *Impressions That Remained* (2 vols., 1919; new ed., 1945); *Streaks of Life* (1921); *As Time Went On* (1936); *What Happened Next* (1940); also some humorous essays and reminiscences, *A Three-legged Tour in Greece* (1927); *A Final Burning of Boats* (1928); *Female Pipings in Eden* (1934); *Beecham and Pharaoh* (1935); *Inordinate (?) Affection* (1936).

BIBL.: C. St. John, *E. S.: A Biography* (N.Y., 1959); L. Collis, *Impetuous Heart: The Story of E. S.* (London, 1984).

Snel, Joseph-François, Belgian violinist, conductor, teacher, and composer; b. Brussels, July 30, 1793; d. Koekelberg, near Brussels, March 10, 1861. He studied violin with Corneille Vander Nicolas in Brussels, and then continued his training with Baillot and Dourlen at the Paris Cons. In 1818 he founded in Brussels the Académie de Musique et de Chant (with Mees). He popularized in Belgium the instructional singing methods of Galin and Wilhem; he was an inspector of army music schools (1829). He conducted at the Théâtre Royal de la Monnaie (1831–34) and was made conductor of the Société Royale de la Grande-harmonie (1831), maître de chapelle at the Church of St. Michel et Ste. Gudule (1835), and head of the music of the Civic Guard (1837). In 1847 he became a member of the Classe des Beaux-arts of the Belgian Royal Academy. Among his works were the ballets (all 1st perf. in Brussels): *Frisac, ou La double noce* (Feb. 13, 1825), *Le page inconstant* (June 27, 1825), *Le cinq juillet* (July 9, 1825; in collaboration with C.-L. Hanssens, Jr.), Pourceaugnac (Feb. 3, 1826), *Les enchantements de Polichinelle* (March 8, 1829), and *Les barricades* (Feb. 3, 1830).

Sobinov, Leonid (Vitalievich), celebrated Russian tenor; b. Yaroslavl, June 7, 1872; d. Riga, Oct. 14, 1934. He was an offspring of a middle-class family with peasant roots (his grandfather was an emancipated serf). He studied law at the Univ. of Moscow, where he also sang in a student choir. In 1892 he began to study voice with Dodonov and appeared professionally in a traveling Italian opera company in Moscow without interrupting his univ. study (1893–94); he graduated in law in 1894, and was appointed assistant advocate to a Moscow lawyer. Turning decisively to singing, he made his debut at the Bolshoi Theater in Moscow in 1897, and retained his connection with it during almost his entire career. In 1901 he also joined the Imperial Maryinsky Theater in St. Petersburg. His successes on the European stage were no less outstanding; he sang at La Scala in Milan (1904–06); from 1909 he also appeared in London, Paris, and Berlin. He was eloquent in the roles of Alfredo in *La Traviata*, Des Grieux in *Manon*, and Faust in Gounod's opera. His performance of Lensky in *Eugene Onegin* remained an unsurpassed model of Russian operatic lyricism. In his solo recitals he could squeeze the last fluid ounce out of Tchaikovsky's melancholy songs. No wonder that he was idolized by Russian audiences, particularly among the young and female; a whole tribe of "Sobinovites" appeared, and long queues formed before his concerts, willing to stand in line for hours in the hope of obtaining scarce tickets. He served as director of the Bolshoi Theater in 1917–18. In 1918–19 he gave recitals in and around Kiev, N. Slonimsky serving occasionally as his accompanist. He retired from the stage in 1924.

BIBL.: M. Lvov, *L. S.* (Moscow, 1951).

Sobolewski, Edward (Johann Friedrich Eduard), German-born American violinist, conductor, and composer of Polish descent; b. Königsberg, Oct. 1, 1804; d. St. Louis, May 17, 1872. He was a composition pupil of Zelter in Berlin and of Weber in Dresden (1821–24). He became an opera conductor in Königsberg (1830), and was founder-conductor of the orch. of the Philharmonische Gesellschaft (from 1838) and conductor of the choir of the Academy of Music (from 1843); he subsequently was director of music at the Bremen Theater (from 1854). In 1859 he emigrated to the United States, settling in Milwaukee, then a center of German musical immigrants; he was founder-conductor of the Milwaukee Phil. Soc. Orch. (1860). He then settled in St. Louis, where he conducted the Phil. Soc. (1860–66); he was prof. of vocal music at Bonham's Female Seminary (from 1869). His works include the operas *Imogen* (1833), *Velleda* (1836), *Salvator Rosa* (1848), *Komala* (Weimar, Oct. 30, 1858), *Mohega, die Blume des Waldes*

(Milwaukee, Oct. 11, 1859, to his own libretto, in German, on an American subject dealing with an Indian girl saved by Pulaski from death), and *An die Freude* (Milwaukee, 1859); also oratorios.

Socor, Matei, Romanian composer; b. Iaşi, Sept. 28, 1908; d. Bucharest, May 30, 1980. He studied theory with Castaldi at the Bucharest Cons. (1927–29) and composition with Karg-Elert at the Leipzig Cons. (1930–33). He then was active as a composer and teacher in his homeland. Among his works is the opera *Conu Leonida faţă cu reactiunea* (1976; Bucharest, Dec. 28, 1978).

Söderblom, Ulf, Finnish conductor; b. Turku, Feb. 5, 1930. He received his training from Swarowsky at the Vienna Academy of Music (graduated, 1957). In 1957 he made his debut as a conductor at the Finnish National Opera in Helsinki, where he subsequently conducted regularly. From 1973 to 1993 he was its music director. During his long tenure, he became particularly known for his championship of contemporary operas. In 1983 he took the Finnish National Opera to the United States for performances at the Metropolitan Opera in New York. He also appeared as a guest conductor with many orchs. in Finland and abroad. On Feb. 25, 1992, he conducted the premiere of Sallinen's *Kullervo* at the Los Angeles Opera.

Söderlind, Ragnar, Norwegian composer; b. Oslo, June 27, 1945. He was a student of Baden (counterpoint), Hukvari (conducting), and Ulleberg (horn) at the Oslo Cons. (1966–67), of Bergman and Kokkonen (composition) at the Sibelius Academy in Helsinki (1967–68), and of Fladmoe (conducting) at the Oslo Cons. (graduate degree, 1976). For all practical purposes, he was autodidact in composition. Söderlind eschewed the predominant avant-garde course blazed by his contemporaries to embrace a style akin to the new Romanticist persuasion. Programmatic elements are found in several of his scores.

WORKS: DRAMATIC: *Esther and the Blue Serenity*, opera (1971–72); *Hedda Gabler*, symphonic/choreographic drama (1978); *Kristin Lavransdatter*, ballet (1982); *Victoria*, ballet music (1985–86); *Rose og Ravn*, opera (1989).

Söderman, (Johan) August, Swedish composer; b. Stockholm, July 17, 1832; d. there, Feb. 10, 1876. He studied piano and composition at the Stockholm Cons. (1847–50), then joined Stjernstrom's theater company as director of music and toured with it in Sweden and Finland. Following further studies with E. F. Richter in Leipzig (1856–57), he resumed his post with the Stjernstrom company; later he was chorusmaster and deputy director at Stockholm's Royal Theater. He was particularly influenced by the lyric works of Schumann, Wagner, and Liszt, an influence that is combined with Swedish national elements in his theater music. Among his works were the operettas *Urdur, eller Neckens dotter Zigenarhofdingen Zohrab* (Zohrab, the Gypsy Chief; Helsinki, 1852) and *Hin Ondes första lärospan* (The Devil's First Lesson; Stockholm, Sept. 14, 1856); also incidental music to some 80 plays.

BIBL.: G. Jeanson, *A. S.: En svensk tondiktares liv och verk* (Stockholm, 1926).

Sodero, Cesare, Italian-American conductor and composer; b. Naples, Aug. 2, 1886; d. N.Y., Dec. 16, 1947. He studied with Alessandro Longo (piano) and Martucci (composition) at the Naples Cons. In 1907 he emigrated to the United States and settled in New York; he was a music director of the Edison Phonograph Co., the National Broadcasting Co., and the Mutual Broadcasting Co.; he conducted the San Carlo Grand Opera Co. and the Philadelphia Grand Opera. He wrote an opera, *Ombre russe* (Venice, June 19, 1930), and ballets.

Söderström (-Olow), (Anna) Elisabeth, prominent Swedish soprano; b. Stockholm, May 7, 1927. She studied voice with Andreyeva von Skilondz in Stockholm; she also took courses in languages and literary history at the Univ. of Stockholm, and received a thorough musical education at the Stockholm Royal Opera School. She made her operatic debut as Bastienne in Mozart's *Bastien und Bastienne* at the Drottningholm Court Theater in Stockholm in 1947; she became a member of the Royal Opera there in 1950. She made her first appearance in Salzburg as Ighino in Pfitzner's *Palestrina* in 1955, then at the Glyndebourne Festival as the Composer in *Ariadne auf Naxos* in 1957, becoming one of its most noted singers. She made her Metropolitan Opera debut in New York as Susanna in *Le nozze de Figaro* on Oct. 30, 1959, and remained on its roster until 1964; subsequently she pursued her career mainly in Europe until returning to the United States in 1977 to sing the title role in *Kat'a Kabanova* at the San Francisco Opera; she returned to the Metropolitan Opera in 1983 as Ellen Orford in *Peter Grimes*. In 1988 she sang in the premiere of Argento's *The Aspern Papers* in Dallas. In 1990 she was appointed artistic director of the Drottningholm Court Theater. In 1991 she was awarded the Stora Culture Prize. Her extraordinary command of languages made her an outstanding concert and lieder artist, both in Europe and in North America. Among her notable roles were Fiordiligi, Tatyana, Sophie, Marie in *Wozzeck*, the Countess in *Capriccio*, Jenůfa, Emilia Marty in *The Makropoulos Affair*, and the Governess in *The Turn of the Screw*. She publ. a lighthearted autobiography, *I Min Tonart* (1978; Eng. tr., 1979, as *In My Own Key*).

Soffel, Doris, German mezzo-soprano; b. Hechingen, May 12, 1948. She received training in voice from Marianne Schech in Munich (1968–73). After singing in *Das Liebesverbot* at the Bayreuth Youth Festival in 1972, she sang in Stuttgart from 1973 to 1976. In 1976 she made her first appearance at the Bayreuth Festival as Waltraute, and returned there as Fricka in 1983. She appeared as Puck in *Oberon* at the Bregenz Festival in 1977. She was engaged as Monteverdi's Poppea in Toronto and as Sextus in *La Clemenza di Tito* at London's Covent Garden in 1983. After singing in the premiere of Reimann's *Troades* in Munich in 1986, she portrayed Angelina in *La Cenerentola* at the Berlin State Opera in 1987. In 1991 she appeared in Munich in the premiere of Penderick's *Ubu Rex*, returning there in 1994 as Preziosilla. She sang Judith in *Bluebeard's Castle* at the Deutsche Oper in Berlin and as Charlotte in *Werther* in Parma in 1995. In 1997 she appeared in recital in London.

Soffredini, Alfredo, Italian writer on music, teacher, and composer; b. Livorno, Sept. 17, 1854; d. Milan, March 12, 1923. He studied with Mazzucato and Sangalli at the Milan Cons. He ed. Milan's influential *Gazzetta Musicale* (1896–1912), and also taught composition, numbering among his students Mascagni. He composed 8 operas to his own librettos: *Il Saggio* (Livorno, Feb. 3, 1883), 2-act children's opera, *Il piccolo Haydn* (Faenza, Nov. 24, 1889), *Salvatorello* (Pavia, March 25, 1894), *Tarcisio* (Milan, Nov. 23, 1895), *Aurora* (Pavia, April 21, 1897), *La coppa d'oro* (Milan, Jan. 27, 1900), *Graziella* (Pavia, Nov. 15, 1902), and *Il leone* (Cesena, 1914).

Sokola, Miloš, Czech composer; b. Bučovice, Moravia, April 18, 1913; d. Malé Kyšice, Sept. 27, 1976. He studied composition with Petrželka and violin with O. Vávra at the Brno Cons. (1929–38); he had further composition studies at the Prague Cons. with Novák (1938–40) and Křička (1942–44). From 1942 to 1973 he was a violinist in the Prague National Theater orch. His works include the opera *Marnotratný syn* (The Prodigal Son; 1948; Olomouc, 1963).

Soler (Ramos), Antonio (Francisco Javier Josê), important Catalan composer and organist; b. Olot, Gerona (baptized), Dec. 3, 1729; d. El Escorial, near Madrid, Dec. 20, 1783. He entered the Montserrat monastery choir school in 1736, where his mentors were the maestro Benito Esteve and the organist Beninto Valls. About 1750 he was made maestro de capilla in Lérida; in 1752, was ordained a subdeacon, and also became a member of the Jeronymite monks in El Escorial, taking the habit, and then being professed in 1753; he was made maestro de capilla in 1757. He also pursued studies with José de Nebra and D. Scarlatti. Soler was a prolific composer of both sacred and secular vocal music, as well as instrumental music. His writings include *Llave de la* *modulación, y antigüedades de la música en que se trata del fundamento necessario para saber modular: Theórica, y prática para el más claro conocimiento de qualquier especie de figuras, desde el tiempo de Juan de Muris, hasta hoy, con albunos cánones enigmáticos, y sus resoluciones* (Madrid, 1762; ed. and tr. by M. Crouch, diss., Univ. of Calif., Santa Barbara, 1978), *Satisfacción a los reparos precisos hechos por D. Antonio Roel del Rio, a la Llave de la modulación* (Madrid, 1765), *Carta escrita a un amigo en que le da parte de un diálogo ultimamente publicado contra su Llave de la modulación* (Madrid, 1766), and *Combinación de Monedas y Cálculo manifiesto contra el Libro anónimo inititulado: Correspondencia de la Moneda de Cataluña a la de Castilla* (Barcelona, 1771).

BIBL.: F. Carroll, *An Introduction to A. S.* (diss., Univ. of Rochester, 1960); T. Espinosa, *Selected Unpublished Villancicos of Padre Fray A. S.* (diss., Univ. of Southern Calif., 1969).

Soler, Josep, Catalan composer; b. Barcelona, March 25, 1935. He studied composition with Leibowitz in Paris (1959) and with Taltabull in Barcelona (1960–64). In 1977 he was appointed to the staff of the Barcelona Cons. Among his compositions are the operas *Agamemnon* (1960), *Edipo y Iocasta* (1972; Barcelona, Oct. 30, 1974), and *Jesús de Nazaret* (1974–78).

Solerti, Angelo, Italian philologist and music scholar; b. Savona, Sept. 20, 1865; d. Massa Carrara, Jan. 10, 1907. He studied at the Istituto di Studi Superiori in Florence and at the Univ. of Turin (arts degree, 1887). His contributions to the early history of opera are valuable: *Le origini del melodramma: Testimonianze dei contemporanei* (a collection of contemporary documents and prefaces to the earliest operas; Turin, 1903), *Gli albori del melodramma* (3 vols., Milan, 1904–05), *Musica, ballo e drammatica alla corte medicea dal 1600 al 1637: Notizie tratte da un diario (tenuto da Cesare Tinghi), con appendice di testi inediti e rari* (Florence, 1905), and *Ferrara e la Corte Estense nella second metà del secolo XVI* (Città di Castello, 1891).

Sollertinsky, Ivan (Ivanovich), brilliant Russian musicologist and music critic; b. Vitebsk, Dec. 3, 1902; d. Novosibirsk, Feb. 11, 1944. He studied Hispanic philosophy at the Univ. of Petrograd (1919–24) and drama at the Inst. for the History of the Arts (graduated, 1923), subsequently pursuing postgraduate courses (1926–29); he also took conducting lessons with Malko. He was active as a lecturer and music critic in Leningrad, where he later taught at the Cons. (from 1936). He showed profound understanding of the problems of modern music and was one of the earliest supporters of Shostakovich; publ. numerous articles dealing with Soviet music in general. M. Druskin ed. 4 vols. of his writings (Leningrad, 1946; 1956, 2d ed., 1963; 1973; 1973).

BIBL.: L. Mikheeva, *I. I. S.* (Leningrad, 1988).

Solomon, Maynard (Elliott), American recording executive and writer on music; b. N.Y., Jan. 5, 1930. He was educated in New York at the High School of Music and Art and at Brooklyn College (A.B., 1950), then pursued postgraduate studies at Columbia Univ. (1950–51). He was cofounder and coowner of the Vanguard Recording Soc., Inc., of N.Y. (1950–86), was on the faculty of the City Univ. of N.Y. (1979–81), and served as a visiting prof. at the State Univ. of N.Y. at Stony Brook (1988–89), Columbia Univ. (1989–90), Harvard Univ. (1991–92), and Yale Univ. (1994–95). In 1978 and 1989 he won ASCAP–Deems Taylor Awards. He contributed many articles on Beethoven, Schubert, and other composers to the *Musical Quarterly, Music & Letters, 19th Century Music, Beethoven Studies*, the *Beethoven-Jahrbuch*, the *Journal of the American Musicological Society*, and other publications, and also served as assoc. ed. of *American Imago*. He ed. "Beethoven's Tagebuch 1812–1818," in *Beethoven Studies 3* (London, 1982).

WRITINGS: *Marxism and Art* (1973); *Beethoven* (1977); *Myth, Creativity and Psychoanalysis* (1978); *Beethoven Essays* (1988); *Mozart: A Life* (1994).

Soloviev, Nikolai (Feopemptovich), Russian music critic, teacher, and composer; b. Petrozavodsk, May 9, 1846; d. Petrograd, Dec. 27, 1916. After completing his studies in composition at the St. Petersburg Cons. (1868–72), he joined its faculty as a teacher of theory (1874–85) and a prof. of composition (1885–1909); he also was active as a music critic (from 1870), acquiring a reputation as a determined opponent of the contemporary scene and being highly critical of Tchaikovsky and the national school of composers. He composed the operas *Vakula the Smith* (1875; concert perf., St. Petersberg, 1880), *Cordelia* (St. Petersburg, Nov. 24, 1885; rev. as *Vengeance*, 1898), and *The House at Kolomna* (n.d.). He also orchestrated Act 5 and part of Act 1 of Serov's opera *The Evil Power*.

Soloviev-Sedoy, Vasili (Pavlovich), Russian composer; b. St. Petersburg, April 25, 1907; d. Moscow, Dec. 2, 1979. He learned to play the balalaika, guitar, and piano before pursuing studies at the Mussorgsky Music School (1929–31) and the Leningrad Cons. (1931–36). He was active as a pianist, playing improvisations on the radio and accompanying exercises in the Leningrad Studio of Creative Gymnastics. During World War II, he organized a series of theatrical productions for the Soviet Army. He was a member of the Supreme Soviet in the 3d, 4th, and 5th congresses. In 1975 he was awarded the order of Hero of Socialist Labor. He was regarded in Russia as one of the most expert composers of Soviet songs, some of which acquired immense popularity; one of them, "Evenings at Moscow," became a musical signature of daily news broadcasts on the Soviet radio. In all, he wrote over 700 songs. He was able to synthesize the melos of Russian folk songs with revolutionary ballads and marching rhythms. His other works include an opera, several operettas, and the ballet *Taras Bulba* (Leningrad, Dec. 12, 1940; rev. 1953); also film scores.

BIBL.: A. Sokhor, *V. P. S.-S.* (Leningrad and Moscow, 1952; 2d ed., 1967); Y. Kremlyov, *V. P. S.-S.: Ocherk zhizni i tvorchestva* (V. P. S.-S.: Outline of His Life and Work; Leningrad, 1960).

Soltesz, Stefan, Hungarian-born Austrian conductor; b. Nyiregyhaza, Jan. 6, 1949. He was a student of Dieter Weber, Hans Swarowsky, Reinhold Schmidt, and Friedrich Cerha at the Vienna Academy of Music. He was a conductor at the Theater an der Wien (1971–73) and the Vienna State Opera (1973–83), and also was an assist. conductor at the Salzburg Festival (1978–79; 1983). After holding the position of 1st conductor at the Graz Opera (1979–81), the Hamburg State Opera (1983–85), and the Deutsche Opera in Berlin (1985–88), he was Generalmusikdirektor in Braunschweig from 1988 to 1993. In 1992 he made his U.S. debut at the Washington (D.C.) Opera conducting *Otello*. He became music director of the Flanders Opera and principal guest conductor of the Leipzig Opera in 1992. From 1997 he was Generalmusikdirektor in Essen. As a guest conductor, he led various opera companies and orchs. in Europe.

Solti, Sir Georg (real name, **György Stern**), eminent Hungarian-born English conductor; b. Budapest, Oct. 21, 1912; d. Antibes, Sept. 5, 1997. He began to study the piano when he was 6, making his first public appearance in Budapest when he was 12; at 13 he enrolled there at the Franz Liszt Academy of Music, studying piano with Dohnányi and, briefly, with Bartók; he took composition courses with Kodály. He graduated at the age of 18, and was engaged by the Budapest Opera as a répétiteur; he also served as an assist. to Bruno Walter (1935) and Toscanini (1936, 1937) at the Salzburg Festivals. On March 11, 1938, he made a brilliant conducting debut at the Budapest Opera with Mozart's *Le nozze di Figaro*; however, the wave of anti-Semitism in Hungary under the reactionary military rule forced him to leave Budapest (he was Jewish). In 1939 he went to Switzerland, where he was active mainly as a concert pianist; in 1942 he won the Concours International de Piano in Geneva; finally, in 1944, he was engaged to conduct concerts with the orch. of the Swiss Radio. In 1946 the American occupation authorities in Munich invited him to conduct *Fidelio* at the Bavarian State Opera; his success led to his appointment as its Generalmusikdirektor, a position he held from 1946 to 1952. In 1952 he became Generalmusikdirektor in Frankfurt am Main, serving as director of the Opera and conductor of the Museumgesellschaft Concerts. He made his U.S. debut with the San Francisco Opera on Sept. 25, 1953, conducting *Elektra*; he later conducted the Chicago Sym. Orch., the N.Y. Phil., and at the Metropolitan Opera in New York, where he made his first appearance on Dec. 17, 1960, with *Tannhäuser*. He was then engaged as music director of the Los Angeles Phil., but the project collapsed when the board of trustees refused to grant him full powers in musical and administrative policy. In 1960–61 he was music director of the Dallas Sym. Orch. In the meantime, he made his Covent Garden debut in London in 1959; in 1961 he assumed the post of music director of the Royal Opera House there, retaining it with great distinction until 1971. In 1969 he became music director of the Chicago Sym. Orch., and it was in that capacity that he achieved a triumph as an interpreter and orch. builder, so that the "Chicago sound" became a synonym for excellence. He showed himself an enlightened disciplinarian and a master of orch. psychology, so that he could gain and hold the confidence of the players while demanding from them the utmost in professional performance. Under his direction the Chicago Sym. Orch. became one of the most celebrated orchs. in the world. He took it to Europe for the first time in 1971, eliciting glowing praise from critics and audiences; subsequently he led it on a number of acclaimed tours there; he also took it to New York for regular appearances at Carnegie Hall. He held the additional posts of music adviser of the Paris Opéra (1971–73) and music director of the Orch. de Paris (1972–75), which he took on a tour of China in 1974; he served as principal conductor and artistic director of the London Phil. from 1979 to 1983 and was then accorded the title of conductor emeritus. During all these years, he retained his post with the Chicago Sym. Orch., while continuing his appearances as a guest conductor with European orchs. In 1983 he conducted the *Ring* cycle at the Bayreuth Festival, in commemoration of the 100th anniversary of the death of Richard Wagner. Solti retained his prestigious position with the Chicago Sym. Orch. until the close of the 100th anniversary season in 1990–91, and subsequently held the title of Laureate Conductor. In 1992–93 he served as artistic director of the Salzburg Festival. In 1968 he was made an honorary Commander of the Order of the British Empire; in 1971 he was named an honorary Knight Commander of the Order of the British Empire. In 1972 he became a British subject and was knighted, assuming the title of Sir Georg. In 1992 he was awarded Germany's Grosses Verdienstskreuz mit Stern und Schulterband. In honor of his 80th birthday in 1992 the Vienna Phil. awarded him the first Hans Richter Medal. In 1993 President Clinton awarded him the National Medal of Arts and he was accorded honors at the Kennedy Center in Washington, D.C. Solti was generally acknowledged as a superlative interpreter of the symphonic and operatic repertoire. He was renowned for his performances of Wagner, Verdi, Mahler, Richard Strauss, and other Romantic masters; he also conducted notable performances of Bartók, Stravinsky, Schoenberg, and other composers of the 20th century. His recordings received innumerable awards.

BIBL.: W. Furlong, *Season with S.: A Year in the Life of the Chicago Symphony* (N.Y. and London, 1974); P. Robinson, *S.* (London, 1979).

Soltys, Mieczyslaw, Polish conductor, teacher, and composer; b. Lemberg, Feb. 7, 1863; d. there (Lwów), Nov. 12, 1929. He studied in Lemberg and Paris. Returning to Lemberg in 1899, he was director of the Cons. and of the Musical Soc.; he also wrote music criticism. His son was the Polish pedagogue and composer Adam Soltys (b. Lemberg, July 4, 1890; d. there [Lwów], July 6, 1968).

WORKS: OPERAS: *Rzeczpospolita Babińska* (Republic of Babin; 1894; Lemberg, April 27, 1905); *Panie Kochanku* (1890; Lwów, May 3, 1924) *Opowieśč kresowa* or *Opowiéšč ukraińska* (A Ukraine Story; 1909; Lemberg, March 8, 1910); *Nieboska komedia* (1925).

Somers, Harry (Stewart), outstanding Canadian composer and pianist; b. Toronto, Sept. 11, 1925. He studied piano with Dorothy Hornfelt (1939–41), Reginald Godden (1942–43), Weldon Kilburn (1945–48), and E. R. Schmitz (1948) in Toronto; he also attended classes in composition with John Weinzweig (1941–43; 1945–49), then studied with Milhaud in Paris (1949–50). Returning to Canada, he eked out a meager living as a music copyist, finally receiving commissions in 1960; he also became active as a broadcaster. In 1972 he was made a Companion of the Order of Canada. His historical opera, *Louis Riel*, was performed at the Kennedy Center in Washington, D.C., on Oct. 23, 1975, as part of America's bicentennial celebration. His musical idiom is quaquaversal, absorbing without prejudice ancient, national, and exotic resources, from Gregorian chant to oriental scales, from simple folkways to electronic sound, all handled with fine expertise.

WORKS: DRAMATIC: *The Fool*, chamber opera for 4 Soloists and Chamber Orch. (1953; Toronto, Nov. 15, 1956); *The Homeless Ones*, television operetta (CBC-TV, Toronto, Dec. 31, 1955); *The Fisherman and His Soul*, ballet (Hamilton, Nov. 5, 1956); *Ballad*, ballet (Ottawa, Oct. 29, 1958); *The House of Atreus*, ballet (1963; Toronto, Jan. 13, 1964); *Louis Riel*, historical opera (Toronto, Sept. 23, 1967); *Improvisation*, theater piece for Narrator, Singers, Strings, any number of Woodwinds, 2 Percussionists, and Piano (Montreal, July 5, 1968); *And*, choreography for Dancers, Vocal Soloists, Flute, Harp, Piano, and 4 Percussionists (CBC-TV, Toronto, 1969); *Death of Enkidu: Part I*, chamber opera, after the epic of Gilgamesh (Toronto, Dec. 7, 1977); *Mario and the Magician*, opera (1991; Toronto, May 19, 1992).

BIBL.: B. Cherney, *H. S.* (Toronto, 1975).

Somigli, Franca (real name, **Maria Bruce Clark**), American-Italian soprano; b. Chicago, March 17, 1901; d. Trieste, May 14, 1974. She was a pupil of Malatesta, Votto, and Storchio in Milan. After making her operatic debut as Mimi in Rovigo (1926), she sang at Milan's La Scala (1933–44), in Chicago (debut as Maddalena in *Andrea Chénier*, 1934), in Rome (1934–43), at the Salzburg Festivals (1936–39), at Buenos Aires's Teatro Colón (1936–39), and at the Metropolitan Opera in New York (debut as Cio-Cio-San, March 8, 1937). She was married to **Giuseppe Antonicelli**. Among her most prominent roles were Kundry, Sieglinde, Fedora, the Marschallin, Arabella, and Salome.

Sommer, Hans (real name, **Hans Friedrich August Zincke**), German teacher, writer on music, and composer; b. Braunschweig, July 20, 1837; d. there, April 26, 1922. He studied mathematics at the Univ. of Göttingen (Ph.D., 1858), where he became a prof. of physics; he taught mathematics at Braunschweig's Technische Hochschule (1859–84), serving as its director (from 1875). He then devoted himself to music. In 1898 he helped to found the Genossenschaft Deutscher Komponisten, which became the Genossenschaft Deutscher Tonsetzer in 1903. His lyric songs were greatly appreciated in Germany and England. He also composed the operas *Der Nachtwächter* (Braunschweig, Nov. 22, 1865), *Der Vetter aus Bremen* (1865; not perf.), *Loreley* (Braunschweig, April 11, 1891), *Saint Foix* (Munich, Oct. 31, 1894), *Der Meermann* (Weimar, April 19, 1896), *Augustin* (1898; not perf.), *Münchhausen* (1896–98; not perf.), *Rübezahl und der Sackpfeifer von Neisse* (Braunschweig, May 15, 1904), *Riquet mit dem Schopf* (Braunschweig, April 14, 1907), and *Der Waldschratt* (Braunschweig, March 31, 1912).

BIBL.: E. Valentin, *H. S.* (Braunschweig, 1939).

Somogi, Judith, American conductor; b. N.Y., May 13, 1937; d. Rockville Centre, N.Y., March 23, 1988. She studied violin, piano, and organ at the Juilliard School of Music in New York (M.M., 1961) and attended courses at the Berkshire Music Center in Tanglewood; she later was an assistant to Schippers at the Spoleto Festival and to Stokowski at the American Sym. Orch. in New York. In 1974 she made a successful debut with the New York City Opera conducting *The Mikado*, and subsequently conducted in San Francisco, San Diego, San Antonio, and Pittsburgh. She made her European debut in Saarbrücken in 1979. After conducting *Madama Butterfly* at the Frankfurt am Main Opera in 1981, she held its position of 1st conductor from 1982 to 1987.

Sondheim, Stephen (Joshua), brilliant American composer and lyricist; b. N.Y., March 22, 1930. Of an affluent family, he received his academic education in private schools; he composed a school musical at the age of 15. He then studied music at Williams College, where he wrote the book, lyrics, and music for a couple of college shows; he graduated magna cum laude in 1950. In quest of higher musical learning, he went to Princeton Univ., where he took lessons in modernistic complexities with Babbitt and acquired sophisticated techniques of composition. He made his mark on Broadway when he wrote the lyrics for Bernstein's *West Side Story* (1957). His first success as a lyricist-composer came with the Broadway musical *A Funny Thing Happened on the Way to the Forum* (1962), which received a Tony award. His next musical, *Anyone Can Whistle* (1964), proved unsuccessful, but *Company* (1970), for which he wrote both lyrics and music, established him as a major composer and lyricist on Broadway. There followed *Follies* (1971), for which he wrote 22 pastiche songs; it was named best musical by the N.Y. Drama Critics Circle. His next production, *A Little Night Music*, with the nostalgic score harking back to the turn of the century, received a Tony, and its leading song, "Send in the Clowns," was awarded a Grammy in 1976. This score established Sondheim's characteristic manner of treating musicals; it is almost operatic in conception, and boldly introduces dissonant counterpoint *à la moderne*. In 1976 he produced *Pacific Overtures*, based on the story of the Western penetration into Japan in the 19th century, and composed in a stylized Japanese manner, modeled after the Kabuki theater; he also wrote the score to the musical *Sunday in the Park with George*, inspired by the painting by Georges Seurat entitled *Sunday Afternoon on the Island of La Grande Jatte* (1982; N.Y., May 1, 1984), which received the Pulitzer Prize for drama in 1985. In 1987 his musical *Into the Woods*, based on 5 of the Grimm fairy tales, scored a popular success on Broadway. It was followed by the musical *Assassins* in 1990. In 1992 he was selected to receive the National Medal of Arts, but he rejected the medal by stating that to accept it would be an act of hypocrisy in light of the controversy over funding of the NEA. After the inauguration of Bill Clinton as president in 1993, Sondheim accepted the National Medal of Arts and was honored at the Kennedy Center in Washington, D.C. His musical *Passion* was premiered in New York on April 28, 1994.

BIBL.: C. Zadan, *S. & Co.* (N.Y., 1974; 2d ed., rev., 1994); M. Adams, *The Lyrics of S. S.: Form and Function* (diss., Northwestern Univ., 1980); D. Cartmell, *S. S. and the Concept Musical* (diss., Univ. of Calif., Santa Barbara, 1983); S. Wilson, *Motivic, Rhythmic, and Harmonic Procedures of Unification in S. S.'s "Company" and "A Little Night Music"* (diss., Ball State Univ., 1983); J. Gordon, *Art Isn't Easy: The Achievement of S. S.* (Carbondale, Ill., 1990; rev. ed., 1992); M. Gottfried, *S.* (N.Y., 1993); M. Secrest, *S. S.: A Life* (N.Y., 1998).

Sonninen, Ahti, Finnish composer; b. Kuopio, July 11, 1914; d. Helsinki, Aug. 27, 1984. Following graduation from the Kajaani training college, he took courses in theory and composition with Palmgren, Merikanto, Ranta, and Funtek at the Sibelius Academy in Helsinki (1939–47). He taught elementary school (1936–43), then taught in the school music dept. of the Sibelius Academy (from 1957). He followed the tenets of international musical modernism in his technique of composition, but also adhered to subjects from Finnish folklore.

WORKS: DRAMATIC: *Merenkuninkaan tytär* (Daughter of Neptune), opera (1949); *Pessi and Illusia*, ballet (1952); *Ruususolmu* (Wreath of Roses), ballet (1956); *Karhunpeijaiset* (Feast to Celebrate the Killing of a Bear), ritual opera (1968); *Se* (It), ballet farce (Helsinki, Feb. 24, 1972); *Haavruuva* (Lady of the Sea), opera (1971); film scores.

Sonnleithner, family of Austrian musicians and writers:

(1) Christoph Sonnleithner, composer; b. Szegedin, May 28, 1734; d. Vienna, Dec. 25, 1786. He was 2 when he was taken to Vienna, where he received his musical training from his uncle, Leopold Sonnleithner, a choirmaster; he took courses in law and served as a barrister in the employ of Prince Esterházy, becoming associated with Haydn. His daughter Anna was the mother of the famous poet Grillparzer. He also had 2 sons who were active in music.

(2) Joseph Sonnleithner, librettist and archivist; b. Vienna, March 3, 1766; d. there, Dec. 25, 1835. He acquired material for the emperor's private library, and was ed. of the *Wiener Theater-Almanach* (1794–96). He served as secretary of the Court theaters (1808–14), and also was manager of the Theater an der Wien (until 1807); he was one of the founders of the Gesellschaft der Musikfreunde (1812). He wrote some librettos and adapted others, including *Fidelio* for Beethoven and *Faniska* by Cherubini. In 1827 he discovered the famous Antiphonary of St. Gall of the 9th century, in neume notation, probably a copy of the one sent there by Charlemagne in 790. He bequeathed his collection of opera librettos to the Vienna Cons. and his instrument collection and library to the Gesellschaft der Musikfreunde. He was a close friend of Schubert and Grillparzer.

(3) Ignaz (von) Sonnleithner, bass, doctor, and scientist; b. Vienna, July 30, 1770; d. there, Nov. 27, 1831. He appeared as principal bass with the Gesellschaft der Musikfreunde. He held musical soirées in his home (1815–24), at which Schubert tried out several of his vocal works. His son was Leopold von Sonnleithner (b. Vienna, Nov. 15, 1797; d. there, March 4, 1873). A barrister, he was a staunch friend of Schubert and enabled him to publ. the *Erlkönig* (Schubert's 1st publ. work). A great lover of music, he was active with the Gesellschaft der Musikfreunde, to which he left his musical papers.

Sontag, Henriette (real name, **Gertrude Walpurgis Sonntag**), celebrated German soprano; b. Koblenz, Jan. 3, 1806; d. Mexico City, June 17, 1854. Her father was the actor Franz Sonntag and her mother the actress and singer Franziska (née Martloff) Sonntag (1798–1865). She studied with her mother, and began appearing in stage plays and operas at age 5. In 1815 she was admitted to the Prague Cons., where she received instruction in singing from Anna Czegka, theory from Josef Triebensee, and piano from Pixis. In 1821 she made her formal operatic debut as the princess in Boieldieu's *Jean de Paris* in Prague; in 1822 she went to Vienna, where she appeared in German and Italian opera. She was chosen by Weber to create the title role in his *Euryanthe* (Oct. 25, 1823), and then was chosen by Beethoven to sing in the first performances of his 9th Sym. and *Missa solemnis* (May 7 and 13, 1824, respectively). She sang in Dresden in 1825, and that same year made her Berlin debut at the Königstädter Theater as Isabella in *L'Italiana in Algeri* (Aug. 3). On May 15, 1826, she made a stunning debut at the Théâtre-Italien in Paris as Rosina in *Il Barbiere di Siviglia*; following engagements in Germany, she returned to Paris in 1828 to win further accolades as Donna Anna and Semiramide. During a visit to Weimar, she won the approbation of Goethe, who penned the poem *Neue Siren* for the "fluttering nightingale" of the operatic stage. On April 19, 1828, she chose the role of Rosina for her British debut at the King's Theatre in London; during her British sojourn, she married Count Carlo Rossi, a Sardinian diplomat, secretly (so as not to jeopardize his career); after the king of Prussia ennobled her as Henriette von Lauenstein, she was able to publicly join her husband in The Hague, her low birth no longer a matter of concern; however, she quit the stage in 1830, and then appeared only in private and concert settings in the cities where her husband was stationed. After her husband lost his diplomatic post at the abdication of the king of Sardinia in 1849, she resumed her stage career with appearances at Her Majesty's Theatre in London. She toured England that same year, and then created the role of Miranda in Halévy's *La tempesta* at Her Majesty's Theatre on June 8, 1850; after further appearances in London and Paris in 1851, she toured with great success in Germany, then appeared in the United States in 1852. In 1854 she toured Mexico as a member of an Italian opera company; on June 11 of that year she made her last appearance as Lucrezia Borgia; the next day she was stricken with cholera and died 5 days later. Her beautiful voice, which ranged from a to e^3, her striking physical appearance, and her natural acting abilities led to her reputation as the equal or superior to all other divas of the age. She was a matchless interpreter of roles in operas by Mozart, Rossini, Donizetti, and Bellini.

BIBL.: T. Gautier, *L'Ambassadrice, Biographie de la comtesse Rossi* (Paris, 1850); J. Gundling, *H. S.* (2 vols., Leipzig, 1861); H. Stümcke, *H. S.* (Berlin, 1913); E. Pirchan, *H. S.: Die Sängerin des Biedermeier* (Vienna, 1946); F. Russell, *Queen of Song: The Life of H. S., Countess de Rossi* (N.Y., 1964).

Sonzogno, Giulio Cesare, Italian composer; b. Milan, Dec. 24, 1906; d. there, Jan. 23, 1976. He was related to the family of the music publishers Sonzogno. He studied cello and composition in Milan; he composed mostly for the stage.

WORKS: DRAMATIC: OPERAS: *Regina Uliva* (Milan, March 17, 1949); *I Passeggeri* (1961); *Il denaro del Signor Arne* (1968); *Boule de suif*, after Maupassant (1970); *Mirra* (1970). BALLET: *L'amore delle tre melarancie* (Milan, Feb. 1, 1936).

Soomer, Walter, German bass-baritone; b. Liegnitz, March 12, 1878; d. Leipzig, Aug. 1955. He was a student of Hermann Stoeckert and Anna Uhlig in Berlin. In 1902 he made his operatic debut in Kolmar. After singing in Halle (1902–06), he was a member of the Leipzig Opera (1906–27). He also appeared at the Bayreuth Festivals (1906; 1908–14; 1924–25). On Feb. 18, 1909, he made his Metropolitan Opera debut in New York as Wolfram, remaining on its roster until 1911. From 1911 to 1915 he sang in Dresden. In 1927 he became director of his own vocal and opera school in Leipzig. Soomer was best known as a Wagnerian, singing such roles as Hans Sachs, Wotan, Gurnemanz, Kurwenal, and Amfortas.

Soot, Fritz (Friedrich Wilhelm), distinguished German tenor; b. Wellesweiler-Neunkirchen, Saar, Aug. 20, 1878; d. Berlin, June 9, 1965. He first pursued a career as an actor in Karlsruhe (1901–07), then studied voice with Scheidemantel in Dresden. He made his operatic debut with the Dresden Court Opera as Tonio in *La Fille du régiment* in 1908, remaining on its roster until 1918; during his tenure there he sang in the first performance of *Der Rosenkavalier* as the Italian Singer (Jan. 26, 1911). His subsequent engagements were in Stuttgart (1918–22), at the Berlin State Opera (1922–44; 1946–52), and at the Berlin Städtische Oper (1946–48). He sang in the premieres of Berg's *Wozzeck*, as well as in works by Pfitzner and Schreker. He excelled in such Wagnerian roles as Tristan, Siegmund, and Siegfried.

Sopeña (Ibáñez), Federico, Spanish musicologist; b. Valladolid, Jan. 25, 1917; d. Madrid, May 22, 1991. He studied in Bilbao and Madrid; later he obtained a doctorate in theology at the Università Gregoriana in Rome. He was active as a music critic; from 1951 to 1956 he was director of the Madrid Cons., and was also the founder and publisher of the music magazine *Música*. He publ. (in Madrid) a number of useful monographs of Spanish composers, including *Joaquín Turina* (1943; 2d ed., 1952) and *Joaquín Rodrigo* (1946; 2d ed., rev. 1970); also *Historia de la música* (1946; 5th ed., 1974), *La música europea contemporánea* (1952), *Historia de la música española contemporánea* (1958; 2d ed., 1967), and *Música y literatura* (1974).

Soproni, József, Hungarian composer and pedagogue; b. Sopron, Oct. 4, 1930. He studied with Viski at the Budapest Academy of Music (1949–56). In 1957 he became a teacher at the Béla Bartók School in Budapest. In 1962 he joined the faculty of the Budapest Academy of Music, where he was a prof. from 1977. From 1988 to 1994 he served as its rector. Among his works is the opera *Antigone* (1987).

Sor (real name, **Sors**), **(Joseph) Fernando (Macari),** celebrated Catalan guitarist and composer; b. Barcelona, Feb. 13, 1778; d. Paris, July 10, 1839. At the age of 11 he entered the school of the monastery of Montserrat, where he studied music under the direction of Anselmo Viola. He wrote a Mass, then attended the Barcelona military academy. In 1799 he went to Madrid, subsequently holding administrative sinecures in Barcelona (from 1808); he also was active in the battle against France, but about 1810 accepted an administrative post under the French. When Bonapartist rule was defeated in Spain in 1813, he fled to Paris. There he met Cherubini, Méhul, and others, who urged him to give concerts as a guitarist, and he soon acquired fame. His ballet *Cendrillon* (London, 1822) became quite popular and was given more than 100 times at the Paris Opéra; it was heard at the gala opening of the Bolshoi Theater in Moscow in 1823. Sor was active in Russia from 1823; he wrote funeral music for the obsequies of Czar Alexander I in 1825. He returned to Paris via London in 1826, and subsequently devoted himself to performing and teaching. An outstanding guitar virtuoso, he also garnered recognition as a composer; in all, he wrote over 65 works for the guitar, including a number of standard pieces. He also wrote the most important guitar method ever penned.

WORKS: DRAMATIC: OPERAS: *Telemaco nell'isola de Calipso* (Barcelona, Aug. 25, 1797); *Don Trastullo* (unfinished; not extant). BALLETS: *La Foire de Smyrne* (London, 1821; not extant); *Le Seigneur généreux* (London, 1821; not extant); *Cendrillon* (London, 1822); *L'Amant peintre* (London, 1823); *Hercule et Omphale* (Moscow, 1826); *Le Sicilien* (Paris, 1827); *Hassan et le calife* (London, 1828; not extant).

BIBL.: M. Rocamora, *F. S.* (Barcelona, 1957); B. Jeffery, *F. S.: Composer and Guitarist* (London, 1977).

Soresina, Alberto, Italian composer and teacher; b. Milan, May 10, 1911. He studied with Paribeni and Bossi at the Milan Cons., graduating in 1933; he then took a course in composition in Siena with Frazzi. He subsequently was on the faculty of the Milan Cons. (1947–60) and the Turin Cons. (1963–66), then again at the Milan Cons. (from 1967). His works include the operas *Lanterna rossa* (1942), *Cuor di cristallo* (1942), *L'amuleto* (Bergamo, Oct. 26, 1954), and *Tre sogni per Marina* (1967).

Sormann, Alfred (Richard Gotthilf), German pianist and composer; b. Danzig, May 16, 1861; d. Berlin, Sept. 17, 1913. He studied at the Hochschule für Musik in Berlin with Barth, Spitta, and Bargiel; in 1885 he studied with Liszt. He made his debut in 1886, giving successful concerts in the chief German towns. He composed the operas *Die Sibylle von Tivoli* (Berlin, 1902) and *König Harald* (Stettin, 1909).

Sotin, Hans, notable German bass; b. Dortmund, Sept. 10, 1939. He was a student of F.W. Hetzel and then of Dieter Jacob at the Dortmund Hochschule für Musik. In 1962 he made his operatic debut as the Police Commissioner in *Der Rosenkavalier* in Essen. After joining the Hamburg State Opera in 1964, he quickly became one of its principal members singing not only traditional roles but creating new roles in works by Blacher, Einem, Penderecki et al. His success led to his being made a Hamburg Kammersänger. In 1970 he made his first appearance at the Glyndebourne Festival as Sarastro. He made his debut at the Chicago Lyric Opera as the Grand Inquisitor in *Don Carlos* in 1971. That same year he sang for the first time at the Bayreuth Festival as the Landgrave, where he subsequently returned with success in later years. On Oct. 26, 1972, he made his Metropolitan Opera debut in New York as Sarastro. From 1973 he sang at the Vienna State Opera. He made his debut at London's Covent Garden as Hunding in 1974. In 1976 he sang for the first time at Milan's La Scala as Baron Ochs. He also appeared as a soloist with the leading European orchs. In 1986 he returned to Covent Garden as Baron Ochs. In 1988 he sang Lodovico in *Otello* at the Metropolitan Opera. In 1992 he appeared as the Landgrave in Berlin. His portrayals of Tannhäuser, Lohengrin, and Gurnemanz at the 1993 Bayreuth Festival elicited critical accolades. He returned there as the Landgrave and Gurnemanz in 1995. In 1998 he was engaged as Pogner at the Metropolitan Opera. In addition to his varied operatic repertoire, Sotin has won distinction for his concert repertoire, most particularly of the music of Bach, Haydn, Beethoven, and Mahler.

Soubre, Etienne-Joseph, Belgian composer; b. Liège, Dec. 29, 1813; d. there, Sept. 8, 1871. He studied at the Liège Cons., and became its director (1862). He composed the opera *Isoline, ou Les chaperons blancs* (Brussels, 1855).

Soukupová, Věra, Czech mezzo-soprano; b. Prague, April 12, 1932. She was a student in Prague of Kadeřábek and Mustanová-Linková. In 1957 she made her debut at the J. K. Tyl Theater in Plzeň, where she sang until 1960. From 1960 to 1963 she was a member of the Prague National Theater. After capturing 1st prize in the Rio de Janeiro competition in 1963, she pursued a major career as an opera and concert singer. In 1966 she sang at the Bayreuth Festival. She made her first appearance in Hamburg in 1968. Thereafter she sang with major European opera houses and at major festivals. She became particularly known for her idiomatic performances of roles in 19th- and 20th-century Czech operas.

Souliotis, Elena, Greek soprano and mezzo-soprano; b. Athens, May 28, 1943. She studied in Buenos Aires with Alfredo Bonta, Jascha Galperin, and Bianca Lietti, and in Milan with Mercedes Llopart. In 1964 she made her operatic debut as Santuzza at the Teatro San Carlo in Naples. In 1965 she made her U.S. debut as Elena in Boito's *Mefistofele* in Chicago. In 1966 she sang Abigaille in *Nabucco* at Milan's La Scala, appeared as Luisa Miller in Florence, and made her N.Y. debut as Anna Bolena in a concert performance at Carnegie Hall. Her London debut followed in 1968 as Abigaille in a concert performance. She returned to London in 1969 to make her Covent Garden debut as Lady Macbeth, and continued to sing there until 1973. In subsequent years, she sang in various European operatic centers. Among her other roles were Norma, Gioconda, Manon Lescaut, Desdemona, Leonora in *Il Trovatore*, and Aida.

Šourek, Otakar, Czech writer on music; b. Prague, Oct. 1, 1883; d. there, Feb. 15, 1956. He was trained as an engineer, and although he was employed in the Prague City Council works dept. (1907–39), music was his avocation. He wrote music criticism for several publications, including Prague's *Venkov* (1918–41). However, it was as an authority on the life and music of Dvořák that he gained distinction; he devoted fully 40 years to Dvořák research, and served as the first ed. of the composer's collected works.

WRITINGS: *Život a dilo Antonína Dvořáka* (The Life and Works of Dvořák; 4 vols., Prague, 1916–33; vols. 1-2, 3d ed., 1955–56; vols. 3-4, 2d ed., 1957–58; in Ger. as *Dvořák: Leben und Werk*, one vol., abr. by P. Stefan, Vienna, 1935; Eng. tr. by Y. Vance as *Anton Dvořák*, N.Y., 1941); *Dvořák's Werke: Ein völlstandiges Verzeichnis in chronologischer, thematischer und systematischer Anordnung* (Berlin, 1917; rev. Czech ed., Prague, 1960); *Výlety pana Broučka* (Mr. Brouček's Excursions; Prague, 1920); *Antonín Dvořák* (Prague, 1929; 4th ed., 1947; Eng. tr., Prague, 1952, as *Antonín Dvořák: His Life and Work*); *Dvořákova citanka* (A Dvořák Reader; Prague, 1929; 3d ed., 1946; Eng. tr., Prague, 1954); *Dvořák ve vzpomínkach a dopisech* (Prague, 1938; 9th ed., 1951; Eng. tr., Prague, 1954, as *Dvořák: Letters and Reminiscences*; Ger. tr., 1955; Russian tr., 1964); *Smetanova Ma vlast* (Prague, 1940); *Antonin Dvořák přátelům doma* (Dvořák to His Friends at Home; 395 letters; Prague, 1941); *Antonín Dvořák a Hans Richter* (Letters to Richter; Prague, 1942).

Sousa, John Philip, famous American bandmaster and composer; b. Washington, D.C., Nov. 6, 1854; d. Reading, Pa., March 6, 1932. He was the son of a Portuguese father and a German mother. He studied violin and orchestration with John Esputa Jr. and violin and harmony with George Felix Benkert in Washington, D.C.; he also acquired considerable proficiency on wind instruments. After playing in the Marine Band (1868–75), he was active in theater orchs.; in 1876 he was a violinist in the special orch. in Philadelphia conducted by Offenbach during his U.S. tour. In 1880 he was appointed director of the Marine Band, which he led with distinction until 1892. He then organized his own band and led it in its first concert in Plainfield, N.J., on Sept. 26, 1892. In subsequent years he gave successful concerts throughout the United States and Canada; he played at the Chicago World's Fair in 1893 and at the Paris Exposition in 1900; he made 4 European tours (1900, 1901, 1903, and 1905), with increasing acclaim, and finally a tour around the world, in 1910–11. His flair for writing band music was extraordinary; the infectious rhythms of his military marches and the brilliance of his band arrangements earned him the sobriquet "The March King"; particularly celebrated is his march "The Stars and Stripes Forever," which became famous all over the world; in 1987 a bill was passed in the U.S. Congress and duly signed by President Ronald Reagan making it the official march of the United States. During World War I, Sousa served as a lieutenant in the Naval Reserve. He continued his annual tours almost to the time of his death. He was instrumental in the development of the Sousaphone, a bass tuba with upright bell, which has been used in bands since the 1890s.

WORKS (in alphabetical order): DRAMATIC: OPERETTAS: *The American Maid* (1909; Rochester, N.Y., Jan. 27, 1913); *The Bride Elect* (New Haven, Conn., Dec. 28, 1897); *El Capitan* (1895; Boston, April 13, 1896); *The Charlatan* (Montreal, Aug. 29, 1898); *Chris and the Wonderful Lamp* (New Haven, Conn., Oct. 23, 1899); *Desirée* (1883; Washington, D.C., May 1, 1884); *The Free Lance* (1905; Springfield, Mass., March 26, 1906); *The Irish Dragoon* (1915; unfinished); *Katherine* (1879); *The Queen of Hearts* (1885; Washington, D.C., April 12, 1886); *The Smugglers* (Washington, D.C., March 25, 1882). Also incidental music.

WRITINGS: AUTOBIOGRAPHICAL: *Through the Years with Sousa* (1910); *Marching Along* (1928). MANUALS: *The Trumpet and Drum* (1886); *National Patriotic and Typical Airs of All Lands* (1890). NOVELS: *The Fifth String* (1902); *Pipetown Sandy* (1905); *The Transit of Venus* (1919).

BIBL.: M. Simon, *J. P. S., the March King* (N.Y., 1944); A. Lingg, *J. P. S.* (N.Y., 1954); K. Berger, *The March King and His Band* (N.Y., 1957); P. Bierley, *J. P. S.: American Phenomenon* (N.Y., 1973; 2d ed., rev., 1986); idem, *J. P. S.: A Descriptive Catalog of His Works* (Urbana, Ill., 1973; 2d ed., rev. and aug., 1984, as *The Works of J. P. S.*); J. Newsom, ed., *Perspectives on J. P. S.* (Washington, D.C., 1983).

Soustrot, Marc, French conductor; b. Lyons, April 15, 1949. He studied at the Lyons Cons. (1962–69) and then was a student at the Paris Cons. (1969–76) of Paul Bernard (trombone), Christian Lardé (chamber music), Claude Ballif (analysis), and Manuel Rosenthal and Georges Tzipine (conducting). In 1974 he won the Rupert conducting competition in London, and was Previn's assistant with the London Sym. Orch. from 1974 to 1976. In 1975 he won the Besançon conducting competition. He was made 2d conductor of l'Orchestre Philharmonique des Pays de la Loire in Angers in 1976, and then was its music director from 1978. From 1986 to 1990 he concurrently served as artistic director of the Nantes Opera. From 1995 he was music director of the Brabant Phil. in Eindhoven and from 1997 he was Generalmusikdirektor of the Orchester der Beethovenhalle and the Opera in Bonn. As a guest conductor, Soustrot appeared with various orchs. and opera houses in Europe.

Souzay, Gérard (real name, **Gérard Marcel Tisserand**), distinguished French baritone; b. Angers, Dec. 8, 1918. He studied voice with Pierre Bernac, Claire Croiza, Vanni Marcoux, and Lotte Lehmann, and was a student at the Paris Cons. (1940–45). He made his recital debut in Paris in 1945, his U.S. debut in a recital at N.Y.'s Town Hall in 1950, and his operatic debut as Count Robinson in Cimarosa's *Il Matrimonio segreto* at the Aix-en-Provence Festival in 1957. He made his Metropolitan Opera debut in New York as Count Almaviva in *Le nozze di Figaro* on Jan. 21, 1965. In subsequent years, he toured extensively, mainly as a recitalist. In 1985 he joined the faculty of the Indiana Univ. School of Music in Bloomington; he taught at the Univ. of Texas in Austin in 1986. Souzay won renown as a concert artist; after Bernac, he was esteemed as the foremost interpreter of French art songs; equally acclaimed were his performances of German lieder, which received encomiums from German critics and audiences.

BIBL.: M. Morris, *The Recorded Performances of G. S.: A Discography* (N.Y., 1991).

Soyer, Roger (Julien Jacques), French bass; b. Paris, Sept. 1, 1939. He began his training with Daum, and then studied with

Jouatte and Musy at the Paris Cons., where he won premiers prix in singing (1962) and opera (1963). In 1962 he made his debut at the Piccola Scala in Milan as Poulenc's Tiresias. From 1963 he sang at the Paris Opéra. In 1964 he appeared as Pluto in Monteverdi's *Orfeo* at the Aix-en-Provence Festival, where he sang with much success in subsequent years. In 1968 he made his U.S. debut in Miami as Friar Lawrence in *Roméo et Juliette*, and also appeared at the Wexford Festival in England in *La Jolie Fille*. He made his Metropolitan Opera debut in New York in one of his finest roles, Don Giovanni, on Nov. 16, 1972. He also chose that role for his first appearance at the Edinburgh Festival in 1973. In subsequent years, he sang with principal European opera houses and festivals. He also appeared widely as a concert artist. Among his other admired roles were Don Basilio, Méphistophélès, Ferrando, Colline, and Sulpice.

Spadavecchia, Antonio (Emmanuilovich), Russian composer; b. Odessa, June 3, 1907; d. Moscow, Feb. 7, 1988. He was of Italian descent. After training with Shebalin at the Moscow Cons. (graduated, 1937), he completed his studies with Prokofiev (1944).

WORKS: DRAMATIC: OPERAS: *Ak-Buzat* (The Magic Steed; Ufa, Nov. 7, 1942; rev. 1952; in collaboration with Zaimov); *Khozyaka gostinitis* (The Inn Hostess; Moscow, April 24, 1949); *Khozhdeniye po mukam* (Pilgrimage of Sorrows; Perm, Dec. 29, 1953); *Ovod* (The Gadfly; Perm, Nov. 8, 1957); *Braviy soldat Shveky* (1963); *Yukki* (1970); *Ognenniye godi* (Ordeal by Fire; 1971). BALLETS: *Vragie* (Enemies; Moscow, May 20, 1938); *Bereg schastya* (The Shore of Happiness; Moscow, Nov. 6, 1948; rev. 1955). Also musical comedies, incidental music, and film scores.

Spani, Hina (real name, **Higinia Tunon**), Argentine soprano; b. Puan, Feb. 15, 1896; d. Buenos Aires, July 11, 1969. She studied in Buenos Aires and Milan. She made her operatic debut at La Scala in Milan in 1915 as Anna in Catalani's *Loreley*; she also sang in Turin, Naples, and Parma; she made many appearances at the Teatro Colón in Buenos Aires (1915–40). From 1946 she taught voice in Buenos Aires, and from 1952 served as director of the School of Music at the Univ. of Buenos Aires. She was highly regarded as a dramatic soprano; her repertoire included more than 70 roles.

Spano, Robert, American conductor and pianist; b. Conneaup, Ohio, May 7, 1961. He studied conducting with Robert Baustian at the Oberlin (Ohio) College-Cons. of Music, where he also received training in piano, violin, and composition; he later completed his conducting studies with Max Rudolf at the Curtis Inst. of Music in Philadelphia. In 1989 he became music director of the Opera Theater at Oberlin College. From 1990 to 1993 he was assistant conductor of the Boston Sym. Orch.; he subsequently toured widely as a guest conductor of major orchs. throughout North America, Europe, and Asia. In 1994 he received the Seaver/NEA conductors award. During the 1994–95 season, he made his debut at London's Covent Garden conducting *Billy Budd*. He was music director designate (1995–96) and then music director (from 1996) of the Brooklyn Phil. In 1999 he became director of the Tanglewood Music Center conducting program.

Speaks, Oley, American baritone and song composer; b. Canal Winchester, Ohio, June 28, 1874; d. N.Y., Aug. 27, 1948. He studied singing with Emma Thursby and composition with Max Spicker and W. Macfarlane. He sang at various churches in New York (1898–1906), then devoted himself entirely to concert singing and composition. He wrote some of the most popular songs in the American repertoire of his day: "On the Road to Mandalay" (1907), "Morning" (1910), "To You" (1910), "Sylvia" (1914), and "The Prayer Perfect" (1930).

Spelman, Timothy (Mather), American composer; b. Brooklyn, Jan. 21, 1891; d. Florence, Italy, Aug. 21, 1970. He studied with H. R. Shelley in New York (1908), W. R. Spalding and E. B. Hill at Harvard Univ. (1909–13), and Walter Courvoisier at the Munich Cons. (1913–15); he returned to the United States in 1915 and was active as director of a military band. After 1918 he went back to Europe with his wife, the poetess Leolyn Everett, settling in Florence. He returned to the United States in 1935; in 1947 he went back to Florence. His music was performed more often in Europe than in America; indeed, his style of composition is exceedingly European, influenced by Italian Romanticism and French Impressionism.

WORKS: DRAMATIC: *Snowdrop*, pantomime (Brooklyn, 1911); *The Romance of the Rose*, "wordless fantasy" (Boston, 1913; rev., St. Paul, Minn., Dec. 4, 1915); *La Magnifica*, music drama after Leolyn Everett-Spelman (1920); *The Sea Rovers*, opera (1928); *The Sunken City*, opera (1930); *Babakan*, fantastic comedy (1935); *The Courtship of Miles Standish*, opera after Longfellow (1943).

Spendiarov, Alexander (Afanasii), significant Armenian composer; b. Kakhovka, Crimea, Nov. 1, 1871; d. Yerevan, May 7, 1928. He studied violin as a child; in 1896 he went to St. Petersburg and took private lessons with Rimsky-Korsakov. In his works, he cultivated a type of Russian orientalism in which the elements of folk songs of the peripheral regions of the old Russian empire are adroitly arranged in the colorful harmonies of the Russian national school. His best work in this manner was an opera, *Almast*, the composition of which he undertook a decade before his death. It was completed and orchestrated by Maximilian Steinberg, and performed posthumously in Moscow on June 23, 1930. A complete ed. of his works was publ. in Yerevan (1943–71).

BIBL.: A. Shaverdian, *A. S.* (Moscow, 1929); G. Tigranov, *A. S.* (Moscow, 1959; 2d ed., 1971); R. Atadjan, *A. S.* (Yerevan, 1971).

Sperry, Paul, American tenor; b. Chicago, April 14, 1934. He studied psychology at Harvard Univ., then attended the Sorbonne in Paris; returning to the United States, he took courses at the Harvard Business School. He then decided upon a career in music, and proceeded to take vocal lessons from a number of coaches, among them Olga Ryss, Michael Trimble, Randolph Mickelson, Martial Singher, Pierre Bernac, Jennie Tourel, and Hans Hotter. He made his debut at Alice Tully Hall in New York on Oct. 8, 1969, then toured throughout the United States and Europe. He became chiefly known for his performances of contemporary scores. From 1989 to 1992 he served as president of the American Music Center in N.Y.

Spies, Hermine, eminent German contralto; b. Lohneberger Hutte, near Weilburg, Feb. 25, 1857; d. Wiesbaden, Feb. 26, 1893. She was a pupil of Stockhausen in Frankfurt am Main, and in 1883 began to give song recitals in Germany. In 1889 she made an appearance in England with excellent success; she also sang in Austria, Denmark, and Russia. She excelled as an interpreter of songs by Brahms, who had a high regard for her.

BIBL.: M. Spies, *H. S.: Ein Gedenkbuch für ihre Freunde* (Stuttgart, 1894).

Spies, Leo, German conductor and composer; b. Moscow, June 4, 1899; d. Ahrenshoop an der Ostsee, May 1, 1965. He studied with Oskar von Riesemann (1913–15), then continued his training with Schreyer in Dresden and with Kahn and Humperdinck at the Berlin Hochschule für Musik (1916–17). He worked as a répétiteur and conductor in German theaters and with the Universum Film AG; he then was in Berlin as conductor of the ballet at the State Opera (1928–35) and the Deutsche Opernhaus (1935–44); subsequently he was director of studies and conductor at the Komische Oper (1947–54). In 1956 he was awarded the National Prize of the German Democratic Republic. His compositions followed Romantic lines. Among his works are the ballets *Apollo und Daphne* (1936), *Der Stralauer Fischzug* (1936), *Seefahrt* (1937), *Die Sonne lacht* (1942), *Pastorale* (1943), *Die Liebenden von Verona* (1944), and *Don Quijote* (1944); also incidental music.

Spiess, Ludovic, Romanian tenor; b. Cluj, May 13, 1938. He studied in Braşov, Bucharest, and with Antonio Narducci in Milan (1965–66). In 1962 he made his operatic debut as the Duke of Mantua in Galaţi. After singing at the Bucharest Operetta Theater (1962–64), he made his first appearance at the Bucharest Opera as Cavaradossi in 1964, where he subsequently sang regularly. In

1967 he made his debut at the Salzburg Festival as Dmitri in *Boris Godunov*. In 1968 he made his first appearances in Zürich as Radames and at the Vienna State Opera as Dalibor. He sang Calaf at the Verona Arena in 1969. On June 3, 1971, he made his Metropolitan Opera debut in New York as Manrico. He sang Radames at his Covent Garden debut in London in 1973. He also appeared with many other opera houses in Europe and North and South America. Among his other roles were Florestan, Lohengrin, Otello, Don José, and Rodolfo.

Spilka, František, Czech choral conductor, pedagogue, and composer; b. Štěken, Nov. 13, 1887; d. Prague, Oct. 20, 1960. He studied at the Prague Cons. with Stecker, Knittl, and Dvořák. In 1918 he was appointed administrative director of the Prague Cons. He established the Prague Teachers' Choral Soc. in 1908, of which he remained choirmaster until 1921, and gave concerts with it in France and England; he later directed the Prague singing ensemble Smetana. Spilka developed, together with Ferdinand Vach, a new approach to choral performance, emphasizing sound color. Among his works are the operas *Stará práva* (Ancient Rights; 1915; Prague, June 10, 1917) and *Cain or The Birth of Death* (1917); also *Jan Hus at the Stake*, oratorio (1907).

Spinelli, Nicola, Italian pianist, conductor, and composer; b. Turin, July 29, 1865; d. Rome, Oct. 17, 1909. He studied with Sgambati in Rome and at the Naples Cons. under Serrao. In 1889 his opera *Labilia* took 2d prize in the famous competition instituted by the publisher Sonzogno, when Mascagni won the 1st prize with *Cavalleria rusticana*; Spinelli's opera was produced in Rome on May 7, 1890, with indifferent success. His next opera, *A basso porto*, was more fortunate; after its initial production in Cologne on April 18, 1894 (in a German version), it was staged in Rome, in Italian (March 11, 1895), and then in Budapest, St. Petersburg, etc.; it was also produced in the United States (St. Louis, Jan. 8, 1900; N.Y., Jan. 22, 1900). He toured widely as a pianist from 1889 to 1894. He was then active as a conductor until becoming mentally ill.

Spink, Ian (Walter Alfred), noted English musicologist; b. London, March 29, 1932. He studied at London's Trinity College of Music (B.Mus., 1952) and pursued postgraduate studies at the Univ. of Birmingham (diss., 1957–58, *The English Declamatory Ayre, c. 1620–60*). He served as an overseas examiner for Trinity College of Music (1958–60), then was senior lecturer at the Univ. of Sydney (1962–69); subsequently he was head of the music dept. of Royal Holloway College at the Univ. of London (from 1969), where he was a reader (1971–74) and a prof. (from 1974); he also was dean of the Faculty of Arts (1973–75; 1983–85) and of the Faculty of Music (1974–78). A learned authority on English lute songs, he ed. the valuable collection English Songs, 1625–1660 for the Musica Britannica series, XXXIII (1971); he also authored *An Historical Approach to Musical Form* (London, 1967) and *English Song: Dowland to Purcell* (London, 1974; rev. 1986), and ed. vol. 3, *The Seventeenth Century*, in *The Blackwell History of Music in Britain* (1992).

Spisak, Michal, eminent Polish composer; b. Dabrowa Górnicza, Sept. 14, 1914; d. Paris, Jan. 29, 1965. He studied violin and composition at the Katowice Cons. (diplomas in both, 1937), and composition with Sikorski in Warsaw (1935–37). He completed his training with Boulanger in Paris, where he lived for the rest of his life although he continued to be closely associated with his homeland. In 1964 he was awarded the Polish Composers' Union Prize. He was greatly influenced by Boulanger and by the music of Stravinsky. Among his works was the opera *Marynka* (1955).

Spitzmüller (-Harmersbach), Alexander, Freiherr von, Austrian composer; b. Vienna, Feb. 22, 1894; d. Paris, Nov. 12, 1962. His father was the last finance minister of Austria-Hungary. He studied law at the Univ. of Vienna (D.Jur., 1919); he later took lessons in composition with Alban Berg and Hans Apostel. In 1928 he went to Paris, where he taught at the Schola Cantorum; he also was active in radio broadcasting and as a music critic. In 1959 he was awarded the music prize of the city of Vienna. His early works are in the neoclassical vein; eventually he followed the method of composition with 12 tones, following its usage by Berg and Webern. His works included the opera *Der Diener zweier Herren* (1958) and the ballets *Le premier amour de Don Juan* (1954), *L'impasse* (1956), *Die Sackgasse* (1957), *Le journal* (1957), and *Construction humaine* (1959).

Spohr, Louis (Ludewig), celebrated German violinist, composer, and conductor; b. Braunschweig, April 5, 1784; d. Kassel, Oct. 22, 1859. His name is entered in the church registry as Ludewig, but he used the French equivalent, Louis. The family moved to Seesen in 1786; his father, a physician, played the flute, and his mother was an amateur singer and pianist. Spohr began violin lessons at the age of 5 with J. A. Riemenschneider and Dufour, a French émigré. In 1791 he returned to Braunschweig, where he studied with the organist Carl August Hartung and the violinist Charles Louis Maucourt; he also composed several violin pieces. Duke Carl Wilhelm Ferdinand admitted him to the ducal orch. and arranged for his further study with the violinist Franz Eck. In 1802 Eck took him on a tour to Russia, where he met Clementi and Field; he returned to Braunschweig in 1803 and resumed his post in the ducal orch. The violin technique and compositional traits of Pierre Rode, whom Spohr met on his return, were major influences on both his compositions and his violin technique. In 1804 Spohr made his first official tour as a violinist to Hamburg (his 1st actual tour to Hamburg in 1799 proved a failure, and a 2d, early in 1804, was aborted when his Guarnerius violin was stolen); he gave concerts in Berlin, Leipzig, and Dresden. In 1805 he became concertmaster in the ducal orch. at Gotha. On Feb. 2, 1806, he married the harpist Dorette (Dorothea) Scheidler (1787–1834); he wrote many works for violin and harp for them to perform together, and also toured with her in Germany (1807). His reputation as a virtuoso established, he began writing compositions in every genre, all of which obtained excellent success. In 1812 he gave a series of concerts in Vienna and was acclaimed both as a composer and as a violinist; he was concertmaster in the orch. of the Theater an der Wien until 1815. He then made a grand tour of Germany and Italy, where Paganini heard him in Venice. In 1816 Spohr's opera *Faust*, skillfully employing many devices that foreshadowed developments in later German operas, was performed by Weber in Prague. After a visit to Holland in 1817, he became Kapellmeister of the Frankfurt am Main Opera, where he produced one of his most popular operas, *Zemire und Azor*. In 1820 he and his wife visited England and appeared at several concerts of the London Phil. Soc.; this was the first of his 6 visits to England, where he acquired an immense reputation as a violinist, composer, and conductor; his works continued to be performed there long after his death. On his return trip to Germany, he presented concerts in Paris; his reception there, however, failed to match his London successes, and he proceeded to Dresden, where Weber recommended him for the Kapellmeistership at the court in Kassel; attracted by the lifetime contract, Spohr accepted the post and settled there in 1822, producing his operatic masterpiece, *Jessonda*, which remained popular throughout the rest of the 19th century, in 1823. Following this success were performances of his oratorio *Die letzten Dinge* (1826) and his 4th Sym., *Die Weihe der Töne* (1832), both of which elicited great praise. The *Violinschule*, a set of 66 studies covering every aspect of his violin style, was publ. in 1831. Spohr's wife died on Nov. 20, 1834, and on Jan. 3, 1836, he married the pianist Marianne Pfeiffer, the sister of his friend Carl Pfeiffer, librettist of *Der Alchymist*. In 1837 Spohr began having difficulties with the electoral prince of Kassel, who caused the cancellation of a festival in Kassel and forbade Spohr from making a trip to Prague, which the composer made nevertheless to conduct *Der Berggeist*; on his return he visited Mozart's widow and birthplace in Salzburg. He traveled to England in 1839 for the Norwich Festival, but could not obtain permission from the prince to return for the performance of his *Fall of Babylon* in 1842. In 1841, returning from the Lucerne Festival, he received the suggestion from his wife to use 2 orchs. for his 7th Sym. in 3 parts, portraying the mundane and divine elements in life. In 1843, in England, his success was so great that a special concert was given by royal command; it was the first time a reigning English monarch attended a Phil. Concert. In 1844 he received the silver medal from the Société des Concerts in Paris, and a festival honoring him was held in Braunschweig. Spohr never visited the United States, in spite of the fact that his daughter lived in New York and an invitation to hold a festival in his honor was issued. In 1845 he received a golden wreath from the Berlin Royal Opera. In 1847 he visited England for the 3d time, then went to Frankfurt am Main for the German National Assembly. Returning to Kassel, he found himself in an increasingly difficult position because of his dissident political views. The elector of Hesse refused him further leaves of absence, but Spohr ignored the ban, traveling to Switzerland and Italy. In the litigation that followed with the Kassel court, Spohr was ordered to forfeit part of his yearly income. He was retired from Kassel on Nov. 22, 1857, on a pension despite his lifetime contract. In 1853 he appeared at the New Phil. Concerts in London. Although he fractured his left arm in a fall on Dec. 27, 1857, he conducted *Jessonda* in Prague in July 1858. He conducted his last performance in Meiningen (1859).

Spohr's compositional style was characteristic of the transition period between Classicism and Romanticism. He was technically a master; while some of his works demonstrate a spirit of bold experimentation. In his aesthetics he was an intransigent conservative. He admired Beethoven's early works but confessed total inability to understand those of his last period; he also failed to appreciate Weber. It is remarkable, therefore, that he was an early champion of Wagner; in Kassel he produced *Der fliegende Holländer* (1843) and *Tannhäuser* (1853), despite strenuous opposition from the court. He was a highly esteemed teacher, numbering among his students Ferdinand David and Moritz Hauptmann. His memoirs were publ. posthumously as *Louis Spohrs Selbstbiographie* (2 vols., Kassel, 1860–61; abr. version in Eng., London, 1865, 1878, and 1969; different tr. by H. Pleasants as *The Musical Journeys of Louis Spohr*, Norman, Okla., 1961). A new ed., edited by F. Göthel using the autograph, was publ. as *Lebenserinnerungen* (Tutzing, 1968). The Spohr Soc. was founded in Kassel in 1908, disbanded in 1934, and revived in 1952. A new ed. of his works, *Neue Auswahl der Werke*, edited by F. Göthel, was begun in 1963 (Kassel, Verlag der Spohr-Gesellschaft). A *Thematisch-bibliographisches Verzeichnis der Werke von Louis Spohr*, compiled by F. Göthel, was publ. in Tutzing in 1981.

WORKS: DRAMATIC (all 1st perf. in Kassel unless otherwise given): OPERAS: *Die Prüfung* (1806); *Alruna, die Eulenkönigin* (1808); *Der Zweikampf mit der Geliebten* (Hamburg, Nov. 15, 1811); *Faust* (1813; Prague, Sept. 1, 1816; rev. 1852; London, July 15, 1852); *Zemire und Azor* (Frankfurt am Main, April 4, 1819); *Jessonda* (July 28, 1823); *Der Berggeist* (March 24, 1825); *Pietro von Abano* (Oct. 13, 1827); *Der Alchymist* (July 28, 1830); *Die Kreuzfahrer* (Jan. 1, 1845). ORATORIOS: *Das jüngste Gericht* (Erfurt, Aug. 15, 1812); *Die letzten Dinge* (March 25, 1826); *Des Heilands letzte Stunden* (Easter 1835); *Der Fall Babylons* (Norwich Festival, Sept. 14, 1842).

BIBL.: W. Neumann, *L. S.* (Kassel, 1854); H. Giehne, *Zur Erinnerung an L. S.* (Karlsruhe, 1860); A. Malibran, *L. S.* (Frankfurt am Main, 1860); L. Stierlin, *L. S.* (2 vols., Zürich, 1862–63); M. Hauptmann, *Briefe von M. Hauptmann an L. S. und andere* (Leipzig, 1876; Eng. tr., London, 1892); H. Schletterer, *L. S.* (Leipzig, 1881); L. Nohl, *S.* (Leipzig, 1882); C. Robert, *L. S.* (Berlin, 1883); R. Wassermann, *L. S. als Opernkomponist* (diss., Univ. of Rostock, 1910); E. von Salburg, *L. S.* (Leipzig, 1936); F. Göthel, *L. S.: Briefwechsel mit seiner Frau Dorette* (Kassel, 1957); D. Mayer, *The Forgotten Master: The Life and Times of L. S.* (London, 1959); D. Greiner, *L. S.: Beiträge zur deutschen romantischen Oper* (diss., Univ. of Kiel, 1960); C. Brown, *The Popularity and Influence of S. in England* (diss., Oxford Univ., 1980); P. Katow, *L. S.: Persönlichkeit und Werk* (Luxembourg, 1983); C. Brown, *L. S.: A Critical Biography* (Cambridge, 1984); H. Peters, *Der Komponist, Geiger, Dirigent und Pädagoge L. S. (1784–1859) mit einer Auswahlbibliographie zu Leben und Schaffen* (Braunschweig, 1987).

Spontini, Gaspare (Luigi Pacifico), significant Italian opera composer; b. Majolati, Ancona, Nov. 14, 1774; d. there, Jan. 24, 1851. His father, a modest farmer, intended him for the church and gave him into the charge of an uncle, a priest at Jesi, who attempted to stifle his musical aspirations. Spontini sought refuge at Monte San Vito with another relative, who not only found a competent music teacher for him, but effected a reconciliation so that, after a year, he was able to return to Jesi. In 1793 he entered the Cons. della Pietà de' Turchini in Naples, where his teachers were Tritto (singing) and Sala (composition). When he failed to obtain the position of maestrino there in 1795, he quit the Cons. without permission. He rapidly mastered the conventional Italian style of his time; some of his church music performed in Naples came to the attention of a director of the Teatro della Pallacorda in Rome, who commissioned him to write an opera. This was *Li puntigli delle donne*, produced during Carnival in 1796. He served as maestro di cappella at Naples's Teatro del Fondo during Carnival in 1800, and that same year went to Palermo to produce 3 operas. Returning to the mainland in 1801, he produced operas for Rome and Venice before going to Paris in 1803. After eking out an existence as a singing teacher, he found a patron in Joséphine. He first gained success as a composer in Paris with a revised version of his *La finta filosofa* (Feb. 11, 1804); it was followed by *La Petite Maison* (May 12, 1804), which proved unsuccessful. All the same, the poet Etienne de Jouy now approached Spontini to write the music to his libretto *La Vestale*, a task previously turned down by Boieldieu, Cherubini, and Méhul. In the meantime, Spontini brought out 2 more operas without much success: *Milton* (Nov. 27, 1804) and *Julie, ou Le Pot de fleurs* (March 12, 1805). However, he won appointment as composer of Joséphine's private music in 1805; for her he wrote several occasional pieces, including the cantata *L'eccelsa gara* (Feb. 8, 1806), celebrating the battle of Austerlitz. Thanks to Josephine's patronage, *La Vestale* won a triumphant success at its premiere on Dec. 15, 1807, in spite of virulent opposition. Spontini's next opera, *Fernand Cortez* (Nov. 28, 1809), failed to equal his previous success, although the 2d version (May 8, 1817) won it a place in the repertoire. In 1810 he was awarded the prix décennal for having composed the finest grand opera of the preceding decade; that same year he married Céleste Erard, daughter of Jean-Baptiste Erard, and accepted the post of director of the Théâtre-Italien. Although his artistic policies were successful, his personality clashed with those of his superiors and he was dismissed in 1812. On Aug. 23, 1814, his opera *Pélage, ou Le Roi et la paix*, celebrating the Restoration, was successfully produced. The following month he was named director of Louis XVIII's private music and of the Théâtre-Italien, although soon after he sold his privilege to the latter to Catalani. Having become a favorite of the Bourbons, he was made a French citizen by the king in 1817 and was granted a pension in 1818. In spite of his favored position, his grand opera *Olimpie* proved a dismal failure at its premiere on Dec. 22, 1819. The next year he went to Berlin as Generalmusikdirektor, scoring an initial success with the revised version of *Olimpie* on May 14, 1821. However, his position of eminence quickly waned. He had been placed on an equality with the Intendant of the Royal Theater, and there were frequent misunderstandings and sharp clashes of authority, not mitigated by Spontini's jealousies and dislikes, his overweening self-conceit, and his despotic temper. Partly through intrigue, partly by reason of his own lack of self-control, he was formally charged in criminal court with lèse-majesté in Jan. 1841. On April 2, 1841, while he was conducting the overture to *Don Giovanni*, a riot ensued and Spontini was compelled to leave the hall in disgrace. In July 1841 he was sentenced to 9 months in prison, and soon thereafter was dismissed as Generalmusikdirektor by the king, although he was allowed to retain his title and salary. In May 1842 his sentence was upheld by an appeals court, but the king pardoned him that same month. He then went to Paris, where illness and growing deafness overtook him. In 1844 he was raised to the papal nobility as the Conte di San Andrea. In 1850 he retired to his birthplace to die. Spontini's importance to the lyric theater rests upon his effective blending of Italian and French elements in his serious operas, most notably in *La Vestale* and *Fernand Cortez*. His influence on Berlioz was particularly notable.

WORKS: DRAMATIC: OPERAS: *Li puntigli delle donne*, farsetta (Rome, Carnival 1796); *Il finto pittore* (Rome?, 1797 or 1798); *Adelina Senese, o sia L'amore secreto*, dramma giocoso (Venice, Oct. 10, 1797); *L'eroismo ridicolo*, farsa (Naples, Carnival 1798); *Il Teseo riconosciuto*, dramma per musica (Florence, 1798); *La finta filosofa*, commedia per musica (Naples, 1799; rev. as a dramma giocoso per musica, Paris, Feb. 11, 1804); *La fuga in maschera*, commedia per musica (Naples, Carnival 1800); *I quadri parlante*, melodramma buffo (Palermo, 1800); *Gli Elisi delusi*, melodramma serio (Palermo, Aug. 26, 1800); *Gli amanti in cimento, o sia Il Geloso audace*, dramma giocoso (Rome, Nov. 3, 1801); *Le metamorfosi di Pasquale, o sia Tutto è illusione nel mondo*, farsa giocosa (Venice, Carnival 1802); *La Petite Maison*, opéra comique (Paris, May 12, 1804); *Milton*, opéra comique (Paris, Nov. 27, 1804); *Julie, ou Le Pot de fleurs*, opéra comique (Paris, March 12, 1805); *La Vestale*, tragédie-lyrique (Paris, Dec. 15, 1807); *Fernand Cortez, ou La Conquête du Mexique*, tragédie-lyrique (Paris, Nov. 28, 1809; 2d version, Paris, May 8, 1817; 3d version, Berlin, Feb. 1832); *Pélage, ou Le Roi et la paix*, opera (Paris, Aug. 23, 1814); *Les Dieux rivaux ou Les Fêtes de Cythère*, opéra ballet (Paris, June 21, 1816; in collaboration with Kreutzer, Persuis, and Berton); *Olimpie*, tragédie-lyrique (Paris, Dec. 22, 1819; rev. as a grosse Oper, Berlin, May 14, 1821); *Nurmahal, oder Das Rosenfest von Caschmir*, lyrisches Drama (Berlin, May 27, 1822); *Alcidor*, Zauberoper (Berlin, May 23, 1825); *Agnes von Hohenstaufen*, lyrisches Drama (Act 1 only, Berlin, May 28, 1827; 2d version as a grosse historisch-romantische Oper, Berlin, June 12, 1829; rev. version, Berlin, Dec. 6, 1837). OTHER: *L'eccelsa gara*, cantata (Paris, Feb. 8, 1806); *Tout le monde a tort*, vaudeville (Malmaison, March 17, 1806); *Lalla Rûkh*, Festspiel (Berlin, May 27, 1822).

BIBL.: L. Rellstab, *Über mein Verhältnis als Kritiker zu Herrn S. als Componist und General Musikdirektor* (Leipzig, 1827); E. Oettinger, *S.* (Leipzig, 1843); D. Raoul-Rochette, *Notice historique sur la vie et les oeuvres de M. S.* (Paris, 1852); C. Bouvet, *S.* (Paris, 1930); K. Schubert, *S.s italienische Schule* (Strasbourg, 1932); A. Ghizlanzoni, *G. S.* (Rome, 1951); P. Fragapane, *S.* (Bologna, 1954); A. Belardinelli, *Documenti s.ani inediti* (Florence, 1955); F. Schlitzer, *La finta filosofa di G. S.* (Naples, 1957); P. Fragapane, *S.* (Florence, 1983).

Spoorenberg, Erna, Dutch soprano; b. Yogyakarta, Java, April 11, 1926. She studied in Hilversum and Amsterdam. She made her debut in an appearance with Radio Hilversum in 1947. In 1958 she became a leading member of the Netherlands Opera in Amsterdam. She made occasional appearances at various European music centers, but principally was associated with the musical life of the Netherlands; she made her first appearance at the Vienna State Opera in 1949 and her U.S. debut in New York in 1967. She was especially esteemed for her roles in operas by Mozart and for her portrayal of Mélisande. She also pursued a successful career as a concert singer.

Spratlan, Lewis, American composer and teacher; b. Miami, Sept. 5, 1940. He studied composition with Wyner, Schuller, and Powell at Yale Univ. (B.A., 1962; M.M., 1965), then studied with Rochberg and Sessions at the Berkshire Music Center in Tanglewood (1966); he held a Guggenheim fellowship (1980–81). He taught at Bay Path Junior College (1965–67), Pennsylvania State Univ. (1967–70), and at Amherst College (from 1970), where he was made a prof. in 1980; he also served as chairman of its music dept. (1977–80; 1984; 1985–88; 1992; 1994). Among his works is the opera *Life Is a Dream* (1975–77); also *Unsleeping City*, dance music (1967).

Šrámek, Vladimír, Czech composer; b. Košice, March 3, 1923. He was a student of Picha at the Prague Cons. After working in the music division of the National Museum in Prague, he joined the staff of the Opera at the National Theater in Prague. In 1977 he became ed. of music at the FILIA. In his early works, Šrámek composed in a traditional style. Later he embraced avant-garde techniques. In his orch. score *The Astronauts* (1959), he introduced the Monophon, an electronic device of his own creation.

WORKS: DRAMATIC: *Driver to Aristofana*, opera (1955); *Flower of Cobalt*, radio opera (1963); *The Pit*, pantomime (1963); *Spectrum I* (1964), *II* (1964), and *III* (1965), music theater; *Light of the World*, pantomime (1964); *The Last Forest*, musical television play (1965).

Stabile, Mariano, prominent Italian baritone; b. Palermo, May 12, 1888; d. Milan, Jan. 11, 1968. He studied voice at the Accademia di Santa Cecilia in Rome. He made his operatic debut as Amonasro in Palermo (1909). For a number of seasons he sang in provincial opera houses in Italy. The turning point in his career came when he was engaged by Toscanini to sing Falstaff in Verdi's opera at La Scala (Dec. 26, 1921). He triumphed and the role became his major success; he sang it more than 1,000 times. His guest engagements took him to London's Covent Garden (1926–31), the Salzburg Festivals (1935–39), the Glyndebourne Festivals (1936–39), again in London (1946–49), and the Edinburgh Festival (1948). He retired in 1960. Among his other notable roles were Don Giovanni, Mozart's and Rossini's Figaro, Don Alfonso, Dr. Malatesta, Iago, Rigoletto, and Scarpia.

Stabinger, Mathias, German flutist, clarinetist, conductor, and composer; b. *c.*1750; d. Venice, *c.*1815. He was a flutist and clarinetist in Lyons in 1772, and then made his first appearance in Paris that same year. In 1777 he went to Italy, where he brought out the highly successful opera buffa *Le astuzie di Bettina* (Genoa, 1780), which subsequently was performed throughout Europe. In 1781 he was maestro al cembalo at the Warsaw Opera; in 1782 he was active with the Mattei-Orecia opera troupe in St. Petersburg, and then was associated with the Petrovsky Theater in Moscow. After another Italian sojourn (1783–85), he returned to Moscow as director of the orch. at the Petrovsky Theater, where he produced such successful stage works as *Schastlivaya Tonia* (Lucky Tonia; Jan. 14, 1786), *Baba Yaga* (Dec. 2, 1786), *Zhenitba neudachnaya* (The Unfortunate Marriage; Feb. 19, 1788), and *Orphée traversant l'enfer à la recherche d'Eurydice* (Feb. 22, 1792). About 1800 he returned once more to Italy, finally settling in Venice in 1814. He also wrote an oratorio, *Betulia liberata* (Moscow, March 26, 1783).

Stade, Frederica von. See **Von Stade, Frederica.**

Stader, Maria, noted Hungarian-born Swiss soprano; b. Budapest, Nov. 5, 1911. She studied voice with Keller in Karlsruhe, Durigo in Zürich, Lombardi in Milan, and T. Schnabel in New York; she won the Geneva International Competition (1939). After a brief career as an opera singer, she devoted herself to a distinguished concert career after World War II; she toured extensively in Europe, North America, and the Far East; following her retirement in 1969, she was active as a teacher. She was particularly esteemed as an interpreter of Mozart, in both operatic and concert settings.

Stadler, Abbé Maximilian (Johann Karl Dominik), prominent Austrian keyboard player, music historian, and composer; b. Melk, Aug. 4, 1748; d. Vienna, Nov. 8, 1833. He began his musical training with Johann Leuthner, a bass at the Melk Benedictine abbey, then went as a choirboy in 1758 to Lilienfeld, where he received instruction in violin, clavichord, and organ; he concurrently took music lessons with Albrechtsberger in Melk, and completed his education at the Jesuit College in Vienna in 1762. In 1766 he returned to Melk and became a novice; he took his vows in 1767 and was made a priest in 1772, then was head of the abbey's theological studies. After being made chaplain in Wullersdorf in 1783, he was elected prior of Melk in 1784. In 1786 he became abbot of Lilienfeld and in 1789 in Kremsmünster. After a sojourn in Linz (1791–96), he settled in Vienna. In 1803 he was secularized and was given the titular canonry of Linz; he was parish priest in Alt-Lerchenfeld (1803–10) and Grosskrut (1810–15), then was again active in Vienna. He was esteemed as a keyboard player and composer by his contemporaries; his oratorio *Die Befreyung von Jerusalem* (1813) was widely performed in his day. His *Materialen zur Geschichte der Musik unter den österreichischen Regenten* (*c.*1816–25) is duly recognized as the first Austrian history of music. He was a friend of Mozart, and took care of Mozart's MS of the Requiem, which he copied at Mozart's death. When the authenticity of the work was called into question by Gottfried Weber and others, Stadler publ. a pamphlet in its defense, *Vertheidigung der Echtheit des Mozartschen Requiems* (Vienna, 1825; supplement, 1826). His own compositions include, in addition to the above-cited oratorio, a Singspiel, *Das Studenten-Valete* (Melk, Sept. 6, 1781), and incidental music; also completions and arrangements of works by other composers.

WRITINGS: *Anleitung zur musikalischen Composition durch Würfelspiel* (MS, *c.*1780); *Erklärung, wir man aus . . . Ziffer-und Notentabellen eine Menuet herauswürfeln könne* (Vienna, 1781); *Priorats-Ephemeriden* (MS, 1784–86); *Beschreibung der Fragmente aus Mozart's Nachlass* (MS, *c.*1798); *Fragmente von Singstücken* (MS, *c.*1798); *Fragmente einiger Mozartischen Klavierstucke, die von einem Liebhaber der Musik vollendet worden* (MS; ed. in *Österreichische Musikzeitschrift*, XXI, 1966); *Materialen zur Geschichte der Musik unter den österreichischen Regenten* (MS, *c.*1816–25; ed. by K. Wagner, Kassel, 1974); *Eigenhändig geschriebene Selbst-Biographie des Hochwürdigen Herrn Maximilian Stadler* (MS, *c.*1816–26; ed. in *Mozart-Jahrbuch* 1957); *Vertheidigung der Echtheit des Mozartschen Requiems* (Vienna, 1825; supplement 1826); *Nachtrag zur Vertheidigung* (Vienna, 1827); *Zweyter und letzter Nachtrag zur Vertheidigung . . . sammt Nachbericht über die Ausgabe . . . durch Herrn André in Offenbach, nebst Ehrenrettung Mozart's und vier fremden Briefen* (Vienna, 1827); *Biographische Notizen über Abbé Maximilian Stadler von ihm selbst aufgezeichnet* (MS, *c.*1833; ed. in *Mozart-Jahrbuch* 1964).

BIBL.: H. Sabel, *M. S.s weltliche Werke und seine Beziehungen zur Wiener Klassik* (diss., Univ. of Cologne, 1941); K. Wagner, *A. M. S.* (Kassel, 1974).

Stadtfeld, Alexandre, composer; b. Wiesbaden, April 27, 1826; d. Brussels, Nov. 4, 1853. He studied with Fétis at the Brussels Cons., winning the Belgian Prix de Rome in 1849. He composed the operas *Hamlet* (Darmstadt, 1857), *Abu Hassan, L'Illusion*, and *La Pedrina*.

BIBL.: M. Weber, *A. S.: Leben und Werk* (Bonn, 1969).

Staempfli, Edward, Swiss composer, pianist, and conductor; b. Bern, Feb. 1, 1908. He received training in composition from Jarnach and Maler in Cologne (1929–30) and Dukas in Paris (1930), and in conducting from Scherchen in Brussels (1935). After living in Paris (1930–39), he returned to Switzerland. He went to Heidelberg in 1951 before settling in Berlin in 1954. He made occasional appearances as a pianist and conductor, usually in hs own works. His early music reflected his Parisian sojourn, but later he embraced 12-tone writing. Among his works are the operas *Ein Traumspiel* (1943), *Medea* (1954), and *Caligula* (1981–82) and several ballets.

Stagno, Roberto (real name, **Vincenzo Andriolo**), Italian tenor; b. Palermo, Oct. 11, 1840; d. Genoa, April 26, 1897. He studied with Giuseppe Lamperti in Milan, making his operatic debut as Rodrigo in Rossini's *Otello* in Lisbon (1862), then sang with notable success in Madrid (from 1865), Moscow (1868), and Buenos Aires (from 1879), and throughout Italy. While in Buenos Aires, he became the mentor of the soprano Gemma Bellincioni; their teacher-pupil relationship developed into intimacy, and they subsequently toured widely together. Their daughter, Bianca Stagno-Bellincioni (b. Budapest, Jan. 23, 1888; d. Milan, July 26, 1980), became a singer. Stagno was engaged for the first season of the Metropolitan Opera in New York, making his debut there as Manrico in *Il Trovatore* on Oct. 26, 1883; he remained there for only that season. In 1884 he appeared at the Paris Théâtre-Italien. He was chosen to create the role of Turiddu in *Cavalleria rusticana* opposite Bellincioni's Santuzza in Rome (1890).

BIBL.: B. Stagno-Bellincioni, *R. S. e Gemma Bellincioni, intimi* (Florence, 1943).

Stahlman, Sylvia, American soprano; b. Nashville, Tenn., March 5, 1933; d. St. Petersburg, Fla., Aug. 19, 1998. She studied voice at the Juilliard School of Music in New York. She then went to Europe and pursued her budding career under a suitably Italianate pseudonym, Giulia Bardi; she made her debut in Brussels in 1951; she then sang regularly in Frankfurt am Main (1954–72). In 1956, under her own name, she joined the N.Y. City Opera, then sang at San Francisco (1958) and Chicago (1960). She also toured as a concert artist.

Standford, Patric (John Patric Standford Gledhill), English composer and teacher; b. Barnsley, Feb. 5, 1939. He was a student of Edmund Rubbra and Raymond Jones at the Guildhall School of Music in London (1961–63); after receiving the Mendelssohn Scholarship in 1964, he continued his studies with Malipiero in Italy and with Lutoslawski. He taught at the Guildhall School of Music (1968–80) and also served as chairman of the Composer's Guild of Great Britain (1977–79). He was director of the music school at Bretton Hall College (Univ. of Leeds) in Wakefield (1980–93). In 1983 he was awarded the Ernest Ansermet prize of Geneva for his Sym. No. 3, *Toward Paradise* for Chorus and Orch. (1982; Geneva, June 11, 1986). Other works include the opera *Villon* (1972–85) and the ballets *Celestial Fall* (1968; orch. suite, 1971) and *Reflections* (1980).

Stanford, Sir Charles Villiers, eminent Irish organist, conductor, pedagogue, and composer; b. Dublin, Sept. 30, 1852; d. London, March 29, 1924. Brought up in an intellectual atmosphere, he was a diligent student in his early youth; he studied piano, organ, violin, and composition with Michael Quarry at St. Patrick's Cathedral, and with Robert Stewart and Joseph Robinson at the Royal Irish Academy of Music in Dublin; in 1862 he was sent to London, where he studied piano with Ernst Pauer and composition with Arthur O'Leary. In 1870 he entered Queen's College, Cambridge, as a choral scholar (B.A., 1874); he then studied composition with Reinecke in Leipzig (1874–76) and with Kiel in Berlin (1876); he was awarded the M.A. degree from Cambridge (1877). In 1883 he was appointed prof. of composition at the Royal College of Music and conductor of the orch. there. In 1887 he also became a prof. of music at Cambridge, holding both positions until his death. He was conductor of the Leeds Festivals from 1901 to 1910, and appeared as guest conductor of his own works in Paris, Berlin, Amsterdam, and Brussels. From 1885 to 1902 he conducted the London Bach Choir. He was knighted in 1902. Stanford was an extremely able and industrious composer in a distinctly Romantic style, yet unmistakably national in musical materials, both Irish and English. In recent years there has been renewed interest in and appreciation of his music, both in England and abroad.

WORKS: DRAMATIC: OPERAS: *The Veiled Prophet of Khorassan* (1877; Hannover, Feb. 6, 1881); *Savonarola* (Hamburg, April 18, 1884); *The Canterbury Pilgrims* (London, April 23, 1884); *Lorenza* (c.1894; not perf.); *Shamus O'Brian* (London, March 2, 1896); *Christopher Patch (The Barber of Bath)* (c.1897; not perf.); *Much Ado about Nothing* (London, May 30, 1901); *The Critic, or An Opera Rehearsed* (London, Jan. 14, 1916); *The Traveling Companion* (1919; amateur perf., Liverpool, April 30, 1925; professional perf., Bristol, Oct. 25, 1926). ORATORIO: *Eden* (Birmingham, 1891); *Mass* (London, 1893). Also incidental music.

WRITINGS (all publ. in London): *Studies and Memories* (1908); *Musical Composition: A Short Treatise for Students* (1911; 6th ed., 1950); *Brahms* (1912); *Pages from an Unwritten Diary* (1914); *Interludes: Records and Reflections* (1922).

BIBL.: J. Porte, *Sir C. V. S.* (London and N.Y., 1921); J. Fuller Maitland, *The Music of Parry and S.* (Cambridge, 1934); H. Plunket Greene, *C. V. S.* (London, 1935); G. Norris, *S., The Cambridge Jubilee and Tchaikovsky* (Newton Abbot, 1980).

Stanislavsky (real name, **Alexeiev**), **Konstantin (Sergeievich),** famous Russian actor and theater and opera director; b. Moscow, Jan. 17, 1863; d. there, Aug. 7, 1938. He received practical experience by performing in and directing operettas in his family's private theater; he studied voice with Komisarzhevsky, but gave up all hope of a career in opera when his voice proved inadequate. Then, with Nemirovich-Danchanko, he founded the Moscow Art Theater in 1898; it became an innovative setting for both stage plays and operas. In 1918 he founded the Bolshoi Theater Opera Studio, which became an independent studio in 1920; it was named the Stanislavsky Opera Theater in his honor in 1926. The Stanislavsky method as applied to opera concentrates upon the musical score as the guiding force of a production, allowing all elements to evolve naturally to present a realistic work of art. He wrote several books on his theater methods.

BIBL.: G. Kristi, *Rabota Stanislavskovo v opernom teatre* (S.'s Work in the Opera Theater; Moscow, 1952); I. Vinogradskaya, ed., *Zhizn i tvorchestvo K. S. Stanislavskovo: Letopis* (The Life and Work of K. S. S.: A Chronicle; Moscow, 1973); E. Hapgood, ed., *S. on Opera* (N.Y., 1975).

Stanley, John, prominent English organist and composer; b. London, Jan. 17, 1712; d. there, May 19, 1786. Blind from early childhood, he studied organ with Maurice Greene, and soon was able to fill church positions. He composed theater music, and publ. a number of instrumental works. He was the youngest individual ever to take the B.Mus. degree at the Univ. of Oxford in 1729. In 1779 he succeeded Boyce as Master of the King's Band of Musicians. He enjoyed the friendship and esteem of Handel, after whose death he conducted performances of Handel's oratorios with J. C. Smith. He especially distinguished himself as a composer of keyboard music and cantatas.

WORKS: DRAMATIC: OPERA: *Teraminta* (not perf.). MASQUE: *The Tears and Triumphs of Parnassus* (London, Nov. 17, 1760). PASTORAL: *Arcadia, or The Shepherd's Wedding* (London, Oct. 26, 1761). INCIDENTAL MUSIC: to J. Hawkesworth's *Oroonoko* (London, Dec. 1, 1759). ORATORIOS: *Jephtha* (c.1751–52); *Zimri* (London, March 12, 1760); *The Fall of Egypt* (London, March 23, 1774).

BIBL.: G. Williams, *The Life and Works of J. S. (1712–86)* (diss., Univ. of Reading, 1977).

Stapp, Olivia, American soprano; b. N.Y., May 31, 1940. She studied at Wagner College in Staten Island, N.Y. (B.A.) and received vocal training from Oren Brown in New York and Ettore Campogalliani and Rodolfo Ricci in Italy. In 1960 she made her debut as Beppe in *L'Amico Fritz* at the Spoleto Festival, and then appeared in various operatic centers in Europe and the United States. In 1972 she made her first appearance at the N.Y. City Opera as Carmen, and subsequently sang there with fine success. In 1981 she appeared as Elvira in *Ernani* in Barcelona. She sang Norma in Montreal and Lady Macbeth at the Paris Opéra in 1982. On Dec. 7, 1982, she made her Metropolitan Opera debut in New York as Lady Macbeth. In 1983 she appeared as Turandot at Milan's La Scala. She again sang Lady Macbeth in Geneva and in Venice in 1986. In 1990 she appeared as Shostakovich's Katerina Ismailova in Hamburg. Among her other prominent roles were Lucrezia Borgia, Aida, Elektra, and Tosca.

Starek, Jiří, Czech conductor; b. Mocovice, March 25, 1928. He was educated at the Prague Academy of Music (graduated, 1950). In 1953 he became a conductor with the Czech Radio in Prague, and was concurrently chief conductor of the Collegium Musicum Pragense chamber orch. (1963–68). From 1975 to 1997 he was a prof. and head of the conducting class at the Frankfurt am Main Hochschule für Musik. He was artistic director of the RIAS Sinfonietta in Berlin (1976–80), chief conductor of the Trondheim Sym. Orch. in Norway (1981–84), and principal guest conductor of the West Australian Sym. Orch. in Perth (1988–90). In 1996 he became chief conductor of the Prague State Opera. His guest conducting engagements took him to many opera companies and orchs.

Starer, Robert, esteemed Austrian-born American composer and pedagogue; b. Vienna, Jan. 8, 1924. He entered the Vienna Academy of Music at 13 and studied piano with Victor Ebenstein. Shortly after the Anschluss in 1938, he went to Jerusalem and pursued his training at the Cons. with Rosowsky, Tal, and Partos (until 1943). After service in the British Royal Air Force (1943–46), he emigrated to the United States and became a naturalized American citizen in 1957. He pursued postgraduate studies under Jacobi at the Juilliard School of Music in New York (1947–49) and studied with Copland at the Berkshire Music Center in Tanglewood (summer, 1948). From 1949 to 1974 he taught at the Juilliard School of Music; he also taught at the N.Y. College of Music (1959–60) and the Jewish Theological Seminary in New York (1962–63). In 1963 he became an assoc. prof. of music at Brooklyn College of the City Univ. of N.Y., where he was made a full prof. in 1966 and a Distinguished Prof. in 1986. He retired in 1991. He publ. the vol. *Rhythmic Training* (1969) and the autobiography *Continuo: A Life in Music* (1987). In 1957 and 1963 he held Guggenheim fellowships, and he also received grants from the NEA and the Ford Foundation. In 1994 he was elected to membership in the American Academy of Arts and Letters. Starer's music reflects his grounding in the 20th-century Viennese tradition and his study of Arabic scales and rhythms. In some of his works, he utilized aleatory techniques and collage. His output is particularly distinguished by its craftsmanship.

WORKS: DRAMATIC: OPERAS: *The Intruder* (N.Y., Dec. 4, 1956); *Pantagleize* (1967; N.Y., April 7, 1973); *Apollonia* (1978). MUSICAL MORALITY PLAY: *The Last Lover* (1974; Katonah, N.Y., Aug. 2, 1975). BALLETS: *The Story of Esther* (1960); *The Dybbuk* (1960); *Samson Agonistes* (1961); *Phaedra* (1962); *The Sense of Touch* (1967); *The Lady of the House of Sleep* (1968); *Holy Jungle* (N.Y., April 2, 1974).

Starokadomsky, Mikhail, Russian composer; b. Brest-Litovsk, June 13, 1901; d. Moscow, April 24, 1954. He studied composition with Miaskovsky at the Moscow Cons., graduating in 1928. He remained in Moscow, where he became a prof. of orchestration. His works follow the traditional line of Russian nationalism, but several of his early orch. scores are purely neoclassical, and in this respect parallel the European developments. He was once known in his homeland for his songs for children. Other works include the opera *Sot* (1933) and the operettas *3 Encounters* (1942), *The Gay Rooster* (1944), and *The Sun Flower* (1947).

Starzer, Josef, outstanding Austrian composer; b. 1726 or 1727; d. Vienna, April 22, 1787. By about 1752 he was a violinist in Vienna's Burgtheater orch., where he began his career as a composer of ballets. During the winter of 1758–59, he went to Russia, where he was active at the Imperial court in St. Petersburg; he gave concerts and later was made Konzertmeister and then deputy Kapellmeister and composer of ballet music; he served as maitre de chapelle et directeur des concerts in 1763. Returning to Vienna about 1768, he composed several notable ballets; with Gassmann, he helped in 1771 to organize the Tonkünstler-Sozietat, for which he wrote a number of works. In 1779 he retired as a violinist and in 1785 gave up his duties with the society. Starzer was one of the leading Austrian composers of his day, winning distinction not only for his ballets but for his orch. and chamber music; his string quartets have been compared favorably with those of Haydn.

WORKS: DRAMATIC: SINGSPIEL: *Die drei Pachter*. BALLETS: *Diane et Endimione* (Vienna, c.1754); *Les Bergers* (Laxenburg, 1755); *Le Misantrope* (Vienna, 1756); *L'Amour venge* (Laxenburg, 1759); *L'Asile de le vertu* (St. Petersburg, 1759; in collaboration with H. Raupach); *Les Nouveaux Lauriers* (St. Petersburg, c.1759; in collaboration with H. Raupach); *La Victoire de Flore su Borée* (St. Petersburg, 1760); *Siroe* (St. Petersburg, 1760); *Le Jugement de Paris* (St. Petersburg, 1761); *Prométhée et Pandore* (St. Petersburg, 1761); *Le Pauvre Yourka* (Moscow, 1762); *Le Seigneur de village moqué* (Moscow, 1762); *Le Vengeance du dieu de l'amour* (Moscow, 1762); *Apollon et Daphne, ou Le Retour d'Apolon au Parnasse* (St. Petersburg, 1763); *Apollon et Diane* (Vienna, 1763); *Le Retour de la déesse du printemps en Arcadie* (Moscow, 1763); *Les Fêtes hollandoises* (Vienna, 1763); *Pygmalion, ou La Statue animée* (St. Petersburg, 1763); *Acis et Galatée* (St. Petersburg, 1764); *Le Triomphe du printemps* (St. Petersburg, 1766); *Don Quichotte* (Vienna, c.1768); *Les Moissonneurs* (Vienna, 1770); *Agamemnon* (Vienna, 1771); *Atlante* (Vienna, 1771); *Les Cinque Sol-*

tanes (Vienna, 1771); *Roger et Bradamante* (Vienna, 1771); *Adèle de Ponthieu* (Vienna, 1773); *El Cid* (Vienna, 1774); *Le Ninfe* (Vienna, 1774); *Les Horaces et les Curiaces* (Vienna, 1774); *Les Moissonneurs* (Vienna, 1775); Montezuma (Vienna, 1775); *Teseo in Creta* (Vienna, 1775); etc. ORATORIO: *La passione di Gesù Christo* (Vienna, 1778). Also arrangements.

Stasny, Ludwig, popular Bohemian bandmaster and composer; b. Prague, Feb. 26, 1823; d. Frankfurt am Main, Oct. 30, 1883. He studied at the Prague Cons., then was bandmaster in the Austrian army. He settled in Frankfurt am Main in 1871. He produced 2 operas in Mainz: *Liane* (1851) and *Die beiden Grenadiere* (1879). He was noted for his popular dances (211 opus numbers) and for his potpourris from Wagner's music dramas.

Stasov, Vladimir (Vasilievich), famous Russian writer on music; b. St. Petersburg, Jan. 14, 1824; d. there, Oct. 23, 1906. He studied foreign languages and art, and also received instruction in music from Antoni Gerke, then continued his training with Adolf Henselt at the so-called Law School for civil servants (1836–43). From 1847 he was active as a book and music reviewer. After an Italian sojourn as secretary to Prince A. N. Demidov (1851–54), he became active at the St. Petersburg Public Library; he was made personal assistant to the director in 1856 and then head of the art dept. in 1872. Stasov played a very important role in the emergence of the Russian national school, and was to the end of his days an ardent promoter of Russian music. It was Stasov who first launched the expression "Moguchaya Kuchka" ("mighty little company," in an article publ. on May 24, 1867, in a St. Petersburg newspaper); although he did not specifically name the so-called "Five" (Balakirev, Borodin, Cui, Mussorgsky, and Rimsky-Korsakov), these composers became identified with the cause championed by Stasov. When young Glazunov appeared on the scene, Stasov declared him a natural heir to the Five. His numerous writings, including biographies of Glinka, Mussorgsky, and others, have the value of authenticity. Those publ. between 1847 and 1886 were reissued in book form in honor of his 70th birthday (3 vols., St. Petersburg, 1894); a 4th vol. was brought out in 1905, containing essays written between 1886 and 1904; among them, "Russian Music during the Last 25 Years" and "Art in the 19th Century" are particularly important. His collected works, including articles on art and other subjects, were publ. in Moscow in 1952. Some of his *Selected Essays on Music* were publ. in English (London, 1968).

BIBL.: V. Komarova (his niece), *V. V. S.* (2 vols., Leningrad, 1927); A. Lebedev and A. Solodovnikov, *V. S.* (Moscow, 1966); Y. Olkhovsky, *V. S. and Russian National Culture* (Ann Arbor, 1983).

Staudigl, (I), Joseph, distinguished Austrian bass, father of **Joseph Staudigl (II);** b. Wöllersdorf, April 14, 1807; d. Michaelbeueangrund, near Vienna, March 28, 1861. He was admitted in 1816 to the Wiener Neustadt Gymnasium, where he made his mark as a boy soprano; after studying at the Krems philosophical college (1823–25), he entered the Melk monastery to commence his novitiate, then went to Vienna as a medical student in 1827, but lack of funds soon compelled him to join the chorus of the Kärnthnertortheater. He subsequently sang minor roles before assuming a position as its principal bass; he was a member of the Theater an der Wien (1845–48) and the Court Opera (1848–54); he appeared at London's Drury Lane (1841), Covent Garden (1842), and Her Majesty's Theatre (1847). He also had a notable career as an oratorio and concert singer, both at home and abroad; he sang Elijah in the premiere of Mendelssohn's oratorio (1846). He died insane.

Staudigl (II), Joseph, Austrian baritone, son of **Joseph Staudigl (I)**; b. Vienna, March 18, 1850; d. Karlsruhe, April 1916. He studied with Rokitansky at the Vienna Cons. He sang at the Karlsruhe Court Theater (1875–83), then made his Metropolitan Opera debut in New York as Fernando in *Fidelio* on Nov. 19, 1884; there he also sang Pogner in the U.S. premiere of *Die Meistersinger von Nürnberg* (Jan. 4, 1886). He appeared as Don Giovanni in Salzburg in 1886, then sang in opera and oratorio in Germany. In 1885 he married the Austrian contralto Gisela (née Koppmayer) Staudigl (b. Vienna, date unknown; d. 1929); she studied with Marchesi in Vienna, where she made her debut in a concert in 1879; she sang opera in Hamburg (1882–83) and Karlsruhe (1883–84) and at Bayreuth (1886–92), where she appeared as Brangane and Magdalene; she also toured as Adriano and the Queen of Sheba with the Metropolitan Opera of New York in 1886; she later made another U.S. tour with the Damrosch-Ellis Opera Co. in 1897–98.

Steber, Eleanor, eminent American soprano; b. Wheeling, W.Va., July 17, 1914; d. Langhorne, Pa., Oct. 3, 1990. She studied singing with her mother; then with William Whitney at the New England Cons. of Music in Boston (Mus.B., 1938) and with Paul Althouse in New York. She won the Metropolitan Opera Auditions of the Air in 1940; she made her debut with the Metropolitan Opera in New York as Sophie in *Der Rosenkavalier* on Dec. 7, 1940, and remained with the company until 1962; altogether she appeared 286 times in New York and 118 times on tour; she sang 28 leading roles in an extremely large repertoire. She performed brilliantly in the roles of Donna Anna in *Don Giovanni*, Pamina in *Die Zauberflöte*, and the Countess in *Le nozze di Figaro*, as well as in other Mozart operas; her other roles were Violetta, Desdemona, Marguerite, Manon, Mimi, and Tosca; in Wagner's operas she sang Eva in *Die Meistersinger von Nürnberg* and Elsa in *Lohengrin*; she also performed the challenging part of Marie in Berg's opera *Wozzeck*. She sang the title role in the premiere of Samuel Barber's opera *Vanessa* on Jan. 15, 1958. After several years of absence from the Metropolitan Opera, she took part in the final gala performance in the old opera building on April 16, 1966. Her European engagements included appearances at Edinburgh (1947), Vienna (1953), and the Bayreuth Festival (1953). After partial retirement in 1962, she was head of the voice dept. at the Cleveland Inst. of Music (1963–72); she taught at the Juilliard School in New York and at the New England Cons. of Music (both from 1971); also at the American Inst. of Music Studies in Graz (1978–80; 1988). She established the Eleanor Steber Music Foundation in 1975 to assist young professional singers. With R. Beatie, she publ. the study *Mozart Operatic Arias* (N.Y., 1988). Her autobiography, written in collaboration with M. Sloat, was publ. posthumously (Ridgewood, N.J., 1992).

Štědroň, Bohumír, eminent Czech musicologist, uncle of **Miloš Štědroň**; b. Vyškov, Oct. 30, 1905; d. Brno, Nov. 24, 1982. He studied theory with Josef Blatný (1925–28) and piano with Vilém Kurz (1926–28); he also took courses in history and geography at the Univ. of Brno (graduated, 1929), where he attended Helfert's lectures in musicology; after further training in Italy (1931), he returned to the Univ. of Brno to take his Ph.D. in 1934 with the diss. *Sólové chrámové kantáty G. B. Bassaniho* (G.B. Bassani's Solo Church Cantatas) and to complete his Habilitation in 1945 with his *Chrámová hudba v Brně v XVIII. století* (Church Music in Brno in the XVIIIth Century). He taught music education at a teacher-training college (1931–39), and also was an assistant to Helfert (1932–38); he then taught music history at the Brno Cons. (1939–45; 1950–52); in 1945 he became a teacher at the Univ. of Brno, where he subsequently was made assistant lecturer in 1950, lecturer in 1955, and prof. in 1963. He was an authority on the life and music of Janáček. In addition to his important books, he contributed many articles to scholarly journals. His brother was the Czech composer Vladimir Štědroň (1900–1982).

WRITINGS: *Leoš Janáček a Luhačovice* (Leoš Janáček and Luhačovice; Luhacovice, 1939); *Leoš Janáček ve vzpominkách a dopisech* (Prague, 1945; rev. Ger. tr., 1955; rev. Eng. tr., 1955, as *Leoš Janáček: Letters and Reminiscences*); *Josef Bohuslav Foerster a Moravia* (Brno, 1947); ed. with G. Černušák and Z. Nováček, *Československý hudební slovník osob a instituci* (Czechoslovak Music Dictionary of Places and Institutions; Prague, 1963–65); *Vítežlav Novák v obrazech* (Vitežlav Novák in Pictures; Prague, 1967); *Zur Genesis von Leoš Janáček's Oper Jenůfa* (Brno, 1968;

2d ed., rev., 1971); *Leoš Janáček: K jeho lidskému a uměleckému profilu* (Leoš Janáček: Personal and Artistic Profile; Prague, 1976).

BIBL.: *Sbornik praci filosofické fakulty brněnské univerzitě* (Brno, 1967; dedicated to S. on his 60th birthday).

Štědroň, Miloš, significant Czech composer and musicologist, nephew of **Bohumír Štědroň**; b. Brno, Feb. 9, 1942. Another uncle was the Czech composer Vladimir Štědroň (1900–1982). He studied musicology with Racel, Vysloužil, and his uncle Bohumír at the Univ. of Brno (Ph.D., 1967); he also studied composition at the Janáček Academy of Music in Brno (1965–70). After working in the music dept. of Brno's Moravian Museum (1963–72), he taught theory at the Univ. of Brno (from 1972). Among his books is a monograph on Monteverdi (Prague, 1985) and a study on Josef Berg (Brno, 1992). He contributed important articles to various journals, many of which deal with the music of Janáček. His own works range from traditional scores to pieces utilizing jazz and pop elements or tape.

WORKS: DRAMATIC: OPERAS: *Aparát* (The Apparatus), chamber opera after Kafka's *In the Penal Colony* (1967); *Kychýnské starosti* (1977); *Josef Fouché-Chameleon* (1984); *Več Cage aneb Anály avantgardy dokořán* (The Cage Affair, or the Avant-Garde Chronicles Flung Open; Brno, Oct. 6, 1995; in collaboration with I. Medek and A. Piňos); *Anály předchůdců avantgardy aneb Setkání slovanských velikánů* (Annals of the Predecessors of the Avant-Garde, or the Meeting of the Slavonic Giants; Brno, Oct. 1997; in collaboration with I. Medek and A. Piňos). BALLETS: *Justina* (1969); *Ballet macabre* (1986). CANTATA ORATORIO: *Ommaggio a Gesualdo: Death of Dobrovský* for 2 Solo Voices, Chorus, and Orch. (1988).

Steel, Christopher (Charles), English composer and teacher; b. London, Jan. 15, 1939; d. Cheltenham, Dec. 31, 1991. He studied composition with John Gardner at the Royal Academy of Music in London (1957–61) and with Harald Genzmer at the Staatliche Hochschule für Musik in Munich (1961–62). He taught at Cheltenham College Junior School (1963–66); he was assistant director (1966–68) and director (1968–81) of music at Bradfield College, also serving as an instructor; he taught at North Hennepin Community College in Brooklyn Park, Minn. (1977–78); he accepted private students from 1982.

WORKS: OPERAS: *The Rescue*, chamber opera (1974); *The Selfish Giant* for Baritone and Children (Westclife-on-Sea, July 1981); *The Angry River*, chamber opera for 7 Soloists, Chorus, and Orch. (1989).

Stefan (Stefan-Grünfeldt), Paul, Austrian writer on music; b. Brünn, Nov. 25, 1879; d. N.Y., Nov. 12, 1943. He settled in Vienna, where he studied law (doctorate, 1904), philosophy, and art history at the Univ.; he also received instruction in theory with Hermann Grädener and Schoenberg. He was employed as a municipal functionary, and at the same time became associated with the modern group of musicians in Vienna; he ed. the progressive music periodical *Musikblätter des Anbruch* (1921–38), and was a founder of the Ansorge-Verein (1903) and the ISCM (1922). After the Anschluss in 1938, he went to Switzerland, and later to Lisbon, eventually emigrating to the U.S. in 1941.

WRITINGS: *Gustav Mahler* (Munich, 1910; 7th ed., 1921; Eng. tr., N.Y., 1913); *Das neue Haus: Ein Halbjahrhundert Weiner Opernspeil* (Vienna, 1919); *Die Feindschaft gegen Wagner* (Regensburg, 1919); *Neue Musik und Wien* (Leipzig, 1921); *Arnold Schönberg: Wandlung, Legende, Erscheinung, Bedeutung* (Vienna, 1924); *Franz Schubert* (Berlin, 1928); *Geschichte der Wiener Oper* (Vienna, 1932); *Arturo Toscanini* (Vienna, 1936; Eng. tr., N.Y., 1936; Italian tr., Milan, 1937); *Bruno Walter* (Vienna, 1936); *Georges Bizet* (Zürich, 1952).

Stefani, Jan, significant Polish composer of Bohemian descent, father of **Józef Stefani**; b. Prague, 1746; d. Warsaw, Feb. 24, 1829. He studied at Prague's Benedictine school. After an Italian sojourn, he went to Vienna about 1765 as a violinist in Count G. Kinski's orch.; in 1779 he settled in Warsaw as a violinist and conductor in King Stanislaw August Poniatowski's Court Orch.; he also was Kapellmeister at the Cathedral and a conductor at the National Theater and later a violinist in its orch. (1799–1811). Stefani's importance rests upon his notable contribution to Polish opera; his masterpiece is *Cud mniemany czyl: Krakowiacy ī Górale* (The Supposed Miracle or Krakovians and Highlanders; Warsaw, March 1, 1794). He also was a fine composer of polonaises.

WORKS: DRAMATIC: (all 1st perf. in Warsaw): OPERAS: *Król w kraju rozkoszy* (The King of Cockaigne; Feb. 3, 1787); *Cud mniemany czyli Krakowiacy ī Górale* (The Supposed Miracle or Krakovians and Highlanders; March 1, 1794); *Wdzieczni poddani czyli Wesele wiejskie* (Thankful Serfs or The Country Wedding; July 24, 1796, also known as *Przjazd pana czyli Szczęśliwi wieśniacy* [The Arrival of the Lord or Happy Country Folk]); *Drzewo zaczarowane* (The Magic Tree; 1796); *Frozyna czyli Siedem razy jedna* (Frozine or 7 Times Dressed Up; Feb. 21, 1806); *Rotmistrz Görecki czyli Oswodobodzenie* (Captain Gorecki or The Liberation; April 3, 1807); *Polka czyli Obleeżnie* (The Polish Woman or The Siege of Trembowla; May 22, 1807); *Stary myśliwy* (The Old Huntsman; Jan. 31, 1808); *Papirius czyli Ciekawość dawnych kobiet* (Papyrus or The Curiosity of Women in Ancient Times; May 15, 1808). BALLET: *Milość każdemu wiekowi przstoi* (Love Becomes Every Age; Nov. 4, 1785).

Stefani, Józef, Polish composer and conductor, son of **Jan Stefani**; b. Warsaw, April 16, 1800; d. there, March 19, 1867. He was a pupil of his father and of Elsner in Warsaw (1821–24). He conducted ballet at the Warsaw Opera, and wrote a number of light operas, which enjoyed a modicum of success during his lifetime: *Dawne czasy* (April 26, 1826), *Lekcja botaniki* (March 15, 1829), *Figle panien* (Aug. 6, 1832), *Talizman* (Dec. 7, 1849), *Zyd wieczny tulacz* (Jan. 1, 1850), *Piorun* (May 21, 1856), and *Trwoga wieczorna* (posthumous, July 25, 1872). He also wrote church music, which was often performed in religious services in Poland. Many of his works are lost.

Steffani, Agostino, eminent Italian composer, churchman, and diplomat; b. Castelfranco, near Venice, July 25, 1654; d. Frankfurt am Main, Feb. 12, 1728. He most likely received his early musical training in Padua, where he was probably a choirboy. In 1667 Elector Ferdinand Maria of Bavaria took him to his court in Munich, where Steffani became a ward of Count von Tattenbach; he sang in *Le pretensioni del sole* (1667) by J. K. Kerll, the court Kapellmeister, who gave him organ lessons (1668–71); he then studied composition with Ercole Bernabei, maestro di capella at St. Peter's in Rome (1672–74). In 1674 he returned to Munich with Bernabei, who assumed the post of Kapellmeister; Steffani appears to have taken on the duties of court and chamber organist in 1674, although the court records only list him as such from 1678. In 1680 he became a priest. With the accession of the elector Maximilian II Emanuel in 1680, he found great favor at the court. In 1681 the position of director of the court chamber music was especially created for him; that same year his first opera, *Marco Aurelio*, to a libretto by his brother Ventura Terzago, was premiered; it was also about this time that he became active as a diplomat for the court. He was made Abbot of Lepsingen in 1683. In 1688 he was called to Hannover by Duke Ernst August to serve as court Kapellmeister; he was in charge of the first permanent Italian opera company there (1689–97); he subsequently was mainly active as a diplomat for the Hannoverian court. In 1691 he was sent to Vienna to assist in creating Hannover as the 9th electorate. In 1693 he was made envoy extraordinary to the Bavarian court in Brussels, where he worked diligently to persuade the elector Maximilian to support the emperor rather than Louis XIV as the War of the Spanish Succession loomed in the background; however, his mission failed, and he returned to Hannover in 1702. In 1703 he entered the service of Johann Wilhelm, Palatine elector, in Düsseldorf; since he had virtually given up composing, a number of his works were circulated from 1709 under the name of one of his copyists, Gregorio Piva. He began his duties in Düsseldorf in 1703 as privy councillor and president of the Spiritual Council for the Palatinate and the duchies of Julich and Berg; later that year he was named general president of the

Palatine government; he also was the 1st rector magnificus (1703–05) and then a curator (from 1705) of the Univ. of Heidelberg. In 1706 he was elected Bishop of Spiga in partibus infedelium (Asia Minor). In 1708–09 he was in Rome to mediate the war between the Pope and the emperor, which resulted in the Pope making him a domestic prelate and assistant to the Throne. In 1709 he was appointed apostolic vicar in northern Germany, and later that year settled in Hannover. He continued to be active at the court there as well, having served as minister and grand almoner to the elector Johann Wilhelm from 1706. His ecclesiastical duties were particularly onerous, but he carried them out faithfully until retiring to Padua in 1722. However, at the insistence of Rome, he returned to Hannover in 1725. In 1727 he received the honor of being elected president of the Academy of Vocal Music in London, the forerunner of the Academy of Ancient Music. This honor renewed his interest in composing, but ill health soon intervened. He died while on his way to Italy. Steffani was an important composer of operas, notably influential in the development of the genre in northern Germany. All the same, his most significant achievement was as a composer of outstanding chamber duets for 2 Voices and Continuo, which had a major impact on Handel.

WORKS: DRAMATIC (all operas unless otherwise given): *Marco Aurelio* (Munich, 1691); Serenata for the wedding of Countess von Preysing (Munich, 1682); *Solone* (Munich, 1685); *Audacia e rispetto* (Munich, 1685); *Servio Tullio* (Munich, 1686); *Alarico il Baltha, cioè L'audace rè de' gothi* (Munich, 1687); *Niobe, regina di Tebe* (Munich, 1688); *Henrico Leone* (Hannover, 1689; German version by G. Schürmann, Braunschweig, 1716); *La lotta d'Hercole con Acheloo*, divertimento drammatico (Hannover, 1689); *La superbia d'Alessandro* (Hannover, 1690); *Orlando generoso* (Hannover, 1691); *Le Rivali concordi* (Hannover, 1692); *La libertà contenta* (Hannover, 1693); *Baccanali*, favola pastorale (Hannover, 1695); *I trionfi del fato* or *Le glorie d'Enea* (Hannover, 1695); *Arminio*, pasticcio (Düsseldorf, 1707); *Amor vien del destino* (Düsseldorf, 1709); *Il Tassilone* (Düsseldorf, 1709).

BIBL.: (J. Hawkins), *Memoirs of the Life of A. S.* (London, *c.*1749–52); F. Woker, *Aus den Papieren des kurpfälzischen Ministers A. S., Bischofs von Spiga, spätern apostolischen Vicars von Norddeutschland . . . 1703–1709: Erste Vereinsschrift der Görresgesellschaft* (Cologne, 1885); idem, *A. S., Bischof von Spiga, i.p.i., apostolischer Vikar von Norddeutschland 1709–28: Dritte Vereinsschrift der Görresgesellschaft* (Cologne, 1886); A. Neisser, *Servio Tullio: Eine Oper aus dem Jahr 1685 von A. S.* (Leipzig, 1902); W. Baxter, Jr., *A. S.: A Study of the Man and His Work* (diss., Eastman School of Music, 1957); G. Croll, *A. S. (1654–1728): Studien zur Biographie, Bibliographie der Opern und Turnierspiele* (diss., Univ. of Münster, 1960).

Steffek, Hanny (Hannelore), Austrian soprano; b. Biala, Galicia, Dec. 12, 1927. She received her training at the Vienna Academy of Music and the Salzburg Mozarteum. In 1949 she made her concert debut at the Salzburg Festival, and returned there in 1950 to make her operatic debut in a minor role in *Die Zauberflöte*. She also sang in Graz and Frankfurt am Main, and then was a member of the Bavarian State Opera in Munich (1957–72). In 1959 she made her debut at London's Covent Garden as Sophie. From 1964 to 1973 she sang at the Vienna State Opera. In 1965 she appeared with the visiting Bavarian State Opera at the Edinburgh Festival singing Christine in the first British performance of *Intermezzo*. She also sang with various other European opera houses. In addition to her noted portrayal of Christine, she was admired for such roles as Despina, Blondchen, Papagena, and Ilia. She also was highly successful in Viennese operetta.

Stegmann, Carl David, German tenor, harpsichordist, conductor, and composer; b. Staucha, near Meissen, 1751; d. Bonn, May 27, 1826. He studied with the Staucha organist, then went to Dresden to study with J. F. Zillich; he also attended the Kreuzschule there (1766–70) and received instruction from Homilius and H. Weisse. He was active at theaters in Breslau (1772) and Königsberg (1773). After serving as court harpsichordist to the Bishop of Ermeland in Heilsberg (1774), he was active again in Königsberg and then in Gotha. From 1778 to 1783 he won success as a harpsichordist in Hamburg, then went to Bonn as a member of the Grossmann theater company and later was active at the Mainz Court Theater. Stegmann was a skillful composer of both vocal and instrumental works.

WORKS: DRAMATIC: OPERAS: *Sultan Wampum oder Die Wünsche* (Mainz, March 7, 1791); *Der Roseninsel* (Hamburg, Nov. 24, 1806). COMIC OPERAS: *Der Kaufmann von Smirna* (Königsberg, 1773); *Die Rekruten auf dem Lande* (Danzig, 1775); *Das redende Gemahlde* (Königsberg, 1775). SINGSPIELS: *Heinrich der Löwe* (Frankfurt am Main, July 15, 1792); *Der Triumph der Liebe oder Das kühne Abentheuer* (Hamburg, Feb. 27, 1796). OPERETTA: *Der Deserteur* (Danzig, 1775). BALLET: *Die herrschaftliche Küche* (Danzig, 1775). Also incidental music.

Stegmayer, Ferdinand, Austrian pianist, conductor, and composer, son of **Matthäus Stegmayer**; b. Vienna, Aug. 25, 1803; d. there, May 6, 1863. He studied with Seyfried, then was chorusmaster in Linz and Vienna. In 1825 he was made music director of Berlin's Königstädtisches Theater, then was conductor of a German opera troupe in Paris (1829–30). After filling various engagements as a theater conductor in Leipzig, Bremen, and Prague, he settled in Vienna in 1848; he was a teacher of singing at the Vienna Cons., and cofounded, with August Schmidt, the Vienna Singakademie (1858). He wrote church music, piano pieces, and songs.

Stegmayer, Matthäus, Austrian singer, poet, actor, and composer, father of **Ferdinand Stegmayer**; b. Vienna, April 29, 1771; d. there, May 10, 1820. He was a chorister in the Dominican church in Vienna. About 1792 he became a member of the Theater in der Josefstadt, where he assumed major roles and was active as a composer; in 1796 he joined Schikaneder's Freihaus-Theater. He joined the court theater in 1800, where he was active as chorus director and producer; in 1804 he became an actor, chorusmaster, and composer at the Theater an der Wien, for which he wrote the text to the enormously successful quodlibet *Rochus Pumpernickel* (Jan. 28, 1809) with music provided by Haibel and Seyfried; it was widely performed in German-speaking countries, and was followed by at least 3 sequels.

BIBL.: F. Blitzenetz, *M. S.* (diss., Univ. of Vienna, 1929).

Stehle, Adelina, outstanding Austrian soprano; b. Graz, 1860; d. Milan, Dec. 24, 1945. She studied in Milan. She made her operatic debut in Broni in 1881 as Amina, then sang in Bologna, Florence, and Venice. In 1890 she joined La Scala in Milan, where she created roles in *Falstaff* as Nanetta, in *Guglielmo Ratcliff* as Maria, and others; she also sang in Berlin, Vienna, St. Petersburg, South America, and the United States. After her marriage to **Edoardo Garbin**, she appeared under the name of Stehle Garbin.

Stehle, Sophie, German soprano; b. Hohenzollern-Sigmaringen, May 15, 1838; d. Schloss Harterode, near Hannover, Oct. 4, 1921. She made her operatic debut as Emmeline in Weigl's *Schweizerfamilie* in Munich (1860). She was a prominent member of the Munich Court Opera, where she created the roles of Fricka in *Das Rheingold* (Sept. 22, 1869) and Brünnhilde in *Die Walküre* (June 26, 1870). She also distinguished herself in other Wagnerian parts (Elisabeth, Elsa, Eva).

Steibelt, Daniel, renowned German pianist and composer; b. Berlin, Oct. 22, 1765; d. St. Petersburg, Oct. 2, 1823. He studied with Kirnberger (piano and theory), then joined the Prussian Army only to desert and flee his homeland in 1784. He publ. sonatas for Piano and Violin, as opp. 1 and 2 (Munich, 1788), then gave concerts in Saxony and Hannover before proceeding to Paris in 1790. There he found himself in strong competition with Ignaz Pleyel, but won out, and became a favorite piano teacher. His opera *Roméo et Juliette* was produced at the Théâtre Feydeau on Sept. 10, 1793, and, despite the revolutionary turmoil of the time, achieved excellent success. After defrauding his publisher, he left Paris in 1796, going to the Netherlands and then to London. He became a soloist at Salomon's Concerts; played the solo part of his 3d Piano Concerto (March 19, 1798), with its rousing finale

L'Orage, précédé d'un rondeau pastoral, which as a piano solo became as popular as *Koczwara's Battle of Prague*; then produced the pasticcio *Albert and Adelaide, or The Victim of Constancy* at Covent Garden (Dec. 11, 1798), to which Attwood also contributed. After returning to Germany in 1799, he was granted an official pardon for his army desertion. In 1800 he visited Dresden, Prague, Berlin, and Vienna, where he challenged Beethoven to a contest of skill, but was easily bested. His next destination was Paris, where he produced Haydn's *Creation* (Dec. 24, 1800), with an orch. of 156 players, in an arrangement by Steibelt himself; Napoleon was present at that performance. A ballet by Steibelt, *Le retour de Zéphire*, was produced at the Paris Opéra on March 3, 1802. He then went to London, where he staged 2 ballets, *Le jugement du berger Paris* (May 24, 1804) and *La belle laitère* (Jan. 26, 1805). Returning once more to Paris, he wrote a festive intermezzo, *La fête de Mars*, to celebrate Napoleon's victory at Austerlitz; it was produced at the Opéra on March 4, 1806. In 1808–09 he presented concerts in Frankfurt am Main, Leipzig, Breslau, and Warsaw on his journey to St. Petersburg to assume his appointment as director of the French Opéra. In 1810 he was made maître de chapelle to the czar. He composed several works for the French Opéra, but devoted himself mainly to teaching and giving occasional concerts. On March 16, 1820, he gave the premiere of his 8th Piano Concerto in St. Petersburg. His last years were marked by ill health. Although he acquired great wealth during his career, he squandered his money and died in relative poverty. Much of his large output is now of little interest, although several of his piano concertos and his 3 quintets for Piano and Strings are worthy of note.

BIBL.: K. Hagberg, *D. S.'s Cendrillon: A Critical Edition with Notes on S.'s Life and Works* (diss., Eastman School of Music, 1975).

Steiger, Anna, American soprano; b. Los Angeles, Feb. 13, 1960. She studied at the Guildhall School of Music and Drama in London (1977–83), the National Opera Studio (1985–86), and with Vera Rozsa and Irmgard Seefried. She won the Sir Peter Pears Award in 1982, the Richard Tauber Prize in 1984, and the John Christie Award in 1985. In 1984 she made her operatic debut with Opera 80 as Dorabella. In 1985 she sang Micaëla with the Glyndebourne Touring Opera, and in 1986 she made her Glyndebourne Festival debut as Poppea. She sang Musetta at Opera North in Leeds in 1986. In 1987 she returned to Glyndebourne to create the role of Sashka in the premiere of Osborne's *The Electrification of the Soviet Union*. Following her debut as a Flower Maiden in *Parsifal* at London's Covent Garden in 1987, she portrayed Kristine in *The Makropulos Affair* at the English National Opera in London in 1989. In 1989 she also sang Weill's Jenny in Los Angeles, and in 1990 Ravel's Conception at the N.Y. City Opera and Despina at the Netherlands Opera in Amsterdam. In 1994 she appeared in Verdi's *Un Giorno di Regno* at the Dorset Opera. She is the daughter of the acclaimed actor Rod Steiger.

Stein, Erwin, Austrian conductor and editor; b. Vienna, Nov. 7, 1885; d. London, July 19, 1958. He studied composition with Schoenberg in Vienna (1906–10) and became Schoenberg's early champion. From 1910 to 1914 he conducted various theater orchs. in Austria and Germany; returning to Vienna, he was a member, with Schoenberg, Berg, and Webern, of the famous Verein für musikalische Privataufführungen (Soc. for Musical Private Performances), which excluded music critics from attendance (1920–22). He then became an ed. for Universal Edition in Vienna, where he was instrumental in bringing out works by the composers of the Second Viennese School. From 1924 to 1930 he ed. the journal *Pult und Taktstock*. He also conducted a tour with a Vienna group named Pierrot Lunaire Ensemble. After the Anschluss in 1938, he went to London and joined the music publ. firm of Boosey & Hawkes. He contributed a fundamental paper on Schoenberg's method of composition with 12 tones, "Neue Formprinzipien," publ. in *Anbruch* (1924). He publ. a selective collection of Schoenberg's letters (Mainz, 1958; Eng. tr., London, 1964); a collection of essays, *Orpheus in New Guises* (London, 1953); his theoretical monograph *Musik, Form und Darstellung* was publ. posthumously, first in Eng. as *Form and Performance* (London, 1962) and later in German (Munich, 1964).

Stein, Horst (Walter), German conductor; b. Elberfeld, May 2, 1928. He studied at the Hochschule für Musik in Cologne, and at age 23 was engaged as a conductor at the Hamburg State Opera; he then was on the staff of the State Opera in East Berlin (1955–61). He was deputy Generalmusikdirektor at the Hamburg State Opera (1961–63); after serving as Generalmusikdirektor of the Mannheim National Theater (1963–70), he returned to the Hamburg State Opera as Generalmusikdirektor (1972–77); he also was Generalmusikdirektor with the Hamburg State Phil. (1973–76). He subsequently was chief conductor of the Orchestre de la Suisse Romande in Geneva (1980–85), the Bamberg Sym. Orch. (from 1985), and the Basel Sym. Orch. (1987–94). He made many guest conducting appearances in Europe and in North and South America.

Stein, Leon, American composer, teacher, and conductor; b. Chicago, Sept. 18, 1910. He studied violin at the American Cons. in Chicago (1922–27), and theory at Crane Junior College in Chicago (1927–29); he took private lessons in composition with Sowerby, in orchestration with DeLamarter, and in conducting with Stock and Lange (1937–40); he also studied at De Paul Univ. (B.M., 1931; M.M., 1935; Ph.D., 1949; diss. publ. as *The Racial Thinking of Richard Wagner*, 1950), where he served on its faculty (1931–78); he served as dean of its school of music (1966–76) and also was director of the Inst. of Music of the College of Jewish Studies (1952–59) and a conductor of various community orchs. He publ. *Structure and Style: The Study and Analysis of Musical Form* (Evanston, Ill., 1962; 3d ed., rev. and enl., 1979) and *Anthology of Musical Forms* (Evanston, Ill., 1962). In 1982 he received Chicago's Hall of Fame Award. His music is academic, but not devoid of occasional modernities.

WORKS: DRAMATIC: OPERAS: *The Fisherman's Wife* (1953–54; St. Joseph, Mich., Jan. 10, 1955); *Deirdre*, after Yeats (1956; Chicago, May 18, 1957). BALLETS FOR PIANO: *Exodus* (Chicago, Jan. 29, 1939); *Doubt* (Chicago, Jan. 21, 1940).

Stein, Peter, German opera and theater producer; b. Berlin, Oct. 1, 1937. He was educated in Frankfurt am Main and in Munich. In 1964 he joined the staff of the Munich Kammerspiele. In 1970 he cofounded the Schaubühne in Berlin, and subsequently was its artistic director until 1985. He produced his first opera, *Das Rheingold*, in Paris in 1976. In 1986 he staged *Otello* at the Welsh National Opera in Cardiff, and returned there to produce *Falstaff* in 1988 and *Pelléas et Mélisande* in 1992. From 1992 to 1997 he was director of drama at the Salzburg Festival, where his production of Schoenberg's *Moses und Aron* was mounted in 1996.

BIBL.: M. Patterson, *P. S.: Germany's Leading Theatre Director* (Cambridge, 1981).

Steinberg, Pinchas, American conductor; b. N.Y., Feb. 12, 1945. He studied violin in New York, then pursued musical training at Tanglewood and at Indiana Univ. In 1967 he became a conductor at the Chicago Lyric Opera; in 1971 he conducted in Berlin; subsequently he conducted opera in Frankfurt am Main, Stuttgart, Hamburg, London, Paris, and San Francisco. From 1985 to 1989 he was Generalmusikdirektor in Bremen. In 1989 he became chief conductor of the Austrian Radio Sym. Orch. in Vienna, a position he held until 1996.

Steinberg, William (Hans Wilhelm), eminent German-born American conductor; b. Cologne, Aug. 1, 1899; d. N.Y., May 16, 1978. He studied piano and violin at home, conducted his own setting for chorus and orch. of a poem from Ovid's *Metamorphoses* in school at the age of 13, then took lessons in conducting with Hermann Abendroth, in piano with Lazzaro Uzielli, and in theory with Franz Bölsche at the Cologne Cons., graduating in 1920, with the Wüllner Prize for conducting. He subsequently became assistant to Otto Klemperer at the Cologne Opera, and in 1924 became principal conductor. In 1925 he was engaged as conductor of the German Theater in Prague; in 1929 he was appointed Generalmusikdirektor of the Frankfurt am Main Opera, where he brought out several modern operas, including Berg's *Wozzeck*. With the advent of the Nazi regime in 1933, he was removed from his position and became conductor for the Jewish Culture League, restricted to Jewish audiences. In 1936 he left Germany and became one of the conductors of the Palestine Orch., which he rehearsed and prepared for Toscanini, who subsequently engaged him as an assistant conductor of the NBC Sym. Orch. in New York in 1938. His career as an orch. conductor was then connected with major American orchs. He became a naturalized American citizen in 1944. He was music director of the Buffalo Phil. (1945–52); in 1952 he was appointed music director of the Pittsburgh Sym. Orch.; concurrently, he served as music director of the London Phil. (1958–60) and of the Boston Sym. Orch. (1969–72); he retired from his Pittsburgh post in 1976. He also made many guest conducting appearances with major U.S. and European orchs. His performances were marked by impeccable taste and fidelity to the music; in this respect he was a follower of the Toscanini tradition.

Steiner, Emma, American composer and conductor; b. 1850; d. N.Y., Feb. 27, 1928. Her grandfather led the Maryland 16th Brigade, which won the battle of North Point (near Fort McHenry, Baltimore) on Sept. 13, 1814, enabling Francis Scott Key to finish the last stanza of "The Star-Spangled Banner." She wrote 7 light operas, plus ballets, overtures, and songs; purportedly she was also the first woman ever to receive payment for conducting. Conried, the manager of the Metropolitan Opera, is said to have declared that he would have let her conduct a performance had he dared to put a woman armed with a baton in front of a totally male orch. According to unverifiable accounts, she conducted 6,000 performances of 50 different operas. She also organized an Emma R. Steiner Home for the Aged and Infirm Musicians at Bay Shore, Long Island. On Feb. 28, 1925, she conducted a concert at the Metropolitan Opera to commemorate the 50th anniversary of her first appearance as conductor. Her works, of different genres and light consistency, aggregate more than 200 opus numbers.

Steiner, Max(imilian Raoul Walter), Austrian-born American composer; b. Vienna, May 10, 1888; d. Los Angeles, Dec. 28, 1971. He studied at the Vienna Cons. with Fuchs and Gradener, and also had some advice from Mahler. At the age of 14, he wrote an operetta. In 1904 he went to England; in 1911 he proceeded to Paris. In 1914 he settled in the United States; after conducting musical shows in New York, he moved in 1929 to Hollywood, where he became one of the most successful film composers. His music offers a fulsome blend of lush harmonies artfully derived from both Tchaikovsky and Wagner, arranged in a manner marvelously suitable for the portrayal of psychological drama on the screen. Among his film scores, of which he wrote more than 200, are *King Kong* (1933), *The Charge of the Light Brigade* (1936), *Gone with the Wind* (1939), and *The Treasure of the Sierra Madre* (1948).

BIBL.: G. Lazarou, *M. S. and Film Music: An Essay* (Athens, 1971).

Steingruber, Ilona, Austrian soprano; b. Vienna, Feb. 8, 1912; d. there, Dec. 10, 1962. She studied piano before taking up vocal training at the Vienna Academy of Music. She sang in performances broadcast by the Austrian Radio (1939–42); she made her operatic debut in Tilsit (1942); after World War II she toured as a concert artist; she also sang at the Vienna State Opera (1948–51), then taught in Darmstadt. In 1946 she married **Friedrich Wildgans**.

Steinpress, Boris (Solomonovich), erudite Russian musicologist; b. Berdyansk, Aug. 13, 1908; d. Moscow, May 21, 1986. He studied piano with Igumnov at the Moscow Cons., graduating in 1931, and took a postgraduate course there in musicology with Ivanov-Boretsky, completing it in 1936; he was a member of its faculty (1931; 1933–36); in 1938 he received the title of candidate of fine arts for his diss. on Mozart's *Le nozze di Figaro*. He taught at the Urals Cons. in Sverdlovsk (1936–37; 1942–43), served as head of the music history dept. of the Central Correspondence Inst. for Musical Education (1939–41), and was senior lecturer and dean of the faculty of history and theory (from 1940). In 1942 he joined the Communist Party. Although engaged primarily in musical encyclopedic work, Steinpress also composed; his patriotic songs were popular in the USSR during World War II. From 1938 to 1940 and from 1943 to 1959 he was chief contributor to the music section of the *Great Soviet Encyclopedia*. His publications are particularly important in musical biography; he decisively refuted the legend of Salieri's poisoning Mozart. His biography of Aliabiev clarifies the story of Aliabiev's life and his internal exile on the false charge of murder in a duel. With I. Yampolsky, he ed. an extremely valuable and accurate one-vol. encyclopedic musical dictionary (Moscow, 1959; 2d ed., 1966); also with Yampolsky he compiled a useful brief dictionary for music lovers (Moscow, 1961; 2d ed., 1967). In 1963 he publ. a partial vol. of a monumental work on opera premieres covering the period 1900–40, giving exact dates and names of theaters for all opera productions worldwide.

Stekke, Léon, Belgian composer and teacher; b. Soignies, Oct. 12, 1904; d. Anderlecht, near Brussels, Jan. 24, 1970. He studied with Joseph Jongen and Paul Gilson in Brussels. From 1942 until his death he taught at the Royal Cons. in Brussels. His works include the opera *Les Cornes du Croissant* (Brussels, 1952).

Stella, Antonietta, Italian soprano; b. Perugia, March 15, 1929. She studied voice with Aldo Zeetti in Perugia. She made her operatic debut in Rome as Leonore in *La forza del destino* in 1951; in 1953 she sang at La Scala in Milan; further engagements were at Covent Garden in London (1955) and at the Vienna State Opera. She made her American debut at the Metropolitan Opera in New York on Nov. 13, 1956, as Aida; after remaining on its roster until 1960, she pursued her career in Europe.

Stenborg, Carl, Swedish tenor, impresario, and composer; b. Stockholm, Sept. 25, 1752; d. Djurgarden, Aug. 1, 1813. His father, Petter Stenborg, was a theater manager. He began appearing in concerts in Stockholm when he was 14; he studied vocal and instrumental music with F. Zellbel, the court Kapellmeister. He appeared as Peleus in F. Uttini's *Thetis och Pelée* for the opening of the Royal Swedish Opera in 1773; he was made a court singer and a member of the Academy of Music in 1782; he also was active as a conductor and composer at his father's theater, which he managed from 1780 until it was closed in 1799. After leaving the court in 1806, he ran his own theater. His major work was the Singspiel *Gustaf Ericsson i Dalarna* (1784); he also wrote incidental music to the dramas *Caspar och Dorothea* (1775) and *Konung Gustaft Adolfs jagt* (1777).

BIBL.: J. Flodmark, *S.ska skadebanorna* (Stockholm, 1893); idem, *Elisabeth Olin och C. S.* (Stockholm, 1903).

Stenhammar, (Karl) Wilhelm (Eugen), eminent Swedish pianist, conductor, and composer; b. Stockholm, Feb. 7, 1871; d. there, Nov. 20, 1927. His father was the Swedish composer Per Ulrik Stenhammar (b. Törnvalla, Feb. 20, 1828; d. Stockholm, Feb. 8, 1875). He began to play the piano and to compose in childhood; he attended Richard Andersson's music school and then studied theory with Joseph Dente and organ with Heintze and Lagergren (1888–89); he passed the organists' examination privately (1890) and later pursued theory lessons with Emil Sjögren and Andreas Hallén; he completed his piano training with Heinrich Barth in Berlin (1892–93). He subsequently toured as a pianist, appearing as a soloist and frequently with the Aulin Quartet. His first large work for Solo Voices, Chorus, and Orch., *I rosengård* (In a Rose Garden; 1888–89; after K. A. Melin's collection of fairy tales, *Prinsessan och svennen*), was performed in Stockholm on Feb. 16, 1892, attracting considerable attention; his love for the theater prompted him to compose 2 music dramas, *Gildet på Solhaug* (1892–93) and *Tirfing* (1897–98), neither of which was successful; he did, however, compose much outstanding incidental music. He made his conducting debut with a performance of his overture *Excelsior!* in 1897. After serving as artistic director of the Phil. Soc. (1897–1900), the Royal Theater (1 season), and the New Phil. Soc. (1904–06) in Stockholm, he went to Göteborg as artistic director of the Orch. Soc.; during his tenure (1906–22), he elevated the musical life of the city, then returned to Stockholm, where he again took charge of the Royal Theater (1924–25) before ill health compelled him to retire. Stenhammar's early compositions reflect his preoccupation with the Romantic movement; the influence of Wagner and Liszt is quite perceptible, but he later developed an individual style based on his detailed study of Classical forms. His ability to absorb and transmute authentic folk melodies is a notable characteristic of many of his works.

WORKS: DRAMATIC: OPERAS: *Gildet på Solhaug* (The Feast at Solhaug), op. 6, after Ibsen (1892–93; 1st perf. in Ger. as *Das Fest auf Solhaug*, Stuttgart, April 12, 1899; 1st perf. in Swedish, Stockholm, Oct. 31, 1902); *Tirfing*, op. 15 (Stockholm, Dec. 9, 1898). INCIDENTAL MUSIC TO: Strindberg's *Ett drömspel*; H. Bergman's *Lodolezzi sjunger*; Tagore's *Chitra*; Shakespeare's *Romeo and Juliet*.

BIBL.: B. Wallner, *W. S. och hans tid* (3 vols., Stockholm, 1991).

Stenz, Markus, German conductor; b. Bad Neuenahr, Feb. 28, 1965. He studied at the Cologne Hochschule für Musik and with Gary Bertini and Noam Sheriff. From 1989 to 1992 he was music director of the Montepulicano Festival. In 1990 he conducted the premiere of Henze's *Das verratene Meer* in Berlin. He was engaged to conduct *Le nozze di Figaro* at the Los Angeles Opera in 1994. From 1994 to 1998 he served as principal conductor of the London Sinfonietta. In 1995 he made his debut with the English National Opera conducting *Don Giovanni*, and in 1996 he appeared at the Hamburg State Opera. In 1997 he conducted the premiere of Henze's *Venus und Adonis* in Munich. From 1998 he was chief conductor of the Melbourne Sym. Orch. He also appeared as a guest conductor with many European and North American orchs.

Stenzl, Jürg (Thomas), prominent Swiss musicologist; b. Basel, Aug. 23, 1942. He began instruction in recorder and violin in 1949 in Bern, then studied the oboe with Huwiler at the Bern Cons. in 1961; he attended the Univ. of Bern as a student of musicology with Geering and Dickenmann (Ph.D., 1968, with the diss. *Die vierzig Clausulae der Handschrift Paris, Bibliothèque Nationale, latin 15139 [Saint Victor-Clauselae]*; publ. in Bern, 1970); he also worked with Chailley at the Univ. of Paris (1965) and later completed his Habilitation at the Univ. of Fribourg (1974), where he was a prof. from 1980 to 1992. He was engaged as a visiting prof. at the univs. of Geneva (1976–77; 1979–80), Neuchâtel (1982), Bern (1986–87), and Basel (1987–88); subsequently he served at the Technical Univ. in Berlin (1988–89). In 1992–93 he was artistic director of Universal Edition in Vienna. He was secretary of the Société Suisse de Musicologie (1972–80) and ed. of the *Schweizerische Musikzeitung* (1975–83); he contributed valuable articles and music criticism to various publications, including *Sohlmans Musiklexikon* (1975–79) and *The New Grove Dictionary of Music and Musicians* (1980); he was author of *Von Giacomo Puccini zu Luigi Nono: Italienische Musik, 1922–1952: Faschismus, Resistenza, Republik* (Buren, 1990). His expertise ranges from the Middle Ages to contemporary music.

Stepanian, Aro (Levoni), Armenian composer; b. Elizavetpol, April 24, 1897; d. Yerevan, Jan. 9, 1966. He studied with Gnessin in Moscow (1923–27) and with Shcherbachev and Kushnarian at the Leningrad Cons. (1926–30). He then settled in Yerevan, where he served as president of the Armenian Composers' Union (1938–48). He was one of the leading Armenian composers of his generation. Among his works were the operas *Brave Nazar* (1934; Yerevan, Nov. 29, 1935), *David of Sasun* (1936), *At the Dawn* (1937), *Nune* (1947), and *Heroine* (1950).

BIBL.: M. Kazakhian, *A. S.* (Yerevan, 1962); G. Tigranov, *A. S.* (Moscow, 1967).

Stephan, Rudi, German composer; b. Worms, July 29, 1887; d. in battle near Tarnopol, Galicia, Sept. 29, 1915. He studied counterpoint with Sekles at the Hoch Cons. in Frankfurt am Main (1905), then went to Munich, where he received instruction in composition from Rudolf Louis and in piano from Heinrich Schwartz (1906–08); he also studied philosophy at the Univ. His output is marked by a secure command of harmony and counterpoint with a fine feeling for orch. color. Stephan's tragic death was greatly lamented. His works included the opera *Die ersten Menschen* (1911–14; Frankfurt am Main, July 1, 1920).

BIBL.: K. Holl, *R. S.: Studie zur Entwicklungsgeschichte der Musik am Anfang des 20. Jahrhunderts* (Saarbrücken, 1920; 2d ed., 1922); A. Machner, *R. S.s Werk* (diss., Univ. of Breslau, 1943).

Stephănescu, George, noted Romanian conductor, teacher, and composer; b. Bucharest, Dec. 13, 1843; d. there, April 25, 1925. He studied harmony and piano with Wachmann at the Bucharest Cons. (1864–67), then pursued his training at the Paris Cons. (1867–71), where he studied harmony with Reber, composition with Auber and Thomas, piano with Marmontel, and singing with Delle Sedie. Returning to Bucharest, he taught singing and opera at the Cons. (1872–1904); he was a conductor of the Romanian Opera at the National Theater (from 1877), for which he wrote several works in an effort to produce native scores for the stage; he also was active as a music critic. Stephanescu was one of the foremost figures in Romanian musical life of his era. He composed the first Romanian sym. (1869). His output reflects his interest in Romanian folk tunes, although he did not directly quote from such sources. Other works include the opera *Petra* (1902), the operettas *Peste Dunăre* (Across the Danube; 1880), *Scaiul bărbaţilor* (Men's Burr; 1885), and *Cometa* (1900), and the musical fairy tale *Sînziana şi Pepelea* (1880).

BIBL.: G. Stephănescu, *G. S.: Viata în imagini* (G. S.: Life in Pictures; Bucharest, 1962).

Stephens, Catherine, noted English soprano and actress; b. London, Sept. 18, 1794; d. there, Feb. 22, 1882. She studied voice with Gesualdo Lanza. After appearing in the English provinces, she sang minor roles with an Italian opera company at London's Pantheon (1822); following additional vocal training with Thomas Welsh, she made her debut at London's Covent Garden as Mandane in Arne's *Artaxerxes* (Sept. 23, 1813); she sang there with much success until 1822. After singing at Drury Lane (1822–28), she returned to Covent Garden and appeared there until her retirement in 1835. In 1838 she married the Earl of Essex. She was highly successful as a concert and oratorio singer, as well as a singer and actress in the theater; she sang Susanna in the first performance in English of *Le nozze di Figaro* (1819). Weber's last work, the song *From Chindara's warbling fount I come* (1826), was written for her.

Steptoe, Roger (Guy), English composer, teacher, and pianist; b. Winchester, Hampshire, Jan. 25, 1953. He studied at the Univ. of Reading (B.A., 1974) and received training in composition from Alan Bush at the Royal Academy of Music in London (1974–76). After serving as composer-in-residence at Charterhouse School, Surrey (1976–79), he was a prof. of composition at the Royal Academy of Music (1980–91), where he served as administrator of its International Composers Festivals (1986–93). In 1993 he became artistic director of the Landmark Festivals Assn. He also was active as a pianist. Among his works is the opera *King of Macedon* (Surrey, Oct. 18, 1979).

Sterkel, Johann Franz Xaver, prominent German pianist, teacher, and composer; b. Würzburg, Dec. 3, 1750; d. there, Oct. 12, 1817. He received a thorough training in music from A. Kette, the court organist, and from Weismandel in Würzburg; he also attended the Univ. there. In 1768 he was tonsured and named organist in the collegiate chapter of Neumünster, where he subsequently was made subdeacon (1772), deacon (1773), and priest (1774). In 1778 he was called to Mainz to serve the Liebfrauen chapter and as court chaplain; the elector then sent him to Italy, where he toured widely as a pianist (1779–82) and produced the opera *Il Farnace* (Naples, Jan. 12, 1782); he subsequently returned to Mainz to serve as a canon of his chapter. Beethoven heard him play in Aschaffenburg in 1791 and was greatly impressed by him as a pianist and composer. The French invasion of 1792 wreaked havoc with the Mainz court, but when the city was regained in 1793, Sterkel was named court Kapellmeister; however, continued warfare led to the closing of the royal chapel in 1797 and Sterkel returned to Würzburg, where he was active at the court. About 1802 he went to Regensburg, where he found a patron in Karl Theodor von Dalberg; he founded his own choir school. When his patron was made grand duke of Frankfurt am Main in 1810, Sterkel went with him to Aschaffenburg as his music director. The court was disbanded in 1814 and he returned once more to Würzburg in 1815. Sterkel was a prolific composer; his most important works are his chamber music and keyboard pieces.

BIBL.: A. Scharnagl, *J. F. X. S.: Ein Beitrag zur Musikgeschichte Mainfrankens* (Würzburg, 1943).

Sterling, Antoinette, American contralto; b. Sterlingville, N.Y., Jan. 23, 1850; d. London, Jan. 9, 1904. She studied with Abella in New York, Mathilde Marchesi in Cologne, and Pauline Viardot-García in Baden; she also took lessons with Manuel García in London. Returning to America (1871), she sang in Henry Ward Beecher's church in Brooklyn; she then went to London, where she made her debut at a Covent Garden Promenade Concert (Nov. 5, 1873). She introduced many favorite songs (most of which were composed especially for her), such as Arthur Sullivan's "Lost Chord" (Jan. 31, 1877) and Barnby's "When the Tide Comes In." In 1875 she toured the United States; her permanent home was in London.

BIBL.: M. MacKinlay (her son), *A. S. and Other Celebrities* (London, 1906).

Sternberg, Erich Walter, German-born Israeli composer; b. Berlin, May 31, 1891; d. Tel Aviv, Dec. 15, 1974. He studied law at the Univ. of Kiel (graduated, 1918), and then received training in composition from Leichtentritt and in piano from Praetorius in Berlin. In 1932 he emigrated to Palestine. In 1936 he was a cofounder of the Palestine Orch. (later the Israel Phil.). Many of his works were inspired by biblical subjects. Among his works are *Dr. Dolittle*, children's opera (1937; orch. suite, 1941), and *Pacificia, the Friendly Island*, opera for "children and others" (1972–74).

Sternberg, Jonathan, American conductor; b. N.Y., July 27, 1919. He studied at the Juilliard School of Music (1929–31), N.Y. Univ. (B.A., 1939; graduate study, 1939–40), and the Manhattan School of Music (1946); he took conducting lessons with Monteux at his summer school (1946, 1947). In 1947 he made his conducting debut with the Vienna Sym. Orch., then toured extensively as a guest conductor in Europe, North America, and the Far East. He was music director of the Royal Flemish Opera in Antwerp (1961–62), the Harkness Ballet in New York (1966–68), and the Atlanta Opera and Ballet (1968–69), then was a visiting prof. of conducting at the Eastman School of Music in Rochester, N.Y. (1969–71), a prof. of music at Temple Univ. (1971–89), and a lecturer at Chestnut Hill College (from 1989).

Sternefeld, Daniël, Belgian conductor, teacher, and composer; b. Antwerp, Nov. 27, 1905; d. Brussels, June 2, 1986. He studied flute and theory at the Antwerp Cons. (1918–24), then composition with Gilson and conducting with van der Stücken (1928); he subsequently took lessons in conducting with Paumgartner, Krauss, and Karajan at the Mozarteum in Salzburg. He was a flutist in the orch. of the Royal Flemish Opera in Antwerp (1929–38), then was its 2d conductor (1938–44) and principal conductor (1944–48); subsequently he was chief conductor of the Belgian Radio and Television Orch. in Brussels (1948–72) and also appeared as a guest conductor in Europe and South America. He taught conducting at the Antwerp Cons. (1949–71). His own works include the opera *Mater Dolorosa* (1934; Antwerp, 1935) and the ballets *Pierlala* (1937), *Antwerpia* (1975), and *Rossiniazata* (1982); also incidental music to various plays.

Sternfeld, F(riedrich) W(ilhelm), Austrian-born English musicologist; b. Vienna, Sept. 25, 1914; d. Brightwell-cum-Sotwell, near Wallingford, Jan. 13, 1994. He took courses with Lach and Wellesz at the Univ. of Vienna (from 1933), then pursued his training with Schrade at Yale Univ. (Ph.D., 1943, with the diss. *Goethe and Music*); he held a Guggenheim fellowship (1954). He taught at Wesleyan Univ. (1940–46) and Dartmouth College (1946–56) and also was a member of the Inst. for Advanced Studies at Princeton Univ. (1955). In 1956 he joined the faculty of the Univ. of Oxford, where he served as a reader in music history (1972–81). He also became a naturalized British subject. He was ed. of *Renaissance News* (1946–54) and of the *Proceedings of the Royal Musical Association* (1957–62); he publ. the books *Goethe's Relationship to Music: A List of References* (N.Y., 1954), *Music in Shakespearean Tragedy* (London, 1963; 2d ed., 1967), *Songs from Shakespeare's Tragedies* (London, 1964), and *The Birth of Opera* (Oxford, 1993). He also ed. *A History of Western Music* (London, 1973); with Wellesz, the 7th vol. of *The New Oxford History of Music: The Age of Enlightenment 1745–1790* (Oxford, 1973); and with others, *Essays on Opera and English Music in Honour of Sir Jack Westrup* (Oxford, 1975).

Stevens, Denis (William), distinguished English violinist, musicologist, and conductor; b. High Wycombe, Buckinghamshire, March 2, 1922. He studied music with R. O. Morris, Egon Wellesz, and Hugh Allen at Jesus College, Oxford (M.A., 1947). He played violin and viola in the Philharmonia Orch. of London (1948–49), then was a program planner in the music dept. of the BBC (1949–54). He served as a visiting prof. of music at Cornell Univ. (1955) and Columbia Univ. (1956), and taught at the Royal Academy of Music in London (1956–61). He subsequently was a visiting prof. at the Univ. of Calif. at Berkeley (1962) and at Pa. State Univ. (1963–64). He was prof. of musicology at Columbia Univ. (1964–76). He was also a visiting prof. at the Univ. of Calif. at Santa Barbara (1974) and at the Univ. of Wash. at Seattle (1976–77). As a conductor, he was cofounder of the Ambrosian Singers in 1952 and served as president and artistic director of the Accademia Monteverdiana from 1961; in his programs, he emphasized early polyphonic works. He ed. several important collections, including *The Mulliner Book*, vol. 1 in the Musica Britannica series (1951; 3d ed., rev., 1962); *Early Tudor Organ Music*, in the Early English Church Music series (1969); and works by Monteverdi. He was made a Commander of the Order of the British Empire in 1984.

WRITINGS: *The Mulliner Book: A Commentary* (London, 1952); *Tudor Church Music* (N.Y., 1955; 3d ed., 1966); *Thomas Tomkins 1572–1656* (London, 1957; 2d ed., 1967); ed. *A History of Song* (London, 1960; 2d ed., 1970); coed., with A. Robertson, *The Pelican History of Music* (3 vols., Harmondsworth, 1960–68); *Plainsong Hymns and Sequences* (London, 1965); *Claudio Monteverdi: Sacred, Secular and Occasional Music* (N.Y., 1977); ed. and tr. *The Letters of Claudio Monteverdi* (London, 1980; rev. ed., 1995); ed. *Ten Renaissance Dialogues* (Seven Oaks, 1981); T. Lewis, ed., *Musicology in Practice: Collected Essays*, vol. 1, 1948–1970 (N.Y., 1987).

Stevens, Horace (Ernest), Australian bass-baritone; b. Melbourne, Oct. 26, 1876; d. there, Nov. 18, 1950. He studied at St. Kilda in Melbourne, and then sang as a lay clerk at St. Paul's Cathedral in Melbourne. In 1919 he made his London debut in a Queen's Hall concert, and subsequently became a popular favorite at major English festivals. He also sang in oratorios in the United States and appeared with the British National Opera Co. and other English companies. Stevens was particularly successful as a concert artist, excelling as Elijah. In opera he won accolades for his Wagnerian roles.

Stevens, John (Edgar), distinguished English musicologist; b. London, Oct. 8, 1921. He studied classics (1940–41) and English (B.A., 1948) at Magdalene College, Cambridge, then pursued training with Dart at the Univ. there (Ph.D., 1953, with the diss. *Early Tudor Song Books*); he served on the univ. faculty as a teacher of English (1952–74), reader in English and music history (1974–78), and prof. of medieval and Renaissance English (from

1978). He was made a Commander of the Order of the British Empire in 1980. An erudite scholar, he contributed greatly to the understanding of music from the medieval and Renaissance periods. In addition to his books and articles, he ed. works for the Musica Britannica series. His writings include *Music and Poetry in the Early Tudor Court* (London, 1961; 2d ed., rev., 1979), *Medieval Romance* (London, 1973), and *Words and Music in the Middle Ages* (London, 1986).

Stevens, Risë, noted American mezzo-soprano; b. N.Y., June 11, 1913. The original family surname was Steenberg. She studied voice with Orry Prado; after graduating from high school, she sang minor roles with the N.Y. Opera-Comique Co. The enterprise soon went bankrupt, and for a while she had to earn her living by dress modeling before she was offered free singing lessons by Anna Schoen-René at the Juilliard School of Music. She was subsequently sent to Salzburg to study with Marie Gutheil-Schoder at the Mozarteum, and later entered classes in stage direction with Herbert Graf. In 1936 she was engaged by Szell for the Prague Opera as a contralto; she prepared several roles from standard operas, coaching with George Schick. She went on a tour to Cairo, Egypt, with a Vienna opera group, and then sang at the Teatro Colón in Buenos Aires. She made her American debut as Octavian in *Der Rosenkavalier* with the Metropolitan Opera in Philadelphia on Nov. 22, 1938. She greatly extended her repertoire, and added Wagnerian roles to her appearances with the Metropolitan. On Jan. 9, 1939, she married in New York the Czech actor Walter Surovy, who became her business manager. In 1939 she sang at the Glyndebourne Festival in England; on Oct. 12, 1940, she appeared with the San Francisco Opera as Cherubino; in 1941 she joined Nelson Eddy in a film production of the operetta *The Chocolate Soldier*, and in 1944 acted in the movie *Going My Way*, in which she sang the Habanera from *Carmen*; on Dec. 28, 1945, she appeared as Carmen at the Metropolitan Opera, scoring a fine success. Carmen became her most celebrated role; she sang it 75 times with the Metropolitan. She remained with the Metropolitan until 1961. On March 24, 1954, she appeared for the first time at La Scala in Milan. She retired from the stage in 1964. In 1975 she joined the teaching staff at the Juilliard School in New York. She also served as president of the Mannes College of Music in New York (1975–78).

BIBL.: K. Crichton, *Subway to the Met: R. S.' Story* (N.Y., 1959).

Stewart, Thomas (James), distinguished American baritone; b. San Saba, Texas, Aug. 29, 1928. He studied electrical engineering in Waco; he later went to New York, where he became a student of Mack Harrell at the Juilliard School of Music. He made his debut there in 1954 as La Roche in *Capriccio* by Richard Strauss; he then sang with the N.Y. City Opera and the Chicago Opera in bass roles. In 1957 he received a Fulbright grant and went to Berlin and was engaged as a baritone with the Städtische Oper; he made his debut there as the Don Fernando in *Fidelio* on March 28, 1958; he remained on its roster until 1964 and also sang regularly at London's Covent Garden (1960–78) and at the Bayreuth Festivals (1960–75). He made his Metropolitan Opera debut in New York on March 9, 1966, as Ford in Verdi's *Falstaff*; in 1981 he sang the title role in the American premiere of Reimann's *Lear* with the San Francisco Opera. His other roles were Don Giovanni, Count di Luna in *Il Trovatore*, Escamillo in *Carmen*, Iago in *Otello*, and Wotan. In 1955 he married **Evelyn Lear**, with whom he often appeared in opera and concert settings.

Stich-Randall, Teresa, admired American soprano; b. West Hartford, Conn., Dec. 24, 1927. She received her training at the Hartt School of Music in Hartford and at Columbia Univ. In 1947 she made her operatic debut as Gertrude Stein in the premiere of Thomson's *The Mother of Us All* in New York. She was chosen to create the title role in Luening's *Evangeline* in New York in 1948. She then was engaged to sing with Toscanini and the NBC Sym. Orch. in New York. After winning the Lausanne competition in 1951, she made her European operatic debut that year as the Mermaid in *Oberon* in Florence. In 1951–52 she sang at the Basel Opera. In 1952 she made her first appearance at the Salzburg Festival and at the Vienna State Opera. In 1955 she made her debut at the Chicago Lyric Opera as Gilda. From 1955 she appeared regularly at the Aix-en-Provence Festivals. On Oct. 24, 1961, she made her Metropolitan Opera debut in New York as Fiordiligi, remaining on its roster until 1966. She also sang widely in the United States and Europe as a concert artist. Her success in Vienna led her to being the first American to be made an Austrian Kammersängerin in 1962. She retired in 1971. Stich-Randall was especially esteemed for her roles in Mozart's operas.

Stiedry, Fritz, eminent Austrian-born American conductor; b. Vienna, Oct. 11, 1883; d. Zürich, Aug. 9, 1968. He studied jurisprudence in Vienna and took a course in composition with Mandyczewski. Mahler recommended him to Schuch in Dresden, and he became his assistant conductor (1907–08); he subsequently was active as a theater conductor in the German provinces, and in Prague. He conducted at the Berlin Opera (1916–23), then led the Vienna Volksoper (1923–25). After traveling as a guest conductor in Italy, Spain, and Scandinavia (1925–28), he returned to Berlin as conductor of the Städtische Oper (1929–33). With the advent of the Nazi regime in 1933, he went to Russia, where he conducted the Leningrad Phil. (1934–37). In 1938 he emigrated to the United States and became a naturalized American citizen; he conducted the New Friends of Music Orch. in New York; on Nov. 15, 1946, he made his Metropolitan Opera debut in New York conducting *Siegfried*, remaining on its roster as one of its most distinguished conductors until 1958. As a conductor, he championed the 2d Viennese School of composition. He was a close friend of Schoenberg; he conducted first performances of his opera *Die glückliche Hand* in Vienna (1924) and his 2d Chamber Sym. in N.Y. (1940). He also gave fine performances of the operas of Wagner and Verdi.

Stigelli, Giorgio (real name, **Georg Stiegele**), celebrated German tenor; b. 1815; d. Boschetti, near Monza, July 3, 1868. He made extensive concert tours in Europe, and appeared in America in 1864–65. He composed many songs, among them the popular "Die schönsten Augen."

Stignani, Ebe, esteemed Italian mezzo-soprano; b. Naples, July 11, 1904; d. Imola, Oct. 6, 1974. She studied voice with Agostino Roche at the Naples Cons. She made her operatic debut as Amneris at the Teatro San Carlo in Naples (1925), then joined Milan's La Scala in 1926, winning great distinction for her roles in Italian operas as well as Gluck's Orfeo, Brangäne, and Ortrud. She made guest appearances at London's Covent Garden, winning success as Amneris (1937, 1939, 1955), Azucena (1939, 1952), and Adalgisa (1952, 1957); she also sang in San Francisco (1938, 1948). In 1958 she made her operatic farewell as Azucena at London's Drury Lane.

Still, William Grant, eminent black American composer; b. Woodville, Miss., May 11, 1895; d. Los Angeles, Dec. 3, 1978. His father was bandmaster in Woodville; after his death when Still was in infancy, his mother moved the family to Little Rock, Ark., where she became a high school teacher. He grew up in a home with cultured, middle-class values, and his stepfather encouraged his interest in music by taking him to see operettas and buying him operatic recordings; he was also given violin lessons. He attended Wilberforce College in preparation for a medical career, but became active in musical activities on campus; after dropping out of college, he worked with various groups, including that of W. C. Handy (1916), then attended the Oberlin (Ohio) College-Cons. During World War I, he played violin in the U.S. Army band, afterward he returned to work with Handy, and became oboist in the Shuffle Along orch. (1921), then studied composition with Varèse, and at the New England Cons. of Music in Boston with Chadwick. He held a Guggenheim fellowship in 1934–35 and was awarded honorary doctorates by Howard Univ. (1941), Oberlin College (1947), and Bates College (1954). Determined to develop a symphonic type of Negro music, he wrote an *Afro-American Symphony* (1930). In his music he occasionally made use of actual Negro folk songs, but mostly he invented his thematic materials. He married the writer Verna Arvey, who collaborated with him as librettist in his stage works.

WORKS: DRAMATIC: OPERAS: *Blue Steel* (1934); *Troubled Island* (1941); *A Bayou Legend* (1940; PBS, 1981); *A Southern Interlude* (1943); *Costaso* (1950); *Mota* (1951); *The Pillar* (1956); *Minette Fontaine* (1958); *Highway 1, U.S.A.* (1962; Miami, May 13, 1963). BALLETS: *La Guiablesse* (1927); *Sahdji* (1930); *Lennox Avenue* (1937); *Miss Sally's Party* (1940). INCIDENTAL MUSIC: *The Prince and the Mermaid* (1965).

BIBL.: V. Arvey, *W. G. S.* (N.Y., 1939); R. Simpson, *W. G. S.: The Man and His Music* (diss., Michigan State Univ., 1964); R. Haas, ed., *W. G. S. and the Fusion of Cultures in American Music* (Los Angeles, 1972); A. Arvey, *In One Lifetime* (Fayetteville, Ark., 1984).

Stillman-Kelley, Edgar. See **Kelley, Edgar Stillman.**

Stilwell, Richard (Dale), outstanding American baritone; b. St. Louis, May 6, 1942. After studying English at Anderson (Ind.) College, he appeared as Silvio in *Pagliacci* with the St. Louis Grand Opera (1962), then studied voice with F. St. Leger and P. Mathen at the Indiana Univ. School of Music in Bloomington (B.A., 1966) and with D. Ferro in N.Y. On April 7, 1970, he made a successful debut as Pelléas with the N.Y. City Opera. In 1973 he made his British debut as Ulysses in *Il ritorno d'Ulisse in Patria* at the Glyndebourne Festival. He was chosen to create the role of Constantine in Pasatieri's *The Seagull* (Houston, 1974) and the title role in Pasatieri's *Ines de Castro* (Baltimore, 1976). On Oct. 15, 1976, he made his Metropolitan Opera debut in New York as Guglielmo in *Così fan tutte*; he scored a major success there as Billy Budd in 1978; he also appeared at the Paris Opéra, the Netherlands Opera, the Chicago Lyric Opera, the Washington (D.C.) Opera Soc., and the Berlin Deutsche Oper; likewise he sang in concerts with the major U.S. orchs. In 1988 he sang in the premiere of Argento's *The Aspern Papers* in Dallas. In 1990 he appeared as Sharpless in Lyons. He sang Don Alfonso in Seattle in 1992. In 1994 he was engaged to sing in Barber's *Vanessa* in Dallas. He appeared in *The Ballad of Baby Doe* at the Washington (D.C.) Opera in 1997. In addition to his remarkable portrayal of Pelléas, he also excels as Papageno, Don Giovanni, Figaro in *Il Barbiere di Siviglia*, Don Pasquale, Eugene Onegin, Rodrigo in *Don Carlos*, and Ford in *Falstaff*.

Stock, Frederick (Friedrich August), respected German-born American conductor; b. Jülich, Nov. 11, 1872; d. Chicago, Oct. 20, 1942. He was first trained in music by his father, a bandmaster, then studied violin with G. Japha and composition with Wüllner, Zöllner, and Humperdinck at the Cologne Cons. (1886–91). From 1891 to 1895 he was a violinist in the Cologne municipal orch. In 1895 he was engaged as a violist in Theodore Thomas's newly organized Chicago Orch., becoming his assistant conductor in 1901; following Thomas's death in 1905, he inherited the orch., which took the name of the Theodore Thomas Orch. in 1906; it became the Chicago Sym. Orch. in 1912, with Stock serving as its conductor until his death, the 1918–19 season excepted. In 1919 he became a naturalized American citizen. As a conductor, Stock was extremely competent, even though he totally lacked that ineffable quality of making orch. music a vivid experience in sound; but he had the merit of giving adequate performances of the classics of Wagner and of the German Romantic school. He also programmed several American works, as long as they followed the Germanic tradition. The flowering of the Chicago Sym. Orch. was to be accomplished by his successors Reiner and Solti. Stock was also a composer, numbering among his works a Violin Concerto (Norfolk Festival, June 3, 1915, E. Zimbalist soloist, composer conducting).

Stockhausen, family of prominent German musicians:

(1) Franz (Anton Adam) Stockhausen, harpist, teacher, and composer; b. Cologne, Sept. 1, 1789; d. Colmar, Sept. 10, 1868. He went to Paris about 1812, and from 1825 toured Europe in concerts with his wife, the soprano Margarethe (née Schmuck) Stockhausen (b. Gebweiler, March 29, 1803; d. Colmar, Oct. 6, 1877), who had been a pupil of Gioseffo Catrufo at the Paris Cons. In 1840 they settled in Alsace. They had 2 sons who became musicians.

(2) Julius (Christian) Stockhausen, esteemed baritone, conductor, and pedagogue; b. Paris, July 22, 1826; d. Frankfurt am Main, Sept. 22, 1906. He began his musical training at an early age with his parents; he studied piano with Karl Kienzl and also received instruction in organ, violin, and cello; in 1843 he went to Paris to study with Cramer, then continued his training at the Cons. (from 1845), and also received private lessons in harmony from Matthäus Nagillers and in singing from Manuel García. In 1848 he sang in Elijah in Basel, and in the next year sang before Queen Victoria in London, then toured widely in Europe as a concert singer. He was 2d baritone at the Mannheim Court Theater (1852–53), then was a member of the Paris Opéra Comique (1856–59). In 1863 he became conductor of the Hamburg Phil. Soc. and Singakademie, positions he held until 1867, then was conductor of the Berlin Sternscher Gesangverein (1874–78). Settling in Frankfurt am Main, he taught voice at the Hoch Cons. (1878–80; 1883–84); he also taught at his own school (from 1880). He publ. *Gesangs-methode* (2 vols., 1886–87; also in Eng.). He was a distinguished interpreter of the lieder of Schubert and Brahms; the latter was a close friend.

BIBL.: J. Wirth-Stockhausen, *J. S.: Der Sänger des deutschen Liedes* (Frankfurt am Main, 1927).

(3) Franz Stockhausen, pianist, conductor, and teacher; b. Gebweiler, Jan. 30, 1839; d. Strasbourg, Jan. 4, 1926. He began his musical studies with his parents, and after piano lessons from Alkan in Paris, he pursued training with Moscheles, Richter, Hauptmann, and Davidov at the Leipzig Cons. (1860–62). He was music director in Thann, Alsace (1863–66), then went to Strasbourg, where he was conductor of the Société de Chant Sacré (1868–79), music director at the Cathedral (from 1868), and director of the Cons. and city concerts (1871–1908).

Stockhausen, Karlheinz, outstanding German composer; b. Modrath, near Cologne, Aug. 22, 1928. He was orphaned during World War II and was compelled to hold various jobs to keep body and soul together; all the same, he learned to play the piano, violin, and oboe; he then studied piano with Hans Otto Schmidt-Neuhaus (1947–50), form with H. Schröder (1948), and composition with Frank Martin (1950) at the Cologne Staatliche Hochschule für Musik; he also took courses in German philology, philosophy, and musicology at the Univ. of Cologne. After studies in Darmstadt (1951), he received instruction in composition from Messiaen in Paris (1952); subsequently he studied communications theory and phonetics with Werner Meyer-Eppler at the Univ. of Bonn (1954–56). He was active at the electronic music studio of the West German Radio in Cologne (from 1953) and also was a lecturer at the Internationalen Ferienkurse für Musik in Darmstadt (until 1974) and was founder-artistic director of the Cologne Kurse für Neue Musik (1963–68); likewise he served as prof. of composition at the Cologne Hochschule für Musik (1971–77). He was made a member of the Swedish Royal Academy (1970), the Berlin Academy of Arts (1973), and the American Academy and Inst. of Arts and Letters (1979); he also was made a Commandeur dans l'Ordre des Arts et des Lettres of France (1985) and an honorary member of the Royal Academy of Music in London (1987). He investigated the potentialities of *musique concrète* and partly incorporated its techniques into his own empiric method of composition, which from the very first included highly complex contrapuntal conglomerates with uninhibited applications of noneuphonious dissonance as well as recourse to the primal procedures of obdurate iteration of single tones; all this set in the freest of rhythmic patterns and diversified by constantly changing instrumental colors with obsessive percussive effects. He further perfected a system of constructivist composition, in which the subjective choice of the performer determines the succession of given thematic ingredients and their polyphonic simultaneities, ultimately leading to a totality of aleatory procedures in which the ostensible application of a composer's commanding function is paradoxically reasserted by the inclusion of prerecorded materials and by recombinant uses of electronically altered thematic ingredients. He evolved energetic missionary activities in behalf of new music as a lecturer and master of ceremonies at avant-garde meetings all over the world; having mastered the intricacies of the English language, he made a lecture tour of Canadian and American Univs. in 1958; in 1965 he was a visiting prof. of composition at the Univ. of Pa. and a visiting prof. at the Univ. of Calif. at Davis in 1966–67; in 1969 he gave highly successful public lectures in England that were attended by hordes of musical and unmusical novitiates. Stockhausen is a pioneer of "time-space" music, marked by a controlled improvisation, and adding the vectorial (i.e., directional) parameter to the 4 traditional aspects of serial music (pitch, duration, timbre, and dynamics), with performers and electronic apparatuses placed in different parts of the concert hall; such performances, directed by himself, were often accompanied by screen projections and audience participation; he also specified the architectural aspects of the auditoriums in which he gave his demonstrations. His annotations to his own works were publ. in the series entitled *Texte* (6 vols., Cologne, 1963–88). See also R. Maconie, ed., *Stockhausen on Music: Lectures and Interviews* (London and N.Y., 1989).

WORKS: DRAMATIC: *Originale*, music theater (1961); *Sternklang*, "park music" for 5 Groups (1971); *Trans* for Orch. (1971); *"Atmen gibt das Leben . . . ,"* choral opera with Orch. or Tape (1975–77); *Licht*, projected cycle of 7 operas, 1 for each day of the week: *Dienstag aus Licht* (1977–91; Leipzig, May 28, 1993); *Donnerstag aus Licht* (1978–80; Milan, April 3, 1981); *Samstag aus Licht* (1981–83; Milan, May 25, 1984); *Montag aus Licht* (1985–88; Milan, May 7, 1988); *Freitag aus Licht* (Leipzig, Sept. 12, 1996).

BIBL.: K. Wörner, *K. S., Werk und Wollen* (Cologne, 1963; Eng. tr. as *S., Life and Work*, London, 1973); C. Cardew, *S. Serves Imperialism* (London, 1974); J. Cott, *S., Conversations with the Composer* (N.Y., 1973, and London, 1974); J. Harvey, *The Music of S.* (London, 1975); R. Maconie, *S.* (London, 1976); B. Sullivan and M. Manion, *S. in Den Haag* (The Hague, 1983); H.-J. Nagel, ed., *S. in Calcutta* (Calcutta, 1984); M. Tannenbaum, *Intervisto sul genio musicale* (Rome, 1985; Eng. tr., 1987, as *Conversations with S.*); *S.: 60. Geburtstag: 22. August 1988* (n.p., 1988); M. Kurtz, *S.: Eine Biographie* (Kassel and Basel, 1988; Eng. tr., 1992, as *S.: A Biography*); C. von Blumröder, *Die Grundlegung der Musik K. S.s* (Stuttgart, 1993).

Stoessel, Albert (Frederic), distinguished American violinist, conductor, teacher, and composer; b. St. Louis, Oct. 11, 1894; d. (fatally stricken while conducting the premiere of Walter Damrosch's *Dunkirk*) N.Y., May 12, 1943. He began his musical studies in St. Louis, then received training in violin with Willy Hess and in theory with Kretzschmar at the Berlin Hochschule für Musik, where he also studied conducting. In 1914 he appeared as a violin soloist in Berlin; after touring in Europe, he returned to St. Louis and performed as a soloist there. During World War I he was a military bandmaster in the U.S. Army (1917–19), serving as director of the school for bandmasters of the American Expeditionary Force in France. Returning to the United States, he appeared as a violin soloist with the Boston Sym. Orch. and toured with Caruso in 1920. He settled in New York in 1921 as Walter Damrosch's successor as conductor of the Oratorio Soc.; he also was named director of music at the Chautauqua Institution (1923) and conductor of the Worcester (Mass.) Music Festival (1925); likewise he appeared widely as a guest conductor. In 1923 he founded the music dept. at N.Y. Univ., which he headed until 1930; he was director of the opera and orch. depts. at the Juilliard Graduate School (from 1927), where he conducted a number of premieres of American works. He was elected a member of the National Inst. of Arts and Letters in 1931. He publ. *The Technic of the Baton* (N.Y., 1920; 2d ed., rev. and enl., 1928). His compositions included an opera, *Garrick* (1936; N.Y., Feb. 24, 1937).

BIBL.: C. McNaughton, *A. S., American Musician* (diss., N.Y. Univ., 1957).

Stöhr, Richard, Austrian-American pedagogue and composer; b. Vienna, June 11, 1874; d. Montpelier, Vt., Dec. 11, 1967. He studied medicine in Vienna (M.D., 1898), but then turned to music and studied with Robert Fuchs and others at the Vienna Cons. In 1903 he was appointed instructor in theory there, and during his long tenure had many pupils who later became celebrated (Artur Rodzinski, Erich Leinsdorf et al.). In 1938 he was compelled to leave Vienna and settled in the United States, where he taught at the Curtis Inst. of Music in Philadelphia (1939–42); he then taught music and German at St. Michael's College in Winooski, Vt. (1943–50). He wrote 4 operas. He publ. a popular manual, *Praktischer Leitfaden der Harmonielehre* (Vienna, 1909; 21st ed., 1963); also *Praktischer Leitfaden des Kontrapunkts* (Hamburg, 1911) and *Musikalische Formenlehre* (Leipzig, 1911; rev. 1933, as *Formenlehre der Musik*); *Modulationslehre* (1932).

BIBL.: H. Sittner, *R. S.: Mensch, Musiker, Lehrer* (Vienna, 1965).

Stojanovič, Peter Lazar, Yugoslav violinist, teacher, and composer; b. Budapest, Sept. 6, 1877; d. Belgrade, Sept. 11, 1957. He studied violin with Hubay at the Budapest Cons. and with J. Grün at the Vienna Cons., where he also received training in composition. In 1913 he established his own school for advanced violin playing in Vienna. In 1925 he settled in Belgrade and became a prof. at the Stankovič Music School; he was its director from 1925 to 1928; from 1937 to 1945 he was a prof. of violin at the Belgrade Academy of Music. He publ. *Schule der Skalentechnik* for Violin. His works include the operas *A Tigris* (The Tiger; Budapest, Nov. 14, 1905), *Das Liebchen am Dache* (Vienna, May 19, 1917), and *Der Herzog von Reichsstadt* (Vienna, Feb. 11, 1921); also 2 ballets.

Stoker, Richard, English composer and author; b. Castleford, Yorkshire, Nov. 8, 1938. He attended the Huddersfield School of Music and School of Art in Yorkshire (1953–58) and studied with Eric Fenby. After further training with Berkeley at the Royal Academy of Music in London (1958–62), he completed his studies with Boulanger in Paris (1962–63). From 1963 to 1987 he taught composition at the Royal Academy of Music. He also was ed. of the journal *Composer* (1969–80). He publ. the autobiographical vols. *Open Window—Open Door* (1985) and *Between the Lines* (1994). His other writings include novels *Tanglewood* (1993) and *Diva* (1995), as well as a collection of short stories (1995). Stoker has composed in various genres producing scores of both a serious and more popular nature. He has utilized a modified serial technique in some of his works, but tonal elements are always in evidence.

WORKS: DRAMATIC: *Johnson Preserv'd*, opera (1966; London, July 4, 1967); *My Friend—My Enemy*, ballet (1970); *Garden Party*, ballet (1973); *Thérèse Raquin*, opera (1979); *Prospero's Magic Island*, musical (1980); film and television scores.

Stokes, Eric (Norman), iconoclastic American composer and teacher; b. Haddon Heights, N.J., July 14, 1930. He studied at Lawrence College (B.Mus., 1952) and with Carl McKinley and Francis Judd Cooke at the New England Cons. of Music (M.Mus., 1956); he completed his education with Argento and Fetler at the Univ. of Minnesota (Ph.D., 1964), where he taught (from 1961; prof. from 1977); he founded its electronic music laboratory and contemporary music ensemble, 1st Minnesota Moving and Storage Warehouse Band (1971). Stokes has been variously described as a crusty, eccentric, wonderfully humorous, very healthy and resourceful American composer of gentle, witty, lyrically accessible music, with a taste for folkloric Americana and a "Whitmanesque" ear. Some of his works (e.g., the series *Phonic Paradigms*) call for unusual instruments that produce unforeseen effects; his *Rock & Roll (Phonic Paradigm I)* (1980) is executed by 5 players hitting rocks together and rolling them across the floor.

WORKS: DRAMATIC: OPERAS: *Horspfal* (1969); *Happ or Orpheus in Clover* (1977); *The Jealous Cellist & Other Acts of Misconduct* (1979); *Itaru the Stonecutter* (1982); *The Further Voyages of the Santa Maria* (1984); *Apollonia's Circus* (1984). Also musicals and theater pieces, including *The Shake of Things to Come (Phonic Paradigm V)* for Mime and 3 Percussionists (1983) and *We're Not Robots, You Know* for Vocal Quintet and Optional Matching Vocal

Quintet and Instrumental Ensemble (1986; Banff, Canada, Dec. 1990).

Stokowski, Leopold (Anthony), celebrated, spectacularly endowed, and magically communicative English-born American conductor; b. London (of a Polish father and an Irish mother), April 18, 1882; d. Nether Wallop, Hampshire, Sept. 13, 1977. He attended Queen's College, Oxford, and the Royal College of Music in London, where he studied organ with Stevenson Hoyte, theory with Walford Davies, and composition with Sir Charles Stanford. At the age of 18, he obtained the post of organist at St. James, Piccadilly. In 1905 he went to America and served as organist and choirmaster at St. Bartholomew's in New York; he became a naturalized American citizen in 1915. In 1909 he was engaged to conduct the Cincinnati Sym. Orch.; although his contract was for 5 years, he obtained a release in 1912 in order to accept an offer from the Philadelphia Orch. This was the beginning of a long and spectacular career as a sym. conductor; he led the Philadelphia Orch. for 24 years as its sole conductor, bringing it to a degree of brilliance that rivaled the greatest orchs. in the world. In 1931 he was officially designated by the board of directors of the Philadelphia Orch. as music director, which gave him control over the choice of guest conductors and soloists. He conducted most of the repertoire by heart, an impressive accomplishment at the time; he changed the seating of the orch., placing violins to the left and cellos to the right. After some years of leading the orch. with a baton, he finally dispensed with it and shaped the music with the 10 fingers of his hands. He emphasized the colorful elements in the music; he was the creator of the famous "Philadelphia sound" in the strings, achieving a well-nigh bel canto quality. Tall and slender, with an aureole of blond hair, his figure presented a striking contrast with his stocky, mustachioed German predecessors; he was the first conductor to attain the status of a star comparable to that of a film actor. Abandoning the proverbial ivory tower in which most conductors dwelt, he actually made an appearance as a movie actor in the film *One Hundred Men and a Girl.* In 1940 he agreed to participate in the production of Walt Disney's celebrated film *Fantasia*, which featured animated characters; Stokowski conducted the music and in one sequence engaged in a bantering colloquy with Mickey Mouse. He was lionized by the Philadelphians; in 1922 he received the Edward Bok Award of $10,000 as "the person who has done the most for Philadelphia." He was praised in superlative terms in the press, but not all music critics approved of his cavalier treatment of sacrosanct masterpieces, for he allowed himself to alter the orchestration; he doubled some solo passages in the brass, and occasionally introduced percussion instruments not provided in the score; he even cut out individual bars that seemed to him devoid of musical action. Furthermore, Stokowski's own orch. arrangements of Bach raised the pedantic eyebrows of professional musicologists; yet there is no denying the effectiveness of the sonority and the subtlety of color that he succeeded in creating by such means. Many great musicians hailed Stokowski's new orch. sound; Rachmaninoff regarded the Philadelphia Orch. under Stokowski, and later under Ormandy, as the greatest with which he had performed. Stokowski boldly risked his popularity with the Philadelphia audiences by introducing modern works. He conducted Schoenberg's music, culminating in the introduction of his formidable score *Gurre-Lieder* on April 8, 1932. An even greater gesture of defiance of popular tastes was his world premiere of *Amériques* by Varèse on April 9, 1926, a score that opens with a siren and thrives on dissonance. Stokowski made history by joining the forces of the Philadelphia Orch. with the Philadelphia Grand Opera Co. in the first American performance of Berg's masterpiece *Wozzeck* (March 31, 1931). The opposition of some listeners was now vocal; when the audible commotion in the audience erupted during his performance of Webern's Sym., he abruptly stopped conducting, walked off the stage, then returned only to begin the work all over again. From his earliest years with the Philadelphia Orch., Stokowski adopted the habit of addressing the audience, to caution them to keep their peace during the performance of a modernistic score, or reprimanding them for their lack of progressive views; once he even took to task the prim Philadelphia ladies for bringing their knitting to the concert. In 1933 the board of directors took an unusual step in announcing that there would be no more "debatable music" performed by the orch.; Stokowski refused to heed this proclamation. Another eruption of discontent ensued when he programmed some Soviet music at a youth concert and trained the children to sing the Internationale. Stokowski was always interested in new electronic sound; he was the first to make use of the Theremin in the orch. in order to enhance the sonorities of the bass section. He was instrumental in introducing electrical recordings. In 1936 he resigned as music director of the Philadelphia Orch.; he was succeeded by Eugene Ormandy, but continued to conduct concerts as coconductor of the orch. until 1938. From 1940 to 1942 he took a newly organized All-American Youth Orch. on a tour in the United States and South America. During the season 1942–43 he was assoc. conductor, with Toscanini, of the NBC Sym. Orch.; he shared the season of 1949–50 with Mitropoulos as conductor of the N.Y. Phil.; from 1955 to 1960 he conducted the Houston Sym. Orch. In 1962 he organized in New York the American Sym. Orch. and led it until 1972; on April 26, 1965, at the age of 83, he conducted the orch. in the first complete performance of the 4th Sym. of Charles Ives. In 1973 he went to London, where he continued to make recordings and conduct occasional concerts; he also appeared in television interviews. Stokowski was married 3 times: his 1st wife was **Olga Samaroff**, whom he married in 1911; they were divorced in 1923; his 2d wife was Evangeline Brewster Johnson, heiress to the Johnson and Johnson drug fortune; they were married in 1926 and divorced in 1937; his 3d marriage, to Gloria Vanderbilt, produced a ripple of prurient newspaper publicity because of the disparity in their ages; he was 63, she was 21; they were married in 1945 and divorced in 1955. Stokowski publ. *Music for All of Us* (N.Y., 1943), which was translated into the Russian, Italian, and Czech languages.

BIBL.: E. Johnson, ed., *S.: Essays in Analysis of His Art* (London, 1973); P. Robinson, *S.* (N.Y., 1977); A. Chasins, *L. S.: A Profile* (N.Y., 1979); O. Daniel, *S.: A Counterpoint of View* (N.Y., 1982); P. Opperby, *L. S.* (Tunbridge Wells and N.Y., 1982); W. Smith, *The Mystery of L. S.* (Rutherford, N.J., 1990).

Stoltz, Rosine (real name, **Victoire Noël**), famous French mezzo-soprano; b. Paris, Feb. 13, 1815; d. there, July 28, 1903. She was the daughter of a janitor, and was sent by Duchess de Berri to a convent, and in 1826 to the Choron School, which she entered under the name of Rosine Niva; it was under that name that she began her career as a concert artist; she then used the name of Mlle. Ternaux, and later Mlle. Héloise Stoltz (the latter being derived from her mother's maiden name, Stoll). In 1832 she made her stage debut as Victoire Ternaux at the Théâtre Royal de la Monnaie in Brussels; after appearances in Spa, Antwerp, Amsterdam, and Lille, she obtained her first important engagement as Alice in *Robert le diable* at the Théâtre Royal de la Monnaie in Brussels in 1835; the next year she sang Rachel in *La Juive* there, and in 1837 married Alphonse Lescuyer, the theater's director. She made her debut at the Paris Opéra as Rachel on Aug. 25, 1837; subsequently she appeared there in many premieres, including operas by Halévy; she also created the roles of Ascanio in Berlioz's *Benvenuto Cellini* (Sept. 3, 1838), and Léonore in *La Favorite* (Dec. 2, 1840) and Zaida in *Dom Sébastien* (Nov. 13, 1843), both by Donizetti. She became intimate with Leon Pillet, manager of the Opéra from 1844, and through him wielded considerable influence on appointments of new singers; after a series of attacks in the press, accusing her of unworthy intrigues, she resigned in March 1847. She fought for vindication through 3 obviously inspired pamphlets (C. Cantinjou, *Les Adieux de Madame Stoltz*; E. Perignon, *Rosine Stoltz*; and J. Lemer, *Madame Rosine Stoltz*), all publ. in 1847. At the invitation of the Brazilian emperor Don Pedro (who was romantically attached to her) she made 4 tours of Brazil between 1850 and 1859, at a salary of 400,000 francs a season. In 1854 and 1855 she once again sang at the Paris Opéra. In 1860 she made her farewell operatic appearance in Lyons, and then sang in concerts for several seasons before retiring. Ernst II of Württemberg named her Baroness Stoltzenau and countess of Ketschendorf in 1865. She subsequently was made duchess of Lesignano upon her marriage to Duke Carlo Lesignano in 1872, and then married the Spanish prince Manuel Godoi Bassano de la Paix in 1878. She publ. 6 songs (not composed by her, in all probability), and her name (as Princesse de Lesignano) was used as author of a learned vol., *Les Constitutions de tous les pays civilisés* (1880), which was written in her behalf.

BIBL.: G. Bord, *R. S.* (Paris, 1909).

Stolz, Robert (Elisabeth), noted Austrian conductor and composer; b. Graz, Aug. 25, 1880; d. Berlin, June 27, 1975. His father was the conductor and pedagogue Jacob Stolz and his mother the pianist Ida Bondy; after initial studies with them, he was a pupil of R. Fuchs at the Vienna Cons. and of Humperdinck in Berlin. He became a répétiteur in Graz in 1897; after serving as 2d conductor in Marburg an der Drau (1898–1902), he was 1st conductor in Salzburg (1902–03) and at the German Theater in Brünn (1903–05). From 1905 to 1917 he was chief conductor of the Theater an der Wien, where he conducted the premieres of many Viennese operettas. He became successful as a composer of popular songs in the Viennese tradition; his first success as an operetta composer came with his *Der Tanz ins Glück* (Vienna, Oct. 18, 1921). In 1924 he went to Berlin, where he eventually won success as a composer for film musicals. His disdain for the Nazi regime led him to leave Germany in 1936 and then Austria in 1938, but not before he helped to smuggle numerous Jews out of the clutches of the Nazis prior to leaving for Paris in 1938. In 1940 he went to the United States and was active as a conductor and as a composer for Hollywood films. In 1946 he returned to Vienna, where he conducted and composed until his last years. He possessed an extraordinary facility for stage music and composed about 65 operettas and musicals in a typical Viennese manner; of these the most famous is *2 Herzen im 3/4 Takt* or *Der verlorene Walzer* (Zürich, Sept. 30, 1933). Other operettas are *Die lustigen Weiber von Wien* (Munich, 1909); *Das Glücksmädel* (1910); *Das Lumperl* (Graz, 1915); *Lang, lang, ist's her* (Vienna, March 28, 1917); *Die Tanzgräfin* (Vienna, May 13, 1921); *Mädi* (Berlin, April 1, 1923); *Ein Ballroman oder Der Kavalier von zehn bis vier* (Vienna, Feb. 29, 1924); *Eine einzige Nacht* (Vienna, Dec. 23, 1927); *Peppina* (1931); *Wenn die kleinen Veilchen bluhen* (The Hague, April 1, 1932); *Venus im Seide* (Zürich, Dec. 10, 1932); *Der verlorene Walzer* (Zürich, Sept. 30, 1933); *Gruzi* (Zürich, 1934); *Frühling im Prater* (Vienna, Dec. 22, 1949); *Karneval in Wien* (1950); *Trauminsel* (Bregenz, July 21, 1962); *Frühjahrs-Parade* (Vienna, March 25, 1964). He wrote about 100 film scores and nearly 2,000 lieder. His other works include waltzes, marches, and piano pieces. After he was forced to leave Austria, he composed a funeral march for Hitler (at a time when Hitler was, unfortunately, very much alive).

BIBL.: G. Holm, *Im Dreivierteltakt durch die Welt* (Linz, 1948); W.-D. Brümmel and F. van Booth, *R. S.: Melodie eines Lebens* (Stuttgart, 1967); O. Herbrich, *R. S.: König der Melodie* (Vienna and Munich, 1975).

Stolz, Teresa (real name, **Teresina Stolzová**), renowned Bohemian soprano; b. Elbekosteletz, June 5, 1834; d. Milan, Aug. 23, 1902. She was born into a musical family; her twin sisters, Francesca and Ludmila, also became sopranos; they were intimate with the composer Luigi Ricci, who had a child by each of them; Ludmila later became his wife. Teresa studied at the Prague Cons. and then with Ricci in Trieste (1856), making her operatic debut in 1857 in Tiflis, where she sang regularly during the next 5 seasons; she also appeared in Odessa and Constantinople. In 1863 she sang in Turin, and thereafter appeared with brilliant success in the major Italian opera centers. She was closely associated with Verdi from 1872 to 1876, leading some writers to speculate that she was his mistress. She was without question one of the greatest interpreters of Verdi's heroines, excelling particularly as Aida and Leonora; she also sang in the premiere of his Requiem (1874). After singing in St. Petersburg (1876–77), she made her farewell appearance as a soloist in the Requiem at Milan's La Scala on June 30, 1879. Her vocal gifts were extraordinary and her range extended from g to c#³.

BIBL.: J. Šolín, *T. S.ová: První a nejslavější Aida* (T. S.: The First and Most Celebrated Aida; Mlnik, 1944; 2d ed., 1946); U. Zoppi, *Mariani, Verdi e la S.* (Milan, 1947).

Stolze, Gerhard, German tenor; b. Dessau, Oct. 1, 1926; d. Garmisch-Partenkirchen, March 11, 1979. He studied voice in Dresden and Berlin. He made his operatic debut as Augustin Moser in *Die Meistersinger von Nürnberg* at the Dresden State Opera in 1949. From 1951 he made regular appearances at the Bayreuth Festivals; he also sang at the Vienna State Opera, and from 1953 to 1961 at the Berlin State Opera. He established his reputation as a Wagnerian singer, but also sang leading parts in German contemporary operas, including Satan in Martin's *Le Mystère de la Nativité* (1960).

Storace, family of Italian-English musicians:

(1) Stephen (Stefano) Storace, double-bass player; b. Torre Annunziata, *c.*1725; d. *c.*1781. By 1748 he was in Dublin, where he played in the Smock Alley Theatre band. By 1758 he was in London, where he tr. several works for performance at Marylebone Gardens. He played in the band at the King's Theatre, and also at the 3 Choirs Festival (1759–70), then took his family to Italy in 1778. He had 2 children who became musicians.

(2) Stephen (John Seymour) Storace, noted composer; b. London, April 4, 1762; d. there, March 19, 1796. He entered the Cons. di S. Onofrio in Naples about 1776, where he studied violin, then followed his sister to Vienna, where he became acquainted with Mozart. Two of his operas to Italian librettos were produced in Vienna with satisfying success: *Gli sposi malcontenti* (June 1, 1785) and *Gli equivoci* (Dec. 27, 1786). In 1787 he returned to London, where he produced another Italian opera, *La Cameriera astuta* (March 4, 1788), and a number of English operas, among which *The Haunted Tower* (Nov. 24, 1789) became extremely successful. His finest work for the stage, *The Pirates*, was premiered at the King's Theatre on Nov. 21, 1792. During the 1792–93 season, he was in charge of the Italian opera productions at the Little Theatre and at Drury Lane.

BIBL.: J. Girdham, *English Opera in Late Eighteenth-Century London: S. S. at Drury Lane* (Oxford, 1997).

(3) Nancy (Ann or **Anna Selina) Storace,** celebrated soprano; b. London, Oct. 27, 1765; d. there, Aug. 28, 1817. She studied in London with Sacchini and Rauzzini. She began her career singing in concerts as a child, and appeared at Hereford's 3 Choirs Festival in 1777; the following year she was taken by her parents to Italy, where she began her operatic career in Florence in 1780; she then sang in Parma (1781) and Milan (1782). In 1783 she went to Vienna as prima donna, excelling in the performance of comic operas. She married the English composer John Abraham Fisher, but the marriage did not last. She created the role of Susanna in Mozart's *Le nozze di Figaro* (May 1, 1786). In 1787 she returned to London and sang at the King's Theatre until it was destroyed by fire in 1789; she then sang at Drury Lane until 1796, appeared in Handel's oratorios, and sang at the King's Theatre in 1793. In 1797 she toured Europe with the tenor John Braham, who became her lover. She continued to sing in London playhouses until her retirement from the stage in 1808. She and Braham lived together until 1816.

BIBL.: G. Brace, *Anna . . . Susanna: Anna Storace, Mozart's First Susanna: Her Life, Times, and Family* (London, 1991).

Storch, M. Anton, Austrian conductor and composer; b. Vienna, Dec. 22, 1813; d. there, Dec. 31, 1888. He was conductor at the Carl and Josephstadt theaters in Vienna, where he produced several of his operettas and opera burlesques: *Romeo und Julie* (Oct. 31, 1863), *Das Festkleid* (April 1, 1865), *Löwen im Dorfe* (Sept. 27, 1866), *Wiener Zugstücke* (April 26, 1868), and *Prinz Taugenichts* (March 8, 1870), the last being successful.

Storchio, Rosina, Italian soprano; b. Venice, May 19, 1876; d. Milan, July 24, 1945. She studied at the Milan Cons., then made her operatic debut at Milan's Teatro del Verme as Micaëla in *Carmen* in 1892. In 1895 she made her first appearance at Milan's La Scala as Sophie in *Werther*; in 1897 she sang in the premiere of Leoncavallo's *La Bohème* in Venice; returning to Milan, she appeared in the title role of Leoncavallo's *Zazà* at the Teatro Lirico in 1900; she then appeared at La Scala (from 1902), where she sang in the premieres of several operas, including the title role of *Madama Butterfly* (Feb. 7, 1904); she continued to appear there until 1918. After a series of tours in South America and in Europe, she was briefly engaged at N.Y.'s Manhattan Opera House and at the Chicago Grand Opera (1920–21); she then retired from the stage. She was paralyzed during the last years of her life as a result of an apoplectic stroke.

Storck, Karl G(ustav) L(udwig), Alsatian writer on music; b. Dürmenach, April 23, 1873; d. Olsberg, Westphalia, May 9, 1920. He studied at the Univs. of Strasbourg and Berlin (Ph.D., 1895). He wrote music criticism for the *Deutsche Zeitung* (Berlin). He publ. a unique ed., *Musik und Musiker in Karikatur und Satire* (Oldenburg, 1911), richly illustrated by numerous reproductions of caricatures on musical subjects; other publications include: *Der Tanz* (1903); *Geschichte der Musik* (1904; 6th ed., 1926); *Das Opernbuch* (1905); *Die Kulturelle Bedeutung der Musik* (1906); *Mozart: Sein Leben und Schaffen* (1908; 2d ed., 1923); *Musik-Politik* (1911); *Emil Jaques-Dalcroze: Seine Stellung und Aufgabe in unserer Zeit* (1912).

Stoyanov, Veselin, Bulgarian composer; b. Shumen, April 20, 1902; d. Sofia, June 29, 1969. He studied piano with his brother Andrei Stoyanov at the Sofia Cons, graduating in 1926, then went to Vienna, where he studied with Joseph Marx and Franz Schmidt. In 1937 he was appointed prof. at the Cons. in Sofia; he was director of the Cons. in 1943–44 and from 1956 to 1962. Among his works were the operas *Jensko zarstwo* (Kingdom of Women; Sofia, April 5, 1935), *Salambo* (Sofia, May 22, 1940), and *Hitar Petar* (The Wise Peter; 1952; Sofia, 1958); also the ballet *Papessa Joănna* (1966; Sofia, Oct. 22, 1968).

Stracciari, Riccardo, Italian baritone; b. Casalecchio di Reno, near Bologna, June 26, 1875; d. Rome, Oct. 10, 1955. He studied with Ulisse Masetti in Bologna, where he made his operatic debut as Marcello in 1898. He was a member of La Scala in Milan (1904–06) and also sang at Covent Garden in London (1905). He made his debut at the Metropolitan Opera in New York on Dec. 1, 1906, as Germont *père*; he remained on the roster until 1908, then returned to Europe, continuing his career there and in South America. He returned to the United States to sing with the Chicago Opera (1917–19) and in San Francisco (1925); he continued to make appearances in Italy until 1944; he also was active as a teacher from 1926, his most eminent student being Boris Christoff. He sang all the major baritone roles in the operatic repertoire, his most famous being Rossini's Figaro, which he sang more than 900 times.

Strada, Anna Maria, famous Italian soprano who flourished in the first half of the 18th century, also known under her married name as **Anna Maria Strada del Pò.** She was born in Bergamo. After serving Count Colloredo, governor of Milan, and singing in Venice (1720–21), she appeared in Naples (1724–26). She then was engaged by Handel for his opera and oratorio seasons in England, making her debut in London as Adelaide in the premiere of his *Lotario* in 1729, and remaining as his principal soprano until 1737. Handel also composed the following roles for her: Partenope (1730), Cleofide in *Poro* (1731), Fulvia in *Ezio* (1732), Elmira in *Sosarme* (1732), Angelica in *Orlando* (1733), Deborah (1733), Josabeth in *Athalia* (1733), Arianna (1734), Erato in *Terpsicore* (1734), Ginevra in *Ariodante* (1735), Alcina (1735), the soprano part in *Alexander's Feast* (1736), Atalanta (1736), Tusnelda in *Arminio* (1737), Arianna in *Giustino* (1737), Berenice (1737), and Bellezza in *Il trionfo del tempo* (1737). In 1738 she was called to Breda to sing for the Princess of Orange; after appearances with Senesino in Naples (1739–40), she retired to Bergamo.

Stradella, Alessandro, important Italian composer; b. Nepi, near Viterbo, 1639; d. (murdered) Genoa, Feb. 25, 1682. He was a scion of nobility, and received his early training in Bologna. In 1667 he went to Rome, where he composed oratorios, prologues, intermezzos for opera, etc. He led a tempestuous life, replete with illicit liaisons, flights from personal vendettas, and some criminal acts. In Rome he attempted to embezzle funds from the Roman Catholic church, and in 1669 fled the city to avoid exposure. He returned to Rome after the affair calmed down, but again got in trouble when he aroused the enmity of Cardinal Alderan Cibo. In 1677 he was forced to flee Rome again, and he went to Venice, where he became involved in a torrid affair with the fiancée of the Venetian nobleman Alvise Contarini; he persuaded the lady to accompany him to Turin, and the outraged bridegroom and a band of assassins followed in hot pursuit. Stradella escaped and fled to Genoa. There he became entangled with a married woman, a sister of the Lomellini brothers, who had a high social standing in the town. This time Stradella failed to evade the vengeful brothers, who hired an experienced murderer to kill him; the bloody deed was done on Feb. 25, 1682. A rather successful opera, *Alessandro Stradella* by Flotow (Hamburg, 1844), dramatized his stormy life and death; other operas on Stradella were composed by Niedermeyer (Paris, 1837) and Sinico (Lugo, 1863).

As a composer, Stradella left an important legacy, both in opera and in instrumental writing. His operas *La forza dell'amor paterno, Le gare dell'amore eroico*, and *Il Trespole tutore* were staged in Genoa (1678–79); he also composed the oratorio *La Susanna* and a wedding serenade, *Il barcheggio*, for Duke Francesco d'Este of Modena (1681). Other operas were *Il moro per amore, Il Corispero*, and *Doriclea*. His oratorios include *S. Giovanni Battista* and *S. Giovanni Crisostomo*; another oratorio, *S. Editta, vergine e monaca, regina d'Inghilterra*, remained unfinished. An ed. of his oratorios was begun in 1969, under the editorship of L. Bianchi.

BIBL.: A. Catelani, *Delle opere di A. S. esistenti nell'archivio musicale della R. Biblioteca Palatina di Modena* (Modena, 1866); H. Hess, *Die Opern A. S.'s*, in *Publicationen der Internationalen Musik-Gesellschaft*, supplement, II/3 (1906); F. Crawford, *S.* (London, 1911); A. Gentili, *A. S.* (Turin, 1936); G. Roncaglia, *Il genio novatore di A. S.* (Modena, 1941); O. Jander, *A Catalogue of the Manuscripts of Compositions by A. S. Found in European and American Libraries* (Wellesley, Mass., 1960; 2d ed., rev., 1962); R. Giazotto, *Vita di A. S.* (2 vols., Milan, 1962); O. Jander, *A. S. and His Minor Dramatic Works* (diss., Harvard Univ., 1962); L. Bianchi, *Carissimi, S., Scarlatti e l'oratorio musicale* (Rome, 1969); C. Gianturco, *The Operas of A. S. (1644–1682)* (diss., Univ. of Oxford, 1970); idem, ed., *A. S. e Modena* (Modena, 1983); C. Gianturco and E. McCrickard, *A. S. (1639–1682): A Thematic Catalog of His Compositions* (Stuyvesant, N.Y., 1991).

Straesser, Joep, Dutch composer and teacher; b. Amsterdam, March 11, 1934. He studied musicology at the Univ. of Amsterdam (1952–55), then took organ lessons with Van der Horst (1956–59) and theory lessons with Felderhof (1959–61) at the Amsterdam Cons.; he also received instruction in composition from Ton de Leeuw (1960–65). He was a church organist (1953–61). From 1962 to 1989 he taught at the Utrecht Cons. Among his many works is *Ueber Erich M.*, Singspiel (1985–86); also *Adastra*, music for ballet (1967).

Strakosch, Maurice, Bohemian pianist and impresario; b. Gross-Seelowitz, near Brünn, Jan. 15, 1825; d. Paris, Oct. 9, 1887. He studied with Sechter at the Vienna Cons., then traveled as a pianist in Europe. He went to New York in 1848 as a teacher, and from 1856 he was active mainly as an impresario. He was the brother-in-law of **Adelina Patti**, and managed her concerts; he, his wife, and Ole Bull toured the United States (1852–54). Returning to New York, he, his brother Max Strakosch (b. Gross-Seelowitz, Sept. 27, 1835; d. N.Y., March 17, 1892), and Bull organized a brief opera season at the Academy of Music in 1855. He then ran his own company (1856–57), which merged with Bernard Ullman's company in 1857; their partnership lasted until 1860, when he again became Patti's manager. In 1861 he went to Europe with the Pattis, and remained Patti's manager until 1868; he also continued to work with his brother, who remained in the United States. Maurice remained active as a pianist, making tours of Europe and the United States with Bull. He also composed, producing the opera *Giovanna di Napoli*. He wrote *Souvenirs d'un impresario* (Paris, 2d ed., 1887) and *Ten Commandments of Music for the Perfection of the Voice* (1896).

Stransky, Josef, Bohemian conductor; b. Humpoletz, near Deutschbrod, Sept. 9, 1872; d. N.Y., March 6, 1936. While studying medicine (M.D., Univ. of Prague, 1896), he also studied music in Leipzig with Jadassohn and in Vienna with R. Fuchs, Bruckner, and Dvořák. In 1898 he was engaged by A. Neumann as 1st Kapellmeister at the Landestheater in Prague; in 1903 he went in a similar capacity to the Stadttheater in Hamburg; in 1910 he resigned from the Hamburg opera to devote himself to concert work; in the autumn of 1911 became Mahler's successor as conductor of the N.Y. Phil. Soc.; a position he held until 1923. A bequest of $1,000,000 to the society (by Joseph Pulitzer, 1912) enabled Stransky to carry out successfully the sweeping reforms instituted by his illustrious predecessor (chief of which was a system of daily rehearsals during the season of 23 weeks). In 1924 he gave up his musical career and spent the rest of his life as an art dealer. He wrote an operetta, *Der General*, which was produced in Hamburg.

Straram, Walther, French conductor; b. London (of French parents), July 9, 1876; d. Paris, Nov. 24, 1933. He was educated in Paris. He played violin in Paris orchs., then was choirmaster at the Opéra Comique there; he later traveled to America as assistant to André Caplet at the Boston Opera Co. Returning to Paris, he established the Concerts Straram, which enjoyed a fine reputation. He conducted the first performance of Ravel's *Bolero* for Ida Rubinstein (dance recital, Nov. 22, 1928).

Stratas, Teresa (real name, **Anastasia Stratakis**), outstanding Canadian soprano; b. Toronto, May 26, 1938. She was born into a family of Greek immigrant restaurateurs. At 12, she began voice training and, at 13, appeared on the radio singing pop songs. In 1954 she entered the Royal Cons. of Music of Toronto to study with Irene Jessner, and in 1959 was awarded her Artist Diploma. In 1958 she sang Nora in Vaughan Williams's *Riders to the Sea* in Toronto. On Oct. 13, 1958, she made her professional operatic debut as Mimi at the Toronto Opera Festival. In 1959 she was a cowinner in the Metropolitan Opera Auditions, which led to her debut with the company in New York on Oct. 28, 1959, as Poussette in *Manon*. She continued to sing at the Metropolitan, winning her first notable success as Liù in 1961. On Aug. 19, 1961, she created the title role in Peggy Glanville-Hicks's *Nausicaa* in Athens. On June 18, 1962, she made her debut at Milan's La Scala as Queen Isabella in the posthumous premiere of Falla's *Atlántida*. She appeared as Desdemona in *Otello* at Expo '67 in Montreal in 1967. In 1974 she starred as Salome in the film version conducted by Karl Böhm. On May 28, 1979, she sang the title role in the first performance of the complete version of Berg's *Lulu* in Paris. She sang Violetta in Zeffirelli's film version of *La Traviata* in 1983. In 1986 she appeared on Broadway. On Dec. 19, 1991, she sang Marie Antoinette in the premiere of Corigliano's *The Ghosts of Versailles* at the Metropolitan Opera. In 1992 she appeared as Mélisande in Chicago. Stratas was made an Officer of the Order of Canada in 1972. A film portrait of her was made by Harry Rasky as *StrataSphere*. Stratas's remarkable lyric voice made her interpretations of such roles as Cherubino, Zerlina, Lisa in *The Queen of Spades*, Marguerite in *Faust*, Micaëla, Liù, and Weill's Jenny particularly memorable.

BIBL.: H. Rasky, *S.: An Affectionate Tribute* (Oxford, 1989).

Straus, Oscar (Nathan), noted Austrian-born French operetta composer and conductor; b. Vienna, March 6, 1870; d. Bad Ischl, Jan. 11, 1954. (His name was spelled "Strauss" on his birth certificate; he cut off the 2d *s* to segregate himself from the multitudinous musical Strausses.) He studied privately in Vienna with A. Prosnitz and H. Gradener, and with Max Bruch in Berlin. From 1893 to 1900 he conducted at various theaters in Austria and Germany. In 1901 he became conductor of the artistic cabaret Uberbrettl in Berlin, and wrote a number of musical farces for it. He remained in Berlin until 1927, then lived in Vienna and Paris; on Sept. 3, 1939, he became a naturalized French citizen. In 1940 he went to America; lived in New York and Hollywood until 1948, when he returned to Europe. He was one of the most successful composers of Viennese operettas. His most celebrated production was *Der tapfere Soldat*, based on G. B. Shaw's play *Arms and the Man* (Vienna, Nov. 14, 1908; in N.Y. as *The Chocolate Soldier*, Nov. 13, 1909; London, Sept. 10, 1910; numerous perfs. all over the world). Other operettas were *Die lustigen Nibelungen* (Vienna, Nov. 12, 1904); *Hugdietrichs Brautfahrt* (Vienna, March 10, 1906); *Ein Walzertraum* (Vienna, March 2, 1907; rev. 1951); *Didi* (Vienna, Oct. 23, 1909); *Das Tal der Liebe* (Berlin and Vienna, simultaneously, Dec. 23, 1909); *Mein junger Herr* (Vienna, Dec. 23, 1910); *Die kleine Freundin* (Vienna, Oct. 20, 1911); *Love and Laughter* (London, 1913); *Rund um die Liebe* (Vienna, Nov. 9, 1914; in N.Y. as *All around Love*, 1917); *Die himmelblaue Zeit* (Vienna, Feb. 21, 1914); *Die schöne Unbekannte* (Vienna, Jan. 15, 1915; in N.Y. as *My Lady's Glove*, 1917); *Der letzte Walzer* (Berlin, Feb. 12, 1920); *Mariette, ou Comment on écrit l'histoire* (Paris, Oct. 1, 1928); *Eine Frau, die weiss was sie will* (Berlin, Sept. 1, 1932); *Drei Walzer* (Zürich, Oct. 5, 1935); *Die Musik kommt* (Zürich, 1948; rev. as *Ihr erster Walzer*, Munich, May 16, 1952); *Božena* (Munich, May 16, 1952). Among his other works were ballets, film scores, orch. music, chamber pieces, choruses, about 500 cabaret songs, and piano pieces.

BIBL.: B. Grun, *Prince of Vienna: The Life, the Times, and the Melodies of O. S.* (London, 1955); F. Mailer, *Weltburger der Musik: Eine O.-S.-Biographie* (Vienna, 1985).

Strauss, family of celebrated Austrian musicians:

(1) Johann (Baptist) Strauss (I), violinist, conductor, and composer, known as "The Father of the Waltz"; b. Vienna, March 14, 1804; d. there, Sept. 25, 1849. He was born into a humble Jewish family of Hungarian descent; called "black Schani," he made a concerted effort to conceal his Jewish origins (when the ancestry of the family was realized by the chagrined Nazis a century later, they falsified the parish register at St. Stephen's Cathedral in 1939 to make the family racially pure). His father was an innkeeper who apprenticed him to a bookbinder, but his musical talent revealed itself at an early age; after Strauss ran away, his parents consented to his becoming a musician. He studied the violin under Polyschansky and harmony under Seyfried; at 15 he became a violist in Michael Pamer's dance orch., where he found a friend in Josef Lanner; in 1819 he became a member of the latter's small band, and later served as 2d conductor of Lanner's orch. (1824–25). In 1825 he organized his own orch., which quickly became popular in Viennese inns. He composed his first waltz, "Täuberln-Walzer," in 1826; his reputation was secured with his appearances at the Sperl, where Pamer served as music director. His renown spread, and his orch. increased rapidly in size and efficiency; from 1833 he undertook concert tours in Austria, and in 1834 was appointed bandmaster of the first Vienna militia regiment. His tours extended to Berlin in 1834, and to the Netherlands and Belgium in 1836; in 1837–38 he invaded Paris with a picked corps of 28, and had immense success both there and in London. In 1846 he was named k.k. (i.e., kaiserlich und königlich, or imperial and royal) Hofballmusikdirektor. After catching scarlet fever from one of his children, he died at the age of 45. Among his publ. waltzes, the "Lorelei-," "Gabrielen-," "Taglioni-," "Cäcilien-," "Victoria-," "Kettenbrücken-," and "Bajaderen-Walzer" are prime favorites; also popular are his "Elektrische Funken," "Mephistos Höllenrufe", and the "Donau-Lieder." He had 3 sons who carried on the family musical tradition.

(2) Johann (Baptist) Strauss (II), greatly renowned violinist, conductor, and composer, known as "The Waltz King"; b. Vienna, Oct. 25, 1825; d. there, June 3, 1899. His father intended him for a business career, but his musical talent manifested itself when he was a mere child; at 6 he wrote the first 36 bars of waltz music that later was publ. as *Erster Gedanke.* While he was still a child, his mother arranged for him to study secretly with Franz Amon, his father's concertmaster; after his father left the family in 1842, he was able to pursue violin training with Anton Kohlmann; he also studied theory with Joseph Drechsler until 1844. He made his first public appearance as conductor of his own ensemble at Dommayer's Casino at Hietzing on Oct. 15, 1844. His success was instantaneous, and his new waltzes won wide popularity. Despite his father's objections to this rivalry in the family, Johann continued his concerts with increasing success; after his father's death in 1849, he united his father's band with his own; subsequently he made regular tours of Europe (1856–86). From 1863 to 1871 he was k.k. Hofballmusikdirektor in Vienna. In 1872 he accepted an invitation to visit the United States, and directed 14 "monster concerts" in Boston and 4 in New York. He then turned to the theater. His finest operetta is *Die Fledermaus*, an epitome of the Viennese spirit that continues to hold the stage as one of the masterpieces of its genre. It was first staged at the Theater an der Wien on April 5, 1874, and within a few months was given in New York (Dec. 29, 1874); productions followed all over the world. It was performed in Paris with a new libretto as *La Tzigane* (Oct. 30, 1877); the original version was presented there as *La Chauve-souris* on April 22, 1904. Also very successful was the operetta *Der Zigeunerbaron* (Vienna, Oct. 24, 1885). All his operettas were first produced in Vienna, with the exception of *Eine Nacht in Venedig* (Berlin, Oct. 3, 1883). A complete list of the Vienna productions includes *Indigo und die vierzig Räuber* (Feb. 10, 1871); *Der Carneval in Rom* (March 1, 1873); *Cagliostro in Wien* (Feb. 27, 1875); *Prinz Methusalem* (Jan. 3, 1877); *Blindekuh* (Dec. 18, 1878); *Das Spitzentuch der Königin* (Oct. 1, 1880); *Der lustige Krieg* (Nov. 25, 1881); *Simplicius* (Dec. 17, 1887); *Ritter Pázmán* (Jan. 1, 1892); *Fürstin Ninetta* (Jan. 10, 1893); *Jabuka, oder Das Apfelfest* (Oct. 12, 1894); *Waldmeister* (Dec. 4, 1895); *Die Göttin der Vernunft* (March 13, 1897). Although Strauss composed extensively for the theater, his supreme achievement remains his dance music. He wrote almost 500 pieces of it (498 opus numbers); of his waltzes the greatest popularity was achieved by "An der schönen blauen Donau," op. 314 (1867), whose main tune became one of the best known in all music. Brahms wrote on a lady's fan the opening measures of it, and underneath: "Leider nicht von Brahms" ("Alas, not by Brahms"); Wagner, too, voiced his appreciation of the music of Strauss. He contracted 3 marriages: to the singer Henriette Treffz, the actress Angelika Dittrich, and Adele Strauss, the widow of the banker Anton Strauss, who was no relation to Johann's family. F. Racek began editing a complete ed. of his works in Vienna in 1967.

(3) Josef Strauss, conductor and composer; b. Vienna, Aug. 22, 1827; d. there, July 21, 1870. He studied theory with Franz Dolleschal and violin with Franz Anton. He was versatile and gifted, and at various times wrote poetry, painted, and patented inventions. He first appeared in public conducting in Vienna a set of his waltzes (July 23, 1853); later he regularly appeared as a conductor with his brother Johann's orch. (1856–62); their younger brother, Eduard, joined them in 1862, but Johann left the orch. in 1863 and Josef and Eduard continued to conduct the family orch. He wrote 283 opus numbers, many of which reveal a composer of remarkable talent. Among his outstanding waltzes are "Perlen der Liebe," op. 39 (1857), "5 Kleebald'ln," op. 44 (1857), "Wiener Kinder," op. 61 (1858), "Schwert und Leier," op. 71 (1860), "Friedenspalmen," op. 207 (1867), and "Aquarellen," op. 258 (1869).

(4) Eduard Strauss, conductor and composer; b. Vienna, March 15, 1835; d. there, Dec. 28, 1916. He studied theory and composition with Gottfried Preyer and Simon Sechter, violin with Amon, and harp with Parish-Alvars and Zamara. After playing harp in his brother Johann's orch., he made his debut as a conductor and composer with it at the Wintergarten of the Dianabad-Saal on April 6, 1862; after Johann left the orch. in 1863, Eduard and his other brother, Josef, shared the conductorship of the orch. until the latter's death in 1870. From 1870 to 1878 he was k.k. Hofballmusikdirektor; subsequently he made annual tours of Europe as a guest conductor, and also with his own orch. In 1890 and 1900–1901 he toured throughout the United States, after which he retired. He wrote some 300 works, but they failed to rival the superior works of his brothers. His memoirs were publ. in 1906. His son, Johann (Maria Eduard) Strauss (III) (b. Vienna, Feb. 16, 1866; d. Berlin, Jan. 9, 1939), was also a conductor and composer; after working as an accountant in the education ministry, he won success as a composer with the operetta *Katze und Maus* (Vienna, Dec. 1898); from 1900 he was active as a conductor, serving as k.k. Hofballmusikdirektor (1901–05); subsequently he pursued his career mainly in Berlin. He also wrote some waltzes, the most popular being "Dichterliebe." His nephew, Eduard (Leopold Maria) Strauss (b. Vienna, March 24, 1910; d. there, April 6, 1969), was a conductor and the last representative of the great family tradition; he studied at the Vienna Academy of Music; he made his conducting debut in Vienna in 1949, and subsequently led concerts there regularly he also toured with the Vienna Johann Strauss Orch. and as a guest conductor.

BIBL.: L. Scheyrer, *Johann S.'s musikalische Wanderung durch das Leben* (Vienna, 1851); L. Eisenberg, *Johann S.: Ein Lebensbild* (Vienna, 1894); C. Flamme, *Verzeichnis der sämtlichen im Druck erschienenen Kompositionen von Johann S. (Vater), Johann S. (Sohn), Josef S. und Eduard S.* (Leipzig, 1898); R. von Procházka, *Johann S.* (Berlin, 1900; 2d ed., 1903); F. Lange, *Joseph Lanner und Johann S.: Ihre Zeit, ihr Leben und ihre Werke* (Vienna, 1904; 2d ed., 1919); R. Specht, *Johann S.* (Berlin, 1909; 2d ed., 1922); F. Lange, *Johann S.* (Leipzig, 1912); E. Neumann, *Die Operetten von Johann S.: Ihre Formen und das Verhältnis von Text und Musik* (diss., Univ. of Vienna, 1919); J. Schnitzer, *Meister Johann: Bunte Geschichten aus der Johann S.-Zeit* (Vienna, 1920); E. Decsey, *Johann S.* (Stuttgart, 1922; 2d ed., rev., 1948, by E. Rieger); K. Kobald, *Johann S.* (Vienna, 1925); S. Loewy, *Rund um Johann S.: Momentbilder aus einen Künstlerleben* (Vienna, 1925); H. Jacob, *Johann S. und das neunzehnte Jahrhundert: Die Geschichte einer musikalischen Weltherrschaft* (Amsterdam, 1937; 3d ed., rev., 1962); H. Sündermann, *Johann S.: Ein Vollender* (Brixlegg, 1937; 3d ed., 1949); W. Jaspert, *Johann S.: Sein Leben, sein Werk, seine Zeit* (Vienna, 1939; 2d ed., 1949); M. Kronberg, *Johann S.* (Paris, 1939); A. Witeschnik, *Die Dynastie S.* (Vienna and Leipzig, 1939; 3d ed., 1958); E. Schenk, *Johann S.* (Potsdam, 1940); D. Ewen, *Tales from the Vienna Woods: The Story of Johann S.* (N.Y., 1944); P. Ruff, *Johann-S.-Festschrift: Juni-September 1949* (Vienna, 1949); W. Reich, ed., *Johann S.-Brevier: Aus Briefen und Erinnerungen* (Zürich, 1950); J. Pastene, *Three-quarter Time: The Life and Music of the S. Family of Vienna* (N.Y., 1951); H. Jacob, *Johann S. Vater und Sohn* (Hamburg, 1953); M. Schönherr and K. Reinöhl, *Johann S. Vater: Ein Werkverzeichnis* (Vienna, 1954); A. Weinmann, *Verzeichnis sämtlicher Werke von Johann S. Vater und Sohn* (Vienna, 1956); F. Grasberger, *Die Walzer-Dynastie S.: Eine Ausstellung zum Neujahrskonzert der Wiener Philharmoniker* (Vienna, 1965–66); H. Jäger-Sustenau, *Johann S.: Der Walzerkönig und seine Dynastie, Familiengeschichte, Urkunden* (Vienna, 1965); A. Weinmann, *Verzeichnis sämtlicher Werke von Josef und Eduard S.* (Vienna, 1967); H. Fantel, *Johann S.: Father and Son, and Their Era* (Newton Abbot, 1971); O. Schneidereit, *Johann S. und die Stadt an der schönen blauen Donau* (Berlin, 1972); J. Wechsberg, *The Waltz Emperors* (London, 1973); F. Endler, *Das Walzer-Buch: Johann S.: Die Aufforderung zum Tanz* (Vienna, 1975); F. Mailer, *Das kleine Johann S. Buch* (Salzburg, 1975); M. Prawy, *Johann S.: Weltgeschichte im Walzertakt* (Vienna, 1975); F. Racek, *Johann S. zum 150. Geburtstag: Ausstellung der Wiener Stadtbibliothek 22. Mai bis 31. Oktober 1975* (Vienna, 1975); F. Mailer, *Joseph S.: Genie wider Willen* (Vienna and Munich, 1977; Eng. tr. as *Joseph S.: Genius against His Will*, Oxford, 1985); M. Schönherr, *S., Ziehrer: Synoptic Handbook of the Dances and Marches* (Vienna, 1982); P. Kemp, *The S. Family: Portrait of a Musical Dynasty* (Tunbridge Wells, 1985); N. Linke, *Musik erobert die Welt, oder, Wie die Wiener Familie S. die "Unterhaltungsmusik" revolutionierte* (Vienna, 1987); M. Prawy, *J. S.* (Vienna, 1991).

Strauss, Richard (Georg), great German composer and distinguished conductor, one of the most inventive music masters of the modern age, son of **Franz (Joseph) Strauss**; b. Munich, June 11, 1864; d. Garmisch-Partenkirchen, Sept. 8, 1949. Growing up in a musical environment, he studied piano as a child with August Tombo, harpist in the Court Orch., then took violin lessons from Benno Walter, its concertmaster, and later received instruction from the court conductor, Friedrich Wilhelm Meyer. According to his own account, he began to improvise songs and piano pieces at a very early age; among such incunabula was the song "Weihnachtslied," followed by a piano dance, *Schneiderpolka*. On March 30, 1881, his first orch. work, the Sym. in D minor, was premiered in Munich under Hermann Levi. This was followed by the Sym. in F minor, premiered on Dec. 13, 1884, by the N.Y. Phil. under Theodore Thomas. Strauss also made progress as a performing musician; when he was 20 years old, Hans von Bülow engaged him as assistant conductor of his Meiningen Orch. About that time, Strauss became associated with the poet and musician Alexander Ritter, who introduced him to the "music of the future," as it was commonly called, represented by orch. works of Liszt and operas by Wagner.

In 1886 Strauss received an appointment as the 3d conductor of the Court Opera in Munich. On March 2, 1887, he conducted in Munich the first performance of his symphonic fantasy, *Aus Italien*. This was followed by the composition of his first true masterpiece, the symphonic poem *Don Juan*, in which he applied the thematic ideas of Liszt; he conducted its premiere in Weimar on Nov. 11, 1889; it became the first of a series of his tone poems, all of them based on literary subjects. His next tone poem of great significance in music history was *Tod und Verklärung*; Strauss conducted it for the first time in Eisenach on June 21, 1890, on the same program with the premiere of his brilliant *Burleske* for Piano and Orch., featuring Eugen d'Albert as soloist. There followed the first performance of the symphonic poem *Macbeth*, which Strauss conducted in Weimar on Oct. 13, 1890. In these works, Strauss established himself as a master of program music and the most important representative of the nascent era of musical modernism; as such, he was praised extravagantly by earnest believers in musical progress and damned savagely by entrenched traditionalists in the press. He effectively adapted Wagner's system of leading motifs (leitmotifs) to the domain of symphonic music. His tone poems were interwoven with motifs, each representing a relevant programmatic element. Explanatory brochures listing these leading motifs were publ. like musical Baedekers to guide the listeners. Bülow, ever a phrasemaker, dubbed Strauss "Richard the 3d," Richard the 1st being Wagner but no one worthy of direct lineage as Richard the 2d in deference to the genius of the master of Bayreuth.

Turning to stage music, Strauss wrote his first opera, *Guntram*, for which he also composed the text; he conducted its premiere in Weimar on May 10, 1894, with the leading soprano role performed by **Pauline de Ahna**; she was married to Strauss on Sept. 10, 1894, and remained with him all his life; she died on May 13, 1950, a few months after Strauss himself. While engaged in active work as a composer, Strauss did not neglect his conducting career. In 1894 he succeeded Bülow as conductor of the Berlin Phil., leading it for a season. Also in 1894 he became assistant conductor of the Munich Court Opera; he became chief conductor in 1896. In 1896–97 he filled engagements as a guest conductor in European music centers. His works of the period included the sparkling *Till Eugenspiegels lustige Streiche* (Cologne, Nov. 5, 1895), *Also sprach Zarathustra*, a philosophical tone poem after Nietzsche (Frankfurt am Main, Nov. 27, 1896, Strauss conducting), and *Don Quixote*, variations with a cello solo, after Cervantes (Cologne, March 8, 1898). In 1898 Strauss became a conductor at the Berlin Royal Opera; in 1908 he was made its Generalmusikdirektor, a position he held until 1918. He conducted the first performance of his extraordinary autobiographical tone poem *Ein Heldenleben* in Frankfurt am Main on March 3, 1899; the hero of the title was Strauss himself, while his critics were represented in the score by a cacophonous charivari; for this exhibition of musical self-aggrandizement, he was severely chastised in the press. There followed his first successful opera, *Feuersnot* (Dresden, Nov. 21, 1901).

In June 1903 Strauss was the guest of honor of the Strauss Festival in London. It was also in 1903 that the Univ. of Heidelberg made him Dr.Phil., *honoris causa*. For his first visit to the United States, he presented to the public the premiere performance of his *Symphonia domestica* at Carnegie Hall in New York on March 21, 1904. The score represented a day in the Strauss household, containing an interlude describing, quite literally, the feeding of the newly born baby. The reviews in the press reflected aversion to such a musical self-exposure. There followed his opera *Salome*, to the German tr. of Oscar Wilde's play. Schuch led its premiere in Dresden on Dec. 9, 1905. *Salome* had its American premiere at the Metropolitan Opera in New York on Jan. 22, 1907; the ghastly subject, involving intended incest, 7-fold nudity, and decapitation followed by a labial necrophilia, administered such a shock to the public and the press that the Metropolitan Opera took it off the repertoire after only 2 performances. Scarcely less forceful was Strauss's next opera, *Elektra*, to a libretto by the Austrian poet and dramatist Hugo von Hofmannsthal, in which the horrors of matricide were depicted with extraordinary force in unabashedly dissonant harmonies. Schuch conducted its premiere in Dresden on Jan. 25, 1909.

Strauss then decided to prove to his admirers that he was quite able to write melodious operas to charm the musical ear; this he accomplished in his next production, also to a text of Hofmannsthal, *Der Rosenkavalier*, a delightful opéra bouffe in an endearing popular manner; Schuch conducted its premiere in Dresden on Jan. 26, 1911. Turning once more to Greek mythology, Strauss wrote, with Hofmannsthal again as librettist, a short opera, *Ariadne auf Naxos*, which he conducted for the first time in Stuttgart on Oct. 25, 1912. In June 1914 Strauss was awarded an honorary D.Mus. degree from the Univ. of Oxford. His next work was the formidable, and quite realistic, score *Eine Alpensinfonie*, depicting an ascent of the Alps, and employing a wind machine and a thunder machine in the orch. to illustrate an Alpine storm. Strauss conducted its first performance with the Dresden Court Orch. in Berlin on Oct. 28, 1915. Then, again with Hofmannsthal as librettist, he wrote the opera *Die Frau ohne Schatten* (Vienna, Oct. 10, 1919), using a complex plot, heavily endowed with symbolism.

In 1917 Strauss helped to organize the Salzburg Festival and appeared there in subsequent years as conductor. In 1919 he assumed the post of codirector with Franz Schalk of the Vienna State Opera, a position he held until 1924. In 1920 he took the Vienna Phil. on a tour of South America; in 1921 he appeared as a guest conductor in the United States. For his next opera, *Intermezzo* (Dresden, Nov. 4, 1924), Strauss wrote his own libretto; then, with Hofmannsthal once more, he wrote *Die ägyptische Helena* (Dresden, June 6, 1928). Their last collaboration was *Arabella* (Dresden, July 1, 1933).

When Hitler came to power in 1933, the Nazis were eager to persuade Strauss to join the official policies of the 3d Reich. Hitler even sent him a signed picture of himself with a flattering inscription, "To the great composer Richard Strauss, with sincere admiration." Strauss kept clear of formal association with the Führer and his cohorts, however. He agreed to serve as president of the newly organized Reichsmusikkammer on Nov. 15, 1933, but resigned from it on July 13, 1935, ostensibly for reasons of poor health. He entered into open conflict with the Nazis by asking Stefan Zweig, an Austrian Jew, to provide the libretto for his opera *Die schweigsame Frau*; it was duly produced in Dresden on June 24, 1935, but then taken off the boards after a few performances. His political difficulties grew even more disturbing when the Nazis found out that his daughter-in-law was Jewish. Zweig himself managed to escape Nazi horrors, and emigrated to Brazil, but was so afflicted by the inhumanity of the world that he and his wife together committed suicide.

Strauss valiantly went through his tasks; he agreed to write the "Olympische Hymne" for the Berlin Olympic Games in 1936. On Nov. 5, 1936, he was honored with the Gold Medal of the Royal Phil. Soc. in London; the next day he conducted the visiting Dresden State Opera in a performance of his *Ariadne auf Naxos* at

Covent Garden. For his next opera, he chose Joseph Gregor as his librettist; with him Strauss produced *Daphne* (Dresden, Oct. 15, 1938), which was once more a revival of his debt to Greek mythology. For their last collaboration, Strauss and Gregor produced the opera *Die Liebe der Danae*, also on a Greek theme. Its public dress rehearsal was given in Salzburg on Aug. 16, 1944, but by that time World War II was rapidly encroaching on devastated Germany, so that the opera did not receive its official premiere until after Strauss's death. The last opera by Strauss performed during his lifetime was *Capriccio*. Its libretto was prepared by the conductor Clemens Krauss, who conducted its premiere in Munich on Oct. 28, 1942. Another interesting work of this period was Strauss's Horn Concerto No. 2, first performed in Salzburg on Aug. 11, 1943.

During the last weeks of the war, Strauss devoted himself to the composition of *Metamorphosen*, a symphonic work mourning the disintegration of Germany; it contained a symbolic quotation from the funeral march from Beethoven's *Eroica* Sym. He then completed another fine score, the Oboe Concerto. In Oct. 1945 he went to Switzerland.

In Oct. 1947 Strauss visited London for the Strauss Festival and also appeared as a conductor of his own works. Although official suspicion continued to linger regarding his relationship with the Nazi regime, he was officially exonerated of all taint on June 8, 1948. A last flame of creative inspiration brought forth the deeply moving *Vier letzte Lieder* (1948), for Soprano and Orch., inspired by poems of Herman Hesse and Eichendorff. With this farewell, Strauss left Switzerland in 1949 and returned to his home in Germany, where he died at the age of 85. Undeniably one of the finest master composers of modern times, Strauss never espoused extreme chromatic techniques, remaining a Romanticist at heart. His genius is unquestioned as regards his tone poems from *Don Juan* to *Ein Heldenleben* and his operas from *Salome* to *Der Rosenkavalier*, all of which have attained a permanent place in the repertoire, while his *Vier letzte Lieder* stand as a noble achievement of his Romantic inspiration. In 1976 the Richard-Strauss-Gesellschaft was organized in Munich.

WORKS: DRAMATIC: OPERAS: *Guntram*, op. 25 (1892–93; Weimar, May 10, 1894, composer conducting; rev. version, with score cut by one 3d, 1934–39; Weimar, Oct. 29, 1940); *Feuersnot*, op. 50 (1900–01; Dresden, Nov. 21, 1901, Ernst von Schuch conducting); *Salome*, op. 54 (1903–05; Dresden, Dec. 9, 1905, Schuch conducting); *Elektra*, op. 58 (1906–08; Dresden, Jan. 25, 1909, Schuch conducting); *Der Rosenkavalier*, op. 59 (1909–10; Dresden, Jan. 26, 1911, Schuch conducting); *Ariadne auf Naxos* "zu spielen nach dem *Bürger als Edelmann* des Molière," op. 60 (1911–12; Stuttgart, Oct. 25, 1912, composer conducting; rev. version, with prologue, 1916; Vienna, Oct. 4, 1916, Franz Schalk conducting); *Die Frau ohne Schatten*, op. 65 (1914–18; Vienna, Oct. 10, 1919, Schalk conducting); *Intermezzo*, op. 72 (1918–23; Dresden, Nov. 4, 1924, Fritz Busch conducting); *Die ägyptische Helena*, op. 75 (1923–27; Dresden, June 6, 1928, Fritz Busch conducting; rev. version, 1932–33; Salzburg, Aug. 14, 1933); *Arabella*, op. 79 (1929–32; Dresden, July 1, 1933, Clemens Krauss conducting; rev. version, Munich, July 16, 1939); *Die schweigsame Frau*, op. 80 (1933–34; Dresden, June 24, 1935, Karl Böhm conducting); *Friedenstag*, op. 81 (1935–36; Munich, July 24, 1938, Krauss conducting); *Daphne*, op. 82 (1936–37; Dresden, Oct. 15, 1938, Böhm conducting); *Die Liebe der Danae*, op. 83 (1938–40; public dress rehearsal, Salzburg, Aug. 16, 1944, Krauss conducting; official premiere, Salzburg, Aug. 14, 1952, Krauss conducting); *Capriccio*, op. 85 (1940–41; Munich, Oct. 28, 1942, Krauss conducting). BALLETS AND OTHER DRAMATIC WORKS: *Romeo und Julia*, incidental music to Shakespeare's drama (Munich, Oct. 23, 1887); *Josephslegende*, op. 63 (1912–14; Paris, May 14, 1914, composer conducting); *Der Bürger als Edelmann*, incidental music to Hofmannsthal's version of Molière's drama, op. 60 (1917; Berlin, April 9, 1918); *Schlagobers*, op. 70 (1921–22; Vienna, May 9, 1924, composer conducting); *Verklungene Feste*, after Couperin (1940; Munich, April 5, 1941, Krauss conducting); *Des Esels Schatten*, comedy for music (1949; Hellbrunn Castle, near Salzburg, July 31, 1982, Ernst Märzendorfer conducting). ARRANGEMENTS, ETC.: Strauss prepared a cadenza for Mozart's C-minor Piano Concerto, K.491 (1885); arranged Gluck's *Iphigénie en Tauride* (1899; Weimar, June 9, 1900); made a new version of Beethoven's *Die Ruinen von Athen* with Hugo von Hofmannsthal (Vienna, Sept. 20, 1924, composer conducting); made a new version of Mozart's *Idomeneo* with Lothar Wallerstein (1930; Vienna, April 16, 1931, composer conducting).

BIBL.: WORKS: SOURCE MATERIAL: There is no complete ed. of Strauss's works. The standard thematic catalog was prepared by E. H. Mueller von Asow, *R. S.: Thematisches Verzeichnis* (3 vols., Vienna, 1954–74). Many of his writings may be found in W. Schuh, ed., *R. S.: Betrachtungen und Erinnerungen* (Zürich, 1949; Eng. tr., N.Y., 1953; 2d Ger. ed., rev., 1957). The major bibliographical source is *R.-S.-Bibliographie* (2 vols., Vienna; Vol. 1, 1882–1944, ed. by O. Ortner, 1964; Vol. 2, 1944–1964, ed. by G. Brosche, 1973). Other sources include the following: R. Specht, *R. S.: Vollständiges Verzeichnis der im Druck erschienen Werke* (Vienna, 1910); J. Kapp, *R. S. und die Berliner Oper* (Berlin, 1934–39); E. Wachten, *R. S., geboren 1864: Sein Leben in Bildern* (Leipzig, 1940); R. Tenschert, *Anekdoten um R. S.* (Vienna, 1945); idem, *R. S. und Wien: Eine Wahlverwandtschaft* (Vienna, 1949); E. Roth, ed., *R. S.: Bühnenwerk* (text in Ger., Eng., and French; London, 1954); W. Schuh, *Das Bühnenwerke von R. S. in den unter Mitwirkung des Komponisten geschaffenen letzten Münchner Inszenierungen* (Zürich, 1954); F. Trenner, *R. S.: Dokumente seines Lebens und Schaffens* (Munich, 1954); R. Petzoldt, *R. S.: Sein Leben in Bildern* (Leipzig, 1962); F. Dostal, ed., *Karl Böhm: Begegnung mit R. S.* (Vienna, 1964); F. Grasberger and F. Hadamowsky, eds., *R.-S.-Ausstellung zum 100. Geburtstag* (Vienna, 1964); F. Hadamowsky, *R. S. und Salzburg* (Salzburg, 1964); W. Schuh, *Ein paar Erinnerungen an R. S.* (Zürich, 1964); W. Schuh and E. Roth, eds., *R. S.: Complete Catalogue* (London, 1964); W. Thomas, *R. S. und seine Zeitgenössen* (Munich, 1964); F. Grasberger, *R. S.: Höhe Kunst, erfülltes Leben* (Vienna, 1965); W. Deppisch, *R. S. in Selbstzeugnissen und Bilddokumenten* (Reinbek, 1968); F. Grasberger, *R. S. und die Wiener Oper* (Vienna, 1969); A. Jefferson, *R. S.* (London, 1975); F. Trenner, *Die Skizzenbücher von R. S. aus dem R.-S.-Archiv in Garmisch* (Tutzing, 1977); idem, *R. S. Werkverzeichnis* (Vienna, 1985). CORRESPONDENCE: F. Strauss, ed., *R. S.: Briefwechsel mit Hugo von Hofmannsthal* (Berlin, 1925; Eng. tr., N.Y., 1927); *R. S. et Romain Rolland: Correspondance, fragments de journal* (Paris, 1951; Eng. tr., 1968); F. von Schuch, *R. S., Ernst von Schuch und Dresdens Oper* (Leipzig, 1952; 2d ed., 1953); W. Schuh, ed., *R. S. und Hugo von Hofmannsthal: Briefwechsel: Gesamtausgabe* (Zürich, 1952; 2d ed., rev., 1955; Eng. tr., 1961, as *A Working Friendship: The Correspondence between R. S. and Hugo von Hofmannsthal*); idem, ed., *R. S.: Briefe an die Eltern 1882–1906* (Zürich, 1954); R. Tenschert, ed., *R. S. und Joseph Gregor: Briefwechsel 1934–1949* (Salzburg, 1955); W. Schuh, ed., *R. S., Stefan Zweig: Briefwechsel* (Frankfurt am Main, 1957; Eng. tr., 1977, as *A Confidential Matter: The Letters of R. S. and Stefan Zweig 1931–1935*); D. Kämper, ed., *R. S. und Franz Wüllner im Briefwechsel* (Cologne, 1963); G. Kende and W. Schuh, eds., *R. S., Clemens Krauss: Briefwechsel* (Munich, 1963; 2d ed., 1964); A. Ott, ed., *R. S. und Ludwig Thuille: Briefe der Freundschaft 1877–1907* (Munich, 1969); W. Schuh, ed., *R. S.: Briefwechsel mit Willi Schuh* (Zürich, 1969). BIOGRAPHICAL: E. Urban, *R. S.* (Berlin, 1901); R. Batka, *R. S.* (Charlottenburg, 1908); E. Newman, *R. S.* (London, 1908); M. Steinitzer, *R. S.* (Berlin, 1911; final ed., enl., 1927); H. Finck, *R. S.: The Man and His Works* (Boston, 1917); R. Specht, *R. S. und sein Werk* (2 vols., Leipzig, 1921); R. Muschler, *R. S.* (Hildesheim, 1924); S. Kallenberg, *R. S.: Leben und Werk* (Leipzig, 1926); W. Hutschenruyter, *R. S.* (The Hague, 1929); F. Gysi, *R. S.* (Potsdam, 1934); W. Brandl, *R. S.: Leben und Werk* (Wiesbaden, 1949); E. Bücken, *R. S.* (Kevelaer, 1949); K. Pfister, *R. S.: Weg, Gestalt, Denkmal* (Vienna, 1949); C. Rostand, *R. S.* (Paris, 1949; 2d ed., 1965); O. Erhardt, *R. S.: Leben, Wirken, Schaffen* (Olten, 1953); E. Krause, *R. S.: Gestalt und Werk* (Leipzig, 1955; 3d ed., rev., 1963; Eng. tr., 1964); I. Fabian, *R. S.* (Budapest, 1962); H. Kralik, *R. S.: Weltbürger der Musik* (Vienna, 1963); W. Panofsky, *R. S.: Partitur eines Lebens* (Munich, 1965); G. Marek, *R. S.: The Life of a Non-Hero* (N.Y., 1967); A. Jefferson, *The Life of R. S.* (Newton Abbot, 1973); M. Kennedy, *R. S.* (London, 1976; 2d ed., rev., 1983; rev. and aug., 1995); W. Schuh, *R. S.: Jugend und Meisterjahre: Lebenschronik 1864–98* (Zürich, 1976; Eng. tr. as *R. S.: A Chronicle of the Early Years 1864–98*, Cambridge, 1982); K. Wilhelm, *R. S. persönlich: Eine Bildbiographie* (Munich, 1984). CRITICAL, ANALYTICAL: G. Jourissenne, *R. S.: Essai critique et biographique* (Brussels, 1899); E. Urban, *S. contra Wagner* (Berlin, 1902); O. Bie, *Die moderne Musik und R. S.* (Berlin, 1906); L. Gilman, *S.' Salome: A Guide to the Opera* (N.Y., 1906); J. Manifarges, *R. S. als Dirigent* (Amsterdam, 1907); E. Schmitz, *R. S. als Musikdramatiker: Eine aesthetisch-kritische Studie* (Munich, 1907); E. von Ziegler, *R. S. und seine dramatischen Dichtungen* (Munich, 1907); E. Fischer-Plasser, *Einführung in die Musik von R. S. und Elektra* (Leipzig, 1909); G. Gräner, *R. S.: Musikdramen* (Berlin, 1909); F. Santoliquido, *Il dopo-Wagner: Claude Debussy e R. S.* (Rome, 1909); O. Hübner, *R. S. und das Musikdrama: Betrachtungen über den Wert oder Unwert gewisser Opernmusiken* (Leipzig, 1910); E. Hutcheson, *Elektra by R. S.: A Guide to the Opera with Musical Examples from the Score* (N.Y., 1910); M. Steinitzer, *S.iana und Anderes* (Stuttgart, 1910); H. Daffner, *Salome: Ihre Gestalt in Geschichte und Künst* (Munich, 1912); A. Seidl, *S.iana: Aufsätze zur R.S.—Frage auf drei Jahrzehnten* (Regensburg, 1913); M. Steinitzer, *R. S. in seiner Zeit, mit einem Abdruck der auf der S.woche zu Stuttgart im. Kgl. Hoftheater gehaltenen Rede und einem Bildnis* (Leipzig, 1914; 2d ed., 1922); O. Bie, *Die neuere Musik bis R. S.* (Leipzig, 1916); H. von Waltershausen, *R. S.: Ein Versuch* (Munich, 1921); R. Rosenzweig, *Zur Entwicklungsgeschichte des S.'schen Musikdramas* (diss., Univ. of Vienna, 1923); W. Schrenk, *R. S. und die neue Musik* (Berlin, 1924); E. Blom, *The Rose Cavalier* (London, 1930); G. Röttger, *Die Harmonik in R. S.' Der Rosenkavalier: Ein Beitrag zur Entwicklung der romantische Harmonik nach Richard Wagner* (diss., Univ. of Munich, 1931); K.-J. Krüger, *Hugo von Hofmannsthal und R. S.: Versuch einer Deutung des künstlerisschen Weges Hugo von Hofmannsthals, mit einem Anhang; erstmalige Veröffentlichung der bischer ungedruckten einzigen Vertonung eines Hofmannsthalschen Gedichtes durch R. S.* (Berlin, 1935); H. Röttger, *Das Formproblem bei R. S. gezeigt an der Oper Die Frau ohne Schatten, mit Einschluss von Guntram und Intermezzo* (diss., Univ. of Munich, 1935; publ. in an abr. ed., Berlin, 1937); J. Gregor, *R. S.: Der Meister der Oper* (Munich, 1939; 2d ed., 1942); G. Becker, *Das Problem der Oper an Hand von R. S.' Capriccio* (diss., Univ. of Jena, 1944); R. Tenschert, *Dreimal sieben Variationen über das Thema R. S.* (Vienna, 1944; 2d ed., 1945); O. Gatscha, *Librettist und Komponist: Dargestellt an den Opern R. S.'* (diss., Univ. of Vienna, 1947); A. Pryce-Jones, *R. S.: Der Rosenkavalier* (London, 1947); W. Schuh, *Über Opern von R. S.* (Zürich, 1947); F. Trenner, *Die Zusammenarbeit von Hugo von Hofmannsthal und R. S.* (diss., Univ. of Munich, 1949); D. Lindner, *R. S./Joseph Gregor: Die Liebe der Danae: Herkunft, Inhalt und Gestaltung eines Opernwerkes* (Vienna, 1952); R. Schopenhauer, *Die antiken Frauengestalten bei R. S.* (diss., Univ. of Vienna, 1952); G. Hausswald, *R. S.: Ein Beitrag zur Dresdener Operngeschichte seit 1945* (Dresden, 1953); W. Wendhausen, *Das stilistische Verhältnis von Dichtung und Musik in der Entwicklung der musikdramatischen Werke R. S.'* (diss., Univ. of Hamburg, 1954); G. Kende, *R. S. und Clemens Krauss: Eine Künstlerfreundschaft und ihre Zusammenarbeit an Capriccio (op. 85): Konversationsstück für Musik* (Munich, 1960); N. Del Mar, *R. S.: A Critical Commentary on His Life and Works* (3 vols., London, 1962, 1969, and 1972; reprint with corrections, 1978); A. Jefferson, *The Operas of R. S. in Britain, 1910–1963* (London, 1963); A. Natan, *R. S.: Die Opern* (Basel, 1963); A. Berger, *R. S. als geistige Macht: Versuch eines philosophischen Verständnisses* (Gisch, 1964); L. Lehmann, *Five Operas and R. S.* (N.Y., 1964; publ. in London, 1964, as *Singing with R. S.*); W. Mann, *R. S.: A Critical Study of the Operas* (London, 1964); K. Pörnbacher, *Hugo von Hofmannsthal/R. S.: Der Rosenkavalier* (Munich, 1964); W. Schuh, *Hugo von Hofmannsthal und R. S.: Legende und Wirklichkeit* (Munich, 1964); A. Goléa, *R. S.* (Paris, 1965); R. Gerlach, *Tonalität und tonale Konfiguration im Oeuvre von R. S.: Analysen und Interpretationen als Beiträge zum Verständnis von tonalen Problemen und Formen in sinfonischen Werken und in der "Einleitung" und ersten Szene des Rosenkavalier* (diss., Univ. of Zürich, 1966; publ. as *Don Juan und Rosenkavalier*, Bern, 1966); R. Schäfer, *Hugo von Hofmannsthals Arabella* (Bern, 1967); W. Gruhn, *Die Instrumentation in den Orchesterwerken von R. S.* (diss., Univ. of Mainz, 1968); W. Schuh, *Der Rosenkavalier: 4 Studien* (Olten, 1968); J. Knaus, *Hugo von Hofmannsthal und sein Weg zur Oper Die Frau ohne Schatten* (Berlin, 1971); W. Schuh, ed., *Hugo von Hofmannsthal, R. S.: Der Rosenkavalier: Fassungen, Filmszenarium, Briefe* (Frankfurt am Main, 1971); A. Abert, *R. S.: Die Opern: Einführung und Analyse* (Hannover, 1972); D. Daviau and G. Buelow, *The "Ariadne auf Naxos" of Hugo von Hofmannsthal and R. S.* (Chapel Hill, 1975); K. Forsyth, *Ariadne auf Naxos by Hugo von Hofmannsthal and R. S.: Its Genesis and Meaning* (Oxford, 1982); R. Hartmann, *R. S.: The Staging of His Operas and Ballets* (Oxford, 1982); R. Schlötter, *Musik und Theater im "Rosenkavalier" vom R. S.* (Vienna, 1985); H. Wajemann, *Die Chorkompositionen von R. S.* (Tutzing, 1986); G. Splitt, *R. S. 1933–1935: Ästhetik und Musikpolitik zu Beginn der nationalsozialistischen Herrschaft* (Pfaffenweiler, 1987); C. Osborne, *The Complete Operas of R. S.* (London, 1988); E.-M. Axt, *Musikalische Form als Dramaturgie: Prinzipien eines Spätstils in der Oper "Friedenstag" von R. S. und Joseph Gregor* (Munich, 1989); B. Gilliam, *R. S.'s Elektra* (Oxford, 1991); D. Greene, *Listening to S. Operas: The Audience's Multiple Standpoints* (N.Y., 1991); W. Krebs, *Der Wille zum Rausch: Aspekte der musikalischen Dramaturgie von R. S.' "Salome"* (Munich, 1991); B. Gilliam, ed., *R. S. and His World* (Princeton, 1992); idem, ed., *R. S.: New Perspectives on the Composer and His Work* (Durham, N.C., 1992); B. Meier, *Geschichtliche Signaturen der Musik bei Mahler, S. und Schönberg* (Hamburg, 1992); A. Unger, *Welt, Leben und Kunst als Themen der "Zarathustra-Kompositionen" von R. S. und Gustav Mahler* (Frankfurt am Main, 1992); J. Williamson, *S.: Also sprach Zarathustra* (Cambridge, 1993).

Stravinsky, Igor (Feodorovich), great Russian-born French, later American composer, one of the supreme masters of 20th-century music, whose works exercised the most profound influence on the evolution of music through the emancipation of rhythm, melody, and harmony, son of **Feodor (Ignatievich)**; b. Oranienbaum, near St. Petersburg, June 17, 1882; d. N.Y., April 6, 1971. His son was the Russian-American pianist, teacher, and composer Soulima (Sviatoslav) Stravinsky (b. Lausanne, Sept. 23, 1910; d. Sarasota, Fla., Nov. 28, 1994). Igor was brought up in an artistic atmosphere; he often went to opera rehearsals when his father sang, and acquired an early love for the musical theater. He took piano lessons with Alexandra Snetkova, and later with Leokadia Kashperova, who was a pupil of Anton Rubinstein; but it was not until much later that he began to study theory, first with Akimenko and then with Kalafati (1900–03). His progress in composition was remarkably slow; he never entered a music school or a cons., and never earned an academic degree in music. In 1901 he enrolled in the faculty of jurisprudence at Univ. of St. Petersburg, and took courses there for 8 semesters, without graduating; a fellow student was Vladimir Rimsky-Korsakov, a son of the composer. In the summer of 1902 Stravinsky traveled in Germany, where he met another son of Rimsky-Korsakov, Andrei, who was a student at the Univ. of Heidelberg; Stravinsky became his friend. He was introduced to Rimsky-Korsakov, and became a regular guest at the latter's periodic gatherings in St. Petersburg. In 1903–04 he wrote a piano sonata for the Russian pianist Nicolai Richter, who performed it at Rimsky-Korsakov's home. In 1905 he began taking regular lessons in orchestration with Rimsky-Korsakov, who taught him free of charge; under his tutelage, Stravinsky composed a sym. in E-flat major; the 2d and 3d movements from it were performed on April 27, 1907, by the Court Orch. in St. Petersburg, and a complete performance of it was given by the same orch. on Feb. 4, 1908. The work, dedicated to Rimsky-Korsakov, had some singularities and angularities that showed a deficiency of technique; there was little in this work that presaged Stravinsky's ultimate development as a master of form and orchestration. At the same concert, his *Le Faune et la* *bergère* for Voice and Orch. had its first performance; this score revealed a certain influence of French Impressionism. To celebrate the marriage of Rimsky-Korsakov's daughter Nadezhda to the composer Maximilian Steinberg on June 17, 1908, Stravinsky wrote an orch. fantasy entitled *Fireworks*. Rimsky-Korsakov died a few days after the wedding; Stravinsky deeply mourned his beloved teacher and wrote a funeral song for Wind Instruments in his memory; it was first performed in St. Petersburg on Jan. 30, 1909. There followed a *Scherzo fantastique* for Orch., inspired by Maeterlinck's book *La Vie des abeilles*. As revealed in his correspondence with Rimsky-Korsakov, Stravinsky had at first planned a literal program of composition, illustrating events in the life of a beehive by a series of descriptive sections; some years later, however, he gratuitously denied all connection of the work with Maeterlinck's book.

A signal change in Stravinsky's fortunes came when the famous impresario Diaghilev commissioned him to write a work for the Paris season of his company, the Ballets Russes. The result was the production of his first ballet masterpiece, *The Firebird*, staged by Diaghilev in Paris on June 25, 1910. Here he created music of extraordinary brilliance, steeped in the colors of Russian fairy tales. There are numerous striking effects in the score, such as a glissando of harmonics in the string instruments; the rhythmic drive is exhilarating, and the use of asymmetrical time signatures is extremely effective; the harmonies are opulent; the orchestration is coruscating. He drew 2 orch. suites from the work; in 1919 he reorchestrated the music to conform to his new beliefs in musical economy; in effect he plucked the luminous feathers off the magical firebird, but the original scoring remained a favorite with conductors and orchs. Stravinsky's association with Diaghilev demanded his presence in Paris, which he made his home beginning in 1911, with frequent travels to Switzerland. His 2d ballet for Diaghilev was *Pétrouchka*, premiered in Paris on June 13, 1911, with triumphant success. Not only was the ballet remarkably effective on the stage, but the score itself, arranged in 2 orch. suites, was so new and original that it marked a turning point in 20th-century music; the spasmodically explosive rhythms, the novel instrumental sonorities, with the use of the piano as an integral part of the orch., the bold harmonic innovations in employing 2 different keys simultaneously (C major and F-sharp major, the "Pétrouchka Chord") became a potent influence on modern European composers. Debussy voiced his enchantment with the score, and young Stravinsky, still in his 20s, became a Paris celebrity. Two years later, he brought out a work of even greater revolutionary import, the ballet *Le Sacre du printemps* (Rite of Spring; Russian title, *Vesna sviashchennaya*, literally Spring the Sacred); its subtitle was "Scenes of Pagan Russia." It was premiered by Diaghilev with his Ballets Russes in Paris on May 29, 1913, with the choreography by Nijinsky. The score marked a departure from all conventions of musical composition; while in Petrouchka the harmonies, though innovative and dissonant, could still be placed in the context of modern music, the score of *Le Sacre du printemps* contained such corrosive dissonances as scales played at the intervals of major sevenths and superpositions of minor upon major triads with the common tonic, chords treated as unified blocks of sound, and rapid metrical changes that seemingly defied performance. The score still stands as one of the most daring creations of the modern musical mind; its impact was tremendous; to some of the audience at its first performance in Paris, Stravinsky's "barbaric" music was beyond endurance; the Paris critics exercised their verbal ingenuity in indignant vituperation; one of them proposed that *Le Sacre du printemps* should be more appropriately described as *Le Massacre du printemps*. On May 26, 1914, Diaghilev premiered Stravinsky's lyric fairy tale *Le Rossignol*, after Hans Christian Andersen. It too abounded in corrosive discords, but here it could be explained as "Chinese" music illustrative of the exotic subject. From 1914 to 1918 he worked on his ballet *Les Noces* (Russian title, *Svadebka*; literally, Little Wedding), evoking Russian peasant folk modalities; it was scored for an unusual ensemble of chorus, soloists, 4 pianos, and 17 percussion instruments.

The devastation of World War I led Stravinsky to conclude that the era of grandiose Romantic music had become obsolete, and that a new spirit of musical economy was imperative in an impoverished world. As an illustration of such economy, he wrote the musical stage play *L'Histoire du soldat*, scored for only 7 players, with a narrator. About the same time, he wrote a work for 11 instruments entitled *Ragtime*, inspired by the new American dance music. He continued his association with Diaghilev's Ballets Russes in writing the ballet *Pulcinella*, based on themes by Pergolesi and other 18th-century Italian composers. He also wrote for Diaghilev 2 short operas, *Renard*, to a Russian fairy tale (Paris, May 18, 1922), and *Mavra*, after Pushkin (Paris, June 3, 1922). These 2 works were the last in which he used Russian subjects, with the sole exception of an orch. *Scherzo à la russe*, written in 1944. Stravinsky had now entered the period usually designated as neoclassical. The most significant works of this stage of his development were his Octet for Wind Instruments and the Piano Concerto commissioned by Koussevitzky. In these works, he abandoned the luxuriant instrumentation of his ballets and their aggressively dissonant harmonies; instead, he used pandiatonic structures, firmly tonal but starkly dissonant in their superposition of tonalities within the same principal key. His reversion to old forms, however, was not an act of ascetic renunciation but, rather, a grand experiment in reviving Baroque practices, which had fallen into desuetude. The Piano Concerto provided him with an opportunity to appear as soloist; Stravinsky was never a virtuoso pianist, but he was able to acquit himself satisfactorily in such works as the Piano Concerto; he played it with Koussevitzky in Paris on May 22, 1924, and during his first American tour with the Boston Sym. Orch., also under Koussevitzky, on Jan. 23, 1925. The Elizabeth Sprague Coolidge Foundation commissioned him to write a pantomime for string orch.; the result was *Apollon Musagète*, given at the Library of Congress in Washington, D.C., on April 27, 1928. This score, serene and emotionally restrained, evokes the manner of Lully's court ballets. He continued to explore the resources of neo-Baroque writing in his *Capriccio* for Piano and Orch., which he performed as soloist, with Ansermet conducting, in Paris, on Dec. 6, 1929; this score is impressed by a spirit of hedonistic entertainment, harking back to the style galant of the 18th century; yet it is unmistakably modern in its polyrhythmic collisions of pandiatonic harmonies. Stravinsky's growing disillusionment with the external brilliance of modern music led him to seek eternal verities of music in ancient modalities. His well-nigh monastic renunciation of the grandiose edifice of glorious sound to which he himself had so abundantly contributed found expression in his opera oratorio *Oedipus Rex*; in order to emphasize its detachment from temporal aspects, he commissioned a Latin text for the work, even though the subject was derived from a Greek play; its music is deliberately hollow and its dramatic points are emphasized by ominous repetitive passages. Yet this very austerity of idiom makes *Oedipus Rex* a profoundly moving play. It had its first performance in Paris on May 30, 1927; its stage premiere took place in Vienna on Feb. 23, 1928. A turn to religious writing found its utterance in Stravinsky's *Symphony of Psalms*, written for the 50th anniversary of the Boston Sym. Orch. and dedicated "to the glory of God." The work is scored for chorus and orch., omitting the violins and violas, thus emphasizing the lower instrumental registers and creating an austere sonority suitable to its solemn subject. Owing to a delay of the Boston performance, the world premiere of the *Symphony of Psalms* took place in Brussels on Dec. 13, 1930. In 1931 he wrote a violin concerto commissioned by the violinist Samuel Dushkin, and performed by him in Berlin on Oct. 23, 1931. On a commission from the ballerina Ida Rubinstein, he composed the ballet *Perséphone*; here again he exercised his mastery of simplicity in formal design, melodic patterns, and contrapuntal structure. For his American tour he wrote *Jeu de cartes*, a "ballet in 3 deals" to his own scenario depicting an imaginary game of poker (of which he was a devotee). He conducted its first performance at the Metropolitan Opera in New York on April 27, 1937. His concerto for 16 instruments entitled *Dumbarton Oaks*, named after the Washington, D.C., estate of Mr. and Mrs. Robert Woods Bliss, who commissioned the work, was first performed in Washington, on May

8, 1938; in Europe it was played under the noncommittal title Concerto in E flat; its style is hermetically neo-Baroque. It is germane to note that in his neoclassical works Stravinsky began to indicate the key in the title, e.g., *Serenade* in A for Piano (1925), Concerto in D for Violin and Orch. (1931), Concerto in E flat (*Dumbarton Oaks*, 1938), Sym. in C (1938), and Concerto in D for String Orch. (1946).

With World War II engulfing Europe, Stravinsky decided to seek permanent residence in America. He had acquired French citizenship on June 10, 1934; in 1939 he applied for American citizenship; he became a naturalized American citizen on Dec. 28, 1945. To celebrate this event, he made an arrangement of "The Star-Spangled Banner," which contained a curious modulation into the subdominant in the coda. He conducted it with the Boston Sym. Orch. on Jan. 14, 1944, but because of legal injunctions existing in the state of Massachusetts against intentional alteration, or any mutilation, of the national anthem, he was advised not to conduct his version at the 2d pair of concerts, and the standard version was substituted. In 1939–40 Stravinsky was named Charles Eliot Norton lecturer at Harvard Univ.; about the same time, he accepted several private students, a pedagogical role he had never exercised before. His American years form a curious panoply of subjects and manners of composition. He accepted a commission from the Ringling Bros. to write a *Circus Polka* "for a young elephant." In 1946 he wrote *Ebony Concerto* for a swing band. In 1951 he completed his opera *The Rake's Progress*, inspired by Hogarth's famous series of engravings, to a libretto by W. H. Auden and C. Kallman. He conducted its premiere in Venice on Sept. 11, 1951, as part of the International Festival of Contemporary Music. The opera is a striking example of Stravinsky's protean capacity for adopting different styles and idioms of composition to serve his artistic purposes; *The Rake's Progress* is an ingenious conglomeration of disparate elements, ranging from 18th-century British ballads to cosmopolitan burlesque. But whatever transmutations his music underwent during his long and productive career, he remained a man of the theater at heart. In America he became associated with the brilliant Russian choreographer Balanchine, who produced a number of ballets to Stravinsky's music, among them his *Apollon Musagète*, Violin Concerto, Sym. in 3 movements, *Scherzo à la russe*, *Pulcinella*, and *Agon*. It was in his score of *Agon* that he essayed for the first time to adopt the method of composition with 12 tones as promulgated by Schoenberg; *Agon* (the word means "competition" in Greek) bears the subtitle "ballet for 12 tones," perhaps in allusion to the dodecaphonic technique used in the score. Yet the 12-tone method had been the very antithesis of his previous tenets. In fact, an irreconcilable polarity existed between Stravinsky and Schoenberg even in personal relations. Although both resided in Los Angeles for several years, they never met socially; Schoenberg once wrote a canon in which he ridiculed Stravinsky as Herr Modernsky, who put on a wig to look like "Papa Bach." After Schoenberg's death, Stravinsky became interested in examining the essence of the method of composition with 12 tones, which was introduced to him by his faithful musical factotum Robert Craft; Stravinsky adopted dodecaphonic writing in its aspect of canonic counterpoint as developed by Webern. In this manner he wrote his *Canticum sacrum ad honorem Sancti Marci nominis*, which he conducted at San Marco in Venice on Sept. 13, 1956. Other works of the period were also written in a modified 12-tone technique, among them *The Flood*, for Narrator, Mime, Singers, and Dancers, presented in a CBS-TV broadcast in New York on June 14, 1962; its first stage performance was given in Hamburg on April 30, 1963.

Stravinsky was married twice; his 1st wife, Catherine Nosenko, whom he married on Jan. 24, 1906, and who bore him 3 children, died in 1939; on March 9, 1940, Stravinsky married his longtime mistress, Vera, who was formerly married to the Russian painter Serge Sudeikin. She was born Vera de Bosset in St. Petersburg, on Dec. 25, 1888, and died in New York on Sept. 17, 1982, at the age of 93. An ugly litigation for the rights to the Stravinsky estate continued for several years between his children and their stepmother; after Vera Stravinsky's death, it was finally settled in a compromise, according to which 2/9 of the estate went to each of his 3 children and a grandchild and 1/9 to Robert Craft. The value of the Stravinsky legacy was spectacularly demonstrated on Nov. 11, 1982, when his working draft of *Le Sacre du printemps* was sold at an auction in London for the fantastic sum of $548,000. The purchaser was Paul Sacher, the Swiss conductor and philanthropist. Even more fantastic was the subsequent sale of the entire Stravinsky archive, consisting of 116 boxes of personal letters and 225 drawers containing MSS, some of them unpubl. Enormous bids were made for it by the N.Y. Public Library and the Morgan Library, but they were all outbid by Sacher, who offered the overwhelming purse of $5,250,000, which removed all competition. The materials were to be assembled in a specially constructed 7-story Sacher Foundation building in Basel, to be eventually opened to scholars for study.

In tribute to Stravinsky as a naturalized American citizen, the U.S. Postal Service issued a 2-cent stamp bearing his image to mark his centennial in 1982, an honor theretofore never granted to a foreign-born composer (the possible exception being Victor Herbert, but his entire career was made in America).

Few composers escaped the powerful impact of Stravinsky's music; ironically, it was his own country that had rejected him, partly because of the opposition of Soviet ideologues to modern music in general, and partly because of Stravinsky's open criticism of Soviet ways in art. But in 1962 he returned to Russia for a visit, and was welcomed as a prodigal son; as if by magic, his works began to appear on Russian concert programs, and Soviet music critics issued a number of laudatory studies of his works. Yet it is Stravinsky's early masterpieces, set in an attractive colorful style, that continue to enjoy favor with audiences and performers, while his more abstract and recursive scores are appreciated mainly by specialists.

WORKS: DRAMATIC: *L'Oiseau de feu* (The Firebird), ballet (Paris Opéra, June 25, 1910; 3 suite versions: 1911, 1919, and 1945; 2 sections arranged for Violin and Piano, 1926); *Pétrouchka*, ballet (Paris, June 13, 1911, Monteux conducting; rev. 1946; excerpts officially designated as a "suite" in 1946); *Le Sacre du printemps*, ballet, "scenes of pagan Russia" (1911–13; Paris, May 29, 1913, Monteux conducting; 1st concert perf., Moscow, Feb. 18, 1914, Serge Koussevitzky conducting; 1st Paris concert perf., April 5, 1914, Monteux conducting); *Le Rossignol*, "lyric tale" in 3 acts, after Hans Christian Andersen (1908–14; Paris Opéra, May 26, 1914, Monteux conducting; in 1917 the 2d and 3d acts were scored as a ballet, *Le Chant du rossignol*; Paris Opéra, Feb. 2, 1920; also, in 1917, fragments from the 2d and 3d acts were used for a symphonic poem under the same title); *Renard*, burlesque chamber opera (1915–16; Paris, May 18, 1922); *L'Histoire du soldat*, ballet with Narrator and 7 Instrumentalists (Lausanne, Sept. 28, 1918; concert suite with original instrumentation, London, July 20, 1920, Ansermet conducting; also *Petite suite* for Violin, Clarinet, and Piano extracted from the score, 1919); *Pulcinella*, ballet "after Pergolesi" with solos, trios, and a duet for Soprano, Tenor, and Bass (Paris Opéra, May 15, 1920; an orch. suite was extracted from it in 1922, and 1st perf. in Boston, Dec. 22, 1922, rev. 1947; 2 chamber pieces, Suite italienne); *Mavra*, comic opera, after Pushkin (Paris Opéra, June 3, 1922); *Les Noces* (The Wedding), ballet cantata, subtitled "choreographic Russian scenes," revision for Soloists, Chorus, 4 Pianos, and 17 Percussion Instruments (1921–23; Paris, June 13, 1923; orig. scored with Full Orch., 1914–17); *Oedipus Rex*, opera oratorio, after Sophocles (concert perf., Paris, May 30, 1927; 1st stage perf., Vienna, Feb. 23, 1928; rev. 1948); *Apollon Musagète*, classic ballet for String Orch. (Washington, D.C., April 27, 1928; rev. 1947); *Le Baiser de la fée*, ballet on themes of Tchaikovsky (Paris Opéra, Nov. 27, 1928; in 1934 several sections were collected for an independent symphonic piece called *Divertimento*; entire ballet rev. 1950); *Perséphone*, melodrama in 3 parts for Female Narrator, Tenor, Chorus, and Orch., after André Gide (1933; Paris Opéra, April 30, 1934; rev. 1949); *Jeu de cartes*, "ballet in 3 deals" (1935–37; N.Y., April 27, 1937); *Orpheus*, ballet (1946–47; N.Y., April 28, 1948); *The Rake's Progress*, opera after Hogarth's engravings, with libretto by W. H. Auden and C. Kallman (1948–51; Venice, Sept. 11, 1951, composer conducting); *Agon*, ballet for 12 Dancers (1954–57; Los Angeles, June 17, 1957); *Noah and the Flood*, also called *The Flood*, biblical spectacle narrated, mimed, sung, and danced (CBS-TV, N.Y., June 14, 1962; 1st stage perf., Hamburg, April 30, 1963).

WRITINGS: *Chroniques de ma vie* (2 vols., Paris, 1935; Eng. tr., 1936, as *Chronicles of My Life*); *Poetique musicale*, the Charles Eliot Norton Lectures at Harvard Univ. (Paris, 1946; Eng. tr., 1948, as *Poetics of Music*); with R. Craft, 6 vols. of revelatory autobiographical publications: *Conversations with Igor Stravinsky* (N.Y., 1958), *Memories and Commentaries* (N.Y., 1959), *Expositions and Developments* (N.Y., 1962), *Dialogues and a Diary* (N.Y., 1963), *Themes and Episodes* (N.Y., 1967), and *Retrospections and Conclusions* (N.Y., 1969); *Themes and Conclusions*, amalgamated and ed. from *Themes and Episodes* and *Retrospections and Conclusions* (1972); also R. Craft, ed., *Stravinsky: Selected Correspondence* (2 vols., N.Y., 1982 and 1984).

A sharp debate raged, at times to the point of vitriolic polemical exchange, among Stravinsky's associates as to the degree of credibility of Craft's reports in his dialogues, or even of the factual accounts of events during Stravinsky's last years of life. Stravinsky was never a master of the English language; yet Craft quotes him at length as delivering literary paragraphs of impeccable English prose. Craft admitted that he enhanced Stravinsky's actual words and sentences (which were never recorded on tape), articulating the inner, and at times subliminal, sense of his utterances. Craft's role was made clear beyond dispute by Stravinsky himself, who, in a letter to his publishing agent dated March 15, 1958, urged that the title of the book be changed to *Conversations with Igor Stravinsky* by Robert Craft, and emphatically asserted that the text was in Craft's language, and that in effect Craft "created" him.

BIBL.: B. de Schloezer, *I. S.* (Paris, 1926); A. Casella, *S.* (Rome, 1926); J. Vainkop, *I. S.* (Leningrad, 1927); V. Belaiev, *I. S.'s Les Noces: An Outline* (London, 1928); I. Glebov, *S.* (Leningrad, 1929); C. Ramuz, *Souvenirs sur I. S.* (Paris, 1929; rev. ed., Lausanne, 1946); P. Collaer, *S.* (Brussels, 1930); E. White, *S.'s Sacrifice to Apollo* (London, 1930); H. Fleischer, *S.* (Berlin, 1931); A. Schaeffner, *I. S.* (Paris, 1931); J. Handschin, *I. S.* (Zürich, 1933); E. Evans, *The Firebird and Pétrouchka* (London, 1933); D. de Paoli, *I. S.* (Turin, 1934); M. Fardell, *S. et les Ballets Russes* (Nice, 1941); G. Malipiero, *S.* (Venice, 1945); A. Casella, *S.* (Brescia, 1947, different from his 1926 book); E. White, *S.: A Critical Survey* (London, 1947; N.Y., 1948); T. Stravinsky, *Le Message d'I. S.* (Lausanne, 1948; Eng. tr. as *The Message of I. S.*, London, 1953); A. Tansman, *I. S.* (Paris, 1948; Eng. tr., 1949); E. Corle, ed., *I. S.* (N.Y., 1949); M. Lederman, ed., *S. in the Theater* (N.Y., 1949); F. Onnen, *S.* (Stockholm, 1949; Eng. tr.); R. Myers, *Introduction to the Music of S.* (London, 1950); W. H. Auden et al., *I. S.* (Bonn, 1952); H. Strobel, *I. S.* (Zürich, 1956; Eng. tr., 1956, as *S.: Classic Humanist*); *I. S.: A Complete Catalogue of His Published Works* (London, 1957); H. Kirchmeyer, *I. S.: Zeitgeschichte im Persönlichkeitsbild* (Regensburg, 1958); R. Vlad, *S.* (Rome, 1958; Eng. tr., London, 1960; 3d ed., 1979); R. Siohan, *S.* (Paris, 1959; Eng. tr., London, 1966); F. Herzfeld, *I. S.* (Berlin, 1961); *S. and the Dance: A Survey of Ballet Productions, 1910–1962* (N.Y. Public Library, 1962); P. Lang, ed., *S.: The Composer and His Works* (London, 1966); E. White, *S.: The Composer and His Works* (Berkeley, Calif., 1966; 2d ed., 1979); A. Boucourechliev, ed., *S.* (Paris, 1968); A. Dobrin, *I. S.: His Life and Time* (London, 1970); B. Boretz and E. Cone, eds., *Perspectives on Schoenberg and S.* (N.Y., 1972); P. Horgan, *Encounters with S.* (N.Y., 1972; rev. ed., 1989); L. Libman, *And Music at the Close: S.'s Last Years, A Personal Memoir* (N.Y., 1972); D. De Lerma, *I. S., 1882–1971, A Practical Guide to Publications of His Music* (N.Y., 1974); T. Stravinsky, *Catherine and I. S.: A Family Album* (N.Y., 1973); B. Yarustovsky, ed., *I. S.: Articles and Materials* (Moscow, 1973); V. Stravinsky and R. Craft, *S.* (N.Y., 1975); idem, *S. in Pictures and Documents* (N.Y., 1976); A. Boucourechliev, *I. S.* (Paris, 1982; Eng. tr., 1987); P. Griffiths, *I. S.: The Rake's Progress* (Cambridge, 1982); H. Keller and M. Cosman, *S. Seen and Heard* (London, 1982); A. Schouvaloff and V. Borovsky, *S. on Stage* (London, 1982); M. Ruskin, *I. S.: His Personality, Works and Views* (Cambridge, 1983); V. Scherliess, *I. S. und seine Zeit* (Laaber, 1983); P. van den Toorn, *The Music of I. S.* (London, 1983); J. Pasler, ed., *Confronting S.: Man, Musician, and Modernist* (Berkeley, 1986); E. Haimo and P. Johnson, eds., *S. Retrospectives* (Lincoln, Nebr., 1987); J. Kobler, *Firebird: A Biography of S.* (N.Y., 1987); S. Walsh, *The Music of S.* (London and N.Y., 1988); L. Andriessen and E. Schönberger, *The Apollonian Clockwork: On S.* (Oxford, 1989); A. Pople, *Skryabin and S. 1908–1914: Studies in Theory and Analysis* (N.Y. and London, 1989); C. Goubault, *I. S.* (Paris, 1991); V. Stemann, *Das epische Musiktheater bei S. und Brecht: Studien zur Geschichte und Theorie* (N.Y., 1991); P. Stuart, *I. S.—the Composer in the Recording Studio: A Comprehensive Discography* (N.Y., 1991); C. Migliaccio, *I balletti di I. S.* (Milan, 1992); G. Vinay, ed., *S.* (Bologna, 1992); S. Walsh, *S.: Oedipus Rex* (Cambridge, 1993); M. Marnat, *S.* (Paris, 1995); J. Cross, *The S. Legacy* (Cambridge, 1998).

Strehler, Giorgio, Italian opera director; b. Trieste, Aug. 14, 1921; d. Lugano, Dec. 25, 1997. He studied at the Accademia di Filodrammatici in Milan. In 1940 he launched an acting career and in 1943 directed his first theater production. With Paolo Grassi, he founded the Piccolo Teatro in Milan in 1947, the same year he staged his first opera, *La Traviata*. In 1955 he helped organize the Piccola Scala in Milan, where he was regularly engaged as an opera director; he also worked at Milan's La Scala. In 1956 he staged a remarkable production of *Die Dreigroschenoper* at the Piccola Scala, winning the praise of Brecht. Strehler first gained wide notice outside Italy with his production of *Die Entführung aus dem Serail* at the Salzburg Festival in 1965. While he continued to work regularly in Milan, he became closely associated with the Théâtre de l'Europe at the Odéon in Paris. Strehler's background as an actor was instrumental in forging his vision of the serious and comic elements of theatrical scores; his productions of Mozart and Verdi were particularly acclaimed. Conversations on his works with the drama critic Ugo Ronfani were publ. as *Io, Strehler* (Milan, 1986).

BIBL.: F. Battistini, *G. S.* (Rome, 1980).

Streich, Rita, noted German soprano; b. Barnaul, Russia, Dec. 18, 1920; d. Vienna, March 20, 1987. She studied with Erna Berger, Maria Ivogün, and Willi Domgraf-Fassbänder. She made her operatic debut as Zerbinetta in Aussig in 1943; from 1946 she sang with the Berlin State Opera; in 1951 she joined the Berlin Städtische Oper. She also appeared in Vienna, Bayreuth, Salzburg, and Glyndebourne; she made her U.S. debut as Zerbinetta with the San Francisco Opera in 1957. In 1974 she became a prof. at the Folkwang-Hochschule in Essen. She was a leading interpreter of parts in Mozart operas.

Strelnikov, Nikolai, Russian composer; b. St. Petersburg, May 14, 1888; d. there (Leningrad), April 12, 1939. He studied composition with Liadov in St. Petersburg. In 1922 he became music director of the Young People's Theater in Leningrad. He wrote 2 operas, *A Fugitive* (Leningrad, May 26, 1933) and *Count Nulin*, after Pushkin (1935); but he is chiefly remembered for his operettas: *The Black Amulet* (Leningrad, 1927), *Luna-Park* (Moscow, 1928), *The Heart of a Poet* (Leningrad, 1934), and *Presidents and Bananas* (1939). He also publ. monographs on several Russian composers.

Strens, Jules, Belgian organist and composer; b. Ixelles, near Brussels, Dec. 5, 1892; d. there, March 19, 1971. He studied with Gilson. In 1925 was one of 8 founders of the Group des Synthétistes (all Gilson pupils), endeavoring to establish a modern style of composition within the formal categories of early music; he was active mainly as an organist. Among his works were the operas *Le Chanteur de Naples* (1937) and *La Tragédie d'Agamemnon* (1941).

Strepponi, Giuseppina (Clelia Maria Josepha), prominent Italian soprano, 2d wife of **Giuseppe Verdi**; b. Lodi, Sept. 8, 1815; d. Sant' Agata, near Busseto, Nov. 14, 1897. She was the daughter of Felician Strepponi (1797–1832), organist at Monza Cathedral and a composer of operas. She studied piano and singing at the Milan Cons. (1830–34), taking 1st prize for bel canto. After making her operatic debut in *Adria* (Dec. 1834), she scored her first success in Rossini's *Matilda di Shabran* in Trieste (1835); that same year she sang Adalgisa and the heroine in *La Sonnambula* in Vienna, the latter role becoming one of her most celebrated portrayals. She subsequently toured widely with the tenor Napoleone Moriani, who became her lover. In 1839 she made her debut at Milan's La Scala; she created Donizetti's Adelia in Rome in 1841; returning to La Scala, she created Verdi's Abigaille on March 9, 1842, but by then her vocal powers were in decline. All the same, she continued to sing in Verdi's operas, having become a favorite of the composer. In 1846 she retired from the opera stage. From 1847 she lived with Verdi, becoming his wife in 1859.

BIBL.: M. Mundula, *La Moglie di Verdi: G. S.* (Milan, 1938); G. Servadio, *Traviata: Vita di G. S.* (Milan, 1994).

Strickland, Lily (Teresa), American composer; b. Anderson, S.C., Jan. 28, 1887; d. Hendersonville, N.C., June 6, 1958. She studied at Converse College in Spartanburg, S.C. (1901–04) and then with Albert Mildenberg, William Henry Humiston, Daniel Gregory Mason, and Percy Goetschius at the Inst. of Musical Art in New York; she also received private lessons from Alfred John Goodrich. She married J. Courtney Anderson of New York in 1912; she traveled in the Orient between 1920 and 1930, and spent several years in India, then returned to the United States. Among her works were several operettas, including *Jewel of the Desert* (1933) and *Laughing Star of Zuni* (1946).

BIBL.: A. Howe, *L. S.: Her Contribution to American Music in the Early Twentieth Century* (diss., Catholic Univ. of America, 1968).

Striegler, Kurt, German conductor, teacher, and composer; b. Dresden, Jan. 7, 1886; d. Wildthurn, near Landau, Aug. 4, 1958. He studied with Draeseke at the Dresden Cons. He became répétiteur at the Dresden Opera in 1905, and then conductor there in 1912; he was associated with the company until 1945, and also taught at the Dresden Hochschule für Musik (1905–45). In 1945 he became director of the Coburg Cons. He went to Munich in 1950. He wrote the operas *Der Thomaskantor* and *Hand und Herz* (Dresden, 1924).

Striggio, Alessandro, eminent Italian instrumentalist and composer; b. Mantua, c.1540; d. there, Feb. 29, 1592. By the 1560s he was the major composer at the court of Cosimo I de' Medici, Duke of Florence. In 1584 he was active at the court of Alfonso II d'Este in Ferrara, but that same year went to Mantua as court composer; all the same, he remained associated with the courts in Ferrara and Florence until his death; he also wrote works for the Munich court. His importance rests upon his music for intermedi, stage works, and madrigals, including the 3 musical intermezzi *Psiche ed Amore* (1565). He publ. several books of madrigals and *Il cicalamento delle donne* (1567; descriptive songs in the manner of Janequin); many compositions by Striggio are found in collections of the period. His son, Alessandro, known as Alessandrino (b. Mantua, c.1573; d. Venice, June 15, 1630), was a librettist, musician, diplomat, and nobleman; he studied law in Mantua and then was a diplomat in the service of the Gonzaga family there; he was made secretary to Duke Vincenzo I in 1611 and later was ambassador to Milan; he died of the plague while on a diplomatic mission to Venice. He wrote the librettos to Monteverdi's *Orfeo* (Mantua, 1607), *Lamento d'Apollo* (not extant), and probably *Tirsi e Clori* (1615).

BIBL.: R. Tadlock, *The Early Madrigals of A. S.* (diss., Univ. of Rochester, 1958).

Stringfield, Lamar (Edwin), American flutist, conductor, and composer; b. Raleigh, N.C., Oct. 10, 1897; d. Asheville, N.C., Jan. 21, 1959. He served in the U.S. Army during World War I; after the Armistice, he studied theory with Goetschius and flute with Barrère at the Inst. of Musical Art in New York; he also took lessons in conducting with Chalmers Clifton. In 1930 he organized the Inst. of Folk Music at the Univ. of North Carolina, and conducted its orch.; he was conductor of the Knoxville (Tenn.) Sym. Orch. (1946–47), then of the Charlotte Sym. Orch. (1948–49). The source material of his compositions is largely derived from the folk songs of the U.S. South. He learned the trade of printing and was able to publ. his own works. Among his compositions were *The 7th Queue*, ballet (1928), *The Mountain Song*, opera (1929), and *Carolina Charcoal*, musical folk comedy (1951–53). He wrote *America and Her Music* (Chapel Hill, 1931) and a *Guide for Young Flutists* (MS, c.1945; included in the Nelson diss. listed in the bibliography below).

BIBL.: D. Nelson, *The Life and Works of L. S. (1897–1959)* (diss., Univ. of North Carolina, 1971).

Strobel, Otto, German musicologist; b. Munich, Aug. 20, 1895; d. Bayreuth, Feb. 23, 1953. He studied at the Univ. of Munich (Ph.D., 1924, with the diss. *Richard Wagner über sein Schaffen: Ein Beitrag zur "Künstlerasthetek"*; publ. in Munich, 1924). After working as an archivist of the Wahnfried Archives in Bayreuth (from 1932), he was director of the short- lived Richard Wagner Forschungsstätte (1938). He publ. *Richard Wagner: Skizzen und Entwürfe zur Ring-Dichtung* (Munich, 1930), *Genie am Werk: Richard Wagners Schaffen und Wirken im Spiegel eigenhandschriftlicher Urkunden: Führer durch die einmalige Ausstellung einer umfassenden Auswahl von Schätzen aus dem Archiv des Hauses Wahnfried* (Bayreuth, 1933; 2d ed., rev., 1934), and *Richard Wagner: Leben und Schaffen: Eine Zeittafel* (Bayreuth, 1952).

Stroe, Aurel, Romanian composer; b. Bucharest, May 5, 1932. He studied harmony with Negrea, composition with Andricu, and orchestration with Rogalski at the Bucharest Cons. (1951–56); he had a course in electronic music in Munich (1966) and attended the annual summer courses in new music given in Darmstadt (1966–69) by Kagel, Ligeti, and Stockhausen. In 1962 he joined the faculty of the Bucharest Cons.; he also worked at the Bucharest Computing Center (1966–69). His early music is rooted in folklore, but in his later period he experimented with sonoristic constructions, some of which were put together by computerized calculations.

WORKS: DRAMATIC: OPERAS: *Ça n'aura pas le Prix Nobel* (*Această piesă nu va primi premiul Nobel*; 1969; Kassel, Nov. 28, 1971); *De Ptolemaeo*, mini-opera for Tape (1970); *Aristophane: La Paix* (1972–73); *Orestia II* (*Purtatoarele de prinoase*), chamber opera (1974–77; Bucharest, Nov. 14, 1978). MUSIC THEATER: *Agamemnon (Orestia I)* (1979–81; Bucharest, March 1, 1983).

Strohm, Reinhard, German musicologist; b. Munich, Aug. 4, 1942. He studied with Georgiades at the Univ. of Munich and Dahlhaus at Berlin's Technical Univ. (Ph.D., 1971, with the diss. *Italienische Opernarien des frühen Settecento [1720–1730]*, 2 vols., Cologne, 1976). He was assistant ed. of the Richard-Wagner-Ausgabe (1970–81) and also lectured on music at King's College, Univ. of London (1975–83), then was prof. of music history at Yale Univ. (from 1983). In 1990 he rejoined the faculty of King's College, where he served as director of its Inst. for Advanced Musical Studies from 1991. He publ. several valuable books, among them *Music in Late Medieval Bruges* (1985), *Essays on Handel and Italian Opera* (1985), *Music in Late Medieval Europe* (1987), and *The Rise of European Music, 1380–1500* (1993).

Strozzi, Piero, amateur Italian composer; b. Florence, *c.*1550; d. there, after Sept. 1, 1609. He was a nobleman. He was a member of the Bardi circle in Florence, and one of the creators of the "stile rappresentativo," leading to the development of opera. With Caccini, Merulo, and Striggio, he wrote the festival music for the wedding of Francesco de' Medici in 1579. In 1596 he set to music Rinuccini's libretto *La mascherata degli accecati*. Two madrigals by Strozzi are in Luca Bati's *Secondo libro di madrigali* (Venice, 1598).

Strube, Gustav, German-American violinist, conductor, music educator, and composer; b. Ballenstedt, March 3, 1867; d. Baltimore, Feb. 2, 1953. He was taught the violin by his father, and later by Brodsky at the Leipzig Cons.; he was a member of the Gewandhaus Orch. of Leipzig until 1891, when he emigrated to America. He was a violinist in the Boston Sym. Orch. from 1891 to 1913; he also conducted the Boston Pops Orch. (1898; 1900–

02; 1905–12), then taught theory and conducting at the Peabody Cons. in Baltimore (from 1913), where he also was its director (1916–46). In 1916 he was appointed conductor of the newly organized Baltimore Sym. Orch., which he led until 1930. He publ. a useful manual, *The Theory and Use of Chords: A Textbook of Harmony* (Boston, 1928). Among his works was the opera *Ramona*, later renamed *The Captive* (1916).

Strungk, Nicolaus Adam, prominent German violinist, organist, and composer; b. Braunschweig (baptized), Nov. 15, 1640; d. Dresden, Sept. 23, 1700. He studied with his father, the esteemed German organist and composer Delphin Strungk (b. 1600 or 1601; d. Braunschweig [buried], Oct. 12, 1694), whose assistant he became at the age of 12 at the Church of St. Magnus in Braunschweig. He also studied violin at Lübeck under Schnittelbach while attending Helmstedt Univ. At 20 he became 1st violinist in the Wölfenbuttel court chapel; a short time later he went to the Celle court. After appearing as a violinist at the Vienna court chapel in 1661, he decided to pursue his career there until 1665, then was in the service of the Hannover court chapel. In 1678 Strungk became music director of Hamburg's Cathedral and of the city; he wrote and produced operas in German (in keeping with the nationalist trend of the time), among them *Der glücklich-steigende Sejanus* and its sequel, *Der unglücklich-fallende Sejanus* (1678), *Alceste* (1680), *Die Liebreiche, durch Tugend und Schönheit erhöhete Esther* (1680), *Doris, oder der königliche Sklaue* (1680), *Semiramis* (1681), *Theseus* (1681), and *Floretto* (1683). From 1682 to 1686 he was court organist and composer in Hannover; he also visited Italy in 1685, meeting Corelli in Rome. In 1688 he became vice Kapellmeister and chamber organist in Dresden, succeeding Carlo Pallavicino, whose unfinished opera *L'Antiope* he completed and produced there in 1689. In this post he was beset with difficulties arising from friction with Italian musicians, and only managed to maintain his authority through the intervention of his patron, the elector Johann Georg III; when Bernhard, Kapellmeister in Dresden, died in 1692, Strungk was appointed to succeed him. In 1693 he organized an opera company in Leipzig; between 1693 and 1700 he wrote 16 operas for it, among them *Alceste* (perf. at the inauguration of the Leipzig opera house, May 18, 1693), *Nero* (1693), *Syrinx* (1694), *Phocas* (1696), *Ixion* (1697), *Scipio und Hannibal* (1698), *Agrippina* (1699), and *Erechtheus* (1700). Financially, the enterprise was a failure, but Strungk continued to receive his salary from Dresden until his retirement on a pension in 1697. He publ. the important manual *Musicalische Übung auf der Violine oder Viola da Gamba in etlichen Sonaten über die Festgesänge, ingleichen etlichen Ciaconen mit 2 Violinen bestehend* (1691). A selection of airs from his operas was publ. in Hamburg under the title *Ein hundert auserlesenen Arien zweyer Hamburgischen Operen, Semiramis und Esther. Mit beigefügten Ritornellen* (1684).

BIBL.: F. Zelle, *J. Theile und N. A. S.* (Berlin, 1891); F. Berend, *N. A. S., 1640–1700: Sein Leben und seine Werke. Mit Beiträgen zur Geschichte der Musik und des Theater in Celle, Hannover, und Leipzig* (Freiburg im Breisgau, 1915).

Strunk, (William) Oliver, distinguished American musicologist; b. Ithaca, N.Y., March 22, 1901; d. Grottaferrata, Italy, Feb. 24, 1980. He studied at Cornell Univ. (1917–19); in 1927 he took a course in musicology with Otto Kinkeldey there, then entered the Univ. of Berlin to study musicology with J. Wolf (1927–28). Returning to America, he served as a member of the staff of the Music Division at the Library of Congress in Washington, D.C. (1928–34), and then was head of its music division (1934–37). In 1937 he was appointed to the faculty of Princeton Univ.; after retirement in 1966, he lived mostly in Italy. He was a founding member of the American Musicological Soc., serving as the first ed. of its journal (1948) and as its president (1959–60), then was director of Monumenta Musicae Byzantinae (1961–71). He publ. *State and Resources of Musicology in the U.S.* (Washington, D.C., 1932) and the extremely valuable documentary *Source Readings in Music History* (N.Y., 1950). Collections of his writings were publ. as *Essays on Music in the Western World* (N.Y., 1974) and *Essays on Music in the Byzantine World* (N.Y., 1977).

BIBL.: H. Powers, ed., *Studies in Music History: Essays for O. S.* (Princeton, N.J., 1968).

Stuck, Jean-Baptiste, distinguished Italian-born French cellist and composer of German descent; b. probably in Livorno, 1680; d. Paris, Dec. 8, 1755. He began his career as a cellist in Italy, then went to France in the service of the prince of Carignam. He was in the service of Elector Max Emanuel of Bavaria about 1714. Returning to France, he was ordinaire de la musique du Roy until being pensioned in 1748; he also appeared at the Concert Spirituel. In 1733 he became a naturalized French citizen. He won great renown as a cellist and was also a notable composer of cantatas, of which he publ. 4 books (1706, 1708, 1711, 1714). His other works include 3 insignificant operas: *Méléagre* (Paris, May 24, 1709), *Manto la fée* (1709; Paris, Jan. 29, 1711), and *Polidore* (Paris, Feb. 15, 1720); also ballets for the Versailles court.

Stückenschmidt, Hans Heinz, eminent German music critic and writer on music; b. Strasbourg, Nov. 1, 1901; d. Berlin, Aug. 15, 1988. He studied violin, piano, and composition. He was chief music critic of Prague's *Bohemia* (1928–29) and of the *Berliner Zeitung am Mittag* (1929–34); he also was active as a lecturer on contemporary music. In 1934 he was forbidden to continue journalism in Germany, and went to Prague, where he wrote music criticism until 1941, when his activities were stopped once more by the occupation authorities; then he was drafted into the German army. In 1946 he became director of the dept. for new music of the radio station RIAS in Berlin; he also was a lecturer (1948–49), reader (1949–53), and prof. (1953–67) of music history at the Technical Univ. there. With Josef Rufer, he founded and ed. the journal *Stimmen* (Berlin, 1947–49).

WRITINGS: *Arnold Schönberg* (Zürich and Freiburg im Breisgau, 1951; 2d ed., 1957; Eng. tr., 1960); *Neue Musik zwischen den beiden Kriegen* (Berlin and Frankfurt am Main, 1951); *Strawinsky und sein Jahrhundert* (Berlin, 1957); *Schöpfer der neuen Musik* (Frankfurt am Main, 1958); *Boris Blacher* (Berlin, 1963); *Oper in dieser Zeit* (Velber, 1964); *Johann Nepomuk David* (Wiesbaden, 1965); *Maurice Ravel: Variationen über Person und Werk* (Frankfurt am Main, 1966; Eng. tr., 1968); *Ferruccio Busoni: Zeittafel eines Europäers* (Zürich, 1967; Eng. tr., 1970); *Twentieth Century Music* (London, 1968; Ger. original, 1969); *Twentieth Century Composers* (London, 1970; Ger. original, 1971); *Schönberg: Leben, Umwelt, Werk* (Zürich, 1974; Eng. tr., 1976); *Die Musik eines halben Jahrhunderts: 1925–1975* (Munich, 1976); *Schöfer klassischer Musik: Bildnisse und Revisionen* (Berlin, 1983).

BIBL.: W. Burde, ed., *Aspekte der neuen Musik: Professor H.H. S. zum 65. Geburtstag* (Kassel, 1968).

Stückgold, Grete (née **Schneidt**), German soprano; b. London (of a German father and an English mother), June 6, 1895; d. Falls Village, Conn., Sept. 13, 1977. She studied voice with **Jacques Stückgold**, whom she married (divorced in 1928); she later married **Gustav Schützendorf**. She commenced her career as a concert and oratorio singer, made her operatic debut in Nuremberg in 1917, and joined the Berlin State Opera in 1922. On Nov. 2, 1927, she made her Metropolitan Opera debut in New York as Eva in *Die Meistersinger von Nürnberg*; she continued to make appearances there until 1939; she also sang in San Francisco, Philadelphia, and Chicago. She later taught voice at Bennington (Vt.) College.

Stückgold, Jacques, Polish singing teacher; b. Warsaw, Jan. 29, 1877; d. N.Y., May 4, 1953. He studied in Venice and taught voice in Germany (1899–1903), where **Grete** (née **Schneidt**) **Stückgold** became his pupil and wife (divorced, 1928); he settled in New York in 1933. He publ. *Der Bankrott der deutschen Gesangskunst* and *Über Stimmbildungskunst*.

Studer, Cheryl, American soprano; b. Midland, Mich., Oct. 24, 1955. She received her training in Ohio, at the Univ. of Tenn., and from Hans Hotter at the Vienna Hochschule für Musik. After appearing in concerts in the United States, she made her debut at the Bavarian State Opera in Munich as Mařenka in *The Bartered Bride* in 1980. From 1983 to 1985 she sang at the Darmstadt Opera. In 1984 she made her U.S. operatic debut as Micaëla at the Chicago Lyric Opera. From 1985 she sang at the Deutsche Oper in Berlin. She made her Bayreuth Festival debut in 1985 as Elisabeth in *Tannhäuser*. In 1986 she sang Pamina at her debut at the Paris Opéra. In 1987 she made her first appearance at London's Covent Garden as Elisabeth, and also sang at Milan's La Scala. She made her Metropolitan Opera debut in New York in 1988 as Micaëla, and subsequently sang there with success. In 1989 she made her first appearance at the Salzburg Festival as Chrysothemis. In 1990 she sang Elsa at the Vienna State Opera. She appeared as Giuditta at the Vienna Volksoper in 1992. On May 4, 1994, she made her Carnegie Hall recital debut in New York. In 1996 she was engaged as Beethoven's Leonore at the Salzburg Festival. She has won particular distinction for such Strauss roles as Salome, the Empress in *Die Frau ohne Schatten*, and Daphne. Among her other admired roles are Donna Anna, Lucia, Aida, and Singlinde.

Sturzenegger, (Hans) Richard, Swiss cellist, teacher, and composer; b. Zürich, Dec. 18, 1905; d. Bern, Oct. 24, 1976. He studied cello with Fritz Reitz at the Zürich Cons., and then continued his training in Paris (1924–27) with Alexanian and Casals (cello) and Boulanger (harmony and counterpoint). He completed his training in Berlin (1929–35) with Feuermann (cello) and Toch (composition), during which time he served as solo cellist of the Dresden Phil. From 1935 to 1949 he played in the Bern String Quartet, and from 1935 to 1963 he was solo cellist of the Bern Musikgesellschaft. He also taught cello and chamber music at the Bern Cons. From 1954 to 1963 he likewise taught cello in Zürich. In 1963 he became director of the Bern Cons. Among his works was the opera *Atalante* (1963–68).

BIBL.: *R. S., Werkverzeichnis* (Zürich, 1970); E. Hochuli, ed., *Variationen: Festgabe für R. S. zum siebzigsten Geburtstag* (Bern, 1975).

Stutzmann, Nathalie, French contralto; b. Suresnes, May 6, 1965. She studied at the Nancy Cons. and with Hans Hotter, Christa Ludwig, and Daniel Ferro in Paris. After becoming a laureate at the Brussels vocal competition in 1983, she attracted notice at her operatic debut in *Dido and Aeneas* at the Paris Opéra in 1986. She subsequently concentrated on a career as a soloist with the leading orchs. on both sides of the Atlantic and as a recitalist. Her engagements in opera took her to many of the major French music centers. She was particularly known for her portrayal of Debussy's Geneviève, which she sang not only in France but in Bonn (1991), Venice (1995), and Brussels (1996).

Subirá (Puig), José, eminent Spanish musicologist; b. Barcelona, Aug. 20, 1882; d. Madrid, Jan. 5, 1980. He studied piano and composition at the Madrid Cons. and simultaneously qualified for the practice of law (Dr.Jur., 1923), then held various government posts in Madrid while pursuing musicological research. In 1952 he was elected a member of the Real Academia de Bellas Artes de San Fernando in Madrid. Apart from his scholarly pursuits, he publ. a novel, *Su virginal pureze* (1916), and a historical account, *Los Españoles en la guerra de 1914–1918* (4 vols.).

WRITINGS: *Enrique Granados* (Madrid, 1926); *La música en la Casa de Alba* (Madrid, 1927); *La participación musical en el antiguo teatro español* (Barcelona, 1930); *Tonadillas teatrales inéditas: Libretos y partituras* (Madrid, 1932); *"Celos aun del aire matan": Opera del siglo XVII, texto de Calderón y música de Juan Hidalgo* (Barcelona, 1933); *La tonadilla escénica: Sus obras y sus autores* (Barcelona, 1933); *Historia de la música teatral en España* (Barcelona, 1945); with H. Anglès, *Catálogo musical de la Biblioteca Nacional de Madrid* (Barcelona, 1946–51); *La ópera en los teatros de Barcelona* (Barcelona, 1946); *Historia de la música Salvat* (Barcelona, 1947; 3d ed., enl., 1958); *Historia y anecdotario del Teatro Real* (Madrid, 1949); *El compositor Iriarte (1750–1791) y el cultivo español del melólogo (melodrama)* (Barcelona, 1949–50); *La música, etapas y aspectos* (Barcelona, 1949); *El teatro del Real palacio (1849–1851), con un bosquejo preliminar sobre la música palatina desde Felipe V hasta Isabel II* (Madrid, 1950); *Historia de la música española e hispanoamericana* (Barcelona, 1958); *Temas musicales madrileños* (Madrid, 1971).

Subotnick, Morton, American composer and teacher; b. Los Angeles, April 14, 1933. He studied at the Univ. of Denver (B.A., 1958) and with Milhaud and Kirchner at Mills College in Oakland, Calif. (M.A., 1960), then was a fellow of the Inst. for Advanced Musical Studies at Princeton Univ. (1959–60). He taught at Mills College (1959–66), N.Y. Univ. (1966–69), and the Calif. Inst. of the Arts (from 1969) and also held various visiting professorships and composer-in-residence positions. In 1979 he married **Joan La Barbara**. His compositions run the gamut of avant-garde techniques, often with innovative use of electronics; his *Silver Apples of the Moon* (1967) became a classic. In 1995, working with programmer Mark Coniglio at the Institute for Studies in the Arts at Arizona State Univ. in Tempe, he completed *Making Music*, an interactive CD-ROM composition program for children; his *All My Hummingbirds Have Alibis*, an "imaginary ballet" set to a series of Max Ernst's paintings for Flute, Cello, Midi Piano, Midi Mallets, and Electronics (1991), was also later converted into a critically appraised CD-ROM.

WORKS: DRAMATIC: OPERA: *Jacob's Room* (Philadelphia, April 20, 1993). INCIDENTAL MUSIC TO: Genet's *The Balcony* (1960); Shakespeare's *King Lear* (1960); Brecht's *Galileo* (1964) and *The Caucasian Chalk Circle* (1965); Büchner's *Danton's Death* (1966).

Sucher, Josef, Hungarian conductor and composer, husband of **Rosa** (née **Hasselbeck**) **Sucher**; b. Döbör, Nov. 23, 1843; d. Berlin, April 4, 1908. He studied in Vienna with Sechter, and was made a répétiteur (1870) and an assistant conductor (1873) at the Court Opera there, and then was conductor at the city's Komische Theater (1874–76). He was conductor of the Leipzig City Theater (1876–78), where he married Rosa Hasselbeck in 1877; they were at the Hamburg Stadttheater from 1878 to 1888, at which time Sucher became conductor of the Berlin Royal Opera, his wife being engaged there as prima donna. He left the Berlin post in 1899. Sucher was especially distinguished as an interpreter of the Wagnerian repertoire.

Sucher, Rosa (née **Hasselbeck**), German soprano, wife of **Josef Sucher**; b. Velburg, Feb. 23, 1849; d. Eschweiler, April 16, 1927. She received her early musical training from her father, a chorusmaster. She sang in provincial operas, then in Leipzig, where she married Josef Sucher in 1877; they subsequently were engaged at the Hamburg Stadttheater (1878–88). In 1882 she made her London debut as Elsa in *Lohengrin*; in 1886 she appeared in Vienna. She made regular visits to the Bayreuth Festivals (1886–96) and was a principal member of the Berlin Royal Opera (1888–98). On June 8, 1892, she made her Covent Garden debut in London as the *Siegfried* Brünnhilde; on Feb. 25, 1895, she made her American debut as Isolde at the Metropolitan Opera in New York, under the sponsorship of the Damrosch Opera Co. In 1903 she gave her farewell operatic performance in Berlin as Sieglinde. In 1908 she settled in Vienna as a voice teacher. She publ. her memoirs, *Aus meinem Leben* (Leipzig, 1914). Among her other fine roles were Euryanthe, Elisabeth, and Senta.

Suchoff, Benjamin, distinguished American music educator and musicologist; b. N.Y., Jan. 19, 1918. He studied at Cornell Univ. (B.S., 1940), then took courses in composition with Vittorio Giannini at the Juilliard School of Music in New York (1940–41). After serving in the U.S. Army in Europe and Asia in World War II, he resumed his studies, first at Juilliard (1946–47) and then at N.Y. Univ. (M.A., 1949; Ed.D., 1956, with the diss. *Guide to Bartók's Mikrokosmos*; publ. in London, 1957; 3d ed., N.Y., 1982). From 1950 to 1978 he was administrator of music at Hewlett-Woodmere Union Free School on Long Island, where he also taught electronic music. From 1973 to 1984 he was adjunct prof. of arts and letters at the State Univ. of N.Y. at Stony Brook; he also was director of its special collections and of the Center for Contemporary Arts and Letters, where he guided the fortunes of the COMMPUTE Program, a consortium of institutions active in research and development of computer-oriented music studies. In 1953 he became curator of the N.Y. Bartók Archive. From 1968 until the death of Bartók's widow in 1982 he was successor-trustee of the Bartók estate. In 1992 he became adjunct prof. in the dept. of ethnomusicology and systematic musicology at the Univ. of Calif., Los Angeles. He was the ed. of the N.Y. Bartók Archive edition of Bartók's writings in English trans. in its Studies in Musicology series; he also was ed. of its edition of Bartók's compositions, known as *The Archive Edition*.

Suchoň, Eugen, significant Slovak composer and pedagogue; b. Pezinok, Sept. 25, 1908; d. Bratislava, Aug. 5, 1993. He studied piano and composition with Kafenda at the Bratislava School of Music (1920–28), then took a course in advanced composition with V. Novák at the Master School of the Prague Cons. (1931–33). He taught composition at the Bratislava Academy of Music (1933–48) and music education at the Univ. of Bratislava (1949–60); he was a prof. of theory there from 1959 to 1974; in 1971 he was appointed prof. at the College of Music and Dramatic Art in Bratislava. In 1958 he was named National Artist of the Republic of Czechoslovakia. He was one of the creators of the modern Slovak style of composition, based on authentic folk motifs and couched in appropriately congenial harmonies. His works include the operas *Krútňava* (The Whirlpool; 1941–49; Bratislava, Dec. 10, 1949) and *Svätopluk* (1952–59; Bratislava, March 10, 1960).

BIBL.: E. Zavarský, *E. S.* (Bratislava, 1955); J. Kresánek, *Národný umelec E. S.* (National Artist E. S.; Bratislava, 1961).

Suchý, František, Czech teacher, conductor, and composer; b. Březové Hory u Příbrami, April 21, 1891; d. Prague, June 13, 1973. He studied at the local teaching inst. (1906–10); after studies with Horník and Stecker at the Prague Cons. (1913–14), he received lessons in conducting from Nikisch in Leipzig (1914–16); subsequently he was active as a teacher, conductor, and composer. His works include the operas *Lásky div* (The Wonder of Love; 1923) and *Havéři* (The Miners; 1947–57) and the ballet *Porcelánové království* (The Porcelain Kingdom; 1922).

Suchý, František, Czech oboist, pedagogue, and composer; b. Libina u Šumperka, April 9, 1902; d. Brno, July 12, 1977. He studied oboe with Wagner and composition with Kvapil at the Brno Cons. (graduated, 1927), then attended Novák's master classes at the Prague Cons. (until 1937). He was 1st oboist in the Brno Radio Orch. (1927–47), then was a prof. of oboe at the Cons. and a prof. of oboe and theory at the Academy in Brno. His works include the opera *Maryla* (1956); also *V. Gethsemaně*, oratorio (1933).

Suitner, Otmar, Austrian conductor; b. Innsbruck, May 16, 1922. He studied piano at the Innsbruck Cons. and then piano with Ledwinka and conducting with Krauss at the Salzburg Mozarteum (1940–42). In 1945 he conducted at the Innsbruck Landestheater; he was then music director in Remscheid (1952–57) and Generalmusikdirektor in Ludwigshafen (1957–60). From 1960 to 1964 he served as Generalmusikdirektor of the Dresden State Opera and Dresden State Orch.; from 1964 to 1971, conducted at the East Berlin State Opera, and from 1974 to 1991 was its Generalmusikdirektor. He also conducted in the United States.

Suk, Josef, eminent Czech violinist, pedagogue, and composer; b. Křečovice, Jan. 4, 1874; d. Benešov, near Prague, May 29, 1935. He received training in piano, violin, and organ from his father, Josef Suk (1827–1913), the Křečovice school- and choirmaster, then took courses in violin with Bennewitz, in theory with Foerster, Knittl, and Stecker, and in chamber music with Wihan at the Prague Cons. (1885–91); after graduating in 1891, he pursued additional training in chamber music with Wihan and in composition with Dvořák at the Cons. (1891–92). In 1898 he married Dvořák's daughter Otilie. He began his career playing 2d violin in Wihan's string quartet, which became known as the Czech Quartet in 1892; he remained a member of it until his retirement in 1933. He also was a prof. of composition at the Prague Cons. (from 1922), where he was head of its master classes; he also served as its rector (1924–26; 1933–35). Suk's early works were greatly influenced by Dvořák; in later years his lyrical Romantic style evolved into an individual style characterized by polytonal writing and harmonic complexity bordering on atonality. His numerous works include incidental music: *Radúz a Mahulena* for Alto, Tenor, Reciters, Chorus, and Orch., op. 13 (Prague, April 6, 1898; rev. 1912); *Pod jabloní* (Beneath the Apple Tree) for Alto, Reciters, Chorus, and Orch., op. 20 (1900–01; rev. 1911, 1915; Prague, Jan. 31, 1934).

BIBL.: J. Šach, ed., *J. S.: Vzpomínková mozaika* (J. S.: A Mosaic of Reminiscences; Prague, 1941); V. Štěpán, *Novák a S.* (Prague, 1945); J. Květ, ed., *Živá slova J. a S. a* (In J. S.'s Own Words; Prague, 1946); J. Květ, *J. S.* (Prague, 1947); J. Berkovec, *J. S. (1874–1935): Život a dílo* (J. S. [1874–1935]: Life and Works; Prague, 1956; 2d ed., 1962; rev. and abr. ed., 1968, as *J. S.*; Eng., Ger., French, and Russian trs., 1968); J. Květ, *J. S. v obrazech* (J. S. in Pictures; Prague, 1964); Z. Sádecký, *Lyrismus v tvorbě J. a S. a* (Lyricism in J. S.'s Works; Prague, 1966); M. Svobodová, *J. S.: Tematický Katalog* (Jinočany, 1993).

Suk, Váša (Ivanovich), noted Russian conductor and composer of Czech parentage; b. Kladno, Nov. 16, 1861; d. Moscow, Jan. 12, 1933. He studied violin at the Prague Cons. and composition privately with Fibich. He was concertmaster of the Kiev Opera orch. (1880–82) and a violinist in the Bolshoi Theater orch. in Moscow (1882–87); in 1885 he launched a conducting career, and subsequently appeared throughout Russia; he was a conductor of the Bolshoi Theater (1906–32) and principal conductor of the Stanislavsky Opera Theater in Moscow (from 1927). He was appreciated in Russia for his thoroughness in drilling the singers and the orch.; he achieved a fine reputation as an operatic conductor. He wrote an opera, *Lord of the Forests*, which he conducted in Kharkov on Feb. 16, 1900.

BIBL.: I. Remezov, *V. I. S.* (Moscow and Leningrad, 1951).

Sukegawa, Toshiya, Japanese composer; b. Sapporo, July 15, 1930. He studied with Ikenouchi from 1951; he graduated in composition from the Univ. of Arts in Tokyo in 1957. His works include a television opera, *Pôra no Hiroba* (1959).

Šulek, Stjepan, prominent Croatian violinist, conductor, teacher, and composer; b. Zagreb, Aug. 5, 1914; d. there, Jan. 16, 1986. He studied violin with Huml at the Zagreb Academy of Music; he was largely self-taught in composition, although he succeeded in becoming a composer of considerable merit. He was active as a violinist, became best known as a conductor, conducted the Zagreb Radio Chamber Orch. on many tours of Europe, and was prof. of composition at the Zagreb Academy of Music (from 1945). His compositions reveal a strong individual profile. They include the operas *Koriolan*, after Shakespeare (Zagreb, Oct. 12, 1958) and *Oluja* (The Tempest), after Shakespeare (Zagreb, Nov. 28, 1969).

BIBL.: K. Šipuš, *S. Š.* (Zagreb, 1961).

Sullivan, Sir Arthur (Seymour), famous English composer and conductor; b. London, May 13, 1842; d. there, Nov. 22, 1900. His father, Thomas Sullivan, was bandmaster at the Royal Military College, Sandhurst, and later prof. of brass instruments at the Royal Military School of Music, Kneller Hall; his musical inclinations were encouraged by his father, and in 1854 he became a chorister in the Chapel Royal, remaining there until 1858 and studying with the Rev. Thomas Helmore. In 1855 his sacred song "O Israel" was publ. In 1856 he received the 1st Mendelssohn Scholarship to the Royal Academy of Music in London, where he studied with Sterndale Bennett, Arthur O'Leary, and John Goss; he then continued his training at the Leipzig Cons. (1858–61), where he received instruction in counterpoint and fugue from Moritz Hauptmann, in composition from Julius Rietz, in piano from Ignaz Moscheles and Louis Plaidy, and in conducting from Ferdinand David. He conducted his overture *Rosenfest* in Leipzig (May 25, 1860), and wrote a String Quartet and music to *The Tempest* (Leipzig, April 6, 1861; rev. version, London, April 5, 1862). His cantata *Kenilworth* (Birmingham Festival, Sept. 8, 1864) stamped him as a composer of high rank. In 1864 he visited Ireland and composed his *Irish Symphony* (London, March 10, 1866). In 1866 he was appointed prof. of composition at the Royal Academy of Music in London. About this time he formed a lifelong friendship with Sir George Grove, whom he accompanied in 1867 on a memorable journey to Vienna in search of Schubert MSS, leading to the discovery of the score of *Rosamunde*. The year 1867 was also notable for the production of the first of those comic operas upon which Sullivan's fame chiefly rests. This was *Cox and Box* (libretto by F. C. Burnand), composed in 2 weeks and performed on May 13, 1867, in London. Less successful were *The Contrabandista* (London, Dec. 18, 1867) and *Thespis* (London, Dec. 26, 1871), but the latter is significant as inaugurating Sullivan's collaboration with Sir W. S. Gilbert, the celebrated humorist, who became the librettist of all Sullivan's most successful comic operas, beginning with *Trial by Jury* (March 25, 1875). This was produced by Richard D'Oyly Carte, who in 1876 formed a company expressly for the production of the "Gilbert and Sullivan" operas. The first big success obtained by the famous team was *H.M.S. Pinafore* (May 25, 1878), which had 700 consecutive performances in London, and enjoyed an enormous vogue in "pirated" productions throughout the United States. In an endeavor to protect their interests, Gilbert and Sullivan went to New York in 1879 to give an authorized performance of *Pinafore*, and while there they also produced *The Pirates of Penzance* (Dec. 30, 1879). On April 23, 1881, came *Patience*, a satire on exaggerated esthetic poses exemplified by Oscar Wilde, whose American lecture tour was conceived as a "publicity stunt" for this work. On Nov. 25, 1882, *Iolanthe* began a run that lasted more than a year. This was followed by the comparatively unsuccessful *Princess Ida* (Jan. 5, 1884), but then came the universal favorite of all the Gilbert and Sullivan operas, *The Mikado* (March 14, 1885). The list of these popular works is completed by *Ruddigore* (Jan. 22, 1887), *The Yeomen of the Guard* (Oct. 3, 1888), and *The Gondoliers* (Dec. 7, 1889). After a quarrel and a reconciliation, the pair collaborated in 2 further works, of less popularity: *Utopia Limited* (Oct. 7, 1893) and *The Grand Duke* (March 7, 1896).

Sullivan's melodic inspiration and technical resourcefulness, united with the delicious humor of Gilbert's verses, raised the light opera to a new height of artistic achievement, and his works in this field continue to delight countless hearers. Sullivan was also active in other branches of musical life. He conducted numerous series of concerts, most notably those of the London Phil. Soc. (1885–87) and the Leeds Festivals (1880–98). He was principal of and a prof. of composition at the National Training School for Music from 1876 to 1881. He received the degree of Mus.Doc. honoris causa from Cambridge (1876) and Oxford (1879), he was named Chevalier of the Légion d'honneur (1878), and was grand organist to the Freemasons (1887); etc. He was knighted by Queen Victoria in 1883. Parallel with his comic creations, he composed many "serious" works, including the grand opera *Ivanhoe* (Jan. 31, 1891), which enjoyed a momentary vogue. His songs were highly popular in their day, and "The Lost Chord," to words by Adelaide A. Proctor (publ. 1877), is still a favorite. Among his oratorios, *The Light of the World* (Birmingham Festival, Aug. 27, 1873) may be mentioned. Other stage works (all 1st perf. in London unless otherwise given) include *The Zoo* (June 5, 1875); *The Sorcerer* (Nov. 17, 1877; rev. version, Oct. 11, 1884); *Haddon Hall* (Sept. 24, 1892); *The Chieftain* (Dec. 12, 1894); *The Martyr of Antioch* (Edinburgh, Feb. 15, 1898; a stage arrangement of the cantata); *The Beauty-Stone* (May 28, 1898); romantic opera, *The Rose of Persia* (Nov. 29, 1899); *The Emerald Isle* (completed by E. German, April 27, 1901); 2 ballets: *L'Ile enchante* (May 14, 1864) and *Victoria and Merrie England* (May 25, 1897).

BIBL.: A. Lawrence, *Sir A. S.: Life Story, Letters and Reminiscences* (London, 1899); W. Wells, *Souvenir of Sir A. S., Mus.Doc., M.V.O.* (London, 1901) B. Findon, *Sir A. S.: His Life and Music* (London, 1904; 2d ed., rev., 1908, as *Sir A. S. and His Operas*); F. Cellier and C. Bridgeman, *Gilbert, S., and D'Oyly Carte* (London, 1914; 2d ed., 1927); H. Walbrook, *Gilbert and S. Opera* (London, 1922); A. Godwin, *Gilbert and S.* (London, 1926); H. Wyndham, *A. S. S.* (London, 1926); N. Flower and H. Sullivan, *Sir A. S.: His Life, Letters and Diaries* (London, 1927; 2d ed., 1950); T. Dunhill, *S.'s Comic Operas: A Critical Appreciation* (London, 1928); I. Goldberg, *The Story of Gilbert and S.* (London, 1929); H. Pearson, *Gilbert and S.* (London, 1935); G. Dunn, *A Gilbert and S. Dictionary* (N.Y., 1936); C. Purdy, *Gilbert and S.: Masters of Mirth and Melody* (N.Y., 1947); W. Darlington, *The World of Gilbert and S.* (N.Y., 1950); A. Jacobs, *Gilbert and S.* (London, 1951); L. Bailey, *The Gilbert and S. Book* (N.Y., 1952; 3d ed., 1966); A. Williamson, *Gilbert and S. Operas: A New Assessment* (N.Y., 1953); A. Powers-Waters, *The Melody Maker: The Life of Sir A. S.* (N.Y., 1959); M. Green, *Treasury of Gilbert and S.* (London, 1961); N. Wymer, *Gilbert and S.* (London, 1962); C. Bulla, *Stories of Gilbert and S. Operas* (N.Y., 1968); J. Helyar, ed., *Gilbert and S. International Conference: Kansas 1970* (Lawrence, Kans., 1971); P. Young, *Sir A. S.* (London, 1971); L. Ayre, *The Gilbert & S. Companion* (N.Y., 1972); M. Hardwick, *The Osprey Guide to Gilbert and S.* (Reading, 1972); P. Kline, *Gilbert and S. Production* (N.Y., 1972); L. Baily, *Gilbert & S. and Their World* (London, 1973); R. Allen and G. D'Luhy, *Sir A. S.: Composer & Personage* (N.Y., 1975); I. Bradley, ed., *The Annotated Gilbert and S.* (2 vols., London, 1982, 1984); A. Williamson, *Gilbert & S. Opera* (London, 1983); A. Jacobs, *A. S.: A Victorian Musician* (Oxford, 1984; 2d ed., rev. and enl., 1992); J. Wolfson, *S. and the Scott Russells* (Chichester, 1984); D. Eden, *Gilbert & S.: The Creative Conflict* (Rutherford, N.J., 1986); C. Hayter, *Gilbert and S.* (N.Y., 1987); I. Asimov, ed., *Asimov's Annotated Gilbert & S.* (N.Y., 1988); M. Ffinch, *Gilbert and S.* (London, 1993); M. Saremba, *A. S.: Ein Komponistenleben im viktorischen England* (Wilhelmshaven, 1993).

Sumac, Yma (real name, **Emperatriz Chavarri**), Peruvian-born American singer of a phenomenal diapason, whose origin is veiled in mystical mist; b. Ichocan, Sept. 10, 1927. She was reared in the Andes; it is credible that she developed her phenomenal voice of 5 octaves in range because her lungs were inflated by the necessity of breathing through oxygen at the high altitude. However that might be, she married Moises Vivanco, who was an arranger for Capitol Records and who launched her on a flamboyant career as a concert singer; with him and their cousin, Cholito Rivero, she toured South America as the Inca Taky Trio (1942–46), then settled in the United States and became a naturalized American citizen in 1955. She was billed by unscrupulous promoters as an Inca princess, a direct descendant of Atahualpa, the last emperor of the Incas, a Golden Virgin of the Sun God worshiped by the Quechua Indians. On the other hand, some columnists spread the scurrilous rumor that she was in actuality a Jewish girl from Brooklyn whose real name was Amy (retrograde of Yma) Camus (retrograde of Sumac). But Sumac never spoke with a Brooklyn accent. She exercised a mesmeric appeal to her audiences, from South America to Russia, from California to Central Europe; expressions such as "miraculous" and "amazing" were used by Soviet reviewers during her tour of Russia in 1962; "supersonic vocal skill" was a term applied by an American critic. Her capacity did not diminish with age; during her California appearances in 1984 and again in 1988 she still impressed audiences with the expressive power of her voice.

Sumera, Lepo, esteemed Estonian composer; b. Tallinn, May 8, 1950. He was educated at the Tallinn State Cons. (1968–73), where he subsequently was a prof. (from 1976) and chairman of its composition dept. (1988–89); he also attended summer courses in new music in Darmstadt (1988–89). He was a recording supervisor for Estonian Radio (1973–78). From 1989 to 1990 he was deputy minister of culture and from 1990 minister of culture for the Republic of Estonia. He received many Estonian Music Prizes for best composition of the year, including those for his film scores (1978), his Sym. No. 1 (1982), his Sym. No. 2 (1985), and his *Saare Piiga laul merest* (The Island Maiden; 1989).

WORKS: DRAMATIC: *Anselmi lugu*, ballet (1977–78); *Ja'st'eritsa*, ballet (1986–88); *Saare Piiga laul merest* (The Island Maiden), *Linda matab Kalevit* (Linda Buries Kalev), and *Linda soome Tuuslar* (Linda Becomes Stone), multimedia dance drama for

Chamber Chorus, Actors, and Shaman Drum (1988); also more than 40 scores for film, television, animation, and theater.

Summers, Jonathan, Australian baritone; b. Melbourne, Oct. 2, 1946. Following training in Melbourne (1964–74), he studied with Otakar Kraus in London (1974–80). In 1975 he made his operatic debut with the Kent Opera as Rigoletto. He sang Falstaff with the Glyndebourne Touring Opera in 1976, and in 1977 he made his first appearance at London's Covent Garden as Kilian in *Der Freischütz*. He also sang with the English National Opera in London, Opera North in Leeds, and the Scottish Opera in Glasgow. In 1981 he sang Germont père with the Australian Opera. He made his Metropolitan Opera debut in New York as Marcello on Jan. 22, 1988. In 1990 he sang Enrico in *Lucia di Lammermoor* at his debut with the Lyric Opera in Chicago, and then returned there in 1994 to sing in *Fedora*. In 1997 he portrayed Mozart's Figaro at the English National Opera.

Summers, Patrick, American conductor and musicologist; b. Washington, Ind., Aug. 14, 1963. He received his education at Indiana Univ. From 1989 to 1994 he was music director of the San Francisco Opera Center, where he conducted the U.S. premiere of Reimann's *Die Gespenstersonate* in 1990. He also conducted its touring company, the Western Opera Theater, throughout the United States and Canada. He likewise made frequent appearances as a conductor with the San Francisco Opera. In 1994 he made his first appearance with Opera Australia conducting *La Cenerentola*. In 1996 he was engaged to conduct Hoiby's *The Tempest* at the Dallas Opera. He conducted his own realization of Monteverdi's *L'incoronazione di Poppea* at the San Francisco Opera in 1997, the same year he led the English Chamber Orch. on a tour of Europe with Olga Borodina and Dmitri Hvorostovsky as guest soloists. In 1998 he became music director of the Houston Grand Opera, and concurrently served as principal guest conductor of the San Francisco Opera. He made his Metropolitan Opera debut in New York that same year on Dec. 24 conducting *Die Fledermaus*. His repertoire is expansive, encompassing scores from the Baroque era to the contemporary period.

Sunnegårdh, Thomas, Swedish tenor; b. Stockholm, July 11, 1949. He received vocal instruction in Stockholm. After appearing with the Swedish National Touring Opera, he made his debut as Albert Herring in 1982 at the Royal Opera in Stockholm, where he subsequently sang such roles as Tamino, Fra Diavolo, Ferrando, Lohengrin, and Taverner. In 1983 he created the title role in Nørgard's *Siddharta* in Stockholm. He appeared as Macduff at the Bregenz Festival in 1988, and in 1990 as Lohengrin in Moscow and Stuttgart. In 1991 he made his debut at London's Covent Garden as Erik. He sang Lohengrin in Barcelona in 1992, and in Düsseldorf in 1994. In 1993 he portrayed Walther von Stolzing at the Bavarian State Opera in Munich. In 1996 he was engaged as Paul in Korngold's *Die tote Stadt* in Stockholm.

Supervia, Conchita, famous Spanish mezzo-soprano; b. Barcelona, Dec. 9, 1895; d. London, March 30, 1936. She studied at the Colegio de las Damas Negras in Barcelona. She made her operatic debut with a visiting opera company at the Teatro Colón in Buenos Aires on Oct. 1, 1910, in Stiattesi's opera *Blanca de Beaulieu*. She then sang in the Italian premiere of *Der Rosenkavalier* in Rome in 1911, as Carmen in Bologna in 1912, and as a member of the Chicago Opera (1915–16). She appeared frequently at La Scala in Milan from 1924; she also sang in other Italian music centers, and at London's Covent Garden (1934–35). She endeared herself to the Italian public by reviving Rossini's operas *L'Italiana in Algeri* and *La Cenerentola*; she also attracted favorable critical attention by performing the part of Rosina in *Il Barbiere di Siviglia* in its original version as a coloratura contralto. In 1931 she married the British industrialist Sir Ben Rubenstein. She died as a result of complications following the birth of a child.

Suppé, Franz (von) (real name, **Francesco Ezechiele Ermenegildo, Cavaliere Suppé-Demelli**), famous Austrian composer; b. Spalato, Dalmatia (of Belgian descent), April 18, 1819; d. Vienna, May 21, 1895. At the age of 11 he played the flute, and at 13 wrote a Mass. He was then sent by his father to study law at Padua. On his father's death, he went with his mother to Vienna in 1835, and continued serious study at the Cons. with Sechter and Seyfried. He conducted at theaters in Pressburg and Baden, then at Vienna's Theater an der Wien (1845–62), Kaitheater (1862–65), and Carltheater (1865–82). All the while, he wrote light operas and other theater music of all degrees of levity, obtaining increasing success rivaling that of Offenbach. His music possesses the charm and gaiety of the Viennese genre, but also contains elements of more vigorous popular rhythms. His most celebrated single work is the overture to *Dichter und Bauer*, which still retains a firm place in the light repertoire. His total output comprises about 30 comic operas and operettas and 180 other stage pieces, most of which were brought out in Vienna; of these the following obtained considerable success: *Dichter und Bauer* (Aug. 24, 1846); *Das Mädchen vom Lande* (Aug. 7, 1847); *Dame Valentine, oder Frauenräuber und Wanderbursche* (Jan. 9, 1851); *Paragraph 3* (Jan. 8, 1858); *Das Pensionat* (Nov. 24, 1860); *Die Kartenaufschlägerin* (April 26, 1862); *Zehn Mädchen und kein Mann* (Oct. 25, 1862); *Die flotten Burschen* (April 18, 1863); *Das Corps der Rache* (March 5, 1864); *Franz Schubert* (Sept. 10, 1864); *Die schöne Galatea* (Berlin, June 30, 1865); *Die leichte Kavallerie* (March 24, 1866); *Die Tochter der Puszta* (March 24, 1866); *Die Freigeister* (Oct. 23, 1866); *Banditenstreiche* (April 27, 1867); *Die Frau Meisterin* (Jan. 20, 1868); *Tantalusqualen* (Oct. 3, 1868); *Isabella* (Nov. 5, 1869); *Cannebas* (Nov. 2, 1872); *Fatinitza* (Jan. 5, 1876); *Der Teufel auf Erden* (Jan. 5, 1878); *Boccaccio* (Feb. 1, 1879); *Donna Juanita* (Feb. 21, 1880); *Der Gascogner* (March 21, 1881); *Das Herzblättchen* (Feb. 4, 1882); *Die Afrikareise* (March 17, 1883); *Des Matrosen Heimkehr* (Hamburg, May 4, 1885); *Bellmann* (Feb. 26, 1887); *Die Jagd nach dem Glücke* (Oct. 27, 1888); *Das Modell* (Oct. 4, 1895); *Die Pariserin, oder Das heimlische Bild* (Jan. 26, 1898).

BIBL.: G. Sabalich, *F. S. e l'operetta* (Zara, 1888); O. Keller, *F. v.S.: Der Schöpfer der deutschen Operette* (Leipzig, 1905).

Suratno, Nano, prolific Indonesian composer, known as **Nano S.**; b. Pasar Kemis Tarogong, West Java, April 4, 1944. He earned degrees from the Akademi Seni Tari Indonesia (A.S.T.I.) Bandung (1978) and Sekolah Tinggi Seni Indonesia (S.T.S.I.) Surakarta (1989); he also studied with Daeng Sutikna (music), Syafei (literature), Tjetje Somantri (choreography and dance), and, especially, Mang Koko (music). He formed his own dance company and then performed with Koko's group, Ganda Mekar. He began composing experimental works for degung, a traditional Sundanese chamber ensemble of tuned gongs, drums, and bamboo flute; in 1979 his *Sangkuriang* was performed at the important national festival Pekan Komponis Muda (Young Composers' Festival); he also began composing highly expressive instrumental music ("karawitan total"), and in 1985 mounted *Umbul-umbul*, involving 75 players in a mixture of over 15 Sundanese styles, on Indonesian TV. Nano S. sees many of his songs as a means of making traditional music more accessible to Sundanese youths; he often recasts classical melodies in forms that conform to popular music styles of the West. Even in his more experimental instrumental works, which he calls "musik total" or "musik murni" (i.e., "absolute" music), he neither borrows from foreign sources nor uses diatonic tuning; while such works have not yet found a place in the standard repertoire of Sunda, audiences abroad have been receptive; in 1989, on a commission from the American Gamelan Inst. in Hanover, N.H., he composed and recorded *Jemplang Polansky*, inspired by his confusion upon listening to the computer music of Larry Polansky, and *Galura* (Emotion; 1988), an instrumental solo piece for kecapi (plucked zither). In 1986 he toured in Canada and the United States; after appearing in Japan (1988), he became a guest lecturer and composer at the Univ. of Calif. at Santa Cruz (1989). In 1990 he directed the touring program "Sunda: From Village to City," presented in the United States at its Festival of Indonesia. Nano S. is best known in Indonesia as a song composer; his texts are often about young love, cast in the regional language of Sundanese, modern Indonesian, or English. More than 200 audiotapes of his works have been released, several of them distributed by the American Gamelan Inst. Among his publications are a book of songs, *Haleuang Tondang* (Bandung, 1975), and *Mengolah Seni Pertunjukan Sebagai Media Penergangan* (Development of the Performing Arts as an Information Medium; 1989); also some 15 operetta librettos. In 1978 he married the Indonesian singer Dheniarsah; their home in Bandung is a fertile international meeting ground for artists of all disciplines. Other works include the operettas *Ki Lagoni* (1967) and *Raja Kecit* (1974).

Surdin, Morris, Canadian composer; b. Toronto, May 8, 1914; d. there, Aug. 19, 1979. He learned to play piano, violin, cello, horn, and trombone and studied composition with Gesensway in Philadelphia (1937) and with Brant in New York (1950). He worked as a music arranger for the CBC and CBS. From 1954 he worked in Canada, primarily in scoring for musicals, radio, television, and films. His works include *The Remarkable Rocket*, ballet, after Oscar Wilde (1960–61), *Look Ahead*, musical comedy (1962), and *Wild Rose*, opera musical (1967).

Surette, Thomas Whitney, American music educator; b. Concord, Mass., Sept. 7, 1861; d. there, May 19, 1941. He studied piano with Arthur Foote and composition with J. K. Paine at Harvard Univ. (1889–92), but failed to obtain a degree. Deeply interested in making musical education accessible and effective in the United States, he founded the Concord Summer School of Music in 1915, which continued to operate until 1938; with A. T. Davison, he ed. the Concord Series of educational music, which found a tremendously favorable acceptance on the part of many schools, particularly in New England; the series provided an excellent selection of good music that could be understood by most music teachers and performed by pupils. He was also largely responsible for the vogue of music appreciation courses that swept the country and spilled over into the British Isles. He publ. *The Appreciation of Music* (with D. G. Mason; 5 vols., of which vols. 2 and 5 were by Mason alone; N.Y., 1907; innumerable subsequent printings), and, on a more elevated plane, *Course of Study on the Development of Symphonic Music* (Chicago, 1915) and *Music and Life* (Boston, 1917). Among his works were 2 light operas, *Priscilla, or The Pilgrim's Proxy*, after Longfellow (Concord, March 6, 1889), which had more than 1,000 subsequent perfs. in the United States, and *The Eve of Saint Agnes* (1897), and a romantic opera, *Cascabel, or The Broken Tryst* (Pittsburgh, May 15, 1899).

BIBL.: C. Heffernan, *T. W. S.: Musician and Teacher* (diss., Univ. of Mich., 1962).

Surinach, Carlos, Spanish-born American composer and conductor; b. Barcelona, March 4, 1915; d. New Haven, Conn., Nov. 12, 1997. He studied in Barcelona with Morera (1936–39) and later with Max Trapp in Berlin (1939–43). Returning to Spain in 1943, he was active mainly as a conductor. In 1951 he went to the United States; he became a naturalized American citizen in 1959. Surinach was a visiting prof. of music at Carnegie-Mellon Inst. in Pittsburgh in 1966–67. He won particular success as a composer for the dance.

WORKS: DRAMATIC: OPERA: *El Mozo que casó con mujer brava* (Barcelona, Jan. 10, 1948). BALLETS: *Monte Carlo* (Barcelona, May 2, 1945); *Ritmo jondo* (1953); *Embattled Garden* (1958); *Acrobats of God* (1960); *David and Bathsheba* (1960); *Apasionada* (1962); *Los renegados* (1965); *Venta quemada* (1966); *Agathe's Tale* (1967); *Suite española* (1970); *Chronique* (1974); *The Owl and the Pussycat* (1978); *Blood Wedding* (1979).

Susa, Conrad, American composer; b. Springdale, Pa., April 26, 1935. He studied theory with Lopatnikoff, musicology with Dorian, counterpoint with Leich, flute with Goldberg, and cello with Eisner at the Carnegie Inst. of Technology in Pittsburgh (B.F.A., 1957); he completed his training in composition with Bergsma and Persichetti at the Juilliard School of Music in New York (M.S., 1961). In 1959 he became composer-in-residence at the Old Globe Theatre in San Diego, where he was active for over 30 years; he also was music director of the APA-Phoenix Repertory Co. in New York (1961–68) and the American Shakespeare Festival in Stratford, Conn. (1969–71) and dramaturge at the Eugene O'Neill Center in Connecticut (from 1986).

WORKS: DRAMATIC: OPERAS: *Transformations* (Minnesota Opera, May 5, 1973); *Black River* (Minnesota Opera, Nov. 1, 1975); *The Love of Don Perlimplin* (1983); *Dangerous Liaisons* (San Francisco, Sept. 10, 1994). Also incidental music; television scores.

Susskind (originally, **Süsskind**), **(Jan) Walter,** distinguished Czech-born English conductor; b. Prague, May 1, 1913; d. Berkeley, Calif., March 25, 1980. He studied composition with Suk and Karel Hába and piano with Hoffmeister at the Prague Cons.; he also studied conducting with Szell at the German Academy of Music in Prague, where he made his debut as a conductor in 1934 with *La Traviata* at the German Opera; he also was pianist with the Czech Trio (1933–38). After the German occupation in 1938, he went to London, where he continued to serve as pianist with the exiled Czech Trio until 1942; he became a naturalized British subject in 1946. He was music director of the Carl Rosa Opera Co. in London (1943–45), then went to Glasgow in that capacity with the Scottish Orch. in 1946, remaining with it after it became the Scottish National Orch. in 1950. After serving as music director of the Victoria Sym. Orch. in Melbourne (1953–55), he was music director of the Toronto Sym. Orch. (1956–65), the Aspen (Colo.) Music Festival (1962–68), the St. Louis Sym. Orch. (1968–75), and the Mississippi River Festival in Edwardsville, Ill. (1969–75); he also taught at the Univ. of Southern Ill. (1968–75). His last position was that of music adviser and principal guest conductor of the Cincinnati Sym. Orch. from 1978 until his death. Susskind was a highly accomplished conductor, being a technically secure and polished musician. He also composed; among his works are 4 songs for Voice and String Quartet (Prague, Sept. 2, 1935); *9 Slovak Sketches* for Orch.; *Passacaglia* for Timpani and Chamber Orch. (St. Louis, Feb. 24, 1977).

Süssmayr, Franz Xaver, Austrian composer; b. Schwanenstadt, 1766; d. Vienna, Sept. 17, 1803. He studied composition with Maximilian Piessinger and Georg von Pasterwiz. He went to Vienna in 1788 as a music teacher; about 1790 he was befriended by Mozart, who gave him composition lessons; Mozart utilized his talents, employing him as a composer and collaborator. After Mozart's death, Sussmayr took lessons in vocal composition from Salieri, then was a harpsichordist and acting Kapellmeister at the National Theater (1792–94). From 1794 until his death he was Kapellmeister of the National Theater's German opera productions. His most successful stage works were the Singspiel *Der Spiegel von Arkadien* (1794) and the ballet *Il noce di Benevento* (1802). After Mozart's death, his widow entrusted the completion of his Requiem to Sussmayr; he was clever in emulating Mozart's style of composition, and his handwriting was so much like Mozart's that it is difficult to distinguish between them. Süssmayr wrote a number of operas and operettas, which he produced in Vienna, among them: *Moses oder Der Auszug aus Ägypten* (May 4, 1792); *L'incanto superato* or *Der besiegte Zauber* (July 8, 1793); *Idris und Zenide* (May 11, 1795); *Die edle Rache* (Aug. 27, 1795); *Die Freiwilligen* (Sept. 27, 1796); *Der Wildfang* (Oct. 4, 1797); *Der Marktschreyer* (July 6, 1799); *Soliman der Zweite, oder Die drei Sultaninnen* (Oct. 1, 1799); *Gülnare oder Die persische Sklavin* (July 5, 1800); *Phasma oder Die Erscheinung im Tempel der Verschwiegenheit* (July 25, 1801). He also wrote secco recitatives for Mozart's opera *La clemenza di Tito* (Prague, Sept. 6, 1791) and composed several numbers for the Vienna production of Grétry's *La Double Épreuve*, given there under the title *Die doppelte Erkenntlichkeit* (Feb. 28, 1796).

BIBL.: G. Sievers, *Mozart und S.* (Mainz, 1829); W. Lehner, *F. X. S. als Opernkomponist* (diss., Univ. of Vienna, 1927); J. Winterberger, *F. X. S.: Leben, Umwelt und Gestalt* (diss., Univ. of Innsbruck, 1946).

Suter, Robert, Swiss composer and teacher; b. St. Gallen, Jan. 30, 1919. In 1937 he entered the Basel Cons., where he received instruction in piano from Paul Baumgartner, in theory from Gustav Güldenstein, Walter Müller von Kulm, and Ernst Mohr, and in composition from Walther Geiser; he later took private composition lessons with Wladimir Vogel (1956). He taught at the Bern Cons. (1945–50) and at the Basel Academy of Music (1950–84). His works include *Konrad von Donnerstadt*, musical fairy tale (1950; Basel, May 5, 1954), and *Der fremde Baron*, musical comedy (1951; Basel, March 23, 1952).

BIBL.: D. Larese and J. Wildberger, *R. S.* (Amriswil, 1967).

Sutermeister, Heinrich, prominent Swiss composer; b. Feuerthalen, Aug. 12, 1910; d. Vaux-sur-Morges, March 16, 1995. He received training in music history from Karl Nef and in piano from Charlotte Schrameck, and also took courses in philology at the Univs. of Basel and Paris (1930–31). After further studies with Walter Courvoisier (harmony and counterpoint) and Hugo Röhr (conducting) at the Munich Akademie der Tonkunst (1931–34), he returned to Switzerland and devoted himself principally to composition. He also was president of the Swiss Copyright Soc. (1958–80) and a teacher of composition at the Hannover Hochschule für Musik (1963–75). In 1965 he won the opera prize of the City of Salzburg and in 1967 the prize of the Swiss Composers Union. In 1977 he was made a member of the Bavarian Akademie der Schönen Künste in Munich. In his music, Sutermeister placed prime importance upon the composer's responsibility to communicate directly with his listeners. While he utilized discordant combinations of sounds as a legitimate means of expression, he rejected what he considered artificial doctrines and opted instead for an effective and melodic style of wide appeal.

WORKS: DRAMATIC: OPERAS: *Die schwarze Spinne*, radio opera (1935; Bern Radio, Oct. 15, 1936; 1st stage perf., St. Gallen, March 2, 1949); *Romeo und Julia* (1938–40; Dresden, April 13, 1940; orch. suite, Berlin, April 9, 1941); *Die Zauberinsel* (1941–42; Dresden, Oct. 31, 1942); *Niobe* (1943–45; Zürich, June 22, 1946); *Raskolnikoff* (1945–47; Stockholm, Oct. 14, 1948); *Der rote Stiefel* (1949–51; Stockholm, Nov. 22, 1951); *Titus Feuerfuchs, oder Liebe, Tücke und Perücke*, burlesque opera (1956–58; Basel, April 14, 1958); *Seraphine, oder Die stumme Apothekerin*, opera buffa (Swiss TV, Zürich, June 10, 1959; 1st stage perf., Munich, Feb. 25, 1960); *Das Gespenst von Canterville*, television opera (1962–63; ZDF, Sept. 6, 1964); *Madame Bovary* (Zürich, May 26, 1967); *Der Flaschenteufel*, television opera (1969–70; ZDF, 1971); *Le Roi Bérenger* (1981–83; Munich, July 22, 1985). BALLETS: *Das Dorf unter dem Gletscher* (1936; Karlsruhe, May 2, 1937); *Max und Moritz* (Bern Radio, 1951).

BIBL.: D. Larese, *H. S.* (Amriswil, 1972).

Suthaus, (Heinrich) Ludwig, eminent German tenor; b. Cologne, Dec. 12, 1906; d. Berlin, Sept. 7, 1971. He received his training in Cologne. In 1928 he made his operatic debut as Walther von Stolzing in Aachen. After singing in Essen (1931–33) and Stuttgart (1933–41), he was a member of the Berlin State Opera (1941–49). In 1943 he made his debut at the Bayreuth Festival as Walther von Stolzing, and sang there again in 1944, 1956, and 1957. From 1948 to 1961 he was a member of the Berlin Städtische Oper, and then of its successor, the Deutsche Oper, from 1961 to 1965. In 1949 he appeared as the Emperor in *Die Frau ohne Schatten* at the Teatro Colón in Buenos Aires. He made his U.S. debut as Aegisthus at the San Francisco Opera in 1953, and that same year made his Covent Garden debut in London as Tristan. Suthaus was one of the outstanding Heldentenors of his day. In addition to his Wagnerian roles, he also excelled as Florestan, Tchaikovsky's Hermann, Verdi's Otello, and Janáček's Števa.

Sutherland, Dame Joan, celebrated Australian soprano; b. Sydney, Nov. 7, 1926. She first studied piano and voice with her mother; at age 19 she commenced vocal training with John and Aida Dickens in Sydney, making her debut there as Dido in a concert performance of *Dido and Aeneas* in 1947; she then made her stage debut there in the title role of Judith in 1951; subsequently she continued her vocal studies with Clive Carey at the Royal College of Music in London and also studied at the Opera School there. She made her Covent Garden debut in London as the 1st Lady in *Die Zauberflöte* in 1952; she attracted attention there when she created the role of Jenifer in *The Midsummer Marriage* (1955) and as Gilda (1957); she also appeared in the title role of Alcina in the Handel Opera Soc. production (1957). In the meantime, she married **Richard Bonynge** (1954), who coached her in the bel canto operatic repertoire. After making her North American debut as Donna Anna in Vancouver (1958), she scored a triumph as Lucia at Covent Garden (Feb. 17, 1959). From then on she pursued a brilliant international career. She made her U.S. debut as Alcina in Dallas in 1960. Her Metropolitan Opera debut in New York as Lucia on Nov. 26, 1961, was greeted by extraordinary acclaim. She continued to sing at the Metropolitan and other major opera houses on both sides of the Atlantic; she also took her own company to Australia in 1965 and 1974; during her husband's music directorship with the Australian Opera in Sydney (1976–86), she made stellar appearances with the company. On Oct. 2, 1990, she made her operatic farewell in *Les Huguenots* in Sydney. Sutherland was universally acknowledged as one of the foremost interpreters of the bel canto repertoire of her time. She particularly excelled in roles from operas by Rossini, Bellini, and Donizetti; she was also a fine Handelian. In 1961 she was made a Commander of the Order of the British Empire and in 1979 was named a Dame Commander of the Order of the British Empire. In 1992 she was honored with the Order of Merit. With her husband, she publ. *The Joan Sutherland Album* (N.Y., 1986). Her autobiography appeared in 1997.

BIBL.: R. Braddon, *J. S.* (London, 1962); E. Greenfield, *J. S.* (London, 1972); B. Adams, *La Stupenda: A Biography of J. S.* (London, 1981); Q. Eaton, *S. & Bonynge: An Intimate Biography* (N.Y., 1987); M. Oxenbould, *J. S.: A Tribute* (1991); N. Major, *J. S.: The Authorized Biography* (Boston, 1994).

Sutherland, Margaret (Ada), Australian pianist, teacher, and composer; b. Adelaide, Nov. 20, 1897; d. Melbourne, Aug. 12, 1984. She was a student of Edward Goll (piano) and Fritz Hart (composition) at the Marshall Hall Cons. in Melbourne (1914), and then she pursued her training at the Univ. of Melbourne Conservatorium. In 1916 she launched her career as a pianist. In 1923 she went to Europe to study, receiving additional training in Vienna and London. In 1935 she returned to Australia and pursued a pioneering role in new music circles as a pianist, teacher, and composer. In 1970 she was made an Officer of the Order of the British Empire. While she was at her best as a composer of chamber music, she also composed *Dithyramb*, ballet (1937), *A Midsummer Night's Dream*, incidental music to Shakespeare's play (1941), and *The Young Kabbarli*, opera (1964).

Svanholm, Set (Karl Viktor), celebrated Swedish tenor; b. Västerås, Sept. 2, 1904; d. Saltsjö-Duvnäs, near Stockholm, Oct. 4, 1964. He was first active as a church organist in Tillberga (1922–24) and Säby (1924–27). After training at the Royal Cons. in Stockholm (1927–29), he was precentor at St. James's Church in Stockholm. He then pursued vocal studies with Forsell at the Royal Cons. Opera School (1929–30). In 1930 he made his operatic debut in the baritone role of Silvio at the Royal Theater in Stockholm. In 1936 he made his debut there as a tenor singing Radames, and subsequently was one of the Royal Theater's most eminent members until 1956. In 1938 he appeared as Walther von Stolzing at the Salzburg Festival, and also sang at the Vienna State Opera that year. In 1941–42 he sang at Milan's La Scala. He made his Bayreuth Festival debut as Siegfried in 1942. He appeared as Tristan in Rio de Janeiro and as Lohengrin in San Francisco in 1946, and continued to sing in the latter city until 1951. On Nov. 15, 1946, he made his Metropolitan Opera debut in New York as Siegfried. During his 10 seasons at the Metropolitan, he appeared in 105 performances and 17 roles. He was acclaimed not only for his Wagnerian Heldentenor roles, but also for such roles as Florestan, Herod, Eisenstein, and Aegisth. His farewell to the Metropolitan came on March 4, 1956, when he sang Parsifal. From 1948 to 1957 he also appeared at London's Covent Garden. He served as director of the Royal Theater in Stockholm from 1956 to 1963.

Švara, Danilo, Slovenian conductor and composer; b. Ricmanje, near Trieste, April 2, 1902; d. Ljubljana, April 25, 1981. He studied piano with Troste in Vienna (1920–22); he pursued training in politics and law at the Univ. of Frankfurt am Main (1922–25) and concurrently took piano lessons from Malata and studied conducting with Scherchen; he attended the Frankfurt am Main Hochschule für Musik (1927–30), where he took courses in composition with Sekles, in conducting with von Schmiedel and Rottenberg, and in stage direction with Wallerstein. He began his career as répétiteur and conductor at the Ljubljana Opera in 1925; later he conducted there regularly, serving as its director (1957–59); he also wrote music criticism and taught conducting at the Ljubljana Academy of Music. His compositions are cast in a modern idiom. They include the operas *Kleopatra* (1937), *Veronika Deseniska* (1943), *Slovo od mladosti* (Farewell to Youth; 1952), and *Ocean* (1963) and the ballet *Nina* (1962).

Svéd, Sándor, Hungarian baritone; b. Budapest, May 28, 1904; d. Vienna, June 9, 1979. He studied violin at the Budapest Cons.; then went to Milan for vocal studies with Sammarco and Stracciari. He made his operatic debut as Count Luna in Budapest in 1930; he was a member of the Vienna State Opera (1936–39); he also sang at Covent Garden in London and the Salzburg Festival. On Dec. 2, 1940, he made his debut under the name of Alexander Sved at the Metropolitan Opera in New York as Renato in *Un ballo in maschera*; he remained on its roster until 1948, and then returned for the 1949–50 season. He subsequently sang in Rome, in Paris, and at the Bayreuth Festival; he also made appearances with the Budapest Opera, and later toured as a concert singer. In 1956 he went to Stuttgart as a vocal teacher.

Sveinsson, Atli Heimer, Icelandic composer, teacher, conductor, and administrator; b. Reykjavík, Sept. 21, 1938. After studying piano at the Reykjavík College of Music, he took courses in theory and composition with Raphael, Petzold, and Zimmermann at the Cologne Staatliche Hochschule für Musik (1959–62). He also attended composition courses in Darmstadt and Cologne under Stockhausen and Pousseur, and took a course in electronic music in Bilthoven under Koenig. Upon returning to Reykjavík, he played a prominent role in Iceland's musical life. In addition to composing prolifically, he was active as a radio producer, conductor, and organizer. He also taught at the College of Music. From 1972 to 1983 he served as chairman of the Soc. of Icelandic Composers. In 1976 he won the Nordic Council Music Prize for his Flute Concerto. In his music, he has developed a style along Romantic-Expressionistic lines. Among his works are *The Silken Drum*, opera (Reykjavík, June 6, 1982), *Vikivaki*, television opera (1989–90), and *Dernier Amour*, chamber opera (1992).

Svenden, Birgitta, Swedish mezzo-soprano; b. Porjus, March 20, 1950. She was educated at the Royal Opera School in Stockholm. After appearing at the Royal Opera in Stockholm, she sang a minor role in the *Ring* cycle at the Bayreuth Festival in 1983. In 1986 she was chosen to create the role of Queen Christina in the premiere of Gefor's *Christina* in Stockholm. She sang Erda at the Metropolitan Opera in New York in 1988. Following an engagement as Wagner's Magdalena in Seattle in 1989, she made her debut at London's Covent Garden as Erda in 1990. She portrayed Octavian at the Théâtre du Châtelet in Paris in 1993. In 1994 she sang at the Bayreuth Festival, where she returned in 1996. In 1995 she was made a Royal Court Singer by the King of Sweden.

Svetlanov, Evgeny (Feodorovich), prominent Russian conductor and composer; b. Moscow, Sept. 6, 1928. He studied composition with Mikhail Gnessin and piano with Mariya Gurvich at the Gnessin Inst. in Moscow (graduated, 1951); he took courses in composition with Shaporin and in conducting with Gauk at the Moscow Cons. (graduated, 1955). In 1953 he made his debut as a conductor with the All-Union Radio orch. in Moscow; he was a conductor at the Bolshoi Theater there from 1955, serving as its chief conductor (1962–64). In 1965 he was appointed chief conductor of the State Sym. Orch. of the USSR; from 1979 he was a principal guest conductor of the London Sym. Orch. Following the collapse of the Soviet Union in 1991, the USSR State Sym. Orch. became the Russian State Sym. Orch. Svetlanov retained his position as its chief conductor, and also served as chief conductor of the Residentie Orch. in The Hague from 1992 and of the Swedish Radio Sym. Orch. in Stockholm from 1997 to 1999. He also made appearances as a pianist. In 1968 he was named a People's Artist of the USSR; in 1972 he was awarded the Lenin Prize and in 1975 the Glinka Prize. He has won particular distinction for his compelling performances of the Russian repertoire. His works include several incidental music for plays and film scores. He is married to **Larissa Avdeyeva**.

BIBL.: L. Krylova, *E. S.* (Moscow, 1986).

Sviridov, Georgi (Vasilevich), Russian composer and pianist; b. Fatezh, near Kursk, Dec. 16, 1915; d. Moscow, Jan. 5, 1998. After studies in Kursk (1929–32), he was a student of Yudin (composition) at the Leningrad Central Music College (1932–36) and of Shostakovich (composition and orchestration) at the Leningrad Cons. (graduated, 1941). From 1945 he made appearances as a pianist but devoted much time to composition. In 1970 he was made a People's Artist of the USSR. His *Oratorio pathétique* (1959) was one of the most successful works by a Soviet composer as per the tenets of socialist realism. Other works included *The Decembrists*, oratorio (1955), *Othello*, incidental music to Shakespeare's play (1944), *Twinling Lights*, operetta (1951), and film scores.

BIBL.: D. Frishman, ed., *G. S.* (Moscow, 1971); A. Sokhor, *G. S.* (Moscow, 1972).

Svoboda, Josef, influential Czech opera designer and producer; b. Čáslav, May 10, 1920. He studied architecture in Prague. In 1947 he made his debut in the theater with a production of *Kát'a Kabanová* at the 5th of May Theater in Prague. His *Halka* was seen at the Prague National Theater in 1951, and he subsequently served as its chief designer and technical director until 1956. After working on the premiere of Nono's *Intolleranza 1960* in Venice (1961), his *Cardillac* was seen in Milan in 1964. In 1966 he brought out *Die Frau ohne Schatten* at London's Covent Garden, where he returned with *Pelléas et Mélisande* in 1969, *Nabucco* in 1972, and the *Ring* cycle in 1974–76. In 1969 his *Der fliegende Holländer* was seen at the Bayreuth Festival, his *Die Soldaten* was produced in Munich, and his *Les Vêpres siciliennes* was staged in Hamburg. In 1970 his innovative production of *Die Zauberflöte* was mounted in Munich. He staged *Wozzeck* in Milan in 1971 and *Carmen* at the Metropolitan Opera in New York in 1972. After producing *Les Vêpres siciliennes* in London (1984), *Elektra* in Bonn (1986), and *Salome* in Berlin (1990), he staged *La Sonnambula* at the Macerata Festival in 1992. His *Attila* was mounted at the Macerata Festival in 1996. Svoboda's innovative stage design and production concepts are centered on his creative use of lighting as the crucial element in what he describes as a "psychoplastic" theater experience.

Swarowsky, Hans, noted Austrian conductor and pedagogue; b. Budapest, Sept. 16, 1899; d. Salzburg, Sept. 10, 1975. He studied in Vienna with Schoenberg and Webern, with whom he formed a friendly association; he also was in close relationship with Richard Strauss. He occupied posts as opera conductor in Hamburg (1932), Berlin (1934), and Zürich (1937–40); after conducting the Kraków orch. (1944–45), he was conductor of the Vienna Sym. Orch. (1946–48) and the Graz Opera (1947–50); from 1957 to 1959 he was conductor of the Scottish National Orch. in Glasgow; from 1959 he appeared mainly as guest conductor of the Vienna State Opera. He became especially well known as a pedagogue; he was head of the conducting class at the Vienna Academy of Music from 1946, where his pupils included Claudio Abbado and Zubin Mehta. As a conductor, he demonstrated notable command of a large symphonic and operatic repertoire, ranging from Haydn to the 2d Viennese School. He was also a highly competent ed. of music by various composers; he also tr. a number of Italian librettos into German. M. Huss ed. his book *Wahrung der Gestalt* (Vienna, 1979).

Swarthout, Gladys, American mezzo-soprano; b. Deepwater, Mo., Dec. 25, 1900; d. Florence, July 7, 1969. She received her training at the Bush Cons. in Chicago. In 1924 she made her operatic debut as the Shepherd in *Tosca* with the Chicago Civic Opera. In 1925 she sang Carmen with the Ravinia Opera Co. in Chicago. On Nov. 15, 1929, she made her Metropolitan Opera debut in New York as La Cieca; she sang that role there often until her farewell in 1945. She was particularly admired for her Carmen and Mignon, but she also sang Adalgisa, Maddalena, and Preziosilla with success. She also sang Carmen in Chicago (1939) and San Francisco (1941), and made appearances in films. Swarthout's career was ended by a severe heart attack, and in 1954 she settled in Florence. Her autobiography appeared as *Come Soon, Tomorrow* (N.Y., 1945). Swarthout was admired for the warmth of her vocal technique.

Swayne, Giles (Oliver Cairnes), English composer; b. Stevenage, June 30, 1946. He began composing as a teenager, receiving encouragement from his cousin, Elizabeth Maconchy, then pursued training with Leppard and Maw at the Univ. of Cambridge (1963–68); he subsequently studied piano with Gordon Green and composition with Birtwistle, Bush, and Maw at the Royal Academy of Music in London (1968–71) and later attended Messiaen's classes in composition in Paris (1976–77). In 1982 he visited West Africa to study the music of the Jola people of Senegal and the Gambia. In common with many other British composers of his generation, he resolutely eschewed musical gourmandise in favor of writing music in an avant-garde, yet accessible style. Among his compositions are *A World Within*, ballet for Tape (Stoke-on-Trent, June 2, 1978), and *Le Nozze di Cherubino*, opera (1984; London, Jan. 22, 1985).

Sweet, Sharon, American soprano; b. N.Y., Aug. 16, 1951. She was a student at the Curtist Inst. of Music in Philadelphia and of Marinka Gurewich in New York. Following appearances as a recitalist in Philadelphia, she sang Aida in a concert performance in Munich (1985). In 1986 she made her formal operatic debut as Elisabeth in *Tannhäuser* at the Dortmund Opera. In 1987 she joined the Deutsche Oper in Berlin, with which she toured Japan; she also appeared as Elisabeth de Valois at the Paris Opéra and the Hamburg State Opera. Other engagements during the 1987–88 season included appearances at the Salzburg Festival and the Vienna State Opera. In 1989 she made her U.S. operatic debut as Aida at the San Francisco Opera, a role she also sang in Dallas in 1992. On Oct. 21, 1993, she sang Lina in the first staging of Verdi's *Stiffelio* by the Metropolitan Opera in New York. After appearing as Aida at London's Covent Garden in 1995, she returned there as Turandot in 1997. She sang Aida at the Metropolitan Opera in 1997. She also toured as a concert artist.

Swenson, Ruth Ann, American soprano; b. Bronxville, N.Y., Aug. 25, 1959. She studied at the Academy of Vocal Arts in Philadelphia. In 1981 and 1982 she won the San Francisco Opera Auditions, which led to her professional opera debut with the company in 1983 as Despina. In subsequent seasons, she appeared there as Gounod's Juliette, Handel's Dorinda, Meyerbeer's Ines, Verdi's Nannetta and Gilda, and Donizetti's Adina. In 1988 she made her first appearance at the Lyric Opera in Chicago as Nannetta. She made her debut at the Opéra de la Bastille in Paris as Mozart's Susanna in 1990. On Jan. 27, 1991, she sang in the gala concert commemorating the 200th anniversary of Mozart's death with Raymond Leppard conducting the N.Y. Phil. in a program telecast live to the nation over PBS. She sang Mozart's Constanze at her debuts at the Munich and Schwetzingen festivals, and at the Cologne Opera in 1991. On Sept. 24, 1991, she made her Metropolitan Opera debut in New York as Mozart's Zerlina; she returned there as Gilda in 1992, as Adina and Zerbinetta in the 1992–93 season, and as Rosina and Susanne in the 1993–94 season. In 1993 she won the Richard Tucker Music Foundation Award and made her debut at the Berlin State Opera as Gilda. During the 1994–95 season, she returned to the Lyric Opera in Chicago as Anne Trulove. In 1997 she was engaged as Gilda at the San Francisco Opera. After portraying Adina at the Metropolitan Opera in 1998, she returned there in 1999 as Lucia. As a concert artist, she sang in principal North American and European music centers. Among her other operatic roles are Cleopatra in Handel's *Giulio Cesare*, Lucia, Martha, and Massenet's Manon.

Swert, Jules de, eminent Belgian cellist, pedagogue, and composer; b. Louvain, Aug. 15, 1843; d. Ostend, Feb. 24, 1891. He commenced his musical training with his father, the Louvain Cathedral choirmaster, and by the time he was 10 he was performing in public; he then pursued studies with Servais at the Brussels Cons., where he graduated with the premier prix in 1858. After touring as a virtuoso, he became Konzertmeister in Düsseldorf in 1865, appearing there in trio recitals with Clara Schumann and Auer, then went to Weimar as soloist in the Hofkapelle in 1868, and subsequently was royal Kapellmeister in Berlin, where he taught at the Hochschule für Musik (1869–73). He was active in Wiesbaden (1873–76), and also made occasional tours; he made his London debut with notable acclaim in 1875. In 1876 Wagner called him to Bayreuth to engage the musicians for his new orch. During the next few years he devoted much time to composition; in 1881 he went to Leipzig. He settled in Ostend in 1888 as director of its music school; he also was a prof. at the conservatories in Ghent and Bruges. He wrote 2 operas, *Die Albigenser* (Wiesbaden, Oct. 1, 1878) and *Graf Hammerstein* (Mainz, 1884). His brother, Isidore (Jean Gaspar) de Swert (b. Louvain, Jan. 6, 1830; d. Brussels, Sept. 1896), was a cellist and teacher; he studied with François de Munck at the Brussels Cons., where he graduated with the premier prix in 1846; he went to Bruges in 1850 as a teacher at its music school and solo cellist at the theater, then became solo cellist at the Théâtre Royal de la Monnaie in Brussels in 1856; he was named a teacher at the Louvain Cons. in 1866, and that same year joined the faculty of the Brussels Cons.

Swieten, Gottfried (Bernhard), Baron van, Dutch-born Austrian diplomat, music patron, librettist, and composer; b. Leiden, Oct. 29, 1733; d. Vienna, March 29, 1803. His father was appointed personal physician to Empress Maria Theresa in 1745 and settled in Vienna. After attending the Theresianum Jesuit school, Gottfried entered the Austrian civil service; he subsequently was active in the foreign diplomatic service from 1755 to 1777, serving as ambassador to Berlin from 1770 to 1777. Upon his return to Vienna, he was made prefect of the Imperial Library. In his early years he wrote some opéras comiques and at least 10 syms., 3 of which were printed under Haydn's name. Van Swieten's significance rests upon his activities as a music patron; he did much to promote the music of J. S. Bach, C. P. E. Bach and Handel. He founded a group of aristocratic patrons, the Associierte, which supported private performances of oratorios. This group commissioned Mozart to prepare his arrangements of Handel oratorios and also sponsored Haydn's *7 Last Words* (choral version, 1796), *The Creation* (1798), and *The Seasons* (1801), the latter 2 works utilizing librettos by van Swieten. Beethoven also found a patron in van Swieten and dedicated his 1st Sym. to him.

BIBL.: D. Olleson, *G., Baron v. S. and His Influence on Haydn and Mozart* (diss., Univ. of Oxford, 1967).

Swift, Richard, American composer, teacher, and writer on music; b. Middlepoint, Ohio, Sept. 24, 1927. He studied with Grosvenor Cooper, Leonard Meyer, and Leland Smith at the Univ. of Chicago (M.A., 1956). In 1956 he joined the faculty of the Univ. of Calif. at Davis, retiring as prof. of music emeritus in 1991; he also was chairman of the music dept. (1963–71); in 1977 he was a visiting prof. at Princeton Univ. He held editorial positions with the journal *19th Century Music* (from 1981); he also contributed articles to various other journals and to reference works. In his compositions, he applies a variety of functional serial techniques, including electronic and aleatory devices. His works include the opera *The Trial of Tender O'Shea* (Davis, Calif., Aug. 12, 1964), as well as incidental music to various plays.

Sydeman, William (Jay), American composer; b. N.Y., May 8, 1928. He studied at the Mannes College of Music in New York with Salzer and Travis (B.S., 1955) and with Franchetti at the Hartt

School of Music in Hartford, Conn. (M.M., 1958); he also had sessions with Sessions and Petrassi. He taught at the Mannes College of Music (1959–70) and at Rudolph Steiner College in Fair Oaks, Calif. (1980–82). His early style of composition tended toward atonal Expressionism invigorated by spasmodic percussive rhythms in asymmetrically arranged meters. In his later works, he moved toward tonal scores with elements of folk, pop, and jazz infusions. Among his scores is the opera *Aria da capo* (1982), and also incidental music: *Encounters* (1967), *Anti-Christ* (1981), and *A Winter's Tale* (1982).

Symonds, Norman, Canadian clarinetist, saxophonist, and composer; b. near Nelson, British Columbia, Dec. 23, 1920. He took up the clarinet as a teenager and played in a Dixieland band. After training in clarinet, piano, theory, and harmony at the Toronto Cons. (1945–48), he studied composition with Delamont. Between 1949 and 1966 he was active as a clarinetist, alto and baritone saxophonist, and as an arranger with Toronto dance bands. He also led his own jazz octet from 1953 to 1957. Symonds was one of Canada's early champions of the "3d stream" idiom. In addition to scores composed in this manner, he also wrote works in an Expressionist vein. Among his works are *Age of Anxiety*, radio play (1959), *Opera for 6 Voices*, radio opera (1962), *Tensions*, ballet (1966), *Man, Inc.*, mixed media piece (1970), *"Charnisay Versus LaTour"* or *The Spirit of Fundy*, opera (1972), *Laura and the Lieutenant*, musical play for children (1974), *The Canterville Ghost*, music theater (1975), *Lady of the Night*, opera (1977), *Episode at Big Quill*, radio theater (1979), *The Fall of the Leaf*, oratorical music drama (1982), and *Sylvia*, music theater (1990).

Szabados, Béla Antal, Hungarian pedagogue and composer; b. Pest, June 3, 1867; d. there (Budapest), Sept. 15, 1936. He studied with Erkel and Volkmann. He became an accompanist and coach at the Academy of Music and Dramatic Art (1888); in 1893 he was made a piano teacher and coach at the reorganized Academy of Music, where he was promoted to prof. of singing in 1920; in 1922 he became director of the dept. for the training of profs. of singing; he served as head of the National Cons. from 1927. He wrote 2 operas: *Maria* (Budapest, Feb. 28, 1905; in collaboration with Arpád Szendy) and *Fanny* (Budapest, Feb. 16, 1927), as well as 11 musical comedies. His brother, Karóly Szabados (b. Pest, Jan. 28, 1860; d. there [Budapest], Jan. 25, 1892), was a pianist, conductor, and composer who studied with Liszt, Erkel, and Volkmann; he became conductor at the Klausenburg National Theater (1880) and then assistant conductor at the Royal Hungarian Opera in Budapest. His most successful score was the ballet *Vióra* (1891).

Szabó, Ferenc, distinguished Hungarian composer and teacher; b. Budapest, Dec. 27, 1902; d. there, Nov. 4, 1969. He studied with Kodály, Siklós, and Léo Weiner at the Budapest Academy of Music (1922–26). In 1926 he became aligned with the labor movement in Hungary and joined the outlawed Communist party in 1927; in 1932 he went to Russia, where he became closely associated with the ideological work of the Union of Soviet Composers. In 1944 he returned to Hungary as an officer in the Red Army, then was prof. of composition (1945–67) and director (1958–67) of the Budapest Academy of Music. He was awarded the Kossuth Prize in 1951 and 1954, and in 1962 was named an Eminent Artist of the Hungarian People's Republic. His music initially followed the trends of central European modernism, with strong undertones of Hungarian melorhythms, but later he wrote music in the manner of socialist realism; his choruses are permeated with the militant spirit of the revolutionary movement. His works include *Lúdas Matyi*, ballet (Budapest, May 16, 1960), and *Légy jó mindhalálig* (Be Faithful until Death), opera (1968–69; completed by A. Borgulya; Dec. 5, 1975); also *Föltámadott a tenger* (In Fury Rose the Ocean), oratorio (Budapest, June 15, 1955).

BIBL.: A. Pernye, *S. F.* (Budapest, 1965); J. Maróthy, *S. F. indulása* (Budapest, 1970).

Szabolcsi, Bence, eminent Hungarian music scholar; b. Budapest, Aug. 2, 1899; d. there, Jan. 21, 1973. He studied jurisprudence at the Univ. of Budapest; concurrently he was a student of Kodály, Weiner, and Siklós at the Budapest Academy of Music (1917–21) and of Abert at the Univ. of Leipzig, where he received his Ph.D. in 1923 with the diss. *Benedetti und Saracini: Beiträge zur Geschichte der Monodie*. He was a prof. of music history at the Budapest Academy of Music from 1945 until his death. He was ed. of the Hungarian music periodical *Zenei Szemle* (with D. Bartha) from 1926 to 1929. With A. Toth, he brought out a music dictionary in the Hungarian language (1930–31); he publ. a history of music (Budapest, 1940; 5th ed., 1974), a monograph on Beethoven (Budapest, 1944; 5th ed., 1976), and a number of valuable papers in various European magazines. His greatest contribution as a scholar is found in his valuable study *A melódia története* (A History of Melody; Budapest, 1950; 2d ed., 1957; Eng. tr., 1965); he also made valuable contributions to research on the life and works of Béla Bartók. On his 70th birthday he was presented with a Festschrift, ed. by Bartha, *Studia musicologica Bence Szabolcsi septuagenario* (Budapest, 1969). Of his writings on Bartók, the most important are *Bartók: Sa vie et son oeuvre* (Budapest, 1956; 2d ed., 1968), *Béla Bartók* (Leipzig, 1968), and *Béla Bartók, Musiksprachen* (Leipzig, 1972). Two of his books were publ. in Eng.: *The Twilight of Ferenc Liszt* (Budapest, 1959) and *A Concise History of Hungarian Music* (Budapest, 1964).

Sze, Yi-Kwei, Chinese bass-baritone; b. Shanghai, June 1, 1919. He received his musical training at the Shanghai Cons., then emigrated to the United States, where he studied with Alexander Kipnis. He toured widely in Europe, South America, and Asia.

Székely, Endre, Hungarian composer; b. Budapest, April 6, 1912; d. there, April 14, 1989. He studied with Siklós at the Budapest Academy of Music (1933–37), then joined the outlawed Communist party, and was active as a conductor and composer with various workers' choral groups; he ed. the periodicals *Eneklö Munkás* (The Singing Worker) and *Éneklö Nép* (The People Sing). In 1960 he was appointed to the faculty of the Budapest Training College for Teachers. His works include the operas *Vizirózsa* (Water Rose; 1959; Budapest Radio, 1962) and *Kőzene* (Stone Music; 1981) and the operetta *Aranycsillag* (The Golden Star; Budapest, 1951); also 3 oratorios: *Dózsa György* (1959; rev. 1974), *Nenia* (1968–69), and *Justice in Jerusalem* (1986).

Székely, Mihály, noted Hungarian bass; b. Jászberény, May 8, 1901; d. Budapest, March 6, 1963. He studied in Budapest. He made his operatic debut as Weber's Hermit at the Budapest Municipal Theater in 1923; that same year, he made his first appearance at the Budapest Opera as Ferrando in *Il Trovatore*, remaining on its roster until his death; he also made guest appearances throughout Europe. On Jan. 17, 1947, he sang the role of Hunding in *Die Walküre* at his Metropolitan Opera debut in New York; he continued on the roster until 1948, and then returned for the 1949–50 season. He subsequently sang in Europe, appearing at the Glyndebourne Festival, the Holland Festival, the Bavarian State Opera in Munich, and other music centers. He was renowned for such roles as Sarastro, Osmin, King Marke, Boris Godunov, Rocco, and Bluebeard.

BIBL.: P. Várnai, *S. M.* (Budapest, 1967).

Szekelyhidy, Ferenc, Hungarian tenor; b. Tövis, April 4, 1885; d. Budapest, June 27, 1954. He received vocal training in Klausenburg. In 1909 he became a member of the Budapest Opera, where he sang both lyric and dramatic roles with success. He also toured widely as an oratorio and recital artist.

Szelényi, István, Hungarian composer and musicologist; b. Zólyom, Aug. 8, 1904; d. Budapest, Jan. 31, 1972. He studied at the Budapest Academy of Music with Kodály. He toured as a concert pianist (1928–30); returning to Budapest, he taught at the Cons. (from 1945), later serving as its director; he also taught at the Academy of Music (1956–72) and ed. the journal *Új Zenei Szemle* (1951–56). In 1969 he was awarded the Erkel Prize. Among his compositions were the pantomimes *A tékozlo fiú* (The Prodigal

Son; 1931) and *Babiloni vásár* (The Fair at Babylon; 1931) and the operetta *Hidavatás* (1936); also oratorios, including *Virata* (1935), *Spartacus* (1960), *10 Days That Shook the World* (1964), and *Pro Pace* (1968).

WRITINGS (all publ. in Budapest): *Rendszeres modulációtan* (Methodical Theory of Modulation; 1927; 2d ed., 1960); *A zenetörténet és bölcselettörténet kapcsolatai* (The Interrelations of the History of Music and That of Philosophy; 1944); *Liszt élete képekben* (Liszt's Life in Pictures; 1956); *A romantikus zene harmóniavílága* (The Harmonic Realm of Romantic Music; 1959); *A magyar zene története* (The History of Hungarian Music; 1965); *A népdalharmónizálás alapelvei* (Principles of Folk-Song Harmonization; 1967).

Szeligowski, Tadeusz, notable Polish composer and pedagogue; b. Lemberg, Sept. 12, 1896; d. Poznan, Jan. 10, 1963. He studied piano with Kurz in Lemberg (1910–14) and composition with Wallek-Walewski in Kraków, where he also took a doctorate in law at the Univ.; after further studies with Boulanger in Paris (1929–31), he taught in Poznan (1932–39; 1947–62) and in Warsaw (1951–62). From 1951 to 1954 he served as president of the Polish Composers' Union.

WORKS: DRAMATIC: OPERAS: *Bunt Żaków* (Rebellion of Clerks; Wrocław, July 14, 1951); *Krakatuk*, after E. T. A. Hoffmann (1955; Gdansk, Dec. 30, 1956); *Theodor gentleman* (1960; Wrocław, 1963). BALLETS: *Paw i dziewczyna* (The Peacock and the Maiden; 1948; Wrocław, Aug. 2, 1949); *Mazeppa* (1957; Warsaw, 1959).

BIBL.: *T. S.: W 10 rocznice śmierci* (T. S.: On the 10th Anniversary of His Death; Gdansk, 1973).

Szell, George (György), greatly distinguished Hungarian-born American conductor; b. Budapest, June 7, 1897; d. Cleveland, July 30, 1970. His family moved to Vienna when he was a small child. He studied piano with Richard Robert and composition with Mandyczewski; also composition in Prague with J. B. Foerster. He played a Mozart piano concerto with the Vienna Sym. Orch. when he was 10 years old, and the orch. also performed an overture of his composition. At the age of 17, he led the Berlin Phil. in an ambitious program that included a symphonic work of his own. In 1915 he was engaged as an assistant conductor at the Royal Opera of Berlin, then conducted opera in Strasbourg (1917–18), Prague (1919–21), Darmstadt (1921–22), and Düsseldorf (1922–24). He held the position of 1st conductor at the Berlin State Opera (1924–29), then conducted in Prague and Vienna. He made his U.S. debut as guest conductor of the St. Louis Sym. Orch. in 1930. In 1937 he was appointed conductor of the Scottish Orch. in Glasgow; he was also a regular conductor with the Residentie Orkest in The Hague (1937–39). He then conducted in Australia. At the outbreak of war in Europe in 1939 he was in America, which was to become his adoptive country by naturalization in 1946. His American conducting engagements included appearances with the Los Angeles Phil., NBC Sym. Orch., Chicago Sym. Orch., Detroit Sym. Orch., and Boston Sym. Orch. In 1942 he was appointed a conductor of the Metropolitan Opera in New York, where he received high praise for his interpretation of Wagner's music dramas; he remained on its roster until 1946. He also conducted performances with the N.Y. Phil. in 1944–45. In 1946 he was appointed music director of the Cleveland Orch., a post he held for 24 years; he was also music adviser and senior guest conductor of the N.Y. Phil. from 1969 until his death. He was a stern disciplinarian, demanding the utmost exertions from his musicians to achieve tonal perfection, but he was also willing to labor tirelessly at his task. Under his guidance, the Cleveland Orch. rose to the heights of symphonic excellence, taking its place in the foremost rank of world orchs. Szell was particularly renowned for his authoritative and exemplary performances of the Viennese classics, but he also was capable of outstanding interpretations of 20th-century masterworks.

Szendrei, Aladár, Hungarian-American conductor, musicologist, and composer who Americanized his name to **Alfred Sendrey**; b. Budapest, Feb. 29, 1884; d. Los Angeles, March 3, 1976. He studied with Koessler at the Budapest Academy of Music (1901–05) and later took courses in musicology at the Univ. of Leipzig (Ph.D., 1932). After serving as a theater conductor in Germany, he went to the United States, where he conducted opera in Philadelphia and Chicago (1911–12); he appeared with N.Y.'s Century Co. (1913–14). He returned to Europe in 1914 and served in the Austrian army during World War I; after the Armistice he conducted opera in Leipzig (1918–24) and sym. concerts there (1924–32). In 1933 he left Germany and went to Paris, where he conducted at Radiodiffusion Française; he also taught conducting; Charles Munch took private lessons in conducting with him (1933–40); after the fall of Paris, Szendrei emigrated to the United States and settled in Los Angeles. He was prof. of Jewish music at the Univ. of Judaism in Los Angeles (1962–73). Among his works was the opera *Der türkisenblaue Garten* (Leipzig, Feb. 7, 1920) and the ballet *Danse d'odalisque*. His son, Albert Richard Sendrey (b. Chicago, Dec. 26, 1911), was also a composer.

Szenkar, Eugen (Jenő), Hungarian conductor; b. Budapest, April 9, 1891; d. Düsseldorf, March 28, 1977. He studied music with his father, a prominent organist; later he attended classes at the Academy of Music in Budapest. He conducted at the German Theater in Prague (1911–13), the Budapest Volksoper (1913–15), the Salzburg Mozarteum (1915–16), in Altenburg (1916–20), the Frankfurt am Main Opera (1920–23), the Berlin Volksoper (1923–24), and the Cologne Opera (1924–33). With the advent of the Nazi regime, as a Jew he was forced to leave Germany in 1933; he lived in Russia until 1937; subsequently he conducted the Brazilian Sym. Orch. in Rio de Janeiro (from 1944). He returned to Germany in 1950; he was Generalmusikdirektor in Düsseldorf from 1952 to 1960.

Szokolay, Sândor, Hungarian composer and teacher; b. Kunágota, March 30, 1931. He studied with Szabó (1950–52) and Farkas (1952–56) at the Budapest Academy of Music (graduated, 1957), concurrently teaching at the Municipal Music School (1952–55); he then was music reader and producer for the Hungarian Radio (1955–59) and a teacher (1959–66) and prof. (from 1966) at the Budapest Academy of Music. He received the Erkel Prize (1960, 1965) and the Kossuth Prize (1966); in 1976 he was made a Merited Artist and in 1986 an Outstanding Artist by the Hungarian government. In 1987 he received the Bartók-Pásztory Award.

WORKS: DRAMATIC: OPERAS: *Vérnász* (Blood Wedding; Budapest, Oct. 30, 1964); *Hamlet* (1965–68; Budapest, Oct. 19, 1968); *Sâmson* (Budapest, Oct. 23, 1973); *Ecce homo*, passion opera (1984); *Szâvitri* (1987–89); *Margit, a hazának szentelt áldozat* (Margit, Victim Sacrificed for the Country; Budapest, Dec. 21, 1995); also 2 children's operas. BALLETS: *Orbân és as ördög* (Urban and the Devil; 1958); *Az iszonyat balladája* (The Ballad of Terror; 1960); *Tetemrehivás* (Ordeal of the Bier; 1961–71); *Az áldozat* (The Victim; 1971). ORATORIO: *Istâr pokoljárása* (Isthar's Descent to Hell) for Soprano, Alto, Baritone, Bass, Chorus, and Orch. (1960–61).

Szönyi, Erzsébet, Hungarian composer and music educator; b. Budapest, April 25, 1924. She studied piano and composition at the Budapest Academy of Music, graduating in 1947; then she went to Paris, where she took courses at the Cons. with Aubin and Messiaen; she also took private lessons in composition with Boulanger. Returning to Budapest, she taught at the Academy of Music from 1948 to 1981. In 1959 she was awarded the Erkel Prize. She played a major role in promoting Kodály's educational methods in Hungary and elsewhere. Her writings include *A zenei írás-olvasás módszertana* (Methods of Musical Reading and Writing; 4 vols., Budapest, 1953–65; Eng. tr., 1972) and a study on Kodály's teaching methods (Budapest, 1973; numerous trs.). Among her compositions are the operas *Dalma* (1952), *The Stubborn Princess* (1955), *Firenzei tragédie* (1957), *The Little Bee with the Golden Wing* (1974), *A Gay Lament* (1979), *The Truth-telling Shepherd* (1979), *Break of Transmission* (1980), and *Elfrida* (1985).

Szulc, Józef Zygmunt, Polish pianist and composer; b. Warsaw, April 4, 1875; d. Paris, April 10, 1956. He studied at the Warsaw Cons. with Noskowski, then took piano lessons in Paris with Moszkowski. He remained in Paris as a piano teacher, then turned to composition of light operas. His first work in this genre, *Flup* (Brussels, Dec. 19, 1913), was successful and had numerous performances in Europe; he continued to produce operettas at regular intervals; the last one was *Pantoufle* (Paris, Feb. 24, 1945). He also wrote a ballet, *Une Nuit d'Ispahan* (Brussels, Nov. 19, 1909).

Szymanowski, Karol (Maciej), eminent Polish composer; b. Timoshovka, Ukraine, Oct. 6, 1882; d. Lausanne, March 28, 1937. The son of a cultured landowner, he grew up in a musical environment. He began to play the piano and compose very early in life. His first teacher was Gustav Neuhaus in Elizavetgrad; in 1901 he went to Warsaw, where he studied harmony with Zawirski and counterpoint and composition with Noskowski until 1904. With Fitelberg, Rózycki, and Szeluto, he founded the Young Polish Composer's Publishing Co. in Berlin, which was patronized by Prince Wladyslaw Lubomirski; the composers also became known as Young Poland in Music, publishing new works and sponsoring performances for some 6 years. Among the works the group publ. was Szymanowski's op. 1, *9 Piano Preludes* (1906). He was greatly influenced by German Romanticism, and his first major orch. works reveal the impact of Wagner and Strauss. His 1st Sym. was premiered in Warsaw on March 26, 1909; however, he was dissatisfied with the score, and withdrew it from further performance. In 1911 he completed his 2d Sym., which demonstrated a stylistic change from German dominance to Russian influences, paralleling the harmonic evolution of Scriabin; it was played for the first time in Warsaw on April 7, 1911. After a Viennese sojourn (1911–12) and a trip to North Africa (1914), he lived from 1914 to 1917 in Timoshovka, where he wrote his 3d Sym.; he appeared in concert with the violinist Paul Kochański in Moscow and St. Petersburg, giving first performances of his violin works; it was for Kochański that he composed his violin triptych, *Mythes (La Fontaine d'Aréthuse* in this cycle is one of his best-known compositions). About this time, his music underwent a new change in style, veering toward French Impressionism. During the Russian Revolution of 1917, the family estate at Timoshovka was ruined, and Szymanowski lost most of his possessions. From 1917 to 1919 he lived in Elizavetgrad, where he continued to compose industriously, despite the turmoil of the Civil War. After a brief stay in Bydgoszcz, he went to Warsaw in 1920. In 1920–21 he toured the United States in concerts with Kochański and Rubinstein. Returning to Warsaw, he gradually established himself as one of Poland's most important composers. His international renown also was considerable; his works were often performed in Europe, and figured at festivals of the ISCM. He was director of the Warsaw Cons. (1927–29) and reorganized the system of teaching along more liberal lines; was rector of its successor, the Warsaw Academy of Music (1930–32). His *Stabat Mater* (1925–26) produced a profound impression, and his ballet pantomime *Harnasie* (1923–31), based on the life and music of the Tatra mountain dwellers, demonstrated his ability to treat national subjects in an original and highly effective manner. In 1932 he appeared as soloist in the first performance of his 4th Sym., *Symphonie concertante* for Piano and Orch., at Poznan, and repeated his performances in Paris, London, and Brussels. In April 1936, greatly weakened in health by chronic tuberculosis, he attended a performance of his *Harnasie* at the Paris Opéra. He spent his last days in a sanatorium in Lausanne. Szymanowski developed into a national composer whose music acquired universal significance.

WORKS: DRAMATIC: *Loteria na mezós* (The Lottery for Men), operetta (1908–09; not perf.); *Hagith*, op. 25, opera (1913; Warsaw, May 13, 1922); *Mandragora*, op. 43, pantomime (Warsaw, June 15, 1920); *Król Roger* (King Roger), op. 46, opera (1918–24; Warsaw, June 19, 1926); *Kniaź Patiomkin* (Prince Potemkin), op. 51, incidental music to T. Micínski's play (Warsaw, March 6, 1925); *Harnasie*, op. 55, ballet pantomime (1923–31; Prague, May 11, 1935).

WRITINGS: *Wychowawcza rola kultury muzycznej w spoleczenstwie* (The Educational Role of Musical Culture in Society; Warsaw, 1931); T. Bronowicz-Chylińska, ed., *Z pism* (From the Writings; Kraków, 1958).

BIBL.: Z. Jachimecki, *K. S.: Zarys dotychczasowej twórczości* (K. S.: An Outline of His Output; Kraków, 1927); S. Golachowski, *K. S.* (Warsaw, 1948; 2d ed., 1956); S. Lobaczewska, *K. S.: Zycie i twórczośc (1882–1937)* (K. S.: Life and Work [1882–1937]; Kraków, 1950); T. Bronowicz-Chylińska, ed., *S. K.: Z listow* (S. K.: From the Letters; Kraków, 1957); J. Chomiński, *Studia nad twórczóscia K.a S.ego* (Kraków, 1969); A. Wightman, *The Music of K. S.* (diss., Univ. of York, 1972); J. Samson, *The Music of S.* (London, 1980); C. Palmer, *S.* (London, 1983); M. Bristiger et al., eds., *K. S. in seiner Zeit* (Munich, 1984); Z. Sierpiński, ed., and E. Harris, tr., *K. S.: An Anthology* (Warsaw, 1986); T. Chylińska, *K. Z.: His Life and Works* (Los Angeles, 1993).

T

Tabachnik, Michel, Swiss conductor and composer; b. Geneva, Nov. 10, 1942. He received training in piano, composition, and conducting at the Geneva Cons. After attending the summer courses in new music given by Pousseur, Stockhausen, and Boulez in Darmstadt (1964), he served as assistant to Boulez in Basel. He was conductor of the Gulbenkian Foundation Orch. in Lisbon (1973–75), the Lorraine Phil. in Metz (1975–81), and the Ensemble Européen de Musique Contemporaine in Paris (1976–77). As a guest conductor, he appeared with principal orchs. of the world. He became particularly known for his interpretations of contemporary music. His compositions followed along advanced lines. Among his works is the opera *La Légende de Haïsha* (Paris, Nov. 1989).

Tabuteau, Marcel, outstanding French oboist and pedagogue; b. Compiegne, July 2, 1887; d. Nice, Jan. 4, 1966. He studied oboe with Georges Gillet at the Paris Cons.; he won a premier prix at the age of 17. In 1905 he went to the United States, where he played in the N.Y. Sym. Orch. until 1914; he also was a member of the orch. of the Metropolitan Opera (from 1908). In 1915 Stokowski engaged him as 1st oboist in the Philadelphia Orch., where he remained until 1954; he was also on the faculty of the Curtis Inst. of Music in Philadelphia (from 1924).

Tacchinardi, Nicola (Niccolò), famous Italian tenor and singing teacher; b. Livorno, Sept. 3, 1772; d. Florence, March 14, 1859. He played cello in the orch. of Florence's Teatro della Pergola (1789–97). After vocal studies, he began his operatic career with appearances in Livorno, Pisa, Florence, and Venice in 1804. In 1805 he sang at Milan's La Scala, where he participated in the coronation performances for Napoleon as King of Italy. He scored a triumph in Zingarelli's *La distruzione di Gerusalemme* at the Paris Odéon on May 4, 1811; until 1814 he sang at the Théâtre-Italien, where his performances in Paisiello's *La bella molinara* were particularly acclaimed. After appearances in Spain (1815–17) and Vienna (1816), he returned to Italy; he was made primo cantante of the Florence Grand Ducal Chapel in 1822, while continuing his appearances in Italian opera houses; he also revisited Vienna in 1823. He retired in 1831 and devoted himself to teaching; one of his students was his daughter, **Fanny** (née **Tacchinardi**) **Persiani**. His most celebrated role was that of Otello in Rossini's *Otello*. He composed vocal exercises and publ. *Dell'opera in musica sul teatro italiano e de' suoi difetti* (Florence, 2d ed., 1833). His son, Guido Tacchinardi (b. Florence, March 10, 1840; d. there, Dec. 6, 1917), was a conductor, music critic, and composer and was director of the Florence Istituto Musicale (1891–1917).

Taddei, Giuseppe, noted Italian baritone; b. Genoa, June 26, 1916. He studied in Rome, where he made his debut at the Teatro Reale dell'Opera as the Herald in *Lohengrin* in 1936; he sang there until he was drafted into the Italian Army in 1942. After World War II, he appeared at the Vienna State Opera (1946–48); he made his London debut at the Cambridge Theatre in 1947 and his Salzburg Festival debut in 1948. He sang at Milan's La Scala (1948–51; 1955–61) and at London's Covent Garden (1960–67); he also appeared in San Francisco, Chicago, and other music centers. On Sept. 25, 1985, at the age of 69, he made his long-awaited debut at the Metropolitan Opera in New York as Falstaff. In 1986 he appeared as Scarpia at the Vienna State Opera. He sang Falstaff in Stuttgart in 1990. He excelled in both lyrico-dramatic and buffo roles.

Tadolini, Eugenia (née **Savonari**), noted Italian soprano, wife of **Giovanni Tadolini**; b. Forli, 1809; d. Naples, after 1851. She received vocal training from her husband. After making her operatic debut in Florence in 1828, she made her first appearance outside her homeland at the Paris Théâtre-Italien in Rossini's *Ricciardo e Zoraide* on Oct. 23, 1830; she continued to sing in Paris until 1833. On Oct. 1, 1833, she made her debut at Milan's La Scala in Donizetti's *Il furioso all'isola di San Domingo*, and in 1834 she sang as his Adina in Vienna, returning there as his Antonina in 1836. Donizetti chose her to sing in the premiere of his *Linda di Chamounix* there on May 19, 1842, and she returned to create the title role in his *Maria di Rohan* on June 5, 1843. She was an early champion of Verdi, creating the title role in his *Alzira* in Naples (Aug. 12, 1845); she returned there to sing Lady Macbeth in 1848. Verdi found her voice beautiful but was dubious about her dramatic talent. On May 20, 1848, she made her London debut in *Linda di Chamounix* at Her Majesty's Theatre. She retired from the operatic stage in 1851.

Tadolini, Giovanni, Italian composer and singing teacher, husband of **Eugenia** (née **Savonari**) **Tadolini**; b. Bologna, Oct. 18, 1785; d. there, Nov. 29, 1872. He studied composition with Mattei and singing with Babini. From 1811 to 1814 he was on the staff of the Théâtre-Italien in Paris, then returned to Italy, where he produced a succession of operas: *La fata Alcina* (Venice, 1815), *Le Bestie in uomini* (Venice, 1815), *La principessa di Navarra ossia Il Gianni di Parigi* (Bologna, 1816), *Il credulo deluso* (Rome, 1817), *Tamerlano* (Bologna, 1818), *Moctar, Gran Visir di Adrianopoli* (Bologna, 1824), *Mitridate* (Venice, 1826), and *Almanzor* (Trieste, 1827); from 1829 to 1839 he was again at his post at the Théâtre-Italien. He settled in Bologna in 1848 and founded his own singing school.

Tagliabue, Carlo, noted Italian baritone; b. Mariano Comense, Jan. 12, 1898; d. Monza, April 5, 1978. He studied with Gennai and Guidotti. He made his debut as Amonasro in 1922 in Lodi. After singing in Italian provincial opera houses, he joined La Scala in Milan in 1930; he continued to appear there regularly until 1943, and again from 1946 to 1953; he also sang in Florence and Rome, at the Teatro Colón in Buenos Aires, and at Covent Garden in London (1938, 1946). On Dec. 2, 1937, he made his Metropolitan Opera debut in New York as Amonasro; he continued on its roster until 1939. He retired in 1960. He was a distinguished interpreter of Verdi and a fine Wagnerian.

Tagliafico, (Dieudonné) Joseph, distinguished French bass-baritone; b. Toulon, Jan. 1, 1821; d. Nice, Jan. 27, 1900. He studied with Piermarini and Lablache in Paris, making his debut there in 1844 at the Théâtre-Italien. In 1847 he joined the new Royal Italian Opera company at Covent Garden in London, remaining on its roster until 1876, then was its stage manager until 1882. He appeared as a guest artist in France, Russia, and the United States. He was best known for his French and Italian roles.

Tagliapietra, Gino, Italian pianist, teacher, and composer; b. Ljubljana, May 30, 1887; d. Venice, Aug. 8, 1954. He studied piano with Julius Epstein in Vienna and with Busoni in Berlin. In 1906 he was appointed to the faculty of the Liceo Benedetto Marcello in Venice; he retired in 1940. His compositions include a fiaba musicale, *La bella addormentata* (Venice, March 11, 1926). He ed. *Antologia di musica antica e moderna per il pianoforte* (Milan, 1931–32) and *Raccolta di composizioni dei secoli XVI e XVII* (Milan, 1937).

BIBL.: F. Vadala, *G. T.* (diss., Univ. of Messina, 1976).

Tagliapietra, Giovanni, Italian baritone; b. Venice, Dec. 24, 1846; d. N.Y., April 11, 1921. He studied naval architecture and graduated from the Univ. of Padua. After a study of singing with Giovanni Corsi, he appeared in various Italian opera houses. He made a tour of South America, and in 1874 was engaged as member of Max Strakosch's company and sang in the United States. In 1876 he married **Teresa (Maria) Carreño**, but they divorced.

Tagliavini, Ferruccio, prominent Italian tenor; b. Reggio Emilia, Aug. 14, 1913; d. there, Jan. 28, 1995. He received his training from Brancucci in Parma and Bassi in Florence. In 1938 he won 1st prize for voice at the Maggio Musicale in Florence, where he made his operatic debut as Rodolfo in Oct. of that year. He then sang in various Italian opera houses. In 1942 he became a member of Milan's La Scala, where he sang with distinction until 1953. In 1946 he toured South America and made his U.S. operatic debut as Rodolfo in Chicago. He made his Metropolitan Opera debut in New York on Jan. 10, 1947, again as Rodolfo, and remained on its roster until 1954. In 1961–62 he was again on the roster of the Metropolitan Opera. Among the roles he sang there were Count Almaviva, Edgardo, the Duke of Mantua, Alfredo, Cavaradossi, and Nemorino. In 1948–49 and again in 1952 he appeared at the San Francisco Opera. In 1950 he sang Nemorino with the visiting La Scala company at London's Covent Garden, and returned there in 1955–56. After retiring from the operatic stage as Werther in Venice in 1965, he made some appearances as a concert artist. In 1941 he married **Pia Tassinari.**

BIBL.: U. Bonafini, *F. T.: L'uomo, la voce* (Reggio Emilia, 1993).

Täglichsbeck, Thomas, German violinist and composer; b. Ansbach, Dec. 31, 1799; d. Baden-Baden, Oct. 5, 1867. He became a violinist in the Isarthortheater orch. in 1817, and in 1819 its music director. In 1822 he was made solo violinist to the Munich court; he also toured in Switzerland and Italy. He was named Kapellmeister to Prince Hohenlohe-Hechingen in 1827, and continued to serve his successor, Prince Constantine (1838–48); when the latter reorganized his Court Orch. in Lowenberg in 1852, Täglichsbeck resumed his duties, retiring in 1857. He then taught at the Dresden Cons. until 1859. Among his works were the operas *Webers Bild* (Munich, Aug. 24, 1823), *König Enzio* (Karlsruhe, May 14, 1843), and *Guido oder Das Jägerhaus im Walde Sila* (not perf.).

Tailleferre (real name, **Taillefesse**), **(Marcelle) Germaine,** fine French composer; b. Parc-St.-Maur, near Paris, April 19, 1892; d. Paris, Nov. 7, 1983. She studied harmony and solfège with H. Dallier (premier prix, 1913), counterpoint with G. Caussade (premier prix, 1914), and accompaniment with Estyle at the Paris Cons.; she also had some informal lessons with Ravel. She received recognition as the only female member of the group of French composers known as Les Six (the other members were Honegger, Milhaud, Poulenc, Auric, and Durey). Her style of composition was pleasingly, teasingly modernistic and feministic (Jean Cocteau invoked a comparison with a young French woman painter, Marie Laurencin, saying that Tailleferre's music was to the ear what the painter's pastels were to the eye). Indeed, most of her works possess a fragile charm of unaffected *joie de jouer la musique*. She was married to an American author, Ralph Barton, in 1926, but soon divorced him and married a French lawyer, Jean Lageat. She visited the United States in 1927 and again in 1942. In 1974 she publ. an autobiographical book, *Mémoires dè l'emporte piece*.

WORKS: DRAMATIC: *Le Marchand d'oiseaux*, ballet (Paris, May 25, 1923); *Paris-Magie*, ballet (Paris, June 3, 1949); *Dolorès*, operetta (1950); *Il était un petit navire*, lyric satire (Paris, March 1951); *Parfums*, musical comedy (1951); *Parisiana*, opéra comique (1955); *Monsieur Petit Pois achète un château*, opéra bouffe (1955); *Le Bel ambitieux*, opéra bouffe (1955); *La Pauvre Eugénie*, opéra bouffe (1955); *La Fille d'opéra*, opéra bouffe (1955); *La Petite Sirène*, chamber opera (1957); *Mémoires d'une bergère*, opéra bouffe (1959); *Le Maître*, chamber opera (1959).

BIBL.: J. Roy, *Le groupe des six: Poulenc, Milhaud, Honegger, Auric, T., Durey* (Paris, 1994); R. Shapiro, *G. T.: A Bio-Bibliography* (Westport, Conn., 1994).

Tajo, Italo, Italian bass and teacher; b. Pinerolo, April 25, 1915; d. Cincinnati, March 29, 1993. He studied at the Turin Cons. He made his operatic debut as Fafner at the Teatro Regio in Turin in 1935, then was a member of the Rome Opera (1939–48) and of La Scala in Milan (1940–41; 1946–56). He made his U.S. debut in Chicago in 1946. On Dec. 28, 1948, he appeared at the Metropolitan Opera in New York as Don Basilio in *Il barbiere di Siviglia*; he remained on its roster until 1950 and also sang with the San Francisco Opera (1948–50; 1952–53; 1956); he then appeared on Broadway and in films. In 1966 he was appointed prof. at the Univ. of Cincinnati College-Cons. of Music. He returned to the Metropolitan Opera after an absence of 30 years in 1980, and delighted audiences in buffo roles; he made his operatic farewell there as the Sacristan in *Tosca* on April 20, 1991. He was equally adept in dramatic and buffo roles from the standard repertory, and also proved himself an intelligent interpreter in contemporary operas by Milhaud, Malipiero, Pizzetti, and Nono.

Takata, Saburô, Japanese composer and teacher; b. Nagoya, Dec. 18, 1913. He studied with Nobutkoki and Pringsheim at the

Tokyo Music School (graduated, 1939). He was a prof. at the Kunitachi Music College in Tokyo (from 1953); he also served as president of the Japanese Society for Contemporary Music (1963–68). Among his works is the opera *Aoki-ōkami* (The Dark Blue Wolf; 1970–72; Tokyo, Oct. 15, 1972).

Taktakishvili, Otar (Vasilievich), Russian composer and teacher; b. Tiflis, July 27, 1924; d. there (Tbilisi), Feb. 22, 1989. He studied at the Tbilisi Cons., graduating in 1947; he was on its faculty as a teacher of choral literature (from 1947) and of counterpoint and instrumentation (from 1959), serving as its rector (1962–65); he was a prof. (from 1966). In 1974 he was made a People's Artist of the USSR. In 1982 he was awarded the Lenin Prize. His music is imbued with the characteristic melorhythms of the Caucasus; he had a natural knack for instrumental color. Among his works are the operas *Mindia* (Tbilisi, July 23, 1961), *Sami novela* (3 Stories; 1967), *Chikor* (1972), and *Mtvaris Motatseba* (The Abduction of the Moon; 1976); also oratorios; film scores.

BIBL.: L. Polyakova, *O. T.* (Moscow, 1956); L.V. Polyakova, *O. T.* (Moscow, 1979).

Taktakishvili, Shalva (Mikhailovich), Russian conductor, teacher, and composer; b. Kvemo-Khviti, Aug. 27, 1900; d. Tbilisi, July 18, 1965. He studied at the Tiflis Cons. He then taught theory at the Batumi Music School, of which he was a cofounder; he then served as conductor at Tbilisi Radio. From 1952 until his death he conducted the Georgian State Orch. His works include the operas *Rassvet* (Sunrise; 1923), *Deputat* (The Delegate; 1939), and *Otarova vdnova* (1942).

BIBL.: P. Hukua, *S. T.* (Tbilisi, 1962).

Tal, Josef (real name, **Joseph Gruenthal**), prominent German-born Israeli composer, pianist, conductor, and pedagogue; b. Pinne, near Posen, Sept. 18, 1910. He took courses with Tiessen, Hindemith, Sachs, Trapp, and others at the Berlin Staatliche Hochschule für Musik (1928–30). In 1934 he emigrated to Palestine, settling in Jerusalem as a teacher of piano and composition at the Cons. in 1936; when it became the Israel Academy of Music in 1948, he served as its director (until 1952); he also lectured at the Hebrew Univ. (from 1950), where he was head of the musicology dept. (1965–70) and a prof. (from 1971); likewise was director of the Israel Center of Electronic Music (from 1961). He appeared as a pianist and conductor with the Israel Phil. and with orchs. in Europe. In 1971 he was awarded the State of Israel Prize and was made an honorary member of the West Berlin Academy of Arts; in 1975 he received the Arts Prize of the City of Berlin, and in 1982 he became a fellow of its Inst. for Advanced Studies. His autobiography was publ. as *Der Sohn des Rabbiners: Ein Weg von Berlin nach Jerusalem* (Berlin, 1985). A true musical intellectual, Tal applies in his music a variety of techniques, being free of doctrinal introversion and open to novel potentialities without fear of public revulsion. Patriotic Hebrew themes often appear in his productions.

WORKS: DRAMATIC: *Saul at Ein Dor*, opera concertante (1957); *Amnon and Tamar*, opera (1961); *Ashmedai*, opera (1968; Hamburg, Nov. 9, 1971); *Massada 967*, opera (1972; Jerusalem, June 17, 1973); *Die Versuchung*, opera (1975; Munich, July 26, 1976); *Else-Hommage*, chamber scene for Mezzo-soprano, Narrator, and 4 Instruments (1975); Scene from Kafka's diaries for Soprano or Tenor Solo (1978); *Der Turm*, opera (1983; Berlin, Sept. 19, 1987); *Der Garten*, chamber opera (1987; Hamburg, May 29, 1988); *Die Hand*, dramatic scene for Soprano and Cello (1987); *Josef*, opera (1993–95; Tel Aviv, June 27, 1995). TAPE: *Exodus II*, ballet (1954); *Ranges of Energy*, ballet (1963); *From the Depth of the Soul*, ballet (1964); *Ashmedai*, overture to the opera (1970); *Variations*, choreographic piece (1970); *Backyard*, choreographic piece (1977).

BIBL.: W. Elias, *J. T.* (Tel Aviv, 1987).

Talbot (real name, **Munkittrick**), **Howard,** English conductor and composer; b. Yonkers, N.Y., March 9, 1865; d. Reigate, Sept. 12, 1928. He was taken to England at the age of 4, and studied at the Royal College of Music in London under Parry, Bridge, and Gladstone. From 1900 he was active as a conductor in various London theaters. He was a prolific composer of light operas, all produced in London; his greatest success was *A Chinese Honeymoon* (1899); his last work was *The Daughter of the Gods* (1929). Other operettas included *Monte Carlo* (1896); *3 Little Maids* (1902); *The Blue Moon* (1905); *The White Chrysanthemum* (1905); *The Girl behind the Counter* (1906); *The 3 Kisses* (1907); *The Belle of Brittany* (1908); *The Arcadians* (1909); *A Narrow Squeak* (1913); *The Pearl Girl* (1913); *A Lucky Miss* (1914); *A Mixed Grill* (1914); *The Light Blues* (1915).

Talich, Václav, eminent Czech conductor; b. Kroměříž, May 28, 1883; d. Beroun, March 16, 1961. He received his early musical training from his father, Jan Talich (1851–1915), a choirmaster and music teacher; he then studied violin with Mařák and Ševčik and chamber music with Kàan at the Prague Cons. (1897–1903). He was concertmaster of the Berlin Phil. (1903–04) and of the orch. of the Odessa Opera (1904–05); he then taught violin in Tiflis (1905–06). He conducted the Slovenian Phil. in Ljubljana (1908–12); he also took courses in composition with Reger and Sitt and in conducting with Nikisch at the Leipzig Cons. and also studied with Vigna in Milan. He was then opera conductor at Pilsen (1912–15). Talich held the post of 2d conductor (1918–19) of the Czech Phil. in Prague, and subsequently served as its chief conductor from 1919 to 1931; in 1931–33 he was conductor of the Konsertforeningen in Stockholm, then in 1933 returned as chief conductor of the Czech Phil. (until 1941), which he brought to a high degree of excellence. He was director and conductor of the National Theater in Prague from 1935 to 1944, when the theater was closed by the Nazis; with the defeat of the Nazis, he resumed his activities there but was dismissed in 1945 after disagreements with the state authorities; he was recalled in 1947, but was dismissed once more in 1948 after conflicts with the new communist regime. He then moved to Bratislava, where he conducted the Slovak Phil. (1949–52); he returned as guest conductor of the Czech Phil. (1952–54); he retired from concert appearances in 1954. He also taught conducting in Prague and Bratislava; among his pupils were Ančerl and Mackerras. He was renowned for his idiomatic performances of the Czech repertory. He was made a National Artist in 1957.

BIBL.: O. Šourek, ed., *V. T.* (Prague, 1943); V. Pospíšil, *V. T.: Několik kapitol o dile a životě českého umělce* (V. T.: Some Chapters on the Life and Work of a Czech Artist; Prague, 1961); H. Masaryk, ed., *V. T.: Dokument života a dila* (V. T.: A Document of His Life and Work; Prague, 1967); M. Kuna, *V. T.* (Prague, 1980).

Tallat-Kelpša, Juozas, Lithuanian conductor, teacher, and composer; b. Kalnujai, Jan. 1, 1889; d. Vilnius, Feb. 5, 1949. He studied cello at the Vilnius Music School before completing his music education at the St. Petersburg Cons. (1907–16). In 1920 he settled in Kaunas and founded its Opera, which he conducted until 1941 and again from 1944 to 1948. He also taught at the music school (1920–33) and at the Cons. (from 1933). In 1948 he was awarded the Stalin Prize. He also composed several scores, and prepared folk song arrangements.

Talley, Marion, American soprano; b. Nevada, Mo., Dec. 20, 1906; d. Los Angeles, Jan. 3, 1983. She sang in churches in Kansas City, Mo., and at 16 appeared in *Mignon* there. Following training from Frank La Forge in New York, she completed her studies in Europe. On Feb. 17, 1926, she made her Metropolitan Opera debut in New York as Gilda and created a stir as an American find. However, her success was short-lived. She sang at the Metropolitan for only 3 seasons and then made sporadic opera and recital appearances. In 1936 she sang on the radio and then returned to opera in 1940, but her career soon waned.

Talma, Louise (Juliette), American composer and teacher; b. Arcachon, France, Oct. 31, 1906; d. Yaddo, N.Y., Aug. 13, 1996. She studied at the Inst. of Musical Art in New York (1922–30) and took courses at N.Y. Univ. (B.M., 1931) and at Columbia Univ. (B.Mus., 1933); she took piano lessons with Philipp and composition with Boulanger in Fontainebleau (summers 1926–39). She taught at Hunter College (1928–79) and was the first American to teach at the Fontainebleau School of Music (summers, 1936–39; 1978; 1981–82). She received 2 Guggenheim fellowships (1946, 1947) and was the first woman composer to be elected to the National Inst. of Arts and Letters in 1974. In her music, she adopted a strongly impressionistic style. Her works include the opera *The Alcestiad* (1955–58; Frankfurt am Main, March 1, 1962) and the oratorio *The Divine Flame* (1946–48). She publ. *Harmony for the College Student* (1966) and *Functional Harmony* (with J. Harrison and R. Levin, 1970).

Talvela, Martti (Olavi), remarkable Finnish bass; b. Hiitola, Feb. 4, 1935; d. Juva, July 22, 1989. He received training at the Lahti Academy of Music (1958–60). After winning the Finnish lieder competition in 1960, he studied voice with Carl Martin Ohmann in Stockholm. He made his operatic debut there at the Royal Theater as Sparafucile in *Rigoletto* in 1961. He made his first appearance at the Bayreuth Festival in 1962 as Titurel; that same year he joined the Deutsche Oper in Berlin, where he sang leading bass roles. In 1968 he made his U.S. debut in a recital at Hunter College in New York. He made his Metropolitan Opera debut in New York as the Grand Inquisitor in *Don Carlos* on Oct. 7, 1968; he appeared there in succeeding years with increasing success, being especially acclaimed for his dramatic portrayal of Boris Godunov. From 1972 to 1980 he served as artistic director of the Savonlinna Festival. He was to have assumed the post of artistic director of the Finnish National Opera in Helsinki in 1992, but death intervened. In 1973 he received the Pro Finlandia Award and the Finnish State Prize. A man of towering dimensions (6′ 7″), his command of the great bass roles was awesome. Among his outstanding portrayals, in addition to Boris Godunov, were Hagen, Hunding, Gurnemanz, the Commendatore, and Sarastro. He also was effective in contemporary roles.

Tamagno, Francesco, famous Italian tenor; b. Turin, Dec. 28, 1850; d. Varese, near Turin, Aug. 31, 1905. He studied with Pedrotti in Turin and Vannuccini in Milan, making his debut in Palermo in 1869. After appearances in Turin, he scored a major success with his portrayal of Riccardo in *Un ballo in maschera* in Palermo in 1874. He made his debut at Milan's La Scala as Vasco da Gamba in *L'Africaine* in 1877, establishing himself as its leading tenor; he created the role of Azaele in Ponchielli's *Il Figliuol prodigo* (1880), appeared as Gabriele Adorno in the revised version of Verdi's *Simon Boccanegra* (1881), and was the 1st Didier in Ponchielli's *Marion Demore* (1885). He then won international acclaim when Verdi chose him to create the title role in *Otello* (1887), a role he sang in London in 1889 and in Chicago and New York in 1890; he also chose it for his Covent Garden debut in London on May 13, 1895. He made his Metropolitan Opera debut in New York as Arnold in Rossini's *Guillaume Tell* on Nov. 21, 1894, remaining on the company's roster for a season. In 1901 he returned to Covent Garden and also sang at La Scala. He made his final stage appearance at Milan's Teatro dal Verme in 1904; his last appearance as a singer took place in Ostend that same year. Tamagno was one of the greatest tenors in the history of opera; in addition to his Othello, he was celebrated for his portrayals of Don Carlos, Radames, Alfredo, Manrico, Don José, John of Leyden, Faust, Ernani, and Samson.

BIBL.: E. de Amicis, *F. T.* (Palermo, 1902); M. Corsi, *T.* (Milan, 1927).

Tamberg, Eino, Estonian composer and pedagogue; b. Tallinn, May 27, 1930. He studied composition with E. Kapp at the Tallinn Cons., graduating in 1953. He then was a music supervisor with the Estonian Radio; he was a teacher (from 1967) and a prof. (from 1983) at the Tallinn Cons. In 1975 he was made a People's Artist of the Estonian SSR.

WORKS: DRAMATIC: OPERAS: *The House of Iron* (Tallinn, July 15, 1965); *Cyrano de Bergerac* (1974; Tallinn, July 2, 1976); *Flight* (1982; Tallinn, Dec. 30, 1983); *Creatures*, chamber opera (1992). BALLETS: *Ballet-Symphony* (1959; Schwerin, March 10, 1960); *The Boy and the Butterfly* (Tallinn, Nov. 30, 1963); *Joanna tentata* (1970; Tallinn, Jan. 23, 1971). ORATORIO: *Moonlight Oratorio* for 2 Narrators, Soprano, Baritone, Chorus, and Orch. (1962; Tartu, Feb. 17, 1963).

Tamberlik, Enrico, celebrated Italian tenor; b. Rome, March 16, 1820; d. Paris, March 13, 1889. He studied singing with Zirilli in Rome and with Guglielmi in Naples, where he made his stage debut in 1841 as Tybalt in *I Capuleti e i Montecchi*. On April 4, 1850, he made his first London appearance, as Masaniello in Auber's *La Muette de Portici*, at the Royal Italian Opera, Covent Garden, and sang annually in London until 1864, with the exception of 1857, when he undertook an extensive European tour, including Spain and Russia. In 1860 he settled in Paris, and lived there most of his life. Verdi admired him, and wrote the part of Don Alvaro in *La forza del destino* for him; Tamberlik sang in its world premiere in St. Petersburg on Nov. 22, 1862, and this role became one of his most famous interpretations. He appeared at the Academy of Music in New York on Sept. 18, 1873, but his American season was a brief one; he later toured the United States with Maretzek's company. He excelled in many Italian, French, and German roles, being especially renowned as Florestan, John of Leyden, Manrico, Arnold, and Rossini's Otello.

Tamburini, Antonio, esteemed Italian baritone; b. Faenza, March 28, 1800; d. Nice, Nov. 8, 1876. He was a pupil of A. Rossi and B. Asioli, making his operatic debut in Generali's *La Contessa di colle* in Cento in 1818. In 1822 he first sang at Milan's La Scala in Rossini's *Matilde di Shabran*, returning there that same year to take part in the premiere of Donizetti's *Chicara e Serafin*. Following engagements in Trieste and Vienna, he went to Rome and sang in the first performance of Donizetti's *L'ajo nell'imbarazzo* (1824). After singing in Naples and Venice, he appeared in Palermo, where he sang in the premiere of Donizetti's *Alahor di Granata* (1826). Returning to La Scala, he created Ernesto in Bellini's *Il Pirata* (Oct. 27, 1827); after appearing in the first performance of Donizetti's *Alina, regina di Golconda* in Genoa (1828), he went to Naples and sang in the premieres of Donizetti's *Gianni di Calais* (1828), *Imelda de' Lammbertazzi* (1830), *Francesca di Foix* (1831), *La Romanziera* (1831), and *Fausta* (1832). On Feb. 14, 1829, at La Scala, he created Valdeburgo in Bellini's *La Straniera*, a role he repeated at the King's Theatre in London on June 23, 1832; that same year he made his first appearance at the Théâtre-Italien in Paris, and subsequently appeared regularly in London and Paris during the next 11 years. On Jan. 24, 1835, he created the role of Sir Richard Forth in Bellini's *I Puritani* at the Théâtre-Italien; he returned there to create Israele in Donizetti's *Marino Failiero* (March 12, 1835) and Malatesta in his *Don Pasquale* (Jan. 3, 1843). After singing in St. Petersburg, he returned to London to appear as Assur in *Semiramide* in the first production mounted by the Royal Italian Opera at Covent Garden. In 1855 he retired from the operatic stage; however, in 1860 he sang Rossini's Figaro in Nice. In 1822 he married the mezzo-soprano Marietta Goja (1801–66).

BIBL.: J. de Biez, *T. et la musique italienne* (Paris, 1877); H. Gelli-Ferraris, *A. T. nel ricordo d'una nipote* (Livorno, 1934).

Tamkin, David, Russian-American composer; b. Chernigov, Aug. 28, 1906; d. Los Angeles, June 21, 1975. He was taken to the United States as an infant; the family settled in Portland, Oreg., where he studied violin with Henry Bettman, a pupil of Ysaÿe; he took lessons in composition with Bloch. In 1937 he settled in Los Angeles; from 1945 to 1966 he was principal composer at Universal Pictures in Hollywood. His music is deeply permeated with the melodic and rhythmic elements of the Hassidic Jewish cantillation. His magnum opus is the opera *The Dybbuk* (1928–31; N.Y., Oct. 4, 1951); he also wrote the opera *The Blue Plum Tree of Esau* (1962).

Tan Dun, significant Chinese composer; b. Si Mao, central Hunan Province, Aug. 18, 1957. While working among peasants during the Chinese Cultural Revolution, he began collecting folk songs. After playing viola in the Beijing Opera orch. (1976–77), he entered the recently reopened Central Cons. in Beijing in 1978 to study composition (B.A.; M.A.). In the 1980s he attended guest lectures given by Goehr, Henze, Crumb, et al. In 1983 his String Quartet won a prize in Dresden, the first international music prize won by a Chinese composer since 1949. His Western compositional leanings led to a 6-month ban on performances or broadcasts of his music soon thereafter. In 1986 he settled in New York, where he accepted a fellowship at Columbia Univ. and studied with Chou Wen-Chung, Mario Davidovsky, and George Edwards. In 1998 he received the Grawemeyer Award for his opera *Marco Polo*. His early works are romantic and florid; after 1982, they reveal a progressing advancement of dissonance and sophistication, while retaining Chinese contexts. Many of his compositions require instrumentalists to vocalize in performance. Included in his catalog of works are *9 Songs*, ritual opera for 20 Singers/Performers (N.Y., May 12, 1989), and *Marco Polo*, opera (1993–94; Munich, May 7, 1996).

Tanev, Alexander, Bulgarian composer and teacher; b. Budapest (of Bulgarian parents), Oct. 23, 1928. He studied law at the Univ. of Sofia (1946–50) and composition with Veselin Stoyanov at the Bulgarian State Cons. in Sofia (graduated, 1957). He was a teacher of composition at the latter institution (from 1970), and dean of the faculty of composition and conductor (from 1986). He also served as secretary of the Union of Bulgarian Composers (1972–76). Among his works are *Prasnik v Tsaravets* (Festival of Tsaravets), ballet (1968), and *Gramada*, music drama (1977); also 3 oratorios: *Annals of Freedom* for Soloists, Chorus, and Orch. (1975–76), *Testament* for Bass, Reader, Chorus, Children's Chorus, and Orch. (1977–78), and *Native Land* for Bass, Reader, Chorus, Children's Chorus, and Orch. (1984–85).

Taneyev, Alexander (Sergeievich), Russian composer; b. St. Petersburg, Jan. 17, 1850; d. there (Petrograd), Feb. 7, 1918. He was educated at the Univ. of St. Petersburg, and also studied composition with F. Reichel in Dresden; upon his return to St. Petersburg, he took lessons with Rimsky-Korsakov. Music was his avocation; he followed a government career, advancing to the post of head of the Imperial Chancellery. The style of his music is Romantic, lapsing into sentimentalism; the main influence is that of Tchaikovsky. Among his works were the operas *Cupid's Revenge* (concert perf., St. Petersburg, May 19, 1899) and *The Snowstorm* (Petrograd, Feb. 11, 1916).

Taneyev, Sergei (Ivanovich), greatly significant Russian composer and pedagogue; b. Vladimir district, Nov. 25, 1856; d. Dyudkovo, Zvenigorodsk district, June 19, 1915. He began taking piano lessons at the age of 5, and when he was only 9 when he entered the Moscow Cons.; after academic training for a year, he reentered the Cons. in 1869 as a piano pupil of Eduard Langer; he also received instruction in theory from Nikolai Hubert and in composition from Tchaikovsky, who became his lifelong friend; in 1871 Nikolai Rubinstein became his piano mentor. On Jan. 29, 1875, he made his formal debut as a pianist as soloist in the Brahms D-minor Concerto in Moscow; on Dec. 3, 1875, he was soloist in the Moscow premiere of the Tchaikovsky 1st Concerto, and subsequently was soloist in all of Tchaikovsky's works for piano and orch. He graduated from the Cons. in 1875 as the first student to win the gold medal in both performance and composition. In 1876 he toured his homeland with Leopold Auer. In 1878 he succeeded Tchaikovsky as prof. of harmony and orchestration at the Moscow Cons.; after the death of N. Rubinstein in 1881, he took over the latter's piano classes there; in 1883 he succeeded Hubert as prof. of composition; after serving as its director (1885–89), he taught counterpoint (1889–1905). Taneyev was a 1st-class pianist, and Tchaikovsky regarded him as one of the finest interpreters of his music. His position as a composer is anomalous: he is one of the most respected figures of Russian music history, and there is a growing literature about him; his correspondence and all documents, however trivial, concerning his life are treasured as part of the Russian cultural heritage; yet outside Russia his works are rarely heard. He wrote a treatise on counterpoint, *Podvizhnoi kontrapunkt strogavo pisma* (1909; Eng. tr, Boston, 1962, as *Convertible Counterpoint in the Strict Style*). The style of his compositions presents a compromise between Russian melos and Germanic contrapuntal writing; the mastery revealed in his 4 syms. (1873–1897) and 5 string quartets (1890–1903) is unquestionable. His most ambitious work was the trilogy *Oresteia*, after Aeschylus, in 3 divisions: *Agamemnon, Choëphorai, and Eumenides*, first performed in St. Petersburg on Oct. 29, 1895. After his death, an almost-completed treatise *Uchenie o kanone* (The Study of Canon) was found and was ed. for publ. by V. Velaiev (Moscow, 1929).

BIBL.: K. Kuznetzov, ed., *S. I. T.* (Moscow and Leningrad, 1925); V. Yakovlev, *S. I. T.: Evo muzikalnaya zhizn* (S. I. T.: His Musical Life; Moscow, 1927); V. Protopopov, ed., *Pamyati S. I. T. a 1856–1946: Sbornik statey i materialov k 90-letiyu so dnya rozhdeniya* (In Memory of S. I. T.: A Collection of Articles and Materials for the 90th Anniversary of His Birth; Moscow and Leningrad, 1947); G. Bernandt, *S. I. T.* (Moscow and Leningrad, 1950); V. Kiselyov et al., eds., *S. I. T.: Materiali i dokumenti* (Moscow, 1952); T. Khoprova, *S. I. T.* (Leningrad, 1968); N. Bazhanov, *T.* (Moscow, 1971); L. Korabelnikova, *S. I. T. v Moskovskoy konservatorri* (S. I. T. at the Moscow Conservatory; Moscow, 1974).

Tangeman, Nell, American mezzo-soprano; b. Columbus, Ohio, Dec. 23, 1917; d. Washington, D.C., Feb. 15, 1965. She studied violin at Ohio State Univ. (M.A., 1937) and received vocal instruction at the Cleveland Inst. of Music and from Fritz Lehmann, Schorr, and Matzenauer in New York. In 1945 she made her debut as a soloist in *Das Lied von der Erde* with Goossens and the Cincinnati Sym. Orch. In 1948 she made her N.Y. recital debut, and then spent a year studying in Italy on a Fulbright scholarship. She created the role of Mother Goose in Stravinsky's *The Rake's Progress* in Venice in 1951. In subsequent years, she sang throughout the United States and Europe in a repertoire extending from the 16th century to the contemporary era.

Tango, Egisto, Italian conductor; b. Rome, Nov. 13, 1873; d. Copenhagen, Oct. 5, 1951. He studied engineering before pursuing musical training at the Naples Cons. He made his debut as an opera conductor in Venice (1893), then conducted at La Scala in Milan (1895) and at Berlin (1903–08). He conducted at the Metropolitan Opera in New York (1909–10), in Italy (1911–12), and in Budapest (1913–19), where he gave the earliest performances of stage works by Bartók. From 1920 to 1926 he was active in Germany and Austria. In 1927 he settled in Copenhagen. He was distinguished for the technical precision and interpretative clarity of his performances.

Tansman, Alexandre, Polish-born French pianist, conductor, and composer; b. Łódz, June 12, 1897; d. Paris, Nov. 15, 1986. He studied at the Łódz Cons. (1902–14), then pursued training in law and philosophy at the Univ. of Warsaw; he also received instruction in counterpoint, form, and composition from Rytel in Warsaw. In 1919 he went to Paris, where he appeared as a soloist in his own works (Feb. 17, 1920). In 1927 he appeared as a soloist with the Boston Sym. Orch., and then played throughout Europe, Canada, and Palestine. He later took up conducting; he made a tour of the Far East (1932–33). After the occupation of Paris by the Germans in 1940, he made his way to the United States; he lived in Hollywood, where he wrote music for films; he returned to Paris in 1946. His music is distinguished by a considerable melodic gift and a vivacious rhythm; his harmony is often bitonal; there are some impressionistic traits that reflect his Parisian tastes. He publ. *Stravinsky* (Paris, 1948; Eng. tr., 1949, as *Igor Stravinsky: The Man and His Music*).

WORKS: DRAMATIC: OPERAS: *La Nuit kurde* (1925–27; Paris Radio, 1927); *La toisson d'or*, opéra bouffe (1938); *Sabbataï Zevi, le faux Messie*, lyric fresco (1953; Paris, 1961); *Le serment* (1954; Brussels, March 11, 1955); *L'usignolo di Boboli* (1962); *Georges Dandin*, opéra comique (1974). BALLETS: *Sextuor* (Paris, May 17, 1924); *La Grande Ville* (1932); *Bric-à-Brac* (1937); *Train de nuit* (London, 1950); *Les Habits neufs du roi* (Venice, 1959); *Resurrection* (Nice, 1962).

BIBL.: I. Schwerke, *A. T., compositeur polonais* (Paris, 1931).

Tappy, Eric, Swiss tenor; b. Lausanne, May 19, 1931. He studied with Fernando Carpi at the Geneva Cons. (1951–58), Ernst Reichert at the Salzburg Mozarteum, Eva Liebenberg in Hilversum, and Boulanger in Paris. In 1959 he made his concert debut as the Evangelist in Bach's St. Matthew Passion in Strasbourg. His operatic stage debut followed in 1964 as Rameau's Zoroastre at the Paris Opéra Comique. After singing in Geneva (1966) and Hanover (1967), he made his debut at London's Covent Garden as Mozart's Tito in 1974. He made his U.S. debut in 1974 as Don Ottavio at the San Francisco Opera, where he returned to sing Poppea and Idomeneo in 1977–78. In 1980 he appeared as Tito in Rome. He retired in 1982. Tappy was esteemed for the extraordinary range of his concert and operatic repertoire, which ranged from early music to the avant-garde.

Taranov, Gleb (Pavlovich), Ukrainian composer and teacher; b. Kiev, June 15, 1904; d. there, Jan. 25, 1989. He studied composition with Mikhail Chernov at the Petrograd Cons. (1917–19) and composition with Glière and Liatoshinsky and conducting with Blumenfield and Malko at the Kiev Cons. (1920–25). He served on the faculty of the Kiev Cons. (1925–41; 1944–74). In 1957 he was named Honored National Artist of the Ukraine. His works were cast in the accepted Soviet mold, with emphasis on the celebration of historical events. Among them was the opera *The Battle on the Ice*, depicting the victory of Alexander Nevsky over the Teutonic Knights at Lake Peipus on April 5, 1242 (1943; rev. 1979).

BIBL.: M. Mikhailov, *G.P. T.* (Kiev, 1963); S. Miroshnichenko, *G. T.* (Kiev, 1976).

Tăranu, Cornel, Romanian composer and teacher; b. Cluj, June 20, 1934. He was a student of Toduţă and Muresianu at the Cluj Cons. (1951–57), and he then joined its faculty. He also studied with Boulanger and Messiaen in Paris (1966–67) and attended the summer courses in music given by Ligeti and Maderna in Darmstadt (1968, 1969, 1972). His music is austerely formal, with atonal sound structures related through continuous variation with permissible aleatory interludes. Among his works is the opera *Secretul lui Don Giovanni* (The Secret of Don Giovanni; Cluj, July 8, 1970).

Tarchi, Angelo, Italian composer; b. Naples, c.1755; d. Paris, Aug. 19, 1814. He studied at the Cons. dei Turchini in Naples with Fago and Sala. He was music director and composer at the King's Theatre in London in 1787–88 and again in 1789, and then was active in Italy until settling in Paris in 1797. He wrote about 45 operas in Italian, and 6 in French; of these the following were produced at La Scala in Milan: *Ademira* (Dec. 27, 1783), *Ariarte* (Jan. 1786), *Il Conte di Saldagna* (June 10, 1787), *Adrasto rè d'Egitto* (Feb. 4?, 1792), *Le Danaidi* (Dec. 26, 1794), and *L'impostura poco dura* (Oct. 10, 1795). In Paris he produced the French version of *Il Conte di Saldagna* as *Bouffons de la foire St. Germain* (1790), *D'Auberge en auberge* (Opéra Comique, April 26, 1800), etc. He acquired a certain notoriety by his attempt to rewrite the 3d and 4th acts of Mozart's *Le nozze di Figaro* (1787); regarding this episode, see A. Einstein, "Mozart e Tarchi," *Rassegna Musicale* (July 1935); also C. Sartori, "Lo Zeffiretto di Angelo Tarchi," *Rivista Musicale Italiana* (July 1954).

Tardos, Béla, Hungarian composer; b. Budapest, June 21, 1910; d. there, Nov. 18, 1966. He studied with Kodály at the Budapest Academy of Music (1932–37). Upon graduation, he was active as a concert manager and music publisher. He composed much choral music for mass singing employing the modalities of Hungarian folk songs. His works include the opera *Laura* (1958, rev. 1964; Debrecen, Dec. 11, 1966).

BIBL.: P. Várnai, *T. B.* (Budapest, 1966).

Tariol-Baugé, Anne, French singer; b. Clermont-Ferrand, Aug. 28, 1872; d. Asnières, near Paris, Dec. 1, 1944. She made her operatic debut in Bordeaux, then went to Russia; returning to France, she sang in Toulouse and Nantes; she then settled in Paris, where she appeared mainly in light opera. She sang the title role at the premiere of Messager's opera *Véronique* at the Bouffes-Parisiens (Dec. 10, 1898); distinguished herself especially in Offenbach's operettas. She was married to the baritone Alphonse Baugé.

Tarp, Svend Erik, Danish composer; b. Thisted, Jutland, Aug. 6, 1908; d. Copenhagen, Oct. 19, 1994. He studied theory with Jeppesen and music history with Simonson at the Copenhagen Cons. (1929–31), then was on its faculty (1936–42); concurrently he lectured at the Univ. of Copenhagen (1939–47) and the Royal Theater Opera School (1936–40); subsequently he was an administrator with Edition Dania (1941–60).

WORKS: DRAMATIC: OPERAS: *Princessen i det Fjerne* (The Princess at a Distance, 1952; Copenhagen, May 18, 1953); *9,90*, burlesque television opera (Copenhagen, Aug. 12, 1962). BALLETS: *Skyggen* (The Shadow, after Hans Christian Andersen, 1941–44; Copenhagen, April 1, 1960); *Den detroniserede dyretoemmer* (The Dethroned Tamer; Copenhagen, Feb. 5, 1944). Also film scores.

Taruskin, Richard, influential American musicologist and music critic; b. N.Y., April 2, 1945. He was educated at Columbia Univ., where he took his Ph.D. in historical musicology (1975); he also held a Fulbright-Hayes traveling fellowship, which enabled him to conduct research in Moscow (1971–72). In 1975 he became an assistant prof. at Columbia Univ., then was assoc. prof. there (1981–87). In 1985 he was a visting prof. at the Univ. of Pa. and in 1987 he was the Hanes-Willis visiting prof. at the Univ. of N.C. at Chapel Hill. In 1986 he was made an assoc. prof. at the Univ. of Calif. at Berkeley, subsequently becoming a prof. there in 1989. He held a Guggenheim fellowship in 1986. In 1987 he was awarded the Dent Medal of England. In 1989 he received the ASCAP–Deems Taylor Award. He contributed many valuable articles on Russian music and composers to *The New Grove Dictionary of Opera* (1992); he also contributed articles and/or reviews to the Journal of *Musicology*, the *Journal of the American Musicological Society, Notes, 19th Century Music*, the *N.Y. Times*, the *New Republic*, and other publications. In addition to his ed. and commentary of Busnoys's *The Latin-Texted Works* (2 vols., N.Y., 1990), he publ. the books *Opera and Drama in Russia* (Ann Arbor, 1981; new ed., 1994), *Mussorgsky: Eight Essays and an Epilogue* (Princeton, N.J., 1993), *Stravinsky and the Russian Traditions: A Biography of the Works Through Mavra* (2 vols, Berkeley and Los Angeles, 1995), and *Text and Act: Essays on Music and Performance* (N.Y., 1995).

Taskin, (Emile-) Alexandre, French baritone; b. Paris, March 8, 1853; d. there, Oct. 5, 1897. His grandfather was the French organist and composer Henri-Joseph Taskin (b. Versailles, Aug. 24, 1779; d. Paris, May 4, 1852). He was a pupil of Ponchard and Bussine at the Paris Cons., making his debut at Amiens in 1875. He sang in Lille and Geneva, then returned to Paris in 1878, where he was engaged at the Opéra Comique in 1879, and created important parts in many new operas. He retired in 1894, and from then until his death was prof. of lyrical declamation at the Cons. On the night of the terrible catastrophe of the burning of the Opéra Comique (May 25, 1887) he was singing in *Mignon*; through his calmness and bravery many lives were saved, and the government decorated him with a medal.

Tassinari, Pia, Italian soprano and mezzo-soprano; b. Modigliana, Sept. 15, 1903; d. Faenza, May 15, 1996. She received her musical training in Bologna and Milan. She made her operatic debut as Mimi at Castel Monferrato in 1929, then sang at La Scala in Milan (1931–37; 1945–46) and at the Rome Opera (1933–44; 1951–52). She made her American debut at the Metropolitan Opera in New York on Dec. 26, 1947, as Tosca. Although she began her career as a soprano, in later years she preferred to sing mezzo-soprano parts. Her repertoire included both soprano and mezzo-soprano roles, e.g., Mimi, Tosca, Manon, and Marguerite, and also Amneris and Carmen. She was married to **Ferruccio Tagliavini**.

Tate, Jeffrey, talented English conductor; b. Salisbury, April 28, 1943. Although a victim of spina bifida, he pursued studies at the

Univ. of Cambridge and at St. Thomas's Medical School; he then attended the London Opera Centre (1970–71). He was a member of the music staff at the Royal Opera, Covent Garden, London (1971–77); he also served as an assistant conductor at the Bayreuth Festivals (1976–80). In 1978 he made his formal conducting debut with Carmen at the Göteborg Opera; on Dec. 26, 1980 he made his first appearance at the Metropolitan Opera in New York conducting Berg's *Lulu*; his debut at Covent Garden followed with *La clemenza di Tito* on June 8, 1982. He appeared as a guest conductor at the Cologne Opera (1981), the Geneva Opera (1983), the Paris Opéra (1983), the Hamburg State Opera (1984), the San Francisco Opera (1984), the Salzburg Festival (1985), and the Vienna State Opera (1986). In 1983 he made his first appearance with the English Chamber Orch., being named its principal conductor in 1985; he led it on tours abroad, including one to the United States in 1988. In 1986 he also became principal conductor at Covent Garden. In 1990 he was made a Commander of the Order of the British Empire. He was chief conductor of the Rotterdam Phil. from 1991 to 1994. In 1997 he became principal conductor of the Minnesota Orch. Viennese Sommerfest. His extensive operatic and concert repertoire encompasses works from the Classical to the contemporary era.

Tate, Phyllis (Margaret Duncan), English composer; b. Gerrards Cross, Buckinghamshire, April 6, 1911; d. London, May 27, 1987. She was a student of Harry Farjeon at the Royal Academy of Music in London (1928–32), and then devoted herself fully to composition. In 1935 she married **Alan Frank**. She was a composer of fine craftsmanship, excelling in works for voices and small ensembles. Her compositions include *The Lodger*, opera (1959–60; London, July 14, 1960), *Dark Pilgrimage*, television opera (1963), and *Scarecrow*, operetta (1982).

Tattermuschová, Helena, Czech soprano; b. Prague, Jan. 28, 1933. She was a pupil of Vlasta Linhartová at the Prague Cons. In 1955 she made her operatic debut as Musetta in Ostrava. In 1959 she became a member of the Prague National Theater, where she won esteem for her portrayals of roles in operas by Mozart, Smetana, Janáček, Puccini, and Strauss. She also toured with the company abroad and made guest appearances in various European opera houses. She also pursued a concert career.

Taube, Michael, Polish-born Israeli conductor, teacher, and composer; b. Łódz, March 13, 1890; d. Tel Aviv, Feb. 23, 1972. He studied at the Leipzig Cons. and with Neitzel (piano), Strässer (composition), and Abendroth (conducting) in Cologne. In 1918 he founded the Bad Godesberg Concert Soc. In 1924 he became a conductor at the Berlin Städtische Oper, and also was founder-conductor of the his own chamber orch. and choir (from 1926). In 1935 he emigrated to Palestine. After appearing as a conductor with the Palestine Sym. Orch., he founded the Ramat Gan Chamber Orch., which he took on tours abroad. He also appeared as a guest conductor in Europe and was active as a teacher of voice and conducting. Taube composed orch. pieces and chamber music.

Tauber, Richard, eminent Austrian-born English tenor; b. Linz, May 16, 1891; d. London, Jan. 8, 1948. He was the illegitimate son of the actor Richard Anton Tauber; his mother was a soubrette singer. He was christened Richard Denemy after his mother's maiden name, but he sometimes used the last name Seiffert, his mother's married name. He took courses at the Hoch Cons. in Frankfurt am Main and studied voice with Carl Beines in Freiburg im Breisgau. He made his operatic debut at Chemnitz as Tamino in *Die Zauberflöte* (March 2, 1913) with such success that he was engaged in the same year at the Dresden Court Opera; he made his first appearance at the Berlin Royal Opera as Strauss's Bacchus in 1915, and later won particular success in Munich and Salzburg for his roles in Mozart's operas. About 1925 he turned to lighter roles, and won remarkable success in the operettas of Lehár. He made his U.S. debut on Oct. 28, 1931, in a N.Y. recital. In 1938 he settled in England, where he appeared as Tamino and Belmonte at London's Covent Garden. In 1940 he became a naturalized British subject. He wrote an operetta, *Old Chelsea*, taking the leading role at its premiere (London, Feb. 17, 1943). He made his last American appearance at Carnegie Hall in New York on March 30, 1947.

BIBL.: H. Ludwigg, ed., *R. T.* (Berlin, 1928); D. Napier-Tauber (his 2d wife), *R. T.* (Glasgow, 1949); W. Korb, *R. T.* (Vienna, 1966); C. Castle and D. Napier-Tauber, *This Was R. T.* (London, 1971).

Taubert, (Carl Gottfried) Wilhelm, German pianist, conductor, teacher, and composer; b. Berlin, March 23, 1811; d. there, Jan. 7, 1891. He was a piano pupil of Neithardt, later of L. Berger, and for composition, of Bernhard Klein. He appeared early as a concert player, and also taught music in Berlin. He became assistant conductor of the court orch. in 1831, then was Generalmusikdirektor of the Royal Opera, Berlin, from 1845 to 1848; also court Kapellmeister from 1845 to 1869; he continued to conduct the court orch. until 1883. He conducted his 1st Sym. in Berlin at the age of 20 (March 31, 1831). Among his works were the operas (all 1st perf. in Berlin): *Die Kirmes* (Jan. 23, 1832), *Marquis und Dieb* (Feb. 1, 1842), *Der Zigeuner* (Sept. 19, 1834), *Joggeli* (Oct. 9, 1853), *Macbeth* (Nov. 16, 1857), and *Cesario*, after Shakespeare's *Twelfth Night* (Nov. 13, 1874); also incidental music to 8 plays.

BIBL.: W. Neumann, *W. T. und Ferdinand Hiller* (Kassel, 1857).

Taubman, Howard, American music and drama critic; b. N. Y., July 4, 1907; d. Sarasota, Fla., Jan. 8, 1996. He studied at Cornell Univ. (A.B., 1929). He joined the staff of the *N.Y. Times* in 1929, where he was its music ed. (1935–55), music critic (1955–60), drama critic (1960–66), and critic-at-large (1966–72). His writings include *Opera: Front and Back* (N.Y., 1938), *The Maestro: The Life of Arturo Toscanini* (N.Y., 1951), and *The Making of the American Theater* (N.Y., 1965; rev. in *Musical Comedy*, XII, 1967).

BIBL.: L. Weldy, *Music Criticism of Olin Downes and H. T. in "The New York Times," Sunday Edition, 1924–29 and 1955–60* (diss., Univ. of Southern Calif., 1965).

Taucher, Curt, German tenor; b. Nuremberg, Oct. 25, 1885; d. Munich, Aug. 7, 1954. He studied with Heinrich Hermann in Munich. He made his operatic debut as Faust in Augsburg in 1908, then sang in Chemnitz (1911–14) and Hannover (1915–20). In 1920 he joined the Dresden State Opera, remaining there until 1934; during his tenure there, he created the role of Menelaus in Strauss's opera *Die Äegyptische Helena*. On Nov. 23, 1922, he sang the role of Siegmund in *Die Walküre* at his Metropolitan Opera debut in New York; he continued on its roster until 1927. He made guest appearances at Covent Garden in London (1932), at the Berlin State Opera, and at the Bavarian State Opera in Munich. He was noted for his roles in Wagner's operas.

Tauriello, Antonio, Argentine composer and conductor; b. Buenos Aires, March 20, 1931. He studied piano with Paul Spivak and Walter Gieseking, and composition with Alberto Ginastera. While still a youth, he was engaged to conduct opera and ballet at the Teatro Colón in Buenos Aires. He often appeared in the United States as an opera rehearsal coach, working at the Lyric Opera in Chicago, the Opera Soc. in Washington, D.C., and the N.Y. City Opera in the 1960s. In the 1970s he led Verdi opera festivals in San Diego. His early works, several of which were suppressed, were in a neoclassical mold. His works composed after 1962 embrace the foundations of the international avant-garde, among them the opera *Les Guerres Picrocholines* (1969–70).

Tausinger, Jan, Romanian-born Czech conductor, teacher, and composer; b. Piatra Neamt, Nov. 1, 1921; d. Prague, July 29, 1980. He studied composition with Cuclin, Jora, and Mendelsohn at the Bucharest Cons., graduating in 1947; he then went to Prague, where he had lessons in conducting with Ančerl; concurrently he took courses in advanced harmony with Alois Hába and Bořkovec at the Prague Academy of Music (1948–52). He was active as a conductor of radio orchs. in Bucharest, Ostrava, and Plzeň; he also taught at the Ostrava Cons., where he was director (1952–58); after working for the Czech Radio in Prague (1969–70), he served as director of the Prague Cons. His music was greatly diversified in style, idiom, and technique, ranging from neoclassical modalities to integral dodecaphony; he made use of optical representational notation when justified by the structure of a particular piece. Among his works were *Dlouhá noc* (The Long Night), ballet (1966), and *Ugly Nature*, opera, after Dostoyevsky (1971).

Tauwitz, Eduard, German conductor and composer; b. Glatz, Silesia, Jan. 21, 1812; d. Prague, July 25, 1894. He was made Kapellmeister at theaters in Vilnius (1837), Riga (1840), Breslau (1843), and Prague (1846), being pensioned in 1863. He wrote more than 1,000 compositions, including 3 operas: *Trilby* (Vilna, 1836), *Bradamante* (Riga, 1844), and *Schmolke und Bakel* (Breslau, 1846).

Tavener, John (Kenneth), remarkable English composer; b. London, Jan. 28, 1944. He was a student of Berkeley at the Royal Academy of Music in London (1961–65) and of Lumsdaine (1965–67). In 1960 he became organist at St. John's, Kensington. From 1969 he served as a prof. of music at Trinity College of Music in London. Tavener's use of total serialism and electronics has been effectively demonstrated in many of his works. After his conversion to the Greek Orthodox faith in 1976, the spiritual and even mystical elements in his output grew apace as he created an important body of both sacred and secular works marked by expert craftsmanship.

WORKS: DRAMATIC: *The Cappemakers*, music drama (Alfriston, June 14, 1964; based on the choral piece); *Thérèse*, opera (1973–76; London, Oct. 1, 1979); *A Gentle Spirit*, chamber opera (1976–77; Bath, June 6, 1977); *Eis Thanaton* (1986; Cheltenham, July 5, 1987); *Mary of Egypt*, chamber opera (1990–91).

Tavrizian, Mikhail (Arsenievich), Armenian conductor; b. Baku, May 27, 1907; d. Yerevan, Oct. 17, 1957. He studied viola (diploma, 1932) and conducting with Gauk (diploma, 1934) at the Leningrad Cons. After playing viola in the Maly Opera orch. in Leningrad (1928–35), he pursued a conducting career. From 1938 he was principal conductor of the Yerevan Opera and Ballet Theater, where he conducted the premieres of many Armenian works. He also was active as a sym. conductor. In 1956 he was made a People's Artist of the USSR.

Tawaststjerna, Erik (Werner), eminent Finnish musicologist; b. Mikkeli, Oct. 10, 1916; d. Helsinki, Jan. 22, 1993. He studied piano with Hannikainen and Bernhard at the Helsinki Cons. (1934–44), with Leygraf in Stockholm, with Neuhaus in Moscow (1946), and with Cortot and Gentil in Paris (1947); he later pursued musicological studies at the Univ. of Helsinki (Mag.Phil., 1958; Ph.D., 1960). After a brief career as a concert pianist, he devoted himself to musicology; he was a prof. at the Univ. of Helsinki (1960–83).

WRITINGS (all publ. in Helsinki unless otherwise given): *Sibeliuksen pianosävellykset ja muita esseitä* (Sibelius's Piano Works; 1955; Eng. tr., 1957); *Sergei Prokofjevin ooppera Sota ja rauha* (Sergei Prokofiev's War and Peace; 1960); *Jean Sibelius* (5 vols., 1965–88; Eng. tr. by R. Layton, 1976–); *Esseitä ja arvosteluja* (Essays and Criticism; 1976); *Voces intimae: Minnesbilder från barndomen* (1990); *Scenes historiques: Kirjoituksia vuosilta 1945–58* (Helsingissä, 1992); *Jean Sibelius: Aren 1865–1893* (1992).

BIBL.: E. Salmenhaara, ed., *Juhlakirja E. T.lle* (Helsinki, 1976).

Taylor, Clifford, American composer and teacher; b. Avalon, Pa., Oct. 20, 1923; d. Abington, Pa., Sept. 19, 1987. He studied composition with Lopatnikoff at the Carnegie-Mellon Univ. in Pittsburgh, and with Fine, Hindemith, Piston, and Thompson at Harvard Univ. (M.A., 1950). He taught at Chatham College in Pittsburgh (1950–63); in 1963 he joined the faculty of Temple Univ. in Philadelphia. Among his works is the opera *The Freak Show* (1975).

Taylor, (Joseph) Deems, greatly popular American composer and writer on music; b. N. Y., Dec. 22, 1885; d. there, July 3, 1966. He graduated from N.Y. Univ. (B.A., 1906) and studied harmony and counterpoint with Oscar Coon (1908–11). After doing editorial work for various publishers and serving as war correspondent for the *N.Y. Tribune* in France (1916–17), he was music critic for the *N.Y. World* (1921–25), ed. of *Musical America* (1927–29), and music critic for the *N.Y. American* (1931–32). He was an opera commentator for NBC (from 1931) and intermission commentator for the N.Y. Phil. national broadcasts (1936–43); he also served as director (1933–66) and president (1942–48) of ASCAP. In 1924 he was elected a member of the National Inst. of Arts and Letters and in 1935 of the American Academy of Arts and Letters. In 1967 the ASCAP–Deems Taylor Award was created in his memory for honoring outstanding writings on music. Following the success of his orch. suite *Through the Looking-Glass*, after Lewis Carroll's tale (1923), he was commissioned by Walter Damrosch to compose a symphonic poem, *Jurgen* (1925). Meanwhile, 2 widely performed cantatas, *The Chambered Nautilus* and *The Highwayman*, had added to his growing reputation, which received a strong impetus when his opera *The King's Henchman*, to a libretto by Edna St. Vincent Millay and commissioned by the Metropolitan Opera, was premiered in that house on Feb. 17, 1927. Receiving 14 performances in 3 seasons, it established a record for American opera at the Metropolitan Opera, but it was surpassed by Taylor's next opera, *Peter Ibbetson* (Feb. 7, 1931); this attained 16 performances in 4 seasons. These successes, however, proved ephemeral, and the operas were allowed to lapse into unmerited desuetude. Other works included the operas *Ramuntcho* (Philadelphia, Feb. 10, 1942) and *The Dragon* (N.Y., Feb. 6, 1958), the comic opera, *Cap'n Kidd & Co.* (1908), a musical play, *The Echo* (1909), an operetta, *The Breath of Scandal* (1916), and incidental music.

WRITINGS (all publ. in N.Y.): *Of Men and Music* (1937); *The Well Tempered Listener* (1940); *Walt Disney's Fantasia* (1940); ed., *A Treasury of Gilbert and Sullivan* (1941); *Music to My Ears* (1949); *Some Enchanted Evenings: The Story of Rodgers and Hammerstein* (1953).

BIBL.: J. Howard, *D. T.* (N.Y., 1927; 2d ed., 1940).

Taylor, Janis (Janice Kathleen née **Schuster**), American-born Canadian mezzo-soprano; b. Westfield, N.Y., March 10, 1946. She studied piano and clarinet before going to Montreal in 1967. In 1972 she became a naturalized Canadian citizen. Following vocal studies with Bernard Diamant, she studied with Lina and Antonio Narducci, Stevenson Barrett, Gérard Souzay, and Danielle Valin. In 1971 she made her recital debut in Montreal. Her orch. debut followed in 1973 as a soloist in *Messiah* with the Toronto Sym. She made her operatic debut as the Queen in Somer's *The Fool* at the Stratford (Ontario) Festival in 1975, and thereafter appeared with various Canadian and American opera houses. In 1979 she made her U.S. orch. debut as a soloist in *Messiah* with the National Sym. Orch. in Washington, D.C. Her European operatic stage debut came that same year when she appeared in Shostakovich's *Lady Macbeth of the District of Mtzensk* at the Spoleto Festival. In 1980 she made her first appearance as an orch. soloist in Europe in *Messiah* with the RAI Orch. in Milan. She sang Handel's Alessandro in a concert performance in N.Y.'s Carnegie Hall in 1985. In 1989 she made her London debut as a soloist in Verdi's *Requiem* with the London Sym. Orch. In 1990 she was the center of attention when she starred in Schoenberg's *Erwartung* at the Holland Festival in Amsterdam. Taylor has won particular distinction for her varied concert repertoire, being especially admired for her performances of the music of Mahler.

Taylor, Raynor, English-American singer, organist, teacher, and composer; b. London, 1747; d. Philadelphia, Aug. 17, 1825. He received his early training as a chorister in the Chapel Royal, and in 1765 became organist of a church in Chelmsford; that same year he was also appointed music director at Marylebone Gardens and at Sadler's Wells Theatre, London. In 1792 he emigrated to the United States. He presented musical entertainments in Richmond, Va., Baltimore, and Annapolis, where he was organist at St. Anne's Church. Moving to Philadelphia in 1793, he was organist of St. Peter's Church (1795–1813); in 1820 he was one of the founders of the Musical Fund Society. A gifted singer, he gave humorous musical entertainments that he called "olios," and in 1796 conducted an orch. concert that included several of his own compositions. In collaboration with A. Reinagle, who had been his pupil in London, he composed a monody on the death of Washington (Philadelphia, Dec. 23, 1799), and a ballad opera, *Pizarro, or the Spaniards in Peru* (1800). Some of his song MSS are in the N.Y. Public Library.

BIBL.: J. Cuthbert, *R. T. and Anglo-American Musical Life* (diss., West Virginia Univ., 1980).

Tchaikovsky, Boris (Alexandrovich), Russian composer; b. Moscow, Sept. 10, 1925; d. Feb. 1996. He studied at the Moscow Cons. with Shostakovich, Shebalin, and Miaskovsky (1941–49). His later works made use of expanded tonality. Among his works was the opera *The Star* (1949; unfinished), as well as much music for films, radio, and plays.

Tchaikovsky, Modest, Russian playwright and librettist, brother of **Piotr Ilyich Tchaikovsky**; b. Alapaevsk, Perm district, May 13, 1850; d. Moscow, Jan. 15, 1916. He was the closest intimate of Tchaikovsky, and the author of the basic biography. His plays had only a passing success, but he was an excellent librettist. He wrote the librettos of Tchaikovsky's last 2 operas, *The Queen of Spades* and *Iolanthe*.

Tchaikovsky, Piotr Ilyich, famous Russian composer, brother of **Modest Tchaikovsky**; b. Votkinsk, Viatka district, May 7, 1840; d. St. Petersburg, Nov. 6, 1893. The son of a mining inspector at a plant in the Urals, he was given a good education; he had a French governess and a music teacher. When he was 10 the family moved to St. Petersburg and he was sent to a school of jurisprudence, from which he graduated at 19, becoming a government clerk; while at school he studied music with Lomakin, but did not display conspicuous talent as either a pianist or composer. At the age of 21 he was accepted in a musical inst., newly established by Anton Rubinstein, which was to become the St. Petersburg Cons. He studied with Zaremba (harmony and counterpoint) and Rubinstein (composition), graduating in 1865, winning a silver medal for his cantata to Schiller's *Hymn to Joy*. In 1866 he became prof. of harmony at the Moscow Cons. As if to compensate for a late beginning in his profession, he began to compose with great application. His early works reveal little individuality. With his symphonic poem *Fatum* (1868) came the first formulation of his style, highly subjective, preferring minor modes, permeated with nostalgic longing and alive with keen rhythms. In 1869 he undertook the composition of his overture-fantasy *Romeo and Juliet*; not content with what he had written, he profited by the advice of Balakirev, whom he met in St. Petersburg, and revised the work in 1870, but this version proved equally unsatisfactory; Tchaikovsky laid the composition aside, and did not complete it until 1880; in its final form it became one of his most successful works. The Belgian soprano Désirée Artôt, a member of an opera troupe visiting St. Petersburg in 1868, took great interest in Tchaikovsky, and he was moved by her attentions; for a few months he seriously contemplated marriage, and so notified his father (his mother had died of cholera when he was 14 years old). But this proved to be a passing infatuation on her part, for soon she married the Spanish singer Padilla; Tchaikovsky reacted to this event with a casual philosophical remark about the inconstancy of human attachments. Throughout his career Tchaikovsky never allowed his psychological turmoil to interfere with his work. Besides teaching and composing, he contributed music criticism to Moscow newspapers for several years (1868–74), made altogether 26 trips abroad (to Paris, Berlin, Vienna, N.Y.), and visited the first Bayreuth Festival in 1876, reporting his impressions for the Moscow daily *Russkyie Vedomosti*. His closest friends were members of his own family, his brothers (particularly Modest, his future biographer), and his married sister, Alexandra Davidov, at whose estate, Kamenka, he spent most of his summers. The correspondence with them, all of which was preserved and eventually publ., throws a true light on Tchaikovsky's character and his life. His other close friends were his publisher, Jurgenson, Nikolai Rubinstein, and several other musicians. The most extraordinary of his friendships was the epistolary association with Nadezhda von Meck, a wealthy widow whom he never met but who was to play an important role in his life. Through the violinist Kotek she learned about Tchaikovsky's financial difficulties, and commissioned him to write some compositions, at large fees, then arranged to pay him an annuity of 6,000 rubles. For more than 13 years they corresponded voluminously, even when they lived in the same city (Moscow, Florence); on several occasions she hinted that she would not be averse to a personal meeting, but Tchaikovsky invariably declined such a suggestion, under the pretext that one should not see one's guardian angel in the flesh. On Tchaikovsky's part, this correspondence had to remain within the circumscribed domain of art, personal philosophy, and reporting of daily events, without touching on the basic problems of his existence. On July 18, 1877, he contracted marriage with a conservatory student, Antonina Milyukova, who had declared her love for him. This was an act of defiance of his own nature; Tchaikovsky was a homosexual, and made no secret of it in the correspondence with his brother Modest, who was also a homosexual. He thought that by flaunting a wife he could prevent the already rife rumors about his sexual preference from spreading further. The result was disastrous, and Tchaikovsky fled from his wife in horror. He attempted suicide by walking into the Moskva River in order to catch pneumonia, but suffered nothing more severe than simple discomfort. He then went to St. Petersburg to seek the advice of his brother Anatol, a lawyer, who made suitable arrangements with Tchaikovsky's wife for a separation. (They were never divorced; she died in an insane asylum in 1917.) Von Meck, to whom Tchaikovsky wrote candidly of the hopeless failure of his marriage (without revealing the true cause of that failure), made at once an offer of further financial assistance, which he gratefully accepted. He spent several months during 1877–78 in Italy, Switzerland, Paris, and Vienna. During these months he completed one of his greatest works, the 4th Sym., dedicated to von Meck. It was performed for the first time in Moscow on Feb. 22, 1878, but Tchaikovsky did not cut short his sojourn abroad to attend the performance. He resigned from the Moscow Cons. in the autumn of 1878, and from that time dedicated himself entirely to composition. The continued subsidy from von Meck allowed him to forget money matters. Early in 1878 he completed his most successful opera, *Evgeny Onegin* ("lyric scenes," after Pushkin); it was first produced in Moscow by a cons. ensemble, on March 29, 1879, and gained success only gradually; the first performance at the Imperial Opera in St. Petersburg did not take place until Oct. 31, 1884. A morbid depression was still Tchaikovsky's natural state of mind, but every new work sustained his faith in his destiny as a composer, despite many disheartening reversals. His Piano Concerto No. 1, rejected by Nikolai Rubinstein as unplayable, was given its world premiere (somewhat incongruously) in Boston, on Oct. 25, 1875, played by Bülow, and afterward was performed all over the world by famous pianists, including Nikolai Rubinstein. The Violin Concerto, criticized by Leopold Auer (to whom the score was originally dedicated) and attacked by Hanslick with sarcasm and virulence at its world premiere by Brodsky in Vienna (1881), survived all its detractors to become one of the most celebrated pieces in the violin repertoire. The 5th Sym. (1888) was successful from the very first. Early in 1890 Tchaikovsky wrote his 2d important opera, *The Queen of Spades*, which was produced at the Imperial Opera in St. Petersburg in that year. His ballets *Swan Lake* (1876) and *The Sleeping Beauty* (1889) became famous on Russian stages. But at the peak of his career, Tchaikovsky suffered a severe psychological blow; von Meck notified him of the discontinuance of her subsidy, and with this announcement she abruptly terminated their correspondence. He could now well afford the loss of the money, but his pride was deeply hurt by the manner in which von Meck had acted. It is indicative of Tchaikovsky's inner strength that even this desertion of one whom he regarded as his staunchest friend did not affect his ability to work. In 1891 he undertook his only voyage to America. He was received with honors as a celebrated composer; he led 4 concerts of his works in New York and one each in Baltimore and Philadelphia. He did not linger in the United States, however, and returned to St. Petersburg in a few weeks. Early in 1892 he made a concert tour as a conductor in Russia, and then proceeded to Warsaw and Germany. In the meantime he had purchased a house in the town of Klin, not far from Moscow, where he wrote his last sym., the *Pathétique*. Despite the perfection of his technique, he did not arrive at the desired form and substance of this work at once, and discarded his original sketch. The title *Pathétique* was suggested to him by his brother Modest, and the score was dedicated to his nephew, Vladimir Davidov. Its music is the final testament of Tchaikovsky's life, and an epitome of his philosophy of fatalism. In the first movement, the trombones are given the theme of the Russian service for the dead. Remarkably, the score of one of his gayest works, the ballet *The Nutcracker*, was composed simultaneously with the early sketches for the *Pathétique*. Tchaikovsky was in good spirits when he went to St. Petersburg to conduct the premiere of the *Pathétique*, on Oct. 28, 1893 (which was but moderately successful). A cholera epidemic was then raging in St. Petersburg, and the population was specifically warned against drinking unboiled water, but apparently he carelessly did exactly that. He showed the symptoms of cholera soon afterward, and nothing could be done to save him. The melodramatic hypothesis that the fatal drink of water was a defiance of death, in perfect knowledge of the danger, since he must have remembered his mother's death of the same dread infection, is untenable in the light of publ. private letters between the attendant physician and Modest Tchaikovsky at the time. Tchaikovsky's fatalism alone would amply account for his lack of precaution. Almost immediately after his death a rumor spread that he had committed suicide, and reports to that effect were publ. in respectable European newspapers (but not in Russian publications), and repeated even in some biographical dictionaries (particularly in Britain). After the grim fantasy seemed definitely refuted, a ludicrous paper by an emigré Russian woman was publ., claiming private knowledge of a homosexual scandal involving a Russian nobleman's nephew (in another version a member of the Romanov imperial family) that led to a "trial" of Tchaikovsky by a jury of his former school classmates, who offered Tchaikovsky a choice between honorable suicide or disgrace and possible exile to Siberia; a family council, with Tchaikovsky's own participation, advised the former solution, and Tchaikovsky was supplied with arsenic; the family doctor was supposed to be a part of the conspiracy, as were Tchaikovsky's own brothers. Amazingly enough, this outrageous fabrication was accepted as historical fact by some biographers, and even found its way into the pages of *The New Grove Dictionary of Music and Musicians* (1980). In Russia, the truth of Tchaikovsky's homosexuality was totally suppressed, and any references to it in his diary and letters were expunged.

As a composer, Tchaikovsky stands apart from the militant national movement of the "Mighty Five." The Russian element is, of course, very strong in his music, and upon occasion he made use of Russian folk songs in his works, but this national spirit is instinctive rather than consciously cultivated. His personal relationship with the St. Petersburg group of nationalists was friendly without being close; his correspondence with Rimsky-Korsakov, Balakirev, and others was mostly concerned with professional matters. Tchaikovsky's music was frankly sentimental; his supreme gift of melody, which none of his Russian contemporaries could match, secured for him a lasting popularity among performers and audiences. His influence was profound on the Moscow group of musicians, of whom Arensky and Rachmaninoff were the most talented. He wrote in every genre, and was successful in each; besides his stage works, syms., chamber music, and piano compositions, he composed a great number of lyric songs that are the most poignant creations of his genius. By a historical paradox, Tchaikovsky became the most popular Russian composer under the Soviet regime. His subjectivism, his fatalism, his emphasis on melancholy moods, even his reactionary political views (which included a brand of amateurish anti-Semitism), failed to detract from his stature in the new society. In fact, official spokesmen of Soviet Russia repeatedly urged Soviet composers to follow in the path of Tchaikovsky's aesthetics. His popularity is also very strong in Anglo-Saxon countries, particularly in America; much less so in France and Italy; in Germany his influence is insignificant.

WORKS: DRAMATIC: OPERAS: *Voyevoda*, op. 3 (1867–68; Moscow, Feb. 11, 1869; destroyed by Tchaikovsky; reconstructed by Pavel Lamm); *Undine* (destroyed by Tchaikovsky; only fragments extant); *Oprichnik* (1870–72; St. Petersburg, April 24, 1874); *Kuznets Vakula* (Vakula the Smith; 1874; St. Petersburg, Dec. 6, 1876); *Evgeny Onegin* (1877–78; Moscow, March, 29, 1879); *Orleanskaya deva* (The Maid of Orleans; 1878–79; St. Petersburg, Feb. 25, 1881; rev. 1882); *Mazepa* (1881–83; Moscow, Feb. 15, 1884); *Cherevichki* (The Little Shoes; 1885; Moscow, Jan. 31, 1887; rev. version of *Kuznets Vakula*); *Charodeyka* (The Sorceress; 1885–87; St. Petersburg, Nov. 1, 1887); *Pikovaya dama* (The Queen of Spades), op. 68 (St. Petersburg, Dec. 19, 1890); *Iolanta*, op. 69 (1891; St. Petersburg, Dec. 18, 1892). BALLETS: *Lebedinoye ozero* (Swan Lake), op. 20 (1875–76; Moscow, March 4, 1877); *Spyashchaya krasavitsa* (The Sleeping Beauty), op. 66 (1888–89; St. Petersburg, Jan. 15, 1890); *Shchelkunchik* (The Nutcracker), op. 71 (1891–92; St. Petersburg, Dec. 18, 1892).

BIBL.: COLLECTED WORKS: SOURCE MATERIAL: An exhaustive ed. of his compositions was publ. in Moscow and Leningrad (1940–71). His diaries for the years 1873–91 were publ. in Moscow and Petrograd (1923; Eng. tr., 1945). He wrote a treatise that was publ. in an Eng. tr. as *Guide to the Practical Study of Harmony* (Leipzig, 1900). A complete ed. of his literary works and correspondence commenced publ. in Moscow in 1953. The *New Edition of the Complete Works* began publ. in Moscow and Mainz in 1993. BIOGRAPHICAL, ANALYTICAL, AND CRITICAL: H. Laroche, *Na pamyat o P. I. T.* (In Memory of P. I. T.; St. Petersburg, 1894); idem, *Pamyati T.* (Memories of T.; St. Petersburg, 1894); V. Baskin, *P. I. T.* (St. Petersburg, 1895); R. Newmarch, *T.: His Life and Works* (London, 1900); M. Tchaikovsky, *Zhizn P. I. T.* (The Life of P. I. T.; 3 vols., Moscow, 1900–2; abr. Eng. tr. by R. Newmarch as *The Life and Letters of P. I. T.*, London, 1906); E. Evans, *T.* (London, 1906; 2d ed., rev., 1935); I. Glebov, *P. I. T.: evo zhizn i tvorchestvo* (P. I. T.: Life and Works; Petrograd, 1922); idem, *T.: opit kharakteristiki* (T: An Attempt at a Characterization; Petrograd, 1923); G. Abraham, ed., *T.: A Symposium* (London, 1945); H. Weinstock, *T.* (N.Y., 1946); B. Yarustovsky, *Opernaya dramaturgiya T.* (T.'s Operatic Dramatury; Moscow and Leningrad, 1947); D. Zhitmorsky, *Baleti P. T.* (P. T.'s Ballets; Moscow and Leningrad, 1950; 2d ed., 1958); V. Protopopov and N. Tumanina, *Opernoye tvorchestvo T.* (T.'s Operas; Moscow, 1957); A. Alshvang, *P. I. T.* (Moscow, 1959); N. Tumanina, *T.* (Moscow, 1962–68); A. Alshvang, *P. I. T.* (Moscow, 1967) E. Garden, *T.* (London, 1973; 2d ed., rev., 1984); J. Warrack, *T.* (London, 1973); V. Volkoff, *T.* (Boston and London, 1974); D. Brown, *T.: A Biographical and Critical Study; Vol. I: The Early Years (1840–1874)* (London, 1978), *Vol. II: The Crisis Years (1874–1878)* (London, 1982), and *Vol. III: The Years of Wandering (1878–1885)* (London, 1986); J. Warrack, *T. Ballet Music* (London, 1979); W. Strutte, *T.* (Sydney, 1983); R. Wiley, *T.'s Ballets* (Oxford, 1985); E. Yoffe, *T. in America: The Composer's Visit to Celebrate the Opening of Carnegie Hall in New York City* (N.Y., 1986); H. Zajaczkowski, *T.'s Musical Style* (Ann Arbor, 1987); N. John, ed., *T.: Eugene Onegin* (London, 1988); A. Kendall, *T.: A Biography* (London, 1988); A. Orlova, *T. Day by Day: A Biography in Documents* (ed. by M. Brown and tr. by F. Jonas; Ann Arbor, 1988); idem, *T.: A Self-Portrait* (Oxford, 1990); J. Brenner, *T., ou, La nuit d'octobre: 1840–1893* (Monaco, 1993); C. Casini and M. Delogu, *T.: La vita tutte le composizioni* (Milan, 1993); E. Garden and N. Gotteri, eds., and G. von Meck, tr., *"To my Best Friend": Correspondence Between T. and Nadezha von Meck, 1876–1878* (Oxford, 1993); A. Lischke, *P. I. T.* (Paris, 1993); A. Poznansky, *T.'s Last Days: A Documentary Study* (Oxford, 1996); L. Kearney, ed., *T. and His World* (Princeton, 1998).

Tchaikowsky, André, Polish pianist and composer; b. Warsaw, Nov. 1, 1935; d. Oxford, June 26, 1982. Most of his family fell victim to the Nazis, but he and his grandmother were hidden by a Catholic family in Warsaw (1942–45). After the liberation, he studied piano at the Łódz State Music School (1945–47) and with Emma Tekla Altberg at the Warsaw Cons. (1947–48); he then took an advanced piano course with Lazare Lévy at the Paris Cons. (premier prix, 1950); he subsequently studied piano with Stanislaw Szpinalski and composition with Kazimierz Sikorski at the Warsaw Cons. (1950–55); he made his debut as a pianist in 1955. He went to Paris to study composition with Boulanger (1957), and then to England to continue his studies with Musgrave and later with Hans Keller. Although he continued to make appearances as a pianist, he gave increasing attention to his work as a composer from 1960. An eccentric to the end, he bequeathed his skull to the Royal Shakespeare Co. for use in the graveside scene in *Hamlet* ("Alas, poor André, A fellow of infinite jest"); it made its debut in 1984. His works include the opera *The Merchant of Venice* (1960–82).

Tchakarov, Emil, Bulgarian conductor; b. Burgas, June 29, 1948; d. Paris, Aug. 4, 1991. He received his training at the Bulgarian State Cons. in Sofia, where he conducted its youth orch. (1965–72). From 1968 to 1970 he also was conductor of the Bulgarian TV Chamber Orch. After capturing 3d prize in the Karajan Competition (1971), he pursued training in conducting with Ferrara (1972) and Jochum (1974). In 1974 he became conductor of the Plovdiv State Phil. On Sept. 27, 1979, he made his Metropolitan Opera debut in New York conducting *Eugene Onegin*, and remained on its roster until 1983. In 1985–86 he was chief conductor of the Flanders Phil. in Antwerp. As a guest conductor, he appeared in many music centers around the globe.

Tcherepnin, Alexander (Nikolaievich), distinguished Russian-born American pianist, conductor, and composer, son of **Nikolai (Nikolaievich)**; b. St. Petersburg, Jan. 20, 1899; d. Paris, Sept. 29, 1977. He studied piano as a child with his mother; he was encouraged by his father in his first steps in composition, but did not take formal lessons with him. He composed a short comic opera when he was 12, and a ballet when he was 13; he then produced a number of piano works; composed 14 piano sonatas before he was 19. In 1917 he entered the Petrograd Cons., where he studied theory with Sokolov, and piano with Kobiliansky, but remained there only one school year; then joined his parents in a difficult journey to Tiflis during the Civil War; he took lessons in composition there with Thomas de Hartmann. In 1921 the family went to Paris, where he continued his studies, taking lessons in piano with Philipp and in composition with Vidal. In 1922 he played a concert of his own music in London; in 1923 he was commissioned by Anna Pavlova to write a ballet, *Ajanta's Frescoes*, which she produced in London with her troupe. Tcherepnin progressed rapidly in his career as a pianist and a composer; he played in Germany and Austria and made his first American tour in 1926. Between 1934 and 1937 he made two journeys to the Far East; he gave concerts in China and Japan; numerous Chinese and Japanese composers studied with him; he organized a publishing enterprise in Tokyo for the publication of serious works by young Japanese and Chinese composers. He married a Chinese pianist, Lee Hsien-Ming. Despite his wide travels, he maintained his principal residence in Paris, and remained there during World War II. He resumed his concert career in 1947; he toured the United States in 1948. In 1949 he and his wife joined the faculty of De Paul Univ. in Chicago, and taught there for 15 years. In the meantime, his music became well known; he appeared as a soloist in his piano concertos with orchs. in the United States and Europe. He became a naturalized American citizen in 1958. In 1967 he made his first visit to Russia after nearly a half century abroad. He was elected a member of the National Inst. of Arts and Letters in 1974. In his early works, he followed the traditions of Russian Romantic music; characteristically, his Piano Sonata No. 13, which he wrote as a youth, is entitled *Sonatine romantique*. But as he progressed in his career, he evolved a musical language all his own; he derived his melodic patterns from a symmetrically formed scale of 9 degrees, subdivided into 3 equal sections (e.g., C, D, E flat, E, F sharp, G, G sharp, A sharp, B, C); the harmonic idiom follows a similar intertonal formation; his consistent use of such thematic groupings anticipated the serial method of composition. Furthermore, he developed a type of rhythmic polyphony, based on thematic rhythmic units, which he termed "interpunctus." However, he did not limit himself to these melodic and rhythmic constructions; he also explored the latent resources of folk music, both oriental and European; he was particularly sensitive to the melorhythms of Russian national songs. A composer of remarkable inventive power, he understood the necessity of creating a communicative musical language, and was primarly concerned with enhancing the lyric and dramatic qualities of his music. At the same time, he showed great interest in new musical resources, including electronic sound. His sons, Ivan (Alexandrovich) (1943–98) and Serge (Alexandrovich) (b. Issy-les-Moulineaux, near Paris, Feb. 2, 1941) Tcherepnin, were both noteworthy composers.

WORKS: DRAMATIC: OPERAS: *Ol-Ol* (1925; Weimar, Jan. 31, 1928; rev. 1930); *Die Hochzeit der Sobeide* (1930; Vienna, March 17, 1933); *The Farmer and the Nymph* (Aspen, Colo., Aug. 13, 1952). BALLETS: *Ajanta's Frescoes* (London, Sept. 10, 1923); *Training* (Vienna, June 19, 1935); *Der fahrende Schüler mit dem Teufelsbannen* (1937; score lost during World War II; reconstructed, 1965); *Trepak* (Richmond, Va., Oct. 10, 1938); *La Légende de Razine* (1941); *Le Déjeuner sur l'herbe* (Paris, Oct. 14, 1945); *L'Homme à la peau de léopard* (Monte Carlo, May 5, 1946; in collaboration with A. Honegger and T. Harsányi); *La Colline des fantômes* (1946); *Jardin persan* (1946); *Nuit kurde* (Paris, 1946); *La Femme et son ombre* (Paris, June 14, 1948); *Aux temps des tartares* (Buenos Aires, 1949); *Le gouffre* (1953).

BIBL.: W. Reich, *A. Tscherepnine* (Bonn, 1959; 2d ed., rev., 1970); C.-J. Chang, *A. T., His Influence on Modern Chinese Music* (diss., Columbia Univ. Teachers College, 1983); E. Arias, *A. T.: A Bio-Bibliography* (Westport, Conn., 1988).

Tcherepnin, Nikolai (Nikolaievich), noted Russian conductor, pedagogue, and composer, father of **Alexander (Nikolaievich) Tcherepnin**; b. St. Petersburg, May 15, 1873; d. Issy-les-Moulineaux, near Paris, June 26, 1945. He was a student of Rimsky-Korsakov at the St. Petersburg Cons. (1895–98); in 1905 he was appointed to its faculty; he taught orchestration and conducting; Prokofiev was among his students. In 1908 he became a conductor at the Marinsky Theater and the Imperial Opera in St. Petersburg; he was conductor of the initial season of the Ballets Russes in Paris in 1909. After the Russian Revolution in 1917, he served as director of the Tiflis Cons. (1918–21); he then settled in Paris, where he was director of the Russian Cons. (1925–29; 1938–45). His music embodies the best elements of the Russian national school; it is melodious and harmonious; lyrical and gently dynamic; in some of his works, there is a coloristic quality suggesting French impressionistic influence.

WORKS: DRAMATIC: OPERAS: *Svat* (1930); *Vanka* (1932; Belgrade, 1935). BALLETS: *Le pavillon d'Armide* (St. Petersburg, Nov. 25, 1907); *Narcisse et Echo* (Monte Carlo, April 26, 1911); *Le Masque de la Mort Rouge* (Petrograd, Jan. 29, 1916); *Dionysus* (1922); *Russian Fairy Tale* (1923); *Romance of the Mummy* (1924). OTHER: Realization and completion of Mussorgsky's opera *The Fair at Sorochinsk* (Monte Carlo, March 17, 1923).

Tear, Robert, distinguished Welsh tenor and conductor; b. Barry, Glamorgan, March 8, 1939. He was a choral scholar at King's College, Cambridge, where he graduated in English (1957–61); he received vocal instruction from Julian Kimbell. He became a lay vicar at St. Paul's Cathedral in London in 1960; he also was active with the Ambrosian Singers. In 1963 he made his operatic debut as Quint in Britten's *The Turn of the Screw* with the English Opera Group in London, where he made regular appearances until 1971; he also sang at London's Covent Garden, where he created the role of Dov in Tippett's *The Knot Garden* in 1970; he was chosen to sing the role of the Painter in the first complete performance of Berg's *Lulu* in Paris in 1979; in 1984 he appeared in the premiere of Tippett's *The Mask of Time* in Boston; in 1991 he sang the title role in Penderecki's *Ubu rex* in Munich. He made guest appearances with various opera houses at home and abroad; he also won particular renown as a concert artist; after making his debut as a conductor in Minneapolis in 1985, he appeared as a guest conductor with many orchs. In 1986 he was appointed to the International Chair of Vocal Studies at the Royal Academy of Music in London. From 1992 to 1994 he was artistic director of the vocal faculty of the London Royal Schools of Music. In 1984 he was made a Commander of the Order of the British Empire. His autobiography was publ. as *Tear Here* (London, 1990).

Tebaldi, Renata, celebrated Italian soprano; b. Pesaro, Feb. 1, 1922. Her mother, a nurse, took her to Langhirano after the breakup of her marriage to a philandering cellist. Renata was stricken with poliomyelitis when she was 3. After initial vocal training from Giuseppina Passani, she studied with Ettore Campogaliani at the Parma Cons. (1937–40) and with Carmen Melis at the Pesaro Cons. (1940–43). She made her operatic debut in Rovigo as Elena in Boito's *Mefistofele* in 1944. In 1946 Toscanini chose her as one of his artists for the reopening concert at La Scala in Milan, and she subsequently became one of its leading sopranos. She made her first appearance in England in 1950 with the visiting La Scala company at London's Covent Garden as Desdemona; also in 1950 she sang Aida with the San Francisco Opera. On Jan. 31, 1955, she made her Metropolitan Opera debut in New York as Desdemona in Verdi's *Otello*; she continued to appear regularly there until 1973. She toured Russia in 1975 and 1976. Her repertoire was almost exclusively Italian; she excelled in both lyric and dramatic roles and was particularly successful as Violetta, Tosca, Mimi, and Madame Butterfly. She also sang the role of Eva in *Die Meistersinger von Nürnberg*. On Nov. 3, 1958, she was the subject of a cover story in *Time* magazine.

BIBL.: K. Harris, *R. T.: An Authorized Biography* (N.Y., 1974); C. Casanova, *R. T.: The Voice of an Angel* (Dallas, 1995).

Tebaldini, Giovanni, Italian conductor, music scholar, and composer; b. Brescia, Sept. 7, 1864; d. San Benedetto del Tronto, May 11, 1952. He studied with Ponchielli, Panzini, and Amelli at the Milan Cons. (1883–85) and with Haller and Haberl at the Regensburg School for Church Music (1888). He served as maestro of the Schola Cantorum at San Marco in Venice (1889–93), maestro di cappella at the Basilica of S. Antonio in Padua (1894–97), and director of the Parma Cons. (1897–1902). After teaching at the Cons. di San Pietro a Majella in Naples (1925–30), he went to Genoa, where he was appointed director of the Ateneo Musicale (1931). His specialty was Italian sacred music, but he gained sensational prominence when he publ. an article provocatively entitled "Telepatia musicale" (*Rivista Musicale Italiana*, March 1909), in which he cited thematic similarities between the opera *Cassandra* (1905) by the relatively obscure Italian composer Vittorio Gnecchi and *Elektra* by Richard Strauss, written considerably later, implying a "telepathic" plagiarism on the part of Strauss. However, the juxtaposition of musical examples from both operas proved specious and failed to support Tebaldini's contention.

WRITINGS: *La musica sacra in Italia* (Milan, 1894); *Gasparo Spontini* (Recanati, 1924); *Ildebrando Pizzetti* (Parma, 1931); also *Metodo teorico pratico per organo* (with Enrico Bossi; Milan, 1897).

Teed, Roy (Norman), English pianist, organist, teacher, and composer; b. Herne Bay, Kent, May 18, 1928. He studied composition with Lennox Berkeley, piano with Virginia McLean, and harmony and counterpoint with Paul Steinitz at the Royal Academy of Music in London (1949–53); from 1966 to 1992 he was on its faculty; he also taught at the Colchester Inst. Music School (1966–79). Among his works is the opera *The Overcoat* (1988–93).

Te Kanawa, Dame Kiri, brilliant New Zealand soprano; b. Gisborne, March 6, 1944. Her father was an indigenous Maori who traced his ancestry to the legendary warrior Te Kanawa; her mother was Irish. She attended Catholic schools in Auckland, and was coached in singing by a nun. She was sent to Melbourne to compete in a radio show; she won 1st prize in the Melbourne *Sun* contest. In 1966 she received a grant for study in London with Vera Rozsa. She made her operatic debut at the Camden Festival in 1969 in Rossini's *La Donna del Lago*; she first appeared at London's Covent Garden in a minor role that same year, and then as the Countess in *Le nozze di Figaro* in 1971. She made her U.S. debut in the same role with the Santa Fe Opera in 1971; it became one of her most remarkable interpretations. She sang it again with the San Francisco Opera in 1972. A proverbial *coup de théâtre* in her career came on Feb. 9, 1974, when she was called upon to substitute at a few hours' notice for the ailing Teresa Stratas in the part of Desdemona in Verdi's *Otello* at the Metropolitan Opera in New York; it was a triumphant achievement, winning for her unanimous praise. She also sang in the film version of *Le nozze di Figaro*. In 1977 she appeared as Pamina in *Die Zauberflöte* at the Paris Opéra. On Dec. 31, 1977, she took the role of Rosalinde in a Covent Garden production of *Die Fledermaus*, which was televised in the United States. In 1990 she sang Strauss's Countess at the San Francisco Opera. She was a soloist in the premiere of Paul McCartney's *Liverpool Oratorio* in 1991. After singing Mozart's Countess at the Metropolitan Opera in 1992, she returned there in that role in 1997. In 1998 she sang Strauss's Countess at the Glyndebourne Festival.

Te Kanawa excelled equally as a subtle and artistic interpreter of lyric roles in Mozart's operas and in dramatic representations of Verdi's operas. Among her other distinguished roles were the Marschallin and Arabella. She also won renown as a concert artist. In later years she expanded her repertoire to include popular fare, including songs by Cole Porter and Leonard Bernstein's *West Side Story*. Hailed as a prima donna assoluta, she pursued one of the most successful international operatic and concert careers of her day. In 1981 she sang at the royal wedding of Prince Charles and Lady Diana Spencer in London, a performance televised around the globe. In 1973 she was made an Officer of the Order of the British Empire; in 1982 she was named a Dame Commander of the Order of the British Empire.

BIBL.: D. Fingleton, *K. T. K.* (N.Y., 1983).

Telemann, Georg Philipp, greatly significant German composer; b. Magdeburg, March 14, 1681; d. Hamburg, June 25, 1767. He received his academic training at a local school, and also learned to play keyboard instruments and the violin; he acquired knowledge of music theory from the cantor Benedikt Christiani. He subsequently attended the Gymnasium Andreanum in Hildesheim, where he became active in student performances of German cantatas. In 1701 he entered the Univ. of Leipzig as a student of jurisprudence; in 1702 he organized a collegium musicum there; later he was appointed music director of the Leipzig Opera, where he used the services of his student singers and instrumentalists. In 1705 he went to Sorau as Kapellmeister to the court of Count Erdmann II of Promnitz. In 1708 he was appointed Konzertmeister to the court orch. in Eisenach; later he was named Kapellmeister there. In 1709 he married Louise Eberlin, a musician's daughter, but she died in 1711 in childbirth. In 1712 Telemann was appointed music director of the city of Frankfurt am Main; there he wrote a quantity of sacred music as well as secular works for the public concerts given by the Frauenstein Society, of which he served as director. In 1714 he married Maria Katharina Textor, the daughter of a local town clerk. They had 8 sons and 2 daughters, of whom only a few survived infancy. His wife later abandoned him for a Swedish army officer. In 1721 he received the post of music director of 5 churches in Hamburg, which became the center of his important activities as composer and music administrator. In 1722 Telemann was appointed music director of the Hamburg Opera, a post he held until 1738. During his tenure he wrote a number of operas for production there, and also staged several works by Handel and Keiser. In 1737–38 he visited France. His eyesight began to fail as he grew older; his great contemporaries Bach and Handel suffered from the same infirmity. An extraordinarily prolific composer, Telemann mastered both the German and the Italian styles of composition prevalent in his day. While he never approached the greatness of genius of Bach and Handel, he nevertheless became an exemplar of the German Baroque at its grandest development. According to Telemann's own account, he composed about 20 operas for Leipzig, 4 for Weissenfels, 2 for Bayreuth, and 3 operettas for Eisenach. He lists 35 operas for Hamburg, but included in this list are preludes, intermezzi, and postludes. His grandson, Georg Michael Telemann (b. Plon, April 20, 1748; d. Riga, March 4, 1831), was also a composer and writer on music.

WORKS: DRAMATIC: OPERAS (all 1st perf. in Hamburg): *Der gedultige Socrates* (Jan. 28, 1721); *Ulysses* (1721; in collaboration with Vogler); *Sieg der Schönheit* (1722; later performed as *Gensericus*); *Belsazar* (July 19, 1723; 2d version, Sept. 30, 1723); *Der Beschluss des Carnevals* (1724; in collaboration with Campara and Conti); *Omphale* (1724); *Der neu-modische Liebhaber Damon* (June 1724); *Cimbriens allgemeines Frolocken* (Feb. 17, 1725); *Pimpinone oder Die ungleiche Heyrath*, intermezzo (Sept. 27, 1725); *La Capricciosa e il Credula*, intermezzo (1725); *Adelheid* (Feb. 17, 1727); *Buffonet und Alga*, intermezzo (May 14, 1727); *Calypso* (1727); *Sancio* (1727); *Die verkehrte Welt* (1728); *Miriways* (May 26, 1728); *Emma und Eginhard* (1728); *Aesopus* (Feb. 28, 1729); *Flavius Bertaridus, König der Langobarden* (Nov. 23, 1729); *Margaretha, Königin in Castilien* (Aug. 10, 1730); *Die Flucht des Aeneas* (Nov. 19, 1731); *Judith, Gemahlin Kayser Ludewig des Frommen* (Nov. 27, 1732; in collaboration with Chelleri); *Orasia oder Die rachgierige Liebe* (Oct. 1736). ORATORIOS: *Der königliche Prophete David als ein Fürbild unseres Heilands Jesu* (1718; not extant); *Freundschaft geget über Liebe* (1720; not extant); *Donnerode* (1756–60); *Sing, unsterbliche Seele, an Mirjam und deine Wehmut*, after Klopstock's *Der Messias* (1759); *Das befreite Israel* (1759); *Die Hirten bei der Krippe zu Bethlehem* (1759); *Die Auferstehung und Himmelfahrt Jesu* (1760); *Der Tag des Gerichts* (1762).

BIBL.: Telemann's autobiography of 1718 was publ. in J. Mattheson, *Grosse Generalbassschule* (Hamburg, 1731); his autobiography of 1739 was publ. in J. Mattheson, *Grundlage einer Ehren-Pforte* (Hamburg, 1740; new ed. by M. Schneider, Berlin, 1910); both of these, plus his autobiographical letter to Walther of 1729, have been republ. in W. Kahl, *Selbstbiographien deutscher Musiker des XVIII. Jahrhunderts* (Cologne, 1948). See also the following: B. Schmid, ed., *Herr G. P. T.: Lebenslauf* (Nuremberg, c.1745; in Ger. and Fr.); M. Frey, *G. P. T.s Singe-, Spiel- und Generalbass-Übungen* (Zürich, 1922); E. Valentin, *G. P. T.* (Burg, 1931; 3d ed., 1952); W. Menke, *Das Vokalwerk G. P. T.s* (Kassel, 1942); C. Rhea, *The Sacred Oratorios of G. P. T.* (diss., Florida State Univ., 1958); E. Valentin, *T. in seiner Zeit* (Hamburg, 1960); R. Petzoldt, *T. und seine Zeitgenossen* (Magdeburg, 1966); R. Petzoldt, *G. P. T.: Leben und Werk* (Leipzig, 1967; in Eng., 1974); K. Zauft, *T.s Liedschaffen und seine Bedeutung für die Entwicklung des deutschen Liedes in der 1. Hälfte des 18. Jahrhunderts* (Magdeburg, 1967); *G. P. T., Leben und Werk: Beiträge zur gleichnamigen Ausstellung* (Magdeburg, 1967); M. Peckham, *The Operas of G. P. T.* (diss., Columbia Univ., 1969); I. Allihn, *G. P. T. und J. J. Quantz* (Magdeburg, 1971); H. Grosse and H. Jung, eds., *G. P. T., Briefwechsel* (Leipzig, 1972); W. Maertens, *T. Kapitänsmusiken* (diss., Univ. of Halle, 1975); E. Klessmann, *T. in Hamburg* (Hamburg, 1980); B. Stewart, *G. P. T. in Hamburg: Social and Cultural Background and Its Musical Expression* (diss., Stanford Univ., 1985); W. Hirschmann, *Studien zum Konzertschaffen von G. P. T.* (Kassel and N.Y., 1986); W. Menke, *G. P. T.: Leben, Werk und Umwelt in Bilddokumenten* (Wilhelmshaven, 1987).

Temirkanov, Yuri, outstanding Russian conductor; b. Nalchik, Dec. 10, 1938. He received his training at the Leningrad Cons., where he graduated as a violinist in 1962 and as a conductor in 1965. In 1965 he made his first appearance as a conductor at the Leningrad Opera. After capturing 1st prize in the All-Union Conductors' Competition in 1966, he appeared as a guest conductor with many Russian orchs. and opera houses. From 1968 to 1976 he was music director of the Leningrad Sym. Orch. He also appeared as a guest conductor abroad, making his Salzburg Festival debut in 1971 with the Vienna Phil. In 1977 he made his London debut as a guest conductor with the Royal Phil., and subsequently appeared with the major British orchs. From 1977 to 1988 he was artistic director of the Kirov Opera and Ballet, which he also led on tours. In 1978 he made a tour of the United States. In 1979 he was named principal guest conductor of the Royal Phil. In 1988 he became chief conductor of the Leningrad (later St. Petersburg) Phil. In 1992 he was made principal conductor of the Royal Phil. while retaining his position in St. Petersburg. During the 1992–93 season, he conducted the St. Petersburg Phil. on a tour of Europe and Japan and the Royal Phil. on a tour of the United States and Germany. In 1994 he became principal guest conductor of the Dresden Phil. He also was music director designate (1998–2000) and music director (from 2000) of the Baltimore Sym. Orch. Temirkanov has won particular renown for his brilliant and idiomatic performances of works from the Russian repertoire.

Templeton, John, Scottish tenor; b. Riccarton, near Kilmarnock, July 30, 1802; d. New Hampton, near London, July 2, 1886. He sang in various churches in Edinburgh, then went to London, where he took lessons in singing with Welch, De Pinna, and Tom Cooke. On Oct. 13, 1831, he made his London debut at Drury Lane as Belville in Sheild's *Rosina*; subsequently he was a regular member there. Maria Malibran selected him as tenor for her operatic appearances in London (1833–35). In 1842 he was in Paris; during the season of 1845–46, he made an American tour announced as "Templeton Entertainment," singing folk songs of Great Britain. His commentaries and reminiscences were publ. as *A Musical Entertainment* (Boston, 1845). He retired in 1852.

BIBL.: W. Husk, ed., *T. and Malibran. Reminiscences* (London, 1880).

Tenducci, Giusto Ferdinando, celebrated Italian castrato soprano, nicknamed "Triorchis" (triple-testicled); b. Siena, c.1735; d. Genoa, Jan. 25, 1790. He made appearances in Venice and Naples before going to London in 1758, where he sang at the King's Theatre until 1760; after a stay in a debtor's prison, he resumed his career and secured a notable success as Arbaces in the premiere of Arne's *Artaxerxes* in 1762; he was again active at the King's Theatre (1763–66). He then went to Ireland, where he contracted a marriage with his 16-year-old pupil Dora Maunsell in Cork; outraged members of her family had him jailed and his new bride spirited away; shortly afterward, however, the 2 were reunited and allegedly produced 2 children. After a sojourn in Edinburgh, he returned to England in 1770 and sang at the Worcester Three Choirs Festival; he then was a featured artist in the Bach-Abel Concerts in London. By 1778 he was in Paris; he sang again in London in 1785. He adapted 4 operas for the Dublin stage, and also wrote English, French, and Italian songs. His wife is reputed to have been the author of the book *A True Genuine Narrative of Mr and Mrs Tenducci* (1768).

Tennstedt, Klaus, brilliant German conductor; b. Merseburg, June 6, 1926; d. Kiel, Jan. 11, 1998. He studied piano, violin, and theory at the Leipzig Cons. In 1948 he became concertmaster in Halle an der Saale, beginning his career as a conductor there in 1953; after serving as a conductor at the Dresden State Opera (1958–62), he was conductor in Schwerin (1962–71); he also appeared as a guest conductor throughout East Germany, Eastern Europe, and the Soviet Union. In 1971 he settled in the West; after guest engagements in Sweden, he served as Generalmusikdirektor of the Kiel Opera (1972–76). In 1974 he made a remarkable North American debut as a guest conductor with the Toronto Sym. Orch., and also appeared with the Boston Sym. Orch., which led to numerous engagements with other major U.S. orchs. In 1976 he made his British debut as a guest conductor of the London Sym. Orch. He was chief conductor of the North German Radio Sym. Orch. in Hamburg (1979–81); he was also principal guest conductor of the Minnesota Orch. in Minneapolis (1979–83). From 1980 to 1983 he was principal guest conductor of the London Phil., and then served as its principal conductor from 1983 until a diagnosis of throat cancer compelled him to give up his duties in 1987. He continued to make guest appearances in subsequent seasons. On Dec. 14, 1983, he made his Metropolitan Opera debut in New York conducting *Fidelio*. In 1994 his worsening health compelled him to announce that he would no longer conduct in public. His appearances around the globe elicited exceptional critical acclaim; he was ranked among the foremost interpreters of the Austro-German repertoire of his day.

Tenschert, Roland, Austrian musicologist; b. Podersam, Bohemia, April 5, 1894; d. Vienna, April 3, 1970. He studied at the Leipzig Cons. (1913–15) and received instruction in musicology from Adler at the Univ. of Vienna (Ph.D., 1921); he also studied composition with Schoenberg and conducting with L. Kaiser. He was librarian at the Salzburg Mozarteum (1926–31) and prof. of music history at the Vienna Academy of Music (from 1945).

WRITINGS: *Mozart: Ein Künstlerleben in Bildern und Dokumenten* (Leipzig, 1931); *Mozart* (Leipzig, 1931); *Joseph Haydn* (Berlin, 1932); *Musikerbrevier* (Vienna, 1940); *Mozart: Ein Leben für die Oper* (Vienna, 1941); *Dreimal sieben Variationen über das Thema Richard Strauss* (Vienna, 1944; 2d ed., 1945); *Frauen um Haydn* (Vienna, 1946); *Salzburg und seine Festspiele* (Vienna, 1947); *Vater Hellmesberger: ein Kapitel Wiener Musikerhumor* (Vienna, 1947); *Richard Strauss und Wien, Eine Wahlverwandtschaft* (Vienna, 1949); *Wolfgang Amadeus Mozart* (Salzburg, 1951; Eng. tr., 1952); *Christoph Willibald Gluck: der grosse Reformer der Oper* (Olten and Freiburg im Breisgau, 1951).

BIBL.: *E. Tenschert, Musik als Lebensinhalt* (Vienna, 1971).

Teodorini, Elena, Romanian soprano; b. Craiova, March 25, 1857; d. Bucharest, Feb. 27, 1926. She studied piano with Fumagalli and voice with Sangiovanni at the Milan Cons.; she also received vocal instruction from G. Stephănescu at the Bucharest Cons. In 1877 she commenced her career with appearances in Italian provincial theaters as a contralto, but her voice gradually changed to a mezzo-soprano of wide range. She made her debut at Milan's La Scala as Gounod's Marguerite on March 20, 1880; she subsequently sang in various South American music centers; she was particularly associated with the Italian Opera and the National Opera in Bucharest. In 1904 she retired from the operatic stage and became a teacher in Paris; after teaching in Buenos Aires (1909–16) and Rio de Janeiro (1916–23), she settled in Bucharest. Her most notable pupil was Bidú Sayão. Among her prominent roles were Rosina, Donna Anna, Amelia, Lucrezia Borgia, Amneris, and Gioconda. In 1964 the Romanian government issued a postage stamp in her honor bearing her stage portrait.

BIBL.: V. Cosma, *Cîtăreata E. T.* (Bucharest, 1962).

Terentieva, Nina (Nikolaievna), Russian mezzo-soprano; b. Kusa, Jan. 9, 1946. She received vocal training at the Leningrad Cons. From 1971 to 1977 she was a member of the Kirov Opera in Leningrad, and then appeared with the Bolshoi Theater in Moscow from 1979. She appeared at the Vienna State Opera from 1987. In 1990 she sang Eboli in Los Angeles, a role she reprised at her Metropolitan Opera debut in New York on March 19, 1992, and at the San Francisco Opera that same year. In 1995 she was engaged as Amneris at London's Covent Garden, a role she sang in San Francisco in 1997. She also was a guest artist of opera houses in Milan, Berlin, Hamburg, Munich, Bordeaux, and Buenos Aires. Among her other roles were Marta, Lubasha, Lubava, Marina, Azucena, Dalila, and Santuzza.

Terfel, Bryn, outstanding Welsh bass-baritone; b. Pantglas, Nov. 9, 1965. He was a student of Arthur Reckless and Rudolf Piernay at the Guildhall School of Music in London (1984–89), winning the Kathleen Ferrier Memorial Scholarship (1988) and the Gold Medal (1989). After winning the Lieder Prize at the Cardiff Singer of the World Competition in 1989, he made his operatic debut as Guglielmo with the Welsh National Opera in Cardiff in 1990. In 1991 he sang Mozart's Figaro at his first appearance with the English National Opera in London, a role he also sang that same year at his U.S. debut in Santa Fe. In 1992 he appeared for the first time at the Salzburg Easter Festival as the Spirit Messenger in *Die Frau ohne Schatten*; that same year he also made his Salzburg Festival debut as Jochanaan and his first appearance at London's Covent Garden as Massetto. In 1993 he made his debut with the Lyric Opera of Chicago as Donner and at the Vienna State Opera as Mozart's Figaro; he also appeared as Verdi's Ford with the Welsh National Opera. In 1994 he returned to the Vienna State Opera as Offenbach's 4 villains, at Covent Garden as Mozart's Figaro, and at the Salzburg Festival as Leporello. In 1994 he made an impressive appearance in the closing night gala concert of the 100th annivesary season of the London Promenade Concerts as soloist with Andrew Davis and the BBC Sym. Orch. His highly acclaimed Metropolitan Opera debut in New York followed on Oct. 19, 1994, as Mozart's Figaro. On Oct. 24, 1994, he made his N.Y. recital debut at Alice Tully Hall. In 1995 he returned to the Lyric Opera of Chicago and at the Metropolitan Opera as Leporello. He portrayed Nick Shadow at the Welsh National Opera in 1996. In 1997 he was engaged as Mozart's Figaro at Milan's La Scala and the San Francisco Opera, and as Jochanaan at Covent Garden. He appeared as Mozart's Figaro at the Metropolitan Opera and as Scarpia at the Netherlands Opera in Amsterdam in 1998. In addition to his operatic repertoire, Terfel has won a wide following for his concert engagements, in a repertoire extending from Bach to Walton.

Ternina, Milka, outstanding Croatian soprano; b. Doljnji, Moslavina, Dec. 19, 1863; d. Zagreb, May 18, 1941. She studied with Ida Winterberg in Zagreb and then with Gansbacher at the Vienna Cons. (1880–82). She made her operatic debut as Amelia in *Un ballo in maschera* in Zagreb (1882), then sang in Leipzig (1883–84), Graz (1884–86), and Bremen (1886–89). In 1889 she appeared as a guest artist at the Hamburg Opera, joining its roster in 1890; she also was a member of the Munich Court Opera (1890–99), where she distinguished herself as a Wagnerian singer. She was engaged by Walter Damrosch for his German Opera Co. in New York, and made her American debut as Elsa in *Lohengrin* in Boston on March 4, 1896; she also appeared at Covent Garden, London, as Isolde (June 3, 1898); after a series of successes at the Bayreuth Festivals (1899), she made her Metropolitan Opera debut in New York as Elisabeth on Jan. 27, 1900, and sang there until 1904 (1902–03 season excepted); she sang Tosca at the American premiere (Feb. 4, 1901) and Kundry in *Parsifal* (Dec. 24, 1903). She made her farewell stage appearance as Sieglinde in Munich on Aug. 19, 1906. In subsequent years, she was active as a teacher, giving instruction at the Inst. of Musical Art in New York and later in Zagreb, where she was the mentor of Zinka Milanov. She was renowned for her portrayals of Isolde and Beethoven's Leonore.

Terradellas, Domingo (Miguel Bernabe), distinguished Spanish composer who became best known via his Italianized name of Domenico Terradeglias; b. Barcelona (baptized), Feb. 13, 1713; d. Rome, May 20, 1751. He began his musical training in Barcelona, then studied at the Cons. dei Poveri di Gesù Cristo in Naples (1732–38); while still a student, he produced his first significant score, the oratorio *Giuseppe riconosciuto* (1736). He gained an outstanding success with his opera *Merope* (Rome, Jan. 3, 1743). From 1743 to 1745 he was active at the Spanish church of Santiago y S. Ildefonso in Rome, and devoted much time to writing sacred music. During the 1746–47 season, he composed 2 operas for the King's Theatre in London; he then returned to the Continent; he was again in Italy by 1750. His last opera, *Sesostri re d'Egitto*, scored a major success at its premiere in Rome (Carnival 1751).

WORKS: DRAMATIC: OPERAS: *Astarto* (Rome, Carnival 1739); *Gli intrighi delle cantarine* (Naples, 1740); *Issipile* (Florence, 1741 or 1742); *Merope* (Rome, Jan. 3, 1743); *Artaserse* (Venice, Carnival 1744); *Semiramide riconosciuta* (Florence, Carnival 1746); *Mitridate* (London, Dec. 2, 1746); *Bellerofonte* (London, March 24, 1747); *Didone abbandonata* (Turin, Carnival 1750); *Imeneo in Atene* (Venice, May 6, 1750); *Sesostri re d'Egitto* (Rome, Carnival 1751); other stage works; 2 oratorios (Naples, 1736 and 1739).

Terrasse, Claude (Antoine), French composer; b. Grand-Lemps, near Grenoble, Jan. 27, 1867; d. Paris, June 30, 1923. He studied at the Lyons Cons. and at the École Niedermeyer in Paris. From 1888 to 1895 he was church organist in Arcachon, then in Paris until 1899, where he began to write for the stage, producing a series of successful operettas. The best known are *Les Travaux d'Hercule* (March 7, 1901), *Le Sire de Vergy* (April 16, 1903), *Monsieur de la Palisse* (Nov. 2, 1904), *La Marquise et le marmiton* (Dec. 11, 1907), *Le Coq d'Inde* (April 6, 1909), *Le Mariage de Télémaque* (May 4, 1910), *Les Transatlantiques* (May 20, 1911), and *Cartouche* (March 9, 1912). His other works include the ballet *Les lucioles* (Dec. 28, 1910).

Tervani, Irma, Finnish mezzo-soprano; b. Helsinki, June 4, 1887; d. Berlin, Oct. 29, 1936. She received her primary training with her mother, the soprano Emmy Strömer-Ackté, then studied voice in Paris and Dresden. She made her operatic debut with the Dresden Court Opera in 1908 as Dalila, remaining on its roster until 1932. She gained renown through her appearance in the role of Carmen opposite Caruso in Frankfurt am Main in 1910.

Terzakis, Dimitri, Greek composer and teacher; b. Athens, March 12, 1938. He studied composition with Iannis Papaioannou at the Hellenic Cons. in Athens (1957–64), then pursued studies with Bernd Alois Zimmermann at the Cologne Hochschule für Musik (diploma, 1970); he also studied Byzantine music and at Mount Athos. He was cofounder of the Greek Soc. for Contemporary Music (1966). He lectured on Byzantine music and instrumentation at the Robert Schumann Inst. in Düsseldorf (from 1974), where he taught composition at the Hochschule für Musik (1987–93). From 1990 he taught composition at the Bern Hochschule für Musik and from 1994 he was prof. of composition at the Leipzig Hochschule für Musik. In 1980 he founded the International Inst. of Research on the Relations Between Occidental and Southeast-European Music in Nauplia, Greece. Terzaki's music steers a resolute course in the cosmopolitan avant-garde, leaving no tonal stone unturned; ancestral Grecian ethos is present, however, both in the titles and in the modalities of his output. In 1994 he began to compose monophonic scores. Among his works are *Torquemada,* opera (1974–76), *Circus Universal,* chamber opera (1975), and *Hermes,* opera (1983–84); also *Passionen*, oratorio (1978–79).

Terziani, Eugenio, Italian conductor, teacher, and composer; b. Rome, July 29, 1824; d. there, June 30, 1889. He studied with Mercadante at the Naples Cons. and later with Baini in Rome. At the age of 19 he produced an oratorio, *La caduta di Gerico* (Rome, March 31, 1844), followed by the operas *Giovanna regina di Napoli* (Ferrara, 1844) and *Alfredo* (Rome, Feb. 21, 1852). He was conductor in Rome at the Teatro Apollo (1847–69), at La Scala in Milan (1867–71), and again in Rome (1871–75), where he then taught composition and singing at the Liceo Musicale di S. Cecilia (from 1875). He also wrote the opera *L'assedio di Firenze* (Rome, Feb. 24, 1883), 2 ballets, including *Una Silfide a Pechino* (Rome, Dec. 26, 1859).

Teschemacher, Margarete, German soprano; b. Cologne, March 3, 1903; d. Bad Wiesse, May 19, 1959. She was trained in Cologne. After making her operatic debut in Cologne as Micaela (1924), she sang in Aachen (1925–27), Dortmund (1927–28), Mannheim (1928–31), and Stuttgart (1931–34). From 1935 to 1946 she was a member of the Dresden State Opera, where Strauss chose her to create his Daphne in 1938. She also made appearances at London's Covent Garden (debut as Pamina, 1931) and at Buenos Aires's Teatro Colón (1934). From 1947 to 1952 she sang in Düsseldorf. Among her other roles were Donna Elvira, Countess Almaviva, Sieglinde, Senta, Jenůfa, and Arabella.

Tesi-Tramontini, Vittoria, famous Italian contralto, known as **La Moretta**; b. Florence, Feb. 13, 1700; d. Vienna, May 9, 1775. She received her instruction in Florence and Bologna, appearing on the stage at the age of 16 in Parma in Dafni; she then was engaged in Venice (1718–19). She sang in Italy every year, and also appeared in Madrid (1739). In 1748 she sang the title role in Gluck's *Semiramide riconosciuta* in Vienna, where she continued to appear until 1751; she then devoted herself to teaching. She was married to one Tramontini, a barber by trade, and adopted the professional name Tesi-Tramontini. She was remarkably free in her morals, and many stories, in which it is impossible to separate truth from invention, were circulated about her life. Her letters to a priest were publ. by Benedetto Croce in his book *Un Prelato e una cantante del secolo XVIII* (Bari, 1946).

Tess (real name, **Tesscorolo**), **Giulia,** noted Italian mezzo-soprano, later soprano; b. Verona, Feb. 9, 1889; d. Milan, March 17, 1976. She studied with Bottagisio in Verona. She made her operatic debut as a mezzo-soprano in 1904 in Prato; she later sang soprano roles after being encouraged by Battistini. In 1922 she was invited by Toscanini to sing at La Scala in Milan, where she created the role of Jaele in Pizzetti's *Debora e Jaele*. She continued to sing there with great distinction until 1936; she then was director of stage craft at the Florence Centro di Avviamento al Teatro Lirico (1940–42), at the Bologna Cons. (1941–46), and at the La Scala opera school (from 1946). Her students included Tagliavini and Barbieri; she also produced opera at La Scala and other Italian opera houses. She was married to the conductor Giacomo Armani (1868–1954). In addition to the Italian repertoire, she gained distinction as an interpreter of roles by Richard Strauss, excelling as Salome and Elektra.

Tetrazzini, Eva, Italian soprano, sister of **Luisa Tetrazzini**; b. Milan, March, 1862; d. Salsomaggiore, Oct. 27, 1938. She studied with Ceccherini in Florence, where she made her operatic debut in 1882 as Marguerite in *Faust*. She sang Desdemona in Verdi's *Otello* at its first American production (N.Y., April 16, 1888). On May 15, 1887, she married the conductor Cleofonte Campanini. She sang with the Manhattan Opera in New York in 1908; then returned to Italy.

Tetrazzini, Luisa (Luigia), celebrated Italian soprano, sister of **Eva Tetrazzini**; b. Florence, June 28, 1871; d. Milan, April 28, 1940. She learned the words and music of several operas by listening to her sister; she then studied at the Liceo Musicale in Florence with Ceccherini. She made her operatic debut as Inez in *L'Africaine* in Florence (1890), then sang in Europe and traveled with various opera companies in South America. In 1904 she made her U.S. debut at the Tivoli Opera House in San Francisco. She made her London debut at Covent Garden as Violetta on Nov. 2, 1907. She was then engaged by Hammerstein to sing with his Manhattan Opera House in New York, where she sang Violetta on Jan. 15, 1908; she remained with the company until it closed in 1910; she subsequently appeared for a single season at the Metropolitan Opera (1911–12), making her debut there on Dec. 27, 1911, as Lucia. After singing at the Chicago Grand Opera (1911–13), she toured as a concert artist. She made the first broadcast on the British radio in 1925; her last American appearance was in New York in 1931. She then taught in Milan. Her fame was worldwide, and her name became a household word, glorified even in food, as in Turkey Tetrazzini. She publ. *My Life of Song* (London, 1921) and *How to Sing* (N.Y., 1923). She acquired a great fortune, but died in poverty.

BIBL.: C. Gattley, *L. T.: The Florentine Nightingale* (Portland, Oreg., 1995).

Teyber, family of Austrian musicians:

(1) Matthäus Teyber, violinist; b. Weinzettel, c.1711; d. Vienna, Sept. 6, 1785. He settled in Vienna, where he entered the Kapelle of the Empress Elisabeth Christine in 1741; he was a court musician from 1757. His family, who became friendly with the Mozart family, included 4 children who distinguished themselves as musicians.

(2) Elisabeth Teyber, soprano; b. Vienna (baptized), Sept. 16, 1744; d. there, May 9, 1816. She was a pupil of Haase and Tesi, appearing in Haase's *Partenope* in Vienna in 1767, then was successful in Naples, Bologna, Milan, Turin, and other Italian opera centers; she also sang in Russia.

(3) Anton Teyber, pianist, organist, cellist, and composer; b. Vienna, Sept. 8, 1754; d. there, Nov. 18, 1822. He studied in Vienna and with Padre Martini in Bologna. After touring with his sister in Italy, and appearing in Spain and Portugal, he returned to Vienna about 1781. He was 1st organist at the Dresden Hofkapelle (1787–91), then went again to Vienna as Weigl's deputy at the National-Hoftheater, a position that was soon abolished; however, he petitioned the emperor and was named court composer and keyboard teacher to the imperial children in 1793. His compositions include a melodrama, *Zermes (Zerbes) und Mirabelle* (Vienna, July 15, 1779).

(4) Franz Teyber, organist, conductor, cellist, bass singer, and composer; b. Vienna, Nov. 15, 1756; d. there, Oct. 22, 1810. He studied with his father and with Wagenseil. After touring in Swabia, Switzerland, and Baden, he became a conductor and composer with Schikaneder's itinerant opera troupe in 1786. After pursuing his career in Karlsruhe (1788–89), in Cologne (1791–93), and in Regensburg, Augsburg, and Bern (1796–98), he returned to Vienna. He wrote the successful opera *Alexander* for the opening of the Theater an der Wien (June 13, 1801), where he was active until 1805; he composed for the Leopoldstadt Theater (1807–10); he was made organist at St. Stephen's Cathedral in 1809 and court organist in 1810.

WORKS: DRAMATIC (all 1st perf. in Vienna unless otherwise given): *Laura Rosetti*, opera (Pressburg, Aug. 1785); *Die Dorfdeputierten*, comic opera (Dec. 18, 1785); *Abelheid von Veltheim*, Singspiel (Karlsruhe, 1788); *Fernando und Jariko oder Die Indianer*, Singspiel (Sept. 5, 1789); *Alexander*, grand opera (June 13, 1801); *Der Schlaftrunk*, Singspiel (Nov. 12, 1801); *Der Neuigkeitskramer oder Der Telegraph*, Singspiel (May 12, 1802); *Pfändung und Personalarrest*, Singspiel (Dec. 7, 1803); *Der Zerstreute*, comic opera (Jan. 29, 1805); *Andrassek und Jurassek*, pantomime (Feb. 20, 1807); *Ruthards Abenteuer oder Die beiden Sänger*, comic opera (July 26, 1808); *Pumphia und Kulikan*, caricature opera (Oct. 8, 1808); *Der bezauberte Blumenstrauss*, pantomime (Aug. 29, 1809); *Der lebendige Postillonstiefel oder Die Luftreise des Arlequin und der Columbina*, pantomime (July 7, 1810).

(5) Therese Teyber, soprano; b. Vienna (baptized), Oct. 15, 1760; d. there, April 15, 1830. She studied with Bonno and Tesi, making her operatic debut as Fiametta in Ulbrich's *Frühling und Liebe* at the Vienna Court Theater (Sept. 8, 1778). She continued to sing there regularly and also in concerts of the Tonkünstler-Sozietät, creating the role of Blondchen in *Die Entführung aus dem Serail* (July 16, 1782); she retired in 1791. Her husband was the tenor Ferdinand Arnold.

Teyte (real name, **Tate**), **Dame Maggie,** distinguished English soprano; b. Wolverhampton, April 17, 1888; d. London, May 26, 1976. She studied in London; then was a pupil of Jean de Reszke in Paris (1903–07). In 1906 she made her debut at a Mozart Festival in France under her real name. In order to ensure correct pronunciation of her name in France, she changed the original spelling Tate to Teyte. She made her operatic debut as Tyrcis in Offenbach's *Myriame et Daphne* in Monte Carlo in 1907; she was very successful as a concert singer in Paris, and appeared with Debussy at the piano; Debussy also selected her as successor to Mary Garden in the role of Mélisande (1908). She sang at the Paris Opéra Comique (1908–10), with Beecham's Opera Co. in London (1910–11), with the Chicago Opera Co. (1911–14), and with the Boston Grand Opera Co. (1914–17). She made appearances at London's Covent Garden (1922–23; 1930; 1936–38); she then sang in operetta and musical comedies in London and later devoted herself mainly to French song recitals there. In 1951 she made her farewell appearance in opera as Purcell's Belinda in London; she gave her last concert there in 1955. She was made a Chevalier of the French Légion d'honneur in 1957 and a Dame Commander of the Order of the British Empire in 1958. In addition to her famous portrayal of Mélisande, she won notable distinction for such roles as Cherubino, Blondchen, Marguerite, Nedda, Madama Butterfly, and Mimi; she also created the Princess in Holst's *The Perfect Fool*. She had 2 indifferent husbands and 2 prominent lovers: Sir Thomas Beecham in London and Georges Enesco in Paris. She publ. a book of memoirs, *Star on the Door* (London, 1958).

BIBL.: G. O'Connor, *The Pursuit of Perfection, A Life of M. T.* (N.Y., 1979).

Thalberg, Sigismond (Fortuné François), celebrated Swiss-born pianist and composer; b. Pâquis, near Geneva, Jan. 8, 1812; d. Posillipo, near Naples, April 27, 1871. His parents were Joseph Thalberg of Frankfurt am Main and Fortunée Stein, also of Frankfurt am Main, but resident in Geneva. Thalberg, however, pretended to be the natural son of Count Moritz Dietrichstein and Baroness von Wetzlar, who took charge of his education. At age 10 he was sent to Vienna to prepare himself for a career as a diplomat; however, he also received instruction in music from Mittag, 1st bassoonist in the orch. of the Court Opera; he subsequently studied piano with Hummel and theory with Sechter. He played as a precocious pianist in the aristocratic salons of Vienna, and began to compose. In 1830 he made a successful concert tour of England and Germany. After further training with J. Pixis and F. Kalkbrenner in Paris and with Moscheles in London, he returned to Paris in 1836 and set himself up as a serious rival to Liszt; the 2 eventually became friends, and Thalberg went on to pursue a brilliant career as a virtuoso, performing mostly his own works. In 1843 he married the widow of the painter Boucher. In 1855 he set out on a concert tour through Brazil and then visited the United States (1856); he made a 2d Brazilian tour in 1863, and in 1864 retired to Naples. Thalberg was unexcelled as a performer of fashionable salon music and virtuoso studies. He possessed a wonderful legato, eliciting from Liszt the remark "Thalberg is the only artist who can play the violin on the keyboard." His technical specialty was to play a central melody with the thumb of either hand, surrounding it with brilliant arpeggios and arabesques. To present this technique graphically in notation, he made use of the method initiated by Francesco Pollini of writing piano music on 3 staves. He wrote 2 operas, *Florinda* (London, July 3, 1851) and *Cristina di Suezia* (Vienna, June 3, 1855), which were not successful, but his brilliant piano pieces were the rage of his day, easily eclipsing in popular favor those of Chopin, his close contemporary. Among them were fantasies on operas by Rossini, Bellini, Meyerbeer, Weber, Verdi, and others.

BIBL.: R. Lott, *The American Concert Tours of Leopold de Meyer, Henri Herz, and S. T.* (diss., City Univ. of N.Y., 1986).

Thebom, Blanche, American mezzo-soprano; b. Monessen, Pa., Sept. 19, 1918. She studied singing with Margaret Matzenauer and Edyth Walker in New York. She made her concert debut there in 1941 and her operatic debut, with the Metropolitan Opera, as Fricka on Dec. 14, 1944; she remained on its roster until 1959, and sang there again from 1960 to 1967; she also sang in various opera houses in America and Europe, with increasing success. In 1967 she was appointed head of the Southern Regional Opera Co. in Atlanta; it folded in 1968; in 1980 she was appointed director of the opera workshop of San Francisco State Univ. Among her best roles were Ortrud, Azucena, Amneris, Laura in *La Gioconda*, and Carmen.

Theil, Johann, distinguished German composer, teacher, and music theorist; b. Naumburg, July 29, 1646; d. there (buried), June 24, 1724. He began his musical training with Johann Scheffler, Kantor in Magdeburg, then pursued the study of law at the Univ. of Leipzig; he also received musical instruction from Schütz. In 1673 he was appointed Kapellmeister to Duke Christian Albrecht in Gottorf; after the duke lost his position in 1675, Theile followed him to Hamburg, where he was chosen to compose the inaugural opera for the new opera house in the Gansemarkt in 1678. He was Kapellmeister in Wölfenbuttel (1685–91), where he also acquired a fine reputation as a teacher; he then held that position at the court of Duke Christian I in Merseburg (1691–94), where he continued to be active as a teacher. About 1718 he settled with his son in Naumburg. Theil was a notable composer of sacred music, known by his contemporaries as "the father of contrapuntists." His theoretical works are also of value.

WORKS (all 1st perf. in Hamburg): DRAMATIC: *Adam und Eva,*

oder Der erschaffene, gefallene und auffgerichtete Mensch (Jan. 2, 1678); *Orontes* (1678); *Die Geburth Christi* (1681).

WRITINGS (all in MS): *Musikalisches Kunst-Buch; Curieuser Unterricht von den gedoppelten Contrapuncten; Contrapuncta praecepta; Von den dreifachten Contrapuncten; Gründlicher Unterricht von den gedoppelten Contrapuncten; Von dem vierfachen Contrapunct alla octava.*

BIBL.: F. Zelle, *J. T. und N. A. Trungk* (Berlin, 1891); W. Maxton, *J. T.* (diss., Univ. of Tübingen, 1926).

Theodorakis, Mikis (Michael George), Greek composer; b. Chios, July 29, 1925. He studied at the Athens Cons. During the German occupation of his homeland, he was active in the resistance; after the liberation, he joined the Left but was arrested and deported during the civil war. In 1953 he went to Paris and studied with Messiaen; soon after he began to compose. After returning to Greece in 1961, he resumed his political activities and served as a member of Parliament in 1963. Having joined the Communist Party, he was arrested after the military coup in 1967 and incarcerated. During this period, he wrote the music for the film *Z*, dealing with the police murder of the Socialist politician Gregory Lambrakis in Salonika in 1963. The film and the music were greatly acclaimed in Europe and America, and the fate of Theodorakis became a cause célèbre. Yielding to pressure from international public opinion, the military Greek government freed Theodorakis in 1970. In 1972 he quit the Communist Party and was active in the United Left; returning to the Communist Party, he served in Parliament in 1981 and again in 1985–86 before quitting it once more. In 1989 he became an ambassador of conservatism in Greece, going so far as to enter the race for the legislature on the New Democracy ticket; with 416 like-minded painters, writers, musicians, singers, and actors, Theodorakis signed his name to a manifesto (Nov. 3, 1989) condemning the divisive policies of the former Socialist government of Andreas Papandreou; he also ended 4 years of musical silence by appearing on an Athens stage before a crowd of 70,000 people, singing songs of protest and love in the name of national unity. From 1990 to 1992 he served in the Greek government as a Minister without Portfolio. In 1993 he became general director of the orch. and chorus of the Greek State Radio in Athens. His 4-vol. autobiography was publ. in Athens (1986–88).

WORKS: DRAMATIC: OPERAS: *Kostas Kariotakis* (1985); *Zorbas*, ballet opera (1988); *Medea* (1990); *Elektra* (1993). BALLETS: *Carnaval* (1953; rev. as *Le Feu aux Poudres*, 1958); *Les Amants de Teruel* (1958); *Antigone* (1958); *Antigone II* (1971); *Elektra* (1976); *Mythologie* (1976); *Zorba* (1976); *7 danses grecques* (1982). Also incidental music to various dramas; film scores, including *Zorba the Greek* (1962) and *Z* (1973). OTHER: *Canto General*, oratorio for 2 Soloists, Chorus, and Orch. (1971–74); *Dionysos*, religious drama for Voice, Chorus, and Chamber Ensemble (1984).

BIBL.: J. Coubard, *M. T.* (Paris, 1969); G. Giannaris, *M. T.: Music and Social Change* (London, 1973); G. Host, *T.: Myth and Politics in Modern Greek Music* (Amsterdam, 1981).

Thern, Kâroly, Hungarian composer of German birth; b. Iglau, Aug. 13, 1817; d. Vienna, April 13, 1886. After studies at the Univ. of Pest, he worked as assistant conductor at the National Theater (1841). He taught at the National Cons. (1853–64), and later settled in Vienna. He wrote the operas *Giyul* (1841), *Tihany ostroma* (The Siege of Tihany; 1845), and *A képzelt beteg* (The Imaginary Invalid; 1855). His sons, Vilmos (1847–1911) and Lajos (1848–1920), studied with Reinecke and Moscheles at the Leipzig Cons., and later with Liszt; after winning distinction as a duo-piano team in Europe, they settled in Vienna as teachers.

Thévenard, Gabriel-Vincent, esteemed French singer; b. Orléans or Paris, Aug. 10, 1669; d. Paris, Aug. 24, 1741. He settled in Paris in 1690. Following training from Destouches, he was a principal singer with the Académie Royale de Musique from 1698 until 1729. He created roles in many operas, including those by Destouches, Campra, Marais, and Desmarets.

Thielemann, Christian, German conductor; b. Berlin, April 1, 1959. He received training in Berlin. In 1979 he became an assistant to Karajan in Berlin and Salzburg. After working in opera houses in Gelsenkirchen, Karlsruhe, Hannover, and Düsseldorf (1982–85), he served as Generalmusikdirektor in Nuremburg (1988–92). In 1991 he conducted at the San Francisco Opera and at the Deutsche Oper in Berlin. He conducted at the Hamburg State Opera in 1992, the same year he made his Metropolitan Opera debut in New York conducting *Der Rosenkavalier*. In 1995 he appeared as a guest conductor with the N.Y. Phil. From 1997 he was Generalmusikdirektor of the Deutsche Oper in Berlin.

Thienen, Marcel van, French composer and sculptor; b. Paris, Oct. 3, 1922. He studied in Paris, receiving instruction in violin at the Ecole Normale de Musique and at the Cons. (graduated, 1940); he also studied composition at the Cons. Russe. After serving as director of the Haiti Cons. (1954–57), he returned to Paris and founded an electronic music studio; in the mid-1960s he turned to sculpture. Among his works is *Le Ferroviaire*, opera farce (1951).

Thill, Georges, distinguished French tenor; b. Paris, Dec. 14, 1897; d. Draguignan, Oct. 17, 1984. He studied at the Paris Cons. and with Fernando De Lucia in Naples. Returning to Paris, he sang at the Opéra Comique; made his first appearance at the Opéra as Nicias in *Thaïs* (Feb. 4, 1924), and continued to sing there regularly until 1940. He appeared at London's Covent Garden (1928, 1937); he made his Metropolitan Opera debut in New York as Romeo (March 20, 1931), remaining on the company's roster until 1932. His farewell appearance was as Canio at the Opéra Comique in 1953. His outstanding roles included Don José, Romeo, Julien in *Louise*, Aeneas, and Samson; he was also a fine singer of Italian and German roles.

BIBL.: R. Mancini, *G. T.* (Paris, 1966); A. Segond, *Album G. T.* (Aix-en-Provence, 1991).

Thiriet, Maurice, French composer; b. Meulan, May 2, 1906; d. Puys, near Dieppe, Sept. 28, 1972. He began his training at the Paris Cons. with Charles Silver, and later studied with Koechlin (counterpoint and fugue) and Roland-Manuel (composition and orchestration). He was a composer of much dramatic music.

WORKS: DRAMATIC: *Le Bourgeois de Falaise*, opéra bouffe (1933; Paris, June 21, 1937); *La Véridique Histoire du docteur* (1937); *La Locandiera*, opéra comique (1959); 16 ballets; film scores; radio music. Also *Oedipe-Roi*, oratorio for Men's Chorus and Orch. (1940–41).

Thomas, Augusta Read, American composer; b. Glen Grove, N.Y., April 24, 1964. She was a student of Karlins and Stout at Northwestern Univ. (1983–87) and of Druckman at Yale Univ. (M.M., 1988) before completing postgraduate studies at the Royal Academy of Music in London (1988–89). She received numerous awards and honors, among them ASCAP prizes (1987–91), NEA fellowships (1988, 1992), a Guggenheim fellowship (1989), the International Orpheus Prize for Opera of Spoleto, Italy (1994), and the Charles Ives Fellowship (1994). In addition to composing, she taught at the Eastman School of Music in Rochester, N.Y. Her works include *Ligeia*, chamber opera (1991–94), and *Conquering the Fury of Oblivion*, theatrical oratorio (1994–95). She is married to the remarkable English-born American composer Bernard Rands (b. Sheffield, March 2, 1934).

Thomas, (Charles Louis) Ambroise, noted French composer and teacher; b. Metz, Aug. 5, 1811; d. Paris, Feb. 12, 1896. He entered the Paris Cons. in 1828, where his teachers were Zimmerman (piano) and Dourlen (harmony and accompaniment); he also studied privately with Kalkbrenner (piano) and Barbereau (harmony), and subsequently studied composition with Le Sueur at the Cons., where he won the Grand Prix de Rome with his cantata *Hermann et Ketty* (1832). After 3 years in Italy, and a visit to Vienna, he returned to Paris and applied himself with great energy to the composition of operas. In 1851 he was elected to the Académie, and in 1856 became a prof. of composition at the Paris Cons.; in 1871 he became director there. As a composer of melodious operas in the French style, he was second only to Gounod; his masterpiece was *Mignon*, based on Goethe's *Wilhelm Meister* (Paris, Nov. 17, 1866), which became a mainstay of the repertoire all over the world; it had nearly 2,000 performances in less then 100 years at the Opéra Comique alone. Equally successful was his Shakespearean opera *Hamlet* (Paris, March 9, 1868). In 1845 he was made a Chevalier of the Légion d'honneur, being the first composer to receive its Grand Croix in 1894.

WORKS (all 1st perf. in Paris): DRAMATIC (all opéras comiques unless otherwise given): *La double échelle* (Aug. 23, 1837); *Le perruquier de la régence* (March 30, 1838); *Le panier fleuri* (May 6, 1839); *Carline* (Feb. 24, 1840); *Le comte de Carmagnola* (April 19, 1841); *Le guerillero* (June 22, 1842); *Angélique et Medor* (May 10, 1843); *Mina, ou Le Ménage à trois* (Oct. 10, 1843); *Le caïd* (Jan. 3, 1849); *Le songe d'une nuit d'été* (April 20, 1850); *Raymond, ou Le secret de la reine* (June 5, 1851); *La Tonelli* (March 30, 1853); *La cour de Célimène* (April 11, 1855); *Psyché* (Jan. 26, 1857); *Le carnaval de Venise* (Dec. 9, 1857); *Le roman d'Elvire* (Feb. 4, 1860); *Mignon* (Nov. 17, 1866); *Hamlet,* opera (March 9, 1868); *Gille et Gillotin,* opera (April 22, 1874); *Françoise de Rimini,* opera (April 14, 1882). BALLETS: *La gipsy* (Jan. 28, 1839; in collaboration with F. Benoist and M. Marliani); *Betty* (July 10, 1846); *La tempête* (June 26, 1889).

BIBL.: H. Delaborde, *Notice sur la vie et les œuvres de M.A. T.* (Paris, 1896); H. de Curzon, *A. T.* (Paris, 1921).

Thomas, David (Lionel Mercer), English bass; b. Orpington, Kent, Feb. 26, 1943. He was educated at St. Paul's Cathedral Choir School, King's School, Canterbury, and King's College, Cambridge. He first gained recognition as a soloist with Rooley's Consort of Musicke, Hogwood's Academy of Music, and other early music groups in England; subsequently appeared throughout Europe. In 1982 he made his U.S. debut at the Hollywood Bowl. In later years, he pursued an international career, specializing in the Baroque and Classical concert and operatic repertoires. He won particular distinction for his performances of works by Monteverdi, Purcell, Bach, Handel, and Mozart.

Thomas, Jess (Floyd), American tenor; b. Hot Springs, S.Dak., Aug. 4, 1927; d. San Francisco, Oct. 11, 1993. After studying psychology at the Univ. of Nebr. and at Stanford Univ., he turned to singing; he had formal study with Otto Schulman. He made his formal operatic debut as Malcolm at the San Francisco Opera in 1957, then continued his training with Emmy Seiberlich in Germany. He was a member of the Karlsruhe Opera (1958–61); he sang Parsifal at the Bayreuth Festival (1961) and appeared in other German music centers. On Dec. 11, 1962, he made his Metropolitan Opera debut in New York as Walter von Stolzing. In 1963 he joined the Bavarian State Opera in Munich, and was honored with the title of Kammersänger; he also made guest appearances in Salzburg, Vienna, London's Covent Garden, and other major opera centers.

Thomas, John Charles, American baritone; b. Meyersdale, Pa., Sept. 6, 1891; d. Apple Valley, Calif., Dec. 13, 1960. He studied at the Peabody Cons. of Music in Baltimore. From 1913 he sang in musical comedy in New York. He made his operatic debut as Amonasro in Washington, D.C. (March 3, 1924). In 1925 he made his European operatic debut as King Herod in Massenet's *Hérodiade* at the Théâtre Royal de la Monnaie in Brussels, where he sang until 1928; he made his Covent Garden debut in London as Valentin in *Faust* (June 28, 1928). He then sang opera in Philadelphia (1928), San Francisco (1930, 1943), and Chicago (1930–32; 1934–36; 1939–42); he made his Metropolitan Opera debut in New York as the elder Germont on Feb. 2, 1934, and remained on the company's roster until 1943. Throughout these years, he toured widely in the United States as a concert artist; he also appeared regularly on the *Bell Telephone Hour* radio program. Among his other roles were Rossini's Figaro, Scarpia, and Strauss's Jochanaan.

Thommessen, Olav Anton, imaginative Norwegian composer and teacher; b. Oslo, May 16, 1946. He studied composition with Bernhard Heiden at the Indiana Univ. School of Music in Bloomington (B.M., 1969), where he also attended the lectures of Xenakis; he continued his training in Warsaw, and then pursued studies in electronic music with Werner Kaegi and Otto Laske at the Instituut voor Sonologie at the Univ. of Utrecht. In 1973 he joined the faculty of the Norwegian State Academy of Music in Oslo. In his compositions, he utilizes Western and non-Western elements in a contemporary style mainly within the tonal tradition.

WORKS: DRAMATIC: *Hermaphroditen* (The Hermaphrodite), chamber opera comprising the following 6 works: *Det Hemmelige Evangeliet* (The Secret Gospel; Bergen, May 24, 1976), *Hermaphroditen* (1975; Vadstena, Sweden, July 28, 1976), *Et Konsert-Kammer* (A Concert-Chamber; 1971; Warsaw, Feb. 6, 1972), *Ekko av et ekko* (Echo of an Echo; Malmö, Oct. 26, 1980), *Gjensidig* (Mutually; 1973; Luleå, Sweden, July 4, 1974), and *Overtonen* (The Overtone; Bergen, May 31, 1977); *Melologer og Monodramaer* (Wordless Chamber Opera; Vadstena, July 20, 1982); *Hertuginnen dør* (The Duchess Dies), chamber opera (1987); incidental music.

Thompson, Oscar, American music critic and editor; b. Crawfordsville, Ind., Oct. 10, 1887; d. N.Y., July 3, 1945. He was educated at the Univ. of Wash., Seattle; he also studied music with G. Campanari and others. He took up journalism and in 1919 joined the staff of *Musical America*, later becoming assoc. ed. and finally ed. (1936–43). He was music critic for the *N.Y. Evening Post* (1928–34); from 1937 to his death he was music critic for the *N.Y. Sun*. In 1928 he established the first class in music criticism in the United States at the Curtis Inst. of Music in Philadelphia; he also gave courses at Columbia Univ. and the N.Y. College of Music. In 1939 he brought out *The International Cyclopedia of Music and Musicians* in one vol. of more than 2,000 pages, with feature articles by eminent authorities; it went through 11 eds. and reprints. He wrote the books *Practical Musical Criticism* (1934); *How to Understand Music* (1935; 2d ed., enl., 1958); *Tabulated Biographical History of Music* (1936); *The American Singer* (1937); *Debussy, Man and Artist* (1937); ed. *Plots of the Operas* (1940) and *Great Modern Composers* (1941), both vols. being extracts from the *Cyclopedia*.

Thompson, Randall, eminent American composer and pedagogue; b. N.Y., April 21, 1899; d. Boston, July 9, 1984. He was a member of an intellectual New England family; he studied at Lawrenceville School in N.J., where his father was an English teacher; he began taking singing lessons and received his rudimentary music training from the organist Francis Cuyler Van Dyck. When he died, Thompson took over his organ duties in the school. Upon graduation, he went to Harvard Univ., where he studied with Walter Spalding, Edward Burlingame Hill, and Archibald T. Davison (B.A., 1920; M.A., 1922). In 1920–21 he had some private lessons in New York with Bloch. In 1922 he submitted his orch. prelude *Pierrot and Cothurnus*, inspired by the poetical drama *Aria da Capo* by Edna St. Vincent Millay, for the American Prix de Rome, and received a grant for residence in Rome; he conducted it there at the Accademia di Santa Cecilia on May 17, 1923. Encouraged by its reception, he proceeded to compose industriously, for piano, for voices, and for orch. He returned to the United States in 1925. From 1927 to 1929 he taught at Wellesley College, and again from 1936 to 1937; in 1929 he was appointed a lecturer in music at Harvard Univ.; in 1929–30 he held a Guggenheim fellowship. On Feb. 20, 1930, his 1st Sym. had its premiere in Rochester, N.Y., with Howard Hanson conducting, and on March 24, 1932, Hanson conducted in Rochester the first performance of Thompson's 2d Sym., which was destined to become one of the most successful symphonic works by an American composer; it enjoyed repeated performances in the United States and also in Europe. Audiences found the work distinctly American in substance; the unusual element was the inclusion of jazz rhythms in the score. Equally American and equally appealing, although for entirely different reasons, was his choral work *Americana*, to texts from Mencken's satirical column in his journal, the *American Mercury*. There followed another piece of

Americana, the nostalgic choral work *The Peaceable Kingdom*, written in 1936, and inspired by the painting of that name by the naturalistic fantasist Edward Hicks; for it, Thompson used biblical texts from the Prophets. Another piece for chorus, deeply religious in its nature, was *Alleluia* (1940), which became a perennial favorite in the choral literature; it was first performed at Tanglewood, Mass., at the inaugural session of the Berkshire Music Center, on July 8, 1940. In 1942 Thompson composed his most celebrated piece of choral writing, *The Testament of Freedom*, to words of Thomas Jefferson; it was first performed with piano accompaniment at the Univ. of Virginia on April 13, 1943. A version with orch. was presented by the Boston Sym. Orch. on April 6, 1945. With this work Thompson firmly established his reputation as one of the finest composers of choral music in America. But he did not limit himself to choral music. His 1st String Quartet in D minor (1941) was praised, as was his opera, *Solomon and Balkis*, after Kipling's *The Butterfly That Stamped*, a parody on Baroque usages, broadcast over CBS on March 29, 1942. In 1949 Thompson wrote his 3d Sym., which was presented at the Festival of Contemporary American Music at Columbia Univ. in New York on May 15, 1949. Thompson's subsequent works included an opera, *The Nativity According to St. Luke* (Cambridge, Mass., Dec. 13, 1961), and an oratorio, *The Passion According to St. Luke* for Soloists, Chorus, and Orch. (1964–65; Boston, March 28, 1965). During all this time, he did not neglect his educational activities; he taught at the Univ. of Calif. at Berkeley (1937–39); the Curtis Inst. of Music in Philadelphia, where he served as director from 1939 to 1941; the School of Fine Arts at the Univ. of Virginia (1941–46); Princeton Univ. (1946–48); and Harvard Univ. (1948–65), where he retired as prof. emeritus in 1965. He also publ. a book, *College Music* (N.Y., 1935). In 1938 he was elected a member of the National Inst. of Arts and Letters; in 1959 he was named "Cavaliere ufficiale al merito della Repubblica Italiana." In his compositions, Thompson preserved and cultivated the melodious poetry of American speech, set in crystalline tonal harmonies judiciously seasoned with euphonious discords, while keeping resolutely clear of any modernistic abstractions. Other works include the opera *Solomon and Balkis*, after Kipling's *The Butterfly That Stamped* (CBS, N.Y., March 29, 1942; 1st stage perf., Cambridge, Mass., April 14, 1942), the ballet *Jabberwocky* (1951), and incidental music to *Torches* (1920), *Grand Street Follies* (N.Y., June 25, 1926; not extant), *The Straw Hat* (N.Y., Oct. 14, 1926), and *The Battle of Dunster Street* (1953).

BIBL.: C. Benser and D. Urrows, *R. T.: A Bio-Bibliography* (Westport, Conn., 1986).

Thomson, Virgil (Garnett), many-faceted American composer of great originality and a music critic of singular brilliance; b. Kansas City, Mo., Nov. 25, 1896; d. N.Y., Sept. 30, 1989. He began piano lessons at age 12 with local teachers; he received instruction in organ (1909–17; 1919) and played in local churches; he took courses at a local junior college (1915–17; 1919), then entered Harvard Univ., where he studied orchestration with E. B. Hill and became assistant and accompanist to A. T. Davison, conductor of its Glee Club; he also studied piano with Heinrich Gebhard and organ with Wallace Goodrich in Boston. In 1921 he went with the Harvard Glee Club to Europe, where he remained on a John Knowles Paine Traveling Fellowship to study organ with Boulanger at the Paris École Normale de Musique; he also received private instruction in counterpoint from her. Returning to Harvard in 1922, he was made organist and choirmaster at King's College; after graduating in 1923, he went to New York to study conducting with Clifton and counterpoint with Scalero at the Juilliard Graduate School. In 1925 he returned to Paris, which remained his base until 1940. He established friendly contacts with cosmopolitan groups of musicians, writers, and painters; his association with Gertrude Stein was particularly significant in the development of his aesthetic ideas. In his music, he refused to follow any set of modernistic doctrines; rather, he embraced the notion of popular universality, which allowed him to use the techniques of all ages and all degrees of simplicity or complexity, from simple triadic harmonies to dodecaphonic intricacies; in so doing he achieved an eclectic illumination of astonishing power of direct communication, expressed in his dictum "jamais de banalité, toujours le lieu commun." Beneath the characteristic Parisian persiflage in some of his music there is a profoundly earnest intent. His most famous composition is the opera *Four Saints in Three Acts*, to the libretto by Gertrude Stein, in which the deliberate confusion wrought by the author of the play (there are actually 4 acts and more than a dozen saints, some of them in duplicate) and the composer's almost solemn, hymnlike treatment, create a hilarious modern opera buffa. It was first introduced at Hartford, Conn., on Feb. 8, 1934, characteristically announced as being under the auspices of the "Society of Friends and Enemies of Modern Music," of which Thomson was director (1934–37); the work became an American classic, with constant revivals staged in America and Europe. In 1940 Thomson was appointed music critic of the *N.Y. Herald-Tribune*; he received the Pulitzer Prize in music in 1948 for his score to the film *Louisiana Story*. Far from being routine journalism, Thomson's music reviews are minor masterpieces of literary brilliance and critical acumen. He resigned in 1954 to devote himself to composition and conducting. He received the Légion d'honneur in 1947; he was elected to membership in the National Inst. of Arts and Letters in 1948 and in the American Academy of Arts and Letters in 1959. In 1982 he received an honorary degree of D.Mus. from Harvard Univ. In 1983 he was awarded the Kennedy Center Honor for lifetime achievement. He received the Medal of Arts in 1988.

WORKS: DRAMATIC: OPERAS: *Four Saints in Three Acts* (1927–28; orchestrated 1933; Hartford, Conn., Feb. 8, 1934); *The Mother of Us All*, to a libretto by Gertrude Stein on the life of the American suffragist Susan B. Anthony (N.Y., May 7, 1947); *Lord Byron* (1961–68; N.Y., April 13, 1972). BALLETS: *Filling Station* (1937; N.Y., Feb. 18, 1938); *The Harvest According* (N.Y., Oct. 1, 1952; based on the *Symphony on a Hymn Tune*, the Cello Concerto, and the Suite from *The Mother of Us All*); *Parson Weems and the Cherry Tree* (Amherst, Mass., Nov. 1, 1975). FILM SCORES: *The Plow that Broke the Plains* (N.Y., May 25, 1936; orch. suite, Philadelphia, Jan. 2, 1943); *The River* (New Orleans, Oct. 29, 1937; orch. suite, N.Y., Jan. 12, 1943); *The Spanish Earth* (1937; in collaboration with M. Blitzstein); *Tuesday in November* (1945); *Louisiana Story* (Edinburgh, Aug. 22, 1948; orch. suite as *Acadian Songs and Dances*, Philadelphia, Jan. 11, 1951); *The Goddess* (1957; Brussels, June 1958); *Power among Men* (1958; N.Y., March 5, 1959; orch. suite as *Fugues and Cantilenas*, Ann Arbor, May 2, 1959); *Journey to America* (N.Y., July 1964; orch. suite as *Pilgrims and Pioneers*, N.Y., Feb. 27, 1971).

WRITINGS (all publ. in N.Y.): *The State Of Music* (1939; 2d ed., rev., 1961); *The Musical Scene* (1945); *The Art of Judging Music* (1948); *Music Right and Left* (1951); *Virgil Thomson* (1966); *Music Reviewed, 1940–1954* (1967); *American Music Since 1910* (1971); *A Virgil Thomson Reader* (1981); *Music with Words: A Composer's View* (1989).

BIBL.: K. Hoover and J. Cage, *V. T.: His Life and Music* (N.Y., 1959); K. Ward, *An Analysis of the Relationship between Text and Musical Shape and an Investigation of the Relationship between Text and Surface Rhythmic Detail in "Four Saints in Three Acts" by V. T.* (diss., Univ. of Texas, Austin, 1978); M. Meckna, *The Rise of the American Composer-critic: Aaron Copland, Roger Sessions, V. T., and Elliott Carter in the Periodical Modern Music, 1924–1946* (diss., Univ. of Calif., Santa Barbara, 1984); A. Tommasini, *The Musical Portraits of V. T.* (N.Y., 1985); M. Meckna, *V. T.: A Biography* (Westport, Conn., 1986); T. and V. Page, eds., *Selected Letters of V. T.* (N.Y., 1988).

Thooft, Willem Frans, Dutch composer; b. Amsterdam, July 10, 1829; d. Rotterdam, Aug. 27, 1900. He studied with A. Dupont in Brussels and with Hauptmann at the Leipzig Cons., then went to Rotterdam, where he organized the German Opera. Among his works was the opera *Aleida von Holland* (Rotterdam, 1866).

Thorborg, Kerstin, noted Swedish contralto; b. Venjan, May 19, 1896; d. Falun, Dalarna, April 12, 1970. She studied at the Royal Cons. in Stockholm. She made her operatic debut there as Ortrud at the Royal Theater in 1924, remaining on its roster until 1930; she sang in Prague (1932–33), at the Berlin Städtische Oper (1933–35), at the Salzburg Festivals (1935–37), at the Vienna State Opera (1935–38), and at London's Covent Garden (1936–39). On Dec. 21, 1936, she made her Metropolitan Opera debut in New York as Fricka, remaining on the company's roster until 1946; she sang there again from 1947 to 1950 and also appeared in concerts. In 1944 she was made a Swedish court singer; she taught voice in Stockholm from 1950. She was particularly esteemed as a Wagnerian; she also excelled as Gluck's Orfeo, Saint-Saëns's Delilah, and Strauss's Herodias and Clytemnestra.

Thoresen, Lasse, Norwegian composer and teacher; b. Oslo, Oct. 18, 1949. He was a student of Mortensen at the Oslo Cons. (graduated, 1972) and then of Kaegi at the Inst. of Sonology at the Univ. of Utrecht. In 1975 he joined the faculty of the Norwegian State Academy of Music in Oslo. His *Stages of the Inner Dialogue* for Piano was named the Norwegian composition of the year in 1981, an honor he received again in 1993 with his *Ab Uno* for Flute, Clarinet, String Quartet, Percussion, and Synthesizer. His music reflects the influence of French spectral music, Harry Partch's microtonal system, and Norwegian folk music. He was the first composer in Norway to incorporate the nontempered intervals of folk music into concert music. His Bahai faith is reflected in his choice of titles for many of his scores. Among his works are *Skapelser*, television ballet (1977), and *Vidunderlampen* (The Wonder Lamp), children's operetta (1984).

Thorne, Francis, American composer; b. Bay Shore, Long Island, N.Y., June 23, 1922. Of a cultural heritage (his maternal grandfather was Gustav Kobbé), he absorbed musical impressions crouching under the grand piano while his father, a banker, played ragtime; he received instruction in composition from Donovan and Hindemith at Yale Univ. (B.A., 1942). After working in banking and stock brokerage (1946–54), he was active as a jazz pianist in the United States and Italy (1955–61); he also studied with Diamond in Florence. Impressed, depressed, and distressed by the inhumanly impecunious condition of middleaged atonal composers, he established the eleemosynary Thorne Music Fund (1965–75), drawing on the hereditary wealth of his family, and disbursed munificent grants to those who qualified, among them Wolpe, Weber, Harrison, Trimble, Cage, and Diamond. He served as executive director of the Lenox Arts Center (1972–76) and of the American Composers' Alliance (1975–85); in 1976 he co-founded the American Composers' Orch. in New York, subsequently serving as its president. In 1988 he was elected to membership in the American Academy and Inst. of Arts and Letters. In 1994 he was composer-in-residence at the American Academy in Rome. Thorne's music shares with that of his beneficiaries the venturesome spirit of the cosmopolitan avant-garde, with a prudently dissonant technique serving the conceptual abstractions and titular paronomasia of many modern compositions.

WORKS: DRAMATIC: *Fortuna*, operetta (N.Y., Dec. 20, 1961); *Opera buffa for Opera Buffs* (1965); *After the Teacups*, ballet (N.Y., July 31, 1974); *Echoes of Spoon River*, ballet (N.Y., June 20, 1976); *Mario and the Magician*, opera (1991–93; N.Y., March 12, 1994).

Thorpe Davie, Cedric, Scottish composer and teacher; b. London, May 30, 1913; d. Kirkcudbrightshire, Jan. 18, 1983. He began his training at the Royal Scottish Academy of Music in Glasgow, then studied in London with Craxton, Thiman, and A. Brain at the Royal Academy of Music and with R. O. Morris, Vaughan Williams, and G. Jacob at the Royal College of Music, where he won the Cobbett and Sullivan prizes in composition (1935); he subsequently received instruction in piano from Petri, and also in composition from Kodály in Budapest and from Kilpinen in Helsinki. He taught theory and composition at the Royal Scottish Academy of Music (1936–45), then was master (1945–73) and prof. (1973–78) of music at St. Andrews Univ. In 1955 he was awarded the Order of the British Empire. He publ. *Musical Structure and Design* (London, 1953) and ed. the *Oxford Scottish Song Book* (London, 1968). His compositions include *Gammer Gurton's Needle*, opera (1936), as well as comic operas, operettas, and music for theater, films, and broadcasting.

BIBL.: *C. T. D.: Catalogue of Works* (Fife, 1988).

Thrane, Waldemar, Norwegian violinist, conductor, and composer; b. Christiania, Oct. 8, 1790; d. there, Dec. 30, 1828. He studied violin with Henrik Groth in Christiania, and then with Claus Schall in Copenhagen (1814–15); he then went to Paris, where he was a pupil of Baillot (violin) and of Reicha and Habeneck (composition). Returning to Christiania in 1818, he was made conductor of the orchs. of the Dramatical Society and of the Musical Lyceum; he also toured as a violinist throughout his homeland and made appearances in Stockholm. He is historically important as the composer of the first Norwegian opera, *Fjeldeventyret* (A Mountain Adventure; 1824; Christiania, Feb. 9, 1825).

BIBL.: F. Benestad, *W. T.: En pioner i norsk musikk* (Oslo, 1961).

Thuille, Ludwig (Wilhelm Andreas Maria), renowned Austrian composer and pedagogue; b. Bozen, Tirol, Nov. 30, 1861; d. Munich, Feb. 5, 1907. He studied theory, piano, and organ with Joseph Pembaur in Innsbruck, then went to Munich, where he was a pupil of Karl Bärmann (piano) and Joseph Rheinberger (composition) at the Königliche Musikschule, graduating with honors in 1882; in 1883 he joined its faculty and was promoted to prof. in 1890. Encouraged by Alexander Ritter, he began to compose music in the grand Wagnerian manner. He wrote 3 operas and other works, but he made his mark chiefly as a fine pedagogue. With Rudolf Louis he publ. the well-known manual *Harmonielehre* (1907; abr. ed. as *Grundriss der Harmonielehre*, 1908; 10th ed., rev., 1933 by W. Courvoisier and others).

WORKS: OPERAS: *Theuerdank* (1893–95; Munich, Feb. 12, 1897), *Lobetanz* (1896; Karlsruhe, Feb. 6, 1898); *Gugeline* (1898–1900; Bremen, March 4, 1901); also a melodrama, *Die Tanzhexe* (1899–1900).

BIBL.: F. Munter, *L. T.* (Munich, 1923).

Thursby, Emma (Cecilia), prominent American soprano; b. Williamsburg, N.Y., Feb. 21, 1845; d. N.Y., July 4, 1931. She was trained in the United States and Italy, her principal mentors being Julius Meyer, Achille Errani, Francesco Lamperti, Sangiovanni, and Erminie Rudersdorff. After beginning her career with solo appearances in churches in Brooklyn and Manhattan, she sang with Theodore Thomas and his orch., with Patrick Gilmore and his band, and in Leopold Damrosch's oratorio concerts. She won extraordinary success touring as a concert singer in Europe (1878–82), then gave concerts and recitals in the United States until her farewell in Chicago in 1895. She subsequently was active as a teacher, serving as a prof. at the Inst. of Musical Art in New York (1905–11). Her most celebrated pupil was Geraldine Farrar. Although she declined to appear in operatic productions, she included numerous arias in her concert repertoire, winning acclaim for her coloratura gifts.

BIBL.: R. Gipson, *The Life of E. T., 1845–1931* (N.Y., 1940).

Thursfield, Anne (née **Reman**), English mezzo-soprano; b. N.Y., March 28, 1885; d. London, June 5, 1945. She received her training principally in Berlin, and then developed a fine concert career in England. Thursfield's interpretations of the song literature were particularly admired for their insight in and handling of both German and French texts, as well as those in her native English tongue.

Thybo, Leif, Danish organist, teacher, and composer; b. Holstebro, June 12, 1922. He studied in Copenhagen at the Cons. (1940–45) and the Univ. (1945–48). He taught harmony and counterpoint at the Univ. of Copenhagen (1949–65); he taught theory (from 1952) and organ (from 1960) at the Copenhagen Cons.; he was also active as a church organist. Among his works is the chamber opera *Den odödliga berättelsen* (The Immortal Story; Vadstena, Sweden, July 8, 1971).

Tibaldi, Giuseppe (Luigi), Italian tenor; b. Bologna, Jan. 22, 1729; d. c.1790. He studied voice with Domenico Zanardi and composition with Padre Martini in Bologna, where he joined its Accademia Filarmonica as a singer (1747) and as a composer (1750), later serving as its principe (1759, 1777, 1783). In 1751 he became maestro di cappella at S. Giovanni in Monte in Bologna, a post he gave up a few years later to pursue a distinguished career as a singer. Tibaldi sang in the premieres of Gluck's *Alceste* (Vienna, Dec. 16, 1767) and Mozart's *Ascanio in Alba* (Milan, Oct. 17, 1771). His son, Ferdinando Tibaldi (b. c.1750; d. 1785), was a singer and composer.

Tibbett (real name, **Tibbet**), **Lawrence,** outstanding American baritone; b. Bakersfield, Calif., Nov. 16, 1896; d. N.Y., July 15, 1960. His real name was accidentally misspelled when he appeared in opera, and he retained the final extra letter. His ancestry was connected with the California Gold Rush of 1849; his great-uncle was reputed to be a pioneer in the navel orange industry; Tibbett's father was a sheriff of Bakersfield who was shot dead by one of the outlaws he had hunted. His mother ran a hotel in Long Beach. Tibbett led a typical cowboy life, but dreamed of a stage career; he played parts in Shakespearian productions. During World War I, he served in the U.S. Navy; after the Armistice, he earned a living by singing at weddings and funerals in a male quartet. He also took vocal lessons with Joseph Dupuy, Basil Ruysdael, Frank La Forge, and Ignaz Zitomirsky. He made his operatic debut in New York with the Metropolitan Opera on Nov. 24, 1923, in the minor role of Lovitsky in *Boris Godunov*; he then sang Valentin in *Faust* (Nov. 30, 1923); he achieved a striking success as Ford in Verdi's *Falstaff* (Jan. 2, 1925), and thereafter was one of the leading members on its roster. Among his roles were Tonio in *Pagliacci*, Wolfram in *Tannhäuser*, Telramund in *Lohengrin*, Marcello in *La Bohème*, Scarpia in *Tosca*, Iago in *Otello*, and the title roles in *Rigoletto* and *Falstaff*. He also sang important parts in modern American operas, such as Colonel Ibbetson in Taylor's *Peter Ibbetson*, Brutus Jones in Gruenberg's *The Emperor Jones*, and Wrestling Bradford in Hanson's *Merry Mount*. During his first European tour in 1937, he sang the title role in the premiere of *Don Juan de Mañara* by Eugene Goossens (Covent Garden, London, June 24, 1937); he also sang in Paris, Vienna, and Stockholm. A sincere believer in musical democracy, he did not disdain the lower arts; he often appeared on the radio and in films, among them *The Rogue Song*, *The Southerner*, and *Cuban Love Song*. During World War II, he sang in army camps. He made his farewell appearance at the Metropolitan Opera as Ivan in *Khovanshchina* on March 24, 1950. His last stage appearance was in the musical comedy *Fanny* in 1956. He publ. an autobiography, *The Glory Road* (Brattleboro, Vt., 1933; reprint, 1977, with discography by W. Moran).

BIBL.: A. Farkas, ed., *L. T.: Singing Actor* (Portland, Maine, 1989); H. Weinstat and B. Wechsler, *Dear Rogue: A Biography of the American Baritone L. T.* (Portland, Oreg., 1996).

Tichatschek, Joseph (real name, **Josef Aloys Ticháček**), noted Bohemian tenor; b. Ober-Weckelsdorf, July 11, 1807; d. Blasewitz, Jan. 18, 1886. He was the son of a poor weaver. In 1827 he went to Vienna as a medical student, but then joined the chorus at the Kärnthnertortheater, and had vocal instruction from Ciccimara. He was engaged at Graz in 1837, then sang in Vienna (1837). His career received a new impetus after his highly successful appearance as Auber's Gustavus III in Dresden (Aug. 11, 1837); in 1838 he joined the Dresden Court Opera, where he remained one of its leading members until he was pensioned in 1861; he continued to make appearances there until 1870. He created the roles of Rienzi (Oct. 20, 1842) and Tannhäuser (Oct. 19, 1845) in Wagner's operas. Wagner mentions him often and with great praise in his autobiography.

BIBL.: M. Fürstenau, *J. T.* (Dresden, 1868).

Tiehsen, Otto, German composer; b. Danzig, Oct. 13, 1817; d. Berlin, May 15, 1849. He studied at the Royal Academy in Berlin, where he settled as a teacher. He wrote the comic opera *Annette* (Berlin, 1847).

Tierney, Vivian, English soprano; b. London, Nov. 26, 1957. She studied with Rita Crosby, Eduardo Asquez, and Jeffrey Neilson-Taylor. At age 17, she joined the chorus of the D'Oyly Carte Co., and soon sang principal roles with it at home and abroad. After appearances with the Kent Opera and Opera 80, she made her debut with the English National Opera in London in *Orpheus in the Underworld* in 1986. In 1989 she created the role of Regan in the British premiere of Reimann's *Lear* in London. From 1989 to 1991 to was a member of the Freiburg im Breisgau Opera, where her roles included the Marschallin, Katerina Ismailova, Iduna in Burkhard's *Das Feuerwerk*, and Renata in *The Fiery Angel*. In 1990 she created the title role in Holloway's *Clarissa* in London. She portrayed Rosalinde at the English National Opera in 1991, and then sang Ellen Orford at the Glydnedourne Festival in 1992. In 1993 she was engaged as Berg's Marie with Opera North in Leeds. During the 1994–95 season, she sang the Dyer's Wife in *Die Frau ohne Schatten* in Basel. She appeared as Gutrune at London's Covent Garden in 1995. After appearing as Mrs. Coyle in *Owen Wingrave* at the Glyndebourne Festival in 1997, she returned to London to sing Tatiana in 1998 and Salome in 1999.

Tiersot, (Jean-Baptiste-Elisée-) Julien, French musicologist; b. Bourg-en-Bresse, July 5, 1857; d. Paris, Aug. 10, 1936. He was a pupil of Savard, Massenet, and Franck at the Paris Cons. In 1883 he was appointed assistant librarian at the Cons., and in 1909, chief librarian, retiring in 1921. He was also a prof. at the École des Hautes Études Sociales and president of the Société Française de Musicologie. His also composed various scores, and publ. several folksong eds.

WRITINGS (all publ. in Paris): *Histoire de la chanson populaire en France* (1889); *Musiques pittoresques: Promenades musicales à l'Exposition de 1889* (1889); *Rouget de Lisle, Son oeuvre, sa vie* (1892); *Le messe Douce mémoire de Roland de Lassus* (1894); *Les Types mélodiques dans la chanson populaire française* (1894); *Étude sur les Mâitres-Chanteurs de Nuremberg de Richard Wagner* (1899); *Hector Berlioz et la société de son temps* (1904); *Les Fêtes et les chants de la Révolution française* (1908); *Gluck* (1910); *Beethoven, musicien de la Révolution* (1910); *Jean-Jacques Rousseau* (1912; 2d ed., 1920); *Histoire de la Marseillaise* (1915); *Un Demi-siècle de musique française: Entre deux guerres 1870–1917* (1918; 2d ed., 1924); *La Musique dans la comédie de Molière* (1921); *La Damnation de Faust de Berlioz* (1924); *Les Couperin* (1926; 2d ed., 1933); *Smetana* (1926); *La Musique aux temps romantiques* (1930); *La Chanson populaire et les écrivains romantiques* (1931); *Don Juan de Mozart* (1933); *J.-S. Bach* (1934).

BIBL.: L. de La Laurencie, *Un musicien bressan: J. T.* (Bourg-en-Bresse, 1932).

Tietjen, Heinz, noted German conductor and opera producer; b. Tangier, June 24, 1881; d. Baden-Baden, Nov. 30, 1967. He studied conducting with Nikisch. He was then active as an opera producer in Trier (1904–22) and later was administrator of the Berlin City Opera (1925–27); from 1931 to 1944 he was artistic director of the Bayreuth Festivals, where he also conducted. He was again administrator of the Berlin City Opera (1948–55) and also of the Hamburg State Opera (1956–59); he then retired in Baden-Baden.

Tietjens, Therese (Carolina Johanna Alexandra), famous German soprano; b. Hamburg, July 17, 1831; d. London, Oct. 3, 1877. She was trained in Hamburg and Vienna, and in 1849 made her operatic debut in Altona as Donizetti's Lucrezia Borgia, which became her most celebrated role. After singing in Frankfurt am Main (1850–51), Brünn, and Vienna, she made her London debut as Valentine in *Les Huguenots* at Her Majesty's Theatre on April 13, 1858; subsequently she appeared in London every season until her death, making her Covent Garden debut as Lucrezia Borgia on Oct. 24, 1868. She also sang opera in Paris (1863), at the Teatro San Carlo in Naples (1862–63; 1868–69), and in the United States (1874, 1876); she also became well known as an oratorio singer in England. Stricken with cancer, she made her farewell appearance at Covent Garden as Lucrezia Borgia on May 19, 1877, collapsing on the stage at the close of the performance. Among her other outstanding roles were Mozart's Countess, Pamina, and Donna Anna, Cherubini's Medea, Beethoven's Leonore, Bellini's Norma, Verdi's Leonora, and Wagner's Ortrud.

Tigranian, Armen (Tigran), Armenian composer and teacher; b. Alexandropol, Dec. 26, 1879; d. Tbilisi, Feb. 10, 1950. He studied flute and theory in Tiflis. He returned to Alexandropol in 1902 and organized a choral society, specializing in Armenian music; in 1913 he settled in Tiflis, where he became an esteemed music pedagogue; received the Order of Lenin in 1939. He composed the operas *Anush* (1908–12; Alexandropol, Aug. 17, 1912) and *David-bek* (1949; Yerevan, Dec. 3, 1950); also theater music.
BIBL.: K. Melik-Wrtanessian, *A. T.* (Moscow, 1939); R. Atanian and M. Muradian, *A. T.* (Moscow, 1966).

Tijardović, Ivo, Croatian composer; b. Split, Sept. 18, 1895; d. Zagreb, March 19, 1976. He studied in Zagreb. He began his professional career by conducting theater orchs., then wrote operettas of the Viennese type; of these, *Little Floramy* (1924) became successful in Yugoslavia. His opera *Dimnjiaci uz Jadran* (The Chimneys of the Adriatic Coast; Zagreb, Jan. 20, 1951) depicts the patriotic uprising of Yugoslav partisans during World War II; he also wrote the opera *Marco Polo* (Zagreb, Dec. 3, 1960).
BIBL.: I. Plamenac, *I. T.* (Split, 1954).

Tikka, Kari (Juhani), Finnish conductor and composer; b. Siilinjärvi, April 13, 1946. He received training in oboe (diploma, 1968), in conducting from Panula (diploma, 1979), and in composition from Englund, Kokkonen, and Rautavaara at the Sibelius Academy in Helsinki; he also studied conducting with Arvid Jansons in Leningrad and with Luigi Ricci in Rome. He played oboe in the Helsinki Phil. (1965–67) and the Finnish National Opera Orch. in Helsinki (1967–68). In 1968 he made his conducting debut in Helsinki; subsequently he conducted at the Finnish National Opera there (1970–72), then was a conductor of the Finnish Radio Sym. Orch. (1972–76) and director of the Ensemble for Modern Music of the Finnish Radio. From 1975 to 1977 he was a conductor of the Royal Opera in Stockholm; then again he was a conductor at the Finnish National Opera (from 1979) and also appeared as a guest conductor throughout Europe. His works include a Cello Concerto (1984) and other orch. pieces; *The Prodigal Son*, oratorio for 3 Soloists, Chorus, and Orch. (1985); cantatas; accompanied and unaccompanied choral works; chamber music; and solo songs.

Tikotsky, Evgeni (Karlovich), Russian composer of Polish descent; b. St. Petersburg, Dec. 25, 1893; d. Minsk, Nov. 24, 1970. He studied composition with Volkova-Bonch-Bruievich in St. Petersburg (1912–14) before pursuing the study of physics and mathematics at the Univ. there (1914–15). He taught in a music school in Bobruysk (1927–34), then settled in Minsk, where he taught at the music school (1934–41); he was artistic director of the Belorussian State Phil. (1944–45; 1953–57). In 1944 he received the Order of Lenin and in 1955 was made a People's Artist of the USSR. His works included the operas *Mihas Podhorny* (Minsk, March 10, 1939) and *Alesya* (Minsk, Dec. 24, 1944; rev. 1952–53), as well as incidental music and film scores.
BIBL.: I. Gusin, *E. K. T.* (Moscow and Leningrad, 1965).

Tilmant, Théophile (Alexandre), noted French violinist and conductor; b. Valenciennes, July 8, 1799; d. Asnières, near Paris, May 7, 1878. He studied violin with Rodolphe Kreutzer at the Paris Cons. (premier prix, 1819), then was a member of the orchs. at the Théâtre-Italien (from 1819) and of the Opéra (from 1825). He was deputy conductor of the Société des Concerts du Conservatoire (1818–60), and then its chief conductor (1860–63); he also was deputy conductor (1834–38) and chief conductor (1838–49) of the Théâtre-Italien, as well as conductor of the Opéra Comique (1849–68). With his brother, the cellist Alexandre Tilmant (b. Valenciennes, Oct. 14, 1808; d. Paris, June 13, 1880), he was active in a chamber music society.

Tinel, Edgar (Pierre Joseph), Belgian pianist, pedagogue, and composer; b. Sinaii, East Flanders, March 27, 1854; d. Brussels, Oct. 28, 1912. He was taught at first by his father, a schoolmaster and organist, then entered the Brussels Cons. in 1863 as a pupil of Brassin, Dupont, Gevaert, Kufferath, and Mailly; in 1873 he took 1st prize for piano playing and in 1877 won the Belgian Prix de Rome with the cantata *De Klokke Roeland*. In 1881 he became director of the Malines Inst. of Religious Music; he was appointed to the staff of the Brussels Cons. in 1896, and in 1908 became its director. He publ. *Le Chant grégorien, Théorie sommaire de son exécution* (Mechelen, 1890). Among his works were the operas *Godelieve* (Brussels, July 22, 1897) and *Katharina* (Brussels, Feb. 27, 1909) and the oratorio *Franciscu* (Mechelen, 1888).
BIBL.: A. van der Elst, *E. T.* (Ghent, 1901); P. Tinel, *E. T.: Le récit de sa vie et l'exégèse de son œuvre de 1854 à 1886* (Brussels, 1922); idem, *E. T.* (Brussels, 1946).

Tinsley, Pauline (Cecilia), English soprano; b. Wigan, March 27, 1928. She studied at the Northern School of Music in Manchester, then with Joan Cross at the National School of Opera in London. She made her operatic debut in London in 1951 as Desdemona in Rossini's *Otello*; she sang with the Welsh National Opera in Cardiff (from 1962) and the Handel Opera Soc. She joined the Sadler's Wells Opera in London in 1963; she sang at London's Covent Garden from 1965. In 1969 she made her U.S. debut as Anna Bolena at the Santa Fe Opera, and later sang with other U.S. opera companies. Among her prominent roles were Mozart's Countess and Fiordiligi, Aida, Lady Macbeth, Elektra, and Turandot.

Tintner, Georg (Bernhard), Austrian-born New Zealand conductor; b. Vienna, May 22, 1917. He sang in the Vienna Boys' Choir (1926–30), with which he gained experience as a youthful conductor. He studied composition with Marx (diploma, 1936) and conducting with Weingartner (diploma, 1937) at the Vienna Academy of Music. In 1937 he became an assistant conductor at the Vienna Volksoper, but the Anschluss in 1938 compelled him to flee the Nazis. He settled in New Zealand and became a naturalized New Zealand citizen. He conducted the Auckland Choral Soc. (1946–54) and the Auckland String Players (1947–54), and then was resident conductor of the National Opera of Australia (1954–56) and the Elizabethan Trust Opera Co. (later the Australian Opera; 1956–63; 1965–67). From 1964 to 1968 he was music director of the New Zealand Opera in Wellington. He conducted the Cape Town Municipal Orch. (1966–67) and at the Sadler's Wells Opera in London (1967–70). From 1970 to 1973 he was music director of the West Australian Opera Co. He conducted at the Australian Opera from 1973 to 1976. From 1977 to 1987 he was music director of the Queensland Theatre Orch. in Brisbane. He was music director of Sym. Nova Scotia in Canada from 1987 to 1994, thereafter serving as its conductor laureate.

Tippett, Sir Michael (Kemp), greatly renowned English composer; b. London, Jan. 2, 1905; d. there, Jan. 8, 1998. His family was of Cornish descent, and Tippett never refrained from proclaiming his pride of Celtic ancestry. He was equally emphatic in the liberal beliefs of his family. His father was a free thinker, which did not prevent him from running a successful hotel business. His mother was a suffragette who once served a prison term. Her last name was Kemp, which Tippett eventually accepted as his own middle name. He took piano lessons as a child and sang in his school chorus but showed no exceptional merit as a performer. He studied in London at the Royal College of Music (1923–28), where his teachers in composition were Charles Wood and C. H. Kitson; he took piano lessons there with Aubin Raymar and attended courses in conducting with Boult and Sargent and studied counterpoint and fugue with R. O. Morris (1930–32). He subsequently held several positions as a teacher and conductor; from 1933 to 1940 he led the South London Orch. at Morley College; he then served as director of music there (1940–51). Socially Tippett had difficulties even early in life. He openly proclaimed his extremely liberal political views, his overt atheism, and his strenuous pacifism. His oratorio *A Child of Our Time* was inspired by the case of Henschel Grynsban, a Jewish boy who assassinated a member of the German embassy in Paris in 1938. As a conscientious objector during World War II, he refused to serve even in a noncombatant capacity in the British military forces; for this intransigent attitude he was sentenced to prison for 3 months; he served his term in a Surrey County gaol with the suggestive name Wormwood Scrubs (June 21–Aug. 21, 1943). He regained the respect of the community after the end of the war. In 1951 he initiated a series of broadcasts for the BBC; from 1969 to 1974 he directed the Bath Festival. He received high honors from the British government; in 1959 he was named a Commander of the Order of the British Empire; in 1966 he was knighted; in 1979 he was made a Companion of Honour; in 1983 he received the Order of Merit. He visited the United States in 1965, and thereafter was a frequent guest in America; his symphonic works were often performed by major American orchs. Tippett's works have a grandeur of Romantic inspiration that sets them apart from the prevalent type of contemporary music; they are infused with rhapsodic eloquence and further enhanced by a pervading lyric sentiment free from facile sentimentality. He excelled in large-scale vocal and instrumental forms; he was a consummate master of the modern idioms, attaining heights of dissonant counterpoint without losing the teleological sense of inherent tonality. Yet he did not shun special effects; 3 times in his 4th Sym. he injected episodes of heavy glottal aspiration, suggested to him by viewing a film depicting the dissection of fetuses of pigs. A man of great general culture, Tippett possessed a fine literary gift; he wrote his own librettos for his operas and oratorios. He publ. *Moving into Aquarius* (London, 1958; 2d ed., 1974). M. Bowen ed. *Music of the Angels: Essays and Sketchbooks of Michael Tippett* (London, 1980). Tippett's autobiography was publ. as *Those Twentieth-Century Blues* (London, 1991). M. Bowen ed. the vol. *Tippett on Music* (Oxford, 1995).

WORKS: DRAMATIC: *Don Juan*, incidental music to Flecker's play (Oxted, Feb. 1930); *Robin Hood*, folk song opera (1934); *Robert of Sicily*, children's opera (1938); *The Midsummer Marriage*, opera (1946–52; London, Jan. 27, 1955); *King Priam*, opera (1958–61; Coventry, May 29, 1962); *The Tempest*, incidental music to Shakespeare's play (London, May 29, 1962); *The Knot Garden*, opera (1966–69; London, Dec. 2, 1970); *The Ice Break*, opera (1973–76; London, July 7, 1977); *New Year*, opera (1986–88; Houston, Oct. 27, 1989). ORATORIO: *A Child of Our Time* for Soprano, Alto, Tenor, Bass, Chorus, and Orch., to a text by the composer about a Jewish boy (Henschel Grynsban) who, in 1938, assassinated a Nazi member of the German embassy in Paris (1939–41; London, March 19, 1944).

BIBL.: I. Kemp, ed., *M. T.: A Symposium on His 60th Birthday* (London, 1965); M. Hurd, *T.* (London, 1978); E. White, *T. and His Operas* (London, 1979); M. Bowen, *M. T.* (London, 1982); A. Whittall, *The Music of Britten and T.: Studies in Themes and Techniques* (Cambridge, 1982; 2d ed., 1990); I. Kemp, *T.: the Composer and his Music* (London, 1984); N. John, ed., *Operas of M. T.* (London, 1985); G. Lewis, ed., *M. T. O. M.: A Celebration* (Tunbridge Wells, 1985); G. Theil, *M. T.: a Bio-Bibliography* (Westport, Conn., 1989); M. Scheppach, *Dramatic Parallels in M. T.'s Operas: Analytical Essays on the Musico-Dramatic Techniques* (Lewiston, N.Y., 1990); D. Clarke, *T. Studies* (Cambridge, 1998).

Tishchenko, Boris (Ivanovich), Russian composer and teacher; b. Leningrad, March 23, 1939. He was a student of Salmanov, Voloshinov, and Evlakhov at the Leningrad Cons. (graduated, 1962), and then of Shostakovich (1962–65). In 1965 he joined the faculty of the Leningrad Cons., where he was made an assoc. prof. in 1980 and a full prof. in 1986. In 1978 he was awarded the Glinka Prize and in 1987 was made a People's Artist of the USSR. Tishchenko's music is crafted in a masterly fashion in an advanced idiom without overstepping the bounds of tonality. Among his works are *The 12*, ballet (1963), *Fly-bee*, ballet (1968), *The Stolen Sun*, opera (1968), *A Cockroach*, musical comedy (1968), and *The Eclipse*, ballet (1974); also incidental music.

Tisné, Antoine, French composer; b. Lourdes, Nov. 29, 1932. He studied at the Paris Cons. with Hugon, N. Gallon, Dufourcq, Milhaud, and Rivier, taking premiers prix in harmony, counterpoint, fugue, and composition. In 1962 he won the 2d Grand Prix de Rome and the Lili Boulanger Prize. From 1967 to 1992 he served as an inspector of music for the French Ministry of Culture. He also was a prof. of composition and orchestration at the Univ. of Paris. In 1992 he became inspector of music for the municipal conservatoires of the City of Paris. Among his honors were the Grand Prix musical of the City of Paris (1979) and the prize for composers of the Soc. of Authors, Composers, and Editors of Music (1988). In his music, Tisné has adopted various contemporary techniques.

WORKS: DRAMATIC: *La Ramasseuse de sarments*, music theater (1980); *Point fixe*, ballet (1982); *Les Enfants du Ciel*, children's musical spectacle (1984); *Instant*, ballet (1985); *Le Chemin des bulles*, children's opera (1988); *Pour l'amour d'Alban*, opera (1993). Also *Maryam*, oratorio for Soloists, Chorus, and Orch. (1990).

BIBL.: D. Niemann, *A. T., ou composer c'est exister* (Paris, 1991).

Titl, Anton Emil, Bohemian conductor and composer; b. Pernstein, Oct. 2, 1809; d. Vienna, Jan. 21, 1882. He took counterpoint lessons with Gottfried Rieger in Brünn, and in 1840 went to Vienna as conductor of the Theater in der Josefstadt; from 1850 to 1870 he was conductor at the Burgtheater there. He wrote 2 operas: *Die Burgfrau* (Brunn, 1832) and *Das Wolkenkind* (Vienna, March 14, 1845); also many Singspiels, including the successful *Zauberschleier* (Vienna, 1842), and incidental music.

Titov, Alexei Nikolaievich, Russian violinist and composer, brother of **Sergei Nikolaievich Titov**; b. St. Petersburg, June 24, 1769; d. there, Nov. 20, 1827. He served in the cavalry, reaching the rank of major general at his retirement. He was an amateur violinist, and wrote operas in the traditional Italian style; of these, the following were produced in St. Petersburg: *Andromeda and Perseus* (1802); *The Judgment of Solomon* (1803); *Nurzadakh* (June 7, 1807); *The Wedding of Filatka* (April 25, 1808); *Errant Moment* (July 10, 1812); *Emmerich Tekkely* (Dec. 13, 1812); *Intrigue in the Basket* (May 12, 1817); *Valor of the People of Kiev, or These Are the Russians* (May 12, 1817); *The Feast of the Mogul* (Sept. 15, 1823); also *The Brewer, or The Hidden Ghost of Evil* (Moscow, 1788). A ballet pantomime, *Le Nouveau Werther*, was first given in St. Petersburg, on Jan. 30, 1799. His son, Nikolai Alexeievich Titov (1800–1875), was also a composer.

Titov, Sergei Nikolaievich, Russian violinist, cellist, and composer, brother of **Alexei Nikolaievich Titov**; b. St. Petersburg, 1770; d. 1825. He rose to major general in the army. His best known works were the opera *Krestyane, ili Vstrecha nezvanikh* (The Peasants, or the Party for the Uninvited; 1814) and the ballet *Noviy Verter* (The New Werther). His son, Nikolai Sergeievich Titov (b. probably in St. Petersburg, 1798; d. 1843), also pursued a military career; he also was a fine composer of songs, which included the popular "Talisman" (1829).

Titta, Ruffo Cafiero. See **Ruffo, Titta.**

Titus, Alan (Wilkowski), American baritone; b. N.Y., Oct. 28, 1945. He was a student of Aksel Schiøtz at the Univ. of Colo. and of Hans Heinz at the Juilliard School of Music in New York, where he sang as Rossini's Figaro. In 1969 he made his formal operatic debut as Marcello in Washington, D.C. He first gained wide recognition when he created the role of the Celebrant in Bernstein's *Mass* at the inauguration of the Kennedy Center in Washington, D.C., on Sept. 8, 1971. After appearing with the N.Y. City Opera and the San Francisco Spring Opera in 1972, he made his European debut as Pelléas in Amsterdam in 1973. On March 20, 1976, he made his Metropolitan Opera debut in New York as Harlekin in *Ariadne auf Naxos*. He made his first appearance at the Glyndebourne Festival in 1979 as Guglielmo. In 1984 he sang Don Giovanni at the Deutsche Oper am Rhein in Düsseldorf. In 1985 he appeared as Storch in *Intermezzo* in Santa Fe. In 1987 he sang

Oliviero in *Capriccio* at the Maggio Musicale in Florence. He appeared as Creonte in Haydn's *Orfeo ed Euridice* at the Salzburg Festival in 1990, and that same year sang Storch in the Italian premiere of *Intermezzo* in Bologna. In 1992 he sang Donizetti's Duca d'Alba at the Spoleto Festival. In 1995 he appeared in the title role of Hindemith's *Mathis der Maler* at London's Covent Garden. He portrayed Pizzaro in Rome in 1996.

Titus, Hiram, American pianist and composer; b. Minneapolis, Jan. 28, 1947. He studied with Emil Dananberg (piano) and Richard Hoffman (composition) at Oberlin (Ohio) College (B.A., 1958), with Guy Duckworth (piano) and Dominick Argento (composition) (1957–63), and with Walter Hartley in Interlochen, Mich. (summers 1963–64). In addition to concert and stage works, he composed a number of scores for television and theater productions, winning DramaLogue awards for music (1979, 1980). Among his compositions are the opera *Rosina* (Minneapolis, 1980) and *The Sand Hills*, oratorio for Soloists, Men's Chorus, Tape, and Ensemble (Los Angeles, 1987).

Toch, Ernst, eminent Austrian-born American composer and teacher; b. Vienna, Dec. 7, 1887; d. Los Angeles, Oct. 1, 1964. His father was a Jewish dealer in unprocessed leather, and there was no musical strain in the family; Toch began playing piano without a teacher in his grandmother's pawnshop; he learned musical notation from a local violinist, and then copied Mozart's string quartets for practice; using them as a model, he began to compose string quartets and other pieces of chamber music; at the age of 17, he had one of them, his 6th String Quartet, op. 12 (1905), performed by the famous Rosé Quartet in Vienna. From 1906 to 1909 he studied medicine at the Univ. of Vienna. In 1909 he won the prestigious Mozart Prize and a scholarship to study at the Frankfurt am Main Cons., where he studied piano with Willy Rehberg and composition with Iwan Knorr. In 1910 he was awarded the Mendelssohn Prize; he also won 4 times in succession the Austrian State Prize. In 1913 he was appointed instructor in piano at Zuschneid's Hochschule für Musik in Mannheim. From 1914 to 1918 he served in the Austrian army during World War I. After the Armistice he returned to Mannheim, resumed his musical career, and became active in the modern movement, soon attaining, along with Hindemith, Krenek, and others, a prominent position in the new German school of composition. He also completed his education at the Univ. of Heidelberg (Ph.D., 1921, with the diss. *Beiträge zur Stilkunde der Melodie*; publ. in Berlin, 1923, as *Melodielehre*). In 1929 he went to Berlin, where he established himself as a pianist, composer, and teacher of composition. In 1932 he made an American tour as a pianist playing his own works; he returned to Berlin, but with the advent of the Nazi regime was forced to leave Germany in 1933. He went to Paris, then to London, and in 1935 emigrated to the United States; he gave lectures on music at the New School for Social Research in N.Y.; in 1936, moved to Hollywood, where he wrote music for films. He became a naturalized American citizen on July 26, 1940. In 1940–41 he taught composition at the Univ. of Southern Calif. in Los Angeles; subsequently he taught privately; among his students were many who, like Andre Previn, became well-known composers in their own right. From 1950 until his death, Toch traveled frequently and lived in Vienna, Zürich, the MacDowell Colony in New Hampshire, and Santa Monica, Calif.

Toch's music is rooted in the tradition of the German and Austrian Romantic movement of the 19th century, but his study of the classics made him aware of the paramount importance of formal logic in the development of thematic ideas. His early works consist mostly of chamber music and pieces for piano solo; following the zeitgeist during his German period, he wrote several pieces for the stage in the light manner of sophisticated entertainment; he also composed effective piano works of a virtuoso quality, which enjoyed considerable popularity among pianists of the time. Toch possessed a fine wit and a sense of exploration; his *Geographical Fugue* for speaking chorus, articulating in syllabic counterpoint the names of exotic places on earth, became a classic of its genre. It was not until 1950 that Toch wrote his first full-fledged sym., but from that time on, until he died of stomach cancer, he composed fully 7 syms., plus sinfoniettas for Wind and String Orch. He was greatly interested in new techniques; the theme of his last String Quartet (No. 13, 1953) is based on a 12-tone row. In the score of his 3d Sym. he introduced an optional instrument, the Hisser, a tank of carbon dioxide that produced a hissing sound through a valve.

Among the several honors Toch received were the Pulitzer Prize in Music for his 3d Sym. (1956), membership in the National Inst. of Arts and Letters (1957), and the Cross of Honor for Sciences and Art from the Austrian government (1963). An Ernst Toch Archive was founded at the Univ. of Calif., Los Angeles, in 1966, serving as a depository for his MSS.

WORKS: DRAMATIC: OPERAS: *Wegwende* (1925; unfinished; sketches destroyed); *Die Prinzessin auf der Erbse* (Baden-Baden, July 17, 1927); *Der Facher* (Königsberg, June 8, 1930); *The Last Tale* (1960–62). FILM SCORES: *Peter Ibbetson* (1935); *Outcast* (1937); *The Cat and the Canary* (1939); *Dr. Cyclops* (1940); *The Ghost Breakers* (1940); *Ladies in Retirement* (1941); *First Comes Courage* (1943); *None Shall Escape* (1944); *Address Unknown* (1944); *The Unseen* (1945). Also incidental music for stage and radio plays.

WRITINGS: *The Shaping Forces in Music* (N.Y., 1948; new ed. by L. Weschler, 1977); M. Hood, ed., *Placed as a Link in this Chain: A Medley of Observations by Ernst Toch* (Los Angeles, 1971).

BIBL.: C. Johnson, *The Unpublished Works of E. T.* (diss., Univ. of Calif., Los Angeles, 1973); L. Weschler, *E. T., 1887–1964: A Biographical Essay Ten Years after His Passing* (Los Angeles, 1974); J. Diane, *The Musical Migration and E. T.* (Ames, Iowa, 1989).

Toczyska, Stefania, Polish mezzo-soprano; b. Gdansk, Feb. 19, 1943. She was a pupil of Barbara Iglikovska at the Gdansk Cons. She took prizes in competitions in Toulouse (1972), Paris (1973), and s'Hertogenbosch (1974). In 1973 she made her operatic debut as Carmen at the Gdansk Opera, and then sang throughout Poland. In 1977 she made her Western European operatic debut as Amneris with the Basel Opera. Later that year she made her first appearance at the Vienna State Opera as Ulrica, and returned there to sing Carmen, Azucena, Eboli, and Preziosilla. In 1979 she sang Eboli at the Bavarian State Opera in Munich and at the Hamburg State Opera, and then appeared as Laura in *La Gioconda* at the San Francisco Opera. She made her Covent Garden debut in London in 1983 as Azucena and in 1986 made her first appearance at the Chicago Lyric Opera as Giovanna Seymour in *Anna Bolena*. In 1987 she sang Adalgisa at the Houston Grand Opera and Venus in *Tannhäuser* at the Barcelona Opera. She made her Metropolitan Opera debut in New York as Laura in *La Gioconda* in 1989. In 1990 she sang at the Caracalla Festival in Rome. In 1992 she appeared as Massenet's Dulcinée in Toulouse. She was engaged as Amneris at the Metropolitan Opera in 1997. In addition to her active operatic career, she has also toured widely as a concert artist.

Toda, Kunio (Morikuni), Japanese composer and teacher; b. Tokyo, Aug. 11, 1915. He studied at the Univ. of Heidelberg (1938–39); following diplomatic service in Moscow (1939–41), he returned to Tokyo to study with Saburo Moroi. He was sent to Indochina in 1944; when World War II ended in 1945, he was detained until 1948. Upon his return to Tokyo, he became active in contemporary-music circles; he introduced 12-note serialism to his homeland. He remained active as a diplomat until 1964; he taught at the Toho Gakuen School of Music (from 1955), remaining on its faculty as a prof. when it became a college in 1961; he also was director and a prof. at the Senzolku Gakuen Academy of Music (from 1975); he retired in 1988 from the latter, but continued as a guest prof. until 1991.

WORKS: DRAMATIC: OPERAS: *Akemi* (Tokyo, 1956); *Kyara monogatari* (History of the City of Kyara; Tokyo, 1973). BALLETS: *Atorie no Salome* (Salome in Studio; Tokyo, Nov. 23, 1951); *Akai tenmaku* or *Le Cirque rouge* (Tokyo, Nov. 4, 1953); *Dokutsu* (The

Cave; Tokyo, Nov. 7, 1954); *Miranda* (Tokyo, Oct. 26, 1968). SCENIC-ORATORIO MYSTERY: *Shito Paolo* (St. Paul; 1961–64; concert perf., Tokyo, Feb. 15, 1973). OTHER: *Jochu no Anna* (Anna la Bonne), monodrama for Soprano, 2 Violas, and Tape (Tokyo, Nov. 17, 1978); *Kesa to Morito* (Kesa and Morito), dramatic cantata for Soprano, Baritone, and String Quintet (Tokyo, Nov. 16, 1979).

Todi, Luisa (**Luiza Rosa**, née **d'Aguiar**), famous Portuguese mezzo-soprano; b. Setubal, Jan. 9, 1753; d. Lisbon, Oct. 1, 1833. She made her debut as a comic actress at age 14 in Lisbon, and married the violinist Francesco Saverio Todi, concertmaster of the theater orch., when she was 16. She studied with David Perez, making her opera debut in 1770 in Scolari's *Il Viaggiatore ridicolo* in Lisbon; during the 1777–78 season, she sang comic opera at the King's Theatre in London, then established herself as a serious artist with her debut at the Paris Concert Spirituel (Nov. 1, 1778). After appearances in Germany, Austria, and Italy, she returned to Paris in 1783 and became a rival of Gertrud Elisabeth Mara at the Concert Spirituel; 2 hostile factions squared off, the Todistes and the Maratistes. After singing at Berlin's Royal Opera, she went to St. Petersburg in 1784, winning great acclaim for her appearances in Sarti's *Armida e Rinaldo* (Jan. 1786) and *Castore e Polluce* (Sept. 22, 1786). After singing in Moscow in Pollinia (April 23, 1787), she returned to Berlin (1788–89); she also sang in Mainz, Hannover, and Venice (1790–91). After further engagements in Italy and in Prague (1791), she appeared at the Madrid Opera (1792–93; 1794–95); she then sang at the Teatro San Carlo in Naples (1797–99). In 1803 she retired to Lisbon, where she spent her final years in total blindness.

BIBL.: J. Ribeiro Guimaraes, *Biographia de Luiza de Aguiar T.* (Lisbon, 1872); J. de Vasconcellos, *Luiza T.: Estudo critico* (Oporto, 1873; 2d ed., 1929); M. de Sampayo Ribeiro, *Luisa de Aguiar T.* (Lisbon, 1934).

Toduţă, Sigismund, Romanian composer and teacher; b. Simeria, May 30, 1908; d. Cluj, July 3, 1991. He studied with Negrea at the Cluj Cons. (1931–33), and later at the Accademia di Santa Cecilia in Rome (1936–38) with Pizzetti (composition) and Casella (piano); he also took courses in musicology at the Pontificio Istituto di Musica Sacra in Rome (Ph.D., 1938, with a diss. on G. F. Anerio). In 1946 he was appointed to the faculty of the Cluj Cons. (he was its director from 1962 to 1964); in 1971 he became managing director of the Cluj State Phil. His music was distinguished by a flowing Romantic melody in large rhapsodic sonorities. Among his works was the opera *Meşterul Manole* (Master-builder Manole; 1943–47; as an opera oratorio, 1977–82; Cluj, Oct. 1, 1985) and 3 oratorios: *Mioriţa* (1958–68; Bucharest, Oct. 7, 1968), *Balada steagului* (1961), and *Pe urmele lui Horea* (1976–78; Cluj, Dec. 2, 1978).

Toeschi, family of prominent German musicians of Italian descent, originally named **Toesca**:

(1) Alessandro Toeschi, violinist and composer; b. probably in Rome, before 1700; d. Mannheim (buried), Oct. 15, 1758. He was descended from a family of the nobility. After touring in England and Germany, he served as court musician to the Landgrave Ernst Ludwig of Hesse in Darmstadt (1719–24), then was 2d maître des concerts at the Wurttemberg court in Stuttgart (1725–37). He subsequently settled in Mannheim as Konzertmeister about 1742, and was director of instrumental church music at the Palatine court there from about 1750. He had 2 sons who became musicians.

(2) Carl Joseph Toeschi, violinist and composer, the most outstanding member of the family; b. Ludwigsburg (baptized), Nov. 11, 1731; d. Munich, April 12, 1788. He studied with Johann Stamitz and Anton Filtz, and in 1752 he became a violinist in the Mannheim Court Orch.; he was made its Konzertmeister in 1759, and in 1774 was named music director of the electoral cabinet; he followed the court to Munich in 1778. He was one of the leading composers of the Mannheim school. Among his output were over some 30 ballets.

(3) Johann (Baptist) (Maria) Christoph Toeschi, violinist and composer, known as **Toesca de Castellamonte**; b. Stuttgart (baptized), Oct. 1, 1735; d. Munich, March 3, 1800. He studied with Johann Stamitz and Christian Cannabich; in 1755 became a violinist in the Mannheim Court Orch., and was also director of the Court Ballet there (from 1758); he was named Konzertmeister in 1774. In 1778 he followed the court to Munich, where he was music director (from 1793); he also was director of the court chapel in 1798; that same year his family was granted hereditary Italian nobility and the right to use the title "de Castellamonte." He wrote a melodrama, *Dirmel und Laura* (Munich, 1784), and at least 4 ballets, but they are not among his extant compositions. His son, Karl Theodor Toeschi (b. Mannheim, April 17, 1768; d. Munich, Oct. 10, 1843), was also a composer; he was active at the Munich court (1780–89) and was named Bavarian chamber composer in 1801. Among his works were an opera and a ballet, also not extant.

Tofts, Catherine, English soprano; b. c.1685; d. Venice, 1756. She first gained notice as a singer when she appeared in a series of London concerts (1703–04). In 1704 she sang at London's Drury Lane, where she soon became a leading rival of Margherita de L'Epine. From 1705 until she was stricken with insanity in 1709 she was a member of the company. She apparently recovered sufficiently to marry Joseph Smith, who served as English consul in Venice.

Tokatyan, Armand, Bulgarian tenor of Armenian descent; b. Plovdiv, Feb. 12, 1896; d. Pasadena, Calif., June 12, 1960. He was educated in Alexandria, Egypt, then studied voice with Cairone in Milan and Wolf in Vienna. He made his operatic debut in Milan in 1921, then went to the United States, where he toured with the Scotti Opera Co. He made his debut at the Metropolitan Opera in New York on Nov. 19, 1922, as Turiddu in a concert performance of Cavalleria rusticana, and remained a member of the company, with interruptions, until 1946. He also made appearances in London, Berlin, and Vienna.

Tolbecque, family of Belgian-French musicians:

(1) Jean-Baptiste-Joseph Tolbecque, violinist, conductor, and composer; b. Hanzinne, Namur, April 17, 1797; d. Paris, Oct. 23, 1869. He studied violin with Kreutzer and counterpoint and fugue with Reicha at the Paris Cons. He was a violinist in the orch. of the Opéra Italien (1820–25), and then conductor of the Tivoli gardens orch. in Paris; he subsequently oversaw the court dances for Louis Philippe I and helped to organize the Société des Concerts du Conservatoire, where he was a violist. With Gilbert and Guiraud, he wrote the opéra comique *Charles V et Duguesclin* (1827), and with Deldevez, the ballet *Vert-Vert* (Paris, 1851), but he became best known as a composer of waltzes, galops, quadrilles, polkas, and other popular dances. Three of his brothers were also musicians.

(2) Isidore-Joseph Tolbecque, conductor and composer; b. Hanzinne, April 17, 1794; d. Vichy, Allier, May 10, 1871. He pursued a career as a conductor and composer of dance music.

(3) August-Joseph Tolbecque, violinist; b. Hanzinne, Feb. 28, 1801; d. Paris, May 27, 1869. He was a pupil of Kreutzer at the Paris Cons., where he won the premier prix (1821). He was a member of the Opera orch. (1824–31); he also played in the Société des Concerts du Conservatoire and subsequently performed at Her Majesty's Theatre in London.

(4) Charles-Joseph Tolbecque, violinist, conductor, and composer; b. Paris, May 27, 1806; d. there, Dec. 29, 1835. He studied with Kreutzer at the Paris Cons., taking the premier prix in violin (1823). After playing in the Société des Concerts du Conservatoire, he became conductor at the Théâtre des Variétées (1830). He wrote incidental music for theater productions and songs.

(5) Auguste Tolbecque, cellist, instrument maker, and composer, son of **Auguste-Joseph Tolbecque**; b. Paris, March 30, 1830; d. Niort, Deux Sèvres, March 8, 1919. He studied cello (premier prix, 1849) with Vaslin and harmony with Reber at the Paris Cons. After playing in the orch. of the Grand Théâtre and teaching at the Cons. in Marseilles (1865–71), he returned to Paris and played with the Société des Concerts du Conservatoire, the Lamoureux Quartet, and the Maurin Quartet. He received instruction in instrument making from Victor Rambaux and then settled in Niort, where he devoted himself to restoring early instruments and making copies of same. He ed. *Monde Musical* and publ. the exercise vol. *La Gymnastique du violoncelle* (Paris, 1875). His works include the opéra comique *Après la valse* (Niort, 1894). His son, Jean Tolbecque (b. Niort, Oct. 7, 1857; d. probably in Paris, 1890), was also a cellist; he was a pupil of Alexandre Chevillard at the Paris Cons. (premier prix, 1873) and then was a member of the Opéra Comique orch.

WRITINGS: *Quelques considérations sur la lutherie* (Paris, 1890); *Souvenirs d'un musicien en province* (Niort, 1896); *Notice historique sur les instruments à cordes et à archet* (Paris and Niort, 1898); *L'Art du luthier* (Niort, 1903).

Toldrá, Eduardo, Catalan violinist, conductor, and composer; b. Villanueva y Geltru, Catalonia, April 7, 1895; d. Barcelona, May 31, 1962. He studied violin and composition at Barcelona's municipal music school. He made his debut as a soloist at the Barcelona Ateneo (1912), then was founder-1st violinist of the Quartet Renaixement (1912–21). In 1921 he became a prof. of violin at Barcelona's municipal music school; in 1944 he was appointed conductor of the Municipal Orch. He composed the comic opera *El giravolt de Maig* (Barcelona, 1928).

BIBL.: M. Capdevila Massana, *E. T.* (Barcelona, 1964; 2d ed., rev., 1972); A. Batista, *E. T.: Un assaig sobre la direcció d'orquestra a Barcelona* (Barcelona, 1995).

Tolonen, Jouko (Paavo Kalervo), Finnish musicologist and composer; b. Porvoo, Nov. 2, 1912; d. Turku, July 23, 1986. He studied piano with Linko, composition with Krohn, Madetoja, and Fougestedt, and conducting in Helsinki; he pursued training in musicology at the Univ. there (Ph.D., 1969). He was director of the music dept. of the Finnish Broadcasting Co. (1946–55) and general director of the Finnish National Opera (1956–60); he taught at the Sibelius Academy in Helsinki (1960–66) and at the Univ. of Turku (from 1965), where he was prof. of musicology (1972–77). He composed various scores, including incidental music for plays and films.

Tolstoy, Dmitri, Russian composer, son of the writer Alexei Tolstoy; b. Berlin, Jan. 20, 1923. He went to Russia with his father after the latter's temporary emigration; he studied at the Leningrad Cons., graduating in 1947; he took courses in composition with Shebalin in Moscow and Shostakovich in Leningrad. Among his works were the operas *Masquerade* (1955; Moscow, Jan. 17, 1956) and *Mariuta* (Perm, Dec. 30, 1960).

Tomaschek (Tomášek), Wenzel Johann (Václav Jan Křtitel), important Bohemian composer and pedagogue; b. Skutsch, April 17, 1774; d. Prague, April 3, 1850. He was the youngest of 13 children. He learned the rudiments of singing and violin playing from P. J. Wolf and studied organ with Donat Schuberth. In 1787 he became an alto chorister at the Minorite monastery in Iglau; in 1790 he went to Prague, supporting himself by playing piano in public places; he also took law courses at the Univ. of Prague. From 1806 to 1822 he was attached to the family of Count Georg Bucquoy de Longeval as music tutor. In 1824 he established his own music school in Prague. Among his many pupils were J. H. Woržischek (Voříšek), Dreyschock, Hanslick, and Schulhoff. Tomaschek was the first to use the instrumental form of the rhapsody systematically in a number of his piano pieces, although it was anticipated by W. R. Gallenberg in a single composition a few years earlier; he also adopted the ancient Greek terms "eclogue" and "dithyramb" for short character pieces. He wrote an autobiography, publ. in installments in the Prague journal *Libussa* (1845–50); a modern ed. was prepared by Z. Nmec (Prague, 1941), excerpts of which appeared in the *Musical Quarterly* (April 1946). His works included the operas *Seraphine, oder Grossmut und Liebe* (Prague, Dec. 15, 1811) and *Alvaro* (unfinished).

BIBL.: M. Tarantová, *Václav Jan Tomášek* (Prague, 1946); M. Postler, *V.J. Tomášek: Bibliografie* (Prague, 1960).

Tomasi, Henri (Frédien), French composer; b. Marseilles, Aug. 17, 1901; d. Paris, Jan. 13, 1971. He studied with Paul Vidal at the Paris Cons.; he won the 2d Grand Prix de Rome for his cantata *Coriolan* (1927). He served in the French army (1939–40). Tomasi was awarded the Grand Prix de Musique Française in 1952. His music is marked by impressionistic colors; he was particularly attracted to exotic subjects, depicting in fine instrumental colors scenes in Corsica, Cambodia, Laos, Sahara, Tahiti, etc. He also wrote music inspired by Gregorian chant and medieval religious songs. During his last period he was motivated in his music by political events, and wrote pieces in homage to the Third World and Vietnam.

WORKS: DRAMATIC: OPERAS: *Miguel de Manâra* (1942; Munich, March 29, 1956); *L'Altantide* (1952; Mulhouse, Feb. 26, 1954); *La triomphe de Jeanne* (1955; Rouen, 1956); *Sampiero Corso* (Bordeaux, May 1956); *Il Poverello* (1957); *Le silence de la mer* (1959); *Ulysse* (1961); *L'élixir du révérend père Gaucher* (1962). BALLETS: *La Grisi* (Paris, Oct. 7, 1935); *La Rosière de village* (Paris, May 26, 1936); *Les Santons* (Paris, Nov. 18, 1938); *La Féerie cambodgienne* (Marseilles, Jan. 31, 1952); *Les Folies mazarguaises* (Marseilles, Oct. 5, 1953); *Noces de cendre* (Strasbourg, Jan. 19, 1954); *Les Barbaresques* (Nice, 1960); *Nana*, after Émile Zola (1962). CHOREOGRAPHIC POEM: *Dassine, sultane du Hoggar* for 2 Speakers, Chorus, and Orch. (1959).

Tomlinson, John (Rowland), distinguished English bass; b. Oswaldtwistle, Lancashire, Sept. 22, 1946. He took a B.Sc. degree in civil engineering at the Univ. of Manchester, and also received vocal training at the Royal Northern College of Music in Manchester and from Otakar Kraus in London. In 1970 he became a member of the Glyndebourne Festival Chorus; his first operatic role of consequence was as the 2d Armed Man in *Die Zauberflöte* with the Glyndebourne Touring Opera Co. in 1970, which led to his first major role with the company in 1972 as Colline; he also appeared as Leporello that year with the Kent Opera. After an engagement with the New Opera Co. in London (1972–74), he sang regularly with the English National Opera in London (1975–80), where he distinguished himself as Masetto, King Marke, Rossini's Moses, Méphistophélès, Baron Ochs, and Bartók's Bluebeard. He made his debut at London's Covent Garden in 1979 as Colline, and returned there successfully in such roles as Mozart's Figaro, Leporello, the Commendatore, and Don Basilio. In 1988 he made his first appearance at the Bayreuth Festival as Wotan, a role he sang there regularly for 5 seasons; he also appeared as the Wanderer there (from 1989). In 1992 he sang Gurnemanz at the Berlin State Opera, and in 1993 returned to Covent Garden as Hans Sachs. In 1994 he again appeared as Wotan at the Bayreuth Festival, a role he reprised at the Berlin State Opera in 1996. In 1997 he was engaged as Baron Ochs and as Hans Sachs at Covent Garden. He portrayed Schonberg's Moses at his Metropolitan Opera debut in New York on Feb. 8, 1999. Tomlinson's commanding vocal technique and histrionic abilities have rendered him as one of the leading bassos of his generation. Among his other notable roles are Hunding, Philip II, Boris Godunov, Attila, and John Claggart.

Tommasini, Vincenzo, Italian composer; b. Rome, Sept. 17, 1878; d. there, Dec. 23, 1950. He studied violin with Pinelli, and later theory with Falchi at the Liceo di Santa Cecilia in Rome; he then went to Berlin, where he took lessons with Bruch; after sojourns in Paris, London, and New York, he returned to Rome. He wrote music in the poetic tradition of Italian Romanticism; his operas, symphonic works, and chamber music obtained immediate performances and favorable receptions; however, his most successful piece, *Le Donne di buon umore*, was not an original work but a comedy ballet written on music from sonatas by Domenico Scarlatti, arranged in a series of tableaux and brilliantly orchestrated; this was a commission for the Ballets Russes of Diaghilev, who staged it at Rome in April 1917, and kept it in the repertoire during his tours all over the world. He publ. *La luce invisibile* (1929) and *Saggio d'estetica sperimentale* (1942).

WORKS: DRAMATIC: OPERAS: *Medea* (1902–04; Trieste, April 8,

1906); *Amore di terra lontana* (1907–08); *Uguale fortuna* (1911; Rome, 1913); *Dielja* (c.1935); *Il tenore sconfitto, ovvero La presunzione punita* (Rome, 1950). BALLETS: *Le donne di buon umore* (1916; Rome, April 1917; suite, 1920; based on sonatas by D. Scarlatti); *Le diable s'amuse* (1936; N.Y., 1937); *Tiepolesco* (Naples, 1945).

Tomowa-Sintow, Anna, admired Bulgarian soprano; b. Stara Zagora, Sept. 22, 1941. She studied at the Bulgarian State Cons. in Sofia with Zlatew-Tscherkin and Zpiridonowa. In 1965 she made her operatic debut as Tatiana in Stara Zagora. She made her first appearance at the Leipzig Opera as Abigaille in 1967, and subsequently sang Arabella, Cio-Cio-San, Desdemona, and Violetta there. After winning the Sofia (1970) and Rio de Janeiro (1971) competitions, she made her debut at the Berlin State Opera as Mozart's Countess in 1972. Her career was assured when Karajan chose her to create the role of Sibyl in the premiere of Orff's *De temporum fine comoedia* at the Salzburg Festival in 1973. She continued to sing there with much success in subsequent years, and also appeared at Karajan's Salzburg Easter Festivals. In 1974 she sang Donna Anna at the Bavarian State Opera in Munich, and made her U.S. debut that same year at the San Francisco Opera in the same role. In 1975 she appeared for the first time at London's Covent Garden as Fiordiligi. She made her debut at the Vienna State Opera in 1977 as Mozart's Countess. Her subsequent successes there led to her being made an Austrian Kammersängerin in 1988. On April 3, 1978, she made her Metropolitan Opera debut in New York as Donna Anna. She appeared as Wagner's Elisabeth at the Paris Opéra in 1984. In 1990 she sang Yaroslavna in *Prince Igor* at Covent Garden. In 1992 she appeared as Tosca in Helsinki. She was engaged as Ariadne in Lisbon in 1996. She also sang extensively as a concert artist. Among her other notable roles are Verdi's Amelia and Aida, Wagner's Elsa, and Strauss's Marschallin.

Toni, Alceo, Italian musicologist and composer; b. Lugo, May 22, 1884; d. Milan, Dec. 4, 1969. He was a pupil of L. Torchi and E. Bossi in Bologna. He was director of the Rovereto Cons. (1908–10), technical director of D'Annunzio's Raccolta Nazionale delle Musiche Italiane (1918–21), a critic for the *Popola d'Italia* (1922–43), and president of the Milan Cons. (1936–40). He ed. numerous works by Corelli, Locatelli, Torelli, Monteverdi, Carissimi, and other early Italian composers. His own compositions include the opera *Su un cavallin di legno* (1914) and the ballet *I Fantocci ribelli* (1930). Some of his many articles were collected in a book, *Studi critici di interpretazione* (Milan, 1923; 2d ed., 1955). With Tullio Serafin, he publ. *Stile, tradizioni e convenzioni del melo dramma italiano del Settecento e dell'Ottocento* (2 vols., Milan, 1958–64).

Töpper, Hertha, Austrian mezzo-soprano; b. Graz, April 19, 1924. She received her musical training in Graz, studying violin with her father at the Cons. and voice with Franz Mixa at the opera school. She made her operatic debut in 1945 as Ulrica at the Graz Landestheater, where she sang until 1952. In 1951 she appeared at the Bayreuth Festival; after singing as a guest artist at the Bavarian State Opera in Munich in 1951–52, she joined its roster; was made a Bavarian Kammersängerin in 1955. In 1953 she made her first appearance at London's Covent Garden as Clairon with the visiting Bavarian State Opera, and later returned for guest appearances. She made her U.S. debut at the San Francisco Opera in 1960 as Octavian, a role she repeated for her Metropolitan Opera debut in New York on Nov. 19, 1962. From 1971 to 1981 she was a prof. at the Munich Hochschule für Musik. In 1980 she retired from the operatic stage. Her operatic repertoire included many roles by Wagner, Verdi, and Strauss; as a concert artist, she was particularly noted for her performances of the music of Bach.

Toradze, David (Alexandrovich), noted Russian composer; b. Tiflis, April 14, 1922; d. there (Tbilisi), Nov. 7, 1983. He studied composition with Barkhudarian and piano with Virsaladze at the Tbilisi Cons.; after pursuing composition studies with Glière at the Moscow Cons., he completed postgraduate work at the Tbilisi Cons. (1948–51), then in 1952 joined its faculty; he was made a reader in 1966 and a prof. in 1973. He received various honors, including the State Prize (1951), People's Artist of the Georgian S.S.R. (1961), and the Order of Lenin. His son, Alexander (David) Toradze (b. Tbilisi, May 30, 1952), is a notable pianist and teacher.

WORKS: DRAMATIC: OPERAS: *The Sumarmi Fortress* (1942); *The Call of the Mountains* (Tbilisi, Nov. 20, 1947); *The Bride of the North* (Tbilisi, 1958). BALLETS: *Gorda* (Tbilisi, 1949); *For Peace* (Tbilisi, June 17, 1953; rev. as *The Unsubdued*, 1970). MUSICAL COMEDIES: *Natel* (1948); *The Avengers* (1952). Also film scores.

Torke, Michael, American composer and pianist; b. Milwaukee, Sept. 21, 1961. He began piano lessons at 5 and commenced composing while still a youth. After studying composition with Rouse and Schwantner and piano with Burge at the Eastman School of Music in Rochester, N.Y. (graduated, 1984), he pursued graduate studies with Druckman and Bresnick at Yale Univ. (1984–85). He won the Prix de Rome and held a residency at the American Academy in Rome in 1986. His output reveals an effective blend of serious and pop music genres.

WORKS: DRAMATIC: *Estatic Orange*, ballet (N.Y., May 10, 1985; includes *Verdant*, later renamed *Green*, for Orch., Milwaukee, Nov. 20, 1986, and the ballet *Purple*, N.Y., June 11, 1987); *The Directions*, chamber opera (Iraklion, Crete, Aug. 6, 1986); *Black and White*, ballet (N.Y., May 7, 1988); *Slate*, ballet (N.Y., June 15, 1989); *King of Hearts*, television opera (1993; Channel 4, England, Jan. 1995).

Torrefranca, Fausto (Acanfora Sansone dei duchi di Porta e), eminent Italian musicologist; b. Monteleone Calabro, Feb. 1, 1883; d. Rome, Nov. 26, 1955. Trained as an engineer, he took up music under E. Lena in Turin (harmony and counterpoint) and also studied by himself. It was through his initiative that the first chair of musicology was established in Italy. In 1913 he became a lecturer at the Univ. of Rome; from 1914 to 1924, was a prof. of music history at the Cons. di S. Pietro in Naples, and from 1915, also librarian there; from 1924 to 1938 he was librarian of the Milan Cons. From 1907 he was ed. of the *Rivista Musicale Italiana*. In 1941 he was appointed a prof. of music history at the Univ. of Florence.

WRITINGS: *La vita musicale dello spirito: La musica, le arti, il dramma* (Turin, 1910); *Giacomo Puccini e l'opera internazionale* (Turin, 1912); *Le origine italiane del romanticismo musicale: I primitivi della sonata moderna* (Turin, 1930); *Il segreto del quattrocento: Musiche ariose e poesia popularesca* (Milan, 1939).

Torri, Pietro, Italian composer; b. Peschiera, c.1650; d. Munich, July 6, 1737. He served as court organist and later Kapellmeister at the court in Bayreuth (until 1684), and in 1689 he became organist at the court of Max Emanuel II, elector of Bavaria, in Munich. When the elector became governor of the Spanish Netherlands in 1692, he took Torri with him to Brussels as his maître de chapelle. In 1696 he was conductor for the carnival season at Hannover; in 1701 he was appointed court chamber music director at Munich, following the elector to Brussels upon the latter's exile in 1704; he fled Brussels with the elector (1706). In Brussels he produced the oratorio *La vanitá del mondo* (March 5, 1706); from 1715 he was again in Munich, where he was made Hofkapell-Direktor; later he was named Hofkapellmeister (1732). He composed about 20 operas, 2 of which were produced at the Munich court: *Lucio Vero* (Oct. 12, 1720) and *Griselda* (Oct. 12, 1723), but he became best known in his lifetime for his vocal chamber pieces.

Tosatti, Vieri, Italian composer; b. Rome, Nov. 2, 1920. He studied piano on his own; also composition with Dobici, Ferdinandini, Jachino, and Petrassi at the Rome Cons. (diploma, 1942) and with Pizzetti. In his compositions he often exploits sensational or morbid subjects, setting them to pungent music, with a liberal application of special effects. Among his works are the operas *Dionisio* (1947), *Il sistema della dolcezza* (1949), *La partita a pugni* (Venice, Sept. 8, 1953), *Il giudizio universale* (1955), *L'isola* *del tesoro* (1958), *La fiera della Meraviglie* (1963), and *Il paradiso e il poeta* (1971).

Toscanini, Arturo, great Italian conductor; b. Parma, March 25, 1867; d. N.Y., Jan. 16, 1957. He entered the Parma Cons. at the age of 9, studying the cello with Carini and composition with Dacci; graduated in 1885 as winner of the 1st prize for cello; he received the Barbacini Prize as the outstanding graduate of his class. In 1886 he was engaged as cellist for the Italian opera in Rio de Janeiro; on the evening of June 30, 1886, he was unexpectedly called upon to substitute for the regular conductor, when the latter left the podium at the end of the introduction after the public hissed him; the opera was *Aida*, and Toscanini led it without difficulty; he was rewarded by an ovation and was engaged to lead the rest of the season. Returning to Italy, he was engaged to conduct the opera at the Teatro Carignano in Turin, making his debut there on Nov. 4, 1886, and later conducted the Municipal Orch. there. Although still very young, he quickly established a fine reputation. From 1887 to 1896 he conducted opera in the major Italian theaters. On May 21, 1892, he led the premiere of *Pagliacci* in Milan, and on Feb. 1, 1896, the premiere of *La Bohème* in Turin. He also conducted the first performance by an Italian opera company, sung in Italian, of *Götterdämmerung* (Turin, Dec. 22, 1895) and *Siegfried* (Milan, 1899); he made his debut as a sym. conductor on March 20, 1896, with the orch. of the Teatro Regio in Turin. In 1898 the impresario Gatti-Casazza engaged him as chief conductor for La Scala, Milan, where he remained until 1903, and again from 1906 to 1908. In the interim, he conducted opera in Buenos Aires (1903–4; 1906). When Gatti-Casazza became general manager of the Metropolitan Opera (1908), he invited Toscanini to be principal conductor; Toscanini's debut in New York was in *Aida* (Nov. 16, 1908). While at the Metropolitan, Toscanini conducted Verdi's *Requiem* (Feb. 21, 1909), as well as 2 world premieres, Puccini's *The Girl of the Golden West* (Dec. 10, 1910) and Giordano's *Madame Sans-Gêne* (Jan. 25, 1915); he also brought out for the first time in America Gluck's *Armide* (Nov. 14, 1910), Wolf-Ferrari's *Le Donne curiose* (Jan. 3, 1912), and Mussorgsky's *Boris Godunov* (March 19, 1913). On April 13, 1913, he gave his first concert in New York as a sym. conductor, leading Beethoven's 9th Sym. In 1915 he returned to Italy; during the season of 1920–21, he took the La Scala Orch. on a tour of the United States and Canada. From 1921 to 1929 he was artistic director of La Scala; there he conducted the posthumous premiere of Boito's opera *Nerone*, which he completed for performance (May 1, 1924). In 1926–27 he was a guest conductor of the N.Y. Phil., returning in this capacity through the 1928–29 season; he then was its assoc. conductor with Mengelberg in 1929–30; subsequently he was its conductor from 1930 to 1936; he took it on a tour of Europe in the spring of 1930. He conducted in Bayreuth in 1930 and 1931. Deeply touched by the plight of the Jews in Germany, he acceded to the request of the violinist Huberman, founder of the Palestine Sym. Orch., to conduct the inaugural concert of that orch. at Tel Aviv (Dec. 26, 1936). During this period, he also filled summer engagements at the Salzburg Festivals (1934–37), and conducted in London (1935; 1937–39). He became music director of the NBC Sym. Orch. in New York in 1937, a radio orch. that had been organized especially for him; he conducted his first broadcast on Dec. 25, 1937, in New York. He took it on a tour of South America in 1940, and on a major tour of the United States in 1950. He continued to lead the NBC Sym. Orch. until the end of his active career; he conducted his last concert from Carnegie Hall, N.Y., on April 4, 1954 (10 days after his 87th birthday).

Toscanini was one of the most celebrated masters of the baton in the history of conducting; undemonstrative in his handling of the orch., he possessed an amazing energy and power of command. He demanded absolute perfection, and he erupted in violence when he could not obtain from the orch. what he wanted (a lawsuit was brought against him in Milan when he accidentally injured the concertmaster with a broken violin bow). Despite the vituperation he at times poured on his musicians, he was affectionately known to them as "The Maestro" who could do no wrong. His ability to communicate his desires to singers and players was extraordinary, and even the most celebrated opera stars or instrumental soloists never dared to question his authority. Owing to extreme nearsightedness, Toscanini committed all scores to memory; his repertoire embraced virtually the entire field of Classical and Romantic music; his performances of Italian operas, of Wagner's music dramas, of Beethoven's syms., and of modern Italian works were especially inspiring. Among the moderns, he conducted works by Richard Strauss, Debussy, Ravel, Prokofiev, and Stravinsky, and among Americans, Samuel Barber, whose *Adagio for Strings* he made famous; he also had his favorite Italian composers (Catalani, Martucci), whose music he fondly fostered. In his social philosophy, he was intransigently democratic; he refused to conduct in Germany under the Nazi regime. He militantly opposed Fascism in Italy, but never abandoned his Italian citizenship, despite his long years of residence in America. In 1987 his family presented his valuable private archive to the N.Y. Public Library.

BIBL.: G. Ciampelli, *A. T.* (Milan, 1923); E. Cozzani, *A. T.* (Milan, 1927); T. Nicotra, *A. T.* (tr. from the Italian, N.Y., 1929); D. Bonardi, *T.* (Milan, 1929); P. Stefan, *A. T.* (Vienna, 1936; Eng. tr., N.Y., 1936); L. Gilman, *T. and Great Music* (N.Y., 1938); S. Hoeller, *A. T.* (N.Y., 1943); G. Ciampelli, *T.* (Milan, 1946); A. Della Corte, *T.* (Vicenza, 1946); D. Nives, *A. T.* (Milan, 1946); F. Sacchi, *T.* (Milan, 1951; Eng. tr. as *The Magic Baton: T.'s Life for Music*, N.Y., 1957); H. Taubman, *The Maestro: The Life of A. T.* (N.Y., 1951); S. Chotzinoff, *T.: An Intimate Portrait* (N.Y., 1956); R. Marsh, *T. and the Art of Orchestral Performance* (Philadelphia, 1956); B. Haggin, *Conversations with T.* (N.Y., 1959; 2d ed., enl., 1979); S. Hughes, *The T. Legacy: A Critical Study of A. T.'s Performances of Beethoven, Verdi, and Other Composers* (London, 1959); L. Frassati, *Il Maestro A. T. e il suo mondo* (Turin, 1967); A. Armani, ed., *T. e La Scala* (Milan, 1972); G. Marek, *T.* (N.Y., 1975); H. Sachs, *T.* (Philadelphia, 1978); D. Matthews, *A. T.* (Tunbridge Wells and N.Y., 1982); J. Freeman and W. Toscanini, *T.* (N.Y., 1987); J. Horowitz, *Understanding T.: How He Became an American Culture-God and Helped to Create a New Audience for Old Music* (N.Y., 1987); H. Sachs, *A. T. dal 1915 al 1946: l'arte all'ombra della politica: omaggio al maestro nel 30° anniversario della scomparsa* (Turin, 1987); idem, *Reflections on T.* (N.Y., 1991); G. Marchesi, *A. T.* (Turin, 1993).

Toselli, Enrico, Italian pianist, teacher, and composer; b. Florence, March 13, 1883; d. there, Jan. 15, 1926. He studied with Sgambati and Martucci. He gave concerts in Italy as a pianist. He wrote the operettas *La cattiva Francesca* (1912) and *La principessa bizzarra* (1913). In 1907 he married the former crown princess Luise of Saxony, creating an international furor; following their separation in 1912, he recounted this affair in his book *Mari d'altessee: 4 ans de mariage avec Louise de Toscane, ex-princesse de Saxe* (Paris, 1913; Eng. tr., 1913).

Tosi, Pier Francesco, prominent Italian castrato contralto, teacher, diplomat, and composer; b. Cesena, c.1653; d. Faenza, April 1732. He studied with his father, then sang successfully in Italy and throughout Europe; in 1692 he settled in London, where he gave regular concerts, and was highly esteemed as a vocal teacher. He was a composer at the Viennese court (1705–11), while concurrently serving as an emissary to Count Johann Wilhelm of the Palatinate. About 1723 he returned to London, where he remained until 1727; later he returned to Italy and took holy orders in Bologna in 1730; he finally settled in Faenza. He wrote the valuable treatise *Opinioni de' cantori antichi e moderni, o sieno Osservazioni sopra il canto figurato* (Bologna, 1723; in Eng., 1742, as *Observations on the Florid Song*; in Ger. as *Anleitung zur Singkunst*, 1757; in French as *L'Art du chant*, 1774; the Eng. ed. was republ. in London in 1967).

Tosti, Sir (Francesco) Paolo, Italian-born English singing teacher and composer; b. Ortano sul Mare, April 9, 1846; d. Rome, Dec. 2, 1916. He was a pupil, from 1858, of the Collegio di S. Pietro a Majella, Naples, and was appointed sub-teacher (maestrino) by Mercadante (until 1869). He visited London in 1875, where he had great success in concerts and settled as a teacher, becoming singing master to the royal family in 1880, and prof. of singing at the Royal Academy of Music in 1894. He became a British subject in 1906 and was knighted in 1908; he retired to Rome in 1912. Besides many original songs, in both English and Italian, he publ. a collection of *Canti popolari abruzzesi*. His songs were highly popular; some of the best known are "Goodbye Forever and Forever," "Mattinata," and "Vorrei morire."

BIBL.: E. Mario, *F. P. T.* (Siena, 1947); A. Piovano, *Ommagio a F. P. T.* (Ortona, 1972); J. Little, *Romantic Italian Song in the Works of F. P. T. and some of his Contemporaries* (diss., Univ. of Illinois, 1977).

Tóth, Aladár, eminent Hungarian writer on music and opera administrator; b. Székesfehérvár, Feb. 4, 1898; d. Budapest, Oct. 18, 1968. He received training in piano and composition in his native city; he then studied at the Scientific Univ. of Budapest (Ph.D., 1925, with the diss. *Adatok Mozart zenedrámáinak esztétikájához*; Contribution to the Aesthetics of Mozart's Dramatic Music). He was a music critic for the newspapers *Új nemzedék* (1920–23) and *Pesti napló* (1923–39), and also for the literary journal *Nyugat* (1923–40). After living in Switzerland during World War II, he returned to Budapest to serve as director of the Hungarian State Opera (1946–56). In 1952 he was awarded the Kossuth Prize. He married the distinguished Hungarian pianist Annie Fischer (b. Budapest, July 5, 1914) in 1937.

WRITINGS (all publ. in Budapest unless otherwise given): *Mozart: Figaro lakodalma* (Mozart: Marriage of Figaro; 1928); ed. with B. Szabolcsi, *Zenei lexikon* (1930–31; 2d ed., rev., 1965); *Zoltán Kodály* (Vienna, 1932); *Liszt Ferenc a magyar zene útján* (Franz Liszt on the Trail of Hungarian Music; 1940); with B. Szabolcsi, *Mozart* (1941); *Verdi művészi hitvallása* (Verdi's Artistic Confession; 1941); F. Bónis, ed., *Tóth Aladár válogatott zenekritikái* (Aladár Tóth's Selected Criticisms of Music; 1968).

Toulmouche, Frédéric (Michel), French composer; b. Nantes, Aug. 3, 1850; d. Paris, Feb. 20, 1909. He studied with Victor Massé in Paris, and in 1894 became director of the Menus-Plaisirs theater. He composed the opéras comique *Le Moûtier de St.-Guignolet* (Brussels, 1885), *La Veillée des noces* (Paris, 1888; in London, 1892, as *The Wedding Eve*), *L'Ame de la patrie* (St. Brieuc, 1892), *La Perle du Cantal* (Paris, 1895), and *La St.-Valentin* (Paris, 1895), and about a dozen operettas and some ballets.

Tourangeau, (Marie Jeannine) Huguette, Canadian mezzo-soprano; b. Montreal, Aug. 12, 1940. She studied voice at the Montreal Cons. with Ruzena Herlinger, repertoire with Otto-Werner Mueller, and declamation with Roy Royal. In 1962 she made her debut in Monteverdi's *Vespro della Beata Virgine* at the Montreal Festival; her operatic debut followed as Mercedes in *Carmen* in Montreal in 1964. She toured in the United States as a member of the Metropolitan Opera National Co. (1964–65), then appeared in Seattle, London, San Francisco, and Hamburg. On Nov. 28, 1973, she made her formal Metropolitan Opera debut in New York as Nicklausse in *Les Contes d'Hoffmann*, and returned in later seasons as a guest artist. In 1974 she sang at the Sydney Opera and made her debut at London's Covent Garden as Elisabetta in *Maria Stuarda* in 1977. Her repertory included roles from French, German, and Italian operas.

Tourel (real name, **Davidovich**), **Jennie,** prominent Russian-born American mezzo-soprano; b. Vitebsk, June 22, 1900; d. N.Y., Nov. 23, 1973. She played flute, then studied piano. After the Revolution, her family left Russia and settled temporarily near Danzig; they later moved to Paris, where she continued to study piano and contemplated a concert career; she then began to take voice lessons with Anna El-Tour, and decided to devote herself to professional singing; she changed her last name to Tourel by transposing the syllables of her teacher's name. She made her operatic debut at the Opéra Russe in Paris in 1931, then her debut at the Metropolitan Opera in New York on May 15, 1937, as Mignon. In 1940, just before the occupation of Paris by Nazi troops, she went to Lisbon, and eventually emigrated to the United States; she appeared on the Metropolitan Opera roster in 1943–45 and 1946–47. She became a naturalized American citizen in 1946. In 1951 she created the role of Baba the Turk in Stravinsky's *The Rake's Progress* in Venice. In later years, she devoted herself to recitals and orch. engagements, excelling particularly in the French repertoire. She also taught at the Juilliard School of Music in New York and at the Aspen (Colo.) School of Music.

Tournemire, Charles (Arnould), distinguished French organist and composer; b. Bordeaux, Jan. 22, 1870; d. Arachon, Nov. 3, 1939. He began his training as a child in Bordeaux; he was only 11 when he became organist at St. Pierre, and later was organist at St. Seurin; then went to Paris, where he studied piano with Bériot, harmony with Taudou, and organ (premier prix, 1891) with Widor and Franck at the Cons.; he also studied composition with d'Indy at the Schola Cantorum. He was organist at Ste. Clotilde (from 1898) and a prof. at the Cons. (from 1919) and also toured Europe. His major achievement as a composer was *L'Orgue mystique* (1927–32), comprising 51 Offices for the Roman Catholic liturgy. Among his other works were the operas *Nittetis* (1905–07), *Les Dieux sont morts* (1910–12; Paris, March 19, 1924), *La Légende de Tristan* (1925–26), and *Il Poverello di Assisi* (1936–38).

WRITINGS: *César Franck* (Paris, 1931); *Précis d'exécution, de registration et d'improvisation à l'orgue* (Paris, 1936); *Petite méthode d'orgue* (Paris, 1949).

BIBL.: J.-M. Fauquet, *Catalogue de l'oeuvre de C. T.* (Geneva, 1979).

Tovey, Sir Donald (Francis), eminent English music scholar, pianist, and composer; b. Eton, July 17, 1875; d. Edinburgh, July 10, 1940. He studied privately with Sophie Weisse (piano), Parratt (counterpoint), and James Higgs and Parry (composition) until 1894, when he won the Nettleship scholarship at Balliol College, Oxford; he graduated with Classical Honors (B.A., 1898). In 1894 he appeared as a pianist with Joachim, and subsequently performed regularly with his quartet; in 1900–01 he gave a series of chamber music concerts in London, at which he performed several of his own works; in 1901–02 he gave similar concerts in Berlin and Vienna; he played his Piano Concerto in 1903 under Henry Wood and in 1906 under Hans Richter, then was an active participant in the concerts of the Chelsea Town Hall and of the Classical Concert Society. In 1914 he succeeded Niecks as Reid Prof. of music at the Univ. of Edinburgh; he founded the Reid Orch. in 1917. He made his U.S. debut as a pianist in 1925; he presented a series of concerts with renowned guest artists in Edinburgh in 1927–28. In 1935 he was knighted. Though highly esteemed as a composer, he was most widely known as a writer and lecturer on music, his analytical essays being models of their kind. Besides much chamber music and several piano pieces, he composed an opera, *The Bride of Dionysus* (Edinburgh, April 23, 1929).

WRITINGS (all publ. in London): *A Companion to the Art of the Fugue* (1931); *Essays in Musical Analysis* (6 vols., 1935–39); with G. Parratt, *Walter Parratt: Master of Music* (1941); *A Musician Talks* (1941); H. Foss, ed., *Essays in Musical Analysis: Chamber Music* (1944); idem, ed., *Musical Articles from the Encyclopaedia Britannica* (1944); idem, ed., *Beethoven* (1944); *A Companion to Beethoven's Piano Sonatas* (1948); H. Foss, ed., *Essays and Lectures on Music* (1949).

BIBL.: M. Grierson, *D.F. T.* (London, 1952).

Townsend, Douglas, American composer and musicologist; b. N.Y., Nov. 8, 1921. He studied at the High School of Music and Art in New York, then received lessons in composition from Serly, Wolpe, Copland, Luening, Greissle et al. He taught at Brooklyn College of the City Univ. of N.Y. (1958–69), Lehman College of the City Univ. of N.Y. (1970–71), the Univ. of Bridgeport, Conn. (1973–75), and the State Univ. of N.Y. in Purchase (1973–76); he served as ed. of the *Musical Heritage Review* (1977–80).

WORKS: DRAMATIC: Three 4-minute operas (1947); 3 folk operettas (1947); *Lima Beans*, chamber opera (1954; N.Y., Jan. 7,

1956); *The Infinite*, ballet (1951; N.Y., Feb. 13, 1952); film and television scores.

Toyama, Yuzo, Japanese composer; b. Tokyo, May 10, 1931. He received his training at the Tokyo Academy of Music (graduated, 1951) and in Vienna (1958–60). His works include *Yugen*, ballet (1965), *Gion Festival*, musical (1966), and *Such a Long Absence*, opera (Osaka, April 3, 1972).

Toye, (John) Francis, English writer on music, brother of **(Edward) Geoffrey Toye**; b. Winchester, Jan. 27, 1883; d. Florence, Oct. 31, 1964. He was a pupil of S. P. Waddington and E. J. Dent. He became a critic for various newspapers in London; in 1923 he lectured on modern music in the United States; from 1939 to 1946, lived in Rio de Janeiro; from 1946, in Florence.

WRITINGS (all publ. in London unless otherwise given): *The Well-Tempered Musician* (1925); *Giuseppe Verdi: His Life and Works* (1931; 2d ed., 1962); *Rossini: A Study in Tragi-comedy* (1934; 2d ed., 1954); *For What We Have Received: An Autobiography* (Melbourne, 1950); *Italian Opera* (1952); *Truly Thankful? A Sequel to an Autobiography* (1957).

Toye, (Edward) Geoffrey, English conductor and composer, brother of **(John) Francis Toye**; b. Winchester, Feb. 17, 1889; d. London, June 11, 1942. He studied at the Royal College of Music in London. He became a conductor at various theaters there. He wrote an opera, *The Red Pen* (London, Feb. 7, 1927), and a ballet.

Tozzi, Giorgio (George), gifted American bass; b. Chicago, Jan. 8, 1923. He commenced vocal training when he was 13, and later studied biology at De Paul Univ. while pursuing his vocal studies with Rosa Raisa, Giacomo Rimini, and John Daggett Howell in Chicago. On Dec. 29, 1948, he made his professional debut under the name George Tozzi as Tarquinius in Britten's *The Rape of Lucretia* in New York. After singing in the musical comedy *Tough at the Top* in London in 1949, he received further vocal instruction from Giulio Lorandi in Milan. In 1950 he made his debut as Rodolfo in *La sonnambula* at Milan's Teatro Nuovo. He sang for the first time at Milan's La Scala in 1953 as Stromminger in *La Wally*. On March 9, 1955, he made his Metropolitan Opera debut in New York as Alvise. He remained on its roster until 1975, becoming well known for such roles as Rossini's Basilio, Mozart's Figaro, Pimen, Boris Godunov, Sparafucile, Ramfis, Hans Sachs, and Pogner; he also created the role of the Doctor in Barber's *Vanessa* there in 1958. His career took him to such operatic centers as San Francisco, Hamburg, Salzburg, Florence, and Munich. In 1977 he appeared in the U.S. premiere of Glinka's *Ruslan and Ludmilla* in Boston. A remarkably versatile artist, he was successful not only in opera and concert settings but also in films, television, and musical comedy. His fine vocal technique was complemented by his assured dramatic gifts. From 1991 he taught at the Indiana Univ. School of Music in Bloomington.

Traetta, Filippo, Italian-American teacher and composer, son of **Tommaso (Michele Francesco Saverio) Traetta**; b. Venice, Jan. 8, 1777; d. Philadelphia, Jan. 9, 1854. He was a pupil of Fenaroli and Perillo at Venice, later of Piccinni at Naples. Becoming a soldier in the patriot ranks, he was captured and cast into prison; he escaped 6 months afterward, and sailed to Boston, arriving there in 1799. With Mallet and Graupner, he founded Boston's American Conservatorio in 1801. Shortly after he went to Charleston, S.C., where he was active as a performer and teacher (1808–17). He settled in Philadelphia in 1822 and founded the American Cons. Among his compositions were an opera, *The Venetian Maskers* (n.d.), and 3 oratorios, *Peace* (N.Y., Feb. 21, 1815), *Jerusalem in Affliction* (1828), and *The Daughters of Zion* (1829).

WRITINGS: (all publ. in Philadelphia): *An Introduction to the Art and Science of Music (n.d.); Rudiments of the Art of Singing, written and composed . . . A. D. 1800* (1841–43); *Trajetta's Preludes for the Piano Forte . . . Introductory to his System of Thorough Bass* (1857).

Traetta, Tommaso (Michele Francesco Saverio), esteemed Italian composer, father of **Filippo Traetta**; b. Bitonto, near Bari, March 30, 1727; d. Venice, April 6, 1779. He entered the Cons. di S. Maria di Loreto in Naples at the age of 11, where he studied with Porpora and Durante. After leaving the Cons. in 1748, he wrote his first known opera, *Il Farnace*, which was produced at the Teatro San Carlo with fine success, on Nov. 4, 1751; there followed several more operas in Naples, and later in other Italian cities. In 1758 he was appointed maestro di cappella to the duke of Parma. His *Armida* was staged in Vienna (Jan. 3, 1761) with excellent success, and he was commissioned to write another opera for Vienna, *Ifigenia in Tauride*, which was produced there on Oct. 4, 1763. He settled in Venice in 1765, and was director of the Cons. dell'Ospedaletto S. Giovanni for 3 years. In 1768 he was engaged for the court of Catherine the Great as successor to Galuppi, and arrived in St. Petersburg in the autumn of that year. He staged several of his operas there (mostly versions of works previously performed in Italy); he also arranged music for various occasions (anniversary of the coronation of Catherine the Great, celebration of a victory over the Turkish fleet, etc.). He left Russia in 1775 and went to London, where he produced the opera *Germondo* (Jan. 21, 1776), without much success. By 1777 he had returned to Venice, where he produced his last 2 operas, *La disfatta di Dario* (Feb. 1778) and *Gli eroi dei campi Elisi* (Carnival 1779). In many respects, Traetta was an admirable composer, possessing a sense of drama and a fine melodic gift. In musical realism, he adopted certain procedures that Gluck was to employ successfully later on; he was highly regarded by his contemporaries. Besides operas, he wrote an oratorio, *Rex Salomone* (Venice, 1766).

BIBL.: V. Capruzzi, *T. e la musica* (Naples, 1873); A. Nuovo, *T. T.* (Rome, 1922); F. Schlitzer, ed., *T. T., Leonardo Leo, Vincenzo Bellini: Notizie e documenti*, Chigiana, IX (1952); E. Saracino, *T. T.: cenni biografico-artistici* (Bitonto, 1954); F. Casavola, *T. T. di Bitonto (1727–1779): la vita e le opere* (Bari, 1957); D. Binetti, *T. T. nella vita e nell'arte* (1972).

Trambitsky, Victor (Nikolaievich), Russian pianist, conductor, teacher, and composer; b. Brest-Litovsk, Feb. 12, 1895; d. Leningrad, Aug. 13, 1970. He went to Petrograd, where he began training with Kalafati in 1915, and then became his pupil at the Cons. in 1917. In 1930 he moved to Sverdlovsk; he taught at the Cons. from 1933. He composed the operas *Gadfly* (Sverdlovsk, 1929), *Orlena* (1934; rev. as *For Life*, 1937), *The Storm* (1941; rev. 1957), *Days and Nights* (1950), and *The Laceworker Nastia* (Leningrad, 1963).

Tranchell, Peter (Andrew), English composer and teacher; b. Cuddalore, India, July 14, 1922; d. Bishops Waltham, Sept. 14, 1993. He studied at King's College, Univ. of Cambridge (B.A., 1946; Mus.B., 1949; M.A., 1950); he taught at the Univ. from 1950 to 1989; he was made a Fellow and director of music at Gonville and Caius College, Cambridge, in 1960.

WORKS: DRAMATIC: OPERAS: *The Mayor of Casterbridge* (Cambridge, July 30, 1951); *Zuleika* (1954); *Bacchae* (1956); *Troades* (1957); *Antigone* (1959). BALLETS: *Falstaff* (1950); *Fate's Revenge* (1951); *Euridice* (1952); *Spring Legend* (1957); *Images of Love* (1964). CONCERT ENTERTAINMENTS: *Daisy Simpkins* for Solo Voices, Chorus, and 2 Pianos (1954); *Murder at the Towers* for Solo Voices, Chorus, and 2 Pianos (1955; rev. 1986); *Aye, aye, Lucian!* for Men's Voices, Men's Chorus, and Piano (1960); *The Mating Season* for Solo Voices, Men's Chorus, and Piano (1962; rev. 1969); *His 1st Mayweek* for Solo Voices, Men's Chorus, and 2 Pianos (1963); *The Robot Emperor* for Men's Voices, Men's Chorus, and Orch. (1965).

Traubel, Helen (Francesca), noted American soprano; b. St. Louis, June 20, 1899; d. Santa Monica, Calif., July 28, 1972. She studied with Vetta Karst. She made her concert debut as soloist in Mahler's 4th Sym. with the St. Louis Sym. Orch. on Dec. 13, 1923. On May 12, 1937, she made her Metropolitan Opera debut in New York as Mary Rutledge in Damrosch's *The Man without a Country*; her first major role there was Sieglinde on Dec. 28, 1939; subsequently she became the leading American Wagnerian soprano on its roster, excelling especially as Isolde, Elisabeth, Brünnhilde, Elsa, and Kundry. In 1953 she made appearances in N.Y. nightclubs; this prompted objections from the Metropolitan Opera management, and as a result she resigned from the Metropolitan. She also appeared on Broadway in *Pipe Dream* (1955), in films, and on television. She publ. the mystery novels *The Ptomaine Canary* and *The Metropolitan Opera Murders* (N.Y., 1951), and an autobiography, *St. Louis Woman* (N.Y., 1959).

Travis, Roy (Elihu), American composer and teacher; b. N.Y., June 24, 1922. He studied with William J. Mitchell and Luening at Columbia Univ. (B.A., 1947; M.A., 1951); he also studied privately with Salzer (1947–50), with Wagenaar at the Juilliard School of Music in New York (B.S., 1949; M.S., 1950), and with Milhaud on a Fulbright scholarship in Paris (1951–52). He taught at Columbia Univ. (1952–53), the Mannes College of Music (1952–57), and at the Univ. of Calif. at Los Angeles (from 1957), where he was a prof. (from 1968). In 1972–73 he held a Guggenheim fellowship. Among his works are the operas *The Passion of Oedipus* (1965; Los Angeles, Nov. 8, 1968) and *The Black Bacchants* (1982).

Traxel, Josef, German tenor; b. Mainz, Sept. 29, 1916; d. Stuttgart, Oct. 8, 1975. He studied at the Hochschule für Musik in Darmstadt. He made his operatic debut as Don Ottavio in Mainz in 1942; in 1946 he joined the Nuremberg Opera; from 1952 he was a member of the Württemberg State Theater in Stuttgart; he later taught at the Hochschule für Musik there. He also sang at Salzburg, Bayreuth, Berlin, Vienna, and Munich; he toured North America as well. His operatic repertoire ranged from Mozart to Wagner; he was also a concert singer.

Trebelli, Zelia (real name, **Gloria Caroline Gillebert**), noted French mezzo-soprano; b. Paris, 1838; d. Étretat, Aug. 18, 1892. She took up the study of voice at 16 with Wartel, and in 1859 made her operatic debut as Rosina in *Il Barbiere di Siviglia* in Madrid; she sang at the Berlin Royal Opera in 1860 and at the Théâtre-Italien in Paris in 1861. On May 6, 1862, she made her first appearance in London in *Lucrezia Borgia* at Her Majesty's Theatre, remaining a London favorite for a quarter of a century. She sang Siebel in *Faust* (June 11, 1863), Taven in *Mireille* (July 5, 1864), and Preziosilla in *La forza del destino* (June 22, 1867) at their London premieres; she appeared at Drury Lane (1868–70), where she sang Frederick in the London premiere of *Mignon* (July 5, 1870); she sang at Covent Garden (1868–71; 1881–82; 1888). She toured the United States with Mapleson's company in 1878; on Oct. 26, 1883, she made her Metropolitan Opera debut in New York as Azucena, remaining on the company's roster until 1884. She retired from the operatic stage in 1888. Her husband was the tenor Alessandro Bettini.

BIBL.: M. de Mensiaux, *T.: A Biographical Sketch* (London, 1890).

Treigle, Norman, remarkable American bass-baritone; b. New Orleans, March 6, 1927; d. there, Feb. 16, 1975. He sang in a church choir as a child; upon graduation from high school in 1943, he served in the navy. After two years in service, he returned to New Orleans and studied voice with Elizabeth Wood. He made his operatic debut in 1947 with the New Orleans Opera as Lodovico in Verdi's *Otello*. He then joined the N.Y. City Opera, making his debut there on March 28, 1953, as Colline in *La Bohème*; he remained with the company for 20 years, establishing himself as a favorite with the public. Among his most successful roles were Figaro in Mozart's *Le nozze di Figaro*, Don Giovanni, Méphistophélès, and Boris Godunov; he also sang in modern operas, including leading roles in the premieres of 3 operas by Carlisle Floyd: *The Passion of Jonathan Wade* (N.Y., Oct. 11, 1962), *The Sojourner and Mollie Sinclair* (Raleigh, N.C., Dec. 2, 1963), and *Markheim* (New Orleans, March 31, 1966). Treigle's other parts in contemporary operas were the title role in Dallapiccola's *The Prisoner* and that of the grandfather in Copland's *The Tender Land*. His untimely death, from an overdose of sleeping pills, deprived the American musical theater of one of its finest talents.

Trento, Vittorio, Italian composer; b. Venice, 1761; d. probably in Lisbon, 1833. He was a pupil of Bertoni at the Cons. dei Mendicanti in Venice. He produced several ballets at Venice, followed by a number of cantatas, farces, and comic operas; he returned to Venice to serve as maestro al cembalo at the Teatro La Fenice. He served as maestro concertatore of the Italian Opera in Amsterdam (from 1806), then took up a similar post in Lisbon in 1809. His most popular stage work was the opera buffa *Quanti casi in un sol giorno, ossia Gli assassini* (Venice, 1801), which was also given in London, as *Roberto l'assassino* (Feb. 3, 1807). Other operas include *Teresa vedova* (Venice, Jan. 13, 1802), *Ines de Castro* (Livorno, Nov. 9, 1803), *Ifigenia in Aulide* (Naples, Nov. 4, 1804), *Andromeda* (Naples, May 30, 1805), and *Le Gelosie villane* (Florence, Nov. 2, 1825).

Treptow, Günther (Otto Walther), German tenor; b. Berlin, Oct. 22, 1907; d. there, March 28, 1981. He studied at the Berlin Hochschule für Musik. He made his operatic debut in 1936 at the Deutsches Opernhaus in Berlin as the Italian Tenor in *Der Rosenkavalier*. Although placed on the forbidden list of non-Aryans by the Nazis, he continued to sing in Berlin until 1942, when he joined the Bavarian State Opera in Munich. After the Nazi collapse, he again sang in Berlin at the Städtische Oper (1945–50) and at the Vienna State Opera (1947–55); he appeared as Siegmund in 1951 and 1952 at the Bayreuth Festival and as Siegfried at London's Covent Garden in 1953. He made his Metropolitan Opera debut in New York as Siegmund in *Die Walküre* on Feb. 1, 1951; he remained on its roster until the close of that season; he continued to sing in Europe until his retirement in 1961. In 1971 he was made a Kammersänger.

Treu, Daniel Gottlob, German composer; b. Stuttgart, 1695; d. Breslau, Aug. 7, 1749. He learned to sing and to play the violin and keyboard as a child, and also received training in composition from Johann Kusser; about 1716 he went to Venice to pursue training with Vivaldi and Biffi. In 1725 he became Kapellmeister to an Italian opera troupe in Breslau, where he brought out 4 of his own operas: *Astaro* (1725), *Caio Martio Coriolano* (1726), *Ulisse e Telemacco* (1726), and *Don Chisciotte* (1727). In 1727 he went to Prague, where he served several families of the nobility as Kapellmeister, instrumentalist, and composer; he also was active at the Viennese and Silesian courts, and in Breslau. In 1740 he was made Kapellmeister to the court of Karl Schaffgotsch of Hirschberg in Silesia; he eventually settled in Breslau. Among his other works were arias, most of which are lost.

Tréville, Yvonne de (real name, **Edyth La Gierse**), American soprano; b. Galveston, Texas (of a French father and an American mother), Aug. 25, 1881; d. N.Y., Jan. 25, 1954. She made her debut in New York as Marguerite (1898); she then went to Paris, where she studied with Madame Marchesi. She appeared at the Opéra Comique as Lakme (June 20, 1902); she sang in Madrid, Brussels, Vienna, Budapest, Cairo, and in Russia; from 1913 she gave concert tours in the United States and sang in light operas. Her voice had a compass of 3 full octaves, reaching high G.

Trial, family of French musicians and actors:

(1) Jean-Claude Trial, violinist and composer; b. Avignon, Dec. 13, 1732; d. Paris, June 23, 1771. A child prodigy, he began playing violin and composing for the instrument at an early age. He settled in Paris as 1st violinist in the Opéra Comique orch. After serving as 2d violinist in the private orch. of Prince Conti, he was made its director; was codirector (with Pierre Berton) of the Paris Opéra (1767–69).

WORKS: DRAMATIC: *Renaud d'Ast*, opéra comique (Fontainebleau, Oct. 12, 1765; in collaboration with P. Vachon); *Silvie*, opéra ballet (Fontainebleau, Oct. 17, 1765; in collaboration with P. Berton); *Escope à Cythère*, comédie (Paris, Dec. 15, 1766; in collaboration with P. Vachon); *Thénois, ou Le Toucher*, pastorale héroïque (Fontainebleau, Oct. 11, 1767; in collaboration with P. Berton and L. Granier); *La Fête de Flore*, pastorale héroïque (Fontainebleau, Nov. 15, 1770); *La Chercheuse d'esprit*, comédie (1771); *Linus*, opera (unfinished; in collaboration with P. Berton and A. Dauvergne); also overtures, divertissements, and ariettes.

(2) Antoine Trial, tenor and actor, brother of the preceding; b. Avignon, 1737; d. (suicide) Paris, Feb. 5, 1795. He received his education at the maîtrise at Avignon Cathedral. He went to Paris and became a member of the Prince of Conti's theater troupe, making his public debut in Paris as Bastien in Philidor's *Le Sorcier* at the Comédie-Italienne (July 4, 1764); he became well known for his portrayal of peasants and simpletons. He was a champion of Robespierre and played a prominent role in the period of the Reign of Terror; after Robespierre's downfall in 1794, he lost his following on the stage and took his own life by poison. His wife was the soprano and actress Marie-Jeanne (née Milon) Trial (b. Paris, Aug. 1, 1746; d. Versailles, Feb. 13, 1818); after vocal training, she made her debut at the Théâtre-Italien in Paris under the name Felicite Mandeville in 1766; following her first husband's death, she married Trial and became a popular favorite on the Parisian stage; poor health led to her retirement in 1786. She was particularly esteemed for her performances in works by Grétry and Monsigny. Their son, Armand-Emmanuel Trial (*fils*) (b. Paris, March 1, 1771; d. there, Sept. 9, 1803), was a pianist and composer; he began composing for the Comédie-Italienne when he was 17; he was director of singing at the Théâtre-Lyrique (from 1797); his dissolute ways led to an early demise. His works, all first performed in Paris, included *Julien et Colette, ou La Milice*, comédie (March 3, 1788), *Adélaide et Mirval, ou La Vengeance paternelle* (June 6, 1791), *Les Deux Petits aveugles*, opéra comique (July 28, 1792), *Cécile et Julien, ou Le Siège de Lille*, comédie (Nov. 21, 1792), *Le Congrès des rois*, opera (Feb. 26, 1793; in collaboration with others), and *La Cause et les effets, ou Le Reveil du peuple*, opéra comique (Aug. 17, 1793).

Trimble, Lester (Albert), American music critic, teacher, and composer; b. Bangor, Wis., Aug. 29, 1920; d. N.Y., Dec. 31, 1986. He began violin studies in Milwaukee when he was 9; he later studied with Lopatnikoff and Dorian at the Carnegie Inst. of Technology in Pittsburgh (B.F.A., 1948; M.F.A.); he also studied with Milhaud and Copland at the Berkshire Music Center at Tanglewood, and then with Boulanger, Milhaud, and Honegger in Paris (1950–52). He began writing music criticism for the *Pittsburgh Post-Gazette* while in school, then was a music critic for the *N.Y. Herald-Tribune* (1952–62), the *Nation* (1957–62), the *Washington Evening Star* (1963–68), and *Stereo Review* (1968–74); he also was managing ed. of *Musical America* (1960–61). He was composer-in-residence of the N.Y. Phil. (1967–68) and at the Wolf Trap Farm Park (1973). He was prof. of composition at the Univ. of Maryland (1963–68) and taught at N.Y.'s Juilliard School (from 1971). His works included *Little Clay Cart*, incidental music (1953), *The Tragical History of Dr. Faustus*, incidental music (1954), and *Boccaccio's Nightingale*, opera (1958–62; rev. 1983); also film scores.

Tritto, Giacomo (Domenico Mario Antonio Pasquale Giuseppe), Italian composer and teacher; b. Altamura, April 2, 1733; d. Naples, Sept. 16, 1824. He studied with Cafaro at the Cons. della Pieta de' Turchini in Naples, becoming maestrino there and Cafaro's assistant; he was made maestro straordinario in 1785, secondo maestro in 1793, and primo maestro in 1799. In 1804 he was appointed maestro of the royal chamber. Bellini, Spontini, Mercadante, Meyerbeer, and Conti were his pupils. He wrote over 50 operas, both comic and serious; many were produced in various Neapolitan theaters, and others in Rome, Madrid, Vienna, and Venice; however, they were generally undistinguished. He also composed much sacred music. He publ. *Partimenti e regole generali per conoscere qual numerica dar si deve ai vari movimenti del basso* (Milan, 1821) and *Scuola di contrappunto, ossia Teoria musicale* (Milan, 1823).

BIBL.: G. de Napoli, *La triade melodrammatica altamurana: G. T., Vincenzo Lavigna, Saverio Mercandante* (Milan, 1931).

Trojahn, Manfred, German composer and teacher; b. Cremlingen, near Braunschweig, Oct. 22, 1949. He received training in orch. music at the Niedersächsische Musikschule in Braunschweig (1966–70; diploma, 1970) and composition with Diether de la Motte at the Staatlichen Hochschule für Musik in Hamburg. In 1975 he won the Bach Prize in Hamburg. In 1979–80 he was in residence at the Villa Massimo in Rome. He was awarded the Niedersächsisches Künstlerstipendium in 1984. In 1991 he became a teacher of composition at the Robert-Schumann-Hochschule in Düsseldorf. Trojahn utilizes various contemporary modes of expression with a subsuming individuality. Among his works are *Enrico*, dramatic comedy (1989–91; Schwetzingen, April 11, 1991), *Das wüste Land*, opera (1994), and *Was ihr wollt*, opera (1997–98; Munich, May 24, 1998).

Trojan, Václav, Czech composer and teacher; b. Pilsen, April 24, 1907; d. Prague, July 5, 1983. He was a student of Wiedermann (organ) and of Ostrčil and Dědeček (conducting) at the Prague Cons. (1923–27) He also attended the master classes in composition given by Suk and Novák (1927–29), and received instruction in quarter tone and 6th tone music in A. Hába's class there. From 1937 to 1945 he was music manager of the Prague Radio, and then lectured on theater and film music at the Prague Academy of Music from 1949. In 1982 he was made a National Artist by the Czech government. His works include *Kolotoč* (The Merry-Go-Round), children's opera (1936–39), *Zlatá brána* (Golden Gate), scenic poem (1971–73), and *Sen noci svatojánské* (A Midsummer Night's Dream), ballet pantomime (1982); also music for puppet films.

Troyanos, Tatiana, brilliant American mezzo-soprano; b. N.Y., Sept. 12, 1938; d. there, Aug. 21, 1993. She studied at the Juilliard School of Music in N.Y. (graduated, 1963) and with Hans Heinz. On April 25, 1963, she made her operatic debut as Hippolyta in *A Midsummer Night's Dream* at the N.Y. City Opera, where she then appeared as Marina, Cherubino, and Jocasta. In 1965 she made her first appearance at the Hamburg State Opera as Preziosilla. She remained on its roster until 1975, winning distinction for such roles as Elisetta, Dorabella, and Baba. She also created the role of Jeanne in *The Devil's of Loudun* there in 1969. In 1966 she sang for the first time at the Aix-en-Provence Festival as Strauss's Composer. In 1969 she made her debut at London's Covent Garden and at the Salzburg Festival as Octavian. In 1971 she sang Ariodante in the first operatic production given at the Kennedy Center in Washington, D.C.; that same year she also made her debut at the Chicago Lyric Opera as Charlotte. In 1975 she sang Bellini's Romeo in Boston. On March 8, 1976, she made a memorable debut at the Metropolitan Opera in New York as Octavian. In subsequent years, Troyanos was one of the leading members of the Metropolitan Opera, excelling in such roles as Amneris, Brangäne, Eboli, the Composer, Kundry, Didon, Santuzza, Orlovsky, Adalgisa, and Geschwitz. In 1992 she created the role of Queen Isabella in Glass's *The Voyage* there. Her death from cancer deprived the Metropolitan Opera of the extraordinary gifts of one of America's finest singers.

Trunk, Richard, German pianist, conductor, music critic, and composer; b. Tauberbischofsheim, Baden, Feb. 10, 1879; d. Herrsching-am-Ammersee, June 2, 1968. He studied with Iwan Knorr at the Hoch Cons. in Frankfurt am Main (1894–95) and with Rheinberger at the Munich Academy of Music (1896–99). He was then active as a choral conductor and music critic in Munich; he went to Cologne in 1925 as director of the Rheinische Hochschule für Musik and as a prof. at the Staatliche Hochschule für Musik; he also was active as a choral conductor; from 1934 to 1945 he was president of the Munich Academy of Music and also director of the Lehrergesangverein (1934–39). He was a prolific composer of choral music; he also wrote a Singspiel, *Herzdame* (Munich, 1917), and over 200 lieder.

BIBL.: A. Ott, *R. T.: Leben und Werk* (Munich, 1964).

Trythall, (Harry) Gil(bert), American composer and teacher, brother of **Richard Trythall**; b. Knoxville, Tenn., Oct. 28, 1930. He studied theory and composition with David Van Vactor at the Univ. of Tenn. (B.A., 1951), composition with Riegger at Northwestern Univ. (M.Mus., 1952), and composition with Palmer and musicology with Grout at Cornell Univ. (D.M.A., 1960). He was assistant prof. at Knox College in Galesburg, Ill. (1960–64); after serving as prof. of theory and composition (1964–75) and chairman of the music school (1973–75) at George Peabody College for Teachers in Nashville, he was prof. of music (from 1975) and dean of the creative arts center (1975–81) at West Virginia Univ. in Morgantown. He publ. *Principles and Practices of Electronic Music* (N.Y., 1974), *Eighteenth Century Counterpoint* (Dubuque, Iowa, 1993), and *Sixteenth Century Counterpoint* (Dubuque, Iowa, 1994). His compositions include the opera buffa *The Music Lesson* (1960) and *The Terminal Opera* (1982; rev. 1987). His brother Richard Trythall (b. Knoxville, Tenn., July 25, 1939), is also a composer and pianist, in the latter role a determined champion of modern music.

Tsintsadze, Sulkhan, Georgian composer, teacher, and cellist; b. Gori, Aug. 23, 1925; d. 1991. He studied cello and composition at the Moscow Cons. In 1963 he joined the faculty of the Tbilisi Cons. In his music, he emphasized ethnic elements, presenting them in congenial modal harmonies. His works include the operas *The Golden Fleece* (1953) and *The Hermit* (1972), and the ballets *The Treasure of the Blue Mountain* (1956) and *The Demon*, after Lermontov (1961); also *Immortality*, oratorio for the centenary of Lenin's birth (1970).

Tsukatani, Akihirô, Japanese composer and pedagogue; b. Tokyo, March 16, 1919. He studied law at the Univ. of Tokyo (graduated, 1941) and received training in theory from Saburo Moroi. He taught economic history at the Univ. of Tokyo before serving on its music faculty.

WORKS: DRAMATIC: OPERAS: *Pongo* (1965); *Ajatasatru* (1966); *Kakitsubata* (Tokyo, May 24, 1967). MUSICAL: *Fairy's Cap* (Tokyo, Dec. 9, 1968). BALLET: *Mythology of Today* (1956).

Tsvetanov, Tsvetan, Bulgarian composer and teacher; b. Sofia, Nov. 6, 1931; d. Paris, April 4, 1982. He studied composition with Hadzhiev and Vladigerov at the Bulgarian State Cons. in Sofia (graduated, 1956); in 1958 he joined its faculty, becoming a prof. in composition and harmony in 1976; he also was its rector (1976–80). He served as secretary of the Union of Bulgarian Composers (1969–75; 1976–80). His works include *Orpheus and Rodopa*, ballet (1960; also an orch. suite), *Immortality*, oratorio (1981), incidental music for plays, and film scores.

Tubb, Carrie (Caroline Elizabeth), English soprano; b. London, May 17, 1876; d. there, Sept. 20, 1976. She studied at the Guildhall School of Music in London. She began her career singing in a vocal quartet during her student days; after winning notice as an oratorio singer, she appeared at Covent Garden and at His Majesty's Theatre in London (1910); however, she soon abandoned opera and pursued a career as a concert artist until her retirement in 1930; in the latter year, she became a prof. at the Guildhall School of Music, where she taught for almost 30 years. She excelled both in Mozart arias and in concert excerpts from Wagner and Verdi.

Tubin, Eduard, Estonian-born Swedish composer and conductor; b. Kallaste, near Tartu, June 18, 1905; d. Stockholm, Nov. 17, 1982. He studied with A. Kapp at the Tartu Cons. and later with Kodály in Budapest. From 1931 to 1944 he conducted the Vanemuine Theater Orch. in Tartu. In 1944 he settled in Stockholm and in 1961 became a naturalized Swedish citizen. In 1982 he was elected to the Royal Swedish Academy of Music. He was at work on his 11th Sym. at the time of his death. Other works include the operas *Barbara von Tisenhusen* (Tallinn, Dec. 4, 1969) and *Prosten fran Reigi* (The Priest from Reigi; 1971), and the ballet *Skratten* (Laughter; 1939–41).

Tucci, Gabriella, Italian soprano; b. Rome, Aug. 4, 1929. She studied at the Accademia di Santa Cecilia in Rome, and then with Leonardo Filoni, who became her husband. In 1951 she made her operatic debut in Lucca. After winning the Spoleto competition that year, she sang Leonora in *La Forza del Destino* at the Spoleto Festival. In 1953 she appeared as Cherubini's Médée in Florence. She made a tour of Australia in 1955. In 1959 she made her first appearance at Milan's La Scala as Mimi. On Sept. 25, 1959, she made her U.S. debut as Giordano's Madeleine at the San Francisco Opera. From 1959 to 1969 she sang regularly at the Verona Arena. She made her Metropolitan Opera debut in New York as Cio-Cio-San on Oct. 29, 1960, and remained on its roster until 1973. Among her most successful roles there were Euridice, Marguerite, both Verdi Leonoras, Aida, Violetta, Alice Ford, and Mimi. She also sang Tosca at her Covent Garden debut in London in 1960. As a guest artist, she sang at the Vienna State Opera, the Deutsche Oper in Berlin, the Bavarian State Opera in Munich, the Bolshoi Theater in Moscow, and the Teatro Colón in Buenos Aires. She later taught at the Indiana Univ. School of Music in Bloomington (1983–86).

Tucker, Richard (real name, **Reuben Ticker**), brilliant American tenor; b. N.Y., Aug. 28, 1913; d. Kalamazoo, Mich., Jan. 8, 1975. He sang in a synagogue choir in New York as a child; he studied voice with Paul Althouse and subsequently sang on the radio. His first public appearance in opera was as Alfredo in *La Traviata* in 1943 with the Salmaggi Co. in N.Y. On Jan. 25, 1945, he made his Metropolitan Opera debut in New York as Enzo in *La Gioconda*; he remained on its roster until his death, specializing in the Italian repertoire. In 1947 he made his European debut at the Verona Arena as Enzo (Maria Callas made her Italian debut as Gioconda in the same performance); he also sang at Covent Garden in London (debut as Cavaradossi, 1958), at La Scala in Milan (1969), in Vienna, and in other major music centers abroad. He died while on a concert tour. He was the brother-in-law of **Jan Peerce**.

BIBL.: J. Drake, *R. T.: A Biography* (N.Y., 1984).

Tudoran, Ionel, Romanian tenor; b. Baragtii de Vede, June 24, 1913. He studied at the Iaşi Cons. He made his operatic debut as Roland in Ziehrer's *Landstreicher* in 1936 in Iaşi, then sang with the Cluj Opera (1937–48) and the Bucharest Opera (1948–63); he also made guest appearances in Prague, Leipzig, Berlin, Dresden, Moscow, and other music centers. He retired in 1963 and taught voice at the Bucharest Cons. until 1972. His finest roles were Don José, Faust, and Cavaradossi.

Tully, Alice, American mezzo-soprano, soprano, and music patroness; b. Corning, N.Y., Sept. 11, 1902; d. N.Y., Dec. 10, 1993. A scion of a family of wealth, she studied voice in Paris with Jean Périer and Miguel Fontecha, where she made her concert debut with the Pasdeloup Orch. in 1927. Returning to the United States, she gave a song recital in New York in 1936, and received critical praise for her interpretation of French songs. She eventually gave up her artistic ambition and devoted herself to various philanthropic endeavors. Her major gift was to Lincoln Center in New York for the construction of a chamber music hall; it was dedicated as Alice Tully Hall in 1969. She also helped to organize the Chamber Music Soc. of Lincoln Center. She received the National Medal of Arts in 1985. Her 90th birthday was celebrated in a N.Y. gala on Sept. 14, 1992, at Lincoln Center.

Turchi, Guido, Italian composer and teacher; b. Rome, Nov. 10, 1916. He studied piano and composition with Dobici, Ferdinandi, and Bustini at the Rome Cons. (diplomas, 1940) and pursued graduate training with Pizzetti at the Accademia di Santa Cecilia in Rome (diploma, 1945). He taught at the Rome Cons. (1941–67; again from 1972); he was artistic director of the Accademia Filarmonica in Rome (1963–66); he served as director of the Parma and Florence cons. (1967–72); he was artistic director of the Teatro Comunale in Bologna (1968–70) and at the Accademia di Santa Cecilia in Rome (from 1970). In his early music, Turchi followed Pizzetti's style of Italian Baroque, with Romantic and impressionistic extensions; he then changed his idiom toward a more robust and accentuated type of music making, influenced mainly by a study of the works of Béla Bartók. Turchi's Concerto for Strings (Venice, Sept. 8, 1948) is dedicated to Bartók's memory. Other works include *Il buon soldato Svejk*, opera (Milan, April 6, 1962), *Dedalo*, ballet (Florence, 1972), incidental music to plays, and film scores.

Turina (y Perez), Joaquín, prominent Spanish composer and teacher; b. Seville, Dec. 9, 1882; d. Madrid, Jan. 14, 1949. He studied with local teachers, then entered the Madrid Cons. as a pupil of Tragó (piano). In 1905 he went to Paris, where he studied composition with d'Indy at the Schola Cantorum and piano with Moszkowski. At the urging of Albéniz, he turned to Spanish folk music for inspiration. Returning to Madrid in 1914, he produced 2 symphonic works in a characteristic Spanish style: *La procesión del rocío* and *Sinfonía sevillana*, combining Romantic and impressionist elements in an individual manner; the same effective combination is found in his chamber music of Spanish inspiration (*Escena andaluza, La oración del torero* et al.) and his piano music (*Sonata romántica, Mujeres españolas* et al.); he also wrote operas and incidental music for the theater. In 1930 he was appointed a prof. of composition at the Madrid Cons.; he also founded the general music commission of the Ministry of Education, serving as its commissioner in 1941.

WORKS: DRAMATIC: *La sulamita*, opera (c.1900); *Fea y con gracia*, zarzuela (1904); *Margot*, lyric comedy (Madrid, Oct. 10, 1914); *Navidad*, incidental music (1916); *La adúltera penitente*, incidental music (1917); *Jardín de oriente*, opera (Madrid, March 6, 1923); *La anunciación*, comedia (1924).

WRITINGS: *Enciclopedia abreviada de la música* (Madrid, 1917); *Tratado de composición* (Madrid, 1946); A. Iglesias, ed., *Escritos de Joaquín Turina* (1982).

BIBL.: F. Sopeña, *J. T.* (Madrid, 1943; 2d ed., rev., 1956); J. Benavente, ed., *Aproximación al Lenguaje Musical de T.* (1982).

Turnage, Mark-Anthony, English composer; b. Grays, Essex, June 10, 1960. He was a student of Knussen in the junior dept. of the Royal College of Music in London (1974–78), where he continued his training as a senior student of John Lambert (diploma, 1982); he then studied with Schuller and Henze at the Berkshire Music Center in Tanglewood (summer, 1983). From 1989 to 1993 he served as composer-in-association with the City of Birmingham Sym. Orch., a position he then held with the English National Opera in London from 1995 to 1998. In his music, Turnage has pursued an eclectic course in an accessible style which has found inspiration in various contemporary modes of expression, including rock and jazz. Among his works are the operas *Greek* (1986–88; Munich, June 17, 1988), *Killing Time*, television opera (1991), and *The Country of the Blind* (Aldeburgh, June 13, 1997).

Turner, Dame Eva, distinguished English soprano; b. Oldham, March 10, 1892; d. London, June 16, 1990. She was a pupil of Dan Roothan in Bristol; Giglia Levy, Edgardo Levy, and Mary Wilson at the Royal Academy of Music in London; and Albert Richards Broad. In 1916 she made her operatic debut as a Page in *Tannhäuser* with the Carl Rosa Opera Co., with which she sang until 1924; she sang with the company at London's Covent Garden in 1920. In 1924 she made her first appearance at Milan's La Scala as Freia in *Das Rheingold*; she then toured Germany with an Italian opera company in 1925. She sang Turandot in Brescia in 1926; she appeared at Covent Garden (1928–30; 1933; 1935–39; 1947–48); she was a guest artist in other European music centers, in Chicago, and in South America. She taught at the Univ. of Okla. (1950–59) and then at the Royal Academy of Music. In 1962 she was made a Dame Commander of the Order of the British Empire. Her other esteemed roles included Agatha, Amelia, Santuzza, Aida, Isolde, Sieglinde, and Cio-Cio-San.

Turner, Robert (Comrie), Canadian composer and teacher; b. Montreal, June 6, 1920. He was a student of Douglas Clarke and Claude Champagne at McGill Univ. in Montreal (B.Mus., 1943; D.Mus., 1953), of Howells and Jacob at the Royal College of Music in London (1947–48), of Roy Harris at the George Peabody College for Teachers in Nashville, Tenn. (1947–50), and of Messiaen at the Berkshire Music Center in Tanglewood (summer, 1949). From 1952 to 1968 he was a music producer for the CBC in Vancouver. He taught at the Univ. of British Columbia in Vancouver (1955–57), Acadia Univ. in Wolfville, Nova Scotia (1968–69), and the Univ. of Manitoba (1969–85). In 1982 he held a Manitoba Arts Council grant. In 1987 he was a fellow at the MacDowell Colony. In 1990–91 he held a Canada Council Artists grant. He was awarded a commemorative medal marking the 125th anniversary of Canadian confederation in 1992. His compositions are couched in an eclectic style that generally adheres to tonal parameters. Among his works are *The Brideship*, lyric drama (1966–67; Vancouver, Dec. 12, 1967), *Vile Shadows*, opera (1982–83; rev. 1986), and music for radio and television.

Turner, W(alter) J(ames Redfern), Australian poet and writer on music; b. Shanghai, Oct. 13, 1889; d. London, Nov. 18, 1946. He studied with his father (who was organist of St. Paul's Cathedral, Melbourne, Australia) and privately in Dresden, Munich, and Vienna. He settled in London, where he was music critic for the *New Statesman* (1916–40); he also was drama critic of the *London Mercury* (1919–23) and literary ed. of the *Daily Herald* (1920–23) and *The Spectator* (from 1942).

WRITINGS (all publ. in London): *Music and Life* (1922); *Variations on the Theme of Music* (1924); *Orpheus, or The Music of the Future* (1926); *Beethoven: The Search for Reality* (1927; new ed., 1933); *Musical Meanderings* (1928); *Music: A Short History* (1932; 2d ed., 1949); *Facing the Music: Reflections of a Music Critic* (1933); *Wagner* (1933); *Berlioz: The Man and His Work* (1934; 2d ed., rev., 1939); *Music: An Introduction to Its Nature and Appreciation* (1936); *Mozart: The Man and His Works* (1938; 2d ed., rev., 1965, by C. Raeburn); *English Music* (1941); *English Ballet* (1944).

Turnovský, Martin, Czech conductor; b. Prague, Sept. 29, 1928. He studied at the Prague Academy of Music (1948–52), his principal mentors being Robert Brock (piano) and Ančerl (conducting); later he pursued private instruction in conducting with Szell (1956). In 1952 he made his debut as a conductor with the Prague Sym. Orch. From 1955 to 1960 he conducted the Czech Army Sym. Orch. In 1958 he captured 1st prize in the Besançon competition. He was music director of the Brno State Phil. (1959–63) and the Plzeň Radio Sym. Orch. (1963–66). In 1966 he became Generalmusikdirektor of the Dresden State Opera and Orch. However, he resigned his position in 1968 when East German troops participated in the Soviet invasion of his homeland. After making his U.S. debut as a guest conductor with the Cleveland Orch. in 1968, Turnovský appeared as a conductor with various orchs. and opera houses. From 1975 to 1980 he was music director of the Norwegian Opera in Oslo. He was music director of the Bonn City Theater from 1979 to 1983. During this time, he also served as co-chief conductor (with Jan Krenz) of the Beethovenhalle Orch. in Bonn. From 1992 to 1995 he was music director of the Prague Sym. Orch. In 1998 he made his U.S. operatic debut conducting *Jenůfa* in Cincinnati.

Turok, Paul (Harris), American composer and music critic; b. N.Y., Dec. 3, 1929. He studied composition at Queens College with Rathaus (B.A., 1950), then at the Univ. of Calif., Berkeley, with Sessions (M.A., 1951) and at the Juilliard School of Music with Wagenaar (1951–53); later he studied at Baruch College (M.S., 1986). He was a lecturer on music at the City College of N.Y. (1960–63) and was a visiting prof. at Williams College in Williamstown, Mass. (1963–64); he then wrote music criticism for the *N.Y. Herald-Tribune* (1964–65), the *Music Journal* (1964–80), *Ovation* (1980–89), and *Fanfare* (from 1980). As a composer, Turok follows the principle of stylistic freedom and technical precision, without doctrinaire adherence to any circumscribed modernistic modus operandi. Among his works are the operas *Scene: Domestic*, chamber opera (1955; Aspen, Colo., Aug. 2, 1973), *Richard III* (1975), and *A Secular Masque* (1979), and the ballet *Youngest Brother* (N.Y., Jan. 23, 1953).

Turski, Zbigniew, Polish composer; b. Konstancin, near Warsaw, July 28, 1908; d. Warsaw, Jan. 7, 1979. He was a student of Rytel (composition) and Bierdiajew (conducting) at the Warsaw Cons. From 1936 to 1939 he was music producer of the Polish Radio in Warsaw. In 1945–46 he was conductor of the Baltic Phil. in Gdansk. His compositions were in an advanced harmonic idiom. They include *Rozmowki* (Chats), micro-opera (1966), *Ty-*

tania i osiol (Titania and the Donkey), ballet (1966), and incidental music for the theater, films, and radio.

Tuukkanen, Kalervo, Finnish conductor and composer; b. Mikkeli, Oct. 14, 1909; d. Helsinki, July 12, 1979. He studied composition with Leevi Madetoja and theory with Krohn in Helsinki. He subsequently conducted local orchs. and choirs; from 1967 to 1969 he was a visiting prof. of music at the Chinese Univ. of Hong Kong. Among his works was the operas *Indumati* (1962). He also publ. a monograph on the life and works of Leevi Madetoja (Helsinki, 1947).

Tuxen, Erik (Oluf), Danish conductor; b. Mannheim (of Danish parents), July 4, 1902; d. Copenhagen, Aug. 28, 1957. After training in architecture, medicine, and philosophy, he pursued studies in music in Copenhagen, Paris, Vienna, and Berlin. He conducted at the Lübeck Opera (1927–29), and then at the Royal Theater in Copenhagen. In 1936 he became conductor of the Danish Radio Sym. Orch. in Copenhagen. During World War II (1939–45), he lived in Sweden. Returning to Copenhagen in 1945, he was again conductor of the Danish Radio Sym. Orch. until his death. He conducted it at the Edinburgh Festival in 1950 in an acclaimed performance of Nielsen's 5th Sym. In 1950–51 he conducted in the United States and in 1954 in South America. Tuxen was a particularly persuasive interpreter of Nielsen.

Tveitt, (Nils) Geirr, Norwegian composer, teacher, and pianist; b. Kvam, Oct. 19, 1908; d. Oslo, Feb. 1, 1981. He learned to play the piano and violin in childhood. Following studies with Grabner and Weninger in Leipzig (1928–32), he pursued his training in Vienna with Wellesz and in Paris with Honegger and Villa-Lobos (1932–35). Returning to Norway, he devoted himself mainly to composition, producing over 300 works. He also made some tours abroad as a pianist. In 1941 the Norwegian government granted him an annual income. However, his activities during the German occupation of Norway led to his loss of the Norwegian government grant after the liberation in 1945. It was finally restored in 1958. In his study *Tonalitätstheorie des parallelen Leittonssystems* (Oslo, 1937), Tveitt attempted to formulate the foundation of his own compositional style by claiming that the modal scales are in actuality old Norse keys. Many of his works employ modal scales.

WORKS: DRAMATIC: OPERAS: *Nordvest—Sud—Nordaust—Nord* (1939); *Dragaredokko* (1940); *Roald Amundsen* (n.d.); *Stevleik*, chamber opera (n.d.); *Jeppe* (1964; Bergen, June 10, 1966; rev. 1968). BALLETS: *Baldurs draumar* (1935); *Birgingu* (1939); *Husguden* (1956). INCIDENTAL MUSIC: *Jonsoknatt* (1936).

BIBL.: R. Storass, *Tonediktaren G. T.: Songjen i fossaduren* (Oslo, 1990).

Twardowski, Romuald, Polish composer and teacher; b. Vilnius, June 17, 1930. He studied composition and piano with Juzeliunas at the Vilnius Cons. (1952–57); after further training with Woytowicz at the Warsaw Cons. (1957–60), he studied medieval polyphony and Gregorian chant with Boulanger in Paris (1963). He later taught at the Warsaw Academy of Music.

WORKS: DRAMATIC: OPERAS: *Cyrano de Bergerac* (1962; Bytom, July 6, 1963); *Tragedyja albo rzecz o Janie i Herodzie* (Tragedy, or Story of John and Herod; 1965; Łódz, April 24, 1969); *Lord Jim* (1972–73); *Upadek ojca Suryna* (The Fall of Father Surin), radio opera (1968; scenic version, Kraków, 1969); *Maria Stuart* (1978); *Story of St. Katherine* (1981; Warsaw, Dec. 14, 1985). BALLETS: *The Naked Prince* (1960); *The Magician's Statues* (1963).

Tyrwhitt-Wilson, Sir Gerald Hugh, Baronet. See **Berners, Lord.**

Tyson, Alan (Walker), esteemed Scottish musicologist; b. Glasgow, Oct. 27, 1926. He was educated at Magdalen College, Oxford; he studied litterae humaniores there (1947–51); in 1952 he was elected a fellow of All Souls College, Oxford; later he pursued training in psychoanalysis and medicine (qualified, 1965). In 1971 he became a senior research fellow at All Souls College, a position he retained until 1994. He also was a visiting prof. of music at Columbia Univ. (1969), the Lyell Reader in Bibliography at the Univ. of Oxford (1973–74), the Ernest Bloch Prof. of Music at the Univ. of Calif., Berkeley (1977–78), a member of the Inst. for Advanced Study at Princeton Univ. (1983–84), and a visiting prof. at the Graduate Center of the City Univ. of N.Y. (1985). In 1989 he was made a Commander of the Order of the British Empire. In 1991 he was made a corresponding member of the American Musicological Soc. He has made extensive textual and bibliographical studies of the period 1770–1850; particularly noteworthy are his contributions to the study of Beethoven.

WRITINGS: *The Authentic English Editions of Beethoven* (London, 1963); with O. Neighbour, *English Music Publishers' Plate Numbers in the First Half of the Nineteenth Century* (London, 1965); *Thematic Catalogue of the Works of Muzio Clementi* (Tutzing, 1967); ed., *Beethoven Studies* (N.Y., 1974), *Beethoven Studies 2* (London, 1977), *Beethoven Studies 3* (London, 1982); *Mozart: Studies of the Autograph Scores* (Cambridge, Mass., 1987); ed. with A. Rosenthal, *Mozart's Thematic Catalogue: A Facsimile* (1990); *Watermarks in Mozart's Autographs* in the *Neue Mozart-Ausgabe* (X/33/Abteilung, 2, 1992).

BIBL.: S. Brandenburg, ed., *Haydn, Mozart, and Beethoven: Studies in the Music of the Classical Period: Essays in Honour of A. T.* (Oxford, 1995).

Tzipine, Georges, French conductor; b. Paris, June 22, 1907; d. there, Dec. 8, 1987. He studied violin at the Paris Cons., winning a premier prix. He made his debut as a violinist with the Paris Radio (1926), then pursued training in harmony, counterpoint, and conducting. In 1931 he began his career as a conductor with the Paris Radio; after further studies with Marc de Rance and Reynaldo Hahn, he appeared as a guest conductor with various Paris orchs. and toured France as a ballet conductor. He was music director of the Cannes Casino (1945–49); he then toured Europe and North and South America as a guest conductor. After serving as music director of the Melbourne Sym. Orch. (1961–65), he taught conducting at the Paris Cons. (from 1966).

Tzybin, Vladimir, Russian flutist, teacher, and composer; b. Ivanovo-Voznesensk, 1877; d. Moscow, May 31, 1949. He played the flute in the orch. of the Bolshoi Theater in Moscow from 1896 to 1907 and from 1921 to 1929. From 1907 to 1920 he was 1st flutist at the Imperial Opera of St. Petersburg. He composed 2 operas: *Flengo* (1918) and *Tale of the Dead Princess and 7 Heroes* (1947). He was esteemed as a pedagogue.

Kurt Herbert Adler at music rehearsal

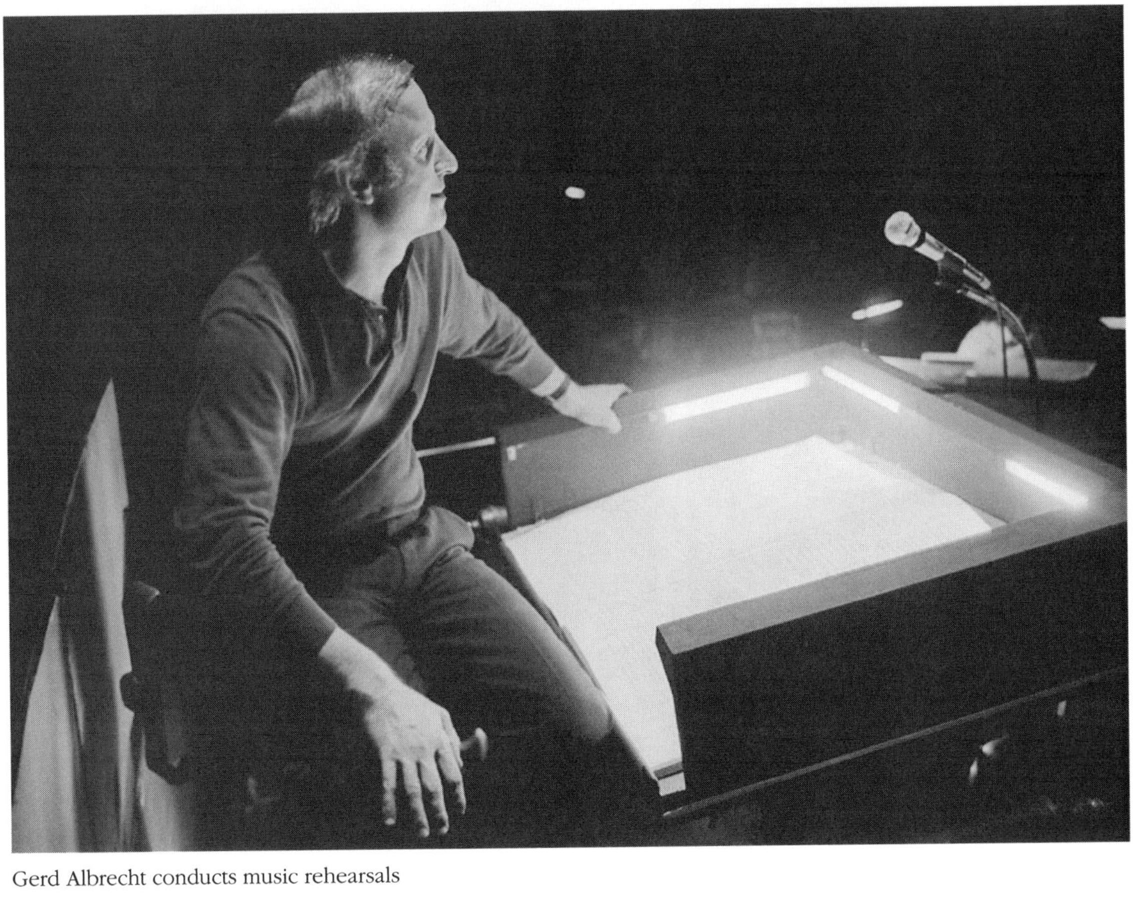

Gerd Albrecht conducts music rehearsals

Ernest Ansermet

Sir John Barbirolli

Bruno Bartoletti conducting rehearsals

Sir Thomas Beecham

Pierre Boulez

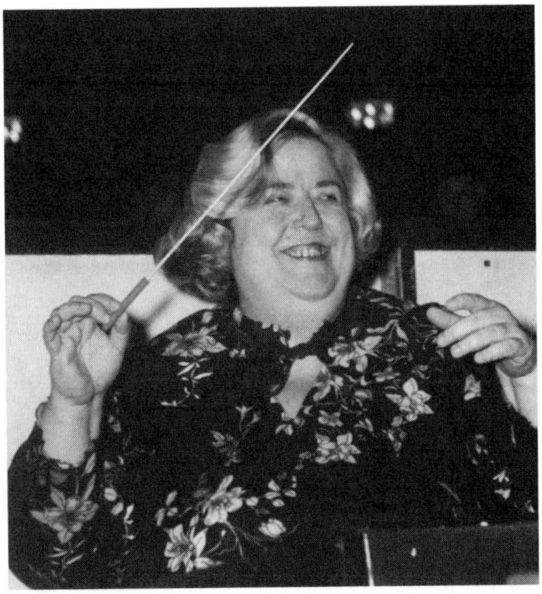

Sarah Caldwell

Cleofonte Campanini

János Ferencsik on the *Der Rosenkavalier* set

Wilhelm Furtwängler

Carlo Maria Gíulini

Reginald Goodall conducts *Peter Grimes*

Bernard Haitink introduces *La Triviata*

Graeme Jenkins reading music score

Herbert von Karajan

Otto Klemperer

Lorin Maazel

Lovro von Matačić

Zubin Mehta

Pierre Monteux

Seiji Ozawa

Giuseppe Patane

Sir John Pritchard

Karl Rankl

Simon Rattle (l.) and Calvin Simmons

Fritz Reiner (seated)

Hans Richter

Artur Rodzinski

Julius Rudel

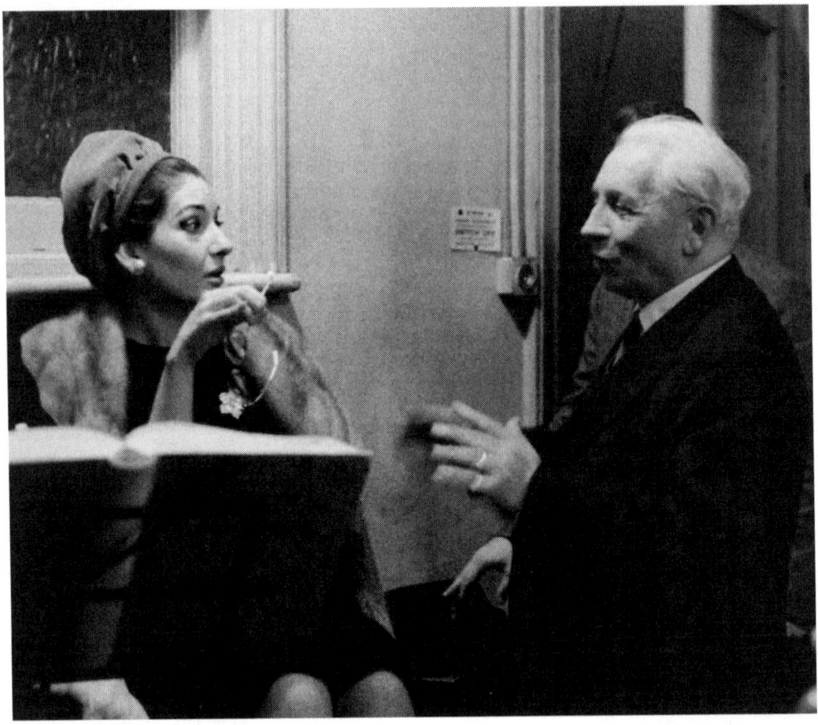
Tullio Serafin with Maria Callas

Sir Georg Solti

Sir Arthur Sullivan

Leopold Stokowski

Arturo Toscanini

Siegfried Wagner conducts rehearsal

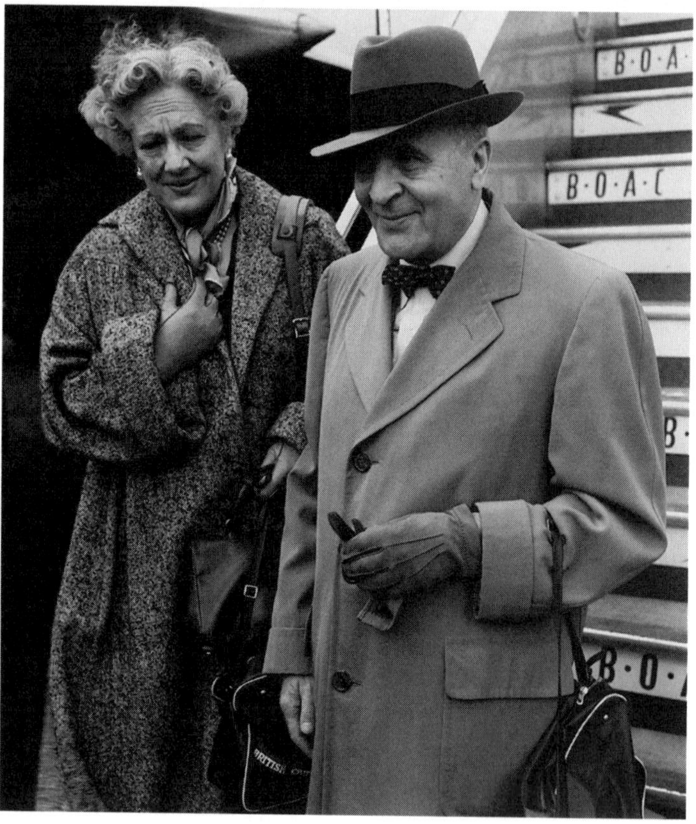

Bruno Walter arrives in London

U

Uber, family of German musicians:

(1) Christian Benjamin Uber, lawyer, glass-harmonica player, and composer; b. Breslau, Sept. 20, 1746; d. there, 1812. He was educated in Halle and Breslau, becoming a civil servant in the latter city in 1772; although an amateur musician, he excelled as a performer on the glass harmonica at concerts he gave in his own home. He wrote a comic opera, *Clarissa oder Das unbekannte Dienstmädchen* (1772). He had 2 sons who became professional musicians.

(2) Christian Friedrich Hermann Uber, violinist, conductor, and composer; b. Breslau, April 22, 1781; d. Dresden, March 2, 1822. After training with his father, he engaged in law studies in Halle; receiving encouragement from D. G. Türk, he decided to pursue a career in music. In 1804 he accompanied Prince Radziwill to Berlin, where he entered the service of Prince Louis Ferdinand, then was a violinist in Braunschweig. He was director of the Kassel Opera (1808–14); after conducting in Mainz (1814–16), he went to Dresden as director of the Seconda company; after a sojourn in Leipzig as a teacher, lecturer, and writer on music, he returned to Dresden in 1818 to serve as cantor at the Kreuzschule and music director of the Kreuzkirche. He composed 2 operas, *Der frohe Tag* (Mainz, 1815) and *Les Marins*, a melodrama, *Der Taucher*, an intermezzo, *Der falsche Werber* (Kassel, 1808), and incidental music to plays; also the oratorio *Die letzten Worte des Erlösers* (1822).

(3) Alexander Uber, cellist and composer; b. Breslau, 1783; d. Carolath, Silesia, 1824. He received initial training from his father in Breslau, where he later studied violin with J. Janetzek, cello with J. Jäger, and theory with J. I. Schnabel; following tours as a virtuoso, he settled as Kapellmeister to the prince of Schönaich-Carolath.

Uberti (real name, **Hubert**), **Antonio**, celebrated Italian castrato soprano, known as "Il Porporino," after his teacher Porpora; b. Verona (of German parents), 1697; d. Berlin, Jan. 20, 1783. He was Porpora's favorite pupil. In 1741 he entered the service of Friedrich II, the Great in Berlin. He was greatly renowned in Germany for his singing of Italian operas. He was the teacher of Gertrud Mara.

Uccellini, Marco, significant Italian composer; b. c.1603; d. Forlimpopoli, near Forli, Sept. 10, 1680. He was educated in Assisi, then went to Modena, where he became head of instrumental music at the Este court in 1641 and maestro di cappella at the Cathedral in 1647; subsequently he was maestro di cappella at the Farnese court in Parma (1665–80). Most of his works for the stage are not extant, but his concertos are preserved and give evidence of excellent knowledge of technique in writing for the violin and other string instruments. He composed the opera *Gli eventi di Filandro ad Edessa* (Parma, 1675) and the ballets *Le navi d'Enea* (Parma, 1673) and *Il Giove d'Elide fulminato* (Parma, 1677).

Udbye, Martin Andreas, distinguished Norwegian organist and composer; b. Trondheim, June 18, 1820; d. there, Jan. 10, 1889. He studied organ with Carl Becker and composition with Hauptmann at the Leipzig Cons. (1851–52); he pursued further studies in Berlin, Leipzig, Dresden, Vienna, and London (1858–59). From 1844 to 1869 he served as organist at the Hospitalskirken in Trondheim, and after 1869 was organist at the church of Our Lady there. He was regarded as one of the finest Norwegian composers of his era. He wrote the first Norwegian opera, *Fredkulla* (The Peacemaker; 1858), as well as the operettas *Hr. Perrichons reise* (1861), *Hjemve* (Homesickness; 1862; Christiania, April 8, 1864), and *Junkeren og flubergrosen* (The Squire and the Rose of Fluberg; 1867; Christiania, Jan. 7, 1872).

Ugalde, Delphine (née **Beaucé**), French soprano; b. Paris, Dec. 3, 1829; d. there, July 19, 1910. She received her first instruction in singing from her mother, an actress, then subsequently studied with Moreau-Sainti, making her debut in Paris in 1848 as Angèle in Auber's *Domino noir*. In 1866 she assumed the management of the Bouffes-Parisiens, taking leading roles in Offenbach's operettas; in 1867 she appeared in her own operetta, *La Halte au* *moulin.* She retired in 1871, and became a successful vocal teacher.

Ugarte, Floro M(anuel), Argentine composer and teacher; b. Buenos Aires, Sept. 15, 1884; d. there, June 11, 1975. He studied in Buenos Aires, and at the Paris Cons. under Pessard, Lavignac, and Fourdrain, with whom he collaborated in writing the ballet *Sigolene.* He returned to Argentina in 1913; in 1924 he became a prof. at the National Cons. in Buenos Aires; he was general director of the Teatro Colón, founder-president of the National Music Soc., prof. at the Escuela Superior de Bellas Artes at La Plata Univ., and director of the Buenos Aires Municipal Cons. His works include the operatic fairy tale *Saika* (1918; Buenos Aires, July 21, 1920).

Uhde, Hermann, noted German bass-baritone; b. Bremen, July 20, 1914; d. during a performance in Copenhagen, Oct. 10, 1965. He studied at Philipp Kraus's opera school in Bremen, making his operatic debut there as Titurel in *Parsifal* in 1936; he appeared in Freiburg im Breisgau and then sang with the Bavarian State Opera in Munich (1940–43) and with the German Opera at The Hague (1943–44). He subsequently was engaged at Hannover (1947–48), Hamburg (1948–50), Vienna (1950–51), Munich (1951–56), Stuttgart (1956–57), and again in Vienna (1957–61). He made his American debut at the Metropolitan Opera in New York as Telramund in *Lohengrin* on Nov. 18, 1955; he was on its roster until 1957, then again from 1958 to 1961 and in 1963–64. He was particularly acclaimed for his performances in Wagnerian roles.

Uhl, Alfred, Austrian composer and pedagogue; b. Vienna, June 5, 1909; d. there, June 8, 1992. He studied composition with Franz Schmidt at the Vienna Academy of Music (diploma, 1932); then in 1940–41, during World War II, he was in the Austrian Army, where he was severely wounded. In 1943 he became a composition teacher at the Vienna Academy of Music; he also served as president of the Austrian copyright society (1970–75). In 1980 he was awarded the Austrian Badge of Honor for Science and Arts. His music was patterned after Classical forms, with emphasis on contrapuntal clarity. Among his compositions were *Katzenmusik*, ballet opera (1957), and *Der Mysteriöse Herr X*, opera (1962–65; Vienna, June 8, 1966); also *Gilgamesh*, oratorio (1954–56; rev. 1967–68; Vienna, June 13, 1969).

BIBL.: A. Witeschnik, *A. U.: Eine biographische Studie* (Vienna, 1966).

Uhl, Fritz, Austrian tenor; b. Matzleinsdorf, near Vienna, April 2, 1928. He studied at the Vienna Academy of Music (1947–52). In 1952 he made his operatic debut in Graz. In 1957 he made his first appearance at the Bayreuth Festival as Vogelsang, and continued to sing there until 1964. In 1958 he became a member of the Bavarian State Opera in Munich, where he was made a Kammersänger in 1962. From 1961 he also sang at the Vienna State Opera. He made his debut at London's Covent Garden as Walther von Stolzing in 1963. In 1968 he sang for the first time at the Salzburg Festival as Florestan, and continued to appear there until 1972. In 1981 he became a prof. at the Vienna Cons. Uhl was particularly known for his Wagnerian portrayals.

Uhlig, Theodor, German violinist, writer on music, and composer; b. Würzen, near Leipzig, Feb. 15, 1822; d. Dresden, Jan. 3, 1853. He studied violin with Schneider in Dessau (1837–40), and in 1841 became a violinist in the Dresden Court Orch. He was one of the most devoted friends and admirers of Wagner; he prepared the vocal score of *Lohengrin*. His death at the age of 30 was lamented. His articles were publ. as *Musikalische Schriften* by L. Frankenstein (Regensburg, 1913).

BIBL.: M. Ahrend, *T. U.: Der früh verstorbene Wagnerianer* (Bayreuth, 1904).

Ujfalussy, József, eminent Hungarian musicologist; b. Debrecen, Feb. 13, 1920. He received training in piano and composition at the Debrecen Music School, and in the classics at the Univ. of Debrecen (Ph.D., 1944, with a diss. on Homer's epics), then studied composition with Veress, conducting with Ferencsik, musicology with Szabolcsi and Bartha, and folk music with Kodály at the Budapest Academy of Music (1946–49). He became a member (1948) and served as head of the music dept. (1951–55) of the Ministry of Culture, then was prof. of aesthetics and theory at the Budapest Academy of Music (from 1955). In 1961 he became associated with the Bartók Archives (the Inst. of Musicology from 1969) of the Hungarian Academy of Sciences; in 1973 he was made a corresponding member of the latter, where he was president of the musicological commission and director of the Inst. of Musicology (from 1973). In 1961 he received the Erkel Prize and in 1966 the Kossuth Prize.

WRITINGS: Ed. *Bartók-breviárium* (Bartók Breviary; Budapest, 1958; 2d ed., rev., 1974; letters, writings, and documents); *Achille-Claude Debussy* (Budapest, 1959); *A valóság zenei képe* (The Musical Image of Reality; Budapest, 1962); *Bartók Béla* (Budapest, 1965; 2d ed., enl., 1970; Eng. tr., 1971); *Az esztétika alapjai és a zene* (The Bases of Aesthetics and Music; Budapest, 1968); *Farkas Ferenc* (Budapest, 1969); ed. *A Liszt Ferenc zeneművészeti föiskola 100 eve* (100 Years of the Franz Liszt Academy of Music; Budapest, 1977).

Ujj, Béla, Hungarian composer; b. Vienna, July 2, 1873; d. there, Feb. 1, 1942. He lost his sight in childhood, but studied music and composed a number of successful operettas, which were premiered in Vienna: *Der Herr Professor* (Dec. 4, 1903), *Kaisermanöver* (March 4, 1905), *Die kleine Prinzessin* (May 5, 1907), *Drei Stunden Leben* (Nov. 1, 1909), *Chanteclee* (Oct. 25, 1910), *Der Turmer von St. Stephan* (Sept. 13, 1912), *Teresita* (June 27, 1914), and *Der Müller und sein Kind* (Oct. 30, 1917).

Ulbrich, Maximilian, Austrian civil servant and composer; b. Vienna, c.1741; d. there, Sept. 14, 1814. He was a student at the Jesuit seminary in Vienna, and also received training in harmony and composition from G. C. Wagenseil and in organ and sacred music from J. G. Reutter. He was a civil servant from 1770 to 1804, and concurrently appeared as a bass singer, cellist, and pianist in chamber music concerts at the court. Among his works were 2 operas: *Frühling und Liebe* (Vienna, 1778) and *Der blaue Schmetterling* (Vienna, April 2, 1782); also an operetta, *Schnitterfreude* (Vienna, 1785), and the oratorio *Die Israeliten in der Wüste* (1779).

Ulfung, Ragnar (Sigurd), Norwegian tenor and opera director; b. Oslo, Feb. 28, 1927. He studied at the Oslo Cons. and in Milan. In 1949 he launched his career singing in concerts. In 1952 he made his stage debut as Magadoff in Menotti's *The Consul* in Stockholm, and then sang in Bergen and Göteborg. In 1958 he became a member of the Royal Opera in Stockholm, where he created the role of the Deaf Mute in Blomdahl's *Aniara* in 1959. In 1959 he also made his British debut as Verdi's Gustavus III with the visiting Royal Opera of Stockholm at the Edinburgh Festival, and returned with it in 1960 in the same role at London's Covent Garden. In 1963 he returned to Covent Garden as Don Carlos. He made his U.S. debut in Santa Fe in 1966, and then appeared at the San Francisco Opera in 1967. In 1969 he sang at the Hamburg State Opera. In 1971 he appeared at the Chicago Lyric Opera. He created the title role in Maxwell Davies's *Taverner* at Covent Garden in 1972, and also made his first appearance at Milan's La Scala. On Dec. 12, 1972, he made his Metropolitan Opera debut in New York as Mime in *Siegfried*, and then returned there for occasional appearances in subsequent years in such roles as Mime, Loge, Herod, Berg's Captain, and Weill's Fatty. In 1973 he made his bow as an opera director with *La Bohème* in Santa Fe, and thereafter directed works there and in Stockholm and Seattle. During the 1974–76 seasons, he sang Mime in the *Ring* cycle at Covent Garden. In 1986 he appeared as Herod in San Francisco. He created the role of Jadidja in *Die schwarze Maske* at its U.S. premiere in Santa Fe in 1988. In 1989 he sang Strauss's Aegisthus in London. In 1990 he appeared as Puccini's Goro in Lyons.

Ullmann, Viktor, Austrian composer, pianist, conductor, and music critic; b. Teschen, Jan. 1, 1898; d. in the concentration camp in Auschwitz, on or about Oct. 15, 1944. After initial training in Teschen, he went to Vienna in 1914, where he later was a student of Schoenberg (1918–19). From 1920 to 1927 he was an assistant to Zemlinsky at the New German Theater in Prague. In 1927–28 he served as director of the Ústí nad Labem Opera. He was active in Germany until the Nazi takeover of 1933 compelled him to return to Prague. He was associated with Czech Radio, wrote music and book reviews, and taught privately. From 1935 to 1937 he attended A. Hába's classes in quarter tone music at the Cons. With the Nazi dismemberment of Czechoslovakia in 1939, Ullmann's life became precarious. In 1942 the Nazis deported him to the Theresienstadt ghetto. In spite of the hardships there, he played an active role in the artistic endeavors of the ghetto. He composed the opera *Der Kaiser von Atlantis* during this time, a work depicting a tyrannical monarch who outlaws death only to beg for its return in order to relieve humanity from the horrors of life. The opera reached its dress rehearsal in 1944, but when the Nazi guards realized that the monarch was a satirical characterization of Hitler, Ullmann was sent to the Auschwitz concentration camp and put to death in the gas chamber. While a number of his works have been lost, several of his surviving scores have been revived. In his early music, Ullmann was influenced by Schoenberg. His later works were classical in form with polytonal textures. His fine songs reveal the influence of Mahler.

WORKS: OPERAS: *Peer Gynt* (1928); *Der Sturz des Antichrist* (1935; Bielefeld, Jan. 7, 1995); *Der zerbrochene Krug* (1941; Weimar, May 17, 1996); *Der Kaiser von Atlantis (oder die Todverweigerung)* (1943; Amsterdam, Dec. 16, 1975).

BIBL.: H.-G. Klein, ed., *V. U., Materialien* (Hamburg, 1992).

Ulrich, Homer, American musicologist; b. Chicago, March 27, 1906; d. Silver Spring, Md., Nov. 28, 1987. He studied bassoon and cello at the Chicago Musical College, and played these instruments in various orchs.; he was bassoonist with the Chicago Sym. Orch. (1929–35); he received his M.A. at the Univ. of Chicago with the thesis *The Penitential Psalms of Lasso* (1939). He was head of the music dept. of Monticello College (1935–38), then taught at the Univ. of Texas (assoc. prof., 1939; prof., 1951); he also played bassoon with the San Antonio Sym. Orch. In 1953 he was appointed head of the music dept. of the Univ. of Maryland; he retired in 1972. Among his publs. was *Famous Women Singers* (N.Y., 1953).

Umlauf, Ignaz, Austrian violist, conductor, and composer, father of **Michael Umlauf**; b. Vienna, 1746; d. Meidling, near Vienna, June 8, 1796. By 1772 he was 4th violist in the Vienna court orch., and by 1775 principal violist in the German Theater orch. there, where he was made Kapellmeister in 1778; by 1782 he was deputy court Kapellmeister under Salieri. He was a highly popular composer of Singspiels. He inaugurated the season of the German Singspiels at the Burg Theater (Feb. 17, 1778) with his piece *Die Bergknappen*. His other Singspiels, all first performed in Vienna, were *Die Insul der Liebe* (1772?), *Die Apotheke* (June 20, 1778), *Die schöne Schusterin oder Die pücefarbenen Schuhe* (June 22, 1779), *Das Irrlicht oder Endlich fand er sie* (Jan. 17, 1782), *Welche ist die beste Nation?* (Dec. 13, 1782), *Die glücklichen Jäger* (Feb. 17, 1786), and *Der Ring der Liebe oder Zemirens und Azors Ehestand* (Dec. 3, 1786). His "Zu Steffan sprach im Traume," an aria from *Das Irrlicht*, enjoyed great popularity; Eberl wrote a set of variations on it that was misattributed to Mozart.

Umlauf, Michael, Austrian violinist, conductor, and composer, son of **Ignaz Umlauf**; b. Vienna, Aug. 9, 1781; d. Baden, near Vienna, June 20, 1842. He joined the Vienna court orch. as a violinist at an early age; he conducted at court theaters from about 1809 to 1825; from 1840 he served as music director of the 2 court theaters. He assisted Beethoven in conducting the 9th Sym. and other works (actually led the performances, with Beethoven indicating the initial tempos). Umlauf had some success as a composer of ballets, the most successful of which was *Paul und Rosette oder Die Winzer* (Vienna, March 5, 1806). Other works include the Singspiel *Der Grenadier* (July 8, 1812), and the ballets *Amors Rache* (Oct. 18, 1804) and *Das eigensinnige Landmädchen* (April 9, 1810).

Unger, Caroline, famous Hungarian contralto; b. Stuhlweissenburg, Oct. 28, 1803; d. near Florence, March 23, 1877. She studied piano as a child, and then received singing lessons from Joseph Mazotti and Ugo Bassi; she then studied voice with Aloysia Weber, J. M. Vogl, and in Milan with D. Roncini. In 1824 she made her operatic debut in Vienna as Dorabella in *Così fan tutte*. Beethoven chose her to sing the contralto part in the first performance of his 9th Sym. (May 7, 1824); long afterward, she recounted that she turned Beethoven around that he might see the applause, which he could no longer hear. She went to Italy, where she changed the spelling of her name to Ungher, to secure proper pronunciation in Italian. Several Italian composers (Donizetti, Bellini, Mercadante) wrote operas especially for her. In 1833 she appeared in Paris. In 1839 she was engaged to be married to the poet Lenau, but the engagement soon was broken; in 1841 she married the French writer François Sabatier (1818–91) and retired from the stage. She publ. an album of 46 songs, *Lieder, Mélodies et Stornelli*.

BIBL.: *Trionfi melodrammatici di Carolina U. in Vienna* (Vienna, 1839); F. Margit Polgar, *U.-Sabatier* (Budapest, 1941).

Unger, Georg, famous German tenor; b. Leipzig, March 6, 1837; d. there, Feb. 2, 1887. He was originally a student of theology, making his operatic debut in Leipzig at the age of 30. Hans Richter heard him in Mannheim and recommended him to Wagner for the role of Siegfried, which he created at the Bayreuth Festival (1876). After appearing in London in a series of Wagner concerts in 1877, he went that year to Leipzig, where he sang with the Opera until 1881. He was the first Wagnerian Heldentenor.

Unger, Gerhard, German tenor; b. Bad Salzungen, Nov. 26, 1916. He received training in Eisenach and at the Berlin Hochschule für Musik. After beginning his career as a concert artist, he joined the Weimar Opera in 1947. From 1949 to 1961 he was a member of the (East) Berlin State Opera. He also appeared as David at the Bayreuth Festivals (1951–52). From 1961 to 1963 he sang in Stuttgart, and in 1962 appeared as Pedrillo at the Salzburg Festival. He then was a member of the Hamburg State Opera (1963–66) and the Vienna State Opera (1966–70). In later years, he became particularly esteemed for his character roles. His last major appearance was as Mime in Stuttgart in 1987. As a concert artist, his repertoire ranged from the Baroque era to contemporary scores.

Unger, (Gustav) Hermann, German composer and writer on music; b. Kamenz, Oct. 26, 1886; d. Cologne, Dec. 31, 1958. He studied classical philology in Freiburg im Breisgau, Leipzig, and Munich (graduated, 1910, with a work on Greek poetry); he also took a course in musicology in Munich with Edgar Istel and Joseph Haas; he subsequently went to Meiningen, where he took lessons with Max Reger (1910–13). He settled in Cologne, where he taught at the Cons. (1919–25) and Univ. (1922–45); he also was prof. at the Staatliche Hochschule für Musik (1925–47) and director of the Rheinische Musikschule (from 1934). Among his compositions were 2 operas: *Der Zauberhandschuh* (1927) and *Richmodis von Aducht* (1928); also *Die Geschichten vom Weihnachtsbaum*, Christmas fairy tale (1943).

WRITINGS: *Max Reger* (Munich, 1921; 2d ed., 1924); *Musikalisches Laienbrevier* (Munich, 1921); *Das Volk und seine Musik* (Hamburg, 1922); *Musikgeschichte in Selbstzeugnissen* (Munich, 1928); *Musikanten gestern und heute* (Siegen, 1935); *Anton Bruckner und seine 7. Sinfonie* (Bonn, 1944); *Harmonielehre* (Frankfurt am Main, 1946); *Die musikalische Widmung* (Munich, 1958).

Unger, (Ernst) Max, German musicologist, conductor, and painter; b. Taura, Saxony, May 28, 1883; d. Zürich, Dec. 1, 1959. He studied at the Leipzig Cons., and also attended Riemann's lectures at the Univ. of Leipzig (Ph.D., 1911, with the diss. *Muzio Clementis Leben*; publ. in Langensalza, 1914). He was conductor of the Vereinigte Leipziger Schauspielhauser in 1906, then was conductor of the Leipzig Madrigal Soc. (1912–14) and ed. of the *Neue Zeitschrift für Musik* (1919–20); after living in Zürich (1932–40), he went to Italy; he returned to Germany after World War II. He devoted his research mainly to Beethoven; he publ. about 150 papers dealing with various aspects of Beethoven's life and works; among his books are *Mendelssohn-Bartholdys Beziehungen zu England* (Langensalza, 1909); *Auf Spuren von Beethovens unsterblicher Geliebten* (Langensalza, 1911); *Beethoven über eine Gesamtausgabe seiner Werke* (Bonn, 1920); *Ludwig van Beethoven und seine Verleger S.A. Steiner und Tobias Haslinger in Wien, Ad. Mart. Schlesinger in Berlin* (Berlin and Vienna, 1921); *Beethovens Handschrift* (Bonn, 1926); *Ein Faustopernplan Beethovens und Goethes* (Regensburg, 1952); he also ed. the catalogue of the Bodmer Beethoven collection in Zürich, under the title *Eine schweizer Beethovensammlung: Katalog* (Zürich, 1939).

Uppman, Theodor, American baritone and teacher; b. San Jose, Calif., Jan. 12, 1920. He received training at the Curtis Inst. of Music in Philadelphia (1939–41) before attending opera workshops at Stanford Univ. (1941–42) and the Univ. of Southern Calif. in Los Angeles (1948–50). In 1941 he made his professional debut with the Northern Calif. Sym. Orch. He first gained notice when he sang Debussy's Pelléas in a concert version with the San Francisco Sym. Orch. in 1947. In 1948 he chose that same role for his debut with the N.Y. City Opera. On Dec. 1, 1951, he created the title role in Britten's *Billy Budd* at London's Covent Garden. He made his Metropolitan Opera debut in New York as Pelléas on Nov. 27, 1953, and then was on its roster from 1955 to 1978, appearing in such roles as Papageno, Marcello, Eisenstein, Guglielmo, Paquillo, Sharpless, et al. He also was a guest artist with other U.S. opera companies and toured as a concert artist. In 1962 he created Floyd's Jonathan Wade at the N.Y. City Opera and in 1983 Bernstein's Bill in *A Quiet Place* at the Houston Grand Opera. He taught at the Manhattan School of Music, the Mannes College of Music in New York, and the Britten-Pears School for Advanced Musical Studies in Aldeburgh.

Upshaw, Dawn, greatly admired American soprano; b. Nashville, Tenn., July 17, 1960. She studied at Illinois Wesleyan Univ. (B.A., 1982) and then pursued vocal training with Ellen Faull at the Manhattan School of Music in New York (M.A., 1984); she also attended courses given by Jan DeGaetani at the Aspen (Colo.) Music School. In 1984 she won the Young Concert Artists auditions and entered the Metropolitan Opera's young artists development program. She was cowinner of the Naumburg Competition in New York (1985). After appearing in minor roles at the Metropolitan Opera in New York, she displayed her vocal gifts in such major roles as Donizetti's Adina and Mozart's Despina in 1988. In 1990 she sang Pamina in a concert performance of *Die Zauberflöte* at the London Promenade Concerts. In 1992 she appeared as the Angel in Messiaen's *St. François d'Assise* at the Salzburg Festival. In 1995 she portrayed Strauss's Sophie in Houston. In 1996 she was engaged as Handel's Theodora at the Glyndebourne Festival. She sang Mozart's Cherubino and Stravinsky's Anne Trulove at the Metropolitan Opera in 1997. She also pursued a notably successful career as a soloist with major orchs. and as a recitalist. Her remarkable concert repertoire ranges from early music to the most intimidating of avant-garde scores.

Urbanner, Erich, Austrian composer, teacher, and conductor; b. Innsbruck, March 26, 1936. He was a student of Schiske and Jelinek (composition), Grete Hinterhofer (piano), and Swarowsky (conducting) at the Vienna Academy of Music (1955–61). He also attended the composition courses of Fortner, Stockhausen, and Maderna in Darmstadt. In 1961 he became an instructor at the Vienna Academy of Music. From 1968 he was also active as a conductor. In 1969 he was named a prof. of composition and harmony at the Vienna Hochschule für Musik. Among his honors were Vienna's Förderungspreis (1962), the City of Innsbruck prize (1980), the Würdigungspreis of the Austrian Ministry of Education and Art (1982), the City of Vienna prize (1984), and the Tiroler Landespreis for the arts (1993). Urbanner's music is strikingly modern without adhering to any particular school.

WORKS: DRAMATIC: *Der Gluckerich, oder Tugend und Tadel der Nützlichkeit*, musical burlesque (1963; Vienna, May 26, 1965); *Ninive, oder Das leben geth weiter*, opera (1987; Innsbruck, Sept. 24, 1988); *Johannes Stein, oder Der Rock des Kaisers*, monodrama (1990–91; Vienna, March 31, 1992); *Die Tochter des Kerensteiners*, musical scenes (1994).

Uribe-Holguín, Guillermo, eminent Colombian composer and pedagogue; b. Bogotá, March 17, 1880; d. there, June 26, 1971. He studied violin with Figueroa at the Bogotá Academy of Music (1890) and with Narciso Garay; taught at the Academy (1905–07). In 1907 he went to Paris, where he studied with d'Indy at the Schola Cantorum; he then took violin lessons with César Thomson and Emile Chaumont in Brussels. He returned to Colombia in 1910 and became director of the newly reorganized National Cons. in Bogotá; he resigned in 1935 and devoted his time to the family coffee plantation. He continued to compose and was active as a conductor; he was again director of the Cons. from 1942 to 1947. In 1910 he married the pianist Lucia Gutiérrez. His music bears the imprint of the modern French style, but his thematic material is related to native musical resources; particularly remarkable are his *Trozos en el sentimiento popular* for Piano, of which he wrote about 350; they are stylizations of Colombian melorhythms in a brilliant pianistic setting. Also among his compositions was an opera, *Furatena*. He publ. an autobiography, *Vida de un músico colombiano* (Bogotá, 1941).

Urlus, Jacques (Jacobus), noted Dutch tenor; b. Hergenrath, near Aachen, Jan. 9, 1867; d. Noordwijk, June 6, 1935. When he was 10, his parents moved to Tilburg, the Netherlands, where he received instruction from an uncle who was a choral conductor; he later studied singing with Anton Averkamp, Hugo Nolthenius, and Cornelie van Zanten. He was a member of the Dutch National Opera (1894–99) and of the Leipzig Opera (1900–14), where he excelled as a Wagnerian. In 1910 he made his London debut at Covent Garden as Tristan, a role he repeated for his U.S. debut in Boston on Feb. 12, 1912, and for his Metropolitan Opera debut in New York on Feb. 8, 1913. He remained on the roster of the Metropolitan Opera until 1917, and in subsequent years toured in Europe and the United States. His other distinguished roles included Parsifal, Tamino, Otello, and Don José. He publ. *Mijn Loopbaan* (My Career; Amsterdam, 1930).

BIBL.: O. Spengler, *J. U.* (N.Y., 1917).

Urner, Catherine Murphy, American singer, teacher, and composer; b. Mitchell, Ind., March 23, 1891; d. San Diego, April 30, 1942. She studied at the Univ. of Calif. at Berkeley and with Koechlin in Paris (1920–21). After serving as director of vocal music at Mills College in Oakland, California (1921–24), she devoted much time to performing, teaching, and composing. She made tours of the United States, France, and Italy. Urner studied Amerian Indian tribal melodies, which she utilized in a number of compositions. She also collaborated with Koechlin on several scores.

Urreta, Alicia, Mexican pianist, teacher, and composer; b. Veracruz, Oct. 12, 1935; d. Mexico City, Dec. 20, 1986. She studied piano with Joaquin Amparán and harmony with Rodolfo Halffter in Mexico City (1948–54), then engaged in teaching. Among her works was a radio opera, *Romance de Doña Balada* (Mexico City, 1972).

Ursuleac, Viorica, noted Romanian soprano; b. Cernăuţi, March 26, 1894; d. Ehrwald, Tirol, Oct. 22, 1985. She studied in Vienna with Franz Steiner and Philip Forstén and in Berlin with Lilli Lehmann. She made her operatic debut as Charlotte in Massenet's *Werther* in Agram in 1922, then sang in Cernăuţi (1923–24) and with the Vienna Volksoper (1924–26). In 1926 she joined the Frankfurt am Main Opera, and then pursued a distinguished career as a member of the Vienna State Opera (1930–34), the Berlin State Opera (1935–37), and the Bavarian State Opera in Munich (1937–44). Richard Strauss held her in the highest esteem; in his operas she created the roles of Arabella (Dresden, July 1, 1933), Maria in *Der Friedenstag* (Munich, July 24, 1938), the Countess in *Capriccio* (Munich, Oct. 28, 1942), and Danae in *Die Liebe der Danae* (public dress rehearsal, Salzburg, Aug. 16, 1944). She was also highly successful in the operas of Mozart, Wagner, and Verdi. She was married to **Clemens Krauss**, with whom she often appeared in concert. After his death in 1954, she settled in Ehrwald.

With R. Schlötterer, she wrote *Singen für Richard Strauss: Erinnerungen und Dokumente* (Vienna, 1986).

Usandizaga, José Maria, Basque composer; b. San Sebastián, March 31, 1887; d. there, Oct. 5, 1915. Encouraged by Planté and d'Indy, he entered the Paris Schola Cantorum when he was 14, where he studied piano with Grovlez and counterpoint with Tricon. In 1906 he returned to his native city and associated himself with the Basque musical movement, to which he gave a great impetus with the production of his stage work *Mendi mendiyan* (High in the Mountains; 1909–10; San Sebastián, 1911), then followed his drama lírico *Las golondrinas* (The Swallows; 1913; Madrid, Feb. 5, 1914; rev. as an opera by his brother, R. Usandizaga, Barcelona, 1929), which obtained excellent success; his last stage work was the drama lírico *La llama* (The Flame; 1915; completed by R. Usandizaga, San Sebastián, 1918). His death from tuberculosis at the age of 28 was deeply lamented by Spanish musicians.

BIBL.: L. Villalba Muñoz, *Ultimos músicos españoles: J. M. U.* (Madrid, 1918); J. de Arozamena, *J. M. U. y la bella época donostiarra* (San Sebastian, 1969).

Usiglio, Emilio, Italian conductor and composer; b. Parma, Jan. 8, 1841; d. Milan, July 7, 1910. He studied in Pisa and Florence, then pursued a successful career as an opera conductor until a wayward lifestyle and abuse of alcohol took its toll. In his last years, he conducted in provincial opera houses before retiring to Milan with his wife, the singer Clementina Brusa. Among his works were the operas *La Locandiera* (Turin, Sept. 5, 1861), *L'eredità in Corsica* (Milan, June 17, 1864), *Le Educande di Sorrento* (Florence, May 1, 1868), *La scommessa* (Florence, July 6, 1870), *Le Donne curiose* (Madrid, Feb. 11, 1879), and *Le nozze in prigione* (Milan, March 23, 1881); also several ballets.

Uspensky, Victor Alexandrovich, Russian composer and ethnomusicologist; b. Kaluga, Aug. 31, 1879; d. Tashkent, Oct. 9, 1949. He was brought up in central Asia, where his father held a government post; he attended the composition classes of Liadov at the St. Petersburg Cons. and graduated in 1913. In 1918 he went to Tashkent. From 1932 to 1948 he was active with the Musical Folklore Division of Uzbekistan, and did valuable research work in native folklore. He also worked on the restoration of Uzbek musical instruments; from these authentic materials he fashioned an Uzbek opera, *Farhad and Shirin*, premiered in Tashkent on Feb. 26, 1936. With V. Belaiev, he publ. a treatise on Turkmenian music (Moscow, 1928).

BIBL.: J. Pekker, *V. A. U.* (Moscow, 1953; 2d ed., 1958).

Ussachevsky, Vladimir (Alexis), innovative Russian-born American composer; b. Hailar, Manchuria, Nov. 3, 1911; d. N.Y., Jan. 2, 1990. His parents settled in Manchuria shortly after the Russo-Japanese War of 1905, at the time when Russian culture was still a powerful social factor there. His father was an officer of the Russian Army, and his mother was a professional pianist. In 1930 he went to California, where he took private piano lessons with Clarence Mader; from 1931 to 1933 he attended Pasadena Junior College; in 1933 he received a scholarship to study at Pomona College (B.A., 1935). He then enrolled in the Eastman School of Music in Rochester in New York in the classes of Hanson, Rogers, and Royce in composition (M.M., 1936; Ph.D., 1939); he also had some instruction with Burrill Phillips. In 1942, as a naturalized American citizen, Ussachevsky was drafted into the U.S. Army; thanks to his fluency in Russian, his knowledge of English and French, and a certain ability to communicate in rudimentary Chinese, he was engaged in the Intelligence Division; subsequently he served as a research analyst at the War Dept. in Washington, D.C. He then pursued postdoctoral work with Luening at Columbia Univ., joining its faculty in 1947; he was prof. of music (1964–80). At various times he taught at other institutions, including several years as composer-in-residence at the Univ. of Utah (from 1970) and was a faculty member there (1980–85). His early works were influenced by Russian church music, in the tradition of Tchaikovsky and Rachmaninoff. A distinct change in his career as a composer came in 1951, when he became interested in the resources of electronic music; to this period belong his works *Transposition, Reverberation, Experiment, Composition* and *Underwater Valse*, which make use of electronic sound. On Oct. 28, 1952, Stokowski conducted in New York the first performance of Ussachevsky's *Sonic Contours*, in which a piano part was metamorphosed with the aid of various sonorific devices, superimposed on each other. About that time, he began a fruitful partnership with Luening; with him he composed *Incantation for Tape Recorder*, which was broadcast in 1953. Luening and Ussachevsky then conceived the idea of combining electronic tape sounds with conventional instruments played by human musicians; the result was *Rhapsodic Variations*, first performed in New York on March 20, 1954. The work anticipated by a few months the composition of the important score *Déserts* by Varèse, which effectively combined electronic sound with other instruments. The next work by Ussachevsky and Luening was *A Poem in Cycles and Bells* for Tape Recorder and Orch., first performed by the Los Angeles Phil. on Nov. 22, 1954. On March 31, 1960, Leonard Bernstein conducted the N.Y. Phil. in the commissioned work by Ussachevsky and Luening entitled *Concerted Piece for Tape Recorder and Orchestra*. On Jan. 12, 1956, Ussachevsky and Luening provided taped background for Shakespeare's *King Lear*, produced by Orson Welles, at the N.Y. City Center, and for Margaret Webster's production of *Back to Methuselah* for the N.Y. Theater Guild in 1958. They also provided the electronic score for the documentary *The Incredible Voyage*, broadcast over the CBS-TV Network on Oct. 13, 1965. Among works that Ussachevsky wrote for electronic sound without partnership were *A Piece for Tape Recorder* (1956), *Studies in Sound, Plus* (1959), and *The Creation* (1960). In 1968 Ussachevsky began experimenting with the synthesizer, with the aid of a computer. One of the works resulting from these experiments was *Conflict* (1971), intended to represent the mystical struggle between 2 ancient deities. In 1959 Ussachevsky was one of the founders of the Columbia–Princeton Electronic Music Center; he was active as a lecturer at various exhibitions of electronic sounds; he also traveled to Russia and to China to present his music. He held 2 Guggenheim fellowships (1957, 1960). In 1973 Ussachevsky was elected to membership in the National Inst. of Arts and Letters.

WORKS: INCIDENTAL MUSIC FOR TAPE: *To Catch a Thief* (sound effects for the film; 1954); *Mathematics* (television score; 1957); *The Boy who Saw Through* (film; 1959); *No Exit* (film; 1962); *Line of Apogee* (film; 1967); *Mourning Becomes Electra* (sound effects for the opera by M. Levy; 1967); *The Cannibals* (play; 1969); *2 Images for the Computer Piece* (film; 1969); *Duck, Duck* (film; 1970); *We* (radio play; 1970). FILM SCORE: *Circle of Fire* (1940). WITH OTTO LUENING: *Of Identity*, ballet for Tape (1954); *Carlsbad Caverns*, television score for Tape (1955); *King Lear*, incidental music (3 versions, 1956); *Back to Methuselah*, incidental music for Tape (1958); *Incredible Voyage*, television score for Tape (1968; also with Shields and Smiley).

Uttini, Francesco Antonio Baldassare, Italian composer and conductor; b. Bologna, 1723; d. Stockholm, Oct. 25, 1795. He studied with Padre Martini, Perti, and Sandoni. In 1743 he became a member of the Accademia dei Filarmonici in Bologna. He first appeared as a singer and conductor with Mingotti's operatic touring group (c. 1752); in 1755, went to Stockholm as conductor of an Italian opera company; he was named Master of the King's Music in 1767, and also was principal conductor at the Royal Opera until his retirement in 1788. Historically he is important as the composer of the earliest operas on Swedish texts; the first, *Thetis och Pelée*, was written for the inauguration of the new Royal Opera in Stockholm (Jan. 18, 1773); another opera to a Swedish libretto, tr. from the French, was *Aline, Drotning uti Golconda* (Aline, Queen of Golconda), produced at the Royal Opera on Jan. 11, 1776. Of Uttini's Italian operas, the best is *Il Re pastore* (Stockholm, July 24, 1755). A great admirer of Gluck, he brought out many of that composer's works in Stockholm. He also wrote the oratorios *La Giuditta* (Bologna, 1742) and *La passione di Gesù* (Stockholm, 1776).

V

Vaccai, Nicola, Italian composer and singing teacher; b. Tolentino, March 15, 1790; d. Pesaro, Aug. 5, 1848. He went to Rome as a youth and took lessons in counterpoint with Jannaconi, then studied with Paisiello in Naples (from 1812). He was a singing teacher in Venice (1818–21), Trieste (1821–23), and in Frohsdorf, near Wiener Neustadt (1822). He taught in Paris (1830) and in England (1830–33) before returning to Italy; later he became vice censore at the Milan Cons., assuming the post of censore in 1838; in 1844 he retired to Pesaro. Although he found little success as a composer for the theater, he won distinction as a singing teacher; his *Metodo pratico di canto italiano per camera diviso in 15 lezioni, ossiano Solfeggi progressivi ed elementari sopra parole di Metastasio* (London, 1832) became a standard work in its field. Among his operas were *Pietro il Grande, ossia Un geloso all tortura* (Parma, Jan. 17, 1824), *La Pastorella feudataria* (Turin, Sept. 18, 1824), and *Giulietta e Romeo*, after Shakespeare (Milan, Oct. 31, 1825), the last scene of which was often used in performances of Bellini's *I Capuletti e i Montecchi*.

BIBL.: G. Vaccai, *La vita di N. V. scritta dal figlio Giulio con prefazione del professore A. Biaggi* (Bologna, 1882).

Vacek, Miloš, Czech composer; b. Horní Roveň, June 20, 1928. He studied organ at the Prague Cons. (1943–47), then took a course in composition with Řídký and Pícha at the Prague Academy of Arts and Music (1947–51). From 1954 he devoted himself totally to composition.

WORKS: DRAMATIC: OPERAS: *Jan Želivský* (1953–56; rev. 1974; Olomouc, April 15, 1984); *Bratr íak* (Brother Jacques; 1976–78; Ostrava, June 12, 1982); *Romance pro křídlovku* (Romance for Bugle Horn; 1980–81; Czech Radio, Plzeň, Oct. 26, 1983; 1st stage perf., České Budějovice, Dec. 12, 1987); *Kocour Mikeš* (Mikeš the Tom Cat; 1981–82; Brno, March 28, 1986). BALLETS: *Komediantská pohádka* (The Comedian's Fairytale; 1957–58); *Vítr ve vlasech* (Wind in the Hair; 1960–61); *Poslední pampeliška* (The Last Dandelion; 1963–64); *Milá sedmi loupežníků* (The Mistress of Seven Robbers; 1966); *Meteor* (1966); *Šťastná sedma* (Lucky Sevens; 1966). MUSICALS: *Noc je můj den* (The Night Is My Day), blues drama about the life of Bessie Smith (1962; Frankfurt am Main, March 15, 1964); *Císařovy nové šaty* (The Emperor's New Clothes; 1962); *Madame Sans Gêne* (1968); *Vítr z Alabamy* (Wind from Alabama; 1970).

Vachon, Pierre, French violinist and composer; b. Arles, June 1731; d. Berlin, Oct. 7, 1803. He studied with Chiabrano in Paris from 1751, first appearing at the Concert Spirituel on Dec. 24, 1756, as soloist in his own concerto. From 1761 he was 1st violinist in the orch. of the Prince de Conti. In 1772 he gave concerts in London and then returned to Paris; by 1775 he was again in London, where he remained for some 10 years. He then went to Germany, and became concertmaster of the royal orch. in Berlin in 1788; he was pensioned in 1798.

WORKS: DRAMATIC: *Renaud d'Ast*, comédie (Fontainebleau, Oct. 12, 1765; in collaboration with J.-C. Trial); *Ésope à Cythère*, comédie (Paris, Dec. 15, 1766; in collaboration with J.-C. Trial); *Les Femmes et le secret*, comédie (Paris, Nov. 9, 1767); *Hippomène et Atalante*, ballet-héroïque (Paris, Aug. 8, 1769); *Sara, ou La Fermière écossaise*, comédie (Paris, May 8, 1773).

Vadé, Jean-Joseph, French poet, dramatist, and composer; b. Ham, Picardy, Jan. 17, 1719; d. Paris, July 4, 1757. He was taken to Paris by his family when he was 5. He was made contrôleur du vingtième arrondissement (a tax-collecting position) in Soissons in 1739; after serving in this capacity in Laon and Rouen, he was made secretary to the Duke of Agenois in Paris in 1743. He began writing for the Comédie-Française in Paris in 1749, scoring success with his first opéra comique, *La Fileuse* (1752); subsequently he brought out other works there. He was awarded a pension by Louis XV (1751). His importance rests upon his creation of the genre poissard, or fish-market style, that permeates his opéras comiques and chansons.

WORKS: OPÉRAS COMIQUES (all 1st perf. in Paris): *La Fileuse* (March 8, 1752); *Le Poirier* (Aug. 7, 1752); *Le Bouquet du roi* (Aug. 24, 1752; in collaboration with J. Fleury and Lattaignant); *Le Suffisant, ou Le Petit Maître dupé* (March 12, 1753); *Le Rien* (April 10, 1753); *Le Trompeur trompé, ou La Rencontre imprévue*

(Feb. 18, 1754); *Il était temps* (June 28, 1754); *La Fontaine de jouvence* (Sept. 17, 1754; in collaboration with Noverre); *La Nouvelle Bastienne* (Sept. 17, 1754; in collaboration with L. Anseaume); *Compliment de clôture* (Oct. 6, 1754); *Les Troyennes en Champagne* (Feb. 1, 1755); *Jérôme et Fanchonette, ou La Pastorale de la grenouillère* (Feb. 18, 1755); *Compliment de clôture* (April 6, 1755); *Le Confidant heureux* (July 31, 1755); *Folette, ou L'Enfant gâté* (Sept. 6, 1755); *Nicaise* (Feb. 7, 1756); *Les Raccoleurs* (March 11, 1756); *L'Impromptu du coeur* (Feb. 8, 1757); *Compliment pour la clôture de l'Opéra-Comique* (April 3, 1757); *Le Mauvais plaisant, ou Le Drôle de corps* (Aug. 17, 1757); also *La Folle raisonnable* (not perf.).

Vaduva, Leontina, Romanian soprano; b. Rosiile, Dec. 1, 1960. She studied at the Bucharest Cons. After winning the Concours de Chant in Toulouse in 1986, she made her operatic debut as Manon in Toulouse and won the 's-Hertogenbosch Competition in the Netherlands in 1987. In 1988 she sang Ninetta in *La gazza ladra* at the Théâtre des Champs-Elysées in Paris and made her debut as Manon at London's Covent Garden. Her subsequent engagements at Covent Garden included Juliette in 1994 and Micaëla in 1996. She also sang in Bordeaux, Avignon, Bonn, Monte Carlo, and other European cities.

Vainberg, Moisei, Polish-born Russian composer; b. Warsaw, Dec. 8, 1919; d. Moscow, Feb. 26, 1996. He studied piano with Turczynski at the Warsaw Cons., graduating in 1939, then studied composition with Zolotarev at the Minsk Cons.; in 1943 he settled in Moscow. In his music he followed the precepts of socialist realism in its ethnic aspects; according to the subject, he made use of Jewish, Polish, Moldavian, or Armenian folk melos, in tasteful harmonic arrangements devoid of abrasive dissonances.

WORKS: DRAMATIC: OPERAS: *The Sword of Uzbekistan* (1942); *The Woman Passenger* (1968); *Love of D'Artagnan*, after Alexandre Dumas (1972). BALLETS: *Battle for the Fatherland* (1942); *The Golden Key* (1955); *The White Chrysanthemum* (1958); *Requiem* (1967).

Vajda, János, Hungarian composer; b. Miskolc, Oct. 8, 1949. He received training in choral conducting from István Párkai and in composition from Emil Petrovics at the Budapest Academy of Music (graduated, 1975); after serving as répétiteur with the Hungarian Radio and Television Choir (1974–79), he completed his composition studies at the Sweelinck Cons. in Amsterdam (1979–80). From 1981 he taught at the Budapest Academy of Music. He won the Erkel Prize in 1981.

WORKS: DRAMATIC: OPERAS: *Barabbás* (1976–77); *Mario és a varázsló* (Mario and the Magician; 1983–85). BALLETS: *Az igazság pillanata* (The Moment of Truth; 1981); *Don Juan árnyéka rajtunk* (Don Juan's Shadow Is Cast on Us; 1981); *Izzó planéták* (Glowing Planets; 1983); *Jön a cirkusz* (Circus Is Coming; 1984).

Valdengo, Giuseppe, Italian baritone; b. Turin, May 24, 1914. He studied cello at the Turin Cons., and also played the oboe, then decided to cultivate his voice, and took singing lessons with Michele Accoriutti. In 1936 he made his operatic debut as Figaro in *Il Barbiere di Siviglia* in Parma; in 1939 he was engaged to sing at La Scala in Milan. On Sept. 19, 1946, he made his N.Y. City Opera debut as Sharpless, remaining on its roster until 1948. On Dec. 19, 1947, he made his Metropolitan Opera debut in New York as Tonio; he continued on the company's roster until 1954; he was also chosen by Toscanini to sing the roles of Amonasro, Renato, Iago, and Falstaff with the NBC Sym. Orch. He made guest appearances in London, Paris, Vienna, and South America. He also acted the part of Antonio Scotti in the film *The Great Caruso*. His association with Toscanini is related in his *Ho cantato con Toscanini* (Como, 1962).

Válek, Jiří, notable Czech composer, writer, and teacher; b. Prague, May 28, 1923. He was a composition student of Řídký at the Prague Cons., graduating from its master school in 1947. He also received private training in philosophy, aesthetics, music history, and theory. After graduating from the Prague College of Higher Education in 1950, he took his Ph.D. at the Charles Univ. in Prague in 1952. From 1949 to 1952 he held the position of creative secretary of the Union of Czech Composers. He was a senior staff member of the state publishing firm Panton from 1959 to 1973. In 1966 he became a prof. at the Prague Cons. He also was artistic director of the state recording firm Supraphon (1974–79) and an assoc. prof. of composition at the Prague Academy of Musical Arts (from 1979). Among his writings are literary works and monographs. In his 17 syms., Válek has traversed an extensive ideological and artistic landscape, embracing both historical and contemporary events. Several of his stage pieces are rich in topical and satirical expression.

WORKS: DRAMATIC: *Shakespearean Variations*, music drama for 9 Actors, Commentator, and Nonet (1967); *Hour of Truth*, opera (1980); *Sonata on Auxiliary Life* for Moderator, Violin, Piano, and Percussion (1983); *Hamlet, our Contemporary*, satirical opera (1985); *Don't Let Us Stone Pygmies*, satirical opera (1991).

Valente, Benita, distinguished American soprano; b. Delano, Calif., Oct. 19, 1934. She began serious musical training with Chester Hayden at Delano High School; at 16 she became a private pupil of Lotte Lehmann, and at 17 received a scholarship to continue her studies with Lehmann at the Music Academy of the West in Santa Barbara; in 1955 she won a scholarship to the Curtis Inst. of Music in Philadelphia, where she studied with Singher. Upon graduation in 1960, she made her formal debut in a Marlboro (Vt.) festival concert. On Oct. 8, 1960, she made her N.Y. concert debut at the New School for Social Research. After winning the Metropolitan Opera Auditions in 1960, she pursued further studies with Margaret Harshaw. She then sang with the Freiburg im Breisgau Opera, making her debut there as Pamina in 1962; after appearances with the Nuremberg Opera (1966), she returned to the United States and established herself as a versatile recitalist, soloist with orchs., and opera singer. Her interpretation of Pamina was especially well received, and it was in that role that she made her long-awaited Metropolitan Opera debut in New York. on Sept. 22, 1973. She won praise for her performances in operas by Monteverdi, Handel, Verdi, Puccini, and Britten. Her extensive recital and concert repertoire ranges from Schubert to Ginastera.

Valente, Giorgio. See **Vitalis, George.**

Valente, Vincenzo, Italian composer; b. Corigliano Calabro, Feb. 21, 1855; d. Naples, Sept. 6, 1921. At the age of 15 he wrote a song, "Ntuniella," which became popular; he continued writing Neapolitan songs of great appeal ("Basta ca po'," "Comme te voglio amà!," "Canzone cafona," "Mugliera comme fa," "Ninuccia, Tiempe felice," "L'acqua," etc.), about 400 in all. He also brought out operettas: *I Granatieri* (Turin, Oct. 26, 1889), *La Sposa di Charolles* (Rome, March 3, 1894), *Rolandino* (Turin, Oct. 15, 1897), *L'usignuolo* (Naples, May 10, 1899), *Lena* (Foggia, Jan. 1, 1918), *L'Avvocato Trafichetti* (Naples, May 24, 1919), and *Nèmesi* (posthumous, Naples, July 23, 1923). His son, Nicola Valente (b. Naples, Aug. 28, 1881; d. there, Sept. 16, 1946), was also a composer of Neapolitan songs and light operas.

Valentin, Erich, distinguished German musicologist; b. Strasbourg, Nov. 27, 1906; d. Bad Aibling, March 16, 1993. He studied music with Courvoisier and Röhr in Munich and took courses in musicology with Sandberger at the Univ. of Munich, where he received his Ph.D. in 1928 with the diss. *Die Entwicklung der Tokkata im 17. und 18. Jahrhundert* (publ. in Munich, 1930). From 1929 to 1935 he taught at the Staatliches Privatmusiklehrer-Seminar in Magdeburg; from 1939 to 1945 he was director of the Zentralinstitut für Mozartforschung. He taught at the Hochschule für Musik in Munich from 1953, where he was a prof. from 1955 and its director (1964–72). From 1950 to 1955 he was ed.-in-chief of the *Zeitschrift für Musik*, and from 1955 to 1959 he was coed. of the *Neue Zeitschrift für Musik*. He became ed.-in-chief of *Acta Mozartiana* in 1954. In addition to his many articles for music journals, he also prepared eds. of works by Mozart, Telemann, and others.

WRITINGS: *Georg Philipp Telemann* (Burg, 1931; 3d ed., 1952); *Richard Wagner* (Regensburg, 1937); *Dichtung und Oper: Eine*

Untersuchung zum Stilproblem der Oper (Leipzig, 1938); *Hans Pfitzner* (Regensburg, 1939); *Wege zu Mozart* (Regensburg, 1941; 4th ed., 1950); *Beethoven* (Salzburg, 1942; Eng. ed., N.Y., 1958); *W. A. Mozart: Wesen und Wandlung* (Hamelin, 1948); *Kleine Bilder grosser Meister* (Mainz, 1952); *Handbuch der Chormusik* (Regensburg, 1953–74); *Handbuch der Instrumentenkunde* (Regensburg, 1954; 6th ed., 1974); *Der früheste Mozart* (Munich, 1956); *Beethoven* (pictorial bibliography; Munich, 1957); *Die Tokkata*, in *Das Musikwerk*, XVII (1958); *Mozart* (pictorial bibliography; Munich, 1959); *Musica domestica: Über Wesen und Geschichte der Hausmusik* (Trossingen, 1959); *Telemann in seiner Zeit* (Hamburg, 1960); *Handbuch der Schulmusik* (Regensburg, 1962); *Die goldene Spur: Mozart in der Dichtung Hermann Hesses* (Augsburg, 1965); with F. Hofmann, *Die evangelische Kirchenmusik* (Regensburg, 1967); with W. Gebhardt and W. Vetter, *Handbuch des Musikunterrichts* (Regensburg, 1970); *Die schönsten Beethoven-Briefe* (Munich, 1973); *Lübbes Mozart-Lexikon* (Bergisch-Gladbach, 1983); *Don-Juan-Reflexionen: Eine Auswahl literarischer Zeugnisse* (Augsburg, 1988).

BIBL.: G. Weiss, ed., *E. V. zum 70. Geburtstag* (Regensburg, 1976).

Valentini, Giuseppe, Italian violinist and composer; b. Florence, c.1680; d. after 1759. He was at Rome in 1700 and in the service of Prince Francesco Maria Ruspoli as a violinist, c.1708–13; he may then have been at Bologna in the service of the Prince di Caserta; from 1735, was at the grand-ducal court of Florence. His violin technique was highly developed (some compositions call for the 6th position). Among his compositions were the operas *La finta rapita* (Cisterna, 1714; in collaboration with N. Romaldi and G. Cesarini) and *La costanza in amore* (Cisterna, 1715); also *Oratorio per l'assunzione della beata vergine* (Rome, 1730).

Valentini-Terrani, Lucia, Italian mezzo-soprano; b. Padua, Aug. 28, 1948; d. Seattle, June 11, 1998. She received training in Padua. In 1969 she made her operatic debut in the title role of Rossini's *La Cenerentola* in Brescia, and then appeared in various Italian operatic centers. From 1973 she sang at Milan's La Scala. On Nov. 16, 1974, she made her Metropolitan Opera debut in New York as Rossini's Isabella. In 1979 she appeared as a soloist in the Verdi *Requiem* with Giulini and the Los Angeles Phil., returning to Los Angeles in 1982 to sing Mistress Quickly under Giulini's direction. From 1984 she sang at the Pesaro Festivals. In 1987 she appeared as Rossini's Rosina at London's Covent Garden. She sang Gluck's Orféo in Naples in 1990. In 1992 she appeared as Rossini's Isabella in Turin. Her guest engagements also took her to the Vienna State Opera, the Paris Opéra, the Bolshoi Theater in Moscow, and the Lyric Opera in Chicago. She was particularly known for her roles in operas by Rossini and Verdi.

Valentino, Henri-Justin-Armand-Joseph, French conductor; b. Lille, Oct. 14, 1785; d. Versailles, Jan. 20, 1865. He began his career as a theater conductor when he was only 14; after working in Rouen, he settled in Paris. In about 1820 he became 2d conductor at the Opéra, where he shared the duties of 1st conductor with Habeneck (1824–30), then was chief conductor of the Opéra Comique (1831–36). After a sojourn in Chantilly (1836–37), he returned to Paris and conducted his own "Concerts Valentino" until 1841; he then retired to Versailles.

Valesi, Giovanni (real name, **Johann Evangelist Walleshauser**), German tenor and singing teacher; b. Unterhattenhofen, Upper Bavaria, April 28, 1735; d. Munich, Jan. 10, 1816. He was a student of Placius von Camerloher. After briefly singing as a bass, he became a tenor and was a court singer to the prince-bishop Johann Theodor of Freising and Liège (1754–56) and subsequently to Duke Clemens in Munich. From 1770 to 1798 he was a leading member of the Munich Court Opera. He also sang in Amsterdam and Brussels (1755), Italy (from 1758), where he adopted the name Giovanni Valesi, and Prague, Dresden, and Berlin (1777–78). Valesi was chosen to create the role of the High Priest of Neptune in Mozart's *Idomeneo* in Munich on Jan. 29, 1781. Among his numerous pupils were 5 of his own children, as well as such notable musicians as Carl Maria von Weber and Valentin Adamberger.

Valkare, Gunnar, Swedish organist, teacher, and composer; b. Norrköping, April 25, 1943. He studied piano with Stina Sundell, organ with Alf Linder, and composition with Ingvar Lidholm at the Stockholm Musikhögskolan (1963–69). He was active as an organist and teacher (1964–79); he served as resident composer in Gislaved (1973) and Kalmar (1977–78). His music is militantly aggressive in its tonal, atonal, and polytonal assault on the most cherished notions of harmonious sweetness. Among his works are *Eld för ett altare* (Fire from an Altar), church drama (1968), *A Play about the Medieval Värend and the Dacke Feud*, musical-dramatic dance for Winds, Violin, Nickelharp, and Xylophone (1971), *Mellan berg och hav, mellan himmel och jard* (Between the Mountains and the Ocean, Between the Sky and the Earth), play on Chinese history, for Singer, Actor, and Instrumental Ensemble (1975), and *Concerto d'incontro*, theater piece (1992).

Vallas, Léon, distinguished French musicologist; b. Roanne, Loire, May 17, 1879; d. Lyons, May 9, 1956. After studying medicine in Lyons, he pursued his musicological training at the univ. there (Ph.D., 1908). In 1902 he became music critic of *Tout Lyon*; in 1903 he founded the *Revue Musicale de Lyon*, which became the *Revue Française de Musique* in 1912 and the *Nouvelle Revue Musicale* in 1920; he also wrote for the *Progrès de Lyon* (1919–54). With G. Witkowski, he founded a schola cantorum in Lyons in 1902; he taught theory at the univ. (1908–11) and the cons. (1912) there, and later at the Sorbonne in Paris (1928–30). He was president of the Société Française de Musicologie (1937–43) and artistic director of Radiodiffusion de Lyon (1938–41).

WRITINGS: *Georges Migot* (Paris, n.d.); *Debussy, 1862–1918* (Paris, 1926); *Les Idées de Claude Debussy, musicien français* (Paris, 1927; 2d ed., 1932; Eng. tr., 1929, as *The Theories of Claude Debussy*); *Claude Debussy et son temps* (Paris, 1932; 2d ed., 1958; Eng. tr., 1933, as *Claude Debussy: His Life and Works*); *Achille-Claude Debussy* (Paris, 1944); *Vincent d'Indy* (2 vols., Paris, 1946, 1949); *César Franck* (London, 1951; in French, 1955, as *La Véritable Histoire de César Franck*).

Vallerand, Jean (d'Auray), Canadian composer, music critic, teacher, and administrator; b. Montreal, Dec. 24, 1915. He received violin lessons from Lucien Sicotte (1921–36); he also studied at the Collège Ste.-Marie de Montréal (B.A., 1935), and was a composition pupil of Claude Champagne (1935–42); he also obtained a diploma in journalism (1938) and a licence ès lettres (1939) from the Univ. of Montreal. He ed. *Quartier Latin* (1937–39), then wrote music criticism for *Le Canada* (1941–46), *Montréal-Matin* (1948–49), *Le Devoir* (1952–61), *Nouveau Journal* (1961–62), and *La Presse* (1962–66). From 1942 to 1963 he was secretary general of the Montreal Cons., where he also taught orchestration. He also taught orchestration and music history at the Univ. of Montreal from 1950 to 1966. After serving as head of radio music for the CBC in Montreal (1963–66), he was cultural attaché for the Quebec government in Paris (1966–70). In 1971 he was named director of music education for the Ministry of Cultural Affairs of Quebec. Following its reorganization that year, he was its director of performing arts until 1975. From 1971 to 1978 he also was director of the Cons. de musique et d'art dramatique du Québec. In 1967 he was awarded the Centenary Medal of Canada, and in 1975 received an honorary doctorate from the Univ. of Ottawa. In 1991 he was made a Chevalier of the Ordre National du Québec. In addition to his many reviews and articles in journals, he publ. the books *Introduction a la musique* (Montreal, 1949) and *La Musique et les tout-petits* (Montreal, 1950). He wrote music in a neo-Romantic manner; in his later compositions he experimented with serial techniques. Among his works was the opera *Le Magicien* (Orford, Quebec, Sept. 2, 1961, with piano; Montreal, May 30, 1962, with orch.).

Valleria (real name, **Schoening**), **Alwina,** noted American soprano; b. Baltimore, Oct. 12, 1848; d. Nice, Feb. 17, 1925. She went to London and entered the Royal Academy of Music in 1867, where she studied piano with W. H. Holmes and voice with Wallworth; after further studies with Arditi, she made her formal debut in a London concert on June 2, 1871. On Oct. 23, 1871, she made her operatic debut with the Italian Opera in St. Petersburg in *Linda di Chamounix*; after appearances in Germany and Italy, she returned to London and sang at the Drury Lane Theatre (1873–75), Her Majesty's Theatre (1877–78), and Covent Garden (1879–82). On Oct. 22, 1879, she made her U.S. debut as Marguerite in New York with Mapleson's company; after appearances with the Carl Rosa company in England (1882–83), she returned to the United States and made her Metropolitan Opera debut in New York as Leonora in *Il Trovatore* on Oct. 26, 1883, remaining on its roster for the season; she then pursued her career in England until retiring in 1886.

Valletti, Cesare, notable Italian tenor; b. Rome, Dec. 18, 1922. He was a student of Tito Schipa. In 1947 he made his operatic debut as Alfredo in Bari. After singing in Rome (1947–48), he appeared as Count Almaviva in Palermo and as Elvino in *La sonnambula* in Naples in 1949. In 1950 he sang Don Narciso in *Il Turco in Italia* at the Eliseo in Rome. Following his London debut as Fenton with the visiting La Scala company of Milan in 1950, he appeared with the company in Milan in such roles as Lindoro in *L'Italiana in Algeri*, Nemorino, and Vladimir in *Prince Igor*. In 1951 he sang Alfredo in Mexico City opposite Callas. He made his U.S. debut as Werther at the San Francisco Opera in 1953. On Dec. 10, 1953, he made his Metropolitan Opera debut in New York as Don Ottavio, where he remained on the roster until 1960 singing such admired roles as Tamino, Ferrando, Count Almaviva, Alfredo, Massenet's Des Grieux, and Alfred in *Die Fledermaus*. In 1958 he sang Alfredo opposite Callas at London's Covent Garden, and appeared as Giacomo in *Donna del lago* at the Florence Maggio Musicale Fiorentino. In 1960 he sang Don Ottavio at the Salzburg Festival. In 1968 he appeared as Nero in *L'incoronazione di Poppea* at the Caramoor Festival in Katonah, N.Y. He retired from the operatic stage that same year. Valletti's admired vocal gifts placed him in the forefront of the bel canto revival of his day.

Vallin, Ninon, French soprano; b. Montalieu-Vercieu, Sept. 8, 1886; d. Lyons, Nov. 22, 1961. She studied at the Lyons Cons. and with Meyriane Heglon in Paris. After appearing in concerts, she attracted the notice of Debussy, who chose her to sing in the premiere of his *Le martyre de Saint Sébastien* in 1911. He later accompanied her in recitals. In 1912 she made her operatic debut as Micaëla at the Paris Opéra Comique, where she sang until 1916. In 1916 she made her first appearance at the Teatro Colón in Buenos Aires, continuing to sing there until 1936. She appeared at Milan's La Scala in 1916 and in Rome in 1917. In 1920 she made her debut at the Paris Opéra as Thaïs. In 1934 she sang at the San Francisco Opera. Thereafter she toured as a concert artist. After teaching at the Montevideo Cons. (1953–59), she settled in Lyons. Among her finest roles were Zerlina, Alceste, Charlotte, Mignon, Juliette, and Mélisande. As a concert singer, she excelled in works by French and Spanish composers.

BIBL.: R. de Fragny, *N. V.: Princesse du chant* (Lyons, 1963).

Valverde, Joaquín, Spanish composer; b. Badajoz, Feb. 27, 1846; d. Madrid, March 17, 1910. He played the flute in bands from the age of 13, then studied at the Madrid Cons. His sym., *Batylo,* won a prize of the Sociedad Fomento de las Artes (1871). He wrote some 30 zarzuelas, some in collaboration with others; his most celebrated was *La gran vía* (Madrid, July 2, 1886; in collaboration with Chueca); it contains the march *Cádiz*, which became immensely popular. He publ. the book *La flauta: Su historia su estudio* (Madrid, 1886). His son, Quinto (Joaquín) Valverde Sanjuán (b. Madrid, Jan. 2, 1875; d. Mexico City, Nov. 4, 1918), was also a composer; he studied with his father and with Irache; he wrote some 250 light pieces for the theater; his zarzuela *El gran capitán* was especially successful. He died during a tour he undertook as conductor of a light opera company.

Van Allan, Richard (real name, **Alan Philip Jones**), English bass; b. Clipstone, Nottinghamshire, May 28, 1935. He studied at the Worcester College of Education and received vocal training from David Franklin at the Birmingham School of Music; he also had private vocal lessons with J. Strasser. In 1964 he became a member of the Glyndebourne Festival Chorus. In 1966 he made his operatic debut at the Glyndebourne Opera in a minor role in *Die Zauberflöte*. In 1969 he joined the Sadler's Wells Opera in London, and later sang there after it became the English National Opera in 1974. In 1970 he created the role of Jowler in Maw's *The Ring of the Moon* at Glyndebourne. He made his debut at London's Covent Garden as the Mandarin in *Turandot* in 1971. In 1976 he sang Baron Ochs at the San Diego Opera. In 1986 he became director of the National Opera Studio. However, he continued to pursue his stage career. In 1990 he sang Don Alfonso at the Metropolitan Opera in New York. In 1992 he created the role of Jerome in the stage premiere of Gerhard's *The Duenna* in Madrid. He appeared as Massenet's Don Quichotte at the Victoria State Opera in Melbourne in 1995. Among his other roles are Osmin, Don Giovanni, Leporello, Mozart's Figaro, the Grand Inquisitor, Philip II, and Verdi's Banquo.

van Appledorn, Mary Jeanne, American composer, pianist, and teacher; b. Holland, Mich., Oct. 2, 1927. She studied piano with Cecile Staub Genhart (B.Mus., 1948), theory (M.Mus., 1950), and composition with Rogers and Hovhaness at the Eastman School of Music in Rochester, N.Y., where she received her Ph.D. in 1966 with the diss. *A Stylistic Study of Claude Debussy's Opera, Pelléas et Mélisande*; she pursued postdoctoral studies at the Mass. Inst. of Technology (1982). She served as prof. and as chairman of the theory and composition dept. in the music school at Texas Technical Univ. in Lubbock (1950–87); she also made appearances as a pianist. Her compositions include the ballet *Set of 7* (N.Y., May 10, 1988).

Van Dam, José (real name, **Joseph Van Damme**), outstanding Belgian bass-baritone; b. Brussels, Aug. 25, 1940. He began to study piano and solfège at 11; he commenced vocal studies at 13, and then entered the Brussels Cons. at 17, graduating with 1st prizes in voice and opera performance at 18; subsequently captured 1st prizes in vocal competitions in Liège, Paris, Toulouse, and Geneva. After making his operatic debut as Don Basilio in *Il Barbiere di Siviglia* in Liège, he gained experience as a member of the Opéra and the Opéra Comique in Paris (1961–65) and of the Geneva Opera (1965–67). In 1967 he joined the Berlin Deutsche Oper, where he established himself as one of its principal artists via such roles as Figaro, Leporello, Don Alfonso, Caspar, and Escamillo. While continuing to sing in Berlin, he pursued a notable international career. In 1973 he made his first appearance at London's Covent Garden as Escamillo, a role he also chose for his Metropolitan Opera debut in New York on Nov. 21, 1975. He was chosen to create the title role in Messiaen's opera *Saint François d'Assise* at the Paris Opéra on Nov. 28, 1983, thereby adding further luster to his reputation. During the 1985–86 season, he appeared as Hans Sachs at the Chicago Lyric Opera. He sang Saint François at the Salzburg Festival in 1992. On Feb. 25, 1994, he made his Carnegie Hall recital debut in New York In 1996 he appeared as Philip II in London and Paris. After singing the Dutchman in Rome in 1997, he portrayed Boris Godunov in Toulouse in 1998. Among his other esteemed roles are Don Giovanni, Verdi's Attila, the Dutchman, Golaud, and Wozzeck. He has also won renown as a concert artist, making appearances with the foremost orchs. of Europe and the United States.

Van der Linden, Cornelis, Dutch conductor and composer; b. Dordrecht, Aug. 24, 1839; d. Amsterdam, May 29, 1918. He studied with Kwast (piano) and F. Böhme (theory). After sojourns in Belgium, Paris, and Germany, he conducted various choral organizations; from 1875, he also led sym. concerts He was conductor of the newly established Nederlandsche Oper in Amsterdam (1888–94), where he produced 2 of his own operas: *Catharina en Lambert* (Nov. 24, 1888) and *Leiden ontzet* (The Relief of Leiden; April 1, 1893).

Vandernoot, André, Belgian conductor; b. Brussels, June 2, 1927; d. there, Nov. 6, 1991. He received training at the Royal Cons. of Music in Brussels and at the Vienna Academy of Music. In 1951 he was a laureate in the Besançon conducting competition. From 1954 he appeared regularly as a conductor with the Orchestre National de Belgique in Brussels. In 1958 he was named to the post of 1st conductor of the Royal Flemish Opera in Antwerp. He was music director of the Théâtre Royal de la Monnaie in Brussels from 1959 to 1973. In 1974–75 he was music director of the Orchestre National de Belgique. From 1976 to 1983 he held the title of 1st guest conductor of the Antwerp Phil. He also was music director of the Noordhollands Phil. in Haarlem in 1978–79. From 1979 to 1989 he was music director of the Brabants Orch. From 1987 he also was chief conductor of the Orchestre Symphonique de la RTBF in Brussels.

Van de Vate, Nancy, American composer; b. Plainfield, N.J., Dec. 30, 1930. She studied piano at the Eastman School of Music in Rochester, N.Y., Wellesley College (A.B., 1952), and with Bruce Simonds at Yale Univ., then concentrated on composition at the Univ. of Mississippi (M.M., 1958) and later at Florida State Univ. (D.M., 1968). She taught at Memphis State Univ. (1964–66), the Univ. of Tenn. (1967), Knoxville College (1968–69; 1971–72), Maryville College (1973–74), the Univ. of Hawaii (1975–76), and Hawaii Loa College (1977–80). She was secretary and then president of the Southeast Composers League (1965–73; 1973–75); in 1975 she founded the International League of Women Composers, and served as chairperson until 1982, when she moved to Indonesia; from 1985 she lived in Vienna. Her music—highly charged and dissonantly colored by way of influences as varied as Prokofiev, Shostakovich, Penderecki, Crumb, and Varèse—has won international awards. Among her works are *A Night in the Royal Ontario Museum*, theater piece for Soprano and Tape (1983; Washington, D.C., April 13, 1984), and *The Saga of Cocaine Lil*, theater piece for Mezzo-soprano, 4 Singers, and Percussion (1986; Frankfurt am Main, April 20, 1988).

Van de Woestijne, David, Belgian composer; b. Llanidloes, Wales, Feb. 18, 1915; d. Brussels, May 18, 1979. He was the son of the painter Gustav van de Woestijne and the nephew of the Flemish poet Karel van de Woestijne. After studies in harmony and counterpoint with Defauw and Gilson, he took lessons with Espla. Van de Woestijne's music reflects the trends of cosmopolitan modernism. His works include *Le Débat de la folie et de l'amour*, opera-ballet (1959), *De zoemende musikant*, television opera (1967), and *Graal 68 ou L'Impromptu de Gand*, opera (Ghent, 1968).

Van Dieren, Bernard. See **Dieren, Bernard van.**

Van Dresser, Marcia, American soprano; b. Memphis, Tenn., Dec. 4, 1877; d. London, July 11, 1937. She studied in Chicago and New York, and sang minor parts at the Metropolitan Opera (1903–04). After further study in Germany, she made her European debut in Dresden (1907). She was a member of the Dessau Opera (1908–10) and the Frankfurt am Main Opera (1911–14). She gave a recital in New York (March 22, 1915), then sang with the Chicago Opera (1915–17).

Van Durme, Jef, Belgian composer; b. Kemzeke-Waas, May 7, 1907; d. Brussels, Jan. 28, 1965. He was a pupil of Alpaerts at the Royal Flemish Cons. of Music in Antwerp and of Berg in Vienna (1931).

WORKS: DRAMATIC: OPERAS: *Remous*, after Weterings (1936); *The Death of a Salesman*, after Arthur Miller (1954–55); *King Lear* (1955–57); *Anthony and Cleopatra* (1957–59); *Richard III* (1960–61). BALLETS: *De dageraad* (1932–33); *Orestes* (1934–35; orch. suite, 1936–40). ORATORIO: *De 14 stonden* (1931).

Van Dyck, Ernest (Marie Hubert), distinguished Belgian tenor; b. Antwerp, April 2, 1861; d. Berlaer-lez-Lierre, Aug. 31, 1923. He studied law, and was a journalist in Paris, where he studied voice with Saint-Yves Bax. He sang at the Lamoureux concerts (from 1883) and made his operatic debut in Lohengrin (May 3, 1887). After further training with Julius Kniese, he appeared at the Bayreuth Festival as Parsifal in 1888, a role he sang there regularly until 1912; he also appeared as Lohengrin there in 1894. From 1888 to 1900 he was a member of the Vienna Court Opera; on May 19, 1891, he made his London debut at Covent Garden, returning there in 1897, 1898, and 1901; he made his first appearance at the Paris Opéra as Lohengrin on Sept. 16, 1891, a role he also sang at his debut at the Théâtre Royal de la Monnaie in Brussels on April 28, 1894. He made his U.S. debut as Tannhäuser in Chicago (Nov. 9, 1898); he made his first appearance at the Metropolitan Opera in New York in the same role (Nov. 29, 1898), and remained with the company until 1902. In 1907 he served as manager of the German Opera season at Covent Garden, where he also sang Tristan and Siegmund; in 1908 he sang Siegfried in *Götterdämmerung* and in 1914 Parsifal at the Paris Opéra. He taught voice in Paris and later in Brussels. He was equally at home in Wagnerian roles and the French repertoire.

Vaness, Carol (Theresa), talented American soprano; b. San Diego, July 27, 1952. She grew up in Pomona, where she took piano lessons; while attending a parochial girls' school, she sang in its choir, then studied English and piano at Calif. State Polytechnic College before concentrating on music at Calif. State Univ. in Northridge (M.A., 1976), where her vocal instructor was David Scott. After serving an apprenticeship at the San Francisco Opera, she made her N.Y. City Opera debut as Vitellia in *La clemenza di Tito* on Oct. 25, 1979, and continued to appear there until 1983, when she scored a major success as Handel's Alcina. On Jan. 9, 1981, she made her European debut as Vitellia in Bordeaux. She made her first appearance at the Glyndebourne Festival in 1982 as Donna Anna in *Don Giovanni*, a role she subsequently sang to much acclaim throughout Europe. In 1982 she also made her debut at London's Covent Garden as Mimi. On Feb. 14, 1984, she made her Metropolitan Opera debut in New York as Armida in Handel's *Rinaldo*, and continued to sing there in later seasons; she also appeared with other U.S. opera houses and toured as a concert artist. In 1988 she made her first appearance at the Salzburg Festival as Vitellia. In 1990 she sang Mozart's Elettra at Milan's La Scala. On Dec. 19, 1991, she made her N.Y. Phil. debut singing excerpts from Strauss's *Daphne* under Leinsdorf's direction. In 1992 she appeared as Rossini's Mathilde in San Francisco. In 1994 she appeared as Desdemona at the Metropolitan Opera, where she returned as Fiordiligi in 1996. She also sang Norma at the Houston Grand Opera in the latter year. In 1997 she portrayed Tosca at the San Francisco Opera. She returned to the Metropolitan Opera as Rosalinde in 1999. Her other roles include Delilah in Handel's *Samson*, Elettra in *Idomeneo*, the Countess in *Le nozze di Figaro*, Rosina, Violetta, Gilda, Nedda, and Mimi.

Van Gilse, Jan. See **Gilse, Jan van.**

Vanhal (also **van Hal, Vanhall, Wanhal**, etc.), **Johan Baptist (Jan Křtitel),** noted Czech composer and teacher; b. Nové Nechanice, Bohemia, May 12, 1739; d. Vienna, Aug. 20, 1813. He was born into a bonded peasant family. He began his musical training as a teacher and organist in Maršov, and then studied organ with the cantor A. Erban in Nové Nechanice. In 1757 he became organist in Opocno; in 1759 he was named choirmaster in Hnevceves. After he won the favor of Countess Schaffgotsch, his patron took him to Vienna about 1761, and he was able to further his training under Dittersdorf. He obtained his release from bondage, and then traveled in Italy (1769–71) before returning to Vienna. Although stricken with mental illness, he recovered and devoted his energies to teaching and composing. He was a prolific composer; some 700 works are extant, of which his 73 syms. (c.1767–85) in the early Classical style were most notable. His output includes works for both professional and amateur performers. He also composed the operas *Il Demofoonte* (Rome, 1770) and *Il trionfo di Clelia* (Rome, 1770); also a Passion Oratorio. He publ. the pedagogical vol. *Anfangsgründe des Generalbasses* (Vienna, 1817).

BIBL.: J. Bušek, *Jansa, Kalivoda, V.* (Prague, 1926).

Van Hoose, Ellison, American tenor; b. Murfreesboro, Tenn., Aug. 18, 1868; d. Houston, March 24, 1936. He studied with Luckstone in New York, Jean de Reszke in Paris, and in Rome and London. He made his operatic debut with the Damrosch Opera Co. in Philadelphia as Tannhäuser (Dec. 11, 1897); he toured with Melba in the United States (1903–05) and with Sembrich (1906–07) and also in Europe (1908–10). He was a member of the Chicago Opera Co. (1911–12), then devoted himself mainly to oratorio singing.

Van Lier, Bertus, Dutch composer, conductor, music critic, and teacher; b. Utrecht, Sept. 10, 1906; d. Roden, Feb. 14, 1972. He was a student of Pijper (composition) in Amsterdam and of Scherchen (conducting) in Strasbourg. After a period as a conductor, music critic, and composer in Utrecht, he taught at the Rotterdam Cons. (1945–60) and then was active in the art history dept. at the Univ. of Groningen. He publ. the vols. *Buiten de maastreep* (Beyond the Bar Line; Amsterdam, 1948) and *Rhythme en metrum* (Groningen, 1967). Van Lier's early compositions were modeled on Pijper's "germ-cell" theory, to which he imparted a literary symbolism. His works include the ballet *Katharsis* (1945; concert version, Utrecht, Nov. 29, 1950) and incidental music to Sophocles's *Ajax* (1932) and *Antigone* (1952); also *5 Mei: Zij* (5th of May: They), oratorio (Radio Hilversum, May 5, 1963).

Van Nes, Jard, Dutch mezzo-soprano; b. Zwollerkarspel, June 15, 1948. Following vocal studies in her homeland, she was active mainly as a concert artist, winning critical acclaim as a soloist in Mahler's 2d Sym. in 1983 with Haitink and the Concertgebouw Orch. in Amsterdam; in subsequent years she became a great favorite with the orch. and toured with it abroad. She made her operatic stage debut also in 1983 as Bertarido in Handel's *Rodelinda* with the Netherlands Opera in Amsterdam, where she returned to sing such successful roles as Handel's Orlando and Wagner's Magdalena; she also sang at the Holland Festivals. During the 1987–88 season she toured North America as soloist with Edo de Waart and the Minnesota Orch. She made her N.Y. recital debut at the Frick Collection during the 1994–95 season. In 1997 she sang in the premiere of the revised version of Ligeti's *Le Grand Macabre* at the Salzburg Festival. Her concert repertoire ranges from Bach to Berio, but she has won greatest acclaim as an interpreter of Mahler.

Vanni-Marcoux. See **Marcoux, Vanni.**

Vannuccini, Luigi, noted Italian singing master; b. Fojano, Dec. 4, 1828; d. Montecatini, Aug. 14, 1911. He studied at the Florence Cons. He became an opera conductor (1848), then turned to the study of the piano, and appeared as a concert pianist with excellent success. He finally settled in Florence, where he devoted himself exclusively to vocal training, and acquired fame as a singing master. He publ. some songs and piano pieces.

Van Raalte, Albert. See **Raalte, Albert van.**

Van Rooy, Anton(ius Maria Josephus), celebrated Dutch bass-baritone; b. Rotterdam, Jan. 1, 1870; d. Munich, Nov. 28, 1932. He studied voice with Julius Stockhausen in Frankfurt am Main. In 1897 he made his first appearance at the Bayreuth Festival as Wotan, a role he sang there each season until 1902; he also appeared there as Hans Sachs in 1899 and as the Dutchman in 1901 and 1902. From 1898 to 1913 he sang at London's Covent Garden. On Dec. 14, 1898, he made his U.S. debut as Wotan in *Die Walküre* at the Metropolitan Opera in New York, remaining on its roster until 1908, except for 1900–1901. In 1908 he was engaged as a regular member of the Frankfurt am Main Opera, retiring in 1913. He was particularly distinguished in Wagnerian roles, but also was noted for his interpretations of Escamillo, Valentin, and Don Fernando in *Fidelio*. He also distinguished himself as a lieder artist.

Van Westerhout, Nicola, Italian pianist and composer of Dutch descent; b. Mola di Bari, Dec. 17, 1857; d. Naples, Aug. 21, 1898. He was a pupil of Nicola d'Arienzo, De Giosa, and Lauro Rossi at the Naples Cons. and of Antonio Tari at the Univ. of Naples, then pursued a fine career as a pianist. He taught harmony at the Naples Cons. (1897–98). Among his works were the operas *Una notte a Venezia* (rev. as *Cimbelino*, Rome, April 7, 1892), *Fortunio* (Milan, May 16, 1895), *Dona Flor* (Mola di Bari, April 18, 1896, on the opening of the Teatro Van Westerhout, named after him), *Colomba* (Naples, March 27, 1923), and *Tilde* (not perf.).

Van Zandt, Marie, American soprano; b. N.Y., Oct. 8, 1858; d. Cannes, Dec. 31, 1919. She studied with her mother, the well-known American soprano Jennie van Zandt, and with Lamperti, making her operatic debut as Zerlina in Turin (Jan. 1879). Her first appearance in London followed later that year as Amina at Her Majesty's Theatre; she then sang with notable success at the Paris Opéra Comique (1880–85). She made her U.S. debut as Amina in Chicago on Nov. 13, 1891, a role she sang at her Metropolitan Opera debut in New York on Dec. 21, 1891, where she sang for one season. She continued to tour as a guest artist until her marriage in 1898. Delibes wrote the role of Lakmé for her, which she created at the Opéra Comique on April 14, 1883. Among her other roles were Cherubino, Dinorah, and Mignon.

Van Zanten, Cornelie, famous Dutch soprano and pedagogue; b. Dordrecht, Aug. 2, 1855; d. The Hague, Jan. 10, 1946. She studied with K. Schneider at the Cologne Cons., and in Milan with Lamperti, who developed her original contralto into a coloratura soprano voice. She made her operatic debut in Turin in 1875 as Leonora in *La Favorite*; she sang in Breslau (1880–82) and Kassel (1882–83), then in Amsterdam (from 1884), and also toured in the United States in 1886–87 as a member of the National Opera Co. under the directorship of Theodore Thomas. She then appeared in special performances of *Der Ring des Nibelungen* in Russia. She taught at the Amsterdam Cons. (1895–1903); subsequently she lived in Berlin, where she became highly esteemed as a singing teacher. She eventually settled in The Hague. Her most distinguished roles were Orfeo, Fidès, Ortrud, Azucena, and Amneris. She publ. songs to German and Dutch texts; with C. Poser, brought out *Leitfaden zum Kunstgesang* (Berlin, 1903).

Varady, Julia, Hungarian-born German soprano; b. Nagyvárad, Sept. 1, 1941. She received training at the Cluj Cons. and the Bucharest Cons. In 1962 she made her operatic debut as Fiordiligi at the Cluj Opera, where she sang until 1970. From 1970 to 1972 she was a member of the Frankfurt am Main Opera. In 1972 she joined the Bavarian State Opera in Munich. In 1974 she made her British debut as Gluck's Alcestis with Glasgow's Scottis Opera during its visits to the Edinburgh Festival. She made her first appearance at the Salzburg Festival in 1976 as Mozart's Elettra. On March 10, 1978, she made her Metropolitan Opera debut in New York as Mozart's Donna Elvira. On July 9, 1978, she created the role of Cordelia in Reimann's *Lear* in Munich. While continuing to sing in Munich, she also appeared as a guest artist in Hamburg, Vienna, Berlin, Paris, and other operatic centers. In 1984 she was engaged as Idomeneo at Milan's La Scala. She portrayed Senta at London's Covent Garden in 1992. In 1997 she sang Aida at the Munich Festival. Among her other roles are Countess Almaviva, Elisabeth de Valois, Tatiana, Desdemona, and Lady Macbeth. Her concert repertoire embraces works from Mozart to Reimann. In 1974 she married **Dietrich Fischer-Dieskau**.

Varcoe, Stephen, esteemed English baritone; b. Lostwithiel, May 19, 1949. He studied at King's College, Cambridge (B.A. in mathematics and land economy, 1970) before pursuing vocal training in London with Arthur Reckless at the Guildhall School of Music (1970–71) and privately with Helga Mott (1972–85) and Audrey Langford (1985–90). In 1970 he made his debut as a soloist at the Wooburn Festival under Richard Hickox's direction. His operatic debut took place in 1971 in Springhead as Purcell's Aeneas. In 1975 he made his first appearance in recital at London's Wigmore Hall, where he frequently returned in subsequent years. He sang in Handel's *Solomon* under Gardiner's direction at the Göttingen Festival in 1983, and then in the St. John Passion under that conductor's direction in London in 1985. In the latter year, he portrayed Apollo in Rameau's *Les Borèades* in Aix-en-Provence and Lyons. He sang Zoroastro in Handel's *Orlando* in Glasgow in 1986. In 1991 he was engaged as a soloist in Bach's Mass in B Minor at London's Royal Albert Hall under Hickox's direction, and also sang Nanni in Haydn's *L'infedeltà delusa* in Antwerp. After appearing as Zossina in Tavener's *Mary of Egypt* at Snape Maltings in 1992, he portrayed the title role in Britten's *Noye's Fludde* in Blackheath in 1993. In 1994 he was engaged to sing in Purcell's *King Arthur* with the Monteverdi Orch. under Gardiner's direction in Paris, Vienna, and London. Following an engagement as Death in Holst's *Sāvitri* in Cambridge in 1997, he appeared as Demetrio in Britten's *A Midsummer Night's Dream* in London in 1998. In 1999 he portrayed Salieri in Rimsky-Korsakov's *Mozart and Salieri* in London.

Varesi, Felice, noted French-Italian baritone; b. Calais, 1813; d. Milan, March 13, 1889. He made his debut in Donizetti's *Furioso all'isola di San Domingo* in Varese in 1834, then sang throughout Italy; he made guest appearances at Vienna's Kärnthnertortheater (1842–47), where he created the role of Antonio in Donizetti's *Linda di Chamounix* (May 19, 1842). He was chosen to create the title roles in Verdi's *Macbeth* (Florence, March 14, 1847) and *Rigoletto* (Venice, March 11, 1851), and Germont père in *La Traviata* (Venice, March 6, 1853). On April 19, 1864, he made his London debut as Rigoletto at Her Majesty's Theatre. His wife was the soprano Cecilia Boccabadati (b. c.1825; d. Florence, 1906); their daughter, Elena Boccabadati-Varesi (b. Florence, c.1854; d. Chicago, June 15, 1920), was also a soprano; she made her London debut as Gilda at Drury Lane (April 17, 1875); after appearing throughout Europe, she settled in Chicago, where she taught voice from 1888; her finest role was Lucia; she was also admired for her portrayals of Zerlina and Amina.

Vargas, Ramón (Arturo), Mexican tenor; b. Mexico City, Sept. 11, 1960. He received vocal training in Mexico City, where he gained experience singing such roles as Fenton, Nemorino, Don Ottavio, and Count Almaviva. In 1987 he appeared at the Vienna State Opera, the Salzburg Festival, and in Pesaro. Following an engagement as Tamino in Mexico City in 1988, he sang in Lucerne (1989–90). In 1991 he appeared as Aménophis in Rossini's *Moïse* in Bologna and as that composer's Leicester in Naples. He sang Count Almaviva in Rome and Rodrigo in *La donna del lago* in Amsterdam in 1992, and on Dec. 18 of that year he made his Metropolitan Opera debut in New York as Edgardo. After singing Fenton at Milan's La Scala in 1993, he portrayed Elvino in San Diego in 1994, where he returned as Edgardo in 1995. He sang Fernand in *La Favorite* at the Teatro Colón in Buenos Aires in the latter year. In 1996 he appeared as Alfredo at London's Covent Garden, as Nemorino in Los Angeles, and as the Duke of Mantua in Paris. He returned to Covent Garden in the latter role in 1997, and to Los Angeles as Werther in 1998.

Varkonyi, Béla, Hungarian-American composer and teacher; b. Budapest, July 5, 1878; d. N.Y., Jan. 25, 1947. He studied with Koessler and Thomán at the Royal Academy of Music in Budapest (Ph.D. in law and M.M. in music, 1902). After winning the Robert Volkmann Competition twice and receiving the Hungarian national scholarship, he studied in London and Paris. He returned in 1907 to Budapest, where he taught at the Royal Academy of Music. At the outbreak of World War I in 1914, he joined the Hungarian army; he was captured by the Russians, and spent 3 years as a prisoner of war; he continued to compose, but his MSS were destroyed when the Danish consulate was burned. After the war, he emigrated to the United States (1923); he taught at Breneau College, Georgia (until 1928), and Centenary College in Tennessee (1928–30); he then settled in New York, where he was active as a teacher and composer. Among his works were the melodramas *Captive Woman* (1911) and *Spring Night* (1912). Varkonyi is reported to have had a fantastic memory; he was able to recount more than 40 years of his life by day and date; S. Rath devotes a chapter to it in his book *Hungarian Curiosities* (1955).

Vârnai, Péter P(ál), Hungarian writer on music; b. Budapest, July 10, 1922; d. there, Jan. 31, 1992. He studied composition with Szervánszky and conducting with Ferencsik at the Budapest Cons. He worked for the Hungarian Radio (1945–50) and was active as a conductor (1951–54). He then devoted himself to music research and criticism; he was an ed. of Editio Musica in Budapest (1956–82). In addition to his writings on contemporary Hungarian music and musicians, he also wrote authoritatively on Verdi.

WRITINGS (all publ. in Budapest): *Goldmark Károly* (1956); *A lengyel zene története* (History of Polish Music; 1959); *Heinrich Schütz* (1959); *Tardos Béla* (1966); *Maros Rudolf* (1967); *Székely Mihály* (1967); *Rösler Endre* (1969); *Oratóriumok könyve* (Book of Oratorios; 1972); *Operalexikon* (1975); *Verdi Magyarországon* (Verdi in Hungary; 1975); *Verdi-operakalauz* (Verdi's Operas; 1978); *Beszélgetések Ligeti György-gyel* (In Conversation with György Ligeti; 1979; Eng. tr., 1983).

Varnay, Astrid (Ibolyka Maria), noted Swedish-born American soprano and mezzo-soprano; b. Stockholm (of Austro-Hungarian parents), April 25, 1918. Her parents were professional singers; she was taken to the United States in 1920, and began vocal studies with her mother, then studied with Paul Althouse, and with the conductor Hermann Weigert (1890–1955), whom she married in 1944. She made her debut as Sieglinde at the Metropolitan Opera in New York (Dec. 6, 1941), substituting for Lotte Lehmann without rehearsal; she appeared at the Metropolitan until 1956, and again from 1974 to 1976; her last performance there was in 1979. From 1962 she sang mezzo-soprano roles, appearing as Strauss's Herodias and Clytemnestra and as Begbick in Weill's *Aufstieg und Fall der Stadt Mahagonny*; however, she was best known for such Wagnerian roles as Isolde, Kundry, Senta, and Brünnhilde.

BIBL.: B. Wessling, *A. V.* (Bremen, 1965).

Varney, Louis, French composer and conductor, son of **Pierre Joseph Alphonse Varney**; b. New Orleans, La., May 30, 1844; d. Paris, Aug. 20, 1908. He was taken to Paris at the age of 7. He studied with his father, then began his career as a conductor at the Théâtre de l'Athénée, where he also brought out several stage works. From 1880 to 1905 he produced some 40 operettas, the best known of which is *Les Mousquetaires au couvent* (Paris, March 16, 1880). Other operettas include *La Femme de Narcisse* (April 14, 1892), *La Fiancée de Thylda* (Jan. 26, 1900), and *Mademoiselle George* (Dec. 2, 1900), all first performed in Paris.

Varney, Pierre Joseph Alphonse, French composer and conductor, father of **Louis Varney**; b. Paris, Dec. 1, 1811; d. there, Feb. 7, 1879. He studied with Reicha at the Paris Cons., then was active as a theater conductor in Belgium, the Netherlands, and France. From 1840 to 1850 he was director of the French Opera Co. in New Orleans, where he married Jeanne Aimée Andry. The family returned to Paris in 1851. Varney set to music a poem by Rouget de Lisle, *Mourir pour la patrie*, which became popular during the Paris revolution of 1848.

Varviso, Silvio, Swiss conductor; b. Zürich, Feb. 26, 1924. He studied piano at the Zürich Cons. and conducting in Vienna with Clemens Krauss. In 1944 he made his debut at St. Gallen, conducting *Die Zauberflöte*, and remained at the theater there until 1950; he then conducted at the Basel Stadttheater, where he later served as its music director (1956–62); he also made guest appearances in Berlin and Paris in 1958, and then made his U.S. debut with the San Francisco Opera in 1959. On Nov. 26, 1961, he made his Metropolitan Opera debut in New York, conducting *Lucia di Lammermoor*; he remained on its roster until 1966, and returned there in 1968–69 and in 1982–83. In 1962 he made his British debut at the Glyndebourne Festival; later that year he made his first appearance at London's Covent Garden; in 1969 he made his Bayreuth Festival debut with *Der fliegende Holländer*. From 1965 to 1972 he was chief conductor of the Royal Theater in Stockholm; after serving as Generalmusikdirektor at the Württemberg State Theater in Stuttgart (1972–80), he was chief conductor of the Paris Opéra (1980–86).

Varvoglis, Mario, Greek composer and teacher; b. Brussels, Dec. 22, 1885; d. Athens, July 30, 1967. He studied in Paris at the Cons. with Leroux and G. Caussade and at the Schola Cantorum with d'Indy. Returning to Athens, he taught at the Cons. (1920–24) and at the Hellenic Cons. (from 1924), where he was codirector in 1947; he served as president of the League of Greek Composers (from 1957). His output was strongly influenced by d'Indy, Fauré, and Ravel. Among his works were the operas *Aya Varvara* (1912; only fragments extant) and *Tó apóyeme tís agápis* (The Afternoon of Love; 1935; Athens, June 10, 1944); also incidental music to 6 Greek dramas.

Vasilenko, Sergei (Nikiforovich), noted Russian conductor, pedagogue, and composer; b. Moscow, March 30, 1872; d. there, March 11, 1956. He studied jurisprudence at the Univ. of Moscow, graduating in 1895, and took private music lessons with Gretchaninoff and G. Conus; in 1895 he entered the Moscow Cons. in the classes of Taneyev, Ippolitov-Ivanov, and Safonov, graduating in 1901. He also studied ancient Russian chants under the direction of Smolensky. In 1906 he joined the faculty of the Moscow Cons.; subsequently he was prof. there (1907–41; 1943–56). From 1907 to 1917 he conducted in Moscow a series of popular sym. concerts in programs of music arranged in a historical sequence. In 1938 he went to Tashkent to help native musicians develop a national school of composition. His music is inspired primarily by the pattern of Russian folk song, but he was also attracted by exotic subjects, particularly those of the East; in his harmonic settings, there is a distinct influence of French Impressionism.

WORKS: DRAMATIC: OPERAS: *Skazaniye o grade velikom Kitezhe i tikhom ozere Svetoyare* (The Legend of the Great City of Kitezh and the Calm Lake Svetoyar), dramatic cantata (Moscow, March 1, 1902; operatic version, Moscow, March 3, 1903); *Sin solntsa* (Son of the Sun; Moscow, May 23, 1929); *Khristofor Kolumb* (Christopher Columbus; 1933); *Buran* (The Snowstorm; 1938; Tashkent, June 12, 1939; in collaboration with M. Ashrafi); *Suvorov* (1941; Moscow, Feb. 23, 1942). BALLETS: *Noyya*, ballet-pantomime (1923); *Iosif prekrasniy* (Joseph the Handsome; Moscow, March 3, 1925); *V solnechnikh luchakh* (In the Rays of the Sun; 1926); *Lola* (1926; rev. version, Moscow, June 25, 1943); *Treugolka* (The Tricorn; 1935); *Tsigani* (The Gypsies; 1936; Leningrad, Nov. 18, 1937); *Akbilyak* (1942; Tashkent, Nov. 7, 1943); *Mirandolina* (1946; Moscow, Jan. 16, 1949).

WRITINGS: *Stranitsi vospominaniy* (Pages of Reminiscences; Moscow and Leningrad, 1948); *Instrumentovka dlya simfonicheskovo orkestra* (vol. 1, Moscow, 1952; ed. with a supplement by Y. Fortunatov, Moscow, 1959); T. Livanova, ed., *Vospominaniya* (Memoirs; Moscow, 1979).

BIBL.: V. Belaiev, *S. N. V.* (Moscow, 1927); G. Polianovsky, *S. N. V.* (Moscow, 1947); idem, *S. N. V.: Zhizn i tvorchestvo* (S. N.V.: Life and Work; Moscow, 1964).

Vasiliev-Buglay, Dmitri, Russian composer; b. Moscow, Aug. 9, 1888; d. there, Oct. 15, 1956. He studied with Kastalsky at the Moscow Synod Seminary (1898–1906). After the Revolution, he became an active member of RAPM (Russian Assn. of Proletarian Musicians), postulating the necessity of creating music for the needs of the class-conscious, socialist proletariat, and also joined the Union of Revolutionary Composers and Musical Workers. He was one of the pioneers of mass Soviet songs, and wrote patriotic ballads and many choruses to revolutionary texts. He also composed the opera *Fatherland's Call*, to promote self-discipline on collective farms.

BIBL.: D. Lokshin, *D. V.-B.* (Moscow, 1958).

Vasseur, Léon (Félix Augustin Joseph), French organist, conductor, and composer; b. Bapaume, Pas-de-Calais, May 28, 1844; d. Paris, July 25, 1917. He studied at the École Niedermeyer in Paris, and in 1870 became organist of the Versailles Cathedral; after a few years, he turned to composing light music and conducting theater orchs. Of his some 30 operettas, the most successful was *La Timbale d'argent* (Paris, April 9, 1872). Others include *Le Voyage de Suzette* (Paris, 1890), *Au premier hussard* (Paris, Aug. 6, 1896), and *La Souris blanche* (Paris, Nov. 9, 1897; in collaboration with de Thuisy).

Vatielli, Francesco, Italian musicologist and composer; b. Pesaro, Dec. 31, 1876; d. Portogruaro, Dec. 12, 1946. He studied in Bologna at the Univ. (arts degree, 1895) and with Mascagni and Antonio Cicognani at the Liceo Musicale. From 1905 to 1906 he was an instructor of music history at the Liceo Musicale in Bologna, then was director of its library until 1945; he also was prof. of music history at the Univ. (from 1908). He was cofounder of the Associazione dei Musicologisti Italiani; he also ed. various music journals. He wrote incidental music for several plays; also piano pieces and songs. Among his important writings were *La civiltà musicale di moda: Ragionamenti di Petronio Isaurico* (Turin, 1913; 2d ed., 1924, as *Ragionamenti e fantasie musicali di Petronio Isaurico*), *Arte e vita musicale a Bologna* (Bologna, 1927), and *Il Principe di Venosa e Leonora d'Este* (Milan, 1941).; he also ed. *Antiche cantate d'amore* (Bologna, 1907–20); *A. Banchieri: Musiche corali*, CMI, I-III (1919); *Antiche cantate bolognesi* (Bologna, 1919); *F. Azzaiolo: Villote del fiore* (Bologna, 1921), and *Madrigali di Carlo Gesualdo, principe de Venosa*, PIISM, Monumenta, II (1942).

Vaucorbeil, Auguste-Emmanuel, French composer; b. Rouen, Dec. 15, 1821; d. Paris, Nov. 2, 1884. He studied with Marmontel and Cherubini at the Paris Cons., joining its faculty as prof. of vocal ensemble in 1871. He became government commissioner of state theaters (1872), and was named Inspector General for the Arts (1878). In 1879 he was appointed director of the Paris Opéra. He wrote the operas *La Bataille d'amour* (Paris, April 13, 1863) and *Mahomet* (not perf.), as well as the lyric scene *La Mort de Diane* (Paris, 1870).

Vaughan, Denis (Edward), Australian conductor and music scholar; b. Melbourne, June 6, 1926. He studied at Wesley College, Melbourne (1939–42), and at the Univ. of Melbourne (Mus.B., 1947), then went to London, where he studied organ with G. Thalben-Ball and double bass with E. Cruft at the Royal College of Music (1947–50); he also studied organ with A. Marchal in Paris. He played double bass in the Royal Phil. in London (1950–54); in 1953 he made his debut as a conductor in London; he served as Beecham's assistant (1954–57), and was founder-conductor of the Beecham Choral Soc.; he also toured in Europe as an organist, harpsichordist, and clavichordist. He made a special study of the autograph scores versus the printed eds. of the operas of Verdi and Puccini, discovering myriad discrepancies in the latter; he proceeded to agitate for published corrected eds. of these works. From 1981 to 1984 he was music director of the State Opera of South Australia.

Vaughan, Elizabeth, Welsh soprano, later mezzo-soprano; b. Llanfyellin, Montgomeryshire, March 12, 1937. She studied with Olive Groves at the Royal Academy of Music in London (1955–58), where she took the gold and silver medals, and also won the Kathleen Ferrier Scholarship (1959); she also studied privately with Eva Turner. In 1960 she sang Abigail in *Nabucco* with the Welsh National Opera in Cardiff. In 1962 she made her debut at London's Covent Garden as Gilda. She made her Metropolitan Opera debut in New York as Donna Elvira on Sept. 23, 1972. She also appeared with other English opera companies and was a guest artist in Vienna, Berlin, Paris, Hamburg, Munich, Prague, and other European opera centers. In 1984 she toured the United States with the English National Opera of London. After singing such roles as Violetta, Liù, Mimi, Tatiana, Tosca, and Cio-Cio-San, she turned to mezzo-soprano roles. In 1990 she appeared as Herodias at Glasgow's Scottish Opera, returning there as Kabanicha in 1993. She also was a prof. of voice at the Guildhall School of Music and Drama in London.

Vaughan Williams, Ralph, great English composer who created the gloriously self-consistent English style of composition, deeply rooted in native folk songs, yet unmistakably participant of modern ways in harmony, counterpoint, and instrumentation; b. Down Ampney, Gloucestershire, Oct. 12, 1872; d. London, Aug.

26, 1958. His father, a clergyman, died when Vaughan Williams was a child; the family then moved to the residence of his maternal grandfather at Leith Hill Place, Surrey. There he began to study piano and violin; in 1887 he entered Charterhouse School in London and played violin and viola in the school orch. From 1890 to 1892 he studied harmony with F. E. Gladstone, theory of composition with Parry, and organ with Parratt at the Royal College of Music in London, then enrolled at Trinity College, Cambridge, where he took courses in composition with Charles Wood and in organ with Alan Gray, obtaining his Mus.B. in 1894 and his B.A. in 1895; he subsequently returned to the Royal College of Music, studying with Stanford. In 1897 he went to Berlin for further instruction with Max Bruch; in 1901 he took his Mus.D. at Cambridge. Dissatisfied with his academic studies, he decided, in 1908, to seek advice in Paris from Ravel in order to acquire the technique of modern orchestration that emphasized color. In the meantime, he became active as a collector of English folk songs; in 1904 he joined the Folk Song Soc.; in 1905 he became conductor of the Leith Hill Festival in Dorking, a position that he held, off and on, until his old age. In 1906 he composed his *3 Norfolk Rhapsodies*, which reveal the ultimate techniques and manners of his national style; he discarded the 2d and 3d of the set as not satisfactory in reflecting the subject. In 1903 he began work on a choral sym. inspired by Walt Whitman's poetry and entitled *A Sea Symphony*; he completed it in 1909; there followed in 1910 *Fantasia on a Theme of Thomas Tallis*, scored for string quartet and double string orch.; in it Vaughan Williams evoked the song style of an early English composer. After this brief work, he engaged in a grandiose score, entitled *A London Symphony* and intended as a musical glorification of the great capital city. However, he emphatically denied that the score was to be a representation of London life. He even suggested that it might be more aptly entitled *Symphony by a Londoner*, which would explain the immediately recognizable quotations of the street song "Sweet Lavender" and of the Westminster chimes in the score; indeed, Vaughan Williams declared that the work must be judged as a piece of absolute or abstract music. Yet prosaically minded commentators insisted that *A London Symphony* realistically depicted in its 4 movements the scenes of London at twilight, the hubbub of Bloomsbury, a Saturday-evening reverie, and, in conclusion, the serene flow of the Thames River. Concurrently with *A London Symphony*, he wrote the ballad opera *Hugh the Drover*, set in England in the year 1812, and reflecting the solitary struggle of the English against Napoleon.

At the outbreak of World War I in 1914, Vaughan Williams enlisted in the British army, and served in Salonika and in France as an officer in the artillery. After the Armistice, he was from 1919 to 1939 a prof. of composition at the Royal College of Music in London; from 1920 to 1928 he also conducted the London Bach Choir. In 1921 he completed *A Pastoral Symphony*, the music of which reflects the contemplative aspect of his inspiration; an interesting innovation in this score is the use of a wordless vocal solo in the last movement. In 1922 he visited the United States and conducted *A Pastoral Symphony* at the Norfolk (Conn.) Festival; in 1932 he returned to the United States to lecture at Bryn Mawr College. In 1930 he was awarded the Gold Medal of the Royal Phil. Soc. of London; in 1935 he received the Order of Merit from King George V. In 1930 he wrote a masque, *Job*, based on Blake's *Illustrations of the Book of Job*, which was first performed in a concert version in 1930 and was then presented on the stage in London on July 5, 1931. His 4th Sym., in F minor, written between 1931 and 1935 and first performed by the BBC Sym. Orch. in London on April 10, 1935, presents an extraordinary deviation from his accustomed solid style of composition. Here he experimented with dissonant harmonies in conflicting tonalities, bristling with angular rhythms. A peripheral work was *Fantasia on Greensleeves*, arranged for harp, strings, and optional flutes; this was the composer's tribute to his fascination with English folk songs; he had used it in his opera *Sir John in Love*, after Shakespeare's *The Merry Wives of Windsor*, performed in London in 1929. He always professed great admiration for Sibelius; indeed, there was a harmonious kinship between the 2 great contemporary nationalist composers; there was also the peculiar circumstance that in his 4th Sym. Sibelius ventured into the domain of modernism, as did Vaughan Williams in his own 4th Sym., and both were taken to task by astounded critics for such musical philandering. Vaughan Williams dedicated his 5th Sym., in D major, composed between 1938 and 1943, to Sibelius as a token of his admiration. In the 6th Sym., in E minor, written during the years 1944 to 1947, Vaughan Williams returned to the erstwhile serenity of his inspiration, but the sym. has its turbulent moments and an episode of folksy dancing exhilaration. Vaughan Williams was 80 years old when he completed his challenging *Sinfonia antarctica*, scored for soprano, women's chorus, and orch.; the music was an expansion of the background score he wrote for a film on the expedition of Sir Robert Scott to the South Pole in 1912. Here the music is almost geographic in its literal representation of the regions that Scott had explored; it may well be compared in its realism with the *Alpine Symphony* of Richard Strauss. In *Sinfonia antarctica* Vaughan Williams inserted, in addition to a large orch., several keyboard instruments and a wind machine. To make the reference clear, he used in the epilogue of the work the actual quotations from Scott's journal. Numerically, *Sinfonia antarctica* was his 7th; it was first performed in Manchester on Jan. 14, 1953. In the 8th Sym. he once more returned to the ideal of absolute music; the work is conceived in the form of a neoclassical suite, but, faithful to the spirit of the times, he included in the score the modern instruments, such as vibraphone and xylophone, as well as the sempiternal gongs and bells. His last sym. bore the fateful number 9, which had for many composers the sense of the ultimate, since it was the numeral of Beethoven's last sym. In this work Vaughan Williams, at the age of 85, still asserted himself as a composer of the modern age; for the first time, he used a trio of saxophones, with a pointed caveat that they should not behave "like demented cats," but rather remain their romantic selves. Anticipating the inevitable, he added after the last bar of the score the Italian word "niente." The 9th Sym. was first performed in London on April 2, 1958; Vaughan Williams died later in the same year. It should be mentioned as a testimony to his extraordinary vitality that after the death of his first wife, he married, on Feb. 7, 1953 (at the age of 80), the poet and writer Ursula Wood, and in the following year he once more paid a visit to the United States on a lecture tour to several American univs.

Summarizing the aesthetic and technical aspects of the style of composition of Vaughan Williams, there is a distinctly modern treatment of harmonic writing, with massive agglomeration of chordal sonorities; parallel triadic progressions are especially favored. There seems to be no intention of adopting any particular method of composition; rather, there is a great variety of procedures integrated into a distinctively personal and thoroughly English style, nationalistic but not isolationist. Vaughan Williams was particularly adept at exploring the modern ways of modal counterpoint, with tonality freely shifting between major and minor triadic entities; this procedure astutely evokes sweetly archaic usages in modern applications; thus Vaughan Williams combines the modalities of the Tudor era with the sparkling polytonalities of the modern age.

WORKS: DRAMATIC: OPERAS: *Hugh the Drover*, ballad opera (1911–14; London, July 14, 1924); *The Shepherds of the Delectable Mountains*, "pastoral episode" after Bunyan's *The Pilgrim's Progress* (1921–22; London, July 11, 1922); *Sir John in Love*, after Shakespeare's *The Merry Wives of Windsor* (1925–29; London, March 21, 1929); *Riders to the Sea*, after the drama by John Millington Synge (1925–32; London, Dec. 1, 1937); *The Poisoned Kiss*, "romantic extravaganza" (1927–29; Cambridge, May 12, 1936; rev. 1934–37 and 1956–57); *The Pilgrim's Progress*, "morality" (includes material from the earlier opera *The Shepherds of the Delectable Mountains*; 1925–36, 1944–51; London, April 26, 1951). BALLETS: *Old King Cole* (Cambridge, June 5, 1923); *On Christmas Night*, masque (1925–26; Chicago, Dec. 26, 1926); *Job, a Masque for Dancing* (1927–30; concert perf., Norwich, Oct. 23, 1930; stage perf., London, July 5, 1931). INCIDENTAL MUSIC TO: Ben Jonson's *Pan's Anniversary* (Stratford-upon-Avon, April 24, 1905); Aristophanes's *The Wasps* (Cambridge, Nov. 26, 1909). FILM MUSIC:

49th Parallel (1940–41); *The People's Land* (1941–42); *Coastal Command* (1942); *The Story of a Flemish Farm* (1943; suite for Orch., London, July 31, 1945); *Stricken Peninsula* (1944); *The Loves of Joanna Godden* (1946); *Scott of the Antarctic* (1947–48; material taken from it incorporated in the *Sinfonia antarctica*); *Dim Little Island* (1949); *Bitter Springs* (1950); *The England of Elizabeth* (1955); *The Vision of William Blake* (1957). OTHER: *The Mayor of Casterbridge*, music for a radio serial after Thomas Hardy (1950). *The Bridal Day*, masque after Edmund Spenser's *Epithalamion* (1938–39; rev. 1952–53; BBC television, London, June 5, 1953, in celebration of the coronation of Elizabeth II; rev. as the cantata *Epithalamion*, London, Sept. 30, 1957).

WRITINGS: *The English Hymnal* (1906; 2d ed., 1933); *Songs of Praise* (with M. Shaw; 1925; 2d ed., 1931); *The Oxford Book of Carols* (with P. Dearmer and M. Shaw; 1928); lectures and articles, reprinted in *National Music and Other Essays* (London, 1963); R. Palmer ed. *Folk Songs Collected by Ralph Vaughan Williams* (London, 1983).

BIBL.: A. Dickinson, *An Introduction to the Music of R. V. W.* (London, 1928); H. Foss, *R. V. W.* (London, 1950); E. Payne, *The Folksong Element in the Music of V. W.* (diss., Univ. of Liverpool, 1953); P. Young, *V. W.* (London, 1953); F. Howes, *The Music of R. V. W.* (London, 1954); J. Bergsagel, *The National Aspects of the Music of R. V. W.* (diss., Cornell Univ., 1957); S. Pakenham, *R. V. W.: A Discovery of His Music* (London, 1957); J. Day, *V. W.* (London, 1961; 2d ed., rev., 1975); A. Dickinson, *V. W.* (London, 1963); M. Kennedy, *The Works of R. V. W.* (London, 1964; 2d ed., rev., 1980); U. Vaughan Williams, *R. V. W.: A Biography* (London, 1964); H. Ottaway, *V. W.* (London, 1966); P. Starbuck, *R. V. W., O.M., 1872–1958: A Bibliography of His Literary Writings and Criticism of His Musical Works* (diss., Library Assn., 1967); M. Hurd, *V. W.* (London, 1970); R. Douglas, *Working with R. V. W.* (London, 1972); U. Vaughan Williams, *R. V. W.: A Biography of R. V. W.* (Oxford, 1988); N. Butterworth, *R. V. W.: A Guide to Research* (N.Y., 1989); W. Mellers, *V. W. and the Vision of Albion* (London, 1989); A. Frogley, ed., *V. W. Studies* (Cambridge, 1996).

Veasey, Josephine, English mezzo-soprano and teacher; b. Peckham, July 10, 1930. She studied with Audrey Langford in London. In 1949 she joined the chorus at London's Covent Garden; she made her Covent Garden debut as the Shepherd Boy in *Tannhäuser* in 1955, and later appeared as Waltraute, Fricka, Brangäne, Berlioz's Dido, Dorabella, et al. there; she created the role of the Emperor in Henze's *We Come to the River* there (1976). From 1957 to 1969 she appeared at the Glynebourne Festivals. On Nov. 22, 1968, she made her Metropolitan Opera debut in New York as Fricka, remaining on the roster until 1969; she also made guest appearances throughout Europe and in South America; likewise she sang in concerts. In 1982 she retired from the operatic stage and became active as a teacher; she taught at the Royal Academy of Music (1983–84), and was a voice consultant to the English National Opera (from 1985) in London. In 1970 she was made a Commander of the Order of the British Empire.

Vecchi, Horatio (Orazio Tiberio), significant Italian composer; b. Modena (baptized), Dec. 6, 1550; d. there, Feb. 19, 1605. He received ecclesiastical training from the Benedictines of S. Pietro in Modena, and also studied music in Modena with the Servite monk Salvatore Essenga; he later took Holy Orders. He was maestro di cappella at Salò Cathedral (1581–84); in 1584 he became maestro di cappella at Modena Cathedral, where he adopted the rendering of Horatio for his first name; within a short time he accepted the post of maestro di cappella in Reggio Emilia, and then became canon at Correggio Cathedral in 1586; he was made archdeacon in 1591. In 1593 he returned to Modena Cathedral as maestro di cappella, and was elevated to mansionario in 1596; he also served in the brotherhood of the Annunciation at the churches of S. Maria and S. Pietro. In 1598 he was named maestro di corte by Duke Cesare d'Este. In 1604 he was dismissed from his duties at the Cathedral for disregarding the bishop's admonition to cease directing music at the Cathedral convent. He was greatly admired in his day for his 6 books of Canzonette. His lasting fame is due above all to his "commedia harmonica" *L'Amfiparnasso*, performed at Modena in 1594 and printed at Venice in 1597; this is a kind of musical farce written not in the monodic style of Peri's *Dafne* but in madrigal style, with all the text sung by several voices (i.e., a chorus a 4–5); it has been called a "madrigal opera," but it was not intended for the theater and stood entirely apart from the path that opera was to take. It was ed. in Publikationen Älterer Praktischer und Theoretischer Musikwerke, XXVI, 1902; in Capolavori Polifonici del Secolo XVI, V (Rome, 1953) and in Early Musical Masterworks (Chapel Hill, 1977). Another important secular work was his *Dialoghi da cantarsi et concertarsi con ogni sorte di stromenti* for 7 to 8 Voices (1608); other works appeared in contemporary collections; some of his works were later included in 19th- and 20th-century collections.

BIBL.: A. Catellani, *Della vita e delle opere di O. V.* (Milan, 1858); J. Hol, *H. V. als weltlicher Komponist* (diss., Univ. of Basel, 1917); idem, *H. V.s weltliche Werke* (Strasbourg, 1934); W. Martin, *The Convito musicale of O. V.* (diss., Univ. of Oxford, 1964); R. Rüegge, *O. V.s geistliche Werke* (Bern, 1967).

Vedernikov, Alexander, Russian bass; b. Mokino, Dec. 23, 1927. He studied voice at the Moscow Cons., graduating in 1955. He won 1st prize at the International Schumann Competition in Berlin in 1956 and, in the same year, 1st prize at the Soviet competition for his performance of songs by Soviet composers. In 1957 he made his debut at the Bolshoi Theater in Moscow as Susanin. In 1961 he entered the La Scala Opera School of Milan as an aspirant; subsequently he toured as a concert singer in France, Italy, England, Austria, and Canada; he also sang with the Bolshoi Theater, with which he made tours abroad. He was particularly noted for his performances of the Russian repertoire; his portrayal of Boris Godunov in Mussorgsky's opera approached Chaliapin's in its grandeur. He also distinguished himself in Italian buffo roles.

Veerhoff, Carlos, Argentine-German composer; b. Buenos Aires, June 3, 1926. He was a student of Grabner at the Berlin Hochschule für Musik (1943–44). After teaching at the National Univ. in Tucumán (1948–51), he returned to Berlin as an assistant to Fricsay (1951–52). After completing his training with Blacher at the Hochschule für Musik (1952) and privately with Thomas and Scherchen, he chose to remain in Germany.

WORKS: DRAMATIC: *Pavane royale*, ballet (1953); *Targusis*, chamber opera (1958); *El porquerizo del ray*, ballet (1963); *Die goldene Maske*, opera (1968; rev. 1978); *Es gibt doch Zebrastreifen*, mini-opera (1971; Ulm, Jan. 20, 1972); *Der Grüne*, chamber opera (1972); *Dualis*, ballet (1978).

Velluti, Giovanni Battista, famous Italian castrato soprano; b. Montolmo, Ancona, Jan. 28, 1781; d. Sambruson di Dolo, Venice, Jan. 22, 1861. He studied with Mattei in Bologna and with Calpi in Ravenna, making his debut in 1801 in Forlì. He then sang in Naples in the premieres of Guglielmi's *Asteria e Teseo* and Andreozzi's *Pirano e Tisbe*. From 1805 to 1808 he was in Rome, where he appeared in the premiere of Nicolini's *Traiano in Dacio*; his La Scala debut in Milan followed in that composer's *Coriolano* (Dec. 26, 1808). After appearances in Venice (1810) and Turin (1811), he sang in Vienna (1812); he also appeared in Munich, where he was named Bavarian court singer. He sang in the premiere of Rossini's *Aureliano in Palmira* in Milan (Dec. 26, 1813), and then toured throughout Italy; he also made appearances in Germany and Russia. On March 7, 1824, he created the role of Armando in Meyerbeer's *Il Crociato in Egitto* in Venice; he chose that same role for his London debut on June 3, 1825, at the King's Theatre, where he continued to sing until 1826, making his farewell to London in 1829. Velluti was the last great castrato of the age.

Veltri, Michelangelo, Argentine conductor; b. Buenos Aires, Aug. 16, 1940; d. there, Dec. 18, 1997. He studied at the Buenos Aires Cons. and with Panizza and Votto in Italy. After conducting in South America, he became music director of the Teatro Liceu in Barcelona in 1966. In 1969 he made his first appearance at

Milan's La Scala conducting *Don Carlos*. On Nov. 10, 1971, he made his Metropolitan Opera debut in New York conducting *Rigoletto*, returning there regularly in performances of the Italian repertory until 1983. From 1972 to 1977 he was artistic director of the Caracas Festival, and thereafter conducted at the opera houses in Santiago and Rio de Janeiro. He was artistic director of the Avignon Opera from 1983 to 1987. In 1986 he conducted *Lucia di Lammermoor* at London's Covent Garden. From 1996 until his death he served as artistic director of the Teatro Colón in Buenos Aires. As a guest conductor, he appeared in Vienna, Berlin, Salzburg, Amsterdam, Paris, Marseilles, Monte Carlo, Turin, Philadelphia, and Washington, D.C.

Venzano, Luigi, Italian cellist, teacher, and composer; b. Genoa, 1814; d. there, Jan. 26, 1878. He played cello in the orch. at the Carlo Felice Theater in Genoa, and taught at the Cons. there. He publ. many songs, including "Valzer cantabile," an operetta, *La notte dei schiaffi* (Genoa, April 25, 1873), and a ballet, *Benvenuto Cellini* (Milan, Aug. 24, 1861).

Veprik, Alexander (Moiseievich), Russian composer and musicologist; b. Balta, near Odessa, June 23, 1899; d. Moscow, Oct. 13, 1958. While still a young boy he went to Leipzig, where he took piano lessons with Karl Wendling, then pursued training in composition with Zhitomirsky at the Petrograd Cons. (1918–21) and with Miaskovsky at the Moscow Cons. (1921–23), where he subsequently taught orchestration (1923–43). He was associated with the Jewish cultural movement in Russia, and composed several works in the traditional ethnic manner of Jewish cantillations. In his harmonic and formal treatment, he followed the "orientalistic" tradition of the Russian national school. Among his works were the operas *Toktogul*, on Kirghiz motifs (1938–39; Frunze, 1940), and *Toktogul* (1949; in collaboration with A. Maldibaiev); also film music.

WRITINGS: *O metodakh prepodavaniya instrumentovki: K voprosu o klassovoy obuslovlennosti orkestrovovo pisma* (Methods of Instrument Teaching: On the Question of the Classification of Orchestral Writing; Moscow, 1931); *Traktovka instrumenov orkestra* (The Treatment of Orchestral Instruments; Moscow, 1948; 2d ed., 1961).

BIBL.: V. Bogdanov-Berezovsky, *A. M. V.* (Moscow and Leningrad, 1964).

Veracini, Francesco Maria, noted Italian violinist and composer; b. Florence, Feb. 1, 1690; d. there, Oct. 31, 1768. He studied violin with his uncle, the esteemed Italian violinist, teacher, and composer Antonio Veracini (1659–1733), with whom he appeared in concerts in Florence; he also received instruction from Giovanni Maria Casini and Francesco Feroci, and from G. A. Bernabei in Germany (1715). In 1711 he went to Venice, where he appeared as a soloist at the Christmas masses at San Marco; in 1714 he gave a series of benefit concerts in London, and in 1716 entered the private service of the elector of Saxony; in 1717 he went to Dresden and entered the court service. In 1723 he returned to Florence, where he was active as a performer and composer of sacred works; he also gave private concerts. In 1733 he returned to London, where he played for the Opera of the Nobility, a rival to Handel's opera company; he also composed operas during his London years. In 1745 he returned to Italy, where from 1755 until his death he was maestro di cappella for the Vallambrosian fathers at the church of S. Pancrazio in Florence; he also held that position for the Teatini fathers at the church of S. Michele agl'Antinori there (from 1758). He acquired a reputation as an eccentric, and some considered him mad. Be that as it may, he was esteemed as a violinist and composer. Among his works were the operas (all 1st perf. in London) *Adriano in Siria* (Nov. 26, 1735), *La clemenza di Tito* (April 12, 1737), *Partenio* (March 14, 1738), and *Rosalinda* (Jan. 31, 1744); also 8 oratorios, all lost.

BIBL.: H. Smith, *F. M. V.'s Il trionfo della pratica musicale* (diss., Indiana Univ., 1963); J. Hill, *The Life and Works of F. M. V.* (diss., Harvard Univ., 1972; rev., Ann Arbor, 1979).

Verdi, Giuseppe (Fortunino Francesco), great Italian opera composer whose genius for dramatic, lyric, and tragic stage music has made him the perennial favorite of a multitude of opera enthusiasts; b. Le Roncole, near Busseto, Duchy of Parma, Oct. 9, 1813; d. Milan, Jan. 27, 1901. His father kept a tavern, and street singing gave Verdi his early appreciation of music produced by natural means. A magister parvulorum, one Pietro Baistrocchi, a church organist, noticed his love of musical sound and took him on as a pupil. When Baistrocchi died, Verdi, still a small child, took over some of his duties at the keyboard. His father sent him to Busseto for further musical training; there he began his academic studies and also took music lessons with Ferdinando Provesi, the director of the municipal music school. At the age of 18 he became a resident in the home of Antonio Barezzi, a local merchant and patron of music; Barezzi supplied him with enough funds so that he could go to Milan for serious study. Surprisingly enough, in view of Verdi's future greatness, he failed to pass an entrance examination to the Milan Cons.; the registrar, Francesco Basili, reported that Verdi's piano technique was inadequate and that in composition he lacked technical knowledge. Verdi then turned to Vincenzo Lavigna, an excellent musician, for private lessons, and worked industriously to master counterpoint, canon, and fugue. In 1834 he applied for the post of maestro di musica in Busseto, and after passing his examination received the desired appointment. On May 4, 1836, he married a daughter of his patron Barezzi; it was a love marriage, but tragedy intervened when their 2 infant children died, and his wife succumbed on June 18, 1840. Verdi deeply mourned his bereavement, but he found solace in music. In 1838 he completed his first opera, *Oberto, conte di San Bonifacio*. In 1839 he moved to Milan. He submitted the score of *Oberto* to the directorship of La Scala; it was accepted for a performance, which took place on Nov. 17, 1839, with satisfactory success. He was now under contract to write more operas for that renowned theater. His comic opera *Un giorno di regno* was performed at La Scala in 1840, but it did not succeed at pleasing the public. Somewhat downhearted at this reverse, Verdi began composition of an opera, *Nabucodonosor*, on the biblical subject (the title was later abbreviated to *Nabucco*). It was staged at La Scala on March 9, 1842, scoring considerable success. Giuseppina Strepponi created the leading female role of Abigaille. *Nabucco* was followed by another successful opera on a historic subject, *I Lombardi alla prima Crociata*, produced at La Scala on Feb. 11, 1843. The next opera was *Ernani*, after Victor Hugo's drama on the life of a revolutionary outlaw; the subject suited the rise of national spirit, and its production in Venice on March 9, 1844, won great acclaim. Not so popular were Verdi's succeeding operas, *I due Foscari* (1844), *Giovanna d'Arco* (1845), *Alzira* (1845), and *Attila* (1846). On March 14, 1847, Verdi produced in Florence his first Shakespearean opera, *Macbeth*. In the same year he received a commission to write an opera for London; the result was *I Masnadieri*, based on Schiller's drama *Die Räuber*. It was produced at Her Majesty's Theatre in London on July 22, 1847, with Jenny Lind taking the leading female role. A commission from Paris followed; for it Verdi revised his opera *I Lombardi alla prima Crociata* in a French version, renamed *Jérusalem*; it was produced at the Paris Opéra on Nov. 26, 1847; the Italian production followed at La Scala on Dec. 26, 1850. This was one of the several operas by him and other Italian composers where mistaken identity was the chief dramatic device propelling the action. During his stay in Paris for the performance of *Jérusalem*, he renewed his acquaintance with Giuseppina Strepponi; after several years of cohabitation, their union was legalized in a private ceremony in Savoy on Aug. 29, 1859. In 1848 he produced his opera *Il Corsaro*, after Byron's poem *The Corsair*. There followed *La battaglia di Legnano*, celebrating the defeat of the armies of Barbarossa by the Lombards in 1176. Its premiere took place in Rome on Jan. 27, 1849, but Verdi was forced to change names and places so as not to offend the central European powers that dominated Italy. The subsequent operas *Luisa Miller* (1849), after Schiller's drama *Kabale und Liebe*, and *Stiffelio* (1850) were not successful. Verdi's great triumph came in 1851 with the production of *Rigoletto*, fashioned after Victor Hugo's drama *Le Roi* *s'amuse*; it was performed for the first time at the Teatro La Fenice in Venice on March 11, 1851, and brought Verdi lasting fame; it entered the repertoire of every opera house around the globe. The aria of the libidinous duke, "La donna + mobile," became one of the most popular operatic tunes sung, or ground on the barrel organ, throughout Europe. This success was followed by an even greater acclaim with the production in 1853 of *Il Trovatore* (Rome, Jan. 19, 1853) and *La Traviata* (Venice, March 6, 1853); both captivated world audiences without diminution of their melodramatic effect on succeeding generations in Europe and America, and this despite the absurdity of the action represented on the stage. *Il Trovatore* resorts to the common device of unrecognized identities of close relatives, while *La Traviata* strains credulity when the eponymous soprano sings enchantingly and long despite her struggle with terminal consumption. The character of Violetta was based on the story of a real person, as depicted in the drama *La Dame aux camélias* by Alexandre Dumas *fils*. The Italian title is untranslatable, *Traviata* being the feminine passive voice of the verb meaning "to lead astray," and it would have to be rendered, in English, by the construction "a woman who has been led astray." Another commission coming from Paris resulted in Verdi's first French opera, *Les Vêpres siciliennes*, after a libretto by Scribe to Donizetti's unfinished opera *Le Duc d'Albe*; the action deals with the medieval slaughter of the French occupation army in Sicily by local patriots. Despite the offensiveness of the subject to French patriots, the opera was given successfully in Paris on June 13, 1855. His next opera, *Simon Boccanegra*, was produced at the Teatro La Fenice in Venice on March 12, 1857. This was followed by *Un ballo in maschera*, which made history. The original libretto was written by Scribe for Auber's opera *Gustave III*, dealing with the assassination of King Gustave III of Sweden in 1792. But the censors would not have regicide shown on the stage, and Verdi was compelled to transfer the scene of action from Sweden to Massachusetts. Ridiculous as it was, Gustave III became Governor Riccardo of Boston; the opera was produced in this politically sterilized version in Rome on Feb. 17, 1859. Attempts were made later to restore the original libretto and to return the action to Sweden, but audiences resented the change of the familiar version. Unexpectedly, Verdi became a factor in the political struggle for the independence of Italy; the symbol of the nationalist movement was the name of Vittorio Emanuele, the future king of Italy. Demonstrators painted the name of Verdi in capital letters, separated by punctuation, on fences and walls of Italian towns (V.E.R.D.I., the initials of Vittorio Emanuele, Re D'Italia), and the cry "Viva Verdi!" became "Viva Vittorio Emanuele Re D'Italia!" In 1861 he received a commission to write an opera for the Imperial Opera of St. Petersburg, Russia; he selected the mystic subject *La forza del destino*. The premiere took place in St. Petersburg on Nov. 10, 1862, and Verdi made a special trip to attend. He then wrote an opera to a French text, *Don Carlos*, after Schiller's famous drama. It was first heard at the Paris Opéra on March 11, 1867, with numerous cuts; they were not restored in the score until a century had elapsed after the initial production. In June 1870 he received a contract to write a new work for the opera in Cairo, Egypt, where *Rigoletto* had already been performed a year before. The terms were most advantageous, with a guarantee of 150,000 francs for the Egyptian rights alone. The opera, based on life in ancient Egypt, was *Aida*; the original libretto was in French; Antonio Ghislanzoni prepared the Italian text. It had its premiere in Cairo on Christmas Eve of 1871, with great éclat. A special boat was equipped to carry officials and journalists from Italy to Cairo for the occasion, but Verdi stubbornly refused to join the caravan despite persuasion by a number of influential Italian musicians and statesmen; he declared that a composer's job was to supply the music, not to attend performances. The success of *Aida* exceeded all expectations; the production was hailed as a world event, and the work itself became one of the most famous in opera history.

After Rossini's death, in 1868, Verdi conceived the idea of honoring his memory by a collective composition of a Requiem, to which several Italian composers would contribute a movement each, Verdi reserving the last section, *Libera me*, for himself. He completed the score in 1869, but it was never performed in its original form. The death of the famous Italian poet Alessandro Manzoni in 1873 led him to write his great *Messa da Requiem*, which became known simply as the "Manzoni" Requiem, and he incorporated in it the section originally composed for Rossini. The *Messa da Requiem* received its premiere on the first anniversary of Manzoni's death, on May 22, 1874, in Milan. There was some criticism of the Requiem as being too operatic for a religious work, but it remained in musical annals as a masterpiece. After a lapse of some 13 years of rural retirement, Verdi turned once more to Shakespeare; the result this time was *Otello*; the libretto was by Arrigo Boito, a master poet who rendered Shakespeare's lines into Italian with extraordinary felicity. It received its premiere at La Scala on Feb. 5, 1887. Verdi was 79 years old when he wrote yet another Shakespearean opera, *Falstaff*, also to a libretto by Boito; in his libretto Boito used materials from *The Merry Wives of Windsor* and *Henry IV*. *Falstaff* was performed for the first time at La Scala on Feb. 9, 1893. The score reveals Verdi's genius for subtle comedy coupled with melodic invention of the highest order. His last composition was a group of sacred choruses, an *Ave Maria, Laudi alla Vergine Maria, Stabat Mater*, and *Te Deum*, publ. in 1898 as *4 pezzi sacri*; in the *Ave Maria*, Verdi made use of the so-called scala enigmatica (C, D♭, E, F♯, G♯, A♯, B, and C).

Innumerable honors were bestowed upon Verdi. In 1864 he was elected to membership in the Académie des Beaux Arts in Paris, where he filled the vacancy made by the death of Meyerbeer. In 1875 he was nominated a senator to the Italian Parliament. Following the premiere of *Falstaff*, the king of Italy wished to make him "Marchese di Busseto," but he declined the honor. After the death of his 2d wife, on Nov. 14, 1897, he founded in Milan the Casa di Riposo per Musicisti, a home for aged musicians; for its maintenance, he set aside 2,500,000 lire. On Jan. 21, 1901, Verdi suffered an apoplectic attack; he died 6 days later at the age of 87.

Historic evaluation of Verdi's music changed several times after his death. The musical atmosphere was heavily Wagnerian; admiration for Wagner produced a denigration of Verdi as a purveyor of "barrel-organ" music. Then the winds of musical opinion reversed their direction; sophisticated modern composers, music historians, and academic theoreticians discovered unexpected attractions in the flowing Verdian melodies, easily modulating harmonies, and stimulating symmetric rhythms; a theory was even advanced that the appeal of Verdi's music lies in its adaptability to modernistic elaboration and contrapuntal variegations. By natural transvaluation of opposites, Wagnerianism went into eclipse after it reached the limit of complexity. The slogan "Viva Verdi!" assumed, paradoxically, an aesthetic meaning. Scholarly research into Verdi's biography greatly increased. The Istituto di Studi Verdiani was founded in Parma in 1959. An American Inst. for Verdi Studies was founded in 1976 with its archive at N.Y. Univ.

WORKS: OPERAS: In the literature on Verdi, mention is sometimes made of 2 early operatic attempts, *Lord Hamilton* and *Rocester*; however, nothing definitive has ever been established concerning these 2 works. The accepted list of his operas is as follows: *Oberto, conte di San Bonifacio* (1837–38; La Scala, Milan, Nov. 17, 1839; libretto rev. by Graffigna and given as *I Bonifazi ed i Salinguerra* in Venice in 1842); *Un giorno di regno* (later known as *Il finto Stanislao*), melodramma giocoso (1840; La Scala, Milan, Sept. 5, 1840); *Nabucodonosor* (later known as *Nabucco*), dramma lirico (1841; La Scala, Milan, March 9, 1842); *I Lombardi alla prima Crociata*, dramma lirico (1842; La Scala, Milan, Feb. 11, 1843; rev. version, with a French libretto by Royer and Vaëz, given as *Jérusalem* at the Paris Opéra, Nov. 26, 1847); *Ernani*, dramma lirico (1843; Teatro La Fenice, Venice, March 9, 1844); *I due Foscari*, tragedia lirica (1844; Teatro Argentina, Rome, Nov. 3, 1844); *Giovanna d'Arco*, dramma lirico (1844; La Scala, Milan, Feb. 15, 1845); *Alzira*, tragedia lirica (1845; Teatro San Carlo, Naples, Aug. 12, 1845); *Attila*, dramma lirico (1845–46; Teatro La Fenice, Venice, March 17, 1846); *Macbeth* (1846–47; Teatro alla Pergola, Florence, March 14, 1847; rev. version, with a French tr. by Nuittier and Beaumont of the Italian libretto, Théâtre-Lyrique, Paris, April 21, 1865); *I Masnadieri* (1846–47; Her Majesty's Theatre, London, July 22, 1847); *Il Corsaro* (1847–48; Teatro Grande, Trieste, Oct. 25, 1848); *La battaglia di Legnano*, tragedia lirica (1848; Teatro Argentina, Rome, Jan. 27, 1849); *Luisa Miller*, melodramma tragico (1849; Teatro San Carlo, Naples, Dec. 8, 1849); *Stiffelio* (1850; Teatro Grande, Trieste, Nov. 16, 1850; later rev. as *Aroldo*); *Rigoletto*, melodramma (1850–51; Teatro La Fenice, Venice, March 11, 1851); *Il Trovatore*, dramma (1851–52; Teatro Apollo, Rome, Jan. 19, 1853; rev. 1857); *La Traviata* (1853; Teatro La Fenice, Venice, March 6, 1853); *Les Vêpres siciliennes* (1854; Opéra, Paris, June 13, 1855); *Simon Boccanegra* (1856–57; Teatro La Fenice, Venice, March 12, 1857; rev. 1880–81; La Scala, Milan, March 24, 1881); *Aroldo* (revision of *Stiffelio*; 1856–57; Teatro Nuovo, Rimini, Aug. 16, 1857); *Un ballo in maschera*, melodramma (1857–58; Teatro Apollo, Rome, Feb. 17, 1859); *La forza del destino* (1861; Imperial Theater, St. Petersburg, Nov. 10, 1862; rev. version, La Scala, Milan, Feb. 27, 1869); *Don Carlos* (1866; Opéra, Paris, March 11, 1867; rev. version, 1883–84, with Italian libretto by Lauzières and Zanardini, La Scala, Milan, Jan. 10, 1884); *Aida* (1870–71; Opera House, Cairo, Dec. 24, 1871); *Otello*, dramma lirico (1884–86; La Scala, Milan, Feb. 5, 1887); *Falstaff*, commedia lirica (1889–93; La Scala, Milan, Feb. 9, 1893).

BIBL.: COLLECTED WORKS, SOURCE MATERIAL: There is still no complete critical ed. of Verdi's works, but Ricordi and the Univ. of Chicago Press are preparing a definitive ed.

Important sources include the following: C. Vanbianchi, *Nel I° centenario di G. V., 1813–1913: Saggio di bibliografia verdiana* (Milan, 1913); C. Hopkinson, *A Bibliography of the Works of G. V., 1813–1901* (2 vols., N.Y., 1973 and 1978); M. Chusid, *A Catalog of V.'s Operas* (Hackensack, N.J., 1974); M. Mila, *La giovinezza di V.* (Turin, 1974); D. Rosen and A. Porter, eds., *V.'s Macbeth: A Sourcebook* (Cambridge, 1984). BIOGRAPHICAL: G. Monaldi, *V. e le sue opere* (Florence, 1878); L. Parodi, *G. V.* (Genoa, 1895); Prince de Valori, *V. et son oeuvre* (Paris, 1895); F. Crowest, *V.: Man and Musician* (London, 1897); G. Cavarretta, *V.: Il genio, la vita, le opere* (Palermo, 1899); G. Monaldi, *V.* (Turin, 1899; Ger. tr. as *G. V. und seine Werke*, Stuttgart, 1898, publ. before the Italian original; 4th Italian ed., 1951); C. Perinello, *G. V.* (Berlin, 1900); M. Basso, *G. V.: La sua vita, le sue opere, la sua morte* (Milan, 1901); O. Boni, *V.: L'Uomo, le opere, l'artista* (Parma, 1901; 2d ed., 1913); E. Checchi, *G. V.* (Florence, 1901); N. Marini, *G. V.* (Rome, 1901); E. Colonna, *G. V. nella vita e nelle opere* (Palermo, 1902); F. Garibaldi, *G. V. nella vita e nell'arte* (Florence, 1904); L. Sorge, *G. V.: Uomo, artista, patriota* (Lanciano, 1904); P. Voss, *G. V.: Ein Lebensbild* (Diessen, 1904); G. Bragagnolo and E. Bettazzi, *La vita di G. V. narrata al popolo* (Milan, 1905); A. Visetti, *V.* (London, 1905); A. d'Angeli, *G. V.* (Bologna, 1910; 2d ed., 1912); C. Bellaigue, *V.: Biographie critique* (Paris, 1912; Italian tr., Milan, 1913); M. Chop, *V.* (Leipzig, 1913); M. Lottici, *Bio-bibliografia di G. V.* (Parma, 1913); A. Mackenzie, *V.* (N.Y., 1913); A. Neisser, *G. V.* (Leipzig, 1914); G. Roncaglia, *G. V.* (Naples, 1914); A. Weissmann, *V.* (Berlin, 1922); A. Bonaventura, *G. V.* (Paris, 1923); E. Gasco Contell, *V.: Su vida y sus obras* (Paris, 1927); F. Ridella, *V.* (Genoa, 1928); F. Bonavia, *V.* (London, 1930; 2d ed., 1947); C. Gatti, *V.* (Milan, 1931; 2d ed., 1951; Eng. tr. as *V.: The Man and His Music*, N.Y., 1955); F. Toye, *G. V.: His Life and Works* (London, 1931); H. Gerigk, *G. V.* (Potsdam, 1932); R. Manganella, *V.* (Milan, 1936); L. d'Ambra, *G. V.* (Milan, 1937); D. Hussey, *V.* (London, 1940; 5th ed., 1973); F. Botti, *G. V.* (Rome, 1941); G. Roncaglia, *G. V.* (Florence, 1941); K. Holl, *V.* (Vienna, 1942); U. Zoppi, Angelo Mariani, *G. V. e Teresa Stolz* (Milan, 1947); D. Humphreys, *V., Force of Destiny* (N.Y., 1948); F. Törnblom, *V.* (Stockholm, 1948); G. Cenzato, *Itinerari verdiani* (Parma, 1949; 2nd ed., Milan, 1955); A. Cherbuliez, *G. V.* (Zürich, 1949); A. Oberdorfer, *G. V.* (Verona, 1949); L. Orsini, *G. V.* (Turin, 1949); F. Abbiati, ed., *G. V.* (Milan, 1951); L. Gianoli, *V.* (Brescia, 1951); G. Monaldi, *V., La vita, le opere* (Milan, 1951); E. Radius, *V. vivo* (Milan, 1951); G. Stefani, *V. e Trieste* (Trieste, 1951); idem, *G. V.* (Siena, 1951); F. Botti, *V. e l'ospedale di Villanova d'Arda* (Parma, 1952); G. Mondini, *Nel cinquantennio della morte di G. V.* (Cremona, 1952); T. Ybarra, *V., Miracle Man of Opera* (N.Y., 1955); M. Mila, *G. V.* (Bari, 1958); P. Petit, *V.* (Paris, 1958); V. Sheean, *Orpheus at Eighty* (N.Y., 1958); F. Abbiati, *G. V.* (4 vols., Milan, 1959); F. Walker, *The Man V.* (N.Y., 1962); G. Martin, *V.: His Music, Life and Times* (N.Y., 1963; 3d ed., rev., 1983); J. Wechsberg, *V.* (N.Y., 1974); W. Weaver, ed., *V.: A Documentary Study* (N.Y. and London, 1977); G. Marchesi, *G. V., l'uomo, il genio, l'artista* (Rozzano, 1982); G. Tintori, *Invito all'ascolto di G. V.* (Milan, 1983); M. Conati, ed., and R. Stokes, tr., *Interviews and Encounters with V.* (London, 1984); J. Budden, *V.* (London, 1985; rev. ed., 1993); C. Osborne, *V.: A Life in the Theatre* (N.Y., 1987); M. Phillips-Matz, *V.: A Biography* (Oxford, 1993); F. Cafasi, *G. V.: Fattore di Sant'Agata* (Parma, 1994). CRITICAL, ANALYTICAL: A. Basevi, *Studio sulle opere di G. V.* (Florence, 1859); G. Bertrand, *Les Nationalités musicales étudiées dans le drame lyrique: V.sme et Wagnérisme* (Paris, 1872); B. Roosevelt, *V., Milan and Otello* (Milan, 1887); V. Maurel, *A propos de la mise-en-scène du drame lyrique "Otello"* (Rome, 1888); E. Destranges, *L'Evolution musicale chez V.: Aïda, Otello, Falstaff* (Paris, 1895); C. Abate, *Wagner e V. Studio critico-musicale* (Mistretta, 1896); P. Bellezza, *Manzoni e V., i due grandi* (Rome, 1901); A. Soffredini, *Le opere di G. V.: Studio critico-analitico* (Milan, 1901); G. Tebaldini, *Da Rossini a V.* (Naples, 1901); J. Hadden, *The Operas of V.* (London, 1910); K. Regensburger, *Über den "Trovador" des García Gutiérrez, die Quelle von V.s "Il Trovatore"* (Berlin, 1911); C. Vanbianchi, *Saggio di bibliografia v.iana* (Milan, 1913); G. Roncaglia, *G. V.: L'ascensione dell'arte sua* (Naples, 1914); P. Berl, *Die Opern V.s in ihrer Instrumentation* (diss., Univ. of Vienna, 1931); G. Menghini, *G. V. e il melodramma italiano* (Rimini, 1931); M. Mila, *Il melodramma di V.* (Bari, 1933); A. Parente, *Il problema della critica v.ana* (Turin, 1933); L. Unterholzner, *G. V.s Operntypus* (Hannover, 1933); R. Gallusser, *V.s Frauengestalten* (diss., Univ. of Zürich, 1936); G. Engler, *V.s Anschauung vom Wesen der Oper* (diss., Univ. of Breslau, 1938); J. Loschelder, *Das Todesproblem in V.s Opernschaffen* (Cologne, 1938); G. Roncaglia, *L'ascensione creatrice di G. V.* (Florence, 1940); G. Mule and G. Nataletti, *V.: Studi e memorie* (Rome, 1941); M. Rinaldi, *V. critico* (Rome, 1951); C. Gatti, *Revisioni e rivalutazioni v.ane* (Turin, 1952); G. Roncaglia, *Galleria v.ana: Studi e figure* (Milan, 1959); M. Mila, *Il melodramma di V.* (Milan, 1960); W. Herrmann, Jr., *Religion in the Operas of G. V.* (diss., Columbia Univ., 1963); P. Pingagli, *Romanticismo di V.* (Florence, 1967); S. Hughes, *Famous V. Operas* (London, 1968); C. Osborne, *The Complete Operas of V.* (London, 1969); G. Baldini, *Abitare la battaglia: La storia di G. V.* (Milan, 1970); J. Budden, *The Operas of V.* (3 vols., London, 1973–81); A. Geck, *"Aïda," die Oper: Schriftenreihe über musikalische Bühnenwerke* (Berlin, 1973); D. Lawton, *Tonality and Drama in V.'s Early Operas* (diss., Univ. of Calif., Berkeley, 1973); V. Godefroy, *The Dramatic Genius of V.: Studies of Selected Operas* (2 vols., London, 1975 and 1977); F. Noske, *The Signifier and the Signified: Studies in the Operas of Mozart and V.* (The Hague, 1977); H. Busch, *V.'s Aida: The History of an Opera in Letters and Documents* (Minneapolis, 1978); W. Weaver and M. Chusid, eds., *The V. Companion* (N.Y., 1979); D. Kimbell, *V. in the Age of Italian Romanticism* (Cambridge, 1981); R. Parker, *Studies in Early V. (1832–1844): New Information and Perspectives on the Milanese Musical Milieu and the Operas from Oberto to Ernani* (diss., King's College, London, 1981); H. Gál, *G. V. und die Oper* (Frankfurt am Main, 1982); A. Duault, *V., la musique et la drame* (Paris, 1986); S. Corse, *Opera and the Uses of Language: Mozart, V., and Britten* (London and Toronto, 1987); J. Hepokoski, *G. V.: Otello* (Cambridge, 1987); J.-F. Labie, *Le cas V.* (Paris, 1987); H. Busch, *V.'s Otello and Simon Boccanegra in Letters and Documents* (Oxford, 1988); M. Engelhardt, *Die Chöre in der frühen Opern G. V.s* (Tutzing, 1988); A. Sopart, *G. V.s "Simon Boccanegra" (1857 and 1881): Eine musikalisch-dramaturgische Analyse* (Laaber, 1988); G. Martin, *Aspects of V.* (London, 1989); G. Marchesi, *V.: Anni, opere* (Parma, 1991); S. Einsfelder, *Zur musikalische Dramaturgie von G. V.s Otello* (Cologne, 1994); R. Parker, *Leonora's Last Act: Essays in V.an Discourse* (Princeton, 1997).

Vere (real name, **Wood de Vere**), **Clémentine Duchene de,** French soprano; b. Paris, Dec. 12, 1864; d. Mount Vernon, N.Y., Jan. 19, 1954. Her father was a Belgian nobleman, and her mother, an English lady. Her musical education was completed under the instruction of Mme. Albertini-Baucardé in Florence, where she made her debut at the age of 16 as Marguerite de Valois in *Les Huguenots*. On Feb. 2, 1896, she made her American debut at the Metropolitan Opera, N.Y., as Marguerite in Gounod's *Faust*; she remained on its roster until 1897; she was again at the Metropolitan from 1898 to 1900; her other roles with it were Violetta, Gilda, and Lucia. In 1892 she married the conductor Romualdo Sapio; taught voice from 1914. Her voice was a brilliant high soprano, and she excelled in coloratura.

Veremans, Renaat, Belgian composer, opera administrator, and teacher; b. Lierre, March 2, 1894; d. Antwerp, June 5, 1969. He received training at the Lemmens Inst. in Mechelen and from De Boeck at the Antwerp Cons., winning the premier prix in organ and piano (1914). From 1921 to 1944 he was director of the Flemish Opera in Antwerp. He also taught at the Antwerp Cons. As a composer, Veremans remained faithful to the Romantic tradition. His works included the operas *Beatrijs* (1928), *Anna-Marie* (Antwerp, Feb. 22, 1938), *Bietje* (1954), and *Lanceloot en Sanderien* (Antwerp, Sept. 13, 1968); also operettas.

Veress, Sándor, eminent Hungarian-born Swiss composer and pedagogue; b. Kolozsvár, Feb. 1, 1907; d. Bern, March 6, 1992. He studied piano with his mother; he also received instruction in piano from Bartók and in composition from Kodály at the Royal Academy of Music in Budapest (1923–27); he obtained his teacher's diploma (1932); he also took lessons with Lajtha at the Hungarian Ethnographical Museum (1929–33). He worked with Bartók on the folklore collection at the Academy of Sciences in Budapest (1937–40); he subsequently taught at the Academy of Music in Budapest (1943–48). In 1949 he went to Switzerland, where he received an appointment as guest prof. on folk music at the Univ. of Bern; then taught at the Bern Cons. from 1950 to 1977; he also was active as a guest lecturer in the United States and elsewhere, and taught musicology at the Univ. of Bern (1968–77). In 1975 he became a naturalized Swiss citizen. His works included the children's opera *Hangjegyek lázadása* (Revolt of the Musical Notes; 1931) and the ballets *Csodafurulya* (The Miraculous Pipe; 1937; Rome, 1941) and *Térszili Katicza* (Katica from Térszil; 1942–43; Stockholm, Feb. 16, 1949).

WRITINGS: With L. Lajtha, *Népdal, népzenegyűtjés* (Folk Song, Folk Music Collecting; Budapest, 1936); *Béla Bartók: The Man and the Artist* (London, 1948); *La raccolta della musica popolare ungherese* (Rome, 1949).

BIBL.: A. Traub, *S. V.: Festschrift zum 80. Geburtstag* (Berlin, 1986).

Veretti, Antonio, Italian composer and music educator; b. Verona, Feb. 20, 1900; d. Rome, July 13, 1978. After initial training in Verona, he studied with Mattioli and Alfano at the Bologna Liceo Musicale (graduated, 1921). He then founded his own Cons. Musicale della Gioventù Italiana in Rome, which he directed until 1943; subsequently he was director of the Pesaro Cons. (1950–52), the Cagliari Cons. (1953–55), and the Florence Cons. (1956–70). While his music generally followed Italian modernist traditions, he later experimented with serial techniques.

WORKS: DRAMATIC: *Il Medico volante*, opera (1928); *Il Favorito del re*, opera (1931; Milan, March 17, 1932; rev. as the opera ballet, *Burlesca*, Rome, Jan. 29, 1955); *Il galante tiratore*, ballet (1932; San Remo, Feb. 11, 1933); *Un favola di Andersen*, ballet (Venice, Sept. 15, 1934); *I sette peccati*, choreographic musical mystery (Milan, April 24, 1956); film music. Also 2 oratorios: *Il Cantico dei Cantici* (1922) and *Il Figliuol prodigo* (Rome, Nov. 21, 1942).

Vergnet, Edmond-Alphonse-Jean, French tenor; b. Montpellier, July 4, 1850; d. Nice, Feb. 25, 1904. He first played violin in the orch. of the Théâtre-Lyrique in Paris, then studied voice in Paris. He made his debut at the Paris Opéra in 1874, continuing as a member there until 1893; he also made guest appearances at La Scala in Milan, Covent Garden in London (1881–82), and in the United States (1885–86). Among the roles he created were Jean in Massenet's *Hérodiade* and Admeto in Catalani's *Dejanice*; his other roles were Faust, Radames, and Lohengrin.

Verikovsky, Mikhail (Ivanovich), Ukrainian conductor, teacher, and composer; b. Kremenetz, Nov. 20, 1896; d. Kiev, June 14, 1962. He was a pupil of Yavorsky at the Kiev Cons. He was conductor of the operas in Kiev (1926–28) and Kharkov (1928–35), and also director of the opera studio of the Kharkov Inst. of Music and Drama (1934–35). In 1946 he became a prof. at the Kiev Cons. He composed the first Ukrainian ballet, *Pan Kanyovsky* (1930). Other works include the operas *Dela nebesniye* (Heavenly Things; 1932), *Sotnik* (The Ensign; 1938), *Naymichka* (For Purchase; 1943), *Batrachka* (The Maid; 1946), *Basnya o chertopolokhe i roze* (The Fable of the Thistle and the Rose; 1948), *Begletsi* (Fugitives; 1948), and *Slava* (Glory; 1961), and the musical comedy *Viy* (1946); also oratorios on political themes.

BIBL.: N. Herasimova-Persidska, *M.I. V.* (Kiev, 1959); N. Shurova, *M. V.* (Kiev, 1972).

Vernon, Ashley. See **Manschinger, Kurt.**

Verrall, John (Weedon), American composer and teacher; b. Britt, Iowa, June 17, 1908. He studied piano and composition with Donald Ferguson, then attended classes at the Royal College of Music in London with R. O. Morris, and took lessons with Kodály in Budapest. Returning to the United States, he studied at the Minneapolis College of Music and Hamline Univ. (B.A., 1932); he received further training at the Berkshire Music Center at Tanglewood, with Roy Harris, and with Frederick Jacobi; he held a Guggenheim fellowship (1947). He held teaching positions at Hamline Univ. (1934–42), at Mount Holyoke College (1942–46), and at the Univ. of Wash. in Seattle (1948–73). His works include the operas *The Cowherd and the Sky Maiden*, after a Chinese legend (1951; Seattle, Jan. 17, 1952), *The Wedding Knell*, after Hawthorne (Seattle, Dec. 5, 1952), and *3 Blind Mice* (Seattle, May 22, 1955).

WRITINGS: *Elements of Harmony* (n.p., 1937); with S. Moseley, *Form and Meaning in the Arts* (N.Y., 1958); *Fugue and Invention in Theory and Practice* (Palo Alto, Calif., 1966); *Basic Theory of Scales, Modes and Intervals* (Palo Alto, Calif., 1969).

Verrett, Shirley, noted black American mezzo-soprano, later soprano; b. New Orleans, May 31, 1931. Her father, a choirmaster at the Seventh-Day Adventist church in New Orleans, gave her rudimentary instruction in singing. Later she moved to California and took voice lessons with John Charles Thomas and Lotte Lehmann. In 1955 she won the Marian Anderson Award and a scholarship at the Juilliard School of Music in New York, where she became a student of Marion Székely-Freschl; while still a student, she appeared as soloist in Falla's *El amor brujo* under Stokowski, and made her operatic debut as Britten's Lucretia in Yellow Springs, Ohio (1957). In 1962 she scored a major success as Carmen at the Festival of Two Worlds at Spoleto, Italy. In 1963 she made a tour of the Soviet Union, and sang Carmen at the Bolshoi Theater in Moscow. In 1966 she made her debut at Milan's La Scala and at London's Covent Garden. On Sept. 21, 1968, she made her debut at the Metropolitan Opera in New York, again as Carmen. On Oct. 22, 1973, she undertook 2 parts, those of Dido and Cassandra, in *Les Troyens* of Berlioz, produced at the Metropolitan. As a guest artist, she also appeared in San Francisco, Boston, Paris, Vienna, and other operatic centers. In 1990 she sang Dido at the opening performance of the new Opéra de la Bastille in Paris. She won distinction in mezzo-soprano roles, and later as a soprano; thus she sang the title role in Bellini's *Norma*, a soprano, and also the role of mezzo-soprano Adalgisa in the same opera. Her other roles included Tosca, Azucena, Amneris, and Delilah. She also showed her ability to cope with the difficult parts in modern operas, such as Bartók's *Bluebeard's Castle*. Her voice is of a remarkably flexible quality, encompassing lyric and dramatic parts with equal expressiveness and technical proficiency. Her concert repertory ranges from Schubert to Rorem, and also includes spirituals.

Verstovsky, Alexei (Nikolaievich), important Russian composer; b. Seliverstovo, March 1, 1799; d. Moscow, Nov. 17, 1862. He was taken as a child to Ufa, and at the age of 17 he was sent to St. Petersburg, where he entered the Inst. of Transport Engineers; he took piano lessons with Johann Heinrich Miller, Daniel Steibelt, and John Field, studied violin with Ludwig Maurer, and voice with Tarquini. He became a member of the flourishing literary and artistic milieu in St. Petersburg; among his friends was Pushkin. In 1823 he went to Moscow; in 1825 he was named inspector of its theater, then was director of all of its theaters (1842–60). Almost all of his compositions for the stage followed the French model, with long scenes of speech accompanied on the keyboard; his first effort was couplets for the vaudeville, *Les perroquets de la mère Philippe* (1819); he also composed popular songs and couplets for various other vaudevilles and stage pieces. He contributed a great deal to the progress of operatic art in Russia, but his music lacked distinction and inventive power. With the advent of Glinka and Dargomyzhsky on the Russian operatic scene, Verstovsky's productions receded into insignificance. His works included the operas (all 1st perf. in Moscow) *Pan Twardowski* (June 5, 1828), *Vadim, ili Probuzhdeniye dvendtsati spyashchikh dev* (Vadim, or The Awakening of the Twelve Sleeping Maidens; Dec. 7, 1832), *Askoldova nogila* (Askold's Grave; Sept. 27, 1835), *Tosko po rodine* (Longing for the Homeland; Sept. 2, 1839), *Churova Dolina, ili Son nayavu* (Chur Valley, or The Waking Dream; Aug. 28, 1841), and *Gromoboy* (Feb. 5, 1858); also incidental music, songs for dramas, and romances for vaudevilles.

BIBL.: B. Dobrohotov, *A.N. V.* (Moscow, 1949).

Vesque von Püttlingen, Johann, Austrian composer; b. Opole, Poland, July 23, 1803; d. Vienna, Oct. 29, 1883. He studied law in Vienna, and became a councillor of state; at the same time he studied with Moscheles (piano) and Sechter (theory), and made his mark as a composer of operas, under the pseudonym J. Hoyen. He also publ. a book on musical copyright, *Das musikalische Autorrecht* (Vienna, 1864). His works include the operas (all 1st perf. in Vienna unless otherwise given) *Turandot* (Oct. 3, 1838), *Johanna d'Arc* (Dec. 30, 1840), *Liebeszauber* (1845), *Ein Abenteuer Carls des Zweiten* (Jan. 12, 1850), and *Der lustige Rat* (Weimar, April 12, 1852).

BIBL.: H. Schultz, *J. V. v.P.* (Regensburg, 1930); H. Ibl, *Studien zu J. v. v. P.s Leben und Opernschaffen* (diss., Univ. of Vienna, 1950).

Vetter, Walther, distinguished German musicologist; b. Berlin, May 10, 1891; d. there, April 1, 1967. He studied at the Leipzig Cons.; subsequently he took a course in musicology with Hermann Abert at the Univ. of Halle, where he received his Ph.D. in 1920 with the diss. *Die Arie bei Gluck*; he completed his Habilitation at the Univ. of Breslau with his *Das frühdeutsche Lied* in 1927 (publ. in Munster, 1928). He taught at the Univs. of Halle, Hamburg, Breslau, and Greifswald before joining the Univ. of Poznan in 1941; from 1946 to 1958 he was a prof. at Humboldt Univ. in Berlin, and also served as director of its Inst. of Musicology. From 1948 to 1961 he was coed. of *Die Musikforschung*; from 1956 to 1966 he was ed. of the *Deutsches Jahrbuch für Musikwissenschaft*.

WRITINGS: *Der humanistische Bildungsgedanke in Musik und Musikwissenschaft* (Langensalza, 1928); *Franz Schubert* (Potsdam, 1934); *Antike Musik* (Munich, 1935); *J. S. Bach: Leben und Werk* (Leipzig, 1938); *Beethoven und die militär-politischen Ereignisse seiner Zeit* (Poznan, 1943); *Der Kapellmeister Bach: Versuch einer Deutung Bachs auf Grund seines Wirkens als Kapellmeister in Köthen* (Potsdam, 1950); *Der Klassiker Schubert* (2 vols., Leipzig, 1953); *Mythos—Melos—Musica: Ausgewählte Aufsätze zur Musikgeschichte* (2 vols., Leipzig, 1957, 1961); *Christoph Willibald Gluck* (Leipzig, 1964).

BIBL.: *Musa—mens—musici: Im Gedenken an W. V.* (Leipzig, 1969).

Vianesi, Auguste-Charles-Léonard-François, Italian-born French conductor; b. Livorno, Nov. 2, 1837; d. N.Y., Nov. 4, 1908. After studying in Italy, he went to Paris in 1857, then became conductor at Drury Lane in London. In 1858–59 he was a conductor in New York; after appearances in Moscow and St. Petersburg, he conducted the Italian, French, and German repertories at London's Covent Garden (1870–80). In 1887 he became principal conductor at the Grand Opéra in Paris. He conducted the performance of *Faust* at the opening night of the Metropolitan Opera House in New York (Oct. 22, 1883), and was on its staff throughout its first season; he also conducted during the season of 1891–92. He then remained in New York as a vocal teacher.

Viardot-García, (Michelle Fedinande) Pauline, celebrated French mezzo-soprano and pedagogue of Spanish descent, daughter of **Manuel del Popolo García** and sister of **Maria Malibran**; b. Paris, July 18, 1821; d. there, May 18, 1910. She commenced vocal training with her mother, then received lessons in piano from Meysenberg and Liszt and in composition from Reicha. Her concert debut was in Brussels in 1837; her stage debut was in London, May 9, 1839, as Desdemona in Rossini's *Otello*. She was then engaged by Louis Viardot, director of the Théâtre-Italien in Paris, where she scored a notable success in her debut as Desdemona on Oct. 8, 1839; she sang there until her marriage to Viardot in 1840, who then accompanied her on long tours throughout Europe. In 1843 she made her first appearances in Russia, where she won distinction singing in both Italian and Russian; in subsequent years she championed the cause of Russian music. She created the role of Fidès in Meyerbeer's *Le Prophète* at the Paris Opéra in 1849, and that of Sapho in Gounod's opera in 1851; after another succession of tours, she took the role of Orphée in Berlioz's revival of Gluck's opera at the Théâtre-Lyrique in Paris (1859), singing the part for 150 nights to crowded houses. She retired in 1863. Her *École classique de chant* was publ. in Paris in 1861. In 1871 she settled in Paris, and devoted herself to teaching and composing. Through her efforts, the music of Gounod, Massenet, and Fauré was given wide hearing. She was one of the great dramatic singers of her era, excelling particularly in the works of Gluck, Meyerbeer, and Halévy. Among her compositions are some operettas. Two of her children were musicians: Louise (Pauline Marie) Héritte (b. Paris, Dec. 14, 1841; d. Heidelberg, Jan. 17, 1918) was a contralto, teacher, and composer; she devoted herself mainly to teaching in St. Petersburg, Frankfurt am Main, Berlin, and Heidelberg; publ. *Memories and Adventures* (London, 1913); she composed a comic opera, *Lindoro* (Weimar, 1879). Paul (Louis Joachim) (b. Courtavenel, July 20, 1857; d. Algiers, Dec. 11, 1941) was a violinist, conductor, and composer; he studied with Léonard; conducted at the Paris Opéra; he wrote the books *Histoire de la musique* (Paris, 1905), *Rapport officiel (mission artistique de 1907) sur la musique en Scandinavie* (Paris, 1908), and *Souvenirs d'un artiste* (Paris, 1910).

BIBL.: La Mara, *P. V.-G.* (Leipzig, 1882); L. Torrigi, *P. V.-G.: Sa biographie, ses compositions, son enseignement* (Geneva, 1901); C. Kaminski, *Lettres à Mlle. V. d'Ivan Tourgéneff* (Paris, 1907); L. Héritte-Viardot, *Memories and Adventures* (London, 1913; tr. from original Ger. MS; Fr. tr., Paris, 1923); A. Rachmanowa (pseud.), *Die Liebe eines Lebens: Iwan Turgenjew und P. V.* (Frauenfeld, 1952); A. FitzLyon, *The Price of Genius: A Life of P. V.* (London, 1964).

Vick, Graham, English opera producer; b. Liverpool, Dec. 30, 1953. He was educated at the Royal Northern College of Music in Manchester. After gaining experience at Glyndebourne and with the English Music Theatre, he produced *Madama Butterfly* at the English National Opera in London in 1984. From 1984 to 1987 he was director of productions at the Scottish Opera in Glasgow. In 1986 he staged *Die Entführung aus dem Serail* in St. Louis. He became artistic director of the City of Birmingham Touring Opera in 1987. In 1989 he produced the British premiere of Berio's *Un re in ascolto* at London's Covent Garden, returning there to stage *Mitridate* in 1992, *Die Meistersinger von Nürnberg* in 1993, *King Arthur* in 1995, and *The Midsummer Marriage* in 1996. In 1992 he produced *The Queen of Spades* at the Glyndebourne Festival, and in 1994 he was made its director of productions. His first staging at the Metropolitan Opera came in 1994 when he produced *Lady Macbeth of the District of Mtsensk*. In 1997 he produced *Parsifal* at the Opéra de la Bastille in Paris. In 1999 he staged Schoenberg's *Moses und Aron* at the Metropolitan Opera. His productions are both innovative and tasteful.

Vickers, Jon(athan Stewart), renowned Canadian tenor; b. Prince Albert, Saskatchewan, Oct. 29, 1926. He began singing as a child. After his voice developed into the tenor range, he acquired experience singing in Baptist church choirs in Prince Albert and Flin Flon. While accepting various singing engagements, he worked in chain stores to make ends meet. After singing major roles in Gilbert and Sullivan and Victor Herbert operettas, he won a scholarship to the Royal Cons. of Music of Toronto in 1950 to study with George Lambert. During this time, he continued to sing in concerts. In 1954 he sang the Duke of Mantua with the Canadian Opera Co. in Toronto, and returned there in such roles as Alfredo in *La Traviata* (1955) and Don José (1956); in the latter year, he appeared in a concert performance of *Medea* in New York. In Jan. 1957 he made his first appearance with the Royal Opera of Covent Garden, London, on tour. It was as Siegmund in *Die Walküre* at the Bayreuth Festival in 1958 that Vickers first won notable acclaim. In 1959 he sang Jason in *Medea* in Dallas and Radames in San Francisco. On Jan. 17, 1960, he made his Metropolitan Opera debut in New York as Canio, where he continued to sing with success in subsequent years. He sang Florestan at Milan's La Scala and Siegmund at the Chicago Lyric Opera in 1961. In 1966, 1967, and 1968 he appeared at Karajan's Easter Festivals. He sang Otello at Expo 67 in Montreal in 1967. In 1975 he appeared as Tristan with the Opéra du Québec. In 1985 Vickers sang Handel's Samson at Covent Garden in a production marking the 300th anniversary of the composer's birth. Throughout the years, he continued to make occasional appearances as a soloist with orchs. and as a recitalist. His remarkable career came to a close with his retirement in 1988. In 1968 Vickers was made a Companion of the Order of Canada. Vickers was acknowledged as one of the principal dramatic and Heldentenors of his era. In addition to roles already noted, he also excelled as Berlioz's Aeneas, Don Alvaro, Don Carlos, Parsifal, and Peter Grimes.

Victory, Gerard (real name, **Alan Loraine**), Irish composer, conductor, and broadcasting administrator; b. Dublin, Dec. 24, 1921; d. there, March 14, 1995. He was educated at Belvedere College, Dublin, the Univ. of Ireland (B.A.), and Trinity College, Univ. of Dublin (B.Mus.). From 1948 to 1953 he was active with the Irish Radio Service. He was a radio (1953–61) and television (1961–62) producer with Radio Telefis Eireann. After serving as its deputy director of music (1962–67), he was its director of music (1967–82). From 1981 to 1983 he was president of UNESCO's International Rostrum of Composers. In 1972 he was awarded an honorary Mus.D. degree from Trinity College. In 1975 he received the Chevalier de l'Ordre des Arts et des Lettres of France and the Order of Merit of the Federal Republic of Germany. Victory created an extensive body of music in various genres and styles. His works were always handsomely crafted and couched in a generally accessible idiom.

WORKS: DRAMATIC: OPERAS: *An Fear a phós Balbhán* (The Silent Wife; 1952; Dublin, April 6, 1953); *Iomrall Aithne* (1955–56); *The Stranger* (1958); *The Music Hath Mischief* (1960); *Chatterton* (1967); *Eloise and Abelard* (1970–72); *Circe 1991*, radio opera (1971); *An Evening for Three* (1975); *The Rendezvous* (1988–89; Dublin, Nov. 2, 1989); *The Wooing of Etain*, children's opera (1994). OPERETTAS: *Nita* (1944); *Once Upon a Moon* (1949); *The 2 Violins* (1955). MUSICAL PLAYS: *Eldorado* (1953); *The Martinique Story* (1960–61). Also incidental music for plays; film music.

Vidal, Paul (Antonin), noted French conductor, pedagogue, and composer; b. Toulouse, June 16, 1863; d. Paris, April 9, 1931. He studied at the Paris Cons., and in 1883 won the Prix de Rome with his cantata *Le Gladiateur*. In 1889 he joined the staff of the Paris Opéra as assistant choral director; later he became chief conductor there (1906). He taught elementary courses at the Paris Cons. from 1894 until 1909, when he was appointed a prof. of composition. He was music director of the Opéra Comique from 1914 to 1919. His brother, Joseph Bernard Vidal (b. Toulouse, Nov. 15, 1859; d. Paris, Dec. 18, 1924), was a conductor and composer; made a name for himself as a composer of operettas.

WORKS: DRAMATIC: *Eros*, fantaisie lyrique (Paris, April 22, 1892); *L'Amour dans les enfers* (1892); *La Maladetta*, ballet (Paris, Feb. 24, 1893); *Fête russe*, ballet (Paris, Oct. 24, 1893); *Guernica*, drame lyrique (Paris, June 7, 1895); *La Burgonde*, opera (Paris, Dec. 23, 1898); *Ramsès*, drame (Paris, June 27, 1900); *L'Impératrice*, ballet (1903); *Zino-Zina* (1908); *Ballet de Terpsichore* (1909); also pantomimes, incidental music to plays.

Vieru, Anatol, distinguished Romanian composer and musicologist; b. Iaşi, June 8, 1926. He was a student of Klepper (composition), Constantinescu (harmony), and Silvestri (conducting) at the Bucharest Cons. (1946–51) before pursuing training with Khachaturian (composition) at the Moscow Cons. (1951–54); later he attended the summer courses in new music at Darmstadt (1967) and subsequently took his Ph.D. in musicology at the Cluj Cons. (1978) with the diss. *De la moduri, spre un model al gîndirii muzicale intervalice* (From Modes Towards a Model of Intervallic Musical Thought; publ. as *Cartea Modurilor* [Book of Modes], Bucharest, 1980; 2d ed., 1993). From 1955 he taught composition at the Bucharest Cons. He was founder-director of the Musiques parallèles concerts (1970–84), at which he presented the first Romanian performances of works by such modern masters as Schoenberg, Varèse, and Ives. In 1973 he was in Berlin under the auspices of the Deutscher Akademischer Austauschdienst. In 1984, 1992, and 1994 he gave courses in Darmstadt and in 1992–93 he was composer-in-residence at N.Y. Univ. Among his honors were the Reine Marie José prize of Geneva (1962), a Koussevitzky Foundation grant (1966), the prize of the Romanian Academy (1967), and the Gottfried von Herder Prize of the Univ. of Vienna (1986). He contributed articles to various journals and publ. the vol. *Cuvinte despre sunete* (Words About Sounds; Bucharest, 1993). Beginning with neomodal models, Vieru has developed a highly personal compositional style in which microstructures serve as the foundation upon which to build scores notable for their inventive handling of modal, tonal, and serial elements.

WORKS (all 1st perf. in Bucharest unless otherwise given): DRAMATIC: OPERAS: *Jonah* (1972–75; concert perf., Oct. 30, 1976); *The Feast of the Cadgers* (1978–81; concert perf., June 24, 1984; 1st stage perf., Berlin, Nov. 10, 1990); 3 "pocket" operas (1982–83): *Telegrams* (Nov. 8, 1983), *Theme and Variations* (Nov. 8, 1983), and *A Pedagogue of the New School* (April 7, 1987); *The Last Days, the Last Hours* (1990–95); film and television scores. Also *Mioritsa*, oratorio for Tenor, Baritone, Chorus, Children's Chorus, and Orch. (1956–57; Feb. 27, 1958).

Vietinghoff-Scheel, Boris, Baron, Russian composer; b. in Latvia, 1829; d. St. Petersburg, Sept. 25, 1901. He was a student of Henselt and Dargomyzhsky in St. Petersburg. Three of his operas were produced in St. Petersburg: *Mazeppa* (May 17, 1859), *Tamara* (May 2, 1886), and *Don Juan de Tenorio* (Nov. 2, 1888); 2 other operas, *Mary Stuart* and *Heliodora*, were not produced. Vietinghoff publ. a book of memoirs (St. Petersburg, 1899).

Vieuille, Félix, French bass; b. Saugéon, Oct. 15, 1872; d. there, Feb. 28, 1953. He was a member of the Paris Opéra Comique from 1898 to 1928, where he created the role of Arkel in Debussy's *Pelléas et Mélisande* (1902). He also appeared with the Manhattan Opera in New York (1908–09).

Viganò, Salvatore, Italian composer and choreographer; b. Naples, March 25, 1769; d. Milan, Aug. 10, 1821. He was the son and pupil of a dancer. He studied music with the famous Italian composer and cellist Luigi (Ridolfo) Boccherini (b. Lucca, Feb. 19, 1743; d. Madrid, May 28, 1805), who was his uncle, then began his career as a dancer at Rome in 1783, and also produced there an opera buffa, *La Vedova scoperta*. In 1789 he went to Madrid, where he married the celebrated ballerina María Medina; they subsequently toured as dancers, winning particular distinction in

Vienna in 1793. After separating from his wife, he served as balletmaster in Vienna (1799–1803). Beethoven wrote the music for Viganò's "heroic ballet" *Die Geschöpfe des Prometheus* (Vienna, March 28, 1801), in which Vigaò danced the leading male role. After producing ballets in several Italian cities, he was active at Milan's La Scala (1811–21)

BIBL.: C. von Ayrenhoff, *Über die theatratischen Tänze und die Ballettmeister Noverre, Muzzarelli, und V.* (Vienna, 1794); C. Ritorni, *Commentarii della vita e delle opere coreodrammatiche di S. V.* (Milan, 1838); A. Levinson, *Meister des Balletts: Stendhal und V.: Eine Seite aus der Geschichte der Romantik* (Potsdam, 1923).

Viglione-Borghese, Domenico, Italian baritone; b. Mondovi, July 3, 1877; d. Milan, Oct. 26, 1957. He studied in Milan and Pesaro. He made his operatic debut as the Herald in *Lohengrin* in Lodi in 1899, and continued to sing in provincial Italian opera companies; he then gave up singing in 1901, and went to the United States, where he earned his living as a railroad worker in San Francisco. There he met Caruso, who recommended him to the impresario Scognamillo, who engaged him for a South American tour (1905–06); he subsequently pursued his career in Italy, retiring in 1940. He sang some 40 roles, the best known being Jack Rance in Puccini's *La Fanciulla del West*, which he first sang in Brescia in 1911 and for the last time in Rome in 1940.

Vignas, Francisco, noted Spanish tenor; b. Moya, near Barcelona, March 27, 1863; d. Barcelona, July 14, 1933. He studied at the Barcelona Cons., and later in Paris. He made his debut in Barcelona in 1888 as Lohengrin, then sang in Italian opera houses; he made his first appearance in London in 1893 at the Shaftesbury Theatre. On Nov. 29, 1893, he made his Metropolitan Opera debut in New York as Turiddu; after only one season there, he returned to Europe.

Vilback, (Alfonse Charles) Renaud de, French organist and composer; b. Montpellier, June 3, 1829; d. Paris, March 19, 1884. He studied piano with Lemoine, organ with Benoist, and composition with Halévy at the Paris Cons., winning the Grand Prix de Rome at the age of 15. In 1856 he became organist at St.-Eugène, Paris, remaining there until 1871. He wrote 2 operas: *Au clair de lune* (Paris, Sept. 4, 1857) and *Almanzor* (Paris, April 16, 1858).

Vilboa, Konstantin, Russian composer of French descent; b. St. Petersburg, May 29, 1817; d. Warsaw, July 16, 1882. He studied in a military school, and was sent by the government to collect folk songs in the country; he also directed various choirs in military establishments. In 1876 he went to Warsaw as a functionary in the ministry of war. His opera *Natasha, or The Volga Brigands* was produced in Moscow on Nov. 12, 1861. His other operas included *Taras Bulba* (after Gogol) and *Tziganka* (The Gypsy).

Vilhar, Franz, Croatian composer; b. Senožeče, Jan. 5, 1852; d. Zagreb, March 4, 1928. He studied music with Skuherský in Prague. After serving as an organist in various churches, he settled in Zagreb, in 1891, as choirmaster at St. Mark's. He composed a Croatian opera, *Smiljana* (Zagreb, Jan. 31, 1897).

Villa, Ricardo, Spanish composer and conductor; b. Madrid, Oct. 23, 1873; d. there, April 10, 1935. He studied at the Madrid Cons. He was founder-conductor of the Madrid municipal band (from 1909). He wrote the operas *El Cristo de la Vega* and *Raimundo Lulio*.

Villa-Lobos, Heitor, remarkable Brazilian composer of great originality and unique ability to recreate native melodic and rhythmic elements in large instrumental and choral forms; b. Rio de Janeiro, March 5, 1887; d. there, Nov. 17, 1959. He studied music with his father, a writer and amateur cello player; after his father's death in 1899, Villa-Lobos earned a living by playing the cello in cafés and restaurants; he also studied cello with Benno Niederberger. From 1905 to 1912 he traveled in Brazil in order to collect authentic folk songs. In 1907 he entered the National Inst. of Music in Rio de Janeiro, where he studied with Frederico Nascimento, Angelo França, and Francisco Braga. In 1912 he undertook an expedition into the interior of Brazil, where he gathered a rich collection of Indian songs. On Nov. 13, 1915, he presented in Rio de Janeiro a concert of his compositions, creating a sensation by the exuberance of his music and the radical character of his technical idiom. He met Artur Rubinstein, who became his ardent admirer; for him Villa-Lobos composed a transcendentally difficult *Rudepoema*. In 1923 Villa-Lobos went to Paris on a Brazilian government grant; upon returning to Brazil in 1930, he was active in São Paulo and then in Rio de Janeiro in music education; he founded a cons. under the sponsorship of the Ministry of Education in 1942. He introduced bold innovations into the national program of music education, with an emphasis on the cultural resources of Brazil; he compiled a *Guia pratico*, containing choral arrangements of folk songs of Brazil and other nations; organized the "orpheonic concentrations" of schoolchildren, whom he trained to sing according to his own cheironomic method of solfeggio. In 1944 he made his first tour of the United States, and conducted his works in Los Angeles, Boston, and New York in 1945. In 1945 he established in Rio de Janeiro the Brazilian Academy of Music, serving as its president from 1947 until his death. He made frequent visits to the United States and France during the last 15 years of his life.

Villa-Lobos was one of the most original composers of the 20th century. He lacked formal academic training, but far from hampering his development, this deficiency liberated him from pedantic restrictions, so that he evolved an idiosyncratic technique of composition, curiously eclectic, but all the better suited to his musical aesthetics. An ardent Brazilian nationalist, he resolved from his earliest attempts in composition to use authentic Brazilian song materials as the source of his inspiration; yet he avoided using actual quotations from popular songs; rather, he wrote melodies that are authentic in their melodic and rhythmic content. In his desire to relate Brazilian folk resources to universal values, he composed a series of extraordinary works, *Bachianas brasileiras*, in which Brazilian melorhythms are treated in Bachian counterpoint. He also composed a number of works under the generic title *Chôros*, a popular Brazilian dance form, marked by incisive rhythm and a ballad-like melody. An experimenter by nature, Villa-Lobos devised a graphic method of composition, using geometrical contours of drawings and photographs as outlines for the melody; in this manner he wrote *The New York Skyline*, using a photograph for guidance. Villa-Lobos wrote operas, ballets, syms., chamber music, choruses, piano pieces, songs; the total number of his compositions is in excess of 2,000.

WORKS: DRAMATIC: OPERAS: *Izaht* (1912–14; rev. 1932; concert premiere, Rio de Janeiro, April 6, 1940; stage premiere, Rio de Janeiro, Dec. 13, 1958); *Magdalena* (1947; Los Angeles, July 26, 1948); *Yerma* (1953–56; Santa Fe, Aug. 12, 1971); *A menina das nuvens* (1957–58; Rio de Janeiro, Nov. 29, 1960); others left unfinished. BALLETS (many converted from symphonic poems): *Uirapuru* (1917; Buenos Aires, May 25, 1935; rev. 1948); *Possessão* (1929); *Pedra Bonita* (1933); *Dança da terra* (1939; Rio de Janeiro, Sept. 7, 1943); *Rudá* (1951); *Gênesis* (1954; as a symphonic poem, 1969); *Emperor Jones* (1955; Ellenville, N.Y., July 12, 1956). ORATORIO: *Vidapura* for Chorus, Orch., and Organ (1918; Rio de Janeiro, Nov. 11, 1922).

BIBL.: V. Mariz, *H. V.-L.* (Rio de Janeiro, 1949; 11th ed., 1990); C. de Paula Barros, *O Romance de V.-L.* (Rio de Janeiro, 1951); *Homenagem a V.-L.* (Rio de Janeiro, 1960); M. Beaufils, *V.-L.: Musicien et poete du Brésil* (Rio de Janeiro, 1967); E. Nogueria França, *V.-L.: Síntese critica e biográfica* (Rio de Janeiro, 1970; 2d ed., 1973); L. Guimarães, *V.-L. visto da plateia e na intimidade (1912–1935)* (Rio de Janeiro, 1972); L. Peppercorn, *H. V.-L.: Leben und Werk des Brasilianischen Komponisten* (Zürich, 1972); F. Pereira da Silva, *V.-L.* (Rio de Janeiro, 1974); P. Carvalho, *V.-L.: Do crépusculo à alvorada* (Rio de Janeiro, 1987); M. Claret, ed., *O Pensamento vivo de H. V.-L.* (São Paulo, 1987); M. Machado, *H. V.-L.: Tradição e renovacão na música brasileira* (Rio de Janeiro, 1987); A. Schic, *V.-L.: Souvenirs de l'indien blanc* (Arles and Paris, 1987); E. Stornio, *V.-L.* (Madrid, 1987); D. Appleby, *H. V.-L.: A Bio-bibliography* (N.Y., 1988); L. Peppercorn, *V.-L.:*

Collected Studies (Aldershot, 1992); S. Wright, *V.-L.* (Oxford, 1992); G. Béhague, *H. V.-L.: The Search for Brazil's Musical Soul* (Austin, Texas, 1994); E. Tarasti, *H. V.-L.: The Life and Works, 1887–1959* (Jefferson, N.C., 1995).

Vinacessi, Benedetto, Italian composer and organist; b. Brescia, c.1670; d. Venice, c.1719. After studies with Pietro Pelli, he was in the service of Prince Ferdinand Gonzaga of Catiglione delle Stiviere, near Mantua, and of Count Alemano Gabara of Brescia. In 1704 he was made a Cavaliere and 2d organist at San Marco in Venice. His successful dramatic works for Venice included *L'innocenza giustificata* (Dec. 1698), *Gli amanti generosi* (Carnival 1703), and *Gli sponsali di giubilo* (1705). Among his other works were 2 books of trio sonatas (1687, 1692), a Mass, 4 oratorios, 2 cantatas, and a book of motets (1714).

BIBL.: M. Talbot, *B. V.: A Musician in Brescia and Venice in the Age of Corelli* (Oxford, 1994).

Vinay, Ramón, Chilean baritone, later tenor; b. Chillán (of French and Italian parents), Aug. 31, 1912; d. Puebla, near Mexico City, Jan. 4, 1996. He was a pupil of José Pierson in Mexico City, where he made his operatic debut as Alfonso in *La Favorite* (1931); after appearances in baritone roles, he pursued further training and turned to the tenor repertory, making his 2d debut as Don José in Mexico City in 1943; he chose that same role for his N.Y. debut in 1945. On Feb. 22, 1946, he made his Metropolitan Opera debut in New York as Don José; he remained on its roster until 1958, and sang there again from 1959 to 1962 and in 1965–66. He also appeared in Europe, opening the 1947–48 season at Milan's La Scala in his most famous role, Otello; he sang at the Bayreuth Festivals (1952–57) and regularly at London's Covent Garden (1953–60). From 1969 to 1971 he was artistic director of the Santiago Opera. Among his other roles were Bartolo, Iago, Falstaff, Scarpia, Telramund, Parsifal, Tristan, Siegfried, and Tannhäuser.

Vincent (real name, **Winzenhörlein**), **Heinrich Joseph,** German tenor, singing teacher, music theorist, and composer; b. Teilheim, near Würzburg, Feb. 23, 1819; d. Vienna, May 19, 1901. He studied law, and also sang in theaters in Vienna (1847), Halle, and Würzburg; eventually he settled in Vienna as a singing teacher. He composed 2 operas, *Die Bettlerin* (Halle, 1864) and *König Murat* (Würzburg, 1870); also operettas and popular songs. He followed the tenets of the Chroma Society in championing the harmonic system based on the functional equality of the 12 notes of the chromatic scale; publ. the studies *Kein Generalbass mehr* (1860), *Die Einheit in der Tonwelt* (1862), *Die Neuklaviatur* (1874), *Die Zwölfzahl in der Tonwelt* (1885), and *Eine neue Tonschrift* (1900).

Vincent, John, American composer and teacher; b. Birmingham, Ala., May 17, 1902; d. Santa Monica, Calif., Jan. 21, 1977. He studied flute with Georges Laurent at the New England Cons. of Music in Boston (1922–26), and composition there with Converse and Chadwick (1926–27), then took courses at the George Peabody College in Nashville, Tenn. (M.A., 1933) and at Harvard Univ., where his principal teacher was Piston (1933–35); he then went to Paris, where he studied at the École Normale de Musique (1935–37), and took private lessons with Boulanger; received his Ph.D. from Cornell Univ. in 1942. He was in charge of music in the El Paso (Texas) public schools (1927–30), then taught at George Peabody College in Nashville (1930–33), at Western Kentucky Teachers College (1937–46), and at the Univ. of Calif., Los Angeles (1946–69). After his death, the John Vincent Archive was established at UCLA. In his music, he evolved a tonal idiom that he termed "paratonality"; fugal elements are particularly strong in his instrumental compositions. He publ. the books *Music for Sight Reading* (N.Y., 1940); *More Music for Sight Reading* (N.Y., 1941); *The Diatonic Modes in Modern Music* (N.Y., 1951; 2d ed., rev., 1974).

WORKS: DRAMATIC: *3 Jacks*, ballet (1942; rev. 1954; rev. as an orch. suite, 1954; rev. as *The House That Jack Built* for Narrator and Orch., 1957); *The Hallow'd Time*, incidental music (1954); *Primeval Void*, opera (1969).

Vinci, Leonardo, noted Italian composer; b. Strongoli, c.1690; d. Naples, May 27, 1730. He studied at the Cons. dei Poveri di Gesù Cristo in Naples, where he was a pupil of Gaetano Greco. In 1719 he served as maestro di cappella to the Prince of Sansevero; he was provicemaestro at the Royal Chapel in Naples from 1725 until his death; in 1728 he was also maestro di cappella at the Cons. dei Poveri di Gesù Cristo. He was highly esteemed by his contemporaries as a composer for the theater. He produced a number of opera serie, including *Silla dittatore* (Naples, Oct. 19, 1723), *L'Astianatte* (Naples, 1725), *La caduta dei Decemviri* (Naples, Oct. 1, 1727), and *Artaserse* (Rome, Feb. 4, 1730); also many commedie musicali, and an oratorio, *Le glorie del Ss. Rosario*.

BIBL.: G. Silvestri Silva, *Illustri musici calabresi: L. V.* (Genoa, 1935).

Vinco, Ivo, Italian bass; b. Verona, Nov. 8, 1927. He studied at the Verona Liceo Musicale and with Ettore Campogalliani in Milan. After making his operatic debut as Ramfis in Verona in 1954, he sang there regularly in succeeding years; he also appeared in virtually all Italian opera centers. On March 19, 1970, he made his Metropolitan Opera debut in New York as Oroveso, remaining on its roster until 1973, and returning for the 1976–78 seasons. Among his prominent roles were the Grand Inquisitor, Mozart's Dr. Bartolo, Alvise, Ferrando, Donizetti's Raimondo, and Sparafucile. In 1958 he married **Fiorenza Cossotto**.

Viotti, Marcello, Italian conductor; b. Vallorbe, June 29, 1954. He received training at the Lausanne Cons. In 1981 he took 1st prize in the Gino Martinuzzi Competition in San Remo. He was permanent guest conductor of the Teatro Regio in Turin from 1985 to 1987. From 1987 to 1990 he was artistic director of the Lucerne Opera. He was Generalmusikdirektor in Bremen from 1990 to 1993. In 1991 he became chief conductor of the Saarland Radio Sym. Orch. in Saarbrücken and was named to the post of 1st guest conductor of the Vienna State Opera. He concurrently served as 1st guest conductor of the Deutsche Oper in Berlin and permanent guest conductor of the Bavarian State Opera in Munich from 1993. In 1998 he became music director of the Munich Radio Orch.

Visconti (di Modrone), Count Luchino, prominent Italian film, theater, and opera director; b. Milan, Nov. 2, 1906; d. Rome, March 17, 1976. After World War II, he assumed a leading position among film directors, producing films notable for their realism. In 1954 he enlarged the scope of his work to include opera, his first production being Spontini's *Le vestale* at Milan's La Scala with Maria Callas; his first production outside his homeland was *Don Carlos* at London's Covent Garden in 1958; that same year, his *Macbeth* opened the Spoleto Festival, where he maintained a close association in subsequent seasons. His opera productions were impressive, particularly for his ability to complement the dramatic qualities of the music with the action on stage to effect a total theatrical experience.

BIBL.: M. Esteve, ed., *L. V.: L'Histoire et l'esthétique* (Paris, 1963); G. Smith, *L. V.* (London, 1967).

Visetti, Alberto Antonio, Italian singing teacher, conductor, and composer; b. Salona, May 13, 1846; d. London, July 10, 1928. He studied at the Milan Cons., first appearing as a pianist. He then went to Paris, where he was appointed a chamber musician to Empress Eugénie. After the fall of the empire in France, he settled in London, where he taught singing; he also conducted the Bath Phil. Soc. (1878–90). He publ. *History of the Art of Singing and Verdi* (1905). The score of his opera *Les Trois Mousquetaires* was lost during the siege of Paris (1871).

Vishnevskaya, Galina (Pavlovna), prominent Russian soprano; b. Leningrad, Oct. 25, 1926. After vocal studies with Vera Garina in Leningrad, she sang in operetta; in 1952 she joined the operatic staff of the Bolshoi Theater in Moscow; there her roles were Violetta, Tosca, Cio-Cio-San, and an entire repertoire of soprano parts in Russian operas. In 1955 she married **Mstislav Rostropovich**, with whom she frequently appeared in concert. She made her debut at the Metropolitan Opera in New York on Nov. 6, 1961, as Aida. Owing to the recurrent differences that developed between Rostropovich and the cultural authorities of the Soviet Union (Rostropovich had sheltered the dissident writer Solzhenitsyn in his summer house), they left Russia in 1974; they settled in the United States when Rostropovich was appointed music director of the National Sym. Orch. in Washington, D.C., in 1977. In March 1978 both he and Vishnevskaya, as "ideological renegades," were stripped of their Soviet citizenship by a decree of the Soviet government. Her autobiography was publ. as *Galina: A Russian Story* (N.Y., 1984). After Gorbachev's rise to power in her homeland, her Soviet citizenship was restored in 1990.

BIBL.: C. Samuel, *Mstislav Rostropovich and G. V.: Russia, Music, and Liberty: Conversations with Claude Samuel* (Portland, Oreg., 1995).

Visse, Dominique, French countertenor; b. Lisieux, Aug. 30, 1955. He was a chorister at Notre Dame Cathedral in Paris, pursued studies in organ and flute at the Versailles Cons., and received training in voice from Alfred Deller, René Jacobs, and Nigel Rogers (1976–78). He founded the Ensemble Clément Janequin, with which he gave performances of works from the medieval and Renaissance periods. In 1982 he made his operatic debut in Monteverdi's *L'incoronazione di Poppea* in Tourcoing. After singing Flora in Vivaldi's *L'incoronazione di Dario* in Grasse in 1984, he portrayed Charpentier's Actéon at the Edinburgh Festival in 1985. In 1987 he sang Nirenus in Handel's *Giulio Cesare* at the Paris Opéra, and then Delfa in Cavalli's *Giasone* in Innsbruck in 1988. He created the role of Geronimo in Claude Prey's *Le Rouge et Noir* in Aix-en-Provence in 1989. In 1991 he sang Annio in Gluck's *La clemenza di Tito* in Lausanne. He portrayed the role of the Nurse in *L'incoronazione di Poppea* in Buenos Airea in 1996.

Vitali, Filippo, Italian composer; b. Florence, c.1590; d. probably there, after April 1, 1653. In 1631 he became a singer in the Pontifical Choir in Rome; he also was a priest in the service of Cardinal Francesco Barberini and Cardinal Antonio Barberini. In 1642 he returned to Florence as maestro di cappella of the grand ducal chapel of S. Lorenzo; in 1648–49 he was also maestro di cappella at S. Maria Maggiore in Bergamo. His "favola in musica" *L'Aretusa*, performed on Feb. 8, 1620, at the home of Monsignor Corsini, is regarded as the first attempt at opera in Rome (publ. there, 1620). In 1622 he composed 6 intermedi for the comedy *La finta mora* by J. Cicognini, performed at the palace of Cardinal de' Medici in Florence (publ. there, 1623). He was highly esteemed by his contemporaries for his mastery of polyphony, his most significant works being the cycle of 34 hymns set to Latin texts and publ. in the *Brevarium romanum* (1632).

BIBL.: J. Pruett, *The Works of F. V.* (diss., Univ. of North Carolina, 1962).

Vitalis, George, Greek composer and conductor; b. Athens, Jan. 9, 1895; d. there, April 27, 1959. He studied with Armani in Milan. He conducted light opera in Athens (1923–36); he went to the United States in 1945 and settled in New York. He composed the operas *Perseus and Andromeda, The Return of the Gods*, and *Golfo* (concert perf., N.Y., Jan. 1, 1949).

Vitale, Edoardo, Italian conductor; b. Naples, Nov. 29, 1872; d. Rome, Dec. 12, 1937. He studied composition with Terziani at the Accademia di Santa Cecilia in Rome, where he then taught harmony (1893–97). He was only 14 when he began conducting operettas at Rome's Teatro Metastasio. From 1897 he conducted throughout Italy. After conducting at Milan's La Scala (1908–10), he was chief conductor of the Rome Opera (1913–26). He conducted the first Italian performances of *Elektra* (1904) and *Boris Godunov* (1909). He also led many premieres, including Mascagni's *Parisina* and Zandonai's *Francesca da Rimini*, and revived many works. In 1897 he married the soprano Lina Pasini.

Vittadini, Franco, Italian composer; b. Pavia, April 9, 1884; d. there, Nov. 30, 1948. He studied at the Milan Cons. After serving as organist and maestro di cappella in Varese, he returned to Pavia, where he was founder-director of the Istituto Musicale (1924–48).

WORKS: DRAMATIC: OPERAS: *Il mare di Tiberiade* (c.1912–14); *Anima allegra* (1918–19; Rome, April 15, 1921); *Nazareth* (Pavia, May 28, 1925); *La Sagredo* (Milan, April 26, 1930); *Caracciolo* (Rome, Feb. 7, 1938); *Fiammetta e l'avvaro* (1942). PASTORAL TRIPTYCH: *Il natale di Gesù* (Bari, Dec. 20, 1933). BALLETS: *Vecchia Milano* (1928); *Fiordisole* (Milan, Feb. 14, 1935); *La Taglioni* (1945). Also film music.

BIBL.: A. Baratti, *Vita del musicista F. V.* (Milan, 1955).

Vittori, Loreto, prominent Italian castrato soprano and composer; b. Spoleto (baptized), Sept. 5, 1600; d. Rome, April 23, 1670. After serving as a chorister at Spoleto Cathedral (1614–17), he went to Rome to pursue his musical training; about 1618 he proceeded to Florence, where he continued his studies and began his operatic career in 1619. Returning to Rome, he was in the service of Cardinal Lodovico Ludovisi (1621–32); he also sang in the papal choir (1622–47), where he was camerlengo (1642–44); likewise he was in the service of Cardinal Antonio Barberini (1637–42). About 1623 he was created Cavaliere della Milizia di Gesù Cristo by Pope Urban VIII; in 1643 he entered the priesthood. He composed both sacred and secular dramatic works, but the music to most of these is lost; his fine pastoral opera, *La Galatea* (Rome, 1639), is extant. He was also a poet; he publ. *Dialoghi sacri, e morali* (Rome, 1652) and *La Troja rapita* (Macerata, 1662).

BIBL.: C. Rau, *L. V.: Beiträge zur historisch-kritischen Würdigung seines Lebens, Wirkens und Schaffens* (Munich, 1916).

Vivaldi, Antonio (Lucio), greatly renowned Italian composer; b. Venice, March 4, 1678; d. Vienna, July 28, 1741. He was the son of Giovanni Battista Vivaldi (b. Brescia, c.1655; d. Venice, May 14, 1736), a violinist who entered the orch. at San Marco in Venice in 1685 under the surname of Rossi, remaining there until 1729; he was also director of instrumental music at the Mendicanti (1689–93). The younger Vivaldi was trained for the priesthood at S. Geminiano and at S. Giovanni in Oleo, taking the tonsure on Sept. 18, 1693, and Holy Orders on March 23, 1703. Because of his red hair he was called "il prete rosso" (the red priest). In 1703 he became maestro di violino at the Pio Ospedale della Pietà, where he remained until 1709; during this period, his first publ. works appeared. In 1711 he resumed his duties at the Pietà, and was named its maestro de' concerti in 1716. In 1711 his set of 12 concerti known as *L'estro armonico*, op. 3, appeared in print in Amsterdam; it proved to be the most important music publication of the first half of the 18th century. His first known opera, *Ottone in Villa*, was given in Vicenza in May 1713, and soon thereafter he became active as a composer and impresario in Venice. From 1718 to 1720 he was active in Mantua, where the Habsburg governor Prince Philipp of Hessen-Darmstadt made him maestro di cappella da (or di) camera, a title he retained even after leaving Mantua. In subsequent years he traveled widely in Italy, bringing out his operas in various music centers. However, he retained his association with the Pietà. About 1725 he became associated with the contralto Anna Giraud (or Giro), one of his voice students; her sister, Paolina, also became a constant companion of the composer, leading to speculation by his contemporaries that the 2 sisters were his mistresses, a contention he denied. His *La cetra*, op. 9 (2 books, Amsterdam, 1727), was dedicated to the Austrian emperor Charles VI. From 1735 to 1738 he once more served as maestro di cappella at the Pietà. He also was named maestro di cappella to Francis Stephen, duke of Lorraine (later the emperor Francis I), in 1735. In 1738 he visited Amsterdam, where he took charge of the musical performances for the centennial celebration of the Schouwburg theater. Returning to Venice, he found little favor with the theatergoing public; as a result, he set out for Austria in 1740, arriving in Vienna in June 1741, but dying a month later. Although he had received large sums of money in his day, he died in poverty and was given a pauper's burial at the Spettaler Gottesacher (Hospital Burial Ground).

Vivaldi's greatness lies mainly in his superb instrumental works, most notably some 500 concertos, in which he displayed an extraordinary mastery of ritornello form and of orchestration. Only 21 of his operas are extant, some missing 1 or more acts.

WORKS: DRAMATIC: OPERAS: *Ottone in Villa* (Vicenza, May 1713); *Orlando finto pazzo* (Venice, 1714); *Nerone fatto Cesare* (Venice, Carnival 1715); *La costanza trionfante degl'amori e de gl'odii* (Venice, Carnival 1716); *Arsilda Regina di Ponto* (Venice, 1716); *L'incoronazione di Dario* (Venice, Carnival 1717); *Tieteberga* (Venice, 1717); *Scanderbeg* (Florence, June 22, 1718); *Armida al campo d'Egitto* (Venice, Carnival 1718); *Teuzzone* (Mantua, Carnival 1719); *Tito Manlio* (Mantua, Carnival 1719); *La Candace o siano Li veri amici* (Mantua, Carnival 1720); *La verità in cimento* (Venice, 1720); *Tito Manlio*, pasticcio (Rome, 1720; in collaboration with G. Boni and C. Giorgio); *Filippo Re di Macedonia* (Venice, Carnival 1721; in collaboration with G. Boneveni); *La Silvia* (Milan, Aug. 26, 1721); *Ercole su'l Termodonte* (Rome, Jan. 23, 1723); *Giustino* (Rome, Carnival 1724); *La virtù trionfante dell'amore e dell'odio overo Il Tigrane* (Rome, Carnival 1724; in collaboration with B. Micheli and N. Romaldi); *L'inganno trionfante in amore* (Venice, 1725); *Cunegonda* (Venice, Carnival 1726); *La Fede tradita e vendicata* (Venice, Carnival 1726); *Dorilla in Tempe* (Venice, 1726); *Ipermestra* (Florence, Carnival 1727); *Siroe, Re di Persia* (Reggio, May 1727); *Farnace* (Venice, 1727); *Orlando (furioso)* (Venice, 1727); *Rosilena ed Oronta* (Venice, Jan. 17, 1728); *L'Atenaide o sia Gli affetti generosi* (Florence, Dec. 29, 1728); *Argippo* (Prague, 1730); *Alvilda, Regina de' Goti* (Prague, 1731); *La fida ninfa* (Verona, Jan. 6, 1732; rev. as *Il giorno felice*); *Semiramide* (Mantua, Carnival 1732); *Motezuma* (Venice, 1733); *L'Olimpiade* (Venice, Carnival 1734); *Griselda* (Venice, May 1735); *Aristide* (Venice, May 1735); *Bajazet* or *Tamerlano* (Venice, Carnival 1735; based on music by other composers); *Ginevra, Principessa di Scozia* (Florence, Jan. 1736); *Didone* (London, April 1737); *Catone in Utica* (Verona, May 1737); *Il giorno felice* (Vienna, 1737); *Rosmira (fedele)* (Venice, Carnival 1738; based on music by other composers); *L'oracolo in Messenia* (Venice, Carnival 1738); *Feraspe* (Venice, 1739). SERENATAS: *Le gare del dovere* for 5 Voices (Rovigo, 1708); *Dall'eccelsa mia Reggia* (1725); *Questa, Eurilla gentil* for 4 Voices (Mantua, July 31, 1726); *L'unione della Pace e di Marte* for 3 Voices (Venice, 1727); *La Sena festeggiante* for 3 Voices (1726); *Il Mopso* (Venice, c.1738); *Le gare della Giustizia e della Pace; Mio cor povero cor* for 3 Voices. ORATORIOS: *La vittoria navale* (Vicenza, 1713); *Moyses Deus Pharaonis* (Venice, 1714); *Juditha triumphans devicta Hoklofernes barbarie* (Venice, 1716); *L'adorazione delli tre re magi* (Milan, 1722).

BIBL.: COLLECTED EDITIONS, SOURCE MATERIAL: G. F. Malipiero et al., eds., *Le opere di A. V.* (Rome, 1947–72). A new critical ed. commenced publication in Milan in 1982 under the auspices of the Istituto Italiano Antonio Vivaldi. P. Ryom edited *Verzeichnis der Werke A. V.s: Kleine Ausgabe* (Leipzig, 1974; 2d ed., 1979) and *Repertoire des oeuvres d'A. V.* (vol. 1, Copenhagen, 1986). See also M. Rinaldi, *Catalogo numerico tematico delle composizioni di A. V.* (Rome, 1945); M. Pincherle, *Inventaire thematique* (Paris, 1948; vol. 2 of *A. V. et la musique instrumentale*); A. Fanna, *A. V.: Catalogo numerico-tematico delle opere strumentali* (Milan, 1968; rev. ed., 1986); P. Ryom, *A. V.: Table de concordances des oeuvres* (Copenhagen, 1973); idem, *Les Manuscrits de V.* (Copenhagen, 1977); M. Talbot, *A. V.: A Guide to Research* (N.Y., 1988). BIOGRAPHICAL, ANALYTICAL: *A. V.: Note e documenti sulla vita e sulle opere*, Chigiana, I (1939); M. Abbado, *A. V.* (Turin, 1942); M. Rinaldi, *A. V.* (Milan, 1943); W. Kolneder, *Aufführungspraxis bei V.* (Leipzig, 1955; 2d ed., 1973); M. Pincherle, *V.* (Paris, 1955; Eng. tr., 1958); G. Malipiero, *A. V., il prete rosso* (Milan, 1958); L. Rowell, *Four Operas of A. V.* (diss., Univ. of Rochester, 1958); R. Giazotto, *V.* (Milan, 1965); W. Kolneder, *A. V.: Leben und Werk* (Wiesbaden, 1965; Eng. tr., 1970); R. de Candé, *V.* (Paris, 1967); R. Giazotto, *A. V.* (Turin, 1973); W. Kolneder, *Melodietypen bei V.* (Berg am Irchel and Zürich, 1973); F. Degrada and M. Muraro, eds., *A. V. da Venezia all'Europa* (Milan, 1978); M. Talbot, *V.* (London, 1978; 4th ed., 1992); W. Kolneder, *A. V.: Dokumente seines Lebens und Schaffens* (Wilhelmshaven, 1979); E. Cross, *The Late Operas of A. V., 1727–1738* (Ann Arbor, 1980); A. Bellini, B. Brizi, and M. Pensa, *I libretti V.ana: Recensione e collazione dei testimoni a stampa* (Florence, 1982); R.-C. Travers, *La Maladie de V.* (Poitiers, 1982); M. Collins and E. Kirk, eds., *Opera and V.* (Austin, Tex., 1984); K. Heller, *A. V.* (Leipzig, 1991); H. Robbins Landon, *V.: Voice of the Baroque* (London, 1993).

Vives, Amadeo, Spanish composer; b. Collbató, near Barcelona, Nov. 18, 1871; d. Madrid, Dec. 1, 1932. He was a pupil of Ribera and then of Felipe Pedrell in Barcelona. With L. Millet, he founded the famous choral society Orfeó Català (1891). In his first opera, *Artus* (Barcelona, 1895), he made use of Catalonian folk songs. Subsequently he moved to Madrid, where he produced his comic opera *Don Lucas del Cigarral* (Feb. 18, 1899); his opera *Euda d'Uriach*, originally to a Catalan libretto, was brought out in Italian at Barcelona (Oct. 24, 1900). Then followed his most popular opera, *Maruxa* (Madrid, May 28, 1914); other operas are *Balada de Carnaval* (Madrid, July 5, 1919) and *Doña Francisquita* (Madrid, Oct. 17, 1923). The style of his stage productions shared qualities of the French light opera and the Spanish zarzuela; he wrote nearly 100 of these; he also composed songs and piano pieces; publ. a book of essays, *Sofia* (Madrid, 1923).

BIBL.: A. Sagardía, *A. V.: Vida y obra* (Madrid, 1971).

Vivier, Albert-Joseph, Belgian music theorist and composer; b. Huy, Dec. 15, 1816; d. Brussels, Jan. 3, 1903. He studied with Fétis at the Brussels Cons. He wrote an interesting *Traité complet d'harmonie* (1862; many later eds.), in which he explained secondary chords as accidental formations through incorporation of auxiliary notes; he also wrote essays on acoustics. His opera *Spadillo le tavernier* was produced in Brussels on May 22, 1857.

Vivier, Claude, Canadian composer; b. Montreal, April 14, 1948; d. (murdered) Paris, March 7, 1983. He studied with Tremblay (composition) and Heller (piano) at the Montreal Cons. (1967–71). From 1971 he lived in Europe on a Canada Council grant, where he studied with Koenig at the Inst. of Sonology at the Univ. of Utrecht, with Stockhausen and Humpert in Germany, and with Méfano in France. His love for the music of the Orient prompted him to tour that region in 1977, where he spent much time on the island of Bali. In 1981 the Canada Music Council named him its composer of the year. In 1982 he went to Paris on another Council grant, where he was brutally murdered by a chance acquaintance. In 1983 Les Amis de Claude Vivier was organized in Montreal to champion his compositions and writings. Vivier developed a thoroughly individual compositional style in which simplicity became its hallmark. In some of his vocal works, he created texts based on his own invented language. His compositions include *Love Songs*, ballet (1977), *Nanti malam*, ballet (1977), and *Kopernicus*, opera (Montreal, May 8, 1980).

Vix, Geneviève, French soprano; b. Nantes, Dec. 31, 1879; d. Paris, Aug. 25, 1939. She studied at the Paris Cons., receiving the premier prix for opera (1908). She sang at the Paris Opéra, in Madrid, and in Buenos Aires; she made her American debut with the Chicago Opera Co. as Manon in Massenet's opera (Dec. 1, 1917); she married Prince Cyril Naryshkin in New York (Feb. 9, 1918). She possessed a fine lyric voice, and was also adept as an actress.

Vlad, Roman, prominent Romanian-born Italian composer, administrator, teacher, pianist, and writer on music; b. Cernăuti, Dec. 29, 1919. After training at the Cernăuti Cons., he went to Rome and studied engineering at the Univ. and attended Casella's master classes at the Accademia di Santa Cecilia (graduated, 1942). He began his career as a pianist and lecturer. In 1951 he became a naturalized Italian citizen. From 1955 to 1958 he was artistic director of the Accademia Filarmonica in Rome. He was president of the Italian section of the ISCM from 1960 to 1963. In 1964 he was artistic director of the Maggio Musicale Fiorentino in Florence, and returned to that city in that capacity with the Teatro Comunale from 1968 to 1973. He also was prof. of composition at the Turin Cons. from 1968. From 1976 to 1980 he was artistic director of the RAI orch. in Turin. From 1982 to 1984 he was president of the International Confederation of the Soc. of Authors and Composers. In 1987 he became president of the Società Italiana Autori ed Composers. From 1994 to 1996 he was artistic director of Milan's La Scala. He was ed. of the journals *Musica e Dossier* and *Lo Spettatore*, and coed. of the journal *Nuova Rivista Musicale*. His scholarly articles appeared in various Italian and foreign publications. He also publ. several books. In his music, Vlad developed a nondogmatic serial technique that respected the role of tradition in the compositional process. In some of his works, he utilized quarter tones and electronics.

WORKS: DRAMATIC: OPERAS: *Storia di una mamma* (Venice, Oct. 5, 1951); *Il dottore di vetro*, radio opera (RAI, Turin, Feb. 23, 1959); *La fantarca*, television opera (1967); *Il Sogno* (Bergamo, Oct. 3, 1973). BALLETS: *La strada sul caffè* (1942–43); *La dama delle camelie* (Rome, Nov. 20, 1945; rev. 1956); *Masques ostendais* (Spoleto, June 12, 1959; rev. 1960); *Die Wiederkehr* (1962; rev. 1968 as *Ricercare*); *Il Gabbiano* (Siena, Sept. 5, 1968). Also incidental music for plays and film scores.

Vladigerov, Pantcho, prominent Bulgarian composer; b. Zürich, March 13, 1899, in a geminal parturition; d. Sofia, Sept. 8, 1978. Distrustful of Bulgarian puerperal skill, his mother sped from Shumen to Zürich as soon as she learned that she was going to have a plural birth. Pantcho's nonidentical twin brother, Luben, a violinist, was born 16 hours earlier than Pantcho, on the previous day, March 12, 1899. Vladigerov studied piano and theory with local teachers in Sofia (1910–12); he then went to Berlin, where he took lessons in composition with Paul Juon and Georg Schumann, and piano with Leonid Kreutzer at the Akademie der Künste. He then served as conductor and composer of the Max Reinhardt Theater (1921–32); subsequently he was a reader (1932–38) and a prof. of piano and composition (1938–72) at the Bulgarian State Cons. of Music in Sofia. His music was rooted in Bulgarian folk songs, artfully combining the peculiar melodic and rhythmic patterns of native material with stark modern harmonies; the method was similar to that of Bartók. Among his works are *Tsar Kaloyan*, opera (1935–36; Sofia, April 20, 1936), and *Legenda za ezeroto* (Legend of the Lake), ballet (1946; Sofia, Nov. 11, 1962). His son, Alexander Vladigerov (b. Sofia, Aug. 4, 1933), was a conductor and composer.

BIBL.: E. Pavlov, *P. V.* (Sofia, 1961); S. Dimitrov, *Slovoto na P. V.* (Sofia, 1988).

Vlasov, Vladimir (Alexandrovich), Russian conductor, ethnomusicologist, and composer; b. Moscow, Jan. 7, 1903; d. there, Sept. 7, 1986. He studied violin at the Moscow Cons., then was active as a teacher. In 1936 he traveled to Frunze, Kirghizia, where he diligently went about collecting authentic songs of the natives. In collaboration with Vladimir Fere, similarly intentioned, he wrote a number of operas based on Kirghiz national melorhythms supplied by local musicians. These included *Altin kiz* (The Golden Girl; Frunze, May 1, 1937); *Aychurek* (Moon Beauty; Frunze, May 1, 1942); *Za schastye naroda* (For the People's Happiness; Frunze, May 1, 1941); *Sin naroda* (A Son of His People; Frunze, Nov. 8, 1947); *Na beregakh Issikh-kulya* (On the Shores of Lake Issik; Frunze, Feb. 1, 1951); *Vedma* (The Witch; 1961); etc. He also composed 2 operettas and several ballets.

BIBL.: V. Vinogradov, *A. Maldibayev, V. V., Vladimir Fere* (Moscow, 1958).

Vlijmen, Jan van, Dutch composer, music educator, and administrator; b. Rotterdam, Oct. 11, 1935. He received training in piano and organ at the Utrecht Cons., where he later studied composition with Kees van Baaren. From 1961 to 1965 he was director of the Amersfoort Music School, and then was a lecturer in theory at the Utrecht Cons. from 1965 to 1967. In 1967 he became deputy director and in 1971 director of the Royal Cons. of Music at The Hague. From 1985 to 1988 he was general manager of the Netherlands Opera in Amsterdam. In 1991 he was director of the Holland Festival.

WORKS: OPERAS: *Reconstructie* (Amsterdam, June 29, 1969; in collaboration with L. Andriessen, R. de Leeuw, M. Mengelberg, and P. Schat); *Axel* (1975–77; Scheveningen, June 10, 1977; in collaboration with R. de Leeuw); *A Wretch Clad in Black* (Amsterdam, Nov. 16, 1990).

Vogel, Adolf, German bass-baritone; b. Munich, Aug. 18, 1897; d. Vienna, Dec. 20, 1969. He studied voice with Anna Bahr-Mildenburg and J. Kiechle. He made his operatic debut as Daland in Klagenfurt (1923), then sang at the Leipzig Opera (1928–30); he was a member of the Bavarian State Opera in Munich from 1930 to 1937; he made his U.S. debut at the Metropolitan Opera in New York as Alberich (Dec. 3, 1937); he remained on its roster until 1939, then taught voice at the Vienna Academy of Music (from 1940). He became best known for his buffo roles.

Vogel, Charles Louis Adolphe, French violinist and composer, grandson of **Johann Christoph Vogel**; b. Lille, May 17, 1808; d. Paris, Sept. 11, 1892. He studied in Lille and then at the Paris Cons. with A. Kreutzer (violin) and Reicha (theory). After winning popularity with his song "Les Trois Couleurs" during the July Revolution (1830), he brought out a series of successful operas: *Le Podestat* (Paris, Dec. 16, 1831), *Le Siège de Leyde* (The Hague, March 14, 1847), *La Moissonneuse* (Paris, Sept. 3, 1853), *Rompons* (Paris, Sept. 21, 1857), *Le Nid de Cigognes* (Baden-Baden, Sept. 1858), *Gredin de Pigoche* (Paris, Oct. 19, 1866), and *La Filleule du roi* (Brussels, April 1875).

Vogel, Jaroslav, Czech conductor and composer; b. Pilsen, Jan. 11, 1894; d. Prague, Feb. 2, 1970. He studied violin with Ševčik and composition with Novák in Prague; after taking courses in Munich (1910–12) and at the Paris Schola Cantorum with d'Indy (1912–13), he completed his training with Novák at the Prague Cons. (graduated, 1919). He was a conductor at the Pilsen Opera (1914–15) and in Ostrava (1919–23); after conducting in Prague (1923–27), he was chief conductor of the Ostrava Opera (1927–43); he then conducted at the Prague National Theater (1949–58), and was chief conductor of the Brno State Phil. (1959–62). In 1964 he was made an Artist of Merit by the Czech government. As a conductor, he championed the music of Smetana, Janáček, and Nováčk. He publ. (in German) the useful study *Leoš Janáček: Sein Leben und Werk* (Prague, 1958; abr. Eng. tr., 1962; Czech original, 1963). He composed the operas *Maréja* (Olomouc, 1923), *Meister Georg or Mistr Jíra* (Prague, 1926), *Jovana* (Ostrava, 1939), and *Hiawatha* (Ostrava, 1974).

Vogel, Johann Christoph, German composer, grandfather of **Charles Louis Adolphe Vogel**; b. Nuremberg (baptized), March 18, 1756; d. Paris, June 27, 1788. He was a pupil of Riepel at Regensburg, then went to Paris in 1776 and was in the service of the duke of Montmorency; later he was in the service of the count of Valentinois. He wrote 2 operas in Gluck's style: *La Toison d'or* (Paris, Sept. 5, 1786) and *Démophon*, which he completed shortly before his untimely death at the age of 32, and which was produced posthumously (Paris, Sept. 22, 1789). He also composed an oratorio, *Jepthe* (1781).

BIBL.: A. Bickel, *J.C. V.: Der grosse Nürnberger Komponist zwischen Gluck und Mozart (1756–1788)* (Nuremberg, 1956).

Vogl, Adolf, German writer on music and composer; b. Munich, Dec. 18, 1873; d. there, Feb. 2, 1961. He was a pupil of Hermann Levi. After a brief career as a conductor in Trier, Saarbrücken, St. Gallen, and Bern, he returned to Munich and devoted his energies to writing and composing. During the Nazi era, he was imprisoned but resumed his activities after the demise of the Third Reich. Among his insightful books were *Tristan und Isolde: Briefe an eine deutsche Künstlerin* (Munich, 1913; 3d ed., 1922) and *Parsifal: Tiefe Schau in die Mysterien des Bühnenweihfestspiels* (Munich, 1914). He composed the operas *Maja* (1908) and *Die Verdammten* (1934).

Vogl, Heinrich, famous German tenor; b. Au, near Munich, Jan. 15, 1845; d. Munich, April 21, 1900. He studied music with Franz Lachner, making a successful debut as Max in *Der Freischütz* at the Munich Court Opera (Nov. 5, 1865), and remained on its roster until his death. He succeeded Schnorr von Carolsfeld as the model Tristan in Wagner's opera, and was for years considered the greatest interpreter of that role. He created the roles of Loge in *Das Rheingold* (Sept. 22, 1869) and of Siegmund in *Die Walküre* (June 26, 1870); he sang Loge in the first complete *Ring* cycle at the Bayreuth Festival (1876). He also appeared as Siegfried in the first Munich mountings of *Siegfried* and *Götterdämmerung* (1878), Loge and Siegmund in the first Berlin *Ring* cycle (1881), and Loge and Siegfried in the first London *Ring* cycle (1882). In 1882 he toured in Europe with Angelo Neumann's Wagner Co.; in 1886 he sang Tristan and Parsifal in Bayreuth. On Jan. 1, 1890, he made his debut at the Metropolitan Opera in New York as Lohengrin, where he appeared later in the season as Tannhäuser, Loge, both Siegfrieds, and Siegmund. On April 17, 1900, just 4 days before his death, he appeared as Canio in his last role in Munich. He was also a composer, numbering among his works an opera, *Der Fremdling*, in which he sang the leading role (Munich, May 7, 1899). In 1868 he married the German soprano Therese Thoma (b. Tutzing, Nov. 12, 1845; d. Munich, Sept. 29, 1921); she was a member of the Munich Court Opera (1866–92), where she appeared as Isolde opposite her husband's Tristan (1869), Wellgunde in the premiere of *Das Rheingold* (1869), and Sieglinde in the premiere of *Die Walküre* (June 26, 1870); she appeared as Brünnhilde in the first complete *Ring* cycles in Munich (1878) and London (1882); she gave her farewell appearance as Isolde in Munich (Oct. 9, 1892).

BIBL.: H. von der Pfordten, *H. V.: Zur Erinnerung und zum Vermächtnis* (Munich, 1900); R. Wünnenberg, *Das Sangerehepaar H. und T. V.: Ein Beitrag zur Operngeschichte des 19. Jahrhunderts* (Tutzing, 1982).

Vogl, Johann Michael, Austrian baritone and composer; b. Ennsdorf, near Steyr, Aug. 10, 1768; d. Vienna, Nov. 19, 1840. He was orphaned at an early age; his vocal gifts were admired by the parish church choirmaster, who gave him his first music lessons. While studying languages and philosophy at the Kremsmünster Gymnasium, he was befriended by his fellow pupil, Franz Xaver Süssmayr; in 1786 he went to Vienna to study law at the Univ. After briefly practicing law, he joined Sussmayr's German opera company, making his debut at the Hofoper on May 1, 1795; he was chosen to sing the role of Pizarro in the revised version of Beethoven's *Fidelio* in 1814. In 1817 he met Schubert, who became his close friend and whose lieder he subsequently championed; he also created the leading role in Schubert's opera *Die Zwillingsbrüder* (1820).

BIBL.: A. Weiss, *Der Schubertsänger J. M. V.* (Vienna, 1915); A. Liess, *J. M. V.: Hofoperist und Schubertsänger* (Graz and Cologne, 1954).

Vogler, Carl, Swiss organist, conductor, pedagogue, and composer; b. Oberrohrdorf, Feb. 26, 1874; d. Zürich, June 17, 1951. He was a pupil of Breitenbach at the Lucerne Organistenschule (1891–93), of Hegar and Kempter at the Zürich Music School (1893–95), and of Rheinberger at the Munich Cons. (1895–97). From 1897 to 1919 he was an organist and music teacher in Baden in Aargau, and also was founder-director of the Gemischter Chor and the Musikkollegium. He taught counterpoint at the Zürich Cons. from 1915, where he was codirector (1919–39) and director (1939–45). From 1907 to 1932 he was president of the Musikpädagogischer Verband, and also of the Schweizerischer Tonkünstlerverein from 1931 to 1941. In 1924 he founded the Gesellschaft für Aufführungsrechte, serving as its president until his death. He ed. the book *Der Schweizerische Tonkünstlerverein* (Zürich, 1925) and publ. the study *Der Schweizer Musiker und seine Berufsbildung* (Zürich, 1942). His music included *Mutter Sybille*, Singspiel (1906), *Rübezsahl*, Märchenspiel (1917), and *Friedelhänschen*, Märchenspiel (1924).

Vogt, Hans, German composer and pedagogue; b. Danzig, May 14, 1911; d. Metternich, May 19, 1992. He studied with Georg Schumann (master class in composition, 1929–34) at the Prussian Academy of Arts and received training in piano, cello, conducting, and music education at the Akademie für Kirchen- und Schulmusik (1930–34) in Berlin. In 1933 he won the Mendelssohn Prize in Berlin. From 1935 to 1938 he was chief conductor of the Detmold Opera, and then was music director in Stralsund from 1938 to 1944. In 1951 he became a teacher of composition at the Mannheim Hochschule für Musik, where he was a prof. from 1971 to 1978. From 1963 to 1984 he was also chairman of the Gesellschaft für Neue Musik in Mannheim. In 1961 and 1969 he won the Prix Reine Elisabeth of Belgium. He won the Prix Rainer III Prince de Monaco in 1961. He received the Premio Città di Trieste in 1968. In 1978–79 he was in residence at the Villa Massimo in Rome. He was a contributor to *Neue Musik seit 1945* (Stuttgart, 1972; 3d ed., 1982) and author of *Johann Sebastien Bachs Kammermusik* (Stuttgart, 1981). His works include *Die Stadt hinter dem Strom*, oratorio opera (1953), and *Athenerkomödie (The Metropolitans)*, comic opera (1962; rev. 1987). Also *Historie der Verkündigung*, chamber oratorio for 3 Women Soloists, Chorus, and 13 Instruments (1955), and *Historie vom Propheten Jona*, chamber oratorio for Alto, Tenor, Chorus, and 6 Instruments (1979).

Voigt, Deborah, outstanding American soprano; b. Chicago, Aug. 4, 1960. She studied on a vocal scholarship at the Crystal Cathedral in Garden Grove, Calif., attended Calif. State Univ. at Fullerton, and graduated from the San Francisco Opera Merola Program. In 1988 she won the Pavarotti Competition and appeared as a soloist in the Verdi Requiem at N.Y.'s Carnegie Hall. In 1989 she won the Verdi Competition in Bussetto, and in 1990 she took 1st prize in the Tchaikovsky Competition in Moscow. Her engagement as Ariadne at the Boston Lyric Opera in 1991 won her critical accolades, which was followed on Oct. 17 of that year by her Metropolitan Opera debut in New York as Amelia. She returned to the Metropolitan Opera in 1992 and scored a major success as Chrysothemis. That same year, she was honored with the Richard Tucker Award. In 1993 she sang Chrysothemis at the London Promenade Concerts. She made her debut at London's Covent Garden as Amelia and appeared as Senta at the Vienna State Opera in 1995. In 1996 she sang Sieglinde at the Metropolitan Opera, and returned there in 1997 as Ariadne. Her Elsa was portrayed at both the Metropolitan Opera and Covent Garden in 1998, and that same year she won further success as soloist in Strauss's *Vier letzte Lieder* with Masur and the N.Y. Phil. On Dec. 31, 1998, she was a soloist with Masur and the N.Y. Phil. in a New Year's Eve Gala Concert televised live to the nation by PBS. In addition to her compelling interpretations of Wagner and Strauss, Voigt has also won notable distinction for her roles in operas by Rossini, Weber, Berlioz, and Verdi. Her concert appearances have also been acclaimed.

Volbach, Fritz, German choral conductor, music scholar, and composer; b. Wipperfürth, near Cologne, Dec. 17, 1861; d. Wiesbaden, Nov. 30, 1940. He studied at the Cologne Cons. with Hiller, Jensen, and Seiss, and in Berlin with Taubert and Löschhorn; completed his education at the Univ. of Bonn (Ph.D., 1899, with the diss. *Die Praxis der Händel-Aufführung*). In 1892 he was appointed conductor of the Liedertafel and the Damengesangverein in Mainz; after serving as music director at the Univ. of Tübingen (1907–18), he went to Munster as prof. at the Univ. and as conductor of the city orch.; he retired to Wiesbaden in 1930. A versatile musician, he had command of almost every orch. instrument. Among his works was an opera, *Die Kunst zu lieben* (1910).

WRITINGS: *Lehrbuch der Begleitung des gregorianischen Gesangs* (Berlin, 1888); *G. F. Händel* (Berlin, 1898; 2d ed., 1907); *Beethoven: Die Zeit des Klassizismus* (Munich, 1905; 2d ed., 1929); *Die deutsche Musik im 19. Jahrhundert* (Kempten, 1909); *Das moderne Orchester in seiner Entwicklung* (Leipzig, 1910; 2d ed., 1919); *Die Instrumente des Orchesters* (Leipzig, 1913; 2d ed., 1921); *Erläuterwungen zu den Klavier-Sonaten Beethovens* (Cologne, 1919; 3d ed., 1924); *Handbuch der Musikwissenschaften* (2 vols., Münster, 1926, 1930); *Die Kunst der Sprache* (Mainz, 1929); *Der Chormeister* (Mainz, 1931); *Erlebtes und Erstrebtes* (autobiography; Mainz, 1956).

BIBL.: J. Hagemann, *F. V.* (Leipzig, 1909); G. Schwake, *F. V.s*

Werke (Münster, 1921); K. Hortschansky, ed., *F. V., 1861–1940: Komponist, Dirigent und Musikwissenschaftler* (Hagen, 1987).

Völker, Franz, gifted German tenor; b. Neu-Isenburg, March 31, 1899; d. Darmstadt, Dec. 5, 1965. He studied in Frankfurt am Main. He made his operatic debut at the Frankfurt am Main Opera as Florestan in 1926; he continued on its roster until 1935; he also sang at the Vienna State Opera (1931–36; 1939–40; 1949–50), the Berlin State Opera (1933–43), and the Bavarian State Opera in Munich (1936–37; 1945–52); he made guest appearances at Covent Garden in London, and in Salzburg and Bayreuth. After his retirement in 1952, he taught voice in Neu-Isenburg; he was a prof. at the Stuttgart Hochschule für Musik from 1958. Among his finest roles were Parsifal, Lohengrin, Siegmund, Florestan, the Emperor in *Die Frau ohne Schatten*, Otello, and Max in *Der Freischütz*.

Vollerthun, Georg, German composer; b. Fürstenau, Sept. 29, 1876; d. Strausberg, near Berlin, Sept. 15, 1945. He studied with Tappert, Radecke, and Gernsheim. He was a theater conductor in Prague, Berlin, Barmen, and Mainz (1899–1905); he went to Berlin as a music critic and teacher in 1910; from 1922 he lived mostly in Strausberg. His works include the operas *Veeda* (Kassel, 1916), *Island-Saga* (Munich, Jan. 17, 1925), *Der Freikorporal* (Hanover, Nov. 10, 1931), and *Das königliche Opfer* (1942).

BIBL.: E. Krieger, *G. V.* (Berlin, 1942).

Voloshinov, Victor, Russian composer and teacher; b. Kiev, Oct. 17, 1905; d. Leningrad, Oct. 22, 1960. He studied composition with Scherbatchev at the Leningrad Cons.; later he became a prof. there. He wrote the operas *Glory* (1939) and *Stronger Than Death* (1942); also incidental music for the theater.

Vomáčka, Boleslav, Czech composer; b. Mladá Boleslav, June 28, 1887; d. Prague, March 1, 1965. He studied law at the Charles Univ. in Prague (LL.D., 1913); he studied organ (1906–09), composition (with Novák; 1909–10), and singing (with Krummer) at the Prague Cons. He was in the service of the Labor Ministry in Prague (1919–50); he wrote music criticism in several newspapers there; he was ed. of *Listy Hudební Matice* (1922–35). In 1955 he was made an Artist of Merit by the Czech government. He publ. *Josef Suk* (Prague, 1922), *Stanislav Suda* (Prague, 1933), and *Sukova sborová tvorba* (Suk's Choral Works; Prague, 1935). He began to compose early in life, developing a strong national style. Among his works were the operas *Vodník* (The Water Spirit; 1934–37; Prague, Dec. 17, 1937), *Čekanky* (Waiting for a Husband; 1939; 1956–57), and *Boleslav I* (1953–55; Prague, March 8, 1957).

BIBL.: H. Doležil, *B. V.* (Prague, 1941).

Vonk, Hans, prominent Dutch conductor; b. Amsterdam, June 18, 1942. He studied law at the Univ. of Amsterdam; he took courses in piano, conducting, and composition at the Amsterdam Cons., then studied conducting with Scherchen and Ferrara. From 1966 to 1973 he was conductor of the Netherlands National Ballet; he also was assistant conductor of the Concertgebouw Orch. in Amsterdam. In 1974 he made his U.S. debut as a guest conductor with the San Francisco Sym. Orch. He was conductor of the Netherlands Radio Phil. in Hilversum (1973–79); he also was assoc. conductor of the Royal Phil. in London (1976–79). He served as chief conductor of the Netherlands Opera in Amsterdam (1976–85) and of the Residentie Orch. in The Hague (1980–85). He appeared regularly as a guest conductor with the Dresden State Orch. and Opera from 1980; he was permanent conductor (1984–85) and chief conductor (1985–91) of the Dresden State Opera, and also chief conductor of the Dresden State Orch. (1985–91). From 1991 to 1997 he was chief conductor of the Cologne Radio Sym. Orch. In 1996 he became music director of the St. Louis Sym. Orch.

Von Stade, Frederica, remarkable American mezzo-soprano; b. Somerville, N.J., June 1, 1945. She was educated at the Norton Academy in Conn.; after an apprenticeship at the Long Wharf Theater in New Haven, she studied with Sebastian Engelberg, Paul Berl, and Otto Guth at the Mannes College of Music in New York. Although she reached only the semifinals of the Metropolitan Opera Auditions in 1969, she attracted the attention of Rudolf Bing, its general manager, who arranged for her debut with the company in New York as the 3d boy in *Die Zauberflöte* on Jan. 11, 1970; she gradually took on more important roles there before going to Europe, where she gave an arresting portrayal of Cherubino at the opera house at the palace of Versailles in 1973. In 1974 she sang Nina in the premiere of Pasatieri's *The Seagull* at the Houston Grand Opera. In 1975 she made her debut at London's Covent Garden as Rosina; subsequently she attained extraordinary success in lyric mezzo-soprano roles with the world's major opera houses and also pursued an extensive concert career, appearing regularly with the Chamber Music Soc. of Lincoln Center in New York. In 1988 she sang the role of Tina in the premiere of Argento's *The Aspern Papers* at the Dallas Opera, and in 1990 appeared in recital in N.Y.'s Carnegie Hall. She celebrated the 25th anniversary of her Metropolitan Opera debut in 1995 as Debussy's Mélisande, a role she reprised at the San Francisco Opera in 1997. In 1999 she appeared in Sondheim's *A Little Night Music* in Houston. Her memorable roles include Dorabella, Idamante, Adalgisa in *Norma*, Charlotte in *Werther*, Mélisande, Octavian, and Malcolm in *La Donna del lago*. She has also proved successful as a crossover artist, especially in Broadway musical recordings.

Vorlová, Sláva (Miroslava Johnova), Czech composer; b. Náchod, March 15, 1894; d. Prague, Aug. 24, 1973. She studied piano with her mother, then received training in voice at the Vienna Academy of Music; she took private lessons in composition with Novák and in piano with Štěpán in Prague. After passing her state examinations in piano and singing (1918), she continued her piano studies with Maxián and her composition studies with Řídký, completing her training with the latter at the Prague Cons. master classes (graduated, 1948). She became interested in writing music for instruments rarely used for solo performances, and wrote one of the few concertos for bass clarinet (1961). Her music is tinted with impressionistic colors. Other works include the operas *Zlaté ptáče* (The Golden Birds; 1949–50), *Rozmarýnka* (Rosemary; 1952; Kladno, 1955), *Náchodská kasace* (The Náchod Cassation; 1955), and *Dva světy* (2 Worlds; 1958).

Vostřák, Zbyněk, Czech composer and conductor; b. Prague, June 10, 1920; d. Strakonice, Aug. 4, 1985. He studied composition privately with Rudolf Karel (1938–43) and attended the conducting classes of Pavel Dědeček at the Prague Cons. In 1963 he became conductor of the Prague chamber ensemble Musica Viva Pragensis. He also worked in an electronic music studio in Prague. His music evolved from the Central European type of modernism; later he annexed serial techniques, electronic sound, and aleatory practices.

WORKS: DRAMATIC: OPERAS: *Rohovín čtverrohý* (The 4-horned Rohovin; 1947–48; Olomouc, 1949); *Kutnohorští havíři* (The King's Master of the Mint; 1951–53; Prague, 1955); *Pražské nokturno* (A Prague Nocturne; 1957–58; Ustí-on-the-Elbe, 1960); *Rozbitý džbán* (The Broken Jug; 1960–61; Prague, 1963). BALLETS: *The Primrose* (1944–45); *Filosofská historie* (A Story of Students of Philosophy; 1949); *Viktorka* (Little Victoria; 1950); *Sněhurka* (Snow White; 1955); *Veselí vodníci* (Jolly Water Sprites; 1978–79).

Votto, Antonino, Italian conductor; b. Piacenza, Oct. 30, 1896; d. Milan, Sept. 9, 1985. He studied piano with Longo and composition with De Nardis at the Cons. di Musica S. Pietro a Majella in Naples. He made his debut as a concert pianist in Trieste in 1919. From 1919 to 1921 he taught piano at the Cons. di Musica G. Verdi in Trieste. In 1921 he became a conductor at the Teatro Colón in Buenos Aires; in 1923 he made his first appearance at Milan's La Scala conducting *Manon Lescaut*, then was a répétiteur and assistant conductor there under Toscanini until 1929. He subsequently made guest conducting appearances throughout Italy, Europe, and South America. From 1948 to 1970 he was a regular conductor at La Scala, during which period he led performances in major productions with Callas and other famous singers; he also conducted at the Chicago Lyric Opera (1960–61; 1970). He was on the faculty of the Milan Cons. (1941–67).

Vreuls, Victor (Jean Léonard), Belgian composer and music educator; b. Verviers, Feb. 4, 1876; d. Brussels, July 27, 1944. He studied at the Verviers Cons., with Dupuis (harmony) and Radoux (counterpoint) at the Liège Cons., and with d'Indy in Paris. After serving as a prof. of harmony at the Schola Cantorum in Paris (1901–06), he was director of the Luxembourg Cons. (1906–26). In 1925 he was elected a member of the Belgian Royal Academy in Brussels. His major works were written in an expansive Romantic style. Among them were the operas *Olivier le simple* (1909–11; Brussels, March 9, 1922) and *Un Songe d'une nuit d'été*, after Shakespeare (1923–24; Brussels, Dec. 17, 1925), and the ballet *Le Loup-garou* (1935).

Vroons, Frans (Franciscus), Dutch tenor; b. Amsterdam, April 28, 1911; d. 's-Hertogenbosch, June 1, 1983. He studied in Amsterdam and Paris. He made his operatic debut as Pelléas in 1937; in 1945 he became the principal tenor at the Netherlands Opera in Amsterdam, where he sang for 2 decades; he also was its codirector (1956–71). In 1948 he made his first appearance at London's Covent Garden as Don José and in 1951 in San Francisco as Massenet's Des Grieux. He taught voice in Amsterdam (from 1971). His other roles included Florestan, Tamino, Hoffmann, and Peter Grimes.

Vuataz, Roger, distinguished Swiss organist, conductor, broadcasting administrator, and composer; b. Geneva, Jan. 4, 1898; d. Chêne-Bougeries, Aug. 2, 1988. He studied at the Collège Calvin and pursued musical training at the Academy of Music and at the Cons. in Geneva, his principal mentors being Delaye, Mottu, and O. Barblan. He later studied Ondes Martenot in Paris (diploma, 1931) and attended the Institut Jaques-Dalcroze in Geneva (rhythm dipoloma, 1936). Vuataz's career was centered on Geneva, where he served as an organist of the Protestant Reformed church from 1917 to 1978. He was founder-director of the Cathedral Choir (1940–60). From 1944 to 1964 he was head of the music dept. of Radio Geneva. From 1961 to 1971 he taught at the Geneva Cons. He was president of the International Music Competition from 1962 to 1969, and also of the Viñes singing competition in Barcelona from 1963 to 1978. In 1967 he was awarded the music prize of the City of Geneva. In 1975 the Assn. of Swiss Musicians gave him its composer's prize. Vuataz's music was well crafted and displayed the influence of the Protestant Reformed tradition in his sacred scores.

WORKS: DRAMATIC: *Le Rhône*, ballet (1929); *Poème méditerranéen pour un ballet* (1938–50); *Monsieur Jabot*, opera-buffa (1957; Geneva, Nov. 28, 1958); *Solitude*, ballet (1962); *L'Esprit du Mal*, lyric drama (1967); *Cora, Amour et Mort*, lyric tragedy (1978–80); radiophonic pieces; film music.

Vysloužil, Jiří, distinguished Czech musicologist; b. Košice, May 11, 1924. He studied musicology with Jan Racek and Bohumír Štědroň, philosophy with Arnošt Bláha and Mirko Novák, and history with Josef Macůrek at the Univ. of Brno (Ph.D, 1949, with the diss. *Problémy a metody hudebního lidopisu* [Problems and Methods of Music Ethnography]; C.Sc., 1959, with the diss. *Leoš Janáček a lidova píseň* [Leos Janáček and Folk Song]; D.Sc., 1974, with the diss. *Alois Hába*; publ. in Prague, 1974). He worked at the Dept. for Ethnography and Folklore in Brno until 1952; after serving as a lecturer and vice dean at the Brno Academy (1952–61), in 1961 he joined the faculty of the Univ. of Brno, where he became a prof. in 1973. He served as head of the editorial board of the complete critical ed. of the works of Janáček, which commenced publication in Prague in 1978. He publ. *Hudobníci 20. storočia* (Musicians of the 20th Century; Bratislava, 1964; 2d ed., 1981), *Leoš Janáček* (Brno, 1978), and *Leoš Janáček: Für Sie porträtiert von Jiří Vysloužil* (Leipzig, 1981).

Vyvyan, Jennifer (Brigit), English soprano; b. Broadstairs, Kent, March 13, 1925; d. London, April 5, 1974. She studied piano and voice at the Royal Academy of Music in London (1941–43), then voice with Roy Henderson. She made her operatic debut as Jenny Diver in *The Beggar's Opera* with the English Opera Group (1947). After further vocal training with Fernando Carpi in Switzerland (1950), she won 1st prize in the Geneva international competition (1951). She gained success with her portrayal of Constanze at London's Sadler's Wells Opera Co. (1952); she then created the role of Penelope Rich in Britten's *Gloriana* at London's Covent Garden (1953). She made guest appearances at the Glyndebourne Festivals, and in Milan, Rome, Vienna, and Paris. She appeared in many contemporary operas, and was closely associated with those of Britten; she created the Governess in his *Turn of the Screw* (1954), Tytania in *A Midsummer Night's Dream* (1960), and Miss Julian in *Owen Wingrave* (1971).

W

Waart, Edo (Eduard) de, noted Dutch conductor; b. Amsterdam, June 1, 1941. He began piano lessons as a child and at 13 began to study the oboe. He pursued training at the Amsterdam Muzieklyceum as an oboe and cello student (1957–62; he graduated, 1962), and also studied conducting with Dean Dixon in Salzburg (summer 1960). In 1962–63 he was an oboist in the Amsterdam Phil., and then played in the Concertgebouw Orch. in Amsterdam. He also studied conducting with Franco Ferrara in Hilversum, where he made his debut as a conductor with the Netherlands Radio Phil. in 1964. That same year he was a cowinner in the Mitropoulos Competition in New York and then served as an assistant conductor of the N.Y. Phil. (1965–66). In 1966 he became assistant conductor of the Concertgebouw Orch., which he accompanied on its 1967 tour of the United States. He first attracted notice with his Netherlands Wind Ensemble, with which he toured and recorded. In 1967 he became a guest conductor of the Rotterdam Phil. In 1969 he made his British debut as a guest conductor with the Royal Phil. of London in Folkestone. In 1971 he toured the United States with the Rotterdam Phil. and also made his first appearance as an opera conductor in the United States in Santa Fe. In 1974 he was a guest conductor with the San Francisco Sym., and in 1975 he was named its principal guest conductor. He made his debut at London's Covent Garden in 1976 conducting *Ariadne auf Naxos*. In 1977 he became music director of the San Francisco Sym., which he conducted in a gala concert at the opening of its new Louise M. Davies Symphony Hall in 1980. In 1979 he made his first appearance at the Bayreuth Festival. He resigned as music director of the San Francisco Sym. in 1986 and served in that capacity with the Minnesota Orch. in Minneapolis until 1995. From 1988 he also was artistic director of the Dutch Radio Orch. in Hilversum. He likewise served as chief conductor of the Sydney Sym. Orch. from 1993. On Jan. 24, 1998 he made his Metropolitan Opera debut in New York conducting *Die Zauberflöte*. From 1999 he was music director of the Netherlands Opera. De Waart's objective approach to interpretation, combined with his regard for stylistic propriety and avoidance of ostentatious conductorial display, makes his performances of the traditional and contemporary repertoire particularly appealing.

Wachtel, Theodor, famous German tenor; b. Hamburg, March 10, 1823; d. Frankfurt am Main, Nov. 14, 1893. The son of a livery-stable keeper, he carried on the business from the age of 17, after his father's death. When his voice was discovered, he was sent to Hamburg for study, and soon appeared in opera. He made his operatic debut in Hamburg (March 12, 1849); he made his debut at London's Covent Garden as Edgardo (June 7, 1862), and sang at the Berlin Royal Opera (1862–79); he also toured the United States (1871–72; 1875–76). His voice was a powerful and brilliant lyric tenor; the role in which he made himself famous was that of the postillion in Adam's *Le Postillon de Longjumeau*, which he sang more than 1,000 times; he also was successful as Manrico, John of Leyden, and Pollione.

Wade, Joseph Augustine, Irish composer; b. Dublin, 1796; d. London, July 15, 1845. He went to London in 1821, and established himself as a highly successful composer of popular ballads. His song "Meet Me by Moonlight Alone" (1826) enjoyed great vogue, as did his vocal duet "I've Wandered in Dreams." He also wrote the comic operas *The Two Houses of Granada* (London, Oct. 31, 1826) and *The Convent Belles* (London, July 8, 1833; in collaboration with W. Hawes), and an operetta, *The Pupil of da Vinci* (London, Nov. 30, 1839).

Wadsworth, Charles (William), American pianist and harpsichordist; b. Barnesville, Ga., May 21, 1929. He studied piano with Tureck and conducting with Morel at the Juilliard School of Music in N.Y. (B.S., 1951; M.S., 1952); he also studied the French song repertoire with Bernac in Paris and German lieder with Zallinger in Munich. In 1960 Menotti invited him to organize the Chamber Music Concerts at the Festival of Two Worlds in Spoleto, Italy; he was its director and pianist for 20 years. In 1969 he helped to found the Chamber Music Society of Lincoln Center in New York, and was its artistic director until 1989; in 1977 he also created the chamber music series for the Charleston, S.C., Spoleto Festival

U.S.A. In addition to numerous appearances as a pianist and harpsichordist with various ensembles, he also appeared in performances with many noted artists of the day, including Dietrich Fischer-Dieskau, Beverly Sills, Hermann Prey, and Shirley Verrett.

Wadsworth, Stephen, American opera producer, librettist, and translator; b. Mount Kisco, N.Y., April 3, 1953. Afer working as a journalist, he turned to opera production. He served as artistic director of the Skylight Opera in Milwaukee, where he oversaw his first production, *L'incoronazione di Poppea*, in 1982. His subsequent stagings there included *Orfeo* and *Il ritorno d'Ulisse in patria*. He wrote the libretto for Bernstein's *A Quiet Place* (1983), which he staged in Milan and Vienna. He then produced *Alcina* in St. Louis (1987), *Partenope* in Omaha (1988), *Der fliegende Holländer* in Seattle (1989), and *Die Entführung aus dem Serail* in San Francisco (1990). In 1991 he produced *Fidelio* and *La clemenza di Tito* at the Scottish Opera in Glasgow, and in 1992 he staged *Alcina* at London's Covent Garden. In 1996 his staging of *Xerxes* was seen in Boston, Los Angeles, and Santa Fe, and in 1999 his *La clemenza di Tito* was mounted in New York. His translations include operas by Monteverdi and Handel.

Waechter, Eberhard, Austrian baritone and opera administrator; b. Vienna, July 9, 1929; d. there, March 29, 1992. He studied at the Univ. of Vienna, the Vienna Academy of Music (1950–53), and with Elisabeth Rado. In 1953 he made his operatic debut as Silvio at the Vienna Volksoper. From 1954 he was a member of the Vienna State Opera, and in 1963 he was named an Austrian Kammersänger. He made his debut at London's Covent Garden as Count Almaviva and his first appearance at the Salzburg Festival as Arbace in *Idomeneo* in 1956. In 1958 he made his debut at the Bayreuth Festival as Amfortas. He sang for the first time at the Paris Opéra as Wolfram in 1959. In 1960 he sang Count Almaviva at his debuts at Milan's La Scala and Chicago's Lyric Opera. On Jan. 25, 1961, he made his Metropolitan Opera debut in New York as Wolfram. In subsequent years, he continued to appear regularly in Vienna, where he created the role of Joseph in Einem's *Jesu Hochzeit* in 1980. In 1987 he became director of the Vienna Volksoper. From 1991 he was also codirector of the Vienna State Opera.

Waelput, Hendrik, Belgian conductor and composer; b. Ghent, Oct. 26, 1845; d. there, July 8, 1885. He studied at the Brussels Cons., winning the Prix de Rome for his cantata *Het woud* (The Forest; 1867). He was assistant director of the Bruges music school (1869–71); he conducted theater orchs. at The Hague, Dijon, Douai, Fécamp, and Lille (1872–76). From 1876 to 1879 he was conductor of the Ghent Theater; in 1879 he was appointed prof. of harmony at the Antwerp Cons.; he became director of the Ghent Opera in 1884. He wrote 3 operas: *La Ferme du diable* (Ghent, 1865), *Berken de diamantslijper* (1868), and *Stella* (Brussels, March 14, 1881).

BIBL.: E. Callaert, *Levensschets van H. W.* (Ghent, 1886); E. De Vynck, *Henry W.* (diss., Univ. of Brussels, 1935).

Wagenaar, Bernard, Dutch-born American composer and teacher, son of **Johan Wagenaar**; b. Arnhem, July 18, 1894; d. York, Maine, May 19, 1971. He was a student of Gerard Veerman (violin), Lucie Veerman-Becker (piano), and his father (composition) in Utrecht. After conducting and teaching in the Netherlands (1914–20), he settled in the United States and became a naturalized American citizen in 1927. He was a violinist in the N.Y. Phil. (1921–23). From 1925 to 1946 he taught fugue, orchestration, and composition at the Inst. of Musical Art in New York and then at its successor, the Juilliard School of Music, from 1946 to 1968. He was made an Officer of the Order of Oranje-Nassau of the Netherlands. His output followed along neoclassical lines, and included the chamber opera *Pieces of Eight* (1943; N.Y., May 9, 1944).

Wagenaar, Johan, distinguished Dutch organist, choral conductor, pedagogue, and composer, father of **Bernard Wagenaar**; b. Utrecht, Nov. 1, 1862; d. The Hague, June 17, 1941. He studied with Richard Hol in Utrecht (1875–85) and with H. von Herzogenberg in Berlin (1889). From 1887 to 1904 he was director of the Utrecht Music School; also was organist at the Cathedral (1887–1919). From 1919 to 1936 he was director of the Royal Cons. in The Hague. Among his works were the operas *De Doge van Venetie* (1901; Utrecht, 1904), *De Cid* (1915; Utrecht, 1916), and *Jupiter Amans*, burlesque opera (Scheveningen, 1925).

Wagenseil, Georg Christoph, Austrian composer and music theorist; b. Vienna, Jan. 29, 1715; d. there, March 1, 1777. He studied with J .J. Fux, and served as the music teacher of the empress Maria Theresa and her children. In 1739 he was appointed court composer; he remained in the Imperial service until his death. He wrote many operas in Italian (all 1st perf. in Vienna): *La generosità trionfante* (1745); *Ariodante* (May 14, 1746); *La clemenza di Tito* (Oct. 15, 1746); *Alexander der Grosse in Indien* (July 7, 1748); *Il Siroe* (Oct. 4, 1748); *L'Olimpiade* (May 13, 1749); *Andromeda* (March 30, 1750); *Antigone* (May 13, 1750); *Armida placato* (Aug. 28, 1750); *Euridice* (July 26, 1750); *Le Cacciatrici amanti* (Laxenburg, June 1755); *Demetrio* (1760); also 3 oratorios.

Waghalter, Ignatz, German conductor and composer; b. Warsaw, March 15, 1882; d. N.Y., April 7, 1949. He studied in Berlin, where he later was conductor of the Komische Oper (1907–11), then conducted in Essen (1911–12), and at the Deutsches Opernhaus in Berlin-Charlottenburg. In 1925 he succeeded Stransky as conductor of the State Sym. Orch. in New York (for one season only); he then returned to Berlin; in 1933 he went to Prague, and in 1934 to Vienna. He settled in New York in 1938.

WORKS: DRAMATIC: OPERAS: *Der Teufelsweg* (Berlin, 1911); *Mandragola* (Berlin, Jan. 23, 1914); *Jugend* (Berlin, 1917); *Der späte Gast* (Berlin, 1922); *Sataniel* (Berlin, 1923). : OPERETTAS*Der Weiberkrieg*; *Wem gehört Helena?*.

BIBL.: H. Leichtentritt, *I. W.* (N.Y., 1924).

Wagner, Cosima, wife of **Richard Wagner**, daughter of **Franz Liszt** and the Countess Marie d'Agoult; b. Bellagio, on Lake Como, Dec. 24, 1837; d. Bayreuth, April 1, 1930. She received an excellent education in Paris, and married **Hans von Bülow** on Aug. 18, 1857. There were 2 daughters of this marriage, Blandine and Daniela; the 3d daughter, Isolde, was Richard Wagner's child, as was the 4th, Eva, and the son, Siegfried. A divorce followed on July 18, 1870; the marriage to Wagner took place in a few weeks, on Aug. 25, 1870. A woman of high intelligence, practical sense, and imperious character, Cosima Wagner emerged after Wagner's death as a powerful personage in all affairs regarding the continuance of the Bayreuth Festivals, as well as the complex matters pertaining to the rights of performance of Wagner's works all over the world. She publ. her reminiscences of Liszt: *Franz Liszt, Ein Gedenkblatt von seiner Tochter* (Munich, 2d ed., 1911). Her diaries were ed. by M. Gregor-Dellin and D. Mack as *Cosima Wagner: Die Tagebücher, 1869–1877* (2 vols., Munich, 1976–77; Eng. tr. by G. Skelton as *Cosima Wagner's Diaries*, 2 vols., N.Y., 1977 and 1980).

BIBL.: M. Strauss, *Wie ich Frau C. W. sehe* (Magdeburg, 1912); W. Siegfried, *Frau C. W.* (Stuttgart, 1930); M. von Waldberg, *C. W.s Briefe an ihre Tochter Daniela von Bülow, 1866–85* (Stuttgart, 1933); P. Pretzsch, *C. W. und H. S. Chamberlain im Briefwechsel, 1888–1908* (Leipzig, 1934); L. Scalero, *C. W.* (Zürich, 1934); M. von Millenkovich (M. Morold), *C. W.: Ein Lebensbild* (Leipzig, 1937); E. Thierbach, ed., *Die Briefe C. W.s an Friedrich Nietzsche* (Weimar, 1938–40); A. Sojoloff, *C. W., Extraordinary Daughter of Franz Liszt* (N.Y., 1969); D. Mack, ed., *C. W.: Das zweite Leben: Briefe und Aufzeichnungen, 1883–1930* (Munich, 1980); G. Marek, *C. W.* (N.Y., 1981); G. Skelton, *Richard and C. Wagner: Biography of a Marriage* (London, 1982).

Wagner, Johanna, German soprano; b. Lohnde, near Hannover, Oct. 13, 1826; d. Würzburg, Oct. 16, 1894. She was a natural daughter of Lieutenant Bock von Wülfingen of Hanover, and was adopted by Richard Wagner's brother, Albert; was thus regarded as Wagner's niece. Of a precocious talent, she acted on the stage as a small child; through Wagner she obtained a position at the Dresden Opera when she was 17, producing an excellent impression as Agathe in *Der Freischütz*, and was engaged as a regular member. She studied the part of Elisabeth in *Tannhäuser* with Wagner, and sang it in the premiere of the opera on Oct. 19, 1845, when she was barely 19 years old. In 1846 she went to Paris for further study with Pauline Viardot-García (1846–48), then was engaged at the Hamburg Opera (1849) and finally at the Court Opera in Berlin (1850–61). In 1856 she made her London debut at Her Majesty's Theatre. In 1859 she married the district judge Alfred Jachmann. After 1862 she acted mainly on the dramatic stage, reappearing in opera at the Bayreuth Festival in 1876 in the parts of Schwertleite and the 1st Norn in the first complete mounting of the *Ring* cycle. She taught at the Royal Music School in Munich (1882–84), then privately.

BIBL.: J. Kapp and H. Jachmann, *Richard Wagner und seine erste "Elisabeth," J. J.-W.* (Berlin, 1927; Eng. tr. as *Wagner and His First Elisabeth*, London, 1944).

Wagner, Joseph (Frederick), American conductor, composer, and teacher; b. Springfield, Mass., Jan. 9, 1900; d. Los Angeles, Oct. 12, 1974. He was a student of Converse (composition) at the New England Cons. of Music in Boston (diploma, 1923). After further training from Casella in Boston (1927), he studied at Boston Univ. (B.M., 1932). In 1934–35 he completed his studies with Boulanger (composition) and Monteux (conducting) in Paris, and with Weingartner (conducting) in Basel. From 1923 to 1944 he was assistant director of music in the Boston public schools. He also was founder-conductor of the Boston Civic Sym. Orch. (1925–44) and a teacher at Boston Univ. (1929–40). He taught at Brooklyn College (1945–47) and at Hunter College (1945–56) in New York, and was conductor of the Duluth Sym. Orch. (1947–50) and the Orquesta Sinfónica Nacional de Costa Rica in San José (1950–54). In 1961 he became a prof. at Pepperdine College in Los Angeles. He publ. the useful books *Orchestration: A Practical Handbook* (N.Y., 1958) and *Band Scoring* (N.Y., 1960). His music was distinguished by excellent craftsmanship, and was set in a fairly advanced idiom, with bitonality as a frequent recourse in his later works. Among his works were the opera *New England Sampler* (1964; Los Angeles, Feb. 26, 1965) and the ballets *The Birthday of the Infanta* (1935), *Dance Divertissement* (1937), and *Hudson River Legend* (1941; Boston, March 1, 1944).

BIBL.: L. Bowling, ed., *J. W.: A Retrospective of a Composer-Conductor* (Lomita, Calif., 1976).

Wagner, Karl Jakob, German oboist, conductor, and composer; b. Darmstadt, Feb. 22, 1772; d. there, Nov. 24, 1822. He was apprenticed to the Darmstadt Hofkapelle when he was 16, becoming a member of its orch. as violinist and horn player at 18; he studied theory with Abbé Vogler. In 1800 he was named master of military music; after touring as a concert artist, he was active in Paris (1805–11), then returned to Darmstadt as Hofkapellmeister (1811–20). He wrote 4 operas for Darmstadt: *Der Zahnarzt* (1803), *Pygmalion* (1809), *Siuph und Nitetis* (1811), and *Chimene* (1821); also incidental music to plays.

Wagner, (Wilhelm) Richard, great German composer whose operas, written to his own librettos, have radically transformed the concept of stage music, postulating the inherent equality of drama and symphonic accompaniment, and establishing the uninterrupted continuity of the action; b. Leipzig, May 22, 1813; d. Venice, Feb. 13, 1883. The antecedents of his family, and his own origin, are open to controversy. His father was a police registrar in Leipzig who died when Wagner was only 6 months old; his mother, Johanna (Rosine), née Pätz, was the daughter of a baker in Weissenfels; it is possible also that she was an illegitimate offspring of Prince Friedrich Ferdinand Constantin of Weimar. Eight months after her husband's death, Johanna Wagner married, on Aug. 28, 1814, the actor Ludwig Geyer. This hasty marriage generated speculation that Geyer may have been Wagner's real father; Wagner himself entertained this possibility, pointing out the similarity of his and Geyer's prominent noses; in the end he abandoned this surmise. The problem of Wagner's origin arose with renewed force after the triumph of the Nazi party in Germany, as Hitler's adoration of Wagner was put in jeopardy by suspicions that Geyer might have been Jewish and that if Wagner was indeed his natural son then he himself was tainted by Semitic blood. The phantom of Wagner's possible contamination with Jewish hemoglobin struck horror into the hearts of good Nazi biologists and archivists; they delved anxiously into Geyer's own ancestry, and much to the relief of Goebbels and other Nazi intellectuals, it was found that Geyer, like Wagner's nominal father, was the purest of Aryans; Wagner's possible illegitimate birth was of no concern to the racial tenets of the Nazi Weltanschauung.

Geyer was a member of the Court Theater in Dresden, and the family moved there in 1814. Geyer died on Sept. 30, 1821; in 1822 Wagner entered the Dresden Kreuzschule, where he remained a pupil until 1827. Carl Maria von Weber often visited the Geyer home; these visits exercised a beneficial influence on him in his formative years. In 1825 he began to take piano lessons from a local musician named Humann, and also studied violin with Robert Sipp. Wagner showed strong literary inclinations, and under the spell of Shakespeare, wrote a tragedy, *Leubald*. In 1827 he moved with his mother back to Leipzig, where his uncle Adolf Wagner gave him guidance in his classical reading. In 1828 he was enrolled in the Nikolaischule; while in school, he had lessons in harmony with Christian Gottlieb Müller, a violinist in the theater orch. In June 1830 he entered the Thomasschule, where he began to compose; he wrote a string quartet and some piano music; his *Overture* in B-flat major was performed at the Leipzig Theater on Dec. 24, 1830, under the direction of the famous musician Heinrich Dorn. Now determined to dedicate himself entirely to music, he became a student of Theodor Weinlig, cantor of the Thomaskirche, from whom he received a thorough training in counterpoint and composition. His first publ. work was a piano sonata in B-flat major, to which he assigned the opus number 1; it was brought out by the prestigious publishing house of Breitkopf & Härtel in 1832. He then wrote an overture to *König Enzio*, which was performed at the Leipzig Theater on Feb. 17, 1832; it was followed by an overture in C major, which was presented at a Gewandhaus concert on April 30, 1832. Wagner's first major orch. work, a sym. in C major, was performed at a Prague Cons. concert in Nov. 1832; on Jan. 10, 1833, it was played by the Gewandhaus Orch. in Leipzig; he was 19 years old at the time. In 1832 he wrote an opera, *Die Hochzeit*, after J. G. Busching's *Ritterzeit und Ritterwesen*; an introduction, a septet, and a chorus from this work are extant. Early in 1833 he began work on *Die Feen*, to a libretto after Carlo Gozzi's *La Donna serpente*. Upon completion of *Die Feen* in Jan. 1834, he offered the score to the Leipzig Theater, but it was rejected. In June 1834 he began to sketch out a new opera, *Das Liebesverbot*, after Shakespeare's play *Measure for Measure*. In July 1834 he obtained the position of music director with Heinrich Bethmann's theater company, based in Magdeburg; he made his debut in Bad Lauschstadt, conducting Mozart's *Don Giovanni*. On March 29, 1836, he led in Magdeburg the premiere of his opera *Das Liebesverbot*, presented under the title *Die Novize von Palermo*. Bethmann's company soon went out of business; Wagner, who was by that time deeply involved with Christine Wilhelmine ("Minna") Planer, an actress with the company, followed her to Königsberg, where they were married on Nov. 24, 1836. In Königsberg he composed the overture *Rule Britannia*; on April 1, 1837, he was appointed music director of the Königsberg town theater. His marital affairs suffered a setback when Minna left him for a rich businessman by the name of Dietrich. In Aug. 1837 he went to Riga as music director of the theater there; coincidentally, Minna's sister was engaged as a singer at the same theater; Minna soon joined her, and became reconciled with Wagner. In Riga Wagner worked on his new opera, *Rienzi, der letzte der Tribunen*, after a popular novel by Bulwer-Lytton.

In March 1839 he lost his position in Riga, and he and Minna, burdened by debts, left town to seek their fortune elsewhere. In their passage by sea from Pillau they encountered a fierce storm, and the ship was forced to drop anchor in the Norwegian fjord of Sandwike. They made their way to London, and then set out for Boulogne; there Wagner met Meyerbeer, who gave him a letter of recommendation to the director of the Paris Opéra. He arrived in Paris with Minna in Sept. 1839, and remained there until 1842.

He was forced to eke out a meager subsistence by making piano arrangements of operas and writing occasional articles for the *Gazette Musicale*. In Jan. 1840 he completed his *Overture to Faust* (later rev. as *Eine Faust-Ouvertüre*). Soon he found himself in dire financial straits; he owed money that he could not repay, and on Oct. 28, 1840, he was confined in debtors' prison; he was released on Nov. 17, 1840. The conditions of his containment were light, and he was able to leave prison on certain days. In the meantime he had completed the libretto for *Der fliegende Holländer*; he submitted it to the director of the Paris Opéra, but the director had already asked Paul Foucher to prepare a libretto on the same subject. The director was willing, however, to buy Wagner's scenario for 500 French francs. Wagner accepted the offer (July 2, 1841). Louis Dietsch brought out his treatment of the subject in his opera *Le Vaisseau fantôme* (Paris Opéra, Nov. 9, 1842).

In 1842 Wagner received the welcome news from Dresden that his opera *Rienzi* had been accepted for production; it was staged there on Oct. 20, 1842, with considerable success. *Der fliegende Holländer* was also accepted by Dresden, and Wagner conducted its first performance there on Jan. 2, 1843. On Feb. 2 of that year, he was named 2d Hofkapellmeister in Dresden, where he conducted a large repertoire of Classical operas, among them *Don Giovanni, Le nozze di Figaro, Die Zauberflöte, Fidelio*, and *Der Freischütz*. In 1846 he conducted a memorable performance in Dresden of Beethoven's 9th Sym. In Dresden he led the prestigious choral society Liedertafel, for which he wrote several works, including the "biblical scene" *Das Liebesmahl der Apostel*. He was also preoccupied during those years in working on the score and music for *Tannhäuser*, completing it on April 13, 1845. He conducted its first performance in Dresden on Oct. 19, 1845. He subsequently revised the score, which was staged to better advantage there on Aug. 1, 1847. Concurrently, he began work on *Lohengrin*, which he completed on April 28, 1848. Wagner's efforts to have his works publ. failed, leaving him again in debt. Without waiting for further performances of his operas that had already been presented to the public, he drew up the first prose outline of *Der Nibelungen-Mythus als Entwurf zu einem Drama*, the prototype of the epic *Ring* cycle; in Nov. 1848 he began work on the poem for *Siegfrieds Tod*. At that time he joined the revolutionary Vaterlandsverein, and was drawn into active participation in the movement, culminating in an open uprising in May 1849. An order was issued for his arrest, and he had to leave Dresden; he made his way to Weimar, where he found a cordial reception from Liszt; he then proceeded to Vienna, where a Prof. Widmann lent him his own passport so that Wagner could cross the border of Saxony on his way to Zürich; there he made his home in July 1849; Minna joined him there a few months later. Shortly before leaving Dresden he had sketched 2 dramas, *Jesus von Nazareth* and *Achilleus*; both remained unfinished. In Zürich he wrote a number of essays expounding his philosophy of art: *Die Kunst und die Revolution* (1849), *Das Kunstwerk der Zukunft* (1849), *Kunst und Klima* (1850), *Oper und Drama* (1851; rev. 1868), and *Eine Mitteilung an meine Freunde* (1851). The ideas expressed in *Das Kunstwerk der Zukunft* gave rise to the description of Wagner's operas as "music of the future" by his opponents; they were also described as Gesamtkunstwerk, "total artwork," by his admirers. He rejected both descriptions as distortions of his real views. He was equally opposed to the term "music drama," which nevertheless became an accepted definition for all of his operas.

In Feb. 1850 Wagner was again in Paris; there he fell in love with Jessie Laussot, the wife of a wine merchant; however, she eventually left Wagner, and he returned to Minna in Zürich. On Aug. 28, 1850, Liszt conducted the successful premiere of *Lohengrin* in Weimar. In 1851 he wrote the verse text of *Der junge Siegfried*, and prose sketches for *Das Rheingold* and *Die Walküre*. In June 1852 he finished the text of *Die Walküre* and of *Das Rheingold*; he completed the entire libretto of *Der Ring des Nibelungen* on Dec. 15, 1852, and it was privately printed in 1853. In Nov. 1853 he began composition of the music for *Das Rheingold*, completing the full score on Sept. 26, 1854. In June 1854 he commenced work on the music of *Die Walküre*, which he finished on March 20, 1856. In 1854 he became friendly with a wealthy Zürich merchant, Otto Wesendonck, and his wife, Mathilde. Wesendonck was willing to give Wagner a substantial loan, to be repaid out of his performance rights. The situation became complicated when Wagner developed an affection for Mathilde, which in all probability remained platonic. But he set to music 5 lyric poems written by Mathilde herself; the album was publ. as the *Wesendonk-Lieder* in 1857. In 1855 he conducted a series of 8 concerts with the Phil. Soc. of London (March 12-June 25). His performances were greatly praised by English musicians, and he had the honor of meeting Queen Victoria, who invited him to her loge at the intermission of his 7th concert. In June 1856 he made substantial revisions in the last dramas of *Der Ring des Nibelungen*, changing their titles to *Siegfried* and *Götterdämmerung*. Throughout these years he was preoccupied with writing a new opera, *Tristan und Isolde*, permeated with the dual feelings of love and death. In April 1857 he prepared the first sketch of *Parzival* (later titled *Parsifal*). In 1858 he moved to Venice, where he completed the full score of the 2d act of *Tristan und Isolde*. The Dresden authorities, acting through their Austrian confederates and still determined to bring Wagner to trial as a revolutionary, pressured Venice to expel him from its territory. Once more Wagner took refuge in Switzerland; he decided to stay in Lucerne; while there he completed the score of *Tristan und Isolde*, on Aug. 6, 1859.

In Sept. 1859 he moved to Paris, where Minna joined him. In 1860 he conducted 3 concerts of his music at the Théâtre-Italien. Napoleon III became interested in his work, and in March 1860 ordered the director of the Paris Opera to produce Wagner's opera *Tannhäuser*; after considerable work, revisions, and a tr. into French, it was given at the Opéra on March 13, 1861. It proved to be a fiasco, and Wagner withdrew the opera after 3 performances. For some reason the Jockey Club of Paris led a vehement protest against him; the critics also joined in this opposition, mainly because the French audiences were not accustomed to the mystically romantic, heavily Germanic operatic music. Invectives hurled against him by the Paris press make extraordinary reading; the comparison of Wagner's music with the sound produced by a domestic cat walking down the keyboard of the piano was one of the favorite critical devices. The French caricaturists exercised their wit by picturing him in the act of hammering a poor listener's ear. A Wagner "Schimpflexikon" was compiled by Wilhelm Tappert and publ. in 1877 in the hope of putting Wagner's detractors to shame, but they would not be pacified; the amount of black bile poured on him even after he had attained the stature of celebrity is incredible for its grossness and vulgarity. Hanslick used his great literary gift and a flair for a striking simile to damn him as a purveyor of cacophony. Oscar Wilde added his measure of wit. "I like Wagner's music better than anybody's," he remarked in *The Picture of Dorian Gray*. "It is so loud that one can talk the whole time without people hearing what one says." In an amazing turnabout, Nietzsche, a worshipful admirer of Wagner, publ. a venomous denunciation of his erstwhile idol in *Der Fall Wagner*, in which he vesuviated in a sulfuric eruption of righteous wrath; Wagner made music itself sick, he proclaimed; but at the time Nietzsche himself was already on the borderline of madness.

Politically, Wagner's prospects began to improve; on July 22, 1860, he was informed of a partial amnesty by the Saxon authorities. In Aug. 1860 he visited Baden-Baden, in his first visit to Germany in 11 years. Finally, on March 18, 1862, he was granted a total amnesty, which allowed him access to Saxony. In Nov. 1861 Wesendonck had invited Wagner to Venice; free from political persecution, he could now go there without fear. While in Venice he returned to a scenario he had prepared in Marienbad in 1845 for a comic opera, *Die Meistersinger von Nürnberg*. In Feb. 1862 he moved to Biebrich, where he began composing the score for *Die Meistersinger*. Minna, after a brief period of reconciliation with Wagner, left him, settling in Dresden, where she died in 1866. In order to repair his financial situation, he accepted a number of concert appearances, traveling as an orch. conductor to Vienna, Prague, St. Petersburg, Moscow, and other cities

(1862–63). In 1862 he gave in Vienna a private reading of *Die Meistersinger*. It is said that the formidable Vienna critic Hanslick was angered when he found out that Wagner had caricatured him in the part of Beckmesser in *Die Meistersinger* (the original name of the character was Hans Lick), and he let out his discomfiture in further attacks on Wagner.

Wagner's fortunes changed spectacularly in 1864 when young King Ludwig II of Bavaria ascended the throne and invited him to Munich with the promise of unlimited help in carrying out his various projects. In return, Wagner composed the *Huldigungsmarsch*, which he dedicated to his royal patron. The publ. correspondence between Wagner and the king is extraordinary in its display of mutual admiration, gratitude, and affection; still, difficulties soon developed when the Bavarian cabinet told Ludwig that his lavish support of Wagner's projects threatened the Bavarian economy. Ludwig was forced to advise him to leave Munich. Wagner took this advice as an order, and late in 1865 he went to Switzerland. A very serious difficulty arose also in Wagner's emotional life, when he became intimately involved with Liszt's daughter Cosima, wife of Hans von Bülow, the famous conductor and an impassioned proponent of Wagner's music. On April 10, 1865, Cosima Bülow gave birth to Wagner's daughter, whom he named Isolde after the heroine of his opera that Bülow was preparing for performance in Munich. Its premiere took place with great acclaim on June 10, 1865, 2 months after the birth of Isolde, with Bülow conducting. During the summer of 1865 he prepared the prose sketch of *Parzival*, and began to dictate his autobiography, *Mein Leben*, to Cosima. In Jan. 1866 he resumed the composition of *Die Meistersinger*; he settled in a villa in Tribschen, on Lake Lucerne, where Cosima joined him permanently in Nov. 1868. He completed the full score of *Die Meistersinger* on Oct. 24, 1867. On June 21, 1868, Bülow conducted its premiere in Munich in the presence of King Ludwig, who sat in the royal box with Wagner. A son, significantly named Siegfried, was born to Cosima and Wagner on June 6, 1869. On Sept. 22, 1869, *Das Rheingold* was produced in Munich. On June 26, 1870, *Die Walküre* was staged there. On July 18, 1870, Cosima and Bülow were divorced, and on Aug. 25, 1870, Wagner and Cosima were married in Lucerne. In Dec. 1870 Wagner wrote the *Siegfried Idyll*, based on the themes from his opera; it was performed in their villa in Bayreuth on Christmas morning, the day after Cosima's birthday, as a surprise for her. In 1871 he wrote the *Kaisermarsch* to mark the victorious conclusion of the Franco-German War; he conducted it in the presence of Kaiser Wilhelm I at a concert in the Royal Opera House in Berlin on May 5, 1871.

On May 12 of that year, while in Leipzig, Wagner made public his plans for realizing his cherished dream of building his own theater in Bayreuth for the production of the entire cycle of *Der Ring des Nibelungen*. In Dec. 1871 the Bayreuth town council offered him a site for a proposed Festspielhaus; on May 22, 1872, the cornerstone was laid; Wagner commemorated the event by conducting a performance of Beethoven's 9th Sym. (this was his 59th birthday). In 1873 Wagner began to build his own home in Bayreuth, which he called "Wahnfried," i.e., "Free from Delusion." In order to complete the building of the Festspielhaus, he appealed to King Ludwig for additional funds. Ludwig gave him 100,000 talers for this purpose. Now the dream of Wagner's life was realized. Between June and Aug. 1876 *Der Ring des Nibelungen* went through 3 rehearsals; King Ludwig attended the final dress rehearsals; the official premiere of the cycle took place on Aug. 13, 14, 16, and 17, 1876, under the direction of Hans Richter. Kaiser Wilhelm I made a special journey from Berlin to attend the performances of *Das Rheingold* and *Die Walküre*. In all, 3 complete productions of the *Ring* cycle were given between Aug. 13 and Aug. 30, 1876. Ludwig was faithful to the end to Wagner, whom he called "my divine friend." In his castle Neuschwanstein he installed architectural representations of scenes from Wagner's operas. Soon Ludwig's mental deterioration became obvious to everyone, and he was committed to an asylum. There, on June 13, 1883, he overpowered the psychiatrist escorting him on a walk and dragged him to his death in the Starnberg Lake, drowning himself as well. Ludwig survived Wagner by 4 months.

The spectacles in Bayreuth attracted music lovers and notables from all over the world. Even those who were not partial to Wagner's ideas or appreciative of his music went to Bayreuth out of curiosity. Tchaikovsky was one such skeptical visitor. Despite world success and fame, Wagner still labored under financial difficulties. He even addressed a letter to an American dentist practicing in Dresden (who also treated Wagner's teeth) in which he tried to interest him in arranging Wagner's permanent transfer to the United States. He voiced disillusionment in his future prospects in Germany, and said he would be willing to settle in America provided a sum of $1 million would be guaranteed to him by American bankers, and a comfortable estate for him and his family could be found in a climatically clement part of the country. Nothing came of this particular proposal. He did establish an American connection when he wrote, for a fee of $5,000, a Grosser Festmarsch for the observance of the U.S. centennial in 1876, dedicated to the "beautiful young ladies of America." In the middle of all this, Wagner became infatuated with Judith Gautier; their affair lasted for about 2 years (1876–78). He completed the full score of *Parsifal* (as it was now called) on Jan. 13, 1882, in Palermo. It was performed for the first time at the Bayreuth Festival on July 26, 1882, followed by 15 subsequent performances. At the final performance, on Aug. 29, 1882, Wagner stepped to the podium in the last act and conducted the work to its close; this was his last appearance as a conductor. He went to Venice in Sept. 1882 for a period of rest (he had angina pectoris). Early in the afternoon of Feb. 13, 1883, he suffered a massive heart attack, and died in Cosima's presence. His body was interred in a vault in the garden of his Wahnfried villa in Bayreuth.

Wagner's role in music history is immense. Not only did he create works of great beauty and tremendous brilliance, but he generated an entirely new concept of the art of music, exercising an influence on generations of composers all over the globe. Richard Strauss extended Wagner's grandiose vision to symphonic music, fashioning the form of a tone poem that uses leading motifs and vivid programmatic description of the scenes portrayed in his music. Even Rimsky-Korsakov, far as he stood from Wagner's ideas of musical composition, reflected the spirit of *Parsifal* in his own religious opera, *The Legend of the City of Kitezh*. Schoenberg's first significant work, *Verklärte Nacht,* is Wagnerian in its color. Lesser composers, unable to escape Wagner's magic domination, attempted to follow him literally by writing trilogies and tetralogies on a parallel plan with his *Ring*; a pathetic example is the career of August Bungert, who wrote 2 operatic cycles using Homer's epics as the source of his libretti. Wagner's reform of opera was incomparably more far-reaching in aim, import, and effect than that of Gluck, whose main purpose was to counteract the arbitrary predominance of the singers; this goal Wagner accomplished through insistence upon the dramatic truth of his music. When he rejected traditional opera, he did so in the conviction that such an artificial form could not serve as a basis for true dramatic expression. In its place he gave the world a new form and new techniques. So revolutionary was Wagner's art that conductors and singers had to undergo special training in the new style of interpretation in order to perform his works. Thus he became the founder of interpretative conducting and of a new school of dramatic singing, so that such terms as "Wagnerian tenor" and "Wagnerian soprano" became a part of the musical vocabulary.

In his many essays and declarations Wagner condemns the illogical plan of Italian opera and French grand opera. To quote his own words, "The mistake in the art form of the opera consists in this, that a means of expression (music) was made the end, and the end to be expressed (the drama) was made a means." The choice of subjects assumes utmost importance in Wagner's aesthetics. He wrote: "The subject treated by the word-tone poet [*Worttondichter*] is entirely human, freed from all convention and from everything historically formal." The new artwork creates its own artistic form; continuous thematic development of basic motifs becomes a fundamental procedure for the logical cohesion of the drama; these highly individualized generating motifs, appearing singly, in bold relief, or subtly varied and intertwined with other motifs, present the ever-changing soul states of the characters of the drama, and form the connecting links for the dramatic situations of the total artwork, in a form of musical declamation that Wagner described as "Sprechsingen." Characters in Wagner's stage works become themselves symbols of such soul states, so that even mythical gods, magic workers, heroic horses, and speaking birds become expressions of eternal verities, illuminating the human behavior. It is for this reason that Wagner selected in most of his operas figures that reflect philosophical ideas. Yet, this very solemnity of Wagner's great images on the stage bore the seeds of their own destruction in a world governed by different esthetic principles. Thus it came to pass that the Wagnerian domination of the musical stage suddenly lost its power with changes in human society and esthetic codes. Spectators and listeners were no longer interested in solving artistic puzzles on the stage. A demand for human simplicity arose against Wagnerian heroic complexity. The public at large found greater enjoyment in the realistic nonsense of Verdi's romantic operas than in the unreality of symbolic truth in Wagner's operas. By the 2d quarter of the 20th century, few if any composers tried to imitate Wagner; all at once his grandeur and animation became an unnatural and asphyxiating constraint.

In the domain of melody, harmony, and orchestration, Wagner's art was as revolutionary as was his total artwork on the stage. He introduced the idea of an endless melody, a continuous flow of diatonic and chromatic tones; the tonality became fluid and uncertain, producing an impression of unattainability, so that the listener accustomed to Classical modulatory schemes could not easily feel the direction toward the tonic; the *Prelude* to *Tristan und Isolde* is a classic example of such fluidity of harmonic elements. The use of long unresolved dominant-ninth-chords and the dramatic tremolos of diminished-seventh chords contributed to this state of musical uncertainty, which disturbed the critics and the audiences alike. But Wagnerian harmony also became the foundation of the new method of composition that adopted a free flow of modulatory progressions. Without Wagner the chromatic idioms of the 20th century could not exist. In orchestration, too, Wagner introduced great innovations; he created new instruments, such as the so-called "Wagner tuba," and he increased his demands on the virtuosity of individual orch. players. The vertiginous flight of the bassoon to the high E in the Overture to *Tannhäuser* could not have been attempted before the advent of Wagner.

Wagner became the target of political contention during World War I when audiences in the Allied countries associated his sonorous works with German imperialism. An even greater obstacle to further performances of Wagner's music arose with the rise of Hitler. Hitler ordered the slaughter of millions of Jews; he was an enthusiastic admirer of Wagner, who himself entertained anti-Semitic notions; ergo, Wagner was guilty by association of mass murder. Can art be separated from politics, particularly when politics become murderous? Jewish musicians in Tel Aviv refused to play the Prelude to *Tristan und Isolde* when it was put on the program of a sym. concert under Zubin Mehta, and booed him for his intention to inflict Wagner on Wagner's philosophical victims.

Several periodicals dealing with Wagner were publ. in Germany and elsewhere; Wagner himself began issuing *Bayreuther Blätter* in 1878 as an aid to understanding his operas; this journal continued publication until 1938. Remarkably enough, a French periodical, *Revue Wagnérienne*, began appearing in 1885, at a time when French composers realized the tremendous power of Wagnerian aesthetics; it was publ. sporadically for a number of years. A Wagner Soc. in London publ., from 1888 to 1895, a quarterly journal entitled, significantly, *The Meister*.

WORKS: OPERAS AND MUSIC DRAMAS: *Die Hochzeit* (1832–33; partly destroyed; introduction, septet, and chorus perf. at the Neues Theater, Leipzig, Feb. 13, 1938); *Die Feen*, romantische Oper (1833–34; Königliches Hof- und Nationaltheater, Munich, June 29, 1888, Fischer conducting); *Das Liebesverbot, oder Die Novize von Palermo*, grosse komische Oper (1834–35; Magdeburg, March 29, 1836, composer conducting); *Rienzi, der Letzte der Tribunen*, grosse tragische Oper (1837–40; Königliches Hoftheater, Dresden, Oct. 20, 1842, Reissiger conducting; rev. 1843); *Der fliegende Holländer*, romantische Oper (1841; Königliches Hoftheater, Dresden, Jan. 2, 1843, composer conducting; reorchestrated in 1846, then rev. in 1852 and 1860); *Tannhäuser und der Sängerkrieg auf Wartburg*, grosse romantische Oper (first titled *Der Venusberg*; "Dresden" version, 1842–45; Königliches Hoftheater, Dresden, Oct. 19, 1845, composer conducting; rev. 1845–47; "Paris" version, a rev. version with additions and a French tr., 1860–61; Opéra, Paris, March 13, 1861, Dietsch conducting; final version, with a German tr. of the French revision and additions, 1865; Königliches Hof- und Nationaltheater, Munich, March 5, 1865); *Lohengrin*, romantische Oper (1845–48; Hoftheater, Weimar, Aug. 28, 1850, Liszt conducting); *Tristan und Isolde* (1856–59; Königliches Hof- und Nationaltheater, Munich, June 10, 1865, Bülow conducting); *Die Meistersinger von Nürnberg* (1st sketch, 1845; 1861–67; Königliches Hof- und Nationaltheater, Munich, June 21, 1868, Bülow conducting); *Der Ring des Nibelungen*, Bühnenfestspiel für drei Tage und einen Vorabend (1st prose outline as *Der Nibelungen-Mythus als Entwurf zu einem Drama*, 1848; Vorabend: *Das Rheingold*, 1851–54; Königliches Hof- und Nationaltheater, Munich, Sept. 22, 1869, Wüllner conducting; erster Tag: *Die Walküre*, 1851–56; Königliches Hof- und Nationaltheater, Munich, June 26, 1870, Wüllner conducting; zweiter Tag: *Siegfried*, first titled *Der junge Siegfried*; 1851–52, 1857, 1864–65, and 1869; Festspielhaus, Bayreuth, Aug. 16, 1876, Richter conducting; dritter Tag: *Götterdämmerung*, first titled *Siegfrieds Tod*; 1848–52 and 1869–74; Festspielhaus, Bayreuth, Aug. 17, 1876, Richter conducting; 1st complete perf. of the *Ring* cycle, Festspielhaus, Bayreuth, Aug. 13, 14, 16, and 17, 1876, Richter conducting); *Parsifal*, Buhnenweihfestspiel (first titled *Parzival*; first sketch, 1857; 1865 and 1877–82; Festspielhaus, Bayreuth, July 26, 1882, Levi conducting). ARRANGEMENTS AND EDITIONS: Aria from Bellini's *Il Pirata*, as orchestrated from the piano score for use in *La Straniera* (1833); arrangement of vocal score for Donizetti's *La Favorite* (1840) and *L'elisir d'amore* (1840); arrangement of vocal score for Halévy's *La Reine de Chypre* (1841) and *Le Guitarrero* (1841); new tr. and new close to the overture of Gluck's *Iphigénie en Aulide* (1846–47; Dresden, Feb. 22, 1847); Palestrina's *Stabat Mater*, with indications for performance (Dresden, March 8, 1848); Mozart's *Don Giovanni*, version of dialogues and recitatives and, in parts, new tr. (Zürich, Nov. 8, 1850; not extant).

WRITINGS: Wagner devoted a large amount of his enormous productive activity to writing. Besides the dramatic works he set to music, he also wrote the following: *Leubald. Ein Trauerspiel* (1826–28); *Die hohe Braut, oder Bianca und Giuseppe*, 4-act tragic opera (prose scenario, 1836 and 1842; music composed by Johann Kittl and produced as *Bianca und Giuseppe, oder Die Franzosen vor Nizza* in Prague, 1848); *Männerlist grösser als Frauenlist, oder Die glückliche Bärenfamilie*, 2-act comic opera (libretto, 1837; some music completed); *Eine Pilgerfahrt zu Beethoven*, novella (1840); *Ein Ende in Paris*, novella (1841); *Ein glücklicher Abend*, novella (1841); *Die Sarazenin*, 3-act opera (prose scenario, 1841–42; verse text, 1843); *Die Bergwerke zu Falun*, 3-act opera (prose scenario for an unwritten libretto, 1841–42); *Friedrich I.*, play (prose scenario, 1846 and 1848); *Alexander der Grosse*, sketch for a play (184?; not extant); *Jesus von Nazareth*, play (prose scenario, 1849); *Achilleus*, sketch for a play (1849–50; fragments only); *Wieland der Schmied*, 3-act opera (prose scenario, 1850); *Die Sieger*, opera (prose sketch, 1856); *Luther* or *Luthers Hochzeit*, sketch for a play (1868); *Lustspiel in 1 Akt* (draft, 1868); *Eine Kapitulation: Lustspiel in antiker Manier*, poem (1870).

Wagner expounded his theories on music, politics, philosophy, religion, etc., in numerous essays; among the most important are *Über deutsches Musikwesen* (1840); *Die Kunst und die Revolution* (1849); *Das Kunstwerk der Zukunft* (1849); *Kunst und Klima* (1850); *Oper und Drama* (1851; rev. 1868); *Eine Mitteilung an meine Freunde* (1851); *Über Staat und Religion* (1864); *Über das Dirigieren* (1869); *Beethoven* (1870); *Über die Anwendung der Musik auf das Drama* (1879); and *Religion und Kunst* (1880). The first ed. of his collected writings, *R. Wagner: Gesammelte Schriften und Dichtungen* (9 vols., Leipzig, 1871–73; vol. 10,

1883), was prepared by Wagner himself; W. A. Ellis ed. and tr. it into Eng. as *Richard Wagner's Prose Works* (8 vols., London, 1892–99). H. von Wolzogen and R. Sternfeld ed. the 5th ed. of the German original as *Samtliche Schriften und Dichtungen*, adding vols. 11 and 12 (Leipzig, 1911); they also prepared the 6th ed., adding vols. 13–14 (Leipzig, 1914).

Wagner's important autobiography, *Mein Leben*, in 4 parts, was privately publ.; parts 1–3, bringing the narrative down to Aug. 1861, were publ. between 1870 and 1875; part 4, covering the years from 1861 to 1864, was publ. in 1881; these were limited eds., being distributed only among his friends; the entire work was finally publ. in an abridged ed. in Munich in 1911 (Eng. tr. as *My Life*, London and N.Y., 1911); the suppressed passages were first publ. in *Die Musik*, 22 (1929–30), and then were tr. into Eng. in E. Newman's *Fact and Fiction about Wagner* (London, 1931); a definitive ed., based on the original MS, was publ. in Munich in 1963, ed. by M. Gregor-Dellin.

Another important source is Wagner's diary-notebook, the so-called *Brown Book*, in which he made entries between 1865 and 1882; it was ed. by J. Bergfeld as *Richard Wagner: Das Braune Buch: Tagebuchaufzeichnungen, 1865–1882* (Zürich, 1975; Eng. tr. by G. Bird as *The Diary of Richard Wagner, 1865–1882; The Brown Book*, London, 1980). See also the diaries of Cosima Wagner; they have been ed. by M. Gregor-Dellin and D. Mack as *Cosima Wagner: Die Tagebucher, 1869–1877* (2 vols., Munich, 1976–77; Eng. tr. by G. Skelton as *Cosima Wagner's Diaries*, 2 vols., N.Y., 1977 and 1980).

BIBL.: COLLECTED EDITIONS, SOURCE MATERIAL: The first collected ed. of his works, *R. W.s Werke*, was ed. by M. Balling (10 vols., Leipzig, 1912–29); the Bayerische Akademie der Schönen Künste of Munich is now publishing a new critical ed., the *Gesamtausgabe der Werke R. W.s*, under the editorship of C. Dahlhaus et al. (Mainz, 1970–). E. Kastner prepared a *W.-Catalog: Chronologisches Verzeichniss der von und über R. W. erschienenen Schriften, Musikwerke* (Offenbach, 1878). J. Deathridge, M. Geck, and E. Voss ed. an exhaustive *Verzeichnis der musikalischen Werke R. W.s und ihrer Quellen* (Mainz, 1983).

Other sources include: N. Oesterlein, *Katalog einer R. W.-Bibliothek: Nach den vorliegenden Originalien zu einem authentischen Nachschlagebuch durch die gesammte insbesondere deutsche W.-Litteratur bearbeitet und veröffentlicht* (describes the treasures of the W.-Museum and contains an extensive bibliography of books and articles publ. about the composer during his life [10,181 titles]; 4 vols., Leipzig, 1882, 1886, 1891, 1895); C. Glasenapp and H. von Stein, *W.-Lexikon. Hauptbegriffe der Kunst und Weltanschauung W.s in wortlichen Ausfuhrungen aus seinen Schriften zusammengestellt* (Stuttgart, 1883); C. Glasenapp, *W.-Enzyklopädie: Haupterscheinungen der Kunst- und Kulturgeschichte im Lichte der Anschauung W.s in wörtlichen Ausführungen aus seinen Schriften dargestellt* (2 vols., Leipzig, 1891); E. Kastner, *Verzeichnis der ersten Aufführungen von R. W.s dramatischen Werken* (Vienna, 1896; 2d ed., Leipzig, 1899); H. Silège, *Bibliographie w.ienne française* (Paris, 1902); P. Pabst, *Verzeichnis von R. W.s Werken, Schriften und Dichtungen, deren hauptsächlichsten Bearbeitungen, sowie von besonders interessanter Litteratur, Abbildungen, Büsten und Kunstblättern, den Meister und seine Schöpfungen betreffend* (Leipzig, 1905); M. Burrell, *Catalogue of the Burrell Collection of W. Documents, Letters and Other Biographical Material* (London, 1929); O. Strobel, *Genie am Werk: R. W.s Schaffen und Wirken im Spiegel eigenhandschriftlicher Urkunden: Führer durch die einmalige Ausstellung einer umfassenden Auswahl von Schätzen aus dem Archiv des Hauses Wahnfried* (Bayreuth, 1933; rev. ed., 1934); E. Terry, *A R. W. Dictionary* (N.Y., 1939); H. Barth, ed., *Internationale W.-Bibliographie: 1945–55* (Bayreuth, 1956; also for 1956–60, publ. 1961, and for 1961–66, publ. 1968); C. von Westernhagen, *R. W.s Dresdener Bibliothek, 1842–1849: Neue Dokumente zur Geschichte seines Schaffens* (Wiesbaden, 1966); H. Kirchmeyer, *Das zeitgenössische W.-Bild* (3 vols., Regensburg; vol. 1, *W. in Dresden*, publ. 1972; vol.2, *Dokumente, 1842–45*, publ. 1967; vol. 3, *Dokumente, 1846–50*, publ. 1968); H.-M. Plesske, *R. W. in der Dichtung: Bibliographie deutschsprachiger Veröffentlichungen* (Bayreuth, 1971); W. Schuler, *Der Bayreuther Kreis von seiner Entstehung bis zum Ausgang der wilhelminischen Ära: W.kult und Kulturreform im Geiste völkischer Weltanschauung* (Münster, 1971); H. Klein, *Erst- und Frühdrucke der Textbücher von R. W.: Bibliographie* (Tutzing, 1979); H. Klein, *Erstdrucke der musikalischen Werke von R. W.* (Tutzing, 1983); U. Müller, ed., *R.-W.-Handbuch* (Stuttgart, 1986; Eng. tr. as *W. Handbook*, Cambridge, 1992); H.-J. Bauer, *R. W. Lexikon* (Bergisch Gladbach, 1988); B. Millington, ed., *The W. Compendium: A Guide to W.'s Life and Music* (N.Y., 1992).

BIOGRAPHICAL: C. Cabrol, *R. W.* (Paris, 1861); A. de Gasperini, *La Nouvelle Allemagne musicale: R. W.* (Paris, 1866); F. Hueffer, *R. W.* (London, 1872; 3d ed., 1912); F. Filippi, *R. W.* (Leipzig, 1876); C. Glasenapp, *R. W.s Leben und Wirken* (2 vols., Leipzig, 1876–77; 3d ed., rev. and enl., as *Das Leben R. W.s*, 6 vols., Leipzig, 1894–1911; Eng. tr. by W. Ellis as *Life of R. W.*, 6 vols., London, 1900–08; vols. 1-3 based on Glasenapp; reprinted N.Y., 1977, with new introduction by G. Buelow; 5th Ger. ed., rev., 1910–23); P. Lindau, *R. W.* (Paris, 1885); A. Jullien, *R. W.: Sa vie et ses oeuvres* (Paris, 1886; Eng. tr., Boston, 1892); G. Kobbé, *W.'s Life and Works* (2 vols., N.Y., 1890); H. Finck, *W. and His Works* (2 vols., N.Y., 1893; 5th ed., 1898); H. Chamberlain, *R. W.* (Munich, 1896; Eng. tr., London, 1897; 9th Ger. ed., 1936); M. Burrell, compiler, *R. W.: Life and Works from 1813 to 1834* (London, 1898); W.J. Henderson, *R. W., His Life and His Dramas* (N.Y., 1901; rev. ed., 1923); R. Burkner, *R. W.: Sein Leben und seine Werke* (Jena, 1906; 6th ed., 1911); M. Koch, *R. W.* (3 vols., Berlin, 1907, 1913, and 1918); J. Kapp, *R. W.* (Berlin, 1910); F. Pfohl, *R. W.: Sein Leben und Schaffen* (Berlin, 1911; 4th ed., Bielefeld, 1924); E. Newman, *W. as Man and Artist* (London, 1914; 2d ed., rev., 1924); L. Barthou, *La Vie amoureuse de R. W.* (Paris, 1925; Eng. tr. as *The Prodigious Lover*, N.Y., 1927); H. Lichtenberger, *W.* (Paris, 1925); W. Wallace, *W. as He Lived* (London, 1925; new ed., 1933); V. d'Indy, *R. W. et son influence sur l'art musical français* (Paris, 1930); M. Morold (pen name of Max von Millenkovitch), *W.s Kampf und Sieg, dargestellt in seinen Beziehungen zu Wien* (Zürich, 1930; 2d ed., 1950); H. Reisiger, *Unruhiges Gestirn; Die Jugend R. W.s* (Leipzig, 1930; in Eng. as *Restless Star*, N.Y., 1932); G. de Pourtalès, *W.: Histoire d'un artiste* (Paris, 1932; Eng. tr., N.Y., 1932; 2d French ed., enl., 1942); P. Lalo, *R. W.* (Paris, 1933); E. Newman, *The Life of R. W.* (4 vols., N.Y., 1933, 1937, 1941, 1946); A. Spring, *R. W.s Weg und Wirken* (Stuttgart, 1933); W. Turner, *W.* (London, 1933); M. Fehr, *R. W.s Schweizer Zeit* (2 vols., Aarau, 1934, 1953); W. Hadow, *R. W.* (London, 1934); R. Jacobs, *W.* (London, 1935; 3d ed., 1947); H. Malherbe, *R. W. Révolutionnaire* (Paris, 1938); E. Kretzschmar, *R. W.: Sein Leben in Selbstzeugnissen, Briefen und Berichten* (Berlin, 1939); O. Strobel, *Neue Urkunden zur Lebensgeschichte R. W.s, 1864–1882* (a supplement to his ed. of *König Ludwig II. und R. W.: Briefwechsel*; Karlsruhe, 1939); M. von Millenkovitch, *Dreigestirn: W., Liszt, Bülow* (Leipzig, 1941); W. Reich, *R. W.: Leben, Fühlen, Schaffen* (Olten, 1948); K. Ipser, *R. W. in Italien* (Salzburg, 1951); L. Strecker, *R. W. als Verlagsgefährte: Eine Darstellung mit Briefen und Dokumenten* (Mainz, 1951); T. Adorno, *Versuch über W.* (Berlin, 1952); P. Loos, *R. W., Vollendung und Tragik der deutschen Romantik* (Munich, 1952); O. Strobel, *R. W.: Leben und Schaffen: Eine Zeittafel* (Bayreuth, 1952); Z. von Kraft, *R. W.: Ein dramatisches Leben* (Munich, 1953); R. Dumesnil, *R. W.* (Paris, 1954); H. Mayer, *R. W.s geistige Entwicklung* (Düsseldorf and Hamburg, 1954); C. von Westernhagen, *R. W.: Sein Werk, sein Wesen, seine Welt* (Zürich, 1956); H. Mayer, *R. W. in Selbstzeugnissen und Bilddokumenten* (Reinbek bei Hamburg, 1959; Eng. tr., 1972); R. Gutman, *R. W.: The Man, His Mind and His Music* (London, 1968); C. von Westernhagen, *W.* (2 vols., Zürich, 1968; 2d ed., rev. and enl., 1978; Eng. tr., Cambridge, 1978); M. Gregor-Martin, *W.-Chronik: Daten zu Leben* (Munich, 1972; 2d rev. ed., 1983); H. Barth, D. Mack, and E. Voss, eds., *W.: Sein Leben und seine Welt in zeitgenössischen Bildern und Texten* (Vienna, 1975; Eng. tr. as *W.: A Documentary Study*, London, 1975); R. Taylor, *R. W.: His Life, Art and Thought* (London, 1979); D. Watson, *R. W.: A Biography* (N.Y. and London, 1979); M. Gregor-Dellin, *R. W.: Sein Leben, sein Werk, sein Jahrhundert* (Munich, 1980; Eng. tr.

as *R. W.: His Life, His Work, His Century*, London, 1983); D. Watson, *R. W.* (N.Y., 1981); G. Skelton, *R. and Cosima W.: A Biography of a Marriage* (London, 1982); M. van Amerongen, *W.: A Case History* (London, 1983); M. Kahane and N. Wild, *W. et la France* (Paris, 1983); E. Voss, compiler, *R. W.: Dokumentarbiographie* (Munich and Mainz, 1983); B. Millington, *W.* (London, 1984; rev. ed., 1992); J. Katz, *The Darker Side of Genius: R. W.'s Anti-Semitism* (Hanover, N.H., and London, 1986); R. Sabor, *The Real W.* (London, 1987); W. Beck, *R. W.: Neue Dokumente zur Biographie. Die Spiritualitat im Drama seines Lebens* (Tutzing, 1988); A. Aberbach, *R. W.: A Mystic in the Making* (Wakefield, N.H., 1991); H.-J. Bauer, *R. W.* (Stuttgart, 1992); M. Schneider, *W.* (Paris, 1995); M. Tanner, *W.* (Princeton, 1996).

CRITICAL, ANALYTICAL: Liszt's essays on *Tannhäuser* (1849), *Lohengrin* (1850), *Der fliegende Holländer* (1854), and *Das Rheingold* (1855) are in vol. 3, 2, of his *Gesammelte Schriften* (Leipzig, 1899); F. Hinrichs, *R. W. und die neuere Musik: Eine kritische Skizze* (Halle, 1854); F. Müller, *R. W. und das Musik-Drama* (Leipzig, 1861); L. Nohl, *Gluck und W. über die Entwicklung des Musikdramas* (Munich, 1870); F. Nietzsche, *Die Geburt der Tragödie aus dem Geiste der Musik* (Leipzig, 1872; Eng. tr. by W. Kaufmann as *The Birth of Tragedy out of the Spirit of Music* in *The Basic Writings of Nietzsche*, N.Y., 1968); E. Dannreuther, *R. W.: His Tendencies and Theories* (London, 1873); F. Hueffer, *R. W. and the Music of the Future* (London, 1874); E. Schuré, *Le Drame musical: I. La Musique et la poésie dans leur développement historique. II. W. Son oeuvre et son idée* (Paris, 1875; 3d ed., aug., 1894); G. Kobbé, *R. W.s "Tristan und Isolde"* (N.Y., 1886); W. Ellis, *R. W. as Poet, Musician and Mystic* (London, 1887); F. Nietzsche, *Der Fall W.* (Leipzig, 1888; Eng. tr. by W. Kaufmann as *The Case of W.* in *The Basic Writings of Nietzsche*, N.Y., 1968); idem, *Nietzsche contra W.* (Leipzig, 1888; Eng. tr. by W. Kaufmann in *The Portable Nietzsche*, N.Y., 1954); H. von Wolzogen, *W.iana: Gesammelte Aufsätze über R. W.s Werke vom Ring bis zum Gral* (Bayreuth, 1888); M. Kufferath, *Parsifal de R. W.: Légende, drame, partition* (Paris, 1890; Eng. tr., 1904); L. Torchi, *Riccardo W.: Studio critico* (Bologna, 1890); H. Krehbiel, *Studies in the W.ian Drama* (N.Y., 1891); M. Kufferath, *Le Théâtre de W. de Tannhäuser à Parsifal: Essais de critique littéraire, esthétique et musicale* (6 vols., Paris, 1891–98); A. Smolian, *The Themes of "Tannhäuser"* (London, 1891); H. Chamberlain, *Das Drama R. W.s: Eine Anregung* (Leipzig, 1892; 5th ed., 1913; Eng. tr., London, 1915); M. Kufferath, *Guide thématique et analyse de Tristan et Iseult* (Paris, 1894); A. Lavignac, *Le Voyage artistique à Bayreuth* (Paris, 1897; Eng. tr. as *The Music-Dramas of R. W.*, N.Y., 1898; new ed., 1932); G. Servières, *R. W. jugé en France* (Paris, 1897); G. B. Shaw, *The Perfect W.ite* (London, 1898; 4th ed., 1923; also in vol. 17 of the complete works, 1932); J. Tiersot, *Études sur les Maîtres-Chanteurs de Nuremberg, de R. W.* (Paris, 1899); A. Smolian, *R. W.'s Bühnenfestspiel Der Ring des Nibelungen: Ein Vademecum* (Berlin, 1901); A. Seidl, *W.iana* (2 vols., Berlin, 1901, 1902); G. Kobbé, *W.'s Music Dramas Analyzed* (N.Y., 1904); W. Dry, *Erläuterungen zur R. W.s Tondramen* (2 vols., Leipzig, 1906, 1907); W. Golther, *Tristan und Isolde in den Dichtungen des Mittelalters und der neuen Zeit* (Leipzig, 1907); S. Hamer, *The Story of "The Ring"* (N.Y., 1907); M. Burckhardt, *Führer durch R. W.s Musikdramen* (Berlin, 1909); E. Istel, *Das Kunstwerk R. W.s* (Leipzig, 1910; 2d ed., 1919); E. Kloss, *R. W. über die "Meistersinger von Nürnberg": Aussprüche des Meisters über sein Werk* (Leipzig, 1910); W. Krienetz, *R. W.s "Feen"* (Munich, 1910); E. Lindner, *R. W. über "Parsifal": Aussprüche des Meisters über sein Werk* (Leipzig, 1913); idem., *R. W. über "Tannhäuser": Aussprüche des Meisters über sein Werk* (Leipzig, 1914); A. Seidl, *Neue W.iana: Gesammelte Aufsätze und Studien* (Regensburg, 1914); H. von Wolzogen, *R. W. über den "Fliegenden Holländer": Die Entstehung, Gestaltung und Darstellung des Werkes aus den Schriften und Briefen des Meisters zusammengestellt* (Leipzig, 1914); E. Kurth, *Romantische Harmonik und ihre Krise in W.s "Tristan"* (Berlin, 1920; 2d ed., 1923); F. Zademack, *Die Meistersinger von Nürnberg: R. W.s Dichtung und ihre Quellen* (Berlin, 1921); W. Wilmshurst, *Parsifal* (London, 1922); P. Bekker, *R. W.: Das Leben im Werke* (Stuttgart, 1924; Eng. tr., London, 1931); A. Coeuroy, *La Walkyrie de R. W.* (Paris, 1924); O. Strobel, *R. W. über sein Schaffen: Ein Beitrag zur "Künstlerästhetik"* (Munich, 1924); H. Wiessner, *Der Stabreimvers in R. W.s "Ring des Nibelungen"* (Berlin, 1924); A. Himonet, *Lohengrin de R. W.* (Paris, 1925); L. Leroy, *W.'s Music Drama of the Ring* (London, 1925); C. Winn, *The Mastersingers of W.* (London, 1925); A. Dickinson, *The Musical Design of "The Ring"* (London, 1926); W. Hapke, *Die musikalische Darstellung der Gebärde in R. W.s Ring des Nibelungen* (Leipzig, 1927); A. Buesst, *R. W., The Nibelung's Ring* (London, 1932; 2d ed., 1952); W. Engelsmann, *W.s klingendes Universum* (Potsdam, 1933); J. Kapp, *Das Liebesverbot, Entstehung und Schicksale des Werkes von R. W.* (Berlin, 1933); idem, *W. und die Berliner Oper* (Berlin, 1933); R. Grisson, *Beiträge zur Auslegung von R. W.'s "Ring des Nibelungen"* (Leipzig, 1934); H. Nathan, *Das Rezitativ der Frühopern R. W.s: Ein Beitrag zur Stilistik des Opernrezitativs in der ersten Hälfte des 19. Jahrhunderts* (diss., Univ. of Berlin, 1934); A. Bahr-Mildenburg, *Tristan und Isolde: Darstellung der Werke R. W.s aus dem Geiste der Dichtung und Musik: Vollständige Regiebearbeitung sämtlicher Partien mit Notenbeispielen* (Leipzig, 1936); L. Gilman, *W.'s Operas* (N.Y., 1937); V. d'Indy, *Introduction à l'étude de Parsifal de W.* (Paris, 1937); R. Schuster, *R. W. und die Welt der Oper* (Munich, 1937); E. Borrelli, *Estetica w.iana* (Florence, 1940); E. Hutcheson, *A Musical Guide to the R. W. Ring of the Nibelung* (N.Y., 1940); J. Barzun, *Darwin, Marx, W.: Critique of a Heritage* (Boston, 1941; rev. ed., 1958); S. Luciani, *Il Tristano e Isolda di R. W.* (Florence, 1942); G. Gavazzeni, *Il Siegfried di R. W.* (Florence, 1944); M. Doisy, *L'Œuvre de R. W. du Vaisseau fantôme à Parsifal* (Brussels, 1945); M. Beaufils, *W. et le w.isme* (Paris, 1947); K. Overhoff, *R. W.s Tristan Partitur: Eine musikalisch-philosophische Deutung* (Bayreuth, 1948); E. Newman, *W. Nights* (London, 1949; American ed. as *The W. Operas*, N.Y., 1949); K. Overhoff, *R. W.s Parsifal* (Lindau im Bodensee, 1951); T. Adorno, *Versuch über W.* (Berlin and Frankfurt am Main, 1952); P. Jacob, *Taten der Musik: R. W. und sein Werk* (Regensburg, 1952); P. Loos, *R. W.: Vollendung und Tragik der deutschen Romantik* (Bern and Munich, 1952); V. Levi, *Tristano e Isotta di Riccardo W.* (Venice, 1958); J. Stein, *R. W. and the Synthesis of the Arts* (Detroit, 1960); H. von Stein, *Dichtung und Musik im Werk R. W.s* (Berlin, 1962); M. Vogel, *Der Tristan-Akkord und die Krise der modernen Harmonie-Lehre* (Düsseldorf, 1962); C. von Westernhagen, *Vom Holländer zum Parsifal: Neue W. Studien* (Freiburg im Breisgau, 1962); J. Bergfeld, *W.s Werk und unsere Zeit* (Berlin and Wunsiedel, 1963); R. Donington, *W.s "Ring" and Its Symbols: The Music and the Myth* (London, 1963; 3rd ed., rev. and enl., 1974); H. Gál, *R. W.: Versuch einer Würdigung* (Frankfurt am Main, 1963; Eng. tr., 1976); H. Scharschuch, *Gesamtanalyse der Harmonik von R. W.s Musikdrama "Tristan und Isolde": Unter spezifischer Berücksichtigung der Sequenztechnik des Tristanstiles* (Regensburg, 1963); E. Zuckerman, *The First Hundred Years of W.'s "Tristan"* (N.Y. and London, 1964); H. Mayer, *Anmerkungen zu W.* (Frankfurt am Main, 1966); W. White, *An Introduction to the Life and Works of R. W.* (Englewood Cliffs, N.J., 1967); K. Overhoff, *Die Musikdramen R. W.s: Eine thematisch-musikalische Interpretation* (Salzburg, 1968); R. Raphael, *R. W.* (N.Y., 1969); C. Dahlhaus, ed., *Das Drama R. W.s als musikalisches Kunstwerk* (Regensburg, 1970); idem, *Die Bedeutung des Gestischen in W.s Musikdramen* (Munich, 1970); E. Voss, *Studien zur Instrumentation R. W.s* (Regensburg, 1970); C. Dahlhaus, *Die Musikdramen R. W.s* (Velber, 1971; Eng. tr. as *R. W.'s Music Dramas*, Cambridge, 1979); idem, *W.s Konzeption des musikalischen Dramas* (Regensburg, 1971); A. Sommer, *Die Komplikationen des musikalischen Rhythmus in den Bühnenwerken R. W.s* (Giebing, 1971); C. von Westernhagen, *Die Entstehung des "Ring," dargestellt an den Kompositionsskizzen R. W.s* (Zürich, 1973; Eng. tr. as *The Forging of the "Ring,"* Cambridge, 1976); K. Kropfinger, *W. und Beethoven: Untersuchungen zur Beethoven-Rezeption R. W.s* (Regensburg, 1975); J. Culshaw, *Reflections on W.'s Ring* (N.Y., 1976); H.-J. Bauer, *W.s Parsifal: Kriterien der Kompositionstechnik* (Munich, 1977); J. Deathridge, *W.'s Rienzi: A Reappraisal Based on a Study of the Sketches and Drafts* (Oxford, 1977); J. Di Gaetani, *Penetrating W.'s Ring: An Anthology* (Cranbury, N.J., 1978); F. Oberkogler, *R. W.: Vom Ring zum Gral: Wiedergewinnung seines Werkes aus Musik und Mythos* (Stuttgart, 1978); P. Wapnewski, *Der traurige Gott: R. W. in seinen Helden* (Munich, 1978); P. Burbridge and R. Sutton, eds., *The W. Companion* (N.Y., 1979); D. Cooke, *I Saw the World End: A Study of W.'s Ring* (London, 1979); L. Rather, *The Dream of Self-Destruction: W.'s Ring and the Modern World* (Baton Rouge, La., 1979); A. Blyth, *W.'s Ring: An Introduction* (London, 1980); L. Beckett, *R. W.: Parsifal* (Cambridge, 1981); D. Borchmeyer, *Das Theater R. W.s* (Stuttgart, 1982; Eng. tr. as *R. W.: Theory and Theatre*, Oxford, 1991); M. Ewans, *W. and Aeschylus: The Ring and the Oresteia* (London, 1982); N. Benvenga, *Kingdom on the Rhine: History, Myth and Legend on W.'s Ring* (Harwich, 1983); A. Aberbach, *The Ideas of R. W.* (Lanham, 1984); S. Fay and R. Wood, *The Ring: An Anatomy of an Opera* (London, 1984); A. Ingenhoff, *Drama oder Epos?: R. W.s Gattungstheorie des musikalischen Dramas* (Tübingen, 1987); H.-M. Palm, *R. W.s 'Lohengrin': Studien zur Sprachbehandlung* (Munich, 1987); L. Shaw, N. Cirillo, and M. Miller, eds., *W. in Retrospect: A Centennial Reappraisal* (Amsterdam, 1987); D. White, *The Turning Wheel: A Study of Contracts and Oaths in W.'s 'Ring'* (Selinsgrove, N.Y., 1988); W. Cord, *The Teutonic Mythology of R. W.'s "The Ring of the Nibelung"* (3 vols., Lewiston, N.Y., 1989–91); P. Buck, *R. W.s Meistersinger: Eine Führung durch das Werk* (Frankfurt am Main and N.Y., 1990); E. Magee, *R. W. and the Nibelungs* (Oxford, 1990); A. Mork, *R. W. als politischer Schriftsteller: Weltanschauung und Wirkungsgeschichte* (Frankfurt am Main and N.Y., 1990); J. Nattiez, *W. androgyne: Essai sur l'interprétation* (Paris, 1990); C. Osborne, *The Complete Operas of R. W.* (London, 1990); P. Peil, *Die Krise des neuzeitlichen Menschen im Werk R. W.s* (Cologne, 1990); H. Brown, *Leitmotiv and Drama: W., Brecht, and the Limits of "Epic" Theatre* (Oxford, 1991); H. Kesting, *Das schlechte Gewissen an der Musik: Aufsätze zu R. W.* (Stuttgart, 1991); H. Richardson, ed., *New Studies in R. W.s The Ring of the Nibelung* (Lewiston, N.Y., 1991); P. Urban, *Liebesdämmerung: Ein psychoanalytischer Versuch über R. W.s "Tristan und Isolde"* (Eschborn, 1991); M. Cicora, *From History to Myth: W.'s Tannhäuser and Its Literary Sources* (Bern and N.Y., 1992); B. Millington and S. Spencer, eds., *W. in Performance* (New Haven, 1992); P. Rose, *W.: Race and Revolution* (New Haven, 1992); G. Skelton, *W. in Thought and Practice* (Portland, Oreg., 1992); W. Darcy, *W.'s Das Rheingold* (Oxford, 1993); H. Hubert, *Götternot: R. W.s grose Dichtungen* (Asendorf, 1993); K. Richter, *R. W.: Visionen* (Vilsbiburg, 1993); B. Benz, *Zeitstrukturen in R. W.s 'Ring'-Tetralogie* (Frankfurt am Main, 1994); B. Heldt, *R. W.: Tristan und Isolde: Das Werk und seine Inszenierung* (Laaber, 1994); J. Warrack, *R. W.: Die Meistersinger von Nürnberg* (Cambridge, 1994); C. Weismüller, *Das Drama der Notation: Ein Philosophischer Versuch zu R. W.s Ring des Nibelungen* (Vienna, 1994); T. Grey, *W.'s Musical Prose: Texts and Contexts* (Cambridge, 1995); E. Roch, *Psychograma: R. W. im Symbol: Mit 34 Abbildungen* (Stuttgart, 1995); M. Weiner, *R. W. and the Anti-Semitic Imagination* (Lincoln, Nebr., 1995); P.-H. Wilberg, *R. W.s mythische Welt: Versuche wider den Historismus* (Freiburg im Breisgau, 1996); M. Bless, *R. W.s Opera "Tannhäuser" im Spiegel seiner geistigen Entwicklung* (Eisenbach, 1997); D. Schneller, *R. W.s "Parsifal" und die Erneuerung des Mysteriendramas in Bayreuth: Die Vision des Gesamtkunstwerks als Universalkultur der Zukunft* (Bern, 1997); D. Scholz, *Ein deutsches Missverständnis: R. W. zwischen Barrikade und Walhalla* (Berlin, 1997); J. McGlathery, *W.'s Operas and Desire* (N.Y., 1998).

Wagner, Siegfried (Helferich Richard), German conductor and composer; b. Triebschen, June 6, 1869; d. Bayreuth, Aug. 4, 1930. He was the son of (Wilhelm) Richard (b. Leipzig, May 22, 1813; d. Venice, Feb. 13, 1883) and Cosima Wagner (b. Bellagio, on Lake Como, Dec. 24, 1837; d. Bayreuth, April 1, 1930), who were married on Aug. 25, 1870, and thus Siegfried was legitimated. Richard Wagner named the *Siegfried Idyll* for him, and it was performed in Wagner's house in Triebschen on Christmas Day, 1870. He studied with Humperdinck in Frankfurt am Main and then pursued training as an architect in Berlin and Karlsruhe; during his tenure as an assistant in Bayreuth (1892–96), he studied with his mother, Hans Richter, and Julius Kniese. From 1896 he was a regular conductor in Bayreuth, where he was general director of the Festival productions from 1906. On Sept. 21, 1915, he married Winifred Williams, an adopted daughter of Karl Klindworth. In 1923–24 he visited the United States in order to raise funds for the reopening of the Bayreuth Festspielhaus, which had been closed during the course of World War I. He conducted from memory, and left-handed. In his career as a composer, he was greatly handicapped by inevitable comparisons with his father. His memoirs were publ. in Stuttgart in 1923.

WORKS: OPERAS: *Der Bärenhäuter* (1898; Munich, Jan. 22, 1899); *Herzog Wildfang* (Munich, March 14, 1901); *Der Kobold* (1903; Hamburg, Jan. 29, 1904); *Bruder Lustig* (Hamburg, Oct. 13, 1905); *Sternengebot* (1907; Hamburg, Jan. 21, 1908); *Banadietrich* (1909; Karlsruhe, Jan. 23, 1910); *Schwarzschwanenreich* (1911; Karlsruhe, Dec. 6, 1917); *Sonnenflammen* (1914; Darmstadt, Oct. 30, 1918); *Der Heidenkönig* (1914; Cologne, Dec. 16, 1933); *Der Friedensengel* (1915; Karlsruhe, March 4, 1926); *An allem ist Hütchen Schuld* (1916; Stuttgart, Dec. 6, 1917); *Der Schmied von Marienburg* (1920; Rostock, Dec. 16, 1923); *Wahnopfer* (1928; unfinished).

BIBL.: L. Karpeth, *S. W. als Mensch und Künstler* (Leipzig, 1902); C. Glasenapp, *S. W.* (Berlin, 1906); idem, *S. W. und seine Kunst* (Leipzig, 1911; essays on the operas; new series, 1913, as *Schwarzschwanenreich*; 2d new series, ed. by P. Pretzsch, 1919, as *Sonnenflammen*); P. Pretzsch, *Die Kunst S. W.s* (Leipzig, 1919); O. Daube, *S. W. und sein Werk* (Bayreuth, 1925); *Festschrift zu S. W.s 60. Geburtstag* (Bayreuth, 1929); H. Rebois, *Lettres de S. W.* (Paris, 1933); O. Daube, *S. W. und die Märchenoper* (Leipzig, 1936); F. Starsen, *Erinnerungen an S. W.* (Detmold, 1942); Z. von Kraft, *Der Sohn: S. W.s Leben und Umwelt* (Graz, 1963); P. Pachl, *S. W.s musikdramatisches Schaffen* (Tutzing, 1979); L. Gunter-Kornagel, *S. W.s Opernschaffen zwischen Mythos, Mystik, und Realität* (Wolfratshausen, 1995).

Wagner, Sieglinde, Austrian mezzo-soprano; b. Linz, April 21, 1921. She studied at the Linz Cons. and with Luise Willer and Carl Hartmann in Munich. In 1942 she made her operatic debut as Erda in Linz. From 1947 to 1952 she sang at the Vienna Volksoper. In 1949 she made her first appearance at the Salzburg Festival as the 2d Lady in *Die Zauberflöte*, and returned there to create the roles of Lady Capulet in Blacher's *Romeo und Julia* (1950), Leda in Strauss's *Die Liebe der Danae* (official premiere, Aug. 14, 1952), and Frau Jensen in Wagner-Régeny's *Das Bergwerk zu Falun* (1961). In 1952 she became a member of the Berlin Städtische Oper. After it became the Deutsche Oper in 1961, she continued as a member until 1986. In 1962 she made her debut at the Bayreuth Festival as Flosshelde, where she made regular appearances until 1973. She also pursued an active career as a concert artist.

Wagner, (Adolf) Wieland (Gottfried), German opera producer and stage designer, son of **Siegfried (Helferich Richard)** and brother of **Wolfgang (Manfred Martin) Wagner**; b. Bayreuth, Jan. 5, 1917; d. Munich, Oct. 16, 1966. He received his general education in Munich, and devoted himself to the problem of modernizing the productions of Wagner's operas. With his brother, Wolfgang Wagner, he served as codirector of the Bayreuth Festivals from 1951 to 1966. Abandoning the luxuriant scenery of 19th-century opera, he emphasized the symbolic meaning of Wagner's music dramas, eschewing realistic effects, such as machinery propelling the Rhine maidens through the wavy gauze of the river, or the bright paper flames of the burning Valhalla. He even introduced Freudian sexual overtones, as in his production of *Tristan und Isolde*, where a phallic pillar was conspicuously placed on the stage.

BIBL.: W. Panofsky, *W. W.* (Bremen, 1964); C. Lust, *W. W. et la survie du théâtre lyrique* (Lausanne, 1969); W. Schäfer, *W. W.: Persönlichkeit und Leistung* (Tübingen, 1970); G. Skelton, *W. W.: The Positive Sceptic* (London, 1971); B. Wessling, *W. W., der Enkel: Eine Biographie* (Cologne, 1997).

Wagner, Wolfgang (Manfred Martin), German opera producer, son of **Siegfried (Helferich Richard)** and brother of **(Adolf) Wieland (Gottfried) Wagner**; b. Bayreuth, Aug. 30, 1919. He studied music privately in Bayreuth, then worked in various capacities at the Bayreuth Festivals and the Berlin State Opera. With his brother, Wieland Wagner, he was codirector of the Bayreuth Festivals from 1951 to 1966; after his brother's death in 1966, he was its sole director. Like his brother, he departed radically from the traditional staging of the Wagner operas, and introduced a psychoanalytic and surrealist mise en scène, often with suggestive phallic and other sexual symbols in the decor. His autobiography was publ. in both Ger. and Eng. in 1994.

Wagner-Régeny, Rudolf, Romanian-born German composer, pedagogue, pianist, and clavichordist; b. Szász-Régen, Transylvania, Aug. 28, 1903; d. Berlin, Sept. 18, 1969. He entered the Leipzig Cons. as a piano pupil of Robert Teichmüller in 1919; in 1920 he enrolled at the Berlin Hochschule für Musik as a student in conducting of Rudolf Krasselt and Siegfried Ochs, in orchestration of Emil Reznicek, and in theory and composition of Friedrich Koch and Franz Schreker. He first gained notice as a composer with his theater pieces for Essen; in 1930 he became a naturalized German citizen, and with the rise of the Nazis was promoted by a faction of the party as a composer of the future; however, the success of his opera *Der Günstling* (Dresden, Feb. 20, 1935) was followed by his supporters' doubts regarding his subsequent output, ending in a scandal with his opera *Johanna Balk* at the Vienna State Opera (April 4, 1941). In 1942 he was drafted into the German Army; after the close of World War II, he settled in East Germany; he was director of the Rostock Hochschule für Musik (1947–50), then was a prof. of composition at the (East) Berlin Hochschule für Musik and at the Academy of Arts. After composing works along traditional lines, he adopted his own 12-note serial technique in 1950.

WORKS: DRAMATIC: OPERAS: *Sganarelle oder Der Schein trügt* (1923; Essen, March 1929); *Moschopulos* (Gera, Dec. 1, 1928); *Der nackte König* (1928; Gera, Dec. 1, 1930); *Der Günstling oder Die letzten Tage des grossen Herrn Fabiano* (1932–34; Dresden, Feb. 20, 1935); *Die Bürger von Calais* (1936–38; Berlin, Jan. 28, 1939); *Johanna Balk* (1938–40; Vienna, April 4, 1941); *Das Bergwerk zu Falun* (1958–60; Salzburg, Aug. 16, 1961). BALLETS: *Moritat* (1928; Essen, March 1929); *Der zerbrochene Krug* (Berlin, 1937). OTHER DRAMATIC: *Esau und Jacob*, biblical scene for 4 Soloists, Speaker, and String Orch. (1929; Gera, 1930); *La Sainte Courtisane* for 4 Speakers and Chamber Orch. (Dessau, 1930); *Die Fabel vom seligen Schlachtermeister* (1931–32; Dresden, May 23, 1964); *Persische Episode* (1940–50; Rostock, March 27, 1963); *Prometheus*, scenic oratorio (1957–58; Kassel, Sept. 12, 1959); incidental music to 7 plays.

BIBL.: A. Burgartz, *R. W.-R.* (Berlin, 1935); T. Müller-Medek, ed., *R. W.-R.: Begegnungen, biographische Aufzeichnungen, Tagebücher und sein Briefwechsel mit Caspar Neher* (Berlin, 1968).

Wahlberg, Rune, Swedish conductor, pianist, and composer; b. Gävle, March 15, 1910. He received training in piano, conducting, and composition at the Stockholm Musikhögskolan (1928–35) and in conducting at the Leipzig Cons. (1936–37; diploma, 1937). He made tours as a pianist. After serving as music director of the Göteborg City Theater (1943–51), he was municipal music director in Kramfors (1953–57), Hofors (1957–64), Härnösand (1964–69), and Hudiksvall (1969–75). His music generally followed along romantic lines with expressionistic infusions, and includes the opera *En Saga* (1952).

Waits, Tom, effective American songwriter and performer; b. Pomona, Calif., Dec. 7, 1949. He began his career playing in Los Angeles clubs as a singer, pianist, and guitarist, sometimes with his group, Nocturnal Emissions. After being signed by Frank Zappa's manager in 1972, he produced his first album, *Closing Time* (1973). He slowly rose from cultdom to stardom through such songs as "Shiver Me Timbers," "Diamonds on My Windshield," and "The Piano Has Been Drinking." He made a number of recordings for the Asylum label, then switched to Island; with *Swordfishtrombones* (1983), he expanded his accompaniment to include a broad spectrum of exotic instruments. He wrote the score for Francis Ford Coppola's film *One from the Heart* (1982), and later made the concert movie *Big Time* (1988). He also appeared frequently as a film and stage actor. He collaborated with his wife, Kathleen Brennan, on the stage show *Frank's Wild Years* (1987), which includes the pastiches *Temptation* and *Innocent When You Dream*. In 1993 he provided music for the first work in Robert Wilson's trilogy of operas, *The Black Rider*; this was followed by his collaborative score with Brennan for the second work in Wilson's trilogy, *Alice*. His contribution to Gavin Bryars's poignant *Jesus' Blood Never Failed Me Yet*, originally composed for tape and ensemble (1971) but refashioned into an orchestral work with tape (1994), in which Waits does raspy vocal duets with the looping, hymnlike verse of a homeless man, became an international success.

Wakasugi, Hiroshi, Japanese conductor; b. Tokyo, May 31, 1935. He studied conducting with Hideo Saito and Nobori Kaneko; in 1967 he was awarded a prize by the Japanese Ministry of Culture. In 1975 he became conductor of the Kyoto Sym. Orch. From 1977 to 1983 he was chief conductor of the Cologne Radio Sym. Orch.; he also was Generalmusikdirektor of the Deutsche Oper am Rhein in Düsseldorf (1982–87). In 1981 he made his U.S. debut as a guest conductor of the Boston Sym. Orch. He was chief conductor of the Tonhalle Orch. in Zürich (1985–91) and the Tokyo Metropolitan Sym. Orch. (1987–95). From 1995 he was permanent conductor of the NHK (Japan Broadcasting Corp) Sym. Orch. in Tokyo.

Wald, Max, American composer and teacher; b. Litchfield, Ill., July 14, 1889; d. Dowagiac, Mich., Aug. 14, 1954. After studying in Chicago, he was active as a theater conductor; he went to Paris in 1922 to study with d'Indy, and remained in Europe until 1936. He then became chairman of the theory dept. of the Chicago Musical College. His symphonic poem *The Dancer Dead* won 2d prize in the NBC competition in 1932, and was broadcast from New York on May 1, 1932. His other works included the operas *Mirandolina* (1936) and *Gay Little World* (1942).

Waldman, Frederic, Austrian-born American conductor and teacher; b. Vienna, April 17, 1903; d. N.Y., Dec. 1, 1995. He studied piano with Richard Robert, orchestration and conducting with Szell, and composition with Weigl. After serving as music director of the Ballet Joos of the Netherlands, he was active in England from 1935 In 1941 he settled in New York and was active as a piano accompanist. After teaching at the Mannes College of Music, he taught at the Juilliard School of Music (1947–67), where, as music director of its Opera Theater, he conducted the American premieres of Strauss's *Capriccio* (1954) and Kodály's *Háry János* (1960). In 1961 he founded the Musica Aeterna Orch. and Chorus, which he conducted in enterprising programs of rarely heard music of the past and present eras, ranging from Monteverdi to Rieti.

Waldmann, Maria, Austrian mezzo-soprano; b. Vienna, 1842; d. Ferrara, Nov. 6, 1920. She studied in Vienna with Passy-Cornet and in Milan with Lamperti, making her debut as Pierotto in *Linda di Chamounix* in Pressburg in 1865. She then sang in Wiesbaden, Amsterdam, Trieste, and Moscow (with the Italian Opera, 1869–70), at La Scala in Milan (1871–72), and in Cairo (1873–76). She retired in 1876. Verdi admired her singing, and chose her for the premiere of his Requiem.

Walker, Alan, English musicologist; b. Scunthorpe, April 6, 1930. He was educated at the Guildhall School of Music in London (ARCM, 1949) and at the Univ. of Durham (B.Mus., 1956; D.Mus., 1965); he also studied with Hans Keller (1958–60). He was prof. of harmony and counterpoint at the Guildhall School of Music (1958–60); after serving as a producer for the BBC music division (1961–71), he was chairman of the music dept. and a prof. at McMaster Univ. in Hamilton, Ontario (from 1971).

WRITINGS (all publ. in London unless otherwise given): *A Study in Musical Analysis* (1962); *An Anatomy of Musical Criticism* (1966); ed., *Frederic Chopin: Profiles of the Man and the*

Musician (1966; 2d ed., rev. and enl., 1978); ed., *Franz Liszt: The Man and His Music* (1970; 2d ed., rev., 1976); Liszt (1971); ed., *Robert Schumann: The Man and His Music* (1972; 2d ed., rev., 1976); *Schumann* (1976); *Franz Liszt: Vol. I, The Virtuoso Years, 1811–1847* (1983; rev. 1987); *Franz Liszt: Vol. II, The Weimar Years, 1848–1861* (1989); with G. Erasmi, *Liszt, Carolyne, and the Vatican: The Story of a Thwarted Marriage* (Stuyvesant, N.Y., 1991).

Walker, Edyth, American mezzo-soprano; b. Hopewell, N.Y., March 27, 1867; d. N.Y., Feb. 19, 1950. She studied singing with Aglaja Orgeni at the Dresden Cons. She made her debut as Fidès in *Le Prophète* at the Berlin Royal Opera on Nov. 11, 1894. She was a member of the Vienna Court Opera (1895–1903); she made her debut at London's Covent Garden as Amneris in 1900. She made her U.S. debut at the Metropolitan Opera in New York. (Nov. 30, 1903), remaining on its roster until 1906, singing soprano as well as mezzo-soprano roles; she also sang both mezzo-soprano and soprano roles at the Hamburg Opera (1903–12); she was the first London Electra (1910). After singing at the Bayreuth and Munich Festivals (1912–17), she turned to private teaching; she was on the faculty of the American Cons. in Fontainebleau (1933–36) before settling in New York.

Walker, Frank, English musicologist; b. Gosport, Hampshire, June 10, 1907; d. (suicide) Tring, Feb. 25?, 1962. He studied telegraphy. In 1926 he went to Rio de Janeiro as a representative of the Western Telegraph Co. From 1931 to 1943 he was in London; in 1944–45 he was in Naples, and later in Vienna, before returning to London. He contributed valuable articles on the composers of the Neapolitan School; he wrote the books *Hugo Wolf: A Biography* (London, 1951; 2d ed., 1968) and *The Man Verdi* (London, 1962).

Walker, Penelope, English mezzo-soprano; b. Manchester, Oct. 12, 1956. She studied at the Guildhall School of Music and Drama in London (1974–78) and the National Opera Studio (1978–80), and received vocal instruction in Munich from Fassbaender and in Paris from Souzay. In 1976 she made her concert debut at London's Royal Albert Hall. After winning the Kathleen Ferrier Prize in 1980, she made her operatic debut at the Paris Opéra Comique in 1982. Her London operatic debut followed in 1983 as Pacini's Maria Tudor with Opera Rara. In 1985 she sang Sosostris in *The Midsummer Marriage* at the English National Opera in London. She portrayed Fricka in the *Ring* cycle at the Welsh National Opera in Cardiff in 1986. In 1989 she made her first appearance at the London Promenade Concerts singing Grimgerde in *Die Walküre*. In 1991 she was engaged at the Zürich Opera. She appeared as Grimgerde at the Théâtre du Châtelet in Paris in 1994, and also sang at Milan's La Scala and at London's Covent Garden. In 1996 she portrayed Handel's Riccardo Primo at the Göttingen Festival. Her concert engagements have taken her to many European music centers. She married **Phillip Joll**.

Walker, Sarah, English mezzo-soprano; b. Cheltenham, March 11, 1943. She studied violin with A. Brosa, cello with H. Philips, and voice with R. Packer and V. Rozsa at the Royal College of Music in London (1961–65). In 1969 she made her operatic debut as Monteverdi's Ottavia with the Kent Opera, and then sang Diana and Jove in Cavalli's *Calisto* at the Glyndebourne Festival in 1970. In 1972 she became a member of the Sadler's Wells Opera in London, and continued to appear there after it became the English National Opera in 1974. She appeared as Magdalene in *Die Meistersinger von Nürnberg* in Chicago in 1977. In 1979 she made her debut at London's Covent Garden as Charlotte. In 1981 she sang Berlioz's Dido in Vienna. On Feb. 3, 1986, she made her Metropolitan Opera debut in New York as Micah in Handel's *Samson*. In 1987 she created the role of Caroline in the British premiere of Sallinen's *The King Goes Forth to War* at Covent Garden. As a concert artist, she appeared throughout Europe and North America. In 1991 she was made a Commander of the Order of the British Empire.

Wallace, Stewart (Farrell), prominent American composer; b. Philadelphia, Nov. 21, 1960. He studied literature and philosophy at the Univ. of Texas at Austin (B.A. with special honors, 1982), and composed his first opera as his thesis. However, he was autodidact in composition. He received various awards and fellowships, and also a MacDowell Colony residency, a Yaddo residency, and a Rockefeller Foundation residency in Bellagio, Italy. In 1998 he was one of the principal figures at the new Institute on the Arts and Civic Dialogue at Harvard Univ. Wallace has demonstrated a particular flair for dramatic composition. His theater scores reveal an imaginative eclecticism that draws upon elements ranging from high art to pop culture. He first attracted widespread notice with his zany opera *Where's Dick?* (Houston, May 24, 1989), which was later transformed into the first feature-length animated opera. It was followed by his opera *Kabbalah* (N.Y., Nov. 14, 1989), whose subject was Jewish mysticism. His *Harvey Milk* (Houston, Jan. 21, 1995), an operatic treatment of the murders of San Francisco mayor George Moscone and city supervisor Harvey Milk by disgruntled ex-city supervisor Dan White, earned Wallace critical encomiums in the United States and abroad. Then followed his opera *Hopper's Wife* (Long Beach, Calif., June 14, 1997), a sexually charged treatment of the American painter Edward Hopper. His subsequent scores include *Yiddisher Teddy Bears* (1999), a "punk-klezmer" opera, and *High Noon* (2000), a "gun" opera. Among his other scores are *Gorilla in a Cage* for Percussion and Orch. (1997), *Kaddish for Harvey Milk* for 3 Soloists, Chorus, and Orch. (1997), *The Cheese and the Worms* for Percussion and Piano (1999), and the film score *Afraid of Everything* (1999).

Wallace, (William) Vincent, Irish violinist, organist, and composer; b. Waterford, March 11, 1812; d. Château de Bagen, Haute-Garonne, France, Oct. 12, 1865. The son of a bandmaster, Wallace was brought up in a musical atmosphere. He was 13 when the family moved to Dublin, and soon entered a professional career, playing violin in theater orchs. and organ in churches. One of his earliest compositions was *The Harp in the Air*, which later became famous when he incorporated it into his opera *Maritana*. In 1831 he married Isabella Kelly. He applied himself to the study of violin, and subsequently was able to give successful concerts. With his wife he traveled in Australia, South America, Mexico, and the U.S. Returning to Europe in 1844, he toured Germany; in 1845 he was in London, where he produced his opera *Maritana* (Drury Lane, Nov. 15, 1845), which obtained excellent success; it was followed by another opera, *Matilda of Hungary* (Drury Lane, Feb. 2, 1847), which was a failure. About 1850 he "married" the American pianist Hélène Stoepel, declaring his first marriage invalid; she made appearances as Mrs. Wallace from 1851. From 1850 to 1853 he visited South and North America. His other operas include *Lurline* (1847; Covent Garden, Feb. 23, 1860), *The Maid of Zürich* (unpubl.), *The Amber Witch* (Haymarket, Feb. 28, 1861), *Love's Triumph* (Covent Garden, Nov. 3, 1862), and *The Desert Flower* (Covent Garden, Oct. 12, 1863); he also wrote the opera *Estrella* (unfinished) and the operettas *Gulnare* and *Olga*.

BIBL.: A. Pougin, *W. V. W.: Étude biographique et critique* (Paris, 1866); W. Flood, *W. V. W.: A Memoir* (Waterford, 1912); R. Phelan, *W. V. W.: A Vagabond Composer* (Waterford, Ireland, 1994).

Wallat, Hans, German conductor; b. Berlin, Oct. 18, 1929. He was educated at the Schwerin Cons. and then conducted in several provincial German music centers. He was music director in Cottbus (1956–58) and 1st conductor of the Leipzig Opera (1958–61), then conducted in Stuttgart (1961–64) and at the Deutsche Oper in West Berlin (1964–65). He was Generalmusikdirektor at the Bremen Opera (1965–70). Wallat made appearances as a guest conductor with various opera houses and orchs. in Europe. On Oct. 7, 1971, he made his Metropolitan Opera debut in New York conducting *Fidelio*. He was Generalmusikdirektor in Mannheim (1970–80), Dortmund (1980–85), and of the Deutsche Oper am Rhein in Düsseldorf (1987–97).

Wallek-Walewski, Boleslaw, Polish conductor, pedagogue, and composer; b. Lemberg, Jan. 23, 1885; d. Kraków, April 9, 1944. He studied theory and composition with Soltys and Niewiadomski and piano with Maliszowa and Zelinger in Lemberg, then continued his training with Zeleński and Szopski at the Kraków Cons.; he completed his studies with Riemann and Prüfer in Leipzig. He became a prof. (1910) and director (1913) of the Kraków Cons.; he was founder-conductor of his own choral society, and also appeared as an operatic and sym. conductor. His compositions followed along Romantic lines. They included the operas *Pan Twardowski* (1911; Kraków, 1915), *Dola* (Lot; Kraków, 1919), *Pomsta Jontkowa* (1926), and *Legenda o królewnie Wandzie* (The Legend of the King's Daughter Wanda; 1936); also oratorios.

Wallen, Errollyn, versatile English composer and formidable pianist; b. Belize City, Belize, April 10, 1958. After studies at Goldsmiths' and King's College, London Univ. (M.Mus.), she worked as a performer and composer in pop, jazz, and classical settings. She also set up her own recording studio in Camden and wrote for film, television, and radio, and studied dance (technique and choreography) in England and the United States (Dance Theatre of Harlem). She wrote and presented "The Music Machine," a youth program for BBC Radio 3 series (April 1994), and also contributed to "Backtracks," a series for London's Channel 4 about music composition for film. She formed Ensemble X, comprised of players from pop, jazz, and classical worlds, to perform her music. Wallen's compositions are remarkably eclectic and range from large orchestral works, choral compositions, and string quartets to ballets, operas, and pop songs. These include *In Our Lifetime* (1990), ballet in celebration of Nelson Mandela's release from prison, choreographed by Christopher Bruce for London's Contemporary Dance Theater, *The Singing Ringing Tree*, musical play to a libretto by Charlotte Keatley (1991), *Heart*, music theater for the Black Mime Theatre (1992), *Waiting*, ballet (1993), *E.D.R.*, music theater for the Black Mime Theatre (1993), *Four Figures with Harlequin*, chamber opera to her own libretto (1993), *LOOK! NO HANDS!*, opera (1996), to a libretto by Cindy Oswin, presented in concert form at the Nottingham Concert Series in a program devoted entirely to her work, *Horseplay*, ballet (1997), and *Nijinska*, musical to a libretto by Kate Westbrook (1999); also the radio plays *Grief* (1993), *The Amazons* (1995), and *The Constant Nymph* (1996). Her first impeccably produced solo album, *Meet Me at Harold Moore's,* appeared in 1998.

Wallenstein, Martin, German pianist and composer; b. Frankfurt am Main, July 22, 1843; d. there, Nov. 29, 1896. He studied with Dreyschock in Prague, and with Hauptmann and Rietz in Leipzig; he made many successful tours as a pianist. His opera, *Das Testament*, was produced at Frankfurt am Main in 1870.

Wallerstein, Lothar, Bohemian-born American pianist and conductor; b. Prague, Nov. 6, 1882; d. New Orleans, Nov. 13, 1949. He studied art and music in Prague and Munich; he also attended the Geneva Cons., where he later taught piano. After serving as accompanist at the Dresden Court Opera (1909), he was conductor and stage director in Posen (1910–14), Breslau (1918–22), Duisberg (1922–24), and Frankfurt am Main (1924–26); he was producer at the Vienna State Opera (1927–38); he conducted at La Scala in Milan (1929). He went to the United States in 1941; he was a producer at the Metropolitan Opera in New York (1941–46). In 1945 he became a naturalized American citizen.

BIBL.: A. Berger, *Über die Spielleitung der Oper: Betrachtungen zur musikalischen Dramaturgie Dr. L. W.s* (Graz, 1928).

Walter, Bruno (full name, **Bruno Walter Schlesinger**), eminent German-born American conductor; b. Berlin, Sept. 15, 1876; d. Beverly Hills, Feb. 17, 1962. He entered the Stern Cons. in Berlin at age 8, where he studied with H. Ehrlich, L. Bussler, and R. Radecke. At age 9, he performed in public as a pianist but at 13 decided to pursue his interest in conducting. In 1893 he became a coach at the Cologne Opera, where he made his conducting debut with Lortzing's *Waffenschmied*; in the following year he was engaged as assist. conductor at the Hamburg Stadttheater, under Gustav Mahler; this contact was decisive in his career, and he became in subsequent years an ardent champion of Mahler's music; conducted the premieres of the posthumous Sym. No. 9 and *Das Lied von der Erde*. During the 1896–97 season, Walter was engaged as 2d conductor at the Stadttheater in Breslau, then became principal conductor in Pressburg, and in 1898 at Riga, where he conducted for 2 seasons. In 1900 he received the important engagement of conductor at the Berlin Royal Opera under a 5-year contract; however, he left this post in 1901 when he received an offer from Mahler to become his assistant at the Vienna Court Opera. He established himself as an efficient opera conductor; he also conducted in England (1st appearance, March 3, 1909, with the Royal Phil. Soc. in London). He remained at the Vienna Court Opera after the death of Mahler. On Jan. 1, 1913, he became Royal Bavarian Generalmusikdirektor in Munich; under his guidance, the Munich Opera enjoyed brilliant performances, particularly of Mozart's works. Seeking greater freedom for his artistic activities, he left Munich in 1922, and gave numerous performances as a guest conductor with European orchs.; he conducted the series "Bruno Walter Concerts" with the Berlin Phil. from 1921 to 1933; from 1925 he also conducted summer concerts of the Salzburg Festival; his performances of Mozart's music there set a standard. He also appeared as pianist in Mozart's chamber works. On Feb. 15, 1923, he made his American debut with the N.Y. Sym. Soc., and appeared with it again in 1924 and 1925. From 1925 to 1929 he was conductor of the Städtische Oper in Berlin-Charlottenburg; in 1929 he succeeded Furtwängler as conductor of the Gewandhaus Orch. in Leipzig, but continued to give special concerts in Berlin. On Jan. 14, 1932, he was guest conductor of the N.Y. Phil., acting also as soloist in a Mozart piano concerto; he was reengaged during the next 3 seasons as assoc. conductor with Toscanini. He was also a guest conductor in Philadelphia, Washington, D.C., and Baltimore. With the advent of the Nazi regime in Germany in 1933, his engagement with the Gewandhaus Orch. was canceled, and he was also prevented from continuing his orch. concerts in Berlin. He filled several engagements with the Concertgebouw Orch. in Amsterdam, and also conducted in Salzburg. In 1936 he was engaged as music director of the Vienna State Opera; this was terminated with the Nazi annexation of Austria in 1938. Walter, with his family, then went to France, where he was granted French citizenship. After the outbreak of World War II in 1939, he sailed for America, establishing his residence in California, and eventually became a naturalized American citizen. He was guest conductor with the NBC Sym. Orch. in New York (1939); he also conducted many performances of the Metropolitan Opera in New York (debut in *Fidelio* on Feb. 14, 1941). From 1947 to 1949 he was conductor and musical adviser of the N.Y. Phil.; he returned regularly as guest conductor until 1960; he also conducted in Europe (1949–60), giving his farewell performance in Vienna with the Vienna Phil. in 1960.

Walter achieved the reputation of a perfect classicist among 20th-century conductors; his interpretations of the masterpieces of the Vienna School were particularly notable. He is acknowledged to have been a foremost conductor of Mahler's syms. His own compositions include 2 syms.; *Siegesfahrt* for Solo Voices, Chorus, and Orch.; String Quartet; Piano Quintet; Piano Trio; several albums of songs. He publ. the books *Von den moralischen Kräften der Musik* (Vienna, 1935); *Gustav Mahler* (Vienna, 1936; 2d ed., 1957; Eng. tr., 1927; 2d ed., 1941); *Theme and Variations: An Autobiography* (N.Y., 1946; Ger. original, 1947); *Von der Musik und vom Musizieren* (Frankfurt am Main, 1957; Eng. tr., 1961); L. Walter-Lindt, ed., *Briefe 1894–1962* (Frankfurt am Main, 1970).

BIBL.: M. Komorn-Rebhan, *Was wir von B. W. lernten* (Vienna, 1913); P. Stefan, *B. W.* (Vienna, 1936); B. Gavoty, *B. W.* (Geneva, 1956).

Walter, David Edgar, American bass-baritone and composer; b. Boston, Feb. 2, 1953. He studied voice with John Powell at Rutgers Univ. (1970–75), Oren Brown, Lois Bove, and Shirley Meier at Trenton (N.J.) State College (M.A., 1978), and Janet Wheeler at the New England Cons. of Music in Boston. He also studied with

Diamond, Luening, and Persichetti at the Juilliard School in New York (B.M. in composition, 1975), Edward Richter and Calvin Hampton (1976–78), and Del Tredici, Mekeel, and John Thow at Boston Univ. (1978–81). Walter subsequently was active as a singer in Boston and N.Y. churches. As a composer, he writes in an accessible style. Among his works are dramatic pieces.

Walter, Georg A., German tenor, pedagogue, and composer; b. Hoboken, N.J., Nov. 13, 1875; d. Berlin, Sept. 13, 1952. He studied singing in Milan, Dresden, Berlin, and London, and composition with Wilhelm Berger in Berlin. He made a career as a singer, particularly distinguishing himself in the works of Bach and Handel. He was a prof. at the Stuttgart Hochschule für Musik (1925–34), then settled in Berlin as a vocal teacher; his most celebrated student was Dietrich Fischer-Dieskau. He brought out new eds. of works by the sons of Bach, Schütz et al.

Walter (also, **Walther** or **Walderth**), **(Johann) Ignaz (Joseph),** German tenor and composer; b. Radonitz, Bohemia, Aug. 31, 1755; d. Regensburg, Feb. 22, 1822. After training from the organist Ignaz Neudörfll, he entered the Univ. of Vienna in 1773; he also received instruction in singing and composition from Starzer. He sang at Vienna's Nationaltheater (1780–82); he was in Prague (1782–84) and in Riga (1784–86), where he married the soprano Juliane Browne Roberts (1759–1835); they appeared at the combined Frankfurt am Main and Mainz theaters (from 1786), serving as court singers (from 1789). They also appeared with Grossmann's company in Hannover and Bremen in 1792, where Walter was named opera director; in 1804 he became director of the new Regensburg theater. He composed some 20 Singspiels, ballet music, and incidental music to plays.

Waltershausen, H(ermann) W(olfgang Sartorius), Freiherr von, German composer, writer on music, and teacher; b. Göttingen, Oct. 12, 1882; d. Munich, Aug. 13, 1954. He began his music studies with M. J. Erb in Strasbourg; although he lost his right arm and leg in an accident when he was 10, he learned to play the piano and conduct with his left hand. He settled in Munich in 1901, where he studied composition with Thuille and piano with Schmid-Lindner; he also studied music history with Sandberger at the Univ. of Munich. In 1917 he established there a seminar for operatic dramaturgy, the Praktisches Seminar für Fortgeschrittene Musikstudierende; he was a prof. and assistant director of the Munich Akademie der Tonkunst (1920–22), then director (1922–33); he later founded his own Seminar für Privatmusiklehrer, which became the Waltershausen-Seminar in 1948. In his music he adopted a neo-Romantic style, rather advanced in harmonic treatment. Among his compositions were 2 operas: *Else Klapperzehen* (Dresden, May 15, 1909) and *Oberst Chabert* (Frankfurt am Main, Jan. 18, 1912); also *Richardis*, dramatic mystery (Karlsruhe, Nov. 14, 1915), *Die Rauensteiner Hochzeit* (Karlsruhe, 1919), and *Die Gräfin von Tolosa* (1934; Bavarian Radio, Munich, 1958).

WRITINGS (all publ. in Munich unless otherwise given): *Der Freischütz: Ein Versuch über die musikalische Romantik* (1920); *Das Siegfried-Idyll oder die Rückkehr zur Natur* (1920); *Die Zauberflöte: Eine operndramaturgische Studie* (1920); *Richard Strauss: Ein Versuch* (1921); *Orpheus und Euridike: Eine operndramaturgische Studie* (1923); *Musik, Dramaturgie, Erziehung* (collected essays; 1926); *Dirigentenerziehung* (Leipzig, 1929); *Die Kunst des Dirigierens* (Berlin, 1942; 2d ed., 1954); *Dramaturgie der Oper* (MS).

BIBL.: K.-R. Danler and R. Mader, *H. W. v.W.* (Tutzing, 1984).

Walthew, Richard Henry, English composer, conductor, and pedagogue; b. London, Nov. 4, 1872; d. East Preston, Sussex, Nov. 14, 1951. He studied with Parry at the Royal College of Music in London (1890–94). After a directorship of the Passmore Edwards Settlement Place (1900–04), he was appointed instructor of the opera class at the Guildhall School of Music in London; in 1907 he became a prof. of music at Queen's College; he also conducted provincial orchs. His works included 2 operettas: *The Enchanted Island* (London, May 8, 1900) and *The Gardeners* (London, Feb. 12, 1906). He was the author of *The Development of Chamber Music* (1909).

Walton, Sir William (Turner), eminent English composer; b. Oldham, Lancashire, March 29, 1902; d. Ischia, Italy, March 8, 1983. Both his parents were professional singers, and Walton himself had a fine singing voice as a youth; he entered the Cathedral Choir School at Christ Church, Oxford, and began to compose choral pieces for performance. Sir Hugh Allen, organist of New College, advised him to develop his interest in composition, and sponsored his admission to Christ Church at an early age; however, he never graduated, and instead began to write unconventional music in the manner that was fashionable in the 1920s. His talent manifested itself in a string quartet he wrote at the age of 17, which was accepted for performance for the first festival of the ISCM in 1923. In London he formed a congenial association with the Sitwell family of quintessential cognoscenti and literati who combined a patrician sense of artistic superiority with a benign attitude toward the social plebs; they also provided Walton with residence at their manor in Chelsea, where he lived off and on for some 15 years. Fascinated by Edith Sitwell's oxymoronic verse, Walton set it to music bristling with novel jazzy effects in brisk, irregular rhythms and modern harmonies; Walton was only 19 when he wrote it. Under the title *Facade*, it was first performed in London in 1923, with Edith Sitwell herself delivering her doggerel with a megaphone; as expected, the show provoked an outburst of feigned indignation in the press and undisguised delight among the young in spirit. But Walton did not pursue the path of facile hedonism so fashionable at the time; he soon demonstrated his ability to write music in a Classical manner in his fetching concert overture *Portsmouth Point*, first performed in Zürich in 1926, and later in the comedy overture *Scapino*. His biblical oratorio *Belshazzar's Feast*, written in 1931, reveals a deep emotional stream and nobility of design that places Walton directly in line from Handel and Elgar among English masters. His symphonic works show him as an inheritor of the grand Romantic tradition; his concertos for violin, for viola, and for cello demonstrate an adroitness in effective instrumental writing. Walton was a modernist in his acceptance of the new musical resources, but he never deviated from fundamental tonality and formal clarity of design. Above all, his music was profoundly national, unmistakably British in its inspiration and content. Quite appropriately, he was asked to contribute to two royal occasions: he wrote *Crown Imperial March* for the coronation of King George VI in 1937 and *Orb and Sceptre* for that of Queen Elizabeth II in 1953. He received an honorary doctorate from the Univ. of Oxford in 1942. King George VI knighted him in 1951. He spent the last years of his life on the island of Ischia off Naples with his Argentine-born wife, Susana Gil Passo.

WORKS: DRAMATIC: OPERAS: *Troilus and Cressida*, after Chaucer (1947–54; London, Dec. 3, 1954; rev. 1963 and 1972–76; London, Nov. 12, 1976); *The Bear*, after Chekhov (1965–67; Aldeburgh, June 3, 1967). BALLETS: *The First Shoot* (1935); *The Wise Virgins*, after J.S. Bach (1939–40; London, April 24, 1940); *The Quest* (1943). ENTERTAINMENT: *Façade* for Reciter and Instrumental Ensemble, after Edith Sitwell (1921; 1st perf. privately at the Sitwell home in London, Jan. 24, 1922; 1st public perf., London, June 12, 1923; rev. 1926, 1928, 1942, and 1951; rev. as *Façade 2*, 1978; arranged as a ballet, 1929, with subsequent changes). INCIDENTAL MUSIC FOR THE THEATER AND RADIO: *A Son of Heaven* (1924–25); *The Boy David* (1935); *Macbeth* (1941–42); *Christopher Columbus* (1942). FILM SCORES: *Escape Me Never* (1934); *As You Like It* (1936); *Dreaming Lips* (1937); *Stolen Life* (1938); *Major Barbara* (1940); *Next of Kin* (1941); *The Foreman Went to France* (1941–42); *The First of the Few* (1942); *Went the Day Well?* (1942); *Henry V* (1943–44); *Hamlet* (1947); *Richard III* (1955); *The Battle of Britain* (1969); *Three Sisters* (1969). ORATORIO: *Belshazzar's Feast* for Baritone, Chorus, and Orch. (1930–31; Leeds, Oct. 8, 1931; rev. 1948 and 1957).

BIBL.: F. Howes, *The Music of W. W.* (2 vols., London, 1942, 1943; new amplified ed., 1965); S. Craggs, *W. W.: A Thematic Catalogue of His Musical Works* (London, 1977; rev. ed., 1990);

A. Poulton, *Sir W. W.: A Discography* (London, 1980); N. Tierney, *W. W.: His Life and Music* (London, 1984); S. Walton, *W. W.: Behind the Facade* (Oxford, 1988); M. Kennedy, *Portrait of W.* (Oxford, 1989); S. Craggs, *W. W.: A Source Book* (Aldershot, 1993).

Waltz, Gustavus, German bass; place and date of birth unknown; d. London, c.1759. His first recorded appearance was at the Little Haymarket Theatre in London in Lampe's Amelia (March 13, 1732). He then sang in the pirated ed. of Handel's *Acis and Galatea* there (May 17, 1732), and subsequently appeared in various London theaters. After accompanying Handel to Oxford in 1733, where he appeared in several of his works, he returned to London as a member of Handel's company until 1736. He created the roles of Minos in *Arianna in Creta* (Jan. 26, 1734), Mars in *Il Parnasso in festa* (April 13, 1734), the King of Scotland in *Ariodante* (Jan. 8, 1735), Melisso in *Alcina* (April 16, 1736), and Nicandro in *Atalanta* (May 12, 1736); he also sang in various oratorio performances. He was subsequently active as a singer in light English theater pieces; however, he continued to make some concert appearances; he sang in performances of Handel's *Messiah* at the Foundling Hospital (1754, 1758, 1759). He is mentioned in the reported acrid comment of Handel on Gluck: "He knows no more of counterpoint than my cook, Waltz."

Wambach, Emile, Belgian composer; b. Arlon, Luxembourg, Nov. 26, 1854; d. Antwerp, May 6, 1924. He studied with Benoit, Mertens, and Callaerts at the Antwerp Cons., and in 1913 became its director. He wrote music in the National Flemish style, following the model of Benoit. He wrote the Flemish opera *Nathans Parabel*, as well as 4 oratorios: *Mozes op den Nijl* (1881), *Yolande* (1884), *Blancefloer* (1889), and *Jeanne d'Arc* (1909).

Wand, Günter, distinguished German conductor; b. Elberfeld, Jan. 7, 1912. He studied in Wuppertal; he attended the Univ. of Cologne and took courses in composition with Philipp Jarnach and in piano with Paul Baumgartner at the Cologne Cons. and Hochschule für Musik; he received instruction in conducting from Franz von Hoesslin at the Munich Academy of Music. After working as a répétiteur and conductor in Wuppertal and other provincial music centers, he became chief conductor in Detmold. He was conductor at the Cologne Opera (1939–44), then of the Salzburg Mozarteum Orch. (1944–45). In 1946 he was appointed Generalmusikdirektor of Cologne, being responsible for both orch. and operatic performances; in 1947 he was named conductor of the Gurzenich Orch. there, a post he retained until 1974; he also was prof. of conducting at the Cologne Hochschule für Musik (from 1948). He appeared as a guest conductor throughout Europe and also in Japan. After leaving Cologne, he conducted in Bern. He subsequently served as chief conductor of the North German Radio Sym. Orch. in Hamburg (1982–91); he also was a principal guest conductor of the BBC Sym. Orch. in London and later of the (West) Berlin Radio Sym. Orch. (1989–90). On Jan. 19, 1989, he made his belated U.S. debut at the age of 77 as a guest conductor with the Chicago Sym. Orch. A conductor in the revered Austro-German tradition, Wand acquired a fine reputation as an interpreter of Mozart, Beethoven, Brahms, and most especially Bruckner; he also did much to foster contemporary music.

BIBL.: F. Berger, *G. W.: Gürzenichkapellmeister 1947–1974* (Cologne, 1974).

Ward, David, esteemed Scottish bass; b. Dumbarton, July 3, 1922; d. Dunedin, New Zealand, July 16, 1983. He was a student of Clive Carey at the Royal College of Music in London and of Hans Hotter in Munich. In 1952 he joined the chorus of the Sadler's Wells Opera in London, where he made his operatic debut as the Old Bard in Boughton's *The Immortal Hour* in 1953. He continued to sing there until 1958. In 1960 he made his debut at London's Covent Garden as Pogner, and returned there as Arkel and Rocco. He also created the role of Morosus in the first British staging of Strauss's *Die Schweigsame Frau* there in 1961. In 1960 he appeared as Titurel at the Bayreuth Festival, where he sang again in 1961 and 1962. In 1964 he sang Wotan at Covent Garden and in 1967 at the Teatro Colón in Buenos Aires. On Jan. 3, 1964, he made his Metropolitan Opera debut in New York as Sarastro, where he remained on the roster until 1966; he was again on its roster from 1973 to 1975 and from 1978 to 1980. Ward also pursued a highly distinguished concert career. In 1972 he was made a Commander of the Order of the British Empire. Among his other roles were Hunding, Fasolt, King Marke, Philip II, and Boris Godunov.

Ward, Robert (Eugene), American composer and teacher; b. Cleveland, Sept. 13, 1917. He studied with Rogers, Royce, and Hanson at the Eastman School of Music in Rochester, N.Y. (B.Mus., 1939) and with Jacobi at the Juilliard Graduate School in New York (certificate, 1946); he also studied conducting with Stoessel and Schenkman and received some training in composition from Copland. He taught at Columbia Univ. (1946–48) and at the Juilliard School of Music (1946–56); he also was music director of the 3d Street Music Settlement (1952–55), then was vice president and managing ed. of the Galaxy Music Corp. (1956–67). After serving as president of the North Carolina School of the Arts in Winston-Salem (1967–74), where he continued as a teacher of composition until 1979, he held the chair of Mary Duke Biddle Prof. of Music at Duke Univ. (1979–87). In 1950, 1952, and 1966 he held Guggenheim fellowships; in 1962 he won the Pulitzer Prize in music and the N.Y. Music Critics' Circle Award for his opera *The Crucible*. In 1972 he was elected a member of the National Inst. of Arts and Letters. He evolved an effective idiom, modern but not aggressively so; composed a number of dramatic and compact stage works on American subjects.

WORKS: DRAMATIC: OPERAS: *He Who Gets Slapped* (1955; N.Y., May 17, 1956; rev. 1973); *The Crucible* (N.Y., Oct. 26, 1961); *The Lady from Colorado* (Central City, Colo., July 3, 1961; rev. as *Lady Kate*, 1981; Wooster, Ohio, June 8, 1994); *Claudia Legare* (1973; Minneapolis, April 14, 1978); *Minutes till Midnight* (1978–82; Miami, June 4, 1982); *Abelard and Heloise* (1981); *Roman Fever* (1993). BALLET: *The Scarlet Letter* (1990).

BIBL.: K. Kreitner, *R. W.: A Bio-Bibliography* (Westport, Conn., 1988).

Ward-Steinman, David, American composer, teacher, and pianist; b. Alexandria, La., Nov. 6, 1936. He studied at Florida State Univ. (B.Mus., 1957); he also received training from Riegger (1954), Milhaud at the Aspen (Colo.) Music School (1956), and Babbitt and Copland at the Berkshire Music Center, Tanglewood (summer, 1957); after further studies at the Univ. of Ill. (M.M., 1958), he pursued private training with Boulanger in Paris (1958–59), then returned to the Univ. of Ill. to complete his education (D.M.A., 1961). In 1961 he became a faculty member and composer-in-residence at San Diego State Univ., where he served as prof. of music (from 1968); he also was the Ford Foundation composer-in-residence of the Tampa Bay area in Florida (1970–72) and the Fulbright Senior Scholar at Victo rian College of the Arts and La Trobe Univ. in Melbourne, Australia (1989–90). In 1995 he was a participant at the Académie d'été at IRCAM in Paris. With S. Ward-Steinman, he publ. *Comparative Anthology of Musical Forms* (2 vols., Belmont, Calif., 1976); he also publ. *Toward a Comparative Structural Theory of the Arts* (San Diego, 1989).

WORKS: DRAMATIC: *Western Orpheus*, ballet (1964; San Diego, Feb. 26, 1965; rev. version, El Cajon, Calif., April 17, 1987); *These Three*, ballet (N.Y., Sept. 13, 1966); *Tamar*, music drama (1970–77); *Rituals* for Dancers and Musicians (Channel 13 TV, Tampa, Dec. 5, 1971).

Ware, Harriet, American pianist and composer; b. Waupun, Wis., Aug. 26, 1877; d. N.Y., Feb. 9, 1962. She received her musical instruction from her father, a choral conductor, then studied piano with William Mason in New York and Sigismund Stojowski in Paris, and composition with Hugo Kaun in Berlin. Her *Women's Triumphal March* was made the national song of the Federation of Women's Clubs in 1927; her symphonic poem *The Artisan* was given by the N.Y. Sym. Orch. in 1929. Some of her songs. She also wrote an operetta, *Waltz for 3*.

Warfield, Sandra, American mezzo-soprano; b. Kansas City, Mo., Aug. 6, 1929. After training at the Kansas City Cons., she began her career singing in operettas. She then pursued her studies in New York with Fritz Lehmann. In 1953 she won the Metropolitan Opera Auditions of the Air and made her debut with the company in New York as a peasant girl in *Le nozze di Figaro* on Nov. 20, 1953. By 1955 she was singing major roles there, most notably Ulrica. When her husband, **James McCracken**, left the Metropolitan Opera in 1957, Warfield did likewise and made her debut at the Vienna State Opera as Ulrica. In 1961 she created the role of Katerina in Martinů's *Greek Passion* at the Zürich Opera. She sang Delilah at the San Francisco Opera in 1963. She was again on the roster of the Metropolitan Opera in 1965–66, 1967–68, and 1971–72. As a guest artist, she sang with various American and European opera houses. She also toured extensively as a concert artist, frequently appearing with her husband. Warfield was especially admired for her dramatic vocal gifts. Among her best roles were Delilah, Amneris, Carmen, Ulrica, Marcellina, and Fricka. With her husband, she publ. the autobiographical vol. *A Star in the Family* (N.Y., 1971).

Warfield, William (Caesar), black American baritone and teacher; b. West Helena, Ark., Jan. 22, 1920. He studied at the Eastman School of Music in Rochester, N.Y. (B.Mus., 1942). Following service in the U.S. Army, he returned to Eastman in 1946 to pursue graduate training. After further studies with Otto Herz and Yves Tinayre, he completed his training with Rosa Ponselle (1958–65). From 1947 he appeared in N.Y. theaters. On March 19, 1950, he made his recital debut at N.Y.'s Town Hall. After a concert tour of Australia in 1950, he sang Joe in *Show Boat* in New York in 1951. In 1952–53 he toured Europe as Porgy in *Porgy and Bess*. He continued to sing in musicals and operas in the United States and abroad, and also made concert tours of Africa and the Middle East (1956), Europe (with the Philadelphia Orch., 1956), and Asia (1958). In 1974 he became a teacher at the Univ. of Ill. In 1984 he was elected president of the National Assn. of Negro Musicians. He married **Leontyne Price** in 1952, but they were divorced in 1974. With A. Miller, he publ. *William Warfield: My Music & My Life* (Champaign, Ill., 1991).

Warlich, Reinhold von, German baritone; b. St. Petersburg, May 24, 1877; d. N.Y., Nov. 10, 1939. His father was an opera conductor active in St. Petersburg; he studied at the Hamburg Cons., in Florence, and in Cologne. He toured in Europe as a singer of German lieder, and was especially distinguished as an interpreter of Schubert, whose song cycles he gave in their entirety. He lived for some time in Canada; later was a singing teacher in Paris and London; made concert tours in the United States from 1909, eventually settling in New York.

Warnots, Henri, Belgian tenor, teacher, and composer; b. Brussels, July 11, 1832; d. Saint-Josse-ten-Noode, Feb. 27, 1893. He studied at the Brussels Cons., making his debut in Liège (1856), then sang in Paris and Strasbourg. In 1867 he became a prof. at the Brussels Cons. In 1870 he established a music school in Saint-Josse-ten-Noode, where he remained until his death. His operetta, *Une heure de mariage*, was produced in Strasbourg on Jan. 24, 1865.

Warrack, John (Hamilton), English writer on music; b. London, Feb. 9, 1928. His father was the Scottish conductor and composer Guy (Douglas Hamilton) Warrack (b. Edinburgh, Feb. 8, 1900; d. Englefield Green, Feb. 12, 1986). He studied at Winchester College, then took up oboe and composition at the Royal College of Music in London; he subsequently played oboe in several ensembles. In 1953 he became music ed. of the Oxford Univ. Press; in 1954 he joined the staff of the *Daily Telegraph*, where he was a music critic; then was chief music critic of the *Sunday Telegraph* (1961–72). After serving as director of the Leeds Festival (1977–83), he was a lecturer in music and a fellow at St. Hugh's College, Oxford (1984–93). He contributed numerous articles and reviews to *Opera* and *Gramophone*. His biography of Weber is the standard modern source.

WRITINGS: *Six Great Composers* (London, 1958); coed. with H. Rosenthal, *The Concise Oxford Dictionary of Opera* (London, 1964; 2d ed., rev., 1979); *Carl Maria von Weber* (London, 1968; also in Ger., 1972; 2d ed., rev., London, 1976); *Tchaikovsky Symphonies and Concertos* (London, 1969; 2d ed., rev., 1974); *Tchaikovsky* (London, 1973); *Tchaikovsky Ballet Music* (London, 1978); ed. *Carl Maria von Weber: Writings on Music* (Cambridge, 1982); coed. with E. West, *The Oxford Dictionary of Opera* (Oxford, 1992); *Richard Wagner: Die Meistersinger von Nürnberg* (Cambridge, 1994).

Warren, Leonard, outstanding American baritone; b. N.Y., April 21, 1911; d. there, on the stage of the Metropolitan Opera House while singing the role of Don Carlos during a performance of *La forza del destino*, March 4, 1960. The original family name was Warenoff; it was Americanized as Warren when his Russian father settled in the United States. He was first employed in his father's fur business in New York; in 1935 he joined the chorus of Radio City Music Hall; he also studied voice with Sidney Dietch and Giuseppe De Luca. In 1938 he won the Metropolitan Opera Auditions of the Air and was granted a stipend to study in Italy, where he took voice lessons with Pais and Piccozi. Returning to America, he made his debut at the Metropolitan Opera in excerpts from *La Traviata* and *Pagliacci* during a concert in New York on Nov. 27, 1938; his formal operatic debut took place there on Jan. 13, 1939, when he sang Paolo in *Simon Boccanegra*. He quickly advanced in public favor, eventually assuming a leading place among the noted baritones of his time. He also sang in San Francisco, Chicago, Canada, and South America. He appeared at La Scala in Milan in 1953; in 1958 he made a highly successful tour of the Soviet Union. His last complete performance at the Metropolitan Opera was as Simon Boccanegra on March 1, 1960, 3 days before his tragic death. He was particularly acclaimed as one of the foremost interpreters of the great Verdi baritone roles; he also sang the parts of Tonio in *Pagliacci*, Escamillo in *Carmen*, and Scarpia in *Tosca*. He collapsed while singing the aria "Urna fatale dal mio destino," underlining the tragic irony of the words, and died of a cerebral hemorrhage backstage. He was reputed to be a person of an intractable character, who always tried to impose his will on stage designers, managers, and even conductors, in matters of production, direction, and tempi. He caused pain, a colleague said, but he had a great voice.

Warren, Raymond (Henry Charles), English composer and teacher; b. Weston-super-Mare, Dec. 7, 1928. He studied with Robin Orr at Corpus Christi College, Cambridge (1949–52; M.A., 1952), continuing his education at the Univ. of Cambridge (M.A., 1955; Mus.D., 1967); he also was a student of Tippett (1952–54) and Berkeley (1958). In 1955 he became a teacher at Queen's Univ. in Belfast, where he was a prof. from 1966 to 1972. From 1972 he was a prof. at the Univ. of Bristol. He publ. *Opera Workshops: Studies in Understanding and Interpretation* (Brookfield, 1995).

WORKS: DRAMATIC: *The Lady of Ephesus*, chamber opera (1958; Belfast, Feb. 16, 1959); *Finn and the Black Hag*, children's opera (Belfast, Dec. 11, 1959); *Graduation Ode*, comic opera (Belfast, Nov. 20, 1963); 3 children's church operas: *Let My People Go* (Liverpool, March 22, 1972), *St. Patrick* (Liverpool, May 3, 1979), and *In the Beginning* (Clifton, July 22, 1982); incidental music for plays. Also 2 oratorios: *The Passion* (Belfast, Dec. 11, 1959) and *Continuing Cities* (Bristol, April 22, 1989).

Warren, Richard Henry, American organist and composer; b. Albany, N.Y., Sept. 17, 1859; d. South Chatham, Mass., Dec. 3, 1933. He studied with his father, the American organist and composer George William Warren (1828–1902), then pursued his training in Europe (1880–86), where his principal mentor was Widor. He was organist and choirmaster in various churches in New York; in 1886 he founded the Church Choral Soc., which he conducted until 1895 and again from 1903 to 1907, producing many important works, including the American premieres of choral compositions by Dvořák, Liszt, Gounod, Saint-Saëns, et al. Horatio Parker wrote his *Hora Novissima* for this society, and

Warren brought it out on May 3, 1893. Among Warren's own compositions are the operettas *Igala* (1880), *All on a Summer's Day* (1882), *Magnolia* (1886), and *The Rightful Heir* (1899); also a "romantic opera," *Phyllis* (N.Y., May 7, 1900).

Wartel, Pierre-François, noted French tenor and teacher; b. Versailles, April 3, 1806; d. Paris, Aug. 3, 1882. In 1825 he entered the Paris Cons. as a pupil of Halévy, but soon thereafter began studies with Choron at the Institut de la Musique Religieuse; in 1828 he returned to the Paris Cons. to pursue vocal training with Davide Banderali and Adolphe Nourrit (premier prix in singing, 1829). He was a member of the Paris Opéra (1831–46), and also made successful concert tours to Berlin, Prague, and Vienna. With Nourrit, he helped create an appreciation of Schubert's lieder in France via his song recitals. He was mainly active as a singing teacher from 1842; his most prominent pupils were Christine Nilsson and Zelia Trebelli. His wife, Atale Thérèse Annette (née Adrien) Wartel (b. Paris, July 2, 1814; d. there, Nov. 6, 1865), was a talented pianist; she studied at the Paris Cons.; after serving as an accompanist there, she was a prof. of piano (1831–38); she composed piano studies and other pieces.

Waters, Edward N(eighbor), American musicologist; b. Leavenworth, Kansas, July 23, 1906; d. Mitchellville, Md., July 27, 1991. He studied piano and theory at the Eastman School of Music in Rochester, N.Y. (B.M., 1927; M.M. in musicology, 1928). In 1931 he joined the staff of the Music Division of the Library of Congress in Washington, D.C.; from 1972 to 1976 he served as chief of the Music Division. He was the program annotator of the National Sym. Orch. in Washington, D.C. (1934–43) and president of the Music Library Assn. (1941–46), later serving as ed. of the latter's journal *Notes* (1963–66); he also wrote many articles and book reviews for professional journals. The Cleveland Inst. of Music conferred upon him the honorary degree of D.Mus. (1973). He wrote a definitive biography of Victor Herbert (N.Y., 1955).

Watkinson, Carolyn, English mezzo-soprano; b. Preston, March 19, 1949. She received her training at the Royal Manchester College of Music and in The Hague. She first established herself as a fine concert singer, especially excelling in Baroque music. In 1978 she sang Rameau's Phèdre at the English Bach Festival at London's Covent Garden. In 1979 she appeared as Monteverdi's Nero with the Netherlands Opera in Amsterdam. In 1981 she made her debut at Milan's La Scala as Ariodante and sang Rossini's Rosina in Stuttgart. She appeared as Gluck's Orfeo with the Glyndebourne Touring Opera in 1982, and then made her formal debut at the Glyndebourne Opera as Cherubino in 1984. In 1987 she made a tour of Australia. She was a soloist in Bach's St. John Passion at Gloucester Cathedral in a performance shown on BBC-TV on Good Friday in 1989. In 1990 she appeared as Purcell's Dido at the Salerno Cathedral and sang Nero at the Innsbruck Festival. She also continued to sing regularly as a concert artist in a repertoire ranging from early music to the contemporary period.

Watson (real name, **McLamore**), **Claire,** American soprano; b. N.Y., Feb. 3, 1924; d. Utting, Germany, July 16, 1986. She studied voice in New York with Elisabeth Schumann and Sergius Kagen; she received further training in Vienna. She made her operatic debut as Desdemona in Graz in 1951; she was a member of the Frankfurt am Main Opera (1956–58) and the Bavarian State Opera in Munich from 1958 until her farewell as the Marschallin in 1976. As a guest artist, she appeared at London's Covent Garden (1958–63; 1964; 1970; 1972), the Glyndebourne Festival (1959), and the Salzburg Festival (1966–68). She also sang in Vienna, Milan, Rome, Chicago, Buenos Aires, and San Francisco. Among her other roles were Donna Elvira, Elisabeth de Valois, Eva, Sieglinde, Ariadne, and Tatiana.

Watson, Lillian, English soprano; b. London, Dec. 4, 1947. She studied at the Guildhall School of Music and Drama in London and at the London Opera Centre, and received private vocal instruction from Vera Rozsa and Jessica Cash. In 1970 she made her formal operatic debut as Cis in *Albert Herring* at the Wexford Festival. She sang Papagena at her first appearance at the Welsh National Opera in Cardiff in 1971, and continued to sing there until 1975. In 1971 she made her debut at London's Covent Gaden as Rossini's Barbarina, where her subsequent roles included Blondchen, Tatiana, Janáček's Vixen, and Tippett's Bella. In 1975 she appeared as Despina with the Glyndebourne Touring Opera, and in 1976 she sang Susanna at the Glyndebourne Festival, which role she also chose for her debut at the English National Opera in London in 1978. In 1982 she made her first appearance at the Salzburg Festival as Marzelline, and then sang Blondchen in Vienna in 1983. She was engaged at the Théâtre des Champs-Elysées in Paris in 1989 as Strauss's Sophie. In 1993 she portrayed the Fairy Godmother in the first British performance of *Cendrillon* at the Welsh National Opera.

Watts, Helen (Josephine), admired Welsh contralto; b. Milford Haven, Dec. 7, 1927. She was a student of Caroline Hatchard and Frederick Jackson at the Royal Academy of Music in London. She began her career singing in the Glyndebourne Festival Chorus and the BBC Chorus in London. Her first appearance as a soloist was in 1953. In 1955 she made her first appearance at the London Promenade Concerts singing Bach arias under Sargent's direction. Thereafter she distinguished herself as a concert artist, appearing in principal European and North American music centers. She also pursued an operatic career. In 1958 she made her operatic debut as Didymus in *Theodora* with the Handel Opera Soc. at the Camden Festival, and continued to appear with the Soc. until 1964. In 1964 she made her debut at the Salzburg Festival as the 1st Maid in *Elektra* and toured Russia with the English Opera Group as Britten's Lucretia. She made her first appearance at London's Covent Garden as the 1st Norn in *Götterdämmerung* in 1965, and continued to sing there until 1971. In 1966 she made her U.S. debut in Delius's *A Mass of Life* in New York. She sang Mistress Quickly at her first appearance with the Welsh National Opera in Cardiff in 1969, where she was a leading member of the company until 1983. In 1978 she was made a Commander of the Order of the British Empire. While she had success in opera, she particularly excelled as a concert artist. Her concert repertoire extended from Bach to the masters of the 20th century.

Watzke, Rudolf, German bass and pedagogue; b. Niemes, April 5, 1892; d. Wuppertal, Dec. 18, 1972. He studied with Kreisel-Hauptfeld in Reichenberg, Kittel in Bayreuth, and Armin in Berlin. After singing at the Karlsruhe Opera (1923–24), the Bayreuth Festivals (1924, 1925, 1927), and the Berlin State Opera (1924–28), he devoted himself principally to a career as a concert artist. He was especially noted for his oratorio and lieder appearances. From 1956 to 1969 he taught at the Dortmund Cons.

Wayditch, Gabriel (real name, **Baron Gabriel Wajditsch Verbovac von Dönhoff**), Hungarian-American composer; b. Budapest, Dec. 28, 1888; d. N.Y., July 28, 1969. He studied piano with Emil von Sauer and composition with Hans Koessler at the Budapest Academy of Music. In 1907 he emigrated to the United States. He wrote 14 lengthy operas to his own libretti in Hungarian, dealing mostly with oriental or religious subjects; of these only one, *Horus*, was performed in his lifetime, at his own expense (Philadelphia, Jan. 5, 1939). His longest opera, *The Heretics*, takes 8 hours to perform; the shortest, *The Caliph's Magician*, in one act, takes 2 hours. The other operas are *Opium Dreams, Buddha, Jesus before Herod, Maria Magdalena, Maria Tesztver, Nereida, Sahara, The Catacombs, Anthony of Padua, The Venus Dwellers*, and *Neptune's Daughter*.

Weathers, Felicia, black American soprano; b. St. Louis, Aug. 13, 1937. She took vocal lessons at the Indiana Univ. School of Music in Bloomington with St. Leger, Kullman, and Manski. She made her operatic debut in Zürich in 1961. In 1963 she sang at the Hamburg State Opera and subsequently was a regular member there (1966–70). In 1965 she made her Metropolitan Opera debut in New York; she also sang at Covent Garden in London in 1970.

Weaver, James (Merle), American harpsichordist, pianist, fortepianist, and teacher; b. Champaign, Ill., Sept. 25, 1937. He was educated at the Univ. of Ill. (B.A., 1961; M.M., 1963), where he received instruction in harpsichord from George Hunter. He also was a student of Leonhardt at the Sweelinck Cons. in Amsterdam (1957–59). In 1967 he became curator of historic instruments at the Smithsonian Institution in Washington, D.C., where he co-founded the period instrument group the Smithsonian Chamber Players in 1976. He also pursued a solo career as a keyboard artist, taught at Cornell Univ. and the American Univ., and gave master classes in 18th-century performance practice.

Weaver, Powell, American pianist, organist, and composer; b. Clearfield, Pa., June 10, 1890; d. Oakland, Calif., Dec. 22, 1951. He studied organ with Dethier, piano with Caroline Beebe, and composition with Goetschius at the Inst. of Musical Art in New York (1909–12); after further organ studies with Pietro Yon in New York, he went to Rome to study organ with Remigio Renzi and later received training in composition with Respighi (1924–25). He was active as an organist at Kansas City's Grand Ave. Temple (1912–37) and the First Baptist Church (1937–51); he was engaged as accompanist to prominent singers; he also gave organ recitals. From 1937 to 1945 he was head of the music dept. at Ottawa Univ. in Kansas City. Among his works is the comic opera pastiche *As We Like It* (1922).

BIBL.: M. Schwartz, *P. W.: His Life and Contributions to Organ Music in Kansas City* (diss., Univ. of Missouri, 1976).

Webber, Andrew Lloyd. See **Lloyd Webber, Andrew.**

Weber, Alain, French composer and teacher; b. Château-Thierry, Dec. 8, 1930. He studied at the Paris Cons. with Robert Dussault (theory), Jules Gentil (piano), Jean Gallon and Henri Challan (harmony), Tony Aubin (composition), and Olivier Messiaen (analysis). In 1952 he won the Premier Grand Prix de Rome and worked at the Villa Medici there. Upon returning to Paris, he taught at the Cons. He was the author of various pedagogical tomes. His opera *La Rivière Perdue* was awarded the Grand Prix Audiovisuel de l'Europe by the Académie du Disque Français in 1982. He also was made an Officier de l'Ordre National du Merite. Among his works are the operas *La Voie Unique* (1957), *La Rivière Perdue* (1981–82), and *Le Rusé Petit Jean* (1984), and the ballets *Le Petit Jeu* (1951) and *Epitome* (1972).

Weber, Bernhard Anselm, German pianist, conductor, and composer; b. Mannheim, April 18, 1764; d. Berlin, March 23, 1821. He commenced keyboard training with Vogler in 1773, and after studying singing with Holzbauer and theory with Einberger, he returned to Vogler to study composition in 1775. He took courses in theology and law at the Univ. of Heidelberg in 1781, then traveled as a performer on the Xanorphica, a keyboard instrument invented by Rölling. In 1787 he became music director of Grossmann's opera troupe in Hanover, touring with it in 1790 in Holland, Germany, and Scandinavia. After a sojourn in Stockholm, he performed in Hamburg. In 1792 he was named joint music director (with Bernhard Wessely) of Berlin's Nationaltheater; in 1796 became its first music director, and in 1803 was elevated to the post of Kapellmeister; he retained his title when the German and Italian theaters merged in 1811. During his Berlin tenure, he championed the music of Gluck, conducting his *Iphigénie en Tauride* on Feb. 24, 1795. Weber distinguished himself as a pianist and conductor. Although he was a prolific composer, only a few songs from his stage works retained their popularity. His incidental music to Schiller's drama *Wilhelm Tell* (1804), however, was long admired.

BIBL.: H. Fischer, *B.A. W.* (diss., Univ. of Berlin, 1923).

Weber, Carl Maria (Friedrich Ernst) von, celebrated German composer, pianist, and conductor; b. Eutin, Oldenburg, Nov. 18, 1786; d. London, June 5, 1826. His father, Franz Anton von Weber (1734?-1812), was an army officer and a good musical amateur who played the violin and served as Kapellmeister in Eutin. It was his fondest wish that Carl Maria would follow in the footsteps of Mozart as a child prodigy (Constanze Weber, Mozart's wife, was his niece, thus making Carl Maria a 1st cousin of Mozart by marriage). Carl Maria's mother was a singer of some ability; she died when he was 11. Franz Anton led a wandering life as music director of his own theater company, taking his family with him on his tours. Although this mode of life interfered with his regular education, it gave him practical knowledge of the stage, and stimulated his imagination as a dramatic composer. Weber's first teachers were his father and his half brother Fritz, a pupil of Haydn; at Hildburghausen, where he found himself with his father's company in 1796, he also received piano instruction from J. P. Heuschkel. The next year he was in Salzburg, where he attracted the attention of Michael Haydn, who taught him counterpoint; he composed a set of *6 Fughetten* there, which were publ. in 1798. As his peregrinations continued, he was taught singing by Valesi (J. B. Wallishauser) and composition by J. N. Kalcher in Munich (1798–1800). At the age of 12, he wrote an opera, *Die Macht der Liebe und des Weins*; it was never performed and the MS has not survived. Through a meeting with Aloys Senefelder, the inventor of lithography, he became interested in engraving; he became Senefelder's apprentice, acquiring considerable skill in the method; he engraved his own *6 Variations on an Original Theme* for Piano (Munich, 1800). His father became interested in the business possibilities of lithography, and set up a workshop with him in Freiberg; however, the venture failed, and the young Carl Maria turned again to music. He composed a 2-act comic opera, *Das Waldmädchen*, in 1800; it was premiered in Freiberg on Nov. 24, 1800, 6 days after his 14th birthday; performances followed in Chemnitz (Dec. 5, 1800) and Vienna (Dec. 4, 1804). In 1801 the family was once more in Salzburg, where he studied further with Michael Haydn; he wrote another opera, *Peter Schmoll und seine Nachbarn* (1801–02). He gave a concert in Hamburg in Oct. 1802, and the family then proceeded to Augsburg; they remained there from Dec. 1802 until settling in Vienna in Sept. 1803; there Weber continued his studies with Abbé Vogler, at whose recommendation he secured the post of conductor of the Breslau Opera in 1804. He resigned this post in 1806 after his attempts at operatic reform caused dissension. In 1806 he became honorary Intendant to Duke Eugen of Württemberg-Öls at Schloss Carlsruhe in Upper Silesia; much of his time was devoted to composition there. In 1807 he was engaged as private secretary to Duke Ludwig in Stuttgart, and also gave music lessons to his children. This employment was abruptly terminated when Weber became innocently involved in a scheme of securing a ducal appointment for a rich man's son in order to exempt him from military service, and accepted a loan of money. This was a common practice at the Stuttgart court, but as a result of the disclosure of Weber's involvement, he was arrested (Feb. 9, 1810) and kept in prison for 16 days. This matter, along with several others, was settled to his advantage, only to find him the target of his many creditors, who had him rearrested on Feb. 17. Finally, agreeing to pay off his debts as swiftly as possible, he was released and then banished by King Friedrich. He then went to Mannheim, where he made appearances as a pianist. He next went to Darmstadt, where he rejoined his former teacher Vogler, for whom he wrote the introduction to his teacher's ed. of 12 Bach chorales. On Sept. 16, 1810, Weber's opera *Silvana* was successfully premiered in Frankfurt am Main; the title role was sung by Caroline Brandt, who later became a member of the Prague Opera; Weber and Brandt were married in Prague on Nov. 4, 1817. Weber left Darmstadt in Feb. 1811 for Munich, where he composed several important orch. works. Weber's 1-act Singspiel, *Abu Hassan*, was successfully given in Munich on June 4, 1811. From Aug. to Dec. 1811, Weber and Bärmann gave concerts in Switzerland; after appearing in Prague in Dec. 1811, they went to Leipzig in Jan. 1812, and then on to Weimar and Dresden. On March 15, 1812, they gave a concert in Berlin, which was attended by King Friedrich Wilhelm III. On Dec. 17, 1812, Weber was soloist at the premiere of his 2d Piano Concerto in Gotha. Upon his return to Prague in Jan. 1813, he was informed that he was to be the director of the German Opera there. He was given extensive authority, and traveled to Vienna to engage singers and also secured the services of Franz Clement as concertmaster. During his tenure, Weber presented a distinguished repertoire, which included Beethoven's *Fidelio*; however, when his reforms encountered determined opposition, he submitted his resignation (1816). On Dec. 14, 1816, he was appointed Musikdirektor of the German Opera in Dresden by King Friedrich August III. He opened his first season on Jan. 30, 1817; that same year, he was named Königlich Kapellmeister, and began to make sweeping reforms. About this time he approached Friedrich Kind, a Dresden lawyer and writer, and suggested to him the idea of preparing a libretto on a Romantic German subject for his next opera. They agreed on *Der Freischütz*, a fairy tale from the *Gespensterbuch*, a collection of ghost stories by J. A. Apel and F. Laun. The composition of this work, which was to prove his masterpiece, occupied him for 3 years; the score was completed on May 13, 1820, and 2 weeks later Weber began work on the incidental music to Wolff's *Preciosa*, a play in 4 acts with spoken dialogue; it was produced in Berlin on March 14, 1821. A comic opera, *Die drei Pintos*, which Weber started at about the same time, was left unfinished. After some revisions, *Der Freischütz* was accepted for performance at the opening of Berlin's Neues Schauspielhaus. There arose an undercurrent of rivalry with Spontini, director of the Berlin Opera, a highly influential figure in operatic circles and at court. Spontini considered himself the guardian of the Italian-French tradition in opposition to the new German Romantic movement in music. Weber conducted the triumphant premiere of *Der Freischütz* on June 18, 1821; the work's success surpassed all expectations and the cause of new Romantic art was won; *Der Freischütz* was soon staged by all the major opera houses of Europe. In English, it was given first in London, on July 22, 1824; translations into other languages followed. Weber's next opera was *Euryanthe*, produced in Vienna on Oct. 25, 1823, with only moderate success. Meanwhile, Weber's health was affected by incipient tuberculosis and he was compelled to spend part of 1824 in Marienbad for a cure. He recovered sufficiently to begin the composition of *Oberon*, a commission from London's Covent Garden. The English libretto was prepared by J. R. Planché, based on a translation of C. M. Wieland's verse-romance of the same name. Once more illness interrupted Weber's progress on his work; he spent part of the summer of 1825 in Ems to prepare himself for the journey to England. He set out for London in Feb. 1826, a dying man. On his arrival, he was housed with Sir George Smart, the conductor of the Phil. Soc. of London. Weber threw himself into his work, presiding over 16 rehearsals for *Oberon*. On April 12, 1826, he conducted its premiere at Covent Garden, obtaining a tremendous success. Despite his greatly weakened condition, he conducted 11 more performances of the score, and also participated in various London concerts, playing for the last time a week before his death. He was found dead in his room on the morning of June 5, 1826. He was buried in London. His remains were removed to Dresden in 1844. On Dec. 14, 1844, they were taken to the Catholic cemetery in Dresden to the accompaniment of funeral music arranged from motifs from *Euryanthe* for wind instruments as prepared and conducted by Wagner. The next day, Weber's remains were interred as Wagner delivered an oration and conducted a chorus in his specially composed *An Webers Grabe*.

Weber's role in music history is epoch making. In his operas, particularly in *Der Freischütz*, he opened the era of musical Romanticism, in decisive opposition to the established Italianate style. The highly dramatic and poetic portrayal of a German fairy tale, with its aura of supernatural mystery, appealed to the public, whose imagination had been stirred by the emergent Romantic literature of the period. Weber's melodic genius and mastery of the craft of composition made it possible for him to break with tradition and to start on a new path, at a critical time when individualism and nationalism began to emerge as sources of creative artistry. His instrumental works, too, possessed a new quality that signalized the transition from Classical to Romantic music. For piano he wrote pieces of extraordinary brilliance, introducing some novel elements in chord writing and passagework. He was himself an excellent pianist; his large hands gave him an unusual command of the keyboard (he could stretch the interval of a twelfth). Weber's influence on the development of German music was very great. The evolutionary link to Wagner's music drama is evident in the coloring of the orch. parts in Weber's operas and in the adumbration of the principle of leading motifs. Finally, he was one of the first outstanding interpretative conducting podium figures.

WORKS: In the list of Weber's works that follows, his compositions are identified by the J. numbers established by F. Jahns in his *Carl Maria von Weber in seinen Werken: Chronologisch-thematisches Verzeichniss seiner sämmtlichen Compositionen* (Berlin, 1871). OPERAS: *Die Macht der Liebe und des Weins,* J. Anh. 6, Singspiel (1798; not perf.; not extant); *Das Waldmädchen*, J. Anh. 1, Romantic comic opera (Freiberg, Nov. 24, 1800; only fragments extant); *Peter Schmoll und seine Nachbarn*, J.8 (1801–02; Augsburg, March 1803?; music not extant, dialogue lost); *Rübezahl*, J.44–46 (1804–05; unfinished; only 3 numbers extant); *Silvana*, J.87, Romantic opera (1808–10; Frankfurt am Main, Sept. 16, 1810, composer conducting); *Abu Hassan*, J.106, Singspiel (1810–11; Munich, June 4, 1811, composer conducting); *Der Freischütz*, J.277, Romantic opera (1817–21; Berlin, June 18, 1821, composer conducting); *Die drei Pintos*, J. Anh. 5, comic opera (begun in 1820; unfinished; libretto rev. by the composer's grandson, Carl von Weber, and Gustav Mahler; extant music completed by adding other works by the composer, with scoring by Mahler; Leipzig, Jan. 20, 1888, Mahler conducting); *Euryanthe*, J.291, grand heroic Romantic opera (1822–23; Vienna, Oct. 25, 1823, composer conducting); *Oberon, or The Elf King's Oath*, J.306, Romantic opera (1825–26; London, April 12, 1826, composer conducting). OTHER WORKS FOR THE THEATER: Overture and 6 numbers for Schiller's tr. of Gozzi's *Turandot, Prinzessin von China*, J.75 (Stuttgart, Sept. 1809); *Rondo alla polacca* for Tenor for Haydn's pasticchio *Der Freibrief*, J.77 (1809); Duet for Soprano and Tenor for Haydn's *Der Freibrief*, J.78 (1809); 4 songs for Voice and Guitar (one with Men's Chorus) for Kotzebue's *Der arme Minnesinger*, J.110–13 (1811); *Scena ed aria* for Soprano for Méhul's opera *Héléna*, J.178 (1815); 2 songs for Baritone and for Soprano and Bass for Fischer's Singspiel *Der travestirte Aeneas*, J.183–84 (1815); 2 songs for Baritone and for Tenor for Gubitz's festspiel *Lieb' und Versöhnen*, J.186–87 (1815); Ballade for Baritone and Harp for Reinbeck's *Gordon und Montrose*, J.189 (1815); Arietta for Soprano for Huber's and Kauer's *Das Sternenmädchen im Maidlinger Walde*, J.194 (1816; text not extant); Romance for Voice and Guitar for Castelli's *Diana von Poitiers*, J.195 (1816); 10 numbers and 1 song for Unaccompanied Mezzo-soprano for Müllner's *König Yngurd*, J.214 (Dresden, April 14, 1817); 6 numbers for Moreto's *Donna Diana*, J.220 (1817); Song for Solo Voices and Chorus for Kind's *Der Weinberg an der Elbe*, J.222 (1817); Romance for Voice and Guitar for Kind's *Das Nachtlager von Granada*, J.223 (1818); 2-part song for Tenor and Bass for Holbein's *Die drei Wahrzeichen*, J.225 (1818); Dance and song for Tenor and Chorus for Hell's *Das Haus Anglade*, J.227 (1818; may not be by Weber); 8 numbers for Gehe's *Heinrich IV, König von Frankreich*, J.237 (Dresden, June 6, 1818); *Scena ed aria* for Soprano for Cherubini's opera *Lodoïska*, J.239 (1818); Chorus for 2 Sopranos and Bass for Grillparzer's *Sappho*, J.240 (1818); Song for Voice and Piano or Guitar for Kind's *Der Abend am Waldbrunnen*, J.243 (1818); 4 vocal numbers, march, and melodrama for Rublack's *Leib' um Liebe*, J.246 (1818); Agnus Dei for 2 Sopranos, Alto, and Wind Instruments for Blankensee's *Carlo*, J.273 (1820); 4 harp numbers for Houwald's *Der Leuchtturm*, J.276 (Dresden, April 26, 1820); Overture and 11 numbers to Wolff's *Preciosa*, J.279 (Berlin, March 14, 1821); Song for 2 Sopranos, Alto, Chorus, and Guitar for Shakespeare's *The Merchant of Venice*, J.280 (1821); one instrumental number (from the adagio of the Sym. No. 1 in C major, J.50) and 5 choruses for Robert's *Den Sachsensohn vermählet heute*, J.289 (1822); Arioso and recitative for Bass and Soprano for Spontini's opera *Olympie*, J.305 (1825). CONCERT ARIAS: "Il momento s'avvicina," recitative and rondo for Soprano and Orch., J.93 (1810); "Misera me!," scena ed aria for Soprano and Orch. for *Atalia* J.121 (1811); "Qual altro attendi," scena ed aria for Tenor, Chorus, and Orch., J.126 (1812); "Signor, se padre sei," scena ed aria for Tenor, Choruses, and Orch. for *Ines de Castro*, J.142 (1812); "Non paventar mia vita," scena ed aria for Soprano and Orch. for *Ines de Castro*, J.181 (1815).

WRITINGS: Weber's critical writings on music are valuable. He also left an autobiographical sketch, an unfinished novel, poems, etc. Editions of his writings include T. Hell, ed., *Hinterlassene Schriften von C. M. v. W.* (3 vols., Dresden and Leipzig, 1828; 2d ed., 1850); G. Kaiser, ed., *Sämtliche Schriften von C. M. v. W.: Kritische Ausgabe* (Berlin and Leipzig, 1908); W. Altmann, ed., *W.s ausgewählte Schriften* (Regensburg, 1928); K. Laux, ed., *C. M. v. W.: Kunstansichten* (Leipzig, 1969; 2d ed., 1975); J. Warrack, ed., and M. Cooper, tr., *C. M. v. W.: Writings on Music* (Cambridge, 1982).

BIBL.: COLLECTED WORKS, SOURCE MATERIAL: There is no complete ed. of Weber's works. A projected collected ed., *C. M. v. W.: Musikalische Werke: Erste kritische Gesamtausgabe*, under the general editorship of H. J. Moser, was abandoned with the outbreak of World War II; only 3 vols. were publ. (vol. 2/1, Augsburg, 1926; vol. 2/2, Augsburg, 1928; vol. 2/3, Braunschweig, 1939). Previously unpubl. works are found in L. Hirschberg, ed., *Reliquienschrein des Meisters C. M. v. W.* (Berlin, 1927). The standard thematic catalogue was prepared by F. Jähns, *C. M. v. W in seinen Werken: Chronologisch-thematisches Verzeichniss seiner sämmtlichen Compositionen* (Berlin, 1871). See also the vols. by H. Dunnebeil, *C. M. v. W.: Verzeichnis seiner Kompositionen* (Berlin, 1942; 2d ed., 1947) and *Schrifttum über C. M. v. W.* (Berlin, 1947; 4th ed., 1957), D. and A. Henderson, *C. M. v. W.: A Guide to Research* (N.Y., 1989), and G. Allroggen and J. Veit, eds., *W.-Studien* (Mainz, 1993 et seq.).

BIOGRAPHICAL: W. Neumann, *W.: Eine Biographie* (Kassel, 1855); M. von Weber (son of the composer), *C. M. v. W.: Ein Lebensbild* (3 vols., Leipzig, 1864–66; abr. Eng. tr. by J. Simpson as *W.: The Life of an Artist*, 2 vols., London, 1865; 2d Ger. ed., abr., by R. Pechel, Berlin, 1912); F. Jähns, *C. M. v. W.: Eine Lebensskizze nach authentischen Quellen* (Leipzig, 1873); J. Benedict, *W.* (London and N.Y., 1881; 5th ed., 1899); L. Nohl, *W.* (Leipzig, 1883); A. Reissmann, *W.: Sein Leben und seine Werke* (Berlin, 1886); H. Gehrmann, *C. M. v. W.* (Berlin, 1899); G. Servières, *W.* (Paris, 1906; new ed., 1925); H. von der Pfordten, *W.* (Leipzig, 1919); A. Cœuroy, *W.* (Paris, 1925; 2d ed., 1953); E. Kroll, *C. M. v. W.* (Potsdam, 1934); W. Saunders, *W.* (London and N.Y., 1940); L. and R. Stebbins, *Enchanted Wanderer: The Life of C. M. v. W.* (N.Y., 1940); H. Moser, *C. M. v. W.: Leben und Werk* (Leipzig, 1941; 2d ed., 1955); P. Raabe, *Wege zu W.* (Regensburg, 1942); W. Zentner, *C. M. v. W.: Sein Leben und sein Schaffen* (Olten, 1952); H. Schnoor, *W.: Gestalt und Schöpfung* (Dresden, 1953); F. Gruniger, *C. M. v. W.: Leben und Werk* (Freiburg im Breisgau, 1954); K. Laux, *C. M. v. W.* (Leipzig, 1966; 2d ed., 1986); J. Warrack, *C. M. v. W.* (N.Y. and London, 1968; 2d ed., 1976); D. Härtwig, *C. M. v. W.* (Leipzig, 1986); K. Höcker, *Oberons Horn: Das Leben von C. M. v. W.* (Berlin, 1986); H. Hoffmann, *C. M. v. W.: Biographie eines realistichen Romantikers* (Düsseldorf, 1986).

CRITICAL, ANALYTICAL: F. Kind, *Freischütz-Buch* (Leipzig, 1843); R. Wagner: articles on W. in his *Gesammelte Schriften und Dichtungen* (Vol. 1, Leipzig, 1871; Eng. tr. by W. Ashton Ellis as *The Prose Works of Richard Wagner*, Vol. 7, London, 1898); A. Jullien, *W. à Paris en 1826* (Paris, 1877); G. Kaiser, *Beiträge zu einer Charakteristik W.s als Musikschriftsteller* (Leipzig, 1910); E. Hasselberg, ed., *Der Freischütz: Friedrich Kinds Operndichtung und ihre Quellen* (Berlin, 1921); M. Degen, *Die Lieder von C. M. v. W.* (Freiburg im Breisgau, 1923); E. Reiter, *W.s künstlerische Persönlichkeit aus seinen Schriften* (Leipzig, 1926); A. Sandt, *W.s Opern in ihrer Instrumentation* (Frankfurt am Main, 1932); P. Listl, *C. M. v. W. als Ouverturenkomponist* (diss., Univ. of Würzburg, 1936); H. Schnoor, *W. auf dem Welttheater: Ein Freischützbuch* (Dresden, 1942; 4th ed., 1963); G. Jones, *Backgrounds and Themes of the Operas of C. M. v. W.* (diss., Cornell Univ., 1972); M. Tusa, *Euryanthe and C. M. v. W.'s Dramaturgy of German Opera* (Oxford, 1991).

Weber, Fridolin, German singer and violinist, uncle of **Carl Maria (Friedrich Ernst) von Weber**; b. Zell, Wiesental, 1733; d. Vienna, Oct. 23, 1779. He served in the Mannheim electoral chapel. He had 4 daughters:

(1) (Maria) Josepha Weber, soprano; b. Zell, c.1759; d. Vienna, Dec. 29, 1819. After appearances in provincial music centers, she settled in Vienna in 1788; that same year, she married the violinist Franz de Paula Hofer (1755–96), one of Mozart's friends. Her 2d husband was the bass and actor (Friedrich) Sebastian Mayer (1773–1835), the creator of the role of Pizarro in Beethoven's *Fidelio*. She was a leading singer in Vienna, being closely associated with Schikaneder's Theater auf der Wieden from 1790; she retired from the stage in 1805. Mozart wrote the aria *Schön lacht der holde Frühling*, K. 580, for her, as well as the role of the Queen of the Night in his opera *Die Zauberflöte*; nevertheless, he disparaged her character in a letter of Dec. 15, 1781.

(2) (Maria) Aloysia (Louise Antonia) Weber, soprano; b. c.1760; d. Salzburg, June 8, 1839. She studied voice with Mozart while he was in Mannheim (1777–78); he fell in love with her, but she left him. After singing in Munich (1778–79), she went to Vienna as a member of the German opera (1779–82) and the Italian opera (1782–92). She married the court actor and painter Joseph Lange (1751–1831) in 1780; she left him in 1795 to pursue a concert career. Mozart wrote a number of concert arias for her, as well as the role of Madame Herz in his *Der Schauspieldirektor*.

(3) (Maria) Constanze (Constantia) (Caecilia Josepha Johanna Aloisia) Weber, soprano; b. Zell, Jan. 4, 1762; d. Salzburg, March 6, 1842. She was the wife of **Wolfgang Amadeus Mozart**.

(4) (Maria) Sophie Weber, soprano; b. Zell, Oct. 1763; d. Salzburg, Oct. 26, 1846. She married **Jakob Haibel** in 1807. She was with Mozart during the last hours of his life, and related her account of his death to her brother-in-law, Georg Nikolaus Nissen, the Danish statesman and music scholar, who wrote a biography of Mozart.

Weber, Friedrich Dionys (actually, **Bedrich Diviš**), Bohemian pedagogue, writer on music, and composer; b. Velichov, near Carlsbad, Oct. 9, 1766; d. Prague, Dec. 25, 1842. He began his musical studies with F. Beier in Velichov; after studies at the Doupov Gymnasium and courses in theology, philosophy, and law in Prague, he completed his musical training with Abbé Vogler; he also met Mozart. He devoted himself mainly to pedagogy; was one of the founders of the Prague Cons., which he served as its 1st director from 1811 until his death; also was director of the Prague Organ School (1839–42). Among his extant works is the opera *König der Genien* (Prague, June 1, 1800).

WRITINGS (all publ. in Prague): *Das Konservatorium der Musik zu Prag* (1817); *Allgemeine theoretisch-praktische Vorschule der Musik* (1828); *Lehrbuch der Harmonielehre und des Generalbasses* (1830–34); *Vollständige Theorie der Musik* (1840); *Allgemeine musikalische Zeichenlehre* (2d ed., 1841); *Harmonielehre* (2d ed., 1841); *Notenbeispiele zu F. D. Webers Vorschule der Musik* (1843); *Theoretisch-praktisches Lehrbuch der Tonsetzkunst* (2d ed., 1843).

Weber, Joseph Miroslav, Czech violinist and composer; b. Prague, Nov. 9, 1854; d. Munich, Jan. 1, 1906. He was taught by his father, and played violin in public as a child, then studied at the Prague Cons. He subsequently occupied posts as concertmaster in Sondershausen (1873–75) and Darmstadt (1875–83), and then assist. conductor (1883–89) and 1st conductor (1889–93) in Wiesbaden. He joined the Court Opera in Munich in 1894 and became its concertmaster in 1901. His works included *Der selige Herr Vetter*, comic opera (Wiesbaden, 1894), *Die neue Mamsell*, operetta (Munich, Nov. 21, 1896), and *Die Rheinnixe*, ballet (Wiesbaden, May 31, 1884).

Weber, Ludwig, German composer and teacher; b. Nuremberg, Oct. 13, 1891; d. Essen-Werden, June 30, 1947. He was mainly autodidact in composition. After teaching school in Nuremberg (1912–25), he taught at the Essen Folkwangschule (from 1927). Among his compositions was *Christgeburt*, chamber play (1925).

Weber, Ludwig, eminent Austrian bass; b. Vienna, July 29, 1899; d. there, Dec. 9, 1974. He studied with Alfred Boruttau in Vienna. He made his operatic debut there at the Volksoper as Fiorello in 1920, then sang in Barmen-Elberfeld (1925–27), Düsseldorf (1927–30), and Cologne (1930–33). After singing at the Bavarian

State Opera in Munich (1933–45), he was one of the principal members of the Vienna State Opera (1945–60); he also appeared at London's Covent Garden (1936–39; 1947; 1950–51) and at the Bayreuth Festivals (1951–60). He was a prof. at the Salzburg Mozarteum (from 1961). He was one of the foremost Wagnerian bass singers of his time, excelling particularly as Daland, Gurnemanz, and Hagen; he also distinguished himself in such roles as Rocco, Kaspar, Baron Ochs, Méphistophélès, and Wozzeck.

Webster, Sir David (Lumsden), Scottish opera administrator; b. Dundee, July 3, 1903; d. London, May 11, 1971. He was educated at the Univ. of Liverpool; then commenced a commercial career while pursuing his various interests in the arts. From 1940 to 1945 he was chairman of the Liverpool Phil. Soc. In 1945 he became general administrator of the Covent Garden Opera Trust; in this capacity he helped to launch the careers of many famous singers, among them Jon Vickers and Joan Sutherland. He was knighted in 1961 and was made a Knight Commander of the Royal Victorian Order in 1970. An account of his career by M. Haltrecht, under the title *The Reluctant Showman*, was publ. in 1975.

Weckerlin, Jean-Baptiste-Théodore, eminent French music scholar and composer; b. Guebwiller, Alsace, Nov. 9, 1821; d. Trottberg, near Guebwiller, May 20, 1910. He ran away from home and settled in Paris in 1843; he entered the Paris Cons. in 1844, where he studied with Ponchard (singing) and Halévy (composition). He wrote a heroic sym., *Roland*, for Soloists, Chorus, and Orch. (1847) while still a student; after graduating in 1849, he took part with Seghers in the direction of the Société Sainte-Cécile (1850–55), which brought out some of his works. He achieved his first success with the 1-act comic opera *L'Organiste dans l'embarras* (Théâtre-Lyrique, 1853). It was followed by 2 comic operas in Alsatian dialect, *Die drifach Hochzitt im Bäsethal* (Colmar, 1863) and *D'r verhäxt' Herbst* (Colmar, 1879), and the 1-act opera *Après Fontenoy* (Théâtre-Lyrique, 1877). In 1863 he became librarian and archivist of the Société des Compositeurs de Musique. He became assistant librarian (1869) and librarian (1876) of the Paris Cons., retiring in 1909. He won distinction as a composer of grand choral works; he also wrote 12 stage works. He ed. various early French stage works and many folk-song collections.

WRITINGS (all publ. in Paris): *Opuscules sur la chanson populaire et sur la musique* (1874); *Musiciana* (1877); *Bibliothèque du Conservatoire national de musique et de déclamation: Catalogue bibliographique . . . de la Reserve* (1885); *La chanson populaire* (1886); *Nouveau musiciana* (1890); *Dernier musiciana* (1899).

BIBL.: H. Expert, *Catalogue de la bibliothèque musicale de M. J. B. W.* (Paris, 1908).

Weede (real name, **Wiedefeld**), **Robert,** American baritone; b. Baltimore, Feb. 11, 1903; d. Walnut Creek, Calif., June 9, 1972. After winning the National Federation of Music Clubs award (1927), he studied at the Eastman School of Music in Rochester, New York, and in Milan. In 1933 he became a soloist at N.Y.'s Radio City Music Hall. On May 15, 1937, he made his Metropolitan Opera debut in New York as Tonio, where he was on the roster until 1942, and then again in 1944–45, 1948–50, and 1952–53. He also sang Rigoletto in Chicago (1939), San Francisco (1940), and at the N.Y. City Opera (1948). In later years he made appearances on Broadway and toured in the musicals *The Most Happy Fella* and *Milk and Honey*. During his operatic career, he sang mainly in operas by Verdi and Puccini.

Wehrli, Werner, Swiss composer and teacher; b. Aarau, Jan. 8, 1892; d. Lucerne, June 27, 1944. He was a student of Hegar and Kempter at the Zürich Cons. and of Knorr at the Frankfurt am Main Cons. He also took courses in musicology and art history at the univs. of Munich, Basel, and Berlin. From 1918 he taught music at the Aarau Lehrerseminar. He also was conductor of the Aarau Cäcilien-Verein (1920–29). His compositions generally followed the precepts of late Romanticism. They include *Das heisse Eisen*, comic opera (Bern, Dec. 11, 1918), *Der Märchenspiegle*, Singspiel (1922), *Das Vermächtnis*, opera (1931), and *Auf dem Mond*, school opera (1933); also 5 festival plays.

Weidemann, Friedrich, German baritone; b. Ratzeburg, Jan. 1, 1871; d. Vienna, Jan. 30, 1919. He studied with Vilmar in Hamburg and Muschler in Berlin, making his debut in 1896 in Brieg; he then sang in Essen (1897–98), Hamburg (1898–1901), and Riga (1901–03). In 1903 he joined the Vienna Court Opera, where he remained until his death. He was highly regarded for his performances in operas by Wagner and Richard Strauss.

Weidinger, Christine, American soprano; b. Springville, N.Y., March 31, 1946. She studied in Phoenix, Wuppertal, and Los Angeles. In 1972 she won the Metropolitan Opera National Auditions and made her operatic debut in Washington, D.C., as Musetta. On Nov. 24, 1972, she made her Metropolitan Opera debut in New York as Ortlinde, remaining on its roster until 1976. From 1981 she made appearances in Europe. In 1989 she sang Amendaide in *Tancredi* in Los Angeles, and then was engaged as Vitellia at Milan's La Scala and as Lucia in Cincinnati in 1990. Following a return to Los Angeles as Elettra and Fiordiligi in 1991, she sang Maria Stuarda in Barcelona in 1992 and in Monte Carlo in 1993. In 1995 she portrayed Donna Anna in Santiago and Elettra at the Welsh National Opera in Cardiff.

Weidt, Lucie, German-born Austrian soprano; b. Troppau, Silesia, c.1876; d. Vienna, July 28, 1940. She studied with her father, and then with Rosa Papier in Vienna. She made her operatic debut in Leipzig in 1900; in 1902 she made her first appearance at the Vienna Opera as Elisabeth, remaining on its roster until 1927. She sang in Munich from 1908 to 1910. On Nov. 18, 1910, she made her first American appearance, as Brünnhilde in *Die Walküre*, at the Metropolitan Opera in New York; after a season there, she sang in Italy. In 1909 she married Baron Joseph von Urmenyi. Her voice was of unusual attractiveness and power, enabling her to perform Wagnerian parts with distinction.

Weigel, Eugene (Herbert), American composer, violist, organist, and teacher; b. Cleveland, Oct. 11, 1910. He studied composition with Arthur Shepherd at Western Reserve Univ. and violin with Maurice Hewitt at the Cleveland Inst. of Music (1930–32); later had composition lessons with Hindemith at Yale Univ. (B.M., 1946) and viola lessons with Hugo Kortschak. He was active as an organist and choirmaster (1929–41); he also was a founding member of the Walden String Quartet (1930–35). While at Yale Univ., he served as music director of its Thomas More Chapel and played viola in the New Haven (Conn.) Sym. Orch.; appeared in various ensembles, including one in New York with Hindemith on the viola d'amore in a performance of Bach's St. John Passion. In 1946–47 he was again a member of the Walden String Quartet during its residency at Cornell Univ.; played in the first performances of Schoenberg's String Trio and Ives's 2d String Quartet; continued to play with the quartet at the Univ. of Ill. (1947–57), where he also taught composition and experimental theory. In 1954–55 he held a Guggenheim fellowship. In 1955 he became composer-in-residence at Montana State Univ. in Missoula, which was renamed the Univ. of Montana that same year; remained there until 1972. He also was a founder-member of the Montana String Quartet (1957–72). In 1972 he retired to Vancouver Island, Canada; conducted the Malespina Chorus and was prof. emeritus at Malespina College (1974–76). In later years, he devoted much time to writing poetry, preparing his memoirs, and pursuing an avid interest in architecture. Among his compositions were the operas *The Lion Makers* (1953) and *The Mountain Child* (1959).

Weigl, family of Austrian musicians:

(1) Joseph (Franz) Weigl, cellist; b. in Bavaria, May 19, 1740; d. Vienna, Jan. 25, 1820. Upon the recommendation of Haydn, he was made a cellist at the Eisenstadt court in 1761; married (Anna Maria) Josepha Scheffstoss, a former singer at the court, in 1764. In 1769 he was named 1st cellist of the Italian Opera orch. at the Kärnthnertortheater in Vienna; in 1792 he became a member of the Hofkapelle.

(2) Joseph Weigl, composer and conductor, son of the preceding; b. Eisenstadt, March 28, 1766; d. Vienna, Feb. 3, 1846. He was taken to Vienna in 1769, where he trained with Sebastian Witzig (singing and thoroughbass) in 1775; he soon became a pupil of Albrechtsberger, with whom he remained until 1782. At age 16 he wrote his first opera, *Die unnütze Vorsicht*, for a marionette theater, winning the esteem of Gluck and Salieri. At 19 he became a pupil in composition of Salieri, who secured a position for him in the Court Theater; he was deputy Kapellmeister by 1790; in 1792 he was made Kapellmeister and composer. From 1827 to 1838 he was vice Kapellmeister at the court, retiring from public life in 1839. His first notable success as a composer for the theater came with his opera *La Principessa d'Amalfi* (Vienna, Jan. 10, 1794), which Haydn described as a masterpiece (in a letter to Weigl after the perf.); it was followed by *Das Waisenhaus* (Vienna, Oct. 4, 1808) and *Die Schweizerfamilie* (Vienna, March 14, 1809; produced in Paris, Feb. 6, 1827, as *Emmeline, ou La Famille suisse*); it was staged in opera houses all over Europe until about 1900, when it disappeared from the repertoire. His ballets also won a wide hearing.

WORKS: DRAMATIC: OPERAS (all 1st perf. in Vienna unless otherwise given): *Die unnütze Vorsicht oder Die betrogene Arglist* (Feb. 23, 1783); *Il Pazzo per forza* (Nov. 14, 1788); *La caffettiera bizzarra* (Sept. 15, 1790); *Der Strassensammler (Lumpensammler) oder Ein gutes Herz ziert jeden Stand*, comic opera (Oct. 13, 1792); *La Principessa d'Amalfi*, comic opera (Jan. 10, 1794); *Das Petermännchen* (part 1, April 8, 1794; part 2, April ?, 1794); *Giuletta e Pierotto* (Oct. 16, 1794); *I solitari*, opera seria (March 15, 1797); *L'amor marinaro ossia Il Corsaro* (Oct. 15, 1797); *Das Dorf im Gebirge*, Singspiel (April 17, 1798); *L'accademia del maestro Cisolfaut* (Oct. 14, 1798); *L'uniforme*, heroic-comic opera (1800); *Die Herrenhuterin*, Singspiel (Nov. 26, 1804; in collaboration with I. Umlauf and F. Devienne); *Vestas Feuer*, heroic opera (Aug. 7, 1805); *Il Principe invisibile* (Oct. 4, 1806); *Kaiser Hadrian* (May 21, 1807); *Ostade oder Adrian von Ostade* (Oct. 3, 1807); *Cleopatra* (Milan, Dec. 19, 1807); *Il Rivale di se stesso* (Milan, April 18, 1808); *Das Waisenhaus*, Singspiel (Oct. 4, 1808); *Die Schweizerfamilie*, Singspiel (March 14, 1809); *Die Verwandlungen*, operetta (Berlin, Feb. 1810); *Der Einsiedler auf den Alpen* (June 13, 1810); *Franciska von Foix*, heroic-comic opera (Feb. 7, 1812); *Der Bergsturz*, Singspiel (Dec. 19, 1813); *Die Jugend (Jugendjahre) Peter des Grossen* (Dec. 10, 1814); *L'imboscata* (Milan, Nov. 8, 1815); *Margaritta d'Anjou ossia L'Orfano d'Inghilterra*, melodramma eroi-comico (Milan, July 26, 1816); *Die Nachtigall und der Rabe* (April 20, 1818); *Daniel in der Löwengrube oder Baals Sturz*, heroic opera (April 13, 1820); *König Waldemar oder Die dänischen Fischer*, Singspiel (May 11, 1821); *Edmund und Caroline* (Oct. 21, 1821); *Die eiserne Pforte*, grand opera (Feb. 27, 1823). Also ballets, incidental music used in several plays, and the oratorio *La passione di Gesù Cristo* (1804).

(3) Thaddäus Weigl, conductor, music publisher, and composer, brother of the preceding; b. April 8, 1776; d. Vienna, Feb. 29, 1844. He studied theory with Albrechtsberger, and then was employed in the Court Theater's music publishing house from 1795. He organized his own publishing concern in 1803; he also was vice Kapellmeister to his brother, becoming a composer at the Court Theater in 1806. His publishing business ended in bankruptcy in 1831. He wrote 5 operettas and 15 ballets.

BIBL.: F. Grasberger, *J. W. (1766–1846): Leben und Werk mit besonderer Berücksichtingung der Kirchenmusik* (diss., Univ. of Vienna, 1938).

Weikert, Ralf, Austrian conductor; b. St. Florian, Nov. 10, 1940. He studied at the Bruckner Cons. in Linz, then took a course in conducting with Swarowsky at the Vienna Academy of Music. In 1965 he won 1st prize in the Nicolai Malko Conducting Competition in Copenhagen. In 1966 he became conductor of the City Theater in Bonn, then was chief conductor there (1968–77). In 1977 he was appointed deputy Generalmusikdirektor of the Frankfurt am Main Opera; he also conducted at the Hamburg State Opera, the Deutsche Oper in Berlin, the Vienna State Opera, and the Zürich Opera. In 1981 he was named chief conductor of the Salzburg Mozarteum Orch. and music director of the Landestheater in Salzburg. He was music director of the Zürich Opera from 1983 to 1992.

Weikl, Bernd, esteemed Austrian baritone; b. Vienna, July 29, 1942. He received his training at the Mainz Cons. (1962–65) and the Hannover Hochschule für Musik (1965–67). In 1968 he made his operatic debut as Ottakar in *Der Freischütz* at the Hannover Opera, where he sang until 1970. From 1970 to 1973 he was a member of the Deutsche Oper am Rhein in Düsseldorf. In 1971 he made his first appearance at the Salzburg Easter Festival as Melot in *Tristan und Isolde*. In 1972 he sang for the first time at the Bayreuth Festival as Wolfram. He appeared at the Hamburg State Opera (from 1973) and at the Berlin Deutsche Opera (from 1974). In 1975 he made his debut at London's Covent Garden as Rossini's Figaro. In 1976 he created the role of Ferdinand in Einem's *Kabale und Liebe* in Vienna. On Dec. 22, 1977, he made his Metropolitan Opera debut in New York as Wolfram, where he returned in such roles as Amfortas, Jochanaan, Beethoven's Don Fernando, and Mandryka. He was a soloist in Bach's St. Matthew Passion at his Salzburg Festival debut in 1984. His portrayal of Hans Sachs was greatly admired, and he sang that role at Milan's La Scala and at Covent Garden in 1990 and at the Metropolitan Opera and the San Francisco Opera in 1993. In 1995 he was engaged as Amfortas at the Bayreuth Festival. He portrayed Jochanaan at the Metropolitan Opera in 1996 and at the San Francisco Opera in 1997. As a concert artist, he appeared widely in oratorio and lieder performances.

Weil, Bruno, German conductor; b. Hahnstätten, Nov. 24, 1949. He studied with Swarowsky in Vienna and Ferrara in Italy. He conducted opera in Wiesbaden (1975–77) and Braunschweig (1977–81). After winning 2d prize in the Karajan conducting competition in 1979, he appeared with the Berlin Phil. In 1980 he conducted at the Deutsche Oper in Berlin. He became Generalmusikdirektor in Augsburg in 1981. In 1984 he was a guest conductor of the Yomiuri Nippon Sym. Orch. in Tokyo. In 1985 he made his debut at the Vienna State Opera conducting *Aida*. He conducted *Don Giovanni* at the Salzburg Festival in 1988, the year he also made his U.S. debut at a N.Y. Schubertiade. During the 1990–91 season, he toured Germany with the English Chamber Orch. In 1991 he became music director of the Carmel (Calif.) Bach Festival. He made his Glyndebourne Festival debut conducting *Così fan tutte* in 1992. In 1994 he became Generalmusikdirektor of the Duisburg Sym. Orch.

Weil, Hermann, German baritone; b. Karlsruhe, May 29, 1876; d. (of a heart attack while fishing in Blue Mountain Lake, N.Y.) July 6, 1949. He studied voice with Adolf Dippel in Frankfurt am Main. He made his operatic debut as Wolfram in *Tannhäuser* at Freiburg, Baden, on Sept. 6, 1901, then sang in Vienna, Brussels, Amsterdam, Milan, and London; he participated in the Bayreuth Festivals (1909–12). On Nov. 17, 1911, he made a successful debut as Kurvenal in *Tristan und Isolde* at the Metropolitan Opera in New York In 1917 he returned to Germany. He sang at the Vienna State Opera (1920–23), toured the United States with the German Opera Co. (1923–24), and appeared at the Bayreuth Festival (1924–25); in 1939 he settled in New York as a vocal teacher. The extensive range of his voice, spanning 3 full octaves, enabled him to undertake bass parts as well as those in the baritone compass. He had about 100 roles in his repertoire, excelling in Wagnerian operas.

Weill, Kurt (Julian), remarkable German-born American composer; b. Dessau, March 2, 1900; d. N.Y., April 3, 1950. He was a private pupil of Albert Bing in Dessau (1915–18); in 1918–19 he studied at the Berlin Hochschule für Musik with Humperdinck (composition), Friedrich Koch (counterpoint), and Krasselt (conducting). He was then engaged as an opera coach in Dessau and was also theater conductor at Ludenscheid. In 1920 he moved to Berlin and was a student of Busoni at the Prussian Academy of Arts until 1923; he also studied with Jarnach there (1921–23). His first major work, the Sym. No. 1, *Berliner Sinfonie*, was composed in 1921. However, it was not performed in his lifetime; indeed, its MS was not recovered until 1955, and it was finally premiered by the North German Radio Sym. Orch. in Hamburg in 1958. Under the impact of new trends in the musical theater, Weill proceeded to write short satirical operas in a sharp modernistic manner: *Der Protagonist* (1924–25) and *Royal Palace* (1925–26). There followed a striking "Songspiel" (a hybrid term of English and German words), *Mahagonny*, to a libretto by Bertolt Brecht, savagely satirizing the American primacy of money (1927); it was remodeled and was presented as the 3-act opera *Aufstieg und Fall der Stadt Mahagonny* (1929). Weill's greatest hit in this genre came with a modernistic version of Gay's *The Beggar's Opera*, to a pungent libretto by Brecht; under the title *Die Dreigroschenoper* (1928), it was staged all over Germany, and was also produced in translation throughout Europe. Marc Blitzstein later made a new libretto for the opera, versified in a modern American style, which was produced as *Threepenny Opera*, the exact translation of the German title. Its hit number "Mack the Knife" became tremendously successful.

After the Nazi ascent to power in Germany, Weill and his wife, **Lotte Lenya**, who appeared in many of his musical plays, went to Paris in 1934. They settled in the United States in 1935; Weill became a naturalized American citizen in 1943. Quickly absorbing the modes and fashions of American popular music, he re-created, with astonishing facility, and felicity, the typical form and content of American musicals; this stylistic transition was facilitated by the fact that in his European productions he had already absorbed elements of American popular songs and jazz rhythms. His highly developed assimilative faculty enabled him to combine this Americanized idiom with the advanced techniques of modern music (atonality, polytonality, polyrhythms) and present the product in a pleasing, and yet sophisticated and challenging, manner. But for all his success in American-produced scores, the great majority of his European works remained to be produced in America only posthumously.

WORKS: DRAMATIC: *Zaubernacht*, ballet (Berlin, Nov. 18, 1922); *Der Protagonist*, opera (1924–25; Dresden, March 27, 1926); *Royal Palace*, ballet-opera (1925–26; Berlin, March 2, 1927; original orchestration not extant; reconstructed as a ballet by Gunther Schuller and Noam Sheriff, San Francisco, Oct. 5, 1968); *Na und?*, opera (1926–27; not perf.; not extant); *Der Zar lasst sich photographieren*, opera (1927; Leipzig, Feb. 18, 1928; U.S. premiere as *The Shah Has Himself Photographed*, N.Y., Oct. 27, 1949); *Mahagonny*, "Songspiel" (Baden-Baden, July 17, 1927; remodeled as a 3-act opera, *Aufstieg und Fall der Stadt Mahagonny*, 1927–29; Leipzig, March 9, 1930; U.S. premiere, N.Y., April 28, 1970); *Happy End*, comedy (Berlin, Sept. 2, 1929; professional U.S. premiere, New Haven, Conn., April 6, 1972); *Der Jasager*, school opera (Berlin radio, June 23, 1930; U.S. premiere as *The One Who Sang Yes*, N.Y., April 25, 1933); *Die Burgschaft*, opera (1930–31; Berlin, March 10, 1932); *Der Silbersee*, musical play (1932–33; simultaneous premiere in Leipzig, Erfurt, and Magdeburg, Feb. 18, 1933; U.S. premiere as *Silverlake*, slightly abr. and with the addition of his 1927 incidental music to Strindberg's play *Gustav III*, N.Y., March 20, 1980); *Die sieben Todsunden der Kleinburger*, ballet (Paris, June 7, 1933; U.S. premiere, N.Y., Dec. 4, 1958); *Der Kuhnhandel*, operetta (1934; Düsseldorf, March 22, 1990; rev. as a musical comedy, *A Kingdom for a Cow*, London, June 28, 1935); *Der Weg der Verheissung*, biblical drama (1934–35; not perf.; rev. by L. Lewisohn as *The Eternal Road*, 1935–36; N.Y., Jan. 7, 1937); *Johnny Johnson*, musical fable (N.Y., Nov. 19, 1936); *Davy Crockett*, musical play (1938; unfinished); *Knickerbocker Holiday*, operetta (Hartford, Conn., Sept. 26, 1938; contains the popular "September Song"); *Railroads on Parade*, historical pageant (1938–39; N.Y. World's Fair, April 30, 1939); *The Ballad of Magna Carta*, scenic cantata (1939; CBS, Feb. 4, 1940); *Ulysses Africanus*, musical play (1939; unfinished); *Lady in the Dark*, musical play (1940; N.Y., Jan. 23, 1941); *One Touch of Venus*, musical comedy (N.Y., Oct. 7, 1943); *The Firebrand of Florence*, operetta (1944; N.Y., March 22, 1945); *Down in the Valley*, folk opera (1945–48; Bloomington, Ind., July 15, 1948); *Street Scene*, opera (1946; N.Y., Jan. 9, 1947); *Love Life*, vaudeville (1947; N.Y., Oct. 7, 1948); *Lost in the Stars*, musical tragedy, after Alan Paton's *Cry, the Beloved Country* (N.Y., Oct. 30, 1949); *Huckleberry Finn*, musical (1950; unfinished). FILM SCORES: *You and Me* (1937–38); *The River Is Blue* (1937–38; discarded); *Where Do We Go from Here?* (1943–44); *Salute to France* (1944).

WRITINGS: S. Hinton and J. Schebera, eds., *Musik und Theater: Gesammelte Schriften* (Leipzig, 1990).

BIBL.: H. Kotschenreuther, *K. W.* (Berlin, 1962); K. Kowalke, *K. W. in Europe* (Ann Arbor, 1979); R. Sanders, *The Days Grow Short: The Life and Music of K. W.* (N.Y., 1980); D. Jarman, *K. W.: An Illustrated Biography* (Bloomington, Ind., 1982); J. Schebera, *K. W.: Leben und Werk* (Leipzig, 1983); K. Kowalke, ed., *A New Orpheus: Essays on K. W.* (New Haven, 1986); S. Cook, *Opera During the Weimar Republic: The Zeitopern of Ernst Krenek, K. W., and Paul Hindemith* (Ann Arbor, 1987); D. Drew, *K. W.: A Handbook* (Berkeley, 1987); S. Hinton, ed., *K. W.: The Threepenny Opera* (Cambridge, 1990); J. Schebera, *K. W. 1900–1950: Eine Biographie in Texten, Bildern und Dokumenten* (Leipzig, 1990); R. Taylor, *K. W.: Composer in a Divided World* (London, 1991); K. Kowalke and H. Edler, eds., *A Stranger Here Myself: K. W.-Studien* (Hildesheim, 1993).

Weinberg, Jacob, Russian-American pianist, teacher, and composer; b. Odessa, July 7, 1879; d. N.Y., Nov. 2, 1956. He studied at the Moscow Cons. with Igumnov (piano) and with Taneyev and Ippolitov-Ivanov (composition); was a private pupil of Leschetizky in Vienna (1910–11). He taught piano at the Odessa Cons. (1915–21); after living in Palestine (1921–26), he emigrated to the United States; he taught piano at Hunter College and the N.Y. College of Music. He composed an opera on a modern Hebrew subject, *Hechalutz* (The Pioneers), fragments of which were performed in Jerusalem, in Hebrew, on April 4, 1925; the complete opera was performed in New York on Nov. 25, 1934, under the title *The Pioneers of Israel*, in English; he also wrote the oratorios *Isaiah* (1948) and *The Life of Moses* (1952). He contributed essays on Russian music to the Musical Quarterly and other periodicals.

Weinberger, Jaromír, Czech-born American composer; b. Prague, Jan. 8, 1896; d. (suicide) St. Petersburg, Fla., Aug. 8, 1967. He was a student of Křička and Hoffmeister in Prague and of Reger in Leipzig. In 1922 he became a teacher of composition at Ithaca (N.Y.) College. Returning to his homeland, he scored a remarkable success with his opera *Švanda dudák* (Schwanda the Bagpiper; Prague, April 27, 1927). It subsequently was performed throughout Europe to critical acclaim. With the dismemberment of his homeland by the Nazis in 1939, Weinberger fled to the United States and later became a naturalized citizen. Weinberger's success with *Švanda dudák* was a signal one. Even though the opera eventually went unperformed, its "Polka and Fugue" became a popular concert piece. He committed suicide, despondent over the lack of interest in his works.

WORKS: DRAMATIC: OPERAS: *Kocourkov* (c.1926); *Švanda dudák* (Schwanda the Bagpiper; Prague, April 27, 1927); *Die geliebte Stimme* (Munich, Feb. 28, 1931); *Lidé z Pokerflatu* (The Outcasts of Poker Flats; Brno, Nov. 19, 1932); *Valdstejn* (Vienna, Nov. 18, 1937). OPERETTAS: *Frühlingssturme* (1933); *Apropo co dela Andula* (n.d.); *Na ruzich ustlano* (Bed of Roses; 1934); *Cisar pan na tresnich* (n.d.).

Weiner, Lazar, Russian-American pianist, conductor, and composer; b. Cherkassy, near Kiev, Oct. 27, 1897; d. N.Y., Jan. 10, 1982. He emigrated to America in 1914, and became associated with numerous Jewish artistic activities in New York; he also took private lessons in composition with Robert Russell Bennett, Frederick Jacobi, and Joseph Schillinger. From 1929 to 1975 he was music director of the Central Synagogue in New York; he conducted classes in the Yiddish art song at Hebrew Union College, the Jewish Theological Seminary, and the 92nd Street Y; he served as music director of the WABC weekly radio program *The Message of Israel* (1934–69). His compositions include an opera, *The Golem* (1956; White Plains, N.Y., Jan. 13, 1957), and 5 ballets. His son, Yehudi Wyner (real name, Weiner) (b. Calgary, June 1, 1929), is a composer, pianist, conductor, and teacher.

Weiner, Leó, eminent Hungarian composer and pedagogue; b. Budapest, April 16, 1885; d. there, Sept. 13, 1960. He was a student of Koessler at the Budapest Academy of Music (1901–06). In 1908 he joined its faculty as a teacher of theory, becoming a prof. of composition in 1912 and of chamber music in 1920. He retired in 1957 but continued to teach there as prof. emeritus until his death. In 1907 he won the Franz-Josef-Jubiläumspreis, and in 1950 and 1960 the Kossuth Prize. In 1953 he was made an Eminent Artist by the Hungarian government. Weiner was particularly influential as a pedagogue. Many outstanding Hungarian composers and performers studied with him, among them Doráti, Foldes, Solti, Starker, and Varga. In his compositions, he generally remained faithful to the precepts of the Austro-German Romantic tradition. His works include *A gondolás* (The Gondolier), opera (n.d.; in collaboration with A. Szirmai; not extant), and *Csongor és Tünde*, incidental music to M. Vörösmarty's play (1913; Budapest, Dec. 6, 1916; as a ballet, Budapest, Nov. 8, 1930; orch. suite, 1937).

WRITINGS (all publ. in Budapest): *Összhangzattanra előkészitő jegyzetek* (Notes inn Preparation for a Harmony Treatise; 1910; 3d ed., 1917, as *Az összhangzattan előkészitő iskolája* [Preparatory School in Harmony]; 6th ed., 1955); *A zenei formák vázlatos ismertetése* (A General Sketch of Musical Forms; 1911); *Elemző összhanszattan: Funkciótan* (Analytic Harmony: Function; 1944); *A hangszeres zene formái* (The Forms of instrumental Music; 1955).

BIBL.: G. Gál, *W. L. Életmüve* (L. W.'s Lifework; Budapest, 1959).

Weingartner, (Paul) Felix, Edler von Münzberg, illustrious Austrian conductor; b. Zara, Dalmatia, June 2, 1863; d. Winterthur, May 7, 1942. After his father's death in 1868, his mother took him to Graz, where he studied music with W. A. Rémy. He publ. some piano pieces when he was 16 years old; Brahms recommended him for a stipend that enabled him to take music courses with Reinecke, Jadassohn, and Paul at the Leipzig Cons. (1881–83). He received the Mozart Prize at his graduation. He was introduced to Liszt, who recommended Weingartner's opera *Sakuntala* for production in Weimar (March 23, 1884), a signal honor for a young man not yet 21 years old. While progressing rapidly as a composer, Weingartner launched a brilliant career as a conductor, which was to become his prime vocation. He conducted in Königsberg (1884–85), Danzig (1885–87), Hamburg (1887–89), and Mannheim (1889–91). In 1891 he was engaged as court conductor in Berlin, where he led the Royal Opera until 1898 and the royal orch. concerts until 1907; also conducted the Kaim Orch. in Munich (1898–1905). His reputation as a fine musician was enhanced by his appearances as an ensemble player in the Weingartner Trio, with himself as pianist, Rettich as violinist, and Warnke as cellist. In 1908 he succeeded Mahler as music director of the Vienna Court Opera, and conducted there until 1911. He also was Mahler's successor as conductor of the Vienna Phil. (1908–27), with which he won great renown. He likewise served as Generalmusikdirektor in Darmstadt (1914–19) and as director of the Vienna Volksoper (1919–24). In 1927 he became director of the Basel Cons. He also conducted sym. concerts in Basel. After serving as a guest conductor of the Vienna State Opera (1934–35), he again was its director (1935–36), then once more was a guest conductor there (1936–38). Throughout the years he had engagements as guest conductor with major European orchs. He made his American debut with the N.Y. Phil. on Feb. 12, 1904, and later conducted the N.Y. Sym. Soc. (Jan.-March 1906). He appeared with the Boston Opera Co. on Feb. 12, 1912, conducting *Tristan und Isolde*; he and his 3d wife, **Lucille Marcel**, were engaged for a season with the Boston Opera Co. in 1913. (His 1st wife was Marie Juillerat, whom he married in 1891; his 2d wife was the Baroness Feodora von Dreifus, whom he married in 1903). He made his debut at Covent Garden in London in 1939 conducting *Parsifal*. He eventually settled in Interlaken, where he established a summer conducting school. Although Weingartner was trained in the Austro-German Romantic tradition, his approach to conducting was notable for its eschewing of Romantic excess. Indeed, he acquired a remarkable reputation for his devotion to the composer's intentions, which he conveyed to his musicians via an unostentatious baton technique. His interpretations of the Austro-German repertoire were acclaimed for their authority and integrity. He was the first conductor to record all the Beethoven syms. Weingartner was also a competent music editor; he was on the editorial board for the complete works of Berlioz (1899) and of Haydn (1907). Despite the pressure of his activities as a conductor, he found time for composition. In addition to his first opera, *Sakuntala*, he wrote the operas *Malawika* (Munich, 1886), *Genesius* (Berlin, Nov. 15, 1892), *Orestes*, a trilogy (Leipzig, Feb. 15, 1902), *Kain und Abel* (Darmstadt, May 17, 1914), *Dame Kobold* (Darmstadt, Feb. 23, 1916), *Die Dorfschule* (Vienna, May 13, 1920), *Meister Andrea* (Vienna, May 13, 1920), and *Der Apostat* (not perf.). He was also an excellent writer on musical subjects, numbering among his publs. *Die Lehre von der Wiedergeburt und das musikalische Drama* (1895), *Über das Dirigieren* (1896; 5th ed., 1913; a fundamental essay on conducting), *Bayreuth* 1876–1896 (1897; 2d ed., 1904), *Die Symphonie nach Beethoven* (1897; 4th ed., 1901; Eng. tr., 1904; new tr. as *The Symphony since Beethoven*, 1926), *Ratschläge für Aufführung der Sinfonien Beethovens* (1906; 3d ed., 1928; Eng. tr., London, 1907), *Akkorde: Gesammelte Aufsätze von Felix Weingartner* (1912); a polemical pamphlet, *Erlebnisse eines kgl. Kapellmeisters in Berlin* (1912; an attack upon the Berlin intendancy; a rebuttal was publ. by A. Wolff in *Der Fall Weingartner*, 1912), *Ratschläge für Aufführung der Sinfonien Schuberts und Schumanns* (1918), *Ratschläge für Aufführung der Sinfonien Mozarts* (1923), *Lebenserinnerungen* (vol. 1, 1923; vol. 2, 1929; Eng. version, London, 1937, as *Buffets and Rewards: A Musician's Reminiscences*), and *Unwirkliches und Wirkliches* (1936).

BIBL.: E. Krause, *F. W. als schaffender Künstler* (Berlin, 1904); P. Riesenfeld, *F. W.: Ein kritischer Versuch* (Breslau, 1906); W. Hutschenruyter, *Levensschets en portret van F. W.* (Haarlem, 1906); J. Lustig, *F. W. Persönlichkeiten* (Berlin, 1908); W. Jacob, *F. W.* (Wiesbaden, 1933); *Festschrift für Dr. F. W. zu seinem siebzigsten Geburtstag* (Basel, 1933); C. Dyment, *F. W.: Recollections and Recordings* (Rickmansworth, 1975).

Weinstock, Herbert, American writer on music; b. Milwaukee, Nov. 16, 1905; d. N.Y., Oct. 21, 1971. He was educated in his native town; later he took courses at the Univ. of Chicago. He was active in New York as a music ed. for the publisher Alfred A. Knopf.

WRITINGS (all publ. in N.Y.): With W. Brockway, *Men of Music* (1939; 2d ed., rev. and enl., 1950); with W. Brockway, *The Opera: A History of its Creation and Performance* (1941; 2d ed., 1962, as *The World of Opera*); *Tchaikovsky* (1943); *Handel* (1946; 2d ed., 1959; also in Ger.); *Chopin: The Man and His Music* (1949; 2d ed., 1959); *Music As an Art* (1953; 2d ed., 1966, as *What Music Is*); *Donizetti and the World of Opera in Italy, Paris and Vienna in the First Half of the Nineteenth Century* (1963); *Rossini: A Biography* (1968); *Vincenzo Bellini: His Life and Operas* (1971).

Weinzierl, Max, Ritter von, Austrian conductor and composer; b. Bergstadtl, Bohemia, Sept. 16, 1841; d. Mödling, near Vienna, July 10, 1898. He served as conductor at various theaters in Vienna; from 1882 he was chorus master of the Männergesangverein. He wrote the operas *Don Quixote* (Vienna, Feb. 15, 1879; with L. Roth), *Die weiblichen Jäger* (Vienna, May 5, 1880), *Moclemos* (Vienna, June 5, 1880), *Fioretta* (Prague, 1886), *Page Fritz* (Prague, 1889), and *Der Schwiegerpapa* (Berlin, 1893), and the oratorio, *Hiob* (Vienna, 1870).

Weir, Judith, Scottish composer; b. Aberdeen, May 11, 1954. After studies with Tavener in London, she received training in computer music from Vercoe at the Mass. Inst. of Technology (1973). From 1973 to 1976 she was a student of Holloway at King's College, Cambridge. She also studied with Schuller and Messiaen at the Berkshire Music Center in Tanglewood (summer 1975). From

1979 to 1982 she taught at the Univ. of Glasgow, and then held a creative arts fellowship at Trinity College, Cambridge, from 1983 to 1985. She was composer-in-residence of the Royal Scottish Academy of Music and Drama in Glasgow from 1988 to 1991. From 1995 to 1997 she was the Fairbairn composer-in-association of the City of Birmingham Sym. Orch. In her diverse output, Weir has effectively utilized both traditional and contemporary techniques in creating a highly individual means of expression.

WORKS: OPERAS: *The Black Spider* (1984; Canterbury, March 6, 1985); *A Night at the Chinese Opera* (1986–87; Cheltenham, July 8, 1987); *Heaven Ablaze in His Breast*, opera ballet (Basildon, Oct. 5, 1989); *The Vanishing Bridegroom* (Glasgow, Oct. 17, 1990); *Supio's Dream* (BBC-TV, Nov. 2, 1991; recomposition of Mozart's *Il Sogno di Scipione*); *Blond Eckbert* (1993–94; London, April 20, 1994).

Weis, Karel, Czech writer on music, ethnomusicologist, and composer; b. Prague, Feb. 13, 1862; d. there, April 4, 1944. He studied violin at the Prague Cons.; also organ with Skuherský and composition with Fibich at the Organ School in Prague. He subsequently filled various posts as organist and conductor in Prague and other cities. He devoted much of his time to collecting Bohemian folk songs, and publ. them in 15 vols. (1928–41).

WORKS: OPERAS: *Viola*, after Shakespeare's *Twelfth Night* (Prague, Jan. 17, 1892; rev. version as *Blíženci* [The Twins], Prague, Feb. 28, 1917); *Der polnische Jude* (Prague, March 3, 1901); *Die Dorfmusikanten* (Prague, Jan. 1, 1905); *Der Revisor*, after Gogol (1907); *Utok na mlýn*, after Zola's *L'Attaque du moulin* (Prague, March 29, 1912); *Lešetínský kovář* (The Blacksmith of Lesetin; Prague, June 6, 1920); *Bojarská nevěsta* (The Boyar's Bride; Prague, Feb. 18, 1943).

BIBL.: L. Firkušný, *K. W.* (Prague, 1949).

Weisgall, Hugo (David), distinguished Moravian-born American composer and pedagogue; b. Eibenschütz, Oct. 13, 1912; d. N.Y., March 11, 1997. He emigrated with his family to the United States and became a naturalized American citizen in 1926. He studied at the Peabody Cons. of Music in Baltimore (1927–32); subsequently he had composition lessons with Sessions at various times between 1932 and 1941; he also was a pupil of Reiner (conducting diploma, 1938) and Scalero (composition diploma, 1939) at the Curtis Inst. of Music in Philadelphia, and pursued academic studies at Johns Hopkins Univ. (Ph.D., 1940, with a diss. on primitivism in 17th-century German poetry). After military service in World War II, he was active as a conductor, singer, teacher, and composer. He was founder-conductor of the Chamber Soc. of Baltimore (1948) and the Hilltop Opera Co. (1952), and was director of the Baltimore Inst. of Musical Arts (1949–51). He taught at Johns Hopkins Univ. (1951–57); he also was made chairman of the faculty of the Cantors' Inst. at the Jewish Theological Center in N.ew York in 1952. He taught at the Juilliard School of Music (1957–70) and at Queens College of the City Univ. of N.Y. (from 1961). He served as president of the American Music Center (1963–73). In 1966 he was composer-in-residence at the American Academy in Rome. He held 3 Guggenheim fellowships and received many prizes and commissions; in 1975 he was elected to membership in the National Inst. of Arts and Letters, and in 1990 became president of the American Academy and Inst. of Arts and Letters, which, in 1994, awarded him its Gold Medal for Music. Weisgall's music constitutes the paragon of enlightened but inoffensive modernism; he is a master of all musical idioms, and bungler of none. His intentions in each of his works never fail in the execution; for this reason his music enjoys numerous performances, which are usually accepted with pleasure by the audiences, if not by the majority of important music critics.

WORKS: DRAMATIC: OPERAS: *Night* (1932); *Lillith* (1934); *The Tenor* (1948–50; Baltimore, Feb. 1, 1952); *The Stronger* (Lutherville, Md., Aug. 9, 1952); *6 Characters in Search of an Author* (1953–56; N.Y., April 26, 1959); *Purgatory* (1958; Washington, D.C., Feb. 17, 1961); *The Gardens of Adonis* (1959; rev. 1977–81; Omaha, Sept. 12, 1992); *Athaliah* (1960–63; N.Y., Feb. 17, 1964); *9 Rivers from Jordan* (1964–68; N.Y., Oct. 9, 1968); *Jennie, or The Hundred Nights* (1975–76; N.Y., April 22, 1976); *Esther* (N.Y., Oct. 6, 1993). BALLETS: *Quest* (Baltimore, May 17, 1938; suite, N.Y., March 21, 1942); *Art Appreciation* (Baltimore, 1938); *One Thing Is Certain* (Baltimore, Feb. 25, 1939); Outpost (1947).

Weismann, Julius, German pianist, conductor, and composer; b. Freiburg im Breisgau, Dec. 26, 1879; d. Singen am Hohentweil, Dec. 22, 1950. He began piano lessons at 9 with Seyffart; later studied composition with Rheinberger in Munich (1892); he received advanced piano training from Dimmler in Freiburg im Breisgau (1893), and took courses at the Univ. of Lausanne; he also studied composition with Bussmeyer, von Herzogenberg in Berlin (1898–99), and Thuille in Munich (1899–1902). He was active as a pianist and conductor in Freiburg im Breisgau from 1906, where he founded (with E. Doflein) the Musikseminar in 1930, subsequently serving as a teacher of harmony and as director of the piano master class; after retiring in 1939, he devoted himself fully to composition. He received the Beethoven Prize (1930), the Bach Prize of Leipzig (1939), and the Ehrenbürgerrecht of Freiburg im Breisgau (1939); he was made an honorary prof. by the government (1936) and by the state of Baden (1950). The Julius Weismann Archive was founded in his memory in Duisburg in 1954.

WORKS: DRAMATIC: OPERAS: *Schwanenweiss* (1919–20; Duisburg, Sept. 29, 1923); *Ein Traumspiel* (1922–24; Duisburg, 1925); *Leonce und Lena* (Mannheim, 1924); *Regina del lago* (Karlsruhe, 1928); *Die Gespenstersonate* (1929–30; Munich, Dec. 19, 1930); *Die pfiffige Magd* (1937–38; Leipzig, Feb. 11, 1939). BALLETS: *Tanzphantasie* (1910; orchestrated from the piano piece); *Die Landsknechte: Totentanz* (1936); *Sinfonisches Spiel* (1937).

BIBL.: F. Herzfeld, *J. W. und seine Generation* (Duisburg, 1965).

Weissberg, Yulia (Lazarevna), Russian composer; b. Orenburg, Jan. 6, 1880; d. Leningrad, March 1, 1942. She studied piano with Rimsky-Korsakov and instrumentation with Glazunov at the St. Petersburg Cons. (1903–05) and continued her musical training with Humperdinck and Reger in Germany (1907–12). She was a coed. of the journal *Muzykalny Sovremennik* (1915–17) and choral director of the Young Workers' Cons. (1921–23). Among her works are the operas *Rusalochka* (1923), *Gulnara* (1935), *Gusilebedi* (Geese Swans; 1937), and *Myortvaya tsarevna* (The Dead Princess; 1937). She married **Andrei Rimsky-Korsakov**.

Weissheimer, Wendelin, German conductor and composer; b. Osthofen, Alsace, Feb. 26, 1838; d. Nuremberg, June 16, 1910. He studied at the Leipzig Cons., and later took lessons in composition with Liszt at Weimar. He served as conductor in Mainz (1858, 1861, and later years), Würzburg (1866–68), Strasbourg (1873–78), and other cities; eventually settled in Nuremberg in 1900. As a composer, he followed the Wagnerian vogue; he wrote 2 operas, *Theodor Körner* (Munich, May 28, 1872) and *Meister Martin und seine Gesellen* (Karlsruhe, April 14, 1879). His book of reminiscences, *Erlebnisse mit Richard Wagner, Franz Liszt und vielen anderen Zeitgenossen, nebst deren Briefen* (Stuttgart, 1898), quotes many letters from Wagner, with whom he maintained a friendship.

Welcher, Dan, American composer, conductor, and teacher; b. Rochester, N.Y., March 2, 1948. He studied bassoon and composition (with Adler and Benson) at the Eastman School of Music in Rochester (B.Mus., 1969). Following further training in composition with Ulehla and Flagello at the Manhattan School of Music in New York (M.M., 1972), he pursued postgraduate studies in electronic music at the Aspen (Colo.) Music School (summer, 1972). He was a bassoonist in the Rochester Phil. (1968–69) and the U.S. Military Academy Band at West Point, N.Y. (1969–72), and then was 1st bassoonist in the Louisville Orch. (1972–78). From 1972 to 1978 he also taught at the Univ. of Louisville. In 1976 he became a member of the artist faculty at the Aspen Music Festival, where he served each summer until 1993. In 1978 he joined the faculty of the Univ. of Texas at Austin, where he was a prof. from 1989. In 1985–86 he was a visiting assoc. prof. at the

Eastman School of Music. From 1980 to 1990 he was assistant conductor of the Austin Sym. Orch. He served as composer-in-residence of the Honolulu Sym. Orch. from 1990 to 1993. His works include the opera *Della's Delight* (1986; Austin, Texas, Feb. 1987).

Weldon, George, English conductor; b. Chichester, June 5, 1906; d. Cape Town, South Africa, Aug. 16, 1963. He studied at the Royal College of Music in London with Sargent. He conducted various provincial orchs.; he traveled as a guest conductor in North Africa, Turkey, and Yugoslavia. He was conductor of the City of Birmingham Sym. Orch. (1943–51); he was 2d conductor of the Hallé Orch. in Manchester under Barbirolli (from 1952); he also conducted the Sadler's Wells Royal Ballet in London (1955–56).

Weldon, Georgina (née **Thomas**), English soprano; b. London, May 24, 1837; d. Brighton, Jan. 11, 1914. She took up singing after her marriage to Capt. Weldon in 1860, and did not appear in public until 1870. She organized an orphan asylum for the purpose of musical education, and also dabbled in music publishing. Special interest attaches to her because of her romantic friendship with Gounod, who during his London sojourn (1870–75) lived at her residence, and whom she assisted in training the Gounod Choir. She translated his autobiography (which goes only as far as 1859) into English (1875). Their relationship deteriorated, leading to a legal entanglement in connection with her claims regarding the copyright of Gounod's choral works; she wrote acrimonious letters to the press, defending her stand. She also publ. some songs of her own (to French texts) and the didactic manuals *Hints for Pronunciation in Singing* (1872) and *Musical Reform* (1875).

Welin, Karl-Erik (Vilhelm), Swedish organist, pianist, and composer; b. Genarp, May 31, 1934; d. Mallorca, May 30, 1992. He studied organ with Alf Linden at the Stockholm Musikhögskolan (graduated, 1961). He also received training in composition from Bucht (1958–60) and Lidholm (1960–64), in piano from Sven Brandel, and at the summer courses in new music in Darmstadt with David Tudor (1960–62). As a performer, he was a proponent of the extreme avant-garde in Sweden. He became well known via many appearances on Swedish TV. In contrast, his compositions followed a mellower path. While he embraced serial techniques, he did so with Romantic elan.

WORKS: DRAMATIC: *Dummerjöns* (Tom Fool), children's television opera (1966–67); *Copelius*, ballet (1968); *Ondine*, theater music (1968); *Vindarnas grotta* (Cave of the Winds), television ballet (Stockholm TV, March 30, 1969); *Drottning Jag* (Queen Ego), opera (1972; Stockholm, Feb. 17, 1973); *Don Quijote*, scenic oratorio (1990–91).

Welitsch (real name, **Veličkova**), **Ljuba,** remarkable Bulgarian-born Austrian soprano; b. Borissovo, July 10, 1913. She studied violin as a child; after attending the Sofia Cons. and the Univ. of Sofia, she studied voice with Lierhammer in Vienna. In 1936 she made her operatic debut at the Sofia Opera; after singing in Graz (1937–40), Hamburg (1942–43), and Munich (1943–46), she joined the Vienna State Opera, having sung there previously at the 80th birthday celebration for Richard Strauss on June 11, 1944, as Salome, which became her most celebrated role. She made her London debut with the visiting Vienna State Opera as Donna Anna in Don Giovanni on Sept. 20, 1947, a role she repeated in 1948 at the Glyndebourne Festival. On Feb. 4, 1949, she made her Metropolitan Opera debut in New York as Salome, remaining on the company's roster until 1952; she sang at London's Covent Garden in 1953. In subsequent years, she appeared in character roles in Vienna; she returned to the Metropolitan Opera in 1972 in a speaking role in *La Fille du régiment*. Among her other notable roles were Aida, Musetta, Minnie, Rosalinde, Jenůfa, and Tosca.

BIBL.: E. Benke, *L. W.* (Vienna, 1994).

Weller, Walter, distinguished Austrian conductor; b. Vienna, Nov. 30, 1939. He received training in violin from Moravec and Samohyl at the Vienna Academy of Music. He also studied conducting with Böhm and Stein, and later received guidance from Krips and Szell. In 1956 he became a violinist in the Vienna Phil., subsequently serving as one of its concertmasters (1964–69). He also was 2d violin in the Wiener Kozerthaus Quartet until founding his own Weller Quartet in 1958, with which he toured with notable success throughout Europe, North America, and Asia. In 1966 he began conducting but it was not until 1968 that he made his professional debut as a conductor of the Vienna Phil. From 1969 he conducted at the Volksoper and State Opera in Vienna. After serving as Generalmusikdirektor in Duisburg (1971–72), he was music director of the Niederösterreichesche Tonkünstlerorchester in Vienna (1975–78). He also began to appear as a guest conductor with major European orchs. and opera houses. From 1977 to 1980 he was principal conductor and musical adviser of the Royal Liverpool Phil., and then was principal conductor of the Royal Phil. in London from 1980 to 1985. From 1991 to 1997 he was music director of the Royal Scottish National Orch. in Glasgow, and he concurrently served as music director of the Theater and Sym. Orch. in Basel from 1994. While Weller is esteemed for his unmannered interpretations of the great Austro-German masterworks, he has also demonstrated a capacity to project modern scores with fine results.

Wellesz, Egon (Joseph), eminent Austrian-born English composer, musicologist, and pedagogue; b. Vienna, Oct. 21, 1885; d. Oxford, Nov. 9, 1974. He studied harmony with Carl Frühling in Vienna and then was a pupil in musicology with Adler at the Univ. of Vienna (graduated, 1908); he also received private instruction from Schoenberg. From 1911 to 1915 he taught music history at the Neues Cons. in Vienna; in 1913 he was engaged as a lecturer on musicology at the Univ. of Vienna, and was a prof. there from 1930 to 1938, when the annexation of Austria by Nazi Germany compelled him to leave. He went to England in 1938; he joined the music dept. of the Univ. of Oxford, which in 1932 had conferred upon him the degree of Mus.Doc. (*honoris causa*). In 1943 he became a lecturer in music history at the Univ. of Oxford; in 1946 he was appointed to the editorial board of the *New Oxford History of Music*, to which he then contributed, and was Univ. Reader in Byzantine music at Oxford (1948–56). Wellesz received the Prize of the City of Vienna in 1953. He was president of the Univ. of Oxford Byzantine Soc. (1955–66). In 1957 he was made a Commander of the Order of the British Empire and was awarded the Grande Médaille d'Argent of the City of Paris. In 1961 he was awarded the Austrian Great State prize. A scholar and a musician of extraordinary capacities, Wellesz distinguished himself as a composer of highly complex musical scores, and as an authority on Byzantine music.

WORKS: DRAMATIC: OPERAS: *Die Prinzessin Girnara* (1919–20; Hannover, May 15, 1921; rev. version, Mannheim, Sept. 2, 1928); *Alkestis* (1922–23; Mannheim, March 20, 1924); *Opferung des Gefangenen* (1924–25; Cologne, April 10, 1926); *Scherz, List und Rache* (1926–27; Stuttgart, March 1, 1928); *Die Bakchantinnen* (1929–30; Vienna, June 20, 1931); *Incognita* (Oxford, Dec. 5, 1951). BALLETS: *Das Wunder der Diana* (1915; Mannheim, March 20, 1924); *Persisches Ballett* (1920; Donaueschingen, 1924); *Achilles auf Skyros* (1921; Stuttgart, March 4, 1926); *Die Nächtlichen* (1923; Berlin, Nov. 20, 1924).

WRITINGS: *Arnold Schönberg* (Vienna, 1921; Eng. tr., 1924); *Byzantinische Kirchenmusik* (Breslau, 1927); *Eastern Elements in Western Chant: Studies in the Early History of Ecclesiastical Music*, Monumenta Musicae Byzantinae, subsidia, II (1947; 2d ed., 1967); *A History of Byzantine Music and Hymnography* (Oxford, 1949; 3d ed., rev., 1963); *Essays on Opera* (London, 1950); *The Origin of Schoenberg's 12-tone System* (Washington, D.C., 1958); *Byzantinische Musik, Das Musikwerk*, I (1959; Eng. tr., 1959); *Die Hymnen der Ostkirche*, Basiliensis de musica orationes, I (Kassel, 1962); *J. J. Fux* (London, 1965); he also ed. *Ancient and Oriental Music*, vol. 1, *The New Oxford History of Music* (Oxford, 1957); ed. with M. Velimirović, *Studies in Eastern Chant*, 1–3 (London, 1966–71); ed. with F. Sternfeld, *The Age of Enlightenment (1745–1790)*, vol. 7, *The New Oxford History of Music* (Oxford, 1973).

BIBL.: R. Schollum, *E. W.* (Vienna, 1964); C. Benser, *E. W.*

(1885–1974): Chronicle of a Twentieth-Century Musician (N.Y., 1985); L. Wedl, *Die Bakchantinnen von E. W.: Oder Das göttliche Wunder* (Vienna, 1992).

Welsh, Thomas, English bass, teacher, and composer; b. Wells, c.1780; d. Brighton, Jan. 24, 1848. He was a grandson of **Thomas Linley Sr.** He became a chorister at Wells Cathedral, and a pupil of J. B. Cramer and Baumgarten. He made his opera debut in London at the age of 12; after his voice changed, he became a bass, and sang in oratorio. He was particularly distinguished as a vocal teacher; he publ. *Vocal Instructor, or the Art of Singing Exemplified in 15 Lessons leading to 40 Progressive Exercises* (London, 1825). His wife and pupil, Mary Anne (née Wilson; 1802–67), whom he married in 1827, was a noted soprano who made her debut at Drury Lane on Jan. 18, 1821, in Arne's *Artaxerxes*. He composed several theater pieces, including the operatic farce *The Green-eyed Monster, or How to Get your Money* (London, Oct. 14, 1811).

Welser-Möst (real name, **Möst**), **Franz,** Austrian conductor; b. Linz, Aug. 16, 1960. He studied at the Munich Hochschule für Musik. After becoming a finalist in the Karajan conducting competition in 1979, he served as principal conductor of the Austrian Youth Orch. In 1985 he was named music director of the Winterthur and Norrköping sym. orchs. He made a successful British debut as a guest conductor with the London Phil. in 1986, and subsequently led it on a tour of Europe. In 1987 he made his debut as an opera conductor in Vienna with *L'Italiana in Algeri*. In 1989 he made his U.S. debut as a guest conductor with the St. Louis Sym. Orch. From 1990 to 1996 he was principal conductor of the London Phil. In 1995 he became music director of the Zürich Opera.

Welting, Ruth, American soprano; b. Memphis, Tenn., May 11, 1949. She received her training from Daniel Ferro in New York, Luigi Ricci in Rome, and Jeanne Reiss in Paris. In 1970 she made her operatic debut as Blondchen at the N.Y. City Opera. As a guest artist, she sang in Houston, San Antonio, Dallas, Sante Fe, and San Francisco. In 1975 she made her first appearance at London's Covent Garden as Zerbinetta, a role she also sang at her Metropolitan Opera debut in New York on March 20, 1976. She continued to make occasional appearances at the Metropolitan Opera until 1982. In 1979 she sang the Fairy Godmother in *Cendrillon* in Ottawa and in 1980 in Washington, D.C. In 1982 she made her first appearance at the Salzburg Festival as Zerbinetta. She sang Marie in *La Fille du régiment* in Barcelona in 1984. In 1990 she appeared as Ophelia in Thomas's *Hamlet* at the Chicago Lyric Opera. Among her other roles are Zerlina, Gilda, Norina, Adele, Sophie, and the Princess in *L'Enfant et les sortilèges*. She has also appeared frequently as a lieder artist.

Wendling, family of German musicians of Alsatian descent:

(1) Johann Baptist Wendling, flutist and composer; b. Rappoltsweiler, Alsace, June 17, 1723; d. Munich, Nov. 27, 1797. He was a flutist in Zweibrücken (1747–50), where he gave lessons to Duke Christian IV and was active in Mannheim as an instructor to the elector, Carl Theodor, and as a member of the Court Orch. In 1752 he married Dorothea Spurni, who often traveled with him on concert tours; among the cities he visited were Paris (played at the Concert Spirituel with Christian IV, 1762, and with Mozart, 1778), London (1771), and Vienna (1776). In 1778 he went with the Mannheim court to Munich, although he spent most of his later years in Mannheim. Mozart orchestrated 1 of his flute concertos (K. 284e).

(2) Dorothea (née **Spurni**) **Wendling,** singer, wife of the preceding; b. Stuttgart, March 21, 1736; d. Munich, Aug. 20, 1811. In 1752 she joined the Mannheim court as a singer, and by 1760 she was its principal member; when the court moved to Munich in 1778, she elected to remain in Mannheim, where she was active mainly as a teacher from 1790. She was held in great repute by her contemporaries; Mozart composed the role of Ilia in *Idomeneo* and the concert aria K. 486a/295a for her.

(3) Elisabeth Augusta Wendling, singer, daughter of **Johann Baptist** and **Dorothea** (née **Spurni**) **Wendling**; b. Mannheim, Oct. 4, 1752; d. Munich, Feb. 18, 1794. She first sang at the Mannheim Court Opera on Nov. 4, 1769, with her mother and her aunt, then appeared in Zweibrücken in 1772 and was a guest artist in Munich (from 1784). Mozart wrote the 2 French ariettas K. 307 and K. 308 for her.

(4) Franz (Anton) Wendling, violinist, brother of **Johann Baptist Wendling**; b. Rappoltsweiler, Oct. 21, 1729; d. Munich, May 16, 1786. In 1755 he became a violinist and in 1774 1st violinist in the Mannheim Court Orch. He went with it to Munich in 1778, where he also appeared as a ballet conductor. In 1764 he married Elisabeth Augusta Sarselli.

(5) Elisabeth Augusta (née **Sarselli**) **Wendling,** singer, wife of the preceding; b. Mannheim, Feb. 20, 1746; d. Munich, Jan. 10, 1786. In 1762 she became a court musician in Mannheim, where, in 1776, she was named 3d soprano; in 1778 she went with the court to Munich. She was greatly admired by her contemporaries; Mozart wrote the role of Elettra in *Idomeneo* for her.

(6) Dorothea Wendling, singer, daughter of **Franz (Anton)** and **Elisabeth Augusta** (née **Sarselli**) **Wendling**; b. Mannheim, Jan. 27, 1767; d. Munich, May 19, 1839. She was a pupil of her aunt, Dorothea (née Spurni) Wendling, in Mannheim, making her debut in 1778 in Munich. She sang mainly in Mannheim before devoting herself to teaching.

(7) (Johann) Karl Wendling, violinist and conductor, nephew of **Johann Baptist Wendling**; b. Zweibrücken, March 30, 1750; d. Mannheim, Nov. 10, 1834. He was a violinist in the Mannheim Court Orch. (from 1765); after the Court Orch. moved to Munich in 1778, he remained in Mannheim and was a violinist in the new National Theater there; he was active as a conductor there from about 1782.

Wenkel, Ortrun, German mezzo-soprano; b. Buttstadt, Oct. 25, 1942. After training at the Franz Liszt Hochschule für Music in Weimar, she attended the master classes of Paul Lohmann at the Frankfurt am Main Hochschule für Musik; she also studied with Elsa Cavelti. While still a student, she made her concert debut in London in 1964. In 1971 she made her operatic debut as Gluck's Orfeo in Heidelberg, and subsequently appeared in opera at Milan's La Scala, London's Covent Garden, Munich, Hamburg, Salzburg, Berlin, Vienna, and Zürich. She also pursued a highly active career as a concert artist, singing with major orchs. and as a recitalist. Her expansive repertoire ranges from the Baroque era to the contemporary period.

Wenkoff, Spas, Bulgarian tenor; b. Tirnovo, Sept. 23, 1928. He received his training from Jossifow in Sofia, Safirowa in Russe, and Kemter in Dresden. In 1954 he made his operatic debut as Kote in Dolidse's *Keto und Kote* in Tirnovo. After singing in Russe (1962–65), Döbeln (1965–68), Magdeburg (1968–71), and Halle (1971–75), he appeared as Tristan at the Dresden State Opera in 1975. From 1976 he sang at the Berlin State Opera. In 1976 he made his debut at the Bayreuth Festival as Tristan, and continued to appear there until 1983. He made his Metropolitan Opera debut in New York as Tristan on Jan. 9, 1981. In 1982 he sang Tannhäuser at the Vienna State Opera. In 1984 he appeared at the Deutsche Oper in Berlin. He sang Tannhäuser in Bern in 1987. In addition to his Heldentenor roles, he also sang roles in operas by Verdi and Puccini.

Werba, Erik, eminent Austrian pianist, teacher, composer, and writer on music; b. Baden, near Vienna, May 23, 1918; d. Hinterbrühl, April 9, 1992. He studied piano with Oskar Dachs and composition with Joseph Marx at the Vienna Academy of Music and musicology with Lach, Wellesz, and Schenk at the Univ. of Vienna (1936–40). He was active as a music critic for various newspapers (1945–65); he also was on the staff of the *Österreichische Musikzeitschrift* (from 1952). In 1949 he commenced touring throughout Europe as an accompanist to leading singers of the day; he also was a prof. of song and oratorio at the Vienna Academy of

Music (from 1949). In addition to numerous articles, he publ. *Joseph Marx* (Vienna, 1964), *Hugo Wolf oder der zornige Romantiker* (Vienna, 1971), *Erich Marckhl* (Vienna, 1972), and *Hugo Wolf und seine Lieder* (Vienna, 1984). He composed a Singspiel, *Trauben für die Kaiserin* (Vienna, 1949).

Werder, Felix, German-born Australian composer and music critic; b. Berlin, Feb. 22, 1922. He acquired early music training from his father, a cantor and composer of liturgical music. He also learned to play piano, viola, and clarinet. Among his teachers were Boas Bischofswerder and Arno Nadel. His family went to England in 1934 to escape Nazi persecution, and then settled in Australia in 1941. He taught music in Melbourne high schools, and was a music critic for the Melbourne newspaper *Age* (1960–77). He was a prolific composer but discarded many of his scores. Werder's musical idiom was determined by the crosscurrents of European modernism, with a gradual increase in the forcefulness of his resources, among them electronics.

WORKS: DRAMATIC: *Kisses for a Quid*, opera (1960); *En passant*, ballet (1964); *The General*, opera (1966); *Agamemnon*, opera (1967); *The Affair*, opera (1969); *Private*, television opera (1969); *The Vicious Square*, opera (1971); *The Conversion*, opera (1973); *Banker*, music theater (1973); *La belle dame sans merci*, ballet (1973); *Quantum*, ballet (1973); *Bellifull*, music theater (1976); *The Director*, music theater (1980); *The Medea*, opera (1984–85; Melbourne, Sept. 17, 1985); *Business Day*, music theater (1988). Also *Francis Bacon Essays*, choral oratorio (1971).

Werle, Lars Johan, Swedish composer; b. Gävle, June 23, 1926. He studied with Bäck (composition) and Moberg (musicology) at the Univ. of Uppsala (1948–51). He held positions at the Swedish Radio (1958–70) and as an instructor at the National School of Music Drama in Stockholm (1970–76), then was resident composer of Göteborg (1976–79). In his music, he employs an amiably modern idiom, stimulating to the untutored ear while retaining the specific gravity of triadic tonal constructions. His theater operas have been received with smiling approbation.

WORKS: DRAMATIC: *Drömmen om Thérèse* (The Dream of Thérèse), opera, after Zola's *Pour une nuit d'amour* (Stockholm, May 26, 1964); *Zodiak*, ballet (1966; Stockholm, Feb. 12, 1967); *Resan* (The Voyage), opera, after J. P. Jersild (Hamburg, March 2, 1969); *En saga om sinnen*, television opera (Swedish TV, June 21, 1971); *Tintomara*, opera, after C. J. L. Almquist's *The Queen's Jewels* (1972; Stockholm, Jan. 18, 1973); *Medusan och djävulen* (Medusa and the Devil), lyrical mystery play (1973); *Animalen*, musical (Göteborg, May 19, 1979); *Är gryningen redan här*, ballet (Göteborg, Sept. 5, 1980); *En midsommarnattsdröm* (A Midsummer Night's Dream), opera, after Shakespeare (1984; Malmö, Feb. 8, 1985); *Gudars skymning eller När kärleken blev blind . . .*, cabaret (1985); *Lionardo*, opera (1985–88; Stockholm, March 31, 1988); *Kvinnogräl*, opera (Göteborg, Oct. 18, 1986); *Tavlan eller En eftermiddag på Prado*, chamber opera (1991–93); *Hercules*, opera (1993); *Appelkriget*, opera (1995; Göteborg, Feb. 10, 1996); *Pandora*, opera (1998).

Wernick, Richard, American composer, teacher, and conductor; b. Boston, Jan. 16, 1934. He was a student in theory and composition of Fine, Shapero, and Berger at Brandeis Univ. (B.A., 1955), in composition of Toch, Blacher, and Copland and in conducting of Bernstein and Lipkin at the Berkshire Music Center at Tanglewood (summers, 1954–55), and in composition of Kirchner at Mills College in Oakland, Calif. (M.A., 1957). In 1957–58 he was music director and composer-in-residence of the Royal Winnipeg Ballet in Canada. In 1964–65 he taught at the State Univ. of N.Y. at Buffalo, and in 1965–66 at the Univ. of Chicago, where he conducted its sym. orch. (1965–68). In 1968 he joined the faculty of the Univ. of Pa., where he conducted its sym. orch. (until 1970); he was also chairman of its music dept. (1969–74), served as prof. of music (1977–86), the Irving Fine Prof. of Music (1986–92), and the Magnin Prof. of Humanities (from 1992). From 1968 he also was music director of the Penn Contemporary Players. He held grants from the Ford Founation (1962–64) and the NEA (1975, 1979, 1982). In 1976 he received a Guggenheim fellowship and an award from the National Inst. of Arts and Letters. He won the Pulitzer Prize in music in 1977 for his *Visions of Terror and Wonder* for Mezzo-soprano and Orch. In 1986 he received a Kennedy Center Friedheim Award for his Violin Concerto. As a composer, Wernick has followed an eclectic course in which he utilizes the most advantageous traditional and modern means of expression.

WORKS: DRAMATIC: OPERA: *Maggie* (1959; unfinished; in collaboration with I. Fine). BALLETS: *The Twisted Heart* (Winnipeg, Nov. 27, 1957); *Fete Brilliante* (Winnipeg, Jan. 13, 1958); *The Emperor's Nightingale* (1958); *The Queen of Ice* (1958); *The Nativity* (1960; CBS-TV, Jan. 1, 1961). Also incidental music to plays and film scores.

Werrenrath, Reinald, American baritone; b. Brooklyn, Aug. 7, 1883; d. Plattsburg, N.Y., Sept. 12, 1953. He was a pupil of his father, a tenor, then of David Bispham and Herbert Witherspoon. He began his career as a concert singer; also in oratorio; he made his operatic debut on Feb. 19, 1919, at the Metropolitan Opera in New York, as Silvio in Pagliacci, and remained with the company until 1921, then devoted himself to teaching and concert singing; he appeared in public for the last time at Carnegie Hall in New York on Oct. 23, 1952. He ed. *Modern Scandinavian Songs* (2 vols., Boston, 1925–26).

Wesendonck, Mathilde (née **Luckemeyer**), German poet; b. Elberfeld, Dec. 23, 1828; d. Traunblick, near Altmünster on the Traunsee, Austria, Aug. 31, 1902. Her first meeting with Richard Wagner took place in Zürich, early in 1852, and soon developed into a deep friendship. She wrote the famous *Fünf Gedichte* (*Der Engel, Stehe still, Träume, Schmerzen*, and *Im Treibhaus*), which Wagner set to music as studies for *Tristan und Isolde*. On May 19, 1848, she married Otto Wesendonck (b. March 16, 1815; d. Berlin, Nov. 18, 1896); in 1857 he gave Wagner the use of a beautiful house on his estate on Lake Zürich, where the first act of *Tristan und Isolde* was written, and the 2d act sketched.

BIBL.: A. Heintz, ed., *Briefe Richard Wagners an Otto Wesendonk* (Charlottenburg, 1898; 2d ed., aug., 1905 by W. Golther; Eng. tr., 1911); idem, ed., *Richard Wagner an M. W.: Tagebuchblätter und Briefe 1853–1871* (Leipzig, 1904; 30th ed., rev., 1906; Eng. tr., 1905); H. Belart, *Richard Wagners Liebestragodie mit M. W.* (Dresden, 1912); J. Kapp, ed., *Richard Wagner an M. und Otto W.* (Leipzig, 1915; 2d ed., 1936); E. Müller von Asow, ed., *Johannes Brahms und M. W.: Ein Briefwechsel* (Vienna, 1943); J. Bergfeld, *Otto und M. W.s Bedeutung für das Leben und Schaffen Richard Wagners* (Bayreuth, 1968).

Wesley-Smith, Martin, Australian composer and teacher; b. Adelaide, June 10, 1945. He was educated at the univs. of Adelaide (B.M., 1969; M.M., 1971) and of York in England (Ph.D., 1974); his mentors in composition were Peter Tahourdin, Peter Maxwell Davies, Sandor Veress, and Jindrich Feld. In 1974 he became a lecturer in electronic music at the New South Wales State Conservatorium of Music in Sydney, where he was senior lecturer in composition and electronic music from 1980; he also was a reader in composition at the Univ. of Hong Kong (1994–95). He was founder-director of watt, an electronic music and audiovisual performing group, with which he toured internationally; he also was founder-musical director of T.R.E.E. (Theatre Reaching Environments Everywhere). With Ian Fredericks, he organized the first computer music studio in mainland China in 1986. In 1987 he was the Australia Council's Don Banks Composer Fellow. In his extensive output, Wesley-Smith follows an imaginative, eclectic course. While he has composed in most genres, he has gained particular notice for his effective computer and audiovisual works, finding particular inspiration in the writings of Lewis Carroll. Some of his works are overtly political.

WORKS: DRAMATIC: *Pi in the Sky*, children's opera (1971); *The Wild West Show*, children's music theater (1971); *Machine*, children's music theater (1972); *Boojum!*, music theater (1985–86); *Quito*, audiovisual music theater (1994); *Encountering Sorro (Ch'ü Yüan Laments)*, radiophonic piece (1994).

Westerberg, Stig (Evald Börje), Swedish conductor; b. Malmö, Nov. 26, 1918. He studied at the Stockholm Musikhögskolan (1937–42) and with Kletzki in Paris. He was a répétiteur at Stockholm's Royal Theater (1943–46), and then conducted at the Oscarsteatern; after conducting the Gävleborg Sym. Orch. (1949–53), he returned to Stockholm as a conductor at the Royal Theater; in 1957 he became chief conductor of the Swedish Radio Sym. Orch.; he taught conducting at the Musikhögskolan from 1969, becoming a prof. there in 1971. From 1978 to 1985 he was chief conductor of the Malmö Sym. Orch. He became well known for his performances of both traditional and contemporary Swedish scores.

Westergaard, Peter (Talbot), American composer, music theorist, and teacher; b. Champaign, Ill., May 28, 1931. He was a student of Piston at Harvard College (A.B., 1953), of Milhaud at the Aspen (Colo.) Music School (summers, 1951–52) and at the Paris Cons. (1953), of Sessions at Princeton Univ. (M.F.A., 1956), and of Fortner in Detmold (1956) and in Freiburg im Breisgau (1957) on a Fulbright fellowship. After serving as a guest lecturer at the Staatliche Hochschule für Musik in Freiburg im Breisgau (1958), he taught at Columbia Univ. (1958–66). In 1966–67 he was a vistiting lecturer at Princeton Univ. In 1967–68 he taught at Amherst College. He became an assoc. prof. at Princeton Univ. in 1968, and a full prof. in 1971. He served as chairman of its music dept. (1974–78; 1983–86). In 1995 he was named the William Shubael Conant Prof. of Music there. He also held the endowed chair at the Univ. of Alabama School of Music in 1995. In addition to various commissions, he held a Guggenheim fellowship (1964–65) and an NEA grant (1990–91). He wrote various articles for journals and publ. the study *An Introduction to Tonal Theory* (N.Y., 1975). In his compositions, Westergaard explored the potentialities of total organization of tones, rhythms, and other compositional elements.

WORKS: DRAMATIC: *Charivari*, chamber opera (1953); *Mr. and Mrs. Discobbolos*, chamber opera (1966); *The Tempest*, opera (1988–90; Lawrenceville, N.J., July 8, 1994); *Chicken Little*, children's opera (1997).

Westerhout, Nicolà van. See **Van Westerhout, Nicolà**.

Westrup, Sir Jack (Allan), eminent English musicologist; b. London, July 26, 1904; d. Headley, Hampshire, April 21, 1975. He received his education at Dulwich College, London (1917–22), and at Balliol College, Oxford (B.A. and B.Mus., 1926; M.A., 1929). He was an assistant classics master at Dulwich College (1928–34), then was a music critic for the *Daily Telegraph* (1934–39); he also was ed. of the *Monthly Musical Record* (1933–45). He gave classes at the Royal Academy of Music in London (1938–40), then was lecturer in music at King's College, Newcastle upon Tyne (1941–44), the Univ. of Birmingham (1944–47), and Wadham College, Oxford (1947–71). In 1946 he received an honorary degree of D.Mus. at the Univ. of Oxford. In 1947 he was named chairman of the editorial board of *The New Oxford History of Music*. In 1959 he succeeded Eric Blom as ed. of *Music & Letters*. From 1958 to 1963 he was president of the Royal Musical Assn. He was also active as a conductor; he conducted the Oxford Opera Club (1947–62), the Oxford Univ. Orch. (1954–63), and the Oxford Bach Choir and Oxford Orch. Soc. (1970–71). He was knighted in 1961. Westrup prepared major revisions of Walker's *A History of Music in England* (Oxford, 3d ed., 1952) and of Fellowes's *English Cathedral Music* (London, 5th ed., 1969); he also supervised rev. eds. of Blom's *Everyman's Dictionary of Music* (4th ed., 1962; 5th ed., 1971). He was coed., with F. Harrison, of the *Collins Music Encyclopedia* (London, 1959; American ed. as *The New College Encyclopedia of Music*, N.Y., 1960).

WRITINGS (all publ. in London unless otherwise given): *Purcell* (1937; 4th ed., rev., 1980); *Handel* (1938); *Liszt* (1940); *Sharps and Flats* (1940); *British Music* (1943; 3d ed., 1949); *The Meaning of Musical History* (1946); *An Introduction to Musical History* (1955); *Music: Its Past and Its Present* (Washington, D.C., 1964); *Bach Cantatas* (1966); *Schubert Chamber Music* (1969); *Musical Interpretation* (1971).

BIBL.: F. Sternfeld et al., eds., *Essays on Opera and English Music in Honour of Sir J. W.* (Oxford, 1975).

Wettergren, Gertrud (née **Pålson**), Swedish contralto; b. Eslöv, Feb. 17, 1897; d. Stockholm, June 1991. She studied at the Stockholm Cons., and later in London. She made her operatic debut as Cherubino at the Royal Opera in Stockholm in 1922, and remained on its roster for 30 years. On Dec. 20, 1935, she appeared at the Metropolitan Opera in New York as Amneris in *Aida*; she sang there until 1938; she also sang with the Chicago Opera (1936–38) and at London's Covent Garden (1936, 1939). In 1925 she married Erik Wettergren, director of the National Museum of Stockholm. Among her most esteemed roles were Venus, Fricka, Brangäne, Dalila, Carmen, Mignon, Marfa, and Herodias; she also sang in many Swedish operas.

Wetz, Richard, German composer, conductor, and teacher; b. Gleiwitz, Feb. 26, 1875; d. Erfurt, Jan. 16, 1935. He studied with R. Hofmann in Leipzig and Thuille in Munich (1899–1900); also attended the Univ. of Munich. He was a theater conductor in Straslund and Barmen; in 1906 he settled in Erfurt as conductor of the Musikverein and the Singakademie; also taught at the Weimar Hochschule für Musik (from 1916). His output was greatly influenced by Bruckner. A Richard Wetz-Gesellschaft was founded in Gleiwitz in 1943 to promote his music, which included an opera, *Das ewige Feuer* (Düsseldorf, March 19, 1907), and the *Weihnachtsoratorio* for Soprano, Baritone, Chorus, and Orch.

WRITINGS: *Anton Bruckner* (Leipzig, 1922); *Franz Liszt* (Leipzig, 1925); *Beethoven* (Erfurt, 1927; 2d ed., 1933).

BIBL.: G. Armin, *Die Lieder von R. W.* (Leipzig, 1911); E. Schellenberg, *R. W.* (Leipzig, 1911; 2d ed., 1914); H. Polack, *R. W.: Sein Werk* (Leipzig, 1935).

Wetzler, Hermann (Hans), American organist, conductor, and composer; b. Frankfurt am Main (of American parents), Sept. 8, 1870; d. N.Y., May 29, 1943. He was taken to the United States as a child, but in 1882 returned to Germany, where he studied at the Hoch Cons. in Frankfurt am Main and studied with Clara Schumann (piano), Iwan Knorr (counterpoint), and Humperdinck (instrumentation). In 1892 he went to New York., where he was organist at Old Trinity Church (1897–1901); in 1903 he established the Wetzler Sym. Concerts, which had considerable success; Richard Strauss conducted a series of 4 concerts of his own works with the Wetzler group (Feb.-March 1904), including the premiere of the *Sinfonia domestica*. In 1905 he returned to Germany and conducted in various German cities and throughout Europe. In 1940 he returned to the United States. He publ. *Wege zur Musik* (Leipzig, 1938). Among his works were the opera *Die baskische Venus* (Leipzig, Nov. 18, 1928; the *Symphonic Dance in the Basque Style* was extracted from this score as a concert piece), and incidental music to Shakespeare's *As You Like It* (1917).

Weyse, Christoph Ernst Friedrich, eminent Danish pianist, organist, pedagogue, and composer of German descent; b. Altona, March 5, 1774; d. Copenhagen, Oct. 8, 1842. He studied with his grandfather, a cantor in Altona, and in 1789 went to Copenhagen, where he studied with J. A. P. Schulz; he remained there the rest of his life. After establishing his reputation as a pianist, he devoted himself to the organ. He was deputy organist (1792–94) and principal organist (1794–1805) at the Reformed Church, and then served as principal organist at the Cathedral from 1805 until his death, winning great renown as a master of improvisation. In 1816 he was named titular prof. at the Univ. and was awarded an honorary doctorate in 1842, the year of his death. In 1819 he was appointed court composer. Through the court conductor Kunzen, he became interested in a movement for the establishment of a national school of Danish opera, for which his works (together with those of Kuhlau) effectively prepared the way. He remains best known for his fine songs.

WORKS: DRAMATIC: OPERAS (all 1st perf. in Copenhagen): *Sovedrikken* (The Sleeping Potion; April 21, 1809); *Faruk* (Jan. 30, 1812); *Ludlams hule* (Ludlam's Cave; Jan. 30, 1816); *Floribella*

(Jan. 29, 1825); *Et eventyr i Rosenborg Have* (An Adventure in Rosenborg Gardens; May 26, 1827); *Festen påa Kenilworth* (Jan. 6, 1836). Also incidental music to Shakespeare's *Macbeth* (1817) and J. Ewald's *Balders død* (The Death of Baldur; 1832).

BIBL.: A. Berggreen, *C. E. F. W.s biographie* (Copenhagen, 1876); J. Larsen, *W.s sange* (Copenhagen, 1942).

White, Clarence Cameron, black American violinist and composer; b. Clarksville, Tenn., Aug. 10, 1880; d. N.Y., June 30, 1960. He studied at the Oberlin (Ohio) Cons. (1896–1901), with Samuel Coleridge-Taylor in London (1906; 1908–10), and with Raoul Laparra in Paris (1930–32). He taught at various institutions while pursuing a concert career; he was director of music at the Hampton (Va.) Inst. (1932–35). In 1919 he helped to organize the National Assn. of Negro Musicians. He won the Bispham Medal for his opera *Ouanga* (concert perf., Chicago, Nov. 1932; stage perf., South Bend, Inc., June 10, 1949) and the Benjamin Award for his *Elegy* for Orch. (1954). His major works were written in a neo-Romantic style with occasional infusions of black folk melos. Other works were the opera *Carnival Romance* (1952), the ballet *A Night in Sans Souci* (1929), and incidental music to J. Matheus's *Tambour* (1929).

White, Eric Walter, English writer on music and administrator; b. Bristol, Sept. 10, 1905; d. London, Sept. 13, 1985. He attended Clifton College, Bristol, and studied English at Balliol College, Oxford (1924–27). After working as a translator for the League of Nations in Geneva (1929–33), he was employed by the National Council for Social Service in London (1935–42); in 1942 he became assistant secretary of the Council for the Encouragement of Music and the Arts, which became the Arts Council of Great Britain in 1946; he retired in 1971. He publ. valuable studies on Stravinsky and an invaluable register of English opera premieres.

WRITINGS (all publ. in London): *Stravinsky's Sacrifice to Apollo* (1930); *Stravinsky: A Critical Survey* (1947); *Benjamin Britten: A Sketch of His Life and Works* (1948; 3d ed., enl., 1970 as *Benjamin Britten: His Life and Operas*); *The Rise of English Opera* (1951); *Stravinsky: The Composer and His Works* (1966; 2nd ed., rev., 1979); *A History of English Opera* (1983); *A Register of First Performances of English Operas and Semi-Operas from the 16th Century to 1980* (1983).

White, Michael, American composer and teacher; b. Chicago, March 6, 1931. He studied at the Chicago Musical College and at the Juilliard School of Music in New York with Peter Mennin. In 1963 he received a Guggenheim fellowship. He taught at the Oberlin (Ohio) College Cons. of Music (1964–66), the Philadelphia College of Performing Arts (1966–79), and the Juilliard School in New York (from 1979). Among his works are several operas, including *Metamorphosis* (1968).

White, Robert, American tenor; b. N.Y., Oct. 27, 1936. He was the son of Joseph White, the "Silver Masked Tenor" of the early radio era in New York. He began his career with appearances on Fred Allen's radio program when he was 9; after studying music at Hunter College, he continued his training with Boulanger and Souzay in France, then completed his studies at the Juilliard School of Music in New York (M.S., 1968), where he found a mentor in Beverley Peck Johnson. He sang with the N.Y. Pro Musica and appeared with various American opera companies before becoming successful as a concert singer. His repertoire ranges from the Baroque to Irish ballads. He sang in a "Homage to John McCormack" at N.Y.'s Alice Tully Hall during the 1985–86 season.

White, Ruth, American composer; b. Pittsburgh, Sept. 1, 1925. She studied composition with Lopatnikoff (B.F.A., 1948; M.F.A., 1949) and received training in piano at the Mellon Inst. in Pittsburgh; she then studied at the Univ. of Calif. at Los Angeles (1951–54) and had private composition lessons with Antheil (1952–54). She specialized in teaching music to children and wrote much didactic music. Her other music followed along conventional lines until she took up electronic composition in 1964. Among her works is the opera *Pinions* (1967); also film and television music.

White, Willard (Wentworth), notable West Indian bass-baritone and actor; b. St. Catherine, Jamaica, Oct. 10, 1946. He studied at the Juilliard School in New York, where he attended Callas's master classes. In 1974 he made his operatic debut in Washington, D.C., as Trulove in *The Rake's Progress*, and then appeared as Colline in *La Bohème* at the N.Y. City Opera. He also made his European operatic debut that year at the Welsh National Opera in Cardiff as Osmin. In 1976 he made his first appearance with the English National Opera in London as Seneca in *L'incoronazione di Poppea*. His debut at the Glyndebourne Festival followed in 1978 as the Speaker in *Die Zauberflöte*, and he also sang Don Diego in *L'Africaine* at his first appearance at London's Covent Garden. After appearing as Plutone in *Orfeo* at the Salzburg Festival in 1980, he returned to the English National Opera as Hunding in 1983 and to the Glyndebourne Festival as Gershwin's Porgy in 1986. In 1989 he sang Wotan at the Scottish Opera in Glasgow and took the title role in Shakespeare's *Othello* at the Royal Shakespeare Co. He returned to Covent Garden as Porgy in 1992, sang Golaud at the San Francisco Opera in 1995, and appeared in Ligeti's *Le Grand Macabre* in Paris and Salzburg in 1997. In 1998 he sang Boris Godunov at the English National Opera. He was made a Commander of the Order of the British Empire in 1995. White has demonstrated a mastery of both vocal and dramatic elements in his varied roles as a singer and as an actor.

Whitehill, Clarence (Eugene), American baritone, later bass-baritone; b. Parnell, Iowa, Nov. 5, 1871; d. N.Y., Dec. 18, 1932. He studied with L. A. Phelps in Chicago; earned his living as a clerk in an express office, and also sang in churches; he then went to Paris in 1896, where he studied with Giraudet and Sbriglia. He made his operatic debut on Oct. 31, 1898, at the Théâtre Royal de la Monnaie in Brussels; he was the first American male singer to be engaged at the Opéra Comique in Paris (1899), then was a member of Henry Savage's Grand English Opera Co. at the Metropolitan Opera in New York in 1900; he went for further study to Stockhausen in Frankfurt am Main, and from there to Bayreuth, where he studied the entire Wagnerian repertoire with Cosima Wagner; after engagements in Germany, he was a member of the Cologne Opera (1903–08).On Nov. 25, 1909, he made his Metropolitan Opera debut in New York with notable success, where he sang for a season. He then was again on its roster from 1914 until his death. He also sang with the Chicago Opera (1911–14; 1915–17). Among his finest roles were Hans Sachs, Gounod's Méphistophélès, and Golaud.

Whitmer, T(homas) Carl, American organist, teacher, and composer; b. Altoona, Pa., June 24, 1873; d. Poughkeepsie, N.Y., May 30, 1959. He studied piano with C. Jarvis, organ with S. P. Warren, and composition with W.W. Gilchrist. He was director of the School of Music, Stephens College, Columbia, Mo. (1899–1909); director of music at the Pa. College for Women in Pittsburgh (1909–16); organist and choirmaster of the Sixth Presbyterian church in Pittsburgh (1916–32), and taught privately at Dramamount, his farm near Newburgh, N.Y. He publ. *The Way of My Heart and Mind* (Pittsburgh, 1920) and *The Art of Improvisation: A Handbook of Principles and Methods* (N.Y., 1934; rev. ed., 1941). His compositions include the opera *Oh, Isabel* (1951); also sacred music dramas.

Whittal, Arnold (Morgan), English musicologist; b. Shrewsbury, Nov. 11, 1935. He took courses at Emmanuel College, Cambridge (B.A., 1959), completing his training at the Univ. there (Ph.D., 1964, with the diss. *La Querelle des Bouffons*). He then taught at the Univ. of Nottingham (1964–69), Univ. College, Cardiff (1969–75), and King's College, London (from 1976).

WRITINGS: *Schoenberg Chamber Music* (London, 1972); *Music since the First World War* (London, 1977; 3d ed., 1988); *Britten and Tippett: Studies in Themes and Techniques* (Cambridge, 1982); *Romantic Music: A Concise History from Schubert to Si-*

belius (London, 1987); with J. Dunsby, *Music Analysis in Theory and Practice* (New Haven, Conn., 1988).

Whyte, Ian, Scottish conductor, broadcasting administrator, and composer; b. Dunfermline, Aug. 13, 1901; d. Glasgow, March 27, 1960. He was a pupil of David Stephen (composition) and Philip Halstead (piano) at the Carnegie Dunfermline Trust Music School, and later was a student of Stanford and Vaughan Williams at the Royal College of Music in London. Upon his return to Scotland, he was made music director to Lord Glentanar in 1923. From 1931 to 1945 he was head of music for the BBC in Glasgow, and then conductor of its orch. from 1945 until his death. His extensive output, which includes operas, operettas, and ballets, reflects his Scottish heritage.

Wich, Günther, German conductor; b. Bamberg, May 23, 1928. He studied flute with Gustav Scheck in Freiburg im Breisgau (1948–52). In 1952 he made his conducting debut there, serving as chief conductor of its Opera until 1959, then was conductor of the Graz Opera (1959–61); he later was Generalmusikdirektor in Hannover (1961–65) and at the Deutsche Oper am Rhein in Düsseldorf (1965–80). In 1982 he joined the faculty of the Würzburg Hochschule für Musik.

Wickham, Florence, American contralto and composer; b. Beaver, Pa., 1880; d. N.Y., Oct. 20, 1962. She studied in Philadelphia, then was a pupil of Franz Emerich in Berlin; she also studied with Mathilde Mallinger. In 1902 she made her operatic debut as Fidès in Wiesbaden; after appearances in Schwerin and Munich, she sang the role of Kundry in *Parsifal* in Henry W. Savage's touring opera troupe in America (1904–05). In 1908 she appeared in Wagnerian roles at London's Covent Garden. On Nov. 17, 1909, she made her Metropolitan Opera debut in New York. as Verdi's Emilia; she remained on its roster until 1912, then sang in concerts and devoted herself to composition. She wrote the operettas *Rosalynd* (1938) and *The Legend of Hex Mountain* (1957).

Widdop, Walter, English tenor; b. Norland, April 19, 1892; d. London, Sept. 6, 1949. He was a student of Dinh Gilly. In 1923 he made his operatic debut as Radames with the British National Opera Co. in Leeds. In 1924 he sang in *Siegfried* at London's Covent Garden, returning there as Siegmund (1932) and Tristan (1933; 1937–38). He was also a guest artist in Spain, Holland, and Germany. In addition to his operatic roles, he also was admired as an oratorio singer. The night before he died he sang Lohengrin's Farewell at a London Promenade concert.

Widor, Charles-Marie (-Jean-Albert), distinguished French organist, pedagogue, and composer; b. Lyons, Feb. 21, 1844; d. Paris, March 12, 1937. His father, an Alsatian of Hungarian descent, was organist at the church of St.-François in Lyons and was active as an organ builder. Widor was a skillful improviser on the organ while still a boy, and became organist at the Lyons lycee when he was 11. After studies with Fétis (composition) and Lemmens (organ) in Brussels, he became organist at St.-François in Lyons (1860), and gained high repute via provincial concerts. In 1870–71 he held a provisional appointment as organist at St.-Sulpice in Paris, where he served as organist from 1871 until 1934. On April 19, 1934, he played his *Pièce mystique* there, composed at age 90. Around 1880 he began writing music criticism under the pen name "Aulétès" for the daily *L'Estafette*. In 1890 he became prof. of organ and in 1896 prof. of composition at the Paris Cons. In 1910 he was elected a member of the Academie des Beaux-Arts, of which he became permanent secretary in 1913. He had many distinguished pupils, including Albert Schweitzer, with whom he collaborated in editing the first 5 vols. of an 8-vol. ed. of J. S. Bach's organ works (N.Y., 1912–14). As a composer, he wrote copiously in many forms but is best known for his organ music, especially his 10 "symphonies" (suites). A master organ virtuoso, he won great renown for his performances of Bach and for his inspired improvisations.

WORKS: DRAMATIC (all 1st perf. in Paris): *Maître Ambros*, opera (May 6, 1886); *Les Pêcheurs de Saint-Jean*, opera (Dec. 26, 1905); *Nerto*, opera (Oct. 27, 1924); *La Korrigane*, ballet (Dec. 1, 1880); *Jeanne d'Arc*, ballet-pantomime (1890). Also incidental music to *Conte d'avril* (Sept. 22, 1885) and to *Les Jacobites* (Nov. 21, 1885).

WRITINGS (all publ. in Paris): *Technique de l'orchestre moderne* (1904; 5th ed., rev. and enl., 1925; Eng. tr., 1906; 2d ed., rev., 1946); *Notice sur la vie et les oeuvres de Camille Saint-Saëns* (1922); *Initiation musicale* (1923); *Académie des Beaux-Arts: Fondations, portraits de Massenet à Paladilhe* (1927); *L'Orgue moderne: La Décadence dans la facture contemporaine* (1928).

BIBL.: H. Reynaud, *L'Œuvre de C.-M. W.* (Lyons, 1900); J. Rupp, *C.-M. W. und sein Werk* (Bremen, 1912); A. Thomson, *The Life and Times of C.-M. W., 1844–1937* (Oxford, 1988).

Wiedemann, Hermann, German baritone; b. 1879; d. Berlin, July 2, 1944. He made his operatic debut in Elberfeld in 1905. After singing in Brünn (1906–10), he was a member of the Hamburg Opera (1910–14), the Berlin Royal Opera (1914–16), and the Vienna Court (later State) Opera (1916–44). He also sang at the Salzburg Festivals (1922–41) and at London's Covent Garden (1933, 1938). Among his best roles were Guglielmo, Beckmesser, Alberich, and Donner.

Wiegand, (Josef Anton) Heinrich, German bass; b. Fränkisch-Crumbach in the Odenwald, Sept. 9, 1842; d. Frankfurt am Main, May 28, 1899. He studied voice privately in Paris, becoming a member of the opera at Zürich in 1870; he then sang in Cologne, and from 1873 to 1877 was the leading bass at the Frankfurt am Main Opera. In 1877 he toured America with the Adams-Pappenheim troupe; he was in Leipzig (1878–82), sang at the Vienna Court Opera (1882–84), and then was engaged at Hamburg. He also appeared in the *Ring* cycle in Berlin (1881) and London (1882).

Wielhorsky, Count Mikhail, Russian arts patron and composer of Polish descent; b. Volhynia, Nov. 11, 1788; d. Moscow, Sept. 9, 1856. His principal mentor in music was Martin y Soler; he learned to play the violin and piano, and began composing at 13. After studying counterpoint in Riga, he completed his studies with Cherubini in Paris (1808). In 1810 he went to St. Petersburg, where his home became the gathering place of many eminent musicians; in 1816 he went to live at his estate in the Kursk province, where he maintained a private orch. After living in Moscow (1823–26) and again in St. Petersburg (1826–56), he spent his last days at his estate near Moscow. His compositions include *Tsigane* (The Gypsies), opera (1838). His brother, Count Matvei Wielhorsky (b. St. Petersburg, April 26, 1794; d. Nice, March 3, 1866), was also a patron of the arts as well as a cellist; he studied cello with Adolph Meinhardt and Bernard Romberg; he toured throughout Russia and in Europe. He lived with his brother in St. Petersburg (1826–56), where he helped to organize the city's branch of the Russian Musical Soc. in 1859. A distant relative, Joseph Wielhorsky (1817–92), was also a musician.

Wiemann, Ernst, German bass; b. Stapelberg, Dec. 21, 1919; d. Hamburg, May 17, 1980. He studied in Hamburg and Munich. After making his operatic debut in Kiel (1938), he sang in provincial German opera houses until joining the Hamburg State Opera in 1955. On Nov. 17, 1961, he made his Metropolitan Opera debut in New York as Heinrich in *Lohengrin*, and remained on its roster until 1969. In 1971 he sang Gurnemanz at London's Covent Garden. He also appeared as a guest artist with opera companies on both sides of the Atlantic. He was best known for his Mozart, Wagner, and Verdi roles.

Wiéner, Jean, French pianist and composer of Austrian descent; b. Paris, March 19, 1896; d. there, June 8, 1982. He studied with Gédalge at the Paris Cons. From 1920 to 1924 he presented the Concerts Jean Wiéner, devoted to the energetic propaganda of new music; he presented several premieres of works by modern French composers; he also performed pieces by Schoenberg, Berg, and Webern. He was the first Frenchman to proclaim jazz as a legitimate art form; he also teamed with Clément Doucet in duo-piano recitals, in programs stretching from Mozart to jazz. His compositions reflect his ecumenical convictions, as exemplified in such works as a desegregationist operetta, *Olive chez les* *nègres* (1926). However, he became famous mainly for his idiosyncratic film music.

Wiener, Otto, Austrian baritone; b. Vienna, Feb. 13, 1913. He was a student in Vienna of Küper and Duhan. In 1939 he began his career as a concert singer. In 1952 he appeared for the first time at the Salzburg Festival, and in 1953 made his operatic stage debut as Simon Boccanegra in Graz. He was a member of the Deutsche Oper am Rhein in Düsseldorf (1956–59). From 1957 to 1963 he sang at the Bayreuth Festivals. From 1957 he also sang at the Vienna State Opera and from 1960 to 1970 at the Bavarian State Opera in Munich. On Oct. 18, 1962, he made his Metropolitan Opera debut in New York as Hans Sachs, remaining on its roster for a season. As a guest artist, he appeared in London, Rome, Milan, and other operatic centers. Throughout the years he continued his concert career as well. Following his retirement in 1976, he served as director of the opera school at the Vienna State Opera. Among his other roles were the Dutchman, Gunther, Wotan, La Roche in *Capriccio*, and Pfitzner's Palestrina.

Wieniawski, Adam Tadeusz, Polish composer and music educator; b. Warsaw, Nov. 27, 1879; d. Bydgoszcz, April 21, 1950. He was the nephew of the famous Polish violinist, teacher and composer Henryk Wieniawski (b. Lublin, July 10, 1835; d. Moscow, March 31, 1880) and of the distinguished Polish pianist, pedagogue, and composer Jozef Wieniawski (b. Lublin, May 23, 1837; d. Brussels, Nov. 11, 1912). He studied in Warsaw with Melcer-Szczawiński and Noskowski, then in Berlin with Bargiel, and in Paris with d'Indy, Fauré, and Gédalge. He fought in the French army during World War I; he returned to Warsaw in 1918 as a teacher at the Chopin School of Music; he was appointed its director in 1928.

WORKS: DRAMATIC: OPERAS: *Megaië* (1910; Warsaw, Dec. 28, 1912); *Zofka*, comic opera (1923); *Wyzwolony* (The Freed Man; Warsaw, July 5, 1928); *Król Kochanek* (The King as Paramour), musical comedy (Warsaw, March 19, 1931). BALLETS: *Lalita* (1922); *Aktea w Jerozolimie* (Actea in Jerusalem; Warsaw, June 4, 1927).

Wiens, Edith, Canadian soprano; b. Saskatoon, Saskatchewan, June 9, 1950. She studied on scholarship at the Hannover Hochschule für Musik (concert performance dipiloma, 1974); she continued her training at the Oberlin (Ohio) College-Cons. of Music (M.A. in music theater, 1976). In 1979 she went to Munich to complete her vocal training with Ernst Haefliger and Erik Werba, taking the gold medal at the Schumann Competition in Zwickau that same year. In 1981 she made her first appearance as a soloist with the Berlin Phil., and thereafter was engaged to sing with principal orchs. of Europe and North America. As a recitalist, she sang in various Canadian cities as well as in New York, Paris, Berlin, Leipzig, Munich, and Vienna. In 1986 she made her operatic debut as Donna Anna with the Glyndebourne Opera; subsequently she sang at the Amsterdam Opera, Milan's La Scala, Buenos Aires's Teatro Colón, and the National Arts Centre in Ottawa. Her concert repertoire extends from Bach to Richard Strauss.

Wieslander, (Axel Otto) Ingvar, Swedish composer and conductor; b. Jönköping, May 19, 1917; d. Malmö, April 29, 1963. He received training in theory from Sven Svensson at the Univ. of Uppsala. He also took some lessons in composition with Lars-Erik Larsson. After training at the Stockholm Musikhögskolan (conducting with Tor Mann; music teacher's diploma, 1945), he completed his studies in Paris on a French scholarship (1947–48) with Tony Aubin (composition) and Eugène Bigot (conducting). From 1949 to 1960 he was director of music at the Malmö City Theater, and then was its chorus master from 1960 to 1963. He was cofounder of the Ars Nova Concert Soc., of which he was chairman (1960–63). In his music, his erstwhile neoclassical style with infusions of 12-tone writing eventually evolved into a highly personal 12-tone style.

WORKS: DRAMATIC: *Nordisk saga*, ballet (1950); *Fröknarna i parken*, radio opera (1953); *Skymningslekar*, ballet (1954); *Skalknallen*, chamber opera (1958; Malmö, Feb. 7, 1959); incidental music.

Wigglesworth, Frank, American composer and teacher; b. Boston, March 3, 1918; d. N.Y., March 19, 1996. He was educated at Columbia Univ. (B.S., 1940) and Converse College, Spartanburg, S.C. (M.Mus., 1942), his principal mentors being Ernest White, Luening, and Cowell; he also studied with Varèse (1948–51). He taught at Converse College (1941–42), Greenwich House, N.Y. (1946–47), Columbia Univ. and Barnard College (1947–51), and Queens College of the City Univ. of N.Y. (1955–56); in 1954 he joined the faculty of the New School for Social Research in New York, where he was chairman of the music dept. (from 1965); also taught at the Dalcroze School in New York (from 1959) and at the City Univ. of N.Y. (1970–76). From 1951 to 1954 he was a fellow and in 1969–70 composer-in-residence at the American Academy in Rome; he held MacDowell Colony fellowships in 1965 and 1972; in 1985 he was composer-in-residence at Bennington College's Chamber Music Conference and Composers' Forum of the East. He was a great-nephew of **Elizabeth Sprague Coolidge**. His output reflects a fine command of orch., instrumental, and vocal writing; he made use of both tonal and atonal techniques.

WORKS: DRAMATIC: *Young Goodman Brown*, ballet (1951); *Between the Atoms and the Stars*, musical play (1959); *Hamlet*, incidental music to Shakespeare's play (1960); *Ballet for Esther Brooks*, ballet (1961); *The Willowdale Handcar*, opera (1969).

Wigglesworth, Mark, English conductor; b. Sussex, July 19, 1964. He was a student of George Hurst at the Royal Academy of Music in London. In 1989 he captured 1st prize in the Kondrashin competition in the Netherlands; that same year he became music director of the Premiere Ensemble of London. In 1990 he conducted *Don Giovanni* with the Opera Factory in London; subsequently served as its music director (1991–94) and appeared as a guest conductor with principal British orchs. as well as those on the Continent. From 1991 to 1993 he was assoc. conductor of the BBC Sym. Orch. in London. In 1992 he made his U.S. debut as a guest conductor with the Dallas Sym. Orch., and subsequently appeared with the Philadelphia Orch., the Chicago Sym. Orch., the Minnesota Orch. in Minneapolis, the St. Louis Sym. Orch., the Los Angeles Phil., and the N.Y. Phil. In 1996 he became music director of the BBC National Orch. of Wales in Cardiff, while retaining his post with the Premiere Ensemble.

Wiklund, Adolf, Swedish conductor, pianist, and composer; b. Långserud, June 5, 1879; d. Stockholm, April 3, 1950. He was the son of an organist. He entered the Stockholm Cons. in 1896, and graduated in 1901 as an organist and music teacher. After studies with Richard Andersson (piano) and Johan Lindegren (composition and counterpoint), he held a state composer's fellowship (1902–04) and the Jenny Lind fellowship (1905–06). During this period, he studied in Paris, where he was organist of the Swedish Church (1903–04), and in Berlin with Kwast (piano). In 1902 he made his formal debut as a piano soloist in his own *Konsertstycke* for Piano and Orch. From 1906 he was principally active as a conductor and composer. After working at the Karlsruhe Opera and then the Berlin Royal Opera (1908–11), he returned to Stockholm as a conductor at the Royal Theater (from 1911), serving as music director (1923–24). From 1924 to 1938 he held the post of 2d conductor of the Concert Soc. He also appeared frequently as a guest conductor throughout Europe. In 1915 he became a member of the Royal Academy of Music in Stockholm. His music, marked by fine workmanship, remained faithful to Nordic Romanticism. He composed 2 fine piano concertos (1906, rev. 1935; 1917), and the popular *Tre stycken* (3 Pieces) for Harp and Strings (1924).

Wildbrunn (real name, Wehrenpfennig), Helene, Austrian soprano; b. Vienna, April 8, 1882; d. there, April 10, 1972. She studied with Rosa Papier in Vienna. She made her operatic debut as a contralto at the Vienna Volksoper in 1906, then sang in Dortmund (1907–14). She began singing soprano roles in 1914, when she joined the Stuttgart Opera, where she remained until 1918; she sang in Berlin at the State Opera (1916–25) and the Deutsche Oper (1926–29); she was a principal member of the Vienna State Opera (1919–32); made guest appearances at Covent Garden in London, La Scala in Milan, and the Teatro Colón in Buenos Aires. After her retirement in 1932, she taught voice at the Vienna Academy of Music (until 1950). Among her finest roles were Kundry, Brünnhilde, Fricka, Isolde, Donna Anna, and Leonore.

Wilder, Alec (Alexander Lafayette Chew), remarkably gifted American composer, distinguished in both popular and serious music; b. Rochester, N.Y., Feb. 16, 1907; d. Gainesville, Fla., Dec. 22, 1980. He studied composition at the Eastman School of Music in Rochester with Herbert Inch and Edward Royce; then moved to New York where he entered the world of popular music; he also wrote excellent prose. His popular songs were performed by Frank Sinatra, Judy Garland, and other celebrated singers; his band pieces were in the repertoire of Benny Goodman and Jimmy Dorsey. He excelled in the genre of short operas scored for a limited ensemble of singers and instruments and suitable for performance in schools, while most of his serious compositions, especially his chamber music, are set in an affably melodious, hedonistic, and altogether ingratiating manner. He publ. a useful critical compilation, *American Popular Song: The Great Innovators* (N.Y., 1972), which included analyses of the songs of Jerome Kern, Vincent Youmans, George Gershwin, Cole Porter, and others. He also publ. the vol. *Letters I Never Mailed* (1975).

WORKS: DRAMATIC: *Juke Box*, ballet (1942); *The Lowland Sea*, folk drama (Montclair, N.J., May 8, 1952); *Cumberland Fair*, a jamboree (Montclair, May 22, 1953); *Sunday Excursion*, musical comedy (Interlochen, Mich., July 18, 1953); *Miss Chicken Little* (CBS-TV, Dec. 27, 1953; stage production, Piermont, N.Y., Aug. 29, 1958); 3 operas: *Kittiwake Island* (Interlochen, Aug. 7, 1954), *The Long Way* (Nyack, N.Y., June 3, 1955), and *The Impossible Forest* (Westport, Conn., July 13, 1958); *The Truth about Windmills*, chamber opera (Rochester, N.Y., Oct. 14, 1973); *The Tattooed Countess*, chamber opera (1974); *The Opening*, comic opera (1975); 3 children's operas: *The Churkendoose, Rachetty Pachetty House*, and *Herman Ermine in Rabbit Town*.

BIBL.: D. Demsey and R. Prather, *A. W.: A Bio-Bibliography* (Westport, Conn., 1993).

Wildgans, Friedrich, Austrian composer and teacher; b. Vienna, June 5, 1913; d. Mödling, near Vienna, Nov. 7, 1965. He studied with J. Marx. He taught at the Salzburg Mozarteum (1934–36). In 1936 he became a clarinetist in the Vienna State Opera orch.; owing to his opposition to the Nazis, he lost his position in 1939 and remained suspect until the destruction of the Third Reich. He then was a teacher (1945–47; 1950–57) and a prof. (1957–65) at the Vienna Academy of Music. In 1946 he married **Ilona Steingruber**. He publ. *Entwicklung der Musik in Österreich im 20. Jahrhundert* (Vienna, 1950) and *Anton Webern* (London, 1966). He wrote in all genres, in an ultramodern style, eventually adopting the 12-tone technique. Among his works were the opera *Der Baum der Erkenntniss* (1932) and the operetta *Der Diktator* (1933); also theater, film, and radio scores.

Wilding-White, Raymond, American composer, teacher, and photographer; b. Caterham, Surrey, England, Oct. 9, 1922. He was a student at the Juilliard School of Music in New York (1947–49), the New England Cons. of Music in Boston (B.M., 1951; M.M., 1953), of Copland and Dallapiccola at the Berkshire Music Center in Tanglewood (summers, 1949–51), and of Read at Boston Univ. (D.M.A., 1962). He taught at the Case Inst. of Technology in Cleveland (1961–67) and at De Paul Univ. in Chicago (1967–88). In 1969 he founded the Loop Group for the performance of 20th-century music, which continued to be active through various transformations until its demise in 1989. He also was active on the radio and prepared numerous programs for WFMT-FM in Chicago, including 366 broadcasts of "Our American Music" for the American bicentennial (1976), "Music Chicago Style" for the Chicago sesquicentennial (1987), and a memorial tribute to John Cage (1992). As a photographer, his work has been exhibited in many settings.

WORKS: DRAMATIC: *The Trees*, ballet (1949); *The Tub*, chamber opera (1952); *The Selfish Giant*, television fable (1952); *The Lonesome Valley*, ballet (1960); *Yerma*, opera (1962); *Encounters*, ballet (1967); *Beth*, musical (1989–90; renamed *Trio* in 1994); *Gifts*, liturgical drama (1993); also "action pieces" entitled *MY aLBUM*.

Wilkes, Josué Teófilo, Argentine composer and teacher; b. Buenos Aires, Jan. 8, 1883; d. there, Jan. 10, 1968. He was a pupil of Williams (harmony and composition), Marchal (cello), and Rinaldi (singing) at the National Cons. in Buenos Aires. After further training with Liapunov in St. Petersburg and studies at the Schola Cantorum in Paris, he taught music in primary schools in Buenos Aires. From 1948 to 1956 he taught music history at the Universidad del Litoral in Santa Fé. With I. Guerrero Cárpena, he publ. *Formas musicales rioplatenses: Cifras, estilas y milongas-su génesis hispánica* (Buenos Aires, 1946). His works include the operas *Nuite persane* (1916–20), *Por el cetro y la corona* (1924), and *El horoscopo* (1926–27); also *La cautiva*, secular oratorio (1930).

Willan, (James) Healey, eminent English-born Canadian composer, organist, choral conductor, and teacher; b. Balham, Oct. 12, 1880; d. Toronto, Feb. 16, 1968. He received training in piano, organ, harmony, and counterpoint at the St. Saviour's Choir School in Eastbourne (1888–95), where he found a mentor in its headmaster and organist-choirmaster Walter Hay Sangster. He then studied organ with William Stevenson Hoyte and piano with Evlyn Howard-Jones in London. Willan began his career as organist of the St. Cecilia Soc. (1895–1900), and then was conductor of the Wanstead Choral Soc. (1904–05) and of the Thalian Operatic Soc. (1906). He also served as organist-choirmaster at St. Saviour's Church, St. Alban's, Herts (1898–1900), Christ Church, Wanstead (1900–03), and St. John the Baptist, Holland Rd., Kensington (1903–13). In 1913 he settled in Toronto as head of theory at the Cons. of Music and as organist at St. Paul's Anglican Church, Bloor Street. In 1914 he also became a lecturer and examiner at the Univ. of Toronto, where he served as music director of its Hart House Theatre (1919–25). From 1920 to 1936 he was vice-principal of the Toronto Cons. of Music. In 1921 he became organist-choirmaster at the Anglican Church of St. Mary Magdalene, a position he retained until his death. From 1932 to 1964 he was the organist of the Univ. of Toronto, where he also taught counterpoint and composition from 1937 to 1950. In 1933 he founded the Tudor Singers, conducting them until 1939. In 1953 he founded the Toronto Diocesan Choir School, which he served as music director. In 1956 the Archbishop of Canterbury conferred upon him the Lambeth Doctorate, the highest honor that can be bestowed upon a musician by the Anglican church. He received the Canada Council Medal in 1961. In 1967 he was made a Companion of the Order of Canada. On July 4, 1980, the Canadian Post Office issued a commemorative stamp bearing his likeness, making Willan the first composer to receive that distinction. As a composer, Willan excelled in music for liturgical use. He was a determined proponent of the Oxford Movement in the Anglican Church, and thus championed the cause of Anglo-Catholicism. Particularly notable in this regard were his 14 settings of the *Missa brevis* (1928–63), the set of 11 *Liturgical Motets* (1928–37), the plainsong-with-fauxbourdons settings of the Canticles, and the *Responsaries for the Offices of Tenebrae* (1956). In 1953 Willan's commissioned homage anthem, *O Lord, Our Governour*, was performed at the coronation of Queen Elizabeth II in London. Willan was thus the first nonresident of Great Britain to receive such an honor. His organ music is also of great distinction. His *Introduction, Passacaglia, and Fugue* (1916) is his masterpiece in that genre. Of his other works, the opera *Deirdre*, the 2 syms., and the Piano Concerto are worthy achievements.

WORKS: DRAMATIC: *The Beggar's Opera*, ballad opera (1927); *The Order of Good Cheer*, ballad opera (1928); *Transit Through Fire: An Odyssey of 1942*, radio opera (1941–42; CBC, March 8, 1942); *Hymn for Those in the Air*, incidental music (1942); *Dier-*

dre, radio opera (1943–45; CBC, April 20, 1946; rev. version for the stage, Toronto, April 2, 1965); *Brebeuf*, pageant (CBC, Sept. 26, 1943); 4 other ballad operas; 14 sets of incidental music, etc.

BIBL.: F. Clarke, *H. W.: Life and Music* (Toronto, 1983).

Williams, Camilla, black American soprano and teacher; b. Danville, Va., Oct. 18, 1922. She studied at Virginia State College (B.S., 1941) and with Marion Szekely-Freschl, Hubert Giesen, Sergius Kagen, and Leo Taubman in Philadelphia; won the Marian Anderson Award twice (1943, 1944), as well as the Philadelphia Orch. Youth Award (1944). On May 15, 1946, she made her operatic debut at the N.Y. City Opera as Cio-Cio-San, remaining on its roster until 1954; she also toured widely as a concert artist. She taught at Brooklyn College of the City Univ. of N.Y. (1970–73) and at the Indiana Univ. School of Music in Bloomington (from 1977).

Williams, Grace (Mary), Welsh composer; b. Barry, Glamorganshire, Feb. 19, 1906; d. there, Feb. 10, 1977. Her father led the local boy's chorus and played the piano in a home trio, with Grace on the violin and her brother on the cello. In 1923 she entered the music dept. of the Univ. of Wales in Cardiff, in the composition class of David Evans. Upon graduation in 1926, she enrolled at the Royal College of Music in London. There she was accepted as a student of Vaughan Williams, who had the greatest influence on her career as a composer, both in idiom and form; she also took classes with Gordon Jacob. She subsequently received the Octavia Traveling Scholarship and went to Vienna to take lessons with Wellesz (1930–31). She did not espouse the atonal technique of the 2d Viennese School, but her distinctly diatonic harmony with strong tertian underpinning was artfully embroidered with nicely hung deciduous chromatics of a decidedly nontonal origin. She marked May 10, 1951, in her diary as a "day of destruction," when she burned all her MSS unworthy of preservation. Among her practical occupations were teaching school and writing educational scripts for the BBC. She was particularly active in her advancement of Welsh music. Her own works include *Theseus and Ariadne*, ballet (1935), and *The Parlour*, opera (1961).

BIBL.: M. Boyd, *G. W.* (Cardiff, 1980).

Williams, Ralph Vaughan. See **Vaughan Williams, Ralph.**

Williamson, Malcolm (Benjamin Graham Christopher), prominent Australian composer, pianist, organist, and conductor; b. Sydney, Nov. 21, 1931. He attended the New South Wales State Conservatorium of Music in Sydney (1944–50), where he received training from Goossens (composition) and Sverjensky (piano). He also studied horn and violin. Settling in London, he pursued his training in composition with Lutyens and Erwin Stein (1953–57). He also studied the organ. As a performing artist, he appeared in his own organ and piano concertos. In 1963 he was awarded the Bax Memorial Prize. In 1970–71 he served as composer-in-residence at Westminster Choir College in Princeton, N.J. Williamson was made Master of the Queen's Musick in 1975. He was named a Commander of the Order of the British Empire in 1976. From 1983 to 1986 he was a visiting prof. at Strathclyde Univ. In his output, Williamson has been influenced by Stravinsky, Britten, and Messiaen along with jazz and popular music. The general accessibility of his works is complemented by fine craftsmanship.

WORKS: OPERAS: *Our Man in Havana* (1962–63; London, July 2, 1963); *The English Eccentrics*, chamber opera (1963–64; Aldeburgh, June 11, 1964); *The Happy Prince*, children's opera (1964–65; Farnham, May 22, 1965); *Julius Caesar Jones*, children's opera (1965; London, Jan. 4, 1966); *The Violins of St. Jacques* (London, Nov. 29, 1966); *Dunstan and the Devil* (Cookham, May 19, 1967); *The Growing Castle*, chamber opera (Dynevor, Aug. 13, 1968); *Lucky Peter's Journey* (London, Dec. 18, 1969); *The Red Sea* (1971–72; Dartington, April 14, 1972). CASSATIONS: *The Moonrakers* (Brighton, April 22, 1967); *Knights in Shining Armour* (Brighton, April 29, 1968); *The Snow Wolf* (Brighton, April 29, 1968); *Genesis* (Black Mountain, N.C., June 1971); *The Stone Wall* (London, Sept. 18, 1971); *The Winter Star* (Holm Cutram, June 19, 1973); *The Glitter Gang* (1973–74; Sydney, Feb. 23, 1974); *La Terre des Rois* (1974); *The Valley and the Hill* (Liverpool, June 21, 1977); *Le Pont du diable* or *The Devil's Bridge* (Angouleme, March 1982). BALLETS: *The Display* (Adelaide, March 14, 1964); *Spectrum* (1964; Bury St. Edmunds, Sept. 21, 1967); *Sun into Darkness* (1965–66; London, April 13, 1966); *Bigfella Toots-Squoodge and Nora* (1967; Manchester, Sept. 25, 1976); *Perisynthyon* (1974); *Heritage* (1985). Also incidental music and film, radio, and television scores.

Wills, Arthur, English organist, teacher, and composer; b. Coventry, Sept. 19, 1926. He was educated at the College of St. Nicholas, Canterbury, and at the Univ. of Durham (D.Mus.). In 1949 he became assist. organist at Ely Cathedral, and then was organist and director of music there from 1958 to 1990. From 1964 to 1992 he was also a prof. at the Royal Academy of Music in London. As a recitalist, he toured throughout Europe, the United States, and the Far East. He was the author of the vol. *Organ* (1984; 2d ed., 1992). In 1990 he was made an Officer of the Order of the British Empire. His works include an opera, *1984* (1988).

Wilson, Charles (Mills), Canadian composer, conductor, and teacher; b. Toronto, May 8, 1931. He studied composition with Ridout at the Royal Cons. of Music of Toronto, and also with Foss (summer, 1950) and Chávez (summer, 1951) at the Berkshire Music Center in Tanglewood. Returning to Toronto, he received his B.Mus. (1952) and later was awarded his D.Mus. (1956). From 1954 to 1964 he was organist-choirmaster at Chalmers United Church in Guelph. He also was founder-conductor of the Guelph Light Opera and Oratorio Co. (1955–74) and conductor of the Bach-Elgar Choir of Hamilton (1962–74). In 1979 he became a teacher at the Univ. of Guelph. In his music, Wilson has adopted many of the prevailing stylistic elements of his era.

WORKS: DRAMATIC: *The Strolling Clerk from Paradise*, chamber opera (1952); *Ballet Score* (1969); *Phrases from Orpheus*, piece for Chorus and Dancers (1970; Guelph, May 10, 1971); *Heloise and Abelard*, opera (1972; Toronto, Sept. 8, 1973); *The Selfish Giant*, children's opera (1972; Toronto, Dec. 20, 1973); *The Summoning of Everyman*, church opera (1972; Halifax, April 6, 1973); *Kamouraska*, opera (1975); *Psycho Red*, opera (1977); *Tim*, radio opera (1990).

Wilson, Ransom, American flutist and conductor; b. Tuscaloosa, Ala., Oct. 25, 1951. He studied with Philip Dunigan at the North Carolina School of the Arts; he also profited from advice given by Rampal. He made a European tour with the Juilliard Chamber Orch. under Maag, and soon established himself as a brilliant virtuoso. In 1980 he founded and served as conductor-soloist with his own ensemble, Solisti New York; he also appeared as guest conductor with other ensembles; served as music director of Opera Omaha and the San Frncisco Chamber Sym. His repertoire as a flutist is catholic, covering all periods and styles; he also commissioned special works for the flute, and arranged music for use in his concerts.

Wilson, Richard (Edward), American composer, pianist, and teacher; b. Cleveland, May 15, 1941. Following lessons in piano, theory, and composition at the Cleveland Music School Settlement (1954–59), he pursued his studies with Moevs (composition) at Harvard Univ. (A.B., 1963), at the American Academy in Rome, and at Rutgers Univ. (M.A. in theory, 1966). He also studied piano with Shure in Aspen, Colo., and New York (1960), and with Wührer in Munich (1963). In 1966 he joined the faculty of Vassar College, where he was made a prof. of music in 1976. He also served as chairman of its music dept. (1979–82; 1985–88; from 1995). In 1992 he became composer-in-residence of the American Sym. Orch. in New York. He received annual ASCAP awards from 1970. In 1986 he received the Walter Hinrichsen Award of the American Academy and Inst. of Arts and Letters. In 1992–93 he held a Guggenheim fellowship. He received the Stoeger Prize of the Chamber Music Soc. of Lincoln Center in 1994. In his output, Wilson has followed a freely atonal course with special attention paid to lyrical expressivity. His works include an opera, *Æthelred the Unready* (1993–94).

Wilson, Robert, notable American theater director, stage designer, and dramatist; b. Waco, Texas, Oct. 4, 1941. After training at the Univ. of Texas (1959–65), he took his B.F.A. in architecture at the Pratt Inst. in New York. In 1969 he began his career as a dramatist. His collaboration with Philip Glass on *Einstein on the Beach* (Avignon Festival and the Metropolitan Opera, N.Y., 1976) brought him wide recognition, and he subsequently collaborated with Gavin Bryars on *Medea* (Lyons, 1984) and with Glass on portions of *The Civil Wars* (1984–87). His later work has been seen to best advantage in *Médée* by Charpentier (Lyons, 1984), *Salome* (Milan, 1987), *Alceste* (Chicago, 1990), *Die Zauberflöte* (Paris, 1991), *Madama Butterfly* (Stuttgart, 1993), and *Prometeo* by Nono (Brussels, 1997). He also created the pop opera trilogy, a "reinvention of H. G. Wells' *The Time Machine*," that includes *The Black Rider* (1993; music by Tom Waits), *Alice* (1995; music by Tom Waits and Kathleen Brennan), and *Time Rocker* (1996; music by Lou Reed). In 1997 he produced Gertrude Stein's *Saints and Singing* at the Hebbel Theater in Berlin, and in 1998 the Berliner Ensemble presented his production of Bertolt Brecht's *Oceanflight*. In 1998 he also mounted his first production, *Lohengrin*, with the Metropolitan Opera in New York. On July 7, 1999, his *The Days Before Death Destruction & Detroit III*, to a libretto after Umberto Eco's *The Island of the Day Before*, with music by Ryuichi Sakamoto (founder of the techno-pop group Yellow Magic Orchestra [YMO] and winner of an Academy Award for his film score for *The Last Emperor*), was given its first perf. in New York. Wilson was engaged for the *Ring* cycle at the Bayreuth Festival in 2000. His provocative productions have elicited great interest and much controversy. He is an acknowledged master of mixed-media forms.

BIBL.: L. Shyer, *R. W. and His Collaborators* (N.Y., 1990).

Wilson-Johnson, David (Robert), English baritone; b. Northampton, Nov. 16, 1950. He studied at the British Inst. in Florence, at St. Catharine's College, Cambridge (B.A., 1973), and at the Royal Academy of Music in London (1973–76). In 1976 he made his operatic debut in the premiere of *We Come to the River* at London's Covent Garden, and then appeared as the Speaker in *Die Zauberflöte* at the Welsh National Opera in Cardiff. He made his recital debut at London's Wigmore Hall in 1977. In 1980 he created the role of Arthur in *The Lighthouse* in Edinburgh, and also appeared with the Glyndebourne Touring Opera. He first sang at the London Promenade Concerts in 1981. In 1988 he created the title role in the British concert premiere of Messiaen's *St. François d'Assise* in London. Following debuts at the Salzburg Festival in Bach's St. John Passion and at the Paris Opéra in *Die Meistersinger von Nürnberg* in 1989, he made his U.S. debut with the Cleveland Orch. in 1990. He appeared for the first time at the English National Opera in London in 1991 in *Billy Budd*, and then made his Netherlands Opera debut in Amsterdam in 1993 in Birtwistle's *Punch and Judy*. He returned to the Netherlands Opera in 1995 to sing in Schoenberg's *Die Glückliche Hand* and *Von Heute auf Morgen*. In 1997 he sang in Pfitzner's *Palestrina* at Covent Garden. His expansive concert repertoire includes works by Purcell, Handel, Bach, Haydn, Mozart, Schubert, and Berlioz, as well as much contemporary music.

Wimberger, Gerhard, Austrian composer, conductor, and pedagogue; b. Vienna, Aug. 30, 1923. He was educated at the Salzburg Mozarteum (1940–41; 1945–47), where he received training in composition from Bresgen and J. N. David and in conducting from Krauss and Paumgartner. From 1948 to 1951 he conducted at the Salzburg Landestheater. In 1953 he joined the faculty of the Salzburg Mozarteum, where he taught conducting until 1968 and composition from 1968 until his retirement in 1991. In 1990 he served as president of the AKM (Staatlich genehmigte Gesellschaft der Autoren, Komponisten, und Musikverleger) of Austria. In 1967 he was awarded the Austrian State Prize for composition. He won the Würdigungspreis for music in 1977, the same year that he was made a corresponding member of the Akademie der Schönen Künste in Munich. In his works, Wimberger makes use of various styles and techniques, including jazz and other popular genres. His dramatic works reveal a penchant for the use of wit and irony.

WORKS: DRAMATIC: *König für einem Tag*, ballet (1951); *Schaubudengeschichte*, opera (1952–53; Mannheim, Nov. 25, 1954); *Der Handschuh*, chamber ballet (1955); *La Battaglia oder Der rote Federbusch*, comic opera (1959–60; Schwetzingen, May 12, 1960); *Hero und Leander*, dance drama (1962–63); *Dame Kobold*, musical comedy (1963–64; Frankfurt am Main, Sept. 24, 1964); *Das Opfer Helena*, chamber musical (1967); *Lebensregeln*, catechism with music (1970–72; Munich, Aug. 27, 1972); *Paradou*, opera (1985); *Fürst von Salzburg—Wolf Dietrich*, scenic chronicle (Salzburg, June 11, 1987); other works for the theater, radio, and television.

BIBL.: H. Goertz, *G. W.* (Vienna, 1991).

Winbergh, Gösta, Swedish tenor; b. Stockholm, Dec. 30, 1943. He studied in Stockholm with Erik Saedén at the Musikhögskolan and pursued training at the Royal Opera School. In 1971 he made his operatic debut as Rodolfo in Göteborg; after singing with the Royal Opera in Stockholm (1973–80), he was a member of the Zürich Opera (from 1981). In 1982 he sang for the first time at London's Covent Garden as Titus. He made his debut at the Metropolitan Opera in New York on Nov. 22, 1983, as Don Ottavio. In 1985 he sang at Milan's La Scala for the first time as Tamino. In 1988 he was engaged as Des Grieux in Houston. He made his first appearance at London's Covent Garden in 1993 as Walther von Stolzing, and returned there in 1997 as Lohengrin. He portrayed Parsifal at the Deutsche Oper in Berlin in 1998. As a concert artist, Winbergh sang widely in Europe and abroad. His other roles include Count Almaviva, Ferrando, Mithridates, Nemorino, Lensky, Massenet's Des Grieux, Alfredo, Faust, and Lohengrin.

Windgassen, Wolfgang (Fritz Hermann), distinguished German tenor; b. Annemasse, Haute Savoie, June 26, 1914; d. Stuttgart, Sept. 8, 1974. He received his early vocal training from his father, Fritz Windgassen (b. Hamburg, Feb. 9, 1883; d. Murnau, April 17, 1963), who was a leading tenor at the Stuttgart Opera; he then continued his studies at the Stuttgart Cons. with Maria Ranzow and Alfons Fischer. He made his operatic debut in Pforzheim in 1941 as Alvaro in *La forza del destino*; after military service in the German army, he joined the Stuttgart Opera in 1945, remaining on its roster until 1972. From 1951 to 1970 he appeared at the Bayreuth Festivals, where he was a leading Heldentenor. He made his Metropolitan Opera debut in New York on Jan. 22, 1957, as Siegmund, but sang there only that season. He sang regularly at Convent Garden in London from 1955 to 1966. He was especially successful in Wagnerian roles, as Tannhäuser, Tristan, Parsifal, Siegfried, and Lohengrin; he also appeared as Radamès and Don José.

BIBL.: B. Wessling, *W. W.* (Bremen, 1967).

Winkelmann, Hermann, notable German tenor; b. Braunschweig, March 8, 1849; d. Vienna, Jan. 18, 1912. He started out as a piano maker, but became interested in singing. He studied voice in Paris and with Koch in Hannover, making his operatic debut in *Il Trovatore* in Sondershausen (1875), and then sang in Altenburg, Darmstadt, and Leipzig. In 1878 he joined the Hamburg Opera, and appeared with the company during its visit to London in 1882 at Drury Lane under Richter's direction in Wagnerian roles. His success induced Richter to recommend him to Wagner, who chose him to create the role of Parsifal at Bayreuth (July 26, 1882). From 1883 to 1906, when he retired on a pension, he was one of the brightest stars of the Vienna Court Opera, where one of his most brilliant achievements was the performance of the role of Tristan (with Materna as Isolde) in the Vienna premiere (Oct. 4, 1883). In 1884 he sang in the United States at the Wagner festivals given by Theodore Thomas in New York, Boston, Philadelphia, Cincinnati, and Chicago.

Winter, Peter (von), German composer; b. Mannheim (baptized), Aug. 28, 1754; d. Munich, Oct. 17, 1825. He was a violinist in the Electoral orch. at the age of 10, and was given permanent employment there in 1776. He studied with Abbé Vogler; went with the court to Munich in 1778 and became director of the Court Orch.; in 1787 he was named court vice Kapellmeister and in 1798 court Kapellmeister. In 1814 he received a title of nobility from the court for his long service. In Munich he brought out a number of operas, of which the most important were *Helena und Paris* (Feb. 5, 1782), *Der Bettelstudent oder Das Donnerwetter* (Feb. 2, 1785), *Der Sturm* (1798), *Marie von Montalban* (Jan. 28, 1800), and *Colmal* (Sept. 15, 1809). Frequent leaves of absence from Munich enabled him to travel, and in Venice he produced his operas *Catone in Utica* (1791), *I sacrifizi di Creta ossia Arianna e Teseo* (Feb. 13, 1792), *I Fratelli rivali* (Nov. 1793), and *Belisa ossia La fedelità riconosciuta* (Feb. 5, 1794). In Prague he produced the opera *Ogus ossia Il trionfo del bel sesso* (1795). In Vienna he brought out *Das unterbrochene Opferfest* (June 14, 1796; his most successful opera; produced all over Europe), *Babylons Pyramiden* (Oct. 25, 1797), and *Das Labirint oder Der Kampf mit den Elementen* (June 12, 1798. In Paris he produced his only French opera, *Tamerlan* (Sept. 14, 1802), and in London the Italian operas *La grotta di Calipso* (May 31, 1803), *Il trionfo dell'amor fraterno* (March 22, 1804), *Il ratto di Proserpina* (May 3, 1804), and *Zaira* (Jan. 29, 1805); in Milan, *Maometto II* (Jan. 28, 1817), *I due Valdomiri* (Dec. 26, 1817), and *Etelinda* (March 23, 1818). He also wrote several ballets and oratorios. He publ. *Vollständige Singschule* (Mainz, 1825; 2nd ed., 1874).

BIBL.: J. Arnold, *P. W.* (Erfurt, 1810); W. Neumann, *P. W.* (Kassel, 1856); V. Frensdorf, *P. W. als Opernkomponist* (diss., Univ. of Munich, 1908); L. Kuckuk, *P. W. als deutscher Opernkomponist* (diss., Univ. of Heidelberg, 1923).

Wintzer, Richard, German composer; b. Nauendorf, near Halle, March 9, 1866; d. Berlin, Aug. 14, 1952. He studied painting, and also music (with Bargiel). He lived mostly in Berlin, where he was active as a painter, composer, and music critic. He wrote 2 operas, *Die Willis* (1895) and *Marienkind* (1905). He also publ. *Menschen von anderem Schlage* (1912) and an autobiography.

Wiora, Walter, renowned German musicologist; b. Kattowitz, Dec. 30, 1906; d. Tutzing, Feb. 8, 1997. He studied in Berlin at the Hochschule für Musik (1925–27) and received training in musicology from Abert, Blume, Hornbostel, Sachs, Schering, and Schünemann; he continued his studies with Gurlitt at the Univ. of Freiburg im Breisgau (Ph.D., 1937, with the diss. *Die Variantenbildung im Volkslied: Ein Beitrag zur systematischen Musikwissenschaft*); he completed his Habilitation there in 1941 with his *Die Herkunft der Melodien in Kretschmers und Zuccalmaglios Sammlung* (publ. in an enl. ed. as *Die rheinisch-bergischen Melodien bei Zuccalmaglio und Brahms*, Bad Godesberg, 1953). He was an assistant at the Deutsches Volksliedarchiv in Freiburg im Breisgau (1936–41); after serving as a reader in musicology at the Univ. of Posen, he returned to Freiburg im Breisgau and was archivist at the Deutsches Volksliedarchiv (1946–58); he then was prof. of musicology at the Univ. of Kiel (1958–64) and at the Univ. of Saarbrücken (1964–72). His principal achievement was his advocacy of a system of "essential research" in musicology that utilizes both traditional and contemporary principles.

WRITINGS: *Die deutsche Volksliedweise und der Osten* (Wolfenbüttel and Berlin, 1940); *Zur Frühgeschichte der Musik in den Alpenlandern* (Basel, 1949); *Das echte Volkslied* (Heidelberg, 1950); *Europäische Volksmusik und abendländische Tonkunst* (Kassel, 1957); *Die geschichtliche Sonderstellung der abendländischen Musik* (Mainz, 1959); *Die vier Weltalter der Musik* (Stuttgart, 1961; Eng. tr., 1965, as *The Four Ages of Music*); *Komponist und Mitwelt* (Kassel, 1964); ed. *Die Ausbreitung des Historismus über die Musik* (Regensburg, 1969); *Das deutsche Lied: Zur Geschichte und Ästhetik einer musikalischen Gattung* (Wolfenbüttel and Zürich, 1971); *Historische und systematische Musikwissenschaft* (Tutzing, 1972); *Ergebnisse und Aufgaben vergleichender Musikforschung* (Darmstadt, 1975); *Das musikalische Kunstwerk* (Tutzing, 1983).

BIBL.: L. Finscher and C.-H. Mahling, eds., *Festschrift für W. W.* (Kassel, 1967); C.-H. Mahling, ed., *Beiträge zu einer musikalischen Gattung: W. W. zum 70. Geburtstag* (Tutzing, 1979).

Wirén, Dag (Ivar), prominent Swedish composer; b. Striberg, Oct. 15, 1905; d. Danderyd, April 19, 1986. He studied at the Stockholm Cons. with Oskar Lindberg and Ernest Ellberg (1926–31), then in Paris with Leonid Sabaneyev (1932–34). He returned to Sweden in 1934, and was music critic for the *Svenska Morgonbladet* (1938–46); was vice president of the Soc. of Swedish Composers (1947–63). His early music was influenced by Scandinavian Romanticism; later he adopted a more sober and more cosmopolitan neoclassicism, stressing the symmetry of formal structure; in his thematic procedures he adopted the method of systematic intervallic metamorphosis rather than development and variation. He ceased composing in 1972.

WORKS: DRAMATIC: *Blått, gult, rott* (Blood, Sweat, Tears), radio operetta (1940); *Den glada patiensen*, radio operetta (1941); *Oscarbalen* (Oscarian Ball), ballet (1949); *Den elaka drottningen* (The Wicked Queen), television ballet (1960; Swedish TV, Nov. 22, 1961); incidental music for plays and films.

Wise, Patricia, American soprano and teacher; b. Wichita, July 31, 1943. She studied in Kansas and Santa Fe, and with Margaret Harshaw in New York. In 1966 she made her operatic debut in Kansas City as Mozart's Susanna, and then joined the N.Y. City Opera. She made her first appearance at London's Covent Garden in 1971 as Rossini's Rosina, and then made her debut as Strauss's Zerbinetta at the Glyndebourne Festival in 1972. From 1976 to 1991 she was a member of the Vienna State Opera, where she became well known for her roles in operas by Mozart and Strauss. She also sang in other European operatic centers, including engagements as Verdi's Nannetta at Milan's La Scala in 1980, the Protagonist in the premiere of Berio's *Un re in ascolto* in Salzburg in 1984, Berg's Lulu in Geneva in 1985, and Verdi's Gilda in Madrid in 1989. From 1995 she taught at the Indiana Univ. School of Music in Bloomington. She was honored as a Kammersängerin of the Vienna State Opera in 1996.

Wishart, Peter (Charles Arthur), English composer and teacher; b. Crowborough, June 25, 1921; d. Frome, Aug. 14, 1984. He received training in composition from Hely-Hutchinson at the Univ. of Birmingham (1938–41) and from Boulanger in Paris (1947–48). He taught at the Univ. of Birmingham (1950–59), the Guildhall School of Music in London (from 1961), King's College, London (1972–77), and the Univ. of Reading (1977–84). He publ. the books *Harmony* (London, 1956) and *Key to Music* (London, 1971). His works include the operas *2 in the Bush* (1956), *The Captive* (1960), *The Clandestine Marriage* (1971), and *Clytemnestra* (1973); also ballets; incidental music.

Wissmer, Pierre, Swiss-born French composer and pedagogue; b. Geneva, Oct. 30, 1915; d. Valcros, France, Nov. 3, 1992. He went to Paris to study with Roger-Ducasse (composition) at the Cons., Daniel-Lesur (counterpoint) at the Schola Cantorum, and Munch (conducting) at the École Normale de Musique. Returning to Geneva, he taught composition at the Cons. (1944–48). He was active as a music critic, and also served as head of the chamber music dept. of the Geneva Radio. After serving as assistant director of programming of Radio Luxembourg (1951–57), he was director of programming of Luxembourg TV (1957–63). In 1958 he became a naturalized French citizen. He was director of the Schola Cantorum in Paris (1957–63) and of the École Nationale de Musique in Le Mans (1969–81), and also was prof. of composition and orchestration at the Geneva Cons. (1973–86). In 1983 he was awarded the Grand Prix Musical of Geneva for his creative efforts. His output reveals an adept handling of traditional and contemporary styles.

WORKS: DRAMATIC: *Le Beau dimanche*, ballet (1939; Geneva, March 20, 1944); *Marion ou la belle au tricorne*, comic opera (1945; Radio Suisse Romande, Geneva, April 16, 1947); *Capitaine Bruno*, opera (Geneva, Nov. 9, 1952); *Léonidas ou la cruauté mentale*, opéra bouffe (Paris, Sept. 12, 1958); *Alerte, puits 21*, ballet (1963); *Christina et les Chimères*, ballet (1964). Also *Le Quatrième Mage*, oratorio for Soli, Chorus, and Orch. (1965).

Wiszniewski, Zbigniew, Polish composer and teacher; b. Lwów, July 30, 1922. He received training in classical philology (1946–49) and in composition, theory, and viola (1946–51) in Łódź. From 1948 to 1957 he was active as a violist. He was an ed. with the Polish Radio in Warsaw from 1957 to 1966, and again from 1968 to 1985. He taught at the Warsaw Academy of Music from 1977 to 1988, and again from 1993. He also served as chief ed. of the music journal *Poradnik Muzyczny* (Music Adviser; 1982–84). Among his works were the radio operas *Neffru* (1958), *Ad If* (1973), and *Pater Noster* (1973); also 2 televisions oratorios: *Genesis* for Baritone, Actor, Chorus, and Orch. (1967) and *The Brothers* for Actor, Men's Chorus, and Orch. (1970).

Witherspoon, Herbert, American bass; b. Buffalo, N.Y., July 21, 1873; d. N.Y., May 10, 1935. He studied composition with Horatio Parker and voice with Gustav Stoeckel at Yale Univ. (graduated, 1895); then was a pupil of MacDowell in New York. He then studied singing with Bouhy in Paris, Henry Wood in London, and G. B. Lamperti in Berlin. Returning to America, he made his operatic debut as Ramfis in *Aida* with Savage's Castle Square Opera Co. in New York in 1898. On Nov. 26, 1908, he made his Metropolitan Opera debut in New York as Titurel in *Parsifal*; he remained on its roster until 1916, where he distinguished himself in such roles as Sarastro, King Marke, Pogner, the Landgrave, and Gurnemanz. In 1922 he founded the American Academy of Teachers of Singing, subsequently serving as its first president. In 1925 he became president of the Chicago Musical College, and in 1931, president of the Cincinnati Cons. of Music; in 1933 he returned to New York, and in May 1935, was chosen to succeed Gatti-Casazza as general manager of the Metropolitan Opera, but he died of a heart attack after only a month in his post. He publ. *Singing: A Treatise for Teachers and Students* (N.Y., 1925) and *36 Lessons in Singing for Teacher and Student* (Chicago, 1930).

Witkowski, Georges-Martin, French conductor, pedagogue, and composer; b. Mostaganem, Algeria (of a French father and a Polish mother), Jan. 6, 1867; d. Lyons, Aug. 12, 1943. He was educated at the military school of St.-Cyr and studied composition with d'Indy at the Paris Schola Cantorum (1894–97); later he left for the army and settled in Lyons, where he founded the Société des Grands Concerts in 1905 for the production of oratorios. In 1924 he was appointed director of the Lyons Cons., retiring in 1941. His works include the opera *La Princesse lointaine*, after Rostand (1928–32; Paris, March 26, 1934).

Witt, Friedrich, German violinist and composer; b. Hallenbergstetten, Württemberg, Nov. 8, 1770; d. Würzburg, Jan. 3, 1836. At the age of 19, he was engaged as violinist in the orch. of Prince von Oettingen. From 1802 he was Kapellmeister at Würzburg, at first to the prince-bishop, then to the grand duke, and finally to the city. It was Witt who composed the so-called *Jena Sym.*, misattributed to Beethoven (see H. C. Robbins Landon's article in the *Music Review*, May 1957). Other works by Witt include the historical opera *Palma* (Frankfurt am Main, 1804), the comic opera *Das Fischerweib* (Würzburg, 1806), and the oratorios *Der leidende Heiland* (Würzburg, 1802) and *Die Auferstehung Jesu*.

Wittassek, Johann Nepomuk August, Bohemian pianist and composer; b. Hořín, March 23, 1770; d. Prague, Dec. 7, 1839. The son of a schoolmaster, he received a good education; took music lessons with F. X. Dušek and J. A. Koželuch in Prague. He succeeded Koželuch in 1814 as music director at the Prague Cathedral; was appointed director of the School for Organists in Prague in 1830. He wrote an opera, *David*, brought out in Prague.

Wittgenstein, Count Friedrich Ernst. See **Sayn-Wittgenstein-Berleburg, Count Friedrich Ernst**.

Wittich, Marie, German soprano; b. Giessen, May 27, 1868; d. Dresden, Aug. 4, 1931. She studied with Otto-Ubridz in Würzburg, making her debut as Azucena at the age of 14 in Magdeburg in 1882, then sang in Düsseldorf, Basel, and Schwerin. In 1889 she became a member of the Dresden Court Opera, remaining on its roster until 1914; while there, she was chosen by Richard Strauss to create the role of Salome in 1905. She also made guest appearances at Covent Garden in London (1905–06) and in Bayreuth (1901–10).

Wittrisch, Marcel, German tenor; b. Antwerp, Oct. 1, 1901; d. Stuttgart, June 3, 1955. He studied at the Munich and Leipzig conservatories. He made his operatic debut as Konrad in *Hans Heiling* in Halle in 1925, then sang in Braunschweig (1927–29); in 1929 he became a member of the Berlin State Opera, where he sang leading roles until 1943; he also made guest appearances at Covent Garden in London (1931) and at Bayreuth (1937); in 1950 he joined the Stuttgart Opera, where he remained until his death. In addition to his operatic career, he gained wide renown as a concert singer.

Wixell, Ingvar, Swedish baritone; b. Luleå, May 7, 1931. He received his training at the Stockholm Musikhögskolan. In 1952 he made his concert debut in Gävle and in 1955 his operatic debut as Papageno at the Royal Theater in Stockholm, where he sang regularly from 1956. In 1960 he sang with the Royal Opera on its visit to London's Covent Garden. He made his first appearance at the Glyndebourne Festival in 1962 as Cuglielmo. In 1966 he made his debut at the Salzburg Festival as Count Almaviva, and continued to sing there until 1969. From 1967 he sang at the Deutsche Oper in Berlin, and made his U.S. debut as Belcore in Chicago that same year. In 1971 he made his first appearance at the Bayreuth Festival as the Herald in *Lohengrin*. In 1972 he made his debut at Covent Garden as Simon Boccanegra, and continued to sing there regularly until 1977. On Jan. 29, 1973, he made his Metropolitan Opera debut in New York as Rigoletto, where he made occasional appearances until 1980. He sang Amonasro in Houston in 1987. From 1987 to 1990 he sang once more at Covent Garden. In 1990 he appeared as Scarpia in Stuttgart, a role he then sang at Earl's Court in London in 1991. Among his other roles were Don Giovanni, Marcello, Germont, and Mandryka.

Wlaschiha, Ekkehard, German baritone; b. Pirna, May 28, 1938. He was trained in Leipzig. In 1961 he made his operatic debut as Don Fernando in *Fidelio* in Gera. After singing in Dresden and Weimar (1964–70), he was a member of the Leipzig Opera from 1970. From 1983 he sang at the Berlin State Opera. In 1985 he appeared as Kaspar in *Der Freischütz* in the reopening of the Semper Opera House in Dresden. He made his debut at the Bayreuth Festival as Kurwenal in 1986. For his first appearance at London's Covent Garden in 1990, he sang Alberich in *Siegfried*, a role he also sang at the Lyric Opera in Chicago in 1996 and at the Metropolitan Opera in 1997. He sang in the premiere of Henze's *Venus und Adonis* in Munich in 1997. Among his other roles are Pizzaro, Tonio, Telramund, Scarpia, and Jochanaan.

Wohl, Yehuda, German-born Israeli composer; b. Berlin, March 5, 1904; d. Tel Aviv, July 12, 1988. He went to Palestine in 1933 and had private studies with Ben-Haim in Tel Aviv; taught until 1972. Under the pseudonym Yehuda Bentow, he wrote popular songs in the ethnic style. Other works include the radio operas *Hagadér* (1947) and *The Circle* (1976).

Woikowski-Biedau, Viktor Hugo von, German composer; b. Nieder-Arnsdorf, near Schweidnitz, Sept. 2, 1866; d. Berlin, Jan. 1, 1935. He studied music with Wilhelm Berger in Berlin. His works include 3 operas: *Helga* (Wiesbaden, 1904), *Der lange Kerl* (Berlin, 1906), and *Das Nothemd* (Dessau, 1913), and 3 melodramas: *Jung Olaf*, *Der Todspieler*, and *Die Mette von Marienburg*.

Wolf, Ernst Wilhelm, German composer; b. Grossenbehringen, near Gotha (baptized), Feb. 25, 1735; d. Weimar (buried), Dec. 1, 1792. After studies at the Eisenach and Gotha Gymnasien, he entered the Univ. of Jena (1755), where he was made director of the collegium musicum. He was active in Naumburg as a music teacher to the von Ponickau family before becoming music tutor to the sons of Duchess Anna Amalia in Weimar; he later was named court Konzertmeister (1761), organist (1763), and Kapellmeister (1772) there. He publ. *Auch eine Reise aber nur eine kleine Musik in den Monaten Junius, Julius und August 1782 zum Vergnügen angestellt und auf Verlangen beschrieben* (Weimar, 1784), *Vorbericht als eine Anleitung zum guten Vortrag beim Klavier-Spielen* (Leipzig, 1785), and *Musikalischer Unterricht für Liebhaber und diejenigen, welche die Musik treiben und lehren wollen* (Dresden, 1788).

WORKS: DRAMATIC (all 1st perf. in Weimar): *Das Gärtnermädchen*, comic opera (1769); *Das Rosenfest*, operetta (1772); *Die Dorfdeputierten*, comic opera (1772); *Die treuen Köhler*, operetta (1772); *Der Abend im Walde*, comic opera (1773); *Das grosse Los*, comic opera (1774); *Ehrlichkeit und Liebe*, Schauspiel (1776); *Le Monde de la lune*, comic opera (n.d.); *Alceste*, opera (1780); 10 others not extant.

BIBL.: J. Brockt, *E. W. W.: Leben und Werke* (diss., Univ. of Breslau, 1927).

Wolf, Hugo (Filipp Jakob), outstanding Austrian composer, one of the greatest masters of the German lied; b. Windischgraz, Styria, March 13, 1860; d. Vienna, Feb. 22, 1903. His father, Philipp Wolf (1828–87), was a gifted musician from whom Hugo received piano and violin lessons at a very early age; he later played 2d violin in the family orch. While attending the village primary school (1865–69), he studied piano and theory with Sebastian Weixler. In 1870 he was sent to the Graz regional secondary school, but left after a single semester and in 1871 entered the St. Paul Benedictine Abbey in Carinthia, where he played violin, organ, and piano; in 1873 he was transferred to the Marburg secondary school and remained devoted to musical pursuits; in 1875 he went to Vienna, where he became a pupil at the Cons.; studied piano with Wilhelm Schenner and harmony and composition with Robert Fuchs and later with Franz Krenn. When Wagner visited Vienna in 1875, Wolf went to see him, bringing along some of his compositions; the fact that Wagner received him at all, and even said a few words of encouragement, gave Wolf great impetus toward further composition. But he was incapable of submitting himself to academic discipline, and soon difficulties arose between him and the Cons. authorities. He openly expressed his dissatisfaction with the teaching, which led to his expulsion for lack of discipline in 1877. He then returned to his native town, but after a few months at home decided to go to Vienna again; there he managed to support himself by giving music lessons to children in the homes of friends. By that time he was composing diligently, writing songs to texts by his favorite poets—Goethe, Lenau, Heine. It was also about that time that the first signs of a syphilitic infection became manifest. An unhappy encounter with Brahms in 1879, who advised him to study counterpoint before attempting to compose, embittered him, and he became determined to follow his own musical inclinations without seeking further advice. That same year he met Melanie (née Lang) Köchert, whose husband, Heinrich Köchert, was the Vienna court jeweller. By 1884 she had become Wolf's mistress and a great inspiration in his creative work. After serving a brief and acrimonious tenure as 2d conductor in Salzburg in 1881, he returned to Vienna in 1882 and in 1883 became music critic of the weekly *Wiener Salonblatt*. He took this opportunity to indulge his professional frustration by attacking those not sympathetic to new trends in music; he poured invective of extraordinary virulence on Brahms, thus antagonizing the influential Hanslick and other admirers of Brahms. But he also formed a coterie of staunch friends, who had faith in his ability. Yet he was singularly unsuccessful in his repeated attempts to secure performances for his works. He submitted a string quartet to the celebrated Rosé Quartet, but it was rejected. Finally, Hans Richter accepted for the Vienna Phil. Wolf's symphonic poem *Penthesilea*, but the public performance was a fiasco, and Wolf even accused Richter of deliberately sabotaging the work; later he reorchestrated the score, eliminating certain crudities of the early version. In 1887 he resigned as music critic of the *Wiener Salonblatt* and devoted himself entirely to composition. He became convinced that he was creating the greatest masterpieces of song since Schubert and Schumann, and stated his conviction in plain terms in his letters. In historical perspective, his self-appraisal has proved remarkably accurate, but psychologists may well wonder whether Wolf was not consciously trying to give himself the needed encouragement by what must have seemed to him a wild exaggeration. However, a favorable turn in his fortunes soon came. On March 2, 1888, Rosa Papier became the first artist to sing one of Wolf's songs in public. On March 23, 1888, Wolf himself played and sang several of his songs at a meeting of the Vienna Wagner-Verein; on Dec. 15, 1888, he made his public debut as accompanist in his songs to the tenor Ferdinand Jäger, which proved the first of many highly successful recitals by both artists. Soon Wolf's name became known in Germany; he presented concerts of his own works in Berlin, Darmstadt, Mannheim, and other musical centers. He completed the first part of his great cycle of 22 songs, *Italienisches Liederbuch*, in 1891, and composed the 2d part (24 songs) in 5 weeks, in the spring of 1896. While Wolf could compose songs with a facility and degree of excellence that were truly astounding, he labored painfully on his orch. works. His early sym. was never completed, nor was a violin concerto; the work on *Penthesilea* took him a disproportionately long time. In 1895 he undertook the composition of his opera, *Der Corregidor*, to the famous tale by Alarcón, *El sombrero de tres picos*, and, working feverishly, completed the vocal score with piano accompaniment in a few months. The orchestration took him a much longer time. *Der Corregidor* had its premiere in Mannheim on June 7, 1896; while initially a success, the opera failed to find wide appeal and was soon dropped from the repertoire. Wolf subsequently revised the score, and in its new version *Der Corregidor* was brought out in Strasbourg on April 29, 1898. He never completed his 2d opera, *Manuel Venegas* (also after Alarcón); fragments were presented in concert in Mannheim on March 1, 1903. In the meantime, his fame grew. A Hugo Wolf-Verein was organized at Berlin in 1896, and did excellent work in furthering performances of Wolf's songs in Germany. Even more effective was the Hugo Wolf-Verein in Vienna, founded by Michel Haberlandt on April 22, 1897 (disbanded in 1906). As appreciation of Wolf's remarkable gifts as a master of lied began to find recognition abroad, tragedy struck. By early 1897, he was a very ill man, both mentally and physically. According to Wolf, Mahler promised to use his position as director of the Vienna Court Opera to mount a production of *Der Corregidor*. When the production failed to materialize, Wolf's mental condition disintegrated. He declared to friends that Mahler had been relieved of his post, and that he, Wolf, had been appointed in his stead. On Sept. 20, 1897, Wolf was placed in a private mental institution; after a favorable remission, he was discharged (Jan. 24, 1898), and traveled in Italy and Austria. After his return to Vienna, symptoms of mental derangement manifested themselves in even greater degree. In Oct. 1898 he attempted suicide by throwing himself into the Traunsee in Traunkirkchen, but was saved and placed in the Lower Austrian provincial asylum in Vienna. (A parallel with Schumann's case forcibly suggests itself.) He remained in confinement, gradually lapsing into complete irrationality. He died at the age of 42, and was buried near the graves of Schubert and Beethoven in Vienna's Central Cemetery; a monument was unveiled on Oct. 20, 1904. His mistress plunged to her death from the 4th-floor window of her home in Vienna on March 21, 1906.

Wolf's significance in music history rests on his songs, about 300 in number, many of them publ. posthumously. The sobriquet "the Wagner of the lied" may well be justified in regard to involved contrapuntal texture and chromatic harmony, for Wolf accepted the Wagnerian idiom through natural affinity as well as by clear choice. The elaboration of the accompaniment, and the incorporation of the vocal line into the contrapuntal scheme of the whole, are Wagnerian traits. But with these external similarities, Wolf's dependence on Wagner's models ceases. In his intimate penetration of the poetic spirit of the text, Wolf appears a legitimate successor to Schubert and Schumann. Wolf's songs are symphonic poems in miniature, artistically designed and admirably arranged for voice and piano, the combination in which he was a master. A complete ed. of his works, ed. by H. Jancik et al., began publ. in Vienna in 1960.

WORKS: DRAMATIC: OPERAS: *König Alboin* (1876–77; fragment); *Der Corregidor* (1895; Mannheim, June 7, 1896); *Manuel Venegas* (1897; fragments perf. in concert, Mannheim, March 1, 1903). INCIDENTAL MUSIC: to Kleist's Prinz *Friedrich von Homburg* (1884; unfinished); Ibsen's *Das Fest auf Solhaug* (Vienna, Nov. 21, 1891).

WRITING: Batka and H. Werner, eds., *Hugo Wolf: Musikalische Kritiken* (Leipzig, 1911; Eng. tr., 1979).

BIBL.: CORRESPONDENCE: E. Hellmer, ed., *H. W.: Briefe an Emil Kauffmann* (Berlin, 1903); M. Haberlandt, ed., *H. W.: Brief an Hugo Faisst* (Stuttgart, 1904); H. Werner, ed., *H. W.: Briefe an Oskar Grohe* (Berlin, 1905); E. Hellmer, ed., *H. W.: Familienbriefe* (Leipzig, 1912); H. Werner, ed., *H. W.: Briefe an Rosa Mayreder, mit einem Nachwort der Dichtetrin des "Corregidors"* (Vienna, 1921); idem, *H. W.: Briefe an Henriette Lang, nebst den briefen an deren Gatten, Prof. Joseph Freiherr von Schey* (Regensburg, 1922); H. Nonveiller, ed., *H. W.: Briefe an Heinrich Potpeschnigg* (Stuttgart, 1923); F. Grasberger, ed., *H. W.: Briefe an Melanie Kochert* (Tutzing, 1964); E. Hilmar and W. Obermaier, eds., *Briefe an Frieda Zerny* (Vienna, 1978). BIOGRAPHICAL: E. Decsey, *H. W.* (Berlin and Leipzig, 1903–06); E. Schmitz, *H. W.* (Leipzig, 1906); E. Newman, *H. W.* (London, 1907); M. Morold, *H. W.* (Leipzig, 1912); E. Decsey, *H. W.: Das Leben und das Lied* (Berlin, 1919; 2nd ed., 1921); K. Grunsky, *H. W.* (Leipzig, 1928); B. Benevisti-Viterbi, *H. W.* (Rome, 1931); H. Hécaen, *Mani et inspiration musicale: Le cas H. W.* (Bourdeaux, 1934); H. Schouten, *H. W.: Mens en componist* (Amsterdam, 1935); A. Ehrmann, *H. W.: Sein Leben in Bildern* (Leipzig, 1937); R. Litterscheid, *H. W.* (Potsdam, 1939); M. Hattingberg-Graedener, *H. W.: Vom Wesen und Werk des grössten Liedschöpfers* (Vienna and Leipzig, 1941; 2d ed., rev., 1953); K. Eickemeyer, *Der Verlauf der Paralyse H. W.s* (diss., Univ. of Jena, 1945); A. Orel, *H. W.* (Vienna, 1947); F. Walker, *H. W.: A Biography* (London, 1951; 2d ed., enl., 1968); N. Loeser, *H. W.* (Antwerp, 1955); D. Lindner, *H. W.* (Vienna, 1960); E. Werba, *H. W. oder der zornige Romantiker* (Vienna, 1971); K. Honolka, *H. W.: Sein Leben, sein Werk, seine Zeit* (Stuttgart, 1988). CRITICAL, ANALYTICAL: *Gesammelte Aufsätze über H. W.* (Berlin, 1898–1900); P. Müller, *H. W.* (Berlin, 1904); K. Heckel, *H. W. in seinem Verhältnis zu Richard Wagner* (Munich, 1905); K. Grunsky, *H. W.-Fest in Stuttgart: Festschrift* (Gutenberg, 1906); W. Salomon, *H. W. als Liederkomponist* (diss., Univ. of Frankfurt am Main, 1925); K. Varges, *Der Musikkritiker H. W.* (Magdeburg, 1934); G. Bieri, *Die Lieder von H. W.* (Bern, 1935); A. Breitenseher, *Der Gesangstechnik in den Liedern H. W.s* (diss., Univ. of Vienna, 1938); E. Sams, *The Songs of H. W.* (London, 1961; 2d ed., rev. and enl., 1981); R. Egger, *Die Deklamationsrhythmik H. W.s in historischer Sicht* (Tutzing, 1963); M. Shott, *H. W.'s Music Criticism* (diss., Indiana Univ., 1964); C. Rostand, *H. W.* (Paris, 1967); P. Boylan, *The Lieder of H. W.* (diss., Univ. of Michigan, 1968); M. Carner, *H. W. Songs* (London, 1982); E. Werba, *H. W. und seine Lieder* (Vienna, 1984); D. Stein, *H. W.'s Lieder and Extensions of Tonality* (Ann Arbor, Mich., 1985); J. Haywood, *The Musical Language of H. W.* (Ilfracombe, 1986); D. Ossenkop, *H. W.: A Guide to Research* (Westport, Conn., 1988); S. Youens, *H. W.: The Vocal Music* (Princeton, 1992).

Wolfe, Jacques (Leon), Romanian-American pianist, teacher, composer, and photographer, father of **Paul (Cecil) Wolfe;** b. Botoshan, April 29, 1896; d. Bradenton, Fla., June 22, 1973. He was taken to the United States in 1898 and studied with Friskin (piano) and Goetschius (composition) at the Inst. of Musical Art in New York (graduated, 1915). After serving as a clarinetist in the 50th Infantry Band during World War I, he taught music in N.Y. public schools and made appearances as a pianist. In 1947 he settled in Miami, where he became well known as a photographer. Wolfe was especially adept at composing songs and making arrangements in the manner of spirituals. Among his most famous were "De Glory Road," "Gwine to Hebb'n," and Shortnin' Bread." He also composed 3 operas, including *John Henry* (1939) and *Mississippi Legend* (1951). His son, Paul (Cecil) Wolfe (b. N.Y., May 8, 1926), is a conductor, harpsichordist, and oboist.

Wolfes, Felix, German-American pianist, conductor, teacher, and composer; b. Hannover, Sept. 2, 1892; d. Boston, March 28, 1971. He was a pupil of Reger (theory) and Teichmüller (piano) at the Leipzig Cons., and of Pfitzner (composition) in Strasbourg. In 1923 he made his debut as a conductor at the Breslau Opera. From 1924 to 1931 he conducted in Essen. In 1931 he became music director of the Dortmund Opera, but when the Nazis came to power in 1933 Wolfes went to Paris. In 1936–37 he conducted the Monte Carlo Opera. In 1938 he emigrated to the United States. He taught at the New England Cons. of Music in Boston, and also made some appearances as a pianist. As a teacher, he was especially admired for his knowledge of the vocal repertoire. He publ. a collection of songs (5 vols., 1962) which reveal him as a gifted composer in the late Romantic lieder tradition.

Wolff, Albert (Louis), French conductor and composer; b. Paris (of Dutch parents), Jan. 19, 1884; d. there, Feb. 20, 1970. He studied with Leroux, Gédalge, and Vidal at the Paris Cons. From 1906 to 1910 he was organist of St. Thomas Aquinas in Paris. In 1908 he became a member of the staff of the Paris Opéra Comique; after serving as its chorus master, he made his conducting debut there, leading the premiere of Laparra's *La Jota*, on April 26, 1911. From 1919 to 1921 he was conductor of the French repertoire at the Metropolitan Opera in N.Y.; he conducted the premiere of his opera *L'Oiseau bleu* there on Dec. 27, 1919. Upon his return to Paris in 1921, he was music director of the Opéra Comique until 1924; in 1925 he became 2d conductor of the Concerts Pasdeloup, and then was principal conductor from 1934 to 1940; he also was conductor of the Concerts Lamoureux from 1928 to 1934. He toured South America from 1940 to 1945, then returned to Paris, where he was director-general of the Opéra Comique in 1945–46; thereafter he continued to conduct occasionally there; also at the Paris Opéra from 1949; in addition, he made appearances as a sym. conductor. He particularly distinguished himself as a champion of French music of his era; he conducted the premieres of Debussy's *La Boîte à joujoux*, Ravel's *L'Enfant et les sortilèges*, Roussel's Sym. No. 4, and Poulenc's *Les Mamelles de Tirésias*. His own works include the operas *Soeur Beatrice* (1911; Nice, 1948), *Le marchand de masques* (Nice, 1914), and *L'Oiseau bleu* (N.Y., Dec. 27, 1919).

Wolff, Beverly, American mezzo-soprano; b. Atlanta, Nov. 6, 1928. She learned to play the trumpet and then played in the Atlanta Sym. Orch.; subsequently she received vocal training from Sidney Dietch and Vera McIntyre at the Academy of Vocal Arts in Philadelphia. In 1952 she won the Philadelphia Youth Auditions and made her formal debut with Ormandy and the Philadelphia Orch.; she also appeared as Dinah in the television premiere of Bernstein's *Trouble in Tahiti*. On April 6, 1958, she made her N.Y. City Opera debut as Dinah, and subsequently sang there regularly until 1971; she also was a guest artist with various other opera companies in the United States and abroad.

Wolff, Fritz, German tenor; b. Munich, Oct. 28, 1894; d. there, Jan. 18, 1957. He studied with Heinrich König in Würzburg. He made his operatic debut as Loge in 1925 at the Bayreuth Festival, where he continued to make appearances until 1941; he also sang in Hagen and Chemnitz. In 1930 he joined the Berlin State Opera, remaining on its roster until 1943; he also made guest appearances at Covent Garden in London (1929–33; 1937–38), and in Vienna, Paris, Chicago, and Cleveland. From 1950 he was a prof. at the Hochschule für Musik in Munich. His finest roles included Parsifal and Lohengrin.

Wolff, Hellmuth Christian, German musicologist and composer; b. Zürich, May 23, 1906; d. Leipzig, July 1, 1988. He studied musicology at the Univ. of Berlin with Abert, Schering, Blume, and Sachs (Ph.D., 1932, with the diss. *Die Venezianische Oper in der zweiten Hälfte des 17. Jahrhunderts*; publ. in Berlin, 1937; 2d ed., 1975). He completed his Habilitation at the Univ. of Kiel in 1942 with his *Die Barockoper in Hamburg 1678–1738* (publ. in Wolfenbüttel, 1957). From 1954 to 1971 he was a prof. of musicology at the Univ. of Leipzig. Beginning in 1956 he devoted a great deal of his time to painting, and exhibited in Leipzig and other German cities. Among his compositions were the operas *Der kleine und der grosse Klaus* (1931; rev. 1940), *Die törichten Wünsche* (1942–43), *Der Tod des Orpheus* (1947), and *Ich lass' mich scheiden* (1950), the ballet *Moresca* (1969), and the scenic oratorio *Esther* (1945); also incidental music.

WRITINGS: *Agrippina, eine italienische Jugendoper von G.Fr. Händel* (Wolfenbüttel and Berlin, 1943); *Die Musik der alten Niederländer (15. und 16. Jahrhundert)* (Leipzig, 1956); *Die Händel-Oper auf der modernen Bühne* (Leipzig, 1957); *Oper: Szene und Darstellung von 1600 bis 1900* (Leipzig, 1968); *Die Oper* (3 vols., Cologne, 1971–72; also in Eng.); *Ordnung und Gestalt: die Musik von 1900 bis 1950* (Bonn, 1977).

Wolf-Ferrari (real name, **Wolf**), **Ermanno,** famous Italian composer; b. Venice, Jan. 12, 1876; d. there, Jan. 21, 1948. His father was a well-known painter of German descent and his mother was Italian; about 1895 he added his mother's maiden name to his surname. He began piano study as a small child but also evinced a talent for art; after studying at the Accademia di Belle Arti in Rome (1891–92), he went to Munich to continue his training but then turned to music and studied counterpoint with Rheinberger at the Akademie der Tonkunst (1892–95). In 1899 he returned to Venice, where his oratorio *La Sulamite* was successfully performed. This was followed by the production of his first major opera, *Cenerentola* (1900), which initially proved a failure; however, its revised version for Bremen (1902) was well received and established his reputation as a composer for the theater. From 1903 to 1909 he was director of the Liceo Benedetto Marcello in Venice; he then devoted himself mainly to composition; he later was prof. of composition at the Salzburg Mozarteum (1939–45). He obtained his first unqualified success with the production of the comic opera *Le donne curiose* (Munich, 1903); the next opera, *I quattro rusteghi* (Munich, 1906), was also well received; there followed his little masterpiece, *Il segreto di Susanna* (Munich, 1909), a one-act opera buffa in the style of the Italian verismo (Susanna's secret being not infidelity, as her husband suspected, but indulgence in surreptitious smoking). Turning toward grand opera, he wrote *I gioielli della Madonna*; it was brought out at Berlin in 1911, and soon became a repertoire piece everywhere; he continued to compose, but his later operas failed to match the appeal of his early creations.

WORKS: DRAMATIC: OPERAS: *Cenerentola* (Venice, Feb. 22, 1900; rev. version as *Aschenbrödel*, Bremen, Jan. 31, 1902); *Le Donne curiose* (1902–03; in Ger. as *Die neugierigen Frauen*, Munich, Nov. 27, 1903; in Italian, N.Y., Jan. 3, 1912); *I quattro rusteghi* (in Ger. as *Die vier Grobiane*, Munich, March 19, 1906); *Il segreto di Susanna* (in Ger. as *Susannens Geheimnis*, Munich, Dec. 4, 1909; in Italian, N.Y., March 14, 1911); *I gioielli della Madonna* (in Ger. as *Der Schmuck der Madonna*, Berlin, Dec. 23, 1911; in Italian, Chicago, Jan. 16, 1912; in Eng. as *The Jewels of the Madonna*, N.Y., Oct. 14, 1913); *L'amore medico* (in Ger. as *Der Liebhaber als Arzt*, Dresden, Dec. 4, 1913; in Italian, N.Y., March 25, 1914); *Gli Amanti sposi* (c.1916; Venice, Feb. 19, 1925); *Das Himmelskleid* (c.1917–25; Munich, April 21, 1927; in Italian as *La veste di cielo*); *Sly, ovvero La leggenda del dormiente risvegliato* (Milan, Dec. 29, 1927); *La vedova scaltra* (Rome, March 5, 1931); *Il campiello* (Milan, Feb. 11, 1936); *La dama boba* (Milan, Feb. 1, 1939); *Gli dei a Tebe* (in Ger. as *Der Kuckuck in Theben*, Hannover, June 5, 1943); also an ed. of Mozart's *Idomeneo* (Munich, June 15, 1931). ORATORIO: *Talitha kumi* (1900).

BIBL.: H. Teibler, *E. W.-F.* (Leipzig, 1906); E. Stahl, ed., *E. W.-F.* (Salzburg, 1936); R. de Rensis, *E. W.-F.: La sua vita d'artista* (Milan, 1937); A. Grisson, *E. W.-F.: Autorisierte Lebensbeschreibung* (Regensburg, 1941; 2d ed., enl., 1958); R. de Rensis and G. Vannini, *In memoria di E. W.-F.* (Siena, 1948); W. Pfannkuch, *Das Opernschaffen E. W.-F.s* (diss., Univ. of Kiel, 1952); A. Suder, ed., *E. W.-F.* (Tutzing, 1986).

Wölfl (Woelfl, Wölffl), Joseph, Austrian pianist and composer; b. Salzburg, Dec. 24, 1773; d. London, May 21, 1812. He was a pupil of Leopold Mozart and Michael Haydn while serving as a chorister at the Salzburg Cathedral (1783–86); he was then in Vienna (1790–92) and Warsaw (1793) and again in Vienna from 1795; he was considered Beethoven's rival as a pianist; in 1798 he married the actress Therese Klemm. Traveling through Germany, he gave numerous concerts as a pianist, reaching Paris in 1801; he produced 2 French operas and was acclaimed as a piano virtuoso. In 1805 he went to London, and almost immediately established himself in the public's favor as a pianist and teacher. He was, however, of an eccentric disposition, and became involved in all sorts of trouble. He died in obscurity at the age of 38. In his professional life, he emphasized the sensational element; he gave fanciful titles to his works; he named one of his piano sonatas *Ne plus ultra*, and claimed that it was the most difficult piece ever written.

WORKS: DRAMATIC: OPERAS: *Der Höllenberg* (Vienna, Nov. 21, 1795); *Das schöne Milchmädchen, oder der Guckkasten* (Vienna, Jan. 5, 1797); *Der Kopf ohne Mann* (Vienna, Dec. 3, 1798); *Das trojanische Pferd* (Vienna, 1797); *L'Amour romanesque* (Paris, 1804); *Fernando, ou Les Maures* (Paris, 1805). BALLETS: *La Surprise de Diane* (London, Sept. 21, 1805); *Alzire* (London, Jan. 27, 1807).

Wolfram, Joseph Maria, Bohemian composer; b. Dobrzan, July 21, 1789; d. Teplitz, Sept. 30, 1839. He studied with J. Koželuch in Prague. He moved to Vienna as a music teacher, then became a government official at Theusing, and mayor of Teplitz (1824). He brought out several successful operas: *Maja und Alpino* (Prague, May 24, 1826), *Der Bergmönch* (Dresden, March 14, 1830), and *Das Schloss Candra* (Dresden, Dec. 1, 1832).

Wolfurt, Kurt von, German composer; b. Lettin, Sept. 7, 1880; d. Munich, Feb. 25, 1957. He studied science at the univs. of Dorpat, Leipzig, and Munich, then took lessons in composition with Reger and in piano with Krause in Munich. He eventually went to Berlin as a teacher at the municipal cons. (1936–45); he later taught in Göttingen (1945–49) and in Johannesburg (1949–52). He publ. monographs on Mussorgsky (Stuttgart, 1927) and Tchaikovsky (Zürich, 1951). Among his works is the opera *Dame Kobold* (Kassel, March 14, 1940).

Wollanck, (Johann Ernst) Friedrich, German composer; b. Berlin, Nov. 3, 1781; d. there, Sept. 6, 1831. He studied with J. A. Gürlich and C. F. C. Fasch. He was a lawyer and held a government position as counselor of the city court in Berlin. His works include an opera, *Der Alpenhirten* (Berlin, Feb. 19, 1811), and a "Liederspiel," *Thibaut von Lowis*.

Wolpe, Stefan, significant German-American composer and pedagogue; b. Berlin, Aug. 25, 1902; d. N.Y., April 4, 1972. He studied theory with Juon and Schreker at the Berlin Hochschule für Musik (1919–24). After graduation, he became associated with choral and theatrical groups in Berlin, promoting social causes; composed songs on revolutionary themes. With the advent of the anti-Semitic Nazi regime in 1933, he went to Vienna, where he took lessons with Webern, then traveled to Palestine in 1934; he taught at the Jerusalem Cons. In 1938 he emigrated to the United States, where he devoted himself mainly to teaching; he was on the faculty of the Settlement Music School in Philadelphia (1939–42); at the Philadelphia Academy of Music (1949–52); at Black Mountain College, N.C. (1952–56); and at Long Island Univ. (1957–68). He also taught privately. Among his students were Elmer Bernstein, Ezra Laderman, Ralph Shapey, David Tudor, and Morton Feldman. He was married successively to Ola Okuniewska, a painter, in 1927, to Irma Schoenberg (1902–84), a Romanian pianist, in 1934, and to Hilda Morley, a poet, in 1948. In 1966 he was elected a member of the National Inst. of Arts and Letters. He contributed numerous articles to German and American music magazines. In his style of composition, he attempted to reconcile the contradictions of triadic tonality (which he cultivated during his early period of writing "proletarian" music), atonality without procrustean dodecaphony, and serialism of contrasts obtained by intervallic contraction and expansion, metrical alteration, and dynamic variegation; super-added to these were explorations of Jewish cantillation and infatuation with jazz. Remarkably enough, the very copiousness of these resources contributed to a clearly identifiable idiom.

WORKS: DRAMATIC: OPERAS: *Schöne Geschichten* (1927–29); *Zeus und Elida* (1928). BALLET: *The Man from Midian* (1942). INCIDENTAL MUSIC TO: *De liegt Hund begraben* (1932); Bertolt Brecht's *The Good Woman of Setzuan* (1953) and *The Exception and the Rule* (1961); *Peer Gynt* (1954); *The Tempest* (1960).

BIBL.: H. Sucoff, *Catalogue and Evaluation of the Work of S. W.* (N.Y., 1969).

Wolpert, Franz Alfons, German composer and music theorist; b. Wiesentheid, Oct. 11, 1917; d. there, Aug. 7, 1978. He sang in the cathedral choir in Regensburg, and studied there at a Catholic church music school; he took lessons in composition with Wolf-Ferrari at the Salzburg Mozarteum (1939–41), where he subsequently taught (1941–44); he was a teacher in Salem, Lake Constance (from 1950). He publ. the useful vol. *Neue Harmonik: Die Lehre von den Akkordtypen* (Regensburg, 1952; 2d ed., rev. and enl., 1972). His compositions include a comic opera, *Der eingebildete Kranke* (1975), and a ballet, *Der goldene Schuh* (1956).

Wood, Charles, Irish pedagogue and composer; b. Armagh, June 15, 1866; d. Cambridge, England, July 12, 1926. He studied at the Royal College of Music in London, and subsequently taught harmony there; he received his Mus.Doc. degree from Cambridge in 1894. He was a univ. lecturer in harmony and counterpoint there from 1897, succeeding Stanford as prof. of music in 1924. His works include a comic opera, *Pickwick Papers* (London, 1922). He also ed. a collection of Irish folk songs (1897). He was the brother of the Irish organist and composer William G. Wood (b. Armagh, Jan. 16, 1859; d. London, Sept. 25, 1895).

Wood, Sir Henry J(oseph), eminent English conductor; b. London, March 3, 1869; d. Hitchin, Hertfordshire, Aug. 19, 1944. Of musical parentage, he was taught to play the piano by his mother; he participated in family musicales from the age of 6; he was equally precocious on the organ; at the age of 10 he often acted as a deputy organist, and gave organ recitals at the Fisheries Exhibition (1883) and at the Inventions Exhibition (1885). In 1886 he entered the Royal Academy of Music in London, where his teachers were Prout, Steggall, Macfarren, and Garcia; he won 4 medals. In 1888 he brought out some of his songs, then composed light operas and cantatas. But soon his ambition crystallized in the direction of conducting; after making his debut in 1888, he was active with various theater companies. On Aug. 10, 1895, he began his first series of Promenade Concerts (the famous "Proms") in Queen's Hall, London, with an orch. of about 80 members. Their success was so conspicuous that a new series of concerts was inaugurated on Jan. 30, 1897, under Wood's direction, and flourished from the beginning. In 1899 he founded the Nottingham Orch.; he also was conductor of the Wolverhampton Festival Choral Soc. (1900), the Sheffield Festival (1902–11), and the Norwich Festival (1908). In 1904 he was a guest conductor of the N.Y. Phil. He was married to Olga Urusova, a Russian noblewoman, and became greatly interested in Russian music, which he performed frequently at his concerts. He adopted a Russian pseudonym, Paul Klenovsky, for his compositions and arrangements, and supplied an imaginary biography of his alter ego for use in program notes. His wife died in 1909, and Wood married Muriel Greatorex in 1911. In 1921 he received the Gold Medal of the Royal Phil. Soc. He was made a Companion of Honour in 1944. In 1918 he was offered the conductorship of the Boston Sym. Orch. as successor to Muck, but declined. In 1923 he was appointed prof. of conducting and orch. playing at the Royal Academy of Music. Wood continued to conduct the Promenade Concerts almost to the end of his life, presenting the last concert on July 28, 1944. He publ. *The Gentle Art of Singing* (4 vols., 1927–28) and *About Conducting* (London, 1945), and ed. the *Handbook of Miniature Orchestral and Chamber Music Scores* (1937); wrote an autobiography, *My Life and Music* (London, 1938). A commemorative postage stamp with his portrait was issued by the Post Office of Great Britain on Sept. 1, 1980.

BIBL.: R. Newmarch, *H. J. W.* (London, 1904); T. Russell et al., eds., *Homage to Sir H. W.: A World Symposium* (London, 1944); W. Thompson et al., *Sir H. W.: Fifty Years of the Proms* (London, 1944); J. Wood, *The Last Years of H. J. W.* (London, 1954); R. Pound, *Sir H. W.: A Biography* (London, 1969); D. Cox, *The H. W. Proms* (London, 1980); A. Jacobs, *H. J. W.: Maker of the Proms* (London, 1994).

Wood, Joseph, American composer and teacher; b. Pittsburgh, May 12, 1915. He was a student of Wagenaar at the Juilliard School of Music (graduated, 1949) and of Luening at Columbia Univ. (M.A., 1950) in New York. From 1950 to 1985 he was a prof. of composition at the Oberlin (Ohio) College-Cons. of Music. He composed in a generally accessible vein with some excursions into serialism. Among his works are *The Mother*, opera (1945), *The Progression*, ballet cantata (1968), and incidental music.

Wooldridge, David (Humphry Michael), English conductor, writer on music, and composer; b. Deal, Aug. 24, 1927. He was the grandson of H. E. Wooldridge and godson of Rachmaninoff. He began violin lessons at 6 and made his conducting debut at 16. After graduating from the Univ. of London (1952), he was apprenticed to Krauss at the Vienna State Opera. In 1954–55 he was at the Bavarian State Opera in Munich. After guest conducting in the United States, he was music director of the Lebanese National Orch. in Beirut (1961–65) and conductor of the Cape Town Sym. Orch. (1965–67). He was the author of *Conductor's World* (N.Y., 1970) and *From the Steeples and Mountains: A Study of Charles Ives* (N.Y., 1974). Among his works were 3 ballets: *Les Parapluies* (1956), *Octet* (1958), and *Movements* (1970); also *The Duchess of Amalfi*, opera (1978), incidental music, and film scores.

Woollen, (Charles) Russell, American composer, pianist, and organist; b. Harford, Conn., Jan. 7, 1923; d. Charlottesville, Va., March 16, 1994. He was educated at St. Mary's Univ. in Baltimore (B.A., 1944) and at the Catholic Univ. of America in Washington, D.C. (M.A., in Romance languages, 1948). He also studied for the priesthood and attended the Pius X School of Liturgical Music in New York. After being ordained a priest in the Hartford Diocese in 1947, he studied Gregorian chant at the Benedictine Abbey in Solesmes in 1948. He also received private training in piano and organ, and also in composition from Franz Wasner. His other mentors in composition were Nabakov at the Peabody Cons. of Music in Baltimore (1949–51), Boulanger in Paris (1951), and Piston at Harvard Univ. (1953–55). From 1948 to 1962 he taught at the Catholic Univ. of America. He was staff keyboard player with the National Sym. Orch. in Washington, D.C., from 1956 to 1980. After leaving the priesthood in 1964, he taught at Howard Univ. in Washington, D.C. (1969–74). In 1982 he became organist at the Arlington (Va.) Unitarian Church. Although considered a minor composer, with the bulk of his manuscripts remaining unpublished at the time of his death, with Robert Evett and Robert Parris, Wollen contributed to the development of the so-called "Washington School of Composers" that flourished in the 1960s and 1970s. His works include *The Decorator*, television opera (N.Y., May 24, 1959).

Worbs, Hans Christoph, German music scholar; b. Guben, Jan. 13, 1927. He studied at the Humboldt Univ. in Berlin (degrees, 1952 and 1958). He subsequently settled in Hamburg, where he was active as a music critic and writer.

WRITINGS: *Der Schlager: Bestandsaufnahme, Analyse, Dokumentation* (Bremen, 1963); *Welterfolge der modernen Oper* (Berlin, 1967); *Felix Mendelssohn-Bartholdy* (Reinbek, 1974); *Modest Mussorgsky* (Reinbek, 1976); *Albert Lortzing* (Reinbek, 1980); *Das Dampkonzert: Musik und Musikleben des 19. Jahrhunderts in der Karikatur* (Wilhelmshaven, 1981).

Wordsworth, Barry, English conductor; b. Worcester Park, Surrey, Feb. 20, 1948. He studied conducting with Boult, winning the Tagore Gold Medal at the Royal College of Music in London in 1970. That same year he was cowinner of the Sargent Conductors' Prize. He received training in harpsichord from Leonhardt in Amsterdam. He appeared as a conductor with the Royal Ballet of

London (1974–84), and with the Australian Ballet and the Ballet of Canada. From 1982 to 1984 he was music director of the New Sadler's Wells Opera in London. In 1989 he became principal conductor of the Brighton Phil. and the BBC Concert Orch. in London. He also was music director of the Royal Ballet in London and of the Birmingham Royal Ballet from 1990. In 1991 he made his debut at London's Covent Garden conducting *Carmen*. In 1993 he was conductor of the Last Night of the Proms gala with the BBC Sym. Orch. in London.

Workman, William, American baritone; b. Valdosta, Ga., Feb. 4, 1940. He studied with Martial Singher at the Curtis Inst. of Music in Philadelphia and at the Music Academy of the West in Santa Barbara, Calif., then went to Europe and took voice lessons with Hedwig Schilling in Hamburg. He made his operatic debut with the Hamburg State Opera in 1965. In 1972 he became a member of the Frankfurt am Main Opera; he also made guest appearances in Stuttgart, Strasbourg, Paris, and Vienna. In 1984 he appeared at London's Covent Garden.

Wörner, Karl(heinz) H(einrich), German musicologist; b. Waldorf, near Heidelberg, Jan. 6, 1910; d. Heiligenkirchen, near Detmold, Aug. 11, 1969. He studied at the Berlin Hochschule für Musik and took courses in musicology with Schünemann, Schering, Blume, Hornbostel, and Sachs at the Univ. of Berlin (Ph.D., 1931, with the diss. *Beiträge zur Geschichte des Leitmotivs in der Oper*). He was music critic of the *Berliner Zeitung am Mittag* (1933–34), then (1935–40) opera conductor at Stettin, Magdeburg, and Frankfurt am Main. He was in the German Army during World War II; in 1944 he was taken prisoner of war by the U.S. Army and spent 2 years in an American internment camp. After his release, he taught at the Heidelberg Hochschule für Musik (1946–54). From 1954 to 1958 he was on the staff of B. Schotts Söhne (Mainz); in 1958, joined the faculty of the Folkwangschule in Essen; from 1961 he taught at the North-West Academy of Music in Detmold.

WRITINGS: *Mendelssohn-Bartholdy* (Wiesbaden, 1947); *Musik der Gegenwart: Geschichte des neuen Musik* (Mainz, 1949); *Robert Schumann* (Zürich, 1949); *Musiker-Worte* (Baden-Baden, 1949); *Geschichte der Musik* (Göttingen, 1954; 6th ed., aug., 1975; Eng. tr., 1973); *Neue Musik in der Entscheidung* (Mainz, 1954); *Gotteswort und Magie: Die Oper "Moses und Aron" von Arnold Schönberg* (Heidelberg, 1959; Eng. tr., aug., 1963); *Karlheinz Stockhausen: Werk und Wollen 1950–1962* (Rodenkirchen, 1963; Eng. tr., aug., 1973); *Das Zeitalter der thematischen Prozesse in der Geschichte der Musik* (Regensburg, 1969); *Die Musik in der Geistesgeschichte: Studien zur Situation der Jahre um 1910* (Bonn, 1970).

Wöss, Josef Venantius von, Austrian editor and composer; b. Cattaro, Dalmatia, June 13, 1863; d. Vienna, Oct. 22, 1943. He received his first musical instruction from his mother and an uncle; he studied theory at the Vienna Cons. with Franz Krenn. He was an ed. for Universal Edition (1908–31) and also ed. the journal *Musica Divina* (1913–34). Among his compositions were the operas *Lenzlüge* (Elberfeld, 1905), *Flaviennes Abenteuer* (Breslau, 1910), and *Carmilhan* (n.d.).

WRITINGS: *Deutsche Meister des Liedes* (Vienna, 1910); *Gustav Mahler, Das Lied von der Erde: Thematische Analyse* (Leipzig, 1912); *Die Modulation* (Vienna, 1921).

Wöss, Kurt, Austrian conductor; b. Linz, May 2, 1914; d. Dresden (while rehearsing the Dresden Phil.), Dec. 4, 1987. He studied conducting with Weingartner in Vienna, and also pursued musicological studies at the Univ. of Vienna with Haas, Lach, Orel, and Wellesz; he taught an orch. class at the Vienna Academy of Music (1938–40). He conducted the Niederösterreichisches Tonkünstlerorchester in Vienna (1948–51) and the Nippon Phil. in Tokyo (1951–54). From 1956 to 1959 he was principal conductor of the Victoria Sym. Orch. in Melbourne and of the Australian National Opera; in 1961 he returned to Linz, where he was chief conductor of the Bruckner Orch. until 1976; he also conducted again in Tokyo. He publ. *Ratschläge zur Aufführung der Symphonien Anton Bruckners* (Linz, 1974).

Wotquenne (-Plattel), Alfred (Camille), Belgian musicologist; b. Lobbes, Jan. 25, 1867; d. Antibes, France, Sept. 25, 1939. He studied at the Royal Cons. in Brussels with Brassin (piano), Mailly (organ; premier prix, 1888), and Dupont and Gevaert (theory). From 1894 to 1896 he was deputy secretary and librarian and from 1896 to 1918 secretary and librarian there. He settled in Antibes as a singing teacher and organist, and subsequently was made maître de chapelle at its cathedral (1921). He prepared a card catalogue of 18,000 Italian "cantate da camera" of the 18th century; ed. *Chansons italiennes de la fin du XVIe siècle* (canzonette *a* 4); continued the collections begun by Gevaert, *Répertoire classique du chant français and Répertoire français de l'ancien chant classique*; and ed. a new collection, *Répertoire Wotquenne* (4 vols. publ.); also ed. violin sonatas of Tartini, Veracini, and others; composed much sacred music. The MSS of several important bibliographies in his collection were bought by the Library of Congress in Washington, D.C., in 1929. A large part of his private music library was also bought by the Library of Congress.

WRITINGS: *Catalogue de la bibliothèque du Conservatoire Royal de Musique de Bruxelles* (vol. 1, 1894; with a supplement, *Libretti d'opéras et d'oratorios italiens du XVIIe siècle*, 1901; 2, 1902; 3, 1908; 4, 1912; 5, 1914); *Étude bibliographique sur les oeuvres de Baldassare Galuppi* (1899; 2d ed., aug., 1902 as *Baldassare Galuppi: Étude bibliographique sur ses oeuvres dramatiques*); *Thematisches Verzeichnis der Werke von Christoph Wilibald von Gluck* (1904); *Alphabetisches Verzeichnis der Stücke in Versen aus den dramatischer Werken von Zeno, Metastasio und Goldoni* (1905); *Thematisches Verzeichnis der Werke von Carl Philipp Emanuel Bach* (1905); *Étude bibliographique sur le compositeur napolitain Luigi Rossi* (1909).

Woyrsch, Felix von, German organist, conductor, and composer; b. Troppau, Silesia, Oct. 8, 1860; d. Altona-Hamburg, March 20, 1944. He studied with E. Chevallier in Hamburg, but was chiefly self-taught. In 1887 he settled in Altona as conductor of the Allgemeine Leidertafel, and from 1893 he led the Kirchenchor, then Singakademie (from 1895), and finally the municipal sym. concerts and Volkskonzerte (from 1903). From 1895 to 1903 he was organist of the Friedenskirche, then of the Johanniskirche until 1926. He retired from public life in 1937. Among his works were the operas *Der Pfarrer von Meudon* (Hamburg, 1886), *Der Weiberkrieg* (Hamburg, 1890), *Wikingerfahrt* (Nuremberg, 1896), and *Faust* (n.d.).

BIBL.: F. Pfohl, *F. W.* (Leipzig, 1934); C. Lerche and A. Feuss, *F. W. (1860–1944)* (Hamburg, 1990).

Wranitzky, Paul, distinguished Bohemian violinist, conductor, and composer; b. Neureisch, Moravia, Dec. 30, 1756; d. Vienna, Sept. 26, 1808. After studying in Moravia, he went in 1776 to Vienna, where he was a pupil of Joseph Martin Kraus and Haydn. Around 1785 he was named music director to Count Johann Nepomuk Esterházy; from about 1790 he served as director of the orchs. at the Court Theaters in Vienna. His opera *Oberon, König der Elfen* was given with excellent success in Vienna on Nov. 7, 1789; other operas and Singspiels produced by him in Vienna were *Rudolf von Felseck* (Oct. 6, 1792), *Merkur, der Heurat-Stifter* (Feb. 21, 1793), *Das Fest der Lazzaroni* (Feb. 4, 1794), *Die gute Mutter* (May 11, 1795), *Johanna von Montfaucon* (Jan. 25, 1799), *Der Schreiner* (July 18, 1799), *Das Mitgefühl* (April 21, 1804), and *Die Erkenntlichkeit* (July 22, 1805). He also produced several successful ballets and wrote incidental music to plays. His brother, Anton Wranitzky (1761–1820), was a violinist, pedagogue, and composer.

BIBL.: J. Pešková, *Vranického Oberon a jeho vliv na rozvoj singspielu* (W.'s Oberon and Its Influence on the Development of the Singspiel; diss., Univ. of Prague, 1955).

Wright, Maurice, American composer and teacher; b. Front Royal, Va., Oct. 17, 1949. He studied with Iain Hamilton at Duke

Univ. (B.A., 1972) and Beeson, Davidovsky, Ussachevsky, and Dodge at Columbia Univ. (M.A., 1974). He taught at Columbia Univ. (1975–77), Boston Univ. (1978–79), and Temple Univ. (from 1980). His works include the opera *The 5th String* (1978–80; also an orch. piece, *Music from the 5th String*).

Wuensch, Gerhard (Joseph), Austrian-Canadian composer and teacher; b. Vienna, Dec. 23, 1925. He received training in musicology at the Univ. (Ph.D., 1950) and in piano and composition at the Academy of Music (diplomas in both, 1952) in Vienna. As a Fulbright fellow, he pursued studies in theory with Pisk and Kennan at the Univ. of Texas (1954–56). After teaching at Butler Univ. in Indianapolis (1956–63), he settled in Canada and taught at the univs. of Toronto (1964–69) and Calgary (1969–73). In 1973 he joined the faculty of the Univ. of Western Ontario in London, where he was chairman of the theory and composition dept. (1973–76) and a prof. (1978–91). In 1991 he was made prof. emeritus. As a composer, his works reveal a familiarity with a wide spectrum of styles and genres.

WORKS: DRAMATIC: *Labyrinth*, ballet (1957); *Il Pomo d'Oro*, comedy-ballet (1958); *Nice People: 3 Scenes from Contemporary Life*, chamber opera (1990; London, Ontario, Nov. 28, 1991).

Wüerst, Richard (Ferdinand), German composer, music critic, and teacher; b. Berlin, Feb. 22, 1824; d. there, Oct. 9, 1881. He studied violin with Ferdinand David at the Leipzig Cons., where he also took lessons with Mendelssohn. He then taught at Kullak's Neue Akademie der Tonkunst in Berlin. As music critic for the *Berliner Fremdenblatt*, he exercised considerable influence; he publ. *Leitfaden der Elementartheorie der Musik* (1867; Eng. tr. as *Elementary Theory of Music and Treatment of Chords*, Boston, 1893). As a composer, he was a follower of Mendelssohn. Among his works were the operas *Der Rotmantel* (Berlin, 1848), *Vineta* (Pressburg, Dec. 21, 1862), *Eine Künstlerreise* (with Winterfeld; Berlin, 1868), *Faublas* (Berlin, 1873), *A-ing-fo-hi* (Berlin, Jan. 28, 1878), and *Die Offiziere der Kaiserin* (Berlin, 1878).

Wüllner, Franz, important German pianist, conductor, and composer, father of **Ludwig Wüllner**; b. Münster, Jan. 28, 1832; d. Braunfels-an-der-Lahn, Sept. 7, 1902. He studied with Schindler in Münster and Frankfurt am Main (1846–50). From 1850 to 1854 he was active as a concert artist; he was a teacher at the Munich music school (1856–58), then music director in Aachen (1858–64). He returned to Munich in 1864, where he became court music director of the church choir; he then taught at the music school (from 1867); he also conducted at the Court Opera. Under unfavorable conditions (against Wagner's wishes), he prepared and conducted the first perf. of *Das Rheingold* (Sept. 22, 1869) and *Die Walküre* (June 26, 1870); his success led to his appointment as principal conductor there in 1871. In 1877 he became court conductor at Dresden, and also director of the Cons.; in 1882 Schuch was promoted to take his place; thereafter Wüllner was one of the conductors of the Berlin Phil. for the 1882–85 seasons. He became conductor of the Gurzenich Concerts in Cologne in 1884, and director of the Cologne Cons., later becoming also municipal music director, posts he held until his death. He was highly regarded as a choral composer; publ. the valuable book of vocal exercises *Chorübungen der Münchener Musikschule* (3 vols., Munich, 1876; new ed. by R. Stephani, 1953–54; Eng. tr., 1882). He was a friend of Brahms.

BIBL.: E. Prieger, *F. W.: Ein Nachruf* (Bonn, 1902); E. Wolff, ed., *Johannes Brahms im Briefwechsel mit F. W.* (Berlin, 1922); D. Kämper, *F. W.: Leben, Wirken und kompositorisches Schaffen* (Cologne, 1963); idem, ed., *Richard Strauss und F. W. im Briefwechsel* (Cologne, 1963).

Wüllner, Ludwig, distinguished German singer, son of **Franz Wüllner**; b. Münster, Aug. 19, 1858; d. Kiel, March 19, 1938. He studied Germanic philology at the univs. of Munich, Berlin, and Strasbourg. He taught Germanic philology at the Akademie in Münster (1884–87), and sang occasionally in concert; his musical training began only in 1887, when he took a course of study at the Cologne Cons. A 2d change of vocation brought him to the Meiningen Court Theater, where he appeared as an actor of heroic parts in the spoken drama (1889–95); he became friendly with Brahms, who commended his singing of German folk songs. In 1895 he gave song recitals in Berlin with such acclaim that he decided to devote himself mainly to lieder. He then made tours of all Europe, arousing tremendous enthusiasm; his first recital in New York (Nov. 15, 1908) was a sensational success, and he followed it by an extensive tour of the United States and then another (1909–10). His peculiar distinction was his ability to give an actor's impersonation of the character of each song, introducing an element of drama on the concert stage.

BIBL.: F. Ludwig, *L. W.: Sein Leben und seine Kunst* (Leipzig, 1931).

Wunderlich, Fritz (Friedrich Karl Otto), outstanding German tenor; b. Kusel, Sept. 26, 1930; d. Heidelberg, Sept. 17, 1966. He was a student of Margarete von Wintenfeld at the Freiburg im Breisgau Hochschule für Musik (1950–55). While still a student, he appeared as a soloist with the Freiburg im Breisgau Choir, and then sang Tamino in a school performance of *Die Zauberflöte* (1954). In 1955 he made his professional operatic debut in Stuttgart as Eislinger in *Die Meistersinger von Nürnberg*, where he sang until 1958. From 1958 to 1960 he was a member of the Frankfurt am Main Opera. In 1958 he sang at the Aix-en-Provence Festival, and then appeared as Henry in *Die schweigsame Frau* at the Salzburg Festival in 1959. In 1960 he became a member of the Bavarian State Opera in Munich and in 1962 was made a Kammersänger. He also was a member of the Vienna State Opera from 1962. In 1965 he made his debut as Don Ottavio at London's Covent Garden. He appeared at the Edinburgh Festival in 1966. Wunderlich was scheduled to make his Metropolitan Opera debut in New York as Don Ottavio on Oct. 8, 1966, but his career of great promise was tragically cut short by his death in a fall at his home. He was acclaimed for the extraordinary beauty of his lyric tenor voice. In addition to his remarkable Mozartian roles, he also was admired for such roles as Alfredo, Lensky, Jeník, Palestrina, and Leukippos. He likewise was noted for his operetta and lieder performances.

BIBL.: W. Pfister, *F. W.: Biographie* (Zürich, 1990).

Wunsch, Hermann, German composer and teacher; b. Neuss, Aug. 9, 1884; d. Berlin, Dec. 21, 1954. He studied in Düsseldorf and Cologne, and later at the Hochschule für Musik in Berlin, where he subsequently taught, becoming a prof. in 1945. He composed 6 syms., of which the 5th won the Schubert Memorial Prize (German section) of the Columbia Phonograph Co. contest (Schubert Centennial, 1928). Other works included the chamber operas *Bianca* (Weimar, May 22, 1927), *Don Juans Sohn* (Weimar, 1928), and *Franzosenzeit* (Schwerin, 1933).

Wuorinen, Charles (Peter), prominent American composer, pedagogue, pianist, and conductor; b. N.Y., June 9, 1938. He was a student of Beeson, Ussachevsky, and Luening at Columbia Univ. (B.A., 1961; M.A., 1963), where he then taught (1964–71). With Harvey Sollberger, he founded the Group for Contemporary Music in 1962, which became a vital force in the propagation of modern music via concerts and recordings. He was a visiting lecturer at Princeton Univ. (1967–68) and the New England Cons. of Music in Boston (1968–71). After serving as adjunct lecturer at the Univ. of South Florida (1971–72), he was on the faculty of the Manhattan School of Music in New York (1972–79). From 1973 to 1987 he was artistic director and chairman of the American Composers Orch. in New York. In 1984 he became a prof. at Rutgers, the State Univ. of N.J. From 1985 to 1989 he served as composer-in-residence of the San Francisco Sym. He was a visiting prof. at the State Univ. of N.Y. at Buffalo from 1989 to 1994. Wuorinen has received numerous prizes, grants, and commissions, among them the Joseph Bearns Prize (1958, 1959, 1961), a National Inst. of Arts and Letters Award (1967), 2 Guggenheim fellowships (1968, 1972), the Pulitzer Prize in Music for his *Times Encomium* (1970), the Brandeis Univ. Creative Arts Award (1970), NEA grants (1974, 1976), Rockefeller Foundation fellowships (1979, 1980, 1981), and a MacArthur Foundation fellowship

(1986–91). He also was elected to membership in the American Academy and Inst. of Arts and Letters. Wuorinen publ. the book *Simple Composition* (N.Y., 1979), which gives insight into his use of 12-tone composition. Wuorinen is one of the most representative of contemporary composers of his generation. His techniques derive from Stravinsky's late period, when stark primitivism gave way to austere linear counterpoint. An even greater affinity in Wuorinen's music is with the agglutinative formations of unrelated thematic statements as practiced by Varèse. A more literal dependence connects Wuorinen's works with the dodecaphonic method of composition as promulgated by Schoenberg. These modalities and relationships coalesce in Wuorinen's writing into a sui generis complex subdivided into melodic, harmonic, and contrapuntal units that build a definitive formal structure. The foundation of his method of composition is serialism, in which pitch, time, and rhythmic divisions relate to one another in a "time point system," which lends itself to unlimited tonal and temporal arrangements, combinations, and permutations. In his prolific output, Wuorinen has explored the entire vocabulary of serial composition.

WORKS: DRAMATIC: *The Politics of Harmony*, masque (1966–67; N.Y., Oct. 28, 1968); *The W. of Babylon (or The Triumph of Love Over Moral Depravity)*, Baroque burlesque (partial perf., N.Y., Dec. 15, 1975; 1st complete perf., San Francisco, Jan 20, 1989); *Delight of the Muses*, ballet (1991; N.Y., Jan. 29, 1992; based on the orch piece). Also *The Magic Art*, instrumental masque, after Purcell (1977–79; St. Paul, Minn., Sept. 26, 1979), and *The Celestial Sphere*, oratorio for Chorus and Orch. (1980; Rock Island, Ill., April 25, 1981).

BIBL.: R. Burbank, *C. W.: A Bio-Bibliography* (Westport, Conn., 1994).

Würfel, Wenzel Wilhelm (actually, **Václav Vilem**), Bohemian pianist, conductor, teacher, and composer; b. Pláňany, near Kolín, May 6, 1790; d. Vienna, March 23, 1832. He made tours as a pianist while still a child, then was a pupil of Tomaschek in Prague. In 1815 he went to Warsaw as prof. of organ and thoroughbass at the Cons.; Chopin was one of his students. After conducting at the Kärnthnertortheater in Vienna (1824–26), he toured as a pianist. His opera *Rübezahl* was first performed in Prague on Oct. 7, 1824, with excellent success, and enjoyed popularity for some years; he also wrote the opera *Der Rotmantel* (1826).

Wykes, Robert (Arthur), American flutist, teacher, and composer; b. Aliquippa, Pa., May 19, 1926. He studied composition with Phillips and Barlow at the Eastman School of Music in Rochester, N.Y. (B.M. and M.M., 1949). He played flute in the Toledo Sym. Orch. while teaching at Bowling Green State Univ. (1950–52); he then taught at the Univ. of Ill. (1952–55). In 1955 he joined the faculty of Washington Univ. in St. Louis, where he was a prof. (1965–88); he also was a flutist with the St. Louis Sym. Orch. (1963–67) and the Studio for New Music in St. Louis (1966–69). In 1990–91 he was a visiting scholar at Stanford Univ. His works include the chamber opera *The Prankster* (1951; Bowling Green, Ohio, Jan. 12, 1952), as well as scores for documentary films, including *Robert Kennedy Remembered* (Academy Award, 1969), *Monument to the Dream, John F. Kennedy 1917–1963*, and *The Eye of Jefferson*.

Wyner, Susan Davenny, American soprano; b. New Haven, Conn., Oct. 17, 1943. She was educated at Cornell Univ., graduating summa cum laude in music and English literature in 1965; then pursued vocal studies with Herta Glaz (1969–75). She received a Fulbright scholarship and a grant from the Ford Foundation; she also won the Walter W. Naumberg Prize. In 1972 she made her Carnegie Recital Hall debut in New York in 1974 she made her orch. debut as a soloist with the Boston Sym. Orch. On Oct. 23, 1977, she made her first appearance at the N.Y. City Opera as Monteverdi's Poppaea. On Oct. 8, 1981, she made her Metropolitan Opera debut in New York as Woglinde in *Das Rheingold*. An exceptionally intelligent singer, she became equally successful as a performer of music in all historic idioms, from early Renaissance works to the most intransigent ultramodern scores. After being struck by a car while bicycling in N.Y. City in 1983, she gave up her vocal career. She joined the faculty of Cornell Univ. and also studied conducting at the Los Angeles Phil. Inst. and at Tanglewood. She married **Yehudi Wyner** in 1967.

Wyschnegradsky, Ivan (Alexandrovich), Russian composer, master of microtonal music; b. St. Petersburg, May 16, 1893; d. Paris, Sept. 29, 1979. He studied composition with Nikolai Sokoloff at the St. Petersburg Cons.; in 1920 he settled in Paris. He devoted virtually his entire musical career to the exploration and creative realization of music in quarter tones and other microtonal intervals; he had a quarter tone piano constructed for him; he also publ. a guide, *Manuel d'harmonie à quarts de ton* (Paris, 1932). On Nov. 10, 1945, he presented in Paris a concert of his music, at which he conducted the first performance of his *Cosmos* for 4 Pianos, with each pair tuned at quarter tones. Bruce Mather took interest in Wyschnegradsky's music and gave a concert of his works at McGill Univ. in Montreal that included 3 premieres (Feb. 10, 1977). But with the exception of these rare concerts, Wyschnegradsky remains a figure of legend; few performances of his music are ever given in Europe or North America. He regarded his *La Journée de l'existence* for Narrator, Orch., and Chorus ad libitum (to his own text; 1916–17; rev. 1927 and 1940) as his germinal work, opening the path to microtonal harmony; he dated this "awakening to ultrachromaticism" as having occurred on Nov. 7, 1918. At his death, he left sketches for a short opera in 5 scenes, *L'Éternel Étranger*, begun in 1939 but never completed. Also unfinished was the ambitious *Polyphonie spatiale*.

Wyttenbach, Jürg, Swiss pianist, conductor, teacher, and composer; b. Bern, Dec. 2, 1935. He studied piano and theory with Fischer and Veress at the Bern Cons. After further studies with Lefébure and Calvet at the Paris Cons. (1955–57), he completed his training in piano with Karl Engel (1958–59). In 1959 he became a teacher at the Biel Music School. In 1962 he became a teacher at the Bern Cons. From 1967 he taught at the Basel Academy of Music. He also appeared frequently as a pianist and conductor, championing particularly the cause of contemporary music. His own music utilizes both aleatory and serialism.

WORKS: DRAMATIC: *Beethoven: Sacré? Sacré Beethoven!* for Singer, Speaker, Musician, and Projection (1977); *Patchwork an der Wäscheleine*, scenic collage (1979); *Chansons ricochets*, madrigal comedy for 5 Singers (1980); *Hors jeux*, "sport-opera" (1981–82).

Y

Yakovlev, Leonid, Russian baritone; b. Kherson government, April 12, 1858; d. Petrograd, June 2, 1919. After training with Ryadnov in Kiev, he completed his studies in Italy. He commenced his career in Tiflis. In 1887 he joined the Maryinsky Theater in St. Petersburg, where he sang in the premiere of Tchaikovsky's *The Queen of Spades* (Dec. 19, 1890). In 1906 he retired from the operatic stage to teach voice. He also was active as an opera producer at the Maryinsky Theater. His most famous role was Onegin, but he also scored success as Escamillo, Nevers, and Wolfram.

Yamada, Kōsaku, eminent Japanese conductor and composer; b. Tokyo, June 9, 1886; d. there, Dec. 29, 1965. He studied vocal music with Tamaki Shibata and cello and theory with Werkmeister at the Tokyo Imperial Academy of Music (1904–08), then composition with Bruch and Karl Leopold Wolf at the Berlin Hochschule für Musik (1908–13). He founded the Tokyo Phil. in 1915; he appeared as a guest conductor with the N.Y. Phil. in 1918 in a program of Japanese music, including some of his own works; conducted in Russia in 1930 and 1933, and then throughout Europe in 1937. His compositions follow in the German Romantic tradition of Wagner and Strauss, with impressionistic overtones. Although most of his MSS were destroyed during the Allied air raid on Tokyo on May 25, 1945, several works have been restored from extant orch. parts.

WORKS: OPERAS: *Ochitaru tennyo* (The Depraved Heavenly Maiden; 1912; Tokyo, Dec. 3, 1929); *Alladine et Palomides* (1913); *Ayame* (The Sweet Flag; Paris, 1931); *Kurofune* (The Black Ships; 1939); *Yoake* (The Dawn; 1939; Tokyo, Nov. 28, 1940); *Hsiang Fei* (1946–47; Tokyo, May 1954).

Yamash'ta, Stomu (real name, **Tsutomu Yamashita**), Japanese percussionist and composer; b. Kyoto, March 10, 1947. He was trained in music by his father; he played piano in his infancy, and drums at puberty; in early adolescence he became a timpanist for the Kyoto Phil. and Osaka Phil.; he also worked in several film studios in Tokyo. At 16, he went to London for further study; he later went to the United States as a scholarship student at the Interlochen (Mich.) Arts Academy; he continued his musical education in Boston, New York, and Chicago. Returning to Japan, he gave solo performances as a percussionist; he developed a phenomenal degree of equilibristic prestidigitation, synchronously manipulating a plethora of drums and a congregation of oriental bells and gongs while rotating 360° from the center of a circle to reach the prescribed percussionable objects. As a composer, he cultivates a manner of controlled improvisation marked by constantly shifting meters. In 1970 he formed the Red Buddha Theater (an ensemble of actors, musicians, and dancers), for which he composed 2 musical pageants, *Man from the East* (1971) and *Rain Mountain* (1973). Other works include a ballet, *Fox* (1968), and percussion scores for many Japanese films, as well as for Ken Russell's *The Devils* (with Peter Maxwell Davies, 1971) and Robert Altman's *Images* (1972).

Yannatos, James, American composer, conductor, and teacher; b. N.Y., March 13, 1929. He was a student of Hindemith and Porter at Yale Univ. (B.M., 1951; M.M., 1952) and of Bezanson at the Univ. of Iowa (Ph.D., 1960). He also studied with Bernstein, Steinberg, Boulanger, Milhaud, and Dallapiccola. From 1964 he taught at Yale Univ. He also was active as a conductor of youth orchs. and choral groups, and conducted various chamber orchs. He was the author of *Explorations in Musical Materials* (1978). Among his works were the opera *The Rocket's Red Glare* (1971) and the ballets *Oedipus* (1960) and *A Suite for Orpheus and Eurydice* (1980).

Yeston, Maury, American composer and music theorist; b. Jersey City, N.J., Oct. 23, 1945. He studied at Yale Univ. with Waite and Forte (B.A., 1967; Ph.D., 1974), subsequently joining the composition faculty there and becoming director of the BMI Musical Theater Workshop in New York. His first major stage work was the Broadway musical *Nine* (1982), based on Fellini's movie *8½*, which won Tony and Drama Desk awards; it includes opulent recollections of Baroque and Romantic styles, continuing the operatic trend in musical theater established by Stephen Sondheim and Andrew Lloyd Webber. He also wrote incidental music for

Caryl Churchill's play *Cloud Nine* and for *Nukata*, a musical written in Japanese and premiered in Tokyo. His theoretical writings are sophisticated; his *Stratification of Musical Rhythm* (New Haven, 1975) elucidates one of the only plausible theories on rhythmic structure yet proposed. He also ed. *Readings in Schenker Analysis* (New Haven, 1977). Among his other compositions are *Goya, a Life in Song* (1987), and another musical, *Grand Hotel* (1989).

Youdin, Mikhail, Russian composer and teacher; b. St. Petersburg, Sept. 29, 1893; d. Kazan, Feb. 8, 1948. He studied at the St. Petersburg Cons. (graduated, 1923), and then was a teacher there (1926–42); he subsequently taught at the Kazan Cons. (1942–48). Among his works were the opera *Farida* (1943) and the *Heroic Oratorio* (1937).

Young (real name, **Youngs**), **(Basil) Alexander,** English tenor; b. London, Oct. 18, 1920. He was a pupil of Steffan Pollmann at the Royal College of Music in London. He sang with the BBC and Glyndebourne choruses (1948–49); in 1950 he made his operatic debut as Scaramuccio in *Ariadne auf Naxos* at the Edinburgh Festival; he sang regularly at London's Covent Garden (1955–70); he also appeared with other English opera companies and in the United States, and toured widely as a concert artist. From 1973 to 1986 he was head of the school of vocal studies at the Royal Northern College of Music in Manchester; he was also founder-conductor of the Jubilate Choir of Manchester (1977). His operatic repertory ranged from Monteverdi to Stravinsky; he was particularly admired for his performances of Handel's music.

Young, Cecilia, English soprano, aunt of **Polly (Mary) Young**; b. London, 1711; d. there, Oct. 6, 1789. She studied with Geminiani, making her 1st public appearance at a benefit concert at the Drury Lane Theatre on March 4, 1730; in 1735 she was engaged by Handel for his opera company. She married **Thomas Augustine Arne** on March 15, 1737, with whom she went to Dublin in 1742. She sang in several of his works there (*Comus, Judgment of Paris, Alfred*, etc.).

Young, Percy M(arshall), English writer on music; b. Northwich, Cheshire, May 17, 1912. He studied English, music, and history as an organ scholar at Selwyn College, Cambridge (B.A., 1933; Mus.B., 1934), then went to Dublin, where he graduated from Trinity College (Mus.D., 1937); upon his return to England, he took courses with C. B. Rootham and E. J. Dent in Cambridge. He subsequently occupied various teaching posts; from 1944 to 1966, was director of music at the College of Technology in Wolverhampton. He publ. a number of arrangements of early English songs, and also composed some vocal pieces and a *Fugal Concerto* for 2 Pianos and Strings (1954); he is known principally for his scholarly biographical studies and essays.

WRITINGS (all publ. in London unless otherwise given): *Samuel Pepys' Music Book* (1942); *Handel* (1947; 3d ed., rev., 1979); *The Oratorios of Handel* (1953); *Messiah: A Study in Interpretation* (1951); *A Critical Dictionary of Composers and Their Music* (1954; U.S. ed. as *Biographical Dictionary of Composers*); Elgar, *O. M.: A Study of a Musician* (1955; 2d ed., 1973); ed. *Letters of Edward Elgar and Other Writings* (1956); *Tragic Muse: The Life and Works of Robert Schumann* (1957; 2d ed., rev., 1961); *The Choral Tradition: An Historical and Analytical Survey from the 16th Century to the Present Day* (1962; 2d ed., rev., 1982); *Zoltán Kodály* (1964); ed. *Letters to Nimrod from Edward Elgar* (1965); *A History of British Music* (1967); *Keyboard Musicians of the World* (1967); ed. *Elgar: A Future for English Music and Other Lectures* (1968); *Debussy* (1969); *The Bachs, 1500–1850* (1970); *Sir Arthur Sullivan* (1971); *A Concise History of Music* (1974); *Beethoven: A Victorian Tribute* (1976); *Alice Elgar: Enigma of a Victorian Lady* (1977); *George Grove* (1980); *Mozart* (1987); *Elgar, Newman and the Dream of Gerontius: In the Tradition of English Catholicism* (Brookfield, Vt., 1995); *Elgar, Newman and the Dream of Gerontius* (1995).

Young, Polly (Mary), English soprano, niece of **Cecilia Young**; b. London, c.1745; d. there, Sept. 20, 1799. She lived in Dublin with her aunt, making her debut as a singer upon her return to London in 1762. In 1766 she married **François-Hippolyte Barthélemon**; their daughter, Cecilia Maria (Mrs. Henslowe), was a talented musician.

Ysaÿe, Eugène (-Auguste), famous Belgian violinist, conductor, and composer; b. Liège, July 16, 1858; d. Brussels, May 12, 1931. At the age of 4, he began to study violin with his father, a theater conductor; at the age of 7, he was enrolled at the Liège Cons. as a pupil of Désiré Heynberg, winning 2d prize in 1867; in 1869 he left the Cons. in a dispute with his mentor, but was readmitted in 1872 as a pupil of Rodolphe Massart, winning 1st prize in 1873 and the silver medal in 1874; he then continued his training on a scholarship at the Brussels Cons. with Wieniawski; he later completed his studies with Vieuxtemps in Paris (1876–79). In 1879 he became concertmaster of Bilse's orch. in Berlin; he appeared as a soloist at Pauline Lucca's concerts in Cologne and Aachen; in Germany he met Anton Rubinstein, who took him to Russia, where he spent 2 winters; he also toured in Norway. In 1883 he settled in Paris, where he met Franck, d'Indy et al., and gave successful concerts; he formed a duo with the pianist Raoul Pugno, and started a long series of concerts with him, establishing a new standard of excellence. On Sept. 26, 1886, he married Louise Bourdeau; Franck dedicated his Violin Sonata to them as a wedding present; Ysaÿe's interpretation of this work made it famous. In 1886 he was named prof. at the Brussels Cons. (resigned in 1898); in 1886 he also organized the Ysaÿe Quartet (with Crickboom, Léon Van Hout, and Joseph Jacob); Debussy dedicated his String Quartet to Ysaÿe's group, which gave its first performance at the Société Nationale in Paris on Dec. 29, 1893. In 1889 Ysaÿe made successful appearances in England. On Nov. 16, 1894, he made his American debut playing the Beethoven Violin Concerto with the N.Y. Phil., and creating a sensation by his virtuosity. He revisited America many times, with undiminished acclaim. He began his career as a conductor in 1894, and established in Brussels his own orch., the Société des Concerts Ysaÿe. When the Germans invaded Belgium in 1914, he fled to London, where he remained during World War I. On April 5, 1918, he made his American debut as a conductor with the Cincinnati Sym. Orch., and also led the Cincinnati May Festival in that year. His success was so great that he was offered a permanent position as conductor of the Cincinnati Sym. Orch., which he held from 1918 to 1922. He then returned to Belgium and resumed leadership of the Société des Concerts Ysaÿe. After the death of his first wife, he married, on July 9, 1927, an American pupil, Jeannette Dincin.

Ysaÿe's style of playing is best described as heroic, but his art was equally convincing in the expression of moods of exquisite delicacy and tenderness; his frequent employment of "tempo rubato" produced an effect of elasticity without distorting the melodic line. He composed many works for and including his instrument. At the age of 70, he began the composition of an opera in the Walloon language, *Piér li Houïeu* (Peter the Miner), which was premiered in Liège on March 4, 1931, in the presence of the composer, who was brought to the theater in an invalid's chair, suffering from the extreme ravages of diabetes, which had necessitated the amputation of his left foot. He began the composition of a 2d Walloon opera, *L'Avierge di Piér* (La Vierge de Pierre), but had no time to complete it. In 1937 Queen Elisabeth of Belgium inaugurated the annual Prix International Eugene Ysaÿe in Brussels; the first winner was David Oistrakh. His brother, Théophile Ysaÿe (1865–1918), was a pianist and a composer.

BIBL.: J. Quitin, *E. Y.: Étude biographique et critique* (Brussels, 1938); E. Christen, *Y.* (Geneva, 1946; 2nd ed., 1947); A. Ysaÿe and B. Ratcliffe, *Y.: His Life, Work and Influence* (London, 1947); A. Ysaÿe, *E. Y.: Sa vie d'après les documents receuillis par son fils* (Brussels, 1948; a considerably altered version of the preceding; Eng. tr., 1980, as *Y., By His Son Antoine*); A. Ysaÿe, *E. Y., 1858–1931* (Brussels, 1972); M. Benoît-Jeannin, *E. Y.: Le dernier romantique ou le sacre du violon* (Brussels, 1989).

Yun, Isang, important Korean-born German composer and teacher; b. Tongyong, Sept. 17, 1917; d. Berlin, Nov. 3, 1995. He studied Western music in Korea (1935–37) and in Japan (1941–43). During World War II, he was active in the anti-Japanese underground; in 1943 he was imprisoned, and then spent the rest of the war in hiding until the liberation in 1945. He became a music teacher in Tongyong in 1946, and later taught in Pusan; in 1953 he became a prof. of composition at the Univ. of Seoul, then studied with Revel at the Paris Cons. (1956–57) and with Blacher, Rufer, and Schwarz-Schilling at the Berlin Hochschule für Musik (1958–59); he also attended the summer courses in new music in Darmstadt. He settled permanently in Berlin, where he produced several successful theatrical works, marked by a fine expressionistic and coloristic quality, and written in an idiom of euphonious dissonance. His career was dramatically interrupted when, on June 17, 1967, he and his wife were brutally abducted from West Berlin by secret police agents of South Korea, and forced to board a plane for Seoul, where they were brought to trial for sedition; he was sentenced to life imprisonment; his wife was given 3 years in jail. This act of lawlessness perpetrated on the territory of another country prompted an indignant protest by the government of West Germany, which threatened to cut off its substantial economic aid to South Korea; 23 celebrated musicians, including Stravinsky, issued a vigorous letter of protest. As a result of this moral and material pressure, South Korea released Yun and his wife after nearly 2 years of detention, and they returned to Germany. In 1969–70 he taught at the Hannover Hochschue für Musik. In 1970 he was appointed lecturer in composition at the Berlin Hochschule für Musik, where he was a prof. from 1973 to 1985. In 1971 he became a naturalized German citizen.

WORKS: OPERAS: *Der Traum des Liu-Tung* (Berlin, Sept. 25, 1965); *Träume* (1965–68; Nuremberg, Feb. 23, 1969; an amalgam of the preceding opera and the following one); *Die Witwe des Schmetterlings* (Bonn, Dec. 9, 1967; Eng. version as *Butterfly Widow*, Evanston, Ill., Feb. 27, 1970); *Geisterliebe* (1969–70; Kiel, June 20, 1971); *Sim Tjong* (1971–72; Munich, Aug. 1, 1972).

BIBL.: H.-W. Heister and W.-W. Sparrer, eds., *Der Komponist I. Y.* (Munich, 1987); H. Bergmeier, ed., *I. Y.: Festschrift zum 75. Geburtstag 1992* (Berlin, 1992).

Z

Zaccaria, Nicola (Angelo), Greek bass; b. Piraeus, March 9, 1923. He received training at the Royal Cons. in Athens. In 1949 he made his operatic debut as Raimondo in *Lucia di Lammermoor* at the Athens Opera. In 1953 he won the La Scala singing competition in Milan, where he made his first appearance as Sparafucile that same year; from then until 1974 he was a member of the company, singing many leading bass roles. He made his first appearance at the Vienna State Opera in 1956. In 1957 he made his debut at the Salzburg Festival as Don Fernando and at London's Covent Garden as Oroveso, where he sang again in 1959. In 1976 he appeared as King Marke in Dallas. He sang Colline in Macerata in 1982. His guest engagements also took him to such operatic centers as Cologne, Geneva, Moscow, Berlin, Edinburgh, Brussels, and Monte Carlo. In addition, he also appeared as a concert artist. Among his other roles were Sarastro, the Commendatore, Creon, Silva, Zaccaria, and Bellini's Rodolfo.

Zádor, Dezső, Hungarian baritone; b. Horna Krupa, March 8, 1873; d. Berlin, April 24, 1931. He studied in Budapest and Vienna. He made his debut as Almaviva in 1898 in Czernowitz, then sang in Elberfeld (1898–1901); he was subsequently a member of the Komische Oper in Berlin (1906–11). In 1911 he joined the Dresden Court Opera, singing there until 1916, then went to the Budapest Opera (1916–19); he was later a member of the Berlin Städtische Oper (1920–24). He made guest appearances at Covent Garden in London and in Paris, Milan, and Chicago. During the last years of his career, he sang bass roles.

Zador, Eugene (real name, **Jenő Zádor**), Hungarian-American composer; b. Bátaszék, Nov. 5, 1894; d. Los Angeles, April 4, 1977. He studied music with a local teacher. In 1911 he enrolled in the Vienna Cons., and studied composition with Heuberger. From 1912 to 1914 he was in Leipzig, where he took a course with Reger; he also attended classes in musicology with Abert and Schering; continued musicological studies with Volbach at the Univ. of Münster (Ph.D., 1921, with the diss. *Wesen und Form der symphonischen Dichtung von Liszt bis Strauss*). He settled in Vienna, and taught at the Neues Konservatorium there. Following the Anschluss of Austria by the Nazi regime in 1938, Zador emigrated to the United States; he settled in Hollywood, where he became successful and prosperous as an orchestrator of film scores; he made some 120 orchestrations in all; at the same time, he continued to compose music in every conceivable genre. Zador was a master of musical sciences, excelling in euphonious modern harmonies, and an expert weaver of contrapuntal voices; his colorful writing for instruments was exemplary. He possessed a special skill in handling Hungarian folk motifs in variation form; in this, he followed the tradition of Liszt. During his European period, he composed some fashionable "machine music," as demonstrated with particular effect in his *Sinfonia tecnica*.

WORKS: DRAMATIC: OPERAS: *Diana* (Budapest, Dec. 22, 1923); *A holtak szigete* (The Island of the Dead; Budapest, March 29, 1928); *Revisor* (The Inspector General; 1928; rev. and reorchestrated, Los Angeles, June 11, 1971); *X-mal Rembrandt* (referring to the multiple copies of Rembrandt's self-portraits; Gera, May 24, 1930); *Asra* (Budapest, Feb. 15, 1936); *Christoph Columbus* (N.Y., Oct. 8, 1939); *The Virgin and the Fawn* (Los Angeles, Oct. 24, 1964); *The Magic Chair* (Baton Rouge, La., May 14, 1966); *The Scarlet Mill* (N.Y., Oct. 26, 1968); *Yehu, a Christmas Legend* (1974). BALLET: *Maschinenmensch* (1934). ORATORIO: *The Judgement* (1974). MELODRAMA: *Cain* for Baritone, Chorus, and Orch. (1976); songs.

BIBL.: L. Zador, *E. Z.: A Catalogue of His Works* (San Diego, Calif., 1978).

Zafred, Mario, Italian conductor, music critic, and composer; b. Trieste, Feb. 21, 1922; d. Rome, May 22, 1987. He was a pupil of Pizzetti at the Accademia di Santa Cecilia in Rome. After serving as music critic of *Unità* (1949–56) and *Giustizia* (1956–63), he was active as a conductor. From 1968 to 1974 he was artistic director of the Rome Opera. In conformity with his communist convictions, he composed in an accessible style. Among his works are the operas *Amleto* (1961) and *Wallenstein* (1965).

Zagiba, Franz, eminent Austrian musicologist; b. Rosenau, Oct. 20, 1912; d. Vienna, Aug. 12,1977. He studied musicology with

Dobroslav Orel and received training in Hungarian and Slavonic studies at the Univ. of Bratislava (Ph.D., 1937, with the diss. *Denkmäler der Musik in den Franziskanerklöstern in der Ostslovakei*; publ. in Prague, 1940, as *Hudobné pamiatky františkánskych kláštorov na východnom Slovensku*); he completed his Habilitation in 1944 at the Univ. of Vienna with his *Geschichte der slowakischen Musik* (publ. in Bratislava, 1943, as *Dejiny slovenskj hudby od najstarších čias až do reformácie*). After serving as director of the musicological inst. of the Bratislava Academy of Sciences, he joined the faculty of the Univ. of Vienna in 1944, where he became a full prof. in 1972. In 1952 he founded the International Chopin Soc. His learned writings ranged from premedieval to 20th-century music.

WRITINGS: *Literárny a hudobný život v Rožňave v 18. a 19. storoči* (Literary and Musical Life in Roznava in the 18th and 19th Centuries; Košice, 1947); *Tvorba sovietskych komponistov* (The Music of Soviet Composers; Bratislava, 1947); *Chopin und Wien* (Vienna, 1951); *Tschaikowskij: Leben und Werk* (Vienna, 1953); *Die ältesten musikalischen Denkmäler zu Ehren des hl. Leopold: Ein Beitrag zur Choralpflege in Österreich am Ausgang des Mittelalters* (Vienna, 1954); *Johann L. Bella (1843–1936) und das Wiener Musikleben* (Vienna, 1955); *Das Geistesleben der Slaven im frühen Mittelalter: Die Anfänge des slavischen Schrifttums aus dem Gebiete des östlichen Mitteleuropa vom 8. bis 10. Jahrhundert* (Vienna, 1971); *Musikgeschichte Mitteleuropas von den Anfängen bis zum Ende des 10. Jahrhunderts* (Vienna, 1976).

Zagortsev, Vladimir, Russian composer; b. Kiev, Oct. 27, 1944. He studied composition with Liatoshinsky and Shtogarenko at the Kiev Cons. Upon graduation, he joined a group of Soviet avant-garde composers who were active in Kiev and who followed the Western techniques. Zagortsev set for himself the task of organizing the elements of pitch, rhythm, dynamics, and tone color in a total serial procedure, but he never abandoned the ethnic resources of Ukrainian folk songs, which remain the thematic source of many of his works, even those written in an extreme modern style. His works include an opera, *Mother* (1985).

Zagrosek, Lothar, German conductor; b. Waging, Nov. 13, 1942. After training in Munich and at the Essen Folkwangschule, he studied conducting with Swarowsky in Vienna; he also received guidance from Karajan, Kertesz, and Maderna. In 1967 he began his career, conducting opera in Salzburg, Kiel, and Darmstadt. In 1972 he became conductor in Solingen. He made his first appearance at the Salzburg Festival in 1973 conducting the Mozarteum Orch. In 1977 he became Generalmusikdirektor in Mönchengladbach. From 1978 he made frequent guest conducting appearances with the London Sinfonietta, establishing a fine reputation as an interpretor of contemporary music. From 1982 to 1987 he was chief conductor of the Austrian Radio Sym. Orch. in Vienna. He made appearances as a guest conductor in the United States from 1984. From 1986 to 1989 he was music director of the Paris Opéra. In 1987 he conducted *Così fan tutti* at the Glyndebourne Festival. He appeared with the English National Opera in London in 1989 conducting *Die Zauberflöte*. From 1990 to 1993 he was Generalmusikdirektor of the Leipzig Opera. He was Generalmusikdirektor of the Stuttgart Opera from 1998.

Zaidel-Rudolph, Jeanne, prominent South African composer; b. Pretoria, July 9, 1948. She began piano instruction at the age of 5 with her aunt, and in her youth began to appear publicly. In 1966 she entered the Univ. of Pretoria, where she studied composition with Johann Potgieter and Arthur Wegelin (B.Mus., 1969; M.Mus., 1972); in 1973 she studied in London with John Lambert (composition), John Lill (piano), and Tristam Carey (electronic music) at the Royal College of Music, where she won the R. O. Morris and Cobbett composition prizes. After further training in composition with Ligeti at the Hamburg Hochschule für Msuik (1974), she returned to South Africa and was a lecturer in the music dept. at the Univ. of the Witwatersand in Johannesburg from 1975 to 1977. She then studied for her D.Mus. degree under Stefans Grove at the Univ. of Pretoria, becoming the first woman in South African history to receive such a degree in composition in 1979. From 1978 to 1982 she again was a lecturer at the Univ. of the Witwatersand; after serving as head of music for the Performing Arts Workshop in Johannesburg (1983–84), she was senior lecturer at the Univ. of the Witwatersand (from 1985). She was also active as a pianist and organist, serving in the latter capacity at the Sydenham/Highlands North Synagogue in Johannesburg. While her compositions utilize various contemporary techniques, she has succeeded in finding a highly personal style, frequently melding Western and African elements. Her Jewish heritage is affirmed in many of her works as well, most notably in the inspiration she has found in the Bible and Jewish mysticism. Among her compositions are *Animal Farm*, opera (1978), *A Rage in a Cage*, rock opera (1983), *The River People—Abantubomlambo*, ballet (Durban, July 1987), and *African Dream*, film score (1988).

Zajc, Ivan. See **Zaytz, Giovanni von.**

Zajick (real name, **Zajic**), **Dolora,** American mezzo-soprano; b. Reno, Nevada, 1960. She took premed courses at the Univ. of Nevada and received some vocal instruction. After joining the Nevada Opera chorus, she studied voice with its artistic director, Ted Puffer. She began her career singing comprimario roles with the Nevada Opera before pursuing training at the Manhattan School of Music in New York. In 1982 she took the Bronze Medal at the Tchaikovsky Competition in Moscow. Following further studies with the San Francisco Opera Merola Program, she made her formal operatic debut as Azucena with the San Francisco Opera in 1985. In 1986 she won the Richard Tucker Award, and then sang at the Houston Grand Opera in 1987. She made her Metropolitan Opera debut in New York on Oct. 8, 1988, as Azucena. In 1989 she portrayed that role again at the Vienna State Opera and sang Amneris at the San Francisco Opera. She returned to San Francisco as Marfa in 1990, the same year she appeared as Amneris at the Lyric Opera of Chicago and as Azucena in Florence. In 1993 she sang Azucena in Barcelona. After singing Ulrica at the Metropolitan Opera in 1995, she returned there as Santuzza in 1997, the same year she appeared as Lady Macbeth in Hamburg. In 1999 she returned to the Metropolitan Opera as Amneris. She also appeared as a soloist with many orchs. and as a recitalist.

Zallinger, Meinhard von, Austrian conductor; b. Vienna, Feb. 25, 1897; d. Salzburg, Sept. 24, 1990. He studied piano and conducting at the Salzburg Mozarteum; he also took music courses at the Univ. of Innsbruck. He conducted at the Mozarteum (1920–22), then was on the staff of the Bavarian State Opera in Munich (1926–29) and the Cologne Opera (1929–35). He returned to the Bavarian State Opera in 1935, conducting there until 1944; he was then made Generalmusikdirektor in Duisburg. In 1947 he became director of the Mozarteum Orch.; he also held the same office at the Salzburg Landestheater. He was music director in Graz (1949–50), of the Vienna Volksoper (1950–53), and the Komische Oper in East Berlin (1953–56). He served again as a conductor at the Bavarian State Opera (1956–73) and was concurrently director of the summer academy at the Mozarteum (1956–68).

Zambello, Francesca, American opera producer; b. N.Y., Aug. 24, 1956. She was educated at Colgate Univ. (B.A., 1978) and received training in opera production from Jean-Pierre Ponnelle. After serving as assistant director at the Lyric Opera in Chicago (1981–82) and the San Francisco Opera (1983–84), she was co-artistic director of the Skylight Opera Theater in Milwaukee from 1985 to 1990. With Ponnelle, she collaborated on a staging of Rossini's *L'occasione fa il ladro* in Pesaro in 1987, a production later mounted at Milan's La Scala in 1989. Her *Beatrice di Tenda* was produced in Venice in 1987. She staged the U.S. premiere of Stephen Oliver's *Mario and the Magician* in Milwaukee in 1989. In 1990 she secured her reputation as one of the leading opera producers of her era with a staging of *War and Peace* in Seattle. In 1991 she produced *Les Troyens* in Los Angeles, and, that same year, became the first American producer to work at the Bolshoi Theater in Moscow where she staged *Turandot*. In 1992 she produced *Lucia di Lammermoor* at the Metropolitan Opera in New

York. She was engaged to stage the premiere of Goehr's *Arianna* at the English National Opera in London in 1995. After producing *Iphigénie en Tauride* at the Glimmerglass Opera in New York in 1997, she mounted *Tristan und Isolde* in Seattle in 1998.

Zamboni, Luigi, noted Italian bass; b. Bologna, 1767; d. Florence, Feb. 28, 1837. He made his debut in 1791 in Ravenna in *Fanatico in Berlina* by Cimarosa, then sang throughout Italy, establishing himself as one of the finest interpreters of buffo roles of his time; in 1816 he created the role of Figaro in Rossini's *Il Barbiere di Siviglia*. He retired from the stage in 1825.

Zandonai, Riccardo, Italian composer; b. Sacco di Rovereto, Trentino, May 30, 1883; d. Pesaro, June 5, 1944. He was a pupil of Gianferrari at Rovereto (1893–98), then studied with Mascagni at the Liceo Rossini in Pesaro. He graduated in 1902; for his final examination he composed a symphonic poem for Solo Voices, Chorus, and Orch., *Il ritorno di Odisseo*. He then turned to opera, which remained his favored genre throughout his career. His first opera was *La coppa del re* (c.1906), which was never performed. After writing the children's opera *L'uccelino d'oro* (Sacco di Rovereto, 1907), he won notable success with his third opera, *Il grillo del focolare*, after Dickens's *The Cricket on the Hearth* (Turin, Nov. 28, 1908). With his next opera, *Conchita*, after the novel *La Femme et le pantin* by Pierre Louÿs (Milan, Oct. 14, 1911), he established himself as an important Italian composer; the title role was created by the soprano Tarquinia Tarquini, whom Zandonai married in 1917. *Conchita* received its American premiere in San Francisco on Sept. 28, 1912; as *La Femme et le pantin* it was given at the Opéra Comique in Paris on March 11, 1929. Zandonai's reputation was enhanced by subsequent works, notably *Francesca da Rimini*, after Gabriele d'Annunzio (Turin, Feb. 19, 1914; Metropolitan Opera, N.Y., Dec. 22, 1916), but a previous opera, *Melenis* (Milan, Nov. 13, 1912), was unsuccessful. During World War I, Zandonai participated in the political agitation for the return of former Italian provinces; he wrote a student hymn calling for the redemption of Trieste (1915). His other operas were *La via della finestra* (Pesaro, July 27, 1919; rev. version, Trieste, Jan. 18, 1923); *Giulietta e Romeo* (Rome, Feb. 14, 1922); *I Cavalieri di Ekebù* (Milan, March 7, 1925); *Giuliano* (Naples, Feb. 4, 1928); *Una partita* (Milan, Jan. 19, 1933); *La farsa amorosa*, after Alarcón's *El sombrero de tres picos* (Rome, Feb. 22, 1933); *Il bacio* (1940–44; unfinished). In 1939 he was appointed director of the Liceo Rossini in Pesaro, remaining there for the rest of his life.

BIBL.: V. Bonajuti Tarquini, *R. Z. nel ricordo dei suoi intimi* (Milan, 1951); G. Barblan, R. Mariani, et al., *A R. Z.* (Trento, 1952); B. Cagnoli, *R. Z.* (Trento, 1978); R. Chiesa, ed., *R. Z.* (Milan, 1984); A. Bassi, *R. Z.* (Milan, 1989).

Zandt, Marie Van. See **Van Zandt, Marie.**

Zanella, Amilcare, Italian composer, pianist, conductor, and pedagogue; b. Monticelli d'Ongina, Piacenza, Sept. 26, 1873; d. Pesaro, Jan. 9, 1949. He studied with Andreotti in Cremona, then with Bottesini at the Parma Cons., graduating in 1891. In 1892 he went to South America as a pianist and opera conductor; returning to Italy in 1901, he organized his own orch., giving sym. concerts in the principal Italian cities and introducing his own works. He then was director of the Parma Cons. (1903–05) and the Liceo Rossini in Pesaro (1905–39); he also served as pianist of the Trio di Pesaro (1927–49). Among his works were the operas *Aura* (Pesaro, Aug. 27, 1910), *La Sulamita* (Piacenza, Feb. 11, 1926), and *Il Revisore*, after Gogol (1938; Trieste, Feb. 20, 1940).

BIBL.: *A. Z.: Artista, uomo, educatore* (Ferrara, 1932); A. Dioli and M. Nobili, *La vita e l'arte di A. Z.* (Bergamo, 1941).

Zanelli (Morales), Renato, esteemed Chilean baritone, later tenor; b. Valparaiso, April 1, 1892; d. Santiago, March 25, 1935. After studies in Neuchâtel and Turin, he pursued a business career in his homeland; his voice was discovered by Angelo Querez, who became his mentor in Santiago; he made his debut as a baritone there as Valentine in 1916. On Nov. 19, 1919, he appeared for the first time with the Metropolitan Opera in New York as Amonasro; he remained on its roster until 1923; he then went to Milan, where he resumed vocal studies; he made his debut as a tenor in the role of Raoul at the Teatro San Carlo in Naples in 1924; he subsequently appeared in Rome, in London (Covent Garden, 1928–30), at La Scala in Milan (1920–32), and at the Teatro Colón in Buenos Aires. He won great distinction with his portrayals of Otello, Lohengrin, and Tristan.

Zanettini, Antonio. See **Gianettini, Antonio.**

Zanten, Cornelie Van. See **Van Zanten, Cornelie.**

Zarinš, Margeris, Latvian composer; b. Jaunpiebalga, May 24, 1910. He studied composition in Riga with Wihtol at the Latvian Cons. (1929–33); he also took lessons in piano and organ. From 1940 to 1950 he was director of music of the Latvian Art Theater. From 1956 to 1968 he was secretary-general of the Union of Latvian Composers. In his works, he stylized the elements of Latvian folk songs. He was particularly successful in his operas on contemporary subjects, often with a satirical tilt. In his *Opera uz lankuma* (Opera in the Town Square; 1970), he attempted to revive the early Soviet attempts to bring theatrical spectacles into the streets.

WORKS: OPERAS: *Kungs un spēlmanitis* (The King and the Little Musician; 1939); *Uz jauno krastu* (To New Shores; 1955); *Zalās dzirnavas* (The Green Mill; 1958); *Nabaqu opera* (Beggar's Opera; 1964); *Sveta Mauricija brinumdarbs* (Miracle of St. Mauritius; 1964); *Opera uz lankuma* (Opera in the Town Square; 1970). Also several oratorios, including *Valmieras varoni* (The Heroes of Valmiera; 1950) and *Mahagoni* (Mahagonny), a propaganda work denouncing the Western colonial policies in Africa (1965).

BIBL.: L. Krasinska, *M. Z.* (Riga, 1960).

Zaslaw, Neal (Alexander), American musicologist; b. N.Y., June 28, 1939. He studied at Harvard Univ. (B.A., 1961), then took flute lessons at the Juilliard School of Music (M.S., 1963); subsequently he studied musicology with Paul Henry Lang at Columbia Univ. (M.A., 1965; Ph.D., 1970, with the diss. *Materials for the Life and Works of Jean-Marie Leclair l'Aine*). He taught at City College of the City Univ. of N.Y. (1968–70); in 1970 he joined the faculty of Cornell Univ. He was ed.-in-chief of *Current Musicology* (1967–70). Zaslaw publ. the vols. *Edward A. MacDowell* (N.Y., 1964) and *Mozart's Symphonies: Context, Performance Practice, Reception* (Oxford, 1990). With W. Cowdery, he ed. *The Complete Mozart: A Guide to the Musical Works of Wolfgang Amadeus Mozart* (N.Y., 1991) and with F. Fein he ed. *The Mozart Repertory: A Guide for Musicians, Programmers, and Researchers* (Ithaca, N.Y., 1991). In 1995 he became editor of the 7th ed. of the Mozart Köchel catalog.

Zavertal, Ladislaw (Joseph Philip Paul; actually, **Josef Filip Pavel),** Czech-born English conductor and composer; b. Milan, Sept. 29, 1849; d. Cadenabbia, Jan. 29, 1942. He was the son of the conductor and composer Wenceslaw (Václav) Hugo Zavrtal (b. Polepy, Aug. 31, 1821; d. Leitmeritz, Sept. 8, 1899) and nephew of the conductor and composer Josef Rudolf Zavrtal (b. Polepy, Nov. 5, 1819; d. Leitmeritz, May 3, 1893). He began his musical training with his father and his mother, the soprano Carlotta Maironi da Ponte, then studied violin with Tosti at the Naples Cons. His first opera, *Tita*, was orchestrated by his father and premiered in Treviso (May 29, 1870); in 1871 he went to Milan as music director of the Teatro Milanese. That same year he went to Glasgow, where he conducted various orch. groups; in 1881 he became bandmaster of the Royal Artillery Band at Woolwich; then was active in London, where he conducted concerts at St. James's Hall and Queen's Hall (1889–95) and Sunday concerts at the Royal Albert Hall (1895–1905); in 1896 he became a British subject; in 1906 he retired to Italy.

WORKS: OPERAS: *Tita* (Treviso, May 29, 1870; orchestrated by his father; rev. 1880 as *Adriana, ovvero Il burratinaro di Venezia*); *I tre perucchi* (Milan, 1871); *La sura palmira sposa* (Milan, 1872); *Una notte à Firenze* (1872–73; in Czech as *Noc ve Florence*, Prague, March 20, 1880); *A Lesson in Magic* (1880; Woolwich, April 27, 1883; rev. as *Love's Magic*, 1889; Woolwich, Feb. 18, 1890); *Mirra* (1882–83; in Czech, Prague, Nov. 7, 1886).

BIBL.: A. Faraone, *Il Commendatore Ladislao Z.* (Treviso, 1929); H. Farmer, *Ladislao Z.: His Life and Work* (London, 1949).

Zaytz, Giovanni von (real name, **Ivan Zajc**), Croatian composer; b. Fiume, Aug. 3, 1831; d. Zagreb, Dec. 16, 1914. He was trained by his father, a bandmaster in the Austrian army, then at the Milan Cons. with Stefano Ronchetti-Monteviti, Lauro Rossi, and Alberto Mazzucato (1850–55). Returning to Fiume, he conducted the municipal band, then was a theater conductor in Vienna (1862–70). Upon entering professional life, he changed his name to Giovanni von Zaytz. In 1870 he settled in Zagreb; he was conductor of the Zagreb Opera (1870–89) and director of the Cons. there (until 1908). He composed about 1,200 works of all descriptions (among them 20 operas), and was the author of the first Croatian national opera, *Nikola Šubrič Zrinski* (Zagreb, Nov. 4, 1876). He also wrote several Italian operas, of which *Amelia, ossia Il Bandito* (Fiume, April 14, 1860) enjoyed considerable popularity. Other operas and operettas (all first perf. in Vienna) were *Mannschaft an Bord* (Dec. 15, 1863), *Fitzliputzli* (Nov. 5, 1864), *Die Lazzaroni vom Stanzel* (May 4, 1865), *Die Hexe von Boissy* (April 24, 1866), *Nachtschwärmer* (Nov. 10, 1866), *Das Rendezvous in der Schweiz* (April 3, 1867), *Das Gaugericht* (Sept. 14, 1867), *Nach Mekka* (Jan. 11, 1868), *Somnambula* (Jan. 21, 1868), *Schützen von Einst und Jetzt* (July 25, 1868), *Meister Puff* (May 22, 1869), and *Der gefangene Amor* (Sept. 12, 1874). In addition, he wrote incidental music for 22 plays.

BIBL.: A. Goglia, *I. Z.* (Zagreb, 1932); H. Pettan, *I. Z.* (Zagreb, 1971).

Zbinden, Julien-François, Swiss composer, pianist, and administrator; b. Rolle, Nov. 11, 1917. He began piano lessons at the age of 8 and later attended the Lausanne Cons. He also studied at the teacher's training college in the canton of Vaud (1934–38; graduated, 1938), and then was active as a pianist. After teaching himself harmony, form, and composition, he pursued training in counterpoint and orchestration with Gerber. In 1947 he joined Radio Lausanne as a pianist and music producer, becoming head of the music dept. in 1956. From 1965 to 1982 he was deputy director of musical broadcasts of the Radio-Télévision Suisse Romande. He served as president of the Swiss Musicians Assn. (1973–79) and of SUISA (the Swiss music copyright society; 1987–91). In 1978 the French government made him an Officier de l'ordre des Arts et des Lettres. His early love of jazz, as well as the influence of Ravel, Stravinsky, and Honegger, was an important factor in the development of his own musical style. Among his works were *La Pantoufle*, farce-ballet (1958), *Fait divers*, opera (1960), and radiophonic scores; also *Terra Dei*, oratorio for Soloists, Chorus, and Orch. (1966–67).

BIBL.: C. Tappolet, *J.-F. Z., compositeur* (1994).

Zeani (real name, **Zahan**), **Virginia,** Romanian soprano; b. Solovastru, Oct. 21, 1928. She studied in Bucharest with Lipkowska and with Pertile in Milan. She made her operatic debut as Violetta in Bologna in 1948, then sang in London (1953), in Rome, at La Scala in Milan (1956), and at Covent Garden in London (1959). She made her Metropolitan Opera debut in New York as Violetta on Nov. 12, 1966, where she sang for only one season. In 1980 she joined the faculty of the Indiana Univ. School of Music in Bloomington, where she was made a Distinguished Prof. in 1994 and Prof. Emeritus in 1995. She married **Nicola Rossi-Lemeni** in 1958. Among her finest roles were Lucia, Elvira, Maria di Rohan, Desdemona, Aida, Leonora, and Tosca.

Zech, Frederick, Jr., American pianist and composer; b. Philadelphia, May 10, 1858; d. San Francisco, Oct. 25, 1926. After preliminary training as a pianist in San Francisco he went to Berlin, where he studied at Kullak's Music School (1878–82). Returning to San Francisco, he held classes in advanced piano playing; he also was director-conductor of his own sym. concerts (1902–03). Among his works were the operas *La Paloma, or The Cruise of the Excelsior* (San Francisco, 1896) and *Wa-Kin-Yon, or The Passing of the Red Man* (San Francisco, 1914).

Zechlin, Ruth, German composer, pedagogue, and harpsichordist; b. Grosshartmannsdorf, June 22, 1926. She studied at the Leipzig Hochschule für Musik (1943–45; 1946–49), where her mentors included J. N. David and Wilhelm Weismann (composition), Anton Rohden and Rudolf Fischer (piano), and Karl Straube and Günther Ramin (organ). In 1950 she went to East Berlin as a teacher at the Hochschule für Musik, and then was a prof. of composition at that city's Hanns Eisler Hochschule für Musik from 1969 to 1986. In 1970 she was made a member of the Akademie der Künste of the German Democratic Republic. From 1990 to 1993 she was vice president of the Akademie der Künste in Berlin. Among her honors were the Goethe Prize of the City of Berlin (1962), as well as the Arts Prize (1965) and 2 National Prizes (1975, 1982) of the German Democratic Republic.

WORKS: DRAMATIC: *Reineke Fuchs*, opera (1967; Berlin, April 1968); *La Vita*, ballet (1983; Berlin, Feb. 2, 1985); *Sommernachtsträume* or *Die Salamandrin und die Bildsäule* (1990); *Die Reise*, chamber opera (1992; Leipzig, Dec. 1994); *Un baiser pour le Roi*, dance piece (Passau, June 16, 1995).

Zeckwer, Camille, American pianist, teacher, and composer; b. Philadelphia, June 26, 1875; d. Southampton, N.Y., Aug. 7, 1924. He was educated by his father, the German-American pianist, teacher, and composer Richard Zeckwer (1850–1922), and also had composition lessons in New York with Dvořák (1893–95), then went to Berlin and studied with Philipp Scharwenka. Returning to Philadelphia, he was active mainly as a teacher. Among his works is an opera, *Jane and Janetta*, which was not produced.

Zedda, Alberto, Italian conductor and musicologist; b. Milan, Jan. 2, 1928. He studied organ with Galliera, conducting with Votto and Giulini, and composition with Fait at the Milan Cons. In 1956 he made his debut as a conductor in Milan. He subsequently went to the United States, where he taught at the Cincinnati College of Music (1957–59). Returning to Europe, he conducted at the Deutsche Oper in West Berlin (1961–63), then conducted at the N.Y. City Opera. With Philip Gossett, he served as coed. of the complete works of Rossini. Zedda was artistic director of the Teatro Comunale in Genoa in 1992 and of Milan's La Scala in 1992–93.

Zednik, Heinz, Austrian tenor; b. Vienna, Feb. 21, 1940. He was a student of Marga Wissmann at the Vienna Cons. In 1963 he made his operatic debut as Trabuco in *La forza del destino* in Graz. In 1965 he became a member of the Vienna State Opera, where he created the role of Kalb in Einem's *Kabale und Liebe* in 1976. His guest engagements took him to such operatic centers as Munich, Paris, Nice, Moscow, and Montreal. In 1970 he made his first appearance at the Bayreuth Festival as David in *Die Meistersinger von Nürnberg*, and he returned there to sing Loge and Mime in the centenary *Ring* cycle in 1976. In 1980 he was made an Austrian Kammersänger. For his first appearance at the Salzburg Festival (1981), he sang Bardolfo in *Falstaff*. On Sept. 22, 1981, he made his Metropolitan Opera debut in New York as Mime in *Das Rheingold*. He returned to Salzburg to create the roles of the Regisseur in Berio's *Un re in ascolto* (1984) and Hadank in Penderecki's *Die schwarze Maske* (1986). In 1987 he appeared as Pedrillo at the Metropolitan Opera, and returned there during the 1989–90 season as Mime. In 1996 he sang Baron Laur in Weill's *Silbersee* at the London Promenade Concerts.

Zeffirelli, Franco (real name, **Gian Franco Corsi**), prominent Italian opera director and designer; b. Florence, Feb. 12, 1923. He began his career as an actor, and then became an assistant to Visconti. His first operatic production was *La Cenerentola* at Milan's La Scala (1953). In 1958 he mounted *La Traviata* in Dallas, and in 1959 *Lucia di Lammermoor* at London's Covent Garden, where he later produced *Falstaff* (1961), *Alcina* and *Don Giovanni* (1962), and *Tosca*. He also worked at the Metropolitan Opera in New York, where he was chosen to produce Barber's *Antony and Cleopatra* as the opening work at the new house at

Lincoln Center in 1966. In later years, he devoted himself to operatic film productions, winning particular acclaim for his filming of *La Traviata* (1983) and *Otello* (1986); he also brought out the film biography *The Young Toscanini* (1988).

Zeidman, Boris, Russian composer and pedagogue; b. St. Petersburg, Feb. 10, 1908; d. Tashkent, Dec. 30, 1981. He studied composition at the Leningrad Cons. with Maximilian Steinberg, graduating in 1931, then taught music in various schools in Russia, Azerbaijan, and Uzbekistan. Among his works were the operas *The People's Wrath* (Baku, Dec. 28, 1941), *Son of the Regiment* (Baku, Feb. 23, 1955), *Zainab and Omon* (1958), and *The Russians* (1970), and the ballets *The Gold Key* (1955) and *The Dragon and the Sun* (1964).

Zeisl, Eric(h), Austrian-born American composer; b. Vienna, May 18, 1905; d. Los Angeles, Feb. 18, 1959. A son of prosperous parents who owned a coffeehouse, he entered the Vienna Academy of Music at 14; he was a pupil of Richard Stöhr, Joseph Marx, and Hugo Kauder; publ. his first songs at 16. In 1934 he won the Austrian State Prize for his *Requiem concertante*. After the seizure of Austria by the Nazis in 1938, he fled to Paris, and at the outbreak of World War II in 1939, went to the United States; in 1941 he settled in Los Angeles; in 1945 he became a naturalized American citizen. He taught at the Southern Calif. School of Music; from 1949 until his death he was on the staff at Los Angeles City College. Increasingly conscious in exile of his Jewish heritage, he selected biblical themes for his stage works; death interrupted the composition of his major work, the music drama *Job*; Hebraic cantillation is basic to this period. His style of composition reflects the late Romantic school of Vienna, imbued with poetic melancholy, with relief provided by eruptions of dancing optimism. He was at his best in his song cycles.

WORKS: DRAMATIC: *Die Fahrt ins Wunderland*, children's opera (Vienna, 1934); *Leonce und Lena*, Singspiel (1937; Los Angeles, 1952); *Job*, opera (1939–41; 1957–59; unfinished); *Pierrot in der Flasche*, ballet (Vienna Radio, 1935); *Uranium 235*, ballet (1946); *Naboth's Vineyard*, ballet (1953); *Jacob und Rachel*, ballet (1954).

BIBL.: M. Cole and B. Barclay, *Armseelchen: The Life and Music of E. Z.* (Westport, Conn., 1984).

Zelenka, Jan Dismas (Lukáš), distinguished Bohemian composer; b. Lounovice, Oct. 16, 1679; d. Dresden, Dec. 22, 1745. He is believed to have studied theory at the Jesuit College Clementinum in Prague, then was in the service of Count Hartig in Prague (1709–10). In 1710 he became a double-bass player in the Dresden Court Orch.; while traveling with the orch., he pursued studies with Fux in Vienna (1715) and with Lotti in Venice (1716); after another sojourn in Vienna (1717–19), he resumed his duties in Dresden, where he later became assistant to the ailing Kapellmeister Heinischen. Upon the latter's death in 1733, J. A. Hasse was named his successor, and the disappointed Zelenka had to wait until 1735 before he received recognition as Kirchen-compositeur. Zelenka was admired by Bach and Telemann. He wrote a large body of sacred vocal music, including the oratorios *Il serpente di bronzo* (1730), *Gesù al Calvario* (1735), and *I Penitenti al sepolchro del Redentore* (1736). His festival opera, *Sub olea pacis et palma virtutis conspicua Orbi regia Bohemia corona or Melodrama de Sancto Wenceslao*, was premiered in Prague on Nov. 12, 1723.

BIBL.: N. Schulzt, *J. D. Z.* (diss., Univ. of Berlin, 1944); W. Reich, *Zwei Z.-Stücken* (Dresden, 1987); W. Horn and T. Kohlhase, *Z.-Dokumentation, Quellen und Materialien* (2 vols., Wiesbaden, 1989); T. Kohlhase, ed., *Z.-Studien I* (Kassel, 1993).

Zelenski, Wladislaw, Polish composer and pedagogue; b. Grodkowice, near Kraków, July 6, 1837; d. Kraków, Jan. 23, 1921. He studied violin with Wojciechowski, then received training in piano from Germasz and in composition from Mirecki in Krakow (1854–59); in 1859 he entered the Jagiellonian Univ. in Prague as a philosophy student (Ph.D., 1862), and pursued training in piano with Dreyschock and in organ and counterpoint with J. Kreiči. After further studies with N. H. Reber at the Paris Cons. (1866), he completed his musical training with Damcke (1868–70). He taught at the Warsaw Music Inst. (1872–81), where he also was music director of the music society. In 1881 he organized the Kraków Cons., and remained its director until his death; he also taught piano and theory there. As a pedagogue, he enjoyed a very high reputation; among his pupils were Stojowski, Opieński, and Szopski. Among his works were the operas *Konrad Wallenrod* (Lemberg, Feb. 26, 1885), *Goplana* (Kraków, July 23, 1896), *Janek* (Lemberg, Oct. 4, 1900), and *Stara baśń* (Lemberg, March 14, 1907).

BIBL.: F. Szopski, *W. Z.* (Warsaw, 1928); Z. Jachimecki, *W. Z.: Zycie i twórczość, 1837–1921* (Kraków, 1952).

Zelinka, Jan Evangelista, Czech composer; b. Prague, Jan. 13, 1893; d. there, June 30, 1969. He studied music with his father, the organist and composer, Jan Evangelista Zelinka (1856–1935), and later with J. B. Foerster, Suk, Novák, and Ostrčil.

WORKS: DRAMATIC: OPERAS: *Dceruška hostinského* (The Tavernkeeper's Little Daughter; 1921; Prague, Feb. 24, 1925); *Devátá louka* (The 9th Meadow; 1929; Prague, Sept. 19, 1931); *Odchod dona Quijota* (Departure of Don Quixote; 1936); *Paličatý švec* (The Stubborn Cobbler; 1940; Prague, March 28, 1944); *Meluzína* (The Wailing Wind; 1947; Plzeň, April 15, 1950); *Námluvy bez konce* (Endless Wooing), radio opera (Czech Radio, Jan. 27, 1950); *Masopustní noc* (Shrovetide Night; 1956); *Lásky žal i smích* (Love's Woe and Laughter), after Goldoni (1958); *Škola pro ženy* (School for Wives), after Molière (1959); *Blouznivé jaro* (A Fanciful Spring; 1960); *Dřevěný kůň* (The Wooden Horse; 1962–63). BALLET PANTOMIME: *Skleněná panna* (The Glass Doll; 1927; Prague, July 2, 1928). SCENIC MELODRAMA: *Srdce na prázdninách* (Heart on a Fishhook; 1932; Brno, Jan. 28, 1938). Also incidental music.

Zeller, Carl (Johann Adam), Austrian composer; b. St. Peter-in-der-Au, June 19, 1842; d. Baden, near Vienna, Aug. 17, 1898. He learned to sing and play various instruments in his youth, and at age 11 became a member of the boy's choir at the Vienna court chapel; he pursued training in law at the Univ. of Vienna and the Univ. of Graz (Dr.Jur., 1869) and in composition from Simon Sechter in Vienna. After practicing law, he was an official in the Austrian Ministry of Education and Culture (from 1873). Although following music only as an avocation, he became one of the most popular operetta composers of the day, winning extraordinary success with his *Der Vogelhändler* (Vienna, Jan. 10, 1891) and *Der Obersteiger* (Vienna, Jan. 5, 1894). Other successful operettas (all produced in Vienna) were *Joconda* (March 18, 1876), *Die Carbonari* (Nov. 27, 1880), *Der Vagabund* (Oct. 30, 1886), and *Der Kellermeister* (Dec. 21, 1901).

BIBL.: C.W. Zeller, *Mein Vater C. Z.* (St. Pölten, 1942).

Zemlinsky, Alexander von, important Austrian composer and conductor of partly Jewish descent (he removed the nobiliary particle "von" in 1918 when such distinctions were outlawed in Austria); b. Vienna, Oct. 14, 1871; d. Larchmont, N.Y., March 15, 1942. At the Vienna Cons. he studied piano with Door (1887–90) and composition with Krenn, Robert Fuchs, and J. N. Fuchs (1890–92). In 1893 he joined the Vienna Tonkünstlerverein. In 1895 he became connected with the orch. society Polyhymnia, and met Schoenberg, whom he advised on the technical aspects of chamber music; Schoenberg always had the highest regard for Zemlinsky as a composer and lamented the lack of appreciation for Zemlinsky's music. There was also a personal bond between them; in 1901 Schoenberg married Zemlinsky's sister Mathilde. Zemlinsky's first opera, *Sarema*, to a libretto by his own father, was premiered in Munich on Oct. 10, 1897; Schoenberg made a Klavierauszug of it. Zemlinsky also entered into contact with Mahler, music director of the Vienna Court Opera, who accepted Zemlinsky's opera *Es war einmal* for performance; Mahler conducted its premiere at the Court Opera on Jan. 22, 1900, and it became Zemlinsky's most popular production. From 1900 to 1906 Zemlinsky served as conductor of the Karlstheater in Vienna; in 1903 he conducted at the Theater an der Wien; in 1904 he was named chief conductor of the Volksoper; in 1910 he orchestrated and conducted the ballet *Der Schneemann* by the greatly talented 11-

year-old wunderkind Erich Korngold. About that time, he and Schoenberg organized in Vienna the Union of Creative Musicians, which performed his tone poem *Die Seejungfrau*. In 1911 Zemlinsky moved to Prague, where he became conductor at the German Opera, and also taught conducting and composition at the German Academy of Music (from 1920). In 1927 he moved to Berlin, where he obtained the appointment of assistant conductor at the Kroll Opera, with Otto Klemperer as chief conductor and music director. When the Nazis came to power in Germany in 1933, he returned to Vienna, and also filled engagements as a guest conductor in Russia and elsewhere. After the Anschluss of 1938, he emigrated to America. As a composer, Zemlinsky followed the post–Romantic trends of Mahler and Richard Strauss. He was greatly admired but his works were seldom performed, despite the efforts of Schoenberg and his associates to revive his music. How strongly he influenced his younger contemporaries is illustrated by the fact that Alban Berg quoted some of Zemlinsky's music from the *Lyric Symphony* in his own *Lyrische Suite*.

WORKS: DRAMATIC: OPERAS: *Sarema* (1894–95; Munich, Oct. 10, 1897); *Es war einmal* (1897–99; Vienna, Jan. 22, 1900); *Der Traumgörge* (1903–06; Nuremberg, Oct. 11, 1980); *Kleider machen Leute* (1907–10; Vienna, Dec. 2, 1910; rev. 1921); *Eine florentinische Tragödie* (1915–16; Stuttgart, Jan. 30, 1917); *Der Zwerg*, after Oscar Wilde's *The Birthday of the Infanta* (1920–21; Cologne, May 28, 1922); *Der Kreidekreis* (1930–32; Zürich, Oct. 14, 1933); *Der König Kandaules* (1935–36; left in short score; completed by A. Beaumont, 1989; Hamburg, Oct. 6, 1996); also 5 unfinished operas: *Malwa* (1902; 1912–13), *Herrn Arnes Schatz* (1917), *Raphael* (1918), *Vitalis* (1926), and *Circe* (1939–41). MIMODRAMA: Ein Lichtstrahl (1903). BALLET: *Das gläsende Herz*, after Hofmannsthal (1901). INCIDENTAL MUSIC TOShakespeare's *Cymbeline* (1914).

BIBL.: H. Weber, *A. Z.: Eine Studie* (Vienna, 1977); O. Biba, *A. Z.: Bin ich ein Wiener?: Ausstellung im Archiv der Gesellschaft der Musikfreunde in Wien: Katalog* (Vienna, 1992).

Zenatello, Giovanni, Italian tenor; b. Verona, Feb. 22, 1876; d. N.Y., Feb. 11, 1949. He was originally trained as a baritone by Zannoni and Moretti in Verona. He made his official operatic debut as such in Belluno in 1898 as Silvio in Pagliacci; he sang in minor opera companies in Italy, then went to Naples, where he sang the tenor role of Canio in 1899. He sang the role of Pinkerton in the first performance of Puccini's *Madama Butterfly* (La Scala, Milan, Feb. 17, 1904). In 1905 he sang at Covent Garden, London. On Nov. 4, 1907, he made his American debut in New York as Enzo Grimaldo in Ponchielli's *La Gioconda*. From 1909 to 1912, and again in 1913–14, he was the leading tenor of the Boston Opera Co.; during the season of 1912–13, he sang with the Chicago Opera Co; he also traveled with various touring opera companies in South America, Spain, and Russia. He eventually settled in New York as a singing teacher, maintaining a studio with his wife, **Maria Gay**, whom he married in 1913. Together, they trained many famous singers, among them Lily Pons and Nino Martini. He retired from the stage in 1928.

Zender, (Johannes Wolfgang) Hans, German conductor, teacher, and composer; b. Wiesbaden, Nov. 22, 1936. He studied at the Frankfurt am Main Hochschule für Musik (1956–59), and then was a student of Fortner and Picht-Axenfeld at the Freiburg im Breisgau Hochschule für Musik. From 1959 to 1963 he was a conductor at the Freiburg im Breisgau City Theater. After further training with Zimmermann in Rome (1963), he was chief conductor of the Bonn City Theater (1964–68). From 1969 to 1972 he was Generalmusikdirektor of Kiel. He was chief conductor of the Saarland Radio Sym. Orch. in Saarbrücken from 1972 to 1984. From 1984 to 1987 he was Generalmusikdirektor of the Hamburg State Opera and Phil. In 1987 he was chief conductor of Radio Hilversum in the Netherlands. From 1988 he was prof. of composition at the Frankfurt am Main Hochschule für Musik. He publ. the vol. *Happy New Ears: Das Abenteuer, Musik zu horen* (Freiburg im Breisgau, 1991). In his compositions, he pursued advanced avenues of expression. His works include *Stephen Climax*, opera (1979–84; Frankfurt am Main, June 15, 1986; concert version as *Dubliner Nachtszenen*, 1987–89), and *Don Quijote*, theatrical adventure (1993).

Zenger, Max, German composer and conductor; b. Munich, Feb. 2, 1837; d. there, Nov. 18, 1911. He studied in Munich and Leipzig, and in 1860 became a theater conductor in Regensburg. In 1869 he became music director of the Munich Court Opera, then was court conductor at Karlsruhe (1872–78) and conductor of the Munich Oratorio Soc. (1878–85) as well as other choral societies in Munich. He wrote *Entstehung und Entwicklung der Instrumentalmusik* (Langensalza, 1906) and *Geschichte der Münchener Oper* (ed. by T. Kroyer, 1923). His works included the operas *Die Foscari* (Munich, 1863), *Ruy Blas* (Mannheim, 1868), *Wieland der Schmied* (Munich, 1880; rev. 1894), and *Eros und Psyche* (Munich, 1901), the oratorio, *Kain*, after Byron (Munich, 1867), and 2 ballets for King Ludwig II of Bavaria, *Venus und Adonis* and *Les Plaisirs de l'île enchantée* (1881); also 2 Gretchen scenes from *Faust* for Soprano and Small Orch. and *Die Kraniche des Ibikus*, melodrama with Orch.

Zeno, Apostolo, famous Italian opera librettist; b. Venice, Dec. 11, 1668; d. there, Nov. 11, 1750. In 1710 he founded the Giornale dei Letterati d'Italia, and in 1718 he was appointed court poet at Vienna; returned to Venice in 1729. The total number of librettos written by him (some in collaboration with Pietro Pariati) is 71; they were collected and ed. by Gasparo Gozzi as *Poesie drammatiche di Apostolo Zeno* (10 vols., Venice, 1744; reprinted in 11 vols., Orléans, 1785–86). A man of great knowledge and culture, he was also an ardent numismatist; his large collection of coins was exhibited at Vienna in 1955.

BIBL.: M. Fehr, *A. Z. und seine Reform des Operntexts* (diss., Univ. of Zürich, 1912); R. Freeman, *Opera Without Drama: Currents of Change in Italian Opera, 1675–1725, and the Roles Played therein by Z., Caldara, and Others* (diss., Princeton Univ., 1967).

Zepler, Bogumil, German composer; b. Breslau, May 6, 1858; d. Krummhübel im Riesengebirge, Aug. 17, 1918. He studied architecture in Berlin, then medicine at the Univ. of Breslau (M.D., 1884); later he began the study of music with H. Urban in Berlin. He attracted attention in 1891 with *Cavalleria Bero lina*, a parody on Mascagni's *Cavalleria rusticana*; he wrote stage music for Ernst von Wolzogen's artistic cabaret, "Uberbrettl" (1901–02); he also wrote a parody on Strauss's *Salome*. He further composed the comic operas *Der Brautmarkt zu Hira* (Berlin, 1892), *Der Vicomte von Letorières* (Hamburg, 1899), *Die Bader von Lucca* (Berlin, 1905), and *Monsieur Bonaparte* (Leipzig, 1911), several operettas (*Diogenes, Pick und Pocket, Die Liebesfestung*, etc.), a serious 1-act opera, *Nacht* (Bern, 1901), and 2 pantomimes: *Die Galgenfrist* and *Die Geisterbraut*.

Zhelobinsky, Valeri (Viktorovich), Russian composer, pianist, and teacher; b. Tambov, Jan. 27, 1913; d. Leningrad, Aug. 13, 1946. He studied in Tambov and with Shcherbachev at the Leningrad Cons. (1928–32). He taught at the Tambov Music School. As a pianist, he performed mainly his own compositions. His operas were written in a fine Romantic manner.

WORKS: DRAMATIC: *Kamarinsky muzhik*, opera (Leningrad, Sept. 15, 1933); *Her Saint's Day*, opera (1934; Leningrad, Feb. 22, 1935); *Mother*, opera, after Maxim Gorky (Leningrad, Dec. 30, 1938); *The Last Ball*, operetta (Leningrad, March 30, 1939); film scores.

Zhiganov, Nazib, Russian composer and music educator of Tatar heritage; b. Uralsk, Jan. 15, 1911; d. Kazan, June 2, 1988. He was reared in an orphan asylum and first studied music in Kazan. He went to Moscow, where he studied at a technological school and then pursued musical training with Litinsky at the Cons. (graduated, 1938). In 1945 he became director and a prof. of the newly founded Kazan Cons. In his music, he attempted to create a new national Tatar school of composition, following the harmonic and instrumental precepts of the Russian national school.

WORKS: DRAMATIC: OPERAS (all 1st perf. in Kazan): *Katchkyn*

(June 17, 1939); *Irek* (Liberty; Feb. 24, 1940); *Altyntchetch* (The Golden Haired; July 12, 1941); *Ildar* (Nov. 7, 1942); *Tulyak* (July 27, 1945); *Namus* (Honor; June 25, 1950); *Dzhalil*, operatic monologue (1950). BALLET: *Zugra* (Kazan, May 17, 1946). Also film music.

BIBL.: Y. Girshman, *N. Z.* (Moscow, 1957).

Zhukovsky, Herman, Ukrainian composer; b. Radzivilovo, Volynya, Nov. 13, 1913; d. Kiev, March 15, 1976. He studied piano and composition at the Kiev Cons., graduating in 1941; from 1951 to 1958 he taught theory there. He wrote operas, ballets, symphonic music, and other works in the approved style of socialist realism, using authentic Ukrainian song patterns for his materials, but a crisis supervened in his steady progress when his opera *From the Bottom of My Heart* (Moscow, Jan. 16, 1951) was viciously attacked by the cultural authorities of the Soviet government for alleged ideological and musical aberrations; he revised the score, and the new version was approved. His other operas were *Marina* (Kiev, March 12, 1939); *The First Spring* (1960); *Contrasts of Centuries*, operatic trilogy (1967); *A Soldier's Wife*, monodrama for Baritone (1968); also 2 ballets: *Rostislava* (1955) and *Forest Song* (Moscow, May 1, 1961).

Ziani, Marco Antonio, Italian composer, nephew of **Pietro Andrea Ziani**; b. Venice, c.1653; d. Vienna, Jan. 22, 1715. In 1686 he was named maestro di cappella at S. Barbara in Mantua. In 1700 he became vice Hofkapellmeister at the Vienna court, and in 1712 he was elevated to Hofkapellmeister. He composed 45 operas and serenades, of which the following were produced in Vienna: *Il Giordano pio* (July 26, 1700), *Gli ossequi della notte* (July 22, 1701), *Il Temistocle* (June 9, 1701), *La fuga dell'invidia* (Nov. 15, 1701), *Il Romolo* (June 9, 1702), *Cajo Popilio* (June 9, 1704), *L'Ercole vincitore dell'invidia* (March 19, 1706), *Il Meleagro* (Aug. 16, 1706), *Chilonida* (April 21, 1709), *Il Campidoglio ricuperato* (July 26, 1709), and *L'Atenaide* (with Negri, Caldara, and F. Conti; Nov. 19, 1714).

Ziani, Pietro Andrea, Italian organist and composer, uncle of **Marco Antonio Ziani**; b. Venice, c.1616; d. Naples, Feb. 12, 1684. He took holy orders in 1640, then was a canon regular and organist at S. Salvatore in Venice. From 1657 to 1659 he served as maestro di cappella at S. Maria Maggiore in Bergamo; in 1662 he became vice Kapellmeister to the dowager empress Eleonora in Vienna. In 1669 he succeeded Cavalli as 1st organist at San Marco in Venice; he went to Naples in 1677, where he was named a teacher at the Cons. S. Onofrio. He also became honorary organist at the Naples court, where he was made maestro di cappella in 1680; he was pensioned in 1684. He wrote 23 operas, including *Le fortune di Rodope, e di Damira* (Venice, Carnival 1657), *L'Antigona delusa da Alceste* (Venice, Jan. 15, 1660), *La congiura del vizio contra la virtù* (Vienna, Nov. 15, 1663), and *La Circe* (Vienna, June 9, 1665).

Zich, Jaroslav, Czech composer and teacher, son of **Otakar Zich**; b. Prague, Jan. 17, 1912. He studied with his father, at the Prague Cons. (1928–31) with Foerster, and at the Charles Univ. in Prague. From 1952 to 1977 he taught at the Prague Academy of Music. Among his compositions is the melodrama *Romance helgolandská* (1934).

Zich, Otakar, Czech composer and musicologist, father of **Jaroslav Zich**; b: Královë Městec, March 25, 1879; d. Ouběnice, near Benešov, July 9, 1934. He studied mathematics at the Univ. of Prague (Ph.D., 1901); he also received training in musicology from Hostinský and in composition from Stecker (1897–1901); he completed his Habilitation at the Univ. of Prague in 1911. After teaching in a secondary school in Domažlice (from 1901), he was made prof. of philosophy at the Univ. of Brno in 1919; from 1924 he was prof. of aesthetics at the Univ. of Prague.

WRITINGS (all publ. in Prague): *Smetanova Hubička* (Smetana's The Kiss; 1911); *Hector Berlioz a jeho Episoda ze života umělcova* (Hector Berlioz and His Episode from the Life of an Artist; 1914); *Česke lidové tance s proměnlivým taktem* (Czech Folkdances with a Changing Beat; 1917); *Symfonické básně Smetanovy* (Smetana's Symphonic Poems; 1924; 2d ed., 1949); *Estetika dramatického umění* (Aesthetics of Dramatic Art; 1931).

WORKS: OPERAS: *Malířský nápad* (Painter's Whim; 1908; Prague, March 11, 1910); *Vina* (Guilt; 1911–15; Prague, March 14, 1922); *Preciézky*, after Molière's *Les Précieuses ridicules* (1924; Prague, May 11, 1926); also cantatas, song cycles, part-songs, etc.

BIBL.: J. Hutter, *O. Z. a jeho "Vina"* (Prague, 1922); J. Burjanek, *O. Z.: Studie k vývoji českého muzikologického myšleni v prvni třetine našeho stoleti* (O. Z.: A Study of the Development of Czech Musicological Thought in the First Third of This Century; Prague, 1966).

Ziegler, Delores, American mezzo-soprano; b. Atlanta, Sept. 4, 1951. She studied at the Univ. of Tenn. After beginning her career with concert engagements, she made her operatic stage debut in Knoxville in 1978 as Verdi's Flora. In 1978–79 she was a member of the Santa Fe Opera apprenticeship program; in 1979 she appeared as Verdi's Maddalena in St. Louis. She made her European operatic debut in Bonn in 1981 as Dorabella. In 1982 she sang for the first time at the Cologne Opera. In 1984 she appeared as Dorabella at her Glyndebourne debut and as Bellini's Romeo at her La Scala debut in Milan. She sang for the first time at the Salzburg Festival in 1985 as Minerva in Henze's setting of *Il Ritorno d'Ulisse*. In 1990 she made her Metropolitan Opera debut as Gounod's Siebel. In 1996 she portrayed Dorabella at the Washington (D.C.) Opera. As a guest artist, she also sang in Munich, Florence, Hamburg, San Diego, Toronto, and elsewhere; she also was widely engaged as a concert artist.

Ziehrer, Carl Michael, Austrian bandleader and composer; b. Vienna, May 2, 1843; d. there, Nov. 14, 1922. Entirely self-taught in music, he organized in 1863 a dance orch., with which he made tours of Austria and Germany, introducing his own pieces; with an enlarged orch. (50 players), he established a regular series of popular concerts in Vienna, which met with great success. In 1908 he was appointed music director of the court balls. He wrote nearly 600 marches and dances for orch. and produced in Vienna a number of operettas: *Wiener Kinder* (Feb. 19, 1881), *Mahomeds Paradies* (Feb. 26, 1866), *König Jerôme* (Nov. 28, 1878), *Ein Deutschmeister* (Nov. 30, 1888), *Der schöne Rigo* (May 24, 1898), *Die Landstreicher*, his best work (July 29, 1899), *Die drei Wünsche* (March 9, 1901), *Der Fremdenführer* (Oct. 11, 1902), *Der Schätzmeister* (Dec. 10, 1904), *Fesche Geister* (July 7, 1905), *Am Lido* (Aug. 31, 1907), *Ein tolles Mädel* (Nov. 8, 1907), *Der Liebeswalzer* (Oct. 24, 1908), *Die Gaukler* (Sept. 6, 1909), *Herr und Frau Biedermeier* (Oct. 5, 1910), *In 50 Jahren* (Jan. 7, 1911), *Fürst Casimir* (Sept. 13, 1913), *Der Husarengeneral* (Oct. 3, 1913), *Das dumme Herz* (Feb. 27, 1914), and *Die verliebte Eskadron* (July 11, 1920).

BIBL.: M. Schönherr, *C. M. Z.: Sein Werk, sein Leben, seine Zeit* (Vienna, 1975).

Zilcher, (Karl) Hermann (Josef), German composer, pianist, and pedagogue; b. Frankfurt am Main, Aug. 18, 1881; d. Würzburg, Jan. 1, 1948. He studied piano with his father, Paul Zilcher, and then continued his training at the Hoch Cons. in Frankfurt am Main (1897–1901) with Kwast (piano) and Knorr and Scholz (composition). After serving on its faculty (1905–08), he was a prof. at the Akademie der Tonkunst in Munich (1908–20). From 1920 to 1944 he was director of the Würzburg Cons. He also made tours as a pianist. His music represents an amalgam of late Romantic and Impressionist elements. Among his compositions were *Fitzebutze*, Traumspiel (1903), *Doktor Eisenbart* (1922), and incidental music.

BIBL.: W. Altmann, *H. Z.* (Leipzig, 1907); H. Oppenheim, *H. Z.* (Munich, 1921).

Zillig, Winfried (Petrus Ignatius), German conductor and composer; b. Würzburg, April 1, 1905; d. Hamburg, Dec. 17, 1963. He studied at the Würzburg Cons. and with Schoenberg in Vienna (1925–26) and in his master classes at the Prussian Academy of Arts in Berlin (1926–28). After working as répétiteur in Oldenburg (1928–32), he conducted in Düsseldorf (1932–37); he was music director of the Essen Opera (1937–40), the Poznań Opera (1940–43), and the Düsseldorf Opera (1946–47), then was chief conductor of the Hesse Radio in Frankfurt am Main (1947–51). He was director of the music division of the North German Radio in Hamburg from 1959 to 1963.

WORKS: DRAMATIC: OPERAS: *Rosse* (Düsseldorf, Feb. 11, 1933); *Das Opfer* (Hamburg, Nov. 12, 1937); *Die Windsbraut* (Leipzig, May 12, 1941); *Troilus und Cressida* (1949; rev. 1963); *Bauernpassion*, television opera (1955); *Die Verlobung in St. Domingo*, radio opera (1956); *Das Verlöbnis* (1962; Linz, Nov. 23, 1963); incidental music.

WRITINGS: *Variationen über neue Musik* (Munich, 1959; 2nd ed., 1963, as *Die neue Musik: Linien und Porträts; Von Wagner bis Strauss* (Munich, 1966).

Zimbalist, Efrem (Alexandrovich), eminent Russian-born American violinist and pedagogue; b. Rostov-na-Donu, April 21, 1889; d. Reno, Nev., Feb. 22, 1985. He studied violin with his father, an orch. musician; from 1901 to 1907 he was a pupil of Leopold Auer at the St. Petersburg Cons., graduating with the gold medal. He made a highly successful European appearance as a soloist in the Brahms Concerto in Berlin, Nov. 7, 1907. In 1911 he emigrated to the United States; he made his American debut with the Boston Sym. Orch. on Oct. 27, 1911, playing the first American performance of Glazunov's Violin Concerto. In 1914 he married **Alma Gluck**, who died in 1938; his 2d wife, whom he married in 1943, was **Mary Louise Curtis Bok**; in 1928 he joined its faculty; he was its director from 1941 to 1968. After Mrs. Zimbalist's death in 1970, he moved to Reno, Nev., to live with his daughter. His son, Efrem Zimbalist Jr. is a well-known actor. Zimbalist was also a composer. He wrote the opera *Landara* (Philadelphia, April 6, 1956) and a musical comedy, *Honeydew* (N.Y., 1920). He publ. *One Hour's Daily Exercise* for the violin.

Zimmer, Ján, significant Slovak composer and pianist; b. Ružomberok, May 16, 1926. He studied with Suchoň at the Bratislava Cons. (graduated, 1948), with Farkas at the Budapest Academy of Music (1948–49), and in Salzburg (1949). After working for Czech Radio in Bratislava (1945–48), he taught at the Bratislava Cons. from 1948 until losing his post in 1952 under the communist regime. In subsequent years, Zimmer devoted himself to composition and made occasional appearances as a pianist, principally in programs of his own works. His music is marked by a mastery of form, technique, and expression. While he has sometimes utilized 12-tone and other modern techniques, he has generally forged his own course as a worthy representative of the Slovak tradition. His works include *Oedipus Rex*, opera (1963–64), *Héraklés*, opera ballet (1972), and *The Broken Line*, opera (1974), all first perf. in Bratislava; also film music.

Zimmerman, Franklin B(ershir), American musicologist; b. Wauneta, Kansas, June 20, 1923. He was educated at the Univ. of Southern Calif. in Los Angeles (B.A., 1949; M.A., 1952; Ph.D., 1958, with the diss. *Purcell's Musical Heritage: A Study of Musical Styles in 17th-century England*) and at Oxford Univ. (B.Litt., 1956). He taught at the State Univ. of N.Y. in Potsdam (1958–59) and at the Univ. of Southern Calif. (1959–64), then was prof. of music at Dartmouth College (1964–67), the Univ. of Kentucky (1967–68), and the Univ. of Pa. (from 1968). He devoted much time to the study of English Baroque music, particularly the life and works of Purcell.

WRITINGS: *Henry Purcell, 1659–1695: An Analytical Catalogue of His Music* (London, 1963); *Henry Purcell, 1659–1695: His Life and Times* (London, 1967; 2d ed., rev., 1983); *Henry Purcell, 1659–1694: Melodic and Intervallic Indexes to His Complete Works* (Philadelphia, 1975); *Henry Purcell: A Guide to Research* (N.Y., 1988).

Zimmerman, Pierre-Joseph-Guillaume, famous French piano teacher and composer; b. Paris, March 19, 1785; d. there, Oct. 29, 1853. The son of a Paris piano maker, he entered the Paris Cons. in 1798, studying under Boieldieu, Rey, Catel, and Cherubini; he won the premier prix for piano in 1800, and for harmony in 1802. He became a prof. of piano there in 1816, and was pensioned in 1848. Among his many pupils were Alkan, Marmontel, Lacombe, Ambroise Thomas, and César Franck. His chief work is the *Encyclopédie du pianiste*, a complete method for piano, part 3 of which is a treatise on harmony and counterpoint. Among his compositions was the opera *L'Enlèvement* (Paris, Oct. 26, 1830).

Zimmermann, Anton, Austrian composer; b. Pressburg, 1741; d. there, Oct. 16, 1781. He was organist at St. Martin's Church in Pressburg, and in 1776 he was named Kapellmeister and court composer to Count Joseph Batthyany, the Archibishop (later cardinal) of Hungary. His works include *Narcisse et Pierre*, Singspiel (Pressburg, 1772; not extant), *Andromeda und Perseus*, melodrama (Vienna, April 23, 1781), and *Zelmor und Ermide*, melodrama (n.d.).

Zimmermann, Bernd (Bernhard) Alois, important German composer and teacher; b. Bliesheim, near Cologne, March 20, 1918; d. (suicide) Königsdorf, near Cologne, Aug. 10, 1970. He studied at the Cologne Hochschule für Musik and at the Univs. of Cologne and Bonn until being drafted for military service. Following his discharge, he pursued training with Lemacher and Jarnach in 1942. Later he attended the summer courses in new music given by Fortner and Leibowitz in Darmstadt (1948–50). He taught at the Univ. (1950–52) and Hochschule für Musik (1957–57) in Cologne. In 1956–57 he served as president of the German section of the ISCM. In 1957 he held a stipend for residence at the Villa Massimo in Rome. In 1958 he was appointed prof. of composition at the Cologne Hochschule für Musik, a position he retained for the rest of his life. In 1966 he was awarded the arts prize of Cologne. Plagued by failing eyesight and obsessed with notions of death, he set his *Requiem für einen jungen Dichter* to texts of poets who had committed suicide. Shortly thereafter, he took his own life. C. Bitter ed. a vol. of Zimmermann's writings as *Intervall und Zeit: Aufsätze und Schriften* (Mainz, 1974). While he made use of serialism and electronics, Zimmermann's works were notable for their distinct individuality. In his later works, he made use of musical quotations, which he called collage, which he borrowed from both Western and non-Western traditions. The result was, in effect, a remarkable musical pluralism.

WORKS: DRAMATIC: *Alagoana (Caprichos brasileiros)*, ballet (1940–43; 1947–50; suite, Hamburg, Nov. 21, 1953; ballet, Essen, Dec. 17, 1955); *Kontraste*, ballet (1953; Bielefeld, April 24, 1954); *Perspektiven*, ballet (1955; Düsseldorf, June 2, 1957); *Die Soldaten*, opera, after J. M. R. Lenz (1958–60; rev. 1963–64; Cologne, Feb. 15, 1965; also used in the Vocal Sym., 1959); *Musique pour les soupers du Roi Ubu*, ballet noir (1966); other theater scores and much radio music.

BIBL.: W. Konold, ed., *B. A. Z.: Dokumente und Interpretationen* (Cologne, 1986); idem, *B. A. Z.:Der Komponist und sein Werk* (Cologne, 1986).

Zimmermann, Udo, noted German composer, conductor, pedagogue, and Intendant; b. Dresden, Oct. 6, 1943. He was a student of Johannes Thilman (composition) and took courses in conducting and voice at the Dresden Hochschule für Musik (1962–68). In 1967 and 1968 he held the Felix-Mendelssohn-Bartholdy-Stipendium. From 1968 to 1970 he attended Kochan's master classes in composition at the Akademie der Künste in East Berlin. In 1970 he became a dramaturg for contemporary music theater at the Dresden State Opera, where he was active until 1984. He became founder-director of Dresden's Studio Neue Musik in 1974. In 1976 he began teaching at the Dresden Hochschule für Musik, where he was made a prof. of composition in 1978 and a prof. of experimental music theater and composition in 1982. He was active as a conductor from 1984, making guest appearances in Europe and abroad. In 1986 he became director of Dresden's Center for Contemporary Music. He became artistic director of Dresden's musica-viva-ensemble in 1988. In 1990 he was made Intendant of the Leipzig Opera. In 1983 he was made a member of the Akademie der Künste in Berlin and of the Freien Akademie der Künste in Hamburg. He served as president of the Freien Akademie der Künste in Leipzig from 1992. Zimmermann's music owes much to the so-called new simplicity style. In his operatic scores, he has brought new life to the genre of Literaturoper.

WORKS: OPERAS: *Die weisse Rose* (1966; Dresden, June 17, 1967); *Die zweite Entscheidung* (1969; Magdeburg, March 10, 1970); *Levins Mühle* (Dresden, March 27, 1973); *Der Schuhu und die fliegende Prinzessin* (Dresden, Dec. 30, 1976); *Die wundersame Schustersfrau* (1981; Schwetzingen, April 25, 1982); *Weisse Rose* (Hamburg, Feb. 27, 1986); *Die Sündflut* (1991).

BIBL.: F. Hennenberg, *U. Z., für Sie porträtiert* (Leipzig, 1983).

Zimmermann, Walter, German composer; b. Schwabach, April 15, 1949. He studied piano, violin, and oboe. While serving as pianist in the "ars-nova-ensemble" of Nuremberg (1968–70), he pursued training in composition with Werner Heider. He then studied with Otto Laske at the Institut voor Sonologie at the Univ. of Utrecht and at the Jaap Kunst Ethnological Center at the Univ. of Amsterdam (1970–73). In 1974 he studied computer music in Hamilton, N.J. In 1977 he founded the Beginner Studio in Cologne, which specialized in concerts of novel music. In 1988 he lectured at the Univ. of The Hague. In 1993 he became a teacher of composition at the Berlin Hochschule für Musik. He publ. the books *Desert Plants* (Vancouver, 1976) and *Insel Musik* (Cologne, 1977), and ed. a vol. of Morton Feldman's essays (Kerpen, 1985). Among his compositions are *Die Blinden*, static drama for 12 Singers and 9 Instruments (1984), *Über die Dörfer*, music theater for Soloists, 3 Choruses, and Organ (1986), *Hyperion*, short opera (1989–90), and *Oedipus Coloneus*, music theater (1995).

Zinck, Hardenack Otto Conrad, German instrumentalist, singer, teacher, and composer; b. Husum, Holstein, July 2, 1746; d. Copenhagen, Feb. 15, 1832. He began his training with his father, the town musician Bendix Friedrich Zinck, and later studied with C. P. E. Bach in Hamburg. In 1777 he became 1st flutist and chamber musician in the Ludwigslust Hofkapelle; in 1787 he was named Singmeister (1st accompanist) in the Copenhagen Hofkapelle; he also was active as a church organist and teacher in Copenhagen, where he founded a Singakademie (1800). He produced an opera to a Danish text, *Selim og Mirza* (Copenhagen, Feb. 1, 1790), and also composed several oratorios. He publ. *Die nördliche Harfe: Ein Versuch in Fragmenten und Skizzen über Musik und ihre Anwendung im Norden* (Copenhagen, 1801) and *Vorlesungen über Musik und ihre nutzlichste Anwendung* (Copenhagen, 1813). His brother, Bendix (Benedikt) Friedrich Zinck (1743–1801), was also an instrumentalist and composer.

Zingarelli, Nicola Antonio, Italian composer and pedagogue; b. Naples, April 4, 1752; d. Torre del Greco, near Naples, May 5, 1837. He studied at the Cons. S. Maria di Loreto in Naples with Fenaroli, Speranza, Anfossi, and Sacchini. His first stage work, *I quattro pazzi*, was performed at the Cons. in 1768. After finishing school in 1772, he earned his living as a violin teacher. He spent much time traveling throughout Italy, supervising the production of his operas. In 1793 he was appointed maestro di cappella at the Cathedral of Milan, in 1794, at the Santa Casa in Loreto, and in 1804, at the Sistine Chapel in the Vatican. In 1811, for refusing to conduct a Te Deum to celebrate the birthday of Napoleon's son, the "King of Rome," he was imprisoned at Civitavecchia, and later transported to Paris by order of Napoleon, who set him at liberty and liberally paid him for a Mass written in Paris. As Fioravanti had meanwhile become maestro di cappella at St. Peter's, Zingarelli went to Naples, and in 1813 became director of the royal Collegio di Musica; in 1816 he succeeded Paisiello as maestro di cappella at the Naples Cathedral. He was renowned as a teacher, numbering Bellini, Mercadante, Carlo Conti, Lauro Rossi, Morlacchi, and Michael Costa among his students. His operas, interpreted by the finest singers of the time (Catalani, Crescentini, Grassini, Marchesi, and Rubinelli), were highly successful. His facility was such that he was able to write an opera in a week. He wrote 37 operas in all.

WORKS: DRAMATIC: OPERAS (all 1st perf. at La Scala in Milan): *Alsinda* (Feb. 22, 1785); *Ifigenia in Aulide* (Jan. 27, 1787); *La morte de Cesare* (Dec. 26, 1790); *Pirro, re d'Epiro* (Dec. 26, 1791); *Il mercato di Monfregoso* (Sept. 22, 1792); *La secchia rapita* (Sept. 7, 1793); *Artaserse* (Dec. 26, 1793); *Giulietta e Romeo*, after Shakespeare (Jan. 30, 1796); *Meleagro* (Jan. 1798); *Il ritratto* (Oct. 12, 1799); *Clitennestra* (Dec. 26, 1800); *Il bevitore fortunato* (Nov. 1803). OTHER OPERAS: *I quattro pazzi* (Naples, 1768); *Montezuma* (Naples, Aug. 13, 1781); *Ricimero* (Venice, May 5, 1785); *Armida* (Rome, Carnival 1786); *Antigono* (Mantua, April 13, 1786); *Artaserse* (Trieste, March 19, 1789); *Antigone* (Paris, April 30, 1790); *Pharamond* (1790); *Annibale in Torino* (Turin, Carnival 1792); *Atalanta* (Turin, Carnival 1792); *L'oracolo sannita* (Turin, Carnival 1792); *La Rossana* (Genoa, Carnival 1793); *Apelle* (Venice, Nov. 18, 1793; rev. as *Apelle e Campaspe*, Bologna, 1795); *Gerusalemme distrutta* (Florence, 1794); *Alzira* (Florence, Sept. 7, 1794); *Quinto Fabio* (Livorno, 1794); *Il conte di Saldagna* (Venice, Dec. 26, 1794); *Gli Orazi e i Curiazi* (Naples, Nov. 4, 1795); *Andromeda* (Venice, 1796); *La morte di Mitridate* (Venice, May 27, 1797); *Ines de Castro* (Milan, Oct. 11, 1798); *Carolina e Mexicow* (Venice, Carnival 1798); *I veri amici repubblicani* (Turin, Dec. 26, 1798); *Il ratto delle Sabine* (Venice, Dec. 26, 1799); *Edipo a Colono* (Venice, Dec. 26, 1802); *La notte dell'amicizia* (Venice, Carnival 1802); *Il ritorno di Serse* (Modena, July 16, 1808); *Baldovino* (Rome, Feb. 11, 1811); *Berenice, regina d'Armenia* (Rome, Nov. 12, 1811); *Malvina* (Naples, Carnival 1829; in collaboration with M. Costa). ORATORIOS: *Pimmalione* (Naples, 1779); *Ero* (Milan, 1786); *Telemaco* (Milan, 1787); *Il trionfo di David* (Naples, 1788); *Francesca da Rimini* (Rome, 1804); *Tancredi al sepolcro di Clorinda* (Naples, 1805); *La fuga in Egitto* (Naples, 1837).

BIBL.: R. Liberatore, *Necrologia di N. Z.* (Naples, 1837); A. Schmid, *Joseph Haydn und N. Z.* (Vienna, 1847).

Zítek, Otakar, Czech music critic and composer; b. Prague, Nov. 5, 1892; d. Bratislava, April 28, 1955. He studied composition with Novák at the Prague Cons. and musicology with Guido Adler and Grädener at the Univ. of Vienna. Upon graduation, he wrote music criticism for the *Hudební Revue* and the *Lidové Noviny* in Prague; he gave lectures on opera at the Prague Cons., then was administrator at the National Theater in Brno (1921–29) and taught at the Brno Cons. (1931–39). From 1939 to 1941 he was in the Buchenwald concentration camp, but was released, and worked as a theater director in Plzeň (1941–43); he supervised opera theaters in Prague and Brno (1946–49). He composed the operas *Vznesene srdce* (The Exalted Heart; 1918) and *Pád Petra Králence* (The Downfall of Peter Kralence; Brno, March 23, 1923); also a ballet after Wilde's *Birthday of the Infanta* (Plzeň [Pilsen], 1942). He publ. *O novou zpevohru* (On New Opera; Prague, 1920).

Ziv, Mikhail, Russian composer; b. Moscow, May 25, 1921. He studied at the Moscow Cons. with Kabalevsky; he graduated in 1947. As a composer, Ziv devoted himself mainly to the musical theater. He wrote the comic operas *Son of a King's Minister* (1973) and *Gentlemen Artists* (1980) as well as several fairy tales for children.

Zoghby, Linda, American soprano; b. Mobile, Ala., Aug. 17, 1949. She studied voice with Elena Nikolaidi at Florida State Univ. She made her professional debut at the Grant Park Festival in Chicago in 1973; subsequently she sang opera in New York, Washington, D.C., Dallas, Santa Fe, Houston, and New Orleans. She received a critical accolade on Jan. 19, 1982, when she substituted on short notice for Teresa Stratas and sang the role of Mimi in the Zeffirelli production of *La Bohème* at the Metropolitan Opera in New York. Her other roles include Pamina, Donna Elvira, and Marguerite in *Faust*.

Zöllner, Heinrich, German organist and composer; b. Öls, Silesia, May 5, 1792; d. Wandsbeck, near Hamburg, July 2, 1836. He toured Germany as an organist, and in 1833 settled in Hamburg. His works include an opera, *Kunz von Kauffungen* (Vienna, March 27, 1826), and a melodrama, *Ein Uhr*.

Zöllner, Heinrich, German composer and conductor; b. Leipzig, July 4, 1854; d. Freiburg im Breisgau, May 4, 1941. His father was the German choral conductor and composer Carl Friedrich Zöllner (1800–1860). He studied at the Leipzig Cons., where his teachers were Reinecke, Jadassohn, Richter, and Wenzel (1875–77); he then went to Tartu, where he was music director at the Univ.; in 1885 he went to Cologne, where he taught at the Cons. and conducted choruses. In 1890 he was engaged to lead the Deutscher Liederkranz in New York; in 1898 he returned to Germany. From 1902 to 1907 he taught composition at the Leipzig Cons., and from 1907 to 1914 he was conductor at the Flemish Opera in Antwerp; subsequently he settled in Freiburg im Breisgau. He wrote 10 operas, of which the following were produced: *Frithjof* (Cologne, 1884); *Die lustigen Chinesinnen* (Cologne, 1886); *Faust* (Munich, Oct. 19, 1887); *Matteo Falcone* (N.Y., 1894); *Der Überfall* (Dresden, Sept. 7, 1895); *Die versunkene Glocke* (Berlin, July 8, 1899); *Der Schützenkönig* (Leipzig, 1903); *Zigeuner* (Stuttgart, 1912); also the musical comedy *Das hölzerne Schwert* (Kassel, 1897).

Zolotarev, Vasili (Andreievich), eminent Russian composer and pedagogue; b. Taganrog, March 7, 1872; d. Moscow, May 25, 1964. He studied violin and theory at the Imperial Court Chapel in St. Petersburg; from 1893 to 1897 he took composition lessons with Balakirev, then entered the St. Petersburg Cons. in the class of Rimsky-Korsakov, graduating in 1900, then received the Rubinstein Prize for his cantata *Paradise and Peri*. He was instructor of violin at the Court Chapel (1897–1900), and teacher of composition at the Rostov Music School (1906–08), the Moscow Cons. (1908–18), the Ekaterinodar Cons. (1918–24), the Odessa Cons. (1924–26), the Kiev Musico-Dramatic Inst. (1926–31), the Sverdlovsk Music School (1931–33), and the Minsk Cons. (1933–41). In 1955 he was awarded the Order of Lenin. Several well-known Soviet composers were his pupils, among them Polovinkin, Dankevich, and Vainberg. In his music, Zolotarev continued the line of the Russian national school of composition, based on broad diatonic melos, mellifluous euphonious harmonies, and, in his operas, a resonant flow of choral singing. Among his works were the operas *The Decembrists* (Moscow, Dec. 27, 1925) and *Ak-Gul* (1942) and the ballet *Lake Prince* (1948; Minsk, Jan. 15, 1949). He publ. a manual on the fugue (Moscow, 1932; 3rd ed., 1965) and a vol. of reminiscences (Moscow, 1957).

BIBL.: S. Nisievich, *V. A. Z.* (Moscow, 1964).

Zoras, Leonidas, Greek composer and conductor; b. Sparta, March 8, 1905; d. Athens, Dec. 22, 1987. He studied law at the Univ. of Athens; at the same time, he took conducting lessons with Mitropoulos, and studied composition with Kalomiris, Lavrangas, and Riadis. From 1926 to 1938 he taught theory at the Odeon Music School in Athens; then studied conducting with Gmeindl, Schmalstich, and F. Stein and composition with Blacher, Grabner, and Hoffer at the Berlin Hochschule für Musik (1938–40). After conducting at the Greek National Opera in Athens (1948–58), he returned to Berlin as a conductor at the Deutsche Opera and RIAS (1958–68). He was director of the Athens National Cons. from 1968. He wrote an opera, *Elektra* (1969), and the ballet *Violanto* (1931).

Zottmayr, Georg, distinguished German bass; b. Munich, Jan. 24, 1869; d. Dresden, Dec. 11, 1941. He studied in Munich, and began his career primarily as a concert singer. In 1906 he made his operatic debut with the Vienna Court Opera; later he was a member of the German Theater in Prague (1908–10). In 1910 he joined the Dresden Court (later State) Opera, where he enjoyed a career of great distinction. He was considered one of the outstanding Wagnerians of his time, numbering among his finest roles King Marke, Hunding, Gurnemanz, Pogner, and Daland.

Zouhar, Zdeněk, Czech composer and teacher; b. Kotvrdovice, Feb. 8, 1927. He was a pupil in Bratislava (1946–51) of Blažek and Kunz before settling in Brno, where he studied with Schaefer at the Janáček Academy of Music (1965–67) and pursued his education at the Univ. (Ph.D., 1962). After serving as head of the music dept. of the Univ. library (1953–61), he taught at the Janáček Academy of Music (from 1962). His music makes multifarious use of modern techniques, including a fairly orthodox dodecaphony. Among his works are *Metamorphosis*, chamber radio opera (1971), *A Great Love*, comic opera (1986), and ballets; also *The Flames of Constance*, oratorio (1988).

Zschau, Marilyn, American soprano; b. Chicago, Feb. 9, 1944. She studied at the Juilliard School of Music in N.Y. (1961–65) and in Montana with John Lester. In 1965–66 she toured as a member of the Met National Co. In 1967 she made her debut as Marietta in *Die Tote Stadt* at the Vienna Volksoper, and in 1971 appeared for the first time at the Vienna State Opera as the Composer in *Ariadne auf Naxos*. She made her N.Y. City Opera debut in 1978 as Minnie in *La Fanciulla del West*, returning there as Cio-Cio-San, Odabella in *Attila*, and Maddalena in *Andrea Chénier*. On Feb. 4, 1985, she made her Metropolitan Opera debut in New York as Musetta. She sang for the first time at Milan's La Scala in 1986 as the Dyer's Wife in *Die Frau ohne Schatten*; thereafter she sang with major opera houses on both sides of the Atlantic. In 1993 she elctrified audiences with her debut at the London Promenade Concerts in a concert performance as Elektra with Andrew Davis conducting the BBC Sym. Orch. She was engaged as Brünnhilde in the *Ring* cycle at the Seattle Opera in 1995. In 1996 she portrayed Elektra in Buenos Aires. Among her many admired roles are Mozart's Countess, Fiordiligi, Aida, Desdemona, Leonora, Tosca, Octavian, the Marschallin, Salome, and Shostakovich's Katerina.

Zubiaurre (y Urionabarrenechea), Valentí, Spanish composer; b. Villa de Garay, Feb. 13, 1837; d. Madrid, Jan. 13, 1914. He was a chorister at Bilbao, and at the age of 16 undertook a voyage to South America. He returned to Spain in 1866, and took music lessons with Hilarión Eslava at the Madrid Cons. He wrote a considerable number of sacred works, then turned to opera, receiving 1st national prize with his *Fernando el Emplazado* (Madrid, May 12, 1871). In 1875 he was named 2d maestro at the Royal Chapel in Madrid, and in 1878 succeeded Eslava as 1st maestro; in the same year, he was appointed a prof. at the Madrid Cons. His 2d opera, *Ledia*, was produced with considerable success in Madrid on April 22, 1877. He also composed several zarzuelas.

Zuelli, Guglielmo, Italian composer; b. Reggio Emilia, Oct. 20, 1859; d. Milan, Oct. 8, 1941. He studied with A. Busi and L. Mancinelli in Bologna. After teaching and conducting in various provincial towns, he was director of the Palermo Cons. (1894–1911), the Parma Cons. (1911–29), and the Liceo Musicale of Alessandria, Piedmont (1929–33). He publ. *Gioacchino Rossini: Pagine segrete* (Bologna, 1922). Among his works is the opera *La Fata del Nord* (Milan, May 4, 1884), for which he won the Sonzogno prize; also the opera ballet *Il Profeta di Korassan*.

Zumpe, Herman, German conductor and composer; b. Oppach, April 9, 1850; d. Munich, Sept. 4, 1903. He studied in Bautzen and Leipzig. In 1872 he joined Wagner at Bayreuth, aiding in the preparation of the performances of *Der Ring des Nibelungen* then conducted opera in Salzburg, Würzburg, Madgeburg, Frankfurt am Main, and Hamburg. After some years spent in teaching and composing, he was appointed court conductor in Stuttgart in 1891; in 1895, was called to Munich to become conductor of the Kaim Orch.. He then was court conductor in Schwerin (1897–1900), returning to Munich in 1900 as Generalmusikdirektor. Among his works is the opera *Anahna* (Berlin, 1881) and the operettas *Farinelli* (Hamburg, 1886), *Karin* (Hamburg, 1888), and *Polnische Wirtschaft* (Hamburg, 1889). Two of his operas were performed posthumously: *Sawitri* (completed by Rössler; Schwerin, Sept. 8, 1907) and *Das Gespenst von Horodin* (Hamburg, 1910).

BIBL.: E. von Possart et al., *H. Z.: Persönliche Erinnerungen nebst Mitteilungen aus seinen Tagebuchblättern und Briefen* (Munich, 1905).

Zumsteeg, Johann Rudolf, German composer and conductor; b. Sachsenflur, Odenwald, Jan. 10, 1760; d. Stuttgart, Jan. 27, 1802. As a pupil at the Carlsschule (near Stuttgart), he was a classmate of Schiller. He studied cello with Eberhard Malterre and cello and composition with Agostino Poli in Stuttgart; in 1781 he became solo cellist in the Court Orch. there, then served as music master at the Carlsschule (1785–94). In 1791 he was made director of German music at the Stuttgart Court Theater, and in 1793 he succeeded Poli as court Konzertmeister, where he championed the works of Mozart. He produced 8 operas at Stuttgart, of which the best was *Die Geisterinsel*, after Shakespeare's *The Tempest* (Nov. 7, 1798); his other stage works included *Zalaor* (March 2, 1787), *Tamira* (June 13, 1788), *Das Pfauenfest* (Feb. 24, 1801), and *Ebondocani* (Dec. 8, 1803). But it is chiefly as the precursor of Loewe and Schubert in the composition of art songs that he is historically important.

BIBL.: I. Arnold, *J. R. Z.: Seine kurze Biographie* (Erfurt, 1810); L. Landshoff, *J. R. Z. (1760–1802): Ein Beitrag zur Geschichte des Liedes und der Ballade* (diss., Univ. of Berlin, 1902); G. Maier, *Die Lieder J. R. Z.s und ihr Verhaltnis zu Schubert* (Goppingen, 1971).

Zur Mühlen, Raimund von, German tenor and pedagogue; b. Livonia, Nov. 10, 1854; d. Steyning, Sussex, Dec. 9, 1931. He began his training at the Berlin Hochschule für Musik, then studied with Stockhausen in Frankfurt am Main and Bussine in Paris; he also took a special course with Clara Schumann, who instructed him in the interpretation of songs by Schumann and Schubert, which gave him the foundation of his career. He had his greatest success in England, where he lived from 1905 until his death. It was he who introduced into London the "song recital" (Liederabend; programs devoted exclusively to songs). He was also a fine teacher.

BIBL.: D. von Zur Mühlen, *Der Sänger R. v.Z. M.* (Hannover, 1969).

Zweig, Fritz, Bohemian-born American conductor and teacher; b. Olmütz, Sept. 8, 1893; d. Los Angeles, Feb. 28, 1984. He received training in theory from Schoenberg in Vienna. After serving on the staff of the Mannheim National Theater (1912–14; 1919–21), he was assist. conductor at the Barmen-Elberfeld Opera (1921–23). In 1923 he went to Berlin as a conductor at the Volksoper, and then was a conductor at the Städtische Oper from 1927. When the Nazis came to power in 1933, Zweig was banned from the Städtische Oper. In 1934 he became a conductor at the German Theater in Prague. In 1938 he fled Prague in the face of the Nazi dismemberment of Czechoslovakia and lived in Paris. With the defeat of France by the Nazis in 1940, he once more fled and made his way to the United States. He subsequently was active as a music teacher in Los Angeles. His most notable student was Lawrence Foster.

Zykan, Otto M., Austrian composer; b. Vienna, April 29, 1935. He received training in piano and composition (with Schiske) at the Vienna Academy of Music. In 1965 he founded the "Salonkonzerte" in Vienna, and appeared as a pianist in many contemporary scores. He also worked in contemporary music theater circles. From 1975 he devoted most of his time to film projects, for which he composed, wrote screenplays, and directed.

WORKS: DRAMATIC: *Sings Nähmaschine ist die beste*, theater piece (1966); *Schön der Reihe nach*, ballet (1966); *Lehrstück am Beispiel Schönbergs*, music theater-action (1974); *Kunst kommt von Gönnen*, opera (1980); *Auszählreim*, opera (1986; rev. 1987); *Wahr ist, dass der Tiger frisst*, choral opera (1994); *Mesmer*, film music (1994).

Zylis-Gara, Teresa, Polish soprano; b. Landvarov, Jan. 23, 1935. She was a student of Olga Ogina at the ódz Academy of Music. After taking 1st prize in the Warsaw Competition in 1954, she sang on the radio and with the Phil. in Kraków. In 1956 she made her operatic debut as Halka in Katowice, and then sang in various Polish music centers. In 1960 she won 1st prize in the Munich Competition, which led to an engagement in Oberhausen. In 1962 she sang in Dortmund and in 1965 in Düsseldorf. In 1965 she made her debut at the Glyndebourne Festival as Octavian. She sang in Paris in 1966. In 1968 she appeared as Donna Elvira at the Salzburg Festival and made her Covent Garden debut in London as Violetta. On Dec. 17, 1968, she made her Metropolitan Opera debut in New York as Donna Elvira, and continued on its roster until 1984. From 1972 she also sang at the Vienna State Opera. In 1973 she appeared in Barcelona. She sang Liù at the Orange Festival in 1979. In 1988 she appeared as Desdemona at the Hamburg State Opera. Throughout the years, she also pursued an active concert career. Among her other operatic roles were Fiordiligi, Tatiana, Manon Lescaut, Elisabeth, Elsa, Anna Bolena, and the Marschallin.

Time Line of Famous Operas*

*Works arranged by composition dates.

1598 *Dafne* (Peri)

1600

1600 *Euridice* (Peri)
Euridice (Caccini)
1607 *La favola d'Orfeo* (Monteverdi)
1624 *Il Combattimento di Tancredi e Clorinda* (Monteverdi)
1640 *Il Ritorno d'Ulisse in patria* (Monteverdi)
1642 *L'Incoronazione di Poppea* (Monteverdi)
1643 *Egisto* (Cavalli)
1644 *L'Ormindo* (Cavalli)
1649 *Orontea* (Cesti)
1651 *La Calisto* (Cavalli)
1662 *Ercole amante* (Cavalli)
1668 *Il Pomo d'oro* (Cesti)
1675 *Thésée* (Lully)
1684 *Amadis* (Lully)
1686 *Armide et Raunaud* (Lully)
1689 *Dido and Aeneas* (Purcell)
1691 *King Arthur, or the British Worthy* (Purcell)
1692 *The Fairy Queen* (Purcell)

1700

1701 *Omphale* (Destouches)
1705 *Almira* (Handel)
1709 *Agrippina* (Handel)
1711 *Rinaldo* (Handel)
1712 *Il Pastor Fido* (Handel)
1718 *Il Trionfo dell'onore* (Alessandro Scarlatti)
1724 *Giulio Cesare* (Handel)
Tamerlano (Handel)
1725 *Rodelinda, regina de'Longobardi* (Handel)
1726 *Alessandro* (Handel)
1727 *Admeto, rè di Tessaglia* (Handel)
1728 *The Beggar's Opera* (Pepusch)
1732 *Demetrio* (Hasse)
1733 *Hippolyte et Aricie* (Rameau)
La Serva padrona (Pergolesi)
1734 *Arianna in Creta* (Handel)
1735 *Alcina* (Handel)
Ariodante (Handel)
Les Indes Galantes (Rameau)
1736 *Atalanta* (Handel)
1737 *Arminio* (Handel)
Castor et Pollux (Rameau)
1738 *Serse* (Xerxes) (Handel)
1739 *Dardanus* (Rameau)
1743 *Demofoonte* (Jommelli)
1745 *Platée* (Rameau)
1760 *La Buona figluola* (Piccinni)
1762 *Orfeo ed Euridice* (Gluck)
1764? *Abaris ou Les Boréades* (Rameau)
1767 *Alceste* (Gluck)
1768 *Bastien und Bastienne* (Mozart)
Lo Speziale (Haydn)
1769 *La Finta semplice* (Mozart)
1770 *Mitridate, rè di Ponto* (Mozart)
Paride ed Elena (Gluck)
1771 *Ascanio in Alba* (Mozart)
Zémire et Azor (Grétry)
1772 *Lucio Silla* (Mozart)
1774 *Iphigénie en Aulide* (Gluck)

1775 *La Finta giardiniera* (Mozart)
Il Rè pastore (Mozart)
1777 *Armide* (Gluck)
Il Mondo della luna (Haydn)
1779 *Iphigénie en Tauride* (Gluck)
1781 *Idomeneo, rè di Creta* (Mozart)
1782 *The Abduction from the Seraglio* (Die Entführung aus dem Serail) (Mozart)
The Barber of Seville (Il Barbiere di Siviglia) (Paisiello)
1784 *Richard Cœur-de-Lion* (Grétry)
1786 *Una Cosa rara* (Martín y Soler)
Doktor und Apotheker (Dittersdorf)
The Marriage of Figaro (Le Nozze di Figaro) (Mozart)
Der Schauspieldirektor (Mozart)
1787 *Don Giovanni* (Mozart)
Tarare (Salieri)
1789 *Nina, o sia La Pazza per amore* (Paisiello)
1790 *Così fan tutte* (Mozart)
Euphrosine (Méhul)
1791 *La Clemenza di Tito* (Mozart)
Lodoïska (Cherubini)
The Magic Flute (Die Zauberflöte) (Mozart)
1792 *Il Matrimonio segreto* (Cimarosa)
1797 *Medée* (Cherubini)
1799 *Ariodant* (Méhul)

1800

1800 *Les Deux journées* (Cherubini)
1807 *Joseph* (Méhul)
La Vestale (Spontini)
1809 *La Mort d'Adam* (Le Sueur)
1812 *Jean de Paris* (Boieldieu)
La Scala di seta (Rossini)
Il Signor Bruschino, ossia Il figlio per azzardo (Rossini)
1813 *L'Italiana in Algeri* (Rossini)
Tancredi (Rossini)
1814 *Fidelio, oder Die eheliche Liebe* (Beethoven)
Il Turco in Italia (Rossini)
1816 *The Barber of Seville* (Il Barbiere di Siviglia) (Rossini)
Otello, ossia Il Moro di Venezia (Rossini)
Undine (E. T. A. Hoffmann)
1817 *La Cenerentola* (Rossini)
La Gazza ladra (Rossini)
1818 *Mosè in Egitto* (Rossini)
1819 *La Donna del lago* (Rossini)
Olimpie (Spontini)
1821 *Der Freischütz* (Weber)
Le Maître de Chapelle (Paër)
1822 *Alfonso und Estrella* (Schubert)
1823 *Euryanthe* (Weber)
Jessonda (Spohr)
Semiramide (Rossini)
1824 *L'Ajo nell'imbarazzo* (Donizetti)
Il Crociato in Egitto (Meyerbeer)
1825 *La Dame blanche* (Boieldieu)
Don Sanche (Liszt)
Il Viaggio a Reims, ossia L'albergo del Giglio d'Oro (Rossini)
1826 *Bianca e Fernando* (Bellini)
Oberon (Weber)
Le Siège de Corinthe (Rossini)
1827 *Agnes von Hohenstaufen* (Spontini)
Il Pirata (Bellini)
1828 *Le Comte Ory* (Rossini)
La Muette de Portici (Auber)
Der Vampyr (Marschner)
1829 *Guillaume Tell* (William Tell) (Rossini)
Der Templer und die Jüden (Marschner)
1830 *Anna Bolena* (Donizetti)
I Capuleti ed i Montecchi (Bellini)
Fra Diavolo (Auber)
1831 *Norma* (Bellini)
Robert le diable (Meyerbeer)
La Sonnambula (Bellini)
Zampa (Hérold)
1832 *L'Elisir d'amore* (Donizetti)
Hans Heiling (Marschner)
1833 *Beatrice di Tenda* (Bellini)
Lucrezia Borgia (Donizetti)
1834 *Die Feen* (Wagner)
Maria Stuarda (Donizetti)
1835 *La Juive* (Halévy)
Das Liebesverbot (Wagner)
Lucia di Lammermoor (Donizetti)
I Puritani (Bellini)
1836 *Les Huguenots* (Meyerbeer)
A Life for the Czar (Zhizn za tsarya) (Glinka)
Le Postillion de Longjumeau (Adam)
1837 *Benvenuto Cellini* (Berlioz)
Le Domino noir (Auber)
Roberto Devereux, ossia Il conte d'Essex (Donizetti)
Zar und Zimmermann (Lortzing)
1839 *Il Bravo* (Mercadante)
1840 *La Favorite* (Donizetti)
La Fille du régiment (The Daughter of the Regiment) (Donizetti)
Rienzi (Wagner)
Saffo (Pacini)
1841 *Der Fliegende Holländer* (The Flying Dutchman) (Wagner)
Nabucco (Verdi)
1842 *Don Pasquale* (Donizetti)
Linda di Chamounix (Donizetti)
I Lombardi alla prima Crociata (Verdi)
Ruslan and Ludmila (Ruslan i Lyudmila) (Glinka)
1843 *The Bohemian Girl* (Balfe)
Caterina Cornaro (Donizetti)
Ernani (Verdi)

1844 *Alessandro Stradella* (Flotow)
Giovanna d'Arco (Verdi)
1845 *Alzira* (Verdi)
Tannhäuser (Wagner)
Undine (Lortzing)
1846 *Attila* (Verdi)
Der Waffenschmied (Lortzing)
1847 *Macbeth* (Verdi)
La Damnation de Faust (Berlioz)
Martha, oder Der Markt von Richmond (Flotow)
I Masnadieri (Verdi)
1848 *La Battaglia di Legnano* (Verdi)
Il Corsaro (Verdi)
Lohengrin (Wagner)
1849 *Genoveva* (Schumann)
Luisa Miller (Verdi)
The Merry Wives of Windsor (Die lustigen Weiber von Windsor) (Nicolai)
Le Prophète (Meyerbeer)
1850 *Stiffelio* (Verdi)
1851 *Rigoletto* (Verdi)
1852 *Si j'étais roi* (Adam)
1853 *La Traviata* (Verdi)
Il Trovatore (Verdi)
1854 *Das Rheingold* (Wagner)
The Sicilian Vespers (Verdi)
1856 *Rusalka* (The Nixie) (Dargomyzhsky)
Die Walküre (Wagner)
1857 *Halka* (Moniuszko)
Simon Boccanegra (Verdi)
1858 *Un Ballo in maschera* (Verdi)
1859 *Dinorah, ou Le pardon de Ploërmel* (Meyerbeer)
Faust (Gounod)
Tristan und Isolde (Wagner)
1860 *Les Troyens* (Berlioz)
1861 *Bànk Bàn* (Erkel)
La Forza del destino (Verdi)
1862 *Béatrice et Bénédict* (Berlioz)
1863 *Les Pêcheurs de perles* (Bizet)
1864 *La Belle Hélène* (Offenbach)
1865 *L'Africaine* (Meyerbeer)
1866 *Barbe-Bleue* (Offenbach)
The Bartered Bride (Prodaná nevěsta, *The Bride Which Is Sold*) (Smetana)
Don Carlos (Verdi)
Mignon (Thomas)
1867 *Dalibor* (Smetana)
La Grande-Duchesse de Gérolstein (Offenbach)
La Jolie fille de Perth (Bizet)
Die Meistersinger von Nürnberg (Wagner)
Roméo et Juliette (Gounod)
1868 *Hamlet* (Thomas)
Mefistofele (Boito)
La Périchole (Offenbach)
The Voyevode (The Voivoda) (Tchaikovsky)
1869 *Prince Igor* (Knyaz Igor) (Borodin)
Siegfried (Wagner)
1871 *Aida* (Verdi)
The Demon (Anton Rubinstein)
1872 *Libue* (Smetana)
The Stone Guest (Kamennyi gost) (Dargomyzhsky)
1874 *Boris Godunov* (Mussorgsky)
Die Fledermaus (Johann Strauss II)
Götterdämmerung (Wagner)
1875 *Carmen* (Bizet)
Die Königen von Saba (Goldmark)
1876 *La Gioconda* (Ponchielli)
The Kiss (Hubička) (Smetana)
1877 *Blaník* (Fibich)
L'Étoile (Chabrier)
Le Roi de Lahore (Massenet)
Samson et Dalila (Saint-Saëns)
1878 *Eugene Onegin* (Tchaikovsky)
1879 *May Night* (Mayskaya noch) (Rimsky-Korsakov)
1880 *Khovanshchina* (Mussorgsky)
1881 *Les Contes d'Hoffmann* (Offenbach)
Hérodiade (Massenet)
The Snow Maiden (Snegurotchka) (Rimsky-Korsakov)
1882 *Il Duca d'Alba* (Donizetti)
Parsifal (Wagner)
1883 *Lakmé* (Delibes)
Mazeppa (Tchaikovsky)
1884 *Manon* (Massenet)
Der Trompeter van Säckingen (Nessler)
1885 *Le Cid* (Massenet)
The Gypsy Baron (Der Zigeunerbaron) (Johann Strauss II)
1886 *Gwendoline* (Chabrier)
Otello (Verdi) 1888
Le Roi d'Ys (Lalo)
1889 *Esclarmonde* (Massenet)
1890 *Cavalleria rusticana* (Mascagni)
Loreley (Catalani)
The Queen of Spades (Pikovaya dama) (Tchaikovsky)
Salammbô (Reyer)
1891 *L'Amico Fritz* (Mascagni)
Iolanta (Yolanta) (Tchaikovsky)
Ivanhoe (Sullivan)
1892 *Irmelin* (Delius)
Pagliacci (Leoncavallo)
La Wally (Catalani)
Werther (Massenet)
1893 *Der Arme Heinrich* (Pfitzner)
L'Attaque du moulin (Bruneau)
Falstaff (Verdi)
Hänsel und Gretel (Humperdinck)
Manon Lescaut (Puccini)
1894 *La Navarraise* (Massenet)
Thaïs (Massenet)
1895 *El Capitan* (Sousa)
Der Corregidor (Wolf)
Oresteia (Taneyev)

1896 *Andrea Chénier* (Giordano)
La Bohème (Puccini)
Sadko (Rimsky-Korsakov)
1897 *La Bohème* (Leoncavallo)
Mozart and Salieri (Rimsky-Korsakov)
Sapho (Massenet)
Šárka (Fibich)
1898 *Fedora* (Giordano)
1899 *The Devil and Kate* (Čert a Káča) (Dvořák)

1900

1900 *Louise* (Charpentier)
Rusalka (The Nixie) (Dvořák)
Tosca (Puccini)
Zazà (Leoncavallo)
1901 *Feuersnot* (Fire-Famine) (Richard Strauss)
Le Maschere (Mascagni)
Saul og David (Nielsen)
A Village Romeo and Juliet (Delius)
1902 *Adriana Lecouvreur* (Cilèa)
Germania (Franchetti)
Le Jongleur de Notre Dame (Massenet)
Pelléas et Mélisande (Debussy)
1903 *Chérubin* (Massenet)
Jenůfa (Janáček)
Tiefland (d'Albert)
1904 *Madama Butterfly* (Puccini)
1905 *Francesca da Rimini* (Rachmaninoff)
The Legend of the Invisible City of Kitezh and the Maiden Fevronia (Skazaniye o nevidimom grade Kitezhe i deve Fevronii) (Rimsky-Korsakov)
The Merry Widow (Die lüstige Witwe) (Lehár)
Salome (Richard Strauss)
1906 *Ariane et Barbe-Bleue* (Dukas)
Maskarade (Nielsen)
I Quatro rusteghi (Wolf-Ferrari)
The Wreckers (Dame Ethel Smyth)
1907 *The Golden Cockerel* (Zolotoy petushok) (Rimsky-Korsakov)
Thérèse (Massenet)
1908 *Elektra* (Richard Strauss)
1909 *Erwartung* (Schoenberg)
L'Heure Espagnole (Ravel)
Monna Vanna (Février)
Il Segreto di Susanna (Wolf-Ferrari)
1910 *Don Quichotte* (Massenet)
La fanciulla del West (The Girl of the Golden West) (Puccini)
Der Ferne Klang (Schreker)
Königskinder (Humperdinck)
Der Rosenkavalier (Richard Strauss)
1911 *Treemonisha* (Joplin)
1912 *Ariadne auf Naxos* (Richard Strauss)
1913 *L'Amore dei tre re* (Montemezzi)
Der Glückliche Hand (Schoenberg)
The Immortal Hour (Boughton)
1914 *Francesca da Rimini* (Zandonai)
Hugh the Drover (Vaughan Williams)
The Nightingale (*Le rossignol*) (Stravinsky)
1915 *Goyescas* (Granados)
Mona Lisa (Schillings)
Palestrina (Pfitzner)
1916 *Nerone* (Boito)
Renard (Stravinsky)
Violanta (Korngold)
1917 *The Excursions of Mr. Brouček* (Výlety páně Broučkovy) (Janáček)
Turandot (Busoni)
1918 *Bluebeard's Castle* (A Kékszakállú herceg vára) (Bartók)
Die Frau ohne Schatten (Richard Strauss)
Gianni Schicchi (Puccini)
Il Tabarro (Puccini)
1919 *The Fiery Angel* (Ognenniy angel) (Prokofiev)
1920 *Die Tote Stadt* (Korngold)
1921 *Kát'a Kabanová* (Janáček)
Le Roi David (Honegger)
1922 *Mavra* (Stravinsky)
The Perfect Fool (Holst)
El Retablo de Maese Pedro (Master Peter's Puppet Show) (Falla)
Wozzeck (Berg)
1923 *The Cunning Little Vixen* (Příhody Liky Bystrouky) (Janáček)
Doktor Faust (Busoni)
Intermezzo (Richard Strauss)
Les Noces (Stravinsky)
1924 *At the Boar's Head* (Holst)
King Roger (Król Roger) (Szymanowski)
1925 *L'Enfant et les Sortilèges* (Ravel)
The Makropulos Affair (Věc Makropulos) (Janáček)
1926 *Cardillac* (Hindemith)
Háry János (Kodály)
Jonny spielt auf (Krenek)
Judith (Honegger)
Turandot (Puccini)
1927 *Oedipus Rex* (Stravinsky)
Schwanda the Bagpiper (Švanda dudák) (Weinberger)
Sly (Wolf-Ferrari)
1928 *Die Ägyptische Helena* (Richard Strauss)
Die Dreigroschenoper (The Threepenny Opera) (Weill)
Four Saints in Three Acts (Thomson)
From the House of the Dead (Z mrtvého domu) (Janáček)
Maschinist Hopkins (Brand)
The Nose (Nos) (Shostakovich)
1929 *Aufstieg und Fall der Stadt Mahagonny* (Rise and Fall of the City of Mahagonny) (Weill)
Von Heute auf Morgen (Schoenberg)
1930 *Christophe Colomb* (Milhaud)
1931 *The Emperor Jones* (Gruenberg)

1932 *Arabella* (Richard Strauss)
Lady Macbeth of the District of Mtzensk (Ledy Makbet Mtsenskovo uyezda) (Shostakovich)
Riders to the Sea (Vaughan Williams)
1933 *Merry Mount* (Hanson)
1934 *Giuditta* (Lehár)
Die Schweigsame Frau (Richard Strauss)
1935 *Lulu* (Berg)
Mathis der Maler (Hindemith)
Porgy and Bess (Gershwin)
1937 *Amelia Goes to the Ball* (Menotti)
The Cradle Will Rock (Blitzstein)
Daphne (Richard Strauss)
1938 *The Devil and Daniel Webster* (Douglas Moore)
Peer Gynt (Egk)
1939 *Night Flight* (Volo di Notte) (Dallapiccola)
1940 *Betrothal in a Convent* (Prokofiev)
Die Liebe der Danae (Richard Strauss)
1941 *Capriccio* (Richard Strauss)
1943 *Der Kaiser von Atlantis* (Ullmann)
1944 *Les Mamelles de Tirésias* (Poulenc)
1945 *Peter Grimes* (Britten)
1946 *Dantons Tod* (Einem)
The Rape of Lucretia (Britten)
1947 *Albert Herring* (Britten)
The Duenna, or The Double Elopement (Gerhard)
1948 *Il Prigioniero* (Dallapiccola)
1950 *The Consul* (Menotti)
1951 *Amahl and the Night Visitors* (Menotti)
Billy Budd (Britten)
Boulevard Solitude (Henze)
Moses und Aron (Schoenberg)
The Pilgrim's Progress (Vaughan Williams)
The Rake's Progress (Stravinsky)
Trouble in Tahiti (Bernstein)
1952 *The Midsummer Marriage* (Tippett)
War and Peace (Voyna i mir) (Prokofiev)
1954 *The Tender Land* (Copland)
Troilus and Cressida (Walton)
The Turn of the Screw (Britten)
1955 *Susannah* (Floyd)
1956 *The Ballad of Baby Doe* (Douglas Moore)
Les Dialogues de Carmélites (Poulenc)
Yerma (Villa-Lobos)
1957 *Assassinio nella cattedrale* (Pizzetti)
Vanessa (Barber)
1958 *Noye's Fludde* (Britten)
La Voix Humaine (Poulenc)
1959 *Aniara* (Blomdahl)
1961 *Elegy for Young Lovers* (Elegie für junge Liebende) (Henze)
Intolleranza 1960 (Nono)
1963 *Montezuma* (Sessions)
1964 *Amerika* (Haubenstock-Ramati)
Curlew River (Britten)
Don Rodrigo (Ginastera)
Der Junge Lord (Henze)
Die Soldaten (Bernd Alois Zimmermann)
1965 *La Passion selon Sade* (Bussotti)
1966 *Antony and Cleopatra* (Barber)
The Burning Fiery Furnace (Britten)
The Visitation (Schuller)
1967 *Bomarzo* (Ginastera)
1968 *Ulisse* (Dallapiccola)
1969 *The Devils of Loudun* (Diably z Loudun) (Penderecki)
The Knot Garden (Tippett)
1970 *Summer and Smoke* (Hoiby)
Taverner (Maxwell Davies)
1971 *Beatrix Cenci* (Ginastera)
Owen Wingrave (Britten)
1972 *Satyrikon* (Maderna)
1973 *Death in Venice* (Britten)
The Master and Margarita (Slonimsky)
1974 *The Seagull* (Pasatieri)
1975 *The Royal Hunt of the Sun* (Hamilton)
1976 *Einstein on the Beach* (Glass)
The Ice Break (Tippett)
Mary, Queen of Scots (Musgrave)
The Voyage of Edgar Allan Poe (Argento)
We Come to the River (Henze)
1978 *Le Grand macabre* (Ligeti)
Lear (Reimann)
Punainen viiva (The Red Line) (Sallinen)
1980 *Jesu Hochzeit* (Einem)
Mary Stuart (Slonimsky)
Perfect Lives (Private Parts) (Ashley)
Where the Wild Things Are (Knussen)
1981 *Abélard and Héloise* (Ward)
The Postman Always Rings Twice (Paulus)
1982 *The Confidence Man* (Rochberg)
1983 *The English Cat* (Henze)
St. François d'Assise (Messiaen)
Un Re in ascolto (Berio)
1984 *The Black Spider* (Weir)
The Mask of Orpheus (Birtwistle)
Stephen Climax (Zender)
1985 *Frederick Douglass* (Kay)
X: The Life and Times of Malcolm X (Anthony Davis)
1987 *The Electrification of the Soviet Union* (Osborne)
Europeras 1 & 2 (Cage)
A Night at the Chinese Opera (Weir)
Nixon in China (John Adams)
Oedipus (Rihm)
Vincent (Rautavaara)
1991 *The Death of Klinghoffer* (John Adams)
The Ghosts of Versailles (Corigliano)
Ubu Rex (Penderecki)
1994 *Rosa* (Louis Andriessen)
1995 *Harvey Milk* (Wallace)
Powder Her Face (Adès)
1996 *Dennis Cleveland* (Mikel Rouse)
1998 *A Streetcar Named Desire* (Previn)

Opera Characters

The following list of entries is not inclusive but rather is intended only to serve as a clarifying aid to the reader when perusing the biographical entries, particularly those in which debut roles (but not always their corresponding operas) are cited. Title characters, for example, Carmen, Aida, Don Giovanni, and others, are not included in this section but may be found in the chapter Opera Synopses.

A

Abigaille. The supposed daughter of Nabucco in Verdi's *Nabucco.*

Abul Hassan. Abul Hassn Ali Ebn Bekar, a barber in Cornelius's *Der Barbier von Bagdad.*

Achilles. The Greek hero in Tippett's *King Priam.*

Adalgisa. Norma's rival, a Druid priestess, in Bellini's *Norma.*

Adele. Eisenstein's maid in Johann Strauss's *Die Fledermaus.*

Adina. The wealthy landowner in Donizetti's *L'elisir d'amore.*

Adolar. The count of Nevers and Euryanthe's lover in Weber's *Euryanthe.*

Adriano. Stefanno Colonna's son in Wagner's *Rienzi.*

Aegisth. Clytemnestra's lover, Aegistheus, in Richard Strauss's *Elektra.*

Aeneas. 1. The Trojan hero of Purcell's *Dido and Aeneas.* 2. Énée in Berlioz's *Les Troyens.*

Aennchen. Agathe's cousin in Weber's *Der Freischütz.*

Agamemnon. The Greek king, father of Iphigénie and husband of Clytemnestre, in Gluck's *Iphigénie en Aulide.*

Agathe. Kuno's daughter and Max's lover in Weber's *Der Freischütz.*

Alberich. A key Nibelung in Wagner's *Der Ring des Nibelungen.*

Alfio. Lola's teamster husband and Turiddu's rival in Mascagni's *Cavalleria rusticana.*

Alfonso. 1. The philosopher Don Alfonso in Mozart's *Così fan tutte.* 2. The duke of Ferrara, Alfonso d'Este, in Donizetti's *Lucrezia Borgia.*

Alphonse. Actually, Alphonse XI, king of Castile, in Donizetti's *La favorite.*

Alfred. Rosalinde's lover in Johann Strauss's *Die Fledermaus.*

Alfredo. Germont *fils,* Violetta's lover, in Verdi's *La traviata.*

Alice. 1. Ford's wife in both Verdi's *Falstaff* and Vaughan Williams's *Sir John in Love.* 2. Robert's foster sister in Meyerbeer's *Robert le diable.*

Almaviva. 1. The count in both Paisiello's and Rossini's *Il barbiere di Siviglia.* 2. The count in Mozart's *Le nozze di Figaro.*

Alvaro. The Peruvian Don Alvaro in Verdi's *La forza del destino.*

Amalia. Count Moor's orphaned niece in Verdi's *I masnadieri.*

Amelia. 1. Boccanegra's daughter in Verdi's *Simon Boccanegra.* 2. Anckarstroem's wife and Gustavus III's lover in Verdi's *Un ballo in maschera.* 3. Menotti's heroine in *Amelia Goes to the Ball.* 4. Donizetti's heroine in *Il Duce d'Alba.*

Amfortas. The Keeper of the Grail, son of Titurel, in Wagner's *Parsifal.*

Amina. The orphaned, adopted daughter of the sleepwalking Teresa in Bellini's *La sonnambula.*

Aminta. Henry Morosus's wife in Richard Strauss's *Die schweigsame Frau.*

Amneris. Daughter of the king of Egypt and Aida's rival in Verdi's *Aida.*

Amonasro. Aida's father and king of Ethiopia in Verdi's *Aida.*

Anckarstroem. King Gustavus III's secretary in the Swedish version of Verdi's *Un ballo in maschera.*

Andrey Khovansky. Son of Prince Ivan Khovansky and Marfa's lover in Mussorgsky's *Khovanshchina.*

Angelina. Cinderella's given name, stepdaughter of Don Magnifico, in Rossini's *La Cenerentola.*

Anne Trulove. Trulove's daughter and Tom Rakewell's lover in Stravinsky's *The Rake's Progress.*

Annio. Servilia's lover and Sesto's friend in Mozart's *La clemenza di Tito.*

Antonia. One of Hoffmann's lovers (the consumptive) in Offenbach's *Les contes d'Hoffmann.*

Antonio. Barbarina's father, a gardener, and Susanna's uncle in Mozart's *Le nozze di Figaro.*

Arkel. The blind king of Allemonde, grandfather of Pelléas and Golaud, in Debussy's *Pelléas et Mélisande.*

Arline. Count Arnheim's daughter in Balfe's *The Bohemian Girl.*

Arnold. Mathilde's lover, Arnold Melcthal, in Rossini's *Guillaume Tell.*

Aron. Moses' brother in Schoenberg's *Moses und Aron.*

Arsace. Semiramide's son in Rossini's *Semiramide.*

Arturo. Lord Arthur Talbot, the cavalier engaged to Elvira, in Bellini's *I Puritani.*

Arvidson. The fortune teller, Mlle Arvidson, in the Swedish (now standard) version of Verdi's *Un ballo in maschera.*

Aschenbach. Gustave Aschenbach ("Brook of Ashes"), the aged writer in Britten's *Death in Venice.*

Arthenaël. The coenobite monk in Massenet's *Thaïs.*

Azucena. A gypsy, Manrico's kidnapper and assumed mother, in Verdi's *Il trovatore.*

B

Baba the Turk. The bearded circus lady in Stravinsky's *The Rake's Progress.*

Bacchus. Ariadne's divine salvation in Richard Strauss's *Ariadne auf Naxos.*

Balducci. Actually, Giacomo Balducci, papal treasurer and father of Teresa in Berlioz's *Benvenuto Cellini.*

Barak the Dyer. Husband of the shadow-bearing (anonymous) Dyer's Wife in Richard Strauss's *Die Frau ohne Schatten.*

Barbarina. The daughter of Antonio the gardener in Mozart's *Le nozze di Figaro.*

Barnaba. The Inquisition spy in Ponchielli's *La Gioconda.*

Beckmesser. The town clerk, Sixtus Beckmesser, in Wagner's *Die Meistersinger von Nürnberg.*

Belcore. The sergeant in Donizetti's *L'elisir d'amore.*

Belfiore. The Cavaliere di Belfiore in Verdi's *Un giorno di regno.*

Belinda. Dido's lady-in-waiting in Purcell's *Dido and Aeneas.*

Belmonte. Constanze's Spanish nobleman lover in Mozart's *Die Entführung aus dem Serail.*

Berendey. The tsar in Rimsky-Korsakov's *The Snow Maiden.*

Bertram. Robert's father (and the Devil) in Meyerbeer's *Robert le diable.*

Bess. Crown's girlfriend and Porgy's lover in Gershwin's *Porgy and Bess.*

Blonde, Blondchen. Constanze's maid in Mozart's *Die Entführung aus dem Serail.*

Boris. Dikoj's nephew and Kát'a's lover in Janáček's *Kát'a Kabanová.*

Bottom. One of the rustics and Titania's weaver lover in Britten's *A Midsummer Night's Dream.*

Brangäne. Isolde's attendant in Wagner's *Tristan und Isolde.*

Brünnhilde. A Valkyrie and Wotan's favorite daughter in Wagner's *Die Walküre, Siegfried,* and *Götterdämerung* in *Der Ring des Nibelugen.*

C

Calaf. A Tartar prince, long-lost son of Timur, who's in love with Turandot, in Puccini's *Turandot.*

Calkas. The High Priest, brother of Pandarus, in Walton's *Troilus and Cressida.*

Canio. Nedda's husband and leader of the strolling players in Leoncavallo's *Pagliacci.*

Captain Vere. The commander of the H.M.S. *Indomitable* in Britten's *Billy Budd.*

Caspar. The huntsman in Weber's *Die Freischütz.*

Cassandre. Priam and Hecuba's Trojan seer daughter in Berlioz's *Les Troyens.*

Cassio. The maligned captain in Verdi's *Otello.*

Cavaradossi. Tosca's lover, Mario Cavaradossi, a painter, in Puccini's *Tosca.*

Chapelou. The postillion, later a famous singer known as Saint-Phar, in Adam's *Le postillon de Lonjumeau.*

Charlotte. Albert's wife in Massenet's *Werther.*

Cherubino. The page of Countess Almaviva in Mozart's *Le nozze di Figaro.*

Chrysothemis. Clytemnestra's daughter and Elektra's sister in Richard Strauss's *Elektra.*

Cio-Cio-San. The Japanese heroine ("Butterfly") in Puccini's *Madama Butterfly.*

Claggart. John Claggart, the master-at-arms in Britten's *Billy Budd.*

Cleopatra. Caesar's lover and, in the end, crowned queen, in Handel's *Giulio Cesare.*

Clytemnestra. Agamemnon's widow and mother of Elektra and Chrysothemis in Richard Strauss's *Elektra.*

Collatinus. Lucretia's Roman husband in Britten's *The Rape of Lucretia.*

Colline. One of the four bohemians (the philosopher) in Puccini's *La bohème.*

Colonna. The patriarch of the Colonna family, Stefano Colonna, in Wagner's *Rienzi.*

Commendatore. The avenging statue that comes to life in Mozart's *Don Giovanni.*

Composer. The idealistic composer (a trouser role) in Richard Strauss's *Ariadne auf Naxos.*

Concepción. The clockmaker Torquemada's wife in Ravel's *L'heure espagnole.*

Count. Among many, 1. Count Almaviva in both Paisiello's and Rossini's *Il barbiere di Siviglia* and in Mo-

Yasuko Hayashi as Cio-Cio-San (*Madama Butterfly*)

Figaro and Susannah (*The Marriage of Figaro*)

Marilyn Horne as Arsace (*Semiramide*)

Turandot and Calaf in dressing room (*Turandot*)

Frederica von Stade as Amina (*La sonnambula*)

Torquemada catches his wife's lover (*L'heure espagnole*)

Carol Neblett as Minnie (*La fanciulla del West*)

Sir John Falstaff and Mistress Quickly (*Falstaff*)

Sheriff Jack Rance confronts Minnie (*La fanciulla del West*)

Allan Monk as Sharpless (*Madama Butterfly*)

Nunzio Todisco as Pollione (*Norma*)

William Neill as Aegisth (*Elektra*)

Janis Martin as Ortrud (*Lohengrin*)

Walter Berry as Leporello (*Don Giovanni*)

Lohengrin kills Telramund (*Lohengrin*)

Giorgio Germont confronts Violetta (*La Traviata*)

James Morris as Wotan (*Die Walkure*)

Anne Evans as Elsa of Brabant (*Lohengrin*)

Anny Schlemm as Clytemnestra (*Elektra*)

Leontyne Price as Leonora
(*La forza del destino*)

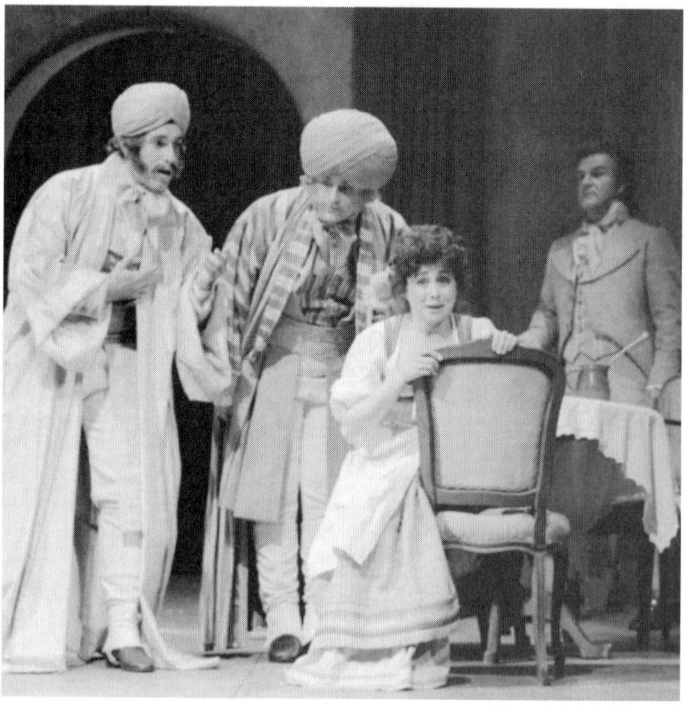

Asking Despina for assistance (*Così fan tutte*)

Don Giovanni seducing Zerlina (*Don Giovanni*)

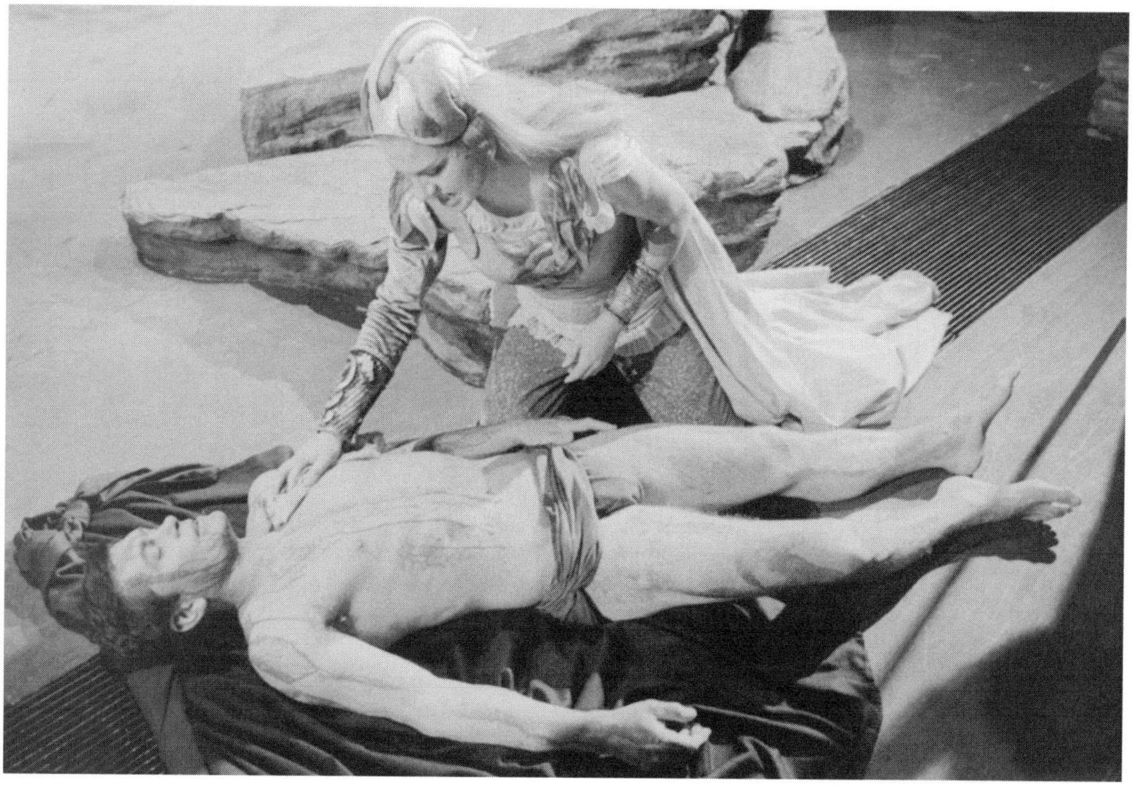
Death of Siegmund (*Die Walkure*)

Bess at Robbins's funeral (*Porgy and Bess*)

Norman Mittelman as Barnaba (*La Giocanda*)

Dr. Malatesta plotting against Don Pasquale (*Don Pasquale*)

zart's *Le nozze di Figaro*. 2. Count Walter in Verdi's *Luisa Miller*.

Countess. Among many, 1. Countess Almaviva in Mozart's *Le nozze di Figaro*. 2. The countess in Tchaikovsky's *The Queen of Spades*. 3. The countess in Strauss's *Capriccio*.

Cressida. Daughter of the Trojan high priest Calkas and (in a later version) Troilus's lover in Walton's *Troilus and Cressida*.

Crown. The tough stevedore and Bess's boyfriend in Gershwin's *Porgy and Bess*.

D

Daland. Senta's father in Wagner's *Die fliegender Holländer*.

Dandini. Don Ramiro's valet in Rossini's *La Cenerentola*.

Dapertutto. The evil sorcerer in Offenbach's *Les contes d'Hoffmann*.

David. Hans Sachs's apprentice in Wagner's *Die Meistersinger von Nürnberg*.

Desdemona. Otello's wife in both Rossini's and Verdi's *Otello*.

Des Grieux. Manon's lover, the chevalier Des Grieux, in Massenet's *Manon* and Puccini's *Manon Lescaut*.

Despina. Maid to Fiordiligi and Dorabella in Mozart's *Così fan tutte*.

Dick Johnson. The western bandit Ramerrez, a.k.a. Dick Johnson, in Puccini's *La fanciulla del West*.

Dikoj. Uncle of Kát'a's lover Boris, Savel Prokofjevič Dikoj, in Janáček's *Kát'a Kabanová*.

Di Luna. The nobleman of Aragon, the Conte di Luna, Manrico's brother, in Verdi's *Il trovatore*.

Dmitry. The pretender to Russia's throne in Mussorgsky's *Boris Godunov*.

Docteur Miracle. The evil doctor in Offenbach's *Les contes d'Hoffmann*.

Doctor Bartolo. The doctor of Seville in both Paisiello's and Rossini's *Il barbiere di Siviglia* and in Mozart's *Le nozze di Figaro*.

Dodon. King Dodon in Rimsky-Korsakov's *The Golden Cockerel*.

Don Alfonso. The engineering philosopher in Mozart's *Così fan tutte*.

Don Basilio. The priest and musicmaster in both Paisiello's and Rossini's *Il barbiere di Siviglia* and in Mozart's *Le nozze di Figaro*.

Don Carlos. Laura's lover and Don Juan's rival in Dargomyzhsky's *The Stone Guest*.

Don Carlos di Vargas. Leonora's brother in Verdi's *La forza del destino*.

Don José. The corporal of dragoons and lover to both Micaëla and Carmen in Bizet's *Carmen*.

Don Magnifico. The stepfather of Cinderella (Angelina) in Rossini's *La Cenerentola*.

Donna Anna. The commendatore's daughter and Don Ottavio's lover in Mozart's *Don Giovanni*.

Donna Elvira. One of Don Giovanni's abandoned lovers, a lady of Burgos, in Mozart's *Don Giovanni*.

Donner. The God of Thunder in Wagner's *Das Rheingold* in *Der Ring des Nibelungen*.

Don Ottavio. Donna Anna's lover in Mozart's *Don Giovanni*.

Dorabella. Fiordiligi's sister in Mozart's *Così fan tutte*.

Dosifey. Leader of the Old Believers, Dositheus, in Mussorgsky's *Khovanshchina*.

Drum-Major. Marie's braggart seducer in Berg's *Wozzeck*.

Duke of Mantua. The licentious duke in Verdi's *Rigoletto*.

Dulcamara. The quack doctor in Donizetti's *L'elisir d'amore*.

Dyer's Wife, The. The anonymous wife of Barak the Dyer in Richard Strauss's *Die Frau ohne Schatten*.

E

Eboli. Princess Eboli, former mistress to King Philip and lady-in-waiting to Elisabeth de Valois, in Verdi's *Don Carlos*.

Edgardo. Lucia's lover, Edgar of Ravenswood, in Donizetti's *Lucia di Lammermoor*.

Eglantine. Lysiart's lover, Eglantine von Puiset, in Weber's *Euryanthe*.

Eisenstein. Rosalinde's husband, Gabriel von Eisenstein, in Johann Strauss's *Die Fledermaus*.

Eléazar. Supposed father of Rachel, a Jewish goldsmith, in Halévy's *La Juive*.

Eletsky. A prince in Tchaikovsky's *The Queen of Spades*.

Elettra. The Greek princess in Mozart's *Idomeneo*.

Elisabeth. 1. Tannhäuser's "sacred" love and the Landgrave's niece in Wagner's *Tannhäuser*. 2. Queen Elisabeth, Mary Stuart's downfall, in Donizetti's *Maria Stuarda*.

Elisabeth de Valois. Queen to King Philip II of Spain and lover to his son Carlos in Verdi's *Don Carlos*.

Elizabeth. Queen Elizabeth, the earl of Essex's downfall, in Donizetti's *Roberto Devereux*.

Ellen Orford. Peter's sympathetic schoolmistress friend in Britten's *Peter Grimes*.

Elsa. Lohengrin's bride, Elsa von Brabant, in Wagner's *Lohengrin*.

Elvino. Amina's young farmer bridegroom in Bellini's *La sonnambula*.

Elvira. 1. Donna Elvira, one of Don Giovanni's abandoned lovers, a lady of Burgos, in Mozart's *Don Giovanni*. 2. The bey of Algiers's scorned wife in Rossini's *L'italiana in Algeri*. 3. Gualtiero Valton's daughter in Bellini's *I Puritani*. 4. Ernani's lover and Silva's kinswoman in Verdi's *Ernani*.

Emilia. 1. Desdemona's companion and Iago's wife in both Rossini's and Verdi's *Otello*. 2. The singer, Emilia Marty, in Janáček's *The Makropulos Affair*.

Enrico. Lucia's brother, Henry Ashton, in Donizetti's *Lucia di Lammermoor*.

Enzo. Laura's lover, Enzo Grimaldi, a Genoese nobleman, in Ponchielli's *La Gioconda.*

Erda. The Earth Goddess and mother of the Valkryies in Wagner's *Rheingold* and *Siegfried* in *Der Ring des Nibelungen.*

Erik. Senta's rejected huntsman lover in Wagner's *Der fliegende Holländer.*

Ernesto. Don Pasquale's nephew in Donizetti's *Don Pasquale.*

Escamillo. The toreador in Bizet's *Carmen.*

Eva. Walther's lover and Pogner's daughter in Wagner's *Die Meistersinger von Nürnberg.*

Ezio. The Roman general in Verdi's *Attila.*

F

Fafner. One of the two giants in Wagner's *Das Rheingold* in *Der Ring des Nibelungen.* In *Siegfried* he appears as a dragon.

Falstaff. Sir John Falstaff in both Nicolai's *Die lustigen Weiber von Windsor* and Vaughan Williams's *Sir John in Love.*

Faninal. Sophie's wealthy and newly ennobled father in Richard Strauss's *Der Rosenkavalier.*

Farlaf. A Varangian warrior in Glinka's *Ruslan and Ludmila.*

Fasolt. One of the two giants in Wagner's *Das Rheingold* in *Der Ring des Nibelungen.*

Fatima. Reiza's attendant in Weber's *Oberon.*

Fenella. The poor and dumb Neapolitan heroine of Auber's *La muette de Portici.*

Fenena. Nabucco's daughter in Verdi's *Nabucco.*

Fenton. Anne's young gentleman lover of Windsor in Nicolai's *Die lustigen Weiber von Windsor,* Verdi's *Falstaff,* and Vaughan Williams's *Sir John in Love.*

Ferrando. Dorabella's officer lover in Mozart's *Così fan tutte.*

Fidès. John of Leyden's mother in Meyerbeer's *Le prophète.*

Fieramosca. The Pope's sculptor and a rival for Teresa's love in Berlioz's *Benvenuto Cellini.*

Fiesco. A Genoese nobleman in Verdi's *Simon Boccanegra.*

Figaro. The barber of Seville in both Paisiello's and Rossini's *Il barbiere di Siviglia* and later Count Almaviva's manservant in Mozart's *Le nozze di Figaro.*

Fiordiligi. Dorabella's sister in Mozart's *Così fan tutte.*

First Lady. The leader of the Three Ladies, attendants to the Queen of the Night, in Mozart's *Die Zauberflöte.*

Flamand. An aspiring musician in Richard Strauss's *Capriccio.*

Florestan. The unjustly imprisoned husband of Leonore, a Spanish nobleman, in Beethoven's *Fidelio.*

Flowermaidens. A group of seductive maidens in Wagner's *Parsifal.*

Ford. 1. Alice's wealthy husband of Windsor in Verdi's *Falstaff* and Vaughan Williams's *Sir John in Love.* 2. Herr Fluth in Nicolai's *Die lustigen Weiber von Windsor.*

Forester. A central human figure, the Moravian forester, in Janáček's *The Cunning Little Vixen.*

Foresto. An Aquileian knight in Verdi's *Attila.*

Fra Melitone. A Franciscan friar in Verdi's *La forza del destino.*

Frasquita. One of the coquettish dancing barmaids in Bizet's *Carmen.*

Freia. The Goddess of Youth in Wagner's *Das Rheingold* in *Der Ring des Nibelungen.*

Frère Laurent. The holy man, confidante to the young lovers, in Gounod's *Roméo et Juliette.*

Fricka. The Goddess of Wedlock and Wotan's wife in Wagner's *Der Ring des Nibelungen.*

Froh. The God of Spring in Wagner's *Das Rheingold* in *Der Ring des Nibelungen.*

Frosch. The jailer (a speaking part) in Johann Strauss's *Die Fledermaus.*

Fyodor. Boris's son, who assumes the throne just prior to his father's death, in Mussorgsky's *Boris Godunov.*

G

Gabriele Adorno. Amelia Grimaldi's Genoese nobleman lover in Verdi's *Simon Boccanegra.*

Galitsky. Igor's sister Yaroslavna's husband, Prince Vladimir Yaroslavich Galitsky, in Borodin's *Prince Igor.*

Gennaro. 1. Lucrezia's young nobleman son in Donizetti's *Lucrezia Borgia.* 2. The blacksmith in Wolf-Ferrari's *I gioielli della Madonna.*

George Brown. Anna's young English officer lover in Boieldieu's *La dame blanche.*

Gérald. Lakmé's English officer lover in Delibes's *Lakmé.*

Gérard. A leader of the revolution in Giordano's *Andrea Chénier.*

Germont. Alfredo's father, Giorgio Germont, in Verdi's *La traviata.*

Gilda. Rigoletto's ill-fated daughter in Verdi's *Rigoletto.*

Giorgetta. Michele's wife in Puccini's *Il tabarro.*

Giulietta. 1. One of Hoffmann's lovers (the courtesan) in Offenbach's *Les contes d'Hoffmann.* 2. Juliet in Bellini's *I Capuleti e i Montecchi* and other Italian Romeo and Juliet operas.

Golaud. Grandson of King Arkel, half brother of Pelléas, and husband of Mélisande in Debussy's *Pelléas et Mélisande.*

Goryanchikov. The political prisoner Alexander Petrovich Goryanchikov in Janáček's *From the House of the Dead.*

Grand Inquisitor, The. The head of the Inquisition in Verdi's *Don Carlos* and Dallapiccola's *Il prigioniero.*

Grane. Brünnhilde's horse in Wagner's *Der Ring des Nibelungen,* although rarely if ever seen onstage anymore.

Gremin. Tatyana's husband, Prince Gremin, in Tchaikovsky's *Eugene Onegin.*

Gretel. Hänsel's wily sister in Humperdinck's *Hänsel und Gretel.*

Guglielmo. Fiordiligi's young officer lover in Mozart's *Così fan tutte.*

Gunther. Gutrune's brother and Hagen's half brother, Lord of the Gibichungs, in Wagner's *Götterdämerung* in *Der Ring des Nibelungen.*

Gurnemanz. The veteran knight of the Grail in Wagner's *Parsifal.*

Gustavus III. The king of Sweden in the Swedish version of Verdi's *Un ballo in maschera.*

Gutrune. Gunther's sister and Hagen's half sister in Wagner's *Götterdämerung* in *Der Ring des Nibelungen.*

H

Hagen. Gunther and Gutrune's half brother, a Gibichung, in Wagner's *Götterdämerung* in *Der Ring des Nibelungen.*

Hannah Glawari. The wealthy "merry widow" in Lehár's *Die Lustige Witwe.*

Hans Sachs. A historically important poet and Mastersinger (1494–1576) who has assumed various roles in operas, including the wise cobbler-poet in Wagner's *Die Meistersinger von Nürnberg.*

Heinrich. The king of Saxony, Heinrich der Vogler, in Wagner's *Lohengrin.*

Hélène. The duchess Hélène, Duke Frederick's sister and Henri's lover, in Verdi's *Les vêpres siciliennes.*

Helen of Troy. A central character, after various classical legends, in Offenbach's *La belle Hélène,* Tippett's *King Priam,* and Richard Strauss's *Die Ägyptische Helena.*

Hermann. A young officer, the object of Lisa's affections, in Tchaikovsky's *The Queen of Spades.*

Herod, Hérode. Salome's stepfather, husband of Herodias (Hérodiade) in Richard Strauss's *Salome* and Massenet's *Hérodiade.*

Herodias, Hérodiade. Herod (Hérode) Antipas's wife in Massenet's *Hérodiade* and Richard Strauss's *Salome.*

Humming Chorus. The hidden chorus that closes the mournful Act II of Puccini's *Madama Butterfly.*

Hunding. Sieglinde's husband, a Neiding, in Wagner's *Die Walküre* in *Der Ring des Nibelungen.*

Huntsmen's Chorus. The chorus in Act III of Weber's *Der Freischütz.*

Huon. Reiza's lover, Sir Huon of Bordeaux, in Weber's *Oberon.*

Hylas. A young sailor in Berlioz's *Les Troyens.*

I

Iago. A Venetian soldier, ensign to Otello, in both Rossini's and Verdi's *Otello.*

Idamante. Ilia's lover and Idomeneo's son in Mozart's *Idomeneo.*

Ilia. A Trojan princess, King Priam's daughter and Idamante's lover, in Mozart's *Idomeneo.*

Inès. 1. Don Diego's daughter in Meyerbeer's *L'Africaine.* 2. Confidante of Léonor in Donizetti's *La favorite.*

Irene. Rienzi's sister and Adriano's lover in Wagner's *Rienzi.*

Isabella. 1. Lindoro's Italian lover in Rossini's *L'italiana in Algeri.* 2. The Princess Isabella, later the duke of Normandy's wife, in Meyerbeer's *Robert le diable.*

Ismaele. The king of Jerusalem's nephew and Fenena's lover in Verdi's *Nabucco.*

Isolde. The Irish princess, King Mark's wife and Tristan's lover, in Wagner's *Tristan und Isolde.*

Isolier. The count's page in Rossini's *Le Comte Ory.*

Ivan Khovansky. Prince Ivan Khovansky, leader of the guards and father of Andrey Khovansky, in Mussorgsky's *Khovanshchina.*

Ivan Susanin. Antonida's peasant father in Glinka's *A Life for the Tsar.*

J

Jack Rance. The sheriff in Puccini's *La fanciulla del West.*

Jacquino. Rocco's assistant in Beethoven's *Fidelio.*

Jason. Medea's former husband, the leader of the Argonauts, in Cherubini's *Médée.*

Jenifer. Mark's young bride in Tippett's *The Midsummer Marriage.*

Jenik. Tobias's son by his first marriage, a young villager, in Smetana's *The Bartered Bride.*

Ježibaba. The Witch in Dvořák's *Rusalka.*

Jochanaan. John the Baptist in Richard Strauss's *Salome.*

John of Leyden. The Anabaptist prophet and self-proclaimed emperor in Meyerbeer's *Le prophète.*

John Sorel. A revolutionary being pursued by the secret police in Menotti's *The Consul.*

Judith. The duke's most recent wife in Bartók's *Bluebeard's Castle.*

Julia. Licinius's lover and the Vestal Virgin in Spontini's *La vestale.*

Juliette. Roméo's lover in Gounod's *Roméo et Juliette.*

K

Kabanicha. The widow of the wealthy merchant Kabanov, Marfa Kabanov, a.k.a. Kabanicha, in Janáček's *Kát'a Kabanová.*

Katerina Izmaylova. Wife of the wealthy merchant and lover of Sergey in Shostakovich's *Lady Macbeth of the District of Mtsensk.*

Kecal. The marriage broker in Smetana's *The Bartered Bride.*

Khan Kontchak. The khan in Borodin's *Prince Igor.*

King Fisher. Jenifer's businessman father in Tippett's *The Midsummer Marriage.*

Klingsor. The magician in Wagner's *Parsifal.*

Kochubey. Maria's rich Cossack father and husband of Lyubov in Tchaikovsky's *Mazeppa.*

Kontchak. The Khan, chief of the Polovtsians, in Borodin's *Prince Igor.*

Kostelnička. Jenůfa's stepmother and caretaker, widow of Toma Buryja, in Janáček's *Jenůfa.*

Kothner. The mastersinger and baker Fritz Kothner in Wagner's *Die Meistersinger von Nürnberg.*

Kovalev. A college assessor, Platon Kuzmich Kovalev, in Shostakovich's *The Nose.*

Kühleborn. Undine's water spirit father in Lortzing's *Undine.*

Kundry. The messenger of the Grail in Wagner's *Parsifal.*

Kurwenal. Tristan's retainer in Wagner's *Tristan und Isolde.*

Kutuzov. Commander of the Russian armies, the field marshal Mikhail Kutuzov, in Prokofiev's *War and Peace.*

L

Laca. Števa Burya's stepbrother, Laca Klemeň, in Janáček's *Jenůfa.*

Lady Billows. An aged autocrat in Britten's *Albert Herring.*

Landgrave. Hermann, landgrave of Thuringia, in Wagner's *Tannhäuser.*

Lauretta. Rinuccio's lover and Schicchi's daughter in Puccini's *Gianni Schicchi.*

Leïla. Nadir's lover, the Brahmin priestess, in Bizet's *Les pêcheurs de perles.*

Lensky. Olga's betrothed, the young poet Vladimir Lensky, in Tchaikovsky's *Eugene Onegin.*

Léonor. King Alphonse XI of Castile's mistress, Léonor de Guzman, in Donizetti's *La favorite.*

Leonora. 1. Oberto's daughter in Verdi's *Oberto.* 2. Manrico's lover, lady-in-waiting to the princess of Aragon, in Verdi's *Il trovatore.* 3. Donna Leonora de Vargas, Don Alvaro's lover, in Verdi's *La forza del destino.*

Leonore. Florestan's wife, a.k.a. Fidelio, in Beethoven's *Fidelio.*

Leporello. Don Giovanni's servant in Mozart's *Don Giovanni* and Dargomyzhsky's *The Stone Guest.*

Lescaut. 1. Manon's cousin and a sergeant in the King's Guards in Massenet's *Manon.* 2. Manon's cousin in Puccini's *Manon Lescaut.*

Lindoro. 1. Isabella's young Italian lover in Rossini's *L'italiana in Algeri.* 2. Count Almaviva's assumed name in Rossini's *Il barbiere di Siviglia.*

Lisa. Hermann's lover and the countess's granddaughter in Tchaikovsky's *The Queen of Spades.*

Liù. A slave girl in Puccini's *Turandot.*

Loge. The God of Fire in Wagner's *Das Rheingold* in *Der Ring des Nibelungen.*

Lola. Alfio's wife and Turiddu's lover in Mascagni's *Cavalleria rusticana.*

Lorenzo. Zerlina's lover in Auber's *Fra Diavolo.*

Lucy Lockit. Polly Peachum's rival in love in Pepusch's *The Beggar's Opera* and Weill's *Die Dreigroschenoper.*

Ludmila. Ruslan's lover and daughter of Prince Svetozar of Kiev in Glinka's *Ruslan and Ludmila.*

Luigi. Giorgetta's young stevedore lover in Puccini's *Il tabarro.*

Lysiart. Eglantine's lover, count of Forest, in Weber's *Euryanthe.*

Lyubov. Maria's mother and wife of the wealthy Cossack Kochubey in Tchaikovsky's *Mazeppa.*

M

Macduff. A Scottish nobleman, Macbeth's assassin in Verdi's *Macbeth.*

Macheath. 1. The highwayman in Pepusch's *The Beggar's Opera.* 2. The highwayman, a.k.a. Mackie Messer (Mack the Knife), in Weill's *Die Dreigroschoper.*

Maddalena. Sparafucile's sister in Verdi's *Rigoletto.*

Madeleine de Coigny. Chénier's lover and daughter of the Comtesse de Coigny in Giordano's *Andrea Chénier.*

Madwoman, The. The dead boy's mother in Britten's *Curlew River.*

Magdalene. David's lover and Eva's nurse in Wagner's *Die Meistersinger von Nürnberg.*

Magda Sorel. John Sorel's ill-fated wife in Menotti's *The Consul.*

Malatesta. Pasquale's friend Dr. Malatesta in Donizetti's *Don Pasquale.*

Mandryka. The rich young landowner in Richard Strauss's *Arabella.*

Manrico. Di Luna's kidnapped brother, supposed son of the gypsy Azucena, in Verdi's *Il trovatore.*

Marcellina. The duenna in Mozart's *Le nozze di Figaro.*

Marcello. Musetta's bohemian lover, a painter, in both Puccini's and Leoncavallo's *La bohème.*

Mařenka. Jeník's betrothed and daughter of Krušina and Ludmila in Smetana's *The Bartered Bride.*

Marfa. A young widow and one of the Old Believers in Mussorgsky's *Khovanshchina.*

Marguerite. Faust's young lover in Gounod's *Faust.*

Marguerite de Valois. Queen to Henri of Navarre in Meyerbeer's *Les Huguenots.*

Maria. Mazeppa's lover and daughter of Kochubey and Lyubov in Tchaikovsky's *Mazeppa.*

Marie. 1. Tonio's lover and the "daughter of the regiment" in Donizetti's *La fille du régiment.* 2. Wozzeck's erring wife in Berg's *Wozzeck.*

Marina. 1. Lover to Dmitry and confessor to Rangoni in Mussorgsky's *Boris Godunov.* 2. Wife of the delusional protagonist of Dvořák's *Dimitrj.*

Mark. 1. Isolde's husband, king of Cornwall, in Wagner's *Tristan und Isolde.* 2. Jenifer's bridegroom in Tippett's *The Midsummer Marriage.*

Marschallin, Die. The field marshal's wife and Octavian's lover, the Princess von Werdenberg, in Richard Strauss's *Der Rosenkavalier.*

Marzelline. The daughter of the jailer Rocco, smitten with Fidelio (a.k.a. Leonore), in Beethoven's *Fidelio.*

Masaniello. Fenella's Neapolitan fisherman brother, Tommaso Aniello, in Auber's *La muette de Portici.*

Masetto. Zerlina's betrothed, a peasant, in Mozart's *Don Giovanni.*

Matteo. The innkeeper, Zerlina's father, in Auber's *Fra Diavolo.*

Max. Agathe's huntsman lover in Weber's *Der Freischütz.*

Melitone. The comic priest, Fra Melitone, in Verdi's *La forza del destino.*

Melot. One of King Mark's courtiers in Wagner's *Tristan und Isolde.*

Méphistophélès. 1. The Devil in Gounod's *Faust* and Berlioz's *La damnation de Faust.* 2. The Devil (Mephistopheles) in Busoni's *Doktor Faust.*

Mercédès. One of the coquettish dancing barmaids in Bizet's *Carmen.*

Mercutio. Prince of Verona, a friend of Roméo, in Gounod's *Roméo et Juliet.*

Micaëla. A peasant girl who loves Don José in Bizet's *Carmen.*

Michele. Giorgetta's husband, a Seine barge driver, in Puccini's *Il tabarro.*

Mime. Alberich's Nibelung brother in Wagner's *Siegfried* in *Der Ring des Nibelungen.*

Mimi. Rodolfo's seamstress lover in both Puccini's and Leoncavallo's *La bohème.*

Minnie. Dick Johnson's lover and owner of the Polka Saloon, a.k.a. "The Girl of the Golden West," in Puccini's *La fanciulla del West.*

Mistress Quickly. A lady of Windsor in Verdi's *Falstaff* and Vaughan Williams's *Sir John in Love.*

Monostatos. A moor in the service of Sarastro in Mozart's *Die Zauberflöte.*

Monterone. A nobleman, Count Monterone, in Verdi's *Rigoletto.*

Mother Goose. The brothel keeper in Stravinsky's *The Rake's Progress.*

Musetta. Marcello's lover in both Puccini's and Leoncavallo's *La bohème.*

Mustafà. The bey of Algiers in Rossini's *L'italiana di Algeri.*

N

Nadir. Zurga's friend and rival in love in Bizet's *Les pěcheurs de perles.*

Nannetta. Fenton's lover and Ford's daughter in Verdi's *Falstaff.*

Narraboth. The young Syrian captain of the guard in Richard Strauss's *Salome.*

Nedda. Canio's wife and Silvio's lover in Leoncavallo's *Pagliacci.*

Neiding. One of Hunding's tribe in Wagner's *Die Walküre* in *Der Ring des Nibelungen.*

Nélusko. The slave, in love with the slave Sélika, in Meyerbeer's *L'Africaine.*

Nemorino. Adina's young peasant lover in Donizetti's *L'elisir d'amore.*

Nero. The Roman emperor, Poppea's lover, in Monteverdi's *L'incoronazione di Poppea.*

Nevers. 1. The Catholic nobleman, the Comte de Nevers, in Meyerbeer's *Les Huguenots.* 2. Adolar, a.k.a. Graf von Nevers, in Weber's *Euryanthe.*

Nicklausse. Hoffmann's friend in Offenbach's *Les contes d'Hoffmann.*

Nick Shadow. The Devil in Stravinsky's *The Rake's Progress.*

Nightwatchman. The nightwatchman in Wagner's *Die Meistersinger in Nürnberg.*

Norina. Ernesto's young widowed lover in Donizetti's *Don Pasquale.*

Nurse. Juliette's caretaker and confidante in Gounod's *Roméo et Juliette.*

O

Oberon. One of the fairies (with Puck and Titania) in Britten's *A Midsummer Night's Dream.*

Ochs. The Marschallin's brother, Baron Ochs auf Lerchenau, in Richard Strauss's *Der Rosenkavalier.*

Octavian. The Knight of the Rose, Count Octavian Rofrano, in Richard Strauss's *Der Rosenkavalier.* His full Christian name, as recited by Sophie in Act II, is Octavian Maria Ehrenreich Bonaventura Fernand Hyacinth. His nickname is Quinquin.

Odabella. The lord of Aquileia's daughter in Verdi's *Attila.*

Olga. Lensky's lover, Olga Larina, in Tchaikovsky's *Eugene Onegin.*

Olivier. A poet and rival in love of the musician Flamand in Richard Strauss's *Capriccio.*

Olympia. Hoffmann's first love (the mechanical doll) in Offenbach's *Les contes d'Hoffmann.*

Ophélie. Polonius's daughter in Thomas's *Hamlet.*

Orest. Elektra's brother, Orestes, in Richard Strauss's *Elektra.*

Orlovsky. The Russian prince in Johann Strauss's *Die Fledermaus.*

Oroveso. The high priest of the Druids in Bellini's *Norma.*

Orsini. A Roman patrician, Paolo Orsini, in Wagner's *Rienzi.*

Ortrud. Telramund's wife in Wagner's *Lohengrin.*

Oscar. King Gustavus III's page in Verdi's *Un ballo in maschera.*

Ottavia. Nero's scorned wife in Monteverdi's *L'incoronazione di Poppea.*

Ottokar. The prince in Weber's *Der Freischütz.*

Ottone. Poppea's scorned and vengeful lover in Monteverdi's *L'incoronazione di Poppea.*

P

Padre Guardiano. Abbot of the monastery of Hornachuelos in Verdi's *La forza del destino.*

Pamina. The Queen of the Night's daughter in Mozart's *Die Zauberflöte.*

Pandarus. The high priest Calkas's brother in Walton's *Troilus and Cressida.*

Pang. One of the three ministers of the court (with Ping and Pong) in Puccini's *Turandot.*

Papageno and **Papagena.** The birdcatcher and his lover in Mozart's *Die Zauberflöte.*

Parasha. The hussar Vasily's village girl lover in Stravinsky's *Mavra.*

Peachum. Actually, J. J. Peachum, Polly Peachum's father and Macheath/Mackie Messer's (Mack the Knife) pursuer in Pepusch's *The Beggar's Opera* and Weill's *Die Dreigroschenoper.*

Pedrillo. Blonde's lover and Belmonte's servant in Mozart's *Die Entführung aus dem Serail.*

Philip. King of Spain, Philip II, in Verdi's *Don Carlos.*

Pimen. The aged chronicler monk in Mussorgsky's *Boris Godunov.*

Ping. One of the three ministers of the court (with Pang and Pong) in Puccini's *Turandot.*

Pinkerton. The American naval lieutenant and faithless husband of Cio-Cio-San ("Butterfly") in Puccini's *Madama Butterfly.*

Pizarro. The prison governor in Beethoven's *Fidelio.*

Pogner. Eva's father, Veit Pogner, a goldsmith and mastersinger, in Wagner's *Die Meistersinger von Nürnberg.*

Pollione. The Roman proconsul lover to both Norma and Adalgisa in Bellini's *Norma.*

Polly Peachum. Lucy Lockit's rival in love in Pepusch's *The Beggar's Opera* and Weill's *Die Dreigroschenoper.*

Pong. One of the three ministers of the court (with Pang and Ping) in Puccini's *Turandot.*

Posa. Rodrigo, marquis of Posa, in Verdi's *Don Carlos.*

Preziosilla. The gypsy girl in Verdi's *La forza del destino.*

Puck. One of the fairies (with Titania and Oberon) in Britten's *A Midsummer Night's Dream.*

Q

Queen of Shemakha, The. King Dodon's seducer in Rimsky-Korsakov's *The Golden Cockerel.*

Queen of the Night, The. Pamina's mother and Sarastro's adversary in Mozart's *Die Zauberflöte.*

R

Rachel. Léopold's lover and Éléazar's daughter, the Jewess in Halévy's *La Juive.*

Radames. Aida's lover and captain of the Egyptian Guard in Verdi's *Aida.*

Ramfis. The high priest in Verdi's *Aida.*

Ramiro. 1. Concepción's muleteer lover in Ravel's *L'heure espagnole.* 2. Don Ramiro, Angelina's (a.k.a. Cinderella) eventual husband, in Rossini's *La Cenerentola.*

Rangoni. Marina's Jesuit confessor in Mussorgsky's *Boris Godunov.*

Raoul. Valentine's Huguenot nobleman lover, Raoul de Nangris, in Meyerbeer's *Les Huguenots.*

Reiza. Huon's lover in Weber's *Oberon.*

Rhinemaidens. The three ocean nymphs who guard the Rheingold in Wagner's *Der Ring des Nibelungen.*

Rinuccio. Lauretta's persistent lover in Puccini's *Gianni Schicchi.*

Rocco. Marzelline's jailer father in Beethoven's *Fidelio.*

Roderigo. A Venetian gentleman in Verdi's *Otello.*

Rodolfo. 1. The count in Bellini's *La sonnambula.* 2. Luisa's lover and Count Walter's son in Verdi's *Luisa Miller.* 3. Mimi's bohemian poet lover in both Leoncavallo's and Puccini's *La bohème.*

Rodrigo. 1. A Venetian gentleman in Rossini's *Otello.* 2. The marquis of Posa in Verdi's *Don Carlos.*

Rosalinde. Eisenstein's wife in Johann Strauss's *Die Fledermaus.*

Rosina. Count Almaviva's lover and ward of Dr. Bartolo in both Paisiello's and Rossini's *Il barbiere di Siviglia.*

Rustics. One of the three groups of characters (comprised of Bottom, Quince, Flute, Snug, Snout, and Starveling) in Britten's *A Midsummer Night's Dream.*

Ruthven. The vampire, Lord Ruthven, in Marschner's *Der Vampyr.*

S

Saint-Bris. A Catholic nobleman, Comte de Saint-Bris, in Meyerbeer's *Les Huguenots.*

Samiel. The devil (a speaking part) in Weber's *Der Freischütz.*

Santuzza. Turiddu's abandoned village girl lover in Mascagni's *Cavalleria rusticana.*

Sarastro. The high priest of Iris and Osiris in Mozart's *Die Zauberflöte.*

Scarpia. Chief of police, Baron Scarpia, in Puccini's *Tosca.*

Schaunard. The bohemian musician in Puccini's *La bohème.*

Sélika. The African slave in love with Vasco de Gama and loved by the slave Nélusko in Meyerbeer's *L'Africaine.*

Seneca. The philosopher Lucius Annaeus Seneca the Younger in Monteverdi's *L'incoronazione di Poppea* in his historically accurate role as Nero's mentor.

Senta. Daland's daughter in Wagner's *Der fliegender Holländer.*

Sergey. Katerina Izmaylova's workman lover in Shostakovich's *Lady Macbeth of the District of Mtsensk.*

Serpina. Uberto's servant, the maid-mistress of Pergolesi's *La serva padrona.*

Servilia. Annio's lover and Sesto's sister in Mozart's *La clemenza di Tito.*

Sesto. 1. Vitelia's young Roman patrician lover and Servilia's brother, Sextus, in Mozart's *La clemenza di Tito.* 2. Caesar's rival in Handel's *Giulio Cesare.*

Sharpless. The American consul in Puccini's *Madama Butterfly.*

Sherasmin. Fatima's lover and Huon's squire in Weber's *Oberon.*

Shuisky. A boyar, Prince Vassily Ivanovich Shuisky, in Mussorgsky's *Boris Godunov.*

Siebel. A village youth in love with Marguerite in Gounod's *Faust.*

Sieglinde. Hunding's wife and Siegmund's sister and (unwitting?) lover in Wagner's *Die Walküre* in *Der Ring des Nibelungen.*

Siegmund. Sieglinde's brother and (unwitting?) lover in Wagner's *Die Walküre* in *Der Ring des Nibelungen.*

Silva. Elvira's uncle and guardian, Don Ruy Gomez de Silva, in Verdi's *Ernani.*

Silvio. Nedda's villager lover in Leoncavallo's *Pagliacci.*

Simpleton. The holy fool (his English name) in Mussorgsky's *Boris Godunov.*

Sophie. 1. Octavian's lover and Faninal's daughter in Richard Strauss's *Der Rosenkavalier.* 2. Charlotte's sister in Massenet's *Werther.*

Sorostris. Actually, Madame Sosostris, a clairvoyant, in Tippet's *The Midsummer Marriage.*

Sparafucile. The hired assassin in Verdi's *Rigoletto.*

Spoletta. The police agent in Puccini's *Tosca.*

Sportin' Life. The drug peddler in Gershwin's *Porgy and Bess.*

Steersman. Daland's steersman in Wagner's *Die fliegende Holländer.*

Števa. 1. Actually, Števa Buryja, Jenůfa's faithless lover and Laca's half brother in Janáček's *Jenůfa.* 2. Jenůfa's ill-fated, short-lived infant in Janáček's *Jenůfa.*

Sulpice. The sergeant of the 21st Grenadiers in Donizetti's *La fille du régiment.*

Susanna. 1. Figaro's betrothed in Mozart's *Le nozze di Figaro.* 2. One of the Old Believers in Mussorgsky's *Khovanshchina.*

Suzel. Fritz's lover, a farmer's daughter, in Mascagni's *L'amico Fritz.*

Suzuki. Butterfly's maidservant in Puccini's *Madama Butterfly.*

T

Tadzio. The adolescent boy (a danced part) contemplated by Aschenbach in Britten's *Death in Venice.*

Tamino. Pamina's lover, an Egyptian prince, in Mozart's *Die Zauberflöte.*

Tarquinius. Sextus Tarquinius, prince of Rome, in Britten's *The Rape of Lucretia.*

Tatyana. Tatyana Larina, in love with Onegin and later the wife of Prince Gremin, in Tchaikovsky's *Eugene Onegin.*

Telramund. Ortrud's husband, Friedrich von Telramund, count of Brabant, in Wagner's *Lohengrin.*

Teresa. Cellini's lover and daughter of the papal treasurer Giacomo Balducci, in Berlioz's *Benvenuto Cellini.*

Timur. The deposed king of Tartary and Calaf's unknown father in Puccini's *Turandot.*

Titania. One of the fairies (with Oberon and Puck) in Britten's *A Midsummer Night's Dream.*

Titurel. Amfortas's father, former ruler of the Kingdom of the Grail, in Wagner's *Parsifal.*

Tom Rakewell. Anne's young lover in Stravinsky's *The Rake's Progress.*

Tonio. 1. Marie's Tyrolean peasant lover in Donizetti's *La fille du régiment.* 2. A clown in Leoncavallo's *Pagliacci.*

Torquemada. The clockmaker and Concepción's husband in Ravel's *L'heure espagnole.*

Turiddu. First Santuzza's young peasant lover and then lover of Lola in Mascagni's *Cavalleria rusticana.*

U

Ulrica. The renowned fortune teller in both the Boston and Naples versions of Verdi's *Ul ballo in maschera,* known as Mlle Arvidson in the (now standard) Swedish version.

Urbain. Marguerite de Valois's page in Meyerbeer's *Les Huguenots.*

V

Valentin. Marguerite's brother in Gounod's *Faust.*

Valentine. The Comte de Nevers's wife, Raoul's lover, and daughter of the Comte de Saint-Bris in Meyerbeer's *Les Huguenots.*

Valzacchi. Annina's Italian crony in Strauss's *Der Rosenkavalier.*

Varlaam. A vagabond friar in Mussorgsky's *Boris Godunov.*

Varvara. Kudrjaš's lover and the Kabanovs' foster-daughter in Janáček's *Kát'a Kabanová.*

Vasco da Gama. Inès's Portuguese naval officer lover in Meyerbeer's *L'Africaine.*

Vašek. Tobias Micha's son, a villager, in Smetana's *The Bartered Bride.*

Vasily. The hussar lover of the village girl Parasha in Stravinsky's *Mavra.*

Venus. Protector and provider of the Venusberg, haven for Tannhäuser until he chooses to return to the earthly world, in Wagner's *Tannhäuser.*

Violetta. Alfredo Germont's lover, Violetta Valéry, the wayward woman in Verdi's *La traviata.*

Vitelia. The deposed daughter of the emperor in Mozart's *La clemenza di Tito.*

W

Walther. Eva's young Franconian knight lover, Walther von Stolzing, in Wagner's *Die Meistersinger von Nürnberg.*

Waltraute. A Valkyrie in Wagner's *Die Walküre* and *Götterdämerung* in *Der Ring des Nibelungen.*

Wanderer. Wotan, disguised, in Wagner's *Siegfried* in *Der Ring des Nibelungen.*

Wolfram. A melodious knight and friend to the hero in Wagner's *Tannhäuser.*

Woodbird. The prophetic bird that warns Siegfried of Mime's treachery and who leads Siegfried to the sleeping Brünnhilde in Wagner's *Siegfried* in *Der Ring des Nibelugen.*

Wotan. The ruler of the gods in Wagner's *Das Rheingold* and *Die Walküre* in *Der Ring des Nibelungen.* In *Siegfried* he appears disguised as the Wanderer.

Wurm. Count Walter's servant in Verdi's *Luisa Miller.*

X

Xenia. Boris's daughter in Mussorgsky's *Boris Godunov.*

Y

Yamadori. A Japanese prince, a suitor for Butterfly's hand, in Puccini's *Madama Butterfly.*

Yaroslavna. Igor's second wife, Princess Yaroslavna, in Borodin's *Prince Igor.*

Yniold. Golaud's young son, a stepson to Mélisande, in Debussy's *Pelléas et Mélisande.*

Z

Zdenka. Arabella's sister in Richard Strauss's *Arabella.*

Zerbinetta. The leader of the Harlequinade in Richard Strauss's *Ariadne auf Naxos.*

Zerlina. 1. The peasant girl betrothed to Masetto in Mozart's *Don Giovanni.* 2. Lorenzo's lover, daughter of the innkeeper Matteo, in Auber's *Fra Diavolo.*

Zuniga. Don José's captain and rival for Carmen's attention in Bizet's *Carmen.*

Zurga. The king of the fishermen in Bizet's *Les pěcheurs des perles.*

Grand Opera Houses of the World

Argentina

Buenos Aires

Teatro Colón
Cerrito 618
1010 Buenos Aires

Building facts:
- 1856 The first Teatro Colón
- 1888 Theater (intentionally) demolished, with land sold to the National Bank
- 1889 Francesco Tamburini and Angelo Ferrari, architects, engaged for the second Teatro Colón, succeeded by:
- 1904 Victor Meano, architect
- 1908 Julio Dormal, architect

Horseshoe auditorium
Capacity: 2,367

Inaugurated (first) on April 25, 1857, with Verdi's *La Traviata*
Inaugurated (second) on May 25, 1908, with Verdi's *Aida*

Australia

Sydney

Sydney Opera House
Bennelong Point
P.O. Box 291
Strawberry Hills, N.S.W. 2012

Building facts:
- 1973 Jørn Utzon, Ove Arup, E. H. Farmer, Peter Hall, Lionel Todd, and David Littlemore, architects and engineers

Capacity: 2,679

Inaugurated September 28, 1973, with Prokofiev's *War and Peace*

Austria

Vienna

Vienna Staatsoper
Opernring 2
A-1015 Vienna

Building facts:
- 1869 Eduard van der Nüll and August Siccard von Siccardsburg, architects
- 1945 Fire damage after Allied aerial bombardment
- 1955 Erich Boltenstern, architect

Horseshoe auditorium
Capacity: 2,276

Inaugurated (first) on May 25, 1869, with Mozart's *Don Giovanni*
Inaugurated (second) on November 5, 1955, with Beethoven's *Fidelio*

Belgium

Brussels

Théâtre Royale de la Monnaie
Place de le Monnaie at Rue neuve
4 Rue Léopold
1000 Brussels

Building facts:
- 1819 Louis Damesne, architect
- 1855 Fire damage
- 1856 Joseph Poelaert, architect
- 1986 A.2R.C., Urbat, and Charles Vandenhove, architects

Horseshoe auditorium
Capacity: 1,770

Inaugurated (second) in 1856 with Halévy's *Jaguarita l'Indienne* Inaugurated (third) on November 12, 1986, with Beethoven's Ninth Symphony

Brazil

Manaus

Teatro Amazonas
Praça São Sebastião SN
69010-240 Manaus

Building facts:
- 1896 Domenico de Angelis, architect
- 1974 Renato Braga, architect
- 1929, 1965, 1990 Restorations

Capacity: 1,600

Inaugurated on December 31, 1896, with excerpts from Italian operas

São Paulo

Teatro Municipal
Praça Ramos de Azevado
01037-010 São Paulo

Building facts:
- 1911 Arthur Ramos de Azevedo, architect

Capacity: 1,750

Inaugurated on July 14, 1909, with the national anthem
Inaugurated (first full season) on September 12, 1911, with Thomas's *Hamlet*

Czech Republic

Prague

Národní Divadlo
P.O. Box 765, Ostrovní 1
112 30 Prague

Building facts:
- 1881 Josef Zitek, architect
- 1881 Fire destroys theater, after 11 performances
- 1883 Josef Schulz, architect
- 1978 Bohuslav Fuchs, architect
- 1983 Pavel Kupka, followed by Karel Progner, architects (3 additional buildings)

U-shaped auditorium
Capacity: 1,554

Inaugurated (first) on June 11, 1881, with Smetana's *Libuše*
Inaugurated (second) in November 18, 1883, with Smetana's *Libuše*

Egypt

Cairo

Cairo Opera House
El Borg, Gezira
Cairo

Building facts:
- 1869 Avoscani and Rossi, architects
- 1971 Fire destroys theater
- 1988 Kuashiro Shikeda, architect

Amphitheatre plan
Capacity: 1,200 (main auditorium)

Inaugurated (first) November 1, 1869, with Verdi's *Rigoletto*
Inaugurated (second) on October 10, 1988, with a program of Egyptian music and Kabuki

England

Glyndebourne

Glyndebourne Opera House
Glyndebourne, Lewes
East Sussex BN8 5UU

Building facts:
- 1994 Michael Hopkins & Partners, architects

Horseshoe auditorium
Capacity: 1,200

Inaugurated on May 28, 1994, with Mozart's *Le nozze di Figaro*

London

Royal Opera House
Covent Garden
London WC2E 9DD

Building facts:
- 1732 Edward Shepherd, architect of the first Covent Garden Theatre

1791 Henry Holland, architect of the reconstructed auditorium
1809 Sir Robert Smirke, architect of the second theatre
1858 E. M. Barry, architect of the third theatre
1899 Edwin O. Sachs, architect of the iron-and-glass Crush Bar
1982 Jeremy Dixon and Edward Jones, architects of the backstage extension and renovation

Horseshoe auditorium
Capacity: 2,174

Inaugurated (third) on May 15, 1858, with Meyerbeer's *Les Huguenots*

Finland

Helsinki

Suomen Kansallisooppera
Helsinginkatu 58
Box 176
00250 Helsinki

Building facts:
1981 Eero Hyvämäki, Jukka Karhunen, and Risto Parkkinen, architects

Horseshoe auditorium (main auditorium)
Capacity: 1,385

Inaugurated on November 30, 1994, with an excerpt from Pacius's *The Hunt of King Charles*, "Gloria" from Beethoven's *Missa Solemnis*, and Sallinen's *Kullervo*

France

Besançon

Opéra-Théâtre (L'Opéra-Théâtre of Nicolas Ledoux)
Place du Théâtre
25000 Besançon

Building facts:
1736– Claude Nicholas Ledoux and Claude Joseph
1806 Alexandre Bertrand, architect
1857 Restoration, Delacroix, architect
1958 Fire damage and restoration Restoration and renaming (Opéra-Théâtre)

Bell-shaped auditorium
Capacity: 2,000

Inaugurated (first) on August 9, 1784, with Piron's *La Métromanie* and Grétry's *Le Tableau parlant*
Inaugurated (third) on November 20, 1958, with Verdi's *Otello*
Inaugurated (fourth) on January 11, 1995, with a performance by the variety singer Claude Nougaro (son of the theatre's former director)

Bordeaux

Grand-Théâtre de Bordeaux
Place de la Comédie
F-33025 Bordeaux

Building facts:
1780 Victor Louis, architect
1837, 1853 Charles-Bernard Burguet, architect
1880, 1915, 1919, 1938, and 1977 Restorations
1990–91 Bernard Fananquerie, architect

Bell-shaped auditorium
Capacity: 1,114

Inaugurated on April 7, 1780, with Act I of Racine's *Athalie*

Lyons

Opéra Nouvel
1 Place de la Comédie, BP 1219
F-69203 Lyons

Building facts:
1756 Jacques-Germain Soufflot, architect
1831 Antoine-Marie Chenavard and Jean-Marie Pollet, architects
1993 Jean Nouvel, architect

Horseshoe auditorium (Italian style)
Capacity: 1,121

Inaugurated (second) on July 1, 1831, with Boieldieu's *La Dame blanche*
Inaugurated (third) on May 14, 1993, with Lully's *Phaéton*

Marseilles

Opéra Municipal
2 Rue Molière
F-13231 Marseilles

Building facts:
1787 Bénard, architect (Salle Beauvau)
1919 Destroyed by fire
1924 Ebrard, Castel, and Raymond, architects

Urn-shaped auditorium
Capacity: 1,800

Inaugurated (first) on October 31, 1787, with Ponteuil's *Tartuffe* and Champein's *Mélomanue*
Inaugurated (second) on December 4, 1924, with Reyer's *Sigurd*

Nantes

Théâtre Graslin
1, Rue Molière
B.P. 287
F-44009 Nantes

Building facts:
1788 Mathurin Crucy, architect

1796 Fire damage
1813 Mathurin Crucy, architect

Fan-shaped auditorium
Capacity: 970

Inaugurated (first) on March 23 (Easter Sunday), 1788, (work unknown)
Inaugurated (second) on May 3, 1813, with Grétry's *Aline ou la reine de Golgonde*

Paris

L'Opéra de la Bastille
120 Rue de Lyon
F-75012 Paris

Building facts:
1989 Carlos Ott, architect

Amphitheatre auditorium
Capacity: 2,723

Inaugurated on July 13, 1989, with a gala entitled "The Night before the Day" (first official season opens in September with Berlioz's *Les Troyens*)

Opéra National de Paris (Palais Garnier)
8 Rue Scribe
F-75009 Paris

Building facts:
1875 Charles Garnier, architect
1959 Bailleau, architect of the first rehearsal studio built under the great dome
1964 Marc Chagall executes the painting for the dome over the auditorium
1988, 1995 Jean-Loup Roubert, architect, renovations

Horseshoe auditorium
Capacity: 1,979

Inaugurated on January 5, 1875, with Halévy's *La Juive* and excerpts from Meyeybeer's *Les Huguenots*

Versailles

Opéra Royal
Château de Versailles
78000 Versailles

Building facts:
1769 Jacques Ange Gabriel, architect

Elliptical auditorium
Capacity: 712

Inaugurated on May 16–17, 1770, with Lully's *Persée*

Germany

Bayreuth

Festspielhaus
Luitpold plat 29
Postfach 100 262
D8580 Bayreuth

Building facts:
1876 Richard Wagner, Otto Brückwald, and Karl Brandt, architects
1962–74 Renovations

Capacity: 1,924

Inaugurated on August 13–17, 1876, with Wagner's *Der Ring des Nibelungen*

Berlin

Deutsche Staatsoper Berlin
Unter den Linden 7
D-10117 Berlin

Building facts:
1742 Georg Wenzeslaus von Knobelsdorff, architect (Berlin Hofoper)
1843 Fire destroys theater
1844 Carl Ferdinand Langhans, architect
1941 Damage from aerial bombardment
1942 Schweizer, Salexki, and Seydel, architects
1945 Damage from aerial bombardment
1955 Reconstruction completed

Horseshoe auditorium
Capacity: 1,396

Inaugurated on December 7, 1942, with Graun's *Cleopatra e Cesare*

Dresden

Staatsoper
Theaterplatz 2
D-01067 Dresden

Building facts:
1841 Gottfried Semper, architect (Semper Theater)
1869 Theater destroyed by fire
1878 Gottfried Semper, architect
1918 Theater renamed Dresden Staatsoper
1945 Theater destroyed by allied bombing
1985 Reconstruction (from Semper's original plans)

Horseshoe auditorium
Capacity: 1,309

Essen

Aalto-Theater
Rolandstrasse 10
D-45128 Essen

Suomen Kansallisooppera (Helsinki, Finland)

Národní Divadlo (Prague, Czech Republic)

Slottstheater Drottningholm (Stockholm, Sweden)

War Memorial Opera House (San Francisco, California)

Teatro alla Scala (Milan, Italy)

Opéra National de Paris (Palais Garnier) (Paris, France)

Vienna Staatsoper (Vienna, Austria)

Teatro Amazonas (Manaus, Brazil)

Royal Opera House (London, England)

Maryinsky Theater (St. Petersburg, Russia)

Magyar Állami Operház (Budapest, Hungary)

Teatro Nacional de São Carlos (Lisbon, Portugal)

Grand-Théâtre de Bordeaux (Bordeaux, France)

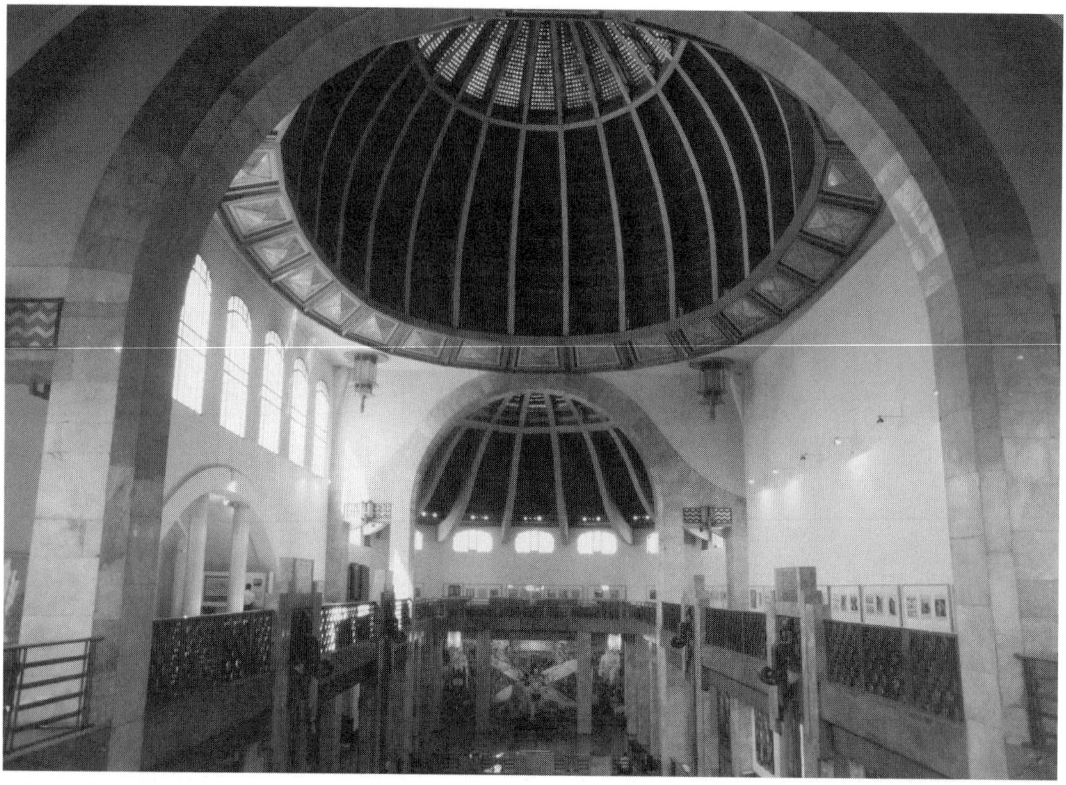

Palacio de Bellas Artes (Mexico City, Mexico)

Sydney Opera House (Sydney, Australia)

Metropolitan Opera House (New York, New York)

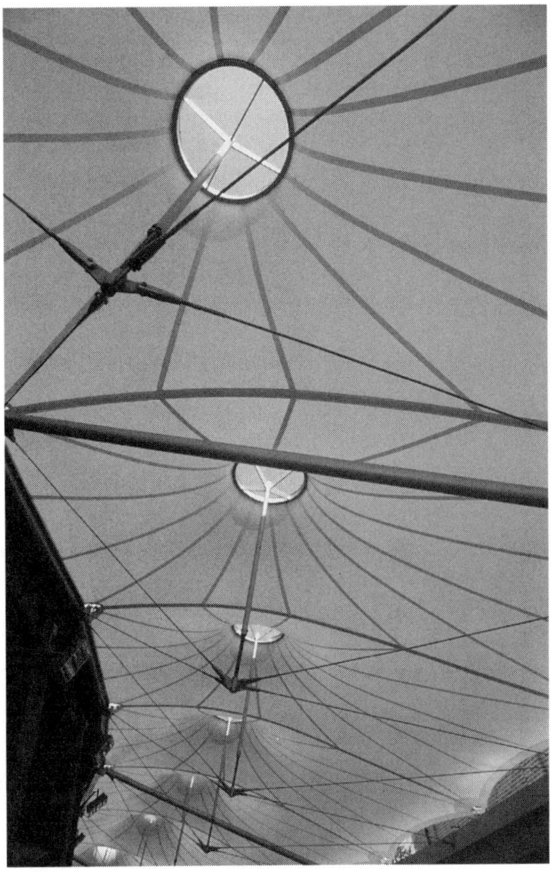

Glyndebourne Opera House (East Sussex, England)

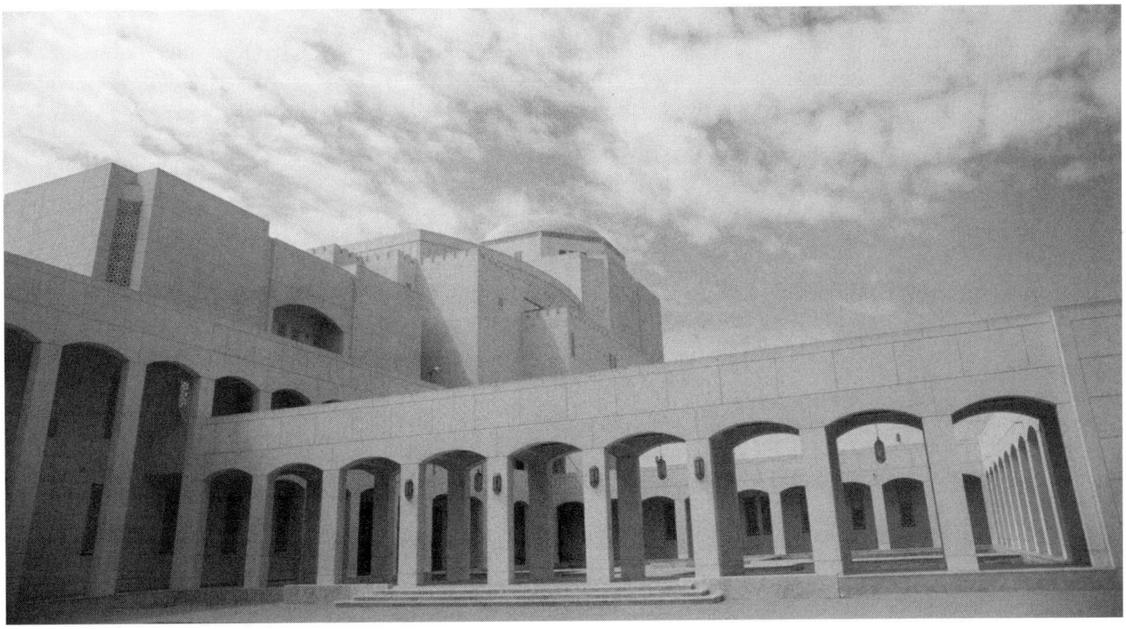

Cairo Opera House (Cairo, Egypt)

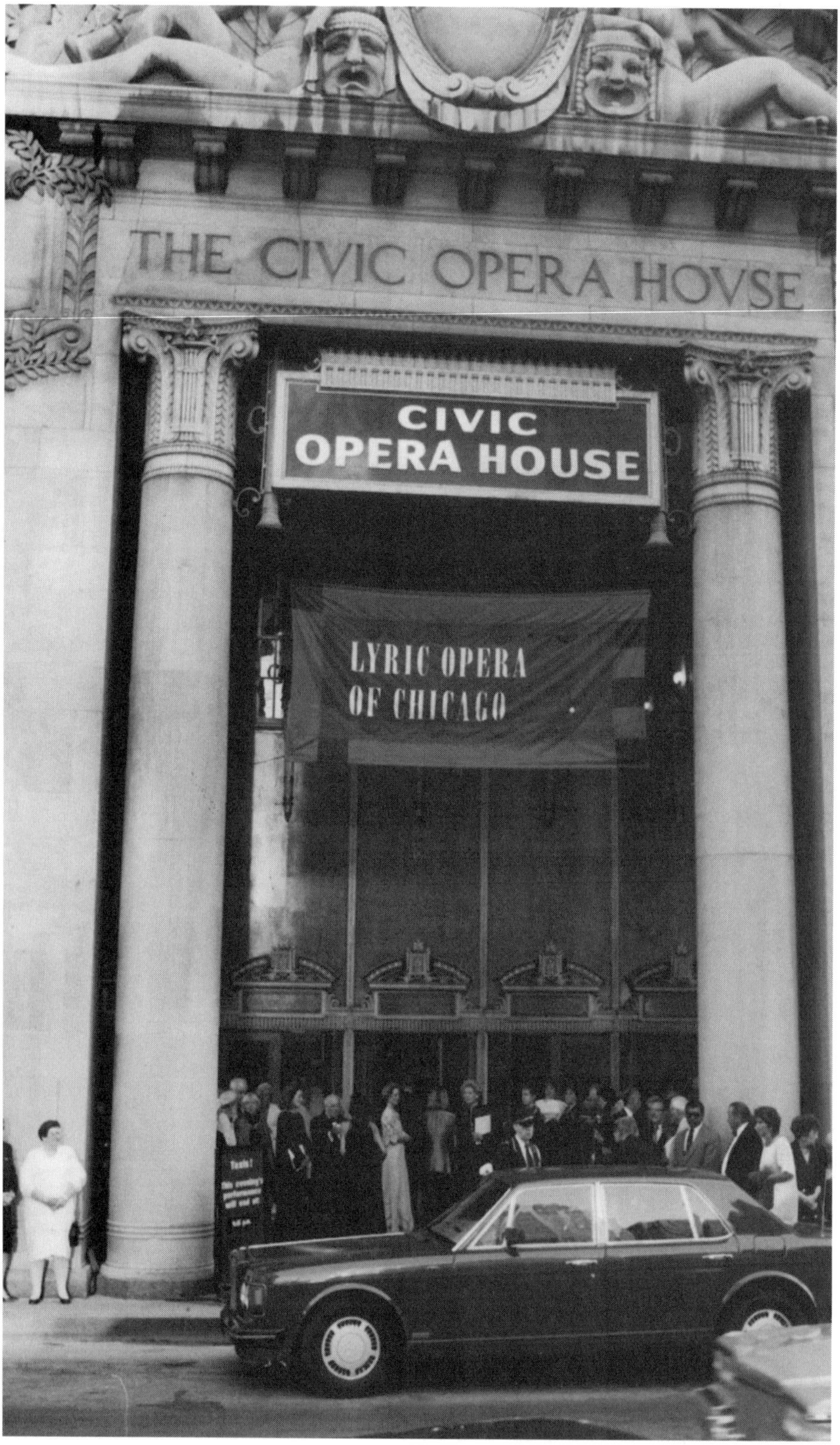

Civic Opera House (Chicago, Illinois)

Building facts:
1988 Alvar Aalto (1898–1976), architect

Fan-shaped auditorium
Capacity: 1,125

Inaugurated on October 2, 1988, with Wagner's *Die Meistersinger von Nürnberg*

Munich

Bayerische Staatsoper
Max Joseph Platz 2
D-80539 Munich

Building facts:
1818 Karl von Fischer, architect
1823 Theater destroyed by fire
1825 Leo von Klenze, architect
1943 Theater destroyed by Allied bombing
1930 Renovations
1963 Gerhard Graaubner, architect (from original plans by Karl von Fischer)

Horseshoe auditorium
Capacity: 2,100

Inaugurated (first) on October 12, 1818, with Ferdinand Fränzel's *Die Weihe*
Inaugurated (second) on November 22, 1963, with Wagner's *Die Meistersinger von Nürnberg*

Hungary

Budapest

Magyar Állami Operaház
Andrassy Út. 22
1061 Budapest

Building facts:
1884 Miklós Ybl, architect
1979–84 Complete renovation

Horseshoe auditorium
Capacity: 2,400

Inaugurated on September 27, 1884, with Act I of Wagner's *Lohengrin* and Act I of Erkel's *Bánk Bán*

Italy

Bologna

Teatro Comunale
Largo Respighi, 1
I-40126 Bologna

Building facts:
1763 Antonio Galli-Bibiena, architect
1820 G. Tubertini, architect (modifications)
1854 C. Parmigiani, architect (modifications)
1931 Fire damages the theater
1935 Umberto Rizzi, architect

Horseshoe auditorium
Capacity: 1,000

Inaugurated (first) on May 14, 1763, with Gluck's *Il Trionfo di Clelia*
Inaugurated (second) on November 14, 1935, with Bellini's *Norma*

Milan

Teatro alla Scala
Piazza della Scala
Via Filodrammatici 2
I-20121 Milan

Building facts:
1778 Giuseppe Piermarini, architect
1943 Damage by allied air raids
1955 Piero Portaluppi, architect, Piccola Scala

Horseshoe auditorium
Capacity: 2,800 (Teatro all Scala)
Capacity: 600 (Piccola Scala)

Inaugurated (Teatro all Scala) on August 3, 1778, with Salieri's *L'Europa Riconosciuta*
Inaugurated (Piccola Scala) in 1955 with Cimarosa'a *Il Matrimonio Segreto*

Naples

Teatro di San Carlo
Via San Carlo, 98f
I-80132 Naples

Building facts:
1737 Giovanni Antonio Medrano and Angelo Carasale, architects
1810 Antonio Niccolini, architect (facade)
1816 Fire destroys the interior of the theater, rebuilt by Niccolini
1944 Damage by Allied aerial bombardment
1946 Repaired and reopened by British occupying forces

Horseshoe auditorium
Capacity: 1,444

Inaugurated on November 4, 1737, with Sarro's *Achille in Sciro*

Venice

Gran Teatro La Fenice
Campo S. Fantin 2519
I-30124 Venice

Building facts:
1792 Gianantonio Selva, architect
1836 Theater destroyed by fire
1837 Tommaso and Giambattista Meduna, architects

1937 Eugenio Miozzi, architect (renovations)
1996 Theater damaged by fire
2000 Anticipated reopening

Horseshoe auditorium
Capacity: 1,500

Inaugurated May 16, 1792, with Paisiello's *I Giuocchi d'Agrigento*

Vicenza

Teatro Olimpico
Piazza Matteotti
36100 Vicenza

Building facts:
1585 Andrea Palladio, architect, succeeded by Vincenzo Scamozzi

Fan-shaped auditorium
Capacity: 496

Inaugurated on March 3, 1585, with Sophocles' *Odeipus the King*

Japan

Tokyo

New National Theatre
1-1-1 Hon-machi
Shibuya-ku
Tokyo 151

Building facts:
1997 Tokahiko Yanagisawa, architect

Horseshoe auditorium
Capacity: 1,810

Inauguration in November 1997 with Wagner's *Lohengrin*

Korea

Seoul

Arts Center
1-5 Tongsung-Dong
Chongno-Gu
South Korea

Building facts:
1992 Seok Chul Kim, architect

2 auditoriums
Capacity: 2,400 and 700

Inaugurated in 1992 with a Korean opera, *The Wedding Day*

Mexico

Mexico City

Palacio de Bellas Artes
Av. Hidalgo 1, 3er piso
06050 Mexico D.F.

Building facts:
1934 Adam Boari, architect, beginning in 1905, followed by Antonio Muñoz, who is followed by Federico E. Mariscal

Horseshoe auditorium
Capacity: 1,987

Inauguration in 1934 by performances by Viennese musicians

The Netherlands

Amsterdam

Musiektheater
Waterlooplein 22
1011 PG Amsterdam

Building facts:
1986 Cees Dam and Wilhelm Holzhauer, architects

Fan-shaped auditorium
Capacity: 1,600

Inaugurated on September 23, 1986, with Ketting's *Ithaka*

Portugal

Lisbon

Teatro Nacional de São Carlos
Rua Serpa Pinta 9
1200 Lisbon

Building facts:
1793 José Da Costa e Silva, architect

Elliptical auditorium
Capacity: 1,100

Inaugurated on June 30, 1793, with Cimarosa's *La Ballerina Amante*

Russia

Moscow

Bolshoi Theater
Theatralnaya Square
103009 Moscow

Building facts:
1825 Ossip Bove and Andrei Mikhailov, architects
1856 Fire damages the theater
1856 Alberto Cavos, architect

Horseshoe auditorium
Capacity: 2,150

Inaugurated (first) on January 7, 1825, with a dance pantomime, *The Triumph of the Muse*
Inaugurated (second) on August 20, 1856, with Bellini's *I Puritani*

St. Petersburg

Maryinsky Theater
Teatralnaya Pl. 1
190000 St. Petersburg

Building facts:
1860 Alberto Cavos, architect

Horseshoe auditorium
Capacity: 1,621

Inaugurated on December 9, 1860, with Glinka's *A Life for the Czar*

Spain

Barcelona

El Gran Teatro del Liceu
Ausias Marc, 56 pral
08010 Barcelona

Building facts:
1847 Miguel Carriga i Roca and Josep Oriol Mestres, architects
1861 Fire destroys the theater
1862 Joseph Oriol Mestres, architect
1994 Fire damages the theater
1997 Ignacio Sola Morales, architect

Horseshoe auditorium
Capacity: 3,000

Inaugurated on April 4, 1847, with a Spanish play, Catalan dances, an Italian cantata, and concert selections

Sweden

Stockholm

Slottstheater Drottningholm
P.O. Box 27050
S-102 51 Stockholm

Building facts:
1766 Carl Frederik Adelcrantz, architect
1791 Jean-Louis Desprez, designer (enlarged foyer)

Capacity: 454

Kungliga Theatern
P.O. Box 16094
S-103 22 Stockholm

Building facts:
1782 Carl Frederik Adelcrantz, architect
1898 Axel Anderberg, architect

Capacity: 1,200

Switzerland

Geneva

Grand-Théâtre
11 Blvd. du Théâtre
CH-1211 Geneva

Building facts:
1879 Jacques-Élysée Goss, architect
1951 Fire damages the theater
1962 Marcello Zavelani-Rossi, Charles Shopfer, and Jacek Stryjenski, architects

Fan-shaped auditorium
Capacity: 1,500

Inaugurated on October 2, 1879, with Rossini's *Guillaume Tell*

United States

California

War Memorial Opera House
301 Van Ness Avenue
San Francisco, California 94102

Building facts:
1932 Arthur Brown, G. Albert Lansburgh, and Willis Polk, architects
1989 Theater damaged by earthquake

Lyre-shaped auditorium
Capacity: 3,176

Inaugurated on October 15, 1932, with Puccini's *Tosca*
Restoration inaugurated on September 5, 1997, with a gala concert

Illinois

Civic Opera House
20 N. Wacker Drive, Suite 860
Chicago, Illinois 60606

Building facts:
1929 Graham, Anderson, Probst, and White, architects
1955, 1993 Renovations

Fan-shaped auditorium
Capacity: 3,563

Inaugurated on December 4, 1929, with Verdi's *Aida*

Louisiana

Theater for the Performing Arts
80 North Rampart Street
New Orleans, Louisiana 70056

Building facts:
- 1973 Edward Mathes of Mathes, Bergman & Associates, and Henry Banker & Associates, architects

Fan-shaped auditorium
Capacity: 2,317

Inaugurated on March 15, 1973, with Puccini's *Madama Butterfly*

New Mexico

Santa Fe Opera
Highway 84-285
P.O. Box 2408
Santa Fe, New Mexico 87504

Building facts:
- 1957 John W. McHugh; Van Dorn Hooker; Bolt Beranek and Newman, architects
- 1967 Fire damages the theater
- 1967 McHugh and Kidder, architects
- 1995–97 James Stewart Polshek and Partners (expansions)

Amphitheatre auditorium
Capacity: 1,889

Inaugurated on July 3, 1957, with Stravinsky's *The Rake's Progress*

New York

Metropolitan Opera House
Lincoln Center
New York, New York 10023

Building facts:
- 1883 Josiah Cleaveland Cady, architect (old Metropolitan Opera House, 39th Street and Broadway)
- 1892 Fire damages the theater, which is quickly rebuilt
- 1965–66 Wallace Harrison, architect (new Metropolitan Opera House, Lincoln Center)

Horseshoe auditorium
Capacity: 3,824

Inaugurated (first) on October 22, 1883, with Gounod's *Faust*
Inaugurated (second) on September 16, 1966, with Barber's *Antony and Cleopatra*

Opera Terms

A

ABA. A symbolic representation of ternary form, in which the 1st section (A) is repeated after the 2 (B). Many classical songs and arias follow this formula, hence ABA is also known as song form.

a cappella (It., as in chapel). Performed in the church style, or choral singing without instrumental accompaniment. Generally, any unaccompanied vocal performance.

accompaniment. Any part or parts (chords, other harmonic units) that attend or support the voices or instruments bearing the principal part or parts in a composition. It is *ad libitum* when the piece can be performed without it, and *obbligato* when it is necessary.

accorde di stupefazione (It., stupefying chord). See *diabolus in musica.*

act (Fr., *acte*; Ger., *Aufzug*; It., *atto*). A primary division of an opera or scenic cantata. In opera each act may be subdivided into several scenes or tableaux.

acte (Fr.). Act.

added number. An aria or other number inserted into an opera, often to commemorate an individual being honored by the performance or to particularize the performance for the occasion at which the opera is being performed. While the practice is now rarely seen, it was widespread in the 18th and 19th centuries. Mozart wrote many arias for insertion into the operas of others, and often singers themselves would add favorite numbers, irrespective of their appropriateness to the work at hand. The Ball Scene of Johann Strauss's *Die Fledermaus* provides a perfect opportunity for such additions.

ad libitum (Lat., at will; abbr. *ad. lib.*; Ger. *Nachgefallen*). 1. Employ the tempo or expression freely. 2. An indication that a vocal or instrumental part may be left out.

agogic (Grk., to lead). A slight deviation from the main rhythm for the purposes of accentuation. This legitimate performing practice may allow melodically important notes to linger without disruption of the musical phrase. *Rubato* is an agogical practice. The term was introduced by Riemann in 1884. In musical rhetoric, it is opposed to the concept of dynamics, which provides accentuation by varying the degree of intensity.

***Aida* trumpet.** A long trumpet specially constructed for use in Verdi's opera *Aida.* The original, manufactured in France, was called *trompette thébaine,* trumpet of Thebes. It produced only four notes: A♭, B♭, B♮, and C.

al fresco (It., in the open air). A description of outdoor concerts, operatic performances, and other events, usually free of charge.

alienation (A-) effect. See *epic opera, epic theater.*

Alt (Ger.). See *alto.*

alti naturali (It., naturally high ones). In the Middle Ages, male falsetto singers, as opposed to *voci artificiali,* the *castratos.*

alto (It., high, from Lat., *altus*). The deeper of the two main divisions of women's or boys' voices, the soprano being the higher; the standard alto gamut ranges from g to c^2; in voices of great range, down to d and up to f^2, or higher. Alto singers possess resonant chest voices. In opera the parts of young swains who unsuccessfully court the heroine are often given to altos (*trouser roles*), e.g., Siebel in Gounod's *Faust.* Also called *contralto.* Alto may also refer to the *countertenor* voice.

antefatto (It., antecedent fact). A device by which the audience is provided necessary information prior to the beginning of an opera that is essential to a full understanding of the plot to come. This may be provided either in narrative form within the opera itself or in printed preparatory notes in a program book.

Anvil Chorus. Popular designation of the scene in Act II of Verdi's *Il trovatore,* in which gypsy camp blacksmiths strike anvils in time with the chorus. Nowhere in Verdi's manuscript does the indication "Anvil Chorus" appear, however. This is one of the most celebrated single passages in all opera.

appaltatore (It., contractor). A theatrical agent.

applause (from Lat., *plaudere,* clap hands). A culturally determined, seemingly instinctive reaction to an excellent artistic performance, often accompanied by shouts of "Bravo!" At the opera, applause often greets the entrance of a favorite singer. When there is an orchestral coda after a particularly successful *aria,* it is often drowned out by intemperate applause, as in the case of the soft instrumental conclusion to the famous tenor aria in Leoncavallo's *Pagliacci.* A tug-of-war can ensue when the conductor makes a serious effort to proceed with the music while the singer is eager to prolong the applause. In the heyday of opera, a singer, expiring at the end of an aria, might have been forced to rise again and bow to the public. Cries of "Bis!" (twice, encore) can bring a repetition of the aria. It was once common practice among opera singers, especially in the 19th century, to hire people to applaud them. The hired group was known as a *claque.*

aria (It., air; from Lat., *aer*; plural *arie*; Ger. *Arie*). An air, song, tune, or melody. A word, common to all European languages, signifying a manner or model of performance or composition. In 17th-century England the spelling *ayre* designated a wide variety of songs, whether serious or popular. Baroque instrumental pieces of a songful character were often called arias. The most common association of *aria,* however, is with a solo song in opera. Specialized categories of arias came to be used in Italian opera, including *aria buffa,* comic or burlesque aria; *aria cantabile,* "songful" aria, expressing sorrow or yearning; *aria da capo, da capo aria*; *aria da chiesa,* church aria, as opposed to secular; *aria da concerto,* aria for concert singing; *aria d'entrata,* aria sung by any operatic character upon her or his 1st entrance; *aria di bravura,* rapid virtuosic song expressing violent passion through florid ornamentation; *aria parlante,* "talking aria," in a declamatory manner; *aria di catalogo, catalog aria.*

Arie (Ger.). *Aria.*

arietta (It.). A short *aria,* lacking the da capo repeat; similar to the *cavatina* found in Baroque Italian opera. The French term *ariette* frequently denotes a short aria or song inserted into French divertissement rather than opera.

arioso (It., like an aria). In vocal music, a term often used to describe a style between full *aria* and lyric *recitative* or a short melodious strain interrupted by or ending in a recitative; invented by the Florentine opera inventors, who called it *recitativo arioso.* It also occasionally refers to an impressive, dramatic style suitable for the *aria grande*; hence, a vocal piece in that style.

arrangement. The adaptation, transcription, or reduction of a composition for performance on an instrument, or by any vocal or instrumental combination, for which it was not originally written. Also, any composition so adapted or arranged.

atto (It.). *Act.*

Aufführung (Ger.). Performance.

Auftritt (Ger.). *Scene.*

Auftrittslied (Ger., entry song). An *aria* in a *Singspiel* through which a character introduces him- or herself to the audience. This may be achieved directly (i.e., character to audience), or through the character addressing himself to another character on the stage, as in Papageno's "Der Vogelfänger bin ich ja" in Mozart's *Die Zauberflöte.*

Aufzug (Ger.). *Act.*

B

ballabile (It., suitable for dancing). A 19th-century term to describe sung dances in Italian opera, e.g., the witches' dance in Act III of Verdi's *Macbeth.*

ballad opera. A musical stage work primarily made up of extant ballads and folk songs, or their tunes, in which spoken dialogue is a component. A genre popular in 18th-century England and its northern colonies, it is stylistically close to the French *vaudeville.* The work that precipitated the genre's heyday was Gay's *The Beggar's Opera* (1728), with music arranged by Pepusch. Subsequent English ballad operas drew freely on arias and choruses of past composers. The genre exhausted itself toward the end of the 18th century and gave way to the fertile development of the German *Singspiel.* More than a century later the ballad opera was revived in Germany by Weill and others who used the mixed English-German designation *Songspiel* (the English *song* having acquired the German meaning for musical entertainment of any kind); the primary difference was that the 20th-century model was usually newly composed.

ballet de cour (Fr., court ballet). A court dance genre of French royalty, from Henry III to Louis XIV, with court members, including the king, participating in the performance. Subject matter included mythology, non-Christian "primitives and savages," and the glory of the royal state. Stylistically, the genre borrowed from the Italian mascherata and intermedio and French courtly pantomimes and *fêtes*; it was similar to the English *masque.* Louis XIV danced from 1651 (at age 13) until 1670; thereafter, the genre began a decline that, except for a brief revival under Louis XV, saw its extinction by the mid-18th century. Composers of music for *ballets de cour* included P. Guérdon, Lully, de Lalande, Destouches, Campra, and Mouret.

barcarola, -e (It.). *Barcarolle.*

Barcarole (Ger.). *Barcarolle.*

barcarolle (*barcarole*; Fr., from It. *barce* + *rollo,* bark-rower; It. *barcarola, barcarole*; Ger. *Gondellied, Barcarole*). 1. A song of the Venetian gondoliers. The genre is inseparably associated with the taxi-boaters who entertained and delighted tourists in the 19th century. The barcarolle is usually set in $\frac{6}{8}$ or $\frac{12}{8}$ time, suggesting the lulling motion of the waters in the Venetian canals. The most famous operatic barcarolle is in Offenbach's *Tales of Hoffmann.* Gilbert and Sullivan turned the gondoliers into sentimental lovers in their operetta *The Gondoliers.* Also called *gondoliera.* 2. A vocal, instrumental, or concert piece imitating the Venetian gondoliers' songs.

baritone (Gr., *barytonos*; deep sound). The medium-range male voice, lower than the tenor and higher than the bass, with a compass from A to about f^1. An ideal baritone voice possesses the character of lyric masculinity. Baritones are rarely given leading operatic roles, usually the property of tenors, yet Mozart entrusted the role of Don Giovanni to a baritone. Character baritones range from villainy to piety, from nefarious Scarpia in *Tosca* to saintly Amfortas in *Parsifal.* The imperious Wotan in Wagner's *Der Ring des Nibelungen* is a *bass-baritone,* a voice generally higher than the bass but lower than the true baritone. The most famous dramatic baritone part is the toreador Escamillo in *Carmen.* Baritones are often given comic parts, e.g., Mr. Lavender-Gas, a professor of literature in Menotti's *Help, Help, The Globolinks!*

bass (It., *basso*; low). 1. The lowest male voice, with an ordinary compass from F to e^1; its extreme compass from C to f^1. Bass parts are usually assigned to the roles of sinners or devils, e.g., Méphistophélès in *Faust,* the villainous usurper Boris Godunov in Mussorgsky's opera of the same name, and the treacherous but victimized Hunding in *Die Walküre.* 2. A singer having such a voice. There have been exceptional bass singers, particularly Russian, who could go below the normal range. Some speculate that the vast expanse of the Russian landscape somehow contributes to the formation of powerful chest cavities, whereas the cerulean waters of the Bay of Naples favor the development of the lyric tenor voice in Italy. The *bass-baritone* voice is generally higher than the true bass, and lower than the *baritone.*

bass-baritone (It., *basso cantante*). See *bass, baritone.*

basse continue (Fr.). *Basso continuo.*

basso (It.). *Bass.*

basso buffo (It.). A comic *bass,* such as the musicmaster Don Basilio in Rossini's *The Barber of Seville.*

basso cantante (It.). See *bass, baritone.*

basso continuo (It., continuous bass, abbr. continuo; Eng. *figured bass, thoroughbass*; Fr. *basse continue, chifrée, figurée*; Ger. *Generalbass, bezifferter Bass*). In Baroque ensemble music, the part played by two instruments: a keyboard or fretted string instrument (harpsichord, organ, lute) and a low-pitched instrument (cello, viola da gamba, bassoon); also, the notational system used for it. Only the bass line is given; the numerical figures located below it indicate the intervals above it to be played, thus spelling out stenographically the harmony within a given tonality. The number of notes, or the position of the voices, is not specifically marked. Historically, the basso continuo developed as an aid to improvisation and as an indicator of the main harmony in the keyboard part, which supplied the accompaniment. Ornamentation and contrapuntal writing could be included in the improvisation, depending on the ability and taste of the player. This method was widely used in the educational system in Baroque music and retained in musical training through the 19th century.

basso profondo (It., profound bass). The lowest *bass* voice, often misspelled *basso profundo.*

beat (It. *ribattuta,* back stroke; Ger. *Takt*). In a *trill,* the pulsation of two consecutive tones.

bel canto (It., beautiful song, beautiful singing). 1. The art of lyrical and virtuosic performance as exemplified by the finest Italian singers of the 18th and 19th centuries, in contrast to *recitative* and the declamatory singing style brought into prominence by Wagner. The term representing the once glorious tradition of vocal perfection for beauty's sake. The secret of bel canto was exclusively the property of Italian singing teachers who spread the technique to Russia, England, and America. It was, above all, applied to lyric singing, particularly in opera. The art of bel canto is still taught in conservatories and music schools as a necessary precondition for an operatic career. 2. The operatic repertoire composed to highlight bel canto singers, notably late Baroque and early Romantic Italian opera. The repertoire fell into disuse until after World War II, when such stellar singers as Callas, Sutherland, and Sills brought new life to the works of Bellini, Donizetti, Handel, and others.

benefit. A special performance whose proceeds go to the singer or director of an opera performance. This was a common practice in the 18th and 19th centuries but declined toward the middle of the 20th century, when benefits were more often given for charitable or patriotic purposes.

bleat. See *goat trill.*

bocca chiusa, con (It., with closed mouth; Fr. *bouche fermée;* Ger., *Brumminstimmen*). Singing without words and with the mouth closed. Famous examples in opera include the mournful "Humming Chorus" in Act II of Puccini's *Madama Butterfly.*

bouche fermée (Fr., with closed mouth). See *bocca chiusa, con.*

break. The point where one *register* of a voice or instrument passes over into another; in the voice, the junction of the head and chest registers.

breeches part. See *trouser role.*

brindisi (It., from Ger. *bring' dir's,* I bring it to you; Ger. *Trinklied*). A salutatory drinking song or toast, not connected to the Italian city of Brindisi. The earliest known operatic brindisi is in Donizetti's *Lucrezia Borgia*; the best known is in *La Traviata* ("Labiamo!").

Brummstimmen (Ger., humming voices). See *bocca chiusa, con.*

brunette (Fr., dark-haired woman). French song genre of the 17th and 18th centuries, similar to the bergerette, containing both authentic traditional and street ballad motives. Lully and Rameau wrote brunettes into their operas.

buca (It.). Prompter's box. See *prompter.*

buffa (It.). Comic or burlesque, as in aria buffa, opera buffa.

buffo (It., from *buffone,* jester). A comic actor or opera singer.

Bühne (Ger.). Stage or theater. *Bühnenmusik* (stage music), incidental music for plays or music performance on the stage, such as the finale to Act II of Mozart's *Don Giovanni.*

burlesque. A dramatic extravaganza or farcical travesty of some serious subject, with more or less music. A popular type of theatrical entertainment that flourished in the 18th century parallel to the *ballad opera,* usually with comic recitatives and songs with original texts set to preexisting popular tunes. In the 19th century the genre was lifted from its vulgar connotations and became a dignified instrumental or vocal form. In the late 19th and 20th centuries burlesque devolved into the *burlesque show,* a popular type of entertainment that became the staple of American musical theater in the second half of the 19th century. Imported from England, the first true burlesque show was an exhibition called *British Blondes.* The burlesque differed from the minstrel show in its emphasis on "sensuality," mostly in the form of scantily clad young women. Indeed, the burlesque had much in common with the musicals of the period, which were more like revues and featured chorus lines.

C

cabaletta (It., rhythmic verse). In 18th-century Italian opera, a *cavatina*-like form. Later, it took the meaning of the concluding section of an aria or duet, forming a summary in rapid tempo and with heightened intensity.

cadenza (It., cadence; from *cadere,* fall; Ger. *Kadenz*). In an *aria* or other accompanied vocal piece, a brilliant improvisatory passage for the soloist in free time, usually near the end. During the "Golden Age of Opera" (18th century and early 19th century) coloratura singers were expected to roll out a formidable line of trills and arpeggios. But composers began to rebel against this sometimes indulgent artistic license, and composers like Berlioz, Wagner, and Verdi did everything they could to prohibit such improvisation. By the 20th century the vocal cadenza was extinct per se, utilized only at the specific direction of the composer.

Camerata (It., society). Historically important Florentine intellectual and artistic group organized by Giovanni de' Bardi, including aristocratic poets, philosophers, and music lovers. Besides functioning as a musical salon, its aim was to reinstate a "pure" singing manner without accompaniment as it was believed to have been practiced in ancient Greek drama. It was thus philosophically allied to the Renaissance. Renouncing the florid art of polyphonic writing, the Camerata cultivated lyric melody and homophonic monody, the basis for the imminent genesis of opera.

cantabile (It.). In a songful manner. This Italian term received currency in the 18th century when it became an aesthetic criterion of beauty in music. As applied to vocal compositions, cantabile appears redundant, for it is obvious that a singer ought to sing singingly, but it became of aesthetic importance as an expression mark in instrumental writing.

cantata (It., work to be sung; Ger. *Kantate*). A vocal work with instrumental accompaniment, eventually written for solo voices (singing recitatives, arias, duets, etc.), chorus, and instruments, which developed parallel to the emergence of *opera* and *oratorio* at the threshold of the 17th century.

caprino (It.). *Goat trill.*

castrato (It.; plur. *castratos, castrati*). A castrated adult male singer with soprano or alto voice. Young males were castrated at puberty in order to inhibit the maturation of their sexual glands, thereby preserving their high voices. This barbaric practice originated in the 16th century, not long before the development of opera, which created the demand for "angelic" voices in such mythological roles as Orpheus. In the 18th century castratos became so famous that they could command large fees to sing in opera houses. Handel wrote special parts for the famous castratos Senesino and Nicolini. Perhaps the most celebrated castrato singer was Carlo Broschi, called Farinelli, who was engaged by the court of Philip II of Spain, who suffered from melancholy. Farinelli sang for him the same four songs every night for 25 years. After 1750 the production of castrato singers became an increasingly hidden affair. It was finally completely forbidden in the latter 19th century. The last castrato singer was Alessandro Moreschi, known as the "Angelo di Roma" because of his celestially pure voice. There are extant recordings of his singing made in 1903.

catalogue aria (It., *aria di catalogo*). An aria form of the 18th-century opera buffa, consisting of a rapid enumeration of a list of names or items. The most famous is that of Leporello in Act I of Mozart's *Don Giovanni,* wherein he counts off his master's sexual conquests country by country.

cavata (It., extraction). An operatic *arioso* epitomizing the sentiment of a scene, in a regular meter and placed at the end of a *recitative* (*recitativo con cavata*). It eventually evolved into the *cavatina.*

cavatina (It.; Ger. *Kavatine*). A short song; an operatic *aria* without a second section or da capo. It is often preceded by an instrumental introduction and concludes with a *cabaletta.*

chamber opera. An opera suitable for performance in a small hall, with a limited number of performers and accompanied by a chamber orchestra.

champagne aria. The name often given to Don Giovanni's aria in Act I of Mozart's eponymous opera, in which he orders Leporello to make preparations for his masked ball.

chest register. The lower register of the male or female voice, the tones of which produce sympathetic vibration in the chest. *Chest tone (voice)*: 1. Vocal quality of the chest register. 2. A manner of voice production recommended by Italian teachers for tenors and basses, subjectively felt as traveling into the chest from the larynx, the corresponding expansion of the lungs producing a richer tone.

chevrotement (Fr.). *Goat trill.*

chorus (Eng.; Fr. *coeur*). Ensemble of voices, consisting of sopranos, altos, tenors, and basses, abbreviated SATB. A female or boys' chorus consists of sopranos and altos, while a male chorus consists of tenors, baritones, and basses. A double chorus often involves a spatially separated ensemble. In any case, there are usually several singers to a part.

church parable. A term coined by Britten and descriptive of various of his works, including *Curlew River* (1964), *The Burning Fiery Furnace* (1966), and *The Prodigal Son* (1968), which derive from Japanese Noh drama. Generally a small group of players presents the dramatic action involving the staging of an opera on a moral subject to a church congregation.

claque (Fr., clapping). Mercenary applause, hired by operatic stars, bosomy prima donnas, self-inflated tenors, and occasionally even seemingly normal pianists and violinists. The practice of engaging a claque began in the early 19th century in Italy, but it rapidly spread into France, even into otherwise snotty Victorian England, and by international infection caught on in America. Claques failed to prosper in Germany, perhaps because Germany took its music seriously. Occasionally, an ambitious opera star would engage in anticlaque to drown out a rival's claque. Well-paid enthusiasm might spill out onto the street, with opera lovers unharnessing the horses of a prima donna's carriage and pulling the carriage to the artist's home by manpower. Claquers were officially banned at the Metropolitan Opera House in New York in 1935 but apparently still prospered as late as 1960, at a cost of up to $100 for a group of vociferous young males on Saturday afternoons.

coeur (It.). *Chorus.*

coloratura (It.; from Ger. *Koloratur*). An internationally recognized term to describe an ornamental passage in opera consisting of diversified, rapid runs and *trills,* often applied in *cadenzas* and occurring in the highest *register.* Coloratura is intended to enhance the brilliancy of a composition and display the singer's skill. A coloratura *soprano* is one capable of performing such virtuoso passages. A famous example is in the aria of the Queen of the Night in Mozart's *Die Zuberflöte.* In modern times Rimsky-Korsakov wrote a highly chromatic coloratura part for the Queen of Shemaka in *Le Coq d'Or.* Tenor roles may also fall into this category.

comédie ballet (Fr., comedy ballet). A type of scenic performance cultivated by Lully and Molière for the court of Louis XIV, e.g., *Les plaisirs de l'ile enchantée* (1664) and *Le bourgeois gentilhomme* (1670). The comédie ballet included, besides the dialogue and ballet, arias and choral pieces.

comédie mêlée d'ariettes (Fr., comedy mixed with ariettes). A form of Italian-influenced French opéra comique, always light and romantic and occasionally involving socially relevant plots, which emerged out of the *Guerre des Bouffons,* in which songs were inserted. Gluck's *Le rencontre imprevue* (1764) is a good example.

comic opera. Opera with a comic subject. In French opéra comique, opera with spoken dialogue. Comic opera does not connote humorous content in the modern sense, but refers to a play in the sense of the Italian *commedia dell'arte* or even Dante's *Commedia divina.* It is applicable to any scenic representation, even a tragedy. In the French opéra comique, a famous example is Bizet's *Carmen,* which, in its original version, included spoken, unaccompanied dialogue, thus fulfilling the requirements of the Opéra Comique Theater in Paris, whose repertory includes tragic operas as well as the type of opera buffa or operetta. In contemporary usage, comic operas must necessarily include elements of comedy. The comic operas of Gilbert and Sullivan are typical in this respect. Historically, comic opera was the opposite of *opera seria.* Composers through the centuries were not consistent in attaching the description of comic opera or opera seria to their works, however, so that even such an unquestionably tragic opera as Mozart's *Don Giovanni* bore the description *dramma giocoso* (jocose drama).

commedia dell'arte (It., artistic play). An Italian genre of theatrical performance that emerged at the time of the Renaissance and incorporated versatile elements of pantomime, acrobatics, masks, music, and dance. Most of the action was improvisational, but the main characters were clearly delineated. They usually included a cuckolded husband, a handsome gallant, an accommodating servant, a wily lawyer, an incompetent doctor, and so on. Later, the stock characters received definite names: a grumbling old Pantalone (Pantalon), his beautiful daughter or ward Columbina (Columbine), her lover Arlecchino (Harlequin), a grotesque clown adorned with a long nose, Pulcinella (Punchinello), and the braggart warrior Scamarella (Scaramouche), characters long familiar from *commedia dell'arte.* Some composers have used these characters or emulated them in their own operas, pantomimes, and plays, e.g., Leoncavallo with *Pagliacci,* and Stravinsky with *Petrouchka* and *Pulcinella.*

commedia per music (It., play with music). An early designation for opera, not necessarily comic.

comparsa (It., extra actor). An "extra" or "walk-on" player in a production. In opera, the comparsa is one who does not have a singing role.

comprimario, -a (It., with the principal). In 19th-century Italian opera, a singer who does not have an individual *aria* to perform. He or she could, however, sing a *romance,* or add his or her voice to an ensemble number.

congiura (It., plot, conspiracy). A term used to denote a conspiratorial scene in an Italian opera, e.g., "Ad augusta!" in Verdi's *Ernani.*

continuo. See *basso continuo.*

contralto (It., against the high voice; Ger. *Alt*). See *alto.*

countertenor. A very high male voice. Ideally, a countertenor sings in the contralto or soprano range, while retaining a masculine tone quality. Highly praised in the Middle Ages, countertenors were replaced in the Baroque era and their function was taken over by the castrati. But when the practice of emasculation came to an end in the 19th century, composers resumed the use of countertenors. They remain in fashion, thanks primarily to the early music movement, and are featured in such modern operas as Britten's *A Midsummer Night's Dream* and Glass's *Akhanaten.*

crescendo (It., growing). A gradual increase in loudness. The abbreviation is *cresc.,* followed by lines or dots to indicate the duration: *cresc.........* The word itself can also be broken up by several dots or hyphens: *cre....scen....do.* The effect of gradual swelling up of the sound was primarily cultivated by the Mannheim school in the 18th century. Crescendo may begin from any dynamic level, including *forte.*

cue. A phrase, from a vocal or instrumental part, occurring near the end of a long pause in another part, and inserted in small notes in the latter to serve as a guide in timing its reentrance.

cycle. Several independent works that collectively narrate a single story. The most famous example is Wagner's tetralogy, *Der Ring des Nibelungen,* although others have followed, including Bungert's tetralogy, *Homerische Welt.*

D

da capo aria (It., to the head). An aria in symmetric ternary form with the third part being the exact repetition (ABA) or slight variation of the first part (ABA^1). This type, also called a *da capo aria,* was popularized by composers of the Neapolitan school in the second half of the 17th century. It became the most common form of the operatic aria, especially among Italian and Italianate composers of the 18th and 19th centuries. In Romantic opera, this type evolved into the *grand aria* (or *aria grande*), divided into (1) the main theme, fully developed; (2) a more tranquil and richly harmonized second section; and (3) a repetition *da capo* of the first theme, with more florid ornamentation.

dark (Fr. *relâche*). In theatrical jargon, a term meaning that there is no performance.

début (Fr.). A first appearance by a performer or work. *Débutant,* a male performer who makes his debut; *débutante,* a female performer who makes her debut.

Deus ex machina (Lat., God from a machine). An archetypal dramaturgical theme in myth, fiction, theater, and epic poetry. In essence, a god would come down from the heavens (or from below) to alter a situation, often at the last moment, and usually to the benefit of the main character(s). When mythical and other stories began to be staged, scenographic technology was developed to permit the descent of actors from above the audience's sightline in the "machine." In opera, an early example can be found in Monteverdi's *Orfeo* (1607). An ironic and multiple use of the device is featured in Glass's *The Voyage* (1992).

diabolus in musica (Lat., devil in music). A nickname, laden with theological connotations found in many medieval treatises on music, for the tritone (an interval of three whole tones), forbidden because it did not fit into the basic hexachord of ancient music theory. It was to be expected that an interval bearing such a satanic designation would be used by composers to characterize sinister forces. Examples are many: the *leitmotif* of the dragon Fafner in Act II of Wagner's *Siegfried,* the motives of the three magical winning cards in Tchaikovsky's *The Queen of Spades,* the devil's motto in Hanson's *Merry Mount,* and so forth. The *diabolus in musica* is the formative interval of the diminished-seventh chord, a favorite device of romantic operas suggesting mortal danger. In appreciation of this dramatic function, the diminished-seventh chord was known in Italian opera circles as the *accorde di stupefazione* (stupefying chord).

diva (It., divine woman). A term introduced by Italian impresarios to describe a female opera singer to whom even the description *prima donna assoluta* (absolutely first lady) seems inadequate. The term was popular in the 19th century, but disappeared from publicity campaigns early in the skeptical 20th century, even as it became part of the vernacular.

division. A "dividing up" of a melodic series of tones into a rapid *coloratura* passage. If a vocal setting, the passage is to be sung in one breath (now obsolete). *To run a division,* to execute such a passage.

Dramaturg (Ger.). A person in a German opera house who manages the requisite and varied printed matter for theatrical productions, including, but not limited to, opera librettos, program booklets, and press materials. He or she may also serve as a producer, and also may occasionally perform as a singer.

drame lyrique (Fr., lyric drama; It., *dramma lirico*). French designation for opera, especially in the 19th century. This genre may be lyric or tragic, and its designation refers only to the use of singing.

dramma giocoso (It., jocular drama). An Italian term current in the 18th century for a comic opera with tragic episodes. It literally means "jocular drama." Mozart's *Don Giovanni* is subtitled a *dramma giocoso.*

dramma lirico (It.). *Drame lyrique.*

dramma per musica (It., drama for music). An early term for opera in Italy about 1600. While the Baroque eventually called such works *opera seria,* Wagner revived the term for his operas (see *music drama*).

Durchkomponiert (Ger.). *Through-composed.*

E

echo (It. *eco*). A subdued repetition of a strain or phrase. In Greek mythology, the nymph Echo languishes in unrequited love for Narcissus, and only her voice remains as an echo. The legend inspired several opera composers. Gluck wrote an opera, *Écho et Narcisse,* in which he made ingenious use of canonic imitation. This effect is used poignantly in the last act of Monteverdi's *Orfeo.*

eco (It.). *Echo.*

Einstudierung (Ger.). Production.

encore (Fr., again). 1. See *applause*; *claque.* 2. The piece or performance repeated at (or added to) the end of a scheduled program.

endless melody (Ger., *Unendliche Melodie*). A term introduced by Wagner to describe an uninterrupted melodic flow unhampered by sectional cadences. Particularly characteristic is the flow of one *leitmotiv* into another with a free interchange of voices and instrumental parts. With the decline of the Wagnerian cult in the 20th century, the endless melody lost much of its attraction. Modern operas now gravitate toward a Verdian concept of well-adorned operatic numbers.

ensemble finale. In opera, summary of all major musical themes and the resolution of tangled threads of the plot, usually with the participation of all principal characters. Wagner and his disciples regarded the finale as a musical supererogation, but composers of the non-Wagnerian ilk still find it useful to construct hell-raising finishes, if for nothing else than for the sake of an effective catalyst for tumultuous applause.

entr'acte (Fr., between acts, interlude). A light instrumental composition or short ballet for performance between acts of theater, music, and dance works. The term is often found in Lully's collaborations with Molière.

epic opera, epic theater. A highly stylized theatrical form in which a technique called the *alienation effect* (A-effect) attempts to keep the audience aware of theatrical artifice and unable to identify with the characters or experience Aristotelian catharsis. The aesthetic was developed most prominently by Bertolt Brecht, who collaborated with Weill, Eisler, and Dessau.

execution. 1. Style, manner of performance. 2. Technical ability.

extended compass. Tones beyond the usual range of a voice or instrument.

F

Fach (Ger., division). A term used much in Germany and sporadically elsewhere to denote the range of operatic roles a singer may be expected to perform when engaged by a company.

Falsett (Ger.). *Falsetto.*

falsetto (It., dim. of *falso*: false, altered; Fr. *fausset*; Ger. *Falsett*). The practice of voice production by using head rather than chest tones, particularly among tenors, thus producing sounds well above the natural range. Falsetto singing was widely practiced in the choirs at the Vatican and Italian cathedrals when the use of female or castrati singers was inappropriate. Falsetto singers were also known as *alti naturali,* natural alto singers, to distinguish them from *voci artificiali,* the artificial voices of the castrati. Another term for falsetto singers was *tenorini,* little tenors. The word *falsetto* itself is a diminutive of the Italian *falso,* because the singer, although not castrated, applies a "false" way of voice production. Falsetto voices are often used in Baroque operas for comic effects. The part of the Astrologer in Rimsky-Korsakov's *Le Coq d'or* is cast in falsetto to indicate that he is a eunuch.

farce. 1. A one-act *opera* or *operetta.* 2. (Lat., stuff). A comic *intermezzo* in medieval plays with music, making use of songs popular at the time, often of lewd, lascivious, libidinous, ultracomical or burlesque character. In modern times, a farce still retains the old meaning of a frivolous comedy of manners.

farewell engagements. These are convenient though rarely truthful announcements issued by famous prima donnas of both sexes at the end of their careers to attract the attention of a long-vanishing public. Long past her prime, Adelina Patti gave an extended series of "farewell" concerts in the United States.

fausset (Fr.). *Falsetto.*

favola per musica (It., fable for music). An early term for an opera *libretto* based on a mythological story.

Festspiel (Ger.). German term for a stage play in which music is included. Wagner called *Der Ring des Nibelungen* a Festspiel.

fiasco. (It., flask or bottle). An utter failure of a theatrical or other performance, although how *fiasco* acquired the meaning of an ignominious failure remains a mystery. Music history abounds in stories of fiascos of great masterpieces that eventually became parts of the standard repertory. The fiasco of Wagner's *Tannhäuser* in Paris in 1861 is notorious. He withdrew the opera after three disastrous performances. The fiasco of the first production of *Madama Butterfly* of Puccini in 1904 was resounding: Puccini and his librettist notified the publishers that inasmuch as the audience showed its disapproval of the opera, they were withdrawing it from further performances. Melodramatic biographies of Bizet describe his anguish at the fiasco of *Carmen,* which drove him to an early grave. Aside from the fact that nobody, not even composers, ever die of chagrin, *Carmen* was anything but a fiasco. It had a continuous run of three months after its initial production, and Bizet died on the night of its 33d performance.

figured bass. *Basso continuo.*

fioritura (It., floral decoration; plur. *fioriture*). An embellishment. An ornamental turn, flourish, or phrase introduced into a melody. It was common practice for Italian singers to embellish their arias with arpeggios, gruppetti, and trills, often obscuring the main melodic line.

fossa d'orchestra (It.). *Orchestra pit.*

fosse d'orchestre (Fr.). *Orchestra pit.*
French overture. See *overture.*

G

Generalbass (Ger.). *Basso continuo.*
Generalintendant (Ger., superintendent). See *Intendant.*
Gesamtkunstwerk (Ger., unified work of art). It was Wagner who promulgated the idea that all arts are interrelated, and that their ultimate synthesis should be the idea of each constituent art, that painting and figurative arts should serve the cause of architecture and stage representations, that poetry should relate to philosophical concepts, and that music should be both the servant and the mistress of its sister arts. In his *music dramas,* he attempted to approximate the ideal of the *Gesamtkunstwerk* by assigning equal importance to the text, orchestra music, singing, acting, and scenic design. This operatic reform aimed at the restoration of the unity of the arts of music, literature, and painting, as was believed to have existed in ancient Greek tragedy.
goat trill (Fr. *chevrotement;* Ger. *Bockstriller*; It. *caprino,* little goat). 1. A curious vocal effect produced when a singer repeats a note very fast and catches a breath after each note. It was introduced by Monteverdi for dramatic purposes. 2. Fanciful 18th-century description of a rasping trill at the interval or a semitone or less. Wagner also used it in *Die Meistersinger.*
gondoliera (It.). *Barcarolle.*
Gondollied (Ger.). *Barcarolle.*
grand opera. 1. A type of opera, usually in five acts, treating a heroic, mythological, or historical subject, sumptuously costumed, and produced in a large opera house. It is most closely associated with 19th-century French works or works performed in Paris during the same period. 2. In English-speaking countries, any serious operatic work without spoken recitatives.
ground bass. An early English form of basso ostinato, with a continually repeated bass phrase of four or eight measures, even notes, a distinct melodic outline, generally symmetrical in structure, serving as the harmonic foundation of variations in the upper voices, along the lines of a passacaglia or chaconne. The technique was first used in the music of the virginalists of the late Renaissance, and became prevalent during the English Baroque, as for example in "When I Am Laid in Earth," Dido's farewell aria in Purcell's *Dido and Aeneas.*
Guerre des Bouffons (*Querelle des Bouffons*). A famous theatrical controversy that erupted in Paris in 1752. That year saw a visit of an Italian opera company (the Bouffons), whose performance of Pergolesi's *La Serva padrona* aroused the admiration of the pro-Italian faction of the Paris intellectuals, including the Encyclopedists. On the other hand, the Italian manner was opposed by the lovers of French opera, fostered by Louis XV. It was followed by a series of polemical pamphlets including Rousseau's historical paper *Lettre sur la musique française.* The controversy subsided when the Bouffons left Paris (1754).

H

happy ending (It., *lieto fine*). In operas and other dramatic works, a morally and emotionally satisfying finale, no matter how improbable or realistic, where virtue triumphs, evil is punished or forgiven magnanimously, and lovers unite after overcoming insurmountable odds.
head voice. Vocal production of notes in the upper register, giving the illusion of being generated from the top of the head.
Heldenbariton (Ger.). Heroic *baritone,* requiring a powerful voice and stamina for difficult operatic parts, particularly in Wagner's *music dramas.*
Heldentenor (Ger.). Heroic *tenor,* requiring a robust voice and stamina for difficult operatic parts, particularly in Wagner's *music dramas.*
historia (It.). See *oratorio.*
Hofkammersänger(in) (Ger.). See *Kammersänger(in).*
Hosenrolle (Ger.). *Trouser role.*

I

imbroglio (It., mixture, confusion). 1. The use of rhythmically contrasting and noncoincident sections within a common meter. A simultaneous use of $\frac{3}{4}$ and $\frac{6}{8}$ in Spanish music is an imbroglio. A similar combination of meters is found in Mozart's opera *Don Giovanni* at the end of the first act, and in the street scene in Wagner's *Die Meistersinger.* 2. Literally, "confusion"; a term used to describe scenes in opera where several groups of singers or instrumental ensembles perform together, each serving a different dramatic purpose.
impresario (from It., *impresa*: undertaking). The agent or manager of an opera or concert company.
incidental music. A set of pieces composed to illustrate selected scenes in a dramatic performance. It is distinguished from an orchestral suite in its subordination of music to dramatic action. It differs from opera because usually there are no vocal parts. In addition to overtures and marches, interludes, songs, and dances may be provided. Exemplary are Beethoven's *Egmont,* part of his music to Goethe's *Egmont,* and Mendelssohn's overture to Shakespeare's *A Midsummer Night's Dream,* written long before the other pieces that he wrote for the play.
Intendant (Ger., superintendent). The administrator of a German opera house.
interlude. See *intermezzo.*
intermède (Fr., interlude). A term of 17th and 18th century France connoting a self-contained musical entertainment inserted between acts of a larger work. Molière used them to good effect. Early examples in opera include Cavalli's *Serse* (1660) and *Ercole amante* (1662).
intermedio (It., interlude). See *intermezzo.*
intermezzo (It., interlude, insertion; Fr., *intermède*; Ger.,

Zwischenspiel). A theatrical genre that dates back to the liturgical drama in the 13th century in which they were interpolated between ritual parts of the religious service. Secular intermezzos served to provide diversions at aristocratic weddings, coronations, and other formal functions. Invariably, they were of a lighter nature than other parts of the occasion, and were not necessarily connected with the action in the drama or religious play into which they were interpolated. The genre eventually developed into independent musical presentations, leading ultimately to the formation of *opera buffa.*

Since intermezzos did not have to be connected with the principal spectacle, their authors strove mainly to please the public by whatever means, and often succeeded in attracting more attention than the stage play itself. Thus, Pergolesi inserted an intermezzo *La Serva padrona* in a performance of his serious opera *Il Prigioniero superbo,* with the result that the intermezzo became extremely popular. Its performances in Paris precipitated the famous *Guerre des Bouffons.* Rousseau, who was an ardent partisan of the Italian type of opera, composed an intermezzo that became quite successful. Richard Strauss wrote an amusing opera of his own in this genre, and pointedly entitled it *Intermezzo.* Within operas, intermezzos are instrumental interludes, usually of short duration, set between scenes. An intermezzo in Mascagni's *Cavalleria rusticana* is often performed as an independent concert piece.

intonation (Ger. *Tonfall*). The production of tone, either vocal or instrumental, with an emphasis on proper pitch.

Italian overture. See *overture.*

K

Kammersänger(in) (Ger., chamber singer). A high honorary title given by the governments in both Germany and Austria to prominent and distinguished singers. When bestowed by the courts in earlier times, the term was *Hofkammersänger(in).*

Kantate (Ger). *Cantata.*

Kapellmeister (Ger., chapel-master; Fr. *maître de chapelle*). Conductor of an orchestra or a choir, especially at central European courts. The *Kapellmeister* was, in effect, in charge of all music at a court, although some employers divided the role into sacred and secular masters.

Korrepetitor(in) (Ger.). *Répétiteur,-euse.*

L

lamento (It., lamentation, complaint). A common regular type of *aria* in Italian opera in which a character expresses unquenchable sorrow. *Lamento d'Arianna,* the only surviving segment from Monteverdi's opera *Arianna* (1608) in which Ariadne laments her painful abandonment by the treacherous Theseus, is an outstanding example.

leitmotiv, leitmotif (Ger., leading motif; from Ger. *leiten,* lead). Any striking musical motive (theme, phrase) associated with or accompanying one of the characters in a musical drama. Also, some particular idea, emotion, or situation therein. The concept is commonly associated with Wagner's *music dramas,* but the term was first used in an annotated catalogue of works by Weber, published in 1871, in which it was described as a "strong delineation of each individual character in an opera." The leitmotiv was aesthetically defined and analyzed by the Wagnerian theorist Wolzogen in 1876. Wagner himself never used the term, but described the identifying motives in his operas as "melodic moments," "thematic motives," "fundamental themes," "idea motives," or "remembrance motives."

The main purpose in Wagner's application of leading motives in his operas was to musically identify characters, emotions, objects, and important ideas. By employing them in contrapuntal combinations, and by varying the rhythm and sometimes the intervallic structure of these motives, Wagner intended to establish "a new form of dramatic music, which possesses the unity of a symphonic movement." This unity can be achieved, Wagner averred, "in a network of basic themes permeating the entire work, analogously to the themes in a sym. They are contrasted with each other, supplement each other, assume new shapes, separate and coalesce . . . according to dramatic action." But Wagner's use of leading motives is not limited to the characters on the stage. He carefully tabulates the motives of material objects, such as the ring and the sword in *Der Ring des Nibelungen,* and abstract concepts such as the Covenant, Conflict, Transformation, Love, and many others.

Wagner was, of course, not the first to introduce identifying themes in opera. Papageno's appearances in Mozart's *Die Zauberflöte* are announced by a scale on his magic bell. And there are definite leading motives in Weber's *Der Freischütz.* Verdi used leading motives in several of his operas. Tchaikovsky can hardly be called a Wagnerian, but the presence of identifying motives in his operas is discerned without difficulty. The true innovation in Wagner's operas is the conscious, philosophical affirmation of unity through plurality, the *Gesamtkunstwerk,* which was Wagner's grand ideal. One of the most fascinating aspects of Wagnerian leading motives is the unexpected musical similarity of the dramatically contrasting characters or ideas. Thus, by a "topological" alteration, the theme of love-death in *Tristan und Isolde* can be converted into the leading motive of the Holy Grail in *Parsifal.*

letter scene. A favored scene in 17th-century opera wherein a character reads aloud a letter or letters, effectively embellishing or enhancing the narrative of the plot, e.g., Charlotte's aria "Air des lettres" in Massenet's *Werther.*

libretto (It., little book, plural, *librettos,* libretti; Fr., *livret*;

Ger., *Textbuch*). The book containing the text or play of an opera. Also, the text or play itself, distributed to the audience in printed form to acquaint them with the subject of the opera. In the 19th century it was common to supply a translation into the language of the country in which the opera was performed. Italian librettos usually carried an *argomento* (not an argument, but a summary), listing the acts and scenes, the cast of characters, and sometimes a *protesta* (a protestation by the author of the libretto that his use of names of pagan deities should not be understood as a lack of Christian faith). A paragon of the art was Metastasio, whose librettos were set to music by some fifty composers, accounting for over 1,000 different Italian operas. Some librettos have independent literary value, such as Boito's rendering of Shakespeare for Verdi, or Hofmannsthal's thoughtful texts for Richard Strauss. Then there were Gilbert and Sullivan, in whose comic operas the merit is distributed equally for literature and music.

lieto fine (It.). *Happy ending.*

liturgical drama. Medieval plays in Latin containing action, dialogue, and occasional singing episodes. One of the most popular types of liturgical drama is the genre of *miracle plays,* reciting stories of saints. During the Renaissance liturgical drama developed into *mystery plays.* Gradually such plays assumed a secular theatrical role while adhering to biblical subjects. Incidental music such as dances, trumpet flourishes, processions—even folk songs—was used. In Italy these dramas with music became known as *sacre rappresentazioni,* and as *autos* (acts) in Spain and Portugal. These festivals were true predecessors of scenic *oratorios* and, by ramification, Wagnerian *music dramas.*

livret (Fr.). *Libretto.*

lyric opera (Fr., *opéra-lyrique*). An opera in which the lyric mode predominates.

M

mad scene. Mad scenes in opera have had since the 17th century extraordinary dramatic currency. Fortunately, most of the victims, most of them female, recover their sanity by work's end, as soon as the dramatic situation turns more favorable. Early examples abound in Cavalli (i.e., *Egisto*) and in countless succeeding works in the *opera seria* genre (Handel's *Orlando*), but the most famous is likely "Ardon gl'incensi" in Donizetti's *Lucia di Lammermoor.* Madness as an overriding condition for operatic characters and their often woeful tales is seen in Richard Strauss's *Elektra,* Berg's *Wozzeck,* and, in gentler fashion, Britten's *Peter Grimes.*

madrigal comedy, madrigal opera. A chain of madrigals united in content and forming a dramatic sequence. A contemporary of the early *dramma per musica.* The best-known composers of madrigal comedy are Vecchi and Banchieri. A distant relative of the *commedia dell'arte,* its origins may be found in Renaissance madrigal collections with a common theme, often found in courtly weddings.

maestro (It., master). An honorary appellation accorded to composers, conductors, and teachers. In Italian, the word conveys little more than a common term for a teacher, but when used by Englishmen, Americans, or Russians in addressing a musical celebrity, it sounds lofty and deferential.

maestro suggeritore (It.). *Prompter.*

maître de chapelle (Fr.). *Kapellmeister.*

masque, mask. An English spectacle or a social assembly during the 16th and 17th centuries that featured a variety of artistic presentations, including poetry, drama, dance, and music. The subjects were usually taken from Greek mythology, and members of the aristocracy were themselves often engaged to perform the parts of shepherds and shepherdesses, benevolent gods and goddesses, etc. Among poets whose masques were produced at the English court were Ben Jonson and Milton. A curious by-product of the masque was the 17th-century *antimasque,* a comic or grotesque interlude between the allegorical scenes, analogous to the *kyōgen* interludes of the medieval Japanese *Noh* drama. When *opera* was introduced into England, masques became integrated with it and disappeared as an independent form.

melodrama. 1. Originally, any musical drama. 2. A form of declamation with musical accompaniment, ranging from piano to full orchestra. 3. A romantic and sensational drama in which music plays a subordinate part. During the 19th century the term *melodrama* acquired the meaning of a theatrical production calculated to excite the sensations of an audience by piling up suspense upon suspense, with natural disasters adding to human conflict and individual misfortunes. The adjective *melodramatic* conveys the derogatory meaning of a cheap exhibition masquerading as a real drama. The text of a typical melodrama corresponds in spirit to Gothic novels. Dramatic dealings, sudden reversals of fortune, mysterious portents and premonitions, often with supernatural overtones, suitably illustrated by chromatic runs or tremolos on the diminished-seventh chord, are potent melodramatic devices.

mélodrame (Fr.). In opera, an orchestral *interlude* between scenes.

melos (Grk., song). The name bestowed by Wagner on the style of *recitative* employed in his later *music dramas.*

metabole (Grk., modification). In rhetoric, a permutation of different words within a sentence. In music, the changed order of notes within a leitmotiv, as well as changes in tempo, rhythm, tonality, or interval structure within a musical period. In its ultimate development, metabole is a variation on a theme.

metteur en scène (Fr.). *Producer.*

mezzo-soprano (It., half-soprano). The female voice between soprano and alto, partaking of the quality of both, and usually of small compass (*a-f* ^{2}, or *a-g* ^{2}), but very full toned in the medium register.

mimodrama. A dramatic or musical spectacle in which performers convey dramatic action by gestures and choreography, without speaking. Mimodrama is the same as pantomime.

miracle plays. Sacred dramas, often with music, popular in England in the Middle Ages. The stories were usually on biblical subjects or parables. Later examples of this genre were called *moralities.*

monodrama. A stage work in which only one actor, speaker, or singer acts, recites, or sings. Schoenberg introduced a type of singing recitation, *Sprechstimme,* a technique that came to its full fruition in his *Pierrot Lunaire.* The classic example of a staged monodrama is his *Erwartung.* Rebikov evolved a novel type of monodrama that he described as psychodrama. In it an actor recites his state of mind with musical accompaniment. In Schoenberg's *Die glückliche Hand,* the central character sings and mimes the story, and a chorus comments on the action in Sprechstimme.

monody (from Lat., single song). Usually, the *recitative*-like *basso continuo* song style of early 17th-century Italy.

moralities. A later form of the *miracle plays.*

motif, motive (Fr., *motif*; Ger., *Motiv*; It., *motivo*). 1. A short phrase or figure used in development or imitation. 2. A leading motive. See *leitmotiv, leitmotif.*

Motiv (Ger.). *Motif, motive.*

motivo (It.). *Motif, motive.*

music drama. The original description of opera as it evolved in Florence early in the 17th century (*dramma per musica*). Wagner adopted this term in order to emphasize the dramatic element in his spectacles (*Musikdrama*).

music theater. Any small to moderate musical stage work involving a dramatic element in its performance, frequently distinguished from opera by its scale and scope.

mystery plays. Medieval Bible plays, often with vocal and instrumental music. In the form called *moralities,* abstract ideas were personified on the stage. Modern versions of the mysteries have been successfully revived in Britain.

N

Nachgefallen (Ger.). *Ad libitum.*

Nachtmusik (Ger.). *Serenade.*

naturalism. In musical usage, naturalism appears as an extreme case of *verismo.* Naturalistic opera emphasizes the negative phenomena of life without the redeeming quality of romance. In Soviet parlance naturalism acquired a pejorative meaning. The word was used as a verbal missile in the attacks on Shostakovich's opera *Lady Macbeth of the District of Mtzensk,* particularly with reference to the scene of adultery illustrated in an orchestral interlude by sliding trombones.

Neapolitan opera. A term used to describe the earliest works in the *opera seria* genre, although neither the formulation nor flowering of the genre, nor its principal composers, were restricted to Naples.

Neuinszenierung (Ger.). New production.

non vibrato (It.). An emphatic negative exhortation often marked as a warning against the natural tendency of string players and singers to play *vibrato* and thus produce what the Baroque considered an *affect,* and what became a standard performance technique of Romantic (and other) music. Other considerations for the use of non vibrato are the period of music being performed (e.g., early music) and the performance of untempered pitch (just intonation).

number opera (Ger., *Nummernoper*). An opera in which the principal ingredients—arias, vocal ensembles, instrumental interludes—are clearly separated from one another, or are connected by recitative or spoken dialogue. Virtually all operas before Wagner were number operas, but an argument can be advanced that transitions between separate numbers create a continuity characteristic of "music drama" of the Wagnerian type. Wagner's theories virtually determined the operatic practice of the second half of the 19th century, but a return to the more formal type of number opera was marked in the 20th century.

Nummernoper (Ger.). *Number opera.*

O

obbligato (It., obligatory). Originally, an instrumental part that was essential in the performance, such as the many sonatas for piano and another instrument *obbligato.* The meaning expanded to any instrumental or vocal part that is a concerted (and therefore essential) part. Through some paradoxical inversion of meaning, *obbligato* began to be used, particularly in popular arrangements, to indicate an optional part; for example, a song with *cello obbligato* would mean that such a part would be a desirable addition to the accompaniment, but not essential.

Oberspiellter (Ger., senior producer). The primary resident producer of an opera company. Sometimes interchanged with the term *Generalintendant.*

ombra scene (It.). Shadow scene; a dramatic operatic episode taking place in the nether regions, in a cemetery, or in a place where ghosts congregate, usually cast in the monodic manner of an accompanied recitative in triadic harmonies. Ombra scenes abound in general pauses, tremolos, exclamations, and other emotional outbursts, the clarinet, horn, and trombone being particularly favored in Baroque operas. Mozart introduces the ghostly statue of the Commendatore in *Don Giovanni* with an ominous trombone passage.

opera (It., work; abbrev. of *opera in musica*). A form of drama, of Italian origin, in which vocal and instrumental music is essential and predominant. The several acts, usually preceded by instrumental introductions, consist of vocal scenes, recitatives, songs, arias, duets, trios, choruses, and so on, accompanied by the orchestra. This is the *grand* or *heroic opera.* A *comic opera* is a versified comedy set to music; an *operetta* or *Singspiel* has spoken interludes.

opéra ballet. A popular dramatic entertainment in early 18th-century France in which operatic elements were combined in equal measure with ballet. While dramatic continuity was not a priority, Campra, with such works as *L'Europe galante* and *Les fêtes vénitiennes,* elevated the lyrical comedy to a level on a par with tragedy for French audiences.

opéra bouffe (Fr.). See *opera buffa.*

opera buffa (It., comic opera; Fr., *opéra bouffe*). *Comic opera,* as opposed to *opera seria.* In a typical cast there are standard comic characters, some of which are borrowed from the *commedia dell'arte.* It thrives on schemes and stratagems found in comedies of Shakespeare, Molière, and other classics of dramatic literature. Such plays are replete with mistaken identities, disguises, deceptions, and intrigues, but virtue triumphs in the end.

opéra comique (Fr., comic opera). French opera with spoken dialogue instead of *recitative.* It is not necessarily humorous in nature. When it became a regular art form in the 18th century, the word *comic* had dignified connotations, on par with Dante's *Divina Commedia,* which, of course, is anything but a comedy. The music of such operas was of a light dramatic texture, often introducing concepts of morality and proper social behavior. The Paris Opéra Comique was originally the theater intended for the production of French dramatic works that contained musical numbers and spoken dialogues in about equal measure. But this opera house also saw productions, such as Bizet's *Carmen,* that could hardly be called comical.

opéra lyrique (Fr., lyric opera). *Lyric opera.*

opera semiseria (It., semiserious opera). Baroque and Classic *opera seria* with a happy ending, sometimes including comic and parodic elements.

opera seria (It., serious opera). Serious (grand, heroic, tragic) opera. It is virtually identical with the concept of *grand opera.* It denotes an eloquent music drama replete with emotional upheavals, tragic conflicts, scenes of triumph and disaster, with insanity, murders, and suicides filling the action. By tradition, an opera seria ought to have at least three acts, but may well extend into five. It can also include ballet. Its opposite is *opera buffa.*

operetta (It., little opera; Fr., *opérette*). A "little opera" in which the *libretto* is in a comic, mock-pathetic, parodistic, or anything-but-serious vein. The music is light and lively, often interrupted by dialogue.

oratorio (It.). An extended, more or less dramatic composition for vocal soloists and chorus, with accompaniment by an orchestra and/or organ and performed without stage play or scenery. The genre, known also as *historia,* tended toward religious subjects, and it developed in 17th-century Italy as a way for operatic composers to keep busy during Lent, when theaters were closed. Many 20th-century composers have composed opera oratorios, with essential elements of both, including Stravinsky (*Oedipus Rex*) and Milhaud (*Orestia*).

Orchestergraben (Ger.). *Orchestra pit.*

orchestra pit (Fr., *fosse d'orchestre*; Ger., *Orchestergraben*; It., *fossa d'orchestra*). The area below and in front of the stage that houses the opera orchestra.

overture (from Fr. *ouverture,* opening). Originally a musical introduction to a play, opera, or ballet, although in the 19th century an independent concert piece, the concert overture. An opera overture served often as a thematic table of contents, with the tunes of the most important arias, choruses, and instrumental interludes passing in review and preparing the listener for the melodic joys to come. As a musical form, the overture made its first appearance in France in the 17th century, and the practice, particularly by Lully, gave rise to a special form of the French overture, which consisted of two contrasting sections, the first being in a slow tempo marked by dotted rhythms and concluding on the dominant of the principal key, and the second in a faster tempo, often culminating in a fugal development. This binary form later expanded into a ternary structure by the simple expedient of returning to the initial slow part, varied at will. The French overture was also much in use in instrumental suites.

In the 18th century the French overture was replaced by the more vivacious Italian overture. The slow movement was placed in the middle between two fast sections. In early Italian operas the overture was called *sinfonia,* that is, an instrumental section without singing, and in more recent times, *preludio.* The type of "summary overture" that incorporates materials from the opera itself is exemplified by Mozart's overtures to *Don Giovanni* and *The Magic Flute,* Beethoven's three *Leonore* overtures, Weber's *Der Freischütz* overture, any overture by Meyerbeer, and virtually all overtures by Russian composers of the 19th century.

Wagner's overtures to his early operas and *Die Meistersinger* belonged to the category of summary overtures, but in his music dramas of the later period, and particularly in *Der Ring des Nibelungen,* he abandoned the idea of using material from the opera itself and returned to the type of prelude, usually of short duration, to introduce the opera. Richard Strauss followed the Wagnerian type of introduction in his own operas, as did a great majority of modern opera composers, including Puccini and composers of the *verismo* school. Only the Russians of the Soviet period remained faithful to the Italian type of summary overture.

In numerous cases, operas, even by famous composers, drop out of the repertory, while their overtures continue to have independent lives on the concert stage. Performances of Beethoven's *Fidelio* are relatively rare, but his *Leonore* overtures are played constantly. Rossini's opera *William Tell* has virtually disappeared from the repertory, but its overture is one of the most popular pieces of the concert repertory. A special case is the *Roman Carnival Overture* by Berlioz, a summary overture based on a previously written opera (*Benvenuto Cellini*).

P

parable aria. A type of aria, much in vogue in the 18th century, in which the singer expresses emotion by way of parable or metaphor. A famous example is the protestation of one of the ladies in Mozart's *Così fan tutte* that she would remain as firm as a rock in resisting temptation. The rock is the crux of the metaphor in the parable.

parody. A parasitic literary or musical genre that emerged in the 18th century and flourished in the 19th century, particularly in opera. It usually followed on the heels of a successful or at least notorious theatrical production. Weber's opera *Der Freischütz* was lampooned in England as "a new muse-sick-all and see-nick performance from the new German uproar, by the celebrated Bunny-bear." Wagner's *Tannhäuser,* which suffered a notorious debacle at its first Paris production, engendered a number of French parodies, among them *Ya-Meine Herr, Cacophonie de l'Avenir.* Occasionally, a parody anticipates the main event. One, *Tristanderl und Süssholde,* was produced in Munich before *Tristan und Isolde* itself.

particella (It., particle). A reduced score. Some composers prefer writing down symphonic scores or even operas in arrangements for two or three staves, one for woodwinds, one for brass, one or two for strings, with the vocal part, if any, in small printing on top. Many publishers now issue abridged scores for conductors, often with optional instrumental parts written in.

partitino (It., little score). Supplementary parts, printed separately, for a work with instruments or vocal part that do not appear often in the score. Examples include the "Turkish" percussion in Mozart's *The Abduction from the Seraglio,* the trombone and the chorus in his *Don Giovanni,* and the children's chorus in Puccini's *La Bohème.* The partitino saves time and paper that would otherwise be wasted on vacuous rests and pauses.

pasticcio (It., pie). A musical medley of extracts from different works, pieced together and provided with new words so as to form a "new" composition. The word is often used disdainfully to designate a motley medley of unrelated tunes by unrelated composers, arranged in a sequence with artificial connective tissue between numbers. Historically, however, the pasticcio performed a useful function in acquainting music lovers with popular opera arias, dance movements, and concert pieces, presented as an appetizing sampler plate of musical desserts, e.g., the *Hexameron* for piano on the march theme from Bellini's opera *I Puritani,* written in 1837 by six composers, including Chopin and Liszt.

patter song. A rapid, syllabic humorous song, particularly effective in comic dialogues. The *tessitura* is in the middle register, and the singing approximates the *parlando* style. Mozart and Rossini excelled in Italian patter song. The greatest master in English was Sullivan in setting Gilbert's witty lines in their comic operas.

portamento (It., carrying). A smooth gliding from one tone to another, differing from the legato in its more deliberate execution and in the actual (though very rapid and slurring) sounding of the intermediate tones.

preghiera (It., prayer). An *aria* or *chorus* of a reverential nature, as Desdemona's "Ave Maria" in Verdi's *Otello.*

prelude (from Lat. *praeludium,* something played before; Fr., *prélude*; Ger., *Vorspiel*; It., *preludio*). A musical introduction to a large work, functionally similar to the *overture* but generally shorter and often running without pause into the main body of the work.

preludio (It.). *Prelude.*

prima donna (It., first lady). The leading *soprano* in opera. *Prima donna assoluta* is an absolute prima donna, superior to the *seconda donna* or *prima donna altra.* The cult of the prima donna reached its height in the 19th century. A typical prima donna was an amply bosomed Italian or German soprano, possessing great lung power. The chronicles of opera are replete with tales about temperamental prima donnas engaging in fistfights and flights of invective with other prima donnas over the size of lettering in their names on theatrical posters, the space allocated in their dressing rooms, the extent of publicity, the efficiency of the hired *claque,* and so on. More than one prima donna has lost an engagement over such seemingly minor matters.

Probe (Ger.). *Rehearsal.*

producer (Fr., *metteur en scène*; Ger., *Spielleiter*; It., *regista*). The person responsible for the dramatic presentation of a performance. At various times in history this has been the composer, the conductor, the balletmaster, or performers themselves. In the late 20th century it was more often a person independent of the production in any artistic sense (although the expression "producer's opera" is sometimes heard in reference to operas whose direction is autocratic in its decisions, without benefit of other, internal artistic input).

prologue. An introductory part of an opera, usually short, sung, or narrated to prepare the audience for the ensuing drama. Wagner described his *music drama Das Rheingold* as the *Vorabend* (literally, the evening before) to the main trilogy of the *Der Ring des Nibelungen.* A typical short prologue is that sung before the beginning of Leoncavallo's *Pagliacci.* Here it is used in a Shakespearean sense, signifying a person who addresses the audience to explain the meaning of the play.

prompter (Fr., *souffleur*; Ger., *Souffleur*; It., *maestro suggeritore*). A rather important person in opera, seated in the proscenium with the score in front of him (or her), who gives cues to singers. The "invisible" place where the prompter stands is called the *prompter's box.* Such a prompter is introduced to the audience in the whimsical opera *Capriccio* by Strauss. In the last act of Wagner's *Tristan und Isolde,* a prompter is sometimes ensconced under the dying Tristan's couch. Depending on the acoustics of the hall, the prompter's voice may unexpectedly carry to some parts of the orchestra seats. Such incautious prompters have also been known to hum.

prompter's box (Fr., *trou de souffleur*; Ger., *Souffleurkasten*; It., *buca*). See *prompter.*

prova (It.). *Rehearsal.*

Q

Querelle des Bouffons (Fr.). *Guerre des Bouffons.*

R

radio opera. The first complete opera broadcast was that of *Hänsel und Gretel,* transmitted from Covent Garden in London in 1923. In 1924 *Aida* was broadcast from the Metropolitan Opera in New York. In 1930 *Fidelio* was broadcast from Dresden by transatlantic radio. But the greatest flowering of opera on radio came by way of the phonograph. With the development of long-playing records, it was possible in the 1950s to air entire operas, even obscure ones, because no royalties had to be paid for broadcasting phonograph records. However, this has since changed. Many composers have written works expressly for the medium. The first appears to be Cadman's *The Willow Tree,* transmitted from New York in 1933. Among the many who have followed his lead are Badings (*Orestes,* 1954, and *Asterion,* 1958), Hambreaus (*Sagan,* 1979), Harsanyi (*Illusion,* 1948), Henze (*Ein Landarzt,* 1951), Egk (*Columbus,* 1933), and Gruenberg (*Green Mansion,* 1937).

It might seem that television would have brought about a real revolution in expanding the walls of an opera house to embrace the entire world. This was not to be, however, because of the cost of television productions. The most successful opera written specially for television to date is *Amahl and the Night Visitors* by Menotti, commissioned by NBC in 1951 and repeated annually (with few omissions) at Christmas time for many years. Badings's television opera *Salto mortale* (1959) was the first opera to be accompanied solely by electronic sound. Many composers have followed suit, Mikel Rouse prominent among them. Numerous composers have taken to video as a viable dramatic element in their operatic productions, in whole or in part, most prominently among them Ashley, e.g., in his *Perfect Lives (Private Parts)* of 1983.

récitatif (Fr.). *Recitative.*

recitative (Fr., *récitative* or *récitatif*; Ger., *Rezitativ*; It., *recitativo*). 1. A musical narrative, as contrasted with *arias* and other formal parts in an opera or *oratorio,* which carries the action from one aria to another. In early opera, *recitativo secco* (dry) was the common practice, with singers reciting a musical phrase following the accents and inflections of the spoken language accompanied by and alternating with a bare minimum of chords played on the harpsichord. In Classic opera, Mozart and others experimented with *recitativo accompagnato* (accompanied), where the vocal line was supported by an economical use of the full orchestra. In the 19th century the demarcation between the accompanied recitative and the aria began to blur, until in Wagner's music dramas they coalesced into the *endless melody.*

recitativo (It.). *Recitative.*

recitativo accompagnato (It.). See *recitative.*

recitativo secco (It.). See *recitative.*

Regie (Ger.). Production.

Regisseur (Fr.). In France, a person engaged in a technical aspect of a production, e.g., lighting.

regista (It.). *Producer.*

register. A portion of the vocal compass, as *high* or *low* register, *chest-* or *head* register.

rehearsal (Fr. *répétition*; It. *prova*; Ger. *Probe,* a tryout). Literally, a rehearing; a practice session. A prerequisite for a fruitful rehearsal is a willingness to achieve a mutual accommodation among the participants so as to achieve proper balance in harmony, fluctuations of tempo, and dynamic equilibration. Basic elements are usually agreed upon in advance, but subtler nuances have to be felt intuitively in the rehearsal setting.

relâche (Fr.). *Dark.*

reminiscence motive. A short motif or theme that recurs throughout a work evoking memory of a previous person, place, object, or idea. Particularly prevalent in late 18th-century French opera and opéra comique, it differs from the *leitmotif* in that its essential shape and character do not change significantly from one appearance to the next.

répétiteur, -euse (Fr.; Ger. *Korrepetitor,-in*). A choral or opera rehearsal assistant. One who conducts rehearsals, sometimes called an opera coach. The répétiteur, humblest of functionaries in the realm of grand opera, often is charged with such tedious duties as training singers to keep time. But this musical menial acquires valuable practice and sometimes rises to conductorship.

répétition (Fr.). *Rehearsal.*

rescue opera. A fanciful term to describe an opera in which the central character is rescued from mortal peril by extraordinary means. A perfect example is Beethoven's *Fidelio,* in which the prisoner's faithful wife comes to his rescue by entering prison service dressed in a man's attire. In Puccini's *Tosca* the rescue of the prisoner seems assured at the risk of the heroine's virtue but a twist of fate turns hope into despair and death. The rescue opera usually involves human activity, rather than the work of a *Deus ex machina.*

Rezitativ (Ger.). *Recitative.*

ribattuta (It.). *Beat.*

romance (Eng.; Fr., *romance*; Ger., *Romanze*; It., *ro-*

manza). Originally a type of Spanish poetic narrative, a ballad or popular tale in verse; later, romance lyrical songs. The French and Russian romance is a short art song or lied composed of several stanzas.

Romanze (Ger.). *Romance.*

romanza (It.). *Romance.*

rubato (It., robbed). Play with a free treatment of the melody; specifically, dwell on and (often) prolong prominent melody tones or chords. This requires an equivalent subsequent acceleration of less prominent tones, which are thus "robbed" of a portion of their time value. The measure remains constant, and the accompaniment is not disrupted.

run. A rapid scale passage. In vocal music, a run is usually sung to one syllable. *Run a division,* perform such a passage, e.g., a dividing up of a melodic phrase into a rapid *coloratura* passage.

S

sacre rappresentazioni (It.). *Liturgical drama.*

sainete (Sp., small farce). Spanish musical comedy popular in the 18th century, eventually displaced by the *zarzuela.*

scena (from Grk., stage). In opera, an accompanied dramatic solo, consisting of *arioso* and *recitative* passages, bearing the character of explanatory narrative, and often ending with an *aria.*

scenario (It., scenery). A concise script outlining the contents of a play, opera, ballet, or other performance work, with an indication of the participating characters/performers.

scene (from Gr. *skene*; lit. tent or booth; Fr. *tableau*; Ger. *Auftritt*). Usually, a part of an act, for example, an opera may contain three acts and seven scenes, which are distributed among the three acts. Sometimes a composer subdivides an opera into scenes without specifying the number of acts, e.g., Prokofiev's *War and Peace* and Mussorgsky's *Boris Godunov.*

scoop. Vocal tones arrived at by a rough and imprecise *portamento* from a lower tone, instead of a firm and just attack.

season (It. *stagione*). Scheduled performances for an operatic or concert music organization over a specific time period up to one calendar year.

semiopera. English works of the late 17th century that, while bringing forth a union of drama and music, differ from genuine opera in that the primary dramatic action is set forth through speech. Examples include Purcell's *King Arthur* (1691) and *The Indian Queen* (1695).

serenade (It., *serenata,* evening song, from *sera*: evening; Ger. *Nachtmusik, Ständchen*). From the 16th century, a song, traditionally performed by a lover before the beloved's window. It was habitually accompanied on the lute or guitar, and delivered at day's end. A serenade is a favorite device in opera. An example of a mock serenade is that of Méphistophélès in Gounod's *Faust.*

serenata (It.). *Serenade.*

servetta (It.). *Soubrette.*

sestet(to) (It.). *Sextet.*

set piece. A separate movement or readily identifiable portion of an opera, etc., formal in structure and cohesive in idiom (as a finale).

sextet (Ger., *Sextett*; Fr., *sextour;* It., *sestet, sestetto*). A concerted composition for six voices or instruments. The most famous operatic vocal sextet is in Donizetti's *Lucia di Lammermoor.*

Sextett (Ger.). *Sextet.*

sextour (Fr.). *Sextet.*

Singspiel (Ger.). From a literary viewpoint, a theatrical piece, usually lighthearted, with interpolated musical numbers. The German Singspiel developed and was particularly popular in the 18th century. From a musical viewpoint, the difference between the Singspiel and a full-fledged opera lies in the use of spoken dialogue (as opposed to *recitative*), but this distinction became less pronounced when purely operatic works began admitting dialogue as part of the action. Many features of the Singspiel were adopted in German Romantic opera.

slumber scene (It., *sonno*). A typical scene in primarily 17th-century Italian opera in which a character is made to fall asleep on the stage. Such slumber may endanger the character's life, or be used as a dramatic means (through the character's talking in sleep) to enlighten the audience of some otherwise "secret" information. Examples are seen in Monteverdi's *Poppea* and Mozart's *Zaide.*

sommeil (Fr., slumber). The French equivalent of the *slumber scene,* seen in Lully's *Atys* (1676) and elsewhere.

sonno (It.). *Slumber scene.*

songspiel. A hybrid English–German designation of a modern satirical opera, cabaret, or vaudeville show that emerged in Germany between the two world wars. The English "song" had a narrowed meaning of "cabaret song" in German. Weill's opera *Aufsteig und Fall der Stadt Mahagonny* bears the designation Songspiel, which is authentic, and not a misprint for *Singspiel.*

Sopran (Ger.). *Soprano.*

soprano (from It., *sopra,* above; Ger. *Sopran*). The highest class of the human voice; the *treble* voice. The normal compass of the soprano voice ranges from c^1 to a^2; solo voices often reach above c^3, some as high as c^4. Some vocal parts call for a boy soprano, meaning a natural voice of an preadolescent boy. *Coloratura soprano* (see separate entry). *Dramatic soprano, soprano drammatico, soprano giusto,* a singer capable of dynamic, dramatic, and tragic qualities; the expectation of a strong upper register is matched by an evenness of power throughout the range; *lyric soprano,* a singer distinguished by a poetic quality of phrasing in bel canto; *soprano leggiero,* a light soprano; *soprano sfogato,* a high soprano.

sortita (It.). The first number sung by any leading character in an opera. An *aria di sortita* is, however, also an air at the conclusion of which the singer makes his or her exit.

sotto voce (It., below the voice). Sung in an undertone, as an aside, under the breath. This is a dramatic lowering of the normal voice, but not necessarily *pp*.

soubrette (Fr., from Old Fr., *soubret*: cunning or shrewd; It. *servetta*). In *comic opera* and *operetta,* a maidservant or lady's maid or an ingenue of intriguing and coquettish character. The term is also applied to light roles of similar type. Susanna in *Le nozze di Figaro* and Papagena in *The Magic Flute* are typical. The *coloratura* soubrette is exemplified by Rosina in *The Barber of Seville* and Zerbinetta in *Ariadne auf Naxos.* Curiously, the term soubrette is used mostly in Germany, the French preferring a term in honor of a famous French singer, Louise Dugazon (1755–1821), who sang such roles: *jeune Dugazon.*

souffleur (Fr.; Ger., *Souffleur*). *Prompter.*

Souffleurkasten (Ger.). Prompter's box. See *prompter.*

sovrintendente (It., superintendent). The administrator of an Italian opera house.

Spielleiter (Ger.). *Producer.*

Spielplan (Ger., performance plan). The published listing, available to the public, of the season's offerings of an opera house.

spinto (It., pushed). A high operatic *soprano* or *tenor* role of a dramatic yet passive type (Cio-Cio-San, Desdemona), as opposed to dramatic and lyric.

Sprechstimme (*Sprechgesang*; Ger., speech song). A type of inflected vocal delivery with pitches indicated only approximately on the staff. The singer follows the pitch contour without actually voicing any notes, and the effect is exaggerated speech. It was popularized by its expressive use by Schoenberg in *Pierrot Lunaire* and later works. The method was used systematically for the first time in 1897 in the operatic melodrama *Königskinder* by Humperdinck. This technique is often used in contemporary opera and song cycles.

SRO. *Standing room only.*

Staatsoper (Ger.). State Opera.

Stabreim (Ger., alliteration). The art of writing verse with alliteration, i.e., with internal, structurally cohesive references with respect to both the meaning and the sounds of words. It developed in Old English and German verse, but was put to effective and elaborate use in mythic opera by Wagner, e.g., in *Tristan und Isolde,* and particularly in *Der Ring des Nibelungen.*

Städtische Oper (Ger.). City Opera.

stagione (It.). *Season.*

Ständchen (Ger.). *Serenade.*

standing ovation. Unanimous and tumultuous applause at the end of a particularly exciting musical performance, when the audience members are so transported by admiration for the performer(s) that through body chemistry, they are impelled by simultaneous and massive production of adrenalin to rise from their seats and clap their hands mightily—sometimes even rhythmically—joyously abandoning themselves to unrestrained vociferation and in extreme cases animalistic ululation. The spontaneity of such manifestations, however, is often suspect (as are similar outbursts of collective enthusiasm for politicians). See *claque.*

Standing Room Only (SRO). An indication in some theaters that all seats for a particular performance are sold out, but that a few places remain where a hardy individual can watch the performance standing up behind the last row of seats.

stalls (U.K.). In a theater, the front rows of the orchestra (seating) section.

stile moderno (It.). See *stile rappresentativo.*

stile monodico (It.). See *stile rappresentativo.*

stile rappresentativo (It., representative style). A dramatic monodic song with instrumental accompaniment in chords. The kind of operatic recitative originating toward the close of the 16th century through the revolutionary ruminations of the composers comprising the Florentine *Camerata* and exemplified early on in the works of Peri, Caccini, and Cavalieri. Eventually this gave way to the clear demarcation between *aria* and *recitative.* The terms *stile moderno, stile monodico, stile recitative,* and *stile rappresentativo* are, in contemporary usage, largely interchangeable.

stile recitative. See *stile rappresentativo.*

Stimme (Ger.). *Voice.*

strette (Fr.). *Stretto,-a.*

stretto, -a (It., straitened, narrowed; Fr. *strette*). A musical climax that usually occurs at the point when thematic and rhythmic elements have reached the point of saturation. A classic example is the finale of Act II in Mozart's *Le nozze di Figaro,* in *prestissimo* tempo. A stretto at the end of an impassioned *aria* or a dramatic *duet* is virtually synonymous with a *cabaletta.*

strophic. Attribute of a song wherein successive stanzas are sung to the same music, with a change, if any, taking place in the final stanza. As opposed to *through-composed.*

summary overture. See *overture.*

surtitles. The screening of the translation of an opera, usually projected above the stage during the course of a production, invented in 1983 by John Leberg. Also known as *supratitles* or *supertitles.* In certain opera houses, such translations are now located in the backs of the seats, in front of each audience member, and may be turned off and on at will.

T

tableau (Fr.). *Scene.*

Takt (Ger.). *Beat.*

teatro (It.). Theater. *Teatro lirico,* opera house.

technic, technique. All that relates to the purely mechanical part of an instrumental or vocal performance. Mechanical training, skill, and dexterity.

tenor (It., *tenore,* holding). Highest and most expressive male voice. Etymologically the word derives from the fact that the cantus firmus in early vocal polyphony was given to a voice called the *tenor,* whose function was to "hold" the melody while other voices moved contrapuntally in relation to it. The voice part gradually became independent of its original function and came to refer simply to the voice range. The ordinary tenor range is two octaves, from the C below middle C to the C above (c^0–c^2). The tenor part is usually notated in the treble clef (from middle C), sounding an octave lower. In some scores the tenor part is indicated by a combined tenor and treble clef. Some singers in the *bel canto* era could go higher in *falsetto,* e.g., Rubini, who regularly hit f^2. The mark of distinction for great tenors is their ability to hold high C for a long time, often ignoring the musical and harmonic reasons to let it go.

Categories include the *dramatic tenor* (It. *tenore di forza*), with a full and powerful quality and a range from c to b^1 (Rodolfo in *La bohème,* Manrico in *Il trovatore*); *heroic tenor* (Ger. *Heldentenor*), with a strong sonority throughout the range (Siegfried in the *Ring,* Otello); *lyric tenor* (It. *tenore di grazia*), sweeter and less powerful, with a range from d to c^2 (or $c\sharp^2$; Gounod's Faust and Almaviva in *The Barber of Seville*); and *Spieltenor* (Ger., acting tenor), a light role in a German company (Pedrillo in Mozart's *Die Entführung aus dem Serail*).

tenorini (It.). See *falsetto.*

tenuto (It., held; abbr. *ten.*). 1. Sustain a tone for its full time value. 2. Use an emphatic and attentive legato.

tessitura (It., texture). Proportionate use of high or low *register* in a given vocal range. If high notes are preponderant, the tessitura is said to be high, as in most coloratura soprano parts; if low notes are especially frequent, as in bass parts of some Russian songs, the tessitura is said to be low. In English a vocal part is said to "lie" high or low.

tetralogy. A thematically connected series of four stage works, e.g., Wagner's *Der Ring des Nibelungen.*

Textbuch (Ger.). *Libretto.*

theater orchestra. Small, flexible ensemble for which arrangements are made, with separate instrumental parts cued into other parts to be used when a particular instrument is not available. For example, an English horn solo might be cued into a clarinet or even violin part. The piano part represents the harmonic skeleton of a theater arrangement.

thematic catalogue. An inventory of works by an individual composer arranged according to genre (operas, symphonies, chamber music, solo works) or chronologically (including opus number) and supplemented by incipits. Such catalogues may be compiled by the composers themselves, their publishers, or subsequent scholars.

thoroughbass. *Basso continuo.*

through-composed (Ger. *durchkomponiert*). Attribute of a song wherein each stanza is written to a different accompaniment, or composed in a developmental, quasi-symphonic manner, the music changing to suit the text. As opposed to *strophic.*

Tonfall (Ger.). *Intonation.*

tragédie ballet (Fr., tragedy ballet). A musico-dramatic form of 17th-century France, similar in form to the *comédie ballet,* although, as its name implies, more serious in its dramatic content. Lully's *Psyché* (1671) is exemplary. It later influenced the development of the *tragédie en musique.*

tragédie en musique (Fr., tragedy in music). A musico-dramatic form of 17th-century France, instituted by Lully's *Cadmus* (1673). The term was quickly replaced by *tragédie lyrique.*

tragédie lyrique (Fr., lyric tragedy). Baroque and Classic French operas on classical subjects. The primary representatives of the genre are Lully and Rameau, although Gluck also contributed to it during his Paris sojourn. In the Romantic era, *drame lyrique* superseded the tragédie lyrique, as Classic subjects became rare in French opera.

travesty (from Fr. *travestir,* to disguise). See *trouser role.*

treble. Voice of soprano *range,* often sung by boys.

tremolo (It., quivering, fluttering). A popular embellishment consisting of a repeated alternation of two notes in rapid tempo, once regarded as a powerful device to produce dramatic tension. However, tremolo is not synonymous with *vibrato.* In singing, a tremulous, somewhat unsteady tone is used.

trilogy. A thematically connected series of three stage works, e.g., Puccini's *Il trittico.*

trill (Fr. *trille*; Ger. *Triller*; It. *trillo*). A melodic embellishment consisting of the even and rapid alternation of two tones a major or minor second apart. The lower tone is the *principal note* (the one being ornamented), the higher tone the *auxiliary note* (the one ornamenting). The practice of trilling was cultivated in France in the 17th century and was sometimes picturesquely described as *tremblement,* translated into English as *shake.* The graphic symbol is a wavy line, sometimes extending according to the duration desired. The abbreviation *tr* is also used. Interpretation of trill performance practice can differ from scholar to scholar and from source to source. Vocal trilling now seems to emerge from the *vibrato* technique in constant use by opera singers, although the technical danger is that one not be used when the other is called for.

Triller (Ger.). *Trill.*

trille (Fr.). *Trill.*

trillo (It.). *Trill.*

Trinklied (Ger.). *Brindisi.*

trou de souffleur (Fr.). Prompter's box. See *prompter.*

trouser role (travesty; U.K., breeches-part; Ger. *Hosenrolle*). In opera, a part sung by a female singer performing the role of a younger man or boy, e.g., Siebel in *Faust,* Cherubino in *The Marriage of Figaro,* Octavian in *Der Rosenkavalier,* and Prince Orlovsky in *Die Fledermaus.*

U

Unendliche Melodie (Ger.). *Endless melody.*

unvocal. 1. Not suitable for singing. 2. Not vibrating with tone. *Unvocal air* is breath escaping with a more or less audible sigh or hiss, due to unskillful management of the voice.

V

vaudeville. A word serving as an umbrella for several genres of French origin, all of which share a satirical, epigrammatic, or comic tone. The term became prevalent in the 17th century, representing simple strophic airs. The genre was very popular; the tunes were so well known that they were not included in manuscripts. The *comédie en vaudevilles* made the vaudeville a theatrical genre in the late 17th and early 18th centuries. These light, often parodic comedies alternated dialogue and pantomime with witty and satirical couplets, generally set to well-known popular airs. The genre gradually gave way to the *opéra comique.* The *vaudeville finale* applied one element of the *comédie en vaudevilles* to comic opera, German and Italian as well as French, in which all the characters of a work came onstage at the end and restored order to the proceedings, expressed their feelings, and gave a moral. Composers as early as Rosseau and as recent as Stravinsky used the form. In the 19th century, the musical comedy evolved increasingly in the direction of a variety show, whether it be the Continental vaudeville, the English music hall, or the American vaudeville and variety show.

vaudeville finale. See *vaudeville.*

vengeance aria. A common device in 18th- and 19th-century opera in which a singer swears, usually in powerful *coloratura,* vengeance against another for a perceived wrong. Examples are many, but exemplary is the Queen of the Night's "Der Hölle Rache" in Mozart's *Die Zauberflöte.*

verismo (from It. *vero,* true). From the 1890s, a type of operatic naturalism exemplified by Mascagni's *Cavalleria rusticana* and Leoncavallo's *Pagliacci.* Soon the vogue spread into France with the production of *Louise* by Charpentier. In Germany verismo assumed satirical and sociological rather than naturalistic forms (Weill, Krenek, Hindemith). In England, Britten's *Peter Grimes* is veristic in both subject and execution. Verismo had no followers in Russia, where nationalistic themes preoccupied the interests of opera composers. However, the USSR's brand of socialist realism could be seen as a verismo of the proletariat.

vibrato (It., vibrated). In singing, a timbral effect achieved by letting the stream of air out of the lungs about eight times per second through the rigid vocal cords. Ideally the pitch should remain the same to avoid an irrelevant *trill.* Vocal and instrumental vibrato assists in the projection of sound. Like temperament, it was the subject of great performance practice debates, as to proper use, prior to the mid-19th century.

virtuosity (from Lat. *virtus,* ability, value). A display of great proficiency by an instrumentalist or vocalist, called a *virtuoso.* The concept dates to the Baroque period, with the loss of religious restrictions on compositional excess and the rise of new monodic textures. A virtuoso must possess above all else superlative technique. Vocal virtuosity developed alongside the growth of opera and certain skills became professional necessities. Virtuoso singers must execute the most difficult passages in rapid tempo. Effortless trills in upper registers can be expected by prima donnas. On the other hand, the physically prepossessing bass should be able to hold his lowest notes with unwavering resonance. A tenor must be able to sustain a "high C" (c^2) at the climax of an aria. All singers must be able to execute flawless *staccato* and maintain a breathtaking *pianissimo* as well as a brilliant *ff.*

vocal. Pertaining to the voice, or suitable for the singing voice. *Vocal cords,* the two opposed ligaments set in the larynx, whose vibration, caused by expelling air from the lungs, produces vocal tones; *vocal glottis,* the aperture between the vocal cords; *vocal quartet,* chamber piece for four singers; group of four solo singers within a larger group.

vocal score. The arrangement of any work for voice(s) and ensemble (up to an orchestra) as a score for voice(s) and piano reduction, for rehearsal purposes and, when resources are limited, actual performance.

vocalise (Fr.). A vocal étude or composition, sung on open vowels, without text. Vocal settings sometimes use vocalise for some duration, e.g., in the "Bell Song" from Delibes's *Lakmé.*

vocalization. Singing exercise comprising a melody sung without words. Scales and arpeggios are common vocalizations used to prepare the vocal cords for performance.

voce (It.). *Voice*

voci artificiali (It.). See *falsetto.*

voice (Fr., *voix*; Ger., *Stimme*; It., *voce*). Human vocal production of musical tone, divided into six principal ranges: *soprano, mezzo-soprano, contralto* (*alto*), *tenor, baritone,* and *bass.* In contemporary scores, such divisions may become irrelevant as composers often call for untraditional sounds, and sometimes (unpitched) speech replaces musical production altogether.

voice production. A pedagogical hypothesis that the human voice can be directed or projected physiologically from the head, the chest, or the epiglottis by conscious effort. Of course, the only source of the human voice is the larynx, and the only resonator is the pharynx, but even serious professional singers are convinced that the lower notes travel from the vocal cords to the thoracic cavity and that the head tone (voice) is monitored from the top of the head. With the invasion of the United States by Italian singing teachers late in the 19th century and by Russian singers after World War

I, the mythology of voice production assumed the status of a science.

voix (Fr.). *Voice.*

Vorspiel (Ger.). *Prelude.*

Z

zarzuela (from Sp. *zarza,* bramble bush). Spanish light opera characterized by dance and spoken dialogue. The name is derived from the Royal Palace La Zarzuela, near Madrid, where zarzuelas were performed before the royal court. The genre appeared in the 17th century. Performances of zarzuelas at the court were interspersed with ballets and popular dances fashioned after the spectacles at Versailles. With the massive intrusion of Italian opera into Spain in the 18th century, the zarzuela lost its characteristic ethnic flavor. But it was revived by nationally minded composers of the second half of the 19th century. Classical composers such as Granados and Falla composed zarzuelas.

Zauberoper (Ger., magic opera). A magic opera in which supernatural forces intervene in human affairs, e.g., Weber's *Der Freischütz.*

Zeitoper (Ger., opera of the time). German operas of the 1920s and early 1930s with distinct sociopolitical themes, driven by a generalized tendency of artists toward the creation of socially relevant art.

Zukunftsmusik (Ger., music of the future). Music of the future. A term coined by Wagner and espoused with equal fervor by Liszt. Their opponents turned this lofty phrase into a derisive description of their music.

Zwischenspiel (Ger.). See *intermezzo.*

Opera Synopses

A

***Abaris ou Les Boréades*.** Opera by Jean-Philippe Rameau, his last, completed by him shortly before his death in 1764. The plot deals with a priest of Apollo in love with the queen of Bactria. However, he cannot marry her because she is a Boréade, a descendant of the wind god Boréas, and must marry a windy relative. A happy dénouement is secured when Abaris opportunely discovers that he, too, is a boreal through his nymph mother. The work was performed 211 years after its composition for the first time by the Monteverdi Choir and Orchestra in London on April 19, 1975.

***Abélard and Héloise*.** Opera by Robert Ward, his fifth, based on the tragic story of the medieval theologian Abélard, who was brutally castrated by the uncle of his secret bride, Héloise. It was first staged in Charlotte, North Carolina, on Feb. 19, 1981.

***Adieux, Les*.** Opera in one act by Marcel Landowski. A young woman refuses to open the door for her lover when he comes for his daily session, realizing that her infatuation with him is not sufficiently compelling. It was first staged in Paris on Oct. 7, 1960.

Admeto, rè di Tessaglia (Admetus, king of Thessaly). Opera in three acts by George Frideric Handel, to a libretto adapted from Ortensio Mauro's *L'Alceste* (1679) after Aureli's *Antigona delusa da L'Alceste* (1660). It is based on the classical myth of Admetus, king of Thessaly, who is saved from death by his loving wife, Alcestis. The opera was first performed in London on Jan. 31, 1727.

***Adriana Lecouvreur*.** Opera in four acts by Francesco Ciléa, his most famous, to a text by Arturo Colautti from the drama *Adrienne Lecouvreur* (1849) by Eugéne Scribe and Legouvé, first performed in Milan on Nov. 6, 1902. It is a highly dramaticized version of the life and loves of the French actress Adrienne Lecouvreur (1692–1730), who undergoes a series of misadventures, including mistaken identities, misdirected letters, mislaid jewels, and misfired amourettes, and dies from the fumes of poisoned violets sent to her by a jealous rival (the real Adrienne died of an internal hemorrhage), with a musical setting luxuriating in sonorous cantilena and throbbing with melodramatic diminished-seventh chords.

Africaine, L' (The African Maid). Opera in five acts by Giacomo Meyerbeer, his last, to a libretto by Eugène Scribe, premiered posthumously in Paris on April 28, 1865. The African of the title is Selika, the Malagasy whom Vasco da Gama brings back to his native Portugal from his African adventures. Realizing that he cannot marry her because of her race, Selika sacrifices her life so that Vasco da Gama can marry his former white mistress. The opera takes nearly six hours to perform, but it attained tremendous popularity with sentimental audiences of the last third of the 19th century. It has exotic flavor, Italianate bel canto, thunderous sunderings of love, and loud orchestration, all qualities that made Meyerbeer the idol of his time.

***Agnes von Hohenstaufen*.** Opera in three acts by Gasparo Spontini, his last, to a text by Ernst Raupach. It deals with Agnes's love for Henry of Brunswick and the various political and courtly maneuvers that ensue to keep them from marrying. A monumental work, it was first produced in its entirety in Berlin on June 12, 1829, and then not until 1954 in Florence in an abridged version.

***Agrippina*.** Opera in three acts by George Frideric Handel, to a text by Vincenzo Grimani. Agrippina, wife of the Roman emperor Claudio (Claudius), fights to ensure that her son by a previous marriage (Nero) takes his rightful place on the throne. It was first produced in Venice on Dec. 26, 1709.

Ägyptische Helena, Die (The Egyptian Helen). Opera in two acts by Richard Strauss, to a Hugo von Hofmannsthal libretto, first performed in Dresden on June 6, 1928. It parodies Greek myths concerning Helen of Troy by suggesting, through sorcery, that there is a phantom Helen and a real one. This was their last collaboration, as Hofmannsthal died the following year.

Aida. Opera in four acts by Giuseppe Verdi, written to the most tragic and most implausible of all librettos ever contrived by Antonio Ghislanzoni from the French prose of Camille Du Locle (1868) with a plot by August Mariette. Radames, commander of the ancient Egyptian army, falls in love with a captive Ethiopian princess, Aida, and inadvertently reveals a crucial military secret to her while her father, Amonsaro, the king of Ethiopia, also captured anonymously, listens from behind the bushes. Amneris, the Egyptian king's daughter, who is affianced to Radames, discovers the treachery but is willing to save Radames if he relinquishes Aida. Radames refuses, and joined by Aida, is buried alive in a stone crypt.

Aida was commissioned for the inauguration of the Cairo Opera House. The outbreak of the Franco-Prussian War delayed the delivery of the costumes from Paris, however, and the production was postponed until Christmas Eve, 1871. The premiere was spectacular, with shiploads of notables and music critics converging on Cairo, but the ever unsocial Verdi declined the invitation to attend. Egyptian scholars regarded *Aida* as quite inauthentic in its story and music, and it didn't enter the repertoire of the Cairo Opera House. Nonetheless, it has remained popular over the years, with many spectacular productions. On May 3, 1987, it was lavishly staged in ancient Luxor, with Plácido Domingo in the role of Radames, and with the participation of some 150,000 Egyptian soldiers and hundreds of singers in the chorus, not to mention the horses. The price of a single ticket was $750, and several supersonic Concorde jets were rented to transport wealthy opera lovers.

Note: *Aïda* with the diaresis is the French spelling.

Aiglon, L' (The Eaglet). Opera in five acts by Arthur Honneger (Acts II–IV) and Jacques Ibert (Acts I and V), to a libretto by Henri Cain after Edmond Rostand's drama, written in 1900, about Napoleon's tubercular son, who was known as the eaglet. It was produced in Monte Carlo on March 10, 1937. The music is written in a style midway between post-Wagnerian expansiveness and ante-Debussyan colorism

Ajo nell'imbarazzo, L' (The Tutor in a Jam). Opera in two acts by Gaetano Donizetti, his first success, to a libretto by Jacopo Ferretti based on Giovanni Giraud's comedy (1807). The Marchese Giulio unsuccessfully tries to keep his sons, one married and one lusting after the housekeeper, ignorant of women. It was premiered in Rome on Feb. 4, 1824.

Akhnaten. Opera by Philip Glass. It tells the story of the 18th-dynasty pharaoh who introduced monotheism to Egypt. It was staged for the first time in Stuttgart on March 24, 1984, with Dennis Russell Davies conducting.

Aladdin. Fairy opera in three acts by Sir Henry Rowley Bishop, to a libretto by G. Soane based on the Oriental tale "Aladdin and his Wonderful Lamp," first performed in London on April 29, 1826, as an unsuccessful rival to Weren's *Oberon.* Also an opera in three acts by Kurt Atterburg, first produced in Stockholm on March 18, 1941.

Albena. Opera in five tableaux by Parashkev Khadzhiev. The story comes from the village life in Dobrudja of the early 20th century. It is based on a true story of an aberrant wife who becomes a passive accomplice in the murder of her husband by her lover. (In real life she was stoned to death by the villagers, but in the opera she is allowed to depart.) It was performed for the first time in Varna on Nov. 2, 1962.

Albert Herring. Comic opera in three acts by Benjamin Britten, to a libretto by Eric Crozier after de Maupassant's story "Le rosier de Madame Husson" (1888). It centers on a contest in a small village for the most virtuous young woman. With none available, the contest is won by Albert, but his immaculate virginity is immediately undermined by alcohol, and he goes morally berserk. The opera was first produced at the Glyndebourne Festival on June 20, 1947, with the composer conducting.

Alceste. Opera in three acts by Christoph Willibald Gluck, to a libretto by Ranieri De'Calzabigi, based on the tragedy of Euripides, first performed in Vienna on Dec. 26, 1767. The mythological story deals with Alcestis, who volunteers to enter Hades in place of her dead husband, Admetus; in a *lieto fine* (happy ending), however, she is saved from the nether region by Hercules. Both Jean-Baptiste Lully and George Frideric Handel wrote an opera on the same story. However, Gluck's remains the most important historically, largely because of the preface to the published score, in which Gluck criticizes the emphasis given to performers, scenery, and costumes, maintaining that the dramatic and poetic content should be a paramount consideration in any artistic stage work. Gluck's approach resulted in "reform opera," the heart of the *querelle des buffons* debate.

Alcestiad, The. Opera by Louise Talma, to a libretto by Thornton Wilder. It is based on the ancient myth of a Greek woman whose devotion to Apollo won her release from Hades. It was performed for the first time in a German translation in Frankfurt am Main on March 1, 1962.

Alcina. Opera in three acts by George Frideric Handel, based on A. Fanzaglia's *Alcina* (1728) after Ariosto's *Orlando Furioso* (1516). It was first produced at Covent Garden in London on April 16, 1735. The story is a typical one of crossed identities, magical spells, and lost relatives, in which all is made right at the end. The title character is an evil sorceress who holds sway over a magical island, where her favorite activity is turning men into wild animals or babbling brooks. The knight Ruggerio falls under her spell, but happily is saved before he too can join the natural landscape. Alcina's powers are crushed, and Ruggerio reunited with his true love.

This was one of the Handel's best and most popular operas. Its powerful music, and the fairy-tale quality of its story, have made it attractive to audiences over the centuries. Joan Sutherland's singing of the title role helped establish the opera in the modern repertory.

Alcione. Opera by Marin Marais, to a libretto by Antoine de Lamotte after Ovid's *Metamorphoses*, produced in Paris on Feb. 18, 1706. Alcione, or Alcyone, was a daughter of Aeolus, the keeper of the winds. She was transformed into a halcyon bird (kingfisher) for defying the gods. The expression "halcyon days" stems from the belief that the seas are becalmed when the halcyon broods on her eggs. The score is noteworthy because it contains a symphonic tempest, the first attempt at realistic effects in the orchestra. The orchestral score also includes, for the first time, a part for the snare drum.

Aleko. Opera in one act by 19-year-old Sergei Rachmaninoff as a graduation piece, to a libretto by Vladimir-Danchenko after Pushkin's poem *The Gypsies* (1824). Aleko runs off with a band of gypsies, falls in love with Zemfira, but she falls in love with another. He kills her, and is subsequently exiled from the gypsy community. It was first produced in Moscow on May 9, 1893.

Alessandro (Alexander). Opera in three acts by George Frideric Handel, his ninth for the Royal Academy of Music, to a libretto by P. A. Rolli after Ortensio Mauro's *La superbia d'Alessandro* (1690), a largely contrived tale of love, jealousy, and treachery revolving around Alexander the Great's Indian campaign. It was first produced in London on May 5, 1726.

Alessandro Stradella. Opera in three acts by Friedrich Flotow, to a libretto by "W. Friedrich" (Friedrich Wilhelm Riese) after a French *comédie mêlée de chants* by P. A. A. Pittaud de Forges and P. Duport. It recounts legends of the loves and the murder of the 17th-century Italian composer Alessandro Stradella (1639–82), whose own operatic output was significant in the development of the Neapolitan school of composition. Stradella was actually murdered by a hired assassin at the behest of a jealous rival in love. In the opera, Stradella soothes the savage breasts of the would-be murderers by singing arias from his operas. They are so deeply moved by the music that they desist from their dastardly deed—hence the subtitle, *The Power of Song*. It was first performed in Hamburg on Dec. 30, 1844, and enjoyed an unusual success in Europe for a spell.

Alfonso und Estrella. Opera in three acts by Franz Schubert, to a libretto by Franz von Schober. It tells of the trials and tribulations of Alfonso, son of the deposed King Froila, and Estrella, daughter of Froila's usurper, Mauregato, who—despite various plots against it—manage to marry happily in the end. It was first produced in Weimar on June 24, 1854, more than 30 years after its completion.

Al gran sole carico d'amore. Panoramic socialistic opera by Luigi Nono. It presents several historic tableaux portraying the French Commune of 1871, czarist Russia shaken by bloody revolt, social upheavals in Cuba and Chile, and culminating in the American debacle in Vietnam. A female quartet comments on the passing events as stages in class struggle. It was first produced in Milan on April 4, 1975. The title, which translates as "In the great sun laden with love," is a line from a poem by Rimbaud.

Alkmene. A twelve-tone opera by Kleve. Zeus assumes the likeness of Amphitryon and materializes in his wife's bedroom to claim his marital right by Olympian proxy. It was performed for the first time at the newly rebuilt Deutsche Oper in West Berlin on Sept. 15, 1961.

Almira. Opera in three acts by George Frideric Handel, his first, to a libretto by Friedrich Christian Feustking after Pancieri's *L'Almira* (1691). Almira, destined to become queen of Castile, manages, through a stroke of operatic fate, to sidestep a prearranged marriage and have both the throne and her lover, too. It was produced in Hamburg on Jan. 8, 1705, when Handel was just 19 years old.

Alpine Ballad. Lyric opera in one act by Andrey Pashchenko. It tells the story of an affectionate international romance spontaneously exfoliating between a Russian soldier and an Italian girl during their flight from a Nazi concentration camp. It was first staged in Leningrad on Jan. 25, 1968.

Alzira. Opera in a prologue and two acts by Giuseppe Verdi, to a text by Salvadore Cammarano, after Voltaire's tragedy *Alzire, ou Les Américains* (1730), first produced in Naples on Aug. 12, 1845. Zamoro, chief of the Incas, is believed to be dead. However, he returns on the wedding day of his betrothed, Alzira, to another, Gusmano, son of the governor of Peru. They duel, and Gusmano is stabbed. He nonetheless pardons Zamoro and returns Alzira to him as he dies. The work is one of Verdi's least-performed operas.

Amadis. Opera in a prologue and five acts by Jean-Baptiste Lully, to a text by Philippe Quinault based on a Spanish chivalric romance by Garcí de Montalvo. The subject was chosen by King Louis XIV from the annals of medieval myth, rather than a classical story, a first for a tragic opera. It was first performed in Paris on Jan. 18, 1684. The story tells of knightly men and courtly maids, specifically the knight Amadis and his beloved Oriane. The expected plot twists and turns keep them apart—including an interlude in a forest where Amadis must overcome a sorceress named Arcabonne who blames him for the murder of her brother—until finally the lovers are united and all is made well.

Amahl and the Night Visitors. Opera in one act by Gian Carlo Menotti, to his own libretto, broadcast on

Christmas Eve, 1951, by NBC television in New York. This is the first operatic work written for television, and its success was such that it became an annual Christmas presentation. Suggested by Bosch's painting *The Adoration of the Magi*, the story deals with the crippled boy Amahl, who is miraculously healed when he gives his crutches to the visiting Three Wise Men as a gift for the Christ child.

Amants captifs, Les. Opera by Pierre Capdevielle. A Vulcan imprisons Venus and Mars in an invisible net on their adulterous bed. It was first performed in Bordeaux on May 20, 1960.

Amelia al bella (Amelia Goes to the Ball). Comic opera by Gian Carlo Menotti, in one act to his own libretto in Italian, first performed in English in Philadelphia on April 1, 1937. The ambitious Amelia is eager to get to the ball on time, but is delayed by a violent encounter between her husband and her lover. She finally is escorted to the ball by a friendly policeman.

Amerika. Opera by Roman Haubenstock-Ramati, after Franz Kafka's unfinished novel. It is written in an advanced serial idiom with electronics, first produced at the Berlin Festival on Oct. 8, 1966.

Amico Fritz, L' (Friend Fritz). Opera in three acts by Pietro Mascagni, to a text by P. Suardon (Nicola Daspuro) after Erckmann-Chatrian's novel (1864). A wealthy confirmed bachelor landowner succumbs to the charms of the daughter of one of his tenants. It was first performed in Rome on Oct. 31, 1891.

Amore dei tre re, L' (The Love of Three Kings). Opera in three acts by Italo Montemezzi, to a text by Sem Benelli, after his own verse tragedy (1910). The story is set in the Middle Ages, just after the barbarians have successfully conquered Italy. One of the barbarian leaders, now old and blind, discovers that his daughter-in-law is having an affair while his son is away at war. He plots to kill her and her lover. First, he strangles the wife, placing her body in the castle crypt; as her lover enters to kiss her cold lips, he swoons and dies. It turns out that the old man has secretly placed poison on her lips. However, before he can stop him, his son also kisses the corpse, and dies. It was first performed in Milan on April 10, 1913.

Amphion. Scenic melodrama in one act by Arthur Honegger, to a libretto by Paul Valéry, first produced in Paris on June 23, 1931, with Ida Rubinstein in the mimed role of Amphion. Apollo orders Amphion to invent music, which he does by creating a scale of two major tetrachords disjunct by a semitone, thus dividing the octave bitonally into tritones, and playing the figure on the lyre so powerfully that stones are moved telekinetically to erect a temple to Apollo in Thebes.

Andrea Chénier. Grand opera in four acts by Umberto Giordano, produced in Milan on March 28, 1896. The libretto by Luigi Illica was inspired by the story of the French poet André Chénier (1762–94), who was condemned to the guillotine by the French revolutionary tribunal in 1793. Set against the background of the French Revolution, the opera addresses issues of aristocratic versus democratic institutions. In this story, neither the idle rich nor the angry mob comes off as ideal governors for the French nation. Meanwhile, the poet—who tries to stand above the fray, critiquing the rich and the mob alike—suffers the ultimate defeat, the loss of his life. His beloved, Maddalena, tries to bribe the jailer to let her take his place, but to no avail.

Andrea del Sarto. Opera in two acts by Daniel-Lesur, his only one. It was inspired by the life of the famous Florentine painter known as "Andrea senza errore" because of his impeccable fresco technique. The opera was performed for the first time in Marseilles on Jan. 24, 1969.

Andzhelo (Angelo). Opera in four acts by César Cui, to a text by Victor Burenin based on Victor Hugo's *Angelo, tyran de Padouse* (1835). It was first performed in St. Petersburg on Feb. 13, 1876. The plot revolves around Angelo, lord of Padua, whose wife and mistress both really love another man, Rodolfo, who just happens to be the son of the former ruling family. Rodolfo leads an insurrection against the tyrant, while the story of love gone wrong unwinds.

Angélique. Opera in one act by Jacques Ibert, to a libretto by Nino (Michel Veber). It is based on the centuries-old folktale of a shrewish wife whom not even the devil himself can tame. It was first produced in Paris on Jan. 28, 1927. It is set to a modernistic score with the inclusion of a jazzy interlude to portray the ethnological consciousness of a voodooistic tribal chief in the African interior.

Aniara. Opera in two acts by Karl-Birger Blomdahl, to a libretto by Erik Lindegren after Harry Martinson's poem (described as "a revue of mankind, in space-time"), first produced in Stockholm on May 31, 1959. After an atomic war, survivors from earth emigrate to Mars in the spaceship *Aniara.* They become demoralized during the long journey and fail to achieve the new way of life that they seek.

Animalen (The Animals). Opera by Lars Johan Werle, to a libretto treating the fateful antagonism between America and Russia. Representatives of both nations hurl their slogans at each other. However, this mutual enmity is unexpectedly challenged by the animals of the world who force both sides to reconcile their differences. It was first staged in Göteborg on May 19, 1979.

Anna Bolena (Anne Boleyn). Opera in two acts by Gaetano Donizetti, to a text by Felice Romani. The story is based loosely on the well-known historical events concerning King Henry VIII's desire to rid himself of his wife. It was first produced in Milan on Dec. 26, 1830. Donizetti's first great success, it was reintroduced to modern audiences by Maria Callas.

Anna Karenina. Opera by Iain Hamilton, after Tolstoy's novel of adulterous passion, the penalty for which was death (the epigraph on the novel was from the Bible: "The Vengeance is Mine, I shall repay"). It was first performed by the English National Opera in London on May 7, 1981.

Antoine et Cléopâtre. Opera by Emmanuel Bondeville, after Shakespeare's play, thematically based on two leading motives, one for Anthony and one for Cleopatra, and immersed in fluid impressionistic harmonies. It was first produced in Rouen, France, on March 8, 1974.

Antony and Cleopatra. Opera in three acts by Samuel Barber, to a text by Franco Zeffirelli based on Shakespeare's drama, commissioned by the Metropolitan Opera for the inauguration of its new house at N.Y.'s Lincoln Center for the Performing Arts and produced there on Sept. 16, 1966. Despite, or perhaps because of, the unabashed romantic flow of operatic cantilena, *Antony and Cleopatra* was generally damned by the critics; but major problems with the stage machinery for an overly elaborate set must also be blamed. Barber revised the score in 1975.

Arabella. Opera in three acts by Richard Strauss, to a Hugo von Hofmannsthal libretto, their last collaboration. It is a Viennese version of a daughter's true love triumphing over a father's mercenary motives, and includes a 19th-century Viennese tradition, the rollicking Coachman's Ball. The work was first produced in Dresden on July 1, 1933.

Arden muss sterben (Arden Must Die). A "political opera about ourselves" in two acts by Alexander Goehr, to a German libretto by Erich Fried after an anonymous 16th-century English play, *Arden of Feversham*. It describes the murder of a faceless businessman by his wife and her lover; after several attempts, they finally succeed. The subsequent trial of the murderers reveals that justice is just as amoral as the guilty lovers themselves. It was performed for the first time by the Hamburg State Opera on March 5, 1967.

Ariadna (Ariadne). Opera in one act by Bohuslav Martinů, to his own libretto based on George Neveux's *Le voyage de hésée*, in turn based on the ancient myth. In this version, Theseus appears as the Freudian *superego* that kills its own *id* personified by the Minotaur with the aid of Ariadne's psychoanalytic umbilical cords. It is set to music in an orderly succession of recitatives, ensembles, and instrumental interludes in a neo-Monteverdian monody. The work was produced posthumously in Gelsenkirchen, Germany, on March 2, 1961.

Ariadne auf Naxos. Opera in one act (later with prelude) by Richard Strauss, to a libretto by Hugo von Hofmannsthal. The first version was given as the second half of a bill with Molière's *Le bourgeois gentilhomme* in Stuttgart on Oct. 25, 1912; the expanded second version was given without the Molière play in Vienna on Oct. 4, 1916. The extremely involved story consists of three superimposed worlds: a nonsinging bourgeois refugee from Molière's play engages an opera seria company and a commedia dell'arte troupe. A philosophical, methodological, and aesthetic imbroglio ensues in which the idealistic composer (a trouser role) is forced to perform his opera seria simultaneously with the commedia play. The opera centers on the mythical Ariadne, abandoned on the island of Naxos, praying for death to release her; she is often interrupted by the commedia players. Bacchus arrives opportunely and takes Ariadne with him to the heavens, to the approval of the onstage spectators.

Ariane et Barbe-bleue (Adriane and Bluebeard). Opera in three acts by Paul Dukas, to a libretto adapted from Maurice Maeterlinck's drama (1901). It tells the familiar story of an uxoricidal castelan in which the last wife outwits her conniving, villainous husband when she discovers the dead bodies of his previous six. It was first performed in Paris on May 10, 1907.

Arianna in Creta (Ariadne in Crete). Opera in three acts by George Frideric Handel, to a libretto after Pariati's text *Teseo in Creta* (1715) set by Leo (1721 and 1729) and Porpora (1727), based loosely on the myth of Theseus and his journey to Crete. It was first produced in London on Jan. 26, 1734.

Ariodant. Opera in three acts by Etienne-Nicolas Méhul, to a text by F. B. Hoffman after Ariosto's poem *Orlando furioso* (1516). It recounts the story of Othon's ill-fated attempts to turn Ina's attentions away from her lover Ariodant and toward himself. It was first produced in Paris on Oct. 11, 1799.

Ariodante. Opera in three acts by George Frideric Handel, to a libretto anonymously adapted from Antonio Salvi's *Ginevra, principessa di Scozia* (1708) after Ariosto's poem *Orlando furioso* (1516). Polinesso, duke of Albany, tries unsuccessfully to win Ginevra away from her betrothed, Ariodante. It was first performed in London on Jan. 8, 1735.

Arme Heinrich, Der (Poor Heinrich). Opera in three acts by Hans Pfitzner, his first, to a text by James Grun after a medieval legend. The knight Heinrich, taken ill through the wrath of God, finds strength in the end to stop his daughter, Agnes (the necessary virgin), from sacrificing herself on his behalf. It was first performed in Mainz on April 2, 1895.

Armide. Lyric tragedy in a prologue and five acts by Jean-Baptiste Lully, first performed in Paris on Feb. 15, 1686. The subject is taken from the famous poem by Tasso *Gerusalemme liberata.* The crusader Renaud is bewitched by the charms of Armide, who lures him to her magic garden. But after lengthy dalliance, Renaud feels a need to perform further heroic deeds and leaves Armide. Despondent, she destroys her garden with its memories of love. This work is regarded as one of the greatest achievements of the French lyric drama.

Armidü. Opera in five acts by Christoph Willibald Gluck, to a text by Quinault after Tasso's *Gerusalemme liberata,* first produced in Paris on Sept. 23, 1777. The plot is essentially the same as that at work in Lully's earlier *Armide* (1686) and many other operas.

Arminio. Opera in three acts by George Frideric Handel, to a text adapted from Antonio Salvi's *Arminio* (1703). It recounts the happy fate of the rebel chieftain Arminius, who, imprisoned by the Roman general Varo, is released through the love of good women (his wife and his sister). It was first produced in London on Jan. 12, 1737.

Ascanio in Alba. Opera in two acts by Wolfgang Amadeus Mozart, to a text by Giuseppe Parini (perhaps after Count Claudio Stampa). The love between Ascanio and Silvia is tried, tested, and found to be true, largely through the intervening efforts of Venus, Ascanio's grandmother. It was first performed in Milan on Oct. 17, 1771.

Ashmedai. Opera by Joseph Tal, first performed in Hamburg on Nov. 9, 1971. Ashmedai, or more commonly Asmodeus, is a minor demon who takes possession of a peaceable kingdom, ostensibly for a year, but who manages to corrupt the populace into voting for him as president for life.

Assassinio nella cattedrale (Murder in the Cathedral). Opera oratorio in two parts with intermezzo by Ildebrando Pizzetti, to a libretto by the composer after T. S. Eliot's dramatic poem *Murder in the Cathedral* (1935). It is based on the historic assassination of Thomas à Beckett on the orders of Henry II of England in 1170. The opera was first staged in Milan on March 1, 1958.

Astuzie femminili, Le. Opera in two acts by Domenico Cimarosa, to a libretto by Giuseppe Palomba. Bellina, promised to an old (and rich) family friend, Don Gianpaolo Lasagna, manages through disguise and deception to wed her real love, the young Filandro. It was first produced in Naples on Aug. 26, 1794.

Atalanta. Opera in three acts by George Frideric Handel, to an anonymous text after Belisario Valeriani's *La caccia in Etolia*, first performed in London on May 12, 1736, on the occasion of the marriage of Frederick, prince of Wales, to Princess Augusta of Saxe-Gotha. Atalanta, a forest denizen, prefers to hunt wild animals than to be domesticated by her lover, Meleager. Meanwhile, a shepherd named Amyntas pines for his beloved, the countrywoman Irene. The usual operatic entanglements ensue—supposed betrayals, misunderstandings, lost gifts—until the two couples are finally united, while Atalanta and Meleager are revealed to be of royal blood. It is a fitting love story, concluding with a visit from Mercury, who brings wedding wishes from Jupiter.

Atlantide, L'. Opera in four acts by Henri Tomasi, to a libretto by F. Didelot after Pierre Denoit's novel (1920). The story deals with the polyandrogynous queen of Atlantis (who has only a dancing part). It premiered in Mulhouse on Feb. 26, 1954.

Atlas. Opera by Meredith Monk, in three sections (*Personal Climate, Night Travel,* and *Invisible Night*). It depicts the misadventures of the fictional explorer Alexandra Daniels (including encounters with spirits from other realms and struggles with personal and societal demons). The work was first staged at the Houston Grand Opera on Feb. 22, 1991, directed by Monk and Pablo Vela and with orchestration by Wayne Hankins.

Atomtod (Atomic Death). Opera by Giacomo Manzoni, to a libretto by Emilion Jona. It depicts in a surrealistically apocalyptic spirit the atomic annihilation of planet earth, with a handful of men surviving in ultrascientific shelters but perishing in the end of mental inanition. It was produced for the first time at Milan's Piccolo Scala on March 27, 1965.

Attaque du moulin, L' (The Attack on the Mill). Opera in four acts by Alfred Bruneau, to a libretto by Louis Gallet after the story in Emile Zola's *Soirées de Médan.* This opera prophetically forecast the senseless destruction of World War I. It centers on the family of an unfortunate miller named Merlier. His daughter, Francoise, falls in love with Dominique, and they are married just as war breaks out. The enemy captain arrives, capturing her father and husband and vowing to kill them at dawn. Her husband escapes, but her father—in the first version of the work—is shot before the French troops arrive. In a second ending later written by Bruneau, the troops arrive in the nick of time to save her father's neck. It was first performed in Paris on Nov. 23, 1893.

At the Boar's Head. Opera in one act by Gustav Holst, to his own libretto after Shakespeare's drama *Henry IV* (parts 1 and 2), with two Shakespeare sonnets, to music derived from old English melorhythms. The action centers on the youthful escapades of the king and his rogue's gallery of friends, including the ever popular drunkard and braggart Sir John Falstaff. It was first produced in Manchester on April 3, 1925.

Attila. Opera in prologue and three acts by Giuseppe Verdi, to a text by Temistocle Solera after Zacharias Werner's drama *Attila, König der Hunnen* (1808), produced in Venice on March 17, 1846. The libretto draws its subject from the final struggle of Rome against the invading hordes of Attila and his Huns. Contemporaneous audiences found a parallel with the subjugation of Italy by Austria in the middle of the 19th century, contributing to the opera's temporary success.

Aufstieg und Fall der Stadt Mahagonny (Rise and Fall of the City of Mahagonny). Opera in three acts by Kurt Weill, to a libretto by Bertolt Brecht, first performed in Leipzig on March 9, 1930. Four workers contend with a Miami-like city in which justice is meted out according to an extreme capitalistic creed, with murder and rape punished lightly and crimes against property penalized by execution. The score includes the pidgin English lament "Alabama Song."

Ausgerechnet und verspielt. "Spiel-Oper" for television by Ernst Krenek, to his own libretto. A mathematician loses a lot of hard-earned money using his highly scientific theory of probability at the roulette table but breaks the bank by playing a series of consecutive numbers taken from the intervals in semitone units in a tone-row selected at random by a humanoid computer. It was performed for the first time on Austrian television in Vienna on June 25, 1962.

Autodafé. Opera in eight episodes with prologue and epilogue by Maurice Ohana, to his own libretto, scored for orchestra, triple chorus, and electronics, "pour le plaisir de brûler les monstres." It features a fiery crackling finale to portray the ritual burning of heretics. It was performed for the first time in Lyons on May 23, 1973.

Ayikuli. Chinese opera composed collectively by a group of communist musicians, adapted from a film entitled *Red Blossom on Tien Shan Mountains.* It deals with a heroic Kazakh woman, a former slave who becomes a revolutionary leader. It was first produced in Beijing on Dec. 24, 1965.

B

Bacchanterna. Opera by Daniel Börtz, after Euripides' play *The Bacchae,* claiming that "all the madness of fundamentalism is contained in the play about the failure of the last great matriarchate." It was given its premiere performance on Nov. 2, 1991, by the Stockholm Opera, directed by the Swedish film director Ingmar Bergman.

Ballad of Baby Doe, The. Folk opera by Douglas Moore to a libretto John Latouche. Baby Doe is a historical figure, the wife of the rich silver mine owner in Colorado who lost his fortune when gold became the official U.S. currency. After his death, she stubbornly remained in her dilapidated house in Leadville, Colorado, where she froze to death in 1935. The world premiere took place appropriately in another ghost city, Central City, Colorado, on July 7, 1956; it was then revised and presented by the New York City Opera on April 3, 1958, with Beverly Sills as Baby Doe.

Ballo in maschera, Un (A Masked Ball). Opera in three acts by Giuseppe Verdi, to a text by Antonio Somma adapted from a Eugène Scribe libretto based on the assassination of King Gustavus III of Sweden in 1792, first produced in Rome on Feb. 17, 1859. Regicide was not regarded as appropriate by the stage censors when Verdi's opera was premiered, so the locale was changed to the distant land of America and the victim of the plot to the "governor of Boston," a nonexistent title. The governor consults a fortune teller, who tells him that he will be murdered. Operatic fortune tellers are never wrong, and the unfortunate governor is stabbed to death at a masked ball by his male secretary with whose wife the governor had been consorting. Recent attempts have been made to restore the original libretto, but they have not been successful, opera audiences preferring romantic invention to historic truth.

Balseros. Opera in four parts by Robert Ashley, accompanied by a synthesized orchestra (in collaboration with Tom Hamilton) and to a libretto, subtitled "Manual for a Desperate Crossing," by Maria Irene Fornes. It deals with actual experiences of the Cuban "rafters" (*balseros*) in their crossing of the Atlantic for refuge in America. The dramatic narrative, drawn largely from interviews from actual *balseros,* is in four parts: (1) the making of the raft; (2) the departure; (3) the events on the sea; and (4) the rescue. First performed in bilingual Miami in 1997, the (two) actors perform (speak) the libretto in Spanish while the (nine) singers perform (sing) their stories in English.

Bánk Bán. Historical opera in three acts by Ferenc Erkel, to a text by Béni Egressy after József Katona's tragedy (1815), first produced in Budapest, March 9, 1861. The contemporaneous political situation is reflected in an allegory of 13th-century German wickedness and patriotic Hungarian vengeance. This work is considered the national opera of Hungary.

Barbe-Bleue (Bluebeard). Opéra bouffe by Jacques Offenbach, produced in Paris on Feb. 5, 1866. The monstrous Bluebeard wins his sixth wife in a lottery. Unaware that his previous wives were merely drugged and not poisoned by an alchemist in his employ, he casts a lustful glance on a potential Wife No. 7. When his former wives make their sudden reappearance, Bluebeard has to be satisfied with Wife No. 6, who is no longer afraid of him now that he has been exposed as a wretched bungler in uxoricide

Barbiere di Siviglia, Il (The Barber of Seville). Opera in two acts by Gioacchino Rossini, to a libretto by Cesare Sterbini after Pierre-Augustin Beaumarchais's *Le barbier de Séville,* originally titled *Almaviva, ossia L'inutile precauzione* (Almaviva, or The Futile Precaution), first produced in Rome, Feb. 20, 1816, the composer conducting. Count Almaviva is in love with Rosina, ward of Doctor Bartolo, who plans to marry her. The versatile barber Figaro arranges various disguises for Almaviva to pursue his quest. After much chicanery, the lovers are united by Bartolo's own notary. Rossini's setting was not the first to be based on the Beaumarchais play; it was preceded by one in four acts by Giovanni Paisiello (St. Petersburg, Sept. 26, 1782), which enjoyed considerable success.

Bartered Bride, The (Prodaná nevěsta, literally, *The Bride Which Is Sold*). Comic opera in three acts by Bedřich Smetana, to a libretto by Karel Sabina, first produced in Prague on May 30, 1866. In early 19th-century Bohemia, the parents of a young woman intend to give her in marriage to a rich man's son, but she loves another. The wily marriage broker attempts to bribe the woman's lover, but he indignantly refuses to trade love for money. All ends well when the lover reveals that he is himself a wealthy prodigal son of the village headmaster. The overture is often performed as a concert piece.

Bassariden, Die. Neo-Grecian opera in one act with intermezzo by Hans Werner Henze, to an English libretto by W. H. Auden and Chester Kallman after Euripides' *The Bacchae,* first produced in Salzburg on Aug. 6, 1966, in a German translation by Maria Basse-Sporleder. The music is in the form of a symphony in four movements, depicting the conflict between the Germanically tense dodecaphonic asceticism of a sexually repressed king of Thebes and the Italianate incandescent sensualism of the multifutuent, yet diatonically conditioned, god of wine Dionysus.

Bastien und Bastienne. Opera in one act by Wolfgang

Amadeus Mozart, to a libretto by F. W. Weiskern, J. Müller, and J. A. Schachtner after M. J. B. and C. S. Favart and H. de Guerville's comedy *Les amours de Bastien et Bastienne* (1753), a simple tale of young love. Bastienne wins the heart of her fickle lover by pretending to be indifferent toward him. It was first produced in Vienna in 1768 when Mozart was only 12 years old, probably at the garden theater in the home of one Dr. Mesmer, the protagonist of the therapeutic method known as mesmerism.

Battaglia di Legnano, La (The Battle of Legano). Opera in three acts by Giuseppe Verdi, to a text by Salvatore Cammarano after Joseph Méry's drama *La battaille de Toulouse* (1828). The story of revolutionary patriotism is set on the battlefields of Milan and Como in 12th-century Italy and concerns, among other things, the tenacious friendship of Rolando and Arrigo, who love the same woman. It was first produced in Rome, Jan. 27, 1849.

Bayou Legend, A. Opera by William Grant Still, to a libretto by his wife, Verna Arvey. It is based on an old legend of the region of Biloxi (within a stone's throw of Still's own birthplace in Woodville, Mississippi) in which a young Cajun falls in love with an astral creature, is hanged for consorting with spirits, but is united with her in the beyond. The opera was first performed 33 years after its composition, on Nov. 15, 1974, by the all-black troupe of Opera/South in Jackson, Mississippi.

Beach of Falesá, The. Opera by Alun Hoddinut, his first, based on a short story by Robert Louis Stevenson. The exotic story is set on a South Seas island, and tells of two English traders, the good Wiltshire and the evil Case. Case has the islanders under his spell, and therefore they will only trade with him. Wiltshire successfully breaks the magical bond, and after Case reveals he has murdered all of his previous trade rivals, successfully kills the evil magician. It was produced in Cardiff, Wales, on March 26, 1974.

Bear, The. Chamber opera in one act by William Walton, to a text by Paul Dehn after Chekhov's play (1888). An ill-mannered intellectual, about to propose to the lady of his heart, nearly ruins their future marital bliss by starting a polemical discussion with her. It was first produced at the Aldeburgh Festival on June 3, 1967, paired with Lennox Berkeley's chamber opera *Castaway.*

Beatrice di Tenda. Opera in two acts by Vincenzo Bellini, to a text by Felice Romani. The story is a tangled web of misplaced affections in which Beatrice, wife of Filippo Visconti, duke of Milan, loves Orombello, who in turn is loved by the duke's mistress, Agnese. The story ends tragically for all when Agnese spitefully reveals the duke's affair. It was first produced in Venice on March 16, 1833.

Béatrice et Bénédict. Opera in two acts by Hector Berlioz, to a text by the composer after the comic romantic subplot in Shakespeare's *Much Ado About Nothing.* The famous ill-matched lovers spar verbally only to be united happily in true love by the drama's end. It was first produced in Baden-Baden on Aug. 9, 1862. The overture is well known and often performed as a concert work.

Béatris. Opera by Jacques Charpentier. It is based on a true story of a 14th-century French matron brought to trial on a charge of consorting with demons and of having carnal relations with a priest. Her eloquent defense saves her from execution. It was first staged in Aix-en-Provence on July 23, 1971.

Beatrix Cenci. Opera by Alberto Ginastera to a libretto by William Shand and Alberto Girri. A patricidal Italian matron, in a plot with her mother and two brothers, exterminates her vicious Roman father. She was beheaded on Sept. 11, 1599, by papal order, despite her claim that her father attempted incest upon her. The work was first produced at the Kennedy Center in Washington, D.C., on Sept. 10, 1971.

Beggar's Opera, The. A satirical ballad opera in three acts to the text by John Gay, with music collated and partly composed in the manner of a pasticcio by the German-born composer John Pepusch. The spectacle was usually introduced by an actor dressed as a beggar announcing the wedding of two popular ballad singers. The musical score mixed English, Irish, and Scottish street tunes with French airs, while the text contained undisguised persiflage of British political figures along with highwaymen and other common criminals.

The first production took place in London on January 29, 1728, at Lincoln's Inn Fields, a venue frequented by the poor rather than the aristocracy that patronized performances of Italian opera. Its tremendous success brought forth countless imitations, and established the popularity of the ballad opera genre in Britain. The satirical impact of the opera moved the Lord Chamberlain to forbid the production of its sequel, *Polly.*

The music historian Sir John Hawkins wrote in all solemnity, "Rapine and violence have been gradually increasing ever since the first representation of *The Begger's Opera,*" while Dr. Johnson opined that there was in the work "such a labefactation of all principles as might be injurious to morality."

Kurt Weill, in collaboration with the radical dramatist Bertolt Brecht, adapted *The Begger's Opera* to a satire on the world conditions in 1928, under the title *Die Dreigroschenoper.* Marc Bliztstein made an adaptation of the opera into the colloquial American, *The Threepenny Opera.*

Belfagor. Comic opera in two acts with prologue and epilogue by Ottopino Respighi, to a libretto by Claudio Guastalla after Ercole Morselli's comedy (c. 1919). The archdemon Belfagor, fittingly characterized in the score by the leading motive of the tritone, is sent to earth to test the theory that wives make marriage a living hell, and flees to real hell to escape impending matrimony. It was first performed at Milan's La Scala on April 26, 1923.

Belisario. Opera seria in three acts by Gaetano Donizetti, to a libretto by Salvadore Cammarano after Jean-

François Marmontel's drama *Bélisaire* (1776). It recounts the hero's untiring defense of Byzantium despite torture, exile, and eventual death. It premiered in Venice on Feb. 4, 1836.

Belle et la Bête, La. Opera by Philip Glass, after the deeply moralistic fable "Beauty and the Beast." It was first mounted in New York on Dec. 7, 1994.

Belle Hélène, La (The Beautiful Helen). Operetta in three acts by Jacques Offenbach to a text by Henri Meihac and Ludovic Halévy. The plot is a farce on the Paris–Helen encounter in Homer's *Illiad.* It was first produced in Paris on Dec. 17, 1864.

Benvenuto Cellini. Opera in two acts by Hector Berlioz, to a text by Léon de Wailly and Auguste Barbier. It is based on the autobiography of the Italian sculptor and libertine. Cellini is beloved of Teresa, the daughter of the papal treasurer, Balducci. Her father, however, wishes her to marry the official papal sculptor, Fieramosca. Balducci is also miffed that Cellini has won a commission from the Pope to create a bronze statue of Perseus. Through a series of mishaps, the lovers are separated; Cellini attempts to kidnap Teresa and ends up murdering an associate of Fieramosca—and he still hasn't completed his statue! Faced with a tight deadline, Cellini miraculously completes the work—and wins a pardon for the murder and the hand of his true love. It was first produced in Paris on Sept. 10, 1838, and revised in 1852.

Bernauerin, Die. Opera by Carl Orff, to his own libretto in the Bavarian dialect, first produced in Stuttgart on June 15, 1947. The story tells of the medieval married woman Agnes Bernauer, commonly known as Bernauerin, who is terrorized and finally drowned by her tyrannical father-in-law.

Besuch der alten Dame, Der (The Visit of the Old Lady). Opera in three acts by Gottfried von Einem, to a surrealistic text by Friedrich Dürrenmatt after his drama of the same name, first performed in Vienna on May 23, 1971. The old lady of the title returns to her native locality in Switzerland, where she had been seduced and abandoned at a tender age by her amoral lover. She becomes rich in the world as Madame Clair Zachanassian (a contraction of millionaire names Zacharoff, Onassis, and Gulbenkian), and promises the impoverished villagers untold riches on condition that they kill her erstwhile seducer, an offer that is ultimately accepted.

Betrothal in a Convent (Obrucheniye v monastïre). Opera in four acts by Sergei Prokofiev, to his own libretto with verses by Mira Mendelson (his second wife), after Sheridan's *The Duenna* (1775). It portrays intersected amours, mistaken identities, and various other embroilments of 18th-century Seville. It was first produced in Prague on May 5, 1946. The work is variously known as *The Duenna, or The Double Elopement* or *The Wedding in the Monastery,* but *Betrothal in a Convent* is the literal translation of the original Russian title.

Bianca e Fernando. Opera in two acts by Vincenzo Bellini, to a libretto by Domenico Gilardoni after Carlo Roti's drama *Bianca e Fernando alla tomba di Carlo IV, Duca di Agrigento* (1820). The evil Filippo has seized power in the dukedom of Agrigento (located in Sicily). He has jailed the legitimate ruler, Carlo, and banished Carlo's son, Fernando. To cement his power, he plans to wed Carlo's daughter, Bianca; a widow, she agrees to the marriage only to protect her own child. Fernando returns to the court disguised as a servant, "Adolfo," winning Filippo's trust. As you might expect, the son saves both his sister from an ill-advised marriage and his father from death; the righteous Carlo is restored to his throne. It was first performed in Naples on May 30, 1826. Note: the original title was *Bianca e Gernando,* owing to the Naples censorship forbidding references to the royal name of Ferdinando.

Bilby's Doll. Opera by Carlisle Floyd, composed for the U.S. bicentennial. Doll, a young French girl brought to America by a sea captain named Bilby, is accused of witchcraft by Bilby's wife (who contends that Doll had caused the fetus to wither in her womb). Doll eventually becomes herself convinced that she is a witch, and prays for Satan to come to her rescue. It was first produced in Houston on Feb. 29, 1976.

Billy Budd. Opera in four acts by Benjamin Britten, to a text by E. M. Forster and Eric Crozier after Herman Melville's highly symbolic novella. It describes a mutiny on the British warship *Indomitable* in 1797, during which the young sailor Billy Budd kills his brutal superior officer and is hanged for it. The work is almost unique as a large-scale opera written for men's voices exclusively. It was first produced in London on Dec. 1, 1951, with the composer conducting.

Black Spider, The. Opera by Judith Weir, to a libretto by Jeremias Gotthelf based on the 1842 novel by the Swiss cleric Albert Bitzius (1797–1854), *Die schwarze Spinne,* and a contemporary news report from Kraków. It was first staged in the crypt of Canterbury Cathedral on March 6, 1985.

Blackwood & Co. Burlesque opera by Armin Schibler, in which a bed manufacturing company of New York City awards a free deluxe bed to a young honeymooning couple as part of a publicity campaign. It was first produced in Zürich on June 3, 1962.

Blaise le savetier (Blaise the Cobbler). Comic opera in one act by François-André Philidor, first performed in Paris on March 9, 1759. The cobbler Blaise is threatened with eviction by his landlord. To evade payment, he accuses the landlord of making illicit advances to his wife. After the landlord is caught in a compromising situation, he is blackmailed into letting Blaise use the apartment rent free.

Blaník. Opera by Zdeněk Fibich, set in 1623, first performed in Prague on Nov. 25, 1881. The libretto is based on the national Czech legend of Czech patriots, followers of the religious reformer Jan Hus. They take refuge on Mt. Blaník, and emerge to liberate the country from Austrian rule.

Blood Moon. Opera by Norman Dello Joio in three acts. It is based on the story of the famed octoroon actress Ada Mencken, who prospered in New Orleans and New York at the time of the Civil War—until her favorite lover discovered the 12 1/2 percent of denigrating Negro blood in her veins. It was performed for the first time in San Francisco on Sept. 18, 1961.

Blood Wedding. Opera by Sándor Szokolay to his own libretto, based on the Spanish poet/playwright Federico Garcia Lorca's *Bodas de sangre.* The plot hinges on interfamily warfare between the families of a bride and bridegroom in a small Spanish village. The bridegroom's mother discovers that the bride has previously been betrothed to another, whose family was responsible in the past for the death of her own husband and elder son. Despite her efforts to control her passion, the bride cannot overcome her feelings for her previous lover, and she elopes with him on her wedding day. In the end, the bridegroom kills his rival, to the grief of both mother and bridegroom. This opera rivals *Bluebeard's Castle* as one of the most popular Hungarian modern works.

Bluebeard's Castle (A Kékszakállú herceg vára). Opera in one act by Béla Bartók, to a libretto by Béla Balázs, first produced in Budapest on May 24, 1918. The justly infamous Bluebeard (possibly a historic character) lets his last bride open the secret doors of his castle that conceal torture chambers and the dead bodies of his previous wives. As Bluebeard proclaims love for his last bride, she joins the dead wives behind the last door.

Blumen von Hiroshima, Die. Musical chamber play by Forrest. A militant American pacifist marries a Japanese girl, survivor of the atomic bombing of Hiroshima, despite the ominous possibility that the genes of their children might be affected by latent radiation. It was first produced in Weimar on June 24, 1967, with the composer conducting.

Boatswain's Mate, The. Opera in one act by Ethel Smyth, to her own libretto after W. W. Jacobs's story. An ex-boatswain asks a friend to fake a burglary of a pub owned by a comely widow, intending to pose as her rescuer and thus impress her into marrying him. The plot miscarries when she surprises the pretend burglar and decides to marry him instead. It was premiered in London on Jan. 28, 1916.

Boghdan Khmel'nyts'ky. Opera by Kostyantyn Fedororych Dan'kevych, first produced in Kiev on Jan. 29, 1951. In deference to criticism in the Soviet press for the erroneous representation of the relationship between the Ukraine and Russia in the 17th century, the composer radically revised the score. The new version was performed for the first time in Kiev on Jan. 21, 1953. Boghdan Khmel'nyts'ky, a historical figure, successfully defeated the then-powerful Polish kingdom and in 1654 effected the reunion of the Ukraine with Russia.

Bohème, La. Opera in four acts by Giacomo Puccini, to a text by Giuseppe Giacosa and Luigi Illica after Henry Murger's novel *Scènes de la vie de Bohème* (1847–49), first produced in Turin on Feb. 1, 1896, and conducted by Toscanini. The opera depicts the life of two impoverished but amorous Paris artists. One, Rodolfo, befriends a neighboring girl, Mimi; they fall in love, but are separated first by poverty and then by her death from consumption. The realism of the subject and the relative modernity of the score made *La Bohème* a scandalous landmark in opera. Ruggero Leoncavallo produced an opera on the same subject with the same French title in Venice (1897), which, although meritorious, was eclipsed by Puccini's masterpiece.

Bohemian Girl, The. Opera in three acts by Michael William Balfe, his greatest success, to a text by Alfred Bunn after the ballet pantomime *The Gypsy* by Jules-Henri Saint-Georges (1839), based on Cervantes's short story *La gitanella* (1614), first produced in London on Nov. 27, 1843. The much revised libretto deals with a girl abducted by gypsies from her socially important father, but finally restored to him and allowed to marry her Polish lover. It includes the nostalgic aria "I Dreamt I Dwelt in Marble Halls."

Bomarzo. Opera by Alberto Ginastera to a libretto by Manuel Láinez, based on the legend of an Italian nobleman who constructed giant statues of volcanic stone in his garden near Rome in the 16th century. It was first mounted in Washington, D.C., on May 19, 1967. Previously, Ginastera wrote a cantata on the same subject, performed for the first time in Washington, D.C., on Nov. 1, 1964.

Boris Godunov. Music drama in four acts with prologue by Modest Mussorgsky, to a text by the composer based on Alexander Pushkin's historical drama *The Comedy of the Distress of the Muscovite State, of Tsar Boris, and of Grishka Otrepiev* (1825), and Nikolai Karamzin's *History of the Russian Empire* (1829). It was composed in 1868–69, revised in 1871–72, and finally premiered, in St. Petersburg, Jan. 27–Feb. 8, 1874. The action takes place during the Russian interregnum of 1598–1605. After his coronation, Boris is tormented by the murder of the young czarevitch Dmitri, lawful heir to the Russian throne, perpetrated on his behalf by assassins. A young monk, Gregory, decides to pretend that he is the "true Dmitri," miraculously saved from Boris's assassins. The Polish government backs the claim and leads its army to Moscow with Gregory as the pretender to the throne. Boris begins to go mad, and demands proof from his henchmen that it was the child Dmitri who was actually slain. The opera ends with Boris's death (after placing his young son, Fyodor, on the throne), and the expectation of the pretender's entry into Moscow.

In its original form, *Boris Godunov* has seven scenes and no act subdivisions. In the four-act revised version, Mussorgsky eliminated one scene, added three new scenes, and altered extant scenes. After his death it was radically reorchestrated by Nickolai Rimsky-Korsakov from 1891 to 1906, and it was in this version that the opera became internationally famous. From the late 1920s, various attempts to restore Mussorgsky's version began, sometimes in a mixture with the Rimsky-Korsakov; others returned to Mussorgsky's notes, but altered the orchestration (K. Rathaus, Shostakovich) to answer the traditional charges against Mussorgsky's orchestrating abilities. The original score was republished in 1928 and 1975, and some recent performances have combined the two Mussorgsky versions into a *Gesamtausführungausgabe.*

Boulevard Solitude. Opera in seven scenes by Hans Werner Henze, to a text by the composer and Grete Weil after Walter Jockisch's play based on Abbé Prévost's novel *L'histoire du chevalier des Grieux et de Manon Lescaut* (1731), first produced in Hanover on Feb. 17, 1952. The libretto is the modern interpretation of the story of Manon Lescaut set in Paris after the end of World War II, in which she is deflowered, debauched, and humiliated, but eventually returned to her now-penitent seducer and dies in his arms.

Brandenburgers in Bohemia, The (Braniboři v Čechách). Opera in three acts by Bedřich Smetana, to a libretto by Karel Sabina recounting the fate of three sisters, daughters of the mayor of Prague, during an attack on their native Bohemia, first performed in Prague on Jan. 5, 1866.

Brautwahl, Die (The Bridal Choice). Opera in three acts and epilogue by Ferruccio Busoni, to a text by the composer after E. T. A. Hoffmann's story, first produced in Hamburg on April 13, 1912. The daughter of a well-to-do merchant must choose between a painter, a government official, and a baron. Eventually, the choice is made through the age-old folkloric trick of selecting among three caskets. The painter wins and immediately takes his betrothed to Rome to further his studies. The work is scored in an opulent polyphonic idiom in which the choice of the bride becomes entangled in inevitable counterpoint.

Bravo, Il. Opera in three acts by Saverio Mercadante, to a text by Gaetano Rossi and M. M. Marcello based on James Fenimore Cooper's novel *The Bravo* and A. Bourgeois's play *La Vénitienne.* The complicated plot is full of mistaken identities and unknown relationships. Set in 16th-century Venice, it centers on the title character, the Bravo, who is the official state assassin. His life is overshadowed by an evil deed committed in his youth, when, in a fit of passion, he killed his wife. However, unbeknownst to him, his wife survived, and now lives in Venice under the name of Teodora. Teodora, in turn, is the mother of the pretty Violetta (although Violetta is unaware of her parentage), whose guardian is the Bravo. Violetta is beloved by the young Pisani, who sadly can't see his loved one because he is banished from Venice. The Bravo, pitying Pisani, lets the youth disguise himself with the clothes of his office so he may visit his beloved; meanwhile, Teodora hires Pisani to kidnap her daughter from the Bravo. The story comes to a fiery end when Teodora unknowingly sets her own palace ablaze; the lovers are reunited, but Teodora commits suicide—leaving the Bravo once again wifeless. The opera's first performance was at La Scala, Milan, on March 9, 1839.

Bremer Stadtmusikanten, Die. Comic opera by Richarel Mohaupt, produced in Bremen on June 25, 1949. The libretto is derived from a folk tale by the Brothers Grimm. Six musically gifted domestic animals (a cat, a dog, a rooster, a hen, a donkey, and a bear) rescue the animal-loving daughter of the burgomaster of Bremen from her abductors. In gratitude, he appoints them *Stadtmusikanten,* "town musicians."

Bride Comes to Yellow Sky, The. Opera by Roger Nixon, from a story by Stephen Crane, written in a songful quastitonal manner descriptive of the purchase of a mail-order wife by an hombre in a western frontier town called Yellow Sky, first produced at Eastern Illinois University on Feb. 20, 1968.

Bridge, The. Opera by Alexander Raichov, to a libretto depicting the communist revolutionary and military action on the eve of the liberation of Sofia by the Soviet Army from the Nazis, first produced in Ruse, Bulgaria, on Oct. 2, 1965.

Bridge, The. "Antiopera" by Japmil Burghauser, to a symbolic libretto placed simultaneously at two points in time, in the revolutionary year of 1848 and in the socialist year of 1963, and located in space on a bridge that divides a town into two parts, first produced in Prague on March 31, 1967.

Brothers Ulyanov. Opera in three acts by Yuli Meitus, first performed in Ufa on Nov. 25, 1967. The libretto traces the early years of the Ulyanov family and the revolutionary development of Vladimir Ulyanov, the future Lenin, whose brother Alexander is implicated in a terrorist conspiracy against the czar. Alexander is offered clemency if he names his accomplices, but he proudly refuses and is hanged. Lenin enters a revolutionary apprenticeship as a university study in Kazan. In the last act of the opera, he predicts the collapse of the Russian monarchy and the rule of the proletariat.

Bunt Zakow (The Rebellion of Students). Opera to a Polish text by Tadeusz Szeligowski, first performed in Wrocław on July 14, 1951. The libretto depicts the rebellion of students and clerks in 1549 in Kraków against the oppressive rule of the Polish king Sigismund II.

Buona figliuola, La (The Good Daughter). Opera in three acts by Niccolò Piccinni, his greatest success, to a text by Carlo Goldoni after Richardson's novel *Pamela, or Virtue Rewarded* (1740). It was first produced in Rome on Feb. 6, 1760. The opera partly follows the plot of the novel. A nobleman falls in love with his servant, who is far below his station; though his sister objects to the match, the nobleman eventually makes the maid his wife. However, in the opera the servant turns out to be of noble blood, so the union is in fact acceptable.

The work was so successful that Piccinni wrote a sequel to it, *La buona figliuola maritata* (The Married Good Daughter). Hoping to capitalize on Piccinni's success, another Italian composer, Gaetano Latilla, continued the series by writing *La buona figliuola supposta la vedova* (Presumed Widow), but it foundered.

Burning Fiery Furnace, The. Church parable by Benjamin Britten, to a text by William Plomer, first performed at the Aldeburgh Festival on June 9, 1966, without a conductor. The score is set for male voices, organ, and instruments, and tells the biblical story of Shadrach, Meshach, and Abednego and their miraculous survival in the Babylonian oven.

C

Calisto (Callisto). Opera in a prologue and three acts by Francesco Cavalli, to a libretto by Giovanni Faustini after Ovid's *Metamorphoses.* The ever-amorous Jupiter (Giove) falls in love with an earthly nymph, Callisto. However, she has taken a vow of chastity as a follower of Diana; not to be put off, the wily God turns himself into Diana, and convinces Callisto to join him in bed. Juno (Giunone), ever angered by her husband's infidelities, turns Callisto into a bear; but Jupiter quickly restores her to a more attractive body, and the two finally are united. As a prize, the God transforms his beloved into a star in the constellation Ursa Minor. It was first produced in Venice on Nov. 28, 1651.

Calzare d'argento, Il (The Silver Shoe). Sacred play in two acts by Ildebrando Pizzetti, dealing with a medieval pauper who is accused of the theft of a sacred relic when a silver shoe falls into his hands from a crucifix in the Lucca Cathedral but who is exonerated by Jesus descending from the cross to testify in his defense, first produced at Milan's La Scala on March 23, 1961.

Cambiale di matrimonio, La (The Bill of Marriage). A "merry farce" in one act by Gioacchino Rossini, to a text by Gaetano Rossi after Camillo Federici's comedy (1791), first performed in Venice on Nov. 3, 1810, when Rossini was only 19 years old. The daughter of a British banker is traded without her consent to a Canadian merchant, but she loves a young employee of her father. When the Canadian, improbably named Slook, arrives in Europe to claim her hand, she explains to him that she is already "mortgaged." Moved, he writes off his own capital to her and her lover as a matrimonial "bill of exchange" (*la cambiale*).

Campana sommersa, La (The Sunken Bell). Opera in four acts by Ottorino Respighi, to a libretto by Claudio Guastalla after Gerhard Hauptmann's fairy-drama *Die versunkene Glocke* (1896) dealing with a bell maker whose masterpiece, a large church bell, falls accidentally into a lake, and who is lured to follow it beneath the murky waters by a mysterious mountain maiden. It was first performed in a German version in Hamburg on Nov. 18, 1927.

Campanello di notte, Il (The Night Bell). Opera in one act by Gaetano Donizetti, to a text by the composer after a vaudeville by Brunswick, Troin, and Lhérie entitled *La sonnette de nuit,* first performed in Naples on June 1, 1836. This is an inconsequential story of Don Annibale Pistacchio, an elderly pharmacist, whose wedding night with his young bride, Serafina, is interrupted by a visit from Serafina's former lover, who, annoyingly ringing the night bell, demands his prescriptions be filled. The opera is also known as *Il campanello dello speziale.*

Campiello, Il (The Small Venetian Square). Opera in three acts by Ermanno Wolf-Ferrari, to a text by Mario Ghisalberti after Goldoni's comedy (1756) detailing a trivially triangular contention among three girls in a three-way intersection for the favors of a handsome stranger, first produced at La Scala, Milan, on Feb. 12, 1936.

Cancelling Dark, The. Radio opera by Christopher Whelen, based on the true story of an aircraft crash-landing in the desert in which the doomed pilot and his sole passenger engage in a philosophical dialogue and self-induced hallucinations of women in their lives, first performed in London on Dec. 5, 1964.

Capitan, El. Comic opera by John Philip Sousa, first produced in Boston on April 13, 1896, the most successful of his ten comic operas. The Viceroy of Peru foils a conspiracy against him by joining it in disguises as El Capitan, a legendary bandit. When he reveals his real identity, the plot against him collapses. Besides the marching chorus "El Capitan," there is a song, "A Typical Tune of Zanzibar."

Capriccio. Opera in one act by Richard Strauss, his last, to a text by Clemens Krauss and the composer, first performed in Munich on Oct. 28, 1942. This is an 18th-century musical play-within-a-play on the evergreen operatic question of the relative importance of words and music. Countess Madeline, a young widow, tries to balance the affections and attitudes of her two suitors, one a poet, the other a composer. Her final meditation is the opera's musical highlight.

Captain's Daughter, The. Opera in four acts by César Cui, first performed in St. Petersburg on Feb. 27, 1911. The libretto by the composer is drawn from a short story by Pushkin and centers on the romance of two Russians helped by the rebellious Cossack chieftain Pugachov. The work was not successful.

Capuleti e i Montecchi, I. Opera in two acts by Vincenzo Bellini to a libretto by Felice Romani, first performed in Venice on March 11, 1830. The text is based on several Italian sources, rather than Shakespeare's *Romeo and Juliet.* (Bel canto arias and conventional Italian recitatives being adaptable to different words and lyrico-dramatic situations, Bellini made use of portions from his earlier unsuccessful operas *Adelson et Salvini* and *Zaira.*) The part of Romeo was written for a female alto, a surrogate for the quondam male castrato of Baroque opera. The spectacle of a richly bosomed female making like Romeo jarred the eyes and ears of literal-minded operagoers of the 19th century, and eventually the part had to be given to a tenor. Attempts to return to the nonrealistic but melodically superior original were made late in the 20th century.

Cardillac. Opera in three acts by Paul Hindemith, after the horrendous tale of E. T. A. Hoffmann (1818) dealing with an insanely possessive Paris goldsmith who murders his customers in order to get back the jewels he sold them, until his daughter's fiancé buys a necklace for her and valiantly resists Cardillac's attempt to murder him too, so that a mob gathers and slays the chronic slayer. It received its first performance in Dresden on Nov. 9, 1926, and was subsequently revised in 1952 according to the composer's later harmonic theory.

Carmen. Opera in four acts by Georges Bizet, to a text by Henri Mailhac and Ludovic Halévy after Prosper Mérimée's novel (1845), first performed in Paris on March 3, 1875. With Gounod's *Faust* and Verdi's *Aida*, *Carmen* became one of the most successful operas in the repertory, continually produced all over the world. Nietzsche counterposed the spirit of *Carmen*, with its Mediterranean gaiety, passion, and drama, to the somber creations of the Nordic Wagner, once his idol.

The action takes place in Seville around 1830. Don José, a soldier, falls in love at first sight with a gypsy cigarette girl, Carmen. He deserts the army for her, but in vain, for Carmen abandons him for a bullfighter. Distraught, Don José stabs her to death. The most famous arias in *Carmen* are the bullfighter's victory song, "Toreador" (from the Sp. *torero*), and Carmen's song "Habanera" (often misspelled Habañera).

Oscar Hammerstein reconceived *Carmen* as a musical play entitled *Carmen Jones*, its score preserved almost intact from the original work. It was first performed in New York on Dec. 2, 1943. Hammerstein shifted the scene from Seville to a southern American town during World War II.

Carry Nation. Opera by Douglas Moore, first performed in the home state of the eponymous heroine, Lawrence, Kansas, on April 28, 1966. Carry Nation was a temperance fanatic who devoted her life to the fight against the "demon rum," carrying a small axe with which she bashed in the glass doors of saloons in her native Kansas. The libretto invents an episode about her marrying an unregenerate alcoholic.

Casanova's Homecoming. Lyrical opera buffa in three acts by Dominick Argento, to an original libretto based on *L'histoire de ma vie* by Jacques Casanova, set in the first week of Carnival season, 1774 Venice. The middle-aged Casanova returns home to his native Venice after nearly two decades of exile. Possessing magical powers, he enchants an elderly dowager into providing a dowry for his godchild—who turns out to be his daughter. Subplots include Casanova's relationship with his benefactor Lorenzo da Ponte and his affair with a young woman, who has disguised herself as a castrato. It was first staged in St. Paul, Minnesota, on April 12, 1985.

Castaway. Chamber opera by Lennox Berkeley, to a libretto by Paul Dehn dealing with the dalliance of Odysseus with Nausicaa, first produced at the Aldeburgh Festival on June 3, 1967, paired with Walton's chamber opera *The Bear*.

Castor et Pollux. Opera in a prologue and five acts by Jean-Phillipe Rameau, to a text by Pierre-Joseph Bernard about the mythical twins, brothers of Helen and Clytamnestra, who ended their days as a constellation, first performed in Paris on Oct. 24, 1737.

Caterina Cornaro. Opera in a prologue and two acts by Gaetano Donizetti, to a text by Giacomo Sacchèro after Vernoy de St. Georges's libretto *La reine de Chypre* for Ludovic Halévy, set in 15th-century Venice and Cyprus and telling the star-crossed love story of Caterina and Gerardo, first produced in Naples on Jan. 18, 1844. The two are finally joined, but in a revised version for Parma, Gerardo is killed in battle.

Catiline Conspiracy, The. Opera in two acts by Iain Hamilton, to a libretto by the composer based on Ben Jonson's play and centered on Cicero's famous apostrophe *Quoque tandem Catilina abutere pantientia nostra?*—(How long then, Catiline, will you abuse our patience?). Failing to gain a place in the government through election, Catiline secretly plans to seize power. Raising a rebel army, Catiline is eventually defeated by Cicero, representing the righteous power of Rome. On his deathbed, the rebel predicts that his loss will be rectified by a triumphant Caesar. The opera was first staged in Stirling, Scotland, on March 16, 1974.

Cavalieri di Ekebù, I. (The Knights of Ekbey). Opera in four acts by Riccardo Zadonai, his seventh, to a text by Arthuro Rossato after Selma Lagerlöf's novel *Gösta Berlings Sign* (1891). The story focuses on the turbulent passion of a disorganized youth who eventually marries a divorced countess, first performed at Milan's La Scala on March 7, 1925, Toscanini conducting.

Cavalleria rusticana (Rustic Chivalry). Opera in one act by Pietro Mascagni, to a text by Guido Menasci and Giovanni Targioni-Tozzetti after Giovanni Verga's drama (1844), first produced in Rome, May 17, 1890. The drama takes place in Sicily and is based on an actual event. A young villager is emotionally torn between his attachment to a local girl and his passion for a married woman. The unfortunate lover is confronted by the husband, a duel ensues, and he is killed. *Cavalleria rusticana* launched the vogue of operatic verismo after its first production in Rome. Because it is unusually short, it is often programmatically paired with Leoncavallo's *Pagliacci*. In America, the two works are affectionately referred to as *Cav* and *Pag*.

Cenerentola, La (Cinderella). Opera in two acts by Gioacchino Rossini, to a text by Jacopo Ferretti after Charles-Guillaume Étienne's text for Nicolas Isouand's opera based on the classic fairy tale by Perrault. Rossini's sparkling work was first produced in Rome on Jan. 25, 1817, and was then enormously popular abroad. Often revived since the 1930s, the opera has become a vehicle for Cecilia Bartoli.

Cents Vierges, Les. Opéra bouffe by Charles Lecocq, first produced in Brussels on March 16, 1872. A bevy of young maidens becomes excited over an advertisement for 100 virgins wanted in marriage by 100 colonists on a tropical island. The plot is complicated by numerous cross-amours, but the bridal ship finally arrives, and the colonists are finally able to gratify their marital impulses.

C'est la guerre (That's War). Opera in one act by Emil Petrovics, to the verisimilitudinous story of a Hungarian deserter given refuge by a friend in Budapest in 1944 who is betrayed to the Nazis by her landlady, avenging the loss of her two sons in battle and who is executed with his host, whose wife, who has in the meantime fallen in love with him, defenestrates herself as the Nazi officer observes in French, "C'est la guerre." It was first performed in concert form on Budapest Radio on Aug. 17, 1961. Its first stage performance followed in Budapest on March 11, 1962.

Chanson de Roland, La. Lyric opera in three acts by Henri Martelli, to his own libretto after the medieval French epic, first produced in Paris on April 13, 1967.

Chaos. Opera by Michael Gordon, to a futuristic libretto by Matthew Maguire dealing with the moral dilemma of two rogue scientists whose discoveries into the realm of chaos threaten their jobs and their lives, with Marie and Pierre Curie making appearances as helpful navigators in the Chaos Zone, first staged in New York on Oct. 7, 1998.

Chérubin. Comic opera in three acts by Jules Massenet to a libretto by Henri Cain, depicting the lighthearted adventures of a youthful amorist who makes love in quick succession to an ingenue, a countess, a baroness, and a famous Spanish ballerina. The work, with an allusive quotation from Mozart's *Don Giovanni* in the finale, was first performed in Monte Carlo on Feb. 14, 1905.

Cheval de bronze, Le (The Bronze Horse). Opera in three acts by Daniel-Françios-Esprit Auber, to a text by Eugène Scribe, set, implausibly, in a Chinese village and on the planet Venus, and wherein a spell is cast, turning three rogues (Yannko, Tao-chin, and Prince Tang-yang) into wooden pagodas after they've disclosed the secrets of Venus (where they rode on a magical bronze horse, hence the title), a happy ending ensuing when the spell is broken by Yanko's betrothed, first produced in Paris on March 28, 1835.

Childhood Miracle, A. Opera in one act by Ned Rorem, to a libretto based on Hawthorne's story "The Snow Image" about the gentle trials of two sisters approaching adolescence, set to music in a simple tonal idiom adorned with the mildest of dissonances, first staged in New York on May 10, 1955.

Chlopi (The Peasants). Opera by Witold Rudziński, depicting the heroic futility of the national Polish insurrection of 1863 against the Russians, first staged in Warsaw on June 30, 1974.

Christophe Colomb (Christopher Columbus). Opera in two parts (27 scenes) by Darius Milhaud, to a Paul Claudel text, first performed in a German version in Berlin on May 5, 1930. There are elements of Greek drama (in the moralistic use of a suasive chorus), mystery play (in allegorical parables), music drama (in the use of identifying through non-Wagnerian musical phrases), surrealistic projection (Columbus conversing with his second self), modern realism (through insertion of cinematic sequences), and symbolistic allusions (doves are released on the stage, the name of Columbus in French being almost identical with *colombe*, a dove).

Christopher Sly. Comic opera by Dominick Argento, to a libretto based on a scene from Shakespeare's play *The Taming of the Shrew*, first produced in Minneapolis on May 31, 1963.

Cid, Le. Opera in four acts by Jules Massenet, to a text by Adolphe D'Ennery, Louis Gallet, and Édourod Blau after Corneille's drama (1637), set in 12th-century Spain and recounting the fine and not so fine deeds of Don Rodrigue, who is celebrated in the end as a master warrior ("Le Cid") and also forgiven by his loving and now politically powerful Chimène. The work was first performed in Paris on Nov. 30, 1885.

Ciro in Babilonia. Opera in two acts by Gioacchino Rossini, to a text by Francesco Aventi in which the king of Persia, Ciro, valiantly rescues his wife, Amaria, and their son from the clutches of Baldassare, king of Babylon, the lives of three Persian captives spared as well when the Persian army finally defeats Babylon. The work was first performed in Ferrara on March 14, 1812.

Cladia Legare. Opera by Robert Ward, his fourth, to a libretto dealing with an American counterpart of Ibsen's independent woman Hedda Gabler, with the action taking place in Charleston, South Carolina, shortly after the Civil War, first staged in St. Paul, Minnesota, on April 14, 1978.

Clemenza di Tito, La (The Clemency of Titus). Opera seria in two acts by Wolfgang Amadeus Mozart, his last, first staged in Prague on Sept. 6, 1791. The libretto by Caterino Mazzolà after Pietro Metastasio's text for Antonio Caldara's opera of the same name (1734) deals with the generous clemency granted by the Roman emperor Titus to those who plotted against him. The libretto was set to music by other composers, before and after Mozart.

Cléopâtre. Opera ("drame passionel") in four acts by Jules Massenet, his last, to a libretto introducing a historically undocumented emancipated Greek slave as Cleopatra's last lover, produced posthumously in Monte Carlo on Feb. 23, 1914.

Clitennestra. Music drama by Ildebrando Pizzetti, to a libretto depicting the classic tragedy of Clytemnestra, from her murder of Agamemnon to her death at the hands of her own children, Electra and Orestes, first produced at Milan's La Scala on March 1, 1965.

Cloches de Corneville, Les (The Bells of Corneville). Opera in three acts by Robert Planquette, his most popular, to a text by Clariville and Gabet concerning Henri, descendant of the duke of Corneville, whose rightful place, to be confirmed by the ringing of the castle bells upon his approach, is thwarted through operatic mishaps, the castle falling into the hands of a servant girl who, in the end, turns out to be Germaine, niece of a wealthy tenant, and who, in the end, loves Henri, who once saved her life. The work was first performed in Paris on April 19, 1877, and had a run of some 461 performances.

Combattimento di Tancredi e Clorinda, Il. Dramatic "madrigal of war" by Claudio Monteverdi, first performed in Venice in 1624, based on the episode from Tasso's *Gerusalemme liberata.* Tancredi is a Christian knight in the first Crusade in the 11th century. Clorinda, whom he loves, is a non-Christian Persian maid who combats the Crusaders. Tancredi mortally wounds her during an encounter near Jerusalem and recognizes her only when he lifts the visor of her armor. He then laments his and her fate. The work is historically important because in it Monteverdi introduces a type of composition that he called *stile concitato* (agitated style), set in the meter of two rapid beats. It was first published in a collection called *Madrigali guerrieri ed amorosi* (Madrigals of War and Love).

Comédie, La. "Antiopera" by Roman Haubenstock-Ramati, scored for one male and two female speech-singers and three percussionists, to a text by Samuel Beckett, performed for the first time in St. Paul de Vence in Alpes-Maritimes, France, on July 21, 1969.

Comte Ory, Le (Count Ory). Comic opera in two acts by Gioacchino Rossini, first produced in Paris on Aug. 20, 1828, the first of Rossini's two operas to French texts. The libretto by Eugène Scribe and Charles-Gaspord Delestre-Poirson is set about the year 1200 and deals with a licentious count's attempt to seduce a woman whose husband is out on a Crusade.

Conchita. Opera in four acts (six scenes) by Riccardo Zandonai, to a libretto by Maurizio Vaucaire and supplemented by Carlo Zangarini based on Pierre Louÿ's *La femme et le pantin* in which a Carmen-like girl, employed in a Seville cigar factory, taunts her wealthy admirer into a rage of unconsummated passion. It was first performed in Milan on Oct. 14, 1911.

Confidence Man, The. Opera by George Rochberg, based on Hermann Melville's satiric novel, produced for the first time at the Santa Fe Opera on July 31, 1982.

Constantine Palaeologus. Opera by Manolis Kalomiris, his last, to a libretto dealing with the emperor of Byzantium whose defeat by the Turks in 1453 marked the end of the eastern empire, first posthumously produced in Athens on Aug. 12, 1962.

Consul, The. Opera in three acts by Gian Carlo Menotti, to his own libretto, first produced in Philadelphia on March 1, 1950, then running for 269 performance on Broadway and winning the N.Y. Drama Critics' award and the Pulitzer Prize for music. This is Menotti's most dramatically powerful work, focused on the desperate effort of a couple to escape from an unidentified Fascist country. They are doomed when the Consul (who never appears on stage) of an unnamed great transoceanic nation refuses to grant their visa.

Contes d'Hoffmann, Les. Opera in three acts with prologue and epilogue by Jacques Offenbach, to a libretto by Jules Barbier and Michel Carré based on stories by the German fabulist. E. T. A. Hoffmann, himself the focus of the opera, telling the stories of his three great loves: a lithe mechanical puppet, a blithe Venetian courtesan, and a tubercular German maiden. In an ideal production not only does Hoffmann appear throughout, but the characters representing the forces of evil, the servant, and in some productions the three beloveds are each acted by one singer. Offenbach died before completing the score, which was finished by Guiraud for its posthumous premiere in Paris on Feb. 10, 1881. The Venice act contains the famous Barcarolle.

Coq d'or, Le (The Golden Cockerel). Opera in three acts by Nikolai Rimsky-Korsakov, his last, produced posthumously in Moscow on Oct. 7, 1909. The libretto is drawn from a fairy tale by Pushkin (1834) involving an indolent czar, his falsetto-singing (but virile) astrologer, the astrologer's magical bird that warns the czar of invading armies, and the exotic queen the two men fight over. The queen sings a famous coloratura hymn to the sun. After the czar angrily murders the astrologer, he is pecked to death. The czarist censor prescribed some modifications in the text to soften the resemblance between the bumbling ruler of the fairy tale and the bungling reigning Czar Nicolas II, who had just lost a war with Japan. Rimsky-Korsakov refused to submit, and the opera was not performed during his lifetime.

Corregidor, Der (The Magistrate). Opera in four acts by Hugo Wolf, to a text by Rosa Mayreder after Alarcón's story *El sombrero de tres picos* (1874), a comedy about intentional and unintentional spouse swapping. A lecherous magistrate, Don Eugenio de Zuniga, hungers for Frasquita, the wife of Lukis, an honest miller. She pretends to encourage him; but then mocks him. Lukas later believes his wife to have betrayed him, but after many plot twists, all's made well when Frasquita's innocence is revealed and she is happily reunited with Lukas. It was first performed in Mannheim on June 7, 1896, but rarely performed since.

Corsaro, Il (The Corsain). Opera in three acts by Giuseppe Verdi, to a text by Francesco Piave after Byron's poem "The Corsair" (1813), first produced in Trieste on Oct. 25, 1848. The story concerns Gulnara, the Pasha Seid's favorite concubine, who is in love with the pirate chieftain Corrado. After she kills the pasha and the couple flee, they soon find themselves back on the Aegean island from whence they came when they learn that Corrado's former lover, Medora, has taken poison and is dying. Gulnara confesses her love for Corrado to Medora, Medora dies in Corrado's arm, and the inconsolable Corrado throws himself into the sea.

Cosa rara, Una (A Rose Thing). Opera in two acts by Martín y Soler, to a libretto by Lorenzo Da Ponte after Luiz Vélez de Guevara's story *La luna della sierra,* first performed in Vienna on Nov. 17, 1786. The score reflects the contemporaneous fascination with exotic subjects. Its libretto is drawn from the history of the Ottoman empire. The opera was probably the first to include a Viennese waltz. Another distinction is the use of the mandolin as an accompanying instrument in a serenade. The opera was so popular that Mozart quoted an aria from the supper scene in *Don Giovanni.*

Così fan tutte (Women Are Like That). Opera in two acts by Wolfgang Amadeus Mozart, first produced in Vienna on Jan. 26, 1790. Lorenzo Da Ponte's original libretto (probably after Ariosto's *Orlando furioso,* 1516) treats the testing of romantic fidelity through two disguised soldiers, Ferrando and Guglielmo, pursuing each other's sweethearts, Fiordiligi and Donatella. Earlier understood as a farce, the opera is now recognized as a masterpiece that explores the darker sides of the human psyche, amid sublime music.

Cradle Will Rock, The. Proletarian opera in two acts by Marc Blitzstein, to his own libretto picturing class warfare between the rapacious Mr. Mister and a group of workers trying to organize a union in Steeltown, U.S.A., given its first performance in New York on June 16, 1937, in a makeshift production without scenery or costumes, with Blitzstein himself at the piano and singers stationed in the hall to circumvent the ban imposed by the Federal Theater, a branch of the Works Progress Administration, on account of the radical nature of the play. It was finally presented as an opera in a Broadway theater in N.Y. on Dec. 27, 1947, and later by the N.Y. City Opera on Feb. 11, 1960.

Crispino e la comare (Crispino and the Fairy). Opera in four acts by Federico and Luigi Ricci, to a libretto by Piave set in 17th-century Venice in which a poor cobbler gains great wealth and fame due to healing powers given to him by a fairy but whose arrogance leads the fairy to change into Death, who's now come to claim him. Happiness is ensured when the cobbler repents of his sins. The opera was first performed in Venice on Feb. 28, 1850.

Crociato in Egitto, Il (The Crusader in Egypt). Opera in two acts by Giacomo Meyerbeer, to a libretto by Gaetano Rossi, first performed in Venice on March 7, 1824. Armando d'Orville, a knight of Rhodes, presumed dead in Egypt during the 6th crusade, resurfaces as Elmireno, confidant of the sultan Aladino. He loves Aladino's daughter, Palmide, and converts her to Christianity, but when his true identity is revealed, he and all other captured Christians are sentenced to die. The sultan has a soft spot for Elmireno, however, who once saved his life, and in the end the couple is united. A peace treaty is also signed.

Crook, The. Comic opera in two acts by Menahem Avidom, the first musical satire on the government of Israel, wherein its fiscal troubles lead to the promulgation of a decree forbidding the population to breathe after the expiration of the deadline for payment of taxes, first staged in Tel Aviv on April 22, 1967.

Cuba's Daughter. Opera by Konstantin Listov, to a libretto depicting in realistically romantic terms the heroic Angela Alonso, Cuban girl guerrilla, who fought in the ranks of Fidel Castro's insurrectionary forces in 1958 and who gave poison to her beloved to save him from torture after he was captured by police, first performed in Voronezh on June 25, 1962.

Cunning Little Vixen, The (Příhody Lišky Bystroušky). Opera in three acts by Leoš Janáček, to a libretto by the composer after Rudolf Těsnohlídek's text for drawings by Stanislav Lolek, first produced in Brno on Nov. 6, 1924. Janáček depicts the natural world anthropomorphically so as to make social commentary in a story of a clever vixen who escapes captivity and raises a family.

Curioso Indiscreto, Il. Opera by Pasquale Anfossi, first performed in Rome in 1777. The libretto is typical of a multitude of operas. A suspicious suitor, desiring to test his fiancée's loyalty, asks a friend to pay court to her. The two promptly fall in love, defeating the suitor's intention. The opera survives in music history because Mozart wrote two special arias to be inserted into the Vienna performancein 1783.

Curlew River. Church parable in one act by Benjamin Britten, first performed at the Aldeburgh Festival on June 12, 1964. The libretto by William Plomen is derived from a Japanese Noh play in which a mother searches for her son who was taken away from her on the Curlew River. He is dead, but his grave becomes an object of pilgrimage. The opening and closing passages are in Latin.

Cyrano de Bergerac. Opera in four acts by Franco Alfano, to a libretto by Henri Cain after Rostand's drama (1897) dealing with the poet's vicarious romance as an epistolary alter ego of an untutored but sexually balanced army soldier, first performed in Rome on Jan. 22, 1936.

D

Dafne. Opera by Jacopo Peri, first presented in 1598, to a libretto by Ottavio Rinuccini, considered the first opera. The music is lost. It was revised and enlarged by Marco da Gagliano in 1608, using basically the same libretto, and presented in Mantua. It tells of the exploits of Apollo as he slays a dragon, and his subsequent unsuccessful pursuit of Daphne, a follower of the virgin goddess Diana.

Daibutsu-Kaigen (The Great Image of Buddha). Opera in three acts by Osamu Shimizu, relating the dramatic events attendant upon the building of the great copper statue of Buddha in A.D. 747 in a Japanese village, first staged in Nissei on Oct. 2, 1970.

Dalibor. Opera in three acts by Bedřich Smetana, to a libretto by Josef Wenzig after the legend translated from German into Czech by Ervín Špindler, first performed in Prague on May 16, 1868. Dalibor is in prison for rebelling against the king of Bohemia. A sister of the Burgrave of Prague, in love with him and determined to rescue him, manages to pass him a handsaw and a violin. When he begins to play as a signal of his readiness to flee, she joins him. There are three variants of the finale, all tragic: (1) both Dalibor and the girl are killed trying to escape; (2) the girl is slain and Dalibor commits suicide over her body; and (3) she is killed and Dalibor is led to execution.

Dame blanche, La (The White Lady). Opera in three acts by Adrien Boieldieu, to a text by Eugène Scribe after Sir Walter Scott's novels *The Monastery* and *Guy Mannering*, first produced in Paris on Dec. 10, 1825 and reaching 1,000 performances by 1862. George Brown, an English officer, purchases a castle on the advice of Anna, who reveals the secret of the castle: treasure hidden in the statue of the White Lady. George turns out to be the rightful heir in any case, and when Anna is unveiled in the statue's place, the two are happily reunited.

Damnation de Faust, La. Opera by Hector Berlioz, based on part 1 of Johann von Goethe's *Faust*, first performed in Paris in concert form on Dec. 6, 1846, and not staged until Feb. 18, 1893, in Monte Carlo.. The reinterpretation of Goethe (found also in Gounod's opera) in which Marguerite goes to Heaven and Faust is sent straight to hell is considered blasphemous by certain German cultural patriots.

Danaïdes, Les. Opera in five acts by Antonio Salieri, to a libretto by F. L. G. Leblanc Roullet and L. T. Tschudi set in Greece in mythological times in which Hypermnestra, the only one of Danaus's 50 daughters to disregard her father's order to kill her husband (like the others, a son of Aegyptus), flees to safety in Memphis as Danaus's palace is struck by lightning and Danaus himself is chained to a rock, tortured for eternity by a vulture, the other Danaïdes also tormented, by both evil spirits and fire. The opera was first performed in Paris on April 26, 1784.

Dantons Tod (Danton's Death). Opera in two parts by Gottfried von Einem, to a text by the composer and Boris Blacher after Georg Büchner's drama (1835), first performed in Salzburg on Aug. 6, 1947. The opera is based on the life and death of a prime mover of the French Revolution. The "Marseillaise" and other revolutionary songs are quoted.

Daphne. Opera in one act by Richard Strauss, to a text by Joseph Gregor after the classical legend about Daphne's metamorphosis into a laurel tree (Daphne means laurel in Greek) to escape Apollo's amorous pursuit and ending with Daphne's voice heard from the branches of a tree, first performed in Dresden on Oct. 15, 1938.

Dardanus. Tragic opera in five acts by Jean-Philippe Rameau, to a text by Charles-Antoine Le Clerc de la Brunère about a son of Jupiter who wins over a beloved princess of Phrygia and gets close to Venus as well, first performed in Paris on Nov. 19, 1739.

Darkened City, The. Opera in three acts by Bernhard Heiden, his only opera to a libretto dealing with the year of the plague, 1319, in East Anglia, during which a lethargic victim, Lazarus, rises from the mass of presumed cadavers, frightening the remaining populace and precipitating ecclesiastical hysteria, first performed by the Indiana University Opera Theater in Bloomington, on Feb. 23, 1963.

David. Opera in five acts by Darius Milhaud, commemorating the city of Jerusalem and its greatest king. The libretto is by Lulel; the first performance, in a concert version, in Hebrew, given in Jerusalem on June 1, 1954, to celebrate the 3,000th anniversary of its founding. A chorus comments on the event from the historical point of view.

Dawns Are Quiet Here, The. Opera by Kirill Molchanov, describing in a series of lachrymogenic scenes the horrors of the Nazi invasion of Russia, contrasted with the heroic patriotic repulse, replete with folk-like tunes and rousing military marches in the finest tradition of Socialist Realism, first staged at the Bolshoi Theater in Moscow on April 11, 1973.

Death in the Family, A. Opera by William Mayer, to a libretto based on the emotionally moving semiautobiographical 1958 Pulitzer Prize-winning novel by James Agree, first staged in Minneapolis on March 11, 1983.

Death in Venice. Opera in two acts by Benjamin Britten, to a libretto by Myfanwy Piper after the novella by Thomas Mann (1912), first performed in Aldeburgh on June 16, 1973, and written for Peter Pears as an aging German writer, Gustav Aschenbach (brook of ashes), who goes to Venice in search of emotional experience. There he admires the Platonic purity and Apollonian beauty of an adolescent Polish boy on vacation with his family. A cholera epidemic breaks out, and Aschenbach listlessly stays on after the boy's departure, falling victim to the dreaded disease.

Death of Klinghoffer, The. Opera in two acts by John Adams, to Alice Goodman's libretto recounting, in postmodern fashion, the murder of the wheelchair-bound American Leon Klinghoffer aboard the kidnapped Italian cruise ship *Achille Lauro* in the Mediterranean in 1985. With direction by Robert Wilson and choreography by Mark Morris, the opera was staged for the first time in Brussels on March 19, 1991.

Deborah e Jaële. Opera in three acts by Pizzetti, constituting the first part of an operatic trilogy (the second and third are *Fra Gherardo* and *Lo Straniero*), written (by the composer) to a biblical story dealing with a patriotic maiden who seduces the hostile chieftain to ruin him but who learns to love him unto death, first produced in Milan on Dec. 16, 1922.

Decembrists, The. Opera in four acts by Shaporin, to a libretto by Vsevolod Rozhdestvensky using verses by Tolstoy and based on events of the December 1825 uprising, first produced in Moscow on June 20, 1953.

Decision, The. Opera in three acts by Thea Musgrave, to a libretto by Maurice Lindsay based on an actual case of a miner entombed for 23 days following a cave-in of rock in Scotland in 1835 (he died three days later), which so shocked the stolid British establishment that a government decision was made to ameliorate the conditions of mine workers and to prohibit the employment of women and children in the Scottish mines. The work was performed for the first time in London on Nov. 30, 1967.

Deidamia. Opera by George Frideric Handel, first produced in London on Jan. 10, 1741, to an Italian libretto, his last opera, and its complete failure made him turn toward oratorio, a felicitous development for Handel and for music. *Deidamia* was revived in London in English more than 200 years after its original production, with a new appreciation. The libretto is taken from Homer. Deidamia was a companion of Achilles who bore him a son.

Demetrio. Opera in three acts by Johann Adolf Hasse, to a libretto by Pietro Metastasio revelatory of the true identity of Demetrio as the son of the exiled king of Syria and his rightful repossession of his father's throne and marriage to Cleonice, daughter of the late usurper Alessandro, who sat temporarily upon it. The opera was first performed in Venice in Jan. 1732 and subsequently revised as *Cleonice* (Vienna, 1734).

Demofoonte. Opera in three acts by Niccolò Jommelli, to a libretto by Pietro Metastasio in which Demophoön, king of Chersonnesus, seeks to end the annual practice of sacrificing a virgin to appease the gods, sparing, at the last minute, both his son and his son's wife, first performed in Padua in 1743, Milan (1753), Stuttgart (1764), and finally Naples.

Demon, The. Opera in three acts by Anton Rubinstein, first produced in St. Petersburg on Jan. 13–25, 1875, to a libretto by Pavel Viskovatov extracted from a romantic poem by Lermontov (1839), now rarely performed outside Russia. Tamara, a beautiful Caucasian princess, is engaged to a brave nobleman who unfortunately perishes, killed by the Demon, who declares his love for her. The Demon pursues her and begs her for a kiss that would redeem his formerly angelic soul. She yields, but his demoniacally virile kiss is lethal, and she dies, though her soul is redeemed, and the Demon is cheated of his redemption.

Dennis Cleveland. The first-ever "talk-show" opera, by Mikel Rouse, the second in a trilogy framed by *Failing Kansas* and *The End of Cinematics*, first performed in New York on Oct. 29, 1996. The idea is inspired and the work divine, capturing the essence of that most banal and bizarre of American pastimes—the TV talk show—while marrying the absolute best of both pop and classical music worlds. The work mimics the form of the talk show, with the obsequious host moving freely among performers seated both on the stage and in the audience, all the while being under the watchful eye of television monitors placed strategically about. Despite its popular theme, this is a deadly serious work, inspired by John Ralston Saul's brilliant 1992 study of the tyranny of reason in the late 20th century, *Voltaire's Bastards*.

Deseret. Television opera by Leonard Kastle, based on a romanticized episode in the life of Brigham Young, founder of the Mormon colony in the Utah desert called Deseret, dealing with his magnanimous surrender of his 25th bride-to-be to a young Union Army officer whom she loves, first broadcast by NBC Television in New York on Jan. 11, 1961.

Deux journées, Les (The Two Days). Opera in three acts by Luigi Cherubini, to a libretto by Jean-Nicolas Bouilly concerning Count Armand and his wife, Constance's, escape from imprisonment, first by being successfully hidden in the house of an old water seller, then by being successfully smuggled into a neighboring village in a water barrel. The work was first produced in Paris on Jan. 16, 1800. It was formerly known in England as *The Water Carrier*.

Devil and Daniel Webster, The. Opera in one act by Douglas Moore, to a libretto by the composer after Stephen Vincent Benét's story (1937) in which the American statesman uses his forensic skills to free a poor artisan from a contract with the devil, first produced on Broadway on May 18, 1939.

Devil and Kate, The (Čert a Káča). Opera in three acts by Antonín Dvořák, to a libretto by Adolf Wenig after the folktale included in Božena Němcová's *Fairy Tales* (1845), first produced in the Czech language in Prague on Nov. 23, 1899. Kate, a middle-aged, garrulous woman, vows to dance with the devil himself if she cannot find a partner at a country fair. The devil obligingly materializes and carries her off to hell, but Kate talks so much that the devil gets a headache and sends her back to earth.

Devils of Loudun, The (Diably z Loudun). Opera in three acts by Krzysztot Penderecki, his first, to a libretto by the composer after John Whiting's drama *The Devils* (1961) based on Aldous Huxley's historical study *The Devils of Loudun* (1952), first produced in Hamburg on June 20, 1969. The story is after an actual event in Loudun, France, in 1634, wherein a handsome and radical lay cleric was accused by hysterical nuns of being a sexual incubus, disturbing their dreams. He was eventually burned at the stake.

Devil's Wall, The (Čertova stčna). Opera in three acts by Bedřich Smetana, to a libretto by Eliška Krásnohorská, first produced in Prague on Oct. 29, 1882. A 13th-century Bohemian ruler, Vok, is convinced by the devil to enter a monastery so as to prohibit his marriage to Hedvika. Hedvika follows him, much to the devil's annoyance, who then attempts to drown the monastery by building a dam. The monastery is saved by the Abbot Beneš, who miraculously collapses the wall with the sign of the cross. The devil is banished, and Vok and Hedvika are free to wed.

Devin du Village, The (The Village Soothsayer). Opera in one act by Jean-Jacques Rousseau, first produced in Fontainebleau on Oct. 18, 1752. In Rousseau's libretto, a village girl suspects her sweetheart of infidelity. She consults a wise friend who advises her to pretend she is in love with another. The stratagem works, and the couple is reunited. The unpretentious score is important historically because it breaks away from the French tradition of mythological grand opera and presents theatrical music as part of common human experience.

Dialogues de Carmélites, Les. Opera in three acts by Francis Poulenc, to his own libretto after Georges Bernanos's play recalling the historical martyrdom of Carmelite nuns during the French Revolution, first produced at Milan's La Scala on Jan. 26, 1957.

Diamonts de la couronne, Les (The Crown of Diamonds). Opera in three acts by Daniel-Franççois-Esprit Auber, to a libretto by Eugéne Scribe and Vernoy de Saint-Georges in which Theophila, heiress to the crown of Portugal, plans to forge her own jewels in an effort to pay off her many debts. When word gets out that the gems have been stolen, she is protected by Don Enriquez, whom she earlier rescued from the band of forgers. When her true identity is disclosed, she chooses him for her husband. The work was first performed in Paris on March 6, 1841.

Diavolo in giardino, Il. "Historical pastoral comedy" in three acts by Franco Mannino, to a libretto centered on the famous swindle of a diamond necklace at the court of Marie Antoinette in Versailles, with the inclusion in the score of some popular airs of the time, produced first in Palermo on Feb. 28, 1963.

Dido and Aeneas. Opera in prologue and three acts by Henry Purcell, to a libretto by Nahum Tate after Book 4 of Vergil's *Aeneid* dealing with the love of Dido, queen of Carthage, for the Trojan hero Aeneas, and her self-immolation when he abandons her. It may have been first performed in Chelsea, London, at Josias Priest's School for Young Gentlewomen in the spring of 1689. "When I am laid in earth" is the opera's best-known piece. About 60 composers of many nations have written operas on the same subject.

Die Entführung aus dem Serail (The Abduction from the Seraglio). Opera in three acts by Wolfgang Amadeus Mozart, to a libretto by Christoph Friedrich Bretznen, adapted by Gottlieb Stephanie the Younger, first performed in Vienna on July 16, 1782. A young woman is captured by a Turkish pasha. A youth in love with her tries to rescue her, but his attempt is foiled by the wily pasha. Eventually, all is made well when the pasha yields in the finale to a sudden magnanimous impulse and lets her go with her lover. Apart from the treasure of Mozartean melodies, the score stylizes "Turkish" tunes and rhythms—movements *alla turca* in slightly syncopated $\frac{2}{4}$ time—with added exotic percussion.

Dimitrj. Opera by Antonín Dvořák, based on the historical life of the false czar (reigned 1603–06) who succeeded the Godunovs, first performed in Prague on Oct. 8, 1882. Here the protagonist has come to believe in his own royalty, and his wife, Marina, reminds him that he is a fugitive monk. He is eventually slain by one of his followers.

Dinorah (ou Le pardon de Ploërmel) (The Pligrimmage of Ploermel). Opera in three acts by Giacomo Meyerbeer, to a libretto by Jules Barbier and Michel Carré, first produced in Paris on April 4, 1859. As a young shepherd takes his bride to their wedding, a local warlock tells him that he can find a buried treasure if he lives for one year in total solitude. His bride, shaken by his sudden disappearance, goes mad. A year passes, and the shepherd has discovered no treasure. He meets his beloved at the dam just as a bolt of lightning destroys it and threatens her. He leaps to her rescue, and she immediately recovers her reason. He realizes that the treasure he sought was she. They finally repair to Ploërmel for their delayed wedding, and he is pardoned for his sin of avarice. The opera enjoyed considerable success for a time, thanks mainly to the effective coloratura part for the heroine, "Ombre légerè qui suis mes pas."

Disappointment, or the Force of Credulity, The. Ballad opera by Andrew Barton, composed in 1767 for the opening of a theater in Philadelphia but canceled by the censors because the text contained satirical references to important colonial officials. The libretto deals with a group of practical jokers who persuade greedy Philadelphians to dig for buried treasure on the banks of the Delaware River. The tunes, popular in colonial times, include an early version of "Yankee Doodle." A reconstructed score, with a specially composed overture, three instrumental interludes, and Baroque orchestration by Samuel Adler, was posthumously produced at the Library of Congress in Washington, D.C., on Oct. 29, 1976, as part of the U.S. bicentennial celebration.

Djamileh. Opera in one act by Georges Bizet, to a libretto by Louis Gallet after Alfred de Musset's poem *Namouna* (1832), set in a 19th-century palace in Cairo and relating the ruse of a mistress to win her lover's heart, first performed in Paris on May 22, 1872.

Dnevnik jednog ludaka (Diary of a Fool). Television opera by Stanoljo Rajičič, to his own libretto after Gogol's tale, first produced on Belgrade Television on April 4, 1981.

Docteur Miracle, Le. Operetta in one act by Georges Bizet, to a libretto by Léon Battu and Ludovic Halévy, first produced in Paris on April 9, 1857, when the composer was only 18 years old. The plot employs an old device: the lover of the town mayor's young daughter introduces himself as a doctor who promises to cure the mayor's gout provided he be allowed to marry the daughter. The mayor signs the necessary contract and then is told the painful truth—the alleged cure is a hoax. Lecocq wrote an operetta on the same subject, competing for a prize that he won jointly with Bizet.

Doctor Faustus Lights the Lights. Opera by David Ahlstrom, to words by Gertrude Stein, first performed in San Francisco on Sept. 17, 1982.

Doktor Faust. Opera in two prologues, interlude, and three scenes by Ferruccio Busoni, left incomplete and performed posthumously, with an ending by Busoni's pupil Philipp Jarnach, in Dresden on May 21, 1925. The composer's libretto is derived from the same medieval sources from which Goethe derived his *Faust,* but here the eponymous character appears as a magician and an artist.

Doktor und Apotheker. Opera in two acts by Carl Ditters von Dittersdorf, to a libretto by Gottlieb Stephanie after a French drama *L'apothicaire de Murcie,* first performed in Vienna on July 11, 1786. A pharmacist's daughter loves the son of a local doctor, but her father wants her to marry a captain of the Austrian army. The libretto resorts to the time-honored ploy of having a marriage contract drawn by a false notary, while the lover puts on a captain's uniform to fool the old man. A happy ending is vouchsafed to all except the pharmacist and the real captain.

Domino noir, Le (The Black Domino). Opera in three acts by Daniel-François-Esprit Auber, to a libretto by Eugéne Scribe relating the escapades of two friends, Horatio and Juliano, who hope to catch a glimpse of a beautiful woman, Angela, who mysteriously appears at the queen's annual Christmas party dressed in a black domino. Angela chooses Horatio as a husband, and also comes into a large inheritance. The work was first performed in Paris on Dec. 2, 1837, with more than 1,200 performances by 1909.

Donauweibchen, Das (The Nixie of the Danube). Opera in three acts by Ferdinand Kauer, his most popular and indeed one of the most popular of all operas in the first half of the 19th century throughout both central and eastern Europe with its romantic elements of love and mysterious apparitions, to a libretto by K. F. Hensler, first performed in Vienna on Jan. 11, 1798.

Don Carlos. Opera in five acts by Giuseppe Verdi, first produced in Paris on March 11, 1867, with libretto by Joseph Méry and Camille Du Locle after Schiller's drama (1787). The opera was revised to four acts for La Scala, Milan, Jan. 10, 1884. Don Carlos, heir to the Spanish throne, is in love with Elisabeth de Valois, but his father, King Philip II, decides to marry her himself. Young Don Carlos continues his clandestine trysts with his stepmother, both appropriately disguised. They are eventually found out, and the sinister Grand Inquisitor directs the king to put his son to death. The final confrontation takes place at the tomb of Philip's father Emperor Charles V, but at the crucial moment the late emperor seems to emerge from behind the tomb, frightening everyone. Don Carlos takes advantage of the confusion and flees. Originally regarded as a confusing story, the opera is now seen as one of Verdi's masterpieces.

Don Giovanni. Wolfgang Amadeus Mozart's greatest opera, in two acts, described as a *dramma giocoso*, although the subject is anything but merry. The libretto, in Italian, is by Lorenzo Da Ponte (his second for Mozart), after the Don Juan legend. The alternative title was *Il Dissoluto Punito* (The Dissolute One Punished). It was first produced on Oct. 29, 1787, in Prague, a city that responded more positively to Mozart's operas than did Vienna. A Vienna production was announced under the title *La Statua parlante* (the speaking statue). Obviously, the producers intended to sensationalize the attraction. The speaking statue was that of the Commendatore, whom Giovanni slew in a duel and whose daughter he debauched. There are many masquerades, charades, disguises, and mistaken identities. Giovanni's servant, Leporello, in a famous "catalogue aria," ticks off the exact number of Giovanni's conquests in various countries, culminating with *mille e tre* (1,003) seductions in Spain. He offers this information to one of Giovanni's most recent conquests. In an act of supreme effrontery, Giovanni challenges the statue of the slain Commendatore to have supper with him. With trombones sounded ominously in the orchestra, the statue accepts Giovanni's defiant invitation, and in a deep bass voice speaks his determination to carry him to Hell. The remaining protagonists gather in happy disbelief, promising to pursue their lives much as they did before meeting Giovanni.

Don Giovanni. Opera in one act by Gian Francesco Malipiero, after Pushkin's drama *The Stone Guest*, first produced in Naples on Sept. 22, 1963.

Donna del lago, La. Opera in two acts by Gioacchino Rossini, to a libretto by Andrea Tottola based on Sir Walter Scott's poem *The Lady of the Lake* (1810), an Arthurian legend in which the king receives his magic sword (Excalibur) from a woman (Morgan le Fay) who lives on an enchanted island (Avalon). It was first produced in Naples on Oct. 24, 1819.

Donne curiose, Le. Opera in three acts by Ermanno Wolf-Ferrari, to a libretto by Luigi Sugana after Goldoni's play of the same name wherein a bevy of inquisitive Venetian wives, intent upon discovering the agenda of an exclusive men's club where their husbands habitually congregate, enter it by ruse only to find that, contrary to their suspicions, the club is indeed womanless. It was first produced in Munich on Nov. 27, 1903.

Don Pasquale. Comic opera in three acts by Gaetano Donizetti, to a text by Giovanni Ruffini and the composer after Angelo Anelli's libretto for Stefano Pavesi's *Ser Marc'antonio* (1810), first staged in Paris on Jan. 3, 1843. An elder is duped into marrying his nephew's intended. However, her shrewish garrulity convinces Pasquale to give her over to the nephew, complete with a considerable dowry.

Don Perlimplin. Radio opera by Bruno Maderna, after a text by Federico García Lorca, broadcast for the first time over RAI Radio in Rome on Aug. 12, 1962. A middle-aged bachelor is persuaded to marry a young woman.

Don Procopio. Opera in two acts by Georges Bizet, to an Italian libretto by Paul Collin and Paul de Choudens, translated from a libretto by Carlo Cambiaggio, in which the miserly old Don Procopio, promised the hand of the young Bettina in marriage, is convinced to give her up to her beloved Eduardo after intimations from her brother and aunt that she will spend all of his money. The work was first produced in a French version in Monte Carlo on March 10, 1906.

Don Quichotte. Opera in five acts by Jules Massenet, to a libretto by Henri Cain after Jacques le Lorrain's play *Le chavalier de la longue figure* (1904), first produced in Monte Carlo on Feb. 19, 1910. The title role was written for the great Russian bass Fyodor Chaliapin.

Don Rodrigo. Opera in three acts by Alberto Ginastera,

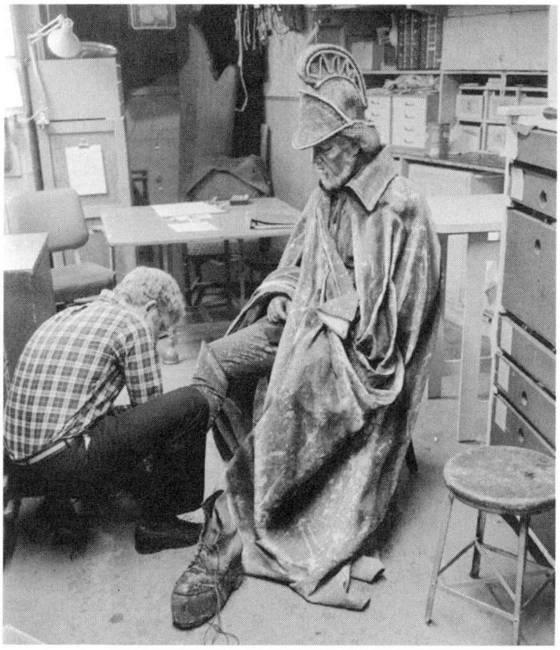

Preparing the Commandant for the final scene
(*Don Giovanni*)

Dennis Cleveland/Photo by Steve Singer

Priest in *Cavalleria rusticana*

Rehearsals for *Lohengrin*

Renata Scotto as La Gioconda

Renato Bruson as Simon Boccanegra

Scene from *Pelléas et Mélisande*

Scene from *Madama Butterfly*

Scene from *The Magic Flute*

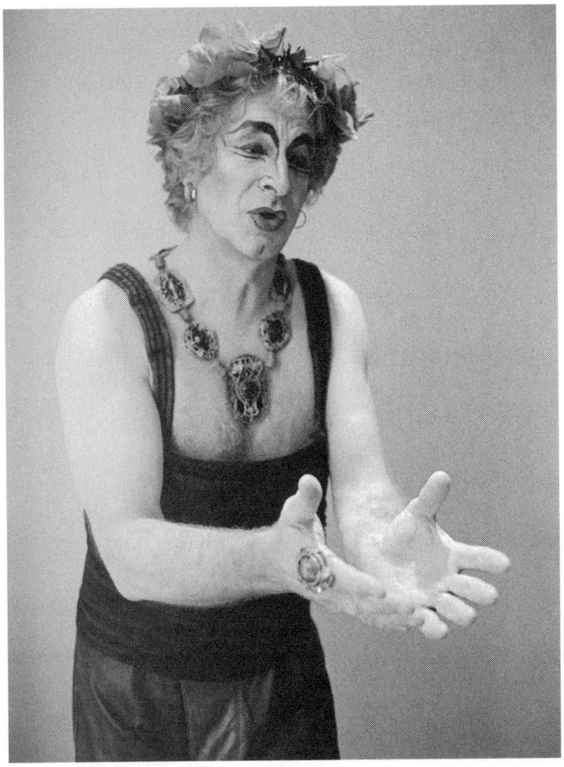

Scene from *Salome*

Sherrill Milnes as Don Carlos in *Ernani*

Scene from *The Flying Dutchman*

Composer Benjamin Britten (l.) with producer Eric Crozier examining set for *Peter Grimes*

Shirley Verrett and Nunzio Todisco in an scene from *Norma*

Eddie Albert in stage makeup for *Turandot*

Dress rehearsal for *Il Prigioniero* with Michael Devlin (l.) as the prisoner

Dress rehearsal for *Billy Budd* (Dale Duesing, left center, in title role)

Crap game in *Porgy and Bess* (Cynthia Haymon, center, as Bess)

Director staging rehearsals for *La Bohème*

Final act of *La Triviata* with Marie McLaughlin as Violetta

Dress rehearsal for *Don Pasquale* with Geraint Evans (r.) in the title role

Giants and Freia (Nancy Gustafson) in *Das Rheingold*

Giuseppi Taddei as Gianni Schicchi

Ashley Putnam in Act II, Scene 2 of *Lucia di Lammermoor*

The Electrification of the Soviet Union with Elizabeth Laurence as Anna Arild

Leonie Rysanek and singers rehearsing *Der Rosenkavalier*

Paul Plishka as Nabucco

Götterdämmerung

to a libretto by Alejandro Casona, first produced in Buenos Aires on July 24, 1964. Don Rodrigo is the Visigoth king in Toledo, Spain, in the 8th century. The governor of Ceuta, whose daughter is raped by Rodrigo in the opening scene, avenges her honor by invading Spain and defeating Rodrigo's army. But the victim forgives Rodrigo, and he dies in her arms.

Don Sanche. Opera in one act by Franz Liszt, his only one and written when he was only 12 years old, to a libretto by Emmanuel Guillaume Théaulon de Lambert and De Rancé after a tale by Florian recounting Don Sanche's attempts to win the love of Princess Elzire and thus gain entrance to a moated castle, access to which is only permitted to those in love and loved. The opera was first produced in Paris on Oct. 17, 1825.

Doppelgängerin, Die. Opera in three acts by Jan Meyerowitz, to a libretto based on Gerhardt Hauptmann's play *Winterballad* telling of murderous violence and preternatural revenge by an alter ego of the victim (hence the title) in 16th-century Sweden, set to music in neomedieval modalities, performed for the first time in Hanover on Jan. 29, 1967.

Dorfbarbier, Der (The Village Begger). Opera in one act by Johann Schenk, his most popular, to a libretto by Josef and Paul Weidmann, first produced in Vienna on Nov. 6, 1796. The tale is of the trickery of a young couple, Suschen and Josef, who wish to be married despite the contrary designs of Suschen's keeper, Lux, who loves Suschen himself. When Josef feigns the taking of poison and names Suschen his beneficiary should she become his wife, Lux consents to the "deathbed" marriage. With this consent, Josef arises, miraculously cured.

Dorian Grey. Opera by Hans Kox, after the novel by Oscar Wilde, in which the portrait of the beauteous English lad painted by one of his admiring friends grows old, while Dorian himself engages in the "love that dares not speak its name." It was first staged in The Hague on March 30, 1974.

Down in the Valley. Folk opera by Kurt Weill, to a libretto by Arnold Sundgaard, first performed at Bloomington, Indiana, School of Music on July 15, 1948. The work is musically centered on the familiar American folk song, telling the tragic tale (in flashbacks) of a young man who is hanged for killing a love rival.

Dreigroschenoper, Die (The Threepenny Opera). Opera in prologue and three acts by Kurt Weill, first produced in Berlin on Aug. 31, 1928, a modern reinterpretation of John Gay's *The Beggar's Opera*, with a new text by Bertolt Brecht, denouncing the social hypocrisy of modern life. The score includes quasi-American fox trots and ragtime. After a happy *deus ex machina* ending, the concluding chorus enjoins the audience to "pursue injustice, but not too much." The production was immensely successful in Germany during the era between the two world wars. *Threepenny Opera*, with an English translation by Blitzstein (1954), was equally popular. Among its many fine songs, the mocking ballad "Mack the Knife" became a perennial favorite in America. Lotte Lenya, Weill's widow, starred in both the German and American premieres.

Drei Pintos, Die. Unfinished comic opera by Carl Maria von Weber, completed and orchestrated by Gustav Mahler, using materials from Weber's other vocal works as well as an interlude composed by Mahler based on themes of the opera. Mahler conducted it for the first time in Leipzig on Jan. 20, 1888. The libretto, by Theodor Hell after Carl Seidel's story *Der Brautkampf* (1819), deals with romantic adventures in Spain in which three pintos (mottled horses) play a part. The opera failed.

Dr. Heidegger's Fountain of Youth. Opera by Jack Beeson, based on the story by Nathaniel Hawthorne, first produced in N.Y. on Nov. 17, 1978.

Duca d'Alba, Il (The Duke of Alba). Opera in four acts by Gaetano Donizetti, to a libretto by Eugéne Scribe. The opera was originally composed for Paris, but not produced. Later, the libretto was revised by Scribe as the text of *Les vêpres siciliennes.* Donizetti's work was recovered in Bergamo in 1875 and completed by Matteo Salvi. Its belated premiere finally took place in Rome on March 22, 1882, nearly 34 years after Donizetti's death.

Due Foscari, I. Opera in three acts by Giuseppe Verdi, to a libretto by Francesco Piave based on Byron's play *The Two Foscari* (1821), first performed in Rome on Nov. 3, 1844. The story recounts a mortal feud between two Venetian families. The two Foscari of the title, father and son, are innocent of suspected murders, but nonetheless die from mental anguish and chagrin.

Due Litiganti, I. Opera in three acts by Giuseppe Sarti, its libretto an altered version of Goldoni's *Le nozze*, first produced in Milan on Sept. 14, 1782. The complete title is *Fra I due litiganti il terzo gode.* The opera was extremely popular in its time. Wolfgang Amadeus Mozart quotes a tune from it in Act II of *Don Giovanni.*

Duenna, The, or The Double Elopement. Opera in three acts by Thomas Linley, father and son, to a libretto by Richard Brinsley Sheridan (1775), first produced in London on Nov. 21, 1775. Although little known, its success was great (even exceeding that of *The Beggar's Opera*), having some 75 performances during its initial run. The libretto, composed of various intersected amours, mistaken identities, and other embroilments of 18th-century Seville, is also the basis of Prokofiev's *Betrothal in a Convent* (1946).

Duenna, or The Double Elopement, The. Opera in three acts by Roberto Gerhard, to his own libretto, first performed in Madrid on Jan. 21, 1992. The text is based on Richard Brinsley Sheridan's libretto for the Linley opera of the same name (1775) and used in Prokofiev's *Betrothal in a Convent* (1946).

During the Storm. Opera in four acts by Tikhon Khrennikov, first produced in Moscow on Oct. 10, 1939, under the title *Brothers.*The action takes places during the decisive phase of agricultural collectivization in Soviet Russia. When an acquisitive and overprosperous kulak treacherously knifes a Bolshevik, young Natasha kills him with a single shot from her trusty rifle. The score introduces, for the first time on the Soviet stage, the character of Lenin in the cast (although he does not sing).

Dybbuk, The (Il Diguk). Opera in prologue and three acts by Lodovico Rocca, to a libretto by R. Simoni after Shelomoh An-Ski's drama (1916), first performed at La Scala, Milan, on March 24, 1934. A rather gruesome story of Chanon, who, through manipulation of the cabala in an effort to win the love of Leah, fails, managing instead to enter her body upon his death. *The Dybbuk* is also the name of an opera by Tamkin, first performed on Oct. 4, 1951, in New York.

E

Edgar. Opera in three acts by Giacomo Puccini, his first full-length work, to a libretto by Ferdinando Fontana after Alfred de Musset's verse drama *La coupe et les lèvres* (1832), first produced at La Scala, Milan, on April 21, 1889. Edgar loves two women, one wild (Tigrana) and one faithful (Fidelia). As Edgar vacillates, Tigrana descends on Fidelia and stabs her to death. The opera lacks distinction, and its rare revivals are in the nature of curiosity to see what kind of music Puccini wrote before *La Bohème.*

Éducation manquée, Une (A Defective Education). Opera in one act by Emmanuel Chabrier, to a libretto by Eugéne Leterrier and Albert Vanloo concerning the sexual inexperience of the count Gontran de Boismassif, who, arriving home with his new bride, Hélène, hasn't the faintest idea how to proceed when a violent storm solves the problem by throwing them into each other's arms. The opera was first performed in Paris on May 1, 1879.

Egisto. Opera in a prologue and three acts by Francessco Cavalli, to a libretto by Giovanni Faustini recounting the struggles of two intertwined couples on the island of Zakynthos during mythological times, Egisto and Clori and Climene and Lidio, first performed in Venice in 1643.

Együtt és egyedül (Together and Alone). Allegorical opera by Mihály, to a libretto in which a perpetual wanderer seeking the location of Dante's Inferno finds it in Hungary under the Nazi-dominated fascistic regime, first performed in Zürich on Nov. 5, 1966.

Einstein. Opera by Paul Dessau, to a Brecht-style libretto in which Einstein laments dodecaphonically that his discoveries resulted in the atomic murder of Hiroshima and Nagasaki and who is actually manhandled by an American military policeman when he resists the attempt by authorities to force him to cooperate in further atomic research and whose colleagues reflect the Manichean polarity of good (communist) and bad (imperialist) states of soul. The opera was first produced in East Berlin on Feb. 16, 1974.

Einstein on the Beach. Opera in four intermissionless acts by Philip Glass, in collaboration with the *enfant terrible* theater director Robert Wilson, involving a surrealistic communion of thematic ingredients and hypnotic repetition of harmonic subjects. It was premiered at the Avignon Festival on July 25, 1976, and subsequently performed throughout Europe. The first American performance was given at the Metropolitan Opera in New York, off regular subscription season, on Nov. 21, 1976, to much acclaim.

Electrification of the Soviet Union, The. Opera by Nigel Osborne, to a libretto by Craig Roine after Boris Pasternak's *The Last Summer*, first mounted in Glyndebourne on Oct. 5, 1987.

Elegy for Young Lovers (Die Elegie für junge Liebende). Chamber opera in three acts by Hans Werner Henze, with an original English libretto by W. H. Auden and Chester Kallman, first performed in Schwetzingen on May 20, 1961, in German translation. The story deals with a poet living in the Swiss Alps who deliberately sends his stepson and his own mistress to the mountains during a raging snowstorm. They die as expected, but their fate gives him the needed inspiration for writing his poem "Elegy for Young Lovers."

Elektra (Electra). Opera in one act by Richard Strauss, to a libretto by Hugo von Hofmannsthal after Sophocles' *Electra,* first produced in Dresden on Jan. 25, 1909. In this work, Strauss reaches greatness. The classical drama of lust and murder, of brother and sister killing their mother to avenge her murder of their father in ancient Greece, is set to a musical score of awesome power.

Eli. Opera in 12 scenes by Walter Steffens, after a story by the Nobel laureate Nelly Sachs dealing with a Jewish boy slain by an ebreocidal Nazi as he plays a tune on his shepherd's pipe in the childish hope of summoning angels from heaven to his aid, first produced in Dortmund on March 5, 1967.

Elisabetta, regina d'Inghilterra (Elizabeth, Queen of England). Opera in two acts by Gioacchino Rossini, to a libretto by Giovanni Schmidt after Carlo Federici's drama (1814) recounting Queen Elizabeth I's harsh actions against Leicester for secretly marrying Mathilde and then refusing to give her up upon the queen's demand, as well as her magnanimous pardoning of them both in the end. The opera was first produced in Naples on Oct. 4, 1815.

Elisir d'amore, L' (The Elixer of Love). Opera in two acts by Gaetano Donizetti, one his most successful, to a libretto by Felice Romani after Eugéne Scribe's libretto for Daniel-François-Esprit Auber's *Le philtre* (1831), first produced in Milan on May 12, 1832. The impecunious nephew of a wealthy man produces an aphrodisiac to charm the girl of his dreams. She rejects him, but he tries again. Opportunely, his uncle dies and he inherits a fortune. The elixir suddenly proves potent as the girl realizes that he is now rich.

Emperor Jones, The. Opera in two acts with a prologue and interlude by Louis Gruenberg, to a libretto after Eugene O'Neill's play (1921) about a former railroad porter who briefly serves as emperor of a West Indian island, first produced at the Metropolitan Opera in New York on Jan. 7, 1933.

Emperor of Ice Cream, The. Music drama by Roger Reynolds, derived from stochastically calculated probabilities of sonic incidence, performed for the first time in New York on March 19, 1965, Schuller conducting.

Enfant et les Sortileges L' (The Child and the Spells). Fantasy opera in two parts by Maurice Ravel, to a libretto by Colette, first produced in Monte Carlo on March 21, 1925. In a dream, broken dishes, mutilated toys, and torn books come to haunt the destructive boy who owns them. There is a duet of meowing cats complaining of ill treatment. When the boy awakens from this nightmare of destruction, he is totally reformed.

English Cat, The. Comic opera by Hans Werner Henze, to a libretto by Edward Bond based on Honoré de Balzac's *Peins de coeur d'une chatte anglaise.* It was performed for the first time in Schwetzingen on June 2, 1983 in German. A story of true love gone wrong among felines.

Equation (x = o), The. Opera in one act by Geoffrey Bush, scored for voices, solo cello, wind ensemble, organ, and percussion, and dealing polyphonically with the incompatibility of war with morality or common sense, first performed in a London church on Jan. 11, 1968.

Ercole amante (Hercules in Love). Opera in prologue and five acts by Francesco Cavalli, to a libretto by Francesco Buti, after Ovid's *Metamorphoses,* in which Diana, representing important royal families, promises Ercole Beauty as his bride if he remains faithful in his chores, with both Ercole and his son Hyllo falling in love with Iole, and ending with each couple properly mated, first produced in Paris on Feb. 7, 1662.

Ernani. Opera in four acts by Giuseppe Verdi, his fifth to a libretto by Francessco Piave after Victor Hugo's drama *Hernani* (1830), first produced in Venice on March 9, 1844. Ernani is a banished scion of the royal house of Aragon. His beloved Elvira is inexorably placed on the apex of a tangled love quadrangle, being loved by Ernani, Silva, her elderly guardian, and the future emperor Charles V. In the end Ernani stabs himself and dies in her arms. The original production of Hugo's play in Paris in 1830 helped give impetus to the Romantic movement in art. But Hugo himself didn't care much for Verdi's opera.

Ero the Joker (Ero s onoga svijeta, literally, Ero from the Other World). Opera in three acts by Jakov Gotovac, to a libretto by Milan Begovič after a Dalmatian folktale wherein a playful revenant causes posthumous mischief in his native village, first performed in Zagreb on Nov. 2, 1935.

Errettung Thebens, Die. Opera in three acts by Rudolf Kelterborn, to his own libretto drawn freely from Aeschylus in which seven princes from Argos assail the seven gates of Thebes, produced in Zürich for the first time on June 23, 1963.

Erwartung (Expectation). Monodrama in one act by Arnold Schoenberg, to a libretto by Marie Pappenheim, first produced in Prague on June 6, 1924. The score has only one singing part, that of a woman who finds the dead body of her faithless lover in a forest and muses (in *Sprechtstimme*) over the circumstances that led to his death.

Esclarmonde. Opera in four acts (eight tableaux) by Jules Massenet, to a libretto by Alfred Blau and Louis de Gramont after a medieval romance, *Partenopeus of Blois,* first performed in Paris on May 14, 1889. Despite her father Phorcas's mandate for her inheritance depending upon her staying away from men, Esclarmonde falls in love with Roland, a French knight. Roland proves heroic, but Esclarmonde is further warned by her father of the dangers of love, and she reluctantly gives him up. When Roland becomes champion of a tournament organized by Phorcas, however, he finally concedes to their seemingly inevitable union.

Esther. Opera in two acts by Hanell, to a libretto in which the non-Aryan animal warmth of a young Jewish girl violinist is used by the Nazi doctors to restore the life of an experimentally frozen Aryan youth, with antifascist love blossoming forth between the two enabling the girl to go to her death in a gas chamber with a renewed hope in the inherent decency of at least one German in a flood of Hitlerian diabolism, first produced at the German State Opera in East Berlin on Oct. 12, 1966.

Étoile, L' (The Star). Opera in three acts by Emmanuel Chabrier, to a libretto by Eugéne Leterrier and Albert Vanloo, first produced in Paris on Nov. 28, 1877. According to the court astrologer, King Ouf's life rests on the life of Lazuli, a peddler in love with his daughter, Princess Laoula, whom the king has chosen for execution and whose demise will magically signal the king's own demise within 24 hours. The king guards the peddler closely, but after Lazuli escapes and survives a shipwreck, the king is so relieved that he finally consents to Lazuli's marriage to Laoula.

Étoile du Nord, L' (The North Star). Opera in three acts by Giacomo Meyerbeer, to a libretto by Eugéne Scribe, first produced in Paris on Feb. 16, 1854. Russia's Peter the Great goes incognito to study carpentry abroad, where he woos a village woman, marries her, and makes her his czarina. The real Peter did study carpentry and shipbuilding incognito in the Netherlands, but the similarity to the opera ends there.

Eugene Onegin (Yeugeny Onegin). Opera in three acts by Pyotr Il'yich Tchaikovsky, to a libretto by the composer and Konstantin Shilovsky after Pushkin's poem (1823–31), first produced in Moscow on March 29, 1879. Two young friends, Onegin and Lensky, are visiting the summer estate of a family with two daughters, Tatiana and Olga. Tatiana is fascinated by Onegin, and confesses her love to him in a passionate and memorable letter aria (in French, then the language of Russian high society). The next day he explains that he is not meant for the simple domestic happiness of marriage. At the family ball he pointedly dances with Olga to taunt Lensky, her fiancé. Lensky angrily challenges him to a duel. Onegin kills him and, torn by remorse, departs on a long journey abroad. Returning to Russia many years later, he meets Tatiana, now the wife of a retired general. He is seized with passion and begs her to go off with him. She rejects his belated entreaty and he leaves her forever. *Eugene Onegin* is a perennial favorite in Russia, and, like Tchaikovsky's *Queen of Spades,* is regularly if not prolifically heard outside of its native land.

Euphrosine. Opera in five (later three and then four) acts by Etienne-Nicholas Méhul, his second, to a libretto by F. B. Hoffman about Euphrosine's successful attempt to win the love of the misogynist Coradin, first produced in Paris on Sept. 4, 1790.

Euridice. Opera in prologue and six scenes by Jacopo Peri, to a libretto by Ottorio Rinuccini loosely following Poliziano's *Orfeo* (1480), but with a happy ending: Orfeo convinces Pluto and Prosperpine to release Euridice, and a chorus of Shades accompany the happy couple on their return to earth. The work was first produced at Florence's Pitti Palace on Oct. 6, 1600. The same plot is at work in Caccini's *Euridice,* also in prologue and six scenes and to Rinuccini's libretto, first produced in Florence on Dec. 5, 1602.

Eurydice. Lyric drama by Jean-Michel Damase, to a play by Jean Anouilh, first staged in Bordeaux on May 26, 1972. A young man disenchanted with the unvirginal condition of a girl with whom he fell in love lets her go after a quarrelsome night in a hotel. She is killed by an automobile, and he spends the rest of his life in fantasies of her being a chaste nymph.

Europeras 1 & 2. Opera in two unequal parts by John Cage, first produced in Frankfurt am Main on Dec. 12, 1987. Its title derives from the words "Europe" and "opera," and its two parts are separated by a 1′50″ looping black and white film of chance-derived moments from both. The work is conceived wholly of chance operations, the musical "content" being the simultaneous presentation of arias and duets heard within a pulverized, decontextualized mass of instrumental fragments drawn from 64 European operas of the past, ranging from Gluck to Puccini. Its cast of players includes 19 singers, 12 dancer/athletes, and a 24-piece orchestra, without the usual body of strings and with the unusual addition to its percussion section of "Truckera," a tape of 101 layered fragments of European operas mixed live at a 1987 broadcast over N.Y.'s WKCR. Each of the opera's elements has been conceived in such a way as to have complete independence, resulting in a work marked by a total absence of intended musical or dramatic interrelationships. There is no intended musical discourse, and thus no managerial hand of a conductor, each of the unconducted soloists governing prescribed actions by digital clock time displayed on video monitors. Even the synopsis, provided in the customary program book, thwarts any attempt to ferret out some hidden narrative thread: each of the 12 different pairs of newly compiled synopses, randomly assigned to one of 12 different program books, is a chance-determined collection of fragmented sentences drawn from the synopses originally intended to accompany the operas upon which Cage's *Europeras 1 & 2* relies.

Cage later produced two diminutive versions in the series: *Europeras 3 & 4* (London, June 17, 1990) and *Europera 5* (Buffalo, N.Y., April 18, 1991).

Euryanthe. Opera in three acts by Carl Maria von Weber, to a libretto by Helmina von Chezy after a medieval French romance, first performed in Vienna on Oct. 25, 1823. The libretto is taken from an old French legend in which the enemies of the virtuous wife Euryanthe attempt to charge her with infidelity, but she withstands their attacks. The opera failed, but its vivacious overture endured.

Eva. Opera in three acts by Josef Foerster, to a libretto by the composer after Gabriela Preissová's drama *Gazdina roba* (The Farm Mistress), first produced in Prague on Jan. 1, 1899. Despite her love for Mánek, the son of a wealthy farmer, Eva, a poor seamstress, marries the tailor Samko. After the loss of her baby, and despite the fact that he is by now married to another, she and Mánek run away together. While Mánek is untroubled by the unhappiness their relationship seems to be causing, Eva begins to have terrifying visions, and in the end throws herself into the Danube.

Evangelimann, Der (The Evangelist). Opera in two acts by Wilhelm Kienzl, his greatest success, to a libretto by the composer after L. F. Meissner's story (1894), first produced in Berlin on May 4, 1895. Two brothers love the same woman, and one of them commits arson and blames the other. The distraught woman commits suicide. The guilty brother belatedly confesses his crimes on his deathbed to his brother.

Excursions of Mr. Brouček, The (Výlety páně Broučkovy). Opera in two acts by Leŏs Janáček, to the composer's own libretto after Čech's novels (1888, 1889), first produced in Prague on April 23, 1920. The opera combines two short works, written at different times, about a 19th-century Czech burgher of average distinction: *Mr. Brouček's Excursion to the Moon,* where he finds life as mundane and stressful as his own, and *Mr. Brouček's Excursion to the 15th Century,* in which he participates in the Hussite nationalist movement.

F

Failing Kansas. Opera by Mikel Rouse, the first in a trilogy followed by *Dennis Cleveland* (1996) and *The End of Cinematics* (2000), first performed in New York on Feb. 2, 1995, and lauded as the first viable music-theater work of the new, post-rock 'n' roll generation of ("totalist") composers. In four large sections linked by five interludes, *Failing Kansas* owes its inspiration to Truman Capote's quasi-documentary novel *In Cold*

Blood, which recounts in vivid detail the heinous Clutter murders. The work is scored for solo singer with a multitude of electronic instruments, a virtual compendium of the possibilities of Rouse's counterpoetry technique.

Fairy-Queen, The. Opera in five acts by Henry Purcell, based on Shakespeare's comedy *A Midsummer Night's Dream,* first produced in London on May 2, 1692.

Fall of the House of Usher, The. Opera by Philip Glass, after Edgar Allan Poe, first mounted in Cambridge, Massachusetts, on May 18, 1988.

Falstaff. Opera in three acts by Giuseppe Verdi, to a libretto by Arrigo Boito traversing the story of Shakespeare's famous fat man, bumbling lover, and cowardly braggart of *The Merry Wives of Windsor* (1600–01). *Falstaff* was Verdi's last opera and only his second comic opera. It was produced at La Scala in Milan, on Feb. 9, 1893, several months short of his 80th birthday. In it Verdi inaugurated a new style, approaching that of music drama. It ends on a magisterial choral fugue with the Shakesperian words "Il mondo e la burla" (All the world's a stage).

Family of Taras, The (Sem'ya Tarasa). Opera by Dmitri Kabelevsky, first performed in Leningrad on Nov. 2, 1947. The action takes place in a Ukranian city occupied by the Nazis in 1942. A group of young partisans, among them a daughter of Taras, is given an assignment to blow up the Nazi headquarters. They succeed, but she is seized by the Germans and hanged. Her sacrifice is not in vain, as Soviet soldiers soon recapture the town. Old Taras vows to live to see that peace again reigns in the world. The opera was written remarkably soon after the events it portrays.

Fanciulla del West, La (The Girl of the Golden West). Opera in three acts by Giacomo Puccini, to a libretto by Guelto Civinini and Carlo Zangarini after David Belasco's drama (1905), commissioned by and produced at the Metropolitan Opera in New York, with Toscanini conducting and Caruso singing the part of the western badman Dick Johnson, on Dec. 10, 1910. Dick and the sheriff are both in love with Minnie, who owns a saloon. When Dick seeks shelter in her quarters, she challenges the sheriff to a poker game, the stake of which is Dick's freedom. She wins by secreting an extra ace in her petticoat. Together Dick and Minnie ride away into the sunset. The score contains one of Puccini's most ambitious orchestrations.

Faust. Grand opera in five acts by Charles Gounod, to a libretto by Jules Barbier and Michel Carré based on Goethe's dramatic poem, first performed in Paris on March 19, 1859. *Faust* is one of the most successful operas of all time. During the first century of its spectacular career, it had more than 2,000 performances in Paris alone. Its libretto emphasizes the mundane aspects of Goethe's great poem. Faust sells his soul to the canny devil Méphistophélès in exchange for the elixir of youth. No sooner is the deal arranged than Faust is shown an image of the virginal weaver Marguerite. He is conducted to the girl's abode, sings an aria extolling the chastity of her retreat, tempts her anonymously with jewels, and, with worldly advice from the ubiquitous devil, seduces her. Marguerite's brother Valentin fights Faust in a duel, but is slain. Faust runs off. Marguerite bears Faust's child, but goes insane and kills her progeny. She is sentenced to die, but a host of cherubim and seraphim carries her to heaven while Faust watches. He goes off with (and to) the devil. The Germans remain so offended by Gounod's earthy treatment of Goethe's text that when the opera is produced in Germany, it is called *Margarete* or *Gretchen.*

Faust III. Operatic trilogy by Niels Bentzon, to his own libretto in which Goethe's Faust, James Joyce's Bloom (*Ulysses*), and Kafka's Josef K. (*The Trial*) are psychologically related through fantasies of feminine projections, produced for the first time in Kiel on June 21, 1964.

Favorite, La. Opera in four acts by Gaetano Donizetti, to a libretto by Alphonse Royer and Gustave Vaëz after Baculard d'Arnauld's drama *Le comte de Comminges* (1764) and other materials, first produced in Paris on Dec. 2, 1840. In Italian it is titled *La Favorita.* The heroine is the favorite mistress of the king of Castile. Unaware of her lofty status, a novitiate monk watches her form in the window. Inflamed with carnal desire, he declares his love to her. The king, eager to rid himself of the embarrassing liaison with his mistress, lets her marry the monk, who soon discovers that he was made a fool by her and returns to the monastery. But she realizes that she really does love the monk and makes her way to his monastic retreat disguised as a young novice. The finale is tragic, as she is overcome by moral scruples and falls dead into his arms.

Fedora. Opera in three acts by Umberto Giordano, to a libretto by Arturo Colautti after Sardou's drama (1882), first produced in Milan on Nov. 17, 1898. A grim morality tale involving Fedora (a Russian countess-to-be), her assassinated intended, his nihilist killer, Fedora's pursuit of and inadvertent falling for the murderer in Paris, their escape to Switzerland, his betrayal of her, and her shock and suicide, dying in his loving arms.

Feen, Die (The Fairies). Opera in three acts by Richard Wagner, his first at age 20, to a libretto by the composer after Gozzi's comedy *La donna serpente* (1762), first produced posthumously in Munich on June 29, 1888. The opera, like Gozzi's comedy, concerns the fate of two lovers, one supernatural, the other not.

Ferne Klang, Der (The Distant Sound). Opera in three acts by Franz Schreker, to the composer's libretto, first produced in Frankfurt am Main on Aug. 18, 1912. A Venetian courtesan is mystically redeemed by assisting her composer lover reach operatic success. In an updating of Sullivan's "The Lost Chord," Schreker's composer dies in his lover's arms upon hearing a supernaturally distant harmony.

Fervaal. Opera in prologue and three acts by Vincent d'Indy, to the composer's libretto set in the Midi of France at the time of the Saracen invasions and that concerns the misconceptions of Guilhen, who, while nursing the Celtic chief Fervaal back to health, unwittingly lures the Celts to their deaths. The opera was first produced in Brussels on March 12, 1897.

Feuersnot (Fire-Famine). Opera in one act by Richard Strauss, to a libretto by Ernst von Wolzogen after a Flemish legend, *The Quenched Fires of Oudenaarde* (1843), first produced in Dresden on Nov. 21, 1901, the composer conducting. It was described by Strauss as a *Singgedicht*, a sung poem. A recluse tries to kiss a girl who ridicules him publicly, unaware of the fact that he possesses magical power. In revenge he creates a fire-famine that extinguishes all lights in the village. The girl quickly repents, and he withdraws his ban.

Fiamma, La (The Flame). Opera in three acts by Ottorino Respighi, to a libretto by Claudio Guastalla after Hans Wiess-Jensen play, dealing with the flaming passion of a woman for her young stepson, first produced in Rome on Jan. 23, 1934.

Fidelio. [Leonore, oder Der Triumph der ehelicher Liebe (Leonore, or The Triumph of Married Love)]. Opera by Ludwig van Beethoven, with premiere performances in three versions in Vienna: first version, Nov. 20, 1805, second version, March 29, 1806, and third version, May 23, 1814. It is based on a German version of Bouilly's libretto *Léonore, ou L'amour conjugal*, the title that Beethoven wished for his opera. Florestan is in a dungeon for his opposition to a tyrannical Spanish governor. His faithful wife, Leonore, enters the jail service in a boy's attire, taking the symbolic name Fidelio and surviving the jailer's daughter's crush on her. Political and marital virtue triumph when a new governor, announced by a resonant fanfare from backstage, orders the release of Florestan and the arrest of his tormentor. The same story was the basis of operas by Ferdinando Paer (*Leonora*, 1804) and Johann Simon Mayr (*L'Amor coniugale*, 1805).

Fiery Angel, The (Ognenniy angel). Opera in five acts by Sergei Prokofiev, to his own libretto after Valery Brysov's historical novel (1907–08), premiered posthumously in Venice on Sept. 14, 1955, two years after the composer's death. A mystical 16th-century girl becomes possessed by the vision of a former lover. Exorcism is initiated by the Grand Inquisitor, and when it fails, the unfortunate maiden is accused of carnal intercourse with the devil and is burned at the stake.

Figaro lässt sich scheiden. Opera in two acts by Giselher Klebe, a non-Mozartian projection wherein characters of the famous Beaumarchais play are placed in the whirlpool of the French Revolution, with Figaro singing atonal arias in a 12-tone idiom, first produced by the Hamburg State Opera on June 28, 1963.

Figlia di Iorio, La. Opera ("pastoral tragedy") in three acts by Ildebrundo Pizzetti, its libretto a literal setting of D'Annunzio's tragedy (1903) wherein the beautiful daughter of a self-styled magus is forced to flee from a massed assault of harvesters and finds refuge in the family of a young bridegroom who, inflamed by her, carries her to an oceanside grotto and kills his own father with an axe when the latter intrudes to ravish her, but is saved from the vengeance of the villagers when she assumes the guilt as a psychological incendiary and goes to her death in the purifying flames of a sacred fire. The work was first produced in Naples on Dec. 4, 1954.

Fille de l'homme, La. Lyric tragedy in three acts by Pierre Capdevielle, to a libretto dealing with an Italian railroad magnate who incites a woman employee to kill her lover, performed for the first time in a complete stage performance in Paris on Dec. 1, 1967.

Fille du régiment, La (The Daughter of the Regiment). Comic opera in two acts by Gaetano Donizetti, to a libretto by Jules-Henri Vernoy de Saint-Georges and Jean-François-Alfred Bayard, first produced in Paris on Feb. 11, 1840. A romantic story tells of Marie, who is brought up by a regiment of soldiers and serves as their army mascot. A crisis occurs when her aunt reclaims her and takes her to her castle. The soldiers lead an assault on her aunt's stronghold, and the girl is reinstated as the "daughter of the regiment." The opera has become a popular vehicle for sopranos, e.g., Lily Pons and Joan Sutherland.

Fille du tambour-major, La (The Drum-Major's Daughter). Comic opera by Jacques Offenbach, first performed in Paris on Dec. 13, 1879, the last work by Offenbach to be produced in his lifetime. The plot resembles Donizetti's *La Fille du régiment*, with the action set in Lombardy in 1806. Napoleon has just crossed the Alps and been welcomed by the Italian populace as liberator from the oppressive Austrian rule. An errant young girl flirts with a French lieutenant, and it develops that she herself is the daughter of a French drum major. After a number of melodramatic imbroglios, the young couple is reunited in Milan as Napoleon enters the city.

Final Ingredient, The. Opera by David Amram, to the story of a Passover celebration by Jewish prisoners in a Nazi concentration camp, performed for the first time as a commissioned work by ABC Television in New York on April 11, 1965, the composer conducting.

Finta giardiniera, La (The Pretended Garden Girl). Comic opera in three acts by Wolfgang Amadeus Mozart, to a libretto possibly by Calzabigi for Anfossi's opera (1774), revised by Coltellini, first produced in Munich on Jan. 13, 1775. An amorous marquise is snubbed by the count she seeks, so she takes on the disguise of a municipal gardener. Further intrigues eventually lead to her success.

Finta semplice, La (The Pretended Simpleton). Comic opera in three acts by Wolfgang Amadeus Mozart, to a libretto by Marco Coltellini after a libretto by Carlo Goldoni wherein three couples—Fracasso and Donna Giacinta, Simone and Ninetta, and Rosina and Cassandro—are finally united after a mishap involving stolen family jewelry. The opera was first performed at the Archbishop's Palace in Salzburg, May 1, 1769.

Finto Stanislao, Il (The False Stanislaus). Opera in two acts by Adalbert Gyrowetz, to a libretto by Romani, first produced in Milan on Aug. 5, 1818. The text is the same as that set by Giuseppe Verdi in *Un giorno di regno* (King for a Day) (1840), but both were preceded by Mosca's opera on the same subject (1812).

Fisherman and His Wife, The. Children's opera by Gunther Schuller, after a grim Grimm fairy tale, staged for the first time in Boston on May 7, 1970, the composer conducting.

Fledermaus, Die (The Bat). Operetta in three acts by Johann Strauss II, to a libretto by Carl Haffner and Richard Genée after a French *spirituel vaudeville* entitled *Le réveillon* (The Midnight Supper Party, 1872), first performed in Vienna on April 5, 1874. The bat of the title is the costume used by one of the characters at a masked ball. An Austrian baron, who is sentenced to prison for a petty offense, eludes the police and goes to a masked ball. His wife, suspicious of his conduct, goes to the same ball disguised as a Hungarian countess. Not recognizing her, the baron flirts with her. A series of mistaken identities reach their climax when the baron exchanges clothes with his own lawyer and enters the jail in order to extract a confession from another suspect and clear himself. A happy ending is vouchsafed when all jail sentences are suspended, and guests from the masked ball join the principals to drink a toast in praise of champagne, the king of wines. *Die Fledermaus* enjoys success everywhere, particularly at New Year's Eve galas with surprise performers.

Fliegende Holländer, Der (The Flying Dutchman). Opera in one act (later three) by Richard Wagner, first produced in Dresden on Jan. 2, 1843. The libretto by Wagner is after a legend recounted in Heine's *Aus den Memoiren des Herren von Schnabelewopski* (1831). Originally Wagner wrote a libretto for an opera, *Le Vaisseau fantôme,* but when another opera of the same name by Louis Dietsch (1808–65) failed, Wagner returned to the legend, rewrote the libretto, and created a minor masterpiece. The "Dutchman" is a mariner doomed to sail until he finds a woman capable of total devotion. Stormy seas drive the ship off course to a Norwegian fjord. The voyager hears a Norwegian girl (Jenta) sing a ballad about the doomed ship, and he realizes that she would redeem him. But in her eagerness, she leaps toward the ship from a cliff and perishes. Her sacrifice is his redemption, however, and together they are lifted to the skies.

Forza del destino, La (The Power of Fate). Opera in four acts by Giuseppe Verdi, to a libretto by Franscesco Piavé after the drama *Don Alvaro, o La fuerza del sino* (1835) by Angel de Saavedra Ramírez de Banquedano, Duke of Rivas, and a scene from Schiller's drama *Wallensteins Lager* (1799). The opera was first produced by an Italian opera company in St. Petersburg on Nov. 10, 1862. The force of destiny decrees that an eager lover accidentally kill the father of his beloved and flee in horror to a monastery. His intended bride follows him there dressed in a man's attire. Her brother, seeking vengeance, tracks him down, too, and, not recognizing his sister under her monastic garb, mortally stabs her before dying himself from a wound inflicted by the now completely disoriented monk.

Fourberies de Scapin, Les. Comic opera in three acts by Yury Falik, after Molière's comedy dealing with an audacious valet, modeled after the rascal servant Scapino in the Italian commedia dell'arte, performed for the first time in Tartu, Estonia, on Dec. 22, 1984.

Four-Note Opera, The. Opera for five voices and piano by Tom Johnson, to his own libretto in which the characters commit mass self-immolation at the end, the entire score based on four notes, A, B, D, and E, in ostentatiously tetraphonic monotony fertilized by rhythmic diversification. It was performed for the first time in New York on May 16, 1972.

Four Saints in Three Acts. "Opera to be sung" in four (*sic*) acts by Virgil Thomson, first produced by the Society of Friends and Enemies of Modern Music in Hartford, Connecticut, on Feb. 8, 1934. The libretto is by Gertrude Stein and follows her unpredictable structuralist tenets. Thus, there are really four acts and a dozen saints, some in duplicate. Her famous nonsensical line "Pigeons on the grass, alas" is emblematic.

Fra Diavolo. Opera in three acts by Daniel-François-Esprit Auber, to a libretto by Eugéne Scribe concerning a notorious and nicknamed bandit who unwittingly involves a woman in a robbery. He is traitorously shot, and in his last breath exonerates her from all his crimes and urges her to marry her law-abiding suitor. The opera was first produced in Paris on Jan. 28, 1830.

Fra Gherardo. Opera in three acts by Ildebrando Pizzetti, to his own libretto after the chronicle of Fra Salimbene da Parma of the 13th century, first performed in Milan on May 16, 1928, Toscanini conducting. The story deals with an actual flagellant friar burned at the stake for heresy about 1260, with fictional additions involving a local girl who is seduced and abandoned by him, and in the end stoned as a witch.

Francesca da Rimini. Short opera by Sergei Rachmaninoff, after Dante, telling the piteous tale of Paolo and Francesca, who is slain by her jealous husband, first staged in Moscow on Jan. 24, 1906, the composer conducting a program that included the world premiere of another of his short operas, *The Miserly Knight.*

Francesca da Rimini. Opera in four acts by Riccardo Zandonai, his fourth and most successful, to a libretto by Tito Ricordi after D'Annunzio's tragedy (1902), itself after Dante's *Inferno,* first performed in Turin on Feb. 19, 1914.

Frankenstein: The Modern Prometheus. Opera by Libby Larsen, performed for the first time in St. Paul, Minnesota, on May 25, 1990.

Frate 'nnamorato, Lo (The Brother in Love). Opera by Giovanni Battista Pergolesi at age 22, to a libretto by Gennaro Antonio Federico in which the twin sisters Nena and Nina love Ascanio rather than their intended husbands, while Ascanio is in love with Lucrezia. Everyone is satisfied (especially Lucrezia!) at the news that Ascanio is actually the twins' brother. It was first produced in Naples on Sept. 27, 1732.

Frau ohne Schatten, Die (The Woman Without a Shadow). Opera in three acts by Richard Strauss, to a libretto by Hugo von Hofmannsthal after his own story, first produced in Vienna on Oct. 10, 1919. An empress, married to an Oriental potentate, is barren because she cannot cast a shadow, a symbol of fertility. Also, her husband's life is in danger. The empress is given a tempting offer to buy a poor woman's shadow. She finally desists, not wishing to deprive her of childbearing. For this noble act she is granted the joy of a shadow so that she can become a mother after all, and her husband is saved.

Frederick Douglass. Opera in three acts by Ulysses Kay, to a fictionalized libretto concerning the post–Civil War activities of the former slave-turned-abolitionist/activist and lecturer, staged for the first time in Newark, New Jersey, on April 14, 1991.

Freischütz, Der (The Freeshooter). Opera in three acts by Carl Maria von Weber, to a libretto by Johann Friedrich Kind after a tale in the *Gespensterbuch* (1811) of Johann Apel and Friedrich Laun, premiered in Berlin on June 18, 1821. Set in Bohemia at the end of the Thirty Years' War, an ambitious freeshooter, in love with a country girl, agrees to trade his soul to the devil for seven magic bullets that would guarantee a victory in a shooting competition. The last bullet must go where the demonic purchaser directs. The shooter hits his six preliminary marks, but the last is aimed at his bride. She is saved by supernatural intervention. The marksman confesses his deal with the devil, but is absolved. *Der Freischütz* is regarded as the first truly Romantic opera.

Friedenstag (Day of Peace). Opera in one act by Richard Strauss, to a libretto by Joseph Gregor after Calderón's drama *La redención de Breda* (1625), first performed in Munich on July 24, 1938. The story deals with the conclusion of the Thirty Years' War, which devastated Europe, and ends with a choral invocation to peace. Its repeated performances on the eve of Hitler's plunge into total war held special meaning for Germans deprived of their freedom of speech.

From the House of the Dead (Z mrtvého domu). Opera in three acts by Leoš Janáček, to his own libretto after Dostoyevsky's partly autobiographical novel describing his Siberian exile (1862), produced posthumously in Brno on April 12, 1930. Its libretto centers on the destiny of the czarist exile who bears traits of Dostoyevsky himself. When he is freed, his fellow prisoners symbolically release an eagle from its cage.

Full Circle. Opera in one act by Robin Orr, to a libretto dealing with an inadvertent killer of a Scottish policeman in 1930 who is tracked down to his middle-class habitat, written in the form of a dramatic ballad, emphasizing the elegiac element in the killer's family life and his devotion to his loyal wife, first performed in Perth, Scotland, on April 10, 1968.

Full Moon in March. Opera by John Harbison, to a text by Yeats, performed for the first time in Cambridge, Massachusetts, on April 30, 1979. The symbolic story deals with a cruel queen and a swineherd who dares to court her.

G

Galileo Galilei. Opera by Ezra Laderman, originally written as an oratorio for television, to a libretto by Joseph Darion, first performed in Binghamton, N.Y., on Feb. 3, 1979.

Gambler, The (Igrok). Opera in four acts by Sergei Prokofiev, to a libretto by the composer after a story by Dostoyevsky (1866), first performed not in Russia (which was twice projected), but in Brussels, on April 29, 1929. The story deals with a Russian general vacationing at a German resort with his very rich grandmother whose fortune he hopes to inherit. But she proceeds to gamble recklessly, and he is in despair. Fortunately, his aide-de-camp manages to break the bank on his own, but this leads to further imbroglios.

Gawain. Opera in two acts by Harrison Birtwistle, to a "poetic libretto" by David Harsent after the anonymous 14th-century English poem *Sir Gawain and the Green Knight* about the supernatural encounter of Gawain and the Green Knight, symbolic of the opposition of Christianity and pagan sorcery, first produced in London on May 30, 1991. After revision, the work was given a second premiere in London on April 14, 1994.

Gazza ladra, La (The Thieving Magpie). Opera semiseria in two acts by Gioacchino Rossini, to a libretto by Giovanni Gherardini, produced at La Scala, Milan, on May 31, 1817. The French play from which the libretto was drawn, *La pie voleuse* (1815) by Baudouin d'Aubigny and Louis-Charles Caigniez, was described as a comedy. It tells of a servant girl who is sentenced to death by hanging on suspicion of stealing a spoon (apparently neither cruel nor unusual punishment in the early 19th century). She is saved from the gallows when the spoon is found in the nest of an errant magpie.

Geheimnis des entwendeten Briefes, Das. Opera by Boris Blacher, after "The Purloined Letter" by Edgar Allan Poe, first produced in Berlin on Feb. 14, 1975.

Genoveva. Opera in four acts by Robert Schumann, to a libretto by Robert Reinick revised by the composer after Ludwig Tieck's tragedy *Das leben und Tod der heiligen Genoveva* (1799) and Frederich Hebbel's tragedy *Genoveva* (1843), first performed in Leipzig on June 25, 1850. The opera is set in 8th century Brabant. Genoveva is the young bride of a warrior who entrusts her to his companion while he is away. But the friend betrays his trust by making advances to Genoveva. She rejects him, and, frustrated, he tells the bridegroom upon his return that she was unfaithful. At first, the husband orders her put to death, but she proves to him medically that she is *virgo intacta.*The "friend" flees and judiciously falls off a cliff. The couple's happiness is ensured.

Gentlemen, Be Seated! Opera in two acts by Jerome Moross, set in the time of the American Civil War and combining elements of a minstrel show, dance, and drama with a "Mister Interlocutor" supplying commentary on the historic, social, and fictional characters and events. The opera was first produced in New York on Oct. 10, 1963.

Gentle Spirit, A. Chamber opera by John Tavener, after a story by Dostoyevsky in which a pawnbroker mourns the suicide death of his young wife. The opera was first staged in London at the Bath Festival on June 6, 1977.

Germania. Opera in prologue, two acts, and epilogue by Alberto Franchetti, to a libretto by Luigi Illica, wherein a German girl, seduced by a university student, marries his comrade in an atmosphere of continued seething rivalry, and in the epilogue conciliates them as they lie dying of patriotic wounds on the battleground of Leipzig on Oct. 19, 1813. The opera was first produced in Milan on March 11, 1902.

Geschäftsbericht. Minimal opera (duration 600 seconds) by Paul Dessau, a "business report" to the text of the indictment of the American aggression in Vietnam by the International Tribunal for War Crimes in Stockholm, with an epilogue in which dead American soldiers curse President Johnson for depriving them of their lives, first produced in Leipzig on April 29, 1967.

Geschichte von einem Feuer, Die. Opera by Dieter Schönbach, a multimedia spectacle for chorus, orchestra, and functional kinetic sculpture cybernetically directed by an electronic computer, to a libretto portraying three anonymous men engaged in quest of instances of nobility through eight periods of time, from ancient Greece to the present, performed for the first time in Kiel on June 23, 1968.

Ghosts of Versailles, The. Grand opera in two acts by John Corigliano, to a libretto by William Hoffman based on Beaumarchais's play *La Mère coupable* written as a sequel to his *Le barbier de Séville* and *Le mariage de Figaro*. The opera brings Beaumarchais himself, Marie Antoinette, Louis XVI, and other French aristocrats of the Revolutionary era back as ghosts to the palace of Versailles, where Beaumarchais stages a Figaro opera-within-an-opera meant to court the queen he has phantomly loved for 200 years and which eventually turns into an attempt by Beaumarchais and Figaro to spare her historic fate (the orchestra plays "La Marseillaise" when her head ultimately rolls again), with the music at times teasingly quoting Rossini's and Mozart's famous Figaro treatments. The work was premiered at N.Y.'s Metropolitan Opera on Dec. 19, 1991 (its first premiere in twenty-five years), with Teresa Stratas, Marilyn Horne, and Håkon Hagegård in leading roles, conducted by James Levine.

Gianni Schicchi. The third of the operatic trilogy *Il Trittico*, by Giacomo Puccini, to a libretto by Giovacchino Forzana after Dante's *Inferno*, in one act, first produced in New York at the Metropolitan Opera on Dec. 14, 1918. The lawyer Schicchi has a daughter who loves the nephew of a wealthy man who dies at the opera's beginning. The will gives his fortune to the church, but Schicchi devises a plan by which he pretends to be the "not quite dead" old man. The greedy family comes to collect, but a disguised Schicchi dictates a will that leaves everyone but himself and the young lovers out in the cold.

Gioconda, La. Opera in four acts by Amikare Ponchielli, to a libretto by "Tobia Gorrio" (Arrigo Boito) after Hugo's drama *Angélo, tyran de Padoue* (1835), first produced at La Scala, Milan, on April 8, 1876. The action takes place in 17th-century Venice. The jocund street singer is in trouble when her blind mother is denounced as a witch by the Inquisition. The local Inquisitor is willing to release her if the girl submits to his licentious desires. She rebukes him, whereupon he carries out his threat to have her mother put to death. Thereupon La Gioconda stabs herself and dies. There are also some murky doings around the Venetian palaces involving, among other things, a cuckolded husband who tries unsuccessfully to poison his wife. Incongruously, the score includes the famous ballet *Dance of the Hours*, as rollicking a piece of rhythmic entertainment as was ever produced by an Italian composer.

Gioielli della Madonna, I (The Jewels of the Madonna). Opera in three acts by Ermanno Wolf-Ferrari, to a libretto by Enrico Golisciani and Carlo Zangarini, a German version of *Der Schmuck der Madonna* by Hans Liebstöckl, first produced in Berlin on Dec. 23, 1911. Two rivals for a woman's love vow to prove their love by an outrageous deed. The winner steals the jewels from a statue of the Holy Virgin and offers them to his beloved. She rejects the blasphemous gift and drowns herself, whereupon the rogue lays the jewels at the statue's feet and stabs himself to death.

Giorno di regno, Un (King for a Day). Opera in two acts by Giuseppe Verdi, to a libretto by Felice Romani after A.V. Pineu-Duval's comedy *Le faux Stanislas* (1808), first performed at La Scala, Milan, on Sept. 5, 1840. Later known as *Il finto Stanislao* (The False Stanislaus). This is Verdi's first comic opera, and yet it was written at the most tragic period of his life when he lost his wife and two children in close succession. The opera tells the story of the courageous act of a Polish officer who travels under the guise of King Stanislaw to expose himself in case of regicide so the real king can travel in safety. He is rewarded by a marital union with a young Polish lady.

Giovanna d'Arco (Joan of Arc). Opera in prologue and three acts by Giuseppe Verdi, to a libretto by Themistocle Solera after Schiller's tragedy *Die Jungfrau von Orleans* (1801), first performed at La Scala, Milan, on Feb. 15, 1845. In it Joan of Arc falls in love with the dauphin, goes to battle against the English, is wounded, and dies in the arms of her royal lover, now King Charles VII. This perversion of the historical story of the sainted virgin infuriated the French at the first Paris performance of the opera.

Giuditta. Opera in five scenes by Franz Léhar, first produced in Vienna on Jan. 20, 1934. The subject of the libretto by Paul Knepler and Fritz Löhner is drawn from the apocryphal Book of Judith about the Hebrew maiden who skillfully decapitates the sleeping Assyrian army leader and carries his severed bearded head back to her city. Finding themselves headless, the Assyrians lift the siege of the Hebrew city. This is the only serious opera Léhar ever wrote, but musically it is much inferior to his sparkling operettas.

Giulio Cesare. Opera in three acts by George Frideric Handel, to a libretto by Nicola Francesco Haym after a libretto by Giacomo Busanni, set by Sartorio (1677) and Kusser (1691), first performed in London on Feb. 20, 1724. The opera with its melodically rich score concentrates on Caesar's encounter with Cleopatra, a role that has attracted such modern sopranos as Beverly Sills and Joan Sutherland.

Gli Spaziali (The Space People). Opera by Wogel, in three interlingual parts—*Leonardo da Vinci* (in Italian and German), *Roman de la Lune*, after Jules Verne (in French and German), and *Present Exploration of the Universe* (in German, English, and Russian)—first staged in Zürich on Dec. 5, 1973.

Gloriana. Opera in three acts by Benjamin Britten, to a libretto by William Plomer after Lytton Strachey's study *Elizabeth and Essex* (1928), commissioned by the Arts Council for the coronation of Elizabeth II and produced at a special gala performance in the queen's presence in Covent Garden, London, on June 8, 1953. The Gloriana of the title was Queen Elizabeth I, and the libretto traverses her romance with the earl of Essex. There is a masque-like dramaturgy, although the work is otherwise entirely 20th century.

Glückliche Hand, Der (The Fortunate Hand). "Drama with music" in one act by Arnold Schoenberg, to the composer's libretto, first performed in Vienna on Oct. 14, 1924. A helpless man, beset by horrible visions, meditates on his search for happiness while a chorus points out the futility of his efforts.

Golden Child, The. Television opera in three sections by Bezanson, to a Christmas libretto by Paul Engle wherein a child's rag doll magically leads a California gold rusher of 1848, his pregnant wife, and a small daughter out of a snowy wilderness to a mining camp, with a subsequent birth of a male child in a manger. It was first performed in a 90-minute broadcast from New York on Dec. 16, 1960.

Golden Cockerel, The (Zolotoy petushok) (Le coq d'on). Opera in three acts by Nikolai Rimsky-Korsakov, his last, to a text by Vladimir Belsky after Pushkin's poem (1834), subtitled "an impersonated fable," concerns a lazy autocrat engaged in a silly war. Its first posthumous production was in Moscow on Oct. 7, 1909.

Goldschmied von Toledo. A pasticcio comprised of music by Jacques Offenbach by Stern and Zamara, to a libretto by Zwerenz afer Hoffmann's story *Das Fräulein von Scuderi* (1818), first performed in Mannheim on Feb. 7, 1919.

Golem, The. Opera in four acts by Abraham Ellstein, to a libretto derived from the famous Jewish legend of a rabbi who by the magic of alchemy creates a destructive human creature, first produced by the N.Y. City Opera, as a commission of the Ford Foundation, on March 22, 1962.

Götterdämmerung (Twilight of the Gods). The final spectacle of Richard Wagner's great tetralogy *Der Ring des Nibelungen,* to his own libretto, first performed at Wagner's Festival Theater in Bayreuth on Aug. 17, 1876. The gods, demigods, heroes, a Valkyrie, and the monstrous offspring of the sinister gnome Nibelung all perish in the final conflagration. The Rhine River overflows the funeral pyre erected for the final rites for Siegfried, the godlike hero of the tetralogy, and the Rhine maidens seize the accursed Ring from the murderous son of the dwarf who made it. Malevolent magic wrought by the Nibelungs makes Siegfried forget his beloved Brünnhilde, transforms him into the image of another Nibelung, then restores his memory and physical shape to him before he is slain. A labyrinthine network of leitmotifs guides, and misguides, the listener trying to trace the principal characters. Even such a confirmed Wagnerite as George Bernard Shaw candidly admitted his inability to penetrate the tangled web of the story.

Goya. Opera by Gian Carlo Menotti, to his own libretto depicting the life of the tortured Spanish artist, first staged at the Kennedy Center Theater in Washington, D.C., on Nov. 11, 1986, Placido Domingo, who commissioned the work, in the title role. It includes Goya's unverified romance with the duchess of Alba (whom he painted both clad and unclad). A dramatic scene describes Goya suddenly going deaf and, to illustrate this, Menotti makes all music stop while the singers continue to silently open and close their mouths, producing a unique effect. At its premiere, and much to Menotti's distress, it was cruelly damned by virtually every music critic as a compendium of mawkish melodies and corny clichés.

Goyescas. Opera in three scenes by Enrique Granados, first performed at the Metropolitan Opera in New York on Jan. 28, 1916. The title refers to the famous Spanish painter Goya, and the libretto (with additions by Fernando Periquet) has a peripheral relationship to the subjects of his paintings. The score was put together from the material of Granados's piano suite of the same name, regarded as one of the finest stylizations of Spanish popular music. Granados attended the performance of his opera and perished tragically on his return trip when the British ship on which he sailed was torpedoed by a German submarine.

Grand macabre, Le. Opera in two acts by György Ligeti, to a libretto by Michael Meschke and the composer after Michel de Ghelderode's play, first produced in Stockholm on April 12, 1978. The action is set in a chimeric town of Breugelland, the story centered on the thanatopherous necro-czar who sexually mutilates local hausfrauen before ordering the world's end. But he shrinks himself into a death mask when the forces of life refuse to stop functioning. A revised version was premiered in Salzburg on July 28, 1997.

Grande-Duchesse de Gerolstein, La. Comic opera by Jacques Offenbach, first presented in Paris on April 12, 1867. The head of a mythical European duchy adores men in uniform, but the commoner soldier she promotes to general marries a milkmaid. The downcast duchess plans a conspiracy to slay him, but another soldier who arouses her interest appears. He is also of royal blood, making the marriage even simpler.

Great Friendship, The (Velikaya druzhba). Opera, 1947, by Vano Il'ich Muradeli, on the Civil War in the Caucasus in 1919. The product of a socialist realist, nationalistic, and (mostly) politically correct Soviet nonentity, the work gained notoriety as the apparent target of a 1948 Communist Central Committee resolution, ostensibly because Muradeli had incorrectly implied that the Chechens had acted in a counter-Bolshevik manner. The attack was a screen for yet another threat to leading Soviet composers (Shostakovich, Prokofiev, and Khachaturian) to respect Party aesthetics. The opera was first presented in Donets'k on Sept. 28, 1947.

Greek Passion, The. Opera by Bohuslav Martinů, his last work, to a libretto after Nikos Kazantzakis's novel *Christ Recrucified*, in which a bearded shepherd, acting Christ in a passion play in a Greek village about 1900, identifies himself so completely with his role that he begins to preach unpopular sermons attacking capitalism and imperialism and is slain by a villager impersonating Judas. It was posthumously produced in Zürich on June 9, 1961, under the direction of Paul Sacher, on whose estate in Switzerland Martinů completed the work on Jan. 15, 1959, shortly before his death.

Griffelkin. Television opera by Lukas Foss, with a libretto from a German fairy tale, first broadcast on NBC Television in New York on Nov. 6, 1955. Griffelkin is a young devil who becomes disloyal to Hell after a visit on earth. An episode includes an entertaining cacophonous ensemble of pupils practicing their scales.

Grisélidis. Opera in prologue and three acts by Jules Massenet, to a libretto by Armand Silvestre and Eugéne Monrand derived from Boccaccio's and later Chaucer's whimsical tale about a submissively acquiescent woman whose sadistically pietistic husband subjects her to a series of calculated humiliations to test her uxorial devotion, first performed in Paris on Nov. 20, 1901.

Growing Castle, The. Opera by Malcolm Williamson, his sixth, to his own libretto after Strindberg's mystical drama *A Dream Play* dealing with a neurotic Scandinavian young woman who lives in an animated world of fantasy, performed for the first time in Dynevor Castle, Wales, on Aug. 13, 1968, as a commissioned work by Lord Dynevor, in concert form, with singers accompanied alternatively at the piano and at the harpsichord by the composer.

Guayana Johnny (The Sugar Reapers). Opera in two acts by Alan Bush, to a libretto by Nancy Bush dealing with the downtrodden sugar plantation workers in British Guiana who successfully overwhelm the British colonial power in 1953, containing an episode of interracial passion of a handsome Negro for a diminutive Hindu maiden, first performed in Leipzig on Dec. 11, 1966.

Guillaume Tell (William Tell). Opera in four acts by Gioacchino Rossini, his last stage work, to a libretto by Étienne de Jouy, Hippolyte Bis, and Armand Marrast, after Schiller's *Wilhelm Tell*, first produced in Paris on Aug. 3, 1829. The opera is rarely performed in its entirety, but its overture is an extremely popular concert piece, and its final section was the theme for *The Lone Ranger* radio and television series. The opera's subject is taken from a turbulent chapter in the history of Switzerland, as retold in Schiller's eponymous play (1804). William Tell is a Swiss patriot and a remarkable archer. The brutal governor of the province tests his marksmanship by ordering him to split an apple placed on the head of his small son with an arrow. William passes the test, then turns the weapon on the tyrant and kills him with a single shot.

Guntram. Opera in three acts by Richard Strauss, to the composer's libretto, first staged in Weimar on May 10, 1894. A medieval German duke is murdered by a minstrel named Guntram. The heiress to the throne loves him, so she absolves him. But she refuses to marry him on account of their class disparity.

Gwendoline. Opera in three acts by Emmanuel Chabrier, to a libretto by Catulle Mendès, first performed in Brussels on April 10, 1886. Gwendoline, the daughter of a prisoner, the Saxon Armel, is loved by the Viking king Harald, her father's oppressor. Armel pretends to give blessing to their marriage, but secretly arranges to have Gwendoline kill Harald. She refuses, and when Harald dies, she commits suicide.

Gypsy Baron, The (Der Zigeunerbaron). Operetta in three acts by Johann Strauss II to a libretto by Ianaz Schnitzer, first produced in Vienna on Oct. 24, 1885. The Ottomans have been forced out of Hungary. Sandor returns to his castle to find it ruined and his fields occupied by Zsupán, a neighbor who is seeking a lost Turkish treasure, and whose daughter Arsena Sandor falls for, but she is in love with her governess's son Ottokar. Now a band of gypsies, led by Czipra, enters the scene. When Sandor, newly anointed as the "gypsy baron," finds out about Arsena and Ottokar, he falls instead for the gypsy beauty Saffi. After all of this breathless action in the first act, two more acts and a war against Spain are necessary to straighten everything out happily for all (except for Zsupán, who never finds the treasure).

H

Hachatur Abovian. Opera in three acts by the Armenian composer Gebork Armenian (who changed from his original name Khachaturian in order to avoid confusion with his famous namesake), to a libretto recounting in romantic tones the life and social activities of the bringer of enlightenment to Armenia in the first half of the 19th century, first staged in Yerevan on Nov. 25, 1960.

Hagith. Opera in one act by Karol Szymanowski, first produced in Warsaw on May 13, 1922. The subject deals with an old king who seeks to regain his youth through the love of a young girl named Hagith.

Halka. Opera in two (later four) acts by Stanislaw Moniuszko, to a libretto by Włodzimierz Wolski after K. W. Wójcicki's story *Góralka*, first produced in its original two-act version in Vilnius on Feb. 18, 1854. The revised four-act version was first given in Warsaw on New Year's Day, 1858. Considered the national Polish opera, its popularity has never abated in Poland, but it is rarely performed in western Europe. The story concerns Halka's eternal love for her seducer. She kills herself when he marries another.

Hamlet. Opera by Humphrey Searle, to a libretto compressed from Shakespeare's play, with the thematic texture derived from melodically and methodically from a 12-tone series, except for the scene of the tragedians, which is set in an ostentatiously tonal idiom in euphonious harmonies, first produced in Hamburg in a German translation on March 4, 1968.

Hamlet. Opera by Sándar Szokolay, after Shakespeare, in a Hungarian translation adapted by the composer, first performed in Budapest on Oct. 19, 1968.

Hamlet. Opera in five acts by Ambroise Thomas, to a libretto by Jules Barbier and Michel Carré after a French version of Shakespeare's tragedy by Dumas *père* and Paul Maurice, first produced in Paris on March 9, 1868. The opera failed to achieve the success of Thomas's *Mignon.*

Hamletmaschine, Die. Opera by Wolfgang Rihm, to his own libretto adapted from a text by Heinrich Müller calling for three Hamlets, first staged in Mannheim on March 25, 1987.

Hänsel und Gretel. Fairy-tale opera in three acts by Engelbert Humperdinck, to a libretto by the composer's sister, Adelheid Wette, after the story in the Grimm brothers' *Kinder- und Hausmärchen* (1812–14), first performed in Weimar on Dec. 23, 1893, and forever forthwith a universal favorite. The subject is grim: a witch lures the siblings Hänsel and Gretel to her gingerbread house, which is built out of baked children. Ingeniously, the two intended victims push the witch into the burning oven. She explodes and the gingerbread children all return to life.

Hans Heiling. Opera in prologue and three acts by Heinrich Marschner, to a libretto by Eduard Devrient after an early folk tale, first produced in Berlin on May 24, 1833. Heiling, a hereditary prince of hell, falls in love with a mortal woman, Anna. However, when she discovers his supernatural essence, she leaves him for a human lover. He plans to slay his rival, but his subterranean mother persuades him to desist, and he vanishes.

Happy Prince, The. Children's opera by Malcolm Williamson, to his libretto after Oscar Wilde, scored for eight soloists, chorus, semi-chorus, piano duet, and percussion, performed for the first time at the Farnham Festival in England on May 22, 1965.

Harmonie der Welt, Die (The Harmony of the World). Opera in five scenes by Paul Hindemith, to his own libretto, first produced in Munich on Aug. 11, 1957. "Harmony of the World" refers to the theological, philosophical, and mathematical theories of planetary motion entertained by the astronomer Johannes Kepler (1571–1630) whose personal life is brought in as a paradigm to his theories.

Harriet, the Woman Called Moses. Opera by Thea Musgrave, to the story of the valiant abolitionist Harriet Tubman, who smuggled Negro slaves to freedom in Canada before the Civil War, performed for the first time by the Virginia Opera in Norfolk on March 1, 1985, conducted by the composer's husband, Peter Mark.

Harvey Milk. Opera in three acts by Stewart Wallace, to a libretto by Michael Korie based on the tragic murders of San Francisco mayor George Moscone and city supervisor Harvey Milk by disgruntled ex-city supervisor Dan White, first performed at the Houston Grand Opera on Jan. 21, 1995.

Háry János. Opera in prologue, five parts, and epilogue by Zoltán Kodály, to a libretto by Béla Paulini and Zsolt Harsányi after János Garay's poems, first produced in Budapest on Oct. 16, 1926. János Háry is in the braggart warrior mold, a fantastic liar who boasts of singlehandedly defeating Napoleon. The opera opens with a deafening orchestral sneeze, which is a protestation of either utter disbelief or total integrity in Hungarian conversational custom.

Hauts de Hurlevent, Les. Opera in seven scenes by Stubbs, to a libretto after Emily Brontë's novel, *Wuthering Heights*, first produced in Rouen on April 16, 1967.

Hell's Angels. Opera by Nigel Osborne, to a libretto paralleling AIDS with corruption in a 15th-century papal court. The work was first staged in London on Jan. 4, 1986.

Help, Help, the Globolinks! Satirical children's opera in one act by Gian Carlo Menotti, to his own libretto, first performed in Hamburg on Dec. 19, 1968. The Globolinks are electronic invaders from outer space bent on converting unwary humans into their own kind. But they are vulnerable to the beautiful sounds of traditional music, and are finally routed by school children led by the exquisite Mme. Euterpova (Euterpe was the Greek musical Muse). The hermaphroditic literature teacher Mr. Lavender-Gas escapes, but the school dean, the unmusical Dr. Stone, becomes a Globolink.

Henry VIII. Opera in four acts by Camille Saint-Saëns, to a libretto by Léon Détroyat and Armand Silvestre concerning the king's love for Anne Boleyn, whom he marries in spite of her love for another and the Pope's disapproval, performed for the first time in Paris on March 5, 1883.

Héritière, L'. Opera by Jean-Michel Damase, after *The Heiress*, the stage adaptation of Henry James's *Washington Square*, in which a rich father who cannot forget that in childbirth his daughter was the unwitting cause of her mother's death and who thwarts her engagement to the man she loves by cutting off her inheritance, first produced in Nancy, France, on March 13, 1974.

Hero, The. Comic opera by Gian Carlo Menotti, to his own libretto, first produced in Philadelphia on June 1, 1976. The hero of the title brings fame to his town as the record-breaking sleeper (actually, he wakes up occasionally), whose wife charges tourists two dollars to see him sleep. (The opera is the first stage work to use the expletive "shit" in its text.)

Hérodiade. Opera in four acts by Jules Massenet, to a text by Paul Millet and "Henri Grémont" (Georges Hartmann) after Gustave Flaubert's story (1877), first produced in Brussels on Dec. 19, 1881. The title, which means "daughter of Herodias," refers to Salome, for whom her uncle Herod, king of Galilee, nurtures an incestuous passion. She rejects him and declares love for the imprisoned John the Baptist. Here the story diverges from Oscar Wilde's *Salome* that served as the libretto for Richard Strauss's opera. In Massenet's opera, Salome wants to die with her adored holy man. When he is executed alone, she stabs herself to death.

Heroine. Opera in two acts by Vangjo Novo, in which an Albanian girl guerrilla heroically refuses, despite inhuman torture, to disclose the names of the communist-led partisans to the Nazi invaders in 1943, culminating in a total liberation of the land and the execution of local traitors, first performed in Tirana on June 17, 1967.

Herr von Hancken. Opera in three acts by Karl-Birger Blomdahl, his second, to a libretto dealing with a Swedish paterfamilias pursued by God for his blasphemy and saved from perdition by the devil, whom he encounters in a European spa in 1806, first mounted in Stockholm on Sept. 2, 1965.

Heure Espagnole, L' (The Spanish Hour). Opera in one act by Maurice Ravel, to a libretto by Franc-Nohain after his own comedy, first produced in Paris on May 19, 1911. The action takes place in Toledo, Spain, during the 18th century. The "Spanish hour" of the title is the period of time during which several successive lovers of the wife of a local clockmaker hide themselves in the cabinets of the large clocks in his shop. When he discovers them, they claim to be bona fide customers, and the greedy clockmaker accepts the explanations, whereupon they all make merry to the sounds of a habanera. The score is one of the finest examples of Ravel's subtle instrumentation and precise rhythms, for the mastery of which he earned the critical sobriquet "the Swiss watchmaker."

Highway No. 1, U.S.A. Opera in one act by William Grant Still, glorifying in epic tones the main north–south automobile artery leading along the coast from Maine to Florida, performed for the first time in Miami on May 11, 1963.

Hin und Zurück (There and Back). "A sketch with music" in one act by Paul Hindemith, to a libretto by Marcellus Schiffer after an English revue sketch, first performed in the Baden-Baden Festival on July 15, 1927. The cuckolded husband kills his cheating wife. Then the action reverses itself, cinema-wise: the adulteress returns to life, her husband empockets the gun, and the situation is restored to the *status quo ante*. In the end, the husband presents his wife with her birthday present.

Hippolyte et Aricie. Lyric tragedy in prologue and five acts by Jean-Philippe Rameau, to a libretto by Simon-Joseph Pellegrin after Racine's *Phèdre* and Euripides' *Hippolyte*, first performed in Paris on Oct. 1, 1733. The plot resembles other operas involving Hippolyte, his absent father, Theseus, and his amorous stepmother, Phaedra. The new element is Aricie, beloved of Hippolyte, who gives a vow of chastity to Phaedra. Theseus returns, hears false rumors, and exiles Hippolyte. Phaedra confesses her guilt and dies, and Hippolyte is reunited with Aricie, thus providing a happier ending than usual for this Greek tragedy.

Historien om en Moder (Story of a Mother). Opera by Herman Koppel, written by him when he was 17 to a sentimental story by Hans Christian Andersen, first produced in Copenhagen on Aug. 25, 1967.

Hochzeit der Sobeide, Die (Sobeide's Wedding). Opera in three acts by Alexander Tcherepnin, after the play by Hugo von Hofmannsthal, first performed in Vienna on March 17, 1933. The beautiful Sobeide, married, falls in love with a muscular youth and, horrified by her own depravity, commits suicide.

Homerische Welt. Operatic tetralogy by August Bungert, each premiered in Dresden: *Kirke* (Jan. 24, 1898), *Nausikaa* (March 20, 1901), *Odysseus' Heimkehr* (Odysseus's Homecoming; Dec. 12, 1896), and *Odysseus' Tod* (Odysseus's Death, Oct. 30, 1903). This epigonic tetralogy, desperately imitating Wagner's *Ring*, soon sank without a trace.

Houdini. Circus opera by Peter Schat, scored for seven soloists, chorus, orchestra, dancers, and, appropriately to its subject, escapologists and acrobats, first produced in Amsterdam on Sept. 29, 1977.

Hra o láske o smrti (Play of Love and Death). Opera in one act by Ján Cikker, after a 1925 play by Romain Rolland. A story of the French Revolution, the opera was first staged in Munich on Aug. 1, 1969.

Huckleberry Finn. Opera by Hall Overton, after selected tales by Mark Twain, performed for the first time in New York on May 20, 1971.

Hugh the Drover. Opera in two acts by Ralph Vaughan Williams, to a libretto by Harold Child, first performed at the Royal College of Music in London on July 4, 1924. True love is opposed by the heroine's father, who favors a rival, John the Butcher, with Hugh the Drover winning out in a boxing match between them, set in England in the year 1812 (political overtones are superinduced when Hugh is unjustly accused of being a spy in Napoleon's pay).

Huguenots, Les. Grand opera in five acts by Giacomo Meyerbeer, to a libretto by Eugéne Scribe and Emile Deschamps, first produced in Paris, Feb. 29, 1836. One of the most spectacular of 19th-century operas, it embraces history, religious strife, and family tragedy. The climatic scene occurs during the St. Bartholomew's Day massacre of French Protestants, the Huguenots, in 1572. A Catholic nobleman leads an assault on the house in which the Huguenots make their last stand, realizing too late that his own daughter is among them. She perishes with her Huguenot lover and her father is left to bemoan his fate.

Hunyadi Lászlô. Historical opera in four acts by Ferenc Erkel, to a libretto by Béni Egressy after Lŏrince Tóth's drama, first performed in Budapest on Jan. 27, 1844. The tragic story is of the leader of the Hungarian Army, László Hunyadi, who is deceived and betrayed by both the new king, László V, and his own father-in-law, leading to his eventual death by beheading.

Huron, Le. Opera in two acts by Andrée-Ernest-Modeste Grétry, to a text by Jean François Marmontel after Voltaire's satric story *L'ingénu* (1767) about the circumvention of a prearranged marriage through half sheer persistence and half miraculous happenstance, first produced in Paris on Aug. 20, 1768.

I

Ice Break, The. Opera in three acts by Michael Tippett, his fourth, to his own highly symbolic libretto dealing with the reunion of a political prisoner with his family after a great many years, involving the estrangement of his son, who questions his father's courage, and his daughter, who offers herself to a black athlete in a gesture of atonement for racial guilt. The work was performed for the first time in London on July 7, 1977.

Idomeneo, rè di Creta (Idomeneus, King of Crete). Opera in three acts by Wolfgang Amadeus Mozart, to a libretto by Giovanni Battista Varesco after Danchet's text for Campra's *Idomenée* and the ancient legend, first produced in Munich on Jan. 29, 1781. Returning from the Trojan War, Idomeneo's ship runs into a storm. To placate the sea god Poseidon, Idomeneo promises to sacrifice the first person who meets his ship at home. As luck would have it, it happens to be his son. When Idomeneo tries to evade his pledge, the gods send a monster to ravage the island of Crete. At this point comes the proverbial *deus ex machina*, which magnanimously arranges a compromise, by forcing Idomeneo's abdication.

Im Weissen Rössl (At the White Horse Inn). Operetta by Ralph Benatzky, his most celebrated, first produced in Berlin on Nov. 8, 1930. It deals with labyrinthine amours in an Austrian hotel, climaxing with the appearance on the scene of Emperor Franz Josef in person.

Immortal Hour, The. Opera in two acts by Rutland Boughton, to a libretto by "Fiona Macleod" (William Sharp), first staged in produced in Glastonbury on Aug. 26, 1914. A Celtic king plans to marry a girl from the fairyland, but she is lured away by one of her own kind to the land of Heart's Desire. The work enjoyed a spell of success during an arid London season.

Incoronazione di Poppea, L' (The Coronation of Poppea). Opera in prologue and three acts by Claudio Monteverdi, his last, to a libretto by Giovanni Francesco Busenello after Tacitus, first performed in Venice in the autumn of 1643. An ambitious Roman matron pressures her lover, the emperor Nero, to divorce his wife and install her as empress. He is made to burn so warmly that he agrees, exiles his wife and his lover's husband, and celebrates with Poppea.

Indes Galantes, Les. Opera ballet by Jean-Philippe Rameau, first produced in Paris on Aug. 23, 1735. The "amorous Indies" of the title stretch through Turkey, Persia, and South America. The score includes some interesting samples of tonal painting, including a storm represented by a drum roll.

Ines de Castro. Opera in three acts by Giuseppe Persiani, to a libretto by Salvadore Cammararo, based loosely on 14th-century history, first performed in Naples on Jan. 28, 1835. Assassins act on behalf of the king. Alfonso wants his son, Don Pedro, to wed Bianca, but instead weds Ines de Castro. The king imprisons the lovers. Bianca later persuades Ines to agree to exile, despite leaving her sons. When they are murdered, she becomes mad and is poisoned by Gonzales, the villianous murderer.

Ines de Castro. Opera by Thomas Pasatieri, to a libretto involving the mistress of Pedro I of Portugal who was assassinated by a court clique in 1355, whose corpse was exhumed by her imperial lover, who forced her assassins to kiss her skeletal remains during her postmortem coronation, first staged in Baltimore on March 30, 1976.

In seinem Garten liebt Don Perlimplin Belisa. Comic opera by Wolfgang Fortner, his third on the subject, drawn from García Lorca's *Bodas de Sangre,* wherein the minifutuent husband of an unusually mobile donna performs a self-induced schizophrenia so that half the time he is a magnificently potent youth, his real self ultimately killing his fantasy ego in a semi-homicidal demisuicide, performed for the first time at the opening of the Music Festival at Schwetzingen, Germany, on May 10, 1962.

Inspector General, The (Der Revisor). Opera by Eugene Zádor, to his own English libretto after the famous Gogol comedy of mutual deception and misrepresentation in czarist Russia, composed in 1928 and later radically revised and orchestrated, first performed on June 11, 1971, in Los Angeles.

Intermezzo. Opera in two acts by Richard Strauss, to his own libretto, performed for the first time in Dresden on Nov. 4, 1924. Based on an incident in the domestic life of Strauss and his wife, Pauline, a composer's wife threatens divorce when a love letter arrives in his mail by misdirection. Fortunately, he proves his total innocence.

Intolleranza 1960. Opera ("scenic action") in two parts by Luigi Nono, to texts Ripellino, Brecht, Sartre, Fucik, and Mayakovsky, first performed in Venice on April 13, 1961. The thoughts of revolutionary poets are integrated into a realistically allegorical continuity of nightmarishly unconnected tableaux, in which a refugee is dodecaphonically tortured by four choruses electronically transmitted from the four points of the compass, and a magnificently irrelevant ballet culminates in the atomic explosion of a polydodecaphonic chord.

Iolanta (Iolanthe). Opera in one act (nine scenes) by Pyotr Il'yich Tchaikovsky, to a text by his brother Modest, after Henrik Hertz's play *Kong René Datter,* itself after Hans Christian Andersen, first performed in St. Petersburg on Dec. 18, 1892. Iolanta is a blind girl living in 15th-century Provence. A Moorish physician promises to cure her if her desire to see is truly passionate, and her love for a Burgundian knight provides the necessary passion. The operation is a success. She sees her knight for the first time, admires the beauty and symmetry of his facial features, and marries him to much jubilation. The work is not among the composer's masterpieces.

Iphigénie en Aulide. Opera in three acts by Christopher Willibald Gluck, to a libretto by Marie François Roullet after a play (1674) by Racine based on Euripides, first produced in Paris on April 19, 1774. The Greek fleet is in doldrums in the port of Aulis and cannot proceed to Troy, for which it is bound, because Agamemnon, king of Crete, had killed a sacred animal in the temple of Artemis, the virgin huntress and moon divinity. A priest warns that the goddess will not be appeased unless Agamemnon sacrifices his daughter, Iphigenia, by immolation. He is willing to yield, but her bridegroom, Achilles, voices objections. In the end, the gods are appeased, and Iphigenia is spared.

Iphigénie en Tauride. Opera in four acts by Christopher Willibald Gluck, to a libretto by Nicolas-François Guillard and after Euripides, first produced in Paris on May 18, 1779. The story is a sequel to the composer's *Iphigénie en Aulide.* The heroine, saved from immolation, travels to Tauris (Greek name for the Crimea), where she joins the local Scythians. When her brother, Orestes (along with his friend Pylades), is seized as an invader, she saves him, rejoins the Greeks, and returns to her native land. The opera is frequently revived in modern times.

Iris. Opera in three acts by Pietro Mascagni, to a text by Luigi Illica, first performed in Rome on Nov. 22, 1898. The action takes place in modern Japan. Iris, pure and innocent, is abducted by a villainous suitor who places her in a bordello. Her blind father curses her, believing her guilty, at which point she throws herself into a ravine. But being innocent, she is lifted by a host of angels to heaven.

Irmelin. Opera in three acts by Frederick Delius, to his own libretto, not performed until May 4, 1953, in Oxford, nearly twenty years after the composer's death. Irmelin is a princess in love with a swineherd who fortuitously turns out to be a prince himself. They meet at a brook, and all ends happily.

Isabeau. Opera in three acts by Pietro Mascagni, to a text by Luigi Illica based on the famous horseback ride of the medieval Lady Godiva wherein the daughter of a tyrannical feudal lord parades through town mounted on a white horse completely naked to protest against being forced into a physically and morally abhorrent marriage. When a fervent swain who throws roses on her unclad figure from a balcony is condemned to death at the stake, she leaps into the flames herself. It was premiered in Buenos Aires on June 2, 1911.

Isle de Merlin, L'. Opera by Christopher Willibald Gluck, first performed on Oct. 3, 1758, in Vienna. Two young Frenchmen find themselves on the island of the magus Merlin and fall in love with his two nieces. To gain their object of matrimony, Merlin insists that they play and win a dice game. The Frenchmen lose, but Merlin helps them win their brides anyway.

Italiana in Algeri, L' (The Italian Girl in Algiers). Opera in two acts by Gioacchino Rossini, to a libretto by Angelo Anelli, produced in Venice on May 22, 1813. The Italian woman in the title seeks her beloved who has been captured by and enslaved by the bey of Algiers. When after some misadventures she finds him, the wily bey professes his carnal desire for her. As he relaxes his controls, she frees her lover and escapes with him.

Ivanhoe. Grand opera in five acts by Arthur Sullivan, his only attempt at serious opera, to a libretto by Julian Sturgis, first produced in London on Jan. 31, 1891, for the inauguration of the short-lived Royal English Opera House. Based on the 1818 novel by Sir Walter Scott, the opera failed with the public.

Ivrogne corrigé, L' (The Drunkard Reformed). Opera in two acts by Christopher Willibald Gluck, to a libretto by Louis Anseaume after La Fontaine's fable *L'ivrogne en Enfer* in which Colette and her lover thwart her uncle's plan for her to marry another, first performed in Vienna in April, 1760.

Izeÿl. Opera by Euger d'Albert from pseudo-Hindu lore, first performed in Hamburg on Nov. 6, 1909. Izeÿl is an Indian princess whose lips are poisonous. She kills her suitors by kissing them until she dies herself when one of her suitors turns out to be immune.

J

Jacobowsky unde der Oberst (Jacobowsky and the Colonel). Opera in four acts by Giselher Klebe, after Franz Werfel's ironic play detailing the tragicomic adventures of a Jewish Pole who saves a snobbish Polish aristocrat after the military debacle in France in 1940, first produced at the Hamburg State Opera on Nov. 2, 1965.

Jacob's Room. Monodrama in two parts by Morton Subotnick, based on Virginia Woolf's novel of the same name and *Eleni* by Nicholas Gage, first performed in San Francisco on Jan. 11, 1985. The work is unstaged, scored for string quartet and voice, and set in an agonizingly permutated quasi-tonal idiom. A third part was added later, to a text by Elie Wiesel, portraying the horrors of Nazi transportation of Jews to their final destination.

Jacobin, The (Jakobín). Opera in three acts by Antonín Dvořák, to a libretto by Marie Červinková-Riegrová, first performed in Prague on Feb. 12, 1889. The action takes place in a small Bohemian town in 1793. Bohuš, a young Bohemian, is denounced by his detractors as a radical "Jacobin," an appellation that bore a particular stigma during the French Revolution. Bohuš is forced to leave Bohemia for several years, but virtue triumphs in the end when the villainous calumniators are exposed, the purported radical returns home with his newly acquired French bride, and he inherits a rich patrimony.

Jasager, Der (The Affirmer). Opera in two acts by Kurt Weill, to a libretto by Bertolt Brecht after a 15th-century Japanese tale of fatalistic feudalism wherein a young boy crossing the mountains into a valley in quest of a miraculously curative herb to combat an epidemic falls ill himself, and, according to a prearranged ritual, does not resist when his companions push him into the precipice so as to enable them to accomplish their laudable purpose. The work was first broadcast over Berlin Radio on June 23, 1930.

Jazavac pred sudom (The Badger before the Jury). The first nationalist opera of Bosnia by Miloje Milosevič, inspired by a folk legend wherein Austro-Hungarian rule in Bosnia is wittily satirized, first produced on Dec. 2, 1978, in Sarajevo (the historic locality where a Bosnian youth assassinated the heir to the Austrian throne in the summer of 1914, precipitating the First World War).

Jean de Paris. Opera in two acts by Adrian Boieldieu, to a libretto by Claude de Saint-Just, first staged in Paris on April 4, 1812. The young widowed princess of Navarre chooses the crown prince of France to be her new husband. He tests her faithfulness by flirting with her, incognito, on the ballroom floor of a Pyranean inn where both of them are guests. She feigns ignorance of his ruse, responds appropriately demurely, and the two are happily united.

Jenůfa. Opera in three acts by Leoš Janáček, to a libretto by the composer after Gabriela Preissová's drama (1890), first produced in Brno under the name *Její pastorkyňa* (Her foster daughter) on Jan. 21, 1904. The subject is grisly, as peasant life in central Europe could be in the 19th century. Jenůfa is heavy with child by a Moravian farmhand. When the child is born, the moralistic female sexton of the local church drowns it to save Jenůfa from disgrace. The truth is found out, the hideous sexton culprit is taken to prison, and Jenůfa marries a stepbrother of her original seducer. The work is one of the most remarkable examples of modern Bohemian music drama. The score underwent several revisions, and it was not until the performance of the final version in Prague, May 26, 1916, that Janáček was recognized as an important international composer.

Jessonda. Opera in three acts by Louis Spohr, to a libretto by E. H. Gehe after Antoine Lemierre's tragedy *La veuve de Malabar*, first performed in Kassel on July 28, 1823. This opera, now a fossil, was once a great favorite, particularly in England. Jessonda is the widow of the rajah of Malabar, and she must immolate herself like a good Brahmin. Portuguese fanfares are sounded and no less a person than Tristan d'Acunha, the explorer, enters the scene. He recognizes in Jessonda his ideal woman, and she sees in him her ideal man. The chorus of Brahmins urges her to take her rightful place at her husband's funerary mound, but now she wants to live. When the Portuguese marines land in force, the Brahmins desist in their foul superstition, and a happy ending is assured.

Jesu Hochzeit (Jesus's Wedding). Opera by Gottfried von Einem, to a libretto in which Christ takes a wife, which scandalized the whole of Christendom, first staged in Vienna on May 18, 1980.

Jeu de Robin et de Marion. Medieval play with music by Adam de la Halle, c.1280. An amorous pastorale with dialogue and songs, this is the first extant secular musical drama.

Joe Hill. Opera by Alan Bush, on the subject of the execution of the labor agitator Joe Hill in Salt Lake City on Nov. 19, 1915, staged for the first time in East Berlin on Sept. 29, 1970.

Johnny Johnson. Musical fable by Kurt Weill, with text by Paul Green first produced on Broadway in New York on Nov. 19, 1936. Weill's first American work concerns the fate of an idealistic soldier who fights Germany in World War I, which he truly believes is the war to end all wars. He tries to immunize the military by channeling laughing gas into them, but in the process of securing world peace he loses his girl and is driven insane. An ideological play, it failed at the box office.

Jolie fille de Perth, La. Opera in four acts by Georges Bizet, to a libretto by Jules-Henri Saint-Georges and Jules Adenis based loosely on Sir Walter Scott's novel *The Fair Maid of Perth* (1832), first performed in Paris on Dec. 26, 1867. The plot involves a betrothed couple, a lecherous duke, a young gypsy woman with her own agenda, and an apprentice who can't hold his drink. The situation almost ends with a fatal duel, but the gypsy saves the day, and the couple is reunited in the nick of time.

Jonah. Opera by Anatol Vieru, to a libretto after the tragedy by Marin Sorescu, first staged in Bucharest on Oct. 31, 1976.

Jongleur de Notre Dame, Le (The Juggler of Notre Dame). Opera in three acts by Jules Massenet, to a libretto by Maurice Léna after a story by Anatole France in *L'étui de nacre* (1892), first produced in Monte Carlo on Feb. 18, 1902. The action takes place in France in the 14th century, focusing on a street juggler who performs for and then collapses in front of a statue of the Holy Virgin. Before he dies, the Virgin silently blesses him with her marmoreal hand, and he becomes, in legend and tradition, "the juggler of Our Lady." This is one of the few operas ever written without (human) female roles.

Jonny spielt auf (Johny Strikes Up). Opera in two parts (11 scenes) by Ernst Krenek, to his own text, first produced in Leipzig on Feb. 10, 1927. The opera was sensationally successful as the first opera to make use of the jazz idiom. Jonny (without an "h" and pronounced Yonny) is a Negro musician who becomes a famous jazz band leader, captivating audiences around the globe. When the opera was first produced by the Metropolitan Opera in New York in 1929, the role of Jonny was changed into that of a blackface musician in order not to offend the segregationist sensitivities of some of the patrons, particularly in scenes when Jonny consorts with white chambermaids.

Joseph. Opera in three acts by Etienne-Nicolas Méhul, to a libretto by Alexandre Duval set in Memphis in biblical times wherein Joseph, disguised as Cleophas, saves Egypt from famine and also reconciles with his estranged father and brothers, first produced in Paris on Feb. 17, 1807.

Jot, oder Wann kommt der Herr zurück? (Jot, or When Does the Man Come Back?) Mock-mystical opera by Klaus Huber, in three parts (*Sandstone Figures, How to Heal Wounds*, and *Concrete Theater)*, with the action of theologically and metaphysical content (the mysterious word *Jot* in the title may be the Berlin dialect for *Gott*, or God), first produced in Berlin on Sept. 27, 1973.

Jubilee. Opera by Ulysses Kay, commissioned for the Bicenntenial to a libretto set on an antebellum plantation in Georgia in which both slave owner and slaves unite in an optimistic jubilee when all men are really equal, first staged in Jackson, Mississippi, on Nov. 20, 1976.

Judas Tree, The. "Musical drama of Judas Iscariot" by Peter Dickinson, to a libretto wherein the tree on which Judas hanged himself is mystically identified with the tree of the true cross, first performed at the College of St. Mark and St. John in London on May 27, 1965.

Judith (Yudit'). Opera by Alexander Serov, first performed in St. Petersburg on May 28, 1863. The libretto is drawn from the Apocrypha. Judith, a patriotic Jewess, risks her virtue by penetrating the tent of the Assyrian chieftain Holofernes, whose army besieges her city. She plies him with wine and, as he sinks into a drunken torpor, she cuts off his head, packs it into a sack, and returns to the city. She holds aloft the richly bearded head of the enemy king at an assembly, and the Jewish people explode in jubilation.

Judith. Opera (opéra serieux) in three acts by Arthur Honegger, based on the same subject as Serov's earlier work, first performed in Monte Carlo on Feb. 13, 1926, the composer conducting. This work was expanded from the incidental music Honegger wrote for a play by René Morax.

Juha. Opera in three acts by Aarre Merikanto, to a libretto Aïno Ackté in which an elderly man kills himself after his more youthful bride lets herself be imprudently impregnated by a transient philanderer, posthumously performed on the stage in the small Finnish locality of Lahti on Oct. 28, 1963, five years after the composer's death.

Juive, La (The Jewess). Grand opera in five acts by Fromentak Halévy, to a libretto by Eugéne Scribe, a study of anti-Semitism and its ill effects on all involved, first produced in Paris on Feb. 23, 1835, in a spectacular production. Éléazar has raised the daughter of a magistrate (now Cardinal Brogni), who thought her lost in a war as Rachel, a Jewess. Cardinal Brogni has been persecuting the Jews of the city for years. Rachel has a lover, Prince Léopold, who pretends to be a Jew named Samuel and, unknown to her, is already married. Eventually, he has to reveal his true status. Rachel denounces him to the court, and both are condemned to death, along with Éléazar. Rachel changes her story to save Léopold's life, but the other two are still burned at the stake. The cardinal pleads to know where his daughter is. "There!" says Éléazar, pointing to Rachel. The two die as the curtain falls.

Julia. Chamber opera by Rudolf Kelterborn, in which the setting of Shakespeare's *Romeo and Juliet* is changed to the west Jordan region and its essential conflict made an Israeli–Palestinian dispute, mounted for the first time in Zürich on April 18, 1991.

Julien. Opera in prologue and four acts by Gustave Charpentier, to the composer's own libretto, a failed sequel to the highly successful *Louise* (1900), first staged in Paris on June 4, 1913. Julien, a painter who figured in the earlier opera, is visited by the deceased Louise's spirit in a vision to encourage him to continue working on his art. Eventually, he follows her to the land of death.

Julietta. Opera in three acts by Bohuslav Martinů, to a libretto by the composer after Georges Neveux's drama *Juliette, ou La clé des songes* (1930) wherein a young man exteriorizes his three dreams about an ethereally beautiful maiden amid oneiristically fluctuating scenes involving Arabian camel riders, pawnbrokers, and blind souvenir vendors. The opera was first produced in Prague on March 16, 1938.

Julius Caesar Jones. Opera in two acts by Malcolm Williamson, to a libretto dealing with imaginative children who conjure up a surrealistic Polynesian fantasy, produced for the first time at a children's theater in London on Jan. 4, 1966.

Junge Lord, Der (The Young Lord). Opera in two acts by Hans Werner Henze, to a libretto by Ingeborg Bachmann after a parable in Wilhelm Hauff's *Der Scheik von Alexandria und seine Sklaven* (1827), first performed in Berlin on April 7, 1965. In a typical Hans Werner Henze musical diatribe against the bourgeoisie, a well-dressed ape arrives with his master in a small German town. The snobbish residents take the ape's simian grunts as the laconic utterances of a British lord. Naturally, the locals get their comeuppance.

K

Kaiser Jovarin. Opera in four acts by Rudolf Kelterborn, to a libretto wherein Jupiter assumes the identity of the ephemeral Roman emperor Jovian (reigned 363–364 A.D.), marries his bride, and ultimately reveals himself and returns to Mt. Olympus, first produced in Karlsruhe on March 4, 1967.

Kaiser von Atlantis, Der (The Emperor of Atlantis). Opera by Viktor Ullmann, to a libretto by Petr Kien about the abdication of Death, written in 1944 at the Theresienstadt concentration camp in Czechoslovakia shortly before his transfer to Auschwitz where he was put to death, the score turning up in 1972 in the hands of the British conductor Kerry Woodward, who restored the barely legible manuscript, produced for the first time in Amsterdam on Dec. 16, 1975.

Karadjordje (Black George) or ***Seme zla*** (The Seed of the Wicked). Television opera by Stanojlo RajičIč, to the text by Ivan Studen depicting psychological aspects of the conflicts between Karadjordje and Miloš Obrenovič, the leaders of the first and second Serbian revolts against Ottoman rule in the early 19th century, ending in Karadjordje's defeat. The work was first broadcast over Belgrade Television on June 26, 1977.

Kashchey, the Immortal. Opera by Nikolai Rimsky-Korsakov, first performed in Moscow on Dec. 25, 1902. Like her father, Kashchei's daughter is sinister. By means of a magic potion she induces Prince Ivan to forget his beloved bride. This done, she sharpens a sword with which she plans to kill him, but at the crucial moment a tempest clears the air and awakens the prince. He returns to his beloved, and Kashchei's evil domain is blown away.

Kát'a Kabanová. Opera in three acts by Leoš Janáček, to a libretto by the composer after Alexander Ostrovsky's tragedy *The Storm* (1859), first produced in Brno on Nov. 23, 1921. The heroine, Kat'a, carries on clandestinely with a friend of her husband's. Internal guilt and external condemnation drive her to suicide during a storm, which she accomplishes by diving into the Volga. The evocative score has become a favorite in modern opera companies.

Kentervilski duh (The Ghost of Canterville). Comic opera by Boris Papandopulo, after the satirically fantastic tale by Oscar Wilde, first staged in Osijek on June 5, 1979.

Kesa and Morito. Opera in three acts by Kan Ishii, a horrendous tale based on a historical incident of medieval Japanese passions in which the reckless suitor of a friend's beauteous wife, scheming to murder the husband in the darkness of the night, severs with his sword the head of his beloved. The opera was first produced in Tokyo on Nov. 20, 1968, by an all-Japanese company.

Khovanshchina (The Khovansky Affair). Music drama in six scenes by Modest Mussorgsky, to a libretto from historical sources by the composer and Vladimir Stasov, posthumously produced in St. Petersburg on Feb. 21, 1886, five years after Mussorgsky's death. The story concerns the rebellious activity of the followers of Prince Khovansky, the leader of the schismatic "Old Believers." Surrounded by Peter the Great's loyal troops, they immolate themselves in fiery death, including Marfa, a seeress, and her fiancé, Khovansky's son, Audrey. The score, left unfinished by Mussorgsky, was completed by Rimsky-Korsakov in 1911, and later reworked by Dmitri Shostakovich in 1960.

Kinder der Heide, Die (The Children of the Steppes). Opera by Anton Rubinstein, first performed in Vienna on Feb. 23, 1861. The story centers on love and intrigue against a background of gypsy life.

King Arthur, or the British Worthy. "Dramatick opera" in prologue, five acts, and epilogue by Henry Purcell, to a libretto by John Dryden wherein Arthur, king of the Britons, and Oswald, king of the Saxons, duel for the hand of Emmeline, first produced in London, probably early June 1691.

King Priam. Opera in three acts by Michael Tippett, to his own libretto based on Homer's *Iliad,* first staged in Coventry on May 29, 1962. Set in the time of the Trojan War the opera focuses on Priam and the Greek hero Achilles. Priam's son, Hector, kills Patroclus and Achilles kills Hector in revenge. Priam comes to gather the body of his son in Achilles' tent, and the old king and the young hero find a moment of understanding among enemies.

King Roger (Król Roger). Opera in three acts by Kurol Szymanowski, to a libretto by Jaroslaw Iwaszkiewicz and the composer, premiered in Warsaw on June 19, 1926. The plot concerns the conversion of a 12th-century Sicilian king to the mystical creed of an Indian holy man.

King Samuel. Opera by Kiril Makedonski, to his own libretto depicting turbulent events in Macedonia in the 10th century, first produced in Skopje on Nov. 5, 1968.

King's Henchman, The. Opera in three acts by Deems Taylor, to a libretto by Edna St. Vincent Millay, commissioned by and first staged at the Metropolitan Opera in New York on Feb. 17, 1927, at the time one of very few American operas given by that institution. Its hero was the messenger of the king of England who was sent to fetch the royal bride from overseas. Instead, he appropriates her for himself and commits suicide when his treachery is revealed.

Kiss, The (*Hubička*). Folk opera in three acts by Bedřich Smetana, to a libretto by Eliška Krásnohorská first performed in Prague on Nov. 7, 1876. A young widower must persuade his fiancée to seal their betrothal with the traditional kiss. He finally tracks her down and forces a kiss.

Kluge, Die (The Clever Young Woman). Opera in six scenes by Carl Orff, to his own libretto after a Grimm fairy tale, first performed in Frankfurt am Main on Feb. 20, 1943. A king marries a peasant woman who is far superior to him in intelligence, so he decides to divorce her, but gives her unqualified permission to take from the palace one thing she values above all else. She takes him to her house. He then restores her to royal status, and they live happily ever after.

Knife, The. Opera in two acts by Daniel Jones, to his own libretto wherein a Negro accused of raping and murdering a white girl in a southern mining town in 1866 is saved from lynching when a conscience-stricken white miner confesses the crime. The opera was first produced at Sadler's Wells in London on Dec. 2, 1963.

Knot Garden, The. Opera in three acts by Michael Tippett, first produced at Covent Garden in London on Dec. 2, 1970. Tippett's libretto, based symbolically on Shakespeare's *The Tempest,* depicts a knotty psychological involvement in which a white musician and a black poet have a homosexual relationship, a feminist revolutionary confronts her hidden lesbianism, and a nubile maiden tries to escape the clutches of a married voluptuary, whose wife has retreated into a perfumed garden of desperate eroticism.

Koanga. Opera in prologue, three acts, and epilogue by Frederick Delius, to a libretto by the composer Charles F. Keary after George Washington Cable's novel *The Grandissimes* (1880), first performed in Elberfeld, on March 30, 1904. A beautiful young mulatto woman on a Mississippi plantation loves the handsome African prince Koanga, but the slave owner lusts after her himself. The lovers organize a voodoo ritual to exorcize their white foes. Eventually Koanga dies, and his beloved stabs herself with his spear.

König Hirsch (The Stag King). Opera in three acts by Hans Werner Henze, to a libretto by Heinz von Cramer, first produced in Berlin on Sept. 23, 1956, and subsequently revised and staged under the original name of Gozzi's 1762 fable *Il Re Cervo,* on which the opera is based. As the title suggests, the king is transformed into a stag, but he eventually sheds his horns, regains his human shape, and returns to his native town.

Königen von Saba, Die (The Queen of Sheba). Opera in four acts by Karl Goldmark, to a libretto by Salomon Mosenthal based on the biblical story of the queen of Sheba's visit to King Solomon, first performed in Vienna on March 10, 1875.

Königskinder (The King's Children). Opera in three acts by Engelbert Humperdinck, to a libretto by "Ernst Rosmer" (Else Bernstein-Porges), first performed at the Metropolitan Opera in New York on Dec. 28, 1910. The libretto reverses the course of events of Humperdinck's famous children's opera *Hänsel und Gretel.* Here the malevolent witch feeds poisonous candy to the young prince and the Goose Girl, whom he loves, and both die. The premiere starred Geraldine Farrar, a popular soprano, as the Goose Girl. The opera is notable for its use of *Sprechstimme* long before Schoenberg.

Krakatit. Opera in two parts by Václav Kaslík, after a novelette of Karel Čapek wherein the inventor of a powerful explosive, Krakatit, has a vivid hallucination that a group of anarchists forces him to use his invention to destroy society, and upon awakening becomes a militant pacifist, first performed on Czechoslovak TV on March 5, 1961.

Krútňavà (Whirlpool). Opera in six scenes by Eugene Suchoň, first performed in Bratislava on Dec. 10, 1949. The title refers to the moral dilemma in which a young village girl finds herself when her lover is killed by an unknown assailant. The killer, tortured by his memories, is finally apprehended and brought to justice. The work is considered one of the most successful Czech operas in the post–Janáček era.

L

Labyrinth. Surrealistic TV opera by Gian Carlo Menotti, to his own libretto, in which a distraught bridegroom misplaces the key to his hotel room on his wedding night and gets lost in a maze of nightmarish corridors and outer space conveyed by special camera effects. The work was performed for the first time as a commissioned work by NBC Television in New York on March 3, 1963.

Lächeln am Füsse der Leiter. Opera by Antonio Bibalo, his first after Henry Miller's story "The Smile at the Foot of the Ladder," first produced with a German libretto translated from the original Italian (*Sorrisi ai piedi d'una scala*) at the Hamburg State Opera on April 6, 1965.

Lady Macbeth of the Mtzensk District (Ledi Makbet Mtsenskoao uyezda). Opera in four acts by Dmitri Shostakovich, to a libretto by Alexander Preys and the composer after Leskov's story (1865), first performed in Leningrad on Jan. 22, 1934. The story depicts adultery and murder in Russia in the middle of the 19th century. The title is hardly justified, since the protagonist conspires with her lover to murder her husband, not her husband's potential rival, as in Shakespeare's tragedy. The culprits are convicted and sent to Siberia. When he takes another mistress there, she kills both her rival and herself. Unexpectedly, *Pravda,* the official organ of the Soviet Communist Party, attacked the opera as a product of bourgeois decadence. Shostakovich apologized abjectly for his musical sins and stopped writing operas for a number of years. The opera was eventually revived in a sanitized version under the title *Katerina Izmaylova* (the name of its heroine), minus the naturalistic sexual intermezzo in the orchestra, in Moscow on Jan. 8, 1963.

Lake Ukereve. Opera in five scenes by Otmar Mácha, to his own libretto dealing with the medical missionaries combating the effects of sleeping sickness in central Africa in 1900, first produced in Prague on May 27, 1966.

Lakmé. Opera in three acts by Léo Delibes, to a libretto by Edmond Gondinet and Philippe Gille after Pierre Loti's novel *Le mariage de Loti*, first performed in Paris on April 14, 1883. Lakmé, the daughter of a priest of Brahma, is loved by a British officer. He inadvertently profanes the Buddhist temple by entering it with his shoes on, whereupon he is denounced by the priest. In the end, Lakmé realizes the futility of her love, plucks a poisonous flower, and dies. Lakmé's "Bell Song" is a perennial favorite with coloratura sopranos.

Last Savage, The (Le dernier sauvage). Comic opera by Gian Carlo Menotti, to his own libretto, first performed (not in its original Italian, but in French) in Paris on Oct. 21, 1963, and later in English in an elaborate Metropolitan Opera production on Jan. 23, 1964. An eccentric Chicago millionairess goes to India in quest of the Abominable Snowman. Scheming individuals produce a tall human whom they declare to be the Snowman. Delighted, the heiress imports him to America, but he is appalled by modern life and abominates the snows of Chicago. When he hears a concert of dodecaphonic music, he decides to quit, and goes back to the Himalayas.

Lear. Opera by Aribert Reimann, after Shakespeare, first staged in Munich on July 9, 1978, Dietrich Fischer-Dieskau in the atonally cast leading role.

Legend of the Invisible City of Kitezh and the Maiden Fevronia, The (Skazaniye o nevidimom grade Kitezhe i deve Fevronii). Mystical opera in four acts by Nikolai Rimsky-Korsakov, to a libretto by Vladimir Belsky, first produced in St. Petersburg on Feb. 20, 1907. Because of its sustained devotional character and the hymn-like quality of its theme, it was often described as "the Russian *Parsifal.*" The action takes place at the time of the Tartar invasion of Russia. Fevronia, the bride of the prince of Kitezh, prays that the city of Kitezh be made invisible so as to be saved from the invaders. Her prayer is answered. As the city vanishes, only the pealing of the church bells reveals its existence.

Leili and Medzhnun. Opera by Hadzhibekov, first performed in Baku on Jan. 25, 1908. Leili loves a youth who is nicknamed Medzhnun (madman) because of his unrestrained passion for her. When she is forced to marry a wealthy merchant, Medzhnun seizes every occasion to tell her of his misery, until her heart breaks and she expires in her husband's arms. Medzhnun visits her tomb, now that she belongs to him alone, and he too dies.

Lembitu. Opera in two acts by Villem Kapp, relating the defeat administered to the crusading German Knights by the Estonians in the 12th century, produced in Tallinn on Aug. 23, 1961.

Leonora. Opera by William Fry, based on a popular play by Bulwer-Lytton, first produced in Philadelphia on June 4, 1845. After a brief flurry of publicity, *Leonora* sank into the footnotes of music history.

Let's Build a Nut House. Chamber opera in memory of Hindemith by Robert Moran, a wistfully perverse homage to the modern German creator of *Gebrauchmusik* who himself wrote a children's opera, *Wir bauen eine Stadt* (Let's Build a City). Moran's work was first performed in San Jose, California, on April 19, 1969.

Let's Make an Opera. "Entertainment for young people" in two parts by Benjamin Britten, to a text by Eric Crozier, first performed at the Aldeburgh Festival on June 14, 1949, incorporates as its third act the opera *The Little Sweep*, ostensibly planned in front of the audience. The story recounts the inhumane practice of sweeping chimneys in Victorian England by lowering children from the roof into the fireplace to clean the soot with their little bodies.

Letze Schuss, Der (The Last Shot). Opera by Siegfried Matthus, to a libretto dealing with the romance between a Red Army girl guerrilla and a captured White Army officer during the civil war in central Asia in 1919, whom she is assigned to guard and whom she shoots down. The opera was first staged in East Berlin as part of the celebration of the semicentennial of the Soviet Revolution on Nov. 5, 1967.

Leviathan. Lyric-fantastic chamber opera by Detlev Glanert, after Thornton Wilder's "Leviathan," published as one of sixteen plays in his 1928 collection *The Angel That Troubled the Waters*, chronicling a young shipwrecked prince who encounters a mermaid who asks for his soul in return for whatever he wishes and who is devoured by a sea monster when he refuses to trade, first staged in Hamburg on Oct. 2, 1991.

Libuše. Opera in three acts by Bedřich Smetana, to an originally German libretto by Josef Wenzig, translated into Czech by Ervín Spindler, first produced at the inauguration of the National Theater in Prague on June 11, 1881. The eponymous queen of Bohemia searches for a worthy consort, someone who will be able to contribute his masculine strength to governance. She finds a satisfactory candidate and marries him. He becomes king.

Liebe der Danae, Die (The Love of Danae). Opera in three acts by Richard Strauss, first given in a public dress rehearsal in Salzburg on Aug. 16, 1944. It was given its official premiere posthumously in Salzburg on Aug. 14, 1952, nearly three years after the composer's death. The libretto is by Josef Gregor, after a sketch by Hugo von Hofmannsthal. In a newly invented episode, the mortal Danae is in a quandary: she must choose between Jupiter and Midas for a lover. She chooses Midas, and does not yield even when Jupiter assumes the shape of Midas to deceive her. Jupiter is compelled to accept defeat.

Liebesverbot, Das (The Ban on Love). Early opera in two acts by Richard Wagner, to the composer's libretto after Shakespeare's *Measure for Measure*, first performed in Magdeburg on March 29, 1836. Unmarried love being a capital crime, an incautious youth is sentenced to death for fornication. But his liberal-minded sister arouses the populace against the brutality of the law, and her brother is saved.

Life for the Czar, A (Zhizn' za tsarya). Opera in four acts and epilogue by Mikhail Glinka, to a libretto by Baron Georgy Fyodorovich Rosen, first produced in St. Petersburg on Dec. 9, 1836, the first Russian opera to enter the standard repertory. The czar of the opera is young Michael Romanov, elected in 1612 to rule Russia after a long period of social unrest. The Poles, intermittently warring with Russia, send a group of soldiers to kill him. Losing their way, they ask the peasant Ivan Susanin to guide them to the czar's house, but he instead leads them into an impenetrable forest. The invaders kill him, but the czar is saved.

Lily. Opera by Leon Kirchner, based on the novel *Henderson the Rain King* by Saul Bellow (Lily is Henderson's lissom wife), first staged by the N.Y. City Opera on April 14, 1977.

Lily of Killarney, The. Opera in three acts by Julius Benedict, to a libretto by John Oxenford and Dion Boucicault after Boucicault's drama *The Colleen Bawn* (1860), first produced in London on Feb. 10, 1862. Hardress Cregan is being encouraged to marry the heiress Ann Shute for her money, despite the fact that he is already married to a peasant, Eily O'Connor. Mrs. Cregan schemes to have Eily killed, but when Eily and her rescuer reappear, the truth of their marriage is finally disclosed.

Linda di Chamounix. Opera in three acts by Gaetano Donizetti, to a libretto by Gaetano Rossi, first produced in Vienna on May 19, 1842. Linda is coveted by the Marchese de Boisfleury but instead goes to work in Paris, where she meets the painter Carlo, who proposes marriage. Linda is wary, however, for Carlo turns out to be the Visconti di Sirval, nephew of the Marchese. She therefore avoids Carlo's advances, but nonetheless is troubled by the news that he is to marry a rich girl. When Linda returns dejectedly to Chamounix, Carlo follows. Having rejected his mother's choice for a bride, with her blessing he has come to ask for Linda's hand.

Lion, the Witch and the Wardrobe, The. Opera in four acts by John McCabe, his first, to a libretto from a Christian parable by C. S. Lewis with a cast of characters on three hypostatic levels, human (four schoolboys), preternatural (a leonine Christ figure), and a bestiary (of superanimals), performed for the first time at the Manchester (England) Cathedral Festival on April 29, 1969.

Lizzie Borden. Opera by Jack Beeson, to a libretto drawn from the famous parenticidal case of the 1890s in New England ("[she] gave her mother forty whacks, [and] when she saw what she had done, she gave her father forty-one"), first produced by the New York City Opera on March 25, 1965.

Loca, La. Opera by Gian Carlo Menotti, written as a farewell vehicle for Beverly Sills, based on the true story of 15th-century Juana of Castile, daughter of Ferdinand and Isabella, who goes mad after her husband, father, and son try to usurp her throne and contrive to have her incarcerated for nearly fifty years. The work was first produced in San Diego on June 3, 1979, with Sills in the leading role.

Lodger, The. Opera in two acts by Phyllis Tate, relating in nostalgically somber tones the predicament of an elderly couple who discover that their lodger is Jack the Ripper and who charitably let him leave and vanish into the London fog as a young detective on his trail takes time off to pay court to their daughter, performed for the first time in London on July 14, 1960.

Lodoïska. Opera in three acts by Luigi Cherubini, to a libretto by Claude-François Fillette-Loraux after Louvet de Couvrai's *Les amours du chevalier de Faublas*, successfully produced in Paris on July 18, 1791. The eponymous heroine loves a political prisoner held by a medieval Polish warlord who covets her himself. When his castle is besieged by the invading Tartar army, Lodoïska escapes with her lover.

Lodoletta. Opera in three acts by Pietro Mascagni, to a libretto by G. Forzano after Ouida's novel *Two Little Wooden Shoes* (1874), first produced in Rome on April 30, 1917. The story tells of an innocent Dutch girl who is seduced and then abandoned by a Parisian painter. When, seized by scruples, he goes to Holland to find her, she is dead and her native wooden shoes are all that is left.

Lohengrin. Opera in three acts by Richard Wagner, his first great masterpiece, to his own libretto, first performed in Weimar on Aug. 28, 1850. Franz Liszt conducted it in Wagner's absence, Wagner being at the time in exile in Switzerland as a fugitive from Saxony, sought by authorities for his rather nominal involvement in the 1848 revolution. In *Lohengrin*, as always, Wagner shows his fascination with Nordic legends. The opera begins with a glowing prelude symbolizing the Holy Grail. Elsa of Brabant has a mystic dream of a noble knight who would defend her from a monstrous accusation of fratricide. Her dream knight arrives in a boat drawn by a swan. She marries him to the strains of the famous bridal chorus. Although he adjures her never to ask his name and origin, she does, and he reveals that he is Lohengrin, the Knight of the Holy Grail, son of Parsifal; his swan is Elsa's brother, believed to be dead. The swan's human shape is restored, but Lohengrin must leave now that his identity is known. Swanless, he summons a dove to draw the boat away.

Lombardi alla prima Crociata, I (The Lombards on the First Crusade). Opera in four acts by Giuseppe Verdi, to a libretto by Temistocle Solera dealing with two crusading brothers from Lombardy who are rivals in love, first produced at La Scala, Milan, on Feb. 11, 1843. The more ambitious one plans to kill the other, but slays their father by mistake. To expiate his sin, he goes to Jerusalem and becomes a hermit. His niece is captured by the infidels, but falls in love with her captor's son. Her lover is wounded, but is baptized by the hermit just in time to save his expiring heathen soul. As the battle rages, the brothers are reunited, the parricide hermit forgiven by his brother and dying in peace. After its premiere the opera was revised as *Jerusalem*.

Long Christmas Dinner, The. Opera by Paul Hindemith, to an English libretto by Thornton Wilder, based on Wilder's play, first performed in Mannheim (in German, as *Das lange Weihnachtsmahl*) on Dec. 17, 1961, the composer conducting. The dinner is indeed long: 90 Christmas dinners in a single American family through several generations between 1840 and 1930, the dead departing and the newly born arriving

Lord Byron. Opera in three acts by Virgil Thomson, to a libretto by Jack Larson focused on the controversy over the erection of a monument to Lord Byron at Westminster Abbey, set to a characteristically Thomsonian, disarmingly bland melody, with candid allusions to such popular songs as "Auld Lang Syne," "Act du lieber Augustin," and "Three Blind Mice," performed for the first time in New York on April 20, 1972.

Loreley. Opera in three acts by Alfredo Catalani, to a libretto by Angelo Zanardini, first staged in Turin on Feb. 16, 1890. Loreley loves Walter, but he loves Anna, so Loreley makes a pact with Alberich, god of the Rhine, to give herself to him if he will make her irresistibly seductive. So transformed, Loreley manages to interrupt the marriage of Walter and Anna. Anna dies of grief, and Loreley, to her surprise, is spirited away by spirits to a rock, where she forever lures sailors to their deaths. Walter, left all alone, throws himself into the Rhine.

Louise. "Roman musical" in four acts by Gustave Charpentier, to his own libretto, first performed in Paris on Feb. 2, 1900. The work was an immediate success, with nearly 1,000 performances during the first half of the century, a counterpart of the Italian verismo, and including imitated cries of vegetable vendors on Parisian streets. Louise is a poor seamstress who yields to the passion of Julien, a young Paris artist. Her fate is uncertain at the end of the opera, and in its sequel, *Julien*, she is spoken of as dead.

Louis Riel. Opera in three acts by Harry Somers, to a bilingual libretto centered on the dramatic career of the French-Canadian rebel who espoused the cause of the Metizo Indians in 1869, tried to overthrow the government, and was hanged in 1886, first staged in Toronto on Sept. 23, 1967.

Love for Three Oranges, The (Lyubov' k tryom apel'sinam). Opera in four acts by Sergei Prokofiev, first produced, in a French version by the composer and Vera Janacopoulos, in Chicago on Dec. 30, 1921, the composer conducting. A witch, Fata Morgana, condemns the young Prince of Clubs to wander the earth in search of three oranges. The prince steals large oranges from a castle cook, and he and his companion Truffaldino rest in the desert with them. While the prince sleeps, the thirsty Truffaldino slices open an orange, out of which a princess steps, begs for water, and dies. Truffaldino repeats his tragic mistake, and runs away. The prince awakens and opens the last orange. This time Princessa Ninetta steps out, but she and the prince undergo trials, and are eventually victorious. Fata Morgana is led away to prison, and the royal couple celebrates.

Love of Don Perlimplín. Opera in one act by Conrad Susa, after the eponymous play by García Lorca, who described it as an "erotic lace-paper valentine," first produced at the State University of N.Y. at Purchase on Aug. 2, 1984.

Love's Labour's Lost. Opera in three acts by Nicolas Nabokov, to a libretto by W. H. Auden and Chester Kallman after Shakespeare, first performed in its original English version by the West Berlin Deutsche Oper at its visiting appearance in Brussels on Feb. 7, 1973.

Lucia di Lammermoor. Opera in three acts by Gaetano Donizetti, to a libretto by Salvadore Cammarrano based on Sir Walter Scott's novel *The Bride of Lammermoor* (1819), first produced in Naples on Sept. 26, 1835. Edgar loves Lucia, but her ambitious brother wants her to marry Arthuro, a British lord. When Edgar goes to war, Lucia is told that he was unfaithful to her. When Edgar returns, he finds her engaged to the lord. He pronounces a curse on the whole family, after taking part in the famous sextet, the other five singers being Lucia, her brother, Lucia's husband, his chaplain, and Lucia's lady-in-waiting. On her wedding night Lucia murders her husband and goes insane. In this celebrated "mad scene" she imagines herself married to Edgar. She then swoons and dies. Vowing to join her in eternity, Edgar stabs himself to death. For all its long-winded narrative, *Lucia di Lammermoor* is one of the most mellifluous products of Italian bel canto.

Lucio Silla. Opera in three acts by Wolfgang Amadeus Mozart, at age 16, to a libretto by Giovanni de Gamerra revised by Metastasio (possibly after Plutarch's *Parallel Lives*), first performed in Milan, Dec. 26, 1772. Silla was the Roman general who reached the highest power after he was elected consul in 81 B.C. and then proclaimed himself dictator of Rome. In Mozart's opera he renounces his power and returns it to the people.

Luck of Ginger Coffey, The. Opera in three acts by Raymond Pannell, to a libretto after Brian Moore's novel, retailing the vicissitudes of an Irishman in search of a newspaper job in Canada, first mounted in Toronto on Sept. 15, 1967.

Lucrezia Borgia. Opera in prologue and two acts by Gaetano Donizetti, to a libretto by Felice Romani, first produced at La Scala, Milan, on Dec. 26, 1833, and popular throughout the 19th century. Lucrezia, the most infamous of the historical Borgia family in 16th-century Italy, shelters her illegitimate son in the Borgia castle and helps him elude arrest by her husband's henchmen. While handing out cups of poisoned wine to some, she unwittingly passes poison to her son, who dies as she faints by his corspe.

Luisa Miller. Opera in three acts by Giuseppe Verdi, to a libretto by Salvadore Cammarano after Schiller's tragedy *Kabale und Liebe* (1784), first produced in Naples on Dec. 8, 1849. Luisa loves Rodolfo, whose father wants him to marry a duchess and forces Luisa to write him a letter renouncing her love. Rodolfo poisons her and himself, but Luisa has just enough singing breath in her to tell him that she has been coerced. With his dying strength, he kisses the coercer, a henchman of his father's.

Luisella. Opera in four acts by Franco Mannino, expanded from his original one-act opera, to a libretto from a short story by Thomas Mann in which a cuckolded husband dressed as a woman at a beer party in a German provincial town in 1897 suffers a fatal cardiac arrest while singing the song "Luisella" composed by his wife's lover. The opera was performed for the first time in Palermo on Feb. 28, 1969, conducted by the composer.

Lulu. Opera by Alban Berg, with a libretto by the composer after Wedekind's dramas *Erdgeist* (1895) and *Die Büchse der Pandora* (1901), produced posthumously in Zürich on June 2, 1937. Berg, a slow worker, was only able to complete two of its three acts, although one section of the third act was included in the orchestral *Lulu Suite* that premiered in 1934. Lulu, a prodigiously magnetic if promiscuous woman, spares neither young nor old, man nor woman. Directly or otherwise, she leads many of them to death. She meets her own doom when, reduced to prostitution, she is disemboweled by Jack the Ripper in London.

In a true tale of mystic mania and musical mystery, Berg in fact had virtually finished a short score of the third act, and a vocal score had been drawn up. But Berg's widow banned its publication. Unknown to her, Friedrich Cerha was surreptitiously orchestrating the third act under the auspices of Berg's publisher. After years of work, Cerha completed the third act (1962–74), and after Berg's widow's death in 1976, the premiere of the complete version took place at the Paris Opéra on Feb. 24, 1979. Evelyn Lear and Teresa Stratas have specialized in the title role.

Lysistrata. Comic opera with serious pacifist intent by Ghersase Dendrino, loosely after Aristophanes and ending with a realistic release of actual white doves and cast in a Viennese manner with a lot of waltzing tunes, performed for the first time in Bucharest on Dec. 15, 1960, under the composer's direction.

M

Macbeth. Opera in four acts by Giuseppe Verdi, to a libretto by Francesco Piave after Shakespeare's tragedy, first performed in Florence on March 14, 1847, revised for Paris, April 21, 1865. The opera set a dramatic standard for Verdi and is notable for Lady Macbeth's sleepwalking aria.

Macbeth. Opera by Ernst Bloch, after Shakespeare, first performed in Paris on Nov. 30, 1910.

Madama Butterfly. Opera in two acts by Giacomo Puccini, to a libretto by Giuseppe Giacosa and Luigi Illica after David Belasco's drama (1900) based on a short story by John Luther Long in turn based on Pierre Loti's *Madame Chrysanthème*, first produced at La Scala, Milan, on Feb. 17, 1904. Pinkerton, a lieutenant in the U.S. Navy on a visit to Nagasaki, becomes enraptured with a local 15-year-old Japanese girl nicknamed Cio-Cio (butterfly). She is also formally referred to as Cio-Cio-San, the last word corresponding to Madame. She and Pinkerton go through a Japanese marriage ceremony, which he knows (for him) is not legally binding. He then sails to the United States, leaving her barefoot and pregnant. But she has faith in him, expressing her feelings in an aria ("Un bel di vedremo"), which has become a favorite of the soprano repertory. A son is born, and when Pinkerton returns with his American wife, Cio-Cio-San yields to the American Mrs. Pinkerton's entreaties to let her have him. After the Pinkertons leave, she commits a ritual harakiri.

Madame Bovary. Opera in two acts by Heinrich Sutermeister, after Flaubert's famous novel analyzing the adulterous life and pitiful death of a provincial Frenchwoman, first performed in Zürich on May 26, 1967.

Madame Chrysanthème. Opera in prologue, four acts, and epilogue by André Messager, to a libretto by Hartmann and André Alexandre after Pierre Loti's novel (1888) about the short-lived marriage of Pierre, a French naval officer, to Madame Chrysanthème, a Japanese geisha, first staged in Paris on Jan. 30, 1893. The story was later used by Puccini for *Madama Butterfly.*

Mädchen aus Domrémy, Das. Opera by Giselher Klebe, to a libretto based on Schiller's play dealing with Joan of Arc, performed for the first time in Stuttgart on June 19, 1976.

Magic Flute, The (Die Zauberflöte). Opera in two acts by Wolfgang Amadeus Mozart, his penultimate stage work, produced in Vienna on Sept. 30, 1791, less than ten weeks before his death. The German libretto is by Emanuel Schikaneder, and its labyrinthine entanglements, drawn from various sources (including "Lulu" in Wieland's collection of Oriental fairy tales *Dschinnistan* [1786] and the Abbé Terrasson's *Sethos* [1731]), are prodigious. An earnest youth (Tamino) falls in love with the portrait of the daughter (Pamina) of the Queen of the Night. He is given a magic flute to enable him to penetrate the fortress in which she is held in captivity somewhere in Egypt. His companion is a comical birdcatcher (Papageno), who owns a set of magic bells (in the score, an *instrumento d'acciacio*), capable of paralyzing any foe. After a series of perilous adventures and tests, Tamino and Pamina are united under the guidance of Sarastro, the father of Pamina, who serves as the light to the queen's darkness. The queen and her forces are defeated, and Tamino and Panima sing a hymn to the sun symbolizing the conquest of love and art over the powers of darkness. Even Papageno finds himself a wife, Papagena.

The Magic Flute is not only the favorite opera of many Mozart aficionados but perhaps the most complex, both musically and dramatically. A partial clue to the story may lie in its heavy pseudo-Oriental symbolism, such as was cultivated in the Masonic Order, of which both Mozart and Schikaneder were members. At the beginning, Tamino is pursued by a serpent, which is killed by the female messengers of the protective Queen of the Night. The multiheaded serpent was a well-known Masonic symbol. The lovers undergo an initiation similar to that of the Masonic Order, and give a vow of silence, commonly administered in the French Order of Masons in the 18th century. Various theatrical scenes are modeled after the rituals of Masonic lodges. The Egyptian pyramid, which is the locale of one of the scenes, is a famous Masonic symbol (reproduced on the reverse side of the Great Seal of the U.S. and on the $1 bill). The similarity between the symbols used in the libretto and the Masonic ritual may have angered members of Mozart and Schikaneder's lodge, but the tale that the Masons resolved to put Mozart to death for the revelation of their secrets is pure fantasy.

Maid of Orleans, The (Orleanskaya deva). Opera in four acts by Pyotr Il'yich Tchaikovsky, first performed in St. Petersburg on Feb. 25, 1881, to a libretto by the composer loosely based on Zhukovsky's version of Schiller's romantic tragedy. Joan of Arc, the maid of Orleans, hears mysterious voices urging her to save France from the English, who approach the city of Orleans. Joan helps the pusillanimous French king Charles VII to win the battle, but she is accused of consorting with the devil, and turned over to the authorities who sentence her to be burned at the stake as an incorrigible heretic. The libretto follows history a little more closely than Giuseppe Verdi's *Giovanni d'Arco,* but like the Verdi, unwarranted amorous episodes are included. In reality, Joan was condemned for, among other things, cutting her hair short and wearing masculine attire, not for heterosexual behavior.

Maid of Pskov, The (Pskovityanka). Opera in four acts by Nikolai Rimsky-Korsakov, to a libretto by the composer after Lev Mey's drama (1860), first produced in St. Petersburg on Jan. 13, 1873, also known as *Ivan the Terrible.* The action takes place in Pskos, 1570, where Ivan the Terrible, accompanied by his dreaded henchmen, enters the city to subdue an incipient rebellion. He discovers that a girl betrothed to a rebel is his natural daughter Olga, born to Vera Sheloga. As his soldiers are about to lay waste Pskov, Ivan orders them to desist to spare Olga, but she runs out into the streets and is slain. Rimsky-Korsakov later wrote a one-act opera called *Boyarina Vera Sheloga* (1898), depicting the original affair between Vera and Ivan.

Maître de Chapelle, Le (The Chapelmaster). Opera in two parts by Ferdinando Paër, to a libretto by Sophie Gay after Duval's comedy *Le souper imprévu* (The Unexpected Supper) (1796), a little farce about a lovable French cook, Gertrude, who agrees to sing, but then tries not to sing, in the first performance of her employer's opera *Cléopâtre,* first staged in Paris on March 29, 1821.

Making of the Representative for Planet 8, The. Opera in three acts by Philip Glass, to a libretto adapted from Doris Lessing's book of the same name, first mounted in Houston on July 8, 1988.

Makropulos Affair, The (Věc Makropulos). Opera in three acts by Leoš Janáček, to a libretto by the composer after Karel Čapek's drama (1922), first performed in Brno on Dec. 18, 1926. An opera singer made immortal by her alchemist father in the 17th century is living in Prague under the name Emilia Marty, bewitching all while desperately searching for the cabalistic formula that her father wrote down before she turns 300 and dies. An accusation of forgery on an old document forces her to reveal her identity as the nearly 300-year-old Elena Makropulos to a shocked coterie. She regains the formula but, weary of life and unable to give it away, burns the paper and dies with its destruction.

Malheurs d'Orphée, Les (The Misfortunes of Orpheus). Opera in three minuscule acts by Darius Milhaud, to a libretto by Armand Lunel in which Orpheus is pictured as "having long hair and wearing a sheepskin cloak" and Euridice as a "jeune Bohémianne," first produced in Brussels on May 7, 1926.

Malin: The Doors of History Open Wide. Opera by Torsten Nilsson, to an archeologist's libretto recounting a museum tour that entices a young girl's imagination to recreate historical Swedish environments from the bronze age to the medieval period as she moves from site to site, with the orchestra augmented by ancient percussion instruments, staged in its entirety for the first time at the Historical Museum on Narvavägen in Stockholm on Aug. 30, 1991.

Mamelles de Tirésias, Les (The Breasts of Tiresias). Opera buffa in two acts by Francis Poulenc, to his own libretto after Guillaume Apollinaire, first produced in Paris on June 3, 1947. The libretto deals with transsexual transformation. Tirésias (Thérèse) is weary of being a woman, so she ignites her bulging breasts, which rise and pop like balloons. Her husband, on the other hand, wants to be a woman. He succeeds brilliantly and gives birth to 40,000 children. In the end, they return to their original genders and appeal to the audience to breed energetically in order to repopulate the French countryside devastated by war.

Manon. Opera in five acts by Jules Massenet, to a libretto by Henri Meilhac and Philippe Gille after Antoine-François Prévost's novel *L'histoire du chevalier des Grieux et de Manon Lescaut* (1731), first produced in Paris on Jan. 19, 1884. Manon, an emotionally perturbed 18th-century French girl, intends to become a nun but is diverted from her purpose by a dashing cavalier who carries her off to Paris. His father urges him to renounce the ways of the world and join the priesthood. Manon is arrested on suspicion of moral turpitude, and although her lover secures her freedom by bribing the authorities, she has no more strength to live, and dies of inanition. In *Manon,* Massenet is at his sentimental best. Its libretto differs from that of Puccini's *Manon Lescaut,* but both are drawn from Prévost's novel.

Manon Lescaut. Opera in four acts by Giacomo Puccini,

to a text by Luigi Illica and Domenico Oliva after Prévost's novel *L'histoire du chevalier des Grieux et de Manon Lescaut* (1731), first produced in Turin on Feb. 1, 1893. A beautiful French girl intends to enter a convent, but a traveling companion induces her to join him in Paris. She becomes debauched by city life but agrees to take a ship to America with her lover. They make the voyage safely, but despite his solicitude, she dies in New Orleans. The libretto differs from that of Massenet's *Manon*, but both are drawn from Prévost's novel.

Manru. Opera in three acts by Ignacy Paderewski, to a libretto by Alfred Nossig after Kraszewski's novel *The Cabin Behind the Wood* (1843), first produced in Dresden on May 29, 1901. Manru is a dissolute gypsy. His wife, unable to bear his constant infidelities, kills herself. Manru is eventually destroyed by a man whose bride he has abducted. Paderewski's only opera, despite his fame as a virtuoso pianist, was rarely produced even in his lifetime.

Man's Destiny, A (Sud'ba cheloveka) Music drama by Ivan Dzerzhinsky, dealing with a Soviet prisoner of war who escapes from Nazi captivity in 1943 and returns to his native village only to find that his wife and daughters were killed in an air raid but saves himself from suicidal despair by adopting an orphan boy, produced for the first time at the Bolshoi Theater in Moscow on Oct. 17, 1961.

Man Who Mistook His Wife for a Hat, The. Opera by Michael Nyman, based on one of several neurological case histories documented in Oliver Sacks's best-selling book of the same name, first staged in London on Oct. 27, 1986, the composer conducting from the keyboard.

Man without a Country, The. Opera in two acts by Walter Damrosch, his last, to a libretto by Arthur Guiterman based on Edward Everett Hale's famous story (1863) of an American navy lieutenant who insolently damns the United States and is sent away to maritime exile on the high seas with an injunction to everyone in his entourage never to mention America in his presence. The opera was first produced at the Metropolitan Opera in New York on May 12, 1937, the composer conducting, but not revived.

Mara. Opera by Hastie, to a libretto dealing with a sea nymph who induces a nonaqueous prince to marry her, produced for the first time in Croydon, England, on Dec. 14, 1965.

Märchen von der schönen Lilie, Das. Opera in two acts by Giselher Klebe, after Goethe's tale of pastoral love, first produced in Schwetzinger on May 15, 1969.

Margot la Rouge. Opera in one act by Frederick Delius, composed in 1902 but laid aside for 80 years before it was unearthed from a dusty heap of forgotten manuscripts, to a story dealing with an originally virtuous girl becoming a *fille de joie et de détresse* on Paris boulevards, and her pimp, who is eventually killed by her fiancé. It was broadcast by the BBC Orchestra and Chorus in London on Feb. 21, 1982. The first stage performance was given in St. Louis on June 8, 1983, Eric Fenby conducting.

Mari à la Porte, Un. Operetta in one act by Jacques Offenbach, first staged in Paris on June 22, 1859. The composer of an unperformed opera called *The Midnight Corpse* invades the flat of a newly married Parisian housewife. When her husband appears at the door, the intruding composer escapes through the window.

Maria di Rudenz (Maria of Rudenz). Opera by Gaetano Donizetti, first performed in Venice on Jan. 30, 1838. A fortune hunter seeks to marry an heiress of the Count di Rudenz. Her sister, Maria, suddenly returns to Rudenz, and asserts her rights to the inheritance. Complications set in when she herself falls in love with the dashing fortune hunter and in order to eliminate competition she stabs her sister and pretends to inflict a lethal wound on herself. But she miscalculates and begins to die in earnest.

Maria di Rohan (Maria of Rohan). Opera in three acts by Gaetano Donizetti, to a libretto by Cammarano and Lillo after Lockroy's *Un duel sous le cardinal de Richelieu* (originally *Il Conte de Chalais*), the sad story of Maria, who is secretly married to one man (Henri, duc de Chevreuse) while secretly loving another (the comte de Chalais). Chevreuse and Chalais duel, and when Chalais is killed, Maria wants to die as well. Chevreuse, however, demands that she live to face her disgrace. It was first produced in Vienna on June 5, 1843.

Maria Padilla. Opera by Gaetano Donizetti, first performed in Milan on Dec. 26, 1841. The eponymous heroine, mistress of King Pedro the Cruel of Castile, threatens suicide unless he marries her. For reasons of state he weds a Bourbon princess. Maria invades the palace and snatches the crown from her rival's head, and then kills herself. (In a censored version, she dies overwrought by emotion.)

Maria Stuarda (Mary Stuart). Opera in three acts by Gaetano Donizetti, to a libretto by Giuseppe Bardari after Schiller's tragedy (1800), first performed in Naples on Oct. 18, 1834, under the title *Buondelmonte,* with the historical characters of Mary Stuart and Queen Elizabeth changed to pacify the queen of Naples, who was horrified to learn that the opera represented the death of a revered Catholic queen of Scots. But outside the kingdom of Naples, the original libretto was restored, and the opera as originally conceived was produced at La Scala in Milan on Dec. 30, 1835. The plot, largely borrowed from Schiller's famous romanticized drama, rewrites history. When Mary calls Elizabeth the bastard offspring of Henry VIII, Elizabeth sings "Then you die" and signs the death warrant. The work's popularity is a typical result of the post–World War II bel canto revival.

Marino Faliero. Opera in three acts by Gaetano Donizetti, to a text by Giovanni Bidera after Casimir Delavigne's (1829) and Byron's (1821) tragedies surrounding the love life of the Doge Marino Faliero and his subsequent sentence of death for conspiracy against the Council, first produced in Paris on March 12, 1835.

Maritana. Opera in three acts by Vincent Wallace, with a libretto by Edward Fitzball after the drama *Don César de Bazan* by Adolphe D'Ennery and Philippe Dumanoir concerning the disguised king of Spain's attraction for the gypsy Maritana, and Don José's ill-fated attraction to the queen of Spain, first produced in London on Nov. 15, 1845.

Mariuta. Opera in three acts by Dmitri Tolstoy, after the story *Forty-First* by Boris Lavrenev dealing with a Soviet girl guerrilla fighter who is left to guard a White Russian officer taken prisoner during the civil war in central Asia, falls in love with him, but despite their intimacy, kills him unhesitatingly when he tries to join the crew of an anti-Bolshevik motorboat on the Aral Sea, performed for the first time in Perm on Dec. 30, 1960.

Markheim. Opera in three acts by Carlisle Floyd, after Robert Louis Stevenson's tale of a pawnbroker who is given a specious promise of a life of pleasure by a diabolical stranger, first mounted in New Orleans on March 31, 1966.

Marko Polo. Opera in three acts by Tijardovič, recounting the epic travels of Marco Polo to China and back to Venice in the years 1271–92, performed for the first time in Zagreb on Dec. 3, 1960.

Mârouf, Savetier du Caire. Opera in five acts by Henri Rabaud, his most successful, to a libretto by L. Népoty after a story in Mardrus's French version of the *1,001 (Arabian) Nights*, first performed in Paris on May 15, 1914. Shipwrecked, Mârouf makes his way to the sultan's palace, pretending to be a wealthy merchant. The sultan gives his daughter to him in marriage. Mârouf robs the palace and flees with his still faithful and credulous wife. He redeems himself by securing a magic ring with which he conjures up a palace of his own.

Marquise de Brinvilliers, La. Opera in three acts by Daniel-François-Esprit Auber, Batton, Berton, Blangini, Boieldieu, Carafa, Cherubini, Hérold, and Paer, to a libretto by Eugéne Scribe and Castil-Blaze, first staged in Paris on Oct. 31, 1831. One of the most famous and successful of all collective operas, it recounts life and love stories of the infamous poisoner.

Marriage, The. Television opera in one act by Bohuslav Martinů, to an English libretto after Gogol's play dealing with a hesitant bridegroom who jumps out of a ground-level window to escape matrimony, televised for the first time over NBC Television in New York on Feb. 7, 1953.

Marriage, The (Zhenit'ba). Opera (unfinished) by Modest Mussorgsky, to a libretto after Gogol's comedy (1842), first produced in a concert performance at Rimsky-Korsakov's home in 1906. The first stage presentation, with piano in a version revised by Rimsky-Korsakov, took place in St. Petersburg, at the Suvorin School, on April 1, 1908. The premiere of the full work, with orchestration by Rimsky-Korsakov and Gauk, was given in Petrograd on Oct. 26, 1917. Completion of Acts II to IV was done by Ippolitov-Ivanov in 1931, and a new completion in one act was done by Tcherepnin in 1933.

Marriage of Figaro, The (Le Nozze di Figaro). Comic opera in four acts by Wolfgang Amadeus Mozart, his most popular, first produced in Vienna on May 1, 1786. The libretto is the first Da Ponte wrote for Mozart, based on Beaumarchais's comedic sequel to his *The Barber of Seville* entitled *La folle journée, ou Le mariage de Figaro* (1784). Count Almaviva is now married to Rosina. Figaro, formerly a cunning barber, is now the count's valet. He wants to marry the countess's maid, Susanna, but the count himself covets her. Particularly insidious is the count's refusal to give up a traditional "right of way" to his female servants just prior to their marriage. The countess laments her husband's flighty ways ("Dove sono"), and Figaro stages complex stratagems to arouse the count's jealousy, in order to bring him closer to his wife. The youthful page, Cherubino, is used by Figaro to play the suitor of the countess. As the count enters the house, the page puts on a maid's dress to hide his sex. (Since the part of Cherubino is entrusted to a mezzo-soprano, the donning of female dress either restores the performer's true gender or gives new meaning to transvestism.) The complications increase exponentially, and the plot reaches the apex of its inspired absurdity when an elderly female housekeeper whom Figaro has promised to marry is revealed as his own mother.

Marriage of Nyakoto, The. Opera in one act by Solomon Mbabi-Katana, to the story of a beautiful country girl, Nyakato, whose family witch doctor correctly interprets, in a psychedelic solo on an indigenous central African long horn, a Freudian dream of her father as a precognitive revelation of her becoming the bride of the tribal king, performed for the first time in city of Kampala in Urganda on May 30, 1968, the composer presiding at the piano.

Martha, oder Der Markt von Richmond (Martha, or The Market at Richmond). Opera in four acts by Friedrich Flotow, to a libretto by W. Friedrich (Friedrich Wilhelm Riese) after Vernoy de Saint-Georges's ballet pantomime *Lady Harriette, ou La servante de Greenwich* (to which Flotow had earlier provided music), first produced in Vienna on Nov. 25, 1847. The action takes place in Richmond, England, under Queen Anne. The queen's maid of honor, Lady Harriet, decides to go to the marketplace dressed as a country girl named Martha. She hires herself as a servant maid to a young farmer, not realizing that the indenture she signed is a legal contract. Her maid signs a similar obligation. Martha sings "The Last Rose of Summer," and at night both girls return to the palace. As Lady Harriet, "Martha" refuses to recognize the farmer but he is revealed to be a hereditary earl. There is a doubly happy ending, since Lady Harriet's maid marries the earl's foster brother.

Martin's Life. Chamber opera by Gian Carlo Menotti, to his own libretto in which a 12-year-old medieval orphan boy shelters a heretic and refuses unto death to reveal his hiding place to the inquisitors, performed for the first time in Bristol Cathedral, England, on June 3, 1964.

Martyrdom of St. Magnus, The. Chamber opera in one act (nine scenes) by Peter Maxwell Davies, to a libretto by the composer drawn from George Mackay Brown's novel *Magnus* recounting the saga of the unnatural murder of the pious Earl Magnus by his own cousin in 1117, first performed in the 12th-century St. Magnus Cathedral in Kirkwall, where Saint Magnus was buried, on June 17, 1977.

Martyred, The. Opera by James Wade, long resident in Korea, to his own libretto dealing with the dramatic events of the Korean War in 1951, first produced in the Korean language in Seoul on April 8, 1970.

Martyrs, Les. Opera in four acts by Gaetano Donizetti, to a libretto by Eugéne Scribe after Corneille's tragedy *Polyeucte*, originally composed to an Italian libretto by Salvadore Cammarano entitled *Poliuoto*, first produced in Paris on April 10, 1840. The protagonist of the story magnanimously yields his wife to her previous lover, a pagan, but is sentenced to death by his father-in-law, the Roman governor of Armenia. After his execution, she joins him in martyrdom. The governor eventually becomes a Christian.

Mary, Queen of Scots. Opera by Thea Musgrave, to her own libretto tracing the tragic life of the queen of Scotland, first produced at the Edinburgh Festival on Sept. 6, 1977.

Mary Stuart. Opera ballade by Sergei Slonimsky, in three tableaux to a historically accurate libretto by Yakov Gordin, wherein the march of events related by folk narrators traces the fate of the tragic queen of Scotland, with the sinister Protestant minister John Knox leading the resistance to the Catholic ruler, first staged in Kuibishev, Russia, on Jan. 31, 1981. It was subsequently produced at Scotland's Edinburgh Festival on Aug. 22, 1986.

Maschere, Le. Opera in prologue and three acts by Pietro Mascagni, to a text by Luigi Illica, with the familiar characters of the commedia dell'arte engaged in traditional encounters. So great were the auguries of success for *Le Maschere* that the opera was premiered on the same day, Jan. 17, 1901, in six Italian cities: Milan (conducted by Toscanini), and Venice, Turin, Verona, Genoa, and Rome (where Mascagni himself conducted). Only half facetiously, Mascagni dedicated the opera "to my distinguished self." But this simultaneous exhibition was a humiliating debacle. In Genoa, the audience hissed and booed so vehemently that the management had to lower the curtain without completing the performance.

Maschinist Hopkins. First opera by Max Brand to his own libretto, an expressionistic score of the "machine era" that served as a significant precursor to Berg's *Lulu*, first mounted in Duisburg on April 13, 1929.

Mascotte, La. Operetta in three acts by Edmond Audran, to a libretto by Duru and Chivot, the "mascot" being the goose girl Bettina, who, loved truly by the shepherd Pippo, is taken away by Prince Laurent, but is subsequently rescued by Pippo after a war in which Laurent fights on the losing side, the two living happily ever after, with the prince's blessing. It was first produced in Paris on Dec. 29, 1880.

Maskarade. Opera in three acts by Carl Nielsen, to a text by Vilhelm Andersen after Ludvig Holberg's play wherein a young man betrothed by parental decision to a young lady he has never met falls in love with a girl behind a mask at a ball and proceeds to arrange a series of illicit meetings with her, only to find that, happily, she is his chosen fiancée, first produced in Copenhagen on Nov. 11, 1906.

Mask of Orpheus, The. Opera in three acts by Harrison Birtwistle, to a libretto by Peter Zinovieff after the classical legend, first performed at the English National Opera in London on May 21, 1986.

Masnadieri, I (The Bandits). Opera in four acts by Giuseppe Verdi, to a libretto by Andrea Maffei after Schiller's drama *Die Räuber* (1781) after C. F. D. Schubart's story (1777), first performed in London on July 22, 1847. Carlo, the disinherited son of Massimiliano, Count Moor, who left home and his lover, Amalia, to join a band of robbers, is announced dead by his brother Francesco, who at the same time announces the death of their father (whom he's actually imprisoned). Amalia learns the truth about both men, and meets Carlo in the forest. Carlo manages to free his father without disclosing his true identity. He is later recognized by his father and kills Amalia to spare her a life with him in crime.

Master i Margarita. Opera by Sergei Slonimsky, after Bulgakov's controversial 1938 novel, a satire of russian society, first mounted in Leningrad on Dec. 1, 1989.

Master of Boyana, The. Opera in four acts by Konstantin Iliev, to a libretto recounting the legendary story of an anonymous painter of 13th-century frescoes in the church at the village of Boyana near Sofia and his artistic victory over iconographic reactionaries who objected to the realistic interpretation of religious subjects and a concomitant consummation of his love for a chosen mate, first produced in Sofia on Oct. 3, 1962.

Mathis der Maler (Mathis the Painter). Opera in seven scenes by Paul Hindemith, to his own libretto inspired by the Colmar triptych of the painter known as Matthias Grünewald (who flourished in the first half of the 16th century), first produced in Zürich on May 28, 1938. In the opera, the artistic career of Mathis is interrupted by a peasant uprising of 1542. Essentially apolitical and beholden to religious authorities, he hides two fleeing rebels and gradually comes to espouse the rebel cause. But realizing that injustice is done in either camp, he withdraws from the materialistic world and dedicates himself to art.

Matrimonio segreto, Il (The secret Marriage). Opera in two acts by Domenico Cimarosa, to a libretto by Giovanni Bertati based on George Colman and David Garrick's comedy *The Clandestine Marriage* (1766). It was first performed in Vienna on Feb. 7, 1792, and was so successful that Emperor Leopold II ordered an immediate encore. A rich man of Bologna tries to arrange a marriage of his older daughter to a titled Britisher, incongruously named Count Robinson. But Robinson likes the proffered bride's younger sister better. However, she is already married secretly to a young lawyer. They plan to run away to escape the complications, aggravated further by the bride's aunt's infatuation with the count. Identities become intentionally falsified, and assorted lovers experience unintended encounters in bedchambers. But in the end the situation is clarified, and the "matrimonio segreto" is finally revealed not to be a secret after all.

Mavra. Comic opera in one act by Igor Stravinsky, to a libretto by Boris Kochno after Pushkin's *The Little House at Kolomna* (1830), first performed in Paris on June 3, 1922. A girl in a suburban community near Moscow is engaged in a clandestine romance with a soldier. When her mother tells her to hire a cook, she brings in her lover disguised as a woman named Mavra. But he is careless and is caught unawares while shaving. He jumps out of the window and never returns.

Maximilien. Opera in three acts by Darius Milhaud, after Franz Werfel's play *Juarez und Maxmilien,* first performed in Paris on Jan. 5, 1932. The libretto follows the historical account of the unfortunate Austrian archduke who was set up as emperor of Mexico in 1864 and then executed by Mexican rebels.

May Night (Mayskaya noch'). Opera in three acts by Nikolai Rimsky-Korsakov, to the composer's libretto after Gogol's story (1831–32), premiered in St. Petersburg on Jan. 21, 1880. In a small Ukrainian town, a young man in love tries to persuade his father to let him marry his beloved. Help arrives from an unexpected source: the water sprites, who suspect that there is a malevolent witch among them. The youth finds her, thus freeing the water sprites from a curse. In return, he receives a magic letter addressed to his father urging him not to stand in the way of his son's love. There is a happy ending.

Mazeppa. Opera in three acts by Pyotr Il'yich Tchaikovsky, to a libretto by the composer and Victor Burenin after Pushkin's poem *Poltava* (1829), a tale of political intrigue and a love triangle between and among Mazeppa, an infamous 17th-century Ukranian separtist, Maria, and Kochubey, first performed in Moscow on Feb. 15, 1884.

Médecin malgré lui, Le (The Doctor Despite Himself). Opera in three acts by Charles Gounod, to a libretto by Jules Barbier, and Michel Carré after a Molière comedy (1666), first staged in Paris on Jan. 15, 1858. A maltreated wife intends to get even with her husband by spreading the rumor that he is a miracle worker in medicine. When he fails to cure the daughter of a wealthy citizen, he is manhandled by the servants. But she is not sick at all, and feigns illness to elope with her lover. Eventually the lovers inherit a fortune, the girl's father is reconciled to her marriage, and the maltreated wife of the hapless "doctor" forgives him

Medée. Opera by Marc-Antoine Charpentier, first produced in Paris on Dec. 4, 1693. The libretto is derived from the ancient Greek myth of Medea, the vengeful wife of Jason, who is enraged by his plan to take a younger wife. She wreaks vengeance by arranging the bride-to-be's death and by murdering their two sons.

Medée. Opera in three acts by Luigi Cherubini, to a libretto by François-Benoît Hoffman after Corneille's tragedy (1635), first performed in Paris on March 13, 1797. It is considered his masterpiece, but it fell into relative obscurity. A century and a half later, the postwar bel canto revival led to the revival of this opera in its Italian form, *Medea,* with Callas and other operatic luminaries in the title role. The early music movement has led to recent performances in its original French version.

Medium, The. Opera in two acts by Gian Carlo Menotti, one of his most successful, to his own libretto, first produced at Columbia University on May 8, 1946, and the next year on Broadway (the first of his "Broadway operas"). The medium Madame Flora arranges for ghosts to speak to bereaved relatives through a hidden microphone. So realistic are the voices, produced by her daughter, that the medium begins to believe in their reality. In a panic, she shoots and kills her deaf-mute helper, whom she finds in the closet.

Mefistofele. Opera in prologue, four acts, and epilogue by Arrigo Boito, first produced in Milan on March 5, 1868. Boito's libretto drew from both parts of Goethe's great philosophical poem *Faust,* unlike Gounod's opera, which ends with the death of Marguerite. Boito adds the encounter with Helen of Troy, and ends with the redemption of Faust. The role of the eponymous devil is one of the great operatic bass roles. *Mefistofele* has excellent musical and literary qualities, but it has never attained the success vouchsafed to Gounod's *Faust.* The opera was not a success at its Milan premiere, but the revised version staged in Bologna on Oct. 4, 1875, fared better.

Meistersinger von Nürnberg, Die (The Mastersingers of Nuremberg). Opera in three acts by Richard Wagner, to his own libretto, his first to include elements of intentional comedy, produced in Munich on June 21, 1868, Bülow conducting. The action takes place in Nuremberg in the 16th century. A singing contest is organized by the Guild of Mastersingers under the guidance of the cobbler Hans Sachs (a historical figure who played an important role in organizing singing societies in Germany in the 16th century). The first prize is the hand of Eva, daughter of the local goldsmith. Von Stolzing, in love with Eva, sings a supremely beautiful song, but the pedantic clerk Beckmesser faults him for violation of rules. (Beckmesser was modeled after Hanslick, a persistent opponent of Wagner; in the early sketches of *Die Meistersinger* Wagner used the name Hans Lick for Beckmesser.) After the prize is given to Walther, Sachs explains the principles underlying the art of German song. The opera is notable for its rich humanism, but criticized by some for anti-Semitism evidenced in the characterization of Beckmesser.

Melusine. Opera by Aribert Reimann, to a libretto based on the medieval legend of a miscegenated Albanian princess who was doomed to change to a serpent from the waist down on Saturdays and who vanished forever after her husband surprised her during one of her weekly metamorphoses, performed for the first time in Schwetzingen on April 29, 1971.

Mercante de Venezia, Il. Grand opera in three acts by Mario Castelnuovo-Tedesco, from Shakespeare's play and equisyllabically translated by the composer into Italian (so that the opera can be performed in English or Italian without rhythmic readjustments) and supplemented by Shakespeare's sonnet "O! Never say that I was false of heart" but with Shylock's forced conversion to Christianity omitted, first mounted in Florence on May 25, 1961.

Mère coupable, La (The Guilty Mother). Opera in three acts by Darius Milhaud, first performed in Geneva on June 13, 1966. The libretto is drawn from Beaumarchais's play, the last in the *Figaro–Barber* trilogy, in which the characters are older and "perhaps more human" according to the composer.

Merrie England. Operetta in two acts by Edward German, to a libretto by Basil Hood lightly picturing the affairs of Sir Walter Raleigh, Queen Elizabeth, et al., first staged in London on April 2, 1902.

Merry Mount. Opera in four acts by Howard Hanson, his only one, based on Hawthorne's *The Maypole of Merry Mount,* first staged at the Metropolitan Opera in New York on Feb. 10, 1934. The action takes place in New England in 1625, where Satan is a living presence in the troubled minds of the inhabitants. A puritan cleric, a victim of unfulfilled desires, is induced by a woman of free morals to take part in pagan games on Merry Mount. When he becomes horrified by his consorting with evil forces, he enters a church set aflame by Indians, and perishes in the inferno together with his seductress.

Merry Widow, The (Die lüstige Witwe). Operetta in three acts by Franz Lehár, to a libretto by Viktor Léon and Leo Stein after Meilhac's comedy *L'attaché d'amtassade,* first produced in Vienna on Dec. 30, 1905. A rich Austrian widow is the object of courtship on the part of a Slavic fortune-seeker, who finally corrals her in Paris. *The Merry Widow* is probably the most popular Viennese operetta of the century. The recitative glorifying Maxim's restaurant in Paris was inserted by Lehár as a token of gratitude to its chef, who allowed him to have free meals there during his impecunious days.

Merry Wives of Windsor, The (Die lustigen Weiber von Windor). Opera in three acts by Otto Nicolai, to a libretto by Salomon Mosenthal after Shakespeare's comedy, first produced in Berlin on March 9, 1849. The libretto follows Shakespeare faithfully, with Falstaff remaining the principal, pathetically comic character.

Metamorforsi di Bonaventura, Le. Fantastic opera in three acts by Gian Francesco Malipiero, tracing the madness of a Seville jester, performed for the first time in Venice on Sept. 4, 1966.

Midsummer Marriage, The. Opera in three acts by Michael Tippett, to his own libretto, first produced in London on Jan. 27, 1955. This romantically lyric but neoclassical work essays archetypal symbolism in a quasi-realistic setting. A young couple quarrels on their wedding day. They reconcile their differences by going through a series of initiations in which a clairvoyant takes part. The bride and groom achieve the needed catharsis, and are spiritually united in marriage. The influence of *The Magic Flute* is palpable.

Midsummer Night's Dream, A. Opera in three acts by Benjamin Britten, to a libretto by the composer and Peter Pears after Shakespeare's comedy, first performed at the Aldeburgh Festival on June 11, 1960.

Mignon. Opera in three acts by Ambroise Thomas, to a libretto by Jules Barbier and Michel Carré after Goethe's novel *Wilhelm Meister Lehrjahre* (1795–96), first performed in Paris on Nov. 17, 1866. The gypsy girl Mignon, maltreated by her people, is rescued by Meister, who makes her his maidservant. They are joined by a wandering minstrel who is searching for his daughter kidnapped by gypsies. The purple threads of the romantic narrative are not nicely intertwined, for Mignon is the kidnapped girl.

Mines of Sulphur, The. Opera by Richard Rodney Bennett, to a libretto by Beverley Cross, in which a band of 18th-century English gypsies murders a rich old man but is driven to terrified confessions when a phantom theatrical troupe performs a play reenacting the murder, in addition contaminating them with plague, first produced in London on Feb. 24, 1965.

Minette Fontaine. Opera by William Grant Still, completed in 1958, depicting the life of the French opera diva in New Orleans in the 1880s, first posthumously performed in Baton Rouge, Louisiana, on Oct. 24, 1984.

Minutes Till Midnight. Opera in two acts by Robert Ward, centered on an idealist atomic scientist who inadvertently invents an annihilating doomsday bomb, performed for the first time at the New World Festival of the Arts in Miami on June 4, 1982.

Mireille. Opera in five acts by Charles Gounod, to a text by Michel Carré after Mistral's poem *Mirèio* (1859) about Mireille's love for Vincent, opposed by Mireille's father, Ramon, and confounded further by the amorous designs on Mireille by the bull tender Ourrias, first performed in Paris on March 19, 1864. The original version of the work ended with Mireille's death, but in the revised version of 1889, Mireille and Vincent live happily ever after.

Miserly Knight, The. Short opera by Sergei Rachmaninoff, after a play of Pushkin, first performed in Moscow on Jan. 24, 1906, the composer conducting a program that included the first performance of another of his short operas, *Francesca di Rimini.* The old miser has accumulated a treasure trove of gold, but he refuses to share with anyone, even his own son. In desperation the youth goes to the duke of the land for help. His father publicly accuses him of planning his murder. But as he utters the monstrous charge, he is seized with mortal pain and dies with the words "Where are the keys to my treasure?" The score exhibits an unpretentious romantic flair.

Miss Julie. Opera by Ned Rorem, after the drama by August Strindberg, first produced at the New York City Opera on Nov. 4, 1965. The play is typical of Strindberg's preoccupations with social contradictions. Miss Julie is of noble birth. Strangely, she falls under the spell of the family majordomo, who dominates her so fully that at his behest she robs her own father. Distressed and repentant, she commits suicide.

Mitridate, re di Ponto (Mithridates, King of Portus). Opera in three acts by Wolfgang Amadeus Mozart, first performed in Milan on Dec. 26, 1770, when Mozart was only 14 years old. The libretto by Vittorio Cigna-Santi after Racine's *Mithridate* (1673) deals with the dramatic story of Mithridates, king of Pontus, who loves a young Greek girl who is loved also by his two sons. All kinds of involvements ensue. Mithridates is fatally wounded in battle and urges his second son to marry the girl they all cumulatively love.

Mlada. Opera ballet in four acts by Nikolai Rimsky-Korsakov, to the composer's libretto based on a text by Viktor Krylov for an earlier opera planned by Borodin, Cui, and Mussorgsky, premiered in St. Petersburg on Nov. 1, 1892. Although the action takes place in the Slavic settlement on the Baltic shore in the 10th century, the cast of characters is mostly preternatural. Mlada herself is a dead princess who visits her fiancé in his dreams. Slavic apparitions tell him that Mlada was murdered by the girl he now plans to marry. He swears vengeance and kills the accused murderess. He dies, too, and is reunited with Mlada in heaven.

Mona. Opera by Horatio Parker, first staged at the Metropolitan Opera in New York on March 14, 1912, as winner of a $10,000 prize for an all-American opera. Despite the emphasis on Americanism (the librettist and the entire cast, with the exception of one minor part, were all Americans), the libretto itself was taken from an old British legend. Mona is the last defender of the Celtic queen Boadicea who fought against the Roman rule. The opera had only four performances, and attempts at revivals have foundered. Yet the music is not all bad. An interesting innovation is the assignment of certain keys to different characters.

Mona Lisa. Opera in two acts by Max von Schillings, first performed in Stuttgart on Sept. 26, 1915. The whimsical libretto by Beatrice Dovsky relates a visit by a married couple in Florence. A local monk tells them the story of Mona Lisa, her husband, Giocondo, and the love she nurtured for a Florentine youth, Giovanni. The smile on the lips of the woman tourist seems strangely familiar, and no wonder, for she is Mona Lisa *rediviva*, traveling with her husband, and the monastic teller of the story is Giovanni.

Mond, Der (The Moon). Opera in three acts by Carl Orff, to his own text after a fairy tale by Grimm, first produced in Munich on Feb. 5, 1939. The story tells of four boys who steal the moon and use it as a bedside lamp. When they die, they arrange to take the moon with them to their graves. The sudden illumination arouses the dead. Saint Peter comes down to restore order, and puts the moon up in the sky where it belongs. Like most of Orff's operas, *Der Mond* is a theatrical spectacle, containing spoken dialogue, a pantomime, and several symphonic interludes in which a plethora of percussion instruments makes interesting noises.

Mondo della luna, Il (The World on the Moon). Opera in three acts by Franz Joseph Haydn, to a libretto by Carlo Goldoni adapted by P. F. Pastor, first performed at the Prince Esterházy estate on Aug. 3, 1777. An astronomer, fittingly named Dr. Ecclittico (ecliptic), drugs a rich Venetian and convinces him that he is on the moon and that the lunar authorities have ordered him to let his daughter marry her impecunious suitor.

Monna Vanna. Opera in four acts by Henry Février, to a text by Maurice Maeterlinck, first performed in Paris on Jan. 13, 1909. The tale is set in 15th-century Italy wherein the virtuous wife of the defender of Pisa offers herself to the commander of the besieging forces as the price of the city's relief, but is spared defilement as the latter recognizes in her his childhood sweetheart and she decides to remain with him.

Monsieur de Pourceaugnac. Opera by Frank Martin, his last, after Molière's farce in which a pompous landlord to whom an ambitious bourgeois wants to give his daughter in marriage is beset by machinations organized by the unwilling bride until he is driven back to his country estate and the bride is free to marry her true lover, performed for the first time at the newly rebuilt Grand Thèâtre in Geneva on April 23, 1963, Ansermet conducting.

Montag aus Licht. Opera by Karlheinz Stockhausen, third in a projected series of seven, one for each day of the week, first performed at La Scala, Milan, on May 7, 1988. Others in the series include *Donnerstag aus Licht* (Milan, April 3, 1981) and *Samstag aus Licht* (Milan, May 25, 1984).

Montezuma. Opera in three acts by Roger Sessions, first staged in Berlin on April 19, 1964, to a libretto recounting the Spanish conquest of Mexico led by Cortés and the death of the Aztec emperor Montezuma II (1520).

Mort d'Adam, La. Opera in three acts by Jean-François Le Sueur, to a libretto by Guillard combining Klopstock's drama *Der Tod Adams* (1757) and material from both the Book of Genesis and Milton's *Paradise Lost* (1667) detailing Adam's concerns on his deathbed that his sons Seth and Cain will pay for his sins, Cain's wrath and Adam's forgiveness, and with Adam in the end rising peacefully to heaven. The opera was first produced in Paris on March 21, 1809.

Morvoren. Opera by (Jack) Philip Cannon, to a libretto concerning an attractive Cornish mermaid who lures a susceptible altar boy to her aquatic realm, first staged in London on July 15, 1964.

Mosè in Egitto (Moses in Egypt). Opera in three acts by Gioacchino Rossini, first produced in Naples on March 5, 1818. The libretto by Andrea Tottola after Francesco Ringhieri's tragedy *L'Osiride* (1747) follows the biblical narrative of the escape of the Hebrews across the miraculously distended Red Sea, and the destruction of the pursuing Egyptian Army when the waters converge on them. The opera was selected by Mussolini to be performed at the gala reception for Hitler in Rome in 1935, oblivious to the fact that his anti-Semitic partner could have hardly enjoyed watching Jews escape.

Moses und Aron. Opera in two acts by Arnold Schoenberg, to his own text after the Book of Exodus. Acts I and II were completed, while Act III was probably never started. The libretto is extant, and the work was produced posthumously in Zürich on June 6, 1957, six years after the composer's death. The religious conflict between spirituality and materialism, personified by Moses and his brother, Aaron, underlies the text. Schoenberg gives indications in the score that an orgy staged around the idol of the Golden Calf should include the immolation of four naked virgins and other scenes of ancient depravity. A realistic production along these lines was attempted in London in 1965, but the alleged virgins wore loincloths. Subsequent productions have left the loincloths in the dressing room. Note: the omission of the second *a* in the German title was due to Schoenberg's triskaidecaphobia. If Aaron were spelled with two *a*s, the sum of the letters in the complete title would have been 13.

Most Important Man, The. Opera in three acts by Gian Carlo Menotti, to his own libretto, in which a black man in an unnamed segregated nation invents an ultimate formula to attain total dominion of the world and himself achieves a liaison with an unpigmented woman, strangles his laboratory assistant, and then destroys himself and the formula in a luminous death dance, performed for the first time in New York on March 12, 1971.

Mother, The (Matka). Opera in 10 scenes by Alois Hába, to his own libretto concerning the enmity between the children of the first and second marriages in a Czech family, first performed (in German) in Munich on May 17, 1931.

Mother of Us All, The. Opera in two acts by Virgil Thomson, to a libretto by Gertrude Stein, first produced in New York at Columbia University on May 7, 1947. The universal matriarch is Susan B. Anthony, the American suffragette who fought for women's right to vote. The cast of characters is two modestly abbreviated names, Virgil T. and Gertrude S., the music disarmingly triadic but greatly sophisticated in its seeming simplicity.

Mountaineers, The. The first national opera of the Dagestan in the Caucasus by Shirvani Chalayev, depicting in dramatic colors and stark asymmetrical rhythms the socialist passions in a remote Caucasian village during the civil war of 1920, first produced in Derbent, Dagestan, Russia, on Jan. 30, 1971.

Mourning Becomes Electra. Opera in three acts by Marvin David Levy, to a libretto by Henry Butler condensed from Eugene O'Neill's trilogy in which the action is shifted from ancient Greece to a New England village in 1865. Agamemnon is phonetically anglicized into Ezra Mannon returning home from the Civil War, Clytemnestra becomes Christine, her lover Aegisthus is Adam Brant, Electra is Lavinia, and her brother Orestes is Orin. It was commissioned by and first performed at the Metropolitan Opera in New York on March 17, 1967.

Mozart and Salieri. Opera in two acts by Nikolai Rimsky-Korsakov, to a libretto after Pushkin's "little tragedy" (1830), first produced in Moscow on Dec. 7, 1898. Pushkin's text gives literary sanction to a legend that spread shortly after Mozart's death, accusing the eminently respectable Italian composer Salieri of poisoning Mozart. In Pushkin's poem as in the opera, Salieri declares that were Mozart allowed to live on, other composers—honest, industrious, but not blessed by genius—would be condemned to futility. Rimsky-Korsakov used authentic excerpts from Mozart's compositions as well as musical allusions to Salieri's opera *Tarare*, which Mozart prized highly.

Mr. and Mrs. Discobbolos. Minuscule opera by Peter Westergaard, scored for two singers and six instrumentalists, to the whimsical poem by Edward Lear, with the aleatorically serial idiom of the music illustrating the rhymed glossolalia of the text, performed for the first time at Columbia University in New York on March 21, 1966.

Muette de Portici, La (The Mute Girl of Portici). Opera in five acts by Daniel-François-Esprit Auber, to a libretto by Eugéne Scribe and Delavigne, first performed in Paris on Feb. 29, 1828. The Neopolitan fisherman Masaniello, the brother of the mute girl, Fanella, leads a rebellion against the Spanish rule. He is mysteriously murdered just as he achieves his goal of overthrowing the Spanish viceroy in Naples. His deaf-mute sister throws herself into the crater of Mt. Vesuvius during an eruption.

Mujer y su sombra, La. Opera by Alcazar, to a libretto by Paul Claudel dealing with an Oriental woman who cannot move without her shadow, which possesses a different personality and a different voice, first staged in Mexico City on April 12, 1981.

Muko Erabi (The Marriage Contest). Comic opera in one act by Osamu Shimizu, to a libretto based on a folktale involving a contest of three suitors for the hand of the beautiful daughter of a prosperous landowner, won by a pauper who guesses rightly by choreographic palpation that his dance partner wearing a hideous demon's mask is his nuptial objective. The opera was first staged in Riverside, California, Oct. 3, 1960.

My Kinsman, Major Molineux. Opera in one act by

Bruce Saylor, after Nathaniel Hawthorne, first staged in Pittsburgh on Aug. 28, 1976.

Myshkin. Opera by John Charles Eaton, after *The Idiot* by Dostoyevsky, conceived for television and shown on PBS on April 23, 1973.

N

Nabucco. Opera in four acts by Giuseppe Verdi, to a libretto by Temostocle Solera after the drama by Auguste Anicet-Bourgeois and Francis Cornue, *Nabucodonosor* (1836), first staged at La Scala, Milan, on March 9, 1842. The opera recounts the biblical story of the Hebrews and Nebuchadnezzar (Daniel 1–4), the Babylonian king who defeated them and held them in the "Babylonian captivity." The king eventually goes mad and saves himself by converting to the Judaic religion. The opera was Verdi's first notable success with its dominant chorus, and has had revivals in the 20th century.

Nacht in Venedig, Eine (A Night in Venice). Operetta in three acts by Johann Strauss II, to a libretto by "F. Zell" (Camillo Walzel) and Richard Genée, set during an 18th-century Venice carnival and traversing the various meanderings of four essential characters toward proper marriages for all, first performed in Berlin on Oct. 3, 1883.

Nachtlager von Granada, Die (A Night's Shelter in Granada). Opera in two acts by Conradin Kreutzer, to a text by Karl von Braunthal after Kind's drama wherein the crown prince of Spain, disguised as a hunter, assists the shepherdess Gabriela in achieving her heart's desire—marriage to the shepherd Gomez, despite contrary plans on her uncle Ambrosio's part—first produced in Vienna on Jan. 13, 1834.

Nachtschwalbe, Die. "Dramatic nocturne" in one act by Boris Blacher, to a libretto dealing with the life of a prostitute in a small German town who turns out to be an illegitimate daughter of the head of the vice squad. Its first performance in Leipzig on Feb. 22, 1948, provoked quite a scandal because of its frank staging.

Napoli milionaria. Comic opera by Nino Rota, to a libretto by Eduardo De Filippo making sport of the American occupation of Naples in 1945 that produced black-market Neapolitan millionaires, first presented in Spoleto on June 22, 1977.

Natalia Petrovna. Opera in two acts by Lee Hoiby, to a libretto from Turgenev's play *A Month in the Country* characterizing in romantic modalities distilled in modernistic ambitonalities the emotional turmoils of 19th-century Russian women, first performed at the New York City Opera on Oct. 8, 1964.

Natoma. Opera by Victor Herbert, first produced in Philadelphia on Feb. 25, 1911, his only attempt to write in a grand operatic manner, reminiscent of Wagner. The action takes place in California under Spanish rule. Natoma is an Indian girl in love with a U.S. Navy lieutenant, but she yields him to her rival, a white woman from Santa Barbara, and finds solace in the invocation to the ancestral Great Spirit.

Nausicaa. Opera by Peggy Glanville-Hicks, to a libretto by Robert Graves from his book *Homer's Daughter*, advancing the notion that the epic *Odyssey* was created not by Homer but by his daughter, first performed in Athens, in the Herodes Atticus amphitheater built in 161 A.D., situated on the southern slope of the Acropolis, on Aug. 19, 1961.

Navarraise, La (The Girl from Navarre). Opera by Jules Massenet, to a libretto by Jules Claretie and Henri Cain after Claretie's story *La cigarette*, first staged in London on June 20, 1894. The heroine becomes involved with a royal officer during the dynastic strife of 16th-century Spain. When he is killed, she goes insane.

Nazar Stodolya. Opera in three acts by Konstyantyn Dan'kevych, to a libretto reciting the dramatic story of a valiant young Cossack in love with a glorious girl whose infamous father is bent on leading her to the connubial bed of an unspeakable colonel of the czarist army, with true young love triumphant in the E-flat-major finale, first produced in Kharkiv on May 28, 1960.

Nerone. Opera in four acts by Arrigo Boito, to the composer's libretto, left unfinished after decades of work. It was finished by Vincenzo Tommasini and Antonio Smareglin working under Toscanini, and premiered posthumously at La Scala, Milan, on May 1, 1924. The opera dramatizes the contrast between the pagan world of the Roman emperor Nero and the emerging Christianity. In the finale, Rome has its famous conflagration.

Neues vom Tage (News of the Day). Opera in three acts by Paul Hindemith, to a libretto by Marcellus Schiffer, first produced in Berlin on June 8, 1929. The events of the libretto begin with a marital separation, while another couple also becomes entangled in divorce proceedings. It includes a bathtub aria, which scandalized the critics, as well as a chorus of stenographers at percussive typewriters.

New Year. Opera in three acts by Michael Tippett, to his own text set in a futuristic but ambiguous time and place ("Somewhere, Today, Nowhere, Tomorrow") in which the essential characters of Jo Ann, Nan, Merlin, Regan, and Pelegrin do a lot time traveling, and, in the end, at a nonspecific New Year's celebration, learn to forgive, forget, and remember, first staged in Houston on Oct. 27, 1989.

Night at the Chinese Opera, A. Opera by Judith Weir, first produced in Cheltanham on July 8, 1987, features an "opera within an opera."

Night Blooming Cereus. Chamber opera in two scenes by John Beckwith, in which a gardening lady receives a visit by her daughter's daughter as an act of contrition to expiate her mother's elopement finale as the nocturnal cereus suddenly blossoms forth in the afternoon, first given on radio, then produced in Toronto on April 5, 1960.

Night Flight (Volo di Notte). Opera by Luigi Dallapiccola, based on the autobiographical novel *Vol de Nuit* by Antoine de Saint-Exupéry, first produced in Florence on May 18, 1940. The story deals with a dramatic night flight over the Andes in a single-engine monoplane. The score includes spoken dialogue and a wordless passage of a disembodied voice warning the pilot of dangers ahead.

Nightingale, The (*Le rossignol*). Opera in three acts by Igor Stravinsky, to a libretto by the composer and Stepan Mitusov after Hans Christian Andersen, first produced in Paris on May 26, 1914. The Chinese emperor is dying, and his life is sustained by the singing of a nightingale. But when the Japanese ambassador thoughtlessly presents the emperor with a mechanical nightingale, the real bird flies away, and the emperor's health declines dangerously. As a discordant funeral march is played, the real nightingale is brought in, and the emperor regains his strength. The moral seems to be that human ills ought to be left to natural cure. The compositional history of the work reveals that the first two acts were composed before the groundbreaking ballets *Petrouchka* and *The Rite of Spring*. The last act was composed afterward, and Stravinsky struggled to maintain consistency (as Wagner had to do in *Siegfried*).

Night of the Moonspell. Opera in three acts by Elie Siegmeister, based on Shakespeare's *A Midsummer Night's Dream*, with the action transferred to a festive mardi gras in Louisiana c.1900 and including Cajun voodoo rites, first produced as a commissioned U.S. bicentennial work in Shreveport, Louisiana, on Nov. 14, 1976.

Nina, o sia La pazza per amore (Nina, or The Love-Distressed Maid). Opera in two acts by Giovanni Paisiello, to a libretto by Giambattista Lorenzi, about Nina's madness over true love lost (Lindoro) and false love gained (Lindoro's rival in a duel), with Nina's sanity magnificently restored in the end when Lindoro recovers from his wounds, first staged in Caserta, at the Royal Palace, on June 25, 1789.

Nine Rivers from Jordan. Opera in three acts by Hugo Weisgall, to a libretto saturated with religious symbolism in which a Christ-like British soldier in World War II lets a Judas-like German war prisoner escape, the first opera in history to employ four-letter words for sexual intercourse in its dialogue, set to music in intransigently dissonant counterpoint, with some topical insertions, such as the singing of "Lili Marlene," a song popular with both sides in conflict, first produced by the N.Y. City Opera on Oct. 9, 1968.

Nixon in China. Modern historical opera in two acts by John Adams, to a libretto by Alice Goodman, depicting, in fancifully realistic scenes, President Richard Nixon's trip to China in 1972, with Nixon's role assigned to a baritone, Mao Zedung to a Wagnerian Heldentenor, and Nixon's wife to a mindless ingenue. The world premiere was given at the 8th annual New Music America Festival in Houston on Oct. 22, 1987, directed by Peter Sellars. Two orchestral excerpts from the work, "Short Ride in a Fast Machine" and "The Chairman Dances," are frequently programmed separately.

Noces, Les. "Choreographic scenes with singing and music" by Igor Stravinsky, scored for chorus, soloists, four pianos, and 17 percussion instruments, first produced by Diaghilev's Ballets Russes in Paris on June 13, 1923. Despite its instrumentation and because it is performed on the stage, it occupies an intermediate position between cantata and opera. The libretto consists of four scenes, tracing the rituals of a peasant betrothal and wedding. The Russian title is *Svadebka* (Little Wedding).

Norma. Opera in two acts by Vincenzo Bellini, his most melodious and harmonious, to a libretto by Felice Romani after Alexandre Soumet's tragedy (1831), first produced in Milan on Dec. 26, 1831. Norma is the high priestess of the Druid temple in ancient Gaul during its occupation by the Romans. Here, not only Norma herself becomes involved with a Roman proconsul and bears him a couple of clandestine children, but a virgin of the temple also loves him, in violation of her vow of chastity. The proconsul is caught desecrating the temple of the Druids, but Norma cannot bring herself to put him to death as she ought to do in her capacity as high priestess. She confesses her own unchastity, and ascends the punitive pyre with the proconsul for ritual incineration. *Norma* is a perennial favorite. The aria "Casta diva," in which Norma appeals to the goddess of the moon, is a paragon of melodic beauty. Even Wagner professed his admiration.

Nose, The (Nos). Opera in three acts by Dmitri Shostakovich, to a libretto by Alexander Preis, Yevgeny Zamyatin, Georgy Yonin, and the composer after the fantastic tale by Gogol (1835), first produced in Leningrad on Jan. 18, 1930. The story deals with the nose of a government functionary that mysteriously disappears from his face during shaving and goes off as an independent individual. All sorts of absurdities occur, interspersed with satirical darts at czarist bureaucracy. In the end, the nose resumes its rightful place, above the mouth and under the eyes, much to the owner's relief. The score includes an octet of janitors in dissonant counterpoint, gigantic orchestral sneezes, and other effects. The production was greeted with great exhilaration by Soviet musicians, but received a chilly reception by the Kremlin bureaucracy, and Shostakovich was charged with imitating decadent Western models. Many years elapsed before *The Nose* was revived on the Soviet stage.

Nouveau locataire, Le. Opera in one act by Milko Kelemen, after a whimsical play by Eugène Ionesco, first staged in Münster on Sept. 20, 1964.

Noye's Fludde. Miracle play in one act by Benjamin Britten to his own libretto, based on the medieval Chester Miracle Play, first performed in Oxford on June 18, 1958. Except for Noye (Noah), the roles are to be filled by children.

Nuit foudroyée, La. Opera in four acts by Jacques Bondon, to a libretto in which a diurnal man is held in thrall by a nocturnal woman who disintegrates in his arms with the dawn, performed for the first time on the stage in Metz on Feb. 10, 1968.

O

1330. Opera by Jacques Bondon, set in the 30th century to a libretto after the 1920 sociofutural novel *We* by the Russian expatriate author Eugene Zamiatine wherein humans of a remote future are forbidden to make love or to think, and are identified only by number and code letter under the rule of a "benefactor," first staged in Nantes on May 20, 1975.

Oberon. Opera in three acts by Carl Maria von Weber, to a libretto by James Robinson Planché after William Sotheby's translation (1798) of Wieland's *Oberon* (1780), first produced in London on April 12, 1826, the composer conducting. The plot is vaguely reminiscent of Shakespeare's *A Midsummer Night's Dream.* Oberon is King of the Elves, and Titania his Queen, with numerous exotic characters springing up here and there. Oberon's appointed task in life is to find a pair of lovers undeterred by misadventure, and he succeeds with the help of his magic horn. There is a grand reunion at the end, at the court of Charlemagne. The English libretto is magnificent in its absurdity. The glorious overture survives on the concert podium, but the opera is never (well, hardly ever) performed in its entirety.

Oberto, conte di San Bonifacio. Opera in two acts by Giuseppe Verdi, his first to be performed, to a libretto by Antonio Piazza, revised by Temistocle Solera, produced at La Scala, Milan, on Nov. 17, 1839. Oberto is killed by his daughter's lover in a duel. The murderous seducer leaves Italy never to return, and the abandoned girl is left to her futile lamentations. The opera was successful, and still maintains a spark of life at its infrequent revivals on the Italian stages.

Ocean. Opera by Danilo Švara, employing 12-note technique after the drama by Leonid Andreyev, first staged in Ljubljana on March 3, 1969.

Occurrence at Owl Creek Bridge, An. Radio opera for baritone, three speakers, tape, and orchestra by Thea Musgrave, to her own libretto after Ambrose Bierce's story, first performed in London on Dec. 20, 1981.

Ochsenmenuett, Die. Light opera by Ignaz Seyfried, first produced in Vienna on New Year's Eve, 1823. The silly libretto tells an unsubstantiated anecdote about Haydn's composing a minuet for his favorite butcher, who sent him an ox as a token of his gratitude. The tune of the minuet was by Seyfried, but the rest of the opera was arranged from various authentic tunes by Haydn. Fortunately, Haydn was long dead when the opera was produced.

October. Opera by Vano Il'ich Muradeli, to a libretto depicting in heroic Russian modalities the glorious Bolshevik Revolution of Oct. 25, 1917, according to the Julian calendar of old Russia, corresponding to Nov. 7, Gregorian style, performed for the first time in its complete stage version at the Palace of Congresses in the Kremlin in Moscow on April 22, 1964. (A concert version was first heard on Moscow Radio on Dec. 5, 1962.) The score represents the first attempt by a Soviet composer to portray Lenin in opera in a singing part.

Oedipe. Lyrical tragedy in four acts by George Enescu, first performed in Paris on March 13, 1936. The subject is drawn from the tragedies of Aeschylus and Sophocles, with the basic events of Greek mythology preserved. Oedipus inadvertently kills his father and mistakenly marries his mother. But he is vindicated in the end as a victim of fate. The peculiarity of the score is that Enesco does not resort to stylization, but internationalizes the theme, even to the point of making use of Rumanian melorhythms and briefly making use of quarter tones.

Oedipus. Opera by Wolfgang Rihm, after Hölderlin's translation of the drama by Sophocles, first mounted in Berlin on Oct. 4, 1987.

Oedipus Rex. Opera oratorio in two acts by Igor Stravinsky, to a libretto by Jean Cocteau after Sophocles' tragedy, the sung portions translated into Latin by Jean Daniélou, first performed in concert in Paris on May 30, 1927. The stage premiere took place in Vienna on Feb. 23, 1928.

Of Mice and Men. Opera by Carlisle Floyd, after John Steinbeck's celebrated novel, first staged in Seattle on Jan. 22, 1970. Two brothers (friends in the novel) working on a farm dream of buying a ranch of their own. One of them, a simple-minded boy, commits murder, and his normal brother shoots him dead to save him from execution. The title is taken from Robert Burns's famous line "The best laid schemes o' mice and men."

Oh, Mr. Fogg. Comic chamber opera by Jan Fischer, satirizing the hero of Jules Verne's novel *Around the World in Eighty Days,* first staged in Saarbrücken on June 27, 1971.

Old Maid and the Thief, The. Opera by Gian Carlo Menotti, to his own libretto in English, depicting in 14 episodes in merry Rossinian tones the picaresque adventures of a sexy intruder in the bedroom of an American spinster who becomes fascinated by his physique and joins him in his kleptophilic profession. The work was heard first in concert form over the NBC Radio Network in New York on April 22, 1939. Its first stage performance took place in Philadelphia on Feb. 11, 1941.

Olimpie. Opera in three acts by Gaspare Spontini, to a libretto by M. Dieulafoy and C. Brifaut after Voltaire's tragedy (1762) first staged in Paris on Dec. 22, 1819.

Olympians, The. Opera in three acts by Arthur Bliss, first produced by London on Sept. 29, 1949. The libretto, by J. B. Priestley, depicts the pathetic destiny of once-powerful Greek gods who are reduced to the status of itinerant actors and are allowed to return to Mt. Olympus only for a vacation once a year.

Omphale. Opera by André Cardinal Destouches, first performed in Paris on Nov. 10, 1701. Its premiere passed without particular notice, but it became a *cause célèbre* in 1752 when the Alsatian diplomat Friedrich Melchior Grimm published a *Lettre sur Omphale,* adding to the dispute between advocates of Rameau vs. those of Lully. He was an advocate of Rameau and a critic of earlier French opera. He included *Omphale* in the latter group, although he was not totally critical of this opera. The libretto of *Omphale* took the subject from Greek mythology as was the ingrained habit of French Baroque opera makers. But the formidable Omphale captures Hercules and makes him spin the yarn in her spindle while she struts in a lion's skin, in a light rather than heroic manner, and therefore anticipated the development of French light opera.

One Man Show. Chamber opera by Nicholas Maw, to a libretto by Arthur Jacobs, dealing with an impecunious young art student whose back is discovered to be tattooed in a theoretically abstract pattern (actually it spells JOE, upside down), and who therefore becomes the target of covetous art dealers, first performed in London on Nov. 12, 1964.

Opera (Works). Mixed media spectacle by Luciano Berio, in which calculated chaos is integrated into an oxymoronic theatrical action, performed for the first time in Santa Fe on Aug. 12, 1970.

Opéra de Poussière, L'. Opera in two acts by Marcel Landowski, to a libretto dealing with an ironic fate of an opera composer who kills himself when his fiancée leaves after a series of fruitless attempts to have his opera produced, with the attendant publicity arousing sudden interest in his work, which is then produced posthumously with sensational success, performed for the first time in Avignon on Oct. 25, 1962, under the composer's direction.

Opéra des Oiseaux, L'. Opera by Antoine Duhamel, after *The Birds* of Aristophanes, featuring a wide mixture of singing and spoken word with soloists and orchestra dressed as birds. The work was first produced in Lyons on May 19, 1971.

Opera Flies. Opera by Helim El-Dabh, to a libretto dealing with the tragic occurrence on the campus of Kent (Ohio) State University when four students were killed by National Guardsmen during an antiwar demonstration in 1970, the "flies" of the title referring to the victims, first staged in Washington, D.C., on May 5, 1971.

Opsadno stanje (The Stage of Siege). Opera by Milko Kelemen, after the surrealistic tale *The Plague* by Camus, with the entire tonal fabric evolving out of a single motive, first produced in Hamburg under the German title *Der Belagerungszustand* on Jan. 13, 1970.

Oresteia. Opera-oratorio trilogy by Darius Milhaud, to texts by Paul Claudel based on Aeschylus's tragedies. The first work, based on *Agamemnon*, was first staged in Paris on April 16, 1927. The second, based on *Les Choéphores*, was first staged in Paris on March 8, 1927. The third and last, based on *Les Euménides*, was first staged in Berlin in April of 1963.

Oresteya. Operatic trilogy by Sergei Taneyev, first performed in St. Petersburg on Oct. 29, 1895. The libretto, in three parts, follows Aeschylus's tragedies. After the murder of Agamemnon by his wife, Clytemnestra, their son swears vengeance, and kills her and her lover. The Furies pursue him but he finds refuge in the temple of Apollo.

Orfeide, L'. Operatic triptych by Gian Francesco Malipiero, to a libretto by the composer, comprising three independent works: *La morte delle maschere, Sette canzoni*, and *Orfeo, ovvero L'ottava canzone.* The complete work, traversing the fine line between fact (life) and fiction (theatricality) in its themes and drawing upon characters from commedia dell'arte as well as early, mostly Renaissance, Italian sources, was first performed in Düsseldorf on Oct. 31, 1925.

Orfeo. "Fable in music" in prologue and five acts by Claudio Monteverdi, to a text by Alessandro Striggio after Ovid, first performed privately in Mantua on Feb. 22, 1607, and publicly two days later at the Mantua Court. The libretto follows the familiar legend of Orpheus trying to recover his beloved Euridice from the Kingdom of the Dead. For aesthetic reasons, Monteverdi omitted the original ending, the dismembering of Orpheus by a crazed mob. Instead, Orpheus is taken to Elysium by Apollo as the *deus ex machina.* The historical significance of *L'Orfeo* lies in its colorful instrumentation and its skillful alternation of monody and more old-fashioned textures, providing the first balanced approach to early opera.

Orfeo. Opera by Luigi Rossi, first produced in Paris on March 2, 1647. The work, to a libretto after the classical legend and among Rossi's finest, is significant as the first Italian opera written expressly for a Paris production.

Orfeo ed Euridice. Opera in three acts by Christopher Willibald Gluck, to a libretto by Ranieri De'Calzabigi after the classical legend, first produced in Vienna in Italian, on Oct. 5, 1762, with the part of Orfeo sung by the famous castrato Gaetano Guadagni. The work acquired its greatest historical significance after its performance with a French libretto in Paris on Aug. 2, 1774. The work demonstrates Gluck's doctrine of subordinating music to text so as to achieve the maximum degree of dramatic verity. The story follows the Greek myth of the singer Orpheus trying to recover his beloved Euridice from the land of death, and losing her when he fails to obey the injunction not to look back at hell's entrance. Unlike the myth, a happy ending is provided. The customary ballet required of all works at the Paris Opéra is fulfilled by the famous *Dance of the Blessed Spirits.*

Ormindo. Opera by Francesco Cavalli, premiered in Venice in 1644 at carnival time. Two young army men are in love with the queen of the land. The king discovers the intrigue, but forgives the youthful adventurers. *Ormindo* is one of the earliest extant monodic operas.

Orontea. Opera by Antonio Cesti, his first, premiered in Venice on Jan. 20, 1649. The story deals with a seriocomic confusion between princely characters and their lowly servants, one of whom, Orontea, turns out to be a princess in her own right who was registered in the wrong column in the church birth records. The style is monodic, the dialogue mostly in recitative. There is no chorus.

Orphée. Opera by Philip Glass, after Cocteau's film, first staged in Cambridge, Massachusetts, on May 14, 1993.

Orphée aux enfers (Orpheus in the Underworld). Operetta in two (later four) acts by Jacques Offenbach, to a libretto by Hector-Jonathan Crémieux and Ludovic Halévy, first produced in its two-act version in Paris on Oct. 21, 1858, his first major success, and in its four-act version in Paris on Feb. 7, 1874. In this parody, the gods of Olympus are exposed as bumbling creatures intent on having their pleasure on earth rather than in heaven. Orpheus is in love with a shepherdess, and Jupiter is attracted by Euridice, the wife of Orpheus, abducted by Hades. Eventually she becomes a Bacchante. The score includes a can-can, which shocked the sensibilities of some proper Parisians.

Orpheus in Pecan Springs. Ballad opera by William Latham, to a libretto by Thomas Holliday, first performed in Denton, Texas, on Dec. 4, 1980.

Ossian, ou Les bardes (Ossian, or The Bards). Opera in five acts by Jean-François Le Sueur, to a libretto by Palat-Dercy and Jacques-Marie Deschamps set in Scotland in medieval times in which battles between the Scandinavians and the Caledonians thwart the desire of Rosmala to marry Ossian (both Caledonians), a happy ending ensuing when the Caledonians rescue them both from the evil clutches of Duntalmo (a Scandinavian), first staged in Paris on July 10, 1804.

Ostrav Afrodité (The Island of Aphrodite). Opera in three acts by Jiří Dvořáček, to his own libretto after a play by Alexis Parnis, performed for the first time in a German version in Dresden on Feb. 13, 1971. The libretto depicts the tense 1955 struggle between the British colonial authorities and the rebellious nationalistic Greek populace on the island of Cyprus, the legendary birthplace of Aphrodite.

Otello. Opera in four acts by Giuseppe Verdi, first produced in Milan on Feb. 5, 1887. The masterly libretto by Arrigo Boito is generally faithful to Shakespeare's play, and the Italian text is exemplary. (The spelling Otello, without an *h*, is proper in Italian.) Otello is a Moor who leads the Venetian army to victories over the Turks. Provoked by Iago, his malicious aide-de-camp, he suspects his wife, Desdemona, of infidelity and strangles her. When he finds out his monstrous error, he stabs himself to death. The opera, which Verdi completed at the age of 73, is remarkable for its departure from the style and idiom of his previous operas, toward the modern concept of music drama.

Otello, ossia Il Moro di Venezia. Opera by Gioacchino Rossini, after Shakespeare, first produced in Naples on Dec. 4, 1816. While revivals have occurred on occasion, it cannot match the musical and popular success of Verdi's opera *Otello* on the same source.

Ottone, rè di Germania (Ottone, King of Germany). Opera by George Frideric Handel, first produced at the King's Theatre in London on Jan. 12, 1723. Revised versions were subsequently given there on Feb. 8, 1726, and on Nov. 13, 1733. The story is set in Rome and concerns the difficulties faced by Ottone on his way to marry Teofane.

Our Man in Havana. Opera in three acts by Malcolm Williamson, after the melodramatic novel by Graham Greene, with spies and counterspies matching wits in wry atonalities over ostentatious pseudo-Cuban rhythms, first produced in London on July 2, 1963.

Outcasts of Poker Flat, The. Opera in one act by Samuel Adler, after a tragic story by Bret Harte, performed for the first time in Dallas, Texas, in April, 1961.

Owen Wingrave. Television opera by Benjamin Britten, to a libretto by Myfanny Piper based on a short story by Henry James dealing with a pacifist youth who suffers social reprehension for his conviction (as Benjamin Britten himself had during World War II), first broadcast over the BBC on May 16, 1971, later staged at Covent Garden, London, May 10, 1973.

P

Padmâvatî. Opera ballet in two acts by Albert Roussel, to a libretto by Louis Laloy after an event in 13th-century history, premiered in Paris on June 1, 1923. The eponymous heroine is the beautiful wife of the king of Ichitor in 13th-century India. The Mongol Khan warring on Ichitor is willing to conclude peace provided the king turns Padmâvatî over to him. To save her husband from a painful dilemma, she stabs him to death and, as behooves any traditional Hindu widow, dies with him on his funeral pyre.

Padrone, The. Opera in two acts by George Chadwick, composed in 1912, to a libretto in which the figure of the padrone, in the period of Italian and Irish immigration in the late 19th century, symbolizes human corruption in the exploitation of poor immigrants, musically based "on the union of Wagner's symphonic recitative and Italian lyricism," with its four principal characters singing in Italian and all others in English, first produced in an abridged concert version at N.Y.'s Carnegie Hall on Dec. 6, 1961, and later given its first complete stage production in Boston on April 10, 1997.

Pagliacci (Players). Opera in two acts by Ruggero Leoncavallo, to his own libretto, first performed in Milan on May 21, 1892, Arturo Toscanini the conductor. Here, Leoncavallo made a deliberate effort to emulate the success of Mascagni's *Cavalleria rusticana*, produced about two years before, succeeding beyond all expectations. Since the two operas are short, they are invariably paired like symmetric twins on operatic playbills, affectionately referred to as *Cav* and *Pag*. With these two works, Leoncavallo and Mascagni inaugurated a realistic movement in opera that came to be known as verismo. The correct title of Leoncavallo's opera is *Pagliacci*, not *I pagliacci*, as often listed.

The story of *Pagliacci* is derived from an actual event when an actor killed his unfaithful wife after a theatrical performance in which they both took part. (Leoncavallo's father was the judge at the murder trial.) The opera is set as a play within a play, with a group of traveling actors performing in a booth in the center of the stage. The cast of characters is that of the commedia dell'arte. Just before the curtain rises in the booth, Canio learns that his wife, Nedda, who plays Columbina in the play within the play, has a lover. He sings his famous aria, "Vesti la giubba" (with which Caruso moved a generation of operagoers to tears), lamenting the necessity of putting on a clown's garb when his heart is breaking. As the play progresses, he begins to identify with his character, and demands to know the name of his wife's lover. She refuses, and he stabs her to death. Her lover rushes in from the stage audience, and is killed in turn. The clown then announces to the shocked spectators, "La commedia e finita" (the play is over).

Palestrina. Opera in three acts by Hans Pfitzner, considered his masterpiece, to his own libretto, first performed in Munich on June 12, 1917. It is subtitled *Musikalische Legende*, to account for its notion that Palestrina wrote his famous *Missa Pape Marcelli* at the behest of angels in order to convince skeptical members of the Council of Trent that polyphony ought to be an integral part of church music. The score has moments of academic grandeur.

Pantagleize. Opera in three acts by Robert Starer, to an ironic political drama by the Belgian playwright Michel de Ghelderode in which a bumbling colonial general precipitates a revolution in an unnamed Belgian colony in west Africa by unwittingly uttering a secret signal, "Oh, what a lovely day!," first staged at Brooklyn College in New York on April 7, 1973.

Paradise Lost. "Sacra rappresentazione" by Krzysztot Penderecki, after Milton's poem, originally planned for production during the 1976 American bicentennial but finally first performed by the Lyric Opera of Chicago on Nov. 29, 1978.

Paride ed Elena (Paris and Helen). Opera in five acts by Christopher Willibald Gluck, to a libretto by Ranieri de Calzabigi, first performed in Vienna on Nov. 3, 1770. The libretto is based on the classical tale of Paris of Troy who kidnaps Helen, the beautiful wife of the king of Sparta. The legend has been set to music by a number of composers. This is the fourth opera by Gluck in which he formulated his basic principle that music should be the handmaid of the text, not its mistress.

Parisina. Opera in three acts by Gaetano Donizetti, to a libretto by Felice Romani after Byron's verse tale (1816), first staged in Florence on March 17, 1833. In this tragic romance, Parisina loves her stepson. The young lovers try to flee but the enraged cuckold intercepts and has his son executed. Parisina dies when she sees the lifeless body of her beloved.

Parsifal. "Sacred festival drama" in three acts by Richard Wagner, to his own libretto after Wolfram von Eschenbach's poem *Parzival*, produced in Bayreuth on July 26, 1882, less than one year before his death. Wagner's libretto is drawn from the legend of the Holy Grail, the chalice from which Jesus drank at the Last Supper. The religious symbolism of *Parsifal* requires some explanation. Before the opera begins, Amfortas, the King of the Grail, allows himself to be seduced by the sorceress Kundry in the service of Klingsor, the magician, who inflicts a grievous wound on the king. The wound can be healed only by the touch of the sacred spear, and only one pure of heart who has acquired wisdom through pity can take the spear away from Klingsor, who has it in his possession.

Young Parsifal satisfies these requirements. He is sent by the Knights of the Holy Grail to Klingsor's domain. Realizing the danger, Klingsor mobilizes a gardenful of flower maidens to lure and confuse Parsifal, and as a further inducement, Kundry kisses him on the lips. This elicits from Parsifal the most unexpected response in all operatic literature, "Amfortas! The spear wound!" Whatever hematological connection may exist between Kundry's lips and the king's wound, she instantly grasps its significance, and suddenly changes from a sorceress into a humble supplicant for salvation, having been cursed for laughing at Jesus on his way to Golgotha. Parsifal seizes the spear that Klingsor has hurled at him and makes the sign of the cross with it. The power of the Christian symbol utterly destroys Klingsor's kingdom. Parsifal makes his way to the Temple of the Holy Grail, where Kundry precedes him. He is named King of the Grail. Amfortas bares his wound and Parsifal heals it with the touch of the sacred spear. Parsifal then raises the Holy Grail in the air; at the sight of it Kundry collapses and dies, free of her curse at last.

Both the score and story of *Parsifal* are invitingly mysterious and elusive. Wagner's music is perhaps his most sublime.

Partizanka Ana (Freedom Fighter Anna). Opera in one act by Rado Simoniti, to a libretto depicting the Yugoslav people's fight again Nazi forces, first produced in Ljubljana on June 18, 1975.

Passion of Jonathan Wade, The. Opera in three acts by Carlisle Floyd, first performed at the New York City Opera on Oct. 11, 1962. The composer's libretto depicts life during Reconstruction in the American south, during which the hero falls victim to the bigotry and vindictiveness of the Ku Klux Klan.

Passion selon Sade, La (The Passion According to Sade). Theatrical action for mixed media by Sylvano Bussotti, evolving from a dodecaphonic motto and ramifying into varied atonal, polytonal, rhythmically dispersed, serialistically surrealistic musical motion purported to portray the sadistic bedroom philosophy of Marquis de Sade (1740–1814), first produced in Palmero on Sept. 5, 1965.

Pastor Fido, Il (The Faithful Shepherd). Opera by George Frideric Handel, first produced at the Queen's Theatre in London on Nov. 22, 1712. This simple pastorale about the archetypal faithful shepherd was one of the composer's first works for the English stage.

Paučina (The Weaving). Opera by Prošev, a sociopsychological drama portraying the lives of Slavic emigrants in America, first produced in Rijeka on June 12, 1964.

Paul Bunyan. Short, light opera in prologue and two acts by Benjamin Britten, to a libretto by W. H. Auden, first performed at Columbia University, N.Y., on May 5, 1941, during a time when both men were in America. The story recounts the exploits of the legendary American lumberjack Paul Bunyan in a series of tuneful episodes. After being laid aside for 35 years, the opera was revived at the 29th Musical Festival at Aldeburgh, England, 1976, as a bicentennial tribute to America.

Pauvre matelot, Le (The Poor Sailor). A "complaint in three acts" in the form of an opera by Darius Milhaud, to a libretto by Jean Cocteau wherein a sailor returning home after many years at sea represents himself to his wife as a stranger to test her fidelity and is murdered by her for his money, which she hopes to save for her husband's return. The work was first staged in Paris on Dec. 16, 1927.

Pêcheurs de perles, Les (The Pearl Fishers). Opera in three acts by George Bizet, to a libretto by Eugène Cormon (Pierre-Étienne Piestre) and Michel Carré, premiered in Paris on Sept. 30, 1863. Two fishermen in Ceylon are rivals in love, but their object of adoration is a priestess bound to chastity. One of the suitors is elected a tribal chief and promises her a priceless pearl if she remains chaste. She spurns the pearl and flees the island with the other fisherman.

Peer Gynt. Opera by Werner Egk, first produced in Berlin on Nov. 24, 1938. The libretto, drawn from Ibsen's great philosophical drama, traverses Peer Gynt's travels in search of adventure and pleasure. He visits Algiers where Anitra dances for him, and he courts the daughter of the King of the Trolls in his mountain palace. In the end, he returns to his ever-faithful Solvieg and dies in her arms. Egk's opera was unexpectedly praised by Hitler, who attended its first performance, thus assuring its success for a few years. However, Egk survived Hitler and his deadly accolade, and *Peer Gynt* resurfaced with its reputation for solidity and vitality intact.

Pelerins de la Mecque, Les. See ***Rencontre imprévue, La.***

Pelléas et Mélisande. Lyric drama in five acts (12 tableaux) by Claude Debussy, to a libretto drawn from Maurice Maeterlinck's tragedy of the same name. It was first performed in Paris on April 30, 1902, André Messager conducting and Mary Garden singing Mélisande, a premiere of historical significance, for Debussy's operatic masterpiece changed the face of the musical theater and inaugurated a new genre of music drama.

Golaud finds Mélisande wandering in a forest. He marries her, but soon an affectionate though innocent alliance develops between Mélisande and Golaud's half brother, Pelléas. When Mélisande lets her long hair fall from her window, Pelléas caresses it. Golaud's jealousy is aroused, and he becomes violent. In a famous scene he drags Mélisande on the floor by her hair, and in a triumph of understatement she whispers, "I am not happy today." When Golaud finds her with Pelléas at the fountain in the park, he kills Pelléas. Mélisande is about to bear Golaud's child; dying in childbirth, she forgives her husband for his crime.

So unusual is the music, so dramatic its departure from traditional French opera, that Paris music critics were bewildered. When Richard Strauss attended a performance of *Pelléas et Mélisande* in Paris, he turned to a friend during the first act and asked: "Is it going to go on and on like this?" To an uninitiated listener Debussy's music appears static and monotonous. A Paris critic, whose physiological aversion to Debussy's music was irrepressible, admitted by way of a compliment, "True, this music makes little noise, but it is a nasty little noise." Debussy's free use of unresolved dissonances, frequent progressions of dominant-ninth chords, and unstable tonality, all contributed to critical incomprehension. It took many years for *Pelléas et Mélisande* to take its rightful place among operatic masterpieces.

Pénélope. Lyric drama in three acts by Gabriel Fauré, first performed in Monte Carlo, in the principality of Monaco, on March 4, 1913. The libretto is drawn from Homer's *Odyssey,* dealing with the faithful wife of Ulysses. She kept weaving during his long sea voyages and never yielded to the importunities of her many suitors. Pénélope is represented in the score by strings, Ulysses mostly by wind instruments, and their music is mostly modal.

Penny for a Song, A. Comic opera by Richard Rodney Bennett, to a story about a British eccentric who dresses up like Napoleon to issue the counterorder canceling the imagined invasion of southern England by the French Army in 1804, precipitating a number of military alarms and absurdities, first produced in London on Oct. 31, 1967.

Perfect Fool, The. Comic opera in one act by Gustav Holst, to his own libretto, first produced in London on May 14, 1923. In it Holst ridicules, by means of stylistic allusions, both German and Italian opera.

Perfect Lives (Private Parts). Video opera by Robert Ashley, in seven acts each lasting exactly twenty-five minutes and fifty seconds, with the composer narrating his song in quasi-singing vocal inflections, televised for the first time from New York on Nov. 19, 1983.

Périchole, La. Operetta in three acts by Jacques Offenbach, one of his most popular, to a libretto by Henri Meilhac and Ludovic Halévy after Mérimée's comedy *Le carrosse de Saint-Sacrement* (1829), first performed in Paris on Oct. 6, 1868. The eponymous heroine is a Peruvian street singer in the 18th century, when the country was under Spanish rule. She loves her singing partner, but the Spanish viceroy hires her as a staff member at his court. She undergoes all kinds of temptations, but in the end returns to her lover.

Peter Grimes. Opera in prologue and three acts by Benjamin Britten, his most popular, first produced in London on June 7, 1945. The libretto by Montagu Slater is taken from George Crabbe's 19th-century poem *The Borough* (1810). The music is alternately lyric and tragic. The symphonic interludes, descriptive of the sea, and particularly one imitating the cries of the gulls, are very fine. Peter Grimes is a fisherman whose apprentice is lost at sea. Everyone suspects Grimes of murder, and he is enjoined at the inquest not to hire other apprentices. He disobeys the order and hires a new helper, who falls off a cliff to his death. A sympathetic sea captain advises the by-now demented Grimes to sail off and "sink the boat" so that he perishes at sea.

Peter Ibbetson. Opera in three acts by Deems Taylor, to a text by the composer and Constance Collier after Collier's play based on George du Maurier's novel (1892), first performed at the Metropolitan Opera, N.Y., on Feb. 7, 1931. The plot involves Peter and his childhood sweetheart Mary, who live separate lives but have vivid dreams of each other. Peter is sentenced to life imprisonment for murder, while Mary marries, is widowed, and dies. Either in dreams, or in anticipated reality, the lovers are reunited.

Photo of the Colonel, The. Opera in three acts by Humphrey Searle, to a play by the Romanian-Parisian dramatist of the theater of the absurd Eugène Ionesco about a maniacal killer who terrorizes the townspeople by inquiries about "the photo of the colonel" and then murdering them, performed for the first time in Frankfurt am Main on June 3, 1964.

Photographer, The. Opera in three acts by Philip Glass, portraying in vivid colors the extraordinary life of the pioneer motion-analyzing photographer Eadweard Muybridge, who was the first to prove that, like a galloping horse, a trotting horse had at moments all four hooves off the ground, who killed the lover of his wife but won an acquittal in a sensational trial, first performed in Amsterdam on May 30, 1982, then a new version, subtitled *Far From the Truth*, at the Brooklyn Academy of Music on Oct. 4, 1983.

Piccolo Marat, Il. Opera in three acts by Pietro Mascagni, to a text by Giovacchio Forzano, first staged in Rome on May 2, 1921. At the time of the French Revolution, a young aristocrat earns the sobriquet "the little Marat" for his revolutionary eloquence, worthy of the great Marat assassinated in his bath by Charlotte Corday. But his political extremism is only a cover for his passion for the niece of the president of the dreaded Comité de Salut Publique. He finally flees France with his beloved.

Piers Powman. Opera oratorio in two acts by Gerard Schurmann, based on the poem by William Langland, performed for the first time at the Three Choirs Festival in Gloucester Cathedral on Aug. 22, 1980.

Pietra del paragone, La (The Touchstone). Opera in two acts by Gioacchino Rossini, to a libretto by Luigi Romanelli set in an early 19th-century Tuscan village in which the wealthy Count Asdrubale tests the worthiness of three young widows for his hand in marriage, with the most faithful among them, Clarice, who tests him in return, winning out in the end, first staged in Milan at La Scala on Sept. 26, 1812.

Pilgrim's Progress, The. Morality play in prologue, four acts, and epilogue by Ralph Vaughan Williams, to a text by the composer after John Bunyan's allegory and the Bible, first performed in London on April 26, 1951. The score contains several scenes passed by the Pilgrim on his journey: the City of Destruction, Valley of Humiliation, Vanity Fair, and the Delectable Mountains.

Pimmalione. Opera in one act by Luigi Cherubini, to a libretto by Stefano Vestris after Antonio Sografi's Italian version of Rousseau's *Pygmalion* (1770), after the classical legend, first performed in Paris on Nov. 30, 1809.

Pipe of Desire, The. "Romantic grand opera" in one act by Frederick Converse, to a diffusely symbolic libretto by George Edward Burton dealing with an old man with a magical pipe ruling over a forestful of sylphs, a riverful of undines, and a swampful of salamanders, who wreaks dire punishment upon a defiant shepherd who seizes the pipe (corno di bassetto) and by playing tunes disastrously harmonized by inverted major-seventh chords and augmented triads, inadvertently causes his young bride to wither and die of malaria. The work was first staged in Boston on Jan. 31, 1906. It was also the first American opera to be produced at the Metropolitan Opera in New York, which took place on March 18, 1910, in a double bill with *Pagliacci.*

Pirata, Il (The Pirate). Opera in two acts by Vincenzo Bellini, to a libretto by Felice Romani after Raimond's drama *Berram ou Le pirate* (1826) and Maturin's *Bertram* (1816), first produced at La Scala, Milan, on Oct. 27, 1827. The heroine of the opera is deserted by her lover, who, *en passant,* murders her husband. The adulterous slayer is caught and sentenced to hang, and the poor woman goes insane. But who is the pirate?

Platée. Opera by Jean-Philippe Rameau, to a libretto by Adrien Le Valois d'Orville, recounting, in its prologue, the birth of comedy by Thespis's establishing of a form of theatrical entertainment in which the gods are mocked and whereby humans are reformed in their behavior, and in its three acts a story of Jupiter's arousing the jealousy of Junon (Juno) by feigning love for an ugly nymph, with the two reconciling happily in the end. It was first performed in Versailles on March 31, 1745.

Plough and the Stars, The. Opera in three acts by Elie Siegmeister, based on the play by Sean O'Casey depicting the agonies, joys, and humor of the dramatic days during the Irish rebellion of 1915 and 1916 against British domination, performed for the first time in St. Louis as *Dublin Song* on May 15, 1963, then revised at the 26th Festival of Contemporary Music of Louisiana State University in Baton Rouge on March 16, 1969.

Poisoned Kiss, The. Romantic extravaganza in three acts by Ralph Vaughan Williams, to a libretto by Evelyn Sharp after Richard Garnett's story "The Poison Maid" in the collection *The Twilight of the Gods* (1888), first performed in Cambridge, England, on May 12, 1936. A sorcerer's daughter thrives on a diet of assorted poisons. Not realizing that her lips are venomous, an unlucky few meet their end. She manages to detoxify her lips when she meets a man she actually loves, and a happy ending is ensured.

Poliuto. See ***Martyrs, Les.***

Pollicino, or ***The New Adventures of Tom Thumb.*** "Community opera" by Hans Werner Henze, first staged in Montepulciano, Italy, on Aug. 2, 1980.

Pomo d'oro, Il (The Golden Apple). "Festa teatrale" by Antonio Cesti, performed in Vienna on July 13–14, 1668, during Carnival, comprised of a prologue and five acts, broken into 66 "scenes." The production involved 24 set changes, and lasted eight or more hours. As one can imagine, the expense was immense. The plot is based on the mythological choice of Paris between three goddesses for their beauty. Choosing Aphrodite, he gets Helen, whom he kidnaps to Troy, whence the war described in Homer's *Iliad.* The music that has survived reveals a skillful use of monody. The work was never revived, unsurprisingly. As it is, *Il pomo d'oro* could have literally been the opera to end all operas.

Porgy and Bess. Folk opera in three acts by George Gershwin, to a libretto by Dubose Heyward after his novel *Porgy,* with lyrics by Heyward and Ira Gershwin, first performed in Boston on Sept. 30, then on Broadway on Oct. 10, 1935. The startling innovation of the opera was its selection of a subject from Negro life, with its cast of characters consisting almost exclusively of African Americans. Porgy is a cripple, and Bess is his girl. He kills her former convict lover and is arrested, but is released for lack of evidence. In the meantime, Bess is spirited away to New York by a worldly gent with an engaging nickname, Sporting Life. At the end of the opera, Porgy is still looking for Bess. Several songs from the opera have become American classics, including "Summertime," "A Woman Is a Sometime Thing," "My Man's Gone Now," "I Got Plenty o' Nuthin'," "Bess You Is My Woman Now," and "It Ain't Necessarily So." The work has entered the standard operatic repertory.

Port Town. Opera in one act by Jan Meyerowitz, to a libretto by Langston Hughes telling a symbolic tale of the platonic love of a sailor in port for a dreamy schoolgirl quickly squelched by horrified townsfolk, performed for the first time at the Berkshire Music Center at Tanglewood, Massachusetts, on Aug. 4, 1960.

Postillion de Lonjumeau, Le (The Coachman of Lonjumeau). Opera in three acts by Adolphe Adam, to a libretto by Adolphe De Leuven and Brunswick telling the tale of the postillion Chapelou, who becomes a great singer and remarries his former wife, Madeline, now rich but previously only the hostess of a village inn, first performed in Paris on Oct. 13, 1836.

Postman Always Rings Twice, The. Opera by Stephen Paulus, after the novel by James M. Cain about amoral lovers who plan a murder, first staged in St. Louis on June 17, 1982.

Powder Her Face. Chamber opera in eight scenes by Adès, to a libretto by the maverick novelist Philip Hensher based on the scandalous life of Margaret, duchess of Argyll (1912–93), the beautiful and alluring English socialite whose marriage to the duke of Argyll ended in a sensational trial in which she was charged with slander, forgery, and various adulteries, premiered at the Cheltenham Festival on July 1, 1995. (*Powder Her Face* boasts the first-ever onstage oral sex act in opera history.)

Pozzi e il Pendolo, Il. Opera by Bertinelli, after Edgar Allan Poe, performed for the first time in Bergamo on Oct. 24, 1967.

Pré aux clercs, Le. Opera in three acts by Ferdinand Hérold, to a libretto by François de Planard after Mérimée's novel *Chronique du règne de Charles IX* (1829) in which the ambassador Mergy successfully thwarts the intended marriage of his childhood sweetheart, Isabelle, to Comminge by killing his rival, in the end marrying Isabelle himself, first staged in Paris on Dec. 15, 1832.

Preussisches Märchen. Ballet opera by Boris Blacher, after a famous play, *Captain of Koepnick,* wherein a humble and frustrated government clerk successfully impersonates a captain of the guard and arrests the mayor of his hometown for corruption. The satiric work was first produced in Berlin on Sept. 23, 1952.

Prigioniero, Il (The Prisoner). Opera in prologue and one act by Luigi Dallapiccola, to a libretto by the composer after Villiers de l'Isle-Adam's *La torture par l'espérance* (1883) and Charles De Coster's *La légende d'Ulenspiegel et de Lamme Goedzak,* first heard in a concert version in a broadcast over Turin radio on Dec. 1, 1949. Its first stage performance followed in Florence on May 20, 1950. A prisoner is deliberately allowed to escape into the garden, but his freedom is a fraud perpetrated by the Grand Inquisitor, who tortures prisoners with hope, only to crush it.

Prima la musica e poi le parole (First the Music and then the Words). Opera in one act by Antonio Salieri, to a text by Giovanni Casti, commissioned by Emperor Joseph II and premiered at the Schönbrunn Palace, Vienna, on Feb. 7, 1786, on the same bill with Mozart's *Der Schauspieldirektor.* The comic plot tackles the age-old conflict between composers and librettists: Which should take precedence, music or words?

Prince Igor (Knyaz' Igor). Opera in prologue and four acts by Alexander Borodin, to a libretto by the composer after a sketch by Vladimir Stasov, produced posthumously in St. Petersburg on Nov. 4, 1890. Borodin, a professor of chemistry, failed to complete many scores, among them *Prince Igor.* This task devolved on Rimsky-Korsakov and Glazunov. The libretto is based on a Russian 12th-century chronicle recounting the story of the heroic Russian warrior prince Igor. He is about to lead his army against the Mongol invaders, the Polovtzi, when an unpredicted eclipse of the sun throws his superstitious soldiers into disarray. (*Prince Igor* is the only opera with a solar eclipse.) The celestial phenomenon is of sinister import. Igor suffers defeat and is captured.

The Polovtzian Khan treats him royally in captivity, however, and is willing to let him go free provided he promises not to go to war against him again. The Khan also offers him a choice of beautiful slave girls who stage the famous Polovtzian dances. Igor rejects all these allurements, eventually escapes, and rejoins his loving wife.

Princesse de Clèves, La. Opera in five acts by Jean Françaix, reviving in a hedonistically modernistic neoclassical idiom the age of royal France, performed for the first time in Rouen on Dec. 11, 1965.

Prinz von Homburg, Der. Opera in three acts by Hans Werner Henze, to a libretto by Ingeborg Bachmann after the play by Heinrich von Kleist (1821), premiered in Hamburg on May 22, 1960. The prince dallies with an alien princess instead of attending to his military duties. For his dereliction he is sentenced to death by the relentlessly militant king, but he is eventually reprieved and leads his army to victory, as he had done before.

Prinzessin auf der Erbse, Die. Opera by Ernst Toch, after the fable by Hans Christian Andersen about a highly sensitive princess who is able to feel a pea through twenty layers of mattresses, performed for the first time in Baden-Baden on July 17, 1927.

Prodigal Son, The. Church parable in one act by Benjamin Britten, first performed at the Orford Church, Suffolk, on June 10, 1968. The text, by William Plomer, is based on the biblical parable of a wandering son who is welcomed home by his lenient father, to the dismay of the prodigal's brother.

Professor Mamlock. Opera by Ludislav Holoubek, to a libretto inspired by the European resistance movement against the Nazi occupation written in an angst-filled dodecaphonic idiom, first performed in Bratislava on May 21, 1966, under the composer's direction.

Prometheus. Opera by Carl Orff, the third part of his trilogy of Greek tragedies, after *Prometheus Bound* by Aeschylus, set to the original ancient Greek text, in one continuous act, constituting a series of homophonic monologues, dialogues, trialogues, tetralogues, and choruses in neo-Grecian diatonic modalities, scored for large orchestra, including some 70 percussion instruments. It was first performed in Stuttgart on March 24, 1968.

Prophete, Le (The Prophet). Opera in five acts by Giacomo Meyerbeer, to a libretto by Eugéne Scribe, first performed in Paris on April 16, 1849. The prophet here is based on the historical John of Leyden, leader of the Anabaptist sect in the 16th century. In order to maintain his self-proclaimed divine status, he denies his identity and repudiates his mother. When his beloved Bertha realizes what he has become, she stabs herself to death. The army of the Holy Roman Emperor advances on Leyden. They set John's palace afire, and he perishes in the cataclysm, along with his forgiving mother.

Protagonist, Der. Opera in one act by Kurt Weill, premiered in Dresden on March 27, 1926. In a play within a play set in Elizabethan England, the leading actor kills the leading actress out of jealousy, while the spectators admire the realism of their acting.

Prozess, Der (The Trial). Opera by Gottfried von Einem, to a libretto drawn by Boris Blacher from the morbid novel by Kafka, first performed in Salzburg on Aug. 17, 1953. The opera comments on the fate of the victim of a monstrous bureaucracy tried on unnamed charges. A recurrent rhythmic pulse serves as a sinister leitmotif.

Punainen viiva (The Red Line). Opera by Aulis Sallinen, to his own libretto based on a Finnish novel by Ilmari Kianto (1874–1970) dealing with an unexpected victory of women's suffrage in Finland in 1907 (the red line of the title was the mark of support on the new social order to be put on the ballot), performed for the first time in Helsinki on Nov. 30, 1978.

Puntila. Opera in 12 scenes with prologue and epilogue by Paul Dessau, after a play by Bertolt Brecht dealing with four resolute women who expose the wickedness of an alcoholic landlord, written in a burlesque manner, first produced in East Berlin on Nov. 15, 1966.

Purgatory. Opera in one act by Gordon Crosse, to a libretto after William Butler Yeats dealing with posthumous retribution wherein a remorseful old man kills his son to end his family's crime-ridden history (he killed his father to avenge his brutal treatment of his mother, who died during his childbirth) and to secure the entrance to purgatory for all of them, first produced at the Cheltenham Festival on July 7, 1966.

Purgatory. Opera in one act by Hugo Weisgall, to a libretto from the Yeats play at work in Crosse's opera of the same name (see above), performed for the first time in concert form at the Library of Congress in Washington, D.C., on Feb. 17, 1961.

Puritani, I. Opera in three acts by Vincenzo Bellini, first performed (as *I Puritani e i Cavalieri*) in Paris on Jan. 24, 1835, a few months before Bellini's untimely death. The libretto by Carlo Pepoli is derived, after several translations and retranslations from French and Italian, from Sir Walter Scott's novel *Old Mortality* (1816). The Puritans are the Roundheads, fanatical followers of Oliver Cromwell. The action takes place in 1649 after the execution of the Stuart king Charles I of England. A noble cavalier, faithful to the king's cause, is engaged to Elvira, the daughter of a Puritan, but fails to appear at the altar in order to get the widowed queen out of Cromwell's murderous clutches. His bride is bewildered by his unexplained defection and goes insane. Her mad scene rivals in effectiveness that of Donizetti's *Lucia di Lammermoor*, which is also derived from Scott, a showcase for the soprano. Having saved the queen, the faithful bridegroom returns to his beloved, causing her to regain her mental faculties. Cromwell's soldiers surprise them and carry the hapless youth to the execution block. Once more his bride-to-be lapses into madness. A trumpet fanfare announces a new victory for Cromwell and his magnanimous decision to grant amnesty to his foes. Once more the situation is saved. The bride regains her senses, and a happy chorus congratulates them.

Purloined Happiness. Opera in three acts by Yuli Meitus, wherein a rural damsel, believing her bridegroom to be dead, marries another and finds herself in a painful dilemma when her first husband returns to claim his purloined happiness, first produced in Lvov on Sept. 10, 1960.

Q

Quatro rusteghi, I (The Four Curmudgeons). Opera in three acts by Ermanno Wolf-Ferrari, to a libretto by Luigi Sugana and Pizzolato after Goldoni, first performed in Munich (in German as *Die vier Grobiane*) on March 19, 1906. Four gross and arrogant married men try to rule their households like feudal lords. They are outwitted by their wives and daughters, however, who arrange the marriage of the daughter of one of the most intransigent of them against his will.

Queen of Spades, The (Pikovaya dama). Opera in three acts by Pyotr Il'yich Tchaikovsky, to a libretto by his brother Modest Tchaikovsky, after Pushkin's tale (1834), first produced in St. Petersburg on Dec. 19, 1890. A Russian army officer tries to elicit the secret of three winning cards from an old woman who had received them from the magician Cagliostro. His strange demand frightens the old woman and she dies, but her ghost appears to him in a lifelike hallucination and gives him the 3 winning cards: 3, 7, and ace. He gambles on these cards, and wins on the first two. But instead of picking up the winning ace, he draws the queen of spades for the last card and loses all. The card face of the queen grimaces at him and he recognizes the old woman in it. He goes out and kills himself. The score is in constant repertory in Russia and elsewhere.

Quiet Place, A. Opera in one act by Leonard Bernstein, to a libretto by Stephen Wadsworth, first staged in Houston on June 17, 1983. A flashback within the work yields a performance of Bernstein's earlier one-act opera *Trouble in Tahiti*. The stories of both concern alienation within a family.

R

Rain. Chamber opera by Boris Arapov, based on Somerset Maugham's short story, first staged in Leningrad on April 25, 1967.

Rake's Progress, The. Opera in three acts and epilogue by Igor Stravinsky, first performed in Venice on Sept. 11, 1951. The libretto, in English, was written by W. H. Auden and Chester Kallman, its title taken from a series of eight satirical engravings by the 18th-century artist Hogarth. The story is a parable, and Tom Rakewell is led into a series of adventures. He marries a bearded circus lady and invests a fortune in a device that grinds stones into flour and makes bread. He gambles for his soul with the devil, and though the devil loses, the rake loses his mind, and his beloved Anne Trulove. The moral pronounced in the epilogue is very much in the manner of 18th-century fabulists: "For idle hearts and hands and minds, the devil finds work to do."

Rape of Lucretia, The. Chamber opera in two acts by Benjamin Britten, to a libretto by Ronald Duncan based on André Obey's play *Le viol de Lucrèce* (1931), first performed at the Glyndebourne Festival on July 12, 1946. Based on an ancient legend, the opera glorifies the "Christian" virtue of Lucretia, who, awaiting her husband's return from war, is confronted by Tarquinius, the Roman commander. Imperiously he demands that she submit to him. When she refuses, he rapes her. Later, when her husband returns, she recounts her tragedy and shame to him before sinking a dagger into her breast.

Rappresentazione di Anima e di Corpo, La (Drama of the Soul and Body). Rappresentazione sacra by Emilio de'Cavalieri (1600). This monodic work represents the first theatrical application of the seconda prattica to religious themes. The title reflects the content, a dramatic parable of the soul and body, in which metaphysical and abstract entities such as Virtue and Valor take part, much like a medieval mystery play.

Regina. Opera in three acts by Marc Blitzstein, to his own libretto based on Lillian Hellman's play *The Little Foxes*, first performed in Boston on Oct. 11, 1949, then on Broadway on Oct. 31. The play recounts the mutual deceptions and self-destructive hatreds among members of a family in the south at the turn of the century.

Rehearsal Call. Opera buffa in three acts by Vittorio Giannini, retailing the vicissitudes of three boys and three girls trying to find menial operatic jobs in New York, with bits from Wagner and atonal arias illustrating their aspirations, performed for the first time at the Juilliard School of Music in New York on Feb. 15, 1962.

Reine de Saba, La (The Queen of Sheba). Opera in four acts by Charles Gounod, to a text by Jules Barbier and Michel Carré after Gérard de Nerval's "Les nuits de Ramazon" (in his *Le voyage en Orient*, 1851), itself based on the Arab legend, first produced in Paris on Feb. 28, 1862. The queen of Sheba falls in love with a wandering minstrel and decides to leave King Solomon and follow her lover. But as she rejoins him, he is slain by one of his own followers. The score is not a major work of Gounod's.

Reine morte, La. Lyric drama by Renzo Rossellini, to a libretto after Henri de Montherland dealing with political and emotional upheavals at a Renaissance court, first staged in Monte Carlo on July 7, 1973.

Resan (The Journey). Opera by Lars Werle, his second, representing a dichotomy of reality and fantasy showing the psychological experiences of a man and a woman, first performed in Hamburg on March 2, 1969.

Renard. Musical fable in two parts by Igor Stravinsky, to a libretto by the composer after Russian folktales, translated into French by C. F. Ramuz, first staged in Paris on

May 18, 1922. Subtitled "a fable about a fox, a rooster, a cat, and a ram, a merry spectacle with singing and music after popular Russian fairy-tales," it tells of a fox outfoxed by other, less sophisticated animals.

Rencontre imprévue, La (The Unexpexted Meeting). Opéra comique by Christopher Willibald Gluck, to a French libretto, his most popular production in the genre, first staged in Vienna on Jan. 7, 1764. It was also performed under the title *Les Pèlerins de la Mecque.*

Re pastore, Il (The Shepherd King). Opera in two acts by Wolfgang Amadeus Mozart, 1775, to a text by Metastasio for Bonno (1751) revised by Varesco, premiered in Salzburg at the Archbishop's Palace on April 23, 1775. The setting follows the conventional pastoral drama in which true love is tested by obstacles. Not a major work of Mozart's, but it has some fine set numbers.

Retablo de Maese Pedro, El (Master Peter's Puppet Show). Puppet opera in one act by Manuel de Falla, to a libretto by the composer after Cervantes's *Don Quixote* (1615), first performed in Paris at the home of Princess Edmond de Polignac on June 25, 1923. The Knight of the Woeful Countenance watches a puppet show in which a young damsel keeps being throttled by disasters. Finally Quixote can no longer bear it and he demolishes the puppet theater.

Revisor, Der. Comic opera in five acts by Werner Egk, to his own libretto after Gogol's comedy *The Inspector General* (1836), first performed in Schwetzingen on May 9, 1957. The story describes the confusion created in a small Russian town by the arrival of a supposed secret investigator sent by the czar. When the deception is exposed, a real investigator makes his appearance, plunging the various functionaries into even greater consternation.

Rheingold, Das. Music drama in prologue and one act by Richard Wagner, designated as the *Vorabend* (fore-evening) to the great tetralogy *Der Ring des Nibelungen*, to his own loftily poetical text strewn with evocative Germanic neologisms, first performed in Munich on Sept. 22, 1869.

The maidens of the river Rhine guard a horde of gold, which in this case is not just a precious yellow metal, but a magical substance. Whoever forges a ring out of the Rhine gold will be master of the world. The Nordic gods who mill around their castle in their abode of Valhalla are no less quarrelsome than the gods of Mt. Olympus, and are beset as much as the Greeks by trouble with disobedient underlings. The dwarf Alberich of the Nibelung clan renounces his love in order to obtain the gold, and from it he forges the baneful ring of the Nibelung. Wotan, the Nordic Jupiter, succeeds in abstracting the ring from the incautious Alberich, who then pronounces a curse upon it. But Wotan has to contend with an annoying couple of giants, Fasolt and Fafner, who demand payment for their work in building Valhalla. Although Wotan offers them the goddess of youth, Freia, in partial payment, they demand the gold as well. Having obtained it, the giants quarrel among themselves and the more vicious of them, Fafner, slays the other.

Realizing that Valhalla must be protected against foes, Wotan procreates nine Valkyries, the stallion-riding warrior maidens generously endowed with brass-plated bosoms. Their main task is to take the bodies of slain heroes to Valhalla where they could be restored to life and protect the stronghold. Wotan also begets human children, Siegmund and Sieglinde, who in time will beget Siegfried. Wotan's hope is that Siegfried, the ideal of a Nordic hero, will track down the giant Fafner, recapture the ring, and return it to the Rhine maidens. A whole encyclopedia of leitmotives is unfolded in *Das Rheingold* and stored away for future use in the remaining tetralogy. Not only the gods, giants, and dwarfs are characterized by these leitmotives, but also objects or ideas involved in the action: the ring itself, the curse imposed upon it, the magic helmet that can transform a person into any human or animal shape, and the sword Nothung, the Nordic equivalent of King Arthur's Excalibur.

Richard Cœur-de-Lion (Richard the Lionheart). Opera in three acts by André-Ernest-Modeste Grétry, to a libretto by Michele-Jean Sedaine after a 13th-century fable, first performed in Paris on Oct. 21, 1784. Richard I of England led the 3d Crusade into the Holy Land. While returning he was captured and held for several years in Austria. The opera focuses on the exploits of the king's jester, who successfully plots his deliverance.

Riders to the Sea. Opera in one act by Ralph Vaughan Williams, based on the 1904 play by J. M. Synge, first performed in London on Dec. 1, 1937. The drama is a lament on the fate of an Irishwoman who has lost all her sons at sea.

Rienzi. Opera in five acts by Richard Wagner, to his own libretto after Mary Russell Mitford's drama (1828) and Bulwer Lytton's novel (1835), first produced in Dresden on Oct. 20, 1842. The original title was *Rienzi, der letzte der Tribunen* (Rienzi, the Last of the Tribunes). Rienzi is a member of a powerful Roman family in the 14th century. He is trying to restore Roman self-government but is caught up in the framework of the internecine struggle between his and other leading families. In the opera, as in the novel and actual history, Rienzi, his sister, and a handful of his adherents perish in a fire at the capitol. This is one of Wagner's early Italianate operas.

Rigoletto. Opera in three acts by Giuseppe Verdi, to a libretto by Francesco Piave based on Victor Hugo's play *Le roi s'amuse* (1832), first performed in Venice on March 11, 1851. The original title was *La maledizione.* Rigoletto, a hunchbacked court jester, mocks an aggrieved father whose daughter was seduced by the libidinous Duke of Mantua, and is cursed by the victim of his insensitive raillery. The curse is prophetic, for his own daughter, Gilda, is debauched in turn by the despicable rake. Incensed, Rigoletto hires an assassin with the task of killing the duke and delivering his body in a sack at the door of a tavern. But when he arrives there at midnight he hears the ineffable duke repeat his immortal and immoral misogynist aria "La Donna è mobile." Horrified, he opens the sack and finds his dying daughter, who had been stabbed when she disguised herself and voluntarily took the knife intended for the duke, whom she still loves. "Maledizione!" Rigoletto cries out, recalling the curse. The opera is regarded as the first of Verdi's mature works, and is a perennial favorite, the duke's aria sung by tenors everywhere. There is also a magnificent vocal quartet.

Riket är ditt (Thine Is the Kingdom). Comic chamber opera by Jonas Forssell, after the stage play by Kim Procopé about a Chilean refugee family hidden from Swedish police by nuns in a convent, in three acts and twelve scenes each dedicated to one of the apostles, a mélange of tragedy and farce and the sacred and the profane, first staged in Vadstena, Sweden, on July 7, 1991.

Rinaldo. Opera in three acts by George Frideric Handel, to a libretto by Giacomo Rossi, based on an incident in Tasso's epic poem *Gerusalemme liberata,* premiered at the Queen's Theatre in London on Feb. 24, 1711. Rinaldo is a Crusader engaged to Almira, daughter of the leader of the Crusaders, who are besieging Islamic Jerusalem. The enchantress Armida is determined to seduce Rinaldo and kill Almira. With the aid of a benign magus, the crusaders destroy Armida's magic garden, so that Rinaldo can now marry Almira without obstacles placed by evil forces. After major revisions the work was performed at the King's Theatre in London on April 6, 1731.

Ring des Nibelungen, Der (The Ring of the Nibelung). Operatic tetralogy by Richard Wagner, described by him as "a stage festival play for three days and a preliminary evening." The entire cycle was produced for the first time at the first Bayreuth Festspiele over four evenings, Aug. 13–17, 1876. The individual titles are *Das Rheingold, Die Walküre, Siegfried,* and *Gotterdämmerung* (see separate entries). The cycle is musically united by a whole encyclopedia of leitmotives identifying personages involved, objects, and ideas. Wagnerian statisticians have counted as many as 90 such leading motives, and special manuals have been published to guide the listener through the Wagnerian jungle.

Ring des Polykrates, Der. Opera in one act by Eric Wolfgang Korngold, to a libretto inspired by Schiller's ballad about the tyrant of Samos whose ill-starred ring that he throws into the ocean returns to him inside a fish he caught, with the action transferred to Saxony in 1797 and centered on a married kapellmeister, his drummer, and an attractive maidservant embroiled in an imbroglio of triangular emotions. The work was first staged in Munich on March 28, 1916, coupled with another one-act opera by Korngold, *Violanta.*

Ritorno d'Ulisse in patria, Il (The Return of Ulysses to His Homeland). Opera in prologue and five acts by Claudio Monteverdi, to a libretto by Giacomo Badoaro, first performed in Venice in Feb. 1640. The libretto traces the return after ten years of Ulysses (Odysseus) from the Trojan War.

Robert le diable (Robert the Devil). Opera in five acts by Giacomo Meyerbeer, tremendously successful in the 19th century, to a libretto by Eugène Scribe and Germain Delavigne, premiered in Paris on Nov. 21, 1831. Robert, a medieval duke in Palermo, is actually half devil, half human. When he falls in love with a young Sicilian woman, his father, the devil-in-chief, keeps him from winning a crucial tournament, the prize of which is her hand. But he is aided by his virtuous half sister (who is all human), and wins his bride after all.

Roberto Devereux, ossia Il conte d'Essex (Robert Devereux, or the Earl of Essex). Opera in three acts by Gaetano Donizetti, to a text by Salvadore Cammarano after François Ancelot's tragedy *Elisabeth d'Angleterre,* first produced in Naples on Oct. 28, 1837. The melodramatic plot concerns the fateful infatuation of Queen Elizabeth I of England with Robert Devereux, the married second earl of Essex, who, after many brilliant victories over Spain, is accused of treason and executed. The role of Queen Elizabeth has been a notable success for sopranos Beverly Sills and Montserrat Caballé.

Robin Hood. Operetta by Reginald De Koven, his best known work, premiered in Chicago on June 9, 1890. Its libretto is based on the exploits of the legendary English highwayman who robbed the rich to enrich the poor. It was produced in London on Jan. 5, 1891, as *Maid Marian.* Its most famous song, "O Promise Me!," was inserted into the score shortly after the London premiere.

Rodelinda, regina de'Longobardi (Rodelinda, Queen of the Lombards). Opera by George Frideric Handel, one of his finest, first produced at the King's Theatre in London on Feb. 13, 1725, based on an apparently historical incident. Rodelinda is the dethroned queen of the Lombards, coveted by the usurper king who threatens to murder her child if she does not yield to his desires. But the lawful ruler returns and Rodelinda's virtue and bravery are rewarded. The quasi-historic libretto has elements of a rescue opera.

Roi, Arthus, Le. Opera by Ernest Chausson, his only completed one, to his own libretto based on the life of the legendary King Arthur, first posthumously produced in Brussels on Nov. 30, 1903.

Roi Carotte, Le. Comic opera by Jacques Offenbach, based on the play by Victorien Sardou, first staged in Paris on Jan. 15, 1872. This is a satire of the recently defunct Second Empire of Napoléon III. Prince Fridolin XXIV of Krokodyne is overthrown by the revolutionary vegetable Carotte. Monkeys, bees, and ants attack Fridolin, but the lovely Rosée-du-Soir rescues him, while the usurper Carotte is eaten by a monkey.

Roi David, Le (King David). Biblical music drama by René Morax with incidental music by Arthur Honegger, first performed in Mézières, near Lausanne, on June 11, 1921, and later revised as a symphonic psalm and oratorio, presented for the first time as an opera at the Paris

Opéra, arranged in 31 scenes interspersed by choral numbers and supplied with additional dialogue.

Roi de Lahore, Le (The King of Lahore). Opera in five acts by Jules Massenet, first performed in Paris on April 27, 1877, to a libretto by Louis Gallet drawn from the Indian epic *Mahabharata.* The king of Lahore is murdered by an official coveting his favorite wife, but the king returns to earth reincarnated as a beggar. His beloved recognizes him under his rags and kills herself in the hope of joining him in the world beyond.

Roi d'Ys, Le (The King of Ys). Opera in three acts by Edouard Lalo, to a libretto by Edouard Blau, premiered in Paris on May 7, 1888. Two daughters of the King of Ys (a town in Brittany) are in love with the same handsome youth. The one who loses out in the contest opens the floodgates and lets the sea inundate the town. Horrified by her deed, she kills herself.

Roi l'a dit, Le (The King Said It). Comic opera by Léo Delibes, first performed in Paris on May 24, 1873. A marquis of the court of Louis XVI boasts falsely of the valor of his male heir, when in fact he has only daughters. When the king commands him to bring his son to the palace, the marquis brings in a peasant boy whom he dresses up to play the role of his son. But the benighted rustic makes one *faux pas* after another, and the marquis marries him off to a conveniently available young damsel. The opera falls below the excellence of Delibes's ballet scores.

Roi malgré lui, Le (The King in Spite of Himself). Opera in three acts by Emmanuel Chabrier, to a libretto by Emile De Najac, and Paul Burani, premiered in Paris on May 18, 1887. The labyrinthine 16th-century plot involves a conspiracy against Henri de Valois, a reluctant candidate for the throne of France. To find out what the plotters have against him, he joins the conspiracy in disguise. In the end the plotters are foiled and willy-nilly Henri becomes King Henri II.

Roland. Tragic opera by Jean-Baptiste Lully, premiered in Versailles on Jan. 8, 1685. The libretto by Philippe Quinault is drawn from the well-known Italian epic *Orlando furioso* by Ariosto, suggested by King Louis XIV himself. The central episode concerns the passion of Roland, knight of Charlemagne, for a young woman who rejects his love. He finds consolation in his victorious battles. This story is the subject of many other operas, including Haydn's *Orlando paladino* (1782) and Handel's *Orlando* (1733).

Roméo et Juliette. Opera by Charles Gounod, after Shakespeare, premiered in Paris on April 27, 1867. Like other works by this composer, the music possesses a peculiar quality of sweetness that delights Gounod's admirers and repels his detractors. It was tremendously successful from the outset and almost equaled his *Faust* in popularity.

Rondine, La (The Swallow). Opera in three acts by Giacomo Puccini, to a text by Giuseppe Adami translated from a German libretto by A. M. Willner and Heinz Reichert, premiered in Monte Carlo on March 27, 1917. A loving and lovable young woman of the Second Empire becomes the mistress of a banker, but she finds time to dally with a youthful admirer. Eventually, like a swallow, she returns to her older, safer, and more reliable protector. The music's quality, though harmonically bold, falls far below the dramatic excellence of Puccini's other operas.

Rosa. "Horse drama" in two acts (12 scenes) by Louis Andriessen, to a libretto by Peter Greenaway set in the 1950s and concerning a fictitious Brazilian pianist who lives in a former slaughterhouse, is devoted to his favorite horse, and writes only music for Wild West films. It was first mounted in Amsterdam on Nov. 2, 1994.

Rosamunde Floris. Opera in three acts by Boris Blacher, to a libretto wherein a promiscuous damsel premaritally impregnated by an unscrupulous gallant and abandoned by him, marries an aspiring librarian, after the latter defenestrates his previous fiancée, first mounted at the Berlin Music Festival on Sept. 21, 1960.

Rose-Marie. Operetta by Rudolf Friml, extremely popular, first performed on Broadway on Sept. 2, 1924. The story concerns Rose-Marie La Flamme, a young French-Canadian woman who is adored by a multitude of competing males. But her true love is a Royal Canadian Mountie falsely accused of murder. He is cleared, and Rose-Marie's faith in him is vindicated. Includes the famous duet "Indian Love Call."

Rosenkavalier, Der (The Knight of the Rose). Opera in three acts by Richard Strauss, to a libretto by his most imaginative collaborator, Hugo von Hofmannsthal, first produced in Dresden on Jan. 26, 1911. The intricacy of the plot, with its manifold entanglements, amatory crosscurrents, transvestism, and contrived mistaken identities, is in the most extravagant manner of 18th-century farce. The action takes place in Vienna in Mozart's time. The personages embroiled in the comedy are the Feldmarschallin (the wife of the fieldmarshal), a young count (Octavian) whom she takes as a sporadic lover, an aging baron (Ochs), and an innocent young woman (Sophie) whom the ineffable baron proposes to marry.

According to the quaint custom of the time, the prospective bridegroom must send to his betrothed a young messenger carrying a rose, and the Feldmarschallin selects her young lover for this role. Naturally, the Rose Cavalier and the young lady fall in love. The scene becomes further confused when the Feldmarschallin orders the young cavalier to put on a servant girl's dress to conceal his presence in her bedroom. Dressed as a girl, he attracts the attention of the foraging baron, and to save the situation, agrees to a tryst with him. As if this were not enough, the part of the Rosenkavalier is entrusted to a mezzo-soprano, so that when he/she changes his/her dress, the actress singing the role actually engages in double transvestitude (as does the actress playing Cherubino in Mozart's *The Marriage of Figaro*). The finale unravels the knotted strands of the plot. The music is almost Mozartean in its melodious involvement, with Viennese waltzes enlivening the score, and a sublime trio for three principal female singers.

Rossignol de Boboli, Le (The Nightingale of Boboli). Opera in one act by Alexandre Tansman, to a libretto in which a nightingale, accidentally mutated into a human, is restored to his original avian identity thanks to the efforts of a devoted love bird, first staged in Nice on July 22, 1965.

Royal Hunt of the Sun, The. Opera by Iain Hamilton, to his own libretto arranged from Peter Shaffer's play dealing with the fall of the Inca empire and the death of the Inca sun king Atahualpa, first produced in London on Feb. 2, 1977.

Rusalka (The Nixie). Opera in four acts by Alexander Dargomïzhsky, to a text by the composer based on Pushkin's dramatic poem (1832), first performed in St. Petersburg on May 16, 1856. A miller's daughter is seduced and impregnated by a local prince who marries a lady of his own station. The wronged girl throws herself into the river Dnieper, thus becoming a Rusalka (nixie, a female water sprite). In her submarine existence, she continues to exercise profound emotional influence on the prince, who often comes to the riverbank to evoke memories of his tragic love. The Rusalka sends her daughter, who was born in the Dnieper, to the prince, asking him to visit her mother, who is now queen of the waters. The prince follows his daughter and rejoins her in the river. The opera is important for its use of natural inflections of Russian speech. It is a classic in Russia, but almost never receives performances elsewhere.

Rusalka (The Nixie). Opera in three acts by Antonín Dvořák, to a libretto by Jaroslav Kvapil based on Fouqué's *Undine*, with materials from Hans Christian Andersen's *The Little Mermaid*, first performed in Prague on March 31, 1901. A nixie (water sprite) leaves her watery realm and falls in love with a normal prince. But because of the disparity of their ranks, marriage is impossible. She returns to her lake, but the prince realizes he really loves her. He follows her to the watery deep and expires in her arms. The opera is very popular in Czech lands, and is probably the most performed Dvořák opera in the non-Slavic world, especially notable for the aria "Song to the Moon."

Ruslan and Ludmila (Ruslan i Lyudmila). Opera in five acts by Mikhail Glinka, first produced in St. Petersburg on Dec. 9, 1842. The libretto by Valerian Shirkov and others follows Pushkin's fairy tale of the same name (1820). Ludmila, daughter of the grand duke of Kiev, is betrothed to the valiant Russian knight Ruslan, but during the wedding feast she mysteriously vanishes as the scene is darkened and lightning and thunder rend the skies. The grand duke promises her hand to anyone who will find her. Two suitors, besides Ruslan, take part in the hunt, but Ruslan is helped by a benign magician. He discovers that Ludmila was abducted by the sinister magus Chernomor (the name means Black Mortifier), whose might resides in his long beard; this presents an obvious clue to the resolution of the problem. Ruslan is confronted with horrendous obstacles, most spectacularly a huge severed head guarding Chernomor (the part of the head is sung by a vocal quartet), but of course he regains his beloved in the end.

S

Sabbataï Zévi, le faux Messie. Opera in four acts with prologue by Alexandre Tansman, to a libretto dealing with a 17th-century Jewish cabalist who inflames his Zionist followers with faith in him as a Messiah destined to assume the throne of Zion in the fatidic year 1666, but is arrested by the sultan as he tries to enter the Holy Land, then part of the Ottoman empire, and embraces the Islamic faith to save himself. It was first mounted in Paris on March 3, 1961.

Sadko. Opera legend in seven scenes by Nikolai Rimsky-Korsakov, first produced in Moscow on Jan. 7, 1898. The libretto, by the composer and Vladimir Belsky, is based on an ancient Russian epic. Sadko is a popular minstrel in Novgorod, the first capital of Russia. He has mercantile dreams of selling wares abroad, dreams that are fanatically realized when a flock of swans on Lake Ilmen, in reality the feathered daughters of the King of the Ocean, take him to their abode on the bottom of the lake. He catches magic goldfish that turn out to be made of real gold, and he returns to Novgorod a rich man. *Sadko* is a paradigm of the Russian fairy-tale opera, its "Song of India," sung by a Hindu merchant visiting Novgorod, a perennial concert favorite.

Saffo (Sappho). Opera by Giovanni Pacini, his dramatic masterpiece, purportedly composed in 28 days, first staged in Naples on Nov. 29, 1840.

Saint François d'Assise (St. Francis of Assisi). Opera in eight scenes by Olivier Messiaen, produced at the Paris Opéra on Nov. 28, 1983. Messiaen's only opera, to his own libretto, is based on the mystical life of St. Francis, whose devotion was not limited to humans alone but embraced the adoration of birds and other of God's creatures. Messiaen himself was a religious birdman who collected songs of the flying species and fused them with melodic twits, twirls, and trills of his own.

Saint Louis, Roi de France. Opera oratorio in two parts by Darius Milhaud, to the poem by Paul Claudel, dramatically evolving as an operatic panorama of eleven scenes tracing the regal course of the canonized French king, first performed in Rio de Janeiro on April 14, 1972.

Saint of Bleecker Street, The. Music drama in three acts by Gian Carlo Menotti, to his own libretto, first produced on Broadway on Dec. 27, 1954. The action takes place on Bleecker Street in an Italian section of N.Y.'s Greenwich Village. An Italian girl believes she has the sacred stigmata, but her agnostic brother derides her. He himself is ridiculed by his girlfriend for his devotion to his sister, and in an argument accidentally kills her. He flees, returning to Bleecker Street as his sister enters the convent. But now she becomes overwrought emotionally and dies as she pledges her vow.

Salambo. Opera by Josef Hauer, composed in 1929 after Flaubert's novel, first posthumously performed over Austrian Radio in Vienna on March 19, 1983.

Salammbô. Unfinished opera by Modest Mussorgsky, composed 1863–66, after Flaubert's novel (1862), orchestrated by Zeltán Peskó and premiered over RAI, Milan, 1980. The plot resembles that of Vincenzo Bellini's *Norma.* Here it is Mathô, the Libyan, falling for Salammbô, priestess of the goddess Tanit. The locale is Carthage, and the result is death for both. Mussorgky wrote about half the opera, although crucial events (e.g., the love and scenes) were never set. When asked why he didn't finish a work that was going well, Mussorgsky burst out laughing, and then, becoming serious, said, "We have already had enough of the Orient with [Alexander] Serov's *Judith.* Art is not a pastime; time is precious."

Salammbô. Opera in five acts by Ernest Reyer, to a libretto by Camille Du Locle after Flaubert's novel (1862) in which Matho, condemned to die after stealing the sacred veil from the shrine of the Carthaginian goddess Tanit, takes his own life after the priestess Salammbô kills herself in his place, first produced in Brussels on Feb. 10, 1890.

Salome. Opera in one act by Richard Strauss, to a libretto based on Hedwig Lachmann's German translation of Oscar Wilde's tragedy (1893), first performed in Dresden on Dec. 9, 1905. The story, obliquely connected with the biblical narrative, is centered on Salome, stepdaughter of Herod, tetrach of Judea. John the Baptist, imprisoned by Herod, is brought to the palace at Salome's request. She is fascinated by him, even though he curses her, and brazenly cries, "I want to kiss your mouth!" Herod, who lusts after Salome, asks her to dance for him. She agrees on condition that he will fulfill her unspoken wish, and performs the provocative "Dance of the Seven Veils." The reward she demands is the severed head of John the Baptist. Herod tries to dissuade her from her monstrous intention, but yields in the end. When the head is brought out on a platter, Salome mocks it: "You wouldn't let me kiss your mouth!" she cries, and kisses it passionately on the lips. Provoked beyond endurance by this act of depravity, Herod commands the guards to kill her.

The score is a masterpiece of stark realism, set to music of overwhelming power, ranging from exotic melodiousness to crashing dissonance. The opera aroused unusually vehement opposition when it was staged at the Metropolitan Opera in New York (1907). The moralistic uproar in the public and press was such that the management was compelled to cancel further performances. It took two decades for the American public to mature sufficiently to absorb it. Strauss also wrote a French version (*Salomé*).

Samson et Dalila. Opera in three acts by Camille Saint-Saëns, to a libretto by Ferdinand Lemaire after Judges 14–16, first performed in Weimar (in German) on Dec. 2, 1877. It tells the biblical story of Delilah, the priestess of the Philistine temple, who entices the Hebrew warrior Samson, and during his sleep cuts his hair, the source of his physical power. He is then blinded, chained, and taken to the Philistine temple in Gaza. There, summoning his remaining strength, he breaks the pillars supporting the roof, bringing the temple down on himself and the miscreant worshipers. On account of the restrictions with respect to theatrical representation of biblical characters, the opera was not performed on the stage in France until 1892, and not in England until 1909.

Sapho (Sappho). Opera by Charles Gounod, his first, premiered in Paris on April 16, 1851. The libretto describes in melodramatic terms the life of the Greek poetess who flourished on the island of Lesbos.

Sapho. Opera in five acts by Jules Massenet, based on a story by Alphonse Daudet, first produced in Paris on Nov. 27, 1897. The heroine poses as an artist's model in this role. A young man from the country falls in love with her, but their differences are such that they eventually go their separate ways. The score is not one of Massenet's best.

Šárka. Opera by Zdeněk Fibich, premiered in Prague on Dec. 28, 1897. After the death of the legendary queen of Bohemia, Libuše, the power passes to her husband, much to the chagrin of the women warriors of the land. When the king refuses to restore their civil rights, they declare war on all men. Šárka challenges a masculine knight to a duel, but he scornfully rejects her proposal. She then resorts to a ruse. Her companions tie her to a tree, and when he enters the forest, he finds her and hears her false story about the maltreatment she has suffered at their hands. Fascinated by her muscular charms, he releases her. But now she herself is fascinated by him and warns him that her companions lie in ambush. Boldly he defies the women but is captured. Desperate to save him from imminent execution, Šárka goes to the king for help. His soldiers arrive, kill most of the women, and liberate Šárka's beloved. He wants to take her to his castle, but she is tormented by her treason and hurls herself from a cliff. This was Fibich's penultimate opera, his most popular in Czechoslovakia, and he would soon turn to composing melodramas.

Šárka. Opera in three acts by Leoš Janáček, to a libretto by Julius Zeyer after his own drama (1887), first performed in its final version in Brno on Nov. 11, 1925. Libuše has died, and her husband, Přemysl, decides to dissolve her council of women. Šárka leads their revolt, falling in love with the warrior hero Ctirad along the way. She nevertheless brings about his death, throwing herself onto his funeral pyre.

Satyagraha. Opera in three acts by Philip Glass, dedicated to the political theory of *Satye* and *agraha* (truth and resolution in the original Sanskrit) and adapted from the Indian epic *Bhagavad Gita*, the libretto dealing with the life of Mahatma Gandhi in South Africa before his ascent to glory as a prophet of nonviolence, in six ritualistic tableaux with timeless, motionless, largely changeless music (at one point Gandhi walks at night singing a scale E to E thirty times, and at another a progression of second inversions of a triad is repeated 143 times). It was first produced in Rotterdam on Sept. 5, 1980.

Satyri'kon. Opera by Bruno Maderna, after Petronius, first staged in Scheveningen, Holland, on March 16, 1973.

Saul og David (Saul and David). Opera in four acts by Carl Nielsen, his first, to a libretto by Elinar Christiansen, first staged in Copenhagen on Nov. 28, 1902. The work is conceived in a grandly oratorical manner and articulated into a series of symphonically designed dramatic tableaux in which the biblical characters assume a veristic psychological coloration.

Sāvitri. Chamber opera in one act by Gustav Holst, to a libretto by the composer drawn from the Hindu epic *Mahabharata,* first performed in London on Dec. 5, 1916. Death calls on the eponymous heroine's husband, but she succeeds in staving off the fateful visitor by ingratiating wiles.

Scala di seta, La (The Silken Ladder). Opera in one act by Gioacchino Rossini, to a libretto by Giuseppe Foppa after the play *L'échelle de soie* by François-Antoine-Eugène de Palnard and perhaps a libretto from it made for Gaveaux (1808), first produced in Venice on May 9, 1812. A youthful couple is united in a *matrimonio segreto,* and the bridegroom is compelled to use a ladder every time he goes to her room upstairs in her father's house.

Schauspieldirektor, Der (The Impressario). "Comedy with music" in one act by Wolfgang Amadeus Mozart, to a text by Gottlieb Stephanie the younger, commissioned by Emperor Joseph II and first performed at the Imperial Palace at Schönnbrunn, Vienna, on Feb. 7, 1786, along with another commissioned opera, *Prima la Musica e poi le parole,* by Antonio Salieri. Mozart's opera concerns an impresario who has to deal with two rival prima donnas contending for the same role, one of whom is a mistress of the banker who finances the season. The libretto has been variously revised, and several versions are in circulation.

Schwanda the Bagpiper (Švanda dudák). Opera in two acts by Jaromín Weinberger, to a libretto by Miloš Kareš and Max Brod after the folktale by Tyl, first performed in Prague on April 27, 1927. It subsequently proved to be one of the most successful 20th-century operas. Schwanda's expertise on the bagpipe is such that he wins the affection of the frosty queen, nicknamed Ice Heart. But when she learns that he has a wife, she sentences him to death. He flees from her wrath, but because of a thoughtless blasphemy he commits, he is sent to hell. A friendly magician wins his soul in a rather dishonest card game with the devil, and Schwanda is freed.

Schwarze Spinne, Die (The Black Spider). Opera in three acts by Josef Hauer, composed in 1932 after a mystical tale (1842) by the Swiss cleric Albert Bitzius (1797–1854) dealing with a peasant woman who attempts to outwit the devil incarnate by pretending to submit to his hideous proposal to surrender to him her unbaptized child for his iniquitous purposes but who is transformed into a black spider and brings forth a proliferation of horrible arachnids instead, first performed posthumously in Vienna on May 23, 1966.

Schweigsame Frau, Die (The Silent Woman). Opera in three acts by Richard Strauss, to a libretto by Stefan Zweig after Ben Jonson's drama *Epicœne* (1609), first produced in Dresden on June 24, 1935. A cantankerous old man, appropriately named Morosus, is looking for a wife who would keep silent. His nephew turns up with a theatrical group that includes his own wife, whom he introduces to his uncle as "the silent woman." A fraudulent marriage contract is drawn between her and the old man, but as soon as she moves into his house she becomes a garrulous shrew. The old man is distraught by this transformation and is only too glad to restore her to her lawful husband, his nephew, and even give him money.

Seagull, The. Opera by Thomas Pasatieri, to a libretto based on a play by Chekhov centered on the character of a young woman who is unloved and has to feed herself emotionally on psychological debris like a seagull in the wake of a brilliantly lit ship, produced for the first time in Houston on March 5, 1974.

Second Hurricane, The. Children's opera by Aaron Copland, his first, and first performed in New York on April 21, 1937, directed by Orson Welles. The work was written for performance by nonprofessional young musicians. The libretto bears the imprint of a newspaper story. A group of children organize aid to victims of a flood in the Ohio Valley after a hurricane. They charter a plane and fly there with food and medicine. But the hurricane strikes for the second time in the same location, and the rescuers themselves have to be rescued. The opera is not Copland's best.

Secret, The (Tajemství). Comic opera in three acts by Bedřich Smetana, to a libretto by Eliška Krásnohorská recounting the story of Rose and Councillor Kalina, who, separated, find each other again when Kalina seeks a promised treasure and ends up in Rose's house, first performed in Prague on Sept. 18, 1878.

Segreto di Susanna, Il (Susanna's Secret). Opera in one act by Ermanno Wolf-Ferrari, to a libretto by Enrico Golisciani, first performed (in German as *Susannas Geheimnis*) in Munich on Dec. 4, 1909. The momentous secret is the presence of cigarette butts in Susanna's room, which makes her husband suspect that during his absence she was receiving a male visitor. He is both relieved and shocked when he discovers that Susanna herself indulges in tobacco, a horrendous breach of feminine mores at the turn of the 20th century. The opera's overture is often played.

Selma sedlák (The Sly Peasant). Comic opera by Antonín Dvořák, first performed in Prague on Jan. 27, 1878. The beautiful Betrushka, daughter of a rich peasant, loves a hired hand, but her father wants her to marry a prosperous villager. Enter new characters: the duke and duchess. The duke is struck by the beauty of Betrushka. Her lover then conceives the idea of securing ducal help for his own marriage. Betrushka persuades the duchess to put on her dress. When the duke makes amorous advances to the disguised duchess, she slaps his face. Thereupon all false identities are straightened out, everybody forgives everybody, and the two young people are united in happy matrimony. What with subplots involving the duke's servants, there are obvious similarities in the story to Mozart's *The Marriage of Figaro*, but Dvořák's music can hardly be compared.

Semiramide. Opera in two acts by Gioacchino Rossini, to a libretto by Gaetano Rossi after Voltaire's tragedy *Sémiramis* (1748), first produced in Venice on Feb. 3, 1823. Semiramide is the queen of Babylon. She conspires with her lover to kill the king. This done, she takes another lover, a young barbarian, but to her horror discovers that he is her own son by a previous union. When her first lover attacks her son, she intercepts his dagger and dies. Thereupon, her son slays her first lover and by hereditary rights becomes king. A number of other composers wrote operas on this subject, among them Porpora, Gluck, Salieri, Cimarosa, Meyerbeer, and, in the 20th century, Respighi.

Semyon Kotko. Opera in five acts by Sergei Prokofiev, to a text by Valentin Katayev and the composer after Katayev's story, first performed in Moscow on June 23, 1940. Kotko was a revolutionary soldier demobilized in 1918 after the conclusion of an armistice between the Soviet government and Germany. The opera is written in an energetic manner, typical of Prokofiev, and contains fine lyrical episodes. There is also a characteristically operatic mad scene, enacted by the young bride of a Bolshevik sailor slain by the counterrevolutionary Ukrainian nationalists.

Serse (Xerxes). Opera by George Frideric Handel, first produced in London on April 15, 1738. Two brothers in ancient Persia are in love with the same woman, but Xerxes loses out despite his royal stature. The opera opens with the celebrated aria "Ombra mai fù," known to the musical multitudes simply as "Handel's Largo."

Servant of Two Masters, The. Opera by Vittorio Giannini, after the play by Carlo Goldoni, written in an effusively euphonious, harmonious, and melodious idiom as a legacy of the composer's Italian legacy, first produced posthumously by the N.Y. City Opera on March 9, 1967, less than one year after the composer's death.

Servants, The. Opera by William Mathias, to a libretto by Iris Murdoch, first produced by the Welsh National Opera in Cardiff on Sept. 15, 1980.

Serva padrona, La (The Maid as Mistress). Opera in two parts by Giovanni Pergolesi, as an intermezzo to his opera *Il Prigionier superbo,* to a libretto by Gennaro Federico, first performed in Naples on Sept. 5, 1733. The opera itself is forgotten, but the intermezzo became a *cause célèbre* in the thundering polemical exchange between the advocates of Italian and French opera after its performance in Paris, 1752. Amazingly, Rousseau sided with the Italian concept of operatic universalism cultivating bel canto. He later reversed his position. The plot, a typical 18th-century farce, involves a scheming servant girl (la serva) who sets her sights on her middle-aged master. To prove that she is desirable to men of higher rank, she induces his valet to don the uniform of an army captain and pretend to be in love with her. The master is impressed and decides to marry her, and she thus becomes "la padrona," the mistress of the house.

Servilia. Opera in five acts by Nikolai Rimsky-Korsakov, first performed in St. Petersburg on Oct. 14, 1902, set in Rome in A.D. 67. A young tribune, Valery, loves Servilia, daughter of a Roman senator who is accused of treason by the emperor Nero and exiled. Servilia is crushed by the internecine domestic fights and expires in the arms of her lover. This is one of only two operas by Rimsky-Korsakov not based on a national Russian story (the other was *Mozart and Salieri*).

17 Tage und 4 Minuten. Opera buffa in three acts by Werner Egk, a fanciful version of Calderón's comedy *El mayor encanto amor,* with wandering Ulysses and nymphomaniacal Circe making love for exactly 17 days and 4 minutes surrounded by half-mythological, quarter-realistic, and quarter-surrealistic creatures, first mounted in Stuttgart on June 2, 1966.

Sganarelle. Comic opera in one act by Violet Archer, to her own libretto based on the first of the several plays by Molière wherein Sganarelle appears as an old duped fool, first staged in Edmonton, Canada, on Feb. 5, 1974.

Shunkan (The Banishment). Opera in one act by Osamu Shimizu, based on the kabuki play about a rebellious priest exiled in 1177 to a desert island by the Japanese feudal lords, first produced in Tokyo on March 9, 1965.

Sì. Operetta in three acts by Pietro Mascagni, described as a "duetto americano" and caricaturing the modern dances of transatlantic provenance, with the purported aim of "safeguarding light Italian music from the enslavement by alien fashions," first performed in Rome on Dec. 13, 1919.

Shivaree, The. Chamber opera by John Beckwith, to a libretto dealing with a successful if maddening shivaree (i.e., chiari, a wedding-night mock serenade) staged by the young lover of the third wife of a middle-aged merchant in rural Ontario c. 1900, first performed in Toronto on April 3, 1982.

Siberia. Opera in three acts by Umberto Giordano, to a text by Luigi Illica, first staged at La Scala, Milan, on Dec. 19, 1903. The libretto deals with the deepest passions in darkest czarist Russia, wherein the lover of the mistress of a St. Petersburg nobleman nearly kills him in a duel and is dispatched to Siberia, whither she follows him and stabs herself to death after a failure to engineer his escape. The musical setting constitutes a veritable anthology of Russian songs and dances wherein the doleful Volga Boatmen's song ungeographically serves as a Siberian motto and a complete rendition of the czarist national anthem is given by a police band during the hero's arrest. The composer's own contribution is limited to Italianate mimicry of Russian sentimental ballads and to instrumental interludes such as a chromatic blizzard in the Siberian "Hungry Steppes."

Sicilian Vespers, The. Opera in five acts by Giuseppe Verdi, first produced in Paris at the Grande Exposition under the French title *Les Vêpres siciliennes* on June 13, 1855. The subject of the libretto by Eugéne Scribe and Chalres Duveyrier was not the most politic choice for a French audience, as it dealt with the expulsion of the French from Sicily in the 13th century. The vespers of the title are the church bells rung by a patriotic Sicilian noblewoman as a signal for the expected uprising. The opera ends in a massacre of the French. Not a major Giuseppe Verdi opera, but surprisingly tenacious in the world's opera houses.

Siddhartha. Opera by Per Nørgård, after Hermann Hesse, first produced in Stockholm on March 18, 1983.

Siège de Corinthe, Le (The Siege of Corinth). Opera by Gioacchino Rossini, first performed in Paris on Oct. 9, 1826. The story deals with a daughter of the governor of Corinth who refuses to submit to the commander of the Turkish army besieging Corinth as the price of its relief. She dies with her father in the city ruins. Since the first production of the opera happened to take place during the uprising against the Ottoman rulers by Greek nationalists, to whom the French were highly sympathetic, it won a particularly warm reception. Actually the score was a revision of an opera on a similar subject that was first produced in Naples, 1820, under the title *Maometto II.*

Siegfried. Music drama in three acts by Richard Wagner, the third part of the tetralogy *Der Ring des Nibelungen,* to his own libretto, first produced on Aug. 16, 1876, as part of the inaugural Bayreuth Festival. Siegfried is the incestuous child of Siegmund and Sieglinde, children of Wotan. He is guarded by the Nibelung dwarf Mime. Wotan predicts that a hero will emerge who will make the mighty sword with which to kill the murderous giant Fafner, magically transformed into a dragon. Siegfried fulfills Wotan's prophecy, forges the sword, and slays Fafner. Inadvertently, he touches the hot gore of the slain dragon, and, putting his finger to his lips, he suddenly becomes aware that he can understand the language of the birds. Siegfried also reads the mind of Mime, and realizes that he plots his death. He kills the malevolent dwarf, and goes forth to his next adventure, to rescue Brünnhilde, the disobedient Valkyrie who was punished by Wotan and placed on a rock surrounded by a ring of fire. He reaches her as she lies in deep sleep, and puts the fateful ring of the Nibelung, now in his possession, on her finger. He awakens her with a kiss.

Signor Bruschino, Il, ossia Il figlio per azzardo (Mr. Bruschino, or Son by Accident). Opera in one act by Gioacchino Rossini, to a libretto by Giuseppe Foppa after a French comedy by de Chazet and Ourry, a tried and true opera tale of true love (Sofia and Florville) winning out over a prearranged marriage (Sofia and her employer's son), first staged in Venice on Jan. 27, 1813.

Si j'étais roi (If I Were King). Opera in three acts by Adolphe Adam, to a libretto by Adolphe d'Ennery and Jules Brésil, first produced in Paris on Sept. 4, 1852. The action unfolds in the Indian port of Goa in the 16th century, before its capture by Portugal. A fisherman saves a young girl from drowning, not realizing that she is a royal princess of Goa. When he recognizes her on the beach he tells of his exploits to the king's nephew who orders him never to mention it again under penalty of death. Aggrieved, the fisherman traces the words on the sand, "Si j'étais roi," and falls asleep. The king, touched by this sight, orders the sleeping man transferred to the royal palace and lets him rule Goa for a day. The fisherman discovers that the king's nephew treacherously conducted negotiations with the Portuguese, preparing to surrender the city. The king expels the traitor, and the Portuguese are repelled. The fisherman marries the princess.

Silas Marner. Opera in three acts by John Joubert, after the novel of the same name by George Eliot dealing with an unjustly maligned village weaver who is vindicated through industry, prosperity, and love for a foundling, produced at the South African College of Music in Capetown on May 20, 1961.

Silence de la Mer, Le. Lyric drama in one act by Henri Tomasi, to a dramatic libretto from the time of Nazi occupation of France in which a German officer of uncommon sensibilities who lodges in a French home tells the story of his life to an old man of the house and his niece, and then kills himself, first produced in Strasbourg on June 15, 1963.

Simon Boccanegra. Opera in prologue and three acts by Giuseppe Verdi, to a libretto by Francesco Piave based on the drama by Antonio García Gutiérrez, premiered in Venice on March 12, 1857. A revised version was premiered in Milan on March 24, 1881. Boccanegra (black mouth) was a historical Doge of Genoa in the 14th century. He lives with the memory of a daughter he had by a Genoese noblewoman. The mistress is now deceased, and the child has disappeared. Many years elapse before the opera takes place. As it turns out, his daughter has been raised by his father. Her romance with a young patrician is temporarily thwarted by a jealous rival. The true identities and relationships between grandfather, father, and daughter/granddaughter are disclosed in the last act. Before his natural death, Boccanegra proclaims his daughter's lover as the new Doge. The opera, although less significant than Verdi's masterpieces, nevertheless retains a hold on the major opera houses. The work is notable for its powerful Council Chamber scene.

Singing Skeleton, The. Opera in one act by Osamu Shimizu, based on a harrowing horror tale of old Japan, first performed in Osaka on March 15, 1962.

Sir John in Love. Opera in four acts by Ralph Vaughan Williams, first produced in London on March 21, 1929. The story deals mainly with Falstaff, the text selected from various sources, including Shakespeare's *The Merry Wives of Windsor, Love's Labour's Lost,* and *Much Ado about Nothing.*

Sly. Opera in two acts by Ermanno Wolf-Ferrari, to a libretto by Giovacchino Forzana developed from an idea in the induction of Shakespeare's *The Taming of the Shrew,* first performed in Milan on Dec. 29, 1927. Christopher Sly is found in a drunken stupor by the lord of the mansion, who decides to play a trick on him by ordering his servants to treat him like an honored guest before returning him to reality. All kinds of Shakespearean imbroglios result from this situation.

Snow Maiden, The (*Snegurotchka*). Opera in prologue and four acts by Nikolai Rimsky-Korsakov, to a libretto by the composer after Alexander Ostrovsky's drama (1873) itself based on a folktale, first produced in St. Petersburg on Feb. 10, 1882. The Snow Maiden is the delicate offspring of incompatible parents, Frost and Spring. At the peril of her life she must not let warmth, physical or emotional, enter her heart. A young villager is captivated by her icy beauty and follows her wherever she goes. Her mother warns her to keep away from the destructive rays of the sun as summer approaches. She ignores her warnings, and melts away like spring snow. The opera is one of the most poetic productions of the Russian operatic stage, but is rarely, if ever, staged elsewhere.

Sogno di Scipione, Il (The Dream of Scipio). Opera in one act by Wolfgang Amadeus Mozart, to a libretto by Pietro Metastasio based on Cicero's "Somnium Scipionis" in *De Republica* (54 B.C.) concerning Scipio's imagined travels through life guided first by the Goddess of Fortune and then by the Goddess of Constancy, both of whom reveal themselves to him in his dreams and who force him to choose between them (he chooses Constancy), first performed in Salzburg, possibly in early May 1772.

Sojourner and Mollie Sinclair, The. Comic opera in one act by Carlisle Floyd, to his own libretto delineating the conflict between an old-fashioned clan chieftain and a progressive-minded lass among the early Scottish settlers in the Carolinas, commissioned by the Charter Tercentenary Commission, first produced in Raleigh, North Carolina, on Dec. 2, 1963.

Soldaten, Die (The Soldiers). "Pluralistic opera" in four acts (15 scenes) by Bernd Alois Zimmermann, to a libretto by the composer from the drama by Jakob Michael Reinhold Lenz (1776), first performed in Cologne on Feb. 15, 1965. The story tells of a naive provincial girl whose unquenchable ambition to meet influential people leads her to yield to the psychological needs of every officer of the local garrison. Dramatic pluralism is emphasized by the subdivision of the stage into simultaneous, separate compartments.

Soldier Boy, Soldier. Opera by T. J. Anderson, to a libretto by Leon Forrest dealing with a black Vietnam veteran's return home, performed for the first time in Bloomington, Indiana, on Oct. 23, 1982.

Sonnambula, La (The Sleepwalker). Opera in two acts by Vincenzo Bellini, first produced in Milan on March 6, 1831. The libretto is by Felice Romani after Eugéne Scribe. The somnambulist of the title is a young orphaned woman betrothed to a villager in Switzerland early in the 19th century. The marriage is nearly wrecked when she wanders in her sleep into the bedroom of a visiting nobleman who is there to court the proprietess of the local tavern. Nobody believes that she wandered into the visitor's room in her sleep, but as they argue pro and con, she appears on the ledge of the house singing a sad aria. Her bridegroom is reassured of her fidelity. The opera is considered an example of Bellini's mature style.

Speziale, Lo (The Apothecary). Comic opera in three acts by Joseph Haydn, to a libretto by the composer based on a libretto by Carlo Goldoni, first performed in Esterháza in the autumn of 1768. A ward of an apothecary is loved by both a rich old man and a youth. Naturally her guardian prefers the rich man. Both are outwitted when the young suitor dons the cloak of a notary and writes out a marriage contract with his own name as the bridegroom. As a counteraction, the rich contender appears dressed in Turkish disguise and offers the post of an ambassador in Turkey to the bewildered apothecary. When the other rejects the scheme the exasperated suitor wrecks his shop. After that the apothecary is only too glad to yield his ward to her beloved.

Spring (Pranvera). Opera in two acts by Tish Daija, set in Albania in the spring of 1944 and centered on a heroic partisan dying "with the name of the Communist Party on his lips" before the firing squad of the Nazi occupying forces, betrayed by an Albanian fascist who failed in love rivalry for the hand of the beautiful mountain maiden, first produced in Tirana on June 12, 1960.

St. Anthony's Great Temptation. Short opera by Louis de Meester, a modernistic interpretation of the horror-laden painting of Hieronymous Bosch, with electronic jazz symbolizing the agony of seduction, performed for the first time in the Flemish language in Antwerp on Nov. 11, 1961.

Stephen Climax. Opera by Hans Zender, first staged in Frankfurt am Main on June 15, 1986. It was preceded by a concert version, entitled *Dubliner Nachtszenen* (1987–89). The work parallels the search for truth by St. Simeon the Stylite and Joyce's hero Stephen Dedalus.

Stiffelio. Opera in three acts by Giuseppe Verdi, to a libretto by Francesco Piave after the play by Émile Souvestre and Eugène Bourgeois, *Le pasteur, ou L'évangile et le foyer* (1849), first produced in Trieste on Nov. 16, 1850. It failed miserably, and no wonder—the uncharacteristically static libretto. Stiffelio, an evangelical minister, faces a problem: his wife allowed herself to be seduced by a local reprobate. As a Christian, should he forgive her? As a man, should he throw her out? The Italian censors stepped in, and their intervention gave the opera its coup de grâce. Still, there was music to salvage, and Verdi grafted it to another opera, *Aroldo*, but it also failed there.

Stone Guest, The (*Kamennyï gost*). Opera in three acts by Alexander Dargomízhsky, to a libretto based on Pushkin's "little tragedy" (1830), left unfinished at Dargomízhsky's death, and completed by Nikolai Rimsky-Korsakov and César Cui. The first performance took place posthumously in St. Petersburg on Feb. 28, 1872, three years after the composer's death. Pushkin's story is based on the same story as Da Ponte's *Don Giovanni* libretto for Mozart. The stone guest of the title is the statue of the commendatore slain by Don Juan. Not only does Don Juan try to seduce his widow, but he also invites the statue to supper. The marble handshake of the Stone Guest crushes Don Juan, and he falls dead. The opera is of importance because of Dargomyzhsky's fruitful attempt to treat the inflections of Russian speech realistically rather than in a conventional operatic style.

Story of a Real Man, The (Povest' o nastoyashchem cheloveke). Opera in four acts by Sergei Prokofiev, to a text by the composer and Mira Mendelson after the story by Boris Polevoy, first performed in an unofficial preview in Leningrad on Dec. 3, 1948. The libretto was based on an actual episode in World War II in which a Soviet flyer lost both feet in combat but was patriotically determined to continue on active duty even though he had to wear prostheses. He succeeded brilliantly in aerial combat. Prokofiev hoped to vindicate himself with this opera against official Soviet critics who accused him of pursuing decadent Western ways. This was a false hope, for the opera was attacked by Soviet spokesmen as failing to achieve the correct line of socialist realism. The opera was revived in Moscow in a posthumous gesture of rehabilitation on Dec. 8, 1960, with the hero glorified in the opera in attendance.

Story of Vasco, The. Opera by Gordon Crosse, to a libretto dealing with an Italian barber caught in a European war in the middle of the 19th century who, unwittingly recruited as a spy for the losing side, is unexpectedly proclaimed a hero and dies in dodecaphonic glory, first performed in London on March 13, 1974.

Strange Story of Arthur Rowe, The. Opera by Ivan Jirko, after Graham Greene's novel *Ministry of Fear*, first mounted in Liberec on Oct. 25, 1969.

Straniera, La (The Stranger). Opera in two acts by Vincenzo Bellini, to a libretto by Felice Romani after Victor-Charles Prévot's, novel *L'étrangère*, perhaps from its dramatization by G. C. Cosenza (1827), premiered in Milan on Feb. 14, 1829. The stranger of the title is Agnese, the first wife of King Philippe of France, who has banished her. She lives in a château in self-inflicted solitude until a romantic lord seeks her out and wins her love. The king is then deposed and Agnese proclaimed queen, putting her out of nuptial reach of the mere lord. Thwarted, he stabs himself to death, and she prays for death herself.

Street Scene. Dramatic folk opera by Kurt Weill, based on a play by Elmer Rice, with lyrics by Langston Hughes, premiered on Broadway on Jan. 9, 1947. The somber story portrays in idiomatically functional tones the drab life in a N.Y. tenement district tragically disrupted when a jealous husband kills his wife and her milkman lover. The work is probably the most ambitious attempt of Weill to recreate his Berlin-Brecht style, integrating popular music with classical sonorities.

Streetcar Named Desire, A. Opera in three acts by Andre Previn, to a libretto by Philip Littell after the play by Tennessee Williams, first performed at the San Francisco Opera on Sept. 19, 1998, under the composer's direction.

Stronger Than Death. Opera in three acts by Kirill Molchanov, focused on a Soviet hero of the defense of Brest-Litovsk against the Nazi assault in June 1941, first produced in Voronezh in the presence of the actual prototype of the story, Pyotr Gavrilov, on March 23, 1967.

Summer and Smoke. Opera in two acts by Lee Hoiby, after a play by Tennessee Williams dealing with the unrequited love of a Mississippi girl who refuses to face reality and seeks refuge in a fantasy world, first performed in St. Paul on June 19, 1971.

Suor Angelica (Sister Angelica). Opera in one act by Giacomo Puccini, to a libretto by Giovacchino Forzano, first produced by the Metropolitan Opera in New York on Dec. 14, 1918, as the second part of his operatic triptych *Il Trittico* (the first part was *Il Tabarro* and the third *Gianni Schicchi*). Sister Angelica, who abandoned her own child, enters the convent to redeem her sin. When she learns that the child is dead, she takes poison. Because of the sincerity of her repentance, the Madonna appears to her holding Angelica's transfigured child in her arms, and Angelica receives absolution. Puccini's own sister was a nun, and when he finished the vocal score, he played it for her at her convent.

Susannah. Music drama in two acts by Carlisle Floyd, to his own libretto, premiered in Tallahassee, Florida, on Feb. 24, 1955. A pious minister succumbs to the charms of a pretty sinner. When her brother discovers them together, he kills the minister. A menacing mob forms near Susannah's, but she takes a resolute stand at the porch with a shotgun, and the villagers disperse.*Susannah* was later staged in New York on Sept. 27, 1956, winning the N.Y. Music Critics Circle Award.

Svätopluk. Historical opera by Eugen Suchoň, premiered in Bratislava on March 10, 1960. In 9th-century Moravia, Svätopluk is an ambitious prince who takes part in a conspiracy against his father the king. His plot is foiled, but the king, shaken by this treachery, dies. Svätopluk's younger brother ascends to the throne.

Sweeney. Opera by Stephen Sondheim, ingeniously arranged from his successful musical *Sweeney Todd* after a grisly tale, *The String of Pearls, or the Fiend of Fleet Street,* published serially in a London newspaper in 1846 dealing with a mad barber who cut the throats of his unsuspecting customers for his even madder landlady who used the most meaty parts for her culinary concoctions ("Man eats man," Sweeney sings). It was first produced in Houston on July 14, 1984.

Symphonie pastorale, La. Opera by Guillaume Landré, after the autumnal novel by André Gide dealing with the crepuscular passion of an aging Swiss minister for a blind orphan adopted by him, who recovers her sight and selects his son as her spiritual bridegroom, dying of mystical inanition just as the world of sight and love is uncovered for her, first staged in Rouen on March 31, 1968.

Székely fonó (The Transylvanian Workshop). Lyrical play by Zoltán Kodály, comprised of a series of 27 connected authentic songs of Transylvanian Szeklers (known, in Magdar, as Székely, descendants of Attila's Huns or of Black Ugrians), first performed in Budapest on April 24, 1932. The texts employed are madrigal-like salutes to love as a socially liberating force, scored for chorus and orchestra and applying the composer's favorite device of "Hungarian counterpoint," wherein two different songs are combined canonically. The story is simple: a landlady's fiancé is forced to flee the country because of an unjust accusation of crime, but is arrested and brought back in chains. Fortunately, an old woman at the workshop recognizes the real criminal among those present. The landlady's beloved is freed, and a happy ending is celebrated by all.

T

Tabarro, Il (The Cloak). Opera in one act by Giacomo Puccini, to a libretto by Giuseppe Adami after Didier Gold's tragedy *La houppelande* (1910), produced as the first part of *Il Trittico* (Triptych) by the Metropolitan Opera in New York on Dec. 14, 1918. The story deals with a love triangle along the Seine River. A barge owner suspects his helper of conducting an affair with his wife. He kills him, covers the body with his wife's cloak, and then kills her, too.

Tale of Tzar Saltan, The (Skazka o Tsare Saltane). Opera in prologue and four acts by Nikolai Rimsky-Korsakov, to a libretto by Vladimir Belsky after a fairy tale by Pushkin (1832), first produced in Moscow on Nov. 3, 1900. The mythical czar Saltan is searching for a bride, and three sisters compete. He selects and marries the youngest, and she bears him a son. But her envious sisters tell the czar that the child is a monster. Horrified, he orders both mother and child put in a barrel to sail the ocean on their own. The prince grows up quickly. The barrel lands on an island, where he saves a swan from a hawk. The swan turns out to be a magic princess, and she endows him with the power to transform himself into any living creature. He turns himself into a bumblebee, flies back to his hometown, and, spotting his treacherous aunts in the garden, stings them viciously. (The orchestral representation of the "Flight of the Bumblebee" is very famous.) The denouement is happy: the heir to the throne marries the magic princess, his mother is reinstated, and even her evil sisters are forgiven.

Tamerlano. Opera by George Frideric Handel, first performed at the King's Theatre in London on Oct. 31, 1724. The central character is Tamerlane (Tamburlaine), the powerful Mongol conqueror, who is preparing to be married but who meanwhile falls in love with a captive Turkish woman. However, she is in love with a Greek prince. Multilateral jealousies ensue, but in the end the conqueror returns to his betrothed and yields the Turkish woman to her prince.

Tamu-Tamu. Chamber opera in two acts by Gian Carlo Menotti, commissioned by the 9th International Congress of Anthropological and Ethnological Sciences, with a libretto by the composer, its title meaning "guests" in Indonesian, sung and partly spoken in both English and Indonesian, the plot dealing with victims of American air attacks in southeast Asia. It was first staged in Chicago on Sept. 5, 1973.

Tancredi. Opera (melodramma eroico) in two acts by Gioacchino Rossini, his first marked success as an opera composer, to a libretto derived from Tasso's poem *Gerusalemme liberata* combined with Voltaire's *Tancrède* (1760), premiered in Venice on Feb. 6, 1813. The story deals with Tancredi, a crusader who took part in the siege of Jerusalem. He is emotionally torn between two loves: a devoted Syrian girl and a Persian woman warrior, Clorinda, whom he loves profoundly. But as he encounters her wearing full armor, he mistakes her for a masculine enemy and fatally wounds her. This tragic episode is also the subject of Monteverdi's dramatic madrigal *Il combattimento di Tancredi e Clorinda* (1624) and of Campra's tragédie lyrique *Tancrede* (1702).

Tannhäuser. Opera in three acts by Richard Wagner, to his own libretto, first produced in Dresden on Oct. 19, 1845. Wagner described the score as a *Handlung* (action). The complete title is *Tannhäuser und der Sängerkrieg auf Wartburg* (Tannhauser and the Singers' Contest on the Wartburg). Tannhäuser was a historical figure, a German Minnesinger who led a wandering life in the 13th century and participated in a Crusade. In Wagner's opera Tannhäuser succumbs to the pleasures of the flesh in the Venusberg, a mountain in central Germany in whose caves, according to medieval legends, the goddess Venus herself holds court. But he yearns to return to his own world and to his beloved Elisabeth. He joins a group of pilgrims in the valley of the Wartburg, which includes his friend Wolfram (also a historical figure). A singing contest is held in the castle, and Tannhäuser shocks the assembly with his song in praise of Venus. He is expelled from the Wartburg and joins the pilgrims on their journey to Rome, where he hopes to obtain absolution from the Pope. Wolfram sings a song appealing to the evening star (that is, Venus) for protection of Elisabeth. Having failed to obtain forgiveness in Rome, Tannhäuser returns home, and encounters a funeral procession, that of Elisabeth. He collapses before her coffin and dies. He achieves redemption when the papal staff, brought back from Rome by the pilgrims, sprouts leaves.

Tarare. Opera in prologue and five acts by Antonio Salieri, first produced in Paris on June 8, 1787. The libretto, written especially for Salieri by Pierre-Augustin Beaumarchais after a Persian tale, deals with a soldier of fortune named Tarare who is involved in mortal combat with the king of the fabled town of Ormuz (Hormuz) in the Persian Gulf. Tarare wins the battle and becomes king. The opera was immensely successful in its first production in Paris and later in an Italian version, *Azur, Re d'Ormus,* in Vienna. *Tarare* was one of the earliest operas to introduce an element of pseudo-oriental mysticism. Mozart liked it very much, and his own *The Magic Flute* (1791) had a similar libretto.

Taras Shevchenko. Opera in four acts by Maiboroda, to his own Ukrainian libretto on the subject of the revolutionary life of the Ukrainian poet Shevchenko (1814–61), first produced in Kiev on May 28, 1964.

Tartuffe. Opera by Arthur Benjamin, his fourth and last, completed shortly before his death in 1960 in vocal score, written in a relaxed opéra-bouffe manner to suit Molière's comedy of hypocrisy, performed for the first time in London on Nov. 30, 1964, under the direction of Alan Boustead, who completed the orchestration.

Taverner. Opera by Peter Maxwell Davies, first performed at London's Covent Garden on July 12, 1972. It is based on the life of John Taverner, the English composer and organist who was incarcerated for a while for Protestant persuasions in the still Popish England in the early 16th century. A dramatic climax is achieved when the soldiers of Henry VIII erupt at the Mass while the monks sing Taverners's own *Benedictus.*

Telephone, The. Opera in one act by Gian Carlo Menotti, to his own libretto, first produced on Broadway in New York on Feb. 18, 1947. Menotti describes the opera as "l'amour à trois," the third member being the telephone itself, which is constantly in use because its female owner is a compulsive talker. After many attempts to get her full attention, her desperate suitor leaves her apartment and calls her on the telephone from the corner drugstore to propose marriage. The story is trifling but *The Telephone* has become a popular success.

Telltale Heart, The. Chamber opera by Daniel Kessner, after the scary tale by Edgar Allan Poe, performed for the first time in Utrecht on March 12, 1982.

Templer und die Jüden, Der (The Templar and the Jewess). Opera in three acts by Heinrich August Marschner, quite popular in its time, first produced in Leipzig on Dec. 22, 1829, to a libretto based on Sir Walter Scott's novel *Ivanhoe,* with concentration on Ivanhoe's abortive love for a Jewess.

Tender Land, The. Opera in two acts by Aaron Copland, to a libretto by Horace Everett (Erik Johns) after James Agee's *Let Us Now Praise Famous Men,* first performed in New York on April 1, 1954. The tender land of the title is the American midwest. A young harvest worker has a summer romance with a farm girl, but he is indecisive about marriage. Eventually he leaves the farm. Her love is more profound, and she sets forth in search of him.

Thaïs. Opera in three acts by Jules Massenet, to a libretto by Louis Gallet drawn from the ironic novel by Anatole France (1890), first performed in Paris on March 16, 1894. A monk in Egypt is horrified by the depravity of the courtesan Thaïs and dreams of converting her. He succeeds rather well. He conducts Thaïs through the desert, where they reach the convent and she takes her vow as the bride of Christ. But the monk himself undergoes a reversal and now craves not her spirit but her flesh. To exorcise the obsession he flagellates himself violently, but in vain. Meanwhile, Thaïs attains spiritual perfection and dies a true Christian. The instrumental solo "Méditation" from the score is a perennial favorite.

Thérèse. Music drama in two acts by Jules Massenet, premiered in Monte Carlo on Feb. 7, 1907. Thérèse loves a French royalist who flees from Paris during the Terror. She marries a Girondiste who is no more acceptable to the revolutionary regime. He is arrested and sentenced to die on the guillotine. Meanwhile, her exiled lover recklessly returns to Paris and is also seized. As the cart carrying them to the execution passes by her window she shouts, "Vive le Roi!" a suicidal outcry, and joins her husband and lover in death.

Thésée. Opera by Jean-Baptiste Lully, first performed in Paris on Jan. 11, 1675. Theseus is the legendary hero who vanquishes the bull Minotaur in Crete, whose annual diet was seven youths and seven maidens. Although a hero in Crete, Theseus proves to be a reprobate when he abandons Ariadne, who had helped him find the way out of the Minotaur's labyrinth by giving him a thread ("Ariadne's thread") to guide him. Numerous epics and dozens of operas have been written with Theseus as the central character.

Three Musketeers, The. Operetta by Rudolf Friml, based on the romance by Alexandre Dumas *fils,* first produced in New York on March 13, 1928, to much acclaim. Like the book, the operetta centers on the fourth musketeer, D'Artagnan, a historical figure and guardsman of Louis XIII. His most notable exploit is the recovery of the queen's jewels from a wily English duke.

Three Sisters. Opera by Thomas Pasatieri, after Chekhov's sad play dealing with a family's tragic triple indecision, first staged in Columbus, Ohio, on March 13, 1986.

Three Sisters Who Are Not Sisters. Chamber opera by David Ahlstrom, to words by Gertrude Stein, first performed in Cincinnati on March 1, 1953.

Three Mysteries. Opera triptych by Niccolò Castiglioni, based on three separate *texts—Silence,* inspired by a Japanese Noh play, *Chordination,* in a setting of a medieval English morality play, and *The Fall of Lucifer and Aria*, developed from a scene in Shakespeare's *Romeo and Juliet*—first performed in Rome on Oct. 2, 1968.

Tiefland (The Lowlands). Opera in prologue and two acts by Eugen d'Albert, to a libretto by Rudolf Lothar after the Catalan play *Terra baixa* by Angel Guimerá, first produced in Prague (in German) on Nov. 15, 1903. A young shepherd descends from his mountain pastures into the valley to marry a village maiden only to find that she is his master's mistress, a revelation that drives him to such homicidal fury that he strangles her seducer as he once strangled a prowling wolf, and carries her body to the highlands where they can breathe the unpolluted air and enjoy unviolated love.

Time Rocker. Opera in prologue and thirty (some subdivided) scenes by Lou Reed, to a futuristic libretto by the composer with text by Darryl Pinckney, directed and designed by Robert Wilson, first staged at the Thalia Theater in Hamburg on June 12, 1996.

Tintomara. Opera by Lars Johan Werle, dealing with a mystical creature named Tintomara and bearing reference to the regicide in Sweden in 1792 (also the subject of Giuseppe Verdi's *Un ballo in maschera*), first produced in Stockholm on Jan. 18, 1973.

Tkalci (The Weavers). Opera in two acts by Vít Nejedlý, completed by Jan Hanašafter Gerhard Hauptmann's drama *Die Weber* dealing with the desperate sabotage action of German weavers, who destroy not only the factory of their oppressive employer but also his private house, posthumously produced in Plzén on May 7, 1961.

Tobias and the Angel. Television opera in two acts by Sir Arthur Bliss, on the biblical subject wherein the Archangel Raphael exorcises the demon who has been annoying the bride of Tobias, broadcast on BBC on May 19, 1960.

Tod des Empedokles, Der (The Death of Empedoclest). "Scenic concerto" in one act by Hermann Reutter, to the romantic poem by Friedrich Hölderlin in which the ancient wise philosopher finds his private truth in a voluntary death in the crater of the volcano Aetna, performed for the first time in Schwetzingen on May 29, 1966, on the same program as the revised version of Reutter's one-act opera buffa *Die Witwe von Ephesus.*

Tom Jones. Comic opera by François-André Philidor, first performed in Paris on Feb. 27, 1765. The libretto is taken from the novel by Henry Fielding, *Tom Jones, The History of a Foundling* (1749). Tom is a scalawag who takes pleasure where he finds it, but he loves Sophia Western in earnest. Her father, however, plans a rich marriage for her. It turns out in the end that Tom is really the nephew of a country squire and therefore belongs to nobility. As such, he is qualified to marry Sophia. Byron called the character of Tom Jones "an accomplished blackguard," but in the opera he appears as a romantic lover.

Tomorrow. Lyric drama in one act by Tadeusz Baird, to a libretto after Joseph Conrad's story of dark passions in a fishermen's village, ending with the murder of a seaman by his own father for attempting to violate a girl who was the object of the father's senescent adoration, first produced in Warsaw on Sept. 18, 1966.

Torch of Prometheus, The. Opera by Jan Hanuš, to a libretto wherein a modernized Prometheus steals atomic fire from heaven thus challenging the power of the monopoly of the dictatorial and imperialistic Olympus, first produced in Prague on April 30, 1965.

Torquato Tasso. Opera in three acts by Gaetano Donizetti, to a libretto by Jacopo Ferretti after Giovanni Rosini's drama *Torquato Tasso* (1832), Goldoni's drama *Tasso* (1755), Goethe's drama *Tasso* (1790), and Byron's poem *The Lament of Tasso* (1817), first produced in Rome on Sept. 9, 1833. The central character is the famous poet of the Italian Renaissance. The duchess Eleonora falls in love with him when he reads poetry to her, but her brother, the reigning duke of Ferrara, wants her to marry a duke of Mantua and divests himself of Tasso by putting him in a madhouse. Torquado eventually succumbs to his new surroundings, especially after the Pope announces his intention to make him poet laureate.

Tosca. Opera in three acts by Giacomo Puccini, first produced in Rome on Jan. 14, 1900. The libretto by Giuseppe Giacosa and Luigi Illica is derived from a semi-historical drama by Victorier Sardou, *La Tosca* (1887). The action takes places during the turbulent events in Rome in the summer of 1800. Napoleon's army advances into Italy and is greeted by Italian patriots as liberators from the oppressive Austrian rule. Floria Tosca is a famous opera singer. Her lover, the painter Mario Cavaradossi, shelters a political refugee and becomes the target of persecution by the sinister chief of the Roman police, Scarpia. Captivated by Tosca's generous feminine endowments, Scarpia seeks to bargain her favors against Cavaradossi's release from prison. In desperation she agrees to submit to him, whereupon Scarpia issues an order for a pretended execution of Cavaradossi, using blank cartridges, "as in the case of Palmieri," he adds ominously. Confident of her lover's escape, Tosca takes advantage of Scarpia's amorous relaxation and stabs him to death. But Scarpia has outwitted Tosca: "in the case of Palmieri" was a code message to the soldiers to make the pretended execution real. Cavaradossi falls at the firing squad. After the soldiers are gone Tosca rushes to him, but he does not rise. Distraught, she hurls herself to her death from the prison's parapet. The opera is a perennial favorite with its magnificent title role for a soprano.

Toten Augen, Die (The Dead Eyes). Opera in prologue and one act by Eugen d'Albert, after *Les yeux morts* by M. Henry (translated by H. Ewers), first performed in Dresden, quite successfully, on March 5, 1916. The bleak story deals with a blind woman miraculously cured by Christ. But the miracle has its disadvantage, for as she regains her sight she realizes how ugly her husband is. Disappointed, she yields her favors to a Roman centurion. Her husband kills himself, and she, too, commits suicide.

Tote Stadt, Die (The Dead City). Opera in three acts by Erich Wolfgang Korngold, to a libretto by "Paul Schott" (the composer and his father), after Georges Rodenbach's novel *Bruges la morte* (1892), premiered in Hamburg and Cologne simultaneously on Dec. 4, 1920. The libretto is Germanically morbid, the ending a dramaturgical smirk, but the score is one of the most effective operas of the post–Wagner era. A widower faithful to the memory of his wife is struck by a resemblance to her in a young dancer whom he learns to love. In her desire to please him the dancer thoughtlessly makes a wig of his late wife's hair. Provoked by this act of sacrilege, he strangles the woman. But welcome relief is vouchsafed: the whole sequence of events was but a dream.

Tovarish Andrei. Opera oratorio in ten scenes with prologue and epilogue by Gibalin, a series of musical tableaux illustrating the revolutionary life of Jacob Svedlov, known in the czarist underground as "Tovarishch Andrei," performed for the first time in Sverdlovsky, the Ural city, formerly Ekaterinburg, renamed Sverdlovsky after Sverdlovk, who died in 1919, on Nov. 6, 1967.

Toyon of Alaska (The Lord of Alaska). Historical pageant opera in three acts by Straight, dealing with the Russian overlord of the Arctic Alexander Baranov, who established the first settlement in Alaska in 1792, produced for the first time in Anchorage on July 7, 1967, during the centennial celebration of the purchase of Alaska by the United States from the Russian government.

Transfjädrarna (The Crane Feathers). Opera by Sven-Erik Bäck, from a Japanese Noh drama dealing with a bride who is really a bird, performed for the first time on the Stockholm radio on Feb. 28, 1957.

Transformations. Opera by Conrad Susa, his first, inspired by a poem by Anne Sexton, with symbolic themes illustrating the characters and events of children's fairy tales transmuted into surrealistic images, first staged in Minneapolis on May 5, 1973.

Transatlantic. Opera by George Antheil, to his own libretto, first performed in Frankfurt am Main on May 25, 1930. In it an American candidate for the presidency is searching for a suitable bride in various N.Y. locales. The divided staging with action occurring on several levels was revolutionary in its time.

Transposed Heads, The. Opera by Peggy Glanville-Hicks, to her own libretto drawn from Thomas Mann's novel, first performed in Louisville, Kentucky on April 3, 1954. A Hindu woman, unsure of her choice between her genius of a husband and her handsome simpleton lover, proposes that they decapitate themselves and transpose their heads to their respective torsos. Bewildered by the resulting severed heads and decapitated torsos, she commits suicide.

Traum des Liu-Tung, Der. Opera in four dream sequences by Isang Yun, after a medieval Taoist fable centered on a Zen-starred youth who lapses into catalepsy and awakens 16 years later, scored for a modern orchestra with a large array of oriental instruments, with singers oscillating between tempered intonation and oriental sing-song, first produced in West Berlin on Sept. 25, 1965.

Traumspiel Ein. Opera by Aribert Reimann, his first, after August Strindberg's symbolically realistic psychological drama *Ett Drömspiel* (The Dream Play), first mounted in Kiel on June 20, 1965.

Traviata, La. Opera in three acts by Giuseppe Verdi, first performed in Venice on March 6, 1853. The libretto by Francesco Piave is drawn from the French play *La dame aux camélias* by Alexandre Dumas *fils*. The title is nearly untranslatable. While some choose "The Wayward One," this obviates the morally important point that the heroine was not wanton by nature. Perhaps a more accurate if unwieldy translation is "The Woman Diverted from the Righteous Way" or "The Woman Led Astray."

La Traviata is Violetta Valery, a courtesan. She meets a dashing gentleman, Alfredo Germont, who proclaims his ardent love for her. They take lodgings together near Paris without benefit of clergy. Alfredo's father, Giorgio Germont, is dismayed by his son's misalliance and begs Violetta to let him go. She complies and contrives a way to end her affair with Alfredo. After a period of anger, Alfredo learns she is ill. He rushes to her side, finding her dying of consumption. After some bittersweet vocalizing and lots of guilt on Alfredo and Germont's part, Violetta dies in her lover's arms.

La Traviata is one of the most tuneful of Verdi's operas. There is a famous scene of drinking a toast, the brindisi "Libiamo," as well as many poignant arias and duets. The subject of the opera shocked the sensibilities of some mid-19th-century operagoers. The London papers expressed outrage that "the ladies of the aristocracy" should be allowed to attend the production "to see an innocent young lady impersonate the heroine of an infamous French novel who varies her prostitution by a frantic passion." But *La Traviata* survived, an unusually contemporary opera for its composer. It was the major inspiration for verismo in general and Puccini's operas especially. Violetta is a role highly regarded by sopranos, especially for its variety of vocal opportunities.

Treemonisha. Opera in three acts by Scott Joplin, to a libretto by the composer describing the life of an abandoned black baby girl found under a tree near Texarkana by a compassionate woman named Monisha and therefore christened Monisha of the Tree, or Treemonisha. It was performed in concert form in 1915, two years before Joplin's death, and did not receive its first stage performance until Jan. 28, 1972, in Atlanta, by an all-black cast as the final event of the Afro-American Musical Workshop Festival at Morehouse College.

Trial of Lucullus, The. Opera by Roger Sessions, first performed in Berkeley, California, on April 18, 1947.

The libretto, by Bertolt Brecht, was originally intended for a radio play as an allegorical indictment of Hitler. The Roman general Lucullus is dead, but before entering the Elysian Fields he must defend himself against the accusations of being a mass murderer. The jury is not impressed by his recital of military victories and unanimously condemns him. An adaptation of the same text was set by Dessau in German as *Das Verhör des Lukullus* (1951).

Trial of Mary Lincoln, The. Opera by Thomas Pasatieri, based on the true story of the trial of Lincoln's widow, on the suspicion of Confederate sympathies, staged for the first time on the National Educational Television network across the United States on Feb. 14, 1972.

Trionfo dell'onore, Il (The Triumph of Honor). Opera by Alessandro Scarlatti, first performed in Naples on Nov. 26, 1718. The antihero of the opera courts two ladies at once. When the honest suitor of one of them nicks him in a duel, he decides to marry the unattached lady. It is historically important as one of the earliest examples of the Neapolitan opera buffa.

Tristan und Isolde. Opera in three acts by Richard Wagner, to his own libretto, first performed in Munich on June 10, 1865. The story is derived from an ancient Cornish legend. King Mark of Cornwall sends his nephew Tristan to fetch his chosen bride, Isolde, a princess of Ireland. During a sea voyage, Isolde falls in love with Tristan so deeply that only death can save her from disgrace. She asks her lady attendant to give her poison, but she prepares a love potion instead. After drinking it, both Tristan and Isolde become consumed with passion. Isolde marries Mark but continues to keep secret trysts with Tristan; their love duet is surpassingly moving in its chromatic sensuousness. Tristan, wounded by the king's henchman, is taken to his castle in Brittany. Isolde comes to visit him; a shepherd plays a tune on his wooden trumpet that is signal that Isolde's ship is approaching. Tristan, still bleeding from his wound, rushes to meet her and expires lovingly. The concluding scene is Isolde's own "Liebestod" (love death), expressing a mystical belief that the deepest light of love can be fulfilled only in the deepest night of death.

Tristan und Isolde is the apotheosis of Wagner's system of leitmotivs. Wagner's annotators have painstakingly compiled the themes of love, death, day and night, and love potion, and of soul states such as fidelity, suspicion, exaltation, impatience, and malediction. *Tristan und Isolde* is couched in a highly chromaticized idiom. The Vienna Opera House accepted the opera for performance, but after 53 rehearsals canceled the production. For some modernists the prelude to *Tristan und Isolde* is a prophetic vision of atonality.

Trittico, Il (Triptych). A group of three short operas by Giacomo Puccini—*Il Tabarro*, *Suor Angelica*, and *Gianni Schicchi*—performed for the first time at the Metropolitan Opera in New York on Dec. 14, 1918.

Triumph of Bacchus, The. Opera ballet by Alexander Dargomïzhsky, first produced in Moscow on Jan. 23, 1867. The libretto is based on a Pushkin poem that glorifies Bacchus as the god of wine and fertility.

Triumph of St. Joan, or The Trial at Rouen, The. Opera by Norman Dello Joio. The plot is the familiar one in which the French maiden warrior is captured, tried, sentenced, and executed, but not without a great wave of spirituality and angelic conversation. What is far more complicated is this work's history. A Dello Joio opera entitled *The Triumph of St. Joan* was premiered in Bronxville, N.Y., in 1950. He then took some of the music and created *The Triumph of St. Joan* Symphony (which he at first entitled *Seraphic Dialogue*) the following year. In 1956 a new opera on the same subject was premiered on NBC Television under the title *The Trial at Rouen*. Finally, on April 12, 1959, the N.Y. City Opera gave the first performance of a second opera called *The Triumph of St. Joan*, but with new music (making it his third Joan of Arc opera). In Dello Joio's eyes, there was no stopping the saint from Orléans.

Troilus and Cressida. Opera in three acts by William Walton, to a libretto by Christopher Hassall derived from Chaucer's *Troilus and Criseyde* (c.1385) and Boccaccio's *Filostrato* (c.1350), premiered in London on Dec. 3, 1954. The story recounts the tragic love affair between the Trojan prince Troilus and Cressida. When Troy is captured by the Greeks, Troilus is slain and Cressida is taken to the Greek camp as a slave. In desperation she stabs herself to death with Troilus's sword.

Trompeter van Säckingen, Der (The Trumpeter of Säckingen). Opera in four acts by Viktor Nessler, to a text by Rudolf Bunge after Scheffel's poem (1854), first performed in Leipzig on May 4, 1884.

Tronkrävarna (The Pretenders). Opera in two acts by Bucht, to a libretto after Ibsen's play *Kongsemnerne*, first mounted by the Royal Opera of Stockholm on Sept. 10, 1966.

Troquers, Les. Comic opera in one act by Antoine Dauvergne, based on a LaFontaine tale, first performed in Paris on July 30, 1753. Two young men try to outwit their girl companions, who in turn outwit them by arousing unjustified jealousy. The piece is a trifle, but it made history as the opening of the famous literary and aesthetic squabble known as the *guerre des bouffons*. *Les Troquers* was the response of the nationalistic group of French men of the theater, supported by the king himself and his mistress Marquise de Pompadour, to the proponents of Italian opera. It was supposed to prove that the French could also write intermezzos *dans le goût Italien*, as opposed to the relatively tedious lyric operas of Lully and Rameau, full of Greek mythology and opaque allegory. The success of the opera gave impetus to the composition of light, short theatrical pieces with music. However, the director of the opera house, fearful that a purely French product would not attract the public accustomed to the Italian type of entertainment, did not reveal the name of the composer until *Les Troquers* became a definite success.

Trouble in Tahiti. Opera by Leonard Bernstein, first produced at Brandeis University in Waltham, Massachusetts, on June 12, 1952. The composer's own libretto describes a disgruntled wife, constantly squabbling with her uncongenial husband. She proposes that they go to a movie about a quarreling couple on the Pacific island of Tahiti as a form of therapy. The stratagem succeeds, and they live happily—for a few months. The entire opera was incorporated into Bernstein's revised *A Quiet Place* of 1984.

Trovatore, Il (The Troubador). Opera in four acts by Giuseppe Verdi, to a libretto by Salvadore Cammarano and Leone Bardare after the drama *El trovador* (1836) by Gutiérrez, first produced in Rome on Jan. 19, 1853. In a genre known for its absurd storylines, *Il Trovatore* probably takes the prize for the most ludicrous libretto in the history of opera. But the score contains some of Giuseppe Verdi's finest inventions, among them the celebrated "Anvil Chorus." The troubador Manrico leads the rebellion against the king of Aragon, whose army is commanded by Manrico's brother, the Count di Luna. However, the brothers are not aware that they are kith and kin. To complicate matters further, they love the same woman, Leonora. (She chooses Manrico.) Enter a mysterious gypsy woman named Azucena who tells Manrico the dreadful story that her own mother was burnt as a witch, so she decided to steal and slay the baby brother of di Luna. She informs Manrico that the baby killed was actually her own. (She doesn't mention that the other was saved, and that Manrico was that baby.)

Azucena is arrested as a spy and condemned to die the same fiery death as her mother. Manrico, who believes Azucena to be his mother, tries to save her life, but is captured by di Luna. Leonora begs di Luna to release him, and the unspeakable count agrees provided she give herself to him. She submits, but takes a slow working poison to escape her unwelcome lover. She goes to the tower where Manrico is kept and brings him the message of his freedom. The poison begins to work, and she dies in his arms. At that moment di Luna arrives and orders Manrico executed after all. Just before she dies, Azucena reveals to di Luna that he has just executed his brother, and she dies avenged.

Troyens, Les (The Trojans). Grand opera in five acts by Hector Berlioz, to a libretto by the composer after the *Aeneid* of Vergil. The complete score was so long that, at Liszt's suggestion, Berlioz split it into two parts. Only the second part, *Les Troyens à Carthage*, was performed during his lifetime, in Paris, on Nov. 4, 1863. The first part, entitled *Le Prise de Troie*, was produced posthumously in Karlsruhe, on Dec. 6–7, 1890. While there were performances of both parts together with major cuts thereafter, the first uncut complete performances occurred as late as 1969 (Glasgow and London).

The libretto begins with the last days of Troy and ends with the suicide of Dido, the queen of Carthage, after her abandonment by Aeneas. As so often happens with Hector Berlioz's vocal works, the best known excerpt from *Les Troyens* is orchestral, namely, the "Royal Hunt and Storm" in the second part, when Dido and Aeneas avoid a downpour by sheltering in a cave. The rest is mythology.

Trumpet Major, The. Opera by Alva Hoddinott, after Thomas Hardy, first produced in Manchester on April 1, 1980.

Turandot. Opera in two acts by Ferruccio Busoni, first performed in Zürich on May 11, 1917, the composer conducting. In 1905, Busoni had composed incidental music for an imaginary production of Gozzi's commedia dell'arte "fable," which had its premiere in Berlin that same year. He decided to turn this music into an opera after seeing a production of the play in London. Although the outline of Busoni's version is essentially the same as Puccini's, the earlier opera maintains the commedia dell'arte aspect of the original, with its comic and masked characters. Crucially, there is neither torture nor suicide (there are two unsuccessful suicide attempts in the Gozzi, one successful suicide attempt in the Puccini). The opera is probably best known for its instrumental piece "Turandot's Frauengemach," which is none other than the old English tune "Greensleeves." The question comes down to whether Busoni knew what he was up to.

Turandot. Opera in three acts by Giacomo Puccini, left unfinished at his death and first performed incomplete at Milan's La Scala on April 25, 1926. The work was subsequently completed by Franco Alfano, using Puccini's thematic material, and it is in this form that *Turandot* is usually performed. The score is remarkable in many respects: in it Puccini attempted bold experimentation, approaching polytonality and atonality. Since Turandot is a Chinese princess, Puccini made use of pentatonic scales.

The libretto is based on an 18th-century play by Carlo Gozzi, perhaps after the *1,001 (Arabian) Nights.* Princess Turandot announces that she will marry only a man wise enough to solve three riddles proposed by her, the price of failure being death. Her palace begins to look like a mortuary, as one after another contender fails the quiz. But she meets her match in the person of Calaf, an exiled prince of Tatary, a Mongol group at war with China. He solves all her riddles, ludicrous as they are, and she begs him to release her from the obligation to marry. He agrees if she can guess his own name by the next morning. The only person who knows his name is Liù, a Tatar slave girl who has followed Calaf and loves him secretly. She is tortured on Turandot's order and stabs herself to death to avoid the disclosure. After Calaf gives her a clue in the form of an embrace, Turandot guesses that his name is Love. This realization makes it possible for her to marry him, and the opera concludes with a sumptuous oriental celebration.

Turco in Italia, Il (The Turk in Italy). Opera in two acts by Gioacchino Rossini, to a libretto by Felice Romani after Caterino Mazzolà, first produced in Milan on Aug. 14, 1814. The commander of a Turkish ship visiting Naples in the 18th century is attracted to a married Neapolitan woman. At a masked ball he mistakes a gypsy woman for the object of his infatuation and urges her to elope with him. He soon discovers his error but finds his new companion pleasant and tractable. Concurrently the Neapolitan matron discovers to her surprise that she really loves her husband, and this double change of hearts results in a conveniently happy ending. Not a major work by Rossini, *Il Turco*'s popularity was helped by the fact that it was once banned in England as immoral.

Turn of the Screw, The. Opera in prologue and two acts by Benjamin Britten, to a libretto by Myfanuy Piper after the somewhat somber psychological novel by Henry James (1898), first produced in Venice on Sept. 14, 1954. A governess is placed in charge of a young boy and girl, in a dismal house in the English countryside. Two former servants, now dead, seem to exercise a mysterious hold on the children's minds, and the governess herself entertains a neurotic belief in their strange posthumous influence. In questioning the boy she brings him to break his alliance with the ghosts, but in the process his heart gives way and he dies. The opera, like the novel, leaves the mystery of reality and superstition unsolved. The thematic "screw" is turned in 15 interludes (variations on the opening thematic fourth) connecting the opera's eight scenes

200,000 Taler. Opera by Boris Blacher, after a tale by Sholom Aleichem, first mounted in Berlin on Sept. 25, 1969.

Two Widows, The (Dvě vdovy). Opera in two acts by Bedřich Smetana, to a libretto by E. Züngel after Pierre Mallefille's comedy *Les deux veuves* (1860), first performed in Prague on March 27, 1874.

Tycho. Chamber opera by Poul Ruders, to a libretto inspired by the last days of the Danish astronomer of the 16th century, mounted for the first time in Århus on May 16, 1987.

U

Ubu Rex. Opera by Krzysztof Penderecki, to a libretto adapted from Alfred Jarry's 1986 proto-surrealist play *Ubu Roi*, in two one-hour-long acts incorporating quotations from the composer's earlier sacred works, first mounted at the Munich Opera Festival on July 6, 1991.

Ugo, Conte di Parigi (Hugo, Count of Paris). Opera by Gaetano Donizetti, first performed at La Scala, Milan, on March 13, 1832. Ugo is Hugh Capet, who remains faithful to King Louis V (the Sluggard), the last of the Carolingians, despite the efforts of dissidents to install the house of Anjou on the throne of France. A love quadrangle complicates the libretto when the king's bride begs Ugo to give her his love. She drinks poison and expires when he marries her sister. In historical fact, Louis V was France's nominal king only, and reigned for one year. Hugh Capet, already the duke of France (and thereby holding *de facto* power), was elected to replace Louis in 987, and ruled until his death in 996 as the first of the Capetian dynasty.

Ulisse. Opera in two acts with prologue by Luigi Dallapiccola, to his own libretto after Homer's *Odyssey*, centering on Princess Nausicaa's insular interlude with Ulysses, first performed in a German version entitled *Odysseus* in Berlin on Sept. 29, 1968, Lorin Maazel conducting.

Under Western Eyes. Opera in three acts by John Joubert, to a libretto fashioned from Joseph Conrad's tale of Russian revolutionary exiles in Geneva early in the 20th century, first performed during the Camden (England) Music Festival on May 29, 1969.

Undine. Opera in three acts by E. T. A. Hoffmann, to a libretto by Friedrich Fouqué, first produced in Berlin on Aug. 3, 1816. The story follows the plot described in the Lortzing opera of the same name.

Undine. Opera in four acts by Albert Lortzing, to a libretto by the composer after Friedrich Fouqué, first first performed in Magdeburg on April 21, 1845. A water nymph marries a mortal by which act she is assured of gaining an immortal soul. But her husband betrays her with a human female. She avenges herself by enticing her husband to join her in her native watery realm, and he perishes.

Unicorn, the Gorgon, and the Manticore, The. Madrigal fable by Gian Carlo Menotti, first performed in Washington, D.C., on Oct. 21, 1956. The story, by Menotti himself, tells of a poet who takes out on three successive Sundays a pet unicorn, a gorgon (Medusa was one), and a manticore (1/3 man, 1/3 lion, and 1/3 scorpion).

Uno Sguardo dal Ponte. Opera by Renzo Rossellini, to a libretto after Arthur Miller's play *A View from the Bridge* dealing with a tragedy of concupiscence among illicit Italian immigrants in New York, first produced in Rome on March 11, 1961.

Un Re in ascolto. "Musical action" in two parts by Luciano Berio, first performed in Salzburg on Aug. 7, 1984, Lorin Maazel conducting. The protagonist is a dying impresario.

Unter dem Milchwald. Opera by Walter Steffens, to a libretto fashioned from the poem *Under Milkwood* by Dylan Thomas, first produced in Hamburg on Oct. 5, 1973.

V

Vaisseau fantôme, Le (The Phantom Ship). Opera by Pierre-Louis Dietsch, first performed in Paris on Nov. 9, 1842. It is of historic interest because Wagner wrote his own opera on the same story, performed under the title *Der fliegende Holländer.*

Vakula the Smith. Opera in three acts by Pyotr Il'yich Tchaikovsky, first produced in St. Petersburg on Dec. 6, 1876. The libretto, by Yakov Polonsky after Gogol's fairy tale "The Night Before Christmas" (1832), is a mixture of rustic merrymaking in the Ukraine, interfered with by unruly demons who wreak havoc on the lives and amatory pursuits of the peasants involved. Tchaikovsky later revised the opera as *Cherevichki* (The Little Shoes), which received its first performance in Moscow on Jan. 31, 1887.

Valis. Video opera for actors, vocalists, keyboards, percussion/electronic percussion, computer-generated tape, and video projections by Tod Machover, to an original libretto adapted from the science fiction novel of the same name by Phillip K. Dick, first given in its installation form in Paris on Dec. 1, 1987.

Vampuka, the African Bride. Satirical opera by an obscure Russian composer, Vladimir Ehrenberg, first produced in a Russian cabaret, the Crooked Mirror, in St. Petersburg on Jan. 30, 1909. It derides the conventions of grand opera on exotic subjects, with numerous director quotations from *Aida* and *L'Africaine.* The satire had an extraordinary success in the sophisticated circles of old Russia, and its popularity was such that the name Vampuka entered the language, signifying operatic nonsense.

Vampyr, Der (The Vampire). Opera in two acts by Heinrich August Marschner, to a libretto by Wilhelm Wohlbrück after the story *The Vampyre* (1819), first produced in Leipzig on March 29, 1828. A Scottish lord, Lord Ruthren, is a vampire under his cloak, who can maintain his existence only through an annual sacrifice of a young women pure of heart. After dispatching two sopranos in succession, he is duly struck dead by lightning.

Vanessa. Opera by Samuel Barber, to a libretto by Gian Carlo Menotti, inspired by Isak Denisen's *Seven Gothic Tales* first produced at the Metropolitan Opera, N.Y., on Jan. 15, 1958. During a stormy night Vanessa awaits the return of her lover, Anatol, as she has done for 20 years. A young man appears seeking shelter, the son of her lover, now dead, named also Anatol. Over the chasm of a generation, Vanessa falls in love with him, and actually marries him. In the meantime, Anatol spends a perilous night with Vanessa's niece, Erika, who subsequently suffers a miscarriage. As her aunt departs for Paris with her young lover, the niece settles down for long years of waiting for his return. Barber was awarded the Pulitzer Prize in 1948.

Van Gogh Video Opera. Video opera by Michael Gordon, to a libretto in which the painter is schizophrenically portrayed by three singers against a backdrop of twenty-four video monitors, accompanied by a chamber ensemble and a raucous rock band, first performed in New York on May 28, 1991.

Venus d'Ille, La. Lyric drama in two acts by Henri Büsser, to his own libretto relating the story of a statue of Venus found in the French provincial town of Ille, which stuns a youth to death with a bracelet he playfully places on her hand, first produced in Lille on April 15, 1964.

Vera Sheloga, Boyarynia (The Noblewoman Vera Sheloga). Opera by Nikolai Rimsky-Korsakov, first performed in Moscow on Dec. 27, 1898. This work was developed out of the prologue to *The Maid of Pskov* (1873), and helps to explain the relationship between the young Ivan the Terrible and a young married Pskov woman. She later gives birth to Ivan's daughter, who in turn becomes a leading character in *The Maid of Pskov*, in which Ivan also figures.

Vera Storia, La (The True Story). Veristic opera by Luciano Berio, employing singers, actors, dancers, and acrobats, and featuring an offstage chorus and a wordless soprano, performed for the first time at Milan's La Scala on March 9, 1982, under the composer's direction.

Verbör des Lukullus, Das (The Trial of Lucullus). Opera by Paul Dessau, first performed in Berlin, on March 17, 1951. The libretto, by Bertolt Brecht, was originally intended for a radio play as an allegorical indictment of Hitler. The Roman general Lucullus has accumulated a fortune during his military exploits. After his death, he is put on trial to decide whether he should go to Hades or the Elysian Fields. He is accused of uncounted murders, but he defends himself by claiming that he undertook his military actions in order to exalt Rome. The judges sentence him to total annihilation. An adaptation of the same text was set by Sessions in English as *The Trial of Lucculus* (1947).

Verlobung in San Domingo, Die (The Betrothal in San Domingo). Opera by Werner Egk, first performed in Munich on Nov. 27, 1963. The libretto, after Kleist, has historical foundation, the action taking place on the island of Santo Domingo (now Hispaniola) in 1803 during the French occupation. A French officer has a love affair with a mulatto woman and proposes his intention to marry her, but he coldly orders her execution on suspicion of treason.

Vérnász (Blood Wedding). Opera in three acts by Sándor Szokolay, after the mystical play *Bodas de Sangre* by García Lorca dealing with a bloody feud between two village families and culminating in an elopement of a married man with his rival's lethal bride (she is a symbol of death incarnate) on her wedding day, leading to the death of both contenders and the retribution in blood dealt to her as well, first produced in Budapest on Oct. 31, 1964.

Veronique. Operetta by André Messager, first produced in Paris on Dec. 10, 1898, one of the most successful Viennese-influenced French operettas.

Verschworenen, Die (The Conspirators). Opera in one act by Franz Schubert, to a libretto by Ignaz Castelli, produced posthumously in Frankfurt on Aug. 29, 1861. The subject follows the plot of *Lysistrata* by Aristophanes. Here the wives of the Crusaders announce a marital strike until their husbands formally repudiate war. It is not a major work of Schubert (opera not being his best medium), but anything by Schubert deserves attention.

Veselohra na mostě (The Comedy on a Bridge). Radio opera in one act by Bohislev Martinů, to a libretto by the composer after Klicpera dealing with a group of civilians trapped on a bridge between two opposing armies, with the resulting stalemate giving an opportunity for social satire and amorous gunplay. The work was first broadcast over Radio Prague on March 18, 1937. The work was performed with an English libretto under the title *Comedy on the Bridge* at Hunter College in New York on May 28, 1951.

Vestale, La (The Vestal Virgin). Opera in three acts by Gaspare Spontini, to a libretto by Etienne de Jouy, first produced in Paris on Dec. 15, 1807. A Roman captain, Licinio, is busy conquering Gaul. In distress, his betrothed applies for a position as a vestal virgin. Upon examination she is found to be *virgo intacta* and is allowed to join the vestals. But Licinio refuses to guard her virginity and upon return to Rome invades the vestal premises, extinguishing the holy flame in the process. The poor bride is sentenced to death for her failure to protect the flame, but at the last moment before her execution, a bolt of lightning strikes the scene and relights the sacred fire. This celestial intervention is interpreted as of divine origin, and the lovers are reunited in unholy matrimony.

The opera was highly successful. Hector Berlioz considered it a masterpiece in the Gluckian and Cherubinian traditions. It held the stage for over a century, before its harmonious and melodious flame, maintained mainly by arpeggios of the chord of the diminished-seventh (accorde di stupefazione), gave up its illumination. Ironically, *La Vestale* has been staged anew as part of the bel canto revival begun in the 1950s, although its aesthetic is quite opposed to that of Bellini, Donizetti, and their contemporaries.

Viaggio a Reims, ossia L'albergo del Giglio d'Oro, Il (The Journey to Reims, or The Hotel of the Golden Lilly). Opera by Gioacchino Rossini, premiered in Paris on June 19, 1825, on the occasion of the coronation of Charles X. The work aroused little interest, and Rossini made use of its materials in a better and more successful opera, *Le Comte Ory* (1828).

Victory. Opera by Richard Rodney Bennett, after the novel by Joseph Conrad, first staged at London's Covent Garden on April 13, 1970.

Vida Breve, Il. Opera in two acts by Falla, to a text by Carlos Fernandez Shaw, first produced (in French) in Nice on April 1, 1913. The story is typical of the romantic preoccupation with bifurcated love. A young gypsy woman loves a man, but he marries another. She curses him, her heart breaks, and she collapses and dies. The opera is rarely performed in its entirety, but it has a couple of Spanish dances that have achieved universal popularity in arrangements.

Vie Parisienne, La (The Parisian Life). Opéretta in five (later four) acts by Jacques Offenbach, to a libretto by Henri Meilhac and Ludovic Halévy, first performed in Paris on Oct. 31, 1866. Two swains await the arrival by train of their mutual object of adoration, but she spurns them both. Frustrated, one tries to seduce a Swedish baroness, while the other assumes the role of an admiral in the Swiss Navy. Secret trysts are held, and a traveling Brazilian sings an infectious matchiche (*maxixe*). There are easily penetrable disguises, but at the end each swain finds a complementary damsel. *La Vie Parisienne* is an affectionate spoof on life under the emperor Napoleon III.

Viimeiset Kiusaukset (The Last Temptations). Opera by Joonas Kokkonen, to a libretto dealing with the Finnish evangelist Paavo Ruotsalainen, who revived the purity of the Finnish Lutheran church in the first half of the 19th century, first performed in Helsinki on Sept. 2, 1975.

Village Romeo and Juliet, A. Opera in prologue and three acts by Frederick Delius, to a libretto by the composer after the story by Gottfried Keller in his *Leute von Seldwyla*, first performed (in German, as *Romeo und Julia auf dem Dorfe*) in Berlin on Feb. 21, 1907.

Villi, Le (The Willis). Opera in two acts by Giacomo Puccini, his first stage work, to a libretto by Ferdinando Fontana after Alphonse Karr's *Les Willis*, first produced in Milan on May 31, 1884. The subject is Teutonically romantic: in the tenebrous Black Forest, a villager, intent on making a fortune in the city, deserts his betrothed, who languishes and dies of the ever-present romantic complaint, a broken heart. When he returns home, her spirit reproaches him bitterly. Worse still, a horde of willies (spirits of fiancéed women who die before their wedding) pursues him with obscene mimicry until he collapses and dies.

Vincent. Opera by Einujuhani Rautavaara, based on letters written by Vincent van Gogh to his brother, Theo, first staged in Helsinki on May 17, 1990.

Violanta. Opera in one act by Erich Wolfgang Korngold, to a libretto wherein a young Venetian matron intent on avenging the violation of her sister's chastity arranges a clandestine assignation with its perpetrator and asks her husband to come, too, and slay him with impunity vouchsafed by the Venetian adultery law, but is overcome at the critical moment by an overwhelming sexual desire for the seducer and throws herself between him and her husband, receiving a mortal dagger blow. The work was first staged in Munich on March 28, 1916, paired with another one-act opera by the composer, *Der Ring des Polykrates.*

Violins of Saint-Jacques, The. Opera in three acts by Malcolm Williamson, his fifth, to a libretto by William Chappel in which phantom violins emerge from the sea on each anniversary of the cataclysmic eruption in 1902 of Mont Pelée on the Island of Martinique, with assorted zombies, among them a convertible lesbian and an effeminate captain, arising from the foam in voodoo rituals, first produced in London on Nov. 29, 1966.

Virineya. Music drama by Sergei Slonimsky, to a libretto depicting the social and personal upheavals in the Russian countryside during the first year of the Russian Revolution, in seven ideologically and politically significant scenes (*The End of the Autocracy, The End of the Family, The End of Religious Faith, The Night, The Dawn, Political Meetings,* and *Farewell*) centering on the fate of a simple Russian woman, Virineia, who breaks away from the chains of dull matrimony and obsolete religious faith. It was first mounted in Leningrad on Sept. 30, 1967.

Vision of Therese, A. Opera in two acts by Lars Johan Werle, after Emile Zola's short story "Pour une nuit d'amour" dealing with a provincial femme fatale who brings passion into the life of a flute-playing postal clerk, with realistic effects contributed by phonograph records, performed for the first time in Stockholm on May 26, 1964.

Visita meravigliosa, La (The Wonderful Visit). Opera by Nino Rota, after H. G. Wells, first performed in Palermo on Feb. 6, 1970.

Visitation, The. Opera in three acts (10 scenes) and epilogue by Gunther Schuller, inspired by the faceless terrors of Kafka's *The Trial* and dedicated to "all men who, through hate, injustice, and oppression are denied freedom in their pursuit of happiness," with the action transferred to the American South and focused on the tragic fate of a black student suspected of harboring a miscegenating sentiment toward a white girl. The work was first staged in Hamburg on Oct. 12, 1966, the composer conducting.

Voice of Ariadne, The. Chamber opera by Thea Musgrave, after a novella by Henry James, *The Last of the Valerii,* with the action, taking place in Rome in 1870, concerned with Marco Valeri, who digs up an ancient statue of the goddess Juno on his Roman estate and becomes so infatuated with it that his American wife decides to rebury it, the "voice of Ariadne" symbolizing Valeri's neglected wife. It was first staged in Aldeburgh on June 11, 1974, the composer conducting.

Voix Humaine, La (The Human Voice). Opera in one act by Francis Poulenc, to a libretto by Jean Cocteau, first produced in Paris on Feb. 6, 1959. This is a modern melodramatic monodrama, featuring a young woman speaking on the telephone to her lover, who has apparently just announced the end of their affair.

Volpone. Opera in three acts by George Antheil, first produced in Los Angeles on Jan. 9, 1953. The libretto is adapted from Ben Jonson's famous comedy in which a sly Venetian miser spreads a rumor that he is dying, which encourages hopeful aspirants to his fortune to lavish attention, affection, and gifts on him. He then stages a miraculous recovery, leaving his would-be heirs in a state of chagrin and financial loss.

Von A bis Z. Abecedarian opera by Bruno Maderna, first staged in Darmstadt on Feb. 22, 1970.

Von Heute auf Morgen. Opera in one act by Arnold Schoenberg, to a libretto by Max Blonda (the composer's then-wife, Gertrud), first produced in Frankfurt am Main on Feb. 1, 1930. The score makes use of the full-fledged method of composition with 12 tones. The plot describes the daily effort of a housewife to retain the affections of her indifferent husband.

Votre Faust. Opera by Posseur, treating the Faust legend in contemporary terms, with audience participation in the form of a vote in favor of one of the four proffered dénouements, performed for the first time in concert form in Buffalo on March 17, 1968.

Voyage of Edgar Allan Poe, The. Opera by Dominick Argento, his third stage work, written in an expansively romantic and ingratiating songful manner, first produced in St. Paul on April 24, 1976. The libretto, with copious quotations from Poe's poem "Annabel Lee," imagines a dream of Poe's in which he recapitulates nostalgic and painful memories of his life, focusing mainly on his child bride who died before him.

Voyevode, The (The Provincial Governor). Opera by Pyotr Il'lich Tchaikovsky, his first, to a libretto based on Ostrovsky's play *A Dream on the Volga,* first performed in Moscow on Feb. 11, 1869. The story deals with the attempt by the head of a Volga community to abduct a young woman engaged to another. He has a prophetic dream of his downfall, which comes true when he is dismissed from office by the czar. His intended victim is now free to marry her beloved. Tchaikovsky destroyed the opera, but orchestral parts were later discovered, and Pavel Lamm, the great restorer of fragmentary Russian operas, reconstructed the work.

Voz del Silencio, La. Opera in one act by Mario Perusso, to a symbolistic libretto, with indeterminate characters described only by gender or age colliding and rotating on the stage in aleatory motion, set to an appropriately atonal score, produced for the first time at the Teatro Colón in Buenos Aires on Nov. 27, 1969.

Vskriesenie (Resurrection). Opera in three acts by Ján Cikker, after Tolstoy's moralistic novel centered on the sufferings of a debauched orphan girl in 1886, set to music in an expressionistically atonal idiom to reflect the psychic contradictions of her reformed seducer, produced first in Prague on May 18, 1962.

V studni (In the Well). Comic opera in one act by Vilém Blodek, first performed in Prague on Nov. 17, 1867. A village woman who enjoys a reputation for wisdom advises a young girl who is in a quandary as to whether to wed a rich widower or an impecunious but handsome youth, to look in the well to see whose face is reflected in the water. Both contenders find out about it, and both climb a tree next to the well to make sure that his face appears. The old widower falls into the well, but the youth keeps his balance and gains the girl's hand. In Germany it was given under the title *Im Brunnen* (1893).

W

Waffenschmied, Der (The Armorer). Comic opera in three acts by Albert Lortzing, to a libretto by the composer after Ziegler's *Liebhaber und Nebenbuhler in einer Person* (1790), premiered in Vienna on May 30, 1846. In the city of Worms, the local gunsmith despises aristocracy. But a local count dons a disguise and hires himself out as an apprentice to the gunsmith in order to woo his daughter. The two young people finally get married.

Wahrer Held, Ein. Opera by Giselher Klebe, after Synge's play *The Playboy of the Western World*, first staged in Zürich on Jan. 18, 1975.

Walküre, Die (The Valkyrie). The second music drama of Wagner's cycle, *Der Ring des Nibelungen*, in three acts, premiered in Munich on June 26, 1870, and, within the cycle at the first Bayreuth Festival, on Aug. 14, 1876. *Die Walküre* begins with the meeting of Siegmund and Sieglinde, the long-separated mortal children of Wotan. Unaware of their kinship they feel a sensuous attraction toward each other. When Sieglinde shows Siegmund the magical sword Nothung, which Wotan drove deep into a tree, and which can be pulled out only by a hero, Siegmund performs the task. Sieglinde becomes enraptured, and she abandons her brutal husband, Hunding, and flees with her brotherly lover. But Wotan comes to the aid of Hunding, and orders his nine warlike daughters, the Valkyries, not to lend support to the lovers. Wotan's favorite Valkyrie, Brünnhilde, disobeys Wotan's orders by trying to help Siegmund, who is killed by Hunding when Wotan shatters the magic sword in Siegmund's hands. (Wotan rewards Hunding by killing him with a wave of his hand.) As Brünnhilde's punishment, Wotan takes her immortality away, places her on a high rock, puts her to sleep, and surrounds the rock by a ring of fire. Only a hero can break through the fire and rescue her. As the following opera of the *Ring* (*Siegfried*) relates, this hero will be Siegfried, son of Sieglinde, who died in childbirth.

The most famous symphonic episode from the opera is "The Ride of the Valkyries," in which the sturdy Teutonic amazons disport themselves on top of cloud-covered rocks. Wagner's thematic use of the arpeggiated augmented triads here is notable. "The Magic Fire," illustrating Brünnhilde's imprisonment by fiery ring, is another popular tableau in the opera. In it, the most important leading motives of the opera, including Wotan's imperious command, Brünnhilde's lament, the slumber motive, and the sparkling magic fire itself, are all combined in a gorgeous Wagnerian panoply.

Wally, La. Opera in four acts by Alfredo Catalani, to a libretto by Luigi Illica after Wilhelmine von Hillern's novel *Die Geyer-Wally*, premiered in Milan on Jan. 20, 1892. The libretto is drawn from the morbid Teutonic tales dealing with strange calamities and unnatural passions in dark and isolated places. A maddened suitor tries to kill the lover of a young Swiss girl. They escape murder but perish in a mountain avalanche. The music is exceedingly mellifluous in the finest Italian manner. Toscanini admired Catalani and conducted *La Wally* often after Catalani died (1893).

Wandering Scholar, The. Chamber opera in one act by Gustav Holst, to a libretto by Clifford Bax based on an incident in Helen Waddell's *The Wandering Scholars* (1928), first performed in Liverpool on Jan. 31, 1934.

War and Peace (Voyna i mir). Opera in five acts by Sergei Prokofiev, to a libretto by the composer and Myra Mendelson (Prokofiev's second wife) after Tolstoy's novel (1869), with a cast of characters numbering 72 singing and acting *dramatis personae.* The score attempts with considerable success to embrace the epic breadth of Tolstoy's great novel, and the work went through more or less continuous revision until 1952. The last version of the opera contains 13 scenes, with the first seven concentrating on Peace, and the last six on War. The work opens with a choral epigraph, summarizing the significance of Napoleon's invasion of Russia in 1812. It was performed for the first time in Leningrad on April 1, 1955. Interlaced with military events are the destinies of the Rostov family and the dramatic story of Pierre Bezuhov. The concluding words of the victorious Field Marshal Kutuzov, "Russia is saved," were unquestionably intended to echo the recent Russian experience in fighting off another invasion, that of Hitler. The musical idiom is profoundly Russian in spirit, but there are no literal quotations from folk songs.

We Come to the River. "Action for music" by Hans Werner Henze, centered on a murderous army general attacked by demented pacifists who gouge his eyeballs, set to a score ranging from insanely inappropriate bel canto to planned pandemonium as the musicians invade the stage to the deafening sounds of a marching band, with celestial diaphony superimposed on an infernal cacophony, produced for the first time at Covent Garden in London on July 12, 1976.

Werther. Opera in four acts by Jules Massenet, to a libretto by Édouard Blau, Paul Milliet, and Georges Hartmann after Goethe's novel *Die Leiden des jungen Werthers* (1774), first performed in Vienna on Feb. 16, 1892. Werther is a young man who is prey to a single overpowering passion for a young woman who reciprocates his affection on a philosophical level but marries a more pragmatic person. Werther does not cease to express his adoration for her. Then he borrows a pistol from her husband and shoots himself. She rushes to his side, and he has the ultimate satisfaction of dying in her arms while proclaiming the eternal validity of his deathless passion. A wave of suicides among young males in the throes of unrequited love followed the publication of Goethe's novel. In some countries, it was banned.

What Where. Opera by Holliger, after Beckett, first mounted in Frankfurt am Main on May 19, 1989.

Where the Wild Things Are. Fantasy opera in one act by Oliver Knussen, after Maurice Sendak, the central character being a small boy confronted with monsters singing in "pidgin Yiddish" and the whole score a mosaic of some 25 interdependent microforms, performed for the first time, in its first version, in Brussels on Nov. 28, 1980, then in final form in London on Jan. 9, 1984.

White Night. "Musical chronicle" by Tikhon Khrennikov, a pasquinade satirizing the last years of czarist rule in Russia, with a cast of historical characters including the last czar, Nicholas II, his czarina, and her coterie maneuvered by the sinister monk Gregory Rasputin (his last name derives from the Russian word for debauchery), performed for the first time in Moscow on Nov.

23, 1967. (The title refers to the subhorizontal sunlight during the summer nights in subarctic St. Petersburg.)

Wildschütz, Der (The Poacher). Opera in three acts by Albert Lortzing, to a libretto by the composer after Kotzebue's comedy *Der Rehbock*, first performed in Leipzig on Dec. 31, 1842. The poacher is a schoolteacher who accidentally kills an animal on the estate of a feudal aristocrat. He is threatened with dismissal from his job, and sends his bride to plead with the lord of the manor, known for his lecherous inclinations. As a result of multiple transsexual changes of attire, a baroness takes her place. In the end class divisions are preserved, with aristocrats pairing up with their equals. The teacher regains his bride undamaged and is freed of accusations of poaching when it develops that the animal he shot was his own ass.

Willie Stark. Opera by Carlisle Floyd, modeled after the career of Huey Long, with marginal participation by other American demagogues such as Bilbo, Talmadge, Wallace, and McCarthy, first produced in Houston on April 24, 1981.

Wings of the Dove, The. Opera in two acts by Douglas Moore, premiered at the New York City Opera on Oct. 12, 1961. The libretto, after a psychological novel by Henry James (1902), deals with a rich young American woman dying in London of a debilitating disease. She falls in love with a young writer of dubious morality, and he is associated with a woman of even lower moral principles. At her suggestion he proposes to marry the dying woman in order to inherit her fortune. Although the intended learns about the plan, she bequeaths her fortune to him anyway. He is deeply struck by this demonstration of nobility, and becomes alienated from his scheming paramour.

Winter's Tale, The. Opera by John Harbison, after Shakespeare, first performed in San Francisco on Aug. 20, 1979.

Witwe des Schmetterlings, Die. Opera in three scenes by Isang Yun, to an oneiric libretto in German based on an old Chinese tale about a defunct functionary whose metempsychotic memory of having been a giant butterfly is reified when he emerges from his coffin as from a chrysalis and scares away his perfidious "butterfly widow" and her lover, first mounted in Nuremberg on Feb. 23, 1969.

W. of Babylon, The. Opera by Charles Wuorinen, a "Baroque burlesque" composed in 1975, first staged in San Francisco on Jan. 20, 1989.

Women in the Garden, The. Chamber opera by Vivian Fine, her second, scored for five singers and nine instruments, to her own feminist libretto portraying Emily Dickinson, Isadora Duncan, Gertrude Stein, and Virginia Woolf, first staged in San Francisco on Feb. 12, 1978.

Wozzeck. Opera in three acts (15 scenes) by Alban Berg, first performed in Berlin on Dec. 14, 1925, heroically conducted by Erich Kleiber (heroically because rehearsals of the enormously complicated atonal score required months of time and portended much trouble on the part of the orchestra, singers, and audience). Berg fashioned the libretto from an obscure unfinished play by an obscure young German dramatist, Georg Büchner, who died of typhus in 1837 at the age of 23. The subject was taken from real life, the tragic story of an ordinary army barber named Woyzeck (Wozzeck was a misspelling, a result of Büchner's illegible handwriting). Woyzeck was content living with his unwedded girlfriend, Marie, who bore him a child. But she becomes a temporary mistress of the dashing drum major of the army, and in a fit of jealousy Wozzeck stabs her to death. The actual soldier Woyzeck was sentenced to death for his crime. In Büchner's drama, as in Berg's opera, he drowns himself in a lake. The opera concludes with a poignant scene wherein their child rocks on his wooden horse, uncomprehending of the tragedy.

Wozzeck is a milestone in the history of modern musical theater. It is a tour de force of formal organization, the entire score being programmed as a series of Baroque dance forms and variations. The idiom is tensely atonal. Although *Wozzeck* is now acknowledged as a modern masterpiece, at its first performances German music critics described it as a cacophonous monstrosity. Curiously, another composer, Manfred Gurlitt (1890–1972), chose the same subject for an opera. His *Wozzeck* was produced in Bremen in 1926, four months after Berg's masterpiece, but could not withstand the comparison and soon faded from the musical scene.

Wreckers, The. Grand opera by Dame Ethel Smyth, originally set to a French libretto as *Les Naufrageurs*, and first produced in a German version as *Strandrecht* in Leipzig on Nov. 11, 1906. The story deals with the inhumanity of villagers on the Cornish coast of Britain (the wreckers of the title) who asserted their right to rob and murder the shipwrecked sailors (the Strandrecht of the German title).

X

X: The Life and Times of Malcolm X. Opera in three acts by Anthony Davis, to a libretto derived from the black leader's autobiography, first staged in a full-scale production in Philadelphia on Oct. 9, 1985. The "official" world premiere was claimed for the N.Y. City Opera production of Sept. 28, 1986.

Y

Yaroslav the Wise. Opera by Yuli Meitus, to a libretto glorifying an early Russian prince, first staged in Donetsk on March 3, 1973.

Yerma. Opera by Heitor Villa-Lobos, to a symbolic drama by Frederico García Lorca depicting the inner torment of a woman remaining barren (*yerma*) because of her husband's inexplicable refusal to have martial relations with her, and her equally inexplicable refusal to find another man, culminating in her superhuman and successful effort to strangle her inactive mate to death, given its first posthumous performance with the original Spanish libretto in Santa Fe on Aug. 12, 1971.

Yolimba, oder Die Grenzen der Magie. Opera in "one act and four love songs" by Wilhelm Killmayer, dealing with a televisionary robotesse scientifically furnished with supernumerary aphrodisiac organs, who shoots every man uttering or muttering the word love but who reaches the limits of her magic (hence the title) in her encounter with a sexless technician and retreats to her native electronic world, first produced in Wiesbaden on March 25, 1964.

Yvonne, Prinzessin von Burgund. Opera by Boris Blacher, to a libretto in which a sadomasochistic prince weds the ugliest bride he can find, with a score designed to express "the agony of suffering in the language of Euclid," first produced in Wuppertal on Sept. 15, 1973.

Z

Zaide. Opera (unfinished) in two acts by Wolfgang Amadeus Mozart, to a libretto by Johann Schachtner after Franz Joseph Sebastiani's *Das Serial*, first performed in Frankfurt am Main on Jan. 27, 1866.

Zampa. Comic opera in three acts by Ferdinand Hérold, to a libretto by Mélesville, first staged in Paris on May 3, 1831.

Zar und Zimmermann. Opera in three acts by Albert Lortzing, to a libretto by the composer after Georg Romers, after Mélesville, Merle, and de Boirie (1818), first produced in Leipzig on Dec. 22, 1837.

Zaubergeige, Die (The Magic Violin). Opera in three acts by Werner Egk, first performed in Frankfurt am Main on May 22, 1935. The libretto derives from a Bavarian folk tale dealing with a peasant who receives a magic violin from an earth spirit that has the power to fulfill any wish except love. When the peasant meets the girl of his dreams, he surrenders the violin.

Zazà. Opera in four acts by Ruggero Leoncavallo, to a libretto by the composer after the play by Charles Simon and Pierre Berton dealing with a Parisian chanteuse whose yearning for matrimonial respectability is shattered by the revelation that her lover is a married man and a father. It was first staged in Milan on Nov. 10, 1900, Toscanini conducting.

Zdravý nemocný (The Hypochondriac). Opera by Jiří Pauer, to his own libretto based on the famous play by Molière, first produced in Prague on May 22, 1970.

Zémire et Azor. Pastorale by Andre-Ernest-Modeste Grétry, first performed in Fontainebleau on Nov. 9, 1771. Azor is a royal prince transformed into a monstrous creature as punishment for his brutal self-conceit and overweening arrogance. Only love can restore his human shape, which he receives from Zémire. Spohr wrote an opera on the same subject, first performed in Frankfurt am Main on April 4, 1819.

Zerrissene, Der. Opera in two acts by Gottfried von Einem, to a libretto arranged by Boris Blacher from a novel by Johann Nestroy dealing with a disillusioned capitalist who finds that money cannot buy happiness, first produced in Hamburg on Sept. 17, 1964.